KU-728-621

D1373051

Shorter Oxford English Dictionary

Shorter Oxford English Dictionary

ON HISTORICAL PRINCIPLES

Sixth edition

VOLUME 1 · A–M

UNIVERSITY PRESS

OXFORD
UNIVERSITY PRESS

Great Clarendon Street, Oxford OX2 6DP

Oxford University Press is a department of the University of Oxford.
It furthers the University's objective of excellence in research, scholarship,
and education by publishing worldwide in

Oxford New York

Auckland Cape Town Dar es Salaam Hong Kong Karachi
Kuala Lumpur Madrid Melbourne Mexico City Nairobi
New Delhi Shanghai Taipei Toronto

With offices in

Argentina Austria Brazil Chile Czech Republic France Greece
Guatemala Hungary Italy Japan Poland Portugal Singapore
South Korea Switzerland Thailand Turkey Ukraine Vietnam

Published in the United States
by Oxford University Press Inc., New York

First edition 1933
Second edition 1936
Third edition 1944
Reprinted with revised etymologies and enlarged addenda 1973
Fourth edition published 1993 as the *New Shorter Oxford English Dictionary*
Fifth edition 2002
Sixth edition 2007

British Library Cataloguing in Publication Data

Data available

Library of Congress Cataloging in Publication Data

Data available

ISBN 978-0-19-920687-2
ISBN 978-0-19-920688-9 (deluxe)
ISBN 978-0-19-923324-3 (US)
ISBN 978-0-19-923325-0 (deluxe leatherbound)

10 9 8 7 6 5 4

Typeset in OUP Swift, OUP Argo, and Capitolium
by Interactive Sciences Ltd, Gloucester
Printed in China through Asia Pacific Offset

Contents

VOLUME 1

VOLUME 2

List of lexicographers

New Shorter Oxford English Dictionary · 1993

EDITOR-IN-CHIEF Lesley Brown

GENERAL EDITORS A. M. Hughes (1984–93), John Sykes (1989–93)

ASSOCIATE EDITOR William R. Trumble (1980–91)

SENIOR EDITORS Georgia Hole (1986–93), Elizabeth M. Knowles (1983–93)
Helen Liebeck (1989–93), Freda J. Thornton (1985–92)

SENIOR ASSISTANT EDITORS Jeremy H. Marshall (1988–93), Richard Palmer (1984–93),
Catherine I. Soanes (1989–93), Angus Stevenson (1988–93)

ASSISTANT EDITORS Gerard O'Reilly (1988–93), David B. Shirt (1990–93), D. B. W. Birk (1983–6),
M. A. Cooper (1983–6), D. Greene (1988–90), H. Kemp (1986–8), F. McDonald (1985–9),
J. Paterson (1986–8), S. C. Rennie (1989–91)

SUPPLEMENTARY EDITING E. S. C. Weiner (1991–3)

SIXTH EDITION · 2007

EDITOR Angus Stevenson

EDITORIAL STAFF Lesley Brown, Georgia Hole, Helen Liebeck, Catherine Soanes

EDITORIAL ASSISTANTS Charlotte Livingstone, Sarah Beattie

ETYMOLOGIES Sarah Ogilvie

DATA PROCESSING James McCracken, Mark Baillie, Orion Montoya

DESIGN Paul Luna

PRODUCTION CONTROL Carol Alexander, Karen Vining

PROOFREADERS Juliet Field, Carolyn Garwes, Sara Hawker, Georgia Hole,
Lucy Hollingworth, Jane Horwood, Jesse Ingham, Susan Jellis, Helen Liebeck,
Duncan Marshall, Bernadette Mohan, Howard Sargeant, Trish Stableford,
George Tulloch, David Wilson, Edmund Wright

Preface to the *New Shorter Oxford English Dictionary* · 1993

The *New Shorter Oxford English Dictionary* is a historical dictionary of modern English. It sets out the main meanings and semantic developments of words current at any time between 1700 and the present day: those which have been in regular literary or colloquial use at some point in their history; slang or dialect words which are nevertheless likely to be generally encountered through accessible literature or the modern mass media; and in addition a wide range of scientific and technical words such as may be of interest to serious amateurs or advanced students. Every headword is traced back to the time of its first known use, however early, in many cases to the manuscript records of the Old and Middle English periods.

Words which have fallen into disuse during the past three centuries are included if they meet the other general criteria. Words which became obsolete before 1700 appear if they are significant in the formation or history of some other headword in the text, or if they remain familiar from the works of Shakespeare, the 1611 Authorized Version of the Bible, and a small number of other influential literary sources (notably the poems of John Milton and Edmund Spenser's *Faerie Queene*).

This work is a replacement for the third edition of the *Shorter Oxford English Dictionary*, but not a direct revision of its text. The *New SOED* editors returned to the *Oxford English Dictionary* itself (in later stages the second edition of 1989, originally the first edition of 1884–1928 and its four-volume *Supplement* of 1972–86), and reabridged, conflated, revised, restructured, added, and updated. Every entry has been written afresh, taking into account the linguistic evidence of the Dictionary Department's extensive quotation files and computer databases. Many new words and senses have been added, and all have been reviewed in the light of social and political changes.

A more strictly chronological basis for entry structure has been adopted than in previous editions (which followed the *OED* more directly). Senses within major semantic and grammatical units are arranged according to the period or date range within which the first known example of each falls (for the definition of date ranges used see p. xxxiv). In many cases dates are at variance with those in the *OED* because earlier and later examples have now been identified. For the *New SOED*, researchers have systematically scrutinized historical dictionaries such as the *Middle English Dictionary* in progress in Ann Arbor, Michigan, the *Dictionary of the Older Scottish Tongue*, the *Scottish National Dictionary*, the *Dictionary of American English*, the *Dictionary of Americanisms*, and the *Australian National Dictionary*, looking for examples which would affect dates or descriptive labels. New information was sought in other known relevant publications, such as Jürgen Schäfer's *Documentation in the O.E.D.* and articles in *Notes and Queries*. Unresolved first dates in the *OED* were pursued and clarified. Several million paper slips in the English Dictionary Department's files were scanned for individual antedatings or postdatings. The editors of the *Middle English Dictionary* have further provided some information from their drafts of later parts of the alphabet which have not yet been published, and a number of unpublished earlier uses have been verified in the files of the *Dictionary of the Older Scottish Tongue*. New significant information will continue to come to light, but every effort has been made to present the most accurate and up-to-date record possible at the time of going to press.

The *New SOED* is founded in the *OED*, and shares its coverage of many words and senses from North America, Australia, New Zealand, South Africa, the Indian subcontinent, and elsewhere within the English-speaking world. Many of the entries for recent vocabulary are based on as yet unpublished additions prepared by members of the *OED*'s New Words section.

The main senses of the headwords are illustrated by 83,000 quotations, drawn from the Dictionary Department's quotation files and computerized databases. Their primary function here is to illuminate semantic distinctions and exemplify possible grammatical constructions. Defined phrases and combinations, and derivatives and minor words related to a headword, cannot receive such expansive treatment and are not illustrated. Where possible and historically appropriate, modern sources have been used, but real examples are notoriously ambiguous or resistant to intelligible abridgement, and the undeniable quotability of Defoe, Macaulay, and Dickens has ensured the use of many earlier quotations directly from the *OED*.

Pronunciations are provided in symbols of the International Phonetic Alphabet, and represent a style of British Received Pronunciation. Coverage of the wide regional, social, and other differences in spoken English in Britain and throughout the world would require more space and a more complex technical apparatus than would be suitable, given the emphases and intended non-specialist readership of the *New SOED*.

Editorial work on this completely new edition of the *SOED* began in 1980, with a build-up of staff from late 1983. Until well into the letter I, entries were handwritten on 6-by-4-inch paper slips. Then in 1987 the availability of the second edition of the *OED* in electronic form prompted a radical revision of editorial procedures. A complex specification was drawn up for the automatic modification of the *OED* text: certain categories of entry and types of information were omitted, senses and structural units were reordered, old-fashioned modes of expression were modified, and many other changes were made to bring it closer to the spirit and style of the *New SOED*. This provisional abridged and transformed *OED* was made a reality as an electronic database and in proofed paper form on editors' desks by members of the Reference Computing team at Oxford University Press and members of the Centre for the New OED at the University of Waterloo in Ontario, Canada. Thereafter a team of keyboarders made the lexicographers' substantial alterations and additions directly to the central database.

Meanwhile International Computaprint Corporation (ICC) in Pennsylvania, who had undertaken data-capture of the second edition of the *OED*, keyed the handwritten slips for *A* to *interwreathe*, converting their conventional typographical mark-up into a generic form which identified the start and end points of the many different elements of dictionary structure. The tagging of the output was then refined and enhanced by programs written within OUP. Soon the sections of dictionary text produced by such contrasting means were formally indistinguishable.

Almost every member of the lexicographical team took part in the first round of editing. Proofs of the results were sent out to advisers for criticisms and suggestions, and many individual entries were also submitted to subject specialists. Comments from both these sources were then fed into a revision of the whole text by senior lexicographers. But for the requirement of publication, this revision could continue for ever.

A project of the size and duration of the *New Shorter Oxford English Dictionary* inevitably draws upon the time and expertise of members of many different departments within Oxford University Press. The editors thank them all. In particular the Reference Computing team helped transform working methods and perceptions and provided the support to sustain the transformation. From outside the organization we wish to mention Hazel Wright and Deborah Honoré, for general critical reading of the text; Dr Clive Upton, for advising on pronunciation and checking phonetic transcriptions; G. Elizabeth Blake, for the programs for preliminary shortening of the *OED*; Julia Cresswell, for historical research in published materials; Ralph Bates, for bibliographical and other library research; Lidie Howes and Barbara Grant, for information from the *Middle English Dictionary* materials; Lorna Pike, for quotations from the *DOST* collections; Helen De Witt, Sara Hawker, Rachel James, Marcia Slater, Jerry Spring, Jeremy Trevett, Penny Trumble, Penny Waddell, Carl Watson, Seren Wildwood, and Jane Windebank, for data-capture and structural tagging; Patricia Moore, for this and on-line regularization of stylistic inconsistencies; Fabia Claris, Louise Keegan, Christina Malkowski-Zaba, Helen Marriage, Margaret McKay, and Coralie O'Gorman, for proofreading and checking of underlying structure; Dorothy McCarthy, for establishing proofreading procedures; Patricia Greene, Lisa Johnston, and Sandy Vaughan, for cross-reference checking; Fred Gill and Peter Gibbs, for checking final page-proofs; Peter Robinson, Catherine Bates, Stephen Shepherd, Lynda Mugglestone, Alexandra Barratt, and Rod McConchie, particularly for searching files for dating and usage information; Margaret Davies, for file-searching and research for the list of authors and publications; Philippa Berry, for work on the authors' list and for identifying potential cross-references for inclusion; Clare Todd, particularly for research for the authors' list, for identifying cross-references, and for quotation abridgement and copying; Kate Batchelor, Mary Burns, and Katie Weale, for quotation copying and for other clerical and administrative help; Colinette Dorey, for file-searching and for filing and clerical help; Kay Pepler, particularly for keying information for the authors' list; Clare Senior, for clerical and filing assistance; Carol Percy, for bibliographical research; Anna Taylor, for distributing proofs. At various earlier stages of the project Karen Cooper, Hania Porucznik, and Annabella Duckit were project administrative assistants, and M. A. Mabe, K. Atherton, and M. C. Palmer contributed to early editorial work.

For specific advice on particular languages and areas of knowledge, we are indebted to Mrs A. J. Allott, Dr Philip Baker, Mr David Barrett, Professor Tomás de Bhaldraithe, Mr R. J. Bowater, Dr Savile Bradbury, Dr Jean Branford, Mr David Bunker, Mr Andrew Burrows, Miss Penelope Byrde, Dr Stanley Chapman, Mr Howard Colvin, Mr Yassin Dutton, Mr Colin Dyson, Mr Elwyn Hartley Edwards, Mr D. H. Fowler, Mr J. B. Franks, Mr Alan J. Gamble, Professor Bryan Garner, Dr Ives Goddard, Mr Noël Goodwin, Mrs Judy Gray, Dr Anne Grinter, Dr P. T. Harries, Mr Andrew Hawke, Professor Tony Honoré, Mr Simon James, Dr W. J. Johnson, Dr Russell Jones, the late Mr Peter Kemp, Professor Harriet Klein, Dr Ann Lackie, M. Pierre-Yves Lambert, Professor J. D. Latham, Professor G. L. Lewis, Professor Robert E. Lewis, Dr Andrew Louth, Professor J. B. McMillan, Dr C. M. MacRobert, Dr F. H. C. Marriott, Professor P. H. Matthews, Dr M. J. Morris, Mr James Mosley, Professor P. Nailor, Mr David Parlett, Professor Andrew Pawley, Ms Jenny Putin, Dr D. A. Roe, Dr H. M. Rosenberg, Captain A. B. Sainsbury, Dr Geoff Sharman, Mr Jonathan Spencer, Professor N. S. Sutherland, Professor M. Twyman, Professor J. O. Urmson, Professor Geza Vermes, Miss Freda Walker, Lord Walton of Detchant, Mr Harry D. Watson, Ms Niki Watts, Dr M. Weitzman, Mr Ken Whyld, Mr Thomas Woodcock, Professor Clifford Wright, Mrs Hazel Wright, and Dr R. David Zorc.

L. B.

March 1993

Preface to the sixth edition

The English language has changed rapidly in the five years since the previous edition of the *Shorter Oxford English Dictionary* was published. This sixth edition takes in new terms from such productive areas as computing, communications, science, and slang while also casting new light on the history of English.

Some 2,500 new entries have been added for words and phrases which have entered the language since the last edition of the *Shorter* was published in 2002. These were identified by our analysis of the new Oxford English Corpus, which contains more than a billion words of real contemporary English from around the world, and the database of the Oxford Reading Programme, now amounting to nearly 100 million words.

More than 1,300 new illustrative quotations have been added, mostly from authors and periodicals of the late 20th and early 21st centuries, in all parts of the English-speaking world. For the first time Internet sources have been used. Professor Paul Luna, of the Department of Typography & Graphic Communication at the University of Reading, has adapted the design he originated for the fifth edition to place illustrative quotations immediately after the sense they relate to, rather than collecting them together in a block at the end of the entry or section. This makes the text easier to navigate and follows the practice of the *Oxford English Dictionary*.

We have taken advantage of the work in progress for the third edition of the *Oxford English Dictionary*, notably by incorporating their discoveries concerning earlier first dates of use. For this edition of the *Shorter* we have been able to antedate nearly 4,500 words and senses, among them *bog-standard*, *maestro*, *muggins*, *mujahideen*, and *phase*. In addition, many etymologies, especially for words of non-European origin, have been revised.

Professor David Crystal has contributed a new essay, 'A Brief History of English', which gives an overview of the development of the language from Old English to the 21st century.

As part of general revision, spelling and orthography have been modernized throughout the text, in many cases by the removal of hyphens in compound nouns. This reflects the evidence of prevailing use and is in line with treatment in the rest of the Oxford dictionaries range. Although the *Shorter* is a historical dictionary that includes words of the past as well as those of today, its definitions are written in contemporary English, and we have updated the defining language where appropriate. Special attention has been given to sensitive terms relating to ethnicity, sexuality, and disability. To this end the usage notes contained in around 1,000 entries have been rewritten, and many new ones added.

A great many people gave generous assistance to the project, both within OUP and outside. We would like to acknowledge the help of the staff of the *Oxford English Dictionary*, in particular Graeme Diamond and his group for their work on new words. Other colleagues deserving special mention are Jude Craft, Anthony Esposito, Gillian Evans, Sara Hawker, Alan Hughes, Nick Rollin, Bill Trumble, and Ben Zimmer. Information on English from outside Britain and the USA was given by Dianne Bardsley, Satarupa Chaudhuri, Tony Deverson, Bruce Moore, Leela Pienaar, and Lise Winer. Stephen Cretney QC advised on our coverage of law terms, and Catherine Sangster of the BBC Pronunciation Unit gave advice on the pronunciation of new entries. We would also like to thank the many people who have corresponded with us, in particular Yukio Ooka of Nagoya, Japan, and V. D. Paulose of Badarpur, India.

A. J. S.

April 2007

A brief history of English by David Crystal

Introduction

Sometime between AD 700 and 800, in Anglo-Saxon England, a scribe compiled a list of 3,200 Latin words and translated 970 of them into Old English. The manuscript is now in the library at Épinal, capital of the Vosges region of north-east France, and is known as the Épinal Glossary. It is in a poor state of preservation: some of the pages are missing, and the tops of several have suffered from wear and damp. But it is a most remarkable document: it is the earliest glossary we have of Old English, and, in its rough-and-ready alphabetical grouping, the earliest known English ancestor of the present Dictionary.

The words come mainly from several Latin Christian sources, such as the Vulgate translation of the Bible, and cover a wide range of topics, as can be seen in these examples from letter A. The Latin word comes first, then the Old English gloss, and I have added a Modern English translation.

LATIN	OLD ENGLISH	MODERN ENGLISH
aleator	*teblere*	gambler
abortus	*misbyrd*	miscarriage
appetitus	*gitsung*	craving
aestuaria	*fleotas*	tidal waters

Glosses are given for plants, animals, illnesses, legal concepts, and many other 'hard words'. It was an important document, influencing several later compilations of a similar kind, and well illustrates the efforts that scribes were taking to bring the latest language to evolve in the British Isles under some sort of practical control.

Where did this language come from? Our main source of information is Bede's *Ecclesiastical History of the English Nation*, written *c.*730:

> This island at present … contains five nations, the English, Britons, Scots, Picts, and Latins, each in its own peculiar dialect cultivating the sublime study of Divine truth. The Latin tongue is, by the study of the Scriptures, become common to all the rest.

Subsequent chapters describe in detail how this situation evolved. The first arrivals, Bede says, were Britons (we would now call them Celts), and they gave their name to the land. The Picts then arrived in the north, from Scythia via northern Ireland, where the resident Scots would not let them stay. The Scots themselves arrived some time later, and secured their own settlements in the Pictish regions. Then, 'in the year of Rome 798' [= AD 43], Emperor Claudius sent an expedition which rapidly established a Roman presence in most of the island.

The Romans ruled there until the early fifth century, when Rome was taken by the Goths, and military garrisons were withdrawn. Attacks on the Britons by the Picts and Scots followed. The Britons appealed to Rome for help, but the Romans, preoccupied with their own wars, could do little. The attacks continued, so the Britons came to a decision. As Bede recounts in Chapters 14 and 15:

> They consulted what was to be done, and where they should seek assistance to prevent or repel the cruel and frequent incursions of the northern nations; and they all agreed with their King Vortigern to call over to their aid, from the parts beyond the sea, the Saxon nation. … Then the nation of the Angles, or Saxons, being invited by the aforesaid king, arrived in Britain with three long ships.

The Anglo-Saxon Chronicle reports their landing in Ebbsfleet (Pegwell Bay, near Ramsgate, Kent) in AD 449. Within 250 years, it would seem from the earliest records, the language we now know as Old English (sometimes called Anglo-Saxon) achieved its distinctive character.

Old English

What was this Germanic language like? Only fragments are immediately intelligible to a modern reader. The orthography devised by missionaries to write the language down made use of a number of symbols and abbreviatory conventions which no longer exist, and these act as a barrier. In the following lines, for example, we see the use of the symbol called 'ash' (æ), a name borrowed from the runic alphabet, representing a sound similar to the vowel sound of *cat* today. And we see the use of another runic symbol called 'thorn' (þ) as well as a symbol (ð) which was later called 'eth' (pronounced as in the first syllable of leather), both of which were used to represent the 'th' sounds in such words as *thin* and *the*. This text is the opening of the Lord's Prayer.

> *fæder ure þu þe eart on heofonum, si þin nama gehalgod, to becume þin rice, gewurþe ðin willa on eorðan swa swa on heofonum.*

If we substitute modern spellings, such as *thu* for *þu* or *eorthan* for *eorðan*, the language becomes a little easier to read—but only a little, because the grammar and vocabulary are still quite alien.

Old English grammar is very different from Modern English, as this literal translation shows:

fæder ure þu þe eart on heofonum
father our thou that art in heaven

si þin nama gehalgod, to becume þin rice,
be thy name hallowed, to become thy kingdom

gewurþe ðin willa on eorðan swa swa on heofonum
be done thy will on earth as as in heaven

The most notable difference is the altered word order, especially the placing of the verb: 'be thy name …', 'become thy kingdom …', 'be done thy will …'. Important too are the endings ('inflections') which appear with some of the nouns: the Old English words for 'heaven' and 'earth' were *heofon* and *eorðe*, but after the preposition *on* we see these words change their form (or 'case'). Certain types of meaning, such as the relationship between words in a sentence, were very largely expressed by inflections. Modern English, by contrast, has very few such inflections; it expresses most meaning relationships either by using extra words or by varying the order of words in a sentence. For example, the meaning of 'who does what to whom' is signalled by changing the order of the words: in 'The man saw the woman', we know that it is the man who is doing the seeing (it is the subject of the clause); in 'The woman saw the man', we know that it is the woman. In Old English, these two sentences would have been like this:

se guma geseah þa cwen	the man saw the woman
seo cwen geseah þone guman	the woman saw the man

Because the endings tell us who did the action and who received the action, the word order can alter without ambiguity. This next sentence is perfectly clear:

geseah þone guman seo cwen	the woman saw the man

Even though the words for 'the woman' appear last, the form of the words tells us that this phrase is nonetheless the subject of the clause.

The other element in the barrier between Old and Modern English is, of course, the alien-looking vocabulary. This is not so noticeable in the Lord's Prayer example, where—*rice* (pronounced 'ree-chuh') and *gewurþe* aside—there are several clear correspondences; but it is immediately obvious in the Épinal glosses, where there is little resemblance to modern usage. And when we take a text that is less familiar, such as the opening lines of the epic poem *Beowulf*, the need for translation is immediately apparent:

Hwæt, we gardena in geardagum,
Lo we of the spear-Danes in days of old

þeodcyninga þrym gefrunon
kings of a people greatness have heard

hu ða æþelingas ellen fremedon.
how the princes deeds of valour carried out.

[Lo! we have heard of the greatness of the kings of the spear-Danes in days of old, how the princes carried out deeds of valour.]

Words like *þeodcyninga*, literally 'people-kings', and *geardagum* 'year-days' illustrate one aspect of Old English vocabulary: two-element words, or 'compounds'. There is another a few lines later: *hronrade* 'whale-road', a vivid metaphor for 'sea'.

Poetic expressions such as *hronrade* illustrate a major feature of Old English linguistic creativity. A ship, for example, might be described straightforwardly as a *scip* or *ceol* ('keel'), but in addition there are descriptions using a variety of compounds—some fairly literal, such as *wægflota* ('wave-floater'), *sægenga* ('sea-goer'), and *brimwudu* ('water-wood'), some more imaginative, such as *merehus* ('sea-house'), *sæhengest* ('sea-steed'), and *yþmearh* ('wave-horse'). Huge leaps of imagination can be seen: the human body is described as a *banhus* or *bancofa* 'bone-house, bone-coffer'; a sword as a *beadoleoma* 'battle-light'; the eye as a *heafodgim* 'head-gem'. The descriptive phrases of Old English are so distinctive that a term from Old Norse poetic treatises, the 'kenning', has been used to describe them.

THE INFLUENCE OF LATIN

In addition to these home-grown creations, Old English borrowed many words from other languages, and from Latin in particular. This trend had begun on the European mainland, where we find dozens of words in the Germanic languages which have come from Latin. They include words for plants and animals (including birds and fish), food and drink, household objects, vessels, coins, metals, items of clothing, settlements, houses, and building materials, as well as several notions to do with military, legal, medical, and commercial matters.

OLD ENGLISH	LATIN ORIGIN	MODERN ENGLISH
butere	*butyrum*	butter
ceaster	*castra*	city
munuc	*monachus*	monk
win	*vinum*	wine

As we move into the period of early Anglo-Saxon settlement in England, we find these semantic areas continuing to expand, with the growing influence of missionary activity reflected in an increase in words to do with religion and learning. This became especially noticeable after the Benedictine revival of the monasteries at the end of the tenth century, when we find such loans as *creda* 'creed' from *credo* and *diacon* 'deacon' from *diaconus*. The emphasis is not surprising: the teaching of the Church had to be communicated to the Anglo-Saxon people, and new vocabulary was needed to express the new concepts, personnel, and organizational procedures.

Borrowing Latin words was not the only way in which the missionaries engaged with this task. Rather more important, in fact, were other linguistic techniques. One method was to take a Germanic word and adapt its meaning so that it expressed the sense of a Latin word: examples include *rod*, originally meaning 'rod, pole', which came to mean 'cross'; and *gast*, originally 'demon, evil spirit', which came to mean 'soul' or 'Holy Ghost'. Another technique, relying on the type of word creation which permeates Old English poetry, was to create new compounds—in this case, by translating the elements of a Latin word into Germanic equivalents: so, *liber evangelii* became *godspellboc* 'gospel book' and *trinitas* became *þriness* 'threeness' = 'trinity'.

THE INFLUENCE OF OLD NORSE

Scandinavia provided another source of words in the Anglo-Saxon period, but only after a considerable passing of time. The Vikings made their presence felt in Britain in the 780s, attacking the south coast, and during the next decade the monasteries in the north. Conflict continued for a century, until the Treaty of Wedmore in 886 between King Alfred and the Danish leader Guthrum established an area of eastern England which, because it was subject to Danish laws, came to be known as the Danelaw. It is evident from the place names which eventually appeared that Danes were present in the whole of the northern and north-eastern third of the country, roughly between Cheshire and Essex. Over 2,000 Scandinavian place names are found throughout the area, chiefly in Yorkshire, Lincolnshire, and the East Midlands. Over 600 end in *-by*, the Old Norse word for 'farmstead' or 'town', as in *Rugby* and *Grimsby*. The other element in such names often refers to a person's name (Hroca's and Grim's farm, in these two cases), but sometimes to general features, as in *Burnby* ('farm by a stream') and *Westerby* ('western farm'). The distribution of Scandinavian family names—such as those that end in *-son* (*Johnson*)—also shows a concentration throughout the Danelaw.

The Treaty of Wedmore contains the first Scandinavian loans known in Old English texts: *healfmarc* 'half a mark' comes from the Scandinavian currency unit, *mǫrk*, and *liesengum*, a variant of *liesing* 'freedmen', comes from *leysingiar*. A few more are found in northern versions of the Anglo-Saxon Chronicle and the Gospels, and in a sprinkling of other sources. But they do not amount to very many. Only about 30 Norse words came into Old English during this period, such as *wrang* 'wrong' from *vrang* and *utlaga* 'outlaw' from *utlagi*. Most are terms reflecting the imposition of Danish law and administration throughout the region, social structure, or cultural objects or practices, such as seafaring and fighting. Very few had enough broad applicability to survive into later periods of English, once Scandinavian culture and power declined. When we count up all the Scandinavian words which entered Old English between the ninth and the twelfth centuries, we arrive at a surprisingly small total—about 150.

But something remarkable was taking place in the period between Old and Middle English. Although there are no written records to show it, a considerable Scandinavian vocabulary was gradually being established in the language. We know that this must have been so because the earliest Middle English literature, from around 1200, shows thousands of Old Norse words being used, especially in texts coming from the northern and eastern parts of the country. They could not suddenly have arrived in the twelfth century, for historically there was no significant connection with Scandinavia at that time; England was under Norman French rule. And as it takes time for loanwords to become established, what we must be seeing is a written manifestation of an underlying current of Old Norse words that had been developing a widespread vernacular use over the course of two centuries or more. There is no doubt that many of these words were well established, because they began to replace some common Anglo-Saxon words. The word for 'take', for example, was *niman* in Old English; Old Norse *taka* is first recorded in an English form, *toc* (= 'took') during the late eleventh century, in the *Anglo-Saxon Chronicle* (year 1072), but by the end of the Middle English period *take* had completely taken over the function of *niman* in general English. The everyday flavour of the Scandinavian loans can be seen in these words, all of which survived into modern Standard English:

cake, dirt, egg, freckle, get, leg, seem, Thursday, window

We must not overrate the impact of Scandinavian words on English: they are only a fraction of the thousands of French words which entered the language during the Middle Ages. Moreover, the majority fell out of use. Modern readers would make no sense of most of the entries in a dictionary of Scandinavian words in Middle English, such as *crus* 'fierce', *goulen* 'scream', and *stor* 'strong'. Yet some of the ones that did survive exercised a disproportionate influence, because (like *take* and *get*) they were very frequently used. And they were supplemented by another set of changes which were even more influential, because they made a permanent impact on the grammar of the language.

The most important of these changes was the introduction of a new set of third person plural pronouns, *they*, *them*, and *their*, which replaced the earlier Old English plural forms *hi*, *him*, and *hira*. Pronouns do not change very often in the history of a language, and to see one set of forms replaced by another is truly noteworthy. Another development was the use of *are* as the third person plural of the verb *to be*. This form had already been used sporadically in northern texts during the late Old English period—for example, in the Lindisfarne Gospels—but in Middle English it steadily moves south, eventually replacing the competing plural forms *sindon* and *be*. *Sindon* disappeared completely by the mid-1200s, but *be* remained in use for several centuries—and indeed may still be encountered today, in such usages as *if they be there* or *the powers that be*.

OTHER INFLUENCES

A few other foreign linguistic elements can be identified in the Old English period. The major impact of French on English would not take place until after the Norman Conquest, but French influence in Britain did not suddenly start in 1066. Trading relationships with the north European mainland had been growing throughout Anglo-Saxon times, and there were religious and political contacts too. During the tenth century there was a renewal of monastic life and learning (the Benedictine revival) which began on the Continent. As a result, we have a sprinkling of French loans recorded in eleventh-century sources: *capun* 'capon' comes from this period, as do a number of words illustrating a more general kind of cultural contact, such as *tumbere* 'dancer', *servian* 'serve', and *prisun* 'prison'.

There is one other source of foreign words in Old English: the other Germanic languages which had been developing in parallel with Old English in other parts of Europe, such as Frisian and Old Saxon. Contacts had been maintained between England and the Baltic territories. English missionaries had worked there, and King Alfred had employed scholars from the European mainland during his cultural revival. A few words in West Saxon have been attributed to that influence, notably *macian* 'make'. And the Old English word for 'island', spelled as *iland* and in other ways, is probably Frisian in origin.

The transition to Middle English

We are lucky to have any evidence of Old English at all. Thousands of manuscripts were destroyed in the Viking invasions. As it is, the surviving material is not very great. Toronto University's *Dictionary of Old English* corpus shows that the entire body of Old English material from 600 to 1150 consists of only 3,037 texts (excluding manuscripts with minor variants), amounting to a mere three million words—not a great deal of data for a period in linguistic history extending over five centuries. A single prolific modern author easily exceeds this total: Charles Dickens's fiction, for example, amounts to over four million. The contrast with the Middle English period, where there is a plethora of texts, is striking.

'Middle English' is a difficult period to identify. Some people define it with reference to historical events, usually selecting the Norman invasion of 1066 as its starting point, and the beginning of the Tudor dynasty, the accession of Henry VII in 1485, as its close. Some use a mixture of literary, linguistic, and cultural criteria, starting with the earliest texts that show significant differences from Old English towards the end of the twelfth century, and finishing with Caxton's introduction of printing towards the end of the fifteenth (1476). Some take 1100 as the starting point; some leave it as late as 1200. But no one feels really comfortable with an identification in terms of boundary points. As the name 'Middle' suggests, we are dealing with a period of transition between two eras that each have stronger definition: Old English and Modern English. Before this period we encounter a language which is chiefly Old Germanic in its character—in its sounds, spellings, grammar, and vocabulary. After this period we have a language which displays a very different kind of structure, with major changes having taken place in each of these areas, many deriving from the influence of French.

However we define it, this period of roughly 300 years is remarkable for its textual fecundity. A huge amount of administrative ephemera built up during the late eleventh century and throughout the twelfth—records of apprenticeship, guild membership, and military conscription (muster rolls), records of assize courts and quarter sessions, enclosure awards, and parish registers. Manorial records, for example, listed such matters as land transfers within a manor, and the names and deaths of tenants. Occasional taxes, or subsidies, were collected by local assessors who kept detailed accounts on behalf of the Exchequer. It might be thought that the vast increase in documentation in Early Middle English is of little importance for the history of English, because they were almost entirely written in Latin. But this is to forget the importance of names—both of people and of places—which can provide a great deal of information about social and regional background. And it would in any case not be long before this documentation began to be written in English.

People often talk about a 'break' between Old and Middle English; but there was never any break. Although the pace of linguistic change between Anglo-Saxon and early medieval times does seem to have been quite rapid, it was still gradual, and we find texts which are amalgams of Old and Middle English and texts which fall 'midway' between Old and Middle English. The eleventh and twelfth centuries have a transitional character of their own. The continuity is mainly to be seen in texts of a religious, political, or administrative character, thousands of which have survived. Most of the surviving material in English is religious in character—about a third are collections of homilies. The writings of Ælfric, in particular, continued to be copied throughout the eleventh and twelfth centuries, and these overlap with sermons from the twelfth century that are very clearly in an early form of Middle English. A copy of the Old English Gospels (Bodleian MS Hatton 38), made in Christ Church, Canterbury, probably in the 1190s, has been called 'the last Old English text'. That is very much later than a manuscript which has been called 'the earliest Middle English text': the *Sermo in festis Sancti Marie uirginis* ('Homily for Feasts of the Blessed Virgin Mary'), a translation of a Latin sermon by Ralph d'Escures, who was Archbishop of Canterbury between 1114 and 1122.

The religious material is of great sociolinguistic significance. If Ælfric's work was still being copied or quoted as late as *c.*1200, this gives us the strongest of hints that the language had not moved so far from Old English as to be totally unintelligible. It is inconceivable that the huge labour involved in copying would have been undertaken if nobody had been able to understand them. On the other hand, we can sometimes sense a growing linguistic difficulty from some of the contemporary decision-making, as when the monks of Worcester requested William of Malmesbury to have the Old English life of Wulfstan translated into Latin—presumably because they found it easier. And sometimes there is a frank admission of failure. Around 1300 we find someone adding the following note in the margin of an Old English text: *non apreciatum propter ydioma incognita*—'not appreciated because unknown language'.

Middle English

Middle English is very different from Old English: it feels familiar. Although the earliest surviving writings in the period are only about a century after the latest writings in Old English, we sense that Middle English texts are very much closer to Modern English. By the time we get to Chaucer, in the fourteenth century, we can find many phrases and sentences which—if we modernize the spelling—look just like an archaic version of Modern English, as in these extracts from *The Reeve's Tale*:

How fares thy fair daughter and thy wife?
And John also, how now, what do ye here?

By contrast, as we saw above, most of the extracts from Old English give the impression of a totally different language, even when the old letters are replaced.

Familiarity is not just a linguistic matter. There is also a continuity of literary content between Middle and Modern English which had not existed previously. English readers today are aware of the subject matter of the Middle English period in a way that they are not in relation to Old English. Chaucer's *Canterbury Tales* have been constantly retold, as has Thomas Malory's account of King Arthur and the knights of the Round Table. Several modern Christmas carols are medieval in origin, and children still learn the verse mnemonic for the number of days in a month, first found in a fifteenth-century collection, albeit in a somewhat different form:

Thirty dayes hath November,
April, June, and September;
Of xxviii is but oon [one],
And all the remenaunt xxx and i.

The difference between Old and Middle English is primarily due to the linguistic changes that took place in grammar. Old English, as we have seen, was a language which contained a great deal of inflectional variation; Modern English has hardly any. And it is during the Middle English period that we see the eventual disappearance of most of the earlier inflections, and the increasing reliance on alternative means of expression, using word order and prepositional constructions rather than word endings to express meaning relationships. All areas of grammar were affected. Among the new kinds of construction were the progressive forms of the verb (as in *I am going*), and the range of auxiliary verbs (*I have seen*, *I didn't go*, etc). The infinitive form of a verb starts to be marked by the use of a particle (*to go*, *to jump*). A new form of expressing relationships such as possession appeared, using *of* (as in *the pages of a book*). In addition, as already noted, several new grammatical forms appeared through the influence of Old Norse.

Other areas of language were also affected. The pronunciation system underwent significant change. We see several consonants and vowels altering their values, and new contrastive units of sound ('phonemes') emerging. In particular, the distinction between the /f/ and /v/ consonants began to differentiate words (e.g. *grief* vs. *grieve*), as did that between /s/ and /z/ (e.g. *seal* vs. *zeal*). The *ng* sound at the end of a word also became contrastive (in Old English the *g* had always been sounded), so we now find such pairs as *sin* vs. *sing*. And at the very end of the period, all the long vowels underwent a series of changes. On top of all this, the way sounds were spelled altered throughout the period, as French scribes introduced their own spelling conventions, such as *ou* for *u* (*house*), *gh* for *h* (*night*), and *ch* for *c* (*church*).

THE INFLUENCE OF FRENCH

The French influence on English in the Middle Ages is second to none—a consequence of the dominance of French power in England and of French cultural pre-eminence in mainland Europe. As a separate tongue, French did not last long in England—by the time of Chaucer it was learned only as a foreign language—and English soon reasserted its position, being used at the opening of Parliament for the first time in 1362. But even though French died out as a language of everyday discourse (at least, by the aristocracy), its influence remained. When English once again came back into public use it had assimilated a great deal of the language which had previously been the medium of power.

By the end of the twelfth century people were already trying to use English to cope with the unfamiliar domains of expression introduced by the Normans. The pressure was growing to use English, but there was no suitable English to use. Writers could not rely on the vernacular varieties available from earlier times, such as had evolved to meet the needs of chronicle history and religion, because the ancient language was no longer in use: Old English had become Middle English. And in the case of the domains most affected by the Norman invaders, such as law, architecture, estate management, music, and literature, there was a new, francophone vision to be expressed. Here, an Anglo-Saxon perspective, with all its associated vocabulary and conceptualization, was irrelevant. People had no alternative but to develop new varieties of expression, adopting Continental models, and adapting traditional genres to cope with the French way of doing things.

The development of new domains of expression involves all aspects of language. A distinctive vocabulary is the most noticeable feature—clusters of words introduced to express sets of related concepts. In ecclesiastical architecture, for example, French architects in England adapted Continental sources for their cathedral designs, so that in due course the buildings are better described as Romanesque or Gothic rather than Early English. The associated specialist terminology needed to express this fundamental shift of vision was very large, covering everything from building tools to aesthetic abstractions. But the 'language of buildings' involves far more than vocabulary. New words from abroad bring new patterns of sound, so pronunciation changes. These pronunciations need to be written down, so new spellings appear. The character of phrases and sentences also changes, with the adoption of foreign compounds, idioms, formulaic expressions, and other multi-word constructions. And individual authors, schools, and genres influence general patterns of style.

A MULTILINGUAL CHARACTER

During the Middle Ages in Britain, educated English people were trilingual as a matter of course. English would have been their mother tongue. They would have learned Latin as the required language of the Church, the Roman Classics, most scholarship, and some politico-legal matters. And they would have found French essential both for routine administrative communication within Britain and in order to be considered fashionable throughout Western European society. The twelfth-century Renaissance reinforced this situation: it affected all areas of knowledge, and new language emerged to express fresh thinking in such domains as theology, philosophy, logic, law, cosmology, medicine, and mathematics. A renewal of interest in the Classics and the nature of ancient learning increased the prestige of Latin; but other languages—notably, Arabic and Greek—also received fresh attention.

The trilingual situation would not last. As the Middle Ages progressed, we find English gradually making inroads into domains of discourse which had previously been the prerogative of Latin or French. Legal English, medical English, philosophical English, literary English, parliamentary English, and other varieties started to appear, and quite quickly evolved the distinctive and sophisticated styles of expression still used today. But in every domain the new vernacular displays the influence of its linguistic antecedents, and by the end of the Middle English period the Germanic element in the English vocabulary had been firmly put in the shade by a Romance and Italic lexical invasion of unprecedented proportions.

The combined influence of French and Latin—with French at the outset by far the more important—radically altered the character of the language. The impact was most noticeable in vocabulary, though all aspects of language were affected to some degree. Around the year 1000, non-Germanic words in English could be numbered in the hundreds; by 1500 the language had incorporated tens of thousands. The words entered English through both written and spoken mediums, and at various stylistic levels within each medium. Many loans were general in character, but some were informal, and others were technical. Large numbers of terms related to specialized domains, such as horse-riding, law, religion, politics, society, and culture.

French words began as a trickle and soon became a stream and then a flood. In the mid-twelfth-century *Peterborough Chronicle* we find only 29 new words, and they belong to just a few domains of discourse. There are religious words such as *cardinal* and *miracle*; words to do with social position such as *duc* 'duke' and *curt* 'court'; administrative words such as *canceler* 'chancellor' and *rent*; and general terms of law and politics such as *iustise* 'justice' and *pais* 'peace'. The numbers quickly increase. In a text probably written less than fifty years later, but with no manuscripts extant earlier than the early thirteenth century, we find nearly 250. This is *Ancrene Riwle* ('Anchorites' Rule'), also known as *Ancrene Wisse* ('Anchorites' Guide'), a lengthy work providing spiritual direction for a group of three female recluses. Of particular note is that the religious subject matter has motivated many specialized terms, such as *grace* and *scrowe* 'scroll'. There is a large increase in abstract words, especially to do with morality and behaviour, such as *chastete* 'chastity', *kurteisie* 'courtesy', and *largesse* 'generosity'. But there are also many everyday words, such as *avancen* 'advance', *broche* 'brooch', *cite* 'city', *flur* 'flower', *jurneie* 'journey', *manere* 'manner', and *tendre* 'tender'.

Middle English also saw a huge increase in the use of affixes (prefixes and suffixes). Excluding inflectional endings, there are just over 100 prefixes and suffixes available for use in everyday English, and at least one of these will be found in 40–50 per cent of all the words in the language. It is during Middle English that we find the first great flood of these affixed words, with French introducing such (Latin-derived) prefixes as *con-*, *de-*, *dis-*, *en-*, *ex-*, *pre-*, *pro-*, and *trans-*, and such suffixes as *-able*, *-ance*/*-ence*, *-ant*/*-ent*, *-ity*, *-ment*, and *-tion* (at the time usually spelled *-cion*). The suffixes were especially productive, as seen in the many words typified by *tournament*, *defendant*, *solemnity*, and *avoidance*. The *-tion* ending alone produced hundreds of creations, such as *damnation*, *contemplation*, and *suggestion*. Prefixes, as seen in *conjoin*, *disobedient*, and *enchant*, were important too, but not so widespread; we have to wait until the end of the Middle English period before we find a comparable explosion in their use.

Each of the major literary works of the Middle English period provides evidence of the way new French loans were continuing to arrive and older loans being consolidated. Some texts contain relatively few such words, and some contain many, but all texts have some. By the time we reach the opening lines of *The Canterbury Tales*, the French lexical content (italicized below) is a major linguistic feature:

> When that *Aprill* with his shoures soote
> The droghte of *March* hath *perced* to the roote,
> And bathed every veyne in swich *licour*
> Of which *vertu engendred* is the *flour* ...
>
> [When April with its sweet showers has pierced the drought of March to the root, and bathed every vein in such liquid from which strength the flower is engendered]

It is difficult to be precise about the number of French words entering English during Middle English, because no dictionary has yet found it possible to take into account the lexical content of the thousands of manuscripts which exist, and many words and senses await identification. We also have to remember that some words which did arrive had a very short lifespan, often being used just once, or having a recorded history of only a few decades or centuries. But in order to assess the general impact of French on English we can nonetheless gain a great deal of relevant information by examining the earliest recorded instances of words contained in the unabridged *Oxford English Dictionary* (*OED*). Between 1250 and 1450 just over 27,000 words are identified as having a first recorded usage in at least one sense in a particular year, and (excluding the derived forms, such as *advisedly* from *advise*) around 22 per cent of these are words of French origin. The peak of borrowing was the last quarter of the fourteenth century, when over 2,500 French words are identified. By the end of the Middle English period we find that—regardless of exactly when the words came into the language, and including the derived forms—around 30 per cent of English vocabulary is French in origin.

The flow of French loanwords into English reduced during the fifteenth century, but the overall rate of foreign borrowing did not, because of the growing influence of Latin. Indeed, thanks chiefly to its role as the language of scholarship and science, Latin words would eventually have a much greater impact on English than French: today, just over 30,000 words (excluding derived forms) have French identified as part of their history in the *OED*; for Latin, the corresponding figure is over 50,000.

As the language of the Church, medieval scholarship, and early political administration, many of these are technical terms or part of a domain's standard nomenclature. Here is a representative sample from some of the chief domains. (In several cases, such as the names of many minerals, Latin is being used as a 'relay' language, re-expressing a term which was originally found in Greek.)

alchemy: dissolve, distillation, elixir, essence, ether, mercury

astronomy: ascension, comet, eccentric, equator, equinox, intercept

biology: asp, cicada, juniper, locust, lupin, pine

language and literacy: allegory, clause, index, neuter, scribe, simile

law: client, debenture, executor, gratis, legitimate, proviso

medicine: diaphragm, digit, dislocate, ligament, orbit, saliva

mineralogy: antimony, arsenic, chrysolite, garnet, lapis lazuli, mineral

religion: collect, diocese, lector, limbo, redemptor, psalm.

In literature a style developed in which authors attempted to emulate the great Classical writers, with intricate sentence patterns and erudite, euphonious vocabulary. The fifteenth-century poet John Lydgate described it as 'aureate'.

Although French and Latin were the major influences on English vocabulary in the Middle Ages, we must not forget that other foreign language sources also contributed to its growing lexical diversity. Scandinavian words had begun to surface in Middle English, as we have seen, and we also find a sprinkling of loanwords from other European languages. Contact with the Netherlands, both abroad and as a result of Flemish settlement by weavers and farmers in England and Wales, brought in some Dutch words from as early as the end of the thirteenth century—*poll* ('head') was one of the first, and later borrowings included *bounce*, *booze*, *dote*, *hobble*, *kit*, and *splint*. Maritime contacts brought in such words as *buoy*, *deck*, *hoist*, and *skipper*. Within the British Isles Celtic words continued to provide a small but steady trickle: Welsh *crag*, Irish *kern* (a type of foot soldier), Scottish Gaelic *clan*. And Celtic words arrived from the Continent, too: *gravel*, *lawn*, *truant*, and *vassal* are some of the Gaulish words which first entered French and thereby came into English.

French found itself in the position of being a relay language very often during the Middle Ages. In the Middle English period virtually all loanwords from languages other than French and Latin were French-mediated. These included words from the other Romance languages, such as *marmalade* from Portuguese, *cordwain* from Spanish, and *brigand* from Italian. *Sable* arrived from Russian. *Bible*, *character*, *horizon*, *tragedy*, and many others came from Greek. A large number came from the Middle East. From Arabic we find a virtual alphabet of forms, from *admiral* to *zenith*, and the distinctive *al-* forms begin to appear, as in *alchemy* and *almanac*. From Persian we find *azure* and *taffeta*, as well as several terms to do with the game of chess: *check*, *rook*, *checkmate*—and *chess* itself. It is not until the sixteenth century, following the growth in continental travel and trade, an increased awareness of European literature and the Italian Renaissance, and a renewed interest in Classical authors, that we find words from a range of other languages coming into English directly.

When we combine all these sources of vocabulary we begin to get a sense of the scale of the lexical change that had taken place during Middle English. At the end of the Old English period the size of the lexicon stood at something over 50,000 different words. Many words then fell out of use, but the rate of replacement was such that by the end of the Middle English period we see this total doubled; and the Early Modern English period would more than double it again. By 1450 something like half of the available word stock was non-Germanic. Thanks to the nature of English grammar, which continued to give a high profile to such words as *the*, *of*, *and*, and *have*, the fundamental Anglo-Saxon character of the language was maintained. And in vocabulary, too, if we were to order Middle English words in terms of their frequency of use, we would find that around half of the most commonly used words were from Old English.

The real importance of the Middle English period was the way in which this additional vocabulary became the primary means of introducing new concepts and new domains of discourse into the language, as well as giving novel ways of expression to familiar concepts within old domains of discourse. The period was offering people a much greater linguistic choice. In 1200 people could only *ask*; by 1500 they could *question* (from French) and *interrogate* (from Latin) as well. What could be done with such new-found linguistic opportunities? During Middle English we see the evolution of a language which is increasingly exploiting the potentialities of regional, social, and stylistic variation. At one extreme there was a learned, literary style, typically formal and elaborate, characterized by a lexicon of French and Latin origin, and employed by the aristocratic and well educated; at the other, there was an everyday, popular style, typically informal and casual, full of words with Germanic roots, and used by ordinary folk.

The poets of the period provide the clearest evidence of the growth in stylistic awareness taking place in Middle English. Chaucer is the primary source because his undisputed pre-eminence in portraying the range of his social milieu has a linguistic reflex in his ability to give so many language varieties of the time a literary presence. Although overlaid with stylistic features of a specifically poetic kind—notably, a remarkable creativity in the use of different metres, verse forms, and rhetorical figures of speech—his characters, belonging to different classes, occupations, and regional backgrounds, come alive in a way that had not previously been seen in English. A little later the poets would be joined by Thomas Malory, whose Arthurian saga raised the level of achievement for narrative prose. And there would be the proliferation of mini-dramas in the play cycles of York, Wakefield, and elsewhere. It was an age, in short, when literary genres were maturing, becoming recognizable and imitable.

THE RISE OF STANDARD ENGLISH

Middle English illustrates an age when all dialects were equal, in the sense that the written language permitted the use of a wide range of variant forms, reflecting the regional backgrounds of the authors, all of which were acceptable. But without a standard to act as a guide, texts present a remarkable number of orthographic variations. A selection of spellings for *day*, for example, includes *dai*, *day*, *daye*, *dæi*, *deai*, *dey*, *dei*, and *dawe*. By 1400 a sense of communicative difficulty must have been present within the literate community. People were trying to work with a written language where variation had become so uncontrolled that words could be spelled in dozens of different ways. A scribe might write a form, and it would be impossible to say whether it was an intentional usage or a mistake. Things could not go on like this. People needed a standard.

The need grew during the fourteenth century, as English became the language of the nation and thus had to be used in a wide range of social settings throughout the country. And by this time a candidate dialect had evolved. The south-east, and in particular the east Midlands area with focal points in London, Oxford, and Cambridge, had become a region of special cultural influence. As a result, the speech of the south-east—or, at least, of those south-easterners in routine contact with the worlds of courtly culture, commerce, and learning—increased in prestige, and began to be evaluated as a more polished, elegant, and altogether more desirable medium of communication than the varieties available elsewhere.

Another indication of the need for a standard is the development of literacy. By the beginning of the fifteenth century the ability to read and write was no longer the province of an aristocratic and scholarly elite, but was becoming widespread among the new middle classes. Some 10 per cent of the male population could sign their names in 1500; this had doubled by 1550 (the corresponding figures for women were 1 and 5 per cent). Although verse was much more popular than prose, and courtly tales in particular, it was not only creative literature which was being read. Homes were acquiring manuscripts of many kinds, as well as producing their own in the form of letters, journals, and business papers. Religious literature was receiving a wide secular circulation. There were manuscripts dealing with medicine, domestic affairs, and pastimes. Ballads, folktales, and secular lyrics were popular. So too were histories, reports of current affairs, and accounts of exotic travel abroad. Educational resources proliferated, such as dictionaries, grammars (of Latin and French), reading primers, and alphabet books. And once printing arrived, in 1476, the availability of home reading material, from Bibles to epic romances, greatly increased. Printing exposed people, far more than had been possible previously, to writing whose source lay outside their locality. The climate needed for the emergence of a standard variety of the language was slowly being formed.

For the basis of a standard language to have emerged so quickly during the fifteenth century, its roots must already have been present in a broad cross-section of society. There must have been a growing sense of shared usage, as individual scribes with different backgrounds came into contact with each other. Language change then will have been no different from language change now, and today sociolinguists have repeatedly drawn attention to the important role social networks play in fostering the diffusion of features throughout a community. Norms quickly grow when a social network is dense—that is, when many people interact regularly and frequently—and the network to which scriveners belonged in fifteenth-century London was, by all accounts, of great density. Large numbers of people were involved in literary activities in the city area.

Individuals belong to more than one network; and literary authors perhaps more than most. When it comes to discussing the sources of influence upon the development of the standard language, it makes no sense to draw sharp dividing lines around the concept of 'literature'. If we wish, we may talk about Chaucer having an influence on the development of the language; but if we do so we must remember that Chaucer was not only a poet, he was also a civil servant—first as a controller of customs in the port of London, later as a clerk of the king's works—as well as a soldier, diplomat, intelligence officer, and parliamentarian. And the same point applies to any of the clusters of scriveners who worked together in those days. If we identify one group as being potentially of great significance, as in the case of the clerks of Chancery, we must not forget that several other groups were also influential. The teaching institutions, in particular, must have been important—the big London grammar schools and convents. Chancery writers would have mixed with teachers, clerics, merchants, and lawyers from the Inns of Court, along with the clerks who worked for them, and been familiar with current linguistic trends.

The influence of the capital made itself increasingly felt throughout the country, through the medium of English. The amount of written record-keeping and correspondence to support a national administrative framework was enormous, especially after the thirteenth century, when the making of copies of important documents became routine. Written material emanating from the civil service, law offices, ecclesiastical bodies, and business centres always operates with a rather special cachet. It is likely to be important and authoritative, and the language in which it is written will be formal. In the fifteenth century most such missives would have originated in London, and whatever linguistic norms were developing there would have been slowly but persistently transmitted around the country. All regions would have been exposed to them, and this would have been the first contact most people had with a written English from outside of their own locality.

By the end of the Middle English period there had been a fundamental change in the literary and linguistic climate in England. There was also a greater consciousness about the nature of English. One consequence was a growing sense that English was not as 'good' as French and Latin, and needed to be improved—a mindset which became a dominant theme of the sixteenth century. And in due course it was the massive borrowing of vocabulary from French which became the chief butt of criticism. The arrival of loanwords may have made the language elegant, in the eyes and ears of some, but it also made it alien. This difference of opinion came to the surface in the sixteenth century, when, for the first time, we see fashion exercising a real influence on the developing standard.

Early Modern English

The linguistic jump from Middle English to Modern English is too great to make in one step, and for this reason scholars have identified a transitional period which usually goes under the name of Early Modern English. It is fairly easy to assign a conventional date to the beginning of this period; less easy to say when it ends. The introduction of the printing press into England is an event of acknowledged significance, and several accounts recognize 1476 for a starting point. Others opt for an earlier onset, such as the death of Chaucer (1400) or the century midpoint (1450); and some a later one, attracted by the nicely rounded appeal of 1500. Candidates for the end point have been even more various, offering the date of the first declaration of American independence (1776), the date of publication of Dr Johnson's *Dictionary* (1755) or some other significant literary work of the time, or the century midpoint (1750). 1700 has appealed to some, as has 1800. A few writers avoid precise dates altogether, preferring a less specific time reference, such as 'fifteenth to eighteenth century', a historical notion such as 'Renaissance English', or a descriptive statement such as 'English from Caxton to Johnson'.

The common focus for the end of the period is evidently the eighteenth century, and from a strictly linguistic point of view it is indeed possible to sense a qualitative difference between 1700 (which plainly is within the Early Modern English period) and 1800 (which plainly is not). The spelling, punctuation, grammar, and vocabulary of Jane Austen or William Hazlitt are appreciably closer to Modern English than is the language of John Dryden or Jonathan Swift. But more important than the structural changes which were taking place in English at the time are the changes in attitude towards the language, in particular the emergence of an explicit prescriptivism midway through what has been called the 'century of manners', and the clear recognition, as a consequence, of what a 'correct English' should be. Publications such as Bishop Robert Lowth's *Short Introduction to English Grammar* (1762) and John Walker's *Pronouncing Dictionary of English* (1774), along with Johnson's *Dictionary* (1755), identify a two-decade period which, sociolinguistically speaking, was a defining moment, after which things were never the same again.

The Early Modern English period is essentially an age of linguistic awareness and anxiety, in which Caxton's writing represents a dawning appreciation that the language is in a mess and needs sorting out, and the rise of the prescriptive movement represents the feeling that the matter is about to be satisfactorily resolved. It was during the sixteenth century that anxiety levels about the nature of the English language rose noticeably. People began to 'notice' the language, and many did not like what they saw. Printers, spelling reformers, and biblical translators were uncertain and confused, both about the state of the language and about the direction in which it seemed to be moving. But the malaise was general, attracting comment from writers of diverse backgrounds. Everyone, whether expert in linguistic matters or not, felt entitled to have an opinion—as indeed they still do today.

The most general worry in the early part of the period was whether English could really carry out the range of communicative functions that French and Latin had previously performed. As early as Caxton's time we find it routine to comment about English being 'symple and rude', whereas French would be described as 'fayr', and although these comments were usually conventional, self-effacing expressions, they helped to inculcate a mindset that the language was inferior. The solution to the problem seemed straightforward. If languages like French and Latin were superior to English, then English would automatically improve its quality by adopting their properties, such as their vocabulary, balanced sentence construction, and features of rhetoric. As early as 1531 we find the writer and diplomat Sir Thomas Elyot (in *The boke named the Gouernour*) commending 'the necessary augmentation of our language', pointing out that once people started using 'strange and darke' words they would soon become 'facile to vnderstande'.

Latin was the chief source of new words. There had been a steady trickle of Latin borrowings into English throughout the Middle English period, but during the fifteenth century their number greatly increased, and in the sixteenth century they became so numerous, along with words from Greek, that the character of the English lexicon was permanently altered. The linguistic development reflected a cultural and cognitive shift. The period from the time of Caxton until around 1650 was later to be called the 'Renaissance'. It included not only a 'rebirth of learning', in the sense of a renewal of connection with classical languages, literatures, and the arts, but also a rethinking of religious and scientific values, as seen in the

Reformation and the discoveries of Copernicus, as well as an expansion of global horizons through the European explorations of Africa, the Americas, and the Far East. There were few words in English to talk precisely about the new perspectives, concepts, techniques, and products which were being seen in Europe or further afield; but the classical languages, increasingly encountered through translations, presented a solution, offering hundreds of Latin and Greek words which could be readily adapted. Writers such as Elyot went out of their way to 'enrich' the language with classically derived words, to enable the new learning to become accessible to the English public.

New varieties of discourse developed as English took over the range of functions previously performed by French and Latin. Legal, scientific, religious, educational, medical, and other 'institutions' developed their distinctive modalities of expression. The 'language of law' is one domain which had begun to develop its own stylistic norms during Middle English, and parallel developments were taking place elsewhere. The glossaries compiled by translators show the range of specialist usage which was emerging, in such fields as alchemy, architecture, fencing, grammar, heraldry, hunting, navigation, and military science. From anatomy, biology, and medicine, for example, we find *larynx*, *pancreas*, *pneumonia*, *skeleton*, *tibia*, and *virus*. Borrowings greatly facilitate stylistic differentiation because they provide synonyms with different sense associations and tonal resonances. Although *hearing* (from the early twelfth century) and *audition* (first recorded use, 1599) basically mean the same thing, the later word came to be used in more intellectual and scientific settings, and developed a greater formality of tone and eventually a distinctive range of meanings.

It is difficult to be definite about the rate at which the neologisms came into Early Modern English. Traditional linguistic indices, such as the *OED*, are only a partial guide because some periods have been covered more thoroughly than others, and a literary bias privileges the later part of the period, when authors such as Spenser, Shakespeare, and Jonson began to write. There is no doubt, however, that this was an age of particularly rapid vocabulary growth, and that Latin was the dominant source: about two-thirds of all borrowing at the time was from that language—a momentum which continued until late in the seventeenth century, when still a third of all borrowing was from Latin. Latin was also the means of entry for many words which ultimately came from Greek. A huge number of words from these two languages entered the general vocabulary, as this short selection illustrates:

> absurdity, adapt, appropriate, benefit, chaos, commemorate, crisis, disability, encyclopedia, exaggerate, fact, habitual, immediate, invitation, malignant, offensive, official, relaxation, relevant, skeleton, species, susceptible, temperature, vacuum.

The presence of suffixes should be noted, and of some suffixes in particular. For example, two-thirds of all verbs which came into the language at the time ended in *-ate*, as did many adjectives.

Elyot had described the classical words as 'strange and darke', and it was precisely those properties which made them appeal to many writers and speakers. But others strongly objected to them, calling them *inkhorn* ('inkpot') terms. In the fifteenth century other words had been used to describe classical borrowings, such as 'ornate' and 'aureate', but the phrase 'inkhorn terms' seemed to appeal more to the imagination, in its scornful suggestion that the words were lengthy and therefore used up more ink. Some people condemned all borrowings, and demanded their removal. Sir John Cheke, for example, writes in a letter (1557):

> I am of the opinion that our tung shold be written cleane and pure, vnmixt and vnmangeled with borowing of other tunges.

He would have been unable to achieve the desired purity even in his own writing. In this sentence alone Cheke used four words of Latin or French origin: *opinion*, *mix*, *mangle*, and *pure*.

In the inkhorn debate both sides won: many Latinate words stayed, and many disappeared. A little-understood system of checks and balances operates in language, as the centrifugal forces which introduce variation and change compete with the centripetal forces which keep people communicating with each other, and we can see it operating in Early Modern English. Over a third of all neologisms which entered the language at that time are not recorded after 1700. They include:

> accersite ('summon'), cohibit ('restrain'), deruncinate ('weed'), dominicall ('lordly'), eximious ('excellent'), suppeditate ('supply').

It remains a lexicological puzzle why some words were accepted and some rejected. Both *impede* and *expede* were introduced during the period, as well as *disabuse* and *disadorn*, but in each of these pairs the first item stayed in the language and the second did not. We do not know how to account for this linguistic 'survival of the fittest'.

As the century progressed, more balanced views began to appear, along with defences of the increasingly mixed character of the language. The matter was put into its historical perspective by William Harrison, in *Description of Britaine* (1587). In Chapter 6, 'Of the languages spoken in this Iland', he sums up the contemporary situation: 'Ours is a meane ['in-between'] language, and neither too rough nor too smooth in vtterance.'

By the end of the century it was widely held that the language had succeeded in making good its deficiencies. Handbooks of rhetoric, modelled on Latin, had shown how English could be made more ornate, and a literature of impressive poetry and drama was accumulating in the work of Shakespeare and his contemporaries. A principle of decorum was widely advocated, characterized by such properties as proportion, harmony, brevity, order, naturalness, and vitality. As a result, a sharper sense of stylistic differentiation emerged. The prestige of the south-east of England was now undisputed. As William Harrison put it, 'This excellencie of the English toong is found in one, and the south part of this Iland.'

A clear sense of a southern standard now existed in people's minds. And during the sixteenth century the use of regional dialect for the literary expression of serious subject matter went into a long period of hibernation.

WIDENING HORIZONS

Latin and Greek were not the only sources of loanwords in the sixteenth century. The Renaissance brought a widening of horizons—indeed, English horizons had never reached so far or in so many directions. Words were introduced from all the major European languages. French continued to be a source of supply, either directly or as a 'relay' language, channelling words from further afield, such as *anatomy*, *detail*, *equip*, *passport*, *ticket*, and *volunteer*. Words which came from or via Italian include *argosy*, *balcony*, *carnival*, *concerto*, *grotto*, *lottery*, *macaroni*, *opera*, *sonnet*, *soprano*, *stanza*, and *volcano*. And there were many from or via Spanish and Portuguese, such as *alligator*, *armada*, *banana*, *cannibal*, *canoe*, *cocoa*, *guitar*, *mosquito*, *mulatto*, *negro*, *potato*, *sherry*, *sombrero*, and *tobacco*. In this last list many of the words ultimately come from South or Central American Indian languages: *canoe* and *potato*, for example, are from the Caribbean languages Carib and Taino via Spanish.

The atmosphere of global exploration is unmistakable. By 1600 there had been plenty of time for words to arrive via Spanish or Portuguese: the first voyages of Columbus and Cabot had been a century before, in 1492 and 1497. Direct loans into English, however, had to wait for the first English settlement. The first expedition from Britain to Virginia was not until 1587, and it took another twenty years before there was a permanent English presence. Even so, that initial contact introduced a few words from North American Indian languages; the first records of *skunk*, *cashaw* (a squash), and *manitou* (a deity) are 1588. After 1607 we find a number of other Algonquian words, such as *totem*, *moose*, *opossum*, *tomahawk*, *caribou*, and *moccasin*.

The explorations on the other side of the world likewise brought in new vocabulary from several languages, in some cases expanding the presence of a language source known from earlier times. Quite a few Arabic words, for example, had come into Middle English, especially reflecting scientific notions, but in the sixteenth century there is a significant expansion, reflecting the contacts with North Africa and the Middle East. In many cases, the Arabic words enter English through another language: *assassin*, for example, is ultimately from Arabic *hashshashin* 'hashish-eaters', but came to English via Italian *assassino*. The new words generally reflect an encounter with the various aspects of culture and religion, as in *alcove*, *civet*, *emir*, *fakir*, *harem*, *hashish*, *hegira*, *jar*, *magazine*, *mameluke*, *muezzin*, *sheikh*, *sherbet*, *sofa*, and *tariff*. Other countries of the region also became a lexical source, sometimes directly, sometimes via another European language or Latin. Such cases include:

> coffee, horde, janissary, kaftan, kiosk, koumiss, pasha, vizier, yogurt (*Turkish*)
>
> hallelujah, midrash, mishna, sanhedrin, shekel, shibboleth, torah (*Hebrew*)
>
> bazaar, caravan, cummerbund, dervish, divan, lascar, shah, turban (*Persian*).

The British East India Company was established in India in 1600, and travel to the region greatly increased. From the north of the Indian subcontinent, where Indo-European languages are spoken, such as Hindi, we accordingly find such seventeenth-century words as *bungalow*, *chintz*, *cot*, *dungaree*, *guru*, *juggernaut*, *punch* (the drink), *pundit*, *rupee*, and *sahib*. And from the south, where Dravidian languages are spoken, such as Tamil, we find such words as *atoll*, *calico*, *catamaran*, *cheroot*, *copra*, *curry*, *mango*, *pariah*, and *teak*. In the Far East, Tibetan, Malay, Chinese, Japanese, and other languages all began to supply new items, such as *bamboo*, *cockatoo*, *gingham*, *ginseng*, *ketchup*, *kimono*, *lama*, *lychee*, *sago*, and *shogun*. The African connection, via the Portuguese or French, was less productive. It did bring a few English loans by the end of the sixteenth century, such as *yam* and *banana*, and during the following century we find a few more, such as *harmattan* and *zebra*. But significant borrowing from African languages does not take place until the 'scramble for Africa' in the nineteenth century.

Although processes of word formation had been much used in previous stages of the language, they were particularly active between 1500 and 1700, accounting for almost a half of all new words. Suffixation was the primary means employed, chiefly in the formation of new nouns and adjectives (e.g. *-ness*, *-er*, *-tion*, *-ment*, *-ship*), but also helping to form verbs (notably with *-ize*) and adverbs (with *-ly*). The *-ness* and *-er* endings (the latter in various senses) were especially popular, appearing in about half of all the new nouns (e.g. *delightfulness*, *bawdiness*, *togetherness*; *caterer*, *villager*, *disclaimer*). The literary authors of the period massively exploited the expressive potential of affixation and compounding. Moreover, affixes were used to coin words even if a perfectly satisfactory word for the same concept already existed, as in the case of *immenseness* (1610) alongside *immensity* (1450), and *delicateness* (1530) alongside *delicacy* (1374). Usually, in such competitions, the earlier form won; but the naturalness of the *-ness* ending still surfaces today: in casual speech, we occasionally hear non-standard forms such as *immediateness* and *immenseness*.

The Early Middle English period is still at an early stage of investigation, compared with Middle English, but it was a period of particular significance, especially in the creation of English vocabulary. The indications are that about four times as many words were introduced between 1500 and 1700 as between 1200 and 1500. The increase is partly a function of the greater number and survivability of texts, as a result of printing: nearly 160,000 early printed titles are listed in the standard catalogues of the period. But it is also a matter of authorial inventiveness, for the late sixteenth and early seventeenth centuries contain some of the most lexically creative authors in English literature. After their attentions, the language emerges with a new and confident character. And several basic linguistic notions—such as dialect, variety, and style—would come to be viewed in a fresh light at the end of the literary 'golden age'.

Whatever the feelings writers expressed about the inferiority of English compared to other languages at the beginning of the sixteenth century, these had largely disappeared by the end. During the Early Modern English period the English lexicon grew from around 100,000 to over 200,000 items. (It would double again, during the eighteenth and nineteenth centuries, as a result of the Industrial Revolution and scientific progress.) The classical origins of much of the new vocabulary sharpened writers' sense of style, widening the range of choices which were available to characterize 'high' and 'low' levels of discourse, and offering the option of intermediate levels. Professional domains, such as science, law, and medicine, developed their expressive capabilities, becoming increasingly standardized. And standardization within the language as a whole made significant progress. All this was reinforced by an increased awareness of the nature of language and of linguistic performance, as seen in such treatises as Philip Sidney's *Defence of Poesie* (1595). The language was undoubtedly richer, in quantitative terms, than it had ever been.

The Elizabethan age had given the language literary eminence, and authors such as Shakespeare, Marston, Nashe, and Spenser created thousands of new words in the process. The Shakespearean ones, such as *assassination* and *incardinate*, are often referred to—there are some 1,700 of them. The other authors are less often illustrated. About 500 or so words have a first recorded use in Spenser, for example. Among those which entered the language are *amenable, baneful, blandishment, chirruping, cheerless, dismay, heart-piercing, heedless, indignant, jovial, lambkin, lawlessness, life-blood, suffused, tambourine,* and *thrilling*. He had a great liking for new adjectives in *-ful*, adding it to verbs as well as the more usual nouns, but hardly any survived:

> adviceful, avengeful, baneful, chanceful, choiceful, corruptful, deviceful, discordful, dislikeful, dueful, dureful, entreatful, gazeful, grudgeful, groanful, listful, mazeful, rewardful, sdeignful, senseful, spoilful, toilful, tradeful, tuneful, vauntful, wreckful.

Spenser is a good example of how an individual author's stylistic preferences do not always have a permanent effect on a language. There can be a big gap between what an author wants to say and what the community thinks is routinely worth saying.

ATTEMPTS AT CONTROL

Today we celebrate the lexical expansion and innovation of the Early Modern English period, but as that period came to a close the opposite opinion was widely expressed. Many people felt that the language was out of control and was descending into chaos. The statesman Philip Stanhope, Earl of Chesterfield, for example, wrote in 1754: 'It must be owned that our language is at present in a state of anarchy.'

And Samuel Johnson, in the Preface to his *Dictionary* (1755) concurred:

> When I took the first survey of my undertaking, I found our speech copious without order, and energetick without rules: wherever I turned my view, there was perplexity to be disentangled, and confusion to be regulated; choice was to be made out of boundless variety, without any established principle of selection.

This impression was partly a reflection of population growth. At the end of the Early Modern English period there was a remarkable doubling of the population of England. From about 2.5 million in 1550, we see a rise to some 5 million by 1650, and a further significant increase to about 6 million by 1700. Immigration to London continued, so that by 1650 the number of people living in the capital had reached 400,000, and 575,000 by 1700, making it the largest city in Western Europe. But more dramatic than this was the rise in urban growth which was beginning to take place outside London. It is in the Hanoverian era (after 1714) that we encounter the rise of cities in Central Scotland and South Wales, the ports of Liverpool, Bristol, and Glasgow, the manufacturing centres of Birmingham, Leeds, and Manchester, and the leisure resorts of Bath, Scarborough, and Brighton. Nor should we forget Ireland, part of Britain at the time: in the seventeenth century Dublin was the second largest city in the British Isles.

Population growth has obvious implications for language. As social groups grow within a township, subgroups proliferate, based on geography, social structure, and social networks. Notions such as 'East End', 'south of the river', and 'well-to-do area' become current. *Ghetto* is first recorded in 1611, with reference to the Jewish quarter of a city; *suburban* in 1625. Differences between townships become more marked, and more noticeable, as people move more about the country and encounter how 'other people' live. In the 1700s we see improved roads and methods of transportation significantly reducing travel times, and increasing the number of journeys.

Britain had never seen such an increase in the numbers of regional speakers as took place in the seventeenth and eighteenth centuries. We might interpret this as a sign of linguistic vitality; but what one person sees as an enriching diversity another person sees as a divisive fragmentation. To the observers of the time, such as Swift and Chesterfield, this was further evidence that the language was headed for disaster.

It was not just the increase in numbers which was significant; it was the increase in the social character of those numbers. These were not all rustics. They were businessmen, merchants, and industrialists, an increasingly powerful sector of society, whose numbers would be further swelled as the Industrial Revolution progressed. They were also an increasingly literate section of society: by 1700 nearly half of the male population and a quarter of the female population of England were able to read and write. And they were an increasingly genteel section of society. The growth of the gentry, a class below the peerage, had been one of the most important developments of the late Middle Ages, and it became a major feature of seventeenth- and eighteenth-century life.

Books of etiquette, conduct guides, and courtesy manuals came to be written, defining gentility. In an era where there is so much emphasis on social hierarchy as part of a stable state, degrees in society become especially important, and social ranks need to be recognized, otherwise they cease to have any value. Far more is involved than being able to demonstrate status through possessions—housing, gardens, furnishing. In the seventeenth century we find special attention being paid to codes of appearance, notably in dress, hairstyle, and body decoration, and in all aspects of behaviour, especially language. There are several words which capture the spirit of the age—'polish', 'refinement', 'propriety', and 'manners'; but the most important watchword for behaviour was 'politeness', recorded in this sense in 1702. 'Polite language' would be a use of English which was widely intelligible and acceptable—polished, elegant, correct. It was the correctness which was the ultimate guarantor of its politeness. 'Every polite tongue has its own rules', affirmed the grammarian Lindley Murray. And it was the job of the grammarians, lexicographers, pronunciation analysts, and usage stylists to make sure that these rules were known, appreciated, and followed.

At the end of the seventeenth century a rigorous approach was perceived to be the only remedy for the 'disease' which was thought to have infected the language. No writers had proved to be immune, no matter how great. Johnson, in his *Dictionary*, focused on the need to institutionalize the lexicon of the standard language. 'I have laboured', he says in *The Rambler*, 'to refine our language to grammatical purity, and to clear it from colloquial barbarisms, licentious idioms, and irregular combinations'. But it was in three other areas that prescriptive opinion was most apparent: in pronunciation, spelling, and grammar. These three domains are central to the definition of a standard language because, as distinct from vocabulary, they are finite and highly rule-governed. There are only so many sounds and letters, and the ways in which they combine to produce syllables and words, although intricate, are limited. Likewise, there are only so many ways in which words vary their grammatical shape, and only so many ways in which they are arranged into sentences. If people are to be persuaded about the value of a standard variety of English, little progress will be made by concentrating on individual words which, by their nature, are only occasionally encountered. It is much better to draw attention to problems which turn up on every page and in every conversation. If standard English is to be a badge of politeness or education, then people need to be able to show it continually in their writing and speech. And that means showing it in spelling, in pronunciation, and in grammar.

Of the three, in the eighteenth century, it was grammar that was considered to be the most powerful means of drawing attention to the importance of linguistic standards. The half-century between 1750 and 1800 saw more English grammars published than in the whole of the previous two centuries. All played their part in fostering a new attitude towards grammar, which in the twentieth century would come to be called the prescriptive or normative approach, because of the way it formulated rules defining what was to count as correct and incorrect usage. One of these grammars had particular influence: Lindley Murray's *English Grammar* of 1795. It became the second best-selling work (after Noah Webster's spelling book) in the English-speaking world, selling over 20 million copies, even more popular in the United States than in Britain, and translated into many languages. Twentieth-century school grammars—at least, until the 1960s—would all trace their ancestry back to Murray.

It took time to build up the accumulation of rules which defined 'correct' grammatical usage. Some of these rules pre-date Murray—such as Dryden's concern about never ending a sentence with a preposition (*That is the man I was talking to*). Some of the rules most widely debated today post-date Murray, such as the one which says it is wrong to split an infinitive by inserting an adverb between the *to* and the verb—to say *I want to really understand what they are saying* rather than *I want really to understand what they are saying* or *I want to understand really what they are saying*. If we count them all up, they do not amount to very many—a few dozen points only, which forms a very small part of the grammar of English. Yet, despite their paucity, the set of rules which comprised the prescriptive element in English grammar proved to be immensely powerful as class discriminators, and by the early nineteenth century they were unquestioned as indicators—along with the rules of the spelling system—of a standard variety of the language. From then on, to speak or write Standard English meant primarily to spell it according to the norms, and to construct sentences according to the norms.

INCREASING DIVERSITY

When might we say with confidence that a standard variety of English arrived? The end of the eighteenth century is usually cited, when influential dictionaries, grammars, and pronunciation manuals had 'institutionalized' the variety, and it had begun to be taught routinely in schools. By then a process of standardization had resulted in a variety whose character was represented throughout the country. The books and teaching were initially influential in America too. For just a few brief decades the English-speaking world—from about 1760 to 1800—was more unified in the way it was taught spelling, grammar, and vocabulary than it had ever been before.

But Standard English, conceived as a uniform mode of linguistic behaviour uniting English speakers everywhere, began to fragment almost as soon as it had appeared. While Johnson, Murray, Walker, and the other prescriptivists were busy inserting the remaining bars into a cage which they thought would keep English under proper control in Britain, on the other side of the Atlantic the cage door was about to be opened by Noah Webster, who was proposing a different set of linguistic norms for American English. Webster saw the arrival of American independence in 1776 as an opportunity to get rid of the linguistic influence of Britain. The new nation needed new language—rationalized and refined as British English had been, but with a fresh identity. In his *Dissertations on the English Language* (1789) he therefore proposed the institution of an 'American standard'. It was hardly possible, he reasoned, for British English to continue to be the model for the American people. It was a matter of honour, he affirmed, 'as an independent nation ... to have a system of our own, in language as well as government'.

As English began its journey around the globe the same pressures of identity which had promoted a standard variety in England began to operate again, except now they operated in different directions. American English, as it soon came to be called, was the first major variety of English to emerge outside of the British Isles, and it was soon followed by others. During the late eighteenth and early nineteenth centuries the geographical horizons of the language steadily expanded as the British Empire grew. To the dialect situation within the British Isles and the USA was now added the foundation of other varieties, as English began to be adapted to meet the communicative demands of new locations. Nothing happened overnight. The power-brokers who took the language around the world—the governors, officers, diplomats, senior civil servants, schoolteachers, missionaries, and their entourages—initially worked through the medium of standard British English, and in many parts of the English-speaking world, 200 years on, still do. But within fifty years of Johnson's *Dictionary* it was possible to see the language adapting in several different directions at once as it came to be taken up by people in the new imperial dominions. The process of expansion would continue throughout the nineteenth century and beyond.

It does not take long for a language to show the effect of being in a new location, when we are dealing with such dramatically different parts of the world as India, West Africa, and Australia. A country's biogeographical uniqueness will generate potentially large numbers of new words for animals, fish, birds, insects, plants, trees, rocks, and rivers. There will be words for foodstuffs, drinks, medicines, drugs, and the practices associated with eating, healthcare, disease, and death. The country's mythology and religion, and practices in astronomy and astrology, will bring forth new names for personalities, beliefs, and rituals. The country's oral and perhaps also written literature will give rise to distinctive names in sagas, poems, oratory, and folktales. There will be a body of local laws and customs, with their own terminology. The culture will have its own technology with its own technical terms—such as for vehicles, house-building, weapons, clothing, ornaments, and musical instruments. The whole world of leisure and the arts will have a linguistic dimension—names of dances, musical styles, games, sports—as will distinctiveness in body appearance (such as hairstyles, tattoos, decoration). Virtually any aspect of social structure can generate complex naming systems—local government, family relationships, clubs and societies. A regionally distinctive English vocabulary involving thousands of items can emerge within just a few years.

As the eighteenth century reached its close English had either been established, or was about to be established, in many regions outside the British Isles and the United States: the Caribbean, Canada, Australia, South Asia, South Africa, West Africa, South-east Asia, and the South Pacific. In each case, a distinctive variety (more accurately, group of varieties) began to emerge, identified chiefly through pronunciation and vocabulary, and some areas would develop norms of educated usage which would eventually attract the designation of 'regional standard'. In the earliest literature of these regions, sparse though it often is, we can see both a backwards-looking and a forwards-looking identity. People who have arrived in a new territory remember their roots, and often incorporate a dialectal dimension into what they write. At the same time they are looking towards a new future for themselves, and their language begins to be shaped by fresh forces.

During the later part of the nineteenth century further expansion took place as British and American colonial interests grew, notably in East Africa and the Pacific. Under the former heading we find the presence of British English in Kenya, Tanzania (formerly Tanganyika and Zanzibar), Uganda, Malawi (formerly Nyasaland), Zambia (formerly Northern Rhodesia) and Zimbabwe (formerly Southern Rhodesia). Under the latter heading we find American English introduced (after the Spanish-American War of 1898) into the Philippines, Guam, and Hawaii, as well as into Puerto Rico in the Caribbean. By the end of the nineteenth century nearly a quarter of the Earth's landmass was part of the British Empire, containing a population of over 400 million.

Modern English

During the nineteenth century processes of linguistic change continued to operate in pronunciation, grammar, and vocabulary, and imperceptibly Early Modern English became Modern English. The changes affected all aspects of English structure. As always, the most noticeable sign of change is in vocabulary, which in this period reflected the multiple social, scientific, technological, and economic developments that cumulatively made up the Industrial Revolution. By 1800 Britain had become the world's leading industrial and trading nation. Most of the innovations of the Industrial Revolution were of British origin: the harnessing of coal, water, and steam to drive heavy machinery; the development of new materials, techniques, and equipment in a wide range of manufacturing industries; and the emergence of new means of transportation. The chief growth areas, in textiles and mining, were producing a range of manufactured goods for export which led to Britain being called the 'workshop of the world'.

The linguistic consequences of this achievement were far-reaching. The new terminology of technological and scientific advance had an immediate impact on the language, adding tens of thousands of words to the English lexicon. Indeed, 'hundreds of thousands' is a better way of expressing this approximation. The bulk of Modern English vocabulary lies in its scientific and technological nomenclature, and most of this arrived during and after the Industrial Revolution. From an examination of any modern professional scientific work in, say, botany, medicine, or chemistry, it is obvious that we are dealing with an unprecedented increase in the size of the English lexicon, which continued into the twentieth century as specialized domains proliferated.

Borrowings from Greek and Latin continued to perform the role they had been assigned in Renaissance English, introducing a large number of forms to science and scholarship, such as *bacillus*, *influenza*, *nickel*, and *rhizome*. More important than borrowing, however, was compounding. Most of the terminological 'monsters' of modern science arise from the stringing together of separate roots—in chemistry, for example:

chlorofluorocarbon	(chloro+fluoro+carbon)
benzoylnitroacetanilide	(benzoyl+nitro+acet+anilide).

The words that tend to get into the record books are usually from chemistry: the full name for *deoxyribonucleic acid* (DNA), cited as the longest scientific name by the *Guinness Book of Records*, contains 16,569 elements. Rather more usual are compounds of just two or three elements, sometimes printed solid or hyphenated:

agoraphobia, crankshaft, daisywheel, kleptomania, radio-isotope, steady-state, turboprop, wavelength

and sometimes spaced:

ammonium chloride, atomic mass unit, bar code, central nervous system, Parkinson's disease, shock absorber, signal-to-noise ratio.

Affixation was also important, using both prefixes and suffixes. Scientific and technical vocabulary of course continued to use everyday prefixes, such as *pre-*, *dis-*, *un-*, and *co-*, and suffixes such as *-al*, *-ful*, *-ous*, and *-less*, but several prefixes were of special scientific relevance:

numerical prefixes, such as bi-, di-, mono-, multi-, poly-, semi-, tri-, uni-

metrical prefixes: micro-, nano-, pico-, femto-, atto-, mega-, giga-, tera-

orientation prefixes, such as anti-, auto-, contra-, counter-, pro-.

Different domains had their 'favourite' suffixes, as can be seen from the following selections of terms:

geology: Pliocene, Miocene, Jurassic, Triassic, Silurian, Cambrian, Cretaceous, Carboniferous

botany: mesocarp, pericarp; fusiform, napiform; anterhozoid, spermatozoid; bacterium, sporangium

chemistry: acetylene, benzene; oxalic, acetic; methane, alkane; ethanol, alcohol; chromium, sodium; chlorine, fluorine; nitrate, sulphate.

Abbreviation has also grown in importance, as we enter the age of modern science. Indeed, abbreviated forms are now so many and varied that their study has evolved its own nomenclature:

initialisms or alphabetisms (spoken as individual letters): BBC, DJ, GM, EU, USA

acronyms (initialisms pronounced as single words): NATO, UNESCO, laser, radar

clippings (part of a word serves as the whole): ad, demo, flu, fridge, max, phone, pub

blends (a word made from two shortened forms): brunch, heliport, infotainment, motel, Muppet (marionette+puppet), Oxbridge, smog.

Everyday usage has employed all these processes, of course, and extended them in various ways. Borrowing has continued from an increasingly diverse range of languages, following the spread of English around the world. Over 350 languages are identified as sources for the present-day lexicon in the *OED*, and the arrival of English in a country where there are many contact languages (over 400 in Nigeria, 10 other official languages in South Africa) immediately increases the rate of lexical borrowing in those countries. Only a small proportion of these words actually end up in standard English, in its British or American incarnations, but they are nonetheless a significant element in the lexical mix. For example, the following words appear towards the beginning of the alphabet in one dictionary of South African English; just two are known in British or American English:

aardvark (*Afrikaans*), abafazi (*Nguni*, 'women'), afdak (*Afrikaans*, 'shed'), agterskot (*Afrikaans*, 'final payment'), amabutho (*Zulu*, 'fighter for a cause'), amadhlozi (*Xhosa*, 'ancestral spirit'), apartheid (*Afrikaans*), askoek (*Afrikaans*, 'dough cake').

The amount of borrowing is always influenced by the number of cultures which coexist, and the status which their languages have achieved. In a highly multilingual country, such as South Africa, Malaysia, or Nigeria, where issues of identity are critical, we might expect a much greater use of loanwords. There is already evidence of this in the range of words collected by lexicographers. In the South African dictionary, depending on the initial letter preferences of the contributing languages, there are long sequences of loanwords: *aandag, aandblom, aap, aar, aardpyp, aardvark, aardwolf, aas*, and *aasvoël* (all from Afrikaans) are immediately followed by *abadala, abafazi, abakhaya, abakwetha, abantu, abaphansi, abathagathi*, and *abelungu* (all from Nguni languages). Only on the next page of the dictionary do we encounter items from British English with local senses, such as *administrator* and *advocate*. The influence of local languages is also apparent in hybrid forms, where a foreign root is given an English affix (as in *Afrikanerdom* and *Afrikanerism*), or where two languages are involved in a blend (as in *Anglikaans*).

Although the amount of borrowing into the two standard varieties was less in the nineteenth and twentieth centuries than it had been in earlier periods, it remained an important feature of lexical growth in English. We find French continuing to exercise its traditional influence, especially on British English, in such loans as *chic, gourmet, art nouveau*, and *voyeurism*. But words continued to arrive from all parts of the world. Of particular note are words from the East, relating to Chinese philosophy and alternative medicine (such as *feng shui, qi*), Indian philosophy and religion (such as *chakra, karma*), and Japanese business, culture, technology, and sport: *aikido, futon, honcho, kanban, karaoke, karate*, and *sushi*. A sense of other regional contributions can be obtained from this mixed bag of examples:

> autobahn (*German*), balti (*Urdu*), bhangra (*Punjabi*), blitz (*German*), bolshy (*Russian*), cappuccino (*Italian*), ciabatta (*Italian*), conga (*Spanish*), dunk (*German*), espresso (*Italian*), fatwa (*Arabic*), flak (*German*), glasnost (*Russian*), intifada (*Arabic*), juggernaut (*Hindi*), kung fu (*Chinese*), lambada (*Portuguese*), latte (*Italian*), lebensraum (*German*), macho (*Spanish*), mah jong (*Chinese*), moussaka (*Turkish*), paparazzo (*Italian*), paso doble (*Spanish*), perestroika (*Russian*), putsch (*German*), robot (*Czech*), rumba (*Spanish*), safari (*Swahili*), schlep, schlock, schmaltz (*Yiddish*), slalom (*Norwegian*), taramasalata (*Greek*), wok (*Chinese*).

GRAMMATICAL FACTORS

Converting one word class into another is a long-standing means of making new words in English. It was a favourite device of Shakespeare, as seen in the Duke of York's 'Grace me no grace nor uncle me no uncle' in *Richard II* or Cleopatra's 'He words me, girls, he words me' in *Antony and Cleopatra*. It continued to be an important process in the nineteenth and twentieth centuries, and is widely encountered today. Modern examples include *spend* as a noun, or *handbag, text, out, spam*, and *surf* as verbs. The process began to incorporate trade names, which developed generic meanings, such as *Filofax, Band-aid, Zimmer, Levi's, Perspex*, and *Xerox*. And there were many instances of personal or place names developing uses as common nouns—*ampere, biro, joule, mae west, ohm, quisling, watt*—or being used as the root for a general concept: *Blairite, Darwinism, Dianamania, Einsteinium, Kremlinology, Leninist, Pinteresque, Reaganomics*.

The modern period is also notable for the way certain types of word formation, sporadic in earlier periods, became widespread. An example is the proliferation of nouns composed of a combination of verb and particle: *knock-out* and *stand-by* are examples from the eighteenth century, *stick-up* and *take-off* from the nineteenth, *check-up* and *fly-past* from the twentieth. The type of word formation known as a 'back-formation' has also become popular. Back-formations occur when a shorter word is made by removing the affix from a longer word. Illustrating from agent nouns, we find *edit* formed from *editor* in the eighteenth century, and *swindle* from *swindler*. Later examples are *shoplift* and *housekeep* in the nineteenth century and *sleepwalk* and *name-drop* in the twentieth.

During the Modern English period the grammar of Standard English continued to change, but at a very much slower rate than in previous centuries. Indeed, a comparison of an early nineteenth-century text with one from the present day seems to show very little difference, from a grammatical point of view. When we read a Jane Austen letter or a Charles Dickens novel we do not feel the need to make regular allowances for points of grammar, such as we do when reading Chaucer or Shakespeare. But some allowances do have to be made, for the grammar is not exactly the same. Whenever we sense that the phrasing of a passage is somewhat 'awkward' or 'old-fashioned', or a conversation is in some way 'stilted' or 'unidiomatic', we are probably noting a difference in grammatical norms between the beginning of the Modern English period and today. For example, there are several differences in the way verbs are used. Keats writes in a letter (1819): *I wonder your Brother don't put a monthly bulleteen in the Philadelphia Papers*; today we would say *doesn't*. And in another letter (1804), Jane Austen writes: *Jenny & James are walked to Charmouth this afternoon*; today we would say *walked* or *have walked*.

PRONUNCIATION CHANGE

In the nineteenth century pronunciation still had some way to go to reach its present-day position. We know this because more information is available about the way words were pronounced at that time, compared with previous periods. Writers were much fuller in their descriptions, and in the last few decades of the century the first cylinder recordings of speech came to be made. Thus we find British observers talking about the pronunciation of *oblige* as *obleege*, *daughters* as *darters*, *gold* as *goold*, *seven* as *sivin*, and *china* as *chayney*, as well as many words where the stress pattern was different from what it is today, as in *balcony* and *compensate*. Probably the most important change during this period affected the pronunciation of *r* after a vowel, in such words as *far* and *heart*. Present in English since Anglo-Saxon times, it weakened during the seventeenth and eighteenth centuries, and by the nineteenth we find rhymes and respellings suggesting that it had actually disappeared: *harm* is said to rhyme with *calm*, and *alms* with *arms*. Also, when people wrote *calm* in a mock-phonetic way they sometimes spelled it *karm*, which they would never have done if the *r* had continued to be sounded.

The most important British development of the nineteenth century, however, was the arrival of a non-regional educated accent—what would later be called 'Received Pronunciation' (or RP), and often described as an 'Oxford accent', a 'BBC accent', the 'King's/Queen's accent', or a 'public-school accent'. This did not exist at the end of the eighteenth century. On the contrary, features of regional pronunciation were a normal characteristic of educated speech, and attracted no comment. But by the 1830s writers were advising provincials to use the RP of fashionable Londoners. RP was never a totally uniform accent, but it was certainly one which was much more widely used than any previous English accent had ever been. The regional neutrality came from a natural process of levelling, with educated people from different regional backgrounds increasingly coming into contact and accommodating to each other's speech. Greater social mobility brought urban and rural dwellers together more than before. University education brought people from many different regional backgrounds together. Schoolteachers were exercising an increased influence on their charges, and a momentum was building up within the schools themselves, especially in the private system. The new accent eventually did come to be associated with a 'public-school education' at such schools as Eton, Harrow, Winchester, and Westminster, followed by higher education at Oxford or Cambridge. And the accent then rapidly spread through the career structure which such an education opened up—in the civil and diplomatic service (especially abroad, as the Empire expanded) and the Anglican Church. It was further institutionalized when it was adopted as the voice of the BBC.

But almost as soon as RP arrived it began to fragment. It already contained a great deal of personal variation, and it was subject to change, as any other accent. By the beginning of the twentieth century it was displaying a range of chiefly age-related differences often described as 'conservative' (used by the older generation), 'general' (or 'mainstream'), and 'advanced' (used by young upper-class and professional people), the latter often being judged as 'affected' by other RP speakers. It retained its upper and upper-middle social-class connotation, as a national standard, but from the 1960s it slowly came to be affected by the growth of regional identities, resulting in the re-emergence of regional colouring—a phenomenon now described as 'modified RP'. There was also a reduction in the extent of the country which recognized the accent as a desirable standard. From a characterization in terms of 'Britain' it came to be restricted to 'England'. And even here, the range of the accent as spoken by the educated class has dramatically altered in recent decades, incorporating a number of features previously associated with local London speech to produce the accent that the media have happily designated 'Estuary English'. The number of people using a non-regionally tinged RP accent has fallen greatly, as a consequence. Estimates of usage in the 1980s were that between 3 and 5 per cent of the British population still used it—around two million. This must be now less than 2 per cent and falling.

A DIVERSE FUTURE

The watchword of the twenty-first century is diversity—in vocabulary, grammar, spelling, and pronunciation. Non-standard forms of English are increasing across the English-speaking world, and being represented in novels, poems, and plays. They illustrate the way people have adapted the language to express new identities and attitudes. Regional accents and dialects have begun to attract a status which previously was associated only with the standard varieties of British and American English. In some countries there are already clear signs of further 'regional standards' emerging, such as Australian English and Indian English. This is not surprising. There is no reason why the same processes which governed the consolidation of a standard variety within Britain and America should not manifest themselves in Australia, India, South Africa, or wherever a country is sufficiently concerned about its linguistic identity to institutionalize its usage in the form of regional dictionaries, grammars, pronunciation guides, and style manuals. Ironically, prescriptive attitudes once again arise, in these circumstances. The debates surrounding a question of what is the 'correct' form of Australian or Indian English can be just as heated as anything seen in eighteenth-century Britain. But there is a difference. In a world where the language is used in dozens of countries, there is no longer a notion of private ownership.

In the twenty-first century no country can be said to 'own' English any more. Or rather: everyone who has opted to use it has come to have a part-ownership in it. That is what happens to a language when it achieves an international or global presence, as English has, with some two billion people using it in 2006. And when people adopt a language they immediately adapt it, to make it suit their needs. As Chinua Achebe once said: 'The price a world language must be prepared to pay is submission to many different kinds of use'. English has now become a language whose norms and functions vary globally and develop independently according to sets of forces that no longer reflect the influence of a single (British or American) point of origin. Even a native-speaking point of origin is becoming less relevant as time goes by. The centre of gravity of the English language is steadily shifting from the native speaker to the non-native speaker. People who use English as a second or foreign language are now very much in the majority, with three non-native speakers in the world for every one native speaker.

The literary implications are profound. Most English literature hitherto has come from people who speak English as a first or second language—that is, they learned their English in a country where the language had some kind of special status arising out of its colonial history. Commonwealth literature was one of the consequences of this situation, with such linguistically distinctive voices as Benjamin Zephaniah and Chinua Achebe. It remains to be seen what contribution will one day be made by those who have learned English as a foreign language—that is, from countries where English has had no colonial history but where fluent levels of competence are increasingly routine, such as Sweden, the Netherlands, and Denmark. Writing in English from such countries is currently always in standard (British or American) English, but it will not always be that way. One day we could be reading Swedish English novels—that is, novels written by people who have Swedish as a mother tongue but who choose to write in a Swedish-coloured variety of English, analogous to those currently found in Commonwealth literature. There could be poetry in Japanese English or Russian English. And English will be pulled in new directions as a consequence.

It is always difficult to predict the future, when it comes to language. Who would have dared suggest, five hundred years ago, that Latin would one day cease to be the language of educated discourse? There are always competing possible scenarios. American English may come to be increasingly dominant. The English spoken in India—a country which has far more speakers of English than any other, mainly as a second language—may come to exercise an increasingly influential role in world affairs. Regional varieties may diverge so much from the standard that one day we may see the emergence of an English 'family of languages'. Mutually unintelligible varieties, historically derived from English, can already be heard in some parts of the world, such as Singapore ('Singlish') and Papua New Guinea ('Tok Pisin').

It is important to emphasize that standard English, as manifested in its two main varieties, is not yet threatened by all these regional developments. That could hardly be, given that the vast majority of the world's printed English output is in either the British or American standard, or in a standard heavily influenced by one or the other (as in the case of Australia and Canada). Nor should we underestimate the common core of linguistic identity which unites them. Every few decades someone predicts that British and American English are one day going to become mutually unintelligible, but there is very little sign of this happening as far as the written language is concerned. When we add up all the differences between these two varieties—all the points of contrast in spelling, grammar, and vocabulary—we are talking about a very small part of the language as a whole. That, of course, is why we usually find the term 'standard English' used without any regional qualification. We sense the common core.

The Internet has added a fresh dimension to these various scenarios. Before the World Wide Web (1991), it would have been difficult to encounter new varieties of English or to interact with them. Now it is easy. We can visit the websites of an English-language newspaper in Tokyo, Cairo, or Athens, read and listen to examples of regional accents and dialects, and through email, chatrooms, and blogging give our own linguistic idiosyncrasies a public presence. The Internet gives us immediate access to national and international Englishes, standard and non-standard alike. We do not know what happens to a language, under such circumstances.

The Internet is changing everything. No one knows exactly how large it is, but the quantity of linguistic data it contains must rival the contents of all the libraries in the world. Much of this content is indexed, by the major search engines, making the Internet the largest corpus of usage that there has ever been. The speed with which additions to the Internet can be circulated is likely to add greatly to the pace of linguistic change. And the lack of centralized control over Internet submissions, in such domains as email, chatrooms, instant messaging, and blogging, is rapidly increasing the amount of diversity that is 'out there'. We have not seen such linguistic spontaneity since the Middle Ages, and nothing then resembles the way we can give our outpourings an elegantly printed shape, as is routinely possible on screen now.

The long-term effects of all this uncontrolled variation are unclear. To take just one area of usage: spelling. Non-standard spelling now has an unprecedented public printed presence. The controls which prevented mis-spelled words getting into print (using copy-editors and proofreaders) are often lacking on the Web, and completely absent in most private interactions, such as blogging, where the language is under the total control of the writer. Type a mis-spelled word into a search engine and you will often find thousands of hits. In due course such popular consensus is bound to alter our perception of what counts as correct—and as many of these 'errors' are phonetically based simplifications, we may find that the Internet will foster a natural kind of spelling reform. Alternatively, there may emerge a neo-prescriptivism which will reassert the norms of traditional standard English.

Checks and balances must continue to operate if we wish to continue understanding each other. On the one hand, the Internet presents unprecedented opportunities for individual self-expression and the public representation of linguistic diversity. On the other hand, there is a pressing need for mutual intelligibility among the millions of people who are the inhabitants of the online 'global village'. Perhaps more than ever before, the English-speaking world needs a standard variety to maintain its role as a lingua franca; but this is likely to be a standard containing rather more variation than has traditionally been the case. It will be interesting to see how these competing pressures manifest themselves in an electronic medium, and how dictionaries and language books cope with the process. One thing is certain: the Internet will present lexicography with one of its greatest challenges.

Guide to the use of the dictionary

1 Purpose

The following guide aims to explain to the user the kind of information that is available in the *Shorter Oxford English Dictionary*, and to assist in the finding of particular information. It outlines the types of entry which appear in the dictionary, lists the possible places where certain kinds of words or phrases may be found, details the different features which may occur in an entry, and explains some of the conventions the dictionary uses.

2 The dictionary entry

2.1 TYPES OF ENTRY

There are five basic types of entry in this dictionary: standard entries, combining entries, letter entries, variant entries, and abbreviation entries.

2.1.1 *Standard entries.* The majority of entries are standard entries. In these the headword, or word being defined, does not belong to any of the other entry types below. The typical standard entry has a headword (in **bold** type), pronunciation (in the International Phonetic Alphabet), part of speech (in *italic* type), date (expressed as a period of part of a century), etymology (in square brackets **[ ]**, introduced by **ORIGIN**), and definition section. The definition section may be accompanied by one or more paragraphs containing illustrative quotations, phrases which contain the headword, compounds whose first element is the headword, or derivatives consisting of the headword and a suffix. Sections containing illustrative quotations are tinted. Usage indicators (labels), variant spellings, and grammatical or other information may also appear in the entry. More information on all these features is given in section 4 below.

2.1.2 *Combining entries.* In these entries the headword either begins or ends with a hyphen, and in use generally occurs joined to another word (either hyphenated or as a solid word). Combining entries include affixes of three types: suffixes (like *-ly, -ness*), prefixes (like *re-, un-*), and combining forms (like *hyper-, kilo-*). See further under section 6 below.

2.1.3 *Letter entries.* Each letter of the alphabet has an entry which contains a brief account of the history of the letter and lists its most important uses as an abbreviation or symbol. See further under section 7 below.

2.1.4 *Variant entries.* A variant entry refers an alternative spelling or grammatical form of a headword to the standard or combining entry with the main form and all other information. See further under section 8 below.

2.1.5 *Abbreviation entries.* Abbreviations and symbols consisting of more than one letter have their own entries. See further under section 9 below.

2.2 ORDERING OF ENTRIES

Entries are listed in strict alphabetical order. Those with hyphens or spaces follow otherwise identical words written solid; a headword with an accent or diacritic over a letter follows one consisting of the same sequence of letters without. Capital and lower-case letters are regarded as equivalent. Strict alphabetical order applies also to prefixes of titles and names (such as *Mc-*) which in other contexts may conventionally be placed elsewhere.

The order of headwords which are spelled the same way but have different parts of speech is as follows:

abbreviation
symbol
noun
pronoun
adjective
verb
adverb
preposition
conjunction
interjection
prefix/combining form
suffix

Entries are positioned in the headword sequence by their first part of speech. The order of headwords with the same spelling and the same (first) part of speech is chronological (according to date ranges: see 4.8 below), with variant entries following any full entries: see 4.4 below.

Subcategorizations of parts of speech, such as participial (*ppl*) of adjectives, verbal of nouns, or personal (*pers.*) of pronouns, are disregarded in determining entry order.

3 How to find a word or phrase

Look in the obvious alphabetical place in the main sequence of entries. If the item sought is not there, consider the following:

(i) Is it formed from a prefix or a combining form (as *dis-*, *Euro-*)? If so, is it included in the entry for that prefix or combining form? It may be listed (in italics) as an example there, or be treated in a small-type paragraph.

(ii) Is it a derivative, i.e. does it end with a suffix (as *-ly*, *-ness*)? If so, is it included at the end of the entry for the word from which it is derived? For example, *befitting* appears under **befit** *verb*, *disclosing* under **disclose** *verb*, and *lacelike* and *lacery* under **lace** *noun & adjective*: none would be found in its own alphabetical place.

(iii) Is it a phrase or combination, or other compound? If so, is it included in a small-type paragraph in the entry for one of the words which it contains? For example, *three cheers* and *sling mud* are respectively under **cheer** *noun*[1] and **mud** *noun*[1], *colour-blind* is under **colour** *noun*, and *infant prodigy* is under **infant** *noun*[1] *& adjective*. Sometimes an entry for one word in a phrase or compound will contain a cross-reference to one of the other elements, under which the definition will be found. For two-word compounds it is generally best to look initially under their first element. For further information see 4.14 below.

(iv) Is it very similar to a word included as a headword? If so, and especially if it is an uncommon or obsolete word, it may also be included in the small-type derivative block at the end of the entry for that word. (See 4.16 below for more information on derivatives.)

4 The features of a standard dictionary entry

This section describes the elements which may appear in a standard dictionary entry, in the order in which they most usually occur. Some, such as labels or phrases, can occur in several places: this is mentioned, and the range of places indicated, later in the guide in the section for the feature in question. Many of the characteristics of standard entries are shared by the other types of dictionary entry.

4.1 HEADWORD

Every entry opens with a headword, printed in bold type. The headword is the word whose meaning, etymology, history, pronunciation, etc., are the subject of the entry.

If the headword is obsolete (i.e. no longer in use in current English) it is preceded by a dagger: †.

If the headword is a word (or phrase) which, although used in English, is still regarded as essentially foreign, it is printed in bold italics. In their normal contexts such items are often written or printed in light italics or within quotation marks, and many may still usually be pronounced in a foreign way.

Where a word has more than one spelling, the spelling used for the headword is usually the one regarded as the dominant or preferred current form. Other spellings may be given later in the entry, as variants (see 4.6 below). Historical considerations occasionally require a form which is less usual for some senses to be chosen as the headword, but in such cases current usage is made clear.

4.2 PRONUNCIATION

4.2.1 The pronunciations shown are those which can safely be regarded as allowable in British English at the present time, within the form of received pronunciation that does not give rise to any negative social judgement when heard by most native speakers. An attempt has been made to represent the English spoken by the current generation, older forms being discarded where necessary, but absence of a variant need not indicate that it is completely unacceptable, and the order of variants need not be one of decreasing frequency.

Pronunciations are given, between slashes, in the symbols of the International Phonetic Alphabet (IPA). The symbols and conventions used are intended to provide sufficient information for accurate production of the appropriate sounds, without needless detail.

4.2.2 *Vowels*. In a conventional vowel diagram (representing the position and degree of raising of the tongue in articulating each sound), the vowel symbols used in this dictionary appear as follows:

	Front	*Central*	*Back*
High	i y		u
	ɪ		ʊ
	e ø	ə	o
Mid	ɛ œ	ʌ	ɔ
Low	a		ɑ ɒ

Lengthening is indicated by ː

Nasality is indicated by the superscript diacritic ˜

The front vowels with lip-rounding, /y/, /ø/, and /œ/, occur only in words which are not fully naturalized. See further the Pronunciation Guide.

The English vowel sounds are

Short		*Long*	
a as in	**cat**	ɑː as in	**arm**
ɛ	**bed**	əː	**her**
ɪ	**sit**	iː	**see**
i	**cosy**	ɔː	**saw**
ɒ	**hot**	uː	**too**
ʌ	**run**	ɛː	**hair**
ʊ	**put**		
ə	**ago**		

Diphthongs

ʌɪ as in	**my**
aʊ	**how**
eɪ	**day**
əʊ	**no**
ɪə	**near**
ɔɪ	**boy**
ʊə	**poor**
ʌɪə	**tire**
aʊə	**sour**

4.2.3 *Consonants and semivowels*. The following sounds are recorded in this dictionary:

Plosives: p, b, t, d, k, ɡ

Fricatives: f, v, θ, ð, s, z, ʃ, ʒ, ç, x, h

Affricates: tʃ, dʒ

Liquids and nasals: l, ʎ, m, n, ɲ, ŋ, r

Semivowels: j, w, ɥ

Of these, b, d, f, h, k, l, m, n, p, r, s, t, v, w, and z have their usual English values. Other symbols are used as follows:

g as in **g**et
tʃ **ch**ip
dʒ **j**ar
ŋ ri**ng**
θ **th**in
ð **th**is
ʃ **sh**e
ʒ vi**s**ion
j **y**es

in some Scottish and foreign words

x as in lo**ch**, German a**ch**

and only in respect of words which are not fully naturalized

ç as in German ni**ch**t
ʎ as in Spanish **ll** or Italian **gl** in *gli*
ɲ as in Spanish **ñ**, French **gn**, Italian **gn** in *gnocco*
ɥ as in French n**u**it.

See further the Pronunciation Guide.

4.2.4 Primary stress is indicated by superscript ˈ before the stressed syllable, secondary stress by subscript ˌ. Primary stress is shown for words with two or more syllables; secondary stress only where its marking is needed to avoid doubt. Word stress is not a significant feature of the French language, and no stress is marked in words retaining a true French pronunciation. See further 4.2.9 below.

4.2.5 Unstressed vowels are reduced to /ə/ unless they are likely to have their full phonetic value when the word is pronounced in isolation.

4.2.6 Optional sounds, sometimes pronounced, sometimes not, are enclosed within round brackets.

E.g. **prompt** /prɒm(p)t/
delivery /dɪˈlɪv(ə)ri/.

The bracketing of schwa, (ə), before /l/, /m/, and /n/ shows that these consonants are often syllabic in the words concerned.

4.2.7 An explicit pronunciation is given for a derivative only if it differs in some unpredictable way from that of the headword or from that usual in combination with the suffix in question. If the derivative bears primary stress on a different syllable from the headword (and consequently has a predictably different pronunciation) this is indicated by a primary stress mark before the stressed syllable within the actual form; any secondary stress is assumed to fall on the syllable bearing primary stress in the headword unless otherwise marked.

E.g. (s.v. FALSIFY) **falsifiable** bears no stress mark so is stressed like falsify on the first syllable, but **falsiˌfiaˈbility**.

Among predictable changes associated with the position of primary stress are

ə or (ə) → a in nouns in *-ality* formed from adjectives in *-al* (e.g. **practiˈcality** and not the full phonetic transcription /praktɪˈkalɪti/ is given under **practical** /ˈpraktɪk(ə)l/);

əʊ or ə(ʊ) → ɒ in derivatives of combining forms in *-o* or words formed from them (e.g. **maˈcropterous** and not the full phonetic transcription /maˈkrɒpt(ə)rəs/ is given under **macro-** /ˈmakrəʊ/).

A final *-r* is pronounced in derivatives formed with a suffix beginning with a vowel.

E.g. **authoress** under **author** /ˈɔːθə/ is to be understood as /ˈɔːθərɪs/.
cellarage under **cellar** /ˈsɛlə/ is to be understood as /ˈsɛlərɪdʒ/.

An exception to this is the suffix *-ed*, which results in a pronunciation /əd/ not /-ərəd/ after /ə/.

The pronunciation of *-icity* in derivatives of adjectives in *-ic* (/-ik/) is /-ɪsɪti/.

4.2.8 A second or subsequent pronunciation is often abbreviated so as to show just the part where it differs from the first; the same applies to pronunciations of variant or inflected forms.

4.2.9 An alternative non-anglicized pronunciation may be given for a word which is largely but not fully naturalized. Such pronunciations are preceded by *foreign*. The first (or only) pronunciation of any non-naturalized word, phrase, or form (printed in italic bold) from one of the more familiar modern European languages will represent the foreign pronunciation but will have no specifying label. A second or subsequent fully anglicized pronunciation will often be given.

4.2.10 A hyphen may be used in a phonetic transcription to clarify or emphasize that the divided sounds are to be separately pronounced, for example where they could be mistaken for a diphthong or single affricate, or where /l/ is repeated when *-less* or *-ly* is added to a word ending in *-l*.

E.g. **Mazdaism** /ˈmazdə-ɪz(ə)m/
potsherd /ˈpɒt-ʃəːd/
drolly /ˈdrəʊl-li/
moralless /ˈmɒr(ə)l-lɪs/.

Most often, however, hyphens simply open or close truncated pronunciations.

4.2.11 Additional examples of words illustrating particular sounds are to be found in the Pronunciation Guide, and the main English sounds are summarized at the foot of the page throughout much of the dictionary.

4.3 PART OF SPEECH

A part of speech is given for all entries, except letter entries. It appears in italics after the pronunciation, or after the headword if no pronunciation is shown.

All the parts of speech of a headword are listed at the beginning of an entry, e.g. ***adjective & adverb***; ***noun, adjective, & verb***. Sometimes parts of speech are treated together, but more often they are in separate sections, in which case each section is headed with a capital initial followed by the part(s) of speech being treated in that section, e.g. **A** *noun*, **B** *adjective*.

If the headword consists of two or more separate words, it may be specified as a phrase (*phr.*). For example, *noun phr.*, or *adjectival phr.*, or (when parts of speech are combined) *noun & adverbial phr.*

If the headword is a verb, the part of speech may be followed by an indication of the verb's transitivity (e.g. *verb intrans.*, *verb trans.*). For more information about transitivity see 4.11.1 below.

Parts of speech are also given for some of the items in combination and other subentry blocks (see 4.14 below) and for derivatives (see 4.16 below).

4.4 HOMONYMS

If two or more headwords have the same spelling and part of speech, but each has a different origin and meaning, the headwords are homonyms. They are distinguished by a superscript number after the relevant part of speech. In this dictionary, homonyms include headwords whose only difference is an initial capital, but not headwords which differ in respect of hyphenation, spacing, or letters with accents or diacritics. If the first part of speech of two or more homonyms is the same, the entries are presented in chronological order (according to date range: see 4.8 below). If successive entries have more than one part of speech, homonym numbers of later parts of speech are allocated in the order in which the entries appear in the text. E.g. if *noun*[1] *& adjective*[1] is followed by *noun*[2] *& adjective*[2], it is to be understood that the second noun is recorded later (or at least no earlier) than the first, but nothing is implied about the relative first dates of the adjectives. Homonyms which are variant entries follow all standard- or combining-entry homonyms of the same (first) part of speech.

E.g. **cupper** ... *noun*[1] ... ME.
cupper ... *noun*[2] ... E20.
cupper *noun*[3] var. of CUPPA.

Only the simple part of speech is relevant in allocating homonym numbers. Qualifications such as *verbal* and *ppl* are disregarded (cf. last paragraph of 2.2 above).

E.g. **picking** *noun*[1]
picking *verbal noun*[2].

In cross-references to combining entries the part of speech is omitted and the homonym number is attached to the small-capital form, e.g. -ER[1], -Y[6].

4.5 LABELS AND SYMBOLS

4.5.1 *Subject and status labels.* Restrictions in the usage of words or senses are frequently conveyed by the use of labels: subject labels in small capitals, regional and other labels in italics. These can show restriction to the English of a particular geographical area (e.g. *dial.*, *Scot.*, *US*, *Austral.*), to a specific style or register of language (e.g. *colloq.*, *poet.*, *slang*), or to a particular branch of knowledge or field of activity (e.g. CRICKET, HERALDRY, LAW, NAUTICAL), or can denote frequency or extent of use (e.g. *rare*).

Subject labels precede any definition (or partial definition) or any variant spelling or form to which they apply. (If they apply to a complete entry they therefore follow the etymology.)

E.g. **infauna** /ɪnˈfɔːnə/ *noun.* E20. [...] ZOOLOGY. The animal life ...
(s.v. COLOUR *noun*) **8** MINING. (A particle of) gold. M19.
(s.v. OCCLUDE *verb*) **5** *verb intrans.* METEOROLOGY. Of a front ...

Geographical, stylistic, and frequency labels (together here referred to as 'status labels') applying to the whole entry appear at the top of the entry after the part of speech.

E.g. **peripherial** /pɛrɪˈfɪərɪəl/ *adjective. rare.* L17.

In a main definition section a status label applying to a complete dated sense follows the definition and immediately precedes the date.

E.g. (s.v. CHIP *verb*[1] 9) ▸**b** *verb trans.* Tease, chaff. *colloq.* L19.

Within dated senses, a status label applying to only part of a definition generally precedes that part to which it applies. If the definition has formal divisions (as (***a***), (***b***), etc.) the label always precedes the part it qualifies; if there is no formal division, the label follows the first part of the definition but precedes any later parts.

E.g. (s.v. OVERLANDER *noun*) **1** A person who drove livestock overland (*Austral. & NZ hist.*); *Austral. hist* a person who journeyed overland; *slang* a tramp.

In small-type subentries (as combinations or derivatives) labels of any kind precede the relevant definition or partial definition.

E.g. (s.v. BASE *noun*[1]) **base hit** BASEBALL a hit enabling the batter to reach a base safely.
(s.v. LOCAL *adjective*) **local talent** the talented people or (*colloq.*) the attractive women or men of a particular locality.
(s.v. PUPPET *adjective & noun*) **puppetish** *adjective* (*rare*) pertaining to ...
(s.v. JESSED) wearing jesses; HERALDRY having jesses of a specified tincture.

Status labels precede any variant spelling or form to which they apply.

E.g. **kiln** /kɪln/ *noun & verb.* Also (now *Scot.*) **kill** ...

Interests of clarity may produce some variation of label positioning, particularly in subentries and individual parts of definitions.

Labels can be combined with other labels, of either the same or a different type. Combined subject and status labels are positioned as for the latter. Labels can also be qualified by words like 'Now' or 'Only'.

E.g. Now *rare* or *obsolete*.
Somewhat *derog.*
Chiefly *US*.
obsolete exc. *hist.*

These are largely self-explanatory. 'Long' (as in 'long *rare* or *obsolete*') implies for several centuries, usually from before the eighteenth.

Certain italic labels can also be used to link or clarify the relationship between (parts of) definitions, e.g. *esp.*, *spec.*, *fig.*, *gen.*, *transf.* The abbreviations used in these labels also appear in other contexts. (The specification *esp.* is in italics if it introduces a complete definition, but in roman if introducing a parenthetical part of a larger definition.)

4.5.2. *Status symbols.* Two symbols are used to express status: a dagger (†) and an asterisk (*).

The dagger indicates that a word, sense, form, or construction is obsolete. It is placed before the relevant word(s) or relevant sense number.

The asterisk indicates that a spelling or form is now used primarily in the United States, and elsewhere where US spelling conventions are followed. The asterisk does not exclude the possibility that the form was standard or common in British use in the past. It is placed before the form it qualifies.

E.g. (s.v. FAVOURITE) Also ***favorite**.

Very occasionally an American pronunciation is given, in which case an asterisk is similarly used.

4.6 VARIANT SPELLINGS

If a headword has a significant alternative spelling, this is given, in bold type, before the date (and inflection if appropriate) at the top of the entry. Variants are generally preceded by 'Also', or sometimes 'Orig.', and are often further qualified in some respect.

E.g. **defence** ... *verb trans.* Also ***defense**.
locale ... *noun.* Also †**local**.
jaunty ... *adjective.* Also (earlier) †**janty**.
disc ... *noun.* Also (*US* & COMPUTING now the usual form) **disk**.
set ... *noun*[1]. Also (now chiefly in senses 16, 23, 24, 32, 33) **sett**.

Frequently the difference from the headword is highlighted by abbreviating the variant to the significant part, the missing part(s) being indicated by a hyphen.

E.g **émigré** ... *noun.* Also **e-**.
dislikeable ... *adjective.* Also **-likable**.
Amerikan ... *adjective.* Also **-kkk-**.

If a variant form is current and has a different pronunciation from the headword, this is given.

E.g. **McCoy** /mə'kɔɪ/ *noun.* ... Also **Mackay** /mə'kʌɪ/.

Variants differing only in initial capitalization are not usually given except for proprietary terms, for nouns from modern German, and for words passing into names or titles. If the capitalization difference applies only to certain senses, it can be specified under those senses.

E.g. **La** /la/ *adjective (def. article).* Also **la**.
(s.v. BEAUTY *noun* 1) ▸**b** (**B-**.) This quality personified.

Many compounds can be (or, in the past, have been) written in several different ways: as two or more words, hyphenated, or (increasingly) as one solid word. In most cases one form (the usual modern form) is given, but this does not mean that the others are unacceptable or even, in some cases, uncommon.

This dictionary follows the tradition of Oxford University Press in using *-ize* (and corresponding *-ization*, *-izer*, etc.) rather than *-ise* for verbs (and corresponding nouns etc.) derived from Greek *-izein* or Latin *-izare*, and for words modelled on these forms. The *-s-* variants are specified for headwords and are to be assumed for derivatives.

Variants with the ligatures *æ* and *œ* are to be assumed for words (usually of classical origin) written in this dictionary with *ae* and *oe*.

Not all possible variants (current or obsolete) of a headword are listed, but only those of particular significance. Among these are variants which are used in the works of a major author (such as Shakespeare), variants which are important for the development or current spelling of the headword or for the etymology of another word, obsolete variants which were widely current up to the modern period, and current variants which are usual in the United States.

A variant entry in the main alphabetical sequence cross-refers the user to the full entry for the word except where the two would be immediately adjacent (see further under 8 below).

4.7 INFLECTIONS

Three kinds of inflected forms may be specified:

1. plurals of nouns (and very occasionally of French adjectives)
2. forms of verbs (according to person, tense, aspect, etc.)
3. comparatives and superlatives of adjectives.

Inflections are specified only if they are unpredictable or irregular in some way, or if there are several alternative inflections for one headword.

4.7.1 *Nouns.* No plural form is given for nouns which simply add *-s* or (in the case of those ending in *-s*, *-x*, *-z*, *-sh*, or soft *-ch*, or in *-j*) *-es*, including those in which final *-y* inflects as *-ies*. Other plural forms are specified, and they include those for:

- nouns ending in *-o* (as the plural may vary between *-os* and *-oes*);
- nouns ending in Latinate forms such as *-a* and *-um*;
- nouns with more than one plural form;
- nouns whose plural involves a change in the stem (as **foot**, **feet**);
- nouns whose plural and singular are the same (as **sheep**; in such cases the formula used is 'Pl. same').

'Pl. pronounced same' with no specified form implies a regular inflection.

4.7.2 *Verbs.* Inflections which are regarded as regular and are not specified are (i) third person singular forms adding *-s* or *-es* (when the stem ends in *-s*, *-x*, *-z*, *-sh*, or soft *-ch*), including most of those in which *-y* inflects as *-ies*; (ii) past tenses and past participles adding *-ed* and, where appropriate, dropping a final silent *-e* (as **changed**, **walked**); (iii) present participles adding *-ing* and, again where appropriate, dropping a final silent *-e* (as **changing**, **walking**); (iv) regular archaic *-est* and *-eth* in older verbs. Other inflections are specified, and they include:

- inflections where a final consonant is doubled (as **bat**, **batted**, **batting**; in such cases the formula used is 'Infl. **-tt-**');
- inflections for the past tense and past participle which involve a change in the stem (as **drink**, **drank**, **drunk** and **go**, **went**, **gone**).

4.7.3 *Adjectives.* Adjectives which add *-er* and *-est* to form the comparative and superlative, including those which drop a final silent *-e* (e.g. **braver**, **bravest**), or replace a final *-y* by *-i-* (e.g. **happier**, **happiest**), are regarded as regular and their inflections are not specified. Single-syllable adjectives which double a final consonant (as **hot**, **hotter**, **hottest**) do have their inflections specified (the formula used is 'Compar. & superl. **-tt-**'), as do adjectives with irregular inflections (as **good**, **better**, **best**).

4.7.4 Inflected forms are given in bold type, usually at the top of the entry before the date. Frequently only the part of a form which differs from the headword is specified. Pronunciations are not given for the most regular forms. The pronunciations of *-ed*, *-s*, and *-es* vary according to the preceding letter(s) or sound(s): for fuller details see the entries for **-ed** *suffix*[1], **-s** *suffix*[2], and **-s** *suffix*[3].

E.g. **hoof** /hu:f/ *noun*. Pl. **hoofs**, **hooves** /hu:vz/.
canephora /kəˈnɛf(ə)rə, -ˈni:-/ *noun*. Pl. **-rae** /-ri:/.
fly /flʌɪ/ *verb*. Pa. t. **flew** /flu:/; pa. pple **flown** /fləʊn/.
learn /lə:n/ *verb*. Pa. t. & pple **learned** /lə:nd/, **learnt** /lə:nt/.
learned ... *adjective*. Compar. (*arch.*) **learneder**; superl. (*arch.*) **learnedest**.

4.7.5 Inflectional information usually follows any variant forms, except where it does not apply to the variant(s).

E.g. **defer** /dɪˈfə:/ *verb*[1]. Infl. **-rr-**. Also †**differ**.

If an entry has several parts of speech and an inflection applies to only one of them, the inflection is usually specified at the beginning of the section for that part of speech.

E.g. **lasso** ... *noun & verb* ... ►**A** *noun*. Pl. **-o(e)s**.

4.8 DATES

Provision of information about the age of all words included, and of their principal senses, is one of the distinctive features of this dictionary. The date of first (and, if relevant, last) recorded uses is given in terms of date ranges: after the Middle English period (and the introduction of printing) according to a tripartite division of centuries into early, middle, and late; in earlier times, where dating depends on less secure manuscript sources, according to broader divisions. The date ranges are defined and abbreviated as follows.

OE Old English -1149
LOE late Old English 1000–1149
ME Middle English 1150–1349 or, in some contexts, 1469
LME late Middle English 1350–1469
L15 late fifteenth century 1470–1499
E16 early sixteenth century 1500–1529
M16 mid sixteenth century 1530–1569
L16 1570–1599
E17 1600–1629
M17 1630–1669
L17 1670–1699
E18 1700–1729
M18 1730–1769
L18 1770–1799
E19 1800–1829
M19 1830–1869
L19 1870–1899
E20 1900–1929
M20 1930–1969
L20 1970–1999
E21 2000–

Every standard entry bears at least one date, indicating the earliest recorded use of the word. Combining entries are also sometimes individually dated for the combining form.

The word's earliest recorded date is given at the top of the entry, immediately before the etymology. Exceptions to this are Old English words which are presumed to be older than the written record (for example because of the existence of parallel words in other Germanic languages) or for which the exact Old English form is considered to be significant. In these cases **OE** (or **LOE**) and a specified form begin the etymology, and the date is not repeated immediately before the opening etymological bracket.

Old English words and senses are usually only specified as 'late' if use earlier in the period (for which written records are scarce) seems unlikely.

Every main numbered or lettered sense in the large-type section of an entry also bears a date, at the end of the definition and after any labels.

4.8.1 *Obsolete words and senses.* If a word or sense is obsolete, the date of its last recorded use is given, linked to the opening date by a dash (e.g. **LME–E18**). If an obsolete headword has only one sense, or if all senses have exactly the same period of currency, a final date is given with the opening date at the top of the entry. In other cases final dates are given after the opening dates at the end of each obsolete sense.

Currency for only one date range, or for one main period or century, is indicated by 'Only in'. For example, 'Only in **L16**', 'Only in **ME**' (either only between 1150 and 1349 or only in the Middle English period as a whole, 1150 to 1469), 'Only in **17**' (in all three parts of the 17th century only). If a word or sense is current for two consecutive date ranges in the same century, the century is given only in the closing date, e.g. **E–M17**; **M–L18**.

4.8.2 *Dates for derivatives.* Derivatives at the end of a standard entry and in most combining entries are also dated. Each bears a single date of first (or, if obsolete, first and last) use at the end of its entry. The dates of individual senses or parts of speech are not distinguished.

4.9 ETYMOLOGY

All entries which are not simply variant entries contain etymological information, explaining the origin and formation of the headword. In standard entries and some combining entries, this information is generally placed in square brackets on a new line after the first date. In some combining entries and all letter entries the etymological information is not formally distinguished, but forms part of a general description of the head form.

Within an entry a particular sense or subentry may also have its own additional etymology.

Etymologies in square brackets frequently contain a great deal of information, sometimes in abbreviated form, with various conventions of presentation. This section aims to explain only those most likely to require clarification.

4.9.1 *Basic etymological forms and facts.* If a word is formed from one or more other words (as by contraction or combination, or by the addition of a prefix or suffix) the etymology gives the words from which it is formed and often explains the nature of the formation.

E.g. **Amerindian** ... *noun*. ... [ORIGIN Contr. of *American Indian*.]
fatuous ... *adjective*. ... [ORIGIN from Latin *fatuus* foolish ... + -OUS.]
initial ... *verb*. ... [ORIGIN from the noun.]
jama ... *noun*[3]. ... [ORIGIN Abbreviation.] Pyjama.
matchmake ... *verb intrans*. ... [ORIGIN Back-form. from MATCHMAKER *noun*.]
outswinger ... *noun*. ... [ORIGIN from OUT- + SWINGER *noun*[1].]

If a word is an adoption from another language, the etymology opens with a specification of the language of origin and, if it differs from the English spelling of the headword, the form of the word in the foreign language.

E.g. **scandal** ... *noun*. ... [ORIGIN Old French & mod. French *scandale* ...]
bigot ... [ORIGIN French, of unknown origin.]

'From' is widely used to open etymologies where the headword is formed from several combined elements or from another headword. The formula 'formed as' (usually followed by a cross-reference) indicates that the headword is from the same principal or initial word as the other word mentioned.

E.g. **anonymity** ... [ORIGIN formed as ANONYMOUS + -ITY.]
—the etymology of **anonymous** is also valid for the *anonym-* part of **anonymity**.

References to other headwords are in the usual cross-reference style of small capitals (see section 5).

A half bracket can be used to exclude part of a word in an etymology that is not represented in the headword.

E.g. **Politbureau** ... [ORIGIN Russian *politbyuro*, from *polit(icheskiĭ* political + *byuro* bureau.]

Foreign forms from languages which do not use the Roman alphabet (as Greek, Russian, Sanskrit, Hebrew, Arabic, and Chinese) are transliterated. The transliteration system used for Chinese is Pinyin, although the Wade–Giles transliteration is also given if it sheds light on the English form. Transliteration tables for Greek and Russian are on p. xlvi.

4.9.2 *References and cross-references in etymologies.* Etymologies often contain cross-references to other entries, frequently at the end of the etymology, preceded by either 'see' or 'cf.'

E.g. **nitrogen** ... [ORIGIN French *nitrogène*, formed as NITRO: see -GEN.]
lecherous ... [ORIGIN Old French *lecheros*, from *lecheor*: see LECHER *noun*[1], -OUS.]
buffalo ... [ORIGIN Prob. immed. from Portuguese *bufalo* ... . Cf. BUFF *noun*[2], BUFFLE.]

If 'see' is used to refer to another entry, the etymology of the entry referred to directly extends or elaborates on the first etymology, and there is usually an identifiable point of contact, often a shared foreign form. For example in **lecherous** above there is a reference 'see LECHER *noun*[1]', and under **lecher** *noun*[1] the etymology runs [Old French *lichiere* (nom.), *lecheor*, *-ur* (accus.), from *lechier* live in debauchery ...]. The point of contact is the form *lecheor* and the etymology of **lecher** *noun*[1] contains more information about that form.

'Cf.' simply draws attention to some parallel or point of interest shared by etymologies.

A reference beginning 'See also' usually refers to a word derived from, or from the same source as, the headword.

4.10 DIVISIONS IN AN ENTRY

Every standard entry has a possible maximum of five hierarchical levels of formal sense division, though in practice two levels (those designated by bold arabic numerals and bold lower-case letters) are most frequent. The five levels are as follows:

▸A, **▸B**, etc.—Bold capital letters are used in entries with more than one part of speech, each of which is treated separately. The section for each is designated by a capital letter. A statement of the part(s) of speech being treated in that section immediately follows the letter: **▸A** *noun*, **▸B** *attrib.* or as *adjective*.

▸I, **▸II**, etc.—Bold capital roman numerals are used to indicate major grammatical or semantic divisions of the same part of speech, especially in long or complex entries. The basis of the division may be specified after the roman numeral.

1, **2**, etc.—Bold arabic numerals divide different basic meanings of the same part of speech. These are the most common sense divisions.

a, **›b**, etc.—Within basic senses identified by arabic numerals, related subsenses are designated by bold lower-case letters. The first division may be unmarked if further subsenses are subdivisions of or subordinate to the first definition.

(***a***), (***b***), etc.—Bold italic lower-case letters in brackets are used to designate minor divisions in a main sense and senses of phrases, derivatives, and other subentries.

The first, third, and fourth of these levels are individually dated, and the second is implicitly dated from the next following sense. Within each dated level senses and divisions are ordered chronologically. The dagger for obsolete uses is usually attached to the highest relevant sense level and not repeated for each of the ranks below.

4.11 GRAMMATICAL INFORMATION

Many definitions (and other parts of entries) contain grammatical information about the word being defined. Much of this information is straightforward, and this section aims only to explain some features which may require further clarification.

4.11.1 *Transitivity of verbs*. All verbs have a specification of transitivity, according to the two main categories transitive and intransitive: ***verb trans.*** and ***verb intrans.*** Fully established uses of fundamentally transitive verbs with an object understood are in this dictionary classed as intransitive.

If a verb has the same transitivity in all its senses, a single indication of transitivity is given. This will be at the top of the entry beside the part of speech if the headword is a verb only, or has no part-of-speech divisions, and after a bold capital if the entry is divided into separate parts of speech. If transitivity varies among senses, it is shown after each relevant sense number or letter, before the definition. Possibilities are ***verb trans.***, ***verb intrans.***, and, where the definition covers both transitive and intransitive uses, ***verb trans. & intrans.*** or ***verb intrans. & trans.*** (either the older or the more frequent being specified first).

Reflexive senses may be marked by ***refl.***, alone if the verb is otherwise only transitive, as ***verb refl.*** if transitivity is mixed.

If a sense of a transitive verb occurs only in the passive, the definition is expressed in the passive form, preceded by 'in ***pass.***'.

If transitivity is the basis of major divisions within an entry, it is specified after each roman numeral, and not at the lower sense divisions.

4.11.2 *Plurality of nouns*. A use or sense of a noun may be specified as 'In ***pl.***'. This means that the following definition relates to the plural form of the noun.

E.g. **acoustic** ***noun***, sense 1 opens 'In ***pl.***' and the definition which follows is of *acoustics*.
gubbin ***noun***, sense 3 opens 'In ***pl.*** (treated as sing.)' and the definition which follows ('A fool') is of *gubbins*.

By contrast ***pl.*** alone implies no change of form (as in **people** ***noun***, **2 a** ***pl.*** The persons belonging to a particular place …, where the use defined is of *people* not *peoples*).

4.11.3 *Constructional information*. Many definitions contain information about the constructions which the headword takes or the contexts in which it is habitually used. Most of this information is in the form of self-explanatory statements of fixed or typical phrases, but in entries for verbs and for limited-set grammatical words (such as determiners) details can be more complex. Often the focus is on what the headword is followed by: either a general category of grammatical construction, for example 'with double object' (as *envied her her job*), 'Foll. by inf. without *to*' (as *shall go*), or a particular word (especially an adverb or preposition) specified in italics, as 'Foll. by *out*'. In these contexts *to do* stands for any infinitive, *doing* stands for any gerund, and *that* stands also for object clauses without explicit *that* ('I said I would' as well as 'I said that I would').

Constructional information can appear before or after a definition, or can form an integral part of it. If the constructional statement precedes the definition, the definition is of the whole construction. If it follows the definition, the definition is of the headword only.

E.g. (s.v. **LAY** ***verb***[1]. **18**) ▸**b** NAUTICAL. Foll. by *aboard*: run into or alongside (a ship), usu. for boarding.
—the definition is of *lay aboard* and in this use *lay* is always followed by *aboard*.

(s. v. **LIVE** ***verb***) **5** ***verb intrans.*** Continue in life … Also foll. by *on*.
—the definition is of *live* but *live on* means the same and is also covered.

(s.v. **REFER** ***verb***) **2** Assign *to* a particular class …
—when *refer* means 'assign' it is always followed by *to*.

(s.v. **ENCLOSE** ***verb***) **3** Surround with or *with* a wall, fence, etc.
—*enclose* means 'surround with a wall etc.' and may or may not be followed by a specifying phrase beginning *with*.

Following elements which occur frequently (but not always) and which extend the meaning of the headword are shown in brackets or preceded by 'Also'.

E.g. (s.v. **PRELUDE** ***verb*** 2 b) be introductory (*to*).
(s.v. **LIKENESS**) **4** The quality or fact of being like … (Foll. by *between*, *to*, †*with*.)
(s.v. **RACKET** ***verb***[2]) **3** ***verb intrans.*** Make a racket, esp. by noisy movement. Also foll. by *about*, *along*, *around*.

Verbal transitivity can be qualified by constructional information.

E.g. (s.v. **HARE** ***verb***[2]) **2** ***verb intrans. & trans.*** (with *it*). Run or move with great speed.
—the verb is used either intransitively, or transitively in the form *hare it*.

(s.v. **LICK** ***verb***[1]) ▸†**b** ***verb trans. & intrans.*** (with *of*, *on*). Lap with the tongue; drink, sip, (a liquid).
—*lick of* and *lick on* mean the same here as *lick* with a direct object.

4.12 USE OF BRACKETS

Brackets are used in many places and for many purposes, and this section does not cover all of these.

A specified direct object of a verb is bracketed.

E.g. (s.v. **LIMB** ***verb trans.***) **3** Remove branches from (a tree).

Definitions in such a form may, when the usage of the verb permits, be designated both transitive and intransitive. In such cases the intransitive definition is to be understood by mentally removing the brackets from around the direct object.

The referent of an adjective or subject of a verb is bracketed when it applies to only part of a sense or to a subsense.

E.g. (s.v. **GREEN** ***adjective***) **2** Covered with herbage or foliage; (of a tree) in leaf.

(s.v. **GO** *verb*) (***b***) (of a firearm etc.) explode.

If the referent applies to a whole main sense it opens the definition and is followed by a colon.

E.g. (s.v. **FOUL** *adjective*) **4** Of speech etc.: indecent, obscene.

Brackets are frequently used in definitions to combine information and avoid repetition.

E.g. (s.v. **CHEEP** *noun*) A shrill feeble sound (as) of a young bird.
(s.v. **LEAVE** *verb*) **1** *verb trans.* **a** (Arrange to) transfer possession of at one's death …
(s.v. **COLOUR** *noun*) **8** *MINING.* (A particle of) gold.
(s.v. **BEEP** *verb trans. & intrans.*) (Cause to) emit a beep or beeps.
(s.v. **MINNESOTAN** *noun & adjective*) (A native or inhabitant) of Minnesota …
(s.v. **LACK** *verb*) **lackland** *adjective & noun* (designating) a person owning no land …
(s.v. **COLOUR** *noun*) **colour-wash** *noun & verb trans.* (paint with) coloured distemper.

In such cases, separate definitions are obtained by including and excluding the bracketed section.

A clarifying or reinforcing part of a definition, which may be useful but is not essential, may also be bracketed.

E.g. (s.v. **CYLINDER** *noun*) **2** A (solid or hollow) body …

4.13 ILLUSTRATION BLOCKS

Any main sense in an entry may be followed by a small-type tinted paragraph containing illustrative quotations and phrases linked to the main sense and its related subsenses.

4.13.1 *Illustrative quotations.* The purpose of the illustrative quotations is to complement the definitions by clarifying sense distinctions, illustrating constructions, and representing common collocations. Consequently, quotations are selective and many words and senses are not illustrated. The first quotation for any use is not the first known example.

If an entry has more than one quotation for a sense, these are arranged in basically chronological order. If a quotation illustrates a type of usage not explicitly covered by the definition, the quotation may be preceded by a qualification, such as *attrib.*:, *fig.*:.

The source of a quotation is given immediately before the quotation text. This is usually either an author (in small capitals except for true capitals) or a published newspaper, journal, etc. (in italics). No quotation from a periodical dates from before the nineteenth century, and the great majority are from the twentieth. With a few exceptions titles of individual works are given only for Shakespeare. Chapter and verse are given for books of the Bible.

E.g. (s.v. **CHEER** *noun*[1] 6) *Times* The market took cheer … and marked the shares up 3p.
(s.v. **RAIN** *verb* 6) SHAKES. *Twel. N.* The rain it raineth every day.
(s.v. **DISCIPLE** *noun* 1) AV *John* 20:20 Then were the disciples glad, when they saw the Lord.

Quotations specified 'OED' reproduce examples included in the *Oxford English Dictionary* but attributed to no particular source and usually described as 'Modern'. They belong to the late nineteenth or early twentieth century.

Omissions from quotations are indicated by ellipses.

See also the list of Authors and Publications Quoted.

4.13.2 *Other illustrative material.* Illustration blocks are sometimes folllowed by defined phrases and cross-references to phrases defined elsewhere. Typical or common types of uses of a headword may be illustrated by italic examples rather than quotations from specified sources.

E.g. (s.v. **ANALYSIS** 2) **bowling analysis** *CRICKET* a statement of a bowler's performance record.
(s.v. **BUTCHER** *noun* 1) *FAMILY* ***butcher***.
(s.v. **RHYME** *noun* 3) ***double rhyme***, ***eye rhyme***, ***imperfect rhyme***, ***treble rhyme***, etc.

4.14 PHRASES AND COMPOUNDS

Phrases and compounds (collectively referred to here as subentries) are usually included (either listed or defined) in small-type blocks in the main entry for one of their significant words. The blocks in which they appear are located after a definition section and any illustration block. These blocks are of several kinds, and each has a heading, as

— **PHRASES**:
— **COMB.**:
— **ATTRIB. & COMB.**:
— **SPECIAL COLLOCATIONS**: (only of adjectives)
— **WITH ADVERBS** (or **PREPOSITIONS**) **IN SPECIALIZED SENSES**: (only of verbs)

or some combination of these. Within such blocks subentries are in alphabetical order. Defined items are in bold type, and there may also be cross-references to similar phrases containing the headword but defined under another entry (see section 5). Subentries in these blocks are not dated. Separate senses or parts of speech of a subentry can be divided by a bracketed bold italic lower-case letter: (***a***), (***b***), etc. Any status labels and symbols at the top of an entry apply also to the subentries in these blocks.

4.14.1 *Phrases.* Phrases can appear in several places in an entry: in a small-type block headed — **PHRASES**:, in an illustration block (see 4.13.2), in a main definition, or (occasionally) in another subentry block as a phrase of a compound. The examples below illustrate the latter two of these:

(s.v. **KIBOSH** *noun*) **1** ***put the kibosh on***, put an end to; dispose of finally.
(s.v. **LEG** *noun*) **leg-of-mutton** *adjective* resembling a leg of mutton, esp. in shape; ***leg-of-mutton sail***, a triangular mainsail; ***leg-of-mutton sleeve***, …

Phrases are usually treated in the entry for their first significant word, but if a later word in the phrase has particular importance, the phrase can be treated under that word.

E.g. **ship of the line** is treated under **line** *noun*[2], not under **ship** *noun*.

4.14.2 *Combinations.* A combination is a compound (usually a two-word compound) the first element of which is the headword. A combination most often consists of two nouns, but may also be made up of a noun and some other part of speech (especially an adjective), a verb plus a noun object or adverb, or an adjective plus any part of speech other than a (separately written) noun (when the formation is classed as a special collocation: see 4.14.3 below). If a combination is a noun only, no part of speech is given. Otherwise a part of speech is specified.

If a noun is particularly frequently used attributively in a certain manner or sense, a combination paragraph may be headed **– ATTRIB. & COMB.**:, and may open with a statement of the headword's attributive use(s) and some italic examples.

E.g. (s.v. **LAND** *noun*[1]) **– ATTRIB. & COMB.**: In the senses ... 'situated or taking place on land ...', 'living on land ...', as ***land battle***, ***-bird***, ... ***-journey***, ***-monster*** ... etc. Special combs., as **land agency** ...

If the first word of the definition of a combination would simply repeat the second word of the combination, a colon may be subsituted.

E.g. (s.v. **CREAM** *noun*[2]) **cream bun**, **cream cake**: filled with cream.

4.14.3 *Special collocations.* A special collocation is a compound (written as two words) consisting of an adjective (the headword) and a following noun used in a fixed way or in a way which is not simply determinable from the separate meanings of its two elements.

No part of speech is given; all special collocations are nouns.

4.14.4 *Verbs with adverbs/prepositions in specialized senses.* A verbal phrase consisting of a verb headword plus a preposition or adverb, whose meaning is not simply the sum of its parts, has a 'specialized sense', and such phrases may be treated (in verb entries) in a block headed

With adverbs in specialized senses:
With prepositions in specialized senses:
With adverbs & prepositions in specialized senses:
etc.

Adverbs in such verbal constructions are sometimes referred to in grammatical literature as 'particles', and with transitive verbs can typically both precede and follow a direct object: *phone her up*, *phone up her father*.

A small-type block like this is normally created only when the uses with adverbs or prepositions are numerous. Isolated or specific examples can be treated under numbered senses or in an illustration block.

E.g. (s.v. **LIGHT** *verb*[1]) **4** *verb trans. & intrans.* NAUTICAL. Move or lift (a sail etc.) *along* or *over*.
11 *verb intrans.* Foll. by *out*: depart, get out.

Transitivity for items in these blocks is not usually specified unless a definition is ambiguous or transitivity varies among senses.

4.15 NOTES

Information of relevance or interest, usually relating to a whole entry, which does not fit obviously into the normal entry structure appears in a small-type note at the end of an entry (but before any derivative block). Such a note opens with **– NOTE**:.

Notes can be on a range of subjects, including dating, pronunciation, etymology, usage, and other relevant entries.

E.g. (s.v. **SERENDIPITY**) **– NOTE**: Rare before 20.
(s.v. **PORT** *noun*[1]) **– NOTE**: See also **CINQUE PORTS**.
(s.v. **MINUSCULE**) **– NOTE**: Spelling *miniscule*, formed by assoc. with **MINI-**, is very common but regarded as erroneous.

4.16 DERIVATIVES

A derivative is formed by adding a suffix (such as *-able*, *-ly*, *-ness*) to a word. Many such formations are treated as main entries, but many others, especially if they are fairly simple, with few senses and without further derivatives or compounds of their own, are placed in a small-type derivative block at the end of an entry.

A derivative block always comes last in its entry. Derivatives themselves are in bold type and always have a part of speech and one date, but regular formations with readily deducible meanings (e.g. those with the adverbial suffix *-ly* or the noun suffix *-ness*) may be left undefined.

Derivatives appear in alphabetical order. Alphabetically adjacent items with the same part of speech, definition, and date may be combined.

E.g. (s.v. **METAPSYCHICS**) **metapsychic**, **metapsychical** *adjectives* **E20**.
(s.v. **NEW JERSEY**) **New Jerseyan**, **New Jerseyite** *nouns* a native or inhabitant of New Jersey **M20**.

If a derivative is divided into formal senses or parts of speech, or if it has a compound definition (i.e. its definition contains a semicolon), its date is separated from its definition(s) by a colon.

A variant of a derivative may be given after the main form, often abbreviated to its differing element.

E.g. (s.v. **CONTEST** *verb*) **contester**, **-or** *noun* a person who contests **L19**.

As long as historically appropriate, any variant spellings specified for the headword occur also in its derivatives. Status and subject labels given at the top of an entry and applying to all its senses are assumed also to apply to any derivatives.

A derivative preceded by 'Also' is a synonym of the headword.

E.g. (s.v. **CONVALESCENCE**) Also **convalescency** *noun* (*rare*) **M17**.

Minor words which are not formal derivatives of the headword but which are etymologically related to it may also be included in the derivative block.

Derivatives are cross-referred to in small capitals (the same style as for headwords).

For pronunciation of derivatives see section 4.2.7.

5 Cross-references

A standard style is used in this dictionary to refer from one dictionary entry to another. For main entries and derivatives (including words defined within combining entries) the word being referred to is represented in small capitals (though any true large capitals are retained). The part(s) of speech may follow in italics (with any homonym number), and a particular branch or sense number may be specified.

E.g. À LA CARTE
FREE *adjective*
ORTHOPTER 1
POST *noun*².

Phrases, combinations, and special collocations which constitute cross-references are given in italic type. Direction to the entry or subentry at which the definition appears is made explicitly by 'see' or implicitly (when the direction is to a unique head form and no individual sense number) by presenting the relevant headword or derivative in small capitals in context within the italic phrase.

E.g. ***abjure the realm***: see ABJURE 3.
FLANDERS ***poppy***.

Explicit cross-references may be made from one subentry to another. The subentry to which direction is made appears in italics followed by 's.v.' (when reference is to another entry) or 'above' or 'below' (when reference is to another subentry or sense within the same entry).

E.g. ***catch cold***: see ***catch a cold*** above.
Cornish moneywort: see ***moneywort*** s.v. MONEY *noun*.

A definition may consist of an equation of one word, sense, or phrase with another. An equals sign is followed by a small-capital or italic cross-reference, as described above.

E.g. (s.v COON *noun*) **1** = RACOON.
(s.v. FIN *noun*¹) **finback** = ***fin whale*** below.
(s.v. GUN *noun*) **6** = ***electron gun*** s.v. ELECTRON *noun*².
(s.v. LINE *noun*² 17) ▸**c** A particular policy ... which a politician may maintain or expect others to follow; = ***party line*** s.v. PARTY *noun*.

When a cross-reference constitutes the only definition, the item cross-referred to is the more common or important one in that sense.

A cross-reference simply to a headword or part of speech equates the item being defined with all senses of that referred to.

6 Combining entries

In combining entries the headword is an affix, either beginning or ending with a hyphen and generally used joined to another word. Combining entries treat affixes of three types: suffixes, prefixes, and combining forms.

The dividing line between prefixes and combining forms is not always clear cut, and for purposes of ordering and cross-reference they are regarded as a single part of speech. In this dictionary combining forms generally represent either (i) modified forms of independent words in English or the source language, often in, or in imitation of, Latin and Greek forms and ending in *-i-* or *-o-* (e.g. **Anglo-**, **auto-**) or (ii) identical and closely related independent English words combining more or less freely with others and in combination not always readily differentiable one from the other (e.g. **after-**, **back-**). All other initial elements that form words are classed as prefixes (e.g. **ex-**, **non-**, **re-**).

7 Letter entries

Each of the twenty-six letters of the alphabet is treated in its own entry. The headword consists of an upper- and lower-case representation of the initial letter, separated by a comma.

E.g. **A, a**

The headword is followed by a pronunciation and a description and brief history of the letter.

This is typically followed by three branches: the first covering senses relating to the letter itself and to its shape or size; the second covering symbolical uses; the third containing the letter used as an abbreviation.

Some digraphs and ligatures, such as **ch**, **ph**, **ae**, and **oe**, are also included as headwords.

8 Variant entries

Variant spellings or inflectional forms specified at the top of an entry will usually also be mentioned in their proper alphabetical sequence. Exceptions are those which would be alphabetically adjacent to the headword, noun plurals in *-os* or *-oes*, regular inflections specified because there is an (irregular) alternative, inflections deducible from statements of consonant doubling, and inflections stated to be the same as those of the root (as in the case of some minor or obsolete words, such †**acknow** which is 'Infl. as KNOW *verb*').

In a variant entry the headword (in bold) is referred to the word under which it is mentioned (in small capitals) by means of the direction 'see' or by means of a statement of its relationship with the word referred to, as 'var. of', 'pa. t. & pple of'.

If a form is obsolete or foreign, this is reflected in the variant entry by a dagger or italicization as appropriate. Other qualifications are restricted to the main entry, which the user is directed to 'see'.

Headwords in variant entries may be combined if they are alphabetically adjacent and are for the same entry or for several correspondingly adjacent entries. If many related words share the same spelling variation, not all will necessarily be listed in the variant entry.

E.g. **honyock**, **honyocker** *nouns* vars. of **hunyak**.
labored *adjective*, **laborer** *noun*, **laboring** *adjective* see LABOURED *adjective* etc.
serjeant, **serjeantcy** *nouns* etc., see SERGEANT etc.

Variant entries which are homonyms follow all the main entries for that homonym.

9 Abbreviation and symbol entries

Abbreviations and symbols consisting of more than one letter have their own entries, which are in many respects similar to standard dictionary entries. The main differences are that no dating information is given, and if there is more than one meaning, these are given in alphabetical rather than chronological order. A pronunciation is only given if it is not simply that of the constituent letters.

E.g. **BAFTA** /ˈbaftə/ ***abbreviation***. British Academy of Film and Television Arts.
Brig. ***abbreviation***. Brigadier.
Cr ***symbol***. CHEMISTRY. Chromium.
DF ***abbreviation***. **1** Latin *Defensor Fidei* Defender of the Faith.

The dividing line between abbreviations *per se* and acronyms and initialisms is not always clear cut, and this dictionary lists as abbreviations a number of formations which will probably come to be considered as nouns or other words in their own right, such as **ISA** and **JPEG**.

Abbreviations are subject to considerable variation of form. For example, they often occur with a full stop after each letter, and those all in capitals may occur with initial capital only, or in lower-case letters. Such variations are not always explicitly covered.

Abbreviations and symbols

In this list the abbreviations are printed in the type and with the capitalization that is normally used for them, but variation according to context will be found. Some general abbreviations, such as those for units of measurement or points of the compass, are not listed here, but can be found in the main dictionary text.

abl.	ablative
abl. absol.	ablative absolute
absol.	in absolute use, absolutely
accus.	accusative
allus.	allusion
allus.	allusively
alt.	altered, alteration
a.m.	ante meridiem, 'before noon'
Amer.	American, America
Ant. & Cl.	Antony and Cleopatra
aphet.	aphetic, aphetized
app.	apparently
approx.	approximately
Arab.	Arabic
arch.	archaic
assim.	assimilated, -ation
assoc.	associated, -ation
attrib.	attributive, -ly
Attrib. & comb.	in attributive uses and combinations
augm.	augmentative
Austral.	Australian, Australia
aux.	auxiliary (verb etc.)
AV	Authorized Version
A.Y.L.	As You Like It
b.	born
back-form(s).	back-formation(s)
Brit.	British
c	*circa*, 'about'
Canad.	Canadian
cap(s).	capital(s)
cent.	century
cents.	centuries
cf.	*confer*, 'compare'
Chron.	Chronicles
cogn.	cognate
Col.	Colossians
collect.	collective, -ly
colloq.	colloquial, -ly
Com.	Comedy
Comb.	(in) combination
combs.	combinations
Com. Err.	Comedy of Errors
compar(s).	comparative(s)
compl.	complement
conf.	confused
contempt.	contemptuous, -ly
contr.	contracted, contraction
Cor.	Corinthians
Coriol.	Coriolanus
correl.	correlative
corresp.	corresponding
corrupt.	corruption
cross-refs.	cross-references
Cymb.	Cymbeline
d.	died
Dan.	Daniel
dat.	dative
def.	definite
demonstr.	demonstrative
deriv(s).	derivative(s), derivation(s)
derog.	derogatory
Deut.	Deuteronomy
devel.	development
dial.	dialect, dialectal, -ly
Dicts.	(in) Dictionaries
dim(s).	diminutive(s)
distrib.	distributive
E	early (in dates)
Eccles.	Ecclesiastes
Ecclus	Ecclesiasticus
elem(s).	element(s)
ellipt.	elliptical, -ly
Encycl. Brit.	Encyclopaedia Britannica
Eph.	Ephesians
equiv.	equivalent
erron.	erroneous, -ly
Esd.	Esdras
esp.	especially
etym.	etymology
euphem.	euphemistic, -ally
exc.	except
exclam(s).	exclamation(s)
Exod.	Exodus
exp.	exponential
expr.	expressing, expressive of
Ezek.	Ezekiel
fem.	feminine
fig.	in figurative use, figuratively
fl.	*floruit*, 'flourished'
foll.	followed
freq.	frequent, -ly
Gal.	Galatians
gen.	general, -ly
Gen.	Genesis
genit.	genitive
Hab.	Habbakuk
Haml.	Hamlet
Heb.	Hebrews
Hen.	Henry
hist.	historical, history
hyperbol.	hyperbolically
imit.	imitative, -ly
immed.	immediately
imper.	imperative, -ly
impers.	impersonal, -ly
indef.	indefinite, -ly
indic.	indicative
inf.	infinitive
infl.	inflected, influenced
instr.	instrumental
interrog.	interrogative, -ly
intrans.	intransitive, -ly
iron.	ironical, -ly
irreg.	irregular, -ly
Isa.	Isaiah
Jer.	Jeremiah
joc.	jocular, -ly
Josh.	Joshua
Judg.	Judges
Jul. Caes.	Julius Caesar
L	late (in dates)
Lam.	Lamentations
lang(s).	language(s)
Ld	Lord
Lev.	Leviticus
lit.	literal, -ly
lit. & fig.	in literal and figurative use, literally and figuratively
L.L.L.	Love's Labour's Lost
LME	late Middle English
LOE	late Old English
Lucr.	Lucrece
M	mid (in dates)
Macb.	Macbeth
Macc.	Maccabees
masc.	masculine
Math.	Mathematics
Matt.	Matthew
ME	Middle English

Meas. for M.	Measure for Measure
Merch. V.	Merchant of Venice
Merry W.	Merry Wives of Windsor
Mids. N. D.	Midsummer Night's Dream
mod.	modern
N. Amer.	North America(n)
NEB	New English Bible
neg.	negative
neut.	neuter
N. Ir.	Northern Ireland, Northern Irish
nom.	nominative
north.	northern
north.	northern (dialect)
Num.	Numbers
NZ	New Zealand
obj.	object, -ive
obs.	obsolete
occas.	occasional, -ly
OE	Old English
OED	Oxford English Dictionary
opp.	opposed (to)
orig.	original, -ly
Oth.	Othello
pa.	past
pa. ppl	past (or passive) participial
pa. pple	past (or passive) participle
pass.	passive, -ly
pa. t.	past tense
Per.	Pericles
perf.	perfect
perh.	perhaps
pers.	personal
Pet.	Peter
Phil.	Philippians
phonet.	phonetic, -ally
phr.	phrase
phrs.	phrases
pl.	plural
pls.	plurals
poet.	poetical
possess.	possessive
ppl	participial
pple	participle
prec.	preceding (headword or main entry)
pred.	predicate
pred.	predicative, -ly
pres.	present
pres. ppl	present participial
pres. pple	present participle
pres. t.	present tense
prob.	probably
prons.	pronouns
pronunc.	pronunciation
Prov.	Proverbs
Ps.	Psalms
redupl.	reduplicated, -ation(s)
ref.	reference
refash.	refashioned, -ing
refl.	reflexive
rel.	relative
rel.	related
repl.	replaced, -ing
repr.	representative (of), represented, representing, representation(s)
Rev.	Revelation
rhet.	rhetorical, -ly
Rich.	Richard
Rom.	Romans
Rom. & Jul.	Romeo and Juliet
RV	Revised Version
S. Afr.	South Africa(n)
Sam.	Samuel
S. Amer.	South America(n)
sc.	*scilicet*, 'that is to say'
Scot.	Scottish, Scots
Shakes.	Shakespeare
sing.	singular
S. of S.	Song of Solomon (or Songs)
Sonn.	Sonnets
sp.	spelling
spec.	specific, -ally
subj.	subject
subjunct.	subjunctive
subord.	subordinate
subsp.	subspecies
superl.	superlative
Suppl.	Supplement
Sus.	Susanna
s.v.	*sub voce*, 'under the word'
syll.	syllable
synon.	synonymous
t.	tense
Tam. Shr.	Taming of the Shrew
techn.	in technical use
Temp.	Tempest
Thess.	Thessalonians
Tim.	Timothy
Times Lit. Suppl.	Times Literary Supplement
Tit. A.	Titus Andronicus
Tr. & Cr.	Troilus and Cressida
trans.	transitive, -ly
transf.	transferred
transf. & fig.	transferred and figurative
Twel. N.	Twelfth Night
Two Gent.	Two Gentlemen of Verona
ult.	ultimate, -ly
unexpl.	unexplained
Univ.	University
Univs.	Universities
unkn.	unknown
US	United States
USA	United States of America
usu.	usually
var.	variant (of), variety
vars.	variants (of)
Ven. & Ad.	Venus and Adonis
voc.	vocative
W. Indies	West Indies
Wint. T.	Winter's Tale
Wisd.	Wisdom of Solomon
Zech.	Zechariah
Zeph.	Zephaniah

Symbols

† obsolete
* now chiefly in the United States (see p. xxxiii)

The printing of hyphens

Hyphens introduced at line breaks in words or formulae not otherwise hyphenated are printed ⁓. The regular form - represents a hyphen which would occur in any circumstance in the text.

Note on proprietary status

This dictionary includes words which have, or are asserted to have, proprietary status as trade marks or otherwise. Their inclusion does not imply that they have acquired for legal purposes a non-proprietary or general significance, nor any other judgement concerning their legal status. In cases where the editorial staff have some evidence that a word has proprietary status this is indicated in the entry for that word, but no judgement concerning the legal status of such words is made or implied thereby.

Pronunciation guide

Vowels

a	*as in*	c**a**t, pl**ai**t
ɛ		b**e**d, d**ea**th
ɪ		s**i**t, m**y**th, beg**i**n, th**e**ology
i		cos**y**, eer**ie**, anemon**e**, *Spanish* s**i**
ɒ		h**o**t, w**a**sh, tr**ou**gh
ʌ		r**u**n, s**o**n, gl**o**ve, r**ou**gh
ʊ		p**u**t, g**oo**d, sh**ou**ld, amb**u**lance
ə		**a**go, gath**er**, flav**our**, cheet**ah**, thor**ough**, lem**o**n, s**u**ccess, mistak**e**n
ɑː		**ar**m, c**al**m, loc**a**le, br**ah**min
əː		h**er**, **ear**n, b**ir**d, sp**ur**, m**yrrh**
iː		s**ee**, p**ea**, s**ei**ze, d**e**cent, f**e**tus, p**ae**on
ɔː		s**aw**, b**a**ll, b**oar**d, h**or**se, th**ough**t, appl**au**d
uː		t**oo**, gl**ue**, fr**ui**t, r**ou**te, thr**ough**, shr**ew**d
ɛː		h**air**, d**are**, p**ear**, th**ere**, v**a**ry

ʌɪ	*as in*	m**y**, h**igh**, **i**ce, s**ig**n, s**ei**smic, bons**ai**
aʊ		h**ow**, pl**ough**, s**ou**nd, kr**au**t
eɪ		d**ay**, g**a**te, d**ai**sy, th**ey**, r**ei**n, d**eig**n
əʊ		n**o**, coc**oa**, s**ou**l, r**oe**, th**ough**, gl**ow**, b**eau**, m**au**ve, y**eo**man
ɪə		n**ear**, b**eer**, th**eo**ry, qu**e**ry, sev**ere**, em**ir**, grenad**ier**
ɔɪ		b**oy**, sp**oi**l, Fr**eu**dian
ʊə		p**oor**, r**u**ral, d**our**, liq**ueur**
ʌɪə		t**ire**, b**yre**, ch**oir**, qu**ie**t, d**ia**phragm
aʊə		s**our**, fl**ower**, c**owar**d

ɑ	*as in*	*French* p**a**s
e		*French* **été**, *Italian* v**e**rde
ɔ		*French* h**o**mme, *Italian* d**o**nna, *German* G**o**tt
o		*French* **eau**, m**o**t, *Italian* figli**o**
u		*French* t**ou**t
ø		*French* bl**eu**, *German* sp**ö**tteln
œ		*French* b**œu**f
y		*French* d**u**, *German* f**ü**nf
eː		*German* **Eh**re
oː		*German* B**oo**t
øː		*German* H**öh**le
œː		*French* doul**eu**r
yː		*German* F**üh**rer
aɪ		*German* **ei**n, fr**ei**
ɔy		*German* H**äu**ser

ː	indicates length
˜	indicates nasality

ɒ̃	*as in*	cord**on** bleu
ɒ̃ː		Ly**ons**
ɑ̃		*French* **en**
ɑ̃ː		*French* bl**an**che
ɛ̃		*French* v**in**
ɛ̃ː		*French* c**in**q
ɔ̃		*French* m**on**
ɔ̃ː		*French* m**on**de
œ̃		*French* **un**

Consonants and semivowels

b, d, f, h, k, l, m, n, p, r, s, t, v, w, and z have their usual English values.

g	*as in*	**g**et
tʃ		**ch**ip, di**tch**, **c**ello, **Cz**ech, cul**t**ure, ques**t**ion
dʒ		**j**ar, he**dg**e, ur**g**e, lo**g**ic, **g**entle, privile**g**e, sol**di**er
ŋ		ri**ng**, ba**n**k, co**n**quer, ju**n**ction
θ		**th**in, **th**rone, bir**th**, heal**th**, too**th**
ð		**th**is, clo**th**e, smoo**th**, swar**th**y
ʃ		**sh**e, a**sh**, **ch**ef, sta**ti**on, mi**ssi**on, spa**ci**ous, herba**ce**ous
ʒ		vi**s**ion, era**s**ure, auber**g**ine, bour**ge**ois
j		**y**es, t**u**ne, n**e**w, **e**ulogy
x		lo**ch**, *German* a**ch**, *Spanish* Rio**j**a
ç		*German* ni**ch**t
ʎ		*Spanish* o**ll**a, **ll**amar, *Italian* **gl**i
ɲ		*French* mi**gn**on, *Spanish* pi**ñ**a, *Italian* **gn**occo
ɥ		*French* n**u**it

Stress

ˈ indicates primary stress on the following syllable
ˌ indicates secondary stress on the following syllable

For further details see pp. xxx–xxxi

Features of dictionary entries

headword (e.g. **messenger**)
see § 4.1, p. xxx

part of speech (e.g. ▸**A** *noun.*)
indicated by arrow and bold letter
see § 4.3, p. xxxi

sense (e.g. **2**, **3**)
indicated by bold numerals
see § 4.10, p. xxxv

date (e.g. LME)
indicates a sense's first recorded use
see § 4.8, p. xxxiv

phrases (e.g. ***express messenger***, **King's messenger**)
introduced by – PHRASES:
see § 4.14, p. xxxvii

combinations (e.g. **messenger-at-arms**, **messenger cable**)
introduced by – COMB.:
see § 4.14, p. xxxvii

derivative (e.g. ■ **messengership**)
introduced by square bullet ■
see § 4.16, p. xxxviii

phrase (e.g. **in mimicry of**)
indicated by bold
see § 4.14, p. xxxvii

cross-reference (e.g. *MERTENSIAN*)
indicated by italic small capitals
see § 5, p. xxxviii

---

messenger /ˈmɛsɪndʒə/ *noun & verb.* ME.

[ORIGIN Old French & mod. French *messager*, formed as MESSAGE: see -ER[2]. For the intrusive *n* cf. *passenger*, *scavenger*, etc.]

▸**A** *noun.* **1** A person who carries a message or goes on an errand for another; a person employed to carry messages. ME. ▸**b** A bearer *of* (a specific message). ME. ▸**c** *BIOLOGY.* A molecule or substance that carries (esp. genetic) information. Freq. *attrib.* M20.

D. CARKEET You can't shoot the messenger for bringing bad news. D. FLANAGAN Jason asked for a cheque to be sent round by messenger.

2 A person sent to prepare the way; a herald, a precursor, a harbinger. *arch.* ME.

fig. SHAKESPEARE Yon grey lines That fret the clouds are messengers of day.

3 A government official employed to carry dispatches and formerly to apprehend state prisoners; a courier. LME. **4 a** Esp. *NAUTICAL.* An endless rope, cable, or chain used with a capstan to haul a cable or to drive a powered winch etc. Also, a light line used to haul or support a larger cable. M17. ▸**b** A device able to be sent down a line, esp. in order to trip a mechanism. M18.

– PHRASES: ***express messenger***: see EXPRESS *adjective.* **King's messenger**, **Queen's messenger** a courier employed by the British Government to carry important official papers within Britain and abroad. ***second messenger***: see SECOND *adjective.*

– COMB.: **messenger-at-arms** *Scot.* an official employed to execute writs from the Court of Session and the High Court of Justiciary; **messenger cable** a cable used to support a power cable or other conductor of electricity; a suspension cable or wire; **messenger RNA** *BIOLOGY* RNA which is synthesized in a cell nucleus with a nucleotide sequence complementary to the coding sequence of a gene (transcription), and passes from the nucleus to a ribosome, where its nucleotide sequence determines the amino-acid sequence of a protein synthesized there (translation); abbreviation ***mRNA***; **messenger wire** = ***messenger cable*** above.

▸**B** *verb trans.* Send by messenger. (*rare* before L20). E19.

■ **messengership** *noun* the position or function of a messenger E17.

mimicry /ˈmɪmɪkri/ *noun.* L17.
[ORIGIN from MIMIC *noun* + -RY.]

1 The action, practice, or art of mimicking; an act, instance, or example of this. L17.

BARONESS ORCZY The mimicry was so perfect, the tone of the voice so accurately produced. DENNIS POTTER When she told them what the wicked old witch said . . her own face twisted and snarled in chilling mimicry. D. FRASER With his gift of mimicry, he also caught the great man's manner perfectly.

in mimicry of in imitation of.

2 *BIOLOGY* A close external resemblance which (part of) one living creature (or occas. a nest or other structure) bears to (part of) another, or to some inanimate object. E19.

R. DAWKINS A remarkable perfection of mimicry on the part of the cuckoo eggs.

MERTENSIAN mimicry. *Müllerian mimicry*: see MÜLLERIAN *adjective*[2].

---

pronunciation (/ˈmɛsɪndʒə/)
see § 4.2, p. xxx

etymology (e.g. [ORIGIN Old French ... etc.])
indicated by bold square brackets and ORIGIN
see § 4.9, p. xxxv

illustrative quotation block
indicated by a tinted box
see § 4.13, p. xxxvii

subsense (e.g. ▸**b**)
indicated by small arrow and bold letter
see § 4.10, p. xxxv

date (e.g. L17)
indicates a word's first recorded use
see § 4.8, p. xxxiv

cross-reference (e.g. MÜLLERIAN)
indicated by small capitals
see § 5, p. xxxviii

†mop *noun*[1]. ME.
[ORIGIN Uncertain: perh. rel. to MOPE *noun*, *verb*.]
1 A fool, a simpleton. ME–L15.
2 A baby or toddler. Also, a rag doll. LME–L16.
– NOTE: Survives as 1st elem. of MOPPET, MOPSY.

mop *noun*[2]. LME–M18.
[ORIGIN Unknown.]
A young fish, esp. a whiting or gurnard. Also ***whiting mop***, ***gurnard mop***.

mop /mɒp/ *noun*[3]. Also (earlier) **†map(p)**. L15.
[ORIGIN Uncertain: perh. ult. connected with Latin *mappa* (see MAP *noun*[1]). In branch II from the verb.]
▸I 1 An implement consisting of a long stick with a bundle of thick loose strings or a piece of foam rubber etc. fastened to one end so as to soak up liquid easily, used in cleaning floors (also ***floor mop***); (in full ***dish mop***), a smaller form of this for washing dishes. L15.

B. REID A lady who was cleaning the floor with a bucket and mop.

2 A thick mass of something, esp. of or *of* hair. E19.

R. CROMPTON Thomas's blue eyes, beneath a mop of curls.

mops and brooms *slang* half-drunk. ***Mrs Mop***: see MRS.
3 Any of various small instruments resembling a mop, as (*a*) a circular pad of cloth used in polishing silver with rouge; (*b*) a surgical instrument with a sponge at the end of a handle, for applying medicated fluids or removing purulent matter. M19.
▸II 4 ***mop-up***, the action or an act of mopping something up. E20.
5 A rub, wipe, or clean with a mop. L20.
– COMB.: **mop-board** *US* a skirting board; **mophead** (*a*) the head of a mop; (*b*) (a person with) a thick head of hair; **mopstick** the handle of a floor mop; ***mop-up***: see sense 4 above.

mop /mɒp/ *noun*[4]. *arch.* L15.
[ORIGIN Rel. to MOP *verb*[1].]
A grimace, orig. esp. as made by a monkey. Chiefly in ***mops and mows***.

mop /mɒp/ *noun*[5]. L17.
[ORIGIN Perh. from a mop (MOP *noun*[1]) carried by maidservants seeking employment.]
ENGLISH HISTORY. An annual fair at which servants seeking to be hired assembled together. Also ***mop fair***.

mop /mɒp/ *verb*[1] *intrans.* *arch.* Infl. **-pp-**. M16.
[ORIGIN Rel. to MOP *noun*[4].]
Make a grimace. Chiefly in ***mop and mow***.

mora /ˈmɔːrə/ *noun*[1]. Pl. **morae** /ˈmɔːriː/. M16.
[ORIGIN Latin = delay.]
1 *SCOTS LAW*. Undue delay in the assertion of a claim etc. M16.
†2 A short space of time; a delay. *rare*. M–L17.
3 a A unit of metrical time equal to the duration of a short syllable. M19. **▸b** *LINGUISTICS*. The minimal unit of duration of a speech sound. M20.

mutatis mutandis /mjuːˌtɑːtɪs njuːˈtandɪs, muː-, -iːs/ *adverbial phr.* E16.
[ORIGIN Latin, lit. 'things being changed that have to be changed'.]
Making the necessary changes; with due alteration of details.

J. BAYLEY Both gifts he shares, *mutatis mutandis*, with the American poets.

---

dagger (†)
indicates a word is obsolete
see § 4.1, p. xxx

date range (e.g. ME–L15)
indicates a sense's first and last recorded usage
see § 4.8, p. xxxiv

note
see § 4.15, p. xxxviii

variant form (e.g. †**map(p)**)
(the dagger indicates that it is obsolete)
see § 4.6, p. xxxiii

major semantic divisions (e.g. ▸I, ▸II)
indicated by arrow and bold roman numeral
see § 4.10, p. xxxv

label (e.g. *slang*)
showing register
see § 4.5, p. xxxii

cross-reference (e.g. MRS)
indicated by small capitals
see § 5, p. xxxviii

label (e.g. *US*)
showing regional distribution
see § 4.5, p. xxxii

homonym numbers (e.g. [4], [5])
indicate different words with the same spelling
see § 4.4, p. xxxii

label (e.g. *arch*)
showing currency
see § 4.5, p. xxxii

inflected form (e.g. **-pp-**)
see § 4.7, p. xxxiii

plural form (e.g. **morae**)
with pronunciation /ˈmɔːriː/
see § 4.7, p. xxxiii

bold italics (e.g. ***mutatis mutandis***)
indicate a word is not fully naturalized in English
see § 4.1, p. xxx

Transliteration guide

Transliteration of Greek

a	α	i	ι	ō	ω	t	τ
b	β	k	κ	p	π	th	θ
d	δ	kh	χ	ph	φ	u	υ
e	ε	l	λ	ps	ψ	x	ξ
ē	η	m	μ	r	ρ	z	ζ
g	γ	n	ν	rh	ῥ		
h	῾ (rough breathing) over a following vowel	o	ο	s	σ, ς		

Transliteration of Russian

a	а	i	и	r	р	ya	я
b	б	ĭ	й	s	с	yu	ю
ch	ч	k	к	sh	ш	z	з
d	д	kh	х	shch	щ	zh	ж
e	е	l	л	t	т	'	ь
é	э	m	м	ts	ц	"	ъ
ë	ё	n	н	u	у		
f	ф	o	о	v	в		
g	г	p	п	y	ы		

Shorter Oxford English Dictionary

Aa

A, a /eɪ/.
The first letter of the modern English alphabet and of the ancient Roman one, corresp. to Greek *alpha*, Hebrew *aleph*. The sound orig. represented by the letter, in English as in Latin, was a low back vowel, articulated with the tongue as low as possible in the mouth, considerable separation of the jaws, and spreading of the lips. For its principal mod. sounds see the Key to the Pronunciation. Pl. **A's**, **As**.
▸**I 1** The letter and its sound.
A per se A by itself, esp. as a word; *fig.* the first, best, or unique person or thing. **A to Z** a comprehensive manual. **from A to Z** over the entire range, completely.
2 The shape of the letter.
A-frame (a house or other structure supported by) a frame shaped like a capital A. **A-line** (a garment) having a narrow waist or shoulders and a somewhat flared skirt. **A-shaped** *adjective* having a shape or a cross-section like the capital letter A. **A tent** a tent with sides sloping down to the ground from a ridge pole.
▸**II** Symbolical uses.
3 Used to denote serial order; applied e.g. to the first group or section, sheet of a book, etc.
4 *MUSIC*. (Cap. A.) The sixth note of the diatonic scale of C major, or the first of the relative minor scale of C. Also, the scale of a composition with A as its keynote.
5 *LOGIC*. (Cap. A.) A universal affirmative proposition.
6 The first hypothetical person or example.
from A to B from any one place to some other place.
7 *MATH*. (Usu. italic *a*.) The first known quantity.
8 (Usu. cap. A.) Designating the first or highest class (of road, academic marks, population as regards affluence, etc.).
A-list (orig. *US*) *noun & adjective* (**a**) a (notional) roster of the most celebrated or sought-after individuals (esp. in the film industry); (**b**) *adjective* pre-eminent, top-ranking. **A No. 1** *US colloq.* excellent, first-rate. **A1** in Lloyd's Register of Shipping, used of ships in first-class condition as to hull (A) and stores (1); *colloq.* excellent, first-rate. **A-side** (the music of) the more important side of a gramophone record. **A Special** *hist.* a member of a full-time special police force in Northern Ireland.
9 (Cap. A.) The blood group characterized by the presence of the agglutinogen designated A and the absence of that designated B.
AB the blood group characterized by the presence of both A and B agglutinogens. **ABO** *adjective* designating or pertaining to the system in which blood is divided into four types (A, AB, B, and O) on the basis of the presence or absence of certain inherited antigens.
10 (Cap. A.) Designating a series of international standard paper sizes with a fixed shape and twice the area of the next size, as *A0*, *A1*, *A2*, *A3*, *A4*, etc.
11 *ANATOMY & ZOOLOGY*. [initial letter of *anisotropic*.] **A band**, a dark transverse band in a myofibril, consisting of interdigitating filaments of actin and myosin.
▸**III 12** Abbrevs.: **A.** = Academician; Academy; Associate. **A** = (*BIOLOGY*) adenine (in DNA sequences); (*hist.*) adult (as a film classification); advanced (in ***A level***, ***A/S level***, of the General Certificate of Education examination); all (in ***A-OK***, ***A-okay*** (colloq.) in perfect order or condition); ampere; atom(ic) (in ***A-bomb*** etc.); attack (in designations of US aircraft types). **a.** = accepted (on bills of exchange); active (of verbs); adjective; [Latin] *ante* before (with dates; also *a*). **a** = (as *prefix*) atto-. **Å** (*PHYSICS*) = angstrom. **@** = at: (**a**) used to indicate cost or rate per unit item; (**b**) used in Internet addresses between the user's name and the domain name.

a /ə/ *pronoun*. *obsolete* exc. *dial.* **ME**.
[**ORIGIN** Unstressed form of *ha* he, *heo* she, *hi* they, etc.]
He, she, it, they.
SHAKES. *Haml.* Now 'a is a-praying. TENNYSON Doctors, they knaws nowt, for a says what's nawways true.

a /ə/; *stressed* eɪ/ *adjective* (usu. called the *indefinite article*; in mod. usage also classed as a *determiner*). Before a vowel sound (see below) **an** /ən/; *stressed* an/.
[**ORIGIN** Old English *ān* one, weakened to proclitic form in early Middle English.]
▸**I 1** One, some, any, (the oneness, or indefiniteness, being implied rather than asserted). **OE**. ▸**b** One like. **LME**.
SHAKES. *Wint. T.* I have . . said many A prayer upon her grave. KEATS I had a dove and the sweet dove died. C. TOMLINSON As good a student As any in the house. M. LASKI They had passed and repassed each other a dozen times. J. BETJEMAN In Ealing on a Sunday Bell-haunted quiet falls. **b** SHAKES. *Merch. V.* A Daniel come to judgment. TENNYSON Shall I weep if a Poland fall?
2 Before quantifiers: some, a matter of, about. *obsolete* exc. *dial.* & in ***a few***, ***a great many***, ***a good many***. **OE**.
WILLIAM TURNER Stepe them a fiue or sixe dayes in vineger.
3 A certain, a particular. **ME**. ▸**b** A single; the same. **M16**.
Notes & Queries It was popularized by a Mr. Trudgen. **b** SHAKES. *Haml.* These foils have all a length? E. DICKINSON I'll tell you how the Sun rose—A ribbon at a time.
▸**II 4** In, to, or for, each. (Orig. the preposition ***a***, Old English *an*, *on*, defining time, as in twice *a* day; afterwards identified with the indef. article, and extended from time to space, measure, weight, number: see **A** *preposition*[1] 3.) **OE**.
DEFOE Four pieces of eight a man. YEATS But always went to chapel twice a week. *Oxford Times* Teams of six a side, each member of the one team fighting a duel with the six members of the other. J. STALLWORTHY Roast chestnuts, a shilling / a bag.
– **NOTE**: *An* was freq. before a consonant to end of **13**, before sounded *h* until **18**. In standard English *an* is now used before a vowel sound (including *h* mute), e.g. *an egg*, *an honour*, and *a* is used before a consonant (including sounded *h* and *eu-*, *u-* pronounced /jʊ, juː/), e.g. *a pen*, *a host*, *a eunuch*, *a unit*. In **18–20** *an* was commonly retained before an unstressed *h* (as in *an historian* and *an hotel*), because the initial *h* was often not pronounced, and less commonly before *eu-*, *u-* (*an university*).

a /ə/ *verb trans. & intrans.* Now chiefly *slang*. **ME**.
[**ORIGIN** Unstressed var.]
= **HAVE** *verb*. Freq. written joined to a preceding aux. verb, as ***coulda***, ***mighta*** (= **-A**[5]).
– **NOTE**: Common **13–17**. After **17** the reduced form of **HAVE** *verb* was freq. written *ha*, *ha'*, though no *h* was pronounced.

a /ə/ *preposition*[1]. *arch. & dial.* See also **A-**[2]. **OE**.
[**ORIGIN** Unstressed form of **ON** *preposition*: cf. **O'** *preposition*[1].]
= **ON** *preposition* in various senses current before the 18th cent.
1 Position or direction: on, on to, at, in, towards. **OE**.
LD BERNERS The quene was brought a bedde. SHAKES. *Hen. V* Stand a tip-toe. C. TOURNEUR That's enow a' conscience!
Compounds: ***aback***, ***abed***, ***aboard***, ***afield***, ***afoot***, ***ashore***, etc.
2 Partition: in, into. **OE**.
SHAKES. *Hen. VIII* Torn a pieces.
Compound: ***asunder***.
3 Time: in, on, by. Esp. with adverbs of repetition (taken as the indef. article: see **A** *adjective* 4). **OE**.
CHAUCER Ful ofte a day. BUNYAN The bold villain . . haunts . . honest men's houses a nights. D. RUNYON A sure thing that is coming up a Monday.
Compound: ***nowadays***.
†**4** Manner: in, with. **OE–L17**.
C. MARLOWE Stands here a purpose.
†**5** Capacity: in (someone's name). **OE–E18**.
SHAKES. *Rich. II* A God's name, let it go.
6 State: in. **OE**.
AV *2 Chron.* 2:18 To set the people a worke.
Compounds: ***afloat***, ***alive***, ***asleep***, etc.
7 Process (with a verbal noun taken pass.): in course of, undergoing. **LME**.
AV *1 Pet.* 3:20 When the Arke was a preparing.
8 Action (with a verbal noun taken actively). With *be*: engaged in. With a verb of motion: to, into. **E16**.
ROBERT BURTON He would burst out a laughing. R. BENTLEY To set them a going. OED Such positions rarely go a begging.

a /ə/ *preposition*[2]. Now chiefly *slang*. **LME**.
[**ORIGIN** Var.]
= **OF** *preposition* (cf. **O'** *preposition*[2]). Now freq. written joined to a preceding word, as ***cuppa***, ***kinda***, ***loadsa***, ***lotsa***, ***lotta***, (= **-A**[6]).

a *interjection* see **AH** *interjection*.

a' /ɔː/ *adjective, noun, & adverb*. *Scot.* Also †**a**; **aw** & other vars. **LME**.
[**ORIGIN** Form of **ALL**, with *l* vocalized.]
= **ALL**.

a- /ə/ *prefix*[1] (not productive).
Old English *ā-*, orig. *ar-*, away, on, up, out, chiefly forming verbs, as ***abide***, ***arise***. Sometimes conf. with **A-**[5].

a- /ə/ *prefix*[2]. **OE**.
[**ORIGIN** Proclitic var.]
= **A** *preposition*[1].

a- /ə/ *prefix*[3] (not productive). **OE**.
Reduced form of Old English *of* off, from, of (see **A** *preposition*[2]), as ***anew***.

a- /ə/ *prefix*[4]. Now *dial.* **ME**.
Reduced form of **I-**[1], **Y-** (from Old English *ġe-*). Also written as a separate word.

a- /ə/ *prefix*[5] (not productive). **ME**.
Repr. French *a-*, *à* from Latin *ad(-)* with the sense of motion to, change into, addition, or intensification, as ***abandon***, ***alarm***, ***amass***, ***avenue***: see **AD-**.

a- /ə/ *prefix*[6] (not productive). **ME**.
Repr. French *a-* from Latin *ab(-)* off, away, from (see **AB-**), as ***abridge***. Sometimes refash., as ***abstain***, or conf. with **A-**[5] and respelt, as ***assoil***.

a- /ə/ *prefix*[7] (not productive). **ME**.
Repr. Anglo-Norman *a-*, Old French *e-*, *es-* from Latin *ex-* out, utterly (see **EX-**[1]), as ***abash***.

a- /ə/ *prefix*[8] (not productive).
Repr. Latin *a-* reduced form of *ad-* before *sc*, *sp*, *st*, as ***ascend***: see **AD-**.

a- /ə/ *prefix*[9] (not productive).
Repr. Latin *a-* reduced form of *ab-* before *v*: see **AB-**.

a- /ə, eɪ, *stressed* a/ *prefix*[10].
Repr. Greek *a-* used before a consonant for *an-* without, not (see **AN-**[5]), as ***abyss***, ***apetalous***. A productive prefix of negation and privation with words of Greek and also Latin origin, as ***agnostic***, ***amoral***.

†**a-** *prefix*[11].
Prefixed (esp. by Spenser and other archaists) to words where it had no historical or etymological basis. Often treated like **A-**[8] and spelt *ad-*, *ac-*, *af-*, etc.

-a /ə/ *suffix*[1].
Repr. Greek & Latin nom. sing. ending of fem. nouns, as ***idea***, ***arena***: cf. **-IA**[1].

-a /ə/ *suffix*[2].
Repr. mod. Romance (Italian, Portuguese, & Spanish) ending of fem. nouns, as ***stanza***, ***duenna***.

-a /ə/ *suffix*[3].
Repr. Greek & Latin pl. ending of neut. nouns, adopted unchanged as English pl., as ***phenomena***, ***data***: cf. **-IA**[2].

-a /ə, ɑː/ *suffix*[4].
Appended to lines in burlesque poetry and other popular verse for metrical reasons.

-a *suffix*[5] see **A** *verb*.

-a *suffix*[6] see **A** *preposition*[2].

AA *abbreviation*.
1 Alcoholics Anonymous.
2 Anti-aircraft.
3 Automobile Association.

aa /ˈɑːɑː/ *noun*. **M19**.
[**ORIGIN** Hawaiian *ʻaʻā*.]
GEOLOGY. Rough, clinkery, scoriaceous lava. Cf. **PAHOEHOE**.

AAA *abbreviation*.
1 Amateur Athletic Association.
2 American or Australian Automobile Association.
3 Anti-aircraft artillery. *US*.

AAAS *abbreviation*.
American Association for the Advancement of Science.

aah *interjection, noun, & verb* var. of **AH**.

aam /ɑːm, ɔːm/ *noun*. *obsolete* exc. *hist.* Also **aum** /ɔːm/. **LME**.
[**ORIGIN** Dutch *aam* = German *Ahm*, *Ohm* ult. from Greek *amē* bucket.]
A Dutch and German liquid measure of varying capacity, 170–200 litres (approx. 37–44 gallons), used in England for Rhine wine.

aandblom /ˈɑːntblɒm/ *noun*. *S. Afr.* Also **avondbloem** /ˈɑːvɒntbluːm/. **L18**.
[**ORIGIN** Afrikaans *aandblom*, from *aand* evening + *blom* flower, Dutch *avondbloem*.]
Any of several sweet-scented plants of the iris family with flowers which tend to open in the evening, *esp.* one belonging to the genus *Hesperantha*. Also = **AFRIKANER** 2.

A & E *abbreviation*.
Accident and emergency.

A & M *abbreviation*.
(Hymns) Ancient and Modern.

A & R *abbreviation*.
Artists and recording (or repertoire).

A

aardvark /ˈɑːdvɑːk/ *noun*. L18.
[ORIGIN Afrikaans *aardvark(en)* (now *erdvark*), from *aarde* earth + *varken* pig.]
A nocturnal, insectivorous, badger-sized mammal, *Orycteropus afer*, having large ears, a long snout, and a long extensile tongue, native to sub-Saharan Africa.

aardwolf /ˈɑːdwʊlf/ *noun*. Pl. **-wolves** /-wʊlvz/. M19.
[ORIGIN Afrikaans, from *aarde* earth + *wolf* wolf.]
A largely insectivorous southern African quadruped, *Proteles cristatus*, related to the hyenas, and having an erectile crest.

Aaronic /ɛːˈrɒnɪk/ *adjective*. M17.
[ORIGIN from *Aaron* (see below) + -IC.]
Pertaining to Aaron, the first Jewish high priest; Levitical; resembling or characteristic of a high priest.
■ **Aaronical** *adjective* E17.

Aaron's beard /ˌɛːr(ə)nz ˈbɪəd/ *noun phr*. E19.
[ORIGIN *Psalms* 133:2.]
Any of various plants suggestive of beards; *esp*. the rose of Sharon, *Hypericum calycinum*, which has tufts of hair-like stamens.

Aaron's rod /ˌɛːr(ə)nz ˈrɒd/ *noun phr*. M18.
[ORIGIN *Numbers* 17:8.]
Any of various tall upright plants; *esp*. the great mullein, *Verbascum thapsus*.

AARP *abbreviation*.
American Association of Retired Persons.

aasvogel /ˈɑːsfəʊɡ(ə)l/ *noun*. *S. Afr*. M19.
[ORIGIN Afrikaans (now *aasvoël*), from *aas* carrion + *vogel* bird.]
A vulture.

AAU *abbreviation*. *US*.
Amateur Athletic Union.

AB *abbreviation*.
1 Able (seaman).
2 Latin *Artium Baccalaureus* Bachelor of Arts. Cf. **BA**. *US*.

Ab /ab/ *noun*[1]. Also **Av** /av/. L18.
[ORIGIN Hebrew *'āḇ*.]
In the Jewish calendar, the eleventh month of the civil and fifth of the religious year, usu. coinciding with parts of July and August. Also, the twelfth month of the Syriac calendar.

ab /ab/ *noun*[2]. *slang*. M20.
[ORIGIN Abbreviation.]
An abdominal muscle. Usu. in *pl*.

ab- /əb, ab/ *prefix*.
Repr. Latin *ab* off, away, from. In mod. formations, = position away from, as ***abaxial***.
■ **ab'apical** *adjective* (BIOLOGY) pertaining to or designating the side or part remote from or opposite to the apex M20.

ABA *abbreviation*.
1 Amateur Boxing Association.
2 American Bar Association. *US*.
3 American Booksellers' Association. *US*.

aba /ˈabə/ *noun*. Also **abba**. E19.
[ORIGIN Arabic *'abā'*.]
A sleeveless outer garment of various forms, worn by Arabs. Cf. **ABAYA**.

abaca /ˈabəkə/ *noun*. M18.
[ORIGIN Spanish *abacá* from Tagalog *abaká*.]
Manila hemp; the plant yielding this.

abaci *noun pl.* see **ABACUS**.

abaciscus /abəˈsɪskəs/ *noun*. Pl. **-sci** /-skʌɪ/, **-scuses**. M18.
[ORIGIN Latin from Greek *abakiskos* dim. of *abakos* **ABACUS**.]
A tile or square in a mosaic pavement.

abacist /ˈabəsɪst/ *noun*. LME.
[ORIGIN medieval Latin *abacista*, formed as **ABACUS**: see **-IST**.]
A person who makes calculations with an abacus.

aback /əˈbak/ *adverb*.
[ORIGIN Old English *on bæc*: see **A** *preposition*[1] 1, **BACK** *noun*[1], and note below.]
1 Backwards; away, to a distance. *arch. & dial.* OE.
2 In the rear, behind; at a distance, aloof. *arch. & dial.* OE.
aback of, **aback o'** *arch. & dial.* at the back of, behind.
3 NAUTICAL. Of square sails: laid back against the mast by a headwind. Of a ship: with sails thus. L17.
take aback disconcert by a sudden check, discomfit. **taken aback** NAUTICAL caught with the sails aback suddenly, through bad steering or a shift of wind, and driven astern.
– NOTE: Orig. written as two words. By 13 the prefix began to be dropped, leaving *back* as the ordinary mod. form of the word, *aback* being chiefly confined to nautical lang. Cf. *adown* and *down*.

abackward /əˈbakwəd/ *adverb*. *arch*. ME.
[ORIGIN from **ABACK** + **-WARD**.]
= **BACKWARD** *adverb*.

abacost /ˈabəkɒst/ *noun*. L20.
[ORIGIN Congolese French, contr. of *à bas le costume* down with the (Western) suit.]
A Congolese man's suit consisting of a short-sleeved collarless jacket and loose trousers.

†**abactor** *noun*. M17–E19.
[ORIGIN Latin, from *abact-* pa. ppl stem of *abigere* drive away: see **-OR**.]
A person who steals cattle in large numbers.

abacus /ˈabəkəs/ *noun*. Pl. **-ci** /-sʌɪ/, **-cuses**. LME.
[ORIGIN Latin from Greek *abakos*, *abax* slab, orig. drawing board covered with dust, from Semitic: cf. Hebrew *'āḇāq* dust.]
†**1** A board strewn with sand, for drawing figures, etc. Only in LME.
2 ARCHITECTURE. The upper member of a capital, supporting the architrave. M16.
3 A calculating frame, *esp*. one with balls sliding on wires. L17.
4 CLASSICAL ANTIQUITIES. A sideboard. L18.

Abaddon /əˈbad(ə)n/ *noun*. LME.
[ORIGIN Hebrew *'ăḇaddōn* (the place of) destruction.]
1 Apollyon, 'the angel of the bottomless pit' (*Revelation* 9:11); the Devil. LME.
2 The pit itself, Hell. L17.

abaft /əˈbɑːft/ *adverb & preposition*. ME.
[ORIGIN from **A** *preposition*[1] 1 + **BAFT** *adverb*.]
Chiefly NAUTICAL. ▶**A** *adverb*. †**1** Backwards. ME–L15.
2 In the rear; in the stern half of the ship. E17.
▶**B** *preposition*. Behind; nearer the stern than. L15.
abaft the beam: see **BEAM** *noun* 10c.

abaht /əˈbɑːt/ *adverb & preposition*. *dial*. M19.
[ORIGIN Repr. a pronunc.]
= **ABOUT**.

†**abaisance** *noun*. L17–M18.
[ORIGIN Old French *abaissance*, formed as **ABASE** + **-ANCE**.]
A low bow.

abalone /abəˈləʊni/ *noun*. M19.
[ORIGIN Amer. Spanish *abulón* from Shoshonean *aulun*.]
An edible gastropod mollusc of the genus *Haliotis*, having an ear-shaped shell lined with mother-of-pearl.

†**aband** *verb trans*. Only in L16.
[ORIGIN Contr.]
= **ABANDON** *verb* 3, 4.

SPENSER Enforst the kingdome to aband.

abandon /əˈband(ə)n, *foreign* abɑ̃dɔ̃/ *noun*. E19.
[ORIGIN French, from *abandonner* **ABANDON** *verb*.]
Surrender to natural impulses; freedom from constraint or convention. Cf. **ABANDONMENT** 4.

abandon /əˈband(ə)n/ *verb trans*. LME.
[ORIGIN Old French *abandoner*, from *à bandon*, from *à* at, to (see **A-**[5]) + *bandon* jurisdiction, control, etc.]
†**1** Bring under control, subdue. LME–M16.

J. SKELTON Fortune to her law cannot abandune me.

2 Give up to the control of another person or agent, surrender *to*. LME.

DRYDEN Abandoning his charge to fate. ARNOLD BENNETT Like a schoolgirl abandoning herself utterly to some girlish grief. J. LE CARRÉ The boiling month of August, when Parisians by tradition abandon their city to the . . bus-loads of packaged tourists.

3 Cease to hold, use, or practise; give up, renounce. LME.

J. BRAINE I might as well abandon that idea. J. GROSS He turned his back on teaching and abandoned mathematics, except as a pastime.

4 Desert; leave behind; leave without help. L15.

C. G. SELIGMAN The aged were abandoned to perish of hunger.

abandon ship take to the lifeboats and leave a ship in imminent danger of sinking, burning, or exploding.
†**5** Banish, expel. M16–M17.

SHAKES. *Tam. Shr.* Abandon'd from your bed.

6 Relinquish a claim to (property insured) to underwriters. M18.
■ **abando'nee** *noun* a person, esp. an underwriter, to whom anything is formally abandoned M19. **abandoner** *noun* L16.

abandoned /əˈband(ə)nd/ *ppl adjective*. LME.
[ORIGIN from **ABANDON** *verb* + **-ED**[1].]
1 Having given oneself up *to* (an impulse); unrestrained, uninhibited. LME. ▸**b** *absol.* Given up to evil influences, profligate. L17.
2 Forsaken, cast off. L15.
■ **abandonedly** *adverb* E18.

abandonment /əˈband(ə)nm(ə)nt/ *noun*. L16.
[ORIGIN Old French *abandonnement*, formed as **ABANDON** *verb* + **-MENT**.]
1 The action or an act of abandoning; the condition of being abandoned. L16.

J. WAIN She had submerged her will in Robert's, but without any abject abandonment of her own personality.

2 LAW. The relinquishment of an interest in property or of a claim for relief in legal proceedings. E19.
3 The surrender of oneself to an influence etc.; lack of inhibition or restraint, abandon. M19.

DISRAELI His manner was frank even to abandonment. A. SILLITOE The hasty abandonment of making love.

abanet *noun* var. of **ABNET**.

abase /əˈbeɪs/ *verb trans*. LME.
[ORIGIN Old French *abaissier*, from **A-**[5] + *baissier* to lower, ult. from late Latin *bassus* short of stature. Infl. by **BASE** *adjective*.]
1 Lower (physically); stoop. *arch*. LME.

SHAKES. *Rich. III* Will she yet abase her eyes on me. A. S. BYATT A half-moon from abased nape to rounded buttocks.

2 Lower in rank, office, etc.; humiliate, degrade. LME.

E. A. FREEMAN This famous refusal of Rolf to abase himself.

†**3** Lower in price or value; debase (coin). M16–M18.
■ **abasedly** /-sɪdli/ *adverb* in an abased manner LME. **abaser** *noun* L16.

abasement /əˈbeɪsm(ə)nt/ *noun*. M16.
[ORIGIN from **ABASE** + **-MENT**, or from French *abaissement*.]
The action or an act of abasing; the condition of being abased.

abash /əˈbaʃ/ *verb*. ME.
[ORIGIN Anglo-Norman *abaiss-* = Old French *esbaïss-* lengthened stem of *e(s)baïr* (mod. *ébahir*), from **ES-** + *baïr* astound: see **A-**[7].]
1 *verb trans*. Destroy the self-possession of, disconcert with sudden shame, consciousness of error or presumption, etc. ME.
†**2** *verb intrans*. Lose self-possession through surprise, shame, etc. LME–L16.
■ **abashedly** /-ʃɪdli/ *adverb* in an abashed manner E19. **abashedness** *noun* (*rare*) the state or quality of being abashed, abashment M16. **abashless** *adjective* (*poet.*) unabashed M19. **abashment** *noun* confusion from shame etc. LME.

abask /əˈbɑːsk/ *adverb & pred. adjective*. M19.
[ORIGIN from **A-**[2] + **BASK** *verb*.]
Basking.

†**abastardize** *verb trans*. Also **-ise**. L16–L17.
[ORIGIN Old French *abastardir*, *-issant*, formed as **A-**[5], **BASTARD**: refashioned after verbs in **-IZE**.]
Render bastard; debase.
■ Also †**abastard** *verb trans*. E–M17.

†**abate** *noun*[1]. LME–L17.
[ORIGIN from **ABATE** *verb*[1].]
= **ABATEMENT** *noun*[1].

abate /əˈbɑːti, *foreign* abˈbaːte/ *noun*[2]. Also **abb-**. E18.
[ORIGIN Italian, from Latin *abbat-* **ABBOT**.]
An Italian abbot or other ecclesiastic. Cf. **ABBÉ**.

abate /əˈbeɪt/ *verb*[1]. ME.
[ORIGIN Old French *abatre* ult. from Latin *batt(u)ere* to beat: see **A-**[5].]
1 *verb trans*. Put an end to. *obsolete* in *gen.* sense. ME. ▸**b** *verb trans. spec.* in LAW. Cause (a nuisance, an action) to cease. ME. ▸**c** *verb intrans*. Become null and void. L15.

c DEFOE Commissions shall not abate by the death of his majesty.

†**2** *verb trans. & intrans.* Bring down (a person) physically, socially, or mentally; depress, humble; fall, be humbled. ME–M17. ▸**b** *verb trans*. Curtail, deprive, *of*. LME–M19.

CHAUCER The hyer that they were in this present lyf, the moore shulle they be abated and defouled in helle. **b** SHAKES. *Lear* She hath abated me of half my train.

3 *verb trans. & intrans.* Reduce in size, amount, or value. *arch*. ME.

AV *Gen.* 8:3 The waters were abated. DEFOE As wages abate to the poor, provisions must abate in the market. J. GALSWORTHY It's much more paying to abate a price than to increase it.

4 *verb trans. & intrans.* Lessen in force or intensity; moderate, diminish. ME.

T. S. ELIOT As soon as relief has abated our rage. A. POWELL The rain had to some extent abated.

5 *verb trans*. Take away (a part of something), deduct. LME. ▸**b** *fig*. Bar, except. L16.

DEFOE Rather than abate a farthing of the price they had asked. B. FRANKLIN She would abate me two shillings a week. **b** S. JOHNSON Abating his brutality, he was a very good master.

6 *verb trans*. Beat down. Formerly also, destroy, level with the ground. LME.

R. FABYAN Ye gates of Bruges . . were abated.

†**7** *verb trans*. Blunt. Cf. **BATE** *verb*[2] 6. M16–L17.

BACON To abate the edge of envy.

– WITH PREPOSITIONS IN SPECIALIZED SENSES: **abate of** *arch.* deduct something from, lessen.
■ **abatable** *adjective* LME. **abater** *noun*[1] E17.

abate /əˈbeɪt/ *verb*[2] *intrans*. & (less commonly) *refl*. LME.
[ORIGIN Anglo-Norman *abatre*, earlier usu. *enbatre*, *em-*. Conf. with **ABATE** *verb*[1].]
LAW (now *hist*.). Enter land after the death of the owner but before the legal heir, thereby keeping that person out of possession.
■ **abater** *noun*[2] M17.

abatement /əˈbeɪtm(ə)nt/ *noun*[1]. LME.
[ORIGIN Old French, formed as **ABATE** *verb*[1] + **-MENT**.]
1 The action of abating; the state of being abated. LME.

O. CROMWELL Much abatement of my hopes. W. BLACKSTONE The abatement, or removal, of Nusances.

2 The result of abating; the amount by which anything is abated; decrease, deduction, drawback. **L15.**
3 *HERALDRY.* A charge representing an offence, dishonour, etc., committed. **E17.**

abatement /əˈbeɪtm(ə)nt/ *noun^2*. **ME.**
[**ORIGIN** Anglo-Norman, formed as **ABATE** *verb^2* + **-MENT**.]
LAW. The action of reducing a legacy which there are insufficient funds to pay in full; *hist.* the action of entering land after the death of the owner but before the legal heir, thereby keeping that person out of possession.

abatis /ˈabətɪs/ *noun*. Also **abattis** /əˈbatɪs/. *Pl. same*, **-es**. **M18.**
[**ORIGIN** French, formed as **ABATE** *verb^1*.]
MILITARY. A defence formed by placing felled trees lengthwise one over the other with their branches towards the enemy's line. Also, a barricade of barbed wire.
■ **abatised** /-st/ *adjective* **M19.**

abator /əˈbeɪtə/ *noun^1*. **L16.**
[**ORIGIN** Late Anglo-Norman *abato(u)r*, formed as **ABATE** *verb^1* + **-OR**.]
A person who or thing which abates; *esp.* in *LAW*, a person who abates a nuisance, an action, etc.

abator /əˈbeɪtə/ *noun^2*. **M16.**
[**ORIGIN** Late Anglo-Norman *abato(u)r*, formed as **ABATE** *verb^2* + **-OR**.]
LAW (now *hist.*). A person who abates in an inheritance.

abattis *noun* var. of **ABATIS**.

abattoir /ˈabətwɑː/ *noun*. **E19.**
[**ORIGIN** French, from *abattre* to fell: see **-ORY^1**.]
A slaughterhouse.

abature /ˈabətjʊə/ *noun*. **L16.**
[**ORIGIN** Old French & mod. French, formed as **ABATE** *verb^1* + **-URE**.]
HUNTING. A trace left by a stag in the underwood. Usu. in *pl.*

abaxial /abˈaksɪəl/ *adjective*. **M19.**
[**ORIGIN** from **AB-** + **AXIAL**.]
BOTANY. Off or away from the axis; (of the surface of a leaf etc.) initially facing away from the stem.

†**abay** *noun*. **ME–L17.**
[**ORIGIN** Old French *abai* (mod. *aboi*): see **BAY** *noun^1*.]
Baying of dogs upon their prey, esp. when closing round it.
stand at abay: said of the dogs. **be at abay**: said of the hunted animal.

abaya /əˈbeɪjə/ *noun*. **M19.**
[**ORIGIN** Arabic *ʿabāya*.]
= **ABA**.

Abaza /əˈbɑːzə/ *noun & adjective*. **E19.**
[**ORIGIN** Abaza.]
▸ **A** *noun*. **1** A member of a people inhabiting the north-west Caucasus. **E19.**
2 The language of this people. **M20.**
▸ **B** *adjective*. Of or pertaining to the Abazas or their language. **M19.**

abb /ab/ *noun*. **OE.**
[**ORIGIN** from **A-^{1}** + **WEB** *noun*.]
(Coarse wool used for) the woof or weft in a web.

Abba /ˈabə/ *noun^1*. **LME.**
[**ORIGIN** ecclesiastical Latin from New Testament Greek from Aramaic *ʾabbā* father.]
CHRISTIAN CHURCH. **1** ***Abba, father***: an invocation to God as Father (*Mark* 14:36 etc.). **LME.**
2 A title given to bishops and patriarchs in the Syrian Orthodox and Coptic Churches. **M17.**

abba *noun^2* var. of **ABA**.

abbacy /ˈabəsi/ *noun*. **LME.**
[**ORIGIN** ecclesiastical Latin *abbacia*, *abbatia*, from *abbat-* **ABBOT**: see **-ACY**.]
The office, jurisdiction, or tenure of an abbot or abbess.
■ Also †**abbatie** *noun* **ME–M17.**

Abbasid /əˈbasɪd, ˈabəsɪd/ *adjective & noun*. Also **-ide** /-ʌɪd/, **-ss-**. **M18.**
[**ORIGIN** from *ʿAbbās* (566–652) uncle of Muhammad + **-ID^3**.]
Of or pertaining to, a member of, the dynasty (750–1258) of caliphs of Baghdad claiming descent from ʿAbbās.

abbate *noun* var. of **ABATE** *noun^2*.

abbatial /əˈbeɪʃ(ə)l/ *adjective*. **L17.**
[**ORIGIN** French, or medieval Latin *abbatialis* from *abbat-* **ABBOT**: see **-IAL**.]
Of or pertaining to an abbacy, abbot, or abbess.
■ Also †**abbatical** *adjective* **M17–M19.**

Abbe /ˈabə/ *noun*. **L19.**
[**ORIGIN** Ernst *Abbe* (1840–1905), German physicist.]
OPTICS. Used *attrib.* and in *possess.* to designate optical instruments and concepts in optical theory introduced or popularized by Abbe.
Abbe condenser a condenser for compound microscopes in the form of a wide-aperture compound lens. **Abbe number** the reciprocal of the dispersive power of a transparent substance. **Abbe refractometer** an instrument for directly determining the refractive index of a small sample of liquid.

abbé /ˈabeɪ, *foreign* abe (*pl. same*)/ *noun*. **M16.**
[**ORIGIN** French from ecclesiastical Latin *abbat-* **ABBOT**.]
In France: an abbot, a secular priest, or *loosely* anyone, with or without official duties, who is entitled to wear ecclesiastical dress.

abbess /ˈabɛs/ *noun*. **ME.**
[**ORIGIN** Old French & mod. French *abbesse* from ecclesiastical Latin *abbadissa*, *-tissa*, from *abbat-* **ABBOT**: see **-ESS^1**.]
1 The female superior of an abbey of nuns. **ME.**
†**2** The mistress of a brothel. *slang*. **L16–L19.**

Abbevillian /abˈvɪlɪən/ *adjective & noun*. **M20.**
[**ORIGIN** French *Abbevillien*, from *Abbeville* in northern France: see **-IAN**.]
(Of) the earliest Palaeolithic period in Europe.

abbey /ˈabi/ *noun*. **ME.**
[**ORIGIN** Old French *ab(b)eïe* (mod. *abbaye*) from medieval Latin *abbatia*: see **ABBACY**, **-Y^3**.]
1 The jurisdiction or office of an abbot or abbess. **ME.**
2 A community of monks governed by an abbot or of nuns governed by an abbess. **ME.**
3 The building(s) occupied by such a community. **ME.** ▸**b** A church or house that was once an abbey or part of one. **M16.**
– **COMB.**: †**abbey-lubber** a lazy monk (used after the Reformation).

abbot /ˈabət/ *noun*. **OE.**
[**ORIGIN** ecclesiastical Latin *abbat-*, *abbas* from Greek *abbas* from Aramaic *ʾabbā* **ABBA** *noun^1*.]
The head or superior of an abbey of monks. After the dissolution of the monasteries also occas., a layman to whom an abbey's revenues were impropriated.
Abbot of Unreason, ***Abbot Unreason***: see **UNREASON** *noun*. ***titular abbot***: see **TITULAR** *adjective* 1.
■ †**abbatess**, **-otess** *noun* [ecclesiastical Latin: see **ABBESS**] = **ABBESS** **OE–L17.** †**abbotric(k)** *noun* [Old English *rīce* realm, rule] = **ABBACY** **OE–E18.** **abbotship** *noun* = **ABBACY** **LME.**

abbreviate /əˈbriːvɪət/ *adjective & noun*. **LME.**
[**ORIGIN** Late Latin *abbreviatus* pa. pple, formed as **ABBREVIATE** *verb*: see **-ATE^2**.]
▸ **A** *adjective*. †**1** Shortened, cut short. **LME–L17.**
2 *BOTANY & ZOOLOGY.* Relatively short. **M19.**
▸ **B** *noun*. An abridgement. Now only *SCOTS LAW*, a brief notice registering a petition for the sequestration of a bankrupt. **M16.**

abbreviate /əˈbriːvɪeɪt/ *verb*. **LME.**
[**ORIGIN** Latin *abbreviat-* pa. ppl stem of *abbreviare*, from *ab* **AB-** or *ad* **AD-** + *breviare*, from *brevis* short, **BRIEF** *adjective*: see **-ATE^3**.]
†**1** *verb trans.* Shorten by omitting details; epitomize. **LME–L17.** ▸†**b** *verb intrans.* Speak or write briefly. **L16–E17.**
2 *verb trans.* Cut short. **LME.** ▸**b** *esp.* Shorten (a word, phrase, or symbol). **L16.**
■ **abbreviatory** *adjective* **M19.**

abbreviation /əbriːvɪˈeɪʃ(ə)n/ *noun*. **LME.**
[**ORIGIN** French *abbréviation* or late Latin *abbreviatio(n-)*, formed as **ABBREVIATE** *verb*: see **-ATION**.]
1 The result of abbreviating; a reduced form; an abridgement. **LME.** ▸**b** *esp.* A shortened form of a word, phrase, or symbol. **L16.**
2 The action of abbreviating. **M16.**

abbreviator /əˈbriːvɪeɪtə/ *noun*. **E16.**
[**ORIGIN** medieval Latin, formed as **ABBREVIATE** *verb*: see **-OR**.]
1 A person who abbreviates. **E16.**
2 *hist.* An officer who composed briefs for the Pope. **M16.**

abbreviature /əˈbriːvɪətjʊə/ *noun*. Now *rare* or *obsolete*. **L16.**
[**ORIGIN** formed as **ABBREVIATE** *verb* + **-URE**. Cf. French †*abréviature*.]
1 **a** An abridgement. **L16.** ▸†**b** *gen.* An abbreviated state or form. **E–M17.** ▸**c** = **ABBREVIATION** 1b. **M17.**
†**2** = **ABBREVIATION** 2. **M–L17.**

ABC *abbreviation*.
1 American Broadcasting Corporation.
2 Australian Broadcasting Corporation (formerly Commission).

ABC /eɪbiːˈsiː/ *noun*. Formerly also as a simple word †**absey** etc. **ME.**
[**ORIGIN** The first three letters of the alphabet.]
1 The alphabet. **ME.**
as easy as ABC *colloq.* very easy.
†**2** An alphabetical acrostic, list, or table. **LME–M17.**
3 **a** A spelling book, a reading primer. **LME–M17.** ▸**b** *fig.* The first elements (*of* a subject). **M16.**

abdabs /ˈabdabz/ *noun pl. slang*. Also **habdabs** /ˈhabdabz/. **M20.**
[**ORIGIN** Unknown.]
Nervous anxiety, the heebie-jeebies. Freq. in ***screaming abdabs***.

abdicate /ˈabdɪkeɪt/ *verb*. **M16.**
[**ORIGIN** Latin *abdicat-* pa. ppl stem of *abdicare* renounce, from *ab* **AB-** + *dicare* proclaim: see **-ATE^3**.]
†**1** *verb trans.* Disown; *esp.* disinherit (a child). **M16–E19.**
†**2** *verb trans.* **a** *refl.* Cut oneself off *from* (an office or dignity); divest oneself of an office. **M16–L17.** ▸**b** Depose. Chiefly as ***abdicated*** *ppl adjective*. **E17–L18.**
†**3** *verb trans.* Discard. **M16–L17.**
4 *verb trans.* Give up (a right, responsibility, trust, office, or dignity) either formally or by default. **M17.**

C. T. ROWAN They've abdicated their judicial function and reduced it to a rubber stamp.

5 *verb intrans.* Renounce sovereignty. **E18.**

A. BARNETT The Queen . . has no intention of abdicating.

■ **abdicable** *adjective* able to be abdicated **L19.** **abdicant** *adjective & noun* (**a**) *adjective* (*rare*) abdicating; (**b**) *noun* a person who abdicates: **M17.** **abdicator** *noun* †(**a**) a person who is in favour of another abdicating; (**b**) a person who abdicates: **L17.**

abdication /abdɪˈkeɪʃ(ə)n/ *noun*. **M16.**
[**ORIGIN** Latin *abdicatio(n-)*, formed as **ABDICATE**: see **-ATION**.]
†**1** The action of formally disowning. **M16–M17.**
2 Resignation or renunciation of something. **E17.** ▸**b** *spec.* Renunciation of sovereignty. **L17.** ▸†**c** *LAW.* = **ABANDONMENT** 2. Only in **M18.**
†**3** Deposition from sovereignty. *rare*. Only in **M17.**

abditory /ˈabdɪt(ə)ri/ *noun*. *rare*. **M17.**
[**ORIGIN** medieval Latin *abditorium*, from *abdere* to hide: see **-ORY^1**.]
A concealed repository.

abdomen /ˈabdəmən, abˈdəʊmən/ *noun*. **M16.**
[**ORIGIN** Latin *abdomen*, *-min-*, of unknown origin.]
†**1** Fat round the belly. **M16–L17.**
2 *ANATOMY.* The belly; the part of the body containing the digestive organs; the cavity of the trunk below the diaphragm, usu. including the pelvic cavity. **E17.**
3 The posterior division of the body in insects, spiders, and some other arthropods. **L18.**

abdominal /əbˈdɒmɪn(ə)l/ *adjective & noun*. **M18.**
[**ORIGIN** mod. Latin *abdominalis*, formed as **ABDOMEN**: see **-AL^1**.]
▸ **A** *adjective*. **1** Of or pertaining to the abdomen. **M18.**
abdominal leg: see **LEG** *noun*.
2 *ICHTHYOLOGY.* **a** Of a fish: having the ventral fins posterior to the pectoral, in the belly region; (of a vertical fin) so situated. **M19.** ▸**b** Of a fin: ventral. **L19.**
▸ **B** *noun*. An abdominal muscle. Usu. in *pl. colloq.* **M20.**
■ **abdominally** *adverb* in the abdomen, with reference to the abdomen **L19.**

abdominoplasty /abˈdɒmɪnəʊˌplasti/ *noun*. **M20.**
[**ORIGIN** from *abdomino-* (combining form of **ABDOMEN**) + **-PLASTY**.]
MEDICINE. A surgical operation involving the removal of excess flesh from the abdomen.

abdominous /əbˈdɒmɪnəs/ *adjective*. **M17.**
[**ORIGIN** formed as **ABDOMEN** + **-OUS**.]
Corpulent.

abduce /əbˈdjuːs/ *verb trans.* **M16.**
[**ORIGIN** Latin *abducere*, from *ab* **AB-** + *ducere* to lead.]
1 = **ABDUCT**. *arch.* **M16.**
2 Infer partly from observation or experience. **M20.**

abducens /abˈdjuːs(ə)nz/ *noun sing.* **E19.**
[**ORIGIN** mod. Latin use as noun of Latin pres. pple: see **ABDUCENT**.]
ANATOMY. An abducent nerve. Also ***abducens nerve***.

abducent /əbˈdjuːs(ə)nt/ *adjective*. **L17.**
[**ORIGIN** Latin *abducent-*, *abducens* pres. pple of *abducere*: see **ABDUCE**, **-ENT**.]
ANATOMY. Of a muscle or nerve: concerned with abduction (sense 2); *spec.* designating or pertaining to the sixth pair of cranial nerves, which supply the muscles concerned with the lateral movement of the eyeballs.

abduct /əbˈdʌkt/ *verb trans.* **E17.**
[**ORIGIN** Latin *abduct-* pa. ppl stem of *abducere* **ABDUCE**.]
1 Lead or take away (a person, esp. a woman or child) by illegal force or fraud. **E17.**
2 *ANATOMY.* Bring about abduction of (a limb etc.). **E17.**

abductee /abdʌkˈtiː/ *noun*. **L20.**
[**ORIGIN** from **ABDUCT** + **-EE^1**.]
A person who has been abducted; *esp.* someone supposedly abducted by aliens.

abduction /əbˈdʌkʃ(ə)n/ *noun*. **E17.**
[**ORIGIN** Late Latin *abductio(n-)*, formed as **ABDUCT**: see **-ION**.]
1 **a** An act or the action of leading away. **E17.** ▸**b** The act of illegally carrying off or leading away a person; *LAW* the illegal removal of a child from its parents or others legally entitled to its care. **M18.**

b *Independent on Sunday* The abduction of unsuspecting young women. *Fortean Times* Genuine eye witness accounts of alien abductions.

2 *ANATOMY.* Movement of a limb etc. outward from the median line. Opp. **ADDUCTION** 2. **M17.**
3 *LOGIC.* A syllogistic argument, with the major premiss certain, the minor only probable. **L17.**

abductive /əbˈdʌktɪv/ *adjective*. **M19.**
[**ORIGIN** from (the same root as) **ABDUCT** + **-IVE**.]
1 Of or pertaining to abduction. **M19.**
2 Chiefly *PHILOSOPHY & LINGUISTICS.* Of, pertaining to, or proceeding by inference from observation or experience; (of an argument) having the major premiss known, the minor only probable. **E20.**
■ **abductively** *adverb* **E20.**

A

abductor /əbˈdʌktə/ *noun*. E17.
[ORIGIN mod. Latin, formed as ABDUCT: see -OR.]
1 *ANATOMY*. A muscle which brings about abduction (sense 2). Also ***abductor muscle***. E17.
2 A person who abducts. M19.

a-be /əˈbiː/ *adverb*. *Scot*. E18.
[ORIGIN Perh. = ***let be*** s.v. BE *verb* on the analogy of *let* (or *leave*) *alone*.]
let a-be, let alone.

abeam /əˈbiːm/ *adverb & pred. adjective*. M19.
[ORIGIN from A-² + BEAM *noun*.]
On a line at right angles to a ship's or aircraft's course; opposite the middle *of* (a ship etc.).

abear /əˈbɛː/ *verb & noun*.
[ORIGIN Old English *aberan*, from A-¹ + BEAR *verb*¹; later prob. a new form. on the analogy of *abide*.]
▸ **A** *verb trans*. Infl. (formerly) as BEAR *verb*¹.
†**1** Bear, carry. OE–ME.
2 Endure, abide. (Now always with *cannot* etc.) Now chiefly *dial*. OE.
DICKENS She couldn't abear the men, they were such deceivers.
†**3** *refl*. Comport oneself. Only in L16.
SPENSER Thus did the . . knight himselfe abeare.
▸ †**B** *noun*. Bearing, behaviour. ME–M17.
H. VAUGHAN Noting well my vain abear.
■ **abearance** *noun* (now *rare*) behaviour M16. †**abearing** *noun* behaviour L15–E18.

abeat /əˈbiːt/ *adverb & pred. adjective*. Chiefly *poet*. L19.
[ORIGIN from A-² + BEAT *noun*¹ or *verb*¹.]
Beating.

abecedarian /ˌeɪbiːsiːˈdɛːrɪən/ *noun & adjective*. E17.
[ORIGIN formed as ABECEDARY: see -ARIAN.]
▸ **A** *noun*. **1** A person learning the alphabet or the rudiments of a subject. E17.
2 A person teaching these. *arch*. E17.
▸ **B** *adjective*. **1** Pertaining to the alphabet; arranged alphabetically. M17.
2 (Pertaining to a person) learning the alphabet. M17.

abecedary /eɪbiːˈsiːdəri/ *noun & adjective*. Now *rare* or *obsolete*. LME.
[ORIGIN Sense A.1 from medieval Latin *abecedarium*, senses A.2 and B. from late Latin *abecedarius*; from the names of the letters *a*, *b*, *c*, *d*: see -ARY¹.]
▸ **A** *noun*. **1** A book containing the alphabet; a primer. Long *rare*. LME.
2 = ABECEDARIAN *noun*. L16.
▸ **B** *adjective*. = ABECEDARIAN *adjective*. L16.

abed /əˈbɛd/ *adverb*. *arch*. ME.
[ORIGIN from A *preposition*¹ 1 + BED *noun*.]
In bed; laid up.

abeigh /əˈbiːx, əˈbeɪx/ *adverb*. *Scot*. Now *rare* or *obsolete*. M16.
[ORIGIN Unknown.]
At a distance because of shyness; aloof.

abele /əˈbiːl, ˈeɪb(ə)l/ *noun*. ME.
[ORIGIN Orig. from Old French *aubel*, *abel* from medieval Latin *albellus* dim. of *albus* white; later (L16) from Dutch *abeel* from Old French.]
The white poplar, *Populus alba*.

abelia /əˈbiːlɪə/ *noun*. M19.
[ORIGIN mod. Latin (see below), from Clarke *Abel* (1780–1826), Brit. botanist: see -IA¹.]
Any of several hardy evergreen shrubs of the genus *Abelia*, of the honeysuckle family, having small pink or white flowers and native to eastern Asia.

abelian /əˈbiːlɪən/ *adjective*. M19.
[ORIGIN from *Abel* (see below) + -IAN.]
MATH. Of a form arising from work by the Norwegian mathematician Niels H. Abel (1802–29); *spec*. designating groups in which the operation is commutative.

Abenaki *noun & adjective* var. of ABNAKI.

abeng /aˈbɛŋ/ *noun*. L19.
[ORIGIN Twi.]
An animal's horn used as a wind instrument to send messages by Maroons of the W. Indies.

Aberdeen /abəˈdiːn/ *noun*. M19.
[ORIGIN A city and former county in NE Scotland.]
1 ***Aberdeen Angus***, (an animal of) a Scottish breed of black polled beef cattle. Also called ***Angus***. M19.
2 ***Aberdeen terrier***, (an animal of) a rough variety of Scottish terrier. L19.

aberdevine /ˈabədəvʌɪn/ *noun*. *dial*. (now *rare* or *obsolete*). M18.
[ORIGIN Unknown.]
The siskin.
– NOTE: Appears to have had little real currency although regularly listed as an alternative name in ornithological texts.

Aberdonian /abəˈdəʊnɪən/ *noun & adjective*. M17.
[ORIGIN from medieval Latin *Aberdonia* ABERDEEN: see -IAN.]
A native of, of or pertaining to, Aberdeen in NE Scotland.

Abernethy /abəˈnɛθi, -ˈniːθi/ *noun*. M19.
[ORIGIN Prob. John *Abernethy*, English surgeon (1764–1831).]
In full ***Abernethy biscuit***. A hard biscuit flavoured with caraway seeds.

aberr /əˈbəː/ *verb*. M16.
[ORIGIN Latin *aberrare*, from *ab* AB- + *errare* wander, err.]
†**1** *verb intrans*. Go astray (chiefly *fig*.). M16–M17.
2 *verb trans*. = ABERRATE 2. *rare*. L19.
G. B. SHAW I should have put on a pair of abnormal spectacles and aberred my vision.

aberrance /əˈbɛr(ə)ns/ *noun*. M17.
[ORIGIN from ABERRANT: see -ANCE.]
The action or an act of straying; (a) vagary.
■ **aberrancy** *noun* the quality or condition of being aberrant, (an) aberrance M17.

aberrant /əˈbɛr(ə)nt/ *adjective*. M16.
[ORIGIN Latin *aberrant-* pres. ppl stem of *aberrare*: see ABERR, -ANT¹.]
†**1** Deviating *from*. M16–E17.
2 Straying from the right path (*lit. & fig*.). M18.
3 Chiefly *BOTANY & ZOOLOGY*. Deviating from the normal type. M19.
■ **aberrantly** *adverb* L19.

aberrate /ˈabəreɪt/ *verb*. M18.
[ORIGIN Latin *aberrat-* pa. ppl stem of *aberrare*: see ABERR, -ATE³.]
1 *verb intrans*. Produce aberration; go astray; deviate *from*. M18.
W. FAULKNER He regrets having to aberrate from being a gentleman.
2 *verb trans*. Distort, cause aberration of. Chiefly as ***aberrated*** *ppl adjective*. L19.

aberration /abəˈreɪʃ(ə)n/ *noun*. L16.
[ORIGIN Latin *aberratio(n-)*, formed as ABERRATE: see -ATION.]
1 A deviation or divergence from the straight, correct, or recognized path (*lit. & fig*.). L16.
SIR W. SCOTT The slightest aberration would plunge him into a morass. GEO. ELIOT A pattern from which she was careful to allow no aberration.
2 The failure of rays of light to converge to a focus. M18. **chromatic aberration**: due to the different refrangibilities of the components of white light. **spherical aberration**: arising from the surface geometry of a spherical lens or mirror.
3 *ASTRONOMY*. An apparent displacement of a celestial object from its true position, arising from the relative motion of the observer and the object. M18.
annual aberration: due to the earth's orbital motion. **diurnal aberration**: due to the earth's axial rotation. **planetary aberration**: due to the motion of a planet during the time taken for its light to reach the earth.
4 An abnormal state of an intellectual faculty. E19.
Midnight Zoo Mental aberrations caused by his witnessing his whole clan being burned to death.
5 Chiefly *BOTANY & ZOOLOGY*. Deviation from the normal type; an instance of this. M19.
J. FOWLES Rare species and aberrations.
■ **aberrational** *adjective* M19. **aberrationally** *adverb* L20.

abessive /əˈbɛsɪv/ *adjective & noun*. L19.
[ORIGIN from Latin *abesse* be away, from *ab* AB- + *esse* be + -IVE.]
GRAMMAR. ▸ **A** *adjective*. Designating, being in, or pertaining to a case in Finnish and other languages expressing the absence of something. L19.
▸ **B** *noun*. *The* abessive case; a word, form, etc., in the abessive case. L19.

†**abet** *noun*. ME.
[ORIGIN Old French, formed as ABET *verb*.]
1 Fraud, cunning. Only in ME.
2 Abetment. LME–E18.

abet /əˈbɛt/ *verb trans*. Infl. **-tt-**. LME.
[ORIGIN Old French *abeter*, from A-⁵ + *beter* hound, urge on, cogn. with BAIT *verb*¹.]
1 †**a** Urge on to do something good or desirable. LME–E17. ▸**b** Incite or encourage (*in* a crime or offence, †*to* commit an offence). LME.
2 a Support, uphold, (a good cause, opinion, etc.). *arch*. L16. ▸**b** Encourage or countenance (a crime, offence, etc.), in *LAW* by active assistance (chiefly in ***aid and abet***). L18.
■ **abettance** *noun* (*rare*) abetment E19. **abetter** *noun* a person who abets an offence or an offender LME.

abetment /əˈbɛtm(ə)nt/ *noun*. LME.
[ORIGIN Anglo-Norman *abetement*, formed as ABET *verb*: see -MENT.]
The action or fact of abetting (usu. an offence).

abettor /əˈbɛtə/ *noun*. LME.
[ORIGIN Anglo-Norman *abettour*, formed as ABET *verb* + -OR.]
1 A person who abets an offender. (In *LAW* preferred to ABETTER.) LME.
2 A supporter, an adherent, an advocate (now almost always of something or someone undesirable or reprehensible). L16.

ab extra /ab ˈɛkstrə/ *adverbial phr*. M17.
[ORIGIN Late Latin.]
From outside.

abeyance /əˈbeɪəns/ *noun*. L16.
[ORIGIN Anglo-Norman *abeiance*, Old French *abeance* aspiration to a title, from *abeer* aspire after: cf. BAY *noun*³ and see -ANCE.]
1 *LAW*. The position of being without, or of waiting for, an owner or claimant but available to the rightful owner. L16.
2 A state of suspension or temporary disuse; dormant condition liable to revival. Chiefly in ***in abeyance*** or ***fall into abeyance***. M17.
■ **abeyant** *adjective* in a state of abeyance M19.

ABH *abbreviation*.
Actual bodily harm.

abhisheka /əb(h)ɪˈʃeɪkə, ʌb-/ *noun*. L19.
[ORIGIN Sanskrit *abhiṣeka*, from *abhi* upon, over + *sic* sprinkle.]
In Hinduism etc.: (a ceremony involving) ritual sprinkling or anointing.

†**abhominable** *adjective*, **abhomination** *noun* vars. of ABOMINABLE, ABOMINATION.

abhor /əbˈhɔː/ *verb*. Infl. **-rr-**. LME.
[ORIGIN Latin *abhorrere*, from *ab* AB- + *horrere* stand aghast. Partly from French *abhorrer*.]
1 *verb trans*. Regard with disgust and hatred. LME.
POPE My soul abhors to stay. R. C. TRENCH To abhor evil is to have it in moral detestation.
†**2** *verb trans*. Cause horror or disgust to. Usu. *impers*. in (*it*) ***abhors*** etc. M16–E17.
SHAKES. *Oth*. It does abhor me.
†**3** *verb intrans*. Shrink with horror or repugnance *from*. M16–M17.
†**4** *verb intrans*. Differ entirely *from*. M16–L17.
EVELYN Abhorring from the genuine and rational sense of the text.
■ **abhorred** *adjective* (**a**) detested; †(**b**) *rare* horrified: L16. **abhorrer** *noun* (**a**) a person who abhors; (**b**) *ENGLISH HISTORY* a person who signed an address of abhorrence: E17. **abhorrible** /əbˈhɒrɪb(ə)l/ *adjective* (now *rare* or *obsolete*) detestable M17. **abhorring** *noun* = ABHORRENCE 1, 3 M16.

abhorrence /əbˈhɒr(ə)ns/ *noun*. M17.
[ORIGIN formed as ABHORRENCY + -ENCE.]
1 The action of abhorring; detestation. M17.
2 An expression of abhorrence; *spec*. any of certain addresses presented to Charles II. *obsolete* exc. *hist*. L17.
3 A detested thing. M18.

†**abhorrency** *noun*. L16.
[ORIGIN from ABHORRENT + -ENCY.]
1 = ABERRANCY. *rare*. Only in L16.
2 The quality of being abhorrent; the feeling of abhorrence. E17–E18.
3 A thing which excites abhorrence. Only in E18.

abhorrent /əbˈhɒr(ə)nt/ *adjective*. L16.
[ORIGIN Latin *abhorrent-* pres. ppl stem of *abhorrere* ABHOR: see -ENT.]
1 (*pred*.) ***abhorrent from***, opposed to, far removed from, inconsistent with. L16.
BURKE The persons most abhorrent from blood, and treason. C. MERIVALE The simple theory of the Gospel . . was . . abhorrent from the prejudices of the heathen.
2 *pred*. Inherently repugnant (*to*); contrary *to*. M17.
F. A. KEMBLE Not abhorrent to nature.
3 Having or showing abhorrence (*of*). *arch*. M18.
GLADSTONE Temperate and abhorrent of excess.
4 Inspiring disgust; detestable. E19.
ISAAC TAYLOR Pride, abhorrent as it is.
■ **abhorrently** *adverb* E19.

Abib /ˈeɪbɪb, ˈɑː-/ *noun*. M16.
[ORIGIN Hebrew *ʾāḇīḇ* ear of corn.]
In the ancient Jewish calendar, = NISAN.

abidance /əˈbʌɪd(ə)ns/ *noun*. E17.
[ORIGIN from ABIDE + -ANCE.]
1 Abiding; dwelling. E17.
2 ***abidance by***, conformity to. E19.

abide /əˈbʌɪd/ *verb*. Pa. t. & pple **abided**, **abode** /əˈbəʊd/; pa. pple also (now *rare*) **abidden** /əˈbɪd(ə)n/.
[ORIGIN Old English *ābīdan*, from A-¹ + BIDE; cogn. with Gothic *usbeidan*.]
▸ **I** *verb intrans*. †**1** Remain in expectation, wait. OE–M17.
AV *Gen*. 22:5 Abide you here with the asse.
†**2** Pause, delay, stop. ME–M17.
3 Stay, remain, (in a place or in some state: with adverb or adjective complement, or absol.). ME. ▸**b** Reside, dwell. *arch*. LME.
LD BERNERS The towne abode frenche. W. COWPER He within his ships Abode the while. TENNYSON Tho' much is taken, much abides. **b** TOLKIEN Ulmo . . abode not in Valinor.
4 Endure, stand firm. LME.
COVERDALE *Ps*. 91:7 But thou Lorde . . abydest worlde without ende.
▸ **II** *verb trans*. **5** Wait for, watch for, expect. OE.

T. ELYOT He abode an answer thereof. TINDALE *Acts* 20:23 Bondes and trouble abyde me.

6 Face, encounter, withstand. ME.

A. THWAITE He [Shakespeare] abides Our questioning syllabus still.

†**7** Suffer, endure. ME–E18.

J. MOXON Not . . strong enough to abide tough Work.

8 Await submissively; submit to. LME.

SHAKES. *Rich. II* To abide Thy kingly doom.

9 Tolerate, put up with. (Chiefly & now only in neg. & interrog. contexts.) L15.

GOLDSMITH I can't abide to disappoint myself. L. LEE They were far more alike than unalike, and could not abide each other.

▸ **III** *verb trans.* [Conf. with ABY.]

10 Pay for, suffer for. Now *arch. rare.* L16.

SHAKES. *Jul. Caes.* Some will dear abide it.

– WITH PREPOSITIONS IN SPECIALIZED SENSES: **abide by** remain with, remain faithful to, (pa. t. & pple now usu. ***abided***).

■ **abider** *noun* LME.

abiding /əˈbʌɪdɪŋ/ *noun.* ME.

[ORIGIN from ABIDE + -ING[1].]

1 The action or state of a person who abides. ME.

†**2** An abode. LME–E17.

– COMB.: **abiding place** place of abode.

abiding /əˈbʌɪdɪŋ/ *adjective.* LME.

[ORIGIN formed as ABIDING *noun* + -ING[2].]

Enduring, permanent.

M. L. KING An abiding faith in America.

■ **abidingly** *adverb* LME. **abidingness** *noun* M19.

abietic /abɪˈɛtɪk/ *adjective.* M19.

[ORIGIN from Latin *abiet-*, *abies* fir + -IC.]

CHEMISTRY. ***abietic acid***, a crystalline terpenoid acid, $C_{20}H_{30}O_2$, that is a component of rosin.

abigail /ˈabɪɡeɪl/ *noun.* Also **A-**. M17.

[ORIGIN A character in *The Scornful Lady* by Beaumont and Fletcher: cf. *1 Samuel* 25.]

A lady's maid.

†**abiliment** *noun* var. of HABILIMENT.

ability /əˈbɪlɪti/ *noun.* Also †**h-**. LME.

[ORIGIN Old French *ablete* from Latin *habilitas*, from *habilis*: see ABLE *adjective*, -ITY.]

†**1** Suitableness. LME–L17.

2 Possession of the means or skill *to do*, †*of doing* something; capacity. LME. ▸**b** Legal competency (to act). M17.

T. S. ELIOT Dryden is distinguished . . by his *poetic* ability. E. HEMINGWAY Cowardice . . is . . a lack of ability to suspend the functioning of the imagination.

to the best of one's ability: see BEST *adjective* etc.

3 Bodily power. Now *Scot. dial.* LME.

E. TOPSELL Complaining of bodily weakness where is no want of ability.

4 Financial means or resources. *arch.* E16.

SHAKES. *Twel. N.* Out of my lean and low ability I'll lend you something.

5 a A special power of the mind, a faculty. Usu. in *pl.* L16. ▸**b** Talent, skill, or proficiency in a particular area. E17.

a J. B. WATSON I'll train him to become any type of specialist . . regardless of his . . abilities. **b** E. GLASGOW Men with ability never stayed in a village.

-ability /əˈbɪlɪti/ *suffix.*

[ORIGIN French *-abilité* from Latin *-abilitas*.]

Forming nouns chiefly from adjectives in -ABLE: see -ITY.

†**abime** *noun* var. of ABYSM.

ab initio /ab ɪˈnɪʃɪəʊ/ *adverbial phr.* E17.

[ORIGIN Latin.]

From the beginning.

ab intra /ab ˈɪntrə/ *adverbial phr.* L17.

[ORIGIN mod. Latin.]

From inside.

abiogenesis /ˌeɪbʌɪəˈdʒɛnɪsɪs/ *noun.* L19.

[ORIGIN from Greek *abios*, from *a-* A-[10] + *bios* life + -GENESIS.]

The production of organic matter or compounds, other than by the agency of living organisms; *esp.* the supposed spontaneous generation of living organisms.

■ **abiˈogenist** *noun* a believer in the spontaneous generation of living organisms L19.

abiogenic /ˌeɪbʌɪəˈdʒɛnɪk/ *adjective.* L19.

[ORIGIN formed as ABIOGENESIS + -GENIC.]

Not involving or produced by living organisms.

■ **abiogenically** *adverb* M20.

abiological /ˌeɪbʌɪəˈlɒdʒɪk(ə)l/ *adjective.* M19.

[ORIGIN from A-[10] + BIOLOGICAL.]

Not associated with living organisms; non-biological.

■ **abiologically** *adverb* L19.

abiotic /eɪbʌɪˈɒtɪk/ *adjective.* L19.

[ORIGIN from A-[10] + BIOTIC.]

Devoid of or inimical to life; inanimate, abiological.

■ **abiotically** *adverb* in the absence of life M20.

Abitur /abiˈtuːr/ *noun.* Also ***a-***. M20.

[ORIGIN German, abbreviation of *Abiturientenexamen* leavers' examination.]

In Germany, a set of examinations taken in the final year of secondary school (success in which formerly ensured a university place).

■ ***Abiturient*** /abituriˈɛnt/ *noun* [German, from mod. Latin *abiturire* wish to leave] a candidate for the *Abitur* M19.

abject /ˈabdʒɛkt/ *adjective, verb, & noun.* LME.

[ORIGIN Latin *abjectus* pa. pple of *abjicere* reject, from *ab* AB- + *jacere* throw.]

▸ **A** *adjective* (orig. *pa. pple*).

†**1** Cast off, rejected. LME–E17.

2 Brought low in position, condition, or status. LME.

F. TROLLOPE The most abject poverty is preferable to domestic service. LD MACAULAY The abject heirs of an illustrious name.

3 In low repute; lacking courage; despicable; self-abasing. LME.

SHAKES. *2 Hen. VI* Paltry, servile, abject drudges. J. THURBER He lived in abject fear of the cold, overbearing, and ruthless police lieutenant. C. HAMPTON He was so abject He kept apologizing all the time.

▸ †**B** *verb trans.* Cast off or down (*lit.* & *fig.*). LME–L17.

▸ **C** *noun.* An outcast; a degraded person. L15.

– NOTE: Orig. stressed on second syllable.

■ **abjectly** *adverb* LME. **abjectness** *noun* L16.

abjection /abˈdʒɛkʃ(ə)n/ *noun.* LME.

[ORIGIN Old French & mod. French, or Latin *abjectio(n-)*, formed as ABJECT: see -ION.]

1 The condition of a person cast down; degradation; low status. LME.

†**2** Something cast off; refuse. Chiefly *fig.* LME–M16.

†**3** The action of casting down. E16–M17.

†**4** The action of casting off; rejection. E–M17.

abjuration /abdʒʊəˈreɪʃ(ə)n/ *noun.* LME.

[ORIGIN Old French & mod. French, or late Latin *abjuratio(n-)*, from *abjurat-* pa. ppl stem of *abjurare*: see ABJURE, -ATION.]

1 (A) renunciation on oath; recantation, esp. of heresies. LME.

2 (An) official repudiation on oath of any ecclesiastical or political principle. M17.

– COMB. & PHRASES: **abjuration oath** (*obsolete* exc. *hist.*) = ***Oath of Abjuration*** below. **abjuration of the realm** etc., an oath taken to leave the realm etc. for ever. **Oath of Abjuration** (*obsolete* exc. *hist.*) an oath disclaiming allegiance to James, son of James II, or his descendants as claimants to the British throne.

abjure /əbˈdʒʊə/ *verb trans.* LME.

[ORIGIN Latin *abjurare* deny on oath, from *ab* AB- + *jurare* swear.]

1 Renounce on oath; recant. LME.

SHAKES. *Temp.* This rough magic I here abjure.

2 Cause to recant. *obsolete* exc. *hist.* LME.

F. THYNNE All such must be burned, or ellis ab-Iuryd.

3 Disclaim solemnly; reject on oath. LME.

absol.: MILTON Say and unsay, feign, flatter, and abjure.

abjure the realm etc., swear to leave the realm etc. for ever.

■ **abjurer** *noun* L18.

Abkhazian /əbˈkɑːzɪən, əbˈkeɪzjən/ *noun & adjective.* Also **-sian**. M19.

[ORIGIN from *Abkhaz(ia)*: see below, -IAN.]

▸ **A** *noun.* A member of a Caucasian people living in Abkhaz, a territory in the Caucasus; the NW Caucasian language of this people. M19.

▸ **B** *adjective.* Of or pertaining to Abkhaz or its inhabitants. M19.

■ **Abkhaz** *noun* = ABKHAZIAN *noun* M19.

ablactation /ablakˈteɪʃ(ə)n/ *noun.* LME.

[ORIGIN Late Latin *ablactatio(n-)*, from *ablactat-* pa. ppl stem of *ablactare* wean, from *ab* AB- + *lactare* suckle: see -ATION.]

1 Weaning. LME.

†**2** HORTICULTURE. Inarching. L17–E19.

†**ablaqueate** *verb trans.* LME–M18.

[ORIGIN Latin *ablaqueat-* pa. ppl stem of *ablaqueare* disentangle: see -ATE[3].]

Expose the roots of (a tree) by loosening or removing soil.

■ †**ablaqueation** *noun* LME–M18.

ablate /əˈbleɪt/ *verb.* L15.

[ORIGIN Latin *ablat-* pa. ppl stem of *auferre* take away: see -ATE[3]. In mod. use as back-form. from ABLATION.]

1 *verb trans.* Take away, remove, *spec.* by ablation (sense 3); erode by ablation. L15.

2 *verb intrans.* Undergo ablation (sense 3). M20.

■ **ablator** *noun* (a layer of) a material which undergoes ablation (sense 3) M20.

ablation /əˈbleɪʃ(ə)n/ *noun.* LME.

[ORIGIN French, or late Latin *ablatio(n-)*, formed as ABLATE: see -ATION.]

1 The action of taking away, removal. *obsolete* in *gen.* sense. LME.

2 MEDICINE. (An instance of) removal by surgical or other means, esp. of a tumour. LME.

3 (An instance of) the wearing away or removal of surface material from a solid body; *esp.* (***a***) the wasting of a glacier, iceberg, etc. by melting and other processes; (***b***) the melting and evaporation of outer surface material from a spacecraft by friction with the atmosphere. M20.

ablative /ˈablətɪv/ *adjective & noun.* LME.

[ORIGIN Old French & mod. French *ablatif*, *-ive* or Latin *ablativus*: see ABLATE, -IVE.]

▸ **A** *adjective.* **1** GRAMMAR. Designating, being in, or pertaining to a case in Latin and other languages expressing direction from a place, or time, and variously also the source, cause, instrument and agent, manner, and sometimes place and time of an action or event. LME.

†**2** Of or pertaining to taking away or removing. M16–E18.

JOSEPH HALL Ablatiue directions are first needfull to vnteach error.

3 Producing, removed by, or pertaining to ablation (senses 2, 3). M20.

▸ **B** *noun.* **1** GRAMMAR. *The* ablative case; a word, form, etc., in the ablative case. LME.

ablative absolute in Latin, an ablative case of a noun or pronoun with a participle (expressed or implied) in concord, grammatically independent of the main clause, and expressing the time, occasion, or circumstance of a fact stated.

2 An ablative material. M20.

■ **ablatival** /-ˈtʌɪv(ə)l/ *adjective* pertaining to the ablative case M19. **ablatively** *adverb* M19.

ablaut /ˈablaʊt/ *noun.* M19.

[ORIGIN German, from *ab* off + *Laut* sound.]

PHILOLOGY. Vowel change in related words, *esp.* that in Indo-European, which survives in English in, e.g., ***sing***, ***sang***, ***sung***, ***song***.

ablaut SERIES.

ablaze /əˈbleɪz/ *adverb & pred. adjective.* E19.

[ORIGIN from A-[2] + BLAZE *noun*[1].]

On fire; *fig.* glittering, excited.

K. HICKMAN The women [were] ablaze with silks and diamonds.

able /ˈeɪb(ə)l/ *adjective.* See also HABILE. LME.

[ORIGIN Old French *(h)able* from Latin *habilis*, from *habere* to hold.]

▸ **I** *pass.* †**1** Easy to handle or use. LME–M18.

T. BETTERTON The Hands are the most habil members of the body.

†**2** Suitable, competent. LME–L18.

R. BROME To the next able Tree with him.

3 *pred.* Liable *to*. *obsolete* exc. *dial.* LME.

MONMOUTH A spectacle able to make a man die for anger.

▸ **II** *active.* **4** Having the qualifications for, and means of, doing something; having sufficient power (*to do*); (*pred.* foll. by *to do* esp. used with parts of *be* to supply the deficiencies of *can*). LME. ▸**b** Legally qualified. E18. ▸**c** Of a seaman: able to perform all duties; *spec.* in the Royal Navy, having a rating between leading and ordinary seaman. L18.

O. FELTHAM An able servant out of imployment. G. M. TREVELYAN A vast population able to read but unable to distinguish what is worth reading. E. O'NEILL You won't be able to drag out the old bottle quick enough.

5 Physically strong; vigorous. *obsolete* exc. *dial.* LME.

SHAKES. *All's Well* Of as able body as when he numbered thirty.

†**6** Wealthy. M16–L19.

S. PEPYS A very able citizen in Gracious Street.

7 Having mental power; talented, clever. M16.

DRYDEN Those able heads expound a wiser way. M. EDGEWORTH By no means so able a boxer. E. HEMINGWAY The bastard must be fairly able to have run this band successfully.

– COMB. & PHRASES: **able-bodied** *adjective* (***a***) having a body free from disability and fit for service; (***b***) = sense 4c above. **able for** *Irish* fit to cope with. ***be able to use***: see USE *verb*. ***be able to wait***: see WAIT *verb*.

■ **ableism** *noun* prejudice or discrimination against disabled persons L20. **ableness** *noun* (now *rare*) LME.

†**able** *verb trans.* ME.

[ORIGIN from the adjective: cf. Old French & mod. French *habiller* in same senses.]

1 Fit, make ready, (esp. *to*). ME–L16.

2 Make capable, enable, (*to do*). Latterly *dial.* LME–L19.

3 Attire, dress. LME–L15.

4 Empower, strengthen, confirm. LME–M17. ▸**b** Warrant; vouch for. L16–E17.

DONNE And life, by this death abled, shall controule Death. **b** SHAKES. *Lear* None does offend, none . . ; I'll able 'em.

-able /əb(ə)l/ *suffix.*

[ORIGIN French from Latin *-abilis* adjectival suffix, the form taken by the suffix *-bilis* (see -BLE) when added to verbs in *-are*, French *-er*; extended in French to verbs of all conjugations and also (as occas. in post-classical Latin, e.g. *amicabilis* AMICABLE, from *amicus* friend) to nouns, as in *charitable*, *équitable*.]

Forming adjectives. Orig. found in English only in words from French or Latin, as ***separable*** (from French *séparable*

A

or Latin *separabilis*), but subsequently used to form many adjectives direct from the stem of English verbs in *-ate*, as ***appreciable*** from ***appreciate***, ***educable*** from ***educate***, ***extricable*** from ***extricate***. Later, prob. by confusion with the unrelated ABLE *adjective*, freely used to form adjectives from verbs of all types, as ***bearable***, ***reliable***, from nouns, as ***clubbable***, ***saleable***, and from verbal phrs., as ***get-at-able***. In new formations now always passive in sense but earlier freq. active, as in ***comfortable***, ***suitable***.

abled /ˈeɪb(ə)ld/ *adjective*. L20.
[ORIGIN Back-form. from DISABLED.]
Able-bodied, not disabled.

ablins /ˈeɪblɪnz/ *adverb*. *Scot. & N. English* (now *literary*). Also **aiblins**. E17.
[ORIGIN from ABLE *adjective*: see -LING².]
Possibly; perhaps.

abloom /əˈbluːm/ *adverb & pred. adjective*. M19.
[ORIGIN from A-² + BLOOM *noun*¹.]
In or into bloom.

ablush /əˈblʌʃ/ *adverb & pred. adjective*. M19.
[ORIGIN from A-² + BLUSH *noun* or *verb*.]
Blushing.

ablute /əˈbluːt/ *verb trans. & intrans. colloq.* L19.
[ORIGIN Back-form. from ABLUTION.]
Wash (oneself).

ablution /əˈbluːʃ(ə)n/ *noun*. LME.
[ORIGIN Old French & mod. French, or late Latin *ablutio(n-)*, from *ablut-* pa. ppl stem of *abluere*, from *ab* AB- + *luere* to wash: see -ION.]
1 The act of washing clean: ▸†**a** ALCHEMY & CHEMISTRY. The purification of substances by the use of liquids. LME–M18. ▸**b** *sing.* & (usu.) in *pl.* The washing of the body as a religious rite. M16. ▸**c** *sing.* & (usu.) in *pl.* Ordinary personal washing. Freq. *joc.* M18. ▸**d** CHRISTIAN CHURCH. The ceremonial washing of sacred vessels after, or of the celebrant's fingers before, during, and after, the Eucharist. L19.
2 The water etc. used in ablution. E18.
3 In *pl.* The building containing washing and toilet facilities in a camp, ship, etc. M20.
■ **ablutionary** *adjective* M19.

ably /ˈeɪbli/ *adverb*. LME.
[ORIGIN from ABLE *adjective*: see -LY².]
In an able manner.

-ably /əbli/ *suffix*.
[ORIGIN from -ABLE: see -LY².]
Forming adverbs corresp. to adjectives in *-able*.

ABM *abbreviation*.
Anti-ballistic missile.

Abnaki /abˈnaki/ *noun & adjective*. Also **Abenaki** /abəˈnaki/. E18.
[ORIGIN French *Abénaqui* from Montagnais *ouabanákionek* people of the eastern country.]
▸ **A** *noun*. Pl. same, **-s**.
1 A member of a grouping of Algonquian peoples living chiefly in Maine and Quebec. E18.
2 Either or both of the two languages (***Eastern Abnaki*** and ***Western Abnaki***) of these peoples. E20.
▸ **B** *adjective*. Of or pertaining to the Abnaki or their languages. E19.

abnegate /ˈabnɪɡeɪt/ *verb trans.* E17.
[ORIGIN Latin *abnegat-* pa. ppl stem of *abnegare*, from *ab* AB- + *negare* deny: see -ATE³.]
1 Deny oneself (something); renounce (a right or privilege). E17.
2 Abjure (a belief etc.). M18.
■ **abnegator** *noun* M17.

abnegation /abnɪˈɡeɪʃ(ə)n/ *noun*. LME.
[ORIGIN French, or Latin *abnegatio(n-)*, formed as ABNEGATE: see -ATION.]
1 Denial; rejection (of a doctrine etc.). LME.

J. KNOX Abnegation of Christe. SOUTHEY Abnegation of the opinion imputed to the heretics. M. BRADBURY A vast degeneration, a major abnegation of any regard for the quality of human life.

2 Self-denial; self-sacrifice; an instance of this. (*Self* now often expressed.) LME.

E. BLUNDEN His gallantry in going through . . the abnegations of service.

abnet /ˈabnət/ *noun*. Also **abanet** /ˈabənət/. E18.
[ORIGIN Hebrew *'aḇnēṭ* belt.]
JEWISH ANTIQUITIES. A girdle of fine linen worn esp. by priests.

Abney level /ˈabnɪ ˌlɛv(ə)l/ *noun phr.* L19.
[ORIGIN Sir William *Abney* (1844–1920), English scientist.]
A kind of clinometer consisting of a sighting tube, spirit level, and graduated scale.

abnormal /əbˈnɔːm(ə)l/ *adjective*. M19.
[ORIGIN Alt. of ANORMAL after Latin *abnormis*: see ABNORMOUS.]
1 Deviating from the type; contrary to the rule or system; unusual. M19.

C. DARWIN The wing of a bat is a most abnormal structure. E. O'NEILL The spell of abnormal quiet.

2 Of or pertaining to what is abnormal. E20.
abnormal psychology: dealing with persons having abnormal (esp. undesirable) traits.
■ **abnorˈmality** *noun* the quality or state of being abnormal; an abnormal feature or act: M19. **abnormalize** *verb trans.* make abnormal L19. **abnormally** *adverb* M19. **abnormalness** *noun* (*rare*) M19.

abnormity /əbˈnɔːmɪti/ *noun*. M18.
[ORIGIN Late Latin *abnormitas*, from *abnormis*: see ABNORMOUS, -ITY.]
1 The quality of being abnormal. M18.
2 A monstrosity. M19.

abnormous /əbˈnɔːməs/ *adjective*. M18.
[ORIGIN from Latin *abnormis*, from *ab* AB- + *norma* rule + -OUS.]
Irregular; misshapen.

Abo /ˈabəʊ/ *noun & adjective*. *Austral. slang* (*offensive*). Pl. of noun **-os**. E20.
[ORIGIN Abbreviation of ABORIGINAL.]
(An) Australian Aboriginal.

aboard /əˈbɔːd/ *adverb & preposition*¹. LME.
[ORIGIN from A *preposition*¹ 1 + BOARD *noun*, partly after Old French & mod. French *à bord*.]
▸ **A** *adverb*. **1** On or on to or into a ship, train, aircraft, etc. LME. ▸**b** On or on to the back of a horse etc. L19. ▸**c** BASEBALL. On base. M20. ▸**d** In or into a group, team, etc.; in an enterprise. M20.
all aboard: the cry to warn passengers to get aboard a vessel, train, etc., about to start.
2 Alongside. LME.

CAPT. COOK Keeping the coast . . aboard.

fall aboard: see FALL *verb*. ***lay aboard***: see LAY *verb*¹ 18b.
▸ **B** *preposition*. **1** On, on to, or into (a ship, train, aircraft, etc.). LME. ▸**b** On or on to the back of (a horse etc.). M20.
†**2** Alongside of. E16–L17.

T. FULLER Hard aboard the shore.

abob /əˈbɒb/ *adverb & pred. adjective*. E20.
[ORIGIN from A-² + BOB *noun*² or *verb*³.]
1 Bobbing, afloat. E20.
2 Foll. by *with*: in which specified objects are bobbing. E20.

abode /əˈbəʊd/ *noun*¹. ME.
[ORIGIN from pa. t. of ABIDE.]
†**1** The action of waiting. ME–E17.

SHAKES. *Merch. V.* Your patience for my long abode.

†**2** A temporary stay. LME–M18.
3 Habitual residence; a house or home. LME.
no fixed abode. ***right of abode***: see RIGHT *noun*¹.

†**abode** *noun*². L16–L17.
[ORIGIN from A-¹ + BODE *noun*².]
An omen, a prognostication.

†**abode** *verb*¹. L16.
[ORIGIN from A-¹ + BODE *verb*¹.]
1 *verb trans.* Presage, forebode. L16–M17.
2 *verb intrans.* Be ominous. M–L17.
■ †**aboding** *noun* (a) foreboding L16–E18.

abode *verb*² *pa. t.* of ABIDE.

†**abodement** *noun*. L16–M17.
[ORIGIN from ABODE *verb*¹ + -MENT.]
An omen; a foreboding.

aboil /əˈbɔɪl/ *adverb & pred. adjective*. M19.
[ORIGIN from A-² + BOIL *noun*² or *verb*.]
Boiling, seething, (*lit. & fig.*).

abolish /əˈbɒlɪʃ/ *verb trans.* LME.
[ORIGIN Old French & mod. French *aboliss-* lengthened stem of *abolir* from Latin *abolere* destroy: see -ISH².]
Put an end to, annul, demolish, destroy; (now only institutions, customs and practices). (Formerly foll. by *from*, *out of*.)
■ **abolishable** *adjective* M17. **abolisher** *noun* M17. **abolishment** *noun* = ABOLITION M16.

abolition /abəˈlɪʃ(ə)n/ *noun*. E16.
[ORIGIN French, or Latin *abolitio(n-)*, from *abolit-* pa. ppl stem of *abolere*: see ABOLISH, -ITION.]
1 The action or an act of abolishing something; the fact or state of being abolished; destruction. E16. ▸**b** *spec.* The abolition of (***a***) *hist.* the slave trade; (***b***) capital punishment; (***c***) AUSTRAL. HISTORY convict transportation. L18.

B. RUSSELL No one would advocate the abolition of competition in games. C. HAMPTON The reintroduction . . , after seventy-five years of abolition, of the death penalty.

†**2** A putting out of memory; an amnesty. E17–E19.
■ **abolitionism** *noun* support for abolition (ABOLITION 1b) E19. **abolitionist** *noun & adjective* (***a***) *noun* a person who favours abolition; (***b***) *adjective* of or pertaining to abolitionists or abolitionism: L18.

abomasum /abəʊˈmeɪsəm/ *noun*. Pl. **-sa** /-sə/. Also †**-sus**, pl. **-si**. L17.
[ORIGIN from AB- + OMASUM.]
The fourth stomach of a ruminant.

abominable /əˈbɒm(ə)nəb(ə)l/ *adjective*. Also †**abhom-**. ME.
[ORIGIN Old French from Latin *abominabilis*, from *abominari*: see ABOMINATE *verb*, -ABLE. Var. with *-h-* (in medieval Latin, Old French, & English) as if from Latin *ab* + *homin-*, *homo* a human, signifying 'inhuman'.]
1 Exciting disgust; offensive; odious. ME.

SHAKES. *Meas. for M.* Their abominable and beastly touches.

Abominable Snowman = YETI.
2 Very unpleasant. *colloq.* M19.

G. B. SHAW What an abominable smell of garlic!

■ **abominableness** *noun* E16. **abominably** *adverb* loathsomely; *colloq.* very badly: LME.

abominate /əˈbɒmɪnət/ *adjective*. Now *rare* or *obsolete*. L16.
[ORIGIN Latin *abominatus* pa. pple, formed as ABOMINATE *verb*: see -ATE².]
Abominable, detested.

abominate /əˈbɒmɪneɪt/ *verb trans.* M17.
[ORIGIN Latin *abominat-* pa. ppl stem of *abominari*, from *ab* AB- + *omin-*, *omen* omen: see -ATE³.]
1 Feel extreme disgust towards; abhor; express abhorrence of. M17.
2 Dislike strongly. *colloq.* L19.

A. S. BYATT He abominated tea. He was a black coffee drinker.

■ **abominator** *noun* L17.

abomination /əbɒmɪˈneɪʃ(ə)n/ *noun*. Also †**abhom-**. ME.
[ORIGIN Old French & mod. French from Latin *abominatio(n-)*, formed as ABOMINATE *verb*: see -ATION.]
1 An abominable act; a degrading vice. ME.

SHAKES. *Ant. & Cl.* Antony, most large In his abominations.

2 A feeling of disgust and hatred; loathing. LME.
†**3** A state exciting disgust; pollution. LME–L15.
4 An object that excites disgust and hatred (*to*, *unto*). LME.

AV *Prov.* 12:22 Lying lippes are abomination to the Lord.

■ †**abominationly** *adverb* abominably L16–E18.

†**abomine** *verb trans.* E16–E18.
[ORIGIN French *abominer* from Latin *abominari*: see ABOMINATE *verb*.]
= ABOMINATE *verb*.

abondance *noun* see ABUNDANCE.

abonnement /abɔnmɑ̃/ *noun*. Pl. pronounced same. L19.
[ORIGIN French, from *abonner* subscribe: see -MENT.]
A subscription, as for a newspaper etc.; a season ticket.
■ ***abonné*** /abɔne (*pl. same*)/ *noun* [pa. pple of *abonner*] a subscriber, a season-ticket holder L19.

aboon *adverb, preposition, & noun* var. of ABUNE.

aboral /abˈɔːr(ə)l/ *adjective*. M19.
[ORIGIN from AB- + ORAL *adjective*.]
ZOOLOGY. Pertaining to the part furthest from the mouth.
■ **aborally** *adverb* L19.

abord /əˈbɔːd/ *noun*. *arch.* E17.
[ORIGIN French, formed as ABORD *verb*.]
Approach; way of approach.

abord /əˈbɔːd/ *verb trans.* Now *rare* or *obsolete*. LME.
[ORIGIN Old French & mod. French *aborder*: see ABOARD.]
†**1** Approach; land on. LME–L17.
2 Accost. E17.

abordage /əˈbɔːdɪdʒ/ *noun*. *rare*. M16.
[ORIGIN French.]
An attack on a ship by boarding it.

aboriginal /abəˈrɪdʒɪn(ə)l/ *adjective & noun*. M17.
[ORIGIN Irreg. from ABORIGINES + -AL¹.]
▸ **A** *adjective*. **1** First or earliest known; primitive; indigenous. M17. ▸**b** Existing in a land before the arrival of (European) colonists. L17.

J. HEATH-STUBBS An aboriginal Filipino pygmy.

2 Of or pertaining to aborigines or their languages, esp. (usu. **A-**) those of Australia. L18.

E. MORRIS Such and such a word is not Aboriginal. F. CLUNE The region is an Aboriginal Reserve, closed to white men.

▸ **B** *noun*. An aboriginal inhabitant or the aboriginal language of a place, esp. (usu. **A-**) of Australia. M18.
■ ˌ**aborigiˈnality** *noun* the quality of being aboriginal M19. **aboriginally** *adverb* from or in the earliest known times E19.

aborigine /abəˈrɪdʒɪniː/ *noun sing.* E19.
[ORIGIN Back-form. from ABORIGINES.]
An aboriginal person, plant, or animal, spec. (**A-**) an aboriginal inhabitant of Australia.

ab origine /ab əˈrɪdʒɪni/ *adverbial phr.* M16.
[ORIGIN Latin, from *ab* from + *origine* abl. of *origo* beginning, source.]
From the beginning; from the creation of the world.

aborigines /abəˈrɪdʒɪniːz/ *noun pl.* E16.
[ORIGIN Latin *aborigines* pl., prob. from AB ORIGINE.]
1 The original inhabitants of a country (orig. of Italy and of Greece). E16.
2 Indigenous plants or animals. L17.
3 The inhabitants of a land before the arrival of (European) colonists, esp. (usu. **A-**) those of Australia. E18.
■ †**aborigen**, **-gin** *noun* = ABORIGINE E17–M19.

aborning /əˈbɔːnɪŋ/ *adverb & pred. adjective*. Chiefly *N. Amer.* M20.
[ORIGIN from A-[2] + *borning* verbal noun of BORN *verb*: see -ING[1].]
(While) being born or produced.

abort /əˈbɔːt/ *noun*. LME.
[ORIGIN Latin ABORTUS.]
†**1** A miscarriage (*lit.* & *fig.*). LME–M17.
2 The product of a miscarriage. Now *rare*. E17.
3 AERONAUTICS & ASTRONAUTICS. An aborted flight by a rocket etc.; a rocket etc. that fails; *transf.* any unsuccessful enterprise. M20.

abort /əˈbɔːt/ *verb*. M16.
[ORIGIN Latin *abort-* pa. ppl stem of *aboriri* miscarry, from *ab* AB- + *oriri* come into being.]
1 a *verb intrans.* Of a pregnant woman: miscarry, with loss of the fetus, esp. (& MEDICINE) in the period before a live birth is possible. (In popular use often with an implication of deliberate induction.) M16. ▸**b** *verb trans.* Cause abortion of; cause to abort; *fig.* bring to a premature or fruitless termination. L16.

b *Church Times* The 800,000 unborn children aborted under the 1967 Abortion Act.

2 *verb intrans.* BIOLOGY. Of an organ: undergo arrestment of development. M19.
3 *verb trans. & intrans.* AERONAUTICS & ASTRONAUTICS. Abandon or fail to complete a flight. M20.

American Speech If trouble develops on the take-off roll . . , it is possible to abort and stop the aircraft.

■ **abor'tee** *noun* a woman who undergoes an abortion M20. **abortifacient** /əbɔːtɪˈfeɪʃ(ə)nt/ *adjective & noun* [-FACIENT] (a drug or other agent) causing abortion M19. †**abortment** *noun* abortion E17–L19. **abortorium** /abɔːˈtɔːrɪəm/ *noun*, pl. **-ia** /-ɪə/, a hospital or hospital department that specializes in performing abortions M20.

aborti *noun pl.* see ABORTUS.

abortion /əˈbɔːʃ(ə)n/ *noun*. M16.
[ORIGIN Latin *abortio(n-)*, formed as ABORT *verb*: see -ION.]
1 The act of giving premature birth with loss of the fetus, esp. (& MEDICINE) in the period before a live birth is possible; (the procuring of) induced termination of pregnancy to destroy a fetus. M16. ▸**b** *fig.* Failure (of an aim, promise, etc.). E18.
contagious abortion: see CONTAGIOUS 3. ***missed abortion***: see MISS *verb*[1].
2 The imperfect offspring or product of a miscarriage; a person or thing dwarfed or misshapen. L16.
3 BIOLOGY. Arrestment of development of any organ, esp. of a seed or fruit. M18.
■ **abortional** *adjective* (*rare*) of abortion, abortive M19. **abortionist** *noun* a person who procures or induces abortion; a person who favours permitting abortion: L19.

abortive /əˈbɔːtɪv/ *noun, adjective, & verb*. ME.
[ORIGIN Old French & mod. French *abortif*, *-ive* from Latin *abortivus*, formed as ABORTION: see -IVE.]
▸ †**A** *noun*. **1** A stillborn child or animal. ME–M18.
2 An imperfect result of an action. E17–E18.
▸ **B** *adjective*. †**1** Of or pertaining to abortion; born prematurely; causing or experiencing abortion. LME–M18.

SHAKES. *Rich. III* If ever he have child, abortive be it.

2 Fruitless, unsuccessful. L16.

SCOTT FITZGERALD An abortive attempt at a laugh. T. PYNCHON An abortive firing, a warhead that didn't explode.

3 BIOLOGY. Arrested in development. M18.

fig.: S. SPENDER An abortive tower at one corner.

▸ †**C** *verb trans.* Cause abortion of; render fruitless. Only in 17.
■ **abortively** *adverb* M16. **abortiveness** *noun* E17.

abortus /əˈbɔːtəs/ *noun*. Pl. **-ti** /-tʌɪ/, **-tuses**. M19.
[ORIGIN Latin = miscarriage: see ABORT *verb*.]
MEDICINE. **1** Abortion. M19.
2 An aborted fetus. E20.
– COMB.: **abortus fever** brucellosis in humans, *spec.* that caused by *Brucella abortus*.

abosom *noun* pl. of OBOSOM.

abought *verb pa. t. & pple* of ABY.

aboulia *noun* var. of ABULIA.

abound /əˈbaʊnd/ *verb intrans*. LME.
[ORIGIN Old French *abunder*, *abonder* from Latin *abundare*, from *ab* AB- + *undare*, from *unda* a wave. 14–16 spelt *hab-* by assoc. with Latin *habere* have.]
1 Overflow, be plentiful. LME.

J. MCCOSH The discontent which abounds in the world. E. WAUGH English titles abounded now in Hollywood.

†**2** Be rich, have possessions to overflowing. LME–M18.

AV *Phil.* 4:18 I have all and abound.

3 Be wealthy *in*; teem *with*. Also foll. by †*of*. LME.

E. M. FORSTER Those grey-brown streets . . in which the eastern quarter of the city abounds. W. STEVENS The vegetation still abounds with forms.

†**4** Be at liberty; revel *in*. LME–L18.
†**abound in one's own sense** follow one's own opinion.
■ **abounder** *noun* a person who has plenty M18. **aboundingly** *adverb* in an abounding manner, plentifully LME.

about /əˈbaʊt/ *adverb & preposition*.
[ORIGIN Old English *onbūtan*, from *on* in, on (see A *preposition*[1] 1) + *būtan* outside of (see BUT *preposition*).]
▸ **A** *adverb*. **1** Around the outside; on or towards every side; all round. OE. ▸**b** In circumference. *arch.* LME.

W. OWEN A mead Bordered about with warbling water brooks. *fig.*: SHAKES. *Rom. & Jul.* Be wary, look about. **b** SHAKES. *Merry W.* In the waist two yards about.

2 Up and down; here and there. OE. ▸**b** On the move, astir; prevailing (as a disease). ME.

YEATS Tumbled and blown about. E. BOWEN About on the low tables stood high alabaster lamps.

know one's way about: see WAY *noun*. **b out and about** (of a person, esp. after an illness) engaging in normal outdoor activity. ***up and about***: see UP *adverb*[2] & *adjective*[2].
3 In rotation or revolution; in the course of events; in succession. OE.

L. STERNE Let the heralds officers twist his neck about if they will.

bring about cause to revolve or happen, bring to pass. **come about** revolve (as time); happen, come to pass. ***turn and turn about***: see TURN *noun*.
4 Near in number, scale, degree, etc., (hovering between adverb and preposition: cf. sense B.4 below); *colloq.* often in iron. understatement or comparison. OE.

DICKENS You're about right respecting the bond. *Tablet* We stopped firing at about seven o'clock. SCOTT FITZGERALD Her family is one aunt about a thousand years old. S. KAUFFMANN Desire and poignant affection, in about equal parts, sprang up in him.

stand about: see STAND *verb*.
5 On any side; somewhere near. ME.
hang about etc.
6 Half round or less; facing in the opposite direction. ME. ▸**b** NAUTICAL. On or to the opposite tack. L15.
right about: see RIGHT *adverb*. ***the other way about***: see WAY *noun*.
7 With inf. (also occas. with verbal noun). ▸†**a** Preparing, planning. ME–L18. ▸**b** (Passing into preposition: cf. sense B.6 below.) On the point of, going *to*. In neg. contexts: intending *to*, prepared *to* (chiefly *N. Amer. colloq.*). E16.

b CARLYLE England seems about deserting him. DYLAN THOMAS The conversation of prayers about to be said. M. RUSS I ain't about to work that hard for no reason.

b †**go about to** endeavour to (do something).
▸ **B** *preposition*. **1** On the outside of; on or towards every side of; all round. OE.

J. HELLER A paisley kerchief . . was knotted rakishly about his neck.

2 Around less definitely: ▸**a** In attendance on. OE. ▸**b** Somewhere on or near the person. ME. ▸**c** Somewhere near *gen.*; in or near. Also *fig.* (in ref. to mental faculties etc.). LME.

a SHAKES. *Jul. Caes.* Let me have men about me that are fat. **b** E. WHARTON You don't happen to have a cigarette about you? **c** CHESTERFIELD Have . . your ears and your eyes about you. R. S. THOMAS There was a coldness / about his heart.

3 Round (as opp. to across, over, into, etc.). *arch.* OE.

W. WOLLASTON Revolution . . about the sun.

beat about the bush: see BUSH *noun*[1].
4 Approximately at; close to. OE.

SHAKES. *Merry W.* Be you in the Park about midnight. J. I. M. STEWART A slight . . figure of about my own age. H. PINTER About the best convenience they had.

about time: see TIME *noun*. ***along about***: see ALONG *adverb* 2b. ***just about***: see JUST *adverb*.
5 Here and there in, over, or upon. ME. ▸**b** Frequenting. L16.

C. MEW She does the work about the house As well as most. K. MANSFIELD Tables and basket chairs scattered about the veranda.

b *man about town*: see TOWN *noun*.
6 In connection with; appertaining to; dealing or occupied with; touching; concerning; on the subject of; in relation to. ME.

AV *Luke* 2:49 I must bee about my fathers businesse. P. LARKIN Scraps of songs about love.

how about what is the news concerning; how do you dispose of the question of; what do you think of; I suggest. **how about that?** isn't that good, surprising, etc.? **how's about** *colloq.* = ***how about*** above. **what about** = ***how about*** above. ***what something is all about***: see ALL *adverb* 1.
■ **aboutness** *noun* E20.

†**aboutes** *adverb & preposition* var. of ABOUTS.

about-face /əbaʊtˈfeɪs/ *verb intrans. & noun*. E20.
[ORIGIN from military command (*right*) *about face!*]
= ABOUT-TURN.

†**abouts** *adverb & preposition*. Also **-tes**. LME–L17.
[ORIGIN from ABOUT + -S[3].]
= ABOUT.
– NOTE: Survives in *hereabouts* etc.

about-turn /əbaʊtˈtəːn/ *noun & verb intrans*. M20.
[ORIGIN from military command (*right*) *about turn!*]
(Make) a reversal of direction, opinion, policy, or behaviour.

above /əˈbʌv/ *adverb, preposition, adjective, & noun*. OE.
[ORIGIN from A *preposition*[1] 1 repr. Old English *on* + *bufan* BOVE. For illustration of senses, *a* and *bove* are here taken together: see note below.]
▸ **A** *adverb*. **1** Overhead; vertically up; on high. OE. ▸**b** In or to heaven. ME.

DICKENS A wooden stair leading above. M. SPARK Mary cast her eyes around her and up above. **b** TENNYSON Trust in things above.

Heavens above: see HEAVEN *noun*.
2 Higher on a sheet or page; earlier in a book or article. OE.
above-cited, ***above-mentioned***, ***above-named***, ***above-quoted***, ***above-said***, ***above-written***, etc.
3 In a higher place; further up. ME.

GEOFFREY HILL The tough pig-headed salmon strove . . To reach the steady hills above.

4 In a higher rank, position, or station. ME.
5 In addition, besides. ME.
OVER AND ABOVE *adverbial phr.*
6 More in number or quantity. (Almost always with numeral following, passing into preposition: see sense B.8 below.) LME. ▸**b** Above zero; above freezing point. M20.
▸ **B** *preposition*. **1** Over; vertically up from; on the top of. OE.

E. ST V. MILLAY Above the world is stretched the sky.

2 In a higher place than; further up from; further north than. OE.

E. HEMINGWAY The attack would cross the river above the narrow gorge.

3 Rising or appearing beyond the level or reach of. ME.

L. HUGHES This college on the hill above Harlem. J. B. PRIESTLEY Even above the screeching . . , voices can be heard.

4 Superior to (the influence of); not condescending to. ME.

M. MOORE Till the poets among us can be . . above insolence and triviality.

5 Higher in rank, position, etc. than. ME.

J. HELLER You'll be marrying far above you.

6 Higher in degree or quality than. ME.
7 In addition to; besides. ME.
8 Surpassing in quantity, amount, or number. (Passing into adverb: see sense A.6 above.) LME.

SHAKES. *Haml.* It was never acted; or, if it was, not above once.

– COMB. & PHRASES: **above all** beyond everything, chiefly. **above and beyond** more than and different from. ***above ground***: see GROUND *noun*. **aboveground** *adjective & noun* (**a**) *adjective* that is above ground; that is not underground (*lit.* & *fig.*); (**b**) *noun* the part of society that is not underground. ***above measure***: see MEASURE *noun*. **above oneself** lacking self-control because of high spirits etc. ***above one's head***: see HEAD *noun*. ***above par***: see PAR *noun*[1]. ***above price***: see PRICE *noun*. ***above reproach***: see REPROACH *noun*. ***above suspicion***: see SUSPICION *noun*. ***above the gangway***: see GANGWAY 3b. ***above the salt***: see SALT *noun*[1]. ***above water***: see WATER *noun*. ***keep one's head above water***: see WATER *noun*. OVER AND ABOVE *prepositional phr.*
▸ **C** *adjective & noun*. **1** Ellipt. after prepositions (chiefly *from*): a higher place; heaven. ME.

AV *James* 1:17 Euery perfect gift is from aboue.

2 Attrib. & absol.: with ellipsis of a pple as *said*, *mentioned*, etc. M18.

G. B. SHAW Reading the above after a lapse of 28 years. T. STOPPARD During the above speech French is becoming increasingly agitated.

– NOTE: In Old English *abufan* was north. and only adverbial, but by the end of 13 it had acquired the prepositional uses of and generally replaced *bufan* BOVE, which became obsolete in 15.

above-board /əbʌvˈbɔːd/ *adverb & pred. adjective*. L16.
[ORIGIN from ABOVE *preposition* + BOARD *noun*.]
Open(ly); fair(ly); without concealment.
– NOTE: Orig. a gambling term.

ab ovo /ab ˈəʊvəʊ/ *adverbial phr.* L16.
[ORIGIN Latin = from the egg.]
From the (very) beginning.

abox /əˈbɒks/ *adverb & pred. adjective*. E19.
[ORIGIN from A-[2] + BOX *verb*[2].]
NAUTICAL. Of head yards: in a position with only the head-sails laid aback.

abracadabra /ˌabrəkəˈdabrə/ *noun*. M16.
[ORIGIN Latin, first found in Q. Serenus Sammonicus (2nd cent.), ult. from Greek.]
Orig., a Kabbalistic word, supposed when written triangularly, or in some other forms, to be a charm against fevers etc. Now, a word said by conjurors when performing a magic trick; a spell; gibberish.

A

abrade /əˈbreɪd/ *verb trans.* L17.
[ORIGIN Latin *abradere*, from *ab* AB- + *radere* to scrape: cf. ABRASE *verb*.]
1 Rub or wear off (a part *from*). L17.
2 Wear down or injure by rubbing. (*lit. & fig.*) M18.
■ **abrader** *noun* something that abrades a surface L19.

Abraham /ˈeɪbrəham/ *noun & adjective*. Also (*arch.*) **Abram** /ˈeɪbrəm/. OE.
[ORIGIN The biblical patriarch (*Genesis* 11:26–25:18 etc.).]
▸ **A** *noun*. **1** ***Abraham's bosom***, †***Abraham's barm*** [*Luke* 16:23], heaven, the place of rest for the souls of the blessed. OE.
2 ***sham Abraham*** [see *Abraham-man* below], feign illness or insanity. L18.
– COMB.: **Abraham-man** (*obsolete* exc. *hist.*) [perh. alluding to the beggar in *Luke* 16], after the dissolution of the religious houses (which had provided charity), a beggar feigning insanity.
▸ †**B** *adjective*. [Alt.] = AUBURN *adjective*. OE–E17.
■ **Abrahamic** /eɪbrəˈhamɪk/ *adjective* of, pertaining to, or characteristic of the patriarch Abraham E19.

†**abraid** *verb*.
[ORIGIN Old English *abreġdan*, from A-[1] + BRAID *verb*[1].]
1 *verb trans.* Wrench out (a sword). OE–ME.
2 *verb intrans. & trans.* Start or startle out of sleep, a faint, etc. ME–E17.
3 *verb intrans. & trans.* Shout out. LME–L16.
4 *verb intrans.* Rise nauseously in the stomach. Chiefly *dial.* M16–M19.

Abram *noun & adjective* see ABRAHAM.

†**abrase** *adjective*. Only in 17.
[ORIGIN Latin *abrasus* pa. pple, formed as ABRASE *verb*.]
Rubbed smooth or clear; blank.

abrase /əˈbreɪz/ *verb trans. rare*. L15.
[ORIGIN Latin *abras-* pa. ppl stem of *abradere* ABRADE.]
= ABRADE.

abrasion /əˈbreɪʒ(ə)n/ *noun*. M17.
[ORIGIN Latin *abrasio(n-)*, formed as ABRASE *verb*: see -ION.]
1 Rubbing or scraping off; wearing away. M17. ▸**b** GEOLOGY. The wearing away of rock by the mechanical action of rock fragments carried by ice, water, or wind. M19.
†**2** Debris. Only in M18.
3 An abraded area; a graze. M19.
■ **abrasional** *adjective* pertaining to or formed by abrasion M20.

abrasive /əˈbreɪsɪv/ *noun & adjective*. M19.
[ORIGIN formed as ABRASE *verb* + -IVE.]
▸ **A** *noun*. An abrasive substance or body. M19.
▸ **B** *adjective*. Abrading; tending to graze the skin; capable of polishing by rubbing or grinding; *fig.* tending to hurt the feelings or cause annoyance. L19.

abrazo /aˈbraθo, əˈbrɑːzəʊ/ *noun*. Pl. **-os** /-ɔs, -əʊz/. E20.
[ORIGIN Spanish.]
An embrace, a hug, esp. as a salutation.

abreaction /abrɪˈakʃ(ə)n/ *noun*. E20.
[ORIGIN from AB- + REACTION, after German *Abreagieren*.]
PSYCHOANALYSIS. The relief of anxiety by the expression and release of a previously repressed emotion, through reliving the experience that caused it; an instance of this.
■ **abreact** *verb trans.* eliminate by abreaction E20. **abreactive** *adjective* M20.

abreast /əˈbrɛst/ *adverb*. LME.
[ORIGIN from A *preposition*[1] 1 + BREAST *noun*.]
1 With chests or fronts in a line; side by side (in advancing). Formerly also after *in, of, on*. LME. ▸**b** NAUTICAL. With ships equally distant, and parallel. L17.

D. H. LAWRENCE They . . passed in on to the grass, four abreast. J. IRVING Three policemen came down the hall abreast, in step.

b line abreast: see LINE *noun*[2].
2 Foll. by *of, with*: parallel to, alongside. Freq. *fig.* M17.
keep abreast: see KEEP *verb*.

†**abrecock** *noun* see APRICOT.

†**abrenounce** *verb trans.* M16–M17.
[ORIGIN from AB- + RENOUNCE *verb*: cf. medieval Latin *abrenunciare*.]
Renounce; contradict.

abrenunciation /ˌabrɪnʌnsɪˈeɪʃ(ə)n/ *noun. arch.* M16.
[ORIGIN Old French *abrenonciation* or late Latin *abrenuntiatio(n-)*, formed as AB- + *renuntiatio(n-)* RENUNCIATION.]
Renunciation; retractation.

abri /əˈbriː/ *noun*. E19.
[ORIGIN French.]
A shelter; *spec.* in ARCHAEOLOGY, an overhanging rock affording shelter.

abridge /əˈbrɪdʒ/ *verb trans.* ME.
[ORIGIN Old French *abreg(i)er* from Latin *abbreviare*: see ABBREVIATE *verb*.]
1 Deprive (a person) *of*; (*rare*) debar *from*. *arch.* ME.
2 Shorten in duration. Now *rare*. LME.

SHAKES. *Two Gent.* Thy staying will abridge thy life.

3 Make shorter in number of words, while retaining the sense; epitomize. (Foll. by *from*.) LME.
4 Cut short; reduce to a small size. Now *rare* of material things. LME.

SIR W. SCOTT To what purpose serve these abridged cloaks?

5 Curtail (rights, privileges, etc.). LME.
■ **abridger** *noun* M16.

abridgement /əˈbrɪdʒm(ə)nt/ *noun*. Also **-dgm-**. LME.
[ORIGIN Old French & mod. French *abrégement*, formed as ABRIDGE: see -MENT.]
1 The act or process of abridging; shortening; curtailment; an instance of this. LME.
2 An epitome or compendium of a larger work, or of a subject that might be treated more fully. LME.

abrim /əˈbrɪm/ *adverb & pred. adjective*. L19.
[ORIGIN from A-[2] + BRIM *noun*[1].]
Full to the brim; brimming.

abrin /ˈeɪbrɪn/ *noun*. L19.
[ORIGIN from mod. Latin *Abrus* (see below) + -IN[1].]
CHEMISTRY. A poisonous protein present in the jequirity bean (*Abrus precatorius*).

abroach /əˈbrəʊtʃ/ *adverb & pred. adjective*. LME.
[ORIGIN Anglo-Norman *abroche*, from Old French *abrochier*, formed as A-[5] + BROACH *noun*[1], *verb*[1].]
Chiefly in ***set abroach***.
1 Of a cask etc.: broached; pierced, so as to let the liquor run. LME.
2 In a state to be diffused or propagated; astir. E16.

SHAKES. *Rom. & Jul.* Who set this ancient quarrel new abroach?

abroad /əˈbrɔːd/ *adverb & noun*. ME.
[ORIGIN from A *preposition*[1] 1 + BROAD *noun*.]
▸ **A** *adverb*. **1** Widely, over a broad surface; widely scattered; widespread. ME.

AV *Rom.* 5:5 The loue of God is shed abroad in our hearts. SHAKES. *Tit. A.* The . . wind Will blow these sands like Sibyl's leaves abroad. LONGFELLOW Stretched abroad on the seashore.

send abroad: see SEND *verb*[1].
2 Out of one's house or abode. ME.

HENRY MILLER The greatest delight . . was . . to walk the streets at night when no one was abroad.

3 In or into foreign countries; out of one's native land. LME.

W. PLOMER A pleasant old buffer, . . Who believed that . . an umbrella might pacify barbarians abroad.

4 At large, freely moving about, (*lit. & fig.*). L15.

LD MACAULAY The suspicions which were abroad.

5 Confused; dazed; astray; wide of the mark. E19.

THACKERAY At the twelfth round the . . champion was all abroad.

▸ **B** *noun*. **1** ***from abroad***, from another country. M19.

Economist The number of . . churches in any small American town astounds visitors from abroad.

2 Somewhere outside one's homeland; foreign countries. Chiefly *joc.* L19.

K. GRAHAME Somewhere over in that beastly abroad.

abrogable /ˈabrəgəb(ə)l/ *adjective*. L16.
[ORIGIN from Latin *abrogare* (see ABROGATE *verb*) + -ABLE.]
Able to be abrogated.

abrogate /ˈabrəgət/ *adjective* (orig. *pa. pple*). *arch.* LME.
[ORIGIN Latin *abrogatus* pa. pple, formed as ABROGATE *verb*: see -ATE[2].]
Repealed; abolished by authority.

abrogate /ˈabrəgeɪt/ *verb trans.* E16.
[ORIGIN Latin *abrogat-* pa. ppl stem of *abrogare*, from *ab* AB- + *rogare* propose a law: see -ATE[3].]
Repeal (a law, custom, etc.); abolish authoritatively or formally; *gen.* do away with.
■ **abrogator** *noun* L16.

abrogation /abrəˈgeɪʃ(ə)n/ *noun*. M16.
[ORIGIN French, or Latin *abrogatio(n-)*, formed as ABROGATE *verb*: see -ATION.]
Repeal; abolition by authority; an instance of this.

†**abrood** *adverb & pred. adjective*. ME–L19.
[ORIGIN from A *preposition*[1] 1 + BROOD *noun*.]
On its brood; hatching eggs, *fig.* mischief etc.

abrook /əˈbrʊk/ *verb trans. rare* (Shakes.). L16.
[ORIGIN from A-[11] + BROOK *verb*.]
Brook, endure.

abrupt /əˈbrʌpt/ *adjective, noun, & verb*. L16.
[ORIGIN Latin *abruptus* broken off, steep, pa. pple of *abrumpere*, from *ab* AB- + *rumpere* break.]
▸ **A** *adjective*. †**1** Broken away (from restraint). *rare*. Only in L16.
2 Characterized by sudden interruption or change; sudden, hasty; curt in manner. L16.

SHAKES. *1 Hen. VI* The cause of your abrupt departure. E. O'NEILL Talking in . . abrupt sentences.

†**3** Broken off. E17–M18.
4 Precipitous, steep. E17.

O. SITWELL The abrupt and mountainous grey background.

5 BOTANY. Truncated. E19.
▸ **B** *noun*. An abrupt place; an abyss. *literary*. M17.

MILTON Upborn with indefatigable wings Over the vast abrupt.

▸ **C** *verb trans.* Break off; interrupt suddenly. M17.

M. INNES To abrupt his journey in a strange town.

■ **abruptly** *adverb* L16. **abruptness** *noun* E17.

abruption /əˈbrʌpʃ(ə)n/ *noun*. E17.
[ORIGIN Latin *abruptio(n-)*, formed as ABRUPT: see -ION.]
1 A breaking off; an interruption. *arch.* E17.
2 A snapping; the sudden breaking away of a portion from a mass. M17.

abruptio placentae /əˌbrʌptɪəʊ pləˈsɛntiː, əˌbrʌpʃɪəʊ/ *noun phr.* E20.
[ORIGIN mod. Latin, formed as ABRUPTION + PLACENTA.]
MEDICINE. Premature separation of the placenta from the uterine wall during pregnancy.

ABS *abbreviation*.
1 Anti-lock braking system (for motor vehicles).
2 Acrylonitrile-butadiene-styrene, a hard composite plastic.

abs- /əbs, abs/ *prefix* (not productive).
Repr. Latin *abs-*, the form of *ab-* AB- used before *c, q, t*.

abscess /ˈabsɪs, -sɛs/ *noun*. M16.
[ORIGIN Latin *abscessus*, from *abscedere*, from ABS- + *cedere* CEDE.]
A localized collection of pus within the body.
■ **abscessed** *adjective* affected by an abscess or abscesses M19.

abscind /əbˈsɪnd/ *verb trans. arch.* E17.
[ORIGIN Latin *abscindere*, from *ab* AB- + *scindere* cut asunder.]
Cut off (*lit. & fig.*).

abscise /əbˈsʌɪz/ *verb*. E17.
[ORIGIN Latin *absciss-* pa. ppl stem of *abscidere*, from ABS- + *caedere* to cut.]
1 *verb trans.* Cut off or away. E17.
2 *verb intrans.* BOTANY. Separate by abscission; fall off. E20.

abscisic /abˈsɪsɪk/ *adjective*. M20.
[ORIGIN from ABSCIS(SION + -IC.]
BIOCHEMISTRY. ***abscisic acid***, a plant hormone which promotes seed and bud dormancy and inhibits germination.

abscision /əbˈsɪʒ(ə)n/ *noun. rare*. LME.
[ORIGIN Latin *abscisio(n-)*, formed as ABSCISE: see -ION.]
A cutting off or away.

absciss /əbˈsɪs/ *verb trans. & intrans.* M19.
[ORIGIN Back-form. from ABSCISSION.]
= ABSCISE.

abscissa /ˈabsɪsə/ *noun*. Pl. **-ssae** /-siː/, **-ssas**. In BOTANY the form is **absciss** /abˈsɪs/. L17.
[ORIGIN mod. Latin, use as noun (sc. *linea* line) of fem. pa. pple of *abscindere*: see ABSCIND.]
1 MATH. Orig., the portion of a line between a fixed point on it and the point of intersection with an ordinate. Now, the distance of a point from the *y*-axis measured parallel to the *x*-axis. L17.
2 BOTANY. ***absciss layer***, a distinctive layer of cells at which separation occurs on leaf fall. L19.

abscission /əbˈsɪʃ(ə)n/ *noun*. E17.
[ORIGIN Latin *abscissio(n-)*, from *absciss-* pa. ppl stem of *abscindere* ABSCIND: see -ION.]
1 The action or process of cutting off or separating something; amputation, removal. E17.
†**2** The state of being cut off from God or the Church; excommunication. Only in M17.
3 BOTANY. The natural separation of a leaf or other part from a plant. L19.

abscond /əbˈskɒnd/ *verb*. M16.
[ORIGIN Latin *abscondere*, formed as ABS- + *condere* put together, stow.]
1 *verb intrans. & refl.* Hide (oneself); leave hurriedly and secretly; flee from justice. M16.
2 *verb trans.* Hide away, conceal. L16.
■ **abscondence** *noun* (*rare*) L19. **absconder** *noun* E18. **absconsion** *noun* (*rare*) M17.

abseil /ˈabseɪl, -zʌɪl/ *noun & verb intrans.* M20.
[ORIGIN German *abseilen*, from *ab* down + *Seil* rope.]
1 MOUNTAINEERING. (Make) a descent of a steep rock face by means of a doubled rope fixed at a higher point. M20.
2 (Make) a similar descent from a helicopter. L20.

absence /ˈabs(ə)ns/ *noun*. LME.
[ORIGIN Old French & mod. French from Latin *absentia*, formed as ABSENT *adjective & noun*: see -ENCE.]
1 The state of being away from a place or person; the time or duration of being away. LME.

B. BEHAN I was . . sentenced to death in my absence, so I said they could shoot me in my absence. B. PYM Her absences . . were spent in mysterious ploys of her own.

leave of absence: see LEAVE *noun*[1].
2 Non-existence or lack *of*. LME.
in the absence of something when or as something is not present or available.
3 Inattention due to thinking of other things. Esp. in ***absence of mind***. E18. ▸**b** MEDICINE. Sudden temporary loss of consciousness occurring without the awareness of the subject, esp. in petit mal; an episode of this (also ***absence seizure***). M20.

ADDISON The little absences and distractions of mankind.

absent /ˈabs(ə)nt/ *adjective, noun, & preposition.* LME.
[ORIGIN Old French & mod. French from Latin *absent-, absens* functioning as pres. pple of *abesse*, from *ab* AB- + *esse* be: see -ENT.]
▸ **A** *adjective.* **1** Away; not present. LME.

JAS. MILL Absent officers were summoned.

2 Not existing; lacking. LME.
3 Preoccupied; paying no attention to present objects etc. E18.

SMOLLETT I . . became absent and thoughtful. I. COMPTON-BURNETT Duncan gave an absent nod towards the bed, as if he hardly heard.

– PHRASES & SPECIAL COLLOCATIONS: **absent from** not present in or at. **absent voter** a person who votes by post because absent from the normal voting place.
▸ †**B** *noun.* = ABSENTEE 1. LME–E19.
▸ **C** *preposition.* In the absence of, without. *N. Amer. formal.* M20.

Chicago Tribune Absent a strong U.S. role, the power balance in Asia would be highly unstable.

■ **absently** *adverb* with absence of mind M19. **absentness** *noun* absent-mindedness M19.

absent /abˈsɛnt/ *verb.* LME.
[ORIGIN Old French & mod. French *absenter* or late Latin *absentare* keep or be away, formed as ABSENT *adjective & noun.*]
1 *verb trans.* Keep away. Now only *refl.* go or stay away. LME.

D. RUNYON If he absents himself from her side.

†**2** *verb intrans.* Stay away; withdraw. LME–L18.
3 *verb trans.* Leave. Long *rare.* LME.
■ **absenˈtation** *noun* the action of absenting oneself E19. **absenter** *noun* a person who absents himself or herself L16.

absentee /abs(ə)nˈtiː/ *noun & adjective.* M16.
[ORIGIN from ABSENT *verb* + -EE[1].]
▸ **A** *noun.* **1** A person who is absent on some occasion. M16. ▸**b** *spec.* An absent voter. E20.
2 A person who lives away from his or her country or home; *esp.* a landowner who lives away from his or her property. E17.
▸ **B** *attrib.* or as *adjective.* That is an absentee; of or pertaining to absentees. M19.

E. A. FREEMAN A foreign and absentee king. *New York Times* Laws governing absentee voting.

■ **absenteeism** *noun* the practice of being an absentee; the practice of workers, pupils, etc., of absenting themselves from work, esp. frequently or without good reason: E19. **absenteeship** *noun* (now *rare*) absenteeism, esp. of landowners L18.

absent-minded /abs(ə)ntˈmʌɪndɪd/ *adjective.* M19.
[ORIGIN from ABSENT *adjective* + MINDED.]
= ABSENT *adjective* 3.
■ **absent-mindedly** *adverb* L19. **absent-mindedness** *noun* L19.

†**absey** *noun* var. of ABC.

absinth /ˈabsɪnθ/ *noun.* Also (in sense 2 usu.) **-the.** LME.
[ORIGIN French *absinthe* from Latin *absinthium* from Greek *apsinthion* wormwood.]
1 Wormwood, the plant *Artemisia absinthium* or its essence; *fig.* bitterness, sorrow. LME.
2 A green liqueur made (at least orig.) from wine and wormwood. M19. ▸**b** A green colour resembling that of the liqueur. L19.

absinthium /əbˈsɪnθɪəm/ *noun.* Now *rare* or *obsolete.* OE.
[ORIGIN Latin: see ABSINTH.]
The plant absinth or wormwood.

†**absis** *noun* see APSIS.

absit omen /ˈabsɪt ˈəʊmən/ *interjection.* L16.
[ORIGIN Latin = may this (evil) omen be absent.]
May the suggested foreboding not become fact.

absolute /ˈabsəluːt/ *adjective & noun.* LME.
[ORIGIN Latin *absolutus* freed, completed, pa. pple of *absolvere* ABSOLVE; partly infl. by Old French *absolu.*]
▸ **A** *adjective.* †**I** Detached, disengaged.
1 Absolved *from.* LME–M17.
2 Disengaged from accidental or special circumstances. Only in LME.
3 Absorbed *in* (an occupation). Only in L15.
▸ **II** In quality or degree.
4 Finished; perfect. *arch.* LME.

G. SANDYS Where mariners be English: who are the absolutest . . in their profession.

5 Pure, mere; in the strictest sense. M16.

P. HAWKER The gale increased to an absolute tornado.

6 Complete, entire, total. L16.

ARNOLD BENNETT Performed with absolute assurance and perfection. N. BLAKE If he wasn't such an absolute ass.

▸ **III** In position or relation.
7 GRAMMAR. Not in the usual grammatical relation or construction; (of a form) uninflected. LME.
8 Of ownership or authority: unrestricted, independent. L15.
9 Having absolute power; arbitrary, despotic. L16.
10 Viewed without relation to or comparison with other things of the same kind; real, actual. E17.
▸ **IV** Without condition or mental limitation.
11 Of a person or prediction: free from doubt or uncertainty. *arch.* E17.

SHAKES. *Cymb.* I am absolute 'Twas very Cloten.

12 Of a statement etc.: free from conditions or reservations. E17.
13 PHILOSOPHY. Existing or able to be thought of without relation to other things. L18.
– SPECIAL COLLOCATIONS ETC.: ***ablative absolute***: see ABLATIVE *noun* 1. **absolute alcohol** ethanol containing less than one per cent of water by weight. ***absolute*** HUMIDITY. ***absolute*** MAGNITUDE. **absolute majority** a majority over all rivals combined, more than half. **absolute music** self-dependent instrumental music without literary or other extraneous suggestions. **absolute pitch** a fixed standard of pitch defined by the rate of vibration; ability to recognize or reproduce the exact pitch of a note. **absolute temperature** temperature measured from absolute zero. ***absolute term***: see TERM *noun.* **absolute title** LAW the guarantee of title to the ownership of a property or lease. **absolute unit** a unit which can be defined in terms of mass, length, and time. **absolute value** MATH. of a real number: its value irrespective of sign; of a complex number $a + ib$: the positive square root of $a^2 + b^2$. ***absolute viscosity***: see VISCOSITY 2. ***absolute zero***: see ZERO *noun* 2b. ***accusative absolute***: see ACCUSATIVE *noun.* ***dative absolute***: see DATIVE *noun.* ***genitive absolute***: see GENITIVE *noun.* ***nominative absolute***: see NOMINATIVE *noun.*
▸ **B** *noun.* **1** *the Absolute*, that which is absolute, that which exists or is able to be thought of without relation to other things. M19.
2 An absolute thing; an absolute principle or truth. M19.
■ **absolutely** *adverb* in an absolute manner or degree; also (stressed on 3rd syll.) used as an emphatic affirmative: yes, quite so: LME. **absoluteness** *noun* M16.

absolution /absəˈluːʃ(ə)n/ *noun.* ME.
[ORIGIN Old French & mod. French from Latin *absolutio(n-)*, formed as ABSOLUTE: see -ION.]
1 Remission of sins, declared by ecclesiastical authority. ME. ▸**b** (An utterance of) the formula by which this is declared. LME.

F. MCCOURT He tells me to kneel, gives me absolution, tells me say three Hail Marys.

2 Forgiveness of sins generally; any absolving or formal setting free (*from* guilt, sentence, or obligation); remission (*of* sin or penance). ME.
3 Esp. ROMAN LAW. A judgement for the defendant. E17.

absolutise *verb* var. of ABSOLUTIZE.

absolutism /ˈabsəluːtɪz(ə)m, -ljuː-/ *noun.* M18.
[ORIGIN from ABSOLUTE *adjective* + -ISM, after French *absolutisme.*]
1 THEOLOGY. The doctrine that God acts absolutely in the matter of salvation. M18.
2 POLITICS. The principle of absolute government; despotism. E19.
3 PHILOSOPHY. The philosophy of the Absolute. L19.

absolutist /ˈabsəluːtɪst, -ljuː-/ *noun & adjective.* M19.
[ORIGIN formed as ABSOLUTISM + -IST, after French *absolutiste.*]
▸ **A** *noun.* **1** POLITICS. A person who is in favour of absolute government. M19.
2 PHILOSOPHY. A person who maintains the absolute identity of subject and object. M19.
3 A person who maintains certain principles to be absolute, an uncompromising person; *spec.* (*hist.*) a conscientious objector in the First World War who refused to perform any compulsory service. E20.
▸ **B** *adjective.* Practising or supporting absolutism; despotic; uncompromising. M19.
■ **absoluˈtistic** *adjective* M19.

absolutize /ˈabsəluːtʌɪz, -ljuː-/ *verb trans.* Also **-ise.** M20.
[ORIGIN from ABSOLUTE *adjective* + -IZE.]
Make absolute.
■ **ˌabsolutiˈzation** *noun* M19.

absolve /əbˈzɒlv/ *verb trans.* LME.
[ORIGIN Latin *absolvere* free, acquit, from *ab* AB- + *solvere* loosen: cf. ASSOIL.]
1 Set free, discharge, (*from* or *of* obligations, liabilities, etc.). LME.

L. A. G. STRONG It absolved him of all responsibility to them in the realm of financial speculation.

†**2** Clear up, solve, resolve. L15–M17.

EVELYN Phenomena already absolved.

3 Pronounce free (*from* blame, guilt, the consequences of crime or sin, etc.). M16.
4 Esp. ROMAN LAW. Pronounce not liable or not guilty. M16.

POPE Absolves the just, and dooms the guilty souls.

5 Give absolution or remission of sins to. M16.

SHAKES. *Rom. & Jul.* To make confession, and to be absolv'd. M. R. MITFORD One's conscience may be pretty well absolved for not admiring this man. C. KINGSLEY I dare not absolve him of robbing a priest.

6 Remit, give absolution for, (a sin or crime). L16.

S. SASSOON Who shall absolve the foulness of their fate?

†**7** Discharge, finish, (a task etc.). L16–E19.

MILTON The work begun, how soon absolved.

■ **absolvable** *adjective* E19. **absolver** *noun* L16.

absolvitor /abˈsɒlvɪtɔː/ *noun.* M16.
[ORIGIN Latin = let him or her be acquitted, 3rd pers. imper. pass. of *absolvere*: see ABSOLVE.]
SCOTS LAW. A judgement for the defender.

absonant /ˈabs(ə)nənt/ *adjective.* Now *rare.* M16.
[ORIGIN from Latin *ab* AB- + *sonant-* pres. ppl stem of *sonare* sound, on the analogy of *consonant, dissonant*, etc.]
Harsh, discordant; *fig.* unreasonable, unnatural.
■ Also †**absonous** *adjective* E17–M18.

absorb /əbˈzɔːb, -ˈsɔːb/ *verb trans.* Pa. pple **absorbed**, (*arch.*) **absorpt** /-ɔːpt/. LME.
[ORIGIN Old French & mod. French *absorber* or Latin *absorbere*, from *ab* AB- + *sorbere* suck in.]
1 Include or take (a thing) in so that it no longer has separate existence; incorporate. LME.

E. O'NEILL The conquered Chinese . . have already begun to absorb their conquerors. G. STEINER The realistic novel reached out to absorb every new quality and locus of experience.

†**2** Of water, mire, etc.: engulf. L15–L18.

T. BURNET To be absorpt . . in a lake of fire and brimstone.

3 Suck or drink in. E17.
4 Take up (a substance, energy, etc.) by chemical or physical action; gain energy from and reduce the intensity of (light or other radiation, sound, etc.). E18.
5 Engross (a person, a person's attention, etc.). L18.
6 Occupy or consume (time). M19.
7 Assimilate mentally. L19.

R. CHURCH Life . . had more to offer me than I could absorb.

■ **absorbaˈbility** *noun* the quality of being absorbable L18. **absorbable** *adjective* able to be absorbed L18. **absorbance** *noun* the logarithm of the reciprocal of transmittance; optical density: M20. **absorbancy** *noun* the ratio of the optical density of a solution to that of a similar body of pure solvent M20. **absorbed** *adjective* that has been absorbed; *esp.* engrossed, intensely interested: M18. **absorbedly** /-bɪdli/ *adverb* M19. **absorbedness** /-bɪdnɪs/ *noun* L19. **absorber** *noun* a person who or thing which absorbs M19. **absorbing** *adjective* that absorbs; *esp.* engrossing, all-engaging: M18. **absorbingly** *adverb* M19.

absorbent /əbˈzɔːb(ə)nt, -ˈsɔːb-/ *adjective & noun.* E18.
[ORIGIN Latin *absorbent-* pres. ppl stem of *absorbere*: see ABSORB, -ENT.]
▸ **A** *adjective.* Absorptive; having a tendency to absorb. E18.
absorbent cotton *N. Amer.* cotton wool.
▸ **B** *noun.* **1** A substance which absorbs. E18.
2 PHYSIOLOGY. In *pl.* The organs through which absorption occurs. Now *rare* or *obsolete.* M18.
■ **absorbency** *noun* †(**a**) the action of absorbing; (**b**) the quality of being absorbent: M19.

absorpt *verb* see ABSORB.

absorptance /əbˈzɔːpt(ə)ns, -sɔːpt(ə)ns/ *noun.* M20.
[ORIGIN from Latin *absorpt-* (see ABSORPTION) + -ANCE, after *reflectance.*]
PHYSICS. The degree to which a surface or object absorbs radiation incident on it, measured by the ratio of the absorbed to the incident flux.

absorptiometer /əbˌzɔːpʃɪˈɒmɪtə, -ˌsɔːp-/ *noun.* L19.
[ORIGIN from ABSORPTION + -OMETER.]
1 An analytical device which measures the amount of gas absorbed by a reagent. L19.
2 An instrument for measuring the absorption of light or other radiation. M20.
■ **abˌsorptioˈmetric** *adjective* E20.

absorption /əbˈzɔːpʃ(ə)n, -ˈsɔːp-/ *noun.* L16.
[ORIGIN Latin *absorptio(n-)*, from *absorpt-* pa. ppl stem of *absorbere* ABSORB: see -ION.]
†**1** The swallowing up or engulfing of bodies. L16–M18.
2 Disappearance through incorporation in something else. M18.
3 The chemical or physical process of absorbing substances, energy, light, etc. M18. ▸**b** PHYSIOLOGY. The taking up of fluids or dissolved substances by living tissue; *esp.* the taking of digested contents of the intestine into the blood and lymphatic system. M18.
4 Engrossment of the mind or faculties. M19.
5 Mental assimilation. M20.
– COMB.: **absorption costing** a method of calculating the cost of a product or enterprise by taking into account indirect expenses (overheads) as well as direct costs; **absorption spectrum** a spectrum of electromagnetic radiation transmitted through a substance, characteristically showing lines or bands due to absorption at particular wavelengths.

absorptive /əbˈzɔːptɪv, -ˈsɔːp-/ *adjective.* M17.
[ORIGIN formed as ABSORPTION + -IVE.]
Having the quality of absorbing.
■ **absorpˈtivity** *noun* the property of being absorptive; a measure of this: M19.

absquatulate /əbˈskwɒtjʊleɪt/ *verb intrans. joc.*, orig. *US.* M19.
[ORIGIN After *abscond, squattle* (depart), *perambulate*, etc.]
Depart, decamp.
■ **absquatuˈlation** *noun* M19.

A

abstain /əbˈsteɪn/ *verb*. LME.
[ORIGIN Anglo-Norman *astener* = Old French *abstenir* from Latin *abstinere*, formed as ABS- + *tenere* to hold.]
†**1** *verb refl.* Keep or withhold oneself (*of, from*). LME–M16.
2 *verb intrans.* Refrain (*from*); *esp.* fast (*obsolete*), refrain from alcohol, decline to use one's vote. LME.
†**3** *verb trans.* Keep back or off. E16–M17.

MILTON Whether he abstain men from marying.

■ **abstainer** *noun* a person who abstains, esp. from eating or drinking particular things; in older religious writings, = NAZIRITE: LME.

abstemious /əbˈstiːmɪəs/ *adjective*. E17.
[ORIGIN from Latin *abstemius*, from ABS- + base of *temetum* intoxicating drink: see -OUS.]
Sparing, moderate, not self-indulgent, esp. in food and drink.

P. MASSINGER Abstemious from base and goatish looseness. SIR W. SCOTT The meal of the Saracen was abstemious. J. UPDIKE The devout and abstemious Muslim he became.

■ **abstemiously** *adverb* E18. **abstemiousness** *noun* E17.

abstention /əbˈstɛnʃ(ə)n/ *noun*. E16.
[ORIGIN French, or late Latin *abstentio(n-)*, from *abstinere* ABSTAIN: see -ION.]
†**1** The act of keeping back or restraining. E16–M17.
2 The act or state of abstaining or refraining (*from*). E17. ▸**b** *spec.* The action or an act of declining to cast one's vote. L19.

M. ARNOLD The character of abstention and renouncement. H. A. L. FISHER The fasting in the month of Ramadan, . . the abstention from wine. **b** H. KISSINGER In 1969 the Important Question resolution had passed by a wide margin of 71 in favor, 48 against, and 4 abstentions.

■ **abstentionism** *noun* the fact or policy of abstaining, *spec.* in a vote E20. **abstentionist** *noun* a person who abstains or believes in abstaining L19.

absterge /əbˈstəːdʒ/ *verb trans.* Now *rare*. E16.
[ORIGIN Old French & mod. French *absterger* or Latin *abstergere*, from ABS- + *tergere* wipe.]
Wipe away; cleanse.
■ **abstergent** *adjective & noun* (**a**) *adjective* cleansing; (**b**) *noun* a cleansing substance: E17.

abstersion /əbˈstəːʃ(ə)n/ *noun*. LME.
[ORIGIN Old French & mod. French, or medieval Latin *abstertio(n-)*, from Latin *absters-* pa. ppl stem of *abstergere*: see ABSTERGE, -ION.]
The act or process of cleansing or purging.
■ **absterse** *verb trans.* (*rare*) = ABSTERGE LME. **abstersive** *adjective & noun* = ABSTERGENT LME. **abstersiveness** *noun* M17.

abstinence /ˈabstɪnəns/ *noun*. ME.
[ORIGIN Old French from Latin *abstinentia*, formed as ABSTINENT: see -ENCE.]
1 Forbearance of any indulgence of appetite; sexual continence (the oldest sense); fasting; abstention from alcohol. ME.
2 *gen.* The action or practice of abstaining *from* (or †*of*) anything. LME.
– COMB. & PHRASES: **abstinence syndrome** MEDICINE the physical symptoms that appear when a person abruptly stops taking a drug to which he or she is addicted. †**abstinence of war** a truce. ***total abstinence***: see TOTAL *adjective*.
■ **abstinency** *noun* the practice of abstaining from pleasure, food, etc.; a fast: L16.

abstinent /ˈabstɪnənt/ *adjective & noun*. LME.
[ORIGIN Old French & mod. French from Latin *abstinent-* pres. ppl stem of *abstinere* ABSTAIN: see -ENT.]
▸ **A** *adjective*. Practising abstinence. LME.
▸ **B** *noun*. A person who abstains; a faster. LME.
■ **abstinently** *adverb* L16.

abstract /ˈabstrakt/ *adjective & noun*. LME.
[ORIGIN Old French, or Latin *abstractus* pa. pple of *abstrahere*, formed as ABS- + *trahere* draw.]
▸ **A** *adjective*. †**1** Derived, extracted. LME–L15.
2 = ABSTRACTED 1. Now *rare* or *obsolete*. LME.
3 Separated from matter, practice, or particular examples; not concrete; ideal; abstruse. LME. ▸**b** Of art etc.: lacking representational qualities. M19.

R. CUDWORTH Pure, Abstract, Incorporeal Substances. E. HEMINGWAY Abstract words, such as glory, honour, courage, or hallow were obscene.

abstract noun: denoting a quality or state. **b abstract expressionism** a movement or style of painting, originating in New York in the 1940s, and often using techniques such as action painting to allow the artist spontaneous freedom of expression.
4 = ABSTRACTED 3. Now *rare*. E16.

D. H. LAWRENCE White and abstract-looking, he sat and ate his dinner.

▸ **B** *noun* **I 1 a** An abridgement or summary of a book, document, etc. LME. ▸**b** *gen.* Something that concentrates in itself the qualities of another greater thing or other things. M16.

b SHAKES. *Ant. & Cl.* A man who is the abstract of all faults That all men follow.

a abstract of title LAW a summary of the contents of the title deeds and documents that prove an owner's right to dispose of land, the summary being sufficient to enable the purchaser to raise questions about the vendor's title to the property.

2 An abstraction; an abstract term. M16.
3 An abstract painting or other work of art. M20.
▸ **II 4** *absol.* That which is abstract; the ideal or theoretical way of regarding things. E17.
– NOTE: At first a pple as well as adjective, stressed on 2nd syllable; as pple replaced by *abstracted*.
■ **abstractly** *adverb* LME. **abstractness** *noun* L16.

abstract /əbˈstrakt/ *verb*. LME.
[ORIGIN Partly from ABSTRACT *adjective & noun*; partly from Latin *abstract-* pa. ppl stem of *abstrahere*: see ABSTRACT *adjective & noun*.]
1 *verb trans.* Separate, disengage, *from*. LME.

A. COWLEY The Importunities of Company or Business, which would abstract him from his Beloved [Poetry].

2 *verb trans.* Withdraw, take away; *euphem.* steal. L15. ▸†**b** *verb trans.* Esp. CHEMISTRY. Extract, distil. E17–E18.

H. MARTINEAU The public burdens, which . . abstract a large proportion of profits and wages. F. HOYLE Living plants abstract carbon dioxide and add oxygen to the atmosphere. **b** J. MARSTON Poison from roses who could e'er abstract?

3 *verb trans.* Summarize, abridge. L16.
4 *verb trans.* Separate in mental conception; consider abstractly. E17.

GIBBON To abstract the notions of time, of space, and of matter. G. W. KNIGHT To abstract the skeleton of logical sequence which is the story of the play.

5 *verb refl. & intrans.* Withdraw oneself, retire *from*, (*lit. & fig.*). M17.
abstracting from *arch.* leaving out of consideration.
■ **abstractable** *adjective* L19. **abstracter** *noun* a person who abstracts; a person who makes an abstract or abstracts: L17. **abstractor** *noun* an abstracter; *spec.* (now *hist.*) as a title of a grade of clerks in the British Civil Service: M17.

abstracta *noun* pl. of ABSTRACTUM.

abstracted /əbˈstraktɪd/ *adjective*. M16.
[ORIGIN from ABSTRACT *verb* + -ED[1].]
1 Drawn off, removed; separate, apart *from*. M16.
2 = ABSTRACT *adjective* 3. Now *rare*. E17.

S. JOHNSON Abstracted ideas of virtue.

3 Withdrawn from the contemplation of present objects; absent in mind. E17.

S. KAUFFMANN Perry turned to him a little thoughtfully, in that abstracted manner which indicates that the subject has to be recalled from a distance.

■ **abstractedly** *adverb* M17. **abstractedness** *noun* M17.

abstraction /əbˈstrakʃ(ə)n/ *noun*. LME.
[ORIGIN Old French & mod. French, or late Latin *abstractio(n-)*, from *abstract-*: see ABSTRACT *verb*, -ION.]
1 The act of taking away; withdrawal; *euphem.* stealing. LME.

C. LAMB He robs . . the revenue,—an abstraction I never greatly cared about.

2 A state of withdrawal from worldly things or things of the senses. LME. ▸**b** Absence of mind. L18.

E. WAUGH Dennis awoke from a deep abstraction. **b** BOSWELL Wrapped up in grave abstraction.

3 a The act of considering something independently of its associations, attributes, or concrete accompaniments; the state of being so considered. L16. ▸**b** A thing so considered; a thing which exists only in idea; something visionary. L16.

a J. WAIN We had been asked to drink a toast to success, in abstraction—not success to this or that person, but success itself. **b** B. RUSSELL 'The State' is an abstraction; it does not feel pleasure or pain, it has no hopes or fears.

a vicious abstraction: see VICIOUS *adjective*.
4 Freedom from representational qualities in art; an abstract work of art. E20.

M. SHADBOLT The paintings were not . . abstractions. They were landscapes, more or less.

■ **abstractional** *adjective* M19. **abstractionism** *noun* the pursuit of abstraction(s); *esp.* the principles or pursuit of abstract art: E20. **abstractionist** *noun* a person who deals with abstractions; an advocate or practitioner of abstract art: M19.

abstractive /əbˈstraktɪv/ *adjective*. LME.
[ORIGIN medieval Latin *abstractivus*, from Latin *abstract-*: see ABSTRACT *verb*, -IVE.]
†**1** GRAMMAR. Of a noun: abstract. Only in LME.
2 Of abstracting character or tendency (in senses 1, 4, 5 of ABSTRACT *verb*). L15.
■ **abstractively** *adverb* (long *rare*) in an abstract manner, in the abstract E17.

abstractum /əbˈstraktəm/ *noun*. Usu. in pl. **-ta** /-tə/. M19.
[ORIGIN mod. Latin, neut. of *abstractus*: see ABSTRACT *adjective & noun*.]
PHILOSOPHY. = ABSTRACT *noun* 2.

abstruse /əbˈstruːs/ *adjective*. L16.
[ORIGIN French *abstrus(e)* or Latin *abstrusus* pa. pple of *abstrudere* conceal, formed as ABS- + *trudere* thrust.]
†**1** Hidden, secret. L16–M18.
2 Difficult to conceive of or apprehend; recondite. L16.
■ **abstrusely** *adverb* E17. **abstruseness** *noun* M17. **abstrusity** *noun* (*arch.*) abstruseness; something abstruse: M17. **abstrusive** *adjective* (*rare*) of abstruse quality or tendency M17.

†**absume** *verb trans.* L16–M18.
[ORIGIN Latin *absumere*, from *ab* AB- + *sumere* take.]
Consume gradually.

absurd /əbˈsəːd/ *adjective & noun*. M16.
[ORIGIN French *absurde* or Latin *absurdus*.]
▸ **A** *adjective*. **1** Out of harmony with reason or propriety; incongruous; inappropriate; unreasonable; ridiculous, silly. M16.
†**2** Inharmonious, out of tune. Only in E17.
▸ **B** *noun*. †**1** An absurd thing. E–M17.
2 *absol.* That which is absurd; *esp.* human existence in a purposeless, chaotic universe. E20.
Theatre of the Absurd: see THEATRE *noun*.
■ **absurdism** *noun* the belief that human beings exist in a purposeless chaotic universe in which attempts to impose order are frustrated M20. **absurdist** *adjective & noun* (**a**) *adjective* of or pertaining to absurdism; (**b**) *noun* an adherent of absurdism; *esp.* a writer who deals with absurdist themes: M20. **absurdly** *adverb* M16. **absurdness** *noun* M16.

absurda *noun* pl. of ABSURDUM.

absurdity /əbˈsəːdɪti/ *noun*. LME.
[ORIGIN French *absurdité* or Latin *absurditas*: see ABSURD, -ITY.]
†**1** Lack of harmony, dissonance. *rare*. LME–L17.
2 Something absurd; an absurd action, statement, etc. L15.
3 The state or quality of being absurd; folly. E16.

absurdum /əbˈsəːdəm/ *noun*. Pl. **-da** /-də/. M19.
[ORIGIN Latin, neut. sing. of *absurdus* ABSURD used as noun.]
An absurd or illogical conclusion or condition. See also REDUCTIO AD ABSURDUM.

abt *abbreviation*.
About.

ABTA /ˈabtə/ *abbreviation*.
Association of British Travel Agents.

abubble /əˈbʌb(ə)l/ *adverb & pred. adjective*. M20.
[ORIGIN from A-[2] + BUBBLE *noun* or *verb*.]
Bubbling over (with excitement etc.).

abuilding /əˈbɪldɪŋ/ *adverb & pred. adjective*. Now *arch.* exc. *US*. M16.
[ORIGIN from A *preposition*[1] 7 + BUILDING *noun*.]
In the process of being built.

abulia /əˈbuːlɪə/ *noun*. Also **aboulia**. M19.
[ORIGIN Greek, from A-[10] + *boulē* will: see -IA[1].]
Absence of willpower, or inability to act decisively, as a symptom of mental illness.
■ **abulic** *adjective* suffering from abulia L19.

Abuna /əˈbuːnə/ *noun*. E17.
[ORIGIN Amharic from Arabic *'abūnā* our father.]
(The title of) the Patriarch of the Ethiopian Orthodox Church.

abundance /əˈbʌnd(ə)ns/ *noun*. In sense 5 also **abon-**. ME.
[ORIGIN Old French *(h)abundance* (mod. *abondance*) from Latin *abundantia*, formed as ABUNDANT: see -ANCE.]
1 A large quantity, plenty; occas. a large number. ME.

DEFOE Abundance of good things for our comfort. HENRY FIELDING There are abundance . . who want a morsel of bread.

2 Overflowing state or condition; superfluity; plentifulness. LME.

AV *Ps.* 105:30 The land brought foorth frogs in abundance. DE QUINCEY My thoughts . . are from the abundance of my heart.

3 Affluence, wealth. LME.

AV *Ecclus* 5:12 The abundance of the rich will not suffer him to sleepe.

4 The relative quantity or number (of a plant, a substance, etc.) present. L19.

S. WEINBERG A truly primordial deuterium abundance.

5 CARDS. A call undertaking to take nine or more tricks in solo whist. L19.
declared abundance: undertaking to take thirteen tricks with no trump suit. **royal abundance**: with the suit of the turned-up card as trumps.
■ **abundancy** *noun* M16.

abundant /əˈbʌnd(ə)nt/ *adjective*. LME.
[ORIGIN Latin *abundant-* pres. ppl stem of *abundare* ABOUND: see -ANT[1].]
1 Overflowing; more than sufficient; plentiful. LME.
2 *pred.* Possessing something in superfluity, wealthy. (Foll. by *in*, †*of*.) LME.
3 MATH. Of a number: exceeded by the sum of its divisors (including 1 but not the number itself). Opp. DEFICIENT *adjective* 3b. M16.
■ **abundantly** *adverb* LME.

abune /əˈbuːn/ *adverb, preposition, & noun*. *Scot. & N. English*. Also **aboon**. LME.
[ORIGIN Alt.]
= ABOVE.

abura /əˈbjuːrə/ *noun*. **E20.**
[ORIGIN Yoruba.]
(A soft pale wood obtained from) the tree *Mitragyna ciliata* of tropical W. Africa.

a-burton *adverb* see BURTON *noun*[1] 2.

abuse /əˈbjuːs/ *noun*. **LME.**
[ORIGIN Old French & mod. French *abus* or Latin *abusus*, formed as ABUSE *verb*.]
1 An improper usage; a corrupt practice. **LME.**
W. R. INGE Dickens was careful to castigate abuses which were being reformed.
2 Improper use, perversion, (*of*). **M16.** ▸**b** *RHETORIC*. Catachresis. Now *rare* or *obsolete*. **L16.**
J. COLLIER The abuse of a thing is no argument against the use of it.
drug abuse etc.
†**3** An imposture; a delusion. **M16–M17.**
SHAKES. *Haml.* Or is it some abuse, and no such thing?
4 Reviling; abusive language. Formerly also, a verbal insult. **M16.**
R. DAHL A torrent of abuse and obscenity as he had never heard before.
5 Injury, maltreatment. **L16.**
child abuse etc.
6 Violation; defilement. Now only in ***self-abuse***. **L16.**
▪ †**abuseful** *adjective* full of abuse, abusive **E17–E18.** **abusefully** *adverb* in an abusive manner **M16.**

abuse /əˈbjuːz/ *verb trans.* **LME.**
[ORIGIN Old French & mod. French *abuser* ult. from Latin *abus-* pa. ppl stem of *abuti*, from *ab* AB- + *uti* to use.]
▸ **I 1** Misuse; make a bad use of; wrongly take advantage of. **LME.** ▸**b** *spec.* Take (a drug) for a purpose other than a therapeutic one. **M20.**
M. FRAYN I'm in a position of trust and privilege . . and I take care not to abuse it.
2 Violate (a person); defile. *arch.* **LME.**
†**3** Misrepresent; adulterate. **LME–M18.**
HENRY FIELDING He hath been . . grossly abused to you.
†**4** Misuse the confidence of; impose upon; deceive. **L15–E19.**
MILTON A misguided and abus'd Multitude.
5 Maltreat, injure, esp. repeatedly; *spec.* assault (esp. a woman or child) sexually. **M16.**
T. FULLER He that abuseth his servants, giving them too little food or sleep. R. S. THOMAS Storming at him/ . . with the eloquence / of the abused heart. *Times* A girl . . was being sexually abused by her father.
6 Speak insultingly or unkindly to or of; malign. **E17.**
YEATS Ever and always curse him and abuse him.
▸ †**II 7** Disuse. *Scot.* **L15–M16.**
▪ **abusable** *adjective* **M17.** **abusage** *noun* abuse, misuse, (*obsolete* after **M17**, revived **M20** by Eric Partridge) **M16.** **abuser** *noun*[1] a person who abuses someone or something **LME.** †**abuser** *noun*[2] [-ER[4]] illegal or wrongful use **M17–M18.**

†**abusion** *noun*. **LME–L17.**
[ORIGIN Old French from Latin *abusio(n-)*, formed as ABUSE *verb*: see -ION.]
= ABUSE *noun*.

abusive /əˈbjuːsɪv/ *adjective*. **M16.**
[ORIGIN Old French & mod. French *abusif*, *-ive* or late Latin *abusivus*, formed as ABUSE *verb*: see -IVE.]
1 Misapplied; improper; *RHETORIC* catachrestic. *arch.* **M16.**
W. HAMILTON The Reproductive Imagination (or Conception, in the abusive language of the Scottish philosophers).
2 Full of abuses. *arch.* **L16.**
T. NASHE The abusive enormities of . . our times.
3 Employing insulting language; scurrilous. **E17.**
†**4** Deceitful. **E–M17.**
S. DANIEL Th' abusive Shews of Sense.
†**5** Given to misusing. Only in **M17.**
▪ **abusively** *adverb* **M16.** **abusiveness** *noun* **M17.**

abustle /əˈbʌs(ə)l/ *adverb & pred. adjective*. **M20.**
[ORIGIN from A-[2] + BUSTLE *noun*[1] or *verb*.]
Bustling (*with*), busy.

abut /əˈbʌt/ *verb*. Infl. **-tt-**. **LME.**
[ORIGIN Sense 1 from Anglo-Latin *abuttare*, formed as A-[8] + BUTT *noun*[2]; sense 2 from Old French & mod. French *abouter*, †*abuter*, formed as A-[5] + BUTT *verb*[1].]
1 *verb intrans.* Of an estate, country, etc.: end at, border on. Foll. by (*up*)*on*, †*to*. **LME.**
2 *verb intrans.* Of part of a building etc.: end *on* or *against*; lean (*up*)*on* at one end. **L16.**
3 *verb trans.* Abut on (in either sense). **M19.**
▪ **abuttal** *noun* abutment; in *pl.*, the parts where land abuts on neighbouring lands: **E17.** **abutter** *noun* a person who or thing which abuts; *spec.* an owner of contiguous property: **L17.**

abutilon /əˈbjuːtɪlɒn/ *noun*. **L16.**
[ORIGIN mod. Latin from Arabic *ūbūtīlūn* Indian mallow.]
A plant or shrub of the chiefly tropical genus *Abutilon* (belonging to the mallow family), of which there are numerous species bearing showy, usu. yellow, red, or mauve flowers.

abutment /əˈbʌtm(ə)nt/ *noun*. **M17.**
[ORIGIN from ABUT + -MENT: cf. Old French & mod. French *aboutement*.]
1 A point of junction, esp. of a support and the thing supported. **M17.**
2 *ARCHITECTURE*. The solid part of a pier, wall, etc., which supports the lateral pressure of an arch. **M18.**
3 Something on which another thing abuts or leans. **M18.**

abuzz /əˈbʌz/ *adverb & pred. adjective*. **M19.**
[ORIGIN from A-[2] + BUZZ *noun*[1] or *verb*[1].]
In a buzz (of excitement); filled with buzzing.

ABV *abbreviation*.
Alcohol by volume.

aby /əˈbʌɪ/ *verb*. *arch.* Also **abye**. Pa. t. & pple **abought** /əˈbɔːt/. (Other forms long *obsolete*.)
[ORIGIN Old English *ābyċġan*, from A-[1] + BUY *verb*, corresp. to Gothic *usbugjan*.]
†**1** *verb trans.* Buy, pay for. **OE–E16.**
2 *verb trans.* Pay the penalty for, atone for. **OE.** ▸†**b** *verb intrans.* Pay the penalty, atone. **ME–L16.**
E. R. EDDISON You shall bitterly aby it.
3 *verb trans.* Pay as a penalty; suffer. **LME.**
W. MORRIS Thou wouldst abye A heavy fate.
4 = ABIDE (with which ***aby*** became formally confused): ▸†**a** *verb intrans.* Endure, remain. **LME–L16.** ▸**b** *verb trans.* Endure, experience; tolerate. *obsolete* exc. *Scot.* **L16.**
a SPENSER Nought that wanteth rest can long aby. **b** R. L. STEVENSON I never could abye the reek of them.

abysm /əˈbɪz(ə)m/ *noun*. Also (earlier) †**abime**. **ME.**
[ORIGIN Old French *abi(s)me* (mod. *abîme*) from medieval Latin *abysmus* alt. of *abyssus* ABYSS by assim. to Greek *-ismos* -ISM.]
1 = ABYSS 1. *arch.* or *poet.* **ME.**
2 = ABYSS 2. Now chiefly *literary*. **L15.**

abysmal /əˈbɪzm(ə)l/ *adjective*. **M17.**
[ORIGIN from ABYSM + -AL[1].]
1 Of, pertaining to, or resembling an abyss. Now *rare* in *lit.* sense. **M17.**
2 *fig.* Bottomless; *colloq.* extremely bad. **E19.**
▪ **abysmally** *adverb* **L19.**

abyss /əˈbɪs/ *noun*. Orig. in Latin form †**abyssus**. **LME.**
[ORIGIN Late Latin *abyssus* from Greek *abussos*, from *a-* A-[10] + *bus(s)os* depth.]
1 The great deep believed in the old cosmogony to lie beneath the earth; the primal chaos; the bowels of the earth; the infernal pit, hell. **LME.**
2 A bottomless chasm; any unfathomable cavity or void space. Freq. *fig.* **L16.**

abyssal /əˈbɪs(ə)l/ *adjective*. **M17.**
[ORIGIN Late Latin *abyssalis*, formed as ABYSS: see -AL[1].]
1 Characteristic of an abyss; unfathomable. **M17.**
2 Of or pertaining to the ocean depths. **M19.**
3 *GEOLOGY*. Pertaining to or occurring at considerable depths in the earth's crust; plutonic. **L19.**

Abyssinia /abɪˈsɪnɪə/ *interjection*. *slang*. **M20.**
[ORIGIN Alt., after the country (see ABYSSINIAN).]
I'll be seeing you! (said on parting).

Abyssinian /abɪˈsɪnɪən/ *noun & adjective*. **M18.**
[ORIGIN from *Abyssinia* (see below) + -AN.]
▸ **A** *noun*. **1** A native or inhabitant of Abyssinia, a country (now officially called Ethiopia) in NE Africa. **M18.**
2 = ***Abyssinian cat*** below. **L19.**
▸ **B** *adjective*. Of or pertaining to Abyssinia or its inhabitants. **L18.**
Abyssinian banana = ENSETE. **Abyssinian cat**: of a breed having long ears and short brown hair flecked with grey.
▪ Earlier †**Abyssian** *noun*: only in **E17.** †**Abyssin(e)** *adjective & noun* **M17–M18.**

†**abyssus** *noun* see ABYSS.

abzyme /ˈabzʌɪm/ *noun*. **L20.**
[ORIGIN from A(NTI)B(ODY + EN)ZYME.]
BIOCHEMISTRY. An antibody (usu. synthetic) having some of the catalytic properties of an enzyme.

AC *abbreviation*.
1 Air-conditioned, -conditioning.
2 Aircraftman.
3 (Also **a.c.**) Alternating current.
4 Athletic club.
5 Latin *ante Christum* 'before Christ'.

Ac *symbol*.
CHEMISTRY. Actinium.

ac- /ak, *unstressed* ək/ *prefix* (rarely productive).
Assim. form of Latin AD- before *c* (*k*) and *qu*. In Old French, Latin *acc-* was reduced to *ac-*, which appears in Middle English adoptions, but in later French, and hence in English, *acc-* was restored by Latinization, as ***account***, ***acquit***. Hence extended to some words of different origin, as ***accloy***, ***accurse***, ***acknowledge***, ***acquaint***.

A/C *abbreviation*.
1 Account current.
2 Air-conditioned, -conditioning.

-ac /ak/ *suffix*. Also †**-ack**, †**-aque**.
[ORIGIN French *-aque* or Latin *-acus* or (the source of both) Greek *-akos*, *-akē*, *-akon* forms of the adjectival suffix *-kos* of or belonging to, in comb. with nouns in *-ia*, *-ios*, *-ion*, as *kardiak-os* of the heart.]
Forming adjectives, as ***elegiac***, ***maniac***, some of which are often also (or only) used as nouns. See also -ACAL.

acacia /əˈkeɪʃə, -sjə/ *noun*. **LME.**
[ORIGIN Latin from Greek *akakia* shittah tree.]
1 Any of numerous freq. thorny leguminous trees and shrubs constituting the genus *Acacia*, found esp. in arid regions of Australia and tropical Africa, with small flowers in spikes or globular clusters. Formerly also (*MEDICINE*), the congealed juice of unripe seed pods of the Egyptian acacia, *A. nilotica*, formerly used as an astringent. Also, a substitute for this made from the juice of green sloes. **LME.** ▸**b** Gum arabic. Also ***gum acacia***. **E19.**
2 More fully ***false acacia***. A robinia tree; spec. *Robinia pseudoacacia*, native to N. America and grown in Britain for its scented white flowers. **M17.**

academe /ˈakədiːm/ *noun*. *literary*. Also **A-**. **L16.**
[ORIGIN Partly from Latin *academia*; partly from transf. use of Greek *Akadēmos*: see ACADEMY.]
1 = ACADEMY 1, 2. **L16.**
SHAKES. *L.L.L.* Our court shall be a little Academe.
2 = ACADEMIA. Esp. in ***the grove of Academe***, ***the groves of Academe***. **M19.**
3 = ACADEMIC *noun* 2. **M20.**

academese /əkadəˈmiːz/ *noun*. Usu. somewhat *derog.* **M20.**
[ORIGIN from ACADEMIC etc. + -ESE.]
The style or language of academic scholarship.

academia /akəˈdiːmɪə/ *noun*. **M20.**
[ORIGIN Latin: see ACADEMY.]
The world of academics; the academic environment or community.

†**academian** *noun*. **M16–L17.**
[ORIGIN formed as ACADEMIA + -AN.]
A disciple of Plato; an academic or academician.

academic /akəˈdɛmɪk/ *noun & adjective*. In senses A.1, B.1 also **A-**. **M16.**
[ORIGIN Old French & mod. French *académique* or Latin *academicus*, from *academia*: see ACADEMY, -IC.]
▸ **A** *noun*. **1** A Platonist. **M16.**
2 A (now *spec.* senior) member of a university or similar institution; a person engaged or excelling in scholarly pursuits. **L16.** ▸**b** In *pl.* = ACADEMICAL *noun* (the more usual term). **E19.**
3 = ACADEMICIAN 1. *rare*. **M18.**
4 In *pl.* Academic studies. *US*. **L20.**
▸ **B** *adjective*. **1** Of the school or philosophy of Plato; sceptical. **L16.**
2 Of or belonging to a university or other institution of higher learning; scholarly. **L16.**
OED Such students wear a distinctive academic dress. H. CECIL The judge had succeeded at the practical side of the law and the professor at the academic.
academic year a period of nearly a year reckoned from the time of the main student intake, usu. from the beginning of the autumn term to the end of the summer term.
3 Abstract, unpractical, merely theoretical. **L19.**
H. G. WELLS All this discussion . . is—academic. The war has begun already. S. HILL Guessing how long they'd been dead as a question of academic interest.
4 *ART*. Conventional; idealizing; excessively formal. **L19.**
E. H. GOMBRICH The programme of idealizing, of 'beautifying' nature, according to the standards set by the classical statues. We call it the neoclassical or 'academic' programme.
▪ **academicism** /-sɪz(ə)m/ *noun* (**a**) a tenet of academic philosophy; (**b**) the state or quality of being academic: **E17.** **academicize** /-sʌɪz/ *verb trans.* render (undesirably) academic **M20.**

academical /akəˈdɛmɪk(ə)l/ *adjective & noun*. **L16.**
[ORIGIN from ACADEMIC + -AL[1].]
▸ **A** *adjective*. **1** = ACADEMIC *adjective* 1. *rare*. **L16.**
2 = ACADEMIC *adjective* 2. **L16.**
▸ **B** *noun*. In *pl.* Academic dress. **E19.**
▪ **academically** *adverb* **L16.**

academician /əkadəˈmɪʃ(ə)n/ *noun*. **M18.**
[ORIGIN French *académicien*, formed as ACADEMIC: see -ICIAN.]
1 A member of an academy (sense 4), esp. of the Royal Academy of Arts, the Académie française, or the former USSR Academy of Sciences. **M18.**
2 = ACADEMIC *noun* 2. *rare*. **M18.**

academy /əˈkadəmi/ *noun*. **LME.**
[ORIGIN French *académie* or Latin *academia* from Greek *akadēm(e)ia* adjective, from *Akadēmos* the man or demigod from whom Plato's garden was named: see -Y[3].]

A

1 (**A-**.) The name of a garden near Athens where Plato taught. **LME.** ▸**b** Plato's followers or philosophical system. **M16.**
2 An institution of higher learning, e.g. a university; also (esp. in Scotland) a secondary school, (in England) an independent publicly run secondary school. **M16.** ▸†**b** *fig.* The knowledge taught in an academy; a treatise on this. **E17–M18.**
3 A place of training, esp. in a special art, as the Royal Military Academy. **L16.**
4 A society for the cultivation of literature, art, science, etc., of which membership is an honour, *esp.* the Royal Academy (of Arts). **E17.**
– **COMB. & PHRASES: Academy award** any of a series of awards of the Academy of Motion Picture Arts and Sciences (Hollywood, US) given annually since 1928 for achievement in the film industry; an Oscar; **Academy figure** a drawing, usu. half life-size, in crayon or pencil, from the nude. **Middle Academy** the school of philosophy of Arcesilaus, head of the Academy in the 3rd cent. BC. **New Academy** the school of philosophy of Carneades of Cyrene, head of the Academy in the 2nd cent. BC. **Old Academy** the school of philosophy founded by Plato in the 4th cent. BC.
– **NOTE:** Formerly stressed on 3rd syllable.
■ **Academism** *noun* †(**a**) *rare* Academic philosophy; (**b**) (**a-**) = **ACADEMICISM** (b): **M18. Academist** *noun* an Academic philosopher; a member or student of an academy: **M17.**

Acadian /əˈkeɪdɪən/ *noun & adjective.* Chiefly *N. Amer.* **E18.**
[**ORIGIN** from *Acadia* (see below), French *Acadie* + **-AN**. Cf. **CAJUN**.]
▸ **A** *noun.* A native or inhabitant of Acadia, a former French colony on the N. American Atlantic coast which included the present Nova Scotia and some adjacent areas; *spec.* a French-speaking descendant of early settlers in Acadia, living esp. in the Maritime Provinces of Canada or in Louisiana. **E18.**
▸ **B** *adjective.* Of, pertaining to, or originating from Acadia. **E19.**

açai /aˈsʌiː, asʌɪˈiː/ *noun.* **E20.**
[**ORIGIN** Portuguese *açaí* from Tupi-Guarani *asaí*.]
Any of various palms of the S. American genus *Euterpe*, used as a source of palm hearts. Also, the edible fruit of these trees, a small blackish-purple berry.

acajou /ˈakəʒuː/ *noun.* **L16.**
[**ORIGIN** French: see **CASHEW**.]
The cashew tree or cashew nut.

-acal /ək(ə)l/ *suffix.*
[**ORIGIN** from **-AC** + **-AL**[1].]
Forming adjectives from adjectives and nouns in **-AC** (as ***hypochondriacal***) and occas. from adjectives with no corresp. noun (as ***heliacal***); often used to distinguish nouns from adjectives (as ***maniac***, ***maniacal***).

acalculia /eɪkalˈkjuːlɪə/ *noun.* **E20.**
[**ORIGIN** from **A-**[10] + Latin *calculare* **CALCULATE** + **-IA**[1].]
MEDICINE. A diminished ability to calculate, as a symptom of cerebral disorder.

acanthamoeba /akanθəˈmiːbə/ *noun.* Pl. **-bae** /-biː/, **-bas. M20.**
[**ORIGIN** mod. Latin (see below), formed as **ACANTHO-** + **AMOEBA** *noun*.]
An amoeba of the genus *Acanthamoeba*, which includes a number that can cause opportunistic infections in humans.

acanthite /əˈkanθʌɪt/ *noun.* **M19.**
[**ORIGIN** formed as **ACANTHO-** + **-ITE**[1].]
MINERALOGY. A monoclinic or orthorhombic form of silver sulphide, occurring as slender black prisms with a metallic lustre.

acantho- /əˈkanθəʊ/ *combining form* of Greek *akantha*: see **ACANTHUS**, **-O-**.
■ **acantho'cephalan** *adjective & noun* [Greek *kephalē* head] **ZOOLOGY** (designating) a parasitic worm of the phylum Acanthocephala, with a thornlike proboscis for attachment to the gut of vertebrates **L19. acan'thodian** *adjective & noun* (designating or pertaining to) a small spiny-finned fossil fish belonging to the subclass Acanthodii, found esp. in Devonian rocks **M19. a,canthopte'rygian** *adjective & noun* [Greek *pterugion* fin, dim. of *pterux* wing] **ZOOLOGY** (designating) a spiny-finned fish belonging to the superorder Acanthopterygii **M19. acan'thosis** *noun* (**MEDICINE**) abnormal thickening of the prickle layer of the skin **L19.**

acanthus /əˈkanθəs/ *noun.* **M16.**
[**ORIGIN** Latin from Greek *akanthos*, from *akantha* thorn, perh. from *akē* sharp point.]
1 Any of several erect herbaceous plants belonging to the genus *Acanthus* (family Acanthaceae), having decorative spiny leaves; esp. *Acanthus spinosus*, native to the Mediterranean region. **M16.**
2 **ARCHITECTURE.** A conventionalized acanthus leaf used to decorate Corinthian and Composite capitals. **M18.**
■ **acan'thaceous** *adjective* of the type of acanthus; of or pertaining to the family Acanthaceae: **M18. acanthine** *adjective* of or pertaining to acanthus **M18.**

a cappella /a kəˈpɛlə, ɑː/ *adjectival & adverbial phr.* **L19.**
[**ORIGIN** Italian = in chapel style.]
Of choral music or choirs: unaccompanied.

acari *noun* pl. of **ACARUS**.

acariasis /akəˈrʌɪəsɪs/ *noun.* Pl. **-ases** /-əsiːz/. **E19.**
[**ORIGIN** from mod. Latin *acari* pl. of **ACARUS** + **-IASIS**.]
MEDICINE. Disease, esp. of the skin, caused by mites.

acaricide /ˈakərɪsʌɪd/ *noun.* **L19.**
[**ORIGIN** formed as **ACARIASIS** + **-CIDE**.]
A substance poisonous to mites or ticks.
■ **acari'cidal** *adjective* poisonous to mites or ticks **M20.**

acarid /ˈakərɪd/ *noun.* **L19.**
[**ORIGIN** formed as **ACARUS** + **-ID**[3].]
A mite of the family Acaridae.

acarine /ˈakərʌɪn/ *adjective & noun.* **E19.**
[**ORIGIN** formed as **ACARID** + **-INE**[1].]
▸ **A** *adjective.* Pertaining to or caused by mites or ticks. **E19.**
▸ **B** *noun.* An arachnid belonging to the order Acari; a mite, a tick. **L19.**

acaroid /ˈakərɔɪd/ *noun.* Also **acc-**. **M19.**
[**ORIGIN** Unknown.]
In full ***acaroid resin***, ***acaroid gum***. A resin obtained in Australia from certain kinds of grass tree or blackboy, and used in making varnish etc.

acarology /akəˈrɒlədʒi/ *noun.* **E20.**
[**ORIGIN** formed as **ACARIASIS** + **-OLOGY**.]
The branch of science that deals with mites and ticks.
■ **acarologist** *noun* **L19.**

acarus /ˈakərəs/ *noun.* Pl. **-ri** /-rʌɪ/. **M17.**
[**ORIGIN** mod. Latin from Greek *akari*.]
A mite, a tick.

ACAS /ˈeɪkas/ *abbreviation.*
Advisory, Conciliation, and Arbitration Service.

acatalectic /a,katəˈlɛktɪk/ *adjective & noun.* **L16.**
[**ORIGIN** Late Latin *acatalecticus*, from Greek *akatalēktos*, or from **A-**[10] + **CATALECTIC**.]
PROSODY. (A line of verse that is) not catalectic, complete in its syllables.

acatalepsy /aˈkatəlɛpsi/ *noun.* **E17.**
[**ORIGIN** medieval Latin *acatalepsis* from Greek *akatalēpsia*, from *a-* **A-**[10] + *kata* thoroughly + *lēpsis* a seizing: see **-Y**[3].]
SCEPTIC PHILOSOPHY. Incomprehensibility, as a property of the thing thought of.
■ **a,cata'leptic** *adjective* (*rare*) relating to acatalepsy; incomprehensible: **M18.**

†**acate** *noun.* Also **ach-**. **LME.**
[**ORIGIN** Early Old French & Anglo-Norman *acat* (later Old French *achat*), from *ac(h)ater* buy, ult. from Latin *captare* seize. Cf. **CATE**.]
1 Purchasing; contract, bargain. **LME–L17.**
2 In *pl.* & *collect. sing.* Things purchased; provisions not made in the house; dainties. **LME–L17.**

†**acater** *noun* see **ACATOUR**.

acathisia *noun* var. of **AKATHISIA**.

†**acatour** *noun.* Also **-ter**, **ach-**. **ME–M18.**
[**ORIGIN** Anglo-Norman & early Old French *acateor* (later Old French *achatour*), from *ac(h)ater*: see **ACATE**, **-OUR**. Cf. **CATER** *noun*[1], *verb*[2].]
A purchaser of provisions; a purveyor; a caterer.
■ †**acatery**, **achatry** *noun* provisions purchased; the storeroom for such provisions: **LME–M18.**

acaulescent /akɔːˈlɛs(ə)nt/ *adjective.* **M19.**
[**ORIGIN** from **A-**[10] + **CAULESCENT**.]
BOTANY. Stemless or apparently so.

acausal /eɪˈkɔːz(ə)l, a-/ *adjective.* **M20.**
[**ORIGIN** from **A-**[10] + **CAUSAL** *adjective*.]
Not causal; not causally related.
■ **acau'sality** *noun* **M20.**

Accadian *adjective & noun* var. of **AKKADIAN**.

accaroid *noun* var. of **ACAROID**.

accede /əkˈsiːd/ *verb intrans.* **LME.**
[**ORIGIN** Latin *accedere*, from *ad* **AC-** + *cedere* **CEDE**: cf. Old French & mod. French *accéder*.]
1 Come forward, approach, arrive (at a place or state). Now *rare* in *gen.* sense. **LME.**
2 Give one's adhesion; join a group, become part of a country etc.; assent or agree (*to*). **LME.**

> C. THIRLWALL Potidæa had already acceded to the confederacy. W. S. MAUGHAM Veiled threats to induce the Florentines to accede to his demands.

3 Enter upon an office or dignity, esp. a throne. (Foll. by *to*.) **L17.**

> J. H. BURTON The Emperor Julian . . had just acceded to the purple. JOYCE Queen Victoria (born 1820, acceded 1837).

■ **accedence** *noun* the action of acceding **L16.**

accelerando /əksɛləˈrandəʊ, ətʃɛl-/ *adverb, adjective, & noun.* **E19.**
[**ORIGIN** Italian.]
MUSIC. ▸**A** *adverb & adjective.* A direction: with gradual increase of speed. **E19.**
▸ **B** *noun.* Pl. **-dos**, **-di** /-di/. A gradual increase of speed; a passage (to be) played with a gradual increase of speed. **L19.**

accelerant /əkˈsɛl(ə)r(ə)nt/ *noun & adjective.* **E20.**
[**ORIGIN** Latin *accelerant-* pres. ppl stem of *accelerare*: see **ACCELERATE**, **-ANT**.]
▸ **A** *noun.* A thing that causes a process to go faster, an accelerator; *spec.* a substance used to aid the spread of fire.
▸ **B** *adjective.* Having an accelerating effect; accelerating.

accelerate /əkˈsɛləreɪt/ *verb.* **E16.**
[**ORIGIN** Latin *accelerat-* pa. ppl stem of *accelerare*, from *ad* **AC-** + *celer* swift: see **-ATE**[3].]
1 *verb trans.* Hasten the occurrence of. **E16.**

> J. B. S. HALDANE A spot of laughter, I am sure, Often accelerates one's cure.

2 *verb trans.* Quicken, increase the speed of, (a motion or a thing in motion). **E17.**

> JAS. WOOD When the successive portions of space . . continually increase, the motion is said to be accelerated. J. CHEEVER Paul accelerated the car happily when they escaped from the narrow streets of the village.

3 *verb intrans.* Become swifter; begin to move more quickly; cause a vehicle etc. to move more quickly. **M17.**

> J. R. SEELEY England's rapidly accelerating decline. A. BURGESS Crabbe accelerated, gave the car all speed.

■ **accelerative** *adjective* tending to increase speed, quickening **E17.**

acceleration /əksɛləˈreɪʃ(ə)n/ *noun.* **L15.**
[**ORIGIN** Old French & mod. French, or Latin *acceleratio(n-)*, formed as **ACCELERATE**: see **-ATION**.]
1 The action of accelerating; the state or condition of being accelerated. **L15.** ▸**b** Increased speed. **M16.** ▸**c** Of a vehicle: ability to gain speed. **E20.**
2 The extent to which anything is accelerated; the rate of change of velocity per unit time. **M17.**

accelerator /əkˈsɛləreɪtə/ *noun.* **M19.**
[**ORIGIN** from **ACCELERATE** + **-OR**.]
▸ **I** *gen.* **1** A person who or thing which accelerates. **M19.**
▸ **II** *spec.* **2** A substance used to increase the rate of a chemical process. **M19.**
3 A device, usu. a pedal, for controlling the speed of the engine of a motor vehicle. **E20.**
4 **PHYSICS.** An apparatus for accelerating charged particles to high energies by means of electric or electromagnetic fields. **M20.**

accelerograph /əkˈsɛlərəgrɑːf/ *noun.* **E20.**
[**ORIGIN** from **ACCELER(ATE** + **-O-** + **-GRAPH**.]
An accelerometer which produces a graphical record of its measurements.
■ **accelerogram** *noun* a graphical record produced by an accelerograph **M20.**

accelerometer /əksɛləˈrɒmɪtə/ *noun.* **E20.**
[**ORIGIN** from **ACCELER(ATE** + **-OMETER**.]
An instrument for measuring the acceleration experienced by a moving or vibrating body.

†**accend** *verb trans.* **LME–M19.**
[**ORIGIN** Latin *accendere* rel. to *candere* to shine: see **AC-**.]
Kindle, set on fire, (*lit.* & *fig.*).

†**accensed** *ppl adjective.* **M16–M18.**
[**ORIGIN** Latin *accensus* pa. pple of *accendere* (see **ACCEND**) + **-ED**[1].]
Kindled, set on fire.

accension /əkˈsɛnʃ(ə)n/ *noun.* Now *rare* or *obsolete*. **M17.**
[**ORIGIN** Latin *accensio(n-)*, formed as **ACCENSED**: see **-ION**.]
The action of kindling; the state of being kindled.

accent /ˈaks(ə)nt/ *noun.* **LME.**
[**ORIGIN** Old French & mod. French, or Latin *accentus*, from *ad* **AC-** + *cantus* song.]
1 The way in which something is said; tone; modulation expressing feeling. **LME.**

> DRYDEN Mild was his accent. L. M. MONTGOMERY Somebody said in muffled accents: 'Merciful goodness!'

2 Prominence given to a syllable by stress or (in some languages) by pitch. **L15.**
3 A mark used with a letter to show the nature and position of the spoken accent of a word, to show metrical stress, to distinguish the quality of a vowel, to distinguish homonyms, etc. **L16.**
acute accent, ***circumflex accent***, ***grave accent***, etc.
4 The mode of pronunciation peculiar to an individual, locality, or nation. **L16.** ▸**b** Without defining word; a regional English accent. **M20.**

> G. GREENE He spoke with the faintest foreign accent. D. ABERCROMBIE R. P. is, within England, a non-regional accent.

5 A significant tone or sound; a word; in *pl.* also, speech, language. *poet.* **L16.**

> SHAKES. *Jul. Caes.* In states unborn and accents yet unknown. BYRON In thy gasping throat The accents rattle.

6 **PROSODY.** Rhythmical stress in verse or prose. **L16.** ▸**b** **MUSIC.** Stress recurring at intervals generally fixed, but variable by syncopation. **M17.**
7 *fig.* **a** Intensity, emphasis; distinctive character; a contrasting detail. **M17.** ▸**b** An accentuating touch of light, colour, etc. **M19.**

a W. GURNALL That which gave accent to Abraham's Faith. F. MEYNELL The design of the components . . will show local accents. **b** E. BOWEN The face had only accents of shadow.

accent /əkˈsɛnt/ *verb.* **M16.**
[**ORIGIN** Old French *accenter*, formed as **ACCENT** *noun*.]
1 *verb intrans.* (*rare*) & *trans.* Pronounce with accent or stress; emphasize; *MUSIC* stress (a note etc.). **M16.**

J. PALSGRAVE I can not accent aryght in the latyn tonge. H. W. FOWLER Accenting the last syllable in the adjective.

2 *verb trans.* Mark with written accents. **M17.**
3 *verb trans.* Pronounce, utter, intone. *arch.* **M17.**

SIR W. SCOTT These solemn sounds, accented by a thousand voices.

4 *verb trans.* = **ACCENTUATE** 3. **M17.**

accentor /əkˈsɛntə/ *noun.* **E19.**
[**ORIGIN** Late Latin, from *ad* **AC-** + *cantor* singer.]
Any bird of the Eurasian genus *Prunella* (formerly *Accentor*), which includes the dunnock and some other small songbirds.

accentual /əkˈsɛntjʊəl/ *adjective.* **E17.**
[**ORIGIN** from Latin *accentus* **ACCENT** *noun* + **-UAL.**]
Of or pertaining to accent.
■ **accentually** *adverb* **M19.**

accentuate /əkˈsɛntjʊeɪt/ *verb trans.* **M18.**
[**ORIGIN** from medieval Latin *accentuat-* pa. ppl stem of *accentuare*, formed as **ACCENTUAL**: see **-ATE**[3]. Cf. French *accentuer*.]
1 = **ACCENT** *verb* 1 (the commoner term). **M18.**
2 = **ACCENT** *verb* 2. *rare.* **M19.**
3 *fig.* Mark emphatically; heighten; make conspicuous. **M19.**

accentuation /əksɛntjʊˈeɪʃ(ə)n/ *noun.* **L15.**
[**ORIGIN** In isolated early use from medieval Latin *accentuatio(n-)*, formed as **ACCENTUAL**; later (**E19**) from **ACCENTUATE** + **-ION.**]
1 The marking of accent or stress in speech. **L15.**

O. JESPERSEN Children . . learn the accentuation as well as the sounds of each word.

2 Mode of pronunciation; vocal modulation. **E19.**

SIR W. SCOTT A strong provincial accentuation.

3 The notation of accents in writing. **M19.**
4 *fig.* Emphasizing, bringing into prominence. **L19.**

accept /əkˈsɛpt/ *verb trans.* & (*arch.*) *intrans.* foll. by *of*. Pa. pple **accepted**, (earlier) †**accept**. **LME.**
[**ORIGIN** Old French & mod. French *accepter* or Latin *acceptare* frequentative of *accipere*, from *ad* **AC-** + *capere* take.]
1 Take or receive with consenting mind; receive with favour or approval. **LME.**

M. PATTISON The husband she had thoughtlessly accepted. JOYCE Mr Mulligan accepted of the invitation. E. O'NEILL Accept my gratitude for your warning. *absol.*: T. S. ELIOT A great many more accepted Than we thought would want to come.

accept the person of, ***accept persons***: see **PERSON** *noun.*
2 Receive as adequate or valid; admit; believe; tolerate; submit to. **LME.**

GEO. ELIOT These fellow-mortals . . must be accepted as they are. G. B. SHAW Parents and priests may forbid knowledge to those who accept their authority. *Times* The report is by a working party . . and has yet to be accepted by the council itself. B. LOVELL The theory of general relativity was accepted half a century ago.

accept a wooden nickel, ***accept wooden money***: see **WOODEN** *adjective.* **accept service of a writ** agree to consider a writ validly served.
3 Undertake (an office), take upon oneself as a responsibility. **E16.**
4 *COMMERCE.* Acknowledge the receipt of and agree to pay (a bill or draft). **M17.**

absol.: T. HOOD I'm free to give my I.O.U., Sign, draw, accept, as majors do.

5 Of an inanimate object: physically receive or accommodate, absorb, (another object, energy, data, etc.). **E20.**

British Medical Bulletin The computer can accept data only in a highly structured (digital) form. *Railway Magazine* The ceiling . . is designed to accept the fluorescent lighting tubes.

■ **accepted**, †**accept** *adjectives* †(**a**) acceptable; (**b**) well received, approved: **LME.** **acceptedly** *adverb* **L16.** **accepter** *noun* **M16.** **acceptingly** *adverb* in an accepting manner **L19.** **acceptive** *adjective* suitable for acceptance; ready to accept, receptive: **L15.**

acceptability /əksɛptəˈbɪlɪti/ *noun.* **M17.**
[**ORIGIN** Late Latin *acceptabilitas*, from *acceptabilis*: see **ACCEPTABLE**, **-ITY**; later from **ACCEPTABLE**: see **-ABILITY.**]
The quality of being acceptable.

acceptable /əkˈsɛptəb(ə)l/ *adjective.* **LME.**
[**ORIGIN** Old French & mod. French from late Latin *acceptabilis*, from *acceptare* **ACCEPT** *verb*: see **-ABLE.**]
Worth accepting; likely to be accepted; pleasing, welcome; tolerable.
the acceptable face of: see **FACE** *noun.*
– **NOTE**: Orig., and in poetry until **20**, stressed on 1st syllable.
■ **acceptableness** *noun* **E17.** **acceptably** *adverb* **M16.**

acceptance /əkˈsɛpt(ə)ns/ *noun.* **M16.**
[**ORIGIN** Old French: see **ACCEPT** *verb*, **-ANCE.**]
1 Favourable reception (of persons, things, or ideas); approval; assent, belief. **M16.**

SHAKES. *Merch. V.* I leave him to your gracious acceptance. M. FARADAY The assertion finds acceptance in every rank of society.

†**acceptance of persons** = ***ACCEPTION of persons.***
2 *gen.* The act or fact of accepting, whether as a pleasure, a satisfaction of claim, or a duty. **L16.**

E. A. FREEMAN William . . may . . have pressed the acceptance of the crown on Eadward. E. O'NEILL Her face now a fatalistic mask of acceptance.

3 Acceptableness. **L16.**

BROWNING A man of such acceptance.

4 The state or condition of being accepted. **M17.**

J. SELDEN She first brought Austin into acceptance with the King.

5 *COMMERCE.* A formal engagement to pay a bill when due; an accepted bill. **L17.**
6 = **ACCEPTATION** 4. *rare.* **E18.**
■ **acceptancy** *noun* favourable reception; willingness to receive: **E19.**

acceptant /əkˈsɛpt(ə)nt/ *noun & adjective.* **L16.**
[**ORIGIN** French, pres. pple of *accepter* **ACCEPT** *verb*: see **-ANT**[1].]
▸ †**A** *noun.* A person who accepts. **L16–L17.**
▸ **B** *adjective.* Willingly accepting (*of*); submissive. **M19.**

acceptation /aksɛpˈteɪʃ(ə)n/ *noun.* **LME.**
[**ORIGIN** Old French & mod. French from late Latin *acceptatio(n-)*, formed as **ACCEPT** *verb*: see **-ATION.**]
1 = **ACCEPTANCE** 1. **LME.**
†**2** = **ACCEPTANCE** 2. **LME–L17.**
3 = **ACCEPTANCE** 4. *arch.* **L16.**
4 A particular sense, or the generally recognized meaning, of a word or phrase. **E17.**
†**5** = **ACCEPTANCE** 5. Only in **E17.**

acceptilation /əksɛptɪˈleɪʃ(ə)n/ *noun.* Now *rare.* **M16.**
[**ORIGIN** Latin *acceptilatio(n-)*, from *acceptum* receipt + *latio(n-)* the formal proposal of a law.]
ROMAN LAW. Release from a debt by an acquittance without payment. Also *fig.*, free remission of sins.

acception /əkˈsɛpʃ(ə)n/ *noun.* Now *rare.* **LME.**
[**ORIGIN** Latin *acceptio(n-)*, formed as **ACCEPT** *verb*: see **-ION.** Partly from Old French.]
1 The action of accepting. **LME.**
†**acception of persons**, †**acception of faces** favourable reception of personal advances, favouritism.
2 = **ACCEPTATION** 4. **M16.**

acceptor /əkˈsɛptə/ *noun.* **LME.**
[**ORIGIN** In earliest use from Anglo-Norman *acceptour* from Latin *acceptor*; later replaced by or refashioned as **ACCEPTER**, but restored esp. in specialized senses: see **ACCEPT** *verb*, **-OR.**]
1 A person who accepts. *rare* in *gen.* sense. **LME.** ▸**b** *spec.* A person who accepts a bill. **M17.**
2 *CHEMISTRY & PHYSICS.* An atom or molecule which receives electrons or which can combine with another (specified) atom or molecule. **E20.** ▸**b** An impurity atom in a semiconductor which has fewer valency electrons than the majority of atoms and effectively contributes a conducting hole to the material. **M20.**
3 *ELECTRICITY.* In full ***acceptor circuit***. A circuit tuned so as to accept signals within a particular range of frequencies. **E20.**

access /ˈaksɛs/ *noun & verb.* **ME.**
[**ORIGIN** Old French & mod. French *accès* or Latin *accessus*, from *access-* pa. ppl stem of *accedere* **ACCEDE.**]
▸ **A** *noun.* **1** A (sudden) coming on of illness. **ME.** ▸†**b** *spec.* An ague fit. (Chiefly *dial.* after **16.**) **LME–L19.**

E. F. BENSON A violent access of hay-fever.

†**2** Coming into the presence of or into contact with (foll. by *to*); approach, entrance. **LME–E19.**

POPE Safe from access of each intruding power.

3 Admittance (*to* the presence or use of). **LME.** ▸**b** *spec.* The action or process of obtaining stored documents, data, etc. **M20.**

D. HALBERSTAM The few favored reporters who gained access to him and to his inner circle. K. AMIS He had access to as much drink as was good for him.

b ***open access***, ***random access***, etc.
4 Being approached. **LME.**

BOSWELL Lord Chesterfield's . . easiness of access.

†**5** Coming to work or business. **L16–M17.**

T. MAY The Accesse and meeting again of the Parliament.

6 A coming as an addition. *arch.* (replaced by **ACCESSION**). **L16.**

MILTON I from the influence of thy looks receive Access in every virtue.

7 Coming towards someone or something; advance. *arch.* **E17.**

J. HEALEY The Sunnes accesse and departure.

8 A way or means of approach or entrance (*lit.* & *fig.*). **E17.**

R. ADAMS The only access to the lower city is through the Peacock Gate. W. STEVENS Knowledge is . . The only access to true ease.

†**9** = **ACCESSION** 6. **M17–M18.**

CHARLES I: Our Accesse to the Crowne.

10 [After French.] An outburst *of* anger or other emotion. **L18.**

J. HELLER An access of powerful fresh feelings.

– **COMB.**: **access broadcasting**, **access television**: undertaken by members of the public by arrangement with broadcasting companies; **access course** an educational course enabling those without traditional qualifications to become eligible for higher education; **access road** a road giving access to a place or to another road; a slip road; ***access television***: see ***access broadcasting*** above; **access time** *COMPUTING* the time needed to retrieve stored information.
▸ **B** *verb trans.* Gain access to (*spec.* data etc. held in a computer or computer-based system, or such a system). **M20.**
– **NOTE**: Stress on the 2nd syllable was prevalent **16–18.**

accessary /əkˈsɛs(ə)ri/ *noun & adjective.* **LME.**
[**ORIGIN** medieval Latin *accessarius*, from Latin *access-*: see **ACCESS**, **-ARY**[1].]
▸ **A** *noun.* **1** = **ACCESSORY** *noun* 2. **LME.**
2 = **ACCESSORY** *noun* 1. **M16.**
▸ **B** *adjective.* †**1** = **ACCESSORY** *adjective* 1. **M16–L17.**
2 = **ACCESSORY** *adjective* 2. **L16.**
– **NOTE**: Etymologically, *accessary* is the noun and *accessory* the adjective, but the two have been used interchangeably in English from the beginning. ***Accessary*** is now largely restricted to legal contexts.

accessible /əkˈsɛsɪb(ə)l/ *adjective.* **LME.**
[**ORIGIN** Old French & mod. French, or late Latin *accessibilis* from Latin *access-*: see **ACCESS**, **-IBLE.**]
1 Able to be reached, entered, influenced, understood, etc. **LME.**
accessible to able to be reached etc. by; open to the influence of.
2 Able to be used as an access. Now *rare.* **E17.**

MILTON With one ascent Accessible from earth.

■ **accessiˈbility** *noun* **M18.** **accessibleness** *noun* **E19.** **accessibly** *adverb* **L19.**

accession /əkˈsɛʃ(ə)n/ *noun & verb.* **L16.**
[**ORIGIN** Old French & mod. French, or Latin *accessio(n-)*, from *access-*: see **ACCESS**, **-ION.**]
▸ **A** *noun.* **I** Result.
1 Something which is added; an augmentation, an increase. **L16.**

S. JOHNSON He will be a very honourable accession [to the club].

2 Adherence; assent; formal acceptance of a treaty etc. **E17.**

S. WILLIAMS Declaring their acquiescence in, and accession to the determination made by Congress.

3 Joining; addition. **M17.**

T. ADAMS The accession of piety to patience.

4 *LAW.* Artificial improvement or natural growth of a property, as of land by the formation of alluvium. **M18.**
▸ **II** Action.
5 The action of coming near, approach; admittance. Formerly also, advance, arrival. **E17.**

T. STANLEY The accession of the Sun from Tropick to Tropick.

6 Entering upon an office or dignity (esp. a throne) or condition. **M17.**
▸ †**III 7** An onset of illness, powerful feeling, etc. **E17–E19.**
▸ **B** *verb trans.* Record the addition of (a book etc.) to a library. **L19.**
■ **accessional** *adjective* **M17.**

accessory /əkˈsɛs(ə)ri/ *noun & adjective.* **LME.**
[**ORIGIN** medieval Latin *accessorius* adjective, from Latin *access-*: see **ACCESS**, **-ORY**[2]. Partly through Old French & mod. French *accessoire*.]
▸ **A** *noun.* **1** An additional or subordinate thing; an adjunct, an accompaniment; a minor fitting or attachment; a small article of (usu. a woman's) dress. Now usu. in *pl.* **LME.**
2 A person who helps in or is privy to any act, esp. a crime. **LME.**
accessory before the fact, **accessory after the fact** *LAW* a person who is criminally involved in the events leading up to or following the commission of a crime (e.g. in concealing evidence).
▸ **B** *adjective.* **1** Of a thing: additional; subordinately contributing, dispensable; adventitious. **E17.**
accessory mineral *GEOLOGY* a constituent mineral present in small quantities and not taken into account in identifying a rock. **accessory nerve** *ANATOMY* either of the eleventh pair of cranial nerves, which supply certain muscles in the neck and shoulder.
2 Of a person: acceding *to*; participant, privy (*to*, esp. a crime). **E17.**
– **NOTE**: See note s.v. **ACCESSARY.**
■ **accessorial** /aksɛˈsɔːrɪəl/ *adjective* of the nature of an accessory; supplementary: **E18.** **accessorily** *adverb* additionally; in the manner of an accessory: **LME.** **accessorize** *verb trans.* & *intrans.* provide or provide (oneself) with an accessory or accessories **M20.**

A

acciaccatura /ətʃakəˈtʊərə, *foreign* aˌtʃakkaˈtuːra/ *noun*. Pl. **-s**, **-ture** /-ˈtuːre/. **E19**.
[**ORIGIN** Italian, from *acciaccare* to crush.]
MUSIC. A grace note performed quickly before an essential note of a melody.

accidence /ˈaksɪd(ə)ns/ *noun*[1]. Now *rare* or *obsolete*. **LME**.
[**ORIGIN** Old French from late Latin *accidentia*: see **ACCIDENCE** *noun*[2], **-ENCE**.]
Chance; a fortuitous circumstance, a mishap.

accidence /ˈaksɪd(ə)ns/ *noun*[2]. **E16**.
[**ORIGIN** Late Latin *accidentia* neut. pl. pres. pple of *accidere* taken as fem. sing.: see **ACCIDENT**, **-ENCE**.]
1 The part of grammar which deals with the variable forms of words (inflections etc.). **E16**.
2 The rudiments of any subject. **M16**.

accident /ˈaksɪd(ə)nt/ *noun*. **LME**.
[**ORIGIN** Old French & mod. French from Latin *accident-* pres. ppl stem of *accidere* happen, from *ad* **AC-** + *cadere* to fall: see **-ENT**.]
▸ **I** A thing that happens.
1 An event. *obsolete* in *gen.* sense. **LME**. ▸**b** An event that is without apparent cause or unexpected; an unfortunate event, *esp.* one causing injury or damage. **LME**.

> **b** C. DAY Our race may be an accident, in a meaningless universe. M. SPARK She . . had been killed in an accident.

2 Chance, fortune. **LME**.

> S. JOHNSON Nature probably has some part in human characters and accident has some part.

†**3** *MEDICINE*. An unfavourable symptom. **LME–L17**.
†**4** A casual appearance or effect. **LME–M18**.
5 An irregularity in the landscape. **M19**.

> J. R. LOWELL Accidents of open green.

▸ **II** Something present but not necessarily so, and therefore non-essential.
6 *LOGIC*. A property or quality not essential to a substance or object. **LME**.
7 *GRAMMAR*. A change of form to which words are subject, as to express number, case, gender, etc. Usu. in *pl. arch.* **M16**.
8 *gen.* A non-essential accompaniment; a mere accessory. **E17**.

> DISRAELI With all the brilliant accidents of birth, and beauty, and fortune. W. W. GREG The 'accidents' of presentation, . . the spelling, punctuation, and other scribal or typographical details.

— **COMB.** & **PHRASES**: **accident-prone** *adjective* predisposed or likely to cause or suffer an accident. **by accident** by chance, unintentionally. **chapter of accidents** an unforeseen course of events.
■ **accidented** *adjective* characterized by accidents **L19**. **accidently** *adverb* (now *rare* exc. as misspelling) accidentally **LME**.

accidental /aksɪˈdɛnt(ə)l/ *adjective* & *noun*. **LME**.
[**ORIGIN** Late Latin *accidentalis*, from *accident-*: see **ACCIDENT**, **-AL**[1].]
▸ **A** *adjective*. **1** *LOGIC*. Not essential to a substance or object. **LME**.
2 *gen.* Incidental; subsidiary. **LME**.

> S. JOHNSON Those accidental benefits which prudence may confer on every state.

accidental sharp, **accidental flat**, **accidental natural** *MUSIC*: signs attached to a single note to mark a temporary change in pitch, not in the key signature.
3 Pertaining to chance; casual; occasional. **E16**.

> SHAKES. *Meas. for M.* Thy sin's not accidental, but a trade.

4 Happening by chance, undesignedly, or unexpectedly. **L16**.

> JOYCE Matthew F. Kane (accidental drowning, Dublin Bay).

▸ **B** *noun*. **1** Something non-essential or subsidiary. **E17**.
2 *MUSIC*. An accidental sharp, flat, or natural. **M19**.
3 *ORNITHOLOGY*. = **VAGRANT** *noun* 3. **M20**.
■ **acciden'tality** *noun* the quality or fact of being accidental **M17**. **accidentally** *adverb* †(*a*) non-essentially; (*b*) by accident: **LME**. **accidentalness** *noun* **L17**.

accidie /ˈaksɪdi/ *noun*. **ME**.
[**ORIGIN** Anglo-Norman = Old French *accide* from medieval Latin *accidia* alt. of late Latin **ACEDIA**.]
Spiritual or mental sloth, apathy.
— **NOTE**: Obsolete after **E16**; revived in **L19**.
■ **accidious** *adjective* (*rare*) **LME**.

accinge /əkˈsɪndʒ/ *verb refl.* Now *rare*. **M17**.
[**ORIGIN** Latin *accingere* gird (oneself).]
Prepare for action; apply oneself.

accipiter /akˈsɪpɪtə/ *noun*. **E19**.
[**ORIGIN** Latin = hawk, bird of prey.]
†**1** A bandage for the nose, resembling a hawk's claw. Only in **19**.
2 *ORNITHOLOGY*. Orig., any bird of prey of the order Accipitres (now called Falconiformes), which excludes owls. Now, any of the relatively short-winged, long-legged birds of prey belonging to the genus *Accipiter* and typified by the sparrowhawk and the goshawk. **E20**.
■ **accipitral** *adjective* hawklike; rapacious; keen-sighted: **M19**.

accipitrine /akˈsɪpɪtrʌɪn/ *adjective*. **M19**.
[**ORIGIN** French, from Latin *accipiter*: see **ACCIPITER**, **-INE**[1].]
1 *ORNITHOLOGY*. Pertaining to or designating birds of the family Accipitridae, which includes most birds of prey other than owls, falcons, and New World vultures. **M19**.
2 Accipitral. **L19**.

†**accite** *verb trans.* **L15**.
[**ORIGIN** Latin *accit-* pa. ppl stem of *accire*, from *ad* **AC-** + *ciere* to call: see **CITE** *verb*.]
1 Summon. **L15–L17**.

> G. CHAPMAN Our heralds . . accited all that were Endamag'd.

2 Excite. **L16–M17**.

> JONSON To accite So ravenous . . an Appetite.

3 Quote. Only in **M17**.

> DONNE Accited for examples . . in the Scriptures.

acclaim /əˈkleɪm/ *verb* & *noun*. **ME**.
[**ORIGIN** Latin *acclamare*, from *ad* **AC-** + *clamare* to shout, with spelling assim. to **CLAIM** *noun*, *verb*.]
▸ **A** *verb*. †**1** *verb trans.* Lay claim to. *Scot.* & *N. English*. **ME–E18**.
2 *verb trans.* Praise enthusiastically and publicly, extol. **M17**. ▸**b** *verb trans.* (with compl.). Hail as. **M18**.

> *Independent* One of the year's most acclaimed dramas. **b** *Sunday Times* Van Gaal was acclaimed as a national hero in Holland.

3 *verb intrans.* Express approval; shout applause. **M17**.
4 *verb trans.* Shout, call out. **L17**.
▸ **B** *noun*. †**1** A claim. *Scot.* **M16–M17**.
2 Acclamation; enthusiastic praise; a shout of applause or welcome. **M17**.

> *Times* The band received widespread critical acclaim for their third album.

■ **acclaimer** *noun* **M19**.

acclamation /akləˈmeɪʃ(ə)n/ *noun*. **M16**.
[**ORIGIN** Latin *acclamatio(n-)*, from *acclamat-* pa. ppl stem of *acclamare*: see **ACCLAIM**, **-ATION**.]
1 An act of acclaiming; a shout of approbation or welcome. Now usu. in *pl.* **M16**. ▸**b** An election by acclamation (see sense 3 below). *N. Amer.* **M20**.
†**2** *RHETORIC*. A brief isolated sentence emphasizing what precedes it. **M16–M17**.
3 The action of acclaiming; loud or eager assent or approval; shouting in a person's honour. **L16**.
by acclamation (chiefly *N. Amer.*) unanimously, without need for a vote.
■ **acclamatory** /əˈklamət(ə)ri/ *adjective* expressing acclamation **L17**.

acclimate /əˈklʌɪmət/ *verb trans.* & *intrans.* Now chiefly *US*. **L18**.
[**ORIGIN** French *acclimater*, formed as **A-**[5] + **CLIMATE**.]
= **ACCLIMATIZE**.
■ **acclima'tation** *noun* (now *rare*) acclimatization **M19**. **acclimatement** *noun* (*rare*) **E19**. **acclimation** /aklɪˈmeɪʃ(ə)n/ *noun* acclimatization **E19**.

acclimatize /əˈklʌɪmətʌɪz/ *verb trans.* & *intrans.* Also **-ise**. **M19**.
[**ORIGIN** formed as **ACCLIMATE** + **-IZE**.]
Habituate, become habituated, to a new climate or environment.
■ **acclimati'zation** *noun* **M19**. **acclimatizer** *noun* **M19**.

acclivity /əˈklɪvɪti/ *noun*. **E17**.
[**ORIGIN** Latin *acclivitas*, from *acclivis*, *-us*, from *ad* **AC-** + *clivus* a slope: see **-ITY**.]
An ascending slope.
■ **acclivitous** *adjective* **E19**. **acclivous** *adjective* (now *rare*) [from Latin *acclivus*: see **-OUS**] **M18**.

accloy /əˈklɔɪ/ *verb trans.* Now *arch. rare*. **LME**.
[**ORIGIN** Old French *encloer* from medieval Latin *inclavare*, from *clavus* a nail.]
†**1** Prick (a horse) with a nail in shoeing; lame. **LME–E18**.
2 Stop up (an aperture); obstruct, clog, choke. **LME**.
†**3** Overfill; burden, oppress. **LME–E17**.
4 Disgust, become offensive to. **M16**.

†**accoast** *verb* var. of **ACCOST** *verb*.

†**accoil** *verb intrans. rare* (Spenser). Only in **L16**.
[**ORIGIN** Old French *acoillir* (mod. *accueillir*).]
Gather together, collect.

accolade /ˈakəleɪd, akəˈlɑːd, -ˈkəʊl-/ *noun* & *verb*. **E17**.
[**ORIGIN** French from Provençal *acolada*, ult. from Latin *ad* **AC-** + *collum* neck: see **-ADE**.]
▸ **A** *noun*. **1** The salutation marking the bestowal of knighthood, at different times an embrace, a kiss, or (now the usual form) a stroke on the shoulder with the flat of a sword; *fig.* the bestowal of praise, an acknowledgement of merit. **E17**.

> M. BEADLE A Nobel Prize is the top accolade a scientist can receive.

2 *MUSIC*. A vertical line or brace, used to couple two or more staves. **E19**.
▸ **B** *verb trans.* **1** Embrace or kiss in salutation. *rare*. **M19**.
2 Confer an accolade on (*lit.* & *fig.*). **M20**.

†**accoll** *verb trans.* **LME–M16**.
[**ORIGIN** Old French *acoler*, (later) *accoller*, (mod. *accoler*): cf. **ACCOLADE**.]
Throw the arms round the neck of, embrace.

accolled /əˈkɒld/ *adjective*. **E18**.
[**ORIGIN** formed as **ACCOLL** + **-ED**[1].]
HERALDRY. Wreathed, esp. about the neck; gorged.

accollée /əˈkɒli/ *adjective*. **E18**.
[**ORIGIN** French, fem. pa. pple of *accoller*: see **ACCOLL**.]
HERALDRY. †**1** = **ACCOLLED**. **E18–L19**.
2 Of two shields: placed side by side. **L19**.

†**accommodate** *adjective*. **E16–L18**.
[**ORIGIN** Latin *accommodatus* pa. pple, formed as **ACCOMMODATE** *verb*: see **-ATE**[2].]
Suited; suitable, fitting.

accommodate /əˈkɒmədeɪt/ *verb*. **M16**.
[**ORIGIN** Latin *accommodat-* pa. ppl stem of *accommodare*, from *ad* **AC-** + *commodus* fitting: see **-ATE**[3].]
†**1** *verb trans.* Ascribe fittingly (a thing to a person). **M16–L17**.
2 *verb trans.* Adapt (one thing or person *to* another). **M16**. ▸†**b** *verb intrans.* Adapt oneself *to*. **L16–L17**. ▸**c** *verb trans.* Adapt to; allow for; take account of; satisfy (a need etc.). **L18**.

> D. BREWSTER The power of accommodating the eye to different distances. R. W. CHAPMAN *Persien* . . was accommodated to the regular *-ian*. C. FREEMAN The reason she had no social life was . . because she couldn't accommodate herself to anyone.

3 *verb trans.* Equip or supply (esp. a person, *with*). **L16**. ▸**b** *verb trans.* Provide lodging or room for; allow space or time for. **L16**. ▸**c** *verb trans.* Oblige, confer a favour on. **M17**.

> DEFOE Wax candles . . to accommodate us with light. **b** J. CONRAD The other buildings . . served only to accommodate the numerous household. B. PYM The space that had once accommodated the four of them. *Independent* Television programmes . . are always about 29 minutes long to accommodate announcements, links, etc. **c** M. L. KING I was having press conferences three times a week—in order to accommodate the reporters and journalists.

4 *verb trans.* Reconcile (things or persons); settle (differences etc.); bring to agreement. **L16**. ▸**b** *verb intrans.* Come to terms. **M17**.

> LD MACAULAY The dispute had been accommodated. **b** EVELYN They must accommodate with His Majesty.

5 *verb trans.* Show the correspondence of (one thing to another); make or make appear consistent. Foll. by *to* (†or *unto*, *with*). **E17**.
†**6** *verb trans.* Fit (a thing) for use; repair. **E17–E19**.
†**7** *verb trans.* Facilitate, aid. **E17–E18**.
■ **accommodable** *adjective* (now *rare*) able to be accommodated, suitable **L16**. **accommodating** *adjective* obliging; easy to deal with; compliant: **L18**. **accommodatingly** *adverb* **E19**. **accommodative** *adjective* tending or able to accommodate **M19**. **accommodativeness** *noun* **M19**. **accommodator** *noun* a person who or thing which accommodates; *US* a temporary domestic help: **M17**. **accommo'datory** *adjective* characterized by accommodation or adaptation **E20**.

accommodation /əkɒməˈdeɪʃ(ə)n/ *noun*. **E17**.
[**ORIGIN** Old French & mod. French, or Latin *accommodatio(n-)*, formed as **ACCOMMODATE** *verb*: see **-ATION**.]
1 Something which supplies a want or ministers to one's comfort. **E17**.

> J. REYNOLDS The regular progress of cultivated life is from necessaries to accommodations, from accommodations to ornaments.

2 *sing.* & (now *US*) in *pl.* Room and provision for the reception of people, lodgings; living premises. **E17**.

> A. POWELL The accommodation was a bit . . squalid.

3 An arrangement of a dispute; a settlement; a compromise. **M17**.

> H. WILSON Trying to reach an accommodation with the Liberal leader.

4 The action of accommodating or the process of being accommodated; adaptation, adjustment. **M17**.

> D. BREWSTER The accommodation of the eye to the distinct vision of external objects.

5 Adaptation to a different purpose, function, or meaning. **E18**.
6 Self-adaptation; obligingness; a favour. **M18**.

> W. FAULKNER Wherever you could take us, it would be a big accommodation.

7 The action of supplying with what is requisite. *rare*. **M18**.
8 Pecuniary aid in an emergency; a loan. **L18**.

> D. RUNYON I do not care to extend such accommodations over any considerable period.

— **COMB.**: **accommodation address**: used on letters to a person unable or unwilling to give a permanent address; **accommodation bill**: for raising money on credit; **accommodation ladder**: allowing access between a ship's decks, or to and from a small boat etc. alongside; **accommodation paddock** *Austral.* & *NZ hist.* a paddock for drovers to keep stock in overnight; **accommodation road**: giving access to a place not on a public road.
■ **accommodational** *adjective* †(*a*) affording (good) accommodation; (*b*) of or pertaining to accommodation: **E19**.

accompaniment /əˈkʌmp(ə)nɪm(ə)nt/ *noun*. **E18**.
[**ORIGIN** Old French & mod. French *accompagnement*, formed as **ACCOMPANIST**: see **-MENT**.]
1 *MUSIC*. The subsidiary part(s), usu. instrumental, supporting a solo instrument or voice, a choir, etc. **E18**.
2 *gen*. Something that accompanies; an appendage. **M19**.

accompanist /əˈkʌmpənɪst/ *noun*. **M19**.
[**ORIGIN** from **ACCOMPANY** + **-IST**.]
A person who or thing which accompanies; *esp*. the performer taking the accompanying part in music.

accompany /əˈkʌmpəni/ *verb*. **LME**.
[**ORIGIN** Old French & mod. French *accompagner*, formed as **A-**[5] + **COMPANION** *noun*[1], later assim. to **COMPANY** *verb*.]
†**1** *verb trans*. Add or join *to*. **LME–L16**.
2 *verb trans*. Join or unite (a thing, †a person) *with*, supplement *with*. **LME**. ▸†**b** *refl*. Associate or unite oneself *with*. **LME–M17**.

JOYCE With what meditations did Bloom accompany his demonstration?

†**3** *verb intrans*. & *trans*. Keep company (*with*); cohabit (*with*). **LME–M18**.

LD BERNERS Suche as accompanyeth with man-killers. P. SIDNEY To bid her go home and accompanie her solitarie father.

4 *verb trans*. Convoy, escort, attend, go with (*lit*. & *fig*.). **LME**.

A. CHRISTIE He got up to accompany his patient to the door. *fig*.: P. G. HAMERTON A . . *déjeuner à la fourchette*, accompanied by half a bottle of . . Bordeaux.

5 *verb trans*. *MUSIC*. Support (a singer, player, melody, etc.) by performing a subsidiary, usu. instrumental, part. **L16**.

DAY LEWIS Knos would sing, accompanying herself on the harmonium. S. HILL A harmonica, which he used to accompany their songs.

6 *verb trans*. Go with as an attribute or attendant phenomenon; characterize. **L17**.
■ **accompanable** *adjective* (now *arch*. *rare*) sociable, companionable **M16**. **accompanied** *adjective* (*a*) *MUSIC* having an instrumental accompaniment; (*b*) escorted; *MILITARY* (of a tour etc.) on which families are allowed to accompany military personnel: **L18**. **accompanier** *noun* **M18**. **accompanyist** *noun* = **ACCOMPANIST** **M19**.

accomplice /əˈkʌmplɪs, əˈkɒm-/ *noun*. **M16**.
[**ORIGIN** Alt. of **COMPLICE**, prob. by assoc. with **ACCOMPANY**.]
An associate in guilt; a partner in crime.

joc.: SHAKES. *1 Hen. VI* Success unto our valiant general, and happiness to his accomplices!

■ **accompliceship** *noun* (*rare*) the state of being an accomplice; criminal assistance: **E19**.

accomplish /əˈkʌmplɪʃ, əˈkɒm-/ *verb*. **LME**.
[**ORIGIN** Old French *acompliss-* lengthened stem of *acomplir* (mod. *acc-*), ult. from Latin *ad* **AC-** + *complere* fill, complete: see **-ISH**[2].]
1 *verb trans*. Fulfil, perform, carry out. **LME**. ▸†**b** *verb intrans*. Carry out a design. *rare*. **L15–E16**.

AV *Prov*. 13:19 The desire accomplished is sweet to the soule. S. KAUFFMANN He had seen the man for only an hour or so, but he'd accomplished enough to make the memorandum sound as if it covered an afternoon.

2 *verb trans*. Bring to an end, complete, (a work). **LME**. ▸**b** Reach the end of (a time, a distance). **L16**.

R. HOLINSHED The abbeie of Abington also he accomplished. **b** AV *Dan*. 9:2 He would accomplish seuentie yeeres in the desolations of Ierusalem. W. H. PRESCOTT He had accomplished half a league or more.

3 *verb trans*. Perfect in mental acquirements or personal graces; finish off. **LME**.

T. FULLER Nothing accomplisheth a man more than learning.

4 *verb trans*. Equip completely. *arch*. **L16**.

SHAKES. *Hen. V* The armourers accomplishing the knights.

■ **accomplishable** *adjective* able to be accomplished **L18**. **accomplished** *adjective* fulfilled; completed; perfect, esp. in acquirements; clever; well trained or educated: **LME**. **accomplisher** *noun* **E17**.

accomplishment /əˈkʌmplɪʃm(ə)nt, əˈkɒm-/ *noun*. **LME**.
[**ORIGIN** from **ACCOMPLISH** + **-MENT**, after French *accomplissement*.]
1 The action of accomplishing; fulfilment, completion. **LME**.
2 Perfection. *arch*. **M16**.
3 An achievement, an attainment; an acquired skill. Also, skill or ability in an activity. **L16**.

Classic CD Their level of technical accomplishment is never in question. D. D'SOUZA Western civilization is a towering human accomplishment.

4 Something that finishes off or equips completely; now usu. a social skill or grace (passing into sense 3). **E17**.

K. THOMAS English was merely to be an extra accomplishment for young middle-class women.

accompt *noun*, *verb*, **accomptant** *adjective* & *noun* see **ACCOUNT** *noun*, *verb*, **ACCOUNTANT**.

accord /əˈkɔːd/ *noun*. **ME**.
[**ORIGIN** Old French *acord* (mod. *acc-*), formed as **ACCORD** *verb*.]
1 Reconciliation; concurrence of opinion, will, or action. **ME**.

W. COWPER Harmony and family accord. WORDSWORTH With due accord Of busy hands and back and forward steps.

†**be of accord** (**with**), †**be at accord** (**with**) agree (with). **with one accord**, †**of one accord** with unanimity.
2 A formal act of reconciliation; a treaty. **ME**.
3 Harmonious correspondence, as of colours or tints; agreement in pitch and tone; harmony. **LME**.

E. BOWEN I did not put place or time of the funeral in *The Times*; in accord with general feeling that it should be strictly private.

4 Assent; consent. Long *obsolete* exc. in ***of one's own accord***, of one's own volition. **LME**.
5 *LAW*. An agreement to accept something in exchange for giving up the right of action. **E17**.
accord and satisfaction the doctrine under which one person agrees with another that the doing of an act shall extinguish his or her claim.

accord /əˈkɔːd/ *verb*. **OE**.
[**ORIGIN** Old French *acorder* (mod. *acc-*), from Latin *ad* **AC-** after *concordare* **CONCORD** *verb*.]
†**1** **a** *verb trans*. Bring (persons) into agreement; reconcile (a person, oneself) *with* another. **OE–E18**. ▸**b** *verb intrans*. Agree, assent, consent, *to*. **ME–E19**.
2 *verb intrans*. Come to an agreement or to terms; be at one; agree. **OE**.

COLERIDGE I warmly accord with W. in his abhorrence of these poetic Licences.

3 *verb trans*. Settle (a quarrel or difference). *arch*. **ME**.
4 *verb intrans*. Of things: be in harmony, be consistent, (*with*). **ME**.

T. KEIGHTLEY Parliament met . . and its acts perfectly accorded with the royal wishes.

†**5** *verb trans*. Agree upon, arrange. **LME–L17**.
6 *verb trans*. Agree to, grant (a request etc., *to* a person); award. **LME**.
†**7** *verb intrans*. *impers*. in ***it accords***, ***it accorded***, it is or was suitable or proper. **LME–M16**.
■ **accordable** *adjective* †(*a*) accordant; (*b*) reconcilable: **LME**. **accorder** *noun* a person who agrees or bestows **M19**. **accordment** *noun* (now *rare*) reconcilement **ME**.

accordance /əˈkɔːd(ə)ns/ *noun*. **ME**.
[**ORIGIN** Old French *acordance*, formed as **ACCORD** *verb*: see **-ANCE**.]
1 Agreement; conformity; harmony. Esp. in ***in accordance with***. **ME**.
2 The action of granting. **M19**.
■ **accordancy** *noun* a condition or state of agreement; harmony: **L18**.

accordant /əˈkɔːd(ə)nt/ *adjective*. **ME**.
[**ORIGIN** Old French *acordant* pres. pple, formed as **ACCORD** *verb*: see **-ANT**[1].]
1 In accordance or agreement *with*; compatible *with*. Also (now *rare*) foll. by *to*. **ME**.
2 *absol*. †**a** Agreeing in character or circumstances; suitable. **ME–E17**. ▸**b** Agreeing in external action or motion; *esp*. (of sounds) harmonious. **LME**. ▸†**c** Agreeing or concurring in mind. Only in **L16**.
■ **accordantly** *adverb* **LME**.

according /əˈkɔːdɪŋ/ *adjective* & *adverb*. **ME**.
[**ORIGIN** from **ACCORD** *verb* + **-ING**[2].]
▸ **A** *adjective*. †**1** *pred*. Corresponding *to*. **ME–M16**.
2 *absol*. Agreeing in nature or action. **LME**.

TENNYSON Harder the times were . . , and the according hearts of men Seemed harder too.

†**3** Appropriate, fitting. **LME–L17**.
▸ **B** *adverb*. **1** ***according to***, in a manner consistent with or a degree proportioned to; as formulated by, as stated by. **LME**. ▸**b** *absol*. According to circumstances. *colloq*. **M19**.
according to Cocker: see **COCKER** *noun*[4]. ***according to plan***: see **PLAN** *noun*.
2 = **ACCORDINGLY** 3. Now *rare*. **L15**.

L. MACNEICE In the second taxi . . the clock showed sixpence extra; he tipped according.

3 ***according as***, exactly as, just as; in proportion as; in a manner depending on which of certain alternatives is true. **E16**.

accordingly /əˈkɔːdɪŋli/ *adverb*. **ME**.
[**ORIGIN** from **ACCORDING** + **-LY**[2].]
†**1** Harmoniously, agreeably. **ME–E16**.
2 Becomingly, duly, properly. Long *rare*. **LME**.
3 In accordance with the particular circumstances; correspondingly. **L16**.

Daily Telegraph The smartcard . . records the mileage and charges an account accordingly.

4 As a result, therefore, so; in due course. **L17**.

C. BROOKMYRE The date was accordingly set for a month hence.

— **PHRASES**: **accordingly as** according as.

accordion /əˈkɔːdɪən/ *noun* & *adjective*. **M19**.
[**ORIGIN** German *Akkordion*, from Italian *accordare* tune (an instrument).]
▸ **A** *noun*. A portable musical instrument consisting of bellows, metal reeds, and a keyboard and/or buttons. **M19**.
piano accordion.
▸ **B** *attrib*. or as *adjective*. Folding like the bellows of an accordion. **L19**.
accordion pleat, ***accordion-pleated*** *adjective*, ***accordion wall***, etc.
■ **accordionist** *noun* **L19**.

accost /əˈkɒst/ *verb* & *noun*. **L16**.
[**ORIGIN** French *accoster* from Italian *accostare*, ult. from Latin *ad* **AC-** + *costa* rib, side. Assoc. with *coast*.]
▸ **A** *verb*. Also †**accoast**.
†**1** *verb intrans*. & *trans*. Lie alongside, border (on). **L16–M17**.
†**2** *verb trans*. Go alongside of. **L16–E17**.
3 *verb trans*. Approach for any purpose; assail, face. *arch*. **L16**.
4 *verb trans*. Approach and speak to, esp. boldly; address. **L16**. ▸**b** Of a prostitute: solicit in the street. **L19**.

T. PARKER He was accosted by two masked men as he walked along a path.

▸ **B** *noun*. An address, a salutation. **E17**.
■ **accostable** *adjective* approachable, accessible **E17**. **accoster** *noun* **M19**.

accouchement /əˈkuːʃmɒ̃, *foreign* akuʃmɑ̃/ *noun*. **L18**.
[**ORIGIN** French, from *accoucher*, formed as **A-**[5] + **COUCH** *verb*: see **-MENT**.]
Childbirth; a confinement.
■ **accouche** *verb intrans*. give birth; act as midwife: **E19**.

accoucheur /akuːˈʃəː; *foreign* akuʃœːr (*pl. same*)/ *noun*. **M18**.
[**ORIGIN** French, formed as **ACCOUCHEMENT** + *-eur* **-OR**.]
A man (formerly also a woman) who acts as midwife.
■ **accoucheuse** /-əːz; *foreign* -øːz (*pl. same*)/ *noun* a midwife **E19**.

account /əˈkaʊnt/ *noun*. Also (*arch*.) **accompt**. **ME**.
[**ORIGIN** Anglo-Norman *acunt*, Old French *acont*, later *a(c)compt*, formed as **ACCOUNT** *verb*.]
1 Counting, reckoning, calculation. **ME**.

T. HARDY My accompt of years outscored her own.

2 A statement of moneys, goods, or services received and expended, or other receipts and outgoings, with calculation of the balance. Also, a business arrangement involving the reckoning of debit or credit; *esp*. (*a*) one involving deferment of payment or (*STOCK EXCHANGE*) deferment of completion of a transaction until the next account day; (*b*) one involving the keeping of money or other assets in a bank etc., with the depositor having the option of withdrawal; (*c*) a credit arrangement with a firm, shop, etc. Also, a sum of money owed or one deposited in a bank etc. but subject to withdrawal. **ME**. ▸**b** A customer having such an arrangement. **M20**. ▸**c** In *pl*. The department of a firm etc. that deals with accounts. **M20**.

THACKERAY Pen thought of opening an account with a banker.

3 A statement as to the discharge of any responsibility; an answering for conduct. **ME**.
4 Estimation, importance; consideration. **LME**.

JONSON A Scholler . . of good accompt. STEVIE SMITH You are only one of many And of small account if any.

5 A particular statement of the administration of money in trust or required by a creditor. **E16**.

GOLDSMITH To give in his accompts to the masters of the temple.

6 *LAW*. A procedure to require an account of monies or property wrongfully received, e.g. by infringing the applicant's copyright or in breach of trust. **E16**.
7 A narration, a report, a description; a performance (*of* a piece of music etc.). **E17**.

E. V. LUCAS Has any reader ever found perfect accuracy in the newspaper account of any event of which he himself had inside knowledge?

8 A reckoning in one's favour; advantage. **E17**.
9 The preparing of a statement of money transactions. **M17**.

GIBBON The actual account employed several hundred persons.

— **PHRASES**: †**account current** = *current account* below. **budget account** an account at a shop etc. with revolving credit and regular payments. **by all accounts** in everyone's opinion. ***call to account***: see **CALL** *verb*. **cast accounts** make calculations. **current account** an account at a bank allowing withdrawal of money on demand, now usu. also providing the depositor with means of authorizing withdrawal of money by others. **deposit account** an account at a bank usu. paying interest and not able to be drawn upon without notice or requiring the depositor to apply for repayment in person. **for account of** to be accounted for to (a person). **for the account** *STOCK EXCHANGE* not for cash, but for settlement on the next account day. **give a good account of** be successful with; do justice to. **go to one's account** die. **joint account**: held by two or more people in conjunction. **keep accounts** record expenditure for comparison with income. **lay one's account with**, **lay one's account on**, **lay one's account for** (orig. *Scot*.) reckon upon, expect. **leave out of account** not take into consideration, disregard. †**make account** reckon, resolve, expect (*that*, *to do*). **make account of** esteem. **money of account** a denomination of money used in reckoning, but not current as coins etc. ***nominal account***: see **NOMINAL** *adjective*. ***numbered account***: see **NUMBER** *verb*. **on account** to be accounted for at the final settlement; not to be paid for immediately; as interim payment. **on account of** (*a*) because of; †(*b*) concerning. **on no account** under no circumstances; certainly not. **on one's own account** for one's own purpose and at one's own risk. **on someone's account** so that it is chargeable to him or her; to benefit him or her. **render an account**, **send in an account** give a statement of money due. **settle accounts**

A

(with), **square accounts (with)** receive or pay the balance due (from or to); *fig.* have revenge (on). **take account of**, **take into account** take into consideration, notice. ***turn to account***, ***turn to good account***: see TURN *verb*. ***unit of account***: see UNIT *noun*[1]. ***vote on account***: see VOTE *noun* 5.

– COMB.: **account book** a book prepared for the keeping of accounts; **account day** a day of reckoning; STOCK EXCHANGE the day on which accounts are settled; **account executive** = ***accounts executive*** below; **accounts department** = sense 2c above; **accounts executive** a business executive, esp. in advertising, who manages a client's account.

account /əˈkaʊnt/ *verb*. Also (*arch.*) **accompt**. ME.
[ORIGIN Old French *acunter*, *aconter*, formed as A-[5] + COUNT *verb*.]
▸ **I** †**1** *verb trans.* Count, enumerate. ME–E17. ▸**b** *verb intrans.* Perform the act of counting. LME–L18.

b ADAM SMITH Able to read, write, and account.

2 *verb intrans.* Render or receive an account. ME. ▸**b** *verb trans.* Render account of. E17.

BURKE Paymasters . . who have never been admitted to account. **b** M. PATTISON All receipts should be accounted to a finance committee.

3 †**a** *verb trans.* Calculate, compute; include in a reckoning. LME–E19. ▸**b** *verb trans.* Reckon, credit, *to*, *unto*. LME.

a TREVISA The Grekes acounte tyme and yeres fro the fyrst Olympias. SOUTHEY Wales, Scotland, and Ireland ought to be accounted with England.

4 *verb trans.* Reckon, estimate (to be so and so), consider, regard as. LME.

AV *Rom.* 8:36 We are accounted as sheepe for the slaughter. A. HECHT Trajan, of his imperial peers Accounted 'the most just'.

▸ †**II 5** *verb trans.* & *intrans.* Recount, narrate. ME–L16.

– WITH PREPOSITIONS IN SPECIALIZED SENSES: **account for** (***a***) give a reckoning of (money held in trust); answer for (conduct, performance of duty, etc.); (***b***) explain the cause of, serve as an explanation of; (***c***) constitute a specified total, proportion, etc., in a reckoning; (***d***) be responsible for the death, defeat, dismissal, etc., of. **account of** esteem, value; think (*much*, *little*, *nothing*, etc.) of; (now only in *pass.*). **account to** put (something) to the credit of, attribute to.

■ †**accounter** *noun* ME–M17.

accountable /əˈkaʊntəb(ə)l/ *adjective*. LME.
[ORIGIN Anglo-Norman *acountable* (Old French *acomptable*): see ACCOUNT *verb*, -ABLE.]
1 Liable to be called to account; responsible (*to* persons, *for* things). LME.

WILKIE COLLINS She is not accountable for her actions. *Economist* Russia's state-owned firms are accountable to nobody for the way they use resources.

†**2** Able to be computed. Only in L16.
†**3** To be counted on. E17–E18.
4 Explicable; able to be accounted *for*. M17.
■ **accountaˈbility** *noun* L18. **accountableness** *noun* M17. **accountably** *adverb* M17.

accountancy /əˈkaʊnt(ə)nsi/ *noun*. M19.
[ORIGIN from ACCOUNTANT: see -ANCY.]
The profession or duties of an accountant.
creative accountancy: see CREATIVE 1.

accountant /əˈkaʊnt(ə)nt/ *adjective* & *noun*. Also (*arch.*) **accompt-**. LME.
[ORIGIN Law French, use of pres. pple of Old French *aconter*: see ACCOUNT *verb*, -ANT[1].]
▸ †**A** *adjective*. Giving or liable to give an account. (*rare* after M17.) LME–E19.
▸ **B** *noun*. **1** A person who is accountable or responsible; LAW the defendant in an action of account. LME.
2 A professional keeper and inspector of accounts; an officer in a public office who has charge of the accounts. LME.
certified public accountant, ***chartered accountant***, etc. ***turf accountant***: see TURF *noun*.
3 *gen.* A person who reckons or calculates. *arch.* M17.
■ **accountantship** *noun* (***a***) the position or employment of an accountant; †(***b***) accountancy: M17.

accounting /əˈkaʊntɪŋ/ *noun*. LME.
[ORIGIN from ACCOUNT *verb* + -ING[1].]
1 Reckoning, counting. Now *spec.* the process or art of keeping and verifying accounts. LME.
cost accounting: see COST *noun*[2]. ***creative accounting***: see CREATIVE 1. ***current cost accounting***: see CURRENT *adjective*.
2 Foll. by *for*: giving a satisfactory explanation of, answering for. L18.

Proverb: There is no accounting for tastes.

– COMB.: **accounting period** a period of time for which accounts are presented.

†**accouple** *verb trans.* L15–M17.
[ORIGIN Old French *acopler* (mod. *accoupler*), formed as A-[5], COUPLE *verb*.]
Join (one thing) to another, couple.

accouplement /əˈkʌp(ə)lm(ə)nt/ *noun*. Now *rare*. L15.
[ORIGIN from ACCOUPLE + -MENT.]
(A) coupling, esp. in marriage.

†**accourage** *verb trans.* M–L16.
[ORIGIN Old French *aco(u)ragier* var. of *encouragier* ENCOURAGE.]
Encourage.

†**accourt** *verb trans. literary*. L16–E17.
[ORIGIN from A-[1] + COURT *verb*.]
Court.

accoutre /əˈkuːtə/ *verb trans.* Also ***-ter**. M16.
[ORIGIN Old French & mod. French *accoutrer*, formed as A-[5] + COUTURE.]
Attire, equip, esp. with special costume. Chiefly as ***accoutred*** *ppl adjective*.

accoutrement /əˈkuːtəm(ə)nt, -trə-/ *noun*. Also ***-ter-** /-tə-/. M16.
[ORIGIN French, formed as ACCOUTRE: see -MENT.]
1 *sing.* & (usu.) in *pl.* Apparel, equipment, trappings; MILITARY a soldier's outfit other than arms and garments. M16.

M. MCCARTHY A mere padded form . . on which clothes and other accoutrements were tried. I. FLEMING The usual accoutrements of a busy organization—In and Out baskets, telephones.

2 The process of accoutring or being accoutred. L16.

†**accoy** *verb trans.* LME–M17.
[ORIGIN Old French *acoier*, formed as A-[5] + COY *adjective*.]
Calm, quiet; coax; daunt.

accra /ˈakrə, əˈkrɑː/ *noun*. Also **akkra**, **akara** /əˈkarə/, & other vars. L19.
[ORIGIN Yoruba *àkàrà* bean cake.]
A W. African and W. Indian fritter made with black-eyed peas or a similar pulse. Also, a W. Indian fritter made with mashed fish.

accredit /əˈkrɛdɪt/ *verb trans.* E17.
[ORIGIN French *accréditer*, formed as A-[5] + CREDIT *noun*.]
1 Gain belief or influence for; set forth as credible; vouch for; recommend to official recognition. E17.
2 Provide (a person) with credentials; authorize as an envoy. L18.
3 Attribute *to*; credit *with*. M19.
■ **accrediˈtation** *noun* recommendation to credit or official recognition E19. **accredited** *adjective* officially recognized; generally accepted, orthodox; having guaranteed quality: M17.

†**accresce** *verb intrans.* Orig. *Scot.* M16.
[ORIGIN Latin *accrescere*, from *ad* AC- + *crescere* grow.]
1 Increase or grow by addition. M16–M18.
2 Fall or accrue *to*. L16–L19.

accrescent /əˈkrɛs(ə)nt/ *adjective*. M19.
[ORIGIN Latin *accrescent-* pres. ppl stem of *accrescere*: see ACCRESCE, -ENT.]
Growing continuously; *spec.* in BOTANY, continuing to grow after flowering.
■ **accrescence** *noun* continuous growth; an accretion: M17. **accrescency** *noun* an accretion M17.

accrete /əˈkriːt/ *verb*. L18.
[ORIGIN Latin *accret-* pa. ppl stem of *accrescere*: see ACCRESCE.]
1 *verb intrans.* Grow together, combine; grow by adhesion or coalescence of or *from* smaller bodies; adhere or become attached *to* or *on to*. L18.
2 *verb trans.* Cause to grow or unite *to*; draw or attract to oneself or itself. L19.
■ **accrete** *adjective* formed by accretion; made up, factitious: E19. **accretive** *adjective* accretionary M17.

accretion /əˈkriːʃ(ə)n/ *noun*. E17.
[ORIGIN Latin *accretio(n-)*, formed as ACCRETE: see -ION.]
1 Growth by organic enlargement. E17.

WILLIAM GIBSON The world's steady accretion of data.

2 Growth or increase by the gradual accumulation of additional layers or matter; a thing formed or added by gradual growth or increase. E17.

Harper's Magazine The slow communal accretion of coral.

3 The growing of separate things into one; the product of such growing together. M17.
4 The adhesion of external matter or things so as to cause increase. E18.
5 LAW. **a** = ACCESSION 4. M19. ▸**b** The increase of an inheritance or legacy by the addition of the share of a failing co-heir or co-legatee. L19.

– COMB.: **accretion disc** ASTRONOMY a rotating disc of matter which may form around a large star etc., esp. one in a binary system, under the influence of gravity.

■ **accretionary** *adjective* characterized or formed by accretion M19.

accroach /əˈkrəʊtʃ/ *verb*. ME.
[ORIGIN Old French *acrochier* (later *acc-*) hook in: see A-[5] and cf. Old French *croche* a hook.]
1 *verb trans.* Draw to oneself, acquire. Now *rare* or *obsolete* exc. in ***accroach to oneself***, seize what is not one's own, usurp (authority etc.). ME.
2 *verb intrans.* Encroach. *rare*. LME.
■ **accroachment** *noun* E17.

accrue /əˈkruː/ *verb*. LME.
[ORIGIN Prob. from Anglo-Norman *accru(e)*, Old French *accreu(e)* pa. pple of *acreistre* from Latin *accrescere*: see ACCRESCE.]
1 *verb intrans.* Of a benefit or sum of money: be received in regular or increasing amounts. Foll. by *to*. LME.

Time Most of the benefits . . would accrue to upper-bracket taxpayers.

2 *verb intrans.* Arise or spring (*from*, †or *by*, *of*) as a natural growth or result. Used esp. of interest on invested money and (LAW) of the coming into existence of a possible cause of action. L16.
3 *verb trans.* Orig., gather up, collect. Now, gain by increment, accumulate; *spec.* make provision for (a charge) at the end of a financial period for work that has been done but not yet invoiced. L16.

Cosmopolitan Missed payments will accrue interest at our standard variable rate.

■ **accrual** *noun* accruement; LAW = ACCRETION 6b: L19. **accruement** *noun* the action of accruing; a thing that accrues or has accrued: E17. **accruer** *noun* (LAW) = ACCRETION 6b M19.

accubation /akjʊˈbeɪʃ(ə)n/ *noun*. M17.
[ORIGIN Latin *accubatio(n-)*, from *ad* AC- + *cubat-* pa. ppl stem of *cubare* to lie: see -ATION.]
†**1** The posture of reclining, esp. at table. M–L17.
2 = ACCOUCHEMENT. *rare*. L19.

acculturation /əkʌltjʊˈreɪʃ(ə)n, -tʃə-/ *noun*. L19.
[ORIGIN from AC- + CULTURE *noun* + -ATION.]
Adoption of or adaptation to an alien culture.
■ **aˌculturaliˈzation** *noun* = ACCULTURATION M20. **aˈcculturate** *verb trans.* & *intrans.* (cause to) undergo acculturation M20. **acculturational** *adjective* M20. **aˈcculturative** *adjective* involving or producing acculturation M20. **aˌccultuurˈzation** *noun* = ACCULTURATION L20. **aˈcculturize** *verb trans.* cause to undergo acculturation L19.

accumbent /əˈkʌmbənt/ *noun* & *adjective*. M17.
[ORIGIN Latin *accumbent-* pres. ppl stem of *accumbere*, from *ad* AC- + *-cumbere*: see CUMBENT.]
▸ **A** *noun*. A person who reclines, or *gen.* is, at table. *rare*. M17.
▸ **B** *adjective*. **1** Reclining at table. *rare*. E18.
2 BOTANY. Of a cotyledon: lying edgewise against the folded radicle in the seed. Cf. INCUMBENT *adjective*. E19.

†**accumber** *verb trans.* ME–M17.
[ORIGIN Var. of ENCUMBER *verb*.]
Encumber, overwhelm, crush.

accumulate /əˈkjuːmjʊlət/ *adjective*. *arch.* M16.
[ORIGIN Latin *accumulatus* pa. pple, formed as ACCUMULATE *verb*: see -ATE[2].]
Heaped up, collected.

accumulate /əˈkjuːmjʊleɪt/ *verb*. L15.
[ORIGIN Latin *accumulat-* pa. ppl stem of *accumulare*, from *ad* AC- + *cumulus* a heap: see -ATE[3].]
1 *verb trans.* Heap up; gradually get an increasing number or quantity of; produce or acquire thus. Freq. *fig.* L15.
2 *verb trans.* Take (degrees) by accumulation. Now *rare*. L17.
3 *verb intrans.* Form an increasing mass or quantity (*lit.* & *fig.*). M18.

accumulation /əkjuːmjʊˈleɪʃ(ə)n/ *noun*. L15.
[ORIGIN Latin *accumulatio(n-)*, formed as ACCUMULATE *verb*: see -ATION. Cf. Old French & mod. French *accumulation*.]
1 The action of accumulating something. L15.
primitive accumulation, ***primitive socialist accumulation***: see PRIMITIVE *adjective* & *noun*.
2 The process of growing in amount or number; *spec.* the growth of capital by the continued addition of interest. L15.
3 An accumulated mass; a quantity formed by successive additions. L15.
4 The combination of several acts or exercises into one; *spec.* the taking of higher and lower university degrees together. M18.

accumulative /əˈkjuːmjʊlətɪv/ *adjective*. M17.
[ORIGIN from ACCUMULATE *verb* + -IVE.]
1 Arising from accumulation; cumulative. M17.
2 Given to accumulating or hoarding. E19.
3 So constituted as to accumulate. M19.
■ **accumulatively** *adverb* M17. **accumulativeness** *noun* M19.

accumulator /əˈkjuːmjʊleɪtə/ *noun*. E17.
[ORIGIN formed as ACCUMULATIVE + -OR.]
1 A person who accumulates things. E17.
2 A person who takes degrees by accumulation. L17.
3 A thing that accumulates something; *spec.* (***a***) a rechargeable electric cell, a secondary battery; (***b***) a storage register in a computer. M19.
4 A bet placed on a sequence of events, the winnings from each being staked on the next. E20.

accuracy /ˈakjʊrəsi/ *noun*. M17.
[ORIGIN from ACCURATE: see -ACY.]
1 The state of being accurate; precision, correctness. M17.
2 The degree of refinement in measurement or specification, as given by the extent of conformity with a standard or true value. Cf. PRECISION *noun* 2C. M20.

accurate /ˈakjʊrət/ *adjective*. L16.
[ORIGIN Latin *accuratus* pa. pple & adjective, from *accurare*, from *ad* AC- + *cura* care: see -ATE[2].]
1 Of a thing or a person: exact or correct, as the result of care. L16.
†**2** *gen.* Executed with care. E17–M18.
3 Of a thing: in exact conformity with a standard or with truth. M17.
■ **accurately** *adverb* with careful exactness; without error or defect: E17. **accurateness** *noun* E17.

†**accurre** *verb intrans. & trans.* M16–M17.
[ORIGIN Latin *accurrere*, from *ad* AC- + *currere* run.]
Run together, meet.

accurse /əˈkɔːs/ *verb trans. arch.* Pa. pple **accursed**, **-st**. ME.
[ORIGIN from A-[1] + CURSE *verb*.]
Utter against (a person or thing) words intended to consign their object to destruction, divine vengeance, misery, etc. (= CURSE *verb* 1).
■ **accursed** /-sɪd, -st/, **-st** *adjective* under a curse; deserving or bringing a curse or misery; execrable, detestable; (= CURSED *adjective* 1, 2, 3): ME. **accursedly** /-ɪdli/ *adverb* E17. **accursedness** /-ɪdnɪs/ *noun* L16.

†**accurtation** *noun*. L15–L18.
[ORIGIN medieval Latin *accurtatio(n-)*, from *accurtat-* pa. ppl stem of *accurtare*, from *ad* AC- + *curtus* short: see -ATION.]
= ABBREVIATION.

accusant /əˈkjuːz(ə)nt/ *noun*. Now *rare*. LME.
[ORIGIN Obsolete French, or Latin *accusant-*, *accusans* pres. pple (used as noun) of *accusare* ACCUSE: see -ANT[1].]
An accuser.

accusation /akjʊˈzeɪʃ(ə)n/ *noun*. LME.
[ORIGIN Old French from Latin *accusatio(n-)*, from *accusat-* pa. ppl stem of *accusare* ACCUSE: see -ATION.]
1 The act of accusing; the state of being accused. LME.
2 A charge of an offence or crime; an indictment. LME.

accusative /əˈkjuːzətɪv/ *adjective & noun*. LME.
[ORIGIN Old French & mod. French *accusatif*, *-ive* or Latin *accusativus* (sc. *casus* case), from *accusat-*: see ACCUSATION, -IVE.]
▸ **A** *adjective*. **1** GRAMMAR. Designating, being in, or pertaining to a case in inflected languages expressing primarily destination, hence a case expressing the object of transitive verbs (i.e. the destination of the verbal action); in uninflected languages occas. designating the relation in which the object stands. LME.
2 [from ACCUSE.] Accusatory. *rare*. LME.
▸ **B** *noun*. GRAMMAR. The accusative case; a word, form, etc. in the accusative case. LME.
accusative absolute (*a*) in German, a construction comprising an accusative noun and a predicate with no finite verb, usu. able to be construed as a modifier of the principal verb; (*b*) in English, a colloquial form of the nominative absolute construction with a pronoun in the objective case. ***cognate accusative***: see COGNATE *adjective*.
■ **accusatival** /-ˈtʌɪv(ə)l/ *adjective* pertaining to the accusative case M19. **accusatively** *adverb* M18.

accusatorial /əkjuːzəˈtɔːrɪəl/ *adjective*. E19.
[ORIGIN formed as ACCUSATORY + -AL[1].]
LAW. Of a system of criminal procedure: in which the facts are ascertained by the judge or jury from evidence presented by the prosecution and the defence. Opp. ***inquisitorial***.
■ **accusatorially** *adverb* in an accusatorial manner; by means of a formal accuser: M19.

accusatory /əˈkjuːzət(ə)ri/ *adjective*. LME.
[ORIGIN Latin *accusatorius*, from *accusat-*: see ACCUSATION, -ORY[2].]
Of the nature of an accusation; accusatorial.

accuse /əˈkjuːz/ *verb & noun*. ME.
[ORIGIN Old French *acuser*, (also mod.) *accuser* from Latin *accusare* call to account, from *ad* AC- + *causa* CAUSE *noun*.]
▸ **A** *verb trans*. **1** Charge with a fault; blame. ME.

> AV *Prov.* 30:10 Accuse not a seruant vnto his master.

2 Charge with the crime or fault *of* (†or *for*, *in*, *upon*, *with*). ME.

> M. DRABBLE You . . accused me of affectation.

3 Betray, disclose. *arch*. LME.

> MILTON This wording . . accuses the whole composure to be conscious of some other Author.

▸ †**B** *noun*. (An) accusation. LME–M17.
■ **accusable** *adjective* liable to be accused; open to an accusation *of*: E16. **accusal** *noun* (an) accusation L16. **accused** *ppl adjective & noun* (*a*) *adjective* charged with a crime or fault; (*b*) *noun the* prisoner at the bar: L15. †**accusèment** *noun* the action of accusing; an accusation: LME–E18. **accuser** *noun* a person who accuses or blames someone; *esp.* a person who accuses someone in a court of justice: ME. **accusing** *adjective* blaming, reproachful L16. **accusingly** *adverb* L16.

accustom /əˈkʌstəm/ *verb & noun*. LME.
[ORIGIN Anglo-Norman *acustumer*, Old French *acost-* (mod. *accout-*), formed as A-[5] + CUSTOM *noun*.]
▸ **A** *verb*. **1** *verb trans*. Foll. by *to*, †*with*: make (oneself or another, or a thing) used to or familiar with. LME. ▸†**b** *verb intrans*. Be wont *to*. M16–M17.

> G. B. SHAW Time to accustom myself to our new relations. V. WOOLF The eyes accustom themselves to twilight and discern the shapes of things in a room. M. MCCARTHY We accustomed him to noise. **b** EVELYN Those . . who . . accustom to wash their heads.

†**2** *verb trans*. Make customary or familiar; practise habitually. Usu. in *pass*. L15–M18.

> C. MARLOWE Such ceremonious thanks, As parting friends accustom on the shore.

†**3** *verb intrans*. Become or be familiar; mix or act familiarly. M16–L17.
†**accustom to** frequent. †**accustom with** consort or cohabit with.

▸ †**B** *noun*. Custom; habituation. LME–M17.
■ †**accustomable** *adjective* habitual, customary LME–M18. †**accustomably** *adverb* habitually, customarily LME–E19. †**accustomance** *noun* customary use or practice LME–M19. **accustomary** *adjective* (*arch*.) usual, customary M16. **accustoˈmation** *noun* (*rare*) habitual practice or use; being accustomed *to*: E17.

accustomed /əˈkʌstəmd/ *adjective*. LME.
[ORIGIN from ACCUSTOM *verb* + -ED[1].]
1 Made customary; wonted, used; usual. LME.

> SHELLEY The accustomed nightingale still broods On her accustomed bough.

accustomed to used to, in the habit of.
†**2** Frequented by customers. L17–L19.

> SMOLLETT A well accustomed shop.

■ **accustomedly** *adverb* E17. **accustomedness** *noun* M17.

AC/DC *abbreviation*.
1 Alternating current/direct current.
2 Bisexual. *slang*.

ace /eɪs/ *noun, verb, & adjective*. ME.
[ORIGIN Old French & mod. French *as* from Latin *as* unity.]
▸ **A** *noun*. **1** The 'one' on dice, later also on playing cards or dominoes; a throw of 'one', or a card etc. so marked (in some card games reckoned as of the highest value). ME. ▸**b** In tennis etc.: an unreturnable shot, now *spec.* a service that an opponent fails to touch; a point scored. E19. ▸**c** GOLF. A hole in one. E20.
AMBS-ACE. **deuce ace** [Old French] two aces at one throw (now taken as ***deuce + ace*** = 2 + 1; so ***trey ace***, ***sice ace***, etc.). **an ace up one's sleeve**, *N. Amer.* **an ace in the hole** something effective in reserve. **play one's ace** use one's best resource.
2 *fig*. A single point; a jot, a particle, an atom; a hair's breadth. E16.
bate an ace *arch*. make the slightest abatement. **within an ace of** on the very point of, within a hair's breadth of.
3 a Esp. in the First and Second World Wars: a pilot who brought down many enemy aircraft. E20. ▸**b** *gen*. A person who excels at something. E20.

> **b** P. G. WODEHOUSE George Bevan's all right. He's an ace.

– COMB.: **ace-high** *adjective* (*N. Amer. colloq.*) highly valued.
▸ **B** *verb*. **1** *verb trans*. **a** In tennis etc.: score an ace against (an opponent). L19. ▸**b** GOLF. Complete (a hole) in one stroke. M20.
2 *verb trans. & intrans*. Achieve the top grade in (an examination etc.). Also foll. by *out*. *N. Amer. slang*. M20.
ace it achieve the top grade.
▸ **C** *adjective*. First-class, excellent. *colloq*. M20.

-acean /ˈeɪʃ(ə)n/ *suffix*.
[ORIGIN from Latin *-acea* neut. pl. of *-aceus* -ACEOUS + -AN.]
Forming adjectives or nouns from names of zoological classes etc. ending in *-acea*, as ***crustacean***.

acedia /əˈsiːdɪə/ *noun*. E17.
[ORIGIN Late Latin *acedia* from Greek *akēdia*, from *a-* A-[10] + *kēdos* care, concern.]
= ACCIDIE.

Acehnese *noun & adjective* var. of ACHINESE.

Aceldama /əˈkɛldəmə, əˈsɛl-/ *noun*. M17.
[ORIGIN Greek *Akeldama* from Aramaic *ḥăqēl dĕmā* field of blood: see *Acts* 1:19.]
A field of bloodshed; a scene of slaughter.

acellular /eɪˈsɛljʊlə/ *adjective*. M20.
[ORIGIN from A-[10] + CELLULAR.]
Not divided into cells.

acentric /eɪˈsɛntrɪk/ *adjective*. M19.
[ORIGIN from A-[10] + CENTRIC.]
Without a centre.

-aceous /ˈeɪʃəs/ *suffix*.
[ORIGIN from Latin *-aceus* of the nature of, belonging to: see -EOUS, -OUS.]
Forming adjectives from Latin words in *-aceus* etc., *spec.* in BOTANY from names of plant families ending in fem. pl. form *-aceae*.

Acephali /əˈsɛfəlʌɪ, -liː/ *noun pl*. L16.
[ORIGIN medieval Latin (Isidore), pl. of *acephalus*: see ACEPHALOUS.]
1 Imaginary men or animals without heads. Now *rare* or *obsolete*. L16.
2 ECCLESIASTICAL HISTORY. Any of various Christian bodies which owned either no leader or no earthly head. L16.

acephalous /eɪˈsɛf(ə)ləs, -ˈkɛf-/ *adjective*. M18.
[ORIGIN from medieval Latin *acephalus* from Greek *akephalos*, from *a-* A-[10] + *kephalē* head: see -OUS.]
1 *gen*. Headless. M18.
2 Having or recognizing no governing head or chief. M18.
3 ZOOLOGY. Having no part of the body organized as a head. M18.
4 Lacking the beginning, as an imperfect manuscript or verse. M18.
■ **aceˈphalic** *adjective* = ACEPHALOUS M17. **acephaly** *noun* absence of a head, esp. as a congenital malformation M20.

acer /ˈeɪsə/ *noun*. L19.
[ORIGIN Latin = maple.]
A tree or shrub of the large genus *Acer*, which includes the maples and the European sycamore.

aceramic /eɪsɪˈramɪk/ *adjective*. M20.
[ORIGIN from A-[10] + CERAMIC *adjective*.]
ARCHAEOLOGY. Of a culture: having no pottery.

acerb /əˈsəːb/ *adjective*. E17.
[ORIGIN Latin *acerbus*: cf. French *acerbe*.]
= ACERBIC.
■ **acerbly** *adverb* M20.

acerbate /əˈsəːbət/ *adjective*. M19.
[ORIGIN formed as ACERBATE *verb*: see -ATE[2].]
Embittered; exasperated.

acerbate /ˈasəbeɪt/ *verb trans*. M18.
[ORIGIN Latin *acerbat-* pa. ppl stem of *acerbare*, formed as ACERB: see -ATE[3].]
Sour, embitter; exasperate.

acerbic /əˈsəːbɪk/ *adjective*. M19.
[ORIGIN formed as ACERB + -IC.]
Astringently sour, harsh-tasting; *fig.* bitter and sharp, esp. in speech, manner, or temper.
■ **acerbically** *adverb* L20.

acerbity /əˈsəːbɪti/ *noun*. L16.
[ORIGIN French *acerbité* or Latin *acerbitas*: see ACERB, -ITY.]
1 Bitterness and sharpness, keen harshness, (of character, manner, speech, etc.). L16.
2 Sourness of taste, with astringency. E17.
3 A bitter experience; a harsh or sharp comment etc. E17.

acerebral /eɪˈsɛrɪbr(ə)l/ *adjective*. M20.
[ORIGIN from A-[10] + CEREBRAL *adjective*.]
Brainless; unintelligent; unthinking.

acerose /ˈasərəʊs/ *adjective*. E18.
[ORIGIN Latin *acerosus*, from *acer-*, *acus* chaff: see -OSE[1]. In sense 2 erron. referred to *acus* needle, or *acer* sharp.]
†**1** Chaffy. Only in Dicts. E18–L19.
2 BOTANY. Needle-shaped and rigid. Now *rare*. M18.

acervation /asəˈveɪʃ(ə)n/ *noun*. L17.
[ORIGIN Latin *acervatio(n-)*, from *acervat-* pa. ppl stem of *acervare* heap up, from *acervus* heap: see -ATION.]
The action of heaping up; an accumulation.
■ **acervate** /əˈsəːvət/ *adjective* heaped, growing in clusters M19. **acervuline** /əˈsəːvjʊlʌɪn/ *adjective* in the form of little heaps M19.

acervulus /əˈsəːvjʊləs/ *noun*. Pl. **-li** /-lʌɪ, -liː/. E19.
[ORIGIN mod. Latin, dim. of Latin *acervus* heap: see -ULE.]
1 ANATOMY. In full ***acervulus cerebri*** /ˈsɛrɪbrʌɪ/. = ***brain-sand*** s.v. BRAIN *noun*. Now *rare* or *obsolete*. E19.
2 BOTANY. A flat mass of fungal conidiophores embedded in the tissue of the host plant. L19.

acescent /əˈsɛs(ə)nt/ *adjective*. M18.
[ORIGIN French, or Latin *acescent-* pres. ppl stem of *acescere* become sour: see -ESCENT.]
Turning sour; tending to turn acid; somewhat sour (*lit.* & *fig.*).
■ **acescence** *noun* the act of turning sour, acetous fermentation L17. **acescency** *noun* tendency to sourness; incipient or slight acidity: M18.

acesulfame /asɪˈsʌlfeɪm/ *noun*. L20.
[ORIGIN Uncertain; see SULF-.]
A white crystalline sulphur-containing heterocyclic compound, $C_4H_5NO_4S$, used as a low-calorie artificial sweetener, esp. in the form of a potassium salt (***acesulfame-K***).

acet- *combining form* see ACETO-.

acetable /ˈasɪtəb(ə)l/ *noun*. Now *rare* or *obsolete*. L15.
[ORIGIN formed as ACETABULUM.]
= ACETABULUM.

acetabulum /asɪˈtabjʊləm/ *noun*. Pl. **-la** /-lə/. LME.
[ORIGIN Latin, from *acetum* vinegar + *-abulum* denoting a container.]
1 ROMAN ANTIQUITIES. A cup to hold vinegar at table; a liquid measure of the capacity of such a cup. LME.
2 ANATOMY. **a** The socket of the hip bone, with which the head of the femur articulates. L16. ▸**b** A sucker possessed by some cephalopods, trematodes, etc. M17.

acetal /ˈasɪtal/ *noun*. M19.
[ORIGIN from ACET(IC + -AL[2].]
CHEMISTRY. **1** An odoriferous liquid, $CH_3CH(OC_2H_5)_2$, formed by reaction of acetaldehyde and ethyl alcohol. Also, any other compound with one hydrogen atom and two alkoxy groups attached to the same carbon atom. Also *gen.* = KETAL. M19.
2 = POLYOXYMETHYLENE. M20.

acetaldehyde /asɪtˈaldɪhʌɪd/ *noun*. M19.
[ORIGIN from ACET(IC + ALDEHYDE.]
CHEMISTRY. A volatile pungent liquid, CH_3CHO, obtained by the oxidation of ethyl alcohol; ethanal.

acetamide /əˈsiːtəmʌɪd, əˈsɛt-/ *noun*. M19.
[ORIGIN from ACET(YL + AMIDE.]
CHEMISTRY. The amide of acetic acid, a crystalline solid, CH_3CONH_2; ethanamide.

acetanilide /asɪtˈanɪlʌɪd/ *noun*. M19.
[ORIGIN from ACET(YL + ANIL(INE + -IDE.]
CHEMISTRY. A crystalline solid, $C_6H_5NHCOCH_3$, obtained by acetylation of aniline.

acetate /ˈasɪteɪt/ *noun*. **L18**.
[ORIGIN from ACET(IC + -ATE¹.]
1 *CHEMISTRY*. A salt or ester of acetic acid. **L18**.
2 The cellulose ester of acetic acid, in the form of an artificial fibre or a plastic. **E20**. ▸**b** A disc coated with cellulose acetate, for direct recording by a cutting stylus; any direct-cut disc. **M20**. ▸**c** A clear plastic film of cellulose acetate, used in photography, as a display medium, etc.; a sheet of this. **M20**.
attrib.: ***acetate fibre***, ***acetate rayon***, ***acetate silk***, etc.

acetic /əˈsiːtɪk, əˈsɛt-/ *adjective*. **L18**.
[ORIGIN French *acétique*, from Latin *acetum* vinegar: see -IC.]
1 *CHEMISTRY*. ***acetic acid***, a weak acid, CH_3COOH, of which vinegar is a crude dilute solution, and which when pure and anhydrous (***glacial acetic acid***) can be obtained as colourless crystals melting at 16.7°C; ethanoic acid. **L18**.
2 Pertaining to or producing acetic acid. **L19**.
acetic anhydride a liquid, $(CH_3CO)_2O$, the anhydride of acetic acid.

acetify /əˈsɛtɪfʌɪ, əˈsiːt-/ *verb trans*. **M19**.
[ORIGIN from Latin *acetum* vinegar + -I- + -FY.]
Subject to fermentation producing acetic acid; convert into vinegar.
■ **acetifiˈcation** *noun* the process of acetifying **M18**. **acetifier** *noun* an apparatus in which vinegar is produced **M19**.

aceto- /əˈsiːtəʊ, ˈasɪtəʊ/ *combining form* of ACETIC, ACETYL: see -O-. Before a vowel also **acet-**.
■ **acetoaˈcetic** *adjective*: ***acetoacetic acid***, an acid, CH_3COCH_2COOH, present in the urine of diabetics, and when pure a viscous unstable liquid **L19**. **acetoˈacetate** *noun* a salt or ester of this acid **L19**. **acetoˈnitrile**, †**-il** *noun* a toxic odoriferous liquid, CH_3CN; methyl cyanide: **M19**.

acetobacter /əˌsiːtə(ʊ)ˈbaktə, asɪ-/ *noun*. **M20**.
[ORIGIN mod. Latin (see below), formed as ACETO- + BACTER(IUM.]
A bacterium that oxidizes organic compounds to acetic acid (as in vinegar formation), *esp*. one of the genus *Acetobacter*.

acetogenic /əˌsiːtə(ʊ)ˈdʒɛnɪk, asɪt-/ *adjective*. **L20**.
[ORIGIN from ACETO- + -GENIC.]
MICROBIOLOGY. Forming or producing acetic acid, esp. as a metabolic by-product.

acetone /ˈasɪtəʊn/ *noun*. **M19**.
[ORIGIN from ACET(IC + -ONE.]
CHEMISTRY. A fragrant volatile liquid ketone, CH_3COCH_3, obtained chiefly by the dehydrogenation of isopropyl alcohol and widely used as a solvent; propanone.
■ **acetoˈnaemia** *noun* (*MEDICINE*) = KETOSIS **M19**. **acetoˈnuria** *noun* (*MEDICINE*) = KETONURIA **L19**.

acetous /əˈsiːtəs/ *adjective*. **LME**.
[ORIGIN from late Latin *acetosus*, from *acetum* vinegar: see -OUS.]
Having the qualities of vinegar; producing vinegar; sour.
– NOTE: Rare before **L18**.

acetyl /ˈasɪtʌɪl, -tɪl/ *noun*. **M19**.
[ORIGIN from ACET(IC + -YL.]
CHEMISTRY. The radical $\cdot COCH_3$, derived from acetic acid. Usu. in *comb*.
– COMB.: **acetylcholine** the acetyl ester of choline and a major neurotransmitter; ***acetylcholinesterase***, a cholinesterase that causes rapid hydrolysis of acetylcholine after transmission of an impulse; **acetyl coenzyme A** the acetyl ester of coenzyme A, involved as an acetylating agent in many biochemical processes; abbreviation ***acetyl CoA***; **acetylsalicylic acid** the acetyl derivative of salicylic acid, $C_9H_8O_4$ (cf. ASPIRIN); **acetyl silk** acetate silk.

acetylation /əsɛtɪˈleɪʃ(ə)n/ *noun*. **L19**.
[ORIGIN from ACETYL + -ATION.]
CHEMISTRY. A reaction or process in which one or more acetyl groups are introduced into a molecule.
■ **aˈcetylate** *verb trans*. subject (a compound) to acetylation **L19**. **aˈcetylator** *noun* (*BIOCHEMISTRY*) an individual capable of metabolic acetylation (at a specified characteristic rate) **M20**.

acetylene /əˈsɛtɪliːn/ *noun*. **M19**.
[ORIGIN formed as ACETYLATION + -ENE.]
CHEMISTRY. A gaseous hydrocarbon, C_2H_2, which burns with a bright flame, used in welding and (esp. formerly) for illumination; ethyne.
■ **acetyˈlenic** *adjective* containing the carbon–carbon triple bond characteristic of acetylene and the alkynes **L19**. **acetylide** *noun* a saltlike derivative of acetylene formed by replacement of one or both of the hydrogen atoms by a metal **M19**.

ach /ɑːx, *foreign* ax/ *interjection*. **L15**.
[ORIGIN Celtic, German, & Dutch.]
Ah!

Achaean /əˈkiːən/ *adjective & noun*. Also **Achaian** /əˈkʌɪən/. **M16**.
[ORIGIN from Latin *Achaeus* from Greek *Akhaios*, from *Akhaia* Achaea, + -AN.]
Of or pertaining to, a native or inhabitant of, Achaea (in Homer a name of Greece generally, later a district of the Peloponnese).

Achaemenian /akɪˈmiːnɪən/ *adjective & noun*. **E18**.
[ORIGIN from Latin *Achaemenius*, from Greek *Akhaimenēs* Achaemenes, reputed ancestor of Cyrus: see -IAN.]
Of or pertaining to, a member of, the dynasty that ruled in ancient Persia from the time of Cyrus the Great (d. 529 BC) until the death of Darius III (330 BC).
■ Also **Achaemenid** /əˈkiːmənɪd/ *adjective & noun* [-ID³] **E20**.

Achaian *adjective & noun* var. of ACHAEAN.

achalasia /akəˈleɪzjə/ *noun*. **E20**.
[ORIGIN from A-¹⁰ + Greek *khalasis*, from *khalan* relax: see -IA¹.]
PHYSIOLOGY. Failure of the muscles of the lower part of the oesophagus to relax, which prevents food from passing into the stomach.

achar /əˈtʃɑː/ *noun*. **L16**.
[ORIGIN Ult. from Persian *āchār*.]
Pickles, as prepared in the Indian subcontinent.

†**a-char** *adverb & pred. adjective* var. of AJAR *adverb*¹ *& pred. adjective*¹.

acharnement /aʃarnəmɑ̃, əˈʃɑːnmɒ̃/ *noun*. **M18**.
[ORIGIN French, from *acharner* give a taste of flesh (to dogs etc.): see -MENT.]
Bloodthirsty fury; ferocity; gusto.

acharya /ɑːˈtʃɑːrjə/ *noun*. **E19**.
[ORIGIN Sanskrit *ācārya* master, teacher.]
In the Indian subcontinent, (a title given to) a spiritual teacher or leader; *transf*. an influential mentor.

achate /ˈakət/ *noun*¹. *arch*. **ME**.
[ORIGIN Old French *ac(h)ate* from Latin *achates*: see AGATE *noun*.]
An agate.

†**achate** *noun*² var. of ACATE.

†**achater** *noun* var. of ACATOUR.

Achates /əˈkeɪtiːz/ *noun*. *literary*. **L16**.
[ORIGIN The faithful friend of Aeneas (Virgil *Aeneid* VI. 158 etc.).]
A devoted follower; a loyal friend and companion. Also FIDUS ACHATES.

†**achatour**, **achatry** *nouns* see ACATOUR.

ache /eɪk/ *noun*¹.
[ORIGIN Old English *æce*, from ACHE *verb*: see note below.]
A continuous or prolonged dull pain, physical or mental.
aches and pains minor ailments and physical discomforts.
– NOTE: See note s.v. ACHE *verb*.

†**ache** *noun*². **ME–E17**.
[ORIGIN Old French & mod. French from Latin *apium* parsley, from *apis* bee (attracted to the plant).]
Smallage; parsley.

†**ache** *noun*³ var. of AITCH.

ache /eɪk/ *verb intrans*. Also (*arch*.) **ake**.
[ORIGIN Old English *acan*, corresp. to forms in West Germanic; possible cognates in other Indo-European langs. are Greek *agos* sin, guilt, Sanskrit *āgas*. See note below.]
1 Suffer or be the source of continuous or prolonged dull pain or mental distress. **OE**.
> S. RICHARDSON Does not your heart ake for your Harriet? T. SHARPE The joints in his knees ached.

2 Feel an intense desire for. **L18**.
> SHERWOOD ANDERSON I ached to see that race.

– NOTE: Historically the verb is *ake*, the noun *ache*. The noun was formerly pronunc. /-tʃ/ (cf. other noun/verb pairs such as *bake/batch* and *speak/speech*). This pronunc. was prevalent until **E19**, though the noun began to be confused with the verb as /-k/ about 1700. Dr Johnson is mainly responsible for the mod. spellings, as he erroneously derived them from Greek *akhos* 'pain' and declared them 'more grammatically written *ache*'.
■ **achingly** *adverb* so as to cause continuous dull pain **M19**.

achene /əˈkiːn/ *noun*. **M19**.
[ORIGIN from mod. Latin *achaenium*, irreg. from Greek *a-* A-¹⁰ + *khainein* gape.]
BOTANY. A small dry one-seeded fruit which does not open to liberate the seed.

Acheron /ˈakərɒn/ *noun*. **E16**.
[ORIGIN Latin *Acheron(t-)* from Greek *Akherōn*.]
In Greek mythology, one of the rivers of Hades; the infernal regions.
■ **Acheˈrontic** *adjective* of or pertaining to Acheron, infernal; gloomy; on the brink of death: **L16**.

Acheulian /əˈʃuːlɪən/ *adjective & noun*. Also **-ean**. **E20**.
[ORIGIN French *Acheuléen*, from St-*Acheul* near Amiens, France.]
(The culture or industry) of an early Palaeolithic period in Europe, the Middle East, Africa, and India, preceding the Mousterian, and distinguished in particular by the manufacture of stone hand axes.

à cheval /a ʃəval, ɑː ʃəˈvɑːl/ *adverbial phr*. **M19**.
[ORIGIN French = on horseback.]
With one foot on each side; in command of two lines of communication; with a stake risked equally on two chances.

achieve /əˈtʃiːv/ *verb*. **ME**.
[ORIGIN Old French & mod. French *achever* come or bring to a head or end, from phr. *a chief*: see A-⁵, CHIEF *noun*.]
1 *verb trans*. Accomplish; carry out successfully. **ME**.
> A. NEWMAN She had achieved a lot in the last twenty-four hours. DAY LEWIS Insurgents who have achieved a revolution before one has even suspected a conspiracy.

†**2** *verb trans*. Finish, terminate. **LME–L16**.
> SHAKES. *Hen. V* Bid them achieve me, and then sell my bones.

†**3** *verb intrans*. Come to an end; result, turn out. **LME–M16**.
> LD BERNERS All your busynes shall acheue the better.

4 *verb trans*. Succeed in gaining; acquire by effort; reach (an end etc.). **LME**.
> SHAKES. *Twel. N.* Some are born great, some achieve greatness. S. GIBBONS All the ingredients for success were present, and success was achieved.

5 *verb intrans*. **a** Be successful; attain a desired end or level of performance. **L15**. ▸†**b** Attain successfully *to*. **L15–L16**.
> **a** *Church Times* Intelligent people . . who had not achieved academically.

■ **achievaˈbility** *noun* the quality or state of being achievable **E20**. **achievable** *adjective* able to be achieved **M17**. **achiever** *noun* **L16**.

achievement /əˈtʃiːvm(ə)nt/ *noun*. **L15**.
[ORIGIN from ACHIEVE + -MENT or from Old French & mod. French *achèvement*.]
1 Completion, accomplishment. **L15**.
2 *HERALDRY*. Orig., an escutcheon or armorial device, *esp*. one granted in memory of a distinguished feat; also = HATCHMENT. Now, a representation of all the armorial devices to which a bearer of arms is entitled. **L16**.
3 Something achieved; a feat. **L16**.
– COMB.: **achievement motivation** motivation to attain a desired end or level of performance, competitiveness.

achillea /akɪˈliːə, aˈkɪlɪə/ *noun*. **L16**.
[ORIGIN Latin *achillea*, *-eos* from Greek *Akhilleios* a plant supposed to have been used medicinally by Achilles (see ACHILLES).]
Any of various plants of the genus *Achillea*, of the composite family, with flower heads usually in corymbs; *spec*. a common garden perennial, *A. filipendulina*, with yellow flower heads on tall stems. Cf. MILFOIL, ***sneezewort*** s.v. SNEEZE, YARROW.

Achilles /əˈkɪliːz/ *noun*. **E17**.
[ORIGIN Latin from Greek *Akhilleus*, a hero in Homer's *Iliad*, invulnerable except in the heel.]
A person like Achilles in point of valour, invulnerability, etc.
– COMB.: **Achilles heel**, **Achilles' heel** a person's only vulnerable spot, a weak point; **Achilles tendon** the tendon attaching the heel to the calf muscles.
■ **Achillean** *adjective* resembling Achilles, invulnerable **L16**.

achimenes /əˈkɪmənɪːz/ *noun*. Pl. same. **M19**.
[ORIGIN mod. Latin (see below) from Greek *akhaimenis* a kind of plant.]
Any of various herbaceous perennial plants of the Central American genus *Achimenes* (family Gesneriaceae), cultivated for their tubular or trumpet-shaped flowers.

Achinese /atʃəˈniːz/ *noun & adjective*. Also **Acehnese**. **L17**.
[ORIGIN from *Acheh*, *Aceh* a territory in northern Sumatra + *-n-* + -ESE.]
▸ **A** *noun*. Pl. same.
1 A member of a Muslim people of northern Sumatra. **L17**.
2 The Austronesian language of this people. **L19**.
▸ **B** *adjective*. Of or pertaining to the Achinese or their language. **L18**.

achiote /atʃɪˈɒti/ *noun*. **M17**.
[ORIGIN Spanish from Nahuatl *achiotl*.]
= ANNATTO.

achiral /eɪˈkʌɪər(ə)l/ *adjective*. **M20**.
[ORIGIN from A-¹⁰ + CHIRAL.]
Of a crystal, molecule, etc.: superposable on its mirror image.
■ **achiˈrality** *noun* **L20**.

achkan /ˈatʃk(ə)n/ *noun*. **E20**.
[ORIGIN Hindi *ackan*.]
A knee-length coat, buttoned in front, worn by men in the Indian subcontinent.

achlamydeous /akləˈmɪdɪəs/ *adjective*. **M19**.
[ORIGIN from A-¹⁰ + Greek *khlamud-*, *khlamus* cloak + -EOUS.]
BOTANY. Of a flower: lacking both calyx and corolla.

achlorhydria /eɪklɔːˈhʌɪdrɪə, a-/ *noun*. **L19**.
[ORIGIN from A-¹⁰ + CHLOR-¹ + HYDRO- + -IA¹.]
MEDICINE. Absence of hydrochloric acid in the gastric secretions.
■ **achlorhydric** *adjective* exhibiting achlorhydria **M20**.

achlorophyllous /eɪklɔːˈrɒfɪləs/ *adjective*. **L19**.
[ORIGIN from A-¹⁰ + CHLOROPHYLLOUS.]
BOTANY. Lacking chlorophyll.

Acholi /əˈtʃəʊli/ *noun & adjective*. Also †**Shooli**. **L19**.
[ORIGIN Acholi.]
▸ **A** *noun*. Pl. same. A member of a farming and pastoral people of northern Uganda and southern Sudan; the Nilotic language of this people. **L19**.
▸ **B** *adjective*. Of or pertaining to the Acholi or their language. **L19**.

acholuric /akəˈljʊərɪk, eɪ-/ *adjective*. **E20**.
[ORIGIN French *acholurique*, from Greek *kholē* bile: see A-¹⁰, -URIC.]
MEDICINE. Designating a form of jaundice characterized by the absence of bile pigments in the urine.

achondrite /əˈkɒndrʌɪt/ *noun*. **E20**.
[ORIGIN from A-¹⁰ + CHONDRITE.]
A stony meteorite containing no chondrules.
■ **achondritic** /akɒnˈdrɪtɪk/ *adjective* **E20**.

achondroplasia /əkɒndrəˈpleɪzjə, eɪˌkɒn-/ *noun*. **L19.**
[ORIGIN from Greek *akhondros*, from *a-* A-[10] + *khondros* cartilage: see -PLASIA.]
MEDICINE. A hereditary disease in which bone growth by production and ossification of cartilage at the epiphyses of the long bones is retarded, and which results in a form of dwarfism, with short limbs, a normal trunk, and a small face.
■ **achondroplasiac**, **achondroplasic**, **achondroplastic** *adjectives & nouns* (**a**) *adjective* affected with or pertaining to achondroplasia; (**b**) *noun* a person with achondroplasia: **E20.**

achromatic /akrəʊˈmatɪk/ *adjective & noun*. **L18.**
[ORIGIN French *achromatique*, formed as A-[10], CHROMATIC.]
▶ **A** *adjective*. Free from colour; transmitting light without decomposing it into its constituent colours. **L18.**
▶ **B** *noun*. An achromatic lens. **L18.**
■ ˈ**achromat** *noun* [-AT[2]] an achromatic lens **E20.** **achromatically** *adverb* **M19.** ˌ**achromaˈticity** *noun* **M19.** **aˈchromatism** *noun* the quality of being achromatic **L18.** **aˈchromatize** *verb trans.* make achromatic **M19.**

achromatopsia /ˌeɪkrəʊməˈtɒpsɪə, ˌa-/ *noun*. Also **-psy** /-psi/. **M19.**
[ORIGIN from Greek *akhrōmatos* without colour (*khrōmat-*, *khrōma* colour) + *-opsia*, from *opsis* sight: see A-[10], -IA[1], -Y[3].]
MEDICINE. Total colour blindness.
■ **achromatopsic** *adjective & noun* (**a**) *adjective* pertaining to or exhibiting achromatopsia; (**b**) *noun* a person with achromatopsia: **L20.**

achromatous /eɪˈkrəʊmətəs/ *adjective*. *rare*. **L19.**
[ORIGIN formed as ACHROMATOPSIA + -OUS.]
Colourless; *esp.* lacking the normal colour.

achromic /eɪˈkrəʊmɪk/ *adjective*. *rare*. **M18.**
[ORIGIN from A-[10] + Greek *khrōma* colour + -IC.]
Free from colour; having no colour except black, white, or intermediate shades of grey.

achronical *adjective* see ACRONYCHAL.

achronological /ˌeɪkrɒnəˈlɒdʒɪk(ə)l/ *adjective*. **L20.**
[ORIGIN from A-[10] + CHRONOLOGICAL.]
Not following chronological order, = UNCHRONOLOGICAL 1.

achy /ˈeɪki/ *adjective*. Also **-ey**. **L19.**
[ORIGIN from ACHE *noun*[1] + -Y[1].]
Full of or suffering from aches.
■ **achiness** *noun* **L20.**

achylia /əˈkʌɪlɪə/ *noun*. **L19.**
[ORIGIN mod. Latin, from Greek *akhulos*, from *a-* A-[10] + *khulos* juice, chyle, + -IA[1].]
MEDICINE. Freq. more fully ***achylia gastrica*** /ˈgastrɪkə/. Absence of gastric secretion.

acicula /əˈsɪkjʊlə/ *noun*. Pl. **-lae** /-liː/, **-las**. Also **-lum** /-ləm/, pl. **-la** /-lə/; **-lus** /-ləs/, pl. **-li** /-lʌɪ, -liː/; & anglicized (esp. *BOTANY*) as **acicle** /ˈasɪk(ə)l/. **M19.**
[ORIGIN Late Latin, dim. of *acus* needle: see -CULE.]
BOTANY & ZOOLOGY. A slender needle-like structure, such as a spine or prickle.

acicular /əˈsɪkjʊlə/ *adjective*. **E18.**
[ORIGIN formed as ACICULA + -AR[1].]
Needle-like (esp. of crystals).
■ **aciculˈlarity** *noun* **M20.** **acicularly** *adverb* in needle-like forms **E18.**

aciculate /əˈsɪkjʊlət/ *adjective*. **M19.**
[ORIGIN formed as ACICULA + -ATE[2].]
Covered with aciculae; marked or striated as if with a needle. Also = ACICULAR.

aciculum *noun* see ACICULA.

acid /ˈasɪd/ *noun*. **L17.**
[ORIGIN from the adjective.]
1 A sour substance; *spec.* in *CHEMISTRY*, any of a large class of substances that contain hydrogen replaceable by metals, and neutralize and are neutralized by alkalis, the most familiar examples being sour corrosive liquids able to dissolve metals. Also, in mod. use, any species capable of donating protons or of accepting pairs of electrons. **L17.**
nitric acid, ***oxalic acid***, ***phosphoric acid***, etc. ***acid of sugar***: see SUGAR *noun & adjective*. **come the acid** *slang* be unpleasant or offensive, speak in a caustic or sarcastic manner. ***conjugate acid***: see CONJUGATE *adjective*. **put the acid on** *Austral. & NZ slang* seek to extract a loan, favour, etc., from.
2 The drug LSD. *slang*. **M20.**
– COMB.: **acid-head** *slang* a user of the drug LSD; **acid house** a kind of popular synthesized dance music with a fast repetitive beat, popular in the 1980s and associated with the taking of drugs such as Ecstasy; **acid jazz** a kind of popular dance music incorporating elements of jazz, funk, soul, and hip hop; **acid rock** a type of rock music associated with the taking of hallucinogenic drugs; **acid test** a test for gold which involves nitric acid; *fig.* a crucial test.
■ **aciˈdaemia** *noun* (*MEDICINE*) a condition of abnormally low pH of the blood **E20.** **aˈcidophil(e)**, **aˌcidoˈphilic**, **aciˈdophilous** *adjectives* readily stained with acid dyes; growing best in acid conditions: **E20.** **acidy** *adjective* resembling or suggestive of acid, somewhat acid, esp. in taste **M20.**

acid /ˈasɪd/ *adjective*. **E17.**
[ORIGIN French *acide* or Latin *acidus*, from *acere* be sour.]
1 Sour, tart, sharp to the taste; tasting like vinegar. **E17.** ▸**b** *fig.* Biting, severe, unpleasant. **L18.** ▸**c** Of a colour: intense. **E20.**

> **b** DISRAELI Rather an acid expression of countenance. W. S. MAUGHAM He had a certain acid humour. **c** D. H. LAWRENCE You acid-blue metallic bird.

acid drop a kind of sweet with an acid taste.
2 *CHEMISTRY.* Having the essential properties of an acid; derived from or characteristic of an acid. **E18.**
acid air air containing a high proportion of acidic pollutants. ***acid AMIDE***. **acid dye** a dye which is a metallic salt of an acid and is usu. applied in an acid medium or as a cytological strain. **acid rain** rain made acidic by atmospheric pollution. **acid salt** a salt derived from an acid by incomplete exchange of the replaceable hydrogen. ***acid tide***: see TIDE *noun*.
3 *GEOLOGY.* Of an igneous rock: rich in silica. **L19.** ▸**b** *METALLURGY.* Pertaining to, resulting from, or designating steel-making processes involving silica-rich refractories and slags. **L19.**
– NOTE: In techn. senses opp. BASIC *adjective*.
■ **acidly** *adverb* sourly **L19.** **acidness** *noun* **M17.**

acidic /əˈsɪdɪk/ *adjective*. **L19.**
[ORIGIN from ACID *noun* + -IC.]
1 *GEOLOGY.* = ACID *adjective* 3. **L19.**
2 *CHEMISTRY.* Of, pertaining to, or having the properties of an acid; having a pH lower than 7. **L19.**

acidify /əˈsɪdɪfʌɪ/ *verb trans.* **L18.**
[ORIGIN formed as ACIDIC + -I- + -FY.]
Convert into an acid (now *rare*); make acid; add acid to.
■ **aˌcidifiˈcation** *noun* the act or process of acidifying **L18.**

acidimetry /asɪˈdɪmɪtri/ *noun*. **M19.**
[ORIGIN formed as ACIDIC + -I- + -METRY.]
CHEMISTRY. The measurement of the strengths of acids.
■ †**acidimeter** *noun* an instrument for acidimetry **M–L19.** **aˌcidiˈmetric**, **aˌcidiˈmetrical** *adjectives* of or pertaining to acidimetry **M19.**

acidise *verb* var. of ACIDIZE.

acidity /əˈsɪdɪti/ *noun*. **E17.**
[ORIGIN French *acidité* or late Latin *aciditas*: see ACID *adjective, noun*, -ITY.]
1 The quality, state, or degree of being acid (*lit. & fig.*). **E17.**

> W. S. MAUGHAM The vicar answered with some acidity.

2 Excess of acid in the stomach. **M18.**

acidize /ˈasɪdʌɪz/ *verb trans.* Also **-ise**. **E20.**
[ORIGIN from ACID *noun* + -IZE.]
Treat with acid; *spec.* pump acid into (an oil well) as a means of stimulating flow.
■ **acidiˈzation** *noun* **M20.**

acidosis /asɪˈdəʊsɪs/ *noun*. Pl. **-doses** /-ˈdəʊsiːz/. **E20.**
[ORIGIN from ACID *noun* + -OSIS.]
MEDICINE. A condition of abnormally low pH of the body fluids.
■ **acidotic** /asɪˈdɒtɪk/ *adjective* **E20.**

acidulate /əˈsɪdjʊleɪt/ *verb trans.* **M18.**
[ORIGIN formed as ACIDULOUS + -ATE[3].]
Make somewhat acid or sour; flavour with an acid.

> *fig.*: LD MACAULAY Scarcely any compliment not acidulated with scorn.

■ **aciduˈlation** *noun* the process or state of being acidulated **M19.**

acidulous /əˈsɪdjʊləs/ *adjective*. **M18.**
[ORIGIN from Latin *acidulus*, from *acidus* sour: see ACID *adjective*, -ULOUS.]
Somewhat sour or acid (*lit. & fig.*).

> CARLYLE He becomes . . gloomy and acidulous.

■ **acidulent** *adjective* = ACIDULOUS **M19.** **acidulously** *adverb* **L19.**

aciduria /asɪˈdjʊərɪə/ *noun*. **M20.**
[ORIGIN from ACID *noun* + -URIA.]
MEDICINE. The presence of excessive acid in the urine.

acinaciform /asɪˈnasɪfɔːm, əˈsɪnə-/ *adjective*. **M18.**
[ORIGIN mod. Latin *acinaciformis*, from Greek *akinakēs* scimitar: see -FORM.]
Chiefly *BOTANY*. Scimitar-shaped.

acinus /ˈasɪnəs/ *noun*. Pl. **-ni** /-nʌɪ/. **M18.**
[ORIGIN Latin = berry growing in a cluster, kernel.]
1 *BOTANY.* A small berry growing in a cluster or as part of a compound fruit; a seed of such a berry. Now *rare* or *obsolete*. **M18.**
2 *ANATOMY.* Any of a number of small rounded terminal sacs in a gland, the cells of whose walls secrete into the central cavity; the small portion of lung tissue served by a single terminal bronchiole. **M18.**
■ **acinar** *adjective* = ACINOUS **M20.** **aˈciniform** *adjective* resembling a grape or a bunch of grapes **M19.** **acinous** *adjective* (*ANATOMY*) consisting of or pertaining to acini **M19.**

-acious /ˈeɪʃəs/ *suffix*.
[ORIGIN Repr. French *-acieux*, or from Latin *-acis*, *-ax* added chiefly to verbal stems to form adjectives + -OUS.]
Forming adjectives meaning 'given to, inclined to' or 'having much', as ***audacious***, ***pugnacious***, ***vivacious***.

-acity /ˈasɪti/ *suffix*.
[ORIGIN French *-acité* or its source Latin *-acitas*, *-tatis*: see -ACIOUS, -TY[1].]
Forming nouns of quality corresp. to adjectives in -ACIOUS.

ack /ak/ *noun*. **L19.**
hist. Arbitrary syllable used for the letter *a* in spoken telephone communications and in the oral spelling of messages.
ack-ack [= *AA*] anti-aircraft (gunfire, regiment, etc.). **ack emma** [= *a.m.*] ante meridiem; air mechanic.

†**-ack** *suffix* var. of -AC.

ackee /ˈaki/ *noun*. Also **akee**. **L18.**
[ORIGIN Prob. from a Kru lang.]
The fruit, edible when cooked, of the tree *Blighia sapida*, native to W. Africa and introduced elsewhere, esp. in the W. Indies; the tree itself.

ackers /ˈakəz/ *noun pl. slang* (orig. *MILITARY*). **M20.**
[ORIGIN Prob. alt. of PIASTRE: orig. used by Brit. and allied troops in Egypt.]
Coins, notes, money; *spec.* piastres.

†**acknow** *verb trans.* Infl. as KNOW *verb*. **OE.**
[ORIGIN from A *preposition*[1] + KNOW *verb*: for the spelling with *ac-* see AC-.]
1 Recognize. **OE–LME.**
2 Acknowledge, confess, (*that*). (*dial.* after **16.**) **OE–M19.**
3 ***be acknown***, be (self-)recognized in relation to anything, avow or confess (*to* a person). **ME–M17.**
– NOTE: Rare after **OE** exc. as *acknown* pa. pple.

acknowledge /əkˈnɒlɪdʒ/ *verb trans.* **L15.**
[ORIGIN Prob. from KNOWLEDGE *verb* on the analogy of the relation of ACKNOW and KNOW *verb*: see AC-.]
1 Recognize or confess (a person or thing to be something); own the claims or authority of. **L15.**

> AV *Wisd.* 12:27 They acknowledged him to be the true God. T. DREISER I acknowledge the Furies, I believe in them.

acknowledge the corn: see CORN *noun*[1].
2 Own with gratitude or as an obligation. **E17.** ▸**b** Announce receipt of (a letter etc.). **M17.** ▸**c** Register recognition of; take notice of. **L19.**

> **c** J. HELLER He acknowledged with a surly nod the greetings of his colleagues.

3 Own the knowledge of; confess; admit the truth of. **M17.**

> SHAKES. *Much Ado* He loved . . your daughter, and meant to acknowledge it this night.

4 Own as genuine, or valid in law; avow or assent to, in legal form. **L19.**
■ **acknowledgeable** *adjective* **M19.** **acknowledged** *ppl adjective* recognized; admitted as true, valid, or authoritative: **L16.** **acknowledgedly** *adverb* **M17.** **acknowledger** *noun* **M16.**

acknowledgement /əkˈnɒlɪdʒm(ə)nt/ *noun*. Also **-dgm-**. **L16.**
[ORIGIN from ACKNOWLEDGE + -MENT.]
1 The act of admitting or confessing; avowal. **L16.**

> SHAKES. *Hen. V* With this acknowledgement, That God fought for us.

2 The act of recognizing the authority or claims of. **L16.**

> JAS. MILL All such places as owe acknowledgement to the Dutch.

3 The owning or due recognition of a gift or benefit received, or of a message etc.; something given or done in return for a favour or message; (esp. in *pl.*) an author's statement of indebtedness to others. **E17.**

> H. E. BATES She waited at the door for a word of acknowledgement, of thanks, of simple recognition, for the things she had done. JOYCE General applause. Edward the Seventh lifts the bucket graciously in acknowledgement.

4 A declaration or avowal of an act or document so as to give it legal validity. **M17.**

aclinic /əˈklɪnɪk/ *adjective*. Now *rare*. **M19.**
[ORIGIN from Greek *aklinēs*, from *a-* A-[10] + *klinein* to bend, lean + -IC.]
aclinic line, = ***magnetic*** EQUATOR.

†**a clock** *adverb* see O'CLOCK.

ACLU *abbreviation*.
American Civil Liberties Union.

acme /ˈakmi/ *noun*. **L16.**
[ORIGIN Greek *akmē* highest point. Long consciously used as a Greek word and written in Greek letters.]
1 *gen.* The highest point; the point or period of perfection. **L16.**
2 *spec.* ▸†**a** The period of full growth; the flower or full bloom of life. **L16–M19.** ▸**b** The crisis of an illness. *arch.* **M17.**

acmite /ˈakmʌɪt/ *noun*. **M19.**
[ORIGIN formed as ACME + -ITE[1].]
MINERALOGY. A variety of aegirine having pointed crystal terminations.

acne /ˈakni/ *noun*. **M19.**
[ORIGIN Erron. Greek *aknas*, a misreading for *akmas* accus. pl. of *akmē* facial eruption, ACME.]
Severe seborrhoea complicated by pustule formation in the hair follicles, esp. of the face.
acne ROSACEA.
■ **acned** *adjective* (*colloq.*) afflicted with acne **M20.**

A

acock /ə'kɒk/ *adverb & pred. adjective*. E19.
[ORIGIN from A-[2] + COCK *noun*[1] or *verb*[1].]
Turned upward; cocked.

fig.: J. FOWLES What had really knocked him a-cock was Mary's innocence.

a-cock-bill *adverb* see COCK-BILL *noun*.

a-cock-horse /ə'kɒkhɔːs, əkɒk'hɔːs/ *adverb*. M16.
[ORIGIN from A *preposition*[1] 1 + COCK-HORSE.]
1 Mounted (as) on a cock-horse; astride; = COCK-HORSE *adverb*. M16.
†**2** In an exalted position, in a place of triumph. M17–E19.

acoelomate /ə'siːləmeɪt/ *adjective*. L19.
[ORIGIN from A-[10] + COELOMATE.]
ZOOLOGY. Lacking a coelom.

Acol /'akɒl/ *noun*. M20.
[ORIGIN *Acol* Road, Hampstead, London, the address of a bridge club in which the system was devised.]
BRIDGE. A commonly used British system of bidding designed to enable partners with weaker hands to find suitable contracts.

acold /ə'kəʊld/ *adjective*. *arch*. ME.
[ORIGIN Prob. orig. pa. pple of ACOOL, with short vowel before two consonants or by assim. to COLD *adjective*.]
Chilled, cold.

acolyte /'akəlʌɪt/ *noun*. ME.
[ORIGIN Old French *acolyt* (mod. *-yte*) or ecclesiastical Latin *acolytus*, *-it(h)us* from Greek *akolouthos* following, follower.]
1 ECCLESIASTICAL. A person who attends a priest and performs subordinate duties as bearing candles etc. ME.
2 An attendant, an assistant, a novice. E19.
■ Also **acolythist** *noun* (*arch.*) E17.

acone /'eɪkəʊn/ *adjective*. L19.
[ORIGIN German: see A-[10], CONE *noun*.]
ENTOMOLOGY. Of an insect's eyes: lacking cones.

aconite /'akənʌɪt/ *noun*. Also in Latin form †**aconitum**. M16.
[ORIGIN French *aconit* or Latin *aconitum* from Greek *akoniton*.]
1 Any of numerous poisonous plants belonging to the genus *Aconitum*; *esp.* monkshood or wolfsbane, *A. napellus*. M16. ▸**b** In full ***winter aconite***. Any small plant of the genus *Eranthis*, esp. *E. hyemalis*, bearing yellow flowers early in the year. L16.
2 An alkaloidal extract from monkshood or the like used as a poison or in pharmacy; *poet.* deadly poison. M16.

aconitine /ə'kɒnɪtiːn/ *noun*. M19.
[ORIGIN from ACONITE + -INE[5].]
CHEMISTRY. A colourless crystalline alkaloid, the toxic principle of monkshood and certain other plants of the genus *Aconitum*.

†**aconitum** *noun* see ACONITE.

à contrecœur /a kɔ̃trəkœːr/ *adverbial phr.* E19.
[ORIGIN French, lit. 'against the heart'.]
Against one's will, reluctantly.

†**acool** *verb intrans. & trans.* OE–M16.
[ORIGIN from A-[1] + COOL *verb*.]
Cool.

acorn /'eɪkɔːn/ *noun*.
[ORIGIN Old English *æcern* = Middle Low German *ackeren* (Dutch *aker*) acorn, Middle High German *ackeran*, *eckern* oak or beech mast, Old Norse *akarn* acorn, Gothic *akran* fruit, produce; rel. to ACRE. Later forms assoc. with OAK and CORN *noun*[1].]
†**1** Fruit generally, mast. OE–E17.
2 The fruit of the oak, an oval nut growing in a cupule. OE. ▸**b** An object or decorative device in the shape of an acorn. LME.
– COMB.: **acorn barnacle** a barnacle that does not possess a stalk; *esp.* a member of the genus *Balanus*; **acorn cup** the cupule of an acorn; **acorn shell** = ***acorn barnacle*** above; **acorn squash** *N. Amer.* a variety of squash with a longitudinally ridged rind; **acorn worm** a wormlike hemichordate of the class Enteropneusta, having an acorn-shaped anterior end to its body.
■ **acorned** *adjective* bearing acorns; fed with acorns: E17. **acorning** *noun* hunting for or gathering acorns E19.

acosmism /ə'kɒzmɪz(ə)m/ *noun*. Also **akosm-**. M19.
[ORIGIN from A-[10] + COSMOS *noun*[1] + -ISM.]
Denial of the existence of the universe, or of a universe distinct from God.
■ **acosmist** *noun* a person who professes acosmism M19.

acotyledon /əkɒtɪ'liːd(ə)n/ *noun*. Now *rare* or *obsolete*. M18.
[ORIGIN from mod. Latin pl. *acotyledones*: see A-[10], COTYLEDON.]
BOTANY. A plant forming no distinct cotyledons, such as a fern, moss, etc.
■ **acotyledonous** *adjective* E19.

acouchi /ə'kuːtʃi/ *noun*. L18.
[ORIGIN French from Tupi.]
A S. American rodent of the genus *Myoprocta*, resembling an agouti.

acoustic /ə'kuːstɪk/ *adjective & noun*. E17.
[ORIGIN Greek *akoustikos*, from *akouein* hear: see -IC.]
▸ **A** *adjective*. **1** Pertaining to the sense of hearing, or to audible sound. E17.
acoustic coupler: see COUPLER 4. ***acoustic* IMPEDANCE**. **acoustic mine** a mine designed to be detonated by sound waves. **acoustic shock** damaged hearing suffered by the user of an earphone as a result of sudden excessive noise in the device.
2 Of a material, a device, etc.: sound-absorbent. E20.
acoustic hood a sound-absorbent cover used esp. to reduce noise from a machine or appliance.
3 Of a musical instrument, gramophone, etc.: not electrically amplified. M20.
▸ **B** *noun*. **1** In *pl.* (usu. treated as *sing.*). The branch of science that deals with sound and the phenomena of hearing. L17.
†**2** A medicine or appliance used to aid hearing. Only in 18.
3 In *pl.* The acoustic properties of a building, room, etc., esp. one in which music or drama is performed. Now also in *sing.*, *esp.* the acoustic properties or ambience of a sound recording or of a recording studio. L19.
■ **acoustician** /-'stɪʃ(ə)n/ *noun* an expert in acoustics M19.

acoustical /ə'kuːstɪk(ə)l/ *adjective*. E19.
[ORIGIN from ACOUSTIC + -AL[1].]
Of or pertaining to audible sound or the science of acoustics.
■ **acoustically** *adverb* L19.

acoustics *noun* see ACOUSTIC *noun*.

acousto- /ə'kuːstəʊ/ *combining form*. M20.
[ORIGIN from ACOUSTIC *adjective* + -O-.]
Forming chiefly adjectives with the sense 'involving acoustic and — effects', as ***acousto-electric***, ***acousto-optic***.

†**acover** *verb* see COVER *verb*[1].

ACP *abbreviation*.
African, Caribbean, and Pacific.

acquaint /ə'kweɪnt/ *adjective* (orig. *pa. pple*). *arch*. ME.
[ORIGIN Old French *acointe*, formed as ACQUAINT *verb*. Cf. QUAINT.]
Acquainted (*with*).

acquaint /ə'kweɪnt/ *verb*. ME.
[ORIGIN Old French *acointier* make known from late Latin *accognitare*, from Latin *accognit-* pa. ppl stem of *accognoscere*, from *ad* AC- + *cognoscere* know.]
†**1** *verb refl.* Make oneself known, become known (*to*). ME–L15. ▸**b** *verb intrans.* Become acquainted or familiar (*with*). LME–L18.

b HOR. WALPOLE Though the Choiseuls will not acquaint with you.

2 *verb refl.* Give or gain for oneself personal knowledge: foll. by *with* a person. Now only in *pass.* as ACQUAINTED. ME.

AV *Job* 22:21 Acquaint now thyselfe with him.

3 *verb trans.* (& *refl.*) Give (oneself or another) experimental knowledge: foll. by *with* a thing. LME.

OED Acquaint yourself with the duties of your new sphere.

4 *verb trans.* Inform, make cognizant or aware. (Foll. by *with*, *that*, †*of*.) M16. ▸†**b** Make known, tell. Only in 17.

HENRY FIELDING He was acquainted that his worship would wait on him. R. B. SHERIDAN I shall certainly acquaint your father. F. RAPHAEL I'm here to acquaint you with the facts. **b** S. ROWLANDS Acquaint thy name in private unto me.

†**5** *verb trans.* Familiarize, accustom. Foll. by *with*, *to do*. L16–M17.

J. BRINSLEY Acquaint them to pronounce some speciall examples.

acquaintance /ə'kweɪnt(ə)ns/ *noun*. ME.
[ORIGIN Old French *acointance*, formed as ACQUAINT *verb*: see -ANCE.]
1 The state of being acquainted; mutual knowledge. Foll. by *with*, †*of*, or with *genit.* (as ***her acquaintance***, ***our acquaintance***). ME.
bowing acquaintance: see BOW *verb*[1] 6. ***nodding acquaintance***: see NOD *verb*. ***scrape acquaintance with***, ***scrape an acquaintance with***: see SCRAPE *verb*.
2 Orig. *collect.*, those with whom one is acquainted. Now usu. (with *pl.*), a person with whom one is acquainted. LME.
casual acquaintance: see CASUAL *adjective*.
3 Knowledge that is more than mere recognition but usu. less than intimacy. (Foll. by *with*, †*of*.) LME.
knowledge by acquaintance, **knowledge of acquaintance** PHILOSOPHY: by direct experience. **make the acquaintance of** come to know.
– COMB.: **acquaintance rape** rape of a woman by a man known to her.
■ **acquaintanceship** *noun* = ACQUAINTANCE 1 E19. †**acquaintant** *noun* = ACQUAINTANCE 2 E17–L18.

acquainted /ə'kweɪntɪd/ *adjective*. ME.
[ORIGIN from ACQUAINT *verb* + -ED[1].]
1 Familiar, through being known. *obsolete* of persons, *arch.* of things. ME.
2 Personally known (to another); having mutual knowledge. (Foll. by *with*.) ME.

Daily Telegraph They had more than enough time to become acquainted.

3 Having personal or experimental knowledge. Foll. by *with*, (occas.) *of*. L15.

P. O'BRIAN A man of some learning, acquainted with Hebrew, Greek, and Latin.

†**4** Accustomed (*with*, *to*). M16–L17.
■ **acquaintedness** *noun* the state or degree of acquaintance M17.

acquest /ə'kwɛst/ *noun*. E17.
[ORIGIN French †*acquest* (Old French *aquest*, mod. *acquêt*), ult. formed as ACQUIRE.]
1 A thing acquired; *spec.* (LAW, now *hist.*) property gained otherwise than by inheritance. E17.
†**2** = ACQUIST 1. E17–L18.

acquiesce /akwɪ'ɛs/ *verb intrans*. E17.
[ORIGIN Latin *acquiescere*, from *ad* AC- + *quiescere* to rest. See also QUIET *adjective*.]
1 Remain at rest or in quiet subjection; rest satisfied. (Foll. by *in*, *under*.) Now *rare*. E17.
2 Agree, esp. tacitly; concur (*in*); raise no objections (*to*). (Also foll. by †*with*.) E17.
■ **acquiescing** *adjective* assenting, silently compliant L18. **acquiescingly** *adverb* M19.

acquiescence /akwɪ'ɛs(ə)ns/ *noun*. E17.
[ORIGIN from ACQUIESCE + -ENCE. Cf. French *acquiescence*.]
1 The action or condition of acquiescing (sense 1); resting satisfied. *arch*. E17.
2 Silent or passive assent to, or compliance with, measures or proposals. (Foll. by *in*, *to*, †*with*.) M17.
■ **acquiescency** *noun* the quality or condition of being acquiescent M17.

acquiescent /akwɪ'ɛs(ə)nt/ *adjective & noun*. E17.
[ORIGIN Latin *acquiescent-* pres. ppl stem of *acquiescere* ACQUIESCE: see -ENT.]
▸ **A** *adjective*. Acquiescing; disposed to acquiesce. E17.
▸ **B** *noun*. A person who acquiesces. *rare*. E19.
■ **acquiescently** *adverb* L17.

acquire /ə'kwʌɪə/ *verb trans*. LME.
[ORIGIN Old French *aquerre*; English spelling Latinized c 1600 under influence of its ult. source Latin *acquirere* get in addition, from *ad* AC- + *quaerere* seek.]
1 Gain or get as one's own, by one's own exertions or qualities. LME.

W. FAULKNER The gun . . which he had acquired . . at the sacrifice of actual food. E. BIRNEY They had acquired piety & table manners.

2 Come into possession of. L16.

S. JOHNSON The Idler acquires weight by lying still.

3 Of radar, a radar operator: begin receiving signals from, locate. M20.
■ **acquirable** *adjective* M17. **acqui'ree** *noun* (chiefly COMMERCE) a person, company, etc., acquired M20. **acquirer** *noun* M18. **acquiring** *noun* the action of obtaining for oneself; the thing obtained: M17.

acquired /ə'kwʌɪəd/ *ppl adjective*. E17.
[ORIGIN from ACQUIRE + -ED[1].]
Obtained by one's own exertion; gained, as opp. to innate or inherited; esp. BIOLOGY & MEDICINE, developed after birth through the influence of the environment.

B. RUSSELL Man has improved in knowledge, in acquired skill, and in social organization, but not . . in congenital intellectual capacity.

acquired immune deficiency syndrome = AIDS. **acquired taste** (an object of) liking gained by experience.

acquirement /ə'kwʌɪəm(ə)nt/ *noun*. M17.
[ORIGIN formed as ACQUIRED + -MENT.]
1 The action of acquiring. M17.
2 Something which is acquired; a personal attainment of body or mind (as opp. to a material ***acquisition***, or a natural ***gift***). M17.

acquis communautaire /aˌki: kɒmjuːnəʊ'tɛː/ *noun*. L20.
[ORIGIN French = body of community legislation.]
The body of EU legislation and judgements of the European Court of Justice by which all EU member states are bound.

†**acquisite** *pple & ppl adjective*. E16–L17.
[ORIGIN Latin *acquisitus* pa. pple, from *acquisit-*: see ACQUISITION.]
Acquired.

acquisition /akwɪ'zɪʃ(ə)n/ *noun*. LME.
[ORIGIN Latin *acquisitio(n-)*, from *acquisit-* pa. ppl stem of *acquirere*: see ACQUIRE *verb*, -ION.]
1 The action of acquiring something or someone. LME.
2 A thing gained or acquired; a useful or welcome addition. L15.
■ **acquisitional** *adjective* L19.

acquisitive /ə'kwɪzɪtɪv/ *adjective*. M17.
[ORIGIN from Latin *acquisit-* (see ACQUISITION) + -IVE; partly through French *acquisitif*, *-ive* from late Latin *acquisitivus*.]
†**1** Belonging to one by acquisition. Only in M17.
2 Acquiring; keen to acquire things. M19.
■ **acquisitively** *adverb* in an acquisitive manner; in a manner expressing acquisition: M16. **acquisitiveness** *noun* the quality of being acquisitive; desire of possession: E19.

acquist /ə'kwɪst/ *noun*. E17.
[ORIGIN Var. of ACQUEST, after Latin *acquisitum*, medieval Latin *acquistum*, Italian *acquisto*.]
1 The action of acquiring, acquisition. E17.
†**2** A thing acquired. M17–M19.

†**acquit** *noun*. LME–L18.
[ORIGIN from the verb.]
The act of acquitting; acquittance.

acquit /ə'kwɪt/ *verb*. Infl. **-tt-**. Pa. pple & ppl adjective **-tted**, (*arch.*) **acquit**. ME.
[ORIGIN Old French *a(c)quiter* (Provençal *aquitar*) from medieval Latin *acquitare*, from *ad* AC- + *quitare* QUIT *verb*.]
1 *verb trans.* **a** Discharge, pay, (a claim, debt, or liability). *arch.* ME. ▸**b** Requite (a benefit or injury). *arch.* ME.
2 †**b** *verb trans.* Pay or cancel the debt of (a person). ME–M17. ▸**b** *verb trans.* Set free, release *of* or *from* a duty, obligation, or burden. *arch.* ME. ▸†**c** *verb refl.* Deliver, rid oneself, *of*. LME–M18. ▸†**d** *verb trans.* Pay off (a person in respect *of* a debt due to him or her); be quits with. LME–L16.
†**3** *verb trans. & intrans.* Atone for (an offence). ME–E17.
4 †**a** *verb trans.* Discharge the duties of (an office), perform, accomplish. LME–L17. ▸**b** *verb refl.* Discharge oneself (*of* duty or responsibility); perform one's part in a specified manner. LME.

b J. MARQUAND George Apley.. acquitted himself well on such occasions.

5 *verb trans.* Clear from a charge; declare not guilty (*of*, †*from*, an offence). LME.

Daily Telegraph Meredith was acquitted of conspiracy to rob.

■ **acquitment** *noun* (now *rare* or *obsolete*) acquittal, release LME. **acquitter** *noun* E17.

acquittal /ə'kwɪt(ə)l/ *noun*. LME.
[ORIGIN from ACQUIT *verb* + -AL[1].]
†**1** Payment, requital, amends. LME–M18.
2 = ACQUITTANCE 2. Now *rare* or *obsolete*. LME.
3 Discharge (of duty); performance. LME.
4 Deliverance from a charge by verdict or other legal process. L15.

acquittance /ə'kwɪt(ə)ns/ *noun & verb*. ME.
[ORIGIN Old French *aquitance*, formed as ACQUIT *verb* + -ANCE.]
▸ **A** *noun*. **1** The action of clearing off debt or other obligation. ME.
2 Release or discharge from a debt or obligation. ME.
3 A release in writing; a receipt in full. LME.
4 = ACQUITTAL 3. *rare*. L15.
▸ †**B** *verb trans.* Give an acquittance to, discharge. *rare*. LME–L16.

acral /'akr(ə)l/ *adjective*. E20.
[ORIGIN formed as ACRO- + -AL[1].]
Pertaining to a tip or apex; *spec.* (MEDICINE & VETERINARY MEDICINE) affecting the extremities.

acraldehyde /ə'kraldɪhʌɪd/ *noun*. M19.
[ORIGIN formed as ACRID + ALDEHYDE.]
CHEMISTRY. Orig., a compound related to acetaldehyde, of formula $C_4H_8O_2$ (probably aldol). Now = ACROLEIN.

acrasia *noun* var. of ACRASY, AKRASIA.

acrasy /ə'kreɪzɪ/ *noun*. Now *rare* or *obsolete*. Also **acrasia** /ə'kreɪzɪə/. L16.
[ORIGIN Greek, confusing two words *akrasia*, (i) lack of proper mixing, from *akratos* unmixed, untempered, intemperate, (ii) lack of self-command, from *akratēs* powerless, incontinent.]
Intemperance, excess; irregularity, disorder.

acrawl /ə'krɔːl/ *adverb & pred. adjective*. M19.
[ORIGIN from A-[2] + CRAWL *noun*[2] or *verb*.]
Crawling (*with*).

acre /'eɪkə/ *noun*.
[ORIGIN Old English *æcer* = Old Frisian *ekker*, Old Saxon *akkar* (Dutch *akker*), Old High German *ackar* (German *Acker*), Old Norse *akr*, Gothic *akrs*, from Germanic from Indo-European base repr. also by Latin *ager*, Greek *agros*, Sanskrit *ajra* field; rel. to ACORN, ACT *verb*.]
1 A piece of tilled or arable land, a field. *obsolete* exc. in ***God's acre*** [from mod. German] a churchyard, in proper names, as ***Great Acre***, and *rhet.* in *pl.*, lands, estates, etc. OE.
2 A measure of land, orig. as much as a yoke of oxen could plough in a day, later limited by statute to a piece 220 yards long by 22 broad (= 4840 sq. yards or about 4047 sq. metres) or of equivalent area (now largely superseded by the hectare); *loosely* a large extent. OE.

CARLYLE Acres of despatches.

Cheshire acre: see CHESHIRE 3. ***land of the broad acres***, ***the broad acres***: see BROAD *adjective* 2.

– COMB.: †**acre breadth** a linear measure equal to 22 yards or about 20 metres; **acre-foot** a unit of volume one acre in area and one foot in depth; †**acre length** a linear measure equal to a furlong or about 201 metres.

■ **acreable** *adjective* (now *rare*) per acre M18. **acreage** *noun* extent of acres; acres collectively or in the abstract: M19. **acred** *adjective* possessing landed estates (mostly in *comb.*, as ***large-acred***) M18.

acrid /'akrɪd/ *adjective*. E18.
[ORIGIN Irreg. from Latin *acri-*, *acer* sharp, pungent + -ID[1], prob. after *acid*.]
1 Bitterly pungent to the organs of taste or smell, or to the skin etc.; irritating; corrosive. E18.
2 Bitterly irritating to the feelings; of bitter and irritating temper or manner. L18.
■ **a'cridity** *noun* the quality of being acrid E19. **acridly** *adverb* L18. **acridness** *noun* (now *rare*) acridity E18.

acridid /'akrɪdɪd/ *noun & adjective*. M20.
[ORIGIN mod. Latin *Acrididae* (see below), from Greek *akrid-*, *akris* locust: see -ID[3].]
ENTOMOLOGY. ▸ **A** *noun*. A grasshopper or locust of the family Acrididae, characterized by the possession of relatively short antennae. M20.
▸ **B** *adjective*. Of, pertaining to, or designating this family. M20.
■ **a'cridian** *noun & adjective* = ACRIDID L19. **a'cridiid** *noun & adjective* = ACRIDID E20.

acridine /'akrɪdiːn/ *noun*. L19.
[ORIGIN German *Acridin*, formed as ACRID: see -IDINE.]
CHEMISTRY. A colourless crystalline heteroaromatic compound, $C_{13}H_9N$, obtained from coal tar and from which the structures of many dyes and pharmaceuticals are derived.

acriflavine /akrɪ'fleɪvɪn, -iːn/ *noun*. E20.
[ORIGIN from ACRI(DINE + FLAVINE.]
PHARMACOLOGY. A bright orange-red derivative of acridine, used as an antiseptic.

Acrilan /'akrɪlan/ *noun*. M20.
[ORIGIN from ACR(YLIC + -I- + Latin *lana* wool.]
(Proprietary name for) a synthetic acrylic fibre used for clothing, blankets, etc.

acrimonious /akrɪ'məʊnɪəs/ *adjective*. E17.
[ORIGIN from ACRIMONY + -OUS.]
1 = ACRID 1. *arch.* E17.

SIR T. BROWNE A rough and acrimonious kinde of salt.

2 Bitter and irritating in tone or manner. L18.

E. WAUGH An acrimonious dispute about the date of the Battle of Hastings.

■ **acrimoniously** *adverb* L18. **acrimoniousness** *noun* E19.

acrimony /'akrɪməni/ *noun*. M16.
[ORIGIN French *acrimonie* or Latin *acrimonia*, formed as ACRID: see -MONY.]
1 Bitter pungency to the organs of taste or smell, or to the skin etc. M16.
2 Bitterness of tone or manner. E17.

†**acrious** *adjective*. L17–E18.
[ORIGIN formed as ACRID + -OUS.]
= ACRID 1.

acritarch /'akrɪtɑːk/ *noun*. M20.
[ORIGIN from Greek *akritos* uncertain, confused + *arkhē* origin.]
PALAEONTOLOGY. Any single-celled fossil whose true affinities are unknown.

†**acritude** *noun*. *rare*. L17–M19.
[ORIGIN Latin *acritudo*, formed as ACRID: see -TUDE.]
Acridity.

acro- /'akrəʊ/ *combining form* of Greek *akros* tip, peak: see -O-.
■ **acro'carpous** *adjective* (of a moss) bearing the archegonia and capsules at the tip of a stem or main branch (opp. PLEUROCARPOUS) M19. **acro'centric** *adjective* (CYTOLOGY) (of a chromosome) having the centromere close to the end M20. **acrodont** *adjective* (ZOOLOGY) having the teeth attached to the ridge of the jaw, as in certain lizards M19. **acrogen** *noun* (BOTANY) a cryptogam with a distinct permanent stem; a fern, a moss: M19. **acrolect** *noun* [-LECT] LINGUISTICS the dialect or variety of any language with the greatest prestige M20. **acrolith** *noun* (GREEK ANTIQUITIES) a statue with the head and extremities of stone, the trunk usu. of wood M19. **acro'lithic** *adjective* of or pertaining to an acrolith M19. **acrome'galic** *adjective & noun* pertaining to acromegaly; (a person) affected with acromegaly: E20. **acro'megaly** *noun* (MEDICINE) abnormal enlargement of the hands, feet, and face; disease caused by excessive growth-hormone secretion, of which this is a symptom: L19. ˌ**acroparaes'thesia**, *-**pares'thesia** *noun* (MEDICINE) paraesthesia of the extremities L19. **a'cropetal** *adjective* [Latin *petere* seek] BOTANY characterized by successive development of parts from below upwards L19. **a'cropetally** *adverb* in an acropetal manner L19. **acrophobe** *noun* a person affected with acrophobia M20. **acro'phobia** *noun* irrational fear of heights L19. **acro'phobic** *adjective* pertaining to or affected with acrophobia M20.

acroamatic /ˌakrəʊə'matɪk/ *adjective & noun*. M17.
[ORIGIN Greek *akroamatikos* adjective, from *akroama(t-)* what is heard, formed as ACROATIC: see -IC.]
▸ **A** *adjective*. Communicated by oral teaching; esoteric. M17.
▸ **B** *noun*. Something so communicated; *spec.* in *pl.* (**A-**), Aristotle's lectures on the esoteric parts of his philosophy. M17.
■ **acroamatical** *adjective* (now *rare*) L16.

acroatic /akrəʊ'atɪk/ *adjective & noun*. M17.
[ORIGIN Greek *akroatikos* adjective, from *akroasthai* hear: see -IC.]
= ACROAMATIC.

acrobat /'akrəbat/ *noun*. E19.
[ORIGIN French *acrobate* from Greek *akrobatēs*, from *akrobatos* walking on tiptoe, formed as ACRO- + base of *bainein* walk.]
A performer of daring gymnastic feats, as rope-walking; a tumbler; *fig.* a person who changes position nimbly in argument, performance, etc.
■ **acrobacy** *noun* (now *rare*) = ACROBATISM E20. **acro'batic** *adjective & noun* (**a**) *adjective* of or characteristic of an acrobat; (**b**) *noun* in *pl.*, (the performing of) acrobatic feats: M19. **acro'batically** *adverb* L19. **acrobatism** *noun* the art of the acrobat; the performing of gymnastic feats: M19.

acrocyanosis /ˌakrəʊsʌɪə'nəʊsɪs/ *noun*. L19.
[ORIGIN from ACRO- + CYANOSIS.]
MEDICINE. A bluish or purple discoloration of the hands and feet caused by slow circulation.

acrolein /'akrəliːn/ *noun*. M19.
[ORIGIN formed as ACRID + *oleum* oil: see -IN[1].]
CHEMISTRY. A colourless, acrid, liquid aldehyde, $CH_2{=}CHCHO$, obtained by dehydration of glycerol; propenal.

acromion /ə'krəʊmɪən/ *noun*. L16.
[ORIGIN Greek *akrōmion*, formed as ACRO- + *ōmos* shoulder.]
ANATOMY. The outer extremity of the posterior projection or spine of the upper part of the shoulder blade. Also ***acromion process***.
■ **acromial** *adjective* of or pertaining to the acromion M19. **acromiocla'vicular** *adjective* of or pertaining to the articulation of the acromion and the lateral end of the clavicle M19.

acronychal /ə'krɒnɪk(ə)l/ *adjective*. Also **achronical** & other vars. (freq. erron. as if from Greek *khronos* time). M16.
[ORIGIN from Greek *akronukhos* at nightfall, formed as ACRO- + *nux* night, + -AL[1].]
Happening at nightfall (applied esp. to the rising or setting of stars).
■ **acronych** *adjective* = ACRONYCHAL M16. **acronychally** *adverb* L16.

acronym /'akrənɪm/ *noun & verb*. M20.
[ORIGIN from ACRO- + -NYM.]
▸ **A** *noun*. A word formed from the initial letters or parts of other words; *loosely* an abbreviation composed of initial letters. M20.
▸ **B** *verb trans.* Abbreviate as an acronym. M20.
■ **acro'nymic** *adjective* M20. **acro'nymically** *adverb* L20. **a'cronymize** *verb trans.* = ACRONYM *verb* M20.

acrook /ə'krʊk/ *adverb & pred. adjective*. LME.
[ORIGIN from A *preposition*[1] 1 + CROOK *noun*.]
In a bend or curve; awry.

acropolis /ə'krɒpəlɪs/ *noun*. E17.
[ORIGIN Greek *akropolis*, formed as ACRO- + *polis* city.]
The citadel or elevated fortified part of a Greek city, esp. of Athens.

acrospire /'akrəspʌɪə/ *verb & noun*. Chiefly *dial.* (orig. *Scot.*). LME.
[ORIGIN from Old English (Northumbrian) *æhher*, *eher* EAR *noun*[2] + SPIRE *verb*[1], assim. to ACRO-.]
▸ **A** *verb intrans.* Of malt: sprout. LME.
▸ **B** *noun*. The first leaf shoot of a cereal plant. L17.

across /ə'krɒs/ *adverb, preposition, & adjective*. ME.
[ORIGIN Old French *a croix*, *en croix*, in, on a cross (see CROSS *noun*), assim. to native formations in A *preposition*[1] 1.]
▸ **A** *adverb*. **1** In the form of a cross, crosswise, crossed. *arch.* ME.

W. H. AUDEN Sheep-dogs.. slumber on with paws across.

2 Transversely; from side to side, or corner to corner. ME. ▸**b** (Filling or to fill spaces) along a horizontal line of a crossword puzzle. Usu. following the number of the word or clue (passing into *adjective*). E20.

G. B. SHAW The nurse rushes across behind the head of the bed. DYLAN THOMAS My heart is cracked across.

come across (**a**) succeed in communicating, convey the desired information or impression, (foll. by *to*); (**b**) *slang* hand over or contribute money, information, etc. **come across as** give the impression of being. **come across with** *slang* hand over, contribute (money, information, etc.). **get across** = ***come across*** (a) above. ***last across*** (***the road***): see LAST *adjective*. ***put across***: see PUT *verb*[1].

3 Obliquely; awry; amiss. *obsolete* exc. *dial.* M16.

JOSEPH HALL The squint-eyed pharisees looke a-crosse at all the actions of Christ.

4 On the other side. E19.

OED At this rate we shall soon be across. SCOTT FITZGERALD I'm right across from you.

across the tracks: see TRACK *noun*.

▸ **B** *preposition*. **1** Motion: from side to side of; over, in any direction but lengthwise. L16.

TENNYSON After dinner talk Across the walnuts and the wine. T. STOPPARD I once took a train journey right across America.

across country: see COUNTRY *noun*. ***across lots***: see LOT *noun*. ***across the board***: see BOARD *noun*.

2 Direction: transverse to; at an angle with; sideways or obliquely against. E17. ▸**b** Indirectly or unintentionally into contact with. E19.

W. STEVENS The shawl across one shoulder.

b ***come across***: see COME *verb*. ***run across***: see RUN *verb*.

3 Position: on the other side of, beyond. M18.

J. CHEEVER The shores of West Chop, across the Sound.

4 Distribution: throughout, all over. *colloq.* M20.

Newsweek Newsweek bureaus across the U.S. reported the story.

▸ **C** *adjective*. Of a crossword clue or answer: that fills or is intended to fill the spaces along a horizontal line of the puzzle. Cf. sense A.2b above. **E20.**

acrostic /əˈkrɒstɪk/ *noun & adjective*. Also †**-ich**. **L16.**
[**ORIGIN** French *acrostiche* from Greek *akrostikhis*, formed as **ACRO-** + *stikhos* row, line of verse: assim. to **-IC**.]
▸ **A** *noun*. **1** A poem or other composition in which the initial (***single acrostic***), the initial and final (***double acrostic***), or the initial, middle, and final (***triple acrostic***) letters of the lines make words. **L16.** ▸**b** A word puzzle so made. **L19.**
†**2** The beginning or end of a verse. **E17–M18.**
3 A poem in which the consecutive lines or verses begin with the successive letters of the alphabet. **L17.**
▸ **B** *adjective*. Of the nature of or in the form of an acrostic. **M17.**
■ **acrostical** *adjective* = **ACROSTIC** *adjective* **M19. acrostically** *adverb* **M19.**

acroterion /akrəˈtɪərɪən/ *noun*. Also **akro-**. Pl. **-ia** /-ɪə/. Also **acroter** /ˈakrətə/, pl. **-ters**; **acroterium** /-ˈtɪərɪəm/, pl. **-ia** /-ɪə/. **M17.**
[**ORIGIN** Greek *akrōtērion* extremity, formed as **ACRO-**. Vars. from French *acrotère* and (its source) Latin *acroterium* from Greek.]
1 ARCHITECTURE. †**a** *collect. sing.* & (usu.) in *pl.* Ornaments in ranges on roofs of classical buildings. **M17–L19.** ▸**b** A pedestal for a statue or the like on the apex or side of a pediment. **E18.**
†**2** MEDICINE. In *pl.* The extremities of the body. **E–M18.**
■ **acroterial** *adjective* (ARCHITECTURE) **E18.**

acrow /əˈkrəʊ/ *adverb & pred. adjective*. *poet.* **L19.**
[**ORIGIN** from **A-**[2] + **CROW** *verb*.]
Crowing.

acrylamide /əˈkrɪləmʌɪd/ *noun*. **L19.**
[**ORIGIN** from **ACRYL(IC + AMIDE.)**]
CHEMISTRY. The amide of acrylic acid, $CH_2{=}CHCONH_2$, a colourless crystalline solid which readily yields water-soluble polymers.

acrylate /ˈakrɪleɪt/ *noun*. **M19.**
[**ORIGIN** from **ACRYLIC** + **-ATE**[1].]
1 CHEMISTRY. A salt or ester of acrylic acid. **M19.**
2 = **ACRYLIC** *noun*. Also ***acrylate resin***. **M20.**

acrylic /əˈkrɪlɪk/ *adjective & noun*. **M19.**
[**ORIGIN** from **ACR(OLEIN** + **-YL** + **-IC.)**]
▸ **A** *adjective*. **1** CHEMISTRY. ***acrylic acid***, a liquid, $CH_2{=}CHCOOH$, orig. obtained by oxidizing acrolein and easily polymerized; propenoic acid. **M19.**
2 Designating or made from resins, plastics, artificial fibres, etc., which are polymers of acrylic acid or its derivatives. **M20.**
▸ **B** *noun*. An acrylic fibre, plastic, etc. **M20.**

acrylonitrile /ˌakrɪləˈnʌɪtrʌɪl/ *noun*. **L19.**
[**ORIGIN** from **ACRYLIC** + **-O-** + **NITRILE.**]
CHEMISTRY. A pungent, toxic liquid, $CH_2{=}CHCN$, the nitrile of acrylic acid, from which artificial fibres and other polymeric materials can be made; propenenitrile.

ACT *abbreviation*.
Australian Capital Territory.

act /akt/ *noun*. **LME.**
[**ORIGIN** Mainly from Latin *actus* doing, playing a part, dramatic action, act of a play, *actum* public transaction, (in pl.) records, register, from *act-* (see **ACT** *verb*); partly through French *acte* from Latin.]
1 A thing done; a deed. **LME.** ▸**b** An operation of the mind. **L17.** ▸**c** A thing done as an outward sign of a condition etc. **M18.**

MILTON Victorious deeds Flam'd in my heart, heroic acts. **b** A. J. AYER The realist analysis of our sensations in terms of subject, act, and object. **c** L. VAN DER POST This . . act of trust between them and the harsh desert earth.

act of contrition a penitential prayer. ***act of faith***: see **FAITH** *noun*. ***act of God***: see **GOD** *noun*. ***act of grace***: see **GRACE** *noun*. **the act** *colloq.* sexual intercourse.

†**2** Fact or reality, as opp. to intention, possibility, etc. **LME–L17.**

SHAKES. *John* If I in act, consent, or sin of thought, Be guilty.

†**3** An active principle. **LME–M18.**
4 Something transacted in council or in a deliberative assembly; a decree passed by a legislative body etc.; a statute. **LME.**
Act of Parliament: see **PARLIAMENT** *noun*. **act of state** an act passed by the executive power of a state, *esp.* an act which relates to foreign affairs or foreign citizens. ***Act of Toleration***: see **TOLERATION** 4. ***Act of Uniformity***: see **UNIFORMITY** 1.
5 A record of decrees etc.; a verificatory document. **LME.**
Acts (of the Apostles) (treated as *sing.*) a New Testament book immediately following the Gospels. **act and deed**: part of a formula used in concluding a legal transaction by signing a document.
6 The process of doing; action, operation. **L15.**
in the act (of) in the process (of), in the very doing of; on the point of.
7 a Each of the main divisions of a play. **E16.** ▸†**b** An interlude in a play. **E–M17.** ▸**c** Each of a series of short performances in a variety programme, circus, etc.; the performer(s) of one of these. **M19.** ▸**d** A piece of acting; a pretence (of being what one is not); a display of exaggerated behaviour; *Austral. slang* a fit of temper, a tantrum. **E20.**

a *fig.*: SCOTT FITZGERALD There are no second acts in American lives. **c** W. TREVOR The act he'd devised for the Spot the Talent competition. **d** D. LODGE Will you stop putting on this concerned parent act.

ca hard act to follow *transf.* a person or thing difficult to be more impressive or successful than. ***do a disappearing act***, ***do the disappearing act***: see **DISAPPEAR**. **get in on the act**, **get into the act** *slang* become a participant, esp. for profit. ***get one's act together***: see **GET** *verb*. **d put on an act** *colloq.* show off, talk for display, pretend.
8 A thesis publicly defended by a candidate for a university degree. *obsolete* exc. *hist.* **M16.**
– **COMB.**: **act-drop** in a theatre, a curtain let down between acts; ***act-tune***: see **TUNE** *noun* 2c.

act /akt/ *verb*. **LME.**
[**ORIGIN** Latin *act-* pa. ppl stem of *agere*: see **AGENT**. Prob. infl. by **ACT** *noun*.]
†**1** *verb trans.* Decide judicially (a case at law). **LME–L15.**
†**2** *verb trans.* Enact, decree; record. Chiefly *Scot.* **L15–M18.**
†**3** *verb trans.* Perform, bring about (a thing or process). **L16–L18.**

DEFOE Had Satan been able to have acted anything by force.

4 *verb trans.* Carry out or represent in mimic action; perform (a play etc.); *fig.* simulate, counterfeit. **L16.**

DAY LEWIS He would act the biblical stories on which he was commenting. J. SQUIRE To ask trite questions and act indifference.

act a lie: see **LIE** *noun*[1]. **act a part**, **act the part of** play the part of (a character in a play); simulate; fulfil the character or duties of.
5 *verb intrans.* Perform a play or part; be an actor or actress. **L16.** ▸**b** *verb intrans.* Of a play: be able to be performed (well, or in a specified manner). **M17.**

T. CORYAT I saw women acte, a thing that I neuer saw before. **b** BYRON My plays won't act . . my poesy won't sell.

6 *verb trans.* Carry out in action. *arch.* **E17.**

SHAKES. *Temp.* To act her . . abhorr'd commands.

†**7** *verb trans.* Put in motion; actuate, animate. **E17–M18.**

POPE Self-love . . acts the soul.

8 *verb trans.* Perform the part of (a character in a play); behave like (a specified kind of person). **M17.**
act the fool: see **FOOL** *noun*[1]. ***act the goat***: see **GOAT**.
9 *verb intrans.* Perform actions; behave. **L17.** ▸**b** *verb intrans.* Do the duties of a particular employment temporarily. **E19.**

T. S. ELIOT What it is to act or suffer. J. D. SALINGER I act quite young for my age.

act on, **act upon** regulate one's conduct according to. **act up to** come up to (an assumed standard), carry out in practice. **b act as** do the work of (a particular employment etc.), serve as. **act for**: on someone's behalf or in his or her absence.
10 *verb intrans.* Of a thing: exert influence (*on*), produce an effect. **M18.**

T. H. HUXLEY A fall of snow . . acts like a mantle.

– **WITH ADVERBS IN SPECIALIZED SENSES**: **act out** (*a*) *verb phr. trans.* translate (ideas etc.) into action, represent in action; (*b*) *verb phr. trans. & intrans.* express (repressed or unconscious feelings) in overt behaviour; (*c*) *US colloq.* misbehave, give trouble. **act up** *colloq.* misbehave, give trouble.

actable /ˈaktəb(ə)l/ *adjective*. **M19.**
[**ORIGIN** from **ACT** *verb* + **-ABLE**. Earlier (**E19**) in the negative **UNACTABLE.**]
Able to be acted (on the stage) or carried out in practice.
■ **actaˈbility** *noun* **M19.**

acte gratuit /akt gratɥi/ *noun phr.* Pl. **-s -s** (pronounced same). **M20.**
[**ORIGIN** French (A. Gide).]
A gratuitous or inconsequent action performed on impulse.

ACTH *abbreviation*.
Adrenocorticotrophic hormone.

actin /ˈaktɪn/ *noun*. **M20.**
[**ORIGIN** from Greek *aktin-*, *aktis* ray + **-IN**[1].]
BIOCHEMISTRY. A protein which with myosin forms the contractile filaments of muscle fibres.

acting /ˈaktɪŋ/ *noun*. **L16.**
[**ORIGIN** from **ACT** *verb* + **-ING**[1].]
1 Performance; execution. **L16.**
2 The performance of deeds; in *pl.*, doings, practices, etc. *arch.* **E17.**

SIR W. SCOTT The great actings which are now on foot.

3 The performing of plays etc.; the art or occupation of performing parts in plays, films, etc.; simulation. **M17.**
4 The putting forth of energy, activity, etc.; operation. **M17.**
– **COMB.**: **acting copy** a copy of a play etc. specially prepared for actors' use, with stage directions, cuts, etc.; **acting part**, **acting play** a part or play with good dramatic qualities; **acting version** = ***acting copy*** above.

acting /ˈaktɪŋ/ *adjective*. **L16.**
[**ORIGIN** from **ACT** *verb* + **-ING**[2].]
1 That acts or has power to act. **L16.**
2 *spec.* (Freq. before a title etc.) Doing duty temporarily (as ***Acting Captain***); doing alone duties nominally shared with others (as ***Acting Manager***). **L18.**

actinia /akˈtɪnɪə/ *noun*. Pl. **-iae** /-ɪiː/, **-ias**. **M18.**
[**ORIGIN** mod. Latin, formed as **ACTIN** + **-IA**[2].]
A sea anemone of the genus *Actinia*, esp. *A. equina*, a common British species; *loosely* any sea anemone.
■ **actinian** *noun* a sea anemone of the genus *Actinia* **L19.**

actinide /ˈaktɪnʌɪd/ *noun*. **M20.**
[**ORIGIN** from **ACTINIUM** + *-ide* after **LANTHANIDE.**]
Any of the series of radioactive chemical elements having atomic numbers between 89 (actinium) and 103 (lawrencium) inclusive, which form part of the group of transition metals.

actinism /ˈaktɪnɪz(ə)m/ *noun*. **M19.**
[**ORIGIN** formed as **ACTIN** + **-ISM.**]
The property by which light or other electromagnetic radiation causes chemical change, as in photography.
■ **acˈtinic** *adjective* of or pertaining to actinism; (of light etc.) having the ability to cause chemical change: **M19.**

actinium /akˈtɪnɪəm/ *noun*. **E20.**
[**ORIGIN** formed as **ACTINISM** + **-IUM.**]
A radioactive metallic chemical element, atomic no. 89, which is the first element of the actinide series and is found in small quantities in pitchblende (symbol Ac).
■ **ˈactinoid** *noun* = **ACTINIDE M20. ˈactinon** *noun* (*a*) HISTORY OF SCIENCE an isotope of radon, radon-219; (*b*) = **ACTINIDE: E20.**

actino- /ˈaktɪnəʊ, akˈtɪnəʊ/ *combining form* of Greek *aktin-*, *aktis* ray: see **-O-**.
■ **ˌactinoˈmorphic** *adjective* (BOTANY) (of a flower) characterized by radial symmetry (opp. ***zygomorphic***) **L19. ˌactinoˈmycin** *noun* an antibiotic obtained from actinomycetes **M20. ˌactinomyˈcosis** *noun* a disease of animals (esp. cattle), and sometimes of people, caused by infection with actinomycetes and most commonly affecting the mouth, jaw, or neck **L19. ˌactinomyˈcotic** *adjective* pertaining to or suffering from actinomycosis **E20. ˌactinopteˈrygian** *adjective & noun* [Greek *pterugion* fin, dim. of *pterux* wing] (designating or pertaining to) a ray-finned fish, a fish belonging to the subclass Actinopterygii, which includes most living bony fishes **L19. ˌactinoˈtherapy** *noun* treatment of disease by means of ultraviolet radiation **E20. ˌactino-uˈranium** *noun* the uranium isotope of mass 235 **E20.**

actinolite /akˈtɪnəlʌɪt/ *noun*. **L18.**
[**ORIGIN** from **ACTINO-** + Greek *lithos* stone: see **-ITE**[1]. Named in ref. to the rayed masses of crystals it often forms.]
MINERALOGY. A green amphibole mineral containing calcium, magnesium, and ferrous iron, forming elongated monoclinic crystals or fibrous masses, and found esp. in many metamorphic rocks and as a form of asbestos.
■ **ˌactinoˈlitic** *adjective* **M19.**

actinometer /aktɪˈnɒmɪtə/ *noun*. **M19.**
[**ORIGIN** from **ACTINO-** + **-METER.**]
An instrument for measuring the heating or actinic power of radiant energy.
■ **ˌactinoˈmetric** *adjective* of or pertaining to actinometers or their use **M19. ˌactinoˈmetrical** *adjective* = **ACTINOMETRIC L19. actinometry** *noun* **M19.**

actinomycete /ˌaktɪnə(ʊ)ˈmʌɪsiːt/ *noun*. Orig. only in pl. **-mycetes** /-ˈmʌɪsiːts, -mʌɪˈsiːtiːz/. **E20.**
[**ORIGIN** Anglicized sing. of mod. Latin *actinomycetes*, formed as **ACTINO-** + Greek *mukētes* pl. of *mukēs* fungus.]
A filamentous bacterium of the order Actinomycetales.

actio /ˈaktɪəʊ/ *noun sing.* **L17.**
[**ORIGIN** Latin.]
(An) action.
actio in distans /ɪn ˈdɪstanz/ [= on something apart] = ***action at a distance*** s.v. **ACTION** *noun*.

action /ˈakʃ(ə)n/ *noun & verb*. **ME.**
[**ORIGIN** Old French & mod. French from Latin *actio(n-)*, formed as **ACT** *verb*: see **-ION.**]
▸ **A** *noun*. **1** The taking of legal steps to establish a claim or obtain remedy; the right to institute a legal process. **ME.** ▸**b** A legal process or suit. **LME.**
2 The process or condition of acting or doing; the exertion of energy or influence; working, agency, operation. **LME.**

JOYCE The corrosive action of copperas. G. SANTAYANA Trust the man who hesitates in his speech and is quick and steady in action.

DELAYED-***action***.
3 A thing done, a deed, an act (usu. viewed as occupying some time in doing); (in *pl.*) freq. habitual or ordinary deeds, conduct. **LME.**
4 Mode of acting. ▸**a** Gesture, esp. in oratory or acting. **M16.** ▸**b** The management of the body or limbs in movement. **L16.** ▸**c** The way in which an instrument acts; the mechanism effecting this. **M19.** ▸**d** A film director's command to begin a scene. **M20.**
†**5** The celebration of a sacrament. Chiefly *Scot.* **M16–L19.**
6 a An engagement with the enemy; a fight. **L16.** ▸**b** Active operation against, or engaging, an enemy; fighting. **E17.**

a S. SASSOON The Division had now been in action for a week. E. BOWEN A month when enemy action was not severe. **b** B. ELTON Jack has seen plenty of action, having served with distinction in Vietnam.

†**7** The acting of plays, performance. **E17–E18.**
†**8** A share in a joint-stock company. **L17–M19.**
9 The event or series of events represented in a drama or forming the subject of a poem or other composition. **L17.**
10 *PHYSICS.* The product (or a corresponding integral) of momentum and distance or (equivalently) of twice the kinetic energy and time. Now also, the product (or integral) of the difference between kinetic energy and potential energy, and time. **E19.**
11 Activity; *the* exciting or important events etc. Freq. in ***where the action is***. *slang.* **M20.**

– **PHRASES**: **action at a distance** the exertion of force by one body on another separated from it by space; *fig.* the exertion of influence from a distance. **action front!**, **action rear!**: commands in an artillery regiment to prepare for action in front of, behind, the guns. **action of a verb**, **verbal action** the thing asserted by the verb, strictly action but also state, existence, etc. ***action of*** DECLARATOR. ***action of*** TROVER. ***action rear!***: see ***action front!*** above. ***chose in action***: see CHOSE *noun*. ***clear the decks for action***: see CLEAR *verb* 8. ***direct action***: see DIRECT *adjective*. **go into action** begin a military action or attack; *gen.* begin work, begin operating. **in action** (*a*) (of property) not in possession, but recoverable by legal process; (*b*) in practical or effective operation, working. ***industrial action***: see INDUSTRIAL *adjective*. ***join action***: see JOIN *verb*. ***live action***: see LIVE *adjective*. ***man of action***: see MAN *noun*. **out of action** not working. ***principle of*** LEAST ***action***. ***suit the action to the word***: see SUIT *verb*. **take action** institute legal proceedings; *gen.* begin to act, act effectively. ***transitory action***: see TRANSITORY 3. ***unity of action***: see UNITY *noun*[1] 8. ***verbal action***: see ***action of a verb*** above.

– **COMB.**: **action committee**: formed to take active steps, esp. in politics; **action figure** a toy figure with movable parts, representing a person or fictional character renowned for adventurous or heroic action; **action group**: formed to take active steps, esp. in politics; **action-noun** *GRAMMAR*: expressing an action; **action-packed** *adjective* (*colloq.*) full of action or excitement; **action painting** (a painting produced by) spontaneous or random application of paint; **action point** a point or issue on which there is a need or a decision to take action; **action potential** *BIOLOGY* the change in electrical potential associated with the passage of an impulse along the membrane of a muscle cell or nerve cell; **action replay** a playback of a televised incident, esp. in a sports match, just after it has taken place; †**action sermon** in the Scottish Presbyterian Church, a discourse at the Eucharist or other sacrament; **action song** a (children's) song involving also some dramatic movement, esp. of the hands; **action stations** positions taken up by troops etc. before going into action; *transf.* positions for beginning any activity.

► **B** *verb trans.* **1** Bring a legal action against. **M18.**
2 Take action on, put into effect. **M20.**
■ **actional** *adjective* (*a*) of or pertaining to action(s); (*b*) actionable: **M17.**

actionable /ˈakʃ(ə)nəb(ə)l/ *adjective.* **L16.**
[**ORIGIN** from ACTION + -ABLE.]
1 Affording ground for an action at law. **L16.**
2 Able to be done or acted on; having practical value. **E20.**
■ **actionaˈbility** *noun* **L19.** **actionably** *adverb* **E19.**

actioner /ˈakʃənə/ *noun.* **L19.**
[**ORIGIN** from ACTION *noun* + -ER[1].]
1 An artisan who makes the action of an instrument, as of a gun, piano, etc. **L19.**
2 A film predominantly consisting of exciting action and adventure. *colloq.* **L20.**

activate /ˈaktɪveɪt/ *verb trans.* **E17.**
[**ORIGIN** from ACTIVE *adjective* + -ATE[3].]
1 Make active, cause to act. Freq. *techn.* **E17.**
activated carbon, **activated charcoal** charcoal which has been treated so as to increase its adsorptive power. **activated sludge** aerated sewage containing aerobic bacteria.
2 *spec.* Make radioactive. **M20.**
■ **activator** *noun* a thing which or (*rare*) a person who activates **E20.**

activation /aktɪˈveɪʃ(ə)n/ *noun.* **E20.**
[**ORIGIN** from ACTIVATE: see -ATION.]
The action of activating; the state of being activated.
– **COMB.**: **activation analysis** *CHEMISTRY* a technique of analysis in which atoms of a particular element in a sample are made radioactive (esp. by irradiation with neutrons) and their concentration is then determined radiologically; **activation energy** *CHEMISTRY* the minimum quantity of energy which a molecule, ion, etc. must possess in order to take part in a specified chemical reaction.

active /ˈaktɪv/ *adjective & noun.* **ME.**
[**ORIGIN** Latin *activus*, formed as ACT *verb* + -IVE; partly from French *actif, -ive*.]
► **A** *adjective.* **1** Given to action rather than contemplation or speculation; practical. **ME.**
active citizen a member of the public who actively takes the initiative in crime prevention etc.
2 Originating or communicating action. **LME.**
3 *GRAMMAR.* Designating, being in, involving, or pertaining to a voice comprising all forms of intransitive verbs, and those forms of transitive verbs that attribute the action of the verb to the person or thing whence it proceeds (the logical subject, in this case coinciding with the grammatical subject). Opp. ***passive***, and in some languages ***middle***. **LME.**
4 Energetic; diligent; brisk; busy. **LME.**

SHAKES. *2 Hen. IV* The most active fellow in Europe. DAY LEWIS Sunday was . . the most active day of the week.

activewear casual, comfortable clothing suitable for sport or exercise, sportswear.
5 Working, effective; not quiescent or extinct. **M17.** ►**b** Radioactive. **E20.** ►**c** *ELECTRONICS.* Of a circuit: containing a source of power. Opp. ***passive***. **M20.** ►**d** *ELECTRONICS & MECHANICS.* Of a system: capable of modifying its state or characteristics automatically in response to input or feedback. **M20.**

BOSWELL Instances of his active benevolence. **d** *Autocar* A sensational prototype with a . . turbo-engine, four-wheel drive, active suspension.

active carbon, **active charcoal** activated carbon. **active driveway** *US*: in use by vehicles etc. **active immunity** *MEDICINE*: resulting from the production of antibodies by the immune system in response to the presence of an antigen. **active layer** *PHYSICAL GEOGRAPHY* a seasonally thawed surface layer above permafrost. **active list** a list of officers in the armed forces liable to be called on for service. **active matrix** *ELECTRONICS* a display system in which each pixel is individually controlled. **active service** actual participation in warfare; full-time service in armed forces. **active site** *BIOCHEMISTRY* a region on an enzyme that binds to and reacts with the substrate during a reaction. **active transport** *BIOLOGY* the movement of ions or molecules across a cell membrane into a region of higher concentration, assisted by enzymes and requiring energy. **active volcano** a volcano that is erupting or has erupted in historical times. ***optically active***: see OPTICALLY.
► **B** *absol.* as *noun.* **1** A person devoted to the active life. **LME.**
2 *GRAMMAR.* *The* active voice; an active form of a verb. **M16.**
■ **actively** *adverb* **LME.** **activeness** *noun* the quality of being active; *esp.* = ACTIVITY 2: **E16.**

activism /ˈaktɪvɪz(ə)m/ *noun.* **E20.**
[**ORIGIN** from ACTIVE *adjective* + -ISM.]
1 *PHILOSOPHY.* The theory that everything whatsoever is active. Now *rare*. **E20.**
2 A policy of vigorous action, esp. in politics. **E20.**
■ **activist** *noun & adjective* (*a*) *noun* an advocate of activism; (*b*) *adjective* of or pertaining to activists or activism: **E20.**

activity /akˈtɪvɪti/ *noun.* **LME.**
[**ORIGIN** French *activité* or late Latin *activitas*, formed as ACTIVE: see -ITY.]
1 The state of being active; the exertion of energy, action. **LME.** ►**b** The degree to which an enzyme or other substance exhibits its characteristic property. **L19.** ►**c** Radioactivity. **E20.** ►**d** *CHEMISTRY.* A thermodynamic quantity which is a measure of the effective concentration of a substance in a system. **E20.**
c specific activity: see SPECIFIC *adjective*.
2 Brisk or vigorous action; energy; diligence; liveliness. **L15.**
optical activity: see OPTICAL.
†**3** Gymnastics, athletics; a gymnastic exercise. **M16–E18.**
4 An active force or operation; an occupation, a pursuit. **M17.** ►**b** In *pl.* Things that a person, animal, or group chooses to do. **E20.**

b H. W. FOWLER A regrettable by-product of their activities. *Listener* The widespread activities of the state security police.

actomyosin /aktə(ʊ)ˈmʌɪəsɪn/ *noun.* **M20.**
[**ORIGIN** from ACTIN + -O- + MYOSIN.]
BIOCHEMISTRY. A complex of actin and myosin.

acton /ˈakt(ə)n/ *noun. obsolete* exc. *hist.* Also **aketon**. **ME.**
[**ORIGIN** Old French *auqueton* (mod. *hoqueton*), ult. from Hispano-Arabic. *alqutūn* the cotton.]
A jacket of quilted cotton worn under mail; a mail-plated jacket of leather etc.

actor /ˈaktə/ *noun.* **LME.**
[**ORIGIN** Latin, formed as ACT *verb* + -OR. Cf. Old French & mod. French *acteur*.]
1 An agent, *esp.* an administrator; a person who acts on behalf of another. *obsolete* exc. *ROMAN LAW* (**15–17** chiefly *Scot.*). **LME.**
†**2** The plaintiff or complainant in a legal action; a pleader. **LME–M18.**
3 A person who performs or takes part in any action; a doer. **M16.**
4 A person whose occupation is acting in plays, films, etc. **L16.**

Daily Telegraph Finney . . was named best supporting actor in the awards.

character actor, ***utility actor***, etc.
■ **actorish**, **actorly** *adjectives* appropriate to or characteristic of a dramatic actor; affectedly theatrical: **M20.** **actorship** *noun* **L16.** **actory** *adjective* = ACTORISH **E20.**

actress /ˈaktrɪs/ *noun.* **L16.**
[**ORIGIN** from ACTOR + -ESS[1].]
†**1** A female doer. **L16–E18.**
2 A female actor in plays, films, etc. **E18.**
■ **actressy** *adjective* pertaining to or characteristic of an actress **L19.**

actual /ˈaktjʊəl, -tʃʊəl/ *adjective & noun.* **ME.**
[**ORIGIN** Old French & mod. French *actuel* from late Latin *actualis* active, practical, from *actus* ACT *noun*: see -AL[1]. The spelling *-al* is by assim. to Latin.]
► **A** *adjective.* **1** Pertaining to or exhibited in acts; practical, active. *obsolete* exc. as below. **ME.**
actual grace *THEOLOGY* a divine influence inspiring some good act. **actual sin** *THEOLOGY* a sin resulting from an individual act of free will (opp. ***original sin***).
2 Existing in act or fact; real. **LME.**

S. HILL He had no illusions about himself as actual or potential soldier. A. BURGESS Too late to attend the actual ceremony.

actual cautery: see CAUTERY 1.
3 In action or existence at the time; present, current. **L16.**

J. BRAINE Husbands were chosen as much on eventual as actual salary.

► **B** *noun.* In *pl.* Actual qualities, actualities. **M16.**
■ **actualism** *noun* (*a*) (now *rare*) the theory that nothing is merely passive; (*b*) realism: **M19.** **actualist** *noun* an advocate of actualism **M19.** **actuaˈlistic** *adjective* of the nature of actualism; realistic: **L19.** **actualness** *noun* actuality **LME.**

actualise *verb* var. of ACTUALIZE.

actuality /aktjʊˈalɪti, -tʃʊ-/ *noun.* **LME.**
[**ORIGIN** Old French *actualité* or medieval Latin *actualitas*, from *actualis*: see ACTUAL, -ITY.]
†**1** Capacity of action, activity. **LME–L17.**
2 Reality; existing objective fact. **M17.**
3 In *pl.* Existing conditions or circumstances. **M17.**
4 Realism in description or presentation. **M19.**

attrib.: L. MACNEICE The radio dramatist . . must select his actuality material with great discrimination.

actualize /ˈaktjʊəlʌɪz, -tʃʊ-/ *verb trans.* Also **-ise**. **E18.**
[**ORIGIN** from ACTUAL *adjective* + -IZE.]
Make actual or real; realize in action or description.
■ **actualiˈzation** *noun* **E19.**

actually /ˈaktjʊəli, -tʃʊ-/ *adverb.* **LME.**
[**ORIGIN** from ACTUAL *adjective* + -LY[2]: partly after late Latin *actualiter*, French *actuellement*.]
†**1** With deeds; actively. **LME–M17.**
2 As a fact; really. **LME.**

GEO. ELIOT With a fixed look, seeing nothing that was actually present.

3 As a present fact, at present, for the time being. **E16.**

OED The party actually in power.

4 As a matter of fact; indeed; even (strange as it may seem). **M18.**

E. O'NEILL You feel no shame, but actually boast you are planning to dishonour yourself and your family. D. HEFFRON We think it's quite all right, actually.

actuarial /aktjʊˈɛːrɪəl, -tʃʊ-/ *adjective.* **M19.**
[**ORIGIN** from ACTUARY + -AL[1].]
Of or pertaining to actuaries or their profession.
■ **actuarially** *adverb* in relation to actuarial principles; on an actuarial basis: **L19.**

actuary /ˈaktjʊəri, -tʃʊ-/ *noun.* **M16.**
[**ORIGIN** Latin *actuarius*, from *actus* ACT *noun*: see -ARY[1].]
1 A registrar, a clerk; an officer who records the acts of a court. *obsolete* exc. in the Convocation of the Province of Canterbury (Ch. of England). **M16.**
2 An officer who manages the deposits in a savings bank. **E19.**
3 A person who compiles statistics of mortality, accidents, etc., and calculates insurance risks and premiums. **M19.**

actuate /ˈaktjʊeɪt, -tʃʊ-/ *verb.* **L16.**
[**ORIGIN** medieval Latin *actuat-* pa. ppl stem of *actuare*, from *actus* ACT *noun*: see -ATE[3].]
†**1** *verb trans.* Carry out in practice. (*rare* after **17.**) **L16–L19.**
2 *verb trans.* Give life to, enliven, vivify; stir into activity, excite. Now *rare* or *obsolete*. **L16.**
3 *verb intrans.* Exert activity, act. **E17.**
4 *verb trans.* Communicate motion to (a machine etc.); cause the operation of (an electrical device etc.); be the motive for (an action). **M17.**
5 *verb trans.* Be the motive for action of (a person). **M18.**
■ **actuator** *noun* a person who or thing which actuates **L19.**

actuation /aktjʊˈeɪʃ(ə)n, -tʃʊ-/ *noun.* **E17.**
[**ORIGIN** In early use from medieval Latin *actuatio(n-)*, formed as ACTUATE; later from ACTUATE: see -ATION.]
A communication of motion; a bringing into action; impulse, movement.

actus reus /ˌaktəs ˈreɪəs/ *noun phr.* **E20.**
[**ORIGIN** Latin = guilty act.]
LAW. The action or conduct which is a constituent element of a crime, as opposed to the *mens rea* or mental guilt which the accused must be shown to have had.

acuate /ˈakjʊət/ *adjective.* **LME.**
[**ORIGIN** medieval Latin *acuatus* pa. pple of *acuare* var. of Latin *acuere*: see ACUTE, -ATE[2].]
Made sharp or pungent; sharp-pointed.

†**acuate** *verb trans.* **M16–M18.**
[**ORIGIN** from ACUATE *adjective*: see -ATE[3].]
Make sharp or pungent.

acuity /əˈkjuːɪti/ *noun.* **LME.**
[**ORIGIN** Old French & mod. French *acuité* or medieval Latin *acuitas*, from *acuere*: see ACUTE, -ITY.]
Sharpness (*lit.* & *fig.*, as of a needle, the sight or hearing, wit, etc.).
visual acuity: see VISUAL *adjective*.

aculeate /əˈkjuːlɪət/ *adjective & noun*. **M17.**
[ORIGIN Latin *aculeatus*, from *aculeus* dim. of *acus* needle: see -ATE[2].]
▸ **A** *adjective* **1 a** ZOOLOGY. Bearing a sting; *spec.* designating hymenopterous insects of the section Aculeata, which comprises bees, ants, and wasps. **M17.** ▸**b** BOTANY. Sharply pointed; prickly; (of a leaf) edged with sharply pointed projections, like a saw. **M17.**
2 *fig.* Pointed, incisive, stinging. **M17.**
▸ **B** *noun*. An aculeate insect. **L19.**
■ **aculeated** /-eɪtɪd/ *adjective* sharply pointed; armed with prickles; incisive: **M17.**

acumen /ˈakjʊmən, əˈkjuːmən/ *noun*. **L16.**
[ORIGIN Latin *acumen*, *-min-* point, acuteness, from *acuere*: see ACUTE.]
1 Sharpness of wit; penetration of perception; keenness of discrimination. **L16.**
2 BOTANY. A tapering point. **L18.**

acuminate /əˈkjuːmɪnət/ *adjective*. **L16.**
[ORIGIN Late Latin *acuminat-* pa. ppl stem of *acuminare* sharpen to a point, formed as ACUMEN: see -ATE[2].]
BOTANY & ZOOLOGY. Tapering to a point.

acuminate /əˈkjuːmɪneɪt/ *verb*. **L16.**
[ORIGIN formed as ACUMEN: see -ATE[3].]
1 *verb trans.* Sharpen; give poignancy or keenness to. **L16.**
2 *verb intrans.* Rise or taper to a point. Chiefly as ***acuminating*** *ppl adjective*. **M17.**
■ **acumiˈnation** *noun* sharpening or giving point to (*lit.* & *fig.*); tending towards a point; a tapering point: **M17.**

acupoint /ˈakjʊpɔɪnt/ *noun*. **L20.**
[ORIGIN from *acu-* as in ACUPUNCTURE + POINT *noun*[1].]
Any of the supposed energy points on the body where acupuncture needles are inserted or manual pressure is applied during acupressure.

acupressure /ˈakjʊprɛʃə/ *noun*. **M19.**
[ORIGIN from Latin *acu* with a needle + PRESSURE *noun*.]
MEDICINE. **1** The prevention of bleeding from an artery by compressing it with one or more needles inserted through the adjacent tissue. **M19.**
2 The application of pressure with the fingers to points on the body, for therapeutic purposes, = SHIATSU. (Now the usual sense.) **M20.**

acupuncture /ˈakjʊpʌŋktʃə/ *noun*. **L17.**
[ORIGIN mod. Latin *acupunctura*, from Latin *acu-*, *acus* needle + *punctura*: see PUNCTURE *noun*.]
Pricking with a needle; *spec.* the insertion of needles into living tissues for remedial purposes, other than for the injection of drugs.
■ **acupunctuˈation** *noun* (now *rare*) = ACUPUNCTURATION **M19.** **acupunctuˈration** *noun* the practice or process of acupuncture **M18.** **acupuncturist** *noun* a person who practises acupuncture **M20.**

acushla /əˈkʊʃlə/ *noun*. *Irish*. **M19.**
[ORIGIN Irish, short for *a chuisle mo chroí* O pulse of my heart. Cf. CUSHLA-MACHREE, MACUSHLA.]
As a form of address: darling, dear heart.

acutance /əˈkjuːt(ə)ns/ *noun*. **M20.**
[ORIGIN from ACUTE *adjective* + -ANCE.]
Sharpness of a photographic or printed image; a measure of this.

acute /əˈkjuːt/ *adjective, noun, & verb*. **LME.**
[ORIGIN Latin *acutus* pa. pple of *acuere* sharpen, from *acus* needle.]
▸ **A** *adjective*. **1** MEDICINE. Of a disease or its symptoms: of short duration (and usu. severe). Cf. CHRONIC *adjective* 1. **LME.** ▸**b** Of a medical facility: designed or reserved for the treatment of acute illness. **M20.**

> *Independent* Nine out of 10 child victims of acute leukaemia survive. **b** *Guardian* The county's one major acute hospital in Truro.

2 a Of an angle: less than a right angle. **M16.** ▸**b** Sharp at the end; coming to a point. **L16.**
3 Of a sound: shrill, high (PHONETICS as a classificatory feature, opp. ***grave***). **M16.**
acute accent the mark ˊ placed over letters in some languages to show quality, vowel length, pronunciation, etc.
4 Of the intellect: penetrating, sharp-witted, shrewd. Cf. CUTE *adjective*[1]. **L16.**
†**5** Of tastes or odours: sharp, pungent. **E–M17.**
6 Of pain, pleasure, etc.: keen, intense. **M17.**

> A. BROOKNER She . . felt acute sadness.

7 Of the senses, the nervous system: responsive or sensitive to impressions; finely strung. **M18.**

> G. MACDONALD His hearing is acute at all times.

8 Of something unpleasant or unwelcome: critical, serious. **M20.**

> *Modern Railways* An acute shortage of suitable rolling stock.

▸ **B** *noun*. An acute illness, tone, etc.; *esp.* an acute accent. **LME.**
▸ †**C** *verb trans.* Sharpen; mark with an acute accent. Chiefly as ***acuted*** *ppl adjective*. **M17–L18.**
■ **acutely** *adverb* **L16.** **acuteness** *noun* **E17.**

ACV *abbreviation*.
Air-cushion vehicle.

ACW *abbreviation*.
Aircraftwoman.

-acy /əsi/ *suffix*.
[ORIGIN A branch of -CY.]
Forming nouns of quality, state, or condition.
1 Repr. Latin *-acia*, from adjectives in *-aci-*, *-ax*, as ***fallacy***.
2 Repr. Latin *-atia* (medieval Latin often *-acia*), from nouns in *-at-*, *-as*, as ***abbacy***, ***primacy***; similarly ***supremacy***.
3 Repr. medieval Latin *-atia*, from nouns in *-atus*, as ***advocacy***, ***prelacy***; hence from nouns in -ATE[1], as ***confederacy***, and adjectives in -ATE[2], as ***accuracy***, ***obstinacy***.
4 Repr. Greek nouns in *-ateia*, as ***piracy***. See also -CRACY.

acyclic /eɪˈsʌɪklɪk, -ˈsɪk-/ *adjective*. **L19.**
[ORIGIN from A-[10] + CYCLIC.]
Not cyclic.

acyl /ˈeɪsʌɪl, ˈasɪl/ *adjective*. **L19.**
[ORIGIN German, from Latin *acidum* acid: see -YL.]
CHEMISTRY. A radical (RCO·) derived from an organic acid by loss of hydroxyl from the carboxy group. Usu. in *comb.*
■ **acylate** *verb trans.* introduce an acyl radical into (a compound) **E20.** **acyˈlation** *noun* **E20.**

AD *abbreviation*.
Latin *anno domini* = in the year of our Lord, of the Christian era.
– NOTE: Usu. written in small capitals and placed before the numerals, as in AD 375 (not 375 AD).

ad /ad/ *noun*. *colloq.* **M19.**
[ORIGIN Abbreviation.]
An advertisement; advertising.
– COMB. & PHRASES: **adman** a person who produces advertisements commercially; **admass** the section of the community regarded as readily influenced by advertising; **adware** (proprietary name for) software for use in the advertising industry; software containing advertising matter such as banners or pop-ups; ***small ad***: see SMALL *adjective*.
■ **adless** *adjective* **E20.**

ad- /ad, *unstressed* əd/ *prefix*.
1 Repr. Latin *ad* preposition 'to', with sense of motion to or direction towards, addition, adherence, increase. The *d* was assim. to following *c*, *f*, *g*, *l*, *n*, *p*, *q*, *r*, *s*, *t* (see AC-, AF-, etc.); *ad-* was reduced to *a-* before *sc*, *sp*, *st* (see A-[8]). In Old French the double consonants of *acc-*, *add-*, etc., were reduced to single ones, and *adv-* became *av-*, and Old French words were adopted with such forms in English; but in the 14th cent. these began to be refashioned after Latin, as ***address***. Opp. to *ab-* away from, as in ***adaxial***, ***abaxial***, *ad-* is recent.
2 At the same time *ad-* was substituted for *a-* of different origin, as in ***advance***, ***addebted***, ***admiral***.

A/D *abbreviation*.
ELECTRONICS. Analogue to digital.

-ad /ad, əd/ *suffix*[1].
[ORIGIN Repr. Latin from Greek *-ad-*, *-as*.]
1 Forming collect. numerals, as ***monad***, ***myriad***, etc.
2 Forming fem. patronymics (var. of -ID[2]) as ***dryad***, ***naiad***, etc.
3 In names of epic poems, as ***Dunciad***, ***Rosciad***, after *Iliad*.
4 BOTANY. Forming names of members of some taxonomic groupings, as ***bromeliad***, ***cycad***.

-ad /əd/ *suffix*[2].
• Repr. French *-ade*, as *ballad*, *salad*, etc.: see -ADE.

-ad /ad/ *suffix*[3]. **E19.**
[ORIGIN from Latin *ad* to: cf. AD-.]
ANATOMY. Invented to form adjectives and adverbs in the sense of 'nearer to' or 'towards' (the part denoted by the main element of the word), as ***dorsad*** etc.

ADA *abbreviation*.
Adenosine deaminase.

Ada /ˈeɪdə/ *noun*. **L20.**
[ORIGIN *Ada* Lovelace (1815–52), English mathematician, who assisted Charles Babbage on his mechanical computer.]
(The name of) a high-level computer programming language used chiefly in real-time computerized control systems, e.g. for aircraft navigation.

†**adad** *interjection*. Also **adod**. **M17–M18.**
[ORIGIN formed as AGAD, EGAD, etc.]
= EGAD.

adage /ˈadɪdʒ/ *noun*[1]. **M16.**
[ORIGIN French from Latin *adagium*, from *ad* AD- + an early form of *aio* I say.]
A traditional maxim, a proverb of common experience.
■ **adagial** /əˈdeɪdʒɪəl/ *adjective* of the nature of an adage **L17.** †**adagy** *noun* [Latin *adagium*] an adage **M16–M18.**

adage /adaːʒ/ *noun*[2]. Pl. pronounced same. **M20.**
[ORIGIN French, formed as ADAGIO.]
= ADAGIO *noun* 2.

adagio /əˈdɑːdʒɪəʊ/ *adverb, adjective, & noun*. **L17.**
[ORIGIN Italian, from *ad agio* at ease.]
MUSIC. ▸**A** *adverb & adjective*. In slow time, leisurely. **L17.**
▸ **B** *noun*. Pl. **-os**.
1 A musical piece or movement in slow time. **M18.**
2 A dance or ballet movement in slow time. **M18.**

Adam /ˈadəm/ *noun*. **ME.**
[ORIGIN Hebrew *'ādām* man, later interpreted as a name.]
1 The first man in Hebrew tradition. **ME.**
2 More fully (now the only form) ***old Adam***. Unregenerate human nature. **E16.**
– COMB. & PHRASES: **Adam-and-Eve** *dial.* any of various plants, *esp.* any of certain orchids (from the supposed resemblance of the tubers to a human couple); **Adam's ale**, (*Scot. & N. English*) **Adam's wine** *joc.* water; **Adam's apple** (*a*) any of various fruits, *esp.* a variety of lime; (*b*) the projection formed in the neck by the thyroid cartilage, esp. when prominent in men; **Adam's needle** yucca, esp. *Y. filamentosa*. **not know from Adam** have no knowledge of (a man). ***second Adam***: see SECOND *adjective*. **would you Adam and Eve it?** *rhyming slang* would you believe it?
■ **Aˈdamic** *adjective* = ADAMICAL **M18.** **Aˈdamical** *adjective* pertaining to or resembling Adam **M17.**

Adam /ˈadəm/ *adjective*. **L19.**
[ORIGIN A surname.]
Designed or built by, or in the style of, the brothers Robert and James Adam, 18th-cent. Scottish architects and designers.
■ **Adaˈmesque** *adjective* resembling the work of the Adam brothers **M20.**

adamant /ˈadəm(ə)nt/ *noun & adjective*. **OE.**
[ORIGIN Old French *adamaunt-* from Latin *adamant-*, *-ma(n)s* from Greek *adamant-*, *-mas* hardest iron or steel, diamond, orig. adjective 'invincible', from *a-* A-[10] + *daman* tame. The sense 'magnet, lodestone' arose from assoc. of medieval Latin *adamas* with Latin *adamare* have a strong liking for. Cf. DIAMOND *noun & adjective*.]
▸ **A** *noun*. An alleged rock or mineral, to which many (often contradictory) properties have been attributed, formerly sometimes identified with the diamond or with the lodestone or magnet. Now only *poet. & rhet.* as an embodiment of impregnable hardness. **OE.**
▸ **B** *adjective*. Unshakeable, unyielding to requests. **M20.**
■ **adamance** *noun* adamantine quality; refusal to yield: **M20.** **adamantly** *adverb* **M20.**

adamantane /adəˈmanteɪn/ *noun*. **M19.**
[ORIGIN French, formed as ADAMANT + -ANE.]
CHEMISTRY. A crystalline alicylic hydrocarbon, $C_{10}H_{16}$, in the molecule of which the carbon atoms are arranged in three six-sided rings as in the crystal structure of diamond.

adamantine /adəˈmantʌɪn/ *adjective*. **ME.**
[ORIGIN Latin *adamantinus* from Greek *adamantinos*, from *adamant-* ADAMANT: see -INE[2].]
Made of, or having the qualities of, adamant; unbreakable, impregnable, unshakeable.

> POPE To count them all, demands . . A throat of brass, and adamantine lungs. C. P. SNOW An adamantine will for success.

■ Also †**adamantean** *adjective* (*rare*, Milton): only in **L17.**

adamellite /adəˈmɛlʌɪt/ *noun*. **L19.**
[ORIGIN from Monte *Adamello* in northern Italy + -ITE[1].]
GEOLOGY. A quartz-bearing plutonic igneous rock containing roughly equal proportions of orthoclase and plagioclase.

Adamite /ˈadəmʌɪt/ *noun*[1] *& adjective*. **M16.**
[ORIGIN ecclesiastical Latin *Adamita*: see ADAM *noun*, -ITE[1].]
▸ **A** *noun*. **1** A person who goes naked like Adam; *esp.* a member of any of various sects advocating nakedness. **M16.**
2 A human being regarded as a descendant of Adam. **M17.**
▸ **B** *adjective*. Descended from Adam; human. **M19.**
■ **Adaˈmitical** *adjective* pertaining to an Adamite or Adamites; naked like Adam: **M17.** **Adamitism** *noun* (*rare*) the beliefs and practices of Adamites **M19.**

adamite /ˈadəmʌɪt/ *noun*[2]. **M19.**
[ORIGIN from G. J. *Adam* (1795–1881), French mineralogist + -ITE[1].]
MINERALOGY. A basic zinc arsenate occurring as yellow, green, or colourless orthorhombic crystals or crystal aggregates.

adance /əˈdɑːns/ *adverb & pred. adjective*. **E19.**
[ORIGIN from A-[2] + DANCE *noun* or *verb*.]
Dancing.

adangle /əˈdaŋɡ(ə)l/ *adverb & pred. adjective*. **M19.**
[ORIGIN from A-[2] + DANGLE *verb*.]
Dangling.

adapt /əˈdapt/ *verb*. Pa. pple & ppl adjective **adapted**, †**adapt**. **LME.**
[ORIGIN French *adapter* from Latin *adaptare*, from *ad* AD- + *aptare*, from *aptus* fit, APT.]
1 *verb trans.* Fit, adjust, (*to*); make suitable (*to* or *for*). **LME.**

> W. S. MAUGHAM She . . was unable to adapt her expenditure to her altered circumstances.

2 *verb trans.* Alter or modify to fit for a new use, new conditions, etc. **L18.**

> C. HAMPTON The account of the Beiços-de-Pau tribe . . is adapted from his diaries.

3 *verb intrans.* Undergo modification to fit a new use, new conditions, etc. **M20.**

> H. WOUK Rhoda adapted merrily to diplomatic life.

■ **adaptative** *adjective* = ADAPTIVE **E19.** **adaptedness** *noun* the state of being adapted **L17.** **adaption** *noun* = ADAPTATION **M17.** **adaptitude** *noun* (*rare*) specially produced aptitude **M19.**

adaptability /ədaptə'bɪlɪti/ *noun*. M17.
[ORIGIN from ADAPT: see -ABILITY.]
The state or quality of being adaptable.

adaptable /ə'daptəb(ə)l/ *adjective*. E19.
[ORIGIN formed as ADAPTABILITY + -ABLE.]
Able to be adapted (*to*, *for*) or to adapt oneself.
■ **adaptableness** *noun* M19.

adaptation /adap'teɪʃ(ə)n/ *noun*. E17.
[ORIGIN French from late Latin *adaptatio(n-)*, from *adaptare*: see ADAPT, -ATION.]
1 The action or process of fitting or suiting one thing *to* another. E17. ▸**b** Modification to fit a new use, new conditions, etc. L18. ▸**c** *BIOLOGY*. Modification by which an organ, organism, or species becomes better fitted for its environment or mode of existence. M19.

b L. BLOOMFIELD Adaptation . . , in which the foreign form is altered to meet the fundamental phonetic habits of the language. **c** B. J. WILLIAMS The pelvis and limbs of *Oreopithecus* indicate an adaptation to upright posture.

2 The condition of being adapted; suitableness. L17.

J. MARTINEAU The adaptation of immortality to our true wants.

3 An instance of adapting; something adapted. M19.

L. HELLMAN *Monserrat*, an adaptation I made from the French play by Emmanuel Roblès.

■ **adaptational** *adjective* L19.

adaptationism /adəp'teɪʃ(ə)nɪz(ə)m/ *noun*. L20.
[ORIGIN from ADAPTATION + -ISM.]
BIOLOGY. A reductionist approach to the study of biological adaptations which considers each character or feature of an organism as having evolved in isolation to fulfil a specific function.
■ **adaptationist** *noun & adjective* L20.

adapter /ə'daptə/ *noun*. Also **-or**. M18.
[ORIGIN from ADAPT *verb* + -ER[1], -OR.]
1 A device allowing connection of pieces of equipment, e.g. chemical apparatus, unable to be connected directly. M18. ▸**b** *spec*. An electrical fitting of this nature, usu. one enabling more than one plug to be connected to the same socket. E20.
2 A person who adapts. E19.
– NOTE: *Adapter* is now more usual for a person, *adaptor* for a device.

adaptive /ə'daptɪv/ *adjective*. E19.
[ORIGIN from ADAPT *verb* + -IVE.]
Characterized by or given to adaptation.
adaptive radiation: see RADIATION 2d.
■ **adaptively** *adverb* by way of adaptation; to suit special conditions: M19. **adaptiveness** *noun* M19. **adap'tivity** *noun* the quality of being adaptive L19.

adaptor *noun* see ADAPTER.

Adar /a'dɑː/ *noun*. LME.
[ORIGIN Hebrew *'ăḏār*.]
In the Jewish calendar, the sixth month of the civil and twelfth of the religious year, usu. coinciding with parts of February and March; in leap years, either of two successive months, ***First Adar*** and ***Second Adar*** (coinciding with parts of March and April).

adat /'adat/ *noun*. L18.
[ORIGIN Malay from Arabic *'āda*.]
Custom, or customary law, in the Islamic regions of SE Asia, esp. in contrast to Islamic religious law. Also ***adat law***.

adatom /'adat(ə)m/ *noun*. M20.
[ORIGIN Contr. of *adsorbed atom*: see ADSORB *verb*, ATOM.]
PHYSICAL CHEMISTRY. An atom adsorbed on a surface.

†**adaunt** *verb trans*. ME–L16.
[ORIGIN Prob. from Anglo-Norman: cf. Anglo-Norman *adant(e)üre* training, breaking in (of a horse) and see DAUNT.]
Quell, subdue.

S. DANIEL Wherewith the Rebell rather was the more Incourag'd than addaunted.

†**adaw** *verb trans*. LME–M17.
[ORIGIN from adverbial phr. *a* (*o*, *of*) *dawe*, from A *preposition*[2] + *dawe* obsolete form of DAY *noun*, = Old English *of dagum* from days, from life.]
Subdue, daunt.

SPENSER Like one adawed with some dreadfull spright.

adaxial /a'daksɪəl/ *adjective*. E20.
[ORIGIN from AD- + AXIAL.]
BOTANY. Towards the axis; (of the surface of a leaf etc.) initially facing towards the stem.

a-day /ə'deɪ/ *adverb*. ME.
[ORIGIN Orig. two words, from A *preposition*[1] 3 + DAY *noun*.]
†**1** By day. Only in ME.
2 Daily. (The *a* now identified with the indef. article: see A *adjective* 4.) See also NOWADAY. ME.

a-days /ə'deɪz/ *adverb*. LME.
[ORIGIN from A *preposition*[1] 3 + genit. sing. of DAY *noun* (used alone adverbially in Old English in sense 'by day', and later blended with A-DAY).]
†**1** By day. LME–M18.
2 At the present time. Chiefly & now only with *now*: see NOWADAYS. LME.

adazzle /ə'daz(ə)l/ *adverb & pred. adjective*. M19.
[ORIGIN from A-[2] + DAZZLE *verb & noun*.]
Dazzling.

ADC *abbreviation*.
1 Aide-de-camp.
2 Analogue–digital converter.

ad captandum vulgus /ad kap'tandəm 'vʌlgəs/ *adverbial & adjectival phr*. M18.
[ORIGIN Latin = for alluring the crowd.]
(Designed) to appeal to the emotions (of the rabble). Also ***ad captandum***.

ADD *abbreviation*.
Attention deficit disorder.

add /ad/ *verb*. LME.
[ORIGIN Latin *addere*, from *ad* AD- + base of *dare* put, give.]
1 *verb trans*. Join or unite (one thing *to* another) as an increase or supplement. LME. ▸†**b** *verb trans*. Give by way of increased possession (*to*). M16–E18.

TENNYSON Yet this grief Is added to the griefs the great must bear. **b** AV *Matt*. 6:33 All these things shalbe added vnto you.

2 *spec*. ▸**a** *verb trans*. Unite (a number *to* another) to get a number equal to their total amount. LME. ▸**b** *verb intrans*. Perform the arithmetical process of addition. L15. ▸**c** *verb trans*. Unite (two or more numbers, freq. *together*) into one sum. L17.
3 *verb trans*. Say or write in addition; go on to say. LME.

POPE But let me add, Sir Robert's mighty dull.

4 *verb intrans*. Foll. by *to*: increase, augment. L16.

S. DELANEY You've got enough bad habits without adding to your repertoire.

– COMB. ETC.: **add in** include in a sum; **add-in** *adjective & noun* (*COMPUTING*) (a device) fitted to a system internally to enhance its capabilities or performance; **add-on** *adjective & noun* (something) that has been or can be added to what already exists; **add up** (*a*) *verb phr. trans. & intrans*. find the sum of (a series of numbers); (*b*) *verb phr. intrans*. make the desired or correct total; amount *to*; *colloq*. make sense.

addax /'adaks/ *noun*. L17.
[ORIGIN Latin from an African word (quoted by Pliny).]
A large, stocky antelope, *Addax nasomaculatus*, with twisted horns, native to the N. African desert.

†**addebted** *pa. pple & ppl adjective*. *Scot*. E16–E19.
[ORIGIN formed as INDEBTED, refashioned with AD-.]
Indebted.

†**addeem** *verb trans*. *literary*. Only in L16.
[ORIGIN from DEEM *verb* after *adjudge*: see A-[11].]
Adjudge.

addend /'adɛnd/ *noun*. L17.
[ORIGIN Latin *addendus* masc. gerundive (sc. *numerus* number) of *addere* ADD: see -END. Cf. ADDENDUM.]
A number which is to be added to another.

addendum /ə'dɛndəm/ *noun*. Pl. **-da** /-də/. L17.
[ORIGIN Latin, neut. gerundive of *addere* ADD: cf. ADDEND.]
1 A thing to be added, esp. because of omission; an appendix, an addition; *sing*. & (esp.) in *pl*. (occas. treated as *sing*.), additional matter at the end of a book. L17.
2 *MECHANICS*. The radial distance from the pitch circle of a cogwheel, wormwheel, etc., to the crests of the teeth or ridge. M19.

adder /'adə/ *noun*[1].
[ORIGIN Old English *nǣd(d)re*, corresp. to Old Saxon *nādra* (Middle Dutch *nadre*, Dutch *adder*), Old High German *nātara* (German *Natter*), and (with a different vowel grade) Old Norse *naðr*, *naðra*, Gothic *nadrs*; perh. rel. to Latin *natrix* water snake, Old Irish *nathir*, Welsh *neidr* snake, viper. The initial *n* was lost in Middle English (14–15) through the erroneous division of *a naddre* as *an addre*, as in *apron*, *auger*, etc.]
†**1** A serpent, a snake; *fig*. *the* Devil. OE–E16.
2 A small poisonous snake, a viper; *spec*. the common European viper, *Vipera berus*. OE. ▸**b** Any of various other poisonous snakes, belonging esp. to the family Viperidae. Usu. with specifying word. See also ***deaf adder*** s.v. DEAF *adjective*. OE.
deaf as an adder completely deaf. **b** ***death adder***, ***night adder***, ***puff adder***, etc.
– COMB.: **adderbolt** (now *dial*.) a dragonfly; **adder-stone** (now *dial*.) an ancient amulet or bead; a perforated stone; **adderwort** bistort; **adder's grass** the early purple orchid, *Orchis mascula*; **adder's mouth** *N. Amer*. an orchid of the genus *Malaxis*; **adder's tongue** any of several plants; *spec*. a fern of the genus *Ophioglossum*.

adder /'adə/ *noun*[2]. L16.
[ORIGIN from ADD + -ER[1].]
A person who or thing which adds (*rare* in *gen*. sense); *spec*. in a computer, a unit which adds together two input variables.

addict /'adɪkt/ *noun*. E20.
[ORIGIN from ADDICT *verb*.]
A person who is addicted to a drug (usu. specified by prefixed word); *colloq*. an enthusiastic devotee of a sport or pastime (usu. specified by prefixed word).
drug addict, *heroin addict*, *jazz addict*, etc.

†**addict** *ppl adjective*. E16.
[ORIGIN Latin *addictus* pa. pple of *addicere*, from *ad* AD- + *dicere* appoint, allot.]
1 Formally made over or bound *to*. Only in 16.
2 Attached by inclination *to*, devoted *to*. M16–L19.

addict /ə'dɪkt/ *verb trans*. M16.
[ORIGIN Back-form. from ADDICTED.]
†**1** *refl*. Attach or devote oneself as a servant or adherent (*to* a person or cause). M16–L17.
2 Devote or apply habitually or compulsively (*to* a practice). L16.

SHAKES. *2 Hen. IV* To addict themselves to sack. SIR W. SCOTT The researches to which your taste addicts you.

†**3** Deliver over formally by judicial sentence *to*; *fig*. make over, give up. L16–L19.
■ **addicting** *adjective* = ADDICTIVE M20.

addicted /ə'dɪktɪd/ *adjective*. M16.
[ORIGIN from ADDICT *ppl adjective* + -ED[1], the verb being inferred later.]
†**1** Voluntarily attached *to* (a person or party). M16–E18.

JAMES II Addicted to the Royal Interest.

2 Attached by inclination *to* (a practice); devoted *to*; doing or using something, esp. a drug, as a habit or compulsively. M16.

L. A. G. STRONG The only form of music to which he was addicted. J. H. BURN Those who are addicted to cocaine often take it in the form of powder like snuff.

†**3** In *ROMAN LAW*, delivered over by judicial sentence *to*; *fig*. destined, bound *to*. M16–L19.

P. HOLLAND Addicted and destined to death.

†**4** *absol*. Devoted (freq. in subscribing letters). L16–M17.

MILTON The same addicted fidelity.

■ **addictedness** *noun* M17.

addiction /ə'dɪkʃ(ə)n/ *noun*. L16.
[ORIGIN Latin *addictio(n-)*, formed as ADDICT *ppl adjective*; later senses from ADDICT *verb*: see -ION.]
1 The way in which one is addicted; inclination; what one is addicted to. Now *rare*. L16.

G. EWART A public whose addiction / is mainly romantic fiction.

†**2** *ROMAN LAW*. A formal giving over by sentence of court; hence, a dedication of a person to a master. E17–L19.
3 The state of being addicted *to* a habit or pursuit; *esp*. the state of dependence on a drug to the extent that it cannot be withdrawn without adverse effects. M17.

addictive /ə'dɪktɪv/ *adjective*. M20.
[ORIGIN from ADDICT *verb* + -IVE.]
Tending to cause addiction or dependence.
■ **addictively** *adverb* L20.

addio /ad'diːo/ *interjection*. L18.
[ORIGIN Italian, from *a* to + *Dio* god: cf. ADIEU, ADIOS.]
Goodbye. (Formerly in general use in the subscription of letters etc.).

Addisonian /adɪ'səʊnɪən/ *adjective*[1]. L18.
[ORIGIN from *Addison* (see below) + -IAN.]
Pertaining to or characteristic of the English essayist, poet, and dramatist Joseph Addison (1672–1719) or his works.

Addisonian /adɪ'səʊnɪən/ *adjective*[2]. E20.
[ORIGIN formed as ADDISON'S DISEASE + -IAN.]
MEDICINE. **1** ***Addisonian anaemia***, pernicious anaemia. E20.
2 Suffering from or pertaining to Addison's disease. M20.

Addison's disease /'adɪs(ə)nz dɪˌziːz/ *noun phr*. M19.
[ORIGIN Thomas *Addison* (1793–1860), English physician.]
MEDICINE. A condition associated with a deficiency of adrenal corticosteroids, which is characterized by weakness, low blood pressure, and brown pigmentation of the skin.

additament /'adɪtəm(ə)nt/ *noun*. LME.
[ORIGIN Old French *additement* or Latin *additamentum*, formed as ADDITION: see -MENT.]
A thing added or appended.

addition /ə'dɪʃ(ə)n/ *noun*. LME.
[ORIGIN Old French & mod. French, or Latin *additio(n-)*, from *addit-* pa. ppl stem of *addere* ADD: see -ION.]
1 The action or process of adding. LME. ▸**b** *CHEMISTRY*. The combination of one molecule with another to form a larger molecule with no other products. L19.

W. S. MAUGHAM A few sums in simple addition.

in addition as an added thing (*to*), as well. **note of addition**, **point of addition** *MUSIC* (now *hist*.) a dot on the right of a note signifying that it is to be lengthened by half (a second dot increasing its value by a further fourth; cf. DOT *noun*[1] 4b, ***double dot*** s.v. DOUBLE *adjective & adverb*.).
2 A thing added; an appendix, an accession. LME. ▸**b** *spec*. A phrase, prefix, etc., added to a person's name to distinguish him or her by rank, place of origin, etc. L15.

E. O'NEILL Expecting an addition to the family.

– COMB.: **addition reaction** *CHEMISTRY*: in which addition occurs.

additional /əˈdɪʃ(ə)n(ə)l/ *noun & adjective*. E17.
[ORIGIN from ADDITION + -AL[1].]
▸ **A** *noun*. Something added; an extra. Now *rare*. E17.
▸ **B** *adjective*. Existing in addition; added; supplementary. M17.
■ **additionally** *adverb* M17.

addititious /adɪˈtɪʃəs/ *adjective*. *rare*. M18.
[ORIGIN Late Latin *additicius* (Tertullian), formed as ADDITION + -ITIOUS[1].]
Due to, or of the nature of, an addition.

additive /ˈadɪtɪv/ *adjective & noun*. L17.
[ORIGIN Late Latin *additivus*, formed as ADDITION + -IVE. Cf. French *additif, -ive*.]
▸ **A** *adjective*. **1** Characterized by addition; to be added. L17. **2** Of or pertaining to the reproduction of colours by the superimposition of primary colours. E20.
▸ **B** *noun*. Something that is added; *esp.* a substance added to another to give it specific qualities, now *spec.* a substance added to food as a colouring, flavouring, or preservative, or for some other non-nutritional purpose. M20.
■ **additively** *adverb* M19. **addiˈtivity** *noun* E20.

additory /ˈadɪt(ə)ri/ *adjective & noun*. Now *rare*. M17.
[ORIGIN from Latin *addit-* (see ADDITION) + -ORY[2].]
(Something) tending to add.

addle /ˈad(ə)l/ *noun, adjective, & verb*[1].
[ORIGIN Old English *adela* = Middle Low German *adele*, Middle Dutch *adel* (Dutch *aal*), German *Adel* mire, puddle, Old Swedish *-adel* in *koadel* cow's urine. *Addle egg* is translation of medieval Latin *ovum urinae* egg of urine, alt. of *ovum urinum* repr. Greek *ourion ōon* wind-egg.]
▸ **A** *noun*. Stinking urine or liquid filth; mire. *obsolete* exc. *dial.* (after Old English in literary use only in the north). OE.
▸ **B** *attrib.* or as *adjective*. **1** Of an egg: rotten or putrid; producing no chicken. ME. **2** *fig.* Empty, idle, muddled, unsound. L15.
J. LYLY His addle head. DRYDEN His brains grow addle.
addle-brained, ***addle-headed***, ***addle-pate***, etc.
▸ **C** *verb*. **1** *verb trans.* Make addle; confuse; make abortive. L16.
HENRY FIELDING My muddy brain is addled like an egg.
2 *verb intrans.* Grow addle (*lit.* & *fig.*). E19.
■ **addleness** *noun* L16.

addle /ˈad(ə)l/ *verb*[2]. *N. English*. ME.
[ORIGIN Old Norse *ǫðla*, refl. *ǫðlask*, from *óðal* property: see UDAL.]
1 *verb trans.* Acquire as one's own; earn. ME.
D. H. LAWRENCE Get thy money, Sam, tha's addled it.
2 *verb intrans.* Of crops: yield. L16.

†**addoom** *verb trans. rare* (Spenser). Only in L16.
[ORIGIN from A-[11] + DOOM *verb*.]
Adjudge.

addorsed /əˈdɔːst/ *adjective*. L16.
[ORIGIN from Latin *ad* to + *dorsum* back + -ED[1]. Cf. French *adossé*.]
Orig. & chiefly HERALDRY. Turned back to back.

address /əˈdrɛs/ *noun*. M16.
[ORIGIN Partly from ADDRESS *verb*, partly from Old French & mod. French *adresse*.]
▸ **I** Direction.
1 The act of approaching or applying to anyone; *esp.* (and now only, in *pl.*) dutiful or courteous approach, courtship. M16.
GOLDSMITH Farmer Williams . . had paid her his addresses.
†**2** The action of sending or dedicating something written. M17–E18.
3 A discourse delivered to an audience; a formal speech of congratulation, thanks, etc. M17.
A. WILSON The judge's address to the jury was . . different.
public address system: see PUBLIC *adjective & noun*.
4 Manner in conversation. *arch.* L17.
W. STEVENS A funny foreigner of meek address.
5 The superscription of a letter etc.; the name of the place to which anyone's letters etc. are directed; one's place of residence. E18. ▸**b** COMPUTING. A sequence of bits which identifies a particular location in a data processing system. M20.
JOYCE The partially obliterated address and postmark. E. HEMINGWAY I got into the cab and gave the driver the address of Simmons.
form of address a name, title, etc., used in addressing a person. **b *direct address***: see DIRECT *adjective*. ***relative address***: see RELATIVE *adjective & noun*. ***symbolic address***: see SYMBOLIC *adjective*.
6 The action of dispatching (esp. a ship, to a person or place). L19.
▸ **II** Preparation.
†**7** Attire, dress. L16–M17.
8 General preparedness; skill, dexterity. L16.
P. G. WODEHOUSE He saved me with the most consummate address from a large shaggy dog.
†**9** The action of making ready; preparation. M17–L18.
MILTON She makes address to speak.
■ **Addressograph** *noun* (proprietary name for) a machine for printing addresses E20.

address /əˈdrɛs/ *verb*. ME.
[ORIGIN Old French & mod. French *adresser*, ult. formed as AD- + DIRECT *adjective*.]
▸ **I** Make straight or right.
†**1** *verb trans.* Erect, raise, set up. ME–E17.
†**2** *verb trans.* Put straight or to rights; set in order. LME–L17.
P. HOLLAND Forced for to addresse themselues, and range a nauall battell in order. MILTON A Parlament being call'd, to addres many things.
†**3** *verb trans.* & *intrans.* Prepare, make ready. (Cf. branch III below.) LME–M19.
ELIZABETH I: We will that you shall . . address several Schedules. SHAKES. *Tr. & Cr.* Let us address to tend on Hector's heels. H. L'ESTRANGE He . . did addresse himself for the stroke of death.
4 *esp.* ▸†**a** *verb trans.* Apparel or attire for a special purpose; (later simply) clothe. LME–L17. ▸**b** *verb trans.* Put on (a garment). *arch.* E16.
J. JEWEL Tecla sometime addressed her selfe in Mans apparell. **b** BROWNING I have addressed a frock of heavy mail.
▸ **II** Direct.
5 *verb trans.* Guide, direct; aim. *obsolete* exc. GOLF, take aim at (the ball). ME.
TENNYSON Bent their . . faces toward us and address'd Their motion.
6 *verb trans.* †**a** *refl.* Betake oneself. LME–L17. ▸**b** Direct to go (*to*); introduce; send, dispatch. *obsolete* exc. with a ship as obj. L15.
EVELYN I addressed him to Lord Mordaunt.
7 *verb trans.* Send as a written message *to* (a person); inscribe. Also, write directions for delivery on (an envelope etc.). LME. ▸**b** COMPUTING. Specify a location in (memory) or location of (data) by means of an address, with a view to transferring data or executing an operation. M20.
G. GREENE All the notes she had once addressed to me. E. BOWEN Recollecting, as she addressed the envelope, that she had no stamp.
8 a *verb trans.* Direct spoken words (*to* a person; with the words or oneself as obj.). L15. ▸†**b** *verb intrans.* Speak directly, present a formal address, pay addresses, *to*. E17–M18. ▸**c** *verb trans.* Speak directly to; deliver a speech to; present a formal address to; pay addresses to. E18.
a SCOTT FITZGERALD To address cordial remarks to the passers-by. G. B. SHAW You should address yourself to His Majesty. **b** SHAKES. *Lear* My Lord of Burgundy, We first address toward you. **c** POPE And, calling Venus, thus address'd his child. E. O'NEILL You'd think you were going to address an audience of literary critics.
9 *verb trans.* Use a particular (specified) form of words in speaking or writing to. L18.
J. MASTERS Subalterns address field officers as 'Sir'. W. TREVOR He wished the boy would address him by his correct name.
▸ **III** from sense 3, infl. by sense 6.
†**10** *verb trans.* Apply or turn to some object or purpose. LME–L16.
11 a *verb refl.* Apply oneself, direct one's skill or energies, *to*. LME. ▸†**b** *verb intrans.* Turn one's attention *to*. M17–M18. ▸**c** *verb trans.* Turn one's attention to (a topic etc.); approach, face, (a problem). E19.
a M. H. ABRAMS Johnson addresses himself to a general examination of Shakespeare's dramas. **b** MILTON Which I shall forthwith addresse to prove. **c** *Guardian Weekly* The agreement . . does not address every aspect of every subproblem.
■ **addressable** *adjective* (COMPUTING) pertaining to or designating a memory unit in which all locations can be separately accessed M20. **addressee** *noun* a person to whom something (esp. a letter) is addressed E19. **addresser** *noun* L17. **addressing** *noun* (*a*) the action of the verb; (*b*) COMPUTING the method of or system for identifying, referring to, or allocating locations in one or more computers: E16. **addressor** *noun* a person who signs a formal address or addresses a formal document M17.

addressed /əˈdrɛst/ *ppl adjective*. Also (*arch.*) **addrest**. LME.
[ORIGIN from ADDRESS *verb* + -ED[1].]
†**1** Prepared. LME–M17.
2 Attired, dressed. *arch.* LME.
†**3** Well ordered; accomplished. L15–L16.
SPENSER Full jolly knight he seemde, and wel addrest.
4 Erect, raised. *arch. rare*. L16.
T. S. ELIOT Sweeney addressed full-length to shave.
5 Directed, dispatched. L16.
SOUTHEY The shaft, unerringly addrest.
6 Superscribed with directions for delivery. L19.

adduce /əˈdjuːs/ *verb trans*. LME.
[ORIGIN Latin *adducere*, from *ad* AD- + *ducere* lead, bring.]
Bring forward for consideration; cite as a proof or instance.
■ **adducer** *noun* E19. **adducible** *adjective* L18.

adducent /əˈdjuːs(ə)nt/ *adjective*. L17.
[ORIGIN Latin *adducent-* pres. ppl stem of *adducere*: see ADDUCE, -ENT.]
ANATOMY. Concerned with adduction (sense 2).

adduct /ˈadʌkt/ *noun*. M20.
[ORIGIN German *Addukt* formed as ADD(ITION + PRO)DUCT *noun*.]
CHEMISTRY. A product of an addition reaction.

adduct /əˈdʌkt/ *verb trans*. M19.
[ORIGIN Back-form. from ADDUCTION.]
ANATOMY. Bring about adduction (sense 2) of (a limb etc.).

adduction /əˈdʌkʃ(ə)n/ *noun*. LME.
[ORIGIN French, or late Latin *adductio(n-)*, from *adduct-* pa. ppl stem of *adducere*: see ADDUCE, -ION.]
1 The action of bringing a thing to something else; *spec.* an alleged bringing of Christ's body and blood into the Eucharistic elements. LME.
2 ANATOMY. Movement of a limb etc. towards the median line. Opp. ABDUCTION 2. M17.
3 The action of adducing. M18.

adductive /əˈdʌktɪv/ *adjective*. Now *rare*. M17.
[ORIGIN from Latin *adduct-* (see ADDUCTION) + -IVE.]
Bringing to something else, *spec.* Christ's body and blood into the elements (see ADDUCTION 1).

adductor /əˈdʌktə/ *noun*. E17.
[ORIGIN mod. Latin, formed as ADDUCTIVE: see -OR.]
ANATOMY. A muscle which brings about adduction towards the median line; *spec.* one which closes the shell of a bivalve mollusc. Also ***adductor muscle***.

†**addulce** *verb trans*. L15–E18.
[ORIGIN Old French *ad(d)oulcir* (mod. *adoucir*) from late Latin *addulcire*, from *ad* AD- + *dulcis* sweet.]
Sweeten, make palatable; soothe, mollify, (a person).

addy /ˈadi/ *noun*. *colloq.* Pl. **-ies**. L20.
[ORIGIN Abbreviation.]
An email address.

-ade /eɪd/ *suffix*.
Forming nouns.
1 Repr. French *-ade* from Provençal, Spanish, Portuguese *-ada*, Italian *-ata*, meaning (i) an action done, as ***crusade***, ***parade***; (ii) the body concerned, as ***brigade***, ***comrade***; (iii) the product of an action or process, as ***arcade***, ***marmalade***. ▸**b** In or after new French formations, as ***cannonade***, ***harlequinade***, ***lemonade***.
2 Repr. French *-ade* from Greek *-ad-a* (nom. *-as*), as in ***decade***.
3 Repr. Spanish, Portuguese *-ado*, Italian *-ato*, masc. of 1, as in ***brocade***, ***renegade***.

adeem /əˈdiːm/ *verb trans*. M19.
[ORIGIN from ADEMPTION, after *redeem*, *redemption*.]
Take away; *spec.* in LAW, revoke (a grant or bequest) by prior disposal.

Adelantado /ˌadelanˈtaðo, ˌadəlanˈtɑːdəʊ/ *noun*. Also ***a-***. Pl. **-os** /-ɔs, -əʊz/. L16.
[ORIGIN Spanish.]
Chiefly *hist.* A Spanish grandee; a Lord Lieutenant or governor of a Spanish province or colony.

adelgid /əˈdɛldʒɪd/ *noun*. E20.
[ORIGIN from mod. Latin *Adelgidae*, perh. from Greek *adelos* unseen + *gē* earth: see -ID[3].]
An insect of the family Adelgidae, which comprises sap-feeding hemipteran insects resembling aphids and usu. covered with white waxy fluff.

-adelic /əˈdɛlɪk/ *suffix*. L20.
[ORIGIN from PSYCHEDELIC.]
Forming adjectives denoting musical genres or styles that incorporate psychedelic music with another element, as ***funkadelic*** etc.

Adélie /ˈadeɪliː/ *noun*. Also **Adelie** /ˈadəli/. E20.
[ORIGIN from *Adélie* Land, in the Antarctic.]
In full ***Adélie penguin***. A small penguin of Antarctic waters, *Pygoscelis adeliae*.

ademption /əˈdɛm(p)ʃ(ə)n/ *noun*. L16.
[ORIGIN Latin *ademptio(n-)*, from *adimere*, from *ad* AD- + *emere* take: see -ION.]
The action of taking away; *spec.* in LAW, revocation of a grant or bequest by prior disposal.

adenine /ˈadɪniːn/ *noun*. L19.
[ORIGIN from Greek *adēn* gland + -INE[5].]
BIOCHEMISTRY. A derivative of purine which is one of the bases of nucleic acids, paired with thymine in double-stranded DNA; 6-aminopurine, $C_5H_5N_5$.

adenitis /adɪˈnʌɪtɪs/ *noun*. M19.
[ORIGIN from Greek *adēn* gland + -ITIS.]
MEDICINE. Inflammation of glands, *spec.* of lymph nodes.

adeno- /ˈadɪnəʊ/ *combining form* of Greek *adēn* gland: see -O-. Before a vowel **aden-**.
■ **adenocarciˈnoma** *noun*, pl. **-mas**, **-mata** /-mətə/, MEDICINE a malignant epithelial tumour of glandular form L19. **adenoˈhyˈpophysis** *noun*, pl. **-physes** /-fɪsiːz/, ANATOMY the anterior lobe of the hypophysis (pituitary gland) M20. **adeˈnoma** *noun*, pl. **-mas**, **-mata** /-mətə/, MEDICINE a benign epithelial tumour of glandular form L19. **adeˈnomatous** *adjective* pertaining to or resem-

bling an adenoma L19. **adeno'virus** *noun* (MEDICINE) any of a class of viruses (the first examples of which were discovered in adenoid tissue), most of which cause respiratory diseases M20.

adenoid /ˈadɪnɔɪd/ *adjective & noun*. M19.
[ORIGIN from Greek *adēn* gland + -OID.]
▸ **A** *adjective*. MEDICINE. Glandular; like a gland. M19.
▸ **B** *noun sing.* (*rare*) & in *pl.* A collection of lymphoid tissue in the wall of the nasopharynx, usu. becoming less prominent in early adult life; *colloq.* an enlarged condition of this tissue, hindering speech and breathing. L19.
■ **ade'noidal** *adjective* (**a**) *rare* = ADENOID *adjective*; (**b**) suffering from enlarged adenoids; characteristic or suggestive of this condition: L19. **adenoi'dectomy** *noun* (an instance of) surgical removal of the adenoids E20. **adenoidy** *adjective* (*colloq.*) = ADENOIDAL (b) E20.

adenosine /əˈdɛnəʊsiːn/ *noun*. E20.
[ORIGIN Blend of ADENINE and RIBOSE.]
BIOCHEMISTRY. A nucleoside (adenine riboside), found in living tissue in the form of nucleotides (see below).
– COMB.: **adenosine deaminase** an enzyme which catalyses the deamination of adenosine to inosine (abbreviation *ADA*); **adenosine diphosphate**, **adenosine monophosphate**, **adenosine triphosphate**: nucleotides involved in many physiological processes, the breakdown of the triphosphate to the diphosphate providing energy, e.g. for muscular contraction.

adenylate /əˈdɛnɪleɪt/ *noun*. M20.
[ORIGIN formed as ADENYLIC + -ATE[1].]
BIOCHEMISTRY. A salt or ester of adenylic acid.
– COMB.: **adenylate cyclase** an enzyme that catalyses the formation of cyclic adenylic acid from adenosine triphosphate.

adenylic /adɪˈnɪlɪk/ *adjective*. L19.
[ORIGIN from ADEN(INE + -YL + -IC.]
BIOCHEMISTRY. ***adenylic acid***, a nucleotide composed of a phosphoric acid ester of adenosine, present in most DNA and RNA.

adeps /ˈadɛps/ *noun*. LME.
[ORIGIN Latin.]
Animal fat; lard.

adept /ˈadɛpt; *as adjective also* əˈdɛpt/ *adjective & noun*. M17.
[ORIGIN Latin *adeptus* pa. pple of *adipisci* attain, acquire.]
▸ **A** *adjective*. Thoroughly proficient (*at*, *in*). M17.
▸ **B** *noun*. (Orig. in Latin form †**adeptus**, pl. **-ti**.) A person who is proficient in or at anything. M17.
■ †**adeption** *noun* obtaining M16–M17. **adeptly** *adverb* M20. **a'deptness** *noun* M19. **adeptship** *noun* (*rare*) thorough proficiency; the state or condition of an adept: E19.

adequacy /ˈadɪkwəsi/ *noun*. E19.
[ORIGIN from ADEQUATE *adjective*: see -ACY. Cf. earlier INADEQUACY.]
The state or quality of being adequate.

adequate /ˈadɪkwət/ *adjective*. E17.
[ORIGIN Latin *adaequatus* pa. pple, formed as ADEQUATE *verb*: see -ATE[2].]
(Foll. by *to*, †*with*.)
†**1** Equal in magnitude or extent. E17–M18.
2 Commensurate in fitness; sufficient, satisfactory. E17. ▸**b** Barely sufficient. E20.
3 LOGIC. Of an idea or concept: fully and clearly representing its object. L17.
■ **adequately** *adverb* E17. **adequateness** *noun* M17. **adequative** *adjective* adequate, equivalent E19.

adequate /ˈadɪkweɪt/ *verb trans*. L16.
[ORIGIN Latin *adaequat-* pa. ppl stem of *adaequare*, from *ad* AD- + *aequus* equal: see -ATE[3].]
Make or be equal or equivalent (*to*).

JOYCE Let them continue as is meet To adequate the balance-sheet. T. EAGLETON No text literally . . adequates its signifiers to some signified distinct from them.

adequation /adɪˈkweɪʃ(ə)n, -ʒ(ə)n/ *noun*. L16.
[ORIGIN Latin *adaequatio(n-)*, formed as ADEQUATE *verb*: see -ATION.]
†**1** The action of equalling. Only in L16.
2 The result of making equal or adequate; an equivalent. E17.
3 The action of equalizing or making equivalent; the fact of being equalized or made equivalent. E17.
4 LINGUISTICS. A change in meaning due to the influence of typical contexts. M20.

adespota /əˈdɛspətə/ *noun pl*. L19.
[ORIGIN Greek, neut. pl. of *adespotos* adjective, from *a-* A-[10] + *despotēs* master.]
BIBLIOGRAPHY. Literary works not attributed to, or not claimed by, an author.

Adessenarian /ədɛsɪˈnɛːrɪən/ *noun*. M18.
[ORIGIN from mod. Latin *adessenarii*, from Latin *adesse* be present: see ADESSIVE, -ARIAN.]
ECCLESIASTICAL HISTORY. A person who believed in the real presence of Christ's body in the Eucharist, but not by transubstantiation.

adessive /əˈdɛsɪv/ *adjective & noun*. M19.
[ORIGIN from Latin *adesse* be present, from *ad* AD- + *esse* be + -IVE.]
GRAMMAR. ▸**A** *adjective*. Designating, being in, or pertaining to a case in Finnish and other languages expressing position in or presence at a place. M19.
▸ **B** *noun*. The adessive case; a word, form, etc., in the adessive case. M19.

ad eundem /ad ɪˈʌndəm/ *adverbial phr*. E18.
[ORIGIN Latin = to the same (degree).]
(Admitted) to the same degree or rank at another university or institution.

à deux /a dø/ *adverbial & adjectival phr*. L19.
[ORIGIN French.]
Of, for, or between, two.

ADF *abbreviation*.
Automatic direction-finder, a device used by pilots to aid navigation.

ADH *abbreviation*.
Antidiuretic hormone.

adhan /ədˈhɑːn/ *noun*. Also **azan** /əˈzɑːn/. M19.
[ORIGIN Arabic *'aḏān* announcement.]
The Muslim call to public prayers, made from the minaret of a mosque.

ADHD *abbreviation*.
Attention deficit hyperactivity disorder.

adhere /ədˈhɪə/ *verb intrans*. L15.
[ORIGIN Old French & mod. French *adhérer* or Latin *adhaerere*, from *ad* AD- + *haerere* to stick.]
1 Attach oneself *to* a person or party; be a follower. L15.

LD MACAULAY These people . . adhered to the Church of Rome.

2 Stick fast (*to* a substance or object). E16.

T. REID The parts of a body adhere so firmly. A. WILSON The ends of her fat, sticky fingers to which the chocolate had adhered. *fig.*: GIBBON Flattery adheres to power.

3 Give support to, or continue to maintain or observe, an opinion, practice, rule, etc. Foll. by *to*. M16.

W. S. MAUGHAM He had adhered scrupulously to the terms of the capitulation.

†**4** Be consistent with itself or circumstances. L16–E17.

SHAKES. *Macb.* Nor time nor place Did then adhere.

■ **adherer** *noun* (now *rare*) M16.

adherence /ədˈhɪər(ə)ns/ *noun*. LME.
[ORIGIN Old French & mod. French *adhérence* from late Latin *adhaerentia*, formed as ADHERE; later from ADHERE: see -ENCE.]
1 The action of adhering (*to*). LME.
2 An instance of adhering; something adherent. (*rare* after 17.) M16.

adherency /ədˈhɪər(ə)nsi/ *noun*. *arch*. L16.
[ORIGIN from ADHERE + -ENCY. Cf. ADHERENCE.]
1 The quality or state of being adherent. L16.
†**2** An adhering party; a following. L16–M17.
†**3** Something adherent. Only in 17.

adherend /ədˈhɪərənd/ *noun*. M20.
[ORIGIN from ADHERE + -END.]
An object bonded to another by an adhesive, or to which an adhesive adheres.

adherent /ədˈhɪər(ə)nt/ *adjective & noun*. LME.
[ORIGIN Old French & mod. French *adhérent* from Latin *adhaerent-* pres. ppl stem of *adhaerere* ADHERE: see -ENT.]
▸ **A** *adjective*. †**1** Attached in sympathy or as a follower (*to*). LME–E17.

W. FULBECKE To be adherent to the King's enemies.

2 Attached materially (*to*); sticking; adhering *to* (an opinion, a rule, etc.). M16.

A. BURGESS A perceptible shaking in the adherent custard.

3 Attached as an attribute or circumstance. L16.
▸ **B** *noun*. **1** A supporter or follower (*of*). LME.

W. S. CHURCHILL He was tried and hanged with four of his adherents.

†**2** Something which adheres. E–M17.

MILTON Not a true limb . . but an adherent.

■ **adherently** *adverb* (*rare*) E17.

adhesion /ədˈhiːʒ(ə)n/ *noun*. L15.
[ORIGIN French *adhésion* or Latin *adhaesio(n-)*, from *adhaes-* pa. ppl stem of *adhaerere* ADHERE: see -ION.]
1 The action of adhering to a person, party, tenet, etc. L15.
2 The action of sticking (together or *to* something); an instance of this; *spec.* in PHYSICS, the sticking together of unlike materials (cf. COHESION). M17. ▸**b** The frictional grip of a wheel on a rail, road surface, etc. M19.
3 MEDICINE. The union of normally separate parts due to inflammation or injury; a mass of tissue joining normally separate parts; *rare* benign union of tissue as in healing. M17.

adhesive /ədˈhiːsɪv, -zɪv/ *adjective & noun*. L17.
[ORIGIN formed as ADHESION + -IVE.]
▸ **A** *adjective*. **1** Apt or tending to adhere (*fig.*), cling to, or persevere in. L17.
2 Having the property of adhering (*lit.*); sticky; prepared so as to adhere. L18.
adhesive tape opaque or transparent paper, plastic, etc., coated with an adhesive and used for fastening, sticking, masking, or insulating.
▸ **B** *noun*. Something which adheres; an adhesive substance. L19.
■ **adhesively** *adverb* M19. **adhesiveness** *noun* M18.

adhibit /ədˈhɪbɪt/ *verb trans*. E16.
[ORIGIN Latin *adhibit-* pa. ppl stem of *adhibere*, from *ad* AD- + *habere* have, hold.]
1 Take in, let in, admit. E16.
2 Put to, put upon, affix. M16.
3 Apply, employ, esp. as a remedy. L16.
■ **adhibition** /adhɪˈbɪʃ(ə)n/ *noun* the action of adhibiting M17.

ad hoc /ad ˈhɒk/ *adverbial & adjectival phr*. M17.
[ORIGIN Latin, lit. 'to this'.]
For this particular purpose; special(ly).
■ **adhocery**, **-ck-** *noun* (*colloq.*) (an) improvisation M20. **adhocism** *noun* the policy of improvisation, adhocery M20.

ad hominem /ad ˈhɒmɪnɛm/ *adverbial & adjectival phr*. L16.
[ORIGIN Latin = to the person.]
Of an argument etc.: directed to the individual, personal; appealing to feeling not reason.

adhort /ədˈhɔːt/ *verb trans*. Now *rare* or *obsolete*. L15.
[ORIGIN Latin *adhortari*, from *ad* AD- + *hortari* incite.]
Urge, exhort.
■ **ˌadhor'tation** *noun* (an) exhortation M16.

adhortative /adˈhɔːtətɪv/ *adjective*. M19.
[ORIGIN formed as ADHORT: see -ATIVE.]
GRAMMAR. Of a verbal mood: expressing exhortation.

adiabatic /ˌeɪdʌɪəˈbatɪk, ˌadɪə-/ *adjective & noun*. L19.
[ORIGIN from Greek *adiabatos* impassable, from *a-* A-[10] + *dia* through + *batos* passable: see -IC.]
PHYSICS. ▸**A** *adjective*. Involving or allowing neither gain nor loss of heat; pertaining to such conditions; (of a curve, line, etc.) obtained by plotting the relative changes in pressure and volume of a gas during a process of this kind. L19.
▸ **B** *noun*. An adiabatic curve; the relationship expressed by an adiabatic curve. L19.
■ **adiabat** /eɪˈdʌɪəbat/ *noun* = ADIABATIC *noun* M20. **adiabatically** *adverb* with neither gain nor loss of heat L19.

adiaphanous /adɪˈaf(ə)nəs/ *adjective*. M17.
[ORIGIN from A-[10] + DIAPHANOUS.]
Not translucent; opaque.

adiaphora *noun* pl. of ADIAPHORON *noun*.

adiaphorist /adɪˈaf(ə)rɪst/ *noun*. M16.
[ORIGIN mod. Latin *adiaphorista*, from Greek *adiaphoros*: see ADIAPHOROUS, -IST.]
1 ECCLESIASTICAL HISTORY. A moderate Lutheran who held some things, condemned by Luther, to be unimportant. M16.
2 A person who is uninterested in points of theological discussion. E17.
■ **adiaphorism** *noun* theological unconcern E17.

adiaphoron /adɪˈaf(ə)rɒn/ *noun & adjective*. *arch*. Pl. of noun **-ra** /-rə/. L16.
[ORIGIN Greek, neut. of *adiaphoros*: see ADIAPHOROUS.]
CHRISTIAN CHURCH. (A thing) inessential in the eyes of the Church.

adiaphorous /adɪˈaf(ə)rəs/ *adjective*. E17.
[ORIGIN Greek *adiaphoros*, from *a-* A-[10] + *diaphoros* differing: see -OUS.]
Making no difference; non-essential; neutral.

ad idem /ad ˈɪdɛm/ *adverbial phr*. L16.
[ORIGIN Latin = to the same thing.]
On the same point, in agreement.

adieu /əˈdjuː/ *interjection & noun*. LME.
[ORIGIN Anglo-Norman *adeu*, Old French & mod. French *adieu*, from *à* to + *Dieu* god: cf. ADDIO, ADIOS.]
▸ **A** *interjection*. Goodbye. *arch*. LME.
▸ **B** *noun*. Pl. **adieus**, **adieux** /əˈdjuːz/. A leave-taking; a parting word; a farewell. LME.

Adi Granth *noun phr*. see GRANTH.

ad infinitum /ad ɪnfɪˈnʌɪtəm/ *adverbial & adjectival phr*. E17.
[ORIGIN Latin, lit. 'to infinity'.]
Without limit, for ever.

ad interim /ad ˈɪntərɪm/ *adverbial & adjectival phr*. L18.
[ORIGIN Latin, *ad* to + *interim* adverb 'meanwhile' used as noun.]
For the meantime.

adios /adɪˈəʊs, adɪˈɒs/ *interjection*. M19.
[ORIGIN Spanish *adiós*, from *a* to + *Dios* god: cf. ADIEU, ADDIO.]
Goodbye.

adipic /əˈdɪpɪk/ *adjective*. M19.
[ORIGIN from Latin *adip-*, ADEPS (from the acid having first been prepared by oxidizing fats) + -IC.]
CHEMISTRY. ***adipic acid***, a crystalline acid, $HOOC(CH_2)_4COOH$, used in the manufacture of nylon.

adipocere /adɪpə(ʊ)ˈsɪə/ *noun*. E19.
[ORIGIN French *adipocire*, formed as ADIPIC + French *cire* wax.]
A greyish-white fatty substance generated in dead bodies subjected to moisture.

adipocyte /ˈadɪpəsʌɪt/ *noun*. M20.
[ORIGIN formed as ADIPOSE + -O- + -CYTE.]
PHYSIOLOGY. A cell specialized for the storage of fat, found in connective tissue.

adipose /ˈadɪpəʊs, -z/ *adjective & noun*. M18.
[ORIGIN mod. Latin *adiposus*, formed as ADIPIC + -OSE[1].]
▸ **A** *adjective*. Of or pertaining to animal fat. Of tissue: concerned with the storage of fat. M18.

adipose fin a small, rayless, fleshy, dorsal fin present in certain fishes, notably in the salmon family.
▸ **B** *noun*. Adipose tissue. M19.
■ **adi'posity** *noun* fatness, obesity M19. **adipous** *adjective* = ADIPOSE *adjective* in less techn. contexts M17.

Adirondack chair /ˌadɪˈrɒndak tʃɛː/ *noun*. *US*. M20.
[ORIGIN from the *Adirondack* Mountains in New York State.]
A wooden armchair for outdoor use, constructed from wide slats.

adit /ˈadɪt/ *noun*. E17.
[ORIGIN Latin *aditus* approach, entrance, from *adit-* pa. ppl stem of *adire*, from *ad* AD- + *ire* go.]
1 A horizontal passage leading into a mine, for the purpose of entrance or drainage. E17.
2 Entrance, access. *rare*. M19.

Adivasi /ɑːdɪˈvɑːsi/ *noun*. Also **a-**. M20.
[ORIGIN mod. Sanskrit (nom.) *ādivāsī*, from *ādi* the beginning + *vāsin* inhabitant.]
A member of any of the aboriginal tribes of India.

adj. /adʒ/ *noun*[1]. M17.
[ORIGIN Abbreviation.]
GRAMMAR. An adjective.

Adj. /adʒ/ *noun*[2]. *colloq*. M20.
[ORIGIN Abbreviation.]
= ADJUTANT *noun* 2.

adjacency /əˈdʒeɪs(ə)nsi/ *noun*. M17.
[ORIGIN Latin *adjacentia* neut. pl. (in sense 2), formed as ADJACENT; in mod. use from ADJACENT: see -ENCY.]
1 A thing which lies near; in *pl.*, adjacent places, environs. M17.
2 The fact, quality, or state of being adjacent. M18.
■ **adjacence** *noun* = ADJACENCY 2 E17.

adjacent /əˈdʒeɪs(ə)nt/ *adjective & noun*. LME.
[ORIGIN Latin *adjacent-* pres. ppl stem of *adjacere*, from *ad* AD- + *jacere* lie down: see -ENT.]
▸ **A** *adjective*. Lying near (*to*), adjoining, contiguous (*to*). LME.
adjacent angles GEOMETRY the two angles defined on the same side of a line when it is intersected by another line.
▸ †**B** *noun*. = ADJACENCY 1. M16–M19.

†**adject** *ppl adjective & noun*. LME.
[ORIGIN Latin *adjectus* pa. pple of *ad(j)icere*, from *ad* AD- + *jacere* lay, throw.]
▸ **A** *ppl adjective*. Annexed, joined. LME–E17.
▸ **B** *noun*. An addition; an adjunct. L17–E18.

adject /əˈdʒɛkt/ *verb trans*. LME.
[ORIGIN Latin *adjectare* frequentative of *ad(j)icere*: see ADJECT *adjective & noun*.]
Add, join, annex.

adjection /əˈdʒɛkʃ(ə)n/ *noun*. ME.
[ORIGIN Latin *adjectio(n-)*, from *adject-*: see ADJECT *ppl adjective & noun*, -ION.]
†**1** A thing which is added; an addition. ME–L18.
2 The action of adding or joining. LME.
■ ˌ**adjec'titious** *adjective* additional M17.

adjectival /adʒɛkˈtʌɪv(ə)l/ *adjective & noun*. L18.
[ORIGIN from ADJECTIVE + -AL[1].]
▸ **A** *adjective*. **1** GRAMMAR. Forming an adjunct to a noun; dependent on a noun and as an attribute; of the nature or quality of an adjective. L18.
2 Of style etc.: characterized by many adjectives. E20.
3 *euphem*. Bloody, damned, etc. *colloq*. E20.

D. L. SAYERS An adjectival . . watering-place like Wilvercombe.

▸ **B** *noun*. GRAMMAR = ADJECTIVE *noun* 1. Also, a phrase, clause, etc., with an adjectival function. L19.
■ **adjectivally** *adverb* M19.

adjective /ˈadʒɪktɪv/ *adjective, noun, & verb*. LME.
[ORIGIN Old French & mod. French *adjectif*, *-ive* from late Latin *adjectivus*, *-iva*, from *adject-*: see ADJECT *ppl adjective & noun*, -IVE. First in *noun adjective* rendering late Latin *nomen adjectivum* (Priscian) translating Greek *onoma epitheton*.]
▸ **A** *adjective*. **1** GRAMMAR. = ADJECTIVAL *adjective* 1. Now *rare*. LME.
noun adjective = sense B.1.
2 *gen*. Dependent; attached. E17.

G. GROTE The women were treated . . as adjective beings. W. H. AUDEN Pastors adjective / to rustic flocks.

adjective dye: needing a mordant to fix it.
3 LAW. Relating to or defining enforcement or procedure, as opp. to rights and duties. Cf. SUBSTANTIVE *adjective* 3a. L18.
4 = ADJECTIVAL *adjective* 3. *colloq*. M19.

DICKENS I won't . . have no adjective police . . in my adjective premises.

▸ **B** *noun*. **1** GRAMMAR. A word designating an attribute and added to a noun, to describe the thing etc. more fully. (One of the parts of speech.) LME.
2 *gen*. A dependent; an accessory. E17.

T. FULLER Subjects should be adjectives, not able to stand without their prince.

▸ **C** *verb trans*. Make adjectival; provide with an adjective. M17.
■ **adjectively** *adverb* in an adjectival manner M16. **adjectivize** *verb trans*. make into an adjective E20.

adjoin /əˈdʒɔɪn/ *verb*. ME.
[ORIGIN Old French *ajoi(g)n-* stem of *ajoindre* (mod. *adj-*) from Latin *adjungere*: see ADJUNCT.]
1 *verb trans*. Join, unite (*to* or *unto*). *arch*. ME. ▸†**b** *verb intrans*. Come into union or contact. LME–L17.

SHAKES. *Haml*. A massy wheel, . . To whose huge spokes ten thousand lesser things Are mortis'd and adjoin'd.

2 *verb intrans*. **a** Lie close, be contiguous *to*, *with*. *obsolete* exc. absol. as ***adjoining*** *ppl adjective*. ME. ▸**b** Lie close to each other. L19.

a POPE Close to the bay great Neptune's fane adjoins. W. FAULKNER He came from the adjoining county. **b** N. SHUTE Two adjoining cabins with a communicating door.

3 *verb trans*. Lie close or be contiguous to. ME.

adjoint /ˈadʒɔɪnt/; *in sense A.2 also foreign* adʒwɛ̃, *pl. same*/ *noun & adjective*. L16.
[ORIGIN French, pa. pple of *adjoindre*: see ADJOIN, ADJUNCT.]
▸ **A** *adjective*. †**1** A helper; an adjunct. L16–E18.
2 A French civil officer who assists the mayor. Also, an assistant professor in a French college. M19.
3 MATH. An adjoint matrix, function, etc. L19.
▸ **B** *adjective*. MATH. Of a function, quantity, etc.: related to a given function, quantity, etc., by a particular process of transposition; *gen*. designating or pertaining to such a relationship; *spec*. (of a matrix) being the transpose of the cofactors of a given square matrix. L19.

adjourn /əˈdʒəːn/ *verb*. ME.
[ORIGIN Old French *ajorner* (mod. *ajourn-*), from phr. *à jorn (nomé)* to a day (appointed).]
†**1** *verb trans*. Appoint (a person) a day to appear; cite or summon for a particular day. ME–M17.
2 *verb trans*. Defer, put off. LME.

R. W. EMERSON I adjourn what I have to say on this topic.

3 *verb trans*. Break off (a meeting etc.) for later resumption. L15.

T. STOPPARD Meeting adjourned for ten minutes.

4 *verb intrans*. Of people met together: suspend proceedings and disperse; transfer a meeting to another place. L15.

D. LODGE They adjourned to a nearby pub to continue the conversation.

■ **adjournal** *noun* (*obsolete* exc. SCOTS LAW) adjournment L15.

adjournment /əˈdʒəːnm(ə)nt/ *noun*. LME.
[ORIGIN Old French *ajornement*, from *ajorner*: see ADJOURN, -MENT.]
The action or an act of adjourning; the state of being adjourned; a period of being adjourned.
– COMB.: **adjournment debate**: on the motion that the House of Commons adjourn (often used as an opportunity to raise various matters).

adjudge /əˈdʒʌdʒ/ *verb trans*. LME.
[ORIGIN Old French *ajuger* (mod. *adj-*) from Latin *adjudicare*: see ADJUDICATE.]
1 Settle or decide (a matter) judicially. LME.
2 Pronounce or decree by judicial sentence (something *to be*, *that* something is). LME.
3 Determine in one's own judgement, consider or declare to be the case. LME.

Radio Times: *The Twilight Zone* has often been adjudged the most innovative American TV series of all time.

4 Condemn (*to* a penalty, *to do*). *arch*. LME.

P. BAYNE By a company of Puritan soldiers . . Charles was adjudged to die.

5 Award, grant, or impose judicially (something *to* a person). L15.
†**6** Try judicially; pass sentence on. E16–M17.
■ **adjudgement**, **-dgm-** *noun* the act of adjudging; a decree, an award: M16. **adjudger** *noun* †(**a**) a person to whom something is adjudged; (**b**) a person who awards judicially: E18.

adjudicate /əˈdʒuːdɪkeɪt/ *verb*. E18.
[ORIGIN Latin *adjudicat-* pa. ppl stem of *adjudicare*, from *ad* AD- + *judic-*, *judex* a judge: see -ATE[3].]
†**1** *verb trans*. Award judicially (SCOTS LAW esp. a debtor's estate). E18–E19.
2 *verb trans*. Try and determine judicially (a claim etc.); pronounce (a person *to be*). L18.
3 *verb intrans*. Act as a judge in a court, a tribunal, a competition, etc. M19.
■ **adjudicative** *adjective* having the character of adjudicating M19. **adjudicator** *noun* a person who settles a question or awards a prize M19. **adjudicature** *noun* the process of adjudicating M19.

adjudication /ədʒuːdɪˈkeɪʃ(ə)n/ *noun*. E17.
[ORIGIN French, or late Latin *adjudicatio(n-)*, formed as ADJUDICATE: see -ATION.]
1 SCOTS LAW. An award of a heritable estate as security or to fulfil an obligation. E17.
2 The act of adjudicating; an awarding or settling by judicial decree. M17.
3 A judicial sentence or award. L18.
4 LAW (now *hist*.). More fully ***adjudication order***. An order declaring bankruptcy. M19.

†**adjument** *noun*. L16–E18.
[ORIGIN Latin *adjumentum* contr. of *adjuvamentum*, from *adjuvare*: see ADJUVANT, -MENT.]
Help; a helper.

adjunct /ˈadʒʌŋkt/ *adjective & noun*. E16.
[ORIGIN Latin *adjunctus* pa. pple of *adjungere*, from *ad* AD- + *jungere* join.]
▸ **A** *adjective*. Joined, added; subordinate. E16.
▸ **B** *noun*. **1** Something joined to something else and auxiliary to or dependent on it, something subordinate or incidental (*to*, *of*). L16.

Mirabella The French newspapers are just an adjunct to the business.

2 A qualifying addition to a word or name. L16.
3 GRAMMAR. A word or words amplifying or modifying the meaning of another word or words in a sentence. L16.
4 LOGIC. A non-essential attribute. L16.
5 A personal addition or enhancement. E17.
6 A person joined to another in some (esp. temporary) service or office. M17.
■ **a'djunctive** *noun & adjective* †(**a**) *noun* = ADJUNCT *noun*; (**b**) *adjective* contributing *to*, forming an adjunct: L17. **a'djunctively** *adverb* as an adjunct E19.

adjunction /əˈdʒʌŋkʃ(ə)n/ *noun*. L16.
[ORIGIN Latin *adjunctio(n-)*, formed as ADJUNCT: see -ION.]
The act of joining on or adding (*to*).

adjuration /adʒʊəˈreɪʃ(ə)n/ *noun*. LME.
[ORIGIN French, or Latin *adjuratio(n-)*, formed as ADJURE: see -ATION.]
The action of adjuring; an earnest appeal, *spec*. in exorcism.
■ **adjuratory** /əˈdʒʊərət(ə)ri/ *adjective* containing a solemn charge or appeal E19.

adjure /əˈdʒʊə/ *verb trans*. LME.
[ORIGIN Latin *adjurare*, from *ad* AD- + *jurare* swear, from *jur-*, *jus* oath.]
†**1** Put (a person) on oath; bind under penalty of a curse. LME–M17.

AV *Josh*. 6:26 Ioshua adiured them . . , saying, Cursed be the man . . that [etc.].

2 Charge or entreat solemnly or earnestly, as if under oath or under the penalty of a curse. Foll. by *to do* (†or *that*). LME.

L. A. G. STRONG Adjuring each other to have fresh cups of tea.

adjust /əˈdʒʌst/ *verb*. E17.
[ORIGIN French †*adjuster* (now *aj-*) refashioned, after *juste* JUST *adjective*, of Old French *ajoster* (mod. *ajouter* add), ult. from Latin *ad* AD- + *juxta* close to.]
1 *verb trans*. Arrange, compose, harmonize, (differences, discrepancies, accounts); assess (loss or damages). E17. ▸†**b** *verb intrans*. Come to terms. M17–M18.
2 *verb trans*. Arrange suitably in relation to something else or to some standard or purpose. (Foll. by *to*.) M17. ▸**b** *verb intrans*. Adapt oneself (*to*); get used to changed circumstances etc. E20.

BURKE They have adjusted the means to that end. S. LEWIS The . . rug was adjusted so that his bare feet would strike it. J. S. HUXLEY The individual . . can adjust himself . . to the ethical standards of his society. **b** S. KING She needs time to adjust.

3 *verb trans*. Arrange (something) suitably in relation to its parts; put in order; regulate. M17. ▸**b** *verb intrans*. Admit of being so arranged. E20.

M. MCCARTHY As he . . adjusted the handkerchief in his pocket.

■ **adjusta'bility** *noun* L19. **adjustable** *adjective* L18. **adjuster** *noun* L17. **adjustive** *adjective* concerned with adjustment L19.

adjustment /əˈdʒʌs(t)m(ə)nt/ *noun*. M17.
[ORIGIN Old French *adjustement* (mod. *aj-*), formed as ADJUST: see -MENT.]
1 The process of adjusting or being adjusted; an arrangement whereby things are adjusted. M17.

Which? All systems have a graphic equaliser allowing adjustment across the frequency range. *Your Horse* You may like to make some small adjustments to her winter diet.

2 COMMERCE. The settlement among various parties of claims, liabilities, or payments. M17.
3 The state of being adjusted; settlement. L17.
– COMB.: **adjustment centre** *US* a section of a prison reserved for the solitary confinement of refractory prisoners.

adjutage /ˈadʒʊtɪdʒ, əˈdʒuːt-/ *noun*. Also **aj-**. E18.
[ORIGIN French *aj(o)utage*, from *ajouter*: see ADJUST, -AGE.]
A tube added to or inserted into an aperture to control the outflow of water, as a pipe at the mouth of an artificial fountain.

adjutant /ˈadʒʊt(ə)nt/ *noun & adjective*. E17.
[ORIGIN Latin *adjutant-* pres. ppl stem of *adjutare* frequentative of *adjuvare*: see ADJUVANT, -ANT[1].]
▸ **A** *noun*. **1** An assistant, a helper. Now *rare* in *gen*. sense. E17.
2 MILITARY. An officer who assists superior officers by communicating orders, conducting correspondence, etc. E17.
Adjutant General a high-ranking Army administrative officer.
3 Either of two large black and white storks of the genus *Leptoptilos*, *L. dubius* (in full ***greater adjutant***), and *L.*

javanicus (in full ***lesser adjutant***), native to India and SE Asia. Also ***adjutant bird***, ***adjutant stork***. L18.

► **B** *adjective*. Helping. *rare*. L17.

■ **adjutancy** *noun* the rank or office of an adjutant M18.

adjutator /ˈadʒʊteɪtə/ *noun*. M17.
[ORIGIN Alt. of AGITATOR after *adjutant* etc.]
ENGLISH HISTORY. = AGITATOR 1.

adjutor /ˈadʒʊtə/ *noun*. Now *rare*. M16.
[ORIGIN Latin *adjutor*, from *adjut-* pa. ppl stem of *adjuvare*: see ADJUVANT, -OR.]
= ADJUTANT *noun* 1.

adjuvant /ˈadʒʊv(ə)nt/ *adjective & noun*. L16.
[ORIGIN French, or Latin *adjuvant-* pres. ppl stem of *adjuvare*, from *ad* AD- + *juvare* help: see -ANT[1].]

► **A** *adjective*. **1** Helpful, auxiliary. L16.

2 *MEDICINE*. Designating therapy applied after the initial treatment of cancer, esp. to suppress secondary tumour formation. L20.

► **B** *noun*. **1** A help; a helper. E17.

2 *MEDICINE*. Something given to augment the effect of a drug or other agent; now *esp*. a substance which enhances the body's immune response to an antigen. M19.

Adlerian /adˈlɪərɪən/ *adjective & noun*. M20.
[ORIGIN from *Adler* (see below) + -IAN.]
Pertaining to, a disciple of, the Austrian psychologist Alfred Adler (1870–1937) or his school of analytic psychology, which was based on such concepts as the inferiority complex and the desire for power.

ad lib /ad ˈlɪb/ *adverbial, adjectival, verb, & noun phr*. Also (esp. as attrib. adjective & verb) **ad-lib**. E19.
[ORIGIN Abbreviation of AD LIBITUM.]

► **A** *adverb*. At one's pleasure; to any desired extent. E19.

► **B** *adjective*. Extemporized; spontaneous. E20.

► **C** *verb trans. & intrans*. Infl. **-bb-**. Speak extempore, improvise. E20.

► **D** *noun*. An ad-lib remark, an extemporized speech; something improvised. M20.

ad libitum /ad ˈlɪbɪtəm/ *adverbial & adjectival phr*. E17.
[ORIGIN Latin = according to pleasure.]
= AD LIB *adverbial & adjectival phr*.

ad litem /ad ˈlʌɪtɛm/ *adverbial & adjectival phr*. M18.
[ORIGIN Latin, lit. 'in relation to the dispute'.]
LAW (now chiefly *hist*.). Of a guardian etc.: appointed to act, in a lawsuit, on behalf of a child or other incapable person.

†**adlocution** *noun* var. of ALLOCUTION.

admeasure /ədˈmɛʒə/ *verb trans*. ME.
[ORIGIN Old French *amesurer* from medieval Latin *admensurare*: see AD-, MEASURE *verb*.]

†**1** Keep in measure; limit, control. ME–E17.

†**2** Apply a measure to; measure out. L15–L19.

3 Apportion; assign in due shares. M17.

admeasurement /ədˈmɛʒəm(ə)nt/ *noun*. Now *rare*. E16.
[ORIGIN Old French *amesurement*, formed as ADMEASURE: see -MENT.]

1 Ascertainment and apportionment of just shares. E16.

2 The process of applying a measure in order to ascertain dimensions. E17.

3 Size, dimensions. L18.

admensuration /ədmɛnsjʊˈreɪʃ(ə)n/ *noun*. Now *rare*. L17.
[ORIGIN Late Latin *admensuratio(n-)*, from *admensurare*, from *ad* AD- + *mensura* a measure: see -ATION.]
= ADMEASUREMENT.

admin /ˈadmɪn/ *noun*. *colloq*. M20.
[ORIGIN Abbreviation.]
Administration.

adminicle /ədˈmɪnɪk(ə)l/ *noun*. M16.
[ORIGIN Latin *adminiculum* prop, support, from *ad* AD- + dim. *-culum* -CULE on an obscure base.]

1 Something that helps. M16.

2 *SCOTS LAW*. Supporting or corroboratory evidence; a writing tending to prove the existence and tenor of a lost deed. L16.

■ ˌadmiˈnicular *adjective* helpful, corroboratory L17.

adminiculate /admɪˈnɪkjʊleɪt/ *verb trans*. M16.
[ORIGIN Latin *adminiculat-* pa. ppl stem of *adminiculare*, formed as ADMINICLE: see -ATE[3].]
Help, support; *SCOTS LAW* support by corroboratory evidence.

administer /ədˈmɪnɪstə/ *verb*. LME.
[ORIGIN Old French *administrer* from Latin *administrare*: see AD-, MINISTER *verb*. Orig. *am-*, refashioned after Latinized Old French & mod. French *administrer*.]

► **I** *verb trans*. **1** Manage as a steward; carry on or execute (an office, affairs, etc.). LME.

W. HOLTBY Once the laws have been passed, we only can administer them. P. G. WODEHOUSE Your aunt . . decided to take over the family finances and administer them herself.

2 *LAW*. Manage and dispose of (the estate of a deceased or incapable person) under a will or by official appointment. LME.

3 Execute or dispense (justice). LME.

4 Provide, supply, give, (orig. something beneficial, *to*). LME.

STEELE The Joy which this Temper of Soul administers. JOYCE Even a fellow on the broad of his back could administer a nasty kick.

5 Execute or perform (offices of religion); dispense (a sacrament). L15.

6 Formerly, apply (a branch of medicine). Now, give (medicine, *to*). M16.

7 Offer (an oath) for swearing (*to* a person). L16.

► **II** *verb intrans*. **8** Act as an administrator. E17.

9 Minister *to*. *arch*. E18.

■ **administrable** *adjective* able to be administered E19. †**administrer** *noun* L15–L17.

administrant /ədˈmɪnɪstr(ə)nt/ *adjective & noun*. *rare*. E17.
[ORIGIN French, pres. pple of *administrer*: see ADMINISTER, -ANT[1].]

► **A** *adjective*. Managing affairs, executive. E17.

► **B** *noun*. An acting officer. E17.

administrate /ədˈmɪnɪstreɪt/ *verb trans. & intrans*. M16.
[ORIGIN Latin *administrat-* pa. ppl stem of *administrare*: see ADMINISTER, -ATE[3].]
= ADMINISTER.

administration /ədmɪnɪˈstreɪʃ(ə)n/ *noun*. ME.
[ORIGIN Old French & mod. French, or Latin *administratio(n-)*, formed as ADMINISTRATE: see -ATION.]

1 The action of administering something to another. ME.

M. FRAYN Ways of speeding up the administration of justice.

2 The action of administering in any office; attendance; performance (*of*). *obsolete* in *gen*. sense. LME.

3 Management (*of* any business); the process or activity of running a business, organization, etc. LME.

A. CROSS She turned out to have a flair for administration.

4 *LAW*. The management and disposal of a deceased person's estate. LME. ▸**b** The management of an insolvent company by an administrator under a court order. L19.

letters of administration authority to administer the estate of an intestate (cf. ***probate***).

5 *ellipt*. The management of public affairs; government. E16.

Parliamentary Commissioner for Administration: see PARLIAMENTARY *adjective*.

6 The executive part of the legislature; the ministry; the government. E18. ▸**b** A period of office of a president of the United States. L18.

J. WILLIAMS The Belgian colonial administration. **b** *Economist* North Korea . . started its uranium-enrichment programme during the Clinton administration.

administrative /ədˈmɪnɪstrətɪv/ *adjective & noun*. M18.
[ORIGIN French *administratif, -ive* or Latin *administrativus*, formed as ADMINISTRATE: see -ATIVE.]

► **A** *adjective*. Pertaining to management of affairs; executive. M18.

► **B** *noun*. An administrative body; an administrator. *rare*. L19.

■ **administratively** *adverb* M19.

administrator /ədˈmɪnɪstreɪtə/ *noun*. LME.
[ORIGIN Latin, formed as ADMINISTRATE + -OR. Cf. French *administrateur*.]

1 A manager of business or public affairs; a person capable of organizing. LME.

2 *LAW*. **a** A person appointed to administer an estate in default of an executor, or to manage an insolvent company. LME. ▸**b** A person authorized to manage an estate for the legal owner during his or her minority, absence, etc.; *SCOTS LAW* (in full ***administrator in law***) a person empowered to act for another, *spec*. for a child. M16.

3 A person who administers something (a sacrament, justice, etc.) to another; an applier or giver (*of*). M16.

■ **administratorship** *noun* L16. **administratress** *noun* (*rare*) a female administrator L18.

administratrix /ədmɪnɪˈstreɪtrɪks/ *noun*. Pl. **-trixes**, **-trices** /-trɪsiːz/. M16.
[ORIGIN from ADMINISTRATOR: see -TRIX. Cf. French *administratrice*.]
A female administrator, *spec*. of an estate in default of an executor.

admirable /ˈadm(ə)rəb(ə)l/ *adjective & adverb*. LME.
[ORIGIN Old French & mod. French from Latin *admirabilis*, from *admirari*: see ADMIRE, -ABLE.]

► **A** *adjective*. **1** To be wondered at. *obsolete* exc. in ***Admirable CRICHTON***. LME.

MILTON Not only strange and admirable, but lamentable to think on.

2 Causing pleased surprise, or wonder united with approbation; (by degrees losing the idea of wonder) excellent, to be warmly approved. L16.

► †**B** *adverb*. Admirably. E17–E18.

■ **admirableness** *noun* E17. **admirably** *adverb* L16.

admiral /ˈadm(ə)r(ə)l/ *noun*. ME.
[ORIGIN Old French & mod. French *amiral*, †*admira(i)l* from (through medieval Latin) Arabic *amīr* commander (see AMIR, EMIR) + *-al* -AL[1]: assoc. with ADMIRABLE.]

†**1** An emir or prince under the Sultan; a Saracen commander. ME–E16.

2 The commander-in-chief of a country's navy. LME.

Lord High Admiral: a title of the British monarch (formerly of an officer who governed the Royal Navy and had jurisdiction over maritime causes).

3 A naval officer of high rank, *spec*. of the rank next below Admiral of the Fleet; the commander of a fleet or squadron. LME.

Admiral of the Fleet, (*US*) **Fleet Admiral**: the highest grade of such officers. ***High Admiral***: see HIGH *adjective*. ***rear admiral***: see REAR *adjective*[1]. VICE ADMIRAL. ***yellow admiral***: see YELLOW *adjective*.

4 The ship which carries the admiral; the flagship. L16.

5 Any of various nymphalid butterflies, *spec*. a red or white admiral. L17.

red admiral: see RED *adjective*. ***white admiral***: see WHITE *adjective*.

■ **admiraˈlissimo** *noun* (*colloq*.) [after GENERALISSIMO] the supreme commander of (combined) naval forces E20. **admiralship** *noun* the position or rank of admiral; ability to perform the duties of an admiral: L16.

admiralty /ˈadm(ə)r(ə)lti/ *noun*. LME.
[ORIGIN Old French *admiral(i)té* (mod. *amirauté*), formed as ADMIRAL: see -TY[1].]

1 The jurisdiction or office of an admiral. LME.

Droit of Admiralty: see DROIT *noun*[1] 1.

†**2** The department under command of the admiral. LME–E17.

3 The department administering the Navy. *obsolete* exc. *hist*. and in titles. LME.

the Admiralty the building from which the Royal Navy is administered. **the Board of Admiralty**, **the Admiralty Board**: formerly appointed to administer the British navy.

4 The maritime branch of the administration of justice. LME.

5 *rhet*. Command of the seas. L19.

R. KIPLING If blood be the price of admiralty Lord God, we ha' paid in full!

admiration /admәˈreɪʃ(ə)n/ *noun*. LME.
[ORIGIN Old French & mod. French, or Latin *admiratio(n-)*, from *admirat-* pa. ppl stem of *admirari*: see ADMIRE, -ATION.]

1 The action of wondering or marvelling; wonder. *arch*. LME.

T. FULLER Admiration is the daughter of ignorance.

note of admiration *arch*. an exclamation mark.

2 An object of admiration. L15.

M. W. MONTAGU The young prince . . is the admiration of the whole court.

3 Wonder mingled with reverence, esteem, approbation; pleased contemplation, warm approval. M16.

mutual admiration society: see MUTUAL *adjective*. **to admiration** in an admirable manner, excellently.

†**4** Admirableness. M16–M17.

SHAKES. *Temp*. Admir'd Miranda! Indeed the top of admiration.

5 An exclamation mark (= ***note of admiration*** above). *arch*. L16.

■ ˈ**admirative** *adjective* characterized by admiration L15.

admire /ədˈmʌɪə/ *verb*. L15.
[ORIGIN Isolated early use from Old French *amirer*; later (L16) from French *admirer* or Latin *admirari*, from *ad* AD- + *mirari* to wonder.]

1 *verb trans*. Regard with pleased surprise, respect, or approval. L15. ▸**b** Express admiration of. M19.

DAY LEWIS I always admired Auden for . . his certainties. J. HELLER You admire money and you idolize the people who have it.

2 *verb intrans*. Feel or express surprise or astonishment. *arch*. L16.

SWIFT She admir'd as much at him. DICKENS Mrs. Chick admires that Edith should be . . such a perfect Dombey.

admire to *US colloq*. be pleased to (do something), like to.

3 *verb trans*. View with wonder or surprise; marvel at. *arch*. L16.

ADDISON How can we sufficiently admire the stupidity or Madness of these Persons?

4 *verb trans*. Astonish, surprise. *rare*. M17.

■ **admirer** *noun* a person who admires; a suitor, a lover: L16. **admiring** *ppl adjective* showing or feeling admiration L16. **admiringly** *adverb* E17.

ad misericordiam /ad mɪzərɪˈkɔːdɪam/ *adverbial & adjectival phr*. E19.
[ORIGIN Latin.]
Of an appeal, argument, etc.: to mercy, to pity.

admissible /ədˈmɪsɪb(ə)l/ *adjective*. E17.
[ORIGIN French, or medieval Latin *admissibilis*, formed as ADMISSION: see -IBLE.]

1 Of an idea or plan: worthy of being accepted or considered. E17. ▸**b** *LAW*. Allowable as evidence. M19.

2 Worthy or able to be admitted (*to* an office or position, or the use of a place). L18.

A

■ **admissable** *adjective* = ADMISSIBLE L19. **admissiˈbility** *noun* L18.

admission /ədˈmɪʃ(ə)n/ *noun*. LME.
[ORIGIN Latin *admissio(n-)*, from *admiss-* pa. ppl stem of *admittere*: see ADMIT, -ION.]
1 The action of admitting or the fact of being admitted (*to* or *into* a place, office or position, class, etc.); a charge or ticket for this. LME.
BACON The admission of poor suitors without fee. R. BRAUTIGAN Fifty-cents admission for their flea circus.
2 The admitting (*of* something) as proper, valid, or true; acknowledging, conceding. M16. ▸**b** A concession, an acknowledgement. E19.
A. G. GARDINER Wars . . only end with the admission of defeat. **b** J. BRAINE Shocking her into an admission that she still cared what happened to him.
■ **admissive** /ədˈmɪsɪv/ *adjective* characterized by admitting, tending to admit L18.

admit /ədˈmɪt/ *verb*. Infl. **-tt-**. LME.
[ORIGIN Latin *admittere*, from *ad* AD- + *mittere* send; but some early forms reflect Old French *ametre*.]
▸ **I** As a voluntary agent.
1 *verb trans. & †intrans.* with *of*. Let in, permit (a person etc.) entrance or access (*to* or *into* a place, office or position, class, etc.), *spec.* in LAW (now *hist.*) into the possession of a copyhold estate. LME.
E. M. FORSTER Admitting into her kindly voice a note of exasperation. B. RUSSELL The Orphic communities . . admitted slaves on equal terms. G. GREENE The office had two waiting-rooms, and I was admitted alone into one.
†**admit of**: into the number or fellowship of. **admit to bail**: see BAIL *noun*¹.
2 *verb trans. & †intrans.* with *of*. Consent to, permit; accept as valid or true; acknowledge, confess (a thing, *doing*, *that*); concede (*that*). LME. ▸**b** *verb intrans.* Foll. by *to*: acknowledge (a weakness etc.), confess to. M20.
SHAKES. *Twel. N.* She will admit no kind of suit. JAS. MILL Tippoo . . had admitted no delay. E. O'NEILL The old veldt has its points, I'll admit, but it isn't home. A. BURGESS I made a mistake, I freely admit it.
▸ **II** As an involuntary agent.
3 *verb†trans. & intrans.* with *of*. Be open to or compatible with; leave room for. M16.
SHAKES. *Tr. & Cr.* My love admits no qualifying dross. G. B. SHAW Public medical work . . admits of organization.
4 *verb trans.* Afford entrance to; have room for. L16.
A. SILLITOE The gap in the fence would have admitted an armoured division.
■ **admittable** *adjective* able to be admitted (now usu. to a place or as a fact) M16. **admittedly** *adverb* as is acknowledged (by a person, or by people generally) to be true E19. **admitter** *noun* L16. †**admittible** *adjective* LME–M17. **admitting** *adjective* that admits someone or something, responsible for the admissions to a hospital etc. E20.

admittance /ədˈmɪt(ə)ns/ *noun*. M16.
[ORIGIN from ADMIT + -ANCE.]
1 The action of admitting or the fact of being admitted (now usu. to a place); entrance given or allowed. M16. ▸**b** = ADMISSION 2. L16.
2 ELECTRICITY. The reciprocal of impedance. L19.

admix /ˈadmɪks/ *noun*. M20.
[ORIGIN from the verb.]
An admixture, a mix.

admix /ədˈmɪks/ *verb trans. & intrans.* Orig. & chiefly as ppl adjective **admixt**, (now) **admixed** /-kst/. LME.
[ORIGIN Orig. ppl adjective from Latin *admixtus* pa. pple of *admiscere*, from *ad* AD- + *miscere* mix; verb (E16) as back-form. or from AD- + MIX *verb*.]
Mingle (*with* something else); add as an ingredient.
■ **admixtion** *noun* (now *rare* or *obsolete*) = ADMIXTURE 1 LME.

admixture /ədˈmɪkstʃə/ *noun*. E17.
[ORIGIN from AD- + MIXTURE.]
1 The action of admixing; the fact of being admixed. E17.
2 Something mixed with something else; a minor ingredient. M17.

admonish /ədˈmɒnɪʃ/ *verb trans.* ME.
[ORIGIN Old French *amonester* ult. from Latin *admonere*, from *ad* AD- + *monere* advise; assim. to -ISH². Early *am-* was Latinized to *adm-*.]
1 Advise or urge earnestly (*to do*, *that* one should do). ME.
Holiday Which? Posters admonish women to dress modestly.
2 *gen.* Put in mind of duties; counsel; warn. Also, reprimand, rebuke. LME.
E. NEWBY She actually descended . . in order to admonish some small boys who were behaving in a rowdy fashion.
3 Warn or caution against danger or error. Usu. foll. by *of*. *arch.* M16.
4 Remind; apprise, inform. *arch.* L16.
■ **admonisher** *noun* L16. **admonishingly** *adverb* in an admonishing manner, so as to admonish M19. **admonishment** *noun* the action of admonishing, the fact of being admonished; a reproof, an admonition. ME.

admonition /admәˈnɪʃ(ә)n/ *noun*. LME.
[ORIGIN Old French *amonition* (mod. *adm-*) from Latin *admonitio(n-)*, from *admonit-* pa. ppl stem of *admonere*: see ADMONISH, -ION.]
1 The action of admonishing; authoritative counsel; warning, reproof. LME.
2 An act of admonishing; a statement of counsel or reproof. LME.

admonitory /ədˈmɒnɪt(ə)ri/ *adjective*. L16.
[ORIGIN medieval Latin *admonitorius*, formed as ADMONITION; in mod. use. from ADMONITION: see -ORY².]
Giving or conveying admonition; warning.
■ **admonitor** *noun* (now *rare*) a person who admonishes M16. **admonitorial** /ədmɒnɪˈtɔːrɪəl/ *adjective* (*rare*) = ADMONITORY M19. **admonitorily** *adverb* M19.

adnate /ˈadneɪt/ *adjective*. M17.
[ORIGIN Latin *adnatus* var. of *agnatus* AGNATE, due to assoc. with AD-.]
Now chiefly BOTANY. Joined by having grown together.
■ **adˈnation** *noun* (BOTANY) adnate condition M19.

ad nauseam /ad ˈnɔːzɪam, -sɪam/ *adverbial phr.* M17.
[ORIGIN Latin, lit. 'to sickness'. Cf. earlier USQUE AD NAUSEAM.]
To a disgusting or tiresome extent.

adnexa /adˈnɛksə/ *noun pl.* L19.
[ORIGIN Latin, neut. pl. of *adnexus* joined, pa. pple of *adnectere*, formed as AD- + *nectere* to tie, fasten: cf. ANNEX *verb*.]
ANATOMY. The parts adjoining an organ.
■ **adnexal** *adjective* E20.

†**adnihilate** *adjective*, *verb*, **adnihilation** *noun*, vars. of ANNIHILATE *adjective & verb*, ANNIHILATION *noun*.

adnominal /adˈnɒmɪn(ə)l/ *adjective & noun*. M19.
[ORIGIN from Latin *adnomin-*, *-men* (var. of AGNOMEN) + -AL¹.]
GRAMMAR. (A word or phrase) modifying a noun.

†**adnoun** *noun*. M18–L19.
[ORIGIN from AD- + NOUN, after *adverb*.]
GRAMMAR. An adjective.

Adnyamathanha /ˈadnjəˌmʌdənə/ *noun*. L19.
[ORIGIN Prob. Adnyamathanha.]
An Aboriginal language of South Australia.

ado /əˈduː/ *noun*. LME.
[ORIGIN from ADO *verb & adjective*, the adverbs in *much ado* etc. being taken as adjectives.]
1 Pl. **ado(e)s**. Action, business; fuss; *rare* a fuss. LME.
without further ado, **without more ado** without any fuss or delay, immediately.
2 Labour, trouble, difficulty. LME.

ado /əˈduː/ *verb (inf.) & adjective*. Now *arch. & dial.* (chiefly *Scot. & N. English*). LME.
[ORIGIN Reduced form of *at do*, from adoption of Old Norse *at* as sign of inf. + DO *verb*, corresp. to native *to-do* (see DO *verb*).]
▸ **A** *verb* (*pres. inf.*). To do. Exc. *N. English* only in ***have ado***. LME.
▸ **B** *adjective*. Being done, in process, astir. M16.

-ado /ˈeɪdəʊ, ˈɑː-/ *suffix*.
Forming nouns.
1 Repr. Spanish & Portuguese *-ado* (from Latin *-atus* -ATE²) masc. pa. ppl ending of verbs in *-ar*, as ***desperado***, ***tornado***.
2 Refash. of French words in *-ade* (see -ADE 1), Spanish words in *-ada*, and Italian words in *-ata*, as ***bravado***.

adobe /əˈdəʊb(ɪ)/ *noun*. M18.
[ORIGIN Spanish, from *adobar* to plaster, from Arabic *aṭ-ṭūb*, from *al* the + *ṭūb* bricks.]
1 An unburnt brick dried in the sun. M18. ▸**b** A house built of such bricks. *US.* E19.
attrib.: I. SHAW A Mexican peasant woman . . sitting in front of an adobe wall.
2 Clay or earth prepared for making into such bricks or suitable for this purpose. L18.

†**adod** *interjection* var. of ADAD.

adoing /əˈduːɪŋ/ *adverb & pred. adjective*. *arch.* M16.
[ORIGIN from A *preposition*¹ 7 + DOING *verbal noun*.]
Being done; in the process of happening.

adolescence /adəˈlɛs(ə)ns/ *noun*. LME.
[ORIGIN Old French & mod. French from Latin *adolescentia*, from *adolescent-*: see ADOLESCENT, -ENCE.]
The process or condition of growing from childhood to manhood or womanhood; the period of growing up.
■ **adolescency** *noun* the quality or state of being adolescent L15.

adolescent /adəˈlɛs(ə)nt/ *noun & adjective*. LME.
[ORIGIN Old French & mod. French from Latin *adolescent-* pres. ppl stem of *adolescere*, from *ad* AD- + *alescere* grow up, from *alere* nourish: see -ENT.]
▸ **A** *noun*. A person in the age of adolescence. LME.
▸ **B** *adjective*. Growing from childhood to maturity; in the age of adolescence. L18.
M. PEAKE Their adolescent faces. *fig.*: E. O'NEILL This adolescent country.
■ **adolesce** *verb intrans.* reach or pass through adolescence E20. **adolescently** *adverb* M20.

Adonai /adɒˈnʌɪ, -ˈneɪʌɪ/ *noun*. LME.
[ORIGIN Hebrew *ʾăḏōnāy*: see JEHOVAH.]
In Judaism (and in the Old Testament): (a name of) God.

Adonic /əˈdɒnɪk/ *adjective & noun*. L16.
[ORIGIN French *adonique* from medieval Latin *adonicus*, from Greek *Adōnis*: see ADONIS, -IC.]
▸ **A** *adjective*. Of or relating to Adonis; CLASSICAL PROSODY designating a metre consisting of a dactyl and a spondee. L16.
▸ **B** *noun*. An Adonic verse or line. L16.
■ **Adonian** /əˈdəʊnɪən/ *adjective* = ADONIC *adjective* M17.

Adonis /əˈdəʊnɪs/ *noun*. L16.
[ORIGIN Greek *Adōnis*, a youth loved by Aphrodite in Greek mythol., ult. from Phoenician *ʾadōnī* my lord, *ʾadōn* lord.]
1 A plant of the genus *Adonis*; pheasant's eye. L16.
2 A handsome young man. E17.
– COMB.: **Adonis blue** a European butterfly, *Lysandra bellargus*.
■ **adonization** /adənʌɪˈzeɪʃ(ə)n/ *noun* (*arch.*) dandification E19. **adonize** *verb trans. & intrans.* (*arch.*) dandify (oneself) E17.

†**a-doors** *adverb*. E16–L19.
[ORIGIN Contr.: see A *preposition*².]
Of doors; at doors.

adopt /əˈdɒpt/ *verb trans.* L15.
[ORIGIN Old French & mod. French *adopter* or Latin *adoptare*, from *ad* AD- + *optare* choose.]
1 Take (a person) voluntarily into a relationship (usu. foll. by *as*), esp. (**a**) as one's child, (**b**) as a candidate for membership of the House of Commons. L15. ▸**b** Of a local authority: accept responsibility for the maintenance of (a road etc.). M19.
SHAKES. *Oth.* I had rather to adopt a child than get it. S. JOHNSON Those whom he happens to adopt as favourites. **b** J. BETJEMAN By roads 'not adopted', by woodlanded ways.
2 Take (a practice, idea, etc.) from someone else. E17. ▸**b** PHILOLOGY. Take (a foreign word) into use without (intentionally) changing its form. L19.
R. GRAVES I adopted the Stoic way of looking at things.
3 Choose for one's own practice, take up, (something, not necessarily another's). M18.
J. BERGER The ruling class adopted new tactics towards the workers and the peasantry.
4 Approve, accept (a report etc.). E20.
J. GALSWORTHY I propose . . that the report and accounts be adopted.
■ **adoptable** *adjective* M19. **adopˈtee** *noun* an adopted person L19. **adopter** *noun* L16.

adoption /əˈdɒpʃ(ə)n/ *noun*. ME.
[ORIGIN Old French & mod. French, or Latin *adoptio(n-)*, formed as *adoptare*: see ADOPT, -ION.]
1 The action of taking or the fact of being taken into any relationship; *esp.* the action of taking a minor who is not one's offspring into the legal relationship of child. ME.
2 The action of taking up and treating as one's own an idea etc.; the fact of being so taken up; an idea etc. so taken. L16. ▸**b** PHILOLOGY. The taking of a foreign word into use without (intentionally) changing its form; a word so taken. L19.
3 Approval, acceptance (of a report etc.). L19.
■ **Adoptionist** *noun & adjective* (ECCLESIASTICAL HISTORY) (**a**) *noun* a person who maintained that Christ is the son of God by adoption only; (**b**) *adjective* of or pertaining to Adoptionists or their beliefs: M19. †**adoptious** *adjective* (*rare*, Shakes.) only in E17.

adoptive /əˈdɒptɪv/ *adjective*. LME.
[ORIGIN Old French & mod. French *adoptif*, *-ive* from Latin *adoptivus*: see ADOPT, -IVE.]
1 Due to adoption; having the specified familial relation by adoption. LME.
adoptive brother, ***adoptive child***, ***adoptive father***, ***adoptive mother***, ***adoptive sister***, etc.
2 Inclined to or in the habit of adopting. *rare*. M19.
G. A. SALA Surely the English language is the . . most swiftly adoptive in the world.
■ **adoptively** *adverb* by way of adoption M19.

adorable /əˈdɔːrəb(ə)l/ *adjective*. E17.
[ORIGIN French, or Latin *adorabilis*, from *adorare* ADORE: see -ABLE.]
1 Worthy of divine worship. Now *rare*. E17.
BURKE The adorable wisdom of God.
2 Worthy of passionate attachment; *colloq.* very pleasing. E18.
New York Times Diane has a wonderful job, a loving husband, and two adorable children. *Independent* Bunny rabbits! Floppy eared, short or long hair, it doesn't matter—they're all adorable.
■ **adoraˈbility** *noun* M17. **adorableness** *noun* L17. **adorably** *adverb* E19.

adoral /adˈɔːr(ə)l/ *adjective*. L19.
[ORIGIN from AD- 1 + ORAL.]
ZOOLOGY. Situated at or near the mouth.
■ **adorally** *adverb* towards or near the mouth L19.

adoration /adəˈreɪʃ(ə)n/ *noun*. E16.
[ORIGIN Old French & mod. French, or Latin *adoratio(n-)*, from *adorare*: see ADORE, -ATION.]
1 The act of worshipping or honouring as divine. E16.
2 (The exhibition of) profound regard or love. L16.
3 ROMAN CATHOLIC CHURCH. A method of electing a pope by a low reverence before the same candidate from two-thirds of the voters present. L16.

adore /əˈdɔː/ *verb*. LME.
[ORIGIN Old French & mod. French *adourer* (now *adorer*), earlier *ao(u)rer* from Latin *adorare*, from *ad* AD- + *orare* speak, pray.]
1 *verb trans.* Worship as divine. Now chiefly *poet.* LME. ▸**b** *verb trans.* ROMAN CATHOLIC CHURCH. Offer reverence to (the Host etc.). L16.

POPE Be crown'd as Monarchs, or as Gods adored.

2 *verb trans.* Regard with deep respect and affection; *colloq.* like greatly. LME.

O. SITWELL Her mother, whom plainly she adored. D. RUNYON If there is one thing he adores it is spare-ribs.

3 *verb intrans.* Offer prayers or entreaties; offer worship. *arch.* E16.

J. M. FAULKNER How the chieftains starlit To Bethlehem came to adore.

■ **adorant** *adjective* (*poet.*) adoring E19. **adorative** *adjective* (now *rare*) pertaining to adoration, adoring M17. **adorer** *noun* a worshipper, an ardent admirer E17. **adoringly** *adverb* E19.

†**adorn** *adjective*. *rare* (Milton). Only in M17.
[ORIGIN Italian *adorno*, ult. formed as ADORN *verb*.]
Adorned, ornate.

adorn /əˈdɔːn/ *verb trans.* LME.
[ORIGIN Old French & mod. French *adorner*, earlier *ao(u)rner* from Latin *adornare*, from *ad* AD- + *ornare* furnish, deck.]
1 Be an ornament to, add beauty or lustre to. LME.

MILTON A garland to adorn her tresses. LEIGH HUNT The following might have adorned the pages of Spenser. CONAN DOYLE A butler who would have adorned a bench of bishops.

2 Provide with ornament(s); embellish (*with*). LME.

SHAKES. *1 Hen. VI* Adorn his temples with a coronet. BURKE The many great vertues with which he has adorned his mind.

■ **adorner** *noun* E16. **adornment** *noun* the action of adorning; a thing which adorns, an ornament: L15.

adown /əˈdaʊn/ *adverb & preposition*. Now *arch.* or *poet.*
[ORIGIN Old English *adūn(e)*, formed as A *preposition*[2], DOWN *adverb & adjective*. Aphet. to DOWN *adverb*.]
▸ **A** *adverb*. Downward, down. OE.
▸ **B** *preposition*. Downwards upon or along. LME.
■ †**adownright** *adverb* straight down, downright (aphet. to DOWNRIGHT): only in ME. †**adownward** *adverb & preposition* (aphet. to DOWNWARD) OE–LME.

adoze /əˈdəʊz/ *adverb & pred. adjective*. M19.
[ORIGIN from A-[2] + DOZE *noun*.]
In a doze, dozing.

ADP *abbreviation*.
1 BIOCHEMISTRY. Adenosine diphosphate.
2 Automatic data processing.

ad personam /ad pəːˈsəʊnam/ *adverbial & adjectival phr.* M20.
[ORIGIN Latin, lit. 'to the person'.]
Personal(ly); on an individual basis.

adpressed /adˈprɛst/ *adjective*. E19.
[ORIGIN from Latin *adpress-* pa. ppl stem of *adprimere*, from *ad* AD- + *premere* press + -ED[1].]
BOTANY. Lying close to the stem, the ground, etc.

ADR *abbreviation*.
1 LAW. Alternative dispute resolution.
2 US STOCK EXCHANGE. American depository receipt.

adrad /əˈdrad/ *adjective*. *arch.* Earlier †**of-**. OE.
[ORIGIN pa. pple of *ofdrǣdan*, from OFF- + base of DREAD *verb*. Weakened to *a-* in Middle English after which *ofdrad* is not recorded.]
Frightened, terrified.

†**adragant** *noun*. Only in 18.
[ORIGIN French *adragant(e)* popular alt. of *tragacanthe* TRAGACANTH. Cf. earlier DRAGANT.]
Tragacanth. Also ***gum adragant***.

†**adread** *verb* see DREAD *verb*.

adream /əˈdriːm/ *adverb & pred. adjective*. *poet.* M19.
[ORIGIN from A-[2] + DREAM *noun*[2].]
In a dream, dreaming.

†**adreamed** *pple & ppl adjective*. M16–L19.
[ORIGIN Prob. from A-[4] + DREAM *noun*[2] or *verb*.]
be adreamed, to dream.

ad referendum /ad rɛfəˈrɛndəm/ *adverbial phr.* L18.
[ORIGIN mod. Latin, lit. 'for reference'.]
Subject to the assent of a higher authority.

ad rem /ad rɛm/ *adverbial & adjectival phr.* L16.
[ORIGIN Latin, lit. 'to the matter'.]
To the point; to the purpose.

adrenal /əˈdriːn(ə)l/ *adjective & noun*. L19.
[ORIGIN from AD- 1 + RENAL.]
ANATOMY. ▸**A** *adjective*. Situated above the kidney, suprarenal; *spec.* designating or pertaining to the adrenals (see sense B. below). L19.
adrenal cortex the outer part of an adrenal gland, secreting corticosteroids and some other hormones. **adrenal medulla** the central part of an adrenal gland, secreting adrenalin and noradrenaline. ***adrenal rest***: see REST *noun*[3] 6.
▸ **B** *noun*. Either of the two small suprarenal glands, which secrete certain hormones, notably adrenalin and corticosteroids. Usu. in *pl.* L19.

■ **adrenaˈlectomy** *noun* (an instance of) surgical removal of the adrenal glands E20. **adrenaˈlectomized** *ppl adjective* that has undergone adrenalectomy E20.

adrenalin /əˈdrɛnəlɪn/ *noun*. Also **-ine**. E20.
[ORIGIN from ADRENAL + -IN[1].]
A hormone, $(HO)_2C_6H_3{\cdot}CHOH{\cdot}CH_2NHCH_3$, secreted by the adrenal medulla of people and animals under stress, which has a range of physiological effects, e.g. on circulation, breathing, muscular activity, and carbohydrate metabolism; (also *US.* **A-** as proprietary name) this hormone extracted from animals or prepared synthetically for medicinal purposes.

adrenalized /əˈdrɛnəlʌɪzd/ *adjective*. Also **-ised**. L20.
[ORIGIN from ADRENALIN + -ED[1].]
Affected with adrenalin; *fig.* (over-)excited, tense.

adrenergic /adrɪˈnəːdʒɪk/ *adjective*. M20.
[ORIGIN from ADREN(ALIN + -ERGIC.]
PHYSIOLOGY. Releasing, involving, or resembling adrenalin or noradrenaline as a neurotransmitter. Cf. CHOLINERGIC.

adreno- /əˈdriːnəʊ, əˈdrɛnəʊ/ *combining form*.
[ORIGIN from ADRENAL and ADRENALIN: see -O-.]
Adrenal; adrenalin.
■ **adrenoˈcortical** *adjective* of, pertaining to, or secreted by the adrenal cortex M20. **aˌdrenocorticoˈtrophic**, **-tropic** *adjective* stimulating or controlling the adrenal cortex; ***adrenocorticotrophic hormone***, a hormone of this nature secreted by the pituitary: M20. **adrenoˈlytic** *adjective* inhibiting the action of adrenalin or the adrenergic transmission of nerve impulses M20.

adret /ˈadreɪ/ *noun*. M20.
[ORIGIN French (orig. dial.) from vars. of *à* to and *droit* straight.]
GEOGRAPHY. A mountain slope which faces the sun. Opp. UBAC.

Adriatic /eɪdrɪˈatɪk/ *adjective & noun*. E17.
[ORIGIN Latin *Adriaticus*, *Ha-*, from *Adria*, *Ha-* Etruscan settlement in NE Italy: see -IC.]
▸ **A** *adjective*. Designating or pertaining to a sea between Italy and the Balkan peninsula (an arm of the Mediterranean). E17.
▸ **B** *noun*. *The* Adriatic Sea. L18.

adrift /əˈdrɪft/ *adverb & pred. adjective*. L16.
[ORIGIN from A *preposition*[1] 1 + DRIFT *noun*.]
Drifting; subject to control by wind and tide, or (*fig.*) by circumstances; *colloq.* unfastened, out of touch, away from what is expected or desired.
cast adrift: see CAST *verb*.

adrip /əˈdrɪp/ *adverb & pred. adjective*. M19.
[ORIGIN from A-[2] + DRIP *noun* or *verb*.]
Dripping.

adrogate /ˈadrəgeɪt/ *verb trans. & intrans.* M17.
[ORIGIN Latin *adrogat-* pa. ppl stem of *adrogare*, from *ad* AD- + *rogare* ask: see -ATE[3] and cf. ARROGATE.]
ROMAN LAW. Adopt (a person who is at the time his or her own master or *sui juris*).
■ **adroˈgation** *noun* E18. **adrogator** *noun* a person who adrogates another L19.

adroit /əˈdrɔɪt/ *adjective*. M17.
[ORIGIN Old French & mod. French, from adverb phr. *à droit* according to right, properly.]
Physically or mentally resourceful; dexterous, skilful.
■ **adroitly** *adverb* M18. **adroitness** *noun* M18.

†**adrop** *noun*. L15–M18.
[ORIGIN Misreading of Arabic *usrubb* lead from Persian †*usrup* (now *surb*).]
ALCHEMY. A substance from which mercury was to be extracted for the philosopher's stone; the philosopher's stone.

adry /əˈdrʌɪ/ *adverb & pred. adjective*. L16.
[ORIGIN from DRY *adjective* after *acold*, *athirst*, etc.]
In a dry condition; thirsty.

†**ads** *noun*. L17–E19.
[ORIGIN Alt.]
God's: used in oaths. Cf. OD *noun*[1].

adscititious /adsɪˈtɪʃəs/ *adjective*. Also (now *rare*) **asc-** /as-/. E17.
[ORIGIN from Latin *a(d)scit-* pa. ppl stem of *adsciscere* admit, adopt + -ITIOUS[1], after *adventitious*.]
Adopted from without; supplemental.

adscript /ˈadskrɪpt/ *noun & adjective*. L17.
[ORIGIN Latin *adscriptus* pa. pple of *adscribere*, from *ad* AD- + *scribere* write.]
▸ **A** *noun*. †**1** MATH. The tangent of an angle. L17–M19.
2 An adscript serf (see sense B.1 below). M19.
3 A comment or note added to a manuscript. L19.
▸ **B** *adjective*. **1** [For medieval Latin *adscriptus glebae* attached to the soil.] Of a feudal serf: hereditarily pertaining to an estate and transferred with it. E19.
2 Written after (opp. ***subscript***). L19.

adscription /adˈskrɪpʃ(ə)n/ *noun*. *rare*. M17.
[ORIGIN Latin *adscriptio(n-)*, formed as ADSCRIPT: see -ION.]
†**1** The circumscribing or inscribing of geometrical figures. Only in M17.
2 = ASCRIPTION. M19.
3 Attachment as an adscript serf. L19.

adsignification /adˌsɪgnɪfɪˈkeɪʃ(ə)n/ *noun*. Now *rare*. E17.
[ORIGIN medieval Latin *adsignificatio(n-)*, from *adsignificare*, from *ad* AD- + *significare* SIGNIFY: see -ATION.]
GRAMMAR & LOGIC. (The signification of) a meaning additional to the basic meaning of a word, phrase, etc.

ADSL *abbreviation*.
COMPUTING & TELECOMMUNICATIONS. Asymmetric (or asynchronous) digital subscriber line (or loop), a technology for the transmission of digital data over standard copper lines which allows high-speed transmission of signals from the telephone network to an individual subscriber, but a slower rate of transmission from the subscriber to the network.

adsorb /ədˈsɔːb/ *verb*. L19.
[ORIGIN Back-form. from ADSORPTION.]
CHEMISTRY. **1** *verb trans.* Collect (a substance) by adsorption. L19.
2 *verb intrans.* Undergo adsorption (*on*, *on to*, *to*, a surface). E20.
■ **adsorbaˈbility** *noun* the degree to which a substance is adsorbable E20. **adsorbable** *adjective* able to be adsorbed E20. **adsorbate** *noun* an adsorbed substance E20. **adsorbent** *noun* a substance on which adsorption occurs E20.

adsorption /ədˈsɔːpʃ(ə)n/ *noun*. L19.
[ORIGIN Blend of AD- and ABSORPTION.]
CHEMISTRY. The adhering of atoms or molecules of gases, liquids, or solutes to exposed surfaces (usu. of solids).
■ **adsorptional**, **adsorptive** *adjectives* E20. **adsorptively** *adverb* M20.

adstratum /ˈadstrɑːtəm, adˈstrɑːtəm/ *noun*. Pl. **-ta** /-tə/. M20.
[ORIGIN mod. Latin, from Latin AD- + *stratum* STRATUM.]
LINGUISTICS. (Elements or features of) a language responsible for change in a neighbouring language. Cf. SUBSTRATUM, SUPERSTRATUM.

†**adstrict** *verb*, **adstriction** *noun* etc., vars. of ASTRICT etc.

†**adstringe** *verb* var. of ASTRINGE.

adsuki *noun* var. of ADZUKI.

adsum /ˈadsʌm/ *interjection*. L16.
[ORIGIN Latin.]
I am present (as an answer in a roll-call etc.).

†**adub** *verb trans.* Infl. **-bb-**. LME.
[ORIGIN Old French *ad(o)ub(b)er*, formed as A-[5] + DUB *verb*[1].]
1 Knight, dub. LME–E17.
2 Equip, array. LME–L16.

adularia /adjʊˈlɛːrɪə/ *noun*. L18.
[ORIGIN from French *adulaire* adjective, from *Adula* a group of peaks in the Lepontine Alps, Switzerland: see -IA[1].]
MINERALOGY. A low-temperature form of potassium feldspar forming colourless or white prisms.

adulation /adjʊˈleɪʃ(ə)n/ *noun*. LME.
[ORIGIN Old French & mod. French, or Latin *adulatio(n-)*, from *adulari* fawn upon: see -ATION.]
Servile flattery; hypocritical praise; an instance of this.
■ ˈ**adulate** *verb trans.* flatter obsequiously M18. ˈ**adulator** *noun* a servile or hypocritical flatterer LME. **adulatory** *adjective* servilely or fulsomely flattering E17.

Adullamite /əˈdʌləmʌɪt/ *noun*. LME.
[ORIGIN from *Adullam* (see below) + -ITE[1] 1.]
1 A native or inhabitant of the Canaanite city of Adullam. LME.
2 A frequenter of the cave of Adullam (see *1 Samuel* 22:1, 2); *fig.* a member of a group of Liberal rebels in the House of Commons in 1866; a member of any dissident political group. M19.

adult /ˈadʌlt, əˈdʌlt/ *adjective & noun*. M16.
[ORIGIN Latin *adultus* pa. pple of *adolescere* (see ADOLESCENT): cf. French *adulte* (L16).]
▸ **A** *adjective*. **1** Grown up; having reached the age of maturity; fully developed. M16.
2 [Orig. attrib. use of noun] Of, pertaining to, or for adults. E19. ▸**b** Sexually explicit. M20.

H. G. WELLS Exhaustive character study is an adult occupation.

adult education: for those over the usual school age.
▸ **B** *noun*. An adult person; a person who has reached maturity. M17.
consenting adult: see CONSENT *verb* 2.
■ **adulthood** *noun* M19. **adultly** *adverb* M20. **adultness** *noun* M18.

†**adulter** *noun*. For early forms see ADULTERER. ME–M17.
[ORIGIN Orig. Old French *a(v)outre* from Latin *adulter*; later assim. to Latin.]
An adulterer.

adulter /əˈdʌltə/ *verb*. Now *rare* or *obsolete*. For earliest forms see ADULTERER. LME.
[ORIGIN Orig. Old French *a(v)outrer* from Latin *adulterare* (see ADULTERATE *verb*); later assim. to Latin.]
1 *verb intrans.* Commit adultery. LME.

R. MACAULAY Ye're nought but an adultering wumman, when all's said.

†**2** *verb trans.* Corrupt, debase. LME–M18.

A

adulterant /əˈdʌlt(ə)r(ə)nt/ *adjective & noun*. **M18.**
[ORIGIN Latin *adulterant-* pres. ppl stem of *adulterare*: see ADULTERATE *verb*, -ANT[1].]
(A substance) used in adulterating.

adulterate /əˈdʌlt(ə)rət/ *adjective*. **E16.**
[ORIGIN Latin *adulteratus* pa. pple, formed as ADULTERATE *verb*: see -ATE[2].]
1 Spurious; base in origin or by admixture. **E16.**
2 Stained by adultery, in origin or conduct; adulterous. **M16.**

adulterate /əˈdʌltəreɪt/ *verb*. **M16.**
[ORIGIN Latin *adulterat-* pa. ppl stem of *adulterare* debauch, corrupt: see -ATE[3].]
1 *verb trans.* Render spurious; debase, esp. by admixture of other substances. **M16.**
†**2** *verb intrans.* Commit adultery (*with*). **L16–M19.**
†**3** *verb trans.* Defile by adultery; debauch. Only in **17.**
■ **adulterator** *noun* a person who adulterates **E17.**

adulteration /ədʌltəˈreɪʃ(ə)n/ *noun*. **E16.**
[ORIGIN Latin *adulteratio(n-)*, formed as ADULTERATE *verb*: see -ATION.]
1 The action of adulterating; debasement. **E16.**
2 An adulterated condition, product, or substance. **M17.**

adulterer /əˈdʌlt(ə)rə/ *noun*. For early forms see below. **LME.**
[ORIGIN from ADULTER *verb* + -ER[1].]
1 A person who commits adultery. **LME.**
†**2** = ADULTERATOR. **LME–M17.**
– NOTE: The series *adulter*, *adulterer*, *adulteress*, *adulterous*, *adultery* emerged in **15** or **16** and superseded earlier *avouter* adulterer, *avoutre* commit adultery, *avout(e)rer* adulterer, *avoutres* adulteress, *avoutrous* adulterous, *avoutrie* adultery, all of which were from regular phonetic derivs. in Old French of Latin *adulterare* (see ADULTERATE *verb*).

adulteress /əˈdʌlt(ə)rɪs/ *noun*. For early forms see ADULTERER. **LME.**
[ORIGIN Orig. Old French *a(v)outresse*, formed as ADULTER *noun* + -ESS[1]; later assim. to Latin.]
A woman who commits adultery.

adulterine /əˈdʌlt(ə)rʌɪn/ *adjective*. **M16.**
[ORIGIN Latin *adulterinus*, from *adulter* adulterous, adulterer: see -INE[1].]
1 Spurious; due to adulteration. **M16.**
2 Illegal, unlicensed. **M17.**
3 Born of adultery. **M18.**
4 Of or pertaining to adultery. **M19.**

adulterize /əˈdʌltərʌɪz/ *verb intrans. arch.* Also **-ise**. **L16.**
[ORIGIN formed as ADULTEROUS + -IZE.]
Commit adultery.

adulterous /əˈdʌlt(ə)rəs/ *adjective*. **L15.**
[ORIGIN from ADULTER *noun* + -OUS.]
1 Pertaining to or characterized by adultery. **L15.** ▸†**b** = ADULTERINE 1. **L16–E17.**
2 Pertaining to or characterized by adulteration. *arch.* **M16.**
■ **adulterously** *adverb* **L16.**

adultery /əˈdʌlt(ə)ri/ *noun*. For early forms see ADULTERER. **ME.**
[ORIGIN Orig. Old French *avout(e)rie*, formed as ADULTER *noun* + -Y[3]; later assim. to Latin.]
1 Voluntary sexual intercourse of a married person other than with his or her spouse. **ME.** ▸**b** Occas. extended in biblical and theological use: any irregular sexual intercourse or forbidden marriage; idolatry. **LME.**

J. GRISHAM I never thought that I was committing adultery. **b** AV *Jer.* 3:9 Shee . . committed adultery with stones and with stockes.

†**2** Adulteration. Only in **17.**

adultescent /adʌlˈtɛs(ə)nt/ *noun*. *colloq.* **L20.**
[ORIGIN Blend of ADULT and ADOLESCENT.]
A middle-aged person whose clothes, interests, and activities are typically associated with youth culture.

adumbrate /ˈadʌmbreɪt/ *verb trans.* **L16.**
[ORIGIN Latin *adumbrat-* pa. ppl stem of *adumbrare*, from *ad* AD- + *umbrare*, from *umbra* shade: see -ATE[3].]
†**1** Shade (a sketch) and so complete it. *rare*. Only in **L16.**
2 Represent in outline, give a faint indication of. **L16.**

JAS. MILL Its duties were . . not defined . . , but only adumbrated.

3 Shadow forth, typify; foreshadow, prefigure. **L16.**

T. GALE Noah . . is adumbrated to us . . in Prometheus.

4 Overshadow; obscure. **L16.**

W. STYRON Her happy reminiscence . . had . . become adumbrated by the consciousness of something else.

■ **aˈdumbrative** *adjective* having the attribute of adumbrating **M19.**

adumbration /adʌmˈbreɪʃ(ə)n/ *noun*. **M16.**
[ORIGIN Latin *adumbratio(n-)*, formed as ADUMBRATE: see -ATION.]
†**1** Shading in painting. *rare*. Only in **M16.**
2 Representation in outline; an outline, a slight sketch or description. **M16.**
3 Symbolic representation typifying or prefiguring the reality. **E17.**
4 Overshadowing; obscuration. **M17.**

adunation /adjʊˈneɪʃ(ə)n/ *noun*. **M16.**
[ORIGIN ecclesiastical Latin *adunatio(n-)*, from *adunat-* pa. ppl stem of *adunare*, from *ad* AD- + *unare*, from *unus* one: see -ATION. Cf. Old French *adunation*.]
Union.

adunc /əˈdʌŋk/ *adjective*. **E17.**
[ORIGIN Latin *aduncus*, from *ad* AD- + *uncus* hook.]
Hooked.
■ **aduncity** /-sɪti/ *noun* (now *rare* or *obsolete*) the state of being hooked or crooked **L16.** **aduncous** *adjective* hooked, incurved **M17.**

†**adure** *verb trans. & intrans.* **LME–M17.**
[ORIGIN Latin *adurere*: see ADUST *adjective & verb*.]
Burn (something) completely, scorch.

adust /əˈdʌst/ *adjective & verb*. *arch.* **LME.**
[ORIGIN French *aduste* or Latin *adustus* pa. pple of *adurere*, from *ad* AD- + *urere* burn.]
▸ **A** *adjective*. **1** Orig. (MEDICINE), exhibiting or pertaining to a supposed hot, dry, atrabilious quality of the body and its humours. Now *obsolete* exc. in *gen.* sense, sallow, melancholic. **LME.**

POPE No meagre muse-rid mope adust and thin.

choler adust: see CHOLER 2.
2 Scorched; calcined; parched. **LME.**

E. BLUNDEN So adust, red-dry / the rock-drift soil was.

3 Brown, as if scorched; sunburnt. **L16.**

SMOLLETT Arabia's scorching sands he crossed . . Conductor of her Tribes adust.

▸ **B** *verb trans.* Scorch, dry up with heat. Chiefly as ***adusted*** *ppl adjective*. Long *arch. rare*. **LME.**
■ †**adustion** *noun* the action of scorching or parching; the state of being scorched or parched: **LME–M19.**

adust /əˈdʌst/ *adverb & pred. adjective*. *rare*. **E19.**
[ORIGIN from A-[2] + DUST *noun*.]
In a dusty condition.

ad valorem /ad vəˈlɔːrɛm/ *adverbial & adjectival phr.* **L17.**
[ORIGIN Latin = according to the value.]
Of taxes: in proportion to the estimated value of goods.

advance /ədˈvɑːns/ *noun & adjective*. **ME.**
[ORIGIN Partly from French *avance*, formed as ADVANCE *verb*; partly from ADVANCE *verb*.]
▸ **A** *noun*. †**1** = ADVANCEMENT 3. Only in **ME.**
2 Progress; a step forward. **LME.**

B. LOVELL The tortuous nature of scientific advance. B. RUSSELL This development . . is indubitably an advance.

3 Payment beforehand, or on security; an anticipatory payment; a loan. **L16.**

G. VIDAL They'll give you an advance for a book. J. CARY An . . advance to enable her to go to Paris and study music.

4 The state or position of being before, to the front, or above. (Usu. as below.) **M17.**
in advance (of) ahead (of) in place or time.
5 Forward motion; progression (in space). **L17.**

CLARENDON The manner of the enemy's advance. H. FAST The fire was brought under control and its advance was halted.

6 A personal approach; a friendly or amorous overture. Freq. in *pl.* **L17.**

LD MACAULAY Frederic had . . made advances towards a reconciliation with Voltaire. L. P. HARTLEY Irma had rejected the crude advances of the three young men.

7 A rise in amount, value, or price. **L17.**

JOYCE Any advance on five shillings?

▸ **B** *attrib.* or as *adjective*. Being, going, supplied, or acquired in advance. **L16.**
advance booking: made before the day of a performance, journey, etc. **advance copy** a copy of a book etc. supplied before the date of publication. **advance directive** LAW a living will which gives durable power of attorney to a surrogate decision-maker, remaining in effect during the incompetency of the person making it. **advance guard**: preceding the main body of an army. **advance man** *N. Amer.*: preparing the way for a visit by a politician etc.

advance /ədˈvɑːns/ *verb*. **ME.**
[ORIGIN Old French & mod. French *avancer*, ult. from late Latin *abante*, from *ab* AB- + *ante* before. For spelling *adv-* see AD- 2.]
1 *verb trans.* Forward, help on, (a process, plan, etc.). **ME.**

M. FONTEYN Those who have advanced the art by contributing to its evolution.

2 *verb trans.* Raise or promote (a person) in rank or office; put in a better position. **ME.**

V. WOOLF At the office they advanced him to a post of considerable responsibility.

3 *verb trans.* LAW. Give as an advancement. **LME.**
4 *verb trans.* Move, put or push, forward (physically, or in time). **LME.**

POPE Who spread their bucklers and advance their spears. E. BROCK All / the family advanced their watches by two minutes.

5 *verb trans.* Raise or lift up (*lit.* & *fig.*). *arch.* **LME.**

SHAKES. *Temp.* The fringed curtain of thine eye advance.

†**6** *verb trans.* Extol; *refl.* boast. **LME–M17.**
7 *verb trans.* Make earlier (an event or date). **L15.**
8 *verb trans.* Bring forward (a statement, claim, etc.) for notice. **E16.**

W. TREVOR She advanced the opinion that the bird wouldn't last much longer.

9 *verb intrans.* Move forward, proceed. **E16.** ▸**b** *fig.* Make progress in life or any course. **L17.** ▸**c** *fig.* Go on towards completion or perfection. **M19.** ▸**d** Of a colour: stand out. **L19.**

A. WILSON His companion . . advanced towards them. ALDOUS HUXLEY In Africa the Sahara is advancing. **b** W. S. GILBERT If you wish in this world to advance, Your merits you're bound to enhance. **c** CONAN DOYLE You will feel even less humorous as the evening advances.

10 *verb trans.* Pay (money) before it is due; lend (money). **L16.**
11 **a** *verb trans.* Raise in rate or price. **L17.** ▸**b** *verb intrans.* Rise in rate or price. **L19.**
■ **advancer** *noun* a person who or thing which advances, *spec.* a second branch of a buck's horn: **L15.**

advanced /ədˈvɑːnst/ *adjective*. **LME.**
[ORIGIN from ADVANCE *verb* + -ED[1].]
†**1** Promoted. **LME–L17.**
2 *fig.* Far on in life or time, or in any course of action, or march of ideas. **M16.**

P. G. WODEHOUSE The day was already well advanced. SCOTT FITZGERALD Everybody thinks so—the most advanced people.

advanced degree: one superior to a bachelor's. **advanced level** an examination (formerly the higher of the two main levels) of the General Certificate of Education in England and Wales. **advanced studies**: in the higher branches of a subject.
†**3** Raised (physically). **L16–E18.**
4 Chiefly MILITARY. Moved forward, being to the front. **E18.**
advanced guard, ***advanced post***, ***advanced works***.
5 Raised in amount, increased. **L18.**

advancement /ədˈvɑːnsm(ə)nt/ *noun*. **ME.**
[ORIGIN Old French & mod. French *avancement*: see ADVANCE *verb*, -MENT.]
1 The raising of a person to a higher rank or position; promotion or preferment. **ME.**

Independent Employees feeling that they have fewer opportunities for advancement.

2 LAW. The promotion of children in life, esp. by the gift of part or all of their prospective share in property to which they would not be entitled until a later date. **LME.**
3 Extolment; boasting. **LME–M17.**
4 The action of promoting a cause or endeavour; furtherance. Also, a development or improvement. **L15.**

K. VONNEGUT Unbridled technological advancements. *Economist* Their real interest is the advancement of their own country.

5 Forward movement. Now *rare*. **M18.**
6 Advancing or advanced condition. Now *rare*. **L18.**

advantage /ədˈvɑːntɪdʒ/ *noun*. **ME.**
[ORIGIN Old French & mod. French *avantage*, from *avant* before: see -AGE. For spelling *adv-* see AD- 2.]
▸ **I** Superior position.
1 The position, state, or circumstance of being ahead of another, or of having the better of him or her; superiority, esp. in contest or debate. **ME.**
get advantage over, **get an advantage over**, **give advantage over**, **give an advantage over** get, give, a better position than (also foll. by *of*, †*on*). **have advantage over**, **have an advantage over** have a better position than (also foll. by *of*, †*on*). **have the advantage of** be in a better position than; *spec.* have a personal knowledge of (another) which is not reciprocal.
2 A favouring circumstance; something which gives one a better position. **ME.**
make an advantage of, **make one's advantage of** = ***take advantage of*** below. **take advantage(s)** avail oneself of circumstances, use one's opportunities, esp. unfairly. **take advantage of** avail oneself of (a circumstance), outwit (a person), esp. unfairly. **take at advantage** *arch.* take (a person) by surprise.
†**3** A good position for defence or attack. **LME–L17.**

W. RALEIGH Upon the advantage of a mountain-side.

†**4** A favourable occasion, a chance. **LME–M17.**

SHAKES. *Ven. & Ad.* Make use of time, let not advantage slip.

5 TENNIS. The next point won after deuce (gaining a temporary superiority, but not the game). **M17.**
▸ **II** The result of a superior position.
6 Benefit; increased well-being or convenience; a resulting benefit. **ME.**

SHAKES. *1 Hen. IV* Those blessed feet Which . . were nail'd For our advantage on the bitter cross. P. SCOTT The advantages people like us enjoy over those who . . have to make do without servants.

mechanical advantage: see MECHANICAL *adjective*. **to advantage** in a way such as to exhibit merits.
†**7** Increased quantity or number; excess. **ME–E18.**

†**8** Pecuniary profit; interest on money lent. LME–M17.

SHAKES. *Merch. V.* You neither lend nor borrow Upon advantage.

– COMB.: **advantage game**, **advantage set**: in which advantage is part of the scoring.

advantage /əd'vɑːntɪdʒ/ *verb trans.* LME.
[ORIGIN from the noun, or from Old French & mod. French *avantager*.]
1 Give an advantage or superiority to; benefit, profit. LME. †**2** Add to the amount or value of. L15–L17. **3** Further the progress of, promote. L16.
■ **advantaged** *adjective* placed at advantage; socially or financially privileged: L16.

advantageous /adv(ə)n'teɪdʒəs/ *adjective.* L16.
[ORIGIN from ADVANTAGE *noun* + -OUS: cf. French *avantageux, -euse*.]
Profitable, opportune, favourable, (*to, for*).
■ **advantageously** *adverb* E17. **advantageousness** *noun* E17.

advection /əd'vɛkʃ(ə)n/ *noun.* E20.
[ORIGIN Latin *advectio(n-)*, from *advehere*, from *ad* AD- + *vehere* carry: see -ION.]
Flow of matter within the atmosphere, the oceans, or in any fluid, esp. horizontally; transfer of heat etc. brought about by such motion.
■ **advect** *verb trans.* convey (fluid, heat, etc.) by advection M20. **advective** *adjective* of, pertaining to, or brought about by advection E20.

advene /əd'viːn/ *verb intrans.* E17.
[ORIGIN Old French *avenir* (mod. *adv-*) or Latin *advenire*: see ADVENT.]
Accede or come (*to*); be superadded.

advenient /əd'viːnɪənt/ *adjective.* L16.
[ORIGIN Latin *advenient-* pres. ppl stem of *advenire*: see ADVENT, -ENT.]
Superadded; adventitious.

advent /'adv(ə)nt, -vɛnt/ *noun.* In sense 1 **A-**. OE.
[ORIGIN Old French, refashioned after Latin of *auvent* (mod. *avent*) from Latin *adventus* arrival, from *advent-* pa. ppl stem of *advenire*, from *ad-* AD- + *venire* come.]
1 The season before Christmas in the ecclesiastical calendar, now four weeks in length. OE. **2** *CHRISTIAN THEOLOGY.* The coming of Christ on earth. LME. ***second advent***: see SECOND *adjective*. **3** The arrival of an important person or thing. M18.
– COMB.: **Advent calendar** a calendar for the days of Advent with a hidden picture or gift to be revealed on each day; **Advent Sunday** the first Sunday in Advent, the Sunday nearest to the 30 November.

Adventist /'adv(ə)ntɪst/ *noun.* M19.
[ORIGIN from ADVENT + -IST.]
A member of any of various sects holding millenarian views.
Second Adventist = MILLERITE *noun*[1]. **Seventh-Day Adventist** a member of a millenarian sect who observe Saturday as the Sabbath.
■ **Adventism** *noun* the beliefs of adventists M19.

adventitia /advɛn'tɪʃə/ *noun.* L19.
[ORIGIN mod. Latin *(tunica) adventitia* additional sheath, formed as ADVENTITIOUS.]
ANATOMY. The outermost layer of the wall of a blood vessel.

adventitious /adv(ə)n'tɪʃəs/ *adjective.* E17.
[ORIGIN from medieval Latin *adventitius* alt. of Latin *adventicius*, from *advent-*: see ADVENT, -ITIOUS[1].]
1 Coming from without, accidental, casual. E17. **2** *LAW.* Of property: coming from a stranger or by collateral, not direct, succession. Opp. ***profectitious***. M17. **3** Formed in an unexpected place anatomically; *esp.* in *BOTANY* (of roots, buds, etc.) arising from a part other than that usual in plants generally. L17.
■ **adventitiously** *adverb* M18.

adventive /əd'vɛntɪv/ *adjective.* E17.
[ORIGIN from Latin *advent-* (see ADVENT) + -IVE, after ADVENTITIOUS.]
1 = ADVENTITIOUS 1. *rare.* E17.

L. DURRELL So . . tenderly had he captured the adventive minute.

2 *BOTANY & ZOOLOGY.* Present spontaneously in a region but not native to it. L19.

adventure /əd'vɛntʃə/ *noun.* ME.
[ORIGIN Old French & mod. French *aventure* ult. from Latin *adventurus* future pple of *advenire*: see ADVENT, -URE. For spelling *adv-* see AD- 2.]
†**1** Chance, fortune, luck. ME–E18.

DRYDEN She . . wished me fair adventure.

†**2** A chance occurrence, an accident. ME–E18.

SWIFT An hope, that this adventure might . . help to deliver me.

3 Chance of danger or loss; risk, jeopardy. *arch.* exc. in maritime insurance. ME. **4** Hazardous activity. ME.

V. WOOLF He, bound for adventure; she, moored to the shore.

5 A hazardous enterprise or performance. ME. ▸**b** An unexpected or exciting incident. L16. ▸**c** An instance of adventurism in foreign policy. M20.

JOYCE Friend Sinbad and his horrifying adventures. **b** C. BRONTË To walk alone in London seemed of itself an adventure.

†**6** A hazard, a venture, an experiment. LME–L18.

SHAKES. *John* To try the fair adventure of to-morrow.

at adventure(s) at hazard, recklessly. **at all adventure(s)** at any risk; at all events.
7 A pecuniary venture, a commercial speculation. L15.

BACON He that puts all vpon Aduentures, doth often times brake, and come to Pouerty.

joint adventure: see JOINT *adjective*.
– COMB.: **adventure playground**: with apparatus for children to climb on and functional materials for building with etc.
■ **adventuresome** *adjective* given to running risks; adventurous: E17.

adventure /əd'vɛntʃə/ *verb.* ME.
[ORIGIN Old French & mod. French *aventurer*, formed as ADVENTURE *noun*.]
1 *verb trans.* Take the chance of; venture upon. *arch.* ME. **2** *verb trans.* Risk the loss of; imperil. *arch.* ME. **3** *verb intrans.* Incur risk; dare to go or come (*into, upon*, etc., a place); dare to enter *(up)on* (an undertaking); go so far as *to do*. ME. ▸**b** *verb trans.* Venture to say. L19.

adventurer /əd'vɛntʃ(ə)rə/ *noun.* L15.
[ORIGIN French *aventurier*, †*adv-*, formed as ADVENTURE *noun*: see -ER[2].]
†**1** A gamester. *rare.* Only in L15. **2** A person who seeks adventures; *esp.* a mercenary soldier. E16. **3** A person who undertakes or shares in commercial adventures; a speculator. E16. **4** A person who lives by his or her wits. M17.
■ **adventuress** *noun* a woman who lives by her wits M18.

adventurism /əd'vɛntʃərɪz(ə)m/ *noun.* M19.
[ORIGIN from ADVENTURE *noun* + -ISM.]
1 The principles and practice of an adventurer. *rare.* M19. **2** A tendency to take risks in foreign policy etc. M20.
■ **adventurist** *noun & adjective* (**a**) *noun* a person inclined to adventurism; (**b**) *adjective* of or pertaining to adventurists or adventurism: E20.

adventurous /əd'vɛntʃ(ə)rəs/ *adjective.* ME.
[ORIGIN Old French *aventureus, -o(u)s*, formed as ADVENTURE *noun*: see -OUS.]
1 In search of adventures; enterprising; full of adventure. Also, involving new ideas or methods. ME.

Daily Telegraph Menus which cater for both conservative and more adventurous palates. A. LURIE Girls who are as brave and adventurous as their brothers.

†**2** Full of risk or peril. ME–M17. **3** Rash, daring. LME. †**4** Fortuitous. LME–L15.
■ **adventurously** *adverb* ME. **adventurousness** *noun* M16.

adverb /'advəːb/ *noun.* LME.
[ORIGIN French *adverbe* or Latin *adverbium*, from *ad* AD- + *verbum* VERB.]
GRAMMAR. A word that qualifies or modifies another, esp. an adjective, a verb, or another adverb, so as to express a relation of place, time, circumstance, manner, cause, degree, etc. (One of the parts of speech.)

adverbial /əd'vəːbɪəl/ *noun & adjective.* L16.
[ORIGIN Late Latin *adverbialis* or French: see ADVERB, -AL[1].]
GRAMMAR. ▸**A** *noun.* A word or phrase of the nature of an adverb. L16.
▸**B** *adjective.* Of, pertaining to, or of the nature of an adverb. L16.
■ **adverbialize** *verb trans.* make (another type of word) into an adverb E19. **adverbially** *adverb* L15.

adversaria /advə'sɛːrɪə/ *noun pl.* E18.
[ORIGIN Latin, use as noun of neut. pl. (sc. *scripta* writings) of *adversarius* facing one (see ADVERSARY).]
Miscellaneous remarks and observations; *collect. sing.* a commonplace book.

adversarial /advə'sɛːrɪəl/ *adjective.* E20.
[ORIGIN from ADVERSARY + -AL[1].]
Of or pertaining to opposition; involving adversaries; adversary.

adversary /'advəs(ə)ri/ *noun & adjective.* ME.
[ORIGIN Old French *adversarie* (mod. *-aire*) from Latin *adversarius* opposed, opponent, from *adversus*: see ADVERSE, -ARY[1].]
▸**A** *noun.* An opponent, an antagonist, an enemy. ME.

S. RUSHDIE He spoke looking his adversary in the eye.

the Adversary the Devil.
▸**B** *adjective.* Opposed, antagonistic. LME.
– NOTE: In Shakes. stressed on 1st syll.; in Milton on 1st or on 2nd.

adversative /əd'vəːsətɪv/ *adjective & noun.* LME.
[ORIGIN French *adversatif, -ive* or late Latin *adversativus* (Priscian), from *adversari*, from *adversus*: see ADVERSE, -ATIVE.]
▸**A** *adjective.* Expressive of opposition, contrariety, or antithesis. LME.
▸**B** *noun.* An adversative word or proposition. M16.
■ **adversatively** *adverb* L16.

adverse /'advəːs/ *adjective.* LME.
[ORIGIN Old French *advers*, earlier *av-* from Latin *adversus* against, opposite, pa. pple of *advertere*: see ADVERT *verb*.]
1 Acting in opposition; actively hostile. (Foll. by *to*.) LME.

www.bbc.co.uk The city's starving population were not adverse to eating anything they could lay their hands on.

adverse possession *LAW* the occupation of land to which another person has title with the intention of possessing it as one's own.
2 Harmful, unfavourable. LME.

Argosy A willingness to toil under the most adverse conditions.

3 Opposite in position. *arch.* E17.
■ **adversely** *adverb* E17. **adverseness** *noun* E17.

adversity /əd'vəːsɪti/ *noun.* ME.
[ORIGIN Old French & mod. French *adversité*, earlier *av-* from Latin *adversitas*, formed as ADVERSE: see -ITY.]
1 The condition of adverse fortune; distress, trial, affliction. ME.

Gay Times She got her act together and triumphed over adversity.

2 An adverse circumstance; a misfortune, a calamity, a trial. ME. †**3** Opposition; contrariety. LME–L15. †**4** Perversity. L15–E17.

advert /'advəːt/ *noun. colloq.* M19.
[ORIGIN Abbreviation.]
An advertisement.

advert /əd'vəːt/ *verb.* LME.
[ORIGIN Old French & mod. French *avertir*, †*adv-* ult. from Latin *advertere*, from AD- + *vertere* to turn. Cf. ANIMADVERT.]
1 *verb trans.* Turn towards. *rare.* LME.

F. R. LEAVIS The facts, to the adverted eye, are obvious.

2 *verb intrans.* Turn one's attention; take heed. Foll. by *to*, †*on*, †*that*. *arch.* LME.

F. O'BRIEN I walked down to the centre of the town without adverting to my surroundings.

†**3** *verb trans.* Take note of, observe, heed, (a thing). LME–L17.

R. SANDERSON Frailties and infirmities . . not hitherto by them adverted, because never suspected.

†**4** *verb trans.* Turn the attention of (another) to, warn of. *rare.* E16–L17. **5** *verb intrans.* Refer *to* in speech or writing. L18.

L. STRACHEY After referring to the death of the Princess, . . the Duke adverted to his own position.

■ **advertent** *adjective* attentive LME. **advertently** *adverb* L19. (Both chiefly repr. in neg. ***inadvertent(ly)***.)

advertence /əd'vəːt(ə)ns/ *noun.* LME.
[ORIGIN Old French *a(d)vertence*, from *a(d)vertir*: see ADVERT *verb*, -ENCE and cf. medieval Latin *advertentia*.]
The action of adverting; observation, attention, consideration. Also, advertency.
■ **advertency** *noun* attentiveness, heedfulness M17.

advertise /'advətʌɪz/ *verb.* LME.
[ORIGIN Old French *a(d)vertiss-* lengthened stem of *a(d)vertir* ADVERT *verb*.]
†**1** *verb intrans.* = ADVERT *verb* 2. LME–E16. †**2** *verb trans.* = ADVERT *verb* 4. LME–E17. **3** *verb trans.* Notify, admonish (a person *of* or *concerning* a thing, *that*; (arch.) *absol.*). LME.

SHAKES. *3 Hen. VI* We are advertis'd . . That they do hold their course toward Tewksbury.

4 *verb trans.* Give notice of; make generally or publicly known. LME. ▸**b** *verb trans.* Call attention to by a published announcement; describe or present (goods, services) publicly with a view to promoting sales. E18.

R. P. WARREN I wouldn't go around advertising this visit. E. BOWEN The . . chintz . . advertised its original delicacy by being . . always a little soiled. **b** JOYCE Corsets . . advertised cheap in the Gentlewoman. J. C. POWYS So widely had John's clever circulars advertised this event, that . . every available lodging . . was crowded.

5 *verb intrans.* Give warning or information (*of*). *obsolete* in *gen.* sense. E17. ▸**b** *verb intrans.* Make an announcement in a public place; describe or present goods publicly with a view to promoting sales. L18.
b advertise for ask for by public notice.
■ **advertiser** *noun* a person who advertises; a journal publishing advertisements: M16. **advertising** *noun* (**a**) the action of the verb; (**b**) the practice or profession of preparing and issuing public advertisements: M18.

advertisement /əd'vəːtɪzm(ə)nt/ *noun.* LME.
[ORIGIN French *avertissement*, †*adv-*, formed as ADVERTISE: see -MENT.]
†**1** Admonition, instruction. LME–E18. †**2** Information, notification. LME–E18. **3** A (written) statement calling attention to something; a notice to readers in a book etc. *arch.* LME. †**4** Attention, observation. L15–M17. **5** A public announcement (formerly by the town crier, now usu. in newspapers, on posters, on television, etc.). L16. ▸**b** Foll. by *for* (with adjective of quality or degree): a means of conveying the merits or demerits of. *colloq.* M20.

b *New Yorker* She has been a splendid advertisement for the benefits of a happy marriage.

small advertisement: see SMALL *adjective*.
■ **advertisemental** *adjective* L18.

advertorial /advəːˈtɔːrɪəl/ *noun*. Orig. *US*. M20.
[ORIGIN Blend of ADVERTISEMENT and EDITORIAL *noun*.]
An advertisement offering information about a commercial or industrial product or activity in the style of editorial comment.

advice /ədˈvʌɪs/ *noun*. ME.
[ORIGIN Old French & mod. French *avis*, ult. from Latin *ad* AD- + *visum* neut. pa. pple of *videre* see. For spelling *adv-* see AD- 2.]
†**1** The way in which a matter is looked at; opinion, judgement. ME–L17.

G. HERBERT All things . . joyn with one advise To honour thee.

†**2** Forethought, wisdom. LME–E16.
†**3** Consideration, consultation, reckoning. LME–M17.

SHAKES. *Merch. V.* Bassanio, upon more advice, Hath sent you here this ring.

4 An opinion given or offered as to action; counsel. LME.

E. O'NEILL I need your advice—your *scientific* advice this time, . . Doctor. JOYCE If I went by his advices.

†**5** The result of consultation; determination, plan. LME–E18.

DRYDEN You may, but 'twill not be your best Advice.

6 Information given, news; formal notice of a transaction; in *pl.* also, communications from a distance. LME.

STEELE A mail from Holland, which brought me several advices.

– PHRASES: ***letter of advice***: see LETTER *noun*[1]. **take advice** †(*a*) deliberate; (*b*) seek advice, esp. from a legal or other expert; (*c*) act upon advice given.
■ †**adviceful** *adjective* thoughtful; skilful as an adviser: LME–E17.

†**adview** *verb* var. of AVIEW.

advisable /ədˈvʌɪzəb(ə)l/ *adjective*. LME.
[ORIGIN Isolated early use from Old French & mod. French *avisable*; later (M17) from ADVISE + -ABLE.]
1 To be recommended; expedient. LME.
2 Open to advice. M17.
■ **advisaˈbility** *noun* the quality of being advisable; expediency: M19. **advisableness** *noun* (*a*) *rare* readiness to be advised; (*b*) advisability: L17. **advisably** *adverb* M19.

advise /ədˈvʌɪz/ *verb*. ME.
[ORIGIN Old French & mod. French *aviser*, ult. from Latin *ad* AD- + *visere* frequentative of *videre* see. For spelling *adv-* see AD- 2.]
†**1** *verb trans.* Look at, observe; watch for. ME–E17.
†**2** *verb trans.* Purpose, devise. ME–E17.
†**3** *verb refl.* & *intrans.* Bethink oneself; consider, reflect. ME–L17.

SHAKES. *Twel. N.* Advise you what you say. MILTON Advise Forthwith how thou oughtst to receive him.

4 *verb trans.* Consider, think of. Now only *SCOTS LAW*, deliberate upon, review, revise, (a case). LME.
5 *verb intrans.* Consider in company, hold a consultation. *obsolete* exc. in ***advise with***, consult with (now chiefly *US*). LME.
6 *verb trans.* **a** Give advice to (a person), caution. LME. ▸**b** Recommend. E17.

a R. ELLISON I am trying to advise you what is best for you. J. HELLER I advised him to put most of the money into an annuity. **b** D. DAVIE The guidebook cheats: the green road it advises In fact misled.

7 *verb intrans.* Offer counsel, give advice. LME.
8 *verb trans.* Inform, notify. Foll. by *of*, *that*. L16.

M. BRADBURY The headlines advise him of many indignities and wrongs.

■ **adviˈsee** *noun* the person advised E19. **adviser** *noun* a person who gives advice E17. **advisor** *noun* (chiefly *N. Amer.*) an adviser L19.

advised /ədˈvʌɪzd/ *adjective*. LME.
[ORIGIN from ADVISE + -ED[1].]
†**1** Having considered something. LME–E17.
†**be advised** consider, reflect.
†**2** Deliberate, wary, cautious. L15–E18.
3 Deliberate, considered, intentional. Also, well considered, judicious; sensible, prudent. LME.

J SPENCER His cool and advised thoughts. *Independent* He would be advised to keep quiet about those weapons of mass destruction he was so certain were going to be found.

ill-advised injudicious, imprudent. **well advised** (*a*) (of a person) prudent, wise; (*b*) (of an action etc.) carefully considered.
4 Counselled. L16.
5 Informed, apprised, warned. L16.
■ **advisedly** /-zɪdli/ *adverb* in an advised manner; *esp.* deliberately: LME. **advisedness** /-zɪdnɪs/ *noun* (now *rare*) LME.

advisement /ədˈvʌɪzm(ə)nt/ *noun*. ME.
[ORIGIN Old French & mod. French *avisement* (later Old French also *adv-*), formed as ADVISE: see -MENT and cf. medieval Latin *a(d)visamentum*.]
†**1** The process of looking at or viewing something. ME–E17.
2 Consideration, deliberation; consultation. *arch.* exc. *N. Amer.* ME.
under advisement under or into (esp. official or formal) consideration.
3 Advice, counsel; an instruction how to act. *arch.* LME.

adviso /ədˈvʌɪzəʊ/ *noun*. Now *arch. rare*. Pl. **-o(e)s**. L16.
[ORIGIN formed as AVISO, infl. by Latin and cognate English words.]
= AVISO.

advisory /ədˈvʌɪz(ə)ri/ *adjective* & *noun*. L18.
[ORIGIN from ADVISE + -ORY[2].]
▸ **A** *adjective*. Giving advice; consisting in giving advice. L18.
▸ **B** *noun*. A statement giving advice or information. *N. Amer.* M20.

advocaat /ˈadvəkɑː, -kɑːt/ *noun*. M20.
[ORIGIN Dutch = ADVOCATE *noun*.]
A liqueur of eggs, sugar, and spirit; a drink of this.

advocacy /ˈadvəkəsi/ *noun*. LME.
[ORIGIN Old French *a(d)vocacie* from medieval Latin *advocatia*, formed as ADVOCATE *verb*[2]: see -ACY.]
The function of an advocate; pleading in support *of*.

advocate /ˈadvəkət/ *noun*. ME.
[ORIGIN Old French & mod. French *avocat* from Latin *advocatus* use as noun of pa. pple of *advocare*: see ADVOKE, -ATE[1]. For spelling *adv-* see AD- 2.]
1 A person whose profession is to plead causes in courts of law (now chiefly *Scot.*); *US* any lawyer. ME.
devil's advocate: see DEVIL *noun*. ***judge advocate***, ***Judge Advocate General***: see JUDGE *noun*. **Faculty of Advocates** the Scottish bar. **Lord Advocate** the principal law officer of the Crown in Scotland.
2 *gen.* A person who pleads, intercedes, or speaks for another. ME.
†**3** = ADVOWEE 2. LME–M18.
4 A person who speaks in favour *of*, †*for*, a proposal etc. M18.
– COMB.: **Advocate Depute** any of several officers assisting the Lord Advocate in prosecutions; **Advocate General** any of several officers assisting the judges in the European Court of Justice.
■ **advocateship** *noun* M16. **advocatess** *noun* a female advocate LME. **advocatory** /ˈadvəkeɪt(ə)ri/ *adjective* of or pertaining to an advocate M19. †**advocatrice** *noun* [Old French] = ADVOCATESS LME–L16.

advocate /ˈadvəkeɪt/ *verb*[1]. E16.
[ORIGIN Latin *advocat-* pa. ppl stem of *advocare*: see ADVOKE, -ATE[3].]
Chiefly *SCOTS LAW*. = ADVOKE.

advocate /ˈadvəkeɪt/ *verb*[2]. L16.
[ORIGIN from ADVOCATE *noun*.]
1 *verb trans.* Plead in favour of, defend; recommend publicly. L16.
2 *verb intrans.* Act as advocate *for*. Now *rare*. M17.

advocation /advəˈkeɪʃ(ə)n/ *noun*. LME.
[ORIGIN Old French *a(d)vocacion* from Latin *advocatio(n-)*, formed as ADVOCATE *verb*[1]: see -ATION.]
†**1** A summoning. LME–L15.
†**2** The function or office of an advocate. LME–M18.
3 The calling of an action before itself by a superior court, *spec.* the papal court or a Scottish criminal (formerly also civil) court. E16.
†**4** An appeal for aid or defence. L16–M18.

advocator /ˈadvəkeɪtə/ *noun*. L15.
[ORIGIN In early use from late Latin *advocator*, formed as ADVOCATE *verb*[1]; in mod. use from ADVOCATE *verb*[2]: see -OR.]
†**1** A patron (saint). L15–L16.
2 A person who advocates something. M18.

advocatus diaboli /advəˌkɑːtəs diːˈabəliː, advəˌkeɪtəs dʌɪˈabəlʌɪ/ *noun phr. sing.* E19.
[ORIGIN mod. Latin.]
= ***devil's advocate*** s.v. DEVIL *noun*.

advoke /ədˈvəʊk/ *verb trans.* M16.
[ORIGIN Latin *advocare*, from *ad* AD- + *vocare* call.]
Call (a cause) to a higher tribunal.

advowee /advaʊˈiː/ *noun*. ME.
[ORIGIN Anglo-Norman *a(d)vowé* patron (mod. French *avoué* solicitor) from Latin *advocatus* ADVOCATE *noun*: assim. to -EE[1].]
†**1** A patron, a protector; *esp.* a patron saint. ME–L15.
2 A person who holds the advowson of an ecclesiastical house or benefice. E17.

advowson /ədˈvaʊz(ə)n/ *noun*. ME.
[ORIGIN Anglo-Norman *a(d)voweson*, *a(d)voeson*, Old French *avoeson* from Latin *advocatio(n-)*: see ADVOCATION.]
Orig., the guardianship or patronage of an ecclesiastical house or benefice. Now, the right of presentation to a benefice.

adytum /ˈadɪtəm/ *noun*. Pl. **-ta** /-tə/. E17.
[ORIGIN Latin from Greek *aduton* use as noun of neut. sing. of *adutos* impenetrable.]
The innermost part of a temple; a private chamber, a sanctum.

adze /adz/ *noun* & *verb*. Also ***adz**.
[ORIGIN Old English *adesa*, of unknown origin.]
▸ **A** *noun*. A tool like an axe with an arched blade at right angles to the handle, for cutting away the surface of wood. OE.
▸ **B** *verb trans.* Cut or dress with an adze. M19.

adzuki /ədˈzuːki/ *noun*. Also **ads-**, **az-**. E18.
[ORIGIN Japanese *azuki*.]
A bushy leguminous plant, *Vigna angularis*, cultivated in China and Japan; the edible bean of this plant. Also ***adzuki bean***.

Æ, æ
A ligature:
1 Old English 'ash' (see ASH *noun*[1] 3), the symbol of a simple vowel intermediate between *a* and *e*. In early Middle English short *æ* was replaced by *a* (sometimes *e*), long *æ* by *e* or *ee*.
2 From the 16th cent. used in forms derived from Latin *æ* and Greek *ai*. When thoroughly anglicized and popularized this becomes *e*; *æ*, now usu. (and in this dictionary) written as a digraph *ae*, is retained only in some Greek and Latin proper names, terms of Greek and Roman Antiquities, and some scientific and techn. terms (where, however, *e* is usual in the US).

-ae /iː/ *pl. suffix*.
Repr. pl. ending of Latin nouns of 1st declension in *-a* and romanized form of Greek (*-ai*) in pl. of nouns. In all words completely popularized it yields to *-as*.

aecidium /ɪˈsɪdɪəm/ *noun*. Pl. **-dia** /-dɪə/. M19.
[ORIGIN mod. Latin, from Greek *aikia* injury + -IDIUM.]
MYCOLOGY. = AECIUM; *spec.* a cup-shaped aecium.
■ **aecidial** *adjective* L19. **aecidiospore** *noun* = AECIOSPORE L19.

aecium /ˈiːsɪəm/ *noun*. Pl. **-cia** /-sɪə/. E20.
[ORIGIN mod. Latin, formed as AECIDIUM + -IUM.]
MYCOLOGY. A fruiting body of a rust fungus, in which aeciospores are produced.
■ **aecial** *adjective* E20. **aeciospore** *noun* any of the first binucleate spores to develop in a rust fungus, often produced on one host and germinating on another E20.

aedicule /ˈiːdɪkjuːl, ˈɛd-/ *noun*. Also **ed-**, & in Latin form **-cula** /-kjʊlə/, pl. **-lae** /-liː/. M19.
[ORIGIN Latin *aedicula* dim. of *aedes* dwelling: see -CULE.]
A small structure or room, *esp.* one used as a shrine; (a small structure over) a niche for a statue etc.
■ **aeˈdicular** *adjective* M20.

aedile /ˈiːdʌɪl/ *noun*. M16.
[ORIGIN Latin *aedilis* adjective & noun, from *aedes*, *-is* building: see -ILE.]
ROMAN HISTORY. Any of several magistrates who superintended public buildings, policing, and other matters.
■ **aedileship**, **aeˈdility** *nouns* the position or term of office of an aedile M16.

AEEU *abbreviation*.
Amalgamated Engineering and Electrical Union.

AEF *abbreviation*.
American Expeditionary Forces (esp. in Europe during the First World War.

Aegean /iːˈdʒiːən, ɪ-/ *adjective*. E17.
[ORIGIN from Latin *Aegaeus* from Greek *Aigaios*: see -EAN.]
Designating, of, or pertaining to the sea between Greece and Asia Minor.

aegirine /ˈiːdʒɪriːn, ˈɛdʒ-/ *noun*. M19.
[ORIGIN from *Aegir*, Norse god of the sea + -INE[5].]
MINERALOGY. A silicate of iron and sodium occurring in many alkaline igneous rocks and belonging to the pyroxene minerals.
■ Also **aegirite** *noun* M19.

aegis /ˈiːdʒɪs/ *noun*. Also ***egis**. E17.
[ORIGIN Latin from Greek *aigis* shield of Zeus.]
1 A shield, defensive armour, *esp.* that of Jupiter or Minerva. E17.
2 *fig.* Protection; an impregnable defence. L18.
under the aegis of under the auspices of.

aegophony /ɪˈɡɒfəni/ *noun*. M19.
[ORIGIN from Greek *aig-*, *aix* goat + -O- + -PHONY.]
MEDICINE. A tremulous nasal resonance of the voice, sometimes heard with the stethoscope in pleurisy.
■ **aegophonic** /iːɡəˈfɒnɪk/ *adjective* M19.

aegrotat /ʌɪˈɡrə(ʊ)tat, ˈiː-, iːˈɡrə(ʊ)-/ *noun*. L18.
[ORIGIN Latin *aegrotat* 3 sing. pres. indic. of *aegrotare* be ill, from *aegr-*, *aeger* sick, ill.]
In universities, a certificate that a student is too ill to attend an examination etc., an examination pass or (*N. Amer.*) a credit awarded to a student having such a certificate.

-aemia /ˈiːmɪə/ *suffix*. Also ***-emia**.
[ORIGIN from Greek *haima* blood + -IA[1].]
Forming nouns denoting conditions of the blood, as ***acidaemia***, ***leukaemia***, ***septicaemia***, etc.

Aeneolithic *adjective* var. of ENEOLITHIC.

†**aenigma** *noun* var. of ENIGMA.

Aeolian /iːˈəʊlɪən/ *adjective*. Also ***Eo-** & (in sense 2) with lower-case initial. L16.
[ORIGIN from Latin *Aeolius* + -IAN.]
1 Of or pertaining to Aeolis or Aeolia, an ancient district of Asia Minor. L16.
Aeolian mode *MUSIC* (*a*) an ancient Greek mode; (*b*) the ninth of the church modes (with A as final and E as dominant).
2 Of or pertaining to Aeolus, mythical god of the winds; of, produced by, or borne on the wind. E17.

A. HOLMES Contrasts between water-laid and Aeolian sands.

Aeolian harp a stringed instrument producing musical sounds on exposure to a current of air.

Aeolic /iːˈɒlɪk/ *adjective & noun*. Also ***Eo-**. L17.
[ORIGIN Latin *Aeolicus* from Greek *Aiolikos*: see AEOLIAN, -IC.]
▸ **A** *adjective*. = AEOLIAN 1. L17.
▸ **B** *noun*. The Greek dialect of Aeolia. E18.

aeolienne *noun* var. of ÉOLIENNE.

aeolipyle /ˈiːə(ʊ)lɪpʌɪl, iːˈɒl-/ *noun*. Also **-pile**. M17.
[ORIGIN French *éolipyle* (16) from Latin *Aeoli pylae* (= Greek *pulai*) the doorway of Aeolus.]
An instrument illustrating the force with which vapour generated by heat in a closed vessel escapes by a narrow aperture.

aeolotropy /iːə(ʊ)ˈlɒtrəpi/ *noun*. Now *rare*. L19.
[ORIGIN from Greek *aiolos* changeful + -TROPY.]
= ANISOTROPY.
■ **aeolotropic** /iːˌəʊləˈtrəʊpɪk, -ˈtrɒpɪk/ *adjective* M19.

aeon /ˈiːən/ *noun*. Also (the usual form in *GEOLOGY*) **eon**. M17.
[ORIGIN ecclesiastical Latin from Greek *aiōn* age.]
1 An age of the universe; an immeasurable period of time; eternity; *colloq*. a very long time. M17. ▸**b** *GEOLOGY*. The largest division of geological time, composed of several eras. M20. ▸**c** *ASTRONOMY & GEOLOGY*. One thousand million years. M20.

P. G. WODEHOUSE Six-thirty seemed æons ahead.

2 The personification of an age; *GNOSTIC PHILOSOPHY* a power existing outside time, an emanation or phase of the supreme deity. M17.
■ **aeonial** /iːˈəʊnɪəl/ *adjective* = AEONIAN M19. **aeonian** /iːˈəʊnɪən/ *adjective* eternal, everlasting M18. **aeonic** /iːˈɒnɪk/ *adjective* lasting an aeon L19.

aepyornis /iːpɪˈɔːnɪs/ *noun*. M19.
[ORIGIN mod. Latin, from Greek *aipus* high + *ornis* bird.]
An extinct giant flightless bird of the genus *Aepyornis*, known from remains found in Madagascar. Also called ***elephant bird***.

†**aequi-** *combining form* var. of EQUI-.

AER *abbreviation*.
Annual Equivalence Rate.

†**aera** *noun* see ERA.

aerate /ˈɛːreɪt/ *verb trans*. L18.
[ORIGIN from Latin *aer* air + -ATE³, after French *aérer*.]
1 Expose to the action of air. L18.
2 Charge with air or another gas (esp. carbon dioxide), usu. so as to produce effervescence. L18.
■ **aerated** *adjective* (*a*) that has been aerated; (*b*) *slang* angry, agitated: E19. **aeˈration** *noun* M19. **aerator** *noun* something which aerates; a device for aerating: M19.

aerenchyma /ɛːˈrɛŋkɪmə/ *noun*. L19.
[ORIGIN from Greek *aēr* air + *egkhuma* infusion.]
BOTANY. Soft cellular tissue containing air spaces, found in many aquatic plants.
■ **aerenˈchymatous** *adjective* L20.

aerial /ˈɛːrɪəl/ *adjective & noun*. L16.
[ORIGIN from Latin *aerius* from Greek *aerios*, from *aēr* air: see -AL¹.]
▸ **A** *adjective*. **1** Thin as air, ethereal; unreal, imaginary. L16.
2 Light as air, airy. E17.
3 Of, pertaining to, or produced in the air; atmospheric. E17.
aerial perspective: in which distant objects are shown as fainter.
4 Existing, moving, or happening in the air. E17. ▸**b** Growing above ground (opp. ***subterranean***). M19. ▸**c** By or from aircraft etc. L19.

A. SILLITOE Full clouds drifting like an aerial continent of milk-white mountains. **b** ANTHONY HUXLEY Aerial roots as in ivy are produced on the dark side of the stem. **c** G. B. SHAW The British refusal to bar aerial bombardment . . made the air battles of the world war lawful.

aerial ping-pong *Austral. slang*. Australian Rules football. ***aerial PLANKTON***. **c aerial top-dressing** *NZ* the spreading of fertilizer from an aircraft. ***aerial torpedo***: see TORPEDO *noun* 2b.
5 Placed at an airy height, elevated (*lit. & fig.*). E17.
aerial cableway, **aerial railway**, **aerial ropeway** a system of overhead cables from which cars or containers are suspended for transport, usu. driven electrically.
6 Composed of air; gaseous. M17.
▸ **B** *noun*. A metal wire, rod, or other structure used to transmit or receive radio waves. Cf. ANTENNA 4. E20.
– NOTE: Formerly with pronunc. /eɪˈɪərɪəl, eɪˈɛːrɪəl/.
■ **aerialist** *noun* (*a*) *rare* a stylite; (*b*) a high-wire or trapeze artist: M19. **aerially** *adverb* E19.

aerie *noun* var. of EYRIE.

aeriferous /ɛːˈrɪf(ə)rəs/ *adjective*. L17.
[ORIGIN from Latin *aer* air + -I- + -FEROUS.]
Bearing or conveying air.

aeriform /ˈɛːrɪfɔːm/ *adjective*. L18.
[ORIGIN formed as AERIFEROUS + -I- + -FORM.]
Of the form of air, gaseous; unsubstantial, unreal.

aero- /ˈɛːrəʊ/ *combining form* of Greek *aēr* air: see -O-.
Often *spec*. with ref. to aeroplanes and aviation.
■ **aeroˈallergen** *noun* an airborne allergen M20. **aerobioˈlogical** *adjective* of or pertaining to aerobiology M20. **aerobiˈologist** *noun* an expert in or student of aerobiology M20. **aerobiˈology** *noun* the branch of knowledge that deals with the nature and distribution of the living organisms, spores, pollen, and seeds carried by the air M20. **aerobraking** *noun* (*ASTRONAUTICS*) a method for slowing down spacecraft by flying through a planet's atmosphere to produce aerodynamic drag M20. **aeroeˈlastic** *adjective* of or pertaining to aeroelasticity M20. **aeroelaˈsticity** *noun* the science of the interaction between aerodynamic forces and non-rigid structures M20. **aeroengine** *noun* an engine for propelling an aircraft M20. **aeroˈgenerator** *noun* a wind-powered electric generator M20. **aerogramme**, ***-gram** *noun* a message sent through the air; esp. = ***air letter*** s.v. AIR *noun*¹: L19. **aeˈrographer** *noun* a meteorologist L19. **aeˈrography** *noun* the description of the atmosphere; meteorology: M18. **aeromagˈnetic** *adjective* of, or pertaining to, or derived from the measurement of the earth's magnetism by means of airborne instruments M20. **ˌaeromagneˈtometer** *noun* an instrument for making aeromagnetic measurements M20. **aeromancy** *noun* divination or augury by the air; later, weather forecasting, meteorology: LME. **aeroˈmedical** *adjective* of or relating to the use of aircraft for medical purposes such as transporting patients to hospital M20. **aeˈrometry** *noun* (*a*) the measurement of the properties of the air; †(*b*) pneumatics: M18. **aeroˈmodelling** *noun* the hobby of building and flying model aircraft M20. **aeˈrophagy** *noun* (*MEDICINE*) the swallowing of air E20. **aerophobe** *noun* a person who is afraid of air travel M20. **aeroˈphobia** *noun* fear of air travel L20. **aeroˈponic** *adjective* of or by means of aeroponics L20. **aeroˈponics** *noun* a hydroponic technique in which the roots of a plant hang suspended in air and nutrient solution is delivered to them in the form of a fine mist M20. **aeroshell** *noun* (*ASTRONAUTICS*) an outer casing designed to protect a spacecraft during travel through an atmosphere M20. **aerospace** *noun* (the technology of flight in) the earth's atmosphere and outer space M20. **aerothermodyˈnamic** *adjective* of or pertaining to aerothermodynamics M20. **ˌaerothermodyˈnamics** *noun* (the branch of science that deals with) the thermodynamic behaviour of flowing gases M20. **aerotowing** *noun* the towing of a glider in the air by a powered aircraft M20.

aerobatics /ɛːrəˈbatɪks/ *noun pl*. E20.
[ORIGIN from AERO- after *acrobatics*.]
Feats of expert aviation; spectacular flying.
■ **ˈaerobat** *noun* a person who performs aerobatics E20. **aerobatic** *adjective* of or pertaining to aerobatics E20.

aerobic /ɛːˈrəʊbɪk/ *adjective*. L19.
[ORIGIN from AERO- + Greek *bios* life + -IC.]
1 *BIOLOGY*. Normally dependent for life upon the presence of free oxygen; taking place in or characterized by the presence of free oxygen. L19.
2 Of, pertaining to, or resulting from aerobics. M20.
■ **ˈaerobe** *noun* any organism that can grow in the presence of free oxygen L19. **aerobically** *adverb* (*a*) in the presence of free oxygen; (*b*) by means of aerobics: L19. **aerobicist** /ɛːˈrəʊbɪsɪst/ *noun* a person who practises aerobics L20. **aerobicized** *adjective* (of a person's body) toned by aerobic exercise L20.

aerobics /ɛːˈrəʊbɪks/ *noun*. M20.
[ORIGIN from AEROBIC: see -ICS.]
(The practice of) physical exercises for producing beneficial changes in the respiratory and circulatory systems by activities which can be sustained by virtue of their low oxygen demand.

aerodrome /ˈɛːrədrəʊm/ *noun*. L19.
[ORIGIN from AERO- + -DROME; in sense 1 from Greek *aerodromos* traversing the air.]
†**1** An aeroplane. L19–E20.
2 An area of open level ground, together with runways, hangars, and other installations, for the take-off, landing, and maintenance of aircraft. E20.

aerodynamics /ˌɛːrə(ʊ)dʌɪˈnamɪks/ *noun pl*. (usu. treated as *sing*.). M19.
[ORIGIN from AERO- + DYNAMICS.]
The branch of science that deals with the properties of air or other gases in motion and the interaction between the air and solid bodies (esp. aircraft) moving through it. Also, the aerodynamic properties of an aircraft etc.
■ **aerodynamic** *adjective* of or pertaining to aerodynamics or the phenomena with which it is concerned L19. **aerodynamical** *adjective* = AERODYNAMIC E20. **aerodynamically** *adverb* as regards aerodynamics E20. **aerodynamicist** /-sɪst/ *noun* an expert in aerodynamics M20.

aerofoil /ˈɛːrəfɔɪl/ *noun*. E20.
[ORIGIN from AERO- + FOIL *noun*¹.]
A structure which gives rise to a lift force when moving through the air, e.g. a wing of an aircraft; a similar structure causing downward pressure on a road vehicle.

aerogel /ˈɛːrədʒɛl/ *noun*. E20.
[ORIGIN from AERO- + GEL *noun*¹.]
CHEMISTRY. A solid material of extremely low density, produced by replacing the liquid component of a conventional gel by air or gas.

aerolite /ˈɛːrəlʌɪt/ *noun*. E19.
[ORIGIN from AERO- + -LITE.]
A meteorite; *spec*. a stony meteorite.
■ **aerolitic** /-ˈlɪtɪk/ *adjective* M19.

aerology /ɛːˈrɒlədʒi/ *noun*. M18.
[ORIGIN from AERO- + -LOGY.]
The branch of knowledge that deals with the atmosphere, now *spec*. with atmospheric conditions away from ground level.
■ **aeroˈlogical** *adjective* M19.

aeronaut /ˈɛːrənɔːt/ *noun*. L18.
[ORIGIN French *aéronaute*, from *aéro-* AERO- + Greek *nautēs* sailor.]
A traveller through the air; a balloonist, a pilot.

aeronautic /ɛːrəˈnɔːtɪk/ *adjective*. L18.
[ORIGIN from AERONAUT + -IC.]
Of or pertaining to aeronauts or aeronautics.
■ **aeronautical** *adjective* E19.

aeronautics /ɛːrəˈnɔːtɪks/ *noun pl*. (usu. treated as *sing*.). E19.
[ORIGIN mod. Latin *aeronautica*, formed as AERONAUTIC: see -ICS.]
The science, art, or practice of controlled flight through the air.

aeronomy /ɛːˈrɒnəmi/ *noun*. M20.
[ORIGIN from AERO- + -NOMY.]
The branch of science that deals with the upper regions of the atmosphere, where dissociation and ionization of air molecules are important.
■ **aeronomer** *noun* an expert in aeronomy M20. **aeroˈnomic**, **aeroˈnomical** *adjectives* of or pertaining to aeronomy M20. **aeronomist** *noun* = AERONOMER M20.

aerophone /ˈɛːrəfəʊn/ *noun*. M20.
[ORIGIN from AERO- + -PHONE.]
A musical instrument which employs a column of air to produce the sound.

aeroplane /ˈɛːrəpleɪn/ *noun & verb*. M19.
[ORIGIN In sense A.1 from AERO- + PLANE *noun*³; in sense A.2 from French *aéroplane*, from *aéro-* AERO- + Greek *-planos* wandering.]
▸ **A** *noun*. †**1** An aerofoil. M19–E20.
2 An aircraft that is heavier than air and has fixed (non-rotating) wings. L19.
▸ **B** *verb intrans*. Fly like or in an aeroplane. E20.
■ **aeroplanist** *noun* (*rare*) a person who flies an aeroplane E20.

aerosol /ˈɛːrəsɒl/ *noun & verb*. E20.
[ORIGIN from AERO- + SOL *noun*⁵.]
▸ **A** *noun*. **1** A colloidal suspension of particles in air or another gas. E20.
2 A substance packed under pressure and able to be released as a fine spray; a container holding such a substance. M20.
▸ **B** *verb trans. & intrans*. Spray with an aerosol. M20.
■ **aerosoliˈzation** *noun* the action of aerosolizing something M20. **aerosolize** *verb trans*. make into an aerosol, disperse as an aerosol M20.

aerostat /ˈɛːrəstat/ *noun*. L18.
[ORIGIN French *aérostat*, from *aéro-* AERO- + Greek *statos* standing.]
1 Any craft which is sustained in the air by buoyancy, e.g. a balloon, an airship. L18.
†**2** An aeronaut. L18–L19.
■ **aerostation** /-ˈsteɪʃ(ə)n/ *noun* (now *rare*) [French] flight by lighter-than-air craft L18.

aerostatic /ɛːrəˈstatɪk/ *adjective*. L18.
[ORIGIN French *aérostatique*, formed as AEROSTAT: see -IC.]
1 Of or pertaining to aerostatics. L18.
2 Of or pertaining to aerostats and their use. L18.
■ **aerostatical** *adjective* (*rare*) L17.

aerostatics /ɛːrəˈstatɪks/ *noun pl*. (usu. treated as *sing*.). L18.
[ORIGIN mod. Latin *aerostatica*, formed as AEROSTAT: see -ICS.]
The science of the equilibrium and pressure of the air and other gases, and of the behaviour of bodies supported in them.

Aertex /ˈɛːtɛks/ *noun*. L19.
[ORIGIN from *aer-* as in AERATE + TEX(TILE).]
(Proprietary name for) a cellular cotton fabric used esp. for leisure wear and underwear.

aeruginous /ɪəˈruːdʒɪnəs/ *adjective*. E17.
[ORIGIN Latin *aeruginosus*, formed as AERUGO: see -OUS.]
Of the nature or colour of verdigris.

aerugo /ɪəˈruːɡəʊ/ *noun*. M16.
[ORIGIN Latin, from *aer-*, *aes* bronze.]
= ***crystallized* VERDIGRIS**.

aery *noun* var. of EYRIE.

aery /ˈɛːri/ *adjective*. *poet*. L16.
[ORIGIN Latin *aerius*, from *aer* air, the suffix assoc. with -Y¹.]
Aerial; ethereal, incorporeal.

Aeschylean /iːskɪˈliːən/ *adjective*. M19.
[ORIGIN from Latin *Aeschylus* from Greek *Aiskhulos*: see -EAN.]
Of, pertaining to, or characteristic of the Athenian tragic poet Aeschylus (525–456 BC), or his works, style, etc.

Aesculapius /iːskjʊˈleɪpɪəs/ *noun*. *joc*. *arch*. L16.
[ORIGIN Latin *Aesculapius*, Roman god of medicine.]
A physician.
■ **Aesculapian** *adjective* of or pertaining to Aesculapius, medicine, or physicians E17.

Aesopian /iːˈsəʊpɪən/ *adjective*. L17.
[ORIGIN from *Aesop* (see AESOPIC) + -IAN.]
1 = AESOPIC 1. L17.
2 [translating Russian *ézopovskiĭ*.] Designating or pertaining to Russian or Soviet Communist language or writing in which (esp. political) dissent is expressed ambiguously or allegorically, to avoid official censorship etc. M20.

Aesopic /iːˈsɒpɪk/ *adjective*. E18.
[ORIGIN Late Latin *Aesopicus*, from *Aesopus* from Greek *Aisōpos*: see -IC.]
1 Pertaining to or characteristic of Aesop, a semi-legendary Greek fabulist of the 6th cent. BC. E18.
2 = AESOPIAN 2. E20.
■ **Aesopical** *adjective* (*rare*) L16.

A

aesthesis /ɛs'θiːsɪs/ *noun*. Also ***es-**. **E18**.
[ORIGIN Greek *aisthēsis* a perceiving: see AESTHETIC.]
The perception of the external world by the senses.
■ **aesthesi'ometer** *noun* an instrument for measuring tactile sensitivity **M19**.

aesthete /'iːsθiːt, 'ɛs-/ *noun*. Also ***es-**. **L19**.
[ORIGIN from AESTHETIC, after *athlete*, *athletic*, or from Greek *aisthētēs* a person who perceives, formed as AESTHETIC.]
A person who professes a superior appreciation of what is beautiful; formerly in British universities, a studious person (opp. ***hearty***).

aesthetic /iːs'θɛtɪk, ɛs-/ *noun & adjective*. Also ***es-**. **M18**.
[ORIGIN Greek *aisthētikos*, from *aisthēta* things perceptible by the senses, from *aisthesthai* perceive: see -IC. Current senses derived through German from A. T. Baumgarten's *Æsthetica* (1750). Senses A.1 & 2 in sing. through German *Ästhetik*, French *esthétique*.]
▸ **A** *noun*. **1** *sing.* & (usu.) in *pl.* (treated as *sing.*). The philosophy of the beautiful or of art; a system of principles for the appreciation of the beautiful etc. **M18**.
M. H. ABRAMS The concept that art is imitation . . played an important part in neo-classic aesthetics. W. STEVENS Tests of the strength of his aesthetic, his philosophy.
2 *sing.* & (usu.) in *pl.* (treated as *sing.*). The science of sensuous perception. (Used only with ref. to the works of Kant.) **E19**.
3 An aesthete; an adherent of the Aesthetic Movement. **L19**.
▸ **B** *adjective*. †**1** Pertaining to perception by the senses. Only in **L18**.
2 Of or pertaining to the appreciation or criticism of the beautiful or of art. **E19**.
3 Of a person: having appreciation of the beautiful; refined. Of a thing: in accordance with the principles of good taste; beautiful. **M19**.
4 *spec.* (**A-**). Designating, of, or pertaining to a 19th-cent. movement of artists and writers who advocated 'art for art's sake'. **M19**.
5 = COSMETIC *adjective* 2. **E20**.
■ **aesthetical** *adjective* = AESTHETIC *adjective* (esp. sense 2) **L18**. **aesthetically** *adverb* **E19**. **aesthetician** /-'tɪʃ(ə)n/ *noun* a person versed in aesthetics **E19**. **aestheticism** /-sɪz(ə)m/ *noun* the quality of being aesthetic; susceptibility to aesthetic influences: **M19**. **aestheticist** /-sɪst/ *noun* an aesthetician **M19**. **aestheticize** /-saɪz/ *verb trans.* render aesthetic **M19**.

aestival /'iːstɪv(ə)l, iː'staɪv(ə)l; ɛ-/ *adjective*. Also ***est-**. **LME**.
[ORIGIN Old French & mod. French *estival* from Latin *aestivalis*, formed as AESTIVE: see -AL[1].]
Belonging to or of summer or the summer solstice; appearing in summer.

aestivate /'iːstɪveɪt, 'ɛst-/ *verb intrans.* Also ***est-**. **E17**.
[ORIGIN Latin *aestivat-* pa. ppl stem of *aestivare*, formed as AESTIVE: see -ATE[3].]
Spend the summer, *spec.* (ZOOLOGY) in a state of torpor. Cf. HIBERNATE.
■ **aestivator** *noun* an animal that aestivates **E20**.

aestivation /iːstɪ'veɪʃ(ə)n, ɛst-/ *noun*. Also ***est-**. **E17**.
[ORIGIN formed as AESTIVATE: see -ATION.]
†**1** The spending of summer; summer residence. **E17–M18**.
2 BOTANY. The arrangement of the parts of a flower inside its bud before opening. Cf. VERNATION 1. **E19**.
3 ZOOLOGY. The act of spending the summer in a state of torpor. Cf. HIBERNATION. **M19**.

aestive /'iːstɪv/ *adjective*. Also ***est-**. **E17**.
[ORIGIN Latin *aestivus*, from *aestus* heat: see -IVE.]
Aestival; hot and burning.

†**aestuary** *noun* var. of ESTUARY.

†**aestuation** *noun*. Also **est-**. **L15–M18**.
[ORIGIN Latin *aestuatio(n-)*, from *aestuare* boil up, from *aestus* heat: see -ATION.]
Feverish disturbance, ebullition.
■ †**aestuate** *verb intrans.* boil; surge up: **E17–M18**.

a.e.t. *abbreviation*.
SOCCER. After extra time.

aetatis /ʌɪ'tɑːtɪs, iː'teɪtɪs/ *adjective*. Usu. abbreviation ***aet.*** /ʌɪt, iːt/, ***aetat*** /'ʌɪtɑːt, 'iːteɪt/. **E19**.
[ORIGIN Latin.]
Of or at the age of.
W. OWEN His son, aetat 13, learned in nothing.

aetheling *noun* var. of ATHELING.

aether *noun* see ETHER *noun*[1].

aethereal, **aetherial** *adjectives* see ETHEREAL.

†**Aethiop**, **Aethiopian** *nouns & adjectives* etc., vars. of ETHIOP etc.

aetiology /iːtɪ'ɒlədʒi/ *noun*. Also **et-**. **M16**.
[ORIGIN medieval Latin *aetiologia* (Isidore) from Greek *aitiologia*, from *aitia* cause + *logia* -LOGY.]
1 The assignment of a cause; (occas.) the cause assigned. **M16**.
2 The philosophy of causation; the part of a science which treats of the causes of its phenomena. Now *rare* or *obsolete*. **M17**.
3 MEDICINE. The causation of disease (usu., of a specified disease), esp. as a subject for investigation. **L17**.
■ ˌ**aetio'logical** *adjective* **M18**. ˌ**aetio'logically** *adverb* **M19**.

aetites /iː'tʌɪtiːz/ *noun*. **L16**.
[ORIGIN Latin from Greek *aetitēs* adjective (used as noun), from *aetos* eagle.]
A stone with a loose nucleus, formerly believed to be found in eagles' nests and to have magical and medicinal properties.

†**aetna** *noun* var. of ETNA.

AEU *abbreviation*.
hist. Amalgamated Engineering Union.

aeviternity /iːvɪ'təːnɪti/ *noun*. Now *rare*. Also **e-**. **L16**.
[ORIGIN from Latin *aeviternus* eternal + -ITY.]
Eternal existence; everlasting duration.

AF *abbreviation*.
Audio frequency.

af- /af, *unstressed* əf/ *prefix* (rarely productive).
Assim. form of Latin *ad-* before *f*. In Old French, Latin *aff-* was reduced to *af-*, which appears in early adoptions, but in later French, and hence in English, *aff-* was restored by Latinization, as ***affair***, ***affront***. Hence extended to some words of different origin, as ***affray***, ***affright***.

afanc /a'vaŋk/ *noun*. **M19**.
[ORIGIN Welsh *afanc* beaver; cogn. with Irish *abac* beaver, dwarf.]
CELTIC MYTHOLOGY. An aquatic monster.

Afar /'afɑː/ *noun & adjective*. Pl. of noun same. **M19**.
[ORIGIN Afar *qafar*.]
= DANAKIL.

afar /ə'fɑː/ *adverb*. **ME**.
[ORIGIN from A *preposition*[1] 1 & A *preposition*[2] + FAR *adverb*.]
1 From a distance. Now only in ***from afar***. **ME**.
2 At or to a distance. Now usu. foll. by *off*. **ME**.

afara /ə'fɑːrə/ *noun*. **E20**.
[ORIGIN Yoruba.]
= LIMBA *noun*[2].

AFB *abbreviation*. *US*.
Air Force Base.

AFC *abbreviation*.
1 Air Force Cross.
2 Association Football Club.

AFDC *abbreviation*.
In the US: Aid to Families with Dependent Children, a welfare benefit paid by the federal government.

afear /ə'fɪə/ *verb trans.* Now *dial.* **OE**.
[ORIGIN from A-[1] + FEAR *verb*.]
Frighten.
■ **afeared**, **afeard** *ppl adjective* (superseded in general use by AFRAID) **OE**.

afebrile /eɪ'fiːbrʌɪl/ *adjective*. **L19**.
[ORIGIN from A-[10] + FEBRILE.]
MEDICINE. Unaccompanied by fever; not feverish.

affable /'afəb(ə)l/ *adjective*. **LME**.
[ORIGIN Old French & mod. French from Latin *affabilis*, from *affari*, from *ad* AF- + *fari* speak: see -ABLE.]
Easy to approach and converse with; courteous, esp. with inferiors; kindly and polite.
■ **affa'bility** *noun* **L15**. **affably** *adverb* **E17**.

affair /ə'fɛː/ *noun*. **ME**.
[ORIGIN Anglo-Norman *afere*, Old French *afaire* (mod. *affaire*), from *à faire* to do: cf. ADO *noun*. See also EFFEIR.]
1 What one has to do; business; a concern, a matter. **ME**.
SHAKES. *Haml.* What is your affair in Elsinore?
affair of honour *arch.* a duel to settle a question of honour.
2 *spec.* In *pl.* Ordinary pursuits of life; business dealings; public matters. **L15**.
S. SMILES Men of affairs, trained to business. N. MITFORD They chatted . . about local affairs.
state of affairs: see STATE *noun*. ***statement of affairs***: see STATEMENT *noun*.
3 A (usu. temporary) sexual relationship outside marriage; a love affair. **E18**.
C. HAMPTON I did have an affair with a gypsy when I was about fifteen.
4 A thing; an incident; an occasion; *spec.* a notorious incident, a scandal. *colloq.* **E19**.
JOYCE The annual dinner you know . . . Boiled shirt affair. R. RENDELL The neighbouring front door, a far more trendy and ambitious affair.

affaire /afɛːr/ *noun*. Pl. pronounced same. **E19**.
[ORIGIN French.]
In full ***affaire de cœur*** /də kœːr/, ***affaire du cœur*** /dy kœːr/ [lit. 'of the heart']. = AFFAIR 3.

affairé /afere/ *adjective*. **E20**.
[ORIGIN French.]
Busy; involved.

†**affamish** *verb trans.* & *intrans.* **M16–M17**.
[ORIGIN French *affamer*: see A-[5], FAMISH.]
Starve.

affamishment /ə'famɪʃm(ə)nt/ *noun*. *arch.* **L16**.
[ORIGIN from AFFAMISH + -MENT.]
Starvation.

affect /'afɛkt/ *noun*. **LME**.
[ORIGIN Latin *affectus* noun of completed action from *afficere*: see AFFECT *verb*[2]. Sense 2 through German *Affekt*.]
†**1** Mental or physical disposition or constitution. **LME–L17**.
2 PSYCHOLOGY. An emotion, a mood. **L19**.
■ **affectless** *adjective* without emotion, incapable of feeling emotion **M20**. **affectlessness** *noun* **M20**.

†**affect** *ppl adjective*. **LME–L17**.
[ORIGIN Latin *affectus* pa. pple of *afficere*: see AFFECT *verb*[2].]
= AFFECTED II, III.

affect /ə'fɛkt/ *verb*[1] *trans.* **LME**.
[ORIGIN French *affecter* or Latin *affectare*, from *affect-*: see AFFECT *verb*[2].]
1 Like, love. *arch.* **LME**. ▸**b** *esp.* Like to use, practise, wear, or frequent. **M16**.
EVELYN Some affect to have it fry'd a little broun and crisp. R. KIPLING [He] . . did not much affect the Major. *absol.*: SHAKES. *Ant. & Cl.* Making peace or war As thou affects. **b** M. BRADBURY He took to wearing the black leather jackets that most of his colleagues . . affected.
†**2** Aim at, seek. **L15–L18**.
SHAKES. *2 Hen. VI* Have I affected wealth or honour? T. JEFFERSON He has affected to render the military independent of . . the civil power.
3 Use or display ostentatiously; assume the character of; take upon oneself (*to do*), profess. **L16**.
POPE Spenser himself affects the obsolete. CARLYLE He affected the freethinker. D. MAHON And once (he affected communism) He brought the whole crew out on strike.
4 Of things: have or display a natural tendency towards. **E17**.
5 Assume a false appearance of; pretend. **E17**.
SIR W. SCOTT He tired, or affected to tire. G. VIDAL I affected an even deeper sincerity.
■ **affecter** *noun* **M16**.

affect /ə'fɛkt/ *verb*[2] *trans.* **LME**.
[ORIGIN French *affecter* or Latin *affect-* pa. ppl stem of *afficere*, from *ad* AD- + *facere* do; sense 1 may be from Latin *affectare* and so a branch of AFFECT *verb*[1].]
1 Attack as a disease. **LME**.
2 Move, touch, (in mind or feelings); influence; make a material impression on. **L16**.
3 In *pass.* Be assigned *to*. *arch.* **E17**.
■ **affecta'bility** *noun* ability to be affected **L19**. **affectable** *adjective* able to be affected **M18**.

affectation /afɛk'teɪʃ(ə)n/ *noun*. **M16**.
[ORIGIN French, or Latin *affectatio(n-)*, from *affectare*: see AFFECT *verb*[1], -ATION.]
†**1** An aiming at; earnest pursuit. **M16–E18**.
2 An ostentatious fondness; studied display. Foll. by *of*. **M16**.
C. BRONTË The studied affectation of coquetry.
3 Pretentious behaviour, speech, or writing that is designed to impress; an instance of this. **L16**.
B. BROPHY Snobberies and titles are to her absurd affectations.
†**4** Affection, liking. (Foll. by *of*.) **E17–L18**.

affected /ə'fɛktɪd/ *adjective*. **M16**.
[ORIGIN Branch I from AFFECT *verb*[1] + -ED[1]; branch II from AFFECT *ppl adjective* + -ED[2]; branch III from AFFECT *verb*[2] + -ED[1]: senses to some extent confused through formal identity.]
▸ **I 1** Artificially assumed or displayed; pretended; (of language) stilted. **M16**.
J. MCCARTHY His real or affected levity.
2 Of a person: full of affectation, artificial. **L16**.
WALKER PERCY A dandyish affected young man.
†**3** Sought after, aimed at. **L16–M17**.
†**4** Fondly held; loved. **L16–E18**.
▸ **II 5** Disposed, inclined (usu. with adverb of manner). **M16**.
†**6** *esp.* Favourably disposed, partial, (*to*). **M16–L17**.
▸ **III 7** Attacked by a disease, afflicted. **E17**.
8 a Mentally influenced; moved, touched in the feelings, (*by*, †*with*). **E17**. ▸**b** Of a thing: influenced, acted upon, (*by*). **M18**.
9 Specially allotted. Now *rare* or *obsolete*. **E17**.
■ **affectedness** *noun* = AFFECTATION 3 **E17**.

affectedly /ə'fɛktɪdli/ *adverb*. **L16**.
[ORIGIN from AFFECTED I + -LY[2].]
†**1** Intentionally, earnestly. **L16–M18**.
†**2** Affectionately. **L16–E17**.
3 With studied art; artificially. **L16**.
4 With studied simulation; hypocritically. **M17**.

affecting /ə'fɛktɪŋ/ *ppl adjective*. **L16**.
[ORIGIN Senses 1 and 2 from AFFECT *verb*[1], sense 3 and 4 from AFFECT *verb*[2] + -ING[2].]
†**1** Using affectation. **L16–E17**.
†**2** Loving, affectionate. Only in **E17**.

†3 Impressive. **M17–L18.**
4 Touching the emotions; moving. **E18.**

J. PRATT She hath an affecting trick of . . shedding tears. *New Republic* An affecting performance of Satie's magnum opus.

■ **affectingly** *adverb* **M18.**

affection /əˈfɛkʃ(ə)n/ *noun.* **ME.**
[**ORIGIN** Old French & mod. French from Latin *affectio(n-)*, from *affect-*: see **AFFECT** *verb*[2], **-ION.**]
► **I** Of the mind.
1 A mental state; an emotion, a feeling. **ME.** ►†**b** *esp.* Feeling as opp. to reason; passion, lust. **ME–M18.**

b SPENSER Most wretched man, That to Affections does the bridle lend!

2 Disposition towards something, bent, inclination. *arch.* **ME.** ►†**b** *gen.* Mental tendency, disposition. **M16–M18.**
3 Goodwill, kindly feeling, love. **LME.**

R. D. LAING Love lets the other be, but with affection and concern. L. P. SMITH Unrequited affections are in youth unmitigated woes.

alienation of affection: see **ALIENATION** 1. ***walk into a person's affections***: see **WALK** *verb*[1].
► **II** Of the body.
4 A bodily state; *esp.* a malady, a disease. **M16.**

A. P. HERBERT Her voice was permanently husky from some old affection of the throat.

► **III** Of substances or essences.
5 A non-essential state; a mode of being; a property or attribute. **M16.**
INJURIOUS affection.
► **IV** *gen.* **6** The action of affecting; the state of being affected. **L16.** ►**b** *CELTIC PHILOLOGY.* Mutation or umlaut of a vowel under the influence of a following sound. **E20.**

J. S. MILL The affection of our bodily organs from without.

► **V** [**AFFECT** *verb*[1] confused with *verb*[2]]
†**7** = **AFFECTATION** 2, 3. **L16–E19.**

COLERIDGE The gaudy affections of style which passed current . . for poetic diction.

■ **affectional** *adjective* of or having affections **M19.** **affectioned** *adjective* (now *rare* or *obsolete*) = **AFFECTIONATE** *adjective* **M16.**

affection /əˈfɛkʃ(ə)n/ *verb trans. arch.* **L16.**
[**ORIGIN** Old French & mod. French *affectionner*, formed as **AFFECTION** *noun.*]
Like, love.

affectionate /əˈfɛkʃ(ə)nət/ *adjective.* **L15.**
[**ORIGIN** from French *affectionné* beloved, or its source medieval Latin *affectionatus* devoted: see **AFFECTION** *noun*, **-ATE**[2].]
†**1** Mentally disposed (*to*). **L15–M17.**
†**2** Biased, prejudiced. **L15–E17.**
†**3** Passionate, wilful. **M16–E18.**
†**4** Well-disposed, favourable, (*to*). **M16–M18.**
5 Loving, fond; expressing or indicating affection. **L16.**

F. MARRYAT Captain Delmar is naturally of a kind and affectionate disposition. MARGARET KENNEDY He was a good and affectionate son.

†**6** Eager, ambitious. **L16–M18.**
■ †**affectionated** *adjective* affectionate **M16–M19.** **affectionately** *adverb* **M16.** **affectionateness** *noun* **M17.**

affective /əˈfɛktɪv/ *adjective.* **LME.**
[**ORIGIN** French *affectif, -ive* from late Latin *affectivus*, from *affect-*: see **AFFECT** *verb*[2], **-IVE.**]
†**1** Tending to affect or influence. **LME–E18.**
2 Of or pertaining to the affections; emotional. **LME.**
■ **affectively** *adverb* **M17.** **affecˈtivity** *noun* emotional susceptibility **E20.**

affectual /əˈfɛktjʊəl, -tʃʊəl/ *adjective.* **L15.**
[**ORIGIN** Old French *affectuel* from medieval Latin *affectualis*, formed as **AFFECT** *noun*: see **-AL**[1].]
†**1** Earnest, ardent. **L15–L16.**
2 = **AFFECTIVE** 2. **M17.**
■ **affectually** *adverb* **LME.**

†**affectuous** *adjective.* **ME–L19.**
[**ORIGIN** French *affectueux*, formed as **AFFECT** *noun*: see **-OUS.**]
Eager, earnest; affectionate; emotional.
■ †**affectuously** *adverb* **LME–E20.**

affeer /əˈfɪə/ *verb trans.* **ME.**
[**ORIGIN** Old French *aforer*, *afeurer*, Anglo-Norman *aferer* from medieval Latin *afforare* fix the price, from *ad* **AF-** + *forum* market.]
hist. Assess (an amercement); reduce to a fair amount.
■ **affeerment** *noun* the action of affeering **M17.** **affeeror** *noun* a person who affeers an amercement **LME.**

affenpinscher /ˈafənpɪnʃə/ *noun.* **E20.**
[**ORIGIN** German, from *Affe* ape, monkey + *Pinscher* terrier.]
(An animal of) a toy breed of dog related to the griffon and having a profuse wiry coat.

afferent /ˈaf(ə)r(ə)nt/ *adjective.* **M19.**
[**ORIGIN** Latin *afferent-* pres. ppl stem of *afferre*, from *ad* **AF-** + *ferre* bring: see **-ENT.**]
ANATOMY. Conducting inwards (of a nerve: towards the central nervous system; of a blood vessel: towards an organ). Opp. **EFFERENT.**

affettuoso /afɛtjʊˈəʊzəʊ, -tʊ-/ *adverb, adjective, & noun.* **E18.**
[**ORIGIN** Italian.]
MUSIC. ►**A** *adverb & adjective.* A direction: with feeling, tender(ly). **E18.**
► **B** *noun.* Pl. **-si** /-zi/, **-sos.** A movement expressing tenderness. *rare.* **L18.**

affiance /əˈfʌɪəns/ *noun. arch.* **ME.**
[**ORIGIN** Old French *afiance*, formed as **AFFY**: see **-ANCE.**]
1 Trust, faith, (*in*, occas. *on*). **ME.**
†**2** Confidence, assurance. **LME–M18.**
3 The pledging of faith, esp. in marriage. **LME.**
†**4** Affinity. **L15–E17.**

affiance /əˈfʌɪəns/ *verb trans.* **L15.**
[**ORIGIN** Old French *afiancer*, formed as **AFFIANCE** *noun.*]
Promise solemnly, esp. in marriage. Usu. in *pass.* foll. by *to.*

affiant /əˈfʌɪənt/ *noun.* **E19.**
[**ORIGIN** French: see **AFFY**, **-ANT**[1].]
US LAW. A person who makes an affidavit.

affiche /afiʃ (*pl. same*); əˈfiːʃ/ *noun.* **E19.**
[**ORIGIN** French.]
A notice affixed to a wall etc.; a poster.

affidavit /afɪˈdeɪvɪt/ *noun.* **M16.**
[**ORIGIN** 3 sing. perf. indic. of medieval Latin *affidare* declare on oath: see **AFFY.**]
LAW. A written statement, confirmed by oath or affirmation, to be used as evidence.

affiliate /əˈfɪlɪət/ *ppl adjective & noun.* **M19.**
[**ORIGIN** Latin *affiliatus* pa. pple, formed as **AFFILIATE** *verb*: see **-ATE**[1].]
► **A** *ppl adjective.* Affiliated. *rare.* **M19.**
► **B** *noun.* Someone or something affiliated; *esp.* an affiliated organization or company. **L19.**

affiliate /əˈfɪlɪeɪt/ *verb.* **E17.**
[**ORIGIN** medieval Latin *affiliat-* pa. ppl stem of *affiliare*, from *ad* **AF-** + *filius* son; prob. after French *affilier*: see **-ATE**[3].]
†**1** *verb trans.* Adopt as a son. Only in Dicts. Only in **E17.**
2 *verb trans.* Adopt as a subordinate member of a society, branch of an organization or company, etc.; attach *to* or connect *with* an organization etc. **M18.** ►**b** *verb intrans.* Connect oneself *with.* **M19.**
3 *verb trans.* In *LAW*, fix the paternity of a child *on* the putative father (esp. to compel the father to pay maintenance); *gen.* ascribe (a child) *to* his or her proper parent; *fig.* father (*up*)*on*, attribute *to.* **E19.**
■ **affiliative** *adjective* pertaining to affiliation or social relationships; sociable, sympathetic: **M20.**

affiliation /əfɪlɪˈeɪʃ(ə)n/ *noun.* **E17.**
[**ORIGIN** French from medieval Latin *affiliatio(n-)*, formed as **AFFILIATE** *verb*: see **-ATION.**]
1 Adoption of a son. *rare.* **E17.**
2 Adoption by a society etc. of branches; union with a central organization. **L18.** ►**b** (A) connection, association. Freq. in *pl.* **M19.**

b F. D. ROOSEVELT I have not the slightest idea what your political affiliations are. S. ROBERTSON The closest affiliations of English . . are . . with the Low German languages.

3 The fixing of the paternity of a child; *fig.* the fathering of a thing upon anyone, the assignment of a thing to its origin. **M19.**
– **COMB.:** **affiliation order** a legal order that the putative father of an illegitimate child must help to support him or her.

affinal /əˈfʌɪn(ə)l/ *adjective.* **M19.**
[**ORIGIN** from Latin *affinis* (see **AFFINITY**) + **-AL**[1].]
Related by marriage; pertaining to marriage.

affine /əˈfʌɪn/ *noun & adjective.* **E16.**
[**ORIGIN** formed as **AFFINAL** or Old French *afin* (mod. *affin*).]
► **A** *noun.* A relation by marriage; a kinsman, a kinswoman. **E16.**
► **B** *adjective.* **1** Closely related. **M17.**
2 *MATH.* That allows of or preserves parallelism. **E20.**

affined /əˈfʌɪnd/ *ppl adjective.* **L16.**
[**ORIGIN** from (the same root as) **AFFINE** + **-ED**[1], perh. after Old French *afiné.*]
1 Related, connected. **L16.**

W. STEVENS Portentous enunciation, syllable To blessed syllable affined.

2 Bound by any tie. *rare.* **E17.**

SHAKES. *Oth.* Whether I . . am affin'd To love the Moor.

affinity /əˈfɪnɪti/ *noun.* **ME.**
[**ORIGIN** Old French *afinité* (mod. *aff-*) from Latin *affinitas*, from *affinis*, from *ad* **AF-** + *finis* border: see **-ITY.**]
► **I** By position.
1 Relationship, esp. by marriage; *collect.* relations, kindred. **ME.**
2 *fig.* Similarity of character suggesting relationship; family likeness. **LME.**
3 Structural resemblance (between languages, animals, plants, etc.) suggestive of a common stock or type. **L16.**
► **II** By inclination or attraction.
†**4** Voluntary social relationship. **LME–E17.**

AV *2 Chron.* 18:1 Jehosaphat . . ioyned affinitie with Ahab.

5 *fig.* Liking, attraction; a person having attraction for another. **E17.**

D. CECIL There is no affinity more perfect than that founded on similar tastes and complementary temperaments. W. FAULKNER A woman's affinity and instinct for secrecy.

6 *CHEMISTRY.* The tendency of a substance to combine with another. **M18.**

JOYCE The incalculable trillions . . of imperceptible molecules contained by cohesion of molecular affinity in a single pinhead.

– **COMB.:** **affinity card** (**a**) *US* a discount card issued to members of an affinity group; (**b**) a bank card for which the bank donates to a specified charity etc. a portion of the money spent using the card; **affinity group** *US* an association of people with a common interest or aim.
■ **affinitive** *adjective* characterized by affinity; closely related: **M17.**

affirm /əˈfəːm/ *verb.* **ME.**
[**ORIGIN** Old French *afermer* (mod. *affirmer*) from Latin *affirmare*, from *ad* **AF-** + *firmus* firm.]
†**1** *verb trans.* Make firm, strengthen; support. **ME–M17.**

LD BERNERS The goddis assure & affirme euerything.

2 *verb trans. LAW.* Confirm or ratify (a judgement, a contract). **LME.**

LD MACAULAY Twenty-three peers voted for reversing the judgment; thirty-five for affirming it.

†**3** *verb trans.* Confirm or maintain (a statement). **LME–M17.**

SHAKES. *Hen. VI* I said so . . and I must not blush to affirm it.

4 *verb trans.* Assert strongly, state as a fact. **LME.** ►**b** *LAW.* Make an affirmation. (Foll. by *that.*) **LME.** ►**c** *LOGIC.* State to be true. **L17.**

A. STORR If a man holds beliefs that are unpopular . . he will look for people with whom he can identify himself in order to affirm his own identity. J. MONTAGUE Against her choice, I still affirm That nothing dies.

5 *verb intrans. GRAMMAR & LOGIC.* Make a statement in the affirmative. *rare.* **M16.**

P. SIDNEY Grammer sayes . . That in one speech two Negatiues affirme.

■ **affirmable** *adjective* **E17.** **affirmant** *adjective & noun* (**a**) *adjective* affirming; (**b**) *noun* a person who affirms: **L16.** **affirmer** *noun* **LME.**

affirmance /əˈfəːm(ə)ns/ *noun.* **LME.**
[**ORIGIN** Old French *af(f)ermance*, formed as **AFFIRM**: see **-ANCE.**]
1 An assertion; a strong declaration. **LME.**
2 A confirming. **E16.**

affirmation /afəˈmeɪʃ(ə)n/ *noun.* **LME.**
[**ORIGIN** French, or Latin *affirmatio(n-)*, from *affirmare*: see **AFFIRM**, **-ATION.**]
1 Confirmation. **LME.**
2 Assertion as true. Also, something which is affirmed; a positive statement. **LME.**
3 *LAW.* A formal declaration with legal effect similar to that of an oath. **L17.**
■ **aˈffirmatory** *adjective* giving affirmation, assertive (*of*) **M17.**

affirmative /əˈfəːmətɪv/ *adjective, noun, & interjection.* **LME.**
[**ORIGIN** Old French & mod. French *affirmatif, -ive* from late Latin *affirmativus*, formed as **AFFIRMATION**: see **-ATIVE.**]
► **A** *adjective.* **1** Assertive; positive. **LME.**
affirmative action positive action towards a goal, esp. the employment of minority groups and women.
2 Asserting that a fact is so; answering 'yes'. **L15.** ►**b** *LOGIC.* Asserting that something is true of the subject of a proposition. **L16.**
†**3** Corroborative, confirmatory. **E16–M17.**

CLARENDON The affirmative advice of all the Judges of England.

► **B** *noun.* Something which affirms; an affirmative word, statement, or proposition; an affirmative reply. **LME.**
answer in the affirmative answer 'yes', or that it is so. **vote in the affirmative** vote in favour of a proposal.
► **C** *interjection.* Yes. Chiefly *N. Amer.* (orig. *MILITARY*). **L19.**
■ **affirmatively** *adverb* **LME.**

affix /ˈafɪks/ *noun.* **L16.**
[**ORIGIN** Latin *affixus* pa. pple of *affigere*, from *ad* **AF-** + *figere* fasten.]
1 An appendage, an addition. **L16.**
†**2** = **AFFICHE. L16–L19.**
3 *GRAMMAR.* A grammatical element prefixed, infixed, or suffixed to the root of a word. **E17.**
■ **affixal** *adjective* (*GRAMMAR*) pertaining to or involving an affix **L19.**

affix /əˈfɪks/ *verb trans.* **LME.**
[**ORIGIN** Old French & mod. French *affixer* or medieval Latin *affixare*, from *ad* **AF-** + *fixare* fix.]
1 Fix, fasten, (*to*, *on*, *upon*). **LME.**

JOYCE An exotically . . accorded . . tinkle gatebell affixed to left lateral gatepost. *fig.*: SPENSER She affixed had Her hart on knight so goodly-glorifyde.

†**2** Fix upon, determine, settle. **E16–E18.**

POPE The land, affix'd . . To end his toils.

3 Impress (a seal, stamp); add in writing (a signature, postscript, etc.). **M17.** ►**b** *fig.* Attach as a stigma (*to*), stigmatize (*with*). **M17.**
■ **affixer** *noun* **M19.**

A

affixation /afɪkˈseɪʃ(ə)n/ *noun.* **E17.**
[**ORIGIN** Sense 1 from **AFFIX** *verb*, sense 2 from **AFFIX** *noun*: see **-ATION**.]
1 Affixture. **E17.**
2 *GRAMMAR.* Addition of an affix. **E20.**

affixture /əˈfɪkstʃə/ *noun.* **L18.**
[**ORIGIN** from **AFFIX** *verb*, after *fixture*.]
The action of affixing; the state of being affixed; attachment.

afflate /əˈfleɪt/ *verb trans. rare.* **L16.**
[**ORIGIN** Latin *afflat-*: see **AFFLATUS**, **-ATE**[3].]
Blow or breathe upon; inspire. Chiefly as ***afflated*** *ppl adjective.*
■ **afflation** *noun* **M17.**

afflatus /əˈfleɪtəs/ *noun.* **M17.**
[**ORIGIN** Latin, from *afflat-* pa. ppl stem of *afflare*, from *ad* **AF-** + *flare* to blow.]
The communication of supernatural knowledge; divine impulse; (esp. poetic) inspiration.

†**afflict** *ppl adjective.* Also **afflight**. **ME–L16.**
[**ORIGIN** Old French *aflit* from Latin *afflictus* pa. pple of *affligere*: see **AFFLICT** *verb.*]
Afflicted.

afflict /əˈflɪkt/ *verb trans.* **LME.**
[**ORIGIN** Latin *afflictare*, or *afflict-* pa. ppl stem of *affligere*, from *ad* **AF-** + *fligere* strike; partly through **AFFLICT** *ppl adjective*. Cf. Old French *afflicter*.]
†**1** Cast down; deject, humble. **LME–M17.**

MILTON Reassembling our afflicted Powers.

2 Distress with bodily or mental suffering; trouble grievously. **M16.**

S. JOHNSON They are afflicted with the head-ach. B. RUSSELL A more general trouble afflicting all large organizations.

■ **afflicter** *noun* **L16.** **afflictingly** *adverb* in an afflicting manner, so as to afflict **E19.**

affliction /əˈflɪkʃ(ə)n/ *noun.* **ME.**
[**ORIGIN** Old French & mod. French from Latin *afflictio(n-)*, from *afflict-*: see **AFFLICT** *verb*, **-ION**.]
†**1** The infliction of grievous pain or trouble; self-mortification. **ME–E17.**
2 The state of being afflicted; misery, distress. **LME.**
3 A pain, a calamity; a cause of misery or distress. **LME.**

afflictive /əˈflɪktɪv/ *adjective.* **E17.**
[**ORIGIN** Old French & mod. French *afflictif, -ive* from medieval Latin *afflictivus*, from *afflict-*: see **AFFLICT** *verb*, **-IVE**.]
Tending to afflict; painful; trying. (Foll. by *to*.)
■ **afflictively** *adverb* **L17.**

†**afflight** *ppl adjective* var. of **AFFLICT** *ppl adjective*.

affluence /ˈafluəns/ *noun.* **LME.**
[**ORIGIN** French from Latin *affluentia*, formed as **AFFLUENT**: see **-ENCE**.]
1 A plentiful flow (*of*); profusion, abundance. **LME.**

LONGFELLOW Winter . . with its affluence of snows.

2 Abundance of worldly possessions, wealth. **L16.**

D. LODGE At a time of increasing general affluence they had to be content with cramped, poorly furnished accommodation.

3 A flowing towards a particular place; a concourse. **L16.**

CARLYLE Great affluence of company.

■ Also **affluency** *noun* (long *rare*) **M17.**

affluent /ˈafluənt/ *adjective.* **LME.**
[**ORIGIN** Old French & mod. French from Latin *affluent-* pres. ppl stem of *affluere*, from *ad* **AF-** + *fluere* flow: see **-ENT**.]
†**1** Flowing towards a particular place. **LME–M18.**
2 Flowing freely; copious, abundant. **LME.**

T. NASHE So affluent an argument. GOLDSMITH Possessed of a very affluent fortune. SOUTHEY O'er his shoulders broad the affluent mane Dishevell'd hung.

3 Having plenty of money; wealthy. **M18.**
affluent society: in which material wealth is widely distributed.
■ **affluently** *adverb* **L17.**

affluenza /afluːˈɛnzə/ *noun.* **L20.**
[**ORIGIN** Blend of **AFFLUENCE** or **AFFLUENT** and **INFLUENZA**.]
A psychological malaise supposedly affecting (esp. young) wealthy people, symptoms of which include a lack of motivation, feelings of guilt, and a sense of isolation.

afflux /ˈaflʌks/ *noun.* **E17.**
[**ORIGIN** medieval Latin *affluxus*, from *afflux-* pa. ppl stem of *affluere*: see **AFFLUENT**. Cf. French *afflux*.]
1 = **AFFLUENCE** 1. **E17.**
2 An accession. *rare.* **M17.**
■ Also **affluxion** *noun* **M17.**

affodill /ˈafədɪl/ *noun.* Now *rare* or *obsolete.* **LME.**
[**ORIGIN** medieval Latin *affodilus* var. of Latin *asphodilus* **ASPHODEL**.]
†**1** = **ASPHODEL** 1. **LME–E17.**
2 = **DAFFODIL** 2. *dial.* **M16.**

afforce /əˈfɔːs/ *verb trans.* **ME.**
[**ORIGIN** Old French *aforcier*, formed as **A-**[5] + **FORCE** *noun*[1].]
†**1** Apply force to; ***refl.*** try. **ME–E16.**
†**2** Add force to. Only in **LME.**
3 Strengthen (a deliberative body etc.) by the addition of new members. **E19.**
■ **afforcement** *noun* †(***a***) a fort; (***b***) reinforcement of a deliberative body etc.: **M18.**

afford /əˈfɔːd/ *verb trans.*
[**ORIGIN** Late Old English *ġeforþian*, from *forþian* to further, formed as **FORTH**: see **A-**[4]. For the change of /θ/ to /d/ cf. *burden*, *murder*.]
†**1** Advance; perform; accomplish. **LOE–LME.**
2 Manage *to do*. With *can*, *be able to*: have the means or be rich enough *to do*, be in a position *to do*; spare; bear the expense of. **LME.**

O. MANNING We cannot afford to go to expensive restaurants every night. G. GREENE I had won the game already, and I could afford to feel a certain pity for my victim. E. O'NEILL I paid a lot of money I couldn't afford. F. M. FORD She could not . . afford a maid . . since every penny was of importance to her.

3 Provide, supply, grant; of things: be capable of yielding, yield naturally. **L16.**

SHAKES. *Rom. & Jul.* The world affords no law to make thee rich. J. IRVING The great privacy afforded us by speaking English in a German-speaking tavern.

■ **afforda'bility** *noun* ability to be afforded **L20.** **affordable** *adjective* able to be afforded **M19.** **affordably** *adverb* **L20.** **afforder** *noun* **L16.**

afforest /əˈfɒrɪst/ *verb trans.* **E16.**
[**ORIGIN** medieval Latin *afforestare*, from *ad* **AF-** + *foresta* **FOREST** *noun*.]
Convert into forest; plant with trees.
■ **afforestable** *adjective* **E20.** **affore'station** *noun* the action or result of converting an area into forest **E17.**

afformative /əˈfɔːmətɪv/ *adjective & noun.* **E19.**
[**ORIGIN** from **AF-** + **FORMATIVE**.]
Chiefly *SEMITIC GRAMMAR.* (A particle) suffixed as a formative element. Cf. **PREFORMATIVE**.

affranchise /əˈfran(t)ʃʌɪz/ *verb trans.* **L15.**
[**ORIGIN** Old French *afranchiss-* lengthened stem of *afranchir* (mod. *aff-*), from *à* **A-**[5] + *franc* free. Cf. **ENFRANCHISE**.]
Release from servitude or from an obligation etc.
■ **affranchisement** *noun* **L18.**

affray /əˈfreɪ/ *noun.* **ME.**
[**ORIGIN** Anglo-Norman *affrai*, Old French *effrei*, *esf-* (mod. *effroi*), formed as **AFFRAY** *verb*.]
†**1** An attack, an assault. **ME–L16.**
†**2** Alarm, fright, terror. **ME–L16.**
3 A disturbance, a noisy outburst; a fray. *obsolete* in *gen.* sense. **ME.** ▸**b** *esp.* A breach of the peace by fighting or rioting. **L15.**

affray /əˈfreɪ/ *verb trans. arch.* Pa. pple & ppl adjective **affrayed**, **AFRAID**. **ME.**
[**ORIGIN** Anglo-Norman *afrayer*, Old French *effreer*, *esf-* (mod. *effrayer*), formed as **A-**[7] + base ult. from Germanic (cogn. with **FRITH** *noun*[1]). Aphet. to **FRAY** *verb*[1].]
1 Disturb, startle. **ME.**
2 Alarm, frighten. **ME.**
3 Frighten away. **LME.**
■ **affrayer** *noun* a person who affrays; a disturber of the peace: **L15.**

affrayed *pred. adjective* see **AFRAID**.

affreightment /əˈfreɪtm(ə)nt/ *noun.* **M18.**
[**ORIGIN** French *affrètement* (earlier written *affrét-*), from *affréter*, from *à* **A-**[5] + *fret* freight; spelling assim. to **FREIGHT** *noun*: see **-MENT**.]
The hiring of a ship to carry cargo.

affricate /ˈafrɪkət/ *noun.* **L19.**
[**ORIGIN** Latin *affricatus* pa. pple, formed as **AFFRICATE** *verb*: see **-ATE**[1].]
PHONETICS. A combination of a plosive with an immediately following homorganic fricative or spirant as one phoneme (as in the first and last consonants of *church* and *judge*).
■ Also **a'ffricative** *noun* **L19.**

affricate /ˈafrɪkeɪt/ *verb trans.* **M17.**
[**ORIGIN** Latin *affricat-* pa. ppl stem of *affricare*, from *ad* **AF-** + *fricare* rub: see **-ATE**[3].]
†**1** Rub (on or against). *rare.* **M17–E18.**
2 *PHONETICS.* Convert into an affricate. **L19.**

affrication /afrɪˈkeɪʃ(ə)n/ *noun.* **E18.**
[**ORIGIN** Latin *affricatio(n-)*, formed as **AFFRICATE** *verb*: see **-ATION**.]
†**1** Rubbing on or against. *rare.* Only in **E18.**
2 *PHONETICS.* Conversion into an affricate; pronunciation as an affricate. **L19.**

†**affriended** *pa. pple & ppl adjective. rare* (Spenser). Only in **L16.**
[**ORIGIN** from **A-**[11] + **FRIEND** *noun* + **-ED**[1].]
Made friends, reconciled.

affright /əˈfrʌɪt/ *noun. arch.* **L16.**
[**ORIGIN** from the verb, on the analogy of *fright* noun & verb.]
1 Terror, fright. **L16.**
2 The action of frightening; a cause of fear. **E17.**
■ **affrightful** *adjective* (*arch.*) frightening, terrifying **E17.**

affright /əˈfrʌɪt/ *ppl adjective.* Long *arch. rare.*
[**ORIGIN** Old English *āfyrhted* pa. pple: see **A-**[1], **FRIGHT** *verb*, **-ED**[1]. Cf. **AFFRIGHT** *verb*.]
Frightened.

affright /əˈfrʌɪt/ *verb trans. arch.* or *poet.* **LME.**
[**ORIGIN** Rare early use formed as **AFFRIGHT** *adjective*; later (**L16**) from **FRIGHT** *verb* by vague form-association.]
Frighten, terrify.
■ **affrighted** *ppl adjective* frightened (replacing **AFFRIGHT** *ppl adjective*) **E17.** **affrightedly** *adverb* **E17.** **affrighten** *verb trans.* = **AFFRIGHT** *verb* **M17.** **affrightment** *noun* †(***a***) = **AFFRIGHT** *noun* 1; (***b***) = **AFFRIGHT** *noun* 2: **L16.**

affront /əˈfrʌnt/ *noun.* **L16.**
[**ORIGIN** from the verb. Cf. French *affront*.]
1 **a** An open insult; an intentionally disrespectful word or act. **L16.** ▸**b** An instance of offence to one's self-respect or modesty. **E17.**

a BUNYAN They had offered great affronts to his person. **b** A. G. GARDINER She . . looked indignant, almost hurt, as though she had received some secret personal affront.

†**2** An encounter; an attack, an assault. **L16–L17.**

MILTON Dreaded On hostile ground, none daring my affront.

†**3** A position of hostility; an obstacle. Only in **M17.**

affront /əˈfrʌnt/ *verb trans.* **ME.**
[**ORIGIN** Old French *afronter* (mod. *aff-*) ult. from Latin phr. *ad frontem* to the face: see **AF-**, **FRONT** *noun*.]
1 Offend the modesty or values of; insult. **ME.**

J. LEES-MILNE I think I affronted her . . with my pacifist tendencies.

2 Face in defiance; confront. **M16.**
3 Face in position; look towards. *arch.* **E17.**
†**4** Put oneself in the way of, accost. **E–M17.**
■ **affronter** *noun* **L16.** **affrontingly** *adverb* in an affronting manner, so as to affront **L17.** **affrontive** *adjective* affronting in character or tendency **M17.**

affronté /əˈfrʌnti/ *adjective.* Also **affronty**. **M16.**
[**ORIGIN** French *affronté* pa. pple of *affronter*: see **AFFRONT** *verb*.]
HERALDRY. Looking towards the spectator.

affronted /əˈfrʌntɪd/ *ppl adjective.* **L16.**
[**ORIGIN** from **AFFRONT** *verb* + **-ED**[1]; sense 2 translating French *effronté*.]
1 Fronted; faced. Also = **AFFRONTÉ**. *rare.* **L16.**
†**2** Impudent; full of effrontery. Only in **M17.**
3 Insulted, offended. **E18.**

Independent Those portrayed . . are so affronted if they feel they are being presented in a misleading manner.

■ †**affrontedly** *adverb* with effrontery **E17–M18.**

affrontee /əfrʌnˈtiː/ *noun. rare.* **E19.**
[**ORIGIN** from **AFFRONT** *verb* + **-EE**[1].]
An affronted person; the person affronted.

affuse /əˈfjuːz/ *verb trans.* Now *rare.* **E17.**
[**ORIGIN** Latin *affus-* pa. ppl stem of *affundere*, from *ad* **AF-** + *fundere* pour.]
Pour (*upon*).
■ **affusion** /-ʒ(ə)n/ *noun* a pouring on or into, as of water on the body in one method of baptism **E17.**

affy /əˈfʌɪ/ *verb. arch.* **ME.**
[**ORIGIN** Old French *afier* (later *aff-*) from medieval Latin *affidare*, from *ad* **AF-** + *fidare* to trust.]
†**1** *verb trans. & intrans.* Trust, confide, (*in*, *on*). **ME–M17.**
†**2** *verb trans.* Affirm on one's faith. **L15–E17.**
3 *verb trans.* Make fast by a solemn promise; espouse; affiance. **L15.**

Afghan /ˈafgan/ *noun & adjective.* **L18.**
[**ORIGIN** Pashto *afghānī*.]
▸ **A** *noun.* **1** A native or inhabitant of Afghanistan, a country lying N. of Pakistan; the language (Pashto) of the people of Afghanistan. **L18.**
2 (**a-**.) A knitted and sewn woollen blanket or shawl; (in the Indian subcontinent) a quilt, a coarse rug. **M19.**
3 = ***Afghan hound*** below. **M20.**
4 = ***Afghan coat*** below. **L20.**
▸ **B** *attrib.* or as *adjective*. Of or pertaining to Afghanistan or the Afghans. **L18.**
Afghan coat a kind of sheepskin coat with the skin side outside, sometimes embroidered and usu. having a shaggy border. **Afghan hound** (an animal of) a tall breed of hunting dog with long silky hair, originating in Afghanistan.
■ **afghani** /afˈgɑːni/ *noun* the basic monetary unit of Afghanistan, equal to 100 puls **E20.**

aficionado /afɪsjəˈnɑːdəʊ, *foreign* afiθjoˈnaðo/ *noun.* Pl. **-os** /-əʊz, *foreign* -os/. **M19.**
[**ORIGIN** Spanish = amateur, use as noun of pa. pple of *aficionar* become fond of, from *afición* from Latin: see **AFFECTION** *noun*.]
1 A devotee of bullfighting. **M19.**
2 An ardent follower of any activity. **L19.**

afield /əˈfiːld/ *adverb.* **ME.**
[**ORIGIN** from **A** *preposition*[1] 1 + **FIELD** *noun*.]
1 In or to the field. **ME.**

SHAKES. *Tr. & Cr.* Æneas is a-field. W. MORRIS Afield he never went, Either to hunting or the frontier war. E. POUND High grain a-field, hundred-fold yield.

2 Away from home; to or at a distance. **LME.**

C. KINGSLEY I had . . never been further afield than Fulham.

afire /əˈfʌɪə/ *adverb & pred. adjective.* **ME.**
[**ORIGIN** from **A** *preposition*[1] 6 + **FIRE** *noun*.]
On fire, burning, (*lit.* & *fig.*).

AFL *abbreviation.*
Australian Football League.

aflame /əˈfleɪm/ *adverb & pred. adjective.* **M16.**
[ORIGIN from A *preposition*[1] 6 + FLAME *noun*.]
In flames; in a glow (*lit. & fig.*).

aflare /əˈflɛː/ *adverb & pred. adjective.* **L19.**
[ORIGIN from A-[2] + FLARE *noun*[1].]
Flaring; spread out; blazing, glowing.

aflat /əˈflat/ *adverb & pred. adjective. arch.* **ME.**
[ORIGIN from A *preposition*[1] 1 + FLAT *noun*[2].]
In a flat position.

aflatoxin /afləˈtɒksɪn/ *noun.* **M20.**
[ORIGIN from mod. Latin *A(spergillus fla(vus)* (see below) + TOXIN.]
Any of a class of carcinogenic toxins produced by moulds of the *Aspergillus flavus* group.

aflaunt /əˈflɔːnt/ *adverb & pred. adjective. arch.* **M16.**
[ORIGIN from A *preposition*[1] 6 + FLAUNT *noun*.]
Flaunting.

afloat /əˈfləʊt/ *adverb & pred. adjective.* **OE.**
[ORIGIN from A *preposition*[1] 6 + FLOAT *noun*; in Middle English partly after Old Norse *á flot(i)*, and Old French *en flot*; from 16 prob. a new formation.]
► **I** *lit.* **1** Floating (as if) in water; at sea; on board ship. **OE.**

S. JOHNSON Whatever is afloat in the stream of time. M. INNES Enough to stock all the smoke-rooms of all the liners afloat.

2 Floating in the air. **M16.**

BROWNING Carelessly passing with your robes afloat.

3 In a state of overflow or submersion. **L16.**

F. MARRYAT The main deck was afloat.

► **II** *fig.* **4** Unembarrassed, out of debt. **M16.**
5 Fully started; in full swing. **M16.**
6 In general circulation; current. **L16.**

J. BRIGHT Various rumours were afloat. J. AUSTEN Whatever money he might come into . . it is, I dare say, all afloat, all employed in his stock, and so forth.

7 Unsettled; adrift. **E17.**

aflow /əˈfləʊ/ *adverb & pred. adjective.* **M19.**
[ORIGIN from A-[2] + FLOW *noun*[1] or *verb*.]
Flowing.

aflower /əˈflaʊə/ *adverb & pred. adjective.* **L19.**
[ORIGIN from A-[2] + FLOWER *noun*.]
Flowering; in bloom.

aflutter /əˈflʌtə/ *adverb & pred. adjective.* **E19.**
[ORIGIN from A-[2] + FLUTTER *noun*.]
Fluttering; in a flutter.

AFM *abbreviation.*
Air Force Medal.

afoam /əˈfəʊm/ *adverb & pred. adjective.* **E19.**
[ORIGIN from A-[2] + FOAM *noun*.]
Foaming.

afocal /eɪˈfəʊk(ə)l/ *adjective.* **M20.**
[ORIGIN from A-[10] + FOCAL.]
OPTICS. Designating or involving a lens or lens system with a focal power of zero (so that rays entering parallel emerge parallel).

à fond /a fɔ̃/ *adverbial phr.* **E19.**
[ORIGIN French, lit. 'to bottom'.]
Thoroughly, fully.

afoot /əˈfʊt/ *adverb & pred. adjective.* **ME.**
[ORIGIN from A *preposition*[1] 1 + FOOT *noun*, partly after Old Norse *á fótum*.]
1 On foot, on one's own feet. *arch.* **ME.**

R. KIPLING The lama and Mahbub Ali, both afoot, walking cautiously.

2 Astir, on the move; in operation or employment. **M16.**

W. S. CHURCHILL The Hungarians were in revolt . . and the Turks were once more afoot. M. SPARK A new plot which is afoot to force me to resign.

afore /əˈfɔː/ *adverb, preposition, & conjunction.* Now chiefly *dial.* & NAUTICAL.
[ORIGIN Old English *onforan*; later (14) from ON *preposition* + FORE *adverb & preposition*.]
► **A** *adverb.* **1** Of place: in front; in or into the forepart. **OE.**
2 Of time: before. **ME.**
– COMB.: With pa. pples forming adjectives, as ***aforesaid***, ***aforementioned***, etc.
► **B** *preposition.* **1** Of time: before. **OE.**
2 Of place: in front of; in advance of; in or into the presence of. **ME.**
3 Of rank etc.: in precedence of. **LME.**
► **C** *conjunction.* Before, sooner than. **ME.**

aforehand /əˈfɔːhand/ *adverb & pred. adjective. arch.* **LME.**
[ORIGIN from AFORE *preposition* + HAND *noun*, after earlier *beforehand*.]
► **A** *adverb.* In anticipation, in advance. **LME.**
► †**B** *pred. adjective.* Prepared or provided for the future. **E16–M18.**

aforethought /əˈfɔːθɔːt/ *noun & ppl adjective.* **ME.**
[ORIGIN from AFORE *adverb* + THOUGHT *noun*[1] and *thought* pa. pple of THINK *verb*[2].]
► **A** *noun.* Forethought, premeditation. *rare.* **ME.**
► **B** *ppl adjective.* Thought before; premeditated. **L15.**
malice aforethought [after *malice prepensed* s.v. PREPENSE *verb*] LAW the intention to kill or harm, which distinguishes murder from unlawful killing.

aforetime /əˈfɔːtʌɪm/ *adverb & adjective. arch.* **LME.**
[ORIGIN from AFORE *preposition* + TIME *noun*, after earlier *beforetime*.]
Before in time; former(ly).
■ **aforetimes** *adverb* (*rare*) **L16.**

a fortiori /eɪ fɔːtɪˈɔːrʌɪ/ *adverbial phr.* **E17.**
[ORIGIN Latin.]
With yet stronger reason; more conclusively.

afoul /əˈfaʊl/ *adverb & pred. adjective.* Now chiefly *N. Amer.* **E19.**
[ORIGIN from A-[2] + FOUL *adjective, noun*.]
In a tangle; in collision; foul. Esp. in ***run afoul of***, ***fall afoul of***.

afraid /əˈfreɪd/ *pred. adjective.* Also (*arch.*) **affrayed**. **ME.**
[ORIGIN pa. pple of AFFRAY *verb* used as adjective after Anglo-Norman *afraye*.]
Frightened, alarmed, in a state of fear. (Foll. by *of* a person or thing, *of doing*; *to do*; *that* or (somewhat *arch.*) *lest* with subjunct. (an unpleasant possibility); *that* with indic. (an unpleasant probability or contemplated reality).)

SWIFT I was affraid of trampling on every traveller that I met. POPE Willing to wound, and yet afraid to strike. J. AUSTEN I am afraid you do not like your pen. G. H. LEWES Afraid lest the poetical spirit should be swept away. J. M. SYNGE A man who is not afraid of the sea will soon be drowned. T. S. ELIOT I have seen the eternal Footman hold my coat, and snicker, And in short, I was afraid. SCOTT FITZGERALD I was afraid . . that my house was on fire. W. STEVENS Mother was afraid I should freeze in the Parisian hotels.

I am afraid (that) *colloq.* I say or admit with regret.
■ **afraidness** *noun* (*rare*) **M17.**

afreet /ˈafriːt/ *noun.* Also **afrit**, **efreet** /ˈɛfriːt/. **L18.**
[ORIGIN Arabic *ʿifrīt*, colloq. *ʿafrīt*.]
A powerful jinn in Arabian stories and Muslim mythology.

afresh /əˈfrɛʃ/ *adverb.* **L15.**
[ORIGIN from A-[3] + FRESH *adjective*, after *anew*.]
Anew; with a fresh beginning.

Afric /ˈafrɪk/ *adjective. arch.* or *poet.* **L16.**
[ORIGIN Latin *Africus*: see AFRICAN.]
African.

African /ˈafrɪk(ə)n/ *noun & adjective.*
[ORIGIN Old English (only pl.) *Africanas* from Latin *Africanus* (Cicero), from *Africa* use as noun of fem. (sc. *terra* land) of *Africus*, from *Afri* pl. (sing. *Afer*) ancient people of N. Africa: see -AN.]
► **A** *noun.* **1** A native or inhabitant of the continent of Africa. **OE.**
2 A black American of African origin or descent. Now rare exc. *hist.* **E18.**
► **B** *adjective.* Of or pertaining to Africa; belonging to or characteristic of African people or (*hist.*) of African Americans. **M16.**
African American an American of African origin or descent; of or pertaining to such people. **African blackwood** = MPINGO. ***African cypress***: see CYPRESS *noun*[1] 1b. **African daisy** a yellow-flowered plant of the composite family, *Lonas annua*, which is native to the Mediterranean region and N. Africa and is a naturalized weed elsewhere. ***African* ELEPHANT**. ***African Eve hypothesis***: see EVE *noun*[1]. **African hemp** = SPARMANNIA. **African mahogany** (the wood of) a W. African tree, *Khaya senegalensis* (family Meliaceae). ***African peach***: see PEACH *noun*[1] 2. ***African pepper***: see PEPPER *noun*. ***African* POMPANO**. ***African* SWINE *fever***. ***African* TEAK**. **African violet** = SAINTPAULIA. **African walnut** (the wood, resembling mahogany, of) a tropical African tree, *Lovoa trichilioides* (family Meliaceae).
■ **Afriˈcana** *noun pl.* publications or other items concerning or associated with Africa **E20.** **Africanism** *noun* an African mode of speech, idiom, etc.; African character; African nationalism: **M17.** **Africanist** *noun & adjective* (*a*) *noun* a specialist in things African; an African nationalist; (*b*) *adjective* of or pertaining to Africanists or Africanism: **L19.** **Afriˈcanity** *noun* = AFRICANNESS **M20.** **Africanize** *verb trans.* make African in character; *spec.* (*a*) place under the control of native African people; (*b*) hybridize (honeybees) with a stock of African origin to give an unusually aggressive strain: **E19.** **Africanness** /-n-n-/ *noun* the quality or condition of being African **M20.**

Afrikaans /afrɪˈkɑːns/ *noun & adjective.* **E20.**
[ORIGIN Dutch = African.]
(Of) a modified form of the Dutch language used in South Africa.

Afrikaner /afrɪˈkɑːnə/ *noun.* Also **Africander**, **-kander** /-ˈkandə/. **E19.**
[ORIGIN Afrikaans, from *Afrikaan* an African + *-(d)er* pers. suffix, after *Hollander* Dutchman.]
1 An Afrikaans-speaking white person in South Africa, *esp.* one of Dutch descent. **E19.**
2 (Also **a-**.) A South African gladiolus belonging to any of several species. **E19.**
3 (Also **a-**.) (An animal of) a long-horned South African breed of cattle, or the indigenous South African breed of sheep. **M19.**
■ **Afrikanerdom**, **Afrikanderdom** *noun* the Afrikaner people; the beliefs of Afrikaners; Afrikaners collectively: **L19.** **Afrikanerism**, **Afrikanderism** *noun* an Afrikaans word or idiom used in South African English **L19.** **Afrikanerize**, **Afrikanderize** *verb trans.* bring under the influence or control of Afrikaners; make like an Afrikaner: **E20.** **Afriˌkaneriˈzation** *noun* the process of Afrikanerizing something **M20.**

afrit *noun* var. of AFREET.

Afro /ˈafrəʊ/ *adjective & noun.* **M20.**
[ORIGIN from AFRO-, or from AFR(ICAN + -O.]
► **A** *adjective.* African, Afro-American; *spec.* (of a hairstyle) long and bushy, as naturally grown by some black people. **M20.**
► **B** *noun.* Pl. **-os**.
1 An Afro-American; a black person. **M20.**
2 An Afro hairstyle. **L20.**

Afro- /ˈafrəʊ/ *combining form.* Before a vowel occas. **Afr-**. **M19.**
[ORIGIN Latin, from *Afr-*, *Afer* African: see -O-.]
Forming adjectives and nouns with the senses 'African (and)', as ***Afro-American***, ***Afro-Brazilian***, ***Afro-Caribbean***, and 'of or pertaining to Africa', as ***Afrocentric***.
■ **Afrobeat** *noun* a style of popular music incorporating elements of African music and jazz, soul, and funk **L20.**

Afro-Asiatic /ˌafrəʊeɪʃɪˈatɪk, -eɪʒ-/ *adjective & noun.* **M20.**
[ORIGIN from AFRO- + ASIATIC *adjective*.]
(Designating or pertaining to) a language family of N. Africa and SW Asia including Semitic languages, Egyptian, Berber, Chadic, and Cushitic.

afront /əˈfrʌnt/ *adverb & preposition.* Now *dial.* or *obsolete.* **LME.**
[ORIGIN from A *preposition*[1] 1 + FRONT *noun*.]
► **A** *adverb.* †**1** Face to face, opposite. **LME–E17.**
†**2** In a front; abreast. **LME–E17.**
3 In front. **L16.**
► **B** *preposition.* In front of. **M16.**

afrormosia /afrɔːˈməʊzɪə/ *noun.* **M20.**
[ORIGIN mod. Latin, formed as AFRO- + *Ormosia*, a related genus, from Greek *hormos* necklace: see -IA[1].]
(The wood of) a N. and W. African leguminous tree of the genus *Pericopsis* (formerly *Afrormosia*).

aft /ɑːft/ *adverb & adjective.* **E17.**
[ORIGIN Prob. alt. of earlier ABAFT, BAFT *adverb*, after Low German, Dutch *achter* abaft, after.]
NAUTICAL & AERONAUTICS. In or near or to or towards the stern or tail.

after /ˈɑːftə/ *noun. colloq.* **L19.**
[ORIGIN Abbreviation.]
Afternoon.

after /ˈɑːftə/ *adjective.*
[ORIGIN Old English *æfter(r)a*, corresp. to Old High German *aftaro*. Later AFTER *adverb* etc. in attrib. use.]
†**1** Second. **OE–ME.**
2 Next, subsequent. Later freq. in *comb.*: see AFTER-. **OE.**
3 Nearer the rear; (chiefly NAUTICAL) nearer the stern. **ME.**
■ **aftermost** *superl. adjective* (NAUTICAL) nearest the stern of a ship **E18.** **afterness** *noun* (now *rare*) the quality of being after or later **L16.**

after /ˈɑːftə/ *adverb, preposition, & conjunction.*
[ORIGIN Old English *æfter*, corresp. to Old Frisian *efter*, Old Saxon, Old High German *aftar*, Old Norse *aptr*, Gothic *aftra*; prob. compar. deriv., rel. to Greek *apo* away from or *opisō* behind.]
► **A** *adverb.* **1** Behind in place or order. **OE.**

J. STALLWORTHY Stiffly he walked out / and his audience shuffled after.

2 Later in time. **OE.** ►**b** *spec.* Contrasted with ***before*** (see BEFORE *adverb* 2b): following an event or (*esp.*) the use of a remedy, cosmetic, or other product. **M18.**

SHAKES. *Jul. Caes.* I do fawn on men . . , And after scandal them. W. STEVENS The lilacs came long after.

► **B** *preposition.* **I** Of place.
1 In the rear of, behind. **OE.**

JOYCE He filed out of the study-hall after the others.

after you: a formula used in yielding precedence.
2 In pursuit or quest of; in the direction of someone or something moving away; about, concerning. **OE.**

LD MACAULAY He was greedy after power. J. WAIN What most of the Sixth were after was a scholarship at Oxford or Cambridge. J. CHEEVER 'Merry Christmas, Charlie!' both the Fullers called after him. J. P. DONLEAVY A Mr. Skully, a former landlord, is after me for money.

be after doing (chiefly *Irish*) (*a*) be intending to do, be on the point of doing; freq. *pleonastic*, be doing; (*b*) have just done. **see after** attend to.
► **II** Of time.
3 Following in time, in succession to. **OE.**

SPENSER Sleep after toil, port after stormy seas, Ease after war, death after life does greatly please. COLERIDGE Day after day, day after day, We stuck, nor breath nor motion.

after you with *colloq.* may I have the next use of. ***time after time***: see TIME *noun*.
4 Following the interval of, at the close of. **OE.**

S. HEANEY After eleven years I was composing Love-letters again.

5 Subsequent to or later than (a point in time). OE. ▸**b** Past, beyond (a specified hour). Now chiefly *dial.* & *N. Amer.* M18.

S. HILL Only a little after ten-thirty. **b** A. MILLER It's twenty after twelve.

after hours after the regular hours of work or of opening (of a public house etc.). ***after the event***: see EVENT *noun*.

6 Subsequent to and in consequence of. OE.

T. S. ELIOT After such knowledge what forgiveness?

7 Subsequent to and notwithstanding. E17.

SHAKES. *Meas. for M.* Hark how the villain would close now, after his treasonable abuses!

after all in spite of all that has happened or been said; in spite of one's exertions, expectations, etc.

▸**III** Of manner.

8 According to; in a manner consistent with. OE.

DICKENS Handsome after its kind.

after a fashion: see FASHION *noun*. ***after a sort***: see SORT *noun*[2].

9 In a manner proportionate to. *arch.* OE.

H. LATIMER Cut thy cloth after the mesure.

10 In imitation of; in allusion to. ME.

GIBBON After his oracle, Dr. Johnson, my friend . . denies all original genius. R. MAYER Van Gogh's drawing after Millet's *The Reapers*. R. BRAUTIGAN It's good to name creeks after people.

after the fashion of: see FASHION *noun*.

11 At (the rate of). *arch.* LME.

▸**IV** Of order.

12 Next to in order or importance. ME.

DRYDEN Codrus after Phœbus sings the best.

▸**C** *conjunction*. **1** In or at the time subsequent to that when. Also (*arch.*) ***after that***. OE.

AV *Jer.* 36:27 After that the king had burnt the roule. LD MACAULAY A few days after the Revolution had been accomplished.

†**2** According as. Also ***after that***, ***after as***. ME–M17.

after- /ˈɑːftə/ *combining form*. OE.

[ORIGIN AFTER *adverb & preposition, adjective*.]

Forming combs., fixed or transitory, with nouns, adjectives, and verbs, in various relations and senses, as 'rear', 'subsequent(ly)', 'eventual(ly)', 'subordinate(ly)'.

after-born *adjective* born after one's father's death or last will; younger. †**after-burden** = AFTERBIRTH. **afterburner** a fitment for burning extra fuel in the exhaust of a jet engine as a means of increasing thrust. **afterburning** the action or use of an afterburner. †**after-burthen** = AFTERBIRTH. **aftercare** attention given after a stay in hospital, prison, etc. **afterclap** an unexpected stroke after the recipient has ceased to be on his or her guard; a surprise happening after a matter is supposed to be at an end. **aftercomer** a successor; in *pl.*, posterity. **after-course** †(*a*) a later course at dinner; (*b*) a subsequent course. **aftercrop** a second crop in one season. **afterdamp** (gas rich in) carbon monoxide occurring in a mine after an explosion. **after-days** later or subsequent days. **afterdeck** an open deck towards the stern of a ship. **after-effect** an effect that follows after an interval or after the primary action of something. **after-game** a second game played to improve on the result of the first; a new plan to meet an unforeseen development. **afterglow** a glow (*lit.* or *fig.*) that remains after the removal or disappearance of its source. **aftergrass** = AFTERMATH 1. **after-growth** (*a*) = AFTERMATH 1; (*b*) growth afterwards. **after-guard** NAUTICAL on a sailing ship, the men stationed on the quarterdeck and poop to work the sails aft of the mainmast. **after-image** an impression of a vivid (esp. visual) sensation retained after the cause has been withdrawn. **after-knowledge** knowledge after the event. **afterlife** life at a later time or after death. **afterlight** an afterglow; hindsight. **aftermarket** (*a*) a market for spare parts and components; (*b*) a market in shares after their original issue. **after-pain** a pain which follows later; *spec.* in *pl.*, uterine contractions occurring after childbirth. **after-party** a party held after another event, esp. a concert or another party. **afterpiece** *hist.* a farce or other short piece after a play; *fig.* a subsequent dramatic event. **after-reckoning** a subsequent or final account. **after-sensation** an after-image (less commonly visual). **aftershave** *adjective & noun* (a lotion) for use after shaving. **aftershock** a lesser shock following the main shock of an earthquake. **aftersight** hindsight. **aftertaste** a taste remaining or recurring after eating or drinking. **afterthought** something that is thought of or added later. **after-time(s)** a later or future time. **aftertouch** MUSIC the resonant effect produced when a pianist sustains the pressure on a key after striking it; (the facility provided by) a programmable device for reproducing this on an electronic keyboard etc. **after-wit** *arch.* wisdom after the event. **afterword** a concluding comment in a book, esp. by a person other than the author. **afterworld** the world later in time; a world after death. †**after-wort** BREWING the second run of beer. **after-years** later years, years to come.

afterbirth /ˈɑːftəbəːθ/ *noun*. M16.

[ORIGIN Perh. directly from German *Afterbürde* (Luther, *Deuteronomy* 28:57), also *Aftergeburt*: cf. Icelandic *eftirburður*, Old Swedish *efterbörd*, Danish *efterbyrd*, and see AFTER-, BIRTH *noun*[1].]

The placenta and fetal membranes expelled from the womb after the birth of offspring.

aftermath /ˈɑːftəmaθ/ *noun*. L15.

[ORIGIN from AFTER- + MATH *noun*[1]. Cf. LATTERMATH.]

1 A second or later mowing; a crop of grass growing after mowing or harvest. Now *dial.* L15.

J. BUCHAN Meadowland from which an aftermath of hay had lately been taken.

2 The effects or conditions arising from an (esp. unpleasant) event. M19.

W. S. CHURCHILL The life and strength of Britain . . will be tested to the full, not only in the war but in the aftermath of war. M. L. KING The aftermath of nonviolence is the creation of the beloved community.

afternoon /ɑːftəˈnuːn/ *noun*. ME.

[ORIGIN from AFTER *preposition* + NOON *noun*: cf. Latin *post meridiem*.]

1 The time from midday or lunchtime to evening; this time spent in a particular way. ME.

TENNYSON In the afternoon they came unto a land In which it seemed always afternoon.

this afternoon (during) the afternoon of today. ***TOMORROW afternoon***. ***YESTERDAY afternoon***.

2 *ellipt.* As *interjection*. Good afternoon. *colloq.* E20.

E. O'NEILL Afternoon, Harriet . . . Afternoon, Ma.

– COMB.: ***afternoon tea***: see TEA *noun* 5(a).

afternoons /ɑːftəˈnuːnz/ *adverb*. *N. Amer.* L19.

[ORIGIN Pl. of AFTERNOON: cf. DAYS, EVENINGS, NIGHTS, etc. (earlier uses of -S[3] being identified with -S[1]).]

During the afternoon, every afternoon.

afters /ˈɑːftəz/ *noun pl. colloq.* E20.

[ORIGIN from AFTER *adverb* or *adjective*.]

The course following the main course of a meal.

afterward /ˈɑːftəwəd/ *adverb*.

[ORIGIN Late Old English *æfterwearde*: see AFTER-, -WARD.]

†**1** Of place: behind; NAUTICAL towards the stern. LOE–E17.

2 = AFTERWARDS. Now chiefly *US*. ME.

†**3** Of order: next. ME–L16.

afterwards /ˈɑːftəwədz/ *adverb*. ME.

[ORIGIN from AFTERWARD: see -WARDS.]

At a later time, subsequently.

AG *abbreviation*.

1 Adjutant General.

2 Attorney General.

Ag *symbol*.

[ORIGIN Latin *argentum*.]

CHEMISTRY. Silver.

ag /ag/ *adjective & noun*. Chiefly *N. Amer. colloq.* E20.

[ORIGIN Abbreviation.]

▸**A** *adjective*. Agricultural. E20.

▸**B** *noun*. Agriculture. M20.

ag /ax/ *interjection*. *S. Afr.* M20.

[ORIGIN Afrikaans from Dutch *ach*.]

= ACH.

ag- /ag, *unstressed* əg/ *prefix* (not productive).

Assim. form of Latin AD- before *g*. In Old French, Latin *agg-* was reduced to *ag-*, which appears in Middle English adoptions, but in later French, and hence in English, *agg-* was restored by Latinization, as ***aggrandize***, ***aggrieve***, except in ***agree***.

aga /ˈɑːgə/ *noun*[1]. Also **agha**. M16.

[ORIGIN Turkish *ağa* master, lord from Mongolian *aqa*.]

An Ottoman title, now abolished, for (orig.) a military commander and (later) officials of various ranks. Now, a title of respect for landowners among Turkish village people.

Aga Khan the spiritual leader of the Khoja branch of Ismaili Muslims.

Aga /ˈɑːgə/ *noun*[2]. M20.

[ORIGIN Acronym, from Swedish Svenska Aktiebolaget Gasackumulator, the original manufacturer.]

(Proprietary name for) a type of large domestic stove for cooking and for heating water.

– COMB.: **Aga saga** [from the Aga stove seen as a status symbol of affluent, traditional middle-class life] a type of popular novel typically set in a semi-rural British location and concerning the domestic and emotional lives of articulate, middle-class characters.

agacerie /agasəri/ *noun*. Pl. pronounced same. E19.

[ORIGIN French.]

(An) allurement; coquetry.

†**agad** *interjection*. L17–M18.

[ORIGIN from AH *interjection* + GAD *noun*[2].]

= EGAD.

Agadic /əˈgadɪk/ *adjective*. L19.

[ORIGIN from *Agada* Latinized form of HAGGADAH + -IC.]

= HAGGADIC.

again /əˈgɛn, əˈgeɪn/ *adverb, preposition, & conjunction*. As preposition also **agen**, (*dial. & joc.*) **agin** /əˈgɪn/.

[ORIGIN Old English (West Saxon) *ongē(a)n*, later *agēn*, (Anglian) *ongægn*, *-gegn*, corresp. to Old Saxon *angegin*, Old High German *ingagan*, *ingegin(i)* (German *entgegen* opposite), Old Norse *í gegn* against. Middle English forms in *aʒ-*, *ay-* were superseded by those in *ag-* from north. dialects (of Scandinavian origin).]

▸**A** *adverb*. **1** In the opposite direction; back to the point of starting. *obsolete* exc. *dial.* & in ***return again***, ***come back again***, etc., (passing into sense 2). OE.

to and again to and fro.

2 Back in or into a former position or state. OE.

S. HILL They have moved us back again to where we were before.

3 In accordance or response; later extended to indicate intensity of action. Now chiefly *arch. & dial.* ME.

DICKENS He laughed till the glasses in the sideboard rang again. WILKIE COLLINS She gallops . . till the horse reeks again.

4 Another time; once more. ME. ▸**b** Once repeated. L16.

A. E. HOUSMAN Now, of my threescore years and ten, Twenty will not come again.

again and again repeatedly. ***BREATHE again***. ***come again***: see COME *verb*. ***ever and again***: see EVER. ***here we go again***: see HERE *adverb*. ***NEVER again!*** **now and again** occasionally. **over again**, **over and over again** repeatedly, many times. ***think again***: see THINK *verb*[2]. **time and again**, **time and time again** repeatedly. **b as much again**, **as many again** twice as much or many. **half as much again**, **half as many again** one-and-a-half times as much or many. ***same again***, ***the same again***: see SAME *pronoun & noun*.

5 Anywhere besides. *arch.* M16.

6 On the other hand; further, besides. M16.

S. RICHARDSON But now again, see what succeeds to this. *English Studies* The use of traditional diction is one thing; improvisation is something else again. B. PYM I might decide to live here, and again I might not.

▸**B** *preposition*. = AGAINST *preposition*. Now chiefly *dial.* OE.

▸**C** *conjunction*. = AGAINST *conjunction*. Now *dial.* ME.

■ †**againward** *adverb* again ME–L16.

against /əˈgɛnst, əˈgeɪnst/ *preposition & conjunction*. ME.

[ORIGIN from AGAIN + -S[3] + *t* as in *amidst*, *amongst*, etc.]

▸**A** *preposition*. **I** Of motion or action in opposition.

1 In hostility or active opposition to; in competition with; to the disadvantage of. ME. ▸**b** BETTING. In expectation of the failure of. With specified odds: with that likelihood of failure of. Also *ellipt.* M19.

AV *Gen.* 16:12 His hand will be against euery man. G. J. WHYTE-MELVILLE I rode a race against Bob Dashwood. E. WAUGH Even his good qualities of geniality and impetuosity counted against him, for his parties . . got talked about. D. H. LAWRENCE Effie sided with Tom against Frank. K. AMIS No Welsh witness would testify against them. **b** DISRAELI I'll take the odds against Caravan. D. RUNYON All life is six to five against.

2 In resistance to, as protection from. ME.

MILTON Here only weak Against the charm of beauty's powerful glance. B. BAINBRIDGE The men with the sacks over their shoulders against the rain.

3 In opposition in tendency or character to; contrary to. ME.

COLERIDGE No power on earth can oblige me to act against my conscience.

4 Towards with hostile intent. *arch.* ME.

AV *Luke* 14:31 To meete him that commeth against him with twentie thousand.

5 In the opposite direction to, counter to. LME.

J. STALLWORTHY Walking against the wind.

▸**II** Of position.

6 Directly opposite, facing. Now chiefly in ***over against*** s.v. OVER *adverb*. ME. ▸†**b** Exposed to (light, cold, etc.). LME–E18.

b SHAKES. *Sonn.* Those boughs which shake against the cold.

†**7** In the sight or presence of. ME–E16.

8 *fig.* With respect to. *arch.* LME.

9 Near, adjoining. Now *dial.* LME.

▸**III** Of mutual opposition or relation.

10 In return for; instead of. ME.

H. MARTINEAU To exchange wheat against bullocks.

11 Weighed in the opposite scale to (*lit. & fig.*). ME.

A. THWAITE Seven hundred years of labour-saving gadgets Weigh little in the balance put against you.

12 *fig.* In contrast with. Also ***as against***. ME.

▸**IV** Of time.

13 Drawing towards, close to. *obsolete* exc. *dial.* ME.

14 In anticipation of, in preparation for. ME.

L. DURRELL Comestibles specially prepared against a feast-day.

▸**V** Of motion towards, or contact with.

15 Towards, to meet. Long *obsolete* exc. *dial.* ME.

16 Into contact with, into collision with. LME.

W. TREVOR Breakers crashed against the wall of the promenade.

17 In contact with, supported by. L16.

W. OWEN Under his helmet, up against his pack, . . Sleep took him by the brow and laid him back. R. CHANDLER There was a bar against the right hand wall.

18 Of something seen: in front of, having as background. E19.

J. BETJEMAN Still I see Twigs and serrated leaves against the sky.

– PHRASES: ***against nature***: see NATURE *noun*. **against the clock**, **against time** so as to complete a task by a certain time, with a time limit. ***against the grain***: see GRAIN *noun*[1]. ***against the hair***: see HAIR *noun*. ***against the world***: see WORLD *noun*. **run up**

against *colloq.* meet accidentally. ***up against***: see UP *adverb*[2] & *adjective*[2].

▸ **B** *conjunction*. Before the time that; in anticipation of the time that. *arch.* ME.

THACKERAY Shutting his shutters . . , against service commenced.

agal /a'gɑːl/ *noun*. M19.
[ORIGIN Repr. Bedouin pronunc. of Arabic *ʿiqāl* bond, rope for hobbling a camel.]
A band worn by Bedouin Arabs to keep the keffiyeh in position.

agallochum /ə'galəkəm/ *noun*. Also **agalloch**. L16.
[ORIGIN Late Latin from Greek *agallokhon*; ult. rel. to AGILA.]
Aloes wood.

agalmatolite /agəl'matəlʌɪt/ *noun*. M19.
[ORIGIN from Greek *agalmat-*, *agalma* statue, image + -O- + -LITE.]
A soapstone or other soft mineral, *esp.* one in which Chinese figures are carved.

agama /ə'gɑːmə/ *noun*. L18.
[ORIGIN Perh. from Carib.]
A lizard resembling an iguana, belonging to *Agama* or a related genus.
– NOTE: Orig. including some American lizards, the genus has been restricted to Old World species by reclassification.
■ **agamid** *adjective & noun* (designating or pertaining to) a lizard of the Old World family Agamidae, to which the agamas belong L19.

agami /ə'gɑːmi/ *noun*. M18.
[ORIGIN French, from Galibi *agamy*.]
The chestnut-bellied heron, *Agamia agami*, of northern S. America.

agamic /ə'gamɪk/ *adjective*. M19.
[ORIGIN from Greek *agamos* unmarried + -IC.]
BIOLOGY. Asexual; reproducing asexually. Formerly also, unfertilized; cryptogamic.
■ Also **agamous** /'agəməs/ *adjective* M19.

agamogenesis /ˌagəmə'dʒɛnɪsɪs/ *noun*. Now *rare*. M19.
[ORIGIN formed as AGAMIC + -GENESIS.]
BIOLOGY. Asexual reproduction; *spec.* parthenogenesis.
■ ˌ**agamoge'netic** *adjective* L19.

agapanthus /agə'panθəs/ *noun*. L18.
[ORIGIN mod. Latin, from Greek *agapē* love + *anthos* flower.]
A lily-like plant of the southern African genus *Agapanthus*, bearing umbels of blue or white flowers.

agape /'agəpi/ *noun*. Pl. **-pae** /-piː/, **-pes**. E17.
[ORIGIN Greek *agapē* brotherly love.]
1 A love feast held by early Christians in connection with the Eucharist; *transf.* a parochial feast at a festival time. E17.
2 Christian love, charity. M19.

agape /ə'geɪp/ *adverb & pred. adjective*. M17.
[ORIGIN from A *preposition*[1] 6 + GAPE *noun*.]
Gaping; open-mouthed with wonder or expectation.

agapemone /agə'piːməni, -'pɛm-/ *noun*. M19.
[ORIGIN Irreg. from Greek *agapē* love + *monē* abode: orig. (with cap. initial) the name of a community founded in Somerset, England, c 1850.]
An abode of love; an establishment where free love is practised.

agar-agar /eɪgɑːr'eɪgɑː/ *noun*. In sense 2 usu. simply **agar**. E19.
[ORIGIN Malay.]
1 Any of certain SE Asian seaweeds from which a gelatinous substance is extracted; *esp.* Ceylon moss, *Gracilaria lichenoides*. E19.
2 The substance itself, used esp. to make soups and to form biological culture media. M19.
■ **agarose** /'agərəʊz, -s/ *noun* [-OSE[2]] *BIOCHEMISTRY* a polysaccharide containing L- and D-galactose residues which is the main constituent of agar and is used in making gels for electrophoresis etc. M20.

agaric /'ag(ə)rɪk, ə'gɑːrɪk/ *noun*. LME.
[ORIGIN Latin *agaricum* (Pliny) from Greek *agarikon* tree fungus. Cf. French *agaric* (15).]
†**1** Any of various bracket fungi having medicinal or other uses; esp. *Fomes officinalis*, a cathartic, and *Phellinus ignarius*, used to check bleeding, etc. LME–M19.
2 A gill-bearing mushroom or toadstool, any member of the order Agaricales. E18.
fly agaric: see FLY *noun*[1].

agasp /ə'gɑːsp/ *adverb & pred. adjective*. E19.
[ORIGIN from A-[2] + GASP *noun*.]
Gasping.

†**agast** *verb trans.* Latterly *dial.* Also **aghast**. Pa. pple & ppl adjective **agast**, AGHAST *adjective*, **agasted**. ME–M19.
[ORIGIN from A-[1] (intensifier) + GAST *verb & adjective*.]
Frighten, terrify.

agate /'agət/ *noun*. L15.
[ORIGIN Old French & mod. French *agate*, †*-the* from Latin *achates* from Greek *akhatēs*. Cf. ACHATE *noun*[1].]
1 A hard semi-transparent variegated chalcedony, having colours usu. arranged in bands. L15.
†**2** *fig.* A diminutive figure (from those cut in agates for seals). Only in L16.
3 *TYPOGRAPHY.* Ruby type. *US.* M19.
4 A coloured toy marble resembling an agate. M19.
– COMB.: **agateware** a kind of pottery coloured to resemble agate.
■ **agatized** *pa. pple & ppl adjective* converted into or made to resemble agate M17.

agate /ə'geɪt/ *adverb & pred. adjective*. *Scot. & N. English.* M16.
[ORIGIN from A *preposition*[1] 1 + GATE *noun*[2].]
On the way; on the road; in motion, astir.

agathodemon /agəθə'diːmən/ *noun*. Also **-daemon**. M18.
[ORIGIN Greek *agathodaimōn*, from *agathos* good + *daimōn* a spirit.]
A good divinity or genius.

agave /ə'geɪvi/ *noun*. L18.
[ORIGIN Latin *Agave* personal name in mythol. from Greek *Agauē* proper fem. of *agauos* illustrious.]
Any of numerous spiny-leaved plants of the American genus *Agave* (family Agavaceae), most members of which, e.g. the American aloe, *Agave americana*, take several years to mature and flower only once.

agaze /ə'geɪz/ *adverb*. LME.
[ORIGIN from A *preposition*[1] 6 + GAZE *noun*.]
Gazing.

†**agazed** *ppl adjective*. LME–E19.
[ORIGIN Perh. var. of *agast* AGHAST *adjective* infl. by AGAZE.]
Frightened; astounded.

agba /'agbə/ *noun*. E20.
[ORIGIN Yoruba.]
(The wood of) a tall W. African leguminous tree, *Gossweilerodendron balsamiferum*.

age /eɪdʒ/ *noun*. ME.
[ORIGIN Old French (mod. *âge*) ult. from Latin *aetat-*, *aetas*, from *aevum* age of time. Cf. AEON.]
▸ **I** A period of existence.
1 The length of past life or of existence; the ordinary duration of life. ME.
act one's age = ***be one's age*** below. **ages with** *Scot.* of the same age as. **be one's age** act sensibly (chiefly as imper.). ***full age***: see FULL *adjective*. ***great age***: see GREAT *adjective*. **look one's age** look as old as one really is. ***mental age***: see MENTAL *adjective*[1]. **of an age to** old enough to. **of an age with** of the same age as. ***reading age***: see READING *noun*[1]. ***the awkward age***: see AWKWARD *adjective* 3b. **the moon's age** the time elapsed since the new moon.
2 The duration of life which naturally or conventionally qualifies for something; *esp.* the duration of life which ordinarily brings maturity, or which by custom or law is fixed as such. ME.
age of consent: see CONSENT *noun* 1. **come of age** reach adult status, in Britain and US usually at 18 (formerly 21) for most purposes. **over age** old enough; too old. **underage** not old enough; *esp.* not yet of adult status.
3 A period or stage of life. ME.

SHAKES. *A.Y.L.* One man in his time plays many parts, His acts being seven ages.

age of DISCRETION. See also MIDDLE AGE, ***old age*** s.v. OLD *adjective* 5, ***third age*** s.v. THIRD *adjective*.
4 *esp.* The latter part of life; old age. ME.

E. WAUGH Having for many years painfully feigned youth, he now aspired to the honours of age.

5 The effects of age; senility; maturity (of things). LME.
▸ **II** A period of time.
6 **a** A distinctive period of human history, real or mythical. ME. ▸**b** *GEOLOGY.* A division of geological time; *spec.* a subdivision of an epoch, corresponding to a stratigraphic stage. M19.
a ***Age of Aquarius***, ***Age of Chivalry***, ***age of gold***, ***brazen age***, ***Bronze Age***, ***Dark Age(s)***, ***golden age***, ***Iron Age***, ***Middle Age(s)***, ***New Age***, ***silver age***, ***Stone Age***, ***three ages***, etc. ***in this day and age***: see DAY *noun*. ***the age of reason***: see REASON *noun*[1]. **b** ***ice age***.
7 The generation to which someone belongs. ME.

ARNOLD BENNETT He had survived into another and a more fortunate age than his own.

8 A long but indefinite period of time (*gen. & colloq.* (esp. in *pl.*) in exaggeration). LME. ▸**b** A century. *rare.* L16.

J. AUSTEN The two ladies . . called it an age since they had met. JOYCE He died of galloping drink ages ago. J. BERRYMAN Across the ages certain blessings swarm.

9 A generation (as a measure of time). E16.

HOBBES The Writers of the New Testament lived all in lesse then an age after Christ's Ascension.

– COMB.: **age gap** a difference in age, esp. as a source of disharmony or misunderstanding; **age group** a number of persons or things classed together as of similar age; **age hardening** *METALLURGY* spontaneous hardening occurring on storage at ambient temperature, or on mild heat treatment, following quenching; **age-long** *adjective* as long as an age; lasting for a very long time; **age-old** *adjective* having existed for a very long time; **age-mate** a person of the same age.
■ **ageism**, **agism** *noun* prejudice or discrimination against people of a particular age, esp. against the elderly M20. **ageist**, **agist** *adjective & noun* (*a*) *adjective* of ageism; (*b*) *noun* a person who practises ageism: L20. **ageless** *adjective* without limits of duration; never growing or appearing old or outmoded: M17. **agelessness** *noun* E20. **ager** *noun* a person living in or having a specified age (as 2nd elem. of comb.) M20.

age /eɪdʒ/ *verb*. Pres. pple **ageing**, **aging**. LME.
[ORIGIN from the noun.]
1 *verb intrans.* Grow old, mature, show the effects of the passage of time; begin to appear older; undergo ageing (see below). LME.
2 *verb trans.* Cause or allow to grow old, mature, begin to appear older, undergo ageing, etc. M16.
3 *verb trans.* Calculate or determine the age of. L19.
■ **ageing**, **aging** *verbal noun* the action or process of growing or causing to grow old etc.; a process of change, usu. gradual and spontaneous, in the properties of a material; age hardening: M19.

-age /ɪdʒ; *in a few words* ɑːʒ/ *suffix*.
[ORIGIN Repr. Old French & mod. French *-age* from late Latin *-aticum* neut. of adjectives in *-aticus* -ATIC. Later a living English formative.]
Forming nouns with gen. sense of appurtenance or collectives. The meanings are typified by ***baggage***, ***carriage***, ***cartage***, ***damage***, ***dotage***, ***hermitage***, ***homage***, ***language***, ***luggage***, ***marriage***, ***passage***, ***tillage***, ***tonnage***, ***vicarage***, ***village***.

aged /*in senses A.1, 2, B,* 'eɪdʒɪd; *in senses A.1b, 3, 4,* eɪdʒd/ *adjective & noun*. LME.
[ORIGIN from AGE *verb* + -ED[1], after French *âgé*.]
▸ **A** *adjective*. **1** Having lived long; old. LME. ▸**b** Of a horse, farm animal, etc.: over a certain age, as (usu.) 6 or 7 for a horse, 3 or 4 for cattle. M19.

DICKENS You don't object to an aged parent, I hope?

2 Belonging to old age. *rare.* L16.

SHAKES. *Tit. A.* The aged wrinkles in my cheeks.

3 Of or at the age of. L16.

DYLAN THOMAS Among those Killed in the Dawn Raid was a Man Aged a Hundred.

4 Of a material: subjected to ageing. M19.
▸ **B** *absol.* as *noun pl. The* people who are old or elderly, as a class. E20.
■ **agedly** /'eɪdʒɪdli/ *adverb* after the manner of an aged person M16. **agedness** /'eɪdʒɪdnɪs/ *noun* the quality of being of advanced age or of a specified age LME.

agee *adverb & pred. adjective* var. of AJEE.

ageing *pres. pple & verbal noun* see AGE *verb*.

agelast /'adʒɪlast/ *noun*. *rare.* L19.
[ORIGIN Greek *agelastos*, from *a-* A-[10] + *gelastos*, from *gelan* to laugh.]
A person who never laughs.

agen *preposition* see AGAIN *preposition*.

agency /'eɪdʒ(ə)nsi/ *noun*. M17.
[ORIGIN medieval Latin *agentia*: see AGENT, -ENCY.]
1 **a** Active operation, action. M17. ▸**b** Intervening action towards an end. M17. ▸**c** Action personified; a source of action towards an end. L18.

a N. SHUTE There may be human agency behind that power. **b** F. M. FORD If he could smile again through her agency. **c** P. H. JOHNSON As though some outside agency is at work.

2 The function or position of an agent (sense 2). M17.
3 The headquarters or business establishment of an agent (sense 2); a specialized department of the United Nations. E19.
adoption agency, ***employment agency***, ***news agency***, etc.
– COMB.: **agency shop** *US* (an establishment operating) a system whereby a recognized trade union receives a sum of money from non-members equivalent to the subscriptions of members.

agenda /ə'dʒɛndə/ *noun*. Also (now *rare*) **agendum** /-dəm/; †**agend**. E17.
[ORIGIN Latin, pl. of *agendum* use as noun of gerundive of *agere*: see AGENT.]
1 As *pl.* Things to be done; matters of practice. E17.
2 A memorandum book. *arch.* M18.
3 A list of items to be discussed at a meeting or to be otherwise attended to. Formerly also as *pl.* L19. ▸**b** The set of underlying motives or ideals of a particular individual or group. L20.

B. BAINBRIDGE She hadn't a spare moment. She had a busy agenda. **b** *www.fictionpress.com* I've got my own agenda. I do what I please and I work for nobody.

4 A diary for listing appointments. *N. Amer.* L20.
– NOTE: Although *agenda* is the pl. of *agendum* in Latin, in modern English it is normally used as a sing. noun with a standard pl. form (*agendas*). The Latinate sing. form *agendum* is now rarely encountered in English. Cf. notes at DATA, MEDIA.

agenesis /ə'dʒɛnɪsɪs, eɪ-/ *noun*. M19.
[ORIGIN from A-[10] + -GENESIS.]
MEDICINE. Congenital absence or imperfect development of a part of the body.

agent /'eɪdʒ(ə)nt/ *noun, adjective, & verb*. LME.
[ORIGIN Latin *agent-* pres. ppl stem of *agere* act, do, cogn. with Greek *agein*, Sanskrit *ajati*: see -ENT. Rel. to ACT *verb*, AGILE, AGONY.]
▸ **A** *noun*. **1** A person who or thing which produces an effect; (the cause of) a natural force or effect on matter. LME.

I. ASIMOV Hydrogen, like carbon, is a reducing agent.

Agent Orange: see ORANGE *noun*. ***uncoupling agent***: see UNCOUPLE 3. ***VACUOLATING agent***. ***V-agent***: see V, V 3b.

A

2 A person who acts for another in business, politics, etc. M16.

P. G. WODEHOUSE Pongo will handle the whole affair, acting as your agent. R. HOGGART Agents for one of the great Clothing or General Credit Clubs. G. VIDAL A special agent of the Central Intelligence Agency.

agent-general the representative of an Australian state or a Canadian province (or, formerly, a South African province) in London or another major foreign city. ***double agent***: see DOUBLE *adjective & adverb*. **law agent** *SCOTTISH HISTORY* a solicitor. ***literary agent***: see LITERARY *adjective*. ***secret agent***: see SECRET *adjective*. ***treble agent***: see TREBLE *adjective*. ***triple agent***: see TRIPLE *adjective & adverb*. ***universal agent***: see UNIVERSAL *adjective*.

3 The material cause or instrument. L16.

R. SCRUTON The Church was the principal agent of charity.

4 A person who or thing which acts or exerts power; *spec.* in *GRAMMAR*, the entity performing the action of the verb. Opp. ***patient*** or ***instrument***. L16. ▸**b** *COMPUTING*. A program that performs background tasks such as information retrieval or processing on behalf of a client or server. L20.

free agent a person whose actions are not subject to another's control.

5 A secret agent, a spy. M20.

– COMB.: **agent noun**, **agent suffix** *GRAMMAR*: denoting an agent or agency.

▸ **B** *adjective*. Acting, exerting power. *arch.* L16.

▸ **C** *verb trans.* Act as agent in. M17.

■ **agential** /ə'dʒɛnʃ(ə)l/ *adjective* of or pertaining to an agent or agency L19. **agentive** /ə'dʒɛntɪv/ *adjective & noun* (*GRAMMAR*) (a noun, suffix, case, etc.) indicating an agent or agency M19. **agentship** *noun* = AGENCY 2 E17.

agent provocateur /ˌaʒɑ̃ prə'vɒkə'təː, *foreign* aʒɑ̃ prɔvɔkatœːr/ *noun phr.* Pl. **-s -s** (pronounced same). L19.
[ORIGIN French = provocative agent.]
An agent employed to tempt suspected persons into committing an incriminating act.

ageostrophic /eɪdʒɪə'strɒfɪk/ *adjective*. M20.
[ORIGIN from A-[10] + GEOSTROPHIC.]
METEOROLOGY. Not geostrophic: *spec.* designating the wind component which when added to a geostrophic wind gives the actual wind.

ageratum /ə'dʒɛrətəm, adʒə'reɪtəm/ *noun*. Sense 1 also †**-ton**. M16.
[ORIGIN mod. Latin from Latin *ageraton* from Greek, neut. of *agēratos*, from *a-* A-[10] + *gērat-*, *gēras* old age.]
1 An everlasting flower, known to the ancients. M16.
2 Any of a number of plants of the American genus *Ageratum*, bearing long-lasting composite flowers. M18.

ageusia /ə'gjuːzɪə, -sɪə/ *noun*. M19.
[ORIGIN from A-[10] + Greek *geusis* sense of taste: see -IA[1] and cf. Greek *ageustia*.]
MEDICINE. Inability to distinguish taste.

agey /'eɪdʒi/ *adjective*. *arch.* Also **agy**. M16.
[ORIGIN from AGE *noun* + -Y[1].]
Aged.

Aggadah *noun* var. of HAGGADAH.

agger /'adʒə/ *noun*. LME.
[ORIGIN Latin.]
ARCHAEOLOGY. A mound; *esp.* the rampart of a Roman camp or a raised Roman road or causeway.

aggeration /adʒə'reɪʃ(ə)n/ *noun*. *rare*. L17.
[ORIGIN Latin *aggeratio(n-)*, from *aggerare* heap up, formed as AGGER: see -ATION.]
The action or an act of raising a heap or mound.

aggiornamento /addʒorna'mento, ədʒɔːnə'mɛntəʊ/ *noun*. M20.
[ORIGIN Italian.]
Bringing up to date, esp. of Roman Catholic Church policy by and after the Second Vatican Council (1962–5).

agglomerate /ə'glɒmərət/ *ppl adjective & noun*. E19.
[ORIGIN Latin *agglomeratus* pa. pple, formed as AGGLOMERATE *verb*: see -ATE[2].]
▸ **A** *ppl adjective*. Collected into a mass. E19.
▸ **B** *noun*. **1** An agglomerated mass. M19.
2 *GEOLOGY*. A coarse mass of pyroclastic fragments, freq. consolidated by heat. Cf. CONGLOMERATE *noun* 1. M19.

agglomerate /ə'glɒməreɪt/ *verb trans. & intrans.* L17.
[ORIGIN Latin *agglomerat-* pa. ppl stem of *agglomerare* add or join to, from *ad* AG- + *glomerare*, from *glomer-*, *glomus* ball: see -ATE[3].]
Collect into a mass; accumulate in a disorderly way.
■ **agglome'ration** *noun* the action of agglomerating; an agglomerated mass: L18. **agglomerative** *adjective* pertaining to agglomeration; tending to agglomerate: E19.

agglutinant /ə'gluːtɪnənt/ *adjective & noun*. Now *rare*. L17.
[ORIGIN Latin *agglutinant-* pres. ppl stem of *agglutinare*: see AGGLUTINATE *adjective*, -ANT[1]. Perh. partly through French.]
(A substance) that agglutinates or causes agglutination.

agglutinate /ə'gluːtɪnət/ *adjective*. *rare*. M16.
[ORIGIN Latin *agglutinatus* pa. pple, formed as AGGLUTINATE *verb*: see -ATE[2].]
1 United as with glue; glued together. M16.
2 *PHILOLOGY*. Of or formed by agglutination. *arch.* M19.

agglutinate /ə'gluːtɪneɪt/ *verb*. M16.
[ORIGIN Latin *agglutinat-* pa. ppl stem of *agglutinare*, from *ad* AG- + *glutinare*, from *gluten* glue: see -ATE[3].]
1 *BIOLOGY & MEDICINE*. **a** *verb trans.* Orig., cause to adhere. Now, cause agglutination of. M16. ▸**b** *verb intrans.* Undergo agglutination. E20.
2 *verb trans. gen.* Unite as with glue. L16.
3 *verb trans.* *PHILOLOGY*. Compound (words) by agglutination. M19.
■ **a,gglutina'bility** *noun* the quality or property of being agglutinable E20. **agglutinable** *adjective* (chiefly *BIOLOGY & MEDICINE*) able to cause or undergo agglutination E20. **agglutinating** *adjective* that agglutinates; *PHILOLOGY* agglutinative: M17.

agglutination /əˌgluːtɪ'neɪʃ(ə)n/ *noun*. M16.
[ORIGIN French, or Latin *agglutinatio(n-)*, formed as AGGLUTINATE *verb*: see -ATION.]
1 The action of agglutinating; the state of being agglutinated. M16. ▸**b** *PHILOLOGY*. The combining of grammatical elements (roots or affixes) into complex words with little or no change of form. M19. ▸**c** *BIOLOGY & MEDICINE*. The induced adhering together or coalescence of cells, esp. bacteria or blood corpuscles. L19.
2 A thing which is agglutinated; a mass, a group. L16.

agglutinative /ə'gluːtɪnətɪv/ *adjective*. L16.
[ORIGIN French *agglutinatif*, *-ive* or from AGGLUTINATE *verb* + -IVE.]
1 Of or pertaining to agglutination; adhesive, cementing. L16.
2 *PHILOLOGY*. Characterized by agglutination. M17.

agglutinin /ə'gluːtɪnɪn/ *noun*. L19.
[ORIGIN from AGGLUTIN(ATE *verb* + -IN[1].]
BIOLOGY & MEDICINE. An antibody, lectin, or other substance which causes agglutination of cells.
■ **agglutinogen** *noun* an antigenic substance present in blood cells, bacteria, etc., which stimulates the formation of an agglutinin in blood serum E20.

aggrace /ə'greɪs/ *verb & noun*. *rare*. L16.
[ORIGIN from A-[1] + GRACE *verb*.]
▸ **A** *verb trans.* †**1** Favour. Only in L16.
2 Grace. *arch.* E19.
▸ †**B** *noun*. Favour, grace. Only in L16.

aggradation /agrə'deɪʃ(ə)n/ *noun*. L19.
[ORIGIN from AG- + DE)GRADATION *noun*[1].]
PHYSICAL GEOGRAPHY. The deposition of material by a river, stream, or current.
■ **aggradational** *adjective* of or pertaining to aggradation L19. **aggrade** /ə'greɪd/ *verb trans. & intrans.* [back-form.] build up by deposition E20.

aggrandise *verb*, **aggrandisement** *noun* vars. of AGGRANDIZE, AGGRANDIZEMENT.

aggrandize /ə'grandʌɪz/ *verb*. Also **-ise**. M17.
[ORIGIN Old French & mod. French *agrandiss-* lengthened stem of *agrandir* prob. from Italian *aggrandire*, from Latin *grandis* GRAND *adjective*[1]; assim. to verbs in -IZE.]
1 *verb trans.* Increase, magnify, intensify. Now *rare* in *gen.* sense. M17.
†**2** *verb intrans.* Become greater. M17–E18.
3 *verb trans.* Increase the power, wealth, or rank of. L17.

J. YEATS Venice was aggrandized by this traffic.

4 *verb trans.* Cause to appear greater than the reality. L17.

R. SHILTS He hoped to aggrandize himself by dying a hero's death.

■ **aggrandi'zation** *noun* (now *rare*) = AGGRANDIZEMENT M17. **aggrandizer** *noun* M18.

aggrandizement /ə'grandɪzm(ə)nt/ *noun*. Also **-ise-**. M17.
[ORIGIN French *agrandissement*: see AGGRANDIZE, -MENT.]
1 The action of aggrandizing. M17.
2 The state or condition of being aggrandized. M18.

†**aggrate** *verb trans.* L16.
[ORIGIN Italian †*aggratare* (Florio, now *aggradare*), from *a* AG- + *grato* pleasing: cf. AGREE.]
1 Gratify. L16–M18.
2 Thank. Only in M17.

†**aggravate** *adjective*. L15.
[ORIGIN Latin *aggravatus* pa. pple, formed as AGGRAVATE *verb*: see -ATE[2].]
1 Weighed down (*lit. & fig.*). L15–E16.
2 Under ecclesiastical censure. Only in L15.
3 Made more serious as an offence. M16–M18.

aggravate /'agrəveɪt/ *verb trans.* M16.
[ORIGIN Latin *aggravat-* pa. ppl stem of *aggravare* from *ad* AG- + *gravare*, from *gravis* heavy (prob. through Old French & mod. French *aggraver*): see -ATE[3].]
†**1** Load (someone or something *with*, something heavy or serious *upon*); bring as a charge (*against*). M16–L18.
2 Strengthen, increase, or magnify. Now usu., increase the gravity of (something bad, an offence, etc.). M16.

Independent on Sunday Climate change may have aggravated the problem.

3 Exaggerate. *obsolete* exc. as an extension of sense 2. M16.
4 Exasperate or annoy (a person). *colloq.* L16.

G. DALY The family maverick, the scapegrace who worried and aggravated his parents.

■ **aggravated** *adjective* (**a**) *colloq.* exasperated, annoyed; (**b**) *LAW* (of an offence) made more serious by attendant circumstances; (of a penalty) made more severe in recognition of the seriousness of an offence: E17. **aggravating** *adjective* that aggravates; *colloq.* exasperating, irritating: M17. **aggravatingly** *adverb* L17. **aggravator** *noun* L16.

aggravation /agrə'veɪʃ(ə)n/ *noun*. L15.
[ORIGIN French from medieval Latin *aggravatio(n-)*, formed as AGGRAVATE *verb*: see -ATION.]
†**1** Oppression. Only in L15.
2 *ROMAN CATHOLIC CHURCH*. An ecclesiastical censure which if repeated can lead to excommunication. M16.
3 The act of increasing or the fact of being increased in gravity or seriousness; a circumstance which increases the gravity of something bad. M16.

Harper's Magazine The wetting caused a fatal aggravation of his gout.

†**4** Exaggeration. E17–M18.
†**5** Accusation. M–L17.
6 The act of irritating, or the state of being irritated; aggressive behaviour; trouble. *colloq.* L19.

L. GOLDING If I should have a son, I should not give him such aggravation.

aggregate /'agrɪgət, -geɪt/ *adjective & noun*. LME.
[ORIGIN Latin *aggregatus* pa. pple, formed as AGGREGATE *verb*: see -ATE[2].]
▸ **A** *adjective*. **1** (Orig. *pple*.) Collected into one body. LME.
2 Constituted by the collection of many particles or units into one body; collective, total. E17.

J. K. GALBRAITH A fall in the aggregate demand . . for buying the output of the economy.

corporation aggregate: see CORPORATION 2.

†**3** *GRAMMAR*. Collective. L17–M18.
4 *TAXONOMY*. That is an aggregate (see sense B.4 below). L19.
▸ **B** *noun*. **1** Sum total. LME. ▸**b** ***on aggregate***, after the calculation of the total score of a player or team in a fixture comprising more than one game or round. E20.

b N. HORNBY In the second game Allen scored again early on, so Spurs were 2–0 up on aggregate.

in aggregate, **in the aggregate** as a whole.

2 A complex whole, mass, or body formed by the union of numerous units or particles; an assemblage. LME.
3 **a** A material, esp. a rock, consisting of fragments or particles grouped or loosely held together. L18. ▸**b** Sand, gravel, or the like used in making concrete etc. L19.
4 *TAXONOMY*. A group of several species elsewhere treated as one species. Cf. SEGREGATE *noun*. M19.
■ **aggregately** *adverb* collectively, in the aggregate M18.

aggregate /'agrɪgeɪt/ *verb*. LME.
[ORIGIN Latin *aggregat-* pa. ppl stem of *aggregare*, from *ad* AG- + *greg-*, *grex* flock: see -ATE[3].]
1 *verb trans. & intrans.* Gather into one whole, mass. LME.
2 *verb trans.* Unite (an individual) *to* an association or company; add as a member. M17.
3 *verb trans.* Amount to (a specified total). *colloq.* M19.
■ **aggregable** *adjective* able to be aggregated (*with*) L16. **aggregator** *noun* (**a**) one who joins himself or herself to something; an adherent; (**b**) a collector or compiler; (**c**) *COMPUTING* (a service providing) a gateway or other device that collects and distributes services to users, organizing this information thematically: M16.

aggregation /agrɪ'geɪʃ(ə)n/ *noun*. LME.
[ORIGIN medieval Latin *aggregatio(n-)*, formed as AGGREGATE *verb*, or from French †*aggrégation* (now *agr-*): see -ATION.]
1 The action of aggregating, or of adding one particle *to* an amount; the state of being aggregated. LME.
2 A whole or mass formed by aggregating items. M16.

aggregative /'agrɪgətɪv/ *adjective*. LME.
[ORIGIN In isolated early use from medieval Latin *aggregativus*; later from French *agrégatif*, *-ive*: see AGGREGATE *verb*, -ATIVE.]
†**1** *MEDICINE*. Having the tendency to close wounds. Only in LME.
2 Of or pertaining to aggregation. M17.
3 Having the tendency to collect particulars into wholes or particles into masses. E18.
4 Associative, social. *rare*. M19.

aggregometer /agrɪ'gɒmɪtə/ *noun*. L20.
[ORIGIN from AGGREGATION + -OMETER.]
An instrument for measuring the rate or degree of spontaneous aggregation of blood platelets.

aggress /ə'grɛs/ *verb*. L16.
[ORIGIN French †*aggresser* (Old French *agr-*) from Latin *aggress-* pa. ppl stem of *aggredi* attack, from *ad* AG- + *gradi* proceed, step.]
†**1** *verb intrans.* Approach. Only in L16.
2 *verb trans.* Attack, assault. M17.
3 *verb intrans.* Make an attack (*on*); begin a quarrel or war (*against*). E18.

aggression /ə'grɛʃ(ə)n/ *noun*. E17.
[ORIGIN French *agression* or Latin *aggressio(n-)*, from *aggress-*: see AGGRESS, -ION.]
1 An unprovoked attack; an assault. Now *rare*. E17.

SIR W. SCOTT An unjust aggression upon their ancient liberties. H. MACMILLAN Egypt had been the victim of an aggression by Israel.

2 The act of beginning a quarrel or war. E18.

G. B. SHAW The protection of Ireland against foreign aggression.

INDIRECT ***aggression***.

3 Behaviour intended to injure another person or animal. **E20.** ▸**b** Self-assertion, forcefulness. **M20.**

A. STORR The most deplorable manifestations of aggression share identical roots with valuable and essential parts of human endeavour.

aggressive /əˈɡrɛsɪv/ *adjective.* **E19.**
[**ORIGIN** from Latin *aggress-* (see **AGGRESS**) + **-IVE**. Cf. French *agressif*, *-ive*.]
1 Of or pertaining to aggression; offensive. **E19.**

E. A. FREEMAN An aggressive war, as distinguished from mere plundering inroads.

2 Disposed to attack others; characterized by aggression (sense 3). **M19.** ▸**b** Self-assertive, forceful. Chiefly *N. Amer.* **M20.**

N. MAILER If he were aggressive, he would swear at her. **b** P. ROTH An ad promising high commissions to aggressive salesmen.

3 Of a chemical: strongly corrosive, promoting corrosion. **M20.**
4 Of a disease or condition: developing or spreading very rapidly within the body. **L20.**
■ **aggreˈssivity** *noun* aggressive quality, aggressiveness **M20.** **aggressively** *adverb* **E19.** **aggressiveness** *noun* **M19.**

aggressor /əˈɡrɛsə/ *noun.* **M17.**
[**ORIGIN** Late Latin, formed as **AGGRESSIVE**: see **-OR**. Cf. French *agresseur*.]
A person who makes an assault or unprovoked attack; the person or nation beginning a quarrel or war.

attrib.: GEORGE VI To continue the fight against the aggressor nations.

aggri *noun* var. of **AGGRY**.

aggrievance /əˈɡriːv(ə)ns/ *noun.* Now *rare* or *obsolete.* **LME.**
[**ORIGIN** Old French *agrevance*, formed as **AGGRIEVE**. Spelling assim. to **AGGRIEVE**.]
†**1** A hardship or burden; a grievance. **LME–M18.**
†**2** Aggravation, making more serious. Only in **E16.**
3 The action of aggrieving or troubling; oppression. **L16.**

aggrieve /əˈɡriːv/ *verb trans.* Now *rare* (exc. as **AGGRIEVED**) or *obsolete.* **ME.**
[**ORIGIN** Old French *agrever* make heavier, ult. from Latin *aggravare*: see **AGGRAVATE** *verb*. Spelling assim. to **GRIEVE** *verb*.]
1 Grieve, distress; oppress, treat unfairly. **ME.**
†**2** Aggravate, make more serious. Only in **16.**
■ **aggrievement** *noun* **M19.**

aggrieved /əˈɡriːvd/ *adjective.* **ME.**
[**ORIGIN** from **AGGRIEVE** + **-ED**[1].]
†**1** Distressed, troubled, grieved. **ME–L16.**
†**2** Aggravated, made more serious. **E–M16.**
†**3** Injured physically. **L16–L18.**
4 Wronged, having a grievance; feeling resentment at having been unfairly treated. **L16.**

I. M. LEWIS He shall pay . . five camels to the aggrieved party. I. T. BOTHAM They were even more aggrieved when Jock was appointed liaison officer at the club.

■ **aggrievedly** /-vɪdli/ *adjective* **L19.**

aggro /ˈaɡrəʊ/ *noun. colloq.* Also **agro**. **M20.**
[**ORIGIN** Abbreviation of **AGGRAVATION** or **AGGRESSION**: see **-O**.]
Deliberate troublemaking; aggression; aggravation.

aggroup /əˈɡruːp/ *verb trans. & intrans.* Now *rare.* **L17.**
[**ORIGIN** French *agrouper*, from Italian *aggroppare*, from *groppa* group.]
Form into a group or groups.
■ **aggroupment** *noun* **M19.**

aggry /ˈaɡri/ *adjective & noun.* Also **-ri**. **E18.**
[**ORIGIN** Prob. from an African lang.]
(Designating) a type of ancient variegated glass bead found buried in the ground in Ghana.

agha *noun* var. of **AGA** *noun*[1].

aghast /əˈɡɑːst/ *adjective.* **LME.**
[**ORIGIN** Var. of *agast* pa. pple & ppl adjective of **AGAST** *verb*, infl. by *ghost* etc.]
Terrified; struck with amazement. (Foll. by *at* the object, *with* the emotion; *to do*.)
■ **aghastness** *noun* the state of being aghast, horror **L19.**

†**aghast** *verb* var. of **AGAST**.

agila /ˈaɡɪlə/ *noun.* Also **aguila**. **L16.**
[**ORIGIN** Portuguese *aguila* from Tamil *akil*. Cf. **AGALLOCHUM**.]
Aloes wood. Also ***agila wood***.

agile /ˈadʒʌɪl/ *adjective.* **LME.**
[**ORIGIN** Old French & mod. French from Latin *agilis*, from *agere* do: see **-ILE**.]
Quick-moving, nimble, active.
agile gibbon a gibbon, *Hylobates agilis*, which has variable coloration and is found in the Malay peninsula, Borneo, and Sumatra.
■ **agilely** *adverb* **L19.**

agility /əˈdʒɪlɪti/ *noun.* **LME.**
[**ORIGIN** Old French & mod. French *agilité* from Latin *agilitat-*, *-tas*, formed as **AGILE**: see **-ITY**.]
The quality of being agile; readiness, nimbleness.

agin *preposition* see **AGAIN** *preposition.*

aging *pres. pple & verbal noun* see **AGE** *verb.*

agio /ˈadʒɪəʊ/ *noun.* Pl. **-os**. **L17.**
[**ORIGIN** Italian *ag(g)io*.]
1 The percentage charged on the exchange of one currency, or form of money, into another that is more valuable; the excess value of one currency over another. **L17.**
2 *loosely.* Money-changing. **E19.**

agiotage /ˈadʒətɪdʒ/ *noun.* **L18.**
[**ORIGIN** French, from *agioter* speculate, from *agio* formed as **AGIO**: see **-AGE**.]
Money-changing business; speculation in stocks; stock-jobbing.

agist /əˈdʒɪst/ *verb.* **LME.**
[**ORIGIN** Old French, Anglo-Norman *agister*, formed as **A-**[5] + *gister*, from *giste* lodging.]
†**1** *verb trans.* Use or grant use of (land etc.) for pasture for a stated time or at a certain rate. **LME–E17.**
2 *verb trans.* Orig., admit (livestock) for a stated time into a forest. Later, take in (livestock) to remain and feed at a certain rate. **L15.**
3 *verb intrans.* Of livestock: remain and feed for a stated time etc. *rare.* **L16.**
4 *verb trans.* Charge (land or its owner) with any public burden. **L17.**

agister /əˈdʒɪstə/ *noun.* Also **-or**. **L15.**
[**ORIGIN** Anglo-Norman *agistour*, formed as **AGIST**: see **-ER**[1].]
A person who agists or supervises the agistment of livestock.

agistment /əˈdʒɪs(t)m(ə)nt/ *noun.* **LME.**
[**ORIGIN** Old French *agistement*, formed as **AGIST**: see **-MENT**.]
1 The action or process of agisting livestock. **LME.**
2 A rate levied upon the owner or occupier of pasture-land. Esp. in ***agistment tithe*** (*hist.*). **E16.**
3 The rate levied or profit made by agisting another's livestock. **L16.**
4 The herbage of a forest, or the right to it. **L16.**

agistor *noun* var. of **AGISTER**.

agitant /ˈadʒɪt(ə)nt/ *noun. rare.* **M17.**
[**ORIGIN** French, use as noun of pres. pple of *agiter* stir up from Latin *agitare*: see **AGITATE** *verb*, **-ANT**[1].]
A person who agitates; a thing which causes agitation.

†**agitate** *adjective* (orig. *pa. pple*). Chiefly *Scot.* **LME–L17.**
[**ORIGIN** Latin *agitatus* pa. pple, formed as **AGITATE** *verb*: see **-ATE**[2].]
Agitated.

agitate /ˈadʒɪteɪt/ *verb.* **LME.**
[**ORIGIN** Latin *agitat-* pa. ppl stem of *agitare* frequentative of *agere* drive: see **-ATE**[3].]
▸**I** Move, excite.
†**1** *verb trans.* Drive away. Only in **LME.**
2 *verb trans.* Disturb, perturb, excite (the thoughts, feelings, etc.). **L16.**

D. J. ENRIGHT Too much coffee agitates the nerves.

3 *verb trans.* Move to and fro, shake (something material). **L16.**

B. PYM He agitated his tea-bag with a spoon.

†**4** *verb trans.* Communicate action or motion to. **E17–M18.**

J. THOMSON Who . . surrounds, informs, and agitates the whole.

5 *verb trans.* Perturb or excite (a person etc.) in mind or feelings. **E19.**

W. S. CHURCHILL Constant bickering agitated the two countries.

▸**II** Be active or busy.
†**6** *verb trans. & intrans.* Manage as an agent. Only in **M17.**
7 *verb trans.* Discuss, debate; push forward as a plan. **M17.**

BURKE Before an appeal was so much as agitated.

8 *verb trans.* Revolve in the mind; contrive busily. *arch.* **M17.**
9 *verb intrans.* Keep a political or other object continually under discussion, keep up an agitation (*for* or *against*). **E19.**
■ **agitatedly** *adverb* in an agitated manner **E19.** **agitating** *ppl adjective* that agitates; *ENGLISH HISTORY* acting as an agitator in the Parliamentary army: **L17.** **agitatingly** *adverb* **E19.** **agitative** *adjective* tending to agitate **E16.**

agitation /adʒɪˈteɪʃ(ə)n/ *noun.* **M16.**
[**ORIGIN** French, or Latin *agitatio(n-)*, formed as **AGITATE** *verb*: see **-ATION**.]
†**1** Action, exercise of activity. **M16–E18.**
2 The action of moving to and fro; brisk stirring or disturbance of a liquid etc. **L16.**
3 Consideration, debate, or discussion of a matter. **L16.**
4 The state of being agitated; anxiety or nervous excitement. **E17.**

D. HUME His whole body was thrown into agitation.

5 The arousing of public concern about an issue and pressing for action on it; *Indian* a public demonstration. **E19.**

Fortune The problem created by the agitation for a Greater Syria.

■ **agitational** *adjective* **M19.**

agitato /adʒɪˈtɑːtəʊ/ *adverb, adjective, & noun.* **E19.**
[**ORIGIN** Italian.]
MUSIC. ▸**A** *adverb & adjective.* A direction: in an agitated manner. **E19.**
▸**B** *noun.* Pl. **-ti** /-ti/, **-tos**. A passage (to be) played or sung in an agitated manner. *rare.* **E19.**

agitator /ˈadʒɪteɪtə/ *noun.* **M17.**
[**ORIGIN** Latin *agitator*, formed as **AGITATE** *verb*: see **-OR**.]
1 *ENGLISH HISTORY.* A delegate of the private soldiers of the Parliamentary army 1647–9. (Also alt. to **ADJUTATOR**.) **M17.**
2 A person who agitates, esp. politically. **M18.**
3 A device for stirring, shaking, or mixing. **E19.**

agitprop /ˈadʒɪtprɒp, ˈaɡ-/ *noun.* Also **A-**. **E20.**
[**ORIGIN** Russian, from *agit(atsiya* agitation + *prop(aganda* propaganda.]
Political (orig. Soviet Communist) propaganda; the system or activity of disseminating this.

aglare /əˈɡlɛː/ *adverb & pred. adjective.* **L19.**
[**ORIGIN** from **A-**[2] + **GLARE** *noun*[1].]
In a glare, glaring.

agleam /əˈɡliːm/ *adverb & pred. adjective.* **L19.**
[**ORIGIN** from **A-**[2] + **GLEAM** *noun*[1].]
Gleaming.

aglet /ˈaɡlət/ *noun.* Also **ai-** /ˈeɪ-/. **LME.**
[**ORIGIN** Old French & mod. French **AIGUILLETTE**.]
1 The metal tag of a lace. **LME.**
2 A metallic tag, pendant, or spangle, worn as an ornament. **E16.** ▸**b** *spec.* A tagged point hanging from the shoulder upon the breast of some uniforms. Now usu. **AIGUILLETTE**. **M19.**
3 A catkin. **L16.**

agley /əˈɡleɪ, əˈɡliː/ *adverb & pred. adjective. Scot.* **L18.**
[**ORIGIN** from **A-**[2] + **GLEY** *verb*.]
Askew, awry.

aglimmer /əˈɡlɪmə/ *adverb & pred. adjective.* **E19.**
[**ORIGIN** from **A-**[2] + **GLIMMER** *noun*[1].]
Glimmering.

aglisten /əˈɡlɪs(ə)n/ *adverb & pred. adjective.* **L19.**
[**ORIGIN** from **A-**[2] + **GLISTEN** *verb*.]
Glistening.

aglitter /əˈɡlɪtə/ *adverb & pred. adjective.* **E19.**
[**ORIGIN** from **A-**[2] + **GLITTER** *noun*.]
In a glitter, glittering.

aglomerular /eɪɡlɒˈmɛrʊlə, a-/ *adjective.* **E20.**
[**ORIGIN** from **A-**[10] + **GLOMERULAR**.]
Chiefly *ICHTHYOLOGY.* Lacking (kidney) glomeruli (as certain fishes).

agloo *noun* see **IGLOO**.

aglow /əˈɡləʊ/ *adverb & pred. adjective.* **E19.**
[**ORIGIN** from **A-**[2] + **GLOW** *noun*.]
In a glow (of warmth, colour, excitement, etc.).

aglu *noun* see **IGLOO**.

aglycone /əˈɡlʌɪkəʊn/ *noun.* Also (see below) **aglu-** /əˈɡluː-/. **E20.**
[**ORIGIN** German *Aglykon*, formed as **A-**[10] + **GLYCO-** + **-ONE**.]
CHEMISTRY. The compound remaining when the sugar is removed from a glycoside. Also called ***aglucone*** when the sugar is glucose.

aglyphous /ˈaɡlɪfəs/ *adjective.* **L19.**
[**ORIGIN** from **A-**[10] + Greek *gluphē* carving + **-OUS**.]
ZOOLOGY. Of a snake's tooth: solid, without a hollow or groove for venom. Of a snake: lacking fangs; not venomous.
■ **aglyph** *noun* an aglyphous snake **E20.**

AGM *abbreviation.*
Annual general meeting.

agma /ˈaɡmə/ *noun.* **M20.**
[**ORIGIN** Late Greek from Greek = fragment.]
The velar nasal consonant /ŋ/; a letter or symbol representing this.

agnail /ˈaɡneɪl/ *noun.*
[**ORIGIN** Old English *angnægl*, corresp. to Old Frisian *ongneil*, Old High German *ungnagel* (German dial. *Anneglen*, *Einnegeln*), from a Germanic base meaning 'compressed, tight, painful' + as **NAIL** *noun*. The application of the word has been much infl. by popular etym.]
†**1** A corn on the toe or foot. **OE–L19.**
2 A painful swelling around the toenail or fingernail. **L16.**
3 A strip of torn skin at the root of the fingernail, a hangnail. **M19.**

agnamed /ˈaɡneɪmd/ *pa. pple & ppl adjective.* Chiefly *Scot.* **M17.**
[**ORIGIN** from **AG-** + *named*, from **NAME** *verb*, on the analogy of **AGNOMEN**.]
Styled or called, in addition to the given personal name and surname; nicknamed.

agnate /ˈaɡneɪt/ *noun & adjective.* **L15.**
[**ORIGIN** Latin *agnatus*, from *ad* **AG-** + *(g)natus* born.]
▸**A** *noun.* Chiefly *LAW.* A descendant, esp. by male links, from the same male ancestor. Cf. **COGNATE**. **L15.**
▸**B** *adjective.* Descended from the same male ancestor, esp. by male links; of the same clan or nation; *fig.* akin. **E17.**
■ **agnatic** /əɡˈnatɪk/ *adjective* pertaining to agnates; related on the father's side: **M18.** **agˈnation** *noun* descent from a common

male ancestor, esp. through male links only; kinship by descent: L16.

agnathan /agˈneɪθ(ə)n/ *noun & adjective*. M20.
[ORIGIN from mod. Latin *Agnatha* (see below), from Greek A-[10] + *gnathos* jaw: see -AN.]
▸ **A** *noun*. A primitive jawless vertebrate of the superclass Agnatha (or Marsipobranchii), which includes the lampreys, the hagfishes, and many fossil fishes. M20.
▸ **B** *adjective*. Of, pertaining to, or characteristic of Agnatha. L20.

agnise *verb* var. of AGNIZE.

agnition /əgˈnɪʃ(ə)n/ *noun*. Now *rare*. LME.
[ORIGIN Latin *agnitio(n-)*, from *agnit-* pa. ppl stem of *agnoscere*, from *ad* AG- + *(g)noscere* know: see -ION.]
Recognition, acknowledgement.

agnize /əgˈnʌɪz/ *verb trans. arch.* Also **-ise**. M16.
[ORIGIN from Latin *agnoscere* (see AGNITION) after *cognize*, *recognize*: see -IZE.]
†**1** Recognize in any capacity, own *for*, *as*, *to be*, etc. M16–M18.
2 Recognize the existence of, confess. M16.
†**3** Own the authority or claims of. L16–M18.
4 Recognize, remember. E17.

Agnoetae /agnəʊˈiːtiː/ *noun pl.* M18.
[ORIGIN medieval Latin *agnoetae* from late Greek *agnoētai*, from *agnoein* be ignorant.]
ECCLESIASTICAL HISTORY. A Monophysite sect of the 6th cent. holding that Jesus was ignorant of some things.
■ **Agnoite** /ˈagnəʊʌɪt/, **Agnoete** /-iːt/ *nouns* a member of the Agnoetae L16.

agnomen /agˈnəʊmɛn/ *noun*. M17.
[ORIGIN Latin, from *ad* AG- + *(g)nomen* name.]
A name given or acquired during the course of one's life, a nickname; ROMAN HISTORY a fourth name occas. given as an honour.

agnominate /agˈnɒmɪneɪt/ *verb trans. rare*. Also **annom-** /aˈnɒm-/. L16.
[ORIGIN Latin *agnominat-* pa. ppl stem of *agnominare*, formed as AGNOMEN; forms with *ann-* from French from medieval Latin: see -ATE[3].]
Give an agnomen to, call, nickname.

agnomination /əgnɒmɪˈneɪʃ(ə)n/ *noun*. Now *rare*. Also **annom-** /ənɒm-/. M16.
[ORIGIN Latin *agnominatio(n-)*, formed as AGNOMEN; forms with *ann-* from French from medieval Latin: see -ATION.]
RHETORIC. **1** (An example of) paronomasia. M16.
2 (An example of) alliteration. M16.

agnosia /əgˈnəʊsɪə/ *noun*. E20.
[ORIGIN Greek *agnōsia* ignorance, from A-[10] + *gnōsis* knowledge: -IA[1].]
MEDICINE. A diminished ability to recognize objects by one or other of the senses.
visual agnosia: see VISUAL *adjective*.
■ **agnosic** *adjective* pertaining to or affected with agnosia M20.

agnostic /agˈnɒstɪk/ *noun & adjective*. M19.
[ORIGIN from A-[10] + GNOSTIC.]
▸ **A** *noun*. A person who holds the view that nothing can be known of the existence of God or of anything beyond material phenomena. Also, a person who is uncertain or non-committal about a particular thing. M19.
▸ **B** *adjective*. Of or pertaining to agnostics or agnosticism. L19.
— NOTE: Coined by T. H. Huxley (OED); but occurs earlier in a letter of 1859 from Isabel Arundell.
■ **agnostical** *adjective* L19. **agnostically** *adverb* L19. **agnosticism** /-sɪz(ə)m/ *noun* the doctrine or tenets of agnostics, an agnostic attitude L19.

Agnus /ˈagnʊs, -nəs, ˈanjʊs/ *noun*. LME.
[ORIGIN Abbreviation.]
= AGNUS DEI.

agnus castus /ˈagnəs ˈkastəs/ *noun phr.* Now *rare* or *obsolete* exc. (with hyphen) as mod. Latin specific epithet. LME.
[ORIGIN Latin, from *agnus* from Greek *agnos*, name of the tree, conf. with *hagnos* chaste, + *castus* chaste.]
The chaste tree, *Vitex agnus-castus*.

Agnus Dei /ˈagnʊs ˈdeiː, *in sense 1 also* ˈanjʊs; ˈagnəs ˈdiːʌɪ/ *noun phr.* LME.
[ORIGIN Latin = Lamb of God.]
CHRISTIAN CHURCH. **1** Part of the Mass beginning with the words *Agnus Dei*; a musical setting of this. LME.
2 A figure of a lamb bearing a cross or flag, as an emblem of Christ. LME. ▸**b** A cake of wax stamped with such a figure and blessed by the Pope. L16.

ago /əˈgəʊ/ *ppl adjective & adverb*. Also (*arch.*) **agone** /əˈgɒn/. ME.
[ORIGIN pa. pple of AGO *verb*, orig. in use as adjective qualifying a noun of time.]
1 *adjective* (now always *postpositive* and also interpreted as *adverb*). Past, gone by. ME.

> SHAKES. *Twel. N.* He's drunk, . . an hour agone. DICKENS Ay, a goodish bit ago. E. BISHOP A slight landslide occurred . . / about an hour ago.

2 *adverb*. In ***long ago*** (†occas. with other adverbs with similar meaning): long since. ME.

†**ago** *verb intrans.* Infl. as GO *verb*. Pa. t. usu. **awent**, pa. pple usu. **agone**. OE.
[ORIGIN from A-[1] + GO *verb*.]
1 Go on, proceed. OE–ME.
2 Of time: pass. OE–M16.
3 Go away. ME–L17.

agog /əˈgɒg/ *adverb & pred. adjective*. M16.
[ORIGIN Prob. (with substitution of A *preposition*[1]) repr. late Old French *en gogues*, from *en* in + pl. of *gogue* merriment, pleasantry.]
In eager readiness, expectant.

agogic /əˈgɒdʒɪk/ *adjective & noun*. L19.
[ORIGIN German *agogisch*, from Greek *agōgos* leading, from *agein* to lead: see -IC.]
MUSIC. ▸**A** *adjective*. Designating or pertaining to accent effected by lengthening the time value of the note. L19.
▸ **B** *noun*. In *pl.* (treated as *sing.*) The theory or use of agogic accents; the deliberate modification of time values in a musical performance. L19.

a gogo /ə ˈgəʊgəʊ/ *adverbial & postpositive adjectival phr. colloq.* M20.
[ORIGIN French *à gogo*.]
In abundance, galore.

agon /ˈagəʊn/ *noun*. Pl. **agones** /əˈgəʊniːz/. E17.
[ORIGIN Greek *agōn* contest.]
GREEK HISTORY. **1** A public celebration of games; a contest for the prize at the games or *transf.* elsewhere. E17.
2 A verbal contest between two characters in a play. L19.

agonal /ˈag(ə)n(ə)l/ *adjective*. L18.
[ORIGIN Sense 1 from AGON, sense 2 from AGONY: see -AL[1].]
1 Pertaining to an agon. L18.
2 Pertaining to or occurring during agony, esp. death agony. E19.

agone *ppl adjective & adverb* see AGO *ppl adjective & adverb*.

†**agone** *verb pa. pple*: see AGO *verb*.

agones *noun* pl. of AGON.

agonic /əˈgɒnɪk/ *adjective*. M19.
[ORIGIN from Greek *agōn(i)os*, from *a-* A-[10] + *gōnia* angle, + -IC.]
agonic line, the imaginary line joining points on the earth's surface where the magnetic declination is zero.

agonise *verb* var. of AGONIZE.

agonism /ˈagənɪz(ə)m/ *noun*. M17.
[ORIGIN In sense 1 from Greek *agōnisma*, from *agōnizesthai* (see AGONIZE); in sense 2 from AGONIST: see -ISM.]
1 A contest; a prize. *rare* (only in Dicts.). M17.
2 BIOCHEMISTRY. The action of an agonist (AGONIST 4). L20.

agonist /ˈagənɪst/ *noun*. E17.
[ORIGIN Greek *agōnistēs* contestant, formed as AGON: see -IST.]
1 A person who competes for prizes. *rare*. E17.
2 A protagonist in a drama (*lit.* & *fig.*). E20.
3 PHYSIOLOGY. A muscle whose contraction is directly responsible for the movement of a part. Cf. ANTAGONIST 2. E20.
4 BIOCHEMISTRY. A chemical which combines with a receptor and initiates a physiological response. Cf. ANTAGONIST 3. M20.

agonistes /agəˈnɪstiːz/ *postpositive adjective*. M20.
[ORIGIN formed as AGONIST.]
Used to designate an agonist, in allus. to Milton's *Samson Agonistes*.

agonistic /agəˈnɪstɪk/ *adjective*. M17.
[ORIGIN Late Latin *agonisticus* from Greek *agōnistikos*, formed as AGONIST: see -IC.]
1 Pertaining to (orig. ancient Greek) athletic contests or to athletic feats. M17.
2 RHETORIC. Polemic, combative. M17.
3 Striving for effect. M19.
4 ZOOLOGY. Of animal behaviour: associated with conflict between individuals. M20.
■ **agonistical** *adjective* (now *rare*) = AGONISTIC 1, 2 M17. **agonistically** *adverb* (*rare*) polemically M19.

agonize /ˈagənʌɪz/ *verb*. Also **-ise**. L16.
[ORIGIN French *agoniser* or late Latin *agonizare* (after Greek *agōnizesthai*, formed as AGON): see -IZE.]
1 *verb trans.* Subject to agony. L16.
2 *verb intrans.* Suffer agony; writhe in anguish. L16.
3 *verb intrans.* Contend in the arena; wrestle. Now chiefly *fig.* L16.
4 *verb intrans.* Worry intensely *about*, *over*, etc.; strive intensely for effect. M19.

> *Woman's Own* You agonised for days over whether or not to cancel it.

■ **agonized** *ppl adjective* subjected to or expressing agony L16. **agonizedly** /-zɪdli/ *adverb* M19. **agonizing** *ppl adjective* causing agony; expressing agony; *arch.* suffering agony: L16. **agonizingly** *adverb* E19.

agonothete /əˈgəʊnəθiːt/ *noun*. Also **-thet** /-θɛt/. E17.
[ORIGIN Greek *agōnothetēs*, formed as AGON + *thetēs* disposer.]
GREEK HISTORY. A director of the public games.

agony /ˈagəni/ *noun*. LME.
[ORIGIN Old French & mod. French *agonie* or late Latin *agonia* from Greek *agōnia*, formed as AGON: see -Y[3].]
1 Extreme mental suffering; a paroxysm of grief or anguish. LME. ▸**b** A paroxysm of pleasure. *arch.* E18.

> COLERIDGE Never a saint took pity on My soul in agony. **b** POPE With cries and agonies of wild delight.

2 *spec.* The mental anguish of Jesus in Gethsemane. LME.
3 The convulsive throes or pangs of death. Exc. MEDICINE now *rare* without specification. LME.
death agony, ***last agony***, ***mortal agony***, etc.
4 Extreme bodily suffering; writhing or throes of the body produced by this. E17.

> MILTON Here in perpetual agony and pain. W. OWEN We hear the mad gusts tugging on the wire, Like twitching agonies of men.

5 A severe struggle or contest. (Usu. with suggestion of sense 4.) L17.
— COMB. & PHRASES: **agony aunt** *colloq.* a female writer of an agony column (sense b); **agony column** (**a**) a personal column of a newspaper etc.; (**b**) a newspaper etc. feature of readers' questions about personal difficulties, with answers and advice; **agony uncle** *colloq.* a male writer of an agony column (sense b). ***pile on the agony***: see PILE *verb*[2].

agora /ˈagɒrə/ *noun*[1]. Pl. **-rae** /-riː/, **-rai** /-rʌɪ/, **-ras**. L16.
[ORIGIN Greek.]
GREEK HISTORY. An assembly; a place of assembly, *esp.* a marketplace.

agora /agəˈrɑː/ *noun*[2]. Pl. **-rot** /-rəʊt/, **-roth** /-rəʊθ/. M20.
[ORIGIN Hebrew *ʾăgōrāh* a small coin.]
A monetary unit of Israel, equal to one-hundredth of a shekel (initially of a pound or lira).

agoraphobia /ag(ə)rəˈfəʊbɪə/ *noun*. L19.
[ORIGIN from Greek AGORA *noun*[1] + -PHOBIA.]
Irrational fear of crowded open or public spaces.
■ **ˈagoraphobe** *noun* = AGORAPHOBIC *noun* M20. **agoraphobic** *adjective & noun* (a person) affected with agoraphobia; pertaining to agoraphobia: L19.

agorot, **agoroth** *nouns* pls. of AGORA *noun*[2].

agouti /əˈguːti/ *noun*. Also **aguti**. M16.
[ORIGIN French, or Spanish *aguti* from Tupi-Guarani *akuti*.]
1 A long-legged rodent belonging to the genus *Dasyprocta*, native to Central and South America. M16.
2 (An animal having) a fur type in which each hair has alternate bands of light and dark pigmentation, usu. producing a grizzled or salt-and-pepper appearance. L19.

AGR *abbreviation*.
Advanced gas-cooled (nuclear) reactor.

agraffe /əˈgraf/ *noun*. M17.
[ORIGIN French *agrafe*, from *agrafer* to hook.]
A hook which fastens to a ring and is used as a clasp.

agrammatism /əˈgramətɪz(ə)m/ *noun*. L19.
[ORIGIN from Greek *agrammatos* illiterate, formed as A-[10] + *grammata* letters, + -ISM.]
MEDICINE. An inability to form sentences grammatically, as a symptom of cerebral disease or mental illness.

agranulocytosis /əˌgranjʊlə(ʊ)sʌɪˈtəʊsɪs/ *noun*. Pl. **-toses** /-ˈtəʊsiːz/. E20.
[ORIGIN from A-[10] + GRANULOCYTE + -OSIS.]
MEDICINE. A deficiency of granulocytes in the blood, causing increased vulnerability to infection.
■ **agranulocytic** /-ˈsɪtɪk/ *adjective* E20.

agrapha *noun* pl. of AGRAPHON.

agraphia /əˈgrafɪə/ *noun*. M19.
[ORIGIN from A-[10] + Greek *-graphia* writing.]
MEDICINE. Inability to write, as a symptom of cerebral disease or damage.
■ **agraphic** *adjective* characterized by agraphia L19.

agraphon /ˈagrəfɒn/ *noun*. Pl. **-pha** /-fə/. L19.
[ORIGIN Greek, neut. of *agraphos* unwritten, formed as A-[10], -GRAPH.]
A saying attributed to Jesus but not in the canonical Gospels. Usu. in *pl.*

agrarian /əˈgrɛːrɪən/ *adjective & noun*. E17.
[ORIGIN from Latin *agrarius*, from *agr-*, *ager* land: see -ARIAN.]
▸ **A** *adjective*. **1** ROMAN HISTORY. Designating a law (Latin *Lex agraria*) for the division of conquered lands. E17.
2 Of or pertaining to landed property. E18.
3 Of or pertaining to cultivated land or the cultivation of land. L18.
▸ **B** *noun*. **1** An agrarian law. *rare*. M17.
2 An advocate of the redistribution of landed property. E19.
■ **agrarianism** *noun* (advocacy of or agitation for) the redistribution of landed property or reform of the conditions of tenure of land E19.

agree /əˈgriː/ *verb*. Pa. t. & pple **agreed**. LME.
[ORIGIN Old French & mod. French *agréer* ult. from Latin *ad* AG- + *gratus* pleasing, agreeable. Cf. GREE *noun*[2].]
▸ **I** Please, be pleased.
†**1** *verb trans.* Please. LME–L15.
†**2** *verb trans.* Be pleased with, accept. LME–M17.
▸ **II** Make agreeable or harmonious.
†**3** *verb trans. & intrans.* Pay (a person); settle an account *with*. Only in LME.
4 *verb trans.* Arrange, settle; reach agreement concerning; consent to, approve of. LME.

> SPENSER Some troublous uprore, Whereto he drew in haste it to agree. POPE Did I for this agree The solemn truce?

†**5** *verb trans.* Reconcile (persons), cause to be friends. L15–L17.
6 *verb trans.* Bring into harmony (things that differ; now only discrepant accounts etc.). M17.
▸ **III** Become well-disposed.
7 *verb intrans.* Give consent, accede. (Foll. by *to, to do, that.*) LME.

SHAKES. *1 Hen. VI* Post . . to France; Agree to any covenants. LD MACAULAY He reluctantly agreed . . that some indulgence should be granted. G. B. SHAW They've agreed to come to the breakfast. SCOTT FITZGERALD 'All right,' I agreed, 'I'll be glad to.'

†**8** *verb refl.* Accede, consent *to.* LME–L16.
†**9** *verb intrans.* Accede *to* the opinion of. E16–M17.
▸ **IV** Come into harmony.
10 *verb intrans.* Come into accord as to something; come to terms. (Foll. by †*for* a payment or price; *on, as to,* †*of* a matter or point; *to do* something; or *that.*) LME.
agree to differ, **agree to disagree** no longer try to convince each other.
11 *verb intrans.* Make up differences; become friends. Now *dial.* LME.
▸ **V** Be in harmony.
12 *verb intrans.* Of things: accord (*together*); coincide in any respect (*with*); be consistent (*with,* †*to*). L15.

SHAKES. *Tam. Shr.* At last . . our jarring notes agree. SWIFT The constitution of the English government . . to which the present establishment of the church doth so happily agree. YEATS If his tale agrees with yours, then I am clear.

13 a *verb intrans.* Be of the same mind as to particular points; concur *with* a person *in, on, as to, about, that,* †such *to be.* L15. ▸**b** *verb intrans.* Feel or state one's thoughts to be in accordance (*with* an opinion or statement). M16. ▸**c** *verb trans.* Say in agreement. M19.
a I couldn't agree more, I couldn't agree with you more *colloq.* I am in complete agreement (with you).
14 *verb intrans.* Do well *with*: ▸**a** Of a person: be suited by (a food, climate, etc.). *obsolete* exc. *dial.* E16. ▸**b** Of food, a climate, etc.: suit the constitution of (a person). E17.

a G. BURNET Fagius, not agreeing with this air, died soon after. **b** K. AMIS Spirits don't seem to agree with you.

†**15** *verb intrans.* Be suitable or appropriate *to.* M16–L17.
16 *verb intrans.* Be in sympathy; live or act together harmoniously. (Foll. by *together, with.*) M16.

T. FULLER It is probable that in Noahs Ark the wolf agreed with the lambe.

17 *verb intrans.* GRAMMAR. Have the same number, gender, case, person, etc. (Foll. by *with.*) M16.
■ **agreeance** *noun* (now *rare*) agreement E16. **agreeing** *ppl adjective* †(*a*) according *to*; (*b*) that agree(s) (*with* etc.): E16. **agreeingly** *adverb* (now *rare*) (*a*) in an agreeing manner; †(*b*) according *to*: M16. **agreer** *noun* a person who or thing which agrees M16.

agreeability /əgriːəˈbɪlɪti/ *noun.* LME.
[ORIGIN Isolated early use from Old French *agreableté*, formed as AGREEABLE; re-formed L18 from AGREEABLE: see -ABILITY.]
Agreeableness, esp. of disposition.

agreeable /əˈgriːəb(ə)l/ *adjective, adverb, & noun.* LME.
[ORIGIN Old French & mod. French *agréable*, formed as AGREE: see -ABLE.]
▸ **A** *adjective.* **1** To one's liking; pleasing (*to*). LME.

W. D. HOWELLS I have met there some agreeable women.

make oneself agreeable to behave so as to please (a person).
2 Conformable, corresponding, suitable, consistent. Foll. by *to, unto,* †*with,* or †*absol.* LME.
3 Kindly disposed; willing to agree (*to* a thing, *to do*). Now *colloq.* LME.

THACKERAY If Ann's agreeable, I say ditto.

†**4** Of one mind. L15–E17.
▸ **B** *adverb.* In a way that corresponds *to*; according *to.* *arch.* M16.
▸ **C** *noun.* †**1** An agreeable person or thing. *rare.* E18–E19.
2 *absol.* A pleasing or polite thing. Esp. in ***do the agreeable.*** *arch.* E19.
■ **agreeableness** *noun* †(*a*) conformity (*to*), consistency (*with*); (*b*) pleasingness, pleasantness: M16. **agreeably** *adverb* (*a*) pleasantly; (*b*) in a manner corresponding *to*; in accordance *with*; †(*c*) correspondingly, in the same way: LME.

agreed /əˈgriːd/ *adjective.* LME.
[ORIGIN from AGREE + -ED[1].]
†**1** Made pleasing. Only in LME.
†**2** Pleased, contented. LME–M16.
3 Arranged or settled by common consent. L15. ▸**b** As a rejoinder: consented to, accepted. M16.

Which? Failing to keep to the agreed credit limit.

4 Of two or more parties: holding the same view or opinion on something; united in feeling or sentiment. Often foll. by *on.* M16.

I. RANKIN Are we agreed on that?

agreement /əˈgriːm(ə)nt/ *noun.* LME.
[ORIGIN Old French (mod. *agrément*), formed as AGREE: see -MENT.]
1 An arrangement or mutual understanding. LME.

S. TUROW They had struck some agreement.

conditional agreement: see CONDITIONAL *adjective* 1. ***gentleman's agreement***, ***gentlemen's agreement***: see GENTLEMAN.
2 A legally binding arrangement between two or more parties. LME.

Big Issue A kind of hire purchase agreement.

Net Book Agreement: see NET *adjective*[2] & *adverb.*
3 Mutual conformity of things; harmony, affinity. LME.
†**4** Pleasing; satisfaction. L15–L16.
†**5** Atonement. E–M16.
6 Accordance in sentiment, opinion, action, etc. E16.

I. RANKIN He nodded as if in agreement.

7 GRAMMAR. The condition of having the same number, gender, case, person, etc. M16.
8 In *pl.* = AGRÉMENT 1. Now *rare* or *obsolete.* L17.

agrément /agremɑ̃/ *noun.* Pl. ***-ments***, ***-mens***, (pronounced same). E18.
[ORIGIN French: see AGREEMENT.]
1 In *pl.* Agreeable qualities, circumstances, etc. E18.
2 MUSIC. In *pl.* Grace notes; embellishments. L18.
3 Official approval given to a diplomatic representative of another country. E20.

agrestal /əˈgrɛst(ə)l/ *adjective.* M19.
[ORIGIN formed as AGRESTIC.]
BOTANY. Growing wild in cultivated fields.

agrestial /əˈgrɛstɪəl/ *adjective.* E17.
[ORIGIN formed as AGRESTIC + -AL[1].]
Of, pertaining to, or inhabiting the fields or open country.

agrestic /əˈgrɛstɪk/ *adjective.* E17.
[ORIGIN from Latin *agrestis*, from *agr-*, *ager* field, + -IC.]
Rural, rustic; uncouth.

agribusiness /ˈagrɪbɪznɪs/ *noun.* M20.
[ORIGIN from AGRI(CULTURE + BUSINESS.]
The production, distribution, etc., of farming produce and agricultural equipment and supplies; (any of) the group of industries engaged in this; agriculture as a business using advanced technology.
– COMB.: **agribusinessman** a man who engages in agribusiness.

agrichemical /agrɪˈkɛmɪk(ə)l/ *adjective & noun.* M20.
[ORIGIN from AGRI(CULTURAL + CHEMICAL.]
▸ **A** *adjective.* Agricultural and chemical; of or pertaining to agrochemicals. M20.
▸ **B** *noun.* A chemical used or produced in agribusiness; an agrochemical. M20.

†**agricole** *noun. rare.* M17–L19.
[ORIGIN Old French & mod. French from Latin *agricola*, from *agr-*, *ager* field + *-cola* tenant.]
A farmer; a rustic.
■ †**agricolist** *noun* an agriculturist M–L18. †**agricolous** *adjective* (*joc.*) agricultural: only in 19.

†**agricultor** *noun. rare.* LME–M19.
[ORIGIN Latin, formed as AGRICULTURE + *cultor* tiller.]
A person who cultivates; a farmer.

agriculture /ˈagrɪkʌltʃə/ *noun.* LME.
[ORIGIN French, or Latin *agricultura*, from *agr-*, *ager* field + *cultura* CULTURE *noun.*]
The science or practice of cultivating the soil and rearing animals; farming; occas. *spec.* tillage.
■ **agriˈcultural** *adjective* of or pertaining to agriculture L18. **agriˈculturalist** *noun* a person engaged in agriculture E19. **agriˈculturally** *adverb* with regard to agriculture E19. †**agriculturer** *noun* an agriculturalist E–M19. **agriˈculturist** *noun* (*a*) a person who studies agriculture; (*b*) an agriculturalist: M18.

agrimensorial /ˌagrɪmɛnˈsɔːrɪəl/ *adjective.* L19.
[ORIGIN from Latin *agrimensor*, formed as AGRICULTURE + *mensor* surveyor, + -IAL.]
Of or pertaining to land-surveying.

agrimi /əˈgriːmi/ *noun.* Pl. **-mia** /-mɪə/, **-mis**. M19.
[ORIGIN mod. Greek.]
In Crete and in Minoan art, the wild goat.

agrimony /ˈagrɪməni/ *noun.* LME.
[ORIGIN Early forms from Old French & mod. French *aigremoine*; later mod. form from Latin *agrimonia* misreading for *argemonia* (Pliny, Celsus) from Greek *argemōnē* poppy.]
1 Any plant of the genus *Agrimonia*; esp. *A. eupatoria*, a common perennial bearing spikes of yellow flowers. LME.
2 Any of a number of other plants, esp. = HEMP ***agrimony.*** L16.

agrin /əˈgrɪn/ *adverb & pred. adjective.* E19.
[ORIGIN from A-[2] + GRIN *noun*[2].]
Grinning.

agriology /agrɪˈɒlədʒi/ *noun.* L19.
[ORIGIN from Greek *agrios* wild, savage + -OLOGY.]
The branch of knowledge that deals with the history and customs of non-literate peoples.
■ **agriologist** *noun* L19.

†**agriot** *noun.* Also **eg-**. E16–L19.
[ORIGIN Old French *agriote* (mod. *griotte*).]
A sour kind of cherry.

agriproduct /ˈagrɪprɒdəkt, -dʌkt/ *noun.* L20.
[ORIGIN from *agri-* in AGRIBUSINESS + PRODUCT *noun.*]
A product of agribusiness.

agriscience /agrɪˈsʌɪəns/ *noun.* L20.
[ORIGIN from AGRI(CULTURE + SCIENCE.]
The application of science to agriculture.
■ **agriscientist** *noun* L20.

†**agrise** *verb.*
[ORIGIN Old English *āgrīsan*, from A-[1] + verb from base also of GRISLY *adjective.*]
1 *verb intrans.* Tremble; be terrified. OE–L16.
2 *verb trans.* Make tremble; terrify. Orig. *impers.* in (*it*) ***agrises*** etc. ME–M17.
3 *verb trans.* Shudder at, loathe. Only in LME.

agritourism /ˈagrɪtʊərɪz(ə)m/ *noun.* L20.
[ORIGIN from AGRI(CULTURE + TOURISM.]
Tourism in which tourists stay with local people in rural areas abroad.

agro *noun* var. of AGGRO.

agro- /ˈagrəʊ/ *combining form.*
[ORIGIN from Greek *agros* land, field: see -O-.]
Agricultural; agriculture and.
■ **agrobioˈlogical** *adjective* of or pertaining to agrobiology M20. **agrobiˈologist** *noun* an expert in or student of agrobiology M20. **agrobiˈology** *noun* the branch of knowledge that deals with soil science and plant nutrition and its application to crop production M20. **agrobusiness** *noun* = AGRIBUSINESS M20. **agroˈchemical** *noun* a chemical used in agriculture; a chemical fertilizer, pesticide, weedkiller, etc.: M20. **agro-cliˈmatic** *adjective* of or pertaining to the relationship between climate and agriculture M20. **agro-ecoˈlogical** *adjective* of or pertaining to the relationship between ecology and agriculture M20. **agro-ˈecosystem** *noun* an ecosystem on agricultural land M20. **agroforestry** *noun* agriculture incorporating the cultivation of trees L20. **agro-inˈdustrial** *adjective* of or pertaining to agro-industry M20. **agro-industry** *noun* (an) industry connected with agriculture; agriculture developed along industrial lines: M20. **agrotechˈnology** *noun* the application of technology in agriculture M20. **agroterrorism** *noun* terrorist acts that are intended to disrupt or damage a country's agriculture L20.

agrology /əˈgrɒlədʒi/ *noun.* E20.
[ORIGIN from AGRO- + -LOGY. Cf. French *agrologie.*]
1 Soil science in relation to crops. *rare.* E20.
2 *Canad.* The application of science to agriculture. M20.
■ **agrologist** *noun* (*Canad.*) M20.

agronomic /agrəˈnɒmɪk/ *adjective & noun.* E19.
[ORIGIN French *agronomique*, from *agronome*: see AGRONOMY, -IC.]
▸ **A** *adjective.* Of or pertaining to agronomy. E19.
▸ **B** *noun.* In *pl.* (usu. treated as *sing.*). = AGRONOMY. M19.
■ **agronomical** *adjective* M19. **agronomically** *adverb* M20.

agronomy /əˈgrɒnəmi/ *noun.* E19.
[ORIGIN French *agronomie*, from *agronome* agriculturist, from Greek *agros* land + *-nomos* arranging, from *nemoein* arrange: see -NOMY.]
The science of soil management and crop production.
■ **agronome** /ˈagrənəʊm/ *noun* [French] an agronomist M19. **agronomist** *noun* a person engaged in agronomy E19.

agrostology /agrəˈstɒlədʒi/ *noun.* M19.
[ORIGIN from Greek *agrōstis* (denoting a kind of grass) + -OLOGY.]
The branch of botany concerned with grasses.

aground /əˈgraʊnd/ *adverb & pred. adjective.* ME.
[ORIGIN from A *preposition*[1] 1 + GROUND *noun.*]
†**1** On the ground; on or to the earth. Latterly *dial.* ME–L19.

J. CLARE She furious stampt her shoeless foot aground.

2 Of a ship: on the bottom of shallow water. Opp. ***afloat.*** L15.

BYRON One bark blew up, a second near the works Running aground, was taken by the Turks.

aguardiente /aˌgwardiˈente, əˌgwɑːdɪˈɛnti/ *noun.* E19.
[ORIGIN Spanish, from *agua* water + *ardiente* fiery, ARDENT.]
Coarse Spanish brandy; in Spanish-speaking areas of America, a similar distilled liquor, *esp.* one made from sugar cane.

ague /ˈeɪgjuː/ *noun & verb.* ME.
[ORIGIN Old French & mod. French from medieval Latin *acuta* use as noun (sc. *febris* fever) of fem. of Latin *acutus* ACUTE.]
▸ **A** *noun.* **1** An acute fever. Now *dial.* rare in *gen.* sense. ME.
2 *esp.* A malarial fever with cold, hot, and sweating stages (at first *esp.* the hot stage, later *esp.* the cold). LME.
WALCHEREN ***ague.***
3 Any shivering fit. L16.
– COMB.: †**ague-cake** the spleen or another organ so enlarged as to be perceptible externally; **ague-tree** sassafras.
▸ **B** *verb trans.* Affect (as) with ague. Chiefly as ***agued*** *ppl adjective.* E17.

aguila *noun* var. of AGILA.

†**aguise** *verb trans.* Only in L16.
[ORIGIN from GUISE *verb*, *a-* opp. *dis-* in *disguise* (cf. *accord, discord,* etc.).]
Dress, array.

SPENSER Sometimes her head she . . would aguize With gaudy girlonds.

aguish /ˈeɪgjuːɪʃ/ *adjective.* E17.
[ORIGIN from AGUE *noun* + -ISH[1].]
1 Subject to ague. E17.
2 Tending to produce ague. E17.
3 Of the nature of or characteristic of an ague; shaky; intermittent. M17.
■ **aguishly** *adverb* M17. **aguishness** *noun* (*rare*) E18.

A

aguti *noun* var. of AGOUTI.

agy *adjective* var. of AGEY.

AH *abbreviation.*
Latin *anno Hegirae* in the year of the Hegira (the Muslim era).

ah /ɑː/ *pers. pronoun. dial. & US black English.* L19.
[ORIGIN Repr. a pronunc.]
= **I** *pers. pronoun.*

ah /ɑː/ *interjection, noun, & verb.* Also **aah**, (as interjection, earlier, now *rare*) **a**. ME.
[ORIGIN Old French *a(h)* (mod. *ah*); cf. Italian, Spanish *ah*, Latin *a(h)*, Greek *a(a)*, etc.]
▸ **A** *interjection.* Expr.: sorrow, regret; entreaty, remonstrance; surprise, pleasure, admiration; realization, discovery; dislike, boredom, contempt, mockery. ME.
SHAKES. *2 Hen. VI* Ah, villain, thou wilt betray me. YEATS Ah me! I cannot reach them. SCOTT FITZGERALD 'Ah,' she cried, 'you look so cool.' T. STOPPARD Ah!—I knew there was something.
▸ **B** *noun.* An utterance of 'ah!' E18.
▸ **C** *verb intrans.* Say 'ah!' L19.

AHA *abbreviation.*
Alpha-hydroxy acid.

aha /əˈhɑː, ɑːˈhɑː/ *interjection.* ME.
[ORIGIN from AH *interjection* + HA *interjection*.]
Expr.: surprise; triumph, satisfaction; mockery, irony.
– COMB.: **aha experience**, **aha moment**, **aha reaction**, etc.: of sudden insight or discovery.

ahead /əˈhɛd/ *adverb.* Orig. NAUTICAL. M16.
[ORIGIN from A *preposition*¹ 1 + HEAD *noun*.]
1 Of motion: straight forwards; headlong. M16.
BROWNING Galloping straight a-head.
go ahead: see GO *verb*. See also GO-AHEAD.
2 Pointing forwards; *fig.* into the future. L16.
J. F. COOPER One who looked on a-head to the wants of posterity.
3 At the head (of a moving company); in advance, in front (*lit. & fig.*). E17.
E. O'NEILL Navy has drawn ahead—half a length—looks like Navy's race. L. HUGHES I am the man who never got ahead, The poorest worker bartered through the years.
4 In the line of one's forward motion; further forward in space or time. L17.
W. H. AUDEN When courage fails, when hopes are fading, Think on the victory ahead.
– PHRASES: **ahead of** in front of, further advanced than (*lit. & fig.*). **ahead of the curve**, **behind the curve** (chiefly *US*) ahead of, or lagging behind, current thinking or trends. ***line ahead***: see LINE *noun*². ***one jump ahead***: see JUMP *noun*¹.

aheap /əˈhiːp/ *adverb & pred. adjective. literary.* E19.
[ORIGIN from A-² + HEAP *noun*.]
In a heap; all of a heap.

a-height /əˈhʌɪt/ *adverb. arch.* E17.
[ORIGIN from A *preposition*¹ 1 + HEIGHT *noun*.]
On high, aloft.

ahem /əˈhɛm/ *interjection.* M18.
[ORIGIN Lengthened form of HEM *interjection*.]
Expr. desire to attract attention, gain time, or show disapproval.

ahey /əˈheɪ/ *interjection.* L17.
[ORIGIN from AH *interjection* + HEY *interjection*.]
Expr. desire to attract attention or show surprise.

ahi /ˈɑːhi/ *noun.* L19.
[ORIGIN Hawaiian *'ahi*.]
In Hawaii: a large tuna, *esp.* the bigeye or yellowfin; the flesh of such a fish as food.

ahigh /əˈhʌɪ/ *adverb. arch.* ME.
[ORIGIN from A *preposition*¹ 1 + HIGH *noun*.]
†**1** In loud tones. ME–L15.
2 On high, aloft. LME.

ahimsa /əˈhɪmsɑː/ *noun.* L19.
[ORIGIN Sanskrit, from *a* non- + *hiṃsā* violence.]
HINDUISM, BUDDHISM, & JAINISM. The doctrine that there should be no violence or killing.

ahind /əˈhɪnd, əˈhʌɪnd/ *adverb & preposition. Scot. & dial.* Also **ahint** /əˈhɪnt/. M18.
[ORIGIN from A-² + *-hind* as in *behind*: see HIND *adjective*.]
Behind.

ahistoric /eɪhɪˈstɒrɪk/ *adjective.* M20.
[ORIGIN from A-¹⁰ + HISTORIC.]
Not historic; unrelated to history.
■ **ahistorical** *adjective* M20.

ahold /əˈhəʊld/ *noun. colloq. & dial.* L19.
[ORIGIN Prob. from A *adjective* + HOLD *noun*¹.]
Hold, grasp, *of*, *on*, etc.

†**ahold** *adverb.* Only in E17.
[ORIGIN from A *preposition*¹ 6 + HOLD *noun*¹.]
NAUTICAL. Close to the wind, so as to hold to it.
SHAKES. *Temp.* Lay her a-hold, a-hold.

-aholic /əˈhɒlɪk/ *suffix.* Also **-oholic**. M20.
[ORIGIN from ALCOHOLIC *noun*.]
Forming nouns with the sense 'a person addicted to —', as ***workaholic*** etc.

a-horseback /əˈhɔːsbak/ *adverb. arch. & dial.* L15.
[ORIGIN from A *preposition*¹ 1 + HORSEBACK.]
On horseback.
■ Also **a-horse** *adverb* E19.

ahoy /əˈhɔɪ/ *interjection.* M18.
[ORIGIN from AH *interjection* + HOY *interjection*.]
NAUTICAL. Used in hailing.
land ahoy!: see LAND *noun*¹.

ahull /əˈhʌl/ *adverb.* L16.
[ORIGIN from A *preposition*¹ 6 + HULL *noun*².]
NAUTICAL. With sails taken in and the helm lashed on the lee side, to weather a storm.

ahunger /əˈhʌŋgə/ *adverb & pred. adjective.* LME.
[ORIGIN from A *preposition*¹ 6 + HUNGER *noun*.]
In a famished state, hungry.

ahungered /əˈhʌŋgəd/ *adjective. arch.* LME.
[ORIGIN Prob. var. of OFHUNGERED.]
Famished, very hungry.
■ **ahungry** *adjective* famished, hungry LME.

ahunt /əˈhʌnt/ *adverb & pred. adjective.* L19.
[ORIGIN from A-² + HUNT *noun*².]
On the hunt.

AI *abbreviation.*
1 Artificial insemination.
2 Artificial intelligence.

ai /ˈɑːɪ/ *noun.* E17.
[ORIGIN Tupi, repr. the animal's cry, prob. through Portuguese *aí*, French *aï* (†*hay*, †*haüt*).]
The three-toed sloth *Bradypus tridactylus*, of S. America.

aiblins *adverb* var. of ABLINS.

AID *abbreviation.*
Artificial insemination by donor.

aid /eɪd/ *noun.* LME.
[ORIGIN Old French *aïde* (mod. *aide*) ult. from pa. pple of Latin *adjuvare*: see ADJUVANT.]
1 Help, succour, relief. LME. ▸**b** ENGLISH LAW (now *hist.*). Help in defending an action, legally claimed from someone who has a joint interest in the defence. E16. ▸**c** Material help given by one country to another. M20.
in aid of in support of; *colloq.* about, concerned with, esp. in ***what's all this in aid of?***, ***what was that in aid of?***, etc. ***legal aid***: see LEGAL *adjective*. ***Voluntary Aid Detachment***: see VOLUNTARY *adjective*. **b** ***pray in aid*** (***of***): see PRAY *verb*.
2 a ENGLISH HISTORY. A grant of a tax or subsidy to the Crown; an exchequer loan. LME. ▸**b** ENGLISH HISTORY. A pecuniary contribution paid by a feudal vassal to his lord. L16. ▸**c** FRENCH HISTORY. In *pl.* Customs dues. E18.
3 A helper, an assistant; an auxiliary. LME. ▸**b** = AIDE. *N. Amer.* L18.
4 Something helpful; a material source of help. L16.
R. HOGGART A life with few modern aids such as vacuum cleaners and electric washers.
visual aid: see VISUAL *adjective*.
– COMB.: **aid climbing** rock climbing using the assistance of objects such as pegs placed in the rock (contrasted with ***free climbing***); **aid-prayer** an appeal for aid.
■ **aidful** *adjective* helpful L16. **aidless** *adjective* E17.

aid /eɪd/ *verb trans.* LME.
[ORIGIN Old French *aïdier* (mod. *aider*) from Latin *adjutare* frequentative of *adjuvare*: see ADJUVANT.]
Help, give support to; further the progress of.
AV *1 Macc.* 8:26 Neither shal they . . aide them with victuals, weapons, money, or ships. SHAKES. *Wint. T.* All the instruments which aided to expose the child. JOYCE Reclining in a state of supine repletion to aid digestion. *absol.*: COLERIDGE Saints will aid if men will call.
■ **aidable** *adjective* (*rare*) †(**a**) helpful; (**b**) able to be helped: L16. **aidance** *noun* aid L16. **aider** *noun* E16.

aida /ˈeɪdə/ *noun.* M20.
[ORIGIN Unknown.]
More fully ***aida cloth***, ***aida fabric***. An openwork fabric used in cross-stitch embroidery.

aidant /ˈeɪd(ə)nt/ *adjective & noun.* LME.
[ORIGIN Old French *ai(d)ant* pres. pple, formed as AID *verb*: see -ANT¹.]
▸ **A** *adjective.* Assisting, auxiliary. LME.
▸ **B** *noun.* A helper, an auxiliary. *rare.* LME.

aid-de-camp *noun* var. of AIDE-DE-CAMP.

aide /eɪd/ *noun.* L18.
[ORIGIN Abbreviation of AIDE-DE-CAMP.]
1 = AIDE-DE-CAMP. L18.
2 *gen.* An assistant, an ancillary worker. Orig. *US.* M19.

aide-de-camp /eɪddəˈkɒ̃, *foreign* ɛddəkɑ̃/ *noun.* Also ***aid-**. Pl. **aides-de-camp**, ***aids-**, /eɪdz-, *foreign* ɛd-/. L17.
[ORIGIN French = camp adjutant.]
MILITARY. An officer acting as a confidential assistant to a senior officer, or assisting on a ceremonial occasion.

aide-memoire /ˌeɪdmɛmˈwɑː; *foreign* ɛdmemwaːr (*pl. same*)/ *noun.* M19.
[ORIGIN French *aide-mémoire*, formed as AID *verb*, MEMORY.]
(A book or document serving as) an aid to the memory; (in diplomats' use) a memorandum.

Aids /eɪdz/ *noun.* Also **AIDS**. L20.
[ORIGIN Acronym, from *acquired immune deficiency syndrome*.]
A syndrome marked by severe loss of cellular immunity as a result of infection with a virus transmitted in sexual fluids and in blood, leaving the patient susceptible to certain opportunistic infections and malignancies.
– COMB.: **Aids-related complex** a set of symptoms including lymphadenopathy, fever, weight loss, and malaise, that seems to precede the full development of Aids.

aiel /ˈeɪ(ə)l/ *noun.* Long *obsolete* exc. *hist.* Also **aile**, **ayle**. LME.
[ORIGIN Old French *aiol*, *aiuel* (mod. *aïeul*) from Proto-Romance dim. of Latin *avus* grandfather. Cf. BESAIEL.]
LAW. A grandfather.
writ of aiel an action by a party based on the seisin of a grandfather for the recovery of land of which that party had been dispossessed.

aiglet *noun* var. of AGLET.

aigre-doux /ɛgrədu, ɛgrəˈduː/ *adjective.* Also ***-douce*** /-dus, -ˈduːs/. LME.
[ORIGIN French.]
Compounded of sweet and sour; bittersweet.

aigrette /ˈeɪgrɛt, eɪˈgrɛt/ *noun.* M18.
[ORIGIN French: see EGRET.]
An egret's plume; a tuft of feathers or hair; a spray of gems etc. worn on the head.

†**aigue-marine** *noun.* L16–M19.
[ORIGIN French formed as AQUAMARINE.]
= AQUAMARINE 1.

aiguille /ˈeɪgwiːl/ *noun.* M18.
[ORIGIN French = needle. Cf. AIGUILLETTE.]
A sharply pointed peak of rock, esp. in the Alps.

aiguillette /eɪgwɪˈlɛt/ *noun.* M16.
[ORIGIN Old French & mod. French, dim. of AIGUILLE: see -ETTE.]
= AGLET, esp. sense 2b.

AIH *abbreviation.*
Artificial insemination by husband.

aikido /ʌɪˈkiːdəʊ/ *noun.* M20.
[ORIGIN Japanese *aikidō*, from *ai* together, unify + *ki* spirit + *dō* way.]
A Japanese form of self-defence and martial art, developed from ju-jitsu and involving holds and throws.

ail /eɪl/ *noun*¹. Long *dial.*
[ORIGIN Old English *egl*, cogn. with German dial. *Egel*, *Agel*.]
The awn of barley or other corn.

ail /eɪl/ *noun*². Now *arch. & dial.* ME.
[ORIGIN from the verb.]
Trouble; illness; an ailment.

ail /eɪl/ *verb.*
[ORIGIN Old English *eġl(i)an* rel. to Gothic *agls* disgraceful, *aglo* oppression, *us)agljan* oppress.]
1 *verb trans.* Trouble, afflict. Chiefly & now only with indef. subj. in ***what ails*** etc. OE.
AV *1 Sam.* 11:5 What aileth the people that they weep? HENRY MILLER He was supposed to be suffering from ulcers of the stomach, though nobody was quite sure exactly what ailed him.
2 *verb intrans.* Be troubled or adversely affected (mentally, *obsolete* or *dial.*); be ill. ME.
G. HEYER They never ail, though they did have the measles . . when they were small. *Times* An improvement in the ailing United States economy.
†**3** *verb trans. impers.* in ***what ails*** etc. Obstruct, prevent. LME–E19.
■ **ailing** *noun* (**a**) the action of the verb; (**b**) an ailment: M19. **ailment** *noun* a disorder, a (usu. slight) illness E18.

ailanthus /eɪˈlanθəs/ *noun.* E19.
[ORIGIN mod. Latin (also *ailantus*) from French *ailanthe*, (usu.) *ailante* from Ambonese *ailanto* lit. 'tree of heaven': infl. by names ending with *-anthus* from Greek *anthos* flower.]
A tree of the mainly Asian genus *Ailanthus* (family Simaroubaceae); esp. the tree of heaven, *A. altissima*, an ornamental and shade tree.

aile *noun* var. of AIEL.

aileron /ˈeɪlərɒn/ *noun.* E20.
[ORIGIN French, dim. of *aile* wing.]
A movable aerofoil used to control the balance of an aircraft in flight, usu. a hinged flap in the trailing edge of a wing.

ailette /eɪˈlɛt/ *noun.* LME.
[ORIGIN French, formed as AILERON: see -ETTE.]
hist. A piece of steel shoulder armour worn by a soldier.

ailurophile /ʌɪˈljʊərəfʌɪl/ *noun.* Also **-phil** /-fɪl/. M20.
[ORIGIN from Greek *ailouros* cat + -PHILE.]
A lover of cats.

ailurophobia /ˌʌɪljʊrəˈfəʊbɪə/ *noun*. **E20.**
[**ORIGIN** formed as **AILUROPHILE** + **-PHOBIA**.]
Irrational fear of cats.
■ **aiˈlurophobe** *noun* a person affected with ailurophobia **E20.** **ailurophobic** *adjective* **E20.**

AIM *abbreviation*.
In the UK: Alternative Investment Market.

aim /eɪm/ *noun*. **ME.**
[**ORIGIN** from the verb.]
1 A thing aimed at, a mark, a butt, (*lit.*). Long *rare*. **ME.**

> **SHAKES.** *Rich. III* A garish flag To be the aim of every dangerous shot.

†**2** Conjecture; a guess. Latterly *dial.* **LME–L19.**

> **SHAKES.** *Jul. Caes.* What you would work me to, I have some aim.

3 The directing of a weapon, missile, etc., at its mark. **LME.**
†**cry aim**: in order to encourage archers about to shoot; *gen.* in encouragement of anything. ***level one's aim***: see **LEVEL** *verb*[1]. **take aim** direct a weapon, a missile, etc., at its mark.
†**4** Course, direction. **M16–L17.**
†**5** Direction given, guidance. **E17–E18.**

> **MILTON** Posts of direction for Travellers . . to give you ayme.

6 An end aimed at, an objective; design, intention, purpose. **E17.**

> **C. HAMPTON** We have kidnapped you in order to achieve certain political aims. **J. BARTH** It is my aim to learn all that can be learned of my father's life.

7 A person who aims in a specified manner. *colloq.* **L19.**
■ **aimful** *adjective* (*rare*) full of purpose **M19.** **aimless** *adjective* without means of taking aim; without purpose: **E17.** **aimlessly** *adverb* **M19.** **aimlessness** *noun* **M19.**

aim /eɪm/ *verb*. **ME.**
[**ORIGIN** Partly from Old French *amer* dial. var. of *esmer* from Latin *aestimare* (see **ESTIMATE** *verb*); partly from Old French *ae(s)mer* ult. from Latin *ad* **AD-** + *aestimare*.]
†**1** *verb trans.* Calculate (a number or value); take account of; esteem; evaluate. Only in **ME.**
†**2** *verb trans.* Guess, conjecture. Long *dial.* **ME–L19.**
3 *verb intrans.* Direct one's course, make it one's object to attain, intend, try, (foll. by *at*, (occas.) *for*, *to do*); *transf.* be directed *at*, be intended *to do*. **ME.**
aim high show ambition.
†**4** *verb trans.* Arrange, plan. **LME–E17.**
5 *verb trans.* & *intrans.* Direct (a missile, blow, remark, act, †missive, etc.) *at*; point or level (a firearm etc., *at*). **LME.**

> **J. RHYS** I asked her who had taught her to aim so well.

■ **aimer** *noun* **L16.**

Aino *noun* & *adjective* var. of **AINU**.

ain't *verb* see **BE** *verb*, **HAVE** *verb*.

Ainu /ˈeɪnuː, ˈʌɪ-/ *noun* & *adjective*. Also **-no** /-nəʊ/. **E19.**
[**ORIGIN** Ainu, lit. 'man', 'person'.]
▸ **A** *noun*. Pl. same, **-s**.
1 A member of (the people descended from) an aboriginal people of Japan, living also in neighbouring parts of Asia. **E19.**
2 The language of this people. **L19.**
▸ **B** *attrib.* or as *adjective*. Of or pertaining to the Ainu or their language. **M19.**

aioli /ʌɪˈəʊli, *foreign* ajɔli/ *noun*. **E20.**
[**ORIGIN** French, from Provençal *ai* garlic + *oli* oil.]
Mayonnaise seasoned with garlic.

AIR *abbreviation*.
All-India Radio.

air /ɛː/ *noun*[1]. Also (*obsolete* exc. as in sense 11b) **ayre**. **ME.**
[**ORIGIN** Branch I from Old French & mod. French *air* from Latin *aer* from Greek *aēr* (rel. to **AURA**); branch II from French *air* prob. repr. Old French *aire* place, site, disposition, from Latin *ager*, *agri-* infl. by Latin *area* **AREA** (rel. to **EYRIE**); branch III repr. Italian **ARIA**.]
▸ **I 1** The invisible gaseous substance which envelops the earth and is breathed by all land animals and plants, one of the four elements of the ancients, now known to be a mixture of oxygen, nitrogen, carbon dioxide, and traces of other gases. **ME.** ▸**b** This considered as a medium for the transmission of radio waves. **E20.**
hot air: see **HOT** *adjective*. ***live on air***: see **LIVE** *verb*. ***thin air***: see **THIN** *adjective*. **tread on air**, **tread as if on air** = ***walk on air*** below. ***upper air***: see **UPPER** *adjective*. ***vital air***: see **VITAL** *adjective*. **walk on air**, **walk as if on air** feel elated. **b off the air** not broadcasting. **on the air** broadcast(ing) by radio or television. **over the air** by means of radio or television broadcast. ***university of the air***: see **UNIVERSITY** 1.
2 A special state or condition of the atmosphere, as affected by contaminating exhalations, temperature, moisture, etc., or as modified by time or place. **ME.** ▸**b** *spec.* The fresh unexhausted air of the outer atmosphere, as opp. to that in confined spaces. **LME.**

> **POPE** Content to breathe his native air In his own ground. **F. NIGHTINGALE** His goods are spoiled by foul air and gas fumes. **A. J. LERNER** All I want is a room somewhere, Far away from the cold night air.

BREATH of fresh air. **change of air** variety of climate, esp. as secured by travel. **b take the air** go out of doors.

3 The body of air surrounding the earth; the (apparently) free or unconfined space in the atmosphere. **ME.** ▸**b** This considered as a medium for operations with aeroplanes etc.; aircraft, aerial power. **E20.**

> **AV** *Eccles.* 10:20 A bird of the aire shall carry the voyce. **LONGFELLOW** The sun is bright—the air is clear.

beat the air: see **BEAT** *verb*[1] 1. **build castles in the air**, **build in the air** form unsubstantial or visionary projects (see also **CASTLE** *noun*[1].). ***CHATEAU in air***. ***clear the air***: see **CLEAR** *verb* 8. **give a person the air** *US slang* dismiss a person. **in the air** (of opinions etc.) spreading about, everywhere met with; (of projects etc.) uncertain, unfixed. ***open air***: see **OPEN** *adjective*. ***saw the air***: see **SAW** *verb*[1] 1. **take air** become widely known. ***with one's nose in the air***: see **NOSE** *noun*. **b by air** in or by aircraft.
†**4** Breath; inspiration; confidential information. **LME–E18.**

> **SHAKES.** *Wint. T.* Still, methinks, There is an air comes from her. What fine chisel Could ever yet cut breath? **BACON** The airs, which the princes and states abroad received from their ambassadors.

5 Now chiefly *SAILING*. A breeze, a light wind. **M16.**

> **POPE** Let vernal airs thro' trembling osiers play. *Times* We've got a yacht which does very well as long as there's reasonable airs.

†**6** Any gas or vapour. **M17–M19.**
▸ **II** Manner, appearance.
7 Outward appearance, manner, style. **L16.**

> **SCOTT FITZGERALD** There was an unmistakable air of natural intimacy about the picture. **S. LEWIS** It had the air of being a very good room in a very good hotel.

8 A person's bearing, gesture, or manner, now usu. as expressive of a specified personal quality or emotion; *absol.* a confident or stylish bearing. **L16.** ▸†**b** Attitude, expression, (*of* a part of the body). **M17–M18.** ▸†**c** Disposition, mood. *rare*. **M17–E18.**

> **SHAKES.** *Wint. T.* Your father's image is so hit in you, His very air. **S. JOHNSON** He . . excites curiosity by an air of importance. **BYRON** But her air, If not her words, tells me she loves another. **D. LODGE** Telling the truth with a jesting air was . . the safest way of protecting your secrets. **b HOR. WALPOLE** The variety of attitudes and airs of heads.

9 *HORSEMANSHIP*. An artificial or practised movement in *haute école*. **E17.**
10 An affected manner. Usu. in *pl.* **M17.**
airs and graces: see **GRACE** *noun*. **give oneself airs**, **put on airs**, etc., be pretentious.
▸ **III** *MUSIC*. **11** An expressive succession of musical sounds, songlike music; a melody; a tune. **L16.** ▸**b** *spec.* A part-song, usu. with lute accompaniment; a light or sprightly tune or song. **L16.**

> **SHAKES.** *Mids. N. D.* Your tongue's sweet air More tuneable than lark to shepherd's ear. **J. THURBER** Two bagpipers were playing Scottish airs near the water's edge.

– **COMB.**: **air bag** a bag (to be) inflated with air; *spec.* one fitted as a safety device in a motor vehicle, which inflates to cushion a driver or passenger in an impact; **air-ball** *arch.* a toy balloon; **airband** a range of frequencies allocated for radio communications involving aircraft; **airbase** a centre for the operation of military aircraft; **air bed** an inflated mattress; **air bell** a small bubble of air; **air bladder** an air-filled sac in an animal or plant; *esp.* a fish's swim bladder; **airboat** a shallow-draught boat powered by an aircraft engine, for use in swamps; **airborne** *adjective* carried through the air; in flight; carried by or employing aircraft; **air brake** (*a*) a brake operated by compressed air; (*b*) a movable flap or other device used to increase the drag of an aircraft; **air brick** a brick perforated for ventilation; **air bridge** a portable bridge used at airports to connect a passenger terminal and an aircraft; **airbrush** *noun* & *verb* (*a*) *noun* a device for spraying paint etc. by means of compressed air; (*b*) *verb trans.* paint or alter with an airbrush; **airburst** the explosion of a bomb etc. in the air; **Airbus** (proprietary name for) an aircraft designed to carry a large number of passengers economically over relatively short routes; **air cavalry** a mobile airborne army unit used esp. to transport troops to a combat area and to provide aerial reconnaissance and support; **air cell** = ***air sac*** (a) below; **Air Chief Marshal**: a high rank in the Royal Air Force, next above Air Marshal; ***air commodore***: see **COMMODORE** 4; **air con** air conditioning; **air-conditioned** *adjective* having air conditioning; **air conditioner** an apparatus for air conditioning; **air conditioning** a system for controlling the humidity, ventilation, and temperature in a building or vehicle, usu. to maintain a cool atmosphere in warm conditions; apparatus for this; **air-cooled** *adjective* cooled by means of a current of air; **air corridor** a route to which aircraft are restricted; **aircrew** an aeroplane's crew; also (pl. same), a member of an aeroplane's crew; **air cushion** a cushion inflated with air; a body of air supporting a vehicle such as a hovercraft; **air-cushioned** *adjective* inflated or cushioned with air, having an air cushion; **airdate** the date on which a particular television or radio programme is scheduled to be broadcast; **airdrome** *US* = **AERODROME** 2; **airdrop** *noun* & *verb* (*a*) *noun* the dropping of supplies, troops, etc., by parachute; (*b*) *verb trans.* & *intrans.* drop (supplies etc.) by parachute; **air-dry** *adjective* not giving off any moisture on exposure to air; **air ferry** a service of aircraft carrying cars etc. across water; **airfield** an area of land set aside for the take-off, landing, and accommodation of (esp. non-commercial) aircraft; ***air-filter***: see **FILTER** *noun* 4; **airflow** the flow of air, *esp.* that encountered by a moving aircraft or vehicle; **airfoil** *US* = **AEROFOIL**; **air force** a large force of warplanes; the branch of a country's armed forces which conducts operations primarily by means of aircraft; (in the UK) ***Royal Air Force*** s.v. **ROYAL** *adjective*; **airframe** the basic structure of an aircraft; **airfreight** *noun* & *verb* (*a*) *noun* freight conveyed by aircraft; (*b*) *verb trans.* convey (freight) by aircraft; **air-freshener** a substance or device for freshening the air in a room; **airglow** radiation emitted by the upper atmosphere; **air guitar** an imaginary guitar mimed to rock music; **airgun** a gun firing pellets etc. by compressed air; **air gunner** an aircrew member whose job is to operate a gun; **airhead** (*a*) an airbase established in enemy territory; (*b*) *slang* a foolish, unintelligent, or empty-headed person; **air hole** a hole admitting air, *esp.* one formed in ice or water; **air hostess** a stewardess in a passenger aircraft; **air-kiss** *verb trans.* & *intrans.* purse the lips as if to kiss, without making contact; simulate a kiss (to); **air lane** a route designated for use or regularly used by aircraft; **air-layering** *HORTICULTURE* a form of layering in which the branch is wrapped in moist earth etc., or potted, to promote root growth; **air letter** a letter conveyed by air; *esp.* (one written on) a special folding sheet of lightweight paper; **airlift** *noun* & *verb* (*a*) *noun* the transportation of supplies, troops, etc. by air; (*b*) *verb trans.* transport (supplies, troops, etc.) by air; **airliner** a large passenger aircraft; **airlock** (*a*) an antechamber giving access to a chamber which is kept at a regulated pressure (usu. above that of its surroundings); (*b*) a stoppage of the flow of liquid in a pipe etc. due to a bubble of air; **airman** a man who is engaged in the operation of aircraft, esp. as a crew member; in Royal Air Force usage, an enlisted man as distinct from a commissioned officer; **airmanship** skill in flying an aircraft; **Air Marshal**: a high rank in the Royal Air Force, equivalent to Lieutenant General and Vice Admiral; the highest rank in the Royal Australian Air Force; **air mass** a body of air with horizontally uniform levels of temperature, humidity, and pressure; **Air Miles** (proprietary name for) points (equivalent to miles of free air travel) accumulated by buyers of airline tickets and other products and redeemable against the cost of air travel with a particular airline; **airmobile** *adjective* (of troops etc.) readily moved about by air; **air officer** any Royal Air Force officer above the rank of Group Captain; **air pipe** a pipe conveying air; a bronchial tube; **air piracy** skyjacking; **air pirate** a skyjacker; **air pistol** a pistol firing pellets etc. by compressed air; **airplane** (now chiefly *N. Amer.*) an aeroplane; **air plant** any epiphytic plant; any plant growing naturally without soil, *spec.* the life-plant, *Kalanchoe pinnata*, which produces young plants from its leaf margins; **airplay** broadcast playing (of recorded music); **air pocket** a local atmospheric condition causing an aircraft to lose height suddenly; **air potato** a yam, *Dioscorea bulbifera*, grown in warm and temperate parts of Asia and Africa for its edible aerial tubers; **air power** ability to defend and attack by means of aircraft etc.; **air pump** (*a*) a device for pumping air in or out; (*b*) (usu. **A-**) *the* constellation Antlia; **air quality** the degree to which the ambient air is pollution-free, assessed by measuring a number of indicators of pollution; **air rage** aggressive or violent behaviour on board an aircraft; **air raid** an attack by aircraft, esp. bombers; **air rifle** a rifle firing pellets etc. by compressed air; **air sac** (*a*) *ANATOMY* a lung compartment containing air; (*b*) *ZOOLOGY* an air-filled extension of a bird's lung or an insect's trachea; **airscrew** an aircraft's propeller; **air-sea rescue** rescue from the sea by aircraft; **air shaft** a straight, usu. vertical passage admitting air into a mine, tunnel, building, etc; **airship** a dirigible powered balloon, *esp.* one having a rigid elongated structure; also occas. (chiefly *N. Amer.*) any aircraft; **air shot** *colloq.* (*a*) a missed stroke at a ball etc.; (*b*) a recording made from broadcast music etc.; **air show** a show at which aircraft are on view and featuring aerial displays; **airsick** *adjective* affected with airsickness; **airsickness** nausea caused by the motion of an aircraft; **airside** *noun, adjective,* & *adverb* (designating or pertaining to, to or towards) the side or sections of an airport to which only passengers and airport personnel have admittance; **airspace** the air above a country etc., esp. considered as subject to its jurisdiction; **airspeed** the speed of an aircraft or other flying body relative to the surrounding air; **air station** an airfield operated by a navy or marine corps; **airstrip** a strip of land on which aircraft may take off and land; **air terminal** a place in a town where facilities for the reception of passengers and transport to and from an airport are provided; **airtight** *adjective* impermeable to air; *fig.* invulnerable, unassailable; **airtime** broadcasting time available for a given purpose; **air-to-air** *adjective* from one aircraft to another in flight; **air-to-ground** *adjective* from an aircraft in flight to the ground; **air-to-surface** *adjective* from an aircraft in flight to the surface of the sea etc.; **air twist** a decorative spiral in the stem of a wine glass; **air vessel** an air-filled vessel, esp. in an animal or plant; **Air Vice-Marshal**: a high rank in the Royal Air Force or Royal Australian Air Force, next below Air Marshal; **airwave** a wave in the atmosphere; *esp.* (in *pl.*) broadcast radio waves; **airwoman** a woman engaged in the operation of aircraft, esp. as a crew member.
■ **airified** *adjective* made airy, given to assuming airs **M19.** **airless** *adjective* without air or other atmosphere; stuffy; breezeless, still: **E17.** **airlessness** *noun* **M19.** **airlike** *adjective* resembling (that of) air **M16.** **airward** *adverb* towards or up into the air **E19.**

air /ɛː/ *noun*[2]. **E18.**
[**ORIGIN** Old Norse *eyrr*.]
A gravelly beach; a sandbank.

air /ɛː/ *verb*. **M16.**
[**ORIGIN** from **AIR** *noun*[1].]
1 *verb trans.* Expose to the open air, ventilate. **M16.**

> **M. EDGEWORTH** To keep the room aired and swept.

2 *verb trans.* Finish drying or warm at a fire, in a heated cupboard, etc. **M16.**

> **D. L. SAYERS** The clean sheets, . . all laying aired and ready.

3 *verb refl.* & (*arch.*) *intrans.* Take the air, go out in the fresh air. **E17.**
4 *verb trans.* Wear openly; parade ostentatiously; make public; talk openly about. **E17.**

> **SHAKES.** *Cymb.* I beg but leave to air this jewel. **E. BLUNDEN** I began to air my convictions that the war was useless and inhuman.

5 *verb trans.* & *intrans.* (Become) broadcast; transmit, be transmitted, by radio or television. **M20.**

> *Publishers Weekly* After the tape was aired . . we received hundreds of calls from listeners. *Broadcasting* Only two episodes have aired.

■ **airer** *noun* a person who or thing which airs; *spec.* a frame for drying off clothes etc.: L18.

air /ɛː/ *adverb. Scot.* LME.
[ORIGIN Parallel to OR *adverb.* Cf. ERE.]
†**1** Formerly. LME–M16.
2 Early, soon. E16.

aircraft /ˈɛːkrɑːft/ *noun.* Pl. **-craft**, †**-crafts**. M19.
[ORIGIN from AIR *noun*[1] + CRAFT *noun.*]
A machine that can be flown in the air; now *spec.* an aeroplane or helicopter; such machines collectively.
– COMB.: **aircraft carrier** a warship designed to serve as a base for aircraft; **aircraftman**, **aircraftwoman** the lowest rank in the (Women's) Royal Air Force (***leading aircraftman***: see LEADING *ppl adjective*).

†**aire** *noun.* ME–E18.
[ORIGIN Old French: see EYRIE.]
= EYRIE.

Airedale /ˈɛːdeɪl/ *noun.* L19.
[ORIGIN A district in West Yorkshire, England.]
In full ***Airedale terrier***. (A dog of) a breed of large terrier having a short dense coat.

airing /ˈɛːrɪŋ/ *noun.* E17.
[ORIGIN from AIR *verb* + -ING[1].]
1 Ventilating; exposure to heat in order to finish drying. E17.
2 A walk, ride, drive, etc., to take air or exercise. E17.

J. AUSTEN I hope you have had a pleasant airing.

3 (An instance of) exposure to public notice. L19. ▸**b** Broadcasting; a radio or television transmission. M20.

Wall Street Journal This subject deserves an airing from a strictly commercial viewpoint. **b** *Listener* An informative and lively series which could certainly stand another airing.

– COMB.: **airing cupboard** a cupboard for airing linen and clothing.

airish /ˈɛːrɪʃ/ *adjective.* LME.
[ORIGIN from AIR *noun*[1] + -ISH[1].]
1 Aerial; like the air. Now *rare.* LME.
2 Cool, fresh, breezy. Now *dial.* M17.

airline /ˈɛːlʌɪn/ *noun.* Also **air-line**. E19.
[ORIGIN from AIR *noun*[1] + LINE *noun*[2].]
1 A direct line, a beeline. *N. Amer.* E19.
2 A regular succession of aircraft plying between certain places; a company or other body operating aircraft in public service. E20.
3 A pipe or tube conveying (compressed) air. E20.

airmail /ˈɛːmeɪl/ *noun & verb.* E20.
[ORIGIN from AIR *noun*[1] + MAIL *noun*[3].]
▸ **A** *noun.* Mail conveyed by air; the conveyance of mail by air. E20.
– COMB.: **airmail paper** etc.: lightweight and suitable for dispatching by air.
▸ **B** *verb trans.* Send (a letter, parcel, etc.) by air. M20.

airport /ˈɛːpɔːt/ *noun.* E20.
[ORIGIN from AIR *noun*[1] + PORT *noun*[1].]
An airfield catering for passenger travel, *esp.* a large one with customs facilities.
– COMB.: **airport art** ethnic art or craft of the type displayed and sold at some airports, viewed dismissively as being copied or mass-produced for the tourist market; **airport novel**: of the type of light, popular fiction sold at airports as ideal for in-flight reading.

airt /ɛːt/ *noun & verb. Scot.* As noun also †**art**. ME.
[ORIGIN Gaelic *àird* from Old Irish *aird.*]
▸ **A** *noun.* A quarter of the compass; a direction. ME.
▸ **B** *verb.* **1** *verb trans.* Direct, guide. L18.
2 *verb intrans.* Direct one's way, make *for.* M19.

airway /ˈɛːweɪ/ *noun.* M19.
[ORIGIN from AIR *noun*[1] + WAY *noun.*]
1 a A passage for ventilation in a mine. M19. ▸**b** MEDICINE. The normal passage for air into the lungs; an artificial device replacing or supplementing this. E20.
2 A route through the air, *esp.* one regularly followed by commercial aircraft. L19. ▸**b** A company etc. operating aircraft, an airline. Usu. in *pl.* E20.
3 A radio broadcasting channel. *N. Amer.* M20.

airworthy /ˈɛːwəːði/ *adjective.* E19.
[ORIGIN from AIR *noun*[1] + -WORTHY.]
Of an aircraft: in a fit condition for flight.
■ **airworthiness** *noun* E20.

airy /ˈɛːri/ *adjective.* LME.
[ORIGIN from AIR *noun*[1] + -Y[1]. Cf. AERY *adjective.*]
▸ **I** Of the atmosphere.
†**1** Atmospheric; living in the air. LME–L17.
2 Placed high in the air; lofty; heavenly. Now *poet.* L16.
3 Exposed to the open air, breezy; spacious and well ventilated. L16.

New Yorker The airy and spacious house on Gordon Square.

4 Performed or taking place in the air. E17.
▸ **II** Of the substance air.
5 Composed of air; of the nature of air. LME.
6 *derog.* Unsubstantial as air, unreal; casual, flippant. L16.

S. JOHNSON Him whose airy negligence puts his friend's affairs . . in continual hazard.

7 Light or buoyant as air; lively; delicate. L16.
▸ **III** [AIR *noun*[1] II.]
8 Assuming airs, pretentious. *rare.* E17.
– COMB.: **airy-fairy** *adjective* (*colloq.*) delicate or light as a fairy; nonchalant; *derog.* fanciful, unsubstantial.
■ **airily** *adverb* M18. **airiness** *noun* L16.

aisle /ʌɪl/ *noun.* Also †**ele** (earliest), †**i(s)le**. LME.
[ORIGIN Old French *ele* (mod. *aile*) from Latin *ala* wing; conf. with *isle*, *island* and infl. by French *aile* wing.]
1 A wing or lateral division of a church; a part parallel to, and usu. divided by pillars from, the main nave, choir, or transept. See also CROSS-AISLE. LME.

fig.: KEATS Through the dark pillars of those sylvan aisles.

2 A passage between rows of pews or seats; a passage between cabinets and shelves of goods in a supermarket etc. M18.
have people in the aisles, **have people rolling in the aisles** *colloq.* make an audience laugh uncontrollably, be very amusing.
3 Any architectural division of a church. M18.
■ **aisled** *adjective* having an aisle or aisles M16. **aisleless** /-l-l-/ *adjective* M19.

ait /eɪt/ *noun*[1]. See also EYOT.
[ORIGIN Old English *iġġaþ*, *iġ(e)oþ*, *iġ(e)þ*, ult. from *ī(e)ġ* island + dim. suffix.]
A small island, esp. in a river.

ait *noun*[2] see OAT *noun.*

aitch /eɪtʃ/ *noun.* Also †**ache**. M16.
[ORIGIN Old French *ache*, perh. from Proto-Romance word exemplifying the sound.]
The letter H, h.
drop one's aitches fail to pronounce initial *h* in words.
■ **aitchless** *adjective* lacking an *h*; (esp. of a person or speech) characterized by a failure to pronounce initial *h*'s: L19.

aitchbone /ˈeɪtʃbəʊn/ *noun.* L15.
[ORIGIN formed as NACHE + BONE *noun*, with loss of *n* as in *adder, apron.*]
(A cut of beef lying over) the buttock or rump bone.

aith *noun* see OATH *noun.*

aiver *noun* var. of AVER *noun.*

aixies /ˈeɪksɪz/ *noun pl. Scot. & N. English.* Also **aixes**, **exies** /ˈɛksɪz/. L16.
[ORIGIN Dial. form of ACCESS *noun.*]
A fit of ague. Also, hysterics.

ajar /əˈdʒɑː/ *adverb*[1] *& pred. adjective*[1]. Also †**a-char**. L17.
[ORIGIN from A *preposition*[1] 6 + CHAR *noun*[1].]
Of a door etc.: partly open.

ajar /əˈdʒɑː/ *adverb*[2] *& pred. adjective*[2]. M19.
[ORIGIN from A-[2] + JAR *noun*[1].]
Out of harmony.

ajee /əˈdʒiː/ *adverb & pred. adjective. Scot. & dial.* Also **agee**. E18.
[ORIGIN from A *preposition*[1] 6 + JEE *noun.*]
Off the straight (*lit.* & *fig.*); aside; ajar; disturbed, mildly deranged.

ajog /əˈdʒɒɡ/ *adverb & pred. adjective.* E17.
[ORIGIN from A *preposition*[1] 6 + JOG *noun*[1].]
Moving mechanically up and down; jogging.

ajowan /ˈadʒəwɒn/ *noun.* E20.
[ORIGIN Hindi *ajvāyn.*]
An umbelliferous annual plant, *Trachyspermum ammi*, with feathery leaves and white flowers, native to India; the aromatic seeds (used as a culinary spice) or essential oil of this plant.

ajuga /əˈdʒuːɡə/ *noun.* L18.
[ORIGIN mod. Latin (see below) from medieval Latin, app. alt. of Latin *abiga* a plant able to cause abortion, from *abigere* drive away.]
A plant of the genus *Ajuga*, of the mint family, which includes several species cultivated as ornamental ground cover.

ajutage *noun* var. of ADJUTAGE.

AK *abbreviation.*
Alaska.

AK-47 /ˌeɪkeɪ-fɔːtiˈsɛv(ə)n/ *noun.* M20.
[ORIGIN Abbreviation of Russian *Avtomat Kalashnikov 1947*, the designation of the original model designed by Mikhail T. Kalashnikov (b. 1919).]
A type of assault rifle originally manufactured in the Soviet Union.

aka *abbreviation.* Also **a.k.a.**
Also known as.

Akali /əˈkɑːliː/ *noun.* E19.
[ORIGIN Punjabi *akālī*, from mod. Sanskrit *Akāla* the Immortal One + Punjabi -*ī* follower of.]
A member of a militant sect of Sikhs; a member of a Sikh political party.

Akan /ˈɑːkən/ *noun & adjective.* Pl. of noun same, **-s**. L17.
[ORIGIN Twi *akaŋ.*]
(A member of, of or pertaining to) a people inhabiting southern Ghana and adjacent parts of Ivory Coast; (of) the group of Twi and Fante languages spoken by this people.

akara *noun* var. of ACCRA.

akasha /ɑːˈkɑːʃə/ *noun.* Also **-sa**. M19.
[ORIGIN Sanskrit *ākāśa.*]
Ether, atmosphere, as one of the five elements in Hindu philosophy.

akathisia /eɪkəˈθɪsɪə, a-/ *noun.* Also **ac-**. E20.
[ORIGIN from A-[10] + Greek *kathisis* sitting + -IA[1].]
MEDICINE. Irrational fear of sitting; restlessness preventing sitting still.

ake *verb* see ACHE *verb.*

ake-ake /ˈakɪaki/ *noun. NZ.* M19.
[ORIGIN Maori.]
A hardwood evergreen tree or shrub, *Dodonaea viscosa*, of the soapberry family. Also, any of certain trees or shrubs of the genus *Olearia* (Compositae), with tinted foliage.

akee *noun* var. of ACKEE.

akela /ɑːˈkeɪlə/ *noun.* E20.
[ORIGIN *Akela*, a wolf in Kipling's *Jungle Book* and *Second Jungle Book.*]
An adult leader of a pack of Cub Scouts.

aketon *noun* var. of ACTON.

akhara /ɑːkˈhɑːrə/ *noun. Indian.* M19.
[ORIGIN Hindi *akhārā.*]
1 A convent or monastery, esp. of ascetics. Also, an order of ascetics or monks. M19.
2 A wrestling ring or pit; a gymnasium or outdoor exercise area. E20.

akimbo /əˈkɪmbəʊ/ *adverb.* LME.
[ORIGIN Prob. from Old Norse phr. = bent in a curve; assim. to A *preposition*[1].]
Of the arms: with hands on hips and elbows turned outwards.

akin /əˈkɪn/ *pred. adjective.* M16.
[ORIGIN from A *preposition*[2] + KIN *noun.*]
1 Of the same kin; related by blood. M16.
2 Of the same kind; similar in character or properties. M17.

akinesia /eɪkɪˈniːsɪə, a-/ *noun.* M19.
[ORIGIN Greek *akinēsia* quiescence, from *a-* A-[10] + *kinēsis* motion.]
MEDICINE. Loss or impairment of the power of voluntary movement.
■ **akinetic** /-ˈnɛtɪk/ *adjective* of, pertaining to, or displaying akinesia L19.

Akita /əˈkiːtə/ *noun.* E20.
[ORIGIN A district in northern Japan.]
(An animal of) a Japanese breed of dog, a kind of spitz.

Akkadian /əˈkeɪdɪən/ *adjective & noun.* Also **Acc-**. M19.
[ORIGIN from *Akkad*, a city and district in ancient Babylonia + -IAN.]
▸ **A** *adjective.* Of or pertaining to an eastern Semitic language of northern Babylonia, known from cuneiform inscriptions, and having two dialects, Assyrian and Babylonian; of or pertaining to the people of northern Babylonia. M19.
▸ **B** *noun.* **1** The Akkadian language. L19.
2 A native or inhabitant of Akkad or northern Babylonia. L19.

akkra *noun* var. of ACCRA.

aknee /əˈniː/ *adverb. arch.* Also †**-s**. ME.
[ORIGIN from A *preposition*[1] + KNEE *noun.*]
On one's knee or knees.

akosmism, **akosmist** *nouns* vars. of ACOSMISM, ACOSMIST.

akrasia /əˈkreɪzɪə, əˈkrasɪə/ *noun.* Also **acrasia**. M19.
[ORIGIN Greek, from *a-* without + *kratos* power, strength: see -IA[1].]
PHILOSOPHY. The state of mind in which one acts against one's better judgement; weakness of will. Used chiefly with ref. to Aristotle's *Nicomachean Ethics.*
■ **akratic** /əˈkratɪk/ *adjective* M20.

akroterion *noun* var. of ACROTERION.

Akubra /əˈkuːbrə/ *noun.* E20.
[ORIGIN Name of a company manufacturing the hats; perh. from an Aboriginal language.]
In full *Akubra hat.* (Proprietary name for) a broad-brimmed hat of a type traditionally worn by Australian farmers and cattlemen.

akvavit *noun* var. of AQUAVIT.

AL *abbreviation.*
1 Alabama.
2 Anglo-Latin.
3 Autograph letter.

Al *symbol.*
CHEMISTRY. Aluminium.

al- /al, *unstressed* əl/ *prefix*[1] (not productive).
Assim. form of Latin AD- before *l.* In Old French, Latin *all-* was reduced to *al-*, which appears in Middle English adoptions, but in later French, and hence in English, *all-* was restored by Latinization, as ***allegation***, ***alliterate***. Hence extended to some words of different origin, as ***allay***.

al- /al/ *prefix*[2] (not productive).
The Arab. def. article *al*, forming an essential element of many words of Romance (esp. Spanish and Portuguese) origin adopted in English, as ***alcohol***, ***alcove***, ***algebra***, ***alkali***.

-al /əl/ *suffix*[1].
1 [Repr. Latin *-alis* adjectival suffix or French *-el* (later refashioned after Latin).] Forming adjectives with the sense 'of the kind of, pertaining to', from Latin (***central***, ***general***, ***oral***, ***providential***, etc.), on Latin bases (***basal*** etc.), from Greek (***baptismal***, ***colossal***, ***tropical***, etc.: cf. **-IAL**, **-ICAL**), or from English nouns (***tidal*** etc.).
2 [Repr. French *-ail(le)*, *-al* or from or after Latin *-alis* etc. used as noun] Forming nouns (***animal***, ***cardinal***, ***rival***, etc.), esp. of verbal action (***arrival***, ***proposal***, ***withdrawal***, etc.).

-al /al, əl/ *suffix*[2].
[**ORIGIN** from **AL**(**COHOL**, **AL**(**DEHYDE**.]
CHEMISTRY. Forming the names of substances which are aldehydes or occas. other derivatives of alcohols, as ***acetal***, ***chloral***, ***retinal***, etc. Also used in *PHARMACOLOGY* with little or no chemical significance, as in ***barbital***, ***Veronal***.

ALA *abbreviation*.
All letters answered (used in personal advertisements).

ala /ˈeɪlə/ *noun*. Pl. **alae** /ˈeɪliː/. **M18.**
[**ORIGIN** Latin = wing.]
1 *ANATOMY.* A winglike process; *esp.* either of the lateral cartilages of the nose, enclosing the nostrils. **M18.**
†**2** *BOTANY.* An axil; also, a lateral petal of a papilionaceous flower, a wing of a seed. **M18–M19.**

Ala. *abbreviation*.
Alabama.

à la /ɑː lɑː, *foreign* a la/ *prepositional phr.* **L16.**
[**ORIGIN** French, abbreviation of **À LA MODE**.]
In the manner, method, or style of (usu. with French, but also in nonce uses with English, nouns). Freq. in *COOKERY*, foll. a noun, cooked or prepared in the specified manner etc.
à la bonne femme: see **BONNE** *adjective*. **à la broche** /brɒʃ, *foreign* brɔʃ/, **à la brochette** /brɒˈʃɛt, *foreign* brɔʃɛt/ (cooked) on a spit or skewer. **À LA CARTE**. **à la daube** /dəʊb, *foreign* doːb/ [**DAUBE**] (of beef etc.) stewed, braised. **à la Florentine** /ˈflɒr(ə)ntiːn, *foreign* flɒrɑ̃tin/ = **FLORENTINE** *adjective* 2. **à la fourchette** /fʊəˈʃɛt, *foreign* furʃɛt/ (of a meal) requiring the use (only) of a fork. **À LA PAGE**. ***à la Portugaise***: see **PORTUGAISE** *noun* 1. **à la reine** /rɛn/ [= queen] cooked or prepared in some special manner. **à la russe** /ruːs, *foreign* rys/ in the Russian manner. ***chicken à la king***: see **CHICKEN** *noun*[1]. ***chicken à la Maryland***: see **MARYLAND** 2. ***meringue à la Chantilly***: see **MERINGUE** *noun*[1].

Alabaman /aləˈbamən/ *noun & adjective*. Also **-mian** /-mɪən/. **M19.**
[**ORIGIN** from *Alabama* (see below) + **-AN**.]
A native or inhabitant of, of or pertaining to, the state of Alabama, USA.

†**alabandine** *noun*. **LME–M17.**
[**ORIGIN** medieval Latin *alabandina* (sc. *gemma* gem), from *Alabanda* a city of Caria in ancient Asia Minor.]
= **ALMANDINE**.

Alabarch /ˈaləbɑːk/ *noun*. **M17.**
[**ORIGIN** Dissimilated form of Latin *arabarches* (Juvenal) from Greek *arabarkhēs*, *ala-*.]
(The title of) the chief magistrate of the Jews at Alexandria under the Ptolemies and Romans.

alabaster /ˈaləbɑːstə, aləˈbɑːstə/ *noun & adjective*. Also †**alablaster**. **LME.**
[**ORIGIN** Old French *alabastre* (mod. *albâtre*) from Latin *alabaster*, *-trum* from Greek *alabastos*, *-tros*.]
▸ **A** *noun*. **1** A fine-grained, translucent, ornamental form of gypsum, usu. white but sometimes tinted or clouded with yellow, red, or other colours; also occas., calcite of similar appearance and use. **LME.**

> *fig.*: E. **LINKLATER** The lovely creature with . . a brow of alabaster.

2 A box made of alabaster, esp. for holding unguents. **LME.**
▸ **B** *adjective*. Of alabaster; like alabaster in whiteness or smoothness. **E16.**
■ **alaˈbastrine** *adjective* of or like alabaster **L16.**

alabastron /aləˈbɑːstrɒn/ *noun*. **M19.**
[**ORIGIN** Greek.]
= **ALABASTER** *noun* 2.

†**alablaster** *noun & adjective* var. of **ALABASTER**.

à la carte /ɑː lɑː ˈkɑːt, *foreign* a la kart/ *adverbial & adjectival phr.* **E19.**
[**ORIGIN** French: see **À LA**, **CARTE** *noun*[1].]
By the bill of fare; ordered as a separately priced item or as separately priced items from a menu, not as part of a table d'hôte meal.

alack /əˈlak/ *interjection*. *arch.* **LME.**
[**ORIGIN** from **AH** *interjection* + **LACK** *noun*[1], after **ALAS**.]
Expr. dissatisfaction, deprecation, regret, surprise. Freq. in ***alack the day***, ***alack-a-day***.

†**alacrious** *adjective*. **E17–E18.**
[**ORIGIN** from Latin *alacris* var. of *alacer* (see **ALACRITY**) + **-OUS**.]
Brisk, lively, active.
■ †**alacriously** *adverb*: only in **17.**

alacrity /əˈlakrɪti/ *noun*. **LME.**
[**ORIGIN** Latin *alacritas*, from *alacr-*, *alacer* brisk: see **-ITY**.]
Briskness, cheerful readiness, liveliness.
■ **alacritous** *adjective* (*rare*) brisk, lively, active **L19.** **alacritously** *adverb* (*rare*) **L19.**

Aladdin /əˈladɪn/ *noun*. **E19.**
[**ORIGIN** Arabic *ʿAlā' al-dīn*, a character in the *Arabian Nights' Entertainments*.]
1 ***Aladdin's lamp***, a talisman enabling the holder to gratify any wish. **E19.**
2 ***Aladdin's cave***, a place of great riches. **L19.**

alalia /əˈleɪlɪə, eɪ-/ *noun*. **M19.**
[**ORIGIN** Greek, from *a-* **A-**[10] + **-LALIA**.]
MEDICINE. Absence or loss of the ability to utter speech sounds.

alameda /aləˈmeɪdə/ *noun*. **L18.**
[**ORIGIN** Spanish.]
In Spain and Spanish-speaking areas: a public walk, shaded with trees.

Alamire /eɪlɑːˈmiːreɪ/ *noun*. *obsolete* exc. *hist.* Also **A la mi re**. **LME.**
[**ORIGIN** from *A* as a pitch letter + *la*, *mi*, *re* designating tones in the solmization of Guido d'Arezzo (*c* 990–1050).]
MEDIEVAL MUSIC. The note A in Guido d'Arezzo's 2nd, 3rd, 4th, 5th, 6th, and 7th hexachords, where it was sung to the syllables *la*, *mi*, or *re*. Cf. **ARE** *noun*[1], **BEFA**, **CEFAUT**, etc.

à la mode /ɑː lɑː ˈməʊd, *foreign* a la mɔd/ *adverbial, adjectival, & noun phr.* Also **alamode**. **L16.**
[**ORIGIN** French = in the fashion.]
▸ **A** *adverbial & adjectival phr.* **1** In or according to the fashion; fashionable. **L16.**
2 *COOKERY.* **a** Of beef: braised or made into a rich stew, usu. with wine. **M17.** ▸**b** Of food: served with ice cream. Chiefly *US*. **E20.**
▸ **B** *noun phr.* Usu. as one word.
†**1** A fashion, a temporary mood. **M–L17.**
2 A thin light glossy usu. black silk. **M17.**
■ **alamoˈdality** *noun* (*rare*) the quality of being à la mode **M18.**

alamort /aləˈmɔːt/ *adverb & adjective*. *arch.* Also ***à la mort*** /a la mɔːr, ɑː lɑː ˈmɔːt/. **L16.**
[**ORIGIN** French *à la mort* to the death. See also **AMORT**.]
▸ **A** *adverb*. To the death; mortally. **L16.**
▸ **B** *adjective*. Mortally sick; dispirited. **L16.**

Alan /ˈalən/ *noun*[1]. Pl. **Alani** /əˈlɑːni, əˈleɪni/, **Alans**. **LME.**
[**ORIGIN** Latin *Alanus*.]
A member of an ancient Scythian people, first mentioned as dwelling near the Caspian Sea.

alan *noun*[2] var. of **ALANT**.

aland *noun* var. of **ALANT**.

aland /əˈland/ *adverb*. *arch.* **OE.**
[**ORIGIN** from **A** *preposition*[1] 1 + **LAND** *noun*[1].]
†**1** In the land, in the country. Long *dial.* **OE–L19.**
2 On dry land. **ME.**
3 To the land or shore. **ME.**

alanine /ˈalənɪːn/ *noun*. **M19.**
[**ORIGIN** German *Alanin*: see **ALDEHYDE**, **-INE**[5]; *-an-* is app. for euphony.]
BIOCHEMISTRY. A crystalline hydrophobic amino acid, $CH_3CH(NH_2)COOH$, which occurs in proteins; 2-aminopropanoic acid.
β-alanine an amino acid, $(NH_2)CH_2CH_2COOH$; 3-aminopropanoic acid.

alannah /əˈlanə/ *noun*. *Irish.* Also **alanna**. **M19.**
[**ORIGIN** Irish *a leanbh* O child.]
My child: used as a form of address or as a term of endearment.

alant /əˈlɑːnt/ *noun*. *obsolete* exc. *HERALDRY.* Also †**alan**, **aland**, †**alaun(t)**. **ME.**
[**ORIGIN** Old French *alan(t)*.]
A large hunting dog; a wolfhound; *HERALDRY* also, a short-eared mastiff.

alap /ɑːˈlɑːp/ *noun*. Also **-pa** /-pə/, **-pana** /-pənə/. **L19.**
[**ORIGIN** Hindi *ālāp*.]
INDIAN MUSIC. An improvisation on a raga as a prologue to its formal expression.

à la page /a la paːʒ, ɑː lɑː ˈpɑːʒ/ *adverbial & adjectival phr.* **M20.**
[**ORIGIN** French, lit. 'at the page'.]
Up to date, up to the minute.

alapana *noun* var. of **ALAP**.

a la plancha /a lə ˈplantʃə/ *adverb & adjective*. **M20.**
[**ORIGIN** Spanish.]
Of meat or fish: cooked on a hotplate or griddle.

Alar /ˈeɪlɑː/ *noun*. **M20.**
[**ORIGIN** Unknown.]
(Proprietary name for) a growth retardant used as a spray on fruit and vegetables to enhance the quality of the crop.

alar /ˈeɪlə/ *adjective*. **M19.**
[**ORIGIN** Latin *alaris*, formed as **ALA**: see **-AR**[1].]
Alary; wing-shaped; *BOTANY* axillary.

alarm /əˈlɑːm/ *noun*. Also (*arch.* exc. in sense 6) **alarum** /əˈlɑːrəm, -ˈlɛːr-, -ˈlar-/. **LME.**
[**ORIGIN** from the adverb in phrs. such as *cry alarm*.]
1 Frightened anticipation of danger; a state of frightened surprise; apprehension. **LME.**

> S. **LEWIS** Babbitt roused, his stomach constricted with alarm.

take alarm: see **TAKE** *verb*.
2 A frightening loud noise or disturbance. *arch.* **E16.**

> **KEATS** What divinity Makes this alarum in the elements?

3 A signal calling upon people to arm; news of approaching hostility. **M16.**

> **SOUTHEY** From east and west . . the breathless scouts Bring swift alarums in. W. **OWEN** No alarms of bugles, no high flags, no clamorous haste.

alarms and excursions, **alarums and excursions** *joc.* [from an old stage direction] confused noise and bustle.
†**4** A sudden attack; a surprise. **L16–L17.**

> **DRYDEN** The doubtful nations watch his arms, With terror each expecting his alarms.

5 A sound to warn of danger or to attract attention, arouse from sleep, etc.; a warning. **L16.**

> V. **SACKVILLE-WEST** The vixen, prick-eared for the first alarm.

false alarm: see **FALSE** *adjective*.
6 A mechanism that sounds the alarm; an apparatus that rings, bleeps, etc., at a set time; an alarm clock. **L16.**

> J. **CHEEVER** The alarm began ringing at six in the morning.

burglar alarm, ***fire alarm***, etc.
– **COMB.**: **alarm bell** a bell rung as a signal of danger; **alarm bird** any of various birds with strident cries; *esp.* (*Austral.*) the kookaburra; **alarm call** (***a***) a bird's or animal's cry when startled; (***b***) a telephone call notifying the person called that a previously agreed time has arrived; **alarm clock**, **alarm watch**: with an apparatus that rings or bleeps at a set time; **alarm-post** *MILITARY* a post appointed to be resorted to in the event of an alarm; ***alarm watch***: see ***alarm clock*** above.
■ **alarmism** *noun* alarmist behaviour or tendency **M19.** **alarmist** *noun & adjective* (***a***) *noun* a person who raises alarm on slight grounds, a panic-monger; (***b***) *adjective* of or pertaining to alarmism or alarmists: **L18.**

alarm /əˈlɑːm/ *verb*. Also †**alarum**. **L16.**
[**ORIGIN** from the noun.]
1 *verb intrans.* & †*trans.* Call to arms. Long *rare*. **L16.**
†**2** *verb trans.* Rouse to action. **E17–M18.**
3 *verb trans.* Rouse to a sense of danger. **M17.**
4 *verb trans.* Agitate with sudden fear or apprehension; disturb. **M17.**

> R. **MEHTA** I don't want to alarm you, but you must face reality.

5 *verb trans.* Fit or protect with an alarm. Chiefly as ***alarmed*** *ppl adjective*. **M20.**

> V. **SETH** All our cars are alarmed.

■ **alarmable** *adjective* liable to be alarmed or excited **E19.** **alarmingly** *adverb* in an alarming manner **L18.**

alarm /əˈlɑːm/ *adverb*. Long *arch.* Also **alarum** /əˈlɑːrəm, -ˈlɛːr-, -ˈlar-/. **LME.**
[**ORIGIN** Old French & mod. French *alarme* from Italian *allarme* = *all' arme* to arms!]
As a call to prepare for fighting.

> **LD BERNERS** The townes all about range their belles alarum. **SHAKES.** *Rich. III* Strike alarum, drums! G. B. **SHAW** *Auxiliaries.* Alarm! Alarm! *Centurion.* What now? Has the old woman attacked you again?

alarum *noun, verb, adverb* see **ALARM** *noun, verb, adverb*.

alary /ˈeɪləri/ *adjective*. **M17.**
[**ORIGIN** Latin *alarius*, formed as **ALA**: see **-ARY**[1].]
Of or pertaining to wings or alae.

alas /əˈlas, əˈlɑːs/ *interjection & noun*. **ME.**
[**ORIGIN** Old French *a las(se)* (mod. *hélas*), from *a* **AH** *interjection* + *las(se)* from Latin *lassus* weary.]
▸ **A** *interjection*. Expr. unhappiness, grief, pity, or concern. **ME.**

> **SHAKES.** *Oth.* Alas the heavy day! Why do you weep. **DAY LEWIS** I had a vision of eternity in my sleep—a vision, alas, far different from Vaughan's 'I saw eternity the other night'. NEB *Luke* 22:22 Alas for that man by whom he is betrayed.

▸ **B** *noun*. An utterance of 'alas!'. **E17.**

Alas. *abbreviation*.
Alaska.

Alaska /əˈlaskə/ *noun*. **L19.**
[**ORIGIN** The northernmost state in the US.]
In full ***baked Alaska***. Sponge cake and ice cream in a rapidly cooked meringue covering; a dish of this.

Alaskan /əˈlask(ə)n/ *adjective & noun*. **M19.**
[**ORIGIN** from **ALASKA** + **-AN**.]
▸ **A** *adjective*. Of or pertaining to Alaska or its inhabitants. **M19.**
▸ **B** *noun*. A native or inhabitant of Alaska. **L19.**

A

Alastor /əˈlaːstə, -ˈlast-/ *noun*. Also **a-**. L16.
[ORIGIN Greek *alastōr*, from *a-* A-[10] + *last-* from *lathein* forget.]
An avenging god, a nemesis.

alate /ˈeɪleɪt/ *adjective*. M17.
[ORIGIN Latin *alatus*, formed as ALA: see -ATE[2].]
Having wings or winglike appendages.

alate /əˈleɪt/ *adverb*. *arch*. LME.
[ORIGIN from A *preposition*[2] + LATE *noun*[2].]
Of late, lately.

alated /ˈeɪleɪtɪd/ *adjective*. L16.
[ORIGIN formed as ALATE *adjective* + -ED[1].]
= ALATE *adjective*.

alaternus /alәˈtәːnәs/ *noun*. Now *rare*. Also †**alatern**. E17.
[ORIGIN Latin: cf. French *alaterne*.]
An evergreen shrub, *Rhamnus alaternus*, of the buckthorn family.

†**alaun(t)** *nouns* vars. of ALANT.

†**alay** *verb* var. of ALLAY *verb*[3].

alb /alb/ *noun*. OE.
[ORIGIN ecclesiastical Latin *alba* use as noun of fem. of Latin *albus* white.]
A white vestment reaching to the feet, worn by Christian priests.

alba /ˈalbə/ *noun*. E19.
[ORIGIN Provençal, ult. from Latin *albus* white.]
A medieval Provençal song at dawn.

albacore /ˈalbәkɔː/ *noun*. L16.
[ORIGIN Portuguese *albacor(a)*, from Arabic *al-bakūra* perh. from *al* the + *bakūr* premature, precocious.]
The long-finned tunny, *Thunnus alalunga*; *loosely* any related fish.

Albanian /alˈbeɪnɪәn/ *noun*[1] & *adjective*[1]. L16.
[ORIGIN from *Albania* (see below) + -AN.]
▸ **A** *noun*. A native or inhabitant of the country of Albania in the western part of the Balkan peninsula; the language of Albania, constituting a separate branch of the Indo-European family. L16.
▸ **B** *adjective*. Of or pertaining to the country of Albania, its inhabitants, or their language. L16.

Albanian /alˈbeɪnɪәn/ *noun*[2] & *adjective*[2]. *hist*. L16.
[ORIGIN from *Albania* (see below) + -AN.]
▸**A** *noun*. A native or inhabitant of Albania, an ancient province on the Caspian Sea; the language of the province of Albania. L16.
▸ **B** *adjective*. Of or pertaining to the province of Albania, its inhabitants, or their language. E17.

albarello /albәˈrɛlәʊ/ *noun*. Pl. **-lli** /-liː/, **-llos**. L19.
[ORIGIN Italian *alberello* pot, phial.]
A majolica jar used esp. as a container for drugs.

albata /alˈbeɪtә/ *noun*. M19.
[ORIGIN Latin, fem. of *albatus* clothed in white, from *albus* white.]
White metal, German silver.

albatross /ˈalbәtrɒs/ *noun*. L17.
[ORIGIN Alt. of ALCATRAS, app. by assoc. with Latin *albus* white.]
1 Any of several large, long-winged, tube-nosed oceanic birds constituting the family Diomedeidae. L17. ▸**b** *fig*. (usu. with allusion to Coleridge's *Ancient Mariner*: see below). A heavy burden, a disadvantage, a hindrance. M20.

COLERIDGE Instead of the cross, the albatross About my neck was hung.

†**2** A frigate bird. Cf. ALCATRAS. Only in M18.
3 GOLF. A hole played in three strokes under par. M20.

†**albe** *conjunction*. LME–E19.
[ORIGIN Contr.]
= ALBEIT.

albedo /alˈbiːdәʊ/ *noun*. Pl. **-os**. M19.
[ORIGIN ecclesiastical Latin = whiteness, from Latin *albus* white.]
The proportion of incident radiation reflected by a surface, esp. of a planet or moon.

albeit /ɔːlˈbiːɪt/ *conjunction*. Now *literary*. LME.
[ORIGIN from ALL *adverb* + BE + IT *pronoun*, = although it be (that).]
Even though (it be *that*).

R. KNOLLES Albeit that a great number of them were slain. M. MEAD In Iatmul a man is a master in his own house, albeit he has to fight for it. M. DRABBLE She was going to Paris, albeit in a school raincoat.

albergo /alˈbɛrgo, alˈbәːgәʊ/ *noun*. Pl. ***-ghi*** /-gi, -giː/. E17.
[ORIGIN Italian: cf. AUBERGE.]
An Italian inn.

Albers-Schönberg disease /albәzˈʃәːnbәːg dɪˌziːz/ *noun phr*. Also **Albers-Schönberg's disease**. E20.
[ORIGIN H. E. *Albers-Schönberg* (1865–1921), German radiologist.]
MEDICINE. Osteopetrosis, esp. in a delayed form.

albert /ˈalbәt/ *noun*. Also **A-**. M19.
[ORIGIN Prince *Albert* (1819–61), consort of Queen Victoria of England.]
1 In full ***albert chain***. A watch chain with a crossbar. M19.
2 ***Albert Medal***: (***a***) instituted in 1864 by the Royal Society of Arts for 'distinguished merit in promoting Arts, Manufactures, and Commerce'; (***b***) instituted in 1866 (though no longer awarded) for 'gallantry in saving life at sea or on land'. M19.

Albertine /ˈalbәtʌɪn/ *adjective*. M18.
[ORIGIN from *Albert* (see below) + -INE[1].]
Designating or pertaining to the younger of the two lines of the house of Frederick the Gentle, Elector of Saxony, which originated with his son Albert III (1443–1500) and to which the electoral title was transferred in 1547. Cf. ERNESTINE.

albertite /ˈalbәtʌɪt/ *noun*. M19.
[ORIGIN from *Albert* County, New Brunswick, Canada + -ITE[1].]
MINERALOGY. A black, almost infusible form of bitumen.

albescent /alˈbɛs(ә)nt/ *adjective*. E18.
[ORIGIN Latin *albescent-* pres. ppl stem of *albescere* become white, from *albus* white: see -ESCENT.]
Growing white; shading into white.

albespine /ˈalbәspʌɪn/ *noun*. *arch*. Also **-yne**. LME.
[ORIGIN Old French *albespine* (mod. *aubépine*) from Latin *alba spina* white thorn.]
Whitethorn, hawthorn.

Albigenses /albɪˈgɛnsiːz, -ˈdʒɛn-/ *noun pl*. E17.
[ORIGIN medieval Latin, from *Albiga* Latin name of Albi, a city in SW France.]
A Manichaean sect in southern France between the 11th and 13th cents.
■ **Albigensian** *noun & adjective* a member of, pertaining to, the Albigenses E17.

albino /alˈbiːnәʊ/ *noun & adjective*. E18.
[ORIGIN Spanish & Portuguese, from *albo* white + *-ino* (-INE[1]): orig. applied by the Portuguese to albinos among black Africans.]
▸ **A** *noun*. Pl. **-os**.
1 A human being having a congenital deficiency of pigmentation in the skin and hair, which are white, and the eyes, which are usu. pink. E18.
2 An abnormally white animal or plant. E19.
▸ **B** *adjective*. Congenitally lacking in pigmentation; abnormally white. E19.
■ **albiness** /-bɪnɛs/ *noun* a female albino E19. **albinism** /ˈalbɪnɪz(ә)m/ *noun* the condition of being an albino M19. **albinistic** /-bɪˈnɪstɪk/ *adjective* = ALBINOTIC L19. **albinoid** /ˈalbɪnɔɪd/ *adjective* being or resembling an albino M20. **albinoism** *noun* = ALBINISM M19. **albinotic** /-bɪˈnɒtɪk/ *adjective* pertaining to, affected with, albinism L19.

Albion /ˈalbɪәn/ *noun*. *poet. & rhet*. OE.
[ORIGIN Latin from Celtic; prob. cogn. with Latin *albus* white (with allus. to the white cliffs of Britain).]
(Orig. the Greek and Roman name for) Britain.
perfidious Albion [translating French *la perfide Albion*] England (with ref. to her alleged treachery to other nations).

albite /ˈalbʌɪt/ *noun*. E19.
[ORIGIN from Latin *albus* white + -ITE[1].]
MINERALOGY. A sodium-rich plagioclase, usu. white, occurring widely in silicate rocks; sodium feldspar.
■ **albitic** /-ˈbɪtɪk/ *adjective* of the nature of or containing albite M19. **albitization** /-bɪtʌɪˈzeɪʃ(ә)n/ *noun* conversion into (a form containing) albite L19. **albitize** /ˈalbɪtʌɪz/ *verb trans*. convert into (a form containing) albite E20.

albitite /ˈalbɪtʌɪt/ *noun*. L19.
[ORIGIN from ALBITE + -ITE[1].]
GEOLOGY. Intrusive rock consisting largely of albite.
■ **albititic** /-ˈtɪtɪk/ *adjective* of the nature of or containing albitite M20.

albondigas /alˈbɒndɪgas/ *noun pl*. L19.
[ORIGIN Spanish.]
In Spanish, Mexican, or South American cookery: small meatballs.

albugo /alˈbjuːgәʊ/ *noun*. Now *rare*. LME.
[ORIGIN Latin *albugo*, *-gin-* whiteness, from *albus* white.]
= LEUCOMA.
■ **albugineous** /albjʊˈdʒɪnɪәs/ *adjective* (now *rare* or *obsolete*) of or pertaining to white fibrous tissue; also, albuminous: M16.

album /ˈalbәm/ *noun*. E17.
[ORIGIN Latin = blank tablet, use as noun of neut. of *albus* white; first in English from German use of Latin phr. *album amicorum* album of friends, and in Latin forms.]
▸ **I** A blank book for the insertion of collected items.
1 A blank book in which people other than the owner insert autographs, memorial verses, etc. E17.
2 A blank book for the insertion of stamps, photographs, etc. M19.
▸ **II 3** A holder for a set of discs or tape recordings; an integral set of discs or tapes; a disc or tape comprising several pieces of music etc. E20.
double album: see DOUBLE *adjective & adverb*.

albumen /ˈalbjʊmɪn/ *noun*. L16.
[ORIGIN Latin *albumen*, *-min-*, from *albus* white.]
1 The white of an egg. L16.
2 BOTANY. = ENDOSPERM. L17.
3 Soluble protein, such as that in egg white. Cf. ALBUMIN. E19.
■ **alˈbumenize** *verb trans*. coat or impregnate with albumen M19.

albumin /ˈalbjʊmɪn/ *noun*. M19.
[ORIGIN French *albumine*, formed as ALBUMEN: see -IN[1].]
BIOCHEMISTRY. Any protein which is readily soluble in water and coagulable by heat; *spec*. (MEDICINE) the soluble protein present in blood serum. Cf. ALBUMEN 3.

albuminoid /alˈbjuːmɪnɔɪd/ *adjective & noun*. M19.
[ORIGIN formed as ALBUMEN + -OID.]
▸ **A** *adjective*. Of the nature of, resembling, or containing albumen. M19.
▸ **B** *noun*. A protein; *esp*. a scleroprotein. L19.

albuminous /alˈbjuːmɪnәs/ *adjective*. M17.
[ORIGIN formed as ALBUMINOID + -OUS.]
Of the nature of, resembling, or containing albumen or albumins.

albuminuria /ˌalbjʊmɪˈnjʊәrɪә/ *noun*. M19.
[ORIGIN formed as ALBUMINOID + -URIA.]
MEDICINE. The presence of albumins or other proteins in the urine.
■ **albuminuric** *adjective* characterized by albuminuria L19.

alburnum /alˈbәːnәm/ *noun*. M17.
[ORIGIN Latin, from *albus* white.]
Sapwood.
■ **alburnous** *adjective* (now *rare*) E19.

alcabala *noun* var. of ALCAVALA.

alcade *noun* var. of ALCALDE.

alcahest *noun* var. of ALKAHEST.

alcaic /alˈkeɪɪk/ *adjective & noun*. Also **A-**. M17.
[ORIGIN Late Latin *alcaicus* from Greek *alkaikos*, from *Alkaios* Alcaeus: see -IC.]
▸ **A** *adjective*. Of or pertaining to Alcaeus, a lyric poet of Mytilene (*c* 600 BC); *esp*. of a verse metre in a four-line stanza invented by him. M17.
▸ **B** *noun*. In *pl*. Alcaic verses. M17.

alcaide /alˈkʌɪdi, *foreign* alˈkaide/ *noun*. Also †**-caid**, **-cayde**. E16.
[ORIGIN Spanish from Arabic *al-qā'id* the leader, the commander: see AL-[2].]
The governor of a Spanish, Portuguese, Moorish, etc., fortress; a jailer.

alcalde /alˈkaldi, *foreign* alˈkalde/ *noun*. Also **alcade** /alˈkɑːd, *foreign* alˈkad/. M16.
[ORIGIN Spanish *alcalde* (French *alcade*) from Arabic *al-qāḍī* the judge: see AL-[2], CADI.]
A mayor, magistrate, or similar administrative officer in Spain, Portugal, and parts of S. America and the southwestern US.

alcanna /әlˈkanә/ *noun*. Also **alk-**. LME.
[ORIGIN Spanish *alcana*, *alcaña* from Arabic *al-ḥinnā'* HENNA.]
Henna; also, alkanet.

alcaptonuria *noun* var. of ALKAPTONURIA.

alcarraza /alkәˈrɑːzә, *foreign* alkaˈrraθa/ *noun*. E19.
[ORIGIN Spanish from Arabic *al-karrāz* the water-cooling jug: see AL-[2].]
A porous earthenware vessel.

alcatras /ˈalkәtras/ *noun*. Now *rare*. M16.
[ORIGIN Spanish *alcatraz* pelican, Portuguese *alcatraz* frigate bird, (formerly) pelican, from Arabic *al-ġaṭṭās* the diver: see AL-[2].]
Any of various large waterbirds, *esp*. a pelican or a frigate bird.

alcavala /alkәˈvɑːlә/ *noun*. Also **-bala** /-ˈbɑːlә/. L16.
[ORIGIN Spanish *alcabala*, Portuguese *-vala* from Arabic *al-qabāla* the tax, duty: see AL-[2]. Cf. GABELLE.]
hist. In Spain and Spanish colonies: an *ad valorem* tax, orig. of ten per cent, chargeable at every sale or exchange of goods.

alcayde *noun* var. of ALCAIDE.

alcazar /alkәˈzɑː, *foreign* alˈkaθar/ *noun*. Pl. **-zars** /-ˈzɑːz/, **-zares** /-θares/. E17.
[ORIGIN Spanish *alcázar* from Arabic *al-qaṣr* the castle: see AL-[2].]
A Spanish palace or fortress.

†**alce** *noun*. M16–L18.
[ORIGIN Latin.]
An elk.

†**alchahest** *noun* var. of ALKAHEST.

alchemical /alˈkɛmɪk(ә)l/ *adjective*. Also †**alchym-**. M16.
[ORIGIN from ALCHEMY + -ICAL.]
Of or pertaining to alchemy.
■ **alchemic** *adjective* = ALCHEMICAL E19. **alchemically** *adverb* E17.

alchemilla /alkәˈmɪlә/ *noun*. M18.
[ORIGIN medieval Latin *alchimilla*, from *alchimia* ALCHEMY + dim. *-illa*, from the belief that dew from the leaves of the plant could turn base metals into gold.]
Any of numerous herbaceous perennials of the genus *Alchemilla*, of the rose family, with palmately lobed leaves and cymes of tiny green or yellowish flowers. Cf. ***lady's mantle*** s.v. LADY *noun & adjective*.

alchemist /ˈalkɪmɪst/ *noun*. Also †**alchym-**. E16.
[ORIGIN Old French *alkemiste*, medieval Latin *alchemista*: see ALCHEMY, -IST.]
A person who studies or practises alchemy.
■ †**alchemister** *noun* = ALCHEMIST LME–L16. **alcheˈmistic** *adjective* L17. **alcheˈmistical** *adjective* M16. †**alchemistry** *noun* alchemy

M16–E19. **alchemize** *verb trans.* [after *baptist, baptize*] change (as) by alchemy L16.

alchemy /ˈalkɪmi/ *noun*. Also †**alchymy**. LME.
[ORIGIN Old French *alkemie*, *-kamie* (mod. *alchimie*) from medieval Latin *alchimia*, *-chemia* from Arabic *al-kīmiyā'*, from *al* AL-² + *kīmiyā'* from Greek *khēm(e)ia* art of transmuting metals. The var. with *-chym-* by assoc. with Greek *khymeia* infusion.]
1 The chemistry of the Middle Ages and the 16th cent.: now usu. connoting the pursuit of the transmutation of baser metals into gold, and the search for the elixir of life, etc. LME. ▸**b** *fig.* Miraculous power of transmutation or extraction. E17.

b SHAKES. *Sonn.* Gilding pale streams with heavenly alchemy.

2 A composition, mainly of brass, imitating gold. *obsolete* exc. *hist.* LME. ▸†**b** *fig.* Glittering dross. L16–M17. ▸†**c** A trumpet made of alchemy or similar metal. *literary*. M17–E19.

b DONNE Compared to this All honour's mimic, all wealth alchemy. **c** MILTON Four speedy cherubim Put to their mouths the sounding alchymie.

alchera /ˈaltʃərə/ *noun*. M20.
[ORIGIN Arrernte *altjerre* dream.]
= ALCHERINGA.

alcheringa /altʃəˈrɪŋgə/ *noun*. L19.
[ORIGIN Arrernte *altjerrenge*, lit. 'in the Dreamtime' from *altjerre* dream + *-nge* from, of.]
A golden age in the mythology of some Australian Aborigines; Dreamtime.

alchymical *adjective*, **alchymist** *noun*, etc., vars. of ALCHEMICAL etc.

alcid /ˈalsɪd/ *noun*. L19.
[ORIGIN from mod. Latin *Alcidae* (see below), from *Alca* genus name, formed as AUK: see -ID³.]
ZOOLOGY. A bird of the auk family, Alcidae. Cf. AUK.

Alclad /ˈalklad/ *noun*. E20.
[ORIGIN from AL(UMINIUM *noun* + CLAD *ppl adjective*.]
(Proprietary name for) a composite material consisting of sheets of aluminium alloy with a corrosion-resistant coating.

Alcmanian /alkˈmeɪnɪən/ *adjective & noun*. M19.
[ORIGIN from Latin *Alcmanius*, from *Alcman* from Greek *Alkman* a Greek lyric poet of the 7th cent. BC: see -AN.]
CLASSICAL PROSODY. (A verse) of four dactyls.
■ Also **Alcmanic** /-ˈmanɪk/ *adjective* M19.

†**alcoate** *noun*. Only in 19.
[ORIGIN Contr.]
Alcoholate.

alcohol /ˈalkəhɒl/ *noun*. M16.
[ORIGIN French (now *alcool*) or medieval Latin from Arabic *al-kuḥl* the kohl: see AL-², KOHL.]
†**1** A fine powder produced by grinding or esp. by sublimation. M16–M18.
†**2** *spec.* = KOHL *noun*. E17–E19.
3 A liquid essence or spirit obtained by distillation. *obsolete* in *gen.* sense. M17.

fig.: COLERIDGE Intense selfishness, the alcohol of egotism.

4 Pure spirit of wine, the intoxicating component of fermented or distilled liquors; = ETHANOL. M17. ▸**b** Intoxicating drink. L19.
absolute alcohol: see ABSOLUTE *adjective* 5.
5 *CHEMISTRY*. Any organic compound containing one or more hydroxyl groups bonded to an aliphatic radical. M19.
ethyl alcohol, *methyl alcohol*, etc.
■ **alcoholate** *noun* an alkoxide; a compound containing alcohol of crystallization: M19.

alcoholic /alkəˈhɒlɪk/ *adjective & noun*. L18.
[ORIGIN from ALCOHOL + -IC.]
▸ **A** *adjective*. **1** Of, pertaining to, or caused by alcohol; containing alcohol. L18.
alcoholic fermentation the type of fermentation, occurring in yeasts, in which glucose is broken down to produce ethanol and carbon dioxide.
2 Suffering from alcoholism. E20.
▸ **B** *noun*. A person addicted to alcoholic drink. L19.
Alcoholics Anonymous an association for the mutual support and rehabilitation of alcoholics.
■ **alcoholically** *adverb* L19.

†**alcoholimeter** *noun* var. of ALCOHOLOMETER.

alcoholise *verb* var. of ALCOHOLIZE.

alcoholism /ˈalkəhɒlɪz(ə)m/ *noun*. M19.
[ORIGIN from ALCOHOL + -ISM.]
The diseased condition caused by chronic over-indulgence in alcoholic drink; addiction to alcohol.
■ **alcoholist** *noun* an alcoholic; a drinker of alcohol: L19.

alcoholize /ˈalkəhɒlʌɪz/ *verb trans*. Also **-ise**; †**alcol-**. M17.
[ORIGIN French *alcooliser*: see ALCOHOL, -IZE.]
†**1** Sublimate, pulverize; refine to an essence, rectify. M17–L18.
2 Saturate or otherwise treat with alcohol. M19.
■ **alcoholiˈzation** *noun* L17.

alcoholometer /alkəhɒˈlɒmɪtə/ *noun*. Also †**-imeter**; **alcoholmeter**, **alcoometer**. M19.
[ORIGIN from ALCOHOL + -OMETER.]
An instrument for measuring the proportion of alcohol in a liquor.
■ ˌ**alcoholoˈmetric** *adjective* M19. **alcoholometry** *noun* M19.

†**alcolize** *verb* var. of ALCOHOLIZE.

alcoometer *noun* var. of ALCOHOLOMETER.

alcopop /ˈalkə(ʊ)pɒp/ *noun*. L20.
[ORIGIN from *alco-* (in ALCOHOLIC *adjective*) + POP *noun*¹.]
A sweet or fruit-flavoured (and freq. carbonated) drink containing alcohol. Also, a bottled ready-mixed spirit and mixer.

Alcoran /alkɔˈrɑːn, ˈalkəran/ *noun*. *arch.* Also **Alkoran**. LME.
[ORIGIN Old French & mod. French from Arabic *al-qur'ān*: see AL-², KORAN.]
The Koran.
■ **Alcoranic** *adjective* M19. †**Alcoranish** *adjective* M17–M18. **Alcoranist** *noun* a person who adheres to the original text of the Koran E17.

alcove /ˈalkəʊv/ *noun*. L16.
[ORIGIN French *alcôve* from Spanish *alcoba* from Arabic *al-qubba* the vault, the vaulted structure: see AL-².]
1 A vaulted or arched recess in a room wall, formerly *esp.* one for a bed. L16.
2 A recess in a garden wall or hedge; *arch.* a bower, a summer house. E18.
■ **alcoved** *adjective* made as an alcove; vaulted, arched: M19.

alcyonarian /alsɪəˈnɛːrɪən/ *noun & adjective*. L19.
[ORIGIN from mod. Latin *Alcyonaria* (see below), from *alcyonium* from Greek *alkuoneion* a coral said to resemble a halcyon's nest (Dioscorides): see HALCYON, -ARIAN.]
ZOOLOGY. ▸**A** *noun*. An anthozoan of the subclass Alcyonaria, which includes colonial soft corals whose polyps bear eight pinnate tentacles. L19.
▸ **B** *adjective*. Of, pertaining to, or designating this subclass. L19.

†**ald** *noun* see OLD *noun*¹.

ald- *combining form* see ALDO-.

aldea /alˈdeɪə, *foreign* alˈdeia/ *noun*. E17.
[ORIGIN Portuguese *aldeia*, †*-ea*, Spanish *aldea* from Arabic *al-ḍay'a*, from *al* AL-² + *ḍay'a* agricultural village, farm.]
A small village or a farm in Portugal, Spain, or one of their former territories.

aldehyde /ˈaldɪhʌɪd/ *noun*. M19.
[ORIGIN from Latin *al(cohol) dehyd(rogenatum)* dehydrogenated alcohol.]
CHEMISTRY. †**1** = ACETALDEHYDE. M–L19.
2 Any of a class of compounds, typified by acetaldehyde, which contain the group ·CH·O and are formed by the partial oxidation of primary alcohols. M19.
■ **aldeˈhydic** *adjective* pertaining to or characteristic of an aldehyde L19.

al dente /al ˈdɛnti, *foreign* al ˈdɛnte/ *adverbial & adjectival phr*. M20.
[ORIGIN Italian, lit. 'to the tooth'.]
Of pasta, vegetables, etc.: (cooked) so as to be still firm when bitten.

alder /ˈɔːldə/ *noun*.
[ORIGIN Old English *alor*, *aler*, rel. to Middle Low German *aller*, Middle Dutch *else*, Old High German *elira*, *erila* (German *Erle*), Old Norse *ǫlr*, connected with Latin *alnus*. Forms with *d* recorded from 14.]
1 Any tree of the genus *Alnus*, related to the birch; esp. *A. glutinosa*, common in wet places. Also ***alder tree***. OE. ▸**b** Any of several similar trees and shrubs of other genera. Also ***alder tree***. L16.
b black alder (*a*) = ***alder buckthorn*** below; (*b*) *N. Amer.* a winterberry, *Ilex verticillata*. **red alder** (*a*) *S. Afr.* = ROOI-ELS; (*b*) a tree of western N. America, *Alnus oregona*. **white alder** (*a*) *N. Amer.* any of several pepperbushes; (*b*) *S. Afr.* a tree, *Platylophus trifoliatus*, allied to the rooi-els but with trifoliate leaves.
2 An alderfly. E19.
– COMB.: **alder buckthorn** a deciduous shrub, *Frangula alnus* (or *Rhamnus frangula*) of the buckthorn family, growing on peaty soils and bearing red or (when ripe) black berries; **alderfly** a neuropteran insect of the genus *Sialis*, found near streams; **alder kitten** a kitten moth, *Furcula bicuspis*; ***alder tree***: see sense 1 above.

†**alder-** *prefix*. ME–M17.
[ORIGIN Later devel. of Old English *alra* genit. pl. of ALL.]
Of all, as *alderliefest* dearest of all.

alderman /ˈɔːldəmən/ *noun*. Also (*hist.*) **ealdor-**. Pl. **-men**.
[ORIGIN Old English *aldormann*, from *aldor*, *ealdor* chief, prince (formed as OLD *adjective*) + MAN *noun*.]
1 A man of noble or high rank. Long *obsolete* exc. *hist.* OE.
2 The chief officer or warden of a guild. Long *obsolete* exc. *hist.* OE.
3 Chiefly *hist.* A magistrate of a borough; a municipal officer next in dignity to a mayor, for a long time (and still in the City of London) representing a ward, more recently (up to 1974) a co-opted member of an English or Welsh county or borough council; *N. Amer.* & *Austral.* an elected member of a city council. (The status and conditions of appointment of aldermen have varied with time and place.) OE.
honorary alderman: a title which, since 1974, can be given to past English or Welsh councillors.
■ **alderˈmanic** *adjective* of, pertaining to, or like an alderman M18. **alderˈmanity** *noun* (*rare*) (*a*) *joc.* aldermanship; (*b*) the body of aldermen: E17. **aldermanlike** *adjective* resembling (that of) an alderman E17. **aldermanly** *adjective* like, or becoming to, an alderman E18. **aldermanry** *noun* (*a*) *hist.* a district having its own alderman; (*b*) the dignity or rank of an alderman: LME. **aldermanship** *noun* the office, position, or quality of an alderman LME. **alderwoman** *noun* (*rare*) †(*a*) an alderman's wife; (*b*) *N. Amer.* a female alderman: M16.

Alderney /ˈɔːldəni/ *adjective & noun*. L18.
[ORIGIN One of the Channel Islands.]
▸ **A** *adjective*. Designating (an animal of) a breed of dairy cattle belonging to Alderney or to the Channel Islands in general. L18.
▸ **B** *noun*. An animal of the Alderney breed. E19.

Aldine /ˈɔːldʌɪn/ *adjective & noun*. E19.
[ORIGIN mod. Latin *Aldinus*, from *Aldus*: see below, -INE¹.]
(A book or edition) printed by Aldus Manutius (1450–1515), a Venetian printer or his successors; (in) a style of printing type made for him, or an imitation of it.

Aldis /ˈɔːldɪs/ *noun*. E20.
[ORIGIN A. C. W. *Aldis* (1878–1953), Brit. inventor.]
In full ***Aldis lamp***. (Proprietary name for) a hand lamp for signalling in Morse code.

aldo- /ˈaldəʊ/ *combining form* of ALDEHYDE: see -O-. Before a vowel **ald-**.
■ **aldoˈsterone** *noun* (*BIOCHEMISTRY*) an adrenocortical steroid hormone important in electrolyte metabolism M20. **aldoˈsteronism** *noun* (*MEDICINE*) excessive secretion of aldosterone M20. **alˈdoxime** *noun* (*CHEMISTRY*) an oxime of an aldehyde, a compound of the general formula RCH=NOH (where R is an alkyl group) L19.

aldol /ˈaldɒl/ *noun*. L19.
[ORIGIN from ALD(EHYDE + -OL.]
CHEMISTRY. A viscous liquid, $CH_3CH(OH)CH_2CHO$, obtained when acetaldehyde dimerizes in dilute alkali or acid; 3-hydroxybutanal.
– COMB.: **aldol condensation** an addition reaction typified by the formation of aldol from acetaldehyde, undergone by most aldehydes and ketones.

aldose /ˈaldəʊz, -s/ *noun*. L19.
[ORIGIN from ALD(EHYDE + -OSE².]
CHEMISTRY. Any sugar which is also an aldehyde.

†**aldress** *noun*. M16–E18.
[ORIGIN Perh. contr. of ALDERMAN + -ESS¹.]
An alderman's wife.

aldrin /ˈɔːldrɪn/ *noun*. M20.
[ORIGIN from K. *Alder* (1902–58), German chemist, + -IN¹.]
A chlorinated polycyclic hydrocarbon, $C_{12}H_8Cl_6$, formerly used as an insecticide.

ale /eɪl/ *noun*.
[ORIGIN Old English *(e)alu* = Old Saxon *alo-*, Old High German *al-*, Old Norse *ǫl*, from Germanic.]
1 Beer, formerly esp. of unhopped or paler-coloured kinds, a type of this, a drink of this, now chiefly in ***real ale*** & as a trade word. Also (usu. with specifying word) a similar drink made from other ingredients. Cf. BEER *noun*¹, PORTER *noun*². OE.
brown ale, ***light ale***, ***mild ale***, ***pale ale***. ***cakes and ale***: see CAKE *noun*. ***ginger ale***: see GINGER *noun*. ***real ale***: see REAL *adjective*². ***twopenny ale***: see TWOPENNY *adjective* 1. ***yard of ale***: see YARD *noun*².
2 Chiefly *hist.* A festival or gathering at which much ale is drunk. OE.
– COMB.: **ale-bench** a bench in or at the front of an alehouse; **aleberry** (*obsolete* exc. *dial.*) ale boiled with spice, sugar, and sops of bread; porridge made with ale; **aleconner** an inspector of ale (still a titular office in some boroughs); **alecost** [COST *noun*¹] = COSTMARY; †**ale-draper** an alehouse-keeper; **ale firkin** a small barrel of ale; an old unit of liquid capacity equal to 9 (earlier 8) gallons; **ale gallon** an old unit of liquid capacity equal to 282 cu. in. (4.62 litres); **alehouse** (chiefly *hist.*) a house where ale is retailed; †**ale-knight** a frequenter of alehouses, a tippler; **ale-taster** an aleconner; **ale-wort** the fermenting infusion of malt.

aleatico /alɪˈatɪkəʊ/ *noun*. Also **A-**. E19.
[ORIGIN Italian.]
A sweet Italian red wine.

aleatory /ˈeɪlɪət(ə)ri/ *adjective*. L17.
[ORIGIN Latin *aleatorius*, from *aleator* dice player, from *alea* a die: see -Y².]
Depending on the throw of a die or on chance; depending on uncertain contingencies; *MUSIC & ART* involving random choice by the composer, performer, or artist.
■ Also **aleatoric** /ˌeɪlɪəˈtɒrɪk/ *adjective* M20.

alec *noun* see SMART ALEC.

alecithal /eɪˈlɛsɪθ(ə)l/ *adjective*. L19.
[ORIGIN from A-¹⁰ + Greek *lekithos* yolk + -AL¹.]
Of an egg or egg cell: having little or no yolk.

aleck *noun* see SMART ALEC.

†**alectoria** *noun*. Also **-ius**. LME–M19.
[ORIGIN Latin, formed as ALECTRYOMANCY.]
A precious stone said to be found in the gizzard of cocks.
■ †**alectorian** *noun & adjective* L16–L19.

A

alectryomancy /əˈlɛktrɪəmansi/ *noun*. Also **-toro-**, †**-tro-**. **M17.**
[ORIGIN from Greek *alektruōn*, *-tōr* cock + -MANCY.]
Divination by means of a cock with grains of corn.

alee /əˈliː/ *adverb & pred. adjective*. **LME.**
[ORIGIN from A *preposition*[1] 1 + LEE *noun*[1], partly after Old Norse *á hlé*.]
NAUTICAL. On the lee or sheltered side of a ship; to leeward.

aleft /əˈlɛft/ *adverb*. *arch*. **ME.**
[ORIGIN from A *preposition*[1] 1 + LEFT *noun*.]
On or to the left.

alegar /ˈeɪlɪɡə/ *noun*. **LME.**
[ORIGIN from ALE, after VINEGAR.]
Sour ale; malt vinegar.

ale-hoof /ˈeɪlhuːf/ *noun*. Now *dial.* **ME.**
[ORIGIN Prob. alt. of earlier ***hayhove*** s.v. HAY *noun*[2].]
Ground ivy, *Glechoma hederacea*.

Alemannic /alɪˈmanɪk/ *adjective & noun*. Also **-manic**, **Alle-**. **L18.**
[ORIGIN Late Latin *Alemannicus*, from *Alemanni* pl. (Greek *Alamanoi*) a Germanic tribe, from Germanic (prob. formed as ALL + MAN *noun*, denoting a wide alliance of peoples): see -IC.]
► **A** *adjective*. Of or pertaining to a confederation of Germanic tribes occupying the territory between the Rhine, the Main, and the Danube, or the (modern representatives of the) dialects of these people. **L18.**
► **B** *noun*. The group of Old High German dialects spoken by these people; the modern representatives of these in Alsace, Switzerland, and SW Germany. **E19.**
■ **Alemannian** *adjective & noun* = ALEMANNIC **L19**. **Alemannish** *adjective & noun* †(**a**) German; (**b**) = ALEMANNIC: **ME.**

alembic /əˈlɛmbɪk/ *noun & verb*. **ME.**
[ORIGIN Old French from medieval Latin *alembicus* from Arabic *al-'anbīq*, the still cap from Greek *ambix*: see AL-[2]. Aphet. to LIMBECK.]
► **A** *noun*. An obsolete kind of still consisting of a gourd-shaped vessel and a cap having a long beak for conveying the products to a receiver; the cap of such a still. **ME.**
fig.: BURKE The hot spirit drawn out of the alembic of hell.
► †**B** *verb trans*. Infl. **-ck-**. Distil (as) in an alembic. Earlier as LIMBECK *verb*. **M17–M18.**
■ **alembicated** *adjective* (of ideas, expression, etc.) over-refined, subtilized **L18**. **alembi'cation** *noun* over-refinement of expression etc.; concentration: **L19.**

alembroth /əˈlɛmbrɒθ/ *noun*. *obsolete* exc. *hist.* **ME.**
[ORIGIN Unknown.]
(A name of the alchemists for) mercury ammonium chloride. Freq. also ***sal alembroth***.

alength /əˈlɛŋθ/ *adverb & pred. adjective*. Now *dial.* **LME.**
[ORIGIN from A *preposition*[1] 1 + LENGTH.]
Lengthwise; forward (freq. *fig.*).

aleph /ˈɑːlɛf/ *noun*. **ME.**
[ORIGIN Hebrew *'ālep* lit. 'ox'. Cf. ALPHA.]
1 The first letter of the Hebrew, Phoenician, and other Semitic alphabets. **ME.**
2 MATH. A transfinite cardinal numeral. **E20.**
– COMB.: **aleph-null**, **aleph-zero** MATH. the smallest transfinite cardinal numeral, the cardinal of the set of positive integers.

†**alepine** *noun*. **M18–M19.**
[ORIGIN French *alépine* from Arabic *ḥalabī* from Aleppo.]
A mixed fabric of wool and silk, or mohair and cotton.

alerce /əˈləːsi/ *noun*. **M19.**
[ORIGIN Spanish = LARCH *noun*[1].]
(The wood of) a Patagonian conifer, *Fitzroya cupressoides*.

alerion /əˈlɪərɪən/ *noun*. Also **alle-**. **L15.**
[ORIGIN French *alérion* = medieval Latin *alario*.]
HERALDRY. An eagle with spread wings but without beak or feet.

alert /əˈləːt/ *adverb, adjective, noun, & verb*. Also †**alerte**. **L16.**
[ORIGIN French *alerte*, earlier *allerte*, *à l'airte* from Italian *all'erta*, from *alla* at the + *erta* lookout (tower).]
► **A** *adverb & adjective*. **1** *adverb & pred. adjective*. Orig. MILITARY. On the lookout; watchful, vigilant. **L16.**
2 *adjective*. Quick in attention or motion; lively, nimble. **E18.**
► **B** *noun*. A sudden attack or surprise; a warning call, an alarm; (the period of) a warning of an air raid etc. **L18.**
on the alert on the lookout against danger or attack. ***red alert***: see RED *adjective*. ***yellow alert***: see YELLOW *adjective*.
► **C** *verb trans*. Make alert, warn. (Foll. by *to*.) **M19.**
■ **alertly** *adverb* **L18**. **alertness** *noun* **E18.**

alethic /əˈliːθɪk/ *adjective*. **M20.**
[ORIGIN from Greek *alētheia* truth + -IC.]
LOGIC. Designating modalities of truth, such as necessity, contingency, or impossibility.

aleuromancy /əˈljʊərəmansi/ *noun*. *rare*. **M17.**
[ORIGIN French *aleuromancie*, formed as ALEURONE: see -MANCY.]
Divination by means of meal or flour.

aleurone /əˈljʊərəʊn/ *noun*. Also **-on** /-ən/. **M19.**
[ORIGIN Greek *aleuron* flour.]
BOTANY. Protein stored as granules within the cells of seeds.

Aleut /əˈljuːt, ˈalɪuːt/ *noun & adjective*. **L18.**
[ORIGIN Unknown.]
► **A** *noun*. **1** A native or inhabitant of the Aleutian Islands (see ALEUTIAN); a speaker of the language of the Aleutian Islands. **L18.**
2 The language of the Aleutian Islands, other islands in the Bering Sea, and parts of western Alaska, related to Inupiaq and Yupik. **L19.**
► **B** *attrib.* or as *adjective*. Of or pertaining to the Aleutian Islands, their inhabitants, or their language. **M20.**

Aleutian /əˈljuːʃ(ə)n/ *adjective & noun*. **L18.**
[ORIGIN from ALEUT + -IAN.]
► **A** *adjective*. Designating a group of islands off the west coast of Alaska; of or pertaining to the Aleutian Islands. **L18.**
► **B** *noun*. = ALEUT *noun*. **E19.**

alevin /ˈaləvɪn/ *noun*. **M19.**
[ORIGIN Old French & mod. French, ult. from Latin *allevare* set up, raise up.]
A young fish fresh from the spawn.

alewife /ˈeɪlwʌɪf/ *noun*. Pl. **-wives** /-wʌɪvz/. **LME.**
[ORIGIN from ALE + WIFE *noun* (in sense 'woman').]
1 A woman who keeps an alehouse. *arch.* **LME.**
2 A fish of the herring family, *Alosa pseudoharengus*, found on the Atlantic coast of N. America. **M17.**

Alexander /alɪɡˈzɑːndə/ *adjective*. **M20.**
[ORIGIN from the surname *Alexander*: see below.]
Designating or pertaining to the principle or technique of using the body and postural alignment advocated by the Australian-born physiotherapist Frederick Matthias Alexander (1869–1955).

†**Alexander** *verb trans*. **M17–E18.**
[ORIGIN formed as ALEXANDRIAN *adjective*[2] & *noun*[2].]
Treat in a manner characteristic of or appropriate to Alexander the Great.

alexanders /alɪɡˈzɑːndəz/ *noun*. **OE.**
[ORIGIN from medieval Latin *alexandrum*; in Middle English also from Old French *alissa(u)ndre*, *-derie*.]
An umbelliferous plant, *Smyrnium olusatrum*, formerly used for salads; *N. Amer.* any of certain other umbellifers.

Alexandrian /alɪɡˈzɑːndrɪən/ *noun*[1] & *adjective*[1]. **M16.**
[ORIGIN from *Alexandria* (see below), founded by Alexander the Great, + -AN.]
1 A native or inhabitant of, of or pertaining to, the Egyptian city of Alexandria. **M16.**
2 Belonging or akin to, a member or follower of, any of the schools of philosophy in ancient Alexandria, *esp.* the Neoplatonic school of Plotinus and others or that of the Christian fathers Clement of Alexandria and Origen. **M18.**
3 Belonging or akin to, a member or imitator of, the school of Greek literature, esp. poetry, which flourished at Alexandria under the Ptolemies; (of a writer) imitative, or fond of recondite learning. **M19.**
■ **Alexandrianism** *noun* the philosophical method or doctrine or the literary style of the Alexandrians **M19.**

Alexandrian /alɪɡˈzɑːndrɪən/ *adjective*[2] & *noun*[2]. In senses A.1, B. also **a-**. **M18.**
[ORIGIN from *Alexander* the Great (356–323 BC), king of Macedonia, + -IAN.]
► **A** *adjective*. **1** = ALEXANDRINE *adjective*[2]. **M18.**
2 Of, pertaining to, or characteristic of Alexander the Great. **E19.**
Alexandrian laurel (**a**) a shrub of SW Asia, *Danae racemosa*, of the lily family, sometimes grown for its evergreen leaves and red berries; (**b**) a large Indo-Malayan evergreen tree, *Calophyllum inophyllum* (family Guttiferae), with glossy leaves, fragrant white flowers, and round green fruit; also called ***poon tree***.
► **B** *noun*. = ALEXANDRINE *noun*[2]. **M18.**

Alexandrine /alɪɡˈzɑːndrɪn, -ʌɪn/ *noun*[1] & *adjective*[1]. **L15.**
[ORIGIN French *alexandrin*, formed as ALEXANDRIAN *noun*[1] & *adjective*[1]: see -INE[1].]
= ALEXANDRIAN *noun*[1] & *adjective*[1]; also, a type of embroidery associated with Alexandria.

alexandrine /alɪɡˈzɑːndrɪn, -ʌɪn/ *adjective*[2] & *noun*[2]. Also **A-**. **L16.**
[ORIGIN French *alexandrin*, from *Alexandre* Alexander (the Great), eponymous hero of a famous Old French romance in which the metre is used.]
PROSODY. ► **A** *adjective*. Designating or pertaining to an iambic line of twelve syllables or six feet. **L16.**
► **B** *noun*. An alexandrine line or verse. **M17.**
POPE A needless Alexandrine ends the song That like a wounded snake, drags its slow length along.

alexandrite /alɪɡˈzɑːndrʌɪt/ *noun*. **M19.**
[ORIGIN from *Alexander* II (1818–81), Tsar of Russia + -ITE[1].]
MINERALOGY. A gem variety of chrysoberyl which appears green in daylight and red in artificial light.

alexia /əˈlɛksɪə, eɪ-/ *noun*. **L19.**
[ORIGIN Irreg. from A-[10] + Greek *lexis* speech (conf. with Latin *legere* read) + -IA[1].]
MEDICINE. Inability to read, or to understand written words, as a result of brain disorder. Cf. DYSLEXIA.
■ **alexic** *adjective* **E20.**

alexin /əˈlɛksɪn/ *noun*. Also **-ine**. **L19.**
[ORIGIN from Greek *alexein* ward off + -IN[1].]
PHYSIOLOGY. = COMPLEMENT *noun* 4e.

alexipharmic /əlɛksɪˈfɑːmɪk/ *noun & adjective*. Now *rare* or *obsolete*. Also †**-mac**. **M17.**
[ORIGIN French *alexipharmaque* from mod. Latin *alexipharmacum* from Greek *alexipharmakon* neut. sing. (as noun) of adjective from *alexein* ward off + *pharmakon* poison: assim. to -IC.]
► **A** *noun*. An antidote against poison. **M17.**
► **B** *adjective*. Having the quality or nature of an antidote. **M17.**
■ **alexipharmacon**, **-cum** *noun* = ALEXIPHARMIC *noun* **M16**. †**alexipharmical**, **-acal** *adjective & noun*: only in **17.**

†**alexiteric** *adjective & noun*. **L17–L19.**
[ORIGIN from medieval Latin *alexiterium* remedy, from Greek *alexitērion* safeguard, + -IC.]
(A substance) having the power to ward off contagion, or act as an antidote.
■ †**alexiterial** *adjective & noun* **E17–M19**. †**alexiterical** *adjective* **M17–L18**. †**alexitery** *adjective & noun* **E17–E18.**

alexithymic /eɪˌlɛksɪˈθʌɪmɪk/ *adjective & noun*. **L20.**
[ORIGIN from A-[10] + Greek *lexis* speech + *thumos* soul + -IC.]
PSYCHOLOGY. (A person) lacking the ability to recognize and express emotions.
■ **alexithymia** *noun* an affective disorder characterized by an inability to recognize and express emotions **L20.**

aley *adjective* var. of ALY.

alfa /ˈalfə/ *noun*. Also **ha-** /ˈha-/. **M19.**
[ORIGIN Arabic *ḥalfā'*, colloq. *ḥalfa*.]
Esparto grass.

alfalfa /alˈfalfə/ *noun*. **M19.**
[ORIGIN Spanish from Arabic *al-fasfaṣa* a green fodder.]
= LUCERNE *noun*[2].

alfaqui /alfəˈkiː, *foreign* alfaˈki/ *noun*. Now *rare*. Pl. **-quis** /-ˈkiːz/, **-quies** /-ˈkiːɛs, *foreign* -ˈkies/. **E17.**
[ORIGIN Spanish *alfaquí* from Arabic *al-faqīh*, from *al* AL-[2] + *faqīh* a person skilled in Islamic jurisprudence.]
A Muslim expert in religious law.

alferez /alˈfɛrəz, *foreign* alˈfereθ/ *noun*. Also †**-res**. Pl. **-rezes** /-rəzɪz/, **-reces** /-rəsɪz, *foreign* -reθes/. **L16.**
[ORIGIN Spanish *alférez*, Old Spanish & Portuguese *-res* from Arabic *al-fāris* the horseman, the skilled fighter on horseback: see AL-[2].]
In Spanish, and formerly in Portuguese, armies: an ensign, a standard-bearer; a second lieutenant.

alfilaria /alfɪləˈriːə/ *noun*. *US*. **M19.**
[ORIGIN Mexican Spanish, from Spanish *alfiler* pin, with ref. to the long-beaked carpels.]
= ***pin clover*** s.v. PIN *noun*[1].

alfin /ˈalfɪn/ *noun*. Long *obsolete* exc. *hist.* Also **-phin**. **LME.**
[ORIGIN Old French *aufin*, later also *alphin* (medieval Latin *alphinus*) from Spanish & Portuguese *alfil* from Arabic *al-fīl* the elephant: see AL-[2].]
A chess piece similar in function to the present-day bishop.

alfisol /ˈalfɪsɒl/ *noun*. **M20.**
[ORIGIN from arbitrary 1st elem. + -SOL.]
SOIL SCIENCE. A soil of an order comprising leached basic or slightly acid soils with a clay-enriched B horizon.

alforja /alˈfɔːhə, *foreign* alˈfɔrxa/ *noun*. Also †**-rge**. **E17.**
[ORIGIN Spanish *alforja*, Portuguese *-rge* from Arabic *al-qurj* saddlebag: see AL-[2].]
1 In Spain, Portugal, Latin America, and other areas of Spanish influence (as the south-western US): a wallet, a saddlebag. **E17.**
†**2** A cheek pouch. **E–M18.**

Alfredian /alˈfriːdɪən/ *adjective*. **E19.**
[ORIGIN from *Alfred* (see below) + -IAN.]
Pertaining to or characteristic of Alfred the Great (849–99), king of the West Saxons, or his writings.

Alfredo /alˈfreɪdəʊ/ *adjective*. **L20.**
[ORIGIN *Alfredo* di Lelio (1893–1959), Italian chef and restaurateur, who invented the sauce.]
Denoting a dressing for pasta, orig. consisting of butter and grated Parmesan cheese but now usu. a sauce incorporating butter, cream, garlic, and Parmesan. Freq. *postpositive*, in ***fettuccine Alfredo***.

al fresco /alˈfrɛskəʊ/ *adverb & adjective*. **M18.**
[ORIGIN Italian *al fresco*: see FRESCO.]
► **A** *adverb*. **1** In the open air. **M18.**
2 ART. In fresco. **M18.**
► **B** *adjective*. Open-air. **E19.**

Alfvén /ˈalfveɪn, -vən/ *noun*. **M20.**
[ORIGIN Hannes *Alfvén* (1908–95), Swedish physicist.]
PHYSICS. Used **attrib.** with ref. to Alfvén's discoveries.
Alfvén speed, **Alfvén velocity** the speed of an Alfvén wave in a plasma of given properties. **Alfvén wave** a transverse magnetohydrodynamic wave travelling in the direction of the magnetic field in a magnetized plasma.

alga /ˈalɡə/ *noun*. Pl. **algae** /ˈaldʒiː, ˈalɡiː/. **M16.**
[ORIGIN Latin = seaweed.]
Orig., seaweed; now, any of a large group of non-vascular mainly aquatic cryptogams capable of photosynthesis, including seaweeds and many unicellular and filament-

ous organisms. Also *collect.*, the mass formed by such organisms.
blue-green alga: see BLUE *adjective*. ***brown alga***: see BROWN *adjective*. ***green alga***: see GREEN *adjective*. ***red alga***: see RED *adjective*.

algal /ˈalg(ə)l/ *adjective & noun*. M19.
[ORIGIN from ALGA + -AL¹.]
▸ **A** *adjective*. Of or pertaining to algae; of the nature of an alga. M19.
▸ **B** *noun*. An alga. *rare*. M19.

algarroba /alɡəˈrəʊbə/ *noun*. L16.
[ORIGIN Spanish from Arabic *al-ḵarrūb(a)*: see AL-², CAROB.]
1 (The pod of) the carob tree. L16.
2 (The fruit of) any of certain mesquites. M18.

algate /ˈɔːlɡeɪt/ *adverb*. Long *obsolete* exc. *dial.* Also **-gates** /-ɡeɪts/. ME.
[ORIGIN from ALL + GATE *noun*²; *-s* analogical.]
†**1** Always, continually. ME–L16.
2 Anyhow; by all or any means. ME.
†**3** At any rate, at all events. ME–E17.
†**4** All the way, altogether. ME–E17.
5 Nevertheless, after all. ME.
6 Everywhere. *N. English*. L19.

algebra /ˈaldʒɪbrə/ *noun*. LME.
[ORIGIN Italian, Spanish, medieval Latin, from Arabic *al-jabr*, from *al* AL-² + *jabr* reunion of broken parts, from *jabara* set broken bones, reunite, restore. The term achieved currency in the title of a book, *ʿilm al-jabr wa'l-muqābala* 'the science of restoring what is missing and equating like with like', by the mathematician al-Ḵwārizmī (cf. ALGORISM).]
†**1** The surgical treatment of fractures. LME–M16.
2 The part of mathematics which investigates the relations and properties of numbers or other mathematical structures by means of general symbols; a system of this based on given axioms. M16.
■ **algebraist** /-breɪɪst/ *noun* a person versed in algebra E17. **algebraize** *verb* (**a**) *verb trans.* express in algebraic form; (**b**) *verb intrans.* perform algebra: M19. †**algebrician** *noun* = ALGEBRAIST L16–L17. **algebrist** *noun* = ALGEBRAIST L17.

algebraic /aldʒɪˈbreɪɪk/ *adjective*. M17.
[ORIGIN from ALGEBRA + -IC.]
Of, pertaining to, or occurring in algebra; *spec.* (of a function, etc.) able to be produced by the simple algebraic operations (opp. TRANSCENDENTAL *adjective*).

C. S. OGILVY The famous equation . . $e^{\pi i} = -1$, is not algebraic.

■ **algebraical** *adjective* of or relating to algebra L16. **algebraically** *adverb* in terms of, by means of, algebra M17. **algebraicize** /-sʌɪz/ *verb trans.* express in algebraic form L19.

algedonic /aldʒɪˈdɒnɪk/ *adjective*. L19.
[ORIGIN from Greek *algos* pain + *hēdonē* pleasure + -IC.]
Pertaining to or characterized by pleasure and pain, or reward and punishment.

Algerian /alˈdʒɪərɪən/ *noun & adjective*. E17.
[ORIGIN from *Algeria* (see below) + -AN.]
▸ **A** *noun*. **1** A native or inhabitant of the country of Algeria or the town of Algiers, in N. Africa. E17.
2 Wine from Algeria. M20.
▸ **B** *adjective*. Of or pertaining to Algeria or Algiers. L19.
■ **Algerine** /ˈaldʒəriːn/ *noun & adjective* (*arch.*) = ALGERIAN; *esp.* (characteristic of) a pirate from Algiers: M17.

-algia /ˈaldʒə/ *suffix*.
[ORIGIN from Greek *algos* pain + -IA¹.]
Forming nouns denoting pain in a specified part, as ***neuralgia***.
■ **-algic** *suffix*: forming corresp. adjectives.

algicide /ˈaldʒɪsʌɪd, ˈalɡɪ-/ *noun*. E20.
[ORIGIN from ALGA + -I- + -CIDE.]
A substance poisonous to algae.

algid /ˈaldʒɪd/ *adjective*. E17.
[ORIGIN Latin *algidus*, from *algere* be cold: see -ID¹.]
Cold, chilly; MEDICINE characterized by a feeling of coldness.
■ **alˈgidity** *noun* (*rare*) M17.

algin /ˈaldʒɪn/ *noun*. L19.
[ORIGIN from ALGA + -IN¹.]
Alginic acid or any of its salts.

alginic /alˈdʒɪnɪk/ *adjective*. L19.
[ORIGIN from ALGIN + -IC.]
CHEMISTRY. ***alginic acid***, an insoluble gelatinous carbohydrate found (chiefly as salts) in many brown algae.
■ ˈ**alginate** *noun* a salt of alginic acid L19.

Algol /ˈalɡɒl/ *noun*. M20.
[ORIGIN from ALGO(RITHMIC *language*.]
(The name of) an early high-level programming language.

algolagnia /alɡəʊˈlaɡnɪə/ *noun*. E20.
[ORIGIN from Greek *algos* pain + *lagneia* lust.]
PSYCHIATRY. The practice of obtaining sexual pleasure from pain inflicted on oneself or another.

algology /əlˈɡɒlədʒi/ *noun*. M19.
[ORIGIN from ALGA + -OLOGY.]
The branch of science that deals with algae.
■ **algoˈlogical** *adjective* M19. **algologist** *noun* M19.

Algonkian /alˈɡɒŋkɪən/ *adjective & noun*. L19.
[ORIGIN Var. of ALGONQUIAN.]
1 GEOLOGY. = PROTEROZOIC. L19.
2 = ALGONQUIAN. E20.

Algonkin *noun & adjective* var. of ALGONQUIN.

Algonquian /alˈɡɒŋkwɪən, -kɪ-/ *adjective & noun*. See also ALGONKIAN. L19.
[ORIGIN Irreg. from ALGONQUIN + -IAN.]
▸ **A** *adjective*. Of or pertaining to a large group of N. American Indian peoples including the Algonquins proper; of or pertaining to (any of) the languages and dialects of these peoples. L19.
▸ **B** *noun*. A member of, any of the languages or dialects of, this group of peoples. L19.

Algonquin /alˈɡɒŋkwɪn, -kɪn/ *noun & adjective*. Also **-kin** /-kɪn/. E17.
[ORIGIN French, contr. of †*Algoumequin*: cf. Micmac *algoomeaking* at the place of spearing fish and eels.]
▸ **A** *noun*. A member of a N. American Indian people of the districts of Ottawa and Quebec; the language of this people; more widely = ALGONQUIAN *noun*. E17.
▸ **B** *attrib.* or as *adjective*. Of or pertaining to the Algonquin or their language; more widely = ALGONQUIAN *adjective*. E18.

†**algor** *noun*. LME–L19.
[ORIGIN Latin.]
Cold, chilliness, esp. at the onset of fever.

algorism /ˈalɡərɪz(ə)m/ *noun*. Also †**augrim** & similar forms. ME.
[ORIGIN Old French *augori(s)me*, *algorisme* from medieval Latin *algorismus* from Arabic *al-Ḵwārazmī* the man of *Ḵwārazm* (Khiva), agnomen of the mathematician Abū Jaʿfar Muḥammad ibn Mūsā (fl. c 800–47), author of widely translated works on arithmetic and algebra.]
1 The Arabic or decimal system of writing numbers; *gen.* arithmetic. ME.
2 = ALGORITHM 2. *rare*. M20.
■ **algoˈrismic** *adjective* (*rare*) M19.

algorithm /ˈalɡərɪð(ə)m/ *noun*. L17.
[ORIGIN Var. of ALGORISM after Greek *arithmos* number.]
1 = ALGORISM 1. L17.
2 A procedure or set of rules for calculation or problem-solving, now esp. with a computer. E19.
■ **algoˈrithmic** *adjective* expressed as or using an algorithm or algorithms L19. **algoˈrithmically** *adverb* L20.

alguacil /alɡwəˈsɪl, *foreign* alɡwaˈθil/ *noun*. Pl. **-cils** /-ˈsɪlz/, ***-ciles*** /-ˈθiles/. Also **-zil** /-ˈzɪl, *foreign* -ˈθil/, pl. **-zils** /-ˈzɪlz/, ***-ziles*** /-ˈθiles/. E16.
[ORIGIN Spanish (earlier *-zil*) from Arabic *al-wazīr*, from *al* AL-² + *wazīr* VIZIER.]
1 In Spain: an officer of justice, a warrant officer, a sergeant. In Latin America or other areas of Spanish influence: a sheriff, a constable. E16.
2 A mounted official at a bullfight. E20.

algum /ˈalɡʌm/ *noun*. Pl. **-im** /-ɪm/, **-s**. L16.
[ORIGIN Hebrew *ʾalgūm*: cf. ALMUG.]
A tree, not definitely identified, mentioned in the Bible. Also ***algum tree***.

Al-Hadj *noun* var. of AL-HAJJ.

alhagi /alˈhɑːdʒi/ *noun*. M18.
[ORIGIN mod. Latin from Arabic *al-ḥāj*: see AL-².]
A spiny leguminous shrub of the genus *Alhagi*, members of which yield a kind of manna.

alhaji /alˈhadʒi/ *noun*. As a title **A-**. M20.
[ORIGIN Hausa, formed as AL-HAJJ.]
In W. Africa: a Muslim who has been to Mecca as a pilgrim.

Al-Hajj /alˈhadʒ/ *noun*. Also **-Hadj**. M19.
[ORIGIN Arabic, formed as AL-² + HAJJ.]
As a title: a Muslim who has undertaken the hajj. Cf. HAJJI.

Alhambresque /alhamˈbrɛsk/ *adjective*. M19.
[ORIGIN from *Alhambra* (see below) + -ESQUE.]
In the architectural style of the Alhambra, the palace of the Moorish kings at Granada in Spain; like the Alhambra.

†**alhidada** *noun* var. of ALIDADE.

alias /ˈeɪlɪəs/ *adverb & noun*. LME.
[ORIGIN Latin = at another time, otherwise.]
▸ **A** *adverb*. Otherwise called or named; called at other times. LME.

E. O'NEILL It sounds to me like Bacchus, alias the Demon Rum, doing the talking.

▸ **B** *noun*. †**1** LAW. A second writ, containing the words *sicut alias praecipimus*, issued after the first has failed. LME–E19.
2 A name by which a person is or has been called on other occasions; an assumed name. E17.
3 PHYSICS & TELECOMMUNICATIONS. Each of a set of signal frequencies which, when sampled at a given uniform rate, would give the same set of sampled values, and thus might be incorrectly substituted for one another when reconstructing the original signal. M20.
4 COMPUTING. An alternative name or label that refers to a file, command, address, etc., and can be used to locate or access it. M20.
■ **aliasing** *verbal noun* (**a**) PHYSICS & TELECOMMUNICATIONS the misidentification of a signal frequency, introducing distortion or error; (**b**) COMPUTING the use of aliases to designate files, commands, addresses, or other items: M20.

Ali Baba /ˈali ˈbɑːbə, ˈbɑːbɑː/ *noun phr*. M20.
[ORIGIN Arabic *ʿAlī Bābā*, a character in the *Arabian Nights' Entertainments*.]
In full ***Ali Baba basket***. A tall basket with a rounded body and a flat base.

alibi /ˈalɪbʌɪ/ *adverb, noun, & verb*. L17.
[ORIGIN Latin = elsewhere.]
▸ †**A** *adverb*. Elsewhere. L17–L18.
▸ **B** *noun*. A plea by the person accused of an act that he or she was elsewhere when it took place; evidence to support such a plea; *colloq.* an excuse of any kind. L18.
▸ **C** *verb trans. & intrans.* Provide an alibi, offer an excuse, (for). E20.

alible /ˈalɪb(ə)l/ *adjective*. *rare*. M17.
[ORIGIN Latin *alibilis*, from *alere* nourish: see -IBLE.]
Nutritive, nourishing.

Alicante /alɪˈkanti/ *noun*. Also †**-cant**, †**-gant**. L15.
[ORIGIN A city in Spain.]
A red wine exported from or produced near Alicante in SE Spain.

Alice /ˈalɪs/ *noun*. E20.
[ORIGIN Female forename.]
1 [*Alice* Roosevelt Longworth, daughter of the US President Theodore Roosevelt.] ***Alice blue***, a light greenish-blue colour. E20.
2 [Heroine of two books by Lewis Carroll.] ▸**a** ***Alice-in-Wonderland*** *adjective*, fantastic, absurd. E20. ▸**b** ***Alice band***, a type of band to hold back the hair. M20.

alick *noun* see SMART ALEC.

alicyclic /alɪˈsʌɪklɪk, -ˈsɪk-/ *adjective*. L19.
[ORIGIN from ALI(PHATIC + CYCLIC.]
CHEMISTRY. Of an organic compound: cyclic but not aromatic. Also, of or pertaining to such a compound.

alidade /ˈalɪdeɪd/ *noun*. Also †**allidatha**, †**alhidada**, †**alidad**. LME.
[ORIGIN Orig. from Arabic *al-ʿiḍāda*, perh. from *al* AL-² + *ʿaḍud* upper arm; in mod. form from French from Spanish.]
A sighting device or pointer for angular measurement, usu. for use with (orig.) a quadrant, astrolabe, etc., or (now) a plane table.

alien /ˈeɪlɪən/ *adjective & noun*. ME.
[ORIGIN Old French from Latin *alienus* belonging to another, from *alius* other.]
▸ **A** *adjective*. **1** Belonging to another person, family, place, context, or world. ME. ▸**b** *esp.* Of a foreign nation, under foreign allegiance. LME. ▸**c** Of a plant: introduced from another country and subsequently naturalized. M19.

KEATS The sad heart of Ruth, when, sick for home, She stood in tears amid the alien corn. *Guardian* Was this an alien attempt to establish life on this planet?

b Alien Priory: owing obedience to a mother abbey in a foreign country.
2 Foreign in nature, character, or origin; out of harmony. LME. ▸**b** Foll. by *from*: differing in nature from, inconsistent with. LME. ▸**c** Foll. by *to*: repugnant to, opposed to; out of character with. E18.

A. G. GARDINER The Fifth Symphony . . creates a state of mind, a spiritual atmosphere, that is destroyed by any intrusive and alien note.

▸ **B** *noun*. **1** A stranger, a foreigner. ME. ▸**b** *esp.* A non-naturalized foreigner. ME. ▸**c** A being from another world. M20.

fig.: SHAKES. *1 Hen. IV* Almost an alien to the hearts Of all the court. **b** M. MCCARTHY It was against the law for an alien to interfere in the domestic affairs of a foreign country. **c** K. AMIS Some excellent stories have been written about non-communicating aliens.

2 A person separated or excluded *from*. *arch.* M16.

J. H. NEWMAN As if aliens from God's mercies.

3 BOTANY. A plant orig. introduced from another country and later naturalized. M19.
4 PHILOLOGY. A word from one language used but not naturalized in another. L19.
– COMB.: **alien-enemy**, **alien-friend** LAW an alien owing allegiance to a country at war with, at peace with, his or her country of residence.
■ **alienage** *noun* the condition or legal standing of an alien E19. **alienness** /-n-n-/ *noun* E20.

alien /ˈeɪlɪən/ *verb trans*. Now *rare*. In sense 2 also **-ene** /-iːn/. LME.
[ORIGIN Old French *aliener* from Latin *alienare*: see ALIENATE *verb*.]
1 = ALIENATE *verb* 1. LME.
2 = ALIENATE *verb* 2. LME.
■ **alieˈnee** *noun* a person to whom the ownership of property is transferred. M16. **alienor** *noun* a person who transfers property to another M16.

alienable /ˈeɪlɪənəb(ə)l/ *adjective*. E17.
[ORIGIN from ALIEN *verb* + -ABLE. Cf. French *aliénable*.]
Able to be alienated.
■ **aliena'bility** *noun* L18.

†**alienate** *adjective & noun*. LME.
[ORIGIN Latin *alienatus* pa. pple, formed as ALIENATE *verb*: see -ATE[2].]
▸ **A** *adjective*. **1** Estranged. LME–E19.
2 Alienated. E16–M17.
3 Foreign in nature or character. M16–M17.
▸ **B** *noun*. An alien, a stranger. L15–M16.

alienate /ˈeɪlɪəneɪt/ *verb trans*. E16.
[ORIGIN Latin *alienat-* pa. ppl stem of *alienare*, from *alienus*: see ALIEN *adjective & noun*, -ATE[3].]
1 Estrange; turn away in feelings or affection. E16.
2 Transfer to the ownership of another. E16.
3 *gen*. Turn away, divert. L16.
■ **alienator** *noun* L17.

alienation /eɪlɪəˈneɪʃ(ə)n/ *noun*. LME.
[ORIGIN Old French, or Latin *alienatio(n-)*, formed as ALIENATE *verb*: see -ATION.]
1 The act of estranging or state of estrangement in feeling or affection. LME. ▸**b** THEATRICAL. Objectivity of a spectator's reaction, sought by some dramatists. M20.

BURKE They grow every day into alienation from this country.

alienation of affection(s) US LAW transfer of a person's affection from one with rights or claims to it to another held responsible for the estrangement.
2 Loss of mental faculties, insanity. Now usu. more fully ***mental alienation***. LME.
3 The action of transferring ownership of anything. LME. ▸**b** The state of being held by other than the proper owner. *arch*. E19.

J. BRAMHALL The alienation of Lands to the Church.

4 Diversion of something to a different purpose. L18.

H. WILSON He [Gladstone] was particularly concerned to strengthen the safeguards against 'alienation', that is, diverting to another purpose . . moneys that had been specifically voted by Parliament for a particular use.

aliene *verb* see ALIEN *verb*.

alienism /ˈeɪlɪənɪz(ə)m/ *noun*. L18.
[ORIGIN from ALIEN *noun* + -ISM.]
1 The position of being an alien; foreign status. Now *rare*. L18.
2 The study and treatment of mental illness. Now *rare* or *obsolete*. L19.

alienist /ˈeɪlɪənɪst/ *noun*. Now chiefly *US*. M19.
[ORIGIN French *aliéniste*: see ALIENATION 2, -IST.]
An expert in mental illness, esp. from a legal standpoint.

†**alife** *adverb*. M16–L17.
[ORIGIN Prob. from LIEF, conf. with LIFE *noun*.]
love alife, love dearly.

aliform /ˈeɪlɪfɔːm/ *adjective*. E18.
[ORIGIN mod. Latin *aliformis*, from Latin *ala* wing: see -FORM.]
Wing-shaped.

†**Aligant** *noun* var. of ALICANTE.

alight /əˈlʌɪt/ *verb intrans*. Pa. t. & pple **alighted**, (*arch*. or *poet*.) **alit** /əˈlɪt/; pa. pple also †**alight**. OE.
[ORIGIN from A-[1] + LIGHT *verb*[1].]
1 Spring lightly down, dismount, *from* (or †*of*) a horse; descend *from* or *out of* a conveyance. OE. ▸†**b** Spring lightly *on* or *upon*. LME–E16.

CLARENDON His Majesty alighted out of his Coach. JOYCE Our travellers . . alighted from their palfreys. B. PYM Elegantly dressed people were alighting from cars.

†**2** *gen*. Go or come down. ME–L15.
3 Get down from a horse or conveyance; land, stop. ME.

SHAKES. *Merch. V.* Madam, there is alighted at your gate A young Venetian.

4 Descend and settle; come to earth from the air. ME.

V. WOOLF That moment . . when if a feather alight in the scale it will be weighed down. G. ORWELL A thrush had alighted on a bough not five metres away. *Times* We were about to alight along the centre-line of the runway. *fig*.: SCOTT FITZGERALD So far his suspicions hadn't alighted on Tom.

5 Descend and strike; fall *on* or *upon*, as a blow. *arch*. ME.
6 Come by chance *on*, *upon*. M19.

S. GILLESPIE His eye immediately alighted on a Degas.

alight /əˈlʌɪt/ *adverb & pred. adjective*. LME.
[ORIGIN Prob. from phr. †*on a light* (= *lighted*) *fire*.]
On fire; lighted up.

†**alighten** *verb trans*. M16–L18.
[ORIGIN Irreg. after LIGHTEN *verb*[1].]
Lighten, relieve.

align /əˈlʌɪn/ *verb*. Also (earlier) **aline**. LME.
[ORIGIN Old French *alignier* (mod. *aligner*), from phr. *à ligne* into line: see A-[5], LINE *noun*[2].]
†**1** *verb trans*. Of a male animal: copulate with (a female animal). Only in LME.
2 *verb trans*. Place or lay in a line or into correct or appropriate relative positions; *esp*. bring (points) into a straight line. L17.

Which? They give a perfectly clean cut provided you keep the blades aligned correctly.

3 *verb intrans*. Fall into line (*with*); come together in agreement or alliance. L19.
4 *verb trans*. Bring into (esp. political) agreement or alliance (*with*). M20.

New York Times Mr. Putin's decision to align Russia squarely with the United States.

alignment /əˈlʌɪnm(ə)nt/ *noun*. Also **aline-**. L18.
[ORIGIN Old French & mod. French *alignement*, formed as ALIGN: see -MENT.]
1 Arrangement in a line or in correct relative positions. L18. ▸**b** *spec*. Arrangement of soldiers in a line or lines; a military line. L18.
2 The drawing of a straight line through a point or points. M19.
3 Bringing into line, straightening. L19.
4 Bringing into (esp. political) agreement or alliance; a grouping of parties, powers, etc. M20.
– COMB.: **alignment chart** = NOMOGRAM.

alike /əˈlʌɪk/ *adjective* (now usu. *pred*.).
[ORIGIN Old English *gelīc* = Old Frisian *gelīk*, Old Saxon *gelīc* (Dutch *gelijk*), Old High German *galīh* (German *gleich*), Old Norse *glíkr*, Gothic *galeiks*, from Germanic: see A-[4], LIKE *adjective*. Reinforced by Old Norse *álíkr* (with prefix as AN-[1]).]
Like one another; similar; indistinguishable.

SHAKES. *Com. Err.* Male twins, both alike. E. BOWEN Their alike profiles. D. PARKER They looked alike, though the resemblance did not lie in their features.

■ **alikeness** *noun* LME.

alike /əˈlʌɪk/ *adverb*.
[ORIGIN Old English *ġelīċe*, formed as ALIKE *adjective* + adverbial suffix *-e* (corresp. forms in Old High German and Gothic): see A-[4], LIKE *adverb*. Reinforced by Old Norse *álíka* (with prefix as AN-[1]).]
In like manner; equally; similarly.

GOLDSMITH Nature, a mother kind alike to all. R. WEST The curtains, . . the wallpapers, which alike were a rich-coloured paste of little flowers.

share and share alike: see SHARE *noun*[2], *verb*[2].

aliment /ˈalɪm(ə)nt/ *noun*. L15.
[ORIGIN French, or Latin *alimentum*, from *alere* nourish: see -MENT.]
1 Nutriment, food. L15.
2 *fig*. Support, mental sustenance. M17.
3 SCOTS LAW & *gen*. Provision for maintenance; alimony. M17.
■ **ali'mental** *adjective* of or pertaining to aliment; nutritive: L16. **ali'mentally** *adverb* (*rare*) M17.

aliment /ˈalɪmɛnt/ *verb trans*. L15.
[ORIGIN French *alimenter* from late Latin *alimentare*, from *alimentum*: see ALIMENT *noun*.]
1 Supply with food. *rare*. L15.
2 SCOTS LAW & *gen*. Make provision for the maintenance of, provide alimony for. E17.
3 *fig*. Sustain, support, nourish. M17.
■ **ali'mentative** *adjective* (*rare*) connected with the supply of aliment L19. **ali'mentativeness** *noun* (*rare*) feeding instinct, desire for food M19. **alimenter** *noun* (*rare*) a person who receives or provides aliment E19. **ali'mentive** *adjective* (*rare*) = ALIMENTATIVE M19. **ali'mentiveness** *noun* = ALIMENTATIVENESS E19.

alimentary /alɪˈmɛnt(ə)ri/ *adjective*. L16.
[ORIGIN Latin *alimentarius*, formed as ALIMENT *verb*: see -ARY[1].]
1 Concerned with or performing functions of nutrition. L16.
alimentary canal the whole passage through the body, from mouth to anus, by which food is received, digested, etc.
2 Of the nature of aliment, nourishing. E17.
3 Concerned with or providing maintenance. M18.

alimentation /ˌalɪm(ə)nˈteɪʃ(ə)n/ *noun*. L16.
[ORIGIN French, or medieval Latin *alimentatio(n-)*, from *alimentare*: see ALIMENT *verb*, -ATION.]
1 Maintenance, support. L16.
2 The process of being nourished; the mode of receiving nourishment. E17.
3 The action or process of nourishing. M17.

alimony /ˈalɪməni/ *noun*. E17.
[ORIGIN Latin *alimonia*, from *alere* nourish: see -MONY.]
1 Nourishment, maintenance; means of subsistence. E17.
2 *spec*. An allowance made to a woman (occas. to a man) by her (or his) (ex-)spouse after divorce or legal separation, or during proceedings for these. Now chiefly *US* (in Britain all such allowances are now called ***maintenance***). M17.

aline *verb*, **alinement** *noun* vars. of ALIGN, ALIGNMENT.

aliphatic /alɪˈfatɪk/ *adjective*. L19.
[ORIGIN from Greek *aleiphat-*, *-phar* unguent, fat + -IC: orig. used of the fatty acids.]
CHEMISTRY. Of an organic compound: having an open-chain structure; not aromatic. Also, of or pertaining to such compounds.

aliquot /ˈalɪkwɒt/ *adjective & noun*. L16.
[ORIGIN French *aliquote* from Latin *aliquot* some, several, from *alius* one of two + *quot* how many.]
Orig. MATH. ▸**A** *adjective*. That is contained in the whole an integral number of times. Chiefly in ***aliquot part***. Cf. QUANTAL *adjective* 1. L16.
▸ **B** *noun*. An aliquot part, integral factor; *loosely* any fraction of a whole, a sample. E17.

alisma /əˈlɪzmə/ *noun*. L16.
[ORIGIN Latin from Greek.]
A plant of the genus *Alisma*; a water plantain.

alisphenoid /alɪˈsfiːnɔɪd/ *adjective & noun*. M19.
[ORIGIN from Latin *ala* wing + SPHENOID *adjective*.]
ANATOMY & ZOOLOGY. (Forming or pertaining to) one of the lateral bones of the cranium (in the human skull either of the greater wings of the sphenoid bone).
■ **alisphe'noidal** *adjective* M19.

alit *verb* see ALIGHT *verb*.

aliter /ˈalɪtə/ *adverb*. L17.
[ORIGIN Latin.]
Chiefly LAW. Otherwise.

aliterate /eɪˈlɪt(ə)rət/ *adjective & noun*. M20.
[ORIGIN from A-[10] + LITERATE.]
▸ **A** *adjective*. Unwilling to read, despite being able to do so. M20.
▸ **B** *noun*. An aliterate person. L20.
■ **aliteracy** *noun* L20.

-ality /ˈalɪti/ *suffix*.
[ORIGIN from -AL[1] + -ITY.]
Forming nouns, with senses as -ITY.

aliunde /alɪˈʌndi/ *adverb*. M17.
[ORIGIN Latin.]
From elsewhere; from another source.

alive /əˈlʌɪv/ *adverb & adjective* (usu. *pred*.).
[ORIGIN Old English phr. *on līfe*: see A *preposition*[1] 6, LIFE *noun*.]
1 Living; in life; while still living. OE.

SHAKES. *Merch. V.* Is my boy—God rest his soul!—alive or dead? STEELE The most contented happy man alive. DICKENS Why, bless my heart alive, my dear, how late you are!

2 Unextinguished, undiminished, unforgotten. E17.

E. F. BENSON For two years she had . . kept that illusion undeniably alive. R. JARRELL This print of mine, that has kept its colour Alive through many cleanings. A. S. BYATT The fire was still alive in the hearth.

3 In a sentient or susceptible condition; fully aware; sensitive or responsive *to*. E17.

A. G. GARDINER You cannot be alive unless you take life gallantly. J. CONRAD I was perfectly alive to the difficulty of stopping him from going there.

4 Full of energy or animation; active, lively, brisk. M18. ▸**b** ELECTRICITY. = LIVE *adjective* 5b. L19.

K. NORWAY Group Captain Hurst is the most alive man I know.

5 In a state of commotion; swarming. Foll. by *with*. L18.

L. VAN DER POST The swamp was alive with crocodile and hippo. T. STOPPARD The air is alive with bells and sirens.

– PHRASES ETC.: **alive and kicking** *colloq*. very active. **alive and well (and living in —)** *colloq*. not (as has been suggested) ill or dead, and to be found in (the place named). **alive oh** [from a fish-sellers' cry] very much alive and active. ***burn alive***: see BURN *verb* 8. ***dead-alive***, ***dead-and-alive***: see DEAD *adjective & adverb*. ***Heavens alive***: see HEAVEN *noun*. **look alive!** *colloq*. be brisk. **man alive!** *colloq*.: an expletive. ***sakes alive!***: see SAKE *noun*[1]. ***snakes alive!***: see SNAKE *noun* 1C.
■ **aliveness** *noun* M19.

aliyah /ˈalɪjə/ *noun*. Pl. **-yoth** /-jəʊt/. E20.
[ORIGIN Hebrew *ʿălīyāh*, lit. 'ascent'.]
JUDAISM. **1** The act or privilege of going up to the reading desk of a synagogue to read from the Torah. E20.
2 Immigration to Israel. Freq. (as ***First Aliyah***, ***Second Aliyah***, etc.), a particular episode of immigration. M20.

alizarin /əˈlɪz(ə)rɪn/ *noun*. Also **-ine**. M19.
[ORIGIN French *alizarine* from *alizari* madder, perh. from colloq. Arabic *al-ʿiṣāra* the juice or sap pressed out: see AL-[2], -IN[1].]
CHEMISTRY. The red colouring matter of madder root; 1,2-dihydroxyanthraquinone, $C_{14}H_8O_4$.
– COMB.: **alizarin red**, **alizarin yellow**: (the colours of) synthetic dyestuffs derived from or resembling alizarin.

Al-kaaba *noun* see KAABA.

alkahest /ˈalkəhɛst/ *noun*. Also †**alc(h)-**. M17.
[ORIGIN Prob. invented by Paracelsus, after Arabic.]
The universal solvent sought by the alchemists. Also *fig*., anything universally applicable.

alkalaemia /alkəˈliːmɪə/ *noun*. E20.
[ORIGIN from ALKALI + -AEMIA.]
MEDICINE. A condition of abnormally raised pH of the blood.

alkalescent /alkəˈlɛs(ə)nt/ *adjective*. Now *rare*. M18.
[ORIGIN from ALKALI + -ESCENT.]
Slightly alkaline; conducive or tending to alkalinity.
■ **alkalescence**, **alkalescency** *nouns* tendency to alkalinity, slight alkaline character M18.

alkali /ˈalkəlʌɪ/ *noun*. Pl. **-s**, **-es**. LME.
[ORIGIN medieval Latin from Arabic *al-qalī* the calcined ashes of *Salsola* etc.: see AL-².]
1 A saline substance extracted from the calcined ashes of plants such as saltwort (genus *Salsola*) or glasswort (genus *Salicornia*); soda ash. LME.
2 A plant from which soda ash is obtained; saltwort, glasswort. Now *rare* or *obsolete*. L16.
3 Any substance which neutralizes or effervesces with acids and forms a caustic or corrosive solution in water; a water-soluble base, *esp.* a hydroxide. E17.
VOLATILE *alkali*.
4 A soluble salt or mixture of such salts existing in excess in the soil; terrain characterized by this. Freq. *attrib*. *N. Amer.* M19.

S. E. WHITE The limitless alkali of the Arizona plains. *attrib.*: J. H. BEADLE Little to see but . . alkali flats and sand-hills.

– COMB.: **alkali metal** *CHEMISTRY* any of the elements occupying group IA of the periodic table (namely lithium, sodium, potassium, rubidium, caesium, francium), which are soft, reactive metals forming soluble hydroxides.
■ **alkalify** /-ɪfʌɪ/ *verb trans.* make alkaline M19. †**alkalious** *adjective* = ALKALINE L17–M18.

alkalic /alˈkalɪk/ *adjective*. M18.
[ORIGIN from ALKALI + -IC.]
1 Alkaline. *rare*. M18.
2 *GEOLOGY*. Of a rock or mineral: richer in alkali metals, esp. sodium and potassium, than the average for the group it belongs to. E20.

alkalide /ˈalkəlʌɪd/ *noun*. L20.
[ORIGIN from ALKALI + -IDE.]
CHEMISTRY. A binary ionic compound in which the anion is an alkali metal.

alkalimetry /alkəˈlɪmɪtri/ *noun*. E19.
[ORIGIN formed as ALKALIDE + -METRY.]
CHEMISTRY. The measurement of the strengths of alkalis.
■ **alkalimeter** *noun* an instrument for alkalimetry E19. **alkaliˈmetric**, **alkaliˈmetrical** *adjectives* M19.

alkaline /ˈalkəlʌɪn/ *adjective*. L17.
[ORIGIN from ALKALI + -INE¹.]
Of, pertaining to, or of the nature of alkalis; rich in alkali; *CHEMISTRY* having a pH greater than 7.
alkaline battery: in which the electrolyte is an alkaline solution. **alkaline earth** *CHEMISTRY* any of the strongly basic oxides of the metals calcium, strontium, barium, and radium; *loosely* any of these elements, which are placed in group IIA of the periodic table. **alkaline metal** = *ALKALI metal*. *alkaline tide*: see TIDE *noun*.
■ **alkalinity** /-ˈlɪnɪti/ *noun* alkaline character or quality L18. **alkalinization** /alkəlɪnʌɪˈzeɪʃ(ə)n/ *noun* making alkaline; reduction of acidity: M20. **alkalinize** /-lɪn-/ *verb trans.* make alkaline E19.

alkalize /ˈalkəlʌɪz/ *verb trans.* Also **-ise**. M17.
[ORIGIN from ALKALI + -IZE.]
Make alkaline, treat with alkali.
■ †**alkalizate** *adjective* alkaline E17–M18. **alkaliˈzation** *noun* L17.

alkaloid /ˈalkəlɔɪd/ *adjective* & *noun*. E19.
[ORIGIN German: see ALKALI, -OID.]
CHEMISTRY. (Designating or pertaining to) any of a class of complex organic bases of vegetable origin which have pronounced physiological actions on humans (e.g. morphine, strychnine, nicotine).
vinca alkaloid: see VINCA *noun*¹.
■ **alkaˈloidal** *adjective* of the nature of an alkaloid; pertaining to alkaloids: L19.

alkalosis /alkəˈləʊsɪs/ *noun*. Pl. **-loses** /-ˈləʊsiːz/. E20.
[ORIGIN from ALKALI + -OSIS.]
MEDICINE. A condition of abnormally raised pH of the body fluids.

alkane /ˈalkeɪn/ *noun*. L19.
[ORIGIN from ALKYL + -ANE.]
CHEMISTRY. Any of the saturated hydrocarbons (e.g. methane, butane) which form a series having the general formula C_nH_{2n+2}. Cf. PARAFFIN.

alkanet /ˈalkənɛt/ *noun*. ME.
[ORIGIN Colloq. Arabic *al-ḥanna(t)* = classical Arab. *al-ḥinnā'* ALCANNA.]
1 A red dye obtained from the roots of certain plants of the genus *Alkanna*, of the borage family, esp. *A. lehmannii*. ME.
2 Any plant of the genus *Alkanna*; any of several related plants having roots which can be used in similar ways, esp. *Anchusa officinalis* of Europe, with violet or occas. yellow or white flowers. Also (more fully ***green alkanet***, ***evergreen alkanet***), a coarse blue-flowered garden plant, *Pentaglottis sempervivens*, native to SW Europe. ME.

alkanna *noun* var. of ALCANNA.

alkaptonuria /alˌkaptəˈnjʊərɪə/ *noun*. Also **alc-**. L19.
[ORIGIN from German *Alkapton*, *Alc-* homogentisic acid, from *alkali* ALKALI + Greek *kapton* neut. pres. pple of *kaptein* swallow greedily, + -URIA.]
MEDICINE. A hereditary metabolic disorder characterized by an accumulation of homogentisic acid in certain tissues and its excretion in the urine.
■ **alkaptonuric** *adjective* & *noun* (a person) suffering from alkaptonuria L19.

alkekengi /alkɪˈkɛndʒi/ *noun*. LME.
[ORIGIN medieval Latin from Arabic *al-* & Persian *kākanj*: see AL-².]
An ornamental plant, *Physalis alkekengi*, native to southern Europe and Asia, bearing red berries enclosed by an inflated orange calyx. Also called ***Chinese lantern***, ***winter cherry***, and other names.

alkene /ˈalkiːn/ *noun*. L19.
[ORIGIN from ALKYL + -ENE.]
CHEMISTRY. Any of the unsaturated hydrocarbons with one double bond, which form a series having the general formula C_nH_{2n}; = OLEFIN.

alkermes /alˈkəːmiːz, -ɪz/ *noun*. M16.
[ORIGIN French *alkermès* from Arabic *al-qirmiz*: see AL-², KERMES.]
1 A confection or cordial containing the kermes insect; a sweet cordial coloured with cochineal. M16.
†**2** = KERMES 2. E17–M18.

alkie *noun* var. of ALKY.

†**alkin** *adjective*. Long *dial.* ME–L19.
[ORIGIN from genit. of ALL + genit. of KIN *noun* & *adjective*, orig. as prenominal phr., later treated as adjective.]
Of every kind; every kind of.

alkine *noun* see ALKYNE.

Alkoran *noun* var. of ALCORAN.

alkoxide /alˈkɒksʌɪd/ *noun*. L19.
[ORIGIN from ALKOXY- + -IDE.]
CHEMISTRY. A salt or simple compound containing an alkoxyl radical.

alkoxy- /alˈkɒksi/ *combining form*. Also as attrib. adjective **alkoxy**. L19.
[ORIGIN from ALKALI + OXY-.]
Used to denote the presence of an alkoxyl group.

alkoxyl /alˈkɒksʌɪl, -sɪl/ *noun*. L19.
[ORIGIN formed as ALKOXY- + -YL.]
The radical RO· derived from an alcohol. Usu. in *comb*.

alky /ˈalki/ *noun*. *slang*. Also **alkie**. M19.
[ORIGIN Abbreviation: see -Y⁶, -IE.]
1 = ALCOHOL. M19.
2 = ALCOHOLIC *noun*. M20.

S. KING They drink because it's what alkies are wired up to do.

alkyd /ˈalkɪd/ *noun*. E20.
[ORIGIN from ALKYL + ACID *noun*.]
CHEMISTRY. Any of a class of synthetic polyester resins. Usu. more fully ***alkyd resin*** etc.

alkyl /ˈalkʌɪl, -kɪl/ *noun*. L19.
[ORIGIN German, from *Alkohol* ALCOHOL: see -YL.]
CHEMISTRY. Any radical derived from an alkane by removal of a hydrogen atom; a compound of a metal, e.g. lead, with a number of such radicals. Freq. in *comb*.
■ **alkylate** *verb trans.* introduce an alkyl radical into (a compound) L19. **alkyˈlation** *noun* E20.

alkyne /ˈalkʌɪn/ *noun*. Orig. **-ine**. E20.
[ORIGIN from ALKYL + -YNE.]
CHEMISTRY. Any of the series of unsaturated hydrocarbons containing one triple bond and having the general formula C_nH_{2n-2}, e.g. acetylene.

all /ɔːl/ *adjective* (in mod. usage also classed as a *determiner*), *pronoun*, *noun*, & *adverb*.
[ORIGIN Old English (*e*)*all* = Old Frisian *al*, *ol*, Old Saxon, Old High German *al* (Dutch *al*, German *all*), Old Norse *allr*, Gothic *als*.]
▸ **A** *adjective*. **1** With *noun sing.* The whole amount, quantity, extent, or compass of. (Preceding the noun and any determiners (the def. article, †the indef. article, demonstratives, possessives, etc.) and other adjectives; following the head noun (always so with pers. prons. without adjunct); or with *be* (*arch. rare* with other verbs) following the verb.) OE.

AV 1 *Pet.* 1:24 All flesh is as grasse. G. WASHINGTON All this looks very well on paper. LD MACAULAY All Devonshire had been gathered together to welcome him. K. MANSFIELD This all sounds very strenuous and serious. E. WAUGH All day the heat had been barely supportable. S. KAUFFMANN I still need all the love I can get. R. MILLAR But one desire—to give all my might to letters. A. AYCKBOURN It was all rather pathetic.

all day (*long*): see DAY *noun*. *all night* (*long*): see NIGHT *noun*. *all that*: see THAT *demonstr. pronoun* etc. *all the best*: see BEST *adjective*, *noun*, & *adverb*. *all the day* (*long*): see DAY *noun*. *all the night* (*long*): see NIGHT *noun*. *all the time*: see TIME *noun*. *all the way*: see WAY *noun*. *all the world and his wife*: see WORLD *noun*. *for all the world*: see WORLD *noun*. *get away from it all*: see GET *verb*. *have seen it all before*: see SEE *verb*. *of all the cheek*, *of all the nerve*: see OF *preposition*.
2 With *noun pl.* The entire number of; the individual constituents of, without exception. (Positioned as for sense 1; after noun (though not pers. pronoun) *poet.*; †preceding *we*.) OE.

AV *Isa.* 53:6 Alle we like sheepe haue gone astray. MILTON Hear all ye Angels. E. YOUNG All men think all men mortal, but themselves. G. CRABBE My senses fail not all. KEATS They are all here to-night. *Daily News* All you who mean to follow in the same old way. YEATS Come gather round me, players all. R. MILNER A fellow from the B.B.C. Symphony Orchestra, of all outfits. J. BOWEN Cast all lean one way. C. HAMPTON May all your troubles be lexicological ones. J. OSBORNE Do you want us to all go? R. MAUGHAM All three men were stone dead when you left?

all and singular: see SINGULAR *adjective* 2. *all comers*: see COMER 1. **All Fools' Day** 1 April, popularly appropriated to practising upon people's credulity. ALL FOURS. ALL HALLOWS. **all kinds of**, **all sorts of** many different kinds of. **All Saints' (Day)** 1 November, on which there is a general commemoration of the saints. **all-sorts** a miscellany, esp. of liquorice sweets. *all sorts of*: see *all kinds of* above. **All Souls' Day** 2 November, on which the Roman Catholic Church makes supplications on behalf of the dead. *all systems go*: see SYSTEM *noun*. *at all costs*: see COST *noun*². *at all hours*: see HOUR *noun*. *at all points*: see POINT *noun*¹. **be all things to all men** be able to please everybody. *fire on all cylinders*, *function on all cylinders*: see CYLINDER 3. *of all others*: see OTHER *pronoun* & *noun*. *of all things*: see THING *noun*¹. *till all hours*: see HOUR *noun*. *to all appearance(s)*: see APPEARANCE. *you-all*: see YOU *pronoun*.
3 With *noun sing.* Every. (Preceding the noun only.) Long *obsolete* exc. as below. OE.
all kind of, **all manner of** = *all kinds of* (sense 2 above). †**all thing** everything; also = ALL *adverb* 1. See also ALKIN, and cf. *all-weather*, *all work* in Comb. below.
4 With *noun sing.* Any whatever. (In universally exclusive sentences or clauses; preceding the noun only.) LME.

LONGFELLOW Without all guile or Suspicion . . was he. C. FRY But by no right does this Briton Break in and ruffle them beyond all hope. J. ORTON If you run into trouble I shall deny all knowledge of you.

5 With *noun sing.* The greatest possible. (Preceding the noun only.) L16.

SHAKES. *Rich. III* I in all haste was sent.

▸ **B** *pronoun* & *noun*. **I** *pronoun*. **1** As antecedent to a relative, in senses A.1, 2 (the earliest use as pronoun); (freq.) the limit of what, the only thing(s) *that*. OE.

SHAKES. *Timon* To have his pomp, and all what state compounds. D. D. EISENHOWER I call upon all who love freedom to stand with us now. DAY LEWIS All I can remember of it is that there was a fire lit in my bedroom and a too heavy eiderdown. B. BERMANGE We will do . . all that our means will allow.

2 *pl.* All people; all persons concerned. OE.

P. BARNES The rest is drowned out as all start shouting angrily.

and all and everything or everyone else (*boots and all*: see BOOT *noun*²). *all aboard*: see ABOARD *adverb* 1. *free-for-all*: see FREE *adjective*.
3 *sing.* Everything; the totality. OE.

MILTON What though the field be lost? All is not lost. S. GRAY I assumed you were coming back, that's all.

above all: see ABOVE *preposition* 6. *after all*: see AFTER *preposition* 7. **all but** *adverbial phr.* everything short of, almost. **all in all** (*a*) *adverbial* taken as a whole; (*b*) *pred.* of supreme importance. *all in a day's work*, *all in the day's work*: see DAY *noun*. *all told*: see TELL *verb*. **at all** in any way, to any extent, on any occasion (usu. in neg., interrog., or hypothetical contexts). BE-ALL. **bugger all**, **damn all**, etc., *coarse slang* absolutely nothing. *crown all*: see CROWN *verb*¹ 5. END-ALL. *first of all*: see FIRST. *for all it is worth*, *for all one is worth*: see WORTH *adjective*. **for all (that)** notwithstanding (that) (with noun passing into adjective, and *that* conjunction into pronoun). *for good and all*: see GOOD *noun*. **in all** in total number. *in all but name*: see NAME *noun*. *least of all*: see LEAST *adjective*, *noun*, & *adverb*. *not at all*: see NOT *adverb*. †**of all** most of all, beyond all. ONCE *and for all*. ONCE *for all*. *the devil and all to do*: see DEVIL *noun*. *warts and all*: see WART. See also WITHAL.
4 Distributed to each member or part of the whole: see phrases below. ME.
all and each *arch.*, **all and every**, **all and some** *arch.*, **all and sundry**, **one and all** all collectively and individually.
5 Foll. by *of*: every one of; the whole of; *colloq.* as much as. L16.

K. LAFFAN It's not all of us have the stuff of martyrdom. A. SHAFFER He wasn't at his cottage all of Saturday. M. TWAIN It must have been all of fifteen minutes . . of dull, homesick silence.

6 In games, of a score: for each side. M18.
▸ **II** *noun*. **7** *The* (or *this*) whole system of things; the universe. L16.

CARLYLE The wide circle of the All where God's Laws are not.

8 (Usu. with possess. pronoun) Everything that one has or that pertains to one; one's whole property, interest, energy, etc. Also in *pl.* in ***pack up one's alls*** (now *dial.*) [perh. alt. of *awls*]. E17.

BURKE We are, as I think, fighting for our all. P. ROTH I gave my all to his cross-examination.

one's little all the little that one has.
9 Whole being, entirety, totality. M17.

J. MASEFIELD Ah, but that ben't the all of love.

▸ **C** *adverb*. **1** Modifying an adjective or adverb (phr.) (orig. the adjective separated from the noun phr. and app. referring to the predicate): wholly, completely; altogether, quite. OE. ▸**b** *hyperbol.* Very. *colloq.* M20.

DISRAELI His Royal Highness all smiles, and his Consort all diamonds. BROWNING All a-gog to have me trespass. JOYCE How, all of a sudden, she had broken out into a peal of laughter. E. O'NEILL She remains like this all during the scene. SCOTT FITZGERALD I'm all out of practice. T. FRISBY This place'll be all empty. **b** ALDOUS HUXLEY We will assume that the Indians have gone all hygienic.

All Blacks the New Zealand international rugby union team. *all ears*: see EAR *noun*¹. *all fingers and thumbs*: see FINGER *noun*. **all for** *colloq.* entirely in favour of. ALL IN. *all in a tremble*, *all of a* *tremble*: see TREMBLE *noun* 1. ***all of a*** —: see OF *preposition*. ***all of a piece***: see PIECE *noun*. **all one** quite the same, a matter of indifference (*to*), (*all* here passing into noun). ALL OUT. ALL RIGHT. ***all square***: see SQUARE *adjective* 6b. **all there** *colloq.* not deficient in intellect etc. ***all the same***: see SAME *adjective, adverb*. ***all together***: see ALTOGETHER *adverb* 2. ***all wool and a yard wide***: see WOOL *noun*. **all yours** *colloq.* your responsibility. ***call all to naught***: see NAUGHT *pronoun & noun*. ***go all unnecessary***: see UNNECESSARY *adjective* 1. ***not all that*** —: see NOT *adverb*. **what something is all about**: its essential nature.

†**2** Modifying a particle combined with a verb, esp. *to-*. Hence ***all to, alto-*** with other verbs: wholly, completely. OE–L17.

3 Modifying an adverb or preposition of place: in all directions, in every part, everywhere. ME.

all along: see ALONG *adverb* 7. ALL OVER. ALL ROUND. ALL UP. ***walk all over***: see WALK *verb*[1].

4 Even *if*, even *though*. Also with conjunction omitted, although. Long *obsolete* exc. in ALBEIT (cf. also ALBE), ALTHOUGH. ME.

5 Just, merely, even. Passing into a mere intensive. *arch.* L16.

SIR W. SCOTT He . . Gave them a chain of twelve marks' weight All as he lighted down.

6 With *the* and compar.: by that amount, to that extent. L16.

V. WOOLF One liked Mr Ramsay all the better for thinking that if his little finger ached the whole world must come to an end.

7 Modifying a verb: wholly, completely. *arch. rare.* E18.

P. J. BAILEY Gazing o'er thee, I all Forget the bounds of being.

– COMB.: With noun in adjective sense (see sense A. above, ALLSPICE, etc.) and in adverbs which were orig. noun phrs. (ALGATE, ALWAYS, etc.); also attrib., as ***all-night***, ***all-time***, etc. With noun in sense 'of all, universal', as ***all-creator***, ***all-destroyer***, ***all-father***, ***all-giver***, etc. With noun (usu. attrib.) in adverbial sense 'wholly, altogether, made wholly of', as ***all-male***, ***all-star***, ***all-wool***, etc. With adjective in adverbial sense 'wholly, infinitely', as ***all-beauteous***, ***all-holy***, ***all-merciful***, ***all-powerful***, etc. With adjective in sense 'representative of the whole of', as ***all-Russian*** etc. With pres. ppl adjective as the obj. of verbal action, sometimes also with the sense 'wholly, infinitely', as ***all-absorbing***, ***all-encompassing***, ***all-judging***, ***all-pervading***, ***all-seeing***, etc. With pa. ppl adjective in adverbial sense 'wholly, completely', also 'by all', as ***all-accomplished***, ***all-honoured***, ***all-praised***, etc. Hence with corresp. and deriv. nouns, as ***all-alikeness***, ***all-pervadingness***, ***all-powerfulness***, ***all-sufficiency***, etc. Special combs., as **all-American** *adjective* (**a**) representing the whole of, or only, America or the USA; (**b**) *colloq.* truly American; **all around** *adjective* (*US*) = ALL ROUND *adjective*; **all-clear** a signal that danger or difficulty is over; **all-electric** *adjective* using only electricity for heating and lighting; **all-fired** *adjective & adverb* (*slang*, chiefly *US*) [euphem. for *hell-fired*] infernal(ly), extreme(ly); **all-firedly** *adverb* (*slang*, chiefly *US*) infernally, extremely; **allgood** = ***Good King Henry*** s.v. GOOD *adjective*; **all hail** *interjection, noun phr.*, & (with hyphen) *verb* (*arch.*) (a greeting of, greet with the words) [I wish you] all health; **allheal** (**a**) any of various plants having medicinal uses, esp. valerian, *Valeriana officinalis*; †(**b**) a panacea; †**all-hid** the game of hide-and-seek; **all-important** *adjective* of vital importance; **all-inclusive** *adjective* including everything or everyone, *spec.* (of a holiday or resort) in which all or most meals, drinks, etc. are included in the overall price; **all-in-one** *noun & adjective* (a garment etc.) made in a single connected piece; **all-might** *arch.* omnipotence; **all-nighter** *colloq.* a task etc. that takes all night; **all-or-none law**, **all-or-nothing law** *PHYSIOLOGY*: that the magnitudes of certain responses (esp. nerve impulses), once evoked, are independent of the strength of the stimuli; **all-points** *adjective* & (without hyphen) *noun* (*N. Amer.*) (a request, bulletin, etc., esp. for the apprehension of a wanted person) issued generally; **all-pro** *adjective & noun* (**a**) *adjective* designating or pertaining to either of two nominated American football teams made up of the best players of the season; (**b**) *noun* a player nominated to an all-pro team; **all-purpose** *adjective* with numerous uses; **all-red** *adjective* (*hist.*) entirely on British territory (usu. coloured red in maps); **allseed** any of a number of small plants producing much seed for their size, esp. *Polycarpon tetraphyllum*, of the pink family, and *Radiola linoides*, of the flax family; **all-terrain** *adjective* designating a robust bicycle or three-wheeled motorbike built to allow it to travel on all kinds of surface. **all-weather** *adjective* suitable for use whatever the weather; **allwhere(s)** *arch.* everywhere; **all work** work, esp. domestic work, of all kinds; ***maid of all work***: see MAID *noun*.

■ **allness** *noun* universality M17.

alla breve /alə 'breɪvɪ, *foreign* alla 'brɛve/ *adverbial, adjectival, & noun phr.* M18.
[ORIGIN Italian = according to the breve.]
MUSIC. With increased speed, at two minim beats in a bar instead of four crotchets; such a tempo or time signature.

alla cappella /ˌalə kə'pɛlə/ *adverbial & adjectival phr.* M18.
[ORIGIN Italian.]
= A CAPPELLA.

Allah /'alə, ə'lɑː/ *noun.* L16.
[ORIGIN Arabic *'allāh* prob. contr. of *al-'ilāh* the god, from *al* AL-[2] + *'ilāh* god.]
The name of God among Arabs and Muslims.

alla marcia /ˌalə 'mɑːtʃə/ *adverbial, adjectival, & noun phr.* L19.
[ORIGIN Italian.]
MUSIC. (A piece, movement, etc.) in the style of a march.

†**allanerly** *adverb & adjective* var. of ALLENARLY.

allanite /'alənʌɪt/ *noun.* E19.
[ORIGIN from T. *Allan* (1777–1833), Scot. mineralogist + -ITE[1].]
MINERALOGY. A brownish-black monoclinic mineral of the epidote group containing rare earth metals, aluminium, and iron.

allantoid /ə'lantɔɪd/ *adjective & noun.* M17.
[ORIGIN Greek *allantoeidēs* (Galen), from *allant-*, *allas* sausage (named from its form in a calf): see -OID.]
ANATOMY. (Of or pertaining to) the allantois.

allantoin /ə'lantəʊɪn/ *noun.* M19.
[ORIGIN from ALLANTOIS + -IN[1]: it was discovered in the allantoic fluid of cows.]
CHEMISTRY. A crystalline base formed in the nitrogen metabolism of many mammals (excluding primates); 5-ureidohydantoin, $C_4H_6N_4O_3$.

allantois /ə'lantəʊɪs/ *noun.* Pl. **-toides** /-təʊɪdiːz/. M17.
[ORIGIN mod. Latin, spurious form evolved from *allantoides* ALLANTOID.]
ANATOMY. The fetal membrane lying beneath the chorion in mammals, birds, and reptiles.
■ **allan'toic** *adjective* of or pertaining to the allantois M19.

allargando /alɑː'gandəʊ/ *adverb, adjective, & noun.* L19.
[ORIGIN Italian = broadening.]
MUSIC. ▸**A** *adverb & adjective.* A direction: getting slower and slower and often also fuller in tone. L19.
▸**B** *noun.* Pl. **-di** /-di/, **-dos**. A passage (to be) so played. M20.

allative /'alətɪv/ *adjective & noun.* M19.
[ORIGIN from Latin *allat-* pa. ppl stem of *afferre* bring to, from *ad* AF- + *ferre* carry + -IVE.]
GRAMMAR. ▸**A** *adjective.* Designating, being in, or pertaining to a case in Finnish and other languages denoting motion to or towards. M19.
▸**B** *noun.* *The* allative case; a word, form, etc., in the allative case. E20.

†**allay** *noun*[1]. ME.
[ORIGIN Old Northern French *aley*, *alai*, formed as ALLAY *verb*[2].]
1 = ALLOY *noun* I. ME–E19.

LD BERNERS Money . . of the same forme and alay as is in Paris. BACON Mixture of Falshood, is like Allay in Coyne of Gold and Siluer. T. D'URFEY Those that know finest metal say, No Gold will coin without Allay.

2 = ALLOY *noun* II. L16–L18.

CLARENDON The Committee . . prepared other Votes of a brighter allay. F. BURNEY Good-nature gives pleasure without any allay.

†**allay** *noun*[2]. LME.
[ORIGIN from ALLAY *verb*[1], infl. by ALLAY *noun*[1].]
1 Dilution. LME–M17.
2 Abatement, tempering of the force of something. LME–M18.
3 Repression, hindrance. M17–E18.
4 Alleviation. Only in M19.

allay /ə'leɪ/ *verb*[1].
[ORIGIN Old English *aleċġan*, from A-[1] + LAY *verb*[1]; = Old High German *irleggen* (German *erlegen*), Gothic *uslagjan*. The sense-development has been infl. by formal identity with (in Middle English) ALLEGE *verb*[1], *verb*[2] and with ALLAY *verb*[2].]
▸**I** *verb trans.* †**1** Lay down, lay aside; annul, abolish; abandon. OE–LME.
†**2** Bring low (a person). OE–LME.
†**3** Put down, quash, (a principle, personal attribute, etc.). OE–M17.
4 Quell (a disturbance, a strong feeling, etc.), appease. ME.

P. GALLICO Had insisted they follow the usual tourist route to allay suspicion.

5 Diminish, weaken, mitigate. ME.

CHESTERFIELD Neither envy, indignation, nor ridicule, will obstruct or allay the applause which you may really deserve.

6 Assuage, relieve, alleviate. LME.

P. G. WODEHOUSE A secret sorrow which the spectacle of Judson did nothing to allay. W. GOLDING The water did not satisfy thirst so much as allay it.

†**7** Temper (iron, steel, etc.). LME–L15.
†**8** Dilute. LME–E19.
9 Make less severe (wind, hot weather, etc.); cause (water, a storm, dust, etc.) to subside. L15.

SHAKES. *Temp.* If by your art . . you have Put the wild waters in this roar, allay them. M. LOWRY The street where no one had allayed the dust.

10 Temper or abate (a pleasure, advantage) by the association of something unpleasant. E16.

S. JOHNSON Benefits are allayed by reproaches.

▸†**II** *verb intrans.* **11** Subside, abate, become mild. E16–E18.
■ **allayer** *noun* E17.

†**allay** *verb*[2]. LME.
[ORIGIN Old Northern French var. of Old French *al(e)ier* ALLY *verb*.]
1 = ALLOY *verb* 2. LME–L18.
2 = ALLOY *verb* 3. LME–M18.
3 = ALLOY *verb* 1: completely identified with ALLAY *verb*[1]. LME.
■ †**allayment** *noun* (*rare*, Shakes.) admixture: only in E17.

allay /ə'leɪ/ *verb*[3] *trans.* Long *arch.* Also †**alay**. L15.
[ORIGIN Unknown.]
Carve (a pheasant).

allective /ə'lɛktɪv/ *noun & adjective.* Now *rare* or *obsolete*. LME.
[ORIGIN medieval Latin *allectivus*, from *allect-* pa. ppl stem of *allicere* allure: see -IVE.]
(Something) alluring or enticing.

allée /ale/ *noun.* Pl. pronounced same. M18.
[ORIGIN French: see ALLEY *noun*[1].]
= ALLEY *noun*[1] 2.

allegate /'alɪgeɪt/ *verb.* LME.
[ORIGIN Sense 1 from Latin *allegat-* pa. ppl stem of *allegare* allege: see -ATE[3]; sense 2 back-form. from ALLEGATION.]
†**1** *verb trans.* = ALLEGE *verb*[1]. LME–M17.
2 *verb intrans.* Argue; make allegations against each other. *Irish.* L19.
■ **allegator** *noun* (*rare*) L17.

allegation /alɪ'geɪʃ(ə)n/ *noun.* LME.
[ORIGIN Old French *allégation* or Latin *allegatio(n-)*, formed as ALLEGATE: see -ATION.]
1 The action of making a charge before a legal tribunal; a charge so made. LME.
†**2** An excuse, a plea, an alleged reason. LME–E17.
3 A claim or assertion of wrongdoing, *esp.* one made without proof. M16.

Economist The allegation that multinationals are exploiting the third world. *Daily Telegraph* An allegation of pension fraud.

†**4** The action of citing an author or document; a quotation. M16–L17.

allege /ə'lɛdʒ/ *verb*[1] *trans.* ME.
[ORIGIN Anglo-Norman *alegier* = Old French *esligier* (see A-[7]), ult. from Latin EX-[1] + *lit-*, *lis* lawsuit; conf. in sense with Latin *allegare*.]
1 Declare upon oath at a tribunal; bring forward as a legal ground or plea. *obsolete* exc. as passing into senses 2 and 4. ME.

T. CROMWELL I have no merits or good works which I may alledge before thee. STEELE The Prosecutor alledged, That he was the Cadet of a very ancient Family.

2 Affirm, assert, esp. without proof. ME.

GIBBON Where much is alleged, something must be true. G. B. SHAW It is simply unscientific to allege or believe that doctors do not under existing circumstances perform unnecessary operations. J. ORTON He is alleged to have misconducted himself with a party of schoolchildren.

3 Cite, quote, (*for* or *against*). *arch.* LME.

MILTON With what face or conscience can they alleage Moses . . for tithes?

4 Advance as an argument or excuse. LME.

GOLDSMITH Refused to lend a farthing, alledging a former resolution against lending. J. R. SEELEY England would give nothing beyond arms and ammunition, alleging that her Spanish enterprise occupied her wholly.

■ **allegeable** *adjective* M16. †**allegeance** *noun* = ALLEGATION 1 LME–E18. **alleged** *ppl adjective* (**a**) *arch.* cited, quoted; (**b**) asserted as provable, asserted but not proved; (**c**) adduced as a legal ground, or as an excuse: LME. **allegedly** /-dʒɪdli/ *adverb* (used esp. in statements for which the author disclaims responsibility) L19. **allegement** *noun* the act of alleging, an allegation E16. **alleger** *noun* L16.

†**allege** *verb*[2] *trans.* ME.
[ORIGIN Old French *alegier* from late Latin *alleviare*: see ALLEVIATE.]
1 Lighten (a person) *of* a burden. ME–L15.
2 Lighten (something); alleviate, diminish, (a burden, grief, pain); abate, repress. (Replaced by ALLAY *verb*[1], some parts of the two verbs being formally identical in Middle English.) ME–L16.

SPENSER The joyous time now nigheth fast, That shall alegge this bitter blast.

allegiance /ə'liːdʒ(ə)ns/ *noun.* LME.
[ORIGIN Anglo-Norman var. of Old French *ligeance* (formed as LIEGE), perh. due to assoc. with Anglo-Latin *alligantia* alliance.]
†**1** The status of a liege lord. Only in LME.
2 The relation or duty of a liegeman to his liege lord; the tie or obligation of a subject to his or her monarch or government. LME.
oath of allegiance: see OATH *noun*.
3 Loyalty; the recognition of the claims which someone or something has to respect or duty. M18.
■ **allegiancy** *noun* L16. **allegiant** *adjective & noun* (**a**) *adjective* giving allegiance, loyal; (**b**) *noun* a person who owes or gives allegiance: M16.

allegoric /alɪ'gɒrɪk/ *adjective.* LME.
[ORIGIN Late Latin *allegoricus* from Greek *allēgorikos*: see ALLEGORY, -IC.]
= ALLEGORICAL (which is now more usual).

allegorical /alɪ'gɒrɪk(ə)l/ *adjective.* E16.
[ORIGIN from ALLEGORIC + -AL[1].]
Of or pertaining to allegory; of the nature of an allegory; consisting of or containing an allegory.
■ **allegorically** *adverb* M16.

allegorise *verb* var. of ALLEGORIZE.

allegorist /ˈalɪg(ə)rɪst/ *noun.* L17.
[ORIGIN French *allégoriste* from Greek *allēgoristēs*: see ALLEGORY, -IST.]
A person who constructs allegories, or writes allegorically; occas., a person who expounds allegorically.
▪ **allegorism** *noun* the use of allegory, allegorical interpretation L19.

allegorize /ˈalɪg(ə)rʌɪz/ *verb.* Also **-ise**. LME.
[ORIGIN Late Latin *allegorizare*, from *allegoria*: see ALLEGORY, -IZE. Cf. French *allégoriser*.]
†**1** *verb trans.* Interpret allegorically. Only in LME.
2 *verb intrans.* Give allegorical explanations, expound allegorically; also, construct allegories. L16.
3 *verb trans.* Make or treat as allegorical; turn into, or explain as, an allegory. L16.
▪ **allegoriˈzation** *noun* M19. **allegorizer** *noun* L17.

allegory /ˈalɪg(ə)ri/ *noun.* LME.
[ORIGIN Old French & mod. French *allégorie* from Latin *allegoria* from Greek *allēgoria*, from *allos* other + *-agoria* speaking.]
1 Narrative description of a subject under the guise of another having points of correspondence with it; symbolic representation. LME.
2 An instance of such description; an extended or continued metaphor. M16.
3 An emblem; a picture in which meaning is symbolically represented. M17.

allégresse /alegrɛs, alɪˈgrɛs/ *noun.* Now *rare.* M17.
[ORIGIN French.]
Gaiety, sprightliness.

allegretto /alɪˈgrɛtəʊ/ *adverb, adjective, & noun.* M18.
[ORIGIN Italian, dim. of ALLEGRO.]
MUSIC. ▸**A** *adverb & adjective.* A direction: in fairly quick time, but not as quick(ly) as allegro. M18.
▸**B** *noun.* Pl. **-ttos**, **-tti** /-ti/. A movement or piece in fairly quick time. Also, a short movement or piece in quick time. L19.

allegro /əˈleɪgrəʊ, -ˈlɛg-/ *adverb, adjective, & noun.* L17.
[ORIGIN Italian = lively, gay.]
MUSIC. ▸**A** *adverb & adjective.* A direction: in quick time; *transf.* (of forms of words and phrases) used in speech and shortened (e.g. *we'll* for *we will*). L17.
▸**B** *noun.* Pl. **-gros**, **-gri** /-griː/. A movement or piece in quick time. M18.

allele /ˈaliːl/ *noun.* M20.
[ORIGIN German *Allel* abbreviation of ALLELOMORPH.]
BIOLOGY. Each of two or more alternative forms of a gene that arise by mutation and are found at the same place on a homologous chromosome.
▪ **aˈllelic** *adjective* of, pertaining to, or of the nature of an allele M20. **aˈllelism** *noun* the occurrence of, or relationship between, alleles M20.

allelochemical /əliːləʊˈkɛmɪk(ə)l/ *noun & adjective.* L20.
[ORIGIN formed as ALLELOMORPH + CHEMICAL *adjective.*]
BIOLOGY. ▸**A** *noun.* Any chemical released into the environment by a living organism (esp. a plant) which exerts a detrimental physiological effect on the individuals of another organism.
▸**B** *adjective.* Of, relating to, or designating such chemicals.
▪ **allelochemic** *noun & adjective* L20.

allelomorph /əˈliːləʊmɔːf/ *noun.* E20.
[ORIGIN from Greek *allēl-* one another + -O- + -MORPH.]
BIOLOGY. = ALLELE.
▪ **alleloˈmorphic** *adjective* E20. **alleloˈmorphism** *noun* E20.

allelopathy /aliːˈlɒpəθi/ *noun.* M20.
[ORIGIN formed as ALLELOMORPH + -PATHY.]
BIOLOGY. The process by which one organism harms or affects others nearby through the release of allelochemicals.
▪ **alleloˈpathic** *adjective* M20.

alleluia /alɪˈluːjə/ *interjection & noun.* Also **-uya**. OE.
[ORIGIN ecclesiastical Latin from (Septuagint) Greek *allēlouia* formed as HALLELUJAH.]
▸**A** *interjection.* Praise the Lord (occurring in many psalms and hymns). OE.
▸**B** *noun.* **1** *ECCLESIASTICAL.* A liturgical chant consisting of or containing the word 'Alleluia'; *spec.* (usu. **A-**) the one that follows the Gradual in the Eucharist. ME.
2 Wood sorrel (in allusion to its flowering between Easter and Whitsun). LME.
3 A song of praise to God. L16.
▪ **alleluˈiatic** *adjective* M19.

allemande /ˈalmɑːnd; almɑ̃d (*pl. same*)/ *noun.* M17.
[ORIGIN French = German (fem.): see ALMAIN.]
†**1** (**A-**.) A German woman. *rare.* Only in M17.
2 A piece of music for a German dance or in its rhythm, *esp.* one which forms a movement of a suite. L17.
3 Any of various German dances. E18. ▸**b** A figure in square dancing in which adjacent dancers link arms or join or touch hands and make a full or partial turn. Also used as a call to dancers to execute this figure turning in the specified direction. E19.

Allemanic, **Allemannic** *adjectives & nouns* vars. of ALEMANNIC.

Allen /ˈalən/ *noun.* M20.
[ORIGIN The *Allen* Manufacturing Co., Hartford, Connecticut, US.]
Allen screw, (proprietary name for) a screw which has a head with a hexagonal recess and can be turned by means of an ***Allen key***, ***Allen wrench***, etc., of corresponding cross-section.

allenarly /aˈlɛnəli/ *adverb & adjective. Scot.* (formerly also *N. English*). Also **-an-**. ME.
[ORIGIN from ALL *adverb* + as ANERLY.]
▸**A** *adverb.* Solitarily, alone; solely, merely. ME.
▸**B** *adjective.* †**1** Only, sole. Only in 16.
2 Alone, lonely. *rare.* E20.

allene /ˈaliːn/ *noun.* L19.
[ORIGIN from ALLYLENE.]
CHEMISTRY. A gaseous hydrocarbon, propadiene, $CH_2{=}C{=}CH_2$. Also, any derivative of this with two adjacent double bonds.

allergen /ˈaləd͡ʒ(ə)n/ *noun.* E20.
[ORIGIN formed as ALLERGIC + -GEN.]
MEDICINE. A substance which produces an allergic reaction.
▪ **allerˈgenic** *adjective* producing an allergic reaction E20.

allergic /əˈləːd͡ʒɪk/ *adjective.* E20.
[ORIGIN from ALLERGY + -IC.]
1 Pertaining to, characterized by, or suffering from allergy. E20.

G. DURRELL He was only allergic to . . the pollen of the lilac flowers, cats, and horses.

2 *fig.* Antipathetic. M20.

S. HEANEY Allergic equally to Pearse and Pope.

allergy /ˈaləd͡ʒi/ *noun.* E20.
[ORIGIN German *Allergie*, from Greek *allos* other, different, after *Energie* ENERGY.]
1 *MEDICINE.* Altered reactivity of the body towards an antigen; *esp.* hypersensitivity towards a particular foreign substance such as a type of food, pollen, or micro-organism. E20.
2 *fig.* Antipathy. M20.
▪ **allergist** *noun* a specialist in the field of allergy M20.

allerion *noun* var. of ALERION.

allers *adverb* see ALLUS.

alleviate /əˈliːvɪeɪt/ *verb trans.* Pa. pple & ppl adjective **-ated**, †**-ate**. LME.
[ORIGIN Late Latin *alleviat-* pa. ppl stem of *alleviare* lighten, from Latin *allevare*, from *ad* AL-[1] + *levare* raise, infl. by *levis* light: see -ATE[3].]
1 Make less burdensome or severe; relieve, mitigate. LME.
†**2** Diminish the weight of. L15–M17.
†**3** Extenuate (an offence). L17–L18.
▪ **alleviative** *adjective & noun* (*rare*) (something) tending to alleviate L16. **alleviator** *noun* a person who or thing which alleviates M17. **alleviatory** *adjective* of an alleviating nature or tendency M19.

alleviation /əliːvɪˈeɪʃ(ə)n/ *noun.* LME.
[ORIGIN Old French, or medieval Latin *alleviatio(n-)*, formed as ALLEVIATE: see -ATION.]
The action of lightening weight, gravity, severity, or pain; relief, mitigation.

alley /ˈali/ *noun*[1]. LME.
[ORIGIN Old French *alee* (mod. ALLÉE) walking, passage, from *aler* (mod. *aller*) go, from Latin *ambulare* to walk.]
†**1** A passageway in or into a house. LME–E17.
2 A walk or passage in a garden, park, etc., usu. bordered by trees or bushes; an avenue. LME.
3 A passage between buildings; a narrow street, a lane. LME. ▸**b** A back lane running parallel with a main street. *US.* E18.
blind alley: see BLIND *adjective.* **up one's alley** *colloq.* = ***down one's street*** s.v. STREET *noun.*
4 A passage between the rows of pews or seats in a church (= AISLE 3). Now *dial.* LME.
5 An enclosure for skittles, bowling, etc. L15.
6 A passage or free space between two lines of any kind. M18.
– COMB.: **alley cat** (chiefly *N. Amer.*) a stray town cat; **alleyway** a narrow passage.
▪ **alleyed** *adjective* laid out as an alley, or with alleys LME.

alley *noun*[2] see ALLY *noun*[2].

alley-oop /alɪˈuːp/ *interjection, noun, & adjective. colloq.* Also **allez-**. E20.
[ORIGIN Uncertain: perh. from French *allez* (imper.) go on! come on! + repr. of a supposedly French pronunc. of UP *adverb.*]
▸**A** *interjection.* Encouraging or drawing attention to the performance of some physical, esp. acrobatic, feat. E20.
▸**B** *noun & adjective. US SPORT.* (Designating) a high lob or pass caught by a leaping teammate, or a score made by the catcher of such a pass. M20.

all fours /ɔːl ˈfɔːz/ *noun phr.* Sense 1 also †**all four**. L15.
[ORIGIN from ALL *adjective* + FOUR, sense 1 sc. limbs etc., sense 2 sc. points.]
1 All four limbs (the legs of a quadruped, the arms and legs of a human etc.). L15.
on all fours (*a*) *esp.* on hands and knees; (*b*) *fig.* even *with*, completely analogous or corresponding.
2 A game of cards, called after the winning four points ('high', 'low', 'Jack', and 'the game'). L17.

All Hallows /ɔːl ˈhaləʊz/ *noun phr. arch.* Also **All Hallow.** OE.
[ORIGIN from ALL *adjective* + HALLOW *noun*[1] + -S[1].]
1 All saints; the saints in heaven collectively. OE.
2 *ellipt.* (Now freq. with hyphen.) All Hallows' Day or Allhallowmass. LME.
– COMB.: **All Hallow Eve** the eve of All Saints (= HALLOWEEN); **Allhallowmass** the feast of All Saints; †**All-hallown summer** (*rare*, Shakes.) a season of fine weather in the autumn, an Indian summer; **All Hallows' Day** All Saints' Day, 1 November; **Allhallowtide** the season of All Saints.

alliable /əˈlʌɪəb(ə)l/ *adjective.* L16.
[ORIGIN from ALLY *verb* + -ABLE. Cf. French *alliable*.]
Able to be allied; able to enter into alliance or union.

alliaceous /alɪˈeɪʃəs/ *adjective.* L18.
[ORIGIN from ALLI(UM + -ACEOUS.]
Characteristic of or resembling garlic.

alliance /əˈlʌɪəns/ *noun & verb.* ME.
[ORIGIN Old French *aliance* (mod. *all-*), formed as ALLY *verb*: see -ANCE.]
▸**A** *noun.* **1** A union by marriage; kinship, consanguinity. ME.

M. LASKI The ladies settled the details of the coming alliance between their two families.

2 Combination in pursuit of common interests, esp. by sovereign states or political groups; a league, an association. ME.

G. ORWELL We were not at war with Eastasia at all. We were in alliance with them. W. S. CHURCHILL An alliance of the four Great Powers already existed.

Holy Alliance: see HOLY *adjective.* **the Alliance (Party)**: *spec.* (*a*) of Roman Catholic and Protestant moderates in Northern Ireland; (*b*) of the British Liberal and Social Democratic Parties. ***triple alliance***: see TRIPLE *adjective & adverb.* ***unholy alliance***: see UNHOLY *adjective* 1.
3 Community in nature or qualities; affinity; a group of related things. LME.

T. SHERLOCK Corrupt Principles . . have no Alliance with Reason. J. LINDLEY Classes, sub-classes, groups, alliances, and orders.

†**4** *collect.* People united by kinship or friendship. LME–M17.
†**5** A kinsman, a kinswoman; an ally. LME–L18.
6 *ECOLOGY.* A group of closely related plant associations. M20.
▸**B** *verb trans. & intrans.* Join in alliance, ally. *rare.* M16.

allice *noun* var. of ALLIS.

allicholly /ˈalɪkəli/ *noun. rare* (chiefly Shakes.). L16.
[ORIGIN Alt.]
Melancholy.

allicient /əˈlɪʃɪənt/ *adjective & noun. rare.* E17.
[ORIGIN Latin *allicient-* pres. ppl stem of *allicere* entice to: see -ENT.]
(A thing) that attracts.
▪ **alliciency** *noun* (long *rare* or *obsolete*) attractive power M17.

†**allidatha** *noun* var. of ALIDADE.

allied /əˈlʌɪd, *esp. attrib.* ˈalʌɪd/ *ppl adjective.* ME.
[ORIGIN from ALLY *verb* + -ED[1].]
1 United, joined, esp. by marriage or kindred or by league or formal treaty; of or pertaining to allied forces or states; *spec.* (usu. **A-**) of or pertaining to the Allies in the First and Second World Wars and later. ME.

LD MACAULAY A German Princess nearly allied to the Imperial House. P. FUSSELL Allied troops landed on the beach at Salerno in September, 1943.

2 Connected by nature or qualities; having affinity. LME.

DRYDEN Great wits are sure to madness near allied. C. HAMPTON Literature and the allied arts.

alligation /alɪˈgeɪʃ(ə)n/ *noun.* Now *rare* or *obsolete*. M16.
[ORIGIN Latin *alligatio(n-)*, from *alligat-* pa. ppl stem of *alligare* bind to: see -ATION.]
1 The action of attaching; the state of being attached. M16.
†**2** *MATH.* The arithmetical solution of problems concerning the mixing of different things. M16–M19.

alligator /ˈalɪgeɪtə/ *noun.* L16.
[ORIGIN Spanish *el lagarto* the lizard, prob. ult. from Latin *lacerta* LIZARD. Cf. LAGARTO.]
1 Either of two crocodilians of the genus *Alligator*, the American *A. mississippiensis*, and *A. sinensis*, native to China. Also *loosely*, any New World crocodilian; (by confusion) a crocodile. L16.
2 Alligator skin. Freq. *attrib.* L19.
– COMB.: **alligator clip** = ***crocodile clip*** s.v. CROCODILE *noun*; **alligator gar** a large holostean freshwater fish of the southern US, *Lepisosteus spatula*; **alligator lizard** a heavily built slow-moving lizard of the genus *Gerrhonotus*, native to North America and Mexico; **alligator pear** *N. Amer.* = AVOCADO; **alligator snapper**, **alligator snapping turtle**, **alligator tortoise**, etc., a large freshwater snapping turtle, *Macroclemys temmincki*, native to the region of the Gulf of Mexico; **alligator weed** an ornamental aquatic plant, *Alternanthera philoxeroides*, native to S. America and introduced elsewhere.

■ **alligatoring** *noun* (the development of) intersecting cracks in paint, varnish, etc., caused by contraction E20.

all in /ɔːl ˈɪn/ *adjectival phr.* Also **all-in**. L19.
[ORIGIN Sense 1 from ALL *noun*, sense 2 from ALL *adverb*, + IN *adverb*.]
1 *attrib.* (With hyphen.) Inclusive of all; *WRESTLING* with few or no restrictions. L19.
2 *pred.* (Without hyphen.) ▸**a** Tired out. *colloq.* E20. ▸**b** Completely or wholeheartedly involved. E20.

allis /ˈalɪs/ *noun.* Also **-ice**, †**alose**. L16.
[ORIGIN Old French & mod. French *alose* from late Latin *alausa* (Ausonius), a small fish in the Moselle.]
An anadromous European fish of the herring family, *Alosa alosa*. Now usu. more fully ***allis shad***.

allision /əˈlɪʒ(ə)n/ *noun.* M17.
[ORIGIN Late Latin *allisio(n-)*, from *allis-* pa. ppl stem of *allido* dash against: see -ION.]
The action of dashing against or striking with violence upon something; now only of one ship upon another stationary ship.

alliterate /əˈlɪtəreɪt/ *verb.* L18.
[ORIGIN Back-form. from ALLITERATION: see -ATE[3].]
1 *verb trans.* Compose with alliteration. Chiefly as ***alliterated*** *ppl adjective.* L18.
2 *verb intrans.* Of a word or words: manifest or produce alliteration. E19.
3 *verb intrans.* Use alliteration, compose alliteratively. E19.
■ **alliterator** *noun* (*rare*) a person who uses alliteration M18.

alliteration /əlɪtəˈreɪʃ(ə)n/ *noun.* E17.
[ORIGIN medieval Latin *alliteratio(n-)*, from Latin *ad* AL-[1] + *littera* letter + -ATION.]
1 *gen.* The commencement of adjacent or closely connected words with the same sound or letter; an instance of this. E17.
2 As a principle of versification: in Old and Middle English and other Germanic poetry, the commencement of certain accented syllables of a verse with the same consonant or consonantal group, or with any vowel sounds; in some Celtic poetry also, commencement with consonants related by mutation. L18.
transverse alliteration: see TRANSVERSE *adjective*.
■ †**alliteral** *adjective* = ALLITERATIVE, as applied to Xhosa languages M19–E20. **alliterational** *adjective* (*rare*) = ALLITERATIVE M19.

alliterative /əˈlɪt(ə)rətɪv/ *adjective.* M18.
[ORIGIN from ALLITERATE *verb* + -IVE.]
Pertaining to or marked by alliteration.
■ **alliteratively** *adverb* E19. **alliterativeness** *noun* (*rare*) E19.

allium /ˈalɪəm/ *noun.* E19.
[ORIGIN Latin = garlic.]
A plant of the genus *Allium*, such as garlic, leek, onion, etc.

allo- /ˈaləʊ/ *combining form.*
[ORIGIN Greek, from *allos* other, different: see -O-.]
Forming words with the sense 'other, different'; *spec.* in *GENETICS*, used in comb. with -PLOID (and also ***-ploidy***) to refer to hybrid individuals whose chromosome sets are derived from different species (cf. AUTO-[1]), as ***allodiploid***, ***allopolyploid***, etc.
■ **alloantibody** *noun* (*IMMUNOLOGY*) = ISOANTIBODY M20. **alloantigen** *noun* (*IMMUNOLOGY*) = ISOANTIGEN M20. **alloˈcentric** *adjective* centred in external objects, interested in objects for themselves E20. **aˈllogamy** *noun* (*BOTANY*) cross-fertilization L19. **allograft** *noun & verb trans.* (*MEDICINE*) (a) graft between genetically dissimilar individuals of the same species M20. **allogrooming** *noun* (*ZOOLOGY*) grooming of an animal by another of the same species M20. **alloˈpatric** *adjective* [Greek *patra* fatherland] (*BIOLOGY*) (of species, speciation, etc.) occurring in different areas; not overlapping in distribution: M20. **alloˈpatrically** *adverb* (*BIOLOGY*) by means of allopatric speciation; in physical isolation: M20. **aˈllopatry** *noun* (*BIOLOGY*) allopatric speciation; the occurrence of allopatric forms: M20. **alloˈpurinol** *noun* [PURINE, -OL] *PHARMACOLOGY* a synthetic purine which inhibits uric acid formation in the body and is used to treat gout and related conditions M20. **alloˈsteric** *adjective* (*BIOCHEMISTRY*) of, pertaining to, or characterized by the alteration of the activity of an enzyme by means of a conformational change induced by a different molecule M20. **allosterically** *adverb* (*BIOCHEMISTRY*) in an allosteric manner M20. **allostery** *noun* (*BIOCHEMISTRY*) allosteric behaviour M20. **alloˈtetraploid** *adjective & noun* (*GENETICS*) (designating) an individual with two diploid sets of chromosomes, each from different species M20. **alloˈtetraploidy** *noun* (*GENETICS*) the condition of being allotetraploid M20.

†**allocate** *ppl adjective & pa. pple. Scot.* M16–M18.
[ORIGIN formed as ALLOCATE *verb*: see -ATE[2].]
Allocated, allotted, assigned.

allocate /ˈaləkeɪt/ *verb trans.* M16.
[ORIGIN medieval Latin *allocat-* pa. ppl stem of *allocare*, from Latin *ad* AL-[1] + *locare* LOCATE: see -ATE[3].]
†**1** Allow (an item) in an account; authorize payment for. M–L16.
2 Assign, allot, devote, (*to* a person as a special share, responsibility, etc.; *to* a special purpose). M17.
> DE QUINCEY That very sum which the Manchester Grammar School allocated to every student. H. R. F. KEATING Determined not to allocate men of the Bombay police to any duties at the mere whim of this Rajah.

3 Assign to a place. *rare.* M19.
4 Fix the locality of. *rare.* L19.
■ **allocable** *adjective* able to be allocated E20. **allocator** *noun* M20.

allocation /aləˈkeɪʃ(ə)n/ *noun.* LME.
[ORIGIN medieval Latin *allocatio(n-)*, formed as ALLOCATE *verb*; later from French or from ALLOCATE: see -ATION.]
†**1** Authorization. Only in LME.
†**2** A contribution levied on revenue etc. for a specific purpose. M16–M17.
3 The action of allowing an item in an account; an item so allowed. Now *rare* or *obsolete*. M17.
4 The action of adding one thing to another. *arch.* M17.
5 The action of apportioning or assigning to a special person or purpose; allotment; a portion so allocated. M19.
> J. K. GALBRAITH Military considerations have induced a large allocation of resources to research. *Times* Allocations will be based on the actual sales made by the butchers.

6 Fixing in position; placing; arrangement. M19.

allochthonous /əˈlɒkθənəs/ *adjective.* E20.
[ORIGIN from German *allochthon*, formed as ALLO- + Greek *khthōn*, *khthonos* earth, soil: see -OUS.]
GEOLOGY. Consisting of or formed from transported material originally accumulated elsewhere; not formed *in situ*.
■ **allochthon** *noun* an allochthonous rock formation M20.

allocution /aləˈkjuːʃ(ə)n/ *noun.* Also †**adl-**. E17.
[ORIGIN Latin *allocutio(n-)*, from *allocut-* pa. ppl stem of *alloqui* address, from *ad* AL-[1] + *loqui* speak: see -ION.]
1 A formal or hortatory address. E17. ▸**b** *spec.* *ROMAN HISTORY.* An address or exhortation by a general to his soldiers. L17.
†**2** An instance of being addressed or spoken to. M17–L18.

allod /ˈalɒd/ *noun.* Also **alod**. L17.
[ORIGIN formed as ALLODIUM.]
= ALLODIUM.

†**allodge** *verb trans. & intrans.* ME–E17.
[ORIGIN Old French *alogier*, formed as A-[5] + LODGE *verb*.]
Lodge; pitch (a tent, camp, etc.).
■ †**allodgement** *noun* [after Italian †*allogiamento* (now *-gg-*)] lodging; in *pl.*, soldiers' quarters: L16–M18.

allodial /əˈləʊdɪəl/ *adjective & noun. hist.* Also **alod-**. M17.
[ORIGIN medieval Latin *al(l)odialis*, formed as ALLODIUM: see -AL[1].]
▸**A** *adjective.* **1** Of an estate etc.: held in absolute ownership. M17.
2 Of or pertaining to the absolute ownership of land. M18.
3 Owning an allodium. M19.
▸**B** *noun.* **1** In *pl.* Allodial lands. L17.
2 = ALLODIALIST. *rare.* L18.
■ **allodialism** *noun* the allodial system of land tenure M19. **allodialist** *noun* an allodial proprietor E19. **allodially** *adverb* by allodial tenure L18.

allodium /əˈləʊdɪəm/ *noun.* Also **alod-**. E17.
[ORIGIN medieval Latin *al(l)odium* (Domesday Book), from Frankish, formed as ALL + *ōd* estate, wealth.]
hist. An estate held in absolute ownership, without acknowledgement to a superior.
■ **allodiary** *noun* = ALLODIALIST L19. **allodifiˈcation** *noun* conversion to allodialism L19.

allogeneic /ˌaləʊdʒəˈniːɪk, -ˈneɪɪk/ *adjective.* M20.
[ORIGIN from ALLO- + Greek *genea* race, stock + -IC.]
IMMUNOLOGY. Genetically dissimilar, and hence immunologically incompatible, although belonging to (individuals of) the same species. Also, involving tissue of this nature.

allogeneous /aləˈdʒiːnɪəs/ *adjective. rare.* Also **allogenous** /əˈlɒdʒɪnəs/. M19.
[ORIGIN from Greek *allogenēs*, formed as ALLO- + *genos* kind, + -OUS.]
Diverse in kind; of a different kind, race, etc.
■ **allogeneity** /-dʒəˈniːɪti/ *noun* (*rare*) difference of nature E19.

allogenic /aləˈdʒɛnɪk/ *adjective.* L19.
[ORIGIN from ALLO- + -GENIC.]
1 *GEOLOGY.* Originating elsewhere (applied esp. to a river or the sediment a river carries). L19.
2 *ECOLOGY.* Caused by external factors. M20.

allograph /ˈaləgrɑːf/ *noun.* M20.
[ORIGIN from ALLO- + GRAPH(EME).]
LINGUISTICS. **1** Each of two or more alternative forms of a minimal distinctive unit of a writing system, as a letter of an alphabet. M20.
2 Either of two or more letters or letter combinations representing a single phoneme in different words etc. M20.
■ **alloˈgraphic** *adjective* M20.

allometry /əˈlɒmɪtri/ *noun.* M20.
[ORIGIN from ALLO- + -METRY.]
BIOLOGY. Growth of a part at a rate different from that of the body as a whole (or of some other standard). Cf. ISOMETRY 2.
■ **alloˈmetric** *adjective* pertaining to or exhibiting allometry M20.

allomone /ˈaləməʊn/ *noun.* M20.
[ORIGIN from ALLO- after PHEROMONE.]
BIOLOGY. A chemical secreted and released by an organism which causes a specific response when detected by an organism of another species, *esp.* one that is to the advantage of the releasing organism (cf. KAIROMONE).

allomorph /ˈaləmɔːf/ *noun.* M20.
[ORIGIN from ALLO- + MORPH(EME).]
LINGUISTICS. Each of two or more alternative forms of a morpheme.
■ **alloˈmorphic** *adjective* M20.

allonge /əˈlɒndʒ; *foreign* alɔ̃ːʒ (*pl. same*)/ *noun.* In sense 1 also †**elonge**. E18.
[ORIGIN French = lengthening, drawing out, from *allonger*, from *long* LONG *adjective*[1].]
1 = LUNGE *noun*[2] 1. (Only in Dicts.) E18.
2 A slip of paper attached to the end of a bill of exchange etc. to give room for further endorsements. M19.

allopathy /əˈlɒpəθi/ *noun.* M19.
[ORIGIN from ALLO- + -PATHY.]
MEDICINE. The treatment of disease by inducing an opposite condition (i.e. in the usual way). Opp. HOMEOPATHY.
■ ˈ**allopath**, **allopathist** *nouns* a person who practises allopathy M19. **alloˈpathic** *adjective* of or pertaining to allopathy M19. **alloˈpathically** *adverb* M19.

allophane /ˈaləfeɪn/ *noun.* E19.
[ORIGIN from ALLO- + Greek *phainein* show, appear: the mineral loses its colour on heating.]
MINERALOGY. An amorphous, usu. pale blue, clay mineral consisting essentially of hydrated aluminium silicate.

allophone /ˈaləfəʊn/ *noun.* M20.
[ORIGIN Sense 1 from ALLO- + PHONE(ME. Sense 2 via Canad. French from ALLO- + -PHONE.]
1 *LINGUISTICS.* Each of two or more alternative sounds realizing a phoneme. M20.
2 In French Canada: a person, esp. an immigrant, whose first language is neither French nor English. L20.

allophonic /aləˈfɒnɪk/ *adjective*[1]. *rare.* E20.
[ORIGIN from ALLO- + Greek *phōnē* voice + -IC.]
Speaking with a different accent etc.

allophonic /aləˈfɒnɪk/ *adjective*[2]. M20.
[ORIGIN from ALLOPHONE + -IC.]
LINGUISTICS. Of or pertaining to an allophone or allophones.

allophylian /aləˈfɪlɪən/ *adjective & noun. arch.* M19.
[ORIGIN from Latin *allophylus* from Greek *allophulos*, formed as ALLO- + *phulē* tribe, + -IAN.]
Of or pertaining to languages, esp. in Europe or Asia, which are neither Indo-European nor Semitic; of or pertaining to, a member of, a people speaking any such language.

allosaurus /aləˈsɔːrəs/ *noun.* Also **allosaur** /aləˈsɔː/. L19.
[ORIGIN mod. Latin (see below), from Greek *allos* other + *sauros* lizard.]
A large bipedal carnivorous dinosaur of the genus *Allosaurus*, of the late Jurassic period.

allot /əˈlɒt/ *verb.* Infl. **-tt-**. L15.
[ORIGIN Old French *aloter* (mod. *allotir*), formed as A-[5] + *lot* LOT *noun*.]
1 *verb trans.* Distribute by lot; apportion authoritatively. L15.
> GOLDSMITH I allotted to each of my family what they were to do. W. S. GILBERT See how the Fates their gifts allot, For A is happy—B is not. S. JOHNSON Ten years I will allot to the attainment of knowledge.

2 *verb trans.* Assign as a lot, appoint, *to* (without the idea of distribution); appropriate to a special purpose. M16.
> W. FAULKNER What the Lord has seen fit to allot you. C. S. LEWIS Three other officers and I were allotted a compartment.

†**3** *verb trans.* Make it the lot of (a person *to do*). L16–L17.
> SHAKES. *1 Hen. VI* Thou art allotted to be ta'en by me.

†**4** *verb trans.* Attribute as due or proper. L16–M18.
> S. JOHNSON Scarce any man is willing to allot to accident, friendship, etc. . . the part that they may justly claim in his advancement.

5 *verb intrans.* Determine *upon*, choose or intend *to*. *colloq.* (orig. *US*). E19.
> D. STOREY Had allotted . . to go in for languages.

■ **allottable** *adjective* M19. **alloˈttee** *noun* a person to whom an allotment is made M19. **allotter** *noun* a person who allots something M17. †**allottery** *noun* (*rare*, Shakes.) an allotted share: only in L16.

allotheism /alə(ʊ)ˈθiːɪz(ə)m/ *noun.* M16.
[ORIGIN from ALLO- + THEISM *noun*[1].]
The abnormal worship of other gods.

allotment /əˈlɒtm(ə)nt/ *noun.* M16.
[ORIGIN from ALLOT + -MENT.]
1 a A share or portion of land assigned to a particular person or appropriated to a special purpose; *spec.* a small portion of usu. public land let out for cultivation. M16. ▸**b** *gen.* A share allotted to someone. E17.
> **a** *attrib.*: DICKENS Certain allotment-gardens by the road-side. **b** W. BLACKSTONE The elder sons . . migrate from their father with a certain allotment of cattle.

2 The action of allotting or assigning as a share; apportionment. L16.
3 One's lot in life. L17.

HENRY FIELDING No man is born into the world without his particular allotment.

■ **allotmen'teer** *noun* a person who holds or rents an allotment of land E20.

allotrope /'alətrəʊp/ *noun*. L19.
[ORIGIN Back-form. from ALLOTROPY.]
CHEMISTRY. An allotropic form of a substance.

allotropy /ə'lɒtrəpi/ *noun*. M19.
[ORIGIN from Greek *allotropos* of another form: see ALLO-, -TROPY.]
CHEMISTRY. The existence in the same state of more than one form of the same element with different properties.
■ **allo'tropic** /-'trəʊpɪk, -'trɒpɪk/ *adjective* pertaining to or displaying allotropy M19. **allotropism** *noun* = ALLOTROPY M19.

allotype /'alətʌɪp/ *noun*. E20.
[ORIGIN from ALLO- + -TYPE.]
1 *TAXONOMY*. A paratype of the opposite sex to the holotype. E20.
2 *IMMUNOLOGY*. An allotypic variant of a protein or antigen. M20.
■ **allo'typic** *adjective* (*IMMUNOLOGY*) of or pertaining to allotypes or allotypy M20. **allotypy** *noun* (*IMMUNOLOGY*) the occurrence of an antibody or other protein in antigenically distinct forms in different individuals of a species M20.

all out /ɔːl 'aʊt/ *adverbial phr. & adjective*. Also **all-out**. ME.
[ORIGIN from ALL *adverb* + OUT *adverb*.]
1 *adverb*. Entirely, completely, quite. Now *arch. & dial.* ME.
2 *adverb* & (with hyphen) *adjective*. To the fullest extent of someone or something's strength, power, resources, etc.; at full speed. L19.

E. F. NORTON Irvine . . was willing . . to 'go all out', as he put it, in an utmost effort to reach the top. M. L. KING The time has come for an all-out world war against poverty.

all over /ɔːl 'əʊvə/ *adverbial & prepositional phr., adjective, & noun*. Also **all-over**, (as noun) **allover**. ME.
[ORIGIN from ALL *adverb* + OVER *adverb, preposition*.]
▸ **A** *adverbial phr.* †**1** To the full extent. Only in ME.
2 Over the whole extent; in every part; in or on one's whole body etc. LME.

H. P. BROUGHAM Such an exertion . . I already *ache all over* with it. JOYCE I often felt I wanted to kiss him all over.

3 In all respects; as regards characteristic attitude, behaviour, etc. E18.

J. GALSWORTHY She's not a bit like me. She's your mother all over. Obstinate as a mule!

4 Completely finished. M18.

H. NELSON I am a dead man, Hardy . . . I am going fast:—it will be all over with me soon. J. LE CARRÉ And then I asked him, 'Is this goodbye?'—whether it was all over.

▸ **B** *prepositional phr.* Everywhere on or in; all through. E17.

DEFOE The People . . began to be allarm'd all over the Town. L. HUGHES In the middle of the winter, Snow all over the ground.

be all over display great affection towards (someone), be excessively attentive to (someone).
▸ **C** *adjective* (*attrib.*) (with hyphen).
1 Generally indisposed. *rare*. M19.

H. MAYHEW An all-over sort of feeling.

2 Covering every part. M19.

Times Lit. Suppl. At least six 'original' bindings, ranging from allover boards with label, through half-cloth and full-cloth.

3 Overall. M20.

Irish Press The Irish people . . have given Fianna Fáil its all-over majority. *Notes & Queries* His all-over conclusion is [etc.].

▸ **D** *noun* (in senses 1 and 2 with hyphen or as one word).
1 (Something with) a pattern that covers every part uniformly, without conspicuous features. M19.
2 In *pl.* ***the all-overs***, a feeling of nervousness or revulsion. *US slang*. L19.
3 After prepositions (chiefly *from*): everywhere, many different places. E20.

Time There were a lot of young people from all over—Colorado, Illinois, Tennessee, Georgia, Brazil, Canada.

■ **all-'overish** *adjective & adverb* (*colloq.*) (**a**) *adjective* generally ill, indisposed all over; nervous; also, ubiquitous; (**b**) *adverb* over the whole extent: M19. **all-'overishness** *noun* (*colloq.*) a general sense of illness or indisposition E19. **all-'overness** *noun* (*colloq.*) (**a**) = ALL-OVERISHNESS; (**b**) the quality of covering every part: E19.

allow /ə'laʊ/ *verb*. ME.
[ORIGIN Old French *alouer* (later *all-*) partly from Latin *allaudare*, formed as AL-[1] + LAUD *verb*, partly from medieval Latin *allocare* ALLOCATE *verb*.]
▸ **I** *verb trans.* †**1** Praise, commend. ME–L18.

G. CRABBE Proud To find the triumphs of his youth allow'd.

2 Approve of, sanction; accept. *arch.* ME.

AV *Luke* 11:48 Truely ye beare witnesse that ye allowe the deeds of your fathers.

†**3** Assign as a right or due. ME–L16.

SHAKES. *Merch. V.* And you must cut this flesh from off his breast. The law allows it and the court awards it.

†**4** Place to someone's credit in an account. ME–L17.

5 Accept as true or valid; acknowledge, admit, grant; concede. LME.

COVERDALE If any man allowe not the vnderstanding of Rome by Babylon. MILTON I suppose it will be allowed us that marriage is a human society. R. B. SHERIDAN They'll not allow our friend . . to be handsome. JOYCE What was their civilisation? Vast, I allow: but vile.

†**6** Give an allowance to, pay. LME–E18.

STEELE The Father who allows his Son to his utmost ability.

7 Give or let have as a share or as appropriate to needs. LME.

POPE Allow him but his plaything of a pen. G. B. SHAW His trustees cannot . . allow him more than £800 a year. B. ENGLAND You really must allow me a moment or two to rest.

†**8** Remit, deduct. LME–M16.
9 Not prevent the occurrence of; not prevent (a person) from doing something; permit. M16. ▸**b** With ellipsis of inf. before adverb (phr.): permit to go, come, be, etc. M19. ▸**c** *PHYSICS*. As ***allowed*** *pa. pple & ppl adjective*: designating or involving a transition between two quantum-mechanical states that conforms to a certain selection rule. E20.

H. S. MERRIMAN He would not allow himself the luxury of being the first arrival. E. F. BENSON We give here plays that the censor would not allow on the London stage. J. B. PRIESTLEY As long as society allows me to hunt, I shall hunt. D. J. ENRIGHT Is it not allowed to stand here? **b** R. BROOKE We were allowed ashore from 5 to midnight.

10 Add or deduct in consideration of something. M17.

BURKE To allow on their account as much as added to the losses of the conqueror, may amount to a million of deaths. A. AYCKBOURN It's only a five minute walk . . . No, but they have to allow a bit longer.

11 *refl.* Indulge oneself *in*. *arch.* E18.

J. RUSKIN It refuses to allow itself in any violent or spasmodic passion.

12 Consider, assert, (*that*). *dial.* E19.

B. HARTE I allows one thing, he allows another, and this yer man gives me the lie and I stabs him!

▸ **II** *verb intrans.* **13** Foll. by *of*: accept the truth or validity of, acknowledge. E16.

J. R. LOWELL Jortin is willing to allow of other miracles.

14 Foll. by *of*, (arch. & dial.) (*up*)*on*: approve of, not prevent the occurrence or existence of, admit of. M16.

S. JOHNSON She tacitly allows of his future visits.

15 Foll. by *for*: make due allowance for, take into consideration. M17.

G. B. SHAW Unfortunately he did not allow for the precession of the equinox. I had to correct some of his results accordingly.

16 *absol.* Give an opportunity, not prevent something. M18.
if circumstances allow, ***if conditions allow***, etc.
■ **allowedly** /ə'laʊɪdli/ *adverb* by general allowance or admission, admittedly E17. **allower** *noun* L16.

allowable /ə'laʊəb(ə)l/ *adjective*. LME.
[ORIGIN Old French *alouable* (later *all-*), formed as ALLOW: see -ABLE.]
†**1** Praiseworthy. LME–E18.
2 Appropriate; satisfactory, acceptable. Long *arch.* LME.
3 Intellectually admissible; valid; probable. LME.
4 Able to be added or deducted in consideration of something. E16.
5 Permissible, tolerable, legitimate. M16.
■ **allowableness** *noun* (now *rare*) L17. **allowably** *adverb* L16.

allowance /ə'laʊəns/ *noun & verb*. LME.
[ORIGIN Old French *alouance* (later *all-*), formed as ALLOW *verb*: see -ANCE.]
▸ **A** *noun* †**1 a** Praise. LME–M17. ▸**b** Approbation; sanction; voluntary acceptance. *arch.* LME.

b G. CRABBE He look'd smiling on And gave allowance where he needed none.

2 The act of allotting a sum as payment or expenses. LME.

BACON Illiberalitie of Parents in allowance towards their children.

3 A limited quantity or sum, esp. of money or food, granted to cover expenses or other requirements. LME.

MILTON In such a scant allowance of starlight. F. MARRYAT They had but their allowance of bread and grog for one day. A. KOESTLER The Committee now paid him a small weekly allowance on which he could manage to live.

at no allowance *arch. & dial.* without stint or limitation. ***compassionate allowance***: see COMPASSIONATE *adjective* 1b. ***family allowance***: see FAMILY *noun*.
†**4** The act of granting as a right or due. Only in L15.
†**5** A balance, remainder. E–M16.
6 a A sum or item put to someone's credit; deduction, discount. M16. ▸**b** *fig.* Addition or deduction in consideration of something; the act of taking (esp. mitigating circumstances) into consideration. Esp. in ***make allowance for***, ***make allowances for***. L17.
†**7** Acknowledgement, admission. L16–M18.

SHAKES. *Haml.* The censure of the which one must, in your allowance, o'erweigh a whole theatre of others.

8 Permission, tolerance (*of*). E17.

E. A. FREEMAN The allowance of slavery in the South. P. V. WHITE I would ask your allowance that I may write to your Uncle . . for your hand.

▸ **B** *verb trans.* **1** Put (a person or animal) on a limited allowance. L18.
2 Limit the amount of (a commodity) supplied. M19.

alloxan /a'lɒks(ə)n/ *noun*. M19.
[ORIGIN from ALL(ANTOIN + OX(ALIC + -AN.]
CHEMISTRY. An acidic heterocyclic compound, $C_4H_2N_2O_4$, obtained by oxidation of uric acid and isolated as an efflorescent crystalline hydrate.

alloy /'alɔɪ, (*in branch II always*) ə'lɔɪ/ *noun*. L16.
[ORIGIN Old French & mod. French *aloi*, from *aloier*, earlier *al(e)ier* ALLY *verb*. Replacing ALLAY *noun*[1].]
▸ **I** *lit.* †**1** Agio of exchange. L16–L17.
2 The comparative purity of gold or silver. E17.
3 Orig., a mixture of a precious metal with a baser one. Now *gen.*, a metallic substance made by combining two or more elements at least one of which is a metal, esp. to give greater strength, resistance to corrosion, etc. M17. ***ferro-alloy***, ***Wood's alloy***, etc.
4 An inferior metal mixed with one of greater value. E18.
▸ **II** *fig.* †**5** Intrinsic standard or character, quality. L16–L17.

SIR T. BROWNE A Soull of the same alloy as our owne.

6 Admixture of something which diminishes character or value; an alien element, something which debases. E17.

J. AUSTEN Disadvantages which threatened alloy to her many enjoyments. V. WOOLF The fatal alloy in his genius, the great clod of clay that has got itself mixed up with the purity of his inspiration.

– COMB.: **alloy steel** steel containing one or more added elements.

alloy /'alɔɪ, ə'lɔɪ/ *verb*. M17.
[ORIGIN French *aloyer*, formed as ALLOY *noun*. Replacing ALLAY *verb*[2].]
1 *verb trans.* Moderate, modify. Cf. ALLAY *verb*[1]. M17.
2 *verb trans.* Mix with a baser metal; *fig.* debase by admixture. L17. ▸**b** *verb trans.* Mix (metals). E19. ▸**c** *verb intrans.* Of a metal or metals: enter into combination (*with*). E19.

all right /ɔːl 'rʌɪt/ *adverbial, adjectival, & noun phr.* Also **alright**. E17.
[ORIGIN from ALL *adverb* + RIGHT *adverb, adjective*.]
▸ **A** *adverbial phr.* As desired; duly; satisfactorily; certainly, indeed. E17.

E. FITZGERALD I got your letter all right. M. LOWRY Boy, but it was hot all right. T. STOPPARD The Minister said up here—he'll find us alright.

▸ **B** *adjectival phr.* **1** In good condition; safe and sound; satisfactory, acceptable. Usu. *pred.* but occas. (with hyphen) *attrib.* E18.

R. CHANDLER *The Big Sleep* is very unequally written. There are scenes that are all right. J. P. DONLEAVY Don't cry anymore now. Its all right. M. PROCTER He seemed an all-right bloke to me.

all right by, **all right with** acceptable to (a person). ***I'm all right, Jack***: see JACK *noun*[1].
2 As *interjection*. Expr. acquiescence, assent, or acknowledgement. M19.

DICKENS 'Stand firm, Sam,' said Mr. Pickwick . . . 'All right, sir,' replied Mr. Weller. A. LURIE 'I want to go. I want to see the animals!' 'All *right*, Markie. I'll take them outside and let them run around for a while, Katherine.'

▸ **C** *noun phr.* ***a bit of all right***, someone or something very pleasing. *colloq.* L19.
– NOTE: The spelling *alright*, dating from L19, is often considered erroneous, although the analogous forms *already*, *although*, etc. have long been accepted.

all round /ɔːl 'raʊnd/ *adverbial, prepositional, & adjectival phr.* Also **all-round**. E18.
[ORIGIN from ALL *adverb* + ROUND *adverb, preposition*.]
▸ **A** *adverbial phr.* Everywhere around; in all respects; for all concerned. E18.

H. P. TRITTON Work was scarce and wages low, and conditions all-round were tough.

▸ **B** *prepositional phr.* Around all the parts of, round in every direction. E19.
▸ **C** *adjective* (*phr.*) (freq. with hyphen). Encompassing everything; affecting everything or everyone; having ability in many departments. M19.

W. JAMES The all-round men like Washington. *Economist* An all-round increase in the rates payable for workmen's compensation. *New Statesman* An excellent all-round performance by the Guildford Repertory Company.

■ **all-'rounder** *noun* †(**a**) a collar which fits all round; (**b**) a person with ability in many departments: M19. **all-'roundness** *noun* L19.

allspice /'ɔːlspʌɪs/ *noun*. E17.
[ORIGIN from ALL + SPICE *noun*, as combining several flavours.]
1 (The aromatic dried ground berry of) the W. Indian tree *Pimenta dioica*, of the myrtle family. Also called ***pimento*** and ***Jamaica pepper***. E17.

A

2 Any of various other aromatic shrubs, esp. *Calycanthus fertilis* and *C. floridus* (both called ***Carolina allspice***). M18.

allude /əˈluːd, əˈljuːd/ *verb*. L15.
[ORIGIN Latin *alludere*, from *ad* AL-[1] + *ludere* to play.]
†**1** *verb trans.* Hint (at), suggest. L15–L17.
2 *verb intrans.* Have or make an oblique, covert, transient, or indirect reference, *to*; *popularly* refer in any manner *to*. M16.

STEELE Quotations which allude to the Perjuries of the Fair. E. M. FORSTER He would allude to her, and hear her discussed, but never mentioned her by name. G. VIDAL He had star quality, an element often alluded to in Arlene's circle of show-biz friends.

†**3** *verb trans.* Play with, mock. M–L16.
†**4** *verb intrans.* & *trans.* Play upon words; refer by play of words ((*un*)*to*); pun. M16–E17.
†**5** *verb trans.* & *intrans.* Refer (something) fancifully or figuratively, have fanciful or figurative reference, *to*. L16–M17.
†**6** Refer (something) as applicable, appropriate, or belonging, *to*. E–M17.

allumette /aluːˈmɛt; *foreign* alymɛt (*pl. same*)/ *noun*. E17.
[ORIGIN French, from *allumer* set light to: see -ETTE.]
A match for lighting or setting things alight.
pommes allumettes: see POMME *noun*.

all up /ɔːl ˈʌp/ *adjectival phr.* Also **all-up**. E19.
[ORIGIN Sense 1 from ALL *adverb*, sense 2 from ALL *noun*, + UP *adverb*[2].]
1 *pred.* Completely done or finished; almost over. Chiefly *impers.* as below. E19.
it is all up with someone: he or she will shortly die, be defeated, etc. **it is all up with something**: it has no prospect of continuation or success.
2 *attrib.* (With hyphen.) ▸**a** Of the weight of an aircraft: total, including crew, passengers, cargo, etc., when in the air. M20. ▸**b** Of a postal service, mail, etc.: (with all items) sent by air though charged at a surface-mail rate. M20.

allure /əˈljʊə/ *noun*[1]. M16.
[ORIGIN from the verb.]
Enticement; personal charm; attractiveness.

allure /alyːr, əˈljʊə/ *noun*[2]. Now *rare*. Pl. pronounced same. M19.
[ORIGIN French.]
Bearing, mien, air.

allure /əˈljʊə/ *verb trans.* LME.
[ORIGIN Anglo-Norman *alurer*, Old French *aloirrier*, *aleurier*, formed as A-[5] + *luere* LURE *noun*[1].]
1 Attract or tempt by something advantageous, pleasant, or flattering; entice, win over. LME.

W. RALEIGH To allure the principall of them to his partie. J. CONRAD He went to Sambir . . allured . . by the fact that there was no Dutch resident on the river. JOYCE Those whose eyes tempted and allured them from the path of virtue. P. G. WODEHOUSE Alluring the public with a rich smell of mixed foods.

†**2** *gen.* Draw or attract towards oneself or itself; elicit. M16–L18.
3 Fascinate, charm. E17.

BURKE Some were allured by the modern, others reverenced the ancient.

■ **allurance** *noun* allurement, enticement L16. **allurer** *noun* M16. **alluring** *adjective* tempting, seductive, attractive L16. **alluringly** *adverb* L16. **alluringness** *noun* (*rare*) E17.

allurement /əˈljʊəm(ə)nt/ *noun*. M16.
[ORIGIN from ALLURE *verb* + -MENT.]
1 The means of alluring; a lure, a bait. M16.
2 The action or process of alluring; temptation, enticement. M16.
3 Alluring faculty or quality; fascination, charm. L16.

allus /ˈɔːləz/ *adverb*. *dial.* Also **allers**. M19.
[ORIGIN Repr. a pronunc.]
Always.

allusion /əˈluːʒ(ə)n, -ˈljuː-/ *noun*. M16.
[ORIGIN French, or late Latin *allusio(n-)*, from *allus-* pa. ppl stem of *alludere* ALLUDE *verb*: see -ION.]
†**1** A play on words, a pun. M16–M18.
†**2** A metaphor, a parable, an allegory. M16–L18.
3 A covert, passing, or indirect reference (*to*); *popularly* any reference *to*. E17.

allusive /əˈluːsɪv, -ˈljuː-/ *adjective*. L16.
[ORIGIN formed as ALLUSION + -IVE.]
1 Symbolical, metaphorical, figurative. *arch.* L16.
2 Containing an allusion (*to*); containing many allusions. E17.
3 Playing on a word, punning. *rare* exc. HERALDRY, designating arms in which the charges suggest or pun on the bearer's name or title. M17.
■ **allusively** *adverb* M17. **allusiveness** *noun* M17.

alluvial /əˈluːvɪəl, -ˈljuː-/ *adjective* & *noun*. E19.
[ORIGIN from ALLUVIUM + -AL[1].]
▸ **A** *adjective*. Of, pertaining to, or consisting of alluvium. E19.
▸ **B** *noun*. An alluvial deposit; alluvium; *Austral.* & *NZ* gold-bearing alluvial soil. M19.

■ **alluvian** *adjective* (*rare*) = ALLUVIAL *adjective* L18. **alluvious** *adjective* (*rare*) = ALLUVIAL *adjective* M18.

alluvion /əˈluːvɪən, -ˈljuː-/ *noun*. *arch.* exc. in sense 4. M16.
[ORIGIN French from Latin *alluvio(n-)*, formed as ALLUVIUM: see -ION.]
1 The wash of water against the shore or a riverbank. M16.
2 An inundation; a flood, esp. when the water carries much suspended material. M16.
3 The matter deposited by a flood or a river; alluvium. M18.
4 LAW. The action of flowing water in forming new land by deposition (cf. AVULSION 3). M18.

alluvium /əˈluːvɪəm, -ˈljuː-/ *noun*. Pl. (now *rare*) **-ia** /-ɪə/, **-iums**. M17.
[ORIGIN Latin, neut. of *alluvius* washed against, from *ad* AL-[1] + *luv-*, *luere* to wash.]
A deposit of clay, silt, sand, etc., left by flowing water, as in a river valley or delta.
■ **alluviate** *verb trans.* cover or build up with deposits of alluvium (chiefly as ***alluviated*** *ppl adjective*) E20. **alluviˈation** *noun* the deposition of alluvium M19.

ally /ˈalʌɪ/ *noun*[1]. LME.
[ORIGIN Partly from Old French *alié* use as noun of pa. pple of *alier* ALLY *verb*; partly from ALLY *verb*.]
†**1** Kinship; confederation, alliance. LME–L16.
†**2** *collect.* Kindred, relatives; associates, confederates. LME–L16.
3 A relative; a kinsman or kinswoman. *arch.* LME.
4 A person, state, etc. united to another by treaty or league or combined with another for a special purpose. LME. ▸**b** ***the Allies***, the states in alliance against Germany and her allies in the First and Second World Wars; Britain and the states in alliance with her in later conflicts. E20.

New York Times The no-flight zones imposed by the United States and its allies.

5 Something similar to another thing in nature or properties, or placed near it in classification. L17.

Nature The other branch . . contains echinoderms (starfishes and allies).

ally /ˈali/ *noun*[2]. Also **alley**. E18.
[ORIGIN Perh. dim. of ALABASTER.]
A kind of toy marble, orig. of marble or alabaster, later also of glass or other material.
make one's ally good *Austral.* & *NZ slang* exploit one's advantage, confirm one's position. **pass in one's ally**, **toss in one's ally** *Austral. slang* give in, die.

ally /əˈlʌɪ, ˈalʌɪ/ *verb*. See also ALLIED. ME.
[ORIGIN Old French *al(e)ier* from Latin *alligare*, from *ad* AL-[1] + *ligare* to bind. Cf. ALLAY *verb*[2], ALLOY *noun*, *verb*.]
1 *verb trans.* Combine or unite, esp. for a special purpose, *to*, *with*. Chiefly of marriage, alliance with foreign states, and union of nature or spirit. ME.
2 *verb intrans.* Unite, enter into alliance. *arch.* ME.
†**3** *verb trans.* Combine or mix (ingredients). LME–L15.

-ally /əli/ *suffix*.
Forming adverbs from adjectives in -AL[1]: see -LY[2].

allyl /ˈalʌɪl, -lɪl/ *noun*. M19.
[ORIGIN from ALLIUM + -YL.]
CHEMISTRY. The monovalent radical $CH_2{=}CHCH_2\cdot$. Freq. in *comb.*
– COMB.: **allyl plastic**, **allyl resin** any synthetic resin which is a polymer of an allyl compound.
■ **allylene** /ˈalɪliːn/ *noun* a gaseous hydrocarbon, $CH_3C{\equiv}CH$, propyne; formerly = ALLENE: M19. **allylic** /əˈlɪlɪk/ *adjective* of or pertaining to an allyl radical or compound M19.

alma /ˈalmə/ *noun*. Also **almah**, **alme**. Pl. same, **-s**. L18.
[ORIGIN Arabic *ʿālima* (colloq.) singer, orig. (fem. adjective) brained, learned, from *ʿalima* know.]
Any of a class of Egyptian singing and dancing girls who entertain at festivals and act as mourners.

almacantar *noun* var. of ALMUCANTAR.

almadia /alməˈdiːə/ *noun*. *obsolete* exc. *hist.* Also **-made** /-ˈmɑːd/, **-madie** /-məˈdiː/. M16.
[ORIGIN Arabic *al-maʿdiya* the ferryboat: see AL-[2]. Vars. from French from Portuguese.]
An African canoe made of bark or of a hollowed tree trunk. Also, a long swift Indian riverboat.

Almagest /ˈalmədʒɛst/ *noun*. LME.
[ORIGIN Old French *almageste* ult. from Arabic *al-mijisti*, formed as AL-[2] + Greek *megistē* greatest (sc. composition).]
A great astronomical treatise by Ptolemy (translated into Arabic in the 9th cent.); any of various other early textbooks of astrology and alchemy.

†**almagra** *noun*. L16–E19.
[ORIGIN Spanish from Arabic *al-maġra*, *-muġra* red ochre: see AL-[2].]
A deep red ochre found in Spain.

almah *noun* var. of ALMA.

Almain /ˈalmeɪn/ *noun* & *adjective*. Now *arch.* or *hist.* Also **-aine**, †**-an**, **-ayn**, & other vars. ME.
[ORIGIN Old French *aleman* (mod. *allemand*) from late Latin *Alemanni*: see ALEMANNIC.]
▸ **A** *noun*. **1** A German. ME.
†**2** The German language. LME–M16.
3 = ALLEMANDE 3. L16.
4 = ALLEMANDE 2. L16.
▸ **B** *adjective*. German. L15.
Almain rivets a kind of flexible light armour with overlapping plates sliding on rivets.

Alma Mater /ˌalmə ˈmɑːtə, ˈmeɪt-/ *noun phr.* Pl. **Alma Maters**, (*rare*) **Almae Matres** /ˌalmʌɪ ˈmɑːtrɛz, ˌalmiː ˈmeɪtriːz/. M17.
[ORIGIN Latin = bounteous mother, a title given to various Roman goddesses, esp. Ceres and Cybele.]
1 Someone or something providing nourishment and care. M17.
2 *esp.* A university or school as regarded by its past and present members. L17.

†**Alman** *noun* & *adjective* var. of ALMAIN.

almanac /ˈɔːlmənak, ˈɒl-/ *noun*. Also (*rare*) **-ack**. LME.
[ORIGIN medieval Latin *almanac(h)* from late Greek *almenikhiaka* of unknown origin.]
An annual table, or book of tables, containing a calendar of months and days, usu. with astronomical data and other information, formerly including astrological and astrometeorological forecasts.
NAUTICAL ***almanac***.

almandine /ˈalməndiːn, -dʌɪn/ *noun*. LME.
[ORIGIN Obsolete French, alt. of ALABANDINE.]
An aluminium iron garnet of a violet or amethyst tint.
■ Also **almandite** *noun* (MINERALOGY) M19.

Almayn *noun* & *adjective* var. of ALMAIN.

alme *noun* var. of ALMA.

almeira(h) *nouns* vars. of ALMIRAH.

almery *noun* see AUMBRY.

almighty /ɔːlˈmʌɪti/ *adjective*, *noun*, & *adverb*.
[ORIGIN Old English *ælmihtig*, from ALL *adverb* + MIGHTY *adjective*; corresp. to Old Frisian *elmachtich*, Old Saxon *alomahtig*, Old High German *alamahtīc* (German *allmächtig*), Old Norse *almáttigr*.]
▸ **A** *adjective*. **1** Having all possible power (orig. as an attribute of God). OE.
God Almighty: see GOD *noun*.
2 Very great. *slang*. E19.
▸ **B** *noun*. ***the Almighty***, God. OE.
▸ **C** *adverb*. Exceedingly. *slang*. M19.
■ **almightiness** *noun* LME. †**almightiship** *noun* (*rare*) M17–E18.

almirah /alˈmʌɪrə/ *noun*. Also **-meira(h)**. E19.
[ORIGIN Urdu *almārī* from Portuguese *almario* from Latin *armarium*: see AUMBRY.]
In the Indian subcontinent: a wardrobe, a movable cupboard.

almoign /alˈmɔɪn/ *noun*. Also **-oin**. ME.
[ORIGIN Late Anglo-Norman *almoin*, Old French *almone* (mod. *aumône*), ult. formed as ALMS.]
†**1** Ecclesiastical possession. Only in ME.
2 Tenure by spiritual service, or by the performance of some religious duty. Chiefly in FRANKALMOIGN. E16.

almond /ˈɑːmənd/ *noun*. ME.
[ORIGIN Old French *alemande*, *a(l)mande* from medieval Latin *amandula* from Greek *amugdalē*.]
1 The kernel, oval with pointed ends, of the stone fruit of the tree *Prunus dulcis*, of which there are two varieties, the sweet and the bitter. ME.
BURNT ***almond***. ***butter of almonds***: see BUTTER *noun*[1] 2.
2 The tree itself, allied to the plum, cherry, etc. Also ***almond tree***. LME.
3 Something having the shape or appearance of an almond. LME. ▸**b** In *pl.* The tonsils; also, the lymph nodes below the ear. Freq. more fully ***almonds of the throat***, ***almonds of the ears***, etc. *arch.* L16.
4 The delicate pink colour of almond blossom or the light brown colour of an almond kernel. Freq. *attrib.* M18.
– ATTRIB. & COMB.: Attrib. in senses 'resembling the almond' as ***almond pink*** etc. (see also sense 4 above); 'made with or containing almonds', as ***almond cake***, ***almond paste***, etc. Special combs., as **almond eye**: with the eyelids forming an almond shape; **almond-eyed** *adjective* having almond eyes; **almond milk** a soothing medicine made with blanched almonds, sugar, and water, or similar ingredients; **almond oil** the expressed oil of bitter almonds, consisting chiefly of benzaldehyde; ***almond tree***: see sense 2 above.
■ **almondy** *adjective* like an almond or almonds M19.

almoner /ˈɑːmənə, ˈalm-/ *noun*. ME.
[ORIGIN Anglo-Norman *aumoner*, Old French *-ier*, earlier *a(u)lmosnier* (mod. *aumônier*) ult. formed as ELEEMOSYNARY; assoc. with words in AL-[1].]
1 An official distributor of alms on behalf of an individual, as a monarch, or an institution, as a religious house. (Holders of particular offices may also have other duties.) ME. ▸**b** A social worker attached to a hospital, seeing to the aftercare of patients and orig. also to patients' payments. (Not now an official title.) L19.

b B. PYM The almoner, or medical social worker as they called it now, at the hospital.

†**2** *gen.* An alms-giver. ME–L19.
■ **almonership** *noun* the position or office of an almoner L16.

almonry /ˈɑːmənri, ˈalm-/ *noun*. LME.
[ORIGIN Orig. from Old French *au(l)mosnerie* (mod. *aumônerie*), formed as ALMONER; later from ALMONER: see -ERY, -RY.]
A place where alms are or were distributed; an office responsible for the distribution of alms.

†almose *noun* var. of ALMS.

almost /ˈɔːlməʊst, -məst/ *adverb & adjective*. OE.
[ORIGIN from ALL + MOST *adverb*.]
†1 *adjective* or *adverb*. Mostly all; for the most part. OE–M17.

R. ASCHAM Thies giuers were almost Northmen.

2 *adverb*. Very nearly; all but; as the nearest thing to. ME. **›b** *adverb* or *adjective*. Close to being, near. *arch.* M16. **›†c** Used to intensify a rhetorical interrogative. L16–M18.

DONNE One might almost say, her body thought. SWIFT Eyes with Reading almost blind. ROBERT WATSON His affairs almost never prospered. BYRON To lose the hour would make her quite a martyr, And they had wasted now almost a quarter. V. WOOLF Almost one might imagine them . . questioning and wondering. E. HEMINGWAY I stood until it had almost passed, then jumped and caught the rear hand-rods. W. TREVOR A single window reached almost to the floor. **b** SOUTHEY I am . . an almost Quaker. **c** R. SOUTH Whom almost can we see who opens his arms to his enemies?

alms /ɑːmz/ *noun*. Also **†almose**, (*Scot. & dial.*) **almous**, (*Scot.*) **awmous**.
[ORIGIN Old English *ælmyssa*, *-messe*, corresp. to Old Norse *almusa*, *ǫlmusa* (from which the Scot. vars. derive), Old Frisian *ielmisse*, Old Saxon *alamosna* (Dutch *aalmoes*), Old High German *alamuosan* (German *Almosen*); Germanic ult. from alt. (prob. through Latin *alimonia* ALIMONY) of Christian Latin *eleemosyna* (see ELEEMOSYNARY).]
1 Charitable relief of the poor, orig. and esp. as a religious duty. As a count noun (infl. pl. long *obsolete*): *sing.* a charitable donation, *pl.* things given in charity. OE.

ADDISON A Beggar Man that had asked an Alms of him. W. S. MAUGHAM Her nuns lived entirely upon alms. W. DE LA MARE This chance-come outcast had Asked for alms a crust of bread.

do alms, ***make alms***, ***work alms***, etc ***give alms***, ***bestow alms***, etc.
†2 A good deed; a charity. Often *iron.* Latterly *Scot.* OE–E19.

R. SANDERSON If he be hungry, it is alms to feed him.

3 = ALMOIGN 2. OE.
free alms = FRANKALMOIGN.
– COMB.: **alms-deed** *arch.* (*a*) an act of almsgiving, a charitable deed; †(*b*) the practice of almsgiving; **almsfee** *hist.* Peter's pence, Rome-scot; **almsfolk** people supported by alms; **almsgiver** a person who gives alms; **almsgiving** the giving of alms; **almshouse** (*a*) a house founded by charity for the reception or support of the poor; †(*b*) a house belonging to a monastery where alms and hospitality were dispensed; **almsman** (*a*) a person supported by alms; (*b*) *arch.* an almsgiver; **almswoman** a woman supported by alms.

almucantar /alməˈkantə/ *noun*. Also **alma-**. ME.
[ORIGIN medieval Latin *almucantarath* or French *†almicantarat*, *†almucantara* from Arabic *al-muqanṭarāt* (pl.) circles of celestial latitude, formed as AL-² + *qanṭara* arch.]
ASTRONOMY. **1** A circle on the celestial sphere parallel to the horizon; a parallel of altitude. Usu. in *pl.* ME.
2 A telescope mounted on a float resting on mercury, used to determine stellar altitude and azimuth. L19.

almug /ˈalmʌg/ *noun*. Pl. **-im** /-ɪm/, **-s**. E17.
[ORIGIN Hebrew *'almug* (Ugaritic *'almg*): cf. ALGUM.]
= ALGUM. Also ***almug tree***.

†almuten *noun*. L16–E18.
[ORIGIN Alt. of (Old French *almutaz* from) Arabic *al-mu'tazz*, from *al* AL-² + *mu'tazz* powerful, proud.]
ASTROLOGY. The ruling planet in the horoscope.

alnage, **alnager** *nouns* vars. of AULNAGE, AULNAGER.

alod *noun*, **alodial** *adjective & noun*, **alodium** *noun*, etc., vars. of ALLOD etc.

aloe /ˈaləʊ/ *noun*.
[ORIGIN Old English *al(e)we* from Latin *aloe* from Greek *aloē*; in LME reinforced by Old French *aloes* (mod. *aloès*) or its source as in LIGN-ALOES, whence freq. use in pl.]
1 In *pl.* The fragrant resin or (also ***aloes wood***) heartwood of the trees *Aquilaria agallocha* and *A. malaccensis*, from the Far East. OE.

NEB *Ps.* 45:8 Your robes are all fragrant with myrrh and powder of aloes.

2 A plant of the genus *Aloe* of the lily family, which includes succulent herbs, shrubs, and trees, bearing erect spikes of flowers and yielding bitter sap. LME.
3 *sing.* & (usu.) in *pl.* A bitter, nauseous purgative, made from the juice of the plant. LME.

fig.: S. HIERON The bitter aloes of the law.

4 Any of several other plants resembling those of the genus *Aloe*; *esp.* (more fully ***American aloe***) a stemless agave, *Agave americana*, with long spiny leaves which flowers only once in many years (also called ***century plant***). M17.
■ **aloetic** /aləʊˈɛtɪk/ *noun & adjective* (now *rare*) (a drug) containing or of the nature of the purgative aloes M17.

aloft /əˈlɒft/ *adverb, pred. adjective, & preposition*. ME.
[ORIGIN Old Norse *á lopt(i)* from *á* in, on, to + *lopt* air, sky, LOFT *noun* (corresp. to Old English LIFT *noun*¹, Old High German *luft*, Gothic *luftus* air).]
► **A** *adverb & pred. adjective*. **1** *gen.* Of position: high up, at a relatively great elevation. ME.
2 *gen.* Of direction: into the air; upward. ME.
3 In or to heaven. *arch.* exc. as below. ME.
go aloft: see GO *verb*.
4 NAUTICAL. On or to a higher part of a ship; into the rigging. ME.
†5 In the sky, above the horizon. ME–L16.
†6 In the ascendant, prevailing. LME–E17.
†7 On the top, on the surface. LME–E18.
†8 In a loud voice; in a lofty tone. LME–E17.
► **B** *preposition*. Above, over; high up in. Long *rare*. LME.

SHAKES. *John* I was amaz'd Under the tide; but now I breathe again Aloft the flood. M. PEAKE A pale sun . . was hung aloft an empty and faded sky.

alogical /eɪˈlɒdʒɪk(ə)l/ *adjective*. L17.
[ORIGIN from A-¹⁰ + LOGICAL *adjective*. Cf. French *alogique*.]
Non-logical; opposed to logic.

aloha /əˈləʊhə/ *interjection & noun*. E19.
[ORIGIN Hawaiian.]
Love, affection: used in Hawaii esp. at greeting or parting; an utterance of this.
– COMB.: **aloha shirt** a loose brightly coloured Hawaiian shirt; **Aloha State** *US* Hawaii.

alone /əˈləʊn/ *adjective* (chiefly *pred.*) *& adverb*. ME.
[ORIGIN from ALL *adverb* + ONE *adjective* etc. Aphet. to LONE *adjective*, *adverb*.]
1 Quite by oneself, itself, or themselves; unaccompanied; without other companions. Occas. *attrib.*, solitary, lonely. ME.

COLERIDGE Alone on a wide wide sea! J. M. FAULKNER I am left alone in the sitting. With none to sit beside. D. H. LAWRENCE This morning Pancrazio and Giovanni had gone off somewhere, Alvina and Cicio were alone on the place. E. BOWEN Two rather alone people. DAY LEWIS The whiteness of the cup, standing alone on the grass, is dazzling.

go it alone act without assistance. **leave alone**, **let alone** (*a*) leave to himself or herself, not have dealings with, not attend to or interfere with; ***leave well alone***, ***let well alone***: see WELL *adjective*; (*b*) in *imper.* (*colloq.*) (now usu. ***let alone***): not to mention, far less or more.
2 Having no one else sharing in one's action, feeling, or position. (Usu. in neg. contexts.) ME.

C. P. SNOW Rose was not alone in that room in having a generalized dislike of scientists.

3 As distinct from anyone or anything else; only, exclusively. ME.

AV *Dan.* 10:7 I Daniel alone saw the vision. SHAKES. *Haml.* 'Tis not alone my inky cloak, good mother, . . That can denote me truly. TENNYSON Wisdom . . which not alone had guided me, But served the seasons that may rise.

4 Taken or acting by itself; of itself, without anything more. †Also *attrib.* LME.

S. JOHNSON He that hopes by philosophy and contemplation alone to fortify himself against that. LD MACAULAY The appointment of a ruined gambler would alone have sufficed to disgust the public.

5 *pred. & attrib.* Having no equal; being the only example; unique, exclusive. Now *rare*. M16.

SHAKES. *Two Gent.* All I can is nothing To her, whose worth makes other worthies nothing; She is alone. G. HERBERT Christ is my onely head, My alone onely heart and breast.

■ **aloneness** *noun* LME.

alonely /əˈləʊnli/ *adverb & adjective*. Long *arch.* ME.
[ORIGIN from ALL *adverb* + ONLY *adjective*.]
1 *adverb & pred. adjective*. Only, solely; without anyone or anything else; solitarily. ME.
†2 *attrib. adjective*. Sole, onely; unique; solitary. L15–E17.

along /əˈlɒŋ/ *adjective*¹. *arch. & dial.*
[ORIGIN Old English *gelang*, corresp. to forms in West Germanic, Old Saxon *gilang* ready, Old High German *gilang* neighbouring: see A-⁴, LONG *adjective*¹.]
Foll. by *of* (*†on*): pertaining to; owing to; on account of; together with.

along /əˈlɒŋ/ *adjective*², *preposition, & adverb*.
[ORIGIN Old English *andlang*, corresp. to Old Saxon *antlang*. See LONG *adjective*¹ and cf. ENDLONG.]
► **†A** *adjective*. Extending lengthwise; livelong. Only in Old English (later merged in ***all long***, as ***all night long***). OE.
► **B** *preposition* (orig. the adjective used absol. or adverbially with genitive). From end to end of; through any part of the length of; parallel to the length of. OE.

SIR W. SCOTT Along the bridge Lord Marmion rode. TENNYSON We roam'd along the dreary coast. T. HARDY Along a shelf at one side were ranged bottles and canisters. W. OWEN He sings along the march Which we march taciturn. S. HILL Men sat along trestle tables lined down the church hall.

► **C** *adverb*. **1** In a line with the length (of something understood); longitudinally. Now only with *by* and as in sense 2. ME.

V. WOOLF They were sailing so fast along by the rocks that it was very exciting.

2 Onward in the course or line of motion or in the course of life etc.; progressively on; further on in a row. ME. **›b** To or at a place, having come from another. M19. **›c** Further on (or *back*) in time. *N. Amer.* M19.

JOYCE Shuffling along for a yard or so . . in an old pair of blue canvas shoes. W. STEVENS As if the sky was a current that bore them along. K. AMIS He bustled round the taxi he had secured, hurrying the baggage-porter along. **b** J. WYNDHAM Any time now they'd be along with pneumatic drills. S. GRAY Mr Keyston says kindly send him along to the office.

c along about at about (a specified time).
†3 At a distance, afar. ME–L16.
†4 At full length. LME–L19.

SHAKES. *Rom. & Jul.* Under yond yew trees lay thee all along.

†5 In full, at length. LME–L16.
6 Foll. by *with*: onward with, in company with; together with, in conjunction with; also *ellipt.*, with a person etc. L16.

YEATS He was seen coming here along with you. E. HUXLEY Along with coal, steel, woollens, whisky and pedigree bulls, for many years we exported people. A. BURGESS Love is something you learn along with the other duties of marriage. G. B. SHAW Bring your sabre along. J. BOWEN Sharks is still there, mind. They're always there. Patient. Tagging along.

play along, ***string along***, etc.
7 ***all along***, all the time, throughout, continuously. E17.

J. IRVING He must be waiting . . for me to tell him he was right all along.

– COMB.: **alongshore** *adverb & adjective* by the shore, along and on the shore (see also LONGSHORE).

alongside /əlɒŋˈsʌɪd/ *adverb & preposition*. E18.
[ORIGIN from ALONG *preposition* + SIDE *noun*.]
► **A** *adverb*. **1** Along, parallel to, or close to the side (of a ship or something else understood). E18.

COLERIDGE The naked hulk alongside came. S. HILL Manor house, it was, and a farm alongside.

2 Foll. by *of*: side by side with (*lit. & fig.*). L18.

N. HAWTHORNE Alongside of a sheet of water. C. HAMPTON Alongside of preaching the Gospel . . there are other ways in which we have to change the lives of these savages.

► **B** *preposition*. Side by side with, parallel to. L18.

alongst /əˈlɒŋst/ *preposition & adverb*. *obsolete* exc. *Scot. & dial.* ME.
[ORIGIN from ALONG *preposition & adverb* + -S³ + *t* as in *against*, *amidst*, etc.]
► **A** *preposition*. **1** Down or through the length of (in contrast to ***across***, ***athwart***). ME.
2 Close by, parallel to. L16.
► **†B** *adverb*. **1** = ALONG *adverb* 1. M–L16.
2 Lengthwise (in contrast to ***athwart***). M16–L18.
3 Foll. by *with*: = ALONG *adverb* 6. E18–E19.

aloo /ˈɑːluː, ˈaluː/ *noun*. Also **alu**. M19.
[ORIGIN Hindi, Urdu *ālū* from Sanskrit.]
INDIAN COOKERY. A potato; a dish consisting of potatoes. Chiefly in names of dishes, as ***aloo saag*** (containing potato and spinach).

aloof /əˈluːf/ *adverb, adjective, & preposition*. M16.
[ORIGIN from A *preposition*¹ 1 + LUFF *noun*¹, prob. after Dutch *te loef*.]
► **A** *adverb*. **1** NAUTICAL. **›†a** As *interjection*. To windward! (expr. an order to turn or keep the ship's head as close as possible to the wind). M16–L18. **›b** Away to windward. M16.

a *fig.*: R. B. SHERIDAN I thought that dragon's front of thine would cry aloof to the sons of gallantry. **b** POPE With all our force we kept aloof to sea.

2 Away at a distance (*from*), apart. M16.
hold aloof (***from***), ***keep aloof*** (***from***), ***sit aloof*** (***from***), ***stand aloof*** (***from***), etc.
3 From a distance. *arch.* M16.

MILTON The lion and fierce tiger glared aloof. TENNYSON Purple cliffs, aloof descried.

► **B** *adjective*. Distant; detached, unsympathetic. E17.

D. CECIL She . . hid her true self behind the shield of an aloof formality. G. MAXWELL Mijbil was neither hostile nor friendly; he was simply aloof and indifferent.

► **†C** *preposition*. Away from, apart from. *rare* (Milton). Only in M17.
■ **aloofly** *adverb* E20. **aloofness** *noun* M17.

alopecia /aləˈpiːʃə/ *noun*. LME.
[ORIGIN Latin from Greek *alōpekia* lit. 'fox-mange', from *alōpek-*, *alōpēx* fox: see -IA¹.]
MEDICINE. Hair loss, baldness.

†alose *noun* var. of ALLIS.

aloud /əˈlaʊd/ *adverb*. ME.
[ORIGIN from A *preposition*¹ 4 + LOUD *adjective*.]
In a loud voice, loudly (*arch.*); audibly, not silently or in a whisper.
think aloud: see THINK *verb*².

à l'outrance *adverbial phr.* var. of À OUTRANCE.

alow /əˈlaʊ/ *adverb*[1]. *Scot. & N. English*. ME.
[ORIGIN from A *preposition*[1] 6 + LOW *noun*[2].]
Ablaze.

alow /əˈləʊ/ *adverb*[2] *& preposition*. LME.
[ORIGIN from A *preposition*[1] + LOW *adjective*; mod. Scot. prob. after BELOW.]
► **A** *adverb* **1 a** *gen.* Low down, below; downwards. Now *arch. & dial.* LME. ►**b** NAUTICAL. In or into a lower part of a vessel. E16.
†**2** *fig.* In a low condition or estate. LME–M16.
†**3** In a low voice. LME–E16.
► **B** *preposition*. Below, low down in or on. *obsolete* exc. *Scot.* M16.

ALP *abbreviation*.
Australian Labor Party.

alp /alp/ *noun*[1]. Also **A-**. LME.
[ORIGIN Orig. pl., from French *Alpes* from Latin from Greek *Alpeis* of unknown origin.]
1 (**A-**.) In *pl.*, the high mountain range occupying much of Switzerland and adjacent regions; *sing.* a peak in this range. LME.
2 Any high, esp. snow-capped, mountain(s). LME.
Southern Alps the high mountain range of the South Island, New Zealand.
3 In Switzerland: an area of green pasture on a mountainside. E19.
– COMB.: **alphorn** = ALPENHORN.

alp /alp/ *noun*[2]. *obsolete* exc. *dial.* LME.
[ORIGIN Unknown.]
A bullfinch.

alpaca /alˈpakə/ *noun*. L18.
[ORIGIN Spanish from Aymara *allpaca*.]
A domesticated Peruvian animal, *Lama pacos*, resembling the llama, with long fine woolly hair and usu. brown and white colouring; the wool of the alpaca; fabric or a garment made from this.

alpargata /alpɑːˈɡɑːtə/ *noun*. E19.
[ORIGIN Spanish from Hispano-Arabic *al-balgha*.]
= ESPADRILLE.

alpeen /ˈalpiːn/ *noun*. Also **-ine**. E19.
[ORIGIN Irish *ailpín*.]
In Ireland: a cudgel, a stout-headed stick.

alpenglow /ˈalpənɡləʊ/ *noun*. L19.
[ORIGIN Partial translation of German *Alpenglühen* lit. 'Alp-glow'.]
The rosy light of the setting or rising sun seen on high mountains.

alpenhorn /ˈalpənhɔːn/ *noun*. L19.
[ORIGIN German = alphorn.]
A long wooden horn used by Alpine herdsmen.

alpenrose /ˈalpənrəʊz/ *noun*. E20.
[ORIGIN German = Alp-rose.]
Either of two pink-flowered rhododendrons, *Rhododendron ferrugineum* and *R. hirsutum*, native to the region of the Alps.

alpenstock /ˈalpənstɒk/ *noun*. E19.
[ORIGIN German = Alp-stick.]
A long iron-tipped staff used in mountain-climbing.

alpha /ˈalfə/ *noun*. ME.
[ORIGIN Latin from Greek.]
1 The first letter (A, α) of the Greek alphabet; the beginning of anything. ME.
alpha and omega the beginning and the end (orig. as a title of God).
2 Denoting the first in a numerical sequence. E17. ►**b** *attrib.* SCIENCE. Freq. written α: (***a***) ASTRONOMY (preceding the genitive of the Latin name of the constellation) designating the chief star in a constellation; (***b***) CHEMISTRY designating the first of a number of isomeric forms of a compound, or of allotropes of an element, etc.; (***c***) designating a positively charged particle now known to be a helium nucleus, which is one of the three main types of decay product emitted by radioactive substances; also designating decay, emission, radiation, rays, etc., associated with such a particle; (***d***) ***alpha rhythm***, ***alpha waves***, the normal rhythmic electrical activity of the conscious brain, consisting of oscillations having a frequency of 8 to 13 hertz; (***e***) MEDICINE. ***alpha receptor***, one of two kinds of adrenergic receptor in the sympathetic nervous system, stimulation of which results esp. in increased blood pressure; ***alpha-adrenergic*** *adjective*, pertaining to or involving alpha receptors; ***alpha blocker***, a drug preventing stimulation of alpha receptors; (***f***) ***alpha test***, a test of machinery, software, etc., in course of development, carried out by the developer before it is made available for beta testing; ***alpha-test*** *verb trans.*, perform an alpha test on. M18. ►**c** A first-class mark in an examination etc. E20.
b *alpha* GLOBULIN. **alpha-hydroxy acid** CHEMISTRY any of a class of organic acids that contain a hydroxyl group bonded to the carbon atom adjacent to the carboxylic acid group, often used in skincare preparations for their exfoliating properties; abbreviation *AHA*. **c alpha minus** a mark just in the first class. **alpha plus** a superlatively good mark.
3 ZOOLOGY. Chiefly *attrib.* Designating the dominant animal within a single-sex group, as ***alpha male***, ***alpha female***, etc.; also (*fig.*) of people. M20.

alphabet /ˈalfəbɛt/ *noun & verb*. LME.
[ORIGIN Late Latin *alphabetum* (Tertullian), *alphabetos*, from Greek from ALPHA, BETA, the first two letters of the alphabet, taken to represent the whole. Cf. ABC.]
► **A** *noun*. †**1** Knowledge acquired from written works. *rare*. Only in LME.
2 A set of letters used in writing a language; a set of symbols or signs used for these letters. E16. ►**b** COMPUTING. A set of characters or symbols used in representing data. M20.
initial teaching alphabet: see INITIAL *adjective*. **phonetic alphabet** a set of symbols used to represent speech sounds (***International Phonetic Alphabet***: see INTERNATIONAL *adjective*).
3 An index in alphabetical order. Now *rare*. M16.
4 *fig.* The key to a branch of knowledge; the first rudiments of a subject. *arch.* L16.
5 *fig.* A long or complete series. L16.
– COMB.: **alphabet soup** clear soup containing letter-shaped pieces of macaroni paste etc.; *fig.* a muddle.
► **B** *verb trans.* = ALPHABETIZE. Chiefly *US*. L17.
■ **alphabetarian** /-ˈtɛːrɪən/ *noun* (now *rare*) (**a**) = ABECEDARIAN *noun* 1; (**b**) a person who studies alphabets: E17. **alphaˈbetic** *adjective* = ALPHABETICAL M17. **alphaˈbetical** *adjective* (of the order of letters or words) corresponding to that of the alphabet; of or pertaining to an alphabet; employing an alphabet: M16. **alphaˈbetically** *adverb* in alphabetical order; by means of an alphabet: M16. **alphaˈbetiform** *adjective* shaped like the letters of an alphabet E20. **alphabetiˈzation** *noun* the process of arranging in alphabetical order; an alphabetical series or list: L19. **alphabetize** *verb trans.* arrange in alphabetical order L18.

alphabetism /ˈalfəbɪˌtɪz(ə)m/ *noun*. M19.
[ORIGIN from ALPHABET + -ISM.]
1 Use of initials as a signature or assumed indication of authorship. *rare*. M19.
2 Symbolization of spoken sounds by means of an alphabet. L19.
3 Prejudice or discrimination resulting from a person's position on a (notional) alphabetical list; *spec.* disadvantage suffered by people whose names begin with letters from the latter part of the alphabet. L20.

alphafetoprotein /ˌalfəfiːtəʊˈprəʊtiːn/ *noun*. L20.
[ORIGIN from ALPHA + *feto-* (from FETUS) + PROTEIN.]
BIOCHEMISTRY. A protein which is produced by a fetus and is present in amniotic fluid and the bloodstream of the mother, and of which levels can be measured to detect congenital conditions such as spina bifida and Down's syndrome.

alphametic /alfəˈmɛtɪk/ *noun*. M20.
[ORIGIN Blend of ALPHABETIC and ARITHMETIC *noun*[1].]
A mathematical puzzle in which numerical values are to be deduced from an equation or the like in which they are represented by letters.

alphanumeric /ˌalfənjuːˈmɛrɪk/ *adjective & noun*. M20.
[ORIGIN from ALPHA(BET + NUMERIC.]
► **A** *adjective*. Consisting of or employing both letters and numerals. M20.
► **B** *noun*. In *pl.* Alphanumeric symbols or expressions. M20.

alphin *noun* see ALFIN.

Alphonsine /alˈfɒnsʌɪn/ *adjective*. M17.
[ORIGIN from *Alphonso* (see below) + -INE[1].]
Designating astronomical tables prepared in Toledo for Alphonso X, 'the Wise' (1226–84), King of Castile.

alphonso /alˈfɒnsəʊ/ *noun*. Pl. **-os**. M20.
[ORIGIN Portuguese.]
A type of mango from western India.

†**alpieu** *noun*. L17–M18.
[ORIGIN French *alpiou* from Italian *al più* for the more, for most.]
In the card game basset: the bending of one corner of a card to indicate that the punter raises the stake on it after winning.

alpine *noun*[1] var. of ALPEEN.

Alpine /ˈalpʌɪn/ *adjective & noun*[2]. Also **a-**. LME.
[ORIGIN Latin *alpinus*: see ALP *noun*[1], -INE[1].]
► **A** *adjective*. **1** Of, pertaining to, or characteristic of the Alps or high mountains in general; growing in or inhabiting such mountains above the tree line; in HORTICULTURE now designating any small plant suitable for rockeries. LME.
Alpine chough: see CHOUGH 2. **Alpine fir** a tall conifer, *Abies lasiocarpa*, native to western N. America. **Alpine rose** = ALPENROSE. *Alpine* STRAWBERRY. *Alpine* WOODSIA.
2 Designating a subgroup of the Caucasoid division of humankind associated mainly with central and eastern Europe. L19.
3 Designating a style of fast downhill skiing first developed in the Alps, or a competition featuring this. Cf. NORDIC *adjective* 2. E20.
► **B** *noun*. **1** An alpine plant. E19.
2 A member of the Alpine division of humankind. E20.

alpinist /ˈalpɪnɪst/ *noun*. L19.
[ORIGIN French *alpiniste*, formed as ALPINE *adjective*: see -IST.]
An Alpine climber.
■ **alpinism** *noun* Alpine climbing L19.

already /ɔːlˈrɛdi/ *adjective & adverb*. ME.
[ORIGIN from ALL *adverb* + READY *adjective*.]
► †**A** *adjective* (*pred. & compl.*). Fully prepared. ME–E16.
► **B** *adverb*. **1** Beforehand, in anticipation; before this or that time; as early as this or that. ME.

> G. ORWELL The best books . . are those that tell you what you know already. G. GREENE He didn't even hear what I said: he was absorbed already.

2 In speech infl. by Yiddish, used at the end of a phrase or sentence as an intensive, to express impatience, etc. *N. Amer.* E20.

> M. SHULMAN 'This story has helped a great many people, and I hope it will help you.' 'So tell it already'.

alright *adjective, adverb, & noun* see ALL RIGHT.

ALS *abbreviation*.
Autograph letter signed.

†**als** *adverb* see ALSO.

†**Alsacian** *adjective & noun* var. of ALSATIAN.

Alsatia /alˈseɪʃə/ *noun*. *obsolete* exc. *hist.* L17.
[ORIGIN medieval Latin = Alsace (as being a much disputed territory).]
The precinct of White Friars in London as a sanctuary for debtors and criminals.

Alsatian /alˈseɪʃ(ə)n/ *adjective & noun*. Also †**-cian**, (in sense B.3) **a-**. L17.
[ORIGIN formed as ALSATIA + -AN.]
► **A** *adjective*. **1** Of or pertaining to White Friars in London or any other place as a sanctuary for debtors and criminals. *obsolete* exc. *hist.* L17.
2 Of or pertaining to Alsace, an area of Europe now forming part of France bordering Germany and Switzerland. L19.
†**Alsatian wolfdog**, **Alsatian wolfhound** = sense B.3 below.
► **B** *noun*. **1** A debtor or criminal in sanctuary. *obsolete* exc. *hist.* L17.
2 A native or inhabitant of Alsace. E19.
3 (An animal of) a breed of wolfhound; a German shepherd dog. E20.

†**alse** *adverb* see ALSO.

al segno /al ˈseɪnjəʊ/ *adverbial phr.* L18.
[ORIGIN Italian = to the sign.]
MUSIC. A direction: go back (= DAL SEGNO) or continue to the point indicated by the sign.

alsike /ˈalsɪk/ *noun*. M19.
[ORIGIN *Alsike* near Uppsala, Sweden.]
In full ***alsike clover***. Clover of the species *Trifolium hybridum*, widely cultivated for fodder.

also /ˈɔːlsəʊ/ *adverb*. Also (chiefly *Scot. & N. English*) †**als(e)**. See also AS *adverb* etc.
[ORIGIN Old English *alswā*, (West Saxon) *ealswā*, from ALL *adverb* + SO; corresp. to Old Frisian *alsa*, Dutch *alzoo* thus, consequently, Old High German *alsō* even so, as (German *also* therefore).]
► **I** Demonstrative.
†**1** In that degree; to that extent; equally. OE–L16.
†**2** Wholly so; in this or that very manner. OE–LME.
3 In like manner, similarly. (Passing into sense 4.) *arch.* OE.

> NEB *Luke* 14:33 So also none of you can be a disciple of mine without parting with all his possessions.

4 Further, in addition, besides, too. ME.

> SHAKES. *1 Hen. IV* I do not only marvel where thou spendest thy time, but also how thou art accompanied. MILTON They also serve who only stand and wait. JOYCE Saturday and Sunday being free days some boys might be inclined to think that Monday is a free day also. SCOTT FITZGERALD Also from New York were the Chromes and Backhyssons.

also-ran *noun* a horse or dog not placed (in the first three, *US* the first two) in a race; a person who fails to win distinction, a failure.
► †**II** Correlative.
5 So, as. Latterly *Scot.* ME–E18.
► †**III** Relative and conjunctive.
6 As, as though. Only in ME.

alstonia /alˈstəʊnɪə/ *noun*. M19.
[ORIGIN mod. Latin, from Charles *Alston* (1683–1760), Scot. botanist and physician + -IA[1].]
A tree or shrub of the genus *Alstonia*, found chiefly in SE Asia and the Pacific islands, some of whose members yield a soft light timber.

alstonite /ˈɔːlstənʌɪt/ *noun*. M19.
[ORIGIN from *Alston*, a town in Cumbria, England + -ITE[1].]
MINERALOGY. A carbonate of barium and calcium, occurring as white, orthorhombic, usu. bipyramidal crystals.

alstroemeria /alstrəˈmɪərɪə/ *noun*. L18.
[ORIGIN mod. Latin, from K. von *Alstroemer* (1736–96), Swedish naturalist + -IA[1].]
Any of various ornamental plants constituting the S. American genus *Alstroemeria*, of the lily family, of which several species are cultivated for their showy lily-like flowers; *esp.* the Chilean *A. aurea*, with bright orange flowers. Also called ***Peruvian lily***.

alt /alt/ *noun*. M16.
[ORIGIN Italian ALTO.]
Mus. ***in alt***, in the octave above G at the top of the treble stave; *fig.* in an exalted mood. Cf. ALTISSIMO.

alt- /ɔːlt/ *prefix*. Also **alt.** L20.
[ORIGIN Abbreviation of ALTERNATIVE, influenced by the *alt.* prefix of some Internet newsgroups.]
Designating a version of something, esp. popular music, that is regarded as being outside the mainstream of its genre.
alt-country, ***alt-rock*** etc.

Alta *abbreviation*.
Alberta.

Altaic /alˈteɪɪk/ *adjective & noun*. M19.
[ORIGIN from *Altai* (see below) + -IC. Cf. French *altaïque*.]
▸ **A** *adjective*. **1** Of or pertaining to the Altai Mountains in central Asia. M19.
2 Of, pertaining to, or designating a group or language family including Turkish, Mongolian, and Tungus, among others. M19.
▸ **B** *noun*. The Altaic group or language family. M20.
■ Also **Altaian** *adjective & noun* E19.

altar /ˈɔːltə, ˈɒl-/ *noun*.
[ORIGIN Old English *altar*, *-er*, corresp. to Old Frisian *altare*, *-er*, Old Saxon, Old High German, Old Norse *altari*, *-eri*; Germanic from late Latin *altar(e)*, *-ium*, from Latin *altus* high.]
1 A flat-topped block or other raised structure on which to make offerings to a god. OE.

fig.: M. L. KING High places where men are willing to sacrifice truth on the altars of their self-interest.

2 CHRISTIAN CHURCH. A raised structure or table at which the Eucharist is celebrated. ME.
high altar: see HIGH *adjective*. **lead to the altar** marry (a woman).
3 (Usu. **A-**.) *The* constellation Ara. M16.
– COMB.: **altar boy** ECCLESIASTICAL a boy acolyte; **altar bread** bread used in celebrating the Eucharist; **altar cloth**: covering an altar during the Eucharist; **altarpiece** a reredos, esp. in the form of a painting; **altar stone** a stone forming part of or used as an altar; **altar tomb** a raised tomb resembling an altar.
■ **altarage** *noun* (*obsolete exc. hist.*) offerings or an endowment for the maintenance of an altar and a priest to say mass LME. **altarist** *noun* a person who prepares an altar for a Eucharist M16. **altarless** *adjective* L19. **altarwise** *adverb* after the manner or in the position of an altar M16.

altazimuth /alˈtazɪməθ/ *noun*. M19.
[ORIGIN from ALT(ITUDE) + AZIMUTH.]
ASTRONOMY. A telescope having a mounting enabling it to move in azimuth about a vertical axis and in altitude about a horizontal axis. Usu. *attrib.*, as ***altazimuth mounting***, ***altazimuth telescope***. Cf. EQUATORIAL.

alter /ˈaltə/ *noun*. L19.
[ORIGIN Latin = other.]
PSYCHOLOGY. The individual's conception of another person; a person with whom one has a social interaction.

alter /ˈɔːltə, ˈɒl-/ *verb*. LME.
[ORIGIN Old French & mod. French *altérer* from late Latin *alterare*, from Latin *alter* other.]
1 *verb trans.* Make otherwise or different in some respect; change in characteristics, position, etc.; modify. LME. ▸**b** *verb trans.* Castrate, spay. *US & Austral.* E19.

SHAKES. *Merch. V.* There is no power in Venice Can alter a decree established. E. M. FORSTER Marriage was to alter her fortunes rather than her character. J. GALSWORTHY She was altering the lace on a collar. L. P. HARTLEY Being with Alec had altered her idea of what became her.

altered chord MUSIC: in which one or more notes are chromatically changed.
2 *verb intrans.* Become otherwise; undergo some change. L15.

AV *Dan.* 6:12 The law of the Medes and Persians which altereth not. A. J. CRONIN Stephen saw his expression alter imperceptibly.

†**3** *verb trans.* Affect mentally, disturb. M16–L17.
■ **alterant** *adjective & noun* (now *rare*) (something) producing alteration; formerly *spec.*, an alterative medicine: E17. †**alterate** *verb trans. & intrans.* = ALTER *verb* LME–E18. **alterer** *noun* a person who or thing which alters or causes alteration LME.

alterable /ˈɔːlt(ə)rəb(ə)l, ˈɒl-/ *adjective*. LME.
[ORIGIN Old French & mod. French *altérable* or medieval Latin *alterabilis*: see ALTER *verb*, -ABLE.]
†**1** Liable to alter or vary. LME–L17.
2 Able to be altered. L16.
■ **alteraˈbility** *noun* L17. **alterableness** *noun* (*rare*) M17.

alteration /ɔːltəˈreɪʃ(ə)n, ɒl-/ *noun*. LME.
[ORIGIN Old French & mod. French *altération* or late Latin *alteratio(n-)* from *alterat-* pa. ppl stem of *alterare*: see ALTER *verb*, -ATION.]
1 The action of altering. LME. ▸†**b** MUSIC. Extension (usu. doubling) of the value of a note. E16–E17.
chromatic alteration: see CHROMATIC *adjective* 1.
2 A change in character or appearance; an altered condition. LME. ▸†**b** *spec.* A change for the worse; a distemper. M16–M17.
– COMB.: **alteration hand** one employed to alter or remake clothes.

alterative /ˈɔːlt(ə)rətɪv, ˈɒl-/ *adjective & noun*. LME.
[ORIGIN medieval Latin *alterativus*, from *alterat-*: see ALTERATION, -ATIVE.]
▸ **A** *adjective*. Tending to produce alteration; MEDICINE (*arch.*) improving bodily function, digestion, etc. LME.
▸ **B** *noun*. An alterative medicine or treatment. *arch.* LME.

altercate /ˈɔːltəkeɪt, ˈɒl-/ *verb intrans.* M16.
[ORIGIN Latin *altercat-* pa. ppl stem of *altercari* wrangle: see -ATE[3].]
Dispute vehemently or angrily; wrangle.
■ †**altercative** *adjective* characterized by altercation M–L18.

altercation /ɔːltəˈkeɪʃ(ə)n, ɒl-/ *noun*. LME.
[ORIGIN Old French & mod. French from Latin *altercatio(n-)*, formed as ALTERCATE: see -ATION.]
1 The action of disputing vehemently or angrily. LME. ▸**b** The conduct of a legal case by question and answer. L18.
2 A vehement or angry dispute; a noisy controversy. LME.

alter ego /ˌaltər ˈɛɡəʊ, ˌɒlt-, ˈiːɡ-/ *noun phr.* Pl. **alter egos**. M16.
[ORIGIN Latin = other self.]
A person's second self; an intimate friend; a representative of another person.

alterity /alˈtɛrɪti, ɒl-/ *noun*. LME.
[ORIGIN Early uses from late Latin *alteritas*, later also from French *altérité*: see ALTER *verb*, -ITY.]
†**1** An alteration. Only in LME.
2 The state of being other or different, otherness. M17.

altern /ɒlˈtəːn; ˈɔːltən, -təːn/ *adjective & adverb*. *arch.* L16.
[ORIGIN Latin *alternus* every other, from *alter* other. Cf. French *alterne*.]
▸ **A** *adjective*. Alternate, alternating. L16.
▸ **B** *adverb*. In turns, one after the other. M17.

alternance /ɔːlˈtəːnəns, ɒl-/ *noun*. E20.
[ORIGIN French, formed as ALTERNANT: see -ANCE.]
Chiefly PHILOLOGY. Alternation, variation; an instance of this.

alternant /ɔːlˈtəːnənt, ɒl-/ *adjective & noun*. M17.
[ORIGIN Latin *alternant-* pres. ppl stem of *alternare*: see ALTERNATE *verb*, -ANT[1].]
▸ **A** *adjective*. Alternating, changing from one to the other. M17.
▸ **B** *noun*. **1** An alternating quantity. *rare*. L19.
2 LOGIC. Either component of an alternation. L19.
3 PHILOLOGY. An alternative form, a variant. E20.

alternate /ɔːlˈtəːnət, ɒl-/ *adjective, adverb, & noun*. E16.
[ORIGIN Latin *alternatus* pa. pple, formed as ALTERNATE *verb*: see -ATE[2].]
▸ **A** *adjective*. **1** Of things of two kinds, from two sources, etc.: coming each after one of the other kind etc. E16.

W. STEVENS A wheel spoked red and white In alternate stripes. A. LURIE The family's alternate feasts and famine whenever his father got work or was laid off.

2 Of things of the same kind: occurring first on one side and then on the other of an axial line. Used *esp.* in BOTANY of leaves (opp. **opposite**) and in GEOMETRY of angles. L16.
3 Alternative. (*rare* before **20**.) Chiefly *N. Amer.* L16.

G. SARTON Modern editions include four books, the fourth having an alternate title. *Dictionaries* The inclusion of numerous alternate spellings.

4 Of a sequence etc.: consisting of things of two kinds etc. coming each after one of the other kind. M17.

G. CRABBE Smooth alternate verse.

5 (With *pl.*) Every other, every second, of a sequence of. L17.

W. FAULKNER Soon he was excused from this on alternate days, which afternoons he spent raking leaves.

6 (With *pl.*) Of things of the same kind etc. in two sets: taken or coming each after a member of the other set. E19.

OED The minister and the people read alternate verses.

▸ **B** *adverb*. One after the other; by turns. *arch.* E18.

POPE Wane and wax alternate like the moon. SIR W. SCOTT Massive arches . . That rose alternate row and row.

▸ **C** *noun*. **1** Something alternative to something else. Now chiefly *N. Amer.* E18.

R. M. PIRSIG The best ones [roads] . . have an alternate that gets you there quicker. *Tucson Magazine* Fresh fruit as an alternate to potatoes with entrees.

2 A deputy; someone to substitute for someone else. Chiefly *N. Amer.* M19.

Transatlantic Review I was the alternate in case he got sick.

alternate /ˈɔːltəneɪt, ˈɒl-/ *verb*. L16.
[ORIGIN Latin *alternat-* pa. ppl stem of *alternare* do things by turns, formed as ALTERN: see -ATE[3].]
1 *verb trans.* Arrange or perform (two different things or two sets of things) alternately; cause to occur in alternation. L16.

MILTON Who in their course Melodious Hymns about the sovran Throne Alternate all night long.

2 *verb intrans.* Of two (occas. more than two) things: succeed each other by turns. E18.

T. STOPPARD Though chickens and eggs may alternate back through the millennia.

3 *verb intrans.* Of a whole: consist of alternations *between*. Of an individual person or thing: move *between*; fluctuate in opinion, resolution, etc., *between*. E19.

DISRAELI A land which alternates between plains of sand and dull ranges of monotonous hills. N. MITFORD He . . had not, like me, alternated between faith and black moods of scepticism.

4 *verb intrans.* Of one thing or one class of things: appear or occur alternately *with* another. M19.

G. MAXWELL Eating them like a stick of Edinburgh rock, always with five crunches of the left-hand side of the jaw alternating with five crunches on the right.

5 *verb trans.* Interchange (one thing) alternately *with* (occas. *by*) another. M19.

F. RAPHAEL Isidore alternated promises of fur coats with threats of excommunication.

alternately /ɔːlˈtəːnətli, ɒl-/ *adverb*. LME.
[ORIGIN formed as ALTERNATE *adjective* + -LY[2].]
1 In alternate order; by turns. LME.
2 In alternate positions; on each side in turn. M18.

alternating /ˈɔːltəneɪtɪŋ, ˈɒl-/ *adjective*. M19.
[ORIGIN from ALTERNATE *verb* + -ING[2].]
1 Occurring alternately with something else. M19.
2 ELECTRICITY. Of a current, potential, etc.: that reverses its polarity at regular intervals, esp. sinusoidally; associated with or producing an alternating current, potential, etc. Cf. DIRECT *adjective* 6. M19.
■ **alternatingly** *adverb* L19.

alternation /ɔːltəˈneɪʃ(ə)n, ɒl-/ *noun*. LME.
[ORIGIN Partly from Latin *alternatio(n-)*, partly from French: see ALTERNATE *verb*, -ATION.]
1 The action of two things succeeding each other by turn; alternate succession, occurrence, or performance. LME.

Isis The alternation of night and day and the motions of astronomic bodies.

alternation of generations BIOLOGY the occurrence in alternate generations of different forms of an organism having different (usu. sexual and asexual) reproductive processes.
2 Successive change because of alternating phenomena. M17.
3 The position or state of being in alternate order. M19.
4 LOGIC. The function of alternative propositions, symbolized by v (Latin *vel* or) and corresponding to the inclusive sense of 'or' (and/or); a statement of such alternatives. L19.

alternative /ɔːlˈtəːnətɪv, ɒl-/ *adjective & noun*. M16.
[ORIGIN French *alternatif*, *-ive* or medieval Latin *alternativus* formed as ALTERNATE *verb*: see -ATIVE.]
▸ **A** *adjective*. **1** Characterized by alternation; alternating; alternate. Now *rare*. M16.
2 Stating or offering either of two things; expressing alternation; disjunctive. L16.
3 Of two things: mutually exclusive. Of one or more things: available in place of another. M19. ▸**b** *spec.* Designating a mode of life, system of knowledge and practice, organization, etc., purporting to represent a preferable and cogent alternative to that of the established social order. M20.
Alternative Service Book: for use in the Church of England as an alternative to the *Book of Common Prayer*. **b *the alternative society***, ***alternative birthing***, ***alternative medicine***, ***alternative technology***, etc. **alternative comedian**, **alternative comedienne**: performing alternative comedy. **alternative comedy**: rejecting certain established (esp. racist and sexist) comic stereotypes and having a strong political component. **alternative energy**: (**a**) not from nuclear fuel; (**b**) not from fossil fuel. **Alternative Investment Market** a secondary market of the London Stock Exchange, dealing chiefly in the shares of small companies (abbreviation *AIM*).
▸ **B** *noun*. **1** A proposition containing two or more mutually exclusive statements; a statement or offer of two or more mutually exclusive things; liberty to choose between two or more things. E17.

J. S. MILL The alternative seemed to be either death, or to be permanently supported by other people, or a radical change in the economical arrangements.

†**2** Alternative course; alternation. M–L18.

J. WEDGWOOD They bear sudden alternatives of heat and cold.

3 Each of the components of an alternative proposition; each of two or more possibilities; the other or remaining course; a thing available in place of another. E19.

T. HARDY Warren's was a sort of clubhouse, used as an alternative to the inn. B. ENGLAND You leave me no alternative. I give you twenty-four hours in which to prove your theories correct. J. ORTON You have the choice. What is it to be? Either madness or death? . . Neither of your alternatives would enable me to continue to be employed by Her Majesty's Government. J. IRVING 'You have four alternatives,' Vigneron said.

■ **alternatively** *adverb* †(*a*) by turns; (*b*) in a way that offers an alternative; as or by way of an alternative: L16. **alternativeness** *noun* (*rare*) M18.

alternator /ˈɔːltəneɪtə, ˈɒl-/ *noun.* M19.
[ORIGIN from ALTERNATE *verb* + -OR.]
1 A person who causes alternation. *rare.* M19.
2 An electric generator producing an alternating power supply. L19.

alternity /ɔːlˈtəːnɪti, ɒl-/ *noun. rare.* M17.
[ORIGIN French *alternité* or medieval Latin *alternitas* formed as ALTERN: see -ITY.]
Being alternate; alternation.

althaea /alˈθiːə/ *noun.* Also **-thea**. LME.
[ORIGIN Latin from Greek *althaia* marshmallow, from *althein* heal.]
A plant of the genus *Althaea* of the mallow family, *esp.* marshmallow. Also, the ornamental shrub *Hibiscus syriacus* (formerly *A. frutex*).

Althing /ˈɔːlθɪŋ, ˈɒl-/ *noun.* L18.
[ORIGIN Icelandic *alþing* from Old Norse *alþingi*, from *allr* ALL *adjective* + *þing* THING *noun*[2].]
hist. The general assembly of Iceland.

altho' *conjunction* see ALTHOUGH.

althorn /ˈalthɔːn/ *noun.* M19.
[ORIGIN German, formed as ALT, HORN *noun*.]
MUSIC. A wind instrument of the saxhorn family.

although /ɔːlˈðəʊ, ɒl-/ *conjunction.* Also (*colloq.*) **altho'**. ME.
[ORIGIN from ALL *adverb* + THOUGH.]
Even though; notwithstanding the fact that; and yet, nevertheless.

> E. O'NEILL I think she's much better, don't you—although she won't admit it. G. EWART Although he giggled Dominic was shocked.

alti *noun* pl. of ALTUS *noun.*

alti- /ˈalti/ *combining form* of Latin *altus* high and *alte* highly: see -I-.
■ **altiplaˈnation** *noun* (*GEOLOGY*) the production of terraces or other flat surfaces by periglacial processes such as solifluction E20.

altimeter /ˈaltɪmiːtə/ *noun.* E19.
[ORIGIN from ALTI- + -METER.]
†**1** An instrument for measuring altitudes geometrically. Only in Dicts. E–M19.
2 An instrument used to determine altitude attained, esp. a barometric or radio-echo device fitted in an aircraft etc. E20.

altimetry /alˈtɪmɪtri/ *noun.* LME.
[ORIGIN medieval Latin *altimetria*: see ALTI-, -METRY.]
The measurement of height or altitude.
■ **altiˈmetric** *adjective* E20.

altiplano /altɪˈplɑːnəʊ, *foreign* altiˈplano/ *noun.* Pl. **-os** /-əʊz, *foreign* -os/. E20.
[ORIGIN Spanish.]
The high tableland of central S. America.

altisonant /alˈtɪsənənt/ *adjective. arch.* E17.
[ORIGIN from Latin *altisonus*, formed as ALTI- + *sonare* to sound + -ANT[1].]
High-sounding, pompous, loud.

altissimo /alˈtɪsɪməʊ/ *noun.* L18.
[ORIGIN Italian, superl. of ALTO.]
Mus. ***in altissimo***, in the second octave above G at the top of the treble stave. Cf. ALT.

†**altitonant** *adjective.* L16–M17.
[ORIGIN Latin *altitonant-*, *-ans*, formed as ALTI- + pres. pple of *tonare* to thunder: see -ANT[1].]
Thundering from on high: an epithet of Jove (Jupiter).

altitude /ˈaltɪtjuːd/ *noun.* LME.
[ORIGIN Latin *altitudo*, *-din-*, from *altus* high: see -TUDE.]
1 *ASTRONOMY.* Angular distance above the horizon. Cf. ZENITH ***distance***. LME.
2 Height or depth, as dimensions of space. LME.
3 Height above the ground or above sea level; great height, loftiness. LME.

> S. HAUGHTON The Himalaya chain . . has a mean altitude of about 18,000 feet. W. DALRYMPLE I could feel the weakening effects of altitude.

4 A height; in *pl.*, great heights. LME. ▸†**b** In *pl. fig.* Lofty feelings, airs, phrases, etc. E17–E19.

> *New Scientist* Conifer forests at high altitudes.

5 *fig.* Eminence; high or exalted position. L15.
6 *GEOMETRY.* The height of a triangle or other figure, measured by a perpendicular from a vertex to the base or base produced. L16.
– COMB.: **altitude sickness** illness caused by ascent to high altitude, characterized chiefly by nausea and exhaustion.
■ **altiˈtudinal** *adjective* relating to height or degree of elevation L18. **altiˈtudinous** *adjective* high, lofty M19.

altivolant /alˈtɪvələnt/ *adjective. rare.* M17.
[ORIGIN Latin *altivolant-*, *-ans*, formed as ALTI- + pres. pple of *volare* to fly: see -ANT[1].]
Flying on high.

alto /ˈaltəʊ/ *noun & adjective.* L16.
[ORIGIN Italian = high (sc. song) from Latin ALTUS.]
MUSIC. ▸**A** *noun.* Pl. **-os**.
1 a The highest adult male voice, with range above the tenor, the counter-tenor voice; a part written for such a voice. L16. ▸**b** A female voice of similar range, a contralto voice; a part written for such a voice. E19.
2 A person who has a counter-tenor or contralto voice. L18.
3 An alto wind instrument (see sense B. below). L19.
▸**B** *adjective.* Designating, pertaining to, or intended for a counter-tenor or contralto voice. Also, designating that member of a group of similar instruments with a range or relative pitch comparable to an alto voice (among wind instruments usu. the second or third highest member of the family). E18.
alto clef: placing middle C on the middle line of the stave. **alto horn** (*a*) = ALTHORN; (*b*) *US* an alto saxophone.

alto- *prefix* see ALL *adverb* 2.

altocumulus /altəʊˈkjuːmjʊləs/ *noun.* Pl. **-li** /-lʌɪ, -liː/. L19.
[ORIGIN from mod. Latin *alto-*, from *altus* high, + CUMULUS.]
METEOROLOGY. A cloud or cloud type resembling cumulus but occurring at medium altitude (usu. 2 to 7 km, 6500 to 23,000 ft).

altogether /ɔːltəˈɡɛðə, ɒl-/ *noun & adverb.* OE.
[ORIGIN from ALL + TOGETHER.]
▸**A** *noun.* †**1** The whole together; the total; everything. OE–E16.

> TINDALE *1 Cor.* 7:19 Circumcision is nothynge . . but the keppynge of the commaundmentes of god is altogether.

2 ***for altogether***, for ever, for good. *arch.* M16.
3 A whole; an overall effect. Now *rare.* M18.
4 *The* nude. *colloq.* L19.
▸**B** *adverb.* **1** Totally; entirely; in all respects. OE.

> H. T. BUCKLE In Greece, we see a country altogether the reverse of India. S. HILL It is getting altogether too hot to walk back to Cliff House.

2 All in one place or in a group; all at once. From 17 usu. ***all together***. ME.

> W. HARRIS The crew began, all together, tugging and hauling the boat.

3 In all; in total amount. L18.

> J. AUSTEN Altogether, they will have five hundred a-year amongst them.

4 On the whole; taking everything into account. E19.

> W. E. COLLINSON Altogether I cannot think of any modern writer who has exercised so far-reaching an influence on our every-day speech.

■ **altogetherness** *noun* (now *rare*) wholeness, unity L17.

alto-relievo /ˌaltəʊrɪˈliːvəʊ/ *noun.* Also **-rilievo** /-rɪˈljeɪvəʊ/. Pl. **-os**. M17.
[ORIGIN Italian *alto-rilievo*: see ALTO, RELIEVO *noun*[1].]
(A sculpture, moulding, carving, etc., in) high relief.

altostratus /altəʊˈstrɑːtəs, -ˈstreɪtəs/ *noun.* L19.
[ORIGIN from mod. Latin *alto-*, from *altus* high, + STRATUS.]
METEOROLOGY. A cloud or cloud type resembling stratus or cirrostratus but occurring at medium altitude (usu. 2 to 7 km, 6500 to 23,000 ft).

altricial /alˈtrɪʃ(ə)l/ *adjective.* L19.
[ORIGIN from mod. Latin *Altrices*, a former division of birds, pl. of *altrix* fem. of *altor* nourisher, from *alere* nourish: see -IAL.]
ZOOLOGY. (Having young which are) helpless at birth; nidicolous. Cf. PRECOCIAL.

altruism /ˈaltrʊɪz(ə)m/ *noun.* M19.
[ORIGIN French *altruisme* (A. Comte), from Italian *altrui* somebody else: see -ISM.]
Regard for others as a principle of action; unselfishness.
■ **altruist** *noun* an altruistic person M19. **altruˈistic** *adjective* of, pertaining to, or practising altruism; unselfish: M19. **altruˈistically** *adverb* M19.

altus /ˈaltʌs/ *noun & adjective.* Pl. of noun **-ti** /-tʌɪ, -tiː/. L16.
[ORIGIN Latin = high.]
EARLY MUSIC. = ALTO.

ALU *abbreviation.*
COMPUTING. Arithmetic and logic unit.

alu *noun* var. of ALOO.

aludel /ˈaljʊdɛl/ *noun.* LME.
[ORIGIN Old French *alutel*, later *aludel*, from Spanish from Arabic *al-ʾuṯāl* the sublimation vessel: see AL-[2].]
A pear-shaped earthenware or glass pot, open at both ends so that a series could be fitted one above another, formerly used in sublimation.

alula /ˈaljʊlə/ *noun.* Pl. **-lae** /-liː/. L18.
[ORIGIN mod. Latin, dim. of *ala* wing.]
1 *ORNITHOLOGY.* A bastard wing. L18.
2 *ENTOMOLOGY.* A small lobe at the base of a wing or elytron, present in certain insects. E19.

alum /ˈaləm/ *noun & verb.* LME.
[ORIGIN Old French from Latin *alumen* rel. to *aluta* tawed leather.]
▸**A** *noun. CHEMISTRY.*
1 A hydrated double sulphate of aluminium and potassium, forming colourless octahedral crystals and having astringent properties; $KAl(SO_4)_2 \cdot 12H_2O$. LME.
2 Any of various substances resembling this; now *spec.* any of a series of isomorphous double sulphates in which other elements or radicals may replace aluminium or potassium. LME.
With specifying word indicating the characteristic element or source, as ***ammonium alum***, ***chrome alum***, ***ferric alum***, ***iron alum***, ***potash alum*** (= sense 1), ***rock alum***, ***Roman alum***, ***soda alum***, etc.
– COMB.: **alum rock** (*a*) = ALUNITE; (*b*) alum shale; **alum root** *N. Amer.* any of various plants with astringent roots, *esp.* heuchera; **alum schist**, **alum shale**, **alum slate** argillaceous rock impregnated with alum; **alum stone** = ALUNITE.
▸**B** *verb trans.* Treat or impregnate with alum. LME.

alumina /əˈluːmɪnə/ *noun.* L18.
[ORIGIN from Latin *alumin-*, *alumen* ALUM, after *soda*, *magnesia*, etc.]
Aluminium oxide, Al_2O_3, a white heat-resistant solid which is a major constituent of many rocks, esp. clays, and is found crystallized as corundum, sapphire, etc.
■ †**alumine** *noun* [French] = ALUMINA L18–M19. **aluminate** *noun* (*CHEMISTRY*) a salt formed (as) from alumina and a base M19.

aluminium /aljʊˈmɪnɪəm/ *noun & adjective.* Also ***aluminum** /əˈluːmɪnəm/. E19.
[ORIGIN from ALUMINA + -IUM.]
▸**A** *noun.* A light silvery ductile and malleable metal, not readily tarnished by air, which is a chemical element, atomic no. 13 (symbol Al). E19.
▸**B** *attrib.* or as *adjective.* Of aluminium; made with or containing aluminium. M19.
aluminium bronze an alloy of aluminium with copper (and sometimes other metals). **aluminium foil** aluminium in very thin sheets, used as wrapping material etc.
■ **aluminize** /əˈljuːmɪnʌɪz/ *verb trans.* coat with aluminium E20.

alumino- /əˈluːmɪnəʊ/ *combining form* of ALUMINA and ALUMINIUM: see -O-.
■ **aluminoˈsilicate** *noun* a silicate containing aluminium, *esp.* one in which aluminium replaces some of the silicon in the ion SiO_4^-; *spec.* any of the numerous minerals of this kind, e.g. the clay minerals and feldspars: E20. **aluminoˈthermic** *adjective* of or pertaining to aluminothermy E20. **aluminoˈthermy** *noun* the production of high temperatures (for welding, smelting, etc.) by means of the oxidation of powdered aluminium E20.

aluminous /əˈluːmɪnəs/ *adjective.* LME.
[ORIGIN from Latin *aluminosus*, from *alumin-*, *alumen* ALUM: see -OUS.]
Of the nature of or containing alum or alumina.

aluminum *noun* see ALUMINIUM.

alumna /əˈlʌmnə/ *noun.* Pl. **-nae** /-niː/. L19.
[ORIGIN Latin, fem. of ALUMNUS.]
A female graduate or former student of a school, college, university, or other educational institution.

alumnus /əˈlʌmnəs/ *noun.* Pl. **-ni** /-nʌɪ/. M17.
[ORIGIN Latin = nursling, pupil, from *alere* nourish.]
Formerly, a pupil. Now *spec.*, a (male) graduate or former student of a school, college, university, or other educational institution.

alunite /ˈaljʊnʌɪt/ *noun.* M19.
[ORIGIN French, from *alun* formed as ALUM + -ITE[1].]
MINERALOGY. A hexagonal basic sulphate of potassium and aluminium, used in alum manufacture.

alunogen /əˈljuːnədʒ(ə)n/ *noun.* M19.
[ORIGIN French *alunogène*, formed as ALUNITE: see -GEN.]
MINERALOGY. A hydrated aluminium sulphate, usu. occurring as masses of feathery or fibrous triclinic crystals.

alure /ˈaljə/ *noun.* Now *arch.* & *dial.* ME.
[ORIGIN Old French *alëor*, later *alëeur*, Anglo-Norman *aleür* passage, gallery, etc., esp. in fortifications.]
A passage, gallery, or cloister to walk in, *esp.* one behind battlements or on the roof of a church.

alveary /ˈalvɪəri/ *noun.* Now *rare* or *obsolete.* L16.
[ORIGIN from Latin *alvearium* set of beehives, from *alveus* beehive: see -ARY[1].]
A beehive.

> *fig.*: J. BARET An alvearie or quadruple dictionarie.

alveolar /alˈvɪələ/ *adjective & noun.* L18.
[ORIGIN from ALVEOLUS + -AR[1].]
▸**A** *adjective.* Of or pertaining to an alveolus or alveoli; *PHONETICS* (of a consonant) articulated with the tip of the tongue at or near the ridge of the upper teeth. L18.
alveolar ridge the ridge that contains the sockets of the upper teeth.
▸**B** *noun.* **1** *ANATOMY.* An alveolar process. *rare.* L19.
2 *PHONETICS.* An alveolar consonant. L19.
■ **alveolarity** /-ˈlarɪti/ *noun* (*PHONETICS*) the quality of being alveolar M20.

alveolitis /ˌalvɪəˈlʌɪtɪs/ *noun.* L19.
[ORIGIN formed as ALVEOLAR + -ITIS.]
MEDICINE. Inflammation of an alveolus or alveoli (now usu. *spec.* of the lungs).

alveolo- /al'vɪələʊ, alvɪ'əʊləʊ/ *combining form*. L19.
[ORIGIN from ALVEOLUS: see -O-.]
Of or pertaining to the sockets of the teeth or the alveolar ridge; PHONETICS alveolar and —, as ***alveolo-palatal***.

alveolus /al'vɪələs, alvɪ'əʊləs/ *noun*. Pl. **-li** /-lʌɪ, -liː/. L17.
[ORIGIN Latin, dim. of *alveus* cavity.]
Chiefly ANATOMY. A small cavity or depression; *esp.* (***a***) the socket of a tooth; (***b***) any of the terminal air sacs of the lungs; (***c***) an acinus.
■ **al'veolate** *adjective* pitted with small cavities E19. **'alveole** *noun* [French] = ALVEOLUS M18.

alveus /'alvɪəs/ *noun*. L17.
[ORIGIN Latin.]
The channel or bed of a river, the trough of the sea. Also, beach ground between the high- and low-water marks.

alvine /'alvʌɪn/ *adjective*. Now *rare*. M18.
[ORIGIN mod. Latin *alvinus*, from *alvus* belly: see -INE[1].]
Of or pertaining to the bowels.

alway /'ɔːlweɪ, ɔːl'weɪ/ *adverb*. Now *arch.* & *poet.* OE.
[ORIGIN Orig. two words, from ALL + WAY *noun* (= *all the way*).]
1 = ALWAYS 2. OE.
2 = ALWAYS 1. LME.
†**3** = ALWAYS 3. LME–L15.

always /'ɔːlweɪz, -ɪz/ *adverb*. ME.
[ORIGIN Prob. distrib. genit., formed as ALWAY + -S[3].]
1 On all occasions; invariably; repeatedly; at every available opportunity; whenever appropriate or possible. ME.

> MILTON And Love hath oft, well meaning, wrought much wo, Yet always pity or pardon hath obtain'd. ADDISON She is always seeing Apparitions. SHELLEY None slow enough for sadness: till we came Homeward, which always makes the spirit tame. YEATS I always said you could not trust these Moors. J. D. SALINGER She was somebody you always felt like talking to on the phone.

2 Throughout all (the) time; for ever; continually; from as far back as can be remembered. LME.

> DONNE But what thy thorny crowne gain'd, that give mee, A crowne of Glory, which doth flower alwayes. F. J. FURNIVALL Since I first saw the Boxes . . , I always meant to have a turn at them. SCOTT FITZGERALD In a real dark night of the soul it is always three o'clock in the morning. W. H. AUDEN It wasn't always like this? Perhaps it wasn't, but it is. DAY LEWIS The smell of bacon and the smell of breadcrumbs have always been closed memories for me.

3 Whatever the circumstances; in any event; anyway. LME.

> GEO. ELIOT Fred had always (at that time) his father's pocket as a last resort.

alwise /'ɔːlwʌɪz/ *adverb*. *arch.* ME.
[ORIGIN from ALL *adjective* + -WISE, = ***in all wise***; assoc. with ALWAYS.]
In every way; in any way; at all events; *Scot.* always.

aly /'eɪli/ *adjective*. Also **aley**. M16.
[ORIGIN from ALE + -Y[1].]
Of or like ale.

alyssum /'alɪs(ə)m, ə'lɪs(ə)m/ *noun*. Also (in sense 2) **alison** /'alɪs(ə)n/. M16.
[ORIGIN mod. Latin (see below), from Latin *alysson* from Greek *alusson*, from *a-* A-[10] + *lussa* rabies.]
1 Any of several cruciferous plants belonging to the chiefly yellow-flowered genus *Alyssum* or formerly included in it. M16.
2 *spec.* In full ***sweet alyssum***. A small Mediterranean plant, *Lobularia maritima*, much grown for its fragrant white flowers. E19.

Alzheimer's disease /'altshʌɪməz dɪˌziːz/ *noun phr.* E20.
[ORIGIN from Alois *Alzheimer* (1864–1915), German neurologist.]
MEDICINE. Mental deterioration occurring in middle or old age, owing to progressive generalized degeneration of the brain; (premature) senile dementia. Also ***Alzheimer's***.

AM *abbreviation*.
1 Amplitude modulation.
2 Latin *anno mundi* in the year of the world.
3 Latin *Artium Magister* Master of Arts. Cf. MA. *US*.
4 Assembly Member (a member of the Welsh Assembly).

Am *symbol*.
CHEMISTRY. Americium.

am *verb* see BE *verb*.

a.m. *abbreviation*.
Ante meridiem.

AMA *abbreviation*.
American Medical Association.

ama /'amə/ *noun*. Pl. same. M20.
[ORIGIN Japanese, lit. 'sea woman'.]
A Japanese woman who dives for shellfish and edible seaweed.

amability /amə'bɪlɪti/ *noun*. Now *rare* or *obsolete*. E17.
[ORIGIN French *amabilité* or Latin *amabilitas*, from *amabilis* lovely, from *amare* to love: see -ITY.]
Lovableness.

amacrine /'aməkrʌɪn, -krɪn/ *adjective* & *noun*. E20.
[ORIGIN from A-[10] + Greek *makros* MACRO- + *in-*, *is* sinew, strip.]
HISTOLOGY. ► **A** *adjective*. Designating a type of small nerve cell within the retina having dendrites but no axon. E20.
► **B** *noun*. An amacrine cell. E20.

amadavat *noun* see AVADAVAT.

amado /'amado/ *noun*. Pl. same. L19.
[ORIGIN Japanese, from *ame* rain + *to* door.]
(Each of) a set of shutters on the outer side of the windows of a Japanese house.

amadou /'amədʊː/ *noun*. L18.
[ORIGIN French, of unknown origin.]
A kind of tinder made from either of the bracket fungi *Fomes fomentarius* and *Phellinus igniarius*, soaked in saltpetre.

amah /'ɑːmə/ *noun*. M19.
[ORIGIN Portuguese *ama* nurse.]
In parts of the Indian subcontinent and the Far East: a wet nurse, children's nurse, or house servant.

†**amain** *verb* var. of AMAINE.

amain /ə'meɪn/ *adverb*. *arch.* M16.
[ORIGIN from A *preposition*[1] 4 + MAIN *noun*[1].]
1 In or with full force; vehemently, violently. M16.
2 At full speed; without delay. M16.
3 Exceedingly, greatly. L16.

†**amaine** *verb*. Also **amain**. M16.
[ORIGIN Old French & mod. French *amener*, formed as A-[5] + *mener* bring.]
1 *verb trans.* Direct, guide. *rare*. Only in M16.
2 NAUTICAL. **a** *verb trans.* Lower (a sail etc., esp. the topsail). Only in E17. ▸**b** *verb intrans.* Lower the topsail as a sign of yielding; *gen.* yield. E17–M19.

Amal /ə'mɑːl, *foreign* 'amal/ *noun*. L20.
[ORIGIN Arabic *'amal* hope.]
A political and paramilitary organization of Shiite Muslims founded in Lebanon in 1975.

amalgam /ə'malgəm/ *noun*. L15.
[ORIGIN French *amalgame* or medieval Latin *amalgama*, prob. ult. from Greek *malagma* emollient.]
1 CHEMISTRY. Orig., a soft mass formed esp. by combination (of gold, etc.) with mercury. Now, any alloy with mercury. L15.

> N. V. SIDGWICK Another peculiarity of mercury is its power of forming liquid metallic solutions or amalgams.

2 An intimate plastic mixture of substances. E17.
3 *fig.* A combination of various elements. L18.

> M. FONTEYN His perfect amalgam of virtuosity and elegance.

4 An ingredient in an amalgam or alloy. Now *rare* or *obsolete*. M19.

> J. H. BURTON No tin or other amalgam.

amalgam /ə'malgəm/ *verb*. *arch.* LME.
[ORIGIN medieval Latin *amalgamare*, formed as AMALGAM *noun*.]
1 *verb trans.* Amalgamate (*lit.* & *fig.*). LME.
†**2** *verb intrans.* Form an amalgam. L16–L17.
■ **amalgamable** *adjective* L17.

amalgamate /ə'malgəmeɪt/ *verb*. Pa. pple & ppl adjective **-ated**, (*arch.*) **-ate** /-ət/. E17.
[ORIGIN medieval Latin *amalgamat-* pa. ppl stem of *amalgamare*: see AMALGAM *verb*, -ATE[3].]
1 CHEMISTRY. **a** *verb trans.* Soften by combining with mercury; alloy with mercury. E17. ▸**b** *verb intrans.* Combine with mercury. M18.
2 *verb trans.* & *intrans.* Unite, mix together; combine in a homogeneous whole. L18.

> COLERIDGE [The Romans] were ordained . . to conquer and amalgamate the materials of Christendom. A. CRUMP Two banks of issue had amalgamated. P. H. GIBBS The old *Daily Post*, afterwards amalgamated with another journal. A. J. P. TAYLOR A reorganization commission was to devise schemes for closing the less efficient pits and amalgamating the others.

■ **amalgamater** *noun* (*rare*) = AMALGAMATOR M19. **amalgamative** *adjective* tending to or characterized by amalgamation M19. **amalgamator** *noun* a person who or thing which amalgamates; an apparatus used in amalgamating; a person involved in an amalgamation: M19.

amalgamation /əmalgə'meɪʃ(ə)n/ *noun*. E17.
[ORIGIN formed as AMALGAMATE, perh. through French: see -ATION.]
1 CHEMISTRY. The action or process of amalgamating; the state of being alloyed with mercury. E17.
2 The action of combining into one uniform whole. L18.

> A. J. P. TAYLOR The amalgamation of public assistance with the local councils. E. F. SCHUMACHER The amalgamation of many small family farms into large agricultural units operated as if they were factories.

3 A homogeneous union. E19.

> G. B. SHAW Her dialect is now a spirited amalgamation of the foreign accents of all the waiters she has known.

amand *noun* see AMEND *noun*.

Amandebele *noun pl.* see NDEBELE *noun*.

amandine /ə'mandʌɪn/ *noun* & *adjective*. M19.
[ORIGIN French, from *amande* ALMOND: see -INE[4].]
(Something) prepared or served with almonds.

amang *preposition* & *adverb* see AMONG.

amanuensis /əˌmanjʊ'ɛnsɪs/ *noun*. Pl. **-enses** /-'ɛnsiːz/. E17.
[ORIGIN Latin (Suetonius), from *a manu* in *servus a manu* slave at hand + *-ensis* belonging to: see -ESE.]
A person who writes from dictation or copies manuscript; a literary assistant.
■ **amanuense** *verb intrans.* (*rare*) act as an amanuensis M19.

Amapondo *noun* & *adjective* see PONDO.

amaracus /ə'marəkəs/ *noun*. Now *rare* or *obsolete*. LME.
[ORIGIN Latin from Greek *amarakos* marjoram.]
An aromatic plant, dittany of Crete (*Origanum dictamnus*).

amaranth /'amərанθ/ *noun*. Also **-ant** /-ant/ & in Latin forms **-ant(h)us** /-ʌs/. M16.
[ORIGIN French *amarante* or mod. Latin *amaranthus*, alt. after names in *-anthus* (Greek *anthos* flower) of Latin *amarantus* from Greek *amarantos* unfading, from *a-* A-[10] + *maran-*, *marainein* wither.]
1 Any of various plants of the family Amaranthaceae and esp. of the genus *Amaranthus*, characterized by chaffy spikes of small flowers and often by coloured foliage. M16.
globe amaranth an erect annual, *Gomphrena globosa*, bearing long-lived globular flower heads. **green amaranth** a pigweed, *Amaranthus hybridus*. **purple amaranth** *Amaranthus cruentus*, bearing purple flowering spikes.
2 An imaginary flower that never fades. E17.
3 The purple colour of *Amaranthus* leaves. L17. ▸**b** A red dye used esp. to colour food. L19.
4 = ***purpleheart*** s.v. PURPLE *adjective*. E20.

amaranthine /amə'ranθʌɪn, -θɪn/ *adjective*. Also **-tine** /-t-/, †**-tin**. M17.
[ORIGIN from AMARANTH + -INE[1].]
1 Of or pertaining to the everlasting flower amaranth. M17.
2 Fadeless, undying. L18.
3 Of the colour amaranth. *rare*. L19.
– NOTE: First recorded in Milton.

amaretto /amə'rɛtəʊ/ *noun*. Pl. **-tti** /-ti/. E20.
[ORIGIN Italian, from *amaro* bitter (almond) + *-etto* dim. suffix (see -ET[1]).]
1 A type of Italian macaroon biscuit. Usu. in *pl.* E20.
2 A sweet almond-flavoured liqueur orig. made at Saronno in northern Italy. M20.

amaryllid /amə'rɪlɪd/ *noun*. M19.
[ORIGIN Latin *Amaryllid-*, *Amaryllis*: see AMARYLLIS, -ID[2].]
BOTANY. Any plant of the large family Amaryllidaceae, which includes many bulbous plants, such as amaryllis, daffodil, snowdrop, etc.
■ ˌ**amaryllі'daceous** *adjective* of or pertaining to the family Amaryllidaceae M19.

amaryllis /amə'rɪlɪs/ *noun*. L18.
[ORIGIN mod. Latin, use of Latin *Amaryllis* from Greek *Amarullis*, a country girl in Theocritus, Virgil, and Ovid.]
A bulbous plant of the genus *Amaryllis*, or formerly of this genus, which now contains only one species (the southern African *A. belladonna*, belladonna lily).

amasi *noun* see MAAS.

amass /ə'mas/ *verb* & *noun*. L15.
[ORIGIN Old French & mod. French *amasser* or medieval Latin *amassare*, ult. formed as AD- + MASS *noun*[2].]
► **A** *verb*. **1** *verb trans.* **a** Accumulate (wealth or other resources) as one's own. L15. ▸**b** *gen.* Heap together, pile up, collect. Now *rare*. L16.

> **a** C. V. WEDGWOOD The son of a small landowner whose family had first amassed, and then lost, considerable wealth. G. GREENE A detective must find it as important as a novelist to amass his trivial material before picking out the right clue. **b** DONNE This last lesson, in which hee amasses and gathers all his former Doctrine. T. BLOUNT Cromwell had amass'd togither a numerous Body of Rebels. M. LASKI The bonfire that the children had been amassing all day.

2 *verb intrans.* Gather, assemble. *arch.* L16.

> D. G. ROSSETTI Billowing skies that scatter and amass.

► †**B** *noun*. An accumulation; a collection. M16–M18.
■ **amasser** *noun* L17. **amassment** *noun* the action or result of amassing M17.

amastigote /eɪ'mastɪgəʊt/ *noun* & *adjective*. *rare*. L20.
[ORIGIN from A-[10] + Greek *mastig-*, *mastix* whip + *-ote* (cf. -OT[2]).]
ZOOLOGY & MEDICINE. (Designating) a parasitic protozoan of the genus *Leishmania* in the leishmanial or non-flagellated form. Opp. PROMASTIGOTE.

†**amate** *verb*[1] *trans.* ME–M19.
[ORIGIN Old French *amater*, ult. formed as MATE *adjective*.]
Cast down; deject.

†**amate** *verb*[2] *trans.* L16–M17.
[ORIGIN from A-[11] + MATE *verb*[2].]
Be a mate to; match, equal.

A

amateur /ˈamətə, -tjʊə/ *noun & adjective*. L18.
[ORIGIN French from Italian *amatore* from Latin *amator* lover (see AMATORY).]
▸ **A** *noun*. **1** A person who is fond *of* something; a person who has a taste for something. L18.
2 A person who practises something, esp. an art or game, only as a pastime; an unpaid player, performer, etc. (opp. ***professional***); also (*derog.*), a dabbler. L18.
▸ **B** *attrib.* or as *adjective*. Done by amateurs, not professional; also (*derog.*), unskilful, amateurish. E19.
■ **amateurish** *adjective* characteristic of an amateur, having the faults of amateur work, unskilful M19. **amateurishly** *adverb* L19. **amateurishness** *noun* M19. **amateurism** *noun* the characteristic practice of an amateur M19. **amateurship** *noun* the quality or character of an amateur E19.

Amati /əˈmɑːti/ *noun*. M19.
[ORIGIN See below.]
In full ***Amati cello***, ***Amati violin***, etc. A stringed instrument from the workshops of the Amati family in Cremona (*c* 1550–1700).

amative /ˈamətɪv/ *adjective*. M17.
[ORIGIN medieval Latin *amativus*, from Latin *amat-* pa. ppl stem of *amare* to love: see -ATIVE.]
Disposed to loving.
■ **amativeness** *noun* (PHRENOLOGY) propensity to love or to sexual passions E19.

amatol /ˈamətɒl/ *noun*. E20.
[ORIGIN Irreg. from AM(MONIUM + TOL(UENE.]
A high explosive consisting of a mixture of TNT and ammonium nitrate.

amatory /ˈamət(ə)ri/ *adjective*. L16.
[ORIGIN Latin *amatorius*, from *amator* lover, from *amare* to love: see -ORY[2].]
Of or pertaining to a lover, lovemaking, or sexual love generally.
■ **amatorial** /-ˈtɔːrɪəl/ *adjective* amatory E17. **amatorious** /-ˈtɔːrɪəs/ *adjective* amatory; amorous: E17.

Amatriciana /ˌamətrɪtʃɪˈɑːnə/ *adjective*. M20.
[ORIGIN Italian *all'Amatriciana* in the style of Amatrice, from *Amatrice*, an Italian town.]
Denoting a spicy sauce made with tomatoes, pancetta or bacon, and basil, typically served with pasta.

amaurosis /amɔːˈrəʊsɪs/ *noun*. M17.
[ORIGIN Greek *amaurōsis*, from *amauroun* darken: see -OSIS.]
MEDICINE. Partial or total blindness, without apparent change in the eye. Freq. in ***amaurosis fugax*** /ˈfjuːgaks/ [see FUGACIOUS], a transient loss of vision.
■ **amaurotic** /-ˈrɒtɪk/ *adjective* affected or characterized by amaurosis E19.

amaze /əˈmeɪz/ *noun*. LME.
[ORIGIN from the verb.]
†**1** = AMAZEMENT 1. LME–M18.
2 = AMAZEMENT 3. Now *arch.* or *poet.* L16.
†**3** = AMAZEMENT 2. E17–M18.
■ †**amazeful** *adjective* causing amazement; struck with amazement: M16–E17.

amaze /əˈmeɪz/ *verb*.
[ORIGIN Old English *āmasian*, from A-[1] + base perh. as in Norwegian, Danish *mase* be busy or active (Norwegian dial. *masast* lose consciousness). Aphet. to MAZE *verb*.]
†**1** *verb trans.* Stun, stupefy; infatuate, craze; bewilder, perplex. OE–E18.
MARVELL How vainly men themselves amaze, To win the palm, the oak, or bays.
†**2** *verb trans.* Terrify, alarm. M16–L18.
I. WALTON The sight of any shadow amazes the fish.
3 *verb trans.* Overwhelm with wonder, astonish greatly. L16.
4 *verb intrans.* Be astounded or stupefied. *arch.* L16.
B. TAYLOR Men amaze thereat.

amazed /əˈmeɪzd/ *adjective*. OE.
[ORIGIN from AMAZE *verb* + -ED[1].]
†**1** Stunned, stupefied; bewildered; thrown into confusion; terrified, alarmed. OE–E18.
2 Lost in wonder or astonishment. L16.
■ **amazedly** /-zɪdli/ *adverb* L16. **amazedness** /-zɪdnɪs/ *noun* M16.

amazement /əˈmeɪzm(ə)nt/ *noun*. L16.
[ORIGIN from AMAZE *verb* + -MENT.]
†**1** *gen.* Loss of one's wits or self-possession; mental stupefaction; bewilderment, perplexity. L16–M18.
†**2** *spec.* Overwhelming fear or apprehension. L16–M18.
3 *spec.* Overwhelming wonder, extreme astonishment. E17.

amazing /əˈmeɪzɪŋ/ *adjective & adverb*. LME.
[ORIGIN from AMAZE *verb* + -ING[2].]
▸ **A** *adjective*. †**1** Causing stupefaction; confusing; terrifying, dreadful. LME–L18.
2 Astonishing, wonderful. E18.
▸ **B** *adverb*. Astonishingly, wonderfully. Now *rare*. L18.
■ **amazingly** *adverb* in an amazing manner; *colloq.* very, exceedingly: L17. **amazingness** *noun* M19.

Amazon /ˈaməz(ə)n/ *noun*. Also (esp. in sense 3) **a-**. LME.
[ORIGIN Latin from Greek *Amazōn*, explained by the Greeks as meaning 'breastless' (as if from A-[10] + *mazos* breast) but prob. of foreign origin. Sense 4 from the River *Amazon*.]
1 Any of a race of female warriors once thought to exist in Scythia and elsewhere. LME.
2 Any female warrior. E16.
3 A very strong, tall, or athletic woman. E17.
4 In full ***Amazon parrot***. Any of several short-tailed, chiefly green Central and South American parrots constituting the genus *Amazona*. L19.
– COMB.: **Amazon ant** an ant of the genus *Polyergus*, the members of which depend on slave ants of other species, captured as pupae; ***Amazon parrot***: see sense 4 above; **Amazon-stone** [from the River *Amazon*] an opaque green variety of microcline, used for amulets, beads, etc.; a piece of this.
■ **Amazonic** /aməˈzɒnɪk/ *adjective* = AMAZONIAN *adjective* 1 L19. **Amazonism** *noun* Amazonian character or condition, in which women are dominant L19.

Amazonian /aməˈzəʊnɪən/ *adjective & noun*. L16.
[ORIGIN from Latin *amazonius*: see AMAZON, -AN.]
▸ **A** *adjective*. **1** Of, pertaining to, resembling, or befitting the Amazons or an Amazon; warlike as a woman; very strong, tall, or athletic as a woman. L16.
2 Of the River Amazon in S. America or its basin. E17.
▸ **B** *noun*. = AMAZON 1. *rare*. E17.

amazonite /ˈaməz(ə)nʌɪt/ *noun*. E17.
[ORIGIN from AMAZON + -ITE[1]; in sense 2 from French.]
†**1** = AMAZON 1. E–M17.
2 Amazon-stone. L19.

ambages /amˈbeɪdʒiːz, ˈambɪdʒɪz/ *noun pl.* Formerly, esp. in sense 1, also sing. †**ambage**. LME.
[ORIGIN Old French & mod. French from Latin *ambages*, from *amb-* both ways + *agere* to drive (cf. AMBIGUOUS). Naturalized from French until 17, but latterly treated as Latin.]
1 Roundabout or indirect modes of speech, for deceit, concealment, or delay. Now *rare* exc. as coinciding with fig. uses of sense 2. LME.
CHAUCER If Calkas lede us with ambages, That is to seyn, with dowble wordes slye. A. BEHN Without more ambages, Sir, I have . . consented to marry him. *Observer* Popular literature is happiest when it can evade the ambages of language and fulfil itself in some unequivocal visual form like the cinema.
2 Indirect or roundabout paths, circuitous ways. Now chiefly *fig.* (lit. *arch.*). M16.
BACON He shall, by Ambages of diets, bathings, anointings, etc. prolong life. SWIFT The other cost me so many strains and traps and ambages to introduce. S. PEGGE You will find it, through the windings and ambages, eight, or perhaps nine miles.
■ **ambagious** /amˈbeɪdʒəs/ *adjective* full of ambages, roundabout L16.

ambari /amˈbɑːri/ *noun*. M19.
[ORIGIN Urdu *ambārā*, *ambārī*.]
In the Indian subcontinent: a hibiscus, *Hibiscus cannabinus*; (more fully ***ambari hemp***) the brown fibre of this plant, used to make ropes and coarse cloth.

ambash *noun* var. of AMBATCH.

†**ambassade** *noun & adverb*. Also **em-**. LME.
[ORIGIN Old French & mod. French (superseding Old French *ambassée* EMBASSY) from Italian *ambasciata* from Provençal *ambaisado* embassy, ult. formed as AMBASSADOR: see -ADE.]
▸ **A** *noun*. **1** The mission, function, or business of an ambassador or embassy. LME–M19.
2 An ambassador; a deputation sent to a monarch etc. LME–E18.
3 A message carried by an ambassador or embassy. LME–L16.
▸ **B** *adverb*. On an embassy. *rare*. Only in 16.
■ Also †**ambassiat(e)** *noun* [medieval Latin *ambassiata*] LME–L16.

ambassador /amˈbasədə/ *noun*. Also (common 17–18, latterly *US*) **em-** /ɛm-/; †**-dour**, †**-to(u)r**, & other vars. LME.
[ORIGIN French *ambassadeur* from Italian *ambasciator* ult. from medieval Latin *ambactia*, *-axia* (Salic and Burgundian Laws) from Germanic (Gothic *andbahts* servant, Old English *ambeht* servant, messenger, Old High German *ambaht*) from Latin *ambactus* servant, vassal (Ennius, Caesar), a Gaulish word.]
1 a An appointed or official messenger. Now *rare* in *gen.* sense exc. *fig.* LME. ▸**b** *spec.* A diplomat sent by one monarch or state on a mission to another. LME.
2 A diplomat of the highest rank permanently representing a monarch or state at a foreign court or government. L16.
– PHRASES & COMB.: **ambassador-at-large** *US*: appointed to perform special duties, and not accredited to any one monarch or state. **ambassador extraordinary** = sense 1b above. †**ambassador leger** = sense 2 above. **ambassador plenipotentiary**: with full powers to sign treaties or otherwise act for the monarch or state. **ordinary ambassador**, **resident ambassador** = sense 2 above.
■ **ambassadorial** /-ˈdɔːrɪəl/ *adjective* of or pertaining to an ambassador M18. **ambassaˈdorially** /ˌambasə-/ *adverb* L19. **ambassadorship** *noun* the position or function of an ambassador M19.

ambassadress /amˈbasədrɪs/ *noun*. Also (now *rare*) **em-** /ɛm-/. L16.
[ORIGIN from AMBASSADOR + -ESS[1].]
1 A female ambassador. L16.
2 The wife of an (esp. resident) ambassador. M17.
■ **ambassadrice** /-driːs/, †**-trice** *noun* (*rare*) an ambassadress M17. **ambassadrix** /-drɪks/, †**-trix** *noun* (*rare*) an ambassadress M17.

ambassage *noun* see EMBASSAGE.

†**ambassato(u)r** *nouns* vars. of AMBASSADOR.

ambassy *noun* see EMBASSY.

ambatch /ˈambatʃ/ *noun*. Also **-ash** /-aʃ/. M19.
[ORIGIN App. of Ethiopic origin.]
The pith tree, *Aeschynomene elaphroxylon*.

amber /ˈambə/ *noun, adjective, & verb*. LME.
[ORIGIN Old French & mod. French *ambre* from Arabic *ʿanbar* (orig.) AMBERGRIS, (later) amber.]
▸ **A** *noun*. †**1** = AMBERGRIS. LME–E18.
2 A translucent, usu. yellow, fossil resin, used for ornaments etc. and easily electrified by rubbing. LME. ▸†**b** An amulet made of amber. Only in 17.
A. ALVAREZ Two lives preserved in amber, unmoving. **b** T. DEKKER Pearles and Ambers, shall not draw me to their Chambers.
fly in amber: see FLY *noun*[1]. **oil of amber** a resinous liquid distilled from amber or colophony.
3 An alloy of four parts of gold with one of silver. LME.
4 = LIQUIDAMBAR 1. Also ***liquid amber***. M16.
5 The yellow colour of amber; a substance having this colour. M18. ▸**b** A yellow road traffic light shown as a caution between green (= *go*) and red (= *stop*). E20.
6 BIOLOGY. [translating German *Bernstein*, app. name of a friend of the discoverers.] The nonsense codon UAG; a mutant fragment of genetic material containing this. Freq. *attrib.* M20.
▸ **B** *adjective*. Having the yellow colour of amber; *spec.* designating the intermediate cautionary light in road traffic signals. E16.
fig.: A. WILSON I regard this as the amber warning.
amber-fish, **amberjack** (chiefly *N. Amer.*) any of a number of brightly coloured marine fishes of the genus *Seriola* (cf. YELLOWTAIL *noun* 2); esp. *S. dumerili*, of the W. Atlantic and *S. lalandi* of S. Africa. **amber fluid**, **amber liquid**, **amber nectar** *slang* (orig. & chiefly *Austral.* & *NZ*) beer.
▸ **C** *verb trans.* *rare*. Chiefly as ***ambered*** *ppl adjective*. [Cf. French *ambrer*, pa. pple *ambré*.]
†**1** Perfume with ambergris. E17–M18.
2 Cause to have the yellow colour of amber. E19.
3 Preserve in amber. L19.

ambergris /ˈambəgrɪs, -iːs/ *noun*. Also †**-grease** & other vars. LME.
[ORIGIN Old French & mod. French *ambre gris* grey amber, as distinct from the later *ambre jaune* yellow amber (the resin): cf. AMBER *noun*.]
An odoriferous pale grey waxlike substance, which originates as a secretion in the intestines of the sperm whale and is found floating in tropical seas.

amberoid /ˈamb(ə)rɔɪd/ *noun*. Also **ambroid**. L19.
[ORIGIN from AMBER *noun* + -OID.]
Amber moulded by heat and pressure.

ambi- /ˈambi/ *combining form*.
[ORIGIN Latin *ambi-*, *ambo*.]
Forming adjectives and nouns with the sense 'both, on both sides, both ways', as ***ambilingual***, ***ambisexual***, ***ambisexuality***, etc.

ambiance /ɑ̃bjɑ̃s/ *noun*. M20.
[ORIGIN French, from *ambiant*: see AMBIENT, -ANCE.]
= AMBIENCE; also *spec.*, the combination of the surrounding and accessory elements of a painting to support the main effect of a piece.

ambidexter /ambɪˈdɛkstə/ *noun & adjective*. Now *rare*. LME.
[ORIGIN Late Latin, from Latin AMBI- + *dexter* right-handed.]
▸ **A** *noun*. **1** A double-dealer; *spec.* in LAW, a person who takes bribes or fees from both sides. LME.
2 A person able to use left and right hands equally well; *fig.* a person of unusual dexterity. L16.
▸ **B** *adjective*. **1** = AMBIDEXTROUS 2. L16.
2 = AMBIDEXTROUS 1. M17.
3 Two-sided. E19.

ambidexterity /ˌambɪdɛkˈstɛrɪti/ *noun*. L16.
[ORIGIN from AMBIDEXTER + -ITY, after DEXTERITY.]
1 The ability to use left and right hands equally well; *fig.* unusual dexterity, many-sidedness. L16.
2 Double-dealing. M18.

ambidextrous /ambɪˈdɛkstrəs/ *adjective*. Also **-terous** /-t(ə)rəs/. M17.
[ORIGIN formed as AMBIDEXTERITY + -OUS.]
1 Able to use left and right hands equally well; *fig.* more than usually dexterous or clever, versatile. M17.
2 Double-dealing; trying to please both parties. M17.
■ **ambidextrously** *adverb* E19. **ambidextrousness** *noun* E18.

ambience /ˈambɪəns/ *noun*. L19.
[ORIGIN from AMBIENT: see -ENCE. Cf. AMBIANCE.]
Environment, surroundings; atmosphere.

ambient /ˈambɪənt/ *adjective & noun*. L16.
[ORIGIN French *ambiant* or Latin *ambient-* pres. ppl stem of *ambire* go round, formed as AMBI- + *ire* go: see -ENT.]
▸ **A** *adjective*. **1** Surrounding, encircling, encompassing; enveloping; pertaining to the immediate surroundings of something. L16.

MILTON Opening to the ambient light. BOSWELL A captive in thy ambient arms. E. F. BENSON A life that should be less idle . . than that of the ambient world. *Nature* The glass remains colourless after rapid cooling to ambient temperature.

2 Moving round (something), circling about (something). *rare*. **M17.**

DISRAELI Ye ambient Winds, That course about the quarters of the globe.

3 Designating atmospheric sound occurring naturally or at random in a particular environment at a particular time. **M20.** ▸**b** Designating or pertaining to a style of gentle, largely electronic instrumental music with no persistent beat. **L20.** ▸**c** Designating or pertaining to advertising that makes use of sites or objects other than the established media. **L20.**

▸ **B** *noun*. **1** An encompassing circle or sphere. **L16.**
2 *ASTROLOGY*. The ambient air or sky. **L17.**

ambiente /ambiˈente, ambɪˈɛnti/ *noun*. **E20.**
[**ORIGIN** Italian & Spanish, from Latin *ambient-*: see **AMBIENT**.]
= **AMBIENCE**.

†**ambigu** *noun*. **L16.**
[**ORIGIN** French, use of adjective = **AMBIGUOUS**.]
1 = **AMBIGUITY** 4. Only in **L16.**
2 A banquet at which a medley of dishes are served together. **L17–M18.**

ambiguity /ambɪˈgjuːɪti/ *noun*. **LME.**
[**ORIGIN** Old French *ambiguité* or Latin *ambiguitas*, formed as **AMBIGUOUS**: see **-ITY**.]
†**1** Hesitation, doubt, uncertainty as to one's course. **LME–L16.**
2 Ability to be understood in more than one way, ambiguousness. **LME.**

New York Review of Books The ambiguity of the word *unheimlich* (unhomelike but also uncanny).

latent ambiguity: see **LATENT** *adjective*. ***systematic ambiguity***: see **SYSTEMATIC** *adjective*.

†**3** An uncertainty. **L16–M17.**
4 An instance of double meaning; an expression having more than one meaning. **L16.**

New Statesman The unresolved ambiguities of Labour policy on the European Community.

ambiguous /amˈbɪgjʊəs/ *adjective*. **E16.**
[**ORIGIN** Latin *ambiguus* doubtful, shifting, from *ambigere* go round, formed as **AMBI-** + *agere* to drive: see **-OUS**, **-UOUS**.]
1 Indistinct, obscure, not clearly defined. **E16.**

J. RUSKIN Even the most dexterous distances of the old masters . . are ambiguous.

2 Admitting more than one interpretation or explanation; having a double meaning or reference; equivocal. **M16.**

MILTON Answers . . dark, Ambiguous, and with double sense deluding. G. GREENE Notes for rendezvous made ambiguous in case they fell into the wrong hands. G. MAXWELL Calum Murdo MacKinnon is always given both his Christian names, for there are so many Calum MacKinnons in the district that Calum alone would be ambiguous.

3 Using words with doubtful or double meaning. **M16.**

POPE Antinous . . Constrain'd a smile and thus ambiguous spoke. E. J. HOWARD 'Well—once more then.' She was deliberately ambiguous about whether it was forgiveness or another cup of tea.

†**4** Uncertain as to course or conduct, hesitating. **M16–M17.**

MILTON Thus shall they be too and fro, doubtfull and ambiguous in all thir doings.

5 Doubtful as regards classification; indeterminate. **E17.**

J. FLORIO Mungrell and ambiguous shapes. T. STOPPARD Four of them carry a machine of ambiguous purpose: it might be a television camera.

6 Uncertain as regards outcome or tendency. **E17.**

SIR W. SCOTT The eddying tides of conflict wheeled Ambiguous.

7 Unreliable. **M18.**

BURKE The taste, that most ambiguous of the senses.

■ **ambiguously** *adverb* **L16.** **ambiguousness** *noun* **L17.**

ambilingual /ambɪˈlɪŋgw(ə)l/ *adjective & noun*. **M20.**
[**ORIGIN** from **AMBI-** + **LINGUAL**.]
(A person who is) bilingual in all situations.

ambisextrous /ambɪˈsɛkstrəs/ *adjective*. *colloq*. **E20.**
[**ORIGIN** Blend of **AMBIDEXTROUS** and **SEX** *noun*.]
= **AMBISEXUAL**.

ambisexual /ambɪˈsɛkʃʊəl/ *adjective*. **M20.**
[**ORIGIN** from **AMBI-** + **SEXUAL** *adjective*. Cf. **AMBOSEXUAL**.]
Sexually attracted to individuals of both sexes.
■ **ambisexuˈality** *noun* **E20.**

ambisonic /ambɪˈsɒnɪk/ *adjective & noun*. **L20.**
[**ORIGIN** from **AMBI-** + **SONIC** *adjective*.]
▸ **A** *adjective*. Designating or pertaining to a high-fidelity audio system that reproduces the directional properties (direct and reverberant) of recorded sound. **L20.**
▸ **B** *noun*. In *pl*. (treated as *sing*.). Ambisonic reproduction. **L20.**
■ **ambisonically** *adverb* **L20.**

ambit /ˈambɪt/ *noun*. **LME.**
[**ORIGIN** Latin *ambitus* circuit, compass, from *ambit-*: see **AMBITION** *noun*.]
1 a A space surrounding a house, castle, town, etc.; precincts. **LME.** ▸**b** A circuit, a compass, a circumference. **L16.** ▸**c** The confines, bounds, or limits of a district etc. **M19.**
2 *fig*. Extent, scope, sphere, (*of*). **L17.**

W. S. CHURCHILL Both motor boats and lawn-mowers came into the ambit of this modest indulgence.

ambition /amˈbɪʃ(ə)n/ *noun*. **ME.**
[**ORIGIN** Old French & mod. French from Latin *ambitio(n-)*, from *ambit-* pa. ppl stem of *ambire*: see **AMBIENT**, **-ION**.]
1 An ardent (orig. inordinate) desire for distinction. **ME.**

SHAKES. *Jul. Caes.* I thrice presented him a kingly crown, Which he did thrice refuse. Was this ambition?

†**2** Ostentatious display, pomp; an instance of this. **LME–M17.**

DONNE Costly and expensive ambitions at Court.

†**3** Personal solicitation of honours. **M16–L17.**

MILTON I, on the other side, Used no ambition to commend my deeds.

4 An aspiration *to be*, *to do* (†*of*, †*for*). **E17.**

BURKE The pitiful ambition of possessing five or six thousand more acres. M. LASKI Sheila's present ambition was to be Senior Mathematics Mistress. G. EWART The ambition of the wealthy was . . to do absolutely nothing but to drink, to ride, to dance, to flirt.

5 An object of ardent desire or aspiration. **E17.**

W. GOLDING A beautiful woman is her own ambition.

■ **ambitionist** *noun* (*rare*) a person who is ruled by ambition **M17.** **ambitionless** *adjective* **E19.**

ambition /amˈbɪʃ(ə)n/ *verb trans*. Now *rare*. **E17.**
[**ORIGIN** French *ambitionner*, formed as **AMBITION** *noun*.]
†**1** Make desirous. Only in **E17.**
2 Be ambitious of, desire strongly. **E17.**

HOR. WALPOLE The Bishop of Chester had ambitioned the Bishopric of Winchester. T. JEFFERSON Who ambitioned to be his correspondent. H. SMART Ambitioning that her lover should make his mark.

ambitious /amˈbɪʃəs/ *adjective*. **LME.**
[**ORIGIN** Old French *ambitieux* or Latin *ambitiosus*, formed as **AMBITION** *noun*: see **-OUS**.]
1 Ardently desiring distinction, full of ambition. **LME.**
2 Strongly desirous *of* or †*for* a thing, *to be* or *to do* something. **LME.**
3 Rising, swelling, towering. *arch*. **E17.**

POPE Helps th' ambitious hill the heav'ns to scale.

4 Showing or requiring ambition. **M18.**

E. O'NEILL You can afford to make bigger, more ambitious plans now. E. WAUGH Sebastian set me to draw it. It was an ambitious subject for an amateur.

■ **ambitiously** *adverb* **LME.** **ambitiousness** *noun* **L15.**

ambivalence /amˈbɪv(ə)l(ə)ns/ *noun*. **E20.**
[**ORIGIN** German *Ambivalenz*, after *Äquivalenz* **EQUIVALENCE**.]
The coexistence in one person or one work of contradictory emotions or attitudes towards the same object or situation; an instance of this.

A. A. BRILL The synchronous laughing and crying are a partial manifestation of schizophrenic ambivalence. L. TRILLING Rousseau's *Confessions* had laid the ground for the understanding of emotional ambivalence. A. L. ROWSE There is much to be said for a certain judicious ambivalence.

■ Also **ambivalency** *noun* **E20.**

ambivalent /amˈbɪv(ə)l(ə)nt/ *adjective*. **E20.**
[**ORIGIN** from **AMBIVALENCE**, after **EQUIVALENT**.]
Of, pertaining to, or characterized by ambivalence.

B. RUSSELL Christianity . . has always had an ambivalent attitude towards the family.

■ **ambivalently** *adverb* **M20.**

ambiversion /ambɪˈvəːʃ(ə)n/ *noun*. **E20.**
[**ORIGIN** from **AMBI-** after *extroversion*, *introversion*.]
PSYCHOLOGY. A condition of balance between extrovert and introvert features in the personality.
■ **ˈambivert** *noun* a person whose personality displays ambiversion **E20.** **ˈambiverted** *adjective* **E20.**

amble /ˈamb(ə)l/ *verb & noun*. **ME.**
[**ORIGIN** Old French & mod. French *ambler* from Latin *ambulare* to walk.]
▸ **A** *verb intrans*. **1** Of a horse, mule, etc.: move lifting each foot individually and both on one side before those on the other; move with a smooth or easy gait. **ME.**
2 Of a person: ride an ambling horse etc.; ride at an easy pace. **LME.**
3 Of a person: move on foot at a smooth or easy pace; proceed in a leisurely fashion. **L16.**

ADDISON She has . . play'd at an Assembly, and ambled in a Ball or two. HARPER LEE They ambled across the square, shuffled in and out of the stores around it, took their time about everything. C. HAMPTON The ability to create essentially frivolous entertainments, which were enjoyed by enough essentially frivolous people for me to be able to amble comfortably through life.

▸ **B** *noun*. **1** The gait of an ambling horse, mule, etc. **LME.**
2 A movement suggestive of the gait of an ambling horse; a leisurely pace. **E17.**
■ **ambler** *noun* a horse, mule, etc., that ambles; an ambling person: **LME.**

ambligon *adjective & noun* var. of **AMBLYGON**.

amblygon /ˈamblɪgɒn/ *adjective & noun*. Now *rare* or *obsolete*. Also **ambli-**. **L16.**
[**ORIGIN** French *amblygone* or late Latin *ambligonius* from Greek *amblugōnios*, from *amblus* blunt + *gōnia* angle.]
▸ †**A** *adjective*. Obtuse-angled. **L16–L18.**
▸ **B** *noun*. Also (earlier) in Latin form †**-gonium**. An obtuse-angled figure, esp. a triangle. **L16.**

amblygonite /amˈblɪg(ə)nʌɪt/ *noun*. **E19.**
[**ORIGIN** formed as **AMBLYGON** + **-ITE**[1].]
MINERALOGY. A triclinic basic phosphate of aluminium, lithium, and sodium occurring as white or faintly coloured prisms.

amblyopia /amblɪˈəʊpɪə/ *noun*. **E18.**
[**ORIGIN** Greek *ambluōpia* dim-sightedness, from *ambluōpos*, from *amblus* blunt: see **-OPIA**.]
MEDICINE. Impaired vision, without apparent change in the eye.
■ **amblyopic** *adjective* **M19.** †**amblyopy** *noun* = **AMBLYOPIA** **E18–E19.**

ambo /ˈambəʊ/ *noun*. Pl. **-os**; also in Latin form **ambones** /amˈbəʊniːz/. **M17.**
[**ORIGIN** medieval Latin *ambo(n-)* formed as **AMBON**.]
The pulpit or reading desk in early Christian churches; an oblong enclosure with steps at both ends.

Amboinese *noun & adjective* var. of **AMBONESE**.

ambon /ˈamb(ə)n/ *noun*. **E18.**
[**ORIGIN** Greek *ambōn* rim or edge of a cup, (medieval Greek) pulpit.]
= **AMBO**.

ambones *noun pl*. see **AMBO**.

Ambonese /ambəˈniːz/ *noun & adjective*. Also **-boin-**, **-boyn-** /-bɔɪ-/. Pl. of noun same. **M19.**
[**ORIGIN** from *Ambon* (see below) + **-ESE**.]
A native or inhabitant of, of or pertaining to, Ambon (Amboina), an island in Indonesia, one of the Molucca Islands. Also, (of) the Austronesian language of Ambon.

ambosexual /ambəʊˈsɛkʃʊəl/ *adjective*. **L18.**
[**ORIGIN** from Latin *ambo* both + **SEXUAL** *adjective*. Cf. **AMBISEXUAL**.]
Of or pertaining to both sexes; bisexual, ambisexual.

amboyna /amˈbɔɪnə/ *noun*. Also **A-**. **M19.**
[**ORIGIN** Var. of *Amboina*: see **AMBONESE**.]
The wood of the SE Asian tree *Pterocarpus indicus*. Also called ***amboyna wood***, ***Burmese rosewood***, ***lingoa***, ***narra***.

Amboynese *noun & adjective* var. of **AMBONESE**.

ambrette /amˈbrɛt/ *noun*. **E18.**
[**ORIGIN** French, formed as **AMBER**: see **-ETTE**.]
†**1** A pear having a musky odour. **E–M18.**
2 The seeds of the musk mallow, *Abelmoschus moschatus*, which yield an oil used in perfumery. Also ***ambrette seed***. **M19.**

ambroid *noun* var. of **AMBEROID**.

†**ambrose** *noun*. **LME.**
[**ORIGIN** Old French & mod. French *ambroise* formed as **AMBROSIA**.]
1 Wood sage, *Teucrium scorodonia*; occas. some other herb. **LME–M19.**
2 = **AMBROSIA** 1. *rare*. Only in **E17.**

ambrosia /amˈbrəʊzjə/ *noun*. **M16.**
[**ORIGIN** Latin from Greek = immortality, elixir of life, from *ambrotos* immortal; in Dioscurides and Pliny applied to one or more herbs.]
▸ **I** **1** *CLASSICAL MYTHOLOGY*. The food, drink, or unguent of the gods. **M16.**
2 A compound of honey and pollen used as food by bees in the nest; bee bread. **E17.**
3 Something very pleasing to taste or smell. **M17.**
4 Water, oil, and fruits mixed as a libation in ancient times. Also, a perfumed or flavoured drink. **L17.**
5 A fungal product which forms the food of the pinhole borer. **L19.**
▸ **II** **6** Any of various plants (cf. **AMBROSE** 1). Now only as mod. Latin name of a genus of plants of the composite family which includes ragweed. **M16.**
– **COMB.**: **ambrosia beetle** the adult form of the pinhole borer.

ambrosial /amˈbrəʊzj(ə)l/ *adjective*. **L16.**
[**ORIGIN** from Latin *ambrosius*, formed as **AMBROSIA** + **-AL**[1].]
Of or like ambrosia; divinely fragrant or delicious. Also, of or pertaining to the immortal gods, heaven, or paradise.
■ **ambrosially** *adverb* (*rare*) **M19.**

ambrosian /amˈbrəʊzj(ə)n/ *adjective*[1]. **E16.**
[**ORIGIN** formed as **AMBROSIA** + **-AN**.]
= **AMBROSIAL**.

A

Ambrosian /am'brəʊzj(ə)n/ *adjective*[2]. **E17.**
[**ORIGIN** Late Latin *ambrosianus*, from *Ambrosius* Ambrose: see **-AN.**]
Of, pertaining to, or instituted by St Ambrose (d. 397), Bishop of Milan.

ambrotype /'ambrətʌɪp/ *noun*. Orig. *US*. **M19.**
[**ORIGIN** from unkn. 1st elem. + **-TYPE.**]
A photograph on glass, with lights given by the silver, and shades by a dark background showing through.

ambry *noun* see **AUMBRY.**

ambs-ace /amz'eɪs/ *noun*. *arch.* **ME.**
[**ORIGIN** Old French *ambes as*, from Latin *ambo* both + *as* **ACE** *noun*.]
A pair of aces, the lowest throw at dice; *fig.* bad luck, worthlessness, next to nothing.
†**within ambs-ace of** on the very verge of.

ambulacrum /ambjʊ'leɪkrəm, -'lakrəm/ *noun*. Pl. **-cra** /-krə/. **E19.**
[**ORIGIN** Latin = walk, avenue, from *ambulare* to walk.]
ZOOLOGY. In an echinoderm, each of the radially arranged bands, together with their underlying structures, through which the double rows of tube feet protrude.
■ **ambulacral** *adjective* of or pertaining to an ambulacrum **E19.**

ambulance /'ambjʊl(ə)ns/ *noun*. **E19.**
[**ORIGIN** French, replacing *hôpital ambulant* mobile (horse-drawn) field ambulance, formed as **AMBULANT**: see **-ANCE.**]
1 A mobile hospital following an army. **E19.**
2 A conveyance for sick or injured persons. **M19.**
– **COMB.**: **ambulance-chaser** *N. Amer. slang* a lawyer who makes a business of raising actions for personal injury.

ambulant /'ambjʊl(ə)nt/ *adjective*. **E17.**
[**ORIGIN** Latin *ambulant-* pres. ppl stem of *ambulare* walk: see **-ANT**[1].]
1 Walking, moving about; *spec.* in *MEDICINE*, walking about or able to walk about although ill or injured. **E17.**

> **BACON** Sir Edward Coke was at Friday's hearing, but in his night-cap; and complained to me he was ambulant and not current. **CARLYLE** An ambulant 'Revolutionary Army' . . shall perambulate the country at large. *fig.*: **COLERIDGE** Discriminating offence from merit by such dim and ambulant boundaries.

2 *MEDICINE*. Of a disease or treatment: not confining the patient to bed. **E20.**

ambulate /'ambjʊleɪt/ *verb intrans.* **E17.**
[**ORIGIN** Latin *ambulat-* pa. ppl stem of *ambulare* walk: see **-ATE**[3].]
Walk, move about.
■ **ambulative** *adjective* (now *rare* or *obsolete*) = **AMBULATORY** *adjective* **LME. ambulator** *noun* (*rare*) a walker **M17.**

ambulation /ambjʊ'leɪʃ(ə)n/ *noun*. **M16.**
[**ORIGIN** Latin *ambulatio(n-)*, formed as **AMBULATE**: see **-ATION.**]
†**1** The spreading of gangrene. **M16–M18.**
2 The action of walking; moving about. Now *rare* exc. *MEDICINE*, after an injury or illness. **L16.**

ambulatory /'ambjʊlət(ə)ri/ *noun*. **M16.**
[**ORIGIN** medieval Latin *ambulatorium* use as noun of neut. of *ambulatorius*: see **AMBULATORY** *adjective*, **-ORY**[1].]
A place for walking; an arcade, esp. in an apse; a cloister.

ambulatory /'ambjʊlət(ə)ri/ *adjective*. **E17.**
[**ORIGIN** Latin *ambulatorius*, formed as **AMBULATE**: see **-ORY**[2].]
1 Moving from place to place; movable. **E17.**

> **JER. TAYLOR** Their ambulatory life. **W. BURKITT** The tabernacle was an ambulatory temple.

2 Of or pertaining to walking. **E17.**

> **A. HELPS** When that man has an object, it is astonishing what ambulatory powers he can develop.

3 *fig.* Shifting, temporary, not fixed, mutable. **E17.**

> **W. LAUD** Nor is this ceremony Jewish or ambulatory, to cease with the law. **H. L. PIOZZI** They learn to think virtue and vice ambulatory.

4 Adapted or fitted for walking. **M19.**

> **J. D. DANA** Feet ambulatory or prehensile.

5 *MEDICINE*. = **AMBULANT** 2. **L19.**
6 = **AMBULANT** 1. **M20.**

> **M. MCCARTHY** The ambulatory mothers who wanted to were allowed to go into the diet kitchen. **A. SHAFFER** 'An ambulatory tun of port with the face of Father Christmas.' That's how I describe him.

ambury *noun* var. of **ANBURY.**

ambuscade /ambə'skeɪd/ *noun* & *verb*. **L16.**
[**ORIGIN** French *embuscade* from Italian *imboscata* or Spanish *emboscada*, Portuguese *embuscada*: see **AMBUSH** *noun*, **-ADE.**]
▸ **A** *noun*. = **AMBUSH** *noun*. **L16.**
▸ **B** *verb intrans.* & *trans.* = **AMBUSH** *verb*. **L16.**
■ **ambuscader** *noun* = **AMBUSHER L17.**

ambuscado /ambə'skeɪdəʊ/ *noun*. *arch.* Pl. **-OS. L16.**
[**ORIGIN** Refashioned from **AMBUSCADE** after Spanish: see **-ADO** 2. Usual in 17.]
= **AMBUSH** *noun*, **AMBUSCADE** *noun*.

ambush /'ambʊʃ/ *noun*. **L15.**
[**ORIGIN** Old French *embusche*, formed as **AMBUSH** *verb*.]
(A military disposition of) troops concealed in a wood or other place in order to surprise an enemy; an attack from such concealment. Also *transf.* & *fig.*, (a disposition of) someone or something lying in wait; a surprise attack from concealment.

> **SHAKES.** *Rich. II* Once did I lay an ambush for your life. **S. JOHNSON** He that perishes in the ambushes of envy. **DAY LEWIS** These flowers . . hummed all day with ambushes of bees and wasps. **S. NAIPAUL** An American congressman . . had been shot and killed in an ambush at a remote jungle airstrip.

ambush /'ambʊʃ/ *verb*. **ME.**
[**ORIGIN** Old French *embuschier*, ult. formed as **IM-**[1], **BUSH** *noun*[1].]
1 *verb trans.* Dispose (troops etc.) in concealment among bushes or elsewhere, in order to surprise an enemy. Now *rare* or *obsolete*. **ME.**

> **COLERIDGE** The ambushed soldier must not fire his musket. *refl.*: **SIR W. SCOTT** To ambush us in greenwood bough.

2 *verb intrans.* Lie in ambush; lie in wait, lurk. **E17.**

> **M. ARNOLD** The archest chin Mockery ever ambush'd in.

3 *verb trans.* Attack from an ambush; waylay. **M17.**

> **A. HALEY** He had organized a war party . . to track and ambush a detachment of the U.S. Army.

■ **ambusher** *noun* a person who lays an ambush **L19.**

ambushment /'ambʊʃm(ə)nt/ *noun*. *arch.* **ME.**
[**ORIGIN** Old French *embuschement*, formed as **AMBUSH** *verb* + **-MENT.**]
= **AMBUSH** *noun*.

AMDG *abbreviation*.
Latin *ad maiorem Dei gloriam* to the greater glory of God.

am-dram /'am dram/ *noun*. *colloq.* **L20.**
[**ORIGIN** Abbreviation.]
Amateur dramatics. Freq. *attrib.* or as *adjective*.

ameba *noun*, **amebean** *adjective*, **amebic** *adjective* see **AMOEBA, AMOEBEAN, AMOEBIC.**

âme damnée /ɑːm dɑne/ *noun phr.* Pl. **-s -s** (pronounced same). **E19.**
[**ORIGIN** French = damned soul.]
A devoted adherent; a tool.

ameer *noun* see **AMIR.**

amel /'am(ə)l/ *noun* & *verb*. Long *arch.* & *dial.* Also **aumail** /ɔː'meɪl/. **LME.**
[**ORIGIN** Anglo-Norman *amail* = Old French *esmail* (see **A-**[7]), from Germanic.]
▸ **A** *noun*. Enamel. **LME.**
▸ †**B** *verb trans.* Infl. **-l(l)-**. = **ENAMEL** *verb*. Chiefly as ***amelled*** *ppl adjective* **LME–E18.**

amelanchier /amə'laŋkɪə/ *noun*. **M18.**
[**ORIGIN** Savoy dial. *amelancier* medlar.]
A tree or shrub of the chiefly N. American genus *Amelanchier*, of the rose family, typified by the juneberry, *A. canadensis*.

amelcorn /'am(ə)lkɔːn/ *noun*. Now *rare* or *obsolete*. **L16.**
[**ORIGIN** Dutch & German *Amelkorn*, from Latin *amylum* starch + *korn* corn.]
= **EMMER** *noun*[1].

ameliorate /ə'miːlɪəreɪt/ *verb*. **M18.**
[**ORIGIN** Alt. of earlier **MELIORATE** after French *améliorer* (refashioning after Latin *melior* better of Old French *ameillorer*, from *meilleur* better).]
1 *verb trans.* Make better, improve. **M18.**
2 *verb intrans.* Become better. **L18.**
■ **ameliorator** *noun* a person who or thing which ameliorates something **M19.**

amelioration /əˌmiːlɪə'reɪʃ(ə)n/ *noun*. **M17.**
[**ORIGIN** French: see **AMELIORATE**, and cf. **MELIORATION.**]
1 The action of making something better; the condition of being made better; improvement; *LINGUISTICS* development of a more favourable meaning or connotation, melioration (opp. ***pejoration***). **M17.**

> **T. PYLES** Amelioration . . is well illustrated by *knight*, which used to mean 'servant'. **E. F. SCHUMACHER** The size of the problem puts it beyond any kind of little amelioration, any little reform, improvement, or inducement.

2 An improvement. *rare*. **L18.**

> **ADAM SMITH** The buildings, drains, enclosures, and other ameliorations.

ameliorative /ə'miːlɪərətɪv/ *adjective* & *noun*. **E19.**
[**ORIGIN** from **AMELIORATE** + **-IVE.**]
▸ **A** *adjective*. Tending to ameliorate something, improving; *LINGUISTICS* meliorative. **E19.**
▸ **B** *noun*. *LINGUISTICS* = **MELIORATIVE** *noun*. **M20.**

ameloblast /ə'mɛləʊblast/ *noun*. **L19.**
[**ORIGIN** from **EN)AMEL** *noun* + **-O-** + **-BLAST.**]
ANATOMY. Any cell in the layer of columnar cells which secrete enamel in the teeth.

amen /ɑː'mɛn, eɪ-/ *interjection, adverb, noun*, & *verb*. **OE.**
[**ORIGIN** ecclesiastical Latin *amen* from Greek *amēn* from Hebrew *'āmēn* certain(ty), from base *'mn* be firm, be certain; adopted in Greek by the Septuagint, whence in New Testament and in early Christian use in Greek and Latin.]
▸ **A** *interjection* or *adverb*. **1** In biblical translations, simply transf. from Latin: finis, the end. **OE.**
2 At the end of a prayer or wish: so be it. Now also used to express general agreement or assent. **ME.**

> **P. LARKIN** 'It is a time of year I dislike more and more as I get older.' Amen to that.

amen corner *US* the part of a meeting house formerly occupied by persons who would affirm the preacher's utterances with occasional responses. **Amen glass** an 18th-cent. drinking glass with part of the Jacobite version of 'God Save the King', concluding with 'Amen', engraved upon the bowl.
3 In translations of the Creed: it is so in truth. **ME.**
4 In biblical translations: truly, verily. **LME.**
▸ **B** *noun*. **1** (The saying of) the word 'amen' at the end of a prayer etc. **ME.**
2 As a title of Christ (*Revelation* 3:14): the faithful one. **LME.**
3 An expression of assent; an assertion of belief. **L16.**
▸ **C** *verb trans.* Pa. t. & pple **amened, amen'd**, pres. pple & verbal noun **amening, amen-ing**. Say 'amen' to (chiefly *fig.*). *rare*. **E19.**

amenable /ə'miːnəb(ə)l/ *adjective*. Also (earlier) †**amesn-**. **L16.**
[**ORIGIN** Presumably legal Anglo-Norman, from Old French *amener* bring to, from *a* **AD-** + *mener* bring, lead from popular Latin *minare* drive (animals) for Latin *minari* threaten: see **MENACE** *noun*, **-ABLE.**]
Foll. by *to* or *absol.*
1 Of a person: liable to answer (*to* a law, tribunal, etc., or *fig.*); responsible, liable, subject, (*to*). **L16.**

> **SPENSER** Not amesnable to Law. **COLERIDGE** The sufficiency of the conscience to make every person a moral and amenable being. **E. MELLOR** The next witness . . is amenable to the same imputation. **JOYCE** Amenable under section two of the Criminal Law Amendment Act.

2 Of a thing (foll. by *to*): liable to the legal authority of; *gen.* subject or liable to. **M18.**

> **JAS. MILL** All offences against the act were rendered amenable to the courts of law. **DICKENS** Your property . . being amenable to all claims upon the company.

3 Disposed to respond or submit (*to*); responsive, susceptible, (*to*); tractable. **E19.**

> **CONAN DOYLE** She is quite amenable to her father's will. **A. J. P. TAYLOR** Churchill determined to restore confidence by changing the leaders. Maybe he hoped, too, to get more amenable ones. **C. SAGAN** The hypothesis . . is amenable to experimental testing. **D. STOREY** You're young, you're flexible, you're amenable to new ideas.

■ **amenaˈbility** *noun* the quality of being amenable (*to*) **L18. amenableness** *noun* the quality or state of being amenable (*to*) **M19. amenably** *adverb* **M19.**

†**amenage** *verb trans.* *rare* (Spenser). Only in **L16.**
[**ORIGIN** French *aménager*, from *a* **AD-** + **MÉNAGE.**]
Domesticate.

†**amenance** *noun*. Also **-aunce. L16–M18.**
[**ORIGIN** Old French, from *amener*: see **AMENABLE, -ANCE.**]
Conduct, bearing, mien.

amend /ə'mɛnd/ *noun*. *obsolete* exc. *hist.* Also (*Scot.*) **amand** /ə'mɑːnd/. Pl. **AMENDS. L15.**
[**ORIGIN** French: see **AMENDE, AMENDS.**]
†**1** Reparation, compensation. **L15–M17.**
2 A fine. Chiefly *SCOTS LAW*. *rare*. **L16.**

amend /ə'mɛnd/ *verb*. **ME.**
[**ORIGIN** Old French & mod. French *amender*, ult. formed as **EMEND** with prefix-substitution. Cf. **MEND** *verb*.]
▸ **I** *verb trans.* †**1** Correct, reform, convert, (a person). **ME–E18.**

> **SHAKES.** *L.L.L.* God amend us, God amend! We are much out o' th' way.

2 Free (a thing) from faults; correct (what is faulty); rectify. *arch.* in *gen.* sense. **ME.** ▸**b** *spec.* Correct errors in (the text of a document etc.); correct (a textual error); emend. **LME.**

> **AV** *Jer.* 7:3 Amend your wayes, and your doings.

3 Repair or make good (what is broken or damaged), restore. (Now **MEND** *verb*.) *arch.* **ME.**
†**4** Heal (a sick person); cure (a disease). **ME–E19.**
†**5** Make amends for. **ME–M17.**
6 Better, improve; *spec.* make minor improvements in (a parliamentary bill, a motion etc. under discussion). **LME.**
†**7** Improve upon, surpass. **LME–L15.**
▸ **II** *verb intrans.* †**8** Recover from illness. **ME–E17.**
†**9** Make amends. **ME–L16.**
10 Reform oneself; abandon one's faults or evil ways. **LME.**
■ **amendable** *adjective* **ME. amendatory** *adjective* (*US*) of or pertaining to amendment; tending to amend: **M19. amender** *noun* a person who or thing which amends (usu. foll. by *of*) **LME.**

amende /amɑ̃ːd/ *noun*. Pl. pronounced same. **E18.**
[**ORIGIN** French: see **AMENDS.** In sense 2 abbreviation of **AMENDE HONORABLE.**]
†**1** A compensatory payment. Only in **E18.**
2 = **AMENDE HONORABLE. E19.**

amende honorable /amɑ̃ːd ɔnɔrabl/ *noun phr.* Pl. **-s -s** (pronounced same). **E17.**
[**ORIGIN** French = honourable reparation.]
Public or open apology and reparation; an instance of this.

amendment /ə'mɛn(d)m(ə)nt/ *noun*. ME.
[ORIGIN Old French & mod. French *amendement*: see AMEND *verb*, -MENT.]
1 Removal of faults or errors; (self-)reformation; correction; emendation. ME.
2 Improvement in health, recovery from illness. *arch.* ME.
3 General improvement; betterment. ME. ▸**b** *spec.* Improvement of the soil; fertilizer, manure. Long *dial.* LME. ▸**c** *spec.* (A) minor improvement in a parliamentary bill, a motion before a meeting, etc.; a proposed alteration, a change or addition to a document. L17.
c ***reasoned amendment***: see REASON *verb* 4b. ***take the Fifth Amendment***: see FIFTH. ***wrecking amendment***: see WRECK *verb*[1].

amends /ə'mɛn(d)z/ *noun sing. & collect. sing.*; in sense 1 also †*pl.*. See also AMEND *noun*. ME.
[ORIGIN Old French *amendes* pecuniary fine, penalties, pl. of *amende* reparation, formed as AMEND *verb*.]
†**1** Moneys paid or things given to make reparation; a fine. ME–L18.
2 Reparation, restitution, compensation, satisfaction. Esp. in ***make amends***. ME.

SOUTHEY I looked forward to an honourable amends.

3 Improvement, betterment. Esp. in ***thole amends***. Now *dial.* L16. ▸†**b** *spec.* Improvement in health, recovery. L16–L17.

amene /ə'miːn/ *adjective*. Now *rare*. LME.
[ORIGIN Old French (implied in *amenement* pleasantly) from Latin *amoenus* pleasant; later directly from Latin.]
Pleasant, agreeable.

amenity /ə'miːnɪti, -'mɛn-/ *noun*. LME.
[ORIGIN Old French & mod. French *aménité* or Latin *amoenitas*, from *amoenus* pleasant: see -ITY.]
1 Pleasantness, agreeableness. LME.

T. CORYAT For amenity of situation . . it doth farre excel all other cities. T. F. DIBDIN Who does not love the amenity of Erasmus? W. S. MAUGHAM The smile died on her lips and she gave me a glance that was totally lacking in amenity.

2 A pleasure; a delight; a pleasant feature; a desirable facility. Usu. in *pl.* M17.

HOR. WALPOLE A country so profusely beautiful with the amænities of nature. DISRAELI Amenities of authors. P. FITZGERALD The new Library was an important amenity.

3 A pleasantry; a civility. Usu. in *pl.* L19.
– COMB.: **amenity bed** a bed available in hospital for a small payment to give more privacy.

amenorrhoea /əmɛnə'riːə/ *noun*. Also *-**rrhea**. E19.
[ORIGIN from A-[10] + MENO- + -RRHOEA.]
MEDICINE. Abnormal absence of menstruation.
■ **amenorrhoeal** *adjective* of, pertaining to, or affected with amenorrhoea E19. **amenorrhoeic** *adjective* of, pertaining to, or affected with amenorrhoea L19.

a mensa et thoro /eɪ ˌmɛnsɑː ɛt 'tɔːrəʊ/ *adverbial & adjectival phr.* E17.
[ORIGIN Latin = from table and bed.]
LAW (now *hist.*). Of a divorce: decreed by an ecclesiastical court on grounds sanctioned by law (having the effect of a modern judicial separation).

ament /ə'mɛnt/ *noun*[1]. Also (earlier) in Latin form **amentum** /-təm/, pl. **-ta** /-tə/. M18.
[ORIGIN Latin *amentum* thong, strap.]
A catkin.
■ **amen'taceous** *adjective* of the nature of or bearing catkins M18. **amental**, **amen'tiferous** *adjectives* bearing catkins M19.

ament /'eɪmɛnt, ə'mɛnt/ *noun*[2]. L19.
[ORIGIN Latin *ament-*: see AMENTIA.]
A person with amentia.

amentia /eɪ'mɛnʃə, ə-/ *noun*. LME.
[ORIGIN Latin = madness, from *ament-*, *amens* mad, from *a-* A-[9] + *ment-*, *mens* mind: see -IA[1].]
MEDICINE. The condition of having a mental disability.

amentum *noun* see AMENT *noun*[1].

Amerasian /amə'reɪʃ(ə)n, -ʒ(ə)n/ *adjective & noun*. M20.
[ORIGIN from AMER(ICAN + ASIAN.]
(A person) of mixed American and Asian parentage; *esp.* (a child) fathered by an American serviceman stationed in Asia.

amerce /ə'məːs/ *verb trans.* Orig. †**amercy**. LME.
[ORIGIN Anglo-Norman *amercier*, orig. in *estre amercié* be placed at the mercy of another (as to the amount of a fine), from *à merci* at (the) mercy.]
Impose a discretionary (as opp. to fixed) fine on (a person); mulct (a person); punish in any way; (with the penalty or amount expressed as second obj. or foll. by *in*, *with*). Also, deprive *of*.
■ **amerciable** *adjective* liable to be amerced E17. †**amerciate** *pa. pple & verb trans.* (*Scot.*) amerce(d) LME–M19.

amercement /ə'məːsm(ə)nt/ *noun*. LME.
[ORIGIN Anglo-Norman *amerciment*, formed as AMERCE: see -MENT.]
1 Imposition of a discretionary penalty or fine (orig. one lighter than a fixed fine). LME.
2 A discretionary penalty or fine. LME.

amerciament /ə'məːsɪəm(ə)nt/ *noun*. Now *rare*. LME.
[ORIGIN medieval Latin *amerciamentum*, from *amerciare* Latinization of Anglo-Norman *amercier* AMERCE: see -MENT.]
= AMERCEMENT.

†**amercy** *verb* see AMERCE.

Amerenglish /'amərɪŋglɪʃ, amər'ɪŋglɪʃ/ *noun*. Also **AmerEnglish**. L20.
[ORIGIN Contr.: see -LISH.]
American English.

American /ə'mɛrɪk(ə)n/ *noun & adjective*. M16.
[ORIGIN mod. Latin *Americanus*, from *America* from Latinized form of the name of *Amerigo* Vespucci (1451–1512), Italian navigator: see -AN.]
▸ **A** *noun*. **1** An aboriginal inhabitant of the continent of America. Now only as ***Native American*** s.v. NATIVE *adjective*. M16.
2 A native or inhabitant of (esp. North) America of Old World descent; a citizen of the United States of America; (with specifying word) a native or inhabitant of the specified part of the continent of America. E18.
Central American: see CENTRAL *adjective*. ***Irish American***: see IRISH *adjective*. ***Latin American***: see LATIN *adjective*. ***Middle American***: see MIDDLE *adjective*. ***North American***: see NORTH *adverb* etc. ***quiet American***: see QUIET *adjective & adverb*. ***South American***: see SOUTH *adverb* etc. ***ugly American***: see UGLY *adjective*.
3 The English language as used in the United States of America. L18.
General American American English with few regional peculiarities.
4 *ellipt.* An American ship etc.; in *pl.*, American stocks, shares, etc. E19.
▸ **B** *adjective*. **1** Of, pertaining to, or characteristic of any part of the continent of America or its inhabitants. L16.
2 *spec.* Of, pertaining to, or characteristic of the United States of America (formerly to the British colonies in N. America) or its inhabitants. M17.
– SPECIAL COLLOCATIONS: ***American aloe***: see ALOE 4. **American bar** a bar serving drinks in an allegedly American style, esp. from a counter at which customers sit. ***American bittersweet***: see BITTERSWEET *noun* 4. **American cheese** a type of mild semi-soft processed cheese made in the US. **American cloth** a cotton cloth with a coated or waterproofed surface. ***American cowslip***: see COWSLIP 1. ***American crow***: see CROW *noun*[1] 1. **American dream** *the* ideal of a democratic and prosperous society, regarded as the aim of the American people. ***American elk***: see ELK *noun*[1]. ***American elm***: see ELM 1. **American English** = sense A.3 above. **American football** football played with an oval ball which may be carried, thrown, or kicked, in which in order to maintain possession of the ball a team must advance at least 10 yards towards the goal in four opportunities. ***American IPECACUANHA***. ***American INDIAN***. ***American jute***: see JUTE *noun*[2]. **American marten** a N. American marten, *Martes americana*, which is brown with a buff throat. ***American MISTLETOE***. ***American olive***: see OLIVE *noun*[1] 1b. **American organ** a reed organ in which the air is drawn inwards to the reeds, instead of being blown outwards. ***American PENNYROYAL***. **American plaice** = ***rough dab*** s.v. ROUGH *adjective*. **American plan** *N. Amer.* a method of charging for a hotel room inclusive of meals. **American Revolution** the overthrow of British supremacy in America by the War of Independence, 1775–81 (***Daughters of the American Revolution***: see DAUGHTER). ***American robin***: see ROBIN *noun*[1] 1b. **American Sign Language** a form of sign language developed for the use of deaf people in the US. **American tea** a social function for raising funds, to which guests contribute by bringing or buying food and drink. **American tiger** the jaguar. **American tournament** a sporting tournament in which each competitor plays all the others in turn. ***American turtle***: see TURTLE *noun*[2] 2. ***American wayfaring tree***: see WAYFARING *noun*. **American whitewood** = ***tulipwood*** (a) s.v. TULIP. ***American woodcock***: see WOODCOCK 1.
■ **Ameri'cana** *noun pl.* publications or other items concerning or associated with America M19. **America'nese** *noun* (somewhat *derog.*) American English, English full of Americanisms L19. **Americanist** *noun* a specialist in or student of subjects pertaining to America L19. **Americanly** *adverb* M19. **Americanness** /-n-n-/ *noun* L19.

Americani /əmɛrɪ'kɑːni/ *noun*. Also **Mer(c)kani** /məː'kɑːni/. M19.
[ORIGIN Kiswahili, alt. of AMERICAN *adjective*.]
In Africa: a kind of (esp. white) cotton cloth.

Americanise *verb* var. of AMERICANIZE.

Americanism /ə'mɛrɪk(ə)nɪz(ə)m/ *noun*. L18.
[ORIGIN from AMERICAN + -ISM.]
1 A word, sense, or phrase peculiar to or originating from the United States of America. L18.
2 Attachment to or sympathy with the United States of America. L18.
3 American quality or character. M19.

Americanize /ə'mɛrɪk(ə)nʌɪz/ *verb*. Also **-ise**. L17.
[ORIGIN formed as AMERICANISM + -IZE.]
1 *verb trans.* Make American in character; naturalize as an American. L17.
2 *verb intrans.* Become American in character. M19.
■ **Americani'zation** *noun* M19.

americium /amə'rɪsjəm/ *noun*. M20.
[ORIGIN from *America* (see AMERICAN) + -IUM.]
A radioactive metallic chemical element of the actinide series, atomic no. 95, which is produced artificially (symbol Am).

Americo- /ə'mɛrɪkəʊ/ *combining form*. L18.
[ORIGIN from *America* (see AMERICAN) + -O-.]
Of America, as ***Americomania***, ***Americophobia***, a passion for, fear of, America or things American.

Amerikan /ə'mɛrɪk(ə)n/ *adjective*. Chiefly *US*. Also **-kkk-**. M20.
[ORIGIN from *Amerik(kk)a* alt. of *America* (see AMERICAN) after German *Amerika*, -*kkk*- after Ku Klux Klan: see -AN.]
Of or pertaining to the United States of America regarded as a racist, fascist, or oppressive country, esp. by black people.

Amerind /'amərɪnd/ *noun & adjective*. L19.
[ORIGIN from (the same root as) AMERINDIAN.]
= AMERINDIAN.

Amerindian /amə'rɪndɪən/ *adjective & noun*. L19.
[ORIGIN Contr. of *American Indian*.]
▸ **A** *adjective*. Of or pertaining to American Indians. L19.
▸ **B** *noun*. An American Indian. E20.

à merveille /a mɛrvɛːj/ *adverbial phr.* M18.
[ORIGIN French = to a marvel.]
Admirably, wonderfully.

âmes damnées *noun phr.* pl. of ÂME DAMNÉE.

Ameslan /'amɪslan/ *noun*. L20.
[ORIGIN Acronym.]
American Sign Language.

†**amesnable** *adjective* see AMENABLE.

Ames test /'eɪmz tɛst/ *noun phr.* L20.
[ORIGIN Named after Bruce N. *Ames* (b. 1928), US biochemist, who devised it.]
MEDICINE. A test for mutagenic activity in which the effect of a substance *in vitro* is observed on certain bacteria in which mutations are readily detected.

amethocaine /a'mɛθə(ʊ)keɪn/ *noun*. M20.
[ORIGIN Perh. from Greek *amethustus* (see AMETHYST) or blend of AMINO- + METHYL: see -O-, -CAINE.]
A cyclic amino ester, $C_{15}H_{24}N_2O_2$, related to procaine which is used as a local anaesthetic, esp. in the eye. Also called ***tetracaine***, ***pantocaine***.

amethyst /'amɪθɪst/ *noun & adjective*. ME.
[ORIGIN Old French *ametiste*, Latin *amethystus* from Greek *amethustos* use as noun (sc. *lithos* stone) of adjective, from *a-* A-[10] + *methuein* be intoxicated: so called because it was supposed to prevent intoxication.]
▸ **A** *noun*. **1** A precious variety of quartz, of a clear purple or bluish-violet colour owing to the presence of iron. ME.
2 HERALDRY. The tincture purpure in the fanciful blazon of arms of peers. *obsolete* exc. *hist.* L16. ▸**b** The colour of amethyst. E19.
▸ **B** *attrib.* or as *adjective*. Of or resembling amethyst; violet-purple. L15.

amethystine /amɪ'θɪstʌɪn/ *adjective*. L17.
[ORIGIN Latin *amethystinus* from Greek *amethustinos*: see AMETHYST, -INE[2].]
1 Of or containing amethyst. L17.
2 Amethyst-coloured, violet-purple. L17.

ametropia /amɪ'trəʊpɪə/ *noun*. M19.
[ORIGIN from Greek *ametres* irregular (formed as A-[10] + *metron* measure) + -OPIA.]
MEDICINE. Any abnormal condition of the refraction of the eye.
■ **ametropic** /-'trəʊpɪk, -'trɒpɪk/ *adjective* M19.

†**ameve** *verb* var. of AMOVE *verb*[1].

AMGOT *abbreviation*.
Allied Military Government of Occupied Territory, an organization first set up in Sicily during the Second World War.

Amharic /am'harɪk/ *noun & adjective*. M18.
[ORIGIN from *Amhara* (see below) + -IC.]
▸ **A** *noun*. **1** A native or inhabitant of Amhara, a central province of Ethiopia. *rare*. M18.
2 The Semitic language of Amhara, the principal language of modern Ethiopia. M19.
▸ **B** *adjective*. Of or pertaining to Amhara, its people, or its language. E19.

amiable /'eɪmɪəb(ə)l/ *adjective*. LME.
[ORIGIN Old French & mod. French from late Latin *amicabilis* AMICABLE; later infl. in sense by mod. French *aimable* lovable, likeable.]
1 Friendly; kind in action. *obsolete* exc. as passing into sense 3. LME.
2 Lovable, lovely. *obsolete* exc. as passing into sense 3. LME.
3 (Combining senses 1 and 2.) Having a friendly disposition that inspires friendliness in return. M18.
■ **amia'bility** *noun* the quality of being amiable E19. **amiableness** *noun* M16. **amiably** *adverb* LME.

amianth /'amɪanθ/ *noun*. Now *poet.* Also **-ant** /-ant/. E17.
[ORIGIN French *amiante* or Latin *amiantus*: see AMIANTHUS.]
= AMIANTHUS.

amianthus /amɪ'anθəs/ *noun*. Also **-tus** /-təs/. E17.
[ORIGIN Latin *amiantus* from Greek *amiantos*, from *a-* A-[10] + *miainein* defile.]
Asbestos, esp. of a fine, silky quality suitable for weaving into cloth.

A

■ **amianthine** *adjective* of the nature of amianthus M17.

amicable /ˈamɪkəb(ə)l/ *adjective*. LME.
[ORIGIN Late Latin *amicabilis*, from Latin *amicus* friend: see -ABLE.]
1 Of a thing: pleasant, kindly, benign. *obsolete* exc. as below. LME.
amicable numbers MATH. any pair of numbers having the property that each is the sum of the factors of the other, e.g. 220 and 284.
2 Friendly; done in a friendly spirit. L15.

POPE Each mild, each amicable guest. P. V. WHITE The most amicable thing about their marriage was their parting.

■ **amicaˈbility** *noun* the quality of being amicable M17. **amicableness** *noun* M17. **amicably** *adverb* LME.

amical /ˈamɪk(ə)l/ *adjective*. Now *rare*. L16.
[ORIGIN Latin *amicalis*, from *amicus*: see AMICABLE, -AL[1].]
Friendly.

amice /ˈamɪs/ *noun*[1]. LME.
[ORIGIN medieval Latin *amicia*, *-sia*, of obscure formation. Superseding AMIT *noun*.]
A scarf, kerchief, or other loose wrap; *spec.* (ECCLESIASTICAL) a white linen vestment worn by celebrant priests, formerly on the head, now on the neck and shoulders.

amice /ˈamɪs/ *noun*[2]. LME.
[ORIGIN Old French *aumusse* from medieval Latin *almucia*, *-ium*, of unknown origin.]
1 A cap, hood, hooded cape, or badge of a religious order, made of or lined with grey fur. LME.
†**2** The fur of the marten or grey squirrel, used for such a garment. M–L16.

amicus curiae /aˌmʌɪkəs ˈkjʊərɪiː/ *noun phr.* Pl. **amici curiae** /aˈmʌɪsʌɪ/. E17.
[ORIGIN mod. Latin = friend of the court.]
LAW. A disinterested adviser who assists the court by drawing attention to points that might otherwise fail to be mentioned.

amid /əˈmɪd/ *adverb & preposition*. ME.
[ORIGIN from A *preposition*[1] 1 + MID *adjective*.]
▸ †**A** *adverb*. In the middle, in the midst. ME–L16.
▸ **B** *preposition*. **1** *lit.* In or near the middle or centre of; in the interior of; surrounded by. Now chiefly *poet.* ME.

LONGFELLOW Like Ruth amid the golden corn. J. S. BLACKIE A certain part of his work . . must be done amid books.

2 *fig.* In the middle of (a state or condition); in the course of. LME.

TOLKIEN It was not easy to get any clear account out of him, amid his mumblings and squeakings, and the frequent interruptions. K. AMIS Mr. Parry sat rock-like amid the storm of introductions.

Amidah /əˈmiːdə/ *noun*. L19.
[ORIGIN Post-biblical Hebrew *ʿămīḏāh*, lit. 'standing'.]
JUDAISM. A prayer, part of the Jewish liturgy, consisting of a varying number of blessings recited by worshippers while standing.

amide /ˈeɪmʌɪd, ˈamʌɪd/ *noun*. M19.
[ORIGIN from AM(MONIA + -IDE.]
CHEMISTRY. A derivative of ammonia in which a hydrogen atom is replaced by an acid radical (orig. by any radical) or a metal. In ORGANIC CHEMISTRY, any compound containing the group $\cdot CO\cdot NH_2$ (which may be further substituted); also ***acid amide***. Cf. AMINE.
■ **amidated** /ˈamɪdeɪtɪd/ *ppl adjective* (now *rare* or *obsolete*) converted into an amide M19. **aˈmidic** *adjective* L19. †**amidogen** *noun* the radical $\cdot NH_2$ M–L19.

†**amidine** *noun*[1]. Also **-in**. M–L19.
[ORIGIN from Latin *amylum* starch + -IN[1], -INE[5].]
CHEMISTRY. The soluble matter in starch granules; dissolved starch.

amidine /ˈamɪdiːn/ *noun*[2]. L19.
[ORIGIN from AMID(E + -INE[5].]
CHEMISTRY. Any compound containing the group $\cdot C(NH_2)NH$, or a substituted derivative of this.

amido- /əˈmʌɪdəʊ/ *combining form* of AMIDE (orig. = AMINO-): see -O-. Also as attrib. adjective **amido**. M19.

amidships /əˈmɪdʃɪps/ *adverb*. Also ***-ship**. L17.
[ORIGIN from A *preposition*[1] 1 + MIDSHIPS *noun*.]
In or into the middle of a ship; *fig.* in or into the middle.

amidst /əˈmɪdst/ *preposition & adverb*. ME.
[ORIGIN from AMID + -S[3] + t as in *against*, *amongst*, etc.]
▸ **A** *preposition*. **1** *lit.* = AMID *preposition* 1. ME.
2 *fig.* = AMID *preposition* 2. LME.
▸ **B** *adverb*. = AMID *adverb* (Foll. by *of*.) *arch.* LME.

amigo /əˈmiːɡəʊ/ *noun*. *colloq.* (chiefly *US*). Pl. **-os**. M19.
[ORIGIN Spanish.]
A friend, a comrade: freq. as a form of address.

amil /ˈɑːmɪl/ *noun*. Now *hist.* Also **aum-** /ˈɔːm-/. M18.
[ORIGIN Urdu & Arabic *ʿāmil* operator, agent, from *ʿamila* do: see AMILDAR.]
= AMILDAR.

amildar /ˈɑːmɪldɑː/ *noun*. Also **aum-** /ˈɔːm-/. L18.
[ORIGIN Persian & Urdu *ʿamal-dār*, from Arabic *ʿamal* work, administration + Persian *-dār* holding, holder. Spelling infl. by AMIL.]
Formerly, a non-European factor in the Indian subcontinent, *esp.* a collector of revenue. Now, the official in charge of a taluk in Karnataka.

aminded /əˈmʌɪndɪd/ *pa. pple & ppl adjective*. Long *dial.*, now *rare*. L16.
[ORIGIN from A-[4] + MINDED.]
Minded, disposed, inclined.

amine /ˈeɪmiːn/ *noun*. M19.
[ORIGIN from AM(MONIA + -INE[5].]
CHEMISTRY. Any derivative of ammonia in which one or more hydrogen atoms are replaced by alkyl or aryl groups.

amino- /əˈmiːnəʊ, əˈmʌɪnəʊ, ˈamɪnəʊ/ *combining form*. Also as attrib. adjective **amino**.
[ORIGIN from AMINE + -O-.]
CHEMISTRY. Designating or containing the group $\cdot NH_2$.
■ **aminoaˈcetic** *adjective* designating the acid glycine L19. **aminobenˈzoic** *adjective*: ***aminobenzoic acid***, an acid, $NH_2\cdot C_6H_4\cdot COOH$, with three isomers, one of which is anthranilic acid E20. **amino-ˈplastic** *noun* any synthetic resin made by copolymerizing urea, melamine, or a related compound with an aldehyde (esp. formaldehyde) M20.

amino acid /əˌmiːnəʊ ˈasɪd, əˌmʌɪn-/ *noun phr.* Also **aminoacid**, **amino-acid**. L19.
[ORIGIN from AMINO- + ACID *noun*.]
CHEMISTRY. An organic compound containing both an amino and a carboxyl group; *spec.* any of about twenty such compounds which occur widely in living organisms and are the building blocks of proteins.

amir /əˈmɪə/ *noun*. Also **ameer**. L16.
[ORIGIN Persian & Urdu from Arabic *ʾamīr* commander, governor, prince, from *amara* to command. Cf. ADMIRAL, EMIR.]
A title of various Muslim rulers.
■ **amirate** *noun* = EMIRATE M20.

Amish /ˈamɪʃ, ˈɑː-, ˈeɪ-/ *adjective & noun*. M19.
[ORIGIN App. from German *amisch*, from Jacob *Amen* or *Amman* a Swiss Mennonite preacher (fl. end of 17): see -ISH[1].]
▸ **A** *adjective*. Of, pertaining to, or characteristic of a strict US Mennonite sect. M19.
▸ **B** *noun pl.* *The* members of the Amish sect. L19.

amiss /əˈmɪs/ *adverb, pred. adjective, & noun*. ME.
[ORIGIN Old Norse *á mis* so as to miss or not to meet, from *á* on + *mis* rel. to MISS *verb*[1].]
▸ **A** *adverb & pred. adjective*. Out of order; astray, awry; erroneous(ly); defective(ly); wrong(ly); inappropriate(ly). ME.

S. JOHNSON It is good to speak dubiously about futurity. It is likewise not amiss to hope. H. MARTINEAU Apt to see wrong and speak amiss. D. H. LAWRENCE Ursula wondered if something was amiss, and if the wedding would yet all go wrong. S. J. PERELMAN I wonder if anything could be amiss with my hearing.

take amiss: now *esp.* take offence at.
▸ †**B** *noun*. An error, a fault, a misdeed. L15–L17.

amissible /əˈmɪsɪb(ə)l/ *adjective*. L17.
[ORIGIN ecclesiastical Latin *amissibilis*, from *amiss-* pa. ppl stem of *amittere* AMIT *verb*: see -IBLE. Cf. earlier INAMISSIBLE.]
Liable to be lost.
■ **amissiˈbility** *noun* (*rare*) M17.

amissing /əˈmɪsɪŋ/ *ppl adjective*. Chiefly *Scot.* L16.
[ORIGIN from A *preposition*[1] 8 + MISSING *ppl adjective*: cf. AWANTING.]
Missing, wanting.

†**amission** *noun*. LME–M18.
[ORIGIN Old French & mod. French, or Latin *amissio(n-)*, from *amiss-*: see AMISSIBLE, -ION.]
Loss, a loss.

†**amit** *noun*. ME–E19.
[ORIGIN Old French (mod. *amict*): see AMICE *noun*[1].]
= AMICE *noun*[1].

†**amit** *verb trans. & intrans.* foll. by *of*. Infl. **-tt-**. E16–M19.
[ORIGIN Latin *amittere*, formed as A-[6] + *mittere* send.]
Lose.

amitotic /eɪmʌɪˈtɒtɪk, am-/ *adjective*. L19.
[ORIGIN from A-[10] + MITOTIC.]
BIOLOGY. Pertaining to or designating the division of a cell nucleus without mitosis.
■ **amitosis** *noun*, pl. **-toses** /-ˈtəʊsiːz/, amitotic division L19. **amitotically** *adverb* L19.

amitriptyline /amɪˈtrɪptɪliːn/ *noun*. M20.
[ORIGIN from AMI(NO- + TRI- + HE)PTYL + -INE[5].]
PHARMACOLOGY. A tricyclic antidepressant and sedative drug, $C_{20}H_{23}N$, given usu. as the hydrochloride.

amity /ˈamɪti/ *noun*. LME.
[ORIGIN Old French & mod. French *amitié*, ult. from Latin *amicus* friend: see -ITY.]
sing. & (*arch.*) in *pl.* Friendship; friendly relations, esp. of a public character between states or individuals.

amlah /ˈamlɑː, ˈʌmlɑː/ *noun*. L18.
[ORIGIN Arabic *ʿumalāʾ*.]
In the Indian subcontinent: the body of officials who staff a courthouse.

amma /ˈʌmɑː/ *noun*. *Indian*. E20.
[ORIGIN Prob. from a child's word, perh. infl. by AMAH.]
Mother.

ammeter /ˈamɪtə/ *noun*. L19.
[ORIGIN from AM(PERE + -METER.]
An instrument for measuring electrical current, esp. in amperes.

ammine /ˈamiːn/ *noun*. L19.
[ORIGIN from AMM(ONIA + -INE[5].]
CHEMISTRY. A coordination compound of ammonia with a metal.

ammo /ˈaməʊ/ *noun*. *colloq.* E20.
[ORIGIN Abbreviation of AMMUNITION: see -O.]
Ammunition, esp. for small arms.

ammocoete /ˈaməsiːt/ *noun*. M19.
[ORIGIN mod. Latin *Ammocoetes*, from Greek *ammos* sand + *koitē* bed.]
The larva of a lamprey (orig. believed to be a distinct creature and given its own genus, *Ammocoetes*).

†**ammodyte** *noun*. E17.
[ORIGIN Latin *ammodytes* from Greek *ammodutēs* sand-burrower, from *ammos* sand + *duein* to dive.]
1 A southern European venomous snake, the sand-natter (*Vipera ammodytes*). E17–L18.
2 A sand eel. (*Ammodytes* is a genus of sand eels.) L17–M19.

ammonal /ˈamən(ə)l/ *noun*. E20.
[ORIGIN from AMMON(IUM + AL(UMINIUM.]
A high explosive consisting chiefly of ammonium nitrate, with some powdered aluminium and occas. other ingredients.

ammonia /əˈməʊnɪə/ *noun*. L18.
[ORIGIN mod. Latin, from *sal ammoniacus* sal ammoniac: see AMMONIAC, -IA[1].]
A colourless pungent gas, NH_3, which is extremely soluble in water giving a strongly alkaline solution; an aqueous solution of this gas.
■ **ammoniate** *verb trans.* treat with ammonia (chiefly as ***ammoniated*** *ppl adjective*) E19.

ammoniac /əˈməʊnɪak/ *adjective & noun*. Also as noun in Latin form **-iacum** /-ɪakəm/; †**arm-**. ME.
[ORIGIN Old French *armoniac* (14), *amm-* (15) from Latin *ammoniacus*, *-um* from Greek *ammōniakos*, *-on* of Ammon, used as noun for the salt and the gum, which were said to be obtained (the former from camel dung) from near the temple of Jupiter Ammon, Siwa, Egypt.]
▸ **A** *adjective*. **1** ***sal ammoniac***, ammonium chloride, a hard white crystalline salt. ME.
2 ***gum ammoniac***, a bitter, odoriferous gum resin obtained from certain N. African or Asian umbelliferous plants, and having some medicinal use; *esp.* that from *Dorema ammoniacum*, native to Persia. LME.
3 Ammoniacal. Now *rare* or *obsolete*. M17.
▸ **B** *noun*. Gum ammoniac. LME.

ammoniacal /amə(ʊ)ˈnʌɪək(ə)l/ *adjective*. M18.
[ORIGIN from AMMONIAC + -AL[1].]
Of the nature of or containing ammonia.

ammoniacum *noun* see AMMONIAC.

ammonification /əˌməʊnɪfɪˈkeɪʃ(ə)n/ *noun*. L19.
[ORIGIN from AMMONIA + -FICATION.]
The production of ammonia or ammonium compounds, esp. by micro-organisms; treatment with or conversion into ammonia.
■ **aˈmmonify** *verb trans.* (freq. as ***ammonifying*** *ppl adjective*) E20.

ammonio- /əˈməʊnɪəʊ/ *combining form*.
[ORIGIN from AMMONIUM: see -O-.]
Indicating the presence of the ammonium ion (esp. in names of minerals).

ammonite /ˈamənʌɪt/ *noun*. M18.
[ORIGIN mod. Latin *ammonites*, from medieval Latin *cornu Ammonis* horn of Ammon, name given to these fossils from their supposed resemblance to the involuted horn of Jupiter Ammon: see -ITE[1].]
PALAEONTOLOGY. Any of numerous fossil cephalopods of the order Ammonoidea, which have a chambered shell usu. coiled into a plane spiral, and occur mainly in Mesozoic rocks.
■ **ammoˈnitic** *adjective* pertaining to or characteristic of ammonites; (of shell suture lines) highly convoluted: M19. **ammoniˈtiferous** *adjective* containing ammonites M19. **ammonoid** *noun* any fossil cephalopod belonging to Ammonoidea, which comprises the ammonites and similar forms M19.

ammonium /əˈməʊnɪəm/ *noun*. E19.
[ORIGIN from AMMONIA + -IUM.]
CHEMISTRY. The ion NH_4^+, which occurs in the salts formed by ammonia and in ammonia solutions.

ammunition /amjʊˈnɪʃ(ə)n/ *noun & verb*. L16.
[ORIGIN French †*am(m)unition*, from division of *la munition* the MUNITION as *l'ammunition*.]
▸ **A** *noun*. **1** Military stores or supplies, formerly of all kinds, now restricted to projectiles (bullets, shells, grenades, etc.) and propellants (powder etc.). L16.
2 *fig.* Facts, arguments, etc., used in attack or defence. M17.

▸ **B** *verb trans.* Supply with ammunition. Chiefly as ***ammunitioned*** *ppl adjective.* **M17.**

amnesia /amˈniːzjə/ *noun.* **L18.**
[ORIGIN Greek *amnēsia* forgetfulness.]
Loss of memory.
■ **amnesiac** *noun* a person suffering from amnesia **E20. amnesic** *adjective* **M19. amnestic** *adjective & noun* (*a*) *adjective* pertaining to, suffering from, or characterized by amnesia; (*b*) *noun* an amnesiac: **L19.**

amnesty /ˈamnɪsti/ *noun & verb.* **L16.**
[ORIGIN French †*amnestie* (now *-istie*) or Latin *amnestia* from Greek *amnēstia* forgetfulness: cf. AMNESIA.]
▸ **A** *noun.* An act of forgetfulness; an intentional overlooking; a general pardon, esp. for a political offence. **L16.**
Amnesty International an organization upholding and campaigning for the human rights of prisoners of conscience.
▸ **B** *verb trans.* Give an amnesty to. **E19.**

amnio /ˈamnɪəʊ/ *noun. colloq.* Pl. **-os.** **L20.**
[ORIGIN Abbreviation.]
An amniocentesis.

amnio- /ˈamnɪəʊ/ *combining form* of AMNION: see -O-.
■ **amniocentesis** /-sɛnˈtiːsɪs/ *noun*, pl. **-teses** /-ˈtiːsiːz/, [Greek *kentēsis* pricking, from *kentein* prick] MEDICINE the sampling of amniotic fluid during pregnancy by insertion of a hollow needle into the uterus **M20. amniˈotomy** *noun* (MEDICINE) rupture of the fetal membranes in order to induce birth **M20.**

amnion /ˈamnɪən/ *noun.* Pl. **-nia** /-nɪə/, **-nions.** **M17.**
[ORIGIN Greek = caul, dim. of *amnos* lamb.]
An inner membrane that forms round a developing fetus in mammals, birds, and reptiles.
■ Also †**amnios** *noun* **M17–M19.**

amniotic /amnɪˈɒtɪk/ *adjective.* **E19.**
[ORIGIN Irreg. from AMNIOS + -OTIC, perh. through French *amniotique*. Cf. *chaos, chaotic*.]
ANATOMY. Of or pertaining to the amnion.
amniotic cavity the fluid-filled cavity inside the amnion, in which the fetus develops. **amniotic fluid** the fluid contained in the amniotic cavity.
■ **amniote** *noun & adjective* (designating or pertaining to) any animal whose embryo develops within an amnion and chorion and possesses an allantois, i.e. a mammal, bird, or reptile **L19.**

amoeba /əˈmiːbə/ *noun.* Also ***ameba.** Pl. **-bas, -bae** /-biː/. **M19.**
[ORIGIN mod. Latin from Greek *amoibē* change, alternation.]
A single-celled aquatic protozoan, characterized by a constantly changing shape.
■ **amoeˈbiasis** *noun*, pl. **-ases** /-əsiːz/, MEDICINE infection with amoebas, esp. as causing dysentery **E20. amoebicide** *noun* a substance that kills amoebas **E20. amoebiform** *adjective* resembling an amoeba **M19. amoebocyte** *noun* a cell resembling an amoeba, *esp.* a leucocyte in some invertebrates **L19. amoeboid** *adjective* resembling or characteristic of an amoeba **M19.**

amoebean /amiːˈbiːən/ *adjective.* Also **-baean**, ***ameb-.** **M17.**
[ORIGIN from Latin *amoebaeus* from Greek *amoibaios* interchanging + -AN. Cf. AMOEBA.]
Esp. of verse dialogue: alternately answering; responsive.

amoebic /əˈmiːbɪk/ *adjective.* Also ***amebic.** **L19.**
[ORIGIN from AMOEBA + -IC.]
Pertaining to, of the nature of, or caused by an amoeba or amoebas.

amok /əˈmɒk/ *adjective, noun, & adverb.* Also **amuck** /əˈmʌk/, (earliest) †**am(o)uco**, pl. **-os.** **E16.**
[ORIGIN (Portuguese *am(o)uco* from) Malay *amuk* fighting furiously, in a homicidal frenzy. See also MUCK *noun*².]
▸ †**A** *adjective.* In a homicidal frenzy. *rare.* Only in **E16.**
▸ **B** *noun.* **1** A Malay in a homicidal frenzy. **M17.**
2 A homicidal frenzy; an act of running amok. **M19.**
▸ **C** *adverb.* ***run amok***, run about in a frenzied thirst for blood; go on a destructive rampage; rush wildly and heedlessly. **L17.**

amole /əˈməʊli/ *noun.* **M19.**
[ORIGIN Mexican Spanish.]
The root of any of several plants of Mexico and the southern US, used as a detergent; any of these plants, *esp.* the soap-plant, *Chlorogalum pomeridianum*, and the lechuguilla, *Agave lecheguilla*.

amomum /əˈməʊməm/ *noun.* **LME.**
[ORIGIN Latin name of some aromatic shrub, from Greek *amōmon*.]
An aromatic plant belonging to the genus *Amomum*, of the ginger family.

among /əˈmʌŋ/ *preposition & adverb.* Also (*obsolete* exc. *N. English*) **amang**; †**emong.**
[ORIGIN Old English *on(ge)mang*, *-mong*, from ON *preposition* (see A *preposition*¹ 6) + *gemang* MONG *noun*¹.]
▸ **A** *preposition.* **1** With *noun pl.*: in the assemblage of, surrounded by and grouped with. With *noun sing.* (exc. *collect.* now chiefly *Scot.* & *Irish*): surrounded by the separate members, components, or particles of; amid. **OE.** ▸**b** Through the assemblage of; through the midst of. **M19.**

SIR W. SCOTT Among the bubbling blood. LONGFELLOW He saw once more his dark-eyed queen Among her children stand. YEATS And saplings root among the broken stone. D. DU MAURIER If I heard it, even among a thousand others, I should recognise her voice. DAY LEWIS There is a screech from among the gooseberry bushes. **b** E. WAUGH Sauntering and skipping among the trim gravel walks. G. GREENE Picking among the dry seaweed for cigarette ends. S. HILL Colds spread like a forest fire among the old.

†**among the hands of** under the charge of, while being attended by.

†**2** During; in the course of. **OE–L17.**

CAXTON Saynt ambrose . . gaue up his ghoost emonge the wordes of his prayers.

3 In company or association with; in the house, city, country, etc., of. **ME.**

G. CRABBE Susan . . had some pride Among our topmost people to preside. SCOTT FITZGERALD It's a great advantage not to drink among hard-drinking people.

4 In the number or class of; in comparison with. **ME.**

TREVISA Amonge all elementes water is prouffytablest. LD BERNERS Your folkes haue brent my house, the whiche I loued among all other. W. STEVENS Among the old men that you know, There is one, unnamed, that broods On all the rest.

5 In the general practice or views of; with or by generally. **ME.**

ADDISON I pass among some for a disaffected Person. J. BOWEN Among the criminal classes, the word 'bird' . . is used to mean 'lady friend' and also a stretch in prison. J. G. FARRELL With a reputation among the young men of that circle.

6 Divided between, to be shared by, (collectively or distributively); in portions to each of. **ME.**

OED That leaves five shillings among us. M. MCCARTHY She was one of many readers he had to distribute manuscripts among.

7 By the joint action of. **ME.**

SHAKES. *Much Ado* You have among you kill'd a sweet and innocent lady.

8 As a reciprocal action of. **ME.**

E. O'NEILL The three girls . . stand around the entrance to the bar, chatting excitedly among themselves.

▸ †**B** *adverb.* **1** Meanwhile, at the same time. **ME–L16.**
2 From time to time, now and then. **ME–E17.**
3 Together, along with something else. Only in **E17.**

amongst /əˈmʌŋst/ *preposition.* **ME.**
[ORIGIN from AMONG + -S³ + *t* as in *against, amidst*, etc.]
= AMONG *preposition.*

amontillado /əmɒntɪˈlɑːdəʊ, -ˈljɑː-/ *noun.* Also **A-.** Pl. **-os.** **E19.**
[ORIGIN Spanish, from *Montilla* a town in southern Spain + -ADO 1. Cf. MONTILLA.]
Formerly, a wine of the sherry type produced in Montilla. Now, a medium sherry of a matured type. Also, a drink or glass of either of these wines.

amora /əˈmɔːrə/ *noun.* Pl. **-im** /-ɪm/. **E18.**
[ORIGIN Hebrew *'ămōrā* interpreter from Aramaic *'āmōrā*.]
JEWISH HISTORY. Any of the religious teachers in the 3rd to 5th cents. who expounded the Mishnah and thus contributed to the completion of the Gemara.
■ **amoraic** /amɔːˈreɪɪk/ *adjective* of or pertaining to the amoraim **E20.**

amoral /eɪˈmɒr(ə)l/ *adjective.* **L19.**
[ORIGIN from A-¹⁰ + MORAL *adjective.*]
Unconcerned with or outside morality; non-moral. Cf. IMMORAL.
■ **amoralism** *noun* the practice of disregarding morality **E20. amoralist** *noun* **E20. amoˈrality** *noun* amoral quality **E20.**

†**amoret** *noun.* **LME.**
[ORIGIN Old French *amoret(te)* (mod. AMOURETTE *noun*) dim. of *amor* from Latin *amor* love: see -ET¹, -ETTE.]
1 A sweetheart; a lover. **LME–L18.**
2 A love-knot. Only in **LME.**
3 A love sonnet or love song. Only in **L16.**
4 In *pl.* Amorous glances; dalliances. **L16–M17.**

amoretto /aməˈrɛtəʊ, *foreign* amoˈretto/ *noun.* Pl. **-tti** /-t(t)i/, **-tto(e)s** /-təʊz/. **L16.**
[ORIGIN Italian, dim. of *amore* love.]
†**1** = AMORET 1, 3. **L16–E18.**
2 A cupid. **E17.**

amorino /aməˈriːnəʊ, *foreign* amoˈriːno/ *noun.* Pl. **-ni** /-ni/, **-nos.** **M19.**
[ORIGIN Italian, dim. of *amore* love.]
= AMORETTO 2.

amorist /ˈamərɪst/ *noun.* **L16.**
[ORIGIN from Latin *amor* or French *amour* love + -IST.]
1 A person who avows (esp. sexual) love. **L16.**
2 A person who writes about love. **M17.**

Amorite /ˈamərʌɪt/ *noun & adjective.* **M16.**
[ORIGIN from Hebrew *'ĕmōrī* from Akkadian *'amurrū* + -ITE¹.]
▸ **A** *noun.* A member of any of a group of Semitic tribes whose semi-nomadic culture flourished in Mesopotamia, Palestine, and Syria in the third millennium BC and who are described in biblical texts as inhabiting the land of Canaan before the arrival of the Israelites; the language of these people. **M16.**
▸ **B** *adjective.* Of or pertaining to the Amorites or their language. **L19.**

amoroso /aməˈrəʊzəʊ/ *noun, adverb, & adjective.* **E17.**
[ORIGIN Spanish & Italian from medieval Latin *amorosus* AMOROUS.]
▸ **A** *noun.* Pl. **-si** /-si/, **-sos.**
†**1** A lover; a gallant. **E17–E19.**
2 A type of sweetened oloroso sherry. **L19.**
▸ **B** *adverb & adjective.* MUSIC. (A direction:) tender(ly). **L18.**

amorous /ˈam(ə)rəs/ *adjective.* **ME.**
[ORIGIN Old French (mod. *amoureux*) from medieval Latin *amorosus*, from Latin *amor* love: see -OUS.]
1 Feeling or showing (esp. sexual) love; enamoured. (Foll. by *of*, †*on*.) **ME.**

J. MCGAHERN As we were getting closer to her house I noticed her growing steadily more amorous.

2 Of or pertaining to (esp. sexual) love. **LME.**

HOR. WALPOLE The poor Princess, and her conjugal and amorous distresses.

†**3** Lovable; lovely. **LME–E17.**
■ **amoˈrosity** *noun* love, fondness **LME. amorously** *adverb* **LME. amorousness** *noun* **LME.**

amorphism /əˈmɔːfɪz(ə)m/ *noun.* **M19.**
[ORIGIN from Greek *amorphos* AMORPHOUS + -ISM.]
Absence of regular form; amorphous quality.
■ Also **amorphy** *noun* (*rare*) **E18.**

amorphous /əˈmɔːfəs/ *adjective.* **M18.**
[ORIGIN mod. Latin *amorphus* from Greek *amorphos*, formed as A-¹⁰ + *morphē* shape: see -OUS.]
1 Having no determinate shape or structure; shapeless; unorganized. **M18.**
2 CHEMISTRY & MINERALOGY. Of a solid: not crystalline, or not apparently so. **E19.**

J. J. LAGOWSKI The so-called amorphous forms of carbon . . are actually composed of microcrystals.

■ **amorphousness** *noun* **L19.**

amort /əˈmɔːt/ *adverb & pred. adjective. arch.* **L16.**
[ORIGIN Misconstruction of French *à la mort* ALAMORT as ALL + *amort*.]
Orig. & chiefly in ***all amort***. As dead; lifeless, inanimate; spiritless, dejected.

amortize /əˈmɔːtʌɪz/ *verb trans.* Also **-ise.** **LME.**
[ORIGIN Old French *amortiss-* lengthened stem of *amortir* ult. from Latin AD- + *mort-*, *mors* death.]
†**1** Deaden; destroy. **LME–M17.**
2 *hist.* Transfer (property) to a corporation in mortmain. **LME.**
3 Extinguish or wipe out (a debt etc.), usu. by means of a sinking fund; gradually write off the initial cost of (assets). **L19.**
■ **amortizable** /-tɪzəb(ə)l/ *adjective* extinguishable as a liability **L19. amortiˈzation** *noun* **M17. amortizement** /-tɪzm(ə)nt/ *noun* = AMORTIZATION **LME.**

amosite /ˈeɪməsʌɪt, ˈam-/ *noun.* **E20.**
[ORIGIN from initial letters of Asbestos Mines of South Africa + -ITE¹.]
MINERALOGY. An iron-rich amphibole asbestos, mined in South Africa.

amotion /əˈməʊʃ(ə)n/ *noun. arch.* **LME.**
[ORIGIN Latin *amotio(n-)*, from *amot-* pa. ppl stem of *amovere* AMOVE *verb*²: see -ION.]
1 Removal, esp. of a person from office; ousting. **LME.**
2 Deprivation of possession. **M17.**

amotivational /ˌeɪməʊtɪˈveɪʃ(ə)n(ə)l/ *adjective.* **M20.**
[ORIGIN from A-¹⁰ + MOTIVATIONAL.]
PSYCHIATRY. Characterized by lack of motivation or goals. Freq. in ***amotivational syndrome***.

†**amouco** *adjective, noun, & adverb* see AMOK.

amount /əˈmaʊnt/ *noun.* **E18.**
[ORIGIN from the verb.]
1 The total to which anything amounts; the total quantity or number. **E18.** ▸**b** *spec.* The sum of the principal and interest on a loan. **L18.**
2 *fig.* The full value, effect, significance, etc. Now *rare.* **M18.**

J. LINGARD What the real amount of that statement may be.

3 A quantity or sum viewed as the total reached. **M19.**

E. A. FREEMAN The amount of resistance which William met with. W. S. MAUGHAM I knew a certain amount of French before. E. BOWEN Quite an amount of people . . have genuinely no idea who I am. A. LURIE Probably the stuff is harmless in small amounts, but what is a small amount?

any amount of *colloq.* a great quantity of. **no amount of** *colloq.* not even the greatest possible amount of.

amount /əˈmaʊnt/ *verb.* **ME.**
[ORIGIN Old French *amunter*, *amo(u)nter*, from *amont* upward from Latin *ad montem*: see AD-, MOUNT *noun*¹.]
†**1** *verb intrans.* Go up, ascend, mount. **ME–M17.**
†**2** *verb intrans.* Mount up, increase. **ME–E18.**
3 *verb* †*trans.* & *intrans.* with *to*. Be equivalent in total to (a specified number or quantity). **ME.**

SHAKES. *Com. Err.* Which doth amount to three odd ducats more Than I stand debted to this gentleman.

4 *verb* †*trans. & intrans.* with *to*. Be equivalent to in significance etc. ME.

D. H. LAWRENCE There was a strange freedom, that almost amounted to anarchy, in the house. STEVIE SMITH Although I collect facts I do not always know what they amount / to. P. NICHOLS We'd gathered that she wasn't ever going to amount to much.

†**5** *verb intrans.* Arise from addition; result. M16–M17.
†**6** *verb trans.* Cause to rise; elevate. M16–M17.

amour /əˈmʊə, *foreign* amuːr/ *noun*. ME.
[ORIGIN Old French & mod. French from Latin *amor* love, rel. to *amare* to love.]
1 Love; affection. Now *rare* exc. in AMOUR COURTOIS, AMOUR PROPRE. ME.

K. AMIS Now and then an ill-printed book, Letters in female hands: the thin Detritus of amour.

†**2** In *pl.* Sexual or romantic love. LME–E18.
3 A love affair, *esp.* a secret one. L16.

DRYDEN Intrigue, that's an old phrase; I have laid that word by: amour sounds better. J. BARTH My high-school amours were limited to hot, open-mouthed kisses and much risqué conversation.

amour courtois /amuːr kurtwa/ *noun phr.* L19.
[ORIGIN French.]
= ***courtly love*** s.v. COURTLY *adjective*.

amourette /amʊəˈrɛt; *foreign* amurɛt (*pl. same*)/ *noun*. E19.
[ORIGIN French: see AMORET.]
1 A brief or unimportant love affair. E19.
2 = AMORETTO 2. M19.

amour fou /amur fu/ *noun phr.* L20.
[ORIGIN French, lit. 'insane love'.]
Uncontrollable or obsessive infatuation or passion.

amour propre /amur prɔpr/ *noun phr.* Also ***amour-propre***. L18.
[ORIGIN French.]
Self-esteem; vanity.

†**amove** *verb*[1]. Long *dial.* Also **ameve**. ME.
[ORIGIN Old French *ameuv-* tonic stem of *amo(u)voir*, from *a* AD- + *moveir* MOVE *verb*; cf. medieval Latin *admovere*, *amm-*. App. infl. by Old French *esmo(u)voir* (see EMOVE).]
1 *verb trans.* Set in motion; stir up; rouse; *esp.* move the feelings of. ME–L19.
2 *verb intrans.* Be roused or moved. ME–L15.

†**amove** *verb*[2] *trans.* LME.
[ORIGIN Old French *amover* or Latin *amovere*, from *a* AB- + *movere* move.]
1 Remove from a position; dismiss (a person) from an office. LME–L19.
2 Remove or put away (abstract things). M16–M17.

amoxycillin /əmɒksɪˈsɪlɪn/ *noun*. L20.
[ORIGIN from AM(INO- + OXY- + PENI)CILLIN, elems. of the chemical name.]
PHARMACOLOGY. A broad-spectrum synthetic penicillin, closely related to ampicillin and with similar properties but better absorbed when taken orally.

Amoy /əˈmɔɪ/ *adjective & noun*. M19.
[ORIGIN The conventional western name for the island of Xiamen (see below).]
(Designating, of, or pertaining to) the form of Chinese of the Min group spoken by the people of Xiamen in Fujian province, China.

AMP *abbreviation*.
Adenosine monophosphate.

amp /amp/ *noun*[1]. *colloq.* L19.
[ORIGIN Abbreviation.]
= AMPERE.

amp /amp/ *noun*[2]. *colloq.* M20.
[ORIGIN Abbreviation.]
= AMPLIFIER 2.

amp /amp/ *verb trans. colloq.* M20.
[ORIGIN Sense 1 from AMPLIFY, prob. infl. by AMPHETAMINE. Sense 2 from AMPHETAMINE.]
1 Connect (a musical instrument) to an amplifier; make (music) louder or more energetic, usu. by using an amplifier or amplified instruments. Freq. with ***up***. M20.

Making Music Their willingness to amp-up Dylan and more traditional songs virtually began the folk-rock genre.

2 Make (a person) very excited or energetic (as if) through the consumption of amphetamines or another stimulant. Freq. with ***up***. L20.

Premiere Crowe . . didn't sleep for days—and not because he was artificially amped.

Ampakine /ˈampəkʌɪn/ *noun*. L20.
[ORIGIN from *AMPA* an acronym denoting certain receptors in the brain (from alpha-amino-3-hydroxy-5-methyl-4-isoxazolepropionic acid) + *-kine* (from Greek *kinein* to move).]
PHARMACOLOGY. (US proprietary name for) any of a class of organic compounds, including benzoyl piperidines and pyrrolidines, which enhance synaptic transmission in the brain and appear to improve memory and learning capacity.

ampelopsis /ampɪˈlɒpsɪs/ *noun*. Pl. same. E19.
[ORIGIN mod. Latin, from Greek *ampelos* vine + *opsis* appearance.]
A climbing plant of the genus *Ampelopsis*, belonging to the vine family.

amper /ˈampə/ *noun*. Long *dial.* OE.
[ORIGIN Unknown: cf. ANBURY.]
A tumour, a swelling; a varicose vein.

ampere /ˈampɛː/ *noun*. L19.
[ORIGIN from André-Marie *Ampère* (1775–1836), French physicist.]
A unit of electric current (now a base unit in the SI) equal to a flow of one coulomb per second. (Symbol A.)
– COMB.: **ampere-hour** a quantity of electricity equivalent to a current of one ampere flowing for one hour; **ampere-turn** a unit of magnetomotive force when expressed as the product of the number of turns in a coil and the current in amperes flowing through it.
■ **amperage** /ˈamp(ə)rɪdʒ/ *noun* the strength of an electric current measured in amperes; the rated current of a fuse or other electrical component: L19.

ampersand /ˈampəsand/ *noun*. M19.
[ORIGIN Alt. of '& per se (i.e. by itself) *and*', the old way of naming and explaining the character.]
The sign & (= *and*, Latin *et*).

amphetamine /amˈfɛtəmiːn/ *noun*. M20.
[ORIGIN from *alpha-methyl-phenethylamine*.]
A synthetic drug, $C_6H_5CH_2CH(CH_3)NH_2$, used as a decongestant and central nervous system stimulant; a tablet of an amphetamine salt. Proprietary name ***Benzedrine***.

amphi- /ˈamfi/ *combining form*.
[ORIGIN Greek.]
Both, of both kinds, about, around.
■ **amphiarˈthrodial** *adjective* (ANATOMY) of or pertaining to amphiarthrosis M19. **amphiarˈthrosis** *noun*, pl. **-throses** /-ˈθrəʊsiːz/, ANATOMY a form of joint which allows limited movement, the bones being joined by fibrous tissue, fibrocartilage, or hyaline cartilage M18. **amphiarˈthrotic** *adjective* = AMPHIARTHRODIAL M20. **amphiˈcoelous** *adjective* (ANATOMY & ZOOLOGY) (esp. of vertebral centra) concave on both sides M19. **amphiˈdiploid** *adjective & noun* (GENETICS) = ALLOTETRAPLOID M20. **amphiˈdiploidy** *noun* (GENETICS) = ALLOTETRAPLOIDY M20. **amphiˈdromic** *adjective* designating a point in a system of tides where the tidal range is zero E20. **amphiˈpathic**, **amphiˈphilic** *adjectives* (CHEMISTRY) having both a hydrophilic and a hydrophobic part; consisting of such molecules: M20. **amphiˈprotic** *adjective* (CHEMISTRY) (of a solvent) able both to accept and to donate protons M20.

amphibia *noun pl.* see AMPHIBIUM.

amphibian /amˈfɪbɪən/ *adjective & noun*. M17.
[ORIGIN from AMPHIBIUM + -AN.]
▸ **A** *adjective*. **1** Of double or doubtful nature. *rare*. M17.

A. TATE Mr. Eliot is amphibian and, if 'neither living or dead', is likewise neither American nor English; he is both.

2 Of or pertaining to the Amphibia. M19.
3 Of a vehicle or other conveyance: able to operate both on land and on water. E20.

H. G. WELLS Enormous amphibian tanks crawl up out of the water. M. INNES An amphibian plane could come and go in darkness.

▸ **B** *noun*. **1** An animal belonging to the class Amphibia. M19.

fig.: G. SARTON The Greeks were . . restless amphibians sailing across the Mediterranean or caravaning across foreign lands.

2 A person having a double nature or mode of existence. E20.
3 A vehicle or other conveyance able to operate both on land and on water. E20.

amphibious /amˈfɪbɪəs/ *adjective*. M17.
[ORIGIN from AMPHIBIUM + -OUS.]
1 Living both on land and in water. M17.
2 Of, pertaining to, or suited for both land and water; (of a vehicle etc.) = AMPHIBIAN *adjective* 3. M17. ▸**b** *spec.* Of a military operation: involving cooperation of sea, land, and air forces. Of forces: trained for such operations. M20.

R. CAMPBELL Since half the country consists of water and reeds, everybody leads an amphibious life.

3 Occupying two positions; having a double nature or mode of existence. M17.

amphibium /amˈfɪbɪəm/ *noun*. Pl. **-bia** /-bɪə/, (in branch I) **-biums**. E17.
[ORIGIN mod. Latin from Greek *amphibion* use as noun of neut. of adjective *amphibios*, from AMPHI- + *bios* life.]
▸ **I 1** A creature that lives both in water and on land. E17.
2 *fig.* A being that has an ambiguous position or a double existence. M17.
▸ **II** In *pl.* only. ZOOLOGY. Also **A-**.
3 a *hist.* The reptiles, including mod. Amphibia (Linnaeus). M18. ▸**b** A class of vertebrates, including frogs, newts, salamanders, etc., which as adults are air-breathing and mainly terrestrial, but whose young have gills and are aquatic. E19.

amphibole /ˈamfɪbəʊl/ *noun*. E17.
[ORIGIN French (both senses) from Latin *amphibolus* ambiguous from Greek *amphibolos*, from AMPHI- + *ballein* to throw.]
†**1** = AMPHIBOLOGY 1. E–M17.
2 MINERALOGY. Orig., hornblende. Now, any of a large class of silicate and aluminosilicate rock-forming minerals which form fibrous or columnar crystals (they are characterized by a crystal structure based on cross-linked double chains of SiO_4 tetrahedra). E19.

amphibolic /amfɪˈbɒlɪk/ *adjective*. E19.
[ORIGIN from AMPHIBOLE or AMPHIBOLY + -IC.]
1 GEOLOGY. Of, pertaining to, or of the nature of amphibole. E19.
2 Ambiguous, equivocal. *rare*. L19.

amphibolite /amˈfɪbəlʌɪt/ *noun*. E19.
[ORIGIN from AMPHIBOLE + -ITE[1].]
GEOLOGY. A metamorphic rock consisting chiefly of hornblende and plagioclase.
■ **amphiboˈlitic** *adjective* E20.

amphibology /amfɪˈbɒlədʒi/ *noun*. Also in Latin form †**-gia**. LME.
[ORIGIN Old French & mod. French *amphibologie* from late Latin *amphibologia* for classical Latin *amphibolia* AMPHIBOLY: see -OLOGY.]
1 An ambiguity; a quibble. LME.
2 Ambiguous wording; equivocation. L16.
■ **amˌphiboˈlogical** *adjective* ambiguous, quibbling L16.

amphiboly /amˈfɪbəli/ *noun*. L16.
[ORIGIN Latin *amphibolia*: see AMPHIBOLE, -Y[3]. Cf. French *amphibolie*.]
1 = AMPHIBOLOGY 2. L16.
2 = AMPHIBOLOGY 1. E17.

amphibrach /ˈamfɪbrak/ *noun*. Orig. in Latin form †**-chus**, †**-chys**. L16.
[ORIGIN Latin *amphibrachys* (later *-us*) from Greek *amphibrakhus* short at both ends, formed as AMPHI- + *brakhus* short.]
PROSODY (orig. CLASSICAL PROSODY). A foot consisting of one long syllable between two short syllables or (in English etc.) one stressed syllable between two unstressed syllables.
■ **amphiˈbrachic** *adjective* E19.

amphictyon /amˈfɪktɪən/ *noun*. Also **-ion**; (GREEK HISTORY) **A-**. L16.
[ORIGIN Greek *amphiktuones* pl. (orig. *-ion-*) dwellers around from *ktizein* to found: see AMPHI-.]
A delegate to an amphictyonic council, orig. and esp. that of ancient Greece. Usu. in *pl.*
■ **amphictyˈonic** *adjective* of or pertaining to an amphictyony M18. **amphictyony** *noun* an association of states for the common interest, orig. and esp. in ancient Greece M19.

amphigouri /amfɪˈgʊəri/ *noun*. Also **amphigory** /ˈamfɪgəri/. E19.
[ORIGIN French, app. a learned (joc.) formation from Greek AMPHI- + *allégorie* ALLEGORY.]
A nonsensical burlesque composition; a piece of nonsense verse.

amphilogy /amˈfɪlədʒi/ *noun*. *rare*. LME.
[ORIGIN Greek *amphilogia* dispute, from *amphilogos* disputed, uncertain: see AMPHI-, -OLOGY.]
Ambiguity, equivocation.

amphimacer /amˈfɪməsə/ *noun*. L16.
[ORIGIN Latin *amphimacrus* from Greek *amphimakros* long at both ends, formed as AMPHI- + *makros* long.]
CLASSICAL PROSODY. A foot consisting of one short syllable between two long syllables (= CRETIC *noun*). Occas. *transf.*, a foot consisting of one unstressed syllable between two stressed syllables.

amphioxus /amfɪˈɒksəs/ *noun*. Pl. **-oxi** /-ˈɒksʌɪ/. M19.
[ORIGIN mod. Latin, from Greek AMPHI- + *oxus* sharp.]
A lancelet of the genus *Branchiostoma* (formerly *Amphioxus*).

amphipod /ˈamfɪpɒd/ *noun & adjective*. M19.
[ORIGIN from mod. Latin *amphipoda* (sc. *animalia*), from Greek AMPHI- + -POD.]
(A crustacean) of the largely marine order Amphipoda, members of which, e.g. sandhoppers, have seven pairs of thoracic legs, some specialized for feeding and others for swimming. Cf. ISOPOD.

amphiprostyle /amˈfɪprəstʌɪl/ *noun & adjective*. E18.
[ORIGIN Latin *amphiprostylus* from Greek *amphiprostulos*, formed as AMPHI- + PROSTYLE.]
ARCHITECTURE. (A building, esp. a temple) with a portico at each end.

amphisbaena /amfɪsˈbiːnə/ *noun*. LME.
[ORIGIN Latin (Pliny) from Greek *amphisbaina*, from *amphis* both ways, AMPHI- + *bainein* go, walk.]
1 A fabled serpent with a head at each end and able to move in either direction. LME.
2 A wormlike burrowing lizard of the genus *Amphisbaena*. M19.
■ **amphisbaenian** *adjective & noun* (being or pertaining to) a reptile of the kind typified by *Amphisbaena* M19. **amphisbaenid** *noun* = AMPHISBAENIAN *noun* L19.

Amphiscii /amˈfɪʃɪʌɪ/ *noun pl. arch.* E17.
[ORIGIN medieval Latin from Greek *amphiskioi*, formed as AMPHI- + *skia* shadow.]
The inhabitants of the tropics (whose shadows at one time fall northward, at another southward).

■ Also *Amphiscians* *noun pl.* (*arch.*) E17.

amphitheatre /ˈamfɪθiːətə/ *noun*. Also ***-theater**. LME.
[ORIGIN Latin *amphitheatrum* from Greek *amphitheatron*, formed as AMPHI- + THEATRE. Cf. French *amphithéâtre*.]
1 An oval or circular building with seats rising in tiers around a central open space. LME. ▸**b** *fig.* The scene of a contest. M17. ▸**c** A semicircular rising gallery in a theatre. M19.
†**2** A joined pair of theatres. E17–E19.
■ **amphitheˈatric** *adjective* = AMPHITHEATRICAL E17. **amphitheˈatrical** *adjective* of, pertaining to, or resembling an amphitheatre L16. **amphitheˈatrically** *adverb* E18.

Amphitryon /amˈfɪtrɪən/ *noun*. M19.
[ORIGIN A character in Molière's play *Amphitryon*.]
A host at dinner.

amphora /ˈamf(ə)rə/ *noun*. Pl. **-rae** /-riː/, **-ras**. Also †**amphore**. ME.
[ORIGIN Latin from Greek *amphoreus*, or French *amphore*.]
1 A Greek or Roman two-handled vessel. ME.
2 A Greek or Roman liquid measure of varying capacity. LME.
■ **amphoral** *adjective* of, pertaining to, or resembling an amphora M17. **amˈphoric** *adjective* (MEDICINE) (of respiratory sounds heard in auscultation) suggesting the resonance produced by blowing across the mouth of an amphora M19.

amphoteric /amfəˈtɛrɪk/ *adjective*. M19.
[ORIGIN from Greek *amphoteros* compar. of *amphō* both + -IC.]
Acting both ways (*rare* in *gen.* sense); *spec.* in CHEMISTRY, having both acidic and basic properties.

amphtrac(k) *nouns* vars. of AMTRAC.

ampicillin /ampɪˈsɪlɪn/ *noun*. M20.
[ORIGIN from AM(INO- + P(EN)ICILLIN.]
PHARMACOLOGY. A semi-synthetic penicillin used esp. to treat infections of the urinary and respiratory tracts. Proprietary name ***Penbritin***.

ample /ˈamp(ə)l/ *adjective & adverb*. LME.
[ORIGIN Old French & mod. French from Latin *amplus* large, capacious, abundant.]
▸ **A** *adjective*. **1** Of abstract things: large in amount, extensive, abundant; (of writing or speech) copious, treating of matters at full length. LME.

T. CLANCY There was ample evidence that people occasionally farmed here.

2 Large in dimensions, capacity, or volume; spacious; capacious; *euphem.* (of a person) stout. L15.

I. RANKIN He patted his ample stomach.

3 Enough to satisfy all demands, plentiful; liberal, unsparing. M16.

Ideal Home There is ample free parking.

▸ †**B** *adverb*. Amply. M16–E17.
■ **ampleness** *noun* (*arch.*) M16. **amply** *adverb* in an ample manner LME.

amplexicaul /amˈplɛksɪkɔːl/ *adjective*. M18.
[ORIGIN from mod. Latin *amplexicaulis*, formed as AMPLEXUS + *caulis* stem.]
BOTANY. Of sessile leaves: embracing the stem.

amplexus /amˈplɛksəs/ *noun*. M20.
[ORIGIN Latin = embrace.]
ZOOLOGY. The mating position of frogs and toads, in which the male clasps the female about the back.

ampliation /amplɪˈeɪʃ(ə)n/ *noun*. *arch.* E16.
[ORIGIN Old French & mod. French, or Latin *ampliatio(n-)*, from *ampliat-* pa. ppl stem of *ampliare*, from *amplus* AMPLE: see -ATION.]
1 Enlarging; amplification. E16.
2 An enlargement, an extension. L16.
3 LAW (now *hist.*). Deferring of judgement for further consideration. M17.

ampliative /ˈamplɪətɪv/ *adjective*. M17.
[ORIGIN French *ampliatif* (medieval Latin *ampliativus*), formed as AMPLIATION: see -ATIVE.]
Amplificatory; *spec.* (LOGIC) enlarging a simple conception by predicating of it something which is not directly implied in it (now chiefly in ***ampliative induction***).

amplification /ˌamplɪfɪˈkeɪʃ(ə)n/ *noun*. E16.
[ORIGIN Old French & mod. French, or Latin *amplificatio(n-)*, from *amplificat-* pa. ppl stem of *amplificare*: see AMPLIFY, -FICATION.]
1 The action of amplifying something; enlargement; augmentation; enhancement; RHETORIC elaboration to increase effect or add importance. E16.
2 The result of amplifying; something which has been extended or elaborated. E16.
3 A thing which amplifies; an addition. E18.
■ **amplificatory** *adjective* tending or serving to amplify something L18.

amplifier /ˈamplɪfʌɪə/ *noun*. M16.
[ORIGIN from AMPLIFY + -ER[1].]
1 A person who amplifies; *esp.* a person who amplifies a statement or narrative. M16.
2 A device for amplifying input electrical signals, esp. in sound reproduction. E20.

amplify /ˈamplɪfʌɪ/ *verb*. LME.
[ORIGIN French *amplifier* from Latin *amplificare* enlarge, from *amplus* AMPLE: see -FY.]
1 *verb trans.* Enlarge, increase, augment; enhance; elaborate on (a statement or narrative); exaggerate. LME. ▸**b** *spec.* Increase the strength or amplitude of (an electrical signal or other physical quantity). E20.
2 *verb intrans.* Expatiate, speak largely, (*arch.* also foll. by *on*, *upon*). M16.
3 *verb intrans.* Become larger, increase. *rare*. E17.

amplitude /ˈamplɪtjuːd/ *noun*. M16.
[ORIGIN French, or Latin *amplitudo*, from *amplus* AMPLE: see -TUDE.]
1 Physical extent; largeness; bulk; *esp.* width, breadth. M16.

T. NASHE It cuts out an Island of some amplitude. C. LAMB An amplitude of form and stature, answering to her mind. T. WALKER And exploiting his great strength, / hurls his amplitude the length / of a pond too small for him.

2 Excellence, grandeur, splendour. *arch.* M16.

R. COKE To the greater amplitude and glory of God.

3 Copiousness; abundance; wide range. M16.

BACON All works are overcommen by amplitude of reward . . and by the conjunction of labours. LD MACAULAY His mind is . . distinguished by the amplitude of its grasp.

†**4** ASTRONOMY. Angular distance from the eastern or western point of the horizon at rising or setting. E17–M19.
5 The maximum extent of vibration or oscillation from an equilibrium position; the maximum extent of deviation from the mean value of an alternating electrical signal or other oscillatory phenomenon. M19.
– COMB.: **amplitude modulation** variation of the amplitude of a radio or other wave as a means of carrying information such as an audio signal.
■ **ampliˈtudinous** *adjective* ample, copious E20.

ampoule /ˈampuːl/ *noun*. M17.
[ORIGIN mod. French: see AMPUL.]
1 = AMPULLA 2. *rare*. M17.
2 A small sealed glass vessel for holding sterilized materials for injection, poisons, air-sensitive chemicals, etc. E20.

ampster /ˈam(p)stə/ *noun*. *Austral. slang.* Also **ams-** /ˈams-/. M20.
[ORIGIN Unknown.]
A showman's or trickster's accomplice who starts the buying of tickets, goods, etc.

amptman *noun* var. of AMTMAN.

ampul /ˈampuːl, -p(ə)l/ *noun*. Now *rare* or *obsolete*. OE.
[ORIGIN Old French *ampo(u)le* (mod. *ampoule*) from Latin AMPULLA.]
†**1** *gen.* A small bottle or flask; a phial. OE–L15.
2 *spec.* = AMPULLA 2. LME.

ampulla /amˈpʊlə/ *noun*. Pl. **-llae** /-liː/. LME.
[ORIGIN Latin, dim. of *ampora* var. of AMPHORA.]
1 ROMAN ANTIQUITIES. A small two-handled globular flask or bottle. LME.
2 A vessel for holding consecrated oil or for other sacred uses. L16.
3 ANATOMY. A vessel or cavity shaped like the ancient ampulla. M19.
ampulla of Lorenzini /lɒr(ə)nˈziːni/ [Stefano *Lorenzini*, 17th-cent. Italian physician] ICHTHYOLOGY a saclike sensory structure sensitive to electric fields, which occurs in numbers in the heads of certain fishes, esp. elasmobranchs. VATER'S ***ampulla***.
■ **ampullar** *adjective* of the form or character of an ampulla (sense 3) M19.

amputate /ˈampjʊteɪt/ *verb*. M16.
[ORIGIN Latin *amputat-* pa. ppl stem of *amputare*, from *am-* for *amb-* around + *putare* prune, lop: see -ATE[3].]
1 *verb trans.* Cut off, lop off; prune. *obsolete* exc. as *fig.* use of sense 2. M16.
2 *verb trans. & intrans. spec.* Cut off from an animal body (some part, esp. a limb because of injury or disease). M17.
■ **amputator** *noun* a person who amputates E19. **ampuˈtee** *noun* a person who has lost a limb or other part of the body by amputation E20.

amputation /ampjʊˈteɪʃ(ə)n/ *noun*. E17.
[ORIGIN formed as AMPUTATE: see -ATION.]
1 A cutting or lopping off; a pruning. *obsolete* exc. as *fig.* use of sense 2. E17.
2 *spec.* The operation of cutting off a limb or other part of an animal body. E17.

AMRAAM *abbreviation*.
Advanced medium-range air-to-air missile.

Amratian /amˈreɪʃ(ə)n/ *adjective*. E20.
[ORIGIN from el-*Amra* a district in Egypt + -*t*- + -IAN.]
Designating or pertaining to an early period of the ancient predynastic culture in Egypt.

amrita /amˈriːtə, *foreign* ˈʌmritə/ *noun*. *poet.* Also **-reeta**. L18.
[ORIGIN Sanskrit *amṛta* an immortal, nectar.]
Ambrosia.

amscray /ˈamskreɪ/ *verb intrans*. *US slang.* Now *rare*. M20.
[ORIGIN Pig Latin.]
= SCRAM *verb*[2].

amster *noun* var. of AMPSTER.

amtman /ˈamtman/ *noun*. Now *hist.* Also **ampt-**. Pl. **-men**. L16.
[ORIGIN German *Amtmann*, Dutch, & Scandinavian.]
In Germany, Scandinavia, etc.: a person in charge; a bailiff, steward, magistrate, etc.

amtrac /ˈamtrak/ *noun*. *US*. Also **amph-** /ˈamf-/; **-ck**. M20.
[ORIGIN from AM(PHIBIOUS + TRAC(TOR.]
An amphibious tracked vehicle for landing assault troops.

amu *abbreviation*. Also **a.m.u.**
Atomic mass unit.

amuck, †**amuco** *adjective, noun, & adverb* see AMOK.

amulet /ˈamjʊlɪt/ *noun*[1]. L16.
[ORIGIN Latin *amuletum* (Varro, Pliny) of unknown origin.]
Something worn as a charm against evil, disease, witchcraft, etc.; *fig.* a preservative, a protection, a charm.
■ **amuletic** /-ˈlɛtɪk/ *adjective* M18.

†**amulet** *noun*[2] see OMELETTE.

amuse /əˈmjuːz/ *verb*. L15.
[ORIGIN Old French & mod. French *amuser* entertain, †deceive, from *à* AD- + *muser* MUSE *verb*[2].]
1 *verb trans.* Divert the attention of (a person) in order to mislead; delude, deceive. (The usual sense 17–18.) *arch.* L15.

H. NELSON Their Fleet was to amuse ours whilst they cross from Leghorn.

†**2** *verb intrans.* Muse intently; gaze in astonishment. M16–L17.
†**3** *verb trans.* **a** Engage the attention of. E17–L18. ▸**b** Confound, puzzle, bewilder. E17–M18.

a P. HOLLAND Why art thou amused upon the course of the stars?

4 *verb trans.* Make (someone) laugh or smile; cause to find something funny. M17.

G. B. SHAW It amuses him to be treated in this fashion: he chuckles secretly. W. SHAWCROSS He would try to amuse everyone by barking like a dog.

5 *verb trans.* Provide interesting and enjoyable occupation for; entertain. L18.

D. DU MAURIER I've a mass of things to see to this morning, do you think you can amuse yourself?

■ **amusable** *adjective* E19. **amusedly** /-zɪdli/ *adverb* in an amused manner, with amusement M19. **amuˈsee** *noun* (*rare*) a person amused or to be amused M19. **amuser** *noun* L16. **amusingly** *adverb* in an amusing manner E19. **amusingness** *noun* the state or quality of being amusing E19.

amuse-bouche /əˌmjuːzˈbuːʃ, *foreign* amyzbuʃ (*pl. same*)/ *noun*. L20.
[ORIGIN French, from *amuser* amuse, gratify + *bouche* mouth.]
= AMUSE-GUEULE.

amuse-gueule /əˌmjuːzˈgəːl, *foreign* amyzgœl (*pl. same*)/ *noun*. L20.
[ORIGIN French, from *amuser* amuse, gratify + *gueule* mouth.]
A cocktail savoury; also *fig.*, a taster.

amusement /əˈmjuːzm(ə)nt/ *noun*. E17.
[ORIGIN French, formed as AMUSE: see -MENT.]
†**1** Musing; mental abstraction. E17–E18.
2 Distraction or diversion of the attention; beguiling, deception; an instance of this. *arch.* E17.
†**3** Distracting bewilderment. M–L17.
4 A pastime; a means of recreation; something amusing. (Orig. *derog.*) M17.

J. H. NEWMAN To take . . pleasure in our families rather than to seek amusements out of doors. V. WELBURN Roll-up, roll-up . . . Amusements . . . Candy-floss . . . Roundabouts.

5 Pleasurable occupation of the attention without seriousness; (orig., idle time-wasting) entertainment, recreation; the causing of laughter or smiles; humour aroused by something droll or grotesque. L17.

POPE Amusement is the happiness of those that cannot think. COLERIDGE The same craving for amusement, i.e. to be away from the Muses for relaxation. G. GREENE His old Italian face showed few emotions but a mild amusement. A. J. P. TAYLOR Lloyd George derived a malicious amusement from the way in which the spokesmen of these two democratic countries . . defied Wilson. S. HILL To the amusement of her mother and sisters. T. STOPPARD A little team I run, mainly for our own amusement.

– COMB.: **amusement arcade** a place for recreation containing automatic game-playing machines, etc.

amusette /amjʊˈzɛt/ *noun*. M18.
[ORIGIN French = plaything: see AMUSE, -ETTE.]
hist. A type of light field cannon.

amusive /əˈmjuːzɪv/ *adjective*. E18.
[ORIGIN from AMUSE + -IVE.]
†**1** Deceitful, illusive. E–M18.
†**2** Affording recreation. Only in M18.
3 Affording pleasing entertainment; causing laughter or smiles. M18.
4 Having amusement as an object. *rare*. L18.
■ **amusively** *adverb* L18. **amusiveness** *noun* (*rare*) E19.

A

amygdala /ə'mɪgdələ/ *noun*. Pl. **-lae** /-liː/. Long anglicized as †**-dal**; also †**-dale**. OE.
[ORIGIN Latin from Greek *amugdalē* almond; some uses & form *-dale* from French.]
†**1** An almond. OE–LME.
2 ANATOMY. Orig. = ALMOND *noun* 3b. Now, either of two of the basal ganglia of the brain adjoining the optic tract. LME.

amygdale /ə'mɪgdeɪl/ *noun*[1]. L19.
[ORIGIN French formed as AMYGDALA.]
GEOLOGY. A vesicle in an igneous rock, containing secondary minerals.
■ **amygdule** *noun* a small amygdale L19.

†**amygdale** *noun*[2] var. of AMYGDALA.

amygdalin /ə'mɪgdəlɪn/ *noun*. M19.
[ORIGIN from Latin AMYGDALA + -IN[1].]
CHEMISTRY. A bitter crystalline glycoside found in bitter almonds and the stones of peaches, apricots, etc.

amygdaline /ə'mɪgdəlʌɪn/ *adjective*. *rare*. L17.
[ORIGIN Latin *amygdalinus* from Greek *amugdalinos* of almonds: see AMYGDALA, -INE[2].]
Of or pertaining to almonds; almond-shaped.

amygdaloid /ə'mɪgdəlɔɪd/ *adjective & noun*. M18.
[ORIGIN from Latin AMYGDALA + -OID.]
▸ **A** *adjective*. Almond-shaped; like almonds; GEOLOGY containing numerous amygdales. M18.
amygdaloid nucleus ANATOMY an amygdala of the brain.
▸ **B** *noun*. GEOLOGY. An igneous rock containing numerous amygdales. L18.
■ **amygda'loidal** *adjective* (GEOLOGY) E19.

amyl /'eɪmʌɪl, 'amɪl/ *noun*. M19.
[ORIGIN from Latin *amylum* starch + -YL.]
CHEMISTRY. Pentyl; *spec*. the primary straight-chain radical $C_5H_{11}\cdot$.
– COMB.: **amyl nitrate** a colourless synthetic liquid, $C_5H_{11}NO_3$, used as an additive in diesel fuel to improve its ignition properties; **amyl nitrite** a yellowish volatile synthetic liquid, $C_5H_{11}NO_2$, used medicinally as a vasodilator, rapidly absorbed by the body on inhalation, and sometimes used for its stimulatory effects.
■ **amylene** *noun* pentene; ***amylene hydrate***, tertiary pentyl alcohol, an anaesthetic: M19.

amylase /'amɪleɪz/ *noun*. L19.
[ORIGIN formed as AMYL + -ASE.]
An enzyme which hydrolyses starch.

amylo- /'amɪləʊ/ *combining form* of Latin *amylum* starch, or of AMYL: see -O-.
■ **amylo'barbitone** *noun* a narcotic and sedative barbiturate, 5-ethyl-5-isopentyl-barbituric acid; (a proprietary name for the drug is AMYTAL): M20. **amy'lolysis** *noun* the breakdown of starch to sugars L19. **amylo'lytic** *adjective* of or pertaining to amylolysis L19. **amylo'pectin** *noun* the amorphous form of starch, consisting of branched polysaccharide chains E20. **amy'lopsin** *noun* a pancreatic enzyme which converts starch to sugars L19. **amylose** *noun* the crystallizable form of starch, consisting of long unbranched polysaccharide chains L19.

amyloid /'amɪlɔɪd/ *adjective & noun*. M19.
[ORIGIN formed as AMYLO- + -OID.]
▸ **A** *adjective*. **1** Resembling (the chemical structure of) starch. M19.
2 MEDICINE. Of or pertaining to amyloid. L19.
▸ **B** *noun*. MEDICINE. A glycoprotein (orig. thought to be akin to starch) deposited in the liver, kidneys, spleen, or other tissues in certain diseases. L19.
■ **amyloi'dosis** *noun* deposition of amyloid in the tissues E20.

amyotrophy /amɪ'ɒtrəfi/ *noun*. L19.
[ORIGIN from A-[10] + Greek *mu-*, *mus* muscle + -O- + -TROPHY.]
MEDICINE. Atrophy of muscle.
■ **amyotrophic** /-'trəʊfɪk, -'trɒfɪk/ *adjective* characterized by amyotrophy; ***amyotrophic lateral sclerosis*** = LOU GEHRIG'S DISEASE: L19.

Amytal /'amɪt(ə)l/ *noun*. E20.
[ORIGIN from AMYL + euphonic *-t-* + -AL[2].]
(Proprietary name for) amylobarbitone.

AN *abbreviation*.
Anglo-Norman.

an *adjective* (*indef. article*) see A *adjective*.

an /an, ən/ *preposition*. *arch*. Also as *prefix* (= AN-[1]). OE.
[ORIGIN Orig. form of ON *preposition*; later a var. of ON *preposition* before vowels: cf. A *preposition*[1].]
= ON *preposition*.

an /(ə)n/ *conjunction & noun*. Now *arch. & dial.* (see also A.1 below). Also **an'**. ME.
[ORIGIN Weakened form of AND *conjunction*[1] & *noun*.]
▸ **A** *conjunction*. **1** = AND *conjunction*[1] I (coordinating). Now *rare* as a written form exc. *an'* as repr. illiterate or dial. use, though the pronunc. is common in informal speech. ME.
2 = AND *conjunction*[1] II (conditional). M16.
▸ **B** *noun*. = AND *noun*. M19.

an- /ən/ *prefix*[1] (not productive). OE.
[ORIGIN Proclitic var.]
= AN *preposition*, as ***anent***, ***anon***. Cf. A-[2].

an- /ən/ *prefix*[2] (not productive). ME.
Repr. Anglo-Norman *an-*, Old French *en-* from Latin *in-* (see IN-[2]), as ***anoint***.

an- /ən/ *prefix*[3] (not productive). ME.
Repr. Latin *an-* assim. form of AD- before *n*, directly, or indirectly through French (Old French *a-* refash. after Latin in French itself or after adoption in English), as ***annex***, ***announce***, ***annul***.

an- /an/ *prefix*[4] (not productive).
Repr. Greek ANA- before a vowel, as ***aneurysm***.

an- /an, *unstressed* ən/ *prefix*[5].
Repr. Greek privative *an-* without, lacking, not, the original form of A-[10] retained before vowels, as ***anecdote***, ***anonymous***. A productive prefix of negation and privation in mod. techn. terms, as ***analgesia***, ***anachoic***, ***anhydrous***.

-an /*in sense* 1 (ə)n, *in sense* 2 -an/ *suffix*.
1 Repr. Latin *-anus*, *-na*, *-num* of or belonging to, as ***urban***, ***sylvan***, directly, or indirectly through French *-ain(e)* later refash. A productive suffix, forming *adjectives* (often used as *nouns*), esp. from names of places (as ***American***, ***Chilean***), systems (as ***Anglican***), zoological classes or orders (as ***crustacean***), and founders (as ***Lutheran***). Already in Latin added so commonly to *-ius*, forming *-ianus*, that -IAN is in use merely a euphonic var. of -AN (as ***Russian***, ***Presbyterian***, ***crocodilian***, ***Christian***).
2 [German: cf. -ANE.] CHEMISTRY. Used more or less arbitrarily to form names of organic compounds, esp. polysaccharides (as ***dextran*** etc.).

ana /'ɑːnə/ *noun*[1]. M18.
[ORIGIN from -ANA.]
1 As *sing*. (with pl. **-s**). A collection of a person's memorable sayings. M18.
2 As *pl*. Publications or other items concerning or associated with a person, place, activity, etc. M18.

ana /'anə/ *adverb & noun*[2]. Long *obsolete* exc. in Dicts. LME.
[ORIGIN medieval Latin from Greek *ana* again.]
▸ **A** *adverb*. In recipes for drugs etc.: of each, of every one alike. LME.
▸ †**B** *noun*. An equal quantity or number (of each ingredient in a recipe); an instruction to use this. M–L17.

ana- /'anə/ *prefix*. Before a vowel usu. **an-**.
Repr. Greek *ana-* up, back, again, anew.
■ **ana'genesis** *noun* (BIOLOGY) species formation without branching of the evolutionary line of descent (cf. CLADOGENESIS) L19. **anage'netic** *adjective* of or pertaining to anagenesis L19. **anaphase** *noun* (BIOLOGY) the stage of cell division in which daughter chromosomes separate towards opposite poles of the spindle L19. **ana'plasia** *noun* (BIOLOGY) loss of specialized characteristics by cells, as in the formation of tumours dedifferentiation E20. **ana'plastic** *adjective* (MEDICINE) †(*a*) of or pertaining to plastic surgery (only in Dicts.); (*b*) pertaining to or characterized by anaplasia: L19. †**anaplasty** *noun* (MEDICINE) plastic surgery (Dicts.): only in L19.

-ana /'ɑːnə/ *suffix*.
[ORIGIN Latin, neut. pl. ending of adjectives in *-anus*: see -AN 1.]
Forming pl. nouns with the sense 'publications or other items concerning or associated with a person, place, or topic', as ***Americana***, ***cricketana***, ***railwayana***, ***Shakespeareana***, ***Victoriana***. Occas. as euphonic var. of -IANA, after Latin words ending in *-iana*.

anabaptise *verb* var. of ANABAPTIZE.

Anabaptism /anə'baptɪz(ə)m/ *noun*. Also (in sense 2 usu.) **a-**. M16.
[ORIGIN ecclesiastical Latin *anabaptismus* (Augustine) from Greek *anabaptismos*, formed as ANA- + *baptismos* BAPTISM.]
1 *hist*. The doctrines of the 16th-cent. Continental Anabaptists or (opprobriously) of the later Baptists (see ANABAPTIST). M16.
2 Rebaptism. Now *rare*. M17.

Anabaptist /anə'baptɪst/ *noun*. Also **a-**. M16.
[ORIGIN French *anabaptiste* or mod. Latin *anabaptista*, formed as ANABAPTISM: see -IST.]
hist. **1** A member of any of various 16th-cent. religious groups in Germany, Switzerland, and the Low Countries, who recognized the baptism of (adult) believers only. M16.
2 (Used more or less opprobriously for) a Baptist (see BAPTIST *noun* 2). Also *loosely*, a person who rejected other Anglican doctrines. L16.
■ ˌ**Anabap'tistic** *adjective* M17. ˌ**Anabap'tistical** *adjective* M16. ˌ**Anabap'tistically** *adverb* M16. †**Anabaptistry** *noun* = ANABAPTISM 1 M16–E18.

anabaptize /anəbap'tʌɪz/ *verb trans*. Now *rare*. Also **-ise**. M17.
[ORIGIN medieval Latin *anabaptizare* from Greek *anabaptizein*, formed as ANA- + *baptizein* BAPTIZE.]
Rebaptize; rechristen; rename.

anabasis /a'nabəsɪs/ *noun*. *literary*. Pl. **-ases** /-əsiːz/. E18.
[ORIGIN Greek = going up, formed as ANA- + *basis* going. Cf. KATABASIS.]
A military advance, an up-country march, *esp*. that of Cyrus the Younger into Asia, as narrated by Xenophon.

anabatic /anə'batɪk/ *adjective*. M19.
[ORIGIN Greek *anabatikos*, from *anabatēs* a person who ascends, from *anabainein* go up: see ANA-, -IC.]
1 MEDICINE. Of or pertaining to the course of a disease to its climax. Only in Dicts. M19.
2 METEOROLOGY. Of a wind: caused by local upward motion of warm air. Opp. KATABATIC. E20.

anabiosis /anəbʌɪ'əʊsɪs/ *noun*. L19.
[ORIGIN Greek *anabiōsis* a return to life, from *anabioein* come to life again: see ANA-, -OSIS.]
BIOLOGY. Revival from a state of suspended animation or apparent lifelessness; a temporary state of greatly reduced metabolism that some organisms can enter.
■ **anabiotic** /-'ɒtɪk/ *adjective* L19.

anabolic /anə'bɒlɪk/ *adjective*. L19.
[ORIGIN formed as ANABOLISM + -IC.]
BIOLOGY. Pertaining to, involved in, or characterized by anabolism. Opp. CATABOLIC.
anabolic steroid any of a class of synthetic steroid hormones used to increase muscle size.

anabolism /a'nabəlɪz(ə)m/ *noun*. L19.
[ORIGIN from Greek *anabolē* a throwing up, ascent, from *anaballein*, formed as ANA- + *ballein* to throw: see -ISM.]
BIOLOGY. Constructive metabolism; the metabolic synthesis of complex substances and their incorporation into body tissue. Opp. CATABOLISM.

anabranch /'anəbrɑːn(t)ʃ/ *noun*. Chiefly *Austral*. M19.
[ORIGIN from *anastomosing* pres. pple of ANASTOMOSE *verb* + BRANCH *noun*.]
A stream that leaves a river and re-enters it downstream.

anacard /'anəkɑːd/ *noun*. Now *rare* or *obsolete*. Also in Latin forms **-dium** /-dɪəm/, †**-dus**. LME.
[ORIGIN medieval Latin *anacardus*, mod. Latin *-dium* from Greek *anakardion*, from *ana* like + *kardion* heart-shaped ornament.]
A cashew nut.

anachoret *noun* see ANCHORITE.

anachronic /anə'krɒnɪk/ *adjective*. E19.
[ORIGIN from ANACHRONISM, after pairs such as *synchronism*, *synchronic*: see -IC. Cf. French *anachronique*.]
Erroneous in date or order; involving anachronism.
■ **anachronically** *adverb* E19.

anachronism /ə'nakrənɪz(ə)m/ *noun*. M17.
[ORIGIN French *anachronisme* or Greek *anakhronismos*, from *anakhronizesthai* refer to a wrong time, formed as ANA- + *khronos* time: see -ISM.]
1 An error in computing time or fixing dates; the relating of an event, custom, or circumstance to a wrong period of time. M17.

> T. HEARNE Virgil making Dido and Æneas Co-temporaries, whereas they lived at Three Hundred Years distance . . committed an Anachronism. H. B. STOWE Some anachronisms with regard to the time of the session of courts have been allowed.

2 Something or someone out of harmony with the time. E19.

> V. SACKVILLE-WEST He had thought of Chevron as a dead thing, an anachronism, an exquisite survival . . with its . . servants and luxury. M. MCCARTHY She herself was a smoldering anachronism, a throwback to one of those ardent young women of the Sixties, Turgenev's heroines. S. J. PERELMAN Anachronisms in the script . . , like penicillin and the atomic bomb.

■ **anachro'nistic** *adjective* of the nature of or involving anachronism L18. **anachro'nistically** *adverb* E20. **anachronous** *adjective* = ANACHRONISTIC E19.

anaclasis /ə'nakləsɪs/ *noun*. Also **-klasis** & (orig.) in Greek characters. Pl. **-ases** /-əsiːz/. L18.
[ORIGIN Greek *anaklasis* bending back, from *anaklaein*: see ANACLASTIC.]
CLASSICAL PROSODY. In Ionic metre: an interchange of the final long syllable of the first foot with the opening short syllable of the second.

anaclastic /anə'klastɪk/ *adjective*. M18.
[ORIGIN from Greek *anaklastos*, from *anaklaein* bend back, refract, formed as ANA- + *klaein* break, + -IC.]
1 Springing back. *rare*. M18.
2 OPTICS. Pertaining to or produced by refraction. *rare*. L18.
3 CLASSICAL PROSODY. Of, pertaining to, or involving anaclasis. L19.

anaclitic /anə'klɪtɪk/ *adjective*. E20.
[ORIGIN from Greek *anaklitos* for reclining, from *anaklinein*, from *klinein* to lean, slope: see -IC. Orig. in phr. *anaclitic type*, translating German *Anlehnungstypus* (Freud).]
PSYCHOANALYSIS. Orig., denoting a person whose choice of a love object is governed by the dependence of the libido on another instinct, e.g. hunger. Now in extended use, relating to or characterized by a strong emotional dependence on another or others.
■ **anaclitically** *adverb* M20.

anacoluthon /anəkə'luːθɒn, -θ(ə)n/ *noun*. Pl. **-tha** /-θə/. E18.
[ORIGIN Late Latin from Greek *anakolouthon* neut. sing. of adjective = lacking sequence, formed as AN-[5] + *akolouthos* following.]
A sentence or construction lacking grammatical sequence.
■ **anacoluthia** *noun* = ANACOLUTHON M19. **anacoluthic** *adjective* M19.

anaconda /anəˈkɒndə/ *noun*. Also †**-do**. M18.
[ORIGIN Unexpl. alt. of Latin *anacandaia* python, for Sinhalese *henakaňdayā* whip snake, perh. from *heňa* lightning + *kaňda* stem.]
Orig., a large python of Ceylon (Sri Lanka). Now, a S. American boa of the genus *Eunectes*, esp. the very large, semi-aquatic *E. murinus*. Also *loosely*, any large constricting snake.

anacreontic /ənakrɪˈɒntɪk/ *adjective & noun*. E17.
[ORIGIN Late Latin *anacreonticus*, from Greek *Anakreōn*, *-ont-* Anacreon: see -IC.]
▸ **A** *adjective*. After the manner of the Greek lyric poet Anacreon (*c* 570–490 BC); convivial, amatory. E17.
▸ **B** *noun*. A poem after the manner of Anacreon; an erotic poem. M17.

anacronym /ənˈakrənɪm/ *noun*. L20.
[ORIGIN from AN-[5] + ACRONYM.]
An acronym of which the majority of people do not know the words from which its constituent letters are taken (e.g. *Nicam*, *scuba*).

anacrusis /anəˈkruːsɪs/ *noun*. Pl. **-cruses** /-ˈkruːsiːz/. M19.
[ORIGIN mod. Latin from Greek *anakrousis* prelude, from *anakrouein*, formed as ANA- + *krouein* to strike.]
1 PROSODY. An unstressed syllable at the beginning of a verse. M19.
2 MUSIC. An unstressed note or unstressed notes before the first strong beat of a phrase. E20.

anadem /ˈanədɛm/ *noun*. *poet*. E17.
[ORIGIN Latin *anadema* from Greek = head-band. Cf. DIADEM.]
A wreath for the head, usu. of flowers; a chaplet, a garland.

anadiplosis /anədɪˈpləʊsɪs/ *noun*. Pl. **-ploses** /-ˈpləʊsiːz/. M16.
[ORIGIN Greek *anadiplōsis*, from *anadiploun* to double: see ANA-, DIPLO-, -OSIS.]
RHETORIC. Reduplication; the beginning of a sentence, line, or clause with the concluding, or any prominent, word of the one preceding; an instance of this.

anadromous /əˈnadrəməs/ *adjective*. M18.
[ORIGIN from Greek *anadromos* running up (of fish entering a river): see ANA-, -OUS.]
ZOOLOGY. Of fish: that ascend rivers from the sea to spawn.

anaemia /əˈniːmɪə/ *noun*. Also ***anemia**. E19.
[ORIGIN mod. Latin from Greek *anaimia*, formed as AN-[5] + *haima* blood: see -IA[1].]
MEDICINE. A deficiency of red blood cells or their haemoglobin, often causing pallor.
pernicious anaemia: see PERNICIOUS *adjective*[1].

anaemic /əˈniːmɪk/ *adjective*. Also ***anemic**. M19.
[ORIGIN from ANAEMIA + -IC.]
Pertaining to or exhibiting anaemia; *fig.* spiritless, weak.

anaerobic /anɛːˈrəʊbɪk/ *adjective*. L19.
[ORIGIN from AN-[5] + AEROBIC.]
BIOLOGY. Living or taking place in the absence of free oxygen; lacking free oxygen.
■ **aˈnaerobe** *noun* any organism that can grow in the absence of free oxygen L19. **anaerobically** *adverb* in the absence of free oxygen L19. **anaerobiˈosis** *noun* life under anaerobic conditions L19.

anaesthesia /anɪsˈθiːzjə/ *noun*. Also ***anes-**. E18.
[ORIGIN mod. Latin from Greek *anaisthēsia*, formed as AN-[5] + *aisthēsis* sensation: see -IA[1].]
Absence of sensation; *esp.* artificially induced inability to feel pain.
general anaesthesia: involving the whole body (with loss of consciousness). **local anaesthesia**: involving a limited part of the body.
■ **anaesthesiˈologist** *noun* an expert in or student of anaesthesiology M20. **anaesthesiˈology** *noun* the branch of knowledge that deals with anaesthesia; the practice of anaesthesia: E20. **anaesthesis** *noun* (*rare*) anaesthesia M19.

anaesthetic /anɪsˈθɛtɪk/ *adjective & noun*. Also ***anes-**. M19.
[ORIGIN from Greek *anaisthētos* without feeling: see ANAESTHESIA, -IC.]
▸ **A** *adjective*. Of, pertaining to, or producing anaesthesia. M19.
▸ **B** *noun*. A substance which produces anaesthesia. M19.

> B. MALAMUD He cut into the pussing sores with a scalpel, without anaesthetic.

general anaesthetic, **local anaesthetic** an agent which produces general, local, anaesthesia.
■ **anaesthetically** *adverb* as or in the manner of an anaesthetic M19.

anaesthetize /əˈniːsθətʌɪz/ *verb trans*. Also ***anes-**; **-ise**. M19.
[ORIGIN formed as ANAESTHETIC + -IZE.]
Deprive of feeling; administer an anaesthetic to.

> *fig.*: A. KOESTLER Deformities . . will only appear as comic if sympathy is anaesthetized.

■ **anaesthetist** *noun* a person who administers anaesthetics L19. **anaesthetiˈzation** *noun* M19.

anagen /ˈanədʒən/ *noun*. E20.
[ORIGIN from ANA- + -GEN]
BIOLOGY. The stage in the life cycle of a hair or hair follicle in which growth takes place.

anaglyph /ˈanəɡlɪf/ *noun*. L16.
[ORIGIN Greek *anagluphē* work in low relief, formed as ANA- + *gluphein* carve.]
1 An embossed ornament in low relief. L16.
2 A composite stereoscopic picture printed in superimposed complementary colours. L19.
■ **anaˈglyphic** *adjective* = ANAGLYPTIC M17.

Anaglypta /anəˈɡlɪptə/ *noun*. Also **a-**. L19.
[ORIGIN Latin *anaglypta* work in low relief: see ANAGLYPTIC.]
(Proprietary name for) a thick embossed wallpaper.

anaglyptic /anəˈɡlɪptɪk/ *adjective*. M17.
[ORIGIN Late Latin *anaglypticus* from Greek *anagluptikos*: see ANAGLYPH, -IC.]
Of or pertaining to embossed anaglyphs or the art of carving in low relief; embossed in low relief.

anagnorisis /anəɡˈnɒrɪsɪs/ *noun*. Pl. **-rises** /-rɪsiːz/. L18.
[ORIGIN Greek *anagnōrisis*.]
Recognition; the denouement in a drama.

†**anagnost** *noun*. E17–E18.
[ORIGIN Latin *anagnostes* from Greek *anagnōstēs* reader.]
A reader, esp. aloud; a prelector.

anagogy /ˈanəɡɒdʒi/ *noun*. LME.
[ORIGIN Analogical alt. of ecclesiastical Latin from Greek *anagōgē* (religious or ecstatic) elevation, mystical feeling, from *anagein* lift up, formed as AN-[4] + *agein* to lead.]
1 Spiritual, mystical, or allegorical interpretation. LME.
†**2** Spiritual elevation, esp. to understand mysteries. *rare*. Only in E18.
■ **anagoge** /anəˈɡəʊdʒi/ *noun* [ecclesiastical Latin] = ANAGOGY 1 M16. **anaˈgogic** *adjective* = ANAGOGICAL LME. **anaˈgogical** *adjective* having a spiritual, mystical, or allegorical interpretation E16. **anaˈgogically** *adverb* L16.

anagram /ˈanəɡram/ *noun & verb*. L16.
[ORIGIN French *anagramme* or mod. Latin *anagramma*, from Greek ANA- + *gramma* letter.]
▸ **A** *noun*. **1** A transposition of the letters of a word or phrase to form another word or phrase. L16.
†**2** *transf.* & *fig.* A transposition; a mutation. M17–E18.
▸ **B** *verb trans*. Infl. **-mm-**. = ANAGRAMMATIZE. *rare*. M17.
■ **anagraˈmmatic** *adjective* = ANAGRAMMATICAL E19. **anagraˈmmatical** *adjective* of or pertaining to an anagram; performed or produced by transposition of letters: E17. **anagraˈmmatically** *adverb* E17. **anaˈgrammatism** *noun* the formation of anagrams E17. **anaˈgrammatist** *noun* a maker of anagrams E17. **anaˈgrammatize** *verb trans.* transpose so as to form an anagram; change into another word or phrase by a different arrangement of letters: L16.

anaklasis *noun* var. of ANACLASIS.

anal /ˈeɪn(ə)l/ *adjective*. M18.
[ORIGIN mod. Latin *analis*: see ANUS, -AL[1]. Cf. French *anal*.]
1 Of or pertaining to the anus; situated near the anus. M18.
2 PSYCHOLOGY. Designating or pertaining to a stage of infantile psychosexual development that is thought to involve a preoccupation with the anus and defecation; of or pertaining to a personality supposed to be the result of fixation at this stage. E20.
– SPECIAL COLLOCATIONS & COMB.: **anal-erotic** *adjective & noun* (PSYCHOLOGY) (**a**) *adjective* pertaining to or characterized by eroticism associated with the anal region; (**b**) *noun* a person characterized by such eroticism. **anal-retentive** PSYCHOLOGY (a person) displaying excessive orderliness and parsimony (interpreted as the result of conflict over toilet-training in infancy). **anal sadism** PSYCHOLOGY abnormal aggressive and destructive tendencies thought to be caused by fixation at the anal stage of development. **anal-sadistic** *adjective* (PSYCHOLOGY) displaying anal sadism.
■ **aˈnality** *noun* (PSYCHOLOGY) anal quality or character M20. **anally** *adverb* via the anus L20.

analcime /əˈnalsiːm/ *noun*. E19.
[ORIGIN French from Greek *analkimos* weak, formed as AN-[5] + *alkimos* stout, brave: the mineral was found to be weakly electrified by friction.]
MINERALOGY. A zeolite occurring as white or faintly coloured trapezohedral crystals.
■ Also **analcite** *noun* M19.

analects /ˈanəlɛkts/ *noun pl*. Also in Latin form **analecta** /anəˈlɛktə/. LME.
[ORIGIN Latin *analecta* from Greek *analekta* things gathered up, from *analegein*, formed as ANA- + *legein* gather.]
†**1** Crumbs, gleanings. LME–E18.
2 *spec.* Literary gleanings. M17.

analemma /anəˈlɛmə/ *noun*. Pl. **-mmae** /-miː/, **-mmas**. M17.
[ORIGIN Latin (Vitruvius) = sundial, from Greek *analēmma* support, (base of a) sundial.]
1 (An astronomical instrument incorporating) an orthographic projection of the sphere on the plane of the meridian. M17.
2 A figure representing the sun's daily declination and the difference between the right ascension of the mean sun and that of the true sun, drawn esp. on terrestrial globes. M19.

analeptic /anəˈlɛptɪk/ *adjective & noun*. L16.
[ORIGIN Late Latin *anale(m)pticus* from Greek *analēptikos* restorative: see -IC. Cf. French *analeptique*.]
MEDICINE. ▸**A** *adjective*. **1** Restorative, strengthening. L16.
2 Able to stimulate the central nervous system. M20.
▸ **B** *noun*. **1** A restorative medicine or food. L17.
2 A stimulant of the central nervous system. M20.

analgesia /an(ə)lˈdʒiːzjə/ *noun*. E18.
[ORIGIN Greek *analgēsia* painlessness, ult. formed as AN-[5] + *algeein* feel pain.]
MEDICINE. Absence or reduction of ability to feel pain; relief of pain, esp. by drugs; medication that acts to relieve pain.
■ **analgesic** /-sɪk/ *adjective & noun* (**a**) *adjective* pertaining to analgesia; (**b**) *noun* an analgesic drug tending to remove pain: L19.

analog *noun* see ANALOGUE.

analogate /əˈnaləɡət/ *noun*. M17.
[ORIGIN from ANALOG(OUS + -ATE[1].]
A thing, concept, etc., shown to be analogous; an analogue.

analogic /anəˈlɒdʒɪk/ *adjective*. M17.
[ORIGIN French *analogique* or Latin *analogicus* from Greek *analogikos*: see ANALOGUE, -IC.]
Of or pertaining to analogy.

analogical /anəˈlɒdʒɪk(ə)l/ *adjective*. L16.
[ORIGIN formed as ANALOGIC + -AL[1].]
†**1** MATH. Proportional; in exact ratio. Only in L16.
2 Of the nature of analogy; according to analogy. E17.
3 Expressing an analogy. E17.
4 = ANALOGOUS 1. *arch.* M17.
5 Of or pertaining to analogy. M19.
■ **analogically** *adverb* L16. **analogicalness** *noun* (*rare*) M18.

analogise *verb* var. of ANALOGIZE.

analogist /əˈnalədʒɪst/ *noun*. M19.
[ORIGIN from ANALOGIZE + -IST.]
A person who argues from or seeks analogies.

analogize /əˈnalədʒʌɪz/ *verb*. Also **-ise**. M17.
[ORIGIN Greek *analogizesthai* reckon up; later from ANALOGY: see -IZE.]
1 *verb intrans.* Employ analogy. M17.
2 *verb trans.* Represent by analogy. M18.
3 *verb intrans.* & *trans.* (Show to) be in harmony *with*. M18.

analogon /əˈnaləɡ(ə)n/ *noun*. Now *rare*. Pl. **-ga** /-ɡə/. E19.
[ORIGIN Irreg. use as noun of neut. sing. of Greek *analogos*: see ANALOGY.]
= ANALOGUE *noun* 1.

analogous /əˈnaləɡəs/ *adjective*. M17.
[ORIGIN from Latin *analogus* (Varro) from Greek *analogos*: see ANALOGY, -OUS.]
1 Having analogy; similar in certain attributes, circumstances, relations, or uses; parallel. (Foll. by *to*, *with*.) M17.
2 = ANALOGICAL 3. *rare*. L17.
■ **analogously** *adverb* in a manner analogous (*to*, *with*); by or according to analogy: M17.

analogue /ˈanəlɒɡ/ *noun & adjective*. Also (*US* & also *gen.* in COMPUTING) **-log**. E19.
[ORIGIN French from Greek ANALOGON.]
▸ **A** *noun*. **1** An analogous or parallel word or thing; a representative in different circumstances; something or someone performing a corresponding part. E19.
2 CHEMISTRY. A compound with a molecular structure closely similar to that of another. M20.
3 A synthetic food product resembling a natural food in taste and texture. L20.
▸ **B** *adjective*. **1** Designating, pertaining to, or operating with signals or information represented by a continuously variable quantity, such as spatial position, voltage, etc. Opp. DIGITAL. M20.
2 Of a clock or watch: showing the time by means of hands or a pointer rather than displayed digits. L20.

analogy /əˈnalədʒi/ *noun*. LME.
[ORIGIN French *analogie* or Latin *analogia* (Varro) from Greek = equality of ratios, proportion (orig. Math.), from *analogos* proportionate, conformable.]
†**1** Appropriateness; correlation; correspondence or adaptation of one thing to another. LME–L18.

> GOLDSMITH Some philosophers have perceived so much analogy to man in the formation of the ocean, that they have not hesitated to assert its being made for him alone.

2 Mathematical proportion; agreement of ratios. M16.
3 Equivalence or likeness of relations; agreement, parallelism; a similarity. (Foll. by *to*, *with*, *between*.) M16.

> BACON Which three parts active have a correspondence and analogy with the three parts speculative. SIR T. BROWNE Who from some analogy of name conceive the Ægyptian Pyramids to have been built for granaries. D. BREWSTER There is still one property of sound, which has its analogy also in light.

4 A figure of speech involving a comparison; a simile, a metaphor. M16.

> HOBBES According to the same analogy, the Dove, and the Fiery Tongues . . might also be called Angels. D. M. THOMAS The Church's dogmas, he said, smiling, were the whalebone of the soul. The analogy delighted her.

5 Grammatical patterning; similarity of formative or constructive linguistic processes. M16. ▸**b** *spec.* Imitation of existing words in forming (the inflections or constructions of) others, without the existence of corresponding intermediate stages of formation. L19.

> **b** JOYCE Unusual polysyllables of foreign origin she interpreted phonetically or by false analogy.

6 *LOGIC.* Resemblance of relations or attributes forming a ground of reasoning; the process of reasoning from parallel cases. E17.

> W. STUBBS Analogy . . is not proof, but illustration.

7 = ANALOGUE *noun* 1. M17.

> LYTTON The child is the analogy of a people yet in childhood.

8 *BIOLOGY.* Resemblance of form or function without fundamental identity. E19.

– PHRASES: **by analogy** after an established pattern or model, by extension. **by analogy with**, **on the analogy of** on the model of, in imitation of. **draw an analogy (between)** make a comparison (between), point out similarities or parallelism (in).

analphabet /an'alfəbɛt/ *adjective & noun. rare.* As noun also **-bete**. L16.

[ORIGIN Latin *analphabetus* from Greek *analphabētos*, formed as AN-[5] + ALPHABET.]

▸ **A** *adjective.* Totally illiterate. L16.

▸ **B** *noun.* A person who is totally illiterate; (in extended use) a person without knowledge of a particular subject etc. L19.

analphabetic /analfə'bɛtɪk/ *adjective.* L19.

[ORIGIN from Greek *analphabētos* (see ANALPHABET) + -IC.]

1 = ANALPHABET *adjective. rare.* L19.

2 *PHONETICS.* Representing sounds by composite signs, not by single letters or symbols. L19.

†**analyse** *noun.* M17–M18.

[ORIGIN French formed as ANALYSIS.]

= ANALYSIS.

analyse /'an(ə)lʌɪz/ *verb trans.* Also ***-lyze**. L16.

[ORIGIN Perh. orig. formed as ANALYSE *noun*; later infl. by French *analyser*.]

1 Ascertain the elements of (something complex); examine minutely the constitution of. L16. ▸**b** Examine critically (a literary or musical composition) in order to bring out essential elements or structure. E17. ▸**c** *CHEMISTRY.* Ascertain the constituents of (a sample of a mixture or compound) or their amounts. M17. ▸**d** *GRAMMAR.* Resolve (a sentence, phrase, etc.) into smaller grammatical elements. E18. ▸**e** *PHILOSOPHY.* Subject to logical or philosophical analysis. E20.

> *New Scientist* Deborah . . has analysed the differences between women's and men's conversational styles. *Which?* The results were then statistically analysed.

†**2** Dissect (material things). E17–L18.

3 *PSYCHOLOGY.* Subject to psychological analysis; *spec.* = PSYCHOANALYSE. E20.

■ **analysa'bility** *noun* the quality of being analysable E20. **analysable** *adjective* able to be analysed M19. **analysand** /ənalɪ'zand/ *noun* a person undergoing psychological analysis M20. **analysandum** /ənalɪ'zandəm/ *noun*, pl. **-da** /-də/, *PHILOSOPHY* that which is to be analysed or clarified E20. **analysans** /ənalɪ'zanz/ *noun* (*PHILOSOPHY*) the clarifying expression in a philosophical analysis M20. **analy'sation** *noun* (now *rare*) analysis M18.

analyser /'an(ə)lʌɪzə/ *noun.* Also ***-lyzer**. E17.

[ORIGIN from ANALYSE *verb* + -ER[1].]

1 A person who analyses; an analyst. E17.

2 An instrument or device for performing analysis; *spec.* a device able to transmit only light polarized in a given direction. M19.

analysis /ə'nalɪsɪs/ *noun.* Pl. **-lyses** /-lɪsiːz/. L16.

[ORIGIN medieval Latin from Greek *analusis*, from *analuein* unloose, formed as ANA- + *luein* loosen.]

▸ **I** *gen.* **1** The resolution or breaking up of something complex into its various simple elements; the exact determination of the elements or components of something complex. L16.

in the final analysis, **in the last analysis**, **in the ultimate analysis** after all due consideration, in the end. ***dimensional analysis***, ***harmonic analysis***, ***linguistic analysis***, ***prosodic analysis***, etc. ***retrograde analysis***: see RETROGRADE *adjective.*

2 A statement of the result of such an operation. M17.

bowling analysis *CRICKET* a statement of a bowler's performance record (overs and maiden overs bowled, runs conceded, wickets taken, etc.).

▸ **II** *spec.* **3** Critical examination of a literary or musical composition in order to bring out essential elements or structure. L16.

4 *PHILOSOPHY.* **a** The resolution, by application of logic etc., of complex structures, facts, propositions, and concepts into their elements. L16. ▸**b** The tracing of things to their source and the resolution of knowledge into its original principles; the discovery of general principles underlying concrete phenomena. E18. ▸**c** The finding of an expression exactly equivalent to a given word, phrase, or sentence, for the purposes of clarification. E20.

a philosophical analysis *spec.* the branch of philosophy that deals with the clarification of existing concepts and knowledge.

5 *GRAMMAR.* The resolution of a sentence, phrase, etc., into smaller grammatical elements. E17.

6 *CHEMISTRY.* The qualitative or quantitative determination by chemical or instrumental means of the constituents of a substance, or of particular components (e.g. contaminants) of a substance. M17.

gravimetric analysis, ***qualitative analysis***, ***quantitative analysis***, ***thermal analysis***, etc.

7 *MATH.* Orig., resolution into simpler propositions already proved or admitted; later, algebra. Now, the part of mathematics which embraces the theory of functions, the use of limits, continuity, and the operations of calculus. M17.

8 *PSYCHOLOGY.* Treatment by the examination of memories, dreams, etc.; *spec.* = PSYCHOANALYSIS. E20.

lay analysis: see LAY *adjective.* ***transactional analysis***: see TRANSACTIONAL 2.

– NOTE: In various senses contrasted with *synthesis*.

analyst /'an(ə)lɪst/ *noun.* M17.

[ORIGIN French *analyste*, from *analyser* ANALYSE *verb*, after nouns in *-iste* -IST from verbs in *-iser* -IZE.]

1 A person engaged or skilled in analysis. M17.

> N. G. CLARK The days are past when every chemist was his own analyst. *Computers & the Humanities* Computational analysts of style. *Times* Analysts say the market may drift for a while.

2 *PSYCHOLOGY.* A person who practises or has been trained in psychological analysis; *spec.* = PSYCHOANALYST. E20.

> W. STYRON My analyst said that my transference problem has passed from the hostile to the affectionate stage.

lay analyst: see LAY *adjective.*

analytic /anə'lɪtɪk/ *noun & adjective.* L16.

[ORIGIN from Latin *analytica* from Greek *analutika* use as noun of neut. pl. adjective by Aristotle as a title of his treatises on logic; as adjective from late Latin *analyticus* from Greek *analutikos*, from *analuein*: see ANALYSIS, -IC.]

▸ **A** *noun sing.* & (usu.) in *pl.* (treated as *sing.*). The use of analysis; *spec.* the part of logic which deals with analysis. Now only with ref. to Aristotle's works. L16.

▸ **B** *adjective.* **1** Of or pertaining to analysis. E17.

analytic proposition *PHILOSOPHY* a proposition the truth of which depends on the definition of the terms employed, a self-evident proposition.

2 = ANALYTICAL 1. E19.

> M. MITCHELL So still was her face as she stared at Stuart that he, never analytic, took it for granted that she was merely surprised.

3 *LINGUISTICS.* Of a language: = ISOLATING. E19.

> M. L. SAMUELS The largest grammatical restructuring known in the history of most European languages—the so-called change from synthetic to analytic structure.

4 *PSYCHOLOGY.* Seeking to analyse ideas and their origins; of, pertaining to, or employing psychological analysis; *spec.* = PSYCHOANALYTIC. M19.

5 *MATH.* = HOLOMORPHIC. L19.

■ **analyticity** /an(ə)lɪ'tɪsɪti/ *noun* the property of being analytic M20.

analytical /anə'lɪtɪk(ə)l/ *adjective.* E16.

[ORIGIN from late Latin *analyticus* (see ANALYTIC) + -AL[1].]

1 Employing analysis; employing the methods of analysis. E16.

analytical geometry geometry involving the use of algebra; coordinate geometry.

2 Of or pertaining to analysis. M17.

3 *LINGUISTICS.* Of a language: = ISOLATING. E19.

4 *PSYCHOLOGY.* = ANALYTIC 4. M19.

analytical psychology: *spec.* that of Jung.

■ **analytically** *adverb* M17.

analyze *verb*, **analyzer** *noun* see ANALYSE *verb*, ANALYSER.

Anamese *adjective & noun* var. of ANNAMESE.

anamnesis /anəm'niːsɪs/ *noun.* Pl. **-neses** /-'niːsiːz/. L16.

[ORIGIN Greek *anamnēsis* remembrance.]

1 The recalling of things past; reminiscence. L16.

2 *CHRISTIAN CHURCH.* That part of the Eucharistic canon in which the sacrifice of Christ is recalled. L19.

3 A patient's account of his or her medical history. L19.

■ **anamnestic** /-'nɛstɪk/ *noun & adjective* †(**a**) *noun* a medicine to aid the memory; (**b**) *adjective* recalling to mind, aiding the memory; pertaining to or of the nature of anamnesis: E18.

anamorphic /anə'mɔːfɪk/ *adjective.* E20.

[ORIGIN from ANA- + Greek *morphē* form + -IC.]

1 Of or pertaining to an anamorphosis. E20. ▸**b** Of a lens: that produces an image distorted in one dimension. M20.

2 *BOTANY & ZOOLOGY.* Characterized by anamorphosis. M20.

anamorphosis /anə'mɔːfəsɪs/ *noun.* Pl. **-phoses** /-fəsiːz/. E18.

[ORIGIN Greek *anamorphōsis* transformation: see ANA-, MORPHOSIS.]

1 A distorted projection or drawing of anything, which appears normal when viewed from a particular point or by means of a suitable mirror. E18.

2 *BOTANY & ZOOLOGY.* Progression to a higher type. Now *spec.* development of the adult form through a series of small changes. M19.

■ **anamorphoscope** *noun* a mirror designed to give a correct image of an anamorphosis L19.

†**anan** *adverb* var. of ANON *adverb.*

ananas /ə'nɑːnəs/ *noun.* L16.

[ORIGIN French & Spanish from Portuguese *ananás* from Guarani *naná*.]

The pineapple plant (*Ananas comosus*) or fruit.

anandamide /ə'nandəmʌɪd/ *noun.* L20.

[ORIGIN from Sanskrit *ā-nandā* happiness, joy + AMIDE.]

BIOCHEMISTRY. An amide of arachidonic acid that is a naturally occurring cannabinid receptor agonist, and is also found in some plant products such as chocolate.

anandrous /ə'nandrəs/ *adjective.* M19.

[ORIGIN from Greek *anandros* without males, from *an-* AN-[5] + *andr-*, *anēr* man + -OUS.]

BOTANY. Having no stamens.

anapaest /'anəpiːst, -pɛst/ *noun.* Also ***-pest**. Also (earlier) in Latin form †**-p(a)estus**. L16.

[ORIGIN Latin *anapaestus* from Greek *anapaistos* reversed, formed as ANA- + *paiein* to strike: so called because it is the reverse of a dactyl.]

PROSODY. **1** A foot consisting of two short syllables followed by one long syllable or, in English etc., of two unstressed syllables followed by a stressed syllable. L16.

2 A verse composed of or containing such feet. M19.

anapaestic /anə'piːstɪk, -'pɛst-/ *adjective & noun.* Also ***-pest-**. L17.

[ORIGIN Late Latin *anapaesticus* from Greek *anapaistikos*: see ANAPAEST, -IC.]

PROSODY. ▸**A** *adjective.* Composed of or containing anapaests; of or pertaining to an anapaest or anapaests. L17.

▸ **B** *noun.* An anapaestic verse or line. Usu. in *pl.* L17.

†**anapaestus** *noun*, **anapest** *noun*, **anapestic** *adjective & noun*, †**anapestus** *noun* see ANAPAEST, ANAPAESTIC *adjective & noun.*

anaphora /ə'naf(ə)rə/ *noun.* L16.

[ORIGIN Branch I from Latin from Greek = repetition, formed as ANA- + *pherein* carry; branch II from late Greek.]

▸ **I 1** *RHETORIC.* The repetition of the same word or phrase in several successive clauses. L16.

2 *LINGUISTICS.* The use of an expression which refers to or stands for an earlier word or group of words. M20.

▸ **II 3** *CHRISTIAN CHURCH.* The part of the Eucharist at which the oblation is made. M18.

■ **anaphoric** /anə'fɒrɪk/, **anaphorical** /anə'fɒrɪk(ə)l/ *adjectives* of, pertaining to, or constituting grammatical anaphora; referring to or standing for an earlier word or words: E20. **ana'phorically** *adverb* M20.

anaphrodisiac /anafrə'dɪzɪak/ *adjective & noun.* E19.

[ORIGIN from AN-[5] + APHRODISIAC.]

(A drug) that reduces sexual desire.

anaphylaxis /anəfɪ'laksɪs/ *noun.* E20.

[ORIGIN mod. Latin, from Greek ANA- + *phulaxis* watching, guarding.]

MEDICINE. An acute allergic reaction to an antigen on reintroduction.

■ **anaphylactic** *adjective* of or pertaining to anaphylaxis; ***anaphylactic shock***, extreme reaction to a second dose of an antigen: E20. **anaphylactoid** *adjective* resembling anaphylaxis or anaphylactic shock E20.

anaplasmosis /anəplaz'məʊsɪs/ *noun.* Pl. **-moses** /-'məʊsiːz/. E20.

[ORIGIN from mod. Latin *Anaplasma* (see below) + -OSIS.]

VETERINARY MEDICINE. A disease of cattle and other animals due to infection with micro-organisms of the genus *Anaplasma*, and characterized chiefly by anaemia.

anaplerosis /anəplɪ'rəʊsɪs/ *noun. rare.* Pl. **-roses** /-'rəʊsiːz/. L17.

[ORIGIN Greek *anaplērōsis*, from *anaplēroun* fill up: see -OSIS.]

The filling up of a deficiency (formerly *spec.* (*MEDICINE*) of tissue).

■ **anaplerotic** *adjective & noun* (**a**) *adjective* promoting anaplerosis; †(**b**) *noun* an anaplerotic medicine: E18.

anapsid /ə'napsɪd/ *adjective & noun.* M20.

[ORIGIN mod. Latin *Anapsida* pl. (see below), formed as AN-[5] + Greek (*h*)*apsid-*, (*h*)*apsis* arch: see -ID[3].]

ZOOLOGY. ▸**A** *adjective.* Of, pertaining to, or characteristic of the subclass Anapsida of reptiles lacking temporal openings in the skull. M20.

▸ **B** *noun.* An anapsid reptile. M20.

anaptyxis /anəp'tɪksɪs/ *noun.* L19.

[ORIGIN mod. Latin from Greek *anaptuxis* unfolding, formed as ANA- + *ptuxis* folding.]

PHONETICS. The development of a vowel between two consonants.

■ **anaptyctic** *adjective* L19.

anarch /'anɑːk/ *noun.* M17.

[ORIGIN Greek *anarkhos* without a chief, formed as AN-[5] + -ARCH.]

1 An instigator of anarchy, a leader of revolt. *poet.* M17.

2 An anarchist. L19.

■ **a'narchal** *adjective* (*rare*) = ANARCHICAL E19.

anarchism /ˈanəkɪz(ə)m/ *noun*. **M17.**
[**ORIGIN** In early use formed as **ANARCH** + **-ISM**; later after French *anarchisme*.]
The principles or practice of anarchy or anarchists.

anarchist /ˈanəkɪst/ *noun*. **M17.**
[**ORIGIN** In early use formed as **ANARCH** + **-IST**; later after French *anarchiste*.]
An advocate of anarchy; a person who believes that all government should be abolished.
■ **anarˈchistic** *adjective* associated with or tending to anarchy **L19.**

anarchy /ˈanəki/ *noun*. **M16.**
[**ORIGIN** medieval Latin *anarchia* from Greek *anarkhia*, formed as **ANARCH**: see **-Y**[3].]
1 Absence of government in a society (orig. as a source of civil disorder, later also as a political ideal); a state of political or social confusion; absolute freedom of the individual. **M16.**

> CARLYLE Without sovereigns, true sovereigns, temporal and spiritual, I see nothing possible but an anarchy; the hatefullest of things. C. V. WEDGWOOD Meanwhile the country, lacking any accepted government, slipped towards anarchy. G. K. ROBERTS *Anarchy* The organisation of society on the basis of voluntary cooperation, and especially without the agency of political institutions, i.e. the state.

2 *transf.* & *fig.* Absence or non-recognition of authority in any sphere; moral or intellectual conflict; a state of disorder; chaos. **M17.**

> A. COWLEY Thousand worse Passions then possesst The Interregnum of my Breast. Bless me from such an Anarchy! CHESTERFIELD Our language is . . in a state of anarchy. M. BEERBOHM An anarchy of small curls.

■ **aˈnarchial** *adjective* (now *rare*) = **ANARCHICAL E18.** **aˈnarchic** *adjective* = **ANARCHICAL L18.** **aˈnarchical** *adjective* of or pertaining to anarchy; disorderly; unregulated: **L16.** **aˈnarchically** *adverb* **L19.** **anarchize** *verb trans.* (*rare*) reduce to anarchy **E19.** **aˈnarcho-** *combining form* [-**O**-] involving anarchy and, used esp. in ***anarcho-syndicalism***, ***anarcho-syndicalist*** *nouns* (a supporter of) a movement aiming at the transfer of the means of industrial production to unions of workers **M20.**

anarthria /əˈnɑːθrɪə/ *noun*. **L19.**
[**ORIGIN** Greek = lack of vigour, formed as **ANARTHROUS**: see **-IA**[1].]
MEDICINE. Inability to articulate in speech, usu. as a result of cerebral disease.

anarthrous /əˈnɑːθrəs/ *adjective*. **E19.**
[**ORIGIN** from Greek **AN-**[5] + *arthron* joint, definite article + **-OUS**.]
GREEK GRAMMAR. Of a noun: used without the article.

anasarca /anəˈsɑːkə/ *noun*. Now *rare*. **LME.**
[**ORIGIN** medieval Latin *anasarc(h)a* from Greek *anasarx* adjective (Galen) = *ana sarka* (*ana-* up, *sarx* flesh).]
MEDICINE. A generalized oedema of subcutaneous tissue, usu. with accumulation of fluid in serous cavities.

> *fig.*: DISRAELI An aged power . . which . . looked with complacency on its own unnatural greatness, its political anasarca.

■ **anasarcous** *adjective* of the nature of or exhibiting anasarca **L17.**

Anasazi /anəˈsɑːzi/ *noun* & *adjective*. **M20.**
[**ORIGIN** Navajo *anaaśází*, lit. 'enemy ancestors'.]
ARCHAEOLOGY. ▸**A** *noun*. Pl. same, **-s**. A member of the Basket Maker and Pueblo peoples of northern Arizona and New Mexico, considered as together forming one continuous civilization; the culture of these peoples, the classic phase of which is dated between *c* 1050 and 1300.
▸**B** *adjective*. Of the Anasazi or their culture.

anastatic /anəˈstatɪk/ *adjective*. *obsolete* exc. *hist.* **M19.**
[**ORIGIN** from Greek *anastatos* ppl formation on *anistanai* set up + **-IC**.]
Designating a lithographic process of printing reproductions from slightly raised metallic plates.

anastigmatic /anəstɪgˈmatɪk/ *adjective*. **L19.**
[**ORIGIN** from **AN-**[5] + **ASTIGMATIC**.]
Of a lens or lens system: free from astigmatism.
■ **aˈnastigmat** *noun* [-**AT**[2]] an anastigmatic lens or lens-system **L19.**

anastomosis /ənastəˈməʊsɪs/ *noun*. Pl. **-moses** /-ˈməʊsiːz/. **L16.**
[**ORIGIN** Greek *anastomōsis*, from *anastomoun* provide with a mouth or outlet, from **ANA-** + *stoma* mouth: see **-OSIS**.]
(A) cross-connection between two vessels, channels, branches, etc. (orig., blood vessels). Also (**MEDICINE**), (a) surgical formation of an interconnecting passage between blood vessels, hollow viscera, etc.
■ **aˈnastomose** *verb trans.* (now *rare*) & *intrans.* connect or communicate by anastomosis **L17.**

anastomotic /ənastəˈmɒtɪk/ *adjective* & *noun*. **M17.**
[**ORIGIN** Greek *anastomōtikos* proper for opening: see **ANASTOMOSIS**, **-OTIC**.]
▸**A** *adjective*. †**1** Of a medicine: designed to open the mouths of vessels. **M17–M19.**
2 Of or pertaining to anastomosis. **M19.**
▸†**B** *noun*. An anastomotic medicine. Only in **E18.**

anastrophe /əˈnastrəfi/ *noun*. **M16.**
[**ORIGIN** Greek *anastrophē* turning back, formed as **ANA-** + *strephein* to turn.]
RHETORIC. Inversion or unusual order of words or clauses.

anatase /ˈanəteɪz/ *noun*. **E19.**
[**ORIGIN** French from Greek *anatasis* extension, formed as **ANA-** + *teinein* to stretch: with allus. to the length of the crystals.]
MINERALOGY. One of the tetragonal forms of titanium dioxide (cf. **RUTILE**), found usu. as brown dipyramidal crystals.

anathema /əˈnaθəmə/ *noun*. Pl. **-mas**, in sense 3 also **anathemata** /anəˈθiːmətə/. **E16.**
[**ORIGIN** ecclesiastical Latin (as senses 1 and 2) from Greek, orig. 'a thing devoted' (sense 3), later 'an accursed thing' (see *Romans* 9:3), orig. var. of *anathēma* votive offering, from *anatithenai* set up.]
1 Something or someone accursed or assigned to damnation; something or someone detested. **E16.**

> BACON He would wish to be an Anathema from Christ, for the Salvation of his Brethren. J. GALSWORTHY Let them go! They are as much anathema to me as I, no doubt, am to them.

anathema maranatha /marəˈnaɪθə/ [Greek *Maran atha* = Aramaic *māran 'ātā* come, Lord] (taken as) a portentously intensified anathema.
2 The formal act or formula of consigning to damnation; the curse of God; the curse of the Church, excommunicating a person or denouncing a doctrine etc.; a denunciation of alleged impiety, heresy, etc.; an imprecation. **L16.**

> BURKE The divine thunders out his anathemas. LYTTON 'Confound the man!' was my mental anathema. GLADSTONE The Pope . . has condemned the slave trade—but no more heed is paid to his anathema than to the passing wind. W. FAULKNER Gaunt, fanaticfaced country preachers thundered anathema from the rustic pulpit at his oblivious and unregenerate head.

3 [Greek *anathēma*.] Something devoted or consecrated to divine use. Now *rare*. **L16.**

> S. BIRCH The little figures . . may have been votive offerings to the gods, such anathemata being offered by the poor.

■ †**anathem** *noun* = **ANATHEMA** 1, 2 **M16–L18.** **anatheˈmatical** *noun* & *adjective* (*rare*) †(**a**) *noun* = **ANATHEMA** 2; (**b**) *adjective* of the nature of an anathema: **L16.** **anathematism** *noun* a statement of anathema, an ecclesiastical denunciation **M16.** ˈ**anatheme** *noun* (now *rare*) = **ANATHEMA** 3 **M17.** **anathemize** *verb trans.* (*rare*) = **ANATHEMATIZE** 1 **L17.**

anathematize /əˈnaθəmətʌɪz/ *verb*. Also **-ise**. **M16.**
[**ORIGIN** Old French & mod. French *anathématiser* from ecclesiastical Latin *anathematizare* from Greek *anathematizein*, from *anathema*: see **ANATHEMA**, **-IZE**.]
1 *verb trans.* Pronounce an anathema against; denounce; curse. **M16.**
2 *verb intrans.* Pronounce anathemas; curse. **M18.**
■ **aˌnathematiˈzation** *noun* **M16.** **anathematizer** *noun* (*rare*) **M17.**

anatocism /əˈnatəsɪz(ə)m/ *noun*. Now *rare* or *obsolete*. **M17.**
[**ORIGIN** Latin *anatocismus* (Cicero) from Greek *anatokismos*, from *tokos* interest: see **ANA-**, **-ISM**.]
Compound interest.

Anatolian /anəˈtəʊlɪən/ *adjective* & *noun*. Also †**Nat-**. **L16.**
[**ORIGIN** from *Anatolia* (cf. Greek *anatolē* east) Asia Minor + **-AN**.]
▸**A** *adjective*. Of or pertaining to Anatolia, now the Asian portion of Turkey, or its inhabitants. **L16.**
▸**B** *noun*. A native or inhabitant of Anatolia. **L16.**
■ Also **Anatolic** *adjective* **M19.**

anatomical /anəˈtɒmɪk(ə)l/ *adjective*. **L16.**
[**ORIGIN** from French *anatomique* or late Latin *anatomicus*: see **ANATOMY**, **-ICAL**.]
1 Of or pertaining to the study or practice of anatomy. **L16.**
2 Of or pertaining to the anatomy; structural. **E18.**
■ **anatomic** *adjective* anatomical **L17.** **anatomically** *adverb* **M17.** **anatomico-** *combining form* [-**O**-] anatomical and —, as ***anatomico-physiological*** *adjective* **L18.**

anatomise *verb* var. of **ANATOMIZE**.

anatomist /əˈnatəmɪst/ *noun*. **M16.**
[**ORIGIN** French *anatomiste* or medieval Latin deriv. of *anatomizare* **ANATOMIZE**: see **-IST**.]
1 A person who dissects dead bodies; a person skilled in (esp. human) anatomy. **M16.**
2 *fig.* A person who dissects or analyses a subject. **L16.**

anatomize /əˈnatəmʌɪz/ *verb*. Also **-ise**. **LME.**
[**ORIGIN** French *anatomiser* or medieval Latin *anatomizare*: see **ANATOMY**, **-IZE**.]
1 *verb trans.* & *intrans.* Dissect; cut up (an animal or vegetable body) in order to display the position, structure, and relations of its various parts. **LME.**
2 *verb trans.* *fig.* Reveal in detail; analyse. **L16.**
†**3** *verb trans.* Analyse chemically. **E–M17.**
■ **anatomiˈzation** *noun* **M17.** **anatomizer** *noun* **M17.**

anatomy /əˈnatəmi/ *noun*. **LME.**
[**ORIGIN** Old French & mod. French *anatomie* from late Latin *anatomia* from Greek, formed as **ANA-** + **-TOMY**.]
1 The science of the structure of the bodies of humans, animals, and plants; a treatise in this field. **LME.**

> C. P. SNOW The anatomy they learn is sheer unscientific nonsense.

MORBID *anatomy*.
2 Anatomical structure. **LME.**
†**3** A body or part anatomized; a subject for dissection. **L15–M18.**
4 The artificial separation of the parts of a human, animal, or vegetable body, in order to discover their position, structure, and relations; dissection. **M16.**

> ADDISON Curious observations which he had lately made in an anatomy of an human body.

5 *fig.* Detailed examination or analysis; structure, organization. **M16.**

> ROBERT BURTON The Anatomy of Melancholy: what it is [etc.]. A. SAMPSON Anatomy of Britain.

†**6** A model or drawing of the human body as dissected. **M16–M18.**
7 A skeleton; a corpse of skin and bone, a mummy; an emaciated being. Cf. **ATOMY** *noun*[1]. *arch.* **L16.**

> DISRAELI Death in the Gothic form of a gaunt anatomy parading through the universe. CARLYLE The thread-paper Duchess of Kendal . . poor old anatomy. *fig.*: J. A. FROUDE What lean and shrivelled anatomies the best of such descriptions would seem!

8 The bodily frame. Chiefly *joc.* **L16.**

> J. G. LOCKHART Brown leathern gaiters buttoned upon his nether anatomy. T. H. WHITE You may grow old and trembling in your anatomies.

†**9** Chemical analysis. **E17–E18.**

anatopism /əˈnatəpɪz(ə)m/ *noun*. *rare*. **E19.**
[**ORIGIN** from Greek **ANA-** + *topos* place + **-ISM**.]
A putting of a thing out of its proper place.

anatropous /əˈnatrəpəs/ *adjective*. **M19.**
[**ORIGIN** formed as **AN-**[5] + **ATROPOUS**.]
BOTANY. Of an ovule: inverted on its funicle.

anatto *noun* var. of **ANNATTO**.

Anaxagorean /anəkˌsagəˈriːən/ *adjective*. **L16.**
[**ORIGIN** from Latin *Anaxagoras* (see below) + **-EAN**.]
Of or pertaining to the Greek philosopher Anaxagoras (fl. during the 5th cent. BC), who taught that matter was eternal but was combined into bodies by a supreme intelligence.

anbury /ˈanb(ə)ri/ *noun*. Now *dial.* Also **am-** /ˈam-/. **L16.**
[**ORIGIN** Perh. from *ang-* in Old English *angnægl* **AGNAIL**, *angseta* carbuncle, pimple + **BERRY** *noun*[1] in the sense of a red mark or pustule.]
1 A soft tumour or spongy wart on horses, oxen, etc. **L16.**
2 Clubroot of turnips or cabbages. **M18.**

ANC *abbreviation*.
African National Congress.

-ance /(ə)ns/ *suffix*.
[**ORIGIN** French from Latin (i) *-antia*, from pres. ppl stems in *-ant-* **-ANT**[1], (ii) *-entia*: see **-ENCE**.]
Forming nouns of quality (or instances of it), as ***arrogance***, ***relevance***, or of action, as ***assistance***, ***penance***. Since the 16th cent. many words ending in *-ance* from French have been altered back to *-ence* after Latin, and more recent words have taken *-ance* or *-ence* according to the Latin vowel (hence much inconsistency, as ***dependence***, ***dependance***, ***resistance***, ***subsistence***). Through such pairs as ***appear***, ***appearance*** it became to some extent a living suffix and was appended to verbs of non-Romance origin, as ***forbear***, ***forbearance***, ***hinder***, ***hindrance***, ***rid***, ***riddance***. Now a common formative element in techn. terms, as ***absorbance***. Cf. **-ANCY**.

ancestor /ˈansɛstə/ *noun*. **ME.**
[**ORIGIN** Old French *ancestre* (mod. *ancêtre*) from Latin *antecessor*, formed as **ANTE-** + *cess-* pa. ppl stem of *cedere* go: assim. to **-OR**.]
1 A person, usu. more remote than a grandparent, from whom one is descended; a forefather. Also *transf.* & *fig.*, an animal from which another is (remotely) descended; a source, a precursor. **ME.**

> H. H. MILMAN St. Peter . . the spiritual ancestor of the Bishop of Rome. M. C. SELF It is believed that his [the Suffolk's] ancestors were the horses of the Norsemen. F. FITZGERALD In the rites of ancestor worship the child imitated the gestures of his grandfather.

2 **LAW.** A person who precedes another in the course of inheritance. **E17.**
3 An animal or other organism from which another has evolved. **M19.**

> B. J. WILLIAMS The reptilian ancestors of mammals.

■ **anceˈstorial** *adjective* (now *rare*) = **ANCESTRAL M17.** **ancestress** *noun* a female ancestor **L16.**

ancestral /anˈsɛstr(ə)l/ *adjective*. **LME.**
[**ORIGIN** Old French *ancestrel* (mod. *-al*), formed as **ANCESTOR** + **-AL**[1].]
1 Of, pertaining to, or inherited from ancestors. **LME.**

> COLERIDGE Kubla heard from far Ancestral voices prophesying war. G. ORWELL Why should one feel it to be intolerable unless one had some kind of ancestral memory that things had once been different?

2 Of, pertaining to, or constituting an evolutionary ancestor; earlier in a line of (evolutionary) development. (Foll. by *to*.) **M19.**

> D. MORRIS In the Old World . . ancestral apes were spreading over a wide forest area.

■ **ancestrally** *adverb* **L19.**

ancestrula /an'sɛstrʊlə/ *noun.* Pl. **-lae** /-liː/, **-las**. E20.
[ORIGIN mod. Latin, irreg. from French ANCESTRAL + Latin *-ula* fem. dim. suffix.]
ZOOLOGY. The original zooecium in a bryozoan colony.

ancestry /'ansɛstri/ *noun.* ME.
[ORIGIN Alt. of Old French *ancesserie* after ANCESTOR: see -Y³, -RY.]
1 Ancestral lineage or descent; *spec.* noble, aristocratic, or ancient descent. Also *fig.*, origin, background. ME.
ADDISON Title and ancestry render a good man more illustrious. W. S. GILBERT I can trace my ancestry back to a protoplasmal primordial atomic globule. M. C. SELF Somewhere in the ancestry of Janus there must have been a happy 'nick' which gave him the peculiar characteristics of the Quarter horse. J. K. GALBRAITH The explanation of consumer behaviour has its ancestry in a much older problem.
2 *collect.* One's ancestors. *arch.* ME.
W. COWPER Our ancestry, a gallant Christian race.
■ **an'cestrial** *adjective* (*rare*) = ANCESTRAL M17.

ancho /'antʃəʊ/ *noun.* Orig. and chiefly *US.* Pl. **-os**. E20.
[ORIGIN from Mexican Spanish (*chile*) *ancho*, lit. 'wide (chilli)', in allusion to its shape.]
A large aromatic variety of chilli, used (usu. dried) in Mexican cuisine; the plant bearing this. Also more fully ***ancho chilli***, ***chile ancho***.

anchor /'aŋkə/ *noun*¹.
[ORIGIN Old English *ancor*, *-cer*, *-cra* (= Old Frisian, Middle & mod. Low German, Middle Dutch *anker*, late Old High German *anchar* (German *Anker*), Old Norse *akkeri*) from Latin *ancora* from Greek *agkura*. In Middle English reinforced by Old French & mod. French *ancre*. The present spelling follows the erron. Latin *anchora*.]
1 An appliance for holding a ship etc. fixed in a particular place by mooring it to the bottom of the sea or river, or for similarly holding a balloon etc. by mooring it to the ground; a heavy metal structure traditionally composed of a long shank with a ring at one end for the cable and at the other end two arms or flukes, tending upwards, with barbs on each side. OE.
kedge anchor, ***mushroom anchor***, etc.
2 *fig.* A ground or source of confidence or security. LME.
3 Any contrivance or instrument that fulfils a purpose similar to that of an anchor. M16. ▸**b** In *pl.* The brakes of a vehicle. *colloq.* M20.
4 Something resembling an anchor in shape, as an architectural moulding. M17.
5 In full ***anchorman***, ***anchorperson***, ***anchorwoman***. A person playing a vital part, as the end member of a tug-of-war team, the last runner in a relay race, the compère of a broadcast programme, etc. E20.
– PHRASES: **at anchor** moored by an anchor. **bring to anchor** moor with an anchor. **cast anchor**, **come to anchor** let down the anchor(s). ***crown and anchor***: see CROWN *noun*. **drop anchor** = ***cast anchor*** above. ***foul anchor***: see FOUL *adjective*. ***fouled anchor***: see FOUL *verb*. SHEET ANCHOR. **weigh anchor** take up the anchor(s).
– COMB.: **anchor-hold** *noun*¹ the hold or grip that an anchor takes; a place for anchoring; *fig.* a firm hold, a point clung to, a ground of confidence, security, etc.; ***anchorman***, ***anchorperson***: see sense 5 above; **anchor plate** a heavy piece of timber or metal serving as a support, e.g. for the cables of a suspension bridge; **anchor ring** (*a*) the ring through which the cable is attached to an anchor; (*b*) GEOMETRY a torus of circular cross-section; ***anchorwoman***: see sense 5 above.
■ **anchorless** *adjective* without an anchor; *fig.* without a firm hold, drifting: M19.

anchor /'aŋkə/ *noun*². Long *arch.* or *hist.*
[ORIGIN Old English *ancra*, *ancor*, *-cer* perh. through Old Irish *anchara*, *angcoire* from ecclesiastical Latin *anchoreta* ANCHORITE.]
An anchorite; an anchoress.
– COMB.: **anchor-hold** *noun*² the cell or retreat of an anchorite.

anchor /'aŋkə/ *verb.* ME.
[ORIGIN Old French & mod. French *ancrer* = medieval Latin *anc(h)orare*: see ANCHOR *noun*¹.]
1 *verb trans.* Secure (a ship etc.) by means of an anchor; place at or bring to anchor. ME.
SOUTHEY It was not possible to anchor the fleet. SCOTT FITZGERALD An enormous couch on which two young women were buoyed up as though upon an anchored balloon.
2 *verb trans. transf. & fig.* Fix as with an anchor, fix firmly. ME.
SHAKES. *Rich. III* Till that my nails were anchor'd in thine eyes. E. O'NEILL Green seaweed anchored to a rock. J. B. PRIESTLEY I didn't feel quite right in my mind, I wasn't firmly anchored to reality.
3 *verb intrans.* Cast anchor; come to anchor; be moored by means of an anchor. L16.
MILTON Sea-faring men . . whose Bark by chance Or Pinnace anchors in a craggy Bay. *fig.*: SHAKES. *Meas. for M.* Heaven hath my empty words, Whilst my invention . . Anchors on Isabel.
4 *verb trans. & intrans.* Act as anchorperson of (a broadcast programme). M20.

anchorage /'aŋk(ə)rɪdʒ/ *noun*¹. ME.
[ORIGIN from ANCHOR *noun*¹ + -AGE. Cf. French *ancrage*.]
1 A toll or charge for anchoring. *arch.* ME.
2 a Conditions admitting of anchoring; a place at which to anchor. L16. ▸**b** *transf. & fig.* A point of support or rest; a hold; something on which to depend or repose. L17.
b J. A. FROUDE The Church anchorage no longer tenable in the change of wind, and the new anchorage in the Bible as yet partially discovered and imperfectly sounded. J. TYNDALL I crossed the fissure, obtained the anchorage at the other side, and helped the others over.
3 A set of anchors. *rare.* L16.
SHAKES. *Tit. A.* The bark . . Returns with precious lading to the bay From whence at first she weigh'd her anchorage.
4 The action or process of anchoring; the condition of lying at anchor. E17.

anchorage /'aŋk(ə)rɪdʒ/ *noun*². Now *arch.* or *hist.* L16.
[ORIGIN from ANCHOR *noun*² + -AGE. Cf. *hermitage*, *parsonage*.]
The cell or retreat of an anchorite.

anchoress /'aŋkərɛs/ *noun.* Also (*arch.*) **ancress** /'aŋkrɛs/. LME.
[ORIGIN from ANCHOR *noun*² + -ESS¹.]
A female anchorite; a nun.

anchorite /'aŋkərʌɪt/ *noun.* Also **anchoret** /'aŋkərɪt/, (esp. in sense 2) **anachoret** /ə'nakərɪt/. LME.
[ORIGIN medieval Latin *anc(h)orita*, ecclesiastical Latin *anchoreta* from ecclesiastical Greek *anakhōrētēs*, from *anakhōrein* retire, retreat, formed as ANA- + *khōrein* withdraw, from *khōra*, *khōros* place. Superseding ANCHOR *noun*².]
1 A person who has withdrawn from the world, usu. for religious reasons; a hermit, a recluse. LME.
2 ECCLESIASTICAL HISTORY. A recluse of the early Eastern Church. L16.
3 *gen.* A person of solitary or secluded habits. E17.
■ **ancho'retic** *adjective* M17. **anchoritic** /-'rɪt-/ *adjective* M19. **anchoritical** /-'rɪt-/ *adjective* M17.

anchoveta /antʃə'vɛtə/ *noun.* M20.
[ORIGIN Spanish, dim. of *anchova*: see ANCHOVY.]
A Pacific anchovy, *Cetengraulis mysticetus*, used as bait or to make fishmeal.

anchovy /'antʃəvi, an'tʃəʊvi/ *noun.* L16.
[ORIGIN Spanish & Portuguese *ancho(v)a*, of unknown origin.]
A small, mainly Mediterranean fish of the herring family, *Engraulis encrasicholus*, which has a rich flavour and is usu. eaten pickled or in pastes, sauces, etc. Also, any of numerous related fishes.
– COMB.: **anchovy pear** (the edible fruit of) the W. Indian tree *Grias cauliflora*.

anchusa /ən'kuːsə, -'tʃuː-/ *noun.* M16.
[ORIGIN Latin (Pliny) from Greek *agkhousa*, *egkh-*.]
Any plant of the genus *Anchusa*, of the borage family; *esp.* the plant *A. azurea*, grown for its deep blue flowers.

anchylose *verb*, **anchylosis** *noun* vars. of ANKYLOSE, ANKYLOSIS.

†**anciency** *noun.* M16–L19.
[ORIGIN Alt. of ANCIENTY as if ANCIENT *adjective* were of ppl origin, after *decent*, *decency*, etc.]
Ancientness; antiquity.

ancien régime /ɑ̃sjɛ̃ reʒim/ *noun phr.* Pl. **-s -s** (pronounced same). L18.
[ORIGIN French = former regime.]
The system of government in France before the Revolution of 1789. Also *transf.*, the old system or style of things.

ancient /'eɪnʃ(ə)nt/ *noun*¹. In senses 2, 6 also **A-**. LME.
[ORIGIN from the adjective.]
1 An old man (or animal); a patriarch. *arch.* LME.
2 A person who lived in times long past; a Greek or Roman of classical antiquity, esp. an author. Freq. in ***the ancients***. L15.
†**3** A senior, *one's* superior in age. M16–M17.
†**4** An ancestor. *rare.* M16–E19.
5 A person holding a senior position, an elder, a dignitary. *arch.* M16.
6 ***the Ancient of Days***, God. M16.

ancient /'eɪnʃ(ə)nt/ *noun*². *arch.* M16.
[ORIGIN Alt. of ENSIGN *noun* by assoc. with early forms of ANCIENT *noun*¹.]
1 A standard or flag; in *pl.*, insignia, colours. M16.
2 A standard-bearer. L16.

ancient /'eɪnʃ(ə)nt/ *adjective.* LME.
[ORIGIN Anglo-Norman *auncien*, Old French & mod. French *ancien*, ult. from Latin ANTE- + *-anus* -AN.]
1 a Belonging to times long past. LME. ▸**b** Former, earlier, bygone, (not necessarily referring to *long* ago). *arch.* L15. ▸**c** *spec.* (Also **A-**.) Belonging or pertaining to the period before the fall of the Western Roman Empire in AD 476. E17.
a D. H. LAWRENCE The grand, pagan twilight of the valleys, . . with a sense of ancient gods. **b** BUNYAN Thy antient kindness. POPE They mourn'd their ancient leader lost. **c** ADDISON Statuary and Architecture both Ancient and Modern.
a ancient Briton: see BRITON *noun* 2. ***ancient Greek***: see GREEK *noun & adjective*. **c ancient history** *fig.* something already long familiar.
2 Having lived long; old, aged; having the experience or wisdom of age; venerable. LME.
SHAKES. *Rom. & Jul.* Farewell, ancient lady. S. JOHNSON The precepts of ancient experience. J. GROSS Saintsbury . . looked the more ancient of the two, with his black skull-cap and his patriarchal beard.
3 That has been many years in some rank, position, or capacity; veteran. *arch.* LME.
K. DIGBY Seuerall of our ancientest seamen . . were sea sicke.
4 Of early origin or formation; going far back in history; long-established; time-worn. L15.
ARNOLD BENNETT The fine and ancient borough. M. PEAKE These dwellings, by ancient law, were granted this chill intimacy. M. DRABBLE They were very upper, but not a bit like an ancient family.
ancient demesne: see DEMESNE *noun*. **ancient lights** ENGLISH LAW the right of access to light of a property, established by custom and used to prevent the construction of adjacent buildings which would obstruct such access. **ancient monument** an old building etc. protected by Act of Parliament from damage or destruction.
■ **anciently** *adverb* (*a*) in ancient times, long ago; (*b*) from ancient times, for a long time: L15. **ancientness** *noun* M16.

ancientry /'eɪnʃ(ə)ntri/ *noun.* *arch.* M16.
[ORIGIN from ANCIENT *noun*¹, *adjective* + -RY.]
†**1** *collect.* Older people, elders. M16–E17.
2 The quality or condition of being ancient. L16.
3 Time long past, antiquity. M18.

†**ancienty** *noun.* LME.
[ORIGIN Anglo-Norman *auncienté*, Old French & mod. French *ancienneté*: see ANCIENT *adjective*, -TY¹.]
1 The quality of having lived or existed for a long time. LME–M17.
2 The time long past; antiquity. Long *rare*. LME–E19.
3 Distance in past time. L15–L16.
4 Seniority, priority. L15–L18.

ancile /an'sʌɪli/ *noun.* Pl. ***-lia*** /-lɪə/. L16.
[ORIGIN Latin.]
The sacred tutelary shield of ancient Rome, said to have fallen from heaven.

ancilla /an'sɪlə/ *noun.* *rare.* Pl. **-llae** /-liː/, **-llas**. L19.
[ORIGIN Latin, fem. dim. of *anculus* servant.]
A maidservant, a handmaid (*lit.* & *fig.*).

ancillary /an'sɪləri/ *adjective & noun.* M17.
[ORIGIN Latin *ancillaris*, formed as ANCILLA: see -ARY².]
▸ **A** *adjective.* **1** Subservient, subordinate; auxiliary, providing support; now *esp.* providing essential support or services to a central function or industry, esp. to hospital medical staff. (Foll. by *to*.) M17.
R. FRY It is an adjectival and ancillary beauty scarcely worthy of our prolonged contemplation. H. WILSON A period of great anxiety in the medical profession and occupations ancillary to medicine. *Financial Times* Its latest offer of 7.5 per cent for nurses and 6 per cent for ancillary staff and other grades.
2 Of or pertaining to maidservants. *rare.* M19.
THACKERAY The ancillary beauty was the one whom the Prince had selected.
▸ **B** *noun.* An auxiliary, an accessory; an ancillary worker. M19.

†**ancle** *noun* var. of ANKLE.

†**ancome** *noun.* L16–L19.
[ORIGIN Prob. var. of ONCOME *noun*. Cf. INCOME *noun*², UNCOME *noun*.]
A boil forming unexpectedly. Also, a whitlow.

ancon /'aŋkɒn, -k(ə)n/ *noun.* Pl. **ancones** /aŋ'kəʊniːz/, **ancons**. E18.
[ORIGIN Latin from Greek *agkōn* nook, bend, elbow.]
ARCHITECTURE. †**1** The corner or quoin of a wall, cross-beam, or rafter. Only in E18.
2 A console, usu. of two volutes, apparently supporting a cornice. M18.

Ancona /an'kəʊnə/ *noun*¹. M19.
[ORIGIN A town in Italy.]
(A bird of) a breed of poultry having black and white mottled plumage.

ancona /an'koːna, an'kəʊnə/ *noun*². Pl. ***-ne*** /-ne, -ni/. L19.
[ORIGIN Italian = medieval Latin, of uncertain origin: perh. alt. of Greek *eikona* accus. of *eikōn* ICON.]
An altarpiece, *esp.* one consisting of a group of paintings connected by architectural structure.

ancone *noun* pl. of ANCONA *noun*².

ancones *noun pl.* see ANCON.

ancress *noun* see ANCHORESS.

-ancy /(ə)nsi/ *suffix.*
[ORIGIN from or after Latin *-antia* -ANCE. Cf. -ENCY.]
Forming nouns of quality, as ***relevancy***, or state, as ***expectancy***, but not of action (cf. -ANCE). Many words orig. in *-ance* have been refash., as ***constancy***.

ancylostomiasis /ˌaŋkɪləʊstə'mʌɪəsɪs, ˌansɪ-/ *noun.* Pl. **-ases** /-əsiːz/. Also **ank-** /ˌaŋk-/. L19.
[ORIGIN from mod. Latin *Ancylostoma* (see below) from Greek *agkulos* crooked + *stoma* mouth, + -IASIS.]
MEDICINE. Hookworm infection of the small intestine, esp. by *Ancylostoma duodenale* or *Necator americanus*, often leading to anaemia. Also called ***uncinariasis***.

and /ənd, (ə)n, *stressed* and/ *conjunction*[1], *adverb*, & *noun*.
[ORIGIN Old English *and*, *ond*, corresp. to Old Frisian *and(a)*, *ande*, *end(a)*, *en*, Old Saxon *ande*, *endi* (Dutch *en*), Old High German *anti*, *enti* (German *und*), Sanskrit *atha* thereupon, also. See also AN *conjunction*.]
▸ **A** *conjunction*. **I** Coordinating. Introducing a word, phr., clause, or sentence which is to be taken side by side with, along with, or in addition to, that which precedes.
1 Simply additive. (When connecting three or more members it is expressed only with the last in ordinary prose but formerly, & still *colloq.* & *rhet.* for emphasis, with every member.) OE. ▸**b** Introducing an adversative clause: on the other hand, yet, but. *arch.* & *rhet.* OE. ▸†**c** Before either of two members connected. ME–E16.

SHAKES. *Com. Err.* My master and his man are both broke loose. AV *Ps.* 90:10 The dayes of our yeres are threescore yeeres and ten. MILTON My three-and-twentieth year. ADDISON We do in our Consciences believe two and two make four. T. MOORE Six hundred and eighty-five ways to dress eggs. KEATS Dance, and Provençal song, and sunburnt mirth! BYRON Through life's road, so dim and dirty, I have dragged to three and thirty. R. KIPLING Oh it's Tommy this, an' Tommy that, an' 'Tommy, go away'. G. B. SHAW My lunch will cost me one [shilling] and sixpence. B. RUSSELL The present holders of power are evil men, and the present manner of life is doomed. JOYCE He saw the priest bend down and kiss the altar and then face about and bless all the people. S. SASSOON Allgood was quiet, thoughtful, and fond of watching birds. P. SCOTT Susy removed the mirror and only set it up again when she had finished. **b** AV *Matt.* 22:30 Hee said, I goe sir, and went not.

and all, ***hit and run***, ***now and then***, ***once and for all***, ***smash and grab***, ***still and all***, ***time and again***, ***to and fro***, etc. ***and/or*** either together or as an alternative. ***but and***: see BUT *conjunction*.
2 Connecting occurrences of the same member, expressing continuous or indefinite repetition. OE.

SHAKES. *2 Hen. IV* A hundred mark is a long one for a poor lone woman to bear; and I have borne, and borne, and borne. BYRON I have lived for months and months on shipboard. YEATS Eternity is passion, girl or boy, Cry at the onset of their sexual joy 'For ever and for ever'.

two and two: see TWO *noun* 1.
3 Introducing a consequence, actual or predicted; after an imperative: in the case or circumstance that you do so. OE.

A. E. HOUSMAN Their shoulders held the sky suspended; They stood, and earth's foundations stay. D. L. SAYERS Spray with Sanfect and you're safe.

4 Introducing an explanation, amplification, or parenthesis. OE.

SHAKES. *Temp.* I heard a humming, And that a strange one too. THACKERAY A regular bang-up chap, and no mistake. DICKENS Scrooge signed it: and Scrooge's name was good upon 'Change. LD MACAULAY He and he alone has done all this. G. K. CHESTERTON The French would certainly have recovered the stolen French provinces whenever they could; and quite right too.

5 Connecting two verbs approaching the sense of *to* with the inf., esp. after *go*, *come*, *try*. OE.

G. B. SHAW Without waiting for them to come and ask for these things. SCOTT FITZGERALD Here's your money. Go and buy ten more dogs with it. E. O'NEILL Try and use your brains!

6 Continuing a narration from a previous sentence or from implied assent to a previous question or opinion. OE.

AV *John* 21:21 Peter seeing him saith to Jesus, Lord, and what shall this man do? C. KINGSLEY And why could not you run away, boy?

7 Expr. a difference of quality between things of the same name or class. M16.

BROWNING Alack, there be roses and roses, John!

8 Connecting two adjectives or an adjective and an adverb, of which the former approaches an adverbial relation to the latter, esp. in ***good and***, ***nice and***. L16.

Blackwood's Magazine They shall drive nice and slowly. J. LONDON The lawyers . . waded into me good and hard for the cash. E. O'NEILL It's nice and quiet out here.

9 Expr. surprise at, or asking the truth of, what one has already heard. L18.

W. J. MICKLE And are ye sure the news is true? And are ye sure he's weel?

▸ **II** Conditional.
10 Provided that; on condition that. Also ***and if***. Now *arch.* & *dial.* ME.
11 Even if; although. Now *arch.* & *dial.* LME.
†**12** As if, as though. LME–E17.
†**13** *indirect interrog.* Whether. L16–E17.
▸ **B** *adverb*. [A Latinism.] Also, even. Long *arch.* LME.
▸ **C** *noun*. **1** An instance of the conjunction 'and' (esp. conditional); an expression of condition or doubt. E16.

J. ASHFORD As my old aunt used to say, 'If ifs and ands were pots and pans, there'd be no work for tinkers' hands.'

2 (Usu. **AND**.) *COMPUTING*. A Boolean operator which gives the value unity if and only if all the operands are unity, and is otherwise zero. Usu. *attrib.* M20.
– COMB.: **AND gate** a circuit which produces an output only when signals are received simultaneously through all input connections.

†**and** *conjunction*[2] (after *compars.*). LME–L16.
[ORIGIN Erron. expansion of north. dial. var. (cf. 'N *conjunction*[2]) of THAN *conjunction*[2], formally conf. with AN *conjunction* = AND *conjunction*[1], *adverb*, & *noun*.]
= THAN *conjunction*[2].

-and /and/ *suffix*.
Repr. Latin *-andus*, *-da*, *-dum* of the gerundive of Latin verbs in *-are*, forming nouns usu. with the sense 'person (or thing) to be treated in a specified way', as ***analysand***, ***multiplicand***. The neut. gerundial ending is sometimes retained, as in ***memorandum***.

Andalusian /andəˈluːzjən, -sjən/ *adjective* & *noun*. Also **-zian**. E17.
[ORIGIN from *Andalusia* (see below) + -AN.]
▸ **A** *adjective*. Of or pertaining to Andalusia, a region in the southernmost part of Spain, its inhabitants, or its language. E17.
Andalusian HEMIPODE.
▸ **B** *noun*. **1** A native or inhabitant of Andalusia. E17.
2 The variety of Spanish spoken in Andalusia. L19.

andalusite /andəˈluːsʌɪt/ *noun*. E19.
[ORIGIN from *Andalusia* (see ANDALUSIAN) + -ITE[1].]
MINERALOGY. A metamorphic aluminium silicate occurring as elongated rhombic prisms sometimes of gem quality.

Andaluzian *adjective* & *noun* var. of ANDALUSIAN.

Andaman /ˈandəmən/ *adjective* & *noun*. E19.
[ORIGIN See below.]
Of or pertaining to the Andaman Islands in the Bay of Bengal or their inhabitants; (of or pertaining to) the Indo-Pacific language of the Andaman Islands.
Andaman Islander a native or inhabitant of the Andaman Islands.
■ **Andaˈmaner** *noun* an Andaman Islander E18. **Andamaˈnese** *noun* & *adjective* = ANDAMAN, ANDAMANER M19.

andante /anˈdanti/ *adverb*, *adjective*, & *noun*. E18.
[ORIGIN Italian, pres. pple of *andare* go.]
MUSIC. ▸**A** *adverb* & *adjective*. A direction: (orig.) distinct(ly); (now) moderately slow(ly). E18.
▸ **B** *noun*. A moderately slow movement or piece. L18.

andantino /andanˈtiːnəʊ/ *adverb*, *adjective*, & *noun*. E19.
[ORIGIN Italian, dim. of ANDANTE.]
MUSIC. ▸**A** *adverb* & *adjective*. A direction: (orig.) rather slower than andante; (now usu.) with less of andante, i.e. rather quicker than andante. E19.
▸ **B** *noun*. Pl. **-os**. A movement or piece rather quicker (orig. slower) than andante. M19.

Andean /ˈandɪən/ *adjective*. M19.
[ORIGIN from *Andes* (see below) + -AN.]
Of, pertaining to, or resembling the Andes, a mountain range in S. America.
Andean CONDOR.

Anderson shelter /ˈandəs(ə)n ˌʃɛltə/ *noun phr.* M20.
[ORIGIN Sir John *Anderson*, UK Home Secretary (1939–40) when the shelter was adopted.]
A small prefabricated air-raid shelter.

andesine /ˈandɪziːn/ *noun*. M19.
[ORIGIN from *Andes* (see ANDEAN) + -INE[5].]
MINERALOGY. A plagioclase occurring in igneous rocks such as andesite and diorite.

andesite /ˈandɪzʌɪt/ *noun*. M19.
[ORIGIN formed as ANDESINE + -ITE[1].]
GEOLOGY. A fine-grained, usu. porphyritic, volcanic rock consisting chiefly of plagioclase and biotite, hornblende, or pyroxene.
■ **andeˈsitic** *adjective* of, pertaining to, or characterized by andesite M19.

andiron /ˈandʌɪən/ *noun*. ME.
[ORIGIN from Old French *andier* with assim. of 2nd syll. to IRON *noun*.]
A metal stand for supporting burning wood on a hearth etc.; a firedog.

Andorran /anˈdɔːr(ə)n/ *adjective* & *noun*. M19.
[ORIGIN from *Andorra* (see below) + -AN.]
Of or pertaining to, a native or inhabitant of, Andorra, a small independent state in the eastern Pyrenees.

andouille /ɑ̃duːj/ *noun*. Pl. pronounced same. E17.
[ORIGIN Old French & mod. French, of unknown origin.]
A kind of pork sausage, usually served as an hors d'oeuvre.

andouillette /ɑ̃dujɛt/ *noun*. Pl. pronounced same. Also †**-llet**. E17.
[ORIGIN French, dim. of ANDOUILLE.]
A sausage made from a paste of minced veal, bacon, and other ingredients.

andr- *combining form* see ANDRO-.

andradite /ˈandrədʌɪt/ *noun*. M19.
[ORIGIN from J. B. de *Andrada* e Silva (c 1763–1838), Brazilian geologist & statesman + -ITE[1].]
MINERALOGY. Calcium iron garnet, occurring in various colours, of which some types are used as gemstones.

Andrew /ˈandruː/ *noun*. *nautical slang*. L16.
[ORIGIN Male forename. Cf. *merry Andrew* s.v. MERRY *adjective*, *St Andrew's cross* s.v. SAINT *noun* & *adjective*.]
In full ***Andrew Millar***, ***Andrew Miller***.
†**1** A ship, *esp.* a warship. L16–M19.
†**2** A government authority. Only in M19.
3 The Royal Navy. E20.

andro- /ˈandrəʊ/ *combining form* of Greek *andr-*, *anēr* man: see -O-. Before a vowel also **andr-**.
■ **androˈcentric** *adjective* having man or the male as its centre E20. **androcracy** /anˈdrɒkrəsi/ *noun* the rule of man or the male, male supremacy E20. **androˈcratic** *adjective* pertaining to or involving androcracy L19. **androdioecious** /-dʌɪˈiːʃəs/ *adjective* (*BOTANY*) having male and hermaphrodite flowers on separate individuals L19. **androdioecism** /-dʌɪˈiːsɪz(ə)m/ *noun* (*BOTANY*) the condition of being androdioecious L19. **androˈgenesis** *noun* fertilization of the egg by the sperm, and development of the embryo, without the participation of the female nucleus and chromosomes; male parthenogenesis: E20. **androgeˈnetic** *adjective* of or pertaining to androgenesis E20. **andromoˈnoecious** *adjective* (*BOTANY*) having male and hermaphrodite flowers on the same individual L19. **andromoˈnoecism** *noun* (*BOTANY*) the condition of being andromonoecious L19. **androsphinx** *noun* a sphinx whose human portion is male E17. **androspore** *noun* the zoospore that in some algae produces the male reproductive organs M19.

androconium /andrəˈkəʊnɪəm/ *noun*. Pl. **-nia** /-nɪə/. L19.
[ORIGIN from ANDRO- + Greek *konia* dust + -IUM.]
ENTOMOLOGY. A scent-producing scale, numbers of which are found on the wings of certain male butterflies and moths.
■ **androconial** *adjective* E20.

androecium /anˈdriːsjəm/ *noun*. Pl. **-cia** /-sjə/. M19.
[ORIGIN mod. Latin from Greek ANDRO- + *oikion* house: see -IUM.]
BOTANY. The stamens of a flower collectively.

androgen /ˈandrədʒ(ə)n/ *noun*. M20.
[ORIGIN from ANDRO- + -GEN.]
A male sex hormone.
■ **androˈgenic** *adjective* of or pertaining to an androgen; of the nature of an androgen: M20.

androgenize /anˈdrɒdʒənʌɪz/ *verb*. Also **-ise**. M20.
[ORIGIN from ANDROGEN + -IZE.]
Treat with or expose to male hormones, typically with the result that male sexual characteristics are produced.
■ **androgenization** *noun* M20.

androgyne /ˈandrədʒʌɪn/ *noun* & *adjective*. M16.
[ORIGIN French, or Latin *androgynus*, *-gyne* from Greek *androgunos*, *-gunē*, formed as ANDRO- + *gunē* woman.]
▸ **A** *noun*. An androgynous individual. M16.
▸ **B** *adjective*. = ANDROGYNOUS. M19.
– NOTE: Recorded in Old English & Middle English in Latin & Greek forms.
■ **anˈdrogynal** *adjective* (*rare*) M17. **anˈdrogyny** *noun* hermaphroditism M19.

androgynous /anˈdrɒdʒɪnəs/ *adjective*. E17.
[ORIGIN from Latin *androgynus* (see ANDROGYNE) + -OUS.]
1 Uniting the (physical) characters of both sexes; hermaphrodite. Also, of ambiguous sex; partly male and partly female in appearance. E17.

Time I heard androgynous characters sing unintelligible lyrics to an endlessly repetitive beat.

2 *ASTROLOGY*. Of a planet: sometimes hot, sometimes cold. M17.
3 *BOTANY*. Bearing stamens and pistils on the same inflorescence, or on the same plant. M18.

android /ˈandrɔɪd/ *noun* & *adjective*. Orig. in Latin form †**-oides**. E18.
[ORIGIN mod. Latin *androides*, from Greek ANDRO- + *-eidēs* -OID.]
▸ **A** *noun*. An automaton resembling a human being; *SCIENCE FICTION* a synthetic human being. E18.
▸ **B** *adjective*. Resembling (that of) a male. L19.

andrology /anˈdrɒlədʒi/ *noun*. L19.
[ORIGIN from ANDRO- + -LOGY.]
The branch of medicine that deals with male reproductive function and with diseases and conditions particular to men.

Andromeda /anˈdrɒmɪdə/ *noun*. M16.
[ORIGIN Latin from Greek *Andromedē*: see PERSEUS.]
1 (The name of) a constellation of the northern hemisphere between Perseus and Pegasus. M16.
2 (**a-**.) Either of two low pink-flowered shrubs of northern bogs, *Andromeda polifolia* and (*N. Amer.*) *A. glaucophylla*, of the heath family. Also called ***bog rosemary***. M18.
■ **Andromedid** *noun* & *adjective* [-ID[3]] *ASTRONOMY* (designating) any of a shower of meteors (now rarely seen) which appear to radiate from the constellation Andromeda L19.

andropause /ˈandrəpɔːz/ *noun*. M20.
[ORIGIN from ANDRO- + PAUSE *noun*, after *menopause*.]
A collection of symptoms, including fatigue and a decrease in libido, experienced by some (esp. older) men and attributed to a gradual decline in androgen levels; the stage of a man's life when this occurs.
■ **andropausal** *adjective* L20.

androsace /anˈdrɒsəsi, -ki/ *noun*. L19.
[ORIGIN medieval Latin *androsaces* from Greek *androsakes* (Dioscurides), name of an unidentified marine plant or zoophyte, formed as ANDRO- + *sakos* shield.]

A

Any of numerous dwarf tufted alpine plants of the genus *Androsace*, belonging to the primula family and bearing red or white flowers.

androsterone /andrə(ʊ)ˈstɪərəʊn, anˈdrɒstərəʊn/ *noun*. M20.
[ORIGIN from ANDRO- + -STERONE.]
BIOCHEMISTRY. A relatively inactive metabolite of testosterone.
■ ˈ**androstane** *noun* [-ANE] a saturated hydrocarbon of which testosterone and related compounds are derivatives M20. ˌ**androstene**ˈ**dione**, **-tendione** *noun* [-ENE + DI-[2] + -ONE] an isomer of testosterone which accompanies the latter in androgenic secretions, in some animals being the predominant male hormone M20.

-androus /ˈandrəs/ *suffix*.
[ORIGIN from mod. Latin *-andrus* from Greek *-andros*, formed as ANDRO-: see -OUS.]
BOTANY. Having male reproductive organs of an indicated kind or number, as ***gynandrous***, ***monandrous***, etc.

ane /eɪn/ *adjective & noun*. *Scot. & N. English*. ME.
[ORIGIN Var. of ONE *adjective* etc.]
= ONE *adjective & noun* (now only as absol. form of the numeral).

-ane /eɪn/ *suffix*.
1 Var. of -AN, usu. with differentiation, as ***humane***, ***urbane***, but also alone, as ***mundane***.
2 CHEMISTRY. Forming names of paraffins and other saturated hydrocarbons, as ***methane***, ***octane***, etc., and of hydrides of other elements, as ***silane***, and more or less arbitrarily of other organic compounds, as ***lindane***.

anear /əˈnɪə/ *verb*. *arch*. M16.
[ORIGIN from A-[1] + NEAR *verb*.]
†1 *verb intrans*. Draw or be near *to*. M–L16.
2 *verb trans*. Approach. L16.

anear /əˈnɪə/ *preposition & adverb*. *arch*. M16.
[ORIGIN from A-[1] + NEAR *adverb*[2] & *preposition*[2].]
▸ A *preposition*. Near to, close to. M16.
▸ B *adverb*. 1 Nearly, almost. E17.
2 Near, close by. L18.

aneath /əˈniːθ/ *preposition & adverb*. *Scot. & N. English*. M18.
[ORIGIN Alt. of *beneath* after *afore* and *before*, *aside* and *beside*.]
= BENEATH.

anecdota *noun pl.* see ANECDOTE.

anecdotage /ˈanɪkdəʊtɪdʒ/ *noun*. L18.
[ORIGIN Sense 1 from ANECDOTE + DOTAGE; sense 2 from ANECDOTE + -AGE.]
1 Garrulous old age. *joc*. L18.
2 Anecdotes; anecdotal literature. E19.

anecdote /ˈanɪkdəʊt/ *noun*. In sense 1 also (earlier) in Latin pl. form **anecdota** /əˈnɛkdə(ʊ)tə/. L17.
[ORIGIN French, or mod. Latin *anecdota* from Greek *anekdota* things unpublished, neut. pl. of *anekdotos*, formed as AN-[5] + *ekdotos*, from *ekdidōnai* publish, give out.]
1 In *pl*. Secret or hitherto unpublished details of history. L17.
2 a A narrative of an amusing or striking incident (orig. an item of gossip). E18. ▸b ART. (The portrayal of) a small narrative incident; a painting portraying a small narrative incident. M20.
■ anecˈ**dotal** *adjective* of, pertaining to, or consisting of anecdotes M19. anecˈ**dotalism** *noun* (*a*) a propensity for telling anecdotes; (*b*) anecdotal quality: E20. anecˈ**dotalist** *noun* a person given to or adept in telling anecdotes E20. anecˈ**dotic** *adjective* (*a*) = ANECDOTAL; (*b*) inclined to tell anecdotes: L18. anecˈ**dotical** *adjective* = ANECDOTIC M18. anecˈ**dotically** *adverb* in an anecdotic manner, with use of anecdotes M19. **anecdotist** /ˈanɪkdəʊtɪst, əˈnɛkdətɪst/ *noun* a teller of anecdotes M19.

anechoic /anɪˈkəʊɪk/ *adjective*. M20.
[ORIGIN from AN-[5] + ECHO *noun* + -IC.]
Free from echo.

anelastic /anɪˈlastɪk/ *adjective*. M20.
[ORIGIN from AN-[5] + ELASTIC.]
PHYSICS. Not elastic.
■ ˌ**anelas**ˈ**ticity** *noun* M20.

anele /əˈniːl/ *verb trans*. *arch*. ME.
[ORIGIN from AN-[1] + *elien* to oil, from Old English *ele* from Latin *oleum* oil.]
Anoint; give extreme unction to.

anemia *noun*, **anemic** *adjective* see ANAEMIA, ANAEMIC.

anemo- /əˈnɛməʊ, anɪˈmɒ/ *combining form* of Greek *anemos* wind: see -O-.
■ aˈ**nemochore** *noun* [Greek *khōrein* to spread] a plant whose seeds are dispersed by the wind E20. aˈ**nemogram** *noun* a record produced by an anemograph L19. aˈ**nemograph** *noun* an instrument for recording the speed, and sometimes also direction, of the wind M19. **anemo**ˈ**graphic** *adjective* of or pertaining to an anemograph L19. aneˈ**mology** *noun* (*rare*) the science of the winds L18. aneˈ**mophilous** *adjective* (BOTANY) wind-pollinated L19. aneˈ**mophily** *noun* pollination by the wind L19. aˈ**nemoscope** *noun* an instrument for indicating wind direction and strength E18.

anemometer /anɪˈmɒmɪtə/ *noun*. E18.
[ORIGIN from ANEMO- + -METER.]
1 An instrument for measuring the speed or force of the wind, or of any gas in motion. E18.
2 An apparatus for indicating wind pressure in an organ. M19.
■ **anemometry** *noun* the measurement of wind speed; the use of anemometers: M19.

anemone /əˈnɛməni/ *noun*. M16.
[ORIGIN Latin from Greek *anemōnē*, from *anemos* wind.]
1 A plant of the genus *Anemone*, of the buttercup family; *esp*. (also ***wood anemone***) *A. nemorosa*, a common woodland plant bearing delicate white flowers in early spring (also called ***windflower***). Also, a flower of such a plant. M16.
Japanese anemone: see JAPANESE *adjective*. PLUMOSE ***anemone***. ***St Brigid anemone***, ***St Brigid's anemone***: see SAINT *noun & adjective*.
2 More fully ***sea anemone***. An anthozoan belonging to the order Actiniaria, having a radiating array of tentacles around the mouth. M18.
– COMB.: **anemone fish** any of a number of damselfishes (esp. of the genus *Amphiprion*), which live in commensal association with sea anemones.

anencephalic /aˌnɛnsɪˈfalɪk, -kɛˈfalɪk/ *adjective*. M19.
[ORIGIN from Greek *anegkephalos* without brain (Galen) (from AN-[5] + *egkephalos* brain) + -IC.]
MEDICINE. Having all or most of the brain congenitally absent.
■ **anen**ˈ**cephalous** *adjective* = ANENCEPHALIC E19. **anen**ˈ**cephaly**, †**-lia** *noun* anencephalic condition M19.

anent /əˈnɛnt/ *preposition & adverb*. Now chiefly *dial*.
[ORIGIN Old English *on efn*, *emn*, formed as ON *preposition* + EVEN *adjective & noun*, = Old Saxon *an eban*, Middle High German *eneben*, *nebent*, (also mod.) *neben*. Form history not fully explained.]
▸ A *preposition*. 1 In line with; in company with. OE.
2 In the sight of, before. ME.
†3 Against, towards, fronting. ME–M19.
4 In respect of; with reference to; concerning, about. Now *arch. & Scot*. ME.
▸ B *adverb*. Opposite. E16.

-aneous /ˈeɪnɪəs/ *suffix*.
[ORIGIN from Latin *-aneus*: see -EOUS, -OUS.]
Forming adjectives from Latin words in *-aneus*, as ***cutaneous***, ***miscellaneous***.

anergy /ˈanədʒi/ *noun*. Orig. in Latin form †**-gia**. L19.
[ORIGIN mod. Latin *anergia* from Greek, from AN-[5] + *ergon* work: see -Y[3].]
MEDICINE. 1 Abnormal lack of energy. L19.
2 (The usual sense.) Absence of response to a given antigen or allergen. E20.
■ aˈ**nergic** *adjective* characterized by anergy L19.

†**anerly** *adverb & adjective*. *Scot. & N. English*. ME–L19.
[ORIGIN from ANE; the *-er-* is unexpl., but cf. FORMERLY, ALLENARLY.]
Alone, only; solitary.

aneroid /ˈanərɔɪd/ *adjective & noun*. M19.
[ORIGIN French *anéroïde*, from Greek A-[10] + *nēros* wet, damp: see -OID.]
(A barometer) that depends on the action of air pressure on the elastic top of a box containing a vacuum.

anesthesia *noun*, **anesthetic** *adjective*, **anesthetize** *verb*, etc., see ANAESTHESIA etc.

anestrus *noun* see ANOESTRUS.

anethole /ˈanɪθəʊl/ *noun*. Also (earlier) †**-ol**. M19.
[ORIGIN from Latin *anethum* anise + -OLE[1].]
CHEMISTRY. An aromatic ether which is the major constituent of certain oils, e.g. anise, fennel; *p*-1-propenylphenyl methyl ether, $C_{10}H_{12}O$.

aneuploid /ˈanjuplɔɪd/ *adjective*. E20.
[ORIGIN from AN-[5] + EUPLOID.]
BIOLOGY. Not euploid.
■ **aneuploidy** *noun* aneuploid condition E20.

aneurin /əˈnjʊərɪn, ˈanjʊrɪn/ *noun*. M20.
[ORIGIN from A(NTI- + POLY)NEUR(ITIS + VITAM)IN.]
= THIAMINE.

aneurysm /ˈanjʊrɪz(ə)m/ *noun*. Also **-ism**. LME.
[ORIGIN Greek *aneurusma* dilatation, from *aneurunein* widen out, from AN-[4] + *eurunein*, from *euros* wide.]
MEDICINE. A morbid dilatation of the wall of a blood vessel, usu. an artery.
dissecting aneurysm: see DISSECT *verb* 1.
■ **aneu**ˈ**rysmal** *noun & adjective* †(*a*) *noun* (*rare*) = ANEURYSM; (*b*) *adjective* characterized by or of the nature of an aneurysm: LME.

anew /əˈnjuː/ *adverb*. ME.
[ORIGIN from A-[3] + NEW *adjective*.]
1 Afresh, once more. ME.
2 In a new way. LME.
†3 Recently. LME–E16.

anfractuosity /anfraktjʊˈɒsɪti/ *noun*. L16.
[ORIGIN French *anfractuosité*, formed as ANFRACTUOUS: see -OSITY.]
Sinuosity, circuitousness, intricacy, (*lit.* & *fig.*); as count noun in *pl*., tortuous passages etc., involutions, intricacies.

anfractuous /anˈfraktjʊəs/ *adjective*. L16.
[ORIGIN from late Latin *anfractuosus*, from Latin *anfractus* a bending: see -OUS. Sense 2 from French *anfractueux*.]
1 Winding, sinuous; roundabout, circuitous. L16.

DAY LEWIS A gorge of a street, anfractuous, narrow.

2 Rugged, craggy. *rare*. E20.

T. S. ELIOT Paint me the bold anfractuous rocks Faced by the snarled and yelping seas.

angareb /ˈaŋgəreɪb/ *noun*. Also **-reeb**, & other vars. M19.
[ORIGIN Yemeni Arabic *ʼangarīb*.]
A stretcher or light bedstead used in Aden, Egypt, Sudan, and Ethiopia.

angary /ˈaŋgəri/ *noun*. L19.
[ORIGIN French *angarie* from Italian or late Latin *angaria* forced service, from Greek *aggareia* from *aggaros* courier from Persian.]
LAW. In full ***right of angary***. A belligerent's right (subject to compensation for loss) to seize or destroy neutral property under military necessity.

angekok /ˈaŋgɪkɒk/ *noun*. M18.
[ORIGIN Inupiaq (Greenlandic) *angakkoq*.]
An Eskimo sorcerer or medicine man.

angel /ˈeɪndʒ(ə)l/ *noun & verb*.
[ORIGIN Old English *engel*, corresp. to Old Frisian *angel*, *engel*, Old Saxon *engil*, Old High German *angil*, *engil* (Dutch, German *Engel*), Old Norse *engill*, Gothic *aggilus* (perh. immed. from Greek), one of the earliest Germanic adoptions from Latin; superseded in Middle English by forms from Old French *angele* from Christian Latin *angelus* from Greek *aggelos* messenger.]
▸ A *noun*. 1 THEOLOGY. A spiritual being more powerful and intelligent than a human being, *esp*. in Jewish, Christian, Muslim, and other theologies, one acting as a messenger, agent, or attendant of God; in Christian theology also *spec*., a member of the ninth and lowest order of the ninefold celestial hierarchy, ranking directly below the archangels (usu. in *pl*.). OE.

SHAKES. *Macb*. Angels are bright still, though the brightest fell. POPE Man seems to be placed as the middle Link between Angels and Brutes. BYRON For the Angel of Death spread his wings on the blast. J. C. OATES The Indians had always feared the Spirit of Lake Noir, as an angel of mischief and death.

on the side of the angels: see SIDE *noun*. ***recording angel***: see RECORD *verb*.
2 THEOLOGY. Any of the fallen spirits who rebelled against God; a devil. *arch*. exc. more fully ***fallen angel***. OE. ▸b In full ***Hell's Angel***. A member of a group of motorcyclists in California, orig. notorious for disturbances of civil order; a member of a similar group elsewhere. M20.

AV *Matt*. 25:41 Euerlasting fire, prepared for the deuill and his angels.

3 A guardian or attendant spirit (used both with and without implication of belief in such). Also *fig*., a person like such a spirit. ME.

ROBERT BURTON Every man hath a good and a bad angel attending him in particular all his life long. TENNYSON I to her became Her guardian and her angel. G. B. SHAW I am sure we all owe you the happiness of our lives. You are our good angel.

familiar angel: see FAMILIAR *adjective* 1. ***guardian angel***. ***ministering angel***: see MINISTER *verb*.
4 A person regarded as a messenger of God; a prophet, a preacher; a pastor or minister, esp. (in biblical translations, as at *Revelation* 2:1) in the early Church, and in some modern sects, as the Catholic Apostolic Church. ME.
5 A messenger. *gen. poet*. (now *rare* exc. as *fig*. use of sense 1). LME.

JONSON The dear good angel of the spring, The nightingale.

6 A conventional representation of a celestial angel, figured with wings and usu. a long robe. LME.

JOYCE Mr Bloom walked . . by saddened angels, crosses, broken pillars, family vaults.

7 *hist*. In full ***angel-noble***. A gold coin having as its device the archangel Michael piercing the dragon (cf. ANGELOT 1). LME.
8 An angelic person; a lovely or innocent being; an obliging or loving person; a person of exemplary conduct. L16.

THACKERAY 'Tis strange what a man may do, and a woman yet think him an angel. V. WOOLF Prue, a perfect angel with the others. P. BARRINGTON I'm no angel . . but I'd never let anyone else swing for a crime they didn't commit.

9 A financial backer of an (esp. theatrical) enterprise. *slang*. L19.
10 In *pl*. An aircraft's altitude (often used with a numeral indicating thousands of feet). *RAF slang*. M20.

J. DICKEY We rendezvous at angels nine.

11 An unexplained radar echo. M20.
– COMB.: **angel cake** a very light and pale sponge cake; **angel dust** *colloq*. the drug phencyclidine; **angelfish** any of various fishes with winglike or elongated fins; *spec*. (*a*) = ***monkfish*** (a) s.v. MONK *noun*[1]; (*b*) a tropical marine fish of the family Pomacanthidae; (*c*) an aquarium fish of the S. American cichlid genus *Pterophyllum*, usu. silver and black; **angel food** = ***angel cake*** above; ***angel-noble***: see sense 7 above; **angel's eye(s)**, **angels' eyes** *dial*. germander speedwell; **angel shark** a shark of the family Squatinidae, with winglike pectoral fins; *spec*. = ***monkfish*** (a) s.v. MONK *noun*[1]; **angels on horseback** simmered oysters individually wrapped in bacon, served on toast; **angel skin** [translating French *peau d'ange*] a fabric with a smooth waxy finish; **angel sleeve** a long loose sleeve; **angel's trumpet** any

of various South American shrubs or small trees of the genus *Brugmansia* (family Solanaceae), with large pendulous trumpet-shaped flowers.

▸ **B** *verb trans.* Infl. **-ll-**, ***-l-**. Back or finance (an enterprise, esp. a theatrical production). **E20.**

■ **angelhood** *noun* **M19.** **angelize** *verb trans.* (*arch.*) = ANGELICIZE **L16.** **ange'lolatry** *noun* the worship of angels **M19.** **ange'lology** *noun* theological doctrine concerning angels **M19.** **ange'lophany** *noun* a visible manifestation of angels **M19.** **angelship** *noun* (**a**) (with possess. adjective, as ***your angelship*** etc.) a mock title of respect for an angel; (**b**) the condition of being an angel: **L16.**

Angeleno /andʒəˈliːnəʊ/ *noun.* Also **-ino**. Pl. **-os**. **L19.**
[ORIGIN Amer. Spanish.]
A native or inhabitant of Los Angeles, California. Cf. LOS ANGELENO.

angelet /ˈeɪndʒ(ə)lɪt/ *noun.* **LME.**
[ORIGIN Alt. of Old French & mod. French ANGELOT: see -ET[1].]
1 *hist.* A gold coin, half the value of an angel. **LME.**
2 A little angel; a cherub. **E19.**

angelic /anˈdʒɛlɪk/ *adjective*[1]. **LME.**
[ORIGIN Old French & mod. French *angélique* from late Latin *angelicus* from Greek *aggelikos*: see ANGEL, -IC.]
1 Of or pertaining to angels; of the angel kind. **LME.** ***the angelic*** SALUTATION.
2 Like an angel; of superhuman beauty; of sublime power. **LME.**
the Angelic Doctor St Thomas Aquinas.
■ **angelicize** *verb trans.* make into or like an angel **M19.**

angelic /anˈdʒɛlɪk/ *adjective*[2]. **M19.**
[ORIGIN from ANGELICA *noun*[1] + -IC.]
CHEMISTRY. ***angelic acid***, an unsaturated acid present as esters in the roots of angelica and related plants; 2-methyl-*cis*-but-2-enoic acid, $C_5H_8O_2$.

angelica /anˈdʒɛlɪkə/ *noun*[1]. **E16.**
[ORIGIN medieval Latin, short for *herba angelica* angelic plant.]
1 A robust umbelliferous plant of northern and eastern Europe, *Angelica archangelica*, grown esp. for its seeds and stems, which are used as flavouring. Also (more fully ***wild angelica***), a related Eurasian plant of streamsides etc., *A. sylvestris*. **E16.**
2 a The root of angelica; an aromatic essence obtained from it. **M16.** ▸**b** The candied stalk of angelica, used in cookery. **L19.**
– COMB.: **angelica tree** a prickly tree, *Aralia spinosa*, of the ginseng family, native to the eastern US.

angelica *noun*[2] var. of ANGÉLIQUE.

angelical /anˈdʒɛlɪk(ə)l/ *adjective.* **LME.**
[ORIGIN from ANGELIC *adjective*[1] + -AL[1].]
= ANGELIC *adjective*[1].
■ **angelically** *adverb* **M17.** **angelicalness** *noun* (*rare*) **M17.**

angelin /ˈandʒ(ə)lɪn/ *noun*[1]. Also **-im** /-ɪm/. **L17.**
[ORIGIN Portuguese *angelim*.]
(The hard wood of) a leguminous tree, *Andira inermis*, native to tropical America and W. Africa.

angelin *noun*[2] var. of ANGILI.

angélique /andʒɪˈliːk, *foreign* ɑ̃ʒelik (*pl. same*)/ *noun.* Also **angelica** /anˈdʒɛlɪkə/. **M17.**
[ORIGIN French & Latin = ANGELIC *adjective*[1].]
EARLY MUSIC. An instrument of the lute family.

Angelman's syndrome /ˈeɪndʒ(ə)lmənz ˌsɪndrəʊm/ *noun phr.* Also **Angelman syndrome**. **L20.**
[ORIGIN from Harry *Angelman* (1915–96), Brit. doctor, who described the condition.]
MEDICINE. A rare hereditary disorder characterized by mental disability and hyperactivity.

angelot /ˈandʒəlɒt/ *noun.* **E16.**
[ORIGIN Old French & mod. French, dim. of Old French *angele* ANGEL: see -OT[1]. Cf. ANGELET.]
1 *hist.* A French gold coin having as its device the archangel Michael piercing the dragon. **E16.**
2 In full ***angelot cheese***. A small rich cheese made in Normandy. Long only in Dicts. **L16.**
3 = ANGÉLIQUE. *rare.* **L17.**

angelus /ˈandʒ(ə)ləs/ *noun.* **M17.**
[ORIGIN Latin, from the opening words *Angelus domini* the angel of the Lord.]
1 A devotional exercise commemorating the Incarnation, said by Roman Catholics at morning, noon, and sunset. **M17.**
2 = ***angelus bell*** below. **M19.**
– COMB.: **angelus bell**: rung at the times for the angelus.

angely *noun* var. of ANGILI.

anger /ˈaŋɡə/ *noun.* **ME.**
[ORIGIN Old Norse *angr* grief, from the base repr. also by Old Norse *ǫngr*, Gothic *aggwus*, and Old English *enge*, Old Saxon, Old High German *engi* (Dutch, German *eng*) narrow. Rel. to Latin *angere* (see ANGUISH *noun*).]
1 Trouble, affliction, vexation, sorrow. Long *obsolete* exc. *Scot.* (now *dial.*). **ME.**
2 Extreme or passionate displeasure, wrath. **ME.**
3 Physical pain, inflamed condition. Long *dial.* **LME.**

■ **angerful** *adjective* (*rare*) †(**a**) careful, anxious, grievous; (**b**) full of anger, wrathful: **ME.** **angerless** *adjective* free from anger **M16.** **angerly** *adverb* †(**a**) hurtfully, painfully; †(**b**) violently, extremely; (**c**) *arch.* = ANGRILY: **LME.** **angersome** *adjective* (*obsolete* exc. *Scot.*) troublesome, irritating **M17.**

anger /ˈaŋɡə/ *verb.* **ME.**
[ORIGIN Old Norse *angra* grieve, vex, formed as ANGER *noun*.]
†**1** *verb trans.* Distress, trouble, vex. **ME–E16.**
2 *verb intrans.* Become angry. Chiefly *Scot.* Now *rare.* **ME.**
3 *verb trans.* Make angry, enrage. **LME.**

POPE It anger'd Turenne . . To see a footman kick'd that took his pay. S. JOHNSON You have both pleased and angered me. SOUTHEY It angers me when people . . depreciate the Spaniards. A. J. P. TAYLOR Some Englishmen were angered at his supposed desertion of the French.

4 *verb trans.* Irritate or inflame (a sore etc.). Long *dial.* **LME.**

Angevin /ˈandʒəvɪn/ *noun & adjective.* **M17.**
[ORIGIN French from medieval Latin *Andegavinus*, from *Andegavum* Angers, capital of Anjou.]
(A native or inhabitant) of Anjou, a former province of France; ENGLISH HISTORY (of, pertaining to, or characteristic of) any of the Plantagenet monarchs descended from Geoffrey, Count of Anjou, i.e. Henry II to Richard III.

angili /ˈandʒɪli/ *noun.* Also **angelin** /ˈandʒ(ə)lɪn/, **angely**. **M17.**
[ORIGIN from Tamil *añcali*.]
A tree of southern India, *Artocarpus hirsuta*, of the mulberry family; (in full ***angili-wood***) the hard timber of this tree.

angina /anˈdʒʌɪnə/ *noun.* **M16.**
[ORIGIN Latin = quinsy from Greek *agkhonē* strangling, assim. to Latin *angere* (see ANGUISH *noun*).]
MEDICINE. **1** A condition marked by a suffocating, oppressive pain or discomfort; *esp.* quinsy. Now *rare.* **M16.**
2 In full ***angina pectoris*** /ˈpɛktərɪs/ [Latin = of the chest]. Severe pain in the chest, and often also the arms and neck, due to inadequate blood supply to the heart muscles. **M18.**
■ **anginal** *adjective* of, pertaining to, or characterized by angina (usu. angina pectoris) **E19.** **'anginoid** *adjective* = ANGINAL **L19.**

angio- /ˈandʒɪəʊ/ *combining form.*
[ORIGIN Greek *aggeio-*, from *aggeion* vessel: see -O-.]
Used chiefly in terms relating to blood vessels or seed vessels.
■ **angioblast** *noun* a cell from which blood vessel tissue evolves **L19.** **angiocardi'ography** *noun* X-ray examination of the thoracic vessels and heart after the intravenous injection of a radio-opaque substance **M20.** **angio'genesis** *noun* the development of new blood vessels **L19.** **angiogram** *noun* a radiograph made by angiography **M20.** **angio'graphic** *adjective* of or pertaining to angiography **M20.** **angi'ography** *noun* radiography of blood and lymph vessels, carried out after introduction of a radio-opaque substance **M20.** **angi'ology** *noun* the branch of anatomy that deals with the blood vessels **E18.** **angi'oma** *noun*, pl. **-mas**, **-mata** /-mətə/, a tumour or swelling produced by a proliferation of blood vessels **L19.** **angi'omatous** *adjective* pertaining to or of the nature of an angioma **L19.** **angioneu'rotic** *adjective* (of oedema) marked by swelling and itching of areas of skin, and usu. allergic in origin **L19.** **angioplasty** *noun* (an instance of) the surgical repair of a damaged blood vessel **E20.**

angiosperm /ˈandʒɪəspəːm/ *noun.* **E19.**
[ORIGIN from ANGIO- + Greek *sperma* seed.]
BOTANY. A plant which bears its seeds enclosed in a seed vessel, i.e. a flowering plant. Cf. GYMNOSPERM.
■ **angio'spermal** *adjective* = ANGIOSPERMOUS **M19.** **angio'spermous** *adjective* pertaining to or being an angiosperm **M18.**

angiostatin /ˌandʒɪə(ʊ)ˈstatɪn/ *noun.* **L20.**
[ORIGIN from ANGIO- + STATIN.]
PHARMACOLOGY. A protein isolated from blood plasma and used as a drug to inhibit the growth of new blood vessels in malignant tumours.

angiotensin /ˌandʒɪə(ʊ)ˈtɛnsɪn/ *noun.* **M20.**
[ORIGIN from ANGIO- + HYPER)TENS(ION + -IN[1].]
BIOCHEMISTRY. A protein whose presence in the blood promotes aldosterone secretion and tends to raise blood pressure.

angle /ˈaŋɡ(ə)l/ *noun*[1]. *arch.*
[ORIGIN Old English *angul* = Old Saxon, Old High German *angul* (German *Angel*), Old Norse *ǫngull*.]
A fishing hook. Also, a rod and line.

I. WALTON I am, Sir, a Brother of the Angle. *fig.*: COVERDALE *Eccles.* 7:26 A woman is bytterer then death: for she is a very angle, hir hert is a nett.

Angle /ˈaŋɡ(ə)l/ *noun*[2]. **OE.**
[ORIGIN Latin *Anglus*, pl. *-li*, in Tacitus *-lii* from Germanic, = the people of *Angul* (mod. *Angeln*), a district of Schleswig (now in northern Germany), so called from its shape, formed as ANGLE *noun*[1]. Cf. ENGLISH *noun*.]
A member of a tribe from Schleswig that invaded and settled in eastern Britain in the 5th cent.

angle /ˈaŋɡ(ə)l/ *noun*[3]. **LME.**
[ORIGIN Old French & mod. French, or Latin *angulus* corner.]
1 The indefinite space between two lines or planes that meet. **LME.**
2 The meeting point of two lines not in the same direction. **LME.**
3 ASTROLOGY. Each of the four mundane houses (the 1st, 4th, 7th, and 10th of the twelve divisions of the heavens) which extend anticlockwise from the cardinal points of the compass. **LME.**
4 A corner viewed internally as a receding space; a sharp-cornered recess; *arch.* an out-of-the-way place, a nook. **LME.**

SHAKES. *Temp.* Whom I left . . In an odd angle of the isle. MILTON To search the tenderest angles of the heart. EDWARD THOMAS I sat among the boughs of the fallen elm That strewed the angle of the fallow.

5 A corner viewed externally or as a projection; a sharp projection. **M16.**

BURKE There is nothing more prejudicial to the grandeur of buildings than to abound in angles. E. K. KANE We trod on the fractured angles of upturned ice.

6 The amount of inclination of two lines to each other, or of one line to a horizontal or vertical baseline. **L16.**

ARNOLD BENNETT The angle of the slatternly bag across his shoulders. B. ENGLAND Thirty feet below the crest, the angle of ascent increased so drastically that they were forced to crawl. J. IRVING He came in at too steep an angle, attempted to correct his position with a weak veer, . . and struck the pond like a stone.

7 The point or direction from which something is viewed or approached (*lit.* & *fig.*); a standpoint; the direction from which a photograph etc. is taken. **L19.**

R. LEHMANN Her face at this new angle had a look of pathos. R. MACAULAY Curious how we always seem to see Waterloo from the French angle and count it a defeat. A. BURGESS I'm concerned with the linguistic angle. Then there's the angle of inter-racial relations.

– PHRASES: ***acute angle***: see ACUTE *adjective* 2b. ***angle of attack***: see ATTACK *noun*. ***angle of*** FRICTION. ***angle of repose***: see REPOSE *noun*. ***angle of weather***: see WEATHER *noun* 3. ***complementary angles***: see COMPLEMENTARY 2. ***conjugate angle***: see CONJUGATE *adjective*. CRITICAL ***angle***. ***exterior angle***: see EXTERIOR *adjective*. ***facial angle***: see FACIAL *adjective* 2. ***interior angle***: see INTERIOR *adjective*. ***reverse angle***: see REVERSE *adjective*. ***right angle***: see RIGHT *adjective*. ***solid angle***: see SOLID *adjective*. SPHERICAL ***angle***. ***straight angle***: see STRAIGHT *adjective*[1]. ***supplementary angle***: see SUPPLEMENTARY *adjective*. ***trihedral angle***: see TRIHEDRAL *adjective*. ***vergence angle***: see VERGENCE 1. ***vertical angle***: see VERTICAL *adjective*. ***visual angle***: see VISUAL *adjective*.
– COMB.: **angle bracket** TYPOGRAPHY etc. a bracket (used alone and in pairs) composed of two lines making an angle, thus 〈 〉; **angledozer** a type of bulldozer with an obliquely set blade; **angle grinder** a device with a rotating abrasive disc, used to grind, polish, or cut metal and other materials; **angle iron** a piece of iron with an L-shaped cross-section used to strengthen a framework; **anglepoise** (proprietary name for) a type of swivelled reading lamp with a sprung and jointed arm; **angle wing** (*N. Amer.*) any of various nymphalid butterflies of the genus *Polygonia*, allied to the comma.
■ **angled** *adjective* [-ED[2]] having an angle or angles; usu. as 2nd elem. of comb. (of the specified type or number): **L16.** **anglewise** *adverb* after the manner of an angle, at an angle; angularly: **L16.**

angle /ˈaŋɡ(ə)l/ *verb*[1]. **LME.**
[ORIGIN from ANGLE *noun*[1].]
1 *verb intrans.* Fish with a hook and bait. (Foll. by *for*, †*to*, a fish.) **LME.**

I. WALTON The fish which we are to Angle for. C. MERIVALE He would . . listlessly angle in the placid waters.

2 *fig.* **a** *verb intrans.* Use artful, indirect, or wily means to obtain something. Foll. by *for*. **L16.** ▸†**b** *verb trans.* Seek to obtain artfully etc. **L16–L17.**

a J. BRAINE If you're hungry and someone's preparing a good meal, you'll naturally angle for an invitation. **b** P. SIDNEY If he spake courteously, he angled the people's hearts.

angle /ˈaŋɡ(ə)l/ *verb*[2]. **LME.**
[ORIGIN from ANGLE *noun*[3].]
1 *verb trans.* Place so as to converge or meet at an angle. *rare.* **LME.**
2 *verb trans.* Drive or direct into an angle or corner; *spec.* in BILLIARDS & SNOOKER etc., cause (a ball) to come to rest behind the cushion in the jaws of a pocket. **L16.**
3 *verb intrans.* Move obliquely; make an angular turn; lie in an oblique direction. **M18.**

R. CHANDLER Two davenports angled across the corners of the room and there was one gold chair.

4 *verb trans.* Move, turn, hit, or direct at an angle; place obliquely. **L19.**

A. UPFIELD Bony had walked like a white man, angling his feet at twenty-five minutes to five. I. ASIMOV He angled the chair so that it faced more away from Baley than towards him.

5 *verb trans.* Present (news etc.) with an inclination towards a particular viewpoint. **M20.**

M. DICKENS You . . almost never see the proprietor, although you feel his presence, because you have to angle your writing his way. C. MACINNES The leader columns are angled at the more intelligent portions of the population.

angleberry /ˈaŋɡ(ə)lb(ə)ri, -bɛri/ *noun.* *Scot.* & *dial.* **L16.**
[ORIGIN Perh. var. of ANBURY or *ang-berry*.]
= ANBURY 1.

A

angler /ˈaŋglə/ *noun*. ME.
[ORIGIN from ANGLE *verb*[1] + -ER[1].]
1 A person who angles (*lit.* & *fig.*). ME.
2 Any of numerous predatory fishes, constituting the order Pediculati (or Lophiiformes), that lure small fish to them by movements of specialized dorsal spines; spec. *Lophius piscatorius*, found in British waters. Usu. more fully ***anglerfish***. M17.

anglesite /ˈaŋg(ə)lʌɪt/ *noun*. M19.
[ORIGIN from *Anglesey*, Wales + -ITE[1].]
MINERALOGY. Lead sulphate, occurring as white or colourless orthorhombic prisms, or in massive form.

Anglian /ˈaŋglɪən/ *adjective* & *noun*. E18.
[ORIGIN from Latin *Angli* (see ANGLE *noun*[2]) + -AN.]
▸ **A** *adjective*. **1** Of or pertaining to the Angles or the Old English dialects of Northumbria and Mercia; ***East Anglian***, of or pertaining to the East Angles or East Anglia, the region now comprising Norfolk and Suffolk, or its dialect. E18.
2 GEOLOGY. Designating or pertaining to a Pleistocene glaciation in Britain, identified with the Elsterian of northern Europe (and perhaps the Mindel of the Alps). M20.
▸ **B** *noun*. **1** The Anglian dialect of Old English; ***East Anglian***, a native or inhabitant, or the dialect, of East Anglia. L19.
2 GEOLOGY. The Anglian glaciation or its deposits. M20.

Anglic /ˈaŋglɪk/ *noun*. M20.
[ORIGIN from ANGL(O- + -IC.]
A simplified form of English spelling devised by the Swedish philologist R. E. Zachrisson (1880–1937) and intended for use as an international auxiliary language.

Anglic /ˈaŋglɪk/ *adjective*. M19.
[ORIGIN from medieval Latin *Anglicus* from Latin *Angli*: see ANGLE *noun*[2], -IC.]
= ANGLIAN *adjective* 1.

Anglican /ˈaŋglɪk(ə)n/ *adjective* & *noun*. E17.
[ORIGIN medieval Latin *Anglicanus* (*Anglicana ecclesia* in Magna Carta), formed as ANGLIC *adjective*: see -AN.]
▸ **A** *adjective*. **1** Of or pertaining to the reformed Church of England or any Church in communion with it. E17.
Anglican Communion the group of Christian Churches derived from or related to the Church of England.
2 *gen*. English. *rare*. M19.
▸ **B** *noun*. An adherent of the reformed Church of England. L18.
■ **Anglicanism** *noun* (adherence to) Anglican doctrine and practice M19. **Anglicanize** *verb trans*. (*a*) *rare* make English; (*b*) make Anglican in doctrine, character, etc.: E19.

anglice /ˈaŋglɪsi/ *adverb*. Also **A-**. E17.
[ORIGIN medieval Latin, from Latin *Anglus*: see ANGLE *noun*[2], -ICE[2].]
In (plain) English.

anglicise *verb* var. of ANGLICIZE.

Anglicism /ˈaŋglɪsɪz(ə)m/ *noun*. M17.
[ORIGIN from medieval Latin *Anglicus* (see ANGLIC *adjective*) + -ISM.]
1 Anglicized language; an English idiom. M17.
2 Englishness; imitation of or support for what is English. L18.
■ **Anglicist** *noun* (*a*) an advocate or favourer of Anglicism; (*b*) = ANGLIST: M19.

anglicize /ˈaŋglɪsʌɪz/ *verb trans*. Also **-ise**, **A-**. E18.
[ORIGIN formed as ANGLICISM + -IZE.]
Make English in form or character. Also, in *pass*., be formed by anglicization (*from*).
■ **angliciˈzation** *noun* L19.

Anglify /ˈaŋglɪfʌɪ/ *verb trans*. Now *rare*. M18.
[ORIGIN from Latin *Angli* (see ANGLE *noun*[2]) + -FY.]
= ANGLICIZE.

Anglist /ˈaŋglɪst/ *noun*. L19.
[ORIGIN German from Latin *Anglus*: see ANGLE *noun*[2], -IST.]
A student of or scholar in English language or literature, esp. on the mainland of Europe.
■ **Anˈglistics** *noun pl*. M20.

Anglo /ˈaŋgləʊ/ *noun* & *adjective*. E19.
[ORIGIN Independent use of ANGLO-.]
▸ **A** *noun*. Pl. **-os**. A person of English or British or N. European origin or descent; a non-Hispanic white American in the south-western US; an English-speaking Canadian. E19.
▸ **B** *adjective*. Of English or British origin or character; of or pertaining to Anglos. M19.

Anglo- /ˈaŋgləʊ/ *combining form*.
[ORIGIN from Latin *Anglus* (see ANGLE *noun*[2]) + -O-.]
English, of English origin; English or British and —, England or Britain in connection with —.
– NOTE: When used of Britain as a whole sometimes offensive to some Scots, Welsh, and N. Irish people.
■ **Anglo-ˈFrisian** *adjective* & *noun* (of or pertaining to) the hypothetical parent language of Old English and Old Frisian L19. **Anglo-ˈGallic** *adjective* pertaining, relating, or common to both England and France M18. **Anglo-ˈGallicism** *noun* a French word or phrase adopted into English E19. **Anglo-ˈLatin** *adjective* & *noun* (of or pertaining to) anglicized Latin or medieval Latin as used in England L18. **Anglo-ˈRoman** *adjective* (*a*) English Roman Catholic; (*b*) of or pertaining to England and Rome: M19. **Anglo-verˈnacular** *adjective* (*Indian*) pertaining to or consisting of English and an Indian language L19.

Anglo-American /aŋgləʊəˈmɛrɪk(ə)n/ *noun* & *adjective*. L18.
[ORIGIN from ANGLO- + AMERICAN.]
▸ **A** *noun*. An American of English or British origin. L18.
▸ **B** *adjective*. **1** Of or pertaining to Americans of English or British origin. L18.
2 Of or belonging to both England (or Britain) and America. E19.

Anglo-Catholic /aŋgləʊˈkaθ(ə)lɪk/ *adjective* & *noun*. M19.
[ORIGIN from ANGLO- + CATHOLIC.]
(A member) of a party holding that the Church of England is a branch of the Catholic Church and rejecting its Protestant elements.
■ **Anglo-Caˈtholicism** *noun* M19.

Anglo-Celt /aŋgləʊˈkɛlt/ *noun*. M19.
[ORIGIN from ANGLO- + CELT *noun*[1].]
A person of British or Irish descent (chiefly used outside Britain and Ireland).
■ **Anglo-Celtic** *adjective* M19.

Anglocentric /aŋgləʊˈsɛntrɪk/ *adjective*. L19.
[ORIGIN from ANGLO- + -CENTRIC.]
Centred on England or Britain.

Anglo-French /aŋgləʊˈfrɛn(t)ʃ/ *noun* & *adjective*. E19.
[ORIGIN from ANGLO- + FRENCH *adjective* & *noun*.]
▸ **A** *noun*. **1** Anglicized French. E19.
2 = ANGLO-NORMAN *noun* 2. E20.
▸ **B** *adjective*. Of or belonging to both England (or Britain) and France. M19.

Anglo-Indian /aŋgləʊˈɪndɪən/ *noun* & *adjective*. E19.
[ORIGIN from ANGLO- + INDIAN.]
▸ **A** *noun*. **1** A person of mixed British and Indian descent resident in the Indian subcontinent. E19.
2 A person of British birth resident, or once long resident, in the Indian subcontinent. M19.
▸ **B** *adjective*. Of, pertaining to, or being an Anglo-Indian or Anglo-Indians; of, pertaining to, or characteristic of India under British rule; (of a word) adopted into English from an Indian language. M19.

Anglo-Irish /aŋgləʊˈʌɪrɪʃ/ *noun* & *adjective*. L18.
[ORIGIN from ANGLO- + IRISH.]
▸ **A** *noun*. **1** *collect*. Persons of English descent born or resident in Ireland or of mixed English and Irish parentage. L18.
2 The English language as used in Ireland. E20.
▸ **B** *adjective*. **1** Of or pertaining to the Anglo-Irish; of mixed English and Irish parentage. M19.
2 Of or belonging to both Britain and the Republic of Ireland. E20.

Economist Off to Dublin to discuss such an Anglo-Irish deal.

Anglomania /aŋgləʊˈmeɪnɪə/ *noun*. M18.
[ORIGIN from ANGLO- + -MANIA, after French *anglomanie*.]
Excessive admiration for what is English.
■ **Anglomaniac** *noun* & *adjective* M19.

Anglo-Norman /aŋgləʊˈnɔːmən/ *noun* & *adjective*. M18.
[ORIGIN from ANGLO- + NORMAN *noun*[1] & *adjective*.]
▸ **A** *noun*. **1** A native or inhabitant of England after the Norman Conquest who was of Norman descent. M18.
2 The variety of Norman French used in England after the Norman Conquest. M19.
▸ **B** *adjective*. Of or pertaining to the Anglo-Normans or Anglo-Norman. M18.
■ **Anglo-Norˈmanic** *adjective* & *noun* (now *rare*) E18.

Anglophile /ˈaŋglə(ʊ)fʌɪl/ *adjective* & *noun*. Also **-phil** /-fɪl/. M19.
[ORIGIN French, formed as ANGLO- + -PHILE.]
(A person who is) friendly to England (or Britain) or to what is English (or British).
■ **Angloˈphilia** *noun* friendliness to England (or Britain) L19.

Anglophobia /aŋglə(ʊ)ˈfəʊbɪə/ *noun*. L18.
[ORIGIN from ANGLO- + -PHOBIA.]
Intense fear or hatred of England (or Britain) or of what is English (or British).
■ ˈ**Anglophobe** *noun* & *adjective* (a person who is) afraid of or hostile to England (or Britain) or what is English (or British) M19. **Anglophobic** *adjective* M19.

anglophone /ˈaŋglə(ʊ)fəʊn/ *noun* & *adjective*. Also **A-**. E20.
[ORIGIN from ANGLO- + Greek *phōnē* voice.]
(A person who is) English-speaking.

Anglo-Saxon /aŋgləʊˈsaks(ə)n/ *noun* & *adjective*. E17.
[ORIGIN mod. Latin *Anglo-Saxones* pl. for medieval Latin *Angli Saxones*, after Old English *Angulseaxe*, *-seaxan*.]
▸ **A** *noun*. **I** Applied to people.
1 An English Saxon (as distinct from one of the Old Saxons of Continental Europe); a (Germanic) native or inhabitant of England before the Norman Conquest. E17.
2 A person of English (or British) descent wherever found. M19.
▸ **II** Applied to language.
3 The language of England before the Norman Conquest; Old English. L18.
4 The English language (of any period); *colloq*. plain, esp. crude, forthright English. M19.
▸ **B** *adjective*. Of or pertaining to the Anglo-Saxons or their language (Old English); *spec*. designating, of, or pertaining to the period between the 5th-cent. conquest of Britain by the Saxons, Jutes, and Angles, and the Norman Conquest. E18.
■ **Anglo-Saxondom** *noun* the collective body of people of English or British descent M19. †**Anglo-Saxonic** *adjective* & *noun* (of) the Anglo-Saxon language L17–L18. **Anglo-Saxonism** *noun* (*a*) the feeling of identity of Anglo-Saxondom; (*b*) a word, idiom, etc., deriving from Anglo-Saxon: M19.

Anglosphere /ˈaŋgləʊsfɪə/ *noun*. L20.
[ORIGIN from ANGLO- + SPHERE *noun*.]
The group of countries where English is the main native language.

angola *noun* & *adjective* see ANGORA.

Angolan /aŋˈgəʊlən/ *noun* & *adjective*. E17.
[ORIGIN from *Angola* (see below) + -AN.]
(A native or inhabitant) of Angola, a country on the SW coast of Africa.

angon /ˈaŋgɒn/ *noun*. L19.
[ORIGIN medieval Latin from Greek *aggōn*.]
ARCHAEOLOGY. A type of iron spear with a double barb.

†**angor** *noun*. LME–M18.
[ORIGIN Old French from Latin = a squeeze, a strangling: see -OR.]
(A feeling of) anguish or constricting pain.

angora /aŋˈgɔːrə/ *noun* & *adjective*. Also **-gola** /-ˈgəʊlə/, **A-**. E19.
[ORIGIN *Angora*, mod. Ankara, in Turkey; *angola* is a corruption.]
▸ **I** **1** In full ***angora cat***. A long-haired variety of cat. E19.
2 In full ***angora goat***. A long-haired variety of goat. E19.
3 In full ***angora rabbit***. A variety of rabbit with long white hair. M19.
▸ **II** *transf*. **4** Fabric made from the hair of the angora goat; mohair. Also designating a garment etc. made from this. M19.
5 Fabric made from a mixture of sheep's wool and angora rabbit hair. Also designating a garment etc. made from this. M20.

angostura /aŋgəˈstjʊərə/ *noun*. Also **-gust-**, **A-**. L18.
[ORIGIN *Angostura*, now Ciudad Bolívar, a town in Venezuela.]
1 ***angostura bark***, an aromatic bark formerly used as a febrifuge and tonic. L18.
2 (**A-**.) In full ***Angostura bitters***. (Proprietary name for) a type of aromatic bitters orig. made in Angostura. L19.

angry /ˈaŋgri/ *adjective* & *verb*. LME.
[ORIGIN from ANGER *noun* + -Y[1].]
▸ **A** *adjective*. †**1** Troublesome, vexatious. LME–M17.
†**2** Troubled, vexed. LME–L15.
3 Feeling anger or resentment, enraged, extremely displeased. (Foll. by usu. *at*, *about* a thing; *at*, *with* a person; *that*.) LME.

JONSON Where it concerns himself, Who's angry at a slander makes it true. H. E. BATES I had never been angry with her before—annoyed sometimes, . . but never more. D. STOREY I was angry with him, angry that he should allow me to talk to him like this. C. HAMPTON I was still very angry about your not letting me stay.

angry young man a young man dissatisfied with and outspoken against existing social and political structures, *spec*. any of several British playwrights and novelists of the 1950s expressing such dissatisfaction.
4 Of a mood or action: moved or excited by anger. LME.

TENNYSON A man's own angry pride Is cap and bells for a fool.

5 Revealing or expressing anger; *fig*. seeming to express anger. LME. ▸**b** Having the colour of an angry face, red. *rare*. M17.

DRYDEN He sheathes his paws, uncurls his angry mane. J. TYNDALL Angry masses of cloud. D. DU MAURIER The angry colour flooded her dead white face. W. FAULKNER His face was not grim and neither cold nor angry. B. MALAMUD He heaved a last angry shovelful into the gutter. **b** C. LAMB His waistcoat red and angry.

6 Hot-tempered, irritable. *arch*. LME.

N. ROWE Honour, This busie, angry thing, that scatters Discord.

7 Of a wound, sore, etc.: inflamed, smarting. L15.
▸ **B** *verb trans*. Make angry. *rare*. LME.
■ **angrily** *adverb* LME. **angriness** *noun* (*rare*) LME.

angst /aŋst/ *noun*. E20.
[ORIGIN German.]
Anxiety, neurotic fear; guilt, remorse.

angstrom /ˈaŋstrəm/ *noun*. Also **ångström**, **A-**, **Å-**. L19.
[ORIGIN A. J. *Ångström* (1814–74), Swedish physicist.]
A unit of length equal to one hundred-millionth of a centimetre; 10^{-10} m. Also ***angstrom unit***.

Anguillan /anˈgwɪlən/ *noun* & *adjective*. M20.
[ORIGIN from *Anguilla* (see below) + -AN.]
(A native or inhabitant) of the island of Anguilla in the W. Indies.

anguilliform /aŋˈgwɪlɪfɔːm/ *adjective*. L17.
[ORIGIN from Latin *anguilla* eel + -I- + -FORM.]
Eel-shaped; eel-like.

anguine /ˈaŋgwɪn/ *adjective*. M17.
[ORIGIN Latin *anguinus*, from *anguis* snake: see -INE[1].]
Of a snake or serpent; snakelike.
■ **anˈguineous** *adjective* (*rare*) M17.

anguish /ˈaŋgwɪʃ/ *noun*. ME.
[ORIGIN Old French *anguis* (mod. *angoisse*) from Latin *angustia*, in pl. straits, distress, from *angustus* narrow, tight, ult. formed as *angere* squeeze, strangle: see -ISH[2]. Cf. ANGER *noun*, ANGINA, ANGOR.]
Severe bodily or mental pain, intense suffering.

A. J. CRONIN The beauty of the scene appeased the anguish of his heart. R. LEHMANN When I went to see her after Rickie's death she was in anguish. I. MURDOCH My head was heavy with pain and any movement brought twinges of anguish.

■ †**anguishous** *adjective* (long *dial.*) (*a*) causing anguish; (*b*) oppressed with anguish; (*c*) anxious: ME–L19.

anguish /ˈaŋgwɪʃ/ *verb*. ME.
[ORIGIN Old French *anguissier* (mod. *angoisser*) from ecclesiastical Latin *angustiare* to distress, from Latin *angustia*: see ANGUISH *noun*, -ISH[2].]
1 *verb trans.* Distress with severe bodily or mental pain. Now chiefly as ANGUISHED *ppl adjective*. ME.
2 *verb intrans.* Suffer severe bodily or mental pain. Now *rare*. ME.
■ **anguished** *ppl adjective* suffering or expressing anguish E17. **anguishment** *noun* (*rare*) severe distress; an affliction: L16.

angular /ˈaŋgjʊlə/ *adjective*. LME.
[ORIGIN Latin *angularis*, from *angulus* ANGLE *noun*[3]: see -AR[1]. Cf. French *angulaire*.]
1 ASTROLOGY. Of or pertaining to each of the four houses at the cardinal points. *rare*. LME.
2 Constituting an angle, sharp corner, or apex; placed in or at an angle; measured by angle. L15.
angular momentum the quantity of rotation of a body, equal to the product of its moment of inertia and angular velocity. **angular velocity** rate of change of angular position.
3 Having an angle or angles; sharp-cornered. L16.
4 Having the joints and bony protuberances prominent; jerky, awkward; lacking suavity, unaccommodating. M19.

J. S. BLACKIE Their movements were slow, their gesticulations abrupt and angular. DICKENS As a particularly angular man, I do not fit smoothly into the social circle. V. WOOLF All well grown, angular, ruthless youngsters.

■ **anguˈlarity** *noun* (*a*) the quality or state of being angular; (*b*) in *pl.*, angular outlines, sharp corners: M17. **angularly** *adverb* in an angular manner; obliquely, diagonally: L15.

angulated /ˈaŋgjʊleɪtɪd/ *adjective*. L15.
[ORIGIN from Latin *angulatus* pa. pple of *angulare*, from *angulus* ANGLE *noun*[3] + -ED[1].]
Chiefly BOTANY & ZOOLOGY. Formed with angles or corners.
■ Also **angulate** *adjective* M18.

angulation /aŋgjʊˈleɪʃ(ə)n/ *noun*. L17.
[ORIGIN formed as ANGULATED: see -ATION.]
†**1** An oblique or diagonal movement. Only in L17.
2 Angular or cornered formation or position. M19.

angulous /ˈaŋgjʊləs/ *adjective*. Long *obsolete* exc. in Dicts. LME.
[ORIGIN from Latin *angulosus* or French *anguleux*: see ANGLE *noun*[3], -ULOUS.]
Having angles or corners; angular.

Angus /ˈaŋgəs/ *noun*. M19.
[ORIGIN A district in NW Scotland.]
= ***Aberdeen Angus*** s.v. ABERDEEN 1.

angustura *noun* var. of ANGOSTURA.

angwantibo /əŋˈgwɒntɪbəʊ/ *noun*. Pl. **-os**. M19.
[ORIGIN Efik.]
A small rare primate, *Arctocebus calabarensis*, related to the potto and loris, and native to western central Africa. Also called ***golden potto***.

anharmonic /anhɑːˈmɒnɪk/ *adjective*. E19.
[ORIGIN from AN-[5] + HARMONIC *adjective*.]
Chiefly PHYSICS. Not harmonic.
■ ˌ**anharmoˈnicity** *noun* deviation from harmonic behaviour E20.

anhedonia /anhɪˈdəʊnɪə/ *noun*. L19.
[ORIGIN French *anhédonie*, from Greek AN-[5] + *hēdonē* pleasure: see -IA[1].]
PSYCHIATRY. Inability to feel pleasure.
■ **anhedonic** *adjective* having little or no capacity to feel pleasure M20.

anhedral /anˈhiːdr(ə)l, -ˈhɛd-/ *adjective & noun*. L19.
[ORIGIN from AN-[5] + -HEDRAL.]
▸ **A** *adjective*. **1** MINERALOGY. Of a crystal: not having plane faces. L19.
2 AERONAUTICS. Negatively dihedral. M20.
▸ **B** *noun*. AERONAUTICS. A downward inclination of a wing, tailplane, etc.; negative dihedral. M20.
■ **anhedron** *noun*, pl. **-dra**, **-drons**, an anhedral crystal L19.

anhelation /anhɪˈleɪʃ(ə)n/ *noun*. Now *rare*. E17.
[ORIGIN French *anhélation* or Latin *anhelatio(n-)*, from *anhelat-* pa. ppl stem of *anhelare* pant: see -ATION.]
Shortness of breath, a difficulty with breathing; *fig.* panting, aspiration (*after* an object of desire).

anhidrosis /anhɪˈdrəʊsɪs/ *noun*. Also **ani-** /anɪ-/. L19.
[ORIGIN Greek *anidrōsis*, from AN-[5] + *hidrōs* sweat: see -OSIS.]
MEDICINE. Abnormal absence of sweating.
■ **anhidrotic** *adjective & noun* characterized by anhidrosis; (a drug) tending to reduce sweating: L19.

anhinga /anˈhɪŋgə/ *noun*. M18.
[ORIGIN Portuguese from Tupi *áyinga*.]
A long-necked fish-eating bird of the genus *Anhinga*; *esp.* the snakebird, *A. anhinga*. Cf. DARTER 4.

an-hua /anˈhwɑː/ *noun & adjective*. E20.
[ORIGIN Chinese *ànhuā*, from *àn* obscure + *huā* flower.]
(Of) a type of decoration of Chinese porcelain or fabrics that is visible only by transmitted light.

anhungered /ənˈhʌŋgəd/ *adjective*. *arch.* ME.
[ORIGIN Alt. of AHUNGERED by prefix-substitution.]
Famished, hungry; *fig.* longing (*for*).

anhydride /anˈhʌɪdrʌɪd/ *noun*. M19.
[ORIGIN formed as ANHYDROUS + -IDE.]
CHEMISTRY. A compound derived from an acid (usu. specified) by the removal of one or more molecules of water; *spec.* (ORGANIC CHEMISTRY) a compound containing the group ·COO·CO·.

anhydrite /anˈhʌɪdrʌɪt/ *noun*. E19.
[ORIGIN formed as ANHYDRIDE + -ITE[1].]
MINERALOGY. Anhydrous calcium sulphate, an orthorhombic mineral which is an important constituent of many evaporites and other sedimentary deposits.

anhydro- /anˈhʌɪdrəʊ/ *combining form* of next, esp. in names of minerals: see -O-.

anhydrous /anˈhʌɪdrəs/ *adjective*. E19.
[ORIGIN from Greek *anudros* waterless, from AN-[5] + *hudr-*, *hudōr* water: see -OUS.]
Chiefly CHEMISTRY. Lacking water, esp. water of crystallization.
■ Also **anhydric** *adjective* (*rare*) L19.

anhypostasia /ˌanhʌɪpəˈsteɪzɪə/ *noun*. L19.
[ORIGIN mod. Latin from Greek *anhupostasia* unsubstantiality, from AN-[5] + as HYPOSTASIS: see -IA[1].]
THEOLOGY. Absence of a substantial or personal existence in the human nature of Christ.
■ **anhypostasis** /-ˈpɒstəsɪs/ *noun* = ANHYPOSTASIA M19. **anhypoˈstatic** *adjective* having no independent or personal existence M20. **anhypoˈstatical** *adjective* = ANHYPOSTATIC M19.

ani /ˈɑːni/ *noun*. E19.
[ORIGIN Spanish *aní* & Portuguese *anum*, from Tupi *anū*.]
Any of several glossy black large-billed birds of the genus *Crotophaga*, of the cuckoo family, found in Central and S. America.

aniconic /anʌɪˈkɒnɪk/ *adjective*. L19.
[ORIGIN from AN-[5] + ICONIC.]
Of an idol, symbol, etc.: not in human or animal form. Of worship: not involving such idols etc.

anicut /ˈanɪkʌt/ *noun*. Also **ann-**. L18.
[ORIGIN Tamil *aṇai-kkaṭṭu* dam-building.]
A river dam in southern India built for irrigation purposes.

anidrosis *noun* var. of ANHIDROSIS.

anigh /əˈnʌɪ/ *adverb & preposition*. *arch.* ME.
[ORIGIN from A-[1] + NIGH *adverb*: cf. AFAR, ANEAR *preposition & adverb*.]
▸ **A** *adverb*. Near. ME.
▸ **B** *preposition*. Near to. L18.
– NOTE: Obsolete or rare after LME; re-formed L18.

anil /ˈanɪl/ *noun*. L16.
[ORIGIN French or Portuguese, from Arabic *an-nīl*, formed as AL-[2] + Arabic & Persian *nīl* from Sanskrit *nīlī* indigo, from *nīla* dark blue. Cf. NIL *noun*[1].]
1 The dye indigo. L16.
†**2** The indigo shrub. E18–M18.
3 CHEMISTRY. Any imine derived from aniline. Orig. more fully ***anil-compound***. L19.

anile /ˈeɪnʌɪl/ *adjective*. M17.
[ORIGIN Latin *anilis*, from *anus* old woman: see -ILE.]
Of or like an old woman.

anilic /əˈnɪlɪk/ *adjective*. M19.
[ORIGIN from ANIL + -IC.]
CHEMISTRY. ***anilic acid***, nitrosalicylic acid, indigotic acid.

aniline /ˈanɪliːn, -lɪn/ *noun*. M19.
[ORIGIN from ANIL + -INE[5]: it was orig. prepared by distilling indigo with alkali.]
CHEMISTRY. A colourless basic oily liquid, $C_6H_5NH_2$, present in coal tar and used in the manufacture of dyes, drugs, and plastics.
aniline black, ***aniline colour***, ***aniline dye***, etc.
■ **anilide** *noun* any substituted amide having a phenyl group bonded to the nitrogen atom M19.

anilingus /eɪmɪˈlɪŋgəs/ *noun*. M20.
[ORIGIN from Latin ANUS + *lingere* to lick.]
Licking or sucking a sexual partner's anus.

anility /əˈnɪlɪti/ *noun*. E17.
[ORIGIN Latin *anilitas*, formed as ANILE: see -ITY.]
Old-womanishness; dotage; (an instance of) foolishness.

anima /ˈanɪmə/ *noun*. E20.
[ORIGIN Latin = (i) air, breath, life; (ii) mind, soul.]
PSYCHOANALYSIS. The inner self (opp. ***persona***). Also, the source of the feminine component of a personality. Cf. ANIMUS.

animadversion /ˌanɪmədˈvəːʃ(ə)n/ *noun*. M16.
[ORIGIN French, or Latin *animadversio(n-)*, from *animadvers-* pa. ppl stem of *animadvertere*: see ANIMADVERT, -ION.]
†**1** Judicial punishment; a penal visitation. M16–M19.

A. ALISON A power whose lightest measure of animadversion would be banishment.

2 Censure, reproof, blame. L16.

S. JOHNSON No weakness of the human mind has more frequently incurred animadversion.

3 A criticism; a (usu. censorious) comment. L16.

W. STYRON His complaints grew louder and his animadversions more serious and cutting.

†**4** The action or faculty of observation. E17–L18.

M. HALE The due animadversion and inspection of their own Minds. J. GLANVILL In an infinite Life as God is, there can be no distraction, his animadversion necessarily being infinite.

†**5** A notice, a warning. M17–E18.

CLARENDON They all knew Caesar's fate, by contemning, or neglecting such animadversions.

animadvert /ˌanɪmədˈvəːt/ *verb*. LME.
[ORIGIN Latin *animadvertere*, from *animum* the mind + *advertere* ADVERT *verb*.]
†**1** *verb trans.* Pay attention to, observe. LME–L17.

I. NEWTON The light.. shall in comparison not be strong enough to be animadverted.

2 *verb intrans.* Pay attention *to*; observe, remark, consider, (*that*). M16.

HENRY FIELDING Animadvert that you are in the house of a great lady.

3 *verb intrans.* Pass criticism or censure *on* (occas. *against*). M17.

POPE Your grace very justly animadverts against the too great disposition of finding faults. H. JAMES He.. inclined a critical head to either quarter, and.. animadverted to his companion on this passage and that.

4 *verb intrans.* Pass judgement, take punitive action, (*against*, (*up*)*on*). *arch.* L17.

JAS. MILL It is for the tribunal before which he offends to animadvert upon his conduct.

■ **animadverter** *noun* M17.

animal /ˈanɪm(ə)l/ *noun & adjective*. ME.
[ORIGIN As adjective from Old French & mod. French, or Latin *animalis* having vital breath, (in medieval Latin) bestial, from ANIMA: see -AL[1]; partly attrib. use of the noun. As noun ult. from Latin *animal* for *animale* use as noun of neut. adjective.]
▸ **A** *noun*. A living organism having sensation and voluntary motion, without rigid cell walls, and dependent on organic substances for food; *spec.* (*a*) an animal other than a human being; (*b*) *colloq.* a land animal as opp. to a fish or a bird; (*c*) *colloq.* a four-legged animal as opp., e.g., to an insect or a worm. Also, a brutish person, a person regarded as without human attributes. ME.
no such animal *colloq.* no such person or thing. **the animal** the animal nature in humans.
▸ **B** *adjective*. †**1** Connected with sensation, innervation, or will. LME–L18.
2 Of, pertaining to, or characteristic of animals; not intellectual, moral, or spiritual. LME.
3 EMBRYOLOGY. Designating or pertaining to that pole of the ovum or embryo that contains the more rapidly dividing cells in the early stages of development. Opp. ***vegetal***, ***vegetative***. M19.
– SPECIAL COLLOCATIONS: **animal black**, **animal charcoal** charcoal obtained from calcined bones. **animal electricity**: that generated within animals, e.g. as nerve impulses. †**animal flower** a sea anemone. ***animal husbandry***: see HUSBANDRY *noun* 2. **animal kingdom** animals collectively, as one of the three (or more) major divisions of the natural world. **animal liberation** the freeing of animals from exploitation by humans. **animal magnetism** *hist.* hypnotism, mesmerism. ***animal oil***: see OIL *noun*. **animal rights** the natural rights of animals to live a free life. **animal spirits** †(*a*) the supposed principle of sensation and voluntary motion; †(*b*) nerve, physical courage; (*c*) natural exuberance.
■ **aniˈmalic** *adjective* (*rare*) L17. **animally** *adverb* E17.

animalcule /anɪˈmalkjuːl/ *noun*. Also in Latin form †**-culum**, pl. **-la**. L16.
[ORIGIN mod. Latin *animalculum*, dim. of *animal*: see ANIMAL, -CULE.]
†**1** A small or tiny animal, as a mouse or an invertebrate. L16–M19.
2 A microscopic animal. L17.
■ **animalcular** *adjective* of or pertaining to animalcules M18.

animalise *verb* var. of ANIMALIZE.

animalism /ˈanɪm(ə)lɪz(ə)m/ *noun*. M19.
[ORIGIN formed as ANIMALCULE + -ISM.]
1 Animal activity, physical exercise and enjoyment; sensuality. M19.
2 The doctrine that humans are merely animals. M19.

A

3 A merely sensual being. *rare*. **M19.**
■ **animalist** *noun* (*a*) a person who practises or adheres to animalism; (*b*) a person who depicts animals; (*c*) a supporter of animal liberation or animal rights: **M19. anima'listic** *adjective* **L19.**

animality /anɪˈmalɪti/ *noun*. **E17.**
[ORIGIN French *animalité*: see ANIMAL, -ITY.]
1 The sum of animal qualities and functions; animal nature; merely animal nature, sensuality. **E17.**
2 The animal kingdom. **L18.**

animalize /ˈanɪm(ə)lʌɪz/ *verb trans*. Also **-ise**. **E17.**
[ORIGIN from ANIMAL + -IZE; partly through French *animaliser*.]
†**1** Inspire, actuate. *rare*. Only in **E17.**
2 Represent in animal form. **M18.**
3 Convert to animal substance. **L18.**
4 Sensualize. **E19.**
■ **animali'zation** *noun* **M18.**

anima mundi /ˌanɪmə ˈmʌndʌɪ, ˈmʊndiː/ *noun phr*. **L16.**
[ORIGIN medieval Latin (Abelard) = soul of the world; app. formed to render Greek *psukhē tou kosmou*.]
A power supposed to organize the whole universe and to coordinate its parts.

†**animastic** *adjective*. **M17–M19.**
[ORIGIN medieval Latin *animasticus* pertaining to the soul, from Latin ANIMA: cf. ONOMASTIC.]
Spiritual (as opp. to ***material***). Also, animate.

animate /ˈanɪmət/ *adjective*. **LME.**
[ORIGIN Latin *animatus* pa. pple, formed as ANIMATE *verb*: see -ATE².]
1 Endowed with life, living. **LME.**

CARLYLE That men should have worshipped . . stocks and stones, and all manner of animate and inanimate objects. F. B. YOUNG A shoal of flying-fish Spurts out like animate spray.

2 Lively; full of activity. **E19.**

SOUTHEY A courser More animate of eye, Of form more faultless never had he seen. B. ENGLAND The entire area was animate with dozens of villagers running about in a state of great excitation.

3 GRAMMAR. Pertaining to or denoting living beings. **E19.**

J. LYONS Most transitive verbs tend to occur with an animate noun as their subject in active sentences.

■ **animatism** *noun* the ascription of psychic qualities to inanimate as well as animate objects **E20.**

animate /ˈanɪmeɪt/ *verb trans*. **L15.**
[ORIGIN Latin *animat-* pa. ppl stem of *animare* give life to, from ANIMA: see -ATE³.]
1 Breathe life into, quicken, vivify, enliven. **L15.** ▸**b** Give (a film, cartoon figure, etc.) the appearance of showing movement, by using a quick succession of gradually varying images. **L19.**

R. W. EMERSON The soul in man is not an organ, but animates and exercises all the organs. O. HENRY Then his eyes get animated, and I see he's got some great scheme in his mind. K. CLARK About ten years later this stiff antiquarian style is animated by a turbine of creative energy.

2 Fill with boldness, courage, or spirit; excite (a person) to action; inspire, actuate. **M16.** ▸**b** Put in motion (a thing). *arch*. exc. as *fig*. use of sense 2. **M17.**

DRYDEN The shouting animates their hearts. SIR W. SCOTT Desperate men, animated by the presence of two or three of the actors in the primate's murder. E. H. GOMBRICH The spirit of creative research that animated the young painters of the nineteenth century. **b** J. TYNDALL Motion . . which animates the bullet projected from the gun.

■ **animated** *adjective* alive; lively, vivacious: **M16. animatedly** *adverb* **L18. animater** *noun* (*rare*) **M17. animator** *noun* a person who or thing which animates something; CINEMATOGRAPHY an artist who prepares animated cartoons: **M16.**

animateur /anɪməˈtɜː, *foreign* animatœːr (*pl. same*)/ *noun*. **M20.**
[ORIGIN French.]
One who coordinates or facilitates a cultural or other activity; freq. a person who works in a school or other community to channel the skills of potential dancers etc.

animatic /anɪˈmatɪk/ *noun*. **L20.**
[ORIGIN from ANIMAT(ED *ppl adjective* + -IC (or possibly a blend with SCHEMATIC).]
A preliminary or test version of a film, esp. of an advertising commercial, produced by shooting successive sections of a storyboard and adding a soundtrack.

animation /anɪˈmeɪʃ(ə)n/ *noun*. **M16.**
[ORIGIN Latin *animatio(n-)*: see ANIMATE *verb*, -ATION.]
†**1** Encouragement, inspiration. **M16–L17.**

HENRY MORE An intimation and animation to us to follow his example.

†**2 a** The action of imparting life, vitality, or motion. **L16–E18.** ▸**b** Preparation or production of animated films, visual images, etc. **L19.**
3 The state of being alive. *arch*. **E17.**

M. SHELLEY Capable of bestowing animation on lifeless matter.

suspended animation: see SUSPENDED *ppl adjective*.
4 Vivacity, ardour. **L18.**

A. FRASER Her attraction lay in her animation and in particular her sparkling black eyes.

5 Enlivenment; enlivening operation or influence. **E19.**

SIR W. SCOTT The animation of the chase and the glow of the exercise.

animato /anɪˈmɑːtəʊ/ *adverb & adjective*. **E18.**
[ORIGIN Italian, from Latin *animatus* filled with life.]
MUSIC. (A direction:) in a lively or spirited manner.

anime /ˈanɪmeɪ/ *noun*. Also **animé**. **L20.**
[ORIGIN Japanese, from French *animé* animated.]
A Japanese genre of animated film, typically science fiction and characterized by violence, eroticism, or anarchy.

animé /ˈanɪmeɪ/ *noun*. **L16.**
[ORIGIN French, from Tupi *wana'ni*.]
Any of various resins; *spec*. that from the W. Indian tree *Hymenaea courbaril*, used in making varnish. Also ***gum animé***.

animism /ˈanɪmɪz(ə)m/ *noun*. **M19.**
[ORIGIN from Latin ANIMA + -ISM.]
1 The doctrine of the ***anima mundi***. **M19.**
2 The attribution of a living soul to plants, inanimate objects, and natural phenomena. **M19.**
■ **animist** *noun* **E19. ani'mistic** *adjective* **M19.**

animosity /anɪˈmɒsɪti/ *noun*. **LME.**
[ORIGIN Old French & mod. French *animosité* or late Latin *animositas*, from *animosus* spirited, formed as ANIMUS: see -OSITY.]
1 Spiritedness, courage. Long *rare*. *dial*. **LME.**
2 A spirit of enmity (*against, between, towards*). **E17.**

animus /ˈanɪməs/ *noun*. **E19.**
[ORIGIN Latin = spirit, mind.]
1 Actuating feeling, animating spirit, usu. hostile; animosity shown in speech or action. **E19.**
2 PSYCHOANALYSIS. The source of the masculine component of a personality. Cf. ANIMA. **E20.**

anion /ˈanʌɪən/ *noun*. **M19.**
[ORIGIN from AN(ODE or ANA- + ION.]
A negatively charged ion, i.e. one which would be attracted to an anode. Opp. CATION.
■ **ani'onic** *adjective* of or pertaining to anions; of the nature of an anion: **E20.**

aniridia /anɪˈrɪdɪə, anʌɪ-/ *noun*. **M19.**
[ORIGIN from Greek AN-⁵ + *irid-*, *iris* IRIS + -IA¹.]
MEDICINE. Congenital or traumatic absence of the iris.

anis /ani(s)/ *noun*. **L19.**
[ORIGIN French: see ANISE.]
A liqueur or aperitif flavoured with aniseed; occas., aniseed.

anis- /ˈanɪs/ *combining form* of Latin *anisum* ANISE, used in CHEMISTRY.
■ **ani'saldehyde** *noun* *p*-methoxybenzaldehyde, a fragrant liquid, $CH_3O{\cdot}C_6H_4{\cdot}CHO$ used in perfumery **M19. anisic** /əˈnɪsɪk/ *adjective*: ***anisic acid***, *p*-methoxybenzoic acid, $CH_3O{\cdot}C_6H_4{\cdot}COOH$, a crystalline acid obtained by oxidizing anethole **M19. anisole** *noun* methoxybenzene, $C_6H_5OCH_3$, a colourless liquid ether **M19. anisyl** *noun* the *p*-methoxybenzyl radical, $CH_3O{\cdot}C_6H_4{\cdot}CH_2{\cdot}$ **M19.**

anise /ˈanɪs/ *noun*. **ME.**
[ORIGIN Old French & mod. French *anis* from Latin *anisum*, from Greek *anison* dill, anise.]
1 (The aromatic seed of) an umbelliferous plant, *Pimpinella anisum*, native to the eastern Mediterranean region. Anciently confused with dill, which was prob. the 'anise' of the Bible. **ME.**
2 Any of several trees and shrubs of the Asian and American genus *Illicium*, which bear fruit with the odour of aniseed; *esp*. (*a*) (more fully ***Japanese anise***, ***Chinese anise***) = SHIKIMI; (*b*) = ***star anise*** s.v. STAR *noun*¹ *& adjective*. Also, the fruit of these plants. **E18.**
■ **anisated** *adjective* mixed or flavoured with aniseed **L17.**

aniseed /ˈanɪsiːd/ *noun*. **LME.**
[ORIGIN from ANISE + SEED *noun*.]
The seed of anise, used to flavour liqueurs and sweets.
– COMB.: **aniseed tree** a tree or shrub of the genus *Illicium* (see ANISE 2).

aniseikonia /ənʌɪsʌɪˈkəʊnɪə/ *noun*. **M20.**
[ORIGIN from ANIS(O- + Greek *eikon-*, *eikōn* image + -IA¹.]
MEDICINE. A defect of vision in which the image seen with one eye is larger than that seen with the other.
■ **aniseikonic** *adjective* **M20.**

anisette /anɪˈzɛt/ *noun*. **M19.**
[ORIGIN French, dim. of ANIS: see -ETTE.]
A liqueur flavoured with aniseed.

aniso- /ˈanʌɪsəʊ/ *combining form* of Greek *anisos* unequal, forming esp. negatives (see AN-⁵) of corresp. terms in ISO-.
■ **aniso'coria** *noun* (MEDICINE) inequality in the sizes of the pupils of the eyes **E20. anisocy'tosis** *noun* (MEDICINE) abnormal variation in the size of red blood cells **E20. aniso'gamete** *noun* (BIOLOGY) either of two unequal gametes **L19. ani'sogamous** *adjective* (BIOLOGY) characterized by anisogamy **L19. ani'sogamy** *noun* (BIOLOGY) union of unequal gametes **L19. anisome'tropia** *noun* inequality of refractive power of the eyes **L19. anisometropic** /-ˈtrəʊpɪk, -ˈtrɒpɪk/ *adjective* characterized by anisometropia **L19.**

anisotropic /ˌanʌɪsəˈtrəʊpɪk, -ˈtrɒp-/ *adjective*. **L19.**
[ORIGIN from ANISO- + Greek *tropos* turn + -IC.]
Of a material, a body: having physical properties which have different magnitudes in different directions. Of a property: varying with direction. Opp. ISOTROPIC.
■ **anisotropically** *adverb* **M20. ani'sotropy** *noun* anisotropic behaviour or quality **L19.**

anker /ˈaŋkə/ *noun*. *obsolete* exc. *hist*. **ME.**
[ORIGIN Low German & Dutch, from medieval Latin *anc(h)eria* of unknown origin.]
(A cask containing) a measure of wines and spirits, about 8 gallons or 36 litres.

ankerite /ˈaŋkərʌɪt/ *noun*. **M19.**
[ORIGIN from M. J. *Anker* (1772–1843), Austrian mineralogist + -ITE¹.]
MINERALOGY. Iron-rich dolomite; *spec*. that in which iron predominates over magnesium.

ankh /aŋk/ *noun*. **L19.**
[ORIGIN Egyptian = life, soul.]
An object resembling a cross, but with a loop in place of the upper limb, used in ancient Egyptian art as a symbol of life. Also called ***crux ansata***.

ankle /ˈaŋk(ə)l/ *noun & verb*. Also †**ancle**.
[ORIGIN Old English *ancléow* superseded in Middle English by forms from Old Norse *ǫkkla*, Old Swedish *ankol* corresp. to Old Frisian *ankel*, Middle Low German *enkel*, Middle Dutch *ankel*, Old High German *anchal*, *enchil* (German *Enkel*), from Indo-European base repr. also by ANGLE *noun*³.]
▸ **A** *noun*. The joint which connects the foot with the leg; the slender part between this and the calf. **OE.**
– COMB.: **ankle bone** ANATOMY = TALUS *noun*¹; **ankle boot**, **ankle sock**: just covering the ankle.
▸ **B** *verb intrans*. **1** Use the ankles to good effect in cycling. **L19.**
2 Walk, go. *slang*. **E20.**

anklet /ˈaŋklɪt/ *noun*. **E19.**
[ORIGIN from ANKLE + -LET, after *bracelet*.]
An ornament or fetter for the ankle; also (*US*) an ankle sock.

ankus /ˈaŋkəs/ *noun*. **L19.**
[ORIGIN Hindi *ãkus*, *aṅkas* from Sanskrit *aṅkuśa*.]
In the Indian subcontinent: an elephant goad.

ankylosaur /ˈaŋkɪləsɔː/ *noun*. **L20.**
[ORIGIN mod. Latin *Ankylosaurus* genus name, from Greek *agkulōsis* ANKYLOSIS: see -SAUR.]
Any of a group of broad short-legged ornithischian dinosaurs with heavy armour of bony plates, of the Jurassic and Cretaceous periods worldwide.
■ **ankylo'saurus** *noun*, pl. **-ruses**, **-ri** /-rʌɪ, -riː/, a large ankylosaur of the late Cretaceous genus *Ankylosaurus* **E20.**

ankylose /ˈaŋkɪləʊz/ *verb*. Also **anch-**. **L18.**
[ORIGIN Back-form. from ANKYLOSIS.]
1 *verb trans*. Join or stiffen by ankylosis. Usu. in *pass*., be solidly united bone to bone. **L18.**
ankylosing spondylitis spinal arthritis that eventually causes ankylosis of vertebral and sacro-iliac joints.
2 *verb intrans*. Become joined or stiffened by ankylosis. **M19.**

ankylosis /aŋkɪˈləʊsɪs/ *noun*. Also **anch-**. Pl. **-loses** /-ˈləʊsiːz/. **E18.**
[ORIGIN Greek *agkulōsis*, from *agkuloun* to crook, from *agkulos* crooked: see -OSIS.]
The stiffening of a joint by fibrosis or by the fusion of the separate bones.

ankylostomiasis *noun* var. of ANCYLOSTOMIASIS.

anlace /ˈanləs/ *noun*. *arch*. **ME.**
[ORIGIN Unknown.]
A short tapering two-edged dagger.

anlage /ˈanlɑːɡə, -leɪdʒ/ *noun*. Pl. **-lagen** /-lɑːɡən/, **-lages** /-leɪdʒɪz/. **L19.**
[ORIGIN German = foundation, basis.]
BIOLOGY. The rudimentary basis of an organ or other part, esp. in an embryo.

anlaut /ˈanlaʊt/ *noun*. **L19.**
[ORIGIN German, from *an* on + *Laut* sound.]
PHILOLOGY. The initial sound of a word.

†**anlet** *noun* var. of ANNULET.

ann /an/ *noun*. **E17.**
[ORIGIN Abbreviation of *annat* ANNATE 1.]
SCOTS LAW (now *hist*.). A half-year's (orig. a year's) salary legally due to the executors of a deceased minister of religion in addition to the ordinary stipend.

anna /ˈanə/ *noun*. **E17.**
[ORIGIN Hindi *ānā* (Punjabi *ānnā*).]
A former monetary unit of the Indian subcontinent, equal to one-sixteenth of a rupee.

annabergite /ˈanəbəːɡʌɪt/ *noun*. **M19.**
[ORIGIN from *Annaberg*, a town in Saxony + -ITE¹.]
MINERALOGY. A monoclinic hydrated nickel arsenate, occurring usu. as an apple-green crust on nickel ores.

annal /ˈan(ə)l/ *verb & noun*. **E17.**
[ORIGIN Back-form. from ANNALS.]
▸ **A** *verb intrans. & trans*. Record (events) in annals, chronicle. *rare*. **E17.**

▸ **B** *noun*. The annals of one year; the record of one item in a chronicle. L17.

annalist /ˈan(ə)lɪst/ *noun*. M16.
[ORIGIN from ANNALS + -IST.]
A writer of annals.
▪ **annaˈlistic** *adjective* M19.

annals /ˈan(ə)lz/ *noun pl.* M16.
[ORIGIN French *annales* or Latin *annales* use as noun of masc. pl. of *annalis* yearly, from *annus* year: see -AL[1].]
1 A narrative of events year by year; historical records. M16.
†**2** ROMAN CATHOLIC CHURCH. Masses said for the space of a year. M16–M18.

Annamese /anəˈmiːz/ *adjective & noun*. Now *hist*. Also **Anam-**. E19.
[ORIGIN from Latin *Annam* (see below) + -ESE.]
▸ **A** *adjective*. Of or pertaining to Annam, a former empire and later French protectorate in SE Asia, its inhabitants, or its language. E19.
▸ **B** *noun*. Pl. same.
1 A native or inhabitant of Annam. E19.
2 The Mon-Khmer language of Annam. L19.
▪ **Annamite** /ˈanəmʌɪt/, **Annamitic** /anəˈmɪtɪk/ *adjectives & nouns* = ANNAMESE M19.

annate /ˈaneɪt/ *noun*. In sense 1 also **annat** /ˈanət/. E16.
[ORIGIN French from medieval Latin *annata* a year's space, work, or proceeds, from *annus* year.]
1 SCOTS LAW (now *hist*.). = ANN. E16.
2 ROMAN CATHOLIC CHURCH. In *pl*. The first year's revenue of a see or benefice, paid to the Pope. M16.

annatto /əˈnatəʊ/ *noun*. Pl. **-os**. Also **anatto**. E17.
[ORIGIN Carib name of the tree.]
An orange-red dye obtained from the seed coat of the tropical American tree *Bixa orellana* and much used as a food colouring. Also, the tree itself; its fruit.

anneal /əˈniːl/ *verb*.
[ORIGIN Old English *onǣlan*, from *on-* (see AN *preposition*) + *ǣlan* kindle, burn, bake, from *āl* fire, burning, = Old Saxon *ēld*, Old Norse *eldr*.]
†**1** *verb trans*. Set on fire, inflame. OE–LME.
†**2** *verb trans*. Subject to the action of fire; fire, bake, fuse, glaze. LME–M17.
†**3** *verb trans*. Burn colours into (glass, earthenware, etc.), enamel by an encaustic process. LME–L18.

> G. HERBERT When thou dost anneal in glasse thy storie.

4 *verb trans*. Toughen (glass or metal) by heating and usu. slow cooling. Cf. TEMPER *verb*[1] 12b. M17. ▸**b** *fig*. Toughen, temper. L17.

> **b** SIR W. SCOTT To press the rights of truth, The mind to strengthen and anneal.

5 *verb trans*. & *intrans*. BIOLOGY. Combine to form double-stranded nucleic acid. M20.
▪ **annealer** *noun* M17.

†**annect** *verb trans*. LME–M18.
[ORIGIN Latin *annectere*: see ANNEX *verb*.]
= ANNEX *verb*.

annectent /əˈnɛkt(ə)nt/ *adjective*. E19.
[ORIGIN formed as ANNECT: see -ENT.]
Chiefly BIOLOGY. Connecting, joining.

annelid /ˈan(ə)lɪd/ *noun & adjective*. M19.
[ORIGIN French *annélide* or from mod. Latin *annelida* (see below), from French *annelés* ringed (sc. *animaux* animals) (Lamarck), use of ppl adjective of *anneler*, from Old French *anel* ring from Latin *anellus* dim. of *anulus*: see ANNULUS, -ID[3].]
ZOOLOGY. ▸**A** *noun*. An animal of the phylum Annelida, members of which (e.g. marine worms, earthworms, and leeches) have bodies made up of annular segments. M19.
▸ **B** *adjective*. Of or pertaining to Annelida or an annelid. M19.
▪ Also **aˈnnelidan** *noun & adjective* M19.

annex *noun* var. of ANNEXE.

annex /əˈnɛks/ *verb trans*. LME.
[ORIGIN Old French & mod. French *annexer*, from Latin *annex-* pa. ppl stem of *annectere*, from *ad* AN-[3] + *nectere* tie, fasten.]
(Foll. by *to*.)
▸ **I** Without the idea of subordination.
1 Join, unite. *arch*. LME.
▸ **II** With the idea of subordination.
2 Append, affix; attach as an accessory or annexe. LME.

> R. BOYLE To which he annexes a Disquisition of the Scurvey. F. A. KEMBLE To each settlement is annexed a cook's shop. N. FREELING This prissy building annexed to the Ministry of Social Affairs.

3 Add (a territory etc.) to existing possessions, esp. (*colloq*.) without right; appropriate to one's use. LME.

> W. BLACKSTONE Appropriators may annex the great tithes to the vicarages. E. M. FORSTER Margaret was all for sightseeing, and . . annexed a motor. G. B. SHAW When Germany annexed Poland in 1939, half of it was snatched out of her jaws by Soviet Russia.

4 Join or attach as an attribute, condition, or consequence. LME.

> HOBBES It is annexed to the Soveraignty, to be Iudge. D. HUME He, though he granted him the commission, annexed a clause, that it should not empower him [etc.]. M. ARNOLD Salvation is not annexed to a right knowledge of geometry.

▪ **annexable**, †**-ible** *adjective* E17. **annexment** *noun* (*rare*) = ANNEXURE E17. **annexure** *noun* something annexed, an adjunct, a supplement L19.

annexation /anɛkˈseɪʃ(ə)n/ *noun*. LME.
[ORIGIN medieval Latin *annexatio(n-)* from *annexat-* pa. ppl stem of *annexare* from Latin *annectere*: see ANNEX *verb*, -ATION.]
The action or an act of annexing; *esp*. the action of attaching as an additional privilege, possession, or territorial dependency.
▪ **annexationist** *noun* a person who advocates the annexation of a territory M19.

annexe /ˈanɛks/ *noun*. Also **annex**. E16.
[ORIGIN French from Latin *annexum* use as noun of pa. pple of *annectere*: see ANNEX *verb*.]
1 SCOTS LAW. An appurtenance. *rare*. E16.
†**2** An adjunct, an accessory. M16–L17.
3 An addition to a document, an appendix. M17.
4 A supplementary building, esp. for extra accommodation. M19.

annexion /əˈnɛkʃ(ə)n/ *noun*. Now *rare*. L15.
[ORIGIN Late Latin *annexio(n-)*, from Latin *annex-*: see ANNEX *verb*, -ION.]
1 = ANNEXATION. L15.
†**2** = ANNEXURE. L16–M18.
▪ **annexionist** *noun* (now *rare*) = ANNEXATIONIST M19.

annicut *noun* var. of ANICUT.

annihilate /əˈnʌɪlət/ *adjective*. *arch*. Also †**adn-**. LME.
[ORIGIN Late Latin *annihilatus* pa. pple of *annihilare* (Jerome), *adn-*, from *ad* AN-[3] + *nihil* nothing: see -ATE[2].]
1 Reduced to nothing, blotted out of existence. LME.
†**2** Made null and void, of no effect. LME–L16.

annihilate /əˈnʌɪleɪt/ *verb*. Also †**adn-**. Pa. pple **-ated**, (*arch*.) **-ate** /-ət/. E16.
[ORIGIN formed as ANNIHILATE *adjective*: see -ATE[3].]
1 *verb trans*. Make null and void, cancel, abrogate (laws, treaties, rights, etc.). *arch*. E16.

> W. FULKE To adnihilate the sacraments ministred by heretikes.

2 *verb trans*. Treat as non-existent, set at naught. *arch*. M16.

> SMOLLETT To usurp your name, and annihilate your exploits.

3 *verb trans*. Destroy largely or completely; blot out of existence. M16.

> DEFOE God can no more be the author of evil, than he can annihilate himself, and cease to be. T. PENNANT The vestiges of the Roman camp . . are almost annihilated. WELLINGTON That event has totally annihilated all order and discipline. M. BORN The human race has today the means for annihilating itself.

4 *verb trans*. *fig*. Reduce to insignificance or powerlessness; silence or humiliate completely. M17.

> BYRON Thou who with thy frown Annihilated senates. J. B. PRIESTLEY All the years between Peter De Wint and myself were annihilated in a flash; he pointed and I saw, he spoke and I heard.

5 *verb trans*. (usu. in *pass*.) & *intrans*. PHYSICS. Convert or be converted into electromagnetic radiation; subject to or undergo annihilation. M20.

> S. WEINBERG Nuclear reactions, in which a fraction of the mass of atomic nuclei is annihilated.

▪ †**annihil** *verb trans*. [Old French & mod. French] = ANNIHILATE *verb* 1, 3 L15–L17. **annihilable** *adjective* L17. **annihilative** *adjective* (*rare*) such as to annihilate, crushing E19. **annihilator** *noun* L17.

annihilation /ənʌɪˈleɪʃ(ə)n/ *noun*. Also †**adn-**. M16.
[ORIGIN Old French & mod. French, formed as ANNIHILATE *adjective*: see -ATION.]
Destruction, complete or effective; PHYSICS the conversion of matter (*esp*. the mutual conversion of a particle and its antiparticle) into electromagnetic radiation.

> BURKE The annihilation of our trade, the ruin of our credit. J. B. MOZLEY When reason itself has opened a view into immortality, to put up contentedly with annihilation,—what a dreadful stupefaction of the human spirit. H. ARENDT The final catastrophe which brought the Jews so near to complete annihilation. H. WOUK Unescorted bombers ran a high risk of annihilation.

▪ **annihilationism** *noun* (THEOLOGY) belief in the destruction of the souls of the wicked as well as their bodies L19. **annihilationist** *noun* (THEOLOGY) an adherent of annihilationism L19.

anniversary /anɪˈvəːs(ə)ri/ *noun & adjective*. ME.
[ORIGIN Latin *anniversarius* returning yearly, from *annus* year + *versus* turning + *-arius* -ARY[1]; used as noun in medieval Latin *anniversaria* (sc. *dies* day), *-arium* (sc. *festum* feast); cf. Old French & mod. French *anniversaire*.]
▸ **A** *noun*. **1** The yearly return of a noteworthy date; the day on which some event of ecclesiastical, national, or personal interest is annually commemorated; the celebration of this. ME.
†**2** ROMAN CATHOLIC CHURCH. A commemorative mass said for the space of a year. E17–M18.
▸ **B** *adjective*. **1** Returning or commemorated on the same date each year; annual, repeated each year. *arch*. L15.
†**2** Enduring for or completed in a year. E17–E18.
▪ **anniversarily** *adverb* at the yearly return M17.

Anno Domini /ˈanəʊ ˈdɒmɪnʌɪ/ *adverbial & noun phr*. M16.
[ORIGIN Latin = in the year of the Lord.]
▸ **A** *adverb*. Of the Christian era. Usu. written AD (see A, A III). M16.
▸ **B** *noun*. **1** A particular year. L17.

> DRYDEN The *Anno Domini* of your new sovereign's coronation.

2 Advanced or advancing age. *colloq*. L19.

> E. V. LUCAS When the time came for A to take the bat he was unable to do so. *Anno Domini* asserted itself.

annominate *verb*, **annomination** *noun* vars. of AGNOMINATE, AGNOMINATION.

annotate /ˈanəteɪt/ *verb*. L16.
[ORIGIN Latin *annotat-* pa. ppl stem of *annotare*, from *ad* AN-[3] + *nota* mark: see -ATE[3].]
†**1** *verb trans*. *gen*. Make a mark on. *rare*. Only in L16.
2 *verb trans*. Add notes to (a book etc.). M18.
3 *verb intrans*. Add or make notes (*on*, *upon*). M18.

annotation /anəˈteɪʃ(ə)n/ *noun*. LME.
[ORIGIN French, or Latin *annotatio(n-)*, formed as ANNOTATE: see -ATION.]
1 A note by way of explanation or comment. LME.

> R. QUIRK Annotations in margins and endpapers.

†**2** Chronological reckoning or notation. L15–M17.

> T. GALE There was anciently no annotation of historie among them [the Grecians].

3 The action of annotating. L16.

annotator /ˈanəteɪtə/ *noun*. M17.
[ORIGIN formed as ANNOTATE + -OR: cf. French *annotateur* (16), medieval Latin *annotator*.]
A person who annotates a text.

announce /əˈnaʊns/ *verb & noun*. L15.
[ORIGIN French *annoncer* from Latin *annuntiare*, from *ad* AN-[3] + *nuntiare*, from *nuntius* messenger.]
▸ **A** *verb trans*. **1** Make publicly known, proclaim as news. L15. ▸**b** Proclaim the arrival or approach of; publicly introduce. M18.

> E. O'NEILL I take this opportunity to publicly announce the betrothal of my daughter. R. ELLISON A huge electric sign announced its message. O. MANNING The wireless announced that the King would address his subjects in Rumanian. **b** SCOTT FITZGERALD Before I could reply that he was my neighbor dinner was announced. P. V. WHITE Do not forget to announce Mr Voss on showing him into the room.

2 Make known (without words) to the senses or mind. L18.

> GIBBON His feeble efforts announced his degenerate spirit. SIR W. SCOTT Gold buckles in his shoes, etc. . . announced him to be a domestic of trust and importance. JOYCE He announced his presence by that gentle . . cough which so many have tried . . to imitate.

▸ †**B** *noun*. = ANNOUNCEMENT. L18–M19.
▪ **announcement** *noun* the action of announcing; a public notice, a proclamation: L18. **announcer** *noun* a person who makes an announcement or announcements, *spec*. in BROADCASTING of the subjects of programmes, and items of news E17.

annoy /əˈnɔɪ/ *noun*. Now *arch*. & *poet*. ME.
[ORIGIN Old French *anui*, *anoi* (mod. *ennui*) ult. from Latin *in odio* in *mihi in odio est* it is hateful to me.]
1 = ANNOYANCE 2. ME.
2 = ANNOYANCE 3. LME.
▪ †**annoyous** *adjective* (latterly *dial*.) troublesome, vexatious, harmful LME–L19.

annoy /əˈnɔɪ/ *verb*. ME.
[ORIGIN Old French *anuier*, *anoier* (mod. *ennuyer*), ult. formed as ANNOY *noun* (cf. late Latin *inodiare*).]
†**1** *verb intrans*. Be hateful *to*, be a cause of trouble *to*. Only in ME.
†**2** *verb trans*. in *pass*. Foll. by *of*: be troubled, irked, or wearied by. ME–M16.
3 *verb trans*. Cause slight anger or mental distress to, irritate. ME.

> H. HOOD They had so far done nothing to annoy or alarm her.

4 Harm or attack repeatedly, harass. *arch*. LME.

> B. MARTIN A gallant Saxon, who annoyed this Coast.

†**5** Damage (something material). Latterly *dial*. LME–L19.
▪ **annoyed** *adjective* somewhat angry *with* a person, *about* or *at* a thing, *that*, or *to do* ME. **annoyer** *noun* L16. **annoying** *adjective* causing annoyance, irritation LME. **annoyingly** *adverb* M19. **annoyment** *noun* (*rare*) = ANNOYANCE 1, 2 L15.

annoyance /əˈnɔɪəns/ *noun*. LME.
[ORIGIN Old French *anoiance*, formed as ANNOY *noun*: see -ANCE.]
1 The action of annoying; vexing, molestation. LME.

> G. WHITE To secure these nests from the annoyance of sheperd boys.

2 The state of being annoyed; vexation, trouble. E16.

> A. NEWMAN Annoyance made her tactless.

3 Something that annoys, a nuisance. E16.

S. BELLOW There are the standard rooming-house annoyances: cooking odours, roaches, and peculiar neighbors.

■ **annoyancer** *noun* (*rare*) a person who or thing which causes annoyance **M17**.

annual /ˈanjʊəl/ *adjective & noun*. **LME**.
[**ORIGIN** Old French & mod. French *annuel* from late Latin *annualis* for Latin *annuus* and *annalis*, from *annus* year: see **-AL**[1].]
▸ **A** *adjective*. **1** Reckoned, payable, or engaged by the year. **LME**.

SHAKES. *Haml.* Gives him threescore thousand crowns in annual fee. JOYCE The balance . . repayable quarterly in equal annual instalments.

2 Lasting for one year. **LME**.

BACON The dying in winter of the roots of plants that are annual. MILTON Whether the Civil Government be an annual Democracy or a perpetual Aristocracy. J. A. FROUDE The annual course of the sun was completed in 365 days and six hours.

annual general meeting: of members or shareholders to elect officers, report on the past year, etc.

3 Pertaining to a year's events. (Now chiefly of publications and freq. interpreted as sense 4.) **E16**.
4 Recurring once every year. **M16**.

P. GALLICO She established the birthday interview as an annual custom.

▸ **B** *noun*. †**1** *ROMAN CATHOLIC CHURCH*. A commemorative mass said for a year after, or on the anniversary of, a person's death; a payment for this. **LME–M18**.
†**2** A yearly payment. Latterly *Scot.* **LME–M19**.
3 A plant that lives for one year only, perpetuating itself by seed. **M17**.
hardy annual: see **HARDY** *adjective*. ***tender annual***: see **TENDER** *adjective*.
4 A book etc. forming part of a series published successively at the same time each year; a book etc. reviewing the events of the past year. **L17**.
■ **annualize** *verb trans.* convert (a quantity) to its value for one year from that for a shorter period **M20**. **annually** *adverb* **L16**.

annuity /əˈnjuːɪti/ *noun*. **LME**.
[**ORIGIN** French *annuité* from medieval Latin *annuitas*, from *annuus*: see **ANNUAL**, **-ITY**.]
1 A yearly grant or allowance; a sum of money payable in respect of a particular year. **LME**.
2 An investment of money entitling the investor to a series of equal annual sums. **L17**.
consolidated annuities: see **CONSOLIDATE** *verb* 1. ***deferred annuity***: see **DEFER** *verb*[1] 2.
■ **annuitant** *noun* [after *accountant*] a person who holds or receives an annuity **E18**. **annuitize** *verb trans.* convert to, or pay in the form of, an annuity or series of regular payments **L18**.

annul /əˈnʌl/ *verb trans.* Infl. **-ll-**. **LME**.
[**ORIGIN** Old French *a(d)nuller* (mod. *annuler*) from late Latin (Vulgate) *annullare*, from *ad* **AN-**[3] + *nullum* nothing, neut. sing. of *nullus* **NULL** *adjective*.]
1 Cause to exist no longer; do away with; abolish; cancel. **LME**.

MILTON Light . . to me is extinct, And all her various objects of delight Annulled. R. W. EMERSON Intellect annuls Fate. So far as a man thinks, he is free. K. AMIS You, Who cannot annul a sparrow's footprint.

2 Declare invalid; *spec.* declare (a marriage) to have had no legal existence. **LME**.

LD MACAULAY A bill, which should at once annul all the statutes passed by the Long Parliament.

■ **annullable** *adjective* (*rare*) **L17**.

annular /ˈanjʊlə/ *adjective*. **L16**.
[**ORIGIN** French *annulaire* or Latin *annularis*, formed as **ANNULUS**: see **-AR**[1].]
1 Of or pertaining to a ring or rings; ringlike. **L16**.
annular eclipse an eclipse of the sun in which the moon, seen projected on the solar disc, leaves a ring of light visible. **annular thickening** *BOTANY* (in the tracheary elements of xylem) a thickening of the cell wall taking the form of isolated rings.
2 Bearing a ring or rings (designating the fourth finger of the left hand). **M17**.
■ **annuˈlarity** *noun* annular condition or form **M19**. **annularly** *adverb* **E18**. **annulary** *adjective & noun* (**a**) *adjective* = **ANNULAR**; (**b**) *noun* the ring finger: **E17**.

annulate /ˈanjʊlət/ *adjective*. **E19**.
[**ORIGIN** Latin *annulatus*, formed as **ANNULUS**: see **-ATE**[2].]
Having or marked with a ring or rings; consisting of rings.

annulated /ˈanjʊleɪtɪd/ *adjective*. **M17**.
[**ORIGIN** formed as **ANNULATE** + **-ED**[1].]
= **ANNULATE**.
■ **annuˈlation** *noun* the formation of rings or ringlike divisions; a ringlike structure: **E19**.

annulene /ˈanjʊliːn/ *noun*. **M20**.
[**ORIGIN** from **ANNULUS** + **-ENE**.]
CHEMISTRY. Any cyclic hydrocarbon whose molecule is a ring having alternate double and single bonds.
Freq. with numeral specifying number of carbon atoms, as **[18]-*annulene***.

annulet /ˈanjʊlɪt/ *noun*. Also †**anlet** & other vars. **LME**.
[**ORIGIN** Old French *anelet* (mod. *ann-*) dim. of *anel* from Latin *anellus* dim. of *anulus*, refashioned (**L16**) after Latin: see **ANNULUS**, **-ET**[1].]
1 *gen.* A small ring. **LME**.
2 *HERALDRY*. A charge in the form of a small ring. **L16**.
3 *ARCHITECTURE*. A small fillet or other flat moulding encircling a column. **E18**.

annulment /əˈnʌlm(ə)nt/ *noun*. **L15**.
[**ORIGIN** from **ANNUL** + **-MENT**.]
1 Total destruction; abolition. **L15**.
2 Invalidation; *spec.* declaration of a marriage as having had no legal existence. Also, a decree of invalidity. **M17**.

M. MCCARTHY In your place, I'd get a divorce or an annulment.

annulose /ˈanjʊləʊs/ *adjective*. **E19**.
[**ORIGIN** mod. Latin *annulosus*, formed as **ANNULUS** + **-OSE**[1].]
Ringlike; annulate.

annulus /ˈanjʊləs/ *noun*. Pl. **-li** /-lʌɪ, -liː/. **M16**.
[**ORIGIN** Latin, late form of *anulus* dim. of *anus* ring (see **ANUS**).]
Chiefly *MATH. & BOTANY*. A ring, a circle that is not filled in; *spec.* a partial veil forming a collar round the stalk in some agarics; the ring of thickened cells surrounding the sporangium of a fern.

†**annumerate** *verb trans.* **LME**.
[**ORIGIN** Latin *annumerat-* pa. ppl stem of *annumerare*, from *ad* **AN-**[3] + *numerare* to number: see **-ATE**[3].]
1 Reckon as an addition *to*. **LME–L18**.
2 Enumerate, adduce. Only in **E19**.

annunciate /əˈnʌnsɪeɪt/ *verb trans.* Also (now *rare*) **-tiate**. Pa. pple †**-ate** (earlier), **-ated**. **LME**.
[**ORIGIN** Orig. pa. pple, from medieval Latin *annunciat-* for Latin *annuntiat-* pa. ppl stem of *annuntiare*: see **ANNOUNCE**, **-ATE**[3].]
Proclaim; indicate as coming or ready.
■ **annunciative** *adjective* (*rare*) characterized by or proper to annunciation **M17**.

annunciation /ənʌnsɪˈeɪʃ(ə)n/ *noun*. **ME**.
[**ORIGIN** Old French & mod. French *annonciation* from late Latin *annuntiatio(n-)*: see **ANNUNCIATE**, **-ATION**.]
1 The action of announcing; an announcement. **ME**.
2 *spec.* (**A-**.) The announcement of the Incarnation, made by Gabriel to Mary; the festival commemorating this, Lady Day, 25 March. **LME**. ▸**b** A picture or representation of the Annunciation. **L18**.

annunciator /əˈnʌnsɪeɪtə/ *noun*. **M18**.
[**ORIGIN** Late Latin *annunciator*: see **ANNUNCIATE**, **-OR**.]
An announcer; an audible or visible indicator of where a bell has been rung, the position of a train, etc.
■ **annunciatory** *adjective* of an announcer or announcing **M19**.

annuntiate *verb* see **ANNUNCIATE**.

annus horribilis /ˌanəs hɒˈriːbɪlɪs/ *noun phr.* **L20**.
[**ORIGIN** mod. Latin = horrible year, suggested by **ANNUS MIRABILIS**.]
A year of disaster or misfortune.

annus mirabilis /ˌanəs mɪˈrɑːbɪlɪs/ *noun phr.* **M17**.
[**ORIGIN** mod. Latin = wonderful year.]
A remarkable or auspicious year.

ano- /ˈeɪnəʊ/ *combining form* of **ANUS**: see **-O-**.
■ **anoˈgenital** *adjective* of or pertaining to the anus and genitals **M20**.

anoa /əˈnəʊə/ *noun*. **M19**.
[**ORIGIN** A name in Sulawesi.]
A small wild bovine, *Anoa depressicornis*, native to Sulawesi, Indonesia.

anode /ˈanəʊd/ *noun*. **M19**.
[**ORIGIN** from Greek *anodos* way up, from **ANA-** + *hodos* way.]
A positive electrode or terminal. Opp. **CATHODE**.
■ **anodal** *adjective* of or pertaining to an anode **L19**. **anodize** *verb trans.* give (a metal, esp. aluminium) a protective oxide coating by means of an electrolytic process in which it forms the anode **M20**. **anodizer** *noun* **M20**.

anodic /əˈnɒdɪk/ *adjective*. **M19**.
[**ORIGIN** from **ANODE** + **-IC**.]
Of or pertaining to an anode or anodizing.
■ **anodically** *adverb* **E20**.

anodyne /ˈanədʌɪn/ *adjective & noun*. **M16**.
[**ORIGIN** Latin *anodynus* (Celsus) from Greek *anōdunos* free from pain, from **AN-**[5] + *odunē* pain; as noun from Greek *anōdunon*, late Latin *anodynum*.]
▸ **A** *adjective*. **1** *MEDICINE*. Having the power of easing pain. **M16**.
2 *fig.* Soothing, comforting; bland, inoffensive. **L18**.
▸ **B** *noun*. **1** *MEDICINE*. A medicine that eases pain. **M16**.
2 *fig.* Something that soothes the feelings, allays anxiety, etc. **M16**.
■ **aˈnodynous** *adjective* (*rare*) **M17**.

anoesis /anəʊˈiːsɪs/ *noun*. **E20**.
[**ORIGIN** from **A-**[10] + Greek *noēsis* understanding.]
PSYCHOLOGY. Consciousness with sensation but without thought and without understanding of the environment.

■ **anoetic** /-ˈɛtɪk/ *adjective* (**a**) (*rare*) unthinkable; (**b**) of or pertaining to anoesis: **M19**.

anoestrus /aˈniːstrəs/ *noun*. Also ***anest-**. **E20**.
[**ORIGIN** from **AN-**[5] + **OESTRUS**.]
A sexually inactive or unreceptive state in animals. Opp. **OESTRUS**.
■ **anoestrous** *adjective* of or pertaining to anoestrus **E20**.

anoint /əˈnɔɪnt/ *verb trans.* **ME**.
[**ORIGIN** Anglo-Norman (see **AN-**[2]), Old French *enoint* pa. pple of *enoindre* from Latin *inungere*, from **IN-**[2] + *ungere* anoint.]
1 Smear or rub over with oil or ointment, esp. as a religious ceremony at baptism or on consecration as a priest or monarch. (Foll. by *with*.) **ME**.

AV *Exod.* 28:41 Thou . . shalt annoint them, and consecrate them . . that they may minister vnto mee in the Priests office. GIBBON The salutary custom of bathing the limbs in water and of anointing them with oil. D. ATTENBOROUGH The bird takes the oil . . with its beak and anoints its feathers individually.

the Lord's Anointed (**a**) Jesus Christ; (**b**) a monarch by divine right.
2 Smear or rub with any other substance. **LME**.

R. CONQUEST While she's proceeding to anoint The sting with sal ammoniac.

3 Thrash soundly, baste. Now *dial.* **L15**.
■ **anointer** *noun* **L16**. **anointment** *noun* (*arch.*) the action of anointing; an ointment: **LME**.

anole /əˈnəʊli/ *noun*. Also **-lis** /-lɪs/. **E18**.
[**ORIGIN** Carib: cf. French *anolis*.]
Any of numerous, chiefly arboreal, iguanid lizards belonging to the American genus *Anolis*, esp. the green anole, *A. carolinensis*.

anomalism /əˈnɒm(ə)lɪz(ə)m/ *noun*. *rare*. **M17**.
[**ORIGIN** formed as **ANOMALISTIC** + **-ISM**.]
Anomalousness; an anomaly.

anomalistic /ənɒməˈlɪstɪk/ *adjective*. **M18**.
[**ORIGIN** from Greek *anōmalos* **ANOMALOUS** + **-ISTIC**.]
ASTRONOMY. Of or pertaining to anomaly.
anomalistic month the period between successive perigees of the moon. **anomalistic year** the period between successive perihelia of the earth or another planet.
■ Also †**anomalistical** *adjective*: only in **18**.

anomalous /əˈnɒm(ə)ləs/ *adjective*. **M17**.
[**ORIGIN** from late Latin *anomalus* from Greek *anōmalos*, from **AN-**[5] + *homalos* even, + **-OUS**.]
1 Unconformable or dissimilar *to*. *arch.* **M17**.
2 Irregular; abnormal. **M17**.
■ **anomalously** *adverb* **M17**. **anomalousness** *noun* **L17**.

anomalure /əˈnɒməljʊə/ *noun*. **L19**.
[**ORIGIN** from mod. Latin *Anomalurus*, from Greek *anōmalos* **ANOMALOUS** + *oura* tail.]
= ***scaly-tailed squirrel*** s.v. **SCALY** *adjective*.

anomaly /əˈnɒm(ə)li/ *noun*. **L16**.
[**ORIGIN** Latin *anomalia* (Varro) from Greek *anōmalia*, from *anōmalos*: see **ANOMALOUS**, **-Y**[3].]
1 Irregularity of condition, motion, behaviour, etc.; an anomalous thing or being, an exceptional circumstance. **L16**.
magnetic anomaly: see **MAGNETIC** *adjective*.
2 *ASTRONOMY*. The angular distance of a planet or the moon from its last perihelion or perigee. **M17**.
eccentric anomaly the actual anomaly in an elliptical orbit. **mean anomaly** the corresponding angle in an imaginary circular orbit.
■ Also †**anomal** *noun* **M16–M17**.

anomer /ˈanəmə/ *noun*. **M20**.
[**ORIGIN** from Greek *anō* upwards + **-MER**.]
Either of two isomers of a cyclic carbohydrate which differ only in the configuration about the hemi-acetal carbon atom.
■ **anoˈmeric** *adjective* **M20**.

anomia /əˈnəʊmɪə/ *noun*. **E20**.
[**ORIGIN** from **A-**[10] + Latin *nomen* name + **-IA**[1].]
MEDICINE. A form of aphasia in which the patient is unable to recall the names of everyday objects.

anomic /əˈnɒmɪk/ *adjective*[1]. **L19**.
[**ORIGIN** Partly formed as **ANOMIE** + **-IC**, partly French *anomique*.]
1 Obeying no known law; not concerned with law. **L19**.
2 Characterized by anomie. **M20**.

anomic /əˈnɒmɪk/ *adjective*[2]. **M20**.
[**ORIGIN** from **ANOMIA** + **-IC**.]
MEDICINE. Characterized by or relating to anomia.

anomie /ˈanəmi/ *noun*. **M20**.
[**ORIGIN** French from Greek *anomia*, from *anomos* lawless: cf. **ANOMY**.]
Lack of the usual social standards in a group or person.

Anomoean /anəˈmiːən/ *adjective & noun*. **L17**.
[**ORIGIN** from mod. Latin *Anomoeus*, from Greek *anomoios*, from **AN-**[5] + *homoios* like, similar, + **-AN**.]
ECCLESIASTICAL HISTORY. Pertaining to, a member of, an extreme Arian sect which held that the Father and the Son are unlike in essence.

anomuran /anəˈm(j)ʊər(ə)n/ *noun & adjective*. L19.
[ORIGIN from mod. Latin *Anomura* (see below), from Greek *anomos* irregular + *oura* tail + -AN: the abdomen in Anomura is irregular in size or form.]
ZOOLOGY. ▸**A** *noun*. Any member of the section Anomura of decapod crustaceans, including certain kinds of crab, notably hermit crabs. L19.
▸**B** *adjective*. Of or pertaining to Anomura or an anomuran. L19.

anomy /ˈanəmi/ *noun*. L16.
[ORIGIN Greek *anomia*: see ANOMIE, -Y³.]
†**1** Disregard of (esp. divine) law. L16–L17.
2 = ANOMIE. M20.

anon /əˈnɒn/ *adjective & noun*. Also **anon.** (point), **A-**. M18.
[ORIGIN Abbreviation.]
Anonymous; (a designation for a person, esp. a writer or composer) whose name is unknown or not stated.

anon /əˈnɒn/ *adverb*. Now *arch. & literary*. In sense 4 also **anan**.
[ORIGIN Old English *on ān* into one, *on āne* in one: see ON *preposition*, ONE *adjective*.]
†**1** In or into one body, state, course, etc. OE–LME.
2 At once, instantly. Long *obsolete* exc. as occas. deliberately revived. OE.

AV *Matt.* 12:20 He that heareth the word, & anon with ioy receiueth it.

3 Soon, in a short time; for a little. LME.

R. L. STEVENSON At our concerts, of which more anon. SCOTT FITZGERALD Good night, Mr. Carraway. See you anon.

4 As *interjection*. (To a person calling for attention) in a moment! coming! Also, at your service!; what did you say? eh? Long *dial.* M16.

SHAKES. *1 Hen. IV* Francis! . . Anon, anon, sir. C. J. LEVER 'Such little events are not unfrequent down here, then?' 'Anan!' said she, not understanding his question.

5 Now again; now at this time (in contrast to another). L16.

J. TYNDALL The avalanche rushed, hidden at intervals, and anon shooting forth.

anonym /ˈanənɪm/ *noun*. Also **-nyme**. E19.
[ORIGIN French *anonyme* from Greek *anōnumos* ANONYMOUS: see -NYM.]
1 An anonymous person or publication. E19.
2 A pseudonym. M19.

anonymity /anəˈnɪmɪti/ *noun*. E19.
[ORIGIN formed as ANONYMOUS + -ITY.]
The state of being anonymous; impersonality.

A. B. GROSART The anonymity of the poem on Felton. K. AMIS Every face Had taken on the flat anonymity of pain. J. FRAME The languorous anonymity of the big overseas cities.

anonymize /əˈnɒnɪmʌɪz/ *verb trans*. Also **-ise**. L20.
[ORIGIN from ANONYMOUS + -IZE.]
MEDICINE. Remove identifying particulars from (test results) for statistical or other purposes. Usu. as ***anonymized*** *ppl adjective*.

anonymous /əˈnɒnɪməs/ *adjective & noun*. L16.
[ORIGIN Late Latin *anonymos*, *-mus* from Greek *anōnumos*, formed as AN-⁵ + *onuma* name (see -NYM) + -OUS.]
▸**A** *adjective*. **1** Nameless; of unknown name; impersonal, not individuated. L16.

ALDOUS HUXLEY No longer anonymous, but named, identified. O. MANNING He could not be recognised among the anonymous dark-clad figures within. D. STOREY Like all the other big towns—impersonal, anonymous. D. LESSING The men making announcements . . had the anonymous voices of officialdom.

Alcoholics Anonymous: see ALCOHOLIC *noun*. **anonymous FTP** *COMPUTING* an implementation of an FTP server that allows anyone who can use FTP to log on to the server, using a general username and without a password check.
2 Of unknown or undeclared source or authorship. L17.

JOYCE A volume . . entitled *Sweets of Sin*, anonymous, author a gentleman of fashion. J. LE CARRÉ Are you used to receiving anonymous gifts of a thousand pounds?

▸**B** *noun*. An anonymous person. Now *rare*. E17.
– NOTE: In earliest uses as a pseudonym; at first freq. in Greek or Latin forms.
■ **anonymously** *adverb* M18. **anonymousness** *noun* E19. **anonyˈmuncule** *noun* [after Latin HOMUNCULUS] a petty anonymous writer M19.

anopheles /əˈnɒfɪliːz/ *noun*. Pl. same. L19.
[ORIGIN mod. Latin from Greek *anōphelēs* unprofitable, useless.]
A mosquito of the genus *Anopheles*, which includes species that carry the parasites of malaria and other diseases.
■ **anopheline** *adjective & noun* (pertaining to or designating) a mosquito of a group that contains this genus but not *Culex* E20.

anoplothere /əˈnɒpləθɪə/ *noun*. Also in Latin form †**-therium**. E19.
[ORIGIN French *anoplothère*, from Greek *anoplos* unarmed, from AN-⁵ + *hoplon* weapon + *thērion* wild animal.]
PALAEONTOLOGY. An extinct hornless artiodactyl of the family Anoplotheriidae, found as fossils of Eocene and Oligocene age.

anopsia /əˈnɒpsɪə/ *noun*. *rare*. Orig. †**-sy**. M17.
[ORIGIN from Greek AN-⁵ + *opsis* sight + -IA¹.]
Sightlessness, blindness.

anorak /ˈanərak/ *noun*. E20.
[ORIGIN Inupiaq (Greenlandic) *annoraaq*.]
1 A skin or cloth hooded jacket worn by Eskimos and so by others in polar regions; a similar weatherproof garment worn elsewhere. E20.
2 A socially inept and studious or obsessive person (caricatured as typically wearing an anorak) with unfashionable and largely solitary interests. *colloq. derog.* L20.

Independent on Sunday With his thick specs . . and grey suit he looks a bit of an anorak. *New Scientist* At the risk of being branded an 'anorak', I felt it natural to consult the Net.

■ **anoraky** *adjective* (in sense 2) L20.

anorectal /eɪnəʊˈrɛkt(ə)l/ *adjective*. L19.
[ORIGIN French *ano-rectal*, from Latin *ano-* (combining form of ANUS) + RECTAL.]
MEDICINE & ANATOMY. Of or relating to the anus and rectum.

anorectic /anəˈrɛktɪk/ *adjective & noun*. L19.
[ORIGIN from Greek *anorektos*, formed as AN-⁵ + *orexein* to desire: see -IC.]
▸**A** *adjective*. Characterized by a lack of appetite, *spec.* by anorexia nervosa; producing a loss of appetite. L19.
▸**B** *noun*. **1** An anorectic agent. M20.
2 A person with anorexia. L20.
■ Also **anoretic** *adjective & noun* E20.

anorexia /anəˈrɛksɪə/ *noun*. Also †**-exy**. L16.
[ORIGIN Late Latin from Greek, from AN-⁵ + *orexis* appetite: see -IA¹.]
MEDICINE. Absence of appetite; *popularly spec.* anorexia nervosa (see below).
anorexia nervosa /nəːˈvəʊsə/ chronic anorexia induced by emotional disturbance.
■ **anorexiant** *adjective & noun* (a drug) producing anorexia M20. **anorexic** *adjective & noun* (**a**) *adjective* = ANORECTIC *adjective*; (**b**) *noun* = ANORECTIC *noun* 2: M20. **anorexiˈgenic** *adjective* producing anorexia M20.

anorgasmia /anɔːˈgazmɪə/ *noun*. L20.
[ORIGIN from AN-⁵ + ORGASM + -IA¹.]
MEDICINE. Persistent inability to achieve orgasm despite responding to sexual stimulation.
■ **anorgasmic** *adjective* L20.

anormal /eɪˈnɔːm(ə)l, ə-/ *adjective*. M16.
[ORIGIN Isolated early use from French, var. of *anomal* (see ANOMALY); later (M19) from A-¹⁰ + NORMAL *adjective*.]
Irregular, not normal or usual.

anorthic /əˈnɔːθɪk/ *adjective*. Now *rare* or *obsolete*. M19.
[ORIGIN from AN-⁵ + Greek *orthos* straight, right + -IC.]
CRYSTALLOGRAPHY. = TRICLINIC.

anorthite /əˈnɔːθʌɪt/ *noun*. M19.
[ORIGIN formed as ANORTHIC + -ITE¹.]
MINERALOGY. A calcium-rich plagioclase occurring in many basic igneous rocks; calcium feldspar.

anorthoclase /əˈnɔːθəkleɪz/ *noun*. L19.
[ORIGIN formed as ANORTHIC + Greek *klasis* breaking, cleavage.]
MINERALOGY. A triclinic sodium-rich alkali feldspar occurring in many alkalic lavas.

anorthosite /əˈnɔːθəsʌɪt/ *noun*. M19.
[ORIGIN from French *anorthose* plagioclase, (now) anorthoclase + -ITE¹: see ANORTHIC.]
GEOLOGY. A granular igneous rock composed largely of a plagioclase (usu. labradorite).
■ **anorthoˈsitic** *adjective* of the nature of anorthosite M20.

anosmia /aˈnɒzmɪə/ *noun*. E19.
[ORIGIN from AN-⁵ + Greek *osmē* smell + -IA¹.]
MEDICINE. Loss of the sense of smell.
■ **anosmic** *adjective & noun* (a person) suffering from anosmia E20.

anosognosia /ənɒsəgˈnəʊsɪə/ *noun*. E20.
[ORIGIN French *anosognosie*: see A-¹⁰, NOSO-, GNOSIS, -IA¹.]
MEDICINE. Unawareness of or failure to acknowledge one's hemiplegia or other disability.

another /əˈnʌðə/ *pronoun & adjective sing.* (in mod. usage also classed as a *determiner*). ME.
[ORIGIN from AN *adjective* (see A *adjective*) + OTHER *adjective*. In two words as late as 16. Cf. NOTHER *adjective*², 'NOTHER.]
1 A second, further, additional (one, specified number (of)). ME. ▸**b** A second in likeness, character, or attributes. L16.

F. M. FORD At meals she would feel an intolerable desire to drink a glass of wine, and then another and then a third. S. BARSTOW Another five minutes goes by while he reckons to look it over. A. THWAITE A stream, a fence, a hedge, another fence. **b** YEATS Another Troy must rise and set, Another lineage feed the crow, Another Argo's painted prow Drive to a flashier bauble yet.

ask me another: see ASK *verb*. ***not give another thought to***: see THOUGHT *noun*. **such another** another of the same sort. ***tell me another***: see TELL *verb*. **you're another** *colloq.*: applying an accusation to the person who makes it; also as a vaguely contemptuous retort.
2 A different (one, specified number (of)); some or any other. ME.

SAKI Do you suppose we shall all get appropriate punishments in another world for our sins in this? V. WOOLF Whose day had slipped past in one quick doing after another. R. G. COLLINGWOOD A patron who buys a picture of a fox-hunt or a covey of partridges does not buy it because it represents that fox-hunt or that covey and not another. G. GREENE He'd got to close her mouth one way or another. D. DU MAURIER I am not she who left him five minutes ago . . . I am another woman, older, more mature. R. P. WARREN Two men, the one who had fired the shot and another, . . ran to the fallen man. T. S. ELIOT One year is a year of rain, Another a year of dryness. I. MURDOCH Well, I'll be off. I can easily see Catherine another time. R. WEST George Willoughby, like many another naval officer, had his reasons for liking a quiet mount.

one and another, ***one another***, ***one with another***: see ONE *adjective* etc. ***one way and another***: see WAY *noun*.
– SPECIAL COLLOCATIONS & COMB.: †**anothergates** *adjective* (*attrib.*) [from genit. of GATE *noun*²] = ***anotherguess*** below. **anotherguess** *adjective* (*attrib.*) *arch.* [alt. of ***anothergates*** above: cf. GUESS *adjective*] of another sort or kind. **another place** the other House of Parliament (used in the Commons to refer to the Lords, and vice versa).

ANOVA /aˈnəʊvə/ *abbreviation*.
Analysis of variance, a statistical method in which the variation in a set of observations is divided into distinct components.

anovulatory /ˌanɒvjʊˈleɪt(ə)ri/ *adjective*. M20.
[ORIGIN from AN-⁵ + OVULATORY.]
MEDICINE. Of menstruation etc.: not accompanied by ovulation.
■ **aˈnovulant** *adjective & noun* (a drug etc.) that suppresses ovulation M20. **anovulation** *noun* absence of ovulation; failure to ovulate: M20.

anoxaemia /anɒkˈsiːmɪə/ *noun*. L19.
[ORIGIN formed as ANOXIA + -AEMIA.]
MEDICINE. = HYPOXAEMIA.

anoxia /aˈnɒksɪə/ *noun*. M20.
[ORIGIN from AN-⁵ + OX- + -IA¹.]
= HYPOXIA.
■ **anoxic** *adjective* characterized by anoxia E20.

ANS *abbreviation*.
Autonomic nervous system.

ansa /ˈansə/ *noun*. Pl. **-sae** /-siː/ Also anglicized as †**anse**. M17.
[ORIGIN Latin = handle (of a vessel).]
ASTRONOMY. Either extremity of Saturn's ring system as seen projecting like a handle from the planet's disc.

Ansafone, **ansaphone** *nouns* see ANSWERPHONE.

ansated /ˈanseɪtɪd/ *adjective*. *rare*. M18.
[ORIGIN from Latin *ansatus* pa. pple of *ansare*, formed as ANSA, + -ED¹.]
Having (something resembling) handles.

ansatz /ˈansats/ *noun*. M20.
[ORIGIN German = approach.]
MATH. An assumption about the form of an unknown function which is made in order to facilitate solution of an equation or other problem.

Anschauung /ˈanʃaʊʊŋ/ *noun*. Pl. ***-en*** /-ən/. M19.
[ORIGIN German = looking at.]
1 *PHILOSOPHY* (esp. KANTIAN PHILOSOPHY). A sense perception, an intuition, an immediate apprehension by sense. M19.
2 An outlook, an attitude, a point of view. E20.

Anschluss /ˈanʃlʊs/ *noun*. E20.
[ORIGIN German, from *anschliessen* join, annex.]
Union, annexation; *spec.* the annexation of Austria by Germany in 1938.

†**anse** *noun* see ANSA.

Anselmian /anˈsɛlmɪən/ *adjective*. L19.
[ORIGIN from St *Anselm* (see below) + -IAN.]
Of or pertaining to St Anselm (1033–1109), Archbishop of Canterbury and scholastic philosopher, esp. to his ontological argument for the existence of God and his view of the atonement.
■ Also **Anselmic** *adjective* L19.

anserine /ˈansərʌɪn/ *adjective*. M19.
[ORIGIN Latin *anserinus*, from *anser* goose: see -INE¹.]
Of or like a goose; silly.
■ Also **anserous** *adjective* E19.

an sich /an zɪç/ *adjectival & adverbial phr.* M19.
[ORIGIN German.]
In itself; in the abstract; not in relation to anything else. See also DING AN SICH.

answer /ˈɑːnsə/ *noun*.
[ORIGIN Old English *andswaru* corresp. to Old Frisian *ondser*, Old Saxon *antswōr*, Old Norse *andsvar*, from Germanic, from prefix meaning 'against, opposite' + base found also in SWEAR *verb*.]
▸**I** Something said or done in order to deal with what has preceded.
1 A reply to a question. OE.

G. VIDAL People started asking him vague questions to which there were no sensible answers.

the short answer is: see SHORT *adjective*.
2 A reply to a charge; a defence. ME.

SHAKES. *2 Hen. VI* Call these foul offenders to their answers.

A

3 A reply to an objection; a rebuttal. ME.

SIR T. MORE The Answer to the First Part of the Poysoned Booke. T. STOPPARD Everything has to begin somewhere and there is no answer to *that*.

4 A reply to an appeal, address, communication, etc.; an acknowledgement; a rejoinder. ME.

AV *Job* 19:16 I called my seruant, and he gaue me no answere. W. FAULKNER I've had no answer to the last two letters. E. WAUGH I wrote long letters to Sebastian and called daily at the post-office for his answers.

not take no for an answer: see NO *noun*[1].

5 The solution of a problem; a response to a test of knowledge etc. ME.

L. HENSLEY The Scholar's Arithmetic, with Answers to the Examples. J. BETJEMAN His written answers . . Pleased the examiners. S. HILL For many people a hospital of this kind is not the answer.

know all the answers *colloq.* be very experienced, be knowing.

▸ **II** Something said or done as a reaction to what has preceded.

6 A reply to an implied question; a decision upon a point at issue. LME.

TENNYSON There must be answer to his doubt. E. O'NEILL Remember our offer. Give us your answer tomorrow.

7 *MUSIC.* A repetition or echoing of a phrase, theme, etc.; also = ANTIPHON 2. LME.

8 A practical reply; a responsive, corresponding, or resulting action. M16. ▸**b** An equivalent or rival *to*. *colloq.* M20.

SHAKES. *Haml.* If Hamlet give the first or second hit, Or quit in answer of the third exchange. C. DARWIN The answer was given by a volley of musketry. **b** *Times* Smirking juveniles being mobilized by a Seattle's answer to Harry Lauder.

▪ **answerless** *adjective* (*rare*) having no answer; unanswerable: M16.

answer /ˈɑːnsə/ *verb*.

[ORIGIN Old English *andswarian*, from ANSWER *noun*: cf. Old Frisian *ondswera*, Old Norse *andsvara*.]

Orig. *verb intrans.* with *dat.*, through levelling of inflections later *verb trans.* in nearly every sense.

▸ **I** Make an answer to a charge.

1 a *verb intrans.* Reply to a charge or accusation. OE. ▸**b** *verb trans.* Defend oneself against (a charge etc.); justify. M16.

a SHAKES. *Much Ado* It is proved already that you are little better than false knaves . . . How answer you for yourselves? **b** C. MARLOWE We were best look that your devil can answer the stealing of this same cup. G. B. SHAW This court has summoned all the dictators to . . answer charges brought against them.

2 *verb intrans.* Be responsible or accountable *for*; vouch *for*. ME.

AV *Gen.* 30:33 So shall my righteousnesse answere for me. E. GASKELL I'll answer for it Mrs. Goodenough saw Molly. G. B. SHAW Waiting nervously in the Hammersmith Police Court to answer for his breach of the peace.

3 *verb intrans.* foll. by *for* (†*to*) & †*trans.* Suffer, atone, make amends, (for). ME.

SHAKES. *Jul. Caes.* If it were so, it was a grievous fault; And grievously hath Caesar answer'd it.

4 *verb* †*intrans.* & *trans.* Rebut (an objection, an argument). ME.

E. O'NEILL He can answer all your arguments easy—with things right out of the Bible!

5 *verb trans.* †**a** Satisfy (a person) *of* or *for* a pecuniary claim. LME–M16. ▸**b** Satisfy (a pecuniary claim), discharge (a debt); be sufficient for (a pecuniary liability). L15.

a LD BERNERS We wolde demaunde good hostages and sufficient, to answere vs of our horses agayne. R. HOLINSHED He would be answered for such summes of monie as king Richard had taken. **b** SHAKES. *1 Hen. IV* This proud king, who studies day and night To answer all the debt he owes to you. H. MARTINEAU A few shillings . . to answer any sudden occasion.

†**6** *verb trans.* Prove a satisfactory return for (an investment) or to (an investor). E16–L18.

SWIFT The maid will . . sell more butter and cheese than will answer her wages.

7 *verb trans.* Satisfy or fulfil (wishes, hopes, expectations, etc.). M16.

8 *verb trans.* Accomplish (an end); suit (a purpose); satisfy the requirements of. M17.

HENRY FIELDING I applied a fomentation . . which highly answered the intention. SIR W. SCOTT He offered him a beast he thought wad answer him weel eneugh.

9 *verb intrans.* Serve the purpose; prove a success; turn out (in a specified manner); be satisfactory *to* (a person). M18.

W. COWPER Their labour was almost in vain before, but now it answers. LYTTON If Beatrice di Negra would indeed be rich, she might answer to himself as a wife. G. B. SHAW I tried the experiment of treating a scarlet fever case with a sample of hydrophobia serum . . , and it answered capitally.

▸ **II** Make an answer to a question, remark, etc.

10 *verb intrans.* & *trans.* Reply to (a question, remark, appeal, request, or other expression of desire or opinion); speak or write in reply (to). OE. ▸**b** Reply impertinently (to). Also (*colloq.*) ***answer back***. E16.

TINDALE *Luke* 13:25 He shall answer and saye vnto you: I knowe you not. AV *Job* 23:5 The words which he would answere me. R. BENTLEY Mr. B. here answers to a Question, that never was ask'd him. POPE The mighty Czar might answer, he was drunk. TENNYSON Will she answer if I call? JOYCE Answering an ad? . . Yes, Mr Bloom said. Town traveller. SCOTT FITZGERALD 'Where is he from, I mean? And what does he do?' 'Now *you're* started on the subject,' she answered with a wan smile. R. GRAVES I wrote, but he did not answer. R. P. WARREN I said I would like to answer any questions they had. S. BELLOW Everybody asks the same questions. You get tired of answering. W. FAULKNER Have they got him? Answer me. L. DURRELL Melissa still writes the spirited nonchalant letters which I have such difficulty in answering. **b** LYTTON Hush, Frank, never answer your father. H. G. WELLS The King . . admonishes him with evident severity . . . Against all etiquette he answers back.

11 *verb trans.* & *intrans.* Respond antiphonally or canonically (to); make a responsive sound, echo. OE.

AV *1 Sam.* 18:7 The women answered one another, as they played. DRYDEN Both alike inspir'd To sing, and answer as the Song requir'd. POPE The woods shall answer, and their echo ring.

12 *verb intrans.* & *trans.* Act in response to (a signal), acknowledge (a signal); react to a summons from (a knock, bell, etc.). L16.

JOYCE Last look at mirror always before she answers the door. S. HILL She went to answer the ringing telephone. A. AYCKBOURN I ring someone up and when they answer I say is that 2467. M. KEANE She pressed the . . bell on the table, and when Breda answered it . . she said: 'What did I want?'

answering machine a tape recorder which supplies a recorded answer to a telephone call and sometimes also takes messages. **answering service** a business that receives and answers telephone calls for its clients. **answer to (the name of)** respond when addressed as, be called.

13 *verb trans.* & *intrans.* Reply favourably to (a petitioner, a petition). L16.

AV *Ps.* 27:7 Haue mercie also vpon mee, and answere me. TENNYSON The Gods have heard it, O Icenian! . . Doubt not ye the Gods have answer'd. O. WILDE When the gods wish to punish us they answer our prayers.

14 *verb trans.* & *intrans.* Solve (a problem); respond to (a test of knowledge etc.). M18.

A. J. CRONIN When he began the written part of the examination . . , he found himself answering the papers with a blind automatism.

▸ **III** Correspond.

15 a *verb intrans.* Correspond *to*. ME. ▸**b** *verb trans.* Correspond to. *arch.* exc. in ***answer the description***. M16.

a AV *Gal.* 4:25 This Agar . . answereth to Ierusalem, which now is. **b** J. LOCKE The Terms of our Law . . will hardly find Words that answer them in the Spanish, or Italian.

†**16** *verb trans.* Return the (esp. hostile) action of. LME–L16.

17 *verb trans.* Give back in kind, return. L16.

SPENSER Well did the squire perceive himselfe too weake To aunswere his defiaunce in the field. J. KEBLE Answering love for love.

18 *verb trans.* & *intrans.* Act in sympathy or conformity (with); be responsive (to). E17.

SHAKES. *Temp.* I come To answer thy best pleasure. DICKENS The girl instantly answered to the action in her sculling.

▪ **answerer** *noun* E16. **answeringly** *adverb* (*rare*) correspondingly LME.

answerable /ˈɑːns(ə)rəb(ə)l/ *adjective*. E16.

[ORIGIN from ANSWER *verb* + -ABLE.]

1 Liable to be answered; able to be answered. E16.

2 Liable to answer, responsible, (*to* an authority, *for* a person or thing). L16.

SHAKES. *1 Hen. IV* If he have robb'd these men He shall be answerable. DEFOE She would be answerable for her on all accounts. SIR W. SCOTT I will be answerable that this galliard meant but some Saint Valentine's jest. E. A. FREEMAN For the good administration of which the magistrate . . was answerable to the power which appointed him.

3 Corresponding (*to*); suitable, fitting, proper, (*to*); commensurate, equivalent, (*to*). *arch.* L16.

J. LYLY If the courtesie of Englande be aunswerable to the custome of Pilgrimes. P. SIDNEY A likeness . . answerable enough in some features and colours, but erring in others. MILTON If answerable style I can obtaine Of my Celestial Patroness. J. REYNOLDS Render your future progress answerable to your past improvement. WELLINGTON The revenue of that Island will [not] be found answerable to its necessary expenditure.

▪ **answeraˈbility** *noun* liability to be called to account, responsibility E20. **answerableness** *noun* (**a**) *arch.* correspondency, conformity; (**b**) = ANSWERABILITY: L16. **answerably** *adverb* in an answerable manner, conformably (*to*) E17.

answerphone /ˈɑːnsəfəʊn/ *noun*. Also (proprietary) **Ansafone**; **ansaphone**. M20.

[ORIGIN from ANSWER *verb* + PHONE *noun*[2].]

= ***answering machine*** s.v. ANSWER *verb*.

ant /ant/ *noun & verb*.

[ORIGIN Old English *ǣmet(t)e* = Middle Low German *āmete*, *ēmete*, Old High German *āmeiza* (German *Ameise*), from West Germanic, from prefix meaning 'off, away' and base meaning 'cut, hew'. The Old English forms gave two Middle English types, (i) *am(e)te*, whence *ant* (the prevailing standard form) and (ii) *emete* (see EMMET).]

▸ **A** *noun*. **1** Any of numerous small hymenopterous insects constituting the family Formicidae, usu. wingless except in the mating season, living in complex social colonies, and proverbial for their industriousness. Cf. ***velvet ant*** s.v. VELVET *noun & adjective*. OE.

black ant, ***honeypot ant***, ***red ant***, ***wood ant***, etc. **have ants in one's pants** *colloq.* be fidgety, be restless.

2 = ***white ant*** (a) s.v. WHITE *adjective*. L17.

– COMB.: **ant bear** (**a**) the giant anteater, *Myrmecophaga tridactyla*; (**b**) = AARDVARK; **antbird** any of numerous insectivorous birds belonging to the neotropical family Formicariidae, usu. with dark plumage; **ant eggs**, **ants'-eggs** pupae or larvae of ants, used as animal food; †**ant fly** a winged ant; **ant heap**, **anthill**, **ant hillock** a nest built by ants or termites in the form of a mound; **ant lion** [translating Greek *murmēko-leōn* in the Septuagint] any of numerous predatory insects of the neuropterous family Myrmeleontidae, whose larvae live beneath pits in which they trap small insects; **ant orchid** a terrestrial Australasian orchid, *Chiloglottis gunnii*, with antlike flowers; **ant plant** any of various plants (e.g. certain acacias) having hollow parts in which ants live in symbiosis with the plant; **ant-thrush** (**a**) orig., any antbird; now, any of several large antbirds; (**b**) each of four African thrushes of the genus *Neocossyphus*; (**c**) = PITTA *noun*[1].

▸ **B** *verb intrans.* & *refl.* Of a bird: rub ants (or occas. other insects or substances) on its plumage. M20.

▪ **antlike** *adjective* resembling (that of) an ant L19.

ant- *prefix* see ANTI-.

an't *verb* see BE *verb*, HAVE *verb*.

-ant /(ə)nt/ *suffix*[1].

[ORIGIN French, or its source Latin *-ant-* pres. ppl stem of verbs of the 1st conjugation, or *-ent-* (see -ENT).]

Forming adjectives denoting existence of action, as ***pendant***, ***repentant***, or state, as ***arrogant***, ***expectant***, and nouns denoting an agent, as ***assistant***, ***celebrant***, ***deodorant***, usu. from verbs. Conflicting English, French, & Latin analogies have produced much inconsistency of use of *-ant* and *-ent*.

-ant /(ə)nt/ *suffix*[2] (not productive).

[ORIGIN Alt. (in Old French & Anglo-Norman) of words in *-an*.]

Forming nouns, as ***pheasant***, ***tyrant***, etc.

anta /ˈantə/ *noun*. Pl. **-tae** /-tiː/, **-tas**. L16.

[ORIGIN Latin.]

ARCHITECTURE. A square pilaster at either side of a door or at the corner of a building. Cf. ANTES.

Antabuse /ˈantəbjuːs/ *noun*. M20.

[ORIGIN from ANTI- + ABUSE *noun*.]

(Proprietary name for) disulfiram.

antacid /antˈasɪd/ *adjective & noun*. M18.

[ORIGIN from ANT- + ACID *noun*.]

(A substance) corrective or preventive of acidity, esp. in the stomach.

antae *noun pl.* see ANTA.

antagonise *verb* var. of ANTAGONIZE.

antagonism /anˈtag(ə)nɪz(ə)m/ *noun*. E19.

[ORIGIN French *antagonisme*: see ANTAGONIST, -ISM.]

1 Mutual resistance of opposing forces; active opposition; a feeling of hostility or opposition. E19. ▸**b** *BIOCHEMISTRY.* Inhibition of or interference with the action of a substance or organism by another. L19.

R. COBDEN The Government had not placed itself in antagonism to them. E. O'NEILL In their whole tense attitudes is clearly revealed the bitter antagonism between them. A. LURIE The antagonism we felt for the audience. A. J. P. TAYLOR The general strike seems to have produced a lessening of class antagonism. **b** M. C. GERALD Atropine's antagonism of acetylcholine.

2 An opposing force or principle. M19.

DE QUINCEY As if resulting from mighty and equal antagonisms.

antagonist /anˈtag(ə)nɪst/ *noun & adjective*. L16.

[ORIGIN French *antagoniste* or late Latin *antagonista* (Jerome) from Greek *antagōnistēs*, formed as ANTAGONIZE: see -IST.]

▸ **A** *noun*. **1** An opponent, an adversary; an opposing force. L16.

E. GLASGOW Some have said that Nature is the antagonist of happiness. C. V. WEDGWOOD The outbreak of the second war convinced the King's more ruthless antagonists that no peace could be made while he lived.

2 *PHYSIOLOGY.* A muscle whose action counteracts that of another. Cf. AGONIST 3. L17.

3 *BIOCHEMISTRY.* A substance or organism which interferes with or inhibits the action of another. Cf. AGONIST 4. L19.

▸ **B** *attrib.* or as *adjective*. = ANTAGONISTIC. Now *rare*. L17.

MILTON None daring to appear antagonist. COLERIDGE Antagonist forces are necessarily of the same kind.

▪ **antagoˈnistic** *adjective* actively opposed, of the nature of an antagonist M17. **antagoˈnistical** *adjective* (*rare*) = ANTAGONISTIC E17. **antagoˈnistically** *adverb* E17.

antagonize /an'tag(ə)nʌɪz/ *verb trans.* Also **-ise**. M17.
[ORIGIN Greek *antagōnizesthai*, formed as ANT- + *agōnizesthai* struggle, formed as AGON: see -IZE.]
†**1** Vie with, rival. Only in M17.
T. HERBERT The Dodo which for shape and rarenesse may antigonize the Phoenix of Arabia.
2 Struggle against, contend with. *arch.* M18.
KEATS Like one huge Python Antagonising Boreas.
3 Counteract, tend to neutralize (a force etc.). M18.
R. W. EMERSON If Fate follows and limits power, power attends and antagonizes Fate. G. H. LEWES The body is balanced by an incessant shifting of the muscles, one group antagonising the other. J. G. FARRELL Our first object must be to antagonize the poison.
4 Render antagonistic, evoke antagonism in. M19.
J. HELLER They conducted their duties humbly and reticently . . and went to great lengths not to antagonize anyone.
■ **antagoni'zation** *noun* L19.

antanaclasis /antə'naklәsɪs/ *noun.* Pl. **-ases** /-əsiːz/. L16.
[ORIGIN Greek: see ANT-, ANACLASIS.]
RHETORIC. Repetition, esp. of a word in different or contrary senses.

antapex /ant'eɪpɛks/ *noun.* Orig. †**anti-apex**. L19.
[ORIGIN from ANT- + APEX *noun*[1].]
ASTRONOMY. The point on the celestial sphere away from which the sun is moving. Cf. APEX *noun*[1] 4.

antaphrodisiac /ˌantafrə'dɪzɪak/ *adjective & noun.* Now *rare* or *obsolete*. M18.
[ORIGIN from ANT- + APHRODISIAC.]
= ANAPHRODISIAC.

†**antapology** *noun.* M17–E18.
[ORIGIN from ANT- + APOLOGY *noun*[1].]
A reply to an apology.

†**antar** *noun* var. of ANTRE.

Antarctic /an'tɑːktɪk/ *adjective & noun.* Also **a-**; orig. †**-art-**. LME.
[ORIGIN Old French *antartique* (mod. *-arct-*) or Latin *antarcticus* from Greek *antarktikos* opposite to the north: see ANT-, ARCTIC.]
▶ **A** *adjective.* **1** Orig., southern. Now usu. opposite to the Arctic; pertaining to the continent of Antarctica or the south polar regions in general. LME.
Antarctic Circle the parallel of latitude 66° 33′ S. **Antarctic convergence** the zone of the Southern Ocean (marking a distinct climatic and ecological boundary) where the cold Antarctic surface water sinks beneath the warmer waters to the north. **Antarctic Ocean** = *Southern Ocean* s.v. SOUTHERN *adjective*.
†**2** *fig.* Opposite, contradictory, (*to*). M17–E18.
▶ **B** *noun. The* south polar regions; Antarctica. LME.

ante /'anti/ *noun & verb.* Chiefly *N. Amer.* E19.
[ORIGIN formed as ANTE-.]
▶ **A** *noun.* **1** In poker and similar games: a stake put up by a player before drawing cards. E19.
penny ante: see PENNY *adjective*.
2 *transf.* An advance payment; a sum of money for a payment. L19.
▶ **B** *verb trans.* Pres. pple & verbal noun **anteing**. Put up as ante; *transf.* bet, stake, pay *up*. M19.

ante- /'anti/ *prefix.*
[ORIGIN Latin *ante* preposition & adverb = before.]
Forming *nouns* and *adjectives* (from adjectives or nouns) with the sense 'before, preceding, (in place, time, or order)'.
■ **antechapel** *noun* the outer part at the west end of a college chapel E18. **Ante-Co'mmunion (Service)** *noun* the earlier portion of the Anglican Communion service said when there is no Eucharist E19. **ante'cubital** *adjective* (*ANATOMY*) of or pertaining to the inner surface of the forearm L19. **ante-post** *adjective* (of racing odds or betting) made before the competitors' starting numbers are known E20. **antetype** *noun* a preceding type, an earlier example E17.

anteater /'antiːtə/ *noun.* M18.
[ORIGIN from ANT *noun* + EATER.]
Any of a number of edentate mammals constituting the neotropical family Myrmecophagidae, having long, sticky, threadlike tongues and feeding chiefly on ants and termites. Also (*popularly*) any of certain other insectivorous mammals (see below).
banded anteater = NUMBAT. **Cape anteater** = AARDVARK. **giant anteater** = TAMANOIR. **scaly anteater** = PANGOLIN. **spiny anteater** = ECHIDNA.

antebellum /antɪ'bɛləm/ *adjective.* M19.
[ORIGIN Latin *ante bellum* before the war.]
Occurring or existing before a particular war, esp. (*US*) the American Civil War.

antebrachial /antɪ'breɪkɪəl/ *adjective.* M19.
[ORIGIN from ANTE- + BRACHIAL.]
ANATOMY. Of or pertaining to the forearm.

antecede /antɪ'siːd/ *verb.* LME.
[ORIGIN Latin *antecedere*, formed as ANTE- + *cedere* go.]
†**1** *verb intrans.* Go before, come first. LME–L17.
2 *verb trans.* Precede in place, time, or order. E17.

antecedence /antɪ'siːd(ə)ns/ *noun.* LME.
[ORIGIN Latin *antecedentia*, formed as ANTECEDE: see -ENCE.]
†**1** Something which precedes; *spec.* = ANTECEDENT *noun* 2a. LME–L16.
†**2** *ASTRONOMY.* Retrograde motion. M17–L18.
3 Precedence, priority. L17.
■ **antecedency** *noun* (**a**) = ANTECEDENCE 3; †(**b**) an antecedent condition or event: L16.

antecedent /antɪ'siːd(ə)nt/ *noun, adjective, & adverb.* LME.
[ORIGIN Old French & mod. French *antécédent* adjective & noun or Latin *antecedent-* pres. ppl stem (also in philosophy as noun) of *antecedere*: see ANTECEDE, -ENT.]
▶ **A** *noun.* **1** *gen.* A preceding thing or circumstance. LME. ▸**b** In *pl.* The ancestors or background of a person. M19.
b S. WINCHESTER One of his antecedents was Mohammed, King of Bokhara.
2 *spec.* ▸**a** *LOGIC.* The statement upon which a consequence logically depends; the part of a conditional proposition on which the other part depends. LME. ▸**b** *GRAMMAR.* A noun, clause, sentence, etc., to which a (usu. following and esp. relative) pronoun or adverb refers. LME. ▸**c** *MATH.* The first of two quantities which are linked by some relationship or operation, e.g. a ratio. L16.
†**3** An usher. E–M17.
▶ **B** *adjective.* **1** Preceding in time or order. Also *pred.* & *adverb*, prior *to*. M16.
2 Presumptive, a priori. L18.
3 *GEOLOGY.* Of (systems of) streams etc.: with courses determined before the establishment of the present topography and essentially unchanged by later geological processes. L19.
■ **antece'dental** *adjective* (*rare*) L18. **antecedently** *adverb* M17.

antecessor /'antɪsɛsə, antɪ'sɛsə/ *noun.* LME.
[ORIGIN Latin: see ANCESTOR.]
A predecessor.

antechamber /'antɪtʃeɪmbə/ *noun.* Orig. †**anti-**. M17.
[ORIGIN French *antichambre* from Italian *anticamera*: see ANTE-, CHAMBER *noun*.]
A room leading to a more important one.

antechinus /antɪ'kʌɪnəs/ *noun.* M20.
[ORIGIN Latin (see below), from Greek *anti-* simulating + *ekhinos* sea urchin, hedgehog.]
Any of various shrew-like marsupial mice of the genera *Antechinus* and *Parantechinus*, found in Australia, New Guinea, and Tasmania.

antedate /'antɪdeɪt/ *noun.* LME.
[ORIGIN from ANTE- + DATE *noun*[2].]
1 A date (affixed to a document, assigned to an event, etc.) earlier than the true one. LME.
†**2** A feeling of anticipation. Only in E17.

antedate /'antɪdeɪt, antɪ'deɪt/ *verb trans.* L16.
[ORIGIN from the noun.]
1 Affix an earlier than the true date to (a document). L16.
G. BURNET He got the king to antedate it, as if it had been signed at Oxford.
2 Carry back to an earlier time or date. *arch.* L16.
E. B. BROWNING That rage Barbaric, antedates the age.
3 Anticipate. *arch.* E17.
POPE Our joys below it can improve, And antedate the bliss above.
4 Assign (an event etc.) to an earlier date; find an earlier instance of. M17.
DONNE Wilt thou then antedate some new-made vow?
5 Bring about at an earlier date, accelerate. *arch.* M17.
SIR W. SCOTT Seem'd . . that Fate Would Camlan's ruin antedate.
6 Precede in time, come before (something) in date. M17.
DEFOE As if design'd by Instinct to be Great, His Judgment seem'd to antidate his Wit. R. V. JONES 'The Hobnails' which . . he had managed to prove antedated (1474) the first mention of hobnails in the Oxford English Dictionary (1594).
■ **antedating** *noun* (**a**) the action of marking with or assigning to an earlier date; anticipating; (**b**) an earlier instance: L16.

antediluvian /ˌantɪdɪ'luːvɪən/ *adjective & noun.* M17.
[ORIGIN from ANTE- + Latin *diluvium* DELUGE + -AN.]
▶ **A** *adjective.* **1** Belonging, referring, or appropriate to the time before the Flood described in Genesis. M17.
2 Utterly out of date, very antiquated. *colloq.* E18.
▶ **B** *noun.* A person who lived before the Flood; an old-fashioned or very old person. L17.
■ Also **antediluvial** *adjective* E19.

antefix /'antɪfɪks/ *noun.* Also in Latin form **-fixum** /-fɪksəm/, pl. **-fixa** /-fɪksə/. M19.
[ORIGIN Latin *antefixum*, formed as ANTE- + use as noun of *fixus*: see FIX *verb*.]
CLASSICAL ARCHITECTURE. An ornament on an eave or cornice to conceal the ends of tiles; also, an ornamental head etc. making a spout from a gutter. Usu. in *pl.*
■ **ante'fixal** *adjective* M19.

anteflexion /antɪ'flɛkʃ(ə)n/ *noun.* M19.
[ORIGIN from ANTE- + FLEXION.]
ANATOMY. = ANTEVERSION.
■ **'anteflexed** *adjective* (of the uterus) anteverted L19.

antelope /'antɪləʊp/ *noun.* Pl. same, **-s**. LME.
[ORIGIN Old French *antelop* or medieval Latin *ant(h)alopus* from medieval Greek *antholops* of unknown origin and meaning.]
1 A fierce mythical creature with long serrated horns, said to haunt the banks of the Euphrates; a heraldic animal resembling this. LME.
2 Any of the more deerlike members of the ruminant family Bovidae (e.g. chamois, gnu, gazelle). Also, the pronghorn of N. America. E17.

antelopine *adjective* var. of ANTILOPINE.

antelucan /antɪ'luːk(ə)n/ *adjective.* M17.
[ORIGIN Latin *antelucanus*, formed as ANTE- + *luc-*, *lux* light: see -AN.]
Of or pertaining to the hours before dawn; happening before dawn.

ante meridiem /ˌanti mə'rɪdɪəm/ *adjectival & adverbial phr.* M16.
[ORIGIN Latin: see MERIDIAN *adjective*.]
Before midday; between midnight and the following noon. Abbreviation ***a.m.***
■ ***anteme'ridian*** *adjective* (*rare*) pertaining or appropriate to the forenoon or morning M17.

†**antemetic** *noun & adjective* var. of ANTI-EMETIC.

ante-mortem /antɪ'mɔːtəm/ *adjective.* L19.
[ORIGIN Latin *ante mortem* before death.]
Made before death.

antemundane /antɪ'mʌndeɪn/ *adjective.* M18.
[ORIGIN from ANTE- + Latin *mundus* world + -ANE 1.]
Existing or occurring before the creation of the world.

antenatal /antɪ'neɪt(ə)l/ *adjective.* E19.
[ORIGIN from ANTE- + NATAL *adjective*[1].]
1 Happening or existing before birth. E19.
2 *MEDICINE.* Pertaining to or concerned with the health and well-being of women during pregnancy. L19.
■ **antenatally** *adverb* L19.

antenna /an'tɛnə/ *noun.* Pl. **-nnae** /-niː/, (esp. sense 4) **-nnas**. M17.
[ORIGIN Latin, alt. of *antemna* sailyard, used in pl. as translation of Aristotle's *keraioi* 'horns' of insects.]
1 *ZOOLOGY.* Either of a pair of sensory appendages on the heads of insects, crustaceans, and some other arthropods; a feeler. M17.
G. DURRELL A weird creature . . , a pear-shaped body, long antennae that twitched indignantly.
2 *fig.* In *pl.* Receptive senses, means of exploration. M19.
E. POUND My soul's antennæ are prey to such perturbations. L. LEE Antennae of eyes and nose and grubbing fingers.
3 *BOTANY.* Either of a pair of projections on the male flowers of certain orchids of the genus *Catasetum*, which when touched cause the ejection of the pollinia. M19.
4 = AERIAL *noun*. Chiefly *US & techn.* E20.
J. CHEEVER A north wind was howling in the television antennas. T. PYNCHON A radio transmitting station was set up on the cliff, antennas aimed at the Continent.
V antenna: see V, V 2.
■ **antennal**, **antennary** *adjectives* of, pertaining to, or of the nature of antennae M19. **ante'nniferous** *adjective* bearing antennae E19. **antenniform** *adjective* of the form of antennae M19. **antennule** *noun* a small antenna M19.

antenuptial /antɪ'nʌpʃ(ə)l/ *adjective.* E19.
[ORIGIN Late Latin *antenuptialis*, formed as ANTE- + NUPTIAL.]
Born, occurring, etc. before marriage.

ante-orbital *adjective* var. of ANTORBITAL.

antepagment /antɪ'pagm(ə)nt/ *noun.* Also in Latin form **-pagmentum** /-pag'mɛntəm/, pl. **-ta** /-tə/. L17.
[ORIGIN Latin *antepagmentum*, formed as ANTE- + *pangere* fasten: see -MENT.]
ARCHITECTURE. Each of the jambs or moulded architraves of a door. Usu. in *pl.*

antepartum /antɪ'pɑːtəm/ *adjective.* L19.
[ORIGIN Latin *ante partum* before birth.]
MEDICINE. Occurring not long before childbirth.

antepast /'antɪpɑːst/ *noun. arch.* L16.
[ORIGIN from ANTE- + Latin *pastus* food: cf. REPAST *noun*, ANTIPASTO.]
A first course to whet the appetite, an hors d'oeuvre; a foretaste.

antependium /antɪ'pɛndɪəm/ *noun.* Also †**anti-**. L16.
[ORIGIN medieval Latin, formed as ANTE- + Latin *pendere* hang.]
A veil or hanging for the front of an altar.

antepenult /antɪpɪ'nʌlt/ *adjective & noun.* L16.
[ORIGIN Abbreviation of ANTEPENULTIMA.]
= ANTEPENULTIMATE.

antepenultima /ˌantɪpɪ'nʌltɪmə/ *noun.* Pl. **-mae** /-miː/, **-mas**. L16.
[ORIGIN Late Latin (*syllaba*) *antepaenultima*, formed as ANTE- + PENULTIMA.]
PROSODY. The last syllable but two of a word or verse.

A

antepenultimate /ˌantɪpɪˈnʌltɪmət/ *adjective & noun*. **L17**.
[ORIGIN formed as ANTE- + PENULTIMATE.]
▸ **A** *adjective*. The last but two. **L17**.
▸ **B** *noun*. = ANTEPENULTIMA **E18**.

anteposition /ˌantɪpəˈzɪʃ(ə)n/ *noun*. *rare*. **M18**.
[ORIGIN from ANTE- + POSITION *noun*, as if from Latin *anteponere* place before: cf. POSTPOSITION.]
The placing of anything in front, *esp*. (GRAMMAR) in front of a word which usually precedes.

anteprandial /antɪˈprandɪəl/ *adjective*. **E19**.
[ORIGIN from ANTE- + Latin *prandium* dinner + -AL[1].]
Done, happening, or taken before dinner or any large meal.

anter *noun & verb* see AUNTER.

ante rem /ˈantɪ rɛm/ *adjectival & adverbial phr*. **L19**.
[ORIGIN medieval Latin (Albertus Magnus) = before the thing.]
PHILOSOPHY. Prior to the existence of something else; *spec*. (of a universal) prior to the particular; of or pertaining to the theory that the universal is logically prior to the particular. Cf. IN RE 2, POST REM.

anterior /anˈtɪərɪə/ *adjective*. **M16**.
[ORIGIN French *antérieur* or Latin *anterior*, compar. from *ante* before: see -IOR.]
1 Fore, more to the front; *esp*. in ANATOMY, situated in the front of the body, or nearer to the head, forepart, etc.; in the case of humans and other erect animals, = VENTRAL. **M16**. ▸**b** BOTANY. Situated further away from the axis. **E19**.
2 Former, earlier, prior (*to*). **L16**.

R. L. STEVENSON News of their anterior home. M. LOWRY From what conceivable standpoint of rectitude did she imagine she could judge what was anterior to her arrival?

■ **anteriˈority** *noun* **E18**. **anteriormost** *adjective* (chiefly BIOLOGY) in the furthest forward position, nearest to the anterior **M20**. **anteriorly** *adverb* **L16**.

antero- /ˈantərəʊ/ *combining form* of ANTERIOR, used (chiefly ANATOMY) to form adjectives and corresp. adverbs: see -O-.
■ **anterograde** *adjective* directed forwards in time; *spec*. (of amnesia) involving inability to remember new information: **L19**. **anteroˈlateral** *adjective* both anterior and lateral **M19**. **anteropoˈsterior** *adjective* pertaining to front and back; directed forwards and backwards: **M19**. **anteroposˈteriorly** *adverb* in an anteroposterior direction, frontwards and backwards **M19**.

anteroom /ˈantɪruːm, -rʊm/ *noun*. **M18**.
[ORIGIN from ANTE- + ROOM *noun*[1], after ANTECHAMBER.]
A room leading to another.

antes /ˈantiːz/ *noun pl*. **L16**.
[ORIGIN French repr. Latin *antae* pl. of ANTA.]
ARCHITECTURE. Antae.

ante-temple /ˈantɪtɛmp(ə)l/ *noun*. **E18**.
[ORIGIN medieval Latin *antetemplum* translating Greek PRONAOS: see ANTE-, TEMPLE *noun*[1].]
A portico of a church or ancient temple.

anteversion /antɪˈvəːʃ(ə)n/ *noun*. **M19**.
[ORIGIN from ANTE- + VERSION.]
ANATOMY. Forward inclination of the uterus.

antevert /ˈantɪvəːt/ *verb trans*. **M17**.
[ORIGIN Latin *antevertere* anticipate, prevent, formed as ANTE- + *vertere* turn.]
1 Avert beforehand, prevent, anticipate. *rare*. **M17**.
2 Turn forward. Chiefly as ***anteverted*** *ppl adjective* (ANATOMY, of the uterus), inclined forward. **M19**.

anth- /anθ/ *prefix* (no longer productive).
Var. of Greek ANTI- before an aspirate.

anthelion /anˈθiːlɪən/ *noun*. Pl. **-lia** /-lɪə/. **L17**.
[ORIGIN Greek *anthēlion* neut. of *anthēlios*, earlier *antēlios* opposite to the sun, from ANTH- + *hēlios* sun.]
A parhelion opposite to the sun in the sky. Also, a glory, a halo.

anthelix /anˈθiːlɪks/ *noun*. Also **antihelix** /ˈantɪhiːlɪks/. Pl. **-lices** /-lɪsiːz/, **-lixes**. **E18**.
[ORIGIN Greek: see ANTH-, HELIX 3.]
ANATOMY. The curved elevation within the helix of the ear.

anthelmintic /anθ(ə)lˈmɪntɪk/ *adjective & noun*. Also **-thic** /-θɪk/. **L17**.
[ORIGIN from ANTH- + Greek *helminth-*, *-mins* worm + -IC.]
MEDICINE. ▸**A** *adjective*. Active against parasitic worms. **L17**.
▸ **B** *noun*. An anthelmintic medicine. **E18**.

anthem /ˈanθəm/ *noun & verb*. **OE**.
[ORIGIN ecclesiastical Latin *antiphona* ANTIPHON: spelling with *-th-* dates from 15.]
▸ **A** *noun*. **1** = ANTIPHON *noun* 1. *arch*. **OE**.
2 A composition in non-metrical prose (usu. from the Scriptures or Liturgy) set to music for sacred use. **LME**.
3 Any song of praise and gladness; *esp*. a song (sometimes strictly a hymn) adopted by a nation to express patriotism or loyalty (usu. more fully ***national anthem***). **LME**.
▸ **B** *verb trans*. Celebrate in an anthem. **E17**.

anthemic /anˈθɛmɪk/ *adjective*. **L20**.
[ORIGIN from ANTHEM + -IC.]
Suggestive of or resembling an anthem; *spec*. (of a popular song or refrain) designed to rouse or stir an audience or assembly. Often mildly *derog*.

S. RUSHDIE The overall effect is oddly affirmative, even anthemic.

anthemion /anˈθiːmɪən/ *noun*. Pl. **-mia** /-mɪə/. **M19**.
[ORIGIN Greek = flower.]
A figure or ornament resembling honeysuckle.

anther /ˈanθə/ *noun*. Orig. in (in sense 1 only in) Latin form †**-era**, pl. **-erae**. **E16**.
[ORIGIN French *anthère* or mod. Latin *anthera*, in classical Latin medicine extracted from flowers, from Greek *anthēra*, fem. of *anthēros* of flowers, from *anthos* flower.]
†**1** A medicine extracted from flowers, used to treat sore gums. **E16–L17**.
2 BOTANY. The part of the stamen in which pollen is contained and from which it is shed when mature. **E18**.
■ **antheral** *adjective* **L18**.

antheridium /anθəˈrɪdɪəm/ *noun*. Pl. **-dia** /-dɪə/. **M19**.
[ORIGIN mod. Latin: see ANTHER, -IDIUM.]
BOTANY. A male reproductive organ in a cryptogam.
■ **antheridial** *adjective* **M19**.

antherozoid /ˌanθ(ə)rəˈzəʊɪd/ *noun*. Also **-zooid** /-ˈzəʊɔɪd/. **M19**.
[ORIGIN from ANTHER + -O- + ZO(O)ID.]
BOTANY. A motile male gamete produced by a cryptogam or gymnosperm.

anthesis /anˈθiːsɪs/ *noun*. **M19**.
[ORIGIN Greek *anthēsis* flowering, from *anthein* to blossom.]
BOTANY. The time when a flower opens, or becomes sexually functional.

antho- /ˈanθəʊ/ *combining form* of Greek *anthos* flower: see -O-.
■ **anˈthography** *noun* (*rare*) scientific description of flowers **L19**. **anthoˈmania** *noun* an extravagant passion for flowers **L18**. **anthoˈmaniac** *noun* (*rare*) a person with anthomania **M19**. **anˈthophilous** *adjective* (of insects etc.) frequenting flowers **L19**. **anthophore** *noun* (BOTANY) a stalk which raises the receptacle above the calyx **M19**. **anthoˈxanthin** *noun* (CHEMISTRY) any yellow flavonoid pigment found in plants **M19**.

anthocyanin /anθəˈsʌɪənɪn/ *noun*. Orig. †**-cyan**. **M19**.
[ORIGIN German *Anthocyan*, from Greek ANTHO- + *kuanos* blue: see -IN[1].]
CHEMISTRY. Any of a large class of blue, violet, or red flavonoid pigments found in plants.
■ **anthocyˈanidin** *noun* any of the pigments of which the anthocyanins are glycosides **E20**.

anthology /anˈθɒlədʒi/ *noun*. **M17**.
[ORIGIN French *anthologie* or medieval Latin *anthologia* from Greek, from *anthos* flower: see -LOGY.]
1 a A collection of poems by various authors, chosen as being especially fine or appropriate. **M17**. ▸**b** A collection of other literary works or of paintings, songs, etc. **L18**.
2 A collection of flowers. *rare*. **M18**.
■ **anthoˈlogical** *adjective* †(**a**) treating of flowers; (**b**) of or relating to an anthology: **E17**. **anthologist** *noun* the compiler of an anthology **E19**. **anthologiˈzation** *noun* the compiling of an anthology; the use of something in an anthology: **M20**. **anthologize** *verb trans. & intrans*. compile an anthology (of); use in an anthology: **E19**.

Anthony /ˈantəni/ *noun*. **LME**.
[ORIGIN Name of the patron saint of swineherds, to whom one of each litter was traditionally vowed.]
The smallest pig of a litter. Also ***Anthony pig***, ***Anthony hog***, etc.
See also ***St Anthony cross***, ***St Anthony's cross***, ***St Anthony's fire*** s.v. SAINT *noun & adjective*, TANTONY.

Anthony Eden /ˌantəni ˈiːd(ə)n/ *noun*. **M20**.
[ORIGIN English statesman, 1897–1977.]
A black Homburg hat.

anthophyllite /anθəˈfɪlʌɪt, anˈθɒfɪlʌɪt/ *noun*. **E19**.
[ORIGIN from mod. Latin *anthophyllum* clove + -ITE[1]: so called from its typical clove-brown colour.]
MINERALOGY. An orthorhombic ferromagnesian amphibole which occurs usu. as fibrous or asbestiform masses.

anthozoan /anθəˈzəʊən/ *noun & adjective*. **L19**.
[ORIGIN from mod. Latin *Anthozoa* (see below), from Greek *anthos* flower + *zōia* animals + -AN.]
▸ **A** *noun*. Any animal of the class Anthozoa of marine coelenterates, which includes sea anemones, corals, and sea pens. **L19**.
▸ **B** *adjective*. Of or pertaining to Anthozoa. **L19**.

anthracene /ˈanθrəsiːn/ *noun*. **M19**.
[ORIGIN from Greek *anthrak-*, *anthrax*, coal + -ENE.]
CHEMISTRY. A tricyclic aromatic hydrocarbon, $C_{14}H_{10}$, found in coal tar and isolated as colourless crystals.

anthracite /ˈanθrəsʌɪt/ *noun & adjective*. **L16**.
[ORIGIN Greek *anthrakitēs*, formed as ANTHRACENE: see -ITE[1].]
†**1** A gem described by Pliny, supposedly hydrophane. **L16–M18**.
2 A hard, non-bituminous kind of coal consisting of relatively pure carbon. Also ***anthracite coal***. **E19**.
3 (Of) the dark grey colour of this coal. **L19**.
■ **anthraˈcitic** *adjective* of, pertaining to, or of the nature of anthracite coal **M19**.

anthracnose /anˈθraknəʊs/ *noun*. **L19**.
[ORIGIN French, from Greek *anthrak-*, *anthrax* coal + *nosos* disease.]
A fungal disease of plants, characterized by dark lesions.

anthracoid /ˈanθrəkɔɪd/ *adjective*. **L19**.
[ORIGIN from Greek *anthrak-*, ANTHRAX + -OID.]
Of a bacterium: of the kind typified by the anthrax bacillus.

anthracosaur /ˈanθrəkəsɔː/ *noun*. **M20**.
[ORIGIN from mod. Latin *Anthracosaurus* genus name, from Greek *anthrak-*, *anthrax* coal + *sauros* lizard.]
PALAEONTOLOGY. Any member of the suborder Anthracosauroideae of labyrinthodont amphibians of the Cretaceous and Permian periods.

anthracosis /anθrəˈkəʊsɪs/ *noun*. Pl. **-coses** /-ˈkəʊsiːz/. **M19**.
[ORIGIN from Greek *anthrak-*, *anthrax* coal + -OSIS.]
MEDICINE. Pneumoconiosis caused by inhalation of coal dust.
■ **anthracotic** *adjective* suffering from anthracosis **M19**.

anthracothere /ˈanθrəkəθɪə/ *noun*. **M19**.
[ORIGIN French *anthracothère* from Greek *anthrak-*, *anthrax* coal + *thērion* wild animal: its remains were first found in coal-bearing strata.]
PALAEONTOLOGY. An extinct artiodactyl of the family Anthracotheriidae, resembling a pig, found as fossils of Middle Tertiary age.

anthranilic /anθrəˈnɪlɪk/ *adjective*. **M19**.
[ORIGIN from Greek *anthrax* coal + ANIL + -IC: app. so called because of a dark blue-black substance intermediate in its first preparation.]
CHEMISTRY. ***anthranilic acid***, a colourless or yellow crystalline compound first obtained by alkaline hydrolysis of indigo; *o*-aminobenzoic acid, $C_7H_7NO_2$.
■ **anˈthranilate** *noun* a salt or ester of this acid **M19**.

anthraquinone /ˈanθrəkwɪnəʊn/ *noun*. **L19**.
[ORIGIN from ANTHRA(CENE + QUINONE.]
CHEMISTRY. A yellow crystalline quinone, $C_{14}H_8O_2$, which is obtained by oxidation of anthracene, and is the basis of many natural and synthetic dyes. Also, any of various other quinones with similar structures.

anthrax /ˈanθraks/ *noun*. **LME**.
[ORIGIN Latin = carbuncle, from Greek *anthrax*, *anthrak-* coal, carbuncle.]
MEDICINE. **1** A carbuncle, a pustule. Now *rare* or *obsolete*. **LME**.
2 Infection with the bacterium *Bacillus anthracis*, which in animals (esp. sheep and cattle) usu. takes the form of a fatal acute septicaemia, and in humans usu. affects the skin, causing development of a pustule, or the lungs, causing wool-sorters' disease, a form of pneumonia. **L19**.

anthropic /anˈθrɒpɪk/ *adjective*. **M19**.
[ORIGIN Greek *anthrōpikos*, formed as ANTHROPO-: see -IC.]
Of or pertaining to humankind; human.
anthropic principle the cosmological principle that theories of the origin of the universe are constrained by the necessity to allow individual human existence.
■ **anthropically** *adverb* **M20**.

anthropo- /ˈanθrəpəʊ/ *combining form* of Greek *anthrōpos* human being: see -O-.
■ **anthropoˈgenic** *adjective* (**a**) of or pertaining to anthropogeny; (**b**) originated by humans: **L19**. **anthropoˈgenically** *adverb* **L20**. **anthroˈpogeny** *noun* the investigation of the origin of humans **M19**. **anthropogeoˈgraphical** *adjective* of or pertaining to anthropogeography **M17**. **anthropogeˈography** *noun* human geography; geographical anthropology: **L19**. †**anthropography** *noun* an anatomical or ethnographic description **L16–M19**. **anthroˈpolatry** *noun* worship of a human being **M17**. **anthroˈponymy** *noun* the study of persons' names **M20**. **anthropoˈpsychism** *noun* the ascription of human mental characteristics to a divine being or agencies at work in nature **L19**. **anthropoˈsophical** *adjective* of or pertaining to anthroposophy **E20**. **anthroˈposophist** *noun* an adherent or advocate of anthroposophy **E20**. **anthroˈposophy** *noun* (**a**) the knowledge of the nature of humans; human wisdom; (**b**) a movement inaugurated by Rudolf Steiner (1861–1925) to develop the faculty of cognition and the realization of spiritual reality: **M18**. **anthropoˈtomical** *adjective* (now *rare*) of or in human anatomy **M19**. **anthroˈpotomist** *noun* (now *rare*) a person who studies human anatomy **M19**. **anthroˈpotomy** *noun* (now *rare*) the anatomy of the human body **M19**.

anthropocentric /anθrəpəˈsɛntrɪk/ *adjective*. **M19**.
[ORIGIN from ANTHROPO- + -CENTRIC.]
Centring in humans; regarding humanity as the central fact of the universe.
■ **anthropocentrically** *adverb* **M20**. **anthropocentricism** /-sɪz(ə)m/, **anthropocentrism** *nouns* an anthropocentric view or doctrine **E20**.

anthropoid /ˈanθrəpɔɪd/ *adjective & noun*. **M19**.
[ORIGIN Greek *anthrōpoeidēs*, formed as ANTHROPO-: see -OID.]
▸ **A** *adjective*. **1** Of human shape; *spec*. of or pertaining to the primate suborder Anthropoidea, comprising humans, apes, and monkeys. **M19**.
anthropoid ape a large ape of the family Pongidae; a gorilla, orang-utan, or chimpanzee.
2 Apelike. *colloq*. **M20**.
▸ **B** *noun*. A being that is human in form only; *esp*. an anthropoid ape. **M19**.
■ **anthroˈpoidal** *adjective* **M19**.

anthropolite /an'θrɒp(ə)lʌɪt/ *noun*. Now *rare* or *obsolete*. L18.
[ORIGIN from ANTHROPO- + -LITE.]
A petrified human being; a human fossil.

anthropological /anθrəpə'lɒdʒɪk(ə)l/*adjective*. E19.
[ORIGIN formed as ANTHROPOLOGY + -ICAL.]
Of, pertaining to, or connected with anthropology; relating to the nature of humankind.
■ **anthropologic** *adjective* anthropological L17. **anthropologically** *adverb* L19.

anthropology /anθrə'pɒlədʒi/ *noun*. L16.
[ORIGIN from ANTHROPO- + -LOGY.]
The science of humankind, in the widest sense.
cultural anthropology = ***social anthropology*** below. **physical anthropology** the science of human zoology, evolution, and ecology. **social anthropology** the science of human social and cultural behaviour and its development.
■ **anthropologist** *noun* L18. **anthropologize** *verb intrans.* (*colloq.*) study anthropology M20.

anthropometric /anθrəpə'mɛtrɪk/ *adjective & noun*. L19.
[ORIGIN from ANTHROPOMETRY + -IC.]
▸ **A** *adjective*. Of or pertaining to anthropometry. L19.
▸ **B** *noun*. In *pl.* (treated as *sing.*). Anthropometry, now esp. as used in designing furniture and machinery. L19.
■ **anthropometrical** *adjective* L19. **anthropometrically** *adverb* L19.

anthropometry /anθrə'pɒmɪtri/ *noun*. M19.
[ORIGIN from ANTHROPO- + -METRY.]
The branch of science that deals with the measurement and proportions of the human body and their variation.
■ **anthropometer** *noun* an instrument used in anthropometry L19. **anthropometrist** *noun* a person engaged in anthropometry L19.

anthropomorph /an'θrɒpəmɔːf, 'anθrə-/ *noun*. L19.
[ORIGIN formed as ANTHROPOMORPHOUS.]
ART. A representation of the human form.

anthropomorphic /anθrəpə'mɔːfɪk/ *adjective*. E19.
[ORIGIN formed as ANTHROPOMORPH + -IC.]
1 Of the nature of anthropomorphism. E19.
2 Having or representing a human form. L19.
■ **anthropomorphical** *adjective* M19. **anthropomorphically** *adverb* M19.

anthropomorphise *verb* var. of ANTHROPOMORPHIZE.

anthropomorphism /anθrəpə'mɔːfɪz(ə)m/ *noun*. M18.
[ORIGIN formed as ANTHROPOMORPHOUS + -ISM.]
Ascription of human form, attributes, or personality to God, a god, an animal, or something impersonal; an instance of this.
■ **anthropomorphist** *noun* a person who uses anthropomorphism M19.

anthropomorphite /anθrəpə'mɔːfʌɪt/ *noun & adjective*. Also **A-**. LME.
[ORIGIN ecclesiastical Latin *anthropomorphitae* pl. from ecclesiastical Greek *anthrōpomorphitai*, formed as ANTHROPOMORPHOUS: see -ITE[1].]
(Designating) a member of a religious sect ascribing a human form to God.
■ **anthropomor'phitic** *adjective* M19. †**anthropomorphitical** *adjective* L17–M18. **anthropomorphitism** *noun* the doctrine of anthropomorphites; anthropomorphism: M17.

anthropomorphize /anθrəpə'mɔːfʌɪz/ *verb*. Also **-ise**. M19.
[ORIGIN formed as ANTHROPOMORPHOUS + -IZE.]
1 *verb trans.* Render or regard as human in form. M19.
2 *verb intrans.* Use anthropomorphism. M19.
■ **anthropomorphi'zation** *noun* L19.

anthropomorphous /anθrəpə'mɔːfəs/ *adjective*. M18.
[ORIGIN from Greek *anthrōpomorphos*, formed as ANTHROPO- + *morphē* form: see -OUS.]
Of human form.

anthropopathy /anθrə'pɒpəθi/ *noun*. M17.
[ORIGIN from ANTHROPO- + -PATHY.]
Ascription of human emotions to God.
■ **anthropopathism** *noun* = ANTHROPOPATHY M19. **anthropo'pathic** *adjective* E19. **anthropo'pathically** *adverb* M19.

anthropophagi /anθrə'pɒfəgʌɪ, -dʒʌɪ/ *noun pl.* Sing. (*rare*) **-gus** /-gəs/. M16.
[ORIGIN Latin *anthropophagus*, *-gi* from Greek *anthrōpophagos* man-eating, formed as ANTHROPO-: see -PHAGOUS.]
Cannibals.
■ †**anthropophaginian** *noun* (*rare*, Shakes.) a cannibal: only in L16. **anthropophagite** *noun* a habitual cannibal M16.

anthropophagy /anθrə'pɒfədʒi/ *noun*. M17.
[ORIGIN Greek *anthrōpophagia*, formed as ANTHROPOPHAGI: see -Y[3].]
Cannibalism.
■ **anthropophagous** /-gəs/ *adjective* cannibal M19.

anthurium /an'θ(j)ʊərɪəm/ *noun*. M19.
[ORIGIN mod. Latin (see below), from Greek *anthos* flower + *oura* tail.]
Any of various tropical American plants of the genus *Anthurium* (family Araceae), several of which are grown for their ornamental foliage or brightly coloured flowering spathes.

†**anthypophora** *noun*. M16–M18.
[ORIGIN Latin from Greek *anthupophora*, formed as ANTH- + *hupophora* allegation.]
RHETORIC. A counter-inference, a contrary allegation.

anti /'anti/ *noun, adjective, & preposition*. L18.
[ORIGIN Independent use of ANTI-.]
▸ **A** *noun*. A person who is antagonistic or opposed to something or someone. L18.
▸ **B** *adjective*. Antagonistic, opposed. M19.
▸ **C** *preposition*. Antagonistic or opposed to, against. M20.

anti- /'anti/ *prefix*. Also **ant-** before a vowel or *h* (see ANTH-).
[ORIGIN Greek = opposite, against, in exchange, instead, representing, rivalling, simulating.]
Used in words adopted (ult.) from Greek and in English words modelled on these, and as a freely productive prefix with the sense 'opposite, against, preventing', forming (***a***) nouns from nouns, as ***antibody***, ***anticlimax***, ***antidemocrat***; also with the senses 'rival, pseudo-', as ***Antichrist***, ***antipope***, 'the reverse of, unlike the conventional', as ***anti-hero***, ***antinovel***, and (with suffix *-ism*, *-ist*) '(the doctrine of) a person opposed to', as ***anti-Americanism***, ***anti-feminism***, ***anti-feminist***, ***anti-imperialism***, ***anti-imperialist*** (those in *-ist* also used attrib. or as adjective); in PHYSICS designating an antiparticle of a specified particle, as ***antineutrino***, ***antineutron***, ***antiproton***, ***antiquark***; in BIOLOGY & MEDICINE designating substances which counteract or inhibit the effect of another substance, as ***anticholinesterase***, ***antihormone***, ***antivitamin***; in CHEMISTRY (usu. italicized) designating geometrical isomers of organic compounds containing C=N or N=N in which the principal atoms or groups attached to the doubly bonded atoms are on opposite sides of the plane of the double bond (opp. *syn-*); (***b***) adjectives from adjectives, the prefix acting as a preposition governing the noun implied, as ***anti-American***, ***anti-colonial***, ***antimalarial***, ***anti-papal***, ***anti-parliamentary***, ***anti-revolutionary***, ***anti-Semitic***, (these can further form adverbs where appropriate); these adjectives can be used ellipt. as nouns, esp. MEDICINE designating a drug or other agent counteracting the noun implied, as ***anticonvulsant***, ***antidepressant***; (***c***) adjectives from nouns in attrib. use, as ***anti-apartheid*** (demonstration etc.), ***anti-combination*** (laws etc.), ***anti-court*** (party etc.), ***anti-missile*** (missile etc.), ***anti-noise*** (regulations etc.), ***anti-roll*** (bar etc.), ***anti-slavery*** (society etc.), ***anti-union*** (feeling etc.), ***anti-war*** (literature, party, etc.).
■ **anti-a'bortion** *adjective* opposed to abortion on demand L20. **anti-a'bortionist** *noun & adjective* (a person who is) anti-abortion L20. **anti-'aircraft** *adjective & noun* (a gun etc.) for defence against hostile aircraft E20. **anti-'aliasing** *noun* (COMPUTING) the process of smoothing curved or inclined lines that have been drawn on a computer screen by means of pixels in a fixed array and therefore appear artificially jagged L20. **anti-'attrition** *noun* (now *rare*) something which resists the effects of friction E19. **antibac'terial** *adjective* active against bacteria E20. **anti'bilious** *adjective* (now *rare*) of use against biliousness E19. **Anti-'Birmingham** *noun* (ENGLISH HISTORY) an opponent of the 1680 Exclusion Bill, a Tory (cf. BIRMINGHAM) L17. **Anti'burgher** *noun* (*hist.*) a member of the section of the Secession Church in Scotland which held it unscriptural to take the burgess oath (cf. BURGHER 2) M18. **anti-'busing**, ***-bussing** /-bʌsɪŋ/ *adjective* (*US*) opposed to the counteracting of racial segregation by transporting pupils in buses to more distant schools M20. **anti'cathode** *noun* in an X-ray tube, the target on which electrons from the cathode impinge, producing X-rays E20. **anti'catholic**, **anti-'Catholic** *adjective & noun* (a person) opposed to what is catholic or (*esp.*) Roman Catholic M17. **anti-'choice** *adjective* opposed to granting choice, *spec.* to granting pregnant women the right to choose abortion L20. **anti'clerical** *adjective & noun* (a person who is) opposed to clerical rule or influence, esp. in politics M19. **anti'clericalism** *noun* opposition to clerical rule or influence L19. **anti'clockwise** *adjective & adverb* in a direction of movement opposite to that of the hands of a clock, moving in a curve from right to left as seen from a central position L19. **anti'codon** *noun* (BIOCHEMISTRY) a triplet of nucleotides forming a unit of genetic code in transfer RNA, corresponding to a complementary codon in messenger RNA. **antico'donic** *adjective* of or pertaining to an anticodon L20. **anticom'petitive** *adjective* tending to suppress (esp. economic) competition M20. **anticon'vulsant** *adjective & noun* (a medicine) that prevents or retards convulsions M20. **antide'pressant** *adjective & noun* (a drug) that alleviates the symptoms of depression M20. **antidia'rrhoeal** *adjective & noun* (a drug) used to alleviate diarrhoea M20. **antidiu'retic** *adjective & noun* (a drug) that tends to inhibit the secretion of urine (***antidiuretic hormone*** = VASOPRESSIN; abbreviation ***ADH***) E20. **antife'brific** *adjective & noun* (now *rare*), **anti'febrile** *noun & adjective* (a medicine) of use against fever M17. **anti'feedant** *noun* a naturally occurring substance in certain plants which adversely affects insects or other animals which eat the plants M20. **antiform** *noun* (GEOLOGY) a fold that is convex upwards, irrespective of the chronological sequence of the strata (opp. ***synform***) M20. **antifouling** *noun* the prevention of fouling of a ship's hull; a paint or other substance applied in order to prevent fouling: M19. **antifreeze** *adjective & noun* (designating) a chemical agent added to water in order to lower the freezing point, esp. for use in the radiator of an engine E20. **anti'friction** *noun & adjective* (a substance) that reduces friction M19. **anti'fungal** *adjective & noun* (a substance) active against fungi or fungal growth M20. **anti-'Gallican** *adjective & noun* (a person) opposed to what is French M18. **anti-'Gallicanism** *noun* opposition or aversion to the French E19. **antiglobali'zation** *noun* opposition to the increase in global power and influence of businesses etc. L20. **anti-god** *noun* (***a***) a rival god; (***b***) an evil demon or devil: M17. **anti-hero** *noun* a person, esp. the chief character in a novel etc., who is the opposite of or unlike a conventional hero E18. **anti-heroine** *noun* an untypical or unconventional heroine E20. **anti'histamine** *noun & adjective* (a drug) that counters the physiological effects of histamine, esp. in some allergies M20. ˌ**antihista'minic** *adjective & noun* = ANTIHISTAMINE M20. **antihy'steric** *noun & adjective* (now *rare*) (a medicine) of use against hysteria M18. **antihy'sterical** *adjective* (*rare*) = ANTIHYSTERIC *adjective* M17. **anti-'Jacobin** *adjective & noun* (a person) opposed to the Jacobins (1789) or to the French Revolution E19. **anti-knock** *noun & adjective* (designating) a substance added to motor fuel to prevent detonation in the engine E20. **anti-life** *noun & adjective* (a principle or attitude) opposed to living fully and harmoniously with the natural order E20. **anti-lock**, **anti-locking** *adjectives* (of a vehicle braking system) designed to prevent the wheels from locking L20. **antima'larial** *adjective & noun* (a drug) of use against malaria M20. **antimatter** *noun* (PHYSICS) matter whose elementary particles are the antiparticles of those (electrons, protons, etc.) making up normal matter M20. **antime'tabolite** *noun* a substance resembling a metabolite and interfering with normal metabolic processes M20. **antimi'crobial** *adjective & noun* (a substance) active against microbes M20. †**antimonarchial** *adjective* = ANTIMONARCHICAL L17–M18. †**antimonarchic** *adjective* = ANTIMONARCHICAL M17–M18. **antimo'narchical** *adjective* opposed to monarchy E17. **anti'monarchist** *noun* a professional opponent of monarchs and monarchy M17. **anti-'national** *adjective* opposed to one's own nation or to a national party E19. **antineo'plastic** *noun & adjective* (a drug) that suppresses neoplasia M20. †**antinephritic** *adjective & noun* (a medicine) of use against kidney disease L17–M19. †**antinephritical** *adjective* of use against kidney disease: only in M17. **antinode** *noun* (PHYSICS) a point or line at which the amplitude of a vibrating system is a maximum L19. **antinovel** *noun* a novel of an unconventional, often experimental, type M20. **anti-'nuclear** *adjective* opposed to nuclear weapons M20. **anti-odon'talgic** *adjective* (*rare*) of use against toothache E19. **anti'oxidant** *noun & adjective* (an agent) that inhibits oxidation M20. **anti'parallel** *adjective* (chiefly PHYSICS) parallel but moving or oriented in opposite directions M17. **antiparticle** *noun* (PHYSICS) an elementary particle having the same mass as a given particle but an opposite electrical charge, or (in the case of an uncharged particle) an opposite magnetic moment; a particle of antimatter: M20. **antiperi'staltic** *adjective* (PHYSIOLOGY) acting contrary to peristaltic motion E18. **anti-perso'nnel** *adjective* (of bombs, weapons, etc.) designed to kill, injure, or obstruct human beings M20. **anti'perspirant** *noun & adjective* (a substance) tending to inhibit perspiration M20. †**antipestilential** *adjective* of use against pestilence M17–E19. **antiphase** *noun* (PHYSICS) opposite phase, when difference in phase is at a maximum (i.e. 180° out of phase) M20. **antipole** *noun* the opposite pole; *fig.* the direct opposite: E19. **antipru'ritic** *noun & adjective* (a substance) that relieves itching L19. **antipsy'chotic** *noun & adjective* (a drug) used to treat psychotic disorders L20. **antipy'retic** *noun & adjective* (a medicine) that tends to reduce fever L17. **antira'chitic** *adjective* (MEDICINE) preventing or curing rickets M19. **anti'retroviral** *noun & adjective* (a drug) that inhibits the activity of retroviruses such as HIV M20. **anti'resonance** *noun* (PHYSICS) a condition in which an interaction or a response has a minimum value E20. ˌ**antisabba'tarian** *adjective & noun* (a person) opposed to the observance of the Sabbath M17. **antiscor'butic** *adjective & noun* (a medicine) that prevents or cures scurvy M17. †**antiscorbutical** *adjective* = ANTISCORBUTIC *adjective* M17–M18. **anti'scriptural** *adjective* opposed to Scripture L17. †**antiscripturist** *noun* a person who denies the truth and authority of Scripture M17–M18. **anti-self** *noun* an adopted persona that is the opposite of the conscious normal self E20. **anti-'Semite** *noun*, **anti-Se'mitic** *adjective* (a person) hostile to Jews L19. **anti-'Semitism** *noun* hostility or opposition to Jews L19. **antiserum** *noun*, pl. **-ra**, **-rums**, MEDICINE a serum containing antibodies, usu. for a particular antigen E20. **antispas'modic** *adjective & noun* (MEDICINE) (a medicine) of use against involuntary-muscle spasm L17. **anti'static** *adjective* counteracting the effects of static electricity M20. ˌ**antisyphi'litic** *noun & adjective* (a medicine) of use against syphilis M19. **anti'terrorism** *noun* opposition to or measures against terrorism L19. **anti'terrorist** *adjective* opposing terrorism M20. **antite'tanic** *noun & adjective* (a drug) that counteracts or prevents tetanus L19. **anti'theism** *noun* opposition to belief in the existence of a god M19. **anti-'theist** *noun* a person opposed to belief in the existence of a god M19. **antithe'istic** *adjective* of or pertaining to antitheists, opposed to belief in a god M19. **anti'toxic** *adjective* (PHYSIOLOGY) of the nature of, pertaining to, or containing an antitoxin L19. **antitoxin** *noun* (PHYSIOLOGY) an antibody effective against an antigenic (usu. bacterial) toxin L19. **antitrade** *noun* (METEOROLOGY) (more fully ***antitrade wind***) orig., any of the prevailing westerly winds of middle latitudes; now, a contrary wind blowing at a high altitude above the trade wind: M19. **antitragus** *noun*, pl. **-gi** /-gʌɪ, -dʒʌɪ/, ANATOMY a small cartilaginous projection above the lobe of the ear, opposite the tragus M19. ˌ**antitrini'tarian** *noun & adjective* (a person) opposed to the doctrine of the Trinity E17. **anti'trust** *adjective* (*US*) opposed to trusts or similar monopolistic combinations L19. **anti'tussive** *adjective & noun* (a drug) that cures or relieves a cough E20. **antive'nene** *noun* an antiserum for a snake venom or other animal poison L19. **anti'venin** *noun* = ANTIVENENE E20. **anti'viral** *adjective* acting against viruses L20. **anti'virus** *noun* an antiviral agent M20.

†**anti-apex** *noun* see ANTAPEX.

antibiosis /ˌantɪbʌɪ'əʊsɪs/ *noun*. L19.
[ORIGIN from ANTI- + SYM)BIOSIS *noun*.]
BIOLOGY. Antagonism between organisms (opp. ***symbiosis***); *esp.* the action of antibiotics.

antibiotic /ˌantɪbʌɪ'ɒtɪk/ *adjective & noun*. M19.
[ORIGIN from ANTI- + Greek *biōtikos* fit for life, from *bios* life: see -OTIC.]
▸ **A** *adjective*. †**1** Doubting the possibility of life (in a particular environment). M–L19.
2 Harmful to or destructive of living matter, esp. micro-organisms; of or pertaining to antibiotics. L19.
▸ **B** *noun*. A substance which is capable of destroying or inhibiting the growth of bacteria or other micro-organisms; *spec.* one that is produced by another micro-organism (or is a synthetic analogue of a microbial product), and is used therapeutically. M20.

– NOTE: Rare before M20.

antibody /ˈantɪbɒdi/ *noun*. E20.
[ORIGIN from ANTI- + BODY *noun*, translating German *Antikörper*.]
PHYSIOLOGY. A protein produced in the body which reacts with a given antigen (whose introduction usu. stimulates its formation).
– COMB.: **antibody-negative**, **antibody-positive** *adjectives* in which antibodies associated with a particular antigen (esp. with HIV) are absent or present.

antic /ˈantɪk/ *noun, adjective, & verb*. Also †**antique**. See also ANTIQUE. E16.
[ORIGIN Italian *antico* ancient, from Latin *antiquus*, *anticus* ANTIQUE, used in English = *grottesco*: see GROTESQUE.]
▸ **A** *noun*. **1** A grotesque or absurd posture or action. Usu. in *pl.* E16.
J. MONTAGUE For an instant / you smile to see / his antics.
†**2** *ARCHITECTURE & ART*. A grotesque or fantastic ornamental representation of a person, animal, or thing; a gargoyle's grotesque face. M16–M19.
C. MARLOWE To make his monks.. stand like apes, And point like antics at his triple crown.
3 A clown; a mountebank's assistant. *arch.* M16.
DEFOE Dancing and hallooing like an antic.
†**4** A grotesque pageant or theatrical representation. L16–L17.
SHAKES. *L.L.L.* Some delightful ostentation, or show, or pageant, or antic, or firework.
▸ **B** *adjective*. **1** Grotesque, bizarre, fantastically incongruous. *arch.* M16.
E. HALL A fountayne of embowed woorke.. ingrayled with anticke woorkes. SHAKES. *Haml.* How strange or odd some'er I bear myself—As I perchance hereafter shall think meet To put an antic disposition on. SWIFT Two rows of guards.. dressed after a very antic manner. WORDSWORTH An antic pair Of monkeys on his back. E. LINKLATER Juan was moved to something between fear and antic laughter.
†**2** Of the face or features: grotesquely distorted (see sense A.2 above). L16–L17.
▸ **C** *verb*. Infl. **-ck-**.
1 *verb intrans. & trans.* with *it*. Perform antics, act as an antic. *arch.* L16.
†**2** *verb trans.* Make grotesque. *rare* (Shakes.). Only in E17.
■ **anticly** *adverb* (*arch.*) grotesquely M16.

†**antichamber** *noun* see ANTECHAMBER.

Antichrist /ˈantɪkrʌɪst/ *noun*. OE.
[ORIGIN Old French *antecrist* (mod. *antéchrist*) or ecclesiastical Latin *antichristus* from Greek *antikhristos* (1 John 2:18), formed as ANTI- + CHRIST.]
1 A great personal opponent of Christ, expected by the early Church to appear before the end of the world. OE.
2 Any opponent of Christ. ME.

antichristian /antɪˈkrɪstʃ(ə)n, -tɪən/ *adjective & noun*. Also **A-**. M16.
[ORIGIN from ANTICHRIST after CHRISTIAN *noun, adjective*; senses A.2 and B.2 with extended meaning, as if from ANTI- + CHRISTIAN *noun, adjective*.]
▸ **A** *adjective*. **1** Of or pertaining to Antichrist. M16.
2 Opposed to what is Christian or to Christianity. L16.
▸ **B** *noun*. †**1** A follower of Antichrist. Only in M16.
2 An opponent of Christianity. E17.
■ **antichristianism** *noun* (*a*) the system of Antichrist; (*b*) the quality of being opposed to Christianity; an antichristian act or belief: L16. **antichristiˈanity** *noun* (long *rare*) = ANTICHRISTIANISM M16. †**antichristianize** *verb intrans.* oppose Christ M17–E18. **antichristianly** *adverb* L16.

†**antichronism** *noun*. E17–E18.
[ORIGIN Greek *antikhronismos* use of one tense for another, formed as ANTI- + *khronos* time, tense + *-ismos* -ISM.]
Contradiction of true chronology; (an) anachronism.

antichthon /anˈtɪkθəʊn/ *noun*. Pl. (in sense 1) †**-ones**. M16.
[ORIGIN Greek *antikhthōn* use as noun of adjective (sc. *gē* earth), formed as ANTI- + *khthōn* earth, ground.]
†**1** The antipodes; in *pl.*, their inhabitants. M16–M18.
2 *HISTORY OF SCIENCE*. A supposed counterpart of the earth in the heavens. M17.

anticipant /anˈtɪsɪp(ə)nt/ *adjective & noun*. *arch.* E16.
[ORIGIN Latin *anticipant-* pres. ppl stem of *anticipare*: see ANTICIPATE, -ANT[1].]
▸ **A** *adjective*. **1** Acting in advance. E16.
2 Apprehending beforehand, expectant. L18.
▸ **B** *noun*. A person who anticipates something. M19.

anticipate /anˈtɪsɪpeɪt/ *verb*. M16.
[ORIGIN Latin *anticipat-* pa. ppl stem of *anticipare*, formed as ANTE- + *cip-* var. of base of *capere* take: see -ATE[3]. Partly after French *anticiper*.]
1 *verb trans.* Take into consideration or mention before the due time. M16. ▸**b** *verb intrans.* Consider something too soon; raise a matter too soon. E18.
R. BAXTER You shall not again tempt me to anticipate the question of effectual Grace. **b** JOYCE I understand you to suggest there was misconduct with one of the brothers... But perhaps I am anticipating?
2 *verb trans.* Observe or practise in advance of the due time; cause (a future event) to be a reality beforehand; cause to happen earlier, accelerate. M16.
SIR W. SCOTT To anticipate by half an hour the usual time of his arrival. BYRON Some leap'd overboard.. As eager to anticipate their grave. C. BRONTË Some real lives do.. actually anticipate the happiness of Heaven. A. J. P. TAYLOR Both British and French tried to anticipate the future.
†**3** *verb intrans.* Occur earlier. L16–M17.
SIR T. BROWNE The Equinoxes had anticipated.
†**4** *verb trans.* Seize or take possession of beforehand. L16–L18.
W. COWPER To soar, and to anticipate the skies.
5 *verb trans.* Take action in advance regarding; forestall. E17.
M. MCCARTHY It was the job of a good servant to read his master's mind and anticipate his wishes. J. LE CARRÉ I'm sorry—do go on. I do not mean to anticipate you. DAY LEWIS To sustain the singer,.. and anticipate every change of volume and tempo.
6 *verb trans.* Use or spend in advance. L17.
CLARENDON To carry on that vast Expence, the Revenue of the Crown had been Anticipated.
7 *verb trans.* Look forward to; *colloq.* expect. M18.
G. K. CHESTERTON The interview which was promised him.. he anticipated with a particular pleasure. S. LEWIS I don't anticipate we'll have any more real cold weather now. A. TOFFLER In the future, we can anticipate networks that broadcast for such specialized occupational groups as engineers, accountants and attorneys. A. EDEN They would anticipate that.. their descendants would work on the estate for many generations.
■ **anticipatingly** *adverb* with anticipation M19. **anticipative** *adjective* (*a*) of the nature of anticipation; (*b*) given to anticipation, expectant: M17. **anticipatively** *adverb* E17. **anticipator** *noun* a person who anticipates something L16. **anticipatorily** *adverb* (*rare*) in anticipation, beforehand L19. **anticipatory** *adjective* of the nature of anticipation M17.

anticipation /antɪsɪˈpeɪʃ(ə)n/ *noun*. LME.
[ORIGIN French, or Latin *anticipatio(n-)*, formed as ANTICIPATE: see -ATION.]
1 Introduction in advance, *spec.* in *MUSIC* of part of a chord which is about to follow. LME.
†**2** Occurrence in advance of the expected time. LME–M19.
3 Action taken beforehand in awareness of a possible or likely event; forestalling. LME.
American Speech Heightened security in anticipation of a terrorist attack.
4 Intuition; presentiment. *arch.* M16.
5 The using of money before it is at one's disposal; a sum so used in advance. M16.
†**6** Prepossession, prejudice. M17–E18.
7 Contemplation or consideration in advance; the action of looking forward to something; (esp. eager or pleasurable) expectation. E18.
T. C. WOLFE He felt a thrill of pleasurable anticipation.

anticlimax /antɪˈklʌɪmaks/ *noun*. E18.
[ORIGIN from ANTI- + CLIMAX *noun*.]
1 *RHETORIC*. The addition of a particular which, against expectation, suddenly lowers the effect; the opposite of climax. E18.
2 An ineffective end where a climax is expected; a descent contrasting with a previous rise. E19.
■ ˌ**anticliˈmactic** *adjective* of the nature of an anticlimax L19. ˌ**anticliˈmactically** *adverb* E20.

anticlinal /antɪˈklʌɪn(ə)l/ *adjective*. E19.
[ORIGIN from ANTI- + Greek *klinein* to lean, slope + -AL[1].]
1 *GEOLOGY*. Pertaining to or of the nature of an anticline. Opp. ***synclinal***. E19.
2 *ANATOMY*. Of a vertebra: having an upright spine, towards which the spines of adjacent vertebrae incline. L19.
3 *BOTANY*. Of a cell wall etc.: perpendicular to the surface of the meristem. Of growth: taking place by the formation of anticlinal walls. Opp. ***periclinal***. L19.
■ **anticlinally** *adverb* M19.

anticline /ˈantɪklʌɪn/ *noun*. M19.
[ORIGIN formed as ANTICLINAL after INCLINE *noun*.]
GEOLOGY. A fold from whose axis the strata incline downwards on either side. Opp. SYNCLINE.
■ **anticliˈnorium** *noun*, pl. **-ria** /-rɪə/, a system of folds which has an overall anticlinal form L19.

anticoagulant /ˌantɪkəʊˈagjʊl(ə)nt/ *adjective & noun*. E20.
[ORIGIN from ANTI- + COAGULANT.]
(A substance) that inhibits coagulation of the blood.
■ **anticoagulate** *verb trans.* treat with an anticoagulant M20. **anticoaguˈlation** *noun* M20.

anticyclone /antɪˈsʌɪkləʊn/ *noun*. M19.
[ORIGIN from ANTI- + CYCLONE.]
METEOROLOGY. A pressure system characterized by a high central barometric pressure and a slow clockwise (northern hemisphere) or anticlockwise (southern hemisphere) circulation.
■ **anticyˈclonic** *adjective* of, pertaining to, of the nature or characteristic of an anticyclone L19. **anticyˈclonically** *adverb* L19.

antidoron /antɪˈdɔːrɒn/ *noun*. M19.
[ORIGIN Greek *antidōron*, formed as ANTI- + *dōron* gift.]
ORTHODOX CHURCH. The unconsecrated bread remaining after the Eucharistic Liturgy, blessed by the priests and given to non-communicants as well as communicants.

†**antidotary** *noun & adjective*. LME.
[ORIGIN medieval Latin *antidotarius*, *-um*, from *antidotum*: see ANTIDOTE *noun*, -ARY[1]. Cf. French *antidotaire*.]
▸ **A** *noun*. A book describing antidotes; also, a dispensary. LME–E18.
▸ **B** *adjective*. Of the nature of an antidote. L16–M17.

antidote /ˈantɪdəʊt/ *noun*. LME.
[ORIGIN French, or Latin *antidotum* from Greek *antidoton* use as noun of neut. of *antidotos*, formed as ANTI- + *do-* stem of *didonai* give.]
1 A medicine given to counteract the effects of a poison (or, formerly, a disease). (Foll. by *against*, *for*, *to*.) LME.
2 *fig.* Something which counteracts an evil. (With constructions as sense 1.) M16.
■ **antidotal** *adjective* pertaining to or of the nature of an antidote M17.

antidote /ˈantɪdəʊt/ *verb trans.* M17.
[ORIGIN from ANTIDOTE *noun*, after medieval Latin *antidotare*, French *antidoter*.]
†**1** Provide with an antidote; fortify against an evil. M17–E18.
2 Administer an antidote against; counteract (a poison, an evil). M17.

antidromic /antɪˈdrəʊmɪk/ *adjective*. E20.
[ORIGIN from ANTI- + Greek *dromos* running + -IC.]
PHYSIOLOGY. Of an impulse: travelling in the opposite direction to that normal in a nerve fibre. Opp. ORTHODROMIC 2.
■ **antidromically** *adverb* E20.

anti-emetic /ˌantɪɪˈmɛtɪk/ *noun & adjective*. Also †**antemetic**. E18.
[ORIGIN from ANTI- + EMETIC.]
(A medicine) serving to prevent vomiting.

antiferromagnetic /ˌantɪfɛrəʊmagˈnɛtɪk/ *adjective*. M20.
[ORIGIN from ANTI- + FERROMAGNETIC.]
PHYSICS. Designating or exhibiting a form of magnetism characterized by an antiparallel alignment of adjacent electron spins in a crystal lattice.
■ ˈ**antiferroˌmagnet** *noun* an antiferromagnetic substance M20. **antiferroˈmagnetism** *noun* M20.

anti-g /antɪˈdʒiː/ *adjective*. M20.
[ORIGIN from ANTI- + *g* = acceleration due to gravity.]
Of clothing (for pilots etc.): designed to counter the effects of high acceleration.

antigen /ˈantɪdʒ(ə)n/ *noun*. E20.
[ORIGIN German from French *antigène*, formed as ANTI-, -GEN.]
PHYSIOLOGY. A foreign substance which, when introduced into the body, stimulates the production of an antibody.
■ **antiˈgenic** *adjective* of the nature of or pertaining to an antigen E20. **antiˈgenically** *adverb* M20. **antigeˈnicity** *noun* M20.

antigorite /anˈtɪgərʌɪt/ *noun*. M19.
[ORIGIN from *Antigorio*, a valley in Piedmont, Italy + -ITE[1].]
MINERALOGY. A magnesium silicate mineral of the serpentine group, occurring usu. as thin green plates.

antigravity /antɪˈgravɪti/ *adjective & noun*. E20.
[ORIGIN from ANTI- + GRAVITY.]
▸ **A** *adjective*. Acting in opposition to the effects of gravity or of high acceleration; (of muscles) serving to maintain the erect posture of the body. E20.
▸ **B** *noun*. A (hypothetical) force opposed to that of gravity. M20.
■ Also **anti-grav** *adjective & noun* (*colloq.*) M20.

Antiguan /anˈtiːg(w)ən/ *adjective & noun*. M19.
[ORIGIN from *Antigua* (see below) + -AN.]
(A native or inhabitant) of the W. Indian island of Antigua, part of the country Antigua and Barbuda.

antihelix *noun* var. of ANTHELIX.

Antillean /anˈtɪlɪən/ *adjective*. L19.
[ORIGIN from *Antilles* (see below) + -AN.]
Of or pertaining to the Antilles, a group of islands in the W. Indies.

antilog /ˈantɪlɒg/ *noun*. *colloq.* E20.
[ORIGIN Abbreviation.]
= ANTILOGARITHM.

antilogarithm /antɪˈlɒgərɪð(ə)m/ *noun*. M17.
[ORIGIN from ANTI- + LOGARITHM.]
MATH. †**1** The logarithm of the complementary trigonometrical function (to a sine etc.), or the complement of the logarithm of a sine etc. *rare*. M17–L18.
2 The number to which a given logarithm belongs. L17.
■ ˌ**antilogaˈrithmic** *adjective* of or pertaining to antilogarithms M18.

antilogism /anˈtɪlədʒɪz(ə)m/ *noun*. E20.
[ORIGIN from Greek *antilogia* (see ANTILOGY) + -ISM: cf. late Greek *antilogismos*.]
LOGIC. A set of three propositions which cannot be true together.

antilogy /an'tɪlədʒi/ *noun*. E17.
[ORIGIN French *antilogie* (= medieval Latin *antilogium*, *-gia*) from Greek *antilogia* contradiction, from ANTI- + *-logia* -LOGY.]
A contradiction in terms or ideas.

antilopine /an'tɪləpʌɪn/ *adjective*. Also **ante-**. E19.
[ORIGIN from mod. Latin *antilopus* ANTELOPE + -INE[1].]
Pertaining to or characteristic of an antelope; of the nature of or resembling an antelope.

antimacassar /,antɪmə'kasə/ *noun*. Now chiefly *hist*. M19.
[ORIGIN from ANTI- + MACASSAR.]
A cover put over the backs (and arms) of chairs etc. as a protection against grease or as an ornament.
■ **antimacassared** *adjective* covered or adorned with an antimacassar E20.

antimasque /'antɪmɑːsk/ *noun*. Also **-mask**. E17.
[ORIGIN from ANTI- + MASQUE *noun*.]
A grotesque interlude as a contrast, given between the acts of a masque.
■ **antimasquer** *noun* a performer in an antimasque M17.

antimeric /antɪ'mɛrɪk/ *adjective*. L19.
[ORIGIN from Greek ANTI- opposite + *meros* part + -IC.]
Characterized by the existence of or designating forms which are mirror images of each other.
■ **'antimer(e)** *noun* either of a pair of antimeric forms; an enantiomorph: L19.

antimonate /'antɪməneɪt, antɪ'məʊneɪt/ *noun*. M19.
[ORIGIN from ANTIMONY + -ATE[1].]
CHEMISTRY. A salt of antimonic acid.
■ Also **anti'moniate** *noun* (now *rare*) E19.

antimonial /antɪ'məʊnɪəl/ *adjective & noun*. E17.
[ORIGIN from ANTIMONY + -AL[1].]
▸ **A** *adjective*. Of or pertaining to antimony; containing antimony. E17.
▸ **B** *noun*. A medicine containing antimony E18.
■ **antimonian** *adjective* = ANTIMONIAL *adjective*; *esp*. (*MINERALOGY*) containing antimony: M17.

antimonic /antɪ'mɒnɪk/ *adjective*. E19.
[ORIGIN from ANTIMONY + -IC.]
CHEMISTRY. Of pentavalent antimony.
antimonic acid a colloidal acid, $HSb(OH)_6$ (approx.), formed e.g. when antimony pentachloride is hydrolysed.

antimonide /'antɪmənʌɪd, antɪ'məʊ-/ *noun*. M19.
[ORIGIN from ANTIMONY + -IDE.]
CHEMISTRY. A compound of antimony with a more electropositive element.

antimonious /antɪ'məʊnɪəs/ *adjective*. E19.
[ORIGIN from ANTIMONY + -OUS.]
CHEMISTRY. Of trivalent antimony.
antimonious acid the hypothetical parent acid of antimonites.

antimonite /'antɪmənʌɪt, antɪ'məʊnʌɪt/ *noun*. E19.
[ORIGIN from ANTIMONY + -ITE[1].]
1 *CHEMISTRY*. A salt formed (as) by reaction of antimony trioxide with alkalis. E19.
2 *MINERALOGY*. = STIBNITE. *rare*. M19.

antimony /'antɪməni/ *noun*. LME.
[ORIGIN medieval Latin *antimonium*, of unknown origin.]
1 The mineral stibnite, Sb_2S_3. *obsolete* exc. as in phrs. below. LME.
2 A brittle silvery-white metalloid chemical element, atomic no. 51, of which stibnite is the chief ore, used in many alloys (e.g. type metal) (symbol Sb). E19.
– PHRASES: **black antimony** (*a*) *arch*. stibnite; (*b*) an unstable nonmetallic allotrope of antimony. ***glass of antimony***: see GLASS *noun*. **grey antimony** *arch*. stibnite. *REGULUS* ***of antimony***. **white antimony** *arch*. antimony trioxide, Sb_2O_3.
– COMB.: **antimony ochre** cervantite or a similar mineral; antimony tetroxide, Sb_2O_4.
■ **anti'moniated** *adjective* combined or impregnated with antimony E18.

antinomian /antɪ'nəʊmɪən/ *adjective & noun*. M17.
[ORIGIN from medieval Latin *Antinomi*, name of the sect, formed as ANTINOMY, + -AN.]
▸ **A** *adjective*. Opposed to the obligatoriness of moral law; of or pertaining to the antinomians. M17.
▸ **B** *noun*. A person who maintains that the moral law is not binding on Christians; *spec*. a member of a 16th-cent. sect in Germany alleged to hold this opinion. M17.
■ **antinomianism** *noun* M17.

antinomy /an'tɪnəmi/ *noun*. L16.
[ORIGIN Latin *antinomia* from Greek, formed as ANTI- + *nomos* law: see -Y[3]. Cf. French *antinomie*.]
1 A contradiction in a law, or between two laws; a conflict of authority. L16.
†**2** A contradictory law or principle. Only in M17.
3 (After Kant.) A paradox; intellectual contradictoriness. L18.
■ **anti'nomic** *adjective* (*rare*) M19. **anti'nomical** *adjective* (*rare*) L19.

Antiochene /an'tʌɪəkiːn/ *noun & adjective*. M19.
[ORIGIN Latin *Antiochenus*, from *Antiochia* Antioch.]
ECCLESIASTICAL HISTORY. (An adherent) of the theological school represented by the church at Antioch in Syria in the 4th and 5th cents.
■ Also **Antiochian** /antɪ'ɒkɪən/ *adjective & noun* M19.

†**antipape** *noun* see ANTIPOPE.

antipasto /antɪ'pɑːstəʊ/ *noun*. Pl. **-ti** /-ti/, **-tos**. M20.
[ORIGIN Italian, formed as ANTEPAST.]
An appetizer, an hors d'oeuvre.

antipathetic /,antɪpə'θɛtɪk/ *adjective*. M17.
[ORIGIN formed as ANTIPATHY, after PATHETIC.]
Having an antipathy or constitutional aversion; opposed in nature or tendency (*to*).
■ **antipathetical** *adjective* E17. **antipathetically** *adverb* M17.

antipathic /antɪ'paθɪk/ *adjective*. M19.
[ORIGIN from ANTIPATHY + -IC.]
Of or pertaining to antipathy; of a contrary nature or character (*to*).

antipathy /an'tɪpəθi/ *noun*. L16.
[ORIGIN French *antipathie* or Latin *antipathia* from Greek *antipatheia*, from *antipathēs* opposed in feeling, formed as ANTI- + PATHOS: see -Y[3].]
†**1** Contrariety of feeling, nature, or disposition (*with* a thing, *between* things). L16–L17.
2 (A) constitutional or settled aversion (*against*, *for*, *to*; *between* persons). E17.
†**3 a** Something contrary to nature. Only in E17. ▸**b** An object of constitutional or settled aversion. L17.
■ **antipathist** *noun* (*rare*) a person possessed by an antipathy, a natural enemy E19. †**antipathize** *verb* (*a*) *verb intrans*. feel or show antipathy; (*b*) *verb trans*. render antipathetic: M17–L18. **antipathous** *adjective* (*rare*) antipathetic E17.

†**antipendium** *noun* var. of ANTEPENDIUM.

antiperistasis /,antɪpə'rɪstəsɪs/ *noun*. *arch*. L16.
[ORIGIN Greek, formed as ANTI- + *peristasis* standing round. Cf. French *antiperistase* (16).]
Opposition or contrast of circumstances; resistance, reaction.

antiphlogistic /,antɪflə'dʒɪstɪk, -'gɪst-/ *adjective & noun*. Now *rare*. M18.
[ORIGIN from ANTI- + PHLOGISTIC.]
▸ **A** *adjective*. **1** *MEDICINE*. Counteracting inflammation. M18.
2 *hist*. Opposed to the theory of phlogiston. L18.
▸ **B** *noun*. A medicine counteracting inflammation. M18.
■ **antiphlo'gistian** *noun & adjective* (*hist*.) (a person) opposed to the theory of phlogiston L18.

Antiphlogistine /,antɪflə'dʒɪstiːn/ *noun*. Also **a-**; **-in** /-ɪn/. E20.
[ORIGIN from ANTIPHLOGISTIC + -INE[5].]
(Proprietary name for) a kind of kaolin poultice.

antiphon /'antɪf(ə)n/ *noun*. LME.
[ORIGIN ecclesiastical Latin *antiphona* fem. sing. from Greek neut. pl. of *antiphōnos* responsive, formed as ANTI- + *phōnē* sound. Cf. ANTHEM.]
1 In traditional Western Christian liturgy: a short sentence sung or recited before or after a psalm or canticle; a musical setting of this. LME.
2 a A versicle or sentence sung by one choir in response to another. M17. ▸**b** *transf*. A response, an echo, an answer. M17.
■ **anti'phonic** *adjective* (*rare*) antiphonal, mutually responsive M19. **anti'phonically** *adverb* M19.

antiphonal /an'tɪfən(ə)l/ *noun & adjective*. E16.
[ORIGIN from ANTIPHON + -AL[1]. Cf. Old French *antiphonal*.]
▸ **A** *noun*. = ANTIPHONARY. E16.
▸ **B** *adjective*. **1** Of the nature of an antiphon; sung alternately. L17.
2 Responsive (*to*). M19.
■ **antiphonally** *adverb* M18.

antiphonary /an'tɪf(ə)nəri/ *noun*. E17.
[ORIGIN ecclesiastical Latin *antiphonarium*, formed as ANTIPHON: see -ARY[1].]
A book of antiphons; a collection of antiphons.

antiphoner /an'tɪf(ə)nə/ *noun*. *arch*. LME.
[ORIGIN Old French *antiphonier* formed as ANTIPHONARY: see -ER[2].]
= ANTIPHONARY.

antiphony /an'tɪf(ə)ni/ *noun*. M16.
[ORIGIN from ANTIPHON + -Y[3], partly through Old French *antiphonie*.]
1 = ANTIPHON 2a. M16. ▸**b** = ANTIPHON 2b. M17.
2 Opposition of sound, antiphonal effect. E17.
3 Antiphonal singing. M18.

antiphrasis /an'tɪfrəsɪs/ *noun*. Pl. **-ases** /-əsiːz/. M18.
[ORIGIN Late Latin from Greek, from *antiphrazein* express by the opposite, formed as ANTI- + *phrazein* indicate, declare, tell.]
RHETORIC. Use of words in a sense opposite to their customary meaning.

antipodal /an'tɪpəd(ə)l/ *adjective & noun*. M17.
[ORIGIN from ANTIPODES + -AL[1].]
▸ **A** *adjective*. **1** Of or pertaining to the antipodes; situated on the opposite side of the earth (*to*). M17.
2 Diametrically opposite (*to*). M17.
3 *BOTANY*. Designating cells formed at the chalazal end of the embryo sac. L19.
▸ **B** *noun*. *BOTANY*. An antipodal cell. M20.

antipode /'antɪpəʊd/ *noun*. Pl. of sense 3 pronounced /'antɪpəʊdz/. E17.
[ORIGIN Back-form. from ANTIPODES.]
†**1** An inhabitant of the opposite side of the earth. (For pl. see ANTIPODES 1.) Only in E17.
2 The exact opposite (*of*, *to*). (For pl. see ANTIPODES 3.) M17.
3 *CHEMISTRY*. An enantiomorphic compound. L19.

Antipodean /,antɪpə'diːən/ *adjective & noun*. M17.
[ORIGIN Irreg. from ANTIPODES + -AN.]
▸ **A** *adjective*. **1** Diametrically opposite (*to*). M17.
2 Using the feet rather than the hands; upside down. E19.
3 Of or pertaining to the opposite side of the earth, *esp*. Australasian. M19.
▸ **B** *noun*. **1** A person who lives on the opposite side of the earth; a native or inhabitant of the Antipodes. M17.
2 A juggler with the feet. L19.
3 An exact opposite (*to*). E20.

antipodes /an'tɪpədiːz/ *noun pl*. (sense 3 also treated as *sing*.). Also **A-**. LME.
[ORIGIN French, or late Latin from Greek pl. of *antipous* having the feet opposite, formed as ANTI- + *pous*, *pod-* foot.]
†**1** Those who live on the opposite side of the earth to each other or to oneself. LME–M19. ▸**b** *fig*. Those in any way resembling the inhabitants of the opposite side of the earth. Only in 17.

> **b** BACON He will neuer be one of the Antipodes, to tread opposite to the present world.

2 Places on the surface of the earth directly or diametrically opposite to each other; a place diametrically opposite to another, *esp*. Australasia as the region on the opposite side of the earth to Europe. M16.

> SHAKES. *Much Ado* I will go on the slightest errand now to the Antipodes. A. R. WALLACE New Zealand, almost the antipodes of Britain.

3 Exact opposites. Also as *sing*., = ANTIPODE 2. (Foll. by *of*, *to*.) E17.

> SIR T. BROWNE Fools . . are antipodes unto the wise. O. HENRY Passengers . . saw them seated together, and wondered at the conflux of two such antipodes. E. B. TITCHENER Common sense is the very antipodes of science.

4 See ANTIPODE 3.
– NOTE: Formerly trisyllabic '*antipodes*.

antipope /'antɪpəʊp/ *noun*. Also **A-**; orig. †**-pape**. LME.
[ORIGIN French *antipape* from medieval Latin *antipapa* (after *antichristus* ANTICHRIST), later assim. to POPE *noun*[1].]
A person set up as Pope in opposition to one (held by others to be) canonically chosen.

antiquarian /antɪ'kwɛːrɪən/ *noun & adjective*. E17.
[ORIGIN formed as ANTIQUARY: see -ARIAN.]
▸ **A** *noun*. = ANTIQUARY *noun* 2. E17.
▸ **B** *adjective*. Of or connected with the study of antiquities or antiques. L18.
■ **antiquarianism** *noun* the profession or pursuits of the antiquarian; taste for or devotion to antiquities: L18. **antiquarianize** *verb intrans*. (*colloq*.) pursue antiquarianism E19.

antiquary /'antɪkwəri/ *noun & adjective*. M16.
[ORIGIN Latin *antiquarius*, from *antiquus*: see ANTIQUE, -ARY[1]. Cf. French *antiquaire*.]
▸ **A** *noun*. **1** An official recorder or custodian of antiquities. Long *obsolete* exc. *hist*. M16.
2 A student or collector of antiquities or antiques. L16.
†**3** A person of great age. *rare*. L16–M17.
▸ **B** *adjective*. Of antiquity; ancient; antique. *rare*. E17.

antiquate /'antɪkwət/ *adjective*. *arch*. LME.
[ORIGIN Latin *antiquatus* pa. pple of *antiquare* restore (a thing) to its former condition, in ecclesiastical Latin make old, from *antiquus*: see ANTIQUE, -ATE[2].]
= ANTIQUATED.

antiquate /'antɪkweɪt/ *verb trans*. Now *rare* exc. as ANTIQUATED. L16.
[ORIGIN from ANTIQUATE *adjective*: see -ATE[3].]
1 Make old or out of date; make obsolete; abolish as out of date. L16.
2 Make conform with earlier usage etc. E19.
■ **anti'quation** *noun* (now *rare*) the action of antiquating; the state of being antiquated: E17.

antiquated /'antɪkweɪtɪd/ *adjective*. L16.
[ORIGIN from ANTIQUATE *verb* + -ED[1].]
1 Grown old, of long standing, inveterate. *arch*. L16.

> ISAAC TAYLOR Prejudice and antiquated jealousy did not easily yield themselves up.

2 Out of use by reason of age; obsolete. *arch*. E17.

> JONSON Neat Terence, witty Plautus now not please; but antiquated and deserted lye.

3 Old-fashioned; out of date. L17.

> J. MARQUAND I paused at the door to grope for the antiquated light switch, for electrical appliances are not modern in Peking. A. KOESTLER We are like children, . . eager to learn from their elders all sorts of useful tricks, while at the same time laughing at their antiquated outlook.

4 Of a person: advanced in age, superannuated. Now *rare* exc. as coinciding with sense 3. L17.

A

ADDISON A maiden Aunt . . one of these Antiquated Sybils.

antique /an'ti:k/ *adjective, noun, & verb.* As adjective & noun also (*arch.*) **antic** /'antɪk/. See also ANTIC. L15.
[ORIGIN French, or Latin *antiquus, anticus,* formed as ANTE-.]
▸ **A** *adjective.* **1** Having existed since old times, old, aged, venerable. L15.

SPENSER A nation so antique, as that no monument remaines of her beginning. D. DUNN They have an antique goldfish, a cat called Sly.

2 Belonging to former times; ancient, olden. E16.

A. H. CLOUGH The antique pure simplicity with which God and good angels communed undispleased. L. LEE The village . . was like a deep-running cave still linked to its antic past. TED HUGHES Not utterly fantastical I expected (As in some antique tale depicted).

3 Of, belonging to, or after the manner of ancient Greece and Rome; in the style of classical antiquity. M16.

BYRON And thus they form a group that's quite antique, Half naked, loving, natural, and Greek. K. CLARK Virgil, that great mediator between the antique and the medieval world.

4 Old-fashioned, antiquated; in the style of an earlier age; archaic. M17.

LONGFELLOW There stood the broad-wheeled wains and the antique ploughs and the harrows. C. BRONTË Looking down on a fine antique street.

▸ **B** *noun.* **1** A relic of ancient art; a relic of old times; an item of furniture, china, etc., valued by collectors because of its age. M16.

GOLDSMITH His own business . . was to collect pictures, medals, intaglios and antiques of all kinds. K. CLARK He made imitations of Graeco-Roman sculpture, one of which . . was actually sold as an antique.

†**2** A person of ancient times; in *pl.* the ancients. M–L16.
▸ **C** *verb trans.* **1** Bind (a book) in the style of an earlier period. M18.
2 Make (furniture etc.) appear antique by artificial means. E20.
■ **antiqueness** *noun* M17.

antiquity /an'tɪkwɪti/ *noun.* ME.
[ORIGIN Old French & mod. French *antiquité* from Latin *antiquitas*, from *antiquus*: see ANTIQUE, -ITY.]
1 The ancient times; *spec.* the period before the Middle Ages. ME.

J. S. BLACKIE The coolest and most practical thinker of all antiquity . . Aristotle. B. RUSSELL In antiquity all large States, except Egypt, suffered from a lack of stability.

Christian antiquity the early period of the Christian era, the early centuries of the Church. **classical antiquity** the time of the ancient Greeks and Romans.
2 *collect.* The people (esp. authors) of ancient times; the ancients. LME.

MILTON That indigested heap, and frie of Authors, which they call Antiquity.

3 The quality of having existed from ancient times; ancientness. LME. ▸†**b** Old age; seniority. L16–L17.

J. I. M. STEWART Anderman was a baronet and his family of some antiquity. **b** SHAKES. *2 Hen. IV* Is not your voice broken, your wind short, . . and every part about you blasted with antiquity?

4 In *pl.* & *collect. sing.* Customs, precedents, or events of ancient times; ancient records. (Formerly also *sing.* of an individual custom etc.) LME.

J. PRIESTLEY Whiston . . was certainly well read in Christian antiquity. K. E. DIGBY The subject belongs entirely to the antiquities of our law.

5 An ancient relic; an antique. Usu. in *pl.* E16.

BACON Antiquities are history defaced, or some remnants of history which have casually escaped the shipwreck of time. T. JEFFERSON The Pont du Gard, a sublime antiquity, and well preserved. D. ASH Reputable dealers in antiquities . . will give a written guarantee of authenticity if required.

■ **an͵tiqui'tarian** *noun* a person attached to the practices or opinions of antiquity M17.

antirrhinum /antɪ'rʌɪnəm/ *noun.* M16.
[ORIGIN Latin from Greek *antirrhinon*, from *anti-* counterfeiting + *rhin-, rhis* nose.]
Any of numerous plants constituting the genus *Antirrhinum*, of the figwort family, bearing usu. showy tubular two-lipped flowers; *spec.* the snapdragon, *A. majus*.

antiscion /an'tɪʃ(ə)n/ *noun.* Pl. **-scia** /-ʃə/, **-scions**. L16.
[ORIGIN App. repr. Greek *antiskion* (sc. *zōidion* sign of the zodiac), formed as ANTI- + *skia* shadow.]
ASTROLOGY. A sign of the zodiac at the same distance from Cancer or Capricorn as another and on the opposite side of it.

antisense /'antɪsɛns/ *adjective.* L20.
[ORIGIN from ANTI- + SENSE *noun*.]
GENETICS. Relating to or designating a sequence of nucleotides complementary to (and hence capable of binding to) a coding or sense sequence, which may be either that of the strand of a DNA double helix which undergoes transcription or that of a messenger RNA molecule.

antisepsis /antɪ'sɛpsɪs/ *noun.* L19.
[ORIGIN from ANTI- + SEPSIS.]
MEDICINE. The practice or principles of antiseptic treatment.

antiseptic /antɪ'sɛptɪk/ *noun & adjective.* E18.
[ORIGIN from ANTI- + SEPTIC.]
▸ **A** *noun.* An antiseptic substance (see sense B.). E18.
▸ **B** *adjective.* Preventing sepsis, esp. by chemically destroying or retarding the growth of bacteria; scrupulously clean, sterile. M18.

fig.: CARLYLE Not divine men, yet useful antiseptic products of their generation.

■ **antiseptically** *adverb* M19.

antisocial /antɪ'səʊʃ(ə)l/ *adjective.* L18.
[ORIGIN from ANTI- + SOCIAL *adjective*.]
1 Averse to society or companionship; not sociable. L18.
2 Opposed or contrary to the practices, principles, and instincts on which society is based. E19.
■ **antisocialism** *noun* = ANTISOCIALITY M19. **antisociality** /͵antɪsəʊʃɪ'alɪti/ *noun* the quality or condition of being antisocial E19. **antisocially** *adverb* E20.

antispastic /antɪ'spastɪk/ *noun & adjective.* E17.
[ORIGIN Greek *antispastikos*, from *antispan* draw in the opposite direction: see ANTI-, SPASTIC.]
CLASSICAL PROSODY. (A foot, line, etc.) composed of, or containing feet composed of, an iamb and a trochee.

antistrophe /an'tɪstrəfi/ *noun.* M16.
[ORIGIN Late Latin from Greek *antistrophē*, from *antistrephein* turn against: see ANTI-, STROPHE.]
1 RHETORIC. The repetition of words in inverse order. M16.
2 The returning movement, from left to right, in Greek choruses and dances, answering to the strophe; the lines of choral song recited during this movement; *transf.* any choral response. E17.
3 An inverse relation or correspondence. E17.
■ **antistrophic** /-'strəʊfɪk/ *noun & adjective* (**a**) *noun* in *pl.*, the lyrical part of Greek dramas; (**b**) *adjective* of or pertaining to antistrophes: E19.

antistrophon /an'tɪstrəf(ə)n/ *noun.* Pl. **-pha** /-fə/. E17.
[ORIGIN Greek, neut. sing. of *antistrophos*, formed as ANTISTROPHE.]
RHETORIC. An argument that is retorted upon an opponent.

antisymmetric /͵antɪsɪ'mɛtrɪk/ *adjective.* E20.
[ORIGIN from ANTI- + SYMMETRIC.]
MATH. & PHYSICS. Of a function: changed in sign but not in magnitude by the exchange of two variables. Also, able to be represented by such a function.
■ **antisymmetrical** *adjective* = ANTISYMMETRIC E20. **anti'symmetrize** *verb trans.* make antisymmetric M20. **anti͵symmetri'zation** *noun* M20. **anti'symmetry** *noun* E20.

antithesis /an'tɪθəsɪs/ *noun.* Pl. **-eses** /-əsiːz/. LME.
[ORIGIN Late Latin from Greek, from *antitithenai*, formed as ANTI- + *tithenai* to set, place: cf. THESIS.]
†**1** GRAMMAR. **a** The substitution of one case for another. Only in LME. ▸**b** The substitution of one sound for another. L16–M17.
2 RHETORIC. (An) opposition or contrast of ideas, expressed by parallelism of words which are the opposites of, or strongly contrasted with, each other. Also, repetition of the same word at the end of successive clauses. E16.
3 The second of two opposed clauses or sentences; a counter-thesis. M16.
4 Direct or striking opposition of character or function (*of, between* two things). E17.

O. CHADWICK The antithesis between Catholic and Protestant.

5 The direct opposite, a complete contrast, (*of, to*). M17.

Times 'Sportswear' . . was always the antithesis of European haute couture.

6 In Hegelian philosophy, the negation of the thesis as the second stage in the process of dialectical reasoning. Cf. SYNTHESIS 2C, THESIS 2. L19.

antithet /'antɪθɛt/ *noun.* E17.
[ORIGIN Latin *antitheton* from Greek, neut. sing. of *antithetos*: see ANTITHETICAL.]
An instance of antithesis; an antithetical statement.

antithetical /antɪ'θɛtɪk(ə)l/ *adjective.* L16.
[ORIGIN from Greek *antithetikos*, from *antithetos* placed in opposition, formed as ANTITHESIS: see -ICAL.]
1 Of the nature of antithesis; containing or using antithesis. L16.
2 Characterized by direct opposition (*to*). M19.
■ **antithetic** *adjective* antithetical E17. **antithetically** *adverb* E19.

antitype /'antɪtʌɪp/ *noun.* E17.
[ORIGIN Late Latin *antitypus* from Greek *antitupos* adjective, corresponding as an impression to the die, formed as ANTI- + *tupos* TYPE *noun*.]
1 Something which a type or symbol represents. E17.
2 A person or thing of the opposite type. E20.
■ **anti'typical** *adjective* of the nature of or pertaining to an antitype M17.

antler /'antlə/ *noun.* LME.
[ORIGIN Anglo-Norman var. of Old French *antoillier* (mod. *andouiller*), of unknown origin.]
A branch of either of the two deciduous outgrowths on the head of a male deer (or a reindeer of either sex), consisting when fully grown of dead bone; orig. *spec.* the lowest (forward-directed) branch. Also, this branched structure as a whole.
– COMB.: **antler-moth** a small noctuid, *Cerapteryx graminis*, with white branched wing markings.
■ **antlered** *adjective* bearing antlers; adorned with stags' horns: E19. **antlerless** *adjective* without antlers L19.

antlia /'antlɪə/ *noun.* E19.
[ORIGIN Latin from Greek = instrument for raising water.]
1 The spiral proboscis of butterflies and moths. E19.
2 (Usu. **A-**.) (The name of) an inconspicuous constellation of the southern hemisphere between Hydra and Vela; = ***air pump*** (b) s.v. AIR *noun*[1]. M19.

†**antoeci** *noun pl.* E17–L18.
[ORIGIN Late Latin from Greek *antoikoi*, formed as ANTI- + *-oikos* dwelling.]
Persons living on the same meridian at equal latitudes on opposite sides of the equator. Cf. PERIOECI.

Antonian /an'təʊnɪən/ *adjective & noun.* E20.
[ORIGIN from Latin *Antonius* Anthony + -IAN.]
= ANTONINE *noun* 1, *adjective* 2.

Antonine /'antənʌɪn/ *noun & adjective.* M16.
[ORIGIN Latin *Antoninus*, formed as ANTONIAN: see -INE[1].]
▸ **A** *noun.* **1** A disciple or follower of St Anthony of Egypt (*c* 251–356). M16.
2 In *pl.* *The* Roman emperors Antoninus Pius (reigned AD 138–161) and Marcus Aurelius Antoninus (161–180). L17.
▸ **B** *adjective.* **1** Of or pertaining to the Antonines (sense A.2 above). L18.
the Antonine Wall a Roman frontier wall in Britain from the Forth to the Clyde, built for Antoninus Pius.
2 Of or pertaining to St Anthony of Egypt. L19.

antonomasia /antənə'meɪzɪə/ *noun.* M16.
[ORIGIN Latin from Greek, from *antonomazein* name instead, formed as ANTI- + *onoma* name: see -IA[1].]
The substitution of an epithet etc. or the name of an office or dignity, for a proper name (e.g. ***the Iron Duke*** for Wellington). Also, conversely, the use of a proper name to express a general idea (e.g. ***a Solomon*** for 'a wise man').

Anton Piller order /͵antɒn 'pɪlə(r) ͵ɔːdə/ *noun phr.* L20.
[ORIGIN from *Anton Piller*, German manufacturers of electric motors, who were involved in legal proceedings (1975) in which such an order was granted.]
ENGLISH LAW. A court order which requires the defendant in proceedings to permit the plaintiff or his or her legal representatives to enter the defendant's premises in order to obtain evidence essential to the plaintiff's case.

antonym /'antənɪm/ *noun.* M19.
[ORIGIN French *antonyme*, from Greek ANTI- + *onuma* name: see -NYM.]
A term of opposite meaning to another.
■ **an'tonymous** *adjective* opposite in meaning M20. **an'tonymy** *noun* M20.

antorbital /an'tɔːbɪt(ə)l/ *adjective.* Also **ante-orbital** /antɪ'ɔːbɪt(ə)l/. M19.
[ORIGIN from ANT(E- + ORBITAL *adjective*.]
ANATOMY. Situated in front of the eyes.

antra *noun* pl. of ANTRUM.

antre /'antə/ *noun. poet.* Also †**antar**. E17.
[ORIGIN French from Latin ANTRUM.]
A cave, a cavern.

antrectomy /an'trɛktəmi/ *noun.* E20.
[ORIGIN from ANTR(UM + -ECTOMY.]
Surgical removal of the walls of an antrum, esp. of the stomach.

antrorse /an'trɔːs/ *adjective.* M19.
[ORIGIN mod. Latin *antrorsus*, from Latin ANTERO- + *versus* towards, after *extrorsus* etc.: see EXTRORSE.]
Directed forward or upward.

antrum /'antrəm/ *noun.* Pl. **antra** /'antrə/. E19.
[ORIGIN Latin from Greek *antron* cave.]
ANATOMY. A cavity, *esp.* one with bony walls. Also, the part of the stomach adjacent to the pylorus.
■ **antral** *adjective* of or pertaining to an antrum L19.

antrustion /an'trʌstjən/ *noun.* E19.
[ORIGIN French, or medieval Latin *antrustio(n-)* (in Salic Law etc.) from Old Frankish (= Old High German *trōst* help, protection).]
A member of the voluntary personal guard of the Merovingian rulers in early medieval Europe.

antsy /'antsi/ *adjective. N. Amer. colloq.* M20.
[ORIGIN from ANT *noun* + -SY.]
Irritated, impatient; fidgety, restless.

J. CASEY Dick had forgot how antsy he got the day before he put to sea.

Antwerp /'antwəːp/ *noun.* M19.
[ORIGIN A city in Belgium.]
1 ***Antwerp blue***, a pale Prussian blue. M19.
2 ***Antwerp edge***, ***Antwerp edging stitch***, (an edge finished with) an embroidery stitch used for decorating and finishing edges and hems. L19.

anucleate /eɪˈnjuːklɪət/ *adjective*. **E20**.
[ORIGIN from A-^{10} + NUCLEATE *adjective*.]
BIOLOGY. Of a cell: having no nucleus.

anudatta /ˈʌnʊdɑːtə/ *noun*. **M19**.
[ORIGIN Sanskrit *anudātta* lit. 'unraised', from *an-* UN-^{1} + *udātta* raised.]
The tone of unaccented syllables in Vedic Sanskrit. Cf. SVARITA, UDATTA.

anuran /əˈnjʊər(ə)n/ *noun & adjective*. **L19**.
[ORIGIN from mod. Latin *Anura* (see below), from Greek AN-^{5} + *oura* tail: see -AN.]
ZOOLOGY. ▸**A** *noun*. Any of the tailless amphibians, constituting the order Anura; a frog, a toad. **L19**.
▸ **B** *adjective*. Of or pertaining to this order. **E20**.

anuria /əˈnjʊərɪə/ *noun*. **M19**.
[ORIGIN from AN-^{5} + -URIA.]
MEDICINE. Failure of the kidneys to produce urine.
■ **anuric** *adjective* displaying or pertaining to anuria **L19**.

anus /ˈeɪnəs/ *noun*. **LME**.
[ORIGIN Latin *anus*, orig. 'ring'.]
The posterior excretory opening of the alimentary canal.

anvil /ˈanvɪl/ *noun & verb*.
[ORIGIN Old English *anfilte* (earlier *onfilti*), *anfealt* = Middle Dutch *aenvilte*, Old High German *anafalz*, ult. from Germanic base of ON *preposition* + verbal stem meaning 'beat' (cf. FELT *noun*).]
▸ **A** *noun*. **1** A block (usu. of iron) on which a smith hammers and shapes metal. **OE**.

fig.: BURKE He has now on the anvil another scheme.

2 a *ANATOMY*. = INCUS *noun* 1. **E17**. ▸**b** *METEOROLOGY*. A horizontally extended top of a cumulonimbus cloud. **L19**.
– COMB.: **anvil cloud** a cloud with a horizontally extended top.
▸ **B** *verb*. Infl. **-ll-**.
1 *verb trans*. Fashion on an anvil. Freq. *fig*. **L16**.
2 *verb intrans*. Work at an anvil. **L19**.

anxiety /aŋˈzʌɪəti/ *noun*. **E16**.
[ORIGIN French *anxiété* or Latin *anxietas*, formed as ANXIOUS: see -TY^{1}.]
1 The quality or state of being anxious; uneasiness, concern; a cause of this. **E16**.

Nature Finance has been a constant anxiety. C. SHIELDS Beth was cold and tense with anxiety.

†**2** *MEDICINE*. A condition of distress accompanied by precordial tightness or discomfort. **M17–M19**.
3 Earnest or solicitous desire *for* a thing, *to do* something. **M18**.
4 *PSYCHIATRY*. A morbid state of excessive or unrealistic uneasiness or dread. **L19**.
attrib.: *anxiety complex*, *anxiety neurosis*, *anxiety state*.

anxiolytic /ˌaŋzɪəˈlɪtɪk/ *adjective & noun*. **M20**.
[ORIGIN from ANXIETY + -O- + -LYTIC.]
MEDICINE. (A drug) that reduces anxiety.

anxious /ˈaŋ(k)ʃəs/ *adjective*. **E17**.
[ORIGIN Latin *anxius*, from *anx-* pa. ppl stem of *angere* choke, oppress: see ANGUISH *verb*, -IOUS.]
1 Troubled in mind about some uncertain event; concerned, solicitous; being in disturbing suspense. (Foll. by *for*, *about*.) **E17**.

LD MACAULAY Anxious for their own safety. G. B. SHAW The most anxious man in a prison is the governor. E. M. FORSTER She was anxious about Leonard, for whom they certainly were responsible.

2 Distressing, worrying; fraught with trouble. **M17**.

A. UTTLEY It was always an anxious time, a slip and a man and mare might be killed.

3 Full of desire and endeavour; eager *for* a thing, *to do* something. **M18**.

K. AMIS All seemed pleased with the performance and anxious for another of the same sort. S. KING You must be anxious to see your folks.

■ **anxiously** *adverb* **L17**. **anxiousness** *noun* (*rare*) **M17**.

any /ˈɛni/ *adjective* (in mod. usage also classed as a *determiner*), *pronoun*, *& adverb*.
[ORIGIN Old English *ǣnig* = Old Frisian *ēnich*, Old Saxon *ēnig*, Middle Low German *einich*, Middle Dutch *ēnich* (Dutch *eenig*), Old High German *einag* (German *einig*), Old Norse *einigr*, Gothic *ainaha*, from Germanic: see ONE *adjective*, *noun*, *& pronoun*, -Y^{1}.]
▸ **A** *adjective*. **1** *gen*. As *sing*., a —, some —, no matter which, or what. As *pl*., some — no matter which, of what kind, or how many: ▸**a** Used primarily in interrogative, hypothetical, and conditional contexts. **OE**. ▸**b** With a preceding negative (expressed or implied): none at all of, no — of any kind; not even one. **OE**. ▸**c** In affirmative senses: every one of (the sort named). **ME**.

AV *John* 1:46 Can there any good thing come out of Nazareth? LD MACAULAY The best governed country of which he had any knowledge. J. STEINBECK If there were any water at all, it would be there. **b** SHAKES. *Haml*. Thou canst not then be false to any man. BURKE It ought not to be done at any time. DAY LEWIS They know so little of any life but their own. E. WAUGH None of these people you go about with pull any weight in their own colleges. **c** I. WALTON I love any discourse of rivers, and fish and fishing. DICKENS Any object they think can lay their thieving hands on. E. BOWEN The two of them would be gabbing up to any hour of the night.

any day: see DAY *noun*. *any old* —, *any old how*: see OLD *adjective*. *any old thing*: see THING *noun*^{1}. **any road** (chiefly *N. English*) = ANYWAY 2. *at any cost*: see COST *noun*^{2}. *at any price*: see PRICE *noun*. **at any rate**, **in any case** whatever the circumstances may be. *in any shape or form*: see SHAPE *noun*^{1}.
2 With quantitative emphasis: ▸**a** A quantity or number of, however great, or however small. **E16**. ▸**b** A large or considerable (number, amount, etc.). *colloq*. **M19**.

a *Daily Chronicle* An animal with little, if any, fat on it. *Nursery rhyme*: Black sheep, have you any wool? **b** R. KIPLING It is not a good idea to live in the East for any length of time. *Academy* The pigeon-hole form of mind collecting any quantity of conclusions and facts.

3 With qualitative emphasis: of any kind or sort whatever; one or some, however imperfect. **M19**.

M. PATTISON The danger is . . that any reform should be adopted because some reform is required.

▸ **B** *pronoun*. **1** Any person; as *pl*., any persons. **OE**.

KEATS Unknown . . to any, but those two alone. T. S. ELIOT I wouldn't have danced like that with any but you. NEB *James* 1:5 If any of you falls short in wisdom, he should ask God for it.

2 One or more, or some, of the noun expressed already or after following *of*. **ME**.

SHAKES. *Wint. T*. If there be any of him left, I'll bury it. W. S. GILBERT He exercises of his brains, that is, assuming that he's got any. A. J. P. TAYLOR The real failure, if any, was his.

not having any *colloq*. wanting no part in something; rejecting a proposition; refusing to tolerate a situation.
3 Either (of two). Long *dial*. **LME**.
▸ **C** *adverb*. **1** With compar. adjectives and adverbs: in any degree, at all. **OE**.

T. HARDY A happy Providence kept it from being any worse. K. AMIS I'm not answering any more questions about whales or tigers.

2 (Not qualifying another word.) At all. *colloq*. **M18**.

M. TWAIN It is a good tune—you can't improve it any. A. CHRISTIE We're used to responsibility. Doesn't worry us any.

anybody /ˈɛnɪbɒdi/ *pronoun*. Orig. two words. **ME**.
[ORIGIN from ANY + BODY *noun*.]
A person, no matter who; whichever person.

JOSEPH PARKER Anybody can attach himself to a mob. J. RUSKIN I am never angry with anybody unless they deserve it.

anybody's game *colloq*. a finely balanced contest. **anybody's guess** *colloq*. a totally unpredictable matter. **anybody who is anybody** (or similar phr.) *colloq*. any person of rank or importance.

anyhow /ˈɛnɪhaʊ/ *adverb*. Orig. two words. **L17**.
[ORIGIN from ANY + HOW *adverb*.]
1 In any way or manner whatever; in any way however imperfect; haphazardly, carelessly. **L17**.

H. G. WELLS His rather crisp brown hair seemed to grow anyhow.

2 At any rate, in any case, at least. **E19**.

G. MACDONALD They went, anyhow, whether they had to do it or not.

any more /ɛnɪ ˈmɔː/ *adverbial phr*. Also **anymore**. **LME**.
[ORIGIN from ANY + MORE *adverb*.]
To any greater extent; any longer.

MRS H. WARD If Westall bullies him any more he will put a knife into him. E. HEMINGWAY I am not lucky anymore. J. P. DONLEAVY Don't cry anymore now. It's all right. A. GLYN It didn't matter any more. The game was over.

anyone /ˈɛnɪwʌn/ *pronoun*. Orig. two words. **E18**.
[ORIGIN from ANY + ONE *noun & pronoun*.]
Any person; = ANYBODY.

anyplace /ˈɛnɪpleɪs/ *adverb*. *N. Amer*. *colloq*. Also as two words. **M20**.
[ORIGIN from ANY + PLACE *noun*^{1}, after ANYWHERE.]
= ANYWHERE.

anything /ˈɛnɪθɪŋ/ *pronoun*, *adverb*, *& noun*. Orig. two words. **OE**.
[ORIGIN from ANY + THING *noun*^{1}.]
▸ **A** *pronoun*. Something, no matter what; whatever thing. **OE**.

E. WAUGH 'Anything wrong?' he asked. IRVING BERLIN Anything you can do I can do better. DAY LEWIS I have never been anything but a poor sight-reader.

anything but *colloq*. by no means, on the contrary. *anything in TROUSERS*. **(as) — as anything** *colloq*. extremely —. **if anything** if in any degree, perhaps even. **like anything** *colloq*. to a great extent etc.; exceedingly. **too — for anything** *colloq*. extremely —. *try anything once*: see TRY *verb*. *would give anything*: see GIVE *verb*.
▸ **B** *adverb*. In any measure; to any extent. *arch*. **OE**.
▸ **C** *noun*. A thing of any kind. **L16**.

SHAKES. *Tam. Shr*. She is my house, . . my ox, my ass, my any thing.

■ **anything'arian** *noun* (*derog*.) a person who professes no creed in particular **E18**.

any time /ˈɛnɪ tʌɪm/ *adverbial phr*. *colloq*. Also **anytime**. **LME**.
[ORIGIN from ANY + TIME *noun*.]
At any time; whenever.

OED I will leave the basket; you can send it round any time. *Guardian* Any time you're stuck for a meal, come around.

Anytown /ˈɛnɪtaʊn/ *noun*. **E20**.
[ORIGIN from ANY + TOWN *noun*.]
A real or fictional place regarded as being typical of a small US town.

New York Times It is difficult to fathom the frenzy that has taken over Anytown U.S.A.

anyway /ˈɛnɪweɪ/ *adverb*. Orig. two words. **ME**.
[ORIGIN from ANY + WAY *noun*: cf. ANYWAYS.]
1 In any way or manner; anyhow. **ME**.

ADDISON All those who are any way concerned in works of literature.

2 At any rate, in any case. (Freq. used in resuming after a digression.) **M19**.

C. P. SNOW She couldn't wish for that. Anyway, she took it for granted that she wouldn't get him.

anyways /ˈɛnɪweɪz/ *adverb*. Now *dial*. Orig. two words. **ME**.
[ORIGIN from ANY + -WAYS.]
= ANYWAY.

anywhen /ˈɛnɪwɛn/ *adverb*. *rare* exc. *dial*. Orig. two words. **M16**.
[ORIGIN from ANY + WHEN.]
At any time, ever.

anywhere /ˈɛnɪwɛː/ *adverb*. Orig. two words. **LME**.
[ORIGIN from ANY + WHERE.]
In or to any place; whichever place.
anywhere from — to — (orig. *N. Amer*.) at any point within specified limits of variation. **not anywhere near** = *nowhere near* s.v. NOWHERE *adverb* 1. **not get anywhere** = *get nowhere* s.v. NOWHERE *adverb* 3. **not go anywhere** = *go nowhere* s.v. NOWHERE *adverb* 3.

anywhither /ˈɛnɪwɪðə/ *adverb*. *arch*. Orig. two words. **E17**.
[ORIGIN from ANY + WHITHER *adverb*.]
To or towards any place.

anywise /ˈɛnɪwʌɪz/ *adverb*. *arch*. Orig. two words. **OE**.
[ORIGIN from ANY + -WISE.]
In any manner, way, or case; at all.

Anzac /ˈanzak/ *noun*. **E20**.
[ORIGIN Acronym of the corps name (see below).]
A member of the Australian and New Zealand Army Corps (1914–18); an Australian or New Zealander, esp. a serviceman.
– COMB.: **Anzac biscuit**: made from wheat flour, rolled oats, desiccated coconut, and golden syrup; **Anzac Day** 25 April, the date of the landing of the corps on the Gallipoli peninsula in 1915.

Anzus /ˈanzəs/ *noun*. Also **ANZUS**. **M20**.
[ORIGIN Acronym of the country names (see below).]
The combination of Australia, New Zealand, and the United States for the security of the Pacific.

AOB *abbreviation*.
Any other business (at the end of the agenda for a meeting).

AOC *abbreviation*.
French *Appellation d'origine contrôlée* (see APPELLATION CONTRÔLÉE).

ao dai /aʊ dʌɪ/ *noun phr*. **M20**.
[ORIGIN Vietnamese.]
A Vietnamese woman's long-sleeved tunic with ankle-length panels at front and back, worn over trousers.

AONB *abbreviation*.
Area of Outstanding Natural Beauty.

Aonian /eɪˈəʊnɪən/ *adjective*. **E17**.
[ORIGIN from Latin *Aonia* (see below) from Greek + -AN.]
Of or pertaining to Aonia, a region of Boeotia in ancient Greece containing Mount Helicon, sacred to the Muses.

AOR *abbreviation*.
Adult-oriented (or album-oriented) rock.

aorist /ˈeɪərɪst/ *adjective & noun*. **L16**.
[ORIGIN Greek *aoristos* indefinite (sc. *khronos* time), from A-^{10} + *horistos* delimited, from *horizein* define: cf. HORIZON.]
GRAMMAR. (Designating) a past tense of verbs, in ancient Greek and some other languages, denoting simple occurrence, with none of the limitations of the other past tenses.
■ **ao'ristic** *adjective* undefined; of or pertaining to the aorist tense: **M19**. **ao'ristically** *adverb* **M17**.

aorta /eɪˈɔːtə/ *noun*. Pl. **-tae** /-tiː/, **-tas**. **M16**.
[ORIGIN Greek *aortē*, by Hippocrates used in pl. for the branches of the windpipe, by Aristotle for the great artery, from base of *aeirein* raise: cf. ARTERY.]
ANATOMY. The great artery or trunk of the arterial system, from its origin in the left ventricle of the heart to its division into the left and right common iliac arteries.
■ **aortal** *adjective* aortic **E19**. **aortic** *adjective* of or pertaining to the aorta; *aortic arch*, the section of the aorta which loops over and behind the heart: **L18**.

A

aortography /eɪɔːˈtɒɡrəfi/ *noun*. M20.
[ORIGIN from AORTA + -O- + -GRAPHY.]
X-ray examination of the aorta.

aoudad /ˈɑːʊdad/ *noun*. Also **udad** /ˈuːdad/. E19.
[ORIGIN French from Berber *udād*.]
A sheep, *Ammotragus lervia*, native to N. Africa. Also called ***Barbary sheep***.

aoul *noun* var. of AUL.

à outrance /a utrɑ̃ːs/ *adverbial phr.* Also ***à l'outrance*** /a l-/, ***à toute outrance*** /a tut/. E17.
[ORIGIN French, from *à* to + OUTRANCE.]
To the death; to the bitter end.

ap- /əp, stressed ap/ *prefix*[1]. (not productive).
Assim. form of Latin AD- before *p*. In Old French, Latin *app-* was reduced to *ap-*, which appears in Middle English adoptions, but in later French, and hence in English, *app-* was restored by Latinization, as *apparel*, *appear*.

ap- *prefix*[2] see APO-.

apace /əˈpeɪs/ *adverb*. Now *literary*. LME.
[ORIGIN Old French *à pas*: see A-[8], PACE *noun*[1].]
1 At a considerable pace; swiftly. LME.

AV *Ps.* 68:12 Kings of armies did flee apace. M. ARNOLD The field . . and the elms Fade into dimness apace. BOSW. SMITH The news . . reached Rome apace.

†**2** At once, promptly. LME–E18.

Apache /*in senses A.1, B.1* əˈpatʃi; *in senses A.2, B.2* əˈpaʃ, *foreign* apaʃ (pl. of noun same)/ *noun & adjective*. Senses A.2, B.2 also **a-**. M18.
[ORIGIN Mexican Spanish, prob. from Zuni *Ápachu* lit. 'enemy'. Senses A.2, B.2 through French.]
▸ **A** *noun*. Pl. same, **-s**.
1 A member of an Athabaskan people of New Mexico and Arizona; the language of this people. M18.
2 A street thug, orig. in Paris. E20.
▸ **B** *attrib.* or as *adjective*. **1** Of or pertaining to the Apache or their language. M19.
2 Designating a vigorous dance for two associated with thugs or apaches. E20.
■ **Apachean** *adjective & noun* (*a*) *adjective* of or pertaining to the Apache Indians or their language; (*b*) *noun* an Apache Indian; the Apache language: M20.

apagoge /apəˈɡəʊdʒi/ *noun*. *rare*. E18.
[ORIGIN Greek *apagōgē* leading away, from *apagein* lead off.]
LOGIC. **1** In Aristotelian logic: = ABDUCTION 3. E18.
2 A *reductio ad absurdum*. M18.
■ **apagogic** *adjective* (*rare*) = APAGOGICAL L17. **apagogical** *adjective* of the nature of apagoge E18.

†**apaid** *verb pa. pple* of APAY.

Apalachee /apəˈlatʃi/ *noun & adjective*. Also **App-**. Pl. **-s**, same. E18.
[ORIGIN Spanish *Apalache* perh. from Choctaw *apelachi* helper, ally.]
A member of, of or pertaining to, a Muskogean people formerly inhabiting parts of Georgia, Alabama, and Florida; (of) the language of this people.

apanage *noun* var. of APPANAGE.

aparejo /apəˈreɪhəʊ/ *noun*. *US*. Pl. **-os**. M19.
[ORIGIN Spanish = preparation, harness, tackle.]
A packsaddle.

apart /əˈpɑːt/ *adverb*. LME.
[ORIGIN Old French (mod. *à part*) from Latin *a parte* at the side: see A-[6], PART *noun*.]
(Foll. by *from*.)
1 To one side, aside; to or at a place removed from the general body. LME.

SHAKES. *Jul. Caes.* Thy heart is big, get thee apart and weep. H. P. BROUGHAM The precise period at which the Commons first sat apart from the Lords is unknown. V. S. PRITCHETT Their experience had set them apart and the effect was to make me feel childish and cut off.

2 Away from each other; parted, separated; in pieces, asunder. LME.

J. M. BARRIE My mother and I were hundreds of miles apart. A. P. HERBERT So far apart were their worlds, though they had slept on the same floor. J. BETJEMAN Red Admirals basking with their wings apart. J. CHEEVER He had the rifle apart and was cleaning it.

poles apart: see POLE *noun*[2]. ***tear apart***: see TEAR *verb*[1].
3 Separately, independently, individually. LME. ▸**b** Used adjectivally, with ellipsis of verb: separate, distinct. L18.

J. SELDEN Their power . . was exercised either collectively, or apart and severally. C. LUCAS Let us view each ingredient apart. **b** G. B. SHAW The passionately religious are a people apart.

tell apart distinguish between.
4 Away from all consideration or use. LME. ▸**b** In absol. phrs.: laid aside, excepted; put out of the question. M18.

AV *James* 1:21 Wherefore lay apart all filthinesse. **b** DISRAELI However, jesting apart, get your hat. A. J. P. TAYLOR His distribution of honours, wartime leaders apart, had been no greater than that of Asquith.

5 Away from common use for a special purpose. E17.

ADDISON Families that set apart an Hour in every Morning for Tea.

– WITH PREPOSITIONS IN SPECIALIZED SENSES: **apart from** other than; except for, in addition to.
■ **apartness** *noun* the quality of standing apart; aloofness: M19.

apartheid /əˈpɑːtheɪt/ *noun*. M20.
[ORIGIN Afrikaans, lit. 'separateness', from Dutch *apart* APART + *heid* -HOOD.]
The South African policy of racial segregation or discrimination on grounds of race (*hist.*). Also *transf. & fig.*, any other form of (esp. racial) segregation.
petty apartheid: see PETTY *adjective*.

aparthotel /əˈpɑːt(h)əʊtɛl/ *noun*. Also **apartotel** /əˈpɑːtəʊtɛl/. M20.
[ORIGIN from APARTMENT + HOTEL.]
An apartment building with privately owned suites available for short-term renting.

apartment /əˈpɑːtm(ə)nt/ *noun*. M17.
[ORIGIN French *appartement* from Italian *appartamento*, from *appartare* to separate, from *a parte* APART: see -MENT.]
1 a A room or suite of rooms allotted to the use of an individual or group. *arch.* M17. ▸**b** A suite of rooms forming one residence in a building containing a number of these; a flat. Chiefly *N. Amer.* L19.
†**2** Place of abode; quarters. L17–E18.
†**3** A compartment. L17–M19.
– COMB.: **apartment block**, **apartment building**, **apartment house** (chiefly *N. Amer.*) a building divided into flats.
■ **apartˈmental** *adjective* (*rare*) E19.

apartotel *noun* var. of APARTHOTEL.

apatheia /apəˈθiːə/ *noun*. L19.
[ORIGIN Greek: see APATHY.]
Stoical apathy.

apathetic /apəˈθɛtɪk/ *adjective*. M18.
[ORIGIN from APATHY after PATHETIC.]
Of or characterized by apathy; not feeling emotion; uninterested, indifferent, (*towards* or *about* something).
■ **apathetically** *adverb* E19.

apathy /ˈapəθi/ *noun*. E17.
[ORIGIN French *apathie* from Latin *apathia* from Greek *apatheia*, from *apathēs* without feeling: see A-[10], PATHOS, -Y[3].]
Insensibility to suffering or emotion; passionless existence; lack of interest or emotion; stolid indifference.

G. H. LEWES Apathy was considered by the Stoics as the highest condition of Humanity. A. TATE A failure resulting from the apathy of responsible classes of society. G. MAXWELL Days when a kind of apathy would settle down upon me.

■ **apathist** *noun* a person habitually given to apathy M17.

apatite /ˈapətʌɪt/ *noun*. E19.
[ORIGIN from Greek *apatē* deceit + -ITE[1]: so named from its diversity of form and colour.]
MINERALOGY. Any of a series of hexagonal calcium phosphate minerals of wide occurrence, having the general formula $Ca_5(PO_4)_3(F, Cl, OH)$; freq. = FLUORAPATITE.

apatosaurus /əpatəˈsɔːrəs/ *noun*. Also **apatosaur** /əˈpatəsɔː/. L19.
[ORIGIN mod. Latin (see below), from Greek *apatē* deceit + *sauros* lizard.]
A large herbivorous sauropod dinosaur of the genus *Apatosaurus* (formerly *Brontosaurus*), having a very long neck and long tail; a brontosaurus.

†**apay** *verb trans.* Pa. pple **apaid**. ME.
[ORIGIN Old French *apaier*, ult. from Latin *ad* A-[5] + *pacare* please, satisfy, (orig.) pacify, from *pac-*, PAX: see PAY *verb*[1].]
Usu. in *pass.* or as *pa. ppl adjective*.
1 Satisfy, please. ME–L19.
2 Repay, requite. LME–M18.

APB *abbreviation*. *US*.
All-points bulletin.

APC *abbreviation*.
Armoured personnel carrier.

ape /eɪp/ *noun, adjective, & verb*.
[ORIGIN Old English *apa* masc., *ape* fem. = Old Saxon *apo* (Dutch *aap*), Old High German *affo*, *affe* (German *Affe*), Old Norse *api*, from Germanic.]
▸ **A** *noun* **1 a** An animal of the monkey tribe (suborder Simiae or Anthropoidea): the generic name before 'monkey', and still occas. so used, esp. with ref. to resemblance to and mimicry of humans. OE. ▸**b** *spec.* A member of the family Pongidae, which includes the gorilla, chimpanzee, orang-utan, and gibbon, and is characterized by the absence of a tail and cheek pouches. L17.
a Barbary ape: see BARBARY *noun*. ***Japanese ape***: see JAPANESE *adjective*. **lead apes in hell** *arch.*: the supposed consequence of dying an old maid. †**play the ape** indulge in (poor) imitation. **b the naked ape** humankind.
2 *fig.* An (esp. inferior or mindless) imitator; a mimic. ME.

SHAKES. *Cymb.* O sleep, thou ape of death. HOR. WALPOLE Every genius has his apes.

3 An apelike person; a fool. Also as a gen. term of abuse. ME.

S. RICHARDSON That she should instigate the titled ape her husband to write to me.

†**4** ***sea-ape***, the thresher or fox-shark, *Alopias vulpinus*. E17–M19.
– COMB.: **apeman** an extinct primate intermediate between ape and human; an apelike human.
▸ **B** *adjective*. †**1** *attrib.* Foolish, silly. Only in LME.
2 *pred.* Crazy. Esp. in ***go ape***, ***go apeshit*** (*slang*, orig. *N. Amer.*). M20.
▸ **C** *verb trans.* Imitate, esp. pretentiously or absurdly. M17.
■ **apelike** *adjective* resembling an ape in appearance or behaviour; resembling that of an ape: M19. ˈ**apeling** *noun* (*rare*) a young or small ape M18.

apeak /əˈpiːk/ *adverb & pred. adjective*. Orig. †**apike**. L16.
[ORIGIN French *à pic*: see A-[5], PEAK *noun*[1].]
NAUTICAL. In a vertical position; vertical; (of an anchor) with the ship directly over it; (of oars) held vertically.

APEC *abbreviation*.
Asia Pacific Economic Cooperation.

Apelles /əˈpɛliːz/ *noun*. Pl. same. E17.
[ORIGIN Greek painter of the 4th cent. BC.]
A master artist.

apepsia /əˈpɛpsɪə/ *noun*. Now *rare* or *obsolete*. Also **-sy** /-si/. L17.
[ORIGIN Greek, from A-[10] + *peptein* to digest: see -IA[1].]
MEDICINE. Lack of digestive power.

aperçu /apɛrsy (*pl. same*), apɛːˈsjuː/ *noun*. E19.
[ORIGIN French.]
A summary, a conspectus; an insight, a revealing glimpse.

aperient /əˈpɪərɪənt/ *adjective & noun*. E17.
[ORIGIN Latin *aperient-* pres. ppl stem of *aperire* to open: see -ENT.]
▸ **A** *adjective*. Opening the bowels; laxative. E17.
▸ **B** *noun*. A laxative medicine or food. L17.

aperiodic /ˌeɪpɪərɪˈɒdɪk/ *adjective*. L19.
[ORIGIN from A-[10] + PERIODIC *adjective*[1].]
Not periodic, esp. owing to strong damping of vibration; irregular.
■ **aperiodically** *adverb* L19. **aperioˈdicity** *noun* L19.

aperitif /əˈpɛrɪtiːf, əpɛrɪˈtiːf/ *noun*. Also ***apéritif*** /aperitif (*pl. same*)/. L19.
[ORIGIN French *apéritif* (noun & adjective) from medieval Latin *aperitivus* (adjective) var. of late Latin *apertivus*, from *apertus*: see APERT, -IVE.]
An alcoholic drink taken as an appetizer.

†**aperitive** *adjective & noun*. E16–M19.
[ORIGIN from medieval Latin *aperitivus*: see APERITIF.]
(A medicine or food) that opens; *spec.* = APERIENT.

apert /əˈpɔːt/ *adjective & adverb*. Long *arch.* ME.
[ORIGIN Old French from Latin *apertus* pa. pple of *aperire* to open: cf. PERT *adjective*.]
▸ **A** *adjective*. **1** Open, public; overt. ME.
†**2** Evident, plain. ME–L17.
†**3** Straightforward; brisk, bold. Only in ME.
†**4** Outspoken; insolent. ME–L17.
†**5** Clever, ready, expert. ME–L16.
▸ †**B** *adverb*. Openly, publicly; plainly. ME–L17.
■ †**apertion** *noun* an opening; the action of opening: L16–M18. †**apertive** *adjective* = APERITIVE *adjective*, APERIENT *adjective* M16–E18. **apertly** *adverb* openly, evidently; boldly: ME. **apertness** *noun* (now *rare* or *obsolete*) openness, frankness E17.

aperture /ˈapətjʊə, -tʃ(ʊ)ə/ *noun*. LME.
[ORIGIN Latin *apertura*, from *apert-* pa. ppl stem of *aperire* to open: see -URE.]
†**1** The process of opening. LME–M18.
2 An opening; a gap, a cleft, a hole. LME.

C. DARWIN The size and shape of the apertures in the sternum. R. L. STEVENSON Raising my head to an aperture among the leaves, I could see clear down into a little green dell. R. P. WARREN She opened the door . . a little way, and slipped through the aperture.

3 A space through which light passes in an optical instrument; *esp.* that provided by the lens diaphragm of a camera. Also, the diameter of this. M17.
■ **aˈpertural** *adjective* (*rare*) M19.

apery /ˈeɪpəri/ *noun*. E17.
[ORIGIN from APE *noun* + -ERY.]
1 Apelike behaviour; pretentious or silly mimicry. Also, an instance of this. E17.
2 A collection or colony of apes. *rare*. E19.

apetalous /eɪˈpɛt(ə)ləs, ə-/ *adjective*. E18.
[ORIGIN from mod. Latin *apetalus* from Greek *apetalos* leafless: see A-[10], PETAL, -OUS.]
BOTANY. Having no petals.

apex /ˈeɪpɛks/ *noun*[1]. Pl. **apexes**, **apices** /ˈeɪpɪsiːz/. E17.
[ORIGIN Latin.]
1 The small rod at the top of a flamen's cap. *rare*. E17.
2 The tip, top, peak, or pointed end of anything; the vertex of a triangle, cone, etc.; *BOTANY* the growing point of a shoot etc. E17.

S. GIBBONS A sick plunge at the apex of your stomach. P. G. WODEHOUSE He sailed in and knocked them base over apex into a pile of Brussels sprouts. M. KEANE Our house stood at the apex of two carriage drives. *fig.*: R. H. TAWNEY A community penetrated from apex to foundation by the moral law.

†**3** A horn on a Hebrew letter; *fig.* a tittle, a jot. **M–L17.**
4 *ASTRONOMY.* The point on the celestial sphere towards which the sun is moving. Also ***solar apex***. **L18.**

Apex /ˈeɪpɛks/ *noun*². Also **APEX**. **L20.**
[ORIGIN from *a*dvance-*p*urchase *ex*cursion.]
A type of reduced-price airline or railway ticket or fare, requiring advance booking and acceptance of certain other limiting conditions.

Apfelstrudel /ˈapf(ə)lʃtruːd(ə)l/ *noun*. **M20.**
[ORIGIN German, from *Apfel* APPLE + STRUDEL.]
= ***apple strudel*** s.v. APPLE *noun*.

Apgar score /ˈapgɑː skɔː/ *noun phr.* **M20.**
[ORIGIN from Virginia *Apgar* (1909–74), US anaesthesiologist.]
MEDICINE. A measure of the physical condition of a newborn infant, obtained by adding points (2, 1, or 0) for heart rate, respiratory effort, muscle tone, response to stimulation, and skin coloration (a score of ten representing the best possible condition).

aphaeresis *noun* see APHERESIS.

aphakia /əˈfeɪkɪə/ *noun*. **M19.**
[ORIGIN from A-¹⁰ + Greek *phakos* lentil + -IA¹.]
MEDICINE. Absence of the lens of the eye.
■ **aphakic** *adjective* pertaining to or displaying aphakia **L19.**

aphanite /ˈaf(ə)nʌɪt/ *noun*. **E19.**
[ORIGIN from Greek *aphanēs* unseen + -ITE¹.]
GEOLOGY. Orig., a very fine-grained diabase. Now, any igneous rock in which crystalline grains cannot be distinguished with the unaided eye.
■ **aphaˈnitic** *adjective* consisting or characteristic of aphanite **M19.**

aphasia /əˈfeɪzɪə/ *noun*. **M19.**
[ORIGIN Greek, from *aphatos* speechless, from A-¹⁰ + *phanai* speak: see -IA¹.]
Loss or impairment of the faculty of speech or of understanding of language (or both), due to cerebral disease or damage.
Broca's aphasia. *SEMANTIC* ***aphasia***. ***sensory aphasia***: see SENSORY *adjective*. ***Wernicke's aphasia***.
■ **aphasiac** *adjective & noun (rare)* = APHASIC **M19.** **aphasic** *adjective & noun* (a person) affected with aphasia; of or pertaining to aphasia: **M19.** **aphasiˈology** *noun* the study and treatment of aphasia **M20.**

aphelion /apˈhiːlɪən, əˈfiːlɪən/ *noun*. Also †**-lium**. Pl. **-lia** /-lɪə/. **M17.**
[ORIGIN Graecized form of mod. Latin *aphelium*, from Greek AP-² + *hēlios* sun, after Latin *apogaeum* APOGEE.]
ASTRONOMY. The point in the orbit of a planet, comet, etc., at which the furthest distance from the sun is reached.

aphemia /əˈfiːmɪə/ *noun*. Now *rare*. **M19.**
[ORIGIN from A-¹⁰ + Greek *phēmē* voice + -IA¹.]
MEDICINE. A form of aphasia in which words can be understood but not uttered.

apheresis *noun* /əˈfɪərɪsɪs/ *noun*. Also **aphaeresis**. Pl. **-eses** /-ɪsiːz/. **M16.**
[ORIGIN Late Latin from Greek *aphairesis*, from *aphairein* take away, from AP-² + *hairein* take.]
The loss of a letter or syllable at the beginning of a word.
■ **apheretic** /afɪˈrɛtɪk/ *adjective* of the nature of apheresis **L19.**

aphesis /ˈafɪsɪs/ *noun*. Pl. **-eses** /-ɪsiːz/. **L19.**
[ORIGIN Greek = letting go, from *aphienai*, from AP-² + *hienai* let go, send.]
Apheresis; *spec.* the loss of an unaccented vowel at the beginning of a word (e.g. of *e* from ***esquire*** to form ***squire***).
■ **aˈphetic** *adjective* pertaining to or resulting from aphesis **L19.** **aˈphetically** *adverb* **L19.** **aphetism** *noun* (a word formed by) aphesis **L19.** **aphetize** *verb trans.* shorten by aphesis **L19.**

apheta /ˈafɪtə/ *noun*. **M17.**
[ORIGIN Latin from Greek *aphetēs* starter, sender off.]
ASTROLOGY. = HYLEG.

aphid /ˈeɪfɪd/ *noun*. **L19.**
[ORIGIN Back-form. from *aphides*, pl. of APHIS.]
A small soft-bodied insect of the homopteran family Aphididae, whose members live on plant juices and include many plant pests, e.g. a greenfly or a blackfly.
rose aphid: see ROSE *noun & adjective*. ***woolly aphid***: see WOOLLY *adjective*.
■ **aphiˈdivorous** *adjective* feeding on aphids **E19.**

aphis /ˈeɪfɪs/ *noun*. Pl. **-ides** /-ɪdiːz/. **L18.**
[ORIGIN mod. Latin from Greek, prob. a misreading (αφ *aph* for κορ *kor*) of *koris* bug.]
= APHID.
■ **aphicide** *noun* an insecticide used against aphids **L19.**

aphonia /eɪˈfəʊnɪə, ə-/ *noun*. Orig. †**aphony**. **L17.**
[ORIGIN mod. Latin from Greek *aphōnia* speechlessness, from A-¹⁰ + *phōnē* voice: see -PHONIA.]
MEDICINE. Loss or absence of voice through a defect in the vocal organs. Cf. ANARTHRIA, APHASIA.
■ **aphonic** *adjective* without voice or sound **E19.**

aphorise *verb* var. of APHORIZE.

aphorism /ˈafərɪz(ə)m/ *noun & verb*. **E16.**
[ORIGIN French *aphorisme* or late Latin *aphorismus* from Greek *aphorismos* definition, from *aphorizein* define, from AP-² + *horizein* set bounds to: see HORIZON, -ISM.]
▶ **A** *noun*. **1** A concise statement of a scientific principle, usu. by a classical author. **E16.**
2 Any pithily expressed precept or observation; a maxim. **L16.**
▶ **B** *verb trans. & intrans.* Utter as an aphorism; aphorize. *rare*. **E17.**
■ **aphorisˈmatic** *adjective* (now *rare*) = APHORISMIC **E19.** **aphoˈrismic** *adjective* of the nature of an aphorism **L18.**

aphorist /ˈafərɪst/ *noun*. **E18.**
[ORIGIN from APHORISM + -IST.]
A person who writes or utters aphorisms.
■ **aphoˈristic** *adjective* of or pertaining to an aphorist; of the nature of an aphorism: **M18.** **aphoˈristical** *adjective (rare)* **L17.** **aphoˈristically** *adverb* in an aphoristic manner **M17.**

aphorize /ˈafərʌɪz/ *verb intrans.* Also **-ise**. **M17.**
[ORIGIN formed as APHORIST + -IZE.]
Write or speak in aphorisms.

aphotic /eɪˈfəʊtɪk, ə-/ *adjective*. **L19.**
[ORIGIN from A-¹⁰ + PHOTIC.]
OCEANOGRAPHY. Not reached by sunlight.

aphrodisiac /afrəˈdɪzɪak/ *noun & adjective*. **E18.**
[ORIGIN Greek *aphrodisiakos*, from *aphrodisios*, from *Aphroditē*: see APHRODITE, -AC.]
▶ **A** *noun*. A food, drug, etc., which stimulates sexual desire. **E18.**
▶ **B** *adjective*. Of the nature of an aphrodisiac; arousing sexual desire. **M19.**
■ **aphrodisiacal** /-ˈzʌɪək(ə)l/ *adjective* **E18.**

Aphrodite /afrəˈdʌɪti/ *noun*. **M17.**
[ORIGIN Greek *Aphroditē* the goddess of love, the Grecian Venus, lit. 'foam-born', from *aphros* foam.]
1 A goddess of love; a beautiful woman. **M17.**
2 = ***SEA mouse***. Now only as mod. Latin genus name. **L18.**

aphtha /ˈafθə/ *noun*. Pl. **-thae** /-θiː/. **M17.**
[ORIGIN Latin from Greek, mostly in pl.; connected with *haptein* set on fire.]
MEDICINE. A small usu. white ulcer occurring in groups in the mouth or on the tongue; *rare* the occurrence of such ulcers. Usu. in *pl.*
■ **aphthous** *adjective* of the nature of or characterized by aphthae **M18.**

aphyllous /əˈfɪləs/ *adjective*. **E19.**
[ORIGIN from mod. Latin *aphyllus* from Greek *aphullos*, from A-¹⁰ + *phullon* leaf: see -OUS.]
Without leaves; *BOTANY* inherently leafless.

API *abbreviation*.
1 American Petroleum Institute (used *spec.* with ref. to a scale for expressing the relative density of oil, with higher values corresponding to lower densities).
2 *COMPUTING.* Application programming interface.

apian /ˈeɪpɪən/ *adjective*. **E19.**
[ORIGIN Latin *apianus*, from *apis* bee: see -AN.]
Of or pertaining to bees.

apiarian /eɪpɪˈɛːrɪən/ *adjective & noun*. **E19.**
[ORIGIN formed as APIARY + -AN.]
▶ **A** *adjective*. Of or pertaining to bee-keeping. **E19.**
▶ **B** *noun*. = APIARIST. Now *rare* or *obsolete*. **E19.**

apiary /ˈeɪpɪəri/ *noun*. **M17.**
[ORIGIN from Latin *apiarium*, from *apis* bee: see -ARY¹.]
A place where bees are kept.
■ **apiarist** *noun* a person who keeps an apiary; a bee-keeper: **E19.**

apical /ˈeɪpɪk(ə)l, ˈap-/ *adjective*. **E19.**
[ORIGIN from Latin *apic-*, APEX *noun*¹ + -AL¹.]
1 Of or pertaining to an apex; situated at the tip or summit. **E19.**
2 *PHONETICS.* Of a sound etc.: made using the tip of the tongue. **L19.**
■ **apically** *adverb* at or towards the apex **L19.**

Apician /əˈpɪʃ(ə)n/ *adjective*. Now *rare*. **E17.**
[ORIGIN from *Apicius* Roman epicure of the early 1st cent. AD + -AN.]
Of or pertaining to luxurious eating; epicurean.

†**a pick-pack** *adverbial phr.* see PIGGYBACK *adverb*.

apico- /ˈeɪpɪkəʊ, ˈap-/ *combining form*. **E20.**
[ORIGIN from APICAL + -O-.]
Forming adjectives & nouns (esp. in *PHONETICS*) with the sense 'apical and —', as ***apico-alveolar***, ***apico-dental***, ***apico-palatal***.

apiculate /əˈpɪkjʊlət/ *adjective*. **E19.**
[ORIGIN formed as APICULUS + -ATE².]
Chiefly *BOTANY.* Terminating in a minute point.

apiculi *noun* pl. of APICULUS.

apiculture /ˈeɪpɪkʌltʃə/ *noun*. **M19.**
[ORIGIN from Latin *apis* bee + -CULTURE.]
Bee-keeping, bee-rearing.
■ **apiˈcultural** *adjective* **L19.** **apiˈculturist** *noun* a person who practises apiculture **L19.**

apiculus /əˈpɪkjʊləs/ *noun*. Now *rare*. Pl. **-li** /-lʌɪ, -liː/. **M19.**
[ORIGIN mod. Latin, dim. of APEX *noun*¹: see -CULE.]
A minute point or tip.

apiece /əˈpiːs/ *adverb*. **LME.**
[ORIGIN from A *adjective* + PIECE *noun*.]
For each piece, article, or person; each, severally.

E. WAUGH Each sold its thousand copies at five guineas apiece. J. T. STORY We now sat up on the bunk, sipping a large scotch apiece.

a-pieces /əˈpiːsɪz/ *adverb*. *obsolete* exc. *dial.* **M16.**
[ORIGIN from A *preposition*¹ 2 + PIECE *noun* + -S¹.]
In pieces; to pieces.

†**apike** *adverb & pred. adjective* see APEAK.

apish /ˈeɪpɪʃ/ *adjective*. **LME.**
[ORIGIN from APE *noun* + -ISH¹.]
1 Of the nature or appearance of an ape. **LME.**
2 Apelike in manner; foolish, silly, affected. **M16.**
3 Unintelligently imitative. **L16.**
■ **apishly** *adverb* **L16.** **apishness** *noun* **M16.**

APL *abbreviation*.
Associative Programming Language (a specific programming language).

aplanatic /apləˈnatɪk/ *adjective*. **L18.**
[ORIGIN from Greek *aplanētos* free from error, from A-¹⁰ + *planan* wander, + -IC.]
Free from spherical aberration.
■ **ˈaplanat** *noun* [-AT²] an aplanatic compound lens **L19.** **aˈplanatism** *noun* freedom from spherical aberration **M19.**

aplasia /əˈpleɪzɪə/ *noun*. **L19.**
[ORIGIN from A-¹⁰ + -PLASIA.]
MEDICINE. Congenital absence or defectiveness of an organ or tissue.
■ **aplastic** /-ˈplas-/ *adjective* pertaining to or characterized by aplasia; unable to form new tissue: **M19.**

aplenty /əˈplɛnti/ *adverb*. **M19.**
[ORIGIN from A-² + PLENTY *noun*.]
In plenty, in abundance.

aplite /ˈaplʌɪt/ *noun*. **L19.**
[ORIGIN German *Aplit*, from Greek *haplous* simple (named on account of its composition): see -ITE¹.]
GEOLOGY. A light-coloured hypabyssal igneous rock having a characteristic saccharoidal texture and usu. granitic composition.
■ **aˈplitic** *adjective* consisting or characteristic of aplite **E20.**

aplomb /əˈplɒm/ *noun*. **L18.**
[ORIGIN French, from *à plomb* according to the plummet.]
1 Perpendicularity; steadiness. Now *rare* or *obsolete*. **L18.**
2 Self-possession, coolness; assurance. **E19.**

aplustre /əˈplʌstri/ *noun*. Pl. **-tra** /-trə/, **-tria** /-trɪə/. **E18.**
[ORIGIN Latin from Greek *aphlaston*.]
The curved and ornamented stern of an ancient Greek or Roman ship.

apneusis /apˈnjuːsɪs/ *noun*. **E20.**
[ORIGIN from A-¹⁰ + Greek *pneusis* breathing.]
MEDICINE. An abnormal type of breathing characterized by long periods of sustained inspiratory effort alternating with brief expirations.

apneustic /apˈnjuːstɪk/ *adjective*. **L19.**
[ORIGIN from Greek *apneustia* holding of the breath + -IC; in sense 1 from German *apneustisch*.]
1 *ENTOMOLOGY.* Lacking functional spiracles. **L19.**
2 *MEDICINE.* Characteristic of or exhibiting apneusis. **M20.**

apnoea /apˈniːə/ *noun*. Also ***apnea**. **E18.**
[ORIGIN mod. Latin from Greek *apnoia*, from *apnous* breathless: see -IA¹.]
MEDICINE. Interruption or cessation of breathing.
■ **apnoeic** *adjective* characterized by or suffering from apnoea **L19.**

apo- /ˈapəʊ/ *prefix*. Before a vowel or *h* usu. **ap-**.
[ORIGIN Repr. Greek *apo-* off, from, away, quite.]
A productive prefix, chiefly in *SCIENCE*, esp. with the senses 'separate', 'away from', 'other than', as ***apocarpous***, ***apocrine***, ***apogamy***. In *ASTRONOMY* forming nouns denoting the point in the orbit of a body at which it is furthest from the primary about which it revolves (opp. PERI-).
■ **aˈpastron** *noun* [Greek *astron* star] *ASTRONOMY* the point furthest from a star in the path of a body orbiting that star **E20.** **apoˈapsis** *noun*, pl. **-apses** /-ˈapsiːz/, *ASTRONOMY* the point in the path of an orbiting body at which it is furthest from the primary **L20.** **apojove** *noun* (*ASTRONOMY*) the point furthest from Jupiter in the orbit of any of Jupiter's satellites **M19.**

Apoc. *abbreviation*.
1 Apocalypse (New Testament).
2 Apocrypha.

Apocalypse /əˈpɒkəlɪps/ *noun*. In sense 2 also **a-**. **OE.**
[ORIGIN Old French & mod. French from ecclesiastical Latin *apocalypsis* from Greek *apokalupsis*, from *apokaluptein* uncover, from APO- + *kaluptein* cover.]
1 The supposed revelation of the future made to St John in the island of Patmos; the book of the New Testament relating this. **OE.**

A

2 Any vision or prophecy, esp. of violent or climactic events comparable with those foretold in the book *Revelation of St John*. Also, the events themselves. LME.
■ **apocalypst** *noun* (*rare*) = APOCALYPTIST E19.

apocalyptic /əpɒkəˈlɪptɪk/ *noun & adjective*. E17.
[ORIGIN French *apocalyptique* adjective from Greek *apokaluptikos*, from *apokaluptein*: see APOCALYPSE, -IC.]
▸ **A** *noun*. **1** The writer of the Apocalypse, St John the Divine; the author or revealer of any comparable vision of the future. E17.
PAUL JOHNSON All societies contain not only creators and builders but apocalyptics.
2 Apocalyptic teaching, philosophy, or literature. L19.
R. H. CHARLES Prophecy and Apocalyptic . . both claim to be a communication through the Divine Spirit of the character and will and purposes of God. *Scrutiny* A periodical which has previously discussed the problems of the relation between culture and the coming social-economic revolution mainly in terms of the crudest Marxian apocalyptic.
▸ **B** *adjective*. **1** Of, pertaining to, or concerned with the Revelation of St John. M17.
D. MASSON Meade was at the head of the Apocalyptic commentators.
2 Of a person: concerned with or given to (similar) visions of the future. M17.
R. SOUTH That some apocalyptick ignoramus . . must . . pick it out of some abused, martyred prophecy of Ezechiel. *Time* As for where the current turmoil is leading Portugal, Lagoa is increasingly apocalyptic.
3 Resembling the Apocalypse; revelatory, prophetic. L17.
A. C. SWINBURNE The recognition of the apocalyptic fact that a workman can only be known by his work.
■ **apocalyptical** *adjective* M17. **apocalyptically** *adverb* after the manner or by means of revelation or of the Apocalypse M18. **apocalypticism** /-sɪz(ə)m/, **apocalyptism** *nouns* belief in an imminent apocalypse L19.

apocalyptist /əpɒkəˈlɪptɪst/ *noun*. M19.
[ORIGIN from Greek *apokaluptein* (see APOCALYPSE) + -IST.]
The author of the Apocalypse or a similarly prophetic work; a commentator on the Apocalypse.

apocarpous /apəˈkɑːpəs/ *adjective*. M19.
[ORIGIN from APO- + Greek *karpos* fruit + -OUS.]
BOTANY. Of a gynoecium: having separated carpels. Opp. SYNCARPOUS.

apocatastasis /ˌapə(ʊ)kəˈtastəsɪs/ *noun*. Also **-kat-**. L17.
[ORIGIN Latin from Greek *apokatastasis* re-establishment, formed as APO- + CATASTASIS.]
Restoration, renewal, return; *spec.* in THEOLOGY, the ultimate salvation of all moral beings.

apocentre /ˈapə(ʊ)sɛntə/ *noun*. Also ***-ter**. E20.
[ORIGIN from APO- + CENTRE *noun*.]
The point in the path of a body revolving round a centre at which it is furthest from the centre.

apochromatic /ˌapə(ʊ)krəˈmatɪk/ *adjective*. L19.
[ORIGIN from APO- + CHROMATIC.]
Corrected for chromatic aberration at three wavelengths. Cf. ACHROMATIC.
■ ˈ**apochromat** *noun* [-AT[2]] an apochromatic lens or lens system E20.

apocope /əˈpɒkəpi/ *noun*. M16.
[ORIGIN Late Latin from Greek *apokopē*, from *apokoptein* cut off, from APO- + *koptein* to cut.]
The loss of one or more letters or syllables at the end of a word.
■ **apocopate** *verb trans*. remove or shorten by apocope E19. **apocoˈpation** *noun* M18.

Apocr. *abbreviation*.
Apocrypha.

apocrine /ˈapəkrʌɪn, -krɪn/ *adjective*. E20.
[ORIGIN from APO- + Greek *krinein* to separate.]
PHYSIOLOGY. Designating or pertaining to glands which lose some of their cytoplasm during secretion, esp. sweat glands opening into hair follicles. Cf. ECCRINE, HOLOCRINE, MEROCRINE.

apocrisiary /apəˈkrɪzɪəri/ *noun*. Also **-sary** /-zəri/. LME.
[ORIGIN medieval Latin *apocrisiarius*, from Greek *apokrisis* answer: see -ARY[1].]
A person appointed as a representative; *spec.* a papal nuncio.

Apocrypha /əˈpɒkrɪfə/ *adjective & noun*. Also **a-**. LME.
[ORIGIN ecclesiastical Latin, neut. pl. (sc. *scripta* writings) of *apocryphus* from Greek *apokruphos* hidden, from *apokruptein* to hide: see APO-.]
▸ †**A** *adjective*. = APOCRYPHAL *adjective* 1, 2. LME–L17.
▸ **B** *noun*. (Usu. treated as *sing.*; rarely as *pl.*, with *sing.* **-phon** /-fɒn/.) A writing or statement of doubtful authorship or authenticity; *spec.* (**a**) those Old Testament books included in the Septuagint and Vulgate which are not included in the Hebrew Scriptures, and which were excluded from the Protestant canon at the Reformation; (**b**) ***New Testament Apocrypha***, various early Christian writings parallel to but excluded from the New Testament canon. LME.

apocryphal /əˈpɒkrɪf(ə)l/ *adjective & noun*. In sense A.2 also **A-**. L16.
[ORIGIN from APOCRYPHA + -AL[1].]
▸ **A** *adjective*. **1** Of a writing, statement, story, etc.: of doubtful authenticity; spurious, false, mythical. L16.
V. BRITTAIN We collected all the tales of her, both authentic and apocryphal, that we could gather together.
2 Of or pertaining to the Apocrypha. E17.
3 Sham, counterfeit. E17.
JONSON A whoreson, upstart, apocryphal captain.
▸ †**B** *noun*. An apocryphal writing. Only in 17.
■ **apocryphally** *adverb* without authenticity M19.

apocynthion /apə(ʊ)ˈsɪnθɪən/ *noun*. M20.
[ORIGIN from APO- + neut. of Greek *Kunthios* (adjective) designating Mount Cynthus: see CYNTHIA.]
ASTRONOMY. The point at which a spacecraft in lunar orbit is furthest from the moon's centre, after having been launched from the earth. Cf. APOLUNE.

†**apod** *adjective*. Also **-ode**. Only in 19.
[ORIGIN formed as APODAL: cf. French *apode*.]
ZOOLOGY. Apodous; apodal.

apodal /ˈapəd(ə)l/ *adjective & noun*. Now *rare* or *obsolete*. M18.
[ORIGIN from Greek *apod-*, *apous* without feet, from A-[10] + *pous* foot, partly through mod. Latin *Apoda*, *Apodes* (taxonomic groupings): see APODAN, -AL[1].]
ZOOLOGY. ▸ **A** *adjective*. Lacking feet; (of fish) lacking ventral fins. M18.
▸ **B** *noun*. = APODAN. M19.

apodan /ˈapəd(ə)n/ *noun*. L19.
[ORIGIN from mod. Latin *Apoda*, an order (usu. called Gymnophiona) + -AN: see APODAL.]
ZOOLOGY. = CAECILIAN.

†**apode** *adjective* var. of APOD.

apodeictic *adjective* etc., **apodeixis** *noun*, see APODICTIC etc., APODIXIS.

apodeme /ˈapədiːm/ *noun*. M19.
[ORIGIN mod. Latin *apodema*, from Greek APO- + *demas* body, frame.]
ZOOLOGY. A hollow invagination of the cuticle of an arthropod, which serves as a point of attachment for muscle.

apodictic /apəˈdɪktɪk/ *adjective*. Also **-deictic** /-ˈdʌɪktɪk/. M17.
[ORIGIN Latin *apodicticus* from Greek *apodeiktikos*, from *apodeiknunai* demonstrate, from APO- + *deiknunai* show.]
Clearly demonstrated or established.
■ **apodictical** *adjective* (*arch.*) based on necessary truth, apodictic L16. **apodictically** *adverb* E17.

apodixis /apə(ʊ)ˈdɪksɪs/ *noun*. *rare*. Also **-deixis** /-ˈdʌɪksɪs/. L16.
[ORIGIN Latin from Greek *apodeiksis*, from *apodeiknunai*: see APODICTIC.]
Demonstration; proof.

apodosis /əˈpɒdəsɪs/ *noun*. Pl. **-oses** /-əsiːz/. E17.
[ORIGIN Late Latin from Greek, from *apodidonai* give back, from APO- + *didonai* give.]
GRAMMAR & RHETORIC. The concluding clause of a sentence; *spec.* the consequent clause of a conditional sentence. Opp. PROTASIS 2.

apodous /ˈapədəs/ *adjective*. E19.
[ORIGIN formed as APODAL + -OUS.]
ZOOLOGY. Without feet; having only rudimentary feet.

apodyterium /ˌapədɪˈtɪərɪəm/ *noun*. Pl. **-ria** /-rɪə/. E17.
[ORIGIN Latin from Greek *apodutērion*, from *apoduein* to strip.]
CLASSICAL HISTORY. A room adjacent to a bath or palaestra where clothes were deposited.

apoenzyme /apəʊˈɛnzʌɪm/ *noun*. M20.
[ORIGIN from APO- + ENZYME.]
BIOCHEMISTRY. The protein part of an enzyme, which is inactive unless combined with a coenzyme.

apogamy /əˈpɒgəmi/ *noun*. L19.
[ORIGIN from APO- + -GAMY.]
BOTANY. Asexual reproduction; *spec.* the production in some ferns etc. of a sporophyte directly from a prothallus without the union of gametes.
■ **apogamous** *adjective* characterized by or of the nature of apogamy L19. **apogamously** *adverb* L19.

apogee /ˈapədʒiː/ *noun*. Formerly also in Latin & Greek forms. L16.
[ORIGIN French *apogée* or mod. Latin *apog(a)eum* from Greek *apogaion*, *-geion* use as noun (sc. *diastēma* distance) of neut. of *apogaios*, *-geios* far from the earth, from APO- + *gaia*, *gē* earth.]
(Opp. PERIGEE.)
1 ASTRONOMY. The point furthest from the earth in the path of a body orbiting the earth. (Orig. also used with ref. to the sun and planets, viewed geocentrically.) L16.
†**2** The point in the sky at which the sun has the highest altitude at noon (i.e. at the summer solstice). E–M17.
3 *fig.* The furthest or highest point; the culmination, the climax. M17.
P. A. SCHOLES Beethoven's Ninth Symphony remains the apogee of the orchestral art. E. BOWEN This conversation we're having now . . seems to me the apogee of bad taste.
■ †**apogaeic**, **-gaic** *adjective* M–L19. **apoˈgeal** *adjective* (now *rare* or *obsolete*) M18. **apoˈgean** *adjective* of or pertaining to apogee (*lit.* or *fig.*) M17.

apograph /ˈapəgrɑːf/ *noun*. M17.
[ORIGIN Greek *apographon*, from *apographein* to copy formed as APO- + *graphein* write.]
An exact copy or transcript.

à point /a pwɛ̃/ *adverbial phr.* E20.
[ORIGIN French = to the point.]
Esp. COOKERY. At or to exactly the right point; just enough, without overcooking or undercooking.

apokatastasis *noun* var. of APOCATASTASIS.

apo koinou /ˌapəʊ ˈkɔɪnuː, ˈkɔɪnaʊ/ *adjectival & adverbial phr.* L19.
[ORIGIN Greek, lit. 'in common'.]
GRAMMAR. Designating a construction comprising two clauses having an unrepeated word or phrase in common; so as to form such a construction.

apolar /eɪˈpəʊlə/ *adjective*. M19.
[ORIGIN from A-[10] + POLAR *adjective*.]
Not polar; having no poles.
■ **apoˈlarity** *noun* E20.

apolaustic /apəˈlɔːstɪk/ *adjective*. M19.
[ORIGIN Greek *apolaustikos*, from *apolauein* enjoy: see -IC.]
1 Given to enjoyment; self-indulgent. M19.
2 Intended for enjoyment. L19.
■ **apolausticism** /-sɪz(ə)m/ *noun* L19.

apolipoprotein /ˌapəʊlɪpəʊˈprəʊtiːn/ *noun*. L20.
[ORIGIN from APO- + LIPO- + PROTEIN.]
BIOCHEMISTRY. Any of several proteins which combine with triglycerides, phospholipids, and cholesterol to form lipoprotein complexes.

apolitical /eɪpəˈlɪtɪk(ə)l/ *adjective*. M20.
[ORIGIN from A-[10] + POLITICAL *adjective*.]
Unconcerned with or detached from politics.

Apollinarian /əpɒlɪˈnɛːrɪən/ *noun & adjective*. L16.
[ORIGIN from Latin *Apollinaris* of Apollo, also as personal name: see -ARIAN.]
▸ **A** *noun*. ECCLESIASTICAL HISTORY. An adherent of the heretical views of Apollinaris of Laodicea (4th cent. AD), who held that Christ assumed a human body but not a human soul. L16.
▸ **B** *adjective*. **1** ECCLESIASTICAL HISTORY. Of or pertaining to Apollinaris or his beliefs. M17.
2 Sacred to or in honour of Apollo. Cf. APOLLONIAN *adjective* 1. M18.
■ **Apollinarianism** *noun* the doctrine of the Apollinarians L19. **Apollinarist** *noun* (now *rare* or *obsolete*) = APOLLINARIAN *noun* LME.

Apollinaris /əpɒlɪˈnɛːrɪs/ *noun*. L19.
[ORIGIN from *Apollinarisburg* (see below).]
An effervescent mineral water from Apollinarisburg in the Rhineland of Germany.

Apolline /əˈpɒlʌɪn, -lɪn/ *adjective*. E17.
[ORIGIN Latin *Apollineus*, from *Apollin-*, *Apollo*.]
Of, pertaining to, or resembling Apollo (see APOLLONIAN *adjective* 1).
■ **Apollinian** /apəˈlɪnɪən/ *adjective* E20.

apollo /əˈpɒləʊ/ *noun*. Pl. **-os**. E19.
[ORIGIN from the Greek god *Apollo* (see APOLLONIAN).]
A large butterfly, *Parnassius apollo*, which has creamy-white wings marked with black and red spots and is found chiefly on the mountains of mainland Europe.

Apollonian /apəˈləʊnɪən/ *adjective & noun*. E17.
[ORIGIN from Latin *Apollonius* from Greek *Apollōnios* of Apollo, also as personal name: see -IAN.]
▸ **A** *adjective*. **1** Of, pertaining to, or resembling Apollo, the sun god of the Greeks and Romans, patron of music and poetry; *spec.* (of character etc.) serene, rational, self-disciplined (opp. ***Dionysian***). E17.
2 MATH. Of Apollonius of Perga, Alexandrine mathematician of the 3rd cent. BC, esp. with ref. to his work on conic sections. E18.
▸ **B** *noun*. A follower or worshipper of Apollo; a person of Apollonian character. E17.
■ **Apoˈllonic** *adjective* = APOLLONIAN *adjective* 1 E19.

Apollonicon /apəˈlɒnɪk(ə)n/ *noun*. E19.
[ORIGIN formed as APOLLONIAN after HARMONICON.]
An organ of great power and complexity, exhibited in London in the early 19th cent.

Apollyon /əˈpɒlɪən/ *noun*. LME.
[ORIGIN Late Latin (Vulgate) from Greek *Apolluōn* destroyer (translating ABADDON, *Revelation* 9:11), use as noun of pres. pple of *apollunai* intensive of *ollunai* destroy.]
The Devil as destroyer.

apologetic /əpɒləˈdʒɛtɪk/ *noun & adjective*. LME.
[ORIGIN French *apologétique* or late Latin *apologeticus* from Greek *apologētikos* fit for defence, from *apologeisthai*: see APOLOGY *noun*[1], -IC.]
▸ **A** *noun*. **1** A formal defence or justification of a person, doctrine, action, etc. LME.
2 *sing.* & (usu.) in *pl.* Reasoned defence, esp. of Christian belief. M18.
▸ **B** *adjective*. **1** Of the nature of a defence; vindicatory. M17.

2 Regretfully acknowledging or excusing fault or failure; diffident. M19.
■ **apologetical** *adjective* L16. **apologetically** *adverb* in an apologetic manner; by way of apology: M17.

apologia /apəˈləʊdʒɪə/ *noun*. L18.
[ORIGIN Latin: see APOLOGY *noun*[1].]
A written defence of one's opinions or conduct.

†**apological** *adjective*. E17–M19.
[ORIGIN formed as APOLOGIA + -ICAL.]
Of the nature of an apology or defence; apologetic.

apologise *verb* var. of APOLOGIZE.

apologist /əˈpɒlədʒɪst/ *noun*. M17.
[ORIGIN French *apologiste*, from Greek *apologizesthai*: see APOLOGIZE, -IST.]
A person who defends another, a belief, etc., by argument; a literary champion.

apologize /əˈpɒlədʒʌɪz/ *verb*. Also **-ise**. L16.
[ORIGIN Greek *apologizesthai* render an account, from *apologos*: see APOLOGUE, -IZE. Now assoc. with APOLOGY *noun*[1].]
1 *verb intrans*. Make an apology (*for* a person, circumstance, action, etc.). L16.

HENRY MORE I can justly apologize for my self that Necessity has no law. E. WAUGH His friends bore him to the gate and . . his host . . returned to apologize. S. NAIPAUL The head waiter, admitting his fault, apologized profusely for the oversight.

2 *verb trans*. †**a** Make an apology for (an action etc.). E17–M18. ▸**b** Acknowledge, and express regret, *that* (something has occurred etc.). M20.

a SWIFT T'apologise his late offence. **b** A. J. P. TAYLOR Lloyd George apologizing to the house of commons that misplaced personal loyalty . . had made him cling to an incompetent minister.

■ **apologizer** *noun* a person who apologizes M17.

apologue /ˈapəlɒɡ/ *noun*. Orig. †**-logy** M16.
[ORIGIN French, or late Latin *apologus* from Greek *apologos* story, account, from APO- + *logos* discourse: see -LOGUE.]
A moral fable, *esp*. one having animals or inanimate things as its characters.

apology /əˈpɒlədʒi/ *noun*[1]. M16.
[ORIGIN French *apologie* or late Latin *apologia* from Greek = speech in defence, from *apologeisthai* speak in one's own defence: see -LOGY.]
1 A formal defence or vindication against an (actual or potential) accusation or imputation. M16.

T. SHERLOCK And before the same great Court of Areopagites Paul made his Apology. C. CONNOLLY The book closes with a long and reasoned apology for the pursuit of happiness.

2 A justification, an explanation, an excuse. L16.

DEFOE The consequence . . will be the best apology for my conduct.

3 A frank acknowledgement of fault or failure, given by way of reparation; an explanation that no offence was intended, with regret for any given or taken. L16.

G. K. CHESTERTON I am afraid my fury and your insult are too shocking to be wiped out even with an apology. G. B. SHAW Sitting down again with a gesture of apology. A. SHAFFER I wonder if all her jewellery was inscribed with apologies for your bully boy behaviour.

with apologies to —: used to introduce a parody or adaptation.
4 *an apology for*, a poor substitute for (a thing), a poor or inadequate specimen of. M18.

C. HAMPTON It never begins to dribble across your apology for a mind that half a million children under five starved to death in Brazil last year.

†**apology** *noun*[2] var. of APOLOGUE.

apolune /ˈapə(ʊ)luːn/ *noun*. M20.
[ORIGIN from APO- + Latin *luna* moon.]
ASTRONOMY. The point at which a spacecraft in lunar orbit (esp. one launched from the moon) is furthest from the moon's centre. Cf. APOCYNTHION.

apomixis /apəˈmɪksɪs/ *noun*. E20.
[ORIGIN from APO- + Greek *mixis*, *mikt-* mingling.]
BOTANY. Asexual reproduction, esp. in a form outwardly resembling a sexual process.
■ ˈ**apomict** *noun* [back-form. from APOMICTIC] a plant which reproduces by apomixis M20. **apomictic** *adjective* characterized by or of the nature of apomixis E20. **apomictically** *adverb* E20.

apomorphine /apəˈmɔːfiːn/ *noun*. L19.
[ORIGIN from APO- + MORPHINE.]
CHEMISTRY. A white crystalline compound, $C_{17}H_{17}NO_2$, which was originally derived from morphine and is used as an emetic and in the treatment of Parkinsonism.
■ Also †**apomorphia** *noun* M–L19.

aponeurosis /apənjʊˈrəʊsɪs/ *noun*. Pl. **-roses** /-ˈrəʊsiːz/. L17.
[ORIGIN mod. Latin from Greek *aponeurōsis*, from APO- + *neuron* sinew + -OSIS.]
ANATOMY. A sheet of pearly-white fibrous tissue which takes the place of a tendon in sheetlike muscles having a wide area of attachment.
■ **aponeurotic** *adjective* pertaining to or of the nature of an aponeurosis M18.

a-poop /əˈpuːp/ *adverb*. L17.
[ORIGIN from A *preposition*[1] 1 + POOP *noun*[1].]
NAUTICAL. On the poop; astern.

apopetalous /apəˈpɛt(ə)ləs/ *adjective*. M19.
[ORIGIN from APO- + PETAL + -OUS.]
BOTANY. Having the petals separate.

apophatic /apəˈfatɪk/ *adjective*. M19.
[ORIGIN Greek *apophatikos* negative, from *apophasis* denial, formed as APO- + *phanai* speak: see -IC.]
THEOLOGY. Of knowledge of God: obtained through negating concepts that might be applied to him. Opp. CATAPHATIC.

†**apophlegmatic** *adjective & noun*. E–M18.
[ORIGIN Greek *apophlegmatikos*, formed as APO- + *phlegmatikos*: see PHLEGMATIC.]
MEDICINE. (An) expectorant.
■ †**apophlegmatism** *noun* an apophlegmatic agent or action E17–M18.

apophony /əˈpɒfəni/ *noun*. L19.
[ORIGIN French *apophonie*, formed as APO-: see -PHONY.]
PHILOLOGY. = ABLAUT.
■ **apoˈphonic** *adjective* M20.

apophthegm /ˈapəθɛm/ *noun*. Also ***apothegm**. M16.
[ORIGIN French *apophthegme* or mod. Latin *apophthegma* from Greek, from *apophtheggesthai* speak one's opinion plainly, formed as APO- + *phtheggesthai* speak.]
A terse saying; a pithy maxim.
■ **apophthegmatic** /-θɛɡˈmat-/ *adjective* = APOPHTHEGMATICAL L18. **apophthegmatical** /-θɛɡˈmat-/ *adjective* pertaining to or of the nature of an apophthegm; pithy, sententious; given to the use of apophthegms: L16. **apophthegmatically** /-θɛɡˈmat-/ *adverb* M17. **apophthegmatize** /-ˈθɛɡmət-/ *verb intrans*. write or speak in apophthegms M17.

apophyge /əˈpɒfɪdʒi/ *noun*. M16.
[ORIGIN Greek *apophugē* lit. 'escape', from *apophugein* flee away.]
ARCHITECTURE. The part of a column where it springs out of its base, or joins its capital, usu. moulded into a concave sweep or cavetto.

apophyllite /əˈpɒfɪlʌɪt/ *noun*. E19.
[ORIGIN from APO- + Greek *phullon* leaf + -ITE[1].]
MINERALOGY. A tetragonal hydrated silicate and fluoride of calcium and potassium, related to zeolites and occurring usu. as white prisms with a vitreous lustre.

apophysis /əˈpɒfɪsɪs/ *noun*. Also †**-physe**. Pl. **-physes** /-fɪsiːz/. L16.
[ORIGIN mod. Latin from Greek *apophusis* offshoot, from APO- + *phusis* growth.]
1 ANATOMY & ZOOLOGY. A protuberance from a bone or other hard tissue. L16.
2 BOTANY. A dilatation of the base of the sporangium in some mosses. L18.
■ **apoˈphyseal**, **-ial** *adjective* pertaining to or of the nature of an apophysis L19.

apoplectic /apəˈplɛktɪk/ *adjective & noun*. E17.
[ORIGIN French *apoplectique* or late Latin *apoplecticus* from Greek *apoplēktikos*, formed as APOPLEXY: see -IC.]
▸ **A** *adjective*. **1** Of or pertaining to apoplexy; causing or conducive to apoplexy. E17.

DICKENS One of your stiff-starched apoplectic cravats.

apoplectic stroke: see STROKE *noun*[1] 2b.
†**2** Of use against apoplexy. L17–M18.
3 Suffering from or liable to apoplexy. E18.

J. AUSTEN A short-necked, apoplectic sort of fellow.

▸ **B** *noun*. A sufferer from apoplexy; a person liable to apoplexy. L17.
■ †**apoplectical** *adjective* E17–E19. **apoplectically** *adverb* L19. **apoplectiform** *adjective* (now *rare* or *obsolete*) having the form of apoplexy M19.

apoplex /ˈapəplɛks/ *noun & verb*. *arch*. M16.
[ORIGIN Late Latin *apoplexis* from Greek, var. of *apoplēxia*: see APOPLEXY.]
▸ **A** *noun*. Apoplexy. M16.
▸ **B** *verb trans*. Strike with apoplexy; benumb. E17.

apoplexy /ˈapəplɛksi/ *noun*. LME.
[ORIGIN Old French & mod. French *apoplexie* from late Latin *apoplexia* from Greek *apoplēxia*, from *apoplēssein* disable by a stroke, from APO- + *plēssein* strike.]
1 A sudden loss of sensation and movement due to a disturbance of blood supply to the brain; a stroke. LME.
2 With specifying word: a haemorrhage or failure of blood supply in another organ or part. Now *rare* or *obsolete*. M19.

apoprotein /ˈapəʊprəʊtiːn/ *noun*. L20.
[ORIGIN from APO- + PROTEIN.]
BIOCHEMISTRY. A protein which together with a prosthetic group forms a particular biochemical molecule such as a hormone or enzyme.

apoptosis /apəpˈtəʊsɪs/ *noun*. E19.
[ORIGIN Greek *apoptōsis* lit. 'falling away or off', formed as APO- + PTOSIS.]
1 MEDICINE. Loosening (of a bandage, ligament, etc.); the loosening and falling off of a scab or crust. *rare* (only in Dicts.). E19.
2 MEDICINE & BIOLOGY. The controlled destruction of cells, as in the growth and development of an organism; the type of cell lysis characteristic of this. L20.
■ **apoptotic** /-ˈtɒtɪk/ *adjective* L20.

aporetic /apəˈrɛtɪk/ *adjective*. E17.
[ORIGIN French *aporétique* from Greek *aporētikos*, from *aporein* be at a loss, from A-[10] + *poros* passage: see -IC.]
Full of doubts and objections; inclined to doubt.

aporia /əˈpɔːrɪə, əˈpɒrɪə/ *noun*. M16.
[ORIGIN Late Latin from Greek, from *aporos* impassable, from A-[10] + *poros*: see APORETIC, -IA[1].]
1 RHETORIC. The expression of doubt. M16.
2 A doubtful matter, a perplexing difficulty. L19.

aport /əˈpɔːt/ *adverb & pred. adjective*. M16.
[ORIGIN from A *preposition*[1] 1 + PORT *noun*[5].]
NAUTICAL. On or towards the port side of the ship.
put the helm aport port the helm, i.e. move the rudder to starboard, causing the vessel to turn to the right.

aposematic /ˌapəʊsɪˈmatɪk/ *adjective*. L19.
[ORIGIN from APO- + SEMATIC.]
ZOOLOGY. Of coloration, markings, etc.: serving to warn or repel.

aposiopesis /ˌapəsʌɪəˈpiːsɪs/ *noun*. Pl. **-peses** /-ˈpiːsiːz/. L16.
[ORIGIN Latin from Greek *aposiōpēsis*, from *aposiōpan* be silent.]
RHETORIC. (A) sudden breaking off in speech.
■ **aposiopetic** /-ˈpɛtɪk/ *adjective* M17.

apospory /əˈpɒsp(ə)ri/ *noun*. L19.
[ORIGIN from APO- + Greek *sporos* seed + -Y[3].]
BOTANY. In some cryptogams: the growth of a gametophyte directly from a sporophyte, without spore production.
■ **aposporous** *adjective* characterized by or of the nature of apospory L19. **aposporously** *adverb* L19.

apostasy /əˈpɒstəsi/ *noun*. Also †**-acy**. ME.
[ORIGIN ecclesiastical Latin *apostasia* from late Greek alt. of *apostasis* defection: see -Y[3].]
1 Abandonment or renunciation of one's religious faith or moral allegiance. ME. ▸**b** Renunciation of religious vows without dispensation. ME.
2 The abandonment of principles, beliefs, or party. L16.

apostate /ˈapəsteɪt/ *noun & adjective*. Also †**-ata**. ME.
[ORIGIN Old French & mod. French, or ecclesiastical Latin *apostata* from late Greek *apostatēs* apostate, runaway slave, formed as APO- + *stat-* rel. to *histanai* cause to stand.]
▸ **A** *noun*. **1** A person who abandons his or her religious faith or moral allegiance. ME. ▸**b** A person who renounces religious vows without dispensation. LME.
2 *gen*. A person who deserts his or her principles or allegiance; a turncoat, a renegade. LME.
▸ **B** *adjective*. **1** Unfaithful to religious principles or creed, or to moral allegiance; unbelieving, infidel. LME.
2 *gen*. Unfaithful, renegade. L17.
■ **apoˈstatic** *adjective* = APOSTATICAL L16. **apoˈstatical** *adjective* of the nature of apostates or apostasy; heretical: M16. **aˈpostatism** *noun* apostasy L16.

apostatize /əˈpɒstətʌɪz/ *verb intrans*. Also **-ise**. M16.
[ORIGIN medieval Latin *apostatizare* (earlier *apostatare*), from *apostata*: see APOSTATE, -IZE.]
1 Become an apostate (*from* a religion etc.). M16.
2 *gen*. Abandon a principle etc.; transfer one's allegiance (*from* a cause, party, etc.). M17.

†**apostem** *noun* var. of APOSTUME.

†**apostemate** *verb*, **apostemation** *noun* vars. of APOSTUMATE, APOSTUMATION.

†**aposteme** *noun* var. of APOSTUME.

a posteriori /eɪ pɒˌstɛrɪˈɔːrʌɪ, pɒˌstɪə-; ɑː pɒ-/ *adverbial & adjectival phr*. E17.
[ORIGIN Latin = from what comes after.]
1 Of reasoning: (by) proceeding from effects to causes; inductive(ly), empirical(ly). Opp. A PRIORI. E17.
2 From behind; on the buttocks. *joc*. M18.

†**aposthumate** *verb*, **aposthumation** *noun* vars. of APOSTUMATE, APOSTUMATION.

†**aposthume** *noun* var. of APOSTUME.

apostil /əˈpɒstɪl/ *noun & verb*. As noun also **-ille**. E16.
[ORIGIN Old French *apostil(le)* noun, from *apostiller* verb, formed as POSTIL *noun*, *verb*.]
▸ **A** *noun*. A marginal note, an annotation. E16.
▸ **B** *verb trans*. Infl. **-l(l)-**. Annotate; inscribe with marginal notes. M17.

apostle /əˈpɒs(ə)l/ *noun*. Also **A-** (the usual spelling in biblical usage & in sense 5). OE.
[ORIGIN ecclesiastical Latin *apostolus* from Greek *apostolos* messenger, from *apostellein* send forth: infl. by Old French *apostle*.]
1 In biblical translations: a person sent, a messenger; *spec*. Christ. OE.

NEB *Heb*. 3:1 Think of the Apostle and High Priest of the religion we profess.

2 Each of the twelve witnesses whom Jesus sent out to preach his gospel. Also, Barnabas or Paul. OE.

A

3 Any person who imitates or is held to resemble the Apostles; a pioneering missionary. LME. ▸**b** An advocate or follower of a cause, activity, etc.; a leader of reform. E19.

> A. MACLAINE Boniface has gained the title of the Apostle of Germany. **b** A. J. P. TAYLOR The members of Milner's kindergarten were, in the nineteen-thirties, apostles of appeasement. M. KEANE When I was twenty, foxhunting was Wholly Holy and everybody was an apostle or disciple.

†**4** Any of the books of Acts and Epistles of the Apostles. LME–M19.

5 *hist.* A member of an exclusive conversazione society ('The Apostles') at Cambridge University. E19.

– COMB.: **apostlebird** *Austral.* any of various birds often seen in flocks of about twelve; *spec.* a grey magpie lark, *Struthidea cinerea*; **Apostles' Creed** the simplest and prob. earliest form of the Christian creed, anciently ascribed to the Apostles; **apostle spoon**: with the figure of an Apostle at the end of the handle.

■ **apostlehood** *noun* OE. **apostleship** *noun* E16. †**apostoless**, **apostless** *noun* a female apostle LME–E19. **apostolize** *verb trans. & intrans.* (*rare*) proclaim (a message); act like an apostle: M17.

apostolate /əˈpɒstəleɪt/ *noun*. LME.
[ORIGIN ecclesiastical Latin *apostolatus* from *apostolus*: see APOSTLE, -ATE[1].]
1 The position or office of an apostle. LME.
2 The Apostles collectively; a group comparable to or associated with the Apostles. LME.

apostolic /apəˈstɒlɪk/ *adjective & noun*. Also **A-**. ME.
[ORIGIN French *apostolique* or ecclesiastical Latin *apostolicus* from Greek *apostolikos*, from *apostolos*: see APOSTLE, -IC.]
▸ **A** *adjective*. **1** Of or pertaining to the Apostles; contemporary with the Apostles. ME.
Apostolic Fathers the early leaders of the Christian Church. **apostolic succession** the uninterrupted transmission of spiritual authority through a succession of Popes and bishops from the Apostles. ***Catholic and Apostolic Church***, ***Catholic Apostolic Church***: see CATHOLIC.
2 Of or pertaining to the Pope as successor of St Peter; papal. LME.
3 Of the nature or character of the Apostles; befitting an apostle. M16.
VICAR ***apostolic***.
4 *hist.* Of or pertaining to the Cambridge Apostles. M19.
▸ **B** *noun*. A member of any of various sects seeking to imitate the Apostles. L16.
■ **apostolical** *adjective* LME. **apostolically** *adverb* E17. **apostolicity** /-ˈlɪsɪti/ *noun* apostolic character or origin E19.

apostrophe /əˈpɒstrəfi/ *noun*[1]. M16.
[ORIGIN Latin from Greek *apostrophē*, from *apostrephein* turn away, formed as APO- + *strephein* to turn.]
RHETORIC. Sudden exclamatory address; an exclamatory passage addressed to a particular person (freq. absent or dead) or thing.

apostrophe /əˈpɒstrəfi/ *noun*[2]. Also †**-phus**. M16.
[ORIGIN French, or late Latin *apostrophus* from Greek *apostrophos* mark of elision, use as noun (sc. *prosōdia* accent) of adjective 'turned away', from *apostrephein*: see APOSTROPHE *noun*[1].]
†**1** The omission of one or more letters in a word. M16–M17.
2 A sign (') used to indicate the omission of one or more letters or numerals (as in ***can't***, ***o'er***, ***'cello***; ***spirit of '76*** (i.e. 1776)), or in marking the possessive case (***man's***, ***boys'***). L16.

apostrophic /apəˈstrɒfɪk/ *adjective*. L18.
[ORIGIN from APOSTROPHE *noun*[1], *noun*[2] + -IC.]
1 Of or pertaining to the sign called an apostrophe. L18.
2 Of or pertaining to a rhetorical apostrophe; given to apostrophe. E19.

apostrophize /əˈpɒstrəfʌɪz/ *verb trans. & intrans.* Also **-ise**. E17.
[ORIGIN from APOSTROPHE *noun*[1], *noun*[2] + -IZE.]
1 Mark the omission of letters in (a word) with an apostrophe; omit one or more letters in a word. *rare*. E17.
2 Address (someone or something) in a rhetorical apostrophe; use apostrophe. E18.

†**apostrophus** *noun* var. of APOSTROPHE *noun*[2].

†**apostumate** *verb*. Also **-tem-**, **-thum-**. Pa. pple & ppl adjective **-ate** (earlier), **-ated**. LME.
[ORIGIN medieval Latin *apostemat-* pa. ppl stem of *apostemari*, from *apostema* APOSTUME: see -ATE[3]. Cf. IMPOSTUMATE.]
1 *verb trans. & intrans.* Form into a cyst or abscess; fester. LME–L17.
2 *verb trans.* In *pass.* Be affected by a cyst or abscess. L16–L17.
■ †**apostematous** *adjective* festering; characterized by abscesses: M17–M19.

†**apostumation** *noun*. Also **-tem-**, **-thum-**. LME.
[ORIGIN Old French *apostemation*, *apostumacion* from medieval Latin *apostematio(n-)*, formed as APOSTUMATE: see -ATION. Cf. IMPOSTUMATION.]
1 The formation of a cyst or abscess; festering. LME–L17.
2 A cyst, an abscess. M16–M18.

†**apostume** *noun*. Also **-tem(e)**, **-thume**. LME–M18.
[ORIGIN Old French *aposteme*, *-ume* from Latin *apostema* from Greek = separation of pus into an abscess, from *aposta-*, *apostēnai* withdraw: cf. IMPOSTUME.]
A gathering of pus; a large abscess.

apotelesmatic /əˌpɒt(ə)ləzˈmatɪk/ *adjective*. M17.
[ORIGIN Greek *apotelesmatikos*, from *apotelesma*, from *apotelein* bring to an end, formed as APO- + *telein* finish: see -IC.]
Of or pertaining to the casting of horoscopes.

apothecary /əˈpɒθɪk(ə)ri/ *noun*. *arch.* LME.
[ORIGIN Old French *apotecaire*, *-icaire* (mod. *apothicaire*) from late Latin *apothecarius* storekeeper, from *apotheca* from Greek *apothēkē* storehouse: see -ARY[1].]
1 A person who prepares and sells drugs and other medicinal substances; a pharmaceutical chemist. LME.
apothecaries' measure, **apothecaries' weight** sets of units formerly used in pharmacy for liquid volume (with one fluid ounce = 8 drachms = 480 minims) and for weight (with one ounce = 8 drachms = 24 scruples = 480 grains) respectively.
†**2** Drugs collectively; a store or list of drugs; treatment by drugs. E16–E17.

apothecium /apəˈθiːsɪəm/ *noun*. Pl. **-ia** /-ɪə/. E19.
[ORIGIN mod. Latin from Greek *apothēkē*: see APOTHECARY, -IUM.]
BOTANY. An open cup- or disc-shaped fruiting body borne by many lichens and ascomycetous fungi.
■ **apothecial** *adjective* L19.

apothegm *noun* etc.: see APOPHTHEGM etc.

apothem /ˈapəθɛm/ *noun*. *rare*. L19.
[ORIGIN from Greek *apotithenai* deposit, after *thema*, from *tithenai* to place: see THEME *noun*.]
GEOMETRY. A perpendicular from the centre of a regular polygon to a side.

apotheosis /əpɒθɪˈəʊsɪs/ *noun*. Pl. **-oses** /-ˈəʊsiːz/. L16.
[ORIGIN ecclesiastical Latin from Greek *apotheōsis*, from *apotheoun* deify, from APO- + *theos* god.]
1 (Elevation to) divine status. L16.

> F. W. FARRAR The early Emperors rather discouraged . . this tendency to flatter them by a premature apotheosis.

2 Glorification or exaltation of a person, principle, or practice; canonization; idealization. E17.

> COLERIDGE The apotheosis of familiar abuses . . is the vilest of superstitions. T. HARDY Thus a mild sort of apotheosis took place in his fancy, whilst she still lived and breathed within his own horizon. T. P. O'CONNOR The meeting developed into an apotheosis of the Marquis of Chandos.

3 Ascension to glory, resurrection, triumph; highest development, culmination. M17.

> C. WALKER His Majesties Speech upon the Scaffold, and His Death or Apotheosis. J. BRAINE An actor-manager whom I knew . . as the apotheosis of wholesome masculinity. J. G. FARRELL At any moment the pageant would begin, the triumphant apotheosis of the Empire's struggle for Peace.

■ **aˈpotheose** *verb trans.* (now *rare*) = APOTHEOSIZE L17. **aˈpotheosize** *verb trans.* deify; exalt; idealize: M18.

†**apotome** *noun*. E16.
[ORIGIN Greek *apotomē* cutting off, from *apotemnein* cut off: see APO-, -TOME.]
1 *MUSIC*. A variety of semitone. E16–E19.
2 *MATH*. A difference of two quantities which are commensurable only when raised to a power, e.g. ($\sqrt{2} - 1$). L16–L18.

apotropaic /apətrəˈpeɪɪk/ *adjective*. L19.
[ORIGIN from Greek *apotropaios* averting evil, from *apotrepein* turn away (see APO-), + -IC.]
Intended to avert evil influence; considered to have the power to avert evil influence or ill luck.

a-pout /əˈpaʊt/ *adverb & pred. adjective*. L19.
[ORIGIN from A-[2] + POUT *verb* & *noun*[3].]
Pouting.

†**apozem** *noun*. LME–L19.
[ORIGIN Old French & mod. French *apozème* or late Latin *apozema* from Greek, from *apozein* boil off, from APO- completely + *zein* to boil.]
MEDICINE. A decoction, an infusion.

app /ap/ *noun*. *colloq.* L20.
[ORIGIN Abbreviation.]
COMPUTING. An application, *esp.* an application program.

†**appair** *verb* see IMPAIR *verb*.

appal /əˈpɔːl/ *verb*. Also †**-pale**; ***-ll**. Infl. **-ll-**. ME.
[ORIGIN Old French *apal(l)ir*, from A-[5] + *palir* (mod. *pâlir*) PALE *verb*[2].]
†**1** *verb intrans.* Grow pale, fade; become enfeebled; lose flavour. ME–M19.
†**2** *verb trans.* Make pale; cause to fade; weaken, impair. LME–E18.
3 *verb trans.* Dismay, terrify; horrify, scandalize. Freq. in *pass.* LME.

> SHAKES. *Macb.* A bold one that dare look on that Which might appal the devil. J. B. PRIESTLEY The waste of money appalled him, but he could not help being delighted by the dash and importance of it all. I. MURDOCH I was utterly appalled that Otto could have laid hands upon his wife. S. HILL I was so appalled at the broken buildings and so little worried by the broken bodies. *absol.*: J. KEBLE Thoughts that awe but not appal.

■ **appalling** *adjective* dismaying, shocking; unpleasant: E19. **appallingly** *adverb* E19. **appalment** *noun* (*rare*) L16.

Appalachee *noun & adjective* var. of APALACHEE.

Appalachian /apəˈleɪtʃ(ə)n/ *adjective & noun*. L17.
[ORIGIN from (the same root as) APALACHEE + -AN.]
▸ **A** *adjective*. **1** Designating the extensive system of mountain ranges in the eastern US. Also, of, pertaining to, or characteristic of this system, its region as a whole, or that region's inhabitants. L17.
Appalachian DULCIMER.
2 Designating the Apalachee and other N. American Indian peoples of the eastern US; pertaining to or characteristic of these peoples. M18.
▸ **B** *noun*. **1** In *pl.* The Appalachian mountains, or the region in general. M19.
2 An Appalachian Indian. L19.

appale, **appall** *verb* see APPAL.

Appaloosa /apəˈluːsə/ *noun*. E20.
[ORIGIN Prob. from *Palouse*, a river in Idaho, USA.]
(An animal of) a N. American breed of horse, usu. white with many spots of colour.

appanage /ˈap(ə)nɪdʒ/ *noun*. Also **apan-**. E17.
[ORIGIN Old French & mod. French *apanage*, from *apaner* dower (a daughter) from medieval Latin *appanare* provide with means of subsistence, from Latin *ad* AP-[1] + *panis* bread: see -AGE.]
1 The provision made for the maintenance of the younger children of kings, princes, etc. (usu. a province, jurisdiction, or office). E17.

> E. A. FREEMAN His son received . . the apanage of Cumberland.

2 A natural accompaniment; a special attribute. M17.

> SWIFT Had he thought it fit, That wealth should be the appennage of wit.

3 A dependent territory or property. E19.

> SYD. SMITH Ireland . . the most valuable appanage of our empire. *fig.*: T. E. HULME Landscape was still a toy or an appanage of figure-painting when Turner and Constable arose to reveal its independent power.

4 A perquisite. M19.

> LYTTON Its revenues and its empire will become the appanage of the hardy soldier.

■ **appanaged** *adjective* endowed with an appanage M18.

apparat /apəˈrɑːt/ *noun*. M20.
[ORIGIN Russian from German, formed as APPARATUS.]
The Communist Party machine in the former USSR and other countries.

apparatchik /apəˈratʃɪk/ *noun*. Pl. **-i** /-i/, **-s**. M20.
[ORIGIN Russian, from APPARAT.]
1 A member of the *apparat*; a Communist agent. M20.
2 *transf.* An implementer of party etc. policy; an executive officer. L20.

apparatus /apəˈreɪtəs/ *noun*. Pl. **-uses**, (*rare*) same. E17.
[ORIGIN Latin, from *apparare* make ready, from *ad* AP-[1] + *parare* PREPARE *verb*.]
1 The things collectively necessary for the performance of some activity or function; the equipment used in doing something; a machine, a device. E17.
2 *spec.* ▸**a** Equipment used for scientific experimentation or processes. M17. ▸**b** The organs etc. by which a natural process is carried on. L17. ▸**c** In full ***critical apparatus***, = APPARATUS CRITICUS. E18. ▸**d** Equipment used in athletic, gymnastic, or sporting activities. L19.
a KIPP'S APPARATUS. **b** ***Weberian apparatus***: see WEBERIAN *adjective*[1].
†**3** Preparation. M17–L18.
4 An organization within a political party or state; *esp.* = APPARAT. M20.

apparatus criticus /apəˌreɪtəs ˈkrɪtɪkəs/ *noun phr.* Pl. **apparatus critici** /apəˌreɪtəs ˈkrɪtɪsʌɪ/. M19.
[ORIGIN mod. Latin: see APPARATUS, CRITICAL.]
A collection of material, as variant readings and other palaeographical and critical matter, for the textual study of a document.

apparel /əˈpar(ə)l/ *noun*. ME.
[ORIGIN Old French *apareil* (mod. *app-*), formed as APPAREL *verb*.]
1 Furnishings, trappings; accoutrements, equipment. *arch.* ME. ▸†**b** The outfit or rigging of a ship. ME–L19.

> J. GALSWORTHY The scarlet and green drawing-room, whose apparel made so vivid a setting for their unaccustomed costumes.

†**2** Physical or moral attributes; bearing, stature. ME–E16.
3 Personal outfit or attire; clothing, raiment. Now *literary*. LME.

> A. G. GARDINER He decked himself out in brave apparel to show the world that he was a person of consequence. J. BALDWIN From their apparel the sinfulness of their lives was evident. *fig.*: ADDISON The rude Stile and evil Apparel of this antiquated Song.

4 †**a** Ornamentation, embellishment. LME–L15. ▸**b** An ornament embroidered on certain ecclesiastical vestments. M19.
†**5** The work of making ready; preparations. LME–L15.

apparel /əˈpar(ə)l/ *verb trans. arch.* Infl. **-ll-**, ***-l-**. ME.
[ORIGIN Old French *apareillier* (mod. *app-*), ult. from Latin *ad-* AP-[1] + dim. of *par* equal.]
†**1** Make ready, prepare (*for*); put into proper order. ME–M17.
2 Provide with necessary things; equip. LME. ▸†**b** *spec.* Equip for fighting. LME–L17.
LONGFELLOW Never.. owned a ship so well apparelled.
3 Array with proper clothing; attire, clothe. LME.
AV *Luke* 7:25 They which are gorgeously apparelled, and liue delicately, are in kings courts. *fig.*: WORDSWORTH When meadow, grove, and stream, To me did seem Apparelled in celestial light.
†**4** Embellish, adorn; trick out, dress up (speciously). LME–M18.
fig.: SHAKES. *Com. Err.* Apparel vice like virtue's harbinger.
■ **apparelment** *noun* (*rare*) clothing, garb; equipment, trappings: LME.

apparency /əˈpar(ə)nsi/ *noun.* Now *rare.* LME.
[ORIGIN from Old French *aparence*, *-a(u)nce*, formed as APPEAR, or from late Latin *apparentia* APPEARANCE: see -ENCY.]
1 Outward appearance. LME.
2 The quality or state of being apparent to the senses, or to the mind; visibility. E17.
3 The position of being heir apparent. M18.

apparent /əˈpar(ə)nt/ *adjective & noun.* LME.
[ORIGIN Old French *aparant*, *-ent* (mod. *apparent*) from Latin *apparent-* pres. ppl stem of *apparere* APPEAR: see -ENT.]
▸ **A** *adjective.* **1** Open to sight; plainly visible. *arch.* LME.
G. WITHER An Owl-eyed buzzard that by day is blinde, And sees not things apparant.
2 Manifest to the understanding; evident, obvious; palpable. LME.
C. HAMPTON The man had no taste at all, as was apparent by the morons he'd already chosen. B. ENGLAND His disapproval of the Court is quite apparent. S. HILL It was not apparent how he died, he seemed to have no injuries.
heir apparent a person whose right of inheritance cannot be superseded by the birth of another (cf. ***heir presumptive*** s.v. PRESUMPTIVE *adjective* 1).
†**3** Likely, probable. E16–M18.
4 Seeming; that appears to the mind or senses, as distinct from (but not necessarily opposed to) what really is. Often contrasted with ***real***. M17.
GIBBON His real merit, and apparent fidelity, had gained the confidence both of the prince and people. D. H. LAWRENCE Her nature, in spite of her apparent placidity and calm, was profoundly restless.
apparent* MAGNITUDE. apparent motion, apparent movement** the perceived movement of a body; *spec.* an illusion of movement perceived when viewing a rapid succession of static images. **apparent solar time**, **apparent time**: as calculated by the apparent motion of the sun (cf. ***mean solar time s.v. MEAN *adjective*[2].).
▸ †**B** *noun.* = ***heir apparent*** above. LME–M17.
■ **apparentness** *noun* (*rare*) L16.

apparently /əˈpar(ə)ntli/ *adverb.* LME.
[ORIGIN from APPARENT *adjective* + -LY[2].]
†**1** Visibly, openly. LME–M17.
HOBBES The Prophets.. who saw not God apparently like unto Moyses.
2 Evidently to the understanding; clearly, plainly. *arch.* E16.
F. QUARLES When thou knowest not apparently, judge charitably.
3 Seemingly; in external appearance; as far as one can judge; (parenthetically or modifying a sentence) it would seem (that); (as a comment on a statement or a reply to a question) so it appears. M16.
T. HARDY An elderly woman, apparently his wife. J. B. PRIESTLEY Winter had set in and apparently taken possession for ever. C. S. FORESTER There was a long delay; apparently the officer had some difficulty in getting up the ship's side. DAY LEWIS The great singer had met something of the same difficulty in this apparently simple song.

apparition /apəˈrɪʃ(ə)n/ *noun.* LME.
[ORIGIN Old French & mod. French, or Latin *apparitio(n-)* attendance, service, from *apparit-* pa. ppl stem of *apparere* APPEAR: see -ITION.]
1 The action of appearing or becoming visible, esp. where this is unexpected or unusual. LME. ▸**b** ASTRONOMY. The appearance of a comet or other body after a period of invisibility; the period during which it is visible. M16. ▸†**c** The Epiphany of Christ; the festival commemorating it. E17–E18.
SIR W. SCOTT Presbyterian divines put to the rout by a sudden apparition of the foul fiend. H. G. WELLS The Arabic chroniclers note their apparition upon the Caspian, and give them the name of Russians. V. WOOLF The silent apparition of an ashen-coloured ship. **b** C. SAGAN In 1301, Giotto.. witnessed another apparition of Comet Halley.
†**2** Semblance, appearance; aspect. LME–M17.
R. BOYLE By their whiteishness, to emulate in some measure the apparition of Light. MILTON A dream, Whose inward apparition gently moved My fancy.
3 Something which appears, esp. if remarkable or unexpected; a phenomenon. L15. ▸**b** *spec.* A ghost, a phantom; a supernatural appearance. L16.
GIBBON So strange an apparition excited his surprise and indignation. **b** SHAKES. *Jul. Caes.* I think it is the weakness of mine eyes That shapes this monstrous apparition. J. CLAVELL I thought that I was seeing another apparition, .. a ghost.
†**4** An illusion; a sham. Only in 17.
■ **apparitional** *adjective* of or pertaining to an apparition; spectral, subjective: E19.

apparitor /əˈparɪtə/ *noun.* ME.
[ORIGIN Latin = public servant, from *apparit-*: see APPARITION, -OR.]
1 A servant or attendant of an ecclesiastical or civil court. ME.
2 ROMAN HISTORY. A public servant of a Roman magistrate. M16.
3 A herald, an usher. M16.

appassionate /əˈpaʃ(ə)nət/ *adjective.* Long *arch.* L16.
[ORIGIN Italian *appassionato* (now rare) adjective, formed as AD- + *passione* PASSION *noun*: see -ATE[2].]
Impassioned.

†**appassionate** *verb trans.* M16–M17.
[ORIGIN formed as APPASSIONATE *adjective*: see -ATE[3].]
Inflame with passion.

appeach /əˈpiːtʃ/ *verb.* Long *arch.* ME.
[ORIGIN Anglo-Norman *enpecher* (see A-[7]), Old French *empechier* IMPEACH *verb*. Aphet. to PEACH *verb*.]
1 *verb trans.* Charge, accuse, impeach (*of* or *with* an offence etc.). ME.
†**2** *verb trans.* Impugn, discredit (a person's honour etc.); denounce, inform against (a crime etc.). LME–E18.
†**3** *verb intrans.* Give accusatory evidence. *rare* (Shakes.). Only in E17.

appeal /əˈpiːl/ *noun.* ME.
[ORIGIN Old French *apel* (mod. *appel*), formed as APPEAL *verb*.]
1 The submission of a case to a higher court in the hope of altering the judgement of a lower one; a request to higher authority for alteration of a decision. ME.
appeal to the country: see COUNTRY *noun*. **Court of Appeal** (in England and Wales) a court of law that hears appeals against both civil and criminal judgements from the Crown Courts, High Court, and County Courts. **court of appeals** *US* a court of law in a federal circuit or state to which appeals are taken. ***Lord Justice of Appeal***: see JUSTICE *noun*. ***Lord of Appeal (in Ordinary)***: see LORD *noun*.
2 A call to an authority for vindication or support, or to a witness for corroboration etc.; a call for help, an entreaty, a supplication. ME. ▸**b** CRICKET. A call to an umpire for a decision, *esp.* a request for a batsman to be given out. M19. ▸**c** A request for public donations to support a charity or cause. L19.
BACON The casting up of the eyes.. is a kind of appeal to the Deity. D. STOREY There was real appeal in her voice... She was crying. J. OSBORNE A very moving appeal to all Christians to do all they can to assist in the manufacture of the H-bomb. **c** C. HAMPTON I saw that TV appeal you did a few weeks ago.
3 A calling to account before a legal tribunal; *spec.* a criminal accusation made by a person undertaking to prove it. *obsolete* exc. *hist.* LME.
†**4** A challenge to defend one's honour by fighting. LME–E19.
5 An address *to* a principle, characteristic, etc., in the expectation of a favourable response. M19.
M. R. MITFORD Slavery.. must not be treated by appeals to the passions. T. FRISBY I like the appeal to my old-fashioned feminine instincts.
6 Attractive power or influence. E20.
W. DEEPING She was standing close to him, .. and Kit was conscious of the sudden shock of her appeal. L. DEIGHTON The shape of his face.. would have little appeal to a portraitist.
– COMB.: **appeal court** = ***Court of Appeal(s)***, sense 1 above.

appeal /əˈpiːl/ *verb.* ME.
[ORIGIN Old French *apeler* (mod. *app-*) call, from Latin *appellare* accost, accuse, impeach, appeal to, from *ad-* AP-[1] + *pell-* stem of *pellere* to drive.]
▸ **I** *verb intrans.* (Foll. by *to* a court, person, etc.)
1 Make request to a higher court or authority for alteration of the decision of a lower one; take a case, question, etc., *from* one court, authority, etc., *to* another; make an appeal *against* a verdict etc. ME.
G. O. TREVELYAN The Revising Barrister's.. decisions have never been appealed against. A. J. P. TAYLOR Thus Lloyd George appealed from the ruling classes to 'the people'.
appeal from Philip drunk to Philip sober: see DRUNK *adjective* 1. ***appeal to the country***: see COUNTRY *noun*.
2 Call on an authority for a decision in one's favour. LME. ▸**b** CRICKET. Call on an umpire for a decision; *esp.* request an umpire to give a batsman out. M18.
A. J. P. TAYLOR The Chinese appealed to the League of Nations against Japan.
appeal to Caesar: see CAESAR 1.
3 Call *to* a witness for corroboration; call attention *to* some evidence for confirmation. LME.
SHAKES. *2 Hen. VI* To heaven I do appeal How I have lov'd my King and common-weal. E. WAUGH Her resistance ended when I appealed to the mysteries of my trade.
4 Make entreaty or earnest request (*to* a person *for* something, *to do* something). M16.
T. CROMWELL I appell to your Highnes for mercy. D. H. LAWRENCE She had managed to get his address, so that she could appeal to him in time of distress. *Daily Telegraph* He appealed for anyone who attended the pool.. to come forward.
5 Address oneself *to* a principle, characteristic, etc., in the expectation of a favourable response from a person or group; seek to be attractive or acceptable *to* a particular group. L18.
G. B. SHAW The Sunday papers.. appealed almost exclusively to the lower middle class. I. MURDOCH Appealing to Dora's better nature may turn out to be a difficult operation.
6 Be attractive or pleasing. L19.
Smart Set The speciousness of Betty's words appealed. T. S. ELIOT I happen to know of a vacancy In my own parish.. If it should appeal to you. V. S. PRITCHETT Gothic inevitably appealed to the disorderly minds of the young.
▸ **II** *verb trans.* **7** Call (a person) to answer before a tribunal; accuse (*of* a crime, esp. treason), impeach. *obsolete* exc. *hist.* LME.
SHAKES. *Rich. II* Hast thou sounded him If he appeal the Duke on ancient malice, Or worthily. W. PRYNNE I.. appeale you to the Tribunall of that high Judge above. T. KEIGHTLEY They came before the king.. and appealed of treason the Archbishop of York.
8 Challenge to defend one's honour by fighting. Long *arch.* LME.
SIR W. SCOTT Man to man will I appeal the Norman to the lists.
9 Submit (a case etc.) to a higher court; make an appeal against (a decision etc.). L15.
C. MARLOWE To patient judgments we appeal our plaud. J. BARTH The young barrister.. didn't even think of appealing the judgment until it was too late.
†**10** Call to witness. Only in M17.
MILTON He hath presum'd to appeale.. the testimony of God.
■ **appealaˈbility** *noun* the state or quality of being appealable M20. **appealable** *adjective* able to be appealed against E17. **appealer** *noun* a person who makes an appeal LME. **appealing** *adjective* that appeals; *esp.* attractive, pleasing: L16. **appealingly** *adverb* imploringly; attractively: M19.

appear /əˈpɪə/ *verb & noun.* ME.
[ORIGIN Old French *aper-* tonic stem of *apareir* (mod. *apparoir*) from Latin *apparere*, from *ad* AP-[1] + *parere* come into view.]
▸ **A** *verb intrans.* **1** Come into view, as from concealment, or from a distance; become visible; become evident. ME.
AV *Luke* 1:11 There appeared vnto him an Angel of the Lord. C. S. FORESTER A row of four or five swarthy faces had appeared at the stern of the galley. P. A. SCHOLES When he was about thirty the first signs of deafness appeared. A. KOESTLER Hipparchus.. had seen a new star appear in the sky. B. MALAMUD Then one day.. there appeared a sign in the empty store window.
2 Be visible; be displayed; be located, occur; manifest itself (*as*). LME.
D. H. LAWRENCE A wide plate-glass door, .. in the round arch of which the words: 'Manchester House' should appear large and distinguished. R. V. JONES It was no artefact for it appeared on two separate photographs.
3 Present oneself formally before an authority; come before a court etc. Also, act as legal representative *for* someone. LME.
STEELE Many.. are known to have Ill-will to him for whom I appear. E. WAUGH Bound over to appear in a week's time. J. LE CARRÉ I supposed he didn't want any mud raked up by Mundt appearing at the Old Bailey.
4 Present oneself publicly; put in an appearance. LME. ▸**b** *spec.* Come before the public as an author. L17. ▸**c** Be published, be issued, become available. E18. ▸**d** *spec.* Come before the public as an actor, performer, participant in a broadcast, etc. E18.
D. DU MAURIER 'You can't possibly not appear' 'No.., I'm not coming down. I can't face them.' S. HILL Kathleen did not appear to tea, and Isabel was sent in search of her. **c** E. WAUGH Many years later, there appeared the first massive volume of his.. work on Byzantine Art. E. F. SCHUMACHER The existence of 'goods' which never appear on the market. **d** A. JACOBS Italian tenor who.. appeared in Britain from 1902, U.S.A. from 1903. A. S. BYATT I think he will ask you to appear on his programme. *Encycl. Brit.* Garrick appeared.. in Thomas Southerne's *Oroonoko* as Aboan, a noble savage.
b appear in print: see PRINT *noun*.
5 Be clear or evident to the understanding; be manifest. LME.
SHAKES. *Merch. V.* It doth appear you are a worthy judge. MILTON Our greatness will appear Then most conspicuous.
6 (In some uses as copular verb.) Seem to the mind, be perceived as, be considered; seem outwardly or superficially (but not be in reality). Foll. by *to be*, *to do*, *that*, *as if*, *as though*. Also *impers.* with *it*. LME.

D. HUME Solely, as it appears, for what you believe to be for our advantage. J. TYNDALL Raindrops which descend vertically appear to meet us when we move swiftly. T. HARDY Oak, not to appear unnecessarily disagreeable, stayed a little while. H. FRENCH They appear as though they had been written in red. G. ORWELL He caught a glimpse of the girl, . . at the far end of the room. She appeared not to have seen him. HARPER LEE He could . . appear tall if height was part of the devilry required. D. STOREY If you must appear the busy executive, you must. S. BARSTOW It appears they live in Essex and this is the first time they've stayed on the Yorkshire coast.

appear in the light of: see LIGHT *noun*.

▸ **B** *noun*. Appearance. *rare*. E17.

■ **appearer** *noun* E17. **appearingly** *adverb* (*obsolete* exc. *dial.*) †(***a***) visibly; (***b***) apparently: LME.

appearance /əˈpɪər(ə)ns/ *noun*. LME.
[ORIGIN Old French *aparance*, *-ence* (mod. *apparence*) from late Latin *apparentia*, from Latin *apparent-* pres. ppl stem of *apparere*: see APPEAR (to which assim. in form). Cf. APPARENCY.]

1 The action of coming into view or becoming visible or evident. LME.

E. A. FREEMAN The appearance of the fleet was unlooked for. J. BUCHAN I had not seen him approach, and the sudden appearance made me start.

2 The action of appearing formally at any proceedings, e.g. in court. LME.

B. ENGLAND His appearance before this court will in no way affect his official knowledge of these proceedings.

3 The action or state of seeming or appearing to be (to the eyes or mind); semblance. LME. ▸†**b** Likelihood, probability. LME–L18. ▸†**c** Viewpoint, opinion. LME–E17.

AV 1 *Thess.* 5:22 Abstaine from all appearance of euill. P. H. JOHNSON They gave every appearance of happiness, of a problem solved, but I felt sure that another problem lay behind it.

4 State or form as perceived; look, aspect; in *pl.*, circumstances as they appear, the look of things in general. LME.

SOUTHEY All appearances Denote alarm and vigilance. A. WILSON Isobel was deeply distressed at her brother's tired, grey appearance. J. LE CARRÉ He took less care of his appearance and less notice of his surroundings.

5 Outward show or aspect (opp. ***reality***). LME.

G. ORWELL We bring him over to our side, not in appearance, but genuinely, heart and soul. S. HILL Alida appears to be a new woman, but is it only an appearance?

6 Something which appears; a phenomenon; an apparition. L15.

SHAKES. *2 Hen. IV* Whose well-labouring sword Had three times slain th' appearance of the King. W. COWPER I am . . a great observer of natural appearances.

†**7** A gathering of people; an attendance. L16–L18.

EVELYN An innumerable appearance of gallants.

8 A conspicuous display; show. L16.

STEELE I gratify the vanity of all who pretend to make an Appearance.

9 The action or an instance of coming before the world or the public in any way; being present, participating. L17. ▸**b** Publication, issue, being made available. L19.

JAMES SULLIVAN 'The first great event in history,' says Berosus, 'was the appearance of Oannes.' B. JAMES The match featured the first appearance of . . Bobby Charlton. G. ABRAHAM Increasing deafness . . inhibited Beethoven's appearances as a virtuoso. **b** F. PALGRAVE The appearance of his first book.

10 Visible occurrence; a manifestation. M19.

E. A. FREEMAN The single appearance of the word in Domesday is the earliest instance.

– PHRASES: **keep up appearances** maintain artificially an outward show of normality etc. so as to conceal the true state of affairs. **make an appearance**, **put in an appearance** be present, esp. briefly; turn up. **save appearances** = ***keep up appearances*** above. **to all appearance(s)** so far as can be seen.
– COMB.: **appearance money**: paid to a performer merely for taking part in a particular event.

appeasable /əˈpiːzəb(ə)l/ *adjective*. M16.
[ORIGIN Old French *apaisable*, from *apaisier*: see APPEASE, -ABLE.]
Able to be appeased.

appease /əˈpiːz/ *verb*. ME.
[ORIGIN Anglo-Norman *apeser*, Old French *apaisier* (mod. *apaiser*), from A-[5] + *pais* PEACE *noun*.]

1 *verb trans.* Settle (strife or disorder); calm or pacify (persons in conflict). ME.

2 *verb trans.* Assuage or allay (anger or displeasure); propitiate (an angry person). LME.

LD MACAULAY The king was silenced, but not appeased.

3 *verb trans.* Relieve or soothe (pain, suffering; †the part suffering, †the sufferer). LME.

4 *verb trans.* Satisfy (a demand, prejudice, etc.); pacify or placate (a person) by acceding to his or her demands etc. LME.

New Statesman He took a different view of the Nazis, whom he thought we could successfully appease.

†**5** *verb intrans.* Be pacified, calmed; abate. LME–M17.

■ **appeaser** *noun* a person who or thing which appeases; *spec.* a person who supports a policy of appeasement: LME. **appeasive** *adjective* tending to appease; propitiatory: E17.

appeasement /əˈpiːzm(ə)nt/ *noun*. LME.
[ORIGIN Old French *apaisement*, from *apaisier*: see APPEASE, -MENT.]

1 The action or process of appeasing. LME. ▸**b** POLITICS. A policy of making concessions to a potential aggressor in order to preserve peace; *spec.* such a policy pursued by Britain towards Nazi Germany prior to the outbreak of war in 1939. Often *derog.* E20.

†**2** A means of appeasing. M16–L17.

3 A state of pacification or satisfaction. *arch.* L16.

appellant /əˈpɛl(ə)nt/ *adjective & noun*. LME.
[ORIGIN Old French *apelant* pres. pple of *apeler* APPEAL *verb*: see -ANT[1].]

▸ **A** *adjective*. **1** Making an appeal; *esp.* appealing to a higher court; *hist.* accusing, challenging. Freq. ***postpositive***. LME.

2 Concerned with appeals; appellate. L18.

▸ **B** *noun*. **1** A person who formally accuses another of treason or felony (*hist.*), or of negligence etc. in a maritime court. LME. ▸†**b** A challenger. LME–L17.

Lords Appellant(s): see LORD *noun*.

2 A person who makes an appeal to a higher court or authority. E17.

3 *gen.* A person who makes an entreaty or request. E18.

appellate /əˈpɛlət/ *adjective*. LME.
[ORIGIN Latin *appellatus* pa. pple, formed as APPELLATE *verb*: see -ATE[2].]

†**1** Appealed against, accused. *rare*. LME–E18.

2 Appealed to; concerned with appeals. M18.

■ †**appellatory** *adjective & noun* (***a***) *adjective* pertaining to an appellant; of the nature of an appeal; (***b***) *noun* a letter of appeal: L16–M18.

appellate /ˈapəleɪt/ *verb trans. rare*. M18.
[ORIGIN Latin *appellat-* pa. ppl stem of *appellare* APPEAL *verb*: see -ATE[3].]
Call, designate.

appellation /apəˈleɪʃ(ə)n/ *noun*. LME.
[ORIGIN Old French & mod. French from Latin *appellatio(n-)*, formed as APPELLATE *verb*: see -ATION.]

1 The action of appealing (esp. in legal senses); an appeal. *arch.* LME.

2 A designation, a name, a title. LME. ▸**b** The action of calling by a name; nomenclature. L16.

appellation contrôlée /apɛlasjɔ̃ kɔ̃trole/ *noun phr.* M20.
[ORIGIN French = controlled appellation.]
(A guarantee of) the description of a bottle of French wine (or other item of food) in conformity with statutory regulations as to its origin. Also ***appellation d'origine contrôlée*** /dɔriʒin/.

appellative /əˈpɛlətɪv/ *adjective & noun*. LME.
[ORIGIN Late Latin *appellativus*, formed as APPELLATE *verb*: see -ATIVE.]

▸ **A** *adjective*. **1** Designating a class of things, people, etc., in general; (of a noun) common (opp. ***proper***). LME.

†**2** Of the nature of a descriptive name or appellation. L16–M17.

3 Of or pertaining to the giving of names. *rare*. M19.

▸ **B** *noun*. **1** A common noun. L16.

2 An appellation or descriptive name. L16.

■ **appellatively** *adverb* as an appellative E17.

appellee /apəˈliː, apɛˈliː/ *noun*. M16.
[ORIGIN from French *appelé* pa. pple of *appeler* APPEAL *verb*: see -EE[1].]
LAW. **1** A person who is formally accused or challenged by another. Now *arch.* exc. in a maritime court. M16.

2 The defendant in a case taken to a higher court. Cf. RESPONDENT. Chiefly *US*. E17.

appellor /apəˈlɔː, əˈpɛlɔː/ *noun*. Now *arch.* or *hist.* LME.
[ORIGIN Anglo-Norman *apelour* = Old French *apeleor* from Latin *appellator*, formed as APPELLATE *verb* + -OR.]
LAW. A person who formally accuses or challenges another.

append /əˈpɛnd/ *verb trans*. LME.
[ORIGIN Latin *appendere* hang to, from *ad* AP-[1] + *pendere* hang.]

1 Hang on, attach as a pendant, affix. LME.

CARLYLE A Conquering Hero, to whom Fate has malignantly appended a tin-kettle of Ambition.

2 Join on, annex. L18.

S. JOHNSON Hales-Owen . . was appended . . to a distant county.

3 Add, esp. in writing. M19.

J. S. MILL Some additional remarks . . are appended. SCOTT FITZGERALD 'They carried him into my house,' appended Jordan, 'because we lived just two doors from the church.' M. MUGGERIDGE He even appended his signature to a memorandum calling for drastic action on the Government's part.

■ †**appension** *noun* the action or process of appending LME–E18.

appendage /əˈpɛndɪdʒ/ *noun*. M17.
[ORIGIN from APPEND + -AGE.]
Something attached; a subsidiary adjunct; an addition; an accompaniment.

W. CAVE Confirmation . . ever was a constant appendage to Baptism. W. DERHAM Clothing, another necessary Appendage of Life. JOYCE A strong suspicion of nose-paint about the nasal appendage. G. B. SHAW Rather than be reduced to a mere appendage of a big American concern, we might fight for our independence.

■ **appendaged** *adjective* having an appendage L18.

appendance /əˈpɛnd(ə)ns/ *noun*. Also **-ence**. E16.
[ORIGIN Old French *apendance*, from *apendre*: see APPENDANT, -ANCE.]

†**1** A dependent possession. E16–M17.

†**2** An appendage. M16–L17.

3 LAW. The fact of being appendant. M19.

■ **appendancy**, **-ency** *noun* (now *rare*) †(***a***) = APPENDANCE 1, 2; (***b***) = APPENDANCE 3: E17.

appendant /əˈpɛnd(ə)nt/ *adjective & noun*. Also **-ent**. LME.
[ORIGIN Old French *apendant* (mod. *app-*), from *apendre* depend on, belong to, formed as APPEND: see -ANT[1].]

▸ **A** *adjective*. (Foll. by *to*, *on*.)

1 LAW. Attached or belonging to a possession or tenure as an additional but subsidiary right. LME.

2 Pertinent, attendant, consequent. E16.

3 Hanging attached. M16.

4 Attached in a subordinate capacity; annexed. L16.

▸ **B** *noun*. *arch.*

1 LAW. A lesser right or property attached by prescription to one more important. L15.

2 An addition, an adjunct, an appendage, an appendix; a dependency. L16.

3 A dependant. L16.

4 A natural consequence; a corollary. L16.

appendectomy /ap(ə)nˈdɛktəmi/ *noun*. Chiefly *N. Amer.* L19.
[ORIGIN from APPENDIX + -ECTOMY.]
MEDICINE. = APPENDICECTOMY.

appendence *noun*, **appendent** *adjective* vars. of APPENDANCE, APPENDANT.

appendical /əˈpɛndɪk(ə)l/ *adjective*. Now *rare*. M19.
[ORIGIN formed as APPENDICECTOMY + -AL[1].]
Of, pertaining to, or of the nature of an appendix.

appendicectomy /əpɛndɪˈsɛktəmi/ *noun*. L19.
[ORIGIN from Latin *appendic-*, APPENDIX *noun* + -ECTOMY.]
Surgical removal of the vermiform appendix; an instance of this.

appendices *noun pl.* see APPENDIX *noun*.

appendicitis /əpɛndɪˈsʌɪtɪs/ *noun*. L19.
[ORIGIN formed as APPENDICECTOMY + -ITIS.]
Inflammation of the vermiform appendix.

appendicle /əˈpɛndɪk(ə)l/ *noun*. E17.
[ORIGIN Latin *appendicula* dim. of *appendic-*, APPENDIX *noun*: see -CULE.]
A small appendix or appendage.

appendicular /ap(ə)nˈdɪkjʊlə/ *adjective*. M17.
[ORIGIN formed as APPENDICLE + -AR[1].]

1 Of, pertaining to, or of the nature of an appendage or appendicle. M17.

2 Of or pertaining to a limb or limbs. L19.

appendicularian /ˌap(ə)ndɪkjəˈlɛːrɪən/ *noun & adjective*. L19.
[ORIGIN from mod. Latin *Appendicularia*, a typical genus, formed as APPENDICLE + -AN.]
ZOOLOGY. ▸**A** *noun*. A member of the class Larvacea of minute free-swimming planktonic tunicates. L19.
▸ **B** *adjective*. Of or pertaining to this class. L19.

appendiculate /ap(ə)nˈdɪkjʊlət/ *adjective*. E19.
[ORIGIN formed as APPENDICLE + -ATE[2].]
BIOLOGY. Having appendages or appendicles; forming an appendage or appendicle.

appendix /əˈpɛndɪks/ *noun & verb*. M16.
[ORIGIN Latin *appendix*, *-dic-*, formed as APPEND.]

▸ **A** *noun*. Pl. **-dices** /-dɪsiːz/, **-dixes**.

1 An addition to a book or document, having some contributory value, but not essential to completeness. M16.

†**2** A subsidiary non-material addition, accompaniment, or consequence. M16–L17.

ROBERT BURTON Idleness is an appendix to nobility.

3 A subsidiary external adjunct; a dependent possession or territory. L16.

CONAN DOYLE I am a brain, Watson. The rest of me is a mere appendix. L. DURRELL The whole island is geologically simply an appendix to the Anatolian continent which has at some time been broken off and set free to float.

4 ANATOMY. A small process developed from the surface of an organ; *spec.* (more fully ***vermiform appendix***) the short thin blind tube extending from the caecum. E17.

SIR T. BROWNE The appendices or beards in the calicular leaves. G. B. SHAW The surgeon . . can remove the appendix or the uvula, and leave the patient none the worse.

▸ **B** *verb trans.* Add as an appendix. *rare*. M18.

apperceive /apəˈsiːv/ *verb trans*. ME.
[ORIGIN Old French *aperceveir* (mod. *apercevoir*) ult. from Latin *ad* AP-[1] + *percipere* perceive.]

1 Observe, notice, perceive. Long *rare*. ME.

2 PSYCHOLOGY. Comprehend by apperception. L19.

apperception /apə'sɛpʃ(ə)n/ *noun*. M18.
[ORIGIN French *aperception* or mod. Latin *apperceptio(n-)* (Leibniz), formed as AP-[1] + PERCEPTION.]
1 The mind's perception of itself. M18.
2 Mental perception, recognition. M19.
3 PSYCHOLOGY. The active mental process of assimilating an idea (esp. one newly perceived) to a body of ideas already possessed, and thereby comprehending it. L19.
Thematic Apperception Test: see THEMATIC *adjective*.
■ **apperceptive** *adjective* (PSYCHOLOGY) of or pertaining to apperception L19.

†**apperil** *noun*. *rare*. E17–M19.
[ORIGIN from A-[11] + PERIL.]
Peril.

appertain /apə'teɪn/ *verb*. LME.
[ORIGIN Old French *apartenir* (mod. *app-*) from Proto-Romance var. of late Latin *appertinere*, formed as AP-[1] + PERTAIN.]
▸ **I** *verb intrans*. Foll. by *to*.
1 Be related, be akin. *arch*. LME.
AV *Num*. 16:32 All the men that appertained vnto Korah.
2 Belong as a possession, right, or privilege. LME.
HOBBES Shall not all Judicature appertain to Christ? R. FIRBANK Prior to the Reformation the farm buildings . . had appertained . . to the Abbots of St. Veronica.
3 Belong naturally, be appropriate. LME.
SHAKES. *Much Ado* Do all rites That appertain unto a burial. D. LESSING Psychological characteristics that are considered as appertaining to one sex rather than another. *absol.*: AV *1 Esd*. 1:12 They rosted the Passeouer with fire, as appertaineth.
4 Pertain, relate. LME.
CHAUCER A certein nombre of conclusions apertenyng to the same instrument. J. CONRAD All that appertained to her haunted me . . , her whole form in the familiar pose, her very substance in its colour and texture.
▸ **II** *verb trans*. †**5** Belong to, become, befit. LME–E17.
■ †**appertainance** *noun* = APPURTENANCE E16–M19.

appertinent *adjective & noun* see APPURTENANT.

appestat /'apɪstat/ *noun*. M20.
[ORIGIN from APPE(TITE + -STAT, perh. after *thermostat*.]
PHYSIOLOGY. A region of the brain (possibly in the hypothalamus) which is believed to control a person's appetite for food.

appetence /'apɪt(ə)ns/ *noun*. E17.
[ORIGIN French *appétence* or formed as APPETENCY: see -ENCE.]
= APPETENCY 2.

appetency /'apɪt(ə)nsi/ *noun*. E17.
[ORIGIN Latin *appetentia* longing after, from *appetere*: see APPETITE, -ENCY.]
1 Natural tendency, affinity; instinctive inclination or propensity. *arch*. E17.
2 The state or action of desiring; passion; an appetite, a craving. (Foll. by *after*, *for*, †*of*.) M17.
I. D'ISRAELI Fanaticism and robbery . . will satiate their appetency for blood and plunder. D. MASSON An appetency after literary distinction. M. INNES The magical and irrational appetencies which make up nine-tenths of the content of the human mind.

appetent /'apɪt(ə)nt/ *adjective*. LME.
[ORIGIN Latin *appetent-* pres. ppl stem of *appetere*: see APPETITE, -ENT.]
Eagerly desirous. (Foll. by *after*, *of*.)

appetible /'apɪtɪb(ə)l/ *adjective*. Now *rare* or *obsolete*. L15.
[ORIGIN Latin *appetibilis* desirable, from *appetere*: see APPETITE, -IBLE.]
†**1** Impelling. Only in L15.
2 Desirable. E17.
■ †**appetibility** *noun* desirableness E17–E19.

appetise *verb*, **appetiser** *noun*, **appetising** *adjective* vars. of APPETIZE etc.

appetite /'apɪtʌɪt/ *noun*. ME.
[ORIGIN Old French *apetit* (mod. *appétit*) from Latin *appetitus* desire towards, from *appetit-* pa. ppl stem of *appetere* seek after, from *ad* AP-[1] + *petere* seek.]
Foll. by *for* (†*of*, †*to*, †*to do*).
1 (A) desire to satisfy a natural need, esp. for food or for sexual pleasure; an instinctive craving; capacity for food, sexual activity, etc. ME.
ADDISON The most violent Appetites in all Creatures are Lust and Hunger. P. G. WODEHOUSE I can't explain till I've had something to eat. You idle rich don't realize it, but working gives one an appetite. J. HERSEY He gained back some of the weight he lost, but his appetite remained only fair. J. HELLER She picked without appetite at her small salad. R. GRAYSON Suji's sexual appetite is formidable.
2 *gen*. A desire, an inclination, a disposition. LME.
J. LYLY I have an appetite it were best for me to take a nap. G. GROTE Obeying without reflection the appetite of the moment. K. TYNAN A pitiful spectacle which has bred in modern audiences an appetite for pathos that amounts to an addiction.
†**3** A natural tendency of a thing towards a state etc. LME–M17.
BACON In all Bodies, there is an Appetite of Union.
4 An object of desire or longing. *arch*. LME.
WORDSWORTH The mountain, and the deep and gloomy wood . . were then to me An appetite.
■ **appe'titious** *adjective* (*rare*) belonging to appetite, appetizing M17.

appetition /apə'tɪʃ(ə)n/ *noun*. E17.
[ORIGIN Latin *appetitio(n-)* strong desire after, from *appetit-*: see APPETITE, -ITION.]
Chiefly PHILOSOPHY. The directing of any kind of desire towards an object or purpose.

appetitive /ə'pɛtɪtɪv/ *adjective*. M16.
[ORIGIN French *appétitif* or medieval Latin *appetitivus*, from *appetit-*: see APPETITE, -IVE.]
Characterized by appetite.

appetize /'apɪtʌɪz/ *verb trans*. Chiefly *Scot*. & *N. English*. Also **-ise**. M18.
[ORIGIN Back-form. from APPETIZING.]
Give an appetite to. Chiefly as ***appetized*** *ppl adjective*.

appetizer /'apɪtʌɪzə/ *noun*. Also **-iser**. M19.
[ORIGIN from APPETIZE + -ER[1].]
Something eaten or drunk to stimulate the appetite.

appetizing /'apɪtʌɪzɪŋ/ *adjective*. Also **-ising**. M17.
[ORIGIN from Old French & mod. French *appétissant* with ending assim. to -IZE, -ING[2].]
Exciting a desire, esp. for food; stimulating the appetite.
■ **appetizingly** *adverb* L19.

applaud /ə'plɔːd/ *verb*. L15.
[ORIGIN Partly from Latin *applaudere*, from *ad* AP-[1] + *plaudere* to clap, partly after French *applaudir*.]
1 *verb trans*. Express approval of, as by clapping hands; approve of, praise. L15.
ADDISON They . . applaud themselves for the Singularity of their Judgment. M. EDGEWORTH I applaud him for standing forward in defence of his friend. A. PATON John Kumalo sits down, and the people applaud him, a great wave of shouting and clapping. J. K. GALBRAITH Audiences of all kinds most applaud what they like best.
†**2** *verb intrans*. Assent *to*; give approbation *to*. M16–L17.
SPENSER The people standing all about . . doe thereto applaud.
3 *verb intrans*. Express approval in a loud or lively manner, esp. by clapping hands. L16.
J. B. PRIESTLEY The enraptured audience would not stop applauding.
■ **applauder** *noun* L16. **applaudingly** *adverb* with applause or loud commendation M18.

applause /ə'plɔːz/ *noun*. LME.
[ORIGIN Latin *applausus*, from *applaus-* pa. ppl stem of *applaudere*: see APPLAUD.]
1 Approbation loudly expressed, esp. by clapping hands; marked approval. LME.
WELLINGTON He has always conducted himself in such a manner as to gain my applause. D. M. THOMAS They took their bows to warm, if not tumultuous, applause.
†**2** An acclamation; a commendation. E17–L18.
POPE Loud applauses rend the vaulted sky.
†**3** An object of approval. *rare*. Only in E17.
JONSON The applause! delight! the wonder of our Stage.
■ **applausive** *adjective* (**a**) (loudly) expressive of approval; †(**b**) worthy of approval: L16. **applausively** *adverb* (*rare*) M18.

apple /'ap(ə)l/ *noun & verb*.
[ORIGIN Old English *æppel*, corresp. to Old Frisian, Old Saxon, Middle Dutch & mod. Dutch *appel*, Old High German *apful* (German *Apfel*), Old Norse *epli*, Crimean Gothic *apel*, from Germanic: cognates in other Indo-European langs.]
▸ **A** *noun*. **1** The round firm fruit of a tree of the rose family, *Malus domestica*, cultivated in innumerable varieties in the temperate zones. Also, an apple tree. OE.
2 Any fruit, *esp*. one which in some respects resembles an apple. Also, a gall. Usu. with specifying word in particular names, e.g. ***oak apple***, ***thorn apple***. OE.
balsam apple, ***crab apple***, ***custard apple***, ***May apple***, ***pineapple***, etc.
3 The forbidden fruit of the tree of knowledge of good and evil (*Genesis* 3:6). OE.
– PHRASES: ***Adam's apple***: see ADAM *noun*. **apple of discord** a subject of dissension (from the golden apple inscribed 'for the fairest' contended for by Hera, Athene, and Aphrodite). ***apple of love***: see LOVE *noun*. **apple of one's eye**, **apple of the eye** †(**a**) the pupil; (**b**) the person or thing most cherished. **apple of Peru** (**a**) a Peruvian plant of the nightshade family, *Nicandra physalodes*, bearing bluish flowers and round brown fruit; (**b**) *N. Amer*. the thorn apple, *Datura stramonium*. **apple of Sodom**, **Sodom apple** = ***DEAD SEA fruit***. **apples (and pears)** *rhyming slang* stairs. **(as) sure as God made little apples** *colloq*. with complete certainty. ***Sodom apple***: see ***apple of Sodom*** above. **the Apple**, **the Big Apple** *US slang* New York City. ***WAGENER apple***. See also APPLES.
– COMB.: **apple-bee** *dial*. a wasp; **apple brandy** spirit distilled from cider; **apple butter** *N. Amer*. a spread of spiced stewed apple, usu. made with cider; **apple cart** a cart for carrying apples; ***upset someone's apple cart***, ***upset the apple cart***, (fig.) spoil someone's plans, ruin an undertaking; **apple green** *adjective & noun* yellowish green; **apple head** a domed head found in certain breeds of small dog; **applejack** (**a**) *N. Amer*. apple brandy; (**b**) *dial*. sliced apple baked in pastry; †**apple-john** [said to be ripe on St John's Day] a kind of apple eaten when much withered; **apple-peru** *N. Amer*. = ***apple of Peru*** (b) above; **apple-polisher** *N. Amer*. a toady; **apple sauce** (**a**) apples stewed to a pulp; (**b**) *N. Amer*. insincere flattery, nonsense; †**apple-squire** a pimp; **apple strudel** baked spiced apples in flaky pastry; **apple tree** (**a**) a tree which bears apples; (**b**) *Austral*. any of various indigenous trees, chiefly eucalypts; **apple woman** a woman who sells apples from a stall.
▸ **B** *verb*. **1** *verb trans. & intrans*. Form or turn into apples; bear apples. OE. ▸**b** Of a turnip: swell into globular shape. Now *rare* or *obsolete*. E18.
2 *verb intrans*. Gather apples. L18.

apple pie /ap(ə)l'pʌɪ; *as adjective* 'ap(ə)lpʌɪ/ *noun & adjective*. L16.
[ORIGIN from APPLE + PIE *noun*[2].]
▸ **A** *noun*. **1** A pie with a filling of apples. L16.
2 The great willowherb, *Epilobium hirsutum*. Also ***apple-pie plant***. (From the odour of its flowers and shoots.) *dial*. M19.
– COMB. & PHRASES: **apple-pie bed** a bed made as a practical joke, with sheets so folded that one's legs cannot be stretched out; **apple-pie order** perfect order; ***MOTHERHOOD and apple pie***.
▸ **B** *attrib*. or as *adjective*. Representing or displaying homespun conservative virtues regarded as traditionally American. M20.

apples /'ap(ə)lz/ *adjective*. *Austral. & NZ slang*. M20.
[ORIGIN Pl. of APPLE *noun*.]
Satisfactory, all right, fine.
T. A. G. HUNGERFORD How's it going, Wally? Everything apples?

applet /'aplɪt/ *noun*. L20.
[ORIGIN from APP(LICATION *noun* + -LET.]
COMPUTING. A small application program, esp. one that executes a single task within a larger application.

Appleton layer /'ap(ə)lt(ə)n ˌleɪə/ *noun phr*. M20.
[ORIGIN Edward V. *Appleton* (1892–1965), Brit. physicist.]
= ***F-layer*** s.v. F, F 7.

appliable /ə'plʌɪəb(ə)l/ *adjective*. *arch*. LME.
[ORIGIN from APPLY + -ABLE.]
†**1** Compliant, accommodating, favourably disposed; ready and willing. Cf. PLIABLE. LME–L17.
2 Able to be applied; having reference, pertinent. L15.

applial /ə'plʌɪəl/ *noun*. *rare*. M16.
[ORIGIN formed as APPLIABLE + -AL[1].]
Application; a request.

appliance /ə'plʌɪəns/ *noun*. M16.
[ORIGIN from APPLY + -ANCE.]
1 The bringing to bear of some technique or agency; application, use, putting into practice. M16.
CARLYLE The human soul . . could be acted-on . . by the appliance of birch-rods.
2 A thing applied as means to an end; a device, a utensil, an apparatus. L16. ▸**b** *spec*. A fire engine. L19.
SHAKES. *Hen. VIII* Ask God for temp'rance; that's th' appliance only Which your disease requires. J. CHEEVER Neither of them understood the mechanics of radio—or of any of the other appliances that surrounded them.
†**3** Compliance; (an act of) subservience. Only in E17.
SHAKES. *Meas. for M*. Too noble to conserve a life In base appliances.
■ **applianced** *adjective* equipped with domestic appliances M20.

†**appliant** *adjective*. LME.
[ORIGIN Old French *apliant* pres. pple of *aplier* APPLY: see -ANT[1].]
1 Favourably disposed, willing, compliant; diligent. LME–M17.
2 Applicable, pertinent *to*. *rare*. M16–M19.

applicable /'aplɪkəb(ə)l, ə'plɪk-/ *adjective*. M16.
[ORIGIN Old French & mod. French, or medieval Latin *applicabilis*, from *applicare*: see APPLY, -ABLE.]
†**1** = APPLIABLE 1. M16–M18.
2 Able to be applied (*to* a purpose etc.); having reference, relevant. L16.
3 Suitable, appropriate. M19.
■ **applica'bility** *noun* the quality of being applicable; pertinence: M17. **applicableness** *noun* (*rare*) M17. **applicably** *adverb* (*rare*) so as to be applied; pertinently, suitably: M18.

applicant /'aplɪk(ə)nt/ *noun*. E19.
[ORIGIN from APPLICATION + -ANT[1].]
A person who applies or makes a formal request.

applicate /'aplɪkət, -keɪt/ *pa. pple & ppl adjective*. *arch*. LME.
[ORIGIN Latin *applicatus* pa. pple, from *applicat-*: see APPLICATION, -ATE[2].]
Applied; applicable.

application /aplɪ'keɪʃ(ə)n/ *noun*. LME.
[ORIGIN Old French & mod. French from Latin *applicatio(n-)*, from *applicat-* pa. ppl stem of *applicare*: see APPLY, -ATION.]
1 The action of bringing something into material or effective contact with something else; *esp*. the putting on or administration of a medicament. Also, a remedy so

A

applied. LME. ▸**b** GEOMETRY. The placing of a line or figure in contact with another. E18.

J. ABERNETHY I began again to try some medicated applications. J. SCOFFERN The application of heat to the bulb. ANTHONY HUXLEY Well-farmed soils . . contain two to four times more phosphate and potassium than is needed by most crops, following past years of regular application.

2 Use with special reference (*to*); use, employment; a specific use or purpose to which something is put. LME.

S. HILL The forceful novelty of this application of such a difficult word, to himself. C. SAGAN The idea of a code, at least in the usual military intelligence application, is to make a message difficult to read.

3 The bringing of a general or figurative statement, a theory, principle, etc., to bear upon a matter; applicability in a particular case, relevance; the bringing of something to bear practically in a matter, practical operation. Also, a practical lesson or moral. LME.

HOBBES The application of the Law to the present case. J. BUTLER A fable or a parable, related without any application or moral. E. O'NEILL He quotes with great sentiment, if with slight application. A. J. P. TAYLOR A lesson . . which had its application in the wider field of international relations. E. F. SCHUMACHER A fascination with novelties . . which insists on their application long before their long-term consequences are even remotely understood.

4 ASTRONOMY & ASTROLOGY. The action of approaching. L16.
5 The action of applying oneself closely (*to* a task etc.); assiduous effort, attention, diligence. E17.

POPE I am obliged . . to give up my whole application to Homer. A. FRASER He was obviously capable of great application when his interest was aroused.

†**6** An obsequious deference or soliciting of favour. Only in E17.
7 (The making of) a request, esp. of a formal nature. M17.

G. BURNET Frequent applications to God in prayer. ALDOUS HUXLEY Applications for bank credit had been rather disappointing. J. LE CARRÉ A firm . . showed interest in his application for the post of assistant manager and personnel officer.

8 COMPUTING. A specific task performed on behalf of the user of a computer system (as distinct from one performed on behalf of the system itself); any program or piece of software that performs such a task. Also as ***application program***. M20.

applicative /ˈaplɪkeɪtɪv, -kətɪv/ *adjective*. M17.
[ORIGIN from Latin *applicat-* (see APPLICATION) + -IVE.]
Characterized by being applied in some way; practical.

applicator /ˈaplɪkeɪtə/ *noun*. M17.
[ORIGIN formed as APPLICATIVE + -OR.]
A thing which or (*rare*) a person who applies; *esp.* a device for the application of a medication or other substance.

applicatory /ˈaplɪkət(ə)ri/ *adjective*. *arch*. M16.
[ORIGIN formed as APPLICATIVE + -ORY[2].]
1 Having the property of applying something to practical use. Also, applicable. M16.
†**2** Making application or request. M–L17.

applied /əˈplʌɪd/ *adjective*. E16.
[ORIGIN from APPLY + -ED[1].]
†**1** Folded. Only in E16.
2 Put to practical use; having or concerned with practical application. (Opp. ***abstract***, ***pure***, or ***theoretical***.) M17.
3 NEEDLEWORK. Laid on as appliqué. L19.

applier /əˈplʌɪə/ *noun*. M16.
[ORIGIN from APPLY + -ER[1].]
A person who or thing which applies.

appliqué /əˈpliːkeɪ/ *noun & verb*. M18.
[ORIGIN French, use as noun of pa. pple of *appliquer* from Latin *applicare*: see APPLY.]
Chiefly NEEDLEWORK. ▸**A** *noun*. (A piece of) ornamental work cut out from one material and affixed to the surface of another; the technique of ornamenting in this way. M18.
▸**B** *verb trans*. Decorate in this way. Chiefly as ***appliquéd*** *ppl adjective*. L19.

applot /əˈplɒt/ *verb trans*. *arch*. Infl. **-tt-**. M17.
[ORIGIN from PLOT *noun*, app. after *lot*, *allot*.]
Divide into plots or parts; apportion.
■ **applotment** *noun* division into plots M17.

apply /əˈplʌɪ/ *verb*. LME.
[ORIGIN Old French *aplier* from Latin *applicare*, from *ad* AP-[1] + *plicare* to fold.]
▸**I** Of a thing in contact with another.
1 *verb trans*. Put close or in contact. (Foll. by *to*.) LME.
▸**b** GEOMETRY. Bring or construct (a figure etc.) in contact. Foll. by *to* (a line etc.). M17.

JOYCE He applies his handkerchief to his mouth.

apply the brakes: see BRAKE *noun*[7].
2 *verb trans*. Place (a plaster, ointment, etc.) in effective contact with the body (foll. by *to*); administer (a remedy etc., *to*); *transf.* & *fig.* bring effectively to bear on something (foll. by *to*). LME.

SPENSER To Guyon . . Their pleasaunt tunes they sweetly thus applyde. BACON He that will not apply new remedies must expect new evils. T. FULLER To apply comfort to him who is not . . ready for it. JAS. MILL They applied coercion to the English resident. M. LEITCH There was . . no real sign on the outside that force had been applied.

†**3** *verb intrans*. Come or be close; come into or be in contact. Foll. by *to*. LME–L18.
4 *verb trans*. Put *to* a special use or purpose; devote, appropriate, *to*; use in special reference *to*. LME.

MARVELL The Poll money hath likewise been applyd to the use of the warre. G. B. SHAW I wonder why the epithet robber is applied only to barons. You never hear of robber dukes.

5 *verb trans*. Put to use; employ; dispose of. LME.

STEELE Knife or a pistol, if he finds stomach to apply them. S. HILL It's not a word you tend to apply.

6 *verb trans*. Give a specific reference to (a general, theoretical, or figurative statement); use as relevant or suitable; bring to bear practically, put into practical operation. (Foll. by *to*.) LME.

S. JOHNSON Knowledge which he cannot apply will make no man wise. W. FAULKNER How false the most profound book turns out to be when applied to life. T. S. ELIOT A test . . which can only be slowly and cautiously applied. A. J. P. TAYLOR His ideas would have had to be applied by civil servants and industrialists who had no faith in them.

†**7** *verb trans*. Refer, ascribe, *to*. LME–E18.

POPE Thus Wit, like Faith, by each man is apply'd To one small sect, and all are damn'd beside.

8 *verb intrans*. Have a practical bearing; have relevance; refer; be operative. (Foll. by *to*, †*for*.) (*rare* before L18.) L15.

W. PALEY This test applies to every supposition. V. WOOLF Perhaps what he was saying did not apply to pictures. E. O'NEILL Arthur hangs back, as if the designation 'kids' couldn't possibly apply to him. M. SPARK She is above the common moral code, it does not apply to her. A. J. P. TAYLOR The Anglo-Polish alliance specifically did not apply against Russia.

†**9** *verb trans*. Compare, liken, *to*. L16–M17.
▸**II** Of a person in close contact with an activity.
10 *verb trans*. Give or devote (a faculty etc., oneself) assiduously *to*, *to do*. LME.

COVERDALE *Ps*. 89:12 That we maye applie oure hertes vnto wyssdome. J. RAY I applyed my mind to consider . . the physical reason of it. V. NABOKOV With rising appetite, Lo applied herself to the fruit.

11 *verb intrans*. Attend assiduously (*to*). *arch*. L15.

SHAKES. *Macb*. Let your remembrance apply to Banquo. C. BRONTË I found my pupil . . disinclined to apply.

†**12** *verb trans*. Devote one's energy to; wield; practise. L15–M17.

T. ELYOT Quintius . . repaired again to his plough and applied it diligently. MILTON The birds thir quire apply.

†**13** *verb trans*. Supply persistently *with*. M16–L16.
▸**III** Bend, direct.
†**14** *verb trans*. Bend (the mind, oneself) *to*; *refl.* conform *to*, be subservient *to*, adapt *to*. LME–E17.

BACON They fail sometimes in applying themselves to particular persons. P. HEYLIN Applying themselves unto the times, they were alwaies favourable to the strongest.

†**15** *verb intrans*. Comply, adapt, *to*. LME–E17.

J. FOXE If she would applie to his request, she should be . . set at libertie. BACON The precedent state or disposition, unto which we do apply.

†**16** *verb intrans*. & *refl*. Land, arrive, (*at*, *to*); steer, proceed, go, (*to*). LME–E19.
†**17** *verb trans*. Go to, visit. *rare*. Only in 16.

G. CHAPMAN He applied each place so fast.

†**18** *verb trans*. Bring (a ship) to land; direct, steer. L16–E17.

SPENSER To whom his course he hastily applide. W. RALEIGH Light things apply themselves upwards.

19 *verb intrans*. & †*refl*. **a** Appeal *to*, address oneself *to*, give attention *to*. *obsolete* in *gen.* sense. M17. ▸**b** Address oneself for information, help, a service, etc., *to*; make a formal request (*to* someone, *for* or *to do* something); make or submit an application (*to* someone, *for* something). M17.

a S. BUTLER Those who apply to Men's Fancies and Humours. J. SMEATON On applying to the bridle . . we found that the chain was dragging upon the rocks. **b** ADDISON An old Woman applied herself to me for my charity. E. WAUGH Sebastian . . had applied to be taken on as a missionary lay-brother. J. LE CARRÉ A notice came round inviting linguists to apply for specialist service abroad . . . I was fed up with soldiering, so I applied. S. HILL There are state agencies to help you, you must apply to them. J. ORTON Have you applied for compensation?

†**20** *verb trans*. Direct (words) *to*. M17–M18.

MILTON God at last To Satan . . his doom apply'd, Though in mysterious terms.

appoggiatura /əpɒdʒəˈtʊərə/ *noun*. M18.
[ORIGIN Italian, from *appoggiare* lean upon, rest.]
MUSIC. A grace note just above or below a primary note, which it precedes and delays; the use of such notes.

appoint /əˈpɔɪnt/ *verb*. LME.
[ORIGIN Old French *apointer*, from *à point* to a point, into condition: see POINT *noun*[1].]
▸**I** Come, or bring matters, to a point.
†**1** *verb trans*. (in *pass.*) & *intrans*. Agree, settle, arrange definitely. Usu. with inf. or *that*. LME–M17.
2 *verb intrans*. & †*refl*. Make up one's mind, resolve, determine. *arch*. LME.

AV 2 *Sam*. 17:14 The Lord had appointed to defeate the good counsell of Ahithophel.

3 **a** *verb intrans*. Make an appointment *to do* something. *arch*. E16. ▸**b** *verb trans*. Arrange the time or place of (a meeting); arrange to meet (a person). *arch*. E16.

a DICKENS Mr. Bentley went away thanking him and appointing to call again. **b** SHAKES. *Tit. A*. Appoint the meeting Even at his father's house. J. GAY I appointed him at this hour.

▸**II** Determine authoritatively; ordain, decree.
4 *verb trans*. Prescribe, fix (a time or place) for an action. Freq. in *pass*. Cf. APPOINTED 1. LME.

SHAKES. 1 *Hen. IV* We will . . appoint them a place of meeting. DEFOE The time appointed for execution.

5 *verb trans*. Decree, prescribe, fix *that* a thing shall be; ordain (something). Freq. in *pass*. LME.

CARLYLE Strangely . . it is appointed that Sound . . should be the most continuing of all things. J. MCCOSH The laws . . are appointed by God.

6 *verb trans*. Nominate, ordain (a person) *to* an office, *to* act in some capacity; give (a person) an official position; nominate, set up someone as (an officer, trustee, etc.). LME.

C. MERIVALE The Roman citizens appointed to all the higher magistracies. W. S. CHURCHILL President Davis appointed him Commander-in-Chief. A. S. NEILL I appoint teachers and ask them to leave if I think they are not suitable.

7 *verb trans*. Destine, ordain, (*to* a fate or purpose, *to* do or suffer something). *arch*. L15.

AV 1 *Thess*. 5:9 God hath not appointed vs to wrath. DEFOE Next day I was appointed to be tried.

†**8** **a** *verb trans*. Assign or grant authoritatively (a thing *to* a person). L15–M18. ▸**b** *verb trans*. & *intrans*. LAW. Determine the destination of (property), in exercise of a power conferred for that purpose. E16.
▸**III** **9** *verb trans*. Put into proper order, make ready; *esp.* equip completely, furnish, accoutre. *obsolete* exc. as *pa. pple*. LME.

BURKE The house of commons . . is miserably appointed for that service. SIR W. SCOTT Thus appointed . . he was in readiness to depart.

▸**IV** †**10** *verb trans*. Point to; point out. Only in M16.

H. SURREY A blazing sterne . . By a long tract appointing vs the way. T. CRANMER As well as if you had appointed me with your finger.

†**11** *verb trans*. Attribute *to*; attribute blame to. *rare*. Only in 17.

MILTON Appoint not heavenly disposition, father. Nothing of all these evils hath befallen me But justly.

■ **appointable** *adjective* M16. **appoin'tee** *noun* †(*a*) [French *appointé*] a long-serving soldier with a special rate of pay; (*b*) a person who is appointed or nominated to an office; (*c*) LAW a person in whose favour a power of appointment is executed: E18. **appointer** *noun* a person who ordains or nominates E16. **appointive** *adjective* (orig. *N. Amer.*) pertaining to appointment; that is filled by appointment: L19. **appointor** *noun* (LAW) a person who exercises the power of appointment L19.

appointed /əˈpɔɪntɪd/ *ppl adjective*. L15.
[ORIGIN from APPOINT + -ED[1].]
1 Settled or fixed beforehand; ordained. L15.

A. KOESTLER Last year's moth which had miraculously and uselessly survived its appointed life-term. R. SUTCLIFF He arrived at the appointed meeting ground . . to find the other waiting for him.

2 (With qualifying adverb.) Equipped, fitted out. M16.

JOYCE They would have a beautifully appointed drawing-room with pictures and engravings . . and chintz covers for the chairs.

appointment /əˈpɔɪntm(ə)nt/ *noun*. LME.
[ORIGIN Old French *apointement*, formed as APPOINT: see -MENT.]
†**1** **a** Agreeing, coming to an arrangement; an agreement, a contract. LME–M18. ▸**b** *spec*. (Terms of) capitulation. LME–E17.
2 An agreement or arrangement for a meeting; a prearranged meeting. LME.

SHAKES. *Merry W*. For missing your meetings and appointments. N. MITFORD If people did not keep their appointments with him well before the specified time he always counted them as being late. J. BARTH I'd like an appointment to see Dr. Rose just before lunch.

appointment in Samarra: see SAMARRA *noun*[2].
3 **a** The action of ordaining or directing what is to be done; ordinance, decree. *arch*. LME. ▸**b** LAW. The act of determining the destination of any property, in exercise of a power conferred for that purpose. E17. ▸**c** The action

of nominating to or placing in an office or post; the position so given. M17.

a J. BUTLER According to a natural order or appointment. c N. SHUTE It meant a new appointment, his first work for five months. H. MACMILLAN My appointment as Chancellor of the Exchequer . . was announced on 21 December 1955.

c by appointment by or as by royal warrant.

†**4** Purpose, resolution. E16–E17.

5 (An item of) equipment; outfit, furnishing. Now usu. in *pl.* L16.

I. MURDOCH The room . . was spartan in its appointments.

†**6** An allowance paid, esp. to a public official. E18–E19.

apport /əˈpɔːt/ *noun & verb.* LME.

[ORIGIN Old French *aport* action of bringing, from *aporter* bring to.]

▸ **A** *noun.* †**1** Demeanour; bearing. LME–E17.

†**2** Something brought; an offering, revenue. Usu. in *pl.* LME–M16.

3 The production of material objects by supposedly occult means at a seance; an object so produced. Usu. in *pl.* L19.

▸ **B** *verb trans.* †**1** Bring. L16–E17.

2 Produce or transport by supposedly occult means. M20.

apportion /əˈpɔːʃ(ə)n/ *verb trans.* L16.

[ORIGIN Old French & mod. French *apportionner* or medieval Latin *apportionare* from *ad* AP-¹ + *portionare*: see PORTION *verb*.]

1 Assign (*to*) as a due portion; allot. L16.

2 Share, portion out. L16.

†**3** Adjust in due proportion. E17–E19.

■ **apportionable** *adjective* E17. **apportionate** *verb trans.* (now *rare* or *obsolete*) = APPORTION E16. **apportioner** *noun* E17. **apportionment** *noun* the action or result of apportioning; *spec.* the determination of the proportional number of members each US state sends to the House of Representatives, based on population figures: M16.

†**appose** *verb*¹ *trans.* ME.

[ORIGIN Old French *aposer* var. of *oposer* OPPOSE. Aphet. to POSE *verb*².]

1 Confront with objections or hard questions: examine, interrogate. ME–M17.

2 *spec.* Examine as to accounts; audit. E17–M18.

■ †**apposal** *noun* a searching question; enquiry, investigation, *esp.* legal examination of accounts: LME–E19. †**apposer** *noun* a person who apposes; *spec.* an Exchequer officer who audited sheriffs' accounts: LME–M19.

appose /əˈpəʊz/ *verb*² *trans.* L16.

[ORIGIN from Latin *apponere* apply after *compose*, *expose*, etc.: see APPOSITE, POSE *verb*¹.]

1 Put or apply (a thing) *to* another. L16.

2 Place in apposition or juxtaposition. E19.

apposite /ˈapəzɪt/ *adjective & noun.* L16.

[ORIGIN Latin *appositus* pa. pple of *apponere* apply, from *ad-* AP-¹ + *ponere* to place, put.]

▸ **A** *adjective.* **1** Well put or applied; appropriate, suitable. L16.

W. S. MAUGHAM He rehearsed to himself a number of apposite speeches.

†**2** Of a person: ready with apt remarks. M17–L18.

▸ **B** *noun.* Something placed beside or in apposition. *rare.* L17.

■ **appositely** *adverb* M17. **appositeness** *noun* M17.

apposition /apəˈzɪʃ(ə)n/ *noun*¹. LME.

[ORIGIN French, or late Latin *appositio(n-)*, from *apposit-* pa. ppl stem of *apponere*: see APPOSITE, -ION.]

1 The action of putting or applying one thing to another; application. *arch.* LME.

J. AYLIFFE By the Apposition of a Publick Seal.

2 GRAMMAR. The placing of a term in syntactic parallelism with another; *esp.* the declarative or distinguishing addition of one noun to another without explicit coordination; the position of the term added. LME.

L. BLOOMFIELD In English we have also *close* apposition without a pause-pitch, as in *King John, John Brown, John the Baptist, Mr. Brown, Mount Everest*. B. RUBENS 'My son, a linguist'—the apposition was a habit with her.

3 *gen.* The placing of things side by side or in close proximity; the fact or condition of juxtaposition or parallelism. E17.

W. S. LANDOR He places strange and discordant ideas in close apposition. C. LYELL These layers must have accumulated one on the other by lateral apposition.

■ **appositional** *adjective & noun* (*a*) *adjective* of, pertaining to, or standing in apposition; (*b*) *noun* a term standing in apposition: L17. **appositionally** *adverb* in apposition L19.

apposition /apəˈzɪʃ(ə)n/ *noun*². E16.

[ORIGIN Old French *aposicion*, *apposition* var. of OPPOSITION: see APPOSE *verb*¹.]

†**1** An objection; opposition. E16–E17.

2 (The name given to) speech day at St Paul's School, London. M17.

appositive /əˈpɒzɪtɪv/ *adjective & noun.* L17.

[ORIGIN Late Latin *appositivus* subsidiary, from *apposit-*: see APPOSITION *noun*¹, -IVE.]

▸ **A** *adjective.* = APPOSITIONAL *adjective.* L17.

▸ **B** *noun.* = APPOSITIONAL *noun.* M19.

■ **appositively** *adverb* = APPOSITIONALLY L16.

appraise /əˈpreɪz/ *verb trans.* LME.

[ORIGIN Alt., by assim. to PRAISE *verb*, of APPRIZE *verb*¹.]

1 Assign a monetary value to, fix a price for, esp. as an official valuer. LME.

2 Estimate the amount, quality, or excellence of; assess; *spec.* conduct a usu. regular formal review of the work performance of (an individual). M19.

■ **appraisable** *adjective* able to be valued or assessed M19. **appraisal** *noun* the act of appraising; a setting of price; an estimate of worth; *spec.* (a) usu. regular formal review of an individual's work performance, an interview or meeting with this purpose or to establish objectives etc.: E19. **appraiˈsee** *noun* a person whose work performance receives a formal review M20. **appraisement** *noun* valuation, estimation; an estimated value: M17. **appraiser** *noun* a person who appraises something or someone; an official valuer of goods or property: LME. **appraisingly** *adverb* so as to make a valuation or assessment L19. **appraisive** *adjective* involving or concerned with appraisal M20.

appreciable /əˈpriːʃəb(ə)l, -ʃɪə-/ *adjective.* LME.

[ORIGIN Old French & mod. French *appréciable*, from *apprécier*: see APPRECIATE, -ABLE.]

†**1** Worth esteeming. Only in LME.

2 Able to be estimated or judged; perceptible; considerable. E19.

■ **appreciably** *adverb* to an appreciable extent, considerably M19.

appreciate /əˈpriːʃɪeɪt, -sɪ-/ *verb.* Also †**-tiate.** M16.

[ORIGIN Late Latin *appretiat-* (medieval Latin *-ciat-*) pa. ppl stem of *appretiare* set a price on, from Latin *ad* AP-¹ + *pretium* PRICE *noun*: see -ATE³. Cf. Old French & mod. French *apprécier*.]

1 *verb trans.* Estimate rightly; perceive the full force of, understand, recognize *that*; be sensible or sensitive to; esteem adequately; recognize as valuable or excellent; be grateful for. M16.

E. O'NEILL You been kind as kind can be to me and I certainly appreciate it—only don't spoil it all now. O. SITWELL It is fatal to be appreciated in one's own time. E. HEMINGWAY You don't appreciate what a fine wife you have. G. GREENE I could appreciate the obstinate stand at Khartoum—the hatred of the safe politicians at home. T. S. ELIOT I'd like to learn about music. I wish you would teach me how to appreciate it. K. AMIS I hope you appreciate these Portuguese wines?

2 *verb trans.* Make or form an estimate of worth, quality, or amount of. *arch.* M18.

BURKE Let us calmly . . appreciate those dreadful and deformed gorgons and hydras.

3 *verb trans.* Raise in value. L18.

H. H. GIBBS The resumption of specie payments in Gold, thus appreciating that metal.

4 *verb intrans.* Rise in value. L18.

R. H. TAWNEY They were compelled to repay loans in an appreciating currency.

■ **appreciatingly** *adverb* with appreciation L19.

appreciation /əpriːʃɪˈeɪʃ(ə)n, -sɪ-/ *noun.* Also †**-tiat-**. LME.

[ORIGIN French *appréciation* from late Latin *appretiatio(n-)*, formed as APPRECIATE: see -ATION.]

†**1** Appraised value. *rare.* Only in LME.

2 Estimation; judgement; an assessment. E17.

A. POWELL There had been a number of appreciations of his work in the literary papers. B. ENGLAND He settled back and tried to make a proper military appreciation of their situation.

3 Adequate or high estimation; sympathetic recognition; perception, understanding; gratitude. M17.

J. GALSWORTHY The appreciation of enough persons of good taste was what gave a work of art its permanent market value. JOYCE His appreciation of the importance of inventions now common but once revolutionary. E. WAUGH In token of her appreciation the chief purser had been asked to our party.

4 The action of setting a money value upon something; valuation. Chiefly *Scot.* L18.

5 A rise in value. L18.

appreciative /əˈpriːʃ(ɪ)ətɪv/ *adjective.* Also †**-tiat-**. L17.

[ORIGIN from APPRECIATE + -IVE.]

Involving (esp. sympathetic) estimation, understanding; showing adequate or great appreciation, grateful.

■ **appreciatively** *adverb* M17. **appreciativeness** *noun* M19.

appreciator /əˈpriːʃɪeɪtə/ *noun.* L18.

[ORIGIN from APPRECIATE + -OR.]

†**1** SCOTS LAW. An appraiser of impounded goods. Only in L18.

2 A person who forms an adequate estimate; a person who recognizes the excellence (*of*); a person with understanding (*of*). E19.

appreciatory /əˈpriːʃ(ɪ)ət(ə)ri/ *adjective.* E19.

[ORIGIN formed as APPRECIATOR + -ORY².]

Of or befitting an appreciator; appreciative.

apprehend /aprɪˈhɛnd/ *verb.* LME.

[ORIGIN French *appréhender* or Latin *apprehendere*, from *ad* AP-¹ + *prehendere* seize.]

▸ **I** Mentally.

†**1** *verb trans. & intrans.* Learn, gain knowledge (of). LME–L17.

S. BUTLER Children . . Improve their nat'ral Talents without Care, And apprehend, before they are aware.

2 *verb trans. & (occas.) intrans.* Perceive with the intellect; understand. L15.

J. WESLEY I apprehended myself to be near death. STEELE I cannot apprehend where lyes the trifling in all this. T. REID What it is to think, to apprehend. LD MACAULAY The nature of the long contest between the Stuarts and their parliaments, was indeed very imperfectly apprehended by foreign statesmen. GLADSTONE The eternal laws, such as the heroic age apprehended them. BROWNING Each man . . avails him of what worth He apprehends in you.

†**3** *verb trans.* Feel emotionally, be sensible of. L16–L17.

JONSON Dead. Lord! how deeply, sir, you apprehend it.

4 *verb trans.* Perceive with the senses, become conscious of (an external impression). E17.

A. BAIN If I see . . two candle flames, I apprehend them as different objects. I. MURDOCH The birds could still be vaguely apprehended, close overhead.

5 *verb trans.* Anticipate, esp. with fear or dread; be apprehensive *that.* E17.

SHAKES. *Meas. for M.* A man that apprehends death no more dreadfully but as a drunken sleep. N. HAWTHORNE I sometimes apprehend that our institutions may perish. I. MURDOCH More danger was to be apprehended from shock than from anything else. D. M. WALKER At common law any private person may arrest where . . a breach of the peace has been or is actually being committed or is reasonably apprehended.

▸ **II** Physically.

†**6** *verb trans.* Lay hold upon, seize or grasp physically. LME–M19.

E. TOPSELL His dogs . . apprehending the garments of passengers. *absol.*: S. RUTHERFORD A lame hand that cannot apprehend.

†**7** *verb trans.* Seize (goods etc.) as a legal act; take possession of. *Scot.* L15–L17.

†**8** *verb trans.* Come upon, find, esp. in wrongdoing or in the wrong place. *Scot.* L15–E17.

9 *verb trans.* Seize (a person) in the name of the law, arrest. E16.

A. FRASER Their priests in particular were in danger of death if apprehended.

†**10** *verb trans.* Seize or embrace (an offer, opportunity, etc.). L16–M17.

■ **apprehender** *noun* M16.

apprehensible /aprɪˈhɛnsɪb(ə)l/ *adjective.* L15.

[ORIGIN Late Latin *apprehensibilis*, from *apprehens-*: see APPREHENSION, -IBLE.]

†**1** Capable of attaining (*to*). Only in L15.

2 Able to be apprehended; able to be grasped by the intellect or senses. (Foll. by *by*, *to*.) E17.

■ **apprehensiˈbility** *noun* E19. **apprehensibly** *adverb* (*rare*) L17.

apprehension /aprɪˈhɛnʃ(ə)n/ *noun.* LME.

[ORIGIN French *appréhension* or late Latin *apprehensio(n-)*, from *apprehens-* pa. ppl stem of *apprehendere* APPREHEND: see -ION.]

▸ **I** Mental.

†**1** The action of learning, acquirement of knowledge. LME–M17.

2 The intellectual faculty; understanding. L16.

T. DEKKER O the quick apprehension of women.

3 The action of perceiving with the intellect, conception. L16.

J. GLANVILL Simple apprehension denotes no more than the soul's naked intellection of an object.

4 A conception, an idea; a view, a notion, an opinion. L16.

R. BAXTER Fix not too rashly upon your first apprehensions. H. JAMES The great question meanwhile was what Chad thought of his sister, which was naturally ushered in by that of Sarah's apprehension of Chad.

5 The action of perceiving with the senses. Long *arch.* L16.

SHAKES. *Mids. N. D.* Dark night, that from the eye his function takes, The ear more quick of apprehension makes.

†**6** Emotional consciousness. E–M17.

7 Anticipation, esp. with fear or dread; uneasiness; an anxiety, a foreboding. E17.

SHAKES. *Meas. for M.* The sense of death is most in apprehension. M. BEERBOHM I had on the way a horrible apprehension What if the Duke . . had taken the one means to forgetfulness. V. BRITTAIN My apprehensions for his safety had been lulled by the long quiescence of the Italian front. L. URIS Each of those dozen people who knew of the scheme went around with hearts heavy with apprehension. A thousand things could go wrong.

▸ **II** Physical.

8 The seizure of a person, a ship, etc., in the name of the law; an arrest. L16.

Scientific American About a million apprehensions were made per year for violations of immigration law.

9 The action of laying hold of physically, prehension. *rare.* M17.

10 LAW. The taking of actual possession. *arch.* M19.

apprehensive /aprɪˈhɛnsɪv/ *adjective*. LME.
[ORIGIN French *appréhensif*, *-ive* or medieval Latin *apprehensivus*, from *apprehens-*: see APPREHENSION, -IVE.]
1 Pertaining to perception by the intellect or the senses. LME.
MILTON Thoughts, my tormentors, armed with deadly stings, Mangle my apprehensive tenderest parts.
2 Intelligent, perceptive, discerning. *arch.* E17.
SHAKES. *Jul. Caes.* Men are flesh and blood, and apprehensive. ROBERT BURTON If the Imagination be very apprehensive, intent, and violent. BROWNING The lower phrase that suits the sense O' the limitedly apprehensive.
3 Realizing, conscious, sensible. Foll. by *of*, *that*. *arch.* E17.
J. SPEED The King apprehensiue of his meaning, called his Lords. J. H. NEWMAN Miracles . . wrought . . by instruments but partially apprehensive that they are such.
4 Anticipative of something adverse; uneasy in mind, fearful. (Usu. foll. by *of*, *that*, *for*.) E17.
R. BOYLE Why should I be more apprehensive for my Body than my Mind. SWIFT Being apprehensive it might spoil the sale of the book. BURKE More apprehensive from his servants . . than from the hired blood-thirsty mob without. CARLYLE Physically of a timid apprehensive nature. ARNOLD BENNETT She was apprehensive about future dangers and her own ability to cope with them; but she was always apprehensive. J. FRAME In spite of our training and position we were . . rather apprehensive of our own safety.
†**5** In the habit of seizing; ready to seize (an offer, opportunity, etc.). E–M17.
■ **apprehensively** *adverb* M17. **apprehensiveness** *noun* E17.

apprentice /əˈprɛntɪs/ *noun & verb*. ME.
[ORIGIN Old French *aprentis* (mod. *apprenti*) nom. of *aprentif*, from *aprendre* learn from Latin *apprendere* contr. of *apprehendere* APPREHEND: see -IVE, -ICE[1].]
▸ **A** *noun*. **1** A learner of a craft, bound to serve, and entitled to instruction from, his or her employer for a specified term. ME.
attrib.: W. OWEN A poor apprentice-tailor.
2 A barrister-at-law of less than sixteen years' standing. *obsolete* exc. *hist.* LME.
3 A beginner, a novice. L15.
▸ **B** *verb trans.* Bind as an apprentice. L16.
■ **apprenticehood** *noun* (now *rare*) = APPRENTICESHIP LME. **apprenticement** *noun* (*rare*) apprenticing, apprenticeship E19.

†**apprenticeage** *noun* see APPRENTISSAGE.

apprenticeship /əˈprɛntɪsʃɪp/ *noun*. L16.
[ORIGIN from APPRENTICE + -SHIP.]
1 The position of an apprentice; service as an apprentice; initiatory training. L16.
articles of apprenticeship: see ARTICLE *noun* 4.
2 The period for which an apprentice is bound; *spec.* (*arch.*) a period of seven years. M17.

†**apprentissage** *noun*. Also **-iceage**. L16–L18.
[ORIGIN French, formed as APPRENTICE + -AGE.]
= APPRENTICESHIP.

appress /əˈprɛs/ *verb trans.* E17.
[ORIGIN Latin *appress-* pa. ppl stem of *apprimere*, from *ad* AP-[1] + *premere* press.]
Press close to each other or to a surface etc. Cf. ADPRESSED.

appressorium /aprɛˈsɔːrɪəm/ *noun*. Pl. **-ria** /-rɪə/. L19.
[ORIGIN formed as APPRESS + -ORIUM.]
BOTANY. A pad of mycelium by which certain parasitic fungi attach themselves to their hosts.

†**appretiate** *verb*, **appretiation** *noun*, etc., vars. of APPRECIATE, APPRECIATION, etc.

apprise /əˈprʌɪz/ *verb*[1] *trans.* Also **-ize**. L17.
[ORIGIN French *appris(e)* pa. pple of *apprendre* teach (causative), learn: see APPRENTICE.]
Inform, acquaint. (Foll. by *of*.)
be apprised of be aware of, know.

apprise *verb*[2] see APPRIZE *verb*[1].

apprize /əˈprʌɪz/ *verb*[1] *trans. arch.* Also (esp. in sense 2) **-ise**. LME.
[ORIGIN Old French *aprisier*, formed as A-[5] + *pris* PRICE *noun*, assim. to PRIZE *noun*[1].]
1 Value; esteem. LME.
2 *SCOTS LAW*. Put a selling price upon; put up for sale to pay a creditor. *obsolete* exc. *hist.* M16.
■ **apprizement**, (esp. *SCOTS LAW*) **-isement** *noun* (now *arch.* & *hist.*) the action of apprizing LME. **apprizer**, (esp. *SCOTS LAW*) **-iser** *noun* (now *arch.* & *hist.*) a person who apprizes LME.

apprize *verb*[2] var. of APPRISE *verb*[1].

appro /ˈaprəʊ/ *noun*. *colloq.* L19.
[ORIGIN Abbreviation of APPROVAL or APPROBATION.]
on appro, on approval.

approach /əˈprəʊtʃ/ *noun*. LME.
[ORIGIN from the verb.]
1 The act of coming near(er) in space. LME. ▸**b** The descent of an aircraft to the landing area. Freq. *attrib.* M20.
W. WHISTON The approach of a Comet to the Earth. GEO. ELIOT Casson's thoughts were diverted by the approach of the horseman. R. P. WARREN Upon nearer approach, he saw that a very dim light showed . . at one window.
b ***missed approach***: see MISS *verb*[1].
2 Power of approaching; access. *arch.* E16.
BACON Honour hath in it . . the approach to kings and principal persons.
3 A drawing near in time or circumstances; a coming near in quality, character, etc.; an approximation. L16.
SHAKES. *2 Hen. VI* Where death's approach is seen so terrible! POPE Thus sung the shepherds till th' approach of night. BURKE Some sort of approach towards infinity. E. O'NEILL The nearest approach to feeling he has shown in many a long night.
4 A movement towards establishing personal relations with someone, an overture, an advance; an application. Freq. in *pl.* M17.
D. ROGERS Thy timorous and weake approaches toward his grace. A. J. P. TAYLOR Harris . . promoted his strategy by personal approach to the minister of defence.
5 A means or way of approaching; a passage, avenue, channel, etc., giving access; (freq. in *pl.*). Also *fig.*, a way of addressing a task, dealing with a subject, etc.; an attitude. M17. ▸**b** *MILITARY*. In *pl.* Entrenchments or other works by which besiegers draw closer to the besieged. *obsolete* exc. *hist.* M17.
W. COWPER Mastiffs in gold and silver lined the approach. K. AMIS Some fishing-boats were doing something in the approaches to Cascais Harbour. J. ORTON The present enlightened approach to the mentally sick.
Western Approaches: see WESTERN *adjective*.
6 *HORTICULTURE*. Inarching. Chiefly in ***by approach***. M17.
7 *GOLF*. The play of the ball (other than from the tee) towards or on to the green. Usu. *attrib.* L19.
– COMB.: **approach road** a road leading up to a place; a slip road leading on to a motorway etc.
■ **approachless** *adjective* (*literary*) unapproachable, inaccessible M17.

approach /əˈprəʊtʃ/ *verb*. ME.
[ORIGIN Old French *aproch(i)er* (mod. *approcher*) from ecclesiastical Latin *appropiare*, from *ad-* AP-[1] + *propius* nearer, compar. of *prope* near.]
▸ **I** *verb trans.* **1** Come near to in space; move towards. ME.
E. WAUGH Two policemen quickened their stride and approached us. A. SHAFFER A minstrels gallery which . . is approached by a winding staircase.
2 Come near(er) to in time, quality, rank, etc.; be nearly equal to; move towards in thought, set about (a problem etc.). LME.
E. A. FREEMAN Vigorous youths fast approaching manhood. C. FRY It was approaching dusk, last evening. T. S. ELIOT Let us approach the question from another angle. S. WEINBERG Velocities approaching that of light.
3 Be so situated or arranged that the parts lie successively nearer to (a line, point, etc.). Also (*arch.*), adjoin, neighbour. LME.
ADDISON Trees rising one higher than another in proportion as they approach the centre. *Encycl. Brit.* The curve and its asymptote approach one another ever more closely but never quite meet except at infinity.
4 Come into the presence of (someone), or (*arch.*) into (someone's presence); seek a meeting or relationship with; make overtures, advances, proposals, etc., to; *spec.* seek to influence or bribe. LME.
STEELE I cannot approach her without Awe. *Congressional Record* Everything that is said about public men being corrupted or approached. J. BUCHAN Twenty days of hiding before I could venture to approach the powers that be. J. P. DONLEAVY I was once approached by a talent scout in summer stock. J. BARTH The Colonel approached me . . on ten different occasions with offers of business. J. BOWEN The sinner approaches your presence, high priest.
5 Bring near(er); make closer in quality, character, etc. *arch.* LME.
SIR W. SCOTT He approached to the fire a three-footed stool. C. MERIVALE His object was . . to approach the Gaulish provincials to Rome.
6 *MILITARY*. Work forward towards by means of entrenchments. *obsolete* exc. *hist.* L17.
▸ **II** *verb intrans.* **7** Come nearer in space; draw near; *arch.* come near(er) *to* a place, person, etc. ME.
AV *2 Sam.* 11:20 Wherefore approched ye so nigh vnto the city when yee did fight? TOLKIEN Before long they saw the marching line approaching: the Ents were swinging along with great strides down the slope towards them.
8 Draw near in time, befall; come near(er) *to* something in quality, magnitude, etc. LME.
G. GASCOIGNE I thinke How ioyes approch, when sorrowes shrinke. B. STEWART The coefficients of dilation . . approach more nearly to equality. SAKI With money behind one, the problem of where to live approaches more nearly to the simple question of where do you wish to live. A. J. P. TAYLOR Perhaps they were conscious that a general election was approaching.
9 Be so situated or arranged that the parts lie successively closer (*to* something). Also (*arch.*), be situated nearby. LME.
D. HARTLEY The ventricles of the brain approach towards each other.
10 Come into someone's presence; make an overture or advance. (Foll. by *to*.) *arch.* LME.
T. J. MATHIAS To the Peers approach with awe.
■ **approacher** *noun* (*arch.*) L16. **approaching** *ppl adjective* & *adverb* (**a**) *adjective* that approaches; (**b**) *adverb* nearly: LME. **approachment** *noun* (now *rare*) the action or state of approaching M16.

approachable /əˈprəʊtʃəb(ə)l/ *adjective*. L16.
[ORIGIN from APPROACH *verb* + -ABLE.]
Able to be approached; accessible (*lit.* & *fig.*), affable.
S. JOHNSON He that regards the welfare of others should make his virtue approachable. HOR. WALPOLE The town was . . approachable only by a narrow causeway. T. ROETHKE Irish writers of the non-sullen and approachable variety.
■ **approachaˈbility** *noun* M19. **approachableness** *noun* (*rare*) M18.

approbate /ˈaprəbeɪt/ *verb trans.* Pa. pple & ppl adjective **-ated**, †**-ate**. LME.
[ORIGIN Latin *approbat-* pa. ppl stem of *approbare*: see APPROVE *verb*[2], -ATE[3].]
1 Approve expressly or formally; sanction, approve of. *obsolete* exc. *N. Amer.* LME.
2 *SCOTS LAW*. Assent to. L18.
approbate and reprobate take advantage of the favourable parts of a deed while repudiating the rest.
■ **approˈbatory** *adjective* = APPROBATIVE M16.

approbation /aprəˈbeɪʃ(ə)n/ *noun*. LME.
[ORIGIN Old French & mod. French from Latin *approbatio(n-)*, formed as APPROBATE: see -ATION.]
†**1** Confirmation, proof. LME–E18.
SHAKES. *Cymb.* Would I had put my estate . . on th' approbation of what I have spoke!
2 The action of formally or authoritatively declaring good or true; sanction, endorsement. LME.
T. KEIGHTLEY Received the royal approbation.
3 Approval or satisfaction expressed or felt. M16.
W. BLAKE Advertisements in Newspapers are no proof of Popular approbation, but often the Contrary. ALDOUS HUXLEY The Controller nodded his approbation. 'I like your spirit, Mr Watson'.
on approbation = *on* APPROVAL.
†**4** Probation, trial. E–M17.
SHAKES. *Meas. for M.* This day my sister should the cloister enter, And there receive her approbation.

approbative /ˈaprəbeɪtɪv/ *adjective*. E17.
[ORIGIN French *approbatif*, *-ive* or medieval Latin *approbativus*, formed as APPROBATE + -IVE.]
Expressing approbation or approval.
■ **approbativeness** *noun* (now *rare*) (**a**) tendency to approve, approbative quality; (**b**) *PHRENOLOGY* love of approbation: M19.

approof /əˈpruːf/ *noun*. *arch.* E17.
[ORIGIN from APPROVE *verb*[1] after PROOF *noun*.]
1 The act of proving, trial; proven quality. E17.
2 Approbation, approval. E17.

appropinquate /aprəˈpɪŋkweɪt/ *verb intrans.* & †*trans.* *arch.* L16.
[ORIGIN Latin *appropinquat-* pa. ppl stem of *appropinquare* to approach, from *ad* AP-[1] + *propinquus* neighbouring, from *prope* near: see -ATE[3].]
Approach; come near *to*.
■ **appropinque** /-ˈpɪŋk/ *verb trans.* & *intrans.* (*rare*) = APPROPINQUATE M17. **appropinquity** *noun* (*rare*) nearness M17.

appropinquation /əprɒpɪŋˈkweɪʃ(ə)n/ *noun*. *arch.* LME.
[ORIGIN Latin *appropinquatio(n-)*, formed as APPROPINQUATE: see -ATION.]
The action of coming or bringing near; approach.

appropriable /əˈprəʊprɪəb(ə)l/ *adjective*. M17.
[ORIGIN from APPROPRIATE *verb* + -ABLE.]
Able to be appropriated.

appropriacy /əˈprəʊprɪəsi/ *noun*. L20.
[ORIGIN from APPROPRI(ATE *adjective* + -ACY.]
Appropriateness, *spec.* in the suitability of a language form or register for a particular context, social situation, etc.

appropriate /əˈprəʊprɪət/ *adjective* (& †*pa. pple*). LME.
[ORIGIN Late Latin *appropriatus* pa. pple, formed as APPROPRIATE *verb*: see -ATE[2].]
1 Attached or belonging (*to*) as an attribute, quality, or right; peculiar (*to*); inherent, characteristic; specially suitable (*for*, *to*); proper, fitting. LME.
COLERIDGE To charm away . . *Ennui*, is the chief and appropriate business of the poet. M. MEAD Some peoples think of women as too weak to work out of doors, others regard women as the appropriate bearers of heavy burdens. J. BOWEN They must behave in a manner appropriate to the myth in which they were participating. A. LURIE Actually, he looks lots better when he isn't dressed as he thinks appropriate for dinner at Illyria. B. ENGLAND At an appropriate moment I shall strike the gong. T. STOPPARD He makes a wordless noise appropriate to male approval of female pulchritude. D. JACOBSON He was dressed in a tweed suit appropriate either to countryman or academic. G. BOYCOTT The music on the radio was turned off; somehow a bit of quiet seemed more appropriate.

2 Annexed or attached (*to*) as a possession, appropriated; *esp.* (ECCLESIASTICAL) annexed as a benefice to a monastery. Now *rare* or *obsolete*. L16.

■ **appropriately** *adverb* †(*a*) specially, peculiarly; (*b*) in an appropriate manner, fittingly: M16. **appropriateness** *noun* M17.

appropriate /əˈprəʊprɪeɪt/ *verb trans.* Pa. pple & ppl adjective **-ated**, †**-ate**. LME.

[ORIGIN Latin *appropriat-* pa. ppl stem of *appropriare* make one's own, from *ad* AP-[1] + *propius* own, proper: see -ATE[3].]

1 Take *to* oneself as one's own property or for one's own use. LME.

G. ANSON Appropriating the whole ships provisions to themselves. E. MELLOR The name 'priesthood' . . was never appropriated by apostles to themselves.

†**2** Make over *to* a person, institution, etc., as his, her, or its own or for his, her, or its use. LME–E18.

COVERDALE *Micah* 4:13 Their goodes shalt thou appropriate vnto the Lorde. T. BLOUNT It was lawful to appropriate the whole Fruits of a Benefice to an Abbey or Priory.

3 Devote, set aside, or assign, *to* the use of a person or institution, *to* or *for* a special purpose or use. LME.

M. PATTISON The revenue is appropriated to the payment of University officers. *Time* Economic Opportunity Act . . appropriates almost $948 million for ten programs including job training, work-study programs, [etc.].

4 Assign or attribute as properly pertaining *to*; attribute specially or exclusively *to*. *arch.* LME.

JOSEPH STRUTT These amusements . . were appropriated to the season of Lent. COLERIDGE The word presumption I appropriate to the internal feeling.

5 Make, or select as, appropriate or suitable (*to*). *arch.* LME.

R. PLOT The best methods of Cultivating, appropriating seeds and manures, and cureing the diseases of land. H. HALLAM The subject chosen is appropriated to the characteristic peculiarities of the poet.

6 Take possession of; use as one's own, esp. without permission. L16.

J. K. JEROME He comes in quietly . . , appropriates the most comfortable chair. P. V. WHITE Some man, a kind of *bushranger*, . . rode up to their vehicle, and appropriated every single valuable the unfortunate couple had upon them. A. J. P. TAYLOR The Conservatives appropriated patriotism.

■ **appropriative** *adjective* of appropriating character or tendency M17. **appropriator** *noun* a person who or thing which appropriates; *esp.* (ECCLESIASTICAL HISTORY) the monastery etc. to which a benefice is assigned: M17. †**approprie**, **appropre** *verb trans.* = APPROPRIATE *verb* ME–E17.

appropriation /əprəʊprɪˈeɪʃ(ə)n/ *noun*. LME.

[ORIGIN Old French & mod. French from late Latin *appropriatio(n-)*, formed as APPROPRIATE *verb*: see -ATION.]

1 The making over (*of* a thing) into one's own or (*arch.*) another's possession; the taking of a thing for one's own use, esp. without permission. LME.

B. UNSWORTH Appropriation of traditional Creek hunting grounds to offer to English settlers. J. COE Apparently he's doing Bob Marley covers now. That's pure cultural appropriation, if you ask me.

2 ECCLESIASTICAL HISTORY. The transference to a body or individual (*spec.* to a monastery) of the tithes and endowments of a parish. LME.

†**3** Attribution, application; a special attribute. LME–L17.

4 The assignment of something to a special purpose. Also, the thing so assigned; *esp.* a sum of money allocated officially for a particular use. M18.

5 ART. The reworking of the images or styles contained in works of art, photographs, etc., esp. well-known ones, in order to encourage critical reinterpretation. L20.

– COMB.: **appropriation bill** a legislative bill allocating public revenue to the purposes for which it may be used.

■ **appropriationist** *noun & adjective* (*a*) *noun* an adherent, supporter, or exponent of appropriation; (in Hindu philosophy) one who holds that the soul is an appropriation of the being of Brahma; (*b*) *adjective* (ART) characterized by appropriation: M19.

approval /əˈpruːv(ə)l/ *noun*. E17.

[ORIGIN from APPROVE *verb*[2] + -AL[1].]

The action of approving; sanction.

on approval (of goods supplied) to be returned if not satisfactory; for examination, without obligation to purchase.

approvance /əˈpruːv(ə)ns/ *noun*. *arch.* L16.

[ORIGIN Old French *aprovance*, formed as APPROVE *verb*[2] + -ANCE.]

= APPROVAL.

approve /əˈpruːv/ *verb*[1] *trans.* Also †**approw**. ME.

[ORIGIN Old French *approver*, *appro(u)er*, from *à* A-[5] + *pro(u)* advantage, profit; later form (17) by interpretation of *u* in *approuer* as = *v*. Cf. IMPROVE *verb*[2].]

LAW. Increase one's profit from (land); *esp.* increase the value of (common land) by appropriation or enclosure, as permitted to the lord of a manor by the Statute of Merton, 1235.

approve /əˈpruːv/ *verb*[2]. ME.

[ORIGIN Old French *aprover* (mod. *approuver*) from Latin *approbare* make good, assent to as good, from *ad* AP-[1] + *probus* good, just.]

▸ **I** †**1** *verb trans.* Show to be true, demonstrate. ME–L17.

T. HEYWOOD This aproves unto us, that order is a cheefe rule in memorie. T. FULLER To approve the truth . . thereof against some one who questioned. MARVELL Mr. Onslow was approved not to have been culpable.

†**2** *verb trans.* Corroborate, attest. LME–M19.

CLARENDON The success has approved this judgement. GIBBON The trembling emperor . . solemnly approved the innocence and fidelity of their assassins.

3 *verb trans.* Confirm authoritatively; sanction. LME.

CHARLES JAMES The colonel or commanding officer approves the sentence of a regimental court-martial. A. J. P. TAYLOR On 28 January the naval plan was approved by the war council.

approved school *hist.* an institution for young offenders, a community home.

4 *verb trans. & intrans.* (foll. by *of*, †*on*). Pronounce or consider to be good or satisfactory; commend; be in sympathy or agreement. LME.

E. HEMINGWAY You cannot marry me and I understand that, although I do not approve it. B. BAINBRIDGE Things go on here that I don't approve of, but I neither interfere nor criticize. *absol.*: J. GALSWORTHY We've never cared whether the world approves or not.

5 *verb trans.* Display, exhibit, make proof of. *arch.* E16. ▸**b** Show (esp. oneself) to be. *arch.* M16.

BYRON 'Tis an old lesson; Time approves it true. LD MACAULAY When he approved himself ripe for military command. R. W. EMERSON Many opportunities to approve his stoutness and worth.

6 *verb trans.* Recommend (oneself, one's qualities, etc.) as worthy of approval. *arch.* E17.

ISAAC TAYLOR If anticipations such as these approve themselves to reason.

▸ †**II 7** *verb trans.* Put to the proof or test of experience. LME–L18.

SHAKES. *1 Hen. IV* Nay, task me to my word; approve me, lord.

8 *verb trans.* Find by experience. L16–M17.

■ **approvable** *adjective* able to be approved; worthy of approval: LME. **approvableness** *noun* (*rare*) E19. **approvedly** /-vɪdli/ *adverb* (*rare*) †(*a*) in a tried and tested manner; (*b*) in a sanctioned or commended manner: LME. **approvingly** *adverb* in an approving manner E19.

approvement /əˈpruːvm(ə)nt/ *noun*[1]. Also †**appowment**. LME.

[ORIGIN Old French *apro(u)ement*, *aprowe-* profit, formed as APPROVE *verb*[1] + -MENT.]

LAW. The action of increasing one's profit by approving land.

approvement /əˈpruːvm(ə)nt/ *noun*[2]. E17.

[ORIGIN Old French *aprovement* (later *approuve-*), formed as APPROVE *verb*[2] + -MENT.]

†**1** A proof. Only in E17.

†**2** Approbation, approval. E17–M19.

3 The action of convicting another by turning informer. Now *arch. & hist.* M18.

†**approver** *noun*[1]. Also **apprower**. LME–M18.

[ORIGIN Anglo-Norman *aprouour*, formed as APPROVE *verb*[1] + -OUR; suffix later interpreted as and replaced by -ER[1].]

A person who manages land for the owner; a steward or bailiff; an agent in any business.

approver /əˈpruːvə/ *noun*[2]. LME.

[ORIGIN from APPROVE *verb*[2] + -ER[1]. Cf. Old French *aproveur*.]

1 A person who proves or offers to prove another guilty, an informer; latterly *spec.* one who turns King's, Queen's, or state's evidence. Now *arch. & hist.* LME.

†**2** A person who proves, tests, or tries someone. M16–L17.

3 A person who confirms, sanctions, pronounces good, or commends something. M16.

†**approw** *verb*, **apprower** *noun*, **approwment** *noun* vars. of APPROVE *verb*[1], APPROVER *noun*[1], APPROVEMENT *noun*[1].

approximant /əˈprɒksɪm(ə)nt/ *adjective & noun*. M17.

[ORIGIN Latin *approximant-* pres. ppl stem of *approximare*: see APPROXIMATE *verb*, -ANT[1].]

▸ †**A** *adjective*. Approaching closely, resembling. *rare*. Only in M17.

▸ **B** *noun*. **1** MATH. A function, series, etc., which is an approximation to the solution of a given problem. E20.

2 PHONETICS. A non-fricative continuant. L20.

approximate /əˈprɒksɪmət/ *adjective & noun*. LME.

[ORIGIN Late Latin *approximatus* pa. pple, from *approximat-*: see APPROXIMATE *verb*, -ATE[2].]

▸ **A** *adjective* (orig. *pa. pple*).

†**1** Brought or placed close. Only in LME.

2 Very near in position or character; close together; similar. *arch.* LME.

3 Fairly or reasonably correct; near to the actual. E19.

very approximate more or less correct; fairly near to the actual.

▸ **B** *noun*. An approximate result or quantity. *rare*. L18.

■ **approximately** *adverb* nearly, with near approach to accuracy M19.

approximate /əˈprɒksɪmeɪt/ *verb*. M17.

[ORIGIN from APPROXIMATE *adjective & noun* or late Latin *approximat-* pa. ppl stem of *approximare* (Tertullian) draw near to, from *ad* AP-[1] + *proximus* very near, next: see -ATE[3].]

1 *verb trans.* Bring close or near, cause to approach or be near (*to*). (Chiefly of non-physical relationships.) M17.

S. JOHNSON Shakespeare approximates the remote, and familiarizes the wonderful. E. H. GOMBRICH He must purify the world of matter, erase its flaws, and approximate it to the idea. J. G. FARRELL A compress . . placed on the palm after the edges of the wound had been evenly approximated.

2 *verb intrans.* Come near or close (*to*, esp. in quality, number, etc., rarely physically). L18.

JOHN ROSS The shores gradually approximate. A. G. GARDINER There are times when the dog approximates so close to our intelligences that he seems to be of us. E. J. HOWARD Pleasing meant approximating to the man's idea of the sort of woman his position and intelligence owed him.

3 *verb trans.* Come close to, approach closely, (used as sense 2). L18.

JAMES SULLIVAN We may yet approximate . . a certainty that is demonstrative. E. POUND Progress lies rather in an attempt to approximate classical quantitative metres (NOT to copy them) than in a carelessness regarding such things.

■ **approximator** *noun* (*rare*) a person who approximates *to* M19.

approximation /əprɒksɪˈmeɪʃ(ə)n/ *noun*. LME.

[ORIGIN Late Latin *approximatio(n-)*, formed as APPROXIMATE *verb*; later from APPROXIMATE *verb*: see -ATION.]

1 The action of bringing or coming near in place, time, or any conception to which ideas of space apply; the state of being near, proximity. LME.

2 A coming or getting near to identity in quantity, quality, or degree; the result of such a process; a value or quantity that is nearly but not exactly correct. M17.

approximative /əˈprɒksɪmətɪv/ *adjective*. E19.

[ORIGIN from APPROXIMATE *verb* + -IVE: cf. French *approximatif*.]

Of approximate character; nearly but not exactly reaching accuracy.

■ **approximatively** *adverb* M19.

appui /əˈpwiː, *foreign* apɥi/ *noun*. *arch.* L16.

[ORIGIN French.]

1 †**a** *gen.* Support; a stay, a prop. L16–L17. ▸**b** MILITARY. Defensive support. L18.

b point of appui = *point d'appui* s.v. POINT *noun*[2] 2.

†**2** HORSEMANSHIP. The tension of the reins; the response of the horse's mouth to the control through the reins. E18–E19.

appulse /əˈpʌls/ *noun*. E17.

[ORIGIN Latin *appulsus* a driving towards, from *appuls-* pa. ppl stem of *appellere*, from *ad* AP-[1] + *pellere* drive.]

1 A driving or energetic motion towards a place; a strong impulse towards something. *arch.* E17.

2 ASTRONOMY. An apparent close approach (falling short of occultation) by a planet etc. to a star or other body. M17.

appurtenance /əˈpəːt(ɪ)nəns/ *noun*. ME.

[ORIGIN Anglo-Norman *apurtenaunce*, Old French *apartenance*, *apert-*, ult. from late Latin *appertinere* (see APPERTAIN) + -ANCE.]

1 LAW. A minor property, right, or privilege, subsidiary or incidental to a more important one; an appendage. Usu. in *pl.* ME.

C. SANDBURG The land and all appurtenances thereto and all deposits of oil and gold.

2 A contributory adjunct, an accessory. Usu. in *pl.* LME.

SHAKES. *Haml.* Th' appurtenance of welcome is fashion and ceremony. L. STRACHEY The bonnet with its jet appurtenances. M. MUGGERIDGE It had now become a grammar school, with all the usual appurtenances in the shape of houses, prefects, blazers, a school song, and so on.

3 The fact or state of appertaining. *rare*. M19.

W. D. WHITNEY The word is a token of the most indefinite appurtenance.

appurtenant /əˈpəːt(ə)nənt/ *adjective & noun*. Also (esp. in sense A.2, *arch.*) **appertinent**. LME.

[ORIGIN Old French *apartenant* pres. pple of *apartenir* APPERTAIN: see -ANT[1].]

▸ **A** *adjective*. **1** Belonging (*to*) as a (subsidiary or incidental) property, right, or privilege. LME.

2 Appertaining (*to*); appropriate (*to*); relating, pertinent. LME.

▸ **B** *noun*. An appurtenance. Now *rare*. LME.

APR *abbreviation*.

Annual percentage rate (of interest on money lent).

Apr. *abbreviation*.

April.

apraxia /əˈpraksɪə/ *noun*. L19.

[ORIGIN German *Apraxie* from Greek *apraxia* inaction.]

MEDICINE. Inability to perform given purposive actions, as a result of cerebral disorder.

après /ˈapreɪ, *foreign* aprɛ/ *preposition*. M19.

[ORIGIN French = after.]

1 ***après coup*** /ku/ [lit. 'after stroke'], after the event; as an afterthought. M19.

2 ***après-ski*** /skiː/ *noun & adjective*, (worn, done, etc., at) the time when skiing is over for the day at a resort. M20. ▸**b** Used with English words in imitation of ***après-ski***, as ***après-bath***, ***après-sex***, etc. M20.

A

apricate /ˈaprɪkeɪt/ *verb. rare.* L17.
[ORIGIN Latin *apricat-* pa. ppl stem of *apricari* bask in the sun, from *apricus* exposed (to the sun): see -ATE[3].]
1 *verb intrans.* Bask in the sun. L17.
2 *verb trans.* Expose to sunlight. M19.

apricot /ˈeɪprɪkɒt/ *noun.* Orig. †**abrecock**, †**apricock**. M16.
[ORIGIN Portuguese *albricoque* or Spanish *albaricoque* from Hispano-Arabic *al-barqūq*, from AL-[2] + *barqūq* from late Greek *praikokion* from Latin *praecoquum* noun, from neut. of var. of *praecox* early-ripe. Assim. to French *abricot* and perhaps infl. by Latin *apricus* ripe.]
1 The juicy stone fruit of the tree *Prunus armeniaca*, of the rose family. M16.
Irish apricot: see IRISH *adjective*.
2 The tree itself, cultivated in the warmer temperate regions and orig. native to China. M16.
3 The pinkish-yellow colour of the ripe fruit. L19.
– COMB.: **apricot plum** (the edible yellow stone fruit of) a tree of the rose family, *Prunus simonii*, which is native to China and bears white blossom.

April /ˈeɪpr(ɪ)l/ *noun.* OE.
[ORIGIN Latin *Aprilis* use as noun of adjective (sc. *mensis* month).]
The fourth month of the year in the Gregorian calendar. Also *fig.*, with allusion to April's position in spring or to bright changeable weather with showers, considered characteristic of the month in Britain and elsewhere in the northern hemisphere.

> TENNYSON Half-opening buds of April. *attrib.*: SHAKES. *Two Gent.* The uncertain glory of an April day. *fig.*: P. SIDNEY In the April of your age. SHAKES. *Ant. & Cl.* The April's in her eyes. It is love's spring.

– COMB.: **April fool** a person upon whom a joke is played on the first of April (called ***April Fool's Day***, †***April Fool Day***).
– NOTE: Rare until LME, before which the usual spelling was *Averil*. At first (and long in dial. use) stressed on 2nd syll., which rhymed with *mile*.

a priori /eɪ prʌɪˈɔːrʌɪ, ɑː priˈɔːri/ *adverbial & adjectival phr.* L16.
[ORIGIN Latin *a priori* from what is before.]
1 Of reasoning: (by) proceeding from causes to effects; deductive(ly). Opp. A POSTERIORI. L16.
2 *loosely.* Presumptive(ly); without previous investigation; as far as one knows. E19.
3 PHILOSOPHY. Of knowledge or concepts: not derived from sensory experience; innate(ly). M19.
■ **apriority** *noun* (*a*) innateness in the mind; (*b*) = APRIORISM: M19.

apriorism /eɪprʌɪˈɔːrɪz(ə)m/ *noun.* L19.
[ORIGIN from A PRIORI + -ISM.]
The doctrine of the existence of a priori knowledge or concepts. Also, (an example of) reasoning a priori.
■ **apriorist** *noun* an adherent of apriorism; a person given to reasoning a priori: L19. **aprioˈristic** *adjective* L19.

apron /ˈeɪpr(ə)n/ *noun & verb.* Orig. †**n-**. ME.
[ORIGIN Old French *naperon* (mod. *napperon*), from *nap(p)e* tablecloth from Latin *mappa* napkin: initial *n* lost by misdivision as in *adder*, *auger*, etc.]
▸ **A** *noun.* **I** An article of dress.
1 A garment, orig. of linen, worn in front of the body to protect the clothes from dirt or damage, or simply as a covering. ME.

> SHAKES. *Jul. Caes.* Where is thy leather apron and thy rule? E. JONG I changed into a blue Gown with my prettiest embroider'd Apron and a Tucker of white Lace.

2 A similar garment worn as part of official dress, e.g. by a bishop, dean, Freemason, etc. LME.
▸ **II** A structure like an apron in form or function.
3 A protective or decorative layer of brickwork etc., esp. beneath a window. E17. ▸**b** A strengthening timber behind the stem of a wooden ship. E18.
4 The skin covering the belly of a roast duck or goose, enclosing the stuffing. M18.
5 A protective covering for the legs in an open carriage. L18.
6 The folded abdomen of a crab. M19.
7 An endless conveyor consisting of overlapping plates (usu. more fully ***apron conveyor***); each of these plates. M19.
8 GEOLOGY. An extensive outspread deposit of sediment, esp. at the foot of a glacier or mountain. L19.
9 THEATRICAL. A projecting strip of stage for playing scenes in front of the curtain. E20.
10 A hard-surfaced area used for the (un)loading, manoeuvring, etc., of aircraft at an airfield. E20.
– COMB.: ***apron conveyor***: see sense 7 above; †**apron-man** a mechanic, a workman; **apron stage** = sense 9.
▸ **B** *verb trans.* Cover with an apron; cover or surround in the manner of an apron. M19.

> DICKENS I mean to apron it and towel it. B. RUBENS All the villas looked exactly alike, red-brick structures, aproned by patios and well laid-out gardens.

■ **aproned** *adjective* having an apron (formerly regarded as a symbol of a working man) E17. **apronful** *noun* the quantity that can be held in an apron M17.

apron-string /ˈeɪpr(ə)nstrɪŋ/ *noun.* M16.
[ORIGIN from APRON *noun* + STRING *noun*.]
A string with which an apron is tied on.
– COMB. & PHRASES: **apron-string hold**, **apron-string tenure** *arch.* tenure of property in virtue of one's wife, or during her lifetime only; **tied to the apron-strings of** unduly controlled by (a wife, mother, etc.).

apropos /aprəˈpəʊ, ˈaprəpəʊ/ *adverb, adjective, noun, & preposition.* Also ***à propos*** /a prɔpo/. M17.
[ORIGIN French *à propos*, from *à* to + *propos* purpose.]
▸ **A** *adverb.* **1** To the point; fitly, opportunely. M17.

> DRYDEN The French . . use them with better judgment, and more àpropos. ADDISON Stanhope and Earl arrived very àpropos.

2 In respect or as a relevant association *of* (now less commonly, *to*). (Cf. sense D. below.) M18. ▸**b** *absol.* Incidentally, by the way. M18.

> G. CLARE Apropos of nothing she declared that love must be wonderful. **b** SMOLLETT But a-propos! Hast thou seen the girl?

▸ **B** *adjective.* Pertinent, appropriate, opportune. (Foll. by *of*, *to*.) M17.

> POPE A tale extremely apropos. J. WOODFORDE Mr. Johnson gave us a very excellent Sermon indeed, very apropos to the times.

▸ **C** *noun.* †**1** An opportune or pertinent occurrence. Only in L18.
2 Relevance, pertinency. M19.

> GEO. ELIOT I fail to see the à propos.

▸ **D** *preposition.* Concerning, with regard to (cf. sense A.2 above). *colloq.* M20.
– PHRASES: ***à propos de bottes*** /də bɔt/ [French = with regard to boots, i.e. to something quite irrelevant] without serious motive, without rhyme or reason.

aprosexia /aprəˈsɛksɪə/ *noun.* L19.
[ORIGIN Greek = lack of attention, from A-[10] + *prosekhein* turn (one's mind): see -IA[1].]
MEDICINE. Abnormal inability to concentrate.

aprosopia /aprəˈsəʊpɪə/ *noun. rare.* M19.
[ORIGIN from Greek A-[10] + *prosōpon* face + -IA[1].]
MEDICINE. Absence or imperfect development of the face.

aprotic /eɪˈprəʊtɪk/ *adjective.* M20.
[ORIGIN German *aprotisch*, formed as A-[10], PROTON, -IC.]
CHEMISTRY. Of a solvent: having little or no ability to exchange protons with the solute.

APS *abbreviation.*
Advanced Photo(graphic) System (proprietary name in the UK).

aps *noun* see ASP *noun*[1].

apsara /ˈʌpsərɑː/ *noun.* Also **up-**. M19.
[ORIGIN Hindi *apsarā* from Sanskrit *apsarās*.]
HINDU MYTHOLOGY. Any of a class of celestial nymphs, freq. regarded as the wives of the gandharvas or heavenly musicians.

apse /aps/ *noun.* E19.
[ORIGIN formed as APSIS.]
1 ASTRONOMY. = APSIS *noun* 2. E19.
2 ARCHITECTURE. A large semicircular or polygonal structure, often roofed with a semi-dome, situated esp. at the end of the choir, nave, or an aisle of a church. M19.

apsidal /ˈapsɪd(ə)l/ *adjective.* M19.
[ORIGIN formed as APSIS + -AL[1].]
1 ARCHITECTURE. Of the form or nature of an apse. M19.
2 ASTRONOMY. Of or pertaining to the apsides. M19.

apsis /ˈapsɪs/ *noun.* Pl. **apsides** /əpˈsʌɪdiːz, ˈapsɪdiːz/. Also †**absis** (orig. the usual spelling), pl. †**absides**. E17.
[ORIGIN Latin *apsis*, *absis*, *-sid-* from Greek *(h)apsis* arch, vault, (rim of a) wheel, perh. from *haptein* fasten, join.]
†**1** Circumference, circuit; orbit (of a planet). E17–E18.
2 ASTRONOMY. Either of the two points in the elliptical orbit of a planet or other body at which it is respectively nearest to and furthest from the primary about which it revolves. M17.
3 ARCHITECTURE. = APSE *noun* 2. Now *rare* or *obsolete*. E18.
■ **apˈsidiole** *noun* (ARCHITECTURE) a small apse L19.

apso /ˈapsəʊ/ *noun.* Pl. **-os**. M20.
[ORIGIN Tibetan *a-sob* /ˈapso/.]
In full ***Lhasa apso***, ***Tibetan apso***. (An animal of) a breed of small long-coated dog, often gold or grey and white, originating at Lhasa.

APT *abbreviation.*
Advanced Passenger Train.

apt /apt/ *adjective.* LME.
[ORIGIN Latin *aptus* pa. pple of *apere* fasten, attach. Cf. French *apte*.]
1 Suited, fitted, adapted, prepared, ready, *for*, †*to*. *arch.* LME.

> SHAKES. *Jul. Caes.* Live a thousand years, I shall not find myself so apt to die. BACON States . . apt to be the Foundations of Great Monarchies. W. MORRIS Tall was he, slim, made apt for feats of war. E. WAUGH The time was apt for reminiscence.

2 Habitually liable, customarily disposed, likely, prone, *to do* something. E16. ▸**b** Inclined, disposed, *to think*, in a particular instance. *arch.* L17.

> N. COWARD I'm so apt to see things the wrong way round. C. MACKENZIE When Hugh did that onlookers were apt to be impressed. R. SUTCLIFF When you get men into that state there is apt to be trouble coming. S. KING Her morning routine was as set as a single person's is apt to be.

3 Suitable, appropriate, apposite. M16.

> SHAKES. *Mids. N. D.* In all the play There is not one word apt. WORDSWORTH To give me human strength, by apt admonishment. DISRAELI The prompt reply or the apt retort. Q. CRISP The day I was there was Columbus day. This I thought was an apt coincidence.

4 Ready to learn, quick-witted, prompt, (*at*). M16.

> DEFOE He was the aptest scholar that ever was. H. MARTINEAU Men . . are . . apt at devising ways of easing their toils.

■ **aptly** *adverb* LME. **aptness** *noun* E16.

apt. *abbreviation.* Chiefly *N. Amer.*
Apartment.

apterous /ˈapt(ə)rəs/ *adjective.* L18.
[ORIGIN from Greek *apteros*, from A-[10] + *pteron* wing: see -OUS.]
Chiefly ENTOMOLOGY. Wingless.

apterygote /apˈtɛrɪgəʊt/ *adjective & noun.* E20.
[ORIGIN mod. Latin *Apterygota* (see below), from Greek A-[10] + *pterugōtos* winged.]
ENTOMOLOGY. ▸**A** *adjective.* Pertaining to or designating insects of the subclass Apterygota, which includes primitive orders in which wings are totally lacking, e.g. bristletails, springtails. E20.
▸ **B** *noun.* An apterygote insect. E20.

apteryx /ˈaptərɪks/ *noun.* Now *rare.* E19.
[ORIGIN mod. Latin, from Greek A-[10] + *pterux* wing.]
= KIWI 1.

aptitude /ˈaptɪtjuːd/ *noun.* LME.
[ORIGIN Old French & mod. French from late Latin *aptitudo* (Boethius), formed as APT: see -TUDE. Cf. ATTITUDE.]
1 Natural tendency, propensity, or disposition. LME.

> R. OWEN The aptitude of the Cheiroptera . . to fall like Reptiles into a state of true torpidity.

2 Fitness, suitability, appropriateness. M16.

> A. HELPS In any comparison so frequently used there must be some aptitude.

3 Natural ability; a talent (*for*); capacity to acquire a particular skill. M16.

> R. CHURCH I had no aptitude for figures. A. TOFFLER People who share the same interests and aptitudes. *attrib.*: M. MCCARTHY By the use of aptitude tests . . he hoped to discover a method of gauging student potential.

†**4** = ATTITUDE 1. M17–E18.

†**aptote** *noun.* L16–L18.
[ORIGIN Late Latin *aptotus* from Greek *aptōtos* without cases, from A-[10] + *ptōsis* case.]
GRAMMAR. An indeclinable noun.

Apulian /əˈpjuːlɪən/ *adjective & noun.* E17.
[ORIGIN from Latin *Apulia* (see below) + -AN.]
▸ **A** *adjective.* Of or pertaining to the ancient province or the modern district of Apulia in southern Italy, or its inhabitants. E17.
▸ **B** *noun.* A native or inhabitant of Apulia. E17.

Apus /ˈeɪpəs/ *noun.* E18.
[ORIGIN Latin *apus* a kind of bird from Greek *apous*.]
(The name of) an inconspicuous circumpolar constellation of the southern hemisphere; = ***bird of paradise*** (b) s.v. BIRD *noun*.

apyretic /eɪpʌɪˈrɛtɪk, apɪ-/ *adjective.* Now *rare.* M19.
[ORIGIN from A-[10] + PYRETIC.]
MEDICINE. = APYREXIAL.

apyrexia /apʌɪˈrɛksɪə, eɪ-/ *noun.* Also †**-exy**. M17.
[ORIGIN mod. Latin from Greek *apurexia*; partly through French *apyrexie* (16).]
MEDICINE. Absence of fever.
■ **apyrexial** *adjective* free from fever L19.

aqua /ˈakwə/ *noun*[1]. LME.
[ORIGIN Latin.]
1 Water, esp. in pharmaceutical and commercial use. LME.
aqua birth, ***aqua park***, ***aqua pool***, etc.
2 CHEMISTRY. The water molecule, H_2O, as a neutral ligand. Usu. *attrib.* Also called **aquo**. M20.
aqua complex, ***aqua salt***, etc.

aqua /ˈakwə/ *noun*[2]. M20.
[ORIGIN Abbreviation.]
The colour aquamarine.

aqua- /ˈakwə/ *combining form.*
[ORIGIN Latin *aqua* water.]
Forming nouns with the sense 'water', esp. with ref. to aquatic entertainment.
■ **aquacade** *noun* (*US*) a spectacle involving swimming and diving, usu. with musical accompaniment M20.

aquaculture /ˈakwəkʌltʃə/ *noun.* Also **aqui-** /ˈakwɪ-/. M19.
[ORIGIN from AQUA- + -CULTURE.]
The rearing of aquatic animals or the cultivation of aquatic plants, for food.
■ **aquaˈcultural** *adjective* L19.

aqua fortis /ˌakwə ˈfɔːtɪs/ *noun phr. arch.* Also **aquafortis**. L15.
[ORIGIN Latin = strong water.]
Nitric acid; orig., any powerful solvent.

aquake /əˈkweɪk/ *adverb & pred. adjective. poet.* L19.
[ORIGIN from A-[2] + QUAKE *noun* or *verb*.]
Quaking.

Aqua Libra /ˌakwə ˈliːbrə/ *noun phr.* L20.
[ORIGIN Latin *aqua* water + *libra* balance.]
(Proprietary name for) a beverage made from flavoured mineral water and fruit juices; a drink of this.

aqualung /ˈakwəlʌŋ/ *noun & verb.* Also (US proprietary name) **Aqua-Lung**. M20.
[ORIGIN from AQUA- + LUNG.]
▸ **A** *noun.* A portable breathing apparatus for divers, comprising cylinders of compressed air strapped on the back, feeding air automatically to a mask or mouthpiece. M20.
▸ **B** *verb intrans.* Use an aqualung. M20.

aquamanile /ˌakwəməˈnʌɪli, -ˈniːli/ *noun.* L19.
[ORIGIN Late Latin from Latin *aquaemanalis* hand-basin, from *aquae* genit. sing. of *aqua* water + *manale* ewer.]
A water vessel or ewer, freq. in the form of an animal or bird.

aquamarine /ˌakwəməˈriːn/ *noun & adjective.* E18.
[ORIGIN from Latin *aqua marina* seawater.]
▸ **A** *noun.* **1** A bluish-green variety of beryl. E18.
2 The colour of this. M19.
▸ **B** *adjective.* Having the colour of aquamarine. M19.

†**aqua mirabilis** *noun phr.* L16–E19.
[ORIGIN Latin = wonderful water.]
A cordial distilled from a mixture of various spices with alcohol.

aquanaut /ˈakwənɔːt/ *noun.* L19.
[ORIGIN from AQUA- + Greek *nautēs* sailor.]
An underwater swimmer or explorer.

aquaphobia /akwəˈfəʊbɪə/ *noun.* M20.
[ORIGIN from AQUA- + PHOBIA.]
Fear of water, spec. of drowning in water (as opp. to ***hydrophobia*** or fear of drinking water).
■ ˈ**aquaphobe** *noun* L20. **aquaphobic** *adjective* L20.

aquaplane /ˈakwəpleɪn/ *noun & verb.* E20.
[ORIGIN from AQUA- + PLANE *noun*[3].]
▸ **A** *noun.* A board on which a person rides, towed behind a speedboat. E20.
▸ **B** *verb intrans.* **1** Ride standing on an aquaplane. E20.
2 Of a vehicle: glide uncontrollably on water covering a road surface. M20.

aqua regia /ˌakwə ˈriːdʒə/ *noun phr.* Also †**aqua regis**. E17.
[ORIGIN Latin = royal water.]
CHEMISTRY. A concentrated mixture of nitric and hydrochloric acids, able to dissolve gold, platinum, etc.

aquarelle /akwəˈrɛl/ *noun.* M19.
[ORIGIN French from Italian *acquarella* watercolour, from *acqua* from Latin *aqua* water.]
A style of painting in thin, usu. transparent, watercolours; a painting in this style.
■ **aquarellist** *noun* an artist in aquarelle L19.

aquaria *noun pl.* see AQUARIUM.

Aquarian /əˈkwɛːrɪən/ *noun & adjective.* L16.
[ORIGIN from Latin *aquarius* pertaining to water, AQUARIUS, from *aqua* water, + -AN.]
▸ **A** *noun.* **1** *ECCLESIASTICAL HISTORY.* A member of an early Christian sect who used water instead of wine at the Eucharist. L16.
2 (**a-**.) = AQUARIST. M19.
3 A person born under the sign Aquarius. E20.
▸ **B** *adjective.* **1** (**a-**.) Of or pertaining to an aquarium. M19.
2 Of or pertaining to the sign Aquarius; (characteristic of a person) born under Aquarius. M20.

aquarist /ˈakwərɪst/ *noun.* Also †**-iist**. L19.
[ORIGIN from AQUARIUM + -IST.]
A person who keeps an aquarium.

aquarium /əˈkwɛːrɪəm/ *noun.* Pl. **-ria** /-rɪə/, **-riums**. M19.
[ORIGIN Use as noun of neut. sing. of Latin *aquarius* (see AQUARIAN), after VIVARIUM.]
An artificial pond or tank (usu. with transparent sides) for keeping live aquatic plants and animals; a place containing such tanks.

Aquarius /əˈkwɛːrɪəs/ *noun.* OE.
[ORIGIN Latin = water-carrier, use as noun of adjective: see AQUARIAN.]
1 (The name of) a constellation on the ecliptic just south of the celestial equator, next to Capricorn; *ASTROLOGY* (the name of) the eleventh zodiacal sign, usu. associated with the period 20 January to 18 February (see note s.v. ZODIAC); the Water-carrier. OE.

attrib.: E. KIRK Aquarius people are remarkable spiritual healers.

Age of Aquarius an astrological age characterized by (esp. sexual) freedom and brotherhood.
2 A person born under the sign Aquarius; = AQUARIAN *noun* 3. M20.

aquarobics /akwəˈrəʊbɪks/ *noun pl.* (treated as *sing.* or *pl.*). L20.
[ORIGIN Blend of AQUA- and AEROBICS.]
(A system of) aerobic exercises performed in water.
– NOTE: Proprietary name in the US.

aquatic /əˈkwatɪk, -ˈkwɒt-/ *adjective & noun.* L15.
[ORIGIN Old French & mod. French *aquatique* or Latin *aquaticus*, from *aqua* water: see -ATIC. Cf. AQUATILE.]
▸ **A** *adjective.* **1** Of or pertaining to water. L15.
2 Growing or living in or near water. M17.
3 Of a sport: conducted on or in water. M19.
▸ **B** *noun.* **1** An aquatic plant or animal. L17. ▸**b** A swimmer, a bather. *joc.* E19.
2 In *pl.* Aquatic sports. M19.

aquatile /ˈakwətʌɪl, -tɪl/ *adjective & noun. arch.* E17.
[ORIGIN Latin *aquatilis*, from *aqua* water: see -ATILE.]
▸ **A** *adjective.* = AQUATIC *adjective* 2. E17.
▸ †**B** *noun.* = AQUATIC *noun* 1. M17–M18.

aquatint /ˈakwətɪnt/ *noun & verb.* As noun also **aquatinta** /akwəˈtɪntə/. L18.
[ORIGIN French *aquatinte*, Italian *acquatinta* coloured water: cf. TINT *verb*[1].]
▸ **A** *noun.* A method of etching on copper with nitric acid, which produces shaded effects as well as lines; an engraving made by this method. L18.
▸ **B** *verb intrans. & trans.* Etch in aquatint. E19.
■ **aquatinter** *noun* M19.

aquavit /akwəˈviːt/ *noun.* Also **akva-** /akvə-/. L19.
[ORIGIN Norwegian, Swedish, Danish *akvavit* AQUA VITAE.]
An alcoholic spirit distilled from potatoes or other starch-containing plants.

aqua vitae /ˌakwə ˈvʌɪtiː, ˈviːtʌɪ/ *noun phr.* Also **aqua-vitae**. LME.
[ORIGIN Latin = water of life: cf. French *eau de vie*, USQUEBAUGH.]
Alcoholic spirits, esp. of the first distillation.

†**-aque** *suffix* var. of **-AC**.

aqueduct /ˈakwɪdʌkt/ *noun.* M16.
[ORIGIN French †*aqueduct* (now *-duc*) or its source Latin *aquae(-)ductus*, from genit. of *aqua* water + *ductus* conveying.]
1 An artificial channel, esp. an elevated structure of masonry, for the conveyance of water. M16.
2 *ANATOMY.* A small fluid-filled canal; *spec.* that connecting the third and fourth ventricles of the brain. E18.

aqueous /ˈeɪkwɪəs/ *adjective & noun.* M17.
[ORIGIN from medieval Latin *aqueus*, from *aqua* water: see -EOUS.]
▸ **A** *adjective.* **1** Of the nature of water; watery. M17.
aqueous humour the clear fluid occupying the space between the lens and cornea of the eye.
2 Connected with or relating to water. M18.
aqueous solution: of a substance dissolved in water.
▸ **B** *noun.* The aqueous humour. L19.

aquiculture *noun* var. of AQUACULTURE.

aquifer /ˈakwɪfə/ *noun.* E20.
[ORIGIN from Latin *aqui-* combining form of *aqua* water + -FER.]
GEOLOGY. A water-bearing stratum of permeable rock.

aquiferous /əˈkwɪf(ə)rəs/ *adjective.* M19.
[ORIGIN formed as AQUIFER: see -FEROUS.]
Conveying or yielding water.

Aquila /ˈakwɪlə, əˈkwɪlə/ *noun.* M16.
[ORIGIN Latin *aquila* eagle.]
(The name of) a constellation on the celestial equator, lying in the Milky Way near Cygnus; the Eagle.

aquilegia /akwɪˈliːdʒə/ *noun.* Also †**-lege**. L16.
[ORIGIN medieval Latin *aquilegia*, *-leia*, prob. from Latin *aquilegus* water-collecting.]
Any plant of the genus *Aquilegia* of the buttercup family, bearing showy flowers whose five petals have backward-directed hollow spurs; a columbine.

aquiline /ˈakwɪlʌɪn/ *adjective.* M17.
[ORIGIN Latin *aquilinus*, from *aquila* eagle, prob. after French *aquilin*: see -INE[1].]
1 Of or belonging to an eagle. M17.
2 Like an eagle; *esp.* (of the nose or features) curved like an eagle's beak. M17.

BURKE A penetrating aquiline eye. ALDOUS HUXLEY The aquiline good looks of a rather long and narrow face. M. DRABBLE She has a . . tall, stiletto . . figure . . . at the worst he could call her aquiline.

†**Aquilon** *noun.* LME–E17.
[ORIGIN Old French & mod. French from Latin *aquilo(n-)*.]
The north or north-north-east wind.

aquiver /əˈkwɪvə/ *adverb & pred. adjective.* L19.
[ORIGIN from A-[2] + QUIVER *noun*[2] or *verb*[1].]
In a quiver, trembling.

aquo /ˈakwəʊ/ *noun.* E20.
[ORIGIN formed as AQUA *noun*[1] + -O-.]
CHEMISTRY. = AQUA *noun*[1] 2. Usu. *attrib.*

aquose /ˈakwəʊs/ *adjective. rare.* LME.
[ORIGIN Latin *aquosus*, from *aqua* water: see -OSE[1].]
Watery; full of fluid.

aquosity /əˈkwɒsɪti/ *noun.* LME.
[ORIGIN Late Latin *aquositas*, formed as AQUOSE: see -ITY.]
1 The quality of being moist or watery. LME.
†**2** Moisture, liquid, fluid. LME–E18.

AR *abbreviation.*
1 Arkansas.
2 Autonomous Republic.

Ar *symbol.*
CHEMISTRY. Argon.

ar /ɑː/ *noun.* LME.
[ORIGIN Repr. pronunc.]
The letter R (r).

ar- /ar, *unstressed* ər/ *prefix* (not productive).
Assim. form of Latin AD- before *r*. In Old French, Latin *arr-* was reduced to *ar-*, which appears in Middle English adoptions, but in later French, and hence in English, *arr-* was restored by Latinization, as ***arrange***, ***arrest***.

-ar /ə/ *suffix*[1].
1 [Repr. Latin *-aris* adjectival suffix, synon. with *-alis* (-AL[1]) but used where *l* preceded, or Old French *-aire*, *-ier* (later refashioned after Latin).] Forming adjectives with the sense 'of the kind of, pertaining to', as ***angular***, ***lunar***, ***molecular***, ***stellar***, ***titular***, etc. Also forming nouns, as ***scholar***.
2 [Repr. Latin *-ar(e)* neut. of *-aris*, or French *-er*.] Forming nouns, as ***pillar***.

-ar /ə/ *suffix*[2] (not productive).
[ORIGIN Repr. Latin *-arius*, *-ium* (usu. repr. by -ER[1], -ARY[1]) or French *-aire*, or *-ier*.]
Forming nouns, as ***bursar***, ***exemplar***, ***vicar***, etc.

-ar /ə/ *suffix*[3] (not productive).
Alt. of -ER[1], -ER[2], or -OR, as ***beggar***, ***liar***, ***pedlar***, etc.

ARA *abbreviation.*
Associate of the Royal Academy.

Ara /ˈɑːrə/ *noun.* M17.
[ORIGIN Latin *ara* altar.]
(The name of) a small constellation of the southern hemisphere in the Milky Way, near Scorpius; the Altar.

Arab /ˈarəb/ *noun & adjective.* In sense A.3 also **a-**. LME.
[ORIGIN French *Arabe* from Latin *Arabs* from Greek *Araps*, *Arab-* from Arabic *ʿarab*.]
▸ **A** *noun.* **1** A member of the Semitic people orig. inhabiting the Arabian peninsula and neighbouring lands, and now the Middle East generally. LME.
2 An Arabian horse (prized for pure breeding and swiftness). M17.
3 More fully ***street Arab***. A homeless vagrant child. *arch.* M19.
▸ **B** *adjective.* Of or pertaining to Arabia or the Arabs; Arabian. E19.
– NOTE: Rare before 17, the usual word being ARABY earlier.
■ **Arabdom** *noun* Arabs collectively; the Arab world: M20.

araba /əˈrɑːbə/ *noun.* E19.
[ORIGIN Turkish from Arabic *ʿarrāda* gun carriage.]
Chiefly *hist.* An ox-drawn or horse-drawn carriage used in Turkey and the Middle East.

arabesque /arəˈbɛsk/ *noun, adjective, & verb.* M17.
[ORIGIN French from Italian *arabesco*, from *arabo* Arab: see -ESQUE.]
▸ **A** *noun.* **1** Decorative work of a kind which originated in Arabic or Moorish art, consisting of flowing lines of branches, leaves, scrollwork, etc., fancifully intertwined; an ornamental design of this kind. M17.

fig.: LONGFELLOW Not Art but Nature . . carved this graceful arabesque of vines.

†**2** Vernacular Arabic. Only in L18.
3 *BALLET.* A posture in which the body is bent forwards and supported on one leg with the other leg extended horizontally backwards, with the arms extended one forwards and one backwards. M19.
4 *MUSIC.* A passage or composition with fanciful ornamentation of the melody. M19.
▸ **B** *adjective.* Of ornamental design: decorated in arabesque, of the nature of arabesque. L18.

fig.: DICKENS Surrounded by this arabesque work of his musing fancy.

▸ **C** *verb trans.* Ornament in arabesque. M19.

Arabian /əˈreɪbɪən/ *adjective & noun.* LME.
[ORIGIN from Old French *arabi* ARABY or Latin *Arab(i)us* from Greek *Arabios*, formed as ARAB: see -AN, -IAN.]
▸ **A** *adjective.* Of or pertaining to Arabia, a large peninsula in SW Asia. LME.
Arabian bird a phoenix, a unique specimen. ***Arabian camel***: see CAMEL 1. ***Arabian*** JASMINE. ***Arabian*** ORYX.
▸ **B** *noun.* **1** A native or inhabitant of Arabia. LME.
2 An Arabian horse. Cf. ARAB *noun* 2. L18.

Arabic /ˈarəbɪk/ *adjective & noun.* Also **a-**. ME.
[ORIGIN Old French (mod. *arabique*) from Latin *Arabicus* from Greek *Arabikos*, formed as ARAB: see -IC.]
▸ **A** *adjective.* **1** From Arabia. Chiefly in ***gum Arabic***, a water-soluble gum exuded by certain acacias (esp. *Acacia senegal*). ME.
2 Of the Arabs; of or pertaining to the language and literature of the Arabs. LME.
arabic numerals the figures 1, 2, 3, 4, etc.

A

► **B** *noun*. The Semitic language originally of the Arabs, now spoken in much of the Middle East and N. Africa. LME.

■ **Arabicism** /əˈrabɪsɪz(ə)m/ *noun* an Arabic idiom or peculiarity of language E19. **Arabicize** /əˈrabɪsʌɪz/ *verb trans.* make like Arabic; make conform to Arabic usage: L19.

arabica /əˈrabɪkə/ *noun*. Also **A-**. E20.
[ORIGIN Latin, specific epithet (see below), fem. of *arabicus*: see ARABIC.]
More fully ***arabica coffee***. A coffee plant of the most widely grown species, *Coffea arabica*; beans or coffee obtained from such a plant.

arabidopsis /aˌrabɪˈdɒpsɪs/ *noun*. L19.
[ORIGIN mod. Latin (see below), from ARABI(S + -*d*- + Greek *opsis* appearance.]
Any of various small plants of the cruciferous genus *Arabidopsis*, found esp. in dry, sandy, stony, or saline habitats; *spec.* thale cress, *A. thaliana*, often used in genetics research.

arabinose /ˈarəbɪnəʊz, -s/ *noun*. L19.
[ORIGIN from ARABICA + -IN[1] + -OSE[2]: it was first obtained from gum arabic.]
CHEMISTRY. A pentose sugar which is a constituent of many plant gums.

arabis /ˈarəbɪs/ *noun*. E17.
[ORIGIN medieval Latin from Greek, use as noun of fem. of *Araps* ARAB.]
A cruciferous plant of the genus *Arabis*, with white, pink, or purple flowers.

Arabise *verb* var. of ARABIZE.

Arabism /ˈarəbɪz(ə)m/ *noun*. E17.
[ORIGIN from ARAB + -ISM.]
1 †**a** Arabic. Only in E17. ►**b** An Arabicism. M18.
2 Arab culture or its influence; (support for) Arab nationalism or political self-assertion. L19.
■ **Arabist** *noun* (**a**) an expert in or student of the Arabic language or other aspects of Arab culture; (**b**) a supporter of Arabism: M18.

Arabize /ˈarəbʌɪz/ *verb trans.* Also **-ise**. L19.
[ORIGIN from ARAB + -IZE.]
Make Arab; give an Arabic character to.
■ **Arabiˈzation** *noun* M20.

arable /ˈarəb(ə)l/ *adjective & noun*. LME.
[ORIGIN Old French & mod. French, or Latin *arabilis*, from *arare* to plough: see -ABLE.]
► **A** *adjective*. Of land: ploughed or fit for ploughing. Also, (of crops) suitable for cultivation on arable land; (of farming) given over largely to growing crops on arable land. LME.
► **B** *noun*. Arable land; arable farming. L16.
■ **araˈbility** *noun* suitability for being used as arable land L19.

Araby /ˈarəbi/ *noun & adjective*. Long *arch. & poet.* ME.
[ORIGIN Old French *ar(r)abi* adjective, prob. from Arabic *ʿarabī* from *ʿarab* ARAB; in sense A.3 from Old French & mod. French *Arabie* from Latin *Arabia* from Greek.]
► **A** *noun*. †**1** An Arabian horse. Cf. ARAB *noun* 2. Only in ME.
†**2** An Arab. LME–L16.
3 Arabia. LME.
► **B** *adjective*. Arabian; Arabic. Now *rare* or *obsolete*. LME.

aracari /arəˈsɑːri, -ˈkɑːri/ *noun*. Also **araçari**. E19.
[ORIGIN Portuguese *araçari* from Tupi *arasaˈri* the name given to any small toucan.]
Any of a number of small toucans of the genus *Pteroglossus*, with a serrated bill and typically a green back and wings, yellow underside, and red rump.

†**arace** *verb trans.* ME–M16.
[ORIGIN Old French *aracier*, formed as A-[6] + *rais* root: see RACE *noun*[2]. Aphet. to RACE *verb*[1].]
Pull up by the roots; pull violently away.

arachide /ˈarəʃiːd/ *noun*. M20.
[ORIGIN French.]
= ARACHIS.

arachidic /arəˈkɪdɪk/ *adjective*. M19.
[ORIGIN from mod. Latin *arachid-*, ARACHIS *noun* + -IC.]
CHEMISTRY. ***arachidic acid***, a straight-chain saturated fatty acid, $C_{19}H_{39}COOH$, present in peanut oil. Also called ***eicosanoic acid***.

arachidonic /arakɪˈdɒnɪk/ *adjective*. E20.
[ORIGIN Unsystematically from ARACHIDIC + -ON(E + -IC.]
CHEMISTRY. ***arachidonic acid***, a polyunsaturated fatty acid, $C_{20}H_{32}O_2$, found in animal fats and considered essential in animal metabolism.

arachis /ˈarəkɪs/ *noun*. M19.
[ORIGIN mod. Latin from Greek *arak(h)os*, *-kis* some leguminous plant.]
The groundnut plant, *Arachis hypogaea*.
– COMB.: **arachis oil** peanut oil.

arachnean /arəkˈniːən/ *adjective*. *rare*. L16.
[ORIGIN from Greek *arakhnaios*, from *arakhnē* spider: see -AN.]
Of spiders or their webs; gossamer.

arachnid /əˈraknɪd/ *noun & adjective*. M19.
[ORIGIN French *arachnide* or mod. Latin *Arachnida* (see below), from Greek *arakhnē* spider: see -ID[3].]
ZOOLOGY. (Designating or pertaining to) an arthropod belonging to the class Arachnida, which includes spiders, scorpions, mites, ticks, etc.
■ Also **arachnidan** *noun & adjective* (now *rare*) E19.

arachnoid /əˈraknɔɪd/ *adjective & noun*. M18.
[ORIGIN mod. Latin *arachnoides* from Greek *arakhnoeidēs* like a cobweb, formed as ARACHNID: see -OID.]
► **A** *adjective*. **1** ANATOMY. Designating or pertaining to a fine delicate membrane which is the middle of the three meninges enveloping the brain and spinal cord. M18.
2 BOTANY. Covered with or consisting of fine hairs resembling a cobweb. E19.
3 Like an arachnid; arachnean. M19.
► **B** *noun*. ANATOMY. The arachnoid membrane. E19.
pia-arachnoid: see PIA *noun*[1].
■ **arachˈnitis** *noun* = ARACHNOIDITIS E19. **arachˈnoidal** *adjective* = ARACHNOID *adjective* 1 M19. **arachnoiˈditis** *noun* inflammation of the arachnoid membrane M19.

arachnology /arəkˈnɒlədʒi/ *noun*. M19.
[ORIGIN from Greek *arakhnē* spider + -OLOGY.]
The branch of zoology that deals with arachnids.
■ **arachnoˈlogical** *adjective* M19. **arachnologist** *noun* E19.

arachnophobia /əraknə(ʊ)ˈfəʊbɪə/ *noun*. E20.
[ORIGIN formed as ARACHNOLOGY + -O- + -PHOBIA.]
Irrational fear of spiders.
■ **aˈrachnophobe** *noun* a person who is frightened of spiders E20. **arachnophobic** *adjective & noun* L20.

†**araeometer** *noun* var. of AREOMETER.

arage *noun* see AVERAGE *noun*[1].

Aragonese /arəgəˈniːz/ *adjective & noun*. Also †**Arr-**. E16.
[ORIGIN Spanish *aragonés*, from *Aragón* Aragon (see below): see -ESE.]
► **A** *adjective*. Of or pertaining to Aragon, a region and former kingdom of NE Spain, its inhabitants, or their dialect. E16.
► **B** *noun*. Pl. same.
1 A native or inhabitant of Aragon. E19.
2 The dialect of Spanish spoken there. L19.

aragonite /ˈarəg(ə)nʌɪt/ *noun*. Also †**arr-**. E19.
[ORIGIN from *Aragon* (see ARAGONESE) + -ITE[1].]
MINERALOGY. A low-temperature orthorhombic form of calcium carbonate.

arahat *noun* var. of ARHAT.

arain /ˈar(ə)n/ *noun*. Long *dial.* Also **arrand** /ˈar(ə)nd/. LME.
[ORIGIN Old French & mod. French *araigne* from Latin *aranea*.]
A spider.

†**araise** *verb trans.* ME–E17.
[ORIGIN from A-[1] + RAISE *verb*.]
Raise, lift up; raise from the dead, arouse.

SHAKES. *All's Well* A medicine . . whose simple touch Is powerful to araise King Pepin.

arak *noun* var. of ARRACK.

Arakanese /arəkəˈniːz/ *adjective & noun*. E19.
[ORIGIN from *Arakan* (see below) + -ESE.]
► **A** *adjective*. Of or pertaining to Arakan, a district on the west coast of Myanmar (Burma), its inhabitants, or their dialect. E19.
► **B** *noun*. Pl. same.
1 A native or inhabitant of Arakan. E19.
2 The dialect of Burmese spoken there. L19.

Araldite /ˈar(ə)ldʌɪt/ *noun*. M20.
[ORIGIN Unknown.]
(Proprietary name for) any of a series of epoxy resins used esp. as strong cements.

aralia /əˈreɪlɪə/ *noun*. M18.
[ORIGIN mod. Latin, of unknown origin.]
A plant of the genus *Aralia* (family Araliaceae), which includes a number of American and Asian trees and shrubs, e.g. wild sarsaparilla *A. nudicaulis*.
■ **araliˈaceous** *adjective* of or pertaining to the family Araliaceae, which includes ivy, ginseng, wild sarsaparilla, and other plants, besides the aralias M19.

Aramaean /arəˈmiːən/ *adjective & noun*. Also **-mean**. M19.
[ORIGIN formed as ARAMAIC + -AN.]
► **A** *adjective*. Of or pertaining to the country or language of Aram (now Syria). M19.
► **B** *noun*. A native or inhabitant of Aram. Also, Aramaic. M19.

Aramaic /arəˈmeɪɪk/ *adjective & noun*. M19.
[ORIGIN from Greek *Aramaios* from Hebrew *ʾărām* Aram, biblical name of Syria: see -IC.]
► **A** *adjective*. Of or pertaining to Aram (now Syria); *spec.* designating or pertaining to a Semitic language of ancient Syria, the official language of the Persian Empire from the 6th cent. BC, widely used as a lingua franca by Jews and others in the Middle East, and later developing into dialects, including Syriac, Mandaean, and one used by Christian Palestinians. M19.
► **B** *noun*. The ancient Aramaic language; any of the dialects developed from it. L19.

arame /ˈarəmi/ *noun*. M20.
[ORIGIN Japanese, from *ara* wild + *me* akin to + *mo* alga.]
An edible Pacific seaweed, *Ecklonia bicyclis*, which has broad brown leaves used in Japanese cookery.

Aramean *adjective & noun* var. of ARAMAEAN.

aramid /ˈaramɪd/ *noun*. L20.
[ORIGIN from AR(OMATIC + POLY)AMID(E.]
Any of a class of synthetic polyamides that are formed from aromatic monomers, and yield fibres of exceptional strength and thermal stability. Freq. *attrib.*, esp. in ***aramid fibre***.
– NOTE: A proprietary name for such a fibre is KEVLAR.

Aran /ˈar(ə)n/ *adjective*. M20.
[ORIGIN The *Aran* islands off the west coast of Ireland.]
Designating a type of knitwear with patterns traditionally used in the Aran islands, esp. involving raised cable stitch and large diamond designs, or a sweater or pullover of this type.

Aranda /əˈrandə/ *noun & adjective*. Also **-ta** /-tə/, **Arunta** /əˈrʌntə/. L19.
[ORIGIN Prob. from a Central Desert Australian Aboriginal language.]
= ARRERNTE.

araneid /əˈreɪnɪɪd/ *noun & adjective*. L19.
[ORIGIN mod. Latin *Araneida* (see below), formed as ARANEOLOGY: see -ID[3].]
ZOOLOGY. (An arachnid) of the order Araneida or the family Araneidae; a spider.
■ Also **araneidan** /arəˈniːɪd(ə)n/ *noun & adjective* = ARANEID M19.

araneology /əreɪnɪˈɒlədʒi/ *noun*. L18.
[ORIGIN from Latin *aranea* spider + -OLOGY.]
The branch of zoology that deals with spiders.
■ **araneologist** *noun* L19.

araneous /əˈreɪnɪəs/ *adjective*. Now *rare* or *obsolete*. M17.
[ORIGIN from Latin *araneosus*, formed as ARANEOLOGY: see -OUS.]
Arachnean; arachnoid.

Aranta *noun & adjective* var. of ARANDA.

Arapaho /əˈrapəhəʊ/ *noun & adjective*. Pl. of noun same, **-s**. E19.
[ORIGIN Crow *alappahó* lit. 'many tattoo marks'.]
A member of, of or pertaining to, an Algonquian people of the plains of N. America; (of) the language of this people.

arapaima /arəˈpʌɪmə/ *noun*. M19.
[ORIGIN Tupi.]
A very large S. American freshwater food fish, *Arapaima gigas*. Also called ***paiche***, ***pirarucú***.

araroba /arəˈrəʊbə/ *noun*. L19.
[ORIGIN Portuguese from Tupi.]
1 PHARMACOLOGY. = ***GOA powder***. L19.
2 A leguminous tree of Brazil, *Andira araroba*, from which Goa powder is obtained. E20.

aration /əˈreɪʃ(ə)n/ *noun*. *rare*. M17.
[ORIGIN Latin *aratio(n-)*, from *arat-* pa. ppl stem of *arare* to plough: see -ATION.]
Ploughing, tillage.

arational /eɪˈraʃ(ə)n(ə)l/ *adjective*. M20.
[ORIGIN from A-[10] + RATIONAL *adjective*.]
Unconcerned with or outside rationality; non-rational.

Araucanian /arɔːˈkeɪnɪən/ *adjective & noun*. E19.
[ORIGIN from Spanish *Araucanía* a region of Chile + -AN.]
= MAPUCHE.

araucaria /arəˈkɛːrɪə/ *noun*. M19.
[ORIGIN mod. Latin, from Spanish *Arauco* a province of Araucanía, Chile: see -ARY[1].]
A member of the genus *Araucaria* of tall evergreen conifers native to the southern hemisphere and including several trees valuable for their timber; *esp.* the monkey-puzzle, *A. araucana*.
■ **araucarian** *adjective* of the genus *Araucaria* M19.

Arawak /ˈarəwak, -ɑːk/ *noun & adjective*. M18.
[ORIGIN Carib *aruac*.]
► **A** *noun*. A member of a group of Arawakan peoples now chiefly inhabiting the NE coast of S. America; the language of these peoples. M18.
► **B** *attrib.* or as *adjective*. Of or pertaining to these peoples or their language. M18.

Arawakan /arəˈwak(ə)n, -wɑːk-/ *adjective & noun*. E20.
[ORIGIN from ARAWAK + -AN.]
► **A** *adjective*. Designating or pertaining to a widespread family of languages of S. America, including Arawak; designating or belonging to a people speaking an Arawakan language. E20.
► **B** *noun*. **1** A member of an Arawakan people. E20.
2 The Arawakan family of languages. M20.

arb /ɑːb/ *noun*. *colloq.* L20.
[ORIGIN Abbreviation.]
= ARBITRAGEUR.

arbalest /ˈɑːbəlɛst/ *noun. obsolete* exc. *hist.* Also **-balist** /-bəlɪst/, **-blast** /-blɑːst/. OE.
[ORIGIN Old French *arbaleste*, *arbe-* (mod. *arbalète*) from late Latin *arcuballista*, from *arcus* bow: see ARC *noun*, BALLISTA.]
1 A crossbow with a wooden shaft and special drawing mechanism, used for discharging arrows, bolts, stones, etc. OE.
2 = ARBALESTER. ME.
■ **arbalester** *noun* a soldier armed with an arbalest; a crossbowman: ME. **arbaˈlestrier** *noun* (*hist.*) = ARBALESTER M19.

†**arber** *noun.* Also **er-**. ME–E18.
[ORIGIN Old French (*h*)*erbier*(*e*), *arb-* (mod. *herbier*), from (*h*)*erbe* rumen.]
The windpipe, the gullet; (sometimes extended to) the whole pluck of an animal.
make the arber HUNTING remove the pluck, the first stage in disembowelling.

arbiter /ˈɑːbɪtə/ *noun.* LME.
[ORIGIN Latin = judge, supreme ruler.]
1 A person whose opinion or decision is authoritative in a matter of debate; a judge, arbitrator, or umpire appointed to decide a dispute. LME.
> W. H. DIXON Appointed arbiter of the dispute. *fig.*: MILTON Twilight.. short Arbiter 'Twixt Day and Night.

2 A person with complete authority over or control *of* (a matter). E17.
> D. HALBERSTAM Her taste was impeccable, she was not so much an arbiter of fashion as she was fashion herself.

– PHRASES: **arbiter elegantiarum** /ˌɛlɪgantɪˈɑːrəm/, **arbiter elegantiae** /ɛlɪˈgantɪʌɪ/ [Latin = judge of elegance] an authority on matters of taste or etiquette.

arbitrable /ˈɑːbɪtrəb(ə)l/ *adjective.* Now chiefly *US.* M16.
[ORIGIN from Latin *arbitrari*: see ARBITRATE, -ABLE.]
Subject to or capable of settlement by an arbiter.

arbitrage /ˈɑːbɪtrɪdʒ; COMMERCE *also* ɑːbɪˈtrɑːʒ, ˈɑːbɪtrɑːʒ/ *noun & verb.* LME.
[ORIGIN Old French & mod. French, from *arbitrer* from Latin *arbitrari*: see ARBITRATE, -AGE. Commercial use from mod. French.]
▸ **A** *noun.* †**1** Exercise of individual authoritative judgement; self-determination. LME–E19.
2 Decision by an arbitrator or arbitrators; the process of arbitration. *arch.* L15.
3 COMMERCE. Trade in bills of exchange or stocks in different markets to take advantage of their different prices. L19.
▸ **B** *verb intrans.* COMMERCE. Engage in arbitrage. E20.

arbitrageur /ˌɑːbɪtrɑːˈʒəː/ *noun.* L19.
[ORIGIN French, formed as ARBITRAGE + *-eur* -OR.]
COMMERCE. A person who engages in arbitrage.

arbitral /ˈɑːbɪtr(ə)l/ *adjective.* L15.
[ORIGIN Old French & mod. French, or late Latin *arbitralis*, formed as ARBITER: see -AL[1].]
Of or pertaining to arbitrators or arbitration.

arbitrament /ɑːˈbɪtrəm(ə)nt/ *noun.* Also **-ement**. LME.
[ORIGIN Old French *arbitrement* from medieval Latin *arbitramentum*, from *arbitrari*: see ARBITRATE, -MENT.]
†**1** The right or capacity to decide for oneself; free will. LME–E19.
> MILTON To stand or fall Free in thine own Arbitrament it lies.

2 The power to decide for others; absolute authority. *obsolete* exc. as approaching sense 3. LME.
> W. S. MAUGHAM He decided to leave the matter to the arbitrament of God.

3 The deciding of a dispute by arbitration. LME.
> GLADSTONE An immediate resort to the arbitrament of war. D. BREWSTER In the arbitraments of science it has always been a difficult task to adjust the rival claims of competitors.

4 The authoritative decision reached or the sentence pronounced by an arbiter. LME.
> LYTTON I will not abide by the arbitrement of a pope.

†**5** Agreement reached by arbitration; amicable compromise. M16–E17.
> BACON As if they would make an Arbitrement, betweene God and Man.

arbitrary /ˈɑːbɪt(rə)ri/ *adjective & noun.* LME.
[ORIGIN Latin *arbitrarius*, formed as ARBITER (perh. after French *arbitraire*): see -ARY[1].]
▸ **A** *adjective.* **1** Dependent on will or pleasure; LAW (now *hist.*) dependent on the decision of a legally recognized authority; discretionary. LME.
> JOSEPH HALL It is not left arbitrary to you that you may doe good if you will.

2 Based on mere opinion or preference as opp. to the real nature of things; capricious, unpredictable, inconsistent. M17.
> H. G. WELLS Those arbitrary standards by which we classify people into moral and immoral. J. HELLER His moods were arbitrary and unpredictable. P. USTINOV His internal policy was as arbitrary as his mother's had been consistent.

3 Unrestrained in the exercise of will or authority; despotic, tyrannical. M17.
> H. MARTINEAU No tyrant, no arbitrary disposer of the fortunes of his inferiors. H. MACMILLAN Arbitrary action without consultation or notice, in breach of solemn undertakings,.. revealed the true character of the regime.

4 PRINTING. Of a character: used occasionally to supplement the letters and other characters which constitute an ordinary font of type. E19.
▸ **B** *noun.* Something arbitrary; *spec.* in PRINTING, an arbitrary character. LME.
■ **arbitrarily** *adverb* E17. **arbitrariness** *noun* M17. †**arbitrarious** *adjective* = ARBITRARY 1, 2, 3 L16–E19.

arbitrate /ˈɑːbɪtreɪt/ *verb.* M16.
[ORIGIN Latin *arbitrat-* pa. ppl stem of *arbitrari* examine, give judgement, formed as ARBITER: see -ATE[3].]
1 *verb trans.* Settle by or submit to arbitration. M16.
> A. MILLER He was called upon to arbitrate disputes as though he were an unofficial judge.

†**2** *verb trans. & intrans.* Give an authoritative decision (*that*). L16–L17.
> H. SWINBURNE He did arbitrate and awarde, that.. the cooke should bee recompensed. R. SOUTH The mind.. with an universal Superintendence, arbitrates.. upon them all.

3 *verb trans.* Give an authoritative decision with regard to. *arch.* E17.
> JOHN TAYLOR Now swordes, not wordes, doe kingdoms arbitrate.

4 *verb intrans.* Mediate or act as arbitrator (*in* a dispute, *between* contending parties). E17.
> R. SANDERSON The blessed Apostle taketh upon him to arbitrate and to mediate in the business. LD MACAULAY He must relinquish all thought of arbitrating between contending nations.

■ **arbitrated** *ppl adjective* settled by arbitration; *spec.* in COMMERCE, determined or conducted by arbitration of exchange: L16.

arbitration /ɑːbɪˈtreɪʃ(ə)n/ *noun.* LME.
[ORIGIN Old French & mod. French from Latin *arbitratio(n-)*, formed as ARBITRATE: see -ATION.]
†**1** = ARBITRAMENT 1, 2. LME–M17.
2 The settlement of a dispute or debate by an arbitrator; the process of arbitrating a dispute. LME.
3 ***arbitration of exchange***, the determination of the rate of exchange to be obtained between two countries or currencies, when the operation is to be conducted through an intermediary or intermediaries, in order to ascertain the most profitable method of drawing bills. Cf. ARBITRAGE 3. E19.

arbitrator /ˈɑːbɪtreɪtə/ *noun.* LME.
[ORIGIN Late Latin, formed as ARBITRATE: see -OR. Cf. Old French *arbitrateur*.]
1 A person chosen by the opposing parties in a dispute to decide the differences between them; an arbiter. LME.
> J. L. MOTLEY In case of their inability to agree, they were to appoint arbitrators.

2 A person who decides according to his or her own absolute pleasure; a supreme ordainer. L16.
> W. WHISTON God is the arbitrator of success in war.

■ **arbitratorship** *noun* the position or function of an arbitrator M17. **arbitratrix** *noun* (now *rare*) a female arbitrator, an arbitress L16.

arbitrement *noun* var. of ARBITRAMENT.

†**arbitrer** *noun.* Also **-or**. LME–E19.
[ORIGIN Anglo-Norman *arbitrour*, Old French *-eor*, formed as ARBITRATOR.]
= ARBITRATOR.

arbitress /ˈɑːbɪtrɪs/ *noun.* ME.
[ORIGIN Old French *arbitresse* fem. of *arbitre* ARBITER: see -ESS[1].]
A female arbiter.
> S. RICHARDSON The arbitress of the quarrels of unruly spirits. DISRAELI The arbitress of fashion is one who is allowed to be singular, in order that she may suppress singularity.

†**arbitror** *noun* var. of ARBITRER.

arblast *noun* var. of ARBALEST.

arbor /ˈɑːbə/ *noun*[1]. M17.
[ORIGIN French *arbre* tree, principal axis, assim. in spelling to Latin *arbor*.]
MECHANICS. An axle, beam, or spindle on which something revolves; *esp.* a tool-holder or mandrel on a lathe.

arbor *noun*[2] see ARBOUR.

Arbor Day /ˈɑːbə deɪ/ *noun phr.* Orig. *US.* L19.
[ORIGIN from Latin *arbor* tree + DAY *noun*.]
A day set apart annually in the US, Australia, New Zealand, and elsewhere for the planting of trees.

arboreal /ɑːˈbɔːrɪəl/ *adjective.* M17.
[ORIGIN from Latin *arboreus*, from *arbor* tree, + -AL[1].]
1 Pertaining to or of the nature of trees. M17.
2 Connected with, haunting, or inhabiting trees. M19.
■ ˈ**arboral** *adjective* (*rare*) = ARBOREAL 1 M17. **arboreˈality** *noun* (ZOOLOGY) the state or condition of living primarily in trees; cf. TERRESTRIALITY: L20.

arboreous /ɑːˈbɔːrɪəs/ *adjective.* M17.
[ORIGIN formed as ARBOREAL + -OUS.]
1 Having many trees, wooded. M17.
2 = ARBOREAL. M17.
3 Treelike. M18.

arborescent /ɑːbəˈrɛs(ə)nt/ *adjective.* L17.
[ORIGIN Latin *arborescent-* pres. ppl stem of *arborescere* grow into a tree, from *arbor* tree: see -ESCENT. Cf. French *arborescent*.]
1 Treelike in growth or size; having a woody stem. L17.
2 a Treelike in appearance; branching. L17. ▸**b** ARCHITECTURE. Of ornamentation: branching from and sustained by its support. M19.
■ **arborescence** *noun* treelike growth or formation M19.

arboret /ˈɑːbərɛt/ *noun. arch.* L16.
[ORIGIN from Latin *arbor* tree + -ET[1].]
A little tree, a shrub.

arboretum /ɑːbəˈriːtəm/ *noun.* Pl. **-ta** /-tə/, **-tums**. E19.
[ORIGIN Latin = place with trees, from *arbor* tree.]
A place devoted to the cultivation and exhibition of rare trees; a botanical tree garden.

arborical /ɑːˈbɒrɪk(ə)l/ *adjective. rare.* M17.
[ORIGIN formed as ARBORICULTURE + -ICAL.]
= ARBOREAL 1.

arboricide /ɑːˈbɔːrɪsʌɪd/ *noun.* L19.
[ORIGIN formed as ARBORICULTURE + -CIDE.]
The wanton destruction of trees.
■ **arboriˈcidal** *adjective* given to arboricide M19.

arboriculture /ˈɑːb(ə)rɪkʌltʃə, ɑːˈbɔːr-/ *noun.* E19.
[ORIGIN from Latin *arbor* tree + -I- + -CULTURE.]
The cultivation of trees and shrubs.
■ ˌ**arboriˈcultural** *adjective* of or pertaining to arboriculture E19. ˌ**arboriˈculturist** *noun* a person who practises arboriculture E19.

arborio /ɑːˈbɔːrɪəʊ/ *noun.* M20.
[ORIGIN Italian.]
COOKERY. A variety of round-grained rice produced in Italy and used in making risotto.

arborisation *noun* var. of ARBORIZATION.

arborist /ˈɑːb(ə)rɪst/ *noun.* L16.
[ORIGIN from Latin *arbor* tree + -IST. Cf. ARBOUR 2.]
†**1** A person who cultivates or studies herbs or other flowering plants. Only in L16.
2 A person who studies or cultivates trees. M17.
3 A person who specializes in the care and maintenance of trees; a tree surgeon. M20.

arborization /ˌɑːb(ə)rʌɪˈzeɪʃ(ə)n/ *noun.* Also **-isation**. L18.
[ORIGIN formed as ARBORIST + -IZATION.]
(The production of) a treelike structure or appearance; *esp.* (ANATOMY) the ramification of the ends of certain nerve cells.
■ ˈ**arborize** *verb* (**a**) *verb trans.* make treelike in structure or appearance (chiefly as ***arborized*** *ppl adjective*); (**b**) *verb intrans.* develop arborization: E19.

arborous /ˈɑːb(ə)rəs/ *adjective.* M17.
[ORIGIN formed as ARBORIST + -OUS.]
Of, belonging to, or consisting of trees.

arborvirus *noun* var. of ARBOVIRUS.

arbor vitae /ˌɑːbə ˈvʌɪtiː, ˈviːtʌɪ/ *noun phr.* Also (esp. in sense 1) **arborvitae**. Pl. same. E17.
[ORIGIN Latin = tree of life.]
1 Any of a number of N. American or Far Eastern evergreen conifers, belonging chiefly to the genus *Thuja*. E17.
oil of arbor vitae = ***oil of thuja*** s.v. THUJA.
2 ANATOMY. The arborescent appearance of the white matter in a sagittal section of the cerebellum. Also called ***tree of life***. E19.

arbour /ˈɑːbə/ *noun.* Also ***arbor**; †**harbour**; (orig.) **herber** (long *obsolete* exc. *hist.*), †**erber**. ME.
[ORIGIN Anglo-Norman *erber*, Old French *erbier* (mod. *herbier*), from *erbe* herb + *-ier* formed as -ARIUM: see -OUR. The mod. spelling was furthered by assoc. with Latin *arbor* tree.]
†**1** A garden lawn or green. ME–L15.
2 A herb or flower garden; a flower bed. Long *obsolete* exc. *hist.* ME.
3 A bower or shady retreat, with sides and roof formed mainly by trees and climbing plants. ME. ▸†**b** A covered alley or walk. L16–E18.
†**4** A garden of fruit trees; an orchard. LME–L16.
†**5** Trees or shrubs trained on trelliswork; espaliers. LME–M17.
■ **arboured** *adjective* arched over or shaded as by an arbour: L16.

arbovirus /ɑːbəˈvʌɪrəs/ *noun.* Also **-bor-** /-bɔː-/. M20.
[ORIGIN from *arthropod-borne* + VIRUS *noun*.]
MEDICINE. Any of a class of pathogenic viruses which are transmitted by arthropods (mainly mosquitoes and ticks).

arbuscle /ˈɑːbʌs(ə)l/ *noun. rare.* M17.
[ORIGIN Latin *arbuscula* dim. of *arbor*, *arbos* tree: see -CULE.]
A dwarf tree, a treelike shrub.

arbutus /ɑːˈbjuːtəs, ˈɑːbjʊtəs/ *noun.* M16.
[ORIGIN Latin.]
1 An evergreen tree or shrub of the genus *Arbutus*, of the heath family, *esp.* the strawberry tree, *A. unedo*. M16.
2 A N. American evergreen trailing shrub, *Epigaea repens*, of the heath family, bearing white or pink flowers. Also more fully ***trailing arbutus***. Also called ***ground-laurel***, ***mayflower***. L18.
■ Also **arbute** /ˈɑːbjuːt/ *noun* (*arch.* & *poet.*) M16.

A

ARC *abbreviation.*
1 Agricultural Research Council.
2 *MEDICINE.* Aids-related complex.

arc /ɑːk/ *noun.* LME.
[ORIGIN Old French & mod. French from Latin *arcus* bow, arch, curve.]
1 *ASTRONOMY.* The part of a circle which a celestial object, esp. the sun, appears to follow from horizon to horizon. Now *rare* or *obsolete.* LME.
diurnal arc, **nocturnal arc** the path of the sun above, below, the horizon.
†**2** An arch. M16–M18.
POPE Turn arcs of triumph to a garden-gate.
3 *gen.* Part of the circumference of a circle or other curve; something having the form or appearance of this. L16.
F. O'BRIEN He lifted it in the air, slowly describing an arc of forty-five degrees. TED HUGHES Porpoises . . With arcs And plungings. B. LOVELL The Moon subtends an angle of 31 minutes of arc.
island arc: see ISLAND *noun.*
4 *ELECTRICITY.* A luminous discharge produced between electrodes in a gas. E19.
5 *PHYSIOLOGY.* The connected set of nerves involved in the production of a reflex action. Usu. more fully ***reflex arc.*** M19.
– ATTRIB. & COMB.: Designating devices and methods using an electric arc as a source of light or heat, as ***arc furnace***, ***arc lamp***, ***arc light***, ***arc welding***; *MATH.* preceding a trigonometrical function, designating the angle having a given value of that function, as ***arc sine*** (also **arcsine**), ***arc tangent*** (**arctangent**). Special combs., as **arc minute** *ASTRONOMY* a unit of angular measure equal to 1/60 degree; **arc second** *ASTRONOMY.* 1/60 arc minute.

arc /ˈɑːk/ *verb intrans.* L19.
[ORIGIN from the noun.]
1 Form an electric arc. Chiefly as ***arcing*** *verbal noun.* L19.
2 Move or fly in an arc. M20.

arcade /ɑːˈkeɪd/ *noun.* L17.
[ORIGIN French from Provençal *arcada* or Italian *arcata*, ult. from Latin *arcus* ARC *noun*: see -ADE.]
1 A passage arched over; any covered walk or avenue, esp. with shops etc. along one or both sides. L17.
WORDSWORTH And shades Of trellis-work in long arcades. THACKERAY A garden, with trim lawns, green arcades and vistas of classic statues. K. CLARK These light, sunny arcades with their round arches . . under their straight cornices.
AMUSEMENT ***arcade***. ***video arcade***: see VIDEO *adjective & noun.*
†**2** An arched opening or recess. M18–E19.
3 *ARCHITECTURE.* A series of arches supporting or along a wall. L18.
■ **arcaded** *adjective* formed into an arcade L18. **arcading** *noun* an arrangement of arcades M19.

Arcades ambo /ˈɑːkədiːz ˈambəʊ/ *noun phr.* Freq. *derog.* E19.
[ORIGIN Latin (Virgil) = both Arcadians, i.e. both pastoral poets or musicians.]
Two people of the same tastes, profession, or character.

Arcadia /ɑːˈkeɪdɪə/ *noun.* Also (*poet.*) **Arcady** /ˈɑːkədi/. LME.
[ORIGIN Latin from Greek *Arkadia* a mountainous district in the Peloponnese.]
(Used as a name for) an ideal region of rural contentment.

Arcadian /ɑːˈkeɪdɪən/ *noun & adjective*[1]. L16.
[ORIGIN from Latin *Arcadius*, formed as ARCADIA, + -AN.]
▸ **A** *noun.* An inhabitant of Arcadia; an ideal rustic. L16.
▸ **B** *adjective.* Of or pertaining to Arcadia; ideally rustic. E17.
■ **Arcadianism** *noun* pastoral simplicity E19.

arcadian /ɑːˈkeɪdɪən/ *adjective*[2]. *rare.* L19.
[ORIGIN from ARCADE + -IAN.]
Of or pertaining to arcades.

Arcadic /ɑːˈkeɪdɪk/ *noun & adjective.* E19.
[ORIGIN from ARCADIA + -IC.]
(Of) the ancient Greek dialect of Arcadia.

Arcady *noun* see ARCADIA.

arcana *noun* pl. of ARCANUM.

arcane /ɑːˈkeɪn/ *adjective.* M16.
[ORIGIN Old French & mod. French, or Latin *arcanus*, from *arcere* shut up, from *arca* chest: see -ANE 1.]
Hidden, secret; mysterious; abstruse.
J. CHEEVER An old Turkey carpet, multicolored and scattered with arcane symbols. W. STYRON Sophie loses track of much of the arcane detail. B. MASON Art was therefore something arcane: if not precisely forbidden, then heavy with the possibility of discovery and guilt.

arcanum /ɑːˈkeɪnəm/ *noun.* Pl. **-na** /-nə/. L16.
[ORIGIN Latin, use as noun of neut. sing. of *arcanus*: see ARCANE.]
Usu. in *pl.* **1** A hidden thing; a mystery, a profound secret. L16.
major arcana (in cartomancy) the 22 trump cards of the tarot pack. **minor arcana** (in cartomancy) the 56 suit cards of the tarot pack.
2 *spec.* Any of the supposed secrets of nature sought by alchemists; a marvellous remedy, an elixir. *arch.* E17.
■ **arcanist** *noun* a person who has knowledge of a secret process of manufacture E20.

arc-boutant /arkbutɑ̃/ *noun.* Pl. pronounced same. M18.
[ORIGIN French.]
ARCHITECTURE. An arched or flying buttress.

arch /ɑːtʃ/ *noun*[1]. ME.
[ORIGIN Old French & mod. French *arche* ult. from Latin *arcus* ARC *noun.*]
▸ **I 1** A curved structure spanning an opening, either acting as a support for a bridge, roof, wall, floor, etc., or as a monument, or as an ornamental feature. ME.
BYRON For *this* the conqueror rears The arch of triumph! E. M. FORSTER The immense viaduct, whose arches span untroubled meadows and the dreamy flow of Tewin Water. L. T. C. ROLT A bridge with two of the largest and flattest arches. J. BRONOWSKI The Romans always made the arch as a semicircle. M. GIROUARD Two large studio windows under the gables, crowned with Gothic pointed arches.
Court of Arches *ECCLESIASTICAL* the court of appeal for the province of Canterbury, orig. held in the church of St Mary-le-bow (or 'of the Arches'). **Dean of the Arches** *ECCLESIASTICAL* the lay judge of the Court of Arches having jurisdiction over thirteen London parishes exempt from the authority of the Bishop of London. ***skew arch***: see SKEW *adjective.* ***straight arch***: see STRAIGHT *adjective*[1] & *adverb*[1]. ***triumphal arch***: see TRIUMPHAL *adjective* 1.
†**2** Any part of a curve. LME–M19.
SIR T. BROWNE An Arch of the Horizon.
3 A thing resembling an arch as described in senses 1 and 2 in form or function; *ANATOMY & ZOOLOGY* = GIRDLE *noun*[1] 4. L16. ▸**b** Each of the arched structures formed by the tarsal and metatarsal bones of the foot. M19.
ADDISON His head is encompassed with . . an arch of glory. J. RUSKIN God's arch, the arch of the rainbow. **b** A. S. BYATT Mrs Bruce said her feet hurt, sat down . . and rubbed her arches.
aortic arch, ***visceral arch***, ***zygomatic arch***, etc. **b fallen arch** an arch of the foot that has flattened.
4 An arched roof, a vault; an archway; *fig.* the heavens. E17.
SIR W. SCOTT While the deep arch with sullen roar Return'd their surly jar.
5 Curvature in the shape of an arch. M19.
F. Y. GOLDING The hollowness or arch of the waist [of a shoe].
▸ **II 6** In *pl.* In names of various moths, as ***buff arches***, ***dark arches***, ***silvery arches.*** M18.
– COMB.: **archway** a vaulted passage, an arched entrance.
■ **archlet** *noun* a little arch E19. **archwise** *adverb* in the form of an arch L16. **archy** *adjective* (*rare*) arched, arching, suggestive of an arch M17.

arch /ɑːtʃ/ *adjective & noun*[2]. M16.
[ORIGIN ARCH- used independently; sense A.2 from use with *rogue*, *wag*, etc.]
▸ **A** *adjective.* **1** Chief, principal, pre-eminent. Now *rare* without hyphen (see ARCH-). M16.
SHAKES. *Rich. III* The most arch deed of piteous massacre. LYTTON Thou mayest have need of thy archest magic to protect thyself.
2 Clever, roguish, waggish; (now usu.) consciously or affectedly playful or teasing. M17.
▸ †**B** *noun.* A chief. *rare.* Only in E17.
SHAKES. *Lear* The noble Duke my master, My worthy arch and patron.
■ **archly** *adverb* M17. **archness** *noun* E18.

arch /ɑːtʃ/ *verb*[1]. ME.
[ORIGIN from ARCH *noun*[1]. Cf. Old French *archer.*]
1 *verb trans.* Form into or provide with an arch. ME.
BACON Fine Deuices, of Arching Water without Spilling. SIR T. BROWNE Dinocrates began to Arche the Temple . . with Load stone. A. SILLITOE The lane was arched with trees. D. M. THOMAS The cat arched her back and spat at the man.
2 *verb intrans.* Form an arch. E17.
BACON The sound . . archeth over the wall. B. MOORE The rainbow arched up and away from this place.
3 *verb trans.* Span like an arch. M17.
SOUTHEY The vine that arch'd His evening seat. R. W. EMERSON The rude bridge that arched the flood.
■ **arching** *noun* an arched structure L16.

arch /ɑːtʃ/ *verb*[2] *intrans.* M17.
[ORIGIN Back-form. from ARCHER, ARCHERY.]
Engage in archery.

arch- /ɑːtʃ/ *prefix.*
[ORIGIN Latin from Greek *arkhi-* etc., from *arkhos* chief, or Old French *arche-* from Latin *arch-*. Cf. ARCHI-.]
1 In titles of office, rank, or dignity, with the sense 'principal, -in-chief, superior', as ***archbishop***, ***archdeacon***, ***archdruid***, ***archduke***, etc.
2 In descriptive appellations of people, with the sense 'a person pre-eminent as, greatest, chief, leading' as ***arch-critic***, ***arch-defender***, etc., and now esp. 'worst of, out-and-out, extremely bad', as ***arch-conspirator***, ***arch-criminal***, ***arch-heretic***, ***arch-rebel***, ***arch-tempter***, ***arch-traitor***, ***arch-villain***, etc. Cf. GRAND *adjective*[1] 2.
3 In descriptive appellations of people, with the sense 'first in time, original', as ***arch-father***, ***arch-founder***. All either *obsolete* or *arch.*
4 Of things: ▸**a** With the sense 'chief, principal, prime', as ***archdiocese*** etc. ▸**b** With the sense 'primitive, original', as ***arch-house***, ***arch-see***, etc. All either *arch.* or *obsolete.*
■ **arch-abbey** *noun* [4a] the head abbey of a Benedictine congregation L19. **arch-abbot** *noun* [1] the chief abbot of a Benedictine congregation L19. **arch-chanter** *noun* (*obsolete* exc. *hist.*) [1] a precentor LME. ˌ**archconfraˈternity** *noun* [1] *ROMAN CATHOLIC CHURCH* a confraternity with power to incorporate or affiliate other similar confraternities M17. **archdean** *noun* (chiefly *Scot.*, *obsolete* exc. *hist.*) [1] a chief dean, an archdeacon LME. **archˈdeanery** *noun* (chiefly *Scot.*, *obsolete* exc. *hist.*) [4a] the jurisdiction, rank, or office of an archdean L15. **archˈdiocese** *noun* [4a] the see or jurisdiction of an archbishop E19. **arch-ˈenemy** *noun* [2] a chief enemy; the Devil: M16. **arch-fiend** *noun* [2] a chief fiend, the Devil M17. **arch-flamen** *noun* (now *arch.* & *hist.*) [medieval Latin *archiflamen*] a chief flamen or priest, an archbishop LME. **arch-foe** *noun* [2] an arch-enemy, the Devil E17. †**arch-poet** *noun* [1] a chief or first poet, a poet laureate E17–M18. **arch-prelate** *noun* [1] a chief prelate, an archbishop L16. **arch-ˈrival** *noun* the chief rival of a person, team, etc. M20.

-arch /ək, ɑːk/ *suffix* (not productive).
[ORIGIN Repr. Greek *-arkhos*, *arkhēs* ruling, rel. to *arkhē* rule, *arkhein* begin, take the lead.]
In nouns denoting kinds of ruler, as ***monarch***, ***ethnarch***, ***tetrarch***, etc.

archaea /ɑːˈkiːə/ *noun pl.* L20.
[ORIGIN mod. Latin *Archaea* from Greek *arkhaios* ancient.]
Micro-organisms of a taxonomic group believed to be of very ancient origin, which are similar to ordinary bacteria in size and structure but radically different in molecular organization.

Archaean /ɑːˈkiːən/ *adjective & noun.* Also ***Archean.** L19.
[ORIGIN from Greek *arkhaios* ancient + -AN.]
GEOLOGY. (Designating or pertaining to) the earlier part of the Precambrian era (before the Proterozoic).

archaebacterium /ˌɑːkɪbakˈtɪərɪəm/ *noun.* Pl. **-ia** /-ɪə/. L20.
[ORIGIN from ARCHAEO- + BACTERIUM.]
A micro-organism of the taxonomic group *Archaea.*
■ **archaebacterial** *adjective* L20.

archaeo- /ˈɑːkɪəʊ/ *combining form.* Also ***archeo-**, †**archaio-**.
[ORIGIN from Greek *arkhaios* ancient, primitive: see -O-.]
Forming terms relating to archaeology or prehistoric times.
■ **archaeoaˈstronomy** *noun* the archaeological investigation of astronomical knowledge in prehistoric cultures L20. **archaeoˈbotany** *noun* the study of plant remains at archaeological sites M20. **archaeography** /ɑːkɪˈɒɡrəfi/ *noun* (*arch.*) the systematic description of antiquities E19. ˌ**archaeomagˈnetic** *adjective* of or pertaining to archaeomagnetism M20. ˌ**archaeoˈmagnetism** *noun* the investigation of the magnetic properties of archaeological remains, esp. for the purpose of dating; magnetism possessed by such materials: M20. **archaeoˈmetric** *adjective* of or pertaining to archaeometry L20. **archaeometry** /ɑːkɪˈɒmɪtri/ *noun* the application of scientific techniques to the dating of archaeological remains M20. **Archaeoˈzoic** *adjective & noun* (*GEOLOGY*) (pertaining to or designating) the Archaean period or (orig.) that part of it in which primitive life existed L19. **archaeozoˈology** *noun* = ZOOARCHAEOLOGY L20.

archaeology /ɑːkɪˈɒlədʒi/ *noun.* Also ***archeo-**, †**archaio-**. E17.
[ORIGIN mod. Latin *archaeologia* from Greek *arkhaiologia*, formed as ARCHAEO- + -LOGY.]
1 Ancient history. *arch.* E17.
2 The systematic description or study of human antiquities, esp. as revealed by excavation. M19.
■ **archaeoˈlogian** *noun* (now *rare*) = ARCHAEOLOGIST M19. **archaeoˈlogic** *adjective* = ARCHAEOLOGICAL M18. **archaeoˈlogical** *adjective* of or pertaining to archaeology L18. **archaeoˈlogically** *adverb* L18. **archaeologist** *noun* E19. **archaeologize** *verb intrans.* study or practise archaeology L19. **archaeologue** /ˈɑːkɪəlɒɡ/ *noun* (*arch.*) [French] an archaeologist, an antiquarian M19.

archaeopteryx /ɑːkɪˈɒptərɪks/ *noun.* M19.
[ORIGIN from ARCHAEO- + Greek *pterux* wing.]
The oldest known fossil bird, dating from the late Jurassic and having several reptilian features such as teeth, forelimb claws, and vertebrate tail.

archaic /ɑːˈkeɪɪk/ *adjective.* M19.
[ORIGIN French *archaïque* from Greek *arkhaikos*, from *arkhaios* ancient: see -IC.]
1 Of a word, language, etc.: no longer in ordinary use though retained by individuals or for special purposes (e.g. poetical, liturgical). M19.
2 Designating or belonging to an early or formative period of culture, art, etc. M19.
3 *gen.* Primitive; antiquated. L19.
■ **archaical** *adjective* (*rare*) archaic; of or pertaining to what is archaic: E19. **archaically** *adverb* in an archaic style; with regard to archaism: L19. **archaicism** /-sɪz(ə)m/ *noun* archaic style or quality M19. **archaicist** /-sɪst/ *noun* (*rare*) a person who employs archaism L19.

†**archaio-** *combining form*, †**archaiology** *noun*, etc., vars. of ARCHAEO-, ARCHAEOLOGY, etc.

archaise *verb* var. of ARCHAIZE.

archaism /ˈɑːkeɪɪz(ə)m/ *noun.* M17.
[ORIGIN mod. Latin *archaismus* from Greek *arkhaismos*, from *arkhaizein* copy the ancients in language etc., from *arkhaios* ancient: see -ISM.]

1 The retention or imitation of what is old or obsolete, esp. in language or art. **M17.**
2 An archaic word or expression; an archaic feature. **M17.**
■ **archaist** *noun* (*a*) *rare* an antiquary; (*b*) a person who employs archaism: **M19. archa'istic** *adjective* of or pertaining to an archaist; imitatively archaic, affectedly antique: **M19. archa'istically** *adverb* **L19.**

archaize /ˈɑːkeɪʌɪz/ *verb*. Also **-ise. M19.**
[ORIGIN Greek *arkhaizein*: see ARCHAISM, -IZE.]
1 *verb intrans.* Imitate the archaic. **M19.**
2 *verb trans.* Render archaistic. **M20.**
■ **archaizer** *noun* **L19.**

archangel /ˈɑːkeɪn(d)ʒ(ə)l, ɑːkˈeɪn-/ *noun*. Also (esp. in titles) **A-. OE.**
[ORIGIN Anglo-Norman *archangele* from ecclesiastical Latin *archangelus* from ecclesiastical Greek *arkhaggelos*, from Greek *arkhi-* ARCH- + *aggelos* (see ANGEL).]
1 An angel of the highest rank; a member of the eighth order of the ninefold celestial hierarchy, ranking directly below the principalities and above the angels (usu. in *pl.*). **OE.**
2 Any of various dead-nettles (genus *Lamium* and allied plants); *esp.* (more fully ***yellow archangel***) *Lamiastrum galeobdolon*, a yellow-flowered woodland plant of Europe and western Asia. **LME.**
■ **archan'gelic** *adjective* of, pertaining to, or resembling archangels; of the nature of an archangel: **LME. archan'gelical** *adjective* = ARCHANGELIC **M17.**

archbishop /ɑːtʃˈbɪʃəp, *esp. in titles* ˈɑːtʃ-/ *noun*. Also (esp. in titles) **A-. OE.**
[ORIGIN from ARCH- (replacing *hēah* high in Old English *hēah-biscop*) + BISHOP *noun*.]
The chief bishop of a province.
■ **archbishophood** *noun* (*rare*) the rank or office of an archbishop **LME. archbishopric** *noun* [Old English *rīce* realm, rule] the diocese or jurisdiction of an archbishop; the rank or office of an archbishop: **OE. archbishopship** *noun* (*rare*) = ARCHBISHOPRIC **M16.**

archdeacon /ɑːtʃˈdiːkən, *esp. in titles* ˈɑːtʃ-/ *noun*. Also (esp. in titles) **A-. OE.**
[ORIGIN ecclesiastical Latin *archidiaconus* (Jerome) from ecclesiastical Greek *arkhidiakonos*: see ARCH-, DEACON *noun*.]
A chief deacon; a member of the Anglican clergy next below a bishop; a dignitary of similar rank in other Churches.
■ **arch'deaconess** *noun* (now *rare*) the wife of an archdeacon **M19. arch'deaconry** *noun* the jurisdiction or district under the ecclesiastical control of an archdeacon; the rank or office of an archdeacon: **LME.**

archducal /ɑːtʃˈdjuːk(ə)l/ *adjective*. Also †**archi-. E17.**
[ORIGIN French *archiducal*: see ARCHDUKE, -AL[1].]
Of or pertaining to an archduke or archduchy.

archduchess /ˈɑːtʃdʌtʃɪs/ *noun*. Also (esp. as a title) **A-. E17.**
[ORIGIN French *archiduchesse*: see ARCH-, DUCHESS.]
hist. The wife of an archduke. Also, a woman with an archducal title in her own right, *spec.* as a daughter of the Emperor of Austria.

archduchy /ˈɑːtʃdʌtʃi/ *noun*. **L17.**
[ORIGIN French †*archeduché* (now *archi-*): see ARCH-, DUCHY.]
hist. The territory subject to an archduke or archduchess.

archduke /ˈɑːtʃdjuːk/ *noun*. Also (esp. as a title) **A-. E16.**
[ORIGIN Old French *archeduc* (mod. *archi-*) from Merovingian Latin *archidux*, *-duc-*: see ARCH-, DUKE *noun*.]
hist. A chief duke; *spec.* (the title of) a son of the Emperor of Austria.
■ **archdukedom** *noun* (now *rare*) = ARCHDUCHY **M16.**

Archean *adjective* & *noun* see ARCHAEAN.

archegonium /ɑːkɪˈɡəʊnɪəm/ *noun*. Pl. **-ia** /-ɪə/. **M19.**
[ORIGIN mod. Latin, from Greek *arkhegonos* progenitor, from *arkhe-* ARCHI- + *gonos* race: see -IUM.]
BOTANY. The female reproductive organ borne by mosses, ferns, and some other plants.
■ **archegonial** *adjective* of or pertaining to an archegonium **M19. archegoniate** *adjective* bearing archegonia **L19.**

archei *noun* pl. of ARCHEUS.

archenteron /ɑːˈkɛntərɒn/ *noun*. **L19.**
[ORIGIN from Greek *arkhē* beginning + *enteron* intestine.]
ZOOLOGY. The rudimentary alimentary cavity of a gastrula.

archeo- *combining form*, **archeology** *noun*, etc., see ARCHAEO-, ARCHAEOLOGY, etc.

archer /ˈɑːtʃə/ *noun*. **ME.**
[ORIGIN Anglo-Norman *archer*, Old French *archier* (mod. *archer*), ult. from Latin *arcus* bow: see -ER[2].]
1 A person who shoots with bow and arrows. **ME.**
2 (Usu. **A-**.) *The* constellation and zodiacal sign Sagittarius. **LME.**
3 *CHESS.* A bishop. Long *obsolete* exc. *hist.* **M16.**
4 Usu. more fully ***archerfish***. Any of several small SE Asian percoid fishes of the genus *Toxotes* (family Toxotidae) which have the ability to knock insect prey off vegetation by spitting water. **M19.**
■ **archeress** *noun* (now *rare*) a female archer **M17.**

archery /ˈɑːtʃəri/ *noun*. **LME.**
[ORIGIN Old French *archerie*, from *archier*: see ARCHER, -ERY.]
1 The practice or art of shooting with bow and arrows; skill as an archer. **LME.**
2 *collect.* An archer's equipment; bows, arrows, etc. Now *rare*. **LME.**
3 *collect.* A company or corps of archers. *arch.* **LME.**

Arches /ˈɑːtʃɪz/ *noun*. Now *rare*. **E17.**
[ORIGIN from ARCH- 4.]
NAUTICAL. ***the Arches***, the Archipelago (the Aegean Sea); any specific archipelago.

archesporium /ɑːkɪˈspɔːrɪəm/ *noun*. Pl. **-ia** /-ɪə/. **L19.**
[ORIGIN from Greek *arkhe-* ARCHI- + SPORE + -IUM.]
BOTANY. A cell or group of cells from which spore-producing or other reproductive cells are developed.
■ **archesporial** *adjective* **L19.**

archetype /ˈɑːkɪtʌɪp/ *noun*. Also (earlier) in Latin form †**-typum. M16.**
[ORIGIN Latin *archetypum* from Greek *arkhetupon* use as noun of neut. of adjective 'first moulded as a model', from *arkhe-* ARCHI- + *tupon* model. Cf. French *archétype*.]
1 The original pattern or model from which copies are made; a prototype; a typical specimen. **M16.**

> LD MACAULAY The House of Commons, the archetype of all the representative assemblies which now meet. A. STORR During the thirty-one years of his residence in Cambridge, he was a recluse; the very archetype of the absent-minded, solitary scholar.

2 *spec.* ▸**a** *ZOOLOGY & BOTANY.* An idealized typical specimen or original form of a particular grouping of living organisms. **M19.** ▸**b** In Jungian psychoanalysis, a primordial mental concept inherited by all from the collective unconscious. **E20.** ▸**c** A pervasive or recurrent idea or symbol in legend, etc. **M20.**
■ **archetypal** *adjective* of the nature of or constituting an archetype; of or pertaining to an archetype; primitive, original: **M17. archetypally** *adverb* **M19. arche'typical** *adjective* = ARCHETYPAL **M18. arche'typically** *adverb* **L19.**

archeus /ˈɑːkɪəs/ *noun*. Pl. **-ei** /-ɪʌɪ/. **M17.**
[ORIGIN mod. Latin *archaeus* from Greek *arkhaios* ancient.]
HISTORY OF SCIENCE. The abstract principle supposed by the Paracelsians to govern animal and vegetable life; a vital force.

archi *noun pl.* see ARCO.

archi- /ˈɑːki/ *prefix*.
[ORIGIN Latin from Greek *arkhi-*: see ARCH-.]
1 = ARCH-: ▸**a** Forming nouns, as ***archiepiscopate***, ***archipresbyter***, etc. ▸**b** Forming adjectives, as ***archiepiscopal*** etc., freq. corresp. to nouns in ARCH-, as ***archidiaconal*** etc.
2 *BIOLOGY.* With the sense 'archetypal, primitive', as ***archinephros*** etc.
3 *ANATOMY.* Designating the phylogenetically oldest parts of the brain, as ***archipallium***, ***archistriatum***, etc.

archiater /ɑːkɪˈeɪtə/ *noun*. **E17.**
[ORIGIN Late Latin from Greek *arkhiatros*, from *arkhi-* ARCHI- + *iatros* physician. Cf. French *archiatre*.]
hist. The chief physician of a monarch; the court physician.

Archibald /ˈɑːtʃɪbɔːld/ *noun*. *slang* (now *hist.*). **E20.**
[ORIGIN Male forename: from the refrain of a popular music hall song.]
An anti-aircraft gun, *esp.* one used by the Germans in the First World War.

archidiaconal /ˌɑːkɪdʌɪˈak(ə)n(ə)l/ *adjective*. **LME.**
[ORIGIN medieval Latin *archidiaconalis*: see ARCHI-, DIACONAL.]
Of, pertaining to, or holding the position of an archdeacon.
■ **archidiaconate** *noun* = ARCHDEACONRY **M18.**

†**archiducal** *adjective* var. of ARCHDUCAL.

Archie /ˈɑːtʃi/ *noun* & *verb*. *slang* (now *hist.*). **E20.**
[ORIGIN Dim. of ARCHIBALD.]
▸ **A** *noun*. = ARCHIBALD. **E20.**
▸ **B** *verb trans.* Pres. pple & verbal noun **Archieing**. Fire at with an anti-aircraft gun. **E20.**

archiepiscopacy /ˌɑːkɪɪˈpɪskəpəsi/ *noun*. **M17.**
[ORIGIN from ecclesiastical Latin *archiepiscopus* from Greek *arkhiepiskopos* (Athanasius) archbishop, formed as ARCHI-, BISHOP *noun*, + -ACY.]
1 The system of Church government by archbishops. **M17.**
2 = ARCHIEPISCOPATE. **M17.**
■ **archiepiscopate** *noun* an archbishop's tenure of office; an archbishopric: **L18.**

archiepiscopal /ˌɑːkɪɪˈpɪskəp(ə)l/ *adjective*. **E17.**
[ORIGIN formed as ARCHIEPISCOPACY + -AL[1].]
Of, pertaining to, or of the nature of an archbishop.
■ **archiepiscopally** *adverb* **M19.**

archil /ˈɑːtʃɪl, ˈɑːkɪl/ *noun*. **M16.**
[ORIGIN Var. of ORCHIL.]
The dye orchil, or any of the lichens which yield this.

Archilochian /ɑːkɪˈləʊkɪən/ *adjective*. **M18.**
[ORIGIN from Latin *Archilochius*, from Greek *Arkhilokhos* Archilochus (see below) + -AN.]
Of, pertaining to, or derived from the Greek satiric poet Archilochus (7th cent. BC), the alleged originator of iambic metre.

archilute *noun* var. of ARCHLUTE.

archimage /ˈɑːkɪmeɪdʒ/ *noun*. Now chiefly *poet.* Also †**-mago**, †**-magus. L16.**
[ORIGIN Greek *arkhimagos* chief of the magi: see ARCHI-, MAGE, MAGUS, and cf. French *archimage*.]
A chief magician; a great wizard.

archimandrite /ɑːkɪˈmandrʌɪt/ *noun*. **M17.**
[ORIGIN French, or ecclesiastical Latin *archimandrita* from ecclesiastical Greek *arkhimandritēs*, from *arkhi-* ARCHI- + *mandra* enclosure, stable, monastery: see -ITE[1].]
The superior of a large monastery in the Orthodox Church; also used as an honorary title of a monastic priest.

Archimedean /ɑːkɪˈmiːdɪən/ *adjective*. **E19.**
[ORIGIN from late Latin *Archimedeus* (formed as ARCHIMEDES) + -AN.]
Of, pertaining to, or invented by Archimedes.
Archimedean drill a drill in which to-and-fro motion along the axis of the drill produces alternating rotary motion of the bit. **Archimedean screw** an instrument for raising water by the turning of an inclined screw within a cylinder.

Archimedes /ɑːkɪˈmiːdiːz/ *noun*. **M17.**
[ORIGIN Greek *Arkhimēdēs*, a celebrated mathematician (c 287–212 BC).]
1 A person like Archimedes, esp. in making scientific discoveries. **M17.**
2 ***Archimedes' principle***, (arch.) ***principle of Archimedes***: that a body immersed in a fluid is subject to an upward force equal in magnitude to the weight of fluid it displaces. **M19.**

archimime /ˈɑːkɪmʌɪm/ *noun*. Also **arch-mime** /ˈɑːtʃ-/. **M17.**
[ORIGIN Latin *archimimus* from Greek *arkhimimos*: see ARCHI-, MIME *noun*.]
ROMAN HISTORY. The chief mimic who imitated the deceased in a funeral procession.

archinephros /ɑːkɪˈnɛfrəs/ *noun*. Pl. **-nephroi** /-ˈnɛfrɔɪ/. **L19.**
[ORIGIN from ARCHI- + Greek *nephros* kidney.]
ZOOLOGY. The archetypal primitive kidney of the earliest vertebrates.
■ **archinephric** *adjective* **L19.**

archipelago /ɑːkɪˈpɛləɡəʊ/ *noun*. Pl. **-o(e)s**. Also †**-gus. E16.**
[ORIGIN Italian *arcipelago* (13), from Greek *arkhi-* ARCHI- + *pelagos* sea.]
1 ***the Archipelago***, the Aegean Sea. *arch.* **E16.**
2 A sea or other stretch of water like the Aegean in having many islands; a group of islands. **M16.**
■ **archipelagic** /-pəˈladʒɪk/ *adjective* **M19.**

archiphoneme /ˈɑːkɪfəʊniːm/ *noun*. **M20.**
[ORIGIN French *archiphonème*: see ARCHI-, PHONEME.]
LINGUISTICS. A phonological unit comprising the sum of distinctive features common to two or more neutralized phonemes.
■ **archipho'nemic** *adjective* **M20.**

archipresbyter /ɑːkɪˈprɛzbɪtə/ *noun*. Also **archpresbyter** /ˈɑːtʃ-/. **M16.**
[ORIGIN Late Latin from Greek *arkhipresbuteros*: see ARCHI-, PRESBYTER.]
= ARCHPRIEST.
■ **ˌarchipres'byterate** *noun* [medieval Latin *archipresbyteratus*] the position or term of office of an archpriest; the order of archpriests: **E20.**

†**archisynagogue** *noun*. **ME–L18.**
[ORIGIN ecclesiastical Latin *archisynagogus* from Greek *arkhisunagōgos* (New Testament): see ARCHI-, SYNAGOGUE.]
A president of a synagogue.

architect /ˈɑːkɪtɛkt/ *noun* & *verb*. **M16.**
[ORIGIN French *architecte* from Italian *architetto*, or their source Latin *architectus* from Greek *arkhitektōn*, from *arkhi-* ARCHI- + *tektōn* builder.]
▸ **A** *noun*. **1** A designer of buildings, who prepares plans, and superintends construction. **M16.** ▸**b** In full ***naval architect***. A designer of ships etc. **M19.**
2 A designer of any complex structure. **L16.**

> T. REID Plato made the causes of things to be matter, ideas, and an efficient architect. G. GROTE The inference that Peisistratus was the first architect of the Iliad and Odyssey.

the Architect the Creator, God.
3 A person who plans, devises, or contrives the achievement *of* a desired result. **L16.**

> MILTON The architects of their own happiness. J. HELLER The architect of an illicit and secret policy of detente.

▸ **B** *verb trans.* Design and build; plan and bring about (a desired result). **M17.**
■ **architective** *adjective* of or pertaining to architecture; fitted for or characterized by construction: **E17.** †**architector** *noun* (*a*) a superintendent; (*b*) = ARCHITECT: **L15–E18. architectress** *noun* (now *rare*) a female architect **E17.**

architectonic /ˌɑːkɪtɛkˈtɒnɪk/ *adjective* & *noun*. **M17.**
[ORIGIN Latin *architectonicus* (Vitruvius) from Greek *arkhitektonikos*, from *arkhitektōn*: see ARCHITECT, -IC.]
▸ **A** *adjective*. **1** Of or pertaining to architecture or architects. **M17.**

2 Of or pertaining to construction. L17.
3 Directive, controlling. L17.
4 Pertaining to the systematization of knowledge. L18.
▸ **B** *noun sing.* & (freq.) in *pl.* (treated as *sing.*).
1 The science of architecture. M17.
2 The science of the systematic arrangement of knowledge. L18.
■ **architectonical** *adjective* (now *rare*) E17. **architectonically** *adverb* with regard or in relation to architectonics M17.

architecture /ˈɑːkɪtɛktʃə/ *noun & verb.* M16.
[ORIGIN French, or Latin *architectura*: see ARCHITECT, -URE.]
▸ **A** *noun.* **1** The art or science of building; *esp.* the art or practice of designing and building edifices for human use, taking both aesthetic and practical factors into account. M16.
marine architecture, **naval architecture** the design and building of ships etc.
2 Architectural work; something built. L16.

J. H. BURTON Architecture, especially if it be of stone. M. PEAKE An eccentric notion translated into architecture.

3 A style of building; mode, manner, or style of construction or organization; structure. E17. ▸**b** The conceptual structure and logical organization of a computer or computer-based system. M20.

J. RUSKIN Many other architectures besides Gothic. *Discovery* The architecture of molecules. D. V. COOKE We speak of the 'architecture' of a symphony. M. GIROUARD They moved on . . to revive elements from the homelier brick architecture of the seventeenth and eighteenth centuries.

4 The action or process of building; construction. *arch.* E17.

SIR T. BROWNE [If] the great Cities Anchiale and Tarsus were built . . both in one day . . Certainely, it was the greatest Architecture of one day.

▸ **B** *verb trans.* Design as architect. E19.
■ **archi'tectural** *adjective* of, relating to, or according to architecture; resembling architecture: L18. **archi'tecturally** *adverb* M19.

architrave /ˈɑːkɪtreɪv/ *noun.* M16.
[ORIGIN French from Italian, from *archi-* ARCHI- + *trave* from Latin *trab-*, *trabs* beam.]
ARCHITECTURE. **1** The lowest part of an entablature, resting immediately upon the abacus on the capital of a column. M16.
2 The various parts surrounding a door or window. M17.
3 Moulding around the exterior of an arch. M19.
■ **architraved** *adjective* having an architrave M17.

archive /ˈɑːkʌɪv/ *noun & verb.* E17.
[ORIGIN French *archives* pl. from Latin *archi(v)a* from Greek *arkheia* public office or records, use as noun of neut pl. of *arkheios* governmental, from *arkhē* government.]
▸ **A** *noun.* **1** *sing.* & in *pl.* A place in which collected public or corporate records are kept; a repository for documents etc.; a databank. E17.
2 In *pl.* & †*sing.* Records so kept. M17.
▸ **B** *verb trans.* Place or store in an archive; *spec.* (COMPUTING) transfer to a store of infrequently used files, or to a memory at a lower hierarchical level (e.g. from disk to tape). L19.
■ **ar'chival** *adjective* of or pertaining to archives M19. **archivist** /ˈɑːkɪvɪst/ *noun* a keeper of archives M18.

archivolt /ˈɑːkɪvəʊlt/ *noun.* Also †**-volto**. M17.
[ORIGIN Italian *archivolto* (whence medieval Latin *archivoltum*) or French *archivolte* ult. formed as ARC *noun* + VAULT *noun*[1].]
ARCHITECTURE. The lower curve of an arch, from impost to impost; the band of mouldings on this.

archlute /ˈɑːtʃl(j)uːt/ *noun.* Also **archi-** /ˈɑːtʃɪ-/. M17.
[ORIGIN French *archiluth*, Italian *arciliuto*: see ARCH-, LUTE *noun*[1].]
A theorbo.

arch-mime *noun* var. of ARCHIMIME.

archon /ˈɑːkən/ *noun.* Pl. **archons**, **archontes** /ɑːˈkɒntiːz/. L16.
[ORIGIN Greek *arkhōn*, *arkhont-* ruler, use as noun of pres. pple of *arkhein* to rule.]
1 The chief magistrate, or, after the time of Solon, each of the nine chief magistrates, of ancient Athens. L16.
2 A ruler, a president. M18.
3 A power subordinate to God, held by some of the Gnostics to have created the world. M18.
■ **archonship** *noun* the position of an Athenian archon L17. **archontate** *noun* the tenure of office of an Athenian archon M18. **ar'chontic** *noun & adjective* (**a**) *noun* a member of a sect of Gnostics who believed that the world was created by archons; (**b**) *adjective* of or pertaining to an archon: L16.

archosaurian /ɑːkəˈsɔːrɪən/ *adjective & noun.* L19.
[ORIGIN from mod. Latin *Archosauria* (see below), from Greek *arkhos* chief or *arkhōn*: see ARCHON, -SAUR, -IAN.]
ZOOLOGY. ▸**A** *adjective.* Belonging to or characteristic of the subclass Archosauria of living and extinct reptiles, which includes the dinosaurs, pterosaurs, and crocodilians. L19.
▸ **B** *noun.* Any archosaurian reptile. E20.
■ Also **'archosaur** *noun* M20.

archpresbyter *noun* var. of ARCHIPRESBYTER.

archpriest /ɑːtʃˈpriːst/ *noun.* LME.
[ORIGIN Old French *archeprestre* (mod. *archiprêtre*) from late Latin ARCHIPRESBYTER, later assim. to ARCH-, PRIEST.]
A chief priest; formerly, a chief assistant or vicar to a bishop in a cathedral. Also, a rural dean.
■ **archpriesthood** *noun* the position or office of an archpriest L17. †**archpriestship** *noun* = ARCHPRIESTHOOD LME–L17.

-archy /əki, ɑːki/ *suffix* (not productive).
[ORIGIN Repr. Greek *arkh(e)ia* government, leadership, formed as -ARCH: see -Y[3].]
In abstract nouns corresp. to personal nouns in **-ARCH**, as ***monarchy***, ***oligarchy***, ***tetrarchy***, etc.

arco /ˈarko, ˈɑːkəʊ/ *noun, adverb, & adjective.* M18.
[ORIGIN Italian.]
MUSIC. ▸**A** *noun.* Pl. ***archi*** /ˈarki/, ***arcos*** /ˈɑːkəʊz/. A bow for a stringed instrument. M18.
▸ **B** *adverb & adjective.* A direction: resuming use of the bow after a pizzicato passage. E19.

arcology /ɑːˈkɒlədʒi/ *noun.* M20.
[ORIGIN Blend of ARCHITECTURE and ECOLOGY.]
A style of urban planning proposed by the Italian-born US architect Paolo Soleri (b. 1919), which envisages fully integrated cities each contained within a massive vertical structure; a city built on these principles.

Arctic /ˈɑːktɪk/ *adjective & noun.* Also **a-**; (earlier) †**Art-**. LME.
[ORIGIN Old French *artique* (mod. *arct-*) from Latin *ar(c)ticus* from Greek *arktikos*, from *arktos* bear, the Great Bear (constellation): see -IC.]
▸ **A** *adjective.* **1** Of or pertaining to the North Pole, or the north polar regions. Formerly also *gen.*, northern. LME. ▸**b** Designating animals and plants of northern species. L18. ▸**c** (Usu. **a-**.) Characterized by or typical of the very cold climate of the north polar regions. L19.
Arctic Circle the parallel of latitude 66° 33′ N. **Arctic Ocean** the (chiefly ice-covered) ocean bounded by the north coasts of Eurasia and N. America. **b** ***Arctic char***, ***Arctic cisco***, ***Arctic grayling***, ***Arctic skipper***, ***Arctic skua***, ***Arctic willow***, etc. **Arctic fox** a small fox, *Alopex lagopus*, whose coat turns white in winter and which occurs on the tundra of Eurasia and N. America; the fur of this fox. **Arctic hare** (**a**) a hare, *Lepus arcticus*, of Greenland and Arctic Canada, whose coat is brown in summer and white in winter; (**b**) = MOUNTAIN ***hare***. **Arctic tern** a migratory tern, *Sterna paradisaea*, which breeds mainly in northern Eurasia and N. America but winters mainly in Antarctic regions.
2 *fig.* Bitterly cold. Formerly also, extreme, remote. L17.
▸ **B** *noun.* **1** *The* north polar regions. LME.
2 In *pl.* (**a-**.) Thick waterproof overshoes. *N. Amer.* M19.

arctophile /ˈɑːktəfaɪl/ *noun.* L20.
[ORIGIN from Greek *arktos* bear + -PHILE.]
A person who collects or is very fond of teddy bears.
■ **arcto'philia** *noun* love of teddy bears L20. **arc'tophilist** *noun* L20. **arc'tophily** *noun* L20.

arcual /ˈɑːkjʊəl/ *adjective.* M17.
[ORIGIN from Latin *arcus* ARC *noun* + -AL[1].]
= ARCUATE.

arcuate /ˈɑːkjʊət/ *adjective.* LME.
[ORIGIN Latin *arcuatus* pa. pple, from *arcuat-*: see ARCUATION, -ATE[2].]
Bent like a bow, curved, arched.
■ **arcuated** /-eɪtɪd/ *adjective* (**a**) = ARCUATE; (**b**) ARCHITECTURE characterized by arches: M18.

arcuation /ɑːkjʊˈeɪʃ(ə)n/ *noun.* LME.
[ORIGIN French, or Latin *arcuatio(n-)* (Frontinus), from *arcuat-* pa. ppl stem of *arcuare* to curve, from *arcus* ARC *noun*: see -ATION.]
1 Curving in the shape of an arch; incurvation. LME.
2 The use of the arch in building; arched work. M18.

arcubalist /ˈɑːkjʊbəlɪst/ *noun. obsolete* exc. *hist.* LME.
[ORIGIN Late Latin *arcuballista*: see ARBALEST.]
= ARBALEST 1.
■ **arcubalister** *noun* = ARBALESTER L16.

arcus senilis /ˌɑːkəs sɪˈnʌɪlɪs/ *noun phr.* L18.
[ORIGIN Latin, lit. 'senile bow'.]
MEDICINE. A narrow opaque band encircling the cornea, common in old age.

ard /ɑːd/ *noun.* M20.
[ORIGIN Old Norse *arðr* plough: see ARDER.]
ARCHAEOLOGY. A primitive light plough.

-ard /əd, *occas.* ɑːd/ *suffix.*
1 Repr. Old & mod. French *-ard*, †*-art* from German *-hart*, *-hard* 'hardy' in nouns, as ***haggard***, ***mallard***, ***placard***, etc., freq. depreciatory, as ***bastard***, ***coward***, etc., and formerly a suffix productive of similar English nouns esp. with the sense 'a person who does to excess, or does what is discreditable', as ***dotard***, ***drunkard***, ***laggard***, ***niggard***, ***sluggard***, ***wizard***. See also -ART.
2 Repr. endings of various origin, as ***bustard***, ***hazard***, ***leopard***, ***standard***, ***tankard***, etc.

ardeb /ˈɑːdɛb/ *noun.* E19.
[ORIGIN Arabic *ʼirdabb*, *ʼar-*, ult. from Greek *artabē*.]
An Egyptian unit of capacity, usu. equal to about 198 litres (5.44 bushels).

ardency /ˈɑːd(ə)nsi/ *noun.* M16.
[ORIGIN from ARDENT + -ENCY.]
Burning quality; *fig.* warmth of feeling or desire, ardour.

ardent /ˈɑːd(ə)nt/ *adjective.* ME.
[ORIGIN Old French *ardant* (mod. *ardent*) from Latin *ardent-* pres. ppl stem of *ardere* to burn: see -ANT[1], -ENT.]
1 Flammable. *obsolete* exc. in ***ardent spirit(s)***, alcoholic spirits (now usu. interpreted as sense 2, with ref. to their taste). ME.
2 Burning, fiery; parching; glowing like fire, gleaming. LME.

POPE From rank to rank she darts her ardent eyes. M. ARNOLD There are some, whom a thirst Ardent, unquenchable, fires.

3 *fig.* Burning with passion or desire; fervent, eager, zealous. LME.

R. BURNS A faltering ardent kiss he stole. W. OWEN Children ardent for some desperate glory. S. LEWIS She passed from a feeble disgust at their closer relations into what promised to be ardent affection. M. MUGGERIDGE We were ardent co-op supporters.

■ **ardently** *adverb* ME.

arder /ˈɑːdə/ *noun.* Long *obsolete* exc. *dial.* E16.
[ORIGIN Prob. from Old Norse *arðr* plough from Latin *aratrum*.]
Ploughing, tilth; land ploughed and left fallow; (a strip of land used for) one stage of a crop rotation.

Ard Fheis /ɑːd ˈɛʃ/ *noun.* E20.
[ORIGIN Irish, from *ard* chief + *feis* convention.]
An Irish party political conference.

ardour /ˈɑːdə/ *noun.* Also ***-or**. LME.
[ORIGIN Old French (mod. *ardeur*) from Latin *ardor*, from *ardere* to burn.]
1 (A feeling of) ardent passion or desire; eagerness, intensity of feeling. LME.

L. STRACHEY Affection, gratitude, . . such feelings possessed him, but the ardours of reciprocal passion were not his. P. H. GIBBS The war had been a horror after the first ardour with which he had come out in time for the Somme. E. F. BENSON His love for her was of an ardour she had not contemplated.

2 (A) fierce or burning heat; fire. *arch.* LME.

C. COTTON To qualifie the excessive ardours of the Sun.

†**3** A radiant spirit. *poet.* Only in M17.

MILTON The wingèd Saint . . from among Thousand Celestial ardors . . up springing light.

arduous /ˈɑːdjʊəs/ *adjective.* M16.
[ORIGIN from Latin *arduus* steep, difficult + -OUS.]
1 Hard to achieve or overcome; difficult, laborious. M16.

LD MACAULAY Such an enterprise would be in the highest degree arduous and hazardous. J. HILTON The next stage . . was less arduous than he had been prepared for, and a relief from the lung-bursting strain of the ascent. M. MUGGERIDGE She found riding or pushing her bicycle uphill too arduous.

2 High; steep. *arch.* E18.

fig.: STEELE To forgive is the most arduous pitch human nature can arrive at.

3 Of an effort etc., or a person making an exertion: energetic, strenuous. M19.

J. TYNDALL An arduous climber. A. J. CRONIN The chapel . . was the product of prolonged and arduous effort. *Partisan Review* The arduous theorists of the SPD were steeped in German pedantry.

■ **arduously** *adverb* laboriously, strenuously; with difficulty: E18. **arduousness** *noun* M18.

ardurous /ˈɑːdjʊrəs/ *adjective. poet. rare.* M18.
[ORIGIN Irreg. formed as ARDUOUS, infl. by ARDOUR.]
Ardent, full of ardour.

Are /eɪˈreɪ/ *noun*[1]. *obsolete* exc. *hist.* Also **A re**. LME.
[ORIGIN from *A* + *re*: see ALAMIRE.]
MEDIEVAL MUSIC. The note A in Guido d'Arezzo's 1st hexachord, where it was sung to the syllable ***re***. Cf. ALAMIRE, BEFA, CEFAUT, etc.

are /ɑː/ *noun*[2]. L18.
[ORIGIN French formed as AREA.]
A metric unit of area equal to 100 sq. metres (about 119.6 sq. yards). Cf. HECTARE.

are *verb* see BE *verb*.

area /ˈɛːrɪə/ *noun.* Pl. **areas**, (occas.) †**areae**. M16.
[ORIGIN Latin = vacant piece of level ground.]
▸ **I** A particular extent of ground or of another surface.
1 A piece of ground, or space within a building, that is not built on or occupied, or is enclosed or reserved for a particular purpose. M16. ▸**b** A sunken enclosure giving access to the basement of a house. E18.

J. LELAND In the west Part of this Street is a large Area invironed with meetly good Buildinges. E. WAUGH One could not normally go further into it than a small roped area around the door. *Lore & Language* The two tarmac play areas would nowadays be considered cramped. **b** DICKENS Pulling the caps from the heads of small boys and tossing them down areas.

2 A particular tract of the earth's (or another planet's) surface; a region; a neighbourhood, a vicinity. M18.

H. GEORGE There are still in India great areas uncultivated. F. RAPHAEL I should have a scout round the area, get your bearings. C. SAGAN We imagined . . that the bright areas that retain frost on Mars are . . low.

3 A particular part of any other surface (e.g. of a living organism), usu. distinguished by coloration, structure, or function. Also, a part of a solid body; *esp.* a region of the brain of specified function. **E19.**

> R. T. PETERSON A very large white stork with . . extensive black wing areas and black tail. A. H. COTTRELL The formation of rust layers on the cathodic areas of the metal surface. J. Z. YOUNG The brain areas involved in speech.

Broca's area, language area, motor area, Wernicke's area, etc.

▸ **II** Extent.

4 Superficial or two-dimensional extent; the amount of this contained within given limits. **L16.**

> STEELE The Area of my Green-House is a Hundred Paces long, Fifty broad. J. UPDIKE In area Kush measures 126,912,180 hectares. F. HOYLE A retreat of the ice sheet at its margin, a shrinkage of its area and decrease in its thickness.

▸ **III** *fig.* **5** A part of anything conceived as having superficial extent; a field (of study etc.), a range of topics etc.; scope, extent. **E17.**

> G. GREENE Whole areas of both our lives were blank like an early map, to be filled in later. D. DAVIE The image serves to indicate roughly the area of experience that the poet is dealing with. G. C. FABER The feeling . . was strongly rooted in a still hateful area of memory.

– PHRASES: ***special area***: see SPECIAL *adjective*. ***twilight area***: see TWILIGHT *adjective*. ***utility area***: see UTILITY *adjective*.

– COMB.: **area bishop** in the Church of England, a bishop who has much of the authority of a diocesan bishop within a particular part of a diocese, by delegation from the diocesan; **area bombing** the indiscriminate bombing of an extended area; **area code** *N. Amer.* a telephone dialling code for another part of the country; ***area dean***: see DEAN *noun*[1] 2. **area defence**: designed to protect an entire area against air attack; **area linguistics** areal linguistics; **areaway** *N. Amer.* a sunken passageway; *esp.* = sense 1b above.

†areach *verb.* Infl. as REACH *verb*[1].
[ORIGIN Old English *arǣcan*, formed as A-[1] + REACH *verb*[1].]
1 *verb trans.* Get at; get possession of. **OE–L16.**

> SPENSER Till his ambitious sonnes vnto them twaine Arraught the rule.

2 *verb trans.* Hand, deliver, (a thing to a person). **OE–M16.**
3 *verb intrans.* Stretch, extend (*to*). **ME–M16.**

aread /əˈriːd/ *verb & noun*. Long *arch.* Also **arede**, **areed**. Pa. t. & pple **areaded**, **ared** /əˈrɛd/.
[ORIGIN Old English *arēdan*, formed as A-[1] + READ *verb*. Branch A.II from A-[1] + READ *verb*.]
▸ **A** *verb trans.* **I †1** Divine, prophesy; make known, declare. **OE–M17.**
2 Divine the meaning of; interpret, solve. **OE.**

> W. MORRIS So is thy dream areded.

3 Guess, conjecture. **ME.**

> SOUTHEY Rightly he ared the Maid's intent.

▸ **II 4** Counsel, advise. **M16.**

> MILTON Let me arreed him, not to be the foreman of any misjudg'd opinion.

5 Decide, adjudge. **L16.**

> SPENSER Thereby Sir Artegall did plaine areed That unto him the horse belong'd.

▸ **†B** *noun.* Counsel, advice. **L16–E19.**

areal /ˈɛːrɪəl/ *adjective*. **L17.**
[ORIGIN from AREA + -AL[1].]
1 Of, pertaining to, or of the nature of an area. **L17.**
2 LINGUISTICS. Of or pertaining to geographical factors as determinants of the relationship or development of languages or dialects. **M20.**
areal linguistics a school of linguistics emphasizing geographical factors in language development and distribution.
■ **areally** *adverb* with regard to area **M20.**

arear /əˈrɪə/ *adverb & pred. adjective*. *rare*. **M19.**
[ORIGIN from A-[2] + REAR *noun*: cf. ARREAR *adverb*.]
In the rear.

areca /ˈarɪkə, əˈriːkə/ *noun*. **L16.**
[ORIGIN Portuguese from Malayalam *aṭekka*.]
(The fruit of) a tropical Asian palm of the genus *Areca*, esp. *A. catechu*, which yields astringent seeds often chewed with betel leaves.
– COMB.: **areca nut** an astringent seed of *A. catechu*.

arecoline /əˈriːkəliːn, -lɪn/ *noun*. **L19.**
[ORIGIN from ARECA after QUINOLINE.]
CHEMISTRY. An alkaloid obtained from areca nuts, which has some use in veterinary medicine as an anthelmintic.

ared, **arede**, **areed** *verb* see AREAD.

areg *noun* pl. of ERG[2].

areligious /eɪrɪˈlɪdʒəs/ *adjective*. **M20.**
[ORIGIN from A-[10] + RELIGIOUS *adjective*.]
Not influenced by or practising religion.

arena /əˈriːnə/ *noun*. **E17.**
[ORIGIN Latin (*h*)*arena* sand, sand-strewn place.]
1 The central part of an amphitheatre, bullring, stadium, etc., in which the action occurs; the building as a whole. **E17.**
2 *fig.* Any scene of open conflict, a sphere of action. **L18.**

> H. ROGERS Howe seldom entered the arena of controversy. J. K. GALBRAITH Economic society was an arena in which men met to compete. N. GORDIMER A landscape without theatricals except when it became an arena for summer storms.

– COMB.: **arena stage** THEATRICAL a stage placed amid the audience; **arena theatre** theatre-in-the-round.

arenaceous /arɪˈneɪʃəs/ *adjective*. **M17.**
[ORIGIN from Latin *arenaceus*, formed as ARENA: see -ACEOUS.]
Having the appearance or consistency of sand; sandy; living or growing in sand.
arenaceous rock = ARENITE.

arenavirus /əˈriːnəvʌɪrəs/ *noun*. Also **areno-**. **L20.**
[ORIGIN from Latin *arenosus* sandy formed as ARENA, + VIRUS.]
MEDICINE. Any of a class of viruses (e.g. that of Lassa fever), which appear under an electron microscope to contain sandlike granules.

arene /ˈariːn/ *noun*. **M20.**
[ORIGIN from AR(OMATIC + -ENE.]
CHEMISTRY. An aromatic hydrocarbon.

arenite /ˈarɪnʌɪt/ *noun*. **E20.**
[ORIGIN formed as ARENA + -ITE[1].]
GEOLOGY. A sandstone or other sedimentary rock made up very largely of sand-sized particles.

arenose /ˈarɪnəʊs/ *adjective*. **LME.**
[ORIGIN Latin *arenosus*, formed as ARENA: see -OSE[1].]
Sandy, gritty.
■ Also **†arenous** *adjective* **LME–M18.**

arenovirus *noun* var. of ARENAVIRUS.

aren't *verb* see BE *verb*.

areo- /ˈarɪəʊ/ *combining form* of Greek *Arēs* Mars: see -O-.
■ **areoˈcentric** *adjective* (ASTRONOMY) having the planet Mars as centre **L19.** **areˈology** *noun* the scientific study of the planet Mars **L19.**

areola /əˈriːələ/ *noun*. Pl. **-lae** /-liː/. **M17.**
[ORIGIN Latin, dim. of AREA.]
Chiefly ANATOMY. **1** A small space or interstice, esp. within body tissue such as bone. **M17.**
2 A small circular area; *spec.* the area of pigmented skin surrounding a nipple. **L17.**
■ **areolar** *adjective* containing many areolae (sense 1); ***areolar tissue***, loose connective tissue found beneath the skin and around muscles. organs, etc.: **E19.** ˈ**areole** *noun* an areola; *esp.* a small area bearing spines or hairs on a cactus: **E19.**

†areometer *noun*. Also **araeo-**. **L17–L19.**
[ORIGIN French *aréomètre*, from Greek *araios* thin: see -METER.]
= HYDROMETER *noun* 1.

Areopagi *noun* pl. of AREOPAGUS.

Areopagite /arɪˈɒpəgʌɪt, -dʒʌɪt/ *noun*. **LME.**
[ORIGIN Latin *areopagites* from Greek *areiopagitēs*: see AREOPAGUS, -ITE[1].]
GREEK HISTORY. A member of the court of Areopagus (see AREOPAGUS).
■ **areopagitic** /ˌarɪɒpəˈdʒɪtɪk/ *noun & adjective* †(**a**) *noun* a speech imitating that of Isocrates addressed to the court of Areopagus; (**b**) *adjective* of or pertaining to the Areopagus or its court: **M17.** **areopagitical** /ˌarɪɒpəˈdʒɪtɪk(ə)l/ *adjective* **L16.**

Areopagus /arɪˈɒpəgəs/ *noun*. Pl. **-gi** /-gʌɪ/. **M17.**
[ORIGIN Latin, from Greek *Areios pagos* hill of Ares (Mars), where the highest judicial court of ancient Athens held its sittings, hence the court itself.]
An important tribunal.

†aret *verb trans.* Also **-tt**. Infl. **-tt-**. **LME.**
[ORIGIN Old French *aret(t)er* from *à* A-[5] + *reter* from Latin *reputare* REPUTE *verb*.]
1 Adjudge, reckon (to be). **LME–L15.**
2 Impute (esp. as a fault) *to*; charge *upon*. **LME–E17.**
3 Accuse, indict, (*of*). **LME–L17.**
4 [orig. a misunderstanding by Spenser of *aret to the charge of*, repr. sense 2.] Entrust, deliver. **L16–E17.**

> SPENSER The charge, which God doth unto me arett, Of his deare safety I to thee commend.

aretalogy /arɪˈtalədʒi/ *noun*. **E20.**
[ORIGIN Greek *aretalogia*, from *aretē* excellence, miracle: see -LOGY.]
A narrative of the miracles performed by a god or semi-divine hero.
■ **aretaˈlogical** *adjective* **L19.**

arête /əˈrɛt, əˈreɪt/ *noun*. **E19.**
[ORIGIN French from Latin *arista* ear of corn, fish-bone or -spine. Cf. ARRIS.]
A sharp mountain ridge with steep sides.

arethusa /arɪˈθjuːzə/ *noun*. **L18.**
[ORIGIN mod. Latin, from Latin *Arethusa* the name of a nymph.]
A rare orchid, *Arethusa bulbosa*, of eastern North America, having a magenta flower. Also called ***dragon's mouth***.

Aretine *adjective* var. of ARRETINE.

†arett *verb* var. of ARET.

'arf /ɑːf/ *noun, adjective, & adverb*. *slang*. **M19.**
[ORIGIN Repr. a pronunc.]
= HALF *noun, adjective & adverb*.

arfvedsonite /ɑːfˈvɛds(ə)nʌɪt/ *noun*. **E19.**
[ORIGIN from J. A. *Arfvedson* (1792–1841), Swedish chemist + -ITE[1].]
MINERALOGY. An iron-rich sodium amphibole which occurs as black or dark green monoclinic crystals.

argal *noun* var. of ARGOL *noun*[2].

argal /ˈɑːg(ə)l/ *adverb*. *arch.* **E17.**
[ORIGIN Alt. of Latin *ergo* therefore.]
Therefore.

> SHAKES. *Haml.* He drowns not himself: Argal, he that is not guilty of his own death shortens not his own life.

†argala *noun*. **M18–M19.**
[ORIGIN Hindi *hargīlā* lit. 'bone-swallower'.]
The greater adjutant stork.

argali /ˈɑːg(ə)li/ *noun*. **L18.**
[ORIGIN Mongolian.]
The large wild sheep of eastern central Asia, *Ovis ammon*; *loosely* the bighorn or other similar animal.

argan /ˈɑːg(ə)n/ *noun*. **E17.**
[ORIGIN Moroccan Arab. from Berber *argān*.]
1 The olive-like fruit of the argan tree (see sense 2). *rare*. **E17.**
2 ***argan tree***, an evergreen tree or shrub, *Argania spinosa*, native to Morocco. **E19.**
3 ***argan oil***, an edible oil from the seeds of the argan tree. **L19.**

Argand /ˈɑːgand/ *noun*. **L18.**
[ORIGIN French surname.]
1 *hist.* [A. *Argand* (1755–1803), French physicist.] ▸**a *Argand burner***, a kind of cylindrical burner for oil or gas, allowing air to pass both inner and outer surfaces of the flame. **L18.** ▸**b** In full ***Argand lamp***. A lamp fitted with such a burner. **E19.**
2 MATH. [J. R. *Argand* (1768–1822), French mathematician.] ***Argand diagram***, a diagram on which complex numbers are represented geometrically using Cartesian axes. **E20.**

argent /ˈɑːdʒ(ə)nt/ *noun & adjective*. **LME.**
[ORIGIN Old French & mod. French from Latin *argentum* silver.]
▸ **A** *noun*. **†1** Silver coin; money, cash. **LME–M18.**
2 The metal silver. Now *arch. & poet.* **M16.**
3 HERALDRY. The tincture silver or white in armorial bearings. **M16.**
▸ **B** *adjective*. Chiefly HERALDRY. Silver, white. **L15.**

> W. DE LA MARE Wan as the argent moon. T. H. WHITE The cognizance was argent, a tall cross gules.

■ **argenˈtiferous** *adjective* yielding silver **L18.** **argentry** *noun* (*rare*) silver plate **E17.**

argentaffin /ɑːˈdʒɛntəfɪn/ *adjective*. **E20.**
[ORIGIN French *argentaffine*, from Latin *argentum* silver + *affinis* akin.]
Readily stained black by silver salts; *spec.* (ANATOMY, now *arch.*) designating numerous isolated endocrine cells situated in the intestinal epithelium.
■ **argentaffiˈnoma** *noun*, pl. **-mas**, **-mata** /-mətə/, MEDICINE an intestinal tumour whose tissue stains like argentaffin cells, from which it is thought to develop **M20.**

argentic /ɑːˈdʒɛntɪk/ *adjective*. **E19.**
[ORIGIN from Latin *argentum* silver + -IC.]
CHEMISTRY. Of or pertaining to divalent silver.
– NOTE: Orig. designating monovalent compounds (cf. ARGENTOUS).

argentine /ˈɑːdʒ(ə)ntʌɪn/ *adjective*[1] *& noun*[1]. **LME.**
[ORIGIN Old French & mod. French *argentin(e)*, formed as ARGENT + -INE[1].]
▸ **A** *adjective*. **1** Of, made of, or containing silver. **LME.**
2 Silvery. **LME.**
▸ **B** *noun*. **1** Silver; material simulating silver. Now *rare* or *obsolete*. **L16.**
2 A small silvery marine fish of the salmoniform genus *Argentina*. **M18.**

Argentine /ˈɑːdʒ(ə)ntʌɪn/ *adjective*[2] *& noun*[2]. **E19.**
[ORIGIN Spanish *Argentina* (in *República*, formerly *Confederación*, *Argentina*) lit. 'silvery', named from the Rio de la Plata (Spanish *plata* silver).]
▸ **A** *adjective*. Of, pertaining to, or designating the federal republic which occupies the greater part of the southern end of S. America, extending from Chile in the west to the Brazilian and Uruguayan borders and the Atlantic Ocean in the east, and bordering Bolivia and Paraguay in the north (now usu. called ***Argentina***). **E19.**
Argentine ant a S. American ant, *Iridomyrmex humilis*, which has been introduced and become a pest elsewhere.
▸ **B** *noun*. **1** A native or inhabitant of Argentina. **E19.**
2 ***the Argentine***, Argentina. **L19.**
■ **Argentinian** /ɑːdʒ(ə)nˈtɪnɪən/ *adjective & noun* (**a**) *adjective* of or pertaining to Argentina; (**b**) *noun* = ARGENTINE *noun*[2] 1: **E20.**

argentite /ˈɑːdʒ(ə)ntʌɪt/ *noun*. **M19.**
[ORIGIN from Latin *argentum* silver + -ITE[1].]
MINERALOGY. A form of silver sulphide crystallizing in the cubic system and occurring as dark grey crystals with a metallic lustre.

argento- /ɑːˈdʒɛntəʊ/ *combining form* of Latin *argentum* silver: see -O-.
■ **argentophil(e)**, **argentoˈphilic** *adjectives* = ARGYROPHILIC **M20.**

argentous /ɑːˈdʒɛntəs/ *adjective.* **M19.**
[**ORIGIN** formed as ARGENTO- + -OUS.]
CHEMISTRY. Of or pertaining to monovalent silver.
– **NOTE:** Orig. designating certain compounds apparently of a lower valency (cf. ARGENTIC).

Argie /ˈɑːdʒi/ *noun & adjective. slang. derog.* Also **Argy. L20.**
[**ORIGIN** Abbreviation of ARGENTINE *adjective*[2] & *noun*[2] or ARGENTINIAN: see -IE.]
(An) Argentine, (an) Argentinian.

argil /ˈɑːdʒɪl/ *noun.* **LME.**
[**ORIGIN** Old French *argille* from Latin *argilla* from Greek *argillos* clay.]
Clay, *esp.* potter's clay.

argillaceous /ɑːdʒɪˈleɪʃəs/ *adjective.* **L17.**
[**ORIGIN** from Latin *argillaceus*, from *argilla* clay, + -OUS: see ARGIL, -ACEOUS.]
Of the nature of clay; largely composed of clay; clayey.

argillite /ˈɑːdʒɪlʌɪt/ *noun.* **L18.**
[**ORIGIN** from Latin *argilla* clay + -ITE[1].]
GEOLOGY. An indurated argillaceous rock that is harder than shale and does not split easily.

arginase /ˈɑːdʒɪneɪz/ *noun.* **E20.**
[**ORIGIN** from ARGININE + -ASE.]
BIOCHEMISTRY. An enzyme which hydrolyses arginine to urea and ornithine.

arginine /ˈɑːdʒɪniːn/ *noun.* **L19.**
[**ORIGIN** German *Arginin*, perh. from Greek *arginoeis* bright-shining, white: see -INE[5].]
BIOCHEMISTRY. A basic amino acid, $HN{=}C(NH_2)NH(CH_2)_3CH(NH_2)COOH$, which occurs in many proteins, is essential in the diet of vertebrates during periods of intensive growth, and is involved in urea synthesis; guanidine aminovaleric acid.

Argive /ˈɑːɡʌɪv, -dʒʌɪv/ *noun & adjective.* **M16.**
[**ORIGIN** Latin *Argivus* (Greek *Argeios*) pertaining to Argos (see below).]
▸ **A** *noun.* A native or inhabitant of Argos, a city state of ancient Greece, or the surrounding territory of Argolis; (in Homeric and later classical use) a Greek. **M16.**
▸ **B** *adjective.* Of or pertaining to Argos or Argolis. Also, Grecian, Greek. **L16.**

argle /ˈɑːɡ(ə)l/ *verb. obsolete* exc. *dial.* **L16.**
[**ORIGIN** Alt. of ARGUE, with *-le* as in *haggle*.]
1 *verb trans.* Argue about. **L16.**
2 *verb intrans.* = ARGY-BARGY *verb.* **E19.**

argle-bargle /ˈɑːɡ(ə)lˈbɑːɡ(ə)l (main stress variable)/ *verb & noun. dial. & colloq.* **E19.**
[**ORIGIN** Redupl. of ARGLE.]
▸ **A** *verb.* **1** *verb trans.* Exchange (words) in argument. *rare.* **E19.**
2 *verb intrans.* = ARGY-BARGY *verb.* **E19.**
▸ **B** *noun.* = ARGY-BARGY *noun.* **L19.**

Argo /ˈɑːɡəʊ/ *noun.* **M16.**
[**ORIGIN** Latin: cf. ARGONAUT.]
(The name of) a large constellation of the southern hemisphere now divided into Carina, Puppis, Vela, and Pyxis; the Ship. Also ***Argo Navis*** /ˈneɪvɪs/ [Latin *navis* ship].

argol /ˈɑːɡɒl, -ɡ(ə)l/ *noun*[1]. **ME.**
[**ORIGIN** Anglo-Norman *argoile*, of unknown origin.]
= TARTAR *noun*[1] 1.

argol /ˈɑːɡ(ə)l/ *noun*[2]. Also **argal. M19.**
[**ORIGIN** Mongolian.]
Dried cattle dung used as fuel in the steppes of central Asia.

argon /ˈɑːɡɒn/ *noun.* **L19.**
[**ORIGIN** Greek, neut. of *argos* idle, inactive, from A-[10] + *ergon* work.]
A colourless odourless gaseous chemical element, atomic no. 18, which is one of the noble gases and is present in air to the extent of about one per cent by volume (symbol Ar).

Argonaut /ˈɑːɡ(ə)nɔːt/ *noun.* **L16.**
[**ORIGIN** Latin *argonauta* from Greek *argonautēs* sailor (*nautēs*) in the ship Argo.]
1 Any of the legendary sailors who travelled with Jason in the Argo in quest of the Golden Fleece. **L16.** ▸**b** *transf.* (Also **a-**.) An adventurer with a quest, esp. for gold; an explorer. **E19.**
2 (Now usu. **a-**.) An octopod of the genus *Argonauta*, the female of which possesses a thin coiled shell into which the eggs are laid. Also called ***paper nautilus.*** **M19.**
■ **argoˈnautic** *noun & adjective* (**a**) *noun* a poem concerning the Argonauts; an epic story; (**b**) *adjective* of or pertaining to the Argonauts; epic: **L16.**

argosy /ˈɑːɡəsi/ *noun.* Now *hist.* exc. *poet.* Also (earlier) †**ragusye. L16.**
[**ORIGIN** App. from Italian *Ragusea* use as noun of fem. adjective (sc. *nave* ship, etc.) 'of Ragusa'.]
A merchant vessel of the largest size and burden, *esp.* one of Ragusa (now Dubrovnik, Croatia) or Venice.

fig.: T. W. HIGGINSON Wagons of sea-weed just from the beach . . each weed an argosy.

argot /ˈɑːɡəʊ/ *noun.* **M19.**
[**ORIGIN** French, of unknown origin.]
The jargon, slang, or peculiar phraseology of a social class or group; orig., criminals' slang.

argue /ˈɑːɡjuː/ *verb.* **ME.**
[**ORIGIN** Old French & mod. French *arguer* from Latin *argutari*, frequentative of *arguere* make clear, prove, assert, accuse.]
▸ **I** Bring reasons, reason, dispute.
1 *verb intrans.* Discuss, reason, debate; contend, dispute. (Foll. by *with*, *against*, an opponent; *for*, *against*, *about*, †*of*, a proposition). **ME.**

MILTON Of good and evil much they argu'd then. M. W. MONTAGU I am not . . arguing for an equality of the two sexes. P. G. WODEHOUSE One cannot argue about personality. Its compelling power has to be accepted as a fact. A. S. EDDINGTON We do not argue with the critic who urges that the stars are not hot enough for this process; we tell him to go and find a hotter place. J. GROSS A well-drilled child of the Scottish Enlightenment, a debater trained to argue back to first principles.

2 *verb trans.* Discuss the pros and cons of; bring forward reasons for or against (a proposition). **L15.**

G. B. SHAW Fifty civilians . . to support two skilled judges in trying her case . . and to argue it out with her at sitting after sitting. J. BUCHAN We refused no challenge, but argued any question anywhere with anyone.

3 *verb trans.* Maintain, by adducing reasons, *that.* **M16.**

M. L. KING A few hours later, before Judge Carter, the city argued that we were operating a 'private enterprise' without a franchise.

4 *verb trans.* Adduce as a reason or argument. *arch.* **E17.**

DEFOE He told me the same thing, which I argued for my staying . . was the strongest Repulse to my Pretensions.

5 *verb trans.* Persuade (a person) *into* or *out of* a course of action, opinion, intention, etc. **M17.**

W. CONGREVE A sort of poetical logic to argue you into a protection of this play.

▸ **II** Bring evidence, prove, indicate.
†**6** *verb trans.* Convict (*of*), prove an accusation against. **LME–E18.**
†**7** *verb trans.* Accuse (*of*); call in question. **LME–L17.**

SIR T. BROWNE Nor would we argue the definitive sentence of God.

8 *verb trans.* Be evidence of; indicate or prove (a thing, a person or thing *to be*, *that* something is). **LME.**

SHAKES. *3 Hen. VI* Which argued thee a most unloving father. J. LOCKE Contrary choices that Men make in the World, do not argue that they do not all pursue Good. H. MAUNDRELL Which seem to argue it to be ancient. J. AGATE The principal star is one Ethel Waters, and her enthusiastic reception argues talent.

– **PHRASES:** ***argue the toss***: see TOSS *noun.* **argue well for** (usu. in neg.) make a good case for.
■ **arguable** *adjective* able to be argued, debatable, open to disagreement **E17. arguably** *adverb* as may be shown by argument or made a matter of argument **L19. arguer** *noun* **LME. arguing** *noun* (**a**) the action or process of the verb; †(**b**) an accusation; (**c**) an argument: **LME.**

arguendo /ɑːɡjʊˈɛndəʊ/ *adverb.* **M18.**
[**ORIGIN** Latin, abl. of *arguendum* gerund of *arguere*: see ARGUE.]
Chiefly *LAW.* In the course of the argument; for the sake of argument.

argufy /ˈɑːɡjʊfʌɪ/ *verb. colloq. & dial.* **L17.**
[**ORIGIN** from ARGUENDO + -FY. Cf. *speechify*.]
†**1** *verb trans.* = ARGUE 2. Only in **L17.**
2 *verb intrans.* Dispute, wrangle, argue. **M18.**
3 *verb intrans.* Prove or be evidence of something; be of importance or consequence; signify. **M18.**
4 *verb trans.* Worry with argumentation. **L18.**
■ **argufier** *noun* **E19.**

argument /ˈɑːɡjʊm(ə)nt/ *noun.* **ME.**
[**ORIGIN** Old French & mod. French from Latin *argumentum*, from *arguere*: see ARGUE, -MENT.]
1 A connected series of statements or reasons intended to establish a position; a process of reasoning or disputation; argumentation. **ME.** ▸**b** *spec.* Any of a number of lines of reasoning that seek to prove the existence of God. **E19.**
b ***argument from design***, ***cosmological argument***, ***ontological argument***, etc.
2 A statement or fact advanced to influence the mind; a reason urged in support of a proposition. Formerly *spec.* in *LOGIC*, the middle term in a syllogism. **LME.**

HENRY MORE But that the Beast that was, and is not, is not the Devil, we shall now evince by other arguments. C. M. YONGE Well provided with golden arguments. F. L. WRIGHT To hold snow on the roof is always a good, wise provision and a good argument for a flat roof.

3 Proof, evidence; a token, an indication. *arch.* **LME.**

T. SHERIDAN Beating the Desk and biting of Nails were Arguments of taking Pains.

4 *MATH.* etc. An independent quantity (orig., *ASTRONOMY*, an angle) on which the value of a function depends or on which an operator acts. **LME.**

5 a Statement of the pros and cons of a proposition; discussion, debate (esp. contentious); a verbal dispute, a quarrel. **L15.** ▸†**b** Subject of contention. **L16–E17.**

a MILTON In argument with men a woman ever Goes by the worse. SHAFTESBURY So intent in upholding their own side of the argument. K. AMIS Just assume for the sake of argument that he's a fake. V. S. PRITCHETT Grandmother, Grandfather and Father were shouting in angry argument across the table, about God and 'that Eddy woman'. A. HAILEY Their discussion . . had quickly developed into an argument. **b** SHAKES. *Hen. V* And sheath'd their swords for lack of argument.

†**6** Subject, theme of debate or discussion, either verbal or written. **L15–M19.**

DISRAELI The throbbing deed Shall make thy name a household argument.

7 A summary of the subject matter of a book; an index, table (of contents), etc. *arch.* **M16.**

POPE Argument to Book the First.

■ **arguˈmental** *adjective* (now *rare*) **L16.**

†**argument** *verb.* **LME.**
[**ORIGIN** from the noun or Old French & mod. French *argumenter* from Latin *argumentari*, from *argumentum*: see ARGUMENT *noun.*]
1 *verb intrans.* Adduce arguments (*for*); argue. **LME–M19.**
2 *verb trans.* Provide proof, establish, (*that*); argue for. **M16–M19.**
3 *verb trans.* Make the subject of debate. **M18–E19.**

argumentation /ˌɑːɡjʊmɛnˈteɪʃ(ə)n/ *noun.* **LME.**
[**ORIGIN** Old French & mod. French from Latin *argumentatio(n-)*, from *argumentat-* pa. ppl stem of *argumentari*: see ARGUMENT *verb*, -ATION.]
1 The action or process of arguing; methodical employment or presentation of arguments; logical or formal reasoning; interchange of argument, discussion, debate. **LME.**
2 An argument advanced; a sequence of arguments, a process of reasoning. **LME.**

argumentative /ɑːɡjʊˈmɛntətɪv/ *adjective.* **LME**
[**ORIGIN** Old French, or late Latin *argumentativus* (Donatus), from *argumentari*: see ARGUMENTATION, -ATIVE.]
1 Characterized by argument; controversial; logical. **LME.**
†**2** Of the nature of an argument (*for*); of weight as evidence (*of*). **M–L17.**
3 Given to argumentation; capable or fond of arguing. **M17.**
■ **argumentatively** *adverb* **M17. argumentativeness** *noun* **M18.**

argumentator /ˌɑːɡjʊmɛnˈteɪtə/ *noun.* Now *rare.* **M17.**
[**ORIGIN** Latin: see ARGUMENT *verb*, -ATOR.]
A person who conducts an argument, a reasoner.

argumentive /ɑːɡjʊˈmɛntɪv/ *adjective. rare.* **M17.**
[**ORIGIN** from ARGUMENT *verb* + -IVE.]
= ARGUMENTATIVE.

argumentum ad hominem /ɑːɡjʊˌmɛntəm ad ˈhɒmɪnɛm/ *noun phr.* **M17.**
[**ORIGIN** Latin: see ARGUMENT *noun*, AD HOMINEM.]
An argument, usu. vilificatory, appealing to the personal circumstances or character of an opponent rather than to sound reasoning.

argumentum e silentio /ɑːɡjʊˌmɛntəm eɪ sɪˈlɛntɪəʊ, -ʃɪəʊ/ *noun phr.* **M20.**
[**ORIGIN** Latin = argument from silence.]
A conclusion based on silence, i.e. on lack of contrary evidence.

Argus /ˈɑːɡəs/ *noun.* In senses 2 & 3 usu. **a-. LME.**
[**ORIGIN** Latin from Greek *Argos*, a mythological person with a hundred eyes.]
1 A very vigilant watcher, a guardian. **LME.**
2 Any of certain butterflies bearing eyespots, esp. *Aricia agestis* (in full ***brown argus***) or *A. artaxerxes* (in full ***Scotch argus***). **L17.**
3 Either of two large SE Asian pheasants, both of which have long tails with numerous eyespots, *Argusianus argus* (in full ***great argus***) and *Rheinardia ocellata* (in full ***crested argus***). **M18.**
– **COMB.**: **Argus eye** (**a**) in *pl.*, sharp eyes, acute observation; (**b**) each of the eyelike markings on the tail of a peacock (to which Argus' eyes were said to be transferred by Hera after his death); **Argus-eyed** *adjective* extremely vigilant, sharp-sighted.

argute /ɑːˈɡjuːt/ *adjective.* Now *literary.* **LME.**
[**ORIGIN** Latin *argutus* pa. pple of *arguere* make clear, ARGUE.]
†**1** Of taste: sharp. Only in **LME.**
2 Of a person, faculty, action, etc.: quick, subtle, shrewd. **L16.**
3 Of sound: shrill. **E18.**
■ **argutely** *adverb* **L16. arguteness** *noun* **M17.**

Argy *noun & adjective* var. of ARGIE.

argy-bargy /ˌɑːɡɪˈbɑːɡi, ˌɑːdʒɪˈbɑːdʒi/ *verb & noun. dial. & colloq.* **L19.**
[**ORIGIN** Alt. & redupl. of ARGUE: cf. ARGLE-BARGLE.]
▸ **A** *verb intrans.* Dispute, wrangle. **L19.**
▸ **B** *noun.* Disputatious argument; a wrangle, a dispute. **L19.**

A

argyle /ɑːˈɡʌɪl/ *noun*. Also **-gyll**, **A-**. L18.
[ORIGIN *Argyll* (*Argyle*), a former county of Scotland and a family name.]
1 A vessel, usu. of silver or other metal and resembling a small coffee pot, in which to serve hot gravy. *obsolete* exc. *hist.* L18.
2 A knitting pattern with diamonds of various colours on a single background colour, based on the tartan of the Argyll branch of the Campbell clan. Also, a garment (esp. in *pl.*, socks) in this pattern. M20.

argyro- /ˈɑːdʒɪrəʊ/ *combining form* repr. Greek *arguro-*, from *arguros* silver: see -O-. Before a vowel also **argyr-**.
■ **arˈgyria** *noun* (MEDICINE) silver poisoning, esp. as causing a greyish-blue discoloration of the skin L19. **arˈgyrodite** *noun* [Greek *argurōdēs* rich in silver] MINERALOGY a sulphide of silver and germanium crystallizing in the cubic system and occurring as black crystals with a metallic lustre L19. **ˈargyrophil(e)** *adjective* = ARGYROPHILIC E20. **argyroˈphilia** *noun* the property of being argyrophilic M20. **argyroˈphilic** *adjective* readily stained black by silver salts M20.

arhat /ˈɑːhat/ *noun*. Also **arahat** /ˈarəhat/. L19.
[ORIGIN Sanskrit *arhat*, Pali *arahat* meritorious.]
BUDDHISM & JAINISM. A saint of one of the highest ranks.
■ **arhatship** *noun* the state of an arhat L19.

arhythmic *adjective* var. of ARRHYTHMIC.

aria /ˈɑːrɪə/ *noun*. E18.
[ORIGIN Italian from Latin *aera* accus. of *aer*: see AIR *noun*[1].]
MUSIC. A long song for one voice usu. with accompaniment; *esp.* such a song in an opera, oratorio, etc.

Arian /ˈɛːrɪən/ *adjective*[1] & *noun*[1]. LME.
[ORIGIN ecclesiastical Latin *Arianus*, from *Arius* from Greek *Arios*, *Areios* (d. 336), a presbyter of Alexandria: see -AN.]
▸ **A** *adjective*. Designating the heretical doctrine of Arius, who denied that Christ was consubstantial with God; of, pertaining to, or holding this doctrine. LME.
▸ **B** *noun*. A holder of this doctrine. LME.
■ **Arianism** *noun* the Arian doctrine L16. **Arianize** *verb* (*a*) *verb intrans.* follow the doctrine of Arius; (*b*) *verb trans.* convert to Arianism: E17. **Arianizer** *noun* L17.

Arian /ˈɛːrɪən/ *adjective*[2] & *noun*[2]. E20.
[ORIGIN from ARIES + -AN.]
▸ **A** *adjective*. Of or pertaining to the zodiacal sign Aries; (characteristic of a person) born under Aries. E20.
▸ **B** *noun*. A person born under Aries. E20.

Arian *adjective*[3] & *noun*[3] var. of ARYAN.

-arian /ˈɛːrɪən/ *suffix*.
[ORIGIN from Latin *-arius* -ARY[1] + -AN.]
Forming adjectives or corresp. nouns of which the earliest are ***disciplinarian***, ***antiquarian***, ***proletarian***; (numeral adjectives) ***quinquagenarian***; commonly in terms denoting religious or moral tenets, as ***Millenarian***, ***sectarian***, ***Unitarian***, on the analogy of which were formed ***humanitarian***, ***utilitarian***, etc., and joc. formations as ***anythingarian***.

arid /ˈarɪd/ *adjective*. M17.
[ORIGIN French *aride* or Latin *aridus*, from *arere* be dry or parched: see -ID[1].]
†**1** Of a substance, the skin, etc.: dry, parched, withered. M17–E19.
2 Of the ground, climate, etc.: dry, parched; barren, bare; GEOGRAPHY too dry to support vegetation. M17.

> A. KOESTLER The mountains underneath were arid as craters on the moon. E. ROOSEVELT It looked like good farming country, in contrast to the arid appearance of the land in so many parts of Greece.

3 *fig.* Uninteresting, dull; unfruitful, barren. E19.

> T. C. WOLFE A dry campaign over an arid waste of Latin prose.

■ **aˈridify** *verb trans.* make arid E20. **aridly** *adverb* L19. **aridness** *noun* M18.

aridisol /əˈrɪdɪsɒl/ *noun*. M20.
[ORIGIN from ARID + -I- + -SOL.]
SOIL SCIENCE. A soil of an order comprising often saline or alkaline soils with very little organic matter, characteristic of arid regions.

aridity /əˈrɪdɪti/ *noun*. L16.
[ORIGIN French *aridité* or Latin *ariditas*, formed as ARID: see -ITY.]
1 Arid state or quality; dryness, barrenness; parched condition. L16.
2 *fig.* Lack of interest, dullness; unproductiveness. L17.

> A. HUSSEIN Another failed relationship, unemployment, the aridity of research and critical writing.

ariel /ˈɛːrɪəl/ *noun*. M19.
[ORIGIN Arabic *ʼaryal*.]
A Middle Eastern and African gazelle, *Gazella arabica*.

Aries /ˈɛːriːz/ *noun*. OE.
[ORIGIN Latin *aries* ram.]
1 (The name of) a constellation of the northern hemisphere, on the ecliptic near Andromeda; ASTROLOGY (the name of) the first zodiacal sign, usu. associated with the period 21 March to 20 April (see note s.v. ZODIAC); the Ram. OE.

> *attrib.*: E. KIRK It is almost impossible to hide anything from an Aries individual who has recognized his or her power of intuition.

first point of Aries the point of the vernal equinox (now actually located in Pisces, owing to precession).
2 A person born under the sign Aries; = ARIAN *noun*[2]. M20.

†**arietation** *noun*. E17–L18.
[ORIGIN Latin *arietatio(n-)*, from *arietat-* pa. ppl stem of *arietare* butt like a ram, from *aries*, *ariet-* ram: see -ATION.]
The action of butting like a ram; ramming, battering, bombardment, (*lit.* & *fig.*).

arietta /arɪˈɛtə/ *noun*. E18.
[ORIGIN Italian, dim. of ARIA.]
MUSIC. A short tune or song.
■ Also **ariette** *noun* [French] E19.

aright /əˈrʌɪt/ *adverb*.
[ORIGIN Old English *on riht*, *ariht*: see A *preposition*[1] 1, RIGHT *noun*[1].]
▸ **I** Of manner.
1 In a right manner, rightly; justly, correctly. OE.

> COVERDALE *Ps.* 77:8 A generacion that set not their herte aright. M. INNES And if I remember aright, sir, it was just then that the horse stopped nodding—sudden-like.

†**2** Immediately; at once. ME–L15.
†**3** Directly; in a straight line. ME–E17.
4 Exactly, just; indeed. Long *arch.* LME.

> E. B. BROWNING Is it true besides—Aright true?

▸ **II** Of direction.
5 On or to the right hand. *arch. rare.* ME.

> SOUTHEY Aright, aleft, The affrighted foemen scatter from his spear.

■ **arightly** *adverb* (now *rare* or *obsolete*) = ARIGHT 1 L16. †**arights** *adverb* (*rare*) = ARIGHT 1: only in L16.

aril /ˈarɪl/ *noun*. Also in Latin form **arillus** /-əs/, pl. **-lli** /-lʌɪ, -liː/. M18.
[ORIGIN mod. Latin *arillus* of unknown origin; medieval Latin *arilli* = dried grape pips.]
BOTANY. An additional envelope, often fleshy, developed around the seed in certain plants (e.g. yew).
■ **arillate** *adjective* having an aril E19.

Arimasp /ˈarɪmasp/ *noun*. Pl. **Arimasps**, **Arimaspi** /arɪˈmaspʌɪ/. L16.
[ORIGIN Latin *Arimaspi* pl., Greek *Arimaspoi*, said to mean 'one-eyed' in Scythian.]
Any of a mythical race of one-eyed men in northern Europe who tried to take gold guarded by griffins.
■ Also **Ariˈmaspian** *noun* M17.

arioso /arɪˈəʊzəʊ, ɑː-/ *adjective*, *adverb*, & *noun*. E18.
[ORIGIN Italian, from ARIA.]
MUSIC. ▸ **A** *adjective*. Melodious, songlike, cantabile; having something of the quality of an aria. Also as *adverb* as a direction. E18.
▸ **B** *noun*. Pl. **-os**. A piece of vocal or instrumental music of this kind. L19.
■ **ariose** /ɑːrɪˈəʊs/ *adjective* = ARIOSO *adjective* E18.

-arious /ˈɛːrɪəs/ *suffix*.
[ORIGIN from Latin *-arius* -ARY[1] + -OUS.]
Forming adjectives, as ***vicarious***, ***gregarious***, etc.

aripple /əˈrɪp(ə)l/ *adverb* & *pred. adjective*. E19.
[ORIGIN from A-[2] + RIPPLE *noun*[3].]
In a ripple, rippling.

arise /əˈrʌɪz/ *verb intrans.* Pa. t. **arose** /əˈrəʊz/; pa. pple **arisen** /əˈrɪz(ə)n/.
[ORIGIN Old English *ārīsan*, (Northumbrian) *arrīsa* = Old Saxon *ārīsan*, Old High German *ur-*, *ar-*, *irrīsan*, Gothic *us-*, *urreisan*: see A-[1], RISE *verb*. Largely replaced by *rise* except in senses in branch III.]
▸ **I** Rise from sitting, repose, inaction, etc. Now *arch.* & *poet.*
1 Get up from sitting or kneeling; stand up. OE.

> AV *John* 14:31 Arise, let us go hence.

†**2** Get up from a fall. OE–M17.

> MILTON Awake, arise, or be for ever fall'n.

3 Get up from sleep or rest. OE.

> GOLDSMITH Nash generally arose early in the morning.

4 Of the sun, moon, etc.: come above the horizon. Of the day, morning, etc.: dawn, begin. OE.

> SHAKES. *Rom. & Jul.* Arise, fair sun, and kill the envious moon.

5 Rise from the dead. OE.

> AV *Matt.* 27:52 Many bodies of the saints which slept arose.

6 Rise from inaction or quiet, esp. in hostility or rebellion. OE.

> SHAKES. *Oth.* Arise, black vengeance, from the hollow hell.

7 Rise in agitation or violence, as the wind, sea, etc.; boil up. OE.

> TENNYSON A wind arose and rush'd upon the South.

8 Of a sound: become audible, be heard. ME.

> AV *Acts* 23:9 There arose a great cry.

▸ **II** Go or come higher.
9 Go or come up; ascend, mount. Now *poet.* OE.

> KEATS A mist arose, as from a scummy marsh.

†**10** Rise in height, eminence, quantity, value, etc.; grow, swell up; amount or attain *to*. ME–L18.

> SWIFT Stocks arose three per cent. upon it in the city. T. R. MALTHUS The number arising annually to the age of puberty.

▸ **III** Spring up; come into existence.
11 Spring out from its source, as a river etc. (*arch.*); originate, result (*from*, †*of*); proceed *out of* as a consequence. OE.

> SHAKES. *Hen. V* Some sudden mischief may arise of it. R. G. COLLINGWOOD Other philosophers discussed problems arising out of distinctions I thought false. F. HOYLE The forces arising from the weight of the ice are . . greatest at the bottom of the glacier.

12 Of a person: be born; come into the world of events. OE.

> COVERDALE *Deut.* 34:10 There arose no prophet more in Israel like vnto Moses. J. BRYCE In the fourteenth century there arose in Italy the first great masters of painting and song.

13 Of a thing: spring up, be raised or built. *poet.* OE.

> TENNYSON So long, that mountains have arisen since With cities on their flanks.

14 Come into existence or notice; present itself, occur. OE.

> LD MACAULAY All questions which arose in the Privy Council. D. ATTENBOROUGH If we want to consider how life arose, we have to look back a further thousand million years.

■ **arisings** *noun pl.* materials forming secondary or waste products of a process E20.

arista /əˈrɪstə/ *noun*. Pl. **-tae** /-tiː/. L17.
[ORIGIN Latin = awn or ear of grain.]
ZOOLOGY & BOTANY. A bristly or beardlike process.
■ **aristate** *adjective* awned, bearded: E19.

Aristarch /ˈarɪstɑːk/ *noun*. Also †**-chus**, pl. **-chi**. M16.
[ORIGIN Latin *Aristarchus* from Greek *Aristarkhos* (2nd cent. BC), a severe critic of Homeric poetry.]
A severe critic.

aristo /əˈrɪstəʊ/ *noun*. *colloq.* Pl. **-os**. M19.
[ORIGIN French, abbreviation of *aristocrate* ARISTOCRAT.]
An aristocrat.

aristocracy /arɪˈstɒkrəsi/ *noun*. L15.
[ORIGIN Old French & mod. French *aristocratie* from Greek *aristokratia*, from *aristos* best: see -CRACY.]
1 The government of a state by its best citizens. L15.
2 Government of a state by those who are most distinguished by birth and wealth; oligarchy; a state so governed. L16.
3 A ruling body of nobles, an oligarchy. E17.
4 The class to which such rulers belong, the nobility; the patrician or privileged class, regardless of the form of government. M17.
5 *transf.* & *fig.* The best representatives of any quality, skill, etc.; any privileged or elite group. M19.

> G. B. SHAW The plays which constitute the genuine aristocracy of modern dramatic literature. G. M. TREVELYAN The working class aristocracy, the engineers and the men of other skilled trades. B. BAINBRIDGE He was convinced that physicians were an ignorant aristocracy kept afloat by witchcraft.

aristocrat /ˈarɪstəkrat, əˈrɪst-/ *noun*. L18.
[ORIGIN French *aristocrate* (a word of the French Revolution) from *aristocratie*, *-tique*: see ARISTOCRACY, ARISTOCRATIC, -CRAT.]
A member of an aristocracy or of the nobility, orig. of the French aristocracy in the French Revolution of 1790 (cf. DEMOCRAT *noun* 1). Also (*rare*), an advocate of aristocratic government.
■ **ariˈstocratism** *noun* aristocratic conduct; haughty exclusiveness: L18. **ariˈstocratize** *verb trans.* make aristocratic L18.

aristocratic /ˌarɪstəˈkratɪk/ *adjective*. E17.
[ORIGIN French *aristocratique* from Greek *aristokratikos*: see ARISTOCRACY, -IC.]
1 Of or pertaining to an aristocracy; attached to or favouring aristocracy. E17.
2 Befitting an aristocrat; grand, stylish, distinguished. M19.
■ **aristocratical** *adjective* oligarchical; aristocratic: L16. **aristocratically** *adverb* L16. **aristocraticalness** *noun* (*rare*) M18.

aristolochia /ˌarɪstəˈləʊkɪə/ *noun*. OE.
[ORIGIN medieval Latin *aristologia*, French *aristoloche*, from Latin *aristolochia* from Greek *aristolokhia*, *-eia*, from *aristolokhos* well-born (from its medicinal repute).]
Any of numerous climbing shrubs or other plants of the genus *Aristolochia* (family Aristolochiaceae), bearing tubular, often bizarre, flowers; esp. *A. clematitis*. Also called ***birthwort***.

aristology /arɪˈstɒlədʒi/ *noun*. M19.
[ORIGIN from Greek *ariston* breakfast, luncheon + -LOGY.]
The art or science of dining.
■ **aristoˈlogical** *adjective* L19. **aristologist** *noun* M19.

A

Aristophanic /ˌarɪstəˈfanɪk/ *adjective & noun*. E19.
[ORIGIN Latin *Aristophanicus*, Greek *Aristophanikos*, from *Aristophanēs* (see below): see -IC.]
▸ **A** *adjective*. Of, pertaining to, or characteristic of the Athenian comic dramatist Aristophanes (d. *c* 380 BC). E19.
▸ **B** *noun*. CLASSICAL PROSODY. A logaoedic tripody beginning with a dactyl. M19.

Aristotelian /ˌarɪstəˈtiːlɪən/ *adjective & noun*. L16.
[ORIGIN from Latin *Aristotelius*, *-eus* from Greek *Aristoteleios*, from *Aristotelēs* Aristotle (see below): see -AN.]
▸ **A** *adjective*. Of or pertaining to the Greek philosopher Aristotle (d. 322 BC) or his philosophical system based on the theory of syllogism, and on the choice of matter, form, potentiality, and actuality as basic concepts; logical, deductive. L16.
▸ **B** *noun*. An adherent or student of Aristotle's philosophy. L16.
■ **Aristotelean** /ˌarɪstɒtɪˈliːən/ *adjective & noun* (now *rare*) = ARISTOTELIAN E17. **Aristotelianism** *noun* the philosophical system or any doctrine of Aristotle E18. **Aristotelic** /ˌarɪstəˈtɛlɪk/ *adjective* = ARISTOTELIAN *adjective* E17. †**Aristotelical** *adjective* L16–L17.

Aristotle's lantern *noun phr.* see LANTERN *noun* 7b.

Arita /əˈriːtə/ *adjective*. L19.
[ORIGIN A town in S. Japan.]
Designating Japanese porcelain of a distinctive style made in or near Arita, typically with unsymmetrical floral designs in blue and white underglaze or polychrome enamel.

arithmancy /ˈarɪθmansi/ *noun*. L16.
[ORIGIN from Greek *arithmos* number + -MANCY.]
Divination by numbers.
■ **arithˈmantical** *adjective* M16.

arithmetic /əˈrɪθmətɪk/ *noun*[1]. Also (earlier) †**arsmet(r)ike** & similar vars. ME.
[ORIGIN Old French *arismetique* ult. from Latin *arithmetica* from Greek *arithmētikē* (*tekhnē*) counting (art), from *arithmein* reckon, from *arithmos* number. Early forms were infl. by Latin *ars metrica* 'measuring art': conformation to orig. Latin and Greek forms took place in 16.]
1 The science of numbers; (the branch of mathematics that deals with) the properties and manipulation of numbers; calculation, reckoning. ME.
BINARY *arithmetic*. *decimal arithmetic*: see DECIMAL *adjective*. *mental arithmetic*: see MENTAL *adjective*[1]. *universal arithmetic*: see UNIVERSAL *adjective*.
2 A treatise on this. L15.
– COMB.: **arithmetic and logic unit**, **arithmetic unit** a unit in a computer which carries out arithmetical and logical operations.

arithmetic /arɪθˈmɛtɪk/ *noun*[2] & *adjective*. M17.
[ORIGIN French *arithmétique*: see ARITHMETIC *noun*[1].]
▸ †**A** *noun*. An arithmetician. Only in M17.
▸ **B** *adjective*. Of, pertaining to, or connected with arithmetic; according to the rules of arithmetic. M17.
arithmetic mean (of *n* numbers): their sum divided by *n*. **arithmetic progression**, **arithmetic series**: in which there is a constant (positive or negative) difference between successive quantities, as 2, 5, 8, 11.

arithmetical /arɪθˈmɛtɪk(ə)l/ *adjective*. M16.
[ORIGIN from Latin *arithmeticus* from Greek *arithmētikos*: see ARITHMETIC *noun*[1], -AL[1].]
= ARITHMETIC *adjective*
arithmetical ratio: see RATIO *noun* 2a.
■ **arithmetically** *adverb* according to arithmetic; by calculation: L15.

arithmetician /ərɪθməˈtɪʃ(ə)n, ˌarɪθ-/ *noun*. M16.
[ORIGIN French *arithméticien* from Latin *arithmetica*: see ARITHMETIC *noun*[1], -ICIAN.]
A person skilled in arithmetic.

arithmetize /əˈrɪθmətʌɪz/ *verb*. Also **-ise**. M17.
[ORIGIN from ARITHMETIC *noun*[1] + -IZE.]
1 *verb intrans. & trans.* Use arithmetic; calculate. *rare*. M17.
2 *verb trans.* Express arithmetically; reduce to arithmetical form. L19.
■ **arithmetiˈzation** *noun* E20.

arithmo- /əˈrɪθməʊ/ *combining form* of Greek *arithmos* number: see -O-.
■ **arithˈmology** *noun* the science of numbers; (a) writing on this subject: L16. **arithmoˈmania** *noun* a pathological desire to count objects or make calculations L19. **arithmoˈmaniac** *noun* a person affected with arithmomania L19. **arithˈmometer** *noun* (now *rare* or *obsolete*) a calculating instrument E19.

arity /ˈarɪti/ *noun*. M20.
[ORIGIN from -ARY[1] (in *binary*, *ternary*, etc.) + -ITY.]
MATH. The number of elements by virtue of which something is unary, binary, etc.

-arium /ˈɛːrɪəm/ *suffix*. Pl. **-ariums**, **-aria** /ˈɛːrɪə/.
[ORIGIN Latin, neut. of adjectives in *-arius*: see -ARY[1].]
Forming nouns with the sense 'a thing connected with or employed in, a place for', as ***herbarium***, ***honorarium***, ***planetarium***, ***vivarium***, etc., freq. (after ***aquarium***) 'a place for keeping and exhibiting something', as ***dolphinarium*** etc.

Ariz. *abbreviation*.
Arizona.

Arizonian /arɪˈzəʊnɪən/ *adjective & noun*. Also **-nan** /-nən/. M19.
[ORIGIN from *Arizona* (see below) + -IAN.]
Of or pertaining to, a native or inhabitant of, the state of Arizona, USA.

arjun /ˈɑːdʒʌn, -uːn/ *noun*. M19.
[ORIGIN Sanskrit *arjuna*.]
= KUMBUK.

ark /ɑːk/ *noun*. In senses 2, 3 also **A-**.
[ORIGIN Old English *ærc* (*eark*) corresp. to Old Frisian *erke*, Old High German *arc(h)a*, Old Norse *ǫrk*, *ark-*, Gothic *arka* from Latin *arca* chest, box, coffer.]
1 A chest, coffer, basket, or similar receptacle; (chiefly *dial.*) a chest or bin for storing meal, fruit, or other foodstuffs. OE.
AV *Exod.* 2:3 She tooke for him an arke of bul-rushes.
2 *spec.* The wooden chest which contained the tables of Jewish law and was kept in the holiest place of the Tabernacle and of the First Temple in Jerusalem (also more fully ***Ark of the Covenant***, ***Ark of Testimony***). Now also, the chest or cupboard housing the Torah scrolls in a synagogue (also more fully ***Holy Ark***). OE.
lay hands on the ark, **touch the ark** treat irreverently what is held to be sacred.
3 The large floating covered vessel in which Noah, his family, and animals were said to be saved from the Flood. Also *fig.*, a place of refuge. OE.
fig.: H. FAST They stood on the deck as the ancient, rusty ship that had been their home and ark for seventeen days wore into Ellis Island.
have come out of the Ark *colloq.* be very antiquated.
4 A ship, boat, etc.; *esp.* (*N. Amer.*) a large flat-bottomed riverboat. L15.
BYRON No more he said: but . . commits him to his fragile ark. M. TWAIN Drifting arks and stone-boats.
– COMB.: **ark shell** (a shell of) a small bivalve belonging to *Arca* or a related genus.
■ **arkite** *adjective* (*rare*) of or pertaining to Noah's ark L18.

Ark. *abbreviation*.
Arkansas.

†**Arkansa** *noun & adjective* var. of ARKANSAS.

Arkansan /ɑːˈkanz(ə)n/ *noun & adjective*. M19.
[ORIGIN from *Arkansas* (see below), formed as ARKANSAS: see -AN.]
A native or inhabitant of, of or pertaining to, Arkansas, a state of the US.
■ Also **Arkansian** *noun & adjective* M19.

Arkansas /ˈɑːk(ə)nsɔː/ *noun & adjective*. Also †**-sa(w)**. Pl. of noun same. L17.
[ORIGIN French from Illinois *akansea*: cf. OZARK.]
= QUAPAW.

†**Arkansaw** *noun & adjective* var. of ARKANSAS.

arkose /ˈɑːkəʊs, -z/ *noun*. M19.
[ORIGIN French, prob. from Greek *arkhaios* ancient.]
GEOLOGY. A coarse-grained sandstone which is at least 25 per cent feldspar.
■ **arˈkosic** *adjective* E20.

arles /ɑːlz/ *noun*. *Scot. & N. English*. ME.
[ORIGIN App. repr. medieval Latin dim. of Latin ARRHA: cf. Old French *ere*, pl. *erres*, *arres*, (16) *arrhes*.]
Money given to bind a bargain; earnest money. Also *fig.*, an earnest, a foretaste.
– COMB.: **arles-penny** a sum of money given as earnest.

arm /ɑːm/ *noun*[1].
[ORIGIN Old English *arm*, *earm* = Old Frisian *arm*, *erm*, Old Saxon, Old High German (Dutch, German) *arm*, Old Norse *armr*, Gothic *arms* from Germanic.]
▸ **I** A limb.
1 Either of the upper limbs of the human body, from the shoulder to the hand (the part from the elbow downwards being the ***forearm***); (in *pl.*) the space enclosed by a person's arms. OE.
G. STEIN He got up and put his arm around her like a brother. J. CONRAD Outside I met Therese with her arms full of pillows and blankets. D. LODGE Allowing his long, gorilla-like arms to hang loosely over the edge of his seat.
2 *fig.* Might, power, authority; a prop, a support. OE.
AV *Jer.* 17:5 Cursed be the man that trusteth in man, and maketh flesh his arme. D. BREWSTER No period of his life can be named when his intellectual arm was shortened.
3 The forelimb of an animal; a flexible limb or other appendage of an invertebrate. LME. ▸**b** FALCONRY. The leg of a hawk from thigh to foot. L16.
D. MORRIS The anthropoid apes differ from the true monkeys in that they are tailless and have elongated arms. D. ATTENBOROUGH These creatures appear to be crinoids that . . are lying in an inverted position with . . their five arms outstretched.
4 A sleeve. L18.
▸ **II** Something resembling an arm.
5 A narrow strip of water or land projecting from a larger body. OE.
C. DARWIN The islands, though in sight of each other, are separated by deep arms of the sea. P. LARKIN I dreamed of an outthrust arm of land Where gulls blew over a wave.
6 Each of the branches into which a main trunk divides, e.g. of a tree, road, nerve, etc. ME.
I. MURDOCH A great tree spread its arms over a circle of grass. D. STOREY The road divided, one arm leading to the Dell, the other to the station.
7 A part of an apparatus which resembles an arm in shape, disposition, or function. See also YARDARM. M16. ▸**b** The middle segment of the bucket of a water wheel. E17.
G. F. FIENNES The arm had fallen off the Up starter at Tottenham. *Encycl. Brit.* That device . . directs the robot's arm and hand to repeat a specific sequence of movements. G. J. KING The modern pickup consists of an arm and a cartridge.
8 A side part of a chair or sofa upon which the sitter's arm may rest. M17.
J. D. SALINGER He came over and sat down on the arm of Stradlater's chair.
9 ASTRONOMY. Any of the luminous bands of stars and gas which form the outer parts of a spiral galaxy. L19.
– PHRASES: **an arm and a leg** *fig.* a large sum, something of high value to one, (esp. in ***cost an arm and a leg***, ***give an arm and a leg for***). **arm in arm** (of two or more people) with arms interlinked. ***a shot in the arm***: see SHOT *noun*[1]. **as long as my arm**, **as long as your arm** *colloq.* very long. **at arm's length** as far as the arm can reach; *fig.* without undue familiarity; (of dealings) with neither party controlled by the other. ***chance one's arm***: see CHANCE *verb* 3. **give one's arm (to)**, **offer one's arm (to)** allow or invite (someone) to walk arm in arm with one, or to lean on one's arm. **have a good arm** (esp. CRICKET) be a strong thrower. **in arms** (of a child) too young to walk (***BABE in arms***). **in a person's arms** embraced by him or her. ***left arm***: see LEFT *adjective*. ***offer one's arm (to)***: see ***give one's arm to*** above. **on one's arm**: supported by it. ***right arm***: see RIGHT *adjective*. ***secular arm***: see SECULAR *adjective*. ***TREM arm***. ***tremolo arm***: see TREMOLO *noun* 2b. ***twist a person's arm***: see TWIST *verb*. **under one's arm**: between it and the body. **within arm's reach** near enough to reach by extending one's arm; *fig.* readily available. **with open arms** cordially, eagerly.
– COMB.: **armband** a band worn round the arm; **arm-bone** (now *rare* or *obsolete*) the humerus; **arm candy** [after ***EYE candy***] *colloq.* a sexually attractive companion accompanying a person, esp. a celebrity, at social events; ARMCHAIR; **armhole** (**a**) (*obsolete* exc. *dial.*) an armpit; (**b**) a hole through which the arm is put into the sleeve of a garment or out of which it is put in a sleeveless garment; **armlock** a close hold by the arm in wrestling or judo; **armpit** (**a**) the hollow under the arm where it is joined to the trunk; the axilla; (**b**) the corresponding region of other animals; (**c**) *fig.* (*N. Amer. colloq.*) a disgusting or contemptible place or part; the lowest place; **armrest** something to support the arm of a seated person; **armstrong** *adjective* (long *arch.*) having strong arms; **arm-twisting** *fig.* (persuasion by) the use of physical force or moral pressure; **arm-wrestle** *verb trans. & intrans.* engage in arm-wrestling (with); **arm-wrestling**: in which two people sit opposite each other at a table, and each places one elbow on the tabletop, grips the other's hand, and tries to force the other's arm down on to the table.
■ **armful** *noun* as much as one arm, or both arms, can hold LME. **armless** *adjective*[1] without arm or branch LME. **armlet** *noun* (**a**) an ornament or band worn round the arm; (**b**) a small arm of the sea, branch of a river, etc.: M16. **armlike** *adjective* resembling (that of) an arm L19.

arm /ɑːm/ *noun*[2]. ME.
[ORIGIN Old French & mod. French *armes* pl. from Latin *arma* (no sing.).]
▸ **I** Something used in fighting.
1 In *pl.* Defensive covering for the body; armour, mail. Now *poet.* ME.
SHAKES. *Rich. II* Boys . . clap their female joints In stiff unwieldy arms.
2 A weapon. Usu. in *pl.*, instruments used in fighting, weapons, armaments. ME.
R. GRAVES As a final arm for use when even the lance failed they carried a heavy broadsword. H. MACMILLAN As regards defence, Pakistan wanted more arms, especially tanks and bombers. *fig.*: SIR T. BROWNE Unable to wield the intellectual arms of reason.
3 In *pl.* Defensive or offensive parts of animals or plants. *rare*. LME.
▸ **II** Elliptical senses.
4 In *pl.* The exercise of arms; fighting, war. ME.
SHAKES. *Rich. II* Thou art a banish'd man, and here art come . . In braving arms against thy sovereign. STEELE It is a barbarous Way to extend Dominion by Arms.
5 In *pl.* The practice or profession of arms; soldiering. ME.
G. B. SHAW A patrician keeping a shop instead of following arms!
6 In *pl.* Feats of arms; valiant deeds. *poet.* LME.
DRYDEN Arms and the man I sing.
7 Each kind of troops in an army, as cavalry, infantry, etc. (orig. these two only); a branch of the armed forces, or (*transf.*) of any organization. (Occas. understood as a fig. use of ARM *noun*[1]) L18.
G. R. GLEIG They numbered about 12,000 of all arms. H. G. WELLS The Emperor . . placed him in control of the new aeronautic arm of the German forces. *Daily Telegraph* Opel, the European arm of General Motors.

▸ **III 8** In *pl.* Heraldic insignia or devices, borne orig. on the shields of knights or barons to distinguish them in battle, which later became the hereditary possessions of their families; armorial bearings. Also, the insignia of a country, corporation, company, etc. (Freq. also in names of inns and public houses.) **ME.**

J. BETJEMAN Balkan Sobranies in a wooden box, The college arms upon the lid. G. HEYER An impressive vehicle which bore its noble owner's arms emblazoned on the door-panels. DYLAN THOMAS It is always opening time at the Sailors Arms.

– PHRASES ETC.: ***assault-at-arms***, ***assault-of-arms***: see ASSAULT *noun* 1. **bear arms** be armed, serve as a soldier; have a coat of arms. ***coat of arms***: see COAT *noun*. ***College of Arms***: see COLLEGE *noun*. ***companion in arms***: see COMPANION *noun*[1]. ***firearms***: see FIREARM *noun*. **in arms** armed, prepared to fight. **in arms with** *HERALDRY* quartered with. ***King at Arms***, ***King of Arms***: see KING *noun*. **lay down arms**, **lay down one's arms** cease fighting, surrender. **man-at-arms** (*arch.*), †**man-of-arms** a soldier, *esp.* one heavily armed. **master-at-arms** the chief police officer on a man-of-war or merchant vessel. ***office of arms***: see OFFICE *noun*. ***passage at arms***, ***passage of arms***: see PASSAGE *noun* 15b. ***place of arms***: see PLACE *noun*[1]. ***small arms***: see SMALL *adjective*. **take up arms** arm oneself, begin fighting. **to arms!** prepare to fight! **under arms** ready for war or battle. **up in arms** actively rebelling; *fig.* strongly protesting.
– COMB.: **arms control** international agreement to limit or reduce armaments; **arms race** competition between nations in the development and accumulation of weapons.
■ **armless** *adjective*[2] (*arch.*) without arms; unarmed: **E17.**

arm /ɑːm/ *verb*[1]. **ME.**
[ORIGIN Old French & mod. French *armer* from Latin *armare*, from *arma*: see ARM *noun*[2].]
▸ **I** *verb trans.* **1** Provide with weapons or (*arch.*) armour; equip for war. **ME.**

G. K. CHESTERTON Enough swords, pistols, partisans, cross-bows, and blunderbusses to arm a whole irregular regiment. P. GALLICO Armed themselves, fought and won battles against their hostile neighbours.

2 Provide with equipment, qualities, advantages, etc., for a task; prepare, make ready. **ME.**

SHAKES. *Mids. N. D.* Look you arm yourself To fit your fancies to your father's will. I. WALTON First you must arm your hook.

3 Provide (an animal etc.) with organs of offence or defence. Usu. in *pass.* **LME.**
4 *HERALDRY.* (Earlier as ARMED *adjective*[1] 2.) Represent as wearing armour; represent (an animal) with distinct teeth, talons, etc. **LME.**
5 Plate, coat, or cover with something providing strength, protection, etc. Usu. in *pass.* **LME.**

DRYDEN Ceres.. armed with Iron Shares the crooked Plough.

arm the lead *NAUTICAL* cover the base of the sounding weight with tallow (to pick up a sample from the bottom).
†**6** Provide (a magnet) with an armature. **M17–M19.**
7 Make (a weapon) ready for immediate use; activate the fuse or firing device of (a bomb etc.). **E20.**

Country Life When the airship made an attack.. it was the pilot who had to arm the bombs, take a sight, and drop them. J. CLAVELL He had broken open some of the crates of muskets and had set those who could to arming them with powder and with shot.

▸ **II** *verb intrans.* **8** Take up arms; provide oneself with weapons or (*arch.*) armour; prepare oneself. **ME.**

BURKE It certainly cannot be right to arm in support of a faction, though it is most laudable to arm in favour of our country. G. B. SHAW Protestant Ulster.. armed against the rest of Ireland and defied the British Parliament. J. KIRKUP If we permit our governments to arm for peace, We sanction war.

■ **arming** *noun* (***a***) the action of the verb; †(***b***) arms, armour; (***c***) a defensive or protective covering; a part which protects, strengthens, or fits for a purpose: **ME.**

arm /ɑːm/ *verb*[2]. **M16.**
[ORIGIN from ARM *noun*[1].]
†**1** *verb intrans.* Project like an arm. Only in **M16.**
2 *verb trans.* Embrace; put one's arm(s) round. *rare.* **E17.**
3 *verb trans.* Give one's arm to; conduct by walking arm in arm. **E17.**

armada /ɑːˈmɑːdə/ *noun*. Also †**-ado**, pl. **-o(e)s**. **M16.**
[ORIGIN Spanish from Proto-Romance *armata* ARMY: see -ADE.]
1 A fleet of warships. **M16.** ▸**b** *spec.* (**A-**.) = ***Spanish Armada*** s.v. SPANISH *adjective*. **L16.**

Time As zero hour approached, an armada of 31 ships swung into position to put them ashore.

†**2** A single warship. **L16–M17.**
– NOTE: Formerly pronounced /ɑːˈmeɪdə/.

armadilla /ɑːməˈdiːljə, *foreign* armaˈðiʎa/ *noun*. Also †**-illo**, pl. **-oes**. **L17.**
[ORIGIN Spanish, dim. of ARMADA.]
A small (Spanish) fighting ship. Also, a small naval squadron.

armadillo /ɑːməˈdɪləʊ/ *noun*[1]. Pl. **-os**. **L16.**
[ORIGIN Spanish, dim. of *armado* armed man, from Latin *armatus* pa. pple of *armare* ARM *verb*[1].]
Any of a number of burrowing edentate mammals native to S. and Central America, which have bodies encased in bony plates and are able to roll themselves into a ball when threatened.

†**armadillo** *noun*[2] var. of ARMADILLA.

†**armado** *noun* var. of ARMADA.

Armageddon /ɑːməˈɡɛd(ə)n/ *noun*. **E19.**
[ORIGIN The place of the last battle at the Day of Judgement: see *Revelation* 16:16 (AV).]
(The scene of) a decisive conflict on a great scale.

Armagnac /ˈɑːm(ə)njak/ *noun*. **M19.**
[ORIGIN Former name of a district of SW France (department of Gers).]
A brandy made in the former Armagnac district.

armalcolite /ɑːˈmalkəlʌɪt/ *noun*. **L20.**
[ORIGIN from Neil A. *Arm*strong, Edwin E. *Al*drin, and Michael *Col*lins, US astronauts, + -ITE[1].]
MINERALOGY. An orthorhombic titanate of iron and magnesium first found in lunar rocks.

Armalite /ˈɑːməlʌɪt/ *noun*. **M20.**
[ORIGIN from ARM *noun*[2] + *-a-* + *-lite* (alteration of LIGHT *adjective*[1]).]
(US proprietary name for) a type of light automatic rifle.

armament /ˈɑːməm(ə)nt/ *noun*. **L17.**
[ORIGIN Latin *armamentum* (in classical Latin only pl.), from *armare* ARM *verb*[1]: see -MENT.]
1 A force (esp. naval) equipped for war. *arch.* **L17.**

TOLKIEN Ar-Pharazôn.. prepared then the greatest armament that the world had seen, and when all was ready he sounded his trumpets and set sail.

2 *sing.* & in *pl.* Military weapons and equipment; (usu. *sing.*) the weapons mounted on a warship, aircraft, tank, etc. **E18.**

M. ARNOLD-FORSTER Throughout the rest of 1940.. Britain imported the food and armaments she needed from the United States in her own ships. J. G. FARRELL Fleury looked to his armament, which.. included a sabre,.. a couple of wavy-bladed daggers from Malaya, and another, Indian, dagger. D. HOWARTH Going in to attack, the *Exeter* drew the fire of the *Graf Spee*'s main armament.

3 The process of equipping for war. **E19.**

A. J. P. TAYLOR Armament on a large scale was begun after the general election of 1935.

armamentarium /ɑːməmɛnˈtɛːrɪəm/ *noun*. Pl. **-ia** /-ɪə/. **L19.**
[ORIGIN Latin = arsenal, armoury.]
The medicines, equipment, and techniques available to a medical practitioner.

armature /ˈɑːmətjə/ *noun*. **LME.**
[ORIGIN French from Latin *armatura*, from *armat-* pa. ppl stem of *armare* ARM *verb*[1]: see -URE.]
1 Arms, armour. *arch.* **LME.**

fig.: SIR T. BROWNE Not the armour of Achilles, but the Armature of St. Paul.

†**2** Armed troops. **LME–M18.**
†**3** The art of fighting with armour. **LME–E18.**
4 Defensive covering (or occas. offensive apparatus) of animals or plants. **E18.**
5 a A keeper for a magnet. **M18.** ▸**b** The iron core of an electromagnetic machine together with the windings which carry the induced electromotive force. Also, the moving part of a relay, electric bell, or similar device. **M19.**
6 An internal framework to support a sculpture during construction. **E20.**

armazine *noun* var. of ARMOZEEN.

armchair /ɑːmˈtʃɛː; *as adjective* ˈɑːmtʃɛː/ *noun* & *adjective*. Also **arm-chair**. **L16.**
[ORIGIN from ARM *noun*[1] + CHAIR *noun*[1].]
▸ **A** *noun*. A chair with arms or side supports. **L16.**
▸ **B** *attrib.* or as *adjective*. Confined to an armchair; *fig.* theorizing rather than participating; lacking or not involving first-hand experience. **E19.**

E. A. POWELL The arm-chair historians have settled down to the task of writing a connected account of the campaign. *Discovery* Armchair travel becomes easier and more pleasant every day. DAY LEWIS We don't want big talk from an armchair critic.

Armco /ˈɑːmkəʊ/ *noun*. Pl. **-os**. **E20.**
[ORIGIN Acronym, from American Rolling Mill Company.]
1 (Proprietary name for) a very pure soft iron. **E20.**
2 (Proprietary name for) a motorway or motor-racing track crash barrier. **M20.**

arme blanche /arm blɑ̃ːʃ/ *noun phr.* Pl. **-s -s** (pronounced same). **L19.**
[ORIGIN French, lit. 'white arm'.]
A cavalry sword or lance; the cavalry.

armed /ɑːmd/ *adjective*[1]. **ME.**
[ORIGIN from ARM *verb*[1] + -ED[1].]
1 Equipped with weapons. **ME.**

fig.: F. RAPHAEL At last she felt armed against the empty bourgeois life of Cricklewood. E. HEATH We were armed with the addresses of youth hostels.

armed bullhead the pogge *Agonus cataphractus*, a fish with a broad spined head and a tapering body covered with bony plates. **armed camp** a town, territory, etc., fully armed for war. ***armed forces***: see FORCE *noun*[1]. **armed neutrality**: with weapons kept available. ***armed services***: see SERVICE *noun*[1]. ***armed to the teeth***: see TOOTH *noun*.
2 *HERALDRY.* Of a charge: having teeth or talons of a specified tincture. **LME.**

armed /ɑːmd/ *adjective*[2]. **E17.**
[ORIGIN from ARM *noun*[1] + -ED[2].]
Having upper limbs, or extensions resembling these. Chiefly as 2nd elem. of comb., as ***long-armed***, ***nine-armed***, ***open-armed***, etc.

Armenian /ɑːˈmiːnɪən/ *adjective* & *noun*. **M16.**
[ORIGIN from Latin *Armenia* from Greek from Old Persian *Armina*, *Arminiya* + -IAN.]
▸ **A** *adjective*. Of or pertaining to Armenia, a country of SW Asia; of or pertaining to the people of this region, their language, or the ancient Christian community established there. **M16.**
Armenian bole: see BOLE *noun*[2] 1.
▸ **B** *noun*. **1** A native or inhabitant of Armenia; a member of the Armenian church. **M16.**
2 The Indo-European language of Armenia. **E18.**
■ **Armeniac** *adjective* = ARMENIAN *adjective* **LME.** **Armenoid** /ˈɑːmənɔɪd/ *adjective* of or pertaining to an eastern branch of the Alpine racial group **L19.**

armes blanches *noun phr.* pl. of ARME BLANCHE.

armet /ˈɑːmɪt/ *noun*. **E16.**
[ORIGIN French (infl. by *armes*: see ARM *noun*[2]) from Spanish *almete* or Italian *elmetto* HELMET.]
hist. A round iron helmet with visor, beaver, and gorget.

armiger /ˈɑːmɪdʒə/ *noun*. **M16.**
[ORIGIN Latin = bearing arms, from *arma* arms: see ARM *noun*[2], -GEROUS.]
An esquire: orig., a person who attended a knight to bear his shield; now, a person entitled to heraldic arms.
■ **arˈmigerous** *adjective* entitled to heraldic arms **M18.**

armil /ˈɑːmɪl/ *noun*. **L15.**
[ORIGIN Partly from Old French & mod. French *armille* from Latin ARMILLA; partly a more recent adaptation of Latin.]
1 A bracelet. *rare.* **L15.**
2 A stole of cloth of gold put on the monarch at the coronation. **L15.**
3 †**a** ***armil sphere***, an armillary sphere. **M16–E17.** ▸**b** = ARMILLA *noun* 1. **M19.**

armilla /ɑːˈmɪlə/ *noun*. Pl. **-llae** /-liː/, **-llas**. **M17.**
[ORIGIN Latin, dim. of *armus* shoulder.]
1 An ancient astronomical instrument consisting of a graduated ring or hoop fixed in the plane of the equator (***equinoctial armilla***), sometimes crossed by another in the plane of the meridian (***solstitial armilla***). **M17.**
2 = ARMIL 2. **L17.**
3 Chiefly *ARCHAEOLOGY.* A bracelet, an armlet. **E18.**

armillaria /ɑːmɪˈlɛːrɪə/ *noun*. **M19.**
[ORIGIN mod. Latin (see below), formed as ARMILLA (so called because of a bracelet-like frill on the stem) + Latin *-aria* -ARY[1].]
An agaric (fungus) of the genus *Armillaria*, which includes a number of species which grow in woodland and can spread over large areas, parasitizing several trees.

armillary /ɑːˈmɪləri/ *adjective* & *noun*. **M17.**
[ORIGIN mod. Latin *armillaris*, from Latin ARMILLA: see -ARY[2].]
▸ **A** *adjective*. Of or pertaining to armillae; ***armillary sphere***, a skeleton celestial globe, consisting of a number of graduated rings or hoops representing the principal celestial circles, which revolves on an axis within a wooden horizon. **M17.**
▸ **B** *noun*. An armillary sphere. **M19.**

Arminian /ɑːˈmɪnɪən/ *adjective* & *noun*. **E17.**
[ORIGIN from *Arminius* Latinized form of *Harmensen* (see below) + -AN.]
▸ **A** *adjective*. Of or pertaining to the Dutch Protestant theologian Arminius (Jakob Harmensen, 1560–1609) or his doctrines, which opposed those of Calvin, esp. regarding predestination. **E17.**
▸ **B** *noun*. An adherent of the doctrines of Arminius. **E17.**
■ **Arminianism** *noun* (adherence to) the Arminian doctrines **E17.** **Arminianize** *verb* (***a***) *verb intrans.* teach Arminianism; (***b***) *verb trans.* make Arminian: **E17.**

armipotent /ɑːˈmɪpət(ə)nt/ *adjective*. **LME.**
[ORIGIN Latin *armipotent-*, *-ens*, from *arma* arms + *potens* powerful, POTENT *adjective*[2].]
Mighty as a warrior (orig. an epithet of the god Mars).

armistice /ˈɑːmɪstɪs/ *noun*. **E18.**
[ORIGIN French, or mod. Latin *armistitium*, from *arma* arms + *-stitium* stoppage, after *solstitium* SOLSTICE.]
A cessation from hostilities; a short truce.
– COMB.: **Armistice Day** (an anniversary of) 11 November 1918, when an armistice was concluded which ended the First World War; (since 1945 superseded by Remembrance Sunday and Veterans Day).

armoire /ɑːˈmwɑː/ *noun*. **L16.**
[ORIGIN French: see AUMBRY.]
A cupboard, a wardrobe; *esp.* one that is ornate or antique.

†**armoniac** *adjective* & *noun* var. of AMMONIAC.

A

armor *noun & verb*, **armored** *ppl adjective*, **armorer** *noun*, see ARMOUR etc.

armorial /ɑːˈmɔːrɪəl/ *adjective & noun*. L16.
[ORIGIN from ARMORY *noun*[1] + -AL[1].]
▸ **A** *adjective*. **1** Pertaining to or of the nature of heraldic arms. L16.
2 Of porcelain etc.: bearing heraldic arms. E20.
▸ **B** *noun*. A book of coats of arms. M18.
■ **armorially** *adverb* E17.

Armorican /ɑːˈmɒrɪk(ə)n/ *adjective & noun*. L15.
[ORIGIN from Latin *Armoricae* (Caesar) the NW provinces of Gaul (mod. Brittany), from Gaulish *are* in front of + *mor* sea, + -AN.]
▸ **A** *adjective*. **1** Of or pertaining to Armorica (Brittany), its inhabitants, or their language (Breton). L15.
2 GEOLOGY. = HERCYNIAN *adjective* 2b. E20.
▸ **B** *noun*. A native or inhabitant of Armorica; the Breton language. *rare*. M17.
■ †**Armoric** *adjective & noun* M17–E19.

armory /ˈɑːməri/ *noun*[1]. LME.
[ORIGIN Old French *armoi(e)rie* (mod. *armoiries* pl.), from *armoier* blazon, from *arme* ARM *noun*[2]: see -Y[3]. Cf. ARMOURY.]
1 Heraldry. LME.
2 Armorial bearings. *arch*. L15.
■ **armorist** *noun* a person skilled in heraldry L16.

armory *noun*[2] see ARMOURY.

armour /ˈɑːmə/ *noun & verb*. Also *-or. ME.
[ORIGIN Old French & mod. French *armure*, earlier *armëure*, from Latin *armatura* ARMATURE: see -OUR.]
▸ **A** *noun*. **I** Corresp. to ARM *noun*[2] I, II.
1 *hist*. Defensive covering for the body worn when fighting; mail. ME.

SHAKES. *Hen. V* The sun doth gild our armour; up, my lords! T. H. WHITE Sir Ector was dressed in 'sensible' leather clothes—it was not considered sporting to hunt in armour. *fig*.: MILTON And also arme With spiritual Armour. BYRON Suspicion is a heavy armour.

hog in armour: see HOG *noun*. ***in armour*** *fig*. (*arch. slang*) wearing a condom. ***shining armour***: see SHINING *adjective*.
†**2** *sing*. & in *pl*. The whole apparatus of war; arms. ME–E19.

R. HOLINSHED The people . . were up in armour against the King.

3 A suit of mail. *arch*. LME.

CAXTON He had . . armours ynowe for to garnysshe with seuen thousand men.

†**4** The exercise of arms; fighting, warfare. LME–E17.
5 Protective or defensive covering of animals or plants. M17.

D. MORRIS In contrast to all other armadillos . . the body armour is connected to the animal's back only down the mid-line.

6 A diver's suit. E19.
7 Sheathing or cladding usu. of metal plates protecting a warship, tank, etc., from projectiles. M19.

C. RYAN Gliders were without protective armour, except in the cockpits. R. V. JONES Such charges could be used in bombs against battleships, where they would easily penetrate the deck armour.

8 Tanks and other armoured vehicles collectively. M20.

M. RICHLER In response to an Egyptian attack, Israeli armour had gone into action.

▸ **II** Corresp. to ARM *noun*[2] III.
9 Blazonry, heraldic arms. *obsolete* exc. in ***coat armour*** s.v. COAT *noun*. LME.
– COMB.: **armour-bearer** *hist*. a person who carried a warrior's armour; a squire; **armour-clad** *adjective* provided with armour, *esp*. armour-plated; **armour-piercing** *adjective* (of a shell etc.) designed to penetrate the armour of a warship, tank, etc., before exploding; **armour plate** (a plate of) the protective metal sheathing of a warship, tank, etc.; **armour-plated** *adjective* provided with armour plate; **armour-plating** (the material of) armour plate.
▸ **B** *verb trans*. Put armour on; provide with protective or defensive covering. Freq. in *pass*. LME.

R. GRAVES In battle the nobler men wear leather coats armoured in front with overlapping plates. *fig*.: N. HAMPSON There are no killers here, whom crusted pride Armours against their own humanity.

■ **armouring** *noun* an external covering, usu. of steel wire, to protect electric cables etc. E20. **armourless** *adjective* without armour, defenceless LME.

armoured /ˈɑːməd/ *ppl adjective*. Also *-ored. E17.
[ORIGIN from ARMOUR *verb* + -ED[1].]
1 Clad in armour; having a natural protective or defensive covering. E17.
2 Of a ship, vehicle, cable, etc.: covered with or protected by armour. M19.
armoured car, **armoured train**: protected with armour plate and usu. equipped with guns.
3 Of glass: toughened. M20.
4 Of a force: equipped with tanks and other armoured vehicles. Of warfare: fought with tanks etc. M20.

armourer /ˈɑːmərə/ *noun*. Also *-orer. ME.
[ORIGIN Anglo-Norman *armurer*, Old French & mod. French *armurier*, formed as ARMOUR *noun*: see -ER[2].]
1 A maker or repairer of armour or weapons. ME.
2 A person who assisted warriors in putting on their armour. *obsolete* exc. *hist*. LME.
3 An official who has charge of the arms of a warship, regiment, etc. M18.

armoury /ˈɑːməri/ *noun*. Also *-ory. ME.
[ORIGIN Old French *armoi(e)rie* ARMORY *noun*[1], assim. to ARMOUR.]
1 Arms or armour collectively (*arch*.); an array of weapons or (*fig*.) resources etc. ME.

WORDSWORTH In our halls is hung Armoury of the invincible Knights of old. *fig*.: J. WAIN It was only the presence of the two visitors . . that stopped her from setting about him with the full armoury of feminine weapons. C. SAGAN I was outfitted under my raincoat with a full armory of shirt, tie, and jacket.

2 A place where arms and armour are kept or (chiefly *US*) made; an arsenal; *N. Amer*. a drill hall. LME.

J. CHEEVER Touch a suit of chain mail in the armory and your hand comes away black with rust. *fig*.: COLERIDGE Language is the armoury of the human mind; it . . contains the trophies of its past and the weapons of its future conquests.

armozeen /ɑːməˈziːn/ *noun*. Also **armazine** & other vars. E16.
[ORIGIN French *armoisin*, (16) *tafetas armoisy*, *armezin*, from Italian *ermesino* from Egyptian Arab. *ʼirmiz*, Arabic *qirmiz* KERMES.]
Orig. †***armozeen taffeta***. A heavy plain silk, usu. black, used esp. for clerical gowns and for mourning.

armure /ˈɑːmjʊə/ *noun*. L19.
[ORIGIN French.]
A fabric made of wool, silk, or both, with a twilled or ribbed surface.

army /ˈɑːmi/ *noun*. In sense 3 also **A-**. LME.
[ORIGIN Old French & mod. French *armée* from Proto-Romance *armata* use as noun of fem. pa. pple of Latin *armare* ARM *verb*[1]: see -Y[5].]
▸ **I** *lit*. †**1** An armed expedition by sea or land. LME–E16.

LD BERNERS They gette the duke of Burgoyne in great desyre to make an armye into Englande.

2 An armed force whether by land or sea; a host. Without qualification, now *spec*. a force equipped to fight on land; an organized body of soldiers. LME.

AV *S. of S.* 6:10 Terrible as an armie with banners. G. B. SHAW Whenever he won an election his opponent raised an army and attempted a revolution. A. J. P. TAYLOR The Russians had just destroyed a German army at Stalingrad.

army of occupation. ***army of reserve***: see RESERVE *noun*. ***land army***: see LAND *noun*[1]. ***private army***: see PRIVATE *adjective*. ***Red Army***: see RED *adjective*. ***regular army***: see REGULAR *adjective*. ***standing army***: see STANDING *adjective*. ***Territorial Army***: see TERRITORIAL *adjective*. ***White Army***: see WHITE *adjective*. ***you and whose army?***
3 *The* entire body of land forces of a country; *the* military service or profession. M17.

SCOTT FITZGERALD A young major just out of the army and covered over with medals he got in the war. E. WAUGH Hooper had no illusions about the Army.

▸ **II** *transf*. & *fig*. **4** A large number, a multitude; an array. L15.

D. LIVINGSTONE An army of locusts. E. BOWEN An army of evening shoes was drawn up under the bureau. E. F. SCHUMACHER The modern man of action may surround himself by ever-growing armies of forecasters.

5 A body of people organized for a cause. M16.

ADDISON Latimer, one of the glorious Army of Martyrs.

Church Army: see CHURCH *noun*. ***Salvation Army***: see SALVATION.
– COMB.: **army ant** = DRIVER 6; **army corps** a main subdivision of an army in the field; **Army List** an official list of commissioned officers in the British army; **army worm** any of various moth or fly larvae occurring in destructive swarms.

Arnaut /ɑːˈnaʊt/ *noun*. *hist*. E18.
[ORIGIN Turkish.]
An Albanian, *spec*. one serving in the Ottoman army.

arnica /ˈɑːnɪkə/ *noun*. M18.
[ORIGIN mod. Latin, of uncertain origin.]
Any plant of the genus *Arnica*, of the composite family; *esp*. mountain tobacco, *A. montana*, native to central Europe. Also, a medicinal tincture prepared from this plant, and used esp. for bruises.

Arnoldian /ɑːˈnəʊldɪən/ *adjective*. L19.
[ORIGIN from *Arnold* (see below) + -IAN.]
Pertaining to or characteristic of either Thomas Arnold (1795–1842), Headmaster of Rugby School, or his son Matthew Arnold (1822–88), poet and critic.
■ ˈ**Arnoldism** *noun* doctrine, theory, or practice formed after the precepts and example of either Thomas or Matthew Arnold M19.

Arnoldist /ˈɑːn(ə)ldɪst/ *noun*. M17.
[ORIGIN from *Arnold* (see below) + -IST.]
ECCLESIASTICAL HISTORY. A follower of Arnold (or Arnaldus) of Brescia, a religious reformer in the 12th cent.

aroar /əˈrɔː/ *adverb & pred. adjective*. *arch*. LME.
[ORIGIN A *preposition*[1] 6 + ROAR *noun*[1].]
In a roar, roaring.

aroha /ˈarəʊhə/ *noun*. *NZ* L18.
[ORIGIN Maori.]
Love, compassion, fellow feeling.

aroid /ˈɛːrɔɪd/ *noun & adjective*. L19.
[ORIGIN from ARUM *noun* + -OID.]
BOTANY. (A plant) belonging to the family Araceae, exemplified by the arums.

aroint /əˈrɔɪnt/ *verb trans*. *arch*. Also **-oynt**. E17.
[ORIGIN Unknown.]
1 ***aroint thee!*** avaunt! begone! E17.

SHAKES. *Macb*. 'Aroint thee, witch!' the rump-fed ronyon cries.

2 Drive away with an execration. M19.

BROWNING That Humbug, whom thy soul aroints.

– NOTE: First recorded in Shakes.

arolla /əˈrɒlə/ *noun*. L19.
[ORIGIN Swiss French *arol(l)e*.]
The Swiss stone pine, *Pinus cembra*. Also ***arolla pine***.

aroma /əˈrəʊmə/ *noun*. Pl. **-mas**, (*rare*) **-mata** /-mətə/. Orig. †**-mat**. ME.
[ORIGIN Latin *aroma*, *-mat-* from Greek *arōma* spice; earlier form from Old French *aromat* (mod. *-ate*) from Latin pl. *aromata*.]
†**1** A fragrant plant, spice. Usu. in *pl*. ME–M18.
2 The distinctive fragrance of a spice, plant, etc., an agreeable odour. E19.
3 A subtle pervasive quality or charm. M19.
– COMB.: **aromatherapeutic** *adjective* of or pertaining to aromatherapy; **aromatherapist** an advocate or promoter of aromatherapy; **aromatherapy** the use of essential oils and other plant extracts to promote personal health and beauty.
■ **aromal** *adjective* M19.

aromatase /əˈrəʊməteɪz/ *noun*. L20.
[ORIGIN from *aromat-* (in AROMATIZATION) + -ASE.]
BIOCHEMISTRY. An enzyme that catalyses an aromatization reaction resulting in the conversion of androgens to oestrogens.

aromatic /arəˈmatɪk/ *adjective & noun*. LME.
[ORIGIN Old French & mod. French *aromatique* from late Latin *aromaticus* from Greek *arōmatikos*: see AROMA, -IC.]
▸ **A** *adjective*. **1** Fragrant, pungent, spicy, sweet-smelling. LME.
2 CHEMISTRY. (Of a compound) possessing one or more planar conjugated rings of the form typified by the benzene molecule; designating or pertaining to such a compound. M19.
▸ **B** *noun*. **1** A substance or plant emitting a spicy odour; a fragrant drug. LME.
2 CHEMISTRY. An aromatic compound. E20.
■ †**aromatical** *adjective* = AROMATIC *adjective* 1 LME–E19. **aromatically** *adverb* with aromatic odour or taste; spicily: E17. **aromaticity** /-ˈtɪsɪti/ *noun* (CHEMISTRY) aromatic character or condition M20. **aromaticness** *noun* the quality of being aromatic LME.

aromatize /əˈrəʊmətʌɪz/ *verb trans*. Also **-ise**. LME.
[ORIGIN Old French & mod. French *aromatiser* from late Latin *aromatizare* from Greek *arōmatizein* to spice: see AROMA, -IZE.]
1 Render aromatic or fragrant; flavour or season with spice. LME.
2 CHEMISTRY. Make aromatic (AROMATIC *adjective* 2). M20.
■ **aromatiˈzation** *noun* (*a*) the action or process of rendering aromatic; CHEMISTRY conversion into an aromatic compound; (*b*) aromatic flavouring: E17. **aromatizer** *noun* L17.

†**aron** *noun* see ARUM.

around /əˈraʊnd/ *adverb & preposition*. ME.
[ORIGIN Prob. from A *preposition*[1] 1 + ROUND *noun*[1]: cf. Old French *a la reond* in the round, French *en rond* in a circle, *au rond de* round about (16).]
▸ **A** *adverb*. **1** In circumference; in a circle; so as to surround. ME.

JOYCE The players closed around, flushed and muddy. W. STEVENS A blue pigeon it is, that circles the blue sky, . . around and round and round.

2 Along the periphery, on or along the circuit or surface, (of something round). ME.

DRYDEN All their heads around With chaplets green of cerrial-oak were crowned.

3 On every side; in every direction or in various directions from a fixed point. E18.

POPE While op'ning blooms diffuse their sweets around. G. B. SHAW Every stick and stone for miles around falling and crumbling.

4 Here and there; at, in, or to various places; all about; at random; with no definite direction or aim. L18.

J. BOWEN If you want to do exercises, then do them. Don't hang around hinting. C. HAMPTON I haven't been sitting around brooding about it for days. T. STOPPARD He has been looking around for a place to put his pants.

go around, ***play around***, ***sleep around***, etc. **have been around** *colloq*. have gained worldly experience.
5 With more or less circular motion; with return to the starting point after such motion; with rotation; with change to the opposite position; with regard to relative position; to a particular place, point, or state. E19.

SCOTT FITZGERALD Turning me around by one arm. DYLAN THOMAS The weather turned around. J. CHEEVER She waited in the rain for him to bring their car around. S. HILL He could not reach around to find his water bottle. S. GRAY I shall find out later which way around it is.

get around (**to**).

A

6 To all points of a circumference or within a given area; to all members of a company etc. L19.
know one's way around: see WAY *noun*.
7 Near at hand; somewhere in the vicinity. *colloq.* L19.

G. VIDAL Well, I'll see you around, Cy. J. F. KENNEDY These very qualities . . have in times of peace caused him to be considered 'dangerous', and a little uncomfortable to have around. J. CHEEVER When I got downstairs, Lawrence wasn't around, but the others were all ready for cocktails.

stick around: see STICK *verb*[1].
▶ **B** *preposition.* **1** On or along the circuit or periphery of; at points on the circumference of; so as to make a circuit of. LME.

MILTON No war or battle's sound Was heard the world around. JOYCE Lifted from the dish the heavy cover pearled around the edge with glistening drops. SCOTT FITZGERALD Her own party . . were spread around a table on the other side of the garden. W. STEVENS Perhaps The truth depends on a walk around a lake. S. GRAY There are a few hard-backed chairs around the walls.

2 On all sides of; in all or various directions from or with regard to; so as to centre or have a basis in. M17.

J. TYNDALL The air around and above us was . . clear. SCOTT FITZGERALD I saw Jordan Baker and talked over and around what had happened to us together. K. AMIS There's a lot of stuff in and around Lisbon we've still got to see. B. LOVELL Planetary systems around stars other than the Sun.

3 So as to surround; enveloping. E19.

E. O'NEILL Tenderly solicitous now, puts an arm around her. A. BURGESS Fussing as if she thought he ought to have rugs around him and his feet in a footcosy. W. TREVOR His short pale hair was plastered around his head.

4 Here and there in or near; to various places in; from one member of (a company) to another; all about. E19.

JOYCE He looked around the little class of students. H. MACLENNAN He had been walking around Halifax all day.

5 So as to double or pass in a curved course; having passed in a curved course; in a position that would result from passing in a curved course. Chiefly *N. Amer.* M19.

P. SHAFFER I know it's just around the corner, that's not the point. ANNE STEVENSON You watch a workman wheel his bicycle around a stile.

get around.
6 In the vicinity of; near; close to. M19.

B. SCHULBERG That's why I took this job, so I can be around writers.

7 At approximately, at about. Chiefly *N. Amer.* L19.

W. G. MCADOO The convention adjourned around four o'clock. E. BOWEN Last May, around that time of the funeral.

arouse /əˈraʊz/ *verb.* L16.
[ORIGIN from A-[11] + ROUSE *verb*[1], after *rise, arise*, etc.]
1 *verb trans.* Raise or stir up (a person or animal) from sleep or inactivity; excite sexually. L16.

D. RUNYON The noise of John Wangle's yelling . . arouses many of the neighbors. R. ELLISON Such an effective piece of eloquence . . you aroused them so quickly to action. P. H. JOHNSON She was still sleeping, and now she looked so serene, so peaceful, that I hated to arouse her.

2 *verb trans.* Stir up into activity (principles of action, emotions, etc.); bring into existence. E18.

G. GREENE I wondered whether Miss Smythe was so convenient a sister as Henry was a husband, and all my latent snobbery was aroused by the name—that y, the final e. T. CAPOTE A case like the Clutter case, crimes of that magnitude, arouse the interest of lawmen everywhere. A. STORR Everyone knows that anger, once thoroughly aroused, takes time to subside.

3 *verb intrans.* Wake up. E19.

J. THURBER Always a deep sleeper, slow to arouse.

■ **arousable** *adjective* L19. **arousal** *noun* the action of arousing or fact of being aroused M19. **arouser** *noun* M19.

arow /əˈrəʊ/ *adverb & pred. adjective.* ME.
[ORIGIN from A *preposition*[1] 1 + ROW *noun*[1].]
1 In a row, rank, or line. ME.
†**2** In succession. ME–L16.

aroynt *verb* var. of AROINT.

ARP *abbreviation.*
Air-raid precautions.

arpeggiate /ɑːˈpɛdʒɪeɪt/ *verb trans.* E20.
[ORIGIN from ARPEGGIO + -ATE[3].]
MUSIC. Play (a chord, theme, etc.) as an arpeggio or arpeggios. Chiefly as ***arpeggiated*** *ppl adjective.*
■ **arpeggiˈation** *noun* L19. **arpeggiator** *noun* L20.

arpeggio /ɑːˈpɛdʒɪəʊ/ *noun.* Pl. **-os**. E18.
[ORIGIN Italian, from *arpeggiare* play on the harp, from *arpa* HARP *noun.*]
MUSIC. The sounding of the notes of a chord in (usu. rapid upward) succession, not simultaneously; a chord so sounded.

arpeggione /ɑːpɛdʒɪˈəʊni, *foreign* arpeˈdʒoːne/ *noun.* L19.
[ORIGIN German, formed as ARPEGGIO.]
An early 19th-cent. bowed musical instrument, resembling a guitar.

arpent /ˈɑːp(ə)nt; *foreign* arpɑ̃ (*pl. same*)/ *noun. obsolete* exc. *hist.* Also **arpen** /-p(ə)n; *foreign* -pɑ̃ (*pl. same*)/. M16.
[ORIGIN Old French & mod. French.]
An old French measure of land, of varying amount but freq. equal to about two-fifths of a hectare (approx. one acre).

arquebus *noun* var. of HARQUEBUS.

arra *noun* var. of ARRHA.

arrabiata /aˈrabɪɑːtə/ *adjective.* L20.
[ORIGIN Italian, lit. 'angry', from *arrabiare* make angry.]
Designating a spicy sauce made with tomatoes and chilli peppers, typically served with pasta.

arrack /ˈarək/ *noun.* Also **arak**. E17.
[ORIGIN Arabic *ʿaraq* sweat, esp. in *ʿaraq at-tamr* fermented and distilled juice of dates. Aphet. to RACK *noun*[7].]
In Eastern countries: an alcoholic spirit of local manufacture, esp. distilled from the sap of the coco palm or from rice.

†**Arragonese** *adjective & noun*, †**arragonite** *noun* vars. of ARAGONESE, ARAGONITE.

arrah /ˈarə/ *interjection. Irish.* L17.
[ORIGIN Irish *ara, arú.*]
Expr. emotion or excitement.

arraign /əˈreɪn/ *verb*[1] *& noun.* LME.
[ORIGIN Anglo-Norman *arainer, areiner*, Old French *araisnier, areisnier*, ult. from Latin *ad* AR- + *ratio(n-)* account, REASON *noun*[1].]
▶ **A** *verb trans.* **1** Call on (a person) to answer a criminal charge before a court; call to account, indict, accuse. LME.

BARONESS ORCZY He was arraigned for treason against the nation, and sent to the guillotine. A. MILLER As though arraigning the entire clock industry, she adds: 'I've got six or eight clocks in this house, and none of them work'.

2 Find fault with, censure, call in question (an action, statement, etc.). L17.

GIBBON He boldly arraigned the abuses of public and private life.

▶ **B** *noun.* = ARRAIGNMENT. M17.
■ **arraigner** *noun* E19. **arraignment** *noun* the act of arraigning or fact of being arraigned; indictment, accusation, censure: LME.

†**arraign** *verb*[2]. LME–E19.
[ORIGIN Anglo-Norman *arraigner, arainer*, alt. of *aramer* = Old French *arami(e)r* from medieval Latin *arramire* guarantee, decide, from *ad* AR- + Frankish *hramjan* appoint a place or time.]
LAW. Appeal to, claim, demand, (an assize).

arrand *noun* var. of ARAIN.

arrange /əˈreɪndʒ/ *verb.* LME.
[ORIGIN Old French *arangier, arengier* (mod. *arranger*), from A-[5] + *rangier* RANGE *verb*[1].]
▶ **I** *verb trans.* **1** Draw up in ranks or in lines of battle. *obsolete* exc. as passing into sense 2. LME.

LD BERNERS There he araynged his men in the stretes.

2 Put into proper or requisite order; dispose; adjust. M18.

J. C. POWYS Helping old Mrs. Robinson arrange the flowers for the church altar. C. ISHERWOOD A plateful of jam tarts arranged in the shape of a star. S. BELLOW The room where the old woman lay, her white hair arranged in a fringe that nearly met her brow. A. WILSON The process of arranging one's thoughts in good order. E. J. HOWARD He . . took off his scarf and arranged it . . round her neck. *Encycl. Brit.* Mendeleyev arranged all the known elements according to their atomic weights on what he called a periodic table.

3 Plan or settle beforehand the details of (something to be done); give instructions for, cause to take place. L18.

LD MACAULAY The details of a butchery were frequently discussed, if not definitely arranged. T. HARDY They had arranged that their meeting should be at the holm-tree. SCOTT FITZGERALD Why didn't he ask you to arrange a meeting?

arranged marriage a marriage planned and agreed by the families or guardians of the couple concerned, who have little or no say in the matter themselves.
4 *MUSIC.* Adapt (a composition) for instruments or voices other than those for which it was written. E19.
5 Settle (a dispute, claim, etc.). M19.

G. B. SHAW I have arranged that little difficulty with Trench. It was only a piece of mischief made by Lickcheese.

6 Adapt (a play etc.) for performance, esp. for broadcasting. M20.
▶ **II** *verb intrans.* **7** Get into order; fall into place. *rare.* E16.
8 Come to an agreement or understanding (*with* a person, *about* something); settle or determine matters, take steps, make plans, (*about, for, to do*). L18.

BURKE We cannot arrange with our enemy in the present conjuncture. J. B. PRIESTLEY I had arranged to go round the Fish Market. B. ENGLAND If you find your duties too arduous . . I can arrange to have you relieved of them.

– NOTE: Rare before L18; not in AV, Shakes., Milton's poetry, or Pope.
■ **arrangeable** *adjective* M19. **arranger** *noun* a person who arranges something (esp. music) L18.

arrangement /əˈreɪndʒm(ə)nt/ *noun.* L17.
[ORIGIN from ARRANGE + -MENT.]
1 The action of arranging; the fact of being arranged. L17.
2 A manner of being arranged; an orderly disposition. M18.

C. DARWIN I believe that the arrangement of the groups within each class . . must be strictly genealogical. E. O'NEILL Her general appearance, the arrangement of her hair and clothes, has the disheveled touch of the fugitive.

3 A disposition or preparation for a future event (freq. in *pl.*); something planned or agreed; a settlement or agreement between parties. M18.

BURKE Arrangements with the Rajah . . for the better government and management of his Zemindary. LD MACAULAY It was impossible to make an arrangement that would please everybody. G. STEIN Mrs. Kreder and Mrs. Haydon . . made all the arrangements for the wedding. A. KOESTLER His staying in the flat was a reasonable and practical arrangement.

4 A number of objects arranged or combined in a particular way. E19.

B. PYM An expensive florist's arrangement of white chrysanthemums had been placed at the side of the altar.

5 A setting of a piece of music for instruments or voices other than those for which it was originally written; a piece so arranged. M19.

arrant /ˈar(ə)nt/ *adjective.* LME.
[ORIGIN Var. of ERRANT *adjective*. Sense 2 developed from its use to designate an outlawed, roving thief.]
†**1** = ERRANT *adjective* 1. LME–M17.
2 Of a thief, wrongdoer, etc., or with gen. terms of opprobrium: openly criminal, professed; public, notorious; downright, unmitigated. (Earlier as ERRANT *adjective* 2a.) M16. ▸**b** Of an (undesirable) action, opinion, quality, etc.: unmitigated, utter, blatant. M17.

SWIFT Every servant an arrant thief as to victuals and drink. HENRY FIELDING The arrantest villain that ever walked upon two legs. W. HOWITT The inhabitants of solitary houses are often most arrant cowards. **b** R. BENTLEY They cover the most arrant Atheism under the mask and shadow of a Deity. W. GERHARDIE The guest, a Russian general, was talking arrant nonsense.

3 (Without opprobrious force.) Thorough, complete; genuine, inveterate. L16.

G. B. SHAW Nobody but an arrant cockney would dream of calling it a brogue now.

†**4** Thoroughly bad, wicked; good-for-nothing. L16–M18.
■ **arrantly** *adverb* L16.

arras /ˈarəs/ *noun.* LME.
[ORIGIN *Arras*, a town in Artois, NE France, famous for the fabric.]
1 A rich tapestry fabric, in which figures and scenes are woven in colours. Freq. *attrib.* LME.
2 *hist.* A screen of this hung round the walls of a room. L16.
■ **arrased** /ˈarəst/ *adjective* hung or covered with arras E17.

array /əˈreɪ/ *noun.* ME.
[ORIGIN Anglo-Norman *arai* from Old French *arei* (mod. *arroi*), formed as ARRAY *verb*.]
1 A state of special preparedness esp. for war, festivities, etc.; preparation. Now *poet.* ME.

POPE The pomp, the pageantry, the proud array.

2 Arrangement in line or ranks, esp. martial order; orderly disposition. LME.

R. HOLINSHED They found them out of araie in following the chase. K. AMIS What howls of dismay From his fans in their dense array. *fig.*: AV *Job* 6:4 The terrors of God doe set themselues in aray against mee.

3 *hist.* The mustering of an armed force; the arming of a militia. LME.
Commission of Array a body of officials responsible for raising a militia.
4 A military force, an armed host; *esp.* (*hist.*) the militia of a county etc. LME.

LD MACAULAY The whole array of the city of London was under arms.

5 Attire, dress; (an) outfit. Now *poet.* LME.

SHAKES. *Tam. Shr.* We will have rings and things, and fine array. T. H. WHITE A Man or a Power set upon Lancelot . . and clothed him in another array which was full of knots.

†**6** Plight, condition; state of affairs. LME–M16.
7 *LAW.* The order of empanelling a jury; the panel itself. L16.
8 An imposing or well-ordered series of persons or things; an assemblage, an arrangement. E19. ▸**b** *MATH.* A matrix or other ordered arrangement of quantities. M19. ▸**c** *COMPUTING.* A set of memory locations or data items of which each member is identified by a common identifier together with one or more subscripts. M20.

Nature An array of particle detectors laid out in a suitable pattern. W. TREVOR He drew back his lips, displaying a small array of teeth. F. WELDON A really magnificent show of sports trophies to join her own array of cups and shields. D. HALBERSTAM He filled his bureau with a stunning array of the best reporters in America.

■ **arrayal** *noun* the process of arraying, muster; array: E19.

A

array /əˈreɪ/ *verb trans.* ME.
[ORIGIN Anglo-Norman *araier*, Old French *areer*, ult. from Latin *ad* AR- + a Germanic base meaning 'prepare' (cf. READY *verb*).]
1 Set or place in order of readiness (orig. esp. for battle); marshal, dispose, arrange. ME.
LD MACAULAY A force of thirteen thousand fighting men were arrayed in Hyde Park. J. LONDON He saw arrayed around his consciousness endless pictures from his life. A. WILSON Three sorts of ink—blue, red and green—were carefully arrayed before her.
†**2** Make ready, prepare; equip, fit out. ME–M16.
3 Attire, dress, esp. with display; *fig.* adorn, embellish (*with*). LME.
K. GRAHAME Mr. Toad, arrayed in goggles, cap, gaiters, and enormous overcoat, came swaggering down the steps. W. S. MAUGHAM I was taking them to a very smart restaurant and expected to find Isabel arrayed for the occasion. W. S. CHURCHILL Mary had arrayed herself superbly for the final scene. *fig.*: EARL RIVERS Arraye you withe iustice. R. ELLISON A panel arrayed with coils and dials.
†**4** Discomfit, thrash; afflict; disfigure, dirty. *iron.* LME–L16.
5 *LAW.* Empanel (a jury). L16.
■ **arrayer** *noun* a person who arrays; *esp.* (*hist.*) a person who musters armed men: LME. **arrayment** *noun* (*a*) dress, accoutrement; an outfit; (*b*) the act of arraying; the state of being arrayed: LME.

arrear /əˈrɪə/ *noun.* ME.
[ORIGIN from the adverb.]
▸ **I** *in arrear(s)*.
†**1** In the past. Only in ME.
2 Behind in time; behind in the discharge of duties or liabilities; *esp.* behindhand in payment. E17.
STEELE The World is in Arrear to your Virtue. A. KNOX I am two or three letters in arrear to different persons. S. RAVEN For years we've had a system whereby we pay tradesmen a term in arrears. A. BRINK Others . . had been evicted from their homes . . because they'd fallen in arrears with the rent.
†**3** Behind in position. Only in M17.
4 Behind as to state or condition. (Foll. by *of*.) M19.
R. FORD The arts of medicine and surgery are somewhat in arrear in Spain.
▸ **II** Without *in*.
5 Something in which one has fallen behind; something remaining to be done; a duty or liability undischarged; an outstanding debt. Now usu. in *pl.* LME.
BURKE Having so faithfully and so fully acquitted towards me whatever arrear of debt was left undischarged. F. MARRYAT To obtain my arrears of pay, and some prize-money which I find due. DICKENS To you . . I owe a long arrear of thanks. J. BUCHAN If I were you I would go to bed, for you must have considerable arrears of sleep to overtake. E. F. BENSON The arrears of general events were soon cleared off, . . and the talk became more intimate.
6 The rear, esp. of a train or procession. Long *arch.* E17.
†**7** A portion held back; something held in reserve. M17–M18.

†**arrear** *adverb.* ME–E19.
[ORIGIN Old French *ar(i)ere* (mod. *arrière*) from medieval Latin *adretro*, from Latin *ad* AR- + *retro* backward, behind. Cf. AREAR.]
In or to the rear; behind; overdue.
arrear-band: see ARRIÈRE-BAN. *arrear-guard*: see ARRIÈRE-GUARD.

arrearage /əˈrɪərɪdʒ/ *noun.* ME.
[ORIGIN Old French *arerage* (mod. *arrérage*), from *arere*: see ARREAR *adverb*, -AGE.]
1 = ARREAR *noun* 5. Now usu. in *pl.* Now *US.* ME.
†**2** The state or condition of being in arrears in payment; indebtedness, debt. ME–L17.
in arrearages in arrears in payment.
3 *gen.* The state or condition of being behind; backwardness. L16.

†**arrear-guard** *noun* var. of ARRIÈRE-GUARD.

arrect /əˈrɛkt/ *ppl adjective. arch.* M17.
[ORIGIN Latin *arrectus* pa. pple of *arrigere* raise up, from *ad* AR- + *regere* straighten.]
Upright, pricked up (as of the ears of an animal); *fig.* attentive, alert.

arrent /əˈrɛnt/ *verb trans.* Now *arch.* & *hist.* LME.
[ORIGIN Old French *arentir*, from *à* A-[5] + *rente* RENT *noun*[1], or French *arrenter*.]
Let out or farm at a rent; *spec.* allow the enclosure of (forest land) for a yearly rent.
■ **arrenˈtation** *noun* the action or the privilege of arrenting land E16.

Arrernte /əˈrʌntə, aˈruːndə/ *noun* & *adjective.* Pl. of noun same. L19.
[ORIGIN Prob. Arrernte.]
A member of, of or pertaining to, an Australian Aboriginal people of central Australia. Also, (of) the language of this people.

arrest /əˈrɛst/ *noun.* LME.
[ORIGIN Old French *areste* stoppage, and *arest* (mod. *arrêt*) act of arresting, formed as ARREST *verb*.]
†**1** The act of standing still or stopping in one's course; halt; delay. LME–L16.
2 The act of stopping something; stoppage; check. LME. ▸**b** *MEDICINE.* A sudden, sometimes temporary, cessation of function of an organ or system, esp. (more fully *cardiac arrest*) the heart. L19.
BACON Some Checke or Arrest in their Fortunes. J. H. BURN Arrest of the patient's respiration might sometimes assist the surgeon.
3 The act of catching and holding, seizure, (*lit.* & *fig.*). LME.
C. LAMB The first arrests of sleep. GEO. ELIOT This strong arrest of his attention made him cease singing.
4 The action of legally arresting a person and taking them into custody; the state of having been arrested; custody, imprisonment, detention. LME.
BYRON The Forty hath decreed a month's arrest. *Spin* One of the officers had made an arrest.
†**5** An abode. LME–L15.
†**6** A resting place for the butt of a lance on a piece of armour. LME–L15.
†**7** = ARRÊT. E16–E18.
– PHRASES: **arrest of judgement** *LAW* a stay of proceedings after a verdict, on the ground of error. *cardiac arrest*: see sense 2b above. *citizen's arrest*: see CITIZEN *noun*. *false arrest*: see FALSE *adjective*. *house arrest*: see HOUSE *noun*[1]. †**under an arrest** = *under arrest* (b) below. **under arrest** (*a*) legally arrested; (*b*) under legal restraint.

arrest /əˈrɛst/ *verb.* LME.
[ORIGIN Old French *arester* (mod. *arrêter*), ult. from Latin *ad* AR- + *restare* stop behind (REST *verb*[3]).]
†**1** *verb intrans.* Stop, stay, remain, rest. LME–E17.
CAXTON Without arestyng for to helpe them. DONNE We must arrest awhile vpon the nature, and degrees, and effects of charity.
2 *verb trans.* Stop; detain; retard. LME. ▸**b** Catch and fix (the attention, mind, etc.); catch and fix the attention of. E19.
DRYDEN My Dogs with better speed Arrest her flight. GIBBON In the pursuit of greatness he was never arrested by the scruples of justice. GEO. ELIOT Her tears were arrested. H. KISSINGER The Soviet advance was first arrested and finally reversed. **b** BYRON The gleaming turret . . and yon solitary palm arrest the eye. T. HARDY He was arrested by the conversation. H. READ A work of art must . . arrest the attention of the onlooker.
arrest judgement *LAW* stay proceedings after a verdict, on the ground of error.
3 *verb trans.* Apprehend (a person, a ship) by legal authority. LME. ▸**b** Seize (property) by legal warrant. Now only *Scot.* & *ADMIRALTY LAW.* L15. ▸†**c** *fig.* Take as security. *rare* (Shakes.). L16–E17.
D. LODGE Sixteen people . . were arrested . . for stealing used bricks from the demolition site. **b** D. H. LAWRENCE The Unholy Inquisition has arrested all my pictures.
4 *verb trans. gen.* Catch, lay hold on. *obsolete* exc. as *fig.* use of sense 3. L15.
SPENSER Whenas Morpheus had with leaden mace Arrested all that courtly company. J. RUSKIN We cannot arrest sunsets nor carve mountains.
†**5** *verb trans.* Fix, engage; keep (one's mind, oneself) on a subject. L15–M17.
JER. TAYLOR We may arrest our thoughts upon the divine mercies.
6 *verb intrans. MEDICINE.* Suffer cardiac arrest. L20.
■ **arrestable** *adjective* (*a*) liable to be arrested; (*b*) *LAW* (of an offence) for which a person can properly be arrested because there is reasonable ground for believing that he or she committed the offence: M16. **arreˈstation** *noun* the action of arresting, an arrest L18. **arreˈstee** *noun* (*a*) *SCOTS LAW* the person in whose hands another's earnings or other assets are attached; (*b*) a person being legally arrested: M18. **arrester** *noun* (*a*) a person who arrests someone or something; (*b*) something which arrests; *esp.* a device for retarding an aircraft by a hook and cable on landing, esp. on an aircraft carrier: LME. **arrestingly** *adverb* in a manner that arrests the attention, strikingly L19. **arrestive** *adjective* tending to arrest the attention etc., striking M19. **arrestor** *noun* = ARRESTER LME.

arrestment /əˈrɛs(t)m(ə)nt/ *noun.* LME.
[ORIGIN Old French *arestement* or medieval Latin *arrestamentum*: see ARREST *verb*, -MENT.]
1 The action of apprehending a person by legal authority; arrest. Chiefly *Scot.* LME.
2 A seizure of property by legal authority; *SCOTS LAW* attachment of earnings or other assets held by a third party. M16.
3 The action or result of stopping or checking. M19.

arrêt /arɛ (*pl. same*), əˈrɛt/ *noun.* M17.
[ORIGIN French: see ARREST *noun*.]
An authoritative sentence or decision, *spec.* of the monarch (*hist.*) or parliament of France.

Arretine /ˈarətʌɪn/ *adjective.* Also **Aret-**. L18.
[ORIGIN Latin *Ar(r)etinus*, from *Ar(r)etium*: see below, -INE[1].]
Of or pertaining to Arretium (mod. Arezzo), an ancient city in central Italy; *spec.* designating fine red pottery made at Arretium and elsewhere from *c* 100 BC until the late 1st cent. AD.

arrha /ˈarə/ *noun.* Also **arra**. Pl. **arr(h)ae** /ˈariː/. L16.
[ORIGIN Latin *arr(h)a* (Gellius) abbreviation of *arr(h)abo* (Plautus) from Greek *arrabōn* earnest money. Cf. ARLES.]
Chiefly *ROMAN* & *SCOTS LAW.* Money given to bind a bargain, earnest money.

arrhenotoky /arɪˈnɒtəki, ˌarənəˈtəʊki/ *noun.* L19.
[ORIGIN from Greek *arrenotokos* bearing male children + -Y[3].]
ZOOLOGY. Parthenogenesis in which unfertilized eggs give rise to males. Cf. THELYTOKY.
■ **arrhenotokous** *adjective* L19.

arrhythmia /əˈrɪðmɪə/ *noun.* L19.
[ORIGIN Greek *arruthmia* lack of rhythm: see A-[10], RHYTHM, -IA[1].]
MEDICINE. Deviation from the normal rhythm of the heart.

arrhythmic /əˈrɪðmɪk/ *adjective.* Also **arh-**. M19.
[ORIGIN from A-[10] + RHYTHMIC, after Greek: see ARRHYTHMIA.]
Not rhythmic; without rhythm or regularity.
■ **arrhythmical** *adjective* L19. **arrhythmically** *adverb* L19.

arrhythmy /ˈarɪðmi/ *noun.* M19.
[ORIGIN formed as ARRHYTHMIA: see -Y[3].]
Lack of rhythm or regularity.

arriage *noun* see AVERAGE *noun*[1].

arride /əˈrʌɪd/ *verb trans. arch.* L16.
[ORIGIN Latin *arridere* smile upon, from *ad* AR- + *ridere* to laugh, smile.]
1 Please, gratify, delight. L16.
†**2** Smile at, laugh at. E–M17.

arrière-ban /arjɛrbɑ̃, ˈarɪəban/ *noun.* Also anglicized as †*arrear-band*. E16.
[ORIGIN French *arrière-ban*, Old French *arierebàn* alt. of *arban*, *herban* from a Frankish word (= Old High German *heriban* call-up for military service), from *hari*, *heri* army + *ban* proclamation, BAN *noun*[1].]
hist. (The order of a Frankish or French king for) the calling together of vassals summoned for military service; the body of vassals thus summoned or liable to be summoned.

arrière-guard /ˈarɪəgɑːd/ *noun.* Also †**arrear-**. L15.
[ORIGIN French †*arrière-guarde* (now *-garde*): see ARREAR *adverb*, GUARD *noun*.]
A rearguard.

arrière-pensée /arjɛrpɑ̃se/ *noun.* Pl. pronounced same. E19.
[ORIGIN French, lit. 'behind-thought'.]
A concealed thought or intention; an ulterior motive; a mental reservation.

arriero /ariˈero/ *noun.* Pl. **-os** /-əs/. E19.
[ORIGIN Spanish.]
In Spain and Spanish-speaking countries: a muleteer.

arris /ˈarɪs/ *noun.* L17.
[ORIGIN Alt. of early mod. French *areste* sharp ridge, ARÊTE.]
Esp. *ARCHITECTURE.* The sharp edge formed by the angular contact of two plane or curved surfaces.
■ **arris-ways** *adverb* (*arch.*) so as to present a sharp edge, diagonally L17.

arrival /əˈrʌɪv(ə)l/ *noun.* LME.
[ORIGIN Anglo-Norman *arrivaile*, formed as ARRIVE: see -AL[1].]
1 The act of arriving; appearance upon the scene. LME.
ADDISON Our Time lies heavy on our Hands till the Arrival of a fresh mail. G. GISSING She had been in the house since her arrival the day before yesterday. OED There was long debate, but no arrival at any agreement. G. B. SHAW The arrival of western civilization in the Balkans. A. C. CLARKE She gave birth to Peter, and with the arrival of his son it seemed to Franklin that the old chapter of his life had finally closed. S. HILL Your sister . . may well be dead upon arrival at the hospital.
2 A person who or thing which has arrived. E19.
E. O'NEILL The crowd of people has been steadily augmented by new arrivals.
new arrival *spec.* (*colloq.*) a newborn child.

arrive /əˈrʌɪv/ *verb.* ME.
[ORIGIN Old French *ariver* (mod. *arriver*), ult. from Latin *ad* AR- + *ripa* shore. Cf. RIVER *noun*[1].]
1 *verb intrans.* Come to the end of a journey (orig. by water); reach one's destination or a specified point on a journey; make one's appearance, come on the scene; (of a child, *colloq.*) be born. (Foll. by *at*, *in*, *(up)on*, †*into*, †*to*.) ME. ▸**b** Of a thing: be brought or conveyed. M17.
P. SIDNEY We arrived upon the verge of his estate. O. CROMWELL Yesterday arrived to me hither your Majesties servants. J. BUCHAN He arrived before eight o'clock every morning and used to depart at seven. D. H. LAWRENCE Already the middle of September was here, and the baby had not arrived. T. S. ELIOT Perhaps she won't even arrive by this plane. DAY LEWIS Arriving at the church, he found it filled with a whole tribe of tinkers. L. HELLMAN Bethe arrived in New Orleans long before I was born. **b** DRYDEN Let the rest arrive to the Audience by narration. R. GRAVES Augustus . . had reached Athens when the news arrived. A. J. CRONIN Parcels of books began to arrive periodically.
†**2** *verb trans.* Bring (orig. a ship, its crew or passengers) to a destination; land. LME–M18.
G. CHAPMAN And made the sea-trod ship arrive them near The grapeful Crissa.

3 *verb intrans.* Come to a position or state of mind; reach an object; attain, achieve, compass, something. Foll. by *at*, †*to*, †*to do*. LME.

SHAKES. *Timon* Many so arrive at second masters Upon their first lord's neck. SWIFT If such gentlemen arrive to be great scholars. H. SPENCER The same conclusion is thus arrived at. T. S. ELIOT Contending and contentious orators, who have not even arrived at the articulation of their differences.

4 *verb intrans.* Come to a certain stage of development by natural growth, lapse of time, etc. Foll. by *at*, †*to*. L16. ▸**b** Of time: come, so as to be present. M18.

SHAKES. *Hen. V* Grandsires, babies, and old women, Either past or not arriv'd to pith and puissance. ADDISON They were each of them arrived at Years of Discretion. **b** SMOLLETT At length the hour arrived.

5 *verb trans.* Come to, reach, land at. *arch.* E17.

MILTON Ere he arrive The happy Ile. SHELLEY While I ask and hear Whence coming they arrive the Ætnean hill.

6 *verb intrans.* Come about, occur, happen. (Foll. by *to*.) *obsolete* exc. as passing into sense 4. M17. ▸†**b** *verb trans.* Happen to, befall. Only in M17.

HOBBES Causes of all things that have arrived hitherto, or shall arrive hereafter. HENRY FIELDING Any such event may arrive to a woman. **b** MILTON Let him also forbear force . . lest a worse woe arrive him.

7 *verb intrans.* [After mod. French.] Be successful, establish one's position or reputation. L19.

English Studies The book was Herrick's greatest success . . . With *Together* Herrick arrived.

■ †**arrivance** *noun* = ARRIVAL E17–L19. **arriver** *noun* E17.

arrivederci /arrivɛˈdɛrtʃi/ *interjection*. L19.
[ORIGIN Italian, lit. 'to the seeing again'.]
Farewell (for the present); goodbye, adieu. Cf. AU REVOIR.

arriviste /ˌariːˈviːst, *foreign* arivist/ *noun*. Pl. pronounced same. E20.
[ORIGIN French, formed as ARRIVE: see -IST.]
An ambitious or self-seeking person.
■ **arrivisme** /-ism/ *noun* the behaviour or character of an arriviste M20.

arroba /əˈrəʊbə/ *noun*. M16.
[ORIGIN Spanish from Arabic *ar-rub'*, from AL-[2] + *rub'* quarter (being a quarter of a quintal).]
A unit of weight formerly used in Spain, Portugal, and Latin America, varying locally between 11 and 16 kg (approx. 24 to 35 lb).

arrogance /ˈarəg(ə)ns/ *noun*. ME.
[ORIGIN Old French & mod. French from Latin *arrogantia*, from *arrogant-*: see ARROGANT, -ANCE.]
Arrogant manner or behaviour; aggressive conceit or presumption.

HELEN FIELDING What a blessing to be born with such Sloaney arrogance.

■ **arrogancy** *noun* (**a**) = ARROGANCE; †(**b**) an arrogant act or assumption: E16.

arrogant /ˈarəg(ə)nt/ *adjective & noun*. LME.
[ORIGIN Old French & mod. French from Latin *arrogant-* pres. ppl stem of *arrogare*: see ARROGATE, -ANT[1].]
▸ **A** *adjective*. Unduly appropriating authority or importance; aggressively conceited or presumptuous; haughty, overbearing. LME.

C. DARWIN The arrogant man looks down on others, and with lowered eyelids hardly condescends to see them. D. H. LAWRENCE Gudrun could see in Gerald an arrogant English contempt for a foreigner. ALDOUS HUXLEY Bernard gave his orders in the sharp, rather arrogant and even offensive tone of one who does not feel himself too secure in his superiority.

▸ **B** *noun*. An arrogant person. *rare*. L15.
■ **arrogantly** *adverb* M16.

arrogate /ˈarəgeɪt/ *verb trans.* M16.
[ORIGIN Latin *arrogat-* pa. ppl stem of *arrogare* claim for oneself, from *ad* AR- + *rogare* ask: see -ATE[3] and cf. ADROGATE.]
1 Appropriate, assume, or claim (*to oneself*) unduly or without justification. M16.

MILTON Will arrogate Dominion undeserv'd Over his brethren. C. STEAD He arrogated every honor to himself, he went out of his way to push into official circles. H. MACMILLAN The illegal but effective authority which the Assembly of the United Nations seemed now to have arrogated to itself.

2 Ascribe or attribute *to* (a person †or thing) without just reason. E17.

COLERIDGE To antiquity we arrogate many things, to ourselves nothing.

†**3** ROMAN LAW. = ADROGATE. Only in M17.
■ **arroˈgation** *noun* †(**a**) ROMAN LAW = ADROGATION; (**b**) the action of claiming and assuming without just reason; an unwarrantable assumption: L16.

arrondissement /arɔ̃dismɑ̃/ *noun*. Pl. pronounced same. E19.
[ORIGIN French, from *arrondiss-* lengthened stem of *arrondir* make round: see -MENT.]
An administrative subdivision of a French city or department.

†**arrouse** *verb trans.* L15–M17.
[ORIGIN French *arrouser* (now *arroser*) from Latin *adrorare*, from *ad* AR- + *ror-*, *ros* dew. Aphet. to ROUSE *verb*[2].]
Sprinkle, moisten.

arrow /ˈarəʊ/ *noun & verb*.
[ORIGIN Old English *ar(e)we* from Old Norse, rel. to Gothic *arhwazna*, from Germanic base from Indo-European, whence Latin *arcus* bow, ARC *noun*.]
▸ **A** *noun*. **1** A slender pointed missile shot from a bow, usu. feathered and barbed. OE. ▸**b** A dart as used in the game of darts. *colloq.* M20.

fig.: S. JOHNSON A mark to the arrows of lurking calumny. E. NEWMAN One wants to have a number of arrows in one's quiver.

arrow of time, **time's arrow**, the direction of travel from past to future in time considered as a physical dimension. ***have an arrow left in one's quiver***: see QUIVER *noun*[1]. ***straight arrow***: see STRAIGHT *adjective*[1] & *adverb*.

2 A mark or symbol shaped like an arrow (e.g. one indicating direction on a map, diagram, etc.) or arrowhead (esp. in ***broad arrow*** s.v. BROAD *adjective*). M16.
3 The leading shoot of a plant or tree, *esp.* the flowering stem of the sugar cane. L16.
4 (Usu. **A-**.) *The* constellation Sagitta. E18.
5 SURVEYING. A metal pin (orig. a real arrow) for driving into the ground at the end of a chain. M18.
– COMB.: **arrow arum** a N. American arum, *Peltandra virginica*, of wet ground, with arrow-shaped leaves; also called ***tuckahoe***, ***wake-robin***; **arrow-back** *N. Amer.* (the back of) a type of Windsor chair with arrow-shaped spindles; **arrow bamboo** = METAKE; **arrowgrass** either of two grasslike marsh plants of the genus *Triglochin*, bearing a slender flowering spike, *T. palustre* (more fully ***marsh arrowgrass***) and *T. maritimum* (more fully ***sea arrowgrass***); **arrowhead** (**a**) the pointed end of an arrow; (**b**) an aquatic or marsh plant of the genus *Sagittaria*, esp. the European *S. sagittifolia*, bearing white flowers and sagittate leaves; **arrow-headed** *adjective* shaped like an arrowhead; *spec.* = CUNEIFORM; **arrow-slit** = LOOPHOLE *noun* 1; **arrowsmith** a maker of iron arrowheads; **arrow-wood** *N. Amer.* any of various shrubs having straight tough shoots, esp. *Viburnum dentatum*; **arrow worm** = CHAETOGNATH.
▸ **B** *verb*. **1** *verb trans.* Pierce, shoot like an arrow. *rare*. E17.
2 *verb intrans.* Move swiftly, like an arrow in flight; dart. E19.
■ **arrowed** *adjective* provided or marked with arrows; *poet.* made into an arrow, pierced with arrows: M17. **arrowy** *adjective* (**a**) consisting of or containing arrows; (**b**) like an arrow, in shape, motion, etc.: E17.

arrowroot /ˈarəʊruːt/ *noun*. L17.
[ORIGIN Alt. of Arawak *aru-aru* lit. 'meal of meals', by assim. to ARROW *noun* and ROOT *noun*[1], the tubers having been used to absorb poison from arrow wounds.]
1 A plant of the genus *Maranta*, *esp.* the W. Indian *M. arundinacea* with fleshy tuberous rhizomes. L17.
2 Pure edible starch prepared from the tubers of *M. arundinacea*, or from other plants. E19.
PORTLAND ***arrowroot***. *TAHITI* ***arrowroot***.

arroyo /əˈrɔɪəʊ/ *noun*. *N. Amer.* Pl. **-os**. M19.
[ORIGIN Spanish.]
A gully, a watercourse.

arse /ɑːs/ *noun*. Now *coarse slang*.
[ORIGIN Old English *ærs* (*ears*) = Old Frisian *ers*, Middle Low German *ars*, *ers*, Middle Dutch *aers*, *e(e)rs* (Dutch *(n)aars*), Old High German *ars* (German *Arsch*), Old Norse *ars*, *rass*, from Germanic from Indo-European. Rel. to Greek *orros* rump.]
1 The buttocks, the rump; the anus. Cf. ASS *noun*[2]. OE. ▸**b** (Women regarded as a source of) sexual gratification. M20.
arse over tip, **arse over tit** head over heels. ***kiss a person's arse***, ***kiss my arse***: see KISS *verb*. ***lick a person's arse***: see LICK *verb*. **not know one's arse from one's elbow** be totally ignorant or incompetent. ***pain in the arse***: see PAIN *noun*[1]. SMART-ARSE. ***tit and arse***, ***tits and arse***: see TIT *noun*[1]. **work one's arse off** work very hard. **b** ***piece of arse***: see PIECE *noun*.
2 *transf.* & *fig.* The lower or hinder end; the bottom; the fag end, the tail. LME. ▸**b** = ***arsehole*** (b) below. M20.
– COMB.: **arse bandit** *coarse slang* a male homosexual; †**arse-foot** *dial.* a grebe, or other bird with feet placed well back; **arsehole** (**a**) the anus; (**b**) *slang* a stupid or despicable person; **arse-kisser** a toady; **arse-kissing** *verbal noun & ppl adjective* toadying; **arse-licker** a toady; **arse-licking** *verbal noun & ppl adjective* toadying; **arsesmart** (now *dial.*) water pepper, *Persicaria hydropiper*.
■ **arsed** *adjective* having buttocks or a rump (of a specified kind) OE. †**arseward(s)** *adverb* & *adjective* backward, perverse(ly) LME–L19.

arse /ɑːs/ *verb*. *slang*. M17.
[ORIGIN from the noun: infl. by ASS *verb*.]
1 *verb intrans.* Fool or mess *about*, *around*, etc. M17.
2 *verb trans.* Mess *up*; make a botched attempt at. L20.
3 *verb trans.* In *pass.* Be bothered to; be willing to make the required effort for (usu. in ***can't be arsed***). L20.

JIMMY BOYLE I couldn't be arsed to give any thought to this.

arsedine /ˈɑːsɪdiːn, -dʌɪn/ *noun*. Also **orsedue** /ˈɔːsɪdjuː/ & other vars. LME.
[ORIGIN Unknown.]
A gold-coloured alloy of copper and zinc, used as leaf.

arsen- *combining form* see ARSENO-.

arsenal /ˈɑːs(ə)n(ə)l/ *noun*. E16.
[ORIGIN French *arsenal*, †*archenal* or its source Italian †*arzanale*, (now) *arsenale*, from Venetian Italian *arzanà* ult. (with unexpl. loss of *d*) from Arabic *dār-(aṣ-)ṣinā'a* workshop, from *dār* house + AL-[2] + *ṣinā'a* art, manufacture, from *ṣana'a* make, fabricate.]
†**1** A dock equipped for the reception, construction, repair, and fitting of ships. E16–M19.
2 A government establishment for the storage or manufacture of weapons and ammunition; a store of weapons (*lit.* & *fig.*). L16.

GIBBON Offensive weapons of all sorts, and military engines, which were deposited in the arsenals. J. K. JEROME I collected a small arsenal—two or three pieces of coal, a few hard pears, . . an empty soda-water bottle, and a few articles of that sort—and . . bombarded the spot from where the noise appeared to come. M. H. ABRAMS Aristotle bequeathed an arsenal of instruments for technical analysis of poetic forms and their elements.

arsenate /ˈɑːs(ə)neɪt/ *noun*. E19.
[ORIGIN from ARSENIC *noun & adjective*[1] + -ATE[1].]
CHEMISTRY. A salt or ester of any oxyacid of arsenic (orig. only of arsenic acid, H_3AsO_4).
■ Also **arseniate** /ɑːˈsiːnɪeɪt/ *noun* (now *rare*) E19.

arsenic /ˈɑːs(ə)nɪk/ *noun & adjective*[1]. LME.
[ORIGIN Old French & mod. French from Latin *arsenicum* from Greek *arsenikon* yellow orpiment, (identified with *arsenikos* male, but in fact) from Arabic *az-zarnīḵ*, formed as AL-[2] + *zarnīḵ* orpiment from Persian, from *zar* gold.]
▸ **A** *noun*. **1** Yellow orpiment, arsenic sulphide, As_2S_3 (more fully ***yellow arsenic***). Also, realgar, AsS (more fully ***red arsenic***). Now *rare*. LME.
2 Arsenic trioxide, As_2O_3 (more fully ***white arsenic***). Also, this or any other arsenic compound used as a poison; *fig.*, poison. LME.
3 The chemical element common to these, in its usual form a brittle steel-grey metalloid, atomic no. 33 (symbol As). E19.
▸ **B** *attrib.* or as *adjective*. Of arsenic, arsenical. LME.
■ **arsenicated** /ɑːˈsɛnɪkeɪtɪd/ *adjective* (now *rare* or *obsolete*) treated, mixed, or combined with arsenic L18. †**arseniuret** *noun* = ARSENIDE M19–E20. **arseniuretted** /ɑːˈsɛnjʊrɛtɪd/ *adjective* (*arch.*) combined with arsenic E19.

arsenic /ɑːˈsɛnɪk/ *adjective*[2]. E19.
[ORIGIN from ARSENIC *noun & adjective*[1], the ending being identified with -IC.]
CHEMISTRY. Of pentavalent arsenic.
arsenic acid a weak acid, H_3AsO_4, with oxidizing properties.

arsenical /ɑːˈsɛnɪk(ə)l/ *adjective & noun*. E17.
[ORIGIN from ARSENIC *noun* + -AL[1].]
▸ **A** *adjective*. Of the nature of, pertaining to, or containing arsenic. E17.
▸ **B** *noun*. A compound (esp. organic) of arsenic. L19.

arsenide /ˈɑːs(ə)nʌɪd/ *noun*. M19.
[ORIGIN from ARSENIC *noun* + -IDE.]
CHEMISTRY. A compound of arsenic with a more electropositive element.

arsenious /ɑːˈsiːnɪəs/ *adjective*. E19.
[ORIGIN from ARSENIC *noun* + -IOUS.]
CHEMISTRY. Of trivalent arsenic.
arsenious acid a weak acid, H_3AsO_3, formed when arsenic trioxide dissolves in water.
■ Also ˈ**arsenous** *adjective* E19.

arsenite /ˈɑːs(ə)nʌɪt/ *noun*. E19.
[ORIGIN from ARSENIC *noun* + -ITE[1].]
CHEMISTRY. A salt of arsenious acid.

arseno- /ˈɑːs(ə)nəʊ, ɑːˈsɛnəʊ/ *combining form*. Also (in some mineral names) **arsen-**.
[ORIGIN from ARSENIC *noun* + -O-.]
Forming names of compounds and derivatives of arsenic.
■ **arˈsenolite** *noun* (MINERALOGY) a form of arsenic trioxide crystallizing in the cubic system, occurring as colourless octahedra M19. **arsenoˈpyrite** *noun* (MINERALOGY) an arsenide and sulphide of iron (and usu. also cobalt), occurring as silvery-grey monoclinic prisms; mispickel: M19.

arses *nouns* pls. of ARSE *noun*, ARSIS.

arsey /ˈɑːsi/ *adjective*. *slang*. Also **arsy**. M20.
[ORIGIN from ARSE *noun* + -Y[1].]
1 Of a person: lucky. Orig. and chiefly *Austral.* M20.

J. WALKER I was real arsy to pick up a job here.

2 Bad-tempered, angry; aggressive, uncooperative. L20.

G. ISON She gets all arsy . . and says something about not being one of his tarts.

3 Arrogant, condescending, self-important, pretentious. L20.

DAVID MITCHELL And what's this about you speaking arsey foreign languages?

arshin /ɑːˈʃiːn/ *noun*. Also **-shine**. M16.
[ORIGIN Russian, of Turkic origin.]
A Russian and Turkish unit of length, equal to about 70 cm.

A

arsine /ˈɑːsiːn/ *noun*. L19.
[ORIGIN from ARS(ENIC *noun* + -INE[5].]
CHEMISTRY. A highly poisonous gas, AsH_3. Also, any substituted derivative of this.

arsis /ˈɑːsɪs/ *noun*. Pl. **arses** /ˈɑːsiːz/. LME.
[ORIGIN Late Latin from Greek = lifting, raising, from *airein* raise.]
The syllable or part of a metrical foot that is stressed (orig., *CLASSICAL PROSODY*, by raised pitch or volume); the unstressed beat in barred music. Opp. THESIS.

†arsmet(r)ike *noun* see ARITHMETIC *noun*[1].

arson /ˈɑːs(ə)n/ *noun*. L17.
[ORIGIN Legal Anglo-Norman & Old French, from medieval Latin *arsio(n-)*, from Latin *ars-* pa. ppl stem of *ardere* to burn.]
The malicious setting on fire of a house, ship, forest, etc.; an instance of this.
■ **arsonist** *noun* a person who commits arson M19.

arsphenamine /ɑːsˈfɛnəmiːn, -ɪn/ *noun*. E20.
[ORIGIN from ARS(ENIC *noun* + PHEN- + AMINE.]
A toxic synthetic bicyclic arsenic compound, $C_{12}H_{12}As_2N_2O_2 \cdot 2HCl$, formerly used to treat syphilis, yaws, etc. Cf. SALVARSAN.

arsy *adjective* var. of ARSEY.

arsy-versy /ɑːsɪˈvəːsi/ *adverb* & *adjective*. Now *dial.* & *coarse slang*. M16.
[ORIGIN from ARSE *noun* + Latin *versus* turned, with -Y[1] added to both elems. to make a jingle.]
▸ **A** *adverb*. Backside foremost; upside down; contrariwise; perversely. M16.
▸ **†B** *adjective*. Contrary; perverse. Only in 17.

art /ɑːt/ *noun*[1]. ME.
[ORIGIN Old French & mod. French from Latin *art-*, *ars*, from a base meaning 'put together, join, fit'.]
▸ **I** Skill. (As a non-count noun)
1 Skill as the result of knowledge and practice. ME. ▸**†b** *spec.* Technical or professional skill. ME–L17. ▸**c** Human skill, as opp. to nature. LME.

POPE The copious accents fall with easy art. LD MACAULAY The potato, a root which can be cultivated with scarcely any art. **b** SHAKES. *Macb.* Tell me, if your art Can tell so much. **c** DRYDEN Art may err, but nature cannot miss.

2 The learning of the schools; scholarship. Now *arch.* & *hist.* ME.

LONGFELLOW Art is long, and time is fleeting.

3 The application of skill according to aesthetic principles, esp. in the production of visible works of imagination, imitation, or design (painting, sculpture, architecture, etc.); skilful execution of workmanship as an object in itself; the cultivation of the production of aesthetic objects in its principles, practice, and results. E17.

T. TRAHERNE Art.. more frequently appears in fiddling and dancing, then in noble deeds. DRYDEN From hence the rudiments of art began, A coal or chalk first imitated man. J. RUSKIN High art differs from low art in possessing an excess of beauty in addition to its truth. A. C. SWINBURNE The well-known formula of art for art's sake.. has, like other doctrines, a true side to it, and an untrue. G. B. SHAW The Renascence of antique literature and art in the sixteenth century.

▸ **II** Something in which skill may be obtained or displayed. (As a count noun.)
4 In *pl.* Certain branches of (esp. university or school) study serving as a preparation for more advanced studies or for later life, now esp. languages, literature, philosophy, history, etc., as distinguished from the sciences or technological subjects. (In the Middle Ages the elements of a course of seven sciences, the trivium, consisting of grammar, logic, and rhetoric, and the quadrivium, consisting of arithmetic, geometry, music, and astronomy.) ME. ▸**†b** *sing.* Each of the subjects of the medieval trivium or quadrivium. Only in ME.

SHAKES. *Per.* My education been in arts and arms. JOYCE Through the matriculation, first arts second arts and arts degree courses at the royal university.

5 A practical application of any science; *esp.* an industrial pursuit of a skilled nature, a craft. LME. ▸**b** A guild or company of craftsmen. *rare*. M19.

ADDISON The Fisher-men can't employ their Art with so much success in so troubled a Sea. E. TERRY Only a great actor finds the difficulties of the actor's art infinite. E. LINKLATER They grew .. technical about such obscure arts as splicing, seizing, gaffing, and pointing. K. CLARK Another development of the art of printing was nourishing the imagination: the woodcut.

6 A pursuit or occupation in which skill is directed towards the production of a work of imagination, imitation, or design, or towards the gratification of the aesthetic senses; the products of any such pursuit. L16.

J. REYNOLDS All arts having the same general end, which is to please. C. MACKENZIE It is a dying art and only to be heard in perfection from old men and old women. K. CLARK The very narrowness of primitive society gives their ornamental art a peculiar concentration and vitality.

7 An acquired faculty; a knack. M17.

A. G. GARDINER The art of the business is to work easily and with a light hand. C. S. FORESTER Curzon had partly acquired the art .. of being uncommunicative without being rude. V. S. PRITCHETT A clever journalist explains to another the art of writing short sketches.

▸ **III** Skilful or crafty conduct.
8 Cunning; artfulness. ME.

POPE Smile without Art, and win without a Bribe.

9 An artifice, a stratagem, a wile, a cunning device. Usu. in *pl.* LME.

J. AUSTEN The arts which ladies sometimes condescend to employ for captivation. LD MACAULAY No art was spared which could draw Monmouth from retreat.

— PHRASES: **art-and-crafty** *adjective* = *ARTSY-craftsy*. ***art and mystery***: see MYSTERY *noun*[2]. **art and part**, **art or part** (orig.) contrivance and/or execution; ***have art or part in***, share in, be involved in; ***be art and part in***, be an accessory or participant in. **arts and crafts** decorative design and handicraft, orig. as encouraged by the Arts and Crafts Exhibition Society. **Bachelor of Arts** (a person who has been awarded) a degree (usu. the lowest, below a master's degree) in an arts subject or arts subjects. ***black art***: see BLACK *adjective*. **decorative arts**: those which involve the production of high-quality objects which are both useful and beautiful. ***fine arts***: see FINE ART. **graphic arts**: those which involve graphic representation or writing, printing, etc. **imitative arts** painting and sculpture. **liberal arts** the medieval trivium and quadrivium; (chiefly *N. Amer.*) arts subjects as opp. to science and technology. *MARTIAL art*. **Master of Arts** (a person who has been awarded) a degree (usu. above a bachelor's degree) for a high level of proficiency in an arts subject or arts subjects. ***object of art***: see OBJECT *noun*. **performing arts**: those, such as drama, dancing, etc., which involve public performance. **plastic arts**: those which involve modelling, as sculpture etc. ***pop art***: see POP *adjective*. ***state of the art***: see STATE *noun*. **the arts** the fine arts (see FINE ART). ***the gentle art***: see GENTLE *adjective*. ***the noble art***: see NOBLE *adjective*. ***will to art***: see WILL *noun*[1]. **work of art** a fine picture, sculpture, poem, building, etc.

— ATTRIB. & COMB.: Pertaining to the use of artistic skill, designed to produce an artistic effect, composed with conscious artistry, as ***art cinema***, ***art film***, ***art furniture***, ***art music***, ***art needlework***, ***art song***, ***art theatre***, etc. Special combs., as ***art DECO***; **art editor** a person who is responsible for illustrations and design, or for the section devoted to the arts, in a book, magazine, etc.; **art form** [cf. German *Kunstform*] (*a*) an established form of composition (e.g. novel, sonata, sonnet, triptych); (*b*) a medium of artistic expression; **art gallery** (a portion of) a building devoted to the exhibition of works of art; **art object** = OBJET D'ART; **art paper** paper coated with china clay or the like to give a smooth surface; **artsman** (*a*) *arch.* = ARTIST; (*b*) a student of or graduate in arts; **art therapy** painting, sculpture, or other artistic activity engaged in as a form of occupational therapy; **art union** a union of people for the purchase of works of art, usu. to be distributed by lottery; *Austral.* & *NZ hist.* any public lottery; **artwork**, **art work** (*a*) a work of art; (*b*) (an example of) graphic art or design; illustrative or decorative matter in a printed text; (*c*) prepared or camera-ready copy.

†art *noun*[2] var. of AIRT.

art /ɑːt/ *verb*[1]. *rare*. E17.
[ORIGIN from ART *noun*[1].]
†**1** *verb trans.* Obtain by art. Only in E17.
†**2** *verb trans.* Make artificial. Only in E17.
†**3** *verb trans.* foll. by *it*. Use art or artifice. Only in M17.
†**4** *verb trans.* Instruct in an art or arts. Only in M17.
5 *verb trans.* & *intrans.* Foll. by *up*: make arty; decorate in an arty fashion. E20.

art *verb*[2] see BE *verb*.

-art /ət/ *suffix*.
Occas. var. of -ARD, as in ***braggart*** etc.

artefact /ˈɑːtɪfakt/ *noun*. Also **arti-**. E19.
[ORIGIN from Latin *arte* abl. of *ars* art + *factum* neut. pa. pple of *facere* make.]
1 A product of human art or workmanship; *ARCHAEOLOGY* a product or by-product of prehistoric or aboriginal workmanship, as opp. to a natural object. E19.
2 Something observed in a scientific investigation, experiment, etc., that is not naturally present but originates in the preparative or investigative procedure or extraneously. L19.
■ **arteˈfactual** *adjective* of or pertaining to an artefact or artefacts M20. **arteˈfactually** *adverb* (*a*) as an artefact; (*b*) by extraneous means: M20.

artel /ɑːˈtɛl/ *noun*. L19.
[ORIGIN Russian *artel'*.]
A Russian or Soviet collective enterprise of craftsmen or skilled workers.

artemisia /ɑːtɪˈmɪzjə/ *noun*. ME.
[ORIGIN Latin from Greek, = wormwood, from *Artemis* the goddess Diana, to whom it was sacred.]
Any of numerous aromatic or bitter-tasting plants of the genus *Artemisia*, of the composite family, which includes wormwood, mugwort, sagebrush, etc.

artemisinin /ɑːtɪˈmiːsɪnɪn/ *noun*. L20.
[ORIGIN from ARTEMISIA + QUININE.]
= QINGHAOSU.

Arte Povera /ˌarte ˈpɔvera, ˌɑːteɪ ˈpɒvərə/ *noun phr.* M20.
[ORIGIN Italian, lit. 'impoverished art'.]
An artistic movement that originated in Italy in the 1960s, combining aspects of conceptual, minimalist, and performance art, and making use of worthless or common materials such as earth or newspaper, in the hope of subverting the commercialization of art.

arterial /ɑːˈtɪərɪəl/ *adjective*. LME.
[ORIGIN medieval Latin *arterialis*: see ARTERY, -AL[1].]
1 Of, pertaining to, or of the nature of an artery; (of blood) oxygenated in the lungs and of a bright red colour (opp. VENOUS). LME.
arterial system the system of arteries by which oxygenated blood is conveyed from the heart and lungs to the various parts of the body. **†arterial vein** the pulmonary artery.
2 Resembling an artery, esp. as a main road or other important route of transport or communication. M19.
■ **arterialiˈzation** *noun* the action or process of arterializing blood M19. **arterialize** *verb trans.* oxygenate (blood) in the lungs M19. **†arterious** *adjective* = ARTERIAL M17–E19.

arterio- /ɑːˈtɪərɪəʊ/ *combining form*.
[ORIGIN Greek *artērio-*: see ARTERY, -O-.]
Of or pertaining to an artery.
■ **arteriˈotomy** *noun* (an instance of) surgical incision into an artery M17. **arterioˈvenous** *adjective* of, pertaining to, or affecting an artery and a vein L19.

arteriography /ɑːˌtɪərɪˈɒgrəfi/ *noun*. M19.
[ORIGIN from ARTERIO- + -GRAPHY.]
MEDICINE. **1** Systematic description of the arteries. Only in Dicts. M19.
2 Radiography of an artery, carried out after injection of a radio-opaque substance. E20.
■ **arˈteriogram** *noun* an image obtained by arteriography E20.

arteriole /ɑːˈtɪərɪəʊl/ *noun*. M19.
[ORIGIN French *artériole* dim. of *artère* ARTERY: see -OLE[1].]
A small artery adjoining capillaries.
■ **arteriˈolar** *adjective* M20.

arteriosclerosis /ɑːˌtɪərɪəʊsklɪəˈrəʊsɪs, -sklə-/ *noun*. Pl. **-roses** /-ˈrəʊsiːz/. L19.
[ORIGIN from ARTERIO- + SCLEROSIS.]
MEDICINE. Abnormal thickening and hardening of the walls of arteries.
■ **arteriosclerotic** *adjective* pertaining to or affected by arteriosclerosis L19.

arteritis /ɑːtəˈrʌɪtɪs/ *noun*. M19.
[ORIGIN from ARTERY + -ITIS.]
MEDICINE. Inflammation of the walls of an artery.

artery /ˈɑːtəri/ *noun*. LME.
[ORIGIN Latin *arteria* from Greek *artēria*, prob. from *airein* raise: see -Y[3].]
†**1** The windpipe. LME–M17.
2 Any of the muscular-walled tubes forming part of the system of vessels by which blood (usu. oxygenated) is conveyed from the heart to all parts of the body. LME.
coronary artery, ***pulmonary artery***, etc.
†**3** A ligament. E–M17.
4 An important channel of communication or transport; a major road, railway, river, etc. M19.

artesian /ɑːˈtiːzjən, -ʒ(ə)n/ *adjective*. M19.
[ORIGIN French *artésien* lit. 'of Artois' (Old French *Arteis*), a region of NE France where wells of this type were first made: see -IAN.]
Of a well: made by a perpendicular boring into a confined aquifer, the water rising spontaneously above the water table (strictly, to the surface). Also, of, pertaining to, or obtainable by such a well.

†artetik *adjective* & *noun* see ARTHRITIC.

Artex /ˈɑːtɛks/ *noun* & *verb*. M20.
[ORIGIN Blend of ART *noun*[1] and TEXTURE *noun*.]
▸ **A** *noun*. (Proprietary name for) a kind of plaster applied to walls and ceilings to give a textured finish. M20.
▸ **B** *verb trans.* Cover with Artex. L20.

artful /ˈɑːtfʊl, -f(ə)l/ *adjective*. E17.
[ORIGIN from ART *noun*[1] + -FUL.]
1 Of a person, action, etc.: skilful, clever, (*arch.*); (passing into) crafty, deceitful. E17.
†**2** Of a person: learned, wise. Only in 17.
3 Of a thing: artificial, imitative, unreal. *arch.* E18.
■ **artfully** *adverb* E17. **artfulness** *noun* E18.

arthame *noun* var. of ATHAME.

art house /ˈɑːt haʊs/ *noun* & *adjectival phr.* M20.
[ORIGIN from ART *noun*[1] + HOUSE *noun*[1].]
▸ **A** *noun*. A cinema which specializes in showing films which are artistic and experimental rather than commercial; the genre or style of film associated with this type of cinema.
▸ **B** *adjective* (**art-house**). Designating, relating to, or associated with such cinemas or films; hence also, arty, pretentious.

JAYNE MILLER I have been to comic conventions .. but they tend to be a bit cliquey and art-house.

arthralgia /ɑːˈθraldʒə/ *noun*. M19.
[ORIGIN from Greek *arthron* joint + -ALGIA.]
MEDICINE. Pain in a joint.

arthritic /ɑːˈθrɪtɪk/ *adjective* & *noun*. Orig. **†artetik** & similar vars. LME.
[ORIGIN Old French *artetique* from medieval Latin *arteticus* from Latin *arthriticus* from Greek *arthritikos*: later assim. to Latin.]
▸ **A** *adjective*. Of, pertaining to, or affected with arthritis. LME.

▸ **B** *noun*. †**1** Disease of the joints. LME–L15.
2 An arthritic person. E19.
■ †**arthritical** *adjective* E16–L18.

arthritis /ɑːˈθrʌɪtɪs/ *noun*. Pl. **-tides** /-tɪdiːz/. M16.
[ORIGIN Latin from Greek, from *arthron* joint: see -ITIS.]
An inflammatory or painful condition of a joint; *spec*. (**a**) = RHEUMATOID ***arthritis***; (**b**) = OSTEOARTHRITIS.

arthro- /ˈɑːθrəʊ/ *combining form* of Greek *arthron* joint: see -O-.
■ **arˈthrodesis** *noun* [Greek *desis* binding together] SURGERY surgical fusion of bones at a joint E20. **arthrogram** *noun* (MEDICINE) a radiographic image of a joint; an investigative procedure in which such an image is made: M20. **arˈthrography** *noun* (**a**) systematic description of the joints (Dicts.); (**b**) examination of joints by radiography: L19. **arˈthropathy** *noun* any disease affecting joints L19. **arthroplasty** *noun* (an instance of) surgical reconstruction of a joint L19.

arthrodia /ɑːˈθrəʊdɪə/ *noun*. L16.
[ORIGIN Greek *arthrōdia*, from *arthrōdēs* well-jointed: see -IA[1].]
ANATOMY & ZOOLOGY. A form of articulation in which bony surfaces slide freely over each other.
■ **arthrodial** *adjective* (of a joint) having this form of articulation M19. **arthrodic** *adjective* = ARTHRODIAL L19.

arthropod /ˈɑːθrəpɒd/ *noun*. L19.
[ORIGIN from mod. Latin *Arthropoda* (see below), from Greek *arthron* joint + -POD.]
ZOOLOGY. Any animal of the phylum Arthropoda, members of which (e.g. insects, arachnids, and crustaceans) are characterized by segmented bodies and jointed limbs.

arthroscope /ˈɑːθrəskəʊp/ *noun*. E20.
[ORIGIN from ARTHRO- + -SCOPE.]
MEDICINE. A type of endoscope used to inspect the interior of a joint cavity, esp. in order to perform a surgical operation inside the joint.
■ **arthroˈscopic** *adjective* involving or relating to arthroscopy; observed using an arthroscope: L20. **arthroˈscopically** *adverb* L20. **arˈthroscopist** *noun* L20. **arˈthroscopy** *noun* the use of an arthroscope to examine the interior of a joint; an operation performed using an arthroscope: E20.

arthrosis /ɑːˈθrəʊsɪs/ *noun*. Pl. **-roses** /-ˈrəʊsiːz/. M17.
[ORIGIN Latin from Greek *arthrōsis*: see ARTHRO-, -OSIS.]
1 Connection by a joint, articulation. M17.
2 MEDICINE. Any disease affecting joints. E20.

Arthurian /ɑːˈθjʊərɪən/ *adjective & noun*. E17.
[ORIGIN from *Arthur* (see below) + -IAN.]
▸ **A** *adjective*. Of, pertaining to, or resembling the legendary British king Arthur, his court, his knights, or the romances in which these figure. E17.
▸ **B** *noun*. A knight of the Round Table, a follower of King Arthur. E20.
– NOTE: Rare before M19.

artic /ˈɑːtɪk/ *noun*[1]. *colloq*. M20.
[ORIGIN Abbreviation.]
An articulated lorry.

†**Artic** *adjective & noun*[2] see ARCTIC *adjective & noun*.

artichoke /ˈɑːtɪtʃəʊk/ *noun*. M16.
[ORIGIN Italian (north.) *articiocco*, *arci-* alt. of Old Spanish *alcarchofa* from Arabic *al-ḵaršūf(a)*.]
1 (The edible flower head of) a plant of the composite family, *Cynara scolymus*, resembling a thistle and native to the Mediterranean region. Also more fully ***French artichoke***, ***globe artichoke***. M16.
2 ***Jerusalem artichoke*** [alt. of Italian *girasole* sunflower], (the edible tuberous root of) a sunflower, *Helianthus tuberosus*. E17.
3 ***Chinese artichoke***, ***Japanese artichoke***, (the edible tuber of) a plant of the mint family, *Stachys affinis*, cultivated esp. in the Far East. E20.

article /ˈɑːtɪk(ə)l/ *noun & verb*. ME.
[ORIGIN Old French & mod. French from Latin *articulus* dim. of *artus* joint, from base also of ART *noun*[1]: see -CLE.]
▸ **A** *noun*. **I** A separate portion of something written.
1 A separate clause or statement of the Apostles' Creed; an item of a summary of faith. ME.
the Thirty-nine Articles statements of doctrine in the *Book of Common Prayer* to which those taking orders in the Church of England had formerly to assent.
2 A separate clause or provision of a statute, constitution, code, etc.; an item in a rule book, a regulation. ME.
Lords of the Articles SCOTTISH HISTORY a standing committee of the Scottish Parliament, who drafted and prepared the measures submitted to the House.
3 Each of the distinct charges or counts of an accusation or indictment. *arch*. LME.
4 Each of the distinct heads or points of an agreement or treaty; in *pl*., a formal agreement, a period of apprenticeship, now esp. as a solicitor. LME. ▸**b** In *pl*. Terms, conditions. *arch*. M17. ▸**c** A formal agreement. *arch*. M18.

HENRY FIELDING Articles of separation were soon drawn up, and signed between the parties. T. JEFFERSON To prepare an article defining the extent of the powers over commerce. A. N. WILSON He had just finished his articles at a London firm of solicitors.

articles of apprenticeship terms of agreement between an apprentice and employer. ***articles of association***: see ASSOCIATION 1. ***articles of*** CONFEDERATION.

5 *gen*. A paragraph, section, or distinct item of any document. LME.
6 A non-fictional literary composition forming part of a newspaper, magazine, or other publication, but independent of others in the same publication. E18.
leading article: see LEADING *adjective*. ***turnover article***: see TURNOVER *adjective*.
▸ **II** A particular item.
7 A particular item of business; a concern, a matter, a subject. *obsolete* exc. in ***in the article of*** (arch.), so far as concerns, with regard to. LME.

S. RICHARDSON To say, there was no article so proper for parents to govern in, as this of marriage.

†**8** An item in an account, list, etc. Only in 18.
9 A particular of a subject, action, or proceeding; a distinct detail. M18.
article of faith a basic point of belief.
10 A particular material thing (*of* a specified class); a commodity; a piece of goods or property. L18. ▸**b** A person regarded (usu. disparagingly) as a commodity etc. E19.

W. C. MACREADY Various articles of furniture. *Spin* He took off every article of clothing. **b** A. TROLLOPE She's the very article for such a man as Peppermint.

article of virtu: see VIRTU *noun* 1. **genuine article** something authentic of its kind.
▸ **III** A portion of time.
11 A specific juncture in time; the critical point or moment. *arch*. LME.

W. WOLLASTON An infirm building, just in the article of falling.

the article of death the moment of death.
▸ **IV** GRAMMAR. **12** A member of a small set of words (in English two, traditionally regarded as adjectives, now also classed as determiners) that give definiteness or indefiniteness and specificness or genericness to the application of a noun. LME.
definite article, ***indefinite article***.
▸ †**V** MATH. **13** The number 10, or any multiple of it. LME–M18.
▸ †**VI** ANATOMY. **14** A joint, a limb. LME–L17.
▸ **B** *verb*. †**1** *verb trans*. Formulate in articles, particularize; claim *that*. LME–E17.
2 **a** *verb trans. & intrans*. Set forth (offences) in articles *against*; make a charge or accusation *against*. *arch*. LME. ▸**b** *verb trans*. Indict, charge. *arch*. E17.
†**3** *verb trans. & intrans*. Arrange by treaty or stipulation (with *direct obj.*, *that*, *to do*; *with* a person, *for* a thing). LME–E19.
4 *verb trans*. Bind by articles of apprenticeship. L18.

Slightly Foxed Young George was articled to a Norwich solicitor but spent little time on the law.

articled clerk a person training to be a solicitor.
5 *verb trans*. Provide with articles of faith. *rare*. E19.

articulable /ɑːˈtɪkjʊləb(ə)l/ *adjective*. M19.
[ORIGIN from ARTICUL(ATE *verb* + -ABLE.]
That can be articulated.

articulacy /ɑːˈtɪkjʊləsi/ *noun*. M20.
[ORIGIN from ARTICULATE *adjective*: see -CY. Cf. earlier INARTICULACY.]
The quality or state of being articulate.

articular /ɑːˈtɪkjʊlə/ *adjective*. LME.
[ORIGIN Latin *articularis*, from *articulus*: see ARTICLE *noun*, -AR[1].]
1 Of or pertaining to the joints. LME.
2 GRAMMAR. Of the nature of an article (ARTICLE *noun* 12); having an article preposed. M18.
■ †**articularly** *adverb* article by article, in separate heads or divisions. LME–M18.

articulate /ɑːˈtɪkjʊlət/ *adjective*. M16.
[ORIGIN Latin *articulatus* pa. pple, formed as ARTICULATE *verb*: see -ATE[2].]
†**1** Charged or specified in articles; formulated in articles. M16–E18.
2 Of sound: with clearly distinguishable parts, each having meaning. Of speech, expression, etc.: fluent and clear. Of a person: able to express himself or herself fluently and clearly. M16. ▸**b** *transf*. Of other sensations: distinct. E17.

MILTON Beasts . . Created mute to all articulate sound. K. GRAHAME The water's own noises . . were more apparent than by day . . ; and constantly they started at what seemed a sudden clear call from an actual articulate voice. M. H. ABRAMS Poetry consists of a sequence of articulate sounds in time rather than of forms and colours fixed in space. H. ARENDT Its most articulate spokesman, Ludwig von der Marwitz . . submitted a lengthy petition to the government. M. SHADBOLT Just a note. Will write again. Not very articulate at present. **b** A. BAIN The discriminative or articulate character of the sense of touch.

3 Jointed; united by a joint; composed of segments united by joints. L16.
4 Distinctly jointed; having the parts distinctly recognizable. M17.

W. IRVING A miserable horse, whose ribs were as articulate as the bars of a gridiron. CARLYLE Added to the firm land of articulate History.

■ **articulately** *adverb* M16. **articulateness** *noun* M18.

articulate /ɑːˈtɪkjʊleɪt/ *verb*. M16.
[ORIGIN Latin *articulat-* pa. ppl stem of *articulare*, from *articulus*: see ARTICLE, -ATE[3].]
▸ **I** Cf. ARTICLE *verb*.
1 *verb trans*. Formulate in an article or articles; particularize. *arch*. M16.

T. NASHE If I articulate all the examples of their absurdeties that I could.

†**2** *verb trans. & intrans*. Charge; bring a charge *against*. M16–E17.

M. DRAYTON Gainst whom, at Pomfret, they articulate.

†**3** *verb intrans*. Come to terms; capitulate. L16–M17.

SHAKES. *Coriol*. Send us to Rome The best, with whom we may articulate For their own good and ours.

†**4** *verb trans*. Arrange by articles or conditions. Only in 17.

W. FULBECKE Articulating peace with the Albanes.

▸ **II** **5** *verb trans*. Pronounce distinctly; give utterance to; express in words; express clearly and fluently. M16.

DISRAELI The lady . . began to articulate a horrible patois. D. H. LAWRENCE 'You do as you like—you can leave altogether if you like,' he managed to articulate. J. CARY Partly from breathlessness, partly from agitation, he could not articulate any single word. R. ELLISON We need a good speaker for this district. Someone who can articulate the grievances of the people. P. GOODMAN There is complaint later that they do not know how to articulate their thoughts. M. FRENCH She discovered only gradually, for Carl never articulated it, just what he expected of her. I. MCEWAN She drew breath sharply, and held it for several seconds, then articulated from the back of her throat a strangled, hard C.

6 *verb trans*. Modify (the air, a pulmonary airstream, etc.) to produce a speech sound, word, etc. *arch*. L16.
7 *verb intrans*. Utter words; speak distinctly; pronounce words. M17.

V. KNOX The capricious modes of dressing, articulating and moving. LD MACAULAY His agitation was so great that he could not articulate.

8 *transf*. Make distinct to sight etc. M19.

L. A. G. STRONG The powerful light . . beat down on it, throwing it into relief, articulating with dark shadow the long slender fingers.

▸ **III** **9** *verb trans*. Attach by a joint; connect with joints; mark with apparent joints; construct (esp. a vehicle) of flexibly connected sections. Usu. in *pass*. Earlier as ARTICULATED 2. E17.

ST G. J. MIVART The most movable joints are those in which the adjacent bones are articulated on the principle either of a pivot, or of a hinge.

10 *verb intrans*. Form a joint (*with*). M19.

T. H. HUXLEY The hollow of the cup articulates with a spheroidal surface furnished by the humerus.

articulated /ɑːˈtɪkjʊleɪtɪd/ *ppl adjective*. M16.
[ORIGIN from ARTICULATE *verb* + -ED[1].]
1 Formulated in an article or articles. *arch*. M16.
2 Attached by a joint; connected by joints; having segments united by joints. L16. ▸**b** Of a vehicle: consisting of flexibly connected sections. E20.

G. ROLLESTON An ossicle articulated to its apex. **b** *Times* Joe had a brand-new articulated truck, . . (where the driving cab is separately joined to the lorry).

3 Uttered as articulate sound; distinctly spoken. E18.

COLERIDGE The same words may be repeated; but in each second of time the articulated air hath passed away.

articulation /ɑːˌtɪkjʊˈleɪʃ(ə)n/ *noun*. LME.
[ORIGIN French, or Latin *articulatio(n-)*, formed as ARTICULATED: see -ATION.]
▸ **I** **1** The action or process of joining; the state of being jointed; a mode of jointing. LME.
2 A joint; *esp*. a structure whereby two bones, or parts of an invertebrate skeleton, are connected in the body, whether rigidly or flexibly. LME.
3 Movement by a flexible joint. *rare*. M16.

E. LINKLATER As if the American hip and knee gave free articulation all round the circle.

4 Each of the segments of a jointed body; the part between two joints. M17.
▸ **II** **5** The production or formation of speech sounds, words, etc.; articulate utterance or expression; speech. E17.

T. S. ELIOT Contending and contentious orators, who have not even arrived at the articulation of their differences. J. LYONS The oldest, and still the most common, method of phonetic description is that made in terms of 'articulation' by the speech-organs. J. BARNES He had a whiny, imprecise voice . . ; what seemed at first a regional inflection turned out to be only casual articulation.

manner of articulation, **mode of articulation** PHONETICS: with or without friction etc. **place of articulation**, **point of articulation** PHONETICS the place at which obstruction of the air passage takes place in the production of a consonant.
6 A speech sound; an articulate utterance. M18.

7 Articulacy, distinctness. *rare*. L18.

W. COWPER The looks and gestures of their griefs and fears Have all articulation in his ears.

articulative /ɑːˈtɪkjʊlətɪv/ *adjective*. E19.
[ORIGIN from ARTICULATE *verb* + -IVE.]
Of or pertaining to articulation.

articulator /ɑːˈtɪkjʊleɪtə/ *noun*. L18.
[ORIGIN from ARTICULATE *verb* + -OR.]
▸ **I 1** A person who articulates words, speech sounds, etc.; a person who gives utterance to or expresses something. L18.

BOSWELL An elderly housekeeper, a most distinct articulator, showed us the house. *Dictionaries* A recent articulator of this need is Professor Fred C. Robinson of Yale University.

2 A mobile organ of speech, as the tongue. M20.
▸ **II 3** A person who articulates bones and mounts skeletons. M19.

articulatory /ɑːˈtɪkjʊlət(ə)ri, ɑːˌtɪkjʊˈleɪt(ə)ri/ *adjective*. E19.
[ORIGIN from ARTICULATOR: see -ORY².]
1 = ARTICULAR 1. *rare*. E19.
2 Of or pertaining to the articulation of speech. M19.

artifact *noun* var. of ARTEFACT.

artifice /ˈɑːtɪfɪs/ *noun*. LME.
[ORIGIN Old French & mod. French from Latin *artificium*, from *arti-*, *ars* ART *noun*¹ + *-fic-* var. of *fac-* stem of *facere* make.]
†**1** Technical skill; art; workmanship; the making of something by art or skill. LME–L18.

SIR T. BROWNE Though they abounded in milk, they had not the Artifice of Cheese. D. HUME Does it not counterwork the artifice of nature?

†**2** Mode or style of workmanship. L16–M18.

BURKE Examine . . into the artifice of the contrivance.

3 Skill in designing and employing expedients; address, cunning, trickery. E17.

DEFOE All the artifice and sleight of hand they were masters of. J. BRAINE A noisy snuffle, without grace or artifice.

4 An ingenious expedient; a cunning trick; a device, a contrivance. E17.

A. G. GARDINER He monopolises the applause as he monopolises the limelight; and by these artifices he has persuaded the public that he is an actor. R. H. TAWNEY Every shift and artifice most repugnant to the sober prudence of plain-dealing men.

†**5** A work of art. Only in 17.
6 (The products of) human skill as opp. to what is natural. M19.

E. H. GOMBRICH Men turned from the admiration of artifice to the worship of nature. R. WILBUR Trusting in God, mistrusting artifice, He would not graft or bud the stock he sold.

artificer /ɑːˈtɪfɪsə/ *noun*. LME.
[ORIGIN Anglo-Norman (cf. medieval Latin *artificiarius*), prob. alt. of Old French *artificien*, formed as ARTIFICE: see -ER².]
1 A person who makes things by art or skill; a craftsman; an artist. LME. ▸**b** *gen*. A maker. *arch*. M17.
†**2** A crafty or artful person; a trickster. LME–E17.
3 A contriver, an inventor, a deviser, (*of*). E17.
4 *MILITARY & NAUTICAL*. A skilled technician. M18.

artificial /ɑːtɪˈfɪʃ(ə)l/ *adjective & noun*. LME.
[ORIGIN Old French & mod. French *artificiel* or Latin *artificialis*, from *artificium*: see ARTIFICE, -AL¹.]
▸ **A** *adjective*. **I** Opp. ***natural***.
1 Made by or resulting from art or artifice; constructed, contrived; not natural (though real). LME.

J. R. MCCULLOCH To give an artificial stimulus to population. J. C. POWYS You are confusing natural, instinctive happiness and the artificial social pride that we get from private property. F. L. WRIGHT Artificial lighting is nearly as important as daylight.

artificial insemination injection of semen into the uterus by other than the natural means. **artificial language** a composite language, esp. for international use, made from the words and other elements in several languages. ***artificial person***: see PERSON *noun* 5. **artificial respiration** the restoration or initiation of breathing by manual or mechanical means.

2 Not real; imitation, substitute. L16.

A. CARTER She made me instant coffee . . there was artificial cream made from corn-syrup solids to go with it. W. MAXWELL When my brother undressed at night he left his artificial leg leaning against a chair. A. GRAY Jam-jars of artificial flowers, some made of plastic, some of coloured wax, some of paper.

artificial horizon a gyroscopic instrument or a fluid (esp. mercury) surface used to provide a horizontal reference plane for navigational measurement. **artificial intelligence** (the field of study that deals with) the capacity of a machine to simulate or surpass intelligent human behaviour. ***artificial KIDNEY***. ***artificial mother***: see MOTHER *noun*¹ 11. **artificial silk** *arch*. rayon. **artificial stone** concrete or a similar substance made to resemble stone, used esp. in building.

3 Affected, insincere; factitious; feigned. L16.

S. JOHNSON Endeavour to kindle in myself an artificial impatience. F. W. ROBERTSON Some will have become frivolous and artificial. T. WILLIAMS Blanche has a tight, artificial smile on her drawn face.

▸ †**II** Displaying special art or skill.
4 Cunning, deceitful. LME–E18.

MILTON This is the artificialest piece of finesse to perswade Men to be Slaves, that the wit of Court could have invented.

5 Displaying skill; skilful. L15–M18.

R. FABYAN An horologe or a clocke . . of a wonder artyficiall makyng. R. HAKLUYT They are very artificiall in making of images.

6 Displaying education or training; scholarly. Only in E17.

DONNE Scholastique and artificiall men use this way of instructing.

▸ †**III** Of art(s).
7 According to the rules of art or science; technical. LME–E19.
▸ **B** *noun*. Something artificial; *spec*. (***a***) an artificial flower; (***b***) an artificial bait used in fishing. E17.
▪ **artificialism** *noun* an artificial principle or practice M19. **artificialize** *verb trans*. L17. **artificially** *adverb* LME. **artificialness** *noun* L16.

artificiality /ˌɑːtɪfɪʃɪˈalɪti/ *noun*. M16.
[ORIGIN from ARTIFICIAL + -ITY.]
†**1** Craftsmanship; artifice. M–L16.
2 The quality or state of being artificial. M18.
3 An artificial thing, characteristic, etc. M19.

artify /ˈɑːtɪfʌɪ/ *verb trans*. L18.
[ORIGIN from ART *noun*¹ + -I- + -FY; mod. uses partly from ARTY *adjective*.]
Modify or adorn by art; render arty.

artillery /ɑːˈtɪləri/ *noun*. LME.
[ORIGIN Old French & mod. French *artillerie*, from *artiller* alt. (after *art*) of Old French *atillier* equip, arm, prob. by-form of *atirier*, from *à* A-⁵ + *tire* order: see TIER *noun*¹, -ERY.]
†**1** Warlike munitions; implements of war. LME–L18.
2 Engines for discharging missiles: formerly including catapults, slings, bows, etc.; now *spec*., large guns used in fighting on land. LME.
†**3** Missiles discharged in war. M16–M19.
4 The science or practice of using artillery. Formerly *spec*., archery, now *spec*. gunnery. M16.
5 Thunder and lightning. *poet*. L16.
6 The branch of the army that uses large guns. L18.
– COMB.: **artilleryman** a man whose military duty it is to serve a large gun, a man who belongs to a regiment of artillery; **artillery plant** a tropical American plant, *Pilea microphylla*, of the nettle family, whose mature anthers throw out clouds of pollen.
▪ **artillerist** *noun* a user of artillery, an artilleryman; a person who studies the principles of artillery: L16.

artiodactyl /ɑːtɪə(ʊ)ˈdaktɪl/ *adjective & noun*. Also (earlier) †**-yle**. M19.
[ORIGIN mod. Latin *Artiodactyla* pl., from Greek *artios* even + *daktulos* finger, toe.]
ZOOLOGY. (Designating or pertaining to) any living or extinct mammal belonging to the order Artiodactyla of even-toed ungulates, including camels, pigs, and ruminants.

artisan /ɑːtɪˈzan, ˈɑːtɪzan/ *noun*. Also **-zan**. M16.
[ORIGIN French from Italian *artigiano*, ult. from Latin *artitus* pa. pple of *artire* instruct in the arts, from *art-*, *ars* ART *noun*¹: see -AN.]
1 A skilled (esp. manual) worker; a mechanic; a craftsman. M16.
†**2** A person who practises or cultivates an art. L16–L18.
▪ **artisanal** *adjective* of or pertaining to artisans; involving manual skill: M20. **artisanate** *noun* artisans collectively, the body or class of artisans M20. **artisanship** *noun* the work and activity of an artisan or of artisans E19.

artist /ˈɑːtɪst/ *noun*. E16.
[ORIGIN Old French & mod. French *artiste* from Italian *artista*, from *arte* ART *noun*¹: see -IST.]
†**1** A person who is master of the liberal arts; a learned person. E16–M18.

SHAKES. *Tr. & Cr.* The wise and fool, the artist and unread.

†**2** A person who is master of a practical science or pursuit; a medical practitioner, astrologer, astronomer, alchemist, professor of occult sciences, chemist, etc. M16–L19.

W. ROWLEY The artists . . That seek the secrets of futurity. MILTON The Moon, whose Orb Through Optic Glass the Tuscan Artist views. SMOLLETT Luckily my wounds were not mortal, and I fell into the hands of a skilful artist.

3 A person who cultivates or practises one of the fine arts, now esp. painting. L16.
artist's proof a copy of an engraving taken for the artist and valued as fresher than ordinary copies.
4 A person who practises one of the performing arts; an artiste. L16.

ADDISON That excellent Artist . . having shewn us the Italian Musick in its Perfection. C. BRONTË He told me his opinion of . . the actress: he judged her as a woman, not an artist.

5 *gen*. A skilled performer; a connoisseur. Now only in a specified or understood activity. L16. ▸**b** A person, a fellow; (usu. with specifying word) a devotee, an indulger in something. *slang*. L19.

I. WALTON I will give you more directions concerning fishing; for I would fain make you an Artist. DEFOE The mate was an excellent sea artist, and an experienced sailor. A. S. BYATT Cassandra was . . an artist in not being on speaking terms. **b** D. M. DAVIN A real artist for the booze, isn't he? HENRY MILLER Neither of us is a booze artist.

6 = ARTISAN 1. *obsolete* exc. as infl. by sense 3, a person who makes his or her craft a fine art. M17.

POPE Then from his anvil the lame artist rose. SOUTHEY Greek artists in the imperial city forged That splendid armour. H. L. MENCKEN And yet the man was a superb artist in words, a master-writer.

†**7** A person who practises artifice; a schemer, contriver. M17–E19.

DEFOE The young artist that has done this roguery.

▪ **artistlike** *adjective & adverb* (in a manner) befitting an artist, artistic(ally) E18. **artistly** *adverb* (now *rare*) artistically, in the manner of an artist M18. **artistry** *noun* artistic ability, artistic characteristics M19.

artiste /ɑːˈtiːst/ *noun*. E19.
[ORIGIN French: see ARTIST.]
A performing artist; a professional singer, dancer, actor, etc.

artistic /ɑːˈtɪstɪk/ *adjective*. M18.
[ORIGIN from ARTIST + -IC.]
Of or pertaining to art or artists; made or done with art; appreciative of or having natural skill in art.
▪ **artistical** *adjective* E19. **artistically** *adverb* in an artistic manner; from an artistic point of view: M19.

artizan *noun* var. of ARTISAN.

artless /ˈɑːtlɪs/ *adjective*. L16.
[ORIGIN from ART *noun*¹ + -LESS.]
1 Without art or skill; unskilled, ignorant; unartistic, uncultured. L16.

S. JOHNSON The work in which I engaged is generally considered . . as the proper toil of artless industry. J. RUSKIN A shadowy life—artless, joyless, loveless.

2 Rude, clumsy, crude. L16.

S. JOHNSON Brogues, a kind of artless shoes.

3 Natural, simple. L17.

C. BROOKS It is like the daffodils, or the mountain brooks, artless, and whimsical, and 'natural' as they.

4 Guileless, ingenuous. E18.

W. IRVING The delightful blushing consciousness of an artless girl.

▪ **artlessly** *adverb* E17. **artlessness** *noun* M18.

art nouveau /ɑː nuːˈvəʊ, *foreign* aːr nuvo/ *noun phr*. E20.
[ORIGIN French, lit. 'new art'.]
An art style of the late 19th cent. characterized by ornamented and flowing lines.

artsy /ˈɑːtsi/ *adjective*. *colloq*. E20.
[ORIGIN Partly from *arts* pl. of ART *noun*¹ + -Y¹; partly from ART *noun*¹ + -SY.]
Of or pertaining to the arts; artistic, *esp*. pretentiously or superficially so.

L. ELLMANN First we went for a drink in an artsy bar.

– COMB.: **artsy-and-craftsy**, **artsy-craftsy** *adjectives* pertaining to or characteristic of the Arts and Crafts Movement, esp. in its more pretentious manifestations; *spec*. (of furniture) remarkable for artistic style rather than for usefulness or comfort; **artsy-fartsy** *adjective* pretentiously artistic.

arty /ˈɑːti/ *noun*. *slang*. M20.
[ORIGIN Abbreviation.]
Artillery.

arty /ˈɑːti/ *adjective*. *colloq*. E20.
[ORIGIN from ART *noun*¹ + -Y¹.]
Pretentiously or quaintly artistic.

G. ORWELL They were arty-looking houses, another of those sham-Tudor colonies. N. FREELING Virulent plastic covers . . : they'd got arty lately in a jazzy style, he had noticed.

– COMB.: **arty-and-craftiness** = ***arty-craftiness*** below; **arty-and-crafty** *adjective* = ***ARTSY-craftsy***; **arty-craftiness** artsy-craftsy quality or characteristics; **arty-crafty** *adjective* = ***ARTSY-craftsy***; **arty-farty** *adjective* = ***ARTSY-fartsy***.
▪ **artily** *noun* M20. **artiness** *noun* E20.

arugula /aˈruːgələ/ *noun*. Chiefly *US*. L20.
[ORIGIN Italian dial. (Calabria) *arucula*, (Sicily) *aruca*, from Italian *rucola*, ult. a dim. of Latin *eruca*.]
The plant rocket, used in salads.

arum /ˈɛːrəm/ *noun*. Also in Greek form †**aron**. LME.
[ORIGIN Latin from Greek *aron*.]
Any of various monocotyledonous plants constituting the genus *Arum* (family Araceae), which have insignificant flowers in a club-shaped spike (or spadix) enclosed in a large leafy bract (or spathe); *esp*. (more fully ***wild arum***) *A. maculatum*, a common plant of woods and hedges.
arrow arum, ***dragon arum***, etc.

– **COMB.**: **arum lily** a plant of the related southern African genus *Zantedeschia*, esp. *Z. aethiopica*, bearing a tall white spadix.

arundinaceous /ərʌndɪˈneɪʃəs/ *adjective*. **M17.**
[**ORIGIN** from Latin *arundinaceus*, from (*h*)*arundo* reed: see **-ACEOUS**.]
Reedlike, reedy.
■ Also **arunˈdineous** *adjective* **M17**.

Arunta *noun & adjective* var. of **ARANDA**.

†**aruspex** *noun* see **HARUSPEX**.

ARV *abbreviation*.
Antiretroviral (drug).

arval /ˈɑːv(ə)l/ *noun*. *N. English*. Also **arvill** /-ɪl/. **LME.**
[**ORIGIN** Old Norse *ervi-ǫl*, from *arfr* inheritance + *ǫl* **ALE**, banquet.]
A funeral feast, a wake.

arvo /ˈɑːvəʊ/ *noun*. *Austral. & NZ slang*. Pl. **-os**. **E20.**
[**ORIGIN** Repr. of voicing of consonants in *af-* of *afternoon* + **-O**.]
= **AFTERNOON**.

-ary /əri/ *suffix*[1].
[**ORIGIN** from Latin *-arius*, (fem.) *-aria*, (neut.) *-arium* connected with, or French *-aire*: see **-Y**[3].]
Forming adjectives, as ***arbitrary***, ***budgetary***, ***contrary***, ***primary***, etc., and nouns, as ***adversary***, ***dictionary***, ***fritillary***, ***January***, etc.

-ary /əri/ *suffix*[2].
[**ORIGIN** from Latin *-aris* **-AR**[1] 1 or French *-aire*: see **-Y**[3].]
Forming adjectives, as ***capillary***, ***military***, etc., and occas. nouns, as ***preliminary***.

Aryan /ˈɛːrɪən/ *noun & adjective*. Also **Arian**. **L15.**
[**ORIGIN** from Sanskrit *ārya* noble (applied earlier as a national name) + **-AN**; sense A.1 through Latin *Ariani* inhabitants of Ariana (see below).]
▸ **A** *noun*. †**1** A native or inhabitant of Ariana, the eastern part of ancient Iran. **L15–E17.**
2 A member of any of the peoples who spoke the parent language of the Indo-European (or esp. Indo-Iranian) family, or one of their descendants. *arch.* **M19.** ▸**b** (Esp. in Nazi Germany) a Caucasian not of Jewish descent. **M20.**
3 The parent language of the Indo-European (or esp. Indo-Iranian) family. **L19.**
▸ **B** *adjective*. **1** Designating or pertaining to the parent language of the Indo-European (or esp. Indo-Iranian) family; *arch.* belonging to the Indo-European (or esp. Indo-Iranian) language family. **M19.**
2 Aryan-speaking; of or pertaining to the Aryan-speaking peoples or their descendants. **M19.** ▸**b** (Esp. in Nazi Germany) of or pertaining to the 'Aryan race'; non-Jewish Caucasian. **M20.**
– **NOTE**: The idea of an 'Aryan race' corresponding to the parent Aryan language was proposed by several 19th-cent. writers. Although the existence of any such race had been generally rejected, the idea was revived by Hitler for political purposes, and became part of the anti-Semitic doctrine of the Nazis.
■ **Aryanism** *noun* belief in an 'Aryan race' and esp. in the theory of its racial and cultural superiority **L19**. **Aryaniˈzation** *noun* the act of Aryanizing, the fact of being Aryanized **L19**. **Aryanize** *verb trans.* make Aryan; *esp.* (in Nazi Germany) bring within 'Aryan' control or status: **M19**.

aryballos /arɪˈbaləs/ *noun*. Pl. **-lloi** /-lɔɪ/. **M19.**
[**ORIGIN** Greek *aruballos* bag, purse, oil flask.]
GREEK ANTIQUITIES. A globular flask with a narrow neck used to hold oil or unguent.

aryl /ˈarʌɪl, -rɪl/ *noun*. **E20.**
[**ORIGIN** from **AR**(**OMATIC** *adjective* + **-YL**.]
CHEMISTRY. Any radical derived from an aromatic hydrocarbon by removal of a hydrogen atom. Usu. in *comb.*

arytenoid /arɪˈtiːnɔɪd/ *adjective & noun*. Also †**-taen-**. **E18.**
[**ORIGIN** mod. Latin *arytaenoides* from Greek *arutainoeidēs*, from *arutaina* funnel: see **-OID**.]
ANATOMY. ▸ **A** *adjective*. Designating, pertaining to, or associated with either of two pyramidal cartilages situated at the back of the larynx and articulating with the cricoid. **E18.**
▸ **B** *noun*. Either of these cartilages. **M19.**
■ **aryteˈnoidal** *adjective* (*rare*) = **ARYTENOID** **L17**.

AS *abbreviation*.
1 Also **A/S**. Advanced supplementary (in ***AS level***, of the General Certificate of Education examination).
2 Anglo-Saxon.

As *symbol*.
CHEMISTRY. Arsenic.

as /as/ *noun*. Pl. **asses** /ˈasɪz/. **M16.**
[**ORIGIN** Latin: see **ACE** *noun*.]
ROMAN ANTIQUITIES. A copper coin which was orig. of twelve ounces but was reduced in stages to half an ounce.

as /əz, *stressed* az/ *adverb, conjunction, & rel. pronoun*. Also **'s** /z/. **ME.**
[**ORIGIN** Reduced form of Old English *alswā* **ALSO**. Cf. Old Frisian *asa*, *as*(*e*), *is*.]
▸ **A** *adverb*. (In a main clause, introducing (with *as*, †*so*) an expressed or understood subord., esp. compar., clause)
†**1** Of manner or quality: in the (same) way that. **ME–L15.**
2 Of quantity or degree: in the same degree; to that extent (in or to which); (with ellipsis of rel. clause) equally. **ME.**

W. WOTTON He was as covetous as cruel. STEELE Chance has . . thrown me very often in her way, and she as often has directed a discourse to me. R. B. SHERIDAN I'd as lieve let it alone. LD MACAULAY He used it, as far as he dared.

(See also similes under B.1.)
▸ **B** *rel. adverb* or *conjunction*. (In a subord. clause.)
▸ **I** Of quantity or degree (preceded by an adjective or adverb).
1 With antecedent *as* or *so* (see sense A.2): in which degree, to what extent; (*arch.*, in comparison with a hypothetical act or state) as if, as though; (in parenthetical clauses) though, however. **ME.**

SHAKES. *John* The day shall not be up so soon as I. S. RICHARDSON To think I should act so barbarously as I did. SOUTHEY As certain of success As he had made a league with victory. SIR W. SCOTT You have never so much as answered me. LONGFELLOW So long as you are innocent fear nothing. BEVERLEY CLEARY As much as he longed to stop . . , he would not let himself. M. BISHOP As tired as he was, he was too hyper to stretch out for some shut-eye.

as black as jet, ***as old as the hills***, ***as safe as houses***, ***as warm as toast***, etc.
2 Without antecedent *as* or *so* (giving emphasis or absoluteness to the attribute or qualification); *esp.* (in parenthetical clauses), though, however. **ME.**

MILTON Soon as they forth were come. G. CRABBE Fair as she is, I would my widow take. T. S. ELIOT Consider Phlebas, who was once handsome and tall as you. J. STALLWORTHY 'Here comes Sir George.' / Yes, here he comes, punctual as nine o'clock.

3 After a compar.: than. *obsolete* exc. *dial.* **LME.**

LD BERNERS They coude do no better . . as to make to their capitayne sir Eustace Damlreticourt. SIR W. SCOTT I rather like him as otherwise.

▸ **II** Of quality or manner (preceded by a verb).
4 With antecedent *so* (†*as*) or equiv. phr. with *such*, *same*, etc.: ▸**a** In the manner that. *arch.* **ME.** ▸**b** With the clauses transposed for emphasis: in what manner . . . (in that manner); in the way that. **LME.** ▸**c** Even as, just as; both . . . and; equally . . . and. *arch.* **E17.**

a AV *Gen.* 18:5 So doe, as thou hast said. OED The committee was not so constituted as he had expected. **b** DRYDEN As the Cold Congeals into a Lump the liquid Gold; So 'tis again dissolv'd by Summer's Heat. **c** W. HAMILTON As some philosophers have denied to vision all perception of extension . . so others have equally refused this perception to touch.

5 Without antecedent *so* etc., in subord. clause: ▸**a** In the way or manner that; to the same extent that; in proportion as; according as. **ME.** ▸**b** Introducing a supposition: as if, as though. *arch.* **ME.** ▸**c** Introducing a clause attesting a statement or adjuring someone: in such manner as befits the prayer, anticipation, belief, profession, etc., that. **LME.** ▸**d** In antithetical or parallel clauses: as on the other hand, even as, whereas, whilst. **E16.**

a AV *John* 15:12 That ye love one another, as I have loved you. G. BERKELEY Which, as they are pleasing or disagreeable, excite the passions of love, hatred, etc. J. CONRAD She turned right round as a marionette would turn. R. DAVIES Boy died as he lived: self-determined and daring. S. MENASHE As streams spread Through a delta Veins on the instep Reach the toes. **b** COLERIDGE He looks as he had seen a ghost. **c** SHAKES. *Rich. II* This swears he, as he is a prince, is just; And as I am a gentleman I credit him. LD MACAULAY Admonished to speak with reverence of their oppressor . . as they would answer it at their peril. **d** THACKERAY It has its prejudices to be sure, as which of us has not?

6 Without antecedent *so* etc., in phr. (part of subord. clause understood): ▸**a** In the same way as, as if, as it were; after the manner of; in the likeness of; like. **ME.** ▸**b** In the character, capacity, function, or role of. **E16.**

a SPENSER His angry steede did chide his foming bitt, As much disdayning to the curbe to yield. AV *Heb.* 12:7 God dealeth with you as with sonnes. BYRON I . . Behold the tall pines dwindled as to shrubs. KEATS To sit upon an Alp as on a throne. TENNYSON His . . hand Caught at the hilt, as to abolish him. W. OWEN What passing-bells for these who die as cattle. H. CORBY Think of them. You did not die as these / caged in an aircraft that did not return. **b** SIR W. SCOTT He as truth received What of his birth the crowd believed. J. RUSKIN The lesson which men receive as individuals, they do not learn as nations. D. H. LAWRENCE When Van Gogh paints sunflowers, he reveals, or achieves, the vivid relationship between himself, as man, and the sunflower, as sunflower, at that quick moment of time. *Times*: *Toad of Toad Hall*, with Mr. Leo McKern as the irrepressible Toad. DAY LEWIS I feel more at home as a guest than as a host. E. BURROWS I come to tell you that my son is dead./ Americans have shot him as a spy.

b ***appear as***, ***rank as***, etc.; ***view as***, ***regard as***, ***represent as***, ***treat as***, ***acknowledge as***, ***know as***, ***consider as***, ***accept as***, etc.
7 Modifying the whole main clause or some part other than its predicate: in accordance with what (is); in the way that. **ME.**

ADDISON This project, as I have since heard, is postponed 'till the Summer Season.

▸ **III** Of time or place.
8 At or during the time that; when, while; whenever. **ME.**

OED The thought occurred to me as I was watching the procession. STEVIE SMITH As I write this / I can hear Arthur roaming overhead. A. MCCOWEN As a small boy I was somewhat tormented by God and Jesus.

9 At the place that, in which, where. *obsolete* exc. as passing into sense 8. **ME.**
▸ **IV** Of reason.
10 In conformity with, in consideration of, the fact that; it being the case that; since. **ME.**

J. MOXON The whole Work will be spoiled, as being smaller than the proposed Diameter. M. DRABBLE She found everything easy, as her memory for facts was remarkable.

▸ **V** Of result or purpose.
11 Without antecedent *so* or with *so* conjoined with *as* in the subord. clause: with the result or purpose that. Foll. by inf. (†finite verb). **ME.**

C. MARLOWE The bright shining of whose glorious acts Lightens the world with his reflecting beams, As . . it grieves my soul I never saw the man. HOBBES He miscarried by unskilfulness so as the loss can no way be ascribed to cowardice. OED Put on your gloves, so as to be ready.

12 With antecedent *so*, †*such*, †*that*, in the main clause: (in such a manner, to such a degree, of such a kind, etc.) that. Foll. by inf. (†finite verb). **LME.**

R. HAKLUYT This so amazed our men . . as they forsooke their Commanders. MILTON I gained a son, And such a son as all men hailed me happy. ADDISON I am not so vain as to think.

▸ **VI** Introducing an attrib. or subord. clause or phr.: passing into *rel. pronoun*.
13 After *such*, *same*, etc.: that, who, which. Also (now *dial. & slang*) with *such* etc. omitted or replaced by *that*, *those*, etc. **ME.** ▸**b** In parenthetic affirmations: that; (referring to the whole statement) a thing or fact which. **M16.**

SHAKES. *Rom. & Jul.* That kind of fruit As maids call medlars. STEELE Such a passion as I have had is never well cured. CARLYLE Never shall we again hear such speech as that was. **b** M. EDGEWORTH He was an Englishman, as they perceived by his accent. LYTTON Crouch! wild beast as thou art!

14 Like and including, such as, for instance. **ME.**

ADDISON I pluck'd aboue Five different Sorts . . as Wild-Time, Lauender, etc. J. P. DONLEAVY 'Yes. And what do you feel now?' 'The good things.' 'As?' 'Joy. Relief.'

15 Added to demonstr. and interrog. adverbs to give conjunctive force. *obsolete* exc. in ***when as*** (arch.) and **WHEREAS** (where the local sense is lost). **ME.**
16 Introducing a subord. clause: that, whether, how. *obsolete* exc. *dial.* **L15.**

STEELE That the Fop . . should say, as he would rather have such-a-one without a Groat, than me with the Indies. H. B. STOWE I don't know as you'll like the appearance of our place.

▸ **VII** Used preceding prepositions and adverbs.
17 Restricting or specially defining the ref. of prepositions; sometimes almost pleonastic. **ME.**

AV *1 Cor.* 8:1 As touching things offered unto idols, we know. *Listener* There are strongly convergent tendencies as between industrial societies.

18 Restricting the force of adverbs Now *dial.* exc. in ***as yet*** below. **ME.**

LD BERNERS I vnderstode so as then.

– **PHRASES**: **as and when** to the extent and at the time that; *absol.* (*colloq.*) if and when, in due time. **as a rule** usually, more often than not. ***as best one can***, ***as best one may***: see **BEST** *adjective, noun, & adverb*. ***as far as***: see **FAR** *adverb*. **as for** with regard to. **as from** from, after, (in formal dating). **as good as** practically. **as how?** *arch.* how? **as if** as the case would be if (with clause containing an explicit or understood past subjunct. or an inf. expressing purpose or destination). **as is**, **as it is** in the existing state, things being what they are. ***as it stands***: see **STAND** *verb*. **as it were** to a certain extent, as if it were actually so. ***as long as***: see **LONG** *adverb*. **as much** that quantity etc.; the same; what practically amounts to that, so. **as of** (orig. *US*) = ***as from*** above. ***as of right***: see **RIGHT** *noun*[1]. ***as per***: see **PER** *preposition*. ***as regards***: see **REGARD** *verb*. ***as soon as***: see **SOON** *adverb*. **as such** as being what has been named. **as that** *arch.* (in such a manner, to such a degree, of such a kind) that. **as though** as if, as the case would be if. **as to** with respect to. **as usual** as is or was usually the case. **as was** in the previously existing state. ***as well*** (***as***): see **WELL** *adverb*. **as who** *arch.* as one would, like one who, as if one. **as yet** up to this or that time (though perhaps not at some later time). **as you were!** (an order, esp. *MILITARY*, to) return to a previous position.
– **COMB.**: **as-new** *adjective* not yet soiled or impaired by use, as good as new; **as-told-to** *adjective & noun* (a book, article, etc.) written with the help of a professional author.

as- /as, *unstressed* əs/ *prefix*[1] (not productive).
Assim. form of Latin **AD-** before *s*. In Old French, Latin *ass-* was reduced to *as-*, which appears in Middle English adoptions, but in later French, and hence in English, *ass-* was restored by Latinization, as ***assent***, ***assign***, etc.

as- /as, *unstressed* əs/ *prefix*[2] (not productive).
Var. of Old French **ES-** from Latin **EX-**[1]. Adoptions with *as-* were usu. altered back or aphetized, but sometimes retained, as ***assay***, ***astonish***.

ASA *abbreviation*.
1 Amateur Swimming Association.
2 American Standards Association.

asafoetida /asəˈfiːtɪdə, -ˈfɛt-/ *noun*. Also **assa-**, ***-fet-**. LME.
[ORIGIN medieval Latin, from *asa* (from Persian *āzā* mastic) + *foetida* (fem.), *-us* FETID *adjective*.]
An acrid gum resin with a strong smell like that of garlic, obtained from certain Asian plants of the umbelliferous genus *Ferula*, and used in condiments. Also, a plant yielding this.

asail /əˈseɪl/ *adverb & pred. adjective*. L19.
[ORIGIN from A-[2] + SAIL *verb*[1].]
Sailing.

asana /ˈasənə/ *noun*. E19.
[ORIGIN Sanskrit *āsana* (manner of) sitting, from *āste* to sit.]
Posture; *spec.* any of the postures adopted in the practice of hatha yoga.

Asante *noun* var. of ASHANTI.

asap *abbreviation*. Also **a.s.a.p.**
As soon as possible.

asarabacca /ˈasərəbakə/ *noun*. E16.
[ORIGIN Syncopated from Latin *asarum* (from Greek *asaron*) + *bacc(h)ar* (from Greek *bakk(h)ar* Lydian name for the same plant) or *bacc(h)aris* (from Greek *bakkaris*) unguent made from it.]
A plant of the birthwort family, *Asarum europaeum*.

ASAT /ˈeɪsat/ *abbreviation*. Also **Asat**.
Anti-satellite (weapon).

ASB *abbreviation*.
Alternative Service Book (of the Church of England).

asbestos /azˈbɛstɒs, as-; -təs/ *noun*. Orig. †**-ton**. Also †**-tus**; (*poet.*) **asbest**. OE.
[ORIGIN Old French *a(l)beston* from Latin from Greek *asbeston* (accus.), *-os* unquenchable (applied by Dioscurides to quicklime), from A-[10] + *sbestos* quenched.]
†**1** A mineral reputed to be unquenchable when set on fire. OE–M18.
2 Any of various fibrous silicate minerals which can be woven, *esp.* chrysotile and certain amphiboles; incombustible fabric or other material made from such minerals. E17.

fig.: K. AMIS Beauty . . is a dangerous thing, Whose touch will burn, but I'm asbestos, see?

blue asbestos: see BLUE *adjective*. ***serpentine asbestos***: see SERPENTINE *noun*.
†**3** An allegedly incombustible flax. E17–M18.
■ **asbestiform** *adjective* having the form or appearance of asbestos L18. **asbestine** *adjective* of, pertaining to, or resembling asbestos; incombustible: M17. **asbestosis** /-ˈstəʊsɪs/ *noun* lung disease caused by inhalation of asbestos particles E20.

ASBO *abbreviation*.
Antisocial behaviour order.

ASC *abbreviation*.
Army Service Corps.

ascariasis /askəˈrʌɪəsɪs/ *noun*. Pl. **-ases** /-əsiːz/. L19.
[ORIGIN from ASCARIS + -IASIS.]
MEDICINE. Disease due to infestation by the nematode *Ascaris lumbricoides*, esp. in the intestine.

ascaris /ˈaskərɪs/ *noun*. Pl. (in use long before sing.) **ascarides** /əˈskarɪdiːz/. LME.
[ORIGIN mod. Latin from Greek *askaris*, pl. *-ides*, intestinal worm.]
A parasitic nematode worm of the genus *Ascaris*; esp. *A. lumbricoides*, parasitic in humans.
■ Also **ascarid** *noun* [back-form. from pl. *ascarides*] L17.

ascend /əˈsɛnd/ *verb*. LME.
[ORIGIN Latin *ascendere*, from *ad* AS-[1] + *scandere* to climb.]
► **I** *verb intrans.* **1** Go up, come up; rise, soar; be raised. Occas. foll. by *up*. LME. ►**b** Of a planet, zodiacal sign, etc.: move towards the zenith, *esp.* come above the horizon; move northwards. LME.

AV *John* 6:62 What and if yee shall see the sonne of man ascend vp where hee was before? MILTON The noise Of riot ascends above their loftiest Towrs. L. DEIGHTON I don't know when you last ascended from your cellar. **b** W. CONGREVE I was born, Sir, when the Crab was ascending.

b ascending node ASTRONOMY the point at which the moon's or a planet's orbit crosses the ecliptic from south to north.
2 Slope or extend upwards; *poet.* rise by growth or construction, be reared. LME.

GOLDSMITH Far to the right, where Apennine ascends. G. B. SHAW On both sides of this passage steps ascend to a landing.

3 Of sound: rise in pitch, go up the scale. LME.
4 Proceed from inferior to superior; rise in quality, station, degree, etc. LME.

J. JORTIN A rash desire to ascend to a rank—for which God's providence has not designed us. J. MCCOSH We shall ascend . . beyond laws to a lawgiver.

5 Go back in time, or in order of genealogical succession. L16.
► **II** *verb trans.* **6** Go up, climb; climb to the summit of; move upstream along (a river etc.). LME.

GIBBON Their galleys ascended the river. C. DARWIN We ascend the lofty peaks of the Cordillera and we find an alpine species of bizcacha. B. MOORE Ascending and descending these winding turret stairs.

7 Get up on to, mount; *arch.* go up into. L16.

SHAKES. *Rom. & Jul.* Go, get thee to thy love, . . Ascend her chamber, hence and comfort her. E. O'NEILL He ascends the dais and places her on the table as on a bier.

ascend the throne become king or queen.
■ **ascendable** *adjective* (*rare*) M18.

ascendancy /əˈsɛnd(ə)nsi/ *noun*. Also **-ency**, (in sense 2) **A-**. E18.
[ORIGIN from ASCENDANT + -ANCY.]
1 Supremacy, paramount influence (*over*), dominant control; the state or quality of being in the ascendant. E18.
2 *spec.* (*hist.*) (Usu. with *the*.) The domination by the Anglo-Irish Protestant minority in Ireland esp. in the 18th and 19th cents.; the dominant class itself. Also more fully ***Protestant ascendancy***. L18.
■ **ascendance** *noun* = ASCENDANCY 1 M18.

ascendant /əˈsɛnd(ə)nt/ *adjective & noun*. Also (now *rare*) **-ent**. LME.
[ORIGIN Old French & mod. French from Latin *ascendent-* pres. ppl stem of *ascendere* ASCEND: see -ANT[1].]
► **A** *adjective*. **1** Of a planet etc.: rising towards the zenith; ASTROLOGY just rising above the eastern horizon. LME.
2 *gen.* Rising, ascending. M16.

BACON A double scale or ladder, ascendent and descendent. SOUTHEY Distended like a ball . . The body mounts ascendant.

3 Having ascendancy; predominant, superior. M17.

A. KNOX To quicken, exalt, and make ascendant all that is rational and noble in us. G. GROTE An ascendent position in public life.

► **B** *noun*. **1** ASTROLOGY. The point of the ecliptic or sign of the zodiac which at a given moment (esp. at a person's birth) is just rising above the eastern horizon. LME.
house of the ascendant the celestial house immediately below the eastern horizon. **lord of the ascendant** a planet within the house of the ascendant.
†**2** *gen.* A person who or thing which ascends or rises; a slope, a rise, a peak; a flight of steps. M16–E18.

T. NASHE Pryde can endure no Superiours, no equals, no ascendants. MILTON A Lordly Ascendant . . from Primate to Patriarch, and so to Pope.

3 = ASCENDANCY *noun* 1. Now only in ***in the ascendant***, supreme, dominating; *popularly* rising; (freq. with fig. reference to sense 1). L16.

MARVELL Having gained this Ascendent upon him. E. A. FREEMAN The star of Harold was fairly in the ascendant. C. S. FORESTER There was one ruling motive still in the ascendant and that was a passionate desire not to make himself conspicuous.

4 A person who precedes in genealogical order; an ancestor. E17.

JOYCE Traces of elephantiasis have been discovered among his ascendants.

ascendency *noun* var. of ASCENDANCY.

ascendent *adjective & noun* see ASCENDANT.

ascender /əˈsɛndə/ *noun*. E17.
[ORIGIN from ASCEND + -ER[1].]
1 A person who or thing which ascends. E17.
2 TYPOGRAPHY & PALAEOGRAPHY. An ascending letter; a part or stroke projecting above letters such as x. M19.

ascending /əˈsɛndɪŋ/ *adjective*. E17.
[ORIGIN from ASCEND *verb* + -ING[2].]
1 Rising, mounting, increasing; sloping upwards. E17.

DRYDEN Bak'd in the Sunshine of ascending Fields. POPE Dark o'er the fields th' ascending vapour flies. F. A. G. OUSELEY The diminished fifth . . should be prepared by a sixth, with an ascending bass. A. J. P. TAYLOR Three tasks in ascending order of difficulty.

ascending letter TYPOGRAPHY & PALAEOGRAPHY a letter with a part or stroke projecting above letters such as x.
2 a ANATOMY. Directed upwards; *spec.* (of a nerve etc.) passing up the spinal cord to the brain. E18. ►**b** BOTANY. Of a stem etc.: inclined upwards, esp. with steepness increasing from the base. M19.
3 Going backwards in genealogical order. E18.

BURKE The ascending collateral branch was much regarded amongst the ancient Germans.

ascension /əˈsɛnʃ(ə)n/ *noun*. In sense 1 also **A-**. ME.
[ORIGIN Old French & mod. French from Latin *ascensio(n-)*, from *ascens-* pa. ppl stem of *ascendere* ASCEND: see -ION.]
1 The ascent of Christ to heaven on the fortieth day after the Resurrection. Also, Ascension Day. ME.
2 ASTRONOMY & ASTROLOGY. The rising of a celestial object; a measure of this. Usu. in special collocations (see below). LME.
oblique ascension (of a star, etc.) the arc intercepted between the first point of Aries and the point of the celestial equator which rises with the star in an oblique sphere. **right ascension** angular distance measured (in hours, minutes, seconds) eastwards along the celestial equator from the first point of Aries.
3 *gen.* The act or process of ascending; ascent, rise; *arch.* a path for ascending. LME.

SOUTHEY Round and round The spiral steps in long ascension wound. C. MACKENZIE We stayed on deck until the funicular had made its last golden ascension and descension. H. F. PRINGLE The ascension to power of Woodrow Wilson. G. SARTON Gigantic mountains, the ascension of which may tax our strength to the limit.

†**4** Distillation, evaporation. LME–E19.
†**5** A going back in genealogical succession; reversion to an ancestor. L16–E17.
– COMB.: **Ascension Day** the day of Christ's Ascension; the Thursday on which this is commemorated; **Ascensiontide** the ten-day period between Ascension Day and the eve of Pentecost.
■ **ascensional** *adjective* of or pertaining to ascension or ascent; tending upwards; ***ascensional difference*** (Astron.), the difference between the right ascension and oblique ascension of a celestial object: L16.

ascensive /əˈsɛnsɪv/ *adjective*. Now *rare*. E17.
[ORIGIN medieval Latin *ascensivus*, from Latin *ascens-*: see ASCENSION, -IVE.]
Characterized by or producing upward movement, rising; progressive, intensive.

ascent /əˈsɛnt/ *noun*. L16.
[ORIGIN from ASCEND *verb* after *descend*, *descent*.]
1 The action or an act of ascending; upward movement, rise (*lit. & fig.*). L16. ►**b** *spec.* The action or an act of climbing or travelling up a mountain, slope, stair, etc. E17.

GIBBON His ascent to one of the most eminent dignities of the republic. J. SIMMONS Stretches of relatively level line to assist the locomotive on the ascent. *Encycl. Brit.* Many manned ascents were made with both hot-air and hydrogen balloons. **b** B. ENGLAND Compared to previous climbs, it was a simple ascent, and in less than two hours they were on the peak.

Song of Ascents: see SONG *noun*[1].
†**2** An eminence, a hill. L16–M18.
3 A means of ascending; a way leading upwards; a way up; an upward slope. E17.

HOR. WALPOLE The ascent of steps from the hall. M. INNES Hudspith puffed as the ascent grew steeper.

4 A going back in time or genealogical order. E17.
■ Earlier †**ascence** *noun* LME–L16.

ascertain /asəˈteɪn/ *verb trans*. LME.
[ORIGIN Old French *acertain-* tonic stem of *acertener* (later *ass-*, *asc-*), formed as A-[5] + CERTAIN.]
†**1** Assure, convince; inform, tell; *refl.* acquire information. LME–L18.

CHARLES CHURCHILL Who may perhaps . . Be ascertained that Two and Two make four. G. MORRIS I wish to be ascertained of the . . intentions of the Court.

†**2** Make certain; prove, demonstrate; ensure, guarantee. L15–L19.

G. HORNE But who shall exactly ascertain to us what superstition is? BOSWELL [This] would ascertain it not to be the production of Johnson. W. GODWIN The intelligence that was brought me by no means ascertained the greatness of the danger. SIR W. SCOTT The squire's influence . . ascertained him the support of the whole class of bucks.

†**3** Fix, determine, limit. L15–L18. ►**b** Destine, doom, (a person) *to*. Only in M17.

SHAFTESBURY To suppress by violence the natural Passion of Enthusiasm or to endeavour to ascertain it. J. STEPHEN Such charters ascertained what were the customs by which the citizens were to be governed.

4 Find out or learn for a certainty; make sure of, get to know. L16.

W. C. WILLIAMS He went to great trouble to ascertain the depth of the water. T. CAPOTE The door was partly open; she opened it . . enough to ascertain that the office was filled only with shadow. C. JACKSON Whether he had ascertained if she was old or young.

■ **ascertainable** *adjective* able to be ascertained L18. **ascertainably** *adverb* in an ascertainable manner; recognizably: M19. **ascertainment** *noun* †(**a**) fixing, settlement; assurance; (**b**) finding out; determination, discovery: M17.

ascesis /əˈsiːsɪs/ *noun*. L19.
[ORIGIN Greek *askēsis* exercise, training, from *askein* to exercise.]
The practice of self-discipline.

ascetic /əˈsɛtɪk/ *adjective & noun*. M17.
[ORIGIN medieval Latin *asceticus* or Greek *askētikos* from *askētēs* monk, hermit, from *askein* to exercise: see -IC.]
► **A** *adjective*. **1** Practising severe abstinence or austerity, esp. for religious or spiritual reasons; characteristic of or suggesting a person dedicated to such existence. M17.

SIR T. BROWNE The old Ascetick christians found a paradise in a desert. R. RENDELL He wore a perfectly plain, almost ascetic dark suit. W. TREVOR His face seeming ascetic until cheered by a smile.

2 = ASCETICAL *adjective* (a) (which is more usual in this sense). E19.
► **B** *noun*. **1** A person who practises extreme self-denial or austerity; *esp.* one of those in the early Church who retired into solitude for this purpose. M17.

ARNOLD BENNETT They discovered the ascetic's joy in robbing themselves of sleep and in catching chills. R. P. JHABVALA He . . was dressed in nothing but an orange robe like an Indian ascetic.

†**2** *sing.* & (usu.) in *pl.* An ascetical treatise. E–M18.

■ **ascetical** *adjective* (*a*) of or pertaining to spiritual exercises intended to lead to perfection and virtue; (*b*) = ASCETIC *adjective* 1 (which is more usual in this sense): E17. **ascetically** *adverb* M19. **asceticism** /-sɪz(ə)m/ *noun* the principles or practice of ascetics; rigorous self-discipline, austerity: M17. **ascetism** *noun* = ASCETICISM M19.

asci *noun* pl. of ASCUS.

ascidian /əˈsɪdɪən/ *noun & adjective*. M19.
[ORIGIN from mod. Latin *Ascidia* pl. (genus name), from Greek *askidion* dim. of *askos* wineskin: see -AN.]
ZOOLOGY. ▶**A** *noun.* Any tunicate belonging to the class Ascidiacea; a sea squirt. M19.
▶ **B** *adjective.* Of or pertaining to this class. M19.

ascidiform /əˈsɪdɪfɔːm/ *adjective.* M19.
[ORIGIN from mod. Latin *ascidium* from Greek *askidion* (see ASCIDIAN) + -I- + -FORM.]
Chiefly *BOTANY.* Shaped like a pitcher or bottle.

ASCII /ˈaski/ *abbreviation.*
American Standard Code for Information Interchange.

ascites /əˈsʌɪtiːz/ *noun.* Pl. same. LME.
[ORIGIN Late Latin from Greek *askitēs* dropsy, from *askos* wineskin.]
MEDICINE. Abnormal accumulation of fluid in the abdomen.
■ **ascitic** /əˈsɪtɪk/ *adjective* of, pertaining to, or affected with ascites L17. **ascitical** *adjective* (now *rare*) = ASCITIC L17.

ascititious *adjective* see ADSCITITIOUS.

asclent *adverb, pred. adjective, & preposition* var. of ASKLENT.

Asclepiad /əˈskliːpɪad/ *noun*[1]. E17.
[ORIGIN from late Latin *asclepiadeus* adjective from Greek *asklēpiadeios*, from *Asklēpiadēs* Greek poet of the 3rd cent. BC, who invented the form.]
CLASSICAL PROSODY. A measure consisting of a spondee, two (or three) choriambi, and an iambus.
■ **Asclepiaˈdean** *adjective* E18.

asclepiad /əˈskliːpɪad/ *noun*[2]. M19.
[ORIGIN from ASCLEPIAS + -AD[1].]
BOTANY. Any plant of the milkweed family Asclepiadaceae.
■ **asclepiaˈdaceous** *adjective* of or pertaining to the family Asclepiadaceae M19.

asclepias /əˈskliːpɪəs/ *noun.* L16.
[ORIGIN Latin = swallowwort from Greek *asklēpias*, from *Asklēpios* AESCULAPIUS.]
Any of various plants now or formerly included in the genus *Asclepias*, of the milkweed family; *esp.* swallowwort, *Vincetoxicum hirundinaria*.

asco- /ˈaskəʊ/ *combining form* of ASCUS: see -O-.
■ **ascocarp** *noun* a fruiting body of an ascomycete, containing a number of asci L19. **aˈscogenous** *adjective* producing asci L19. **ascoˈgonium** *noun*, pl. **-ia** /-ɪə/, a female reproductive organ of an ascomycete L19. **ascospore** *noun* a spore produced in an ascus L19.

ascomycete /ˌaskəˈmʌɪsiːt/ *noun.* Orig. only in pl. **-mycetes** /-ˈmʌɪsiːts, -mʌɪˈsiːtiːz/. M19.
[ORIGIN Anglicized sing. of mod. Latin *Ascomycetes* (see below), from ASCO- + Greek *mukētes* pl. of *mukēs* fungus.]
MYCOLOGY. A fungus of the subdivision Ascomycotina (formerly the class Ascomycetes), bearing asci.
■ **ascomyˈcetous** *adjective* M19.

ascon /ˈaskɒn/ *noun.* L19.
[ORIGIN mod. Latin genus name, from Greek *askos* bag, sac.]
ZOOLOGY. A grade of sponge structure of the asconoid type; a stage in sponge development characterized by this structure; a sponge of this type or stage. Cf. LEUCON, SYCON.
■ **asconoid** *adjective & noun* (*a*) *adjective* of, pertaining to, or designating the simplest sponges, which have a tubelike or baglike structure lined with choanocytes; (*b*) *noun* a sponge of this type: M20.

ascorbic /əˈskɔːbɪk/ *adjective.* M20.
[ORIGIN from A-[10] + SCORB(UT)IC *adjective*.]
BIOCHEMISTRY. **ascorbic acid**, the antiscorbutic vitamin (chemically an enolic lactone, $C_6H_8O_6$), which is found in citrus fruits and green vegetables and is essential in maintaining healthy connective tissue; also called ***vitamin C***.

ascot /ˈaskət/ *noun.* Also **A-**. E20.
[ORIGIN *Ascot* in Berkshire, southern England, where race meetings are held.]
(In full ***ascot tie***) a man's broad silk necktie; a broad scarf looped under the chin.

ascribe /əˈskrʌɪb/ *verb trans.* Branch I orig. also †**-ive**. ME.
[ORIGIN Latin *ascribere*, from *ad* AS-[1] + *scribere* write; forms in *-v-* from Old French *ascriv-* stem of *ascrire* from Italian *ascrivere*.]
▶ **I 1** Assign or impute *to* someone or something as an action, effect, product, etc., or as a quality, characteristic, or property (rarely in a material sense). ME.

R. W. EMERSON There is a depth in those brief moments which constrains us to ascribe more reality to them than to all other experiences. J. N. LOCKYER The invention of clocks is variously ascribed to the sixth and ninth centuries. J. CONRAD I ascribed this behaviour to her shocked modesty. A. KOESTLER You ascribe to me an opinion which I do not hold. W. STYRON Most of the mischief ascribed to the military has been wrought with the advice and consent of civil authority.

†**2** Reckon up, count. LME–E17.

▶ †**II 3** Enrol, register. LME–L17.
4 Dedicate, inscribe, *to*. Only in M16.
5 Subjoin (one's name); subjoin one's name to. E–M17.
■ **ascribable** *adjective* able to be ascribed; attributable: M17.

ascription /əˈskrɪpʃ(ə)n/ *noun.* L16.
[ORIGIN Latin *ascriptio(n-)*, from *ascript-* pa. ppl stem of *ascribere*: see ASCRIBE, -ION.]
The act of ascribing; a statement etc. that ascribes; *spec.* a formula ascribing praise to God, used at the end of a sermon.
■ **ascriptive** *adjective* able to be ascribed; pertaining to ascription: M17.

ascrive *verb* see ASCRIBE.

ascus /ˈaskəs/ *noun.* Pl. **asci** /ˈaskʌɪ/. M19.
[ORIGIN mod. Latin from Greek *askos* bag, sac.]
MYCOLOGY. A sac, usu. cylindrical, in which a number of spores develop in ascomycetes.

Asdic /ˈazdɪk/ *noun.* Also **a-**, **ASDIC**. E20.
[ORIGIN from *ASD*, prob. repr. Anti-Submarine Division + -IC.]
An early form of sonar used to detect submarines.

-ase /eɪz/ *suffix.*
[ORIGIN from DIAST)ASE.]
Forming names of enzymes, as ***lactase***, ***maltase***, etc.

asea /əˈsiː/ *adverb & pred. adjective.* M19.
[ORIGIN from A-[2] + SEA *noun*.]
At sea, to the sea.

ASEAN /ˈasɪan/ *abbreviation.*
Association of South East Asian Nations.

aseismic /eɪˈsʌɪzmɪk/ *adjective.* L19.
[ORIGIN from A-[10] + SEISMIC *adjective*.]
1 Resistant to the effects of earthquakes. L19.
2 *GEOLOGY.* Free from earthquakes. E20.

aseity /eɪˈsiːɪti, ə-/ *noun.* L17.
[ORIGIN medieval Latin *aseitas*, from Latin *a* from + *se* oneself: see -ITY.]
METAPHYSICS. Underived or independent existence.

asepsis /eɪˈsɛpsɪs/ *noun.* L19.
[ORIGIN from A-[10] + SEPSIS.]
MEDICINE. The exclusion or absence of disease-causing micro-organisms in surgery etc.

aseptic /eɪˈsɛptɪk/ *adjective.* M19.
[ORIGIN from A-[10] + SEPTIC *adjective*.]
MEDICINE. Free from sepsis; pertaining to or promoting asepsis.
■ **aseptically** *adverb* E20. †**asepticism** *noun* L19–E20.

asexual /eɪˈsɛksʃʊəl/ *adjective.* M19.
[ORIGIN from A-[10] + SEXUAL.]
Chiefly *BIOLOGY.* Not sexual; without sex or sexuality; (of reproduction) not involving the fusion of gametes.
■ **asexuˈality** *noun* L19. **asexually** *adverb* M19.

ASH *abbreviation.*
Action on Smoking and Health.

ash /aʃ/ *noun*[1].
[ORIGIN Old English *æsc* = Old Saxon *ask* (Dutch *esch*), Old High German *ask* (German *Esche*), Old Norse *askr*, from Germanic.]
1 More fully ***ash tree***. A forest tree, *Fraxinus excelsior*, with grey bark, pinnate foliage, and hard, tough, pale wood. OE. ▸**b** Any of various related or otherwise similar trees; *esp.* any other tree of the genus *Fraxinus*. Usu. with specifying word. LME.
b ***black ash***, ***ground ash***, ***manna ash***, ***mountain ash***, ***red ash***, ***white ash***, etc.
2 More fully ***ash wood***. The wood of the ash. OE. ▸†**b** (The ashen shaft of) a spear. OE–E18.
3 The runic letter ᚨ; its romanized equivalent *æ* (see Æ, *Æ* 1). OE.
– COMB.: **ash key** the one-seeded winged fruit of the ash; **ash plant** an ash sapling used as a stick, whip, etc.; ***ash tree***: see sense 1 above; **ashweed** ground elder, *Aegopodium podagraria*, whose leaves resemble those of ash; ***ash wood***: see sense 2 above.
■ **ashling** *noun* an ash sapling M18.

ash /aʃ/ *noun*[2]. Freq. in pl. **ashes** /ˈaʃɪz/.
[ORIGIN Old English *æsce*, *æxe* = Middle Low German *asche*, Dutch *asch*, Old High German *asca* (German *Asche*), Old Norse *aska*: cf. Gothic *azgo*.]
1 In *pl.* & *collect. sing.* The powdery residue, composed chiefly of earthy or mineral particles, left after the combustion of any substance. (Sometimes as a symbol of grief or repentance.) OE. ▸**b** *sing.* A powdery residue (as above); *spec.* that left after the smoking of tobacco. LME.

E. WAUGH The fire, unattended . . , had sunk to a handful of warm ashes. B. JONES On watering-place islands / our fires of dead wood / sink rapidly to ash. *fig.*: J. A. FROUDE Where the ashes of the Sertorian rebellion were still smouldering. P. GALLICO The triumph suddenly developed the taste of ashes. **b** J. D. DANA Hircite . . after complete combustion leaves an ash.

ash of roses, **ashes of roses** a greyish-pink colour. ***dust and ashes***: see DUST *noun*. ***in sackcloth and ashes***. **lay in ashes** burn to the ground, destroy utterly. **rise from the ashes** be renewed after destruction. **turn to ashes (in a person's mouth)** become utterly disappointing or worthless. ***volcanic ash***: see VOLCANIC *adjective*.

2 Dust of the ground, esp. as symbolizing humanity's mortal nature. OE.
3 That which remains of a human body after cremation; *poet.* mortal remains. ME.

LD MACAULAY Facing fearful odds For the ashes of his fathers And the temples of his Gods.

the Ashes *CRICKET* the mythical trophy held by the winners of a series of test matches between England and Australia (orig. with ref. to the symbolical remains of English cricket, taken to Australia).

4 Powdery matter ejected from volcanoes. M17.
5 The colour of (esp. wood) ashes; pale grey; deathlike pallor. E19.

BYRON The lip of ashes, and the cheek of flame.

– COMB.: **ash-bin** a receptacle for ashes and household refuse, a rubbish bin; **ash blonde** *adjective & noun* (of hair) very fair; (a person) with very fair hair; **ashcan** (chiefly *US*) = ***ash-bin*** above; **ash-coloured** *adjective* of the colour of ashes, pale grey; **ash-hole** a hole beneath a fireplace or furnace into which the ashes fall; **ash pan** a tray, fitted beneath a grate, in which ashes are collected and removed; **ash-pit** = ***ash-hole*** above; **ashtray** a receptacle for tobacco ash; **Ash Wednesday** the first day of Lent (from the custom of sprinkling ashes on or otherwise applying ashes to the heads of penitents).
■ **ashery** *noun* a place for the manufacture of potash or pearl ash M19.

ash /aʃ/ *verb trans.* E16.
[ORIGIN from ASH *noun*[2].]
1 Sprinkle or cover with ashes; mark (a person) with ash as a sign of penitence. E16.
2 *CHEMISTRY.* Remove all combustible components from (a substance) by incineration, in analysis. L19.

ashake /əˈʃeɪk/ *adverb & pred. adjective.* M19.
[ORIGIN from A-[2] + SHAKE *noun* or *verb*.]
Shaking.

ashame /əˈʃeɪm/ *verb. arch.* exc. as next.
[ORIGIN Old English *āscamian*, formed as A-[1] + SHAME *verb*.]
†**1** *verb intrans.* Feel shame. OE–M16.
2 *verb trans.* Put to shame. (Cf. ASHAMED.) L15.

ashamed /əˈʃeɪmd/ *adjective* (usu. *pred.*).
[ORIGIN Old English *āscamod*: see ASHAME, -ED[1].]
Affected, embarrassed, or disconcerted, by shame. (Foll. by *of* or †*for*, †*on*, the cause of shame; *for* a person, on his or her account; *that*. See also ***ashamed to do*** below.)

AV *Jer.* 17:13 All that forsake thee shall be ashamed. M. W. MONTAGU I am ashamed for her who wrote them. STEELE I am ashamed to be caught in this Pickle. TENNYSON Ashamed am I that I should tell it thee. ARNOLD BENNETT Maggie . . felt as though she had done something wrong and was ashamed of it.

ashamed to do (*a*) prevented by shame from doing; (*b*) feeling shame when doing. **not ashamed to do** not prevented or deterred by shame from doing.
■ **ashamedly** /-mɪdli/ *adverb* E17. **ashamedness** /-md-, -mɪd-/ *noun* L16.

Ashanti /əˈʃanti/ *noun & adjective.* Also **Asante** /əˈsanti/. E18.
[ORIGIN Twi *Asante*.]
▶ **A** *noun.* **1** A member of one of the Akan peoples of Ghana. E18.
2 The dialect of Twi spoken by this people. L19.
▶ **B** *adjective.* Of or pertaining to this people or their dialect. M19.
■ Also **Ashantian** *adjective* E18.

ashen /ˈaʃ(ə)n/ *adjective*[1]. ME.
[ORIGIN from ASH *noun*[1] + -EN[4].]
1 Made of ash wood. *arch.* ME.
2 Of or pertaining to an ash tree. L15.

ashen /ˈaʃ(ə)n/ *adjective*[2]. LME.
[ORIGIN from ASH *noun*[2] + -EN[4].]
1 Ash-coloured, deathly pale. LME.
2 Of ashes. M19.

Asherah /əˈʃiːrɑː/ *noun.* Pl. **-rim** /-rɪm/. M19.
[ORIGIN Hebrew *ʾăšērāh*.]
(A tree trunk or wooden post symbolizing) an ancient goddess of Canaan.

ashet /ˈaʃɪt/ *noun.* Chiefly *Scot. & N. English.* M16.
[ORIGIN French ASSIETTE.]
A large plate or dish, esp. for meat.

ashimmer /əˈʃɪmə/ *adverb & pred. adjective.* L19.
[ORIGIN from A-[2] + SHIMMER *noun* or *verb*.]
Shimmering.

ashine /əˈʃʌɪn/ *adverb & pred. adjective.* M19.
[ORIGIN from A-[2] + SHINE *noun* or *verb*.]
Shining.

ashipboard /əˈʃɪpbɔːd/ *adverb & pred. adjective. arch.* M16.
[ORIGIN from A *preposition*[1] 1 + SHIPBOARD.]
On board ship.

ashiver /əˈʃɪvə/ *adverb & pred. adjective.* E19.
[ORIGIN from A-[2] + SHIVER *noun*[3] or *verb*[2].]
Shivering; shivery.

Ashkenazi /aʃkəˈnɑːzi/ *noun.* Pl. **-zim** /-zɪm/. M19.
[ORIGIN mod. Hebrew, from *Ashkenaz* a descendant of Japheth (*Genesis* 10:3).]
A Jew of middle, northern, or eastern Europe, or of such ancestry. Cf. SEPHARDI.
■ **Ashkenazic** *adjective* L19.

ashlar /ˈaʃlə/ *noun & verb*. Also **-ler**. ME.
[ORIGIN Old French *aisselier* from Latin AXILLA dim. of AXIS *noun*[1], *assis*, board, plank.]
▸ **A** *noun*. A square-hewn stone; masonry constructed of such stones laid in horizontal courses with vertical joints; similar masonry used as a facing to rubble or brick. ME.
▸ **B** *verb trans*. Face with ashlar. M19.
■ **ashlaring** *noun* (*a*) upright boarding fixed in attics from the joists to the rafters to cut off the acute angle of the roof and the floor; (*b*) ashlar masonry: E18.

ashore /əˈʃɔː/ *adverb & pred. adjective*. L16.
[ORIGIN from A *preposition*[1] 1 + SHORE *noun*[1].]
1 To the shore, to land. L16.
2 On shore, on land. M17.
Jack ashore: see JACK *noun*[1].

ashram /ˈaʃrəm/ *noun*. E20.
[ORIGIN Sanskrit *āśrama* hermitage.]
1 In the Indian subcontinent: a hermitage, a place of religious retreat. E20.
2 *transf*. Any group with shared spiritual or social aims living together. M20.

ashtanga /aʃˈtɑːŋə/ *noun*. L20.
[ORIGIN Hindi *aṣṭaṅ* or its source, Sanskrit *aṣṭaṅga* having eight parts, from *aṣṭán* eight.]
A type of yoga based on eight principles and consisting of a series of poses executed in swift succession, combined with deep, controlled breathing.

Ashura /ˈaʃʊərə/ *noun*. M19.
[ORIGIN from Arabic *ʿāšūrā* from Aramaic *ʿāśôrā*.]
The tenth of Muharram, celebrated as a holy day by Sunni Muslims and as a day of mourning (the anniversary of the death of Husain) by Shiite Muslims.

ashy /ˈaʃi/ *adjective*. LME.
[ORIGIN from ASH *noun*[2] + -Y[1].]
1 Covered or sprinkled with ashes. LME.
2 = ASHEN *adjective*[2] 1. LME.
> S. KING The ashy afterglow of dusk.

ashy-grey, ***ashy-pale***, etc.
3 Consisting of ashes. L15.

ASI *abbreviation*.
Airspeed indicator.

Asiago /asɪˈɑːɡəʊ/ *noun*. M20.
[ORIGIN A plateau and town in northern Italy, where the cheese was first made.]
A strong-flavoured cow's milk cheese, originally and chiefly made in northern Italy.

Asian /ˈeɪʃ(ə)n, -ʒ(ə)n/ *noun & adjective*. LME.
[ORIGIN Latin *Asianus* from Greek *Asianos*, from *Asia*: see below, -AN.]
▸ **A** *noun*. A native or inhabitant of the continent of Asia; a person of Asian descent. LME.
Kenyan Asian: see KENYAN *adjective*. ***Ugandan Asian***: see UGANDAN *adjective* 1.
▸ **B** *adjective*. Of or pertaining to Asia or its peoples or inhabitants; descended from Asians. E17.
Asian flu a kind of influenza whose virus was first identified at Hong Kong.
– NOTE: In Britain *Asian* is generally used of people who come from (or whose parents came from) the Indian subcontinent, while in North America it denotes people from China, Japan, Korea, etc.
■ **Asianic** /eɪʃɪˈanɪk, eɪʒɪ-/ *adjective* of or pertaining to Asia Minor L19. **Asianize** *verb trans*. make Asian in character etc.; transfer to Asian ownership or control: L19. **Asianness** /-n-n-/ *noun* the fact or quality of being Asian M20.

Asiarch /ˈeɪʃɪɑːk, ˈeɪʒ-/ *noun*. M18.
[ORIGIN Late Latin *asiarcha* from Greek *asiarkhēs*, from *Asia* Asia: see -ARCH.]
An official responsible for religious rites and public games in Asia Minor under Roman rule.

Asiatic /eɪʃɪˈatɪk, eɪʒ-/ *adjective & noun*. E17.
[ORIGIN Latin *Asiaticus* from Greek *Asiatikos*, from *Asia* Asia: see -IC.]
▸ **A** *adjective*. **1** = ASIAN *adjective*. Now usu. considered *offensive* when applied to persons. E17.
Asiatic CHOLERA.
2 Of literary style: florid and imaginative. *arch*. M18.
▸ **B** *noun*. = ASIAN *noun*. Now usu. considered *offensive*. E17.
■ **Asiatically** *adverb* in an Asiatic style or manner E19. **Asiaticism** /-sɪz(ə)m/ *noun* (*arch*.) (a) florid and imaginative expression or usage L18.

ASIC *abbreviation*.
ELECTRONICS. Application specific integrated circuit.

aside /əˈsʌɪd/ *adverb, preposition, & noun*. ME.
[ORIGIN from A *preposition*[1] 1 + SIDE *noun*.]
▸ **A** *adverb*. **1** To or at the side; out of the way, away. ME.
> V. S. NAIPAUL Ganesh stood between the women, but The Great Belcher moved him aside. T. STOPPARD He throws the paper aside and picks up the Guardian.

2 Sideways, obliquely, aslant; towards one side, away from the direct line. ME.
> CHAUCER With that he loked on me asyde, As who sayth nay, that wol not be. J. MCCRAE We have sworn and will not turn aside. K. AMIS Barbara turned the car aside on to an unmade track.

3 Away from the general throng or main body; in or into privacy; so as not to be generally heard (freq. as a stage direction: cf. sense C.1 below). LME.
> SCOTT FITZGERALD Sloane and the lady began an impassioned conversation aside. C. S. FORESTER 'Beggin' your pardon, sir,' said Hunter aside to Hornblower. G. GREENE He . . took my arm and led me a little aside.

4 Away from one's person or thought; out of use or consideration; off, down; excepted, apart. LME.
> SPENSER Her fillet she vndight, And laid her stole aside. E. O'NEILL No, all kiddin' aside, I know he'll run me down first second he sees you. A. WILSON He put aside prejudice. J. HELLER I've put aside my novel, you know.

aside from (chiefly *N. Amer.*) = APART ***from***.
5 Alongside, close by; by the side (*of*). *arch. & dial*. LME.
> SIR W. SCOTT From ancient vessels ranged aside.

▸ **B** *preposition*. †**1** Past, beyond. L16–L19.
2 At the side of, beside. *obsolete* exc. *dial*. E17.
▸ **C** *noun*. **1** Words spoken aside or in an undertone, esp. by an actor in the hearing of the audience but supposedly not of the other actors. E18.
> G. B. SHAW The action is not carried on by impossible soliloquys and asides. M. KEANE The laughing asides grew into a mild kind of persecution.

2 An incidental writing or remark of an author etc. L19.
> O. SACKS Other observations and asides . . have instead been placed in footnotes.

asile /əˈsʌɪl/ *noun*. *arch*. Also **-yle**. LME.
[ORIGIN Old French & mod. French from Latin ASYLUM.]
= ASYLUM *noun*.

asilus /əˈsʌɪləs/ *noun*. L17.
[ORIGIN Latin = gadfly.]
ENTOMOLOGY. A robber fly. Now only as mod. Latin genus name.
■ **asilid** /ˈasɪlɪd/ *adjective & noun* (*a*) *adjective* of or pertaining to the family Asilidae (robber flies); (*b*) *noun* a fly of this family: E20.

†**asinego** *noun*. Also **-igo**, **as(s)inico**. Pl. **-o(e)s**. E17–L19.
[ORIGIN Spanish *asnico* dim. of *asno* ASS *noun*[1].]
A little ass; *fig*. a dolt, a fool.

asinine /ˈasɪnʌɪn/ *adjective*. L15.
[ORIGIN Latin *asininus*, from *asinus* ASS *noun*[1]: see -INE[1].]
Of or pertaining to asses; asslike; stupid, obstinate.
■ **asininity** /asɪˈnɪnɪti/ *noun* M19.

ask /ɑːsk/ *noun*[1]. OE.
[ORIGIN from the verb.]
1 A request; a question. *rare*. OE.
2 The price at which an item, esp. a financial security, is offered for sale. *US*. L20.
3 With specifying word, as ***a big ask***: a difficult demand to fulfill, something which is a lot to ask of someone. *colloq*. (orig. *Austral*.). L20.
> *Bolton Evening News (online ed.)* If we get four wins we will make the play-offs, but it's a big ask.

ask /ask/ *noun*[2]. *Scot. & N. English*. ME.
[ORIGIN App. from Old English *āþexe*, cogn. with Old High German *egidehsa* (German *Eidechse* lizard).]
A newt; occas. (*Scot*.) a lizard.

ask /ɑːsk/ *verb*. Also (now *dial. & W. Indian*) **ax(e)** /aks/.
[ORIGIN Old English *āscian*, *ācsian*, *āhsian*, *āxian* = Old Frisian *āskia*, Old Saxon *ēscon*, Old High German *eiscōn*, from West Germanic.]
▸ †**I 1** *verb trans*. Call for, call upon to come. OE–ME.
▸ **II 2** *verb trans*. Call upon a person, or thing personified, for an answer or for information. As obj. the person, the thing desired (which may take the form of a noun or pronoun, a clause introduced by a rel. pronoun or conjunction, or direct or indirect speech), or both. (Foll. by †*at*, †*to*, or *of* the person; *about*, (arch.) *of* the matter in question; *after* the matter in question, esp. a person absent; *for* esp. a person whom one wishes to see.) OE.
> CAXTON Asking to her why she had trespaced his commaundments. COVERDALE *Ecclus* 21.17 It is axed at the mouth of the wyse. H. LATIMER The other axed ye price, he sayed: xx. nobles. SHAKES. *2 Hen. IV* Knocking at the taverns, And asking every one for Sir John Falstaff. AV *John* 9:19 They asked them, saying, Is this your son? POPE Ask your own heart; and nothing is so plain. GOLDSMITH Ask me no questions and I'll tell you no fibs. TENNYSON Once I ask'd him of his early life. DICKENS I . . asked him what o'clock it was. G. BORROW I asked her her maiden name. GEO. ELIOT Animals are such agreeable friends—they ask no questions, they pass no criticisms. OED A farmer of whom I asked the way. R. KIPLING 'Dost *thou* give news for love, or dost thou sell it?' Kim asked. E. W. ROGERS If you want to know the time, ask a P'liceman! G. STEIN Often Jeff would ask her, did she really love him. V. WOOLF Where was he this morning, for instance? Some committee, she never asked what. G. GREENE If Hitler had come into the conversation she would have interrupted to ask who he was. L. DURRELL It was the question that Nessim asked himself repeatedly. DAY LEWIS I seldom asked my father . . about our relations near or distant. K. LAFFAN Father Patrick asked me if I'd like to be a priest.

ask me another *colloq*. I do not know (the answer to your question). **I ask you** *colloq*.: expr. ridicule, contempt, denial, etc. **if you ask me** in my opinion.
3 *verb intrans*. Enquire, make enquiries. (Foll. by *about*, †*of* the thing desired; *after* a thing missing, a person absent, etc.; *for* esp. a person whom one wishes to see; †*at*, †*of* the person called upon.) OE.
> AV *1 Sam*. 28:16 Wherefore then doest thou aske of me? MILTON Ask for this great deliverer now, and find him Eyeless in Gaza. G. MACDONALD To ask after their health when he met them. T. FRISBY Here, you're not kinky or anything, are you? . . Why do you ask?

▸ **III 4** *verb trans*. Express to someone a desire to obtain a thing. As obj. the person, the thing desired (which may take the form of a noun or pronoun, a clause introduced by *that*, or an inf. phr.), or both. (Foll. by indirect obj. or †*at*, *of*, *from* the person, *for* the thing desired.) ME.
> EARL RIVERS I had delyte & axed to rede some good historye. SHAKES. *Com. Err*. He ask'd me for a thousand marks in gold. MILTON To stand upright Will ask thee thousand skill. HENRY FIELDING I ask Mr. Blifil pardon. R. BURNS I am ashamed to ask another favour of you. J. TYNDALL I asked him to accompany me. M. ARNOLD I ask but that my death may find The freedom to my life denied. G. B. SHAW Thirty crowns is too much to ask from him. T. FRISBY I say, could I ask you a favour? C. HAMPTON I'm sure she'd marry you like a shot if you asked her. A. AYCKBOURN They keep sending them . . . I've asked them not to.

ask a blessing: see BLESSING 1.
5 *verb intrans*. Express a desire to obtain something. (Foll. by †*after* or *for* the thing desired.) ME.
> COVERDALE *Matt*. 6:7 Axe & it shalbe giuen you. SOUTHEY Could hear a famish'd woman ask for food, And feel no pity. J. LE CARRÉ We always ask for a banker's reference before giving credit.

▸ **IV** Pregnant senses and special uses.
†**6** *verb trans. & intrans*. Inquire into, examine, investigate. OE–E17.
7 *verb trans. & intrans*. (foll. by *for*). Predicated of things: need, require; demand; call for. ME.
> SHAKES. *Tam. Shr*. Signior Baptista, my business asketh haste.

8 *verb trans. & intrans*. Call for as by right; demand. (Foll. by direct obj. or *for* the thing demanded; *from* or *of* the person or thing called upon). LME.
> W. FAULKNER Because they don't ask thirty-five cents for it. L. T. C. ROLT Once again he may have asked too much from the manufacturing resources of the day. G. F. FIENNES It would have to be an act of faith that the Pacifics would stand up to what we were going to ask of them, . . almost 500 miles a day. *New Zealand Herald* The unrealistic prices asked for by vendors.

9 *verb trans*. Proclaim in church, calling upon any who have claims or objections to put them forward. Now only in ***ask the banns***. LME.
10 †**a** *verb trans*. Provoke, bring upon oneself. L15–E17. ▸**b** *verb intrans*. Foll. by *for*: provoke, bring upon oneself, lay oneself open to, (trouble etc.). E20.
> **b** *Times* Mr — had behaved as badly as anyone could and a bystander might well have taken the view that he had asked for everything he got.

b ask for it *colloq*.: for trouble. ***ask for trouble***: see TROUBLE *noun*.
11 *verb trans*. Invite. Freq. foll. by adverb. M19.
> DICKENS If I see him . . tomorrow, perhaps I'll ask him down. R. CROMPTON But if he asks you to his you must ask him back. J. LE CARRÉ We'll ask Sam round and perhaps one or two of the old press boys from Berlin. J. BOWEN They asked me to tea at St. Peter's Hall.

ask out invite to accompany one to a restaurant, entertainment, etc.
■ **askingly** *adverb* (*rare*) †(*a*) as a question; (*b*) inquiringly, with entreaty: LME.

askance /əˈskans, əˈskɑːns/ *adverb*[1], *adjective, & verb*. L15.
[ORIGIN Unknown.]
▸ **A** *adverb & (usu. pred.) adjective*. Sideways, oblique(ly); with a side glance, asquint. Now chiefly *fig*., suspicious(ly), with disfavour; esp. in ***look askance (at)***. L15.
> J. BEATTIE They meet, they dart away, they wheel askance. R. L. STEVENSON Looking askance on each other as possible enemies. T. HARDY Down there they are dubious and askance. P. G. WODEHOUSE One looked askance at that habit of his of writing poetry. V. S. PRITCHETT The habit of seeing things askance or out of the corner of his eye.

▸ **B** *verb trans*. Turn (one's eye) aside. *rare*. L16.

†**askance** *conjunction & adverb*[2]. Also **askances**. LME–L16.
[ORIGIN Unknown: not rel. to ASKANCE *adverb*[1], *adjective, & verb*.]
As though, as if; *ellipt*. as much as to say.

askant /əˈskant/ *adverb & pred. adjective*. M17.
[ORIGIN from ASKANCE *adverb*[1], *adjective*, prob. after *aslant*, *asquint*.]
= ASKANCE *adverb*[1], *adjective*.

†**Askapart** *noun*. LME–M18.
[ORIGIN Ult. origin unknown.]
A hardy warrior of a fabled Arabian race.

askari /əˈskɑːri/ *noun*. Pl. **-s**, same. L19.
[ORIGIN Arabic *ʿaskarī* soldier.]
An E. African soldier or police officer.

asker /ˈɑːskə/ *noun*[1]. LME.
[ORIGIN from ASK *verb* + -ER[1].]
1 A person who asks a question; an inquirer. LME.
2 A suppliant, a beggar. LME.

asker /ˈɑːskə/ *noun*^{2}. *dial.* **L17.**
[ORIGIN from ASK *noun*^{2}.]
A newt.

askew /əˈskjuː/ *adverb* & (usu. *pred.*) *adjective*. **M16.**
[ORIGIN from A *preposition*^{1} 1 + SKEW *noun*^{3}.]
Oblique(ly), askance, to one side; awry, crooked(ly).

> SIR W. SCOTT The boy looking askew at him with his sharp gray eyes. L. DEIGHTON His hair was unkempt and his club tie was, as always, askew. B. CHATWIN An old yew-tree whose writhing roots have set the paving slabs askew.

look askew *fig.* (*arch.*) look disdainfully or as if pretending not to see.

asking /ˈɑːskɪŋ/ *noun*. **OE.**
[ORIGIN from ASK *verb* + -ING^{1}.]
▸ **I 1** The action of ASK *verb*. **OE.**
for the asking (available) upon the least request, merely to be asked for.
▸ **II 2** An inquiry, a question. Long *arch. rare*. **ME.**
3 A request, a supplication. *arch.* **ME.**
†**4** A demand; a claim; a price asked. **LME–M17.**
– COMB.: **asking price** the price set by the seller.

asklent /əˈsklɛnt/ *adverb, pred. adjective, & preposition*. *Scot.* Also **ascl-**. **L16.**
[ORIGIN Alt.]
= ASLANT.

ASL *abbreviation*.
American Sign Language.

†**aslake** *verb*.
[ORIGIN Old English *aslacian*: see A-^{1}, SLAKE *verb*^{1}.]
1 *verb intrans.* Become slack or feeble; grow less. **OE–L16.** ▸**b** Grow cool. Only in **E19.**
2 *verb trans.* Mitigate, assuage; reduce, abate. **ME–E19.**

aslant /əˈslɑːnt/ *adverb, pred. adjective, & preposition*. **ME.**
[ORIGIN from A *preposition*^{1} 1 + SLANT *noun*^{1}. See also ASKLENT.]
▸ **A** *adverb & pred. adjective*. On the slant, oblique(ly). **ME.**
▸ **B** *preposition*. Obliquely across; athwart. **E17.**
■ **aslantwise** *adverb* = ASLANT *adverb* **E19.**

asleep /əˈsliːp/ *adverb & pred. adjective*. **ME.**
[ORIGIN from A *preposition*^{1} 6 + SLEEP *noun*.]
1 In a state of sleep, sleeping. **ME.**

> G. GREENE I had told from the irregularity of her breathing that she was not asleep. DAY LEWIS An ass which was lying asleep in the middle of the road.

2 Into a state of sleep. Esp. in ***fall asleep***. **ME.**

> SHAKES. *Tit. A.* A nurse's song Of lullaby to bring her babe asleep. WILFRID GIBSON At last he cursed himself asleep.

3 *fig.* In or into a state of inactivity or quiescence; idle, dormant, inattentive. **ME.**

> SHAKES. *1 Hen. IV* And now their pride and mettle is asleep. ROBERT WATSON Their apprehensions were laid asleep. BYRON During this inquisition Julia's tongue Was not asleep.

asleep at the switch: see SWITCH *noun* 3.
4 *euphem.* Dead. **ME.**

> TINDALE *1 Cor.* 15:18 They which are fallen a slepe in Christ.

5 Of a limb etc.: benumbed by pressure. **LME.**
6 *NAUTICAL.* Of a sail: filled with wind just enough to prevent flapping. Now *rare* or *obsolete*. **M19.**

ASLIB *abbreviation*.
Association of Special Libraries and Information Bureaux.

aslope /əˈsləʊp/ *adverb & pred. adjective*. **LME.**
[ORIGIN Uncertain: earlier than SLOPE *noun*^{1}, *verb*^{1}.]
Inclined, sloping; crosswise, aslant.

ASM *abbreviation*.
1 Air-to-surface missile.
2 Assistant stage manager.

†**asma** *noun* var. of ASTHMA.

†**asmak** *noun* see YASHMAK.

asmoke /əˈsməʊk/ *adverb & pred. adjective*. **E19.**
[ORIGIN from A-^{2} + SMOKE *noun* or *verb*.]
Smoking.

Asmonean *noun & adjective* var. of HASMONEAN.

asoak /əˈsəʊk/ *adverb & pred. adjective*. **E17.**
[ORIGIN from A *preposition*^{1} 8 + SOAK *noun*^{1} or *verb*.]
Soaking.

asocial /eɪˈsəʊʃ(ə)l/ *adjective & noun*. **L19.**
[ORIGIN from A-^{10} + SOCIAL *adjective*.]
▸ **A** *adjective*. Not social; antisocial; inconsiderate or hostile to others. **L19.**
▸ **B** *noun*. An asocial person. *rare*. **M20.**

asomatous /əˈsəʊmətəs/ *adjective*. *rare*. **M18.**
[ORIGIN from late Latin *asomatus* from Greek *asōmatos*, from A-^{10} + *sōmat-*, *sōma* body, + -OUS.]
Disembodied, incorporeal.

ASP *abbreviation*.
Computing. Application service provider, a company providing Internet access to software applications.

asp /asp/ *noun*^{1}. *arch.* Also (long *dial.*) **aps** /aps/.
[ORIGIN Old English *æspe* (corresp. to Old High German *aspa*), *æps* (corresp. to Old Norse *ǫsp*), from Germanic.]
(The wood of) the aspen.

asp /asp/ *noun*^{2}. Orig. in Latin form †**aspis**, pl. †**aspides**, †**aspisses**. **ME.**
[ORIGIN Old French *aspe* or (its source) Latin *aspis*, *-id-* from Greek.]
1 The Egyptian cobra, *Naja haje*, found throughout Africa. Also, a southern European viper, *Vipera aspis*. **ME.**
2 *loosely & poet.* A poisonous snake. **E18.**

aspalathus /əˈspaləθəs/ *noun*. **E17.**
[ORIGIN Latin from Greek *aspalathos*.]
Orig., the Middle Eastern camel thorn, *Alhagi camelorum*, or a similar fragrant shrub. Now, an evergreen thorny leguminous shrub of the African genus *Aspalathus*.

asparagine /əˈsparədʒiːn/ *noun*. Also †**-in**. **E19.**
[ORIGIN from ASPARAGUS + -INE^{5}.]
BIOCHEMISTRY. A hydrophilic amino acid, $CONH_2{\cdot}CH_2CH(NH_2){\cdot}COOH$, which is an amide of aspartic acid and occurs in proteins and (free) in plant tissues.

asparagus /əˈsparəgəs/ *noun*. Orig. †**sp-**. Many popular vars.: see SPARAGE, SPARROW GRASS. **OE.**
[ORIGIN (medieval Latin *sparagus* from) Latin *asparagus* from Greek *asparagos*.]
A plant of the genus *Asparagus*, of the lily family, spec. *A. officinalis*; the young shoots of this plant, eaten as a delicacy.
– COMB.: **asparagus beetle** a small beetle of the genus *Crioceris*, which feeds on the foliage of asparagus; **asparagus fern** *Asparagus setaceus*, native to southern Africa, grown for its decorative fernlike foliage; **asparagus pea** a pea plant, *Tetragonolobus* (or *Lotus*) *purpurea*, which has edible cylindrical pods with four longitudinal wavy flanges; **asparagus stone** yellow-green apatite of gem quality.

asparkle /əˈspɑːk(ə)l/ *adverb & pred. adjective*. **M19.**
[ORIGIN from A-^{2} + SPARKLE *noun* or *verb*^{1}.]
Sparkling.

aspartame /əˈspɑːteɪm/ *noun*. **L20.**
[ORIGIN from ASPARTIC + *-ame* of unknown origin.]
A derivative of phenylalanine that contains the radical of aspartic acid and is used as a low-calorie artificial sweetener.

aspartic /əˈspɑːtɪk/ *adjective*. **M19.**
[ORIGIN French *aspartique*, formed arbitrarily on Latin ASPARAGUS: see -IC.]
BIOCHEMISTRY. ***aspartic acid***, an acidic amino acid, $COOH{\cdot}CH_2{\cdot}CH(NH_2){\cdot}COOH$, which occurs in proteins and esp. in sugar cane, and is important in nitrogen metabolism in animals.

aspect /ˈaspɛkt/ *noun*. **LME.**
[ORIGIN Latin *aspectus*, from *aspect-* pa. ppl stem of *aspicere* look at, from *ad* A-^{8} + *specere* to look.]
▸ **I** The action of looking.
†**1** The action of looking at something; beholding; view, gaze. **LME–E19.**

> BACON The tradition . . that the basilisk killeth by aspect. STEELE The downcast Eye, and the Recovery into a sudden full Aspect.

†**2** Mental looking; consideration, regard. **LME–L17.**

> J. DENHAM Those latter parts . . have not yet received your Majesties favourable Aspect.

3 A look, a glance. *arch.* **L16.**

> SHAKES. *Com. Err.* Some other mistress hath thy sweet aspects. *fig.*: O. W. HOLMES Meeting the cold aspect of Duty.

▸ **II** Way of looking, as to position or direction.
4 *ASTROLOGY.* The relative positions of the planets, etc., or the position of one with respect to the others, as they appear from the earth. **LME.**

> SHAKES. *Tr. & Cr.* The glorious planet Sol . . , whose med'cinable eye Corrects the ill aspects of planets evil. SWIFT He Mars could join To Venus in aspect malign.

5 The direction in which a thing has respect or practical bearing; bearing *upon*; reference *to*. *arch.* **E16.**

> O. CROMWELL Divers things . . which I hope have a public aspect.

6 The looking, facing, or fronting of something in a given direction; the side or surface which fronts or is turned towards a given direction. **M17.**

> MILTON The setting Sun . . with right aspect Against the eastern Gate of Paradise. JOYCE A thatched . . 2 storey dwellinghouse of southerly aspect.

in TRIAN aspect.
7 A point of view (chiefly *fig.*); any of the ways in which something may be looked at or considered. **M17.**

> T. F. DIBDIN Their rarity and intrinsic worth render them acceptable under any aspect. C. S. FORESTER Six months ago he had been inspecting similar arrangements from a regimental aspect.

8 Any of the ways in which something may present itself to the mind; a phase; a particular component or area of something complex. **L17.**

> K. MANSFIELD There are in life as many aspects as attitudes towards it. N. MITFORD We talked about nothing else, too, round and round the subject, every aspect of it. A. WILSON They enjoyed . . showing each other little-known aspects of London—an Italianate Methodist Chapel in Lewisham, a strange formal garden in Highbury. G. VIDAL The third aspect of the one god is Siva, the destroyer. D. HALBERSTAM Lawyers were getting ready to go through every aspect of Murrow's own past, in preparation for McCarthy's counterchallenge.

9 *GRAMMAR.* A group of forms of a verb, expressing inception, duration, completion, repetition, etc.; the quality of a verb by which it represents such features. **M19.**
▸ **III** Appearance.
10 The look a person wears; expression; countenance. **LME.**

> MILTON But soon his cleer aspect Returned. BYRON Ah! he unveils his aspect; on his brow The thunder-scars are graven. J. C. OATES If he did appear, his aspect was so greatly changed she could not recognize him.

11 The appearance presented by an object to the eye; look. **LME.** ▸**b** Any of a number of different lights that can be shown by a railway signal. **E20.**

> R. SUTCLIFF Later that evening the tumble-down shelter bore a much more cheerful aspect.

†**12** A sight. **E17–E18.**

> DEFOE That he saw such Aspects . . I never believ'd.

13 The appearance presented by circumstances etc. to the mind. **E18.**

> W. PENN Matters seem to look of a better aspect.

– COMB.: **aspect ratio** *gen.* a ratio of height or length to width; *spec.* (of an aerofoil or a bird's wing) orig. the ratio of the span to the mean chord, now usu. the ratio of the square of the span to the surface area.
■ **aspected** *adjective* having an aspect (usu. specified) **L16.** **aspectful** *adjective* (*rare*) having favourable aspect, benignant **E17.** **aˈspectual** *adjective* †(*a*) *rare* of or pertaining to a planetary aspect or planetary aspects; (*b*) of or pertaining to grammatical aspect: **L15.**

aspect /əˈspɛkt, ˈaspɛkt/ *verb*. **LME.**
[ORIGIN Latin *aspectare* frequentative of *aspicere*: see ASPECT *noun*.]
1 *verb trans.* *ASTROLOGY.* Of a planet: look upon and exert influence upon (another). Usu. in *pass.* **LME.**
†**2** *verb trans.* Look with favour upon. **L16–M17.**
†**3** *verb trans.* Look at, face; survey, watch. **L16–L17.**
†**4** *verb intrans.* Look; have an aspect or bearing. Only in **M17.**
■ †**aspectable** *adjective* (*a*) able to be seen, visible; (*b*) fit to be beheld, attractive to the eye: **E17–M19.**

aspen /ˈasp(ə)n/ *adjective & noun*. **LME.**
[ORIGIN from ASP *noun*^{1} + -EN^{4}.]
▸ **A** *adjective*. **1** (Now taken to be the noun used *attrib.*) Of or pertaining to the aspen. **LME.**
2 *fig.* Tremulous; timorous. **LME.**

> G. CHAPMAN Possess'd with aspen fear.

▸ **B** *noun*. (The wood of) a European poplar, *Populus tremula*, noted for its tremulous leaves, or any of a number of similar poplars, esp. the N. American *P. tremuloides* (in full ***quaking aspen***). **L16.**

asper /ˈaspə/ *noun*^{1}. *obsolete* exc. *hist.* Also **aspre**. **LME.**
[ORIGIN French *aspre* app. from Turkish from medieval Greek *aspron* from Latin *asper* (*nummus*) newly minted (coin).]
A small silver Byzantine and Ottoman coin; later, as a monetary unit, 1/120 piastre.

asper /ˈaspə/ *noun*^{2}. **L19.**
[ORIGIN Latin (sc. *spiritus* breath): see ASPER *adjective*.]
GREEK GRAMMAR. The sign (ʽ) of rough breathing.

†**asper** *adjective*. Long *dial.* Also **aspre**. **LME–L19.**
[ORIGIN Old French *aspre* (mod. *âpre*) from Latin *asper* rough, harsh.]
Rough; harsh, bitter; severe, stern; fierce.

asperate /ˈaspəreɪt/ *verb trans.* Now *rare*. Pa. pple & ppl adjective **-ate** /-ət/, **-ated**. **L16.**
[ORIGIN Latin *asperat-* pa. ppl stem of *asperare*, from *asper*: see ASPER *adjective*, -ATE^{3}.]
Make rough or harsh.

asperge /əˈspɑːdʒ/ *verb trans.* **E16.**
[ORIGIN French *asperger* or Latin *aspergere*, from *ad* AS-^{1} + *spargere* sprinkle.]
Sprinkle, besprinkle.

Asperger's syndrome /ˈaspɑːdʒəz ˌsɪndrəʊm/ *noun phr.* **L20.**
[ORIGIN from Hans *Asperger* (1906–80), Austrian psychiatrist.]
PSYCHIATRY. A rare and relatively mild autistic disorder which develops in early childhood and persists in adult life, characterized by awkwardness in social interaction, pedantry in speech, and preoccupation with very narrow interests although intellectual development is normal.

asperges /əˈspɑːdʒiːz/ *noun*. **L16.**
[ORIGIN First word (= thou shalt purge) of Latin text of *Psalms* 50(51):7, recited during the sprinkling of holy water before mass.]
ROMAN CATHOLIC CHURCH. The sprinkling of holy water before mass. Also = ASPERGILLUM.

A

aspergill /ˈaspədʒɪl/ *noun*. M19.
[ORIGIN Anglicized from ASPERGILLUM.]
= ASPERGILLUM.

aspergilla *noun pl.* see ASPERGILLUM.

aspergillosis /aspədʒɪˈləʊsɪs/ *noun*. Pl. **-lloses** /-ˈləʊsiːz/. L19.
[ORIGIN from mod. Latin *Aspergillus* (see below), from ASPERGILLUM, + -OSIS.]
MEDICINE. Infection, esp. of the lungs, with a fungus of the genus *Aspergillus*.

aspergillum /aspəˈdʒɪləm/ *noun*. Pl. **-lla** /-lə/, **-llums**. M17.
[ORIGIN mod. Latin, from *aspergere* (see ASPERGE) + *-illum* dim. suffix.]
A kind of brush or other implement for sprinkling holy water.

asperity /əˈspɛrɪti/ *noun*. ME.
[ORIGIN Old French & mod. French *asperité* or Latin *asperitas*, from *asper* rough, harsh: see -ITY.]
1 Hardship; rigour, severity. *arch.* ME.

HENRY MORE To.. minysh the vygour and asperite of the paynes. S. JOHNSON The nakedness and asperity of the wintry world.

2 Harshness to any of the senses; roughness, ruggedness; hardness. *arch.* LME. ▸**b** A rough excrescence. *arch.* M17.

CAXTON Fewe people wente for to see him, for the grete asprete or sharpnesse of the place. G. BERKELEY The asperity of tartarous salts. S. JOHNSON Our language, of which the chief defect is ruggedness and asperity. **b** J. LINDLEY Almost all Delimaceæ have the leaves covered with asperities.

3 Harshness or sharpness of temper, esp. as displayed in tone or manner; bitterness, acrimony; in *pl.*, embittered feelings. M17.

DICKENS Demanded with much asperity what she meant. H. WILSON Intervening also to soften asperities and curb the invocation of personalities.

aspermia /eɪˈspəːmɪə, ə-/ *noun*. M19.
[ORIGIN from A-[10] + Greek *sperma* seed + -IA[1].]
MEDICINE. Failure to produce semen, or absence of sperms from the semen. Cf. AZOOSPERMIA.
■ **aspermic** *adjective* pertaining to or characterized by aspermia E20.

asperous /ˈasp(ə)rəs/ *adjective*. Now *rare*. M16.
[ORIGIN from late Latin *asperosus*, from Latin *asper* rough, harsh: see -OUS.]
1 Rough, rugged. M16.
2 Harsh, bitter. M16.

asperse /əˈspəːs/ *verb trans.* L15.
[ORIGIN Latin *aspers-* pa. ppl stem of *aspergere* ASPERGE.]
1 Besprinkle, bespatter, (a person or thing, *with*). *arch.* L15.

H. L'ESTRANGE The child is thrice to be aspersed with water on the face. M. BEERBOHM Rain! His very mantle was aspersed. In another minute he would stand sodden.

†**2** Sprinkle in as an ingredient; intermingle. M16–E17.

E. TOPSELL Making a plaister thereof with Barley meal and a little Brimstone aspersed.

3 Sprinkle, scatter, (liquid, dust, etc.). *arch.* E17.

SOUTHEY Blood, which hung on every hair, Aspersed like dew-drops.

4 Attack the reputation of (a person) *with* harmful allegations etc. E17.

JAS. MILL The criminations with which the leaders.. appeared desirous of aspersing one another.

5 Spread false and harmful charges against; calumniate; detract from. M17.

SIR W. SCOTT There were foul tongues to asperse a Douglas. L. A. G. STRONG No one is aspersing their honesty.

■ **asperser** *noun* a person who asperses someone, a calumniator E18. **aspersive** *adjective* (*rare*) defamatory M17.

aspersion /əˈspəːʃ(ə)n/ *noun*. LME.
[ORIGIN Latin *aspersio(n-)*, formed as ASPERSE: see -ION.]
▸**I 1** The action of sprinkling or scattering liquid, esp. in baptism. LME.

J. FOXE By the aspersion of the bloud of Jesus Christ.

†**2** The sprinkling in of an ingredient; admixture. E–M17.

BACON Divinity Morality and Policy, with great aspersion of all other artes.

3 Calumniation, defamation. M17.

W. COWPER Aspersion is the babbler's trade, To listen is to lend him aid.

▸**II 4** A calumny, a slander, a false insinuation. L16.
cast aspersions (*on*): see CAST *verb*.
5 A shower, a spray. *arch.* E17.

SHAKES. *Temp.* No sweet aspersion shall the heavens let fall To make this contract grow.

aspersorium /aspəˈsɔːrɪəm/ *noun*. Pl. **-ria** /-rɪə/. M19.
[ORIGIN medieval Latin, formed as ASPERSE: see -ORIUM.]
A vessel for holy water; an aspergillum.

■ **aspersoir** /əˈspəːswɑː/ *noun* [French] = ASPERSORIUM M19. **aspersory** /əˈspəːsəri/ *noun* = ASPERSORIUM L19.

asphalt /ˈasfalt, -əlt/ *noun & verb*. LME.
[ORIGIN (French *asphalte* ult. from) late Latin *asphalton*, *-um* from Greek *asphalton*, of alien origin.]
▸**A** *noun*. Also in Latin form **asphaltum** /asˈfaltəm/.
1 Black or brownish-black, solid or viscous, bituminous pitch, of natural occurrence or produced from petroleum. LME.
2 A mixture of this with sand etc. used for surfacing paths, roads, etc. M19.
▸**B** *verb trans.* Cover or lay (a road etc.) with asphalt. M19.
■ **asphalter** *noun* a person who lays down asphalt L19. **asˈphaltic** *adjective* of the nature of or containing asphalt M17. **asphaltite** *noun* any of the naturally occurring solid forms of asphalt L19.

asphaltene /ˈasfaltiːn, asˈfaltiːn/ *noun*. M19.
[ORIGIN from ASPHALT *noun* + -ENE.]
Any of the solid organic constituents of asphalt, petroleum, etc., which are soluble in carbon disulphide but not in paraffin oil.

asphaltum *noun* var. of ASPHALT *noun*.

aspheric /əsˈfɛrɪk, eɪ-/ *adjective*. E20.
[ORIGIN from A-[10] + SPHERIC *adjective*.]
OPTICS. Not spherical (although curved); (of a lens) having one or more aspheric surfaces.
■ **aspherical** *adjective* E20. **asphericity** /eɪsfɛˈrɪsɪti/ *noun* the state of being aspheric M20.

aspheterism /əsˈfɛtərɪz(ə)m/ *noun*. L18.
[ORIGIN from A-[10] + Greek *spheteros* one's own, after *spheterismos* appropriation: see -ISM.]
The doctrine that there ought to be no private property; communism.

asphodel /ˈasfədɛl/ *noun*. LME.
[ORIGIN from Latin *asphodilus*, *-delus* from Greek *asphodelos*. Cf. AFFODILL.]
1 a Any plant of the genera *Asphodelus* and *Asphodeline*, of the lily family, native to the Mediterranean region, the former with white flowers, the latter (more fully ***yellow asphodel***) with yellow flowers, esp. *Asphodeline lutea*. LME. ▸**b** An immortal flower, said to cover the Elysian fields. *poet.* M17.
2 (With specifying word.) Any of certain other plants of related genera. L16.
bog asphodel a yellow-flowered marsh plant of the genus *Narthecium*, esp. *N. ossifragum*. **false asphodel** *N. Amer.* = *Scotch asphodel* below (in the wider sense). **Scotch asphodel**, **Scottish asphodel** a white-flowered subalpine plant of the genus *Tofieldia*; esp. (in Britain) *T. pusilla*.

asphyxia /əsˈfɪksɪə/ *noun*. E18.
[ORIGIN mod. Latin from Greek *asphuxia*, from A-[10] + *sphuxis* pulsation: see -IA[1].]
MEDICINE. **1** Stoppage of the pulse. Only in Dicts. E18.
2 The condition of defective aeration of the blood caused by failure of the oxygen supply; suffocation. M19.
■ **asphyctic** *adjective* = ASPHYXIAL L19. **asphyxial** *adjective* of, pertaining to, or characterized by asphyxia M19. **asphyxiant** *adjective & noun* (a substance) causing asphyxia L19.

asphyxiate /əsˈfɪksɪeɪt/ *verb trans.* M19.
[ORIGIN from ASPHYXIA + -ATE[3].]
Affect with asphyxia, suffocate.
■ **asphyxiˈation** *noun* the action of asphyxiating; asphyxia: M19.

asphyxy /əsˈfɪksi/ *noun & verb*. Now *rare*. L18.
[ORIGIN French *asphyxie*: see ASPHYXIA, -Y[3].]
▸**A** *noun*. = ASPHYXIA 2. L18.
▸**B** *verb trans.* = ASPHYXIATE. M19.

aspic /ˈaspɪk/ *noun*[1]. Chiefly *poet.* M16.
[ORIGIN Old French & mod. French, var. of Old French *aspide* ASP *noun*[2], prob. infl. by *piquer* to sting.]
= ASP *noun*[2].

aspic /ˈaspɪk/ *noun*[2]. E17.
[ORIGIN French from Provençal *aspic*, *espic* from medieval Latin (*lavandula*) *spica*: see SPIKE *noun*[1].]
Lavender.

aspic /ˈaspɪk/ *noun*[3]. L18.
[ORIGIN French, use of *aspic* asp, ASPIC *noun*[1], the various colours of the jelly being prob. compared to those of the snake.]
A savoury meat jelly used as a garnish or to contain game, eggs, etc.

†**aspides** *noun pl.* see ASP *noun*[2].

aspidistra /aspɪˈdɪstrə/ *noun*. E19.
[ORIGIN mod. Latin, from Greek *aspid-*, *aspis* shield, after *Tupistra* a related genus.]
A plant of the Far Eastern genus *Aspidistra*, of the lily family, with broad tapering leaves (freq. regarded as a symbol of dull middle-class respectability, owing to its former popularity as a house plant).
■ **aspidistral** *adjective* of or pertaining to an aspidistra; decorated with aspidistras: M20.

aspirant /əˈspʌɪər(ə)nt, ˈasp(ɪ)r-/ *noun & adjective*. M18.
[ORIGIN French, or Latin *aspirant-* pres. ppl stem of *aspirare*: see ASPIRE, -ANT[1].]
▸**A** *noun*. A person who aspires (*to*, *for*, *after*); a person who desires and strives to attain a position, acquire a privilege, etc. M18.

LD MACAULAY The way to greatness was left clear to a new set of aspirants. BROWNING Degrade me.. To an aspirant after fame, not truth! B. TAYLOR Aspirants for poetic honors. A. STORR A Catholic aspirant to the priesthood.

▸**B** *adjective*. **1** Aspiring to a higher position, seeking distinction. E19.

SOUTHEY I receive plenty of letters from poets aspirant.

2 Mounting up, ascending. Now *rare*. M19.

A. C. SWINBURNE With flame all round him aspirant Stood flushed.. the tyrant.

aspirate /ˈasp(ə)rət/ *adjective & noun*. M16.
[ORIGIN Latin *aspiratus* pa. pple, formed as ASPIRATE *verb*: see -ATE[2], -ATE[1].]
▸**A** *adjective*. Aspirated, pronounced with a marked flow of breath. M16.
▸**B** *noun*. An aspirate consonant; a consonant followed by or blended with the sound of *h*; the sound of *h*. E17.

aspirate /ˈaspəreɪt/ *verb*. L17.
[ORIGIN Latin *aspirat-* pa. ppl stem of *aspirare* ASPIRE *verb*: see -ATE[3].]
▸**I 1** *verb intrans.* Of a consonant: be pronounced with aspiration. *rare.* L17.

DRYDEN Our *w* and *h* aspirate.

2 *verb trans.* Pronounce with a marked flow of breath. E18.

L. BLOOMFIELD An aspirated *p*, *t*, *k*, (as we usually have it in words like *pin*, *tin*, *kick*).

3 *verb intrans.* Pronounce the sound of *h* at the beginning of a word. E19.

M. EDGEWORTH Londoners [are] always aspirating where they should not, and never aspirating where they should.

▸**II 4** *verb trans.* Remove or draw (esp. a fluid) by suction; remove fluid etc. from (a cavity) by suction. L19.

O. SACKS She.. aspirated a chicken-bone, and choked to death on the spot. *Lancet* The ankle and an ear nodule were aspirated, but no fluid or crystals were found. *Nature* The liquid was directly aspirated into the flame of the atomic absorption spectrometer.

aspiration /aspəˈreɪʃ(ə)n/ *noun*. LME.
[ORIGIN Old French & mod. French from Latin *aspiratio(n-)*, formed as ASPIRATE *verb*: see -ATION.]
▸**I** Corresp. to ASPIRATE *verb*.
1 The action of aspirating a consonant. LME.
2 = ASPIRATE *noun*. Now *rare*. M16.
3 The removal or transfer of fluid etc. by suction. M19.
▸**II** Corresp. to ASPIRE.
†**4** Inspiration. LME–M16.
5 The action of breathing; the drawing of breath; a breath, a sigh. L15.

E. TOPSELL Corrupt inflamation taking away freedom or easinesse of aspiration. R. B. SHERIDAN There is.. not an aspiration of the breeze, but hints some cause. J. F. COOPER She sighed with an aspiration so low that it was scarcely audible.

6 The action of desiring and striving for something; an earnest desire (*to*, *for*, *after*). E17.

I. WATTS A soul inspired with the warmest aspirations after celestial beatitude. L. M. MONTGOMERY Anne's highest pinnacle of aspiration had been a teacher's provincial licence, Class First. B. BAINBRIDGE His entire life, with its small triumphs and disasters, its boundless hopes and aspirations for the future.

■ **aspirational** *adjective* L19.

aspirator /ˈaspɪreɪtə/ *noun*. E19.
[ORIGIN from ASPIRATE *verb* + -OR.]
An instrument or apparatus for aspirating fluid etc.

aspire /əˈspʌɪə/ *verb*. LME.
[ORIGIN Old French & mod. French *aspirer* or Latin *aspirare*, from *ad* AS-[1] + *spirare* breathe.]
▸**I** Desire.
1 *verb intrans.* Have an earnest desire or ambition for something; desire and seek to attain something. (Foll. by *to* (*do*), *after*, *at*, †*for*.) LME.

R. LOVELACE Aspiredst for the everlasting Crowne. GOLDSMITH Ye powers of truth, that bid my soul aspire. V. KNOX He who aspires at the character of a good man. R. LYND It is no wonder that human beings aspire after a standard pronunciation which will reduce as far as possible the chances of misunderstanding. M. L. KING We Americans have long aspired to the glories of freedom while we compromised with prejudice and servitude. *New York Review of Books* He aspired to be a Rhodes Scholar, and thus had to be an all-around man.

†**2** *verb trans.* Have an earnest desire for, be ambitious of. L16–E19.

SOUTHEY And Love aspired with Faith a heavenward flight.

▸†**II 3** *verb trans.* Breathe (*in*)*to*; inspire. L15–M17.
▸**III** Rise (infl. by SPIRE *noun*[1], *verb*[1]).
4 *verb intrans.* Rise up, mount up, tower, rise high, (*lit.* & *fig.*). M16.

A

SHAKES. *Merry W.* Lust is but a bloody fire, . . whose flames aspire, As thoughts do blow them, higher and higher. S. JOHNSON Orgilio sees the golden pile aspire. S. LEWIS The towers of Zenith aspired above the morning mist.

†**5** *verb intrans.* Grow up *to* (a specified age). Only in **L16.**

SPENSER To ryper yeares he gan aspire.

†**6** *verb trans.* Mount up to, reach, attain. **L16–E17.**

SHAKES. *Rom. & Jul.* That gallant spirit hath aspir'd the clouds.

■ **aspirer** *noun* **L16. aspiringly** *adverb* in an aspiring manner, so as to aspire **E17. aspiringness** *noun* the quality of being aspiring **M19.**

aspirin /ˈasp(ə)rɪn/ *noun.* **L19.**
[ORIGIN German, from *acetyli(e)rte Spirsäure* acetylated salicylic acid: see ACETYL, SPIRAEA, -IN[1].]
Acetylsalicylic acid, $C_9H_8O_4$, used as an analgesic and antipyretic drug; a tablet of this.

†**aspis** *noun*, †**aspisses** *noun pl.* see ASP *noun*[2].

asportation /aspɔːˈteɪʃ(ə)n/ *noun.* Now chiefly *LAW.* **L15.**
[ORIGIN Latin *asportatio(n-)*, from *asportat-* pa. ppl stem of *asportare* carry away, from ABS- + *portare* carry: see -ATION.]
The action of carrying off; detachment or movement of property (formerly an essential in the common law crime of larceny).
■ **aˈsport** *verb trans.* carry away, remove feloniously **E17.**

asprawl /əˈsprɔːl/ *adverb & pred. adjective.* **L19.**
[ORIGIN from A-[2] + SPRAWL *noun, verb.*]
Sprawling, in a sprawling posture.

aspre *noun, adjective* vars. of ASPER *noun*[1], *adjective.*

aspread /əˈsprɛd/ *adverb & pred. adjective.* **L19.**
[ORIGIN from A-[2] + SPREAD *verb.*]
Spread out, spread widely.

asquat /əˈskwɒt/ *adverb & pred. adjective.* **L17.**
[ORIGIN from A *preposition*[1] 6 + SQUAT *noun*[1].]
Squatting.

asquint /əˈskwɪnt/ *adverb & pred. adjective.* **ME.**
[ORIGIN Perh. from A-[1] + a Low German or Dutch form now repr. by Dutch *schuinte* obliquity, slant, from *schuin* oblique = Frisian, Low German *schüns*. Aphet. to SQUINT *adjective, verb.*]
1 (Looking) to one side, or out of the corners of the eyes; oblique(ly). **ME.**
2 (Looking) obliquely because of a defect in the eyes, so that they look in different directions; with a squint. **LME.**
3 (Looking) suspiciously, askance; with bias or distortion; furtive(ly), glancing(ly). **LME.**
4 In contexts other than vision: oblique(ly), aslant. *rare.* **L15.**

Asquithian /aˈskwɪθɪən/ *adjective & noun. hist.* **E20.**
[ORIGIN from *Asquith* (see below) + -IAN.]
▸**A** *adjective.* Pertaining to, resembling, or supporting Herbert Henry Asquith (1852–1928), Brit. Prime Minister 1908–16, as leader of the Liberal Party or, later, of a faction of the divided party. **E20.**
▸ **B** *noun.* A supporter of Asquith. **E20.**

ass /as/ *noun*[1].
[ORIGIN Old English *as(s)a* from Celtic (Welsh *asyn* = Old Irish *asan*, Old Cornish *asen*, Breton *azen*) from Latin *asinus*.]
1 A domesticated hoofed mammal of the horse family, *Equus asinus*, used as a beast of burden, a donkey. (Proverbially regarded as the type of clumsiness, ignorance, and stupidity.) **OE.** ▸**b** In full ***wild ass***. A wild animal of the genus *Equus.* **ME.**
make an ass of make (someone, oneself) look absurd or foolish.
2 An ignorant or stupid person. **LME.**
asses' bridge *MATH.* = ***PONS asinorum***. ***silly ass***: see SILLY *adjective.*
– COMB.: **ass-head** *colloq.* a fool.
■ **assifiˈcation** *noun* (*rare*) the action of making an ass of a person, an asinine act **E19. assify** *verb trans.* (*joc.*) make an ass of, turn into an ass **E19. assish** *adjective* asinine, stupid **L16. assishness** *noun* **L16. asslike** *adverb & adjective* (**a**) *adverb* in the manner of an ass; (**b**) *adjective* resembling (that of) an ass: **M16.**

ass /as/ *noun*[2]. *coarse slang* (chiefly *N. Amer.*). **M19.**
[ORIGIN Repr. a pronunc. of ARSE *noun.*]
1 The buttocks; the anus; = ARSE *noun* 1. **M19.** ▸**b** (Women regarded as a source of) sexual gratification. **M20.**
2 ***one's ass***, one's self or person. Freq. in casual use as an intensifier, as in ***you bet your ass***, ***work one's ass off***, etc.; also in other phrs. listed s.v. ARSE *noun.* **M20.**
– PHRASES & COMB.: **asshole** = ***arsehole*** s.v. ARSE *noun.* **ass-kicking** (**a**) *noun* forceful or aggressive behaviour; an instance of this, a beating; (**b**) *adjective* forceful or aggressive: **M20. ass-kisser, -kissing** = ***arse-kisser***, ***-kissing*** s.v. ARSE *noun.* **ass-licker, -licking** = ***arse-licker***, ***-licking*** s.v. ARSE *noun.* **cover one's ass** take steps to protect oneself. **drag ass, haul ass** move fast, hurry, leave. ***kick a person's ass, kick ass***: see KICK *verb*[1].

ass /as/ *verb.* **L16.**
[ORIGIN from ASS *noun*[1]: in recent use infl. by ASS *noun*[2], ARSE *noun.* Cf. ARSE *verb.*]
†**1** *verb trans.* Call ass. Only in **L16.**
2 *verb intrans.* †**a** Play the ass. Only in **M17.** ▸**b** Fool or mess *about, around. slang.* **L19.**

assafoetida *noun* var. of ASAFOETIDA.

assagai *noun & verb* var. of ASSEGAI.

assai /aˈsʌɪ/ *adverb.* **E18.**
[ORIGIN Italian.]
MUSIC. In directions: very.

assail /əˈseɪl/ *verb & noun.* **ME.**
[ORIGIN Old French *asaill-* tonic stem of *asalir* (mod. *assaillir*) from medieval Latin *assalire* (Latin *assilire*), from *ad* AS-[1] + *salire* to leap: infl. by ASSAY *verb*, esp. in sense 3.]
▸ **A** *verb trans.* **1** Attack with physical violence; assault. **ME.**

STEELE It is for the Vulgar to assail one another like brute Beasts. W. S. CHURCHILL Tribal revolts and Scottish raids continually assailed the northern frontier system.

†**2** Attack with temptation, try; woo, court. **ME–E17.**

SHAKES. *Cymb.* I have assail'd her with musics.

†**3** Venture on, attempt; endeavour *to do.* **ME–E17.**
4 Attack with hostile speech, writing, etc.; take action against (a belief, practice, etc.). **LME.**

H. P. BROUGHAM Choosing to assail the religion of the people before he had destroyed their liberty. W. S. CHURCHILL Clive was assailed in the House of Commons. He defended himself in an eloquent speech.

5 Seek to persuade or controvert by reasoning. **LME.**

H. MARTINEAU She assailed her husband on the subject of taking work.

6 Of a mental condition, physical state, or phenomenon: come upon (a person, sense, etc.) strongly; invade, threaten to overcome; dash against, injure. **LME.**

DRYDEN New pangs of mortal fear our minds assail. J. TYNDALL We were assailed by a violent hailstorm. J. LONDON The ever-recurrent fever of expectancy assailed Martin as he took the bundle of long envelopes. M. LEITCH A smell of gun-oil assailed their nostrils.

7 Approach (an obstacle, task, etc.) with the intention of mastering. **L17.**

POPE The thorny wilds the woodmen fierce assail. P. G. WODEHOUSE When a lazy man does make up his mind to assail a piece of work, he is like a dog with a bone. *absol.*: SHAKES. *Lucr.* When shame assail'd, the red should fence the white.

▸ **B** *noun.* (An) attack, (an) assault. *arch.* **ME.**
■ **assailable** *adjective* **E17. assailer** *noun* a person who assails, an assailant **LME. assailment** *noun* (now *rare* or *obsolete*) the action or power of assailing **L16.**

assailant /əˈseɪl(ə)nt/ *noun & adjective.* **M16.**
[ORIGIN from ASSAIL + -ANT[1], after French.]
▸ **A** *noun.* A person who or thing which assails someone or something; an attacker. **M16.**
▸ **B** *adjective.* Assailing, attacking. *arch.* **L16.**

Assam /aˈsam/ *noun.* **M19.**
[ORIGIN See ASSAMESE.]
In full ***Assam tea***. (A) tea grown in Assam in NE India.

Assamese /asəˈmiːz/ *noun & adjective.* **E19.**
[ORIGIN from *Assam* (see below) + -ESE.]
▸ **A** *noun.* Pl. same.
1 A native or inhabitant of Assam, a state of NE India. **E19.**
2 The Indo-Aryan (official) language of Assam. **M19.**
▸ **B** *adjective.* Of or pertaining to Assam, its people, or their language. **E19.**

assart /əˈsɑːt/ *noun. obsolete* exc. *hist.* **LME.**
[ORIGIN Anglo-Norman, formed as ASSART *verb*: cf. ESSART *noun.*]
LAW. **1** A piece of land converted from forest to arable. **LME.**
2 The action of assarting. **L16.**

assart /əˈsɑːt/ *verb trans. obsolete* exc. *hist.* **E16.**
[ORIGIN Anglo-Norman *assarter*, *-ier*, *-ir*, Old French *essarter* from medieval Latin *ex(s)artare*, from EX-[1] + *sart-* pa. ppl stem of *sar(r)ire* to hoe, weed: cf. ESSART *verb.*]
LAW. Make (forest land) arable by grubbing up trees and bushes.

assassin /əˈsasɪn/ *noun.* **M16.**
[ORIGIN French, or medieval Latin *assassinus* from Arabic *ḥašīšī* hashish-eater.]
A person who undertakes to assassinate somebody; *spec.* any of a band of Ismaili Muslim fanatics in the time of the Crusades who were allegedly sent on murder errands by the Old Man of the Mountains or by later leaders.
– COMB.: **assassin bug** any bug of the large family Reduviidae, members of which are predacious or bloodsucking.

†**assassin** *verb trans.* **M17–L18.**
[ORIGIN French *assassiner*, formed as ASSASSIN *noun.*]
= ASSASSINATE *verb.*

†**assassinate** *noun.* **L16.**
[ORIGIN Sense 1 app. from French *assassinat* from medieval Latin *assassinatus*, formed as ASSASSINATE *verb*: see -ATE[1]. Sense 2 is unexpl.]
1 An assassination. **L16–M18.**
2 An assassin. **E17–E19.**

assassinate /əˈsasɪneɪt/ *verb trans.* **E17.**
[ORIGIN medieval Latin *assassinat-* pa. ppl stem of *assassinare*, from *assassinus*: see ASSASSIN *noun*, -ATE[3].]
1 Kill (esp. a public figure such as a political or religious leader) by treacherous violence; commit a planned murder of (freq. by a person hired or instructed to commit the act). **E17.** ▸†**b** Attempt to murder. **L17–E18.**

M. SPARK If the authorities wanted to get rid of her she would have to be assassinated. H. KISSINGER Palestinian guerillas sought . . to assassinate King Hussein, attacking his motorcade.

2 *fig.* Destroy or injure maliciously. **E17.**

E. P. WHIPPLE After his death they tried to assassinate his name.

■ **assassinator** *noun* a person who assassinates someone; an assassin: **M17.**

assassination /əsasɪˈneɪʃ(ə)n/ *noun.* **E17.**
[ORIGIN formed as ASSASSINATE *verb* + -ATION.]
The action of assassinating someone; (a) planned murder, esp. of a public figure.
character assassination: see CHARACTER *noun.*

†**assation** *noun.* **L16–E19.**
[ORIGIN French, or medieval Latin *assatio(n-)*, from *assat-* pa. ppl stem of late Latin *assare* to roast, from Latin *assus* roasted: see -ATION.]
Roasting, baking.

assault /əˈsɔːlt, əˈsɒlt/ *noun.* **ME.**
[ORIGIN Old French *asaut* (mod. *assaut*) ult. from medieval Latin *assalire*: see ASSAIL *verb.*]
1 An attack with blows or weapons; a sudden military raid or offensive. **ME.** ▸**b** *spec.* The charge of an attacking force against the walls of a fortress etc. **ME.**

F. FITZGERALD The imperial armies disintegrated quickly under direct assault. *fig.*: E. F. BENSON The pastry resisted the most determined assaults without showing any sign of fracture. **b** W. S. CHURCHILL Marlborough and the Margrave . . in a bloody assault stormed the strong entrenchments of the Schellenberg.

assault-at-arms, **assault-of-arms** a display of combat by two fencers etc.
2 An attack by spiritual enemies; temptation to evil. *obsolete* exc. as passing into other fig. and transf. senses. **ME.**

MILTON Hear what assaults I had, what snares besides.

3 **a** *LAW.* Conduct (whether deeds or threatening words) which puts a person in fear of physical attack or improper interference. **LME.** ▸**b** *euphem.* Sexual molestation or rape. **M20.**
a assault and battery unlawful attack involving the striking of blows or other menacing physical contact. ***INDECENT assault***.
4 An attempt to overthrow institutions, opinions, etc. **LME.**

W. S. CHURCHILL Fox had made his name by savage personal assaults on North's administration.

5 The hostile onset of a misfortune, harmful natural phenomenon, etc. **LME.**

S. O'CASEY A fine old Georgian house, struggling for its life against the assaults of time.

†**6** An act of wooing. *rare* (Shakes.). **L16–E17.**
– COMB.: **assault course** a course (of instruction or of obstacles) for the training of troops in vigorous attack; **assault craft**, **assault ship** a vessel for carrying and landing attacking troops; **assault rifle** a lightweight rifle developed from the submachine gun, which may be set to fire automatically or semi-automatically.

assault /əˈsɔːlt, əˈsɒlt/ *verb trans.* **LME.**
[ORIGIN Old French *assauter*, ult. from Latin *ad* AS-[1] + *saltare* frequentative of *salire* to leap.]
1 Make a violent hostile attack upon by physical means; storm (a fortress etc.); commit an assault upon the person of (*LAW*: cf. ASSAULT *noun* 3a). **LME.** ▸**b** *euphem.* Molest sexually, rape. **M20.**

AV *Acts* 17:5 But the Iewes which beleeued not . . gathered a company, and . . assaulted the house of Iason. J. K. JEROME George suggested walking back to Henley and assaulting a policeman, and so getting a night's lodging in the station-house.

2 Tempt, try. *arch.* **E16.**
3 Attack with hostile words etc.; seek to persuade or overcome with argument etc. **M16.**

A. TOFFLER The average American adult is assaulted by a minimum of 560 advertising messages each day.

4 = ASSAIL *verb* 6. **L16.**

GIBBON His vessel was assaulted by a violent tempest. D. WALCOTT Each spring, memories Of his own country . . Assaulted him.

■ **assaultable** *adjective* **M16. assaulter** *noun* a person who makes an assault; an assailant: **M16. assaultive** *adjective* liable to commit an assault **M20.**

assay /əˈseɪ/ *noun.* **ME.**
[ORIGIN Old French *assai*, *-ay* var. of *essai* ESSAY *noun.*]
▸ **I** Trial, testing.
1 The trial or testing of the virtue, fitness, etc., of a person or thing. (Now only as fig. use of 2.) **ME.**

SHAKES. *Meas. for M.* He hath made an assay of her virtue to practise his judgment with the disposition of natures. J. RUSKIN A great assay of the human soul.

2 The determination of the quality or purity of an ore or (esp. precious) metal; any (esp. biological) test to

A

measure the content of a preparation. LME. ▸**b** A substance to be assayed. M19.

R. L. STEVENSON Some rock pounded for assay. *Lancet* The identification and quantitative assay of specific antibodies in parasitic and infectious diseases.

†**3** Tribulation, an affliction. LME–L17.

MILTON My way must lie Through many a hard assay even to the death.

†**4** (An) experiment; experience. LME–M18.

TREVISA Schort witted men and litel of assay. L. STERNE 'Tis an assay upon human nature.

5 The trial of food, drink, or other substances by taste. *obsolete* exc. *hist.* LME.

W. PRYNNE Hee made Dukes and Earles to serve him with Wine, with assay taken.

cup of assay a small cup with which wine was tasted before being served to a noble etc.

†**6** Trial of weights and measures etc. by legal standard. E17–M18.

▸ **II 7** (Good) quality or character; standard of purity etc. *arch.* ME.

J. GOWER That outward feignen youthe so And ben within of pouer assay. SPENSER Gold and pearle of rich assay.

▸ **III 8** An attempt, an endeavour; a tentative effort; one's best effort. *arch.* ME.

J. GOWER He hath put all his assay To winne thing which he ne may get. BUNYAN She and her companions made a fresh assay to go past them. A. HECHT Surely the mind in all its brave assays Must put much thinking by.

†**9** An assault, an attack. LME–E18.

SHAKES. *Hen. V* Galling the gleaned land with hot assays.

– COMB.: **assay-master** the master of an assay office; **assay office** an office for the assaying of metals, ores, etc.; *spec.* (with cap. initials) one authorized to award hallmarks on precious metal.

assay /əˈseɪ/ *verb*. ME.

[ORIGIN Old French *assaier* var. of Old French & mod. French *essayer* ESSAY *verb*.]

1 *verb trans.* Put to the proof; test the quality, fitness, etc., of. (Now chiefly as fig. use of 4.) ME. ▸†**b** *verb intrans.* Make trial (*of*). LME–L16.

MILTON I shall . . his strength as oft assay. S. BELLOW I should not venture to assay the merit of the tendency without more mature consideration.

†**2** *verb trans.* Learn or know by experience; examine, inquire into. ME–M17.

CHAUCER Thou hast nat yit assayed al hire wit. CAXTON The auncyent faders wold . . assaye the werkis of our Lord. S. BUTLER He knew . . Which Socrates and Chærophon In vain assaid so long agone.

3 *verb trans.* Attempt (a deed); try *to do* something; do one's best *to do*. *arch.* ME. ▸†**b** *verb intrans.* & *trans.* with inf. Address or apply oneself (*to do*). ME–M17. ▸†**c** Make bold, venture, *to do*. L15–L17.

SIR W. SCOTT Uncertain whether he should demand or assay entrance. E. A. FREEMAN He assayed to show himself in the usual kingly state.

4 *verb trans.* Test chemically the purity of (a metal, ore, etc.); perform an assay on. LME. ▸**b** Yield (a purity, value, etc.) on assay. L19.

N. LUTTRELL The goldsmiths are to meet to assay the new money coyned at the Tower. *Lancet* Drugs . . can be assayed . . by biological methods. J. BRONOWSKI The man who assayed gold was also more than a technician. *fig.*: SOUTHEY Sterling merit . . he can now understand and value, having . . the means of assaying it. **b** *Sunday Times* Ore . . assaying as high as 7.3 dwts.

5 *verb trans.* & *intrans.* (foll. by *of*). Test by tasting. *obsolete* exc. *hist.* LME.

†**6** *verb trans.* Practise by way of trial. LME–E18.

MILTON Let him . . now assay His utmost subtlety.

†**7** *verb trans.* Make trial of with afflictions, temptation, etc. LME–E17.

SPENSER O, how great sorrow my sad soule assaid! W. RALEIGH Then did he assay them with goodly words, accompanied with gifts.

8 *verb trans.* Attack, assault, assail, (*lit.* & *fig.*). Long *arch.* LME. ▸†**b** Challenge. *rare* (Shakes.). Only in E17.

SPENSER Th' other was with Thetis love assaid. M. DRAYTON She the high Mountaynes actively assayes. HOBBES Exhorting them the Trenches to assay. **b** SHAKES. *Haml.* Did you assay him To any pastime?

†**9** *verb trans.* Try the fit or style of (an item of clothing). Also foll. by *on*. L16–M17.

■ **assayable** *adjective* M19. **assayer** *noun* LME.

ass-backwards /asˈbakwədz/ *adverb* & *adjective*. *N. Amer. slang*. Also **ass-backward**. M20.

[ORIGIN from ASS *noun*[2] + BACKWARDS.]

Backwards; in a manner contrary to what is usual, expected, or logical.

WILLIAM GIBSON I never did like to do anything simple when I could do it ass-backwards. S. J. GOULD The variational fallacy has caused us to read some of our most important . . cultural trends in an ass-backwards manner.

†**assecution** *noun*. E16–E18.

[ORIGIN Latin *assecut-* pa. ppl stem of *assequi* obtain from *ad* AS-[1] + *sequi* follow: see -ION.]

Acquisition; attainment.

assegai /ˈasəgʌɪ/ *noun* & *verb*. Also **assa-**. E17.

[ORIGIN French †*azagaie* (now *zagaie*, *s-*) or Portuguese *azagaia*, Spanish *azagaya*, from colloq. Arabic *az-zağāya*, from *az-* AL-[2] + Berber *zağāya* spear.]

▸ **A** *noun*. A slender iron-tipped spear of hard wood, used as a missile by southern African peoples. E17.

– COMB.: **assegai tree** a southern African hardwood tree, *Curtisia dentata*; **assegai wood** the wood of the assegai tree.

▸ **B** *verb trans.* Kill or pierce with an assegai. E19.

asself /əˈsɛlf/ *verb trans. rare*. M17.

[ORIGIN Irreg. from AS-[1] + SELF *noun*.]

Take to oneself, appropriate.

assemblage /əˈsɛmblɪdʒ/ *noun*. L17.

[ORIGIN from ASSEMBLE *verb* + -AGE; partly after French.]

1 A bringing or coming together; the state of being collected together. L17. ▸**b** *spec.* The fitting or joining together of a number of components. E18.

J. LOCKE Wit lying most in the assemblage of Ideas. W. BLACKSTONE In consequence of this lucky assemblage. **b** *Listener* The cutting and assemblage of the recordings under the composer's care.

2 A number of things grouped together; a collection, a cluster. L17. ▸**b** A number of pieces fitted together; *spec.* a work of art consisting of miscellaneous objects fastened together. L19.

G. ANSON Opposite . . is an assemblage of rocks. J. D. CLARK The preservation of more complete faunal assemblages.

3 A number of people gathered together; a gathering, a concourse. M18.

HOR. WALPOLE It was an assemblage of all ages and nations. J. A. MICHENER The vast assemblage prepared to make the move, which all approved.

†**assemblance** *noun*[1]. LME–L16.

[ORIGIN Old French: see ASSEMBLE *verb*, -ANCE.]

Assemblage, assembling.

†**assemblance** *noun*[2]. L15–L16.

[ORIGIN Old French: see AS-[1], SEMBLANCE *noun*.]

Semblance, show.

SHAKES. 2 *Hen. IV* Care I for the limb, the thews, the stature, bulk, and big assemblance of a man?

assemble /əˈsɛmb(ə)l/ *verb*. ME.

[ORIGIN Old French *assembler* (mod. *ass-*), ult. from Latin *ad* AS-[1] + *simul* together.]

▸ **I** *verb trans.* **1** Bring together into one place, company, or mass; collect, convene. ME.

AV 1 *Kings* 8:2 All the men of Israel assembled themselves unto king Solomon. E. LONGFORD The French assembled an army along the Pyrenees. M. AMIS Now, I thought, assembling fountain-pen, inkpot and notes, I'm really going to hit the bastard with everything.

2 Put together the separate component parts of (a machine or other object). M19.

3 COMPUTING. Translate (a program) from a symbolic language into machine code. M20.

▸ **II** *verb intrans.* **4** Come together into one place or company; congregate, meet. ME. ▸**b** *spec.* in ENTOMOLOGY. Of insects: gather together; *esp.* (of male moths) gather for mating in response to a pheromone released by a female. E20.

V. WOOLF The audience was assembling. G. ORWELL It was inconceivable that its members could ever assemble in larger numbers than twos and threes. W. S. CHURCHILL About these two centres there slowly assembled the troops and resources for the waging of civil war.

■ **assembler** *noun* a person who or thing which assembles; *spec.* in COMPUTING (**a**) a program for converting programs in a low-level language into machine code; (**b**) an assembly language: M17. **assembling** *noun* (**a**) the action of the verb; (**b**) ENTOMOLOGY the collecting of male moths by attracting them with a captive female: LME.

assemblé /asɑ̃ble/ *noun*. Pl. pronounced same. L18.

[ORIGIN French, pa. pple of *assembler*: see ASSEMBLE.]

BALLET. A leap in which the feet are brought together before landing.

assemblée /asɑ̃ble/ *noun*. Pl. pronounced same. E18.

[ORIGIN French: see ASSEMBLY.]

= ASSEMBLY (esp. sense 2c).

assembly /əˈsɛmbli/ *noun*. ME.

[ORIGIN Old French *asemblee* (mod. *assemblée*) use as noun of fem. pa. pple of *asembler* ASSEMBLE *verb*: see -Y[5].]

1 Gathering or putting together; the state of being collected or brought together. ME.

J. R. GREEN A Triennial Bill enforced the assembly of the Houses every three years. *Encycl. Brit.* After final assembly it is necessary to test the completed equipment.

2 A gathering of people; a concourse, a throng. ME. ▸**b** *spec.* A deliberative body; a legislative council. LME. ▸**c** *spec.* A gathering (esp. public) for social purposes or recreation. L16. ▸**d** A gathering (esp. of a school) for religious worship; a congregation. E17.

F. FITZGERALD To forbid not only demonstrations but assemblies of over seven people. **b** J. KNOX The General Assembly of the Church . . holden in December after the Queen's Arrival. A. J. P. TAYLOR Chamberlain, Stresemann, and Briand always attended the meetings of the League assembly at Geneva. **c** P. V. WHITE Mr Bright, the dancing instructor, who was experienced in conducting Assemblies and such like. **d** SHAKES. *A.Y.L.* Here we have no temple but the wood, no assembly but horn-beasts. E. BLISHEN At assembly the head announced that it was going to be a fine year.

UNLAWFUL ***assembly***. **b *National Assembly***: see NATIONAL *adjective*.

†**3** A hostile encounter, an attack. LME–M16.

4 A collection of objects; *esp.* a number of component pieces fitted together to form a whole; a device consisting of numerous parts. M17.

D. H. LAWRENCE The whole is a strange assembly of apparently incongruous parts. E. WAUGH A wireless set had now been added to Nanny Hawkins' small assembly of pleasures. L. DEIGHTON With each pull the tail assembly of Sweet's Lancaster rose higher until it was strung up . . suspended from a buttress.

5 A military call to assemble, given by drum or bugle. E18.

– COMB.: **assembly language** COMPUTING a low-level language employing mnemonic symbols which correspond exactly to groups of machine instructions; **assembly line** a group of machines and workers progressively assembling some product; **assemblyman** a (male) member of a legislative assembly; **assembly program** COMPUTING = ASSEMBLER (a); **assembly room** (**a**) a public room in which social functions are held (usu. in *pl.*); (**b**) = ***assembly shop*** below; **assembly shop** a place where a machine or machine parts are assembled.

assent /əˈsɛnt/ *noun*. ME.

[ORIGIN Old French *as(s)ent(e)*, formed as ASSENT *verb*.]

1 Consent to or compliance with a proposal, desire, etc. ME.

G. B. SHAW The assent of the majority is the only sanction known to ethics. K. AMIS Already his silence might have been taken as assent to some proposal that he should cable the British Council in Lisbon.

2 *spec.* Official or judicial sanction; an action or instrument signifying this. ME.

POPE Laws, to which you gave your own assent.

royal assent the formal consent of the British monarch to a bill passed by Parliament.

†**3** Common purpose or feeling; accord. ME–M19.

AV 2 *Chron.* 18:12 The prophets declare good to the king with one assent.

†**4** Opinion. LME–M16.

5 (Expression of) agreement with a statement, opinion, etc.; mental acceptance. L15.

J. S. MILL Our assent to the conclusion being grounded on the truth of the premises. ALDOUS HUXLEY He smiled nervously and nodded a vague and non-committal assent.

assent /əˈsɛnt/ *verb*. ME.

[ORIGIN Old French *as(s)enter*, ult. from Latin *assentire* from *ad* AS-[1] + *sentire* feel, think.]

▸ **I** *verb intrans.* **1** Agree, give one's consent (*to* a proposal, request, etc.). ME.

W. S. CHURCHILL To all the actions of these zealots the King had so far assented.

†**2** Agree together, determine. (Foll. by *to* or *into* a proposal.) ME–E16.

†**3** Conform, submit *to*. ME–M17.

4 Give or express one's agreement (*to* a statement, opinion, etc., †*with*, †*unto*). ME.

G. B. SHAW A Roman Catholic may obey his Church by assenting verbally to the doctrine of indissoluble marriage. J. CONRAD The deep voice on the other side said: 'What an extraordinary thing,' and I assented mentally. E. F. SCHUMACHER An axiom is a self-evident truth which is assented to as soon as enunciated.

▸ †**II** *verb trans.* **5** Agree to, agree upon. LME–L17.

6 *refl.* Agree. LME–L15.

■ **assentant** *adjective* (now *rare* or *obsolete*) = ASSENTIENT *adjective* LME. **assenter** *noun* a person who gives assent LME. **assentingly** *adverb* in a manner expressing assent M16. **assentment** *noun* (*rare*) assent, agreement L15. **assentor** *noun* an assenter; *spec.* a person other than the proposer and seconder who subscribes a candidate's nomination: LME.

assentation /as(ə)nˈteɪʃ(ə)n/ *noun*. Now *rare*. L15.

[ORIGIN French: see ASSENT *verb*, -ATION.]

The (esp. obsequious) expression or act of assent.

■ **assentator** *noun* (*rare*) a person who assents to or connives at something M16.

assentient /əˈsɛnʃ(ə)nt, -ʃɪənt/ *adjective* & *noun*. M19.

[ORIGIN Latin *assentient-* pres. ppl stem of *assentire* assent: see ASSENT *verb*, -ENT.]

▸ **A** *adjective*. Assenting, approving. M19.

▸ **B** *noun*. A person who assents. M19.

assert /əˈsəːt/ *verb trans.* E17.
[ORIGIN Latin *assert-* pa. ppl stem of *asserere* claim, affirm, from *ad* AS-[1] + *serere* join. Cf. medieval Latin *assertare*.]
1 Declare formally and distinctly; aver, affirm. E17.

J. RUSKIN Would you not at once assert of that mistress, that she knew nothing of her duties? E. A. FREEMAN It is not directly asserted, but it seems to be implied. H. SPENCER Common Sense asserts the existence of a reality. P. TILLICH If courage, as he asserts, is the knowledge of 'what is to be dreaded and what dared'. J. THURBER The kind of senator or congressman that boldly asserts he will be glad to repeat his remarks in private and practically never does.

2 Affirm the existence of; draw attention to the existence of. *arch.* M17. ▸**b** Be evidence of. *rare.* E19.

T. S. ELIOT My necktie rich and modest, but asserted by a simple pin. **b** C. LAMB Their air and dress asserted the parade.

3 Vindicate one's claim to (a right etc.); give effect to (a quality etc.). M17. ▸**b** *refl.* Insist that one's rights or opinions be recognized. L19.

J. M. BARRIE Father . . assert your position as the chief person on the island. E. WAUGH I hope to assert my independence early and so get time for a little more writing. **b** J. WAIN If he did not assert himself now his wife would rule him for ever. *fig.*: J. BRAINE Brought out, perhaps, by the music and the dancers . . , a deeply buried instinct asserted itself.

†**4** Lay claim to; claim as belonging *to* oneself or another. M17–M19.

W. COWPER The fourth awarded lot . . Meriones asserted next. W. HAMILTON The few who assert to man a knowledge of the infinite.

†**5** Take the part of; champion, protect. M17–E19.

POPE Sedition silence, and assert the throne.

†**6** Release *to* liberty. M–L17.
■ **asserter** *noun* a person who asserts something M17. **asserti'bility** *noun* ability to be asserted E20. **assertible** *adjective* able to be asserted M19. **assertor** *noun* = ASSERTER LME.

assertation /asəˈteɪʃ(ə)n/ *noun. rare.* M16.
[ORIGIN medieval Latin *assertatio(n-)*, from *assertare* assert, formed as ASSERT: see -ATION.]
(An) assertion, affirmation.
■ **a'ssertative** *adjective* (*rare*) = ASSERTIVE E19.

assertion /əˈsəːʃ(ə)n/ *noun.* LME.
[ORIGIN Old French, or Latin *assertio(n-)* declaration, formed as ASSERT *verb* + -ION.]
1 Positive statement; a declaration. LME.

G. B. SHAW I hear the note of breezy assertion in your voice. E. O'NEILL A profound assertion of joy in living. E. LONGFORD Greville's assertion that the Duke had nothing to do was untrue. T. SHARPE The loud assertions that passed for conversation.

†**2** The action of setting free. M16–E18.
3 The action of maintaining a cause; vindication. *arch.* M16.

SIR W. SCOTT Flinching from the assertion of his daughter's reputation.

4 Insistence upon a right or opinion; effective use of a power etc. M17.

J. R. GREEN An assertion of her right of arbitrary taxation.

■ **assertional** *adjective* (*rare*) M19.

assertive /əˈsəːtɪv/ *adjective.* E17.
[ORIGIN French *assertif*, *-ive* from medieval Latin *assertivus*, formed as ASSERT *verb* + -IVE.]
Of the nature of or characterized by assertion; tending to assert oneself; dogmatic, positive.
■ **assertively** *adverb* LME. **assertiveness** *noun* L19.

assertory /əˈsəːtəri/ *adjective.* E17.
[ORIGIN medieval Latin *assertorius*, formed as ASSERT *verb*: see -ORY[2].]
Of the nature of assertion; assertive, affirmative.
assertory oath: taken in support of a statement.
■ **asser'torial** *adjective* = ASSERTORIC M19. **asser'torially** *adverb* L19. **asser'toric** *adjective* (chiefly LOGIC) of the nature of assertion, affirming that something is L19. **asser'torical** *adjective* = ASSERTORIC M19. **asser'torically** *adverb* M19.

asses *nouns* pls. of AS *noun*, ASS *noun*[1], *noun*[2].

assess /əˈsɛs/ *verb & noun.* LME.
[ORIGIN Old French *assesser*, from Latin *assess-* pa. ppl stem of *assidere* sit by, (in medieval Latin) levy tax, from *ad* AS-[1] + *sedere* sit: cf. ASSIZE *noun*. Aphet. to CESS *verb*[1], SESS *verb*.]
▸ **A** *verb trans.* **1** Fix the amount of (a tax, fine, etc.); impose (a specified tax etc.) (*up*)*on* a person or community. LME.

J. R. GREEN A forced loan was assessed upon the whole kingdom. *Daily Telegraph* The judge assessed total damages at £112,600.

2 Impose a fine or tax on (a person or community). (Foll. by *at*, *in* the amount, or foll. by second obj.) LME.

H. COX John Hampden was assessed twenty shillings.

3 Estimate officially the value of (property, income, etc.) for taxation. E19.
4 *gen.* Estimate the worth or extent of; evaluate. M20.

A. J. CRONIN Material success isn't so important . . . Usually it's assessed by false standards. J. HELLER Dressing at his locker, he assessed the damage to his flesh, bones, and systems. D. LESSING One of my tasks was to observe him, to assess his present state.

▸ †**B** *noun.* = ASSESSMENT. Cf. CESS *noun*[1]. L16–L17.
■ **assessable** *adjective* LME. **asse'ssee** *noun* a person whose property or income is assessed E18.

assession /əˈsɛʃ(ə)n/ *noun.* LME.
[ORIGIN Latin *assessio(n-)* session, (in medieval Latin) assessment, from *assess-*: see ASSESS, -ION.]
1 LAW. Assessment, assessing; *spec.* the action of assessing and leasing the lord's demesnes in the Duchy of Cornwall, done at a special court. LME.
2 A sitting beside or together; a session. Now *rare* or *obsolete.* M16.
■ **assessionable** *adjective* let by a court of assession E19.

assessment /əˈsɛsm(ə)nt/ *noun.* M16.
[ORIGIN from ASSESS *verb* + -MENT.]
1 The determination of the amount of a tax, fine, etc.; a scheme of taxation etc. M16.
2 Official valuation of property, income, etc. for the purpose of taxation. M16.
3 The amount of such a charge or valuation. E17.
4 *gen.* Evaluation, estimation; an estimate of worth, extent, etc. E17.

T. S. ELIOT It is not merely the passage of time . . that makes new assessments necessary.

CONTINUOUS assessment.

assessor /əˈsɛsə/ *noun.* LME.
[ORIGIN Old French *assessour* (mod. *-eur*) from Latin *assessor* assistant judge, (in medieval Latin) assessor of taxes: see ASSESS *verb*, -OR.]
▸ **I 1** A person who sits as assistant or adviser to a judge or magistrate on technical points. LME.
2 *gen.* A person who sits beside another; a person who shares another's position. Now *rare* or *obsolete.* M17.

MILTON Whence to his Son, Th' Assessor of his Throne.

▸ **II 3** A person who makes assessments for the purposes of taxation. LME.
4 *gen.* A person who makes evaluations or estimates. M19.
■ **asse'ssorial** *adjective* of or pertaining to an assessor or assessors E18.

asset /ˈasɛt/ *noun.* Orig. only as *collect. sing.* (now regarded as *pl.*) **assets.** M16.
[ORIGIN Legal Anglo-Norman *as(s)etz* from Old French *asez* (mod. *assez* enough), ult. from Latin *ad* to + *satis* enough, sufficiency.]
1 In *pl.* Sufficient estate or effects for an executor to discharge a testator's debts and legacies. M16.

T. SOUTHERNE I shall fall like an Executor without assets.

2 In *pl.*, any property or effects available to meet the debts of a testator, debtor, or company, whether sufficient or not; *sing.* an item of property or an effect so available. L16.

JAS. MILL The assets or effects of the London Company in India fell short of the debts of that concern. W. PLOMER He felt that the best thing would be to store the picture against better times, as it was a great asset.

tangible assets: see TANGIBLE *adjective* 1. ***wasting asset***: see WASTE *verb* 13.
3 *fig.* A thing or person of use or value. L17.

D. LODGE Philip Swallow's chief social asset at Euphoric State turned out to be his association with Charles Boon. G. CLARE An ability to speak languages would undoubtedly have been a great asset to his work.

current asset: see CURRENT *adjective*.
– COMB.: **asset-backed** *adjective* denoting securities having as collateral the return on a series of mortgages, credit agreements, or other forms of lending; **asset-stripper** an entrepreneur engaged in asset-stripping; **asset-stripping** the piecemeal sale of a company's assets by an entrepreneur for profit.

†**assethe** *noun & verb* see ASSYTHE.

assever /əˈsɛvə/ *verb trans. arch.* L16.
[ORIGIN Latin *asseverare*: see ASSEVERATE.]
= ASSEVERATE.

asseverate /əˈsɛvəreɪt/ *verb trans.* L18.
[ORIGIN Latin *asseverat-* pa. ppl stem of *asseverare*, from *ad* AS-[1] + *severus* grave, SEVERE: see -ATE[3].]
Declare solemnly or emphatically.

asseveration /əsɛvəˈreɪʃ(ə)n/ *noun.* M16.
[ORIGIN Latin *asseveratio(n-)*, formed as ASSEVERATE: see -ATION.]
(A) solemn affirmation; (an) emphatic declaration or confirmation; an oath.

BACON Men ought . . to propound things sincerely, with more or less asseueration, as they stand in a man's own iudgement. SMOLLETT Incensed at this asseveration, which he was not prepared to refute. DICKENS The sergeant rejoined with many choice asseverations that he didn't.

■ **a'sseverative** *adjective* pertaining to or of the nature of asseveration M19.

assibilate /əˈsɪbɪleɪt/ *verb trans.* M19.
[ORIGIN Latin *assibilat-* pa. ppl stem of *assibilare* hiss at, from *ad* AS-[1] + *sibilare* to hiss: see -ATE[3].]
PHONETICS & PHILOLOGY. Pronounce as or change to a sibilant or other fricative.
■ **assibi'lation** *noun* pronunciation as or change to a sibilant or other fricative M19.

Assidean /asɪˈdiːən/ *noun. arch.* E17.
[ORIGIN from Greek *Asidaioi* (formed as HASID) + -AN.]
1 A member of a Jewish group who opposed the attempts of Antiochus Epiphanes to introduce idolatry among them (1 *Macc.* 2:42). E17.
2 A Hasid. M19.

assiduity /asɪˈdjuːɪti/ *noun.* LME.
[ORIGIN Latin *assiduitas*, formed as ASSIDUOUS: see -ITY. Cf. Old French & mod. French *assiduité*.]
1 Persistence, unremitting application, perseverance, diligence. LME. ▸**b** Persistent endeavour to please; in *pl.*, constant attentions. *arch.* M17.
†**2** Continual recurrence; frequency. LME–M17.
– NOTE: Rare before 17.

assiduous /əˈsɪdjʊəs/ *adjective.* M16.
[ORIGIN from Latin *assiduus*, from *assidere* (see ASSESS), + -OUS.]
1 Of an action etc.: unremitting, persistent. M16.

MILTON To wearie him with my assiduous cries. H. MACMILLAN Selwyn Lloyd . . worked with assiduous and skilful diplomacy.

2 Of a person: persevering, diligent; attending closely. E17. ▸**b** Constantly endeavouring to please. *arch.* E18.

ADDISON Those assiduous Gentlemen who employ their whole Lives in the Chace. D. J. ENRIGHT A self-effacing, even shadowy, presence, assiduous without passion, obliging and long-suffering. **b** S. JOHNSON Few can be assiduous without servility.

■ **assiduously** *adverb* E17. **assiduousness** *noun* M17.

†**assiege** *verb trans.* ME–M17.
[ORIGIN Old French *asegier* (mod. *assiéger*) from Proto-Romance, ult. formed as AS-[1] + SIEGE *noun*.]
Besiege, beset.
■ †**assiegement** *noun* L16–M19.

assiento /asɪˈɛntəʊ, *foreign* asiˈento/ *noun.* Pl. **-os** /-əʊz, *foreign* -os/. E17.
[ORIGIN Spanish (now *asiento*).]
hist. A contract or convention between the King of Spain and other powers, esp. for supplying the Spanish dominions in America with black slaves (as that made between Spain and Great Britain at the Peace of Utrecht).
■ **assi'entist** *noun* a party to an assiento, a slave trader for Spain E18.

assiette /asjɛt (*pl. same*), asɪˈɛt/ *noun.* M18.
[ORIGIN French = plate, course of a meal; seat, site; bed, foundation.]
1 A prepared dish of food. M18.
2 BOOKBINDING. A composition laid on the cut edges of books before gilding. M19.

assign /əˈsʌɪn/ *noun.* ME.
[ORIGIN formed as ASSIGNEE, with which early uses are identical.]
1 = ASSIGNEE 1. ME.
†**2** = ASSIGNEE 2. LME–E18.
†**3** An appurtenance. *rare* (Shakes.). Only in E17.

assign /əˈsʌɪn/ *verb trans.* ME.
[ORIGIN Old French *asi(g)ner* (mod. *assigner*) from Latin *assignare*, from *ad* AS-[1] + *signare* SIGN *verb*.]
▸ **I** Allot, appoint, determine.
1 Transfer or make over formally (esp. personal property, *to*). ME.

S. JOHNSON I assign to him the right of copy of an Imitation of the Tenth Satire of Juvenal.

2 Appoint or designate (a person) *to* an office, duty, fate, etc., *to do* a task etc.; set aside or designate (a thing) *for* a purpose. ME. ▸†**b** Appoint or consign (a person) *to* a place. LME–E17.

W. BLACKSTONE If the founder has appointed and assigned any other person to be visitor. G. CRABBE Has a small space for garden-ground assign'd. T. CAPOTE A total of eighteen men were assigned to the case full time, among them three of the F.B.I.'s ablest investigators. D. HALBERSTAM The *New York Times* . . had a large and expensive staff of reporters assigned to cover the world. **b** AV 2 *Sam.* 11:16 He assigned Vriah vnto a place where hee knewe that valiant men were.

3 Fix, determine, or appoint (a time or temporal limit). ME. ▸†**b** Fix the time and place of (a meeting). LME–M16.

SWIFT In this month likewise an ambassador will die in London; but I cannot assign the day.

4 Allot as a share or allowance (*to*); allot or appoint (a place, *to* a person); allocate (a task, office, etc., *to*); allot as a task. LME.

MILTON The work which here God hath assign'd us. GOLDSMITH I was assigned my place on a cushion on the floor. O. HENRY He assigned his men to their respective posts with discretion, and coached them carefully as to their duties. R. LARDNER The Thayers had a very pretty home and the room assigned to us was close to perfection. W. S. CHURCHILL To him was assigned what was then a lowly office, the Presidency of the Board of Trade. D. LODGE We're supposed to discuss some text I've assigned.

5 Appoint (a person) *to* another to assist or act for him or her in some capacity. LME. ▸**b** AUSTRAL. HISTORY. Make over (a convict) as an unpaid servant to a colonist. E19.

JOSEPH HALL The Lords Assigned us five very worthy Lawyers.

†**6** Prescribe (a course of action). LME–E17.
7 Determine, establish. *arch.* M17.

CAPT. COOK Who sailed round it, and assigned its true position.

▸ **II** Point out, show.
8 Designate, specify. ME.

SIR T. MORE Folk whom I neither assigne bi name, nor as yet know not who they be.

†**9** Exhibit, display. Only in LME.
▸ **III** Ascribe, attribute.
10 Ascribe, attribute, refer, as belonging or due *to*. LME.

M. MEAD Sometimes one quality has been assigned to one sex, sometimes to the other.

11 Ascribe (a reason, explanation, etc., *to* or *for*). LME.
12 Bring forward, allege, suggest, as a reason, explanation, etc. LME.

W. PALEY I cannot assign a supposition of forgery.

▸ **IV** After SIGN *verb*.
†**13** Sign. M16–L19.
■ **assignable** *adjective* able to be assigned (*to*, *for*) LME. **assignably** *adverb* (*rare*) LME. **assigner** *noun* †(*a*) = ASSIGNEE; (*b*) a person who assigns: LME. **assignor** *noun* †(*a*) = ASSIGNEE; (*b*) the person for or by whom an assignee is appointed: LME.

assignat /asiɲa (*pl. same*), ˈasɪgnat/ *noun*. L18.
[ORIGIN French from Latin *assignatum* neut. pa. pple of *assignare*: see ASSIGN *verb*.]
A promissory note issued until 1796 by the revolutionary government of France, on security of state lands. Cf. MANDAT 1.

assignation /asɪgˈneɪʃ(ə)n/ *noun*. LME.
[ORIGIN Old French & mod. French from Latin *assignatio(n-)*, from *assignat-* pa. ppl stem of *assignare*: see ASSIGN *verb*, -ATION.]
†**1** A command; bidding. LME–E17.
†**2** Appointment to office. LME–M17.
†**3** The allotment of revenue to meet claims; a mandate granting payment of a claim; a pension, an allowance. LME–M18.
4 Formal transference; a document effecting this; = ASSIGNMENT 6. L16.
5 Allotment; apportionment; allocation; = ASSIGNMENT 4. E17.
6 Attribution as belonging or due *to*; = ASSIGNMENT 10. E17.
7 Appointment of a particular time and place; an appointment; a tryst, an illicit meeting. M17.

JOAN SMITH It was the setting for an assignation with a lover.

8 A promissory note secured by revenue or property; paper currency. Cf. ASSIGNAT. *arch.* L17.

assignee /asɪˈniː, -sʌɪ-/ *noun*. ME.
[ORIGIN Old French & mod. French *assigné* pa. pple of *assigner* ASSIGN *verb*, used as noun: in early use identical with ASSIGN *noun*.]
1 A person (other than the heir-at-law) to whom a right or property is legally transferred. ME.
2 A person appointed to act for another; a deputy, an agent, a representative. LME. ▸**b** *spec.* (*hist.*) A person appointed to administer a bankrupt's property on behalf of the creditors. L17.
■ **assigneeship** *noun* the position or office of assignee E19.

assignment /əˈsʌɪnm(ə)nt/ *noun*. LME.
[ORIGIN Old French *assignement* from medieval Latin *assignamentum*, from Latin *assignare*: see ASSIGN *verb*, -MENT.]
†**1** Command, bidding. LME–M18.
†**2** = ASSIGNATION 2. LME–M19.
†**3** = ASSIGNATION 3. LME–M19.
4 Allotment; apportionment; allocation; = ASSIGNATION 5. LME. ▸**b** AUSTRAL. HISTORY. The making over of a convict to a colonist as an unpaid servant; the condition of such service. E19.
†**5** An assigned measure; a definite amount. E–M16.
6 Legal or other formal transference of a right or property; a document that effects or authorizes this; = ASSIGNATION 4. L16.
†**7** = ASSIGNATION 8. E17–E18.
8 Statement or attribution of a reason etc. M17.
9 Indication; specification. M17.
10 Attribution as belonging or due *to*; = ASSIGNATION 6. L17.

Nature The assignment of each species to one of the three recognized . . families.

11 A task that has been assigned to a person; a commission. M19.

K. AMIS My next journalistic assignment is to write an article on supermarket Scotch.

assimilable /əˈsɪm(ɪ)ləb(ə)l/ *adjective*. M17.
[ORIGIN medieval Latin *assimilabilis*, from Latin *assimilare*: see ASSIMILATE *verb*, -ABLE.]
1 Able to be absorbed and incorporated. M17.
2 Able to be likened or compared *to*. *arch.* M19.
■ **assimilaˈbility** *noun* E19.

assimilate /əˈsɪmɪlət/ *ppl adjective & noun*. *rare*. LME.
[ORIGIN Latin *assimilatus* pa. pple, formed as ASSIMILATE *verb*: see -ATE², -ATE¹.]
▸ †**A** *ppl adjective*. Like, likened, (*to*). LME–L17.
▸ **B** *noun*. †**1** A similar thing. Only in L17.
2 An assimilated substance. M20.

assimilate /əˈsɪmɪleɪt/ *verb*. LME.
[ORIGIN Latin *assimilat-* pa. ppl stem of *assimilare*, from *ad* AS-¹ + *similis* SIMILAR: see -ATE³.]
▸ **I** Absorb and incorporate.
1 *verb trans.* Of a living organism: convert (extraneous material) into fluids and tissues identical with its own; absorb into the system; *fig.* absorb and make one's own (ideas, influences, etc.); incorporate into one's own way of thinking or acting; take in and understand fully. LME.

S. JOHNSON Falsehood by long use is assimilated to the mind, as poison to the body. E. WILSON Marx and Engels . . had assimilated with remarkable rapidity the social and historical thinking of their time. K. CLARK Poussin was a learned artist who had studied and assimilated the poses of antique sculpture. H. WILSON Showed a detailed knowledge of the subject matter which could not have been assimilated within so short a time.

2 *verb intrans.* Become absorbed or incorporated into the system (*lit. & fig.*). E17.

CHARLES CHURCHILL He stands aloof from all . . And scorns, like Scotsmen, to assimilate. J. H. NEWMAN I am a foreign material, and cannot assimilate with the Church of England. DICKENS The nightly pint of beer, instead of assimilating naturally [etc.].

▸ **II** Make or be like. (Earlier as ASSIMILATE *ppl adjective*.)
†**3** *verb trans.* Resemble. L16–M17.

J. GAULE The reason that children . . assimulate their nurses more than their mothers.

4 *verb trans.* Make like (*to*; also, with suggestion of incorporation, as in branch I, *with*). E17. ▸**b** Bring into conformity, adapt, *to*. *arch.* M17. ▸**c** PHONOLOGY. Make (a sound) more like another in the same or a contiguous word. M19.

W. COWPER The downy flakes . . Softly alighting upon all below, Assimilate all objects. DICKENS Observe the dyer's hand, assimilating itself to what it works in. J. S. MILL Whose education and way of life assimilate them with the rich. **b** S. RICHARDSON This lady . . half-assimilates me to her own virtue.

5 *verb trans.* Liken, compare, put into the same class. (Foll. by *to*, *with*.) *arch.* E17.

GOLDSMITH Which we can assimilate with no shells that are known. J. HUTTON To assimilate things upon fallacious grounds. R. G. COLLINGWOOD They have been assimilating a work of art to an artifact, and the artist's work to the craftsman's.

6 *verb intrans.* Be or become like, resemble. Foll. by *to*, (with suggestion of incorporation, as in branch I above) *with*. *arch.* M18. ▸**b** Conform *to*, act in accordance *with*. *arch.* L18.

W. BLACKSTONE Which revenues . . do always assimilate, or take the same nature, with the antient revenues. LYTTON Whose courage assimilated to their own. **b** COLERIDGE With whose prejudices and ferocity their unbending virtue forbade them to assimilate.

■ **assimilative** *adjective* (*a*) of, characterized by, or tending to assimilation; (*b*) *rare* that may be or has been assimilated: LME. **assimilator** *noun* a person who or thing which assimilates M18. **assimilatory** *adjective* = ASSIMILATIVE (a) M19.

assimilation /əsɪmɪˈleɪʃ(ə)n/ *noun*. LME.
[ORIGIN French, or its source Latin *assimilatio(n-)*, formed as ASSIMILATE *verb*: see -ATION.]
1 Conversion into a similar substance; *esp.* conversion by a living organism of extraneous material into fluids and tissues identical with its own; the final part of this process, the incorporation of digested nutriment within the system following absorption. LME. ▸**b** *fig.* Absorption and incorporation (of ideas, influences, etc.); integration with another (dominant) social, racial, or cultural group. L18. ▸**c** PSYCHOLOGY. The process whereby a person acquires new ideas through comparing experience with the existing content of the mind. M19.

b BURKE Which, by a bland assimilation, incorporated into politics the sentiments which beautify and soften private society. G. H. LEWES Interpretation means mental assimilation. MALCOLM X 'Integration' is called 'assimilation' if white ethnic groups alone are involved.

2 The action of making or becoming like; the state of being like. E17. ▸**b** The action of conforming *to*, conformity *with*. *arch.* exc. as passing into sense 1b. L17. ▸**c** PHONOLOGY. The process of assimilating a sound. M19.
c *progressive assimilation*: see PROGRESSIVE *adjective*. *reciprocal assimilation*: see RECIPROCAL *adjective*.
■ **assimilationist** *noun & adjective* (*a*) *noun* an advocate of racial or cultural integration; (*b*) *adjective* of or pertaining to assimilationists or their beliefs: E20.

Assiniboine /əˈsɪnɪbɔɪn/ *noun & adjective*. Also **-boin**, **Assina-**, (earlier) †**-bouet**. Pl. of noun same, **-s**. L17.
[ORIGIN Canad. French from Ojibwa *assini:-pwa:n* lit. 'stone Sioux', from *assin* stone + *pwa:n* (Cree *pwa:t*) Sioux.]
1 A member of, of or pertaining to, a Siouan people of the Great Plains of N. America. L17.
2 (Of) the language of this people. M19.

†**assinico** *noun* var. of ASINEGO.

Assisian /əˈsiːsɪən/ *adjective & noun*. L19.
[ORIGIN from *Assisi* (see below) + -AN.]
(A native or inhabitant) of the town of Assisi in central Italy; *spec.* (of) St Francis of Assisi.

assist /əˈsɪst/ *noun*. L16.
[ORIGIN from the verb.]
1 An act of helping; a help. Now chiefly *US*. L16.
2 In baseball, ice hockey, etc.: a player's action in helping to put out an opponent, score a goal, etc.; a credit for this. Chiefly *N. Amer.* L19.

assist /əˈsɪst/ *verb*. LME.
[ORIGIN Old French & mod. French *assister* from Latin *assistere*, from *ad* AS-¹ + *sistere* take one's stand.]
▸ **I** Help.
1 *verb trans.* Help (a person *in*, *to do*, *with*, etc.; a person in necessity; an action, process, or result); support, further, promote. LME.

STEELE When I assist a friendless person. E. GASKELL May I assist you to potatoes? R. MACAULAY Miss Smith . . was assisted from her hammock. J. C. POWYS Mr. Geard . . permitted John to assist him to mount the platform. P. K. KEMP An assisted take-off with rockets. P. H. JOHNSON Her pelvis is very narrow and they will have to assist the birth. T. CAPOTE A young man who assisted him with the management of the farm.

assisted passage a journey to another country at a fare reduced by a subsidy. **assisted place** a place in a fee-paying school for which state financial assistance is given. **assisted suicide**: effected with the assistance of another person; *esp.* the taking of lethal drugs, provided by a doctor for the purpose, by a patient considered to be incurable.
2 *verb intrans.* Give help or support (*in*, †*to*, (arch.) *to do*, *with*). LME.

DRYDEN If Heav'n assist, and Phœbus hear my call. J. A. FROUDE Barlow . . whose indiscretion had already assisted to ruin Cromwell. E. F. BENSON She had herself assisted in adding to the tediousness.

▸ **II** Be present.
†**3** *verb trans.* Stand by; attend, escort; accompany, join. L15–M17.

SHAKES. *Temp.* The King and Prince at prayers! Let's assist them. R. CRASHAW Three vigorous virgins, waiting still behind, Assist the throne of th' iron-sceptred king.

4 *verb intrans.* Be present (*at*), either as a spectator (*arch.*) or as a participant. M16.

THACKERAY The dinner at which we have just assisted.

■ **assister** *noun* a person who assists; an assistant: E16. **assistful** *adjective* (*arch.*) helpful E17. **assistive** *adjective* giving assistance; *spec.* designating an appliance designed to aid someone whose mobility is impaired: (*rare* before L20) L19. †**assistor** *noun* (chiefly LAW) = ASSISTER LME–L18.

assistance /əˈsɪst(ə)ns/ *noun*. LME.
[ORIGIN Old French & mod. French, or medieval Latin *assistentia*, from Latin *assistere*: see ASSIST *verb*, -ANCE, -ENCE.]
1 *sing.* & †in *pl.* The action of helping; help, aid, support. LME.

New Yorker The Bush administration is sending military assistance to Peru. *Guardian* They are fed and given medical assistance.

be of assistance help, provide help. ***National Assistance***: see NATIONAL *adjective*.
2 *collect. sing.* (occas. *pl.*). Persons present; bystanders. *obsolete* exc. as occas. readopted from French. L15.
3 Presence, attendance. Long *rare*. E16.
†**4** A helper; *collect.* a body of helpers. M16–L17.

assistant /əˈsɪst(ə)nt/ *adjective & noun*. LME.
[ORIGIN Old French & mod. French, or medieval Latin *assistent-* pres. ppl stem of *assistere*: see ASSIST *verb*, -ANT¹, -ENT.]
▸ **A** *adjective*. **1** Helping, auxiliary, subordinate, (*to*). LME.
assistant manager, ***assistant master***, ***assistant mistress***, ***assistant professor***, ***assistant secretary***, etc.
†**2** Standing by, present, accompanying. L15–L17.
▸ **B** *noun*. **1** A helper; a supporter; a subordinate worker. LME.
editorial assistant, ***shop assistant***, etc.
†**2** A person who is present, a bystander, a participant. L15–M19.
■ **assistancy** *noun* = ASSISTANTSHIP E17. **assistantship** *noun* the position or office of an assistant E17.

assize /əˈsʌɪz/ *noun & verb*. *obsolete* exc. *hist.* ME.
[ORIGIN Old French *as(s)ise* use as noun of fem. of *assis* pa. pple of *asseeir* (mod. *asseoir*) sit, settle, assess, from Latin *assidere*: see ASSESS *verb*.]
▸ **A** *noun*. **I** Uses pertaining to legislation or trial.
1 A decree or edict made by a consultative or legislative body. ME.
†**rent of assize** a fixed rent.
2 *hist.* **a** An ordinance regulating weights, measures, and the price of articles of general consumption; the regulation of weights, measures, and prices in accordance with such an ordinance. ME. ▸**b** Statutory weight, measure, or price; customary or prescriptive standard. LME.
3 A legal proceeding of the nature of an inquest or trial; *spec.* (*sing.* & (usu.) in *pl.*) a periodical session in each county of England and Wales for the administration of civil and criminal justice. ME. ▸**b** An action decided at such a trial; a writ instituting such a trial. L16.
the great assize(s), **the last assize(s)** the Last Judgement.
†**4** Judgement; sentence. ME–M17.
5 In Scotland: a trial by jury; a jury, a panel. LME.

▸ †**II** Other uses.
6 Custom, practice; mode, manner, fashion. ME–L15.
7 Site; situation. LME–L15.
8 Measurement, dimensions, size; measure, extent. LME–M17.
▸ †**B** *verb trans.* **1** Decree, ordain. LME–L15.
2 Decide, judge; try. LME–L17.
3 Assess. LME–E17.
4 Regulate (weights, measures, prices, etc.) according to an ordinance or standard. M16–M19.
■ **assizer** *noun* = ASSIZOR (b) L16. **assizor** *noun* (*a*) each of those who constituted an assize or inquest; (*b*) *Scot.* a member of a jury: ME.

associable /əˈsəʊʃɪəb(ə)l, -sɪ-/ *adjective.* M16.
[ORIGIN French, from *associer* from Latin *associare*: see ASSOCIATE *verb*, -ABLE.]
†**1** Companionable. *rare.* M16–L17.
2 That may be associated (*with*) or joined in association. E19.

associate /əˈsəʊʃɪət, -sɪ-/ *adjective & noun.* LME.
[ORIGIN Latin *associatus* pa. pple, formed as ASSOCIATE *verb*: see -ATE², -ATE¹.]
▸ **A** *adjective.* **1** Joined in companionship, function, or dignity; allied; concomitant. LME.

C. MARLOWE With him is Edmund gone associate? R. KNOLLES Christ our Sauiour, equall and associate to his Father. POPE Amphinomus survey'd th' associate band. S. JOHNSON They want some associate sounds to make them harmonious.

2 Sharing in responsibility, function, membership, etc., but with a secondary or subordinate status. E19.

H. F. PRINGLE The *Outlook* office where the ex-President was an associate editor.

associate professor in N. American universities, (a person of) the academic rank immediately below (full) professor.
▸ **B** *noun.* **1** A partner, a comrade; a companion; an ally, a confederate; a colleague. M16.

P. SIDNEY They persuade the king . . to make Plangus his associate in government. LD MACAULAY These men, more wretched than their associates who suffered death. W. IRVING His associates soon turned the tide of the battle. D. W. HARDING To her the first necessity was to keep on reasonably good terms with the associates of her everyday life.

2 A thing placed or found in conjunction with another. M17.
PAIRED *associates.*
3 A person who belongs to an association or institution in a secondary or subordinate degree of membership. E19.
■ **associateship** *noun* the position or status of an associate E19.

associate /əˈsəʊʃɪeɪt, -sɪ-/ *verb.* LME.
[ORIGIN Latin *associat-* pa. ppl stem of *associare*, from *ad* AS-¹ + *socius* sharing, allied: see -ATE³.]
1 *verb trans.* Join, unite, ally, (persons; oneself or another *with*, (arch.) *to* another or others, *in*, †*to* a common purpose, action, or condition); declare (oneself) in agreement *with*. LME. ▸**b** Elect as an associate member. E19.

SWIFT None but papists are associated against him. D. HUME The troops . . associating to them all the disorderly people. E. A. FREEMAN Arnulf associated his son with him in his government. GLADSTONE It is for me . . to associate myself with the answer previously given by the Under-Secretary. **b** SOUTHEY He . . was associated to the royal Academy there.

†**2** *verb trans.* Join oneself to (a person); accompany; keep company with. M16–M17.

J. MARBECK Therfore shal man leaue father and mother and associate his wife. SHAKES. *Rom. & Jul.* A barefoot brother . . to associate me, Here in this city visiting the sick.

3 *verb trans.* **a** *gen.* Join, combine, (things together; one thing *with*, *to* another or others). Chiefly *refl.* or in *pass. arch.* L16. ▸**b** *spec.* Connect as an idea (*with*, †*to*). M18.

A. BAIN The muscles . . act in groups, being associated together by the organization of the nervous centres. T. H. HUXLEY This vapour is intimately associated with the other constituents of the atmosphere. **b** A. S. NEILL The children will leave electric lights on because they do not associate light with electricity bills. JENNIE MELVILLE She associated love and pain.

†**4** *verb trans.* Of things: accompany, join. L16–L17.

T. HEYWOOD Those torturing pangues That should associate death.

5 *verb intrans.* Combine for a common purpose; keep company, have frequent dealings, *with*. M17.

BURKE When bad men combine, good men must associate. D. RUNYON As a rule I do not care to associate with coppers, because it arouses criticism from other citizens.

■ **associater** *noun* (*rare*) = ASSOCIATOR E17. **associator** *noun* a person who or thing which associates; an associate; a confederate: L17. **associatory** *adjective* having the quality of associating L19.

association /əsəʊsɪˈeɪʃ(ə)n, -ʃɪ-/ *noun.* M16.
[ORIGIN French, or medieval Latin *associatio(n-)*, formed as ASSOCIATE *verb*: see -ATION.]
1 The action of joining or uniting for a common purpose; the state of being so joined. M16.

R. COKE A solemn oath of association for the restoring of it. CONAN DOYLE The good Watson had at that time deserted me for a wife, the only selfish action which I can recall in our association.

articles of association, **deed of association** a document giving the regulations of a limited liability company. **memorandum of association** a document giving the name, status, purposes, and capital of a limited liability company.
2 A body of people organized for a common purpose; a society. L16.

F. O'BRIEN The people who attended the College had banded themselves into many private associations.

†**3** A document setting out the common purpose of a number of people and signed by them. L16–M19.

LD MACAULAY Dropping the Association into a flowerpot.

4 Fellowship, companionship; social intercourse (esp. in prison). M17.

SMOLLETT The nobility would be profaned by my association. H. ALLEN To have so pleasant and bright a companion as young Anthony sitting before the fire sped their association mightily.

5 The conjoining or uniting of things or persons with another or others; the state of being so conjoined, conjunction. M17.

J. REYNOLDS The spark that without the association of more fuel would have died. T. CAPOTE A tendency not to experience anger or rage in association with violent aggressive action.

6 Mental connection between related ideas; an idea, recollection, or feeling mentally connected with another. L17.

J. LOCKE On the Association of Ideas. W. HAMILTON Our Cognitions, Feelings, and Desires are connected together by what are called the *Laws of Association* B. RUBENS The theatre, the picnics, the concerts, separately and by association, they triggered off total recall. A. STORR The dreamer's associations to all the images in the dream. B. BETTELHEIM The replacement of a word that has deep emotional associations with one that evokes hardly any.

free association: see FREE *adjective.* PAIRED ***association.***
7 ECOLOGY. A group of dominant plant species occurring together; a plant community characterized by such a group. E20.
– COMB.: **association book**, **association copy** a volume showing some mark of personal connection with the author or a notable former owner; **Association football** football played according to the rules of the Football Association, with a round ball which may not be handled during play except by a goalkeeper; soccer.
■ **associational** *adjective* of or pertaining to (an) association E19. **associationism** *noun* (*a*) *rare* union in an association; (*b*) a theory accounting for mental phenomena by association of ideas: M19. **associationist** *noun & adjective* (*a*) *noun* a member of an association; an adherent of associationism; (*b*) *adjective* = ASSOCIATIONISTIC: M19. **associatioˈnistic** *adjective* of or pertaining to associationism or associationists E20.

associative /əˈsəʊʃɪətɪv, -sɪ-/ *adjective.* E19.
[ORIGIN from ASSOCIATE *verb* + -IVE.]
1 Of, pertaining to, or characterized by association (esp. of ideas). E19.
2 MATH. Governed by or stating the condition that where three or more quantities in a given order are connected together by operators, the result is independent of any grouping of the quantities, e.g. that $(a \times b) \times c = a \times (b \times c)$. M19.

B. RUSSELL The associative, commutative and distributive laws.

■ **associatively** *adverb* L19. **associativeness** *noun* (*rare*) L19. **associaˈtivity** *noun* (esp. MATH.) M20.

assoil /əˈsɔɪl/ *verb trans. arch.* exc. SCOTS LAW (see sense 4b). Also (*Scot.*) **assoilzie** /-l(j)i/. ME.
[ORIGIN Anglo-Norman *as(s)oil(e)r*, from Old French *assoil-* tonic stem of *asoldre* (mod. *absoudre*) from Latin *absolvere* ABSOLVE; the Scot. form derives from Middle English -*lȝ*-.]
▸ **I** With a person as obj.
1 Grant absolution to; absolve *of*, *from* a sin. ME. ▸**b** Release from purgatory. LME.
†**2** Release from excommunication or other ecclesiastical sentence. LME–L17.
†**3** Release *from*, *of* obligations or liabilities. LME–M17.
4 Acquit of a criminal charge. (Foll. by *of*, *from*.) LME. ▸**b** SCOTS LAW (as **assoilzie**). Hold not liable, in a civil action, by decision of court. E17.
5 *gen.* Release, set free, discharge, (*of*, *from*). LME.
▸ **II** With a thing as obj.
†**6** Clear up, solve, resolve. LME–L17.
†**7** Refute (an objection or argument). LME–E18.
8 Expiate, atone for. L16.
†**9** Get rid of, dispel. *rare* (Spenser). Only in L16.
■ **assoilment** *noun* absolution from sin, guilt, censure, accusation, etc. E17.

†**assoin** *noun, verb* see ESSOIN *noun, verb.*

assonance /ˈas(ə)nəns/ *noun.* E18.
[ORIGIN French, from Latin *assonare* respond to, from *ad* AS-¹ + *sonare*, from *sonus* sound: see -ANCE.]
1 Resemblance or correspondence of sound between two syllables. E18.
2 The rhyming of one word with another in accented vowel and those that follow, but not in consonants, or (less usually) in consonants but not in vowels. E19.
3 *transf.* Correspondence more or less incomplete. M19.
■ **assonant** *adjective & noun* (*a*) *adjective* exhibiting assonance; (*b*) *noun* in *pl.*, words exhibiting assonance: E18. **assonantal** /-ˈnant(ə)l/ *adjective* of or pertaining to assonance, exhibiting assonance M19.

assonate /ˈas(ə)neɪt/ *verb intrans.* E17.
[ORIGIN Latin *assonat-* pa. ppl stem of *assonare*: see ASSONANCE, -ATE³.]
†**1** Sound like a bell. *rare.* Only in E17.
2 Correspond in sound; *spec.* exhibit assonance. M17.

assort /əˈsɔːt/ *verb.* L15.
[ORIGIN Old French *assorter* (mod. *-ir*), from *à* A-⁵ (assim. to *as* AS-¹) + *sorte* SORT *noun*².]
1 *verb trans.* Distribute into groups; arrange in sorts. L15. ▸**b** Classify, place in a group, *with*. M19.

Tait's Edinburgh Magazine Merchants . . employ wool-sorters of their own to assort and repack it. **b** DICKENS He would . . assort it with the fabulous dogs . . as a monstrous invention.

2 *verb trans.* Provide with an assortment. *arch.* M18.

OED We have sent orders for some white goods to assort our store.

3 *verb intrans.* Fall into a class *with*; correspond or suit (*well*, *ill*, etc.) *with*. E19.

W. HAMILTON Finding that it is harmonious,—that it dovetails and naturally assorts with other parts. E. LINKLATER Her cold hard voice that assorted so badly with his memory of her.

4 *verb intrans.* Keep company, associate, *with*. *arch.* E19.

C. LAMB I could abide to assort with fisher-swains.

■ **assorted** *adjective* (*a*) matched *to*; (*ill*, *well*, etc.) suited to one another; (*b*) of various sorts put together: L18.

assortative /əˈsɔːtətɪv/ *adjective.* L19.
[ORIGIN from ASSORT + -ATIVE.]
BIOLOGY. Designating mating which is not random, but correlated with the possession by the partners of certain similar (or dissimilar) characteristics.

assortment /əˈsɔːtm(ə)nt/ *noun.* E17.
[ORIGIN from ASSORT *verb* + -MENT, after French *assortiment*.]
1 The action of assorting; the state of being assorted. *arch.* E17.

OED She was engaged in the assortment of her crewels.

2 A set of various sorts put together. M18.

J. BRAINE A confusion of voices and an assortment of minor noises—glasses clinking, matches being struck, the central heating rumbling.

3 A group of things of the same sort. *rare.* M18.

ADAM SMITH Those classes and assortments, which . . are called genera and species.

assot /əˈsɒt/ *verb.* Long *arch. rare.* Infl. **-tt-**. ME.
[ORIGIN Old French & mod. French *assoter*, formed as A-⁵ + *sot* from medieval Latin *sottus*: see SOT *noun*.]
†**1** *verb intrans.* Behave foolishly; become infatuated. Only in ME.
2 *verb trans.* Make a fool of; infatuate. Chiefly as ***assotted*** *ppl adjective.* LME.

ASSR *abbreviation.*
hist. Autonomous Soviet Socialist Republic.

Asst *abbreviation.*
Assistant.

assuage /əˈsweɪdʒ/ *verb.* ME.
[ORIGIN Old French *as(s)ouagier* from Proto-Romance, from Latin *ad* AS-¹ + *suavis* sweet.]
▸ **I** *verb trans.* **1** Mitigate, appease, allay, alleviate, relieve, (feelings, pain, appetite, desire, etc.). ME.

BACON They need medicine . . to assuage the disease. J. LONDON He had once gone three days without water . . in order to experience the exquisite delight of such a thirst assuaged. N. ALGREN Assuaging her fears by day and her lusts by night.

†**2** Relax, moderate, (a harsh law etc.). ME–L15.
3 Pacify, soothe, (a person). LME.

ADDISON Kindling pity, kindling rage At once provoke me, and asswage.

4 *gen.* Abate, lessen, diminish. *arch.* LME.

W. OWEN Of a truth All death will he annul, all tears assuage? W. S. CHURCHILL But in the name of reason irrational forces had been let loose. These were not easily to be assuaged.

▸ **II** *verb intrans.* †**5** Of passion, pain, appetite, etc.: become less violent, abate. ME–E18.

DEFOE The plague being come to a crisis, its fury began to assuage.

6 *gen.* Diminish, fall off, abate, subside. Long *arch.* LME.

AV *Gen.* 8:1 And the waters asswaged.

■ **assuagement** *noun* (*a*) the action of assuaging; the condition of being assuaged; (*b*) (now *rare*) an assuaging medicine or application: M16. **assuager** *noun* M16.

A

assuasive /əˈsweɪsɪv/ *adjective*. Now *rare*. E18.
[ORIGIN from AS-[1] after PERSUASIVE, conf. in sense with ASSUAGE.]
Soothingly persuasive; soothing.

assubjugate /əˈsʌbdʒʊgeɪt/ *verb trans. rare* (chiefly Shakes.). E17.
[ORIGIN from A-[11] (assim. to AS-[1]) + SUBJUGATE.]
Reduce to subjugation.

assuefaction /aswɪˈfakʃ(ə)n/ *noun*. Long *arch. rare*. E17.
[ORIGIN from Latin *assuefact-* pa. ppl stem of *assuefacere* habituate: see -FACTION. Perh. partly through French *assuéfaction*.]
The action of becoming or the state of being accustomed to something; habituation.

assuetude /ˈaswɪtjuːd/ *noun*. E17.
[ORIGIN Latin *assuetudo*, from *assuet-* pa. ppl stem of *assuescere*, from *ad* AS-[1] + *suescere* accustom: see -TUDE.]
Accustomedness; familiarity.

assume /əˈsjuːm/ *verb trans*. LME.
[ORIGIN Latin *assumere*, from *ad* AS-[1] + *sumere* take. Cf. French *assumer*.]
1 Receive (a person) into association, service, or use; adopt; *spec.* receive up into heaven. *arch.* LME. ▸†**b** Choose, elect, to some (elevated) position. E16–L17.

R. C. TRENCH Revealed religion assumes them into her service. **b** F. QUARLES Her Unkles love assum'd her for his own.

2 Take (a thing) into use; use, absorb, consume. Long *rare*. LME.

T. VENNER Let there be assumed a draught of . . Beere. D. H. LAWRENCE The pink young houses show one side bright Flatly assuming the sun.

3 Take for granted; take as being true, for the sake of argument or action; suppose. LME.

E. WILSON Marx had assumed the value of Shakespeare and the Greeks and more or less left it at that. C. S. FORESTER A slight broadening of the high-road, with an avenue of trees, which Hornblower assumed must be the central square of the town. M. AMIS When you're young you assume everybody old knows what they're doing. H. KISSINGER The letter was assumed—quite correctly—to have been drafted by my staff and me.

4 Chiefly LAW. Take it upon oneself, undertake, *to do*. *arch.* LME.
5 Lay claim to, appropriate, arrogate, (*to* oneself). LME. ▸**b** Claim *to do*. L16.

O. FELTHAM Such . . think there is no way to get Honour, but by a bold assuming it. LD MACAULAY The king assumed to himself the right of filling up the chief municipal offices. **b** GIBBON Witnesses who had or assumed to have knowledge of the fact.

6 Take or put on oneself (an aspect, form, or garb); take to oneself, develop, (an attribute); take to oneself formally (the insignia of office or symbol of a vocation); undertake (an office or duty). In early use foll. by *upon* oneself. M16.

DRYDEN The slipp'ry God will . . various Forms assume. E. A. FREEMAN He assumed the monastic habit. D. H. LAWRENCE Gerald assumed responsibility for the amusements on the water. J. B. PRIESTLEY She had dropped the manner she had assumed at lunch. A. WILSON Bill had been the rebel of the family and inevitably had ended by assuming his father's mantle. L. DEIGHTON A line of men had formed and assumed the relaxed attitudes with which Servicemen accept inevitable delay. O. SACKS The attacks were now assuming a most frightening intensity.

7 Simulate, pretend to have. E17.

SHAKES. *Haml.* Assume a virtue, if you have it not. D. CECIL An essay he wrote under the assumed name of Elia.

8 LOGIC. = SUBSUME 2b. *arch.* E17.
■ **assumable** *adjective* M17. **assumedly** /-mɪdli/ *adverb* as is assumed, presumably L19. **assumer** *noun* E17. **assuming** *adjective* taking much upon oneself, presumptuous, arrogant E17. **assumingly** *adverb* in an assuming manner, presumptuously M19.

assumpsit /əˈsʌm(p)sɪt/ *noun*. L16.
[ORIGIN Latin, lit. 'he has taken upon himself', 3 perf. indic. sing. of *assumere* ASSUME.]
1 An undertaking. L16.
2 *spec.* in LAW (now *hist.*). A promise or contract, oral or in writing not sealed, founded upon a consideration. Also (more fully ***action of assumpsit***), an action to recover damages for breach or non-performance of such a contract. M17.

assumpt /əˈsʌm(p)t/ *verb*. Long *arch.* Pa. pple **-ed**, †**assumpt**. LME.
[ORIGIN Latin *assumpt-* pa. ppl stem of *assumere* ASSUME.]
1 *verb trans.* = ASSUME 1. *obsolete* exc. *spec.* receive up into heaven. LME. ▸†**b** = ASSUME 1b. L16–E17.
†**2** *verb trans.* = ASSUME 6. LME–E17.
3 *verb intrans.* Ascend (to heaven). LME.

E. CRISPIN 'B.V.M. assumpting in jakes,' he spluttered.

assumption /əˈsʌm(p)ʃ(ə)n/ *noun*. ME.
[ORIGIN Old French *asompsion* (mod. *assomption*) or Latin *assumptio(n-)*, formed as ASSUMPT: see -ION.]
▸ **I** Reception, adoption.
1 CHRISTIAN CHURCH. (Also **A-**.) The reception of the Virgin Mary bodily into heaven; a feast held annually on 15 August in honour of this. ME. ▸**b** *gen.* (An) ascent to and reception into heaven. L16.

b TENNYSON Can hang no weight upon my heart In its assumptions up to heaven.

†**2** Consumption, absorption. L16–M17.

JONSON The most gentlemanlike use of tabacco . . the delicate sweete formes for the assumption of it.

3 Reception into union or association; incorporation; adoption. *obsolete* exc. SCOTS LAW. E17.

T. WARTON It is evident that the prose psalms of our liturgy were chiefly consulted . . by the perpetual assumptions of their words.

†**4** Elevation to office or dignity. M–L17.
▸ **II** Taking for or upon oneself.
5 The action or an act of laying claim to something; appropriation, arrogation, usurpation. LME.

R. CRASHAW We to the last Will hold it fast, And no assumption shall deny us. BURKE This astonishing assumption of the publick voice of England.

6 The action or an act of taking upon oneself of a form, aspect, or character; formal taking of office or position. L15.

SIR T. BROWNE The assumption of humane shape, had proved a disadvantage unto Sathan. HOR. WALPOLE Before Richard's assumption of the crown. E. WILSON There is something other than romantic perversity in this assumption of a diabolic role.

7 LAW. A promise or undertaking, either oral or in writing not sealed, founded on a consideration. Cf. ASSUMPSIT. Now *rare*. L16.
8 Presumption, arrogance. E17.

SIR W. SCOTT His usual air of haughty assumption.

9 The action or an act of taking of something for granted; the taking of something as being true, for the sake of argument or action; something so assumed; a supposition. E17.

T. STANLEY He used Arguments not by Assumption, but by inference. E. M. FORSTER Improvements that they had made under the assumption that all would be theirs some day. J. G. FARRELL Were the Irish civilized? The Major was not prepared to risk his life on the assumption that they were. B. MAGEE We, all of us, take a great number of things for granted, and many of these assumptions are of a philosophical character.

▸ **III 10** LOGIC. = SUBSUMPTION 1. *arch.* LME.

assumptive /əˈsʌm(p)tɪv/ *adjective*. M16.
[ORIGIN Latin *assumptivus*, formed as ASSUMPT + -IVE.]
1 Characterized by assumption to oneself; adopted. M16.
2 Taken for granted; apt to take things for granted. M17.
3 Appropriative; making undue claims; arrogant. L18.

†**assura** *noun* see SURA *noun*[2].

assurance /əˈʃʊər(ə)ns/ *noun*. LME.
[ORIGIN Old French & mod. French (earlier *aseürance*), formed as ASSURE: see -ANCE.]
1 A formal guarantee, engagement, or pledge. LME. ▸†**b** *spec.* A marriage engagement, a betrothal. LME–M17. ▸**c** *spec.* A pledge of peace; in *pl.*, terms of peace. *obsolete* exc. *hist.* L16.
2 Subjective certainty; confidence, trust. LME.

J. BUCHAN He spoke with assurance, but I could see the dawning of a doubt in his mind. T. C. WOLFE He is exultant in the assurance of his knowledge and his power.

3 Security, safety. *arch.* LME.

W. LAMBARDE To sende . . unto a place of most assuraunce all such as hee had taken prisoners.

†**4** Objective certainty. L15–E17.
5 LAW. The security of a title to property; (legal evidence of) the conveyance of property by deed. *arch.* L16.
6 Insurance, now *esp.* life insurance. L16.
7 Self-confidence, self-reliance; presumption, impudence. L16.

SWIFT Several of my friends had the assurance to ask me, whether I was in jest? B. SPOCK With your second baby you have more assurance.

8 A positive declaration intended to give confidence; encouraging confirmation. E17.

H. MACMILLAN I was able to give sufficient assurances to satisfy the Australian Cabinet. D. LODGE I'd hoped that the roses would have been some assurance that I was . . thinking of you.

assure /əˈʃʊə/ *verb*. LME.
[ORIGIN Old French & mod. French *assurer* (earlier *asseürer*) from Proto-Romance, from Latin *ad* AS-[1] + *securus* SECURE *adjective*.]
†**1** *verb trans.* Guarantee (a thing *to* a person); promise (*that*). LME–L17.
2 *verb trans.* Give confidence to, confirm, encourage. LME. ▸†**b** *verb intrans.* Have confidence or trust *in*. Only in LME.

BACON Man, when he resteth and assureth himselfe, vpon diuine Protection. F. W. ROBERTSON A pure man forgives, or pleads for mercy, or assures the penitent.

3 *verb trans.* Make (a person) sure or certain (*of*, *that*); *refl.* & in *pass.*, feel certain or satisfied. LME.

SPENSER Assure your selfe, I will not you forsake. AV *2 Tim.* 3:14 Continue thou in the things which thou hast learned, and hast been assured of. J. S. MILL To consider how we are to assure ourselves of its truth. R. KIPLING He came in as one assured that thou wouldst not soon return. S. BELLOW I felt obliged to visit her, at first, as though to assure her that I valued her as much as ever.

†**4** *verb trans.* Make safe or secure from attack or danger; secure to oneself. LME–L17.

W. RALEIGH The Romans, the better to assure themselves, cut a deep trench.

5 *verb trans.* Make safe *from* or *against* risks; insure (esp. life). LME.
6 *verb trans.* Make secure from change or overthrow; make stable, establish securely. LME.

LYTTON The two chiefs who most assured his throne.

†**7** *verb trans.* Affiance, betroth. LME–L16.
8 *verb trans.* Tell (a person) confidently (*of* a thing, its being so, *that*) as something that can be relied upon. E16.

OED He assured us of his own willingness to go. J. B. PRIESTLEY Miss Trant . . was assured by Hilary that all was well with her. T. S. ELIOT You'll come to find that I'm right, I assure you.

†**9** *verb trans.* State positively, affirm. M16–E18.

COVERDALE *Jer.* 29:23 This I testifie and assure. SWIFT I cannot . . so confidently assure the events will follow exactly as I predict them.

†**10** *verb trans.* Secure the possession or reversion of; convey (property) by deed. L16–L17.

C. MARLOWE And with my proper blood Assure my soul to be great Lucifers.

11 *verb trans.* Ensure the occurrence, arrival, etc., of (an event). E17.

A. EDEN Vitality, charm, together with a sweeping no-nonsense air . . always assured her an eager welcome and a rapt audience.

12 *verb trans.* Make certain (a thing that was doubtful). *arch.* L17.

DRYDEN Not to assure our doubtful way.

■ **assurer** *noun* (**a**) an insurer, an underwriter; (**b**) a person who or thing which gives assurance; (**c**) a person who insures his or her life: L16. **assuror** *noun* = ASSURER (a) E17.

assured /əˈʃʊəd/ *adjective & noun*. LME.
[ORIGIN from ASSURE + -ED[1].]
▸ **A** *adjective*. †**1** Made safe; secure. LME–E17.
2 Made sure or certain, guaranteed. LME.

F. DONALDSON His place in the history of literature is assured.

†**3** Engaged, covenanted, pledged. LME–L17.
4 Self-possessed, confident, bold; self-satisfied, presumptuous. LME.

Los Angeles You need a secretary who is assured and competent.

5 Satisfied as to the truth or certainty of a matter. E16.
6 Certified, verified. L16.
▸ **B** *noun*. A person whose life or goods are insured. M18.
■ **assuredly** /əˈʃʊərɪdli/ *adverb* (**a**) certainly, undoubtedly; (**b**) confidently: L15. **assuredness** /əˈʃʊədnɪs, əˈʃʊərɪdnɪs/ *noun* (**a**) certainty, confidence, trust; (**b**) self-confidence, audacity: M16.

assurgent /əˈsəːdʒ(ə)nt/ *adjective*. L16.
[ORIGIN Latin *assurgent-* pres. ppl stem of *assurgere*, from *ad* AS-[1] + *surgere* to rise: see -ENT.]
Rising, ascending; BOTANY rising obliquely.
■ **assurgency** *noun* the quality of being assurgent; the disposition to rise: M17.

Assyrian /əˈsɪrɪən/ *noun & adjective*. LME.
[ORIGIN from Latin *Assyrius*, from Greek *Assurios*, from *Assuria* Assyria (see below), + -AN.]
▸ **A** *noun*. **1** A native or inhabitant of Assyria, an ancient empire in Mesopotamia. LME.
2 The Akkadian dialect of Assyria. L19.
▸ **B** *adjective*. Of or pertaining to Assyria or its dialect. L16.

Assyriology /əsɪrɪˈɒlədʒi/ *noun*. L19.
[ORIGIN from Latin *Assyria* from Greek *Assuria* (see ASSYRIAN), + -OLOGY.]
The branch of knowledge that deals with the language, history, and antiquities of Assyria.
■ **Assyriologist** *noun* L19.

†**assythe** *noun & verb*. Also (earlier) **assethe**. LME–E17.
[ORIGIN formed as ASSET.]
▸ **A** *noun*. Compensation, satisfaction. LME–E17.
▸ **B** *verb trans.* Compensate, satisfy. LME–E17.

assythement /əˈsʌɪðm(ə)nt/ *noun*. M16.
[ORIGIN from ASSYTHE + -MENT.]
SCOTS LAW (now *hist.*). Indemnification owed by an unlawful killer to the surviving relatives of the victim.

AST *abbreviation*.
Atlantic Standard Time.

astable /əˈsteɪb(ə)l, eɪ-/ *adjective*. M20.
[ORIGIN from A-[10] + STABLE *adjective*.]
ELECTRONICS. Designating or pertaining to a circuit which oscillates spontaneously between unstable states.

astarboard /əˈstɑːbəd/ *adverb & pred. adjective.* **L15.**
[ORIGIN from A *preposition*[1] 1 + STARBOARD *noun*.]
NAUTICAL. On or towards the starboard side of a ship.
put the helm astarboard starboard the helm, i.e. move the rudder to port, causing the vessel to turn to the left.

astare /əˈstɛː/ *adverb & pred. adjective.* **M19.**
[ORIGIN from A-[2] + STARE *noun*[2] or *verb*.]
Staring; prominent.

astart /əˈstɑːt/ *verb.* Long *arch. rare.* **ME.**
[ORIGIN from A-[1] + START *verb*.]
1 *verb intrans.* Start up, move suddenly. **ME.**
†**2** *verb intrans. & trans.* Escape, get away, (from). **ME–L16.**
†**3** *verb intrans. & trans.* Happen (to), befall. **LME–L16.**

astart /əˈstɑːt/ *adverb.* **E18.**
[ORIGIN from A *preposition*[1] 4 + START *noun*[2].]
With a start, suddenly.

astatic /əˈstatɪk/ *adjective.* **E19.**
[ORIGIN from Greek *astatos* unstable + -IC.]
ELECTRICITY. Having no fixed position of stability; *esp.* not lining up with or otherwise responding to external magnetic fields.

astatine /ˈastətiːn/ *noun.* **M20.**
[ORIGIN formed as ASTATIC + -INE[5].]
An artificial radioactive chemical element, atomic no. 85, which belongs to the halogen group and has no long-lived isotopes. (Symbol At.)

asteer /əˈstɪə/ *adverb & pred. adjective. Scot.* **M16.**
[ORIGIN from A *preposition*[1] 6 + var. of STIR *noun*[1].]
Stirring, aroused; in commotion.

asteism /ˈastiːɪz(ə)m/ *noun.* Also in Latin form **-ismus** /-ˈɪzməs/. **M16.**
[ORIGIN Late Latin *asteismus* from Greek *asteismos* refined, witty talk, from *asteios* polite, from *astu* city.]
RHETORIC. Urbane irony, polite mockery.

aster /ˈastə/ *noun.* **E17.**
[ORIGIN Latin from Greek *astēr* star.]
†**1** A star. **E17–E18.**
2 a Any of numerous plants constituting the genus *Aster*, of the composite family, bearing showy radiated flowers, e.g. Michaelmas daisy; a flower of such a plant. **E18.** ▸**b** ***China aster***, a related plant, *Callistephus chinensis*, native to China and much cultivated for its showy flowers; a flower of this plant. **M18.**
a NEW ENGLAND *aster*.
3 CYTOLOGY. A star-shaped structure formed during division of the nucleus of an animal cell. **L19.**

-aster /ˈastə/ *suffix* (not productive).
[ORIGIN Latin.]
Forming nouns expressing poor quality or incomplete resemblance, as ***pinaster***, ***poetaster***, etc.

astereognosis /əˌstɛrɪɒgˈnəʊsɪs, əˌstɪər-; eɪ-/ *noun.* **E20.**
[ORIGIN from A-[10] + STEREOGNOSIS.]
MEDICINE. Inability to identify the nature, size, and shape of objects by touch, as a symptom of disorder of the central or peripheral nervous system.
■ Also **astereognosia** *noun* **M20.**

asteriated /əˈstɪərɪeɪtɪd/ *adjective.* **E19.**
[ORIGIN from Greek *asterios* starry + -ATE[2] + -ED[1].]
MINERALOGY. Displaying an asterism (ASTERISM *noun* 4).

asterion /əˈstɪərɪən/ *noun.* **OE.**
[ORIGIN Latin from Greek, from *astēr* star.]
†**1** A flower, of unknown identity. **OE–E17.**
2 ANATOMY. The point at which the parietal, occipital, and temporal bones meet, situated behind the mastoid process. **L19.**

asterisk /ˈastərɪsk/ *noun & verb.* Orig. & (sense A.2b) also in Latin form **-iscus** /-ɪskəs/, pl. **-isci** /-ɪskʌɪ/. **LME.**
[ORIGIN Late Latin *asteriscus* from Greek *asteriskos* dim. of *astēr* star.]
▸ **A** *noun.* **1** The figure of a star (*) used in writing and printing as a reference to a footnote, as a distinguishing or dividing mark, or to replace omitted matter. **LME.**
2 *gen.* A little star; something starlike or star-shaped. **L17.** ▸**b** ORTHODOX CHURCH. A star-shaped utensil placed above the chalice and paten to prevent the veil from touching the elements. **L19.**
▸ **B** *verb trans.* Mark with an asterisk. **M18.**

asterism /ˈastərɪz(ə)m/ *noun.* **L16.**
[ORIGIN Greek *asterismos*, from *astēr* star: see -ISM.]
1 A group of stars; a constellation. **L16.**
†**2** A star; something star-shaped. **M17–L18.**
3 An asterisk or group of asterisks, esp. three printed thus (⁂). **M17.**
4 MINERALOGY. A figure of light having the form of a six-rayed star, seen in certain crystals. **M19.**

astern /əˈstəːn/ *adverb, pred. adjective, & preposition.* **LME.**
[ORIGIN from A *preposition*[1] 1 + STERN *noun*[2].]
Chiefly NAUTICAL. ▸**A** *adverb & pred. adjective.* **1** Of position: in or at the stern; in the rear, behind. (Foll. by *of*.) **LME.**

> DICKENS Keeping half his boat's length astern of the other boat. N. HAMPSON Free as the petrels hovering astern. M. LOWRY If he had expected to leave British snobbery astern with his public school he was sadly mistaken.

line astern: see LINE *noun*[2].
2 Of motion: to the rear, backward; stern foremost. **L17.**

> R. DAHL They'd have to put her in reverse and go full speed astern.

▸ **B** *preposition.* At the stern or rear of. *rare.* **L17.**

asteroid /ˈastərɔɪd/ *noun & adjective.* **E19.**
[ORIGIN from Greek *asteroeidēs* starlike, from *astēr* star: see -OID.]
▸ **A** *noun.* **1** ASTRONOMY. Any of the numerous small planetary bodies which orbit the sun, mainly between the orbits of Mars and Jupiter. **E19.**
2 ZOOLOGY. An echinoderm of the class Asteroidea, which includes the starfishes other than the brittlestars. **M19.**
▸ **B** *adjective.* Star-shaped; starlike. **M19.**
■ **asteˈroidal** *adjective* (ASTRONOMY) of or pertaining to an asteroid or asteroids; of the nature of or resembling an asteroid: **E19.**

asthenia /əsˈθiːnɪə/ *noun.* **L18.**
[ORIGIN mod. Latin from Greek *astheneia* weakness, from *asthenēs* weak: see -IA[1].]
MEDICINE. Loss of strength, weakness.

asthenic /əsˈθɛnɪk/ *adjective & noun.* **L18.**
[ORIGIN Greek *asthenikos*, from *asthenēs* weak: see -IC.]
▸ **A** *adjective.* **1** MEDICINE. Of, pertaining to, or characterized by asthenia. **L18.**
asthenic personality PSYCHOLOGY: characterized by low energy, lack of enthusiasm, and oversensitivity to stress.
2 (Of physique) lean, narrow-shouldered, and long-limbed; characterized by or pertaining to such a physique. Cf. STHENIC. **E20.**
▸ **B** *noun.* An asthenic person; *esp.* a person with an asthenic physique. **L19.**

asthenosphere /əsˈθɛnəsfɪə/ *noun.* **E20.**
[ORIGIN from Greek *asthenēs* weak + -O- + -SPHERE.]
GEOLOGY. The upper layer of the earth's mantle, below the lithosphere, characterized by a relatively low resistance to plastic flow.
■ **asthenospheric** /əsθɛnəˈsfɛrɪk/ *adjective* of or pertaining to the asthenosphere **M20.**

asthma /ˈasmə/ *noun.* Also †**asma**. **LME.**
[ORIGIN (medieval Latin *asma* from) Greek *asthma*, *-mat-*, from *azein* breathe hard.]
Difficulty of breathing; *spec.* such a condition characterized by attacks due to bronchial spasm and often of allergic origin.
– COMB.: **asthma herb**, **asthma weed** *Austral.* a common tropical weed, *Euphorbia pilulifera*, used to treat asthma.

asthmatic /asˈmatɪk/ *noun & adjective.* **E16.**
[ORIGIN Latin *asthmaticus* from Greek *asthmatikos*, from *asthmat-*: see ASTHMA, -IC.]
▸ **A** *noun.* A person who suffers from asthma. **E16.**
▸ **B** *adjective.* **1** That suffers from asthma. **E16.**
2 Of or pertaining to asthma. **E17.**
3 Of medicine: of use against asthma. Now *rare.* **E18.**
4 *fig.* Puffing, wheezy. **E19.**

> J. BERESFORD An asthmatic pair of bellows. F. KIDMAN The ferry, powered by an asthmatic diesel engine, shuddered and roared.

■ **asthmatical** *adjective* = ASTHMATIC *adjective* **M17.** **asthmatically** *adverb* **E19.**

asthore /əsˈθɔː/ *noun. Irish.* **E19.**
[ORIGIN Irish, from *a* O *interjection* + *stór* treasure.]
As a form of address: (my) treasure, darling.

Asti /ˈasti/ *noun.* **M19.**
[ORIGIN A province in Piedmont, NW Italy.]
A still or (esp.) sparkling white wine from Asti.
Asti Spumante /spʊˈmanti/ sparkling Asti.

astigmatic /astɪgˈmatɪk/ *adjective.* **M19.**
[ORIGIN formed as ASTIGMATISM + -IC.]
1 Pertaining to or characterized by astigmatism. **M19.**
2 Correcting astigmatism. **L19.**

astigmatism /əˈstɪgmətɪz(ə)m/ *noun.* **M19.**
[ORIGIN from A-[10] + Greek *stigmat-*, *-ma* point + -ISM.]
A defect of the cornea or lens of the eye, or of any lens, mirror, etc., which prevents rays of light from coming to a single focus.

astilbe /əˈstɪlbi/ *noun.* **M19.**
[ORIGIN mod. Latin, from Greek *a-* A-[10] + *stilbē* fem. of *stilbos* glittering.]
A plant of the genus *Astilbe*, of the saxifrage family, bearing small inconspicuous white or pink flowers.

†**astipulation** *noun.* **L16–E18.**
[ORIGIN Latin *astipulatio(n-)*, from *astipulat-* pa. ppl stem of *astipulari*, from *ad* AS-[1] + *stipulari* STIPULATE *verb*: see -ATION.]
Agreement, assent; a confirming statement.

astir /əˈstəː/ *adverb & pred. adjective.* **L18.**
[ORIGIN from A-[2] + STIR *noun*[1] or *verb*: cf. ASTEER.]
Stirring, esp. out of bed; in motion, excited(ly).

†**astone** *verb trans.* Also **astun**, infl. **-nn-**. **ME.**
[ORIGIN Old French *estoner* (mod. *étonner*) from Proto-Gallo-Romance, from Latin EX-[1] + *tonare* to thunder: see ASTOUND *verb*, STUN *verb*. Cf. ASTONY.]
1 Stun, stupefy. **ME–M18.**
2 Amaze, astound; bewilder. **ME–L17.**

astonied *ppl adjective* see ASTONY *verb*.

astonish /əˈstɒnɪʃ/ *verb trans.* **E16.**
[ORIGIN Prob. from ASTONY or ASTONE + -ISH[2]: first recorded as pa. ppl adjective. Cf. ASTOUND *verb*.]
†**1** Stun mentally; drive stupid, bewilder; dismay, terrify. **E16–L18.**

> SHAKES. *Jul. Caes.* The most mighty gods by tokens send Such dreadful heralds to astonish us. MILTON Blind, astonished, and struck with superstition as with a planet.

†**2** Render insensible; paralyse, benumb. **M16–M17.**

> P. HOLLAND The one smote the king upon the head, the other astonished his shoulder.

3 Amaze; surprise greatly. **E17.**

> AV *Matt.* 7:28 The people were astonished at his doctrine. GIBBON The Romans . . astonished the Greeks by their sincere and simple performance of the most burthensome engagements. E. BLYTON Think how astonished the Sticks will be to find the little girl gone—and their dear Edgar shut up in the cave instead!

astonish the natives: see NATIVE *noun* 5.
■ **astonishable** *adjective* †(*a*) calculated to astonish, surprising; (*b*) able to be astonished: **E17.** **astonishedly** *adverb* in an astonished manner, with astonishment **E17.** **astonisher** *noun* **M19.** **astonishingly** *adverb* in an astonishing manner; to an astonishing degree; amazingly: **M17.**

astonishment /əˈstɒnɪʃm(ə)nt/ *noun.* **L16.**
[ORIGIN from ASTONISH + -MENT.]
†**1** Insensibility; paralysis, numbness. **L16–M17.**

> E. TOPSELL Those which are troubled with any deafness or astonishment in any part of their bodies.

†**2** Bewilderment, stupor; consternation, dismay, loss of presence of mind. **L16–M19.**

> AV *Ps.* 60:3 Thou hast made vs to drinke the wine of astonishment.

3 Amazement due to the unexpected or unaccountable; great surprise. **L16.**

> ADDISON We are flung into pleasing astonishment at such unbounded views. J. BARTH I shook my head in astonishment at the whole business.

4 An object or cause of amazement or great surprise. **E17.**

> AV *Deut.* 28:37 Thou shalt become an astonishment, a prouerbe, and a by-worde.

astony /əˈstɒni/ *verb trans. arch.* Now only as **astonied** *ppl adjective.* **ME.**
[ORIGIN Obscure var. of ASTONE *verb*.]
= ASTONISH.

astoop /əˈstuːp/ *adverb & pred. adjective.* **M17.**
[ORIGIN from A *preposition*[1] 4 + STOOP *noun*[2].]
In an inclined position, stooping.

astound /əˈstaʊnd/ *adjective. arch.* **ME.**
[ORIGIN Phonet. devel. of *astoned* pa. pple of ASTONE.]
†**1** Stunned, insensible. **ME–M18.**
2 Astonished, amazed; confounded. **LME.**

astound /əˈstaʊnd/ *verb trans.* **LME.**
[ORIGIN Earliest as *astounded* ppl adjective, from ASTOUND *adjective* + -ED[1]; later back-form. from this.]
†**1** Render insensible, stupefy. **LME–E18.**
2 Shock with alarm or wonder; astonish, amaze. **L16.**
■ **astoundingly** *adverb* in an astounding manner, astonishingly **E19.** **astoundment** *noun* (profound) astonishment **E19.**

astrachan *noun* var. of ASTRAKHAN.

astraddle /əˈstrad(ə)l/ *adverb & pred. adjective.* **M17.**
[ORIGIN from A *preposition*[1] 6 + STRADDLE *noun*.]
In a straddling position; astride (*of*).

astragal /ˈastrəg(ə)l/ *noun.* **M17.**
[ORIGIN from ASTRAGALUS, partly through French *astragale*.]
1 ARCHITECTURE. A small moulding of semicircular section, esp. placed round the top or bottom of a column. Freq. *attrib.* **M17.**
2 A ring or moulding round the barrel of a cannon. **M17.**
3 = ASTRAGALUS 1; in *pl.* also, dice (for which such bones were formerly used). **E18.**
4 A thin bar separating panes of glass in a window. **E19.**

astragalus /əˈstrag(ə)ləs/ *noun.* Pl. **-li** /-lʌɪ, -liː/. **M16.**
[ORIGIN Latin from Greek *astragalos*.]
1 ANATOMY. = TALUS *noun*[1]. *arch.* **M16.**
†**2** = ASTRAGAL 1. Only in **M16.**
3 Any plant of the large leguminous genus *Astragalus*. Also called ***milk-vetch***. **M16.**
■ **astragalar** *adjective* (ANATOMY) of or pertaining to an astragalus **M19.** **astragalomancy** *noun* divination by means of dice or knuckle bones (cf. ASTRAGAL 3) **M17.**

astrain /əˈstreɪn/ *adverb & pred. adjective.* **M18.**
[ORIGIN from A-[2] + STRAIN *noun*[2] or *verb*[1].]
On the strain, straining.

astrakhan /astrəˈkan/ *noun.* Also **-chan**. **M18.**
[ORIGIN *Astrakhan*, a city and region in central Asia.]
The dark furry fleece of very young lambs from Astrakhan; a cloth resembling this.
Red Astrachan: see RED *adjective*.

astral /ˈastr(ə)l/ *adjective & noun*. E17.
[ORIGIN Late Latin *astralis*, from *astrum* star: see -AL[1].]
▸ **A** *adjective*. **1** Of, connected with, or proceeding from the stars. E17.
astral spirits: those formerly thought to inhabit celestial objects.
2 Star-shaped, starlike. L17.
astral lamp *hist.* a kind of Argand lamp.
3 THEOSOPHY. Pertaining to or consisting of an ethereal substance supposed to be next above the material world in refinement and to pervade all space. L19.
astral body the ethereal counterpart of a human or animal body.
4 CYTOLOGY. Of or pertaining to an aster. L19.
▸ **B** *noun*. **1** *hist.* An astral lamp. M19.
2 THEOSOPHY. An astral body. L19.
■ **astrally** *adverb* (**a**) according to the stars; (**b**) in or through the powers of the astral body: L17.

astrand /əˈstrand/ *adverb & pred. adjective*. E19.
[ORIGIN from A-[2] + STRAND *verb*[1].]
Stranded.

astrantia /asˈtrantɪə/ *noun*. M19.
[ORIGIN mod. Latin (see below), perh. from Greek *astēr* star.]
Any of various plants of the genus *Astrantia* (family Umbelliferae, or Apiaceae) with small compact starlike heads of tiny flowers surrounded by prominent bracts, native to Europe and western Asia.

astray /əˈstreɪ/ *adverb & pred. adjective*. ME.
[ORIGIN Anglo-Norman var. of Old French *estraié* pa. pple of *estraier* stray, ult. from Latin *extra* out of bounds + *vagari* wander: see A-[7] and cf. STRAY *adjective*.]
1 Out of the right way, wandering. ME.

> SIR W. SCOTT Why urge thy chase so far astray?

go astray be lost, be mislaid.
2 *fig.* In or into error or sin. LME.

> SHAKES. *Two Gent.* Nay, in that you are astray. E. A. FREEMAN Evil counsellors had led him astray. J. BALDWIN Fathers . . , have you ever had a son who went astray?

astream /əˈstriːm/ *adverb & pred. adjective*. M18.
[ORIGIN from A-[2] + STREAM *noun* or *verb*.]
Streaming; in a stream.

astrict /əˈstrɪkt/ *verb trans.* Pa. pple & ppl adjective **-ed**, (earlier) †**astrict**. Also †**ad-**. LME.
[ORIGIN Orig. pa. pple, from Latin *astrict-* pa. ppl stem of *astringere* ASTRINGE.]
1 Bind, compress, constrict. *arch.* LME.
2 Bind by moral or legal obligation. *arch.* LME.
3 Restrict, limit, (*to*). M16.
4 SCOTS LAW. Restrict in tenure by an obligation to have grain ground at a particular mill. Usu. as ***astricted ppl adjective***. *obsolete* exc. *hist.* M16.
■ **astrictive** *adjective* (now *rare* or *obsolete*) binding; obligatory; astringent: M16.

astriction /əˈstrɪkʃ(ə)n/ *noun*. Also †**ad-**. M16.
[ORIGIN Old French & mod. French, or Latin *astrictio(n-)*, formed as ASTRICT: see -ION.]
†**1** Moral or legal obligation. M16–M17.
2 Binding together; constriction; constipation. *arch.* M16.
†**3** Astringency. M16–M18.
4 Restriction; *spec.* in SCOTS LAW, restriction in tenure by an obligation to have grain ground at a particular mill. *obsolete* exc. *hist.* E17.

astride /əˈstrʌɪd/ *adverb, adjective, & preposition*. E17.
[ORIGIN from A *preposition*[1] 6 + STRIDE *noun*.]
▸ **A** *adverb* & (chiefly *pred.*) *adjective*. With the legs apart or on either side (*of*). E17.

> W. COWPER The playful jockey scow'rs the room . . astride upon the parlour broom. S. SMILES Sitting astride of a house-roof. S. G. GOLDSCHMIDT Some say that astride riding is safer. *fig.*: A. ALISON Napoleon's central position astride on the Elbe.

▸ **B** *preposition*. Bestriding. E18.

> E. M. FORSTER He sat near her, astride the parapet, with one foot in the loggia and the other dangling into the view.

astringe /əˈstrɪn(d)ʒ/ *verb trans.* Also †**ad-**. Pres. pple & verbal noun **astringeing**. E16.
[ORIGIN Latin *astringere*, from *ad* AS-[1] + *stringere* bind, draw tight.]
†**1** Bind morally or legally; oblige. E16–M18.
2 Bind together, constrict; constipate. M16.

astringent /əˈstrɪn(d)ʒ(ə)nt/ *adjective & noun*. M16.
[ORIGIN French from Latin *astringent-* pres. ppl stem of *astringere*: see ASTRINGE, -ENT.]
▸ **A** *adjective*. **1** Causing contraction of the body tissues, styptic. M16.
2 *fig.* Severe, austere. E19.
▸ **B** *noun*. An astringent medicine or substance. E17.
■ **astringency** *noun* astringent quality (*lit.* & *fig.*) E17. **astringently** *adverb* M19.

†**astrion** *noun*. ME–L19.
[ORIGIN Latin, dim. of Greek *astēr* star.]
A certain precious stone, prob. star sapphire.

astro- /ˈastrəʊ/ *combining form* of Greek *astron* star: see -O-.
■ **astro-archaeˈology** *noun* = ARCHAEOASTRONOMY M20. **astrobiˈology** *noun* the branch of science that deals with the search for and investigation of extraterrestrial life M20. **astrobleme** /-bliːm/ *noun* [Greek *blēma* wound produced by a missile] GEOLOGY an eroded remnant of a large impact crater of extraterrestrial origin M20. **astroˈchemistry** *noun* the chemistry of materials present in outer space M20. **astrocompass** *noun* an instrument designed to indicate direction with respect to the stars M20. **astrocyte** *noun* (ANATOMY) a star-shaped glial cell of the central nervous system L19. **astrocyˈtoma** *noun*, pl. **-mas**, **-mata** /-mətə/, MEDICINE a brain tumour derived from astrocytes M20. **astrodome** *noun* (**a**) a domed window in an aircraft for astronomical observations; (**b**) (chiefly *US* in proper names) a stadium with a domed roof: M20. **astrogeˈology** *noun* the science of geology as applied to extraterrestrial bodies M20. **astrohatch** *noun* = ASTRODOME (a) M20. **astrometeoroˈlogical** *adjective* of or pertaining to the investigation of the supposed influence of the celestial objects on the weather etc. L17. **astrometeoˈrologist** *noun* an expert in or student of astrometeorology M19. **astrometeoˈrology** *noun* the investigation of the supposed influence of celestial objects on the weather etc. M19. **astronaviˈgation** *noun* navigation of aircraft or spacecraft by means of the stars M20. **astrophil(e)** *noun* a lover of the stars E18. **astrophotoˈgraphic**, **astrophotoˈgraphical** *adjectives* of or pertaining to astrophotography L19. **astrophoˈtography** *noun* the use of photography in astronomy M19. **astrotheˈology** *noun* theology founded on observation of celestial objects E18.

astrogation /astrəˈgeɪʃ(ə)n/ *noun*. M20.
[ORIGIN from ASTRO- + NAVI)GATION.]
(Chiefly in science fiction) the science or practice of navigating a vehicle through space.
■ **astrogational** *adjective* M20. **ˈastrogator** *noun* M20.

astrography /əˈstrɒgrəfi/ *noun*. M18.
[ORIGIN from ASTRO- + -GRAPHY.]
Orig., the science of describing the stars. Now, the mapping of the heavens.
■ **ˈastrograph** *noun* a telescope designed for photographic astrography M20. **astroˈgraphic** *adjective* of, pertaining to, used in, or produced by astrography L19.

astroid /ˈastrɔɪd/ *noun*. L19.
[ORIGIN from ASTRO- + -OID.]
MATH. A hypocycloid with four cusps (resembling a square with concave sides), defined by the equation $x^{2/3} + y^{2/3} = R^{2/3}$.

†**astroite** *noun*. Freq. in Latin form **astroites**. M16.
[ORIGIN Latin *astroites* from Greek *astroitēs*: see ASTRO-, -ITE[1].]
1 = ASTRION *noun*. M16–M18.
2 A star-shaped mineral or fossil. E17–E18.
3 A kind of coral. L17–M19.

astrolabe /ˈastrəleɪb/ *noun*. LME.
[ORIGIN Old French *astrelabe* from medieval Latin *astrolabium* from Greek *astrolabon* use as noun of neut. of adjective *astrolabos* star-taking.]
An instrument used to make astronomical measurements, esp. of the altitudes of stars.
■ **astroˈlabic** *adjective* of or pertaining to the astrolabe M20. **astroˈlabical** *adjective* (*rare*) = ASTROLABIC E17.

astrolatry /əˈstrɒlətri/ *noun*. L17.
[ORIGIN from ASTRO- + -LATRY.]
The worship of celestial objects.

astrologer /əˈstrɒlədʒə/ *noun*. LME.
[ORIGIN Old French *astrologue* or *-logien* from Latin *astrologus* from Greek *astrologos*: see ASTRO-, -LOGER.]
†**1** An observer of the stars, a practical astronomer. LME–M18.
†**2** ***common astrologer***, the cock. Only in LME.
3 A person who practises astrology (ASTROLOGY *noun* 2). E17.
■ †**astrolog(ue)** *noun* an astrologer LME–E18. †**astrologian** *noun* an astrologer LME–M19.

astrologic /astrəˈlɒdʒɪk/ *noun & adjective*. M16.
[ORIGIN noun from medieval Latin *astrologica* noun pl.; adjective from French *astrologique* or as ASTROLOGICAL.]
▸ †**A** *noun*. In *pl.* Matters or facts of astrology. M16–L17.
▸ **B** *adjective*. = ASTROLOGICAL. M17.

astrological /astrəˈlɒdʒɪk(ə)l/ *adjective*. L16.
[ORIGIN from late Latin *astrologicus* from Greek *astrologikos*, from *astrologia*: see ASTROLOGY, -IC, -AL[1].]
Of or pertaining to astrology.
■ **astrologically** *adverb* E17.

astrologist /əˈstrɒlədʒɪst/ *noun*. Chiefly *N. Amer.* M20.
[ORIGIN from ASTROLOGY + -IST.]
An astrologer.

astrology /əˈstrɒlədʒi/ *noun*. LME.
[ORIGIN Old French & mod. French *astrologie* from Latin *astrologia* from Greek: see ASTRO-, -LOGY.]
†**1** Astronomy, esp. in its practical aspects, as the measurement of time, prediction of natural phenomena, etc. Also more fully ***natural astrology***. LME–M19.
2 The supposed art of foretelling or counselling in human affairs by interpretation of the motions of celestial objects. Also more fully ***judicial astrology***. M16.

astrometry /əˈstrɒmɪtri/ *noun*. M19.
[ORIGIN from ASTRO- + -METRY.]
The measurement of the positions, motions, and magnitudes of stars.
■ **astroˈmetric** *adjective* of or pertaining to astrometry; identified by astrometry: M20. **astroˈmetrical** *adjective* = ASTROMETRIC E20.

astronaut /ˈastrənɔːt/ *noun*. E20.
[ORIGIN from ASTRO- after *aeronaut*.]
A space traveller; a member of the crew of a spacecraft.

astronautics /astrəˈnɔːtɪks/ *noun*. E20.
[ORIGIN from ASTRO- after *aeronautics*.]
The science and technology of the exploration and utilization of space.
■ **astronautical** *adjective* pertaining to or concerned with astronautics or astronauts E20.

astronomer /əˈstrɒnəmə/ *noun*. LME.
[ORIGIN from ASTRONOMY + -ER[1].]
1 A person who studies or practises astronomy. LME.
Astronomer Royal: a title held by two astronomers, one in England and one in Scotland who are usu. also the directors of the Royal Observatories.
†**2** = ASTROLOGER 3. LME–E17.

astronomical /astrəˈnɒmɪk(ə)l/ *adjective*. M16.
[ORIGIN from French *astronomique* or Latin *astronomicus* from Greek *astronomikos*: see ASTRONOMY, -ICAL.]
1 Of or pertaining to astronomy. M16.
astronomical clock: keeping sidereal time. ***astronomical day***: see DAY *noun*. **astronomical telescope** *spec.* a refractor giving an inverted image (opp. ***terrestrial telescope***). **astronomical triangle** a triangle on the celestial sphere whose vertices are the north or south celestial pole, the zenith, and the position of a given celestial object. **astronomical unit** the mean distance of the earth from the sun, equal to 1.496 × 10[8] km or approx. 93 million miles. ***astronomical year***: see YEAR *noun*[1].
2 *fig.* As enormous as the distances, sizes, etc., typically encountered in astronomy; very great. L19.

> P. H. GIBBS Reparations demanded from Germany—astronomical sums. ANTHONY HUXLEY Pollen production is astronomical in wind-pollinated flowers.

■ **astronomic** *adjective* = ASTRONOMICAL E18. **astronomically** *adverb* M17.

astronomy /əˈstrɒnəmi/ *noun*. ME.
[ORIGIN Old French & mod. French *astronomie* from Latin *astronomia* (Seneca) from Greek: see ASTRO-, -NOMY.]
1 The science of celestial objects (including the earth in relation to them), of space, and of the universe as a whole. With specifying word, any of the branches of this subject, as ***radio astronomy***. ME.
†**2** = ASTROLOGY 2. ME–E18.
■ **astronomize** *verb intrans.* pursue astronomy; act or speak astronomically: L17.

†**astrophel** *noun*. *rare* (Spenser). Only in L16.
[ORIGIN Perh. alt. of *astrophyllum* star-leaf from Greek *astron* star + *phullon* leaf.]
A certain unidentified plant.

astrophysics /astrə(ʊ)ˈfɪzɪks/ *noun*. L19.
[ORIGIN from ASTRO- + PHYSICS.]
The branch of astronomy that deals with the physical and chemical properties of celestial objects and interstellar space.
■ **astrophysical** *adjective* of or pertaining to astrophysics L19. **astrophysically** *adverb* as regards or by means of astrophysics L20. **astrophysicist** *noun* an expert in or student of astrophysics M19.

Astroturf /ˈastrətəːf/ *noun*. M20.
[ORIGIN from *Astrodome*, an indoor baseball ground in Houston, Texas, where first used, + TURF *noun*.]
(Proprietary name for) an artificial grasslike surface.

astrut /əˈstrʌt/ *adverb & pred. adjective*. *arch.* ME.
[ORIGIN from A *preposition*[1] 4 + STRUT *noun*[2].]
Sticking out; puffed up; defiant.

astucious /əˈstjuːʃəs/ *adjective*. E19.
[ORIGIN from French *astucieux*, from *astuc(i)e* astuteness + *-eux* -OUS.]
Astute.
■ **astucity** /-sɪti/ *noun* astuteness L18.

†**astun** *verb* var. of ASTONE.

Asturian /əˈstjʊərɪən/ *adjective & noun*. E17.
[ORIGIN Spanish *asturiano*, from *Asturias* (see below). Cf. Latin *Astur*, *-uris* Asturian.]
▸ **A** *adjective*. **1** Of or pertaining to Asturias, a region of northern Spain (formerly a principality and once an independent kingdom), or its inhabitants. E17.
2 *spec.* in ARCHAEOLOGY. Designating or pertaining to a Mesolithic culture whose remains are found in Asturias. E20.
▸ **B** *noun*. **1** A native or inhabitant of Asturias. E17.
2 The Castilian dialect spoken in Asturias. L19.

astute /əˈstjuːt/ *adjective*. E17.
[ORIGIN French †*astut* or Latin *astutus*, from *astus* crafty, cunning.]
Of keen penetration, esp. as to one's own interests; shrewd; sagacious; crafty.

> CONAN DOYLE He made a bad slip when he allowed my astute friend to notice the number of the seat taken for his wife. G. B. SHAW It seemed an astute stroke of German imperial tactics to send Lenin safely through Germany to Russia.

be astute to do LAW (of a court) exercise ingenuity to do, take pains to do.
■ **astutely** *adverb* E19. **astuteness** *noun* M19.

astylar /eɪˈstʌɪlə/ *adjective*. M19.
[ORIGIN from Greek *astulos* without columns, from A-[10] + *stulos* column, + -AR[1].]
Without columns or pilasters.

asudden /əˈsʌd(ə)n/ *adverb*. L19.
[ORIGIN from A-[2] + SUDDEN.]
Suddenly.

asunder /əˈsʌndə/ *adverb*.
[ORIGIN Old English *on sundran*, *-um*: see A *preposition*[1] 2, SUNDER *adjective*.]
†**1** In or into a position separate or apart. OE–M16.
> COVERDALE But me called he a sonder to be his preacher.

2 Apart or separate from one another in position or direction. ME.
> J. A. FROUDE Wide asunder as pole and pole. J. GALSWORTHY He went up to the curtains, and . . drew them asunder.

3 Apart from one another in character, separately as objects of thought. *arch.* LME.
know asunder distinguish.
4 Into separate parts. LME.
> B. BAINBRIDGE A noise . . like a piece of silk being ripped asunder.

asura /ˈʌsʊrə/ *noun*. L18.
[ORIGIN Sanskrit = Lord, spirit, demon, perh. from *ásu* breath, life.]
HINDUISM. In the earliest texts of the Rig Veda, (the title of a) god. Later, (a member of) a class of chiefly malevolent deities or demons.

ASW *abbreviation*.
Anti-submarine warfare.

aswarm /əˈswɔːm/ *adverb & pred. adjective*. M19.
[ORIGIN from A-[2] + SWARM *noun* or *verb*[1].]
Swarming (*with*).
> B. BRYSON The terminal area was aswarm with . . cars and lorries.

asway /əˈsweɪ/ *adverb & pred. adjective*. M19.
[ORIGIN from A-[2] + SWAY *noun* or *verb*.]
Swaying.

asweat /əˈswɛt/ *adverb & pred. adjective*. L19.
[ORIGIN from A-[2] + SWEAT *noun* or *verb*.]
Sweating.

aswim /əˈswɪm/ *adverb & pred. adjective*. M17.
[ORIGIN from A *preposition*[1] 6 + SWIM *noun*.]
Swimming, afloat.

aswing /əˈswɪŋ/ *adverb & pred. adjective*. L19.
[ORIGIN from A-[2] + SWING *noun*[1] or *verb*.]
Swinging.

aswirl /əˈswəːl/ *adverb & pred. adjective*. E20.
[ORIGIN from A-[2] + SWIRL *noun* or *verb*.]
Swirling.

aswoon /əˈswuːn/ *adverb & pred. adjective*.
[ORIGIN Old English *geswōgen*: see A-[4], SWOWN. Later from A-[2] + SWOON *noun* or *verb*.]
In a swoon or faint.

asyle *noun* var. of ASILE.

asyllabic /eɪsɪˈlabɪk, a-/ *adjective*. E19.
[ORIGIN from A-[10] + SYLLABIC *adjective*.]
Not syllabic; not constituting a syllable.
■ **asyllabical** *adjective* (*rare*) M18.

asylum /əˈsʌɪləm/ *noun & verb*. LME.
[ORIGIN Latin from Greek *asulon* refuge, use as noun of neut. of *asulos* inviolable, from A-[10] + *sulē*, *sulon* right of seizure.]
▸ **A** *noun*. Pl. **-lums**, †**-la**.
1 A sanctuary, a place of refuge and safety, orig. and esp. for criminals. LME.
> ANTHONY WOOD He fled to Oxon, the common Asylum of afflicted royalists.

2 Sanctuary, refuge, protection; *spec.* (also ***political asylum***) protection granted by a state to someone who has left their native country as a political refugee. E18.
> E. WILSON Weitling had been expelled from Paris . . and, seeking asylum in Switzerland, had there been convicted of blasphemy. E. LONGFORD Catherine . . had found asylum with her two unmarried sisters.

3 An institution for the shelter and support of disabled (esp. insane) or destitute persons. Now chiefly *colloq.* exc. *hist.* M18.
> L. HELLMAN He had spent much of his childhood in a Philadelphia orphan asylum. *Spectator* She ends up going mad, and Charlie . . has to commit her to an asylum.

LUNATIC ***asylum***.
– COMB.: **asylum seeker** a person seeking refuge, esp. political asylum, in a nation other than his or her own.
▸ **B** *verb trans.* Give asylum to; place in an asylum. *rare*. L18.
■ **asylee** *noun* a person who is seeking, or has been granted, political asylum M20.

asymbolia /asɪmˈbəʊlɪə, eɪ-/ *noun*. L19.
[ORIGIN from A-[10] + SYMBOL *noun*[1] + -IA[1].]
MEDICINE. Inability to understand or use visual, auditory, or other sensory symbols.

asymmetric /asɪˈmɛtrɪk, eɪ-/ *adjective*. L19.
[ORIGIN from A-[10] + SYMMETRIC.]
1 = ASYMMETRICAL. L19.
2 CHEMISTRY. Designating or containing a carbon atom which is bonded to four different substituents and is hence a cause of optical isomerism. Of a synthesis: preferentially yielding a particular optical isomer. L19.

asymmetrical /asɪˈmɛtrɪk(ə)l, eɪ-/ *adjective*. L17.
[ORIGIN from A-[10] + SYMMETRICAL.]
Not symmetrical, with the parts not arranged in symmetry.
asymmetrical warfare: involving surprise attacks by small, simply armed groups on a nation with sophisticated modern armed forces.
■ **asymmetrically** *adverb* L19.

asymmetry /aˈsɪmɪtri, eɪ-/ *noun*. M17.
[ORIGIN Greek *asummetria*: see A-[10], SYMMETRY.]
†**1** MATH. Incommensurability. M17–L18.
2 Absence of symmetry or proportion. M17.
3 CHEMISTRY. The property of being asymmetric. L19.

asymptomatic /əˌsɪmptəˈmatɪk, eɪ-/ *adjective*. M20.
[ORIGIN from A-[10] + SYMPTOMATIC *adjective*.]
MEDICINE. Producing or exhibiting no symptoms.

asymptote /ˈasɪm(p)təʊt/ *noun*. M17.
[ORIGIN mod. Latin *asymptota* (sc. *linea* line) from Greek *asumptōtos* adjective (also used as noun), from A-[10] + *sun-* SYN- + *ptōtos* apt to fall.]
MATH. A straight line which is continually approached by a given curve but does not meet it within a finite distance.
■ **asymptotic** /asɪm(p)ˈtɒtɪk/ *adjective* of, pertaining to, or of the nature of an asymptote; pertaining to the behaviour of a function when its argument takes large values: L17. **asympˈtotical** *adjective* E18. **asympˈtotically** *adverb* in the manner of an asymptote L17.

asynchronous /əˈsɪŋkrənəs, eɪ-/ *adjective*. M18.
[ORIGIN from A-[10] + SYNCHRONOUS.]
Not synchronous.
■ **asynchronously** *adverb* M20. **asynchrony** /eɪˈsɪŋkrəni/ *noun* the quality of being asynchronous M20.

asyndetic /asɪnˈdɛtɪk/ *adjective*. L19.
[ORIGIN formed as ASYNDETON + -IC.]
1 RHETORIC. Characterized by asyndeton, not connected by conjunctions. L19.
2 Of a catalogue, index, etc.: without cross-references. L19.

asyndeton /əˈsɪndɪt(ə)n/ *noun*. M16.
[ORIGIN mod. Latin from Greek *asundeton* use as noun of neut. of *asundetos* unconnected, from A-[10] + *sundetos* bound together.]
RHETORIC. Omission of a conjunction.

asyntactic /asɪnˈtaktɪk, eɪ-/ *adjective*. E19.
[ORIGIN from Greek *asuntaktos* disorganized, ungrammatical + -IC, after SYNTACTIC: see A-[10].]
With loose syntax, ungrammatical.

asystole /əˈsɪstəli/ *noun*. L19.
[ORIGIN from A-[10] + SYSTOLE.]
MEDICINE. Cessation of the contractions of the heart.
■ **asystolic** /asɪˈstɒlɪk/ *adjective* L19.

At *symbol*.
CHEMISTRY. Astatine.

at /ɑːt, at/ *noun*. M20.
[ORIGIN Lao.]
A monetary unit of Laos, equal to one-hundredth of a kip.

at /at, *unstressed* ət/ *preposition*.
[ORIGIN Old English *æt* = Old Frisian *et*, Old Saxon *at*, Old High German *az*, Old Norse, Gothic *at*, a Germanic preposition and verbal prefix, rel. to Latin *ad*.]
▸ **I** Physical position.
1 Expr. exact, approximate, or vague spatial or local position (*lit.* or in *fig.* contexts). OE. ▸**b** With proper names of places, esp. of towns (exc. usu. those of public or private importance, cf. IN *preposition*) and small islands. OE. ▸**c** Expr. position or distance in relation to a point of orientation. E16. ▸**d** Used with cardinal points of the compass to indicate parts of the country or (NAUTICAL) the quarter of the wind. *US*. M17.
> I. BARROW At a point given A, to make a right line AG. E. HEMINGWAY I . . found the major sitting at a table in the bare room. N. BALCHIN The young chimpanzee was sitting at the back of the cage. J. CARY She said no more except to utter a brief thanks when Joanna put her down at her door. S. ULLMANN The dog's scraping at the door. R. QUIRK I have often been at the receiving end of calls for help from this Unit. J. I. M. STEWART The cricket field at the centre of the scene. R. WILLIAMS At the very centre of a major area of modern thought and practice . . is a concept 'culture'. A. BURNETT At the start of the poem the speaker thinks he sees his dead wife brought to him; at the end only his 'night' is brought back. **b** LD MACAULAY The Parliament met at Edinburgh. GERALD MOORE I was born at Watford, Hertfordshire, in 1899. **c** MILTON To save himself against a coward arm'd At one spear's length. H. NELSON The Corsican privateers kept at such a distance.

2 Expr. some practical connection with a place (freq. with article omitted). OE.
> DICKENS What the parson at chapel says. L. GOLDING He would put up at the village pub. A. SILLITOE Winnie enquired: had he had a good time at the camp? H. FAST Thomas was at school in the East. B. MOORE Eileen deserves better, her father was at the university. J. MORTIMER Later she taught drawing in Manchester, at a Lycée in Versailles, and at a girls' school in Natal.

3 Expr. the place of occurrence of an event; assisting or present on the occasion of. OE.
> SHAKES. *Temp.* When we were . . at the marriage of your daughter. STEELE He is at a Play. T. PYNCHON Apt . . to appear at a public function and begin a speech.

4 Defining the point or part, side or direction, where anything is or is applied. OE.
> J. WEEVER The Seale . . hanging at the parchment by a silke string. ADDISON Liberty with Monarchy at her right hand. L. GOLDING Whenever and wherever a farmer died . . , his widow would find Johnnie Hummel at her ear. W. TREVOR Your predecessor would suck at the butt of a cig.

5 Expr. the relation of an attribute to a particular place or part. OE.
> SHAKES. *Haml.* 'Tis bitter cold, And I am sick at heart. J. THOMSON Withered at the root.

6 Defining the point where anything enters or issues; through, by. OE.
> THACKERAY He looked in at the dining-room window. A. BRIDGE The air blowing in at the car windows was chill with the approach of nightfall.

7 Specifying the source from which anything comes and where it is sought. *obsolete* exc. in ***at the mouth of***, ***at the hands of***. OE.
> COVERDALE *Judith* 10:7 They axed no question at her, but let her go.

8 With verbs of motion: expr. attainment of a position or determining the point to which motion extends; as far as. OE.
arrive at, (arch.) ***come at***, ***end at***, ***land at***, ***stop at***, etc.
9 Governing a person: ▸†**a** In personal contact with; in the presence or company of; *fig.* in the eyes of, in the estimation of. ME–L18. ▸**b** Ellipt.: (with the possess.) in the house of; (with the possess. or simply) in the shop etc. of. M16. ▸**c** In active or aggressive contact with; applying to, pestering. E17.
> **b** STEELE We had Yesterday at Sir Roger's a Set of Country Gentlemen who dined with him. P. SCOTT The memsahib was at the hairdresser. **c** OED The midges are at me again. J. HERRIOT She was at me again the next day and I had to rush out to her cottage.

10 In the direction of, towards; so as to reach or attack. LME.
> SHAKES. *2 Hen. VI* Put forth thy hand, reach at the glorious gold. ADDISON The Parson is always preaching at the 'Squire. N. HAWTHORNE The spectator's imagination completes what the artist merely hints at. T. DREISER He had unintentionally struck at her. M. DE LA ROCHE She peered up at him from under her shaggy red brows. S. SASSOON Earth and chalk heaved up at the blue sky. G. STEINER In method and scope I am aiming at something different from literary criticism. W. STYRON Clothes like this have individuality . . . That's why it's fun when people stare at us. A. GRAY He pressed his lips together and frowned at the coffee cup.

▸ **II** Action, engagement, occupation, condition, etc.
11 With things put for the activities of which they are the objects, centres, or instruments. OE.
> S. JOHNSON He must be a great English lawyer, from having been so long at the bar. T. HOOD And my right hand grows raging hot, Like Cranmer's at the stake. J. L. MOTLEY His carpets . . were disposed of at auction. OED To contest it at sword's point.

barrister-at-law, ***serjeant-at-arms***, etc.
12 Connecting adjectives or nouns of occupation and proficiency with a thing or action. OE.
> THACKERAY I am not good at descriptions of female beauty. LD MACAULAY In agility and skill at his weapons he had few equals. G. B. SHAW I'm no good at making money.

13 With actions in or with which one is engaged, before nouns or after verbs expressing such action. ME.
> SHAKES. *Two Gent.* As she sits at supper. G. CRABBE I trace the matron at her loved employ. OED To work hard at clearing a path.

14 Of state or condition of existence, posture, conditioning circumstance, mutual relations, mode, manner, measure, extent, etc. ME.
> HENRY FIELDING Pursue her at the hazard of his life. JOHN PHILLIPS Section at right angles to the axis. E. A. FREEMAN At all risks, at all sacrifices, to keep Normandy in full possession. B. RUSSELL Civilians stood bare-headed and soldiers at the salute. J. HELLER His round white cap was cocked at an insolent tilt.

15 Of relation to someone's will or disposition. ME.
> LD BERNERS To make your marchaundise at your pleasure. LD MACAULAY Their votes were at his disposal.

at the mercy of: see MERCY *noun*.
▸ **III** Of time, order, consequence, cause, object.
16 Of order. OE.
at first, ***at last***, ***at length***, etc.
17 Defining the time of an event, the time indicated by an event, or a person's age at the time of an event. ME.
> DEFOE Our men . . gave them a shout at parting. ARNOLD BENNETT At a quarter to seven he put his boots on. R. FULLER As on a silly marriage, he embarked / at sixty-five on a whole programme of moon / watching. H. FAST She would awaken at night in the darkness. J. JOHNSTON I played a lot of tennis at your age.

A

18 Of nearness or distance in time, interval. ME.

M. SPARK Sandy and Jenny got ink on their blouses at discreet intervals of four weeks. F. FORSYTH At the end of two hours he had secured the name he was looking for.

19 Of the number of times, turns, or occasions. ME.

M. HALE May go far at one Essay to provide a fit law. OED To complete the business at two sittings.

20 Defining the occasion or event on which a fact or occasion ensues, and hence the occasioning circumstance or cause. ME.

E. WHARTON Stooping to pick up the book he had dropped at Lily's approach. J. STEINBECK Tom touched his swollen face . . , and at his movement Al groaned and murmured in his sleep.

21 Defining the occasion or cause (sometimes also the object) of an emotion. ME.

MILTON I sorrow'd at his captive state. E. K. KANE Impatient at the delays. D. TOPOLSKI Weary disgust . . at the self-satisfied imposition of an alien way of life and values on these people. J. CHEEVER I was cross at myself for having forgotten her birthday.

†**22** Defining the reason or consideration. LME–L16.

▸ **IV** Relative position in a series or scale; degree, rate, value.

23 Defining a special point in a series or scale. ME.

COVERDALE *Ezek.* 9:6 Then they begane at the elders, which were in the Temple. G. O. TREVELYAN He was rewarded by seeing Johnson at his very best. K. VONNEGUT Graduating from Cornell Law School at the top of his class. E. PENNING-ROWSELL Some vineyards were practically wiped out at temperatures as low as −24 degrees C. J. GALWAY The whole might of the Berlin Philharmonic at full blast.

24 Of the rate or degree at which a thing is done. ME.

POPE If I am to go on at this rate. R. M. PIRSIG The wind, even at sixty miles an hour, is warm and humid. B. BAINBRIDGE He propelled her at a fast trot up the cobbled ramp.

25 Of price or value. ME.

SHAKES. *Haml.* If my love thou hold'st at aught. K. VONNEGUT Published at twenty-five cents.

at any cost: see COST *noun*[2].

26 Of reference to a standard generally; according to. LME.

LD MACAULAY By land or water at their choice. L. P. HARTLEY They often reversed their roles, at the dictates of the penny.

▸ **V** With inf. (cf. Old Norse *at*).

27 Introducing the inf. of purpose. (See also ADO *verb*.) Long *obsolete* exc. *dial.* ME.

▸ **VI** Before other prepositions and adverbs.

†**28** Before prepositions. LME–L16.

29 Before adverbs. Long *obsolete* exc. *dial.* LME.

– PHRASES: (For the many phrs. in which *at* governs a noun or forms an elem. in a phrasal verb, see the nouns and verbs.) **where it's at** *slang* the (true) scene of action, the (true) state of things.

at- /at, *unstressed* ət/ *prefix* (not productive).
Assim. form of Latin AD- before *t*. In Old French, Latin *att-* was reduced to *at-*, which appears in Middle English adoptions, but in later French, and even more commonly in English, *att-* was restored by Latinization, as ***attainder*** (cf. French *atteindre*), ***attorney*** (French *atourné*), etc.

-at /at/ *suffix*[1] (not productive).
[ORIGIN (French from) as -ATE[1].]
Forming nouns, as ***commisariat***, ***concordat***, ***format***, ***secretariat***, etc.

-at /at/ *suffix*[2].
[ORIGIN Back-form. after German *aplanat(isch* etc.]
Forming nouns denoting lenses, etc., of the kinds specified by adjectives in *-atic*, as ***achromat***, ***aplanat***, etc.

atabal /ˈatəbal/ *noun*. L16.
[ORIGIN Spanish from Arabic *at-tabl* from *at-* AL-[2] + *tabl* drum.]
A Moorish kettledrum.

Atabrine *noun* var. of ATEBRIN.

atacamite /atəˈkɑːmʌɪt/ *noun*. E19.
[ORIGIN from *Atacama* a province of Chile + -ITE[1].]
MINERALOGY. An emerald-green basic chloride of copper, crystallizing in the orthorhombic system, freq. as thin prisms.

atactic /əˈtaktɪk/ *adjective*. M19.
[ORIGIN from Greek *ataktos*, from A-[10] + *taktos* arranged, + -IC.]
1 Of (a) language: without rigid word order, without syntax. Cf. ASYNTACTIC. M19.
2 *MEDICINE*. = ATAXIC *adjective*. L19.
3 *CHEMISTRY*. Having or designating a polymeric structure in which the repeating units have no regular configuration. M20.

ataghan *noun* var. of YATAGHAN.

†**Atalantis** *noun*. L18–E19.
[ORIGIN Short title of an E18 romance (prob. itself named after Bacon's *New Atlantis*) satirizing the movers of the Glorious Revolution.]
A secret or scandalous history.

ataman /ˈatəman/ *noun*. M19.
[ORIGIN Russian.]
A Cossack leader. Cf. HETMAN.

atamasco lily /atəˈmaskəʊ ˌlɪli/ *noun phr*. M18.
[ORIGIN from N. Amer. Indian word + LILY *noun*.]
A plant, *Zephyranthes atamasco*, of the south-eastern US, bearing a single white lily-like flower.

atap *noun* var. of ATTAP.

ataractic /atəˈraktɪk/ *adjective & noun*. M20.
[ORIGIN from Greek *ataraktos* not disturbed, calm + -IC. Cf. ATARAXY.]
MEDICINE. ▸ **A** *adjective*. Of a drug: tranquillizing. M20.
▸ **B** *noun*. A tranquillizing drug. M20.

ataraxia /atəˈraksɪə/ *noun*. M19.
[ORIGIN Greek: see ATARAXY.]
= ATARAXY.

ataraxic /atəˈraksɪk/ *adjective & noun*. M20.
[ORIGIN formed as ATARAXY + -IC.]
▸ **A** *adjective*. **1** Calm, serene. *rare*. M20.
2 *MEDICINE*. = ATARACTIC *adjective*. M20.
▸ **B** *noun*. *MEDICINE*. = ATARACTIC *noun*. M20.

ataraxy /ˈatəraksi/ *noun*. E17.
[ORIGIN French *ataraxie* from Greek *ataraxia* impassiveness, from A-[10] + *tarassein* disturb: see -Y[3], -IA[1].]
Imperturbability; stoical indifference.

ataunt /əˈtɔːnt/ *adverb & pred. adjective*. In sense 2 also **-to** /-təʊ/. LME.
[ORIGIN Sense 1 from Old French & mod. French *autant* as much, ult. from Latin *aliud* (neut.) other + *tantum* (neut.) so great; sense 2 from A *preposition*[1] 6 + TAUNT *adjective*.]
†**1** *adverb*. As much as possible; to the full; thoroughly. LME–E16.
2 *adverb & pred. adjective*. *NAUTICAL*. With all sails set; fully shipshape. L16.

atavism /ˈatəvɪz(ə)m/ *noun*. M19.
[ORIGIN French *atavisme*, from Latin *atavus* great-grandfather's grandfather, forefather, from *at-* beyond + *avus* grandfather: see -ISM.]
Resemblance to more remote ancestors rather than to parents; tendency of animals or plants to revert to an ancestral type.
■ **atavic** /əˈtavɪk/ *adjective* = ATAVISTIC M19. **ata'vistic** *adjective* of, pertaining to, or of the nature of atavism L19. **ata'vistically** *adverb* L19.

ataxia /əˈtaksɪə/ *noun*. L19.
[ORIGIN mod. Latin from Greek, from A-[10] + *-taxia*, *taxis* order: see -IA[1].]
MEDICINE. Lack of coordination of movement, esp. as causing unsteadiness of gait.
locomotor ataxia incoordination of movements, *spec.* due to syphilitic infection of the spinal cord; tabes dorsalis.

ataxic /əˈtaksɪk/ *adjective & noun*. M19.
[ORIGIN from ATAXY, ATAXIA + -IC.]
▸ **A** *adjective*. Of or affected with ataxia or (formerly) ataxy. M19.
▸ **B** *noun*. An ataxic person. L19.

ataxy /əˈtaksi/ *noun*. L16.
[ORIGIN formed as ATAXIC: see -TAXY.]
†**1** Irregularity, disorder. L16–M18.
2 *MEDICINE*. Orig., irregularity of the animal functions or of the symptoms of disease. Later, ataxia. Now *rare*. L17.

ATB *abbreviation*.
All-terrain bike.

at-bat /ətˈbat/ *noun*. M20.
[ORIGIN from AT *preposition* + BAT *noun*[1].]
BASEBALL. A turn at batting.

ATC *abbreviation*.
1 Air traffic control.
2 Air Training Corps.

Ate /ˈeɪti/ *noun*. L16.
[ORIGIN Greek *Atē*.]
Infatuation, rashness, (personified by the Greeks as a destructive goddess).

ate *verb* see EAT *verb*.

-ate /ət, eɪt/ *suffix*[1].
[ORIGIN Latin *-atus*, *-ata* (fem.), *-atum* (neut.) noun suffix or Old French & mod. French *-at*[1] (earlier *-ée*).]
Forming nouns denoting (**a**) office, function, state, etc., or a person, group, or thing having it, as ***curate***, ***doctorate***, ***electorate***, ***magistrate***, ***mandate***, etc.; (**b**) *CHEMISTRY* salts or esters of acids (esp. of acids ending in *-ic*: cf. -ITE[1]), or other derivatives, as ***acetate***, ***alcoholate***, ***hydrate***, ***sulphate***, etc.

-ate /ət, eɪt/ *suffix*[2].
[ORIGIN Latin (fem.) *-atus*, (neut.) *-ata*, *-atum* pa. ppl suffix of verbs in *-are*, or French *-é*.]
Forming adjectives and nouns, as ***affectionate***, ***associate***, ***caudate***, ***delegate***, ***Italianate***, ***precipitate***, ***reprobate***, ***roseate***, ***separate***, etc. Hence forming nouns from English verbs, denoting end products of (esp. chemical) operations or processes, as ***centrifugate***, ***dialysate***, ***homogenate***, etc. Many of the adjectives were orig. ppl and also served as pa. pples of verbs in -ATE[3].

-ate /eɪt/ *suffix*[3].
[ORIGIN After or formed as -ATE[2], orig. on the basis of existing ppl adjectives in -ATE[2], later from any Latin verb in *-are*; also used to anglicize French verbs in *-er* (from Latin *-are*).]
Forming verbs, as ***assassinate***, ***associate***, ***fascinate***, ***felicitate***, ***hydrate***, ***separate***, ***vaccinate***, etc. Some, as ***automate***, repr. back-forms. from nouns in *-ation*.

Atebrin /ˈatɪbrɪn/ *noun*. Also ***Atabrine**. M20.
[ORIGIN Unknown.]
(Proprietary name for) mepacrine.

atelectasis /atɪˈlɛktəsɪs/ *noun*. M19.
[ORIGIN from Greek *atelēs* imperfect + *ektasis* extension.]
MEDICINE. Incomplete dilatation of the lungs; collapse of a lung or part of a lung.
■ **atelectatic** /ˌatɪlɛkˈtatɪk/ *adjective* L19.

ateleiosis /ətɛlɪˈəʊsɪs, ətiːl-/ *noun*. Also **-lio-**. E20.
[ORIGIN from A-[10] + TELEIOSIS.]
MEDICINE. Dwarfism due to pituitary insufficiency.
■ **ateleiotic** /-ˈɒtɪk/ *adjective & noun* (**a**) *adjective* pertaining to, characterized by, or affected with ateleiosis; (**b**) *noun* a person with ateleiosis: E20.

atelier /əˈtɛlɪeɪ/ *noun*. L17.
[ORIGIN French.]
A workshop or studio, esp. of an artist or couturier.

ateliosis *noun* var. of ATELEIOSIS.

Atellan /əˈtɛlən/ *adjective & noun*. E17.
[ORIGIN Latin *Atellanus*, from *Atella* (see below): see -AN.]
▸ **A** *adjective*. Of or pertaining to Atella, a town in Campania, southern Italy, formerly famous for satirical and licentious farces; farcical, ribald. E17.
▸ **B** *noun*. A farcical or ribald dramatic composition. E17.

a tempo /ɑː ˈtɛmpəʊ/ *adverbial phr*. M18.
[ORIGIN Italian = in time.]
MUSIC. A direction: in the tempo indicated previously, before the direction to deviate from it.

atemporal /eɪˈtɛmp(ə)r(ə)l/ *adjective*. L19.
[ORIGIN from A-[10] + TEMPORAL *adjective*[1].]
Not temporal, free from limits of time, timeless.

Atenism /ˈɑːtənɪz(ə)m/ *noun*. E20.
[ORIGIN from *Aten* from Egyptian *itn* a name of the sun (god): see -ISM.]
The worship of the sun in ancient Egypt, esp. in the reign of Amenophis IV (Akhnaten) in the 14th cent. BC.

atenolol /əˈtɛnəlɒl/ *noun*. L20.
[ORIGIN Perh. from *angina* + *tension* + -O- + propran*olol*.]
PHARMACOLOGY. A beta blocker given orally in the treatment of angina and hypertension.

Aterian /əˈtɪərɪən/ *adjective*. E20.
[ORIGIN French *atérien*, from Bir el *Ater* in Algeria + -IAN.]
ARCHAEOLOGY. Designating or pertaining to a form of Middle Palaeolithic culture found in N. Africa.

à terre /a tɛːr/ *adverbial & adjectival phr*. E20.
[ORIGIN French.]
Chiefly *BALLET*. On the ground.

ATF *abbreviation*. *US*.
(Federal Bureau of) Alcohol, Tobacco, and Firearms.

Athabaskan /ˌaθəˈbask(ə)n/ *adjective & noun*. Also **Athapaskan** /ˌaθəˈpask(ə)n/, **-can**. M19.
[ORIGIN from Lake *Athabasca* in western Canada, from Cree *Athapaskaw* lit. 'grass and reeds here and there' + -AN.]
▸ **A** *adjective*. Of or pertaining to a widely spread N. American Indian people speaking various closely related languages. M19.
▸ **B** *noun*. **1** A member of this people. M19.
2 Their language group. L19.

athame /əˈθɑːmeɪ, əˈθeɪmi/ *noun*. Also **arthame** /ɑːˈθeɪmi/. M20.
[ORIGIN Unknown.]
A black-handled ritual dagger used in modern witchcraft.

Athanasian /aθəˈneɪʃ(ə)n/ *adjective & noun*. L16.
[ORIGIN from *Athanasius* (see below) + -AN.]
▸ **A** *adjective*. Of or pertaining to Athanasius (293–373), bishop of Alexandria in the reign of Constantine. L16.
Athanasian Creed: that beginning *Quicunque vult* 'Whosoever will', formerly attributed to Athanasius.
▸ **B** *noun*. An adherent of the doctrines of Athanasius. E18.

athanor /ˈaθənɔː/ *noun*. L15.
[ORIGIN Arabic *at-tannūr*, from *at-* AL-[2] + *tannūr* baker's oven.]
A self-feeding digesting furnace used by the alchemists, capable of maintaining a steady heat for long periods.

Athapascan, **Athapaskan** *adjectives & nouns* vars. of ATHABASKAN.

atheise *verb* var. of ATHEIZE.

atheism /ˈeɪθɪɪz(ə)m/ *noun*. **L16**.
[**ORIGIN** French *athéisme*, from Greek *atheos* without God, denying God, formed as **A-**[10] + *theos* god: see **-ISM**.]
Disbelief in, or denial of, the existence of God or gods (opp. ***theism***, (formerly) ***deism***). Also, godlessness.

atheist /ˈeɪθɪɪst/ *noun & adjective*. **L16**.
[**ORIGIN** French *athéiste* or Italian *atheista*, from Greek *atheos*: see **ATHEISM**, **-IST**.]
▸ **A** *noun*. **1** A person who denies or disbelieves the existence of God or gods. Opp. ***theist***, (formerly) ***deist***. **L16**.
2 A person who denies God morally; a godless person. **L16**.
▸ **B** *adjective*. Denying or disbelieving the existence of God or gods; godless. **L16**.
■ **atheˈistic** *adjective* of the nature of or pertaining to atheism; of or befitting an atheist; godless, impious: **M17**. **atheˈistical** *adjective* = **ATHEISTIC L16**. **atheˈistically** *adverb* **E17**.

atheize /ˈeɪθɪʌɪz/ *verb trans*. Also **-ise**. **L17**.
[**ORIGIN** from Greek *atheos* (see **ATHEISM**) + **-IZE**.]
Make atheistic; convert to atheism.

athel /ˈaθ(ə)l/ *adjective & noun*. Long *arch*. or *hist*. Also **eth-** /ˈɛθ-/.
[**ORIGIN** Old English *æþele* = Old Frisian *ethele*, Old Saxon *eþili*, Old High German *edili* (Dutch, German *edel*) from Germanic.]
▸ **A** *adjective*. Noble; illustrious. **OE**.
▸ **B** *noun*. A lord, a chief. **ME**.

atheling /ˈaθ(ə)lɪŋ/ *noun*. *obsolete* exc. *hist*. Also **aeth-**.
[**ORIGIN** Old English *æþeling* = Old Frisian *etheling*, Old High German *adalung*, from West Germanic, from a base meaning 'race, family': see **-ING**[3].]
An Anglo-Saxon prince or lord, *esp*. (*hist*.) the heir to the throne. Often (**A-**) used as the epithet of Edgar (d. *c* 1125), grandson of Edmund Ironside and putative heir of Harold II.

athematic /aθɪˈmatɪk, eɪ-/ *adjective*. **L19**.
[**ORIGIN** from **A-**[10] + **THEMATIC** *adjective*.]
1 *LINGUISTICS*. Having suffixes attached to the stem without a connecting (thematic) vowel. **L19**.
2 *MUSIC*. Not based on the use of themes. **M20**.

athenaeum /aθɪˈniːəm/ *noun*. Also ***-neum**. **M18**.
[**ORIGIN** Latin *Athenaeum* from Greek *Athēnaion*.]
1 (**A-**.) The temple of the goddess Athene in ancient Athens, which was used for teaching. **M18**.
2 A reading room or library. **L18**. ▸**b** A literary or scientific club. **E19**.
3 (**A-**.) As the title of various periodicals devoted to literature, science, and art. **M19**.

Athenian /əˈθiːnɪən/ *noun & adjective*. **E16**.
[**ORIGIN** Latin *Atheniensis* adjective & noun, from *Athenae*, Greek *Athēnai* Athens.]
▸ **A** *noun*. A native or inhabitant of Athens, the leading city of Greece in antiquity and its modern capital. **E16**.
▸ **B** *adjective*. Of, pertaining to, or characteristic of Athens. **L16**.

atheologian /eɪθɪəˈləʊdʒɪən/ *noun*. *rare*. **E17**.
[**ORIGIN** from **A-**[10] + **THEOLOGIAN**.]
A person who knows no theology; a person opposed to or not admitting theology.

atheology /eɪθɪˈɒlədʒi/ *noun*. **L17**.
[**ORIGIN** from **A-**[10] + **THEOLOGY**.]
Opposition to theology.
■ **atheological** /eɪθɪəˈlɒdʒɪk(ə)l/ *adjective* **M17**.

atheous /ˈeɪθɪəs/ *adjective*. **E17**.
[**ORIGIN** from Greek *atheos* (see **ATHEISM**) + **-OUS**.]
†**1** Atheistic. **E17–M19**.
2 Not concerned with the existence of God. *rare*. **L19**.

atherine /ˈaθərʌɪn/ *noun*. Also in Latin form **-ina** /-ʌɪnə/. **M18**.
[**ORIGIN** mod. Latin *atherina* from Greek *atherinē*: see **-INE**[1].]
= ***silverside*** (b) s.v. **SILVER** *noun & adjective*.

atherogenesis /aθərəʊˈdʒɛnəsɪs/ *noun*. **M20**.
[**ORIGIN** formed as **ATHEROMA** + **-GENESIS**.]
MEDICINE. The formation of fatty deposits in the lining of the arteries; the mechanism or process by which this occurs.
■ **atherogenic** *adjective* of or relating to atherogenesis; causing or promoting atherogenesis: **M20**. ˌ**atherogeˈnicity** *noun* **M20**.

atheroma /aθəˈrəʊmə/ *noun*. Pl. **-mas**, **-mata** /-mətə/. **L16**.
[**ORIGIN** Latin from Greek *athērōma*, from *athērē* = *atharē* groats: see **-OMA**.]
MEDICINE. **1** A sebaceous cyst. Now *rare* or *obsolete*. **L16**.
2 A deposit or the deposition of fatty material on the inside surface of an artery. Cf. **ATHEROSCLEROSIS**. **L19**.
■ **atheromatous** *adjective* of the nature of or characterized by atheroma **L17**.

atherosclerosis /ˌaθərəʊsklɪəˈrəʊsɪs, -sklə-/ *noun*. Pl. **-roses** /-ˈrəʊsiːz/. **E20**.
[**ORIGIN** formed as **ATHEROMA** + **SCLEROSIS**.]
MEDICINE. A form of arteriosclerosis characterized by the deposition of fatty material in the lining of the arteries.
■ **atherosclerotic** /-ˈrɒtɪk/ *adjective* pertaining to or characterized by atherosclerosis **E20**.

athetesis /aθɪˈtiːsɪs/ *noun*. Pl. **-teses** /-ˈtiːsiːz/. **L19**.
[**ORIGIN** Greek *athetēsis*, from *athetein*: see **ATHETIZE**.]
In textual criticism: the rejection of a passage as spurious.

athetize /ˈaθɪtʌɪz/ *verb trans*. Also **-ise**. **L19**.
[**ORIGIN** from Greek *athetos* (see **ATHETOSIS**) + **-IZE**, rendering Greek *athetein*.]
In textual criticism: reject (a passage) as spurious.

athetosis /aθɪˈtəʊsɪs/ *noun*. Pl. **-toses** /-ˈtəʊsiːz/. **L19**.
[**ORIGIN** from Greek *athetos* without position or place, set aside + **-OSIS**.]
MEDICINE. A form of involuntary slow writhing movement of the extremities.
■ **athetoid** /ˈaθɪtɔɪd/, **athetotic** /-ˈtɒtɪk/ *adjectives* of, pertaining to, or characterized by athetosis **L19**.

athirst /əˈθəːst/ *pred. adjective*. Now *literary*.
[**ORIGIN** Old English *ofþyrst* shortened from *ofþyrsted* pa. pple of *ofþyrstan* suffer thirst: formed as **OFF** *adverb* + **THIRST** *verb*.]
Very thirsty; *fig*. eager, longing, (*for*).

athlete /ˈaθliːt/ *noun*. Also in Latin form †**-eta**, pl. **-tae**. **LME**.
[**ORIGIN** Latin *athleta* from Greek *athlētēs*, from *athlein* contend for a prize, from *athlon* prize.]
1 A competitor or performer in physical exercises or games. **LME**.
athlete's foot ringworm infection of the foot.
2 *transf*. & *fig*. A strong competitor; a vigorous performer. **M18**.

J. R. LOWELL The long-proved athletes of debate. R. PEARL Present-day examples of sexual athletes who make Casanova . . seem a somewhat puny performer.

3 A person who is physically strong or fit by training and exercise; a muscular or physically robust person. **E19**.

athletic /aθˈlɛtɪk/ *noun & adjective*. **E17**.
[**ORIGIN** French *athlétique* or Latin *athleticus* from Greek *athlētikos*: see **ATHLETE**, **-IC**.]
▸ **A** *noun*. **1** *sing*. & (now) in *pl*. (often treated as *sing*.). The practice of or competition in physical exercises (running, jumping, throwing, etc.); *N. Amer*. physical sports and games generally. **E17**.
†**2** An athlete. **L17–E19**.
▸ **B** *adjective*. **1** Of or pertaining to athletes or athletics. **M17**.
athletic support, **supporter** = **JOCKSTRAP** 1.
2 Physically powerful or fit; muscular, vigorous. **M17**.
■ **athletical** *adjective* (long *rare*) = **ATHLETIC** *adjective* **L16**. **athletically** *adverb* **M18**. **athleticism** /-sɪz(ə)m/ *noun* athletic quality, physical fitness; the practice of athletics: **L19**.

Athoan /aˈθəʊən/ *adjective*. **M19**.
[**ORIGIN** from Greek *Athōos* of Athos + **-AN**.]
Of or pertaining to Athos, a mountainous peninsula of NE Greece, or the monasteries situated upon it. Cf. **ATHONITE**.

Athole brose /ˌaθ(ə)l ˈbrəʊz/ *noun phr*. Also **Atholl brose**. **L18**.
[**ORIGIN** from *Atholl* (*Athole*) a district in Tayside, Scotland + **BROSE**.]
Honey and whisky, often mixed with meal.

at-home /ətˈhəʊm/ *noun*. **M18**.
[**ORIGIN** from *at home* (see **HOME** *noun*).]
A reception of visitors within certain stated hours, during which the host or hostess or both have announced that they will be at home.

-athon /əθ(ə)n, əθɒn/ *suffix*. After a vowel **-thon**.
[**ORIGIN** from **MARATHON**.]
Forming nouns denoting activities of abnormal length, as ***talkathon***, ***radiothon***, etc.

Athonite /ˈaθənʌɪt/ *noun & adjective*. **L19**.
[**ORIGIN** from *Athon-* taken as stem of Greek *Athos* + **-ITE**[1].]
▸ **A** *noun*. A member of an Athoan monastery. **L19**.
▸ **B** *adjective*. Of or pertaining to Athos or (esp.) its monasteries. **M20**.

athort *preposition & adverb* see **ATHWART**.

athrill /əˈθrɪl/ *adverb & pred. adjective*. *literary*. **L19**.
[**ORIGIN** from **A-**[2] + **THRILL** *noun*[2] or *verb*[1].]
In a thrill, thrilled.

athrob /əˈθrɒb/ *adverb & pred. adjective*. *literary*. **M19**.
[**ORIGIN** from **A-**[2] + **THROB** *noun* or *verb*.]
Throbbing.

athrong /əˈθrɒŋ/ *adverb & pred. adjective*. Now *literary*. **ME**.
[**ORIGIN** from **A** *preposition*[1] 6 + **THRONG** *noun*.]
In a throng; thronged, crowded.

athwart /əˈθwɔːt/ *preposition & adverb*. Also (*Scot*.) **athort** /əˈθɔːt/. **LME**.
[**ORIGIN** from **A** *preposition*[1] 1 + **THWART** *adverb*, prob. after Old Norse *um þvert* over in a transverse direction.]
▸ **A** *preposition*. **1** From side to side of; transversely over, across. **LME**.

SHAKES. *L.L.L.* Nor never lay his wreathed arms athwart His loving bosom, to keep down his heart. J. GALSWORTHY Its . . latticed window athwart which the last of the sunlight was shining. A. E. COPPARD The wind blew strongly athwart the yellow field.

2 Across the course or direction of, freq. so as to oppose or meet; *fig*. in opposition to; to the notice of. **LME**.

R. HAWKINS If this Spanish shippe should fall athwart his King's armado. MILTON I have seen this present work, and finde nothing athwart the Catholick faith. SMOLLETT If you come a-thwart me, 'ware. H. A. L. FISHER The Avars, whose barbarous power . . lay athwart the middle Danube.

athwart the hawse: see **HAWSE** *noun*[1]. **run athwart** *NAUTICAL* pass across the line of a ship's course.
3 Across in various directions; to and fro over, all over. Chiefly *Scot*. **M16**.
▸ **B** *adverb*. **1** Across in various directions, about. *Scot*. **L15**.

R. BAILLIE There goes a speech athort . . dissuading the king from war with us.

2 Across from side to side, transversely. **M16**.

SIR T. BROWNE The Asse having . . a crosse made by a black list down his back, and another athwart, or at right angles down his shoulders. W. FALCONER The fore-sail right athwart they brace. TENNYSON The cloud . . sweeps athwart in storms.

3 Across the course or direction of something; *fig*. in opposition, perversely, awry. **L16**.

SHAKES. *Meas. for M.* The baby beats the nurse, and quite athwart Goes all decorum. W. COWPER And with his spear Advanced athwart pushed back the Trojan van.

– **COMB.**: ***athwart-hawse***: see **HAWSE** *noun*[1]; **athwartship** *adjective*, **athwartships** *adverb* (*NAUTICAL*) (extending, lying) from side to side of the ship.

-atic /ˈatɪk/ *suffix*.
1 [(French *-atique* from) Latin *-aticus* suffix combining **-IC** with verb or noun stems in *-at-*: cf. **-AGE**.] Forming adjectives and derived nouns, as ***aquatic***, ***erratic***, ***lunatic***, etc.
2 [(Late Latin *-aticus* from) Greek *-atikos* suffix combining **-IC** with noun stems in *-at-*.] Forming adjectives and derived nouns, as ***aromatic***, ***idiomatic***, ***problematic***, ***rheumatic***, etc.

-atile /ətʌɪl/ *suffix*.
[**ORIGIN** (French *-atile* from) Latin *-atilis* suffix combining *-ilis* **-ILE** with verb or noun stems in *-at-*.]
Forming adjectives and derived nouns expressing capability or quality, as ***aquatile***, ***volatile***, etc.

atilt /əˈtɪlt/ *adverb & pred. adjective*. **M16**.
[**ORIGIN** Sense 1 from **A** *preposition*[1], sense 2 from *a-* of uncertain origin, + **TILT** *noun*[2].]
1 Tilted up; on the point of falling over. **M16**.

J. HEYWOOD We apply the spigot, till tubbe stande a tilte. D. C. PEATTIE One searched for Saturn and found it, rings a-tilt, tearing out of the field of vision.

2 ***ride atilt***, ***run atilt***, etc.: on horseback with the thrust of a lance. Chiefly *fig*. *arch*. **L16**.

SHAKES. *1 Hen. VI* What will you do, good grey-beard? Break a lance, And run a tilt at death within a chair? H. TAYLOR He rode a-tilt and smote the scaly Dragon. J. H. BURTON A paper in defense of queen Mary's honour, in which he ran atilt with Buchanan.

atingle /əˈtɪŋɡ(ə)l/ *adverb & pred. adjective*. **M19**.
[**ORIGIN** from **A-**[2] + **TINGLE** *verb & noun*[3].]
Tingling.

-ation /ˈeɪʃ(ə)n/ *suffix*.
[**ORIGIN** (Old French *-aci(o)un*, mod. *-ation*, from) Latin *-atio(n-)* suffix combining **-(T)ION** with verb stems in *-a(t)-*.]
Forming nouns denoting verbal action or an instance of it, or a resulting state or thing. Most such English words, as ***creation***, ***moderation***, ***saturation***, etc., have corresp. verbs in **-ATE**[3], but some do not, as ***capitation***, ***constellation***, ***duration***, etc. Others are formed directly on verbs in **-IZE**, as ***civilization***, ***organization***, etc. The remainder correspond to a verb without suffix, derived from French, as ***alteration***, ***causation***, ***formation***, ***vexation***, etc.; the suffix was thence applied to words of various origin, as ***botheration***, ***flirtation***, ***starvation***, etc. Cf. **-FICATION**.

atiptoe /əˈtɪptəʊ/ *adverb & pred. adjective*. **M16**.
[**ORIGIN** from **A** *preposition*[1] 1 + **TIPTOE** *noun*.]
On the tips of one's toes.

atishoo /əˈtɪʃuː/ *interjection & noun*. **L19**.
[**ORIGIN** Imit.]
(Repr.) the characteristic noises accompanying a sneeze; a sneeze.

Ativan /ˈatɪvan/ *noun*. **L20**.
[**ORIGIN** Invented name.]
PHARMACOLOGY. (Proprietary name for) the benzodiazepine tranquillizer lorazepam.

-ative /ətɪv, ˈeɪtɪv/ *suffix*.
[**ORIGIN** from or after French *-atif*, fem. *-ative*, or Latin *-ativus* suffix combining *-ivus* **-IVE** with verb stems in *-at-*.]
Forming adjectives, as ***authoritative***, ***demonstrative***, ***figurative***, ***imitative***, ***qualitative***, ***talkative***, etc.

Atjehnese *noun & adjective* var. of **ACHINESE**.

Atkins diet /ˈatkɪnz/ *noun*. **L20**.
[**ORIGIN** from the name of the American cardiologist Robert C. *Atkins* (1930–2003), who devised the diet.]
A high-protein, high-fat diet in which carbohydrates are severely restricted.
– **NOTE**: Proprietary name in the US.

atlantal /at'lant(ə)l/ *adjective*. **E19**.
[ORIGIN from Greek *atlant-* (see ATLAS *noun*[1]) + -AL[1].]
ANATOMY. †**1** Of or pertaining to the upper half of the body. **E–M19**.
2 Of or pertaining to the atlas vertebra. **M19**.

Atlantean /at'lantɪən, atlən'tiːən/ *adjective*. **M17**.
[ORIGIN from Latin *Atlanteus*, from *Atlant-* (see ATLAS *noun*[1]): see -EAN.]
1 Of or pertaining to the Titan Atlas; having the superhuman strength of Atlas. **M17**.
2 Of or pertaining to Atlantis, a mythical island placed by the ancient Greeks in the far west. **E19**.

atlantes /at'lantiːz/ *noun pl.* **E17**.
[ORIGIN Greek, pl. of ATLAS *noun*[1].]
ARCHITECTURE. Male figures used as pillars to support an entablature.

Atlantic /at'lantɪk/ *adjective & noun*. **LME**.
[ORIGIN Latin *Atlanticus* from Greek *Atlantikos*, from *Atlant-*: see ATLAS *noun*[1], -IC. Branch A.I from the Atlas mountains, II from the Titan Atlas, III from the island of Atlantis.]
▸ **A** *adjective* **I 1** ***Atlantic Ocean***, the ocean separating Europe and Africa in the east from America in the west. Orig. restricted to the seas adjacent to the western shores of Africa (sometimes including parts of the Mediterranean). **LME**.
2 Of or pertaining to the Atlantic Ocean; (of or involving countries or regions) bordering the Atlantic Ocean. Formerly *fig.*, far-reaching, distant. **E17**. ▸**b** Crossing the Atlantic Ocean; transatlantic. **M19**.
Atlantic Charter *hist.* a declaration of common aims and principles drawn up by British Prime Minister Winston Churchill and US President Franklin D. Roosevelt at a meeting in the W. Atlantic in 1941. **Atlantic seal** = *grey seal* s.v. GREY *adjective*. **Atlantic States**: those forming the eastern coastline of the US. **Atlantic time** the standard time used in eastern Canada. ***Middle Atlantic States***: see MIDDLE *adjective*.
3 Designating or pertaining to the climatic period in northern Europe or elsewhere following the boreal period. **L19**.
▸ †**II 4** = ATLANTEAN *adjective* 1. **E17–E18**.
▸ **III 5** Of or pertaining to Atlantis (see ATLANTEAN *adjective* 2); Utopian. *rare*. **M17**.
▸ **B** *noun*. **1** *The* Atlantic Ocean. **LME**.
2 A steam locomotive of 4-4-2 wheel arrangement. **E20**.
■ **Atlanticism** /-sɪz(ə)m/ *noun* belief in or support for NATO or the close political relationship of western Europe and the US generally **M20**. **Atlanticist** /-sɪst/ *noun & adjective* (a person) advocating or favouring Atlanticism **M20**.

atlanto- /at'lantəʊ/ *combining form*. **E19**.
[ORIGIN from Greek *atlant-* (see ATLAS *noun*[1]) + -O-.]
ANATOMY. Forming adjectives with the sense 'atlantal and —', as ***atlanto-axial***, ***atlanto-occipital***, etc.

atlas /'atləs/ *noun*[1] *& verb*. **L16**.
[ORIGIN Latin *Atlas*, *Atlant-* from Greek *Atlas*, *Atlant-*, the Titan supposed to hold up the pillars of the universe, and a mountain range in western N. Africa also regarded mythically as supporting the heavens.]
▸ **A** *noun*. **1** (**A-**.) A person who supports a great burden; a mainstay. **L16**.
2 A collection of maps or charts bound in a volume. (Orig. published with a figure of Atlas at the front.) **M17**. ▸**b** A similar collection of diagrams or illustrations in any subject. **L19**.
3 ANATOMY. More fully ***atlas vertebra***. The first or uppermost cervical vertebra, which articulates with the skull. **L17**.
4 (**A-**.) A large size of drawing paper. **E18**.
– COMB.: **atlas moth** a very large tropical saturniid, *Attacus atlas*; ***atlas vertebra***: see sense 3 above.
▸ **B** *verb trans.* (**A-**.) Infl. **-s(s)-**. Prop up or carry after the manner of Atlas. *rare*. **L16**.

atlas /'atləs/ *noun*[2]. Now *arch.* or *hist.* Also **-ss**. **E17**.
[ORIGIN Ult. from Arabic *'atlas* smooth; smooth silk cloth, satin. Cf. German *Atlas*.]
An oriental satin; a piece of this; a garment made of this.

atlatl /'at(ə)lat(ə)l/ *noun*. **L19**.
[ORIGIN Nahuatl *ahtlatl*.]
A throwing stick used by American Indians and Eskimos.

ATM *abbreviation*[1].
1 TELECOMMUNICATIONS. Asynchronous transfer mode, a method of transmitting data over a network in small packets of a fixed length, at variable speeds and with a variable allocation of bandwidth.
2 Automated or automatic teller machine.

atm *abbreviation*[2].
Atmosphere(s).

atman /'ɑːtmən/ *noun*. **L18**.
[ORIGIN Sanskrit *ātman*.]
HINDUISM. The self as the subject of individual consciousness, the soul; the supreme personal principle of life in the universe.

atmometer /at'mɒmɪtə/ *noun*. **E19**.
[ORIGIN from Greek *atmos* vapour + -METER.]
An instrument for measuring the rate of evaporation of water into the atmosphere.

atmosphere /'atməsfɪə/ *noun & verb*. **M17**.
[ORIGIN mod. Latin *atmosphaera*, from Greek *atmos* vapour + *sphaira* SPHERE *noun*.]
▸ **A** *noun*. **1** The spheroidal gaseous envelope surrounding the earth or a celestial object; the whole quantity of such gas. **M17**. ▸**b** A body of gas or vapour surrounding any object or substance, or occupying a given space. **M19**.

> E. DENISON The earth's atmosphere decreases so rapidly in density, that half its mass is within 3½ miles above the sea; and at 80 miles high there can be practically no atmosphere. B. LOVELL The atmosphere of Mars contains about 95 percent carbon dioxide. W. BOYD It must be . . some trick of the atmosphere, the stillness and dryness of the air. **b** J. K. JEROME A permanent atmosphere of paraffin, however faint, is apt to cause remark. N. CALDER The main batch of samples went into an atmosphere of sterile nitrogen.

upper atmosphere: see UPPER *adjective*.
†**2** A supposed region of influence surrounding a body such as a magnet. **M17–M18**.

> B. FRANKLIN The additional quantity [of 'electrical fluid'] does not enter, but forms an electrical atmosphere.

3 A (unit of) pressure approximately equal to the mean pressure of the atmosphere at sea level; now, 101,325 pascal (about 14.6959 lb per sq. inch). **E18**.
4 The air in any particular place, esp. as regards some characteristic such as temperature, wholesomeness, etc. **M18**.

> N. HAWTHORNE No amount of blaze would raise the atmosphere of the room ten degrees. ANTHONY HUXLEY This plant prefers a very moist atmosphere under glass.

5 *fig.* A pervading tone or mood; associations, effects, sounds, etc., evoking a particular, esp. pleasurable or interesting mood. **L18**.

> J. S. MILL Genius can only breathe freely in an atmosphere of freedom. J. B. PRIESTLEY The town seems to have no atmosphere of its own. N. SHUTE There was an atmosphere of cheerful activity in the garage that warmed his heart. J. D. WATSON These ideas . . did a great deal to liven up the atmosphere of the lab. M. FONTEYN Their [ballets'] special quality lies in their greater dependence on mood and atmosphere than on choreographic exactitude.

▸ **B** *verb trans.* Surround (as) with an atmosphere (*lit.* & *fig.*). Usu. in *pass.* **M19**.

atmospheric /atməs'fɛrɪk/ *adjective & noun*. **L18**.
[ORIGIN from ATMOSPHERE + -IC.]
▸ **A** *adjective*. **1** Of or pertaining to the atmosphere; existing or taking place in the atmosphere; operated or produced by the action of the atmosphere. **L18**.
atmospheric engine a steam engine in which the piston is forced down by atmospheric pressure after the condensation of the steam which has raised it. **atmospheric pressure** *spec.* = ATMOSPHERE *noun* 3. **atmospheric railway**: in which motive power is provided by atmospheric pressure acting against a partial vacuum produced in a pipe laid between the rails.
2 Possessing or evoking a particular or characteristic tone, mood, or set of associations. **E20**.
▸ **B** *noun*. **1** In *pl.* Evocative qualities or effects, esp. in a photograph. **L19**.
2 In *pl.* & (*rare*) *sing.* Electrical disturbances in the atmosphere; interference with telecommunications so caused. **E20**.
■ **atmospherical** *adjective* = ATMOSPHERIC *adjective* **M17**. **atmospherically** *adverb* **L19**.

atole /ə'təʊli/ *noun*. Chiefly *US*. **M17**.
[ORIGIN Amer. Spanish from Nahuatl *atolli*.]
Gruel or porridge made of maize or other meal.

atoll /'atɒl, ə'tɒl/ *noun*. Orig. †**atollon**. **E17**.
[ORIGIN Sinhalese (Maldivian) *atoḷu*.]
A coral island consisting of a ring-shaped reef enclosing a lagoon.

atom /'atəm/ *noun & adjective*. **LME**.
[ORIGIN Old French & mod. French *atome* from Latin *atomus* smallest particle, from Greek *atomos* use as noun of adjective 'indivisible', formed as A-[10] + *temnein* to cut. Sense 1 from medieval Latin: cf. ecclesiastical Greek *atomos* moment (*1 Corinthians* 15:52). Cf. ATOMY *noun*[2].]
▸ **A** *noun*. †**1** The smallest medieval unit of time, equal to 15/94 second. **LME–M16**.
2 *hist.* A hypothetical ultimate particle of matter, so small as to be incapable of further division. **L15**.

> SWIFT That the universe was formed by a fortuitous concourse of atoms.

3 A speck of dust; a mote in a sunbeam. *arch.* **E17**.

> BYRON Moted rays of light Peopled with dusty atoms.

4 A very small portion of anything; a particle, a jot. **M17**.

> HOBBES Casting atomes of Scripture, as dust before mens eyes. E. F. BENSON They haven't succeeded one atom. F. KING She was a sweet girl, there wasn't an atom of badness or meanness in her.

5 Anything relatively very small. *arch.* **M17**.

> G. HERBERT The smallest ant or atome knows thy power.

6 A particle of a chemical element which is the unit in which the elements combine and which cannot be divided into further particles all having the properties of that element now known to consist of a positively charged nucleus, containing most of the mass, surrounded by a number of electrons. **E19**. ▸**b** A corresponding particle of a compound or radical. Now *rare* or *obsolete*. **M19**.
split the atom bring about nuclear fission.
7 An irreducible constituent unit of something. **L19**.

> A. S. EDDINGTON The quantum . . is apparently an atom of action.

logical atom PHILOSOPHY a propositional element which cannot be analysed into simpler elements.
– COMB.: **atom smasher** a particle accelerator.
▸ **B** *attrib.* or as *adjective*. = ATOMIC 1b. **M20**.
atom bomb etc.

atomic /ə'tɒmɪk/ *adjective*. **L17**.
[ORIGIN mod. Latin *atomicus*, from *atomus*: see ATOM, -IC.]
1 Of or pertaining to atoms; about or concerned with atoms. **L17**. ▸**b** *spec.* Of, pertaining to, or connected with atoms as a source of power or destructive force; nuclear; employing or driven by nuclear energy; possessing or employing nuclear weapons. **E20**.

> *Discovery* The quantum of action . . forms the foundation of atomic physics. N. CALDER All geology and all life are a continual reordering of the same atomic ingredients. **b** H. G. WELLS Destined to see atomic energy dominating every other source of power. *Daily Telegraph* How atomic power might be used to maintain the future peace. A. BOYD The arrival of the 'atomic age'. O. BRADLEY The way to win an atomic war is to make sure it never starts. A. KOESTLER The only deterrent against atomic aggression is an atomic stockpile. *Times* The Soviet atomic icebreaker Lenin left Leningrad to-day on her maiden voyage.

2 Adhering to the doctrine of the atomism of matter. **L17**.
3 Like atoms in size; minute. **E19**.

> H. EDIB Flies, with atomic specks of brilliant red and green on their wings.

4 Simple, elemental; *esp.* in PHILOSOPHY, (of a proposition etc.) unanalysable, ultimate. **L19**.

> D. R. HOFSTADTER The dissection can go only so far, and then we hit the 'atomic' nature of reasoning processes.

5 Existing in the form of separate atoms. Opp. ***molecular***. **E20**.
– SPECIAL COLLOCATIONS: **atomic bomb**: deriving its destructiveness from the release of nuclear energy. **atomic clock** an instrument which uses atomic vibrations as a standard of time. **atomic heat** the heat capacity of one gram-atom of an element. **atomic mass** = *relative atomic mass* s.v. RELATIVE *adjective*; ***atomic mass unit***, a unit of relative atomic mass equal to 1/12 the mass of an atom of the isotope carbon-12. **atomic number** the number of protons present in the nucleus of an atom of an element. **atomic particle** a subatomic particle. **atomic philosophy** = ATOMISM 1. **atomic pile** = PILE *noun*[4] 6. **atomic theory** (*a*) = ATOMISM 1; (*b*) the theory that chemical elements consist of atoms of definite relative weight combining with those of other elements in fixed proportions. **atomic volume** the volume occupied by one gram-atom of an element under standard conditions. **atomic weight** = *relative atomic mass* s.v. RELATIVE *adjective*.
■ **atomical** *adjective* (now *rare*) **M17**. **atomically** *adverb* **L17**.

atomicity /atə'mɪsɪti/ *noun*. **M19**.
[ORIGIN from ATOMIC + -ITY.]
1 CHEMISTRY. Orig., combining power, valency. Now, the number of atoms in a molecule of an element. **M19**.
2 The property of existing as atoms or analogous elemental units; PHILOSOPHY the ability to be analysed into atomic propositions. **E20**.

atomise *verb* var. of ATOMIZE.

atomism /'atəmɪz(ə)m/ *noun*. **L17**.
[ORIGIN from ATOM + -ISM.]
1 The theory that all matter consists of minute indivisible particles or atoms. **L17**.
2 Any doctrine or theory which propounds or implies the existence of irreducible constituent units. Also = ATOMICITY 2. **M19**.

> S. BARING-GOULD Liberal atomism, the doctrine that all social and political economy must start from the individual.

logical atomism the theory that all propositions can be analysed into logical atoms. **psychological atomism** the theory that mental states are made up of elementary units.

atomist /'atəmɪst/ *noun*. **E17**.
[ORIGIN formed as ATOMISM + -IST.]
An exponent or adherent of the atomism of matter, or of any atomistic theory.

> J. HEALEY Of the Atomists, some confound all, making bodies of coherent remaynders. JOHN PHILLIPS Symbols of chemical constitution, on which there is still some want of agreement among atomists. P. F. STRAWSON Atomists and Positivists alike accepted the skeleton language of the new mathematical logic.

atomistic /atə'mɪstɪk/ *adjective*. **L17**.
[ORIGIN from ATOMIST + -IC.]
1 Of, pertaining to, or of the nature of atomism, in any field. **L17**.

> COLERIDGE It is the object of the mechanical atomistic philosophy to confound synthesis with synartesis. B. RUSSELL When I say that my logic is atomistic, I mean that I share the common-sense belief that there are many separate things. R. S. WOODWORTH An atomistic psychology attempts to explain any total activity by analysing it into its elements.

2 Consisting or of the nature of atoms or analogous elemental units. **L19.**
▪ **atomistical** *adjective* (*rare*) **E18. atomistically** *adverb* **L19.**

atomize /ˈatəmʌɪz/ *verb.* Also **-ise. L17.**
[ORIGIN from ATOM + -IZE.]
†**1** *verb intrans.* Hold the doctrine of the atomism of matter. *rare.* Only in **L17.**
2 *verb trans.* **a** Reduce to atoms or (*rare*) to an atom. Chiefly *fig.*, divide into small units, fragment, disunite. **M19.** ▸**b** Convert (a liquid or solid) into fine particles or spray. **M19.**

> **a** J. W. N. SULLIVAN Matter, electricity, energy, they have all been atomized. I. DEUTSCHER The atomized mass of Moslem labourers did not lend itself easily to propaganda or organization. **b** D. BAGLEY The rain had slackened and there were no large drops, just an atomized mist.

3 *verb trans.* Damage or destroy with nuclear weapons. *colloq.* **M20.**

> A. WILSON Atomized into eternity.

▪ **atomiˈzation** *noun* **M19. atomizer** *noun* a device for atomizing a liquid or solid **M19.**

atomy /ˈatəmi/ *noun*[1]. *arch.* **L16.**
[ORIGIN from ANATOMY by metanalysis as AN *adjective* (*indef. article*) + *atomy.*]
A skeleton; an emaciated body.

atomy /ˈatəmi/ *noun*[2]. *arch.* **L16.**
[ORIGIN Prob. Latin *atomi* pl. of *atomus* ATOM, but assoc. with ATOMY *noun*[1].]
1 An atom, a mote. **L16.**
2 A tiny being, a pygmy. **L16.**

atonal /eɪˈtəʊn(ə)l, ə-/ *adjective.* **E20.**
[ORIGIN from A-[10] + TONAL *adjective.*]
MUSIC. Not written in any particular key or mode.
▪ **atonalism** *noun* the practice of writing atonal music **E20. atonalist** *noun* **E20. atoˈnality** *noun* atonal style of composition **E20. atonally** *adverb* **M20.**

atone /əˈtəʊn/ *verb & noun.* **ME.**
[ORIGIN Isolated early use from *at one* s.v. ONE *adjective* etc.; later (**M16**) back-form. from ATONEMENT.]
▸**A** *verb.* †**1** *verb intrans.* Become reconciled; come into unity or concord. **ME–E17.**

> SHAKES. *A.Y.L.* Then is there mirth in heaven, When earthly things made even Atone together.

†**2** *verb trans.* Compose, appease, (differences, quarrels); reconcile, bring into unity or concord, (contending persons). **M16–M19.**

> MILTON The king and parliament will soon be attoned. N. ROWE Could I attone The fatal Breach 'twixt thee and Tamerlane.

†**3** *verb trans. & intrans.* Join in one; harmonize. **E17–M19.**

> G. CHAPMAN High built with pines, that heaven and earth attone. LD HOUGHTON Welcome such thoughts! They well atone With this more serious mood.

†**4** *verb trans.* Conciliate, propitiate, appease, (an offended person). **E17–E19.**

> POPE So heaven atoned, shall dying Greece restore.

5 *verb intrans.* Make propitiation or amends (*for* an offence, †an offender). **M17.**

> DRYDEN If sheep or oxen could atone for men. E. WAUGH The stewards . . sought to atone for ten days' neglect with a multitude of un-needed services. W. S. CHURCHILL No administrative achievements, . . no magnitude of personality, could atone to his former friends for his desertion.

6 *verb trans.* Expiate, make amends for (an offence, †an offender). *arch.* **M17.**

> R. B. SHERIDAN I will endeavour to atone the . . errors. LYTTON They endeavoured to atone the loss by the pursuit of Artabazus.

▸†**B** *noun.* Atonement. **L16–M19.**
▪ **atoner** *noun* **E18.**

atonement /əˈtəʊnm(ə)nt/ *noun.* **E16.**
[ORIGIN from *at one* (see ONE *adjective* etc.) + -MENT, after medieval Latin *adunamentum*, from *adunare* unite, and earlier ONEMENT.]
†**1** Unity of feeling; harmony, concord, agreement. **E16–E17.**

> SIR T. MORE Having more regarde to their olde variaunce then their new attonement.

†**2** **a** Restoration of friendly relations between persons, reconciliation. **E16–L17.** ▸**b** THEOLOGY. Reconciliation between God and humankind. **E16.**

> **a** SHAKES. *Rich. III* He desires to make atonement Between the Duke of Gloucester and your brothers. P. MASSINGER A perfect sign of your atonement with me.

†**3** Settlement *of* (differences, strife, etc.). Only in **E17.**
4 Expiation; reparation for wrong or injury; amends; THEOLOGY propitiation of God by expiation of sin. **E17.**

> W. BLACKSTONE No suitable atonement can be made for the loss of life, or limb. N. MOSLEY It is part of Christian mythology . . that without Christ's execution there would be no atonement for the sins of the world.

Day of Atonement the most solemn religious fast of the Jewish year, celebrated on the tenth day of Tishri.

at-oneness /atˈwʌnnɪs/ *noun.* **L19.**
[ORIGIN from *at one* s.v. ONE *adjective* etc. + -NESS.]
The state of being at one (*with*), harmonious relationship.

atonic /eɪˈtɒnɪk/ *noun & adjective.* **M18.**
[ORIGIN from A-[10] + TONIC *adjective*; sense B.1 from ATONY + -IC.]
▸**A** *noun.* PROSODY (esp. GREEK PROSODY). An unaccented word, a proclitic. **M18.**
▸**B** *adjective.* **1** MEDICINE. Lacking tone; characterized by atony. **L18.**
2 PROSODY. Unaccented; not bearing the main stress. **L19.**

atony /ˈat(ə)ni/ *noun.* **L17.**
[ORIGIN Old French & mod. French *atonie* or late Latin *atonia* debility from Greek, from *atonos* lacking tone, formed as A-[10] + *tonos* TONE *noun*: see -Y[3].]
Lack of tone of muscle or other body tissue.

atop /əˈtɒp/ *adverb & preposition.* **M17.**
[ORIGIN from A *preposition*[1] 1 + TOP *noun*[1].]
▸**A** *adverb.* On the top (*of*), above. **M17.**
▸**B** *preposition.* On the top of. **M17.**

atopy /ˈatəpi/ *noun.* **E20.**
[ORIGIN Greek *atopia* unusualness from *atopos* unusual, from A-[10] + *topos* place: see -Y[3].]
MEDICINE. An allergic reaction which is associated with a hereditary predisposition to allergy in some form.
▪ **aˈtopic** *adjective* pertaining to or of the nature of atopy **E20.**

-ator /eɪtə/ *suffix.*
[ORIGIN from or after (French *-ateur*, †*-atour*, from) Latin *-ator* suffix, from pa. ppl stems in *-at-*: see -OR.]
Forming agent nouns, as ***creator***, ***denominator***, ***dictator***, ***mediator***, ***spectator***, ***translator***, etc.; also (esp. from the early 19th cent.) in names of instruments, implements, and machines, as ***detonator***, ***escalator***, ***generator***, ***percolator***, ***refrigerator***, ***ventilator***, etc.

à tort et à travers /a tɔːr e a travɛːr/ *adverbial phr.* **M18.**
[ORIGIN French = wrongly and across.]
At random, haphazardly.

atour /əˈtaʊə/ *preposition & adverb. Scot. & N. English.* **LME.**
[ORIGIN App. from AT *preposition* + OVER *prep, adverb.*]
▸**A** *preposition.* Over; beyond; in addition to. **LME.**
▸**B** *adverb.* Over and above, moreover, in addition. **LME.**

à toute outrance *adverbial phr.* see À OUTRANCE.

ATP *abbreviation.*
1 BIOCHEMISTRY. Adenosine triphosphate.
2 Automatic train protection.

atrabilarious /atrəbɪˈlɛːrɪəs/ *adjective.* **L17.**
[ORIGIN from medieval Latin *atrabilarius* (formed as ATRABILIOUS + -ARY[1]) + -OUS.]
Of or pertaining to choler adust; atrabilious.
▪ **atrabilarian** *adjective* (now *rare*) = ATRABILARIOUS **L17.** †**atrabilary** *adjective* = ATRABILARIOUS **L17–E18.**

atrabilious /atrəˈbɪlɪəs/ *adjective.* **M17.**
[ORIGIN from Latin *atra bilis* choler adust, black bile, translating Greek *melankholia* MELANCHOLY *noun*: see -IOUS.]
Orig., affected by choler adust, one of the four supposed cardinal humours of the body. Now only *gen.*: melancholy, hypochondriac; acrimonious, splenetic.

> R. GRAVES He broke school bounds, he dared defy The Master's atrabilious eye. T. H. WHITE There were atrabilious hawk-masters . . quarrelling with their assistants.

▪ **atrabiliar** *adjective* (*rare*) = ATRABILIOUS **M19. atrabiliary** *adjective* (now *rare* or *obsolete*) = ATRABILARIOUS **E18. atrabiliousness** *noun* **L19.**

atrament /ˈatrəm(ə)nt/ *noun. arch.* **LME.**
[ORIGIN Latin *atramentum*, from *ater* black: see -MENT.]
Blacking; ink; any similar black substance.
▪ **atraˈmental**, **atraˈmentous** *adjectives* of or pertaining to ink, inky, black as ink **M17.**

atraumatic /eɪtrɔːˈmatɪk, a-; -traʊ-/ *adjective.* **M20.**
[ORIGIN from A-[10] + TRAUMATIC.]
MEDICINE. Of surgical techniques or instruments: causing minimal injury to the tissues.
▪ **atraumatically** *adverb* **M20.**

atrazine /ˈatrəziːn/ *noun.* **M20.**
[ORIGIN from A(MINO- + TR(I)AZINE.]
A selective, highly persistent herbicide, used esp. to control annual weeds in crops.

atremble /əˈtrɛmb(ə)l/ *adverb & pred. adjective.* **M19.**
[ORIGIN from A-[2] + TREMBLE *noun* or *verb.*]
Trembling.

atresia /əˈtriːʃə, -zjə/ *noun.* **E19.**
[ORIGIN from A-[10] + Greek *trēsis* perforation + -IA[1].]
MEDICINE. **1** Absence or occlusion, esp. congenital, of a channel or opening of the body. **E19.**
2 Degeneration of non-ovulating ovarian follicles during the menstrual cycle. **E20.**
▪ **atresic** /əˈtriːsɪk, -zɪk/ *adjective* = ATRETIC **L19. atretic** /əˈtrɛtɪk/ *adjective* pertaining to or displaying atresia **E20.**

atria *noun pl.* see ATRIUM.

atrip /əˈtrɪp/ *adverb & pred. adjective.* **E17.**
[ORIGIN from A *preposition*[1] 6 + TRIP *noun*[1].]
NAUTICAL. **1** Of yards: swayed up, ready to have the stops cut for crossing. Of sails: hoisted from the cap, sheeted home, and ready for trimming. **E17.**
2 Of an anchor: just raised perpendicularly from the ground in weighing. **M17.**

atrium /ˈeɪtrɪəm/ *noun.* Pl. **-ia** /-ɪə/, **-iums. L16.**
[ORIGIN Latin.]
1 ARCHITECTURE. A central court, orig. that of an ancient Roman house; a covered court or portico; (a building with) a large light well; a central hall or glassed-in court in a building. **L16.**
2 ANATOMY & ZOOLOGY. Any of various chambers into which one or more passages open; *spec.* (***a***) either of the two upper chambers of the heart (in fish, a single chamber), into which the veins conduct blood (cf. AURICLE 1); (***b***) the tympanic chamber of the ear. **L19.**
▪ **atrial** *adjective* (ANATOMY & ZOOLOGY) of or pertaining to an atrium **M19. atriovenˈtricular** *adjective* (ANATOMY) of or pertaining to the atrial and ventricular chambers of the heart; ***atrioventricular bundle***, a bundle of nerves leading from the right atrium to the ventricles and serving to maintain the heartbeat: **L19.**

atrocious /əˈtrəʊʃəs/ *adjective.* **M17.**
[ORIGIN from Latin *atroc-*, *atrox* fierce, cruel: see -IOUS.]
1 Excessively and wantonly savage or cruel; heinously wicked. **M17.**

> T. PENNANT Here all atrocious criminals were excluded. P. H. GIBBS Your pity for the world's young manhood in that atrocious war. M. LOWRY Spots where diabolical plots must be hatched, atrocious murders planned.

†**2** Stern, fierce; extremely violent. Only in **M18.**

> J. THOMSON The fierce, atrocious frown of sinewed Mars.

3 Very bad; execrable. *colloq.* **L19.**

> B. BAINBRIDGE Her knowledge of German was poor and her accent atrocious. D. M. THOMAS The weather was atrocious, and for three days we couldn't set foot outside because of a snow-storm.

▪ **atrociously** *adverb* **M18. atrociousness** *noun* (now *rare*) **M18.**

atrocity /əˈtrɒsɪti/ *noun.* **M16.**
[ORIGIN Old French & mod. French *atrocité* or Latin *atrocitas*, formed as ATROCIOUS: see -ITY.]
1 Horrible or heinous wickedness; wanton cruelty. **M16.**

> CLARENDON They desired justice might be done upon offenders, as the atrocity of their crimes deserved.

2 Fierceness, sternness. *arch.* **M17.**

> S. BARING-GOULD They besiege it with atrocity, striving to break in the doors.

3 An act of wanton cruelty or extreme heinousness; an atrocious deed. **L18.**

> F. FITZGERALD The extortion rackets, rape, pillage, and outright military atrocities.

4 A repellent act or thing. *colloq.* **L19.**

à trois /a trwa/ *adjective & adverbial phr.* **L19.**
[ORIGIN French.]
Shared by, or in a group of, three people.
ménage à trois: see MÉNAGE 1.

atrophy /ˈatrəfi/ *noun.* **E17.**
[ORIGIN French *atrophie* or late Latin *atrophia* from Greek = lack of food, from A-[10]: see -TROPHY.]
1 MEDICINE. Orig., wasting away of the body from lack of nourishment; emaciation. Now, wasting away of an organ or tissue, through any cause. **E17.**
red atrophy: see RED *adjective*. ***yellow atrophy***: see YELLOW *adjective*.
2 *fig.* Wasting away, enfeeblement. **M17.**
▪ **atrophic** /əˈtrɒfɪk/ *adjective* pertaining to, affected by, or characterized by atrophy **M19.**

atrophy /ˈatrəfi/ *verb.* **L16.**
[ORIGIN French *atrophier* formed as ATROPHY *noun*, or from the noun.]
1 *verb trans.* Affect with atrophy. Chiefly as ***atrophied*** *ppl adjective.* **L16.**

> J. S. MILL Organs are strengthened by exercise and atrophied by disuse. R. FRY The pressure of commercial life has crushed and atrophied that creative impulse completely. B. PYM She was too old to learn anything new and . . her brain had become atrophied.

2 *verb intrans.* Undergo atrophy, waste away. **M19.**

> D. LIVINGSTONE The horns, mere stumps not a foot long, must have atrophied. K. VONNEGUT Foresight and the ability to reason have simply atrophied from long neglect. H. KISSINGER Causing the North Vietnamese forces in the South to atrophy owing to normal attrition.

▪ †**atrophiated** *ppl adjective* atrophied **M17–M19.**

atropine /ˈatrəpiːn, -ɪn/ *noun.* Also **-in** /-ɪn/. **M19.**
[ORIGIN from mod. Latin *Atropa* (*belladonna*) deadly nightshade, fem. from Greek *Atropos* 'Inflexible', one of the Fates, + -INE[5].]
CHEMISTRY & PHARMACOLOGY. A poisonous alkaloid, $C_{17}H_{23}NO_3$, found in deadly nightshade, thorn apple, and other plants, and used medicinally esp. to relax muscles and to inhibit secretion.
▪ †**atropia** *noun* = ATROPINE: only in **19.** ˌ**atropiniˈzation** *noun* treatment or poisoning with atropine **L19. atropinized** *adjective* treated or poisoned with atropine **L19. atropism** *noun* atropine poisoning **L19.**

atropous /ˈatrəpəs/ *adjective*. **M19.**
[ORIGIN from Greek *atropos* not turned from A-[10] + *tropos* a turn, + -OUS.]
BOTANY. Of an ovule: not inverted on its funicle; orthotropous.

ATS /*colloq.* ats/ *abbreviation*.
Auxiliary Territorial Service (for women in Britain, 1938–48); members of this.

Atsina /atˈsiːnə/ *noun & adjective*. Pl. of noun same, **-S**. **L19.**
[ORIGIN Blackfoot, lit. 'good people'.]
A member of, of or pertaining to, an Arapaho people of Montana and Saskatchewan; (of) the Arapaho dialect of this people. Also called ***Gros Ventre***.

atta /ˈatə/ *noun*. **M19.**
[ORIGIN Hindi *āṭā*, Punjabi *āṭṭā*.]
In the Indian subcontinent: wheat flour or meal.

attaboy /ˈatəbɔɪ/ *interjection*. *slang* (chiefly *N. Amer.*). **E20.**
[ORIGIN Prob. repr. a pronunc. of *that's the boy!*]
Expr. encouragement or admiration.

attach /əˈtatʃ/ *verb & noun*. **ME.**
[ORIGIN Old French *atachier* (mod. *attacher*) = Italian *attaccare*, Spanish *atacar*; in sense A.II, III, from Old French *estachier* fasten, fix = Provençal, Spanish *estacar* (see A-[7]); ult. from a Germanic base (see STAKE *noun*[1]).]
▸ **A** *verb*. **I** *verb trans*. **1** *LAW*. Place or take (a person, goods) under the control of a court; seize or arrest by authority. **ME.**

SHAKES. *Hen. VIII* For France.. hath attach'd Our merchants goods at Bordeaux. SIR W. SCOTT I attach thee of the crime of which thou hast but now made thy boast. C. M. YONGE The Earl Marshal attached Gloucester for high treason.

†**2** Indict, accuse. **LME–M17.**

T. NASHE They shall not easily be attached of any notable absurditie.

†**3** Seize, grasp, take hold of. **M16–L17.**

SHAKES. *Temp.* Old lord, I cannot blame thee, Who am myself attach'd with weariness. J. GUILLIM The Lion.. lesse able to attach and rend his Prey.

†**4** Attack. **E–M17.**
▸ **II** *verb trans*. Usu. in *pass.* or *refl.* **5** Fasten or join (a thing *to* another, *to* a point). **LME.**

G. FENNELL The young of the oyster.. attach themselves immediately to the first clean, hard substance they meet with. J. K. JEROME Attached to the boat-hook was a line, which trailed behind them. W. TREVOR Clumps of mistletoe were attached by drawing-pin to the centre of the door-frames.

6 Join or connect functionally *to* (esp. a person *to* a group etc.); join on *to* another person as companion etc. Freq. *refl.* **L17.** ▸**b** Allocate or join for service *to* a particular (orig. military) unit etc. **E19.**

SIR W. SCOTT That I should seriously consider to which department of the law I was to attach myself. J. E. TENNENT A cemetery.. attached to the city. P. G. WODEHOUSE He had never speculated on any possible family that might be attached to her. DAY LEWIS What shall I do this afternoon?—attach myself, probably, to Keyes and follow him around in a daze of pure satisfaction. **b** A. C. CLARKE Since I've been attached to the Pacific branch of the bureau I've more or less adopted Australia as a second home. C. RYAN Ringsdorf's unit was told to report immediately to a command post... There, a major attached them to a company of the 21st *Panzer* Grenadier Regiment.

7 Join in sympathy or affection *to*; bind in friendship, make devoted. Now usu. in *pass.* **M18.**

J. AUSTEN So totally unamiable, so absolutely incapable of attaching a sensible man. D. L. SAYERS She has told us herself, with great candour, how she became deeply attached to Philip Boyes. J. JOHNSTON We'll have to decide what we're going to sell and what we're going to keep... One becomes so attached to things. H. SEGAL Under the influence of a French governess to whom she was very attached.

8 Fix *to* something or someone as a property, description, or other adjunct. **E19.**

J. BRYCE Legends which attached themselves to the name of Charles the Emperor. B. TAYLOR To this treasure a curse is attached.

9 Attribute (importance, a meaning, etc.) *to*. **M19.**

H. KISSINGER The President.. attached the utmost importance to the avoidance of war.

attach credence to: see CREDENCE 1.
▸ **III** *verb intrans*. **10** Be attributable or appertain *to*; fall *upon* as an obligation etc. **L18.**

A. W. KINGLAKE Blame attaches upon Lord Aberdeen's Cabinet for yielding. H. BELLOC There is a flavour of Fame certain to attach to his achievement. N. MITFORD She was clever enough to avoid the ridicule which often attaches to such a situation.

11 Take legal effect; come into legal operation. *arch.* **E19.**

SOUTHEY Wherever they should make their settlement, there the laws of England attached. J. WILLIAMS The wife's right to dower accordingly attached.

▸ †**B** *noun*. **1** An attack (of disease etc.). **LME–L17.**
2 An act of legal seizure; arrest. **E16–M17.**
3 A thing attached; an attachment. **L16–M18.**

■ **attachable** *adjective* liable to be attached; able to be attached (*to*): **L16.** **attacher** *noun* a person who attaches; a means of attaching: **LME.**

attaché /əˈtaʃeɪ/ *noun*. **E19.**
[ORIGIN French, pa. pple of *attacher* ATTACH *verb*.]
1 A junior official attached to the staff of an ambassador etc.; a representative of his or her government in a foreign country. **E19.**
cultural attaché: see CULTURAL 2. ***military attaché***: see MILITARY *adjective*.
2 An attaché case. *N. Amer.* **L20.**
– COMB.: **attaché case** a small rectangular case for carrying documents etc.
■ **attachéship** *noun* **M19.**

attachment /əˈtatʃm(ə)nt/ *noun*. **LME.**
[ORIGIN Old French & mod. French *attachement* from *atachier* ATTACH *verb*: see -MENT.]
1 Apprehension or arrest, esp. for contempt of court; a writ authorizing this. **LME.**

T. SHADWELL I'll follow and apprehend him, and his attachment will secure me. J. GALSWORTHY If you wish to give me your information, you can; otherwise I'm afraid we shall have to get an attachment for contempt.

2 Legal seizure of property. **L16.**
attachment of earnings *ENGLISH LAW* payment of debts by direct deduction from the debtor's earnings, under a court order.
†**3** Confinement. *rare* (Shakes.). Only in **E17.**

fig.: SHAKES. *Tr. & Cr.* Sleep kill those pretty eyes, And give as soft attachment to thy senses As infants' empty of all thought!

4 Affection, devotion; a sympathetic, friendly, or romantic connection. **E18.**

SIR W. SCOTT The lover's eye discovered the object of his attachment. J. GALSWORTHY At the most a flirtation, ending, as all such attachments should, at the proper time. H. A. L. FISHER A fierce attachment to the faith of their ancestors. E. LONGFORD The Duke's romantic attachment to the lovely Marianne Patterson was no fabrication.

5 Something attached, or intended to be attached; an adjunct. **L18.** ▸**b** *COMPUTING*. A file appended to an email. **L20.**

D. NOBBS There was a hand-held shower for washing the back, and he utilized this attachment to the full.

6 The action of fastening, joining, affixing, or attributing; the condition of being fastened etc. **E19.**

R. OWEN The rest of the cranium is modified.. for the attachment of muscles to work the jaw. C. CAUDWELL Their desertion of their class and their attachment to another. F. HOYLE The attachment of mystic significance to symbols, words, and objects is still widespread today.

7 A means of attaching; a fastening, a bond. **E19.**

J. E. TENNENT The falling timber.. dragging those behind to which it is harnessed by its living attachments.

attack /əˈtak/ *noun*. **M17.**
[ORIGIN from the verb or French *attaque* from Italian *attacco*.]
1 An act of attacking with violence or weapons; an attempt to defeat, kill, or injure; offensive action. **M17.**

MILTON The dire attack Of fighting Seraphim. LD MACAULAY A night attack might be attended with success. J. G. FARRELL Not a single day had gone by without news of a raid or shooting or terrorist attack somewhere in Ireland.

2 An assault with hostile words or other actions. **M18.**

H. WILSON The attacks on me in the Press and in politics.

3 *CHESS*. A move or series of moves played with the object of checkmating, gaining a positional advantage, or capturing a man. Also, an opening or opening variation played by White. **M18.**
4 *SPORTS & GAMES*. An attempt to gain a scoring or other significant advantage; play, moves, or tactics aimed at gaining such an advantage; (the function of) those members of a team whose principal responsibility is to mount attacks; *CRICKET* bowling or the bowlers (as opp. to batting or the batsmen). **L18.**
5 A (sudden) bout of an illness, a mental condition, etc. **E19.**

L. M. MONTGOMERY Anne was the victim of an overwhelming attack of stage fright. V. BRITTAIN I had been really ill with a sharp attack of influenza.

heart attack: see HEART *noun*. *VASOVAGAL* ***attack***.
6 The beginning of an arduous task; a determined attempt upon something. **E19.**

A. KOESTLER Kepler's first attack on the problem is described.

angle of attack: between the wing chord of an aircraft in flight and the direction of the airflow.
7 A destructive action by a physical agency; corrosion, eating away, dissolution. **M19.**
8 Chiefly *MUSIC*. The action or manner of beginning a piece, passage, etc.; brilliance or decisiveness of style. **L19.**

A. L. HASKELL Riabouchinska is not a purely classical dancer, lacking the necessary hardness and attack. H. C. SCHONBERG His fortissimo attack had an almost savage quality.

attack /əˈtak/ *verb*. **E17.**
[ORIGIN French *attaquer* from Italian *attaccare* join (battle), ATTACH *verb*.]
▸ **I** *verb trans*. **1** Act against with violence or force of arms; seek to kill or injure. **E17.**

W. S. CHURCHILL 673 horsemen, led by Lord Cardigan, rode up the valley under heavy fire.. to attack the Russian batteries. D. MORRIS Killers [whales] prefer to attack aquatic mammals such as dolphins, porpoises, seals, [etc.]. E. CALDWELL Several teen-age girls and young women had been attacked by a night-time prowler. *fig.*: R. G. COLLINGWOOD I was attacked by a strange succession of emotions.

2 Of disease: begin to affect; seize upon, afflict. **E17.**

F. A. KEMBLE Rheumatism.. attacks indiscriminately the young and old.

3 Act against with hostile words or actions. **M17.**

MILTON Under colour of a pretended partie.. the Parliament is attaqued. G. GREENE There were speakers out on the Common: the I.L.P. and the Communist Party,.. a man attacking Christianity.

4 *CHESS*. Attempt to gain a positional advantage in relation to (a piece or square); threaten to give checkmate to or capture (a man). **M18.**
5 *SPORTS & GAMES*. Attempt to gain a scoring or other significant advantage over (an opponent); attempt to score points, goals, etc., against (an opponent) or in (a particular goal etc.). **L18.**
6 Of a physical agent: act harmfully upon, begin to destroy; corrode, dissolve. **L18.**

B. STEWART Hydrofluoric acid.. attacks the glass where the wax has been scratched off.

7 Begin vigorous work on (a task etc.); *MUSIC* begin (a piece, passage, etc.), esp. decisively or confidently. **E19.**

SHELLEY Mrs. Shelley is attacking *Latin* with considerable resolution. H. C. SCHONBERG Notes of scales could not have been more evenly matched..; chords could not be attacked more precisely.

▸ **II** *verb intrans*. **8** Make or begin an attack; take the offensive; *CHESS* attempt to checkmate, to gain a positional advantage, or to capture an opposing man; *SPORTS & GAMES* attempt to gain a scoring or other significant advantage, be in possession of the ball, puck, etc. **E17.**

DONNE Ere sicknesses attack, yong death is best. A. J. P. TAYLOR On 8 August the British attacked in front of Amiens, in order to protect the railway junction there. *Times* Kent attacked with fire and fury and it seemed impossible that they should fail to score.

■ **attackable** *adjective* **E19.** **attacker** *noun* a person who attacks; an assailant; an attacking player: **M17.**

attain /əˈteɪn/ *verb & noun*. **ME.**
[ORIGIN Anglo-Norman *atain-*, *atein-*, Old French *ataign-*, *ateign-*, stem of *ataindre*, *ateindre* (mod. *atteindre*), from Latin *attingere* touch on, reach, from *ad* AT- + *tangere* to touch.]
▸ **A** *verb*. (See also ATTAINT *pa. pple & ppl adjective*.)
▸ **I** *verb trans*. †**1** Convict, condemn; bring to justice. Only in **ME.**
2 Accomplish, achieve (an end or purpose); reach, gain (a state, rank, or quality). **ME.**

J. WESLEY Let me the Life Divine attain. A. J. TOYNBEE Buenos Aires is a great modern city that has attained its present stature gradually. D. JACOBSON I never came close to attaining any of my goals. R. ADAMS She was a woman.. who had already attained a position of authority and trust.

3 Reach or arrive at by motion in space or time, or by the passage of time. **LME.**

SOUTHEY Now had they almost attain'd The palace portal. S. BELLOW I might be concerned with age merely because I might never attain any great age.

†**4** Encroach on. Only in **LME.**
†**5** Overtake, come up with, catch. **LME–E17.**
6 Come into the possession of, acquire, obtain, (now usu. something abstract, passing into sense 2). **LME.**

LD BERNERS To atteyne thereby the towne of Berwike. J. CONRAD At that moment I attained the knowledge of who it was I had before me. H. J. LASKI A new class of men attained control of the nation's economic power.

†**7** Get to know, find out. **LME–M17.**

CAXTON Secretes that humayne nature may not attayne, knowe, ne understonde.

†**8** Touch, hit, strike. **L15–L16.**

G. CHAPMAN Yet him beneath the eare The sonne of Telamon attain'd.

▸ **II** *verb intrans*. Usu. with *to*, (arch.) *unto*.
9 Succeed in coming or get *to* a state, condition, goal, etc. **LME.**

W. COWPER To see your trees attain to the dignity of timber. H. J. LASKI He had attained to the highest office under Anne at an exceptionally early age. J. HILTON After ten years in various parts of Asia he had attained to a somewhat fastidious valuation of places and happenings.

10 Succeed in coming or get *to* a point in space; live on *to* a time or age. **LME.**

AV *Acts* 27:12 If by any meanes they might attaine to Phenice. SIR W. SCOTT Nor nearer might the dogs attain. OED He has attained to years of discretion.

†**11** Extend, reach; amount; matter. LME–M16.
†**12** Foll. by *to*, *unto*: get to know, find out. M16–E17.
▸ **B** *noun.* Attainment; a thing attained. *rare.* M16.
■ **attaina'bility** *noun* attainableness E19. **attainable** *adjective* able to be attained M17. **attainableness** *noun* M17.

attainder /ə'teɪndə/ *noun.* LME.
[ORIGIN Anglo-Norman *attainder*, *atteinder*, use as noun of inf. *atteinder*, Old French & mod. French *atteindre* ATTAIN *verb*: see -ER[4].]
1 *hist.* The action or process of attainting; *spec.* the legal consequences of a sentence of death or outlawry, i.e. forfeiture of estate, deprivation of rank or title, and loss of civil rights generally. LME.
act of attainder, **bill of attainder**: introduced in Parliament for attainting a person without trial.
†**2** *fig.* Condemnation; dishonour; slander. L16–M18.

SHAKES. *Rich. II* Have mine honour soil'd With the attainder of his slanderous lips. S. JOHNSON A resumption of ancestral claims, and a kind of restoration to blood after the attainder of a trade.

attainment /ə'teɪnm(ə)nt/ *noun.* M16.
[ORIGIN from ATTAIN *verb* + -MENT.]
1 The action or process of attaining, reaching, or gaining. M16.
2 Something which is attained; an achievement, an accomplishment. M17.

T. F. DIBDIN A prelate and poet of very distinguished attainments.

attaint /ə'teɪnt/ *noun.* ME.
[ORIGIN Old French *atainte*, *ateinte* use as noun of fem. pa. pple of *ataindre*, *ateindre* ATTAIN *verb*.]
†**1** Exhaustion, fatigue. (Cf. ATTAINT *pa. pple & ppl adjective* 3.) *rare.* ME–L16.

SHAKES. *Hen. V* He . . freshly looks, and over-bears attaint With cheerful semblance and sweet majesty.

2 The act of touching or hitting, esp. in jousting. Cf. earlier TAINT *noun* 1. *arch.* E16.
†**3** A contusion or wound on the leg of a horse, *esp.* one caused by overreaching. E16–M18.
4 LAW (now *hist.*). The process of convicting a jury for having given a false verdict, and reversing the verdict. E16.
5 †**a** (A temptation to) a dishonourable act. Only in M16. ▸**b** Imputation or touch of dishonour; stain. L16.

b D. G. ROSSETTI Among the faults . . Are two so grave that some attaint is brought Unto the greatness of his soul thereby.

†**6** = ATTAINDER *noun* 1. Only in 17.

†**attaint** *pa. pple & ppl adjective.* ME.
[ORIGIN Old French *ataint*, *ateint* pa. pple of *ataindre*, *ateindre* ATTAIN *verb*: later infl. by TAINT *verb*.]
1 Convicted, attainted. ME–M18.
2 Affected with sickness, passion, etc.; infected. ME–E16.
3 Exhausted, overcome. LME–E16.

attaint /ə'teɪnt/ *verb trans.* ME.
[ORIGIN from ATTAINT *adjective*: infl. by TAINT *verb*.]
†**1** Touch, reach, strike; accomplish, get at. ME–M16.
†**2** Convict, prove guilty. LME–M18.
3 Subject to attainder. LME.

HOBBES To be attainted is, that his Blood be held in Law, as stained and corrupted. H. P. BROUGHAM On Edward IV's victory, they unanimously attainted Henry IV.

4 Accuse *of* crime, dishonour, etc. *arch.* E16.

W. D. HOWELLS Who are you to attaint me of unworthy motives?

5 Affect or infect with disease, contagion, corruption, etc.; sully, taint. E16.

J. SKELTON They be so attaynted With coveytous and ambycyon. SPENSER Lest she with blame her honour should attaint. DRYDEN The same shivering sweat his lord attaints. DE QUINCEY Even to have kicked an outsider might have been held to attaint the foot.

■ **attaintment** *noun* (*rare*) conviction, attainder M16. †**attainture** *noun* conviction; attainder; imputation of dishonour, stain: M16–M17.

†**attame** *verb trans.* ME.
[ORIGIN Old French *atamer* from Latin *attaminare* to attack: see AT-. Aphet. to TAME *verb*[2].]
1 Cut into, pierce. ME–L15. ▸**b** Broach (a cask etc.). Only in LME.
2 Attack; meddle with. Only in LME.
3 Begin, undertake. Only in LME.

attap /'atəp/ *noun.* Also **atap**. E19.
[ORIGIN Malay *atap* roof, thatch.]
Palm fronds used in SE Asia for thatching, *esp.* those of the nipa palm; a thatch made of these. Freq. *attrib.*

attar /'atə/ *noun.* Also (earlier) **otto** /'ɒtəʊ/. M17.
[ORIGIN Persian *'itr*, Arabic *'itr*, colloq. Arabic *'aṭar* perfume, essence.]
A fragrant volatile essence, *esp.* (more fully ***attar of roses***) that obtained from rose petals.

fig.: T. HARDY That buzz of pleasure which is the attar of applause.

– COMB.: **attar-gul** /gʊl/ [Persian *gul* roses] attar of roses.

atteal /'atiːl/ *noun. Scot.* (esp. *Orkney*). L16.
[ORIGIN Unknown.]
A pochard, teal, or other small duck.

attemper /ə'tɛmpə/ *verb trans. arch.* ME.
[ORIGIN Old French *atemprer* (mod. *attremper*) from Latin *attemperare*, from *ad* AT- + *temperare* TEMPER *verb*[1].]
†**1** Regulate, control; order, arrange. ME–L18.

T. CRANMER The Holy Ghost hath so ordered and attempered the Scriptures.

2 Qualify, modify, or moderate by admixture; temper. LME.

HOR. WALPOLE The most perfect taste in architecture, where grace softens dignity, and lightness attempers magnificence.

3 Make warmer or cooler. *obsolete* exc. as passing into sense 2. LME.

EVELYN Attemper the air with a fire of charcoal.

4 Moderate, assuage (passion, harshness); soothe, appease, (a person). LME.

BACON How the . . Habit, To be Angry, may be attempred, and calmed.

†**5** Restrain. Usu. *refl.* LME–M16.
6 Make fit or suitable; accommodate, adapt. Foll. by *to*. LME.

E. B. PUSEY God often attempers Himself and His oracles to the condition of men.

7 Attune, bring into harmony. Foll. by *to*. L16.

POPE High airs, attemper'd to the vocal strings.

■ **attemperament** *noun* the bringing to a proper temper; mixture in due proportions: M17.

attemperate /ə'tɛmpəreɪt/ *verb trans.* M16.
[ORIGIN Latin *attemperat-* pa. ppl stem of *attemperare*: see ATTEMPER, -ATE[3].]
†**1** Moderate, regulate; accommodate or adapt *to*. M16–E18.
2 Modify in temperature as required. E17.
■ **attempe'ration** *noun* (now *rare* or *obsolete*) E17. **attemperator** *noun* (BREWING) a system of water pipes for controlling the temperature of the fermenting wort M19. †**attemperature** *noun* attempered condition M17–M19.

attempt /ə'tɛm(p)t/ *noun.* M16.
[ORIGIN from the verb.]
1 An act of making an effort to accomplish something uncertain or difficult; a trial, an endeavour (esp. when unsuccessful or incomplete). M16.

SHAKES. *Macb.* They have awak'd, And 'tis not done. Th' attempt, and not the deed, Confounds us. J. M. BARRIE [He] flung away his life in a gallant attempt to save a servant who had fallen overboard. J. MARQUAND I tried to smile, but I made a rather poor attempt at it. L. DURRELL All attempts to meet her have failed so far.

make an attempt try.
2 An attack, an assault; an effort to conquer or to kill (now usu. with specification, as ***an attempt on the summit of***, ***an attempt on the life of***). L16. ▸†**b** An endeavour to seduce; a temptation. E–M17.

S. ROHMER I know that Fu-Manchu will make an attempt upon him. J. MASTERS Your adjutant has just told me about the attempt on the Karode bridge. *Encycl. Brit.* Seven successive attempts on the Northeast Ridge . . failed. **b** AV *Ecclus* 9:4 Vse not much the companie of a woman that is a singer, least thou be taken with her attempts.

†**3** Something attempted, an aim. E17–L18.

W. PALEY His design and attempt was to sail . . immediately from Greece.

4 Something produced in an endeavour or effort. L19.

P. V. WHITE The trellis, its attempt at grapes mildewed by the humidity.

■ **attemptless** *adjective* (*rare*) L16.

attempt /ə'tɛm(p)t/ *verb.* LME.
[ORIGIN Old French *attempter*, Latinized form of *atenter* (mod. *attenter*) from Latin *attemptare*, from *ad* AT- + *temptare* TEMPT *verb*.]
1 *verb trans.* Try to accomplish (an action); make an effort, use one's endeavour, *to do* something. LME.

SHAKES. *Oth.* If thou attempt it, it will cost thee dear. D. HUME To embolden her to attempt extorting the right of investitures. R. GRAVES Tiberius answered . . that his troops were not yet fit to attempt the task. W. TREVOR He attempted to smile back at him, but found it difficult.

2 *verb trans.* Attack, assault; try to take by force, overthrow, kill; try to take (a person's life). LME. ▸†**b** Try to ravish or seduce. E17–M18.

DEFOE How I should escape from them, if they attempted me. J. MORSE Those rash hands which attempted his father's crown. J. LANGHORNE They attempted the Capitol by night.

†**3** **a** *verb intrans.* Make an attack *against*, (*up*)*on*. LME–L17. ▸**b** *verb trans.* Venture (hostile action) (*up*)*on*. E17–M18.

a W. CONGREVE Look that she attempt not on her life. **b** SHAKES. *Hen. VIII* If you cannot Bar his access to th' King, never attempt Anything on him.

†**4** *verb trans.* **a** Try with temptations; seek to win over; tempt. LME–M19. ▸**b** Try with afflictions. E16–M17.

a SPENSER Why then will ye, fond dame, attempted bee Unto a stranger's love? MILTON God . . Hinder'd not Satan to attempt the minde of Man. **b** JER. TAYLOR O Pain, in vain do'st thou attempt me.

†**5** *verb trans.* Try to obtain or attract (friendship etc.). LME–M18.

S. JOHNSON Shall . . No cries attempt the mercy of the skies?

†**6** *verb trans.* Try to move by entreaty etc.; address urgently. M16–L17.

MILTON I have attempted . . the lords With supplication prone and father's tears, To accept of ransom for my son.

7 *verb trans. gen.* Try to attain, venture upon, or engage with (the object of any action understood). M16.

J. RAY Courage and Hardiness to attempt the Seas. DAY LEWIS Though I was shamed . . into attempting *The Ambassadors* and the *Recherche*, I rejected these masterpieces. *Encycl. Brit.* This expedition . . was the eighth team in 30 years to attempt Everest.

■ **attemptable** *adjective* (*rare*) M17. †**attemptate** *noun* an attempt; *esp.* a violent or criminal attempt, an attack, an assault: LME–E18. **attempter** *noun* a person who makes an attempt L15. **attemptible** *adjective* (*rare*) attemptable E17.

attend /ə'tɛnd/ *verb.* ME.
[ORIGIN Old French *atendre* (mod. *attendre* wait for) from Latin *attendere*, from *ad* AT- + *tendere* stretch. Aphet. to TEND *verb*[1].]
▸ **I** Give one's attention, efforts, or presence (to).
1 *verb trans.* (*arch.*) & *intrans.* (with *to*, (arch.) *unto*, or absol.). Pay attention, listen, (to); apply one's mind, give thought, (to). ME.

SHAKES. *Cymb.* I do condemn mine ears that have So long attended thee. AV *Ps.* 17:1 O Lord, attend vnto my crie. POPE Thus Chryses pray'd: the favouring power attends. E. M. FORSTER Mrs. Honeychurch started and smiled. She had not been attending. J. W. KRUTCH Everything seems designed to be glanced at rather than attended to.

2 *verb intrans.* (with *to*, †*to do*, (arch.) *unto*, †*upon*) & †*trans.* Turn one's energies, apply oneself practically, (to). ME.

S. DANIEL First, he attends to build a strong conceipt Of his usurped powre. AV *Rom.* 13:6 They are Gods ministers, attending continually vpon this very thing. POPE The maids . . dispersing various tasks attend. I. COMPTON-BURNETT Well, Nance, send the servants to church, and attend to the dinner yourself.

3 *verb trans.* & *intrans.* with *to*. Direct one's care to (a matter); look after, tend, guard, (something). LME.

POPE Leave only two the gally to attend. DAY LEWIS After the hens had been attended to, the sisters would sit . . shelling peas.

4 *verb trans.* & *intrans.* (with *on*, (arch.) *upon*, or absol.). Wait on as a servant or attendant, or in answer to a summons; escort; follow or accompany for the purpose of rendering services. LME.

SHAKES. *Two Gent.* We'll both attend upon your ladyship. DRYDEN Officious Nymphs, attending in a Ring. SOUTHEY Following the deep-veil'd Bride Fifty female slaves attend. D. L. SAYERS The prisoner was brought in, attended by a female wardress. J. BUCHAN The High Commissioner and his wife . . are attended by a lady-in-waiting, by several maids of honour, and by four A.D.C.'s.

5 *verb trans.* & *intrans.* (with *at*, †*on*, or absol.). Be present at or go to (a meeting, function, etc., or its location); go regularly to ((a) school, (a) church, etc.). LME.

Boston Transcript To attend church tomorrow in the Bloomer costume. T. HARDY This fair was frequently attended by the folk of Weatherbury. OED He attends regularly at the City Temple. R. MACAULAY He wanted to know what churches she had been used to attend when in London. J. B. PRIESTLEY She died about ten days later, and I didn't even attend her funeral. J. WAIN He had arranged to attend the hospital as an out-patient. JO GRIMOND He never attended unless personally summoned.

6 *verb trans.* Apply oneself to the care of, tend, (a person, esp. an invalid); visit (a patient) professionally. L16.

DEFOE Hired nurses who attended infected people. G. STEIN He would not let a doctor come in to attend Melanctha.

7 *verb trans.* & (*rare*) *intrans.* (with *on*). Of things (usu. abstract): accompany, occur with or as a result of; follow closely upon. E17.

SHAKES. *Tr. & Cr.* All fears attending on so dire a project. HENRY FIELDING Our food was attended with some ale. E. BOWEN The birth of the third of her little boys, attended by a quite serious illness. J. CHEEVER The song, attended with laughing and clapping, came from the far end of the basement. F. WELDON The shock, dismay and disagreeable nostalgia which attends any untimely and violent death.

†**8** *verb trans.* Follow up or conjoin (a thing) *with* another. E17–L18.

G. ANSON The Governor . . had returned a very obliging answer . . and had attended it with a present of two boats.

†**9** *verb trans.* & *intrans.* (with *to*). Follow in order to counter or defeat. L17–E19.

A

CLARENDON He was . . strong enough to have stopped or attended Waller in his western expedition. H. NELSON Cruizing off Cadiz for the purpose of attending to L'Aigle, and securing the approach of our Convoy.

▸ **II** Wait for.
†**10** *verb trans.* Look forward to, expect. **LME–L17.**

J. RAY So dreadful a Tempest that all the People attended therein the very End of the World.

11 *verb trans.* Look out for, await (an event, time, etc.; †a person). *arch.* **L15.**

SMOLLETT Here I attend The king—and lo! he comes. *fig.*: J. LOCKE The state that attends all men after this.

†**12** *verb intrans.* Wait, tarry. **M16–M18.**

L. STERNE The lady attended as if she expected I should go on.

■ **atten'dee** *noun* = ATTENDANT *noun* 3 **M20. attender** *noun* **LME.**

attendance /ə'tɛnd(ə)ns/ *noun.* **LME.**
[ORIGIN Old French: see ATTEND, -ANCE.]
†**1** = ATTENTION 1. **LME–M19.**
†**2** = ATTENTION 2. **LME–L17.**
3 The action or condition of waiting upon or accompanying someone to render service; ministration, assiduous service. **LME.**

DEFOE Reputation for . . good attendance on his customers.

4 The action or condition of awaiting the leisure, convenience, or decision of a superior. **LME.**
5 The action or fact of being present at a meeting, function, etc., or when summoned. **LME.**

POPE The King in council your attendance waits. D. L. SAYERS Whatever fantastic pictures she had . . conjured up of married life . . , none of them had ever included attendance at village concerts. P. SCOTT Her own attendances had fallen off, and she had not gone to communion for years.

†**6** Waiting; delay; expectation. **LME–M17.**

R. HOOKER That which causeth bitterness in death, is the languishing attendance and expectation thereof. W. RALEIGH Compelled . . to put the matter in hazard without further attendance.

7 A body of attendants, a retinue. *arch.* **LME.**

R. GRAVES He had a meagre attendance of four or five young officers, who clung to him from loyalty.

8 The body or number of people present at any proceedings. **M19.**

B. JAMES The poor attendance, only 35,000, was attributed to the strong counter-attraction of the Oxford-Cambridge Boat Race.

– PHRASES: **dance attendance (on)**, †**wait attendance (on)** follow about obsequiously, be deliberately kept waiting (by). **in attendance** waiting upon someone, attending.
– COMB.: **attendance allowance** a social-security benefit payable to a severely disabled person needing attendance at home (formerly ***constant attendance allowance***); **attendance centre** a place where young delinquents must attend regularly instead of being sent to prison; **attendance officer** a person whose duty it is to see that children attend school.

attendant /ə'tɛnd(ə)nt/ *adjective & noun.* **LME.**
[ORIGIN Old French & mod. French: see ATTEND *verb*, -ANT[1].]
▸ **A** *adjective.* †**1** Attentive. **LME–M17.**
2 Waiting upon, ministering; accompanying in a subordinate capacity. **LME.**

MILTON Other Suns . . With thir attendant Moons thou wilt descrie. LD MACAULAY Fresh meat was never eaten by the gentlemen attendant on a great Earl. R. L. STEVENSON Alone, on the other side of the railway, stands the Springs Hotel, with its attendant cottages.

†**3** LAW. Dependent *on*, owing service *to*. **LME–M17.**
4 Present at a meeting etc. *rare.* **L16.**
5 Closely consequent (*on*, *upon*); resulting, associated. **E17.**

R. D. LAING The anxieties attendant on the schizophrenic's phantasmic omnipotence. H. MACMILLAN The . . revolt in the capital city with all its attendant horrors.

▸ **B** *noun.* **1** A person in attendance or providing service; a servant, assistant, subordinate companion, etc. **M16.**

MILTON Least sin Surprise thee, and her black attendant, Death. BYRON Two . . ladies, who With their attendant aided our escape. SAKI He left all the parcels in charge of the cloak-room attendant. ARNOLD BENNETT An attendant . . was feeding the sheets at one end of the machine and another attendant . . taking them off at the other.

2 A close consequence, an accompanying circumstance etc. **E17.**

POPE The laugh, the jest, attendants on the bowl.

3 A person who is present at a meeting etc. **M17.**

D. H. LAWRENCE She was . . a regular attendant at morning service.

attent /ə'tɛnt/ *noun. arch.* **ME.**
[ORIGIN Old French *atente* (mod. *att-*) use as noun of fem. pa. pple of *atendre* ATTEND *verb*; in Old French conf. with *entente* INTENT *noun*.]
†**1** Intention, purpose. Only in **ME.**
†**2** Attitude. **ME–L15.**
3 Attention; care, heed. **ME.**

attent /ə'tɛnt/ *adjective. arch.* **L15.**
[ORIGIN Latin *attentus* pa. pple of *attendere* ATTEND *verb*.]
Attentive (*to*); intent (*on*).

attentat /*in sense 1 foreign* atɑ̃ta (*pl. same*); *in sense 2* ə'tɛntət/ *noun.* Also (now only in sense 2) **-ate** /-eɪt/. **E17.**
[ORIGIN Old French & mod. French, or medieval Latin *attentatum*, from *attentat-* pa. ppl stem of *attentare* var. of Latin *attemptare* ATTEMPT *verb*.]
1 An attack; an attempted assassination. **E17.**
2 LAW. Something wrongfully done by a judge in a proceeding, pending an appeal. **E18.**

attention /ə'tɛnʃ(ə)n/ *noun.* **LME.**
[ORIGIN Latin *attentio(n-)*, from *attent-* pa. ppl stem of *attendere* ATTEND *verb*: see -ION.]
1 The action, fact, or state of attending or giving heed; the mental faculty of attending, attentiveness; application of the mind, consideration, thought. **LME.**

SHAKES. *Rich. II* The tongues of dying men Enforce attention like deep harmony. W. LINDGREN Brought to my attention three specimens of a mineral. DAY LEWIS I must have weakened my capacity for attention and observation. E. ROOSEVELT Whenever he read anything aloud like this, he acted it straight through, which was why he held the attention of the little children so well.

attract attention; ***draw attention to***; ***give attention (to)***, ***pay attention (to)***, etc. ***call attention to***: see CALL *verb*. SELECTIVE ***attention***.
2 Practical consideration, observant care. **M18.**

Encounter Please address it for the attention of John Hall.

3 The action of attending to the comfort or pleasure of others; ceremonious politeness, courtesy. Freq. in *pl.* **M18.**

CHESTERFIELD Nice and scrupulous, in points of ceremony, respect, and attention. P. ACKROYD He fed my vanity with his attentions.

pay one's attentions to court.
4 Orig. MILITARY. An erect attitude of readiness; chiefly in ***at attention***, ***to attention***. Also as *interjection*, a command to assume such an attitude. **L18.**

G. B. SHAW Remember that you are in the army now . . . Attention! Left turn! Quick march. C. S. FORESTER Each officer in turn came up to attention as his name was spoken.

■ **attentional** *adjective* of or pertaining to the mental faculty of attention **L19.**

attentisme /atɑ̃tism/ *noun.* **M20.**
[ORIGIN French, from *attente* wait, waiting: see ATTENT *noun*, -ISM.]
The policy of waiting to see what happens.

attentive /ə'tɛntɪv/ *adjective.* **LME.**
[ORIGIN Old French & mod. French *attentif*, *-ive*, formed as ATTENT *noun* + -IVE.]
1 Steadily applying one's mind or energies; intent, heedful. **LME.** ▸**b** = ATTENTIONAL *adjective*. **L19.**
2 Assiduously attending to the comfort or wishes of others; polite, courteous. **L16.**
■ **attentively** *adverb* **LME. attentiveness** *noun* **LME.**

†**attenuant** *adjective & noun.* **E17.**
[ORIGIN French *atténuant* from Latin *attenuant-* pres. ppl stem of *attenuare*: see ATTENUATE *adjective*, -ANT[1].]
MEDICINE. ▸**A** *adjective.* Having the property of thinning the secretions. **E17–M19.**
▸ **B** *noun.* A drug or other agent credited with this property. **E18–M19.**

attenuate /ə'tɛnjʊət/ *adjective.* **LME.**
[ORIGIN Latin *attenuatus* pa. pple, formed as ATTENUATE *verb*: see -ATE[2].]
1 Slender, thin; emaciated; tapering to thinness. **LME.**
2 Thin in consistency; weakened, rarefied, refined. *arch.* **LME.**

attenuate /ə'tɛnjʊeɪt/ *verb.* **M16.**
[ORIGIN Latin *attenuat-* pa. ppl stem of *attenuare*, from *ad* AT- + *tenuare* make thin, from *tenuis* thin: see -ATE[3].]
1 *verb trans.* Make thin or slender. **M16.**

E. YOUNG The spider's most attenuated thread.

2 *verb trans.* Make thin in consistency; dilute; rarefy. **M16.**

C. LAMB Attenuated small beer.

3 *verb trans.* Weaken; reduce in force, effect, value, etc. **M16.** ▸**b** PHYSICS. Reduce the amplitude of (an oscillation, esp. an electrical signal). **L19.** ▸**c** MEDICINE. Reduce the virulence of (pathogenic organisms) or of pathogenic organisms in (vaccines). Usu. as ***attenuated*** *ppl adjective.* **L19.**

J. GALSWORTHY 'I expect we shall be sick.' They were, and reached London somewhat attenuated. T. SHARPE My conditions are final . . . I am not prepared to attenuate them. H. ACTON Experience had attenuated and finally extinguished Nancy's Socialist sympathies.

4 *verb intrans.* Become slender, weaker, etc.; *esp.* (PHYSICS) decrease in amplitude. **M19.**
■ †**attenuater** *noun* (MEDICINE) = ATTENUANT *noun* **L17–L18. attenuator** *noun* †(**a**) = ATTENUANT *noun* (Dicts.); (**b**) PHYSICS a device which produces attenuation: **L19.**

attenuation /ətɛnjʊ'eɪʃ(ə)n/ *noun.* **LME.**
[ORIGIN French *atténuation* or Latin *attenuatio(n-)*, formed as ATTENUATE *verb*: see -ATION.]
1 The action of making something thin or slender; diminution of thickness, emaciation. **LME.**
2 The action of making something thinner in consistency; diminution of density, esp. (BREWING) of the wort during fermentation. **L16.**
3 The process of weakening; reduction in force, effect, etc. **M19.** ▸**b** PHYSICS. Reduction of the amplitude of an electrical signal or other oscillation. **L19.** ▸**c** MEDICINE. Reduction of the virulence of a pathogenic organism. **L19.**

atter /'atə/ *noun.* Long *obsolete* exc. *dial.* (*N. English*).
[ORIGIN Old English *ātr*, *āt(t)or* = Old Saxon *ettor*, Old High German *eitar* (German *Eiter*), Old Norse *eitr*.]
1 Poison, venom, *esp.* that of reptiles. **OE.**
2 Gall; bitterness. **OE.**
3 Corrupt matter, pus. **LME.**
■ **attery** *adjective* venomous; spiteful; bitter; purulent: **OE.**

attercop /'atəkɒp/ *noun.* Long *obsolete* exc. *dial.*
[ORIGIN Old English *āttorcoppe*, formed as ATTER + (perh.) COP *noun*[1].]
1 A spider. **OE.**
2 *fig.* A malevolent person. **E16.**
3 A spider's web. **M16.**

†**attermine** *verb trans.* **LME–E19.**
[ORIGIN Old French *aterminer* from late Latin *atterminare*, from *ad* AT- + *terminare* TERMINATE *verb*.]
Settle the term or limit of; set a date for (esp. payment of a debt).

†**atterrate** *verb trans.* **L17–M18.**
[ORIGIN Italian *atterrare*, from *a* to + *terra* earth: see -ATE[3].]
Fill up with (esp. alluvial) earth.
■ †**atterration** *noun* **L17–M18.**

attest /ə'tɛst/ *verb & noun.* **E16.**
[ORIGIN French *attester* from Latin *attestari*, from *ad* AT- + *testari* to witness, from *testis* witness.]
▸ **A** *verb.* **1** *verb trans.* Bear witness to, affirm the truth or validity of; testify, certify formally. **E16.**

SWIFT I will assert nothing here, but what I dare attest. L. A. G. STRONG As if to attest the excellence of her nursing, he began quickly to recover. D. CECIL An oath attesting him to be a member of the Church.

attested cattle, **attested milk**: certified free from disease. ***attesting witness***: see WITNESS *noun* 4.
2 *verb trans.* Of things: be evidence or proof of; testify to, tend to confirm. **L16.**

GIBBON Twenty-two acknowledged concubines, and a library of sixty-two thousand volumes attested the variety of his inclinations. JAMES SULLIVAN Physical appearances attest the high antiquity of the globe.

†**3** *verb trans.* Call to witness. **E17–L19.**

SHAKES. *Tr. & Cr.* But I attest the gods, your full consent Gave wings to my propension.

4 *verb trans.* Put (a person) on oath; *esp.* administer an oath of allegiance to or enrol (a recruit) for military service. **L17.**

WELLINGTON They are to be attested according to the following form . . I, A. B. do make oath [etc.].

5 *verb intrans.* Bear witness, testify, *to*. **L17.**

J. WILKINS To the reasonableness of this, several of the wisest heathens have attested.

6 *verb intrans.* Enrol oneself as ready for military service. **E20.**

Observer I attested for military service but was not called up.

▸ **B** *noun.* Testimony, evidence, attestation. **E17.**
■ **attestant** *noun* a person who makes a formal attestation **L17. attester** *noun* **L16. attestor** *noun* an attester **M17.**

attestation /atɛ'steɪʃ(ə)n/ *noun.* **LME.**
[ORIGIN French, or late Latin *attestatio(n-)*, from *attestat-* pa. ppl stem of *attestari*: see ATTEST, -ATION.]
1 The action of bearing witness, testimony; evidence, proof, confirmation; *spec.* formal confirmation by signature or oath, esp. by a witness in verification of the execution of a will, deed, etc. **LME.**
†**2** The action of calling to witness. **M16–M18.**
3 The administration of an oath of allegiance, esp. to a military recruit. **E19.**
■ **a'ttestative** *adjective* of the nature of or pertaining to attestation **M19. attestator** *noun* an attester **L16.**

Attic /'atɪk/ *adjective*[1] *& noun*[1]. **L16.**
[ORIGIN Latin *Atticus* from Greek *Attikos* of Attica: see -IC.]
▸ **A** *adjective.* Of, pertaining to, or characteristic of Attica, a district of ancient Greece, or Athens, its chief city, or (formerly) Greece generally; (of literary style etc.) refined, elegant, classical. **L16.**

C. THIRLWALL A wooden theatre still sufficed for the Attic drama. M. ARNOLD Addison's prose is Attic prose.

Attic base ARCHITECTURE a column base consisting of an upper and lower torus divided by a scotia and two fillets. **Attic dialect** Greek as used by the ancient Athenians. **Attic order** CLASSICAL ARCHITECTURE a square column or pillar. **Attic salt**, **Attic wit** refined, delicate, poignant wit.

▶ **B** *noun*. A native or inhabitant of Attica or ancient Athens; the Attic dialect. L17.

attic /ˈatɪk/ *adjective*² & *noun*². L17.
[ORIGIN French *attique* formed as ATTIC *adjective*¹ & *noun*¹.]
▶ **A** *adjective*. **1** ARCHITECTURE. Designating a small order above a taller one (see sense B.1 below). *rare*. L17.
2 (Passing into *attrib.* use of the noun) Designating the highest storey of a building, under the beams of the roof, or a room in this. E18.

CARLYLE The attic floor of the highest house. W. FAULKNER Behind a loose board in the wall of his attic room.

▶ **B** *noun*. **1** ARCHITECTURE. A small (usu. Attic) order (column and entablature) placed above another order of much greater height constituting the main facade. M18.
2 The highest storey of a house, usu. immediately under the beams of the roof; a room in this. E19.

E. LINKLATER The servants got it first and in a drove took to their garrets and attics. E. O'NEILL It might be in an old trunk in the attic.

3 ANATOMY. The upper part of the cavity of the middle ear. *arch*. L19.

Atticise *verb* var. of ATTICIZE.

Atticism /ˈatɪsɪz(ə)m/ *noun*. L16.
[ORIGIN Greek *Attikismos*, from *Attikos*: see ATTIC *adjective*¹ & *noun*¹, -ISM.]
1 An ancient Athenian idiom; an instance of elegant Greek; a well-turned phrase. L16.
2 *hist*. Siding with or attachment to Athens. *rare*. E17.

Atticist /ˈatɪsɪst/ *noun*. *hist*. M17.
[ORIGIN Greek *Attikistēs*, from *Attikos*: see ATTIC *adjective*¹ & *noun*¹, -IST.]
A person who affected Attic literary style.

Atticize /ˈatɪsʌɪz/ *verb*. Also **-ise**. E17.
[ORIGIN Greek *Attikizein*, from *Attikos*: see ATTIC *adjective*¹ & *noun*¹, -IZE.]
1 a *verb intrans*. Affect Attic style; conform to Athenian or (in a wider sense) Greek habits, modes of thought, etc. E17. ▸**b** *verb trans*. Make Attic in character. M19.
2 *verb intrans*. Side with or favour Athens. M18.

attingent /əˈtɪndʒ(ə)nt/ *adjective*. *rare*. L16.
[ORIGIN Latin *attingent-* pres. ppl stem of *attingere*: see ATTAIN, -ENT.]
Touching, contiguous (*to*).

†**attirail** *noun*. Also **-al**. E17–L18.
[ORIGIN French, formed as ATTIRE *verb*: see -AL¹.]
Apparatus, gear.

attire /əˈtʌɪə/ *noun*. ME.
[ORIGIN from the verb.]
†**1** A person's complete equipment for war. Only in ME.
2 Dress, apparel; *esp*. fine, formal, or special clothing. ME. ▸**b** An outfit of clothes; a style of dress. *arch*. L16.

SHAKES. *Jul. Caes.* And do you now put on your best attire? And do you now cull out a holiday? G. GISSING Her attire of subdued mourning indicated widowhood. V. S. NAIPAUL He had eaten, dressed—not in English clothes but in his normal Hindu attire. *fig.*: MILTON Earth in her rich attire Consummate lovly smil'd. **b** F. BURNEY Two new attires, one half, the other full dressed. G. K. CHESTERTON It seemed odd to them that men had once worn so elvish an attire.

†**3** Personal adornment or decoration. LME–M17.

T. FULLER Commonly known by her whorish attire: As crisping and curling.

†**4** Covering for the head; a headdress, esp. for a woman. LME–E17.
5 HUNTING & HERALDRY. A deer's antlers. M16.

attire /əˈtʌɪə/ *verb trans*. ME.
[ORIGIN Old French *atir(i)er* arrange, equip, from *a tire*, Provençal *a tieira* in succession or order, of unknown origin.]
†**1** Equip, fit out; make ready, prepare. ME–L15.
2 Dress, esp. in fine, formal, or special clothing; clothe. Now chiefly *refl.* & as ***attired*** *ppl adjective*. ME.

DRYDEN His shoulders large a mantle did attire. R. KIPLING I was . . attired as a Sahib. G. HEYER Nattily attired in the correct town-dress of a gentleman of fashion. *fig.*: BURKE The rose and the apple blossom are both beautiful, and the plants that bear them are most engagingly attired.

3 Adorn, arrange, (the hair, the head). *arch*. LME.

SPENSER Her golden tresses, She dothe attyre vnder a net of gold. TENNYSON The women who attired her head.

4 HUNTING & HERALDRY. Provide with antlers, esp. of a distinct colour. Chiefly as ***attired*** *ppl adjective*. L16.
■ **attirement** *noun* (*a*) an outfit, a dress, apparel; †(*b*) an ornament, an adornment: M16. **attiring** *noun* (*a*) the action of the verb; †(*b*) a dress, an outfit; a headdress; an ornament; in *pl*. trappings: ME.

attitude /ˈatɪtjuːd/ *noun*. L17.
[ORIGIN French from Italian *attitudine*, Spanish *attitud*, fitness, disposition, posture, from late Latin *aptitudo*, *-din-* APTITUDE.]
1 ART. The disposition of a figure in painting, statuary, etc.; the posture given to a figure. *obsolete* exc. as passing into sense 2. L17.
2 The posture of the body proper to or implying some action or mental state. E18. ▸**b** A posture or disposition of the body in dancing. E18. ▸**c** The orientation of an aircraft, spacecraft, etc., relative to the direction of travel. E20.

W. CATHER He stood in an attitude of self-defense, his feet well apart, his hands clenched and drawn up at his sides. P. HESKETH The fox's sculpted attitude was tense With scenting, listening. D. JACOBSON Those portraits of languid houris lying about in attitudes suggestive of inner heats.

strike an attitude: see STRIKE *verb*.
3 Settled behaviour, as representing feeling or opinion; (also ***attitude of mind***) settled mode of thinking. M19.

H. SPENCER Much depends on the attitude of mind we preserve while listening to, or taking part in, the controversy. E. WILSON Michelet's fundamental attitude is . . realistic and not romantic. R. HOGGART Characteristic working-class relationships and attitudes. G. J. WARNOCK A marked capacity for abstract thought is compatible with an 'attitude to life' entirely ordinary, or even dull. T. STOPPARD Her whole attitude in the play is one of innocent, eager willingness to please.

■ **attiˈtudinal** *adjective* of or pertaining to attitudes or attitude M19. **attitudiˈnarian** *noun* a person who uses postures and poses M18. **attitudiˈnarianism** *noun* the (excessive) use of attitudes E19.

attitudinize /atɪˈtjuːdɪnʌɪz/ *verb intrans*. Also **-ise**. L16.
[ORIGIN from Italian *attitudine* (see ATTITUDE) + -IZE.]
Practise or adopt attitudes; strike an attitude; speak, write, or behave affectedly.
■ **attitudinizer** *noun* E19.

attn *abbreviation*.
Attention, for the attention of.

atto- /ˈatəʊ/ *combining form*.
[ORIGIN from Danish or Norwegian *atten* eighteen: see -O-.]
Used in names of units of measurement to denote a factor of 10^{-18}, as ***attowatt*** etc. Abbreviation ***a***.

attorn /əˈtəːn/ *verb*. ME.
[ORIGIN Old French *atorner*, *aturner* assign, appoint, from *a* A-⁵ + *torner* TURN *verb*.]
†**1** *verb trans*. Turn; change, transform; deck out. Only in ME.
2 *verb trans*. Turn over (goods, service, allegiance, etc.) to another; transfer, assign. *arch*. LME.
attorn tenant (to) LAW formally transfer one's tenancy (*to*), make legal acknowledgement of tenancy (*to* a new landlord).
3 *verb intrans*. Transfer one's tenancy, or (*arch.*) homage or allegiance, *to* another; formally acknowledge such transfer. LME.
■ **attornment** *noun* the transference of bailor status, tenancy, or (*arch.*) allegiance, service, etc., to another; formal acknowledgement of such transfer: LME.

attorney /əˈtəːni/ *noun* & *verb*. ME.
[ORIGIN Old French *atorné*, *aturné*, or (branch A.II) *atornée* (fem.), use as noun of pa. pple of *atorner*: see ATTORN.]
▶ **A** *noun* **I 1** LAW. A person formally appointed to act for another in legal or business matters. Also ***attorney-in-fact***, ***private attorney***. ME. ▸†**b** *gen*. A person appointed to act for another; an agent, a deputy, a representative. LME–M17.

b SHAKES. *Com. Err.* I will attend my husband, . . And will have no attorney but myself.

†**Attorney general**: one empowered to act for his principal without restriction to specified matters.
2 A legal practitioner properly qualified to represent a client in a court of law (now chiefly *US*). In English law (*hist.*), a legal practitioner entitled to conduct litigation in lower courts (distinguished from ***counsel***), a solicitor (freq. *derog.*). Also ***attorney-at-law***, ***public attorney***. Also (**A-**), the title of certain law officers of the Crown, councils, etc. ME.
Attorney General the highest legal officer in England and Wales and some other countries, empowered to act for the Crown or state in legal matters. **Attorney-Generalship** the position of Attorney General. ***district attorney***: see DISTRICT *noun*. †**King's Attorney**, †**Queen's Attorney** the Attorney General. ***Scotch attorney***: see SCOTCH *adjective*.
†**3** An advocate, a mediator. LME–L16.

SHAKES. *Rich. III* Therefore, dear mother . . Be the attorney of my love to her.

▶ **II 4** The action or fact of appointing a person to act as one's representative in legal or business matters. Now chiefly in ***power of attorney***, the authority conferred by this action; the legal document conferring such authority. LME.

SHAKES. *Rich. III* I, by attorney, bless thee from thy mother.

letter of attorney the legal document conferring power of attorney. ***warrant of attorney***: see WARRANT *noun*¹.
▶ **B** *verb trans*. Appoint as attorney; perform etc. by attorney or proxy. *rare*. L15.
■ **attorneydom** *noun* M19. **attorneyism** *noun* (*arch.*) the practice of attorneys; unscrupulous cleverness: M19. **attorneyship** *noun* (*a*) acting as attorney, proxy; (*b*) the position of an attorney: L16.

attract /əˈtrakt/ *verb trans*. LME.
[ORIGIN Latin *attract-* pa. ppl stem of *attrahere*, from *ad* AT- + *trahere* draw.]
1 (Tend to) draw to oneself or itself, cause to come near, esp. (***a***) by an invisible force such as gravity, magnetism, or electricity, (***b***) by influencing the will or actions of people or animals, (***c***) by presenting favourable conditions or opportunities. LME.

SIR T. BROWNE Jet and amber attracteth straws. J. A. FROUDE Like all other systems which have attracted followers, it addresses itself, not to the logical intellect, but to the imagination. E. F. SCHUMACHER Neither the successful farmers nor the Soil Association have been able to attract official support or recognition. M. GIROUARD The old red-brick houses and innumerable artistic associations of Hampstead attracted architects, artists, and writers. J. UPDIKE There was no population here, until your contraption attracted it. D. ATTENBOROUGH Some orchids . . attract insects by sexual impersonation.

†**2** Draw or pull in; absorb, inhale. M16–L17.
3 Excite (pleasurable emotions) in a person towards oneself or itself; give or promise pleasure to (a person). E17.

MILTON Adornd She was indeed, and lovely to attract Thy Love. I. FLEMING She had the sort of firm, compact figure that always attracted him. R. DAWKINS The ability to attract loyal friends.

4 Draw out and fix upon oneself or itself (the attention etc. of others). L17.

DRYDEN A wife . . Made to attract his eyes, and keep his heart. E. WAUGH Now and then I noticed him attract curious glances, but most of the party knew him too slightly to see the change in him. M. LEITCH He couldn't have attracted their attention more if he had waved a red, white and blue flag.

5 *euphem*. Come by dishonestly, pilfer. L19.
■ **attractable** *adjective* able to be attracted L18. **attractant** *noun* an agent which attracts; *esp*. a substance used to attract insects: E20. **attractor** *noun* a person who or thing which attracts something or someone else (***GREAT attractor***; ***strange attractor***: see STRANGE *adjective*) M17.

attraction /əˈtrakʃ(ə)n/ *noun*. LME.
[ORIGIN French, or Latin *attractio(n-)*, formed as ATTRACT: see -ION.]
†**1** MEDICINE. The action of a poultice etc. in drawing matter from the tissues; something applied for this purpose. LME–M17.
†**2** Absorption; the taking in of food; inhalation. M16–M17.
3 The action of a body in drawing another towards itself by some physical force such as gravity, magnetism, etc.; the tendency for this to occur. Opp. ***repulsion***. E17.

LONGFELLOW Every arrow that flies feels the attraction of earth. A. KOESTLER Explanation of the tides as an effect of the moon's attraction.

capillary attraction: see CAPILLARY *adjective* 3. ***centre of attraction***: see CENTRE *noun*. **chemical attraction** = AFFINITY 6.
4 An attractive quality. Freq. in *pl*. E17.

SHAKES. *Per.* She, questionless, with her sweet harmony And other chosen attractions, would allure. DAY LEWIS A capacity for relishing the everyday and recognising the attractions in the commonplace. A. J. P. TAYLOR Here, he believed, he could win the war—with the added attraction of doing so before the Americans arrived.

5 The action of causing people or animals to come nearer by influencing their conscious actions, providing favourable conditions, etc. M18.

OED The attraction of the disaffected to his standard. ROGER JOHNSON Sexual attraction has been a frequently suggested function of scent glands.

6 The action or capacity of eliciting interest, affection, sympathy, etc.; attractiveness, charm, fascination. M18.

E. WAUGH She was daily surprised by the things he knew and the things he did not know; both . . added to his attraction. T. STOPPARD What is the attraction or the point in thinking better of oneself? E. F. SCHUMACHER Scientific . . 'solutions' which poison the environment or degrade the social structure . . are of no benefit, no matter how brilliantly conceived or how great their superficial attraction.

7 A thing or feature which attracts visitors, customers, etc. E19.

ANTHONY HUXLEY Another major flowery attraction is nectar, a . . sugar secretion . . which is of course food of a delicious kind to many insects. P. THEROUX There are few tourist attractions in Veracruz; there is an old fort and . . a beach.

8 GRAMMAR. The influence of a word in context causing an adjacent word to be given an incorrect form, as in *one in six have* (for *has*) *this problem*. E20.

attractive /əˈtraktɪv/ *adjective* & *noun*. LME.
[ORIGIN French *attractif*, *-ive* from late Latin *attractivus*, formed as ATTRACT + -IVE.]
▶ **A** *adjective*. †**1** Absorptive. LME–E18.
†**2** MEDICINE. Having the property of drawing bodily humours etc. LME–L18.
3 Having the property or capacity of attracting towards itself by a physical force; of the nature of such attraction. Opp. ***repulsive***. M16.

W. HERSCHEL The sun, by its attractive power, retains the planets . . in their orbits.

4 Having the property or capacity of attracting towards oneself or itself by influencing will and action; having the property of attracting interest, attention, affection, desire, etc.; interesting, pleasing, alluring. L16.

A

SIR W. SCOTT Interesting and attractive for those who love to hear an old man's stories of a past age. W. CATHER A gay young fellow, so attractive that the prettiest Bohemian girl in Omaha had run away with him. S. HILL What an attractive garden you have here! P. SCOTT The proposal could turn out to be financially attractive One might presume to make a small profit.

▸ †**B** *noun*. **1** *MEDICINE*. A preparation used to draw bodily humours etc. **LME–L18.**
2 An attractive thing or quality. **L16–M19.**
■ **attractively** *adverb* **E17. attractiveness** *noun* **M17.**

†**attrahent** *adjective & noun*. **M17–L18.**
[**ORIGIN** Latin *attrahent-* pres. ppl stem of *attrahere* **ATTRACT**: see **-ENT**.]
(Something) that attracts.

attrait /atrɛ/ *noun*. **E20.**
[**ORIGIN** French, from *attraire* attract.]
THEOLOGY. Vocation; inclination.

†**attrap** *verb trans*. Infl. **-pp-**. **L16–L17.**
[**ORIGIN** from **A-**[1] + **TRAP** *verb*[1].]
Provide (a horse) with trappings. Chiefly as ***attrapped*** *ppl adjective*.

attribute /ˈatrɪbjuːt/ *noun*. **LME.**
[**ORIGIN** Old French & mod. French *attribut* or Latin *attributum* use as noun of neut. pa. pple of *attribuere* **ATTRIBUTE** *verb*.]
†**1** *MEDICINE*. A condition of the bodily humours. Only in **LME.**
2 A quality or character ascribed (esp. in common estimation) to a person or thing. Also, an epithet denoting this. **L15.**

SHAKES. *Merch. V.* But mercy is above this sceptred sway, .. It is an attribute to God himself. T. WRIGHT It is surprising how soon historical personages become invested with romantic attributes.

3 A material object recognized as appropriate to or symbolic of a person or office; a conventional symbol serving to identify a figure in a painting etc. **L16.**

WORDSWORTH A crown, an attribute of sovereign power. K. CLARK The Greek philosophers are represented with their attributes, Aristotle, with the severe figure of Dialectic.

4 An inherent characteristic quality or feature of a person or thing; a property; in *STATISTICS* etc., a non-quantifiable property. **E17.** ▸**b** *LOGIC*. That which may be predicated of something. **L18.**

BACON The attributes and acts of God, as far as they are revealed to man. SIR W. SCOTT Beauty was an attribute of the family. H. FAST It had all the attributes and virtues and sins that history requires of a great city. H. KISSINGER At this point I experienced for the first time two of Nixon's distinguishing attributes. S. NAIPAUL Recycling is the highest good, biodegradability the most sought-after attribute.

†**5** Distinguished quality or character; reputation, credit. Only in **17.**

SHAKES. *Tr. & Cr.* Much attribute he hath, and much the reason Why we ascribe it to him.

6 *GRAMMAR*. An attributive word or phrase. **E19.**

†**attribute** *ppl adjective*. **LME–L16.**
[**ORIGIN** Latin *attributus* pa. pple, formed as **ATTRIBUTE** *verb*.]
Attributed; assigned, given.

attribute /əˈtrɪbjuːt/ *verb trans*. **L15.**
[**ORIGIN** Latin *attribut-* pa. ppl stem of *attribuere*, from *ad* **AT-** + *tribuere* allot: cf. **TRIBUTE** *noun*.]
†**1** Assign, give, or concede *to* a person as a right. **L15–L18.**

LD BERNERS These two townes were attributed to Flaunders by reason of gage. BACON What celsitude of honour Plinius Secundus attributeth to Trajan in his funeral oration.

2 Ascribe as belonging or appropriate *to*. **M16.**

MILTON God attributes to place No sanctity, if none be thither brought By men. W. S. CHURCHILL Opposition speakers were pleased to attribute to him an aim he did not possess.

†**attribute much to** attach great importance or value to.
3 Ascribe *to* as an inherent quality or characteristic. **M16.**

E. BISHOP Their gods, to which, in their present historical state of superstition and helplessness, they attribute magical powers.

4 Ascribe *to* as an effect or consequence. **M16.**

R. L. STEVENSON It was the character of the man to attribute nothing to luck and but little to kindness. R. LYND Some writers have attributed the tendency to laugh at mispronunciations to snobbery. G. VIDAL I attributed my condition to the altitude.

5 Ascribe *to* an author, painter, etc., as his or her work. **M16.**

P. GALLICO He repeated the words John had attributed to Jesus. M. GIROUARD Two more houses in Cambridge .. can be attributed to him with reasonable confidence.

6 Assign in one's opinion *to* its proper time and place. **M16.**

F. H. A. SCRIVENER Several copies which may fairly be attributed to the fourth century.

■ **attributable** *adjective* able to be attributed *to*, owing *to* **M17.**

attribution /atrɪˈbjuːʃ(ə)n/ *noun*. **LME.**
[**ORIGIN** Old French & mod. French from Latin *attributio(n-)*, formed as **ATTRIBUTE** *verb*: see **-ION**.]
†**1** Bestowal, awarding. **LME–E19.**
†**2** Something ascribed in estimation or opinion, as a quality, appellation, meaning, etc. **L15–M18.**
3 *LOGIC*. Predication of an attribute. **E17.**
4 Ascription of a quality etc. as belonging or proper to a person or thing. **M17.**
5 Ascription of an effect to a cause, a work to an author, etc. **M17.**
6 An authority or function granted to a ruler, court, etc. **L18.**
– **COMB.**: **attribution theory** *PSYCHOLOGY* a theory which supposes that people attempt to understand the behaviour of others by attributing feelings, beliefs, and intentions to them.

attributive /əˈtrɪbjʊtɪv/ *adjective & noun*. **E17.**
[**ORIGIN** French *attributif*, *-ive*, from *attribut*: see **ATTRIBUTE** *noun*, **-IVE**.]
▸ **A** *adjective*. †**1** Characterized by attributing. *rare* (Shakes.). Only in **E17.**
2 *LOGIC*. That assigns an attribute to a subject. **M19.**
3 *GRAMMAR*. That expresses an attribute; *spec.* (opp. ***predicative***) designating adjectives (or their equivalents) that premodify or occas. immediately follow nouns (e.g. *old* in *the old dog*, *a dog old in years*, but not in *the dog is old*). **M19.**
4 Of a work of art etc.: that is such by attribution. **M19.**
▸ **B** *noun*. *GRAMMAR*. An attributive word or phrase. **M18.**
■ **attributively** *adverb* **M19.**

†**attrist** *verb trans*. **L17–M19.**
[**ORIGIN** French *attrister*, from *à* **A-**[5] + *triste* sad, from Latin *tristis*.]
Make sad, sadden.

attrit /əˈtrɪt/ *verb trans*. *US colloq*. Infl. **-tt-**. **M20.**
[**ORIGIN** Back-form. from **ATTRITION**: cf. **ATTRITE** *verb*.]
Wear down in quality or quantity by military attrition.

attrite /əˈtrʌɪt/ *adjective*. **LME.**
[**ORIGIN** Latin *attritus* pa. pple, formed as **ATTRITE** *verb*.]
†**1** Worn or ground down. **LME–M17.**
2 *THEOLOGY*. Having attrition. **E17.**

attrite /əˈtrʌɪt/ *verb trans*. **M18.**
[**ORIGIN** Latin *attrit-* pa. ppl stem of *atterere*, from *ad* **AT-** + *terere* to rub.]
1 Wear down by continued friction. Chiefly as ***attrited*** *ppl adjective*. **M18.**
2 = **ATTRIT**. *US colloq*. **M20.**
■ **attritive** *adjective* (*rare*) = **ATTRITIONAL M19. attritor** *noun* (*rare*) an agent which wears something down by attrition **E19.**

attrition /əˈtrɪʃ(ə)n/ *noun*. **LME.**
[**ORIGIN** Late Latin *attritio(n-)*, formed as **ATTRITE** *verb*: see **-ION**.]
1 *THEOLOGY*. Regret for sin, e.g. through fear of punishment, falling short of true repentance or contrition. **LME.**
2 *MEDICINE*. Comminution; tearing; excoriation, abrasion (passing into sense 3). Now *rare* or *obsolete*. **LME.**
3 Rubbing away, wearing or grinding down, by friction. **L15.**

C. LYELL Pebbles and sand .. decrease in size by attrition. *fig.*: MAX-MÜLLER Contact with English society exercises a constant attrition on the system of castes.

4 The action of rubbing one thing against another; mutual friction. **E17.**

J. PRIESTLEY Some .. think that heat is produced in the lungs by the attrition of the blood in passing through them.

5 The gradual wearing down of an enemy's forces in sustained warfare; loss of men or material by enemy action; *gen.* gradual loss or reduction. **E20.**

H. WOUK Combat attrition was taking a steep toll, and to send green replacements into the skies was fruitless. P. F. BOLLER He hammered stubbornly away at the enemy and wore him down by sheer attrition.

war of attrition a prolonged war characterized by continual small-scale actions rather than by decisive battles.
■ **attritional** *adjective* characterized by or of the nature of attrition **M19.**

attune /əˈtjuːn/ *verb*. **L16.**
[**ORIGIN** from **AT-** + **TUNE** *verb*.]
1 *verb trans*. Bring into musical accord. (Foll. by *to*.) **L16.**

POPE For Phemius to the lyre attuned the strain.

†**2** *verb trans*. Make tuneful or melodious. **M17–L18.**

MILTON Aires, vernal aires .. attune The trembling leaves.

3 *verb trans*. Bring (an instrument) to the correct pitch; tune. **E18.**
4 *verb trans*. *fig*. Bring into harmony or accord; make perfectly suited or receptive *to*. **E18.**

M. L. KING My hearing was not attuned to the sound of such bitterness. C. SAGAN Life forms developed that were finely attuned to their specific environments. J. CAREY It's curious .. that a novel so attuned to the selfishness and pain behind every face should transmit such an exuberant sense of life.

5 *verb intrans*. Harmonize *with*. **E20.**

fig.: R. LANGBRIDGE This might have been carefully studied so as to attune with his general appearance.

■ **attunement** *noun* **M19.**

Atty *abbreviation*.
Attorney.

atua /ˈatua, əˈtuːə/ *noun*. **M18.**
[**ORIGIN** Maori, & other Polynesian langs.]
A supernatural being, god, or demon.

ATV *abbreviation*.
All-terrain vehicle.

atwain /əˈtweɪn/ *adverb*. Long *arch*. **ME.**
[**ORIGIN** from **A** *preposition*[1] 2 + **TWAIN** *noun*.]
In two; apart, asunder.

atweel /əˈtwiːl/ *adverb*. *Scot*. **M18.**
[**ORIGIN** Prob. contr. of *I wat weel* = I wot well.]
Certainly, for sure; indeed.

atween /əˈtwiːn/ *preposition & adverb*. *arch. & dial.* **LME.**
[**ORIGIN** from **A** *preposition*[1] 1 + stem of **BETWEEN**, on the analogy of *afore*, *before*.]
▸ **A** *preposition*. Between. **LME.**
▸ **B** *adverb*. In between. **LME.**

atwist /əˈtwɪst/ *adverb & pred. adjective*. **M18.**
[**ORIGIN** from **A-**[2] + **TWIST** *noun*[1].]
Twisted, askew.

†**atwit** *verb* see **TWIT** *verb*.

atwitter /əˈtwɪtə/ *adverb & pred. adjective*. **M19.**
[**ORIGIN** from **A-**[2] + **TWITTER** *noun*[2] or *verb*[1].]
Twittering; aflutter.

atwixt /əˈtwɪkst/ *preposition*. *arch. & dial.* **ME.**
[**ORIGIN** from **A** *preposition*[1] 1 + stem of **BETWIXT**: cf. **ATWEEN**.]
Between.

atwo /əˈtuː/ *adverb*. *arch. & dial.* **OE.**
[**ORIGIN** from **A** *preposition*[1] 2 + **TWO**.]
In two; apart, asunder.

atypia /eɪˈtɪpɪə, a-/ *noun*. **M20.**
[**ORIGIN** from **A-**[10] + Greek *tupos* **TYPE** *noun* + **-IA**[1].]
MEDICINE. An atypical condition; irregularity, abnormality.

atypical /eɪˈtɪpɪk(ə)l, a-/ *adjective*. **L19.**
[**ORIGIN** from **A-**[10] + **TYPICAL** *adjective*.]
Not typical; not conforming to type.
■ **atypically** *adverb* **E20.**

AU *abbreviation*.
1 African Union.
2 Angstrom unit.
3 Astronomical unit.

Au *symbol*.
[**ORIGIN** Latin *aurum*.]
CHEMISTRY. Gold.

aubade /əʊˈbɑːd; *foreign* obad (*pl. same*)/ *noun*. **L17.**
[**ORIGIN** French from Spanish *albada*, from *alba* (= French *aube*) dawn.]
A piece of music or a poem written to be heard at or appropriate to dawn.

aubaine /obɛn/ *noun*. **L16.**
[**ORIGIN** French, from *aubain* foreigner, of unknown origin.]
hist. In full ***droit d'aubaine*** /drwa dobɛn/. The right of the French monarch to claim the property of any foreigner who died in France.

auberge /əʊˈbɛːʒ; *foreign* obɛrʒ (*pl. same*)/ *noun*. **L16.**
[**ORIGIN** French from Provençal *alberga* lodging.]
An inn, *esp.* one in France.
■ ***aubergiste*** /obɛrʒist (*pl. same*)/ *noun* the keeper of an auberge **M18.**

aubergine /ˈəʊbəʒiːn/ *noun & adjective*. **L18.**
[**ORIGIN** French from Catalan *alberginia* from Arabic *al-bāḏinjān*, from **AL-**[2] + Persian *bādingān*, *-injān* from Sanskrit *vātimgana*.]
▸ **A** *noun*. **1** The fruit of the eggplant, *Solanum melongena*, eaten as a vegetable; the plant itself. **L18.**
2 A dark purple colour typical of the skin of the fruit. **L19.**
▸ **B** *adjective*. Of the colour aubergine, dark purple. **L19.**

aubretia /ɔːˈbriːʃə/ *noun*. Also **aubrietia**, **-ta** /-tə/. **E19.**
[**ORIGIN** mod. Latin *Aubrieta*, from Claude *Aubriet* (1668–1743), French botanist: see **-IA**[1].]
Any of several dwarf trailing cruciferous plants of the genus *Aubrieta*, usu. bearing violet or purple flowers.
– **NOTE**: *Aubrieta* is the original spelling of the name of the genus, but in ordinary usage forms with *-tia* have been predominant.

auburn /ˈɔːbən, -bɔːn/ *adjective*. **LME.**
[**ORIGIN** Old French *alborne*, *auborne* from medieval Latin *alburnus* whitish, from Latin *albus* white: later assoc. with *brown* by false etymology (through forms with metathesis).]
Orig., of a yellowish- or brownish-white colour. Now, of a golden- or reddish-brown colour. (Used esp. of a person's hair.)

Aubusson /ˈəʊbjʊsɒn, *foreign* obysɔ̃/ *noun*. Pl. pronounced same. **E20.**
[**ORIGIN** A town in central France.]
Tapestry or (esp.) a tapestry carpet woven at Aubusson.

AUC *abbreviation*.
Latin *ab urbe condita* from the foundation of the city (of Rome, in 753 BC), or *anno urbis conditae* in the year of the founding of the city.

aucht /ɔːxt/ *noun*. Long *obsolete* exc. *Scot*. Also **aught**.
[**ORIGIN** Old English *æht* (= Old High German *ēht*, Gothic *aihts*), from *āgan* to own, possess (pa. t. *āhte*).]
Possessions, property.

aucht *verb* see **OUGHT** *verb*.

au contraire /əʊ kɒnˈtrɛː, *foreign* o kɔ̃trɛːr/ *adverb & interjection*. **M18.**
[**ORIGIN** French.]
On the contrary.

au courant /o kurɑ̃/ *adverbial & pred. adjectival phr.* **M18.**
[**ORIGIN** French.]
In an informed position; aware of current developments. (Usu. foll. by *with*, *of*.)

auction /ˈɔːkʃ(ə)n/ *noun & verb*. **L16.**
[**ORIGIN** Latin *auctio(n-)* lit. 'increase', from *auct-* pa. ppl stem of *augere* to increase: see **-ION**.]
▸ **A** *noun*. **1** A (usu. public) sale in which articles are sold to or reserved for the highest bidder. **L16.**
all over the auction *Austral. slang* everywhere. **Dutch auction** a sale in which the price is gradually reduced by the auctioneer until a buyer is found. ***mock auction***: see **MOCK** *adjective*.
2 The bidding in a hand of a card game such as bridge. Also *ellipt.*, = ***auction bridge*** s.v. **BRIDGE** *noun*[2]. **E20.**
auction bridge: see **BRIDGE** *noun*[2].
▸ **B** *verb trans.* Sell by auction. **E19.**

auctioneer /ɔːkʃəˈnɪə/ *noun & verb*. **E18.**
[**ORIGIN** from **AUCTION** + **-EER**.]
▸ **A** *noun*. A person who conducts sales by auction, *esp.* a person whose business is to do this. **E18.**
▸ **B** *verb intrans. & trans.* Sell by auction. Chiefly as ***auctioneering*** *verbal noun*. **M18.**

auctorial /ɔːkˈtɔːrɪəl/ *adjective*. **E19.**
[**ORIGIN** from Latin *auctor* **AUTHOR** *noun* + **-IAL**.]
Of or pertaining to an author. Cf. **AUTHORIAL** *adjective*.

aucuba /ˈɔːkjʊbə/ *noun*. **L18.**
[**ORIGIN** mod. Latin, from Japanese *aokiba*, from *ao* green + *ki*, *ko* tree + *ba*, *ha* leaf.]
A hardy evergreen shrub belonging to the Far Eastern genus *Aucuba*, of the dogwood family; *esp.* the Japanese laurel, *A. japonica*.

aucupate /ˈɔːkjʊpeɪt/ *verb trans.* **M17.**
[**ORIGIN** Latin *aucupat-* pa. ppl stem of *aucupari* lit. 'go bird-catching', from *avis* bird + *capere* to catch: see **-ATE**[3].]
Lie in wait for, gain by craft.

audacious /ɔːˈdeɪʃəs/ *adjective*. **M16.**
[**ORIGIN** from Latin *audac-*, *-ax* bold, from *audere* dare: see **-ACIOUS**.]
1 Daring, bold, confident, intrepid. **M16.**

> A. J. CRONIN Claire began to look at the paintings, seeing little . . but an audacious contrast of brilliant colours. J. BERGER The bold and audacious youth who had the fabulous vision of the Alps conquered and fleeing under his glance.

2 Openly disregarding decorum or morality; impudent, shameless. **L16.**

> SHAKES. *1 Hen. VI* Such is thy audacious wickedness. DEFOE I grew more hardened and audacious than ever.

■ **audaciously** *adverb* **L16.** **audaciousness** *noun* = **AUDACITY** **L16.**

audacity /ɔːˈdasɪti/ *noun*. **LME.**
[**ORIGIN** from medieval Latin *audacitas*, formed as **AUDACIOUS**: see **-ACITY**.]
1 Boldness; reckless daring. **LME.**
2 Effrontery; impudence. **M16.**

Audenesque /ɔːdəˈnɛsk/ *adjective*. **M20.**
[**ORIGIN** from *Auden* (see below) + **-ESQUE**.]
Resembling in matter or style the works of the English poet and critic Wystan Hugh Auden (1907–73).

audible /ˈɔːdɪb(ə)l/ *adjective & noun*. **L15.**
[**ORIGIN** Late Latin *audibilis*, from *audire* hear: see **-IBLE**. Cf. earlier **INAUDIBLE**.]
▸ **A** *adjective*. Able to be heard. **L15.**

> S. RICHARDSON I had rather have their silent Prayers, than their audible ones. R. LARDNER The hubbub must have been audible to Miss Jackson outside. M. FRAYN He could hear a distant banging and shouting, but it was scarcely audible over the noise of the celebration.

▸ **B** *noun*. **1** A thing able to be heard. *rare*. **E17.**
2 *AMER. FOOTBALL*. A play called at the line of scrimmage to replace that previously agreed on. **M20.**
■ **audiˈbility** *noun* the quality of being audible, audible capacity **M17.** **audibleness** *noun* **E17.** **audibly** *adverb* **M17.**

audience /ˈɔːdɪəns/ *noun*. **LME.**
[**ORIGIN** Old French & mod. French, refashioned after Latin of †*oiance* from Latin *audientia*, from *audient-* pres. ppl stem of *audire* hear: see **-ENCE**. Sense 5 from Spanish *audiencia*.]
1 Hearing; attention to what is spoken. *arch.* **LME.**

> SHAKES. *Coriol.* List to your tribunes. Audience! peace, I say. H. F. CARY Thou in his audience shouldst thereof discourse. LD MACAULAY These teachers easily found attentive audience.

give audience give ear, listen.
2 Judicial hearing. Now *arch. & hist.* **LME.**
Court of Audience *hist.* an ecclesiastical court, orig. held by an archbishop, later by his auditors.
3 (A) formal interview, esp. with a monarch or a member of government. (Foll. by *of*, *with*.) **LME.**

> SHAKES. *Hen. V* The French ambassador upon that instant Crav'd audience. *Daily Telegraph* The Rt. Hon. James Callaghan . . had an audience of Her Majesty this evening. M. AMIS I had then had a brief audience with Rachel's guardians.

4 a The persons within hearing; an assembly of listeners. **LME.** ▸**b** *transf.* The readership of a book, newspaper, etc.; the whole group of spectators or viewers of a play, television programme, etc. **M18.**

> **a** E. M. FORSTER The lecturer was a clergyman, and his audience must be also his flock. **b** A. TOFFLER Like radio broadcasters and moviemakers, publishers tended to seek the largest and most universal audience. G. EWART Opposite was the audience, to watch the total effect, / a sort of firework display.

a captive audience: see **CAPTIVE** *adjective* 1.
5 *hist.* (The territory administered by) a Spanish-American court of government or justice. **E18.**
– **COMB.**: **audience chamber** a reception room in a palace etc.; **audience participation** participation by the audience esp. in a broadcast programme; **audience research** investigation into the numbers and opinions of listeners or viewers of broadcast programmes.

†**audiencer** *noun*. **L16–M18.**
[**ORIGIN** Old French & mod. French *audiencier* from medieval Latin *audientiarius*, from *audient-*: see **AUDIENCE**, **-ER**[2].]
An officer in Chancery who dealt with all letters patent.

audient /ˈɔːdɪənt/ *noun & adjective*. **E17.**
[**ORIGIN** As noun from late Latin *audient-*, *-ens* (Cyprian) catechumen; as adjective from Latin *audient-*: see **AUDIENCE**, **-ENT**.]
▸ **A** *noun*. A hearer, a listener; *ECCLESIASTICAL HISTORY* a hearer of the gospel, not yet a member of the Church, a catechumen. **E17.**
▸ **B** *adjective*. Listening. **M19.**

audile /ˈɔːdʌɪl/ *adjective & noun*. **L19.**
[**ORIGIN** Irreg. from Latin *audire* hear + **-ILE**.]
▸ **A** *adjective*. **1** Of, pertaining to, or predominantly involving the sense of hearing. **L19.**
2 *PSYCHOLOGY*. Of, pertaining to, or characterized by responses that involve audile imagery; (of a person) responding to perceptions more readily in terms of audile imagery than in tactile or visual terms. **E20.**
▸ **B** *noun*. *PSYCHOLOGY*. An audile person. **L19.**

audio /ˈɔːdɪəʊ/ *noun*. **E20.**
[**ORIGIN** Independent use of **AUDIO-**: orig. used attrib. or as adjective.]
Audible sound, esp. as electrically reproduced; sound reproduction.
– **COMB.**: **audio frequency**: within the normal frequency range of human hearing; **audio secretary**: who does audio typing; **audio typing** typewriting directly from a tape or other sound recording; **audio typist**: who types directly from a tape or other sound recording.

audio- /ˈɔːdɪəʊ/ *combining form* of Latin *audire* hear: see **-O-**.
■ **audio-active** *adjective* (of language teaching, facilities for this) providing opportunity for listening and response **M20.** **audiobook** *noun* a sound recording of a reading of a book **L20.** **audioˈgenic** *adjective* caused by sound **M20.** **audiogram** *noun* a graphic record of sensitivity of hearing produced by an audiometer **M20.** **audio-lingual** *adjective* pertaining to listening and speaking, as opp. to reading and writing, esp. in language teaching **M20.** **audiophile** *noun* a devotee of high-fidelity sound reproduction **M20.** **audiotape** *noun & verb* (**a**) *noun* (also as two words) magnetic tape on which sound can be recorded; (a sound recording on) a length of magnetic tape; (**b**) *verb trans.* record on audiotape: **M20.** **audioˈvisual** *adjective* (esp. of aids to teaching) using or pertaining to both sight and sound **M20.**

audiology /ɔːdɪˈɒlədʒi/ *noun*. **M20.**
[**ORIGIN** from **AUDIO-** + **-LOGY**.]
The branch of science that deals with hearing.
■ **audioˈlogical** *adjective* **M20.** **audiologist** *noun* **M20.**

audiometer /ɔːdɪˈɒmɪtə/ *noun*. **L19.**
[**ORIGIN** from **AUDIO-** + **-METER**.]
An instrument for measuring the sensitivity of the ear to sounds of different frequencies.
■ **audioˈmetric** *adjective* of or pertaining to audiometry **L19.** **audiomeˈtrician**, **audiometrist** *nouns* a person who specializes in audiometry **M20.** **audiometry** *noun* the measurement and testing of the sense of hearing **L19.**

audion /ˈɔːdɪən/ *noun*. *obsolete* exc. *hist.* **E20.**
[**ORIGIN** from Latin *audire* hear + *-on*.]
A triode valve of the earliest form.

audit /ˈɔːdɪt/ *noun & verb*. **LME.**
[**ORIGIN** from Latin *auditus* hearing, from *audit-* pa. ppl stem of *audire* hear; in medieval Latin *auditus (compoti)* audit (of an account).]
▸ **A** *noun*. **1** An official examination and verification of (orig. orally presented) financial accounts, esp. by an independent body. **LME.**
†**2** A statement of account; a balance sheet. **LME–M17.**
3 A hearing, an inquiry; a methodical and detailed review; *arch.* a judicial hearing or examination. **LME.**

> MILTON With his orisons I meddle not, for hee appeals to a high audit. *Shell Technology* In the safety audit, an independent safety team reviews the design and construction work, concentrating on safety aspects.

4 A periodical settlement of accounts between landlord and tenants. **L15.**
5 *fig.* A searching examination; a reckoning, a settlement; *esp.* the Day of Judgement. **M16.**

> T. DEKKER Those heapes of Siluer . . will be a passing bell . . calling thee to a fearefull Audit.

– **COMB.**: **audit ale** an ale of special quality formerly brewed at certain colleges of English universities, orig. for use on the day of audit; **audit-house**, **audit-room** a building or room attached to a cathedral for the transaction of business; **audit trail** a system allowing tracing of the detailed transactions underlying any part of an audit record.
▸ **B** *verb*. **1** *verb trans.* Conduct an audit of (accounts etc.); *gen.* review methodically and in detail. **LME.**

> J. A. FROUDE With subscribed funds, regularly audited. *Christian Science Monitor* Honeywell . . would audit a building, identify [energy] conservation possibilities, install the equipment, and monitor its operation.

†**2** *verb intrans.* Draw up or render an account. **M17–E18.**
3 *verb trans. & intrans.* Attend (a lecture, course, etc.) without intending to receive credits. *N. Amer.* **M20.**

> A. LURIE She audited his undergraduate lectures; she waylaid him in the department office.

■ **auditaˈbility** *noun* **L20.** **auditable** *adjective* **L20.**

audition /ɔːˈdɪʃ(ə)n/ *noun & verb*. **L16.**
[**ORIGIN** Latin *auditio(n-)*, from *audit-*: see **AUDIT**, **-ION**.]
▸ **A** *noun*. **1** The action, power, or faculty of hearing; listening. **L16.**

> E. POUND All that the critic can do for the reader or audience or spectator is to focus his gaze or audition.

2 Something heard. *rare*. **M17.**

> HOR. WALPOLE I went to hear it for it is not an *apparition* but an audition.

3 A trial hearing or viewing of an applicant for employment as a singer, actor, etc. **L19.**

> J. BERGER She had the impression that everyone was waiting their opportunity to compete, like singers at an audition.

▸ **B** *verb*. **1** *verb trans.* Give an audition to (an applicant); test by means of an audition **M20.**
2 *verb intrans.* Undergo an audition; be tested by means of an audition. **M20.**
■ **auditioˈnee** a person who undergoes an audition **M20.**

auditive /ˈɔːdɪtɪv/ *adjective*. **LME.**
[**ORIGIN** Old French & mod. French *auditif*, *-ive*, from Latin *audit-*: see **AUDIT**, **-IVE**.]
= **AUDITORY** *adjective* 1.

auditor /ˈɔːdɪtə/ *noun*. **ME.**
[**ORIGIN** Anglo-Norman *auditour*, Old French & mod. French *auditeur*, from Latin *auditor*, from *audit-*: see **AUDIT**, **-OR**.]
1 A person who conducts an audit of accounts etc.; *spec.* (more fully ***auditor of court***) a taxing master in a Scottish court. **ME.**

> SHAKES. *Timon* Call me before th'exactest auditors, And set me on the proof.

2 A hearer, a listener. **LME.**

> S. JOHNSON He that long delays a story, and suffers his auditor to torment himself with expectation.

3 A person who listens judicially and tries cases, esp. in an ecclesiastical court. *obsolete* exc. *hist.* **LME.**

> J. AYLIFFE The Auditor, or Official of Causes and Matters in the Court of Audience of Canterbury.

4 A person who learns by oral instruction; a pupil, a disciple; a catechumen. **L15.**

> ANTHONY WOOD Bodley . . was an auditor of Chevalerius in Hebrew.

5 A person who attends a lecture, course, etc., without intending to receive credits. *N. Amer.* **M20.**
■ **auditorship** *noun* the position of an auditor **LME.** **auditress** *noun* (now *rare*) a female auditor **M17.**

auditorial /ɔːdɪˈtɔːrɪəl/ *adjective*. *rare*. **M19.**
[**ORIGIN** Sense 1 from **AUDITORY** *adjective* + **-AL**[1]; sense 2 from **AUDITOR** + **-IAL**.]
1 = **AUDITORY** *adjective* 1. **M19.**
2 Of or pertaining to auditors or an audit. **L19.**
■ **auditorially** *adverb* **L19.**

auditorium /ɔːdɪˈtɔːrɪəm/ *noun*. Pl. **-riums**, **-ria** /-rɪə/. **E17.**
[**ORIGIN** Latin, use as noun of neut. of *auditorius*: see **AUDITORY** *adjective*, **-ORIUM**.]
1 A place for hearing. *rare*. **E17.**
2 The part of a theatre, lecture hall, or other public building occupied by the audience; (*N. Amer.*) such a building as a whole. **M19.** ▸**b** A large room, esp. in a school, used for public gatherings. *N. Amer.* **M19.**

auditory /ˈɔːdɪt(ə)ri/ *noun*. *arch.* **LME.**
[**ORIGIN** from Latin **AUDITORIUM**: see **-ORY**[1].]
1 An assembly of hearers, an audience. **LME.**
2 A place for hearing; an auditorium. **LME.** ▸†**b** A lecture room; a philosophical school. **E17–L18.**

auditory /ˈɔːdɪt(ə)ri/ *adjective*. **L16.**
[**ORIGIN** Late Latin *auditorius*, from Latin **AUDITOR**: see **-ORY**[2].]
1 Pertaining to the sense or organs of hearing. **L16.**
auditory scanning: see **SCANNING** *noun*.
2 Pertaining to an auditorium. *rare*. **M18.**
■ **audiˈtorily** *adverb* by means of hearing or listening **M20.**

auditual /ɔːˈdɪtjʊəl/ *adjective*. Long *rare*. **M17.**
[**ORIGIN** from Latin *auditus* sense of hearing from *audit-* (see **AUDIT**), + **-AL**[1].]
Of or pertaining to the sense of hearing, auditory.

au fait /əʊ feɪ, *foreign* o fɛ/ *adverbial & pred. adjectival phr.* M18.
[ORIGIN French, lit. 'to the fact, to the point'.]
Thoroughly conversant (*with*, †*of*), well instructed (*in*), expert or skilful (*at*).

†**auf(e)** *nouns* see OAF *noun*.

aufgabe /ˈaʊfɡɑːbə/ *noun*. E20.
[ORIGIN German.]
Chiefly PSYCHOLOGY. A task, an assignment. Cf. TASK *noun* 1(d).

Aufklärung /ˈaʊfklɛːrʊŋ/ *noun*. E19.
[ORIGIN German = enlightenment.]
= ENLIGHTENMENT 2.

au fond /o fɔ̃/ *adverbial phr.* L18.
[ORIGIN French.]
At bottom, basically.

Aug. *abbreviation*.
August.

†**auge** *noun*. L16–M18.
[ORIGIN Old French from Arabic *'awj* peak, apogee.]
ASTRONOMY. = APOGEE, APSIS.

Augean /ɔːˈdʒiːən/ *adjective*. L16.
[ORIGIN from Latin *Augeas*, Greek *Augeias* (see below) + -AN.]
Abominably filthy; resembling the stables of Augeas, King of Elis, that had not been cleaned for thirty years until Hercules turned the River Alpheus through them.

augelite /ˈɔːɡəlʌɪt, ˈɔːdʒ-/ *noun*. M19.
[ORIGIN from Greek *augē* lustre + -LITE.]
MINERALOGY. A monoclinic basic aluminium phosphate occurring usu. as colourless or reddish tabular crystals.

augen /ˈaʊɡ(ə)n/ *noun pl.* L19.
[ORIGIN German, pl. of *Auge* EYE *noun*.]
GEOLOGY. Lenticular mineral grains or aggregates present in some metamorphic rocks. Usu. *attrib.* or *comb.*, denoting the presence of these, as ***augen-gneiss***.

augend /ˈɔːdʒ(ə)nd/ *noun*. L19.
[ORIGIN German from Latin *augendus* gerundive of *augere* to increase: see -END.]
The quantity to which an addend is added.

auger /ˈɔːɡə/ *noun*[1]. Also †**n-**.
[ORIGIN Old English *nafogār*, from *nafu* NAVE *noun*[1] + *gār* spear, piercer: corresp. to Old Saxon *nabugēr*, Old High German *nabugēr*, Old Norse *nafarr*. The initial *n* was lost by misdivision as in *adder*, *apron*, etc.]
1 A tool for boring holes in wood, having a long shank with a usu. helical cutting edge, and a transverse handle fixed to the top of the shank by means of which the tool is turned by hand. OE.
2 An instrument for boring in earth, working on a similar principle. L16.
3 More fully ***auger shell***. (The slender tapering spiral shell of) any marine gastropod of the genera *Terebra* and *Turritella*. L18.
4 A helical bit used to convey material, or to mix material and force it through an aperture. M20.
– COMB.: **auger hole** a hole drilled by an auger; ***auger shell***: see sense 3 above.

Auger /ˈəʊʒeɪ/ *noun*[2]. M20.
[ORIGIN P. V. *Auger* (1899–1993), French physicist.]
PHYSICS. **1** ***Auger effect***, the emission of an electron, rather than an X-ray photon, accompanying the filling of a vacancy in an inner electron shell of an atom. M20.
2 ***Auger electron***, an electron emitted in this effect. M20.

aught *noun* var. of AUCHT *noun*.

aught /ɔːt/ *pronoun, adjective, & adverb*. Also **ought**, (*Scot.*) **ocht** /ɒxt/, (*dial.*) **owt** /aʊt/.
[ORIGIN Old English *āwiht*, *āwuht*, *āuht*, *āht*, corresp. to Old Frisian *āwet*, *āet*, Old Saxon *ēowiht*, Old High German *eowiht*, *iewiht*, from West Germanic compound of AYE *adverb*[1] & WIGHT *noun*.]
▸ **A** *pronoun*. Anything whatever; anything. OE.

B. MALAMUD For aught he meant to anyone, Yakov Bok did not exist.

▸ †**B** *adjective*. Worth something; worthy, doughty. Only in ME.
▸ **C** *adverb*. To any extent, in any respect, at all. ME.

W. OWEN Lest aught she be disturbed or grieved at all.

aught *verb* see OUGHT *verb*.

augite /ˈɔːdʒʌɪt/ *noun*. E19.
[ORIGIN Latin *augites* a precious stone, prob. turquoise, from Greek *augitēs*, from *augē* lustre: see -ITE[1].]
MINERALOGY. A monoclinic mineral of the pyroxene group which occurs as black or dark green prisms esp. in many basic igneous rocks.
■ **augitic** /ɔːˈdʒɪtɪk/ *adjective* pertaining to or characterized by augite E19.

augment /ˈɔːɡm(ə)nt/ *noun*. LME.
[ORIGIN Old French & mod. French, or late Latin *augmentum*, from *augere* to increase: see -MENT.]
1 Increase. LME.

W. H. AUDEN April's rapid augment of colour.

2 GRAMMAR. The prefixed vowel marking the past tenses of verbs in the older Indo-European languages. L17.

augment /ɔːɡˈmɛnt/ *verb*. LME.
[ORIGIN Old French & mod. French *augmenter* or late Latin *augmentare*, from *augmentum*: see AUGMENT *noun*.]
▸ **I** *verb trans.* **1** Make greater in size, number, amount, degree, etc.; increase. LME.

SIR W. SCOTT The insurgents were intent upon augmenting and strengthening their forces. W. PLOMER I took on stray jobs of this kind to augment my income. A. J. TOYNBEE Man has been content just to live on Nature's bounty without seeking to augment it.

2 Raise (a person) in estimation or dignity. Now *rare*. M16.

P. H. JOHNSON Certain things Rupert really loved, his wife (when he was not put to the necessity of augmenting her) and his games.

3 HERALDRY. Make an honourable addition to (a coat of arms). M17.
▸ **II** *verb intrans.* **4** Become greater in size, amount, etc.; increase. LME.

DRYDEN The Winds redouble, and the Rains augment. J. TYNDALL The polarizing angle augments with the refractive index of the medium.

■ **augmentable** *adjective* †(*a*) capable of increasing; (*b*) able to be increased: L15. **augmenter** *noun* = AUGMENTOR E18. **augmentive** *adjective & noun* (*rare*) = AUGMENTATIVE E17. **augmentor** *noun* a person who or thing which augments something M16.

augmentation /ɔːɡmɛnˈteɪʃ(ə)n/ *noun*. LME.
[ORIGIN Old French *au(g)mentacion* (mod. *augmentation*) from late Latin *augmentatio(n-)*, from *augmentat-* pa. ppl stem of *augmentare*: see AUGMENT *verb*, -ATION.]
1 The action or process of making or becoming greater in size, amount, etc.; enlargement, increase. LME.
Court of Augmentation(s) *hist.* a court established in the reign of Henry VIII in order to settle the disposal of the property of monasteries upon dissolution.
†**2** The action or process of raising in estimation or dignity; exaltation, honouring. LME–E17.
3 Something by which anything is augmented; an addition, an increase. L15.
4 Augmented or intensified state or condition; increased size etc. M16.
5 HERALDRY. An honourable addition to a coat of arms. L16.
6 MUSIC. The repetition of a subject (esp. in fugues) in notes uniformly longer than those of the original. L16.
7 SCOTS LAW. An increase of clerical stipend obtained through an action in the Court of Teinds. *obsolete* exc. *hist.* M17.

augmentative /ɔːɡˈmɛntətɪv/ *adjective & noun*. LME.
[ORIGIN Old French & mod. French *augmentatif*, *-ive* or medieval Latin *augmentativus*, from *augmentat-*: see AUGMENTATION, -IVE.]
▸ **A** *adjective*. **1** Having the property of increasing or adding to; LOGIC = AMPLIATIVE. LME.
2 GRAMMAR. Of an affix or derivative: intensive; *esp.* indicating something large of its kind (opp. ***diminutive***). M17.
▸ **B** *noun*. GRAMMAR. An augmentative formative or word. L17.

augmented /ɔːɡˈmɛntɪd/ *adjective*. E17.
[ORIGIN from AUGMENT *noun*, *verb*: see -ED[2], -ED[1].]
1 That has been augmented; increased. E17.
augmented reality a form of technology that superimposes a computer-generated image on a user's view of the real world.
2 MUSIC. Of an interval: greater by a semitone than the corresponding major or perfect interval. Of a chord: containing such an interval. Opp. DIMINISHED 2. E19.
3 GRAMMAR. Having an augment. M19.

au grand sérieux /o ɡrɑ̃ serjø/ *adverbial phr.* M19.
[ORIGIN French.]
In all seriousness. Cf. AU SÉRIEUX.

au gratin /o ɡratɛ̃/ *adverbial & pred. adjectival phr.* E19.
[ORIGIN French, from *au* with the + GRATIN.]
COOKERY. Sprinkled with breadcrumbs and/or grated cheese and browned.

†**augrim** *noun* var. of ALGORISM.

augur /ˈɔːɡə/ *noun*. LME.
[ORIGIN Latin.]
A Roman religious official who interpreted omens derived from the behaviour of birds, the appearance of entrails, etc., and gave advice in accordance with them; *gen.* a soothsayer, a diviner, a prophet.
■ **augural** /ˈɔːɡjʊr(ə)l/ *adjective* (*a*) of or pertaining to augurs or augury; (*b*) significant of the future, lucky or ominous: E16. **augurate** *noun* the position of augur M18. **augurous** /ˈɔːɡjʊrəs/ *adjective* (*rare*) full of foreboding, anxious E17. **augurship** *noun* = AUGURATE *noun* E17.

augur /ˈɔːɡə/ *verb*. M16.
[ORIGIN from AUGUR *noun*: cf. Old French & mod. French *augurer* from Latin *augurari*.]
1 *verb trans.* Usher in (or *in*) with auguries; inaugurate. M16.

H. LATIMER Numa Pompilius, who was augured and created king [of] the Romaynes next after Romulus.

2 *verb intrans.* **a** Take auguries; conjecture from signs, have a foreboding. M16. ▸**b** (With *well*, *ill*, etc.) (Of a person) anticipate, (of a thing) portend, a good or bad outcome. L18.

a SIR W. SCOTT Not that he augur'd of the doom, Which on the living closed the tomb. **b** WELLINGTON I augur well from this circumstance. W. H. PRESCOTT A reverential deference, which augured well for the success of his mission. E. J. HOWARD Everything augured badly—they weren't meant to be together.

3 *verb trans.* Divine, forebode, anticipate; portend, give promise of. E17.

JONSON I did augur all this to him beforehand. W. SPARROW He may augur the gust is coming, but cannot prevent it. LYTTON Whose open, handsome, hardy face augured a frank and fearless nature. L. STRACHEY The strange mixture of ingenuous lightheartedness and fixed determination . . seemed to augur a future perplexed and full of dangers.

■ **augurer** *noun* = AUGUR *noun* LME.

auguration /ɔːɡjʊˈreɪʃ(ə)n/ *noun*. Now *rare*. LME.
[ORIGIN Latin *auguratio(n-)*, from *augurat-* pa. ppl stem of *augurari*: see AUGUR *verb*, -ATION.]
Augury; an omen, a token.
■ †**augurate** *verb trans. & intrans.* = AUGUR *verb* L16–M18.

augury /ˈɔːɡjʊri/ *noun*. LME.
[ORIGIN Old French *augurie* or Latin *augurium*, formed as AUGUR *noun*: see -Y[3].]
1 The art of the augur; divination; *arch.* skill in this. LME.
2 An augural observance or rite. E17.
3 An omen, a portent, a token. E17.
4 Foreboding, anticipation; promise, indication. L18.
■ **augurial** /ɔːˈɡjʊərɪəl/ *adjective* (*rare*) E16.

August /ˈɔːɡəst/ *noun*. OE.
[ORIGIN Latin *augustus* (see AUGUST *adjective*): named after *Augustus* Caesar, the first Roman Emperor.]
The eighth month of the year in the Gregorian calendar.

august /ɔːˈɡʌst/ *adjective*. M17.
[ORIGIN Old French & mod. French *auguste* or Latin *augustus* consecrated, venerable.]
1 Inspiring reverence and admiration; solemnly grand, stately. M17.
2 Venerable by birth, status, or reputation; eminent, dignified; (sometimes as an honorific). L17.
■ **augustly** *adverb* M17. **augustness** *noun* M18.

august /ˈɔːɡəst/ *verb trans.* *rare*. L17.
[ORIGIN from AUGUST *noun*, after French *aoûter*.]
Ripen, bring to fruition.

Augustal /ɔːˈɡʌst(ə)l/ *adjective*. M17.
[ORIGIN from Latin *augustalis*, from *Augustus*: see AUGUST *noun*, -AL[1].]
Of or pertaining to Augustus Caesar; imperial Roman.
Augustal Prefect (the title of) the prefect of Roman Egypt.

Augustan /ɔːˈɡʌst(ə)n/ *adjective & noun*. M16.
[ORIGIN Latin (sense A.1 medieval Latin) *Augustanus*, from (sense A.1) *Augusta* (*Vindelicorum*) Augsburg, a city in Bavaria, (sense A.2) *Augustus*: see AUGUST *noun*, -AN.]
▸ **A** *adjective*. **1** ECCLESIASTICAL HISTORY. Of Augsburg, where in 1530 Luther and Melanchthon drew up their confession of Protestant principles. M16.
2 Designating or pertaining to the reign of Augustus Caesar (27 BC–AD 14), esp. as a period of outstanding refinement of Latin literature, or the corresponding period of any national literature; classical; *spec.* designating or pertaining to English literature from the mid 17th to the late 18th cent. E18.
▸ **B** *noun*. **1** Augustan literary style. *rare*. M19.
2 A writer of the Augustan age of any literature. L19.
■ **Augustanism** *noun* Augustan principles, quality, or condition, *spec.* in English literature E20. †**Augustean** *adjective* = AUGUSTAN *adjective* 2: only in L17.

auguste /ˈɔːɡuːst; *foreign* oɡyst (*pl. same*)/ *noun*. E20.
[ORIGIN French from German *August*, male forename, (slang) clown, fool.]
A circus clown wearing ill-fitting or dishevelled clothes.

Augustine /ɔːˈɡʌstɪn/ *noun & adjective*. Also †**-in**. LME.
[ORIGIN Old French & mod. French *augustin*, from Latin *Augustinus* Augustine (see below): cf. AUSTIN.]
▸ **A** *noun*. A member of the monastic order named after St Augustine of Hippo (354–430), a Father of the Church. LME.
▸ **B** *adjective*. Of or pertaining to St Augustine or the Augustines. LME.

Augustinian /ɔːɡəˈstɪnɪən/ *adjective & noun*. M16.
[ORIGIN from AUGUSTINE + -IAN.]
▸ **A** *adjective*. = AUGUSTINE *adjective*. M16.
▸ **B** *noun*. = AUGUSTINE *noun*. Also, an adherent of the doctrines of St Augustine. M16.
■ **Augustinianism** *noun* the doctrines of St Augustine, *esp.* those regarding predestination and grace M19.

auk /ɔːk/ *noun*. L17.
[ORIGIN Old Norse *álka* razorbill (orig. neck) (Swedish *alka*, Danish *alk*).]
Any of several short-winged diving seabirds of the family Alcidae, native to the northern oceans, which includes razorbills, guillemots, and puffins.
great auk a large flightless auk, *Pinguinus impennis*, of the N. Atlantic, now extinct. **little auk** a small Arctic auk, *Alle alle*.
■ **auklet** *noun* any of various small auks, chiefly of the N. Pacific L19.

aul /ˈɑːʊl/ *noun*. Also **aoul**. E19.
[ORIGIN Eastern Turkic.]
A Caucasian or Tatar village or encampment.

aula /ˈɔːlə/ *noun*. Pl. **-lae** /-liː/, **-las**. M18.
[ORIGIN medieval Latin = hall, court, college, from Greek *aulē*.]
1 *hist.* ***aula regis*** /ˈriːdʒɪs/, the King's Court of the Norman kings of England. M18.
2 A hall; an assembly hall, esp. at a German school or university. L19.

aulacogen /ɔːˈlakədʒ(ə)n/ *noun*. L20.
[ORIGIN from Greek *aulak-*, *aulax* furrow + -OGEN.]
GEOLOGY. A sediment-filled trough in continental crust representing the trace of an incipient rift which failed to develop.

aularian /ɔːˈlɛːrɪən/ *noun & adjective*. L17.
[ORIGIN from medieval Latin *aularius* adjective, from AULA: see -ARIAN.]
OXFORD & CAMBRIDGE UNIVS. ▸**A** *noun*. A member of a hall (as opp. to a college). L17.
▸**B** *adjective*. Of, pertaining to, or characteristic of a hall. M19.

auld /ɔːld, ɑːld/ *adjective, noun, & adverb*. *Scot.* LME.
[ORIGIN Var. of OLD *adjective* repr. Old English (Anglian) *ald*.]
= OLD *adjective, noun*[2], *& adverb*.
auld alliance the political alliance between Scotland and France, beginning with the treaty of 1295 and repeatedly renewed until the reign of Mary, Queen of Scots. **auld lang syne** /laŋ sʌɪn/ 'old long since', the days of long ago (esp. as the title and refrain of a song sung at parting etc.). **Auld Reekie** 'Old Smoky', Edinburgh. ***auld*** THIEF.

aulic /ˈɔːlɪk/ *adjective*. E18.
[ORIGIN French *aulique* or Latin *aulicus*, from Greek *aulikos*, from *aulē* court: see -IC.]
Of or pertaining to a court; courtly.
Aulic Council *hist.* the personal council of the German Emperor; later, a council managing the war department of the Austrian Empire.

aulnage /ˈɔːlnɪdʒ/ *noun*. Also **aln-**, **†aun-**. LME.
[ORIGIN Old French *alnage*, (mod.) *aunage*, from *alner*, *auner* measure by the ell, from *alne*, AUNE: see -AGE. Cf. ULNAGE.]
hist. The official measurement and inspection of cloth; the fee paid for this.
■ **aulnager** *noun* an officer appointed to measure and inspect cloth M16.

aum *noun* var. of AAM.

aumail *noun & verb* var. of AMEL.

aumbry /ˈɔːmbri/ *noun*. Also **almery** /ˈɑːm(ə)ri/, **ambry** /ˈambri/. ME.
[ORIGIN Old French *almarie* var. of *armarie* (mod. *armoire*) from Latin *armarium* closet, chest, from *arma* utensils.]
A place for keeping things; *spec.* †(***a***) a library, an archive; (***b***) (now *dial.*) a pantry or store closet; (***c***) a closed recess in the wall of a church; (***d***) *hist.* a small cupboard.

R. MACAULAY The Blessed Sacrament had had to be locked in an aumbry when no one was on guard.

†aumelet *noun* see OMELETTE.

au mieux /o mjø/ *adverbial phr.* M19.
[ORIGIN French = at the best.]
On the best of, or on very intimate, terms *with* (someone).

aumil, **aumildar** *nouns* vars. of AMIL, AMILDAR.

aumônière /omonjɛːr/ *noun*. Pl. pronounced same. E19.
[ORIGIN French, fem. of *aumônier*: see ALMONER.]
A purse carried at the waist.

†aunage *noun* var. of AULNAGE.

au naturel /o natyrɛl/ *adverbial phr.* E19.
[ORIGIN French.]
In the natural state; cooked plainly; uncooked.

auncel /ˈɔːns(ə)l/ *noun*. Long *obsolete* exc. *dial.* ME.
[ORIGIN Anglo-Norman, earlier *aunser*, = Anglo-Latin *auncella*, *a(u)nser* of unknown origin.]
A kind of balance and weight; a steelyard.

aune /ɔːn/ *noun*. *obsolete* exc. *hist.* L15.
[ORIGIN French.]
An ell; a French measure of cloth.

aung *verb* var. of OUNG.

aunt /ɑːnt/ *noun*. Also (esp. as a title) **A-**. ME.
[ORIGIN Anglo-Norman *aunte*, Old French *ante* (mod. *tante*) from Latin *amita*. Cf. NAUNT, TANTE.]
1 The sister of one's father or mother; an uncle's wife. ME. ▸**b** A woman to whom one can turn for help; an unrelated older woman friend, esp. of children. *colloq.* L18.

J. R. ACKERLEY My Aunt Bunny, my mother's younger sister. **b** H. B. STOWE These universally useful persons receive among us the title of 'aunt' by a sort of general consent. J. LE CARRÉ She . . became . . their guide, friend and universal aunt.

Aunt Sally a game in which players throw sticks or balls at a wooden dummy; *fig.* an object of unreasonable attack. ***great-aunt***: see GREAT *adjective*. **my aunt!**, **my giddy aunt!**, ***my*** SAINTED ***aunt!***, etc., expr. surprise, disbelief, etc. ***Welsh aunt***: see WELSH *adjective*. **b** AGONY ***aunt***.
†**2** An old woman; a gossip. Only in L16.

SHAKES. *Mids. N. D.* The wisest aunt, telling the saddest tale.

†**3** A bawd, a procuress; a prostitute. E17–M19.
■ **auntly** *adjective* having or showing the qualities of an aunt M19. **auntship** *noun* (***a***) (with possess. adjective, as ***your auntship*** etc.) a pompous form of address to an aunt; (***b***) the relationship of aunt: E19.

aunter /ˈɔːntə/ *noun & verb trans. & intrans.* Long *obsolete* exc. *Scot. & N. English*. Also (*Scot.*) **anter** /ˈantə/. ME.
[ORIGIN Contr.]
= ADVENTURE *noun, verb*.

auntie /ˈɑːnti/ *noun*. *colloq.* Also **-ty**; (esp. in names) **A-**. L18.
[ORIGIN from AUNTER + -IE, -Y[6].]
1 = AUNT. L18.

R. BURNS My auld Auntie Katie upon me taks pity. W. FAULKNER She began to ask her old schoolmates that their children call her 'cousin' instead of 'aunty'. J. BRAINE Honestly, that woman's magazine stuff, just the sort of advice these damned aunties give. DAY LEWIS You'd better not tell your Auntie.

2 (**A-**.) An institution regarded as conservative in its approach; *spec.* the BBC. M20.

au pair /əʊ ˈpɛː/ *adjectival & noun phr.* L19.
[ORIGIN French = on equal terms.]
▸**A** *adjectival phr.* Of arrangements between two parties: paid for (entirely or largely) by mutual services. Of a person: party to such an arrangement; *spec.* (of a (usu. foreign) girl) undertaking domestic duties in return for room and board. L19.
▸**B** *noun phr.* An au pair girl. M20.

au pied de la lettre /o pje də la lɛtr/ *adverbial phr.* L18.
[ORIGIN French = to the foot of the letter.]
Down to the last detail; literally.

aura /ˈɔːrə/ *noun*. Pl. **-ras**, (*rare*) **-rae** /-riː/. LME.
[ORIGIN Latin from Greek = breath, breeze.]
1 A gentle breeze, a zephyr. *arch. & poet.* LME.

C. PATMORE I *did* respire the lonely auras sweet.

2 A subtle emanation or exhalation; a surrounding glow; *fig.* an atmosphere diffused by or attending a person, place, etc.; a distinctive impression of character or aspect. M18. ▸**b** In arts criticism: the quality of uniqueness or authenticity possessed by an object or artefact, which cannot be present on a reproduction. M20.

COLERIDGE The electrical aura of oxygen. A. MILLER There is an aura of far places about him. J. G. FARRELL A dimly lit table above which a faint aura of exasperation seemed to hang.

3 A premonitory sensation experienced before an attack of epilepsy or migraine. L18.
■ **auˈratic** *adjective* relating to or possessing aura (sense 2b); original, authentic: L20.

aural /ˈɔːr(ə)l/ *adjective*[1]. M19.
[ORIGIN from Latin *auris* ear + -AL[1].]
Of, pertaining to, or received by the ear. Cf. ORAL.
■ **aurally** *adverb* L19.

aural /ˈɔːr(ə)l/ *adjective*[2]. M19.
[ORIGIN from AURA + -AL[1].]
Of or pertaining to an aura.

auramine /ˈɔːrəmiːn, -mɪn/ *noun*. L19.
[ORIGIN from Latin *aurum* gold + AMINE.]
A synthetic yellow dyestuff of the diphenylmethane series.

aurar *noun* pl. of EYRIR.

aurata /ɔːˈreɪtə/ *noun*. E16.
[ORIGIN Latin, use as noun of fem. pa. pple of *aurare* gild, from *aurum* gold.]
A gold-coloured marine fish, *esp.* the gilthead, *Sparus aurata*.

aurate /ˈɔːreɪt/ *noun*. E19.
[ORIGIN from Latin *aurum* gold + -ATE[1].]
CHEMISTRY. A salt derived from auric acid.

aureate /ˈɔːrɪət/ *adjective*. LME.
[ORIGIN Late Latin *aureatus*, from *aureus* golden, from *aurum* gold: see -ATE[2].]
1 Golden, gold-coloured. LME.
2 Resplendent; (of literary style or diction) highly ornamented, elaborate. LME.
■ **aureˈation** *noun* the condition of being aureate in literary style E20.

aureity /ɔːˈriːɪti/ *noun*. E19.
[ORIGIN medieval Latin *aureitas*, from *aureus*: see AUREATE, -ITY.]
The peculiar quality of gold.

aurelia /ɔːˈriːlɪə/ *noun*. L16.
[ORIGIN Italian, fem. of *aurelio* golden; as noun a silkworm in its cocoon.]
†**1** A helichrysum, *Helichrysum stoechas*. L16–E17.
2 A chrysalis. Now *rare* or *obsolete*. E17.
3 A jellyfish of the common genus *Aurelia*, esp. *A. aurita*. L19.

aurelian /ɔːˈriːlɪən/ *adjective & noun*. L18.
[ORIGIN from AURELIA + -AN.]
Of or pertaining to, a student or collector of, butterflies and moths.

aureola /ɔːˈriːələ/ *noun*. Pl. **-lae** /-liː/, **-las**. L15.
[ORIGIN Latin, fem. (sc. *corona* crown) of *aureolus* adjective, dim. of *aureus* golden, from *aurum* gold.]
= AUREOLE.

aureole /ˈɔːrɪəʊl/ *noun & verb*. ME.
[ORIGIN Old French & mod. French *auréole* formed as AUREOLA.]
▸**A** *noun*. **1** ROMAN CATHOLIC CHURCH. The celestial crown won by a martyr, virgin, or doctor as victor over the world, the flesh, and the devil; the special degree of glory which distinguishes these. ME.
2 The glory around the head or body in depictions of divine figures. M19.
3 A halo or ring around the sun or moon. M19.
4 *transf. & fig.* Something that surrounds like a halo; an aura. M19.

O. W. HOLMES The aureole of young womanhood had not yet begun to fade from around her. J. AGATE One of the clowns wearing a flaming aureole of silly yellow hair. A. SILLITOE The glow of her soft features was framed and accentuated by an aureole of silence backed by the sound of the city.

5 GEOLOGY. The zone of metamorphosed rock surrounding an igneous intrusion. L19.
▸**B** *verb trans.* Encircle with or as with an aureole. Chiefly as ***aureoled*** *ppl adjective*. M19.

aureolin /ˈɔːrɪəlɪn, ɔːˈrɪəlɪn/ *noun*. L19.
[ORIGIN formed as AUREOLA + -IN[1].]
Cobalt yellow, a transparent yellow pigment.

Aureomycin /ɔːrɪəˈmʌɪsɪn/ *noun*. Also **a-**. M20.
[ORIGIN from mod. Latin (*Streptomyces*) *aureofaciens*, the source bacterium, from *aureus* golden + *-faciens* -FACIENT, + -MYCIN.]
(Proprietary name for) the antibiotic chlortetracycline.

au reste /o rɛst/ *adverbial phr.* E17.
[ORIGIN French.]
As for the rest.

aureus /ˈɔːrɪəs/ *noun*. Pl. **-rei** /-rɪʌɪ/. E17.
[ORIGIN Latin, use as noun of *aureus* golden, from *aurum* gold.]
A Roman coin of the late republic and the empire, of the value of 25 silver denarii.

au revoir /o rəvwaːr, əʊ rəˈvwɑː/ *interjection & noun phr.* L17.
[ORIGIN French, lit. 'to the seeing again'.]
(Goodbye) until we meet again; a farewell for the present.

auric /ˈɔːrɪk/ *adjective*[1]. E19.
[ORIGIN from Latin *aurum* gold + -IC.]
Of or pertaining to gold, golden; *spec.* (CHEMISTRY) of gold in the trivalent state (cf. AUROUS).
auric acid (***a***) the weakly acidic hydroxide $Au(OH)_3$; †(***b***) auric oxide, Au_2O_3.

auric /ˈɔːrɪk/ *adjective*[2]. L19.
[ORIGIN from AURA + -IC.]
= AURAL *adjective*[2].

aurichalc *noun* var. of ORICHALC.

aurichalcite /ɔːrɪˈkalsʌɪt/ *noun*. M19.
[ORIGIN from Latin *aurichalcum*, *orichalcum*, from Greek *oreikhalkon* 'mountain copper', (brass or copper made from) a yellow ore, + -ITE[1].]
MINERALOGY. An orthorhombic basic carbonate of copper and zinc, occurring usu. as greenish-blue encrustations.

aurichalcum *noun* see ORICHALC.

auricle /ˈɔːrɪk(ə)l/ *noun*. LME.
[ORIGIN from Latin AURICULA: see -CLE.]
1 ANATOMY. A small muscular pouch situated on the upper anterior surface of either atrium of the heart. Formerly also, an atrium of the heart. LME.
2 ANATOMY. The external ear. Formerly also, the lower lobe of the ear. M17.
3 Chiefly ZOOLOGY & BOTANY. A projection or process shaped like an ear or ear lobe. M17.

auricula /ɔːˈrɪkjʊlə/ *noun*. In sense 1 orig. **†-culus**. M17.
[ORIGIN Latin, dim. of *auris* ear: see -CULE.]
1 A primula, *Primula auricula*, having ear-shaped leaves. M17.
†**2** = AURICLE 2. Only in L17.
3 A pulmonate mollusc of the family Ellobiidae, found in brackish marshes. Now *rare* or *obsolete*. L18.
4 ZOOLOGY. A perforated projection from an ambulacral plate of an echinoid, to which jaw muscles are attached. L19.

auricular /ɔːˈrɪkjʊlə/ *adjective & noun*. LME.
[ORIGIN Late Latin *auricularis*, formed as AURICULA: see -AR[1].]
▸**A** *adjective*. **1** Of confession: spoken into the ear, private. LME.
2 Audible. L16.

SHAKES. *Lear* I will place you where you shall hear us confer of this, and by an auricular assurance have your satisfaction.

†**3** Addressing, affecting, or employing the ear only (without mental apprehension). L16–M18.

C. CIBBER Not mere auricular imitators of one another.

4 *gen.* Of or pertaining to the ear. M17.
auricular finger the little finger (see sense B.1 below). **auricular witness**: one who relates what he has heard.

5 Of, pertaining to, or resembling an auricle of the heart. M19.
▸ **B** *noun*. **1** The little finger (as most easily inserted into the ear). M17.
2 Any of the feathers in the tuft covering the orifice of a bird's ear. L18.
3 An ear. *rare*. M19.
■ **auricularly** *adverb* L16.

auriculate /ɔːˈrɪkjʊlət/ *adjective*. E18.
[ORIGIN from AURICULA + -ATE[2].]
BOTANY & ZOOLOGY. Having one or more auricles or earlike processes.
■ Also **auriculated** *adjective* E18.

auriculo- /ɔːˈrɪkjʊləʊ/ *combining form*. M19.
[ORIGIN formed as AURICLE + -O-.]
Forming adjectives with the sense 'of the auricle and —', as ***auriculo-temporal***, ***auriculo-ventricular***.

auriculotherapy /ɔːˌrɪkjələʊˈθɛrəpi/ *noun*. L20.
[ORIGIN French *auriculothérapie*, formed as AURICULO- + THERAPY.]
A form of acupuncture applied to points on the ear in order to treat other parts of the body.

†**auriculus** *noun* see AURICULA.

auriferous /ɔːˈrɪf(ə)rəs/ *adjective*. M17.
[ORIGIN from Latin *aurifer* gold-bearing, from *aurum* gold, + -OUS: see -FEROUS.]
Containing or yielding gold (*lit*. & *fig*.).
■ **auriferously** *adverb* (*rare*) M19.

aurify /ˈɔːrɪfʌɪ/ *verb trans. & intrans*. M17.
[ORIGIN from Latin *aurum* gold + -I- + -FY.]
Turn into gold.

Auriga /ɔːˈrʌɪgə/ *noun*. In sense 1 **a-**. LME.
[ORIGIN Latin *auriga* charioteer, Auriga, from *aureae* bridle + *-iga* from *agere* drive.]
†**1** A charioteer; *fig*. a leader. Only in LME.
2 (The name of) a constellation of the northern hemisphere in the Milky Way, near Orion; the Charioteer, the Wagoner. M16.

aurigation /ɔːrɪˈgeɪʃ(ə)n/ *noun*. *rare*. E17.
[ORIGIN Latin *aurigatio(n-)*, from *aurigat-* pa. ppl stem of *aurigare*, from *auriga* a charioteer: see -ATION.]
The action or art of driving a chariot or coach.

Aurignacian /ɔːrɪˈnjeɪʃ(ə)n, -ɪgˈneɪ-/ *adjective & noun*. E20.
[ORIGIN French *Aurignacien*, from *Aurignac* in SW France, where remains of it were found.]
▸ **A** *adjective*. Designating or pertaining to a culture of the Palaeolithic period in Europe following the Mousterian and preceding the Solutrean. E20.
▸ **B** *noun*. (A person of) this culture. E20.

†**aurigo** *noun*. ME–L18.
[ORIGIN Latin.]
Jaundice.

aurin /ˈɔːrɪn/ *noun*. Also **-ine**. M19.
[ORIGIN from Latin *aurum* gold + -IN[1].]
A red synthetic dyestuff of the triphenylmethane series.

†**auripigment** *noun*. Also in Latin form **-mentum**. LME–E19.
[ORIGIN Latin *auripigmentum*: see ORPIMENT.]
= ORPIMENT.

auriscope /ˈɔːrɪskəʊp/ *noun*. M19.
[ORIGIN from Latin *auris* ear + -SCOPE.]
MEDICINE. An instrument for visual examination of the ear.

aurist /ˈɔːrɪst/ *noun*. L17.
[ORIGIN formed as AURISCOPE + -IST.]
MEDICINE. A specialist with regard to the ear.

aurivorous /ɔːˈrɪv(ə)rəs/ *adjective*. *rare*. L18.
[ORIGIN from Latin *aurum* gold + -I- + -VOROUS.]
Consuming gold; avidly desirous of gold.

auro- /ˈɔːrəʊ/ *combining form*.
[ORIGIN from Latin *aurum* gold: see -O-.]
Used chiefly in *CHEMISTRY & MINERALOGY* to form names of substances containing gold, as ***auro-chloride***.

aurochs /ˈɔːrɒks, ˈaʊ-/ *noun*. L18.
[ORIGIN German, early var. of *Auerochs* (Old High German *ūrohso*, from *ūr* = Old English *ūr* etc. of unknown origin, + *ohso* OX). Cf. URE-OX, UROCHS, URUS.]
The extinct wild ox, *Bos primigenius*, which is the ancestor of domestic cattle in Europe and many parts of the world. Also, the European bison.

aurora /ɔːˈrɔːrə/ *noun*. Pl. **-rae** /-riː/, **-ras**. LME.
[ORIGIN Latin: cf. EAST.]
1 The rising light of the morning; the dawn. Also (**A-**), a goddess in Roman mythology. LME. ▸**b** *fig*. The beginning, the early period. M19.
2 A rich orange colour, as of the sky at sunrise. M17.
3 A luminous phenomenon, often taking the form of variable streamers or resembling drapery, seen in the upper atmosphere in high northern or southern latitudes, and caused by the interaction of charged solar particles with atmospheric gases, under the influence of the earth's magnetic field; orig. with specifying adjective (see below). E18.
aurora australis /ɔːˈstreɪlɪs/ [southern] the aurora of the southern polar regions, the Southern Lights. **aurora borealis** /bɔːrɪˈeɪlɪs/ [northern] the aurora of the northern regions, the Northern Lights. **aurora polaris** /pə(ʊ)ˈlɑːrɪs/ [polar] either of the auroras of the polar regions, the Northern or Southern Lights.
– COMB.: **aurora snake** a non-venomous southern African snake, *Lamprophis aurora*, which is olive green with an orange-yellow stripe.
■ **aurorean** *adjective* belonging to dawn, or like it in hue E19.

auroral /ɔːˈrɔːr(ə)l/ *adjective*. M16.
[ORIGIN Orig. from French, or medieval Latin *auroralis*; later from AURORA + -AL[1].]
1 Of or pertaining to the dawn; eastern; *fig*. of or pertaining to the first period of anything. M16.

> P. BAYNE Auroral splendours of promise . . which accompany all revolutions in their earlier stages. V. NABOKOV An atmosphere of . . barbecue smoke, horseplay, jazz music, and auroral swimming.

2 Like the dawn; dawning, roseate. E19.

> LONGFELLOW Her cheeks suffused with an auroral blush.

3 Of or pertaining to the aurora (borealis or australis). E19.

> E. K. KANE A true and unbroken auroral arch.

4 Resembling the aurora in its bright display. L19.

> F. T. PALGRAVE Auroral flashings of wit.

■ **aurorally** *adverb* L19.

aurothiomalate /ˌɔːrə(ʊ)θʌɪˈɒməleɪt, -θʌɪə(ʊ)ˈmaleɪt/ *noun*. M20.
[ORIGIN from AURO- + THIO- + MALATE.]
PHARMACOLOGY. The sodium salt of a gold- and sulphur-containing derivative of succinic acid, used to treat rheumatoid arthritis.

aurous /ˈɔːrəs/ *adjective*. M19.
[ORIGIN from Latin *aurum* gold + -OUS.]
CHEMISTRY. Of gold in the monovalent state. Cf. AURIC *adjective*[1].

aurum /ˈɔːrəm/ *noun*. *arch*. LME.
[ORIGIN Latin.]
Gold.
†***aurum fulminans*** gold fulminate. ***aurum mosaicum*** /məˈzeɪɪkəm/, **aurum musivum** /mʊˈziːvəm/ stannic sulphide, SnS_2, formerly used as a bronzing powder. †***aurum potabile*** potable gold.

auscultate /ˈɔːsk(ə)lteɪt/ *verb*. M18.
[ORIGIN Latin *auscultat-* pa. ppl stem of *auscultare* hear with attention: see -ATE[3].]
1 *verb intrans*. Listen, hear. *rare*. M18.
2 *verb trans*. *MEDICINE*. Examine by auscultation. M19.
■ **auˈscult** *verb trans. & intrans*. = AUSCULTATE M19. **auˈscultative** *adjective* (*MEDICINE*) of or pertaining to auscultation M19. **auscultator** *noun* (*MEDICINE*) a person who examines by auscultation M19. **auscultatory** *adjective* of or pertaining to listening or (*MEDICINE*) auscultation M17.

auscultation /ɔːsk(ə)lˈteɪʃ(ə)n/ *noun*. M17.
[ORIGIN Latin *auscultatio(n-)*, formed as AUSCULTATE: see -ATION.]
1 The action of listening. M17.
2 *MEDICINE*. The action of listening, usu. with a stethoscope, to the heart, lungs, or other organs, as an aid to diagnosis. E19.

au sérieux /o serjø/ *adverbial phr*. M19.
[ORIGIN French.]
Seriously. Cf. AU GRAND SÉRIEUX.

auslaut /ˈaʊslaʊt/ *noun*. L19.
[ORIGIN German, from *aus-* denoting termination + *Laut* sound.]
PHILOLOGY. The final sound of a syllable or word.

Auslese /ˈaʊsleːzə/ *noun*. Also **a-**. Pl. **-sen** /-zən/, **-ses**. M19.
[ORIGIN German, from *aus* out + *lese* picking, vintage.]
A white wine made (esp. in Germany) from selected bunches of grapes picked later than the general harvest.

Ausonian /ɔːˈsəʊnɪən/ *adjective & noun*. L16.
[ORIGIN from Latin *Ausonia* southern Italy, in poetry Italy, from Greek, from *Ausōn* son of Odysseus, who was said to have settled there, + -AN.]
(A native or inhabitant) of ancient central and southern Italy; (an) Italian.

auspicate /ˈɔːspɪkeɪt/ *verb trans*. Now *rare*. E17.
[ORIGIN Latin *auspicat-* pa. ppl stem of *auspicari*, from *auspicium*: see AUSPICE, -ATE[3].]
1 Prognosticate; predict. E17.
2 Initiate with an auspicious ceremony; give a fortunate start to. E17.
3 Enter upon in a specified way or with specified consequences. E17.
4 Begin; inaugurate. M17.

auspice /ˈɔːspɪs/ *noun*. M16.
[ORIGIN French, or Latin *auspicium* taking omens from birds, from *avis* bird + var. stem of *specere* look.]
1 a An observation of birds for omens; a sign or token given by birds. M16. ▸**b** *gen*. A prophetic token or premonition, esp. of a happy future; a forecast. M17.
2 *sing*. & (now) in *pl*. Patronage, favouring influence. E17. Esp. in ***under the auspices of***.
■ **auˈspicial** *adjective* auspicious; of or pertaining to auspices or augury: E17.

auspicious /ɔːˈspɪʃəs/ *adjective*. L16.
[ORIGIN from AUSPICE + -OUS.]
1 Propitious; favourable, favouring; conducive to success. L16.

> SHAKES. *All's Well* Fortune play upon thy prosperous helm, As thy auspicious mistress! E. CALDWELL You might want to consult Evelyn about the most auspicious date for our wedding.

2 Giving or being an omen; *spec*. of good omen, betokening success. E17. ▸**b** Of a person: predicting or prognosticating good. E18.

> E. YOUNG Beneath auspicious planets born. K. AMIS But such an auspicious debut Was a little too good to be true. A. K. RAMANUJAN A belief/ in auspicious/ snakes in the skylight. **b** C. ROSSETTI The aspect of jubilant auspicious angels.

3 Prosperous, fortunate. E17.
■ **auspiciously** *adverb* L16. **auspiciousness** *noun* M17.

Aussie /ˈɒzi, ˈɒsi/ *noun & adjective*. *colloq*. E20.
[ORIGIN Abbreviation of AUSTRALIAN, *Australia*: see -IE. Cf. OZZIE.]
▸ **A** *noun*. An Australian; Australia. E20.
▸ **B** *adjective*. Australian. E20.

austenite /ˈɒstɪnʌɪt, ˈɔː-/ *noun*. E20.
[ORIGIN from Sir William Roberts-*Austen* (1843–1902), English metallurgist + -ITE[1].]
METALLURGY. A solid solution of carbon in a non-magnetic high-temperature allotropic form of iron.
■ **austeˈnitic** *adjective* pertaining to or consisting principally of austenite E20.

Auster /ˈɒstə, ˈɔː-/ *noun*. LME.
[ORIGIN Latin.]
The south wind, esp. personified; the south.

austere /ɒˈstɪə, ɔː-/ *adjective*. ME.
[ORIGIN Old French & mod. French *austère* from Latin *austerus* from Greek *austēros* severe.]
▸ **I 1** Stern in manner, appearance, or disposition; severe in judgement. ME. ▸**b** Resolute in warfare. ME.

> BROWNING They would be gentle, not austere. E. O'NEILL His mask-like face is . . grimly remote and austere in death. **b** C. M. YONGE Simon, Count de Montfort, an austere warrior.

2 Severe in self-discipline; stringently moral; strict. LME.

> LD MACAULAY To these austere fanatics a holiday was an object of positive disgust. W. S. CHURCHILL He ruled according to the laws, and he made it known that these were to be administered in austere detachment from his executive authority.

3 Severely simple; without any luxury. L16.

> R. MACAULAY I'm afraid our meals are rather austere . . Our meat ration is so tiny. J. K. GALBRAITH An austere community is free from temptation . . . Not so a rich one. L. DEIGHTON The white-painted office was bare and austere.

4 Grave, sober, serious. M17.

> MILTON Eve . . With sweet austeer composure thus reply'd.

▸ **II 5** Harsh to the taste; astringent and bitter or sour. *arch*. LME.

> W. COWPER The bramble, black as jet, or sloes austere.

■ **austerely** *adverb* LME. **austereness** *noun* LME.

austerity /ɒˈstɛrɪti, ɔː-/ *noun*. LME.
[ORIGIN Old French & mod. French *austérité* from Latin *austeritas*, from *austerus*: see AUSTERE, -ITY.]
1 Sternness of manner, appearance, or disposition; severity in judgement. LME. ▸**b** *transf*. Rigour. E18.

> W. RALEIGH He gave presence . . with such austeritie, that no man durst presume to spit or cough in his sight. **b** BYRON Which soften'd down the hoar austerity Of rugged desolation.

2 Severe self-discipline; moral strictness; asceticism; severe simplicity, lack of luxury or adornment; abstinence, economizing, esp. nationwide; in *pl*., ascetic practices, economies. LME.

> SHAKES. *Mids. N. D.* On Diana's altar to protest For aye austerity and single life. BYRON And wherefore blame gaunt wealth's austerities? Because, you'll say, nought calls for such a trial. R. CHURCH The austerity of life in the boys' school did not improve my health. A. J. P. TAYLOR Cripps . . rejoiced at introducing measures of austerity: no petrol for pleasure motoring, the clothes ration cut down. H. ACTON In spite of the prevalent austerities he managed to conjure succulent meals for his guests.

3 Harshness to the taste; astringent bitterness or sourness. *arch*. M17.

Austin /ˈɒstɪn, ˈɔː-/ *noun & adjective*. ME.
[ORIGIN Contr. of Old French & mod. French *augustin*: see AUGUSTINE.]
= AUGUSTINE.
Austin Friars: see FRIAR.

austral /aʊˈstrɑːl/ *noun*. Pl. **-les** /-lɪz/. L20.
[ORIGIN Spanish = southern, formed as AUSTRAL *adjective*.]
A monetary unit of Argentina replacing the peso between 1985 and 1992.

austral /ˈɒstr(ə)l, ˈɔː-/ *adjective*. In sense 2 also **A-**. L15.
[ORIGIN Latin *australis*, from AUSTER: see -AL[1].]
1 Southern; influenced by the south wind. L15.
2 Of or pertaining to Australia or Australasia. E19.

Australasian /ɒstrəˈleɪʒ(ə)n, -ʃ(ə)n; ɔː-/ *adjective & noun*. E19.
[ORIGIN from *Australasia* (see below) from French *Australasie*, formed as *Australia* + *Asia*, + -AN.]
▸ **A** *adjective*. Of or pertaining to Australasia (Australia and the islands of the SW Pacific). E19.
Australasian warbler: see WARBLER 2c.
▸ **B** *noun*. A native or inhabitant of Australasia. E19.

Australian /ɒˈstreɪlɪən, ɔː-/ *noun & adjective*. L17.
[ORIGIN French *australien*, from Latin *australis* in *Terra Australis* southern land (see sense A.1 below), + -AN.]
▸ **A** *noun*. †**1** A native of the *Terra Australis*, the supposed continent and islands lying in the Great Southern Ocean, now identified as including Australasia, Polynesia, and parts of southern S. America. L17–L18.
2 A native or inhabitant of the island continent of Australia. E19.
new Australian: see NEW *adjective*.
▸ **B** *adjective*. Of or pertaining to Australia. E19.
Australian cattle dog *Austral. & NZ* a cattle dog with a dark speckled body. **Australian crawl** a fast swimming stroke originating in Australia. **Australian football** = ***Australian Rules football*** below. ***Australian*** MAGPIE. ***Australian*** PRATINCOLE. **Australian Rules** (the rules governing) a form of football developed in Australia (= ***Australian Rules football*** below). **Australian Rules football** a form of football played on an oval pitch with a rugby ball by teams of 18 players. **Australian salmon** a large green and silver percoid fish, ***Arripis trutta***, found off the coast of New Zealand and SE Australia. **Australian teak** = FLINDOSA. **Australian terrier** a wire-haired terrier of an Australian breed. ***Australian warbler***: see WARBLER 2c.
■ **Australiˈana** *noun pl.* [-ANA] publications or other items concerning or associated with Australia M19. **Australianism** *noun* (*a*) a word or idiom peculiar to Australia; (*b*) = AUSTRALIANNESS: L19. **Australianize** *verb trans.* make Australian in character etc. L19. **Australianness** /-n-n-/ *noun* the state or quality of being Australian M20.

australite /ˈɒstrəlʌɪt, ɔː-/ *noun*. E20.
[ORIGIN from *Australia* + -ITE¹.]
GEOLOGY. A tektite found in the Australian strewn field.

Australoid /ˈɒstrəlɔɪd, ɔː-/ *adjective & noun*. Now considered *offensive*. M19.
[ORIGIN from AUSTRALIAN + -OID.]
(A person) of the ethnological type of the Australian Aborigine.
– NOTE: The terms ***Australoid***, ***Caucasoid***, ***Mongoloid***, and ***Negroid*** were introduced in 19 by anthropologists attempting to classify human racial types, but are now regarded as having little scientific validity and as potentially offensive.
■ **Ausˈtralioid** *adjective* M19.

Australopithecus /ˌɒstrələʊˈpɪθɪkəs, ˌɔː-/ *noun*. E20.
[ORIGIN mod. Latin, from Latin *australis* southern + -O- + Greek *pithēkos* ape.]
Any of various small-brained fossil hominids of the genus *Australopithecus*, known from remains found in Africa and southern Asia.
■ **Auˈstralopith** *noun* = AUSTRALOPITHECUS M20. **australopithecine** /-siːn/ *adjective & noun* M20.

Australorp /ˈɒstrəlɔːp, ɔː-/ *noun*. E20.
[ORIGIN from AUSTRALIAN + ORP(INGTON.]
A black Orpington fowl of an Australian breed.

Austrasian /ɒˈstreɪʃ(ə)n/ *adjective & noun*. L18.
[ORIGIN from medieval Latin *Austrasia*, *Ost-* + -AN.]
(A native or inhabitant) of the eastern part of the Frankish empire in the Merovingian period.

Austrian /ˈɒstrɪən, ɔː-/ *adjective & noun*. E17.
[ORIGIN from *Austria* (= German *Österreich* Eastern kingdom) + -AN.]
(A native or inhabitant) of Austria, a country in central Europe.
Austrian blind a blind made from ruched fabric, which extends about a third of the way down a window. ***Austrian briar***: see BRIAR *noun*¹. **Austrian pine** a very hardy pine, *Pinus nigra*, of Europe and Asia Minor, with a dense branch system.

austringer /ˈɔːstrɪndʒə/ *noun*. Also **ostreger** /ˈɒstrɪdʒə/, **ostringer** /ˈɒstrɪndʒə/. L15.
[ORIGIN Alt. of Old French *ostruchier*, *aust-* OSTREGER: cf. *messenger*, *passenger*.]
FALCONRY. A keeper of goshawks.

Austro- /ˈɒstrəʊ, ˈɔː-/ *combining form*¹ of AUSTRIAN, as ***Austro-Hungarian***, ***Austro-Prussian***, etc.: see -O-.

Austro- /ˈɒstrəʊ, ˈɔː-/ *combining form*² of *Austral* (AUSTRAL *adjective* 2) and AUSTRALIAN, as ***Austro-Asiatic***, ***Austro-Malayan***, etc.: see -O-.

Austronesian /ɒstrə(ʊ)ˈniːzjən, -ʒ(ə)n, ɔː-/ *adjective & noun*. E20.
[ORIGIN from German *austronesisch*, from Latin *australis* southern + -O- + Greek *nēsos* island: see -IAN.]
(Of or pertaining to) a family of agglutinative languages spoken widely in Malaysia, Indonesia, and other parts of SE Asia, and in the islands of the central and southern Pacific.

AUT *abbreviation*.
Association of University Teachers.

aut- *combining form* see AUTO-¹.

autarchic /ɔːˈtɑːkɪk/ *adjective*¹. L19.
[ORIGIN from AUTARCHY *noun*¹ + -IC.]
Absolute, despotic.
■ **autarchical** *adjective*¹ M20.

autarchic *adjective*², **autarchical** *adjective*² vars. of AUTARKIC, AUTARKICAL.

autarchy /ˈɔːtɑːki/ *noun*¹. M17.
[ORIGIN mod. Latin *autarchia* after *monarchia* MONARCHY: see AUTO-¹, -ARCHY.]
Absolute sovereignty, despotism.
■ **autarch** *noun* an absolute ruler, an autocrat E19.

autarchy *noun*² var. of AUTARKY.

autarky /ˈɔːtɑːki/ *noun*. Also **-archy**. E17.
[ORIGIN Greek *autarkeia*, from *autarkēs* self-sufficient, from AUTO-¹ + *arkein* suffice.]
Self-sufficiency, esp. in spiritual or economic matters.
■ **auˈtarkic** *adjective* of, pertaining to, or characterized by autarky; (economically) self-sufficient: L19. **auˈtarkical** *adjective* = AUTARKIC M20. **autarkist** *noun* an advocate of autarky M20.

autecious *adjective* see AUTOECIOUS.

autecology /ɔːtɪˈkɒlədʒi/ *noun*. E20.
[ORIGIN from AUTO-¹ + ECOLOGY.]
BIOLOGY. The ecology of an individual species. Cf. SYNECOLOGY.
■ **autecoˈlogical** *adjective* E20.

auteur /əʊˈtəː, ɔː-/ *noun*. M20.
[ORIGIN French = AUTHOR.]
A film director who so greatly influences the films directed as to be able to rank as their author.
■ **auˈteurism** *noun* M20. **auˈteurist** *noun & adjective* L20.

authentic /ɔːˈθɛntɪk/ *adjective & noun*. LME.
[ORIGIN Old French *autentique* (mod. *authentique*) from late Latin *authenticus* from Greek *authentikos* principal, genuine.]
▸ **A** *adjective*. †**1** Of authority, authoritative; entitled to obedience or respect. LME–M19.

LD BERNERS One of the moost autentyke men of the court of parlyment. SWIFT Some short plain authentick tract might be published.

†**2** Legally valid; legally qualified. LME–E18.

SHAKES. *All's Well* All the learned and authentic fellows. J. FLAVEL What is done by Commission is Authentick.

3 Entitled to belief as stating or according with fact; reliable, trustworthy. LME.

T. NORTON To discredit so many authentike witnesses. A. J. P. TAYLOR The battles of El Alamein or Stalingrad only became fully authentic when they appeared on the [cinema] screen. *Listener* BBC1's *Tenko* was the most authentic representation to date of the Far East prisoner's life.

4 Real, actual, genuine; original, first-hand; really proceeding from its stated source, author, painter, etc. L15.

MILTON Him who had stole Joves authentic fire. E. WAUGH A treasure house of period gems; pure authentic 1914. R. D. LAING To be 'authentic' is to be true to oneself, to be what one is, to be 'genuine'.

†**5** Own, proper. L16–M17.

G. CHAPMAN Then Nestor cut the gears With his new-drawn authentic sword.

6 MUSIC. Of a church mode: having sounds comprised between a final note and its octave (cf. PLAGAL). Of a cadence: perfect. E18.
▸ **B** *noun*. **1** An original or authoritative document. Long *obsolete* exc. as below. L15.
the Authentics a collection of enactments of Justinian.
†**2** An authority. *rare*. Only in E17.
■ **authentical** *adjective* (now *rare* or *obsolete*) = AUTHENTIC *adjective* M16. **authentically** *adverb* L16. †**authenticalness** *noun* M17–M19. †**authenticly** *adverb* LME–M18. **authenticness** *noun* M16.

authenticate /ɔːˈθɛntɪkeɪt/ *verb trans*. E17.
[ORIGIN medieval Latin *authenticat-* pa. ppl stem of *authenticare*, from late Latin *authenticus*: see AUTHENTIC, -ATE³.]
1 Give authority or legal validity to, establish as valid. E17.

R. NORTH Antiquity to authenticate their ceremonies. C. V. WEDGWOOD The minutes read in the form in which Phelps finally authenticated them on the great roll of parchment . . as a perpetual record.

2 Establish the credibility of a statement, reported occurrence, reputed fact, etc. M17.

C. LAMB A room, which tradition authenticated to have been the same. C. DARWIN I doubt whether any case of a perfectly fertile hybrid animal can be considered as thoroughly well authenticated. J. CHEEVER Letters, photographs, diplomas—anything that authenticated the past was always thrown into the fire.

3 Establish as genuine or real; certify the origin or authorship of. M19.

H. T. COCKBURN We went through the whole work, authenticating all his papers. V. WOOLF The authenticated masterpiece by Michael Angelo.

■ **authentiˈcation** *noun* the action or process of authenticating something; the condition of being authenticated: L18. **authenticator** *noun* a person who authenticates something M19.

authenticity /ɔːθɛnˈtɪsɪti/ *noun*. M17.
[ORIGIN from AUTHENTIC *adjective* + -ITY.]
The quality of being authentic.

authigenic /ɔːθɪˈdʒɛnɪk/ *adjective*. L19.
[ORIGIN from Greek *authigenēs* born on the spot, native + -IC.]
GEOLOGY. Originating where found; formed *in situ*.
■ **authigenesis** *noun* formation *in situ* M20.

author /ˈɔːθə/ *noun & verb*. ME.
[ORIGIN Anglo-Norman *autour*, Old French *autor* (mod. *auteur*) from Latin *auctor*, from *augere auct-* increase, promote, originate.]
▸ **A** *noun*. **1** *gen.* The person who originates, invents, gives rise to, or causes something (now only an abstract thing, a condition, an event, exc. of God). ME. ▸†**b** A person who authorizes or instigates. M16–M17.

W. LAMBARDE One Robert Creuequer, the authour of the Castle. J. CHEEVER Embittered by the waste that he himself was the author of. A. HAILEY He was the author of early legislation to protect minorities. **b** SHAKES. *Tit. A.* The gods of Rome forfend I should be author to dishonour you!

the Author (of all), **the great Author** God, the Creator.
2 A father, an ancestor. *arch.* LME.

C. LAMB Certainly old Walter Plumer (his reputed author) had been a rake in his days.

3 The writer of a book, essay, article, etc.; a person who writes books etc. LME. ▸**b** *ellipt.* An author's writings. E17. ▸†**c** The editor of a journal. L17–M18.

b SHAKES. *Twel. N.* I will be proud, I will read politic authors.

4 A person on whose authority a statement is made; an informant. *obsolete* exc. *dial.* LME.

W. DAMPIER Islands that abound with Gold and Cloves, If I may credit my Author Prince Jeoly.

– COMB.: **author-craft** *arch.* (exercise of) skill as an author (of books etc.).
▸ **B** *verb trans*. **1** Originate, bring about, (an action, condition, circumstance, etc.). L16.

M. LOWRY Who would ever have believed that some obscure man . . was authoring their doom.

†**2** State, declare. E–M17.
3 Write, be the author of, (a book, essay, article, etc.). Orig. *US*. E20.

Time Her father . . authored several successful plays and movies.

■ **authoress** *noun* a female author L15. **authorial** /ɔːˈθɔːrɪəl/ *adjective* of or pertaining to an author (of books etc.) L18. **authorially** *adverb* M19. **authorism** *noun* (now *rare* or *obsolete*) the position or character of an author of books etc. M18. **authorless** *adjective* E18. **authorling** *noun* a petty or insignificant writer L18. **authorly** *adjective* proper to or characteristic of an author or authors L18.

authorise *verb*, **authorised** *adjective* vars. of AUTHORIZE, AUTHORIZED.

authoritarian /ɔːθɒrɪˈtɛːrɪən/ *adjective & noun*. L19.
[ORIGIN from AUTHORITY + -ARIAN.]
▸ **A** *adjective*. Favouring or characterized by obedience to (esp. political) authority as opp. to personal liberty; tyrannical, dictatorial. L19.

P. NICHOLS I don't want to sound authoritarian or fascist but there's only one useful approach to any human problem and that's a positive one. A. STORR No one would wish to advocate a return to the authoritarian rule of the Victorian *pater familias*. B. MAGEE A government with Utopian aims has to, and is bound to become authoritarian.

▸ **B** *noun*. A supporter of authoritarian principles or methods. L19.
■ **authoritarianism** *noun* E20.

authoritative /ɔːˈθɒrɪtətɪv, -teɪtɪv/ *adjective*. E17.
[ORIGIN from AUTHORITY + -ATIVE.]
1 Having authority; exercising or assuming power; imperative, commanding. E17.

R. NORTH He was diligent and in acting authoritative. L. W. MEYNELL Above the general chatter, a loud authoritative voice cried, 'Now, then, what's the trouble 'ere?'

2 Possessing or claiming due authority; entitled to deference or acceptance. M17.

HENRY MORE A number sufficient to constitute an Authoritative Church. E. F. SCHUMACHER If the 'rich' populations grow at . . 1¼ per cent and the 'poor' at . . 2½ per cent a year, world population will grow to about 6900 million by AD 2000—a figure not very different from the most authoritative current forecasts.

3 Proceeding from a competent authority. E19.

J. B. MARSDEN An authoritative declaration of pardon.

■ **authoritatively** *adverb* LME. **authoritativeness** *noun* M17.

authority /ɔːˈθɒrɪti/ *noun*. ME.
[ORIGIN Old French & mod. French *autorité* from Latin *auctoritas*, from *auctor*: see AUTHOR, -ITY.]
▸ **I** Power to enforce obedience.
1 Power or right to enforce obedience; moral or legal supremacy; right to command or give a final decision. ME.

J. RUSKIN If ever you find yourselves set in positions of authority. D. LODGE You conspired with the students to weaken the authority of the senior staff.

in authority in a position of power or control.
2 Derived or delegated power; authorization. LME.

A

COVERDALE *Ezra* 7:24 Ye shall have no auctorite to requyre taxinge & custome. CARLYLE He carries in him an authority from God.

3 Those in power or control (treated as *sing.* (abstract) or *pl.*); the governing body; a body exercising power in a particular sphere. **M16.**

Westminster Gazette The Port of London Authority is a thoroughly practical body of men. K. AMIS If you want to get up a charity . . , then you must first get the authorities' permission. C. P. SNOW As a natural conservative, his feelings would be on the side of authority.

local authority: see LOCAL *adjective*.

► **II** Power to influence action, opinion, belief, etc.

4 The book, quotation, etc., acknowledged or alleged to settle a question or give conclusive testimony. **ME.**

SIR T. MORE Hys fyrst authorite be these words of saynte Austyne. J. R. GREEN Giving in detail the authorities for every statement.

5 Power to inspire belief; right to be believed; testimony, statement. **ME.**

OED Do not accept news on the authority of the evening papers. G. B. SHAW I await the decision of the Church. Until that is delivered the story has no authority.

6 Power over the opinions of others; authoritative opinion, intellectual influence. **ME.**

J. S. MILL He is either led by authority, or adopts . . the side to which he feels most inclination. W. H. DIXON I hear on good authority . . that Cardinal Wolsey is not now in favour of a divorce.

7 Power to influence the conduct and actions of others; personal or practical influence, commanding manner etc. **LME.**

V. S. PRITCHETT He was a man of authority with a deep, curt sarcastic voice used to command.

8 A person whose opinion or testimony is to be accepted; an expert in any subject. **M17.**

W. H. PRESCOTT Historians in a season of faction are not the best authorities. LADY BIRD JOHNSON I became an authority on the climate of India. I knew exactly where the rain fell and where it failed to fall.

authorize /ˈɔːθərʌɪz/ *verb trans.* Also **-ise**. **LME.**
[ORIGIN Old French & mod. French *autoriser* from medieval Latin *auctorizare*, from *auctor*: see AUTHOR, -IZE.]

†**1** Set up or acknowledge as having authority. **LME–E17.**
†**2** Make legally valid. **LME–L17.**
3 Give formal approval to; sanction, countenance. **LME.**

ISAIAH BERLIN Why should any conduct be tolerated that is not authorized by appropriate experts?

†**4** Vouch for, confirm. **LME–M17.**

SHAKES. *Macb.* A woman's story at a winter's fire, Authoriz'd by her grandam.

5 Endow (a person, body, etc.) with authority; commission. **LME.**
6 Give legal or formal warrant to (a person or body) *to do*; empower, permit authoritatively. **LME.**

LD MACAULAY A royal message authorizing the Commons to elect another Speaker.

7 Of things: give grounds for, justify. **E17.**

G. ANSON These reasons alone would authorize the insertion of those papers.

8 Of things: give grounds to. **L18.**

JAMES SULLIVAN Nothing which can authorise us to suppose it formed in the sea.

■ **authorizable** *adjective* †(**a**) able to be entrusted with authority; †(**b**) having the power of authorizing; (**c**) able to be authorized: **LME. authoriˈzation** *noun* formal approval or warrant **L15. authorizer** *noun* a person who authorizes something or someone **L16.**

authorized /ˈɔːθərʌɪzd/ *adjective*. Also **-ised**. **LME.**
[ORIGIN from AUTHORIZE + -ED¹.]

1 Acknowledged as authoritative; thoroughly established. *arch.* **LME.**

COLERIDGE Received and authorized opinions.

2 Endowed with authority. **LME.**

OED The arrangement was made by your own authorized agent.

3 Legally or formally sanctioned or appointed. **LME.**
Authorized Version the 1611 English translation of the Bible.

authorship /ˈɔːθəʃɪp/ *noun*. **E18.**
[ORIGIN from AUTHOR *noun* + -SHIP.]

1 Occupation or career as a writer; the dignity or position of an author. **E18.**
2 Literary origin (of a writing); *gen.* origination of any action or circumstance. **E19.**

autism /ˈɔːtɪz(ə)m/ *noun*. **E20.**
[ORIGIN from Greek *autos* self + -ISM.]
PSYCHIATRY. Abnormal withdrawal from the world of reality; *spec.* a condition which has its onset in childhood and is marked by severely limited responsiveness to other persons, restricted behaviour patterns, and usu. abnormal speech development.
■ **auˈtistic** *adjective & noun* (**a**) *adjective* pertaining to, associated with, or affected by autism; (**b**) *noun* a person affected by autism: **E20.**

auto /ˈaʊtəʊ/ *noun*¹. Pl. **-os** /-əʊs/. **M16.**
[ORIGIN Spanish & Portuguese from Latin *actus* ACT *noun*.]
1 = AUTO-DA-FÉ. **M16.**
2 A play (by a Spanish or Portuguese author). **L18.**

auto /ˈɔːtəʊ/ *noun*² *& verb. colloq.* **L19.**
[ORIGIN Abbreviation of AUTOMOBILE.]
► **A** *noun*. Pl. **-os**. A car. **L19.**
– COMB.: ***auto bra***: see BRA *noun*¹ 2; **automaker** *N. Amer.* a manufacturer of motor vehicles, a company that manufactures motor vehicles.
► **B** *verb intrans.* Travel in or drive a car. **E20.**

auto- /ˈɔːtəʊ/ *combining form*¹. Before a vowel also **aut-**.
[ORIGIN Repr. Greek *auto-*, from *autos* self.]
1 Used in words adopted from Greek and in English words modelled on these, and as a freely productive prefix, with the sense 'one's own, of or by oneself, by itself, independent, self-produced, spontaneous, automatic'.
2 GENETICS. Used in comb. with **-PLOID** (and also *-ploidy*) to refer to individuals whose chromosome sets are derived from a single parent species (cf. ALLO-), as ***autodiploid***, ***autopolyploid***, etc.
■ **auto-aˈnalysis** *noun* self-analysis **L19. autoˈantibody** *noun* an antibody produced by an organism in response to a constituent of its own tissues **M20. autoˈbracketing** *noun* a facility on a camera which automatically takes a number of photographs of the desired subject at different exposures **L20. autoˈcentric** *adjective* centred in the self; making oneself the centre: **M19. autoˈcephalous** *adjective* [Greek *kephalē* head] independent of archiepiscopal or patriarchal jurisdiction **M19. autochange, autochanger** *nouns* a mechanism for the automatic substitution of one gramophone record or compact disc for another during use **M20. autocode** *noun* a low-level programming language in which each instruction corresponds to an instruction in machine code **M20. autocomˈplete** *noun* a software function that completes words or strings without the user needing to type them in full **L20. autoˈcritical** *adjective* critical of oneself or one's own work **M17. Autocue** *noun* (proprietary name for) a device which projects a rolling script, out of camera range, in front of a speaker on television **M20. auto-destruct** *noun & verb* (**a**) *noun* self-destruction, esp. as a built-in feature of a machine etc.; (**b**) *verb intrans.* destroy oneself, self-destruct: **L20. auto-destruction** *noun* self-destruction **L20. auto-destructive** *adjective* self-destructive; *spec.* designating or pertaining to art in which the artwork is destroyed as it is created: **M20. autodial** *verb intrans.* (COMPUTING) (esp. of a modem) dial a telephone number automatically; establish a connection with a computer automatically: **L20. autodialler** *noun* (US **autodialer**) COMPUTING a device or facility that dials telephone numbers automatically **L20. autodiˈgestion** *noun* = AUTOLYSIS **L19. autofocus** *noun & adjective* (PHOTOGRAPHY) automatic(ally) focusing **M20. autoˈfocusing** *noun* automatic focusing **M20. autograft** *noun* (SURGERY) a graft of skin or other tissue taken from the same individual **E20. autoharp** *noun* a musical instrument of the zither type, with dampers to facilitate the production of arpeggio effects **L19. auto-inˈfection** *noun* (**a**) self-infection; (**b**) continued infection with parasitic worms owing to their larvae maturing without leaving the body: **L19. auto-inˈfective** *adjective* of or pertaining to auto-infection **L19. auto-intoxiˈcation** *noun* poisoning by a toxin formed within the body **L19. autoland** *noun & verb* (**a**) *noun* automatic landing; (**b**) *verb trans. & intrans.* land automatically: **M20. autolatry** /ɔːˈtɒlətri/ *noun* self-worship **E17. autoload** *noun* (PHOTOGRAPHY) a facility on a camera which, on insertion of a film, automatically feeds it on to its spool and advances it to the first frame (freq. *attrib.*) **L20. autoˈlogical** *adjective* (of a word) having the property which it denotes (opp. HETEROLOGICAL) **E20. autologous** /ɔːˈtɒləgəs/ *adjective* obtained from the same individual **E20. autology** /ɔːˈtɒlədʒi/ *noun* study of oneself, self-knowledge **M17. automath** *noun* (*rare*) = AUTODIDACT **M18. autophagic** /-ˈfeɪdʒɪk/ *adjective* pertaining to or concerned with (lysosomal) autophagy **M20. autophagy** /ɔːˈtɒfədʒi/ *noun* digestion of the body's own tissues; *esp.* breakdown of cell constituents within lysosomes: **L19; autopilot** *noun* = ***automatic pilot*** s.v. AUTOMATIC *adjective* **M20. autoˈplastic** *adjective* of or pertaining to autoplasty **M19. autoˈplastically** *adverb* by means of autoplasty **E20. autoplasty** *noun* plastic surgery using autografts **M19. Autoplate** *noun* (PRINTING, now chiefly *hist.*) (proprietary name for) a machine for making curved stereotype plates; a stereotype plate made by such a machine: **E20. autopsyˈchography** *noun* psychography of oneself **M19. autosave** *noun & verb* (COMPUTING) (**a**) *noun* a software facility which automatically saves a user's word-processed or other work at regular intervals; (**b**) *verb trans.* save (work) automatically using such a facility: **L20. autoseˈmantic** *adjective & noun* (a word or phrase) having meaning outside its context; categorematic: **E20. autoˈsexing** *adjective* (of a breed of poultry) possessing sex-linked characters which enable easy identification of sexes on hatching **M20. autosoteric** /-sə(ʊ)ˈterɪk/ *adjective* [Greek *sōtēria* salvation] relating to salvation by one's own efforts **L19. autotelic** /-ˈtelɪk/ *adjective* having or being an end in itself **E20. autoˈtherapy** *noun* treatment of one's own infirmity **M20. autotransˈformer** *noun* (ELECTRICITY) a zooid transformer having a single winding of which part is common to both primary and secondary circuits **L19. autotransˈfusion** *noun* (MEDICINE) (**a**) a transfer of blood within the body; (**b**) transfusion with a patient's own blood: **E20. autotransˈplant** *verb trans.* transplant (tissue) from one site to another within the same individual **E20. ˌautotransplanˈtation** *noun* transplantation of tissue from one site to another within the same individual **E20. autotune** *noun* a device for tuning something automatically; *spec.* an effect or device which enables a recording engineer to correct an out-of-tune vocal performance **M20. autozooid** /-ˈzəʊɔɪd/ *noun* (ZOOLOGY) a typical zooid of an anthozoan or bryozoan **L19.**

auto- /ˈɔːtəʊ/ *combining form*².
[ORIGIN Abbreviation of AUTOMOBILE *adjective & noun*: cf. AUTO *noun*².]
Forming words relating to motor vehicles.
■ **autobus** *noun* = BUS *noun* 1 **L19. autocade** *noun* (*US*) [after *cavalcade*] a motorcade **M20. autocar** *noun* (*arch.*) = AUTOMOBILE *noun* **L19. autocrime** *noun* theft of motor vehicles or their contents **L20. autocross** *noun* motor racing across country or on unmade roads **M20. autocycle** *noun* (*arch.*) a bicycle with an auxiliary engine **E20. autoworker** *noun* (chiefly *N. Amer.*) a person who works in the motor industry **E20.**

autobahn /ˈɔːtəbɑːn, *foreign* ˈaʊtobaːn/ *noun*. Pl. **-bahns**, **-*bahnen*** /-baːnən/. **M20.**
[ORIGIN German, from *Auto* automobile + *Bahn* road.]
A German, Swiss, or Austrian motorway.

autobiographer /ˌɔːtəbʌɪˈɒgrəfə/ *noun*. **E19.**
[ORIGIN from AUTO-¹ + BIOGRAPHER.]
A person who writes the story of his or her own life.

autobiographical /ˌɔːtəbʌɪəˈgrafɪk(ə)l/ *adjective*. **E19.**
[ORIGIN from AUTO-¹ + BIOGRAPHICAL.]
Of or pertaining to an autobiography; of the nature of autobiography, relating to one's own life story.
■ **autobiographic** *adjective* = AUTOBIOGRAPHICAL **E19. autobiographically** *adverb* **M19.**

autobiography /ˌɔːtəbʌɪˈɒgrəfi/ *noun*. **L18.**
[ORIGIN from AUTO-¹ + BIOGRAPHY.]
The writing of one's own history; a story of a person's life written by himself or herself.
■ **autobiographist** *noun* = AUTOBIOGRAPHER **M19.**

autocatalysis /ˌɔːtə(ʊ)kəˈtalɪsɪs/ *noun*. **L19.**
[ORIGIN from AUTO-¹ + CATALYSIS.]
CHEMISTRY. Catalysis of a reaction by one of its products.
■ **autoˈcatalyst** *noun* a product effecting autocatalysis **M20. autocataˈlytic** *adjective* **E20. autocataˈlytically** *adverb* **M20.**

autochthon /ɔːˈtɒkθ(ə)n, -θəʊn/ *noun*. Pl. **-thons**, (senses 1,2) in Latin form **-thones** /-θəniːz/. **L16.**
[ORIGIN Greek *autokhthōn* indigenous, from AUTO-¹ + *khthōn* earth, soil.]
1 (Usu. in *pl.*) Any of the earliest known dwellers in a region; an original inhabitant, an aboriginal. **L16.**
2 A human being living in his or her place of origin. *rare*. **M17.**
3 GEOLOGY. An autochthonous rock formation. **M20.**
■ **autochthonal** *adjective* = AUTOCHTHONOUS *adjective* 1 **E19. autochˈthonic** *adjective* = AUTOCHTHONOUS *adjective* 1 **M19. autochthony** *noun* autochthonous condition **M19.**

autochthonous /ɔːˈtɒkθənəs/ *adjective*. **E19.**
[ORIGIN from AUTOCHTHON + -OUS.]
1 Indigenous, native, aboriginal. **E19.**
2 MEDICINE. Of a blood clot etc.: that originated where it is found, or without external agency. **L19.**
3 GEOLOGY. Formed *in situ*; consisting of indigenous material. **E20.**
■ **autochthonously** *adverb* **L19.**

autoclave /ˈɔːtəkleɪv/ *noun & verb*. **L19.**
[ORIGIN French, formed as AUTO-¹ + Latin *clavus* nail or *clavis* key: so called because self-fastening.]
► **A** *noun*. **1** A pressure cooker. *rare*. **L19.**
2 A strong vessel used for chemical reactions at high pressures and temperatures, or for high-pressure sterilization using steam. **L19.**
► **B** *verb trans.* Heat in an autoclave. **E20.**

autocorrelation /ˌɔːtə(ʊ)kɒrɪˈleɪʃ(ə)n/ *noun*. **M20.**
[ORIGIN from AUTO-¹ + CORRELATION.]
A correlation between the elements of a series and those respectively separated from them by a given interval.
■ **autoˈcorrelator** *noun* a machine for performing autocorrelations **M20. autoˈcorrelogram** *noun* a graphical representation of an autocorrelation **M20.**

autocracy /ɔːˈtɒkrəsi/ *noun*. **M17.**
[ORIGIN Greek *autokrateia*, formed as AUTOCRAT: see -CRACY.]
†**1** Independent power; autonomy. **M17–M19.**
2 Absolute government; controlling authority or influence. **E19.**
3 Autocrats collectively. **E20.**

autocrat /ˈɔːtəkrat/ *noun*. **E19.**
[ORIGIN French *autocrate* from Greek *autokratēs*, from AUTO-¹ + *kratos* power, authority.]
A monarch of uncontrolled authority, an absolute ruler; a person with dictatorial powers or tendencies.
■ **autoˈcratic**, **autoˈcratical** *adjectives* of the nature of or pertaining to an autocrat; despotic, dictatorial: **E19. autoˈcratically** *adverb* **M19. autocratism** /ɔːˈtɒkrətɪz(ə)m/ *noun* the principles or practices of autocrats **M19.**

autocrator /ɔːˈtɒkrətə/ *noun. arch.* **M18.**
[ORIGIN Late Latin = emperor, from Greek *autokratōr* one's own master, from AUTO-¹ + *kratōr* ruler.]
An absolute monarch.
■ †**autocratorical** *adjective* **M17–E19. autocratrix** *noun* a female autocrator, esp. *hist.* (**A-**) as a title of empresses of Russia ruling in their own right **M18.**

autocrine /ˈɔːtəʊkrʌɪn, ˈɔːtəʊkriːn/ *adjective*. **L20.**
[ORIGIN from AUTO- *combining form*¹ + Greek *krinein* to separate.]
BIOCHEMISTRY. Designating or pertaining to a cell-produced substance that has an effect on the cell by which it is secreted.

auto-da-fé /ˌautodaˈfe; ˌɔːtəʊdɑːˈfeɪ, ˌaʊt-/ *noun.* Pl. **autos-da-fé** /ˌautosdaˈfe; ˌɔːtəʊzdɑːˈfeɪ, ˌaʊtəʊz-/, **auto-da-fés**. E18.
[ORIGIN Portuguese = act of the faith.]
(The execution of) a judicial sentence of the Inquisition; *esp.* the public burning of a heretic.

autodidact /ˈɔːtəʊdɪdakt/ *noun.* M18.
[ORIGIN from Greek *autodidaktos* self-taught: see AUTO-¹, DIDACTIC.]
A person who is self-taught.
■ **autodiˈdactic** *adjective* self-taught; of or pertaining to self-teaching: M19.

autoecious /ɔːˈtiːʃəs/ *adjective.* Also ***autec-**. L19.
[ORIGIN from AUTO-¹ + Greek *oikia* house + -IOUS.]
BOTANY. (Of a parasitic fungus) completing its life cycle on a single host; (of a bryophyte) having antheridia and archegonia on separate branches of the same plant.
■ Also **autoicous** /ɔːˈtɔɪkəs/ *adjective* E20.

auto-erotic /ˌɔːtəʊɪˈrɒtɪk/ *adjective.* L19.
[ORIGIN from AUTO-¹ + EROTIC.]
PSYCHOLOGY. Of or pertaining to auto-eroticism; characterized by or given to auto-eroticism.
■ **auto-erotically** *adverb* E20.

auto-eroticism /ˌɔːtəʊɪˈrɒtɪsɪz(ə)m/ *noun.* E20.
[ORIGIN from AUTO-¹ + EROTICISM.]
PSYCHOLOGY. Sexual arousal or gratification obtained without the involvement of another person; masturbation.

auto-erotism /ɔːtəʊˈɛrətɪz(ə)m/ *noun.* L19.
[ORIGIN from AUTO-¹ + EROTISM.]
PSYCHOLOGY. = AUTO-EROTICISM.

autogamy /ɔːˈtɒgəmi/ *noun.* L19.
[ORIGIN from AUTO-¹ + -GAMY.]
BIOLOGY. Self-fertilization; (in some unicellular organisms) fusion of sister nuclei.
■ **autogamic** /ɔːtəˈgamɪk/, **autogamous** *adjectives* pertaining to or characterized by autogamy L19.

autogenesis /ɔːtə(ʊ)ˈdʒɛnɪsɪs/ *noun.* L19.
[ORIGIN from AUTO-¹ + -GENESIS.]
Self-production; spontaneous formation.

autogenetic /ˌɔːtə(ʊ)dʒəˈnɛtɪk/ *adjective.* L19.
[ORIGIN from AUTOGENESIS: see AUTO-¹, -GENETIC.]
Self-produced; spontaneously formed.
■ **autogenetically** *adverb* L19.

autogenic /ɔːtə(ʊ)ˈdʒɛnɪk/ *adjective.* L19.
[ORIGIN from AUTO-¹ + -GENIC.]
Self-produced, autogenous; *ECOLOGY* self-generated without external influence.
autogenic training a method of learning to hypnotize oneself and then induce physiological changes in the body.

autogenous /ɔːˈtɒdʒɪnəs/ *adjective.* M19.
[ORIGIN from Greek *autogenēs*: see AUTO-¹, -GENOUS.]
Self-produced; *spec.* (**a**) (of a weld, welding) formed by or involving the melting of the joined ends, without added filler; (**b**) (of a vaccine) derived from the patient's own infecting micro-organisms.
■ **autogenously** *adverb* L19.

autogiro /ɔːtəʊˈdʒʌɪrəʊ/ *noun.* Also **-gyro**. Pl. **-os**. E20.
[ORIGIN Spanish, formed as AUTO-¹ + *giro* gyration.]
A type of aircraft having a propeller and freely rotating horizontal rotary blades.

autograph /ˈɔːtəgrɑːf/ *noun, verb, & adjective.* E17.
[ORIGIN French *autographe* or late Latin *autographum* from Greek *autographon* use as noun of neut. of *autographos* written with one's own hand: see AUTO-¹, -GRAPH.]
▸ **A** *noun.* **1** A person's own signature. E17.

DICKENS Left our autographs and read those of other people.

2 A manuscript in an author's own handwriting; a document signed by its author. M17.

W. W. SKEAT The MS. of Piers Plowman .. seems to be an autograph of the author.

3 A person's own handwriting. M19.

N. HAWTHORNE Poems of Tasso in his own autograph.

4 A reproduction made by direct facsimile; *esp.* = AUTOLITHOGRAPH *noun. arch.* M19.
– COMB.: **autograph album**, **autograph book** a book in which a person collects the signatures of various people, often with rhymes etc.; **autograph-hunter** a person who makes a collection of signatures of celebrities.
▸ **B** *verb trans.* **1** Write with one's own hand. E19.
2 Write one's signature on or in; sign. M19.

S. LEACOCK The Prince took the pen and very kindly autographed for us seven photographs of himself. D. WELCH A book that had been signed by Walter de la Mare .. the first autographed book I had ever held.

▸ **C** *adjective.* Written in the author's own handwriting; (of a painting) done by the artist himself, not by a copier. M19.

P. G. WODEHOUSE You will appreciate another capture of mine, the autograph manuscript of Don Juan, Canto Nine. *Times Lit. Suppl.* Some of the Madonnas .. must be wholly or in large part autograph.

autographic /ɔːtəˈgrafɪk/ *adjective.* E19.
[ORIGIN from AUTOGRAPH + -IC.]
1 Written with the author's own hand. E19.
2 Of or pertaining to reproduction by direct facsimile; *esp.* = AUTOLITHOGRAPHIC *adjective. arch.* M19.
■ **autographical** *adjective* †(**a**) = AUTOBIOGRAPHICAL; (**b**) = AUTOGRAPHIC: M17. **autographically** *adverb* L17.

autography /ɔːˈtɒgrəfi/ *noun.* M17.
[ORIGIN from AUTOGRAPH *noun* + -Y³.]
1 The action of writing with one's own hand; the author's own handwriting. M17.
2 = AUTOBIOGRAPHY. Now *rare* or *obsolete.* M17.
3 Reproduction of writing, drawing, etc., by direct facsimile; *esp.* = AUTOLITHOGRAPHY. *arch.* M19.

autogyro *noun* var. of AUTOGIRO.

autohypnosis /ˌɔːtəʊhɪpˈnəʊsɪs/ *noun.* Pl. **-noses** /-ˈnəʊsiːz/. E20.
[ORIGIN from AUTO-¹ + HYPNOSIS.]
(A) self-induced hypnosis; self-hypnotism.
■ **autohypnotic** /-hɪpˈnɒtɪk/ *adjective* E20. **autoˈhypnotism** *noun* self-hypnotism L19.

autoimmunity /ˌɔːtəʊɪˈmjuːnɪti/ *noun.* E20.
[ORIGIN from AUTO-¹ + IMMUNITY.]
MEDICINE. †**1** Immunity produced within the body. Only in E20.
2 The production or presence within the body of autoantibodies. M20.
■ **autoimmune** *adjective* pertaining to, caused or characterized by autoimmunity (sense 2) M20. **ˌautoimmuniˈzation** *noun* †(**a**) = AUTOIMMUNITY 1; (**b**) the induction of autoimmunity (sense 2): E20.

autokinesis /ˌɔːtə(ʊ)kɪˈniːsɪs, -kʌɪ-/ *noun.* M19.
[ORIGIN from AUTO-¹ + Greek *kinēsis* motion.]
1 Spontaneous motion. Only in Dicts. M19.
2 An illusion of the motion of a stationary object in an otherwise empty visual field. M20.
■ **autokinetic** *adjective* L19.

autolithography /ˌɔːtə(ʊ)lɪˈθɒgrəfi/ *noun.* L19.
[ORIGIN from AUTO-¹ + LITHOGRAPHY.]
Lithographic printing done directly from original drawings etc.
■ **autoˈlithograph** *noun & verb* (**a**) *noun* a picture or print made by autolithography; (**b**) *verb trans.* produce or reproduce by autolithography: L19. **autolithoˈgraphic** *adjective* L19.

autolysis /ɔːˈtɒlɪsɪs/ *noun.* E20.
[ORIGIN from AUTO-¹ + -LYSIS.]
BIOLOGY. Destruction of cells or tissues by their own enzymes, esp. as released from lysosomes.
■ **autolysate** *noun* a substance produced by autolysis E20. **ˈautolyse** /-lʌɪz/ *verb intrans. & trans.* (cause to) undergo autolysis E20. **autolysin** *noun* an enzyme causing autolysis E20. **autoˈlytic** *adjective* E20.

automacy /ɔːˈtɒməsi/ *noun. rare.* M19.
[ORIGIN from AUTOMATIC: see -ACY.]
The condition or state of being an automaton; automaticity.

automat /ˈɔːtəmat/ *noun.* L17.
[ORIGIN German from French AUTOMATE *noun.*]
1 = AUTOMATON. L17.
2 A cafeteria in which food is obtained from a slot machine; a slot machine. Chiefly *US.* E20.

automata *noun pl.* see AUTOMATON.

†**automate** *noun & adjective.* M17.
[ORIGIN French from Latin AUTOMATON.]
▸ **A** *noun.* An automaton. M17–M18.
▸ **B** *adjective.* Automatic. Only in E19.

automate /ˈɔːtəmeɪt/ *verb.* M20.
[ORIGIN Back-form. from AUTOMATION.]
1 *verb trans.* Convert to or equip for largely automatic operation. Freq. as **automated** *ppl adjective.* M20.
2 *verb intrans.* Apply or introduce automation. M20.

automatic /ɔːtəˈmatɪk/ *adjective & noun.* M18.
[ORIGIN from Greek *automatos* + -IC: see AUTOMATON.]
▸ **A** *adjective.* **1** Like the action of an automaton; unintelligent, merely mechanical; done without thought, unconscious; occurring as a matter of course without debate. M18.

A. BAIN The winking of the eyes is essentially automatic. J. MASTERS I tossed my head—it is an automatic gesture I cannot help—and went forward again. DAY LEWIS A natural system .. under which the demands of the younger are not given automatic priority over the rights of the older. C. JACKSON The invitation was compulsive and automatic, it sprang from old habit merely. T. BAILEY As a batsman, he would have been an automatic choice for any Test team of any period. *Lancet* Approximately a quarter of narcoleptics have frequent periods of automatic behaviour in the daytime when they are only half-awake.

2 Self-acting; *esp.* (of a machine, device, etc.) working of itself, with little or no direct human actuation; (of a process etc.) working thus, involving such equipment. M18. ▸**b** *spec.* Of a firearm: having a mechanism for continuous loading, firing, and ejecting until ammunition is exhausted or pressure on the trigger is released. L19. ▸**c** *spec.* Of a telephone exchange: operated by automatic switches. L19. ▸**d** *spec.* Of the transmission in a motor vehicle: changing gear automatically according to speed and acceleration. Of a vehicle: equipped with automatic transmission. M20.

OED A Sewing Machine with automatic tension. G. B. SHAW A box of matches will come out of an automatic machine when I put a penny in the slot. T. S. ELIOT She smoothes her hair with automatic hand, And puts a record on the gramophone. J. HEDGECOE Fully automatic metering systems set both aperture and shutter speed automatically.

automatic landing landing of an aircraft under the control or guidance of instruments. **automatic pilot** a device for keeping an aircraft or ship on a set course; ***on automatic pilot*** (*fig.*) acting without conscious thought or careful attention.
3 Of psychic phenomena etc.: occurring subconsciously or unconsciously. L19.
automatic writing: done by means of a planchette etc.
4 Occurring as a necessary consequence; (esp. of a legal sanction) taking effect without further process in set circumstances. E20.

Washington Post Brown was charged with a game misconduct, his fourth, and will sit out the next two games on an automatic suspension.

5 *ART.* Characterized by or pertaining to surrealist automatism. M20.
▸ **B** *noun.* **1** A machine, device, etc., operated automatically; *esp.* (**a**) an automatic firearm; (**b**) a motor vehicle with automatic transmission. L19.
2 *AMER. FOOTBALL.* = AUDIBLE *noun* 2. M20.
■ **automatical** *adjective* (now *rare* or *obsolete*) L16. **automatically** *adverb* M19. **automaticity** /-məˈtɪsɪti/ *noun* automatic condition, nature, or functioning L19.

automation /ɔːtəˈmeɪʃ(ə)n/ *noun.* M20.
[ORIGIN Irreg. from AUTOMATIC + -ATION.]
Automatic control of a manufacturing or other process through a number of successive stages; the use of automatic devices to save mental and manual labour; the introduction of automatic methods or equipment.

automatise *verb* var. of AUTOMATIZE.

automatism /ɔːˈtɒmətɪz(ə)m/ *noun.* M19.
[ORIGIN French *automatisme*, from AUTOMATE *noun*: see -ISM.]
1 The quality of being automatic, or of acting mechanically only; involuntary action; a doctrine ascribing this quality to animals. M19.
2 Mechanical, unthinking routine. L19.
3 The faculty of independently originating action. Now *rare* or *obsolete.* L19.
4 *PSYCHOLOGY.* An action that is, unusually, performed subconsciously or unconsciously; the mental state accompanying such an action. L19.
5 *ART.* A surrealist technique seeking to eliminate conscious thought from the creative process. M20.
■ **automatist** *noun* an adherent or practitioner of, or a person subject to, automatism L19.

automatize /ɔːˈtɒmətʌɪz/ *verb trans.* Also **-ise**. M19.
[ORIGIN French *automatiser*, formed as AUTOMATISM: see -IZE.]
Reduce to an automaton; make automatic; automate.
■ **automatiˈzation** *noun* E20.

automaton /ɔːˈtɒmət(ə)n/ *noun.* Pl. **-matons**, **-mata** /-mətə/. E17.
[ORIGIN Latin (also *-tum*) from Greek, use as noun of neut. of *automatos* acting of itself.]
1 Something having the power of spontaneous motion; *esp.* a living being viewed as a machine. E17.

R. BOYLE These living Automata, Human bodies. BURKE The perfect Drama, an automaton supported and moved without any foreign help, was formed late and gradually. T. H. HUXLEY Such a self-adjusting machine, containing the immediate conditions of its actions within itself, is what is properly understood by an Automaton.

2 A piece of mechanism with concealed motive power, *esp.* one simulating a living being; a robot. M17.

EVELYN Another automaton strikes the quarters. L. MUMFORD The belief that automatons would ultimately displace human labor was common to the new Utopias.

3 A living being whose actions are purely involuntary or mechanical; a person behaving without active intelligence or mechanically in a set pattern or routine. L17.

J. PRIESTLEY Descartes .. made the souls of brutes to be mere automata. J. A. SYMONDS How could a Spartan, that automaton of the state .. excel in any fine art? C. S. FORESTER Last night they had staggered into the village, exhausted automata.

4 *COMPUTING.* A machine whose responses to all possible inputs are specified in advance. M20.

automatous /ɔːˈtɒmətəs/ *adjective.* M17.
[ORIGIN from Greek *automatos* (see AUTOMATON) + -OUS.]
1 Of the nature of an automaton; acting mechanically. M17.
2 Acting spontaneously; having the power of self-motion. M18.

automobile /ˈɔːtəməbiːl/ *adjective, noun, & verb.* Chiefly *N. Amer.* L19.
[ORIGIN French, formed as AUTO-[1] + MOBILE *adjective*.]
▸ **A** *adjective.* **1** Esp. of a vehicle: self-propelling (as opp. to horse-drawn). *arch.* L19.
2 [The noun used attrib.] Of or pertaining to motor vehicles. L19.
▸ **B** *noun.* A motor vehicle; a car. L19.
▸ **C** *verb intrans.* Drive or travel in a motor vehicle. L19.
■ **autoˈmobilism** *noun* (*arch.*) the use of motor vehicles L19. **autoˈmobilist** *noun* (*arch.*) a motorist L19. **automoˈbility** *noun* the use of motor vehicles; mobility based on this: E20.

automorphism /ɔːtəʊˈmɔːfɪz(ə)m/ *noun.* M19.
[ORIGIN from AUTO-[1] + Greek *morphē* form + -ISM.]
1 MATH. Any of various kinds of transformation or correspondence which relate a function etc. to itself or to another of the same kind; *spec.* an isomorphism of a structure with itself. M19.
2 The ascription of one's own characteristics to another. Now *rare* or *obsolete*. L19.
■ **automorphic** *adjective* pertaining to, characterized by, or invariant under automorphism M19.

automotive /ɔːtəˈməʊtɪv/ *noun & adjective.* M19.
[ORIGIN from AUTO-[1] + MOTIVE *adjective*.]
▸ †**A** *noun.* A self-propelled vehicle. Only in M19.
▸ **B** *adjective.* Of or pertaining to an automobile or automobiles. L19.

autonomic /ɔːtəˈnɒmɪk/ *adjective.* M19.
[ORIGIN from AUTONOMY + -IC.]
1 Self-governing, independent. M19.
2 PHYSIOLOGY. Functioning independently of the will; *esp.* denoting the parts of the nervous system serving organs which control the normally involuntary functions of the body. L19.
■ **autonomical** *adjective* (*rare*) = AUTONOMIC M17. **autonomically** *adverb* M19.

autonomous /ɔːˈtɒnəməs/ *adjective.* E19.
[ORIGIN from Greek *autonomos* (see AUTONOMY) + -OUS.]
Of, pertaining to, or characterized by autonomy; self-governing, independent; free of external influence or control.

J. REED At Helsingfors the Finnish Senate . . declared Finland autonomous, and demanded the withdrawal of Russian troops. R. G. COLLINGWOOD Consciousness is absolutely autonomous: its decision alone determines whether a given sensum or emotion shall be attended to or not. J. C. RANSOM English might almost as well announce that it does not regard itself as entirely autonomous, but as a branch of the department of history.

■ **autonomously** *adverb* L19.

autonomy /ɔːˈtɒnəmi/ *noun.* E17.
[ORIGIN Greek *autonomia*, from *autonomos* having its own laws, from AUTO-[1] + *nomos* law: see -NOMY.]
1 The right or condition of self-government (freq. only in specified matters) of a state, community, institution, etc. E17.

C. G. SELIGMAN The village is the administrative unit, to which the most complete autonomy is allowed. *Encycl. Brit.* The national autonomous regions [of China] reflect the CCP policy of seeking to . . accord cultural autonomy—but not political independence—to areas in which national minority peoples predominate.

2 Freedom of the will. L18.
3 *gen.* Independence, freedom from external control or influence; personal liberty. E19.

A. STORR The therapist should not give advice or do anything else which might interfere with the patient's autonomy. U. LE GUIN They preserved autonomy of conscience even at the cost of becoming eccentric.

■ **autonomism** *noun* = AUTONOMY L19. **autonomist** *noun* an advocate of autonomy M19.

autonym /ˈɔːtənɪm/ *noun.* M19.
[ORIGIN from AUTO-[1] + -NYM.]
(A work published under) an author's own name. Opp. PSEUDONYM.

autopista /ɔːtəˈpiːstə, *foreign* autoˈpista/ *noun.* M20.
[ORIGIN Spanish, from *auto* automobile + *pista* track, PISTE.]
A motorway in Spain and Spanish-speaking countries.

autopsy /ˈɔːtɒpsi, ɔːˈtɒpsi/ *noun & verb.* As noun also in Latin form †**-opsia**. M17.
[ORIGIN French *autopsie* or mod. Latin *autopsia* from Greek, from *autoptēs* eyewitness: see AUTO-[1], OPTIC, -Y[3].]
▸ **A** *noun.* **1** Seeing with one's own eyes; personal observation. *rare.* M17.
2 Dissection of a dead body so as to determine the cause of death or the extent of disease; a post-mortem examination; *fig.* a critical dissection. M19.
▸ **B** *verb trans.* Perform an autopsy on (a body). E20.
■ **autopsic** *adjective* of or pertaining to an autopsy L19.

autoptical /ɔːˈtɒptɪk(ə)l/ *adjective.* M17.
[ORIGIN from Greek *autoptikos*, from *autoptēs* (see AUTOPSY), + -AL[1].]
1 Of, pertaining to, or of the nature of an eyewitness; based on personal observation. M17.
2 = AUTOPSIC. L20.
■ **autoptic** *adjective* (*a*) *rare* = AUTOPTICAL 1; (*b*) = AUTOPSIC: M19. **autoptically** *adverb* M17.

autoradiograph /ɔːtəʊˈreɪdɪəgrɑːf/ *noun & verb.* E20.
[ORIGIN from AUTO-[1] + RADIOGRAPH.]
▸ **A** *noun.* A photograph of an object obtained using radiation from radioactive material in the object. E20.
▸ **B** *verb trans.* Make an autoradiograph of. M20.
■ **autoradiogram** *noun* = AUTORADIOGRAPH *noun* M20. **autoradioˈgraphic**, **autoradioˈgraphical** *adjectives* of or pertaining to autoradiography or an autoradiograph M20. **autoradioˈgraphically** *adverb* M20. **autoradiˈography** *noun* the production and interpretation of autoradiographs M20.

autorotation /ˌɔːtə(ʊ)rə(ʊ)ˈteɪʃ(ə)n/ *noun.* E20.
[ORIGIN from AUTO-[1] + ROTATION.]
1 AERONAUTICS. Rotation (esp. of rotor blades) not caused by engine power. E20.
2 Rotation resulting from the shape or structure of an object (e.g. a winged seed). L20.
■ **autorotate** *verb intrans.* undergo autorotation E20.

autoroute /ˈɔːtəruːt, *foreign* otorut (*pl. same*)/ *noun.* M20.
[ORIGIN French, from *auto* automobile + *route* ROUTE *noun*.]
A French motorway.

autoschediastic /ˌɔːtəʊskɛdɪˈastɪk/ *adjective.* E19.
[ORIGIN Greek *autoskhediastikos*, from *autoskhediazein* act or speak extempore, from *autoskhedios* personally near, offhand: see -IC.]
Done on the spur of the moment, improvised.

autoscopy /ɔːˈtɒskəpi/ *noun.* L19.
[ORIGIN from AUTO-[1] + -SCOPY.]
Viewing or examination of oneself; a hallucination of viewing one's own body.
■ **ˈautoscope** *noun* an instrument for self-observation; *esp.* any device which reveals subliminal actions (e.g. a dowsing rod): L19. **autoˈscopic** *adjective* E20.

autos-da-fé *noun pl.* see AUTO-DA-FÉ.

autosome /ˈɔːtəsəʊm/ *noun.* E20.
[ORIGIN from AUTO-[1] + -SOME[3].]
BIOLOGY. A chromosome other than a sex chromosome.
■ **autoˈsomal** *adjective* M20.

autostrada /ɔːtəˈstrɑːdə, *foreign* autoˈstraːda/ *noun.* Pl. **-stradas**, ***-strade*** /-ˈstraːde/. E20.
[ORIGIN Italian, from *auto* automobile + *strada* road from Latin STRATUM.]
An Italian motorway.

auto-suggestion /ˌɔːtə(ʊ)səˈdʒɛstʃ(ə)n/ *noun.* L19.
[ORIGIN from AUTO-[1] + SUGGESTION.]
PSYCHOLOGY. Suggestion to oneself; the hypnotic or subconscious adoption of an idea originating within oneself.
■ **auto-suˈggest** *verb* (*a*) *verb trans.* produce, remove, influence (ideas, feelings), by auto-suggestion; (*b*) *verb intrans.* undergo auto-suggestion: E20. **auto-suˈggestible** *adjective* able to be influenced by auto-suggestion E20. **auto-suˈggestive** *adjective* of the nature of or pertaining to auto-suggestion E20.

autotheism /ɔːtəʊˈθiːɪz(ə)m/ *noun.* L16.
[ORIGIN from eccl. Greek *autotheos* very god, from AUTO-[1] + *theos* god, + -ISM.]
1 THEOLOGY. The doctrine of the self-subsistence of God or (esp.) Christ. L16.
2 Self-deification. E17.
■ **autotheist** *noun* M18. **autotheˈistic** *adjective* M19.

autotomy /ɔːˈtɒtəmi/ *noun.* L19.
[ORIGIN from AUTO-[1] + -TOMY.]
ZOOLOGY. The casting off of a part of the body by some animals (e.g. lizards, crabs) as a means of escape.
■ **autotomize** *verb trans.* lose by autotomy E20.

autotoxin /ɔːtə(ʊ)ˈtɒksɪn/ *noun.* L19.
[ORIGIN from AUTO-[1] + TOXIN.]
A product of an organism's metabolism which is poisonous to the organism itself.
■ **autotoˈxaemia** *noun* toxaemia due to an autotoxin L19. **autotoxic** *adjective* E20.

autotrophic /ɔːtə(ʊ)ˈtrəʊfɪk, -ˈtrɒfɪk/ *adjective.* L19.
[ORIGIN from AUTO-[1] + -TROPHIC.]
BIOLOGY. Of an organism: requiring only simple inorganic compounds for nutrition.
■ **ˈautotroph(e)** *noun* an autotrophic organism M20. **autotrophically** *adverb* M20. **auˈtotrophism** *noun* E20.

autotype /ˈɔːtə(ʊ)tʌɪp/ *noun.* M19.
[ORIGIN from AUTO-[1] + -TYPE.]
1 A reproduction in facsimile; a true representation of an original. M19.
2 (A facsimile produced by) a photographic printing process for monochrome reproduction. M19.

autoxidation /ˌɔːtɒksɪˈdeɪʃ(ə)n/ *noun.* L19.
[ORIGIN from AUTO-[1] + OXIDATION.]
CHEMISTRY. Spontaneous oxidation by molecular oxygen.
■ **auˈtoxidize** *verb intrans.* undergo autoxidation E20. **autoxiˈdizable** *adjective* susceptible to autoxidation L19.

autumn /ˈɔːtəm/ *noun.* LME.
[ORIGIN Old French *autompne* (mod. *automne*), later directly from Latin *autumnus*.]
1 The third season of the year, between summer and winter: in the northern hemisphere freq. regarded as comprising September, October, and November, or (ASTRONOMY) reckoned from the autumnal equinox to the winter solstice; in the southern hemisphere corresponding in time to the northern spring. LME. ▸**b** The fruits of autumn; harvest. *poet.* E17.

b MILTON On her ample square, from side to side, All Autumn pil'd.

2 *fig.* A season of maturity or incipient decay. L16.

J. LANGHORNE The very autumn of a form once fine Retains its beauties.

– COMB.: ***autumn crocus***: see CROCUS *noun*[1]; **autumn equinox** = AUTUMNAL ***equinox***; **autumn gentian** felwort, *Gentianella amarella*; **autumn tints** the brown and gold colours of dying leaves.
■ **autumnity** /ɔːˈtʌmnɪti/ *noun* (*rare*) autumnal quality or conditions L16. **autumny** /ˈɔːtəmi/ *adjective* suggestive or characteristic of autumn E20.

autumn /ˈɔːtəm/ *verb trans. & intrans.* Now *rare.* M17.
[ORIGIN Latin *autumnare* bring on autumn, (medieval Latin) ripen, from *autumnus* AUTUMN *noun*.]
Bring or come to maturity; ripen.

autumnal /ɔːˈtʌmn(ə)l/ *adjective.* L16.
[ORIGIN Latin *autumnalis*, from *autumnus* AUTUMN *noun*: see -AL[1].]
1 Of or pertaining to autumn; characteristic of or appropriate to autumn; maturing or blooming in autumn. L16.

MILTON Thick as Autumnal Leaves that strew the Brooks In Vallombrosa. LD MACAULAY The autumnal rains of Ireland are usually heavy. M. DRABBLE The autumnal colours were deeper . . in the sinking light.

autumnal equinox the point in time at which the sun crosses the celestial equator in a southerly direction (approx. 22 September), or, in the southern hemisphere, in a northerly direction (approx. 21 March).
2 *fig.* Past the prime of life; in decline. E17.

DONNE No Spring, nor Summer Beauty hath such grace, As I have seen in one Autumnall face. *absol.*: DICKENS Melissa might have seen five and thirty summers or thereabouts, and verged on the autumnal.

■ **autumnally** *adverb* M19.

autunite /ˈɔːtʌnʌɪt/ *noun.* M19.
[ORIGIN from *Autun*, a town in eastern France + -ITE[1].]
MINERALOGY. A tetragonal hydrated phosphate of uranium and calcium, occurring usu. as yellow crystal aggregates or encrustations.

Auvergnat /ovɛrɲa/ *noun.* Pl. pronounced same. M19.
[ORIGIN French, from *Auvergne*: see -AT[1].]
A native or inhabitant of the Auvergne, a region of central France; the dialect spoken in the Auvergne.

auxanography /ɔːksəˈnɒgrəfi/ *noun.* E20.
[ORIGIN formed as AUXANOMETER + -OGRAPHY.]
BIOLOGY. A technique for determining the substances required by a micro-organism for growth, in which different nutrients are distributed on a culture of the micro-organism.
■ **auˈxanogram** *noun* a plate culture used in this L19. **ˌauxanoˈgraphic** *adjective* E20.

auxanometer /ɔːksəˈnɒmɪtə/ *noun.* L19.
[ORIGIN from Greek *auxanein* to increase + -OMETER.]
BOTANY. An instrument for measuring growth in plants.

auxesis /ɔːkˈsiːsɪs/ *noun.* L16.
[ORIGIN Late Latin from Greek *auxēsis* increase, amplification.]
1 RHETORIC. Increase in intensity of meaning; hyperbole; amplification. L16.
2 BIOLOGY. Increase, growth; *esp.* increase in size by expansion of cell size or number of cells. M19.
■ **auxetic** /-ˈsɛtɪk/ *adjective* M18.

auxiliary /ɔːgˈzɪlɪəri, ɒg-/ *adjective & noun.* LME.
[ORIGIN Latin *auxiliarius*, from *auxilium* help: see -ARY[1].]
▸ **A** *adjective.* **1** Helpful; giving support or succour; orig., (of foreign troops etc.) assisting an army at war. LME.
2 Subsidiary, additional, ancillary; (freq. in names of military or other service bodies). L17.
3 GRAMMAR. Used in forming words, constructions, etc. Now *spec.* (of a verb) used in forming tenses, moods, aspects, or voices, of other verbs. L17.
▸ **B** *noun.* **1** (A member of) a body of foreign or allied troops etc. in the service of a belligerent nation. E17.
2 A person or thing which assists, supports, or is subsidiary or ancillary. M17.
3 GRAMMAR. An auxiliary verb. L17.
■ †**auxiliar** *adjective & noun* = AUXILIARY L16–M19.

auxin /ˈɔːksɪn/ *noun.* M20.
[ORIGIN from Greek *auxein* to increase + -IN[1].]
BIOCHEMISTRY. Any of a class of compounds that cause the elongation of plant cells in shoots and (with cytokinins) control plant growth and development.

auxo- /ˈɔːksəʊ/ *combining form* of Greek *auxein* to increase: see -O-.
■ **auxochrome** *noun* (CHEMISTRY) a polar group which when introduced into a chromogen produces a dyestuff L19; **auxoˈchromic** *adjective* (CHEMISTRY) of or pertaining to an auxochrome L19. **auxospore** *noun* (BOTANY) a vegetative cell formed by diatoms, usu. sexually L19.

A

auxology /ɔːk'sɒlədʒi/ *noun*. **L19**.
[ORIGIN from AUXO- + -OLOGY.]
The study of growth and development; *spec.* in MEDICINE, the study of physical growth and development in humans on the basis of measurements such as height, weight, and rate of growth.
■ **auxo'logical** *adjective* **M20**. **auxologist** *noun* **L20**.

auxotroph /'ɔːksətrəʊf, -trɒf/ *noun*. **M20**.
[ORIGIN from Latin *auxilium* help + -O- + Greek *trophos* feeder.]
BIOLOGY. A mutant bacterium, fungus, etc., having an additional nutritional requirement compared with the original strain.
■ **auxo'trophic** *adjective* **M20**. **au'xotrophy** *noun* **M20**.

AV *abbreviation*.
1 Audiovisual.
2 Authorized Version (of the Bible).

Av *noun* var. of AB *noun*[1].

ava /'ɑːvə/ *noun*. **L18**.
[ORIGIN Hawaiian *'awa*.]
= KAVA.

ava /ə'vɑː/ *adverb*. *Scot.* **M18**.
[ORIGIN Repr. a pronunc. of *of all*.]
Of all; at all.

avadavat /'avədəvat/ *noun*. Also (earlier) **am-** /'am-/. **L17**.
[ORIGIN from *Ahmadabad*, a city in western India where the birds were sold.]
Either of two southern Asian waxbills, the green *Amandava formosa* and (esp.) the red *A. amandava*.

avail /ə'veɪl/ *noun*. **LME**.
[ORIGIN App. from the verb, but cf. Anglo-Norman *avail*.]
1 Beneficial effect, advantage; assistance; value, estimation. *arch.* exc. in neg. or interrog. phrs. **LME**.
of little avail, ***of no avail***, ***to little avail***, ***to no avail***. ***to what avail?*** ***without avail***.
2 *sing.* & (usu.) in *pl.* Profits, proceeds; remuneration, perquisites. *arch.* **LME**.

avail /ə'veɪl/ *verb*. **ME**.
[ORIGIN from VAIL *verb*[1], app. on the analogy of pairs like *amount*, *mount*.]
1 *verb intrans. & trans.* Be of use, help, value, or advantage, (to); have efficacy; profit. **ME**.
CHAUCER Moore it auaileth a man to haue a good name, than for to haue grete richesses. AV *Esther* 5:13 All this auaileth me nothing, so long as I see Mordecai the Iew sitting at the kings gate. POPE Nor aught the warrior's thundering mace avail'd. SIR W. SCOTT Words avail very little with me, young man. DISRAELI What avail his golden youth, his high blood . . if they help not now? E. M. FORSTER How little, we feel, avails knowledge and technical cleverness against a man who truly feels!
2 *verb refl. & intrans.* Make use *of*, obtain the benefit *of*, take advantage *of*. **LME**.
MILTON Then shall they seek to avail themselves of names, Places, and titles. J. TYNDALL I . . availed myself of my position to make an excursion into North Wales. R. W. EMERSON Power . . must be availed of, and not by any means let off and wasted. D. LESSING This time I availed myself of the invitation to move about.
†3 *verb intrans.* Do well, prosper. **E16–E17**.
4 *verb trans.* Give (a person) the advantage *of*; inform, assure, *of*. *US. arch.* **L18**.
T. JEFFERSON It will rest, therefore, with you, to avail Mr. Barclay of that fund. F. TROLLOPE We should have got no invites, you may be availed of that.
■ **availing** *adjective* advantageous, profitable, of beneficial effect **LME**. **availment** *noun* benefit, efficacy **L17**.

available /ə'veɪləb(ə)l/ *adjective*. **LME**.
[ORIGIN from AVAIL *verb* + -ABLE.]
1 Capable of producing a desired result; effectual, valid; *obsolete* exc. LAW. **LME**.
2 Of advantage (*to*, *unto*). *arch.* **LME**.
3 Able to be used or turned to account; at one's disposal; within one's reach, obtainable; (of a person) free for consultation, service, amorous advances, etc. **E19**.
J. TYNDALL We spent every available hour upon the ice. S. KAUFFMANN He was vividly excited by the renewed evidence that right here in the house was an available female. J. ORTON I'd like another woman present. Is your wife available? J. T. STORY To have a hire car made available for a visiting Member of Parliament. M. BRADBURY Of course Henry would elect to carry a tray when he had only one available hand.
4 Of a political candidate: likely to succeed in gaining office irrespective of ability, because of political associations, personal popularity, etc. *US.* **M19**.
■ **availa'bility** *noun* (**a**) the quality of being available; (**b**) something available: **E19**. **availableness** *noun* **L17**. **availably** *adverb* **LME**.

avalanche /'avəlɑːnʃ/ *noun & verb*. **L18**.
[ORIGIN French from Romansh, alt. of Alpine French dial. *lavanche* (of unknown origin), by blending with *avaler* descend: cf. Provençal *lavanca*, Italian *valanga*.]
▸ **A** *noun*. **1** A large mass of snow, rocks, and ice, moving swiftly down a mountainside. **L18**.
2 *transf. & fig.* A sudden onrush or descent; a rapidly descending mass. **M19**. ▸**b** PHYSICS. A process of cumulative ionization in which each electron and ion generates further charged particles. Also more fully ***Townsend avalanche***. Freq. *attrib.* **M20**.
A. G. GARDINER An avalanche of indignant protests and appeals burst on him. C. MCCULLERS He grasped the scuttle . . and rattled an avalanche of coal on the fire. H. ARENDT The Nazis let loose an avalanche of laws and decrees.
– COMB.: **avalanche lily** *N. Amer.* an erythronium commonly found near the snowline, esp. the yellow *Erythronium grandiflorum*.
▸ **B** *verb*. **1** *verb intrans.* Descend in or like an avalanche. **L19**.
M. TWAIN We avalanched from one side of the stage[-coach] to the other.
2 *verb trans.* Strike, carry, or envelop (as) by an avalanche. **L19**.
Daily Telegraph Just one touch of *rustique* from a designer who used to avalanche us with folklore: cream, Aran-knit coats . . glamorised by lynx collars. P. GILLMAN He and three other men were avalanched.
3 *verb intrans.* PHYSICS. Undergo a rapid increase in conductivity due to an avalanche process. **M20**.
■ **avalanchy** *adjective* susceptible to avalanches **L19**.

†**avale** *verb*. **ME**.
[ORIGIN Old French & mod. French *avaler*, from *à val* at the bottom, down, from Latin *ad vallem*. Cf. AMOUNT *verb*, DEVALL.]
1 *verb intrans.* Sink, drop; flow down; descend, alight. **ME–L16**.
2 *verb trans.* Cause to descend or fall; let down, lower; remove or doff (one's headgear), open (one's visor). **ME–L18**. ▸**b** *fig.* Abase, degrade. **LME–M17**.

avania /avə'niːə/ *noun*. *obsolete* exc. *hist.* Also **-iah**. **L16**.
[ORIGIN Ult. from medieval Greek *abania* perh. from Arabic *'awān* mischievous damage. Cf. Italian *avania*, French *avanie*.]
A tax (esp. an extortionate one) levied by the Turkish authorities.
■ **avanious** *adjective* (*arch.*) extortionate **L17**.

avant- /'avɒ̃/ *combining form*. **L20**.
[ORIGIN French *avant* forward, before, after AVANT-GARDE.]
Esp. with reference to popular music: innovative, avant-garde.
Time Out New York This classically trained vocalist can rock out as a wailing avant-pop angel.

avant-courier /avɒ̃ː'kʊrɪə/ *noun*. **E17**.
[ORIGIN from French *avant* forward, before + COURIER *noun*, after French *avant-coureur*. Cf. earlier VAUNT-COURIER.]
A person who runs or rides before; a herald; a member of the advance guard of an army.

avant-garde /avɒ̃ː(ŋ)'gɑːd/ *noun & adjective*. **LME**.
[ORIGIN French, from *avant* forward, before + *garde* GUARD *noun*.]
▸ **A** *noun*. **1** The vanguard of an army. Now *arch.* or *hist.* **LME**.
2 The pioneering or innovative writers, artists, etc., in a particular period. **E20**.
▸ **B** *adjective*. Of or pertaining to the artistic avant-garde; progressive, ultra-modern. **E20**.
■ **avant-gardism** *noun* the characteristic quality or principles of the artistic avant-garde **M20**. **avant-gardist** *noun* a member of the artistic avant-garde **M20**.

avanturine *noun* var. of AVENTURINE.

Avar /'avɑː, 'ɑː-/ *noun & adjective*. **L18**.
[ORIGIN Avar.]
A member of, of or pertaining to, a people of the NE Caucasus, identified with a people prominent in SE Europe from the 6th to the 9th cent.; (of) the language of this people.
■ **Avarian** /ə'vɑːrɪən, ɑː-/ *adjective & noun* (**a**) *adjective* of or pertaining to the Avars or their language; (**b**) *noun* the language of the Avars: **L19**.

avarice /'av(ə)rɪs/ *noun*. **ME**.
[ORIGIN Old French & mod. French from Latin *avaritia*, from *avarus* greedy: see -ICE[1].]
Greed for gain, cupidity; *fig.* eager desire to get or keep something for oneself.

avaricious /avə'rɪʃəs/ *adjective*. **LME**.
[ORIGIN Old French & mod. French *avaricieux*, formed as AVARICE + *-ieus*, *-ieux* -IOUS.]
Manifesting avarice; grasping; greedy for wealth.
■ **avariciously** *adverb* **M16**. **avariciousness** *noun* **M16**.

avascular /ə'vaskjʊlə, eɪ-/ *adjective*. **E20**.
[ORIGIN from A-[10] + VASCULAR.]
Characterized by or associated with an absence or deficiency of blood vessels.
■ **avascu'larity** *noun* **M20**.

avast /ə'vɑːst/ *interjection*. **E17**.
[ORIGIN from Dutch *hou'vast*, *houd vast* hold fast, with 1st syll. assim. to A *preposition*[1].]
NAUTICAL. Stop! cease! hold!
SMOLLETT Avast there friend, none of your tricks upon travellers. F. MARRYAT 'Avast heaving,' said Gascoigne.

avatar /'avətɑː/ *noun*. **L18**.
[ORIGIN Sanskrit *avatāra* descent, from *ava* off, away, down + *tar-* pass over.]
1 HINDU MYTHOLOGY. The descent of a god to earth in incarnate form. **L18**.
R. K. NARAYAN Krishna was the eighth avatar of Vishnu, incarnated to help the Five Brothers regain their kingdom.
2 An incarnation or embodiment (of another person, an idea, etc.). **E19**.
M. MCCARTHY The classic English butler, of which he personally was the avatar.
3 A manifestation to the world as a ruling power or as an object of worship; *gen.* a manifestation, a phase. **E19**.
L. STEPHEN Wit and sense are but different avatars of the same spirit.
4 COMPUTING. A movable icon representing a person in cyberspace or virtual reality graphics. **L20**.

†**avaunt** *verb*[1] & *noun*[1]. **ME**.
[ORIGIN Old French *avanter*, *avaunter*, formed as A-[5] + VAUNT *verb*.]
▸ **A** *verb*. **1** *verb trans.* Boast or brag of; praise; vaunt (oneself). **ME–L16**.
2 *verb intrans.* Boast, brag. **LME–L16**.
▸ **B** *noun*. Boasting, bragging; a brag, a boast. **LME–L16**.

avaunt /ə'vɔːnt/ *adverb*, *interjection*, *verb*[2], & *noun*[2]. Long *arch.* **LME**.
[ORIGIN Anglo-Norman, Old French & mod. French *avant* to the front, before, onward, ult. from Latin *ab* from + *ante* before.]
▸ †**A** *adverb*. Forward; to the front. **LME–E17**.
▸ **B** *interjection*. Onward! go on! begone! away! **LME**.
▸ †**C** *verb*. **1** *verb intrans.* Advance, go forward; depart, be off. **LME–E17**.
2 *verb trans.* Raise, advance. **LME–E17**.
▸ †**D** *noun*. An order to go away. **L16–E18**.

AVC *abbreviation*.
Additional voluntary contributions (to a pension scheme).

ave /'ɑːvi, 'ɑːveɪ/ *noun & interjection*. **ME**.
[ORIGIN Latin as imper. sing. of *avere* be or fare well, used as an expression of greeting or farewell. In earliest use short for *Ave Maria*.]
▸ **A** *noun*. **1** (Also **A-**.) = AVE MARIA 1. **ME**. ▸**b** A bead on a rosary (as used for counting the number of aves recited). **ME**.
2 A shout of welcome or farewell. **E17**.
– COMB.: **ave bell** a bell rung at the hours when aves are to be said.
▸ **B** *interjection*. Hail! farewell! **LME**.

Ave. *abbreviation*.
Avenue.

avellan /ə'vɛlən, 'avələn/ *noun & adjective*. Also **-l(l)ane** /-leɪn/. **ME**.
[ORIGIN from Latin *Avellanus* of Avella, a town in Campania, Italy: see -AN.]
▸ **A** *noun*. A filbert, a hazelnut. **ME**.
▸ **B** *adjective*. **1** ***avellan nut*** = sense A above. **LME**.
2 HERALDRY. Of a cross: resembling four thin filberts joined together. **E17**.

Ave Maria /ˌɑːvi mə'riːə, ˌɑːveɪ/ *interjectional & noun phr.* Also **Ave Mary** /'mɛːri/. **ME**.
[ORIGIN Latin = hail, Mary!: see AVE.]
1 The angel's greeting to the Virgin Mary combined with that of Elizabeth (cf. *Luke* 1:28 & 42), used as a devotional recitation; the prayer to the Virgin as Mother of God beginning with these words; a recitation of this devotional phrase or prayer. **ME**.
2 (The time of) the ave bell. **L16**.

aven /'eɪv(ə)n/ *noun*. **L19**.
[ORIGIN French dial., of Celtic origin.]
A vertical shaft in limestone, closed or almost closed at the top; a swallow hole.

avener /ə'viːnə/ *noun*. *obsolete* exc. *hist.* **ME**.
[ORIGIN Anglo-Norman *avener*, Old French *avenier*, from medieval Latin *avenarius* use as noun of the Latin adjective, from *avena* oats: see -ARY[1].]
A chief officer of the stable, in charge of provender for the horses.

avenge /ə'vɛndʒ/ *verb & noun*. **LME**.
[ORIGIN Old French *avengier*, from *a* (intensifier) + *vengier* (mod. *venger*) from Latin *vindicare* VINDICATE.]
▸ **A** *verb*. **1** *verb trans.* Take vengeance, inflict retribution, exact satisfaction, on behalf of (another person, oneself), or on account of (a wrong, injury, etc.). Freq. in *pass.* Foll. by (*up*)*on*, †*of*, †*against* the offender. **LME**.
COVERDALE *Ps.* 119:84 When wilt thou be auenged of my aduersaries? MILTON Avenge, O Lord, thy slaughtered saints. W. N. MASSEY Private grudges were avenged. W. F. HOOK Edwy had the power to avenge himself upon Dunstan. A. TROLLOPE Those who offend us are generally punished . . but we so frequently miss the satisfaction of knowing that we are avenged. L. TRILLING Why Hamlet . . did not avenge upon his hated uncle his father's death. D. JACOBSON The ferocity and guile with which Absalom had avenged the rape of his sister.
2 *verb intrans.* Take vengeance. *arch.* **M16**.
AV *Lev.* 19:18 Thou shalt not auenge nor beare any grudge against the children of thy people.
†3 *verb trans.* Take vengeance upon. Only in **M17**.
▸ **B** *noun*. Retribution, vengeance. *arch.* **M16**.
■ †**avengeance** *noun* vengeance **LME–E18**. **avengeful** *adjective* (*arch.*) full of vengeance, taking vengeance **L16**. **avengement** *noun*

(*arch.*) vengeance **L15**. **avenger** *noun* †(**a**) a person who takes vengeance on (an offender); (**b**) a person who avenges (an injured person or an injury): **LME**. **avengeress** *noun* (*rare*) a female avenger **L16**.

avens /ˈeɪv(ə)nz/ *noun*. **ME**.
[**ORIGIN** Old French *avence* = medieval Latin *avencia*, of unknown origin.]
Any of a number of rosaceous plants belonging to the genus *Geum* or a related genus.
mountain avens a creeping alpine, *Dryas octopetala*, bearing white flowers. **water avens** *Geum rivale*, bearing bell-like flowers having dull pink petals and a purple calyx. **wood avens** *Geum urbanum*, bearing small yellow flowers; also called ***herb bennet***.

aventail /ˈav(ə)nteɪl/ *noun*. Also **-ayle**. **ME**.
[**ORIGIN** Anglo-Norman = (see **A-**[7]) Old French *esventail* air hole, from *esventer* (mod. *éventer*), ult. from Latin **EX-**[1] + *ventus* wind: see **-AL**[1].]
hist. The movable front or mouthpiece of a helmet, which may be raised to admit air. Cf. **VENTAIL** 2.

aventure /əˈvɛntʃə/ *noun*. *obsolete* exc. *hist.* **E17**.
[**ORIGIN** Old French = **ADVENTURE** *noun*.]
LAW. Pure accident, as a cause of death (cf. **MISADVENTURE**).

aventurine /əˈvɛntʃərɪn/ *noun*. Also **avan-** /əˈvan-/. **E18**.
[**ORIGIN** French from Italian *avventurino*, from *avventura* chance (from its accidental discovery): see **ADVENTURE** *noun*, **-INE**[1].]
1 A brownish ornamental glass containing sparkling particles of copper or another foreign material. Also ***aventurine glass***. **E18**.
2 A variety of quartz or of feldspar spangled with particles of another mineral (usu. mica or haematite respectively). Also ***aventurine quartz***, ***aventurine feldspar***. **L18**.

avenue /ˈav(ə)njuː/ *noun*. **E17**.
[**ORIGIN** French, use as noun of fem. pa. pple of *avenir* arrive, approach, from Latin *advenire*, from **AD-** + *venire* come.]
1 A way of access or approach. Now chiefly *fig.*, a way, a means. **E17**.
H. BELLOC Cheating on a large scale was an avenue to social advancement in most of the progressive European countries. D. CARNEGIE She had found in making the breakfast food an avenue of self-expression.
EXPLORE ***every avenue***.
2 A tree lined approach to a country house; lines of trees forming such an approach; a broad roadway marked by trees or other objects at regular intervals. **M17**.
GEO. ELIOT Arthur Donnithorne passed under an avenue of limes and beeches. A. P. STANLEY The avenue of sphinxes leading to the huge gateway.
3 A broad street; an urban street with trees. (Freq. in proper names.) **L18**.
D. LESSING I'd better be getting home to 16 Plane Avenue. S. CISNEROS Down the avenue one block past the bright lights.
4 *ZOOLOGY*. = **AMBULACRUM**. Now *rare* or *obsolete*. **M19**.

aver /ˈeɪvə/ *noun* & *verb*[1]. *Scot.* & *N. English*. Also **aiver**.
[**ORIGIN** Old English *eafor*, whence Anglo-Norman *aver*, Anglo-Latin *av(e)ra*, *affrus*.]
▸ **A** *noun*. A draught horse; an old horse, a nag. **OE**.
▸ †**B** *verb trans.* Supply with horse transport. Only in **OE**.

aver /əˈvəː/ *verb*[2] *trans*. Infl. **-rr-**. **LME**.
[**ORIGIN** Old French & mod. French *avérer*, from **A-**[5] + *veir*, *voir* from Latin *verus* true.]
†**1** Declare true. **LME–M17**.
†**2** Prove true; confirm. **LME–L17**.
3 *LAW*. Prove or justify (a plea etc.); make an averment *that*. **LME**.
4 Assert as a fact; state positively, affirm. **L16**.
P. SIDNEY How often doe the Phisitians lye, when they auer things good for sicknesses. R. BENTLEY Which being . . within the reach of my own Knowledge, I do averr to be a Calumny. COLERIDGE They all averr'd I had killed the Bird That brought the fog and mist. G. P. R. JAMES What one author avers upon the subject, another denies. BARONESS ORCZY A brilliant matrimonial prize for which, as all chroniclers aver, there had been many competitors.
5 Assert the existence or occurrence of. *arch.* **E17**.
MILTON Æsop's Chronicles auer many stranger Accidents.
■ **averrable** *adjective* **M16**.

average /ˈav(ə)rɪdʒ/ *noun*[1]. *obsolete* exc. *hist.* Also (*Scot.*) **arage**, **arriage**, /ˈarɪdʒ/. **LME**.
[**ORIGIN** medieval Latin *averagium*, from **AVER** *verb*[1]: see **-AGE**.]
A service (orig. with draught animals) owed by a tenant to a feudal superior.

average /ˈav(ə)rɪdʒ/ *noun*[2]. **L15**.
[**ORIGIN** from French *avarie* damage to ship or cargo, (earlier) customs duty, from Italian *avaria* from Arabic *'awār* damage to goods: *-age* after *damage* etc.]
▸ **I** Maritime use.
1 A minor charge over and above the freight incurred in the shipment of goods, and payable by their owner or consignee. Also ***petty average***. **L15**.
†**2** A duty charged upon goods; a customs duty etc. **E16–M18**.
3 (The equitable apportionment of) liability resulting from loss of or damage to an insured ship or its cargo. **L16**.
general average: arising from the deliberate partial sacrifice of a ship or its cargo in order to avoid total loss. **particular average**: arising from accidental partial damage or loss.
▸ **II** *transf.* **4** The determination of a medial estimate or arithmetic mean. Chiefly in ***on average***, ***on the average***, ***on an average***, as a mean value or general rule, usually, (formerly also with *at*). **M18**.
5 The generally prevailing rate, degree, or amount; the ordinary standard; the arithmetic mean. **M18**. ▸**b** *spec.* In *CRICKET*, the mean number of runs per completed innings scored by a batsman, or the mean cost in runs per wicket achieved by a bowler, during a season, tour, etc.; in *BASEBALL* (more fully ***batting average***), the mean number of safe hits made by a batter per time at bat. **M19**.
I. COMPTON-BURNETT I never can make out whether Father's hearing is below the average or above it. R. HOGGART Those whose husbands earned just a few shillings above the average for the street. R. DAVIES We played an average of five days a week.
law of averages the proposition that the occurrence of one extreme will be matched by that of the other extreme so as to maintain the average. ***weighted average***: see **WEIGHT** *verb* 3c.
– **COMB.**: **average adjustment** the apportionment of liability due to average.

average /ˈav(ə)rɪdʒ/ *noun*[3]. *dial.* **M16**.
[**ORIGIN** Unknown.]
The pasturage of arable land after harvest; land under stubble.

average /ˈav(ə)rɪdʒ/ *adjective*. **L18**.
[**ORIGIN** from **AVERAGE** *noun*[2].]
Estimated or calculated as an average; medium; of the ordinary standard or kind; typical.
ARNOLD BENNETT The average age appeared to be about fifty. E. GLASGOW In a democracy . . it was safer to be average. W. H. AUDEN Average distance run per week: two hundred miles. B. PYM There was something very unattractive about the average man's pyjamas.
■ **averagely** *adverb* to an average degree; ordinarily: **M19**. **averageness** *noun* **E20**.

average /ˈav(ə)rɪdʒ/ *verb*. **M18**.
[**ORIGIN** from **AVERAGE** *noun*[2].]
1 *verb trans.* Amount to on average; do or achieve on average in any activity. **M18**.
D. MASSON The sale of the book . . averaged a thousand copies a year. G. GREENE Over twenty years I have probably averaged five hundred words a day for five days a week. R. LARDNER It averaged about two dollars per day for the two of us.
2 *verb trans.* Work out or estimate the average of. **L18**.
SOUTHEY His Sunday congregation was averaged at about six hundred persons.
3 *verb trans.* & *intrans.* (with *out*). (Cause to) result in or yield on average a moderate value, intermediate level, even distribution, etc.; even or cancel *out*; remove (variation) by calculating an average. **E20**.
Times Lit. Suppl. The particular obstacles will vary from time to time . . but on the whole will average out. D. W. SCIAMA The clustering might then be real, but be averaged out by this procedure. *Accountant* Those who seek to average out profits by taking profit by stages.
■ **averager** *noun* (**a**) a person whose business is average adjustment; (**b**) a small computer designed for the automatic averaging of a series of input signals: **L19**.

avermectin /eɪvəˈmɛktɪn/ *noun*. **L20**.
[**ORIGIN** from mod. Latin *averm(itilis)* (see below), perh. formed as **A-**[10] + Latin *vermis* worm: see **-IN**[1].]
PHARMACOLOGY. Any of a group of compounds, isolated from the bacterium *Streptomyces avermitilis*, which are macrocyclic lactones with a disaccharide ring attached and have anthelmintic and insecticidal properties.

averment /əˈvəːm(ə)nt/ *noun*. **LME**.
[**ORIGIN** Anglo-Norman, Old French *aver(r)ement*: see **AVER** *verb*[2], **-MENT**.]
1 The action of proving, by argument or evidence; *esp.* (*LAW*) a formal statement including an offer of proof or justification. **LME**.
2 Assertion, affirmation; a positive declaration. **E17**.

Avernal /əˈvəːn(ə)l/ *adjective*. **L16**.
[**ORIGIN** Latin *avernalis*, from *avernus* (*lacus*) = Greek *aornos* (*limnē*) birdless (lake), from **A-**[10] + *ornis* bird: see **-AL**[1].]
Of the nature of or pertaining to Avernus, a lake in Campania, Italy, the effluvium from which was anciently said to kill overflying birds; *gen.* infernal, devilish.

Averroist /ˈavərəʊɪst, avəˈrəʊɪst/ *noun*. Also **-rrhoist**. **M18**.
[**ORIGIN** from *Averroës* (see below) + **-IST**.]
Any of a sect of peripatetic philosophers in pre-Renaissance Italy, who adopted the supposed tenets of Averroës (1126–98), a Muslim philosopher from Cordoba, esp. the belief that the individual soul returns after death to a universal, immortal soul.
■ **Averroism** *noun* **M18**. **Averroˈistic** *adjective* **M19**. **Averroˈistical** *adjective* **M17**.

averruncate /avəˈrʌŋkeɪt/ *verb trans.* *rare* exc. in Dicts. **E17**.
[**ORIGIN** Latin *averruncat-* pa. ppl stem of *averruncare* avert, from *a* **AB-** + *verruncare* turn: see **-ATE**[3]. Erron. explained in 17 as from Latin *ab* off + *eruncare* weed out.]
1 Root out, weed; prune. **E17**.
†**2** Avert, ward off. **M–L17**.
■ †**averruncation** *noun* **M17–E19**. †**averruncator** *noun* (*HORTICULTURE*) a long-handled pruning implement: only in **19**.

aversation /avəˈseɪʃ(ə)n/ *noun*. *arch.* **E17**.
[**ORIGIN** Latin *aversatio(n-)*, from *aversat-* pa. ppl stem of *aversari* turn away from, frequentative of *avertere*: see **AVERT**, **-ATION**.]
= **AVERSION**.

averse /əˈvəːs/ *adjective* (usu. *pred.*) & *adverb*. **L16**.
[**ORIGIN** Latin *aversus* pa. pple of *avertere* **AVERT**.]
▸ **A** *adjective*. **1** Turned away in thought or feeling; opposed, disinclined. (Foll. by *to*, (now *rare*) *from*.) **L16**.
AV *Micah* 2:8 As men auerse from warre. E. M. FORSTER Averse to wasting her time, she went on sewing. B. PYM He wasn't averse to a bit of a rest.
†**2** Of things: adverse. Only in **17**.
HOBBES What Opinions and Doctrines are averse, and what conducing to Peace.
†**3** Lying on the opposite side. *rare*. Only in **M17**.
MILTON On the Coast averse From entrance or cherubic watch . . Found unsuspected way.
†**4** Turned away or in the reverse direction. **L17–E18**.
DRYDEN The tracks averse a lying notice gave.
▸ †**B** *adverb*. In the reverse or opposite direction. **E17–E19**.
E. TOPSELL The hair groweth averse . . forward toward his head.
■ **aversely** *adverb* **M17**. **averseness** *noun* **E17**.

aversion /əˈvəːʃ(ə)n/ *noun*. **L16**.
[**ORIGIN** French, or Latin *aversio(n-)*, formed as **AVERSE**: see **-ION**.]
1 The action of turning away oneself, one's eyes, etc. Long *rare*. **L16**.
T. BERGER He might turn no female heads, but neither would he cause the aversion of faces.
2 A mental attitude of opposition or repugnance; a habitual dislike; antipathy, unwillingness. (Foll. by *to*, *from*, *for*, †*towards*, †*against*.) **E17**.
BACON His aversion towards the house of York. ADDISON An unconquerable aversion which some stomachs have against a joint of meat. R. L. STEVENSON She had conceived at first sight a great aversion for the present writer, which she was at no pains to conceal. H. A. L. FISHER Charles had married, and on grounds of personal aversion divorced, the daughter of the Lombard king. J. GALSWORTHY Her aversion from him who had owned her body, but had never touched her spirit or her heart. W. S. CHURCHILL The Tories regarded with aversion the sending of large armies to the Continent. K. A. PORTER He had a moral aversion to poverty, an instinctive contempt and distrust of the swarming poor.
3 An object of dislike or repugnance. **L17**.
M. TWAIN For years my pet aversion had been the cuckoo clock.
– **COMB.**: **aversion therapy** behaviour therapy designed to cause the patient to give up an undesirable habit by associating it with an unpleasant effect.

avert /əˈvəːt/ *verb*. **LME**.
[**ORIGIN** Partly from Old French *avertir*, partly directly from Latin *avertere*, from *a* **AB-** + *vertere* turn.]
1 *verb trans.* Turn away (a person) *from* a place, course of action, etc. *arch.* **LME**.
DRYDEN Mighty Cæsar, whose victorious Arms . . Avert unwarlike Indians from his Rome. A. TROLLOPE How fatal it might be to avert her father from the cause while the trial was still pending.
2 *verb intrans.* Turn away (*from*). *arch.* **L15**.
SOUTHEY And from that hideous man Averting, to Ocellopan he turn'd.
3 *verb trans.* Alienate, estrange. *arch.* **M16**.
L. MORRIS Appease Zeus and the averted Gods.
4 *verb trans.* Turn away (the face, eyes, thoughts, etc.). **L16**.
SHAKES. *Lear* I . . therefore beseech you T'avert your liking a more worthier way. R. G. COLLINGWOOD I could not bear to look at it, and passed with averted eyes. F. RAPHAEL James was asleep . . , his head averted from the light of the door.
5 *verb trans.* Prevent; ward off. **E17**.
J. B. PRIESTLEY Elsie averted the kiss that she knew would inevitably have descended upon her a moment later. A. LURIE Time is of the essence if a frightful disaster is to be averted.
†**6** *verb trans.* Oppose; view with aversion. Only in **M17**.
■ **avertable** *adjective* = **AVERTIBLE** **L19**. **avertible** *adjective* preventable **M17**.

Avesta /əˈvɛstə/ *noun*. **E19**.
[**ORIGIN** Persian.]
(The text of) the Zoroastrian scriptures, compiled by Zoroaster as a means of reforming an older tradition. See also **ZEND-AVESTA**.
■ **Avestan** *adjective* & *noun* (**a**) *adjective* of or pertaining to the Avesta or the ancient Iranian language in which it is written; (**b**) *noun* this language: **M19**. **Avestic** *adjective* & *noun* = **AVESTAN** **L19**.

avgas /ˈavgas/ *noun*. Orig. *US*. **M20**.
[**ORIGIN** from **AV(IATION** + **GAS** *noun*[2].]
Aviation gasoline, petrol for aircraft.

avgolemono /avgəʊˈlɛmənəʊ/ *noun*. Also (earlier) **avgho-**. E20.
[ORIGIN mod. Greek *augolemono*, from *augo* egg + *lemoni* lemon.]
(In Greek cuisine) a sauce made from eggs and lemon juice; a soup made using this sauce.

avian /ˈeɪvɪən/ *adjective*. L19.
[ORIGIN from Latin *avis* bird + -AN.]
Of or pertaining to birds.
avian flu = ***bird flu*** s.v. BIRD *noun*.

aviary /ˈeɪvɪəri/ *noun*. L16.
[ORIGIN Latin *aviarium*, from *avis* bird: see -ARY[1].]
A large cage, building, or enclosure for keeping birds.

aviate /ˈeɪvɪeɪt/ *verb*. L19.
[ORIGIN Back-form. from AVIATION.]
1 *verb intrans*. Pilot or fly in an aeroplane. L19.
2 *verb trans*. Fly (an aeroplane). M20.

aviation /eɪvɪˈeɪʃ(ə)n/ *noun*. M19.
[ORIGIN French, irreg. from Latin *avis* bird: see -ATION.]
The operation of aircraft, aeronautics; the development and manufacture of aircraft.
CIVIL ***aviation***.

aviator /ˈeɪvɪeɪtə/ *noun*. L19.
[ORIGIN French *aviateur*, formed as AVIATION: see -ATOR.]
1 A pilot of an aeroplane; an airman, an airwoman. L19.
†**2** An aeroplane. L19–E20.
■ **aviatrix** *noun* a female aviator E20.

avicide /ˈeɪvɪsʌɪd/ *noun*. *rare*. M19.
[ORIGIN from Latin *avis* bird + -CIDE.]
The slaughter of birds, bird-shooting.

avicularium /əˌvɪkjʊˈlɛːrɪəm/ *noun*. Pl. **-ria** /-rɪə/. M19.
[ORIGIN mod. Latin, from *avicula* dim. of *avis* bird: see -CULE, -ARIUM.]
ZOOLOGY. A specialized member of an ectoproctan colony, having the form of a pair of snapping jaws resembling a bird's head.

aviculture /ˈeɪvɪkʌltʃə/ *noun*. L19.
[ORIGIN from Latin *avis* bird + -CULTURE.]
The breeding and rearing of birds.
■ **aviˈculturist** *noun* a person who breeds and rears birds E20.

avid /ˈavɪd/ *adjective*. M18.
[ORIGIN French *avide* or Latin *avidus*, from *avere* long for: see -ID[1].]
Eager; eagerly desirous, greedy, (*of*, *for*).
■ **avidly** *adverb* M19.

avidin /ˈavɪdɪn/ *noun*. M20.
[ORIGIN from AVID + -IN[1].]
BIOCHEMISTRY. A protein found in raw egg white which combines with and inactivates biotin.

avidious /əˈvɪdɪəs/ *adjective*. *rare*. M16.
[ORIGIN formed as AVID + see -IOUS.]
Avid; greedy, eager.
■ **avidiously** *adverb* LME.

avidity /əˈvɪdɪti/ *noun*. LME.
[ORIGIN French *avidité* or Latin *aviditas*, from *avidus*: see AVID, -ITY.]
1 Extreme eagerness, greediness (*for*, *of*). LME.
2 *spec*. Graspingness, avarice. M17.

†**aview** *verb trans*. Also **ad-**. L15–L16.
[ORIGIN from A-[11] + VIEW *verb*.]
Survey; reconnoitre; view.

SPENSER All which when Artegall . . well advewed . . He could no longer beare.

avifauna /ˈeɪvɪfɔːnə/ *noun*. L19.
[ORIGIN from Latin *avis* bird + FAUNA.]
The birds of a region collectively.
■ **avifaunal** *adjective* L19.

avine /ˈeɪvʌɪn/ *adjective*. *rare*. L19.
[ORIGIN from Latin *avis* bird + -INE[1].]
Avian; birdlike.

avionics /eɪvɪˈɒnɪks/ *noun pl*. M20.
[ORIGIN from AVI(ATION + ELECTR)ONICS.]
1 Treated as *sing*. Electronics as applied to aviation. M20.
2 Electronic equipment fitted in an aircraft. M20.
■ **avionic** *adjective* of or pertaining to avionics M20.

avirulent /eɪˈvɪrjʊl(ə)nt, a-/ *adjective*. E20.
[ORIGIN from A-[10] + VIRULENT.]
Of a micro-organism: not virulent.
■ **avirulence** *noun* M20.

avisandum *noun* var. of AVIZANDUM.

aviso /əˈvʌɪzəʊ/ *noun*. *arch*. Pl. **-os**, †**-oes**. E17.
[ORIGIN Spanish: see ADVICE.]
†**1** Intelligence, information; a notification, a dispatch. E–M17.
2 A boat bringing news, a dispatch boat. E18.

avitaminosis /eɪˌvɪtəmɪˈnəʊsɪs, -ˌvʌɪt-/ *noun*. Pl. **-noses** /-ˈnəʊsiːz/. E20.
[ORIGIN from A-[10] + VITAMIN + -OSIS.]
MEDICINE. A vitamin deficiency disease.

†**avives** *noun pl*. var. of VIVES.

avizandum /avɪˈzandəm/ *noun*. Also **-isa-**. E17.
[ORIGIN medieval Latin, neut. gerund of *avizare*, *-sare* consider, ADVISE.]
SCOTS LAW. Further consideration, esp. out of court; private consideration by a judge etc.

avocado /avəˈkɑːdəʊ/ *noun & adjective*. M17.
[ORIGIN Spanish, alt. (after *avocado* lawyer) from *aguacate* from Nahuatl *ahuacatl*.]
▸ **A** *noun*. Pl. **-os**, ***-oes**.
1 (The rough-skinned pear-shaped edible fruit of) the tree *Persea americana*, of the laurel family, native to Central America and the W. Indies. Also ***avocado pear***. M17.
2 Avocado green. L20.
– COMB.: **avocado green** (of) the green colour of the flesh of the avocado; ***avocado pear***: see sense 1 above.
▸ **B** *adjective*. Of avocado green. L20.

†**avocate** *verb trans*. M16.
[ORIGIN Sense 1 from Latin *avocat-* (see AVOCATION); sense 2 after French †*avoquer* from Latin *advocare* ADVOKE.]
1 Call away, withdraw, (*from*). M16–M18.
2 = ADVOKE. M–L17.

avocation /avəˈkeɪʃ(ə)n/ *noun*. E16.
[ORIGIN Branch I after Latin *advocatio(n-)* ADVOCATION; branch II from Latin *avocatio(n-)*, from *avocat-* pa. ppl stem of *avocare*, from *a-* AB- + *vocare* to call: see -ATION.]
▸ **I** **1** = ADVOCATION 3. E16.
▸ **II** †**2** Diversion of the thoughts. E17–M18.

T. GRAY Try, by every method of avocation and amusement, whether you cannot . . get the better of that dejection.

3 The condition of having one's attention diverted; distraction. *arch*. M17.

S. R. MAITLAND He devoted himself, with less avocation, to prayer.

4 A (less important) distraction; a minor occupation; *colloq*. (a) vocation, (a) calling. M17.

G. B. SHAW It was at the university that I became . . a sky pilot. When the war took me it seemed natural that I should pursue that avocation as a member of the air force. W. FAULKNER A horseman, a groom, merely by accident, but by avocation and dedication a minister of God.

■ **avocational** *adjective* M20.

avocatory /əˈvɒkət(ə)ri, avəˈkeɪtəri/ *adjective*. M17.
[ORIGIN medieval Latin *avocatorius*, from *avocat-*: see AVOCATION, -ORY[2].]
Recalling; that recalls.
letters avocatory *hist*.: by which a monarch recalled subjects from a foreign state or ordered them to desist from illegal proceedings.

avocet /ˈavəsɛt/ *noun*. Also †**-set(ta)** L17.
[ORIGIN French *avocette* from Italian *avosetta*.]
A wading bird of the genus *Recurvirostra*, having a long upturned beak; *esp*. the black and white *R. avosetta* of Europe.

avodiré /avəʊˈdɪəreɪ/ *noun*. M20.
[ORIGIN French.]
(The smooth, light-coloured hardwood of) either of two W. African trees, *Turraeanthus africanus* and *T. vignei*, of the mahogany family.

Avogadro /avəˈgɑːdrəʊ/ *noun*. L19.
[ORIGIN Count Amedeo *Avogadro* (1776–1856), Italian scientist.]
CHEMISTRY. **1** ***Avogadro's law***: that equal volumes of gases under the same conditions of temperature and pressure contain equal numbers of molecules. L19.
2 ***Avogadro's number***, ***Avogadro number***, ***Avogadro's constant***, ***Avogadro constant***, the number of molecules in a mole of material, 6.023×10^{23}. E20.

avoid /əˈvɔɪd/ *verb*. LME.
[ORIGIN Anglo-Norman *avoider* = Old French *esvuidier*, *evuider* (see A-[7]), from *es-* EX-[1] + *vuide* empty, VOID *adjective*.]
▸ **I** Make empty.
†**1** *verb trans*. Empty; clear, free, rid (*of*); depart from, quit (a place). LME–E19.

T. ELYOT Commanded the chambre to be avoided.

2 *verb trans*. Chiefly *LAW*. Make void or of no effect; refute. Formerly also, defeat (pleading); invalidate, quash (a sentence etc.). LME.
†**3** *verb trans*. Clear out, put away; eject, excrete; do away with; get rid of; expel, banish. LME–L17.

R. FABYAN He auoyded yͤ munkys out of the house of Aumbrisbury. R. HAKLUYT It causeth vrine to be avoided in great measure. W. PRYNNE His Images and Pictures . . should be pluckt down and avoided out of all Churches. R. BAXTER There was then no Judge of such controversies . . to avoid and end them.

4 *verb refl*. Leave, withdraw. Long *arch*. LME.

SIR W. SCOTT Avoid thee, Fiend!

†**5** *verb intrans*. Leave, withdraw, depart; retire, retreat. L15–M18. ▸**b** Of things: escape; run out or away. L15–E17.

AV 1 *Sam*. 18:11 Dauid auoided out of his presence. G. SANDYS The Musicians spent so much time in vnseasonable tuning, that he commanded them to auoid. **b** G. MARKHAM If you put a hollow quill therein . . the wind will auoyd the better.

†**6** *verb intrans*. Fall vacant. E16–E18.

J. AYLIFFE If a Person takes a Bishoprick, it does not avoid by Force of that Law of Pluralities, but by the antient Common Law.

▸ **II** Keep (away) from, keep off.
7 *verb trans*. Keep away from; shun; refrain from. Foll. by a person or thing, *doing*, †*to do*. LME.

ALDOUS HUXLEY He always does his best to avoid me; goes out of the room when I come in; . . won't even look at me. L. P. HARTLEY He avoided looking at himself in the glass, so as not to see the circles under his eyes. C. JACKSON Harry Harrison avoided the main highway as tiresome, and took an older, less direct route instead. W. MAXWELL The epidemic was raging and people were told to avoid crowds.

8 *verb trans*. Evade, escape; keep or get out of the way of (something coming towards one or in one's path). LME.

J. GALSWORTHY How, by some sort of settlement, he could best avoid the payment of those death duties which would follow his decease. C. ISHERWOOD A second journey had to be made through the living-room in the dark . . , skirting the table, avoiding the chairs. W. TREVOR A red Post Office van had to swerve to avoid him.

9 *verb trans*. Keep off; prevent; obviate. E17.

CARLYLE That the Body . . be decently interred, to avoid putrescence.

■ **avoidable** *adjective* (**a**) able to be avoided; †(**b**) to be shunned: LME. **avoidably** *adverb* M19. **avoidal** *noun* (*rare*) avoidance L17. **avoidant** *adjective* tending to avoid; *spec*. (*PSYCHOLOGY & PSYCHIATRY*) designating (a person displaying) behaviour which tends towards avoidance of an unpleasant stimulus or situation: L19. **avoider** *noun* E17. **avoidless** *adjective* (*poet*.) that cannot be avoided M17.

avoidance /əˈvɔɪd(ə)ns/ *noun*. LME.
[ORIGIN from AVOID + -ANCE.]
†**1** The action of emptying; ejection, excretion; removal; dismissal; departure (*from*, *out of*). LME–M17.

J. HAYWARD By voluntary avoidance out of the Realme. DONNE The King having made avoydance of those hee esteemed not necessary.

2 The occurrence of a vacancy (of an office, benefice, etc.); the right to fill up a vacancy. *arch*. LME.

G. F. MACLEAR On each avoidance of the abbacy, to fill up the situation from founder's kin.

3 The action of keeping away or refraining from something; escaping, evasion; shunning, holding aloof from someone or something; prevention. LME.

DONNE For avoydance of scandall is Divine law. *Listener* The avoidance of marked peaks and troughs in the amplitude-frequency characteristic. A. LURIE The same avoidance of all topics which might annoy them.

tax avoidance: see TAX *noun*.
4 Chiefly *LAW*. The action of making void or of no effect; invalidation, annulment. E17.

H. H. MILMAN The obsequious clergy . . pronounced at once the avoidance of the marriage.

†**5** An outlet. Only in E17.

avoirdupois /avədəˈpɔɪz, ˌavwɑːdjʊˈpwɑː/ *noun*. ME.
[ORIGIN Old French *aveir de peis* goods of weight, from *ave(i)r* (mod. *avoir*) use as noun of *avoir* have (from Latin *habere*) + *de* of + *peis*, *pois* (mod. *poids*) weight, POISE *noun*[1]. Substitution of *du* for *de* established 17.]
†**1** Merchandise sold by weight. ME–L17.
2 A system of weights based on a pound (the ***avoirdupois pound***) of 16 ounces or 7,000 grains. More fully ***avoirdupois weight***. L15.
3 Weight, heaviness. L16.

†**avolation** *noun*. M17–E19.
[ORIGIN medieval Latin *avolatio(n-)*, from *avolat-* pa. ppl stem of *avolare*, from *a-* AB- + *volare* to fly: see -ATION.]
The action of flying away; exhalation; evaporation.

avondbloem *noun* see AANDBLOM.

†**avoset(ta)** *nouns* vars. of AVOCET.

avouch /əˈvaʊtʃ/ *verb & noun*. *arch*. & *rhet*. L15.
[ORIGIN Old French *avochier* from Latin *advocare*: see ADVOKE. Cf. AVOW *verb*[1].]
▸ **A** *verb*. **1** *verb trans*. Declare as a thing one can prove or, formerly, on which one is an authority; testify to as a personal witness; affirm, assert. L15.

BYRON A report . . Avouch'd his death. C. M. YONGE His own deposition, as three Cardinals avouched that he had made it before them. J. CAREY A locket containing ringlets which he avouches, in confidence, to be relics of a Spanish girl.

2 *verb trans*. & *intrans*. Guarantee; vouch for or *for*. M16.

BACON The seller must bring one to avouch his sale. DEFOE I can avouch for her reputation. H. H. MILMAN The authority of Erasmus avouches the accomplished scholarship of Pace.

3 *verb trans*. Acknowledge; take responsibility for; admit; sanction. M16.

S. DANIEL He for whom thou dost this villanie . . will not avouch thy fact. AV *Deut*. 26:17 Thou hast auouched the Lord this day to be thy God. SIR W. SCOTT The first time that I have heard one with a beard on his lip avouch himself a coward. R. C. TRENCH Milton in his prose works frequently avouches the peculiar affection to the Italian literature and language which he bore.

4 *verb trans*. Establish, prove. L16.

A

C. MARLOWE And will avouch his saying with the sword.

†**5** *verb trans.* Appeal to; cite as warrant, authority, or testimony. L16–E18.

G. HARVEY Reasuns he usid none against me, but only avouchid and maintainid M. Osburns.

†**6** *verb trans.* Establish upon testimony. L16–L17.

F. THYNNE Whiche I will sufficiently advouche, yf Instances be called for at my handes.

▸ **B** *noun.* Guarantee, assurance. E17.

■ **avouchable** *adjective* L16. **avoucher** *noun* L16. **avouchment** *noun* the action of avouching; an assurance, guarantee; a positive declaration: L15.

avoué /avwe/ *noun.* Pl. pronounced same. E19.
[ORIGIN French: see ADVOWEE.]
1 = ADVOWEE 2. E19.
2 *hist.* A French solicitor. E19.

avow /ə'vaʊ/ *noun. arch.* ME.
[ORIGIN from AVOW *verb*[2].]
1 A vow, a solemn promise. ME.
†**2** A votive offering. Only in LME.

avow /ə'vaʊ/ *verb*[1]. ME.
[ORIGIN Old French *avouer* acknowledge, recognize as valid, from Latin *advocare*: see ADVOKE. Cf. AVOUCH.]
†**1** *verb trans.* Acknowledge (a person) as one's own. ME–E17.

R. HAKLUYT Not our subiects, nor by vs any way to be advowed.

†**2** *verb trans.* Authorize, approve. ME–M17.

HOBBES Be contented to avow all the actions he shall do.

3 *verb trans.* Declare as a thing one can vouch for; affirm, maintain. ME.

SIR T. MORE Ryghte worshipful folk, that before me aduowed it in his face. F. WELDON God can be worshipped anywhere, the Reverend Allbright avowed.

4 *verb trans.* Admit, confess; *refl.* reveal one's identity or character. LME.

T. WILLIAMS For the first time . . I saw her beauty, I consciously avowed it to myself. W. S. CHURCHILL By a custom, openly avowed, the Paymaster was permitted to carry his balances to his private account and draw the interest on them.

†**5** *verb refl.* Affiliate oneself *to*; put oneself under the patronage of (foll. by (*up*)*on*). LME–E17.

6 *verb intrans.* LAW. Justify or maintain an act done, esp. a distraining for rent. *arch.* E16.

■ **avowable** *adjective* E17. **avowal** *noun* acknowledgement, unconstrained admission M18. **avowant** *noun* (LAW, now *hist.*) a challenger; a person who admits an act but believes it to be justified: E16. **avowedly** /ə'vaʊɪdli/ *adverb* with open declaration or acknowledgement L16. **avower** *noun*[1] †(*a*) a patron, a protector; (*b*) a person who declares or acknowledges something: LME. †**avower** *noun*[2] [-ER[4]] a vow; avowal: only in 16.

†**avow** *verb*[2]. ME.
[ORIGIN Old French *avo(u)er* vow, formed as A-[5] + VOW *verb*.]
1 *verb trans.* Bind with a vow (*to*, *to do*); devote, consecrate, (*to*). ME–L16.
2 *verb trans.* & *intrans.* Make a vow (*that*, *to* an act, *to do*); undertake solemnly, vow, (something, *to do*). LME–E19.

avowry /ə'vaʊ(ə)ri/ *noun.* ME.
[ORIGIN Anglo-Norman *avowrie*, Old French *avoerie*, from *avoeor* (formed as AVOW *verb*[1] + -OR): see -Y[3], -RY.]
†**1** Acknowledgement as one's own. Only in ME.
†**2** Authorization, approval. Only in ME.
†**3** Patronage, protection. Only in ME.
4 A patron, a protector; a patron saint. LME.
†**5** The right of presentation to a benefice; advowson. LME–M17.
6 The avowal of an act done; *esp.* in LAW (now *hist.*), the plea whereby a person who distrains for rent avows the act and justifies it. L15.

avoyer /ə'vɔɪə; *foreign* avwaje (*pl. same*)/ *noun.* L16.
[ORIGIN Swiss French from Old French *avoié* corresp. to French AVOUÉ.]
hist. In some Swiss cantons: the chief magistrate.

avulse /ə'vʌls/ *verb trans.* M18.
[ORIGIN Latin *avuls-* pa. ppl stem of *avellere*, from *a* AB- + *vellere* to pluck.]
Pull or pluck off; tear away.

avulsion /ə'vʌlʃ(ə)n/ *noun.* E17.
[ORIGIN French, or Latin *avulsio(n-)*, formed as AVULSE: see -ION.]
1 The action of pulling off or tearing away; forcible separation. E17.
2 A part torn off; a detached portion. L17.
3 LAW. The sudden removal of land by a change in the course of a river, floodwater, etc., to another person's estate (the land remaining the property of the original owner: cf. ALLUVION 4). M19.

avuncular /ə'vʌŋkjʊlə/ *adjective.* M19.
[ORIGIN from Latin *avunculus* maternal uncle, dim. of *avus* grandfather, + -AR[1].]
Of, pertaining to, or resembling an uncle.

avunculate /ə'vʌŋkjʊlət/ *noun.* E20.
[ORIGIN formed as AVUNCULAR + -ATE[1].]
ANTHROPOLOGY. The special relationship in some societies between a maternal uncle and his sister's son.

aw *adjective, noun, & adverb* see A'.

aw /ɔː/ *interjection. Scot. & N. Amer.* M19.
[ORIGIN Imit.]
Expr. mild remonstrance, entreaty, commiseration, disgust, or disapproval.

awa' *adverb, adjective, & noun* see AWAY.

Awabakal /ə'wʌbəkəl/ *noun & adjective.* Pl. of noun same. E19.
[ORIGIN Prob. Awabakal.]
A member of, of or pertaining to, an Australian Aboriginal people of an area of New South Wales north of Sydney. Also, (of) the language of this people.

awabi /ə'wɑːbi/ *noun.* E18.
[ORIGIN Japanese.]
The Japanese abalone, *Haliotis gigantea*.

AWACS /'eɪwaks/ *abbreviation.*
MILITARY. Airborne warning and control system, an airborne long-range radar system for detecting other aircraft and controlling weapons directed against them.

†**await** *noun.* LME.
[ORIGIN Anglo-Norman, formed as AWAIT *verb*.]
1 A waylaying with hostile intent; (an) ambush; a plot. Long *rare*. LME–M19.
2 Watching, watchfulness, caution. LME–M16.

await /ə'weɪt/ *verb.* ME.
[ORIGIN Anglo-Norman *awaitier* = Old French *aguaitier*, formed as A-[5] + WAIT *verb*.]
†**1** *verb trans.* & *intrans.* Keep watch (on); lie in wait (for); waylay. ME–L17.

M. DRAYTON Thou seest who doth awaite, T' intrap thy Beautie. MILTON Your ill-meaning politician lords . . Appointed to await me thirty spies.

†**2** *verb trans.* & *intrans.* Look (at), observe. Only in ME.
†**3** *verb intrans.* Remain (in a place); wait (*for*, *on*). ME–E19.

SIR W. SCOTT The acclamations . . of the commons who awaited without.

4 *verb trans.* Wait for (a coming event or person); expect. ME.

J. AGATE On arrival, found Lady H. awaiting us with wonderful cocktails. H. INNES If this were England . . you'd be in a condemned cell awaiting execution.

†**5** *verb trans.* Plot (harm of some kind) *to*. Only in LME.
†**6** *verb trans.* & *intrans.* Attend to; take care, endeavour, (*that*, *to do*). LME–E17.
†**7** *verb trans.* & *intrans.* Wait on (or (*up*)*on*) as a servant, attendant, etc. LME–M18.

H. SURREY Then issued she, awayted with great train. POPE On whom three hundred gold-capt youths await.

8 *verb trans.* Be in store for. L16.

LD MACAULAY Honors and rewards which he little deserved awaited him.

■ **awaiter** *noun* (now *rare*) LME.

awake /ə'weɪk/ *pred. adjective.* ME.
[ORIGIN Use as adjective of obsolete pa. pple of AWAKE *verb*.]
1 No longer or not yet asleep. ME.
2 Vigilant; alert. E17.
awake to fully aware of.

awake /ə'weɪk/ *verb.* Pa. t. **awoke** /ə'wəʊk/, †**awaked**; pa. pple **awoke**, **awoken** /ə'wəʊk(ə)n/, **awaked**.
[ORIGIN Old English *āwæcnan* & *āwacian*: see A *preposition*[1] 6, WAKE *verb*.]
▸ **I** *verb intrans.* **1** Come out of the state of sleep; cease to sleep. OE.

AV *Judg.* 16:20 Hee awoke out of his sleepe. M. MCCARTHY Terrible dreams about money, from which she would awake sweating. F. TUOHY When he awoke it was bright sunshine.

2 Come out of a state resembling sleep; become active. ME.

E. A. FREEMAN The national spirit again awoke.

awake to become fully aware of.

3 Be wakeful; be vigilant. *rare*. LME.
▸ **II** *verb trans.* **4** Rouse from sleep. ME.

DRYDEN No dreadful Dreams awak'd him with affright.

5 Rouse from a state resembling sleep; stir up, make active. ME.

SIR W. SCOTT But morning beam, and wild bird's call, Awaked not Mortham's silent hall. G. ORWELL The young, strong body, now helpless in sleep, awoke in him a pitying, protecting feeling.

■ **awaker** *noun* (*rare*) E17.

awaken /ə'weɪk(ə)n/ *verb.*
[ORIGIN Old English *āwæcn(i)an*: see A *preposition*[1] 6, WAKEN *verb*.]
▸ **I** *verb intrans.* **1** Cease to sleep, wake. OE.
†**2** Come into existence, originate. OE–ME.
3 Become active or lively. E18.
▸ **II** *verb trans.* **4** Rouse from sleep, wake (a person). ME.

Argosy They had been awakened by the disturbance.

5 Stir up, make active, *esp.* arouse *to* a sense of, make aware. ME.

S. WATERS She had awakened particular appetites in me. *English Today* Their aim is to awaken students to the richness of language.

■ **awakener** *noun* L16. **awakening** *noun* (a) rising, (an) arousal, from sleep, inaction, indifference, etc. L16. **awakenment** *noun* (now *rare*) an awakening M19.

awald /'ɑːw(ə)ld/ *adverb & pred. adjective. Scot.* Also **-lt** /-lt/. M18.
[ORIGIN Perh. ult. from Old Norse *af* from + *velta* to rise.]
Of an animal, esp. a sheep: on its back and unable to rise; of a person: incapacitated through intoxication, insensible.

awanting /ə'wɒntɪŋ/ *ppl adjective.* Chiefly *Scot.* L16.
[ORIGIN from A *preposition*[1] 8 + *wanting* ppl adjective of WANT *verb*: cf. AMISSING.]
Missing, wanting.

award /ə'wɔːd/ *noun.* LME.
[ORIGIN Anglo-Norman, formed as AWARD *verb*[1].]
▸ **I 1** A judicial decision. LME.
2 A payment, penalty, etc., appointed by a judicial decision; a prize or other honour assigned by authority. L16.
Tony award: see TONY *noun*[1].
▸ †**II 3** Custody, wardship. LME–L16.
– COMB.: **award wage** *Austral. & NZ* a minimum wage fixed by an industrial court for a particular industry or occupation; **award-winning** *adjective* that has won an award.

award /ə'wɔːd/ *verb*[1] *trans.* LME.
[ORIGIN Anglo-Norman *awarder* var. (see A-[7]) of Old Northern French *eswarder*, Old French *esguarder* consider, ordain: see EX-[1], WARD *verb*.]
†**1** *gen.* Decide or determine (something, *that*, *to do*) after consideration or deliberation. LME–E18.
2 Decide judicially (a process); issue judicially (a document etc.). LME.
3 Grant, assign, (*to* a person); order to be given as a payment, penalty, prize, etc. LME.

SHAKES. *Merch. V.* A pound of that same merchant's flesh is thine, The court awards it and the law doth give it. G. B. SHAW A Court of Discipline, which awarded him two years imprisonment and fifty lashes. A. J. CRONIN For his thesis on Dust Inhalation, he had been awarded his MD.

†**4** Sentence, appoint, (a person, *to* custody etc., *to do*). LME–M17.

■ **awardable** *adjective* able (esp. legally) to be awarded E17. **awar'dee** *noun* a person to whom an award is given M20. **awarder** *noun* M16.

†**award** *verb*[2] *trans.* M16.
[ORIGIN from A-[11] + WARD *verb*.]
1 Guard. Only in M16.
2 Ward off (blows etc.). L16–M19.

aware /ə'wɛː/ *pred. adjective.*
[ORIGIN Old English *gewær* (see A-[4], WARE *adjective*) = Old Saxon *giwar* (Middle Dutch *gheware*), Old High German *gawar*, *gi-* (German *gewahr*) from West Germanic.]
†**1** Vigilant, cautious, on one's guard. (Foll. by *lest*, *of*.) OE–M19.
2 Conscious, sensible, not ignorant, having knowledge, (*of*, *that*); *colloq.* (occas. *attrib.*) well-informed, responsive to conditions etc., (with specifying adverb) informed about current developments. OE.

R. P. WARREN It was cold in the room, and he was aware of the cold, but as knowledge, as it were, not as sensation. E. F. BENSON I am aware there are many different sorts of people in the world. J. STEINBECK Along the road the trackers would become aware that they had missed the path. J. I. M. STEWART He seemed scarcely aware of us when we did turn up. *Gay News* I think a lot of *aware* men influenced fashion. *Chicago Tribune* You'd think people would be more ecologically aware.

■ **awareness** *noun* E19.

†**awarn** *verb trans. rare.* LME–L16.
[ORIGIN from A-[11] + WARN *verb*[1].]
Give notice to; warn.

SPENSER That every bird and beast awarned made To shrowd themselves.

†**awarrant** *verb trans.* LME–L19.
[ORIGIN from A-[11] + WARRANT *verb*.]
Vouch for, warrant, guarantee.

awash /ə'wɒʃ/ *adverb & pred. adjective.* M19.
[ORIGIN from A-[2] + WASH *noun* or *verb*.]
Level with the surface of water, so that it just washes over; flooded (*lit.* & *fig.*); washing about.

C. READE The rising water set everything awash. C. MACKENZIE An unpleasant black reef awash at half tide. A. SETON The glorious singing mingled with the exultant organ and the Abbey was awash with beauty of sound. J. P. DONLEAVY The bar was awash. Uncontrolled pints. *Times* The stock market has suddenly become awash with takeover bids and rumours.

away /ə'weɪ/ *adverb, adjective, & noun.* Also (*Scot.*) **awa'** /ə'wɑː, ə'wɔː/.
[ORIGIN Late Old English *aweg* (earlier *on weg*): see A *preposition*[1] 1, ON *preposition*, WAY *noun*.]
▸ **A** *adverb* **I 1** On one's way; onward, on, along. Long *obsolete* exc. *Scot. & N. English.* LOE.

SHAKES. *Twel. N.* Come away, come away, death; And in sad cypress let me be laid. R. L. STEVENSON And now come awa' to your bed.

2 From this or that place; to a distance (*lit. & fig.*). LOE.

DRYDEN And hungry sent the wily fox away. W. COWPER Away went Gilpin, neck or nought; Away went hat and wig. DYLAN THOMAS I have longed to move away but am afraid. P. LARKIN That Whitsun, I was late getting away: Not till about One-twenty . . Did my . . train pull out. E. ROOSEVELT He had grown away from her in some ways and . . in later years they had often not been in sympathy. M. KEANE I stepped up to my reflection, then away from it.

carry away, drive away, etc. ***go away, run away, slip away, steal away***, etc. **far and away**, **out and away** by far, by a very large amount.

3 From adherence, contact, or inclusion; aside, off. LOE.

LONGFELLOW She folded her work, and laid it away. G. B. SHAW She touches her eyes as if to wipe away a tear.

fall away.

4 From or out of one's personal possession. LOE.

LONGFELLOW This passing traveller, who hath stolen away The brightest jewel of my crown to-day.

give away, put away, take away, throw away, whisk away, etc.

5 Towards or into non-existence; so as to remove, reduce, eliminate, bring to an end, reach the end of, etc., something by the action of the verb. LOE.

AV *Job* 33:21 His flesh is consumed away. YEATS She grew pale as death and fainted away. R. HUGHES The breeze having dropped away almost to a calm. DYLAN THOMAS There could I marvel My birthday Away.

die away, fade away, pine away, waste away, wither away, etc. ***pass away, explain away. idle away*** (time), ***while away*** (time). ***do away with***: see DO *verb*. ***make away with***: see MAKE *verb*.

6 Gone from a place; absent; wanting. ME.

A. COWLEY How could it be so fair and you away? N. COWARD They're away in Tunis.

7 Gone from existence; vanished; consumed; dead, fainted. Now *dial.* ME.

COVERDALE *Jer.* 31:15 Rachel mournynge for hir children, and wolde not be comforted, because they were awaye.

8 At a (stated) distance; in another place. LME. ▸**b** With adverbs with intensive force: a considerable distance or time *back, down, up*, etc. Chiefly *N. Amer.* E19. ▸**c** *SPORT.* On an opponent's ground. L19.

R. D. BLACKMORE His home was some miles away. YEATS Hidden away where nobody can find it. S. HEANEY Kelly's kept an unlicensed bull, well away From the road. B. PYM She had chosen a seat away from the other people.

9 In the other direction, from the place, person, etc., in question. LME.

J. N. LOCKYER The axis of rotation is inclined away from the Sun. A. LOOS Mr Spoffard turned on his heels and walked away. SCOTT FITZGERALD I turned my head away and wept.

10 Continuously, constantly, persistently. M16.

THACKERAY He sat down and worked away, very, very hard. A. HELPS And kept 'pegging away' . . with all my might.

pound away.

11 Without hesitation or delay; forthwith, directly. M16. ***fire away***: see FIRE *verb*. ***right away***: see RIGHT *adverb*. ***straight away***: see STRAIGHT *adverb*[1].

▸ **II** Ellipt. uses (esp. for an imper. or inf.).

12 Go away. ME.

AV *Exod.* 19:24 Away, get thee downe. R. L. STEVENSON I'm weariet, an' here I'm awa to my bed. YEATS We must away, and wait until she dies.

13 Take away; go or get away *with*. LME.

DICKENS In his honest indignation he would reply, 'Away with it!'

14 Get on or along *with*. L15.

CARLYLE Idolatry . . is a thing they cannot away-with.

▸ **B** *adjective.* Played or taking place on an opponent's ground. E20.

– COMB.: **awayday** [first denoting a type of money-saving return rail ticket] (**a**) a day trip; (**b**) a day on which employees meet at a venue away from the workplace to plan strategy or discuss an issue.

away game, away goal, away match, away win, etc.

▸ **C** *noun.* A match or win on an opponent's ground. M20.

■ **aways** *adverb* (long *dial.*) = AWAY *adverb* L15.

†awayward *adverb & adjective.* ME.
[ORIGIN from AWAY *adverb* + -WARD.]
▸ **A** *adverb.* In a different direction; aside; away. ME–L16.
▸ **B** *adjective.* = WAYWARD. Only in ME.

awe /ɔː/ *noun & verb.*
[ORIGIN Old English *ege* = Gothic *agis* fear, from Germanic; replaced in Middle English by forms cognate with Old Norse *agi*.]
▸ **A** *noun.* †**1** Terror, dread. OE–L18.

W. COWPER His voice Shook the delinquent with such fits of awe.

2 Reverential fear or wonder. OE.

J. KEBLE There is an awe in mortals' joy, A deep mysterious fear. A. S. NEILL Some parents taught their children that sex was sacred and spiritual, something to be treated with awe and wonder. V. S. PRITCHETT We walked behind them listening with awe to their astonishing man-of-the-world talk about girls. A. EDEN We boys were in considerable awe of Smitton, whose rules were strict and whose praise was sparing.

3 Power to inspire reverential fear or wonder. *arch.* OE.

D. BAGLEY Clothing himself in the full awe of British majesty.

– COMB.: **awestricken**, **awestruck** *adjectives* suddenly affected with awe.

▸ **B** *verb trans.* Inspire with awe; influence or control by awe. ME.

SHAKES. *Much Ado* Shall quips, and sentences, . . awe a man from the career of his humour? GIBBON He was not awed by the sanctity of the place. J. K. JEROME They awe us, these strange stars, so cold, so clear. J. B. PRIESTLEY He looked so imposing that immediately an awed silence fell on the company. A. SCHLEE Ellie, awed out of ill temper, turned shyly to face them.

■ **aweless** *adjective* (**a**) without feeling awe; †(**b**) without inspiring awe: LME. **awelessness** *noun* (*rare*) L16.

aweary /əˈwɪəri/ *pred. adjective.* M16.
[ORIGIN from A-[11] + WEARY *adjective*.]
Tired, weary, (*of*).
■ Also **awearied** *adjective* E17.

aweather /əˈwɛðə/ *adverb, pred. adjective, & preposition.* L16.
[ORIGIN from A *preposition*[1] 1 + WEATHER *noun*.]
NAUTICAL. Towards the weather or windward side (of).

aweel /əˈwiːl/ *adverb. Scot.* E19.
[ORIGIN Weakened form of *ah well!*]
Well then, well.

aweigh /əˈweɪ/ *adverb & pred. adjective.* E17.
[ORIGIN from A *preposition*[1] 6 + WEIGH *noun*[1].]
NAUTICAL. Of an anchor: just raised perpendicularly above the ground in weighing. Of a ship, crew, etc.: just about to set sail.

†awent *verb pa. t.*: see AGO *verb*.

awesome /ˈɔːs(ə)m/ *adjective.* L16.
[ORIGIN from AWE *noun* + -SOME[1].]
1 Filled with awe. L16.
2 Inspiring awe. L17.
3 Outstanding, remarkable. *colloq.* M20. ▸**b** Excellent, marvellous. *slang.* L20.
■ **awesomely** *adverb* (**a**) so as to inspire awe; (**b**) *colloq.* outstandingly, very: L19. **awesomeness** *noun* L19.

awful /ˈɔːfʊl, *esp. in senses A.4, B* -f(ə)l/ *adjective & adverb.* OE.
[ORIGIN from AWE *noun* + -FUL.]
▸ **A** *adjective.* **I** Objectively.
1 Causing terror or dread; appalling. OE.

W. S. CHURCHILL The grim and awful cataclysm of war.

2 Worthy of or commanding profound respect or reverential fear or wonder. OE.

ADDISON Cato's character . . is rather awful than amiable.

3 Solemnly impressive, sublimely majestic. M17.

ANNE STEVENSON The great trees, as soon as they die, / immediately become ghosts, / stalk upright among the living with awful composure.

4 Notable of its kind (esp. in badness); exceedingly bad, long, etc. *colloq.* E19.

KEATS It is an awful while since you have heard from me. M. DRABBLE He likes such awful people. A. LURIE An awful, vulgar sport shirt . . , made of shiny green material.

▸ **II** Subjectively.
†**5** Terror-stricken; timid. L16–M18.

C. MARLOWE Monarch of hell under whose black survey Great potentates do kneel with awful fear.

6 Profoundly respectful or reverential. *arch.* L16.

GIBBON At an awful distance they cast away their garments. J. KEBLE Towards the East our awful greetings Are wafted.

▸ **B** *adverb.* = AWFULLY 3. *colloq.* E19.

A. TROLLOPE It is awful lonely here, too. R. D. PAINE A prairie town . . that looks awful good to me.

■ **awfulness** *noun* †(**a**) *rare* an awe-inspiring act; †(**b**) profound reverence, awe; (**c**) the quality of inspiring with awe; impressive solemnity; terribleness; *colloq.* poor quality: LME.

awfully /ˈɔːfʊli, *esp. in sense 3* -fli/ *adverb.* LME.
[ORIGIN from AWFUL + -LY[2].]
▸ **I** Objectively.
1 So as to cause terror. LME.
2 So as to cause reverential fear or wonder; majestically. LME.
3 Exceedingly; very much. *colloq.* E19.

G. B. SHAW Thanks awfully, old chap. JOYCE Pretend to want something awfully. SCOTT FITZGERALD I certainly am awfully glad to see you again.

▸ **II** Subjectively.
4 With a feeling of awe; fearfully; reverentially. *arch.* L16.

awhato /əˈwɛtəʊ, əˈwa-/ *noun. NZ.* Also **awheto** /əˈwɛtəʊ/. Pl. same, **-os**. L19.
[ORIGIN Maori.]
A caterpillar infested with a parasitic fungus of the genus *Cordyceps*, which reduces its host to 'mummified' form. Also called ***vegetable caterpillar***.

awheel /əˈwiːl/ *adverb & pred. adjective.* L19.
[ORIGIN from A-[2] + WHEEL *noun*.]
On wheels; on a bicycle.

awhile /əˈwʌɪl/ *adverb.* OE.
[ORIGIN Orig. two words, from A *adjective* + WHILE *noun*.]
For a short time.

awhirl /əˈwəːl/ *adverb & pred. adjective.* L19.
[ORIGIN from A-[2] + WHIRL *noun* or *verb*.]
In a whirl; whirling.

awing /əˈwɪŋ/ *adverb & pred. adjective.* E17.
[ORIGIN from A *preposition*[1] 1 + WING *noun*.]
On the wing; flying (*lit. & fig.*).

†awk *adjective, adverb, & noun.* Long *dial.* LME.
[ORIGIN Old Norse *afugr*, *of-* turned the wrong way, back foremost. For the phonetic devel. cf. HAWK *noun*[1].]
▸ **A** *adjective.* **1** In the wrong direction; back-handed. LME–M16.
2 Perverse; clumsy; awkward. LME–M19.
▸ **B** *adverb.* Backwards, in reverse order, confusedly; esp. in ***ring awk***, ring (bells) as a warning or summons. E17–M19.
▸ **C** *noun.* **1** Awkwardness; back-handedness. M–L17.
2 An awkward person. *rare.* Only in E19.

awkward /ˈɔːkwəd/ *adverb & adjective.* LME.
[ORIGIN from AWK *adjective* + -WARD.]
▸ **A** *adverb.* In the wrong direction; in reverse order; in a backwards direction; upside down. Long *obsolete* exc. *dial.* of an animal: on its back and unable to rise (cf. AWALD). LME.
▸ **B** *adjective.* †**1** Oblique; back-handed. E16–M19.
2 Froward, perverse, cantankerous, (passing into sense 7). Now *dial.* M16.
3 a Of a person: lacking dexterity, clumsy, bungling; ungainly, uncouth. M16. ▸**b** Of things and actions: clumsy; ill-adapted for use; ungainly. E17.

a SWIFT I have not seen a more clumsy, aukward, and unhandy people. J. IRVING Basketball and football players, great big awkward sorts of boys. **b** J. FRAME His body uncontrolled and his gait awkward. F. ORMSBY We laughed at your awkward dress. Your half-hearted passes at a fat waitress.

a awkward squad: see SQUAD *noun*[1] 1. **b the awkward age** adolescence.

†**4** Unfavourable; adverse. L16–M17.

SHAKES. *2 Hen. VI* Twice by awkward wind from England's bank Drove back again.

5 Of things or actions: causing embarrassment; inconvenient; reflecting embarrassment. E18.

J. O'HARA Frances's father . . had caught his daughter and Snyder in an awkward position and had given Snyder the choice of marriage or death. D. LODGE It was the most awkward time, about 6, just as I was about to serve up the dinner. W. TREVOR They didn't say anything, and after a few moments the silence hardened and became awkward.

6 Of a person: embarrassed; ill at ease. E18.

LEIGH HUNT He was . . beginning to feel awkward with his Whig friends.

7 Difficult or dangerous to deal with. M19.

J. TYNDALL We let ourselves down an awkward face of rock. G. ORWELL It was an awkward job getting the wounded down the narrow, crowded trench. B. HINES There's always someone you can't suit, who has to be awkward, who refuses to be interested in anything.

■ **awkwardish** *adjective* (*colloq.*) E17. **awkwardly** *adverb* LME. **awkwardness** *noun* L17.

awl /ɔːl/ *noun.*
[ORIGIN Old English *æl* = Old High German *ala* (German *Ahle*), Old Norse *alr*, of unknown origin.]
A small pointed tool for pricking or piercing holes, *esp.* such a tool used by shoemakers.
cobbler's awls: see COBBLER 1C.
– COMB.: **awl-bird** *dial.* (**a**) the green woodpecker; (**b**) the avocet; **awlwort** a cruciferous aquatic plant, *Subularia aquatica*, having white flowers and awl-shaped leaves.

awmous *noun* see ALMS.

awn /ɔːn/ *noun.* OE.
[ORIGIN Old Norse *agn-* oblique stem of *ǫgn* (Swedish *agn*, Danish *avn*) corresp. to late Old English *ægnan* (pl.), *egenu* husk, chaff, Old High German *agana* (German *Ahne*), Gothic *ahana* chaff.]
BOTANY. A bristle-like projection; *esp.* that terminating the grain sheath of barley, oats, and other grasses.
■ **awned** *adjective*[1] having an awn E19. **awnless** *adjective* L18. **awny** *adjective* (chiefly *Scot.*) bearded, bristly L18.

awn /ɔːn/ *verb*[1] *trans.* E19.
[ORIGIN from the noun.]
Remove the awns from.
■ **awner** *noun* a machine for awning grain. L19.

awn /ɔːn/ *verb*[2] *trans.* M19.
[ORIGIN Back-form. from AWNING.]
Cover with an awning.
■ **awned** *adjective*[2] = AWNINGED L19.

awning /ˈɔːnɪŋ/ *noun.* E17.
[ORIGIN Unknown.]
1 A sheet of canvas etc. forming a shelter against sun or rain, orig. on a ship's deck. E17.
2 The part of the poop deck of a ship which is continued forward beyond the bulkhead of the cabin. M18.
■ **awninged** *adjective* having an awning M19.

awoke, awoken *verbs* see AWAKE *verb.*

AWOL /*colloq.* ˈeɪwɒl/ *abbreviation.*
Absent without (official) leave.

awork /əˈwəːk/ *adverb & pred. adjective.* LME.
[ORIGIN from A *preposition*[1] 6 + WORK *noun.*]
At or to work; in activity.

awrong /əˈrɒŋ/ *adverb.* LME.
[ORIGIN from A *preposition*[1] 4 + WRONG *noun*[2].]
Wrong, in a wrong way.

awry /əˈrʌɪ/ *adverb & (usu. pred.) adjective.* LME.
[ORIGIN from A *preposition*[1] 6 + WRY *noun.*]
1 Oblique(ly); crooked(ly); uneven(ly); askew; askance. LME.

POPE Not Cynthia when her manteau's pinned awry, E'er felt such rage. C. DARWIN Some of our party began to squint and look awry. M. MITCHELL His new coat did not fit very well, for the tailor had been hurried and some of the seams were awry. I. MCEWAN The hair, so tightly drawn back before, was slightly awry.

2 Improper(ly); wrong; distorted(ly); amiss. L15.

E. B. BROWNING Those who think Awry, will scarce act straightly. CARLYLE Far worse, the marriage itself went awry. ARNOLD BENNETT Most invalids got their perspective awry.

AWS *abbreviation.*
Automatic warning system, a system of providing train drivers with audible indications regarding signals and where necessary applying brakes automatically.

aw-shucks /ɔːˈʃʌks/ *interjection, adjective, & verb.* Chiefly *N. Amer.* E20.
[ORIGIN from AW *interjection* + SHUCK *noun*[2] 3.]
▸ **A** *interjection.* Expr. mild disagreement, entreaty, embarrassment, self-deprecation, or similar sensations of unease. E20.

K. ATKINSON Whenever things started to get steamy . . he'd say things like 'Aw shucks,' and look embarrassed.

▸ **B** *adjective.* Of a person's manner etc.: awkward, self-deprecating, unsophisticated; supposedly typical of that of the inhabitants of rural North America. *colloq.* L20.

T. CLANCY The congressman would smile in his aw-shucks way.

▸ **C** *verb trans. & intrans.* Disparage (one's achievements); speak or behave with (esp. affected) awkwardness or self-deprecation. L20.

Sports Illustr. Ryan aw-shucksed his own achievement.

ax /aks/ *noun*[1]. Long *obsolete* exc. *dial.* Also **axe.**
[ORIGIN Old English *eax, æx* = Old Frisian *axe*, Old Saxon, Old High German *ahsa*, also Old Norse *ǫxull* (see AXLE), from Germanic.]
= AXLE.
– COMB.: **axtree** = AXLE-TREE.

ax *noun*[2], *verb*[1] vars. of AXE *noun*[1], *verb*[1].

ax *verb*[2] see ASK *verb.*

axal /ˈaks(ə)l/ *adjective.* Now *rare* or *obsolete.* E19.
[ORIGIN Irreg. from AXIS *noun*[1] + -AL[1].]
= AXIAL.

axe /aks/ *noun*[1]. Also ***ax.**
[ORIGIN Old English *æx* (*eax*), *æces* = Old Frisian *axa*, Old Saxon *akus* (Dutch *aaks*), Old High German *ackus* (German *Axt*), Old Norse *ǫx*, Gothic *aqizi*, from Germanic.]
1 A chopping tool, having a blade usu. of iron with a steel edge and a wooden handle. OE. ▸**b** *hist.* A battleaxe. ME. ▸**c** *hist.* An executioner's axe. LME. ▸**d** ARCHAEOLOGY. A double-edged or wedge-shaped stone implement. M19.
an axe to grind a private end to serve. ***battleaxe, double axe, poleaxe***, etc.
2 *the axe*, drastic reduction or elimination of expenditure, staff, etc.; abolition; dismissal. E20.

Sun David Ginola faces the axe from Aston Villa's squad. *Big Issue* Taxpayers' money . . didn't stop the axe falling on 200 printers.

3 A musical instrument used in jazz and rock music, *esp.* (orig.) a saxophone, (now) a guitar. *slang.* M20.
– COMB.: **axe-breaker** *Austral.* a tree, *Notelaea longifolia*, with very hard timber; **axe-grinding** *verbal noun & ppl adjective* serving a private end; **axe-hammer** a tool consisting of an axe and a hammer combined; **axe head** the cutting blade of an axe; **axeman** a person who works with an axe; *fig.* a man who cuts costs drastically or ruthlessly; *slang* a jazz or rock guitarist; **axemanship** skill in using an axe.

†**axe** *noun*[2]. M16–L18.
[ORIGIN French from Latin AXIS *noun*[1].]
= AXIS *noun*[1].

axe *noun*[3] var. of AX *noun*[1].

axe /aks/ *verb*[1] *trans.* Also ***ax.** L17.
[ORIGIN from AXE *noun*[1].]
1 Shape, trim, or strike with an axe. L17.
2 Cut down drastically (costs, services, etc.); eliminate, remove, abolish, dismiss. E20.

axe *verb*[2] see ASK *verb.*

axel /ˈaks(ə)l/ *noun.* Also **A-.** M20.
[ORIGIN from *Axel* Rudolph Paulser (1885–1938), Norwegian skater.]
SKATING. A 1½-turn jump from the forward outside edge of one skate to the backward outside edge of the other.

axenic /eɪˈzɛnɪk/ *adjective.* M20.
[ORIGIN from A-[10] + Greek *xenikos* alien, strange + -IC.]
BIOLOGY. Free from living organisms of any kind other than that stated or implied.
■ **axenically** *adverb* M20.

axes *nouns* pls. of AX *noun*[1], AXE *noun*[1], AXIS *noun*[1].

axial /ˈaksɪəl/ *adjective.* M19.
[ORIGIN from AXIS *noun*[1] + -AL[1].]
Of or pertaining to an axis; of the nature of or forming an axis; round or about an axis.
axial flow flow parallel to an axis of rotation (usu. (with hyphen) *attrib.* designating turbines etc. in which such flow occurs). ***axial vector***: see VECTOR *noun* 2a.
■ **axiˈality** *noun* L19. **axially** *adverb* M19.

axiate /ˈaksɪət/ *adjective.* E20.
[ORIGIN from AXIS *noun*[1] + -ATE[2].]
ZOOLOGY. = AXIAL.

axil /ˈaksɪl/ *noun.* L18.
[ORIGIN from Latin AXILLA.]
BOTANY. The upper angle between a leaf or petiole and the stem from which it springs, or between a branch and the trunk.

axile /ˈaksʌɪl/ *adjective.* E19.
[ORIGIN from AXIS *noun*[1] + -ILE.]
Axial; *esp.* (BOTANY) growing or occurring along an axis.

axilla /akˈsɪlə/ *noun.* Pl. **-llae** /-liː/. E17.
[ORIGIN Latin, dim. of *ala* wing.]
1 ANATOMY & ZOOLOGY. The region of the armpit; the corresponding part of a bird or other creature. E17.
2 BOTANY. = AXIL. *rare.* M19.

axillant /akˈsɪl(ə)nt/ *adjective.* L19.
[ORIGIN from AXILLA + -ANT[1].]
BOTANY. Of a leaf: growing at a particular axil.

axillar /akˈsɪlə/ *adjective & noun.* M16.
[ORIGIN from Latin AXILLA + -AR[1], after French *axillaire.*]
▸ **A** *adjective.* **1** = AXILLARY *adjective* 1. M16.
2 = AXILLARY *adjective* 2. *rare.* M19.
▸ **B** *noun.* Something axillary; *spec.* †(**a**) ANATOMY an axillary vein; (**b**) ORNITHOLOGY an axillary feather. E18.

axillary /akˈsɪləri/ *adjective & noun.* E17.
[ORIGIN from AXILLA + -ARY[2].]
▸ **A** *adjective.* **1** ANATOMY & ZOOLOGY. Of or pertaining to an axilla. E17.
2 BOTANY. Pertaining to, situated in, or growing from an axil. Opp. ***terminal.*** M18.
▸ **B** *noun.* Something axillary; *esp.* (ORNITHOLOGY) an axillary feather. L19.

axinite /ˈaksɪnʌɪt/ *noun.* E19.
[ORIGIN from Greek *axinē* axe + -ITE[1].]
MINERALOGY. A rock-forming triclinic silicate of the epidote group containing calcium, iron, manganese, aluminium, and boron, and occurring as brown or yellow, often large, crystals.

axinomancy /akˈsɪnəmansi/ *noun.* E17.
[ORIGIN Latin *axinomantia* from Greek *axinomanteia*, from *axinē* axe: see -MANCY.]
Divination by means of an axe head.

axiology /aksɪˈɒlədʒi/ *noun.* E20.
[ORIGIN French *axiologie*, from Greek *axia* value + -OLOGY.]
PHILOSOPHY. The theory of value.
■ **axioˈlogical** *adjective* E20. **axioˈlogically** *adverb* E20. **axiologist** *noun* M20.

axiom /ˈaksɪəm/ *noun.* L15.
[ORIGIN French *axiome* or Latin *axioma* from Greek = what is thought fitting, a self-evident principle (Aristotle), from *axios* worthy.]
1 An established or generally accepted principle; a maxim, a rule. L15.
†**2** LOGIC. A proposition (true or false). L16–M18.
3 MATH. A self-evident truth; a proposition on which an abstractly defined structure is based. L16.

axiomata media /aksɪˌɒmətə ˈmiːdɪə/ *noun phr. pl.* M19.
[ORIGIN mod. Latin (Bacon) = middle principles.]
PHILOSOPHY. Principles above simple empirical laws but below the highest generalizations or fundamental laws.

axiomatic /aksɪəˈmatɪk/ *adjective & noun.* L18.
[ORIGIN Greek *axiomatikos*, from *axiomat-, -ma*: see AXIOM, -ATIC.]
▸ **A** *adjective.* **1** Self-evident; indisputably true; of the nature of a maxim. L18.

H. SPENCER These axiomatic truths are truths recognized by the simplest order of reasoning. N. GORDIMER It's axiomatic the faults you see in others are often your own.

2 Characterized by self-evident principles. E19.

H. DAVY He gave an axiomatic form to the Science.

3 Full of maxims, aphoristic. M19.

SOUTHEY The most axiomatic of English Poets.

▸ **B** *noun.* In *pl.* (usu. treated as *sing.*). A body of axioms; the study or use of axioms. E20.

axiomatical /aksɪəˈmatɪk(ə)l/ *adjective.* Now *rare.* L16.
[ORIGIN formed as AXIOMATIC + -AL[1].]
†**1** LOGIC. Pertaining to, or of the nature of, a simple statement or proposition. L16–L17.
2 Of or pertaining to maxims, self-evident truths, or accepted first principles. L17.
3 = AXIOMATIC *adjective* 1. L17.
4 = AXIOMATIC *adjective* 3. M18.

axiomatically /aksɪəˈmatɪk(ə)li/ *adverb.* L16.
[ORIGIN from AXIOMATIC *adjective* or AXIOMATICAL: see -ICALLY.]
In an axiomatic manner; as an axiom.

axiomatize /aksɪˈɒmətʌɪz/ *verb.* Also **-ise.** E18.
[ORIGIN from AXIOMAT(IC *adjective* + -IZE.]
1 *verb intrans.* Make an axiom or axioms. *rare.* E18.
2 *verb trans.* Render axiomatic; reduce to a system of axioms. M20.
■ **axiomatiˈzation** *noun* M20.

axion /ˈaksɪɒn/ *noun.* L20.
[ORIGIN from AXIAL + -ON.]
PARTICLE PHYSICS. A light neutral pseudoscalar particle postulated in order to account for the rarity of processes which break charge-parity symmetry.

axis /ˈaksɪs/ *noun*[1]. Pl. **axes** /ˈaksiːz/. LME.
[ORIGIN Latin, rel. to Sanskrit *akṣa*, Greek *axōn*, Old Church Slavonic *osĭ*, Lithuanian *aszis*, and AX *noun*[1].]
▸ **I** Of rotation.
1 The imaginary straight line about which a body such as the earth rotates; the prolongation of that of the earth on which the heavens appear to revolve. LME.
2 The imaginary line by rotation about which a plane figure is conceived as generating a solid. L16.
†**3** An axle. E17–E19.
4 *fig.* **a** A central support or pivot. E17. ▸**b** An alliance between countries regarded as a pivot about which they and their associates revolve; *spec.* (**A-**) the alliance of 1939 between Germany and Italy, later extended to Japan and other countries; these countries collectively. Also *transf.*, (a link between) any two or more places, bodies, etc., acting or being considered together. M20.
5 ANATOMY. More fully ***axis vertebra***. The second cervical vertebra, upon which the head is turned. Formerly also, the odontoid process of this vertebra. L17.
▸ **II** A line from pole to pole; a principal direction of extension. (Passing into branch III.)
6 A straight line between the poles of a magnet. M17.
7 A main line of extension or growth, esp. (ANATOMY, ZOOLOGY, etc.) of (a part of) a body or organism; a central structure following this. M18. ▸**b** BOTANY. The central column of an inflorescence or other part; the main stem. L18. ▸**c** GEOLOGY. The direction of a linear feature such as a ridge, mountain range, or valley; *esp.* the line of intersection of the land surface with the plane bisecting a fold. M19.
▸ **III** Of symmetry or reference.
8 A straight line which divides a figure into two symmetrical parts, or with respect to which the parts of a body or system are symmetrically arranged. L17.
conjugate axis, major axis, minor axis, principal axis, etc.
9 Any of various lines or directions defined by the geometry of optical systems, or by the structure and physical properties of crystals. E18.
crystal axis: see CRYSTAL *adjective & noun.* ***optic axis***: see OPTIC *adjective.* ***visual axis***: see VISUAL *adjective.*
10 Each of a set of (usu. mutually perpendicular) lines used to define a system of coordinates, as in a graph. M19.
x-axis, y-axis, etc.

axis /ˈaksɪs/ *noun*[2]. Pl. same. E17.
[ORIGIN Latin (Pliny).]
= CHITAL. Also ***axis deer.***

axisymmetric /ˌaksɪsɪˈmɛtrɪk/ *adjective.* L19.
[ORIGIN from AXIS *noun*[1] + SYMMETRIC.]
Symmetrical with respect to an axis.
■ **axisymmetrical** *adjective* M20. **axiˈsymmetry** *noun* M20.

axle /ˈaks(ə)l/ *noun.* ME.
[ORIGIN formed as earlier AXLE-TREE.]
1 The centrepin or spindle upon which a wheel revolves or which revolves along with it. Also = AXLE-TREE 1. ME.

fig.: F. TUOHY Below them stood the Palace of Culture, an axle with the whole grey city gyrating around it.

axle tramp: see TRAMP *noun* 3b. ***wheel and axle***: see WHEEL *noun.*
†**2** = AXLE-TREE 3. M16–M19.

MILTON The earth . . With inoffensive pace that spinning sleeps On her soft Axle.

■ **axled** *adjective* having an axle (usu. as 2nd elem. of comb., of a specified type) M17.

axle-tooth /ˈaks(ə)ltuːθ/ *noun.* *obsolete* exc. *dial.* Pl. **-teeth** /-tiːθ/. L15.
[ORIGIN from Danish *axel* molar + TOOTH *noun*: cf. Danish *axel-tand*.]
A molar tooth.

axle-tree /ˈaks(ə)ltriː/ *noun.* ME.
[ORIGIN Old Norse *ǫxultré*, from *ǫxull* ult. formed as AX *noun*[1] + as TREE *noun*.]
1 A fixed bar or rod on the ends of which a pair of wheels of a vehicle revolve. ME.
†2 The spindle upon or with which a wheel revolves. LME–L17.
†3 = AXIS *noun*[1] 1; *poet.* the heaven, the sky. LME–M17.

Axminster /ˈaksmɪnstə/ *noun.* E19.
[ORIGIN A town in Devon, SW England.]
In full ***Axminster carpet***, ***Axminster rug***. A carpet or rug with a soft tufted cut pile of a type orig. manufactured at Axminster.

axo- /ˈaksəʊ/ *combining form* of Greek *axōn* axis or of AXON: see -O-.
■ **axolemma** *noun* [Greek *lemma* husk, skin] ANATOMY the plasma membrane of an axon L19. **axoˈnemal** *adjective* (BIOLOGY) of or pertaining to an axoneme M20. **axoneme** *noun* [Greek *nēma* thread] BIOLOGY a central strand of a locomotor organelle such as a cilium or flagellum E20. **axoplasm** *noun* the cytoplasm of an axon E20. **axopod** *noun* = AXOPODIUM M20. **axoˈpodium** *noun*, pl. **-ia** /-ɪə/, ZOOLOGY a rodlike pseudopodium having a central microtubular filament L19. **axostyle** *noun* (ZOOLOGY) a central flexible rod of microtubules present in certain flagellates E20. **aˈxotomous** *adjective* (MINERALOGY, now *rare* or *obsolete*) (having a cleavage) perpendicular to the axis of growth E19.

axolotl /ˈaksəlɒt(ə)l/ *noun.* L18.
[ORIGIN Nahuatl, from *atl* water + *xolotl* servant.]
Any of a number of Central American salamanders of the genus *Ambystoma* (esp. *A. mexicanum*), which live in lakes and retain many larval characters, including external gills, throughout life, although capable in certain conditions of developing full adult form.

axon /ˈaksɒn/ *noun.* Also **-one** /-əʊn/. M19.
[ORIGIN Greek *axōn* axis.]
ANATOMY. †1 The main axis of the body. M–L19.
2 A filamentous extension of a nerve cell, serving to conduct impulses to other cells. L19.
■ **aˈxonal** *adjective* E20. **aˈxonic** *adjective* M20.

axonometric /ˌaks(ə)nə(ʊ)ˈmɛtrɪk/ *adjective.* E20.
[ORIGIN from Greek *axōn* axis + -O- + -METRIC.]
Of a (method of) pictorial representation: using an orthographic projection of the object on a plane inclined to each of the three principal axes of the object.

axunge /ˈaksʌndʒ/ *noun.* Now *rare.* M16.
[ORIGIN French †*axunge* (now *axonge*) from Latin *axungia* axle-grease, formed as AXIS *noun*[1] + *ung-* of *ungere* to grease.]
The internal fat of an animal's kidneys etc.; lard or goose grease; *gen.* fat, grease.

ay *adverb*[1] & *noun*[1] var. of AYE *adverb*[1] & *noun*[1].

ay *adverb*[2], *interjection*[1], & *noun*[2] var. of AYE *adverb*[2], *interjection*, & *noun*[2].

ay /ʌɪ/ *interjection*[2]. Also (earlier) †**ey**. ME.
[ORIGIN Natural exclam.; *ay me* is prob. modelled on Old French *aimi* or Italian *ahimè*, Spanish *ay de mi*.]
1 Expr. surprise or earnestness. Now *N. English.* ME.
2 ***ay me!***: expr. regret, sorrow, or pity. M16.

ayah /ˈʌɪə/ *noun.* L18.
[ORIGIN Portuguese *aia* fem. of *aio* tutor.]
A nurse or maidservant, esp. of Europeans in India, SE Asia, etc.

ayahuasca /ʌɪəˈwaskə/ *noun.* M20.
[ORIGIN S. Amer. Spanish from Quechua *ayawáskha*, from *aya* corpse + *waskha* vine, creeper.]
1 Any of various South American vines of the genus *Banisteriopsis* (family Malpighiaceae), noted for their hallucinogenic properties. M20.
2 A hallucinogenic drink prepared from the bark of such a vine. M20.

ayatollah /ʌɪəˈtɒlə/ *noun.* Also (as a title) **A-**. M20.
[ORIGIN Persian from Arabic *ʾāyatu-llāh* miraculous sign of God.]
A Shiite religious leader in Iran; *fig.* a dogmatic leader, an influential or powerful person.

aye /eɪ, ʌɪ/ *adverb*[1] & *noun*[1]. Now *arch.* & *Scot.* Also **ay**. ME.
[ORIGIN Old Norse *ei*, *ey* = Old English *ā*, Old Saxon *eo*, Old High German *eo*, *io* (German *je*), Gothic *aiws* age, eternity, from Germanic, rel. to Latin *aevum* age, Greek *aie(i)* ever, *aiōn* AEON.]
▸ **A** *adverb.* Ever, always; at all times. ME.

R. BURNS And ay the ale was growing better. OED Things grew ay the longer, the waur [worse]. L. G. GIBBON But poor folk aye have to work.

– COMB.: **aye-green** *dial.* a houseleek.
▸ **B** *noun.* ***for aye***, (expanded ***for ever and aye***), for ever, for all time. ME.

aye /ʌɪ/ *adverb*[2], *interjection*, & *noun*[2]. Also **ay**; orig. †**I**. L16.
[ORIGIN Prob. I *pronoun* expr. assent.]
▸ **A** *adverb & interjection.* Yes. Now *arch.* & *dial.* exc. NAUTICAL & in formal voting. L16.

W. OWEN Proud to see him going, aye, and glad. L. G. GIBBON There were cries *Rob, what about a song now, man?* And Rob said, *Och, ay, I'll manage that fine.* A. L. KENNEDY 'You ready for your tea now?' 'Aye.'

aye, aye, sir! NAUTICAL: I understand and will carry out your order.
▸ **B** *noun.* Pl. **ayes**. An affirmative answer or vote. L16.
the ayes have it affirmative voters are in the majority.

aye-aye /ˈʌɪˌʌɪ/ *noun.* L18.
[ORIGIN French from Malagasy *aiay*.]
An insectivorous tree-dwelling primate of Madagascar, *Daubentonia madagascariensis*, which is closely related to the lemurs and has a narrow elongated finger on each hand for prising insects from bark.

ayle *noun* var. of AIEL.

Aylesbury /ˈeɪlzb(ə)ri/ *noun.* M19.
[ORIGIN A town in Buckinghamshire, central England.]
In full ***Aylesbury duck***. (A bird of) a breed of white domestic duck.

Aymara /ˈʌɪmərɑː/ *noun.* M19.
[ORIGIN Bolivian Spanish: cf. Spanish *aimará*.]
1 A member of a S. American Indian people of Bolivia and Peru near Lake Titicaca. M19.
2 The language of this people, related to Quechua. M19.

†**ayne** *noun* & *adjective* var. of EIGNE.

ayont /əˈjɒnt/ *preposition. dial.* Also **-nd** /-nd/. E18.
[ORIGIN from A-[2] + BEYOND, after *afore*, *before*.]
Beyond, on the other side of.

ayre *noun* see AIR *noun*[1].

Ayrshire /ˈɛːʃə/ *noun.* M19.
[ORIGIN A former county in SW Scotland.]
In full ***Ayrshire bull***, ***Ayrshire cow***, ***Ayrshire cattle***, etc. (An animal of) a breed of mainly white dairy cattle.

Ayurveda /ˌɑːjʊəˈveɪdə, -ˈviːdə/ *noun.* L18.
[ORIGIN Sanskrit *āyur-veda*, from *āyus* life + *veda* (sacred) knowledge.]
The traditional Hindu system of medicine, which is based on the idea of balance in bodily systems and uses diet, herbal treatment, and yogic breathing.
■ **Ayurvedic** *adjective* of or pertaining to the Hindu medical tradition (opp. UNANI) E20.

AZ *abbreviation.*
Arizona.

aza- /ˈeɪzə/ *combining form.*
[ORIGIN from AZO-.]
Used in CHEMISTRY to indicate the presence of a nitrogen atom in a molecular ring or chain.

azalea /əˈzeɪlɪə/ *noun.* M18.
[ORIGIN mod. Latin from Greek, use as noun of fem. of *azaleos* dry (because flourishing in dry soil).]
Any of a large group of rhododendrons, most of which are deciduous.
mountain azalea, **trailing azalea** a pink-flowered evergreen alpine shrub, *Loiseleuria procumbens*, of the heath family.

azan *noun* var. of ADHAN.

Azande *noun* & *adjective* see ZANDE.

azarole /ˈazərəʊl/ *noun.* M17.
[ORIGIN French *azerole*, †*aza-* from Spanish *azarolla*, *acerola* from Hispano-Arabic *az-zaʿrūra*: see AL-[2].]
(The edible fruit of) the tree *Crataegus azarolus*, related to the hawthorn and native to the eastern Mediterranean region.

azedarac /əˈzɛdərak/ *noun.* M18.
[ORIGIN French *azédarac* from Spanish *acedaraque* from Arabic *ʾāzād-diraḵt* from Persian *ʾāzād* free, *diraḵt* tree.]
A tall Asian tree, *Melia azedarach* (family Meliaceae), bearing fragrant lilac flowers. Also called ***bead-tree***, ***China tree***.

azelaic /azɪˈleɪɪk/ *adjective.* M19.
[ORIGIN from AZO- (since nitric acid was involved in its orig. preparation) + Greek *elaion* oil + -IC.]
CHEMISTRY. ***azelaic acid***, a solid fatty acid obtained by oxidizing various fats (such as castor oil) and present in rancid fat; nonanedioic acid, $HOOC(CH_2)_7COOH$.

azeotropic /ˌeɪzɪəˈtrəʊpɪk, -ˈtrɒp-, əˌziːə-/ *adjective.* E20.
[ORIGIN from A-[10] + Greek *zeo-*, *zein* to boil + -TROPIC.]
CHEMISTRY. Of a mixture of liquids: having a constant boiling point during distillation; of or pertaining to such a mixture.
■ **azeotrope** /ˈeɪzɪətrəʊp, əˈziːə-/ *noun* an azeotropic mixture E20. **azeˈotropism**, **azeˈotropy** *nouns* azeotropic behaviour E20.

Azerbaijani /ˌazəbʌɪˈdʒɑːni/ *noun* & *adjective.* L19.
[ORIGIN from *Azerbaijan* (see below) + -I[2].]
▸ **A** *noun.* A member of a people of Azerbaijan, in SW Asia; the Turkic language of this people. L19.
▸ **B** *attrib.* or as *adjective.* Of or pertaining to the Azerbaijanis or their language. L19.

azide /ˈeɪzʌɪd/ *noun.* E20.
[ORIGIN from AZO- + -IDE.]
CHEMISTRY. A salt or ester of hydrazoic acid, HN_3.

azidothymidine /ˌeɪzɪdəʊˈθʌɪmɪdiːn, eɪˌzʌɪdəʊ-/ *noun.* L20.
[ORIGIN from AZIDE + -O- + THYMIDINE.]
= ZIDOVUDINE.

Azilian /əˈzɪlɪən/ *adjective & noun.* L19.
[ORIGIN from Mas d'Azil in the French Pyrenees, where remains were found, + -IAN.]
ARCHAEOLOGY. (Of or pertaining to) a culture of the transition period between the Palaeolithic and Mesolithic ages in southern France and northern Spain, following the Magdalenian.

azimuth /ˈazɪməθ/ *noun.* LME.
[ORIGIN Old French & mod. French *azimut* from Arabic *as-samt*, from AL-[2] + *samt* way, direction: see ZENITH.]
1 An arc of a celestial great circle extending from the zenith to the horizon. Now only in ***azimuth circle***, a great circle passing through the zenith. LME.
2 Horizontal angular distance of such an arc (usu. that passing through a given celestial object) from the north or south point. E17.
3 Horizontal angle or direction; compass bearing. M17.
■ **azimuthal** /azɪˈmjuːθ(ə)l/ *adjective* of, pertaining to, or used in measuring azimuth; measured in azimuth: M17. **aziˈmuthally** *adverb* M19.

azine /ˈeɪziːn/ *noun.* L19.
[ORIGIN from AZO- + -INE[5].]
CHEMISTRY. 1 Any organic compound containing the group =N–N=. L19.
2 Any (usu. polycyclic) organic compound containing a six-membered ring with two nitrogen atoms occupying opposite positions. Usu. *attrib.*, denoting dyestuffs based on such structures. L19.

azo- /ˈeɪzəʊ/ *combining form.*
[ORIGIN from AZOTE.]
CHEMISTRY. Indicating the presence of nitrogen in a compound, *spec.* as the group –N=N– joined to two carbon atoms. Freq. as attrib. adjective **azo**, as ***azo compound***, ***azo group***, etc.
■ **azoˈbenzene** *noun* a synthetic crystalline compound, $(C_6H_5)N{=}N(C_6H_5)$, used chiefly in dye manufacture L19. **azo colour**, **azo dye** *nouns* any of a large class of dyestuffs which contain the azo group, made by coupling of diazonium compounds L19. **azoˈmethine** *noun* any compound having the general formula $R^1R^2C{=}NR^3$; a Schiff base: L19. **azoˈprotein** *noun* (BIOCHEMISTRY) a protein coupled to another molecule by an azo group E20.

azoic /əˈzəʊɪk, eɪ-/ *adjective*[1]. M19.
[ORIGIN from Greek *azōos* + -IC: see A-[10], ZOIC.]
Having no trace of life, or organic remains; *spec.* (GEOLOGY) referring to the early Precambrian era.

azoic /eɪˈzəʊɪk/ *adjective*[2]. L19.
[ORIGIN French *azoïque*: see AZO-, -IC.]
CHEMISTRY. Orig. (*rare*) = AZO- used adjectivally. Now *spec.* designating a class of water-insoluble azo dyes made by coupling their components on the fibre; pertaining to or using such dyes.

azole /ˈeɪzəʊl/ *noun.* L19.
[ORIGIN from AZO- + -OLE[2].]
CHEMISTRY. Any organic compound having a five-membered ring containing at least two hetero-atoms of which at least one is nitrogen.

azolla /əˈzɒlə/ *noun.* L19.
[ORIGIN mod. Latin, from Greek *azein* to dry + *ollunai* slay.]
A floating mosslike fern of the genus *Azolla*.

azonal /eɪˈzəʊn(ə)l, ə-/ *adjective.* L19.
[ORIGIN from A-[10] + ZONAL: cf. AZONIC.]
Having no zonal arrangement or structure; *esp.* (of soils) lacking distinct horizons.

azonic /eɪˈzɒnɪk, ə-/ *adjective.* L18.
[ORIGIN from Greek *azōnos* formed as A-[10] + *zonē* ZONE *noun*, + -IC.]
Not confined to a zone, not local.

azoospermia /ˌeɪzəʊəˈspəːmɪə, əˈzəʊ-/ *noun.* L19.
[ORIGIN from A-[10] + ZOOSPERM + -IA[1].]
MEDICINE. Absence of motile sperms in the semen. Cf. ASPERMIA.

azotaemia /azəˈtiːmɪə/ *noun.* Also *-**temia**. E20.
[ORIGIN from AZOTE + -AEMIA.]
MEDICINE. The presence of excessive urea or other nitrogenous waste products in the blood.
■ **azotaemic** *adjective* pertaining to or affected with azotaemia M20.

azote /ˈazəʊt/ *noun. arch.* L18.
[ORIGIN French, from Greek A-[10] + *zōē* life.]
Nitrogen.
■ †**azotic** *adjective* of, pertaining to, or combined with nitrogen; nitric: L18–M19. **azotize** *verb trans.* (now *rare*) nitrogenize E19.

azotea /aθoˈtea, az-/ *noun.* E19.
[ORIGIN Spanish, from Arabic *saṭḥ* or *suṭayḥa*.]
The flat terrace roof of a house in Spain and Spanish-speaking countries.

azotemia *noun* see AZOTAEMIA.

A

azoth /ˈazəʊθ, ˈazɒθ/ *noun*. L15.
[ORIGIN Hispano-Arabic *az-zūq* from Arabic *az-zāwūq*: see AL-[2].]
(The alchemists' name for) mercury, as the first principle of metals. Also, Paracelsus' universal remedy.

azotobacter /əˈzəʊtəbaktə/ *noun*. E20.
[ORIGIN mod. Latin (see below), formed as AZOTE + -O- + BACTER(IUM.]
An aerobic nitrogen-fixing bacterium of the genus *Azotobacter*.

azoturia /ˌazəˈtjʊərɪə/ *noun*. M19.
[ORIGIN from AZOTE + -URIA.]
MEDICINE. The presence of excessive urea or other nitrogenous substances in the urine.

azoxy- /əˈzɒksi/ *combining form*. Also as attrib. adjective **azoxy**.
[ORIGIN from AZO- + OXY-.]
CHEMISTRY. Designating or containing the group $\cdot N_2O \cdot$.

AZT *abbreviation*.
PHARMACOLOGY. (Proprietary name for) azidothymidine.

Aztec /ˈaztɛk/ *noun & adjective*. L18.
[ORIGIN French *Aztèque* or Spanish *Azteca*, from Nahuatl *aztecatl* person from Aztlan (their legendary place of origin).]
▸ **A** *noun*. **1** A member of the native American people dominant in Mexico until its conquest by Cortes in 1519. L18.
2 The language of the Aztecs. E19.
▸ **B** *adjective*. Of or pertaining to the Aztecs or their language. E19.
Aztec hop, **Aztec revenge**, **Aztec two-step** *colloq*. diarrhoea suffered by visitors to Mexico.
■ **Aztecan** *adjective* L19.

azuki *noun* var. of ADZUKI.

azulejo /azjʊˈleɪhəʊ, aθuˈlexo/ *noun*. Pl. **-os** /-əʊz, -ɔs/. M19.
[ORIGIN Spanish, from *azul* blue (see AZURE *noun & adjective*).]
A kind of glazed coloured tile used in Spanish buildings.

azulene /ˈazjʊliːn/ *noun*. L19.
[ORIGIN from Spanish *azul* blue + -ENE.]
CHEMISTRY. A blue liquid hydrocarbon, $C_{10}H_8$, which has a molecule containing a five- and a seven-membered ring fused together, and occurs in some natural oils. Also, any hydrocarbon having this bicyclic structure.

azuline /ˈazjʊliːn/ *noun*. M19.
[ORIGIN App. from Spanish *azulino* bluish, from *azul* blue.]
A shade of blue, esp. as a fashion colour.

azure /ˈaʒə, -ʒj(ʊ)ə, -zjʊə; ˈeɪ-/ *noun & adjective*. ME.
[ORIGIN Old French *asur*, (also mod.) *azur* (cogn. with Portuguese, Spanish *azul*, Italian *azzurro*) from medieval Latin *azzurum*, *azolum* from Arabic *al-lāzaward*, formed as AL-[2] + Persian *lāžward* lapis lazuli.]
▸ **A** *noun*. **1** A bright blue pigment or dye; ultramarine. Now *rare*. ME.
2 *HERALDRY*. Blue (represented in engraving by horizontal lines). ME.
3 The semi-precious stone lapis lazuli (from which ultramarine is made). *arch*. LME.
4 The blue colour of the unclouded sky (orig. the deep intense blue of more southern latitudes, now the soft clear bright blue of more northern latitudes). L15.
5 The unclouded vault of heaven. M17.

MILTON Not like those steps On Heavens Azure. *fig.*: CARLYLE Borne aloft into the azure of Eternity.

▸ **B** *adjective*. **1** *HERALDRY*. Blue. LME.
2 Of the colour azure. E16.
3 [After Latin *caeruleus*.] Designating or pertaining to a sea god or river god. *poet*. L17.

POPE An azure sister of the main.

4 *fig*. Cloudless; serene. E19.
5 *BOOKBINDING*. Of a tooled or stamped design: composed of horizontal parallel lines. Of a tool: used to produce such a design. (Cf. sense A.2 above.) L19.

■ **azury** *adjective* of a colour resembling azure, tinted with azure E17.

azure /ˈaʒə, -ʒj(ʊ)ə, -zjʊə; ˈeɪ-/ *verb trans*. ME.
[ORIGIN from AZURE *noun & adjective*: cf. French *azurer*, *azuré*.]
1 As ***azured*** *ppl adjective*. = AZURE *adjective*. *obsolete* exc. *BOOKBINDING*. ME.
2 Paint, dye, or colour azure. LME.

azurine /ˈaʒʊrʌɪn, -ʒj(ʊ)ər-, -zjʊər-; ˈeɪ-/ *adjective*. Now *rare*. M16.
[ORIGIN French *azurin*: see AZURE *noun & adjective*, -INE[1].]
Of an azure colour.

azurite /ˈaʒʊrʌɪt, -ʒj(ʊ)ər-, -zjʊər-/ *noun*. E19.
[ORIGIN from AZURE *noun & adjective* + -ITE[1].]
MINERALOGY. †**1** = LAZULITE. Only in E19.
2 A monoclinic basic copper carbonate found as blue prisms or crystal masses, usu. with malachite. E19.

azygos /ˈazɪɡəs/ *noun & adjective*. As adjective also **-gous**. M17.
[ORIGIN from Greek *azugos*, from A-[10] + *zugon* yoke: see -OUS.]
Chiefly *ANATOMY*. (An organic part, esp. a vein) that is not one of a pair.
azygos vein a large vein of the right posterior thorax, draining into the superior vena cava.

azyme /ˈazɪm, -ʌɪm/ *noun*. L16.
[ORIGIN ecclesiastical Latin *azymus* adjective, *-ma* noun pl. from ecclesiastical Greek *azumos*, *ta azuma* noun phr. pl., from A-[10] + *zumē* leaven.]
(A cake or loaf of) unleavened bread, esp. as used by Jews at Passover or by Christians of the Western Church in the Eucharist.

Azymite /ˈazɪmʌɪt/ *noun*. E18.
[ORIGIN medieval Latin *azymita* from medieval Greek *azumitēs*, from *azumos*: see AZYME, -ITE[1].]
ECCLESIASTICAL HISTORY. (A contemptuous name used by the Orthodox Church for) a member of any of the Western Christian Churches which administer the Eucharist with unleavened bread. Cf. PROZYMITE.

Bb

B, b /biː/.
The second letter of the modern English alphabet and of the ancient Roman one, corresp. to Greek *beta*, Hebrew *beth*. The sound normally represented by the letter is a voiced bilabial plosive consonant. Pl. **B's, Bs**.
▸ **I 1** The letter and its sound.
not know a B from a BATTLEDORE.
▸ **II** Symbolical uses.
2 Used to denote serial order; applied e.g. to the second group or section, sheet of a book, etc.
B-DNA *BIOCHEMISTRY* the commonest form of DNA, in which the base pairs are almost at right angles to the axis of the double helix.
3 *MUSIC.* (Cap. B.) The seventh note of the diatonic scale of C major (in German notation repr. by H, B repr. English B flat). Also, the scale of a composition with B as its keynote.
4 The second hypothetical person or example.
from A to B: see A, A 6.
5 *MATH.* (Usu. italic *b*.) The second known quantity.
6 (Usu. cap. B.) Designating the second or second-highest class (of road, academic marks, population as regards affluence, etc.).
B-film, -movie, -picture a film made for use as a supporting feature in a cinema programme. **B-side** (the music of) the less important side of a gramophone record. **B Special** *hist.* a member of a paid occasional special police force in Northern Ireland.
7 (Cap. B.) The blood group characterized by the presence of the agglutinogen designated B and the absence of that designated A.
AB: see A, A 9.
8 (Cap. B.) Designating a series of international standard paper sizes with a fixed shape and twice the area of the next size, as ***B0, B1, B2, B3, B4***, etc.
9 *PHYSIOLOGY.* ***B-lymphocyte*** [from B(URSA, referring to the organ in birds where such cells were first identified], a lymphocyte not processed by the thymus gland, and responsible for producing antibodies.
▸ **III 10** Abbrevs.: **B.** = Bachelor or [Latin] *baccalaureus* (in academic degrees); Blessed; British. **B** = bar (in ***B-girl*** (*US slang*) a bar girl); (*PHYSICS*) bel(s); (*CHESS*) bishop; black (of pencil lead); (*CHEMISTRY*) boron; bomber (in designations of US aircraft types). **b.** = (*colloq.*) bastard, bugger (as a euphemism sometimes printed ***b***—); billion; born; (*CRICKET*) bowled by, bye(s). **b** = (*NUCLEAR PHYSICS*) barn; (*PARTICLE PHYSICS*) beauty, bottom.

BA *abbreviation.*
1 Bachelor of Arts.
2 British Academy.
3 British Airways.
4 British Association (for the Advancement of Science).

Ba *symbol.*
CHEMISTRY. Barium.

ba /bɑː/ *noun.* L19.
[ORIGIN Egyptian.]
The soul of a person or god which, according to the ancient Egyptians, survived after death but had to be sustained with offerings of food, typically represented as a human-headed bird. Cf. KA.

BAA *abbreviation.*
British Airports Authority.

baa /bɑː/ *noun & verb.* E16.
[ORIGIN Imit.]
▸ **A** *noun.* The bleat of a sheep or lamb. E16.
– COMB.: **baa-lamb** (a child's name for) a lamb.
▸ **B** *verb intrans.* Pa. t. & pple **baaed, baa'd**. Esp. of a sheep: bleat. L16.

Baal /ˈbeɪəl/ *noun.* Pl. **-im** /-ɪm/. LME.
[ORIGIN Hebrew *Ba'al* from Canaanite, = lord.]
A Phoenician or Canaanite god; *gen.* a false god.
■ **Baalism** *noun* the worship of Baal; idolatry: E17. **Baalist** *noun* a worshipper of Baal, an idolater E17. **Baalite** *noun* = BAALIST M17.

baal teshuvah /bɑːl təˈʃuːvə/ *noun.* M20.
[ORIGIN Hebrew, lit. 'master returner', from BAAL + *tšuba* returner.]
JUDAISM. A repentant sinner, *esp.* a person who has returned to Judaism; now *spec.*, one who has returned to or taken up Orthodox Judaism.

baas /bɑːs/ *noun.* E17.
[ORIGIN Dutch: see BOSS *noun*[4].]
†**1** A Dutch sea captain; a Dutch foreman etc. E–M17.
2 A (usu. white) employer, master, foreman, etc. Freq. as a form of address. *S. Afr.* Now regarded as *offensive*. L18.

Z. MDA He cannot just summon me as if he is the baas.

baasskap /ˈbɑːskap/ *noun.* *S. Afr.* M20.
[ORIGIN Afrikaans from Dutch *baasschap*, formed as BAAS + *-schap* -SHIP.]
Domination, esp. of non-whites by whites.

Baath /bɑːθ/ *noun.* Also **Ba'ath** & other vars. M20.
[ORIGIN Arabic *ba'ṯ* lit. 'resurrection'.]
More fully ***Baath party*** etc. A pan-Arabic socialist movement founded in Syria in the early 1940s.
■ **Baathism** *noun* the beliefs of the Baath party M20. **Baathist** *noun & adjective* (a member or supporter) of the Baath party M20.

bab *noun* see BABE.

baba /ˈbɑːbɑː/ *noun*[1]. E19.
[ORIGIN French from Polish, lit. 'married (peasant) woman'.]
A rich sponge cake; *spec.* (more fully ***rum baba***) one served in a rum syrup.

Baba /ˈbaba/ *noun*[2]. Also ***b-***. M19.
[ORIGIN Malay.]
In Malaysia, a Straits-born person of Chinese descent.

babaco /bəˈbɑːkəʊ/ *noun.* Pl. **-os**. E20.
[ORIGIN S. Amer. Spanish.]
An Ecuadorian tree, *Carica pentagona*, related to the papaya or pawpaw; the large yellow fruit of this tree, similar in shape to a marrow.

babacoote /ˈbabəkuːt/ *noun.* L19.
[ORIGIN Malagasy *babakoto* lit. 'father-child'.]
= INDRI.

baba ganoush /ˌbɑːbə ɡaˈnuːʃ/ *noun phr.* Also **baba ghanouj** /ɡaˈnuːʒ/ & other vars. M20.
[ORIGIN Arabic *bābā ghannūj* father of coquetry, from *bābā* father + *ghanj* coquetry, flirtation; perh. in reference to its supposed invention by a member of a royal harem.]
A Middle Eastern dish of puréed roasted aubergines, tahini, olive oil, lemon, and garlic.

babalaas /ˈbabəlas, -lɑːs/ *noun & adjective.* *S. Afr. colloq.* M20.
[ORIGIN Afrikaans, from Zulu *ibhabhalazi*.]
▸ **A** *noun.* A hangover. M20.
▸ **B** *adjective.* Suffering from a hangover, hung-over. M20.

babassu /babəˈsuː/ *noun.* Also **babaçú**. E20.
[ORIGIN Brazilian Portuguese *babaçú* from Tupi *ybá* fruit + *guasu* large.]
A palm of the genus *Orbignya*, native to NE Brazil and yielding an edible oil.

babbitt /ˈbabɪt/ *noun*[1] *& verb.* Also **B-**. L19.
[ORIGIN Isaac *Babbitt* (1799–1862), US inventor.]
▸ **A** *noun.* Any of a group of usu. tin-based alloys used for antifriction linings in bearings. Also more fully ***babbitt metal***. L19.
▸ **B** *verb trans.* Line with babbitt. L19.

Babbitt /ˈbabɪt/ *noun*[2]. E20.
[ORIGIN (The hero of) a novel by Sinclair Lewis, 1922.]
A materialistic and complacent businessman conforming to the standards of his set.
■ **Babbittry, -itry** *noun* the Philistine behaviour of a Babbitt E20.

babblative /ˈbablətɪv/ *adjective.* L16.
[ORIGIN from BABBLE *verb* + -ATIVE.]
Inclined to babble, loquacious.

babble /ˈbab(ə)l/ *noun.* Also †**bable**. L15.
[ORIGIN from the verb. Cf. French *babil*.]
1 Idle, foolish, or inopportune talk; (esp. as 2nd elem. of comb.) pretentious jargon. L15.

CARLYLE A great deal of unwise babble on this subject.

psychobabble, ***technobabble***, etc.
2 Confused murmur or noise, as of many voices heard at once, a stream, etc. E17.

W. MORRIS Nought he seemed to hear Save the brook's babble. G. F. NEWMAN The general babble of conversation didn't decrease . . but a few heads turned. P. ACKROYD The babble of voices was indescribable.

3 Inarticulate speech, as of infants. M17.

C. DARWIN Man has an instinctive tendency to speak, as we see in the babble of our young children.

4 *TELEPHONY.* Crosstalk from conversations on other lines. M20.

babble /ˈbab(ə)l/ *verb.* Also †**bable**. ME.
[ORIGIN Prob. from Middle Low German (Dutch) *babbelen*, or a parallel native imit. formation; cf. French *babiller* prattle, from onomatopoeic base *bab-*.]
1 *verb intrans.* Talk childishly, prattle; talk incoherently or foolishly; utter meaningless words. ME.

R. B. SHERIDAN They only babble who practise not reflection.

2 *verb intrans.* Utter inarticulate or indistinct sounds, like a child; (of a stream, bird, etc.) produce a more or less continuous succession of indistinct sounds. LME.

W. JONES Echo babling by the mountain's side.

babbling brook *Austral. & NZ rhyming slang* a cook, esp. for a camp or for an isolated group of shepherds, musterers, etc.
3 *verb intrans.* Talk excessively or inopportunely; prate. LME.

E. F. BENSON Maud sat quite silent, while Lucia babbled on. J. THURBER An eccentric elderly woman who babbled of her recently inherited fortune.

4 *verb trans.* Repeat or utter with meaningless iteration; utter incoherently or foolishly. L15.

QUILLER-COUCH His lips happily babbling the curses that the ships' captains had taught him. R. KIPLING He babbled tales of oppression and wrong till the tears ran down his cheeks.

5 *verb trans.* Reveal (a secret etc.) by talking. M16.

I. D'ISRAELI The queen . . impatiently babbled the plot. R. DAVIES Didn't you yourself babble out all the secrets of your life to me?

■ **babblement** *noun* babble; idle chatter, incoherent or meaningless talk: M17. **babblingly** *adverb* in a babbling manner, with babbling E17.

babbler /ˈbablə/ *noun.* M16.
[ORIGIN from BABBLE *verb* + -ER[1].]
1 A foolish or idle talker, a chatterer. M16.
2 A gossip, a teller of secrets. L16.
3 A foxhound that gives tongue too freely. M18.
4 Any of a large group of Old World passerine birds (belonging to the family Timaliidae) with loud chattering voices. M19.
5 = ***babbling brook*** s.v. BABBLE *verb* 2. *Austral. & NZ slang.* E20.

babby *noun* see BABY *noun*.

babe /beɪb/ *noun.* Also (now *dial.*) **bab** /bab/. LME.
[ORIGIN Prob. a contr. of an imit. form derived from childish utterance, similar to *mama*, *papa*: cf. Middle English *baban*.]
1 A young child, a baby. Chiefly *biblical & arch.* LME.

S. VICKERS Innocent as a new-born babe.

babe in arms a newborn baby. ***babe of clouts***: see CLOUT *noun*[1] 4. ***milk for babes***: see MILK *noun* 3a.
2 A childish, inexperienced, or guileless person. E16.
babe in Christ a person newly converted to Christianity. **babes in the wood** [with ref. to the old ballad *The Children in the Wood*] inexperienced persons.
†**3** A doll or puppet. Cf. BABY *noun* 2. M–L16.
4 An attractive girl or young woman. Also, an affectionate form of address for a lover. *colloq.* E20.

Cosmopolitan A sexy young babe. E. NOBLE I'm not going to make it back, babe, I'm afraid.

babel /ˈbeɪb(ə)l/ *noun & adjective.* Also **B-**. E16.
[ORIGIN *Babel*, the city and tower where the confusion of tongues took place (*Genesis* 11), = Hebrew *bāḇel* Babylon, from Akkadian *bāb ili* gate of God.]
▸ **A** *noun.* **1** A confused medley of sounds; meaningless noise. E16.

ALAN ROSS Their words are a Babel whose meaning is plain— The shadow of Cain has been thrown on to Abel. TOLKIEN There was a hoot of snarling horns and a babel of baying voices.

2 A scene of confusion; a noisy assembly. E17.

SWIFT The whole babel of sectaries joined against the church. S. GIBBONS A babel broke out, in which Aunt Ada could dimly be discerned beating at everybody.

3 (**B-**.) A lofty structure; a visionary project. M17.

MILTON And still with vain designe New Babels, had they wherewithall, would build.

▸ **B** *attrib.* or as *adjective.* Confused, turbulent; lofty, visionary. M17.

DICKENS Babel towers of chimneys. E. H. W. MEYERSTEIN I never thought I should come round to Eliot as a poet. Here he has dropped his Poundian Babel-tongues.

■ **babelish** *adjective* noisily confused E17. **babelism** *noun* noisy confusion of speech; a strange utterance: M19. **babelize** *verb trans.* make a babel of E17.

†**babery** *noun.* LME–L18.
[ORIGIN Perh. var. of BABOONERY, assim. to BABE: see -ERY.]
Absurdity; grotesque ornamentation.

babesiosis /bəbiːzɪˈəʊsɪs/ *noun.* Pl. **-oses** /-ˈəʊsiːz/. E20.
[ORIGIN from mod. Latin *Babesia* (see below), from Victor *Babès* (1854–1926), Romanian bacteriologist: see -IA[1], -OSIS.]
VETERINARY MEDICINE. Tick-borne infection of animals (and rarely of humans) with sporozoans of the genus *Babesia*. Also called ***murrain***, ***red-water*** (***fever***).
■ Also **babesiasis** /bɑːbɪˈzʌɪəsɪs/ *noun*, pl. **-ases** /-əsiːz/. M20.

Babi /ˈbɑːbi/ *noun*. M19.
[ORIGIN Persian, from Arabic *bāb* intermediary, lit. 'gate'. The title *Bāb* was assumed by the founder.]
A member of a Persian eclectic sect founded in 1844, emphasizing the coming of a new prophet or messenger of God, and from which Baha'ism developed.
■ **Babism** *noun* the doctrine or practice of the Babis M19. **Babist** *noun & adjective* (**a**) *noun* a Babi; (**b**) *adjective* of or pertaining to the Babis: M19. **Babite** *noun* a Babi E20.

babiche /bəˈbiːʃ/ *noun*. *N. Amer.* E19.
[ORIGIN Canad. French from Micmac *a:papi:č*.]
Thongs or thread made of rawhide, sinew, etc.

babify /ˈbeɪbɪfʌɪ/ *verb trans.* Also **babyfy**. M19.
[ORIGIN from BABY *noun* + -FY.]
Make baby-like or babyish.

babingtonite /ˈbabɪŋtənʌɪt/ *noun*. E19.
[ORIGIN from William *Babington* (1756–1833), English mineralogist + -ITE¹.]
MINERALOGY. A triclinic basic silicate of iron and calcium, occurring as glassy greenish-black crystals.

Babinski /bəˈbɪnski/ *noun*. E20.
[ORIGIN from J. F. F. *Babinski* (1857–1932), French neurologist.]
Used *attrib.* with ref. to a reflex action in which the big toe remains extended or extends itself when the sole of the foot is stimulated.

babirusa /bɑːbɪˈruːsə/ *noun*. Also **-r(o)ussa**. L17.
[ORIGIN Malay, from *babi* hog + *rusa* deer.]
A wild hog, *Babyrousa babyrussa*, of the Malay archipelago, having upturned hornlike tusks.

babish /ˈbeɪbɪʃ/ *adjective*. *arch.* M16.
[ORIGIN from BABE + -ISH¹.]
Infantile, baby-like; babyish, silly.

babka /ˈbabkə/ *noun*. M20.
[ORIGIN Polish, lit. 'old woman, grandmother', from *baba* BABA *noun*¹ + *-ka* fem. dim. suffix.]
A Polish cake (similar to a baba) made from a yeast dough and usu. containing raisins and almonds.

†**bable** *noun, verb* var. of BABBLE *noun, verb*.

†**baboo** *noun* var. of BABU.

babool *noun* var. of BABUL.

baboon /bəˈbuːn/ *noun*. ME.
[ORIGIN Old French *babuin* gaping figure, manikin, baboon, or medieval Latin *babewynus*; perh. from Old French & mod. French *baboue* muzzle, grimace.]
†**1** A grotesque figure used in architecture etc. ME–L16.
2 Any of a number of large African and Arabian monkeys, having muzzles resembling those of dogs. LME.
chacma baboon, ***gelada baboon***, ***hamadryas baboon***, ***sphinx-baboon***, ***ursine baboon***, ***yellow baboon***, etc.
3 An ugly or uncouth person; a stupid person. Also *gen.* as a term of abuse. L15.
– COMB.: **baboon spider** any of various large, hairy burrowing spiders of *Ceratogyrus*, *Harpactira*, or related genera, found in Africa.
■ **baboonery** *noun* †(**a**) = BABERY; (**b**) *rare* a baboon colony, a place where baboons are kept; (**c**) baboonish behaviour or condition: LME. **baboonish** *adjective* resembling (that of) a baboon E19.

babouche /bəˈbuːʃ/ *noun*. L17.
[ORIGIN French from Arabic *bābūj*, Persian *pāpūš*, from *pā* foot + *pūš* covering.]
A Turkish or oriental heelless slipper.

babu /ˈbɑːbuː/ *noun*. Also †**-oo**; **B-**. L18.
[ORIGIN Hindi *bābū*.]
†**1** Orig., a Hindu title of respect. Later, a Hindu gentleman. L18–E19.
2 *hist.* An Indian clerk or official who could write English; *derog.* an Indian, esp. in Bengal, who had had a superficial English education. M19.
– COMB.: **babu English** *hist.* ornate and unidiomatic English regarded as characteristic of an Indian who had learned the language from books.

babul /bəˈbuːl/ *noun*. Also **-ool**. E19.
[ORIGIN Hindi *babūl*, Bengali *bābul*, from Sanskrit *babbūla*.]
Esp. in the Indian subcontinent: a tropical acacia, *Acacia nilotica*, introduced from Africa and used as a source of fuel, gum arabic, and (formerly) tannin. Cf. KIKAR, NEB-NEB, SUNT.

babushka /bəˈbʊʃkə/ *noun*. M20.
[ORIGIN Russian = grandmother.]
1 In Russia: a grandmother, an old woman. M20.
2 A headscarf folded diagonally and tied under the chin. M20.

baby /ˈbeɪbi/ *noun & adjective*. Also (*dial.*) **babby** /ˈbabi/. LME.
[ORIGIN Prob. formed as BABE: see -Y⁶.]
▸ **A** *noun*. **1** An infant; a very young child, *esp.* one not yet able to walk. LME. ▸**b** *fig.* A person's invention, achievement, or concern. L19.

> **b** J. THURBER I worry about Talk of the Town because it was my baby for so many years.

battered baby: see BATTER *verb*¹ 1. ***blue baby***: see BLUE *adjective*. **carry the baby**, **hold the baby** bear an unwelcome responsibility. ***jelly baby***: see JELLY *noun*¹. ***surrogate baby***: see SURROGATE *adjective*. **throw away the baby with the bathwater** & vars., reject what is essential or valuable along with the inessential or useless. ***wet the baby's head***: see WET *verb*.

†**2** A doll or puppet. E16–E18.

> POPE Sober over her Sampler, or gay over a jointed Baby.

3 A small image of oneself reflected in the pupil of another's eye. *obsolete* exc. as below. L16.
look babies gaze into another's eyes.
4 In *pl.* [perh. orig. ornamental work with cupids etc.] Pictures in books. Now only *N. English*. L16.
5 An unduly childish person. Cf. CRYBABY. E17.
6 A (relatively) tiny or diminutive animal or thing; a small version of something generally larger; *esp.* a small-sized bottle, jar, etc. M19.
7 A person; a thing; a young woman, a girlfriend. Freq. as a form of address. *slang* (chiefly *N. Amer.*). M19.

> C. SANDBURG My baby's going to have a new dress. A. LOMAX Some terrible environments . . inhabited by some very tough babies. *New York Times* You need that left ankle for strength when you hit the brake. That's why I couldn't drive stocks. You got to stay on the brake with those babies.

this baby *slang* I, me.
8 The youngest or most junior member of a family, team, group, etc. L19.
– COMB.: **baby-blue-eyes** a N. American ornamental annual plant, *Nemophila menziesii*, having saucer-shaped blue flowers with a white centre; **baby blues** *colloq.* (**a**) postnatal depression; (**b**) blue eyes; **baby bonus** *Canad. colloq.* a family allowance; **baby boom** (the children born at a time of) a marked increase in the birth rate, esp. that after the Second World War; **baby boomer** a person born during a baby boom; **baby bouncer** = ***baby jumper*** below; **Baby Buggy** (**a**) (proprietary name for) a kind of child's pushchair; (**b**) *N. Amer.* (with lower-case initials) a pram; **baby bust** *colloq.* (orig. *US*) (a period of) a marked decrease in the birth rate; **baby buster** *colloq.* (orig. *US*) a person born during such a period; **baby carriage** a pram; **baby-doll** (**a**) = DOLL *noun*¹; (**b**) an ingenuous girl or woman with pretty features like those of a doll; (**c**) *attrib.* denoting women's clothing resembling that traditionally worn by a doll or young child, esp. short, high-waisted, short-sleeved dresses; **baby-face** (a person with) a smooth rounded face like a baby's; **baby farm** *derog.* a place where baby-farming is carried on; **baby-farmer** *derog.* a person engaged in baby-farming; **baby-farming** *derog.* the lodging and care of babies for payment; **baby food** a milk substitute or light diet suitable for a baby; **Babygro** (proprietary), **babygrow** a kind of all-in-one stretch garment for babies; **baby house** (now *arch.* or *hist.*) a doll's house; **baby jumper** a hanging frame on springs, in which a child is fastened to exercise his or her limbs; **baby-minder** a person who looks after babies for payment, esp. while their parents or guardians are at work; **babymother**, **babyfather** *black English* the mother (or father) of one or more of one's children; **baby nest** a warmly lined pouch, similar to a sleeping bag, designed for a young baby; **baby oil** a mineral oil used to soften babies' skin; **baby powder** a skin powder for babies; **baby's breath** (chiefly *N. Amer.*) any of various scented plants, esp. *Gypsophila paniculata*; **babysit** *verb trans. & intrans.* look after (a child) while his or her parents or guardians are out; *fig.* look after (a thing) while its owner is away; **babysitter** a person engaged to babysit; **baby-snatcher** (**a**) a person who abducts a very young child; (**b**) *colloq.* a person who is sexually attracted to, has an amorous affair with, or marries a much younger person; **baby-snatching** the action of a baby-snatcher; **baby stay** SAILING an additional forestay sometimes used on offshore racing yachts; **baby step** a small tentative step; **baby talk** imperfect or contrived speech used by or to young children; **baby-walker** a device for helping a baby learn to walk.
▸ **B** *attrib.* or as *adjective*. Small or diminutive of its kind; young. E17.

> F. A. FORBES I have in my room a baby rhododendron in full bloom. E. WAUGH Julia always drove herself, in the latest model of mass-produced baby car. *Daily Telegraph* Early pickings of baby carrots.

baby beef flesh of young cattle older than those producing veal. **baby grand** a small grand piano.
■ **babyhood** *noun* infancy; babies collectively: M18. **babyish** *adjective* resembling or characteristic of a baby; unduly childish, silly: M18. **babyishly** *adverb* M19. **babyishness** *noun* L19. **babyism** *noun* babyhood; a babyish phrase or action: M19. **babykins** *noun* (*colloq.*) (a term of endearment for) a baby M20. **baby-like** *adjective* resembling (that of) a baby E19.

baby /ˈbeɪbi/ *verb trans.* M18.
[ORIGIN from the noun.]
Treat as a baby; coddle, pamper.

> M. AMIS Women do adore to be cuddled and babied in the morning.

babyfy *verb* var. of BABIFY.

Babylon /ˈbabɪlən, -lɒn/ *noun*. M17.
[ORIGIN Latin from Greek *Babulōn* (from Hebrew *bāḇel* BABEL), name of the ancient Chaldean capital and also of the mystical city of the Apocalypse.]
1 A great and decadent city. Formerly *esp.* (*derog.*) Rome or the papal power. M17.
2 Among black people, esp. Rastafarians: white society; the representatives of this, *esp.* the police. M20.
■ **Babyˈlonic** *adjective* = BABYLONIAN *adjective* E17. **Babylonish** /babɪˈləʊnɪʃ/ *adjective* (**a**) of or pertaining to Babylon; †(**b**) popish; (**c**) babelish, confused in language: M16.

Babylonian /babɪˈləʊnɪən/ *noun & adjective*. M16.
[ORIGIN from Latin *Babylonius* from Greek *Babulōnios*: see BABYLON, -IAN.]
▸ **A** *noun*. **1** A native or inhabitant of Babylon. M16. ▸†**b** A papist. L17–L18.
2 The Akkadian dialect of Babylon. L19.
▸ **B** *adjective*. Of or pertaining to Babylon or its dialect; *fig.* (**a**) huge, gigantic, †(**b**) popish, (**c**) (with ref. to *Revelation* 17:4) scarlet. L16.

bac /bak/ *noun*. E20.
[ORIGIN Abbreviation.]
Baccarat.

bacalao /bakəˈlaʊ/ *noun*. Also **-lhau** /-ˈʎaʊ/. M16.
[ORIGIN Spanish *bacal(l)ao*, Portuguese *bacalhau*.]
Codfish, esp. dried or salted.

Bacardi /bəˈkɑːdi/ *noun*. E20.
[ORIGIN *Bacardi* & Co., Nassau, Bahamas (orig. based in Cuba).]
(Proprietary name for) a dry white rum; a drink of this.

†**bacare** *interjection* var. of BACKARE.

bacca /ˈbakə/ *noun*. *colloq.* Also **baccer**, **backer**. E19.
[ORIGIN Abbreviation.]
Tobacco. Cf. BACCO, BACCY.

baccalaurean /bakəˈlɔːrɪən/ *adjective*. M19.
[ORIGIN from medieval Latin *baccalaureus* (see BACHELOR) + -AN.]
Of or befitting a bachelor.

baccalaureate /bakəˈlɔːrɪət/ *noun*. M17.
[ORIGIN French *baccalauréat* or medieval Latin *baccalaureatus*, from *baccalaureus*: see BACHELOR, -ATE¹.]
1 The university degree of bachelor. M17.
2 = BACHELOR 4. *rare*. L17.
3 ***International Baccalaureate***, (proprietary name for) a set of internationally recognized academic programmes, *esp.* one intended to qualify successful candidates for higher education; a qualification awarded for satisfactory performance in these programmes. L20.

baccarat /ˈbakərɑː/ *noun*. Also **-ra**. M19.
[ORIGIN French *baccara*, of unknown origin.]
A gambling card game, played between a banker and one punter, or several punters in turn, in which the best one- or two-card hand is that yielding the highest remainder when its total face value is divided by 10.

baccate /ˈbakeɪt/ *adjective*. E19.
[ORIGIN Latin *baccatus*, from *bacca* berry: see -ATE².]
BOTANY. Bearing berries; berry-like.

baccer *noun* var. of BACCA.

Bacchanal /ˈbakən(ə)l, -nal/ *adjective & noun*. Also **b-**. M16.
[ORIGIN Latin *bacchanalis*, from BACCHUS: see -AL¹.]
▸ **A** *adjective*. **1** = BACCHIC 1. M16.
2 = BACCHIC 2. L16.
▸ **B** *noun*. **1** An occasion of drunken revelry; an orgy. M16.
2 A priest, priestess, or devotee of Bacchus. M16.
3 A dance or song in honour of Bacchus; *sing.* & (usu.) in *pl.*, a festival in honour of Bacchus. E17.
4 A scene of revelry painted or sculptured. M18.
5 A noisy or drunken reveller. E19.
■ **bacchanalize** *verb intrans.* indulge in drunken revelry M17.

Bacchanalia /bakəˈneɪlɪə/ *noun pl.* Also **b-**. L16.
[ORIGIN Latin *bacchanalia* neut. pl. of *bacchanalis*: see BACCHANAL.]
1 The Roman festival in honour of Bacchus, the god of wine. L16.
2 Drunken revelry; an orgy. M17.

Bacchanalian /bakəˈneɪlɪən/ *adjective & noun*. Also **b-**. M16.
[ORIGIN from Latin *bacchanalis* BACCHANAL + -IAN.]
▸ **A** *adjective*. **1** Marked by, connected with, or given to drunken revelry; riotously drunken. M16.
2 Connected with or relating to the worship of Bacchus, the Greek and Roman god of wine. E17.
▸ **B** *noun*. A Bacchant; a drunken reveller. E17.

Bacchant /ˈbakənt/ *noun & adjective*. Also **b-**. Pl. **Bacchants**, **Bacchantes** /bəˈkantɪz/. L16.
[ORIGIN French *bacchante*: see BACCHANTE.]
▸ **A** *noun*. A priest, priestess, or devotee of Bacchus, the Greek and Roman god of wine; a drunken reveller, a roisterer. L16.
▸ **B** *adjective*. Bacchus-worshipping; wine-loving. E19.
■ **Bacchantic** /bəˈkantɪk/ *adjective* M19.

Bacchante /ˈbak(ə)nt, bəˈkant, bəˈkanti/ *noun & adjective*. Also **b-**. L18.
[ORIGIN French, from Latin *bacchant-* pres. ppl stem of *bacchari* celebrate the feast of Bacchus (in Latin only in fem. pl. *bacchantes*).]
▸ **A** *noun*. A priestess or female devotee of Bacchus, the Greek and Roman god of wine. L18.
▸ **B** *attrib.* or as *adjective*. Of, pertaining to, or characteristic of a Bacchante. E19.

baccharis /ˈbakərɪs/ *noun*. Also †**bacchar**. M16.
[ORIGIN Latin *baccar*, *bacc(h)aris* from Greek *bakkaris*, *bakkh-*.]
Orig., a plant with an aromatic root, mentioned by the ancients and variously identified; any of several plants identified with this. Now *spec.* any American shrub of the genus *Baccharis*, which includes the groundsel tree, *B. halimifolia*.

Bacchic /ˈbakɪk/ *adjective*. Also **b-**. M17.
[ORIGIN Latin *bacchicus* from Greek *bakkhikos*: see BACCHUS, -IC.]
1 Of or pertaining to Bacchus, the Greek and Roman god of wine, or his worship. M17.
2 Frenzied like a devotee of Bacchus; riotously drunken, roistering. L17.

bacchius /bəˈkʌɪəs/ *noun*. Pl. **bacchii** /bəˈkʌɪʌɪ/. L16.
[ORIGIN Latin from Greek *bakkheios* (*pous* foot).]
PROSODY. A metrical foot of three syllables, one short and two long.
■ **bacchiac** *adjective* M18.

Bacchus /ˈbakəs/ *noun*. LME.
[ORIGIN Latin from Greek *Bakkhos* the god of wine.]
Wine or intoxicating liquor personified.

bacciferous /bakˈsɪf(ə)rəs/ *adjective*. M17.
[ORIGIN from Latin *baccifer* (formed as BACCIVOROUS) + -OUS: see -FEROUS.]
Berry-bearing; producing berries.

baccivorous /bakˈsɪv(ə)rəs/ *adjective*. M17.
[ORIGIN from Latin *bacci-* combining form of *bacca* berry + -VOROUS.]
Berry-eating.

bacco /ˈbakəʊ/ *noun*. *colloq.* L18.
[ORIGIN Abbreviation.]
Tobacco. Cf. BACCA, next.

baccy /ˈbaki/ *noun*. *colloq.* Also **backy**. E19.
[ORIGIN Abbreviation.]
Tobacco. Cf. BACCA, prec.

bach /batʃ/ *noun*[1] & *verb*. *colloq.* Also **batch**. M19.
[ORIGIN Abbreviation of BACHELOR.]
▸ **A** *noun*. **1** A bachelor. *US*. M19.
2 A small makeshift hut; a small holiday house. *Austral. & NZ*. E20.
▸ **B** *verb intrans. & trans.* (with *it*). Live alone and cater for oneself as a bachelor. *N. Amer., Austral., & NZ*. L19.

bach /baːx/ *noun*[2]. *Welsh dial.* L19.
[ORIGIN Welsh, lit. 'little'.]
Dear, beloved; little one; friend. (Chiefly *voc.* and often placed appositionally after personal names.)

> A. BURGESS How different your voice sounds tonight, *bach*. R. DAVIES Time to pay back now, Dicky bach.

Bach /batʃ/ *noun*[3]. L20.
[ORIGIN Edward *Bach* (1886–1936), Brit. physician.]
Bach* (*flower*) *remedy, any of a number of preparations of the flowers of plants used in a system of complementary medicine intended to relieve ill health by influencing underlying emotional states.

Bacharach /ˈbakərak, *foreign* ˈbaxarax/ *noun*. E17.
[ORIGIN A town on the Rhine, western Germany.]
A (usu. white) wine produced in the area of Bacharach.

bachata /baˈtʃata/ *noun*. Pl. **-s**, same. L20.
[ORIGIN Caribbean Spanish = party, good time.]
A style of romantic music originating in the Dominican Republic; a song in this style.

bachelor /ˈbatʃələ/ *noun*. Also †**batch-**. ME.
[ORIGIN Old French *bacheler* young man aspiring to knighthood, from Proto-Romance, of uncertain origin: in academic use the medieval Latin form was *baccalarius*, later altered to *-laureus*, with ref. to *bacca lauri* laurel berry.]
1 *hist.* A young knight who followed the banner of another; a novice in arms. ME.
knight bachelor a knight of the lowest order; the full title of a gentleman who has been knighted.
2 A man who is not and has never been married. ME.
3 A junior member or 'yeoman' of a trade guild. *obsolete* exc. *hist.* LME.
4 A man or woman who has taken a degree below that of Master (usu. a first degree) at a university or other academic institution. LME.
bachelor of arts, ***bachelor of science***, etc. ***determining bachelor***: see DETERMINE 4b.
5 A male animal, esp. a male fur seal, which is prevented from breeding by more dominant males in a social group. L19.
6 An apartment suitable for a bachelor. Chiefly *N. Amer.* M20.
– COMB.: **bachelor apartment**, **bachelor flat**: suitable for an unmarried person; **bachelor girl** a young unmarried woman who lives independently; **bachelor party**: for men only, esp. to mark the end of a man's bachelorhood; **bachelor's button(s)** any of various double-flowered forms of plants grown for ornament, *esp.* a double form of the meadow buttercup, *Ranunculus acris*, or sneezewort, *Achillea ptarmica*; **bachelor's degree** a degree of Bachelor of Arts, Bachelor of Science, etc.; **bachelor's hall** a home presided over by a bachelor (or a man living apart from his wife); **bachelor's wife** the ideal wife of whom a bachelor theorizes or dreams.
■ **bachelordom** *noun* = BACHELORHOOD L19. **bacheloˈrette** *noun* (*N. Amer.*) (**a**) = ***bachelor girl*** above; (**b**) an apartment suitable for a bachelor girl: M20. **bachelorhood** *noun* the state or quality of a bachelor E19. **bachelorism** *noun* a habit or peculiarity of a bachelor; the condition or behaviour of a bachelor: E19. **bachelorly** *adjective* like a bachelor L16. **bachelorship** *noun* = BACHELORHOOD L16.

bachelorize /ˈbatʃələrʌɪz/ *verb intrans.* Also **-ise**. M18.
[ORIGIN from BACHELOR + -IZE.]
1 Take the degree of bachelor. *rare*. M18.
2 Live as a bachelor. M19.

Bachian /ˈbɑːkɪən, ˈbɑːx-/ *noun & adjective*. E20.
[ORIGIN from *Bach* (see below) + -IAN.]
▸ **A** *noun*. An interpreter, student, or admirer of the music of the German composer Johann Sebastian Bach (1685–1750). E20.
▸ **B** *adjective*. Of, pertaining to, or characteristic of Bach or his music. M20.

bacillary /bəˈsɪləri/ *adjective*. M19.
[ORIGIN from late Latin BACILLUS + -ARY[1].]
1 Of, pertaining to, or consisting of little rods. M19.
2 Of, pertaining to, or of the nature of bacilli; caused by bacilli. L19.
bacillary white diarrhoea = PULLORUM DISEASE.
■ **bacillar** *adjective* = BACILLARY 2 L19. **bacilliform** *adjective* rod-shaped M19.

bacillus /bəˈsɪləs/ *noun*. Pl. **-lli** /-lʌɪ, -liː/. L19.
[ORIGIN Late Latin = little rod, dim. of *baculus* rod, stick.]
Any rod-shaped bacterium; *loosely* any pathogenic bacterium.
■ **baciˈlluria** *noun* (MEDICINE) the presence of bacilli in the urine L19.

bacitracin /basɪˈtreɪsɪn/ *noun*. M20.
[ORIGIN from BACILLUS + Margaret *Tracy*, an Amer. child in whom the substance was discovered in a wound + -IN[1].]
An antibiotic obtained from bacteria of the *Bacillus subtilis* group.

back /bak/ *noun*[1].
[ORIGIN Old English *bæc* = Old Frisian *bek*, Old Saxon *bak*, Middle & mod. Low German, Middle Dutch *bak*, Old High German *bah*, Old Norse *bak*, from Germanic.]
▸ **I** Orig. sense.
1 The convex surface of the body of humans and vertebrate animals which is adjacent to the spinal axis and opposite to the belly, and extends from the neck and shoulders to the extremity of the backbone. OE.

> O. HENRY Down his back from his mane to his tail went a line of black. A. SCHLEE She stood with her back against the door feeling the brass handle press against a bone in her spine.

2 Regarded with reference to its position or functions. *spec.* ▸**a** The hinder surface of a person's body, esp. as turned away from someone else. OE. ▸**b** The part of the body which bears burdens. OE. ▸**c** That part of the body which is the special recipient of clothing (often repr. the whole body in this capacity). ME. ▸**d** In animals, the upper surface opposite to that on which they move or rest. LME.

> **a** SHAKES. *Cymb.* The army broken, And but the backs of Britons seen. **b** SHAKES. *Tit. A.* Wrongs more than our backs can bear. R. V. JONES More than one careerist in the Admiralty had climbed on Butterworth's back by exploiting his work. **c** G. B. SHAW Give them the clothes off my back.

▸ **II** *transf.* The surface of things analogous in position to the (human) back; the hinder side.
3 The side or surface of any object which answers in position to the back and is opposite to the face or front, or to the side approached or contemplated, or away from the normal direction of motion; e.g. the outer side of the hand, the underside of a leaf, the convex part of a book, the rear part of a house or vehicle. ME.

> LYTTON At the back of the cottage . . there are some fields. OED The back of the leaf is lighter in colour. F. O'CONNOR He . . wrote down the address on the back of an envelope. A. BURGESS Took three bullets straight in the back of the throat. T. STOPPARD He got into the back of the motor.

4 The side or part of any object that is away from or more remote from the spectator; the further side. M17.

> J. TYNDALL A plate of copper against the back of which a steady sheet of flame is permitted to play. G. B. SHAW Finally comes the band, which posts itself at the back of the square.

5 *ellipt.* = ***backblocks***, ***back country*** s.v. BACK-. L19.
6 In *pl.* (Also **B-**.) The grounds behind some Cambridge colleges bordering on the River Cam. L19.
▸ **III** Parts of things having relation, or analogous in position, to the human back.
7 The hind part, e.g. of a chair, garment, etc. LME.

> LD MACAULAY The back of the chimney did not seem to be firmly fixed. J. CONRAD I grabbed the back of the nearest piece of furniture.

8 A body of followers or supporters; backing. Now only *Scot.* M16.

> J. SPEED Scotland . . was a special backe and second to King Henry.

9 The rear of an armed force. *arch.* L16.

> SHAKES. *2 Hen. IV* He leaves his back unarm'd.

10 FOOTBALL & HOCKEY etc. (The position of) a defending player stationed behind the forwards. L19.
centre back, ***full back***, ***halfback***, ***quarterback***, etc.
▸ **IV** Surfaces or parts of things analogous to the back of animals.
11 The upper surface of anything, esp. as bearing burdens; the ridge of a hill; *poet.* the surface of water, the waves, etc. LME.

> SHAKES. *Temp.* I saw him beat the surges under him, And ride upon their backs: he trod the water. N. HAWTHORNE We now rambled about on the broad back of the hill.

12 The keel and keelson of a ship. L17.

> P. O'BRIAN I drove her on to the rock before Gijon . . . She was hopelessly bilged, her back broken.

– PHRASES ETC. (see also BACK-): **at the back of** behind in support, pursuit, or concealment. **at the back of one's mind** in the memory but not consciously thought of or immediately recalled. ***back and edge***: see EDGE *noun*. **back of Bourke**, **back o' Bourke** [*Bourke*, a town in western New South Wales] *Austral. slang* the most remote outback, the back of beyond. **back-to-back** *adjective* (**a**) (of houses) built in a continuous terrace divided along its length so as to produce two terraces of houses adjoining at the rear; (**b**) *N. Amer.* (of events) consecutive. **behind one's back** in one's absence or without one's knowledge. **break the back of** *fig.* overburden, crush (a person), finish the greatest or hardest part of (a task). ***claw the back of***: see CLAW *verb* 2. ***fall off the back of a lorry***: see LORRY *noun*. **get a person's back up** make a person angry or stubborn. **get off a person's back** *fig.* (*colloq.*) stop annoying or harassing him or her. **give a back** = ***make a back*** below. ***have a monkey on one's back***, ***have the monkey on one's back***: see MONKEY *noun*. **in back** (**of**) *N. Amer.* behind, in or at the back (of). **know like the back of one's hand** be thoroughly familiar or conversant with. ***left back***, ***left half(-back)***: see LEFT *adjective*. ***loose back***: see LOOSE *adjective*. **make a back** bend the body to provide a surface for jumping over, e.g. in leapfrog. ***make a rod for one's own back***: see ROD *noun*. ***not a shirt to one's back***: see SHIRT *noun*. **on one's back** laid up or ill in bed; prostrate, helpless. **on the back of** behind, immediately following; weighing upon as a burden; *fig.* harassing, annoying. ***pat on the back***: see PAT *noun*[1] 3, *verb* 5. **put a person's back up** = ***get a person's back up*** above. **put one's back into** use all one's efforts or strength in (a particular endeavour). ***right back***, ***right half*** (***-back***): see RIGHT *adjective*. ***running back***: see RUNNING *ppl adjective*. ***scratch my back and I will scratch yours***: see SCRATCH *verb*. **see the back of** be rid of. **short back and sides** *colloq.* a short haircut. ***slap on the back***: see SLAP *noun*[1] 1, SLAP *verb*[1]. ***stab in the back***: see STAB *noun*[1] 2, STAB *verb* 3. ***the back of beyond***: see BEYOND *noun*. ***the beast with two backs***: see BEAST *noun*. ***the last straw that breaks the camel's back***: see STRAW *noun*. ***the shirt off one's back***: see SHIRT *noun*. **turn one's back on** turn away from, flee, forsake, abandon. **upon the back of** = ***on the back of*** above. ***watch one's back***, ***watch a person's back***: see WATCH *verb*. WATTEAU **back**. **with one's back to the wall** hard-pressed, at bay.
■ **backed** *adjective* having a back, background, or backing, (usu. as 2nd elem. of a comb., of a specified kind) LME. **backless** *adjective* without a back, having no back; (of a woman's garment) cut low at the back: E19.

back /bak/ *noun*[2]. L16.
[ORIGIN Dutch *bak*, Low German *back* large dish: cf. medieval Latin *bacca* 'vas aquarium' (Isidore).]
A tub, a trough, a vat, esp. as used in brewing, dyeing, or pickling.

back /bak/ *adjective* (*attrib.*) Superl. BACKMOST; compar. (*obsolete* exc. in sense 2) **backer**. Freq. with hyphen (see also BACK-). LME.
[ORIGIN Attrib. use of BACK *noun*[1] or ellipt. use of BACK *adverb*.]
▸ **I** From the noun.
1 Situated at the back, behind, or away from the front; remote, obscure; inferior, subsidiary. LME.

> J. RAY A small flat back claw, or toe. L. STERNE Coming unexpectedly from a back parlour into the shop. J. LE CARRÉ Leamas looked out of the back window, and saw the DKW following them. R. P. JHABVALA She lived off the main shopping district in a back lane. F. FORSYTH They sat over a pot of tea in the back kitchen.

2 PHONETICS. Of a sound: formed at the back of the mouth. M19.
▸ **II** From the adverb.
3 In arrears, overdue; behindhand; belonging to the past. E16.
4 Turned back, reversed. L16.

back /bak/ *verb*. LME.
[ORIGIN from BACK *noun*[1].]
▸ **I** Provide a back; cover the back; support.
1 *verb trans.* †**a** Clothe. Only in LME. ▸**b** Put a back to, line the back of. M16.

> **b** J. SMEATON The ashler walls were backed . . with rubble stone, or with bricks.

2 *verb trans.* Support or help (a person or thing) materially or mechanically; support morally, esp. by argument. Also foll. by *up*. E16.

> E. A. FREEMAN Demands which had been backed by an armed force. W. LIPPMANN Guarantees, backed by the authority of the state. W. S. CHURCHILL Canning had backed the Spanish national rising in 1808.

3 *verb trans.* Mount, ride on, or (now *esp.*) break in (a horse or other animal). L16.
backing dog *Austral. & NZ* a sheepdog that jumps on to the backs of sheep to help move them.
4 *verb trans.* Countersign, endorse; print on the back (as well as the front) of; *Scot. & US* address (a letter). L17.
5 *verb trans.* Support (an opinion or judgement) by a wager; bet on the success of (a horse in a race, an entrant in any contest, etc.); *fig.* be confident of (a stated outcome). L17.

> BYRON Most men (till by losing render'd sager) Will back their own opinions with a wager. E. LONGFORD Bets were laid in the London clubs, many of Brooks's Whigs backing Napoleon for a win.

back the field bet on the rest of the horses against the favourite. **back the wrong horse** *fig.* make a wrong or inappropriate choice.

B

6 a *verb trans.* Form, lie, or stand at the back of. **E19.** ▸**b** *verb intrans.* Be so situated that the back abuts *on* or *on to* a piece of land etc. **L19.**

a T. H. HUXLEY The chalk cliffs which back the beach. M. MITCHELL Turning so that she backed the corpse, she caught a heavy boot under each arm and threw her weight forward. **b** *Edinburgh Review* St. James' Square, on which the club backs. M. BRADBURY The gardens, the houses backing onto them.

7 *verb trans.* Accompany (a singer or instrumentalist, esp. in popular music or jazz). **M20.**

▸ **II** Move or hold back.

8 *verb trans.* Set or lay back; restrain, check; *esp.* (NAUTICAL) lay (a sail or yard) aback to slow the ship down. **LME.**

9 *verb intrans.* Of a person, vehicle, etc.: go or move backwards; retreat. **L15.**

J. STEINBECK Ahead the truck pulled up and then backed slowly. L. P. HARTLEY She did not move towards it—rather, she backed away. E. L. DOCTOROW As the great liner backed into the river he stood at the rail and waved.

back and fill *N. Amer.* move to and fro; *fig.* vacillate.

10 *verb trans.* Cause to move backwards or in the opposite direction; reverse. **M18.**

DICKENS Backing his chair a little. E. WAUGH Dennis locked the office and backed the car from the garage.

back water reverse a boat's forward motion with the oars.

11 *verb intrans.* Of the wind: change in an anticlockwise direction. Opp. ***veer***. **M19.**

– WITH ADVERBS & PREPOSITIONS IN SPECIALIZED SENSES: **back down**, **back off** *fig.* abandon a claim made, stand taken, etc. **back out** move backward out of a place; *fig.* withdraw from a commitment or difficulty. **back up** (*a*) *verb phr. trans.* & *intrans.* (CRICKET) (of a fielder) place oneself in readiness to stop the ball if it is missed by (another fielder); of the batsman at the bowler's end: start in readiness for a possible run made by (the striking batsman); (*b*) *verb phr. intrans.* & *trans.* (orig. *N. Amer.*) of water, traffic, etc.: accumulate behind an obstacle etc.; of a barrier etc.: cause (water, traffic, etc.) to accumulate; (*c*) *verb phr. trans.* & *intrans.* (orig. *N. Amer.*) drive (a vehicle etc.) backwards; move backwards; (*d*) *verb phr. trans.* (COMPUTING) provide backup for; make a duplicate copy of (a disk, file, program, etc.); (see also sense 2 above).

back /bak/ *adverb.* **LME.**

[ORIGIN Aphet. from ABACK.]

▸ **I** Of motion or direction.

1 To the rear (often, esp. in the imper., with the verb *go*, *come*, etc., omitted); away from what is considered to be the front or the normal position. **LME.**

AV *Matt.* 28:2 The angel of the Lord rolled back the stone. SIR W. SCOTT Back, beardless boy! Back, minion! J. D. SALINGER I sort of brushed my hair back with my hand. P. PORTER Looking back when at the gate.

2 In the opposite direction, so as to return to the place originally left; to a former or normal condition, in reversal of progress or in restoration of former circumstances. **M16.** ▸**b** Come, received, put, etc., back. **M17.**

E. A. FREEMAN The whole country fell back into heathenism. E. HEMINGWAY She came back from wherever she had been. S. SPENDER Across the bay, the searchlight beams Swing and swing back across the sky. J. D. SALINGER I started to get up and all, but Mr. Antolini got hold of my jacket and pulled me back down. **b** J. CONRAD She was back from the remoteness of her meditation, very much so indeed. G. B. SHAW She'll come to no harm. She'll be back for tea. A. ROOK Our toys of Monday are scarcely back on their tray. J. P. DONLEAVY Make a fire in the stove. I'll be back.

3 Into the past; backward in time. **L16.**

STEELE If we go back to the days of Solomon. Q. CRISP Old men looking back on their lives.

4 In return or retaliation. **L16.**

SHAKES. *Much Ado* What have I to give you back? J. MICHIE 'That's a dirty crooked question,' back I roared.

answer back, ***pay back***, ***strike back***, etc.

5 Away from a promise or undertaking. **L18.**

▸ **II** Of position:

6 At a distance, to the rear, away (*from* a specified point). **LME.**

SHAKES. *Rich. III* My lord, stand back, and let the coffin pass. OED I left him back at the second milestone. E. BOWEN The intruder had occupied a pew . . some way back from the last of the rows of relatives.

7 In a state of check to forward movement or progress in condition. **M16.**

8 In the past; (a specified time) ago. **L18.**

T. PYNCHON Pierce had died back in the spring. C. CAUSLEY Got into trouble two years back With the local gentry.

– PHRASES ETC. (see also BACK-): **back and forth** to and fro. **back in the day** *colloq.* in the past; some time ago. **back of** (chiefly *N. Amer.*) behind. ***back on one's heels***: see HEEL *noun*[1]. **back to nature** to a simpler and supposedly more 'natural' existence. ***back to square one***: see SQUARE *noun*. **laid-back**: see LAID *ppl adjective* 4.

back- /bak/ *combining form.* **OE.**

[ORIGIN Repr. BACK *noun*[1], *adjective*, *adverb*, or (occas.) *verb*.]

In combs. in various relations (often difficult to distinguish) and senses, as 'of or on the back', 'backwards', 'reverse', 'rearmost'. (Many, esp. when ***back*** has an adjectival function, can be written with or without a hyphen.)

backache pain or discomfort in the back. **back-acter** = *backhoe* below. **back-action** (orig. *US*) backward or reverse action, as in a machine. **back-along** *adverb* (*dial.*) = BACK *adverb* 2, 8. **back-and-forth** exchange, reciprocity. **backband** a broad strap or chain passing over a cart saddle, and serving to support the shafts. †**backbear** LAW the act of carrying game killed illegally (cf. BACK-BERAND *adjective*). **backbeat** MUSIC a strongly accented beat in a position generally unaccented. **back bench** one of the benches in an assembly (esp. the House of Commons) occupied by members not entitled to sit on the front benches. **backbencher** a member who occupies a back bench. **backblocker** *Austral., NZ, & Canad.* a resident in the backblocks. **backblocks** *Austral., NZ, & Canad.* land in the remote and sparsely inhabited interior; land cut off from a river front. †**back-blow** a blow struck at the back or from behind. **back boiler** a boiler behind a domestic fire or cooking range. **back-bond** SCOTS LAW a deed qualifying the terms of another that is apparently absolute. **back-breaking** *adjective* (*fig.*) extremely laborious, exhausting. ***back burner***: see ***on the back burner*** s.v. BURNER 3. **back-cast** *adjective, noun, & verb* (*a*) *adjective* cast or thrown backwards; (*b*) *noun* a backward swing of a fishing line preparatory to casting; (*c*) *verb intrans.* swing a fishing line backwards preparatory to casting. **back catalogue** the totality of all the works previously produced by a recording artist, film director, record company, etc. **back channel** (*a*) *Canad.* a secondary channel of a stream or river, esp. one forming an island; (*b*) POLITICS a means of conveying information without passing it through normal (esp. diplomatic) channels (freq. *attrib.* or as *adjective*); (*c*) LINGUISTICS any of various means, as nods, grunts, etc., by which a listener may indicate attention to a speaker and thereby invite continued speech. **backchat** *colloq.* impertinent or impudent repartee, esp. to a superior. **backcomb** *verb trans.* & *intrans.* comb (the hair) back towards the scalp. **back country** (chiefly *N. Amer., Austral., & NZ*) the country lying towards or in the rear of a settled district. **backcourt** a smaller court to the rear of a house; TENNIS the part of the court behind the service line. **backcrawl** SWIMMING a form of crawl in which the swimmer lies on his or her back. **backcross** *verb & noun phr.* (*a*) *verb trans.* cross (a first-generation hybrid) with one of its parent strains; (*b*) *noun* an instance of back crossing, a hybrid so produced. **backdate** *verb trans.* assign an earlier date to, make retrospectively valid. **back door** (*a*) a door at the back of a building or enclosure; a secondary or private entrance; (*b*) *fig.* a second (usu. secret or less conspicuous) means of entry or approach. **back-door** *adjective* secret, clandestine, underhand. **back-double** *colloq. & dial.* a backstreet, a side road. **backdraught** (*a*) a reverse draught of air or current of water; (*b*) (freq. ***backdraft***) the explosion of a build-up of hot flammable gases produced by incomplete combustion in a confined space, as a result of a sudden influx of oxygen. **backdrop** *noun & verb* (*a*) *noun* (THEATRICAL) (orig. *US*) = BACKCLOTH 1; (*b*) *verb trans.* (*fig.*) provide with a background, set off. **back emf** an electromotive force opposing that driving the current in a circuit. **back-end** (*a*) the hinder of two ends; (*b*) the later part of the year, late autumn; (*c*) the latter stages or outcome of a process, esp. in relation to financial matters such as the profits of a film; (*d*) COMPUTING a specialized part of a computer system with which the user does not interact directly; *spec.* (*attrib.*) designating the interface between a database and the interactive programs used to query that database; **back-fanged** *adjective* (ZOOLOGY) = OPISTHOGLYPH *adjective*. **backfield** AMER. FOOTBALL (the positions occupied by) the players behind the line of scrimmage. **backfill** *verb & noun* (*a*) *verb trans.* fill (an excavation) in again with material removed earlier, e.g. around foundations; (*b*) *noun* earth etc. used for backfilling. **backfist** a karate punch using the back of the fist. **backfit** *verb trans.* fit (an advanced component) to an older product; upgrade (an older product) in this way. **back-flash** the act or process of flashing back; *esp.* = ***flashback*** (b) s.v. FLASH *verb*. **backflip** a backward somersault. **back-formation** PHILOLOGY the formation of what looks like a root word from an already existing word which might be (but is not) a derivative of the former; a word so formed. **back-front** the rear boundary line or elevation of a building. **backhaul** (*a*) the return journey of a vehicle from its original destination to its base; a load carried on such a journey; (*b*) BROADCASTING the satellite signal of an event recorded by a television channel, radio station, etc., as it is returned for editing. **back-heel** (*a*) *verb trans.* kick (esp. a ball) backwards with the heel; (*b*) *noun* such a kick. **backhoe** *N. Amer.* a mechanical excavator which operates by drawing towards itself a bucket attached to a hinged boom. **back-house** (now *dial.*) an outhouse; a privy, a lavatory. **back issue** an edition of a journal, magazine, etc., earlier than the current one. **backland** = ***back country*** above. **backlift** (in various games) a backward lift given to the bat etc. before playing a stroke, or to the leg before kicking the ball. **back-lighting** PHOTOGRAPHY lighting coming from behind the subject. **backline** (*a*) a rearmost line; *esp.* in games, a line marking the limit of play; (*b*) RUGBY the players behind a scrum or line-out lined out across the field. (*c*) the amplifiers used by a popular music group for guitars and other instruments. **backliner** RUGBY a player in the backline. **backlist** (a catalogue of) books still available but no longer recent. **backlit** *adjective* illuminated from behind. **backlot** (orig. *US*) an outdoor area in a film studio where large exterior sets are made and some outside scenes are filmed. **back-marker** one who starts from scratch or has the least favourable handicap in a race; a horse etc. at the rear of the field. **back matter** (in a book or similar publication) the appendices, index, and any other matter following the text; **back number** a number of a periodical earlier than the current one; *colloq.* a person who or a thing which is out of date, behind the times, or useless. **back office** an office or centre in which the administrative work of a business is carried out, as opposed to its dealings with customers; *spec.* (STOCK EXCHANGE) that part of a stockbroking firm which handles settlements and other administration arising from its dealers' work. **backpack** *noun & verb* (chiefly *N. Amer.*) (*a*) *noun* a pack carried on the back, *esp.* a rucksack; (*b*) *verb intrans.* & *trans.* travel with a backpack, esp. for recreation; carry in a backpack. **backpacker** a hiker, camper, etc., with a backpack. **back pass** FOOTBALL a deliberate pass to one's own goalkeeper (who is not now allowed to pick up the ball if the pass was kicked). **back passage** *colloq.* the rectum. **back-pay** pay to cover a past period of time. **back-payment** payment to cover a past period of time. **back-pedal** *verb intrans.* work the pedals of a bicycle backwards; *fig.* (try to) reverse one's previous action. **backpiece** a piece of armour protecting the back; the piece that forms the back of something. **backplane** a board to which the main circuit boards of a computer may be fitted, and which provides connections between them. **backplate** a plate of armour for the back; a plate placed at or forming the back of something. **back-pressure** pressure opposing the normal flow of a liquid or gas. **back-project** display by back-projection. **back-projection** projection on to a translucent screen from the rear, as a means of providing a still or moving background to a scene or performance. **backrest** a support for the back. **back room** a room at the back of a house or other building; *spec.* a room or premises where (esp. secret) research etc. is carried out; ***backroom boy***, a person who does such research or wields influence behind the scenes. **back-rope** NAUTICAL a rope leading inboard from the martingale. **back row** the rear line (of a chorus, rugby scrum, etc.). **back-saw** a saw with a blade strengthened by a metal strip at the rear. **back-scatter** *verb & noun* (PHYSICS) (*a*) *verb trans.* scatter (radiation etc.) with more or less complete reversal of direction; (*b*) *noun* back-scattering; radiation etc. so scattered. **back-scratcher** an implement for scratching one's own back; *fig.* a person who takes part in mutual services for gain. **back-scratching** the performance of such services. **back-set** a setting back, a reverse; an eddy or countercurrent. **backsight** (*a*) SURVEYING a sight or reading taken backwards, or towards the point of starting; (*b*) the rearsight of a gun. **back slang** a form of slang in which words are spelled and pronounced backwards (as *yob* for *boy*). **backslapper** *fig.* a vigorously hearty person. **backslapping** slapping the back, esp. in congratulation or encouragement; *fig.* vigorously hearty behaviour. **backslash** a backward-sloping diagonal line, a reverse solidus. **backspace** *verb intrans.* use the backspacer. **backspacer** a key on a typewriter etc. that moves the printing position one space backward. **backspin** a backward spin on a ball in motion. **backsplash** *N. Amer.* = ***splashback*** s.v. SPLASH *verb*[1]. **back-stabber** *fig.* a person who attacks another unfairly, or behind his or her back. **back stage** THEATRICAL the rear part of a stage; the part of a theatre behind the stage or curtain, *esp.* the wings, dressing rooms, etc. **backstage** *adverb & adjective* at or to the back stage of a theatre; (situated, occurring, etc.) behind the scenes (*lit. & fig.*). **backstair(s)** *noun & adjective* (*a*) *noun* stairs at the back of a house, a secondary staircase; the private stairs in a palace, used for other than state visitors; *fig.* a secret method of approach; (*b*) *adjective* relating to or employing underhand intrigue, back-door. **backstay** NAUTICAL each of a number of ropes extending downwards and aft from the top of the mast towards the stern of the ship (usu. in *pl.*); *gen.* a stay or support at the back (*lit. & fig.*). **backstitch** *noun & verb* (*a*) *noun* a method of sewing with overlapping stitches; (*b*) *verb trans.* & *intrans.* sew in backstitch. **backstop** *noun & verb* (*a*) *noun* something or someone placed at the rear to serve as a barrier or support; CRICKET = ***longstop*** s.v. LONG *adjective*[1]; (*b*) *verb trans.* (chiefly *US*) act as a backstop to (chiefly *fig.*). **backstory** a history or background created for a fictional character in a film or television programme. **back straight** the stretch along the side of a racecourse or racetrack opposite to that on which the races end. **backstreet** *noun & adjective* (*a*) *noun* a street in a quiet part of a town etc., away from the main streets; (*b*) *adjective* taking place in a backstreet, taking place illicitly or illegally. **backstroke** a blow or stroke in return; a back-handed stroke; SWIMMING a stroke in which the swimmer lies on his or her back in the water. **backswimmer** a carnivorous aquatic bug of the family Notonectidae, a water boatman. **back-swing** a backward swing, esp. of the arm or a golf club when about to hit a ball. **back-talk** *colloq.* (orig. *dial.*) = ***backchat*** above. **backtrack** *verb* (orig. *US*) (*a*) *verb intrans.* return, retrace one's steps; *fig.* go back *on*, withdraw; (*b*) *verb trans.* trace, pursue, investigate. **backtracker** a person who backtracks. **backveld** *S. Afr.* primitive rural districts. **backvelder** *S. Afr.* (freq. *derog.*) a dweller in the backveld. **backwater** dammed or still water, *esp.* that beside a stream and fed by the back flow; *fig.* a remote or neglected place, (a place or condition of) intellectual stagnation. **back-way** a way leading to the back, a roundabout way. **backwind** *verb & noun* (SAILING) (*a*) *verb trans.* (of a sail or vessel) deflect a flow of air into the back of (another); (*b*) *noun* a flow of air deflected into the back of a sail. **back-winter** a return of winter after its regular time. **backwoods** wholly or partly uncleared forest; a remote or sparsely inhabited region. **backwoodsman** an inhabitant of the backwoods; *fig.* an uncouth person; a peer who very rarely attends the House of Lords. **back-word** *dial.* withdrawal from a promise or invitation; a contradictory or rude answer. **backyard** a yard or enclosure at the back of a building; *fig.* an adjacent or easily accessible area.

†**backare** *interjection.* Also **bacare**. **M16–M17.**

[ORIGIN Prob. joc. from BACK *adverb* + *-are* Latin inf. ending.]

Go back! Give way!

back-berand /ˈbakbɛr(ə)nd/ *adjective.* Long *rare* or *obsolete*. Also **-ind**.

[ORIGIN Old English *bæc-berende*, formed as BACK *noun*[1] + pres. pple of *beran* BEAR *verb*[1].]

Bearing on the back; LAW (of a thief) apprehended in the possession of stolen goods.

backbite /ˈbakbʌɪt/ *verb trans.* Pa. t. **-bit** /-bɪt/; pa. pple **-bitten** /-bɪt(ə)n/. **ME.**

[ORIGIN from BACK *noun*[1] + BITE *verb*.]

Slander, speak ill of (someone) behind his or her back. Freq. as ***backbiting*** *verbal noun*.

■ **backbiter** *noun* a slanderer, a secret calumniator **ME.**

backboard /ˈbakbɔːd/ *noun & verb.* **OE.**

[ORIGIN from BACK *noun*[1] + BOARD *noun*.]

▸ **A** *noun.* **1** NAUTICAL. = PORT *noun*[5]. Now *Scot.*, *rare* or *obsolete*. **OE.**

2 A board placed at or forming the back of anything; *esp.* (*a*) one fastened across the back of the shoulders to straighten the figure; (*b*) one behind the basket in basketball, off which the ball may rebound; (*c*) one against which tennis strokes may be practised. **M18.**

▸ **B** *verb trans.* Subject to the use of a backboard. **M19.**

backbone /ˈbakbəʊn/ *noun*. ME.
[ORIGIN from BACK *noun*[1] + BONE *noun*.]
1 The vertebral column, the spine. ME.
to the backbone completely, through and through.
2 A central support or axis; the chief substantial part; *N. Amer.* the spine of a book. L17.
3 The main element or support; the mainstay. M19.
> M. BARROWCLIFFE Ordinary, hardworking men and women who are the backbone of this country.

4 Strength of character, stability of purpose, firmness. M19.
5 A primary or central link in a communications network, now *spec.* a high-speed, high-capacity digital connection which forms the axis of a local or wide area network. E20.
■ **backboned** *adjective* having a backbone M19. **backboneless** *adjective* M19.

backcloth /ˈbakˌklɒθ/ *noun*. L19.
[ORIGIN from BACK- + CLOTH *noun*.]
1 THEATRICAL. A painted cloth hung across the back of the stage as the principal part of the scenery. Freq. *fig.* L19.
> *fig.*: G. S. FRASER A river, for a Restoration poet, would be primarily . . a backcloth for pastoral.

2 A cloth placed between a fabric that is being printed and the blanket, to keep the latter clean. L19.

back-down /ˈbakdaʊn/ *noun*. *colloq.* M19.
[ORIGIN from *back down* s.v. BACK *verb*.]
A surrender of a claim or claims made; a retreat from a stand taken.

backen /ˈbak(ə)n/ *verb*. Now *rare*. M17.
[ORIGIN from BACK *adjective*, *adverb* + -EN[5]: cf. LESSEN *verb*.]
1 *verb trans.* Put or throw back; retard. M17.
2 *verb intrans.* Move or draw back; *esp.* = BACK *verb* 11. M18.

backer /ˈbakə/ *noun*[1]. L16.
[ORIGIN from BACK *verb* + -ER[1].]
A supporter, esp. a person who makes a bet; a person who provides financial backing.
backer-up a person who backs (up).

backer *noun*[2] var. of BACCA.

backer *adjective* see BACK *adjective*.

backet /ˈbakɪt/ *noun*. *Scot.* LME.
[ORIGIN Old French & mod. French *baquet* dim. of *bac* BACK *noun*[2]: see -ET[1].]
A shallow wooden trough for carrying ashes, lime, salt, etc.

backfall /ˈbakfɔːl/ *noun*. L17.
[ORIGIN from BACK- + FALL *noun*[1].]
†**1** MUSIC. An accessory note a tone or a semitone above the main note. L17–L19.
2 A fall or throw on the back in wrestling. E19.
3 A lever in the coupler of an organ. L19.

backfire /ˈbakfʌɪə/ *noun*. M19.
[ORIGIN from BACK *adverb* + FIRE *noun*.]
1 A fire deliberately lighted ahead of an advancing prairie fire or bush fire in order to deprive it of fuel and so extinguish it. *N. Amer. & Austral.* M19.
2 A premature ignition or explosion in an internal-combustion engine or its exhaust pipe. L19. ▸**b** *fig.* The recoiling of a plan, scheme, etc., adversely on its originator (see BACKFIRE *verb* 2b). E20.

backfire /bakˈfʌɪə/ *verb*. L19.
[ORIGIN from BACKFIRE *noun*.]
1 *verb intrans.* Light a fire ahead of an advancing prairie fire in order to deprive it of fuel. *N. Amer.* L19.
2 *verb intrans.* Of an internal-combustion engine or its fuel: ignite or explode prematurely; also *transf.* (esp. of a firearm). L19. ▸**b** *fig.* Of a plan, scheme, etc.: recoil adversely on its originator. E20.
3 *verb trans.* Expel backwards in backfiring. E20.

Backfisch /ˈbakfɪʃ/ *noun*. Pl. **-e** /-ə/. L19.
[ORIGIN German, lit. 'fish for frying'.]
A girl in late adolescence, a teenage girl.

backfriend /ˈbakfrɛnd/ *noun*. L15.
[ORIGIN from BACK- + FRIEND *noun*.]
1 A pretended friend; an unavowed enemy. *obsolete* exc. *dial.* L15.
2 A supporter, a backer. L16.

backgammon /ˈbakgamən/ *noun*. M17.
[ORIGIN from BACK *adverb* + an earlier form of GAME *noun* (see GAMMON *noun*[4]).]
1 A game for two played on a special (usu. hinged) double board, with draughtsmen whose moves are determined by throws of the dice. M17.
2 *spec.* The most complete form of win at backgammon. L19.

background /ˈbakgraʊnd/ *noun & verb*. L17.
[ORIGIN from BACK *adjective* + GROUND *noun*.]
▸**A** *noun*. **1** The ground or surface lying at the back of or behind the chief objects and foreground in a scene, picture, or description. L17.
> R. B. SHERIDAN Elvira walks about pensively in the background. J. HEDGECOE The most convenient way to photograph a silhouette is to position the subject some distance in front of a white background.

2 *fig.* A less prominent position; obscurity, retirement. L18.
> LD MACAULAY Political friends thought it best . . that he should remain in the background.

3 *fig.* Surroundings, ambience, the prevailing circumstances; *esp.* (information about) events or facts regarded as a basis on which more particular matters may be considered or apprehended. M19.
> J. LE CARRÉ He told you about Mundt; gave you the background? *attrib.*: M. INNES Do some background reading in published sources.

4 *fig.* A person's cultural knowledge, education, experience, environment, etc.; social surroundings. E20.
> C. JACKSON Who they are and where they came from—their backgrounds, I mean. T. STOPPARD Do you find it incredible that a man with a scientific background should be Archbishop of Canterbury?

5 Adventitious radio, sound, etc., signals; the normal level of radioactivity, electromagnetic radiation, or other phenomena, arising from natural sources. E20.
> J. NARLIKAR Penzias and Wilson found a radiation background which was isotropic . . and which corresponded to a black body temperature of ∼3.5 K.

6 Music or sound effects used as an accompaniment, esp. to a film or broadcast programme. E20.
> L. FEATHER Vocals . . with fine backgrounds and solos by Bird.

– COMB.: **background heater**, **background heating** a heater, heating, intended for general warmth; **background music** music played in the background; *esp.* music accompanying a film etc. (cf. sense 6 above); **background noise** noise in the background; *esp.* adventitious radio etc. signals (cf. sense 5 above).
▸**B** *verb trans.* **1** Form a background to. M18.
2 Put in the background. Chiefly *fig.*, treat as unimportant, give no emphasis to. L19.
3 Provide with background information or knowledge. M20.
■ **backgrounder** *noun* (*N. Amer.*) an official briefing or handout giving background information M20.

backhand /ˈbakhand/ *noun*, *adjective*, & *verb*. M17.
[ORIGIN from BACK- + HAND *noun*.]
▸**A** *noun*. The hand turned backwards in making a stroke; *spec.* in tennis, badminton, and similar games, a stroke played with the arm across the body and the back of the hand facing one's opponent. M17.
on the backhand (on the side on which one must strike a ball etc.) backhanded.
▸**B** *attrib.* or as *adjective*. Of a stroke etc.: played backhanded. Of an area of a tennis or badminton court, etc.: in which it is usually necessary to play backhanded. L17.
▸**C** *verb*. **1** *verb intrans.* Take an extra glass of wine out of turn: see BACKHANDER 2. *rare*. M19.
2 *verb trans.* Hit with the back of one's hand. M20.

backhanded /ˈbakhandɪd/ *adjective & adverb*. E19.
[ORIGIN from BACKHAND + -ED[2].]
▸**A** *adjective*. **1** Of a stroke etc.: made with the back of the hand or with the hand turned backwards; *spec.* in tennis, badminton, and similar games, played as a backhand (BACKHAND *noun*). E19.
2 *fig.* Indirect, ambiguous. E19.
> K. TYNAN Is it a backhanded compliment to say that this actor is best when maddest?

▸**B** *adverb*. With the back of the hand or with the hand turned backwards; with a backhand. L19.
■ **backhandedly** *adverb* L19.

backhander /ˈbakhandə/ *noun*. E19.
[ORIGIN formed as BACKHANDED + -ER[1].]
1 A blow with the back of the hand. E19. ▸**b** *fig.* A hurtful or stinging remark. M19.
2 An extra glass of wine out of turn, the bottle being passed back. *rare*. M19.
3 A backhanded stroke or blow (cf. BACKHANDED *adjective* 1). L19.
4 A tip or bribe made surreptitiously; a secret payment. *slang*. M20.

backing /ˈbakɪŋ/ *noun*. M16.
[ORIGIN from BACK *verb* + -ING[1].]
1 The action of BACK *verb*, *esp.* the action of supporting at the back; motion in a backward direction. M16.
2 *collect.* Something which backs or forms the back, *esp.* a body of supporters; the material used to form the back or support of something. L18. ▸**b** Instrumental or vocal accompaniment, esp. on a recording. M20.
– COMB.: **backing store** COMPUTING secondary storage (usu. disk) supporting the primary storage (usu. volatile); a device for this.

backlash /ˈbaklaʃ/ *noun*. E19.
[ORIGIN from BACK *adverb* + LASH *noun*[1].]
1 An irregular recoil or excessive play in a piece of mechanism. E19.
2 *transf.* & *fig.* An excessive or violent reaction; reactionary attitudes or opinion. E20.
> P. BRICKHILL She learned the police had searched her room. I caught the backlash. M. L. KING The white backlash had always existed underneath and sometimes on the surface of American life.

B

backload /ˈbakləʊd/ *noun & verb*. E18.
[ORIGIN from BACK- + LOAD *noun & verb*.]
▸**A** *noun*. **1** An amount that can be carried on the back. E18.
2 A cargo carried by a vehicle returning to its base. E19.
▸**B** *verb*. **1** *verb intrans.* Of a cargo vehicle: return to its base carrying a new load; be loaded with a cargo for its return journey. M20.
2 *verb trans.* Defer the bulk of (expenditure, fees, etc.) until the latter part of a certain period of time. Chiefly *US*. L20.
■ **backloaded** *adjective* (of payment, etc.) deferred until the latter part of a period of time L20.

backlog /ˈbaklɒg/ *noun*. L17.
[ORIGIN from BACK- + LOG *noun*[1].]
1 A large log placed at the back of a fire. Chiefly *N. Amer., Austral., & NZ*. L17.
2 *fig.* **a** An accumulation, a reserve. L19. ▸**b** Arrears of unfulfilled orders, uncompleted work, etc. M20.

backmost /ˈbakməʊst/ *adjective*. L18.
[ORIGIN from BACK *adjective* after FOREMOST, HINDMOST: see -MOST.]
Furthest to the back, hindmost. Opp. FOREMOST.

back seat /bak siːt/ *noun phr.* M19.
[ORIGIN from BACK *adjective* + SEAT *noun*.]
1 A seat at the back of a vehicle; an inferior seat at the back of a hall etc. M19.
2 A position of comparative obscurity or inferiority. *colloq.* M19.
take a back seat (orig. *US*) occupy a subordinate place.
– COMB.: **back-seat driver** a person who rides in the back seat of a motor vehicle and gives unwanted advice to its driver; *fig.* a person who criticizes or attempts to control without responsibility.

backsheesh *noun & verb* var. of BAKSHEESH.

backside /bakˈsʌɪd/; *in sense 4 also* ˈbaksʌɪd/ *noun*. LME.
[ORIGIN from BACK *adjective* + SIDE *noun*.]
1 The hinder or back part; the back, the rear. LME.
2 The back premises of, or an outbuilding attached to, a dwelling; also, a privy, a lavatory. Now *dial. & US*. LME.
†**3** = BACK *noun*[1] 3. LME–E18.
4 The buttocks. E16.
†**5** *fig.* The reverse or wrong side; the opposite. M–L17.

backslide /ˈbakslʌɪd/ *verb intrans.* Pa. t. & pple **-slid** /-slɪd/. M16.
[ORIGIN from BACK *adverb* + SLIDE *verb*.]
Slide back (in fig. sense); fall away from attained excellence, esp. of religious faith and practice; relapse into sin or error.
■ **backslider** *noun* a person who backslides, an apostate L16.

backstone *noun* var. of BAKESTONE.

backsword /ˈbaksɔːd/ *noun*. *arch.* M16.
[ORIGIN from BACK *noun*[1] + SWORD *noun*.]
1 A sword with only one cutting edge. M16.
2 A single stick used instead of a sword in fencing; (an) exercise using this. L17.
3 A fencer with a backsword. L17.

backup /ˈbakʌp/ *noun*. E20.
[ORIGIN from *back up* s.v. BACK *verb*.]
1 Backward motion of a vehicle. *N. Amer.* E20.
2 An accumulation of water, traffic, etc., behind an obstruction. *N. Amer.* M20.
3 A reserve, a standby or spare; support, backing; COMPUTING (the making of) a duplicate copy of a disk, file, program, etc. Freq. *attrib.* M20.
– COMB.: **backup light** a reversing light.

Backus /ˈbakʌs/ *noun*. M20.
[ORIGIN John W. *Backus* (b. 1924), US computer scientist.]
COMPUTING. ***Backus–Naur*** /naʊə/ [Peter *Naur*, 20th-cent. mathematician] or ***Backus normal form***, a form of notation used to describe context-free programming languages. Abbreviation ***BNF***.

backward /ˈbakwəd/ *adverb*, *adjective*, *verb*, & *noun*. As adverb & (*rare*) adjective also **-wards** /-wədz/. ME.
[ORIGIN Aphet. from ABACKWARD: later assoc. with BACK *noun*[1].]
▸**A** *adverb*. **I** Towards one's back, or the back of anything.
1 Of movement: in the direction of one's back or away from one's front. ME. ▸**b** With verbs of continuous motion: with the back foremost, with the face to the rear. ME.
> S. HILL She had fallen heavily backwards down the stairs. **b** LYTTON He walked backward, as if not to lose the view.

bend over backward(s), **fall over backward(s)**, **lean over backward(s)** *fig.* go to the opposite extreme to avoid possible bias etc., do one's utmost *to* oblige, accommodate, etc.
2 Of position: towards the back or rear of a place; away from the front. *obsolete* or *arch.* LME.
▸**II** Towards what is behind in position or course.

B

3 In the direction which (as regards one's ordinary position) is behind one, or from which one is moving. (Now more usu. expressed by *back* or *behind*.) *arch.* LME.

BROWNING Whom else could I dare look backward for?

4 Of things: towards the place of starting; in the direction opposite to that of previous progress. (Not normally used of people or animals, where ambiguity might arise.) LME.

DRYDEN Like some impetuous flood, which mastered once, With double force bends backward.

backward and forward, backwards and forwards in both directions alternately, to and fro.

5 In the direction of retreat. LME.

BYRON They are beaten backward from the palace.

6 *fig.* Towards or into a worse state; into decline. LME.

G. B. SHAW He regarded that as a step backward in civilization.

7 Of time: towards or in the past. (More usu. expressed by *back*.) *arch.* LME.

M. MITCHELL Bitter-eyed women who looked backward, to dead times, to dead men, evoking memories that hurt and were futile.

▸ **III** In the reverse direction or order.

8 In a direction opposite to the normal, in the reverse way. LME.

L. DURRELL Damn the word [love] . . . I would like to spell it backwards as you say the Elizabethans did God. J. LE CARRÉ Sloping his pen backwards he practised the second signature until he was satisfied with it. M. FRAYN As if in a film of a breaking vase run backwards the pieces flew miraculously together.

know something backward(s) know something thoroughly, be very well versed in something. **ring the bells backward(s)** *arch.* ring bells beginning with the lowest, to give an alarm etc.

▸ **B** *adjective.* [Attrib. (often ellipt.) use of the adverb; but analogous to adjectives in -WARD of Old English origin.]

1 Directed to the back or rear. LME.

R. SUTCLIFF He watched her walking away without a backward glance.

2 Directed in the opposite way; of or pertaining to return. LME.

W. C. BRYANT And takes the backward way with trembling limbs.

†3 Perverse, unfavourable. L16–M18.

4 Turning or hanging back from action; reluctant, chary; shy, bashful. L16.

SHAKES. *Hen. V* Perish the man whose mind is backward now.

backward in coming forward *colloq.* reluctant, shy (to do something), reticent, (freq. in neg. contexts).

5 Placed towards or at the back; *obsolete* exc. CRICKET (of a fielding position) behind the line of the wicket. E17.

S. JOHNSON A lodging in the backward garret of a mean house.

backward point, backward short leg, etc. (in cricket).

6 Reaching into the past; retrospective. M17.

BYRON The soul . . flies unconscious o'er each backward year.

7 Behindhand in respect of progress; late (esp. of the season or crops); slow to learn; having learning difficulties. L17.

G. GREENE I'd have gone to Oxford . . but they are very backward in technology. A. S. NEILL A child who is backward at school. A. J. TOYNBEE To help . . other still backward peoples on the outer edges of Mexico, to find their way into the modern world.

8 Done in the reverse way; reversed. E18.

POPE The backward labours of her faithless hand.

▸ **C** *verb trans. & intrans.* Put or keep back, retard; go backward. Now *rare*. L16.

▸ **D** *noun.* The past portion of time. *rare*. E17.

SHAKES. *Temp.* What seest thou else In the dark backward and abysm of time?

– SPECIAL COLLOCATIONS & COMB.: **backward compatibility** (of new technology) the capacity to interact with products designed to be used with an earlier version of that technology. **backward-compatible** *adjective* having backward compatibility. **backward masking** PSYCHOLOGY a diminution in the response to a stimulus as a result of a second stimulus following closely after it.

– NOTE: In adverbial uses *backward* is the usual form in North American English, while in British English *backwards* is commoner. As an adjective the standard form is *backward*, and *backwards* is rare.

■ **backwardly** *adverb* M16. **backwardness** *noun* L16.

backwardation /bakwəˈdeɪʃ(ə)n/ *noun.* M19.

[ORIGIN from BACKWARD + -ATION.]

COMMERCE. A premium paid by the seller of stock or commodities in some cases where delivery is to be deferred. Cf. CONTANGO *noun*.

backwards *adverb & adjective* see BACKWARD.

backwash /ˈbakwɒʃ/ *noun & verb.* L19.

[ORIGIN from BACK *adverb* + WASH *noun*.]

▸ **A** *noun.* **1** The motion of a receding wave, a backward current; *fig.* repercussions. L19.

2 The process of cleaning a filter by flushing it in the reverse direction to normal flow; the liquid used in this process. E20.

▸ **B** *verb trans.* **1** Move or otherwise affect (a boat etc.) with backwash. L19.

2 Clean (a filter) by flushing it in the reverse direction to normal flow; remove (sediment, an obstruction) using this method. M20.

backy *noun* var. of BACCY.

bacon /ˈbeɪk(ə)n/ *noun & verb.* ME.

[ORIGIN Old French *bacon*, -*un* = Provençal *bacon* from Frankish *bako* ham, flitch = Old High German *bahho* from Germanic, rel. to BACK *noun*[1].]

▸ **A** *noun.* **1** The cured back or side of a pig (formerly also the fresh flesh now called *pork*). ME.

bring home the bacon *fig.* (*colloq.*) achieve success. ***save a person's bacon, save one's bacon***: see SAVE *verb*.

†2 The carcass of a pig. ME–M18.

†3 A rustic. Cf. ***chaw-bacon*** s.v. CHAW *verb*. *rare* (Shakes.). Only in L16.

– COMB.: **bacon beetle** = LARDER ***beetle***.

▸ **B** *verb trans.* Convert into bacon. Chiefly *N. Amer.* E19.

■ **baconer** *noun* a pig fit for being made into bacon and ham M18.

Baconian /beɪˈkəʊnɪən/ *adjective & noun.* E19.

[ORIGIN from *Bacon* (see below) + -IAN.]

▸ **A** *adjective.* **1** Of or pertaining to the English philosopher Francis Bacon (1561–1626) or the experimental or inductive system of philosophy propounded by him. E19.

2 Designating or pertaining to the theory that Bacon wrote the plays attributed to Shakespeare. L19.

▸ **B** *noun.* An adherent of Bacon's philosophical system, or of the Baconian theory of Shakespeare's plays. M19.

bacteraemia /baktəˈriːmɪə/ *noun.* Also ***-remia**, **-riaemia** /-rɪˈiːmɪə/. L19.

[ORIGIN from BACTERIUM + -AEMIA.]

MEDICINE. The presence of bacteria in the blood.

■ **bacteraemic** *adjective* M20.

bacteria *noun* pl. of BACTERIUM.

bacteriaemia *noun* var. of BACTERAEMIA.

bacterial /bakˈtɪərɪəl/ *adjective.* L19.

[ORIGIN from BACTERIUM + -AL[1].]

Of, pertaining to, or caused by bacteria.

■ **bacterially** *adverb* L19.

bactericide /bakˈtɪərɪsʌɪd/ *noun.* L19.

[ORIGIN formed as BACTERIAL + -CIDE.]

A substance able to kill bacteria.

■ **bacteriˈcidal** *adjective* able to kill bacteria L19. **bacteriˈcidally** *adverb* L19.

bacterio- /bakˈtɪərɪəʊ/ *combining form* of BACTERIUM: see -O-.

■ **bacterioˈcidal** *adjective* = BACTERICIDAL *adjective* M20. **bacteriophage** *noun* a virus that causes lysis or prophage formation in bacteria E20. **bacterioˈphobia** *noun* irrational fear of bacteria L19. **bacteriorhoˈdopsin** *noun* (BIOCHEMISTRY) a protein pigment in the bacterium *Halobacterium halobium* which under the action of light transports protons across the cytoplasmic membrane L20. **bacteriˈosis** *noun*, pl. **-oses** /-ˈəʊsiːz/, a bacterial disease of plants L19.

bacteriocin /bakˈtɪərɪəsɪn/ *noun.* M20.

[ORIGIN French *bactériocine*, formed as BACTERIO- + COLICIN.]

BACTERIOLOGY. A protein produced by bacteria of one strain and active against those of a closely related strain.

bacterioid /bakˈtɪərɪɔɪd/ *adjective & noun.* L19.

[ORIGIN from BACTERIUM + -OID.]

= BACTEROID.

bacteriological /bakˌtɪərɪəˈlɒdʒɪk(ə)l/ *adjective.* L19.

[ORIGIN from BACTERIOLOGY + -ICAL.]

Of or pertaining to bacteriology.

bacteriological warfare the deliberate use of bacteria to spread disease among an enemy.

■ **bacteriologic** *adjective* = BACTERIOLOGICAL L19. **bacteriologically** *adverb* L19.

bacteriology /bakˌtɪərɪˈɒlədʒi/ *noun.* L19.

[ORIGIN from BACTERIO- + -LOGY.]

The branch of science that deals with bacteria.

■ **bacteriologist** *noun* L19.

bacteriolysis /bakˌtɪərɪˈɒlɪsɪs/ *noun.* Pl. **-lyses** /-lɪsiːz/. L19.

[ORIGIN from BACTERIO- + -LYSIS.]

†1 Artificial liquefaction of organic waste by bacteria. Only in L19.

2 The destruction of bacteria by an antibody. E20.

■ **bacteriolysin** /-ˈlʌɪsɪn/ *noun* a bacteriolytic antibody E20. **bacteriolytic** /-ˈlɪtɪk/ *adjective* of, pertaining to, or capable of bacteriolysis E20.

bacteriostasis /bakˌtɪərɪəˈsteɪsɪs/ *noun.* Pl. **-stases** /-ˈsteɪsiːz/. E20.

[ORIGIN formed as BACTERIOLYSIS + Greek *stasis* stopping.]

Inhibition of the proliferation of bacteria without killing them.

■ **bacteriostat** /bakˈtɪərɪəstat/ *noun* a bacteriostatic agent E20. **bacteriostatic** /-ˈstatɪk/ *adjective* pertaining to or capable of bacteriostasis E20.

bacterium /bakˈtɪərɪəm/ *noun.* Pl. **-ia** /-ɪə/. M19.

[ORIGIN mod. Latin from Greek *baktērion* dim. of *baktēria* staff, cane.]

Any of the very widely distributed group *Bacteria* of microscopic prokaryotic mainly single-celled organisms, many of which are symbiotic or pathogenic in animals and plants.

iron bacterium: see IRON *noun & adjective*. ***purple bacterium***: see PURPLE *adjective & noun*.

– NOTE: Bacteria were formerly classified as fungi, but are now usu. regarded (with blue-green algae) as constituting a distinct division of plants, or an independent kingdom.

■ **bacterize** /ˈbaktərʌɪz/ *verb trans.* treat with bacteria E20. **bacteriˈzation** *noun* E20.

bacteriuria /bakˌtɪərɪˈjʊərɪə/ *noun.* Also **bacteruria** /baktəˈrʊərɪə/. L19.

[ORIGIN from BACTERIUM + -URIA.]

MEDICINE. The presence of bacteria in the urine.

bacteroid /ˈbaktərɔɪd/ *adjective & noun.* M19.

[ORIGIN formed as BACTERIURIA + -OID.]

▸ **A** *adjective.* Of the nature of or resembling a bacterium. M19.

▸ **B** *noun.* A bacteroid organism or structure; *esp.* a modified cell formed by a symbiotic bacterium in a root nodule of a leguminous plant. L19.

bacteruria *noun* var. of BACTERIURIA.

Bactrian /ˈbaktrɪən/ *noun & adjective.* LME.

[ORIGIN Greek *Baktrianos*, Latin *Bactrianus*, from *Bactria*: see below, -IAN.]

▸ **A** *noun.* **1** *hist.* A native or inhabitant of Bactria, an ancient country of central Asia lying between the Hindu Kush and the Oxus. LME.

2 = ***Bactrian camel*** s.v. CAMEL 1. E17.

▸ **B** *adjective.* Of or belonging to Bactria. E17.

Bactrian camel: see CAMEL 1.

baculine /ˈbakjʊlʌɪn/ *adjective.* *rare.* E18.

[ORIGIN from Latin *baculum*, -*us* rod, stick + -INE[1].]

Of or pertaining to punishment by caning or flogging.

baculovirus /ˈbakjʊlə(ʊ)ˌvʌɪrəs/ *noun.* L20.

[ORIGIN formed as BACULINE + VIRUS.]

Any of a family of DNA viruses which infect arthropods (esp. insects) and include some forms used for pest control.

baculum /ˈbakjʊləm/ *noun.* Pl. **-la** /-lə/. M20.

[ORIGIN mod. Latin: see BACULINE.]

= ***os penis*** s.v. OS *noun*[1].

bad /bad/ *adjective, noun, & adverb.* ME.

[ORIGIN Orig. disyllabic: perh. repr. Old English *bǣddel* hermaphrodite (cf. BADLING *noun*[1]) with loss of *l* as in *much(e)*, *wench(e)* for Old English *myċel*, *wenċel*.]

▸ **A** *adjective.* Compar. WORSE *adjective*, (now *non-standard*) **badder**, superl. WORST *adjective*, (now *non-standard*) **baddest**.

▸ **I** In a privative sense: not good.

1 Of defective quality or worth; worthless, inferior, deficient, deteriorated; debased, counterfeit. ME.

T. R. MALTHUS Children perished . . from bad nourishment. E. GLASGOW All ways are long over bad roads. S. GOLDWYN Why should people go out to see bad films when they can stay at home and see bad television? K. LAFFAN I couldn't do it on the phone—his hearing's bad.

2 Unfortunate, unfavourable; incurring or involving disapproval or dislike. ME.

MILTON Perplexed and troubled at his bad success. E. WAUGH He . . could talk at length of [Vatican] policy and appointments, saying which contemporary ecclesiastics were in good favour, which in bad.

come to a bad end: see COME *verb*.

3 LAW. Not valid. L19.

▸ **II** In a positive sense: evil, noxious.

4 Morally depraved; immoral, wicked; (in weakened sense) naughty, badly behaved, blameworthy. ME.

J. FORDYCE Young people . . are often corrupted by bad books. LD MACAULAY Discreet counsellors implored the royal brothers not to countenance this bad man. S. HILL That is a bad habit which must be cured at once. P. ROTH When I am bad and rotten in small ways she can manage me herself.

5 Of a person: in ill health, sick, unwell; *transf.* distressed, regretful (*about* something). Of the body or a part of it: diseased, injured. ME.

S. RICHARDSON Still very bad with my Gout. W. H. HERNDON Tiger felt bad about the matter. E. O'NEILL You were afraid his heart was bad.

6 Causing inconvenience or trouble; offensive, unpleasant; (of weather) inclement. E16.

A. CHERRY-GARRARD Polar exploration is . . the cleanest and most isolated way of having a bad time. L. URIS The children . . smelled bad from the lack of water to wash with. J. HARVEY Barry's father saw that something serious and bad had happened.

7 Harmful, hurtful, or dangerous (*for* someone); more gen. as an intensifying word in unfavourable contexts: extreme, pronounced. M17.

B

LD MACAULAY He had just had a bad fall in hunting. N. MITFORD He caught a bad cold . . and stayed indoors. B. PYM Too much washing was bad for the skin. K. J. DOVER A trustfulness which admits regretfully that he made some bad mistakes.

► **III 8** Good, excellent. *slang* (chiefly *US*). **M20.**

– SPECIAL COLLOCATIONS, PHRASES, & COMB.: ***a bad sport***: see SPORT *noun*. ***a bad taste in the mouth***: see TASTE *noun*[1]. ***bad bargain***: see BARGAIN *noun* 2. ***bad blood***: see BLOOD *noun*. ***bad break***: see BREAK *noun*[1]. **bad business** an unfortunate matter. ***bad cess to***: see CESS *noun*[2]. ***bad coin***: see COIN *noun* 4. ***bad conscience***. **bad debt**: which cannot be recovered. **bad egg** (*a*) an egg that is inedible through deterioration; (*b*) a person or scheme that comes to no good. ***bad faith***: see FAITH *noun*. ***bad form***: see FORM *noun*. **bad hair day** *colloq.* a day on which one's hair is particularly unmanageable; (in extended use) a day on which everything seems to go wrong. ***bad hat***: see HAT *noun*. ***bad health***: see HEALTH *noun* 5. ***bad job***: see JOB *noun*[1]. **badland**, **badlands** (chiefly *N. Amer.*) barren, inhospitable land with many gullies, ridges, and other erosional features, esp. in certain parts of the western US. ***bad language***: see LANGUAGE *noun*[1] 2d. **bad law**: that is not sustainable or not justifiable. ***bad loser***: see LOSER 2. ***bad lot***: see LOT *noun*. ***bad luck!***, ***bad luck to you!*** etc.: see LUCK *noun*. **badman** (chiefly *N. Amer.*) a desperado, an outlaw. **bad mouth** *N. Amer. slang* malicious gossip or criticism. **bad-mouth** *verb trans.* (*N. Amer. slang*) abuse, criticize maliciously. **bad news** *slang* an unwelcome guest; something undesirable. ***bad penny***: see PENNY *noun*. ***bad scran to —***: see SCRAN 2. ***bad show***: see SHOW *noun*[1]. **bad-tempered** *adjective* having a bad temper; easily angered. ***come to a bad end***: see COME *verb*. ***from bad to worse***: see WORSE *adjective, noun, & adverb*. **go bad** decay, (esp. of food) become mouldy, sour, etc. ***in a bad temper***: see TEMPER *noun*. **in a bad way** ill, in trouble. ***in bad repair***: see REPAIR *noun*[2]. ***in bad stead***: see STEAD *noun*. ***in someone's bad books***: see BOOK *noun*. ***just too bad***: see JUST *adverb*. ***keep bad time***: see TIME *noun*. **not bad**, **not half bad**, **not so bad** better than might have been expected, fairly good. ***throw good money after bad***: see THROW *verb*. **too bad** regrettable (often *iron.*). ***with a bad grace***: see GRACE *noun*.

► **B** *noun*. **1** Something bad; bad condition; ill fortune. **LME.**

SHAKES. *Two Gent.* T'exchange the bad for better.

from bad to worse: see WORSE *noun*. ***get in bad***: see GET *verb*. **in bad** *colloq.* out of favour (*with*). **to the bad** to a bad state, to ruin; in deficit.

2 (As a count noun) A bad thing, quality, or (*rare*) person. **L16.**

3 ***my bad***, used to acknowledge responsibility for a mistake. *US colloq.* **L20.**

Parenting Sorry I lost your CD. It's my bad.

► **C** *adverb*. = BADLY. Now chiefly *N. Amer.* **E17.**

L. HELLMAN I only came cause she's so bad off. M. K. RAWLINGS She's bad hurt. B. SCHULBERG If you needed shoes that bad you could have told me.

have got it bad: see GET *verb*.

■ **baddish** *adjective* **M18.** **baddy** *noun* (*colloq.*) a bad person, a criminal, a villain (esp. in a film or play) **M20.** **badness** *noun* **LME.**

†**bad** *verb* see BID *verb*.

Badarian /bəˈdɛːrɪən, bəˈdɑːrɪən/ *adjective & noun*. **E20.**
[ORIGIN from *Badari* (see below) + -AN.]
ARCHAEOLOGY. ► **A** *adjective*. Designating or pertaining to an early predynastic culture of Upper Egypt, evidence for which was first found in the Badari region. **E20.**
► **B** *noun*. (A person of) the Badarian culture. **M20.**

badass /ˈbadas/ *noun & adjective*. *slang* (orig. and chiefly *US*). **M20.**
[ORIGIN from BAD *adjective* + ASS *noun*[2].]
► **A** *noun*. A tough, aggressive, or uncooperative person; a troublemaker. **M20.**
► **B** *adjective*. Belligerent or intimidating; tough; bad, nasty. Also used approvingly: terrific, excellent. **M20.**

S. KING Elbert was a strange fellow with a badass temper. T. CLANCY This Nikon F-20 was one badass camera.

■ **bad-assed** *adjective* **L20.**

baddeleyite /ˈbad(ə)lɪʌɪt/ *noun*. **L19.**
[ORIGIN from Joseph *Baddeley* (fl. 1892), English traveller + -ITE[1].]
MINERALOGY. Zirconium dioxide, occurring as colourless, yellow, brown, or black monoclinic crystals.

badder *compar. adjective* see BAD *adjective*.

baddest *superl. adjective* see BAD *adjective*.

bade *verb* see BID *verb*.

badge /badʒ/ *noun & verb*[1]. **LME.**
[ORIGIN Unknown: cf. Old French *bage*, Anglo-Latin *bagia*.]
► **A** *noun*. **1** A distinctive device, emblem, or mark (orig. in HERALDRY, a device borne for distinction by all the retainers of a noble house: cf. COGNIZANCE), worn as a sign of office or licensed employment or of membership of a society. **LME.**

T. H. WHITE There were already thousands . . who carried his badge of a scarlet fist clenching a whip. N. HAMILTON Monty's contempt for army regulations was epitomized by his adoption . . of a tank beret with two badges.

rogue's badge: see ROGUE *noun*.

2 A distinguishing sign, token, or emblem; *fig.* a characteristic feature revealing a quality or condition. **E16.**

G. W. KNIGHT Dark secrecy and night are in Shakespeare ever the badges of crime. A. HALEY Every cook . . would walk in a way to make those keys jangle as a badge of how important and trusted she was.

yellow badge: see YELLOW *adjective*.

3 NAUTICAL. An ornamental window surround, or a representation of a window, at the stern of a small sailing vessel. **M18.**

– COMB.: **badge-man** a person who wears an official badge.

► **B** *verb trans*. Mark with or distinguish by a badge. **LME.**

■ **badgeless** *adjective* **L16.**

badge /badʒ/ *verb*[2] *intrans. & trans*. Long *obsolete* exc. *dial.* **M16.**
[ORIGIN Prob. back-form. from BADGER *noun*[1].]
Deal as a badger; trade in (corn etc.) as a badger.

badge *verb*[3] see BAG *verb*[2].

badger /ˈbadʒə/ *noun*[1]. Long *obsolete* exc. *dial.* **ME.**
[ORIGIN Unknown.]
A person who buys and sells grain or other commodities; a huckster.

badger /ˈbadʒə/ *noun*[2] *& verb*. **E16.**
[ORIGIN Perh. from BADGE *noun* + -ARD, with ref. to the distinctive head-markings.]
► **A** *noun*. **1** A nocturnal burrowing Eurasian mammal, *Meles meles*, of the weasel family, having a grey coat and distinctive white facial stripes. **E16.** ►**b** Any of various animals of similar appearance or habits; *esp.* (*a*) the related N. American badger, *Taxidea taxus*; (*b*) *Austral.* the wombat. **M17.**

draw the badger *fig.* entice one's opponent into the open. **b** ***honey badger***: see HONEY *noun*. ***stinking badger***: see STINKING *adjective*.

2 A brush, or a fishing fly, made of badger's hair. **L18.**

– COMB.: **badger-baiting**, **badger-drawing** setting dogs to draw a badger from its set or from a cask; **badger game** *slang* luring men into (esp. sexually) compromising situations in order to blackmail them; **Badger State** *US* Wisconsin.

► **B** *verb trans*. Bait or pester as a dog does a badger; torment, tease, nag. **L18.**

F. O'CONNOR She began to badger him about his health. C. RYAN Badgered by Field Marshal Model to capture the Arnhem bridge quickly. L. VAN DER POST I could easily have been talked, badgered and teased out of my belief.

■ **badgerer** *noun* (*a*) a dog used for badger-baiting; (*b*) a person who badgers another: **L19.**

badian /ˈbɑːdɪən/ *noun*[1]. **M19.**
[ORIGIN French *badiane* from Persian & Urdu *bādyān* fennel, anise.]
The fruit of Chinese anise or star anise.

Badian /ˈbeɪdɪən/ *noun*[2] *& adjective*. **M19.**
[ORIGIN Abbreviation of BARBADIAN. See also BAJAN.]
= BARBADIAN.

badigeon /bəˈdɪdʒ(ə)n/ *noun*. Now *US*. **M18.**
[ORIGIN French, of unknown origin.]
A composition used to fill up gaps in stone or wood.

badinage /ˈbadɪnɑːʒ/ *noun & verb*. **M17.**
[ORIGIN French, from *badiner* to joke, from *badin* fool from Provençal, from *badar* gape from Proto-Romance: see -AGE.]
► **A** *noun*. Humorous banter or ridicule. **M17.**
► **B** *verb intrans. & trans*. Banter playfully. **E19.**

badling /ˈbadlɪŋ/ *noun*[1]. Long *obsolete* exc. *dial.*
[ORIGIN Old English *bǣdling*, from *bǣddel*: see BAD *adjective*, -LING[1].]
An effeminate or homosexual man; a worthless fellow.

badling /ˈbadlɪŋ/ *noun*[2]. **L15.**
[ORIGIN Perh. var. of *paddling* verbal noun of PADDLE *verb*[1].]
A small group of ducks.

badly /ˈbadli/ *adverb & adjective*. **ME.**
[ORIGIN from BAD *adjective* + -LY[2].]
► **A** *adverb*. Compar. WORSE *adverb*, superl. WORST *adverb*.
1 In a bad manner; inadequately; incorrectly; immorally, wickedly; severely. **ME.**

SHAKES. *John* How goes the day with us? . . Badly, I fear. SOUTHEY One of the Indian chiefs was badly wounded. DICKENS A mean and badly-furnished apartment. J. RUSKIN So great a painter . . would never paint badly enough to deceive. G. B. SHAW Think of the temptation to behave badly when he had us all there helpless.

badly off in poor circumstances, lacking money. ***have got it badly***: see GET *verb*.

2 With *want*, *need*, etc.: greatly, very much. **L19.**

E. O'NEILL His blond hair, badly in need of a cut.

► **B** *adjective*. Sick, unwell; regretful. *dial.* **L18.**

D. H. LAWRENCE 'I want my mother.' . . 'Ay, but she's badly'. A. HALEY Kunta felt badly for having wished sometimes that he might strike the man.

badmash /ˈbʌdmɑːʃ/ *noun*. **M19.**
[ORIGIN Urdu from Persian, from *bad* evil + Arabic *maʿāš* means of livelihood.]
In the Indian subcontinent: a disreputable or villainous man.

badminton /ˈbadmɪnt(ə)n/ *noun*. **M19.**
[ORIGIN *Badminton*, a town in SW England and seat of the Duke of Beaufort.]
1 A summer drink of claret, soda, and sugar. **M19.**
2 A game played on a court (usu. indoors) across a net with rackets and a shuttlecock. **L19.**

BAe *abbreviation*.
British Aerospace.

Baedeker /ˈbeɪdɪkə/ *noun*. **M19.**
[ORIGIN See below.]
Any of a series of guidebooks published by Karl Baedeker (1801–59), German publisher, or his successors; *gen.* any guidebook.

– COMB.: **Baedeker raids** *hist.* a series of German reprisal air raids in 1942 on places in Britain of cultural and historical importance.

bael /ˈbeɪl/ *noun*. Also **bel** /bɛl/. **E17.**
[ORIGIN Hindi *bel* from Sanskrit *bilva* from Tamil *vilavu*.]
(The aromatic fruit of) a thorny Indian tree, *Aegle marmelos*. Also called ***Bengal quince***.

baetyl /ˈbiːtɪl/ *noun*. Also in Graecized form **baetylion** /bɪˈtɪlɪən/, pl. **-lia** /-lɪə/. **M19.**
[ORIGIN Latin *baetulus* from Greek *baitulos*.]
A sacred meteoric stone.

baff /baf/ *noun & verb*. *Scot.* **E16.**
[ORIGIN Prob. from Old French *baffe* a slap in the face.]
► **A** *noun*. A blow with something flat or soft. **E16.**
► **B** *verb trans*. Beat, strike; GOLF strike (the ground) with the sole of the club head in making a stroke. **E16.**

baffle /ˈbaf(ə)l/ *verb & noun*. **M16.**
[ORIGIN In sense 1 perh. alt. of BAUCHLE *verb*. In other senses perh. rel. to French *bafouer* (16) ridicule, alt. of Old Provençal *bafar*: cf. French †*beffler* (Rabelais) mock, deceive.]
► **A** *verb*. **I** *verb trans*. †**1** Subject to public disgrace or infamy; treat with scorn. **M16–L17.**

SPENSER He by the heels him hung upon a tree And baffuld so, that all which passed by The picture of his punishment might see.

†**2** Hoodwink, cheat. **L16–E18.**

DEFOE He had not a mind to cheat or baffle the poor man.

3 Bewilder, confuse; reduce to perplexity, puzzle. **M17.**

M. INNES Such incongruities . . had an insidious power to paralyse the will, to baffle the intellect. W. FAULKNER He looked about with a strained, baffled gaze, as if . . trying to remember what it was he wanted to say or to do. H. E. BATES She had been a little sorry for Parker; she had been a little puzzled and baffled by him; and now she was hurt. W. H. AUDEN A murder which has the professionals baffled.

†**4** Confound, bring to nought. **M17–E19.**

G. CRABBE A wish so strong, it baffled his repose.

5 Defeat in one's efforts, thwart, foil (passing into sense 3); (of the weather) impede the progress of (a ship). **L17.**

E. A. FREEMAN The murderer baffled pursuit. R. L. STEVENSON The more they tried, the more obstinately fixed I grew to baffle them. H. ALLEN She had met light, baffling airs from the coast of Puerto Rico onward. W. S. CHURCHILL Hamilton, the baffled peacemaker, returned . . full of self-reproach for the advice he had given to the King.

6 Restrict by means of a baffle; equip with a baffle. **L19.**

► **II** *verb intrans*. †**7** Trifle, quibble. **M17–M18.**

8 Struggle ineffectually or futilely. *rare*. **M19.**

– COMB.: **bafflegab** *colloq.* (chiefly *N. Amer.*) incomprehensible or pretentious verbiage or jargon.

► **B** *noun*. †**1** Confusion, discomfiture; a setback; a disgrace or affront. **E17–E19.**

2 A state of being baffled. **M19.**

3 A plate or other device which serves to restrict or regulate the passage of fluid, gas, etc., or to limit the emission of sound, light, etc. Freq. *attrib.* **L19.**

baffle-board, ***baffle-plate***, etc.

■ **bafflement** *noun* the action of baffling; the state of being baffled: **M19.** **baffler** *noun* (*a*) a person who or thing which baffles; (*b*) = BAFFLE *noun* 3: **E17.** **bafflingly** *adverb* **L19.**

baft /bɑːft/ *noun*. Also **bafta** /ˈbɑːftə/. **L16.**
[ORIGIN Urdu from Persian *bāft* a textile, *bāfta* woven.]
A coarse (usu. cotton) fabric.

baft /bɑːft/ *adverb*. *arch.*
[ORIGIN Old English *beæftan*, from *be* by, at + *æftan* behind. Cf. AFT.]
Behind, in the rear. Latterly only NAUTICAL, astern, aft.

BAFTA /ˈbaftə/ *abbreviation*.
British Academy of Film and Television Arts.

bafta *noun* var. of BAFT *noun*.

bag /bag/ *noun*. **ME.**
[ORIGIN Perh. from Old Norse *baggi* bag, bundle, of unknown origin.]
► **I 1** A receptacle made of flexible material with an open (usu. closable) top (esp. with preceding word indicating its contents or purpose). **ME.**

R. HAWKINS Any man that putteth himself into the enemies port, had need of Argus eyes, and the wind in a bagge. R. LAWLER She's got her bags piled up by the stairs. S. PLATH I cracked open a peanut from the ten-cent bag I had bought.

diplomatic bag, ***gamebag***, ***handbag***, ***mailbag***, ***money bag***, ***paper bag***, ***shoulder bag***, ***sleeping bag***, etc.

2 *spec.* ►**a** A money bag; a handbag. **LME.** ►**b** A small pouch used to hold the back hair of a wig. **E18.** ►**c** A mailbag. **E18.** ►**d** A diplomatic bag. **E19.**

3 *fig.* A concern or preoccupation; one's particular interest or distinctive style. *slang*. **M20.**

E. MCBAIN She developed a new bag after she moved, writing poetry. Wild, huh? A. GLYN He'd never do that. It's just not his bag.

▸ **II 4** A measure of quantity, varying according to the nature of the commodity (*rare* before 17). **ME.**
5 The amount of game a sportsman has shot or caught; *gen.* an amount obtained or achieved in any activity. **M19.**

N. MITFORD A bag of interesting anecdotes. R. V. JONES My bag was mainly rabbits but over the years I had also shot hares, stoats, pigeons, crows, and jays.

6 In *pl.* Much or many (*of*), lots, heaps. *colloq.* **E20.**

J. B. MORTON It's not gay, this life, but it might be bags worse. A. WESKER We 'ad bags o' fun, bags o' it.

▸ **III 7** A fold of skin, esp. under the (human) eye; a dewlap; an udder. **LME.**

E. BOWEN That lamp makes Thomas's face all bags and lines.

8 A sac in the body of an animal, containing poison, honey, etc. **E16.**

fig.: DRYDEN The swelling poison of the several sects Shall burst its bag.

9 In *pl.* (Loosely fitting) trousers. *colloq.* **L16.**

D. L. SAYERS Can't feed with Freddie Arbuthnot in these bags.

OXFORD *bags*.
10 A base in baseball. *N. Amer.* **L19.**
11 A woman, *esp.* one who is unattractive, elderly, or promiscuous. *slang. derog.* **E20.**

M. DICKENS I've never really known a pretty girl like you. At the training college they were all bags. C. JACKSON Heaven knows . . what hell the old bag would give him if she had [waited for him].

— PHRASES: *a hundred in the water bag*: see WATER *noun*. **bag and baggage** (with) all belongings, (of departure) entire, absolute; orig. (*MILITARY*) *march out with bag and baggage*, *march out bag and baggage*, make an honourable retreat, leave with equipment etc. intact. **bag of bones** an emaciated person or animal. **bag of mystery** *slang* a sausage. *bag of nerves*: see NERVE *noun*. **bag of tricks** a stock of resources. **hold the bag**, **be left holding the bag** be (left) in an awkward situation. **in the bag** *colloq.* virtually secured, (as good as) in one's possession or power; captured. *let the cat out of the bag*: see CAT *noun*[1]. MIXED *bag*. *Petty Bag*: see PETTY *adjective*. *rough as bags*: see ROUGH *adjective*. **the whole bag of tricks** everything. *tote bag*: see TOTE *noun*[4].
— COMB.: **bag job** *US slang* an illegal search of a suspect's property by a federal agent, esp. to copy or steal incriminating documents; **bag lady** (chiefly *N. Amer.*) a homeless woman, esp. an elderly one, who carries her possessions in bags; = *SHOPPING-bag lady*; **bagman** †(*a*) a maker of bags or pouches; (*b*) a person who carries a bag; *spec.*: *derog.* a commercial traveller; (*slang*, chiefly *US & Austral.*) a person who collects or distributes the proceeds of illicit activities; *Austral.* a tramp, a vagrant; **bag net** a bag-shaped net for catching fish etc. **bag people** *N. Amer.* homeless people who carry their possessions in bags; **bagpudding** *arch.* a pudding boiled in a bag; **bag-shaped** *adjective* shaped like a bag; *esp.* (of a fishing net) rounded and with an opening at the top; **bagstuffer** (orig. *US*) a piece of promotional literature handed to shoppers, *esp.* one put into shopping bags at a checkout; **bagwash** (a laundry that undertakes) the rough unfinished washing of clothes; **bag-wig** an 18th-cent. wig with the back hair enclosed in an ornamental bag; **bagworm** *US* any of various destructive moth larvae which live within a silken case covered with plant debris.
■ **bagful** *noun* as much or as many as a bag will hold; *colloq.* a lot: **ME. baglike** *adjective* resembling (that of) a bag **M19.**

bag /baɡ/ *verb*[1]. Infl. **-gg-**. **LME.**
[ORIGIN from the noun.]
1 *verb intrans.* Swell out, bulge; *NAUTICAL* drop away from the direct course. **LME.** ▸**b** Hang loosely; *esp.* (of trousers) become out of shape at the knees. **E19.**

F. MARRYAT He was bagging to leeward like a . . barge laden with a hay-stack.

2 *verb trans.* Put into a bag or bags. **LME.**
bag up store up.
3 *verb trans.* Cause to swell; cram full. **LME.**

J. SMEATON Almost all the lights [= windows] in the church, tho' not broke were bagged outward.

4 *verb trans.* Succeed in killing (so much game); *gen.* add to one's 'bag'; seize, catch; steal, appropriate. **E19.** ▸**b** Esp. among children: claim or reserve, usu. on the ground of being the first to do so. Freq. in *bags I*. *slang.* **M19.**

P. HAWKER To bag a dozen head of game without missing. J. DOS PASSOS He was almost bagged by a taxicab crossing the street. T. PYNCHON Slothrop's grandfather . . in typical sarcasm and guile bagged his epitaph from Emily Dickinson, without a credit line. **b** A. A. MILNE Bags I all the presents. B. MARSHALL Bags I do not ask about the room. R. A. KNOX The other girl bagging the hot-water pipes first.

5 *verb trans.* Fit (a patient) with an oxygen mask or other respiratory aid. *N. Amer. colloq.* **L20.**
■ **bagger** *noun*[1] a person who or a machine which puts something into bags **M18.**

bag /baɡ/ *verb*[2] *trans.* Infl. **-gg-**. Also **badge** /badʒ/. **L17.**
[ORIGIN Unknown. Cf. FAG *verb*[2].]
Cut (wheat etc.) with a reaping hook.
■ **bagger** *noun*[2] a person who harvests in this way **M19.**

Baganda /bəˈɡandə/ *noun pl. & adjective.* **L19.**
[ORIGIN Bantu, from *ba-* pl. prefix + *ganda*. Cf. MUGANDA.]
▸ **A** *noun.* Pl. of MUGANDA. **L19.**
▸ **B** *attrib.* or as *adjective.* Of or pertaining to the Baganda. **L19.**

bagarre /baɡaːr/ *noun.* Pl. pronounced same. **L19.**
[ORIGIN French.]
A tumult; a scuffle, a brawl.

bagasse /bəˈɡas/ *noun.* **E19.**
[ORIGIN French from Spanish *bagazo*.]
The residue left after the extraction of juice from sugar cane or sugar beet.
■ **bagassosis** /baɡəˈsəʊsɪs/ *noun* respiratory disease due to inhalation of bagasse dust **M20.**

bagatelle /baɡəˈtɛl/ *noun.* **M17.**
[ORIGIN French from Italian *bagatella* perh. dim. of Latin *baca* berry, or from Italian *baga* baggage.]
1 A trifle, a thing of no value or importance; a negligible amount. **M17.**

C. ISHERWOOD They were well-to-do gentlemen, to whom a miserable fifty-mark note was a mere bagatelle.

2 A piece of verse or music in a light style. **M18.**
3 A game in which small balls are struck (usu. by a mechanical striker operated by the player) towards numbered holes on a board with a semicircular end. **E19.**
RUSSIAN *bagatelle*.

bagel /ˈbeɪɡ(ə)l/ *noun.* Also **beigel** /ˈbʌɪɡ(ə)l/. **E20.**
[ORIGIN Yiddish *beygel*.]
A usu. hard ring-shaped roll of bread.

baggage /ˈbaɡɪdʒ/ *noun.* **LME.**
[ORIGIN Old French & mod. French *bagage*, from *baguer* tie up, or from *bagues* (pl.) bundles (thought to be formed as BAG *noun*): see -AGE.]
Usu. *collect.* in senses 1 and 2 (formerly occas. with *pl.*).
1 Packages of belongings (now usu. suitcases etc.) that a traveller takes on a journey, luggage; *spec.* the portable equipment of an army (= Latin *impedimenta*). **LME.** ▸**b** *fig.* Encumbrances, burdensome matters; (esp. mental) equipment. **E17.**

E. GOWERS Englishmen travel by land with *luggage* and by sea and air with *baggage* Americans, more sensibly, travel everywhere with *baggage*. **b** R. FIRBANK 'Naturally', the lieutenant interposed, 'her intellectual baggage is nil—simply nil.'

bag and baggage: see BAG *noun*.
2 Rubbish, refuse, dirt; pus. Freq. *attrib.* *obsolete* exc. *dial.* **M16.**
3 A disreputable or immoral woman; *joc.* a young woman (usu. with *saucy*, *artful*, etc.). *colloq.* **L16.**

GOLDSMITH Tell them they are two arrant little baggages. DYLAN THOMAS She's tucked her dress in her bloomers—oh, the baggage!

— COMB.: **baggage car** *N. Amer.* a railway luggage van; **baggage check** *N. Amer.* a luggage ticket; **baggage claim** = *baggage reclaim* (b) s.v. RECLAIM *noun* 1; *baggage reclaim*: see RECLAIM *noun* 1; **baggage room** *N. Amer.* a luggage office or cloakroom; **baggage tag** *N. Amer.* a luggage label.
■ **baggager** *noun* a person who carries or has charge of baggage; an animal carrying baggage: **E17.**

Baggie /ˈbaɡi/ *noun.* *N. Amer.* **M20.**
[ORIGIN from BAG *noun*: see -IE.]
(Proprietary name for) a small plastic bag typically used for storing food.

bagging /ˈbaɡɪŋ/ *noun*[1]. *N. English.* **M18.**
[ORIGIN Perh. orig. a verbal noun expressing the act of carrying food in a bag.]
Food eaten between meals; *spec.* a substantial afternoon tea.

bagging /ˈbaɡɪŋ/ *noun*[2]. **M18.**
[ORIGIN from BAG *noun* + -ING[1]: cf. *sacking* etc.]
Coarse woven fabric out of which bags are made.

baggit /ˈbaɡɪt/ *noun.* **M19.**
[ORIGIN Scot. form of *bagged* pa. pple & ppl adjective of BAG *verb*[1].]
A female salmon that has not shed its eggs when the spawning season is over. Cf. KELT *noun*[1].

baggy /ˈbaɡi/ *adjective & noun.* **L18.**
[ORIGIN from BAG *noun* + -Y[1].]
▸ **A** *adjective.* Of clothing: loose and hanging in folds. **L18.**
▸ **B** *noun.* In *pl.* Loose wide-legged swimming trunks, shorts, or trousers. *colloq.* **M20.**
■ **bagginess** *noun* **M19.**

bagne /baɲ/ *noun.* Pl. pronounced same. **M18.**
[ORIGIN French formed as BAGNIO.]
= BAGNIO 1.

bagnio /ˈbɑːnjəʊ/ *noun.* Pl. **-os**. **L16.**
[ORIGIN Italian *bagno* from Latin *balneum* bath.]
1 An Eastern prison; a slave house. *obsolete* exc. *hist.* **L16.**
†**2** A bath, a bathing house. **E17–E19.**
3 A brothel. **E17.**

bagpipe /ˈbaɡpʌɪp/ *noun.* **ME.**
[ORIGIN from BAG *noun* + PIPE *noun*[1].]
1 *sing.* & (freq.) in *pl.* A wind instrument having a bag as a reservoir for air, sound being emitted through a melody pipe (chanter), played with a reed, and from one to three single-note (drone) pipes, now chiefly associated with the Scottish Highlands and Ireland. Also *set of bagpipes*, *pair of bagpipes*. **ME.**
2 *fig.* A long-winded speaker; a windbag. **E17.**
■ **bagpiper** *noun* a person who plays the bagpipes (usu. called a *piper*) **ME. bagpiping** *noun* **L16.**

bagsy /ˈbaɡzi/ *verb trans. slang.* **L20.**
[ORIGIN from *bags I*.]
= BAG *verb*[1] 4b.

ba gua /bɑːˈɡwɑː/ *noun phr.* Also **pa kua** /pɑːˈkwɑː/. **L19.**
[ORIGIN Chinese *bāguà* (Wade–Giles *pā-kua*), from *bā* eight + *guà* divinatory symbols.]
1 *ART.* Any of various decorative and religious motifs incorporating the eight trigrams of *I Ching*; *spec.* an arrangement of these trigrams in a circle round the yin-yang symbol. **L19.**
2 A Chinese martial art in which fighters are arranged around a circle according to the trigram sequence in positions which they must defend. **M20.**

baguette /baˈɡɛt/ *noun.* **E18.**
[ORIGIN French from Italian *bacchetto* dim. of *bacchio* from Latin *baculum* staff.]
1 *ARCHITECTURE.* A small moulding of semicircular section, like an astragal. **E18.**
2 A gem, usu. a diamond, cut in a long rectangular shape. **E20.**
3 A long narrow French loaf. **M20.**
4 A slim rectangular handbag with a short strap. **L20.**

bah /bɑː/ *interjection.* **E19.**
[ORIGIN Prob. after French.]
Expr. contempt, irritation, or annoyance.

bahada *noun* var. of BAJADA.

Bahadur /bəˈhɑːdʊə/ *noun.* Also †**Bahawder**; **b-**. **L18.**
[ORIGIN Urdu & Persian *bahādur* from Mongolian.]
A brave man; a great or distinguished man. Freq. as a title appended to a name.

Baha'i /bɑːˈhɑːi/ *noun & adjective.* **L19.**
[ORIGIN Persian, from Arabic *bahā'* splendour.]
▸ **A** *noun.* A member of a religious faith developed from Babism by Bahā' Allāh (1817–92) and his son 'Abd al-Bahā' (1844–1921), emphasizing the unity of humankind and its religions, and seeking world peace. **L19.**
▸ **B** *attrib.* or as *adjective.* Of or pertaining to the Baha'is or Baha'ism. **E20.**
■ **Baha'ism** *noun* the doctrine or practice of the Baha'is **E20.** **Baha'ist**, **Baha'ite** *nouns* a Baha'i **E20.**

Bahamian /bəˈheɪmɪən/ *noun & adjective.* **M18.**
[ORIGIN from *Bahama* (see below) + -IAN.]
▸ **A** *noun.* A native or inhabitant of the Bahama Islands in the western Atlantic. **M18.**
▸ **B** *adjective.* Of or pertaining to the Bahama Islands or their people. **L19.**

Bahasa /bəˈhɑːsə/ *noun.* **M20.**
[ORIGIN Malay from Sanskrit *bhāṣā* speech, language.]
Malay as the national language of the Indonesian Republic (in full ***Bahasa Indonesia***) or of Malaysia (in full ***Bahasa Malaysia***).

†**Bahawder** *noun* var. of BAHADUR.

Bahiric *noun & adjective* var. of BOHAIRIC.

bahookie /bəˈhʊki/ *noun.* *Scot.* **M20.**
[ORIGIN prob. a blend of BEHIND *noun* and HOUGH *noun* + -IE.]
The buttocks.

Bahraini /bɑːˈreɪni/ *noun & adjective.* Also **-eini**. **L19.**
[ORIGIN from *Bahrain* (see below) + -I[2].]
▸ **A** *noun.* A native or inhabitant of Bahrain, a sheikhdom consisting of a group of islands in the Persian Gulf. **L19.**
▸ **B** *adjective.* Of or pertaining to Bahrain or the Bahrainis. **M20.**

baht /bɑːt/ *noun.* Pl. same. **E19.**
[ORIGIN Thai *bāt*.]
The basic monetary unit of Thailand, equal to 100 satangs.

bahu /ˈbɑːhuː/ *noun.* *Indian.* **L20.**
[ORIGIN Hindi *bahū* daughter-in-law, (son's) wife, from Sanskrit *vadhū*, *vadhukā*.]
A daughter-in-law, *esp.* one who traditionally lives with her husband's family after marriage.

bahut /bay/ *noun.* Pl. pronounced same. **M19.**
[ORIGIN French.]
An ornamental chest or cabinet.

Bahutu *noun* pl. of HUTU.

bahuvrihi /bahʊˈvriːhi/ *adjective & noun.* **M19.**
[ORIGIN Sanskrit *bahuvrīhi*, from *bahu* much + *vrīhi* rice (as a typical compound of this type).]
GRAMMAR. (Designating) an exocentric compound adjective or noun.

baignoire /bɛɲwaːr/ *noun.* Pl. pronounced same. **M19.**
[ORIGIN French = bath tub.]
A box at a theatre on the same level as the stalls.

bail /beɪl/ *noun*[1]. **ME.**
[ORIGIN Old French *bail*, *bail(l)e* power, custody, jurisdiction, delivery, from *baillier* take charge of, receive, hand over, deliver from Latin *bajulare* bear a burden, manage, from *bajulus* carrier. Senses 2–5 are peculiarly English, and their development is uncertain.]
†**1** Custody, charge, jurisdiction. **ME–L16.**

SPENSER Faunus, now within their baile.

†**2** The friendly custody of a person otherwise liable to be kept in prison, upon security given for his or her appearance at a time and place assigned. **LME–E19.**
3 Temporary delivery or release of a prisoner who provides security to appear for trial. **LME.**
4 Security given for the release of a prisoner awaiting trial. **L15.**
5 The person(s) acting as surety (now only by financial guarantee) for a prisoner's appearance for trial. **L16.**

SHAKES. *2 Hen. VI* The sons of York . . Shall be their father's bail. G. GREENE He ought to be brought before a magistrate . . . I will stand bail for any reasonable amount. *fig.*: THACKERAY Ye'll spend it like a man of spirit—I'll go bail for that.

– PHRASES: **admit to bail** allow to be released on bail. **deny bail** = ***refuse bail*** below. **forfeit bail**, **forfeit one's bail**: by failing to appear for trial after release on bail. ***give leg bail***: see LEG *noun*. **grant bail** allow the prisoner to be released on bail. ***hold to bail***: see HOLD *verb*. **jump bail** *colloq.* fail to appear for trial after release on bail. ***justify bail***: see JUSTIFY *verb* 6. **on bail** (with permission to be temporarily released from custody) on provision of security to appear for trial. **refuse bail** not allow the prisoner to be released on bail. ***surrender to one's bail***, ***surrender to bail***: see SURRENDER *verb* 1d.
– COMB.: **bail-bond** the bond or security entered into by a bail; **bail bondsman** = *bailsman* below; **bail-jumper** *colloq.* a person who fails to appear for trial after release on bail; **bail-jumping** *colloq.* failure to appear for trial after release on bail; **bailsman** a person who gives bail for another.

bail /beɪl/ *noun*[2]. **ME.**
[ORIGIN Old French *bail*, *bail(l)e* palisade, enclosure (cf. *baillier* enclose), perh. from Latin *baculum* rod. Cf. BAILEY.]
1 The wall of the outer court of a feudal castle; by extension, a wall of an inner court; one of the courts themselves; in *pl.*, an outer line of fortification formed of stakes, palisades. **ME.**
2 †**a** A crossbar. Only in **L16.** ▸**b** *CRICKET*. Either of two wooden crosspieces (formerly a single crosspiece) placed over the stumps (cf. WICKET 3). **M18.**
3 A bar to separate horses standing in an open stable. **M19.**
4 A framework for securing the head of a cow at milking. *Austral. & NZ.* **M19.**
5 On a typewriter, a hinged bar that holds the paper against the platen. **M20.**
– COMB.: **bail-dock** *hist.* at the Old Bailey, a small open-topped room formed from the corner of the court and used to accommodate accused persons.

†**bail** *noun*[3]. **ME–M19.**
[ORIGIN French *baille* bucket from Proto-Gallo-Romance from Latin *bajulus* carrier: cf. BAIL *noun*[1].]
NAUTICAL. A bucket or scoop for bailing water from a boat.

bail /beɪl/ *noun*[4]. **LME.**
[ORIGIN Prob. from Old Norse *beygla* from *beygja* = Old English *bēgan*, *bygan* bend, bow.]
A hoop or ring, *esp.* a half hoop for supporting the cover of a wagon; the handle of a kettle, pail, etc.

bail /beɪl/ *verb*[1] *trans.* **M16.**
[ORIGIN from BAIL *noun*[1] or (sense 3) immed. from French *baillier*.]
1 Of a magistrate etc.: grant bail to, release on bail. **M16.**
2 Obtain the release of (a person) by providing security for his or her later appearance; provide bail for. **L16.**
bail out release from imprisonment by providing bail; *fig.* release from (esp. financial) difficulty.
3 Deliver (goods) in trust for a specified purpose. **M18.**
■ **bailable** *adjective* entitled to be released on bail; admitting of or providing for bail: **M16.** **bailage** *noun* (*hist.*) a duty on delivery of goods **M16.** **bailment** *noun* (*a*) delivery in trust; (*b*) the action or process of bailing a person: **M16.**

bail /beɪl/ *verb*[2]. Exc. in sense 1, *Austral. & NZ.* **L16.**
[ORIGIN App. from Old French *baillier* enclose, shut, rel. to *baille* BAIL *noun*[2]: the priority of *baille* or *baillier* is uncertain.]
1 *verb trans.* Confine. *rare.* **L16.**
2 *verb trans.* Secure the head of (a cow) in a bail while milking. Usu. foll. by *up*. **M19.**
3 *verb trans.* Make (a person) hold up the arms to be robbed; detain or buttonhole (a person); corner (a wild animal). Usu. foll. by *up*. **M19.**
4 *verb intrans.* Surrender (by throwing up the arms). Usu. foll. by *up*. **M19.**

bail /beɪl/ *verb*[3]. In senses 1, 2 also **bale**. **E17.**
[ORIGIN from BAIL *noun*[3].]
1 *verb trans. & intrans.* Scoop (water) out of a boat; scoop water out of (a boat). Freq. foll. by *out*. **E17.**
2 *verb intrans.* Foll. by *out*: jump out of an aircraft, make an emergency descent by parachute; (of a surfer) leave the surfboard. **M20.**
3 *verb intrans.* Foll. by *on*: let (a person) down. *N. Amer. slang.* **L20.**
– NOTE: The spelling *bale* in senses 1 and 2 is restricted to British English.

Ba-ila *noun & adjective* see ILA.

baile /ˈbʌɪleɪ/ *noun*. **M19.**
[ORIGIN Spanish = dance, dancing.]
In the south-western US and parts of Central and South America: a gathering for dancing. Also, a dancehall.
– COMB.: **baile funk** a type of dance music of Brazilian origin.

bailee /beɪˈliː/ *noun*. **E16.**
[ORIGIN from BAIL *verb*[1] + -EE[1].]
A person to whom goods are delivered in trust.

bailer /ˈbeɪlə/ *noun*[1]. **M19.**
[ORIGIN from BAIL *verb*[3] + -ER[1].]
A utensil or machine for bailing water etc.
– COMB.: **bailer-shell** = *melon-shell* s.v. MELON *noun*[1].

bailer /ˈbeɪlə/ *noun*[2]. Now *rare*. **M19.**
[ORIGIN from BAIL *noun*[2] + -ER[1].]
CRICKET. A ball that hits the bails.

bailer *noun*[3] var. of BAILOR.

bailey /ˈbeɪli/ *noun*. **ME.**
[ORIGIN Prob. from Old French *bail*, *bail(l)e* (whence medieval Latin *ballium*, *ballia*): see BAIL *noun*[2].]
1 The outer wall and first line of defence of a castle; *gen.* any of a castle's defensive circuits. **ME.**
2 The outer court of a castle; any of the courts enclosed between the circuits of walls or defences. **E16.**
Old Bailey the seat of the Central Criminal Court in London, which formerly stood in the ancient bailey of the city wall between Lud Gate and New Gate.

Bailey bridge /ˈbeɪli brɪdʒ/ *noun phr.* **M20.**
[ORIGIN Sir D. Coleman *Bailey* (1901–85), English engineer, its designer.]
A bridge of lattice steel designed for rapid assembly from prefabricated parts, used esp. in military operations.

bailie /ˈbeɪli/ *noun*[1]. Also **-ll-**. **ME.**
[ORIGIN Old French *bailli(s)*: see BAILIFF.]
1 = BAILIFF. *obsolete* exc. *dial.* **ME.**
2 *Scot.* ▸**a** The chief magistrate of a barony or part of a county. Long *obsolete* exc. *hist.* **LME.** ▸**b** A municipal councillor serving as a magistrate. Now *hist.* exc. as an honorary title conferred on a senior councillor. **LME.**
■ **bailiery** /ˈbeɪlɪəri, -lɪri/ *noun* (*Scot.*, *obsolete* exc. *hist.*) the office or jurisdiction of a bailie; the district under the jurisdiction of a bailie: **LME.** **bailieship** *noun* (*obsolete* exc. *hist.*) = BAILIWICK **LME.**

†**bailie** *noun*[2] var. of BAILLIE *noun*[1].

bailiff /ˈbeɪlɪf/ *noun*. **ME.**
[ORIGIN Old French *baillif* oblique case of *bailli(s)* from medieval Latin *bajulivus* (*ballivus*) adjective, from *bajulus* carrier, manager, administrator: cf. BAIL *noun*[1].]
1 *hist.* (exc. in formal titles). A person charged with public administrative authority in a certain district; in England, a representative of the monarch, *esp.* the chief officer of a hundred; in Jersey and Guernsey, the first civil officer, appointed by the Crown. **ME.**
2 An officer of justice under a sheriff, who executes writs and processes, and performs distraints and arrests. **ME.**
3 The agent of the lord of a manor, who collects rents, etc.; the steward or manager of an estate or farm; the agent of a landlord. **ME.**
■ **bailiffship** *noun* the office of bailiff **LME.** †**bailiffwick** *noun* the office of bailiff; the district under a bailiff's jurisdiction: **LME–M18.**

bailiwick /ˈbeɪlɪwɪk/ *noun*. **LME.**
[ORIGIN from BAILIE *noun*[1] + -WICK.]
1 A district or place under the jurisdiction of a bailiff. **LME.** ▸**b** *transf.* A person's concern or sphere of operations. Chiefly *joc.* **M19.**

Encycl. Brit. They [the Channel Islands] are . . grouped into two distinct bailiwicks of Guernsey and Jersey, with differing constitutions. **b** E. ROOSEVELT I established the fairly well-understood pattern that affairs of state were not in my bailiwick.

2 The office or jurisdiction of a bailiff. *obsolete* exc. *hist.* **LME.**

bailliage /ˈbeɪlɪɪdʒ/ *noun*. **LME.**
[ORIGIN French, from *bailli*: see BAILIFF, -AGE.]
The jurisdiction or district of a bailiff (now usu. in a foreign country).

†**baillie** *noun*[1]. Also **bailie**, **-lly**. **ME–M18.**
[ORIGIN Old French, from *baillir* have under one's jurisdiction etc.: cf. medieval Latin *bajulia* tutelage etc.: see BAIL *noun*[1], -Y[3].]
The office or jurisdiction of a bailiff; delegated authority.

baillie *noun*[2] var. of BAILIE *noun*[1].

†**bailly** *noun* var. of BAILLIE *noun*[1].

bailor /beɪˈlɔː/ *noun*. Also **-er** /-ə/. **L16.**
[ORIGIN from BAIL *verb*[1] + -OR.]
A person who delivers goods in trust. Occas. now also = ***bailsman*** s.v. BAIL *noun*[1].

bailout /ˈbeɪlaʊt/ *noun*. In sense 1 also **bale-**. **M20.**
[ORIGIN from ***bail out*** s.v. BAIL *verb*[3] 2, *verb*[1] 2.]
1 An act of bailing out from an aircraft; an emergency descent by parachute. **M20.**
2 An act of bailing out a person or organization; a release from (esp. financial) difficulty. **L20.**

Baily's beads /ˈbeɪlɪz biːdz/ *noun phr.* **M19.**
[ORIGIN Francis *Baily* (1774–1844), English astronomer.]
ASTRONOMY. The appearance of the sun's crescent as a string of brilliant points at the beginning or end of totality in a solar eclipse.

báinín *noun* var. of BAWNEEN.

bain-marie /banməˈriː, *foreign* bɛ̃mari/ *noun*. Pl. **bains-** (pronounced same). **E18.**
[ORIGIN French, translating medieval Latin *balneum Mariae* translating medieval Greek *kaminos Marias* furnace of Maria, a supposed Jewish alchemist.]
A vessel of hot water in which pans and their contents are slowly heated; a double saucepan. Also, a dish prepared in this.

Bairam /bʌɪˈrɑːm/ *noun*. **L16.**
[ORIGIN Turkish †*baïrām* (now *bayram*), ult. from Persian *bazrām*.]
Either of two annual Muslim festivals, the ***Lesser Bairam***, lasting one day, which follows the fast of Ramadan, and the ***Greater Bairam***, lasting three days, marking the culmination of the annual pilgrimage to Mecca. Also called ***Eid***.

bairn /bɛːn/ *noun*. Chiefly *Scot., N. English, & literary.* Also (*N. English*) **barn** /bɑːn/.
[ORIGIN Old English *bearn* = Old Saxon, Old High German, Old Norse, Gothic *barn*, from Germanic, rel. to BEAR *verb*[1].]
A child; a young son or daughter.
– COMB.: **bairn's part** *SCOTS LAW* = LEGITIME *noun* 2; **bairn-team**, **-time** *N. English* a family of children.
■ **bairnly** *adjective* childish, childlike **M16.**

†**baisemain** *noun*. **M17–M18.**
[ORIGIN French.]
A kiss of the hands; in *pl.*, compliments, respects.

bait /beɪt/ *noun*[1]. **ME.**
[ORIGIN Old Norse *beit* (neut.) pasture, *beita* (fem.) food; in part from BAIT *verb*[1].]
1 Food placed on a hook or in a trap to entice fish or animals as prey; *fig.* an allurement, temptation. **ME.**

I. WALTON Let your bait fall gently upon the water. DEFOE The profits of trade are baits to the avaricious shopkeeper. A. HAILEY Nim knew he . . was rising to the bait, probably just as Birdsong intended.

groundbait, ***ledger-bait***, ***spoon bait***, etc. ***smig bait*** etc. ***live bait***: see LIVE *adjective*. **baitfish** a small fish of a kind used as bait to catch larger fish.
2 Food, refreshment, esp. a feed for horses or a meal for travellers on a journey. *obsolete* exc. in *dial.* sense, a snack taken between meals. **L15.**
3 A stop on a journey for refreshment or rest. *arch.* **L15.**

bait *noun*[2] var. of BATE *noun*[4].

bait /beɪt/ *verb*[1]. **ME.**
[ORIGIN Old Norse *beita* hunt or chase with dogs or hawks (= Old English *bǣtan*, Old High German *beizen*, German *beizen*), causative of *bíta* BITE *verb*. Senses 6 & 7 prob. from BAIT *noun*[1].]
1 *verb trans.* Worry or torment (a chained or confined animal) by setting dogs at it; attack with dogs for sport. **ME.**

SHAKES. *2 Hen. VI* We'll bait thy bears to death.

2 *verb trans. fig.* Harass or persecute (a more or less helpless person) persistently; worry or torment; cause (a person) to be troubled or annoyed *with* something. **ME.**

S. JOHNSON I will not be baited with *what* and *why*. R. HUGHES There was not even any fun to be got out of baiting her; nothing seemed to ruffle her temper.

3 *verb trans. & intrans.* Attack and bite and tear, as dogs attack a confined animal. **LME.**

W. SOMERVILLE Raving he foams, and howls, and barks, and bates.

4 *verb trans.* Give food and drink to (an animal), esp. on a journey. *arch.* **LME.** ▸**b** *verb intrans.* Of an animal: feed. *arch.* **LME.**

THACKERAY Whilst their horses were baited, they entered the public room.

5 *verb intrans.* Stop on a journey to take food or rest. **LME.**

R. B. SHERIDAN To bait here a few days longer, to recover the fatigue of his journey. *fig.*: MILTON Evil news rides post, while good news baits.

6 Put bait in or on (a trap, hook, fishing place, etc.). **LME.**

POPE My absent mates . . Bait the barb'd steel. *fig.*: L. DURRELL The Tripartite Conference was . . rumoured to be a trap, baited by an unacceptable constitution.

7 *verb trans.* Offer bait to; allure, entice. Chiefly *fig.* **L16.**

SHAKES. *Merch. V.* Why, . . thou wilt not take his flesh. What's that good for? To bait fish withal. E. ROOSEVELT He would . . bait me into giving an opinion by stating a point of view with which he knew I would disagree.

bait-and-switch a sales technique by which a customer is inveigled into purchasing a more expensive product by the display or advertisement of a cheaper one.
■ **baiter** *noun* **E17.**

bait *verb*[2] var. of BATE *verb*[1].

baittle *adjective* see BATTLE *adjective*.

baity *adjective* var. of BATEY.

baiza /ˈbʌɪzɑː/ *noun*. Pl. same, **-s**. **L20.**
[ORIGIN Arabic.]
A monetary unit of Oman, equal to one thousandth of a rial.

baize /beɪz/ *noun & verb.* L16.
[ORIGIN French *baies* fem. pl., use as noun of *bai* reddish brown, BAY *noun*[7] (so named presumably from its original colour).]
▸ **A** *noun.* **1** A coarse usu. green woollen stuff with a long nap, used for coverings and linings. L16.
2 A curtain or covering of baize. E19.
▸ **B** *verb trans.* Cover or line with baize. M19.
– NOTE: The pl. form *baies* was early taken as a sing.; the form *baize* was not established before 19.

bajada /bəˈhɑːdə/ *noun.* Orig. *US.* Also **bah-**. M19.
[ORIGIN Spanish = descent, slope.]
A broad slope of alluvial material at the foot of an escarpment.

Bajan /ˈbeɪdʒ(ə)n/ *noun & adjective. colloq.* M20.
[ORIGIN Repr. a pronunc. of BADIAN *noun*[2] *& adjective.*]
= BARBADIAN.

Bajau /ˈbadʒaʊ/ *noun & adjective.* M19.
[ORIGIN Unknown.]
▸ **A** *noun.* **1** A member of a nomadic maritime people (formerly notorious as pirates) found throughout the islands and coastal areas of Kalimantan, Sulawesi, and eastern Indonesia to New Guinea and northern Australia (also called ***sea gypsy***). M19.
2 The Austronesian language of this people. M19.
▸ **B** *attrib.* or as *adjective.* Of or pertaining to the Bajaus or their language. L19.

bajra /ˈbɑːdʒrɑː/ *noun.* Also **-ri** /-riː/. E19.
[ORIGIN Hindi *bājrā, bājrī.*]
In the Indian subcontinent: pearl millet or a similar grain.

baju /ˈbɑːdʒuː/ *noun.* E19.
[ORIGIN Malay.]
A short loose jacket worn in Malaysia and Indonesia.

Baka /ˈbaka/ *noun.* Pl. same. M20.
[ORIGIN Perh. from Lingala *Ba-aka* Pygmies.]
1 The Bantu language of a nomadic Pygmy people inhabiting the rainforests of south-eastern Cameroon and northern Gabon. M20.
2 A member of this people. L20.

bake /beɪk/ *noun.* M16.
[ORIGIN from the verb.]
1 The act or process of baking; baked food. M16.
2 A biscuit or small cake. *Scot.* E17.
3 A social gathering, esp. for eating baked food. *US.* M19.
– COMB.: **bake sale** *N. Amer.* a fund-raising sale of home-baked items.

bake /beɪk/ *verb.* Pa. pple **baked**, (*arch. & dial.*) **baken** /ˈbeɪk(ə)n/.
[ORIGIN Old English *bacan* strong verb = Old High German *backan*, Old Norse *baka*, from Germanic from Indo-European; rel. to Greek *phōgein* roast, parch. The weak form *baked* appeared as a pa. t. before 15 and as a pa. pple by 16 (it is the only form in Shakes.).]
▸ **I** *verb trans.* **1** Cook by dry heat acting by conduction and not by radiation, as in an oven or on a heated surface. OE.

> SMOLLETT My bread is . . baked in my own oven. DICKENS We have half a leg of mutton, baked, at a quarter before three. A. THOMAS Bake the aubergines in an oiled dish for about 45 minutes. J. BRONOWSKI The women . . bake bread—in the biblical manner, in unleavened cakes on hot stones.

bake blind: see BLIND *adverb.*
2 Harden by heat. LME.

> F. NORRIS All Tulare County . . was bone-dry, parched, and baked and crisped after four months of cloudless weather. J. C. RICH The clay form that is to be baked hard must be adequately . . dried *before* it is placed in the kiln. *transf.*: SHAKES. *Temp.* Th' earth when it is bak'd with frost.

†**3** Form into a cake or mass. LME–L17.

> DONNE The old dirt is still baked on my hands.

4 Of the sun: ripen (fruit), tan (the skin). L17.

> DRYDEN The Vine her liquid Harvest yields, Bak'd in the Sunshine.

▸ **II** *verb intrans.* **5** Cook a batch of bread, cakes, etc. ME.

> W. FAULKNER Now that she had a stove to bake in.

6 Undergo cooking by dry heat; be cooked, hardened, or tanned by heat; *colloq.* become uncomfortably hot. LME.

> J. R. GREEN The cakes which were baking on the hearth. OED These apples do not bake well. M. SHARP 'I'm going to bake' thought Julia . . and indeed the plain . . shimmered under a heat mist. R. CARRIER The warm and spicy smell of apple pie baking in the oven.

– COMB.: **bakeapple** *Canad.* the (dried) fruit of the cloudberry; **bakehouse** a house or room with an oven for baking bread; †**bake-meat** a pie, pastry; **bake-off** *N. Amer.* a contest in which cooks prepare baked goods such as bread and cakes for judging; *transf.* a contest between companies to win a contract; **bakeware** vessels, trays, etc., used in baking.

baked /beɪkt/ *adjective.* M16.
[ORIGIN from BAKE *verb* + -ED[1].]
Cooked by dry heat; hardened by heat; *colloq.* uncomfortably hot.
baked beans haricot beans baked, and usu. tinned in tomato sauce. †**baked-meat** = ***bake-meat*** s.v. BAKE *verb.* **baked potato** a potato baked in its skin. ***half-baked***: see HALF-.

Bakelite /ˈbeɪkəlʌɪt/ *noun.* Also **b-**. E20.
[ORIGIN from Leo H. *Baekeland* (1863–1944), Belgian-born US chemist + -ITE[1].]
(Proprietary name for) an early form of plastic, characteristically dark brown, made by copolymerization of a phenol with formaldehyde.

baken *verb* see BAKE *verb.*

baker /ˈbeɪkə/ *noun.*
[ORIGIN Old English *bæcere*, formed as BAKE *verb* + -ER[1].]
A person who bakes; *esp.* one who bakes and sells bread.
baker's bread bread baked professionally by a baker. **baker's dozen** thirteen (the 13th loaf representing the retailer's profit). ***the butcher, the baker, the candlestick-maker***: see BUTCHER *noun.*
▪ **bakery** *noun* a baker's work, baked items; a place where baked products are made or sold: M16.

Baker day /ˈbeɪkə deɪ/ *noun phr. colloq.* L20.
[ORIGIN from Kenneth *Baker*, Brit. Education Secretary (1986–9), who introduced the practice.]
(Former name for) any of several days in the normal school year statutorily set aside for in-service training for teachers.

bakestone /ˈbeɪkstəʊn/ *noun. dial.* Also **back-** /ˈbak-/. ME.
[ORIGIN from BAKE *verb* + STONE *noun.*]
A flat stone or metal plate on which cakes are baked in the oven.

Bakewell /ˈbeɪkwɛl/ *noun.* M19.
[ORIGIN A town in Derbyshire, N. England.]
Bakewell pudding, ***Bakewell tart***, a baked tart of pastry lined with jam and filled usu. with an almond paste.

baking /ˈbeɪkɪŋ/ *noun.* ME.
[ORIGIN from BAKE *verb* + -ING[1].]
1 The action of BAKE *verb*; cooking by dry heat, esp. of bread, cakes, etc.; hardening by heat. ME.
2 The product of baking; (a batch of) baked items, esp. bread, cakes, etc. LME.
– COMB.: **baking powder** a mixture of sodium bicarbonate, cream of tartar, etc., used instead of yeast to make cakes etc. rise; **baking sheet** a metal tray used for baking cakes etc.; ***baking soda***: see SODA 2c.

baking /ˈbeɪkɪŋ/ *adjective.* L18.
[ORIGIN from BAKE *verb* + -ING[2].]
That bakes; *colloq.* extremely or uncomfortably hot.
▪ **bakingly** *adverb* M19.

bakkie /ˈbaki, ˈbʌki/ *noun. S. Afr.* L19.
[ORIGIN Afrikaans, from *bak* container + the dim. suffix *-ie.*]
1 A small basin or similar container. L19.
2 A light truck or pickup truck. M20.

> T. BLACKLAWS A Ford bakkie full of jeering Transvalers hoots at me.

baklava /ˈbɑːkləvə/ *noun.* M17.
[ORIGIN Turkish.]
A dessert made of thin pieces of flaky pastry, honey, and nuts.

baksheesh /bakˈʃiːʃ/ *noun & verb.* Also **back-**. M18.
[ORIGIN Ult. from Persian *bakšīš*, from *bakšīdan* give.]
▸ **A** *noun.* In Eastern countries: a gratuity, a tip. M18.
▸ **B** *verb trans.* Give a gratuity to, tip. M19.

bal /bal/ *noun. obsolete* exc. *dial.* E17.
[ORIGIN Cornish = tin mine.]
A mine in Cornwall.

Balaam /ˈbeɪləm/ *noun.* M17.
[ORIGIN The prophet in *Numbers* 22–4.]
1 A person who follows religion for profit. M17.
2 Superfluous or trivial material used to fill up a column. *Journalists' slang.* E19.
– COMB.: **Balaam basket** an editor's container for unwanted material.
▪ **Balaamite** *noun* = BALAAM 1 M16.

balaclava /baləˈklɑːvə/ *noun.* L19.
[ORIGIN *Balaclava*, a village near Sebastopol in the Crimea, site of a battle fought in 1854.]
In full ***balaclava helmet***. A woollen covering for the head and neck, worn orig. by soldiers on active service.

balafon /ˈbaləfɒn/ *noun.* Also (earlier) **balafo** and other vars. L18.
[ORIGIN French, from Manding *bala* xylophone + *fo* to play.]
A large xylophone with hollow gourds as resonators, used in the performance of West African music.

balalaika /baləˈlʌɪkə/ *noun.* L18.
[ORIGIN Russian, of Tartar origin.]
A Russian musical instrument like a guitar, with a triangular body and from two to four strings.

balance /ˈbal(ə)ns/ *noun.* ME.
[ORIGIN Old French & mod. French from Proto-Romance from late Latin *bilanc-, bilanx* (in *libra bilanx* balance having two scales), from *bi-* BI- + *lanx* scale.]
▸ **I** A physical object.
1 An apparatus for weighing, consisting of a beam poised so as to move freely on a central pivot, with a scale pan at each end. ME. ▸**b** Any apparatus used in weighing, *esp.* a spring or lever substitute for the above. E19.
2 (Usu. **B-**.) *The* constellation and zodiacal sign Libra; the Scales. LME.
†**3** Either scale of a balance; in *pl.* (occas. with *sing.* form) scales. LME–M17.
4 A counterpoise. *rare* in *lit.* sense. E17.
5 In full ***balance wheel***. A mechanical device which regulates the speed of a clock or watch. M17.
▸ **II** Gen. *fig.* senses.
6 The metaphorical balance of justice, reason, or opinion, by which actions and principles are weighed or estimated. ME. ▸†**b** Either scale of this. L16–M17.
7 The wavering of fortune or chance, by which issues hang in suspense. ME. ▸†**b** Uncertainty. ME–L17.
8 Power to decide or determine. LME.

> G. B. SHAW The balance is held in my constituency by the tradesmen and shopkeepers.

9 A thing of equal importance; a counterbalancing consideration etc.; a set-off. E17.

> J. R. GREEN If France . . had ceased to be a balance to Spain, she found a new balance in Flanders.

10 Equilibrium; the even distribution of weight or amount (of things ponderable and imponderable). M17.

> W. DERHAM Such alterations in the æquipoise or ballance of the Atmosphere. D. H. LAWRENCE Life is so made that opposites sway about a trembling centre of balance. X. J. KENNEDY Hovering scale-pans . . Settled their balance slow as silt. T. BENN The balance between freedom and security poses special difficulty in political democracies.

11 Stability due to equilibrium between the forces within a system; (ability to maintain) steadiness of position; *transf.* mental stability. M17.

> E. K. KANE If my mind had retained its balance. E. ALBEE Her balance is none too good, and she bumps into or brushes against the door chimes by the door. N. GORDIMER He stands with his hands on his hips, for balance, looking down into the hole.

12 General harmony between the parts of anything; *esp.* in *ART* etc., harmony of proportion and design. M18. ▸**b** *spec.* (The sound produced by) the adjustment of the relative positions, volume levels, etc., of sources of sound. E20.
13 The preponderating weight or amount. M18.

> H. P. BROUGHAM The balance of evidence appears in favour of the due execution.

▸ **III** The adjustment of accounts.
14 (The process of finding) the difference between credits and debits; a statement of the results. L16.

> L. P. HARTLEY This increase of personal worth, which the bank balance so eloquently conveyed.

15 The difference between the debit and credit sides of an account. E17.

> A. CRUMP Such arrangements may continue for years without the balance ever being a credit-balance.

16 An equality between the total of the two sides of an account (cf. sense 10 above). M17.

> GLADSTONE While we exported £8,860,000, we imported £8,509,000. That is very nearly a balance.

17 A sum remaining (either *in hand* or *due*) after the settlement or partial settlement of an account or accounts; *colloq.* the rest, the remainder. E18.

> S. UNWIN I sent for water, and after he had had a drink, spilt the balance over his head. J. CLAVELL We still haven't had a down payment, let alone the balance.

– PHRASES: ***balance due***, ***balance in hand***: see sense 17 above. **balance of mind** sanity. **balance of nature** a state of equilibrium in nature produced by the interaction of living organisms; ecological balance. **balance of payments** the difference of value between the payments into and out of a country, including invisible exports and imports. **balance of power** a state of international equilibrium with no nation predominant. **balance of terror** balance of power based on the possession of terrifying weapons, esp. nuclear weapons. **balance of trade** the difference between a country's exports and imports. **be in the balance**, **hang in the balance** be uncertain. **keep one's balance** not fall; maintain physical or mental stability. **lose one's balance** fall or stumble physically; become upset mentally. **off balance** in danger of falling; confused; unprepared. **on balance** taking everything into consideration. **strike a balance** determine the difference between two sides of an account (*lit. & fig.*); arrive at a medial position or course.
– COMB.: **balance sheet** a written statement of the assets and liabilities of an organization on a particular date; **balance spring** = ***hairspring*** s.v. HAIR *noun*; ***balance wheel***: see sense 5 above.

balance /ˈbal(ə)ns/ *verb.* L16.
[ORIGIN Old French & mod. French *balancer*, formed as BALANCE *noun.*]
▸ **I** *gen.* **1** *verb trans.* Weigh in or with a balance. *rare* in *lit.* sense. L16.
2 *verb trans.* Weigh (two or more arguments, considerations, etc.) against each other; consider with a view to making a choice. L16.

> YEATS I balanced all, brought all to mind, The years to come seemed waste of breath. J. LE CARRÉ Do you think they sit like monks . . balancing the rights and wrongs?

3 *verb trans.* Equal in weight; neutralize the weight of; make up for. L16.

R. LYND The craving for getting things done is balanced . . by the craving for leaving things undone. A. J. P. TAYLOR They were reinforced by Irish immigrants and made a number of intellectual converts, roughly balancing the old Catholics who lapsed.

4 *verb trans.* Counterbalance or match (one thing) *by, with,* or *against* another. **E17.**

J. RUSKIN A mass of subdued colour may be balanced by a point of a powerful one. T. HARDY And don't you know that a woman who loves at all thinks nothing of perjury when it is balanced against her love?

5 *verb trans.* Weigh (a matter or problem); ponder. **M17.**

TENNYSON She balanced this a little, And told me she would answer us to-day.

6 *verb trans.* Bring into or keep in equilibrium (*lit. & fig.*); keep steady or erect. **M17.** ▸**b** *spec.* Adjust (sources of sound) to the correct relative positions, volume levels, etc. **E20.**

DICKENS Strong men . . balancing chests of drawers . . upon their heads. G. MURRAY The future seemed about equally balanced between good and evil. SCOTT FITZGERALD He was balancing himself on the dashboard of his car. F. CHICHESTER I trimmed the tail as delicately as I could to balance the plane, but she would not stabilize. S. HILL Dorothea stood alone, . . balancing the two pots in her hand.

7 *verb intrans.* Waver, deliberate, hesitate. *arch.* **M17.**

C. MERIVALE The same disposition to balance and temporize.

8 *verb intrans.* Keep steady or erect, esp. as a feat of acrobatics or dancing. **E19.**

JOSEPH STRUTT Tumbling and balancing . . exhibited by the gleemen. *fig.*: *Times Lit. Suppl.* The East-West balancing act of Rapallo.

▸ **II** *spec.* Of an account (*lit. & fig.*).
9 *verb trans.* Add up and compare the debit and credit sides of (an account or set of accounts). **L16.**
10 *verb trans.* Make entries in (an account or set of accounts) that will make the two sides equal; of an entry: make the two sides of (an account) equal. **E17.**
11 *verb trans.* Settle (an account) by paying the amount due. **M18.**
12 *verb intrans.* Of an account: have its two sides equal. **L19.**
■ **balanceable** *adjective* **M17.** **balanced** *adjective* poised, in equilibrium; well arranged or disposed; with no constituent lacking or in excess: **L16.** **balancer** *noun* (*a*) a person who balances, *esp.* an acrobat; (*b*) a thing which balances; *spec.* = HALTERE 2: **LME.**

balancé /balɑ̃se/ *noun.* Pl. pronounced same. **L18.**
[ORIGIN French = balanced (sc. *pas* step).]
DANCING. A swaying step from one foot to the other.

balancing /ˈbal(ə)nsɪŋ/ *verbal noun.* **L16.**
[ORIGIN from BALANCE *verb* + -ING[1].]
The action of BALANCE *verb*; an instance of this.
– COMB.: **balancing act** an (acrobatic) act involving feats of balance; *fig.* a maintaining of equilibrium or harmony in difficult circumstances.

balanitis /baləˈnʌɪtɪs/ *noun.* **M19.**
[ORIGIN from Greek *balanos* acorn, glans penis + -ITIS.]
MEDICINE & VETERINARY MEDICINE. Inflammation of the glans penis.

balanoid /ˈbalənɔɪd/ *adjective & noun.* **M19.**
[ORIGIN from mod. Latin *Balanus* genus name from Latin *balanus* from Greek *balanos* acorn, + -OID.]
ZOOLOGY. (Of, pertaining to, or being) an acorn barnacle (see ACORN).

balao /bəˈlaʊ/ *noun.* Also **ballahoo** /baləˈhuː/. **M19.**
[ORIGIN Spanish *balajú*.]
The halfbeak.

balas /ˈbaləs/ *noun.* **LME.**
[ORIGIN Old French & mod. French *balais* from medieval Latin *balascus, -cius* from Arabic *balakš*, from Persian *Badakš(ān)*, a district in Afghanistan, where it is found.]
A delicate rose-red variety of the spinel ruby. Now usu. more fully ***balas ruby***.

balata /ˈbalətə, bəˈlɑːtə/ *noun.* Also **ball-**, (earlier) †**barratta**. **E17.**
[ORIGIN Carib *balatá*.]
(The wood of) any of a number of tropical American trees of the sapodilla family, spec. *Manilkara bidentata*. Also, the dried latex of this tree, used as a substitute for gutta-percha.

balboa /balˈbəʊə/ *noun.* **E20.**
[ORIGIN from Vasco Núñez de *Balboa* (*c* 1475–1519), Spanish explorer and discoverer of the Pacific Ocean.]
The basic monetary unit of Panama, equal to 100 centésimos.

balbriggan /balˈbrɪg(ə)n/ *noun & adjective.* **L19.**
[ORIGIN *Balbriggan*, a town near Dublin in Ireland, where orig. made.]
(Of) a knitted cotton fabric used esp. for underwear.

balcony /ˈbalkəni/ *noun.* **E17.**
[ORIGIN Italian *balcone* (whence also French *balcon*, Spanish *balcón*), prob. from Germanic base repr. by BAULK *noun* with augm. suffix: see -OON.]
1 A railed or balustraded platform projecting from the wall of a building, with access from an upper-floor window. **E17.**
2 In a theatre: formerly, a stage box; now usu. a tier of seats above the dress circle; the gallery; *N. Amer.* the dress circle. In a cinema etc.: an upper tier of seats. **E18.**
– NOTE: Until **E19** usually with pronunc. /balˈkəʊni/.
■ **balconied** *adjective* having a balcony **M18.**

bal costumé /bal kɔstyme/ *noun phr.* Pl. ***bals costumés*** (pronounced same). **E19.**
[ORIGIN French.]
A fancy-dress ball.

bald /bɔːld/ *adjective.* **ME.**
[ORIGIN Prob. from a base meaning orig. 'white patch' + -ED[2]. In branch I perh. from BALL *noun*[1].]
▸ †**I 1** Round, ball-shaped; rotund, corpulent. Only in **ME.**
▸ **II 2** Lacking hair on part or all of the scalp. **ME.**

J. D. SALINGER He was one of those bald guys that comb all their hair over from the side to cover up the baldness. G. VIDAL Completely bald, his neat round head shone pinkly under the indirect lights. L. DEIGHTON The crown of his head was bald, but a natural wave gave him curls across the ears and over his collar.

3 Lacking hair on other parts of the body. Of an animal etc.: hairless, featherless. **ME.**
4 *fig.* Devoid of force; meagre, dull, basic, unadorned; (of bad qualities) undisguised. **LME.**

BOSWELL Tom Davies repeated, in a very bald manner, the story of Dr. Johnson's first repartee to me. H. T. COCKBURN In towns the great modern object has . . been to reduce everything to the dullest and baldest uniformity. J. R. LOWELL A bald egotism which is quite above and beyond selfishness. L. M. MONTGOMERY Just stick to bald facts. Begin at the beginning.

5 Of things: without the usual or natural covering; treeless; leafless; napless; worn bare; (of a tyre, *colloq.*) having lost its tread by wear. **E17.**

SHAKES. *A.Y.L.* Under an oak, whose boughs were moss'd with age, And high top bald with dry antiquity. E. BOWEN A bald patch in the carpet under her desk. L. SIMPSON My right front tyre is as bald as Odysseus. P. THEROUX The bald hills, stripped of all foliage, were rounded on their slopes.

▸ **III 6** Streaked or marked with white (cf. Welsh *ceffyl bal* a horse with a white streak or mark on its face). **LME.**
– PHRASES: **as bald as a coot** completely bald.
– COMB. & SPECIAL COLLOCATIONS: **bald coot**, **baldicoot** a coot (because of its white plate on the forehead); *fig.* a bald-headed person; ***bald cypress***: see CYPRESS *noun*[1] 1b; **bald eagle** a white-headed, white-tailed, fish-eating eagle, *Haliaeetus leucocephalus*, the national emblem of the US; **baldhead** (*a*) a person who has a bald head; (*b*) = ***baldpate*** below; (*c*) (orig. & chiefly *W. Indian*) a person without dreadlocks, a non-Rastafarian; **bald-headed** *adjective* = sense 2 above; ***go bald-headed*** (colloq.), proceed (*at, for, into*) regardless of the consequences; **bald ibis** either of two ibises of the genus *Geronticus*, which have bare heads (cf. WALDRAPP); **baldpate** a white-crowned American wigeon, *Anas americana*.
■ **balding** *adjective* going bald **M20.** **baldish** *adjective* **E19.** **baldly** *adverb* in a bald, basic, or dull manner; meagrely; undisguisedly: **E17.** **baldness** *noun* **LME.** **baldy** *noun & adjective* (*colloq.*) (*a*) *noun* a bald person; a bald head; (*b*) *adjective* (somewhat) bald: **M19.**

baldachin /ˈbaldəkɪn, ˈbɔːld-/ *noun.* Also **-quin.** **L16.**
[ORIGIN Italian *baldacchino*, from (with suffix *-ino* -INE[1]) *Baldacco* Italian form of *Baghdad*, its place of origin. Cf. BAUDEKIN.]
1 A rich embroidered material, orig. woven with woof of silk and warp of gold thread; rich brocade. **L16.**
2 (Now the usual sense.) A canopy (orig. made of the material in sense 1), supported on columns or fixed to a roof or wall, and placed over an altar, throne, or doorway. **M17.**
■ **baldachined** *adjective* covered with a baldachin **E20.**

balderdash /ˈbɔːldədaʃ/ *noun & verb.* **L16.**
[ORIGIN Unknown.]
▸ **A** *noun.* †**1** Frothy liquid. *rare.* Only in **L16.**
†**2** A jumbled mixture of liquors, e.g. of milk and beer, beer and wine, etc. Only in **17.**
3 *transf.* A senseless jumble of words; nonsense, trash (spoken or written). **L17.**
▸ †**B** *verb trans.* Make a jumbled mixture of (liquors); adulterate *with*. **L17–E19.**

baldicoot *noun* see s.v. BALD *adjective*.

baldmoney /ˈbɔːldmʌni/ *noun.* **LME.**
[ORIGIN Unknown.]
1 Gentian. *obsolete* exc. *Scot.* **LME.**
2 = SPIGNEL. **L16.**

baldric /ˈbɔːldrɪk/ *noun.* **ME.**
[ORIGIN Cf. Middle High German *balderich*, of uncertain origin (doubtfully referred to Latin *balteus* belt); occas. early forms from Old French *baudré*.]
1 *hist.* A belt or girdle, usu. richly ornamented, hung from the shoulder across the body to the opposite hip, and used to support a sword, bugle, etc. **ME.**

fig.: SPENSER Those twelve signes which nightly we do see The heavens bright-shining baudricke to enchace.

†**2** A leather strap etc. by which the clapper of a church bell was suspended. **LME–L19.**
†**3** A necklace. **M16–M19.**

bale /beɪl/ *noun*[1]. *arch. & poet.*
[ORIGIN Old English *balu* (*bealu*) = Old Frisian, Old Saxon *balu*, Old High German *balo*, Old Norse *bǫl*, from Germanic.]
1 Evil, esp. as an active and destructive force; a malign influence; woe, harm, injury. In early use freq. *spec.* death. **OE.**
2 Evil as something suffered; physical torment, pain, misery. **ME.**
3 Mental suffering; misery, sorrow, grief. **ME.**
■ **baleless** /-l-l-/ *adjective* (long *arch.*) harmless, innocent **OE.**

bale /beɪl/ *noun*[2]. *arch.*
[ORIGIN Old English *bǣl* = Old Norse *bál* great fire, cogn. with Sanskrit *bhāla* lustre, Greek *phalos* shining, bright. In Middle English and mod. English from Old Norse *bál*. Much confused with BALE *noun*[1], esp. in *balefire* below).]
†**1** *gen.* A great consuming fire, a conflagration. **OE–E19.**
2 *spec.* ▸**a** A funeral pile or pyre. **OE.** ▸**b** A beacon fire. *Scot.* **LME.**
– COMB.: **balefire** a great open-air fire, esp. a funeral pyre; a beacon fire.

bale /beɪl/ *noun*[3] & *verb*[1]. **ME.**
[ORIGIN Prob. from Middle Dutch *bale* (Dutch *baal*) from Old French *bale* (later and mod. *balle*); ult. identical with BALL *noun*[1].]
▸ **A** *noun.* **1** A package of merchandise, orig. round in shape, now usu. compressed, wrapped in canvas etc., and tightly corded or hooped; the quantity in a bale, used varyingly as a measure. **ME.**
†**2** A set of dice. **L15–E19.**
– COMB.: **bale-goods** merchandise in bales.
▸ **B** *verb trans.* Make up into a bale or bales. **M18.**
■ **baler** *noun* **L19.**

bale *verb*[2] see BAIL *verb*[3].

Balearic /balɪˈarɪk/ *adjective.* **M17.**
[ORIGIN Latin *Balearicus*, from *Balearis* adjective (*Baleares insulae* the islands listed below): see -IC.]
Designating, of, or pertaining to a group of islands off the east coast of Spain, comprising Majorca, Minorca, Ibiza, and Formentera, and seven smaller islands.
■ **Balearian** *adjective & noun* (*rare*) (*a*) *adjective* = BALEARIC; (*b*) *noun* a native or inhabitant of the Balearic Islands: **E17.**

balection *adjective & noun* var. of BOLECTION.

baleen /bəˈliːn/ *noun.* **ME.**
[ORIGIN Old French & mod. French *baleine* whale, from Latin *balaena*.]
†**1** A whale. **ME–E17.**
2 Whalebone. **ME.**
†**3** Some kind of fish, perhaps sea bream. **ME–L16.**
– COMB.: **baleen whale** any whale of the suborder Mysticeti, members of which yield whalebone.

baleful /ˈbeɪlfʊl, -f(ə)l/ *adjective.* **OE.**
[ORIGIN from BALE *noun*[1] + -FUL.]
1 Pernicious, destructive, malignant (physically or morally). **OE.**
2 Miserable; distressed, sorrowful. *arch.* **ME.**
■ **balefully** *adverb* **LME.** **balefulness** *noun* **L16.**

baleout *noun* see BAILOUT.

†**balester** *noun* var. of BALISTER.

balibuntal /balɪˈbʌnt(ə)l/ *noun.* **E20.**
[ORIGIN from *Baliuag* in the Philippines, where it originated + BUNTAL.]
A fine close-woven straw, used for hats.

Balinese /bɑːlɪˈniːz/ *adjective & noun.* **E19.**
[ORIGIN from *Bali* (see below) + -ESE, after Dutch *Balinees*.]
▸ **A** *adjective.* Of or pertaining to the island of Bali in Indonesia. **E19.**
▸ **B** *noun.* Pl. same. A native or inhabitant of Bali; the Indonesian language of Bali. **E19.**

balinger /ˈbalɪndʒə/ *noun. obsolete* exc. *hist.* **LME.**
[ORIGIN Anglo-Norman *balyngere* = medieval Latin *balingaria, -gera* whaleboat, *-arius* a kind of warship, MFr. (north.) *balenghier(e)*, *balengier*, Old French & mod. French *baleinier* whaler, formed as BALEEN.]
A small seagoing sailing vessel without a forecastle, used mainly for coastal trade.

†**balister** *noun.* Also **-est-**. **ME–E18.**
[ORIGIN Old French *balestre* = medieval Latin *balistarius, -est-*, from Latin BALLISTA: see -ER[2].]
A crossbowman; = ARBALESTER.

balk *noun, verb* var. of BAULK *noun, verb*.

Balkan /ˈbɒlkən, ˈbɔːl-/ *adjective & noun.* **M19.**
[ORIGIN Turkish *balkan* chain of wooded mountains, name of a chain in Bulgaria: assim. to words in -AN.]
▸ **A** *adjective.* Designating, of, or pertaining to a mountain chain in Bulgaria, and (by extension) the peninsula bounded by the Adriatic, Aegean, and Black Seas, or the countries or peoples of this region. **M19.**
▸ **B** *noun.* In *pl.* *The* Balkan mountains (formerly also *sing.*); *the* Balkan countries. **M19.**
■ **Balkaniˈzation** *noun* the action of Balkanizing an area **E20.** **Balkanize** *verb trans.* divide (an area) into smaller mutually hostile states **E20.**

ball /bɔːl/ *noun*[1]. ME.
[ORIGIN Old Norse *ball-*, *bǫllr* (Old Swedish *baller*, Swedish *båll*) from Germanic.]
1 A globular body. ME. ▸**b** *spec.* A planetary or celestial body. Now always with specifying word. ME.

M. W. MONTAGU The . . tents . . are adorned on the top with guilded balls. R. E. VERNÈDE The sun's a red ball in the oak. R. CAMPBELL A kind of sweet known as Moor Balls, flavoured with anis. D. ATTENBOROUGH All the flagella around the sphere beat in an organised way and drive the tiny ball in a particular direction. **b** ADDISON What, though in solemn silence all Move round the dark terrestrial ball.

ball and chain, **chain and ball** a heavy metal ball secured by a chain to the leg of a prisoner or convict to prevent escape; *fig.* a severe hindrance, *esp.* (*colloq.*, *derog.* & *joc.*) one's wife. ***claw-and-ball***: see CLAW *noun*[1]. ***red ball***: see RED *adjective*. **three balls** a pawnbroker's sign.
2 A spherical or egg-shaped object that is used in games or play, varying greatly in size, material, and degree of hardness, and either inflated or solid. ME. ▸**b** A game played with a ball. ME. ▸**c** A single throw, kick, or other kind of delivery of a ball in the course of a game (freq. with specifying word indicating the nature or quality of the movement); BASEBALL (esp.) a single delivery of the ball by a pitcher outside specified limits and not struck at by the batter. L15.

c S. RAVEN Nigel had sent him down some five or six balls, all of which he played correctly and neatly. C. POTOK He ignored it completely, and the umpire called it a ball.

billiard ball, ***cricket ball***, ***rugby ball***, ***tennis ball***, etc.; (also sense 2b) ***baseball***, ***basketball***, ***football***, ***handball***, ***netball***, ***volleyball***, etc. **have one's eye on the ball** *fig.* be paying attention, be alert. **have the ball at one's feet** *fig.* be able to take advantage of opportunity, be in a controlling position. **keep one's eye on the ball** *fig.* remain alert. **keep the ball rolling** *fig.* play one's part in a conversation, an undertaking, etc. **on the ball** in contact with or playing the ball in football, hockey, etc.; *fig.* (*colloq.*) competent, sharp, alert. **run with the ball** *fig.* take and maintain control, keep the initiative. ***see off the new ball***: see SEE *verb*. ***spot-ball***: see SPOT *noun* 6b. **start the ball rolling** *fig.* initiate a conversation, an undertaking, etc. ***the ball is in your court***: see COURT *noun*[1]. ***trap and ball***: see TRAP *noun*[1]. **b play ball (with)** *fig.* (*colloq.*) act fairly, cooperate, (with). ***c base on balls***: see BASE *noun*[1]. ***no-ball***: see NO *adjective*. ***short ball***: see SHORT *adjective*. ***sinker ball***: see SINKER *noun*[1] 7.
3 A globular or rounded mass of any substance. ME. ▸**b** *spec.* A large pill or capsule of medicine. Now only in VETERINARY MEDICINE. LME.

AV *Sus.* 1:17 Bring me oil & washinge balls. F. MARRYAT You had a ball of twine.

ball of fire (*a*) *slang* a glass of brandy; (*b*) a person of great energy or spirit. SNOWBALL *noun*.
4 In *pl.* The testicles; *fig.* (treated as *sing.*) nonsense, a muddle, an unsuccessful attempt. Now *coarse slang*. ME. ▸**b** Manliness, power, strength; courage, nerve. *slang*. M20.

B. MARSHALL What do you mean by talking all that unpatriotic balls? S. BECKETT I've made a balls of the fly. **b** M. PUZO What gives you the balls to think I'd leave my wife for you?

balls-out *adverb* & *adjective* without moderation or restraint. **balls-up** a confusion or mess, a muddle.
5 Any rounded protuberant part of the body, *esp.* that at the base of the thumb or the big toe. ME.

J. STEINBECK One foot was to the ground, the other rested on the ball.

†**6** An orb as a symbol of sovereignty. LME–E18.

SHAKES. *Hen. V* The balm, the sceptre, and the ball, The sword, the mace, the crown imperial.

7 A solid non-explosive missile (orig. always spherical) fired from a cannon, rifle, pistol, etc. (In small arms now usu. called ***bullet***.) LME.

J. C. OATES A thirty-two-pound ball was fired by the British. F. SMYTH The leaden ball extracted from the dead man by a surgeon. *collect.*: LD MACAULAY A body of troops . . was ordered to load with ball.

8 The eye within the lids and socket (formerly, the pupil). LME.

SIR W. SCOTT Raising his sightless balls to heaven.

EYEBALL.
9 A small wooden or ivory sphere used in voting (cf. BALLOT *noun*). L16.
black ball, ***blackball***: see BLACK *adjective*.
10 A leather-covered pad used by printers for inking type. *obsolete* exc. *hist.* L16.
†**11** A rounded package. Cf. BALE *noun*[3]. L16–L18.
– COMB.: **ball-and-socket joint** a form of joint having a rounded end in a concave cup or socket, allowing great freedom of movement; **ball bearing** a bearing in which friction is reduced by the use of small balls; a ball for this purpose; **ballboy** one who retrieves balls for the players in lawn tennis; **ball-breaker**, **ball-buster** *coarse slang* a sexually demanding woman, a woman who destroys men's self-confidence; **ball clay** a very adhesive clay, *esp.* a fine-textured clay used in the manufacture of earthenware; **ballcock** an automatic device with a floating ball, to control the level of water in a cistern; **ball-court** an area (such as a paved yard) for the playing of ball games; **ball flower** ARCHITECTURE an ornament resembling a ball within the petals of a flower; **ball game** a game played with a ball; *spec.* (*N. Amer.*) a game of baseball; *colloq.* a particular affair or concern (esp. in ***whole new ball game*** & vars.); **ball hawk** *N. Amer. slang* a skilled ball player; a footballer etc. who is quick to get possession of the ball; BASEBALL a defensive outfielder skilled in catching fly balls; **ball-hawk** *verb intrans.* (*N. Amer. slang*) be quick to get possession of the ball in a game of football etc.; **ball joint** = ***ball-and-socket joint*** above; **ball lightning** a rare globular form of lightning; **ballpark** *N. Amer.* a baseball ground; *colloq.* an area, a region, (*lit.* & *fig.*), esp. in ***in the right ballpark***, close to one's objective, approximately correct; ***ballpark figure***, a rough estimate; **ball-peen**, **-pein** *adjective* (of a hammer) having a ball-shaped peen; **ballplayer** *N. Amer.* a baseball player; **ballpoint (pen)** a pen having a tiny ball as its writing point; **ball-proof** *adjective* able to withstand the impact of a cannon etc. ball; **balls-aching** *adjective* (*coarse slang*) annoying, boring; **ball-tampering** CRICKET illegal alteration of the surface or seam of a ball on the field, to affect its motion when bowled.
■ **baller** *noun*[1] (chiefly *US*) a player of a ball game E20. **ball-like** *adjective* resembling (that of) a ball, globular L19.

ball /bɔːl/ *noun*[2]. E17.
[ORIGIN Old French & mod. French *bal* dance, from †*bal(l)er* to dance from late Latin *ballare* rel. to Greek *ballein* to throw (cf. Greek *ballizein* to dance).]
1 A formal social assembly for dancing, usu. with an organized programme and accompanied by special entertainment. E17.
hunt ball: see HUNT *noun*[2]. MASKED ***ball***. **open the ball** *fig.* begin operations.
2 A wildly enjoyable time. Esp. in ***have a ball***, ***have oneself a ball***. *colloq.* M20.
– COMB.: **ball gown** a gown suitable for wearing at a ball; **ballroom** a large room in which balls are held; ***ballroom dancing***, formal social dancing in couples (dances including the foxtrot, waltz, tango, rumba, etc.).

ball /bɔːl/ *noun*[3]. Chiefly *Irish*. E20.
[ORIGIN Unknown.]
A glass *of* (an alcoholic drink).

S. O'CASEY There's nothin' like a ball o' malt occasional like.

ball /bɔːl/ *verb*[1]. L16.
[ORIGIN from BALL *noun*[1].]
1 *verb trans.* Round or swell out. *rare*. L16.
2 *verb trans.* Make into a ball; wind (thread) *off* into a ball; clench or screw up (the fist) tightly; roll *up* into a ball-like mass. M17.

E. K. KANE Brooks balls off twine. P. GALLICO Small hands balled into possessive fists. E. CRISPIN This handkerchief, balled up in Mavis's hand.

3 *verb intrans.* Gather into a ball. E18.

SOUTHEY In clogs . . snow balls under the wooden sole.

4 *verb intrans.* Become clogged or blocked, esp. with snow. Also foll. by *up*; *fig.* make a mess of something, fail. M18.
5 *verb trans.* Clog, block. Also foll. by *up*. M19. ▸**b** Bring into a state of confusion or difficulty; make a mess of. Usu. foll. by *up*. *slang*. L19.

A. BRONTË The snow . . clogged the wheels and balled the horses' feet. J. HERRIOT Not merely a few of the hair-like worms irritating the tubes, but great seething masses of them crawling everywhere, balling up and blocking the vital air passages. **b** N. COWARD You can't even do a straight walk off without balling it up.

6 *verb trans.* & *intrans.* Of a man (*verb intrans.* also of a woman): have sexual intercourse (with). *N. Amer. slang*. M20.

G. VIDAL You can tell the world all about those chicks that you ball.

■ **baller** *noun*[2] a person who or a machine which makes balls E19. **balling** *verbal noun* (*a*) the action of the verb; (*b*) the administration of medicine to an animal in the form of a capsule (usu. *attrib.* as ***balling gun*** etc., an instrument for this purpose): E18.

ball /bɔːl/ *verb*[2]. M17.
[ORIGIN from BALL *noun*[2].]
1 *verb intrans.* Attend a ball or balls. M17.
2 *verb trans.* Entertain at a ball. M19.
3 *verb intrans.* Enjoy oneself greatly, have a wildly enjoyable time. *N. Amer. slang*. M20.

ballabile /baˈlaːbile/ *noun*. Pl. ***-li*** /-li/. M19.
[ORIGIN Italian, from *ballare* to dance.]
A dance by the *corps de ballet* or by the chorus in an opera; a piece of music for this; any piece of instrumental music suggestive of a dance.

ballad /ˈbaləd/ *noun* & *verb*. L15.
[ORIGIN Old French & mod. French *ballade* from Provençal *balada* dance, song or poem to dance to, from *balar* to dance: cf. BALL *noun*[2].]
▸**A** *noun*. **1** A light, simple song; *spec.* †(*a*) a song intended to accompany a dance; (*b*) a sentimental or romantic composition of two or more verses each sung to the same melody. L15. ▸**b** A popular song, *esp.* one attacking persons or institutions. *obsolete* exc. *hist.* M16. ▸**c** A popular narrative song in slow tempo. E20.
†**2** A proverbial saying, usu. in the form of a couplet. E16–E17.
3 A lively poem in short stanzas, in which a popular narrative is graphically told (orig. sung). M18.
– COMB.: **ballad-monger** a person who deals in ballads (used *derog.*, orig. by Shakes.).
▸**B** *verb*. **1** *verb intrans.* Compose or sing a ballad or ballads (*about*, †*against*). Now *rare*. L16.

R. GRAVES The best of all years to ballad about.

†**2** *verb trans.* Compose or sing a ballad about. E17–E18.

SHAKES. *Ant. & Cl.* Scald rhymers [will] Ballad us out o' tune.

■ **balla'deer** *noun* a person who sings or composes ballads M19. **ballader** *noun* a writer of ballads L16. **ba'lladic** *adjective* pertaining to or of the nature of ballads M19. **balladist** *noun* a balladeer M19. **balladize** *verb intrans.* & *trans.* compose a ballad or ballads (about) L16. **balladry** *noun* composition in ballad style L16.

ballade /baˈlɑːd/ *noun* & *verb*. LME.
[ORIGIN formed as BALLAD, with differentiation of application.]
▸**A** *noun*. **1** A poem (orig. for singing with accompaniment) of one or more triplets of stanzas having 7, 8, or 10 lines, each usu. ending with the same refrain line, and an envoy; more *gen.*, a poem divided into stanzas of equal length, usu. of 7 or 8 lines. Also *collect.*, poetry of this form. LME.
ballade royal = ***rhyme royal*** s.v. RHYME *noun*.
2 MUSIC. An extended, usu. dramatic, piece usu. for the piano. M19.
▸†**B** *verb intrans.* Compose ballades. Only in LME.

ballahoo *noun* var. of BALAO.

ballahou /baləˈhuː/ *noun*. M19.
[ORIGIN Spanish *balahú* schooner.]
NAUTICAL. A type of fast two-masted schooner. Also, an ungainly vessel. Cf. BALLYHOO *noun*[1].

ballan /ˈbalən/ *noun*. M18.
[ORIGIN Irish *ballán*, from *ball* spot.]
In full ***ballan wrasse***. A wrasse, *Labrus bergylta*, usu. green or greenish-brown.

ballast /ˈbaləst/ *noun* & *verb*. M16.
[ORIGIN Prob. from Low German or Scandinavian, in Old Swedish and Old Danish *ballast*, *barlast* (taken to be from *bor* bare or *barm* hull (of a ship) + *last* burden).]
▸**A** *noun*. **1** A heavy substance, such as gravel, sand, iron, or lead, placed in the bilge of a ship to ensure its stability. M16. ▸**b** A substance, usu. sand or water, carried in an airship or balloon to stabilize it, and jettisoned for higher flight. L18.
in ballast (of a ship) laden with ballast only.
2 *fig.* That which gives stability in morals or politics; experience or principles regarded as reinforcing character. E17.

I. WALTON Having to his great Wit added the ballast of Learning. H. T. COCKBURN Delay is often the ballast of sound legislation.

3 Gravel or coarse stone used to form the bed of a railway track or the substratum of a road. M19.
4 A passive component used in an electric circuit in order to moderate changes of current. Freq. *attrib.* E20.
– COMB.: **ballast-tank**: that can be flooded with water to allow a submarine to dive.
▸**B** *verb trans.* **1** Provide (a ship etc.) with ballast; fill or steady with ballast. M16.
2 Load with cargo; *fig.* burden or weigh down, steady. Now only *arch.* in *fig.* sense. M16.
3 Form (the bed of a railway line etc.) with ballast. M19.
■ **ballasting** *noun* (*a*) the action of the verb; (*b*) ballast: M16.

ballata /baˈlaːta, bɔˈlɑːtə/ *noun*[1]. Pl. ***-te*** /-te, -ti/. M18.
[ORIGIN Italian from Provençal *balada*: see BALLAD.]
An Italian ballad; an old Italian verse form in which the refrain occurs at the beginning and the end of each stanza.

ballata *noun*[2] var. of BALATA.

ballate *noun* pl. of BALLATA *noun*[1].

ballerina /baləˈriːnə/ *noun*. Pl. **-nas**, †**-ne**. L18.
[ORIGIN Italian, fem. of *ballerino* dancing master, from *ballare* to dance: see BALL *noun*[2].]
A female ballet dancer, *esp.* one who undertakes a leading role in classical ballet.
PRIMA BALLERINA.

ballet /ˈbaleɪ, -li/ *noun*. M17.
[ORIGIN French from Italian *balletto* dim. of *ballo* BALL *noun*[2].]
1 (A theatrical performance of) an artistic dance form using formalized set steps and gestures; a company performing this. Also, a creative work of this form; the music written for it. M17.

Vanity Fair He was terribly lonely and had season tickets to the ballet and invited me. *Daily Telegraph* In three weeks' time, the Kirov Ballet arrives in Britain as part of its world tour.

ballet d'action /bale daksjɔ̃/, pl. ***ballets d'action*** (pronounced same), [French = of action] a dramatic ballet, a ballet with a plot. ***corps de ballet***. ***maître de ballet***: see MAÎTRE 1a. RUSSIAN ***ballet***. ***symphonic ballet***: see SYMPHONIC 3.
†**2** *gen.* A dance. L18–E19.
– COMB.: **ballet dancer** a person who dances in ballets. **ballet master** a trainer of ballet dancers.
■ **balletic** /baˈlɛtɪk/ *adjective* of, pertaining to, or characteristic of ballet M20. **ba'lletically** *adverb* M20. **balletomane** /ˈbalɪtəmeɪn/ *noun* an enthusiast for ballet M20. **balletomania** /ˌbalɪtəˈmeɪnɪə/ *noun* enthusiasm for ballet M20.

ballist /ˈbalɪst/ *noun*. *rare*. LME.
[ORIGIN formed as BALLISTA.]
= BALLISTA.

ballista /bəˈlɪstə/ *noun*. Pl. **-stae** /-stiː/, **-stas**. E16.
[ORIGIN Latin, ult. from Greek *ballein* to throw.]
A military engine used in antiquity for hurling stones and other missiles.

ballistic /bəˈlɪstɪk/ *adjective*. L18.
[ORIGIN from BALLISTA + -IC.]
Of or pertaining to projectiles or their flight; moving under the action of no force except gravity.
ballistic galvanometer: with little or no damping, used to measure transient currents. **ballistic missile**, **ballistic rocket**: moving under gravity only, after an initial period of powered, guided flight. **go ballistic** *colloq.* fly into a rage.
■ **ballistically** *adverb* in a ballistic manner; as regards ballistics: L19. **ballistician** /balɪˈstɪʃ(ə)n/ *noun* an expert in ballistics E20.

ballistics /bəˈlɪstɪks/ *noun*. M18.
[ORIGIN formed as BALLISTIC + -ICS.]
The science of the motion of projectiles; *esp.* that part of the subject connected with firearms.
exterior ballistics, **interior ballistics**: dealing respectively with motion after and during the period when a projectile is subject to propulsive force or guidance. ***terminal ballistics***: see TERMINAL *adjective*.

ballistocardiograph /bəˌlɪstəˈkɑːdɪəɡrɑːf/ *noun*. M20.
[ORIGIN from BALLISTIC *adjective* + -O- + CARDIOGRAPH.]
An instrument for recording the movements of the body caused by ejection of blood from the heart at each beat.
■ **ballistocardiogram** *noun* the record made by a ballistocardiograph M20. **ballistocardioˈgraphic** *adjective* M20. **ballistocardiˈography** *noun* M20.

ballium /ˈbalɪəm/ *noun*. L18.
[ORIGIN medieval Latin formed as BAIL *noun*².]
= BAILEY 1.

ballock /ˈbɒlək/ *noun*. Now *coarse slang*. See also BOLLOCK *noun*.
[ORIGIN Old English *bealluc* dim. of Germanic base of BALL *noun*¹.]
1 A testicle. Usu. in *pl.* OE.
2 *fig.* In *pl.* (treated as *sing.*) Nonsense; a mess, a muddle. Also as *interjection*. M20.

ballock *verb* var. of BOLLOCK *verb*.

ballon /balɔ̃/ *noun*. Pl. pronounced same. M19.
[ORIGIN French: see BALLOON.]
1 Elasticity and buoyancy in dancing; smooth passage from step to step. M19.
2 = BALLOON *noun* 3b. M20.

ballon d'essai /balɔ̃ desɛ/ *noun phr.* Pl. ***ballons d'essai*** (pronounced same). L19.
[ORIGIN French = trial balloon.]
An experiment to see how a new policy or project will be received; a tentative proposal.

ballonet /ˈbalənɛt/ *noun*. Also **-nn-**. E20.
[ORIGIN French *ballonnet* dim. of *ballon* BALLOON *noun*: see -ET¹.]
A compartment in a balloon or airship into which air or another gas can be forced in order to maintain the craft's shape as buoyant gas is released.

ballonné /balɔne/ *noun*. Pl. pronounced same. L18.
[ORIGIN French, pa. pple of *ballonner* swell or puff out, distend.]
A bouncing step in dancing.

ballonnet *noun* var. of BALLONET.

ballons d'essai *noun phr.* pl. of BALLON D'ESSAI.

balloon /bəˈluːn/ *noun* & *verb*. L16.
[ORIGIN French *ballon* or Italian *ballone* augm. of *balla* BALL *noun*¹: see -OON.]
▸ **A** *noun*. †**1** (A game played with) a large inflated leather ball, struck to and fro with the arm protected by a bracer of wood. L16–E19.
†**2** A pasteboard ball filled with combustible matter, projected into the air as a firework. M17–M19.
3 A spherical glass with a narrow neck or mouth; *spec.*: ▸†**a** CHEMISTRY. A receiving vessel of this shape. L17–M19. ▸**b** A brandy goblet of this shape. M20.

> **b** M. GEE Cradling brandy . . in his elegant glass balloon.

4 A usu. round or pear-shaped airtight envelope designed to rise into the air when inflated with hot air or another gas that is lighter than air; *esp.* one carrying a basket or car for passengers. L18. ▸**b** A small rubber pouch with a neck, which is inflated with air for use esp. as a child's toy. M19.

> *fig.*: CARLYLE The hollow balloon of popular applause.

barrage balloon: see BARRAGE *noun*. ***captive balloon***: see CAPTIVE *adjective* 1. **when the balloon goes up** when the action, excitement, or trouble starts.
5 A round or pear-shaped outline containing words, *esp.* those in a cartoon or comic strip representing a person's words or thoughts and shown as issuing from the mouth or head. M19.

> DICKENS Diabolical sentiments . . were represented as issuing from his mouth in fat balloons. D. L. SAYERS I'm afraid it's rather full of marginal balloons and interlineations.

6 *fig.* A high hit or kick given to a ball. *colloq.* E20.
– COMB.: **balloon angioplasty** MEDICINE a technique in which a tiny balloon is passed along a blood vessel and inflated to remove a clot or other blockage; **balloon barrage** a connected system of balloons and cables used as a defence against hostile aircraft; **balloon catheter** MEDICINE an inflatable catheter used in the operation of balloon angioplasty; **balloon fish** a pufferfish; **balloon-flower** = PLATYCODON; **balloon frame** ARCHITECTURE: of light timbers nailed together; **balloon glass**, **balloon goblet** = sense 3b above; **balloon sleeve** a large sleeve puffed out over the upper arm; **balloon tyre** a low-pressure pneumatic tyre with a large cross-section; **balloon vine** a tropical American vine, *Cardiospermum halicacabum*, which bears inflated pods.
▸ **B** *verb*. **1** *verb trans*. Lift up in or as in a balloon. *rare*. L18.
2 *verb intrans*. Travel in a balloon. Chiefly as ***ballooning*** *verbal noun*. L18.
3 *verb intrans.* & *trans*. Swell, puff out; distend. M19.

> I. MURDOCH His shirt ballooned out over his trousers. S. BRETT His face . . , ballooned out with indignation. T. KENEALLY The doctor was forced to work with a ballooning face, now half again its normal size. *fig.*: *Poetry Nation Review* What started with a perfectly defensible basis has ballooned out of all proportion.

4 *verb trans*. Hit or kick (a ball) high in the air. *colloq.* E20.
5 *verb intrans*. Of an aircraft: rise up in the air, esp. as a result of a hard landing. E20.
■ **ballooner**, **balloonist** *nouns* a person who travels in a balloon L18.

ballot /ˈbalət/ *noun*. M16.
[ORIGIN Italian *ballotta* dim. of *balla* BALL *noun*¹.]
1 A small ball used for secret voting; a ticket, paper, etc., so used. M16.
2 The system of or an instance of secret voting, orig. by means of small balls placed in an urn or box; the number of votes thus recorded. M16.

> G. M. TREVELYAN Protected by the ballot, the agricultural labourer could vote as he wished, regardless of farmer and landlord. B. CASTLE In the ballot the railwaymen voted six to one to escalate the dispute into a national strike.

second ballot: see SECOND *adjective*. ***short ballot***: see SHORT *adjective*.
3 Lot-drawing, orig. by taking out small balls etc. from a box. L17.
– COMB.: **ballot box** a box used to contain ballot papers, esp. to preserve secrecy; *fig.* election by ballot; **ballot paper** the voting paper used in a ballot.

ballot /ˈbalət/ *verb*. M16.
[ORIGIN Italian *ballottare*, formed as BALLOT *noun*.]
▸ **I** †**1** *verb trans*. Vote by ballot on (a proposal, candidate, etc.). M16–L17.
2 *verb intrans*. Give a (usu. secret) vote (*for*, *against*). M16.
3 *verb trans*. Take a ballot of (a body of voters). L19.
▸ **II 4** *verb intrans*. Draw lots (*for*). E17.
5 *verb trans*. Select (esp. conscripts) by the drawing of lots. L18.
■ **balloter** *noun* a voter by ballot M18.

ballotin /ˈbalətɪn/ *noun*. L20.
[ORIGIN from French *ballot* small package of merchandise, rel. to BALLOT *verb*.]
A lidless box with a transparent cellophane cover, in which chocolates and other items are sold.

ballotine /ˈbalətiːn/ *noun*. M19.
[ORIGIN French, ult. from *balle* a package of goods.]
A piece of roasted meat which has been boned and stuffed before being folded or rolled into an egg-like shape; a dish of this.

ballotini /baləˈtiːni/ *noun pl*. M20.
[ORIGIN Italian *ballottini*, pl. of *ballottino*, dim. of *ballotta* small ball.]
Small particles or beads of glass, used for a variety of industrial and scientific applications.

ballottement /bəˈlɒtm(ə)nt/ *noun*. M19.
[ORIGIN French.]
MEDICINE. Palpation of a fluid-filled part of the body to detect a floating object, *spec.* of the uterus to discover the presence or position of the fetus.

†**ballow** *noun*. *dial.* *rare*. E17–L19.
[ORIGIN Unknown.]
A cudgel; a truncheon.

> SHAKES. *Lear* Whether your costard or my ballow be the harder.

balls /bɔːlz/ *verb trans*. *slang*. M20.
[ORIGIN from BALL *noun*¹ 4.]
Mess *up*. Cf. BALL *verb*¹ 5b.

ballsy /ˈbɔːlzi/ *adjective*. *slang*. M20.
[ORIGIN from BALL *noun*¹ + -S¹ + -Y¹.]
Manly, powerful; courageous; having or requiring nerve.

bally /ˈbali/ *adjective* & *adverb*. *slang*. L19.
[ORIGIN Alt. of BLOODY *adjective* & *adverb*, perh. from the written form *bl—y*.]
= BLOODY *adjective* & *adverb* as a vague intensive; confounded(ly); unpleasant(ly); very.

ballyhoo /balɪˈhuː/ *noun*¹. M19.
[ORIGIN Perh. formed as BALLAHOU.]
NAUTICAL. More fully ***ballyhoo of blazes***. A vessel that one dislikes.

ballyhoo /balɪˈhuː/ *noun*² & *verb*. Orig. *US*. L19.
[ORIGIN Unknown.]
▸ **A** *noun*. A showman's touting speech; bombastic nonsense; extravagant or brash publicity; noisy fuss. L19.
▸ **B** *verb trans*. Cajole by ballyhoo; praise or advertise extravagantly. E20.

ballyrag *verb* var. of BULLYRAG.

balm /bɑːm/ *noun*¹. ME.
[ORIGIN Old French *ba(s)me* from Latin *balsamum* BALSAM *noun*.]
1 A fragrant and medicinal exudation from certain trees (see sense 5 below). ME.
†**2** An aromatic preparation for embalming. ME–E17.
3 Fragrant oil or ointment; *fig.* fragrance, perfume. LME.

> SHAKES. *Rich. II* Not all the water in the rough rude sea Can wash the balm from an anointed king. J. THOMSON When nought but balm is breathing thro' the woods.

4 Aromatic ointment used for soothing pain or healing wounds; *fig.* a healing or soothing influence, consolation. LME.

> MILTON As Balm to fester'd wounds. D. WELCH The stillness in the room was balm. A. STORR No amount of recognition could have brought balm to that tortured soul.

5 A tree yielding a fragrant and medicinal exudation; *esp.* an Asian and N. African tree of the genus *Commiphora* (family Burseraceae). LME.
6 Any of various fragrant herbs; *spec.* (more fully ***lemon balm***) a labiate herb, *Melissa officinalis*, with lemon-scented leaves. LME.
– PHRASES ETC.: **balm in Gilead** [Jer. 8:22] comfort in distress, succour. **balm of Gilead** [*balm* in Coverdale *Genesis* 37:25, earlier rendered *resin*] (*a*) (a fragrant medicinal gum from) any of various trees, *spec.* of the genus *Commiphora*; (*b*) a balsam poplar, *Populus candicans*; (*c*) ***balm of Gilead fir*** = ***balsam fir*** s.v. BALSAM *noun*. **bastard balm** a labiate herb of European woodland, *Melittis melissophyllum*, with leaves smelling of new-mown hay. ***Molucca balm***.
– COMB.: **balm-apple** = *balsam apple* s.v. BALSAM *noun*. **balmyard** (in the West Indies) a place where the rituals of Pocomania or obeah are practised.

balm *noun*² var. of BARM *noun*².

balm /bɑːm/ *verb*¹ *trans*. *arch*. ME.
[ORIGIN App. from BALM *noun*¹.]
1 Embalm. ME.
2 †**a** Anoint (with oil etc.). LME–E17. ▸**b** Smear with something sticky; daub. *obsolete* exc. *dial.* LME.
3 Soothe or alleviate (pain, sorrow, etc.). LME.

balm *verb*² var. of BARM *verb*.

balmacaan /balməˈkɑːn/ *noun*. E20.
[ORIGIN from the name of *Balmacaan*, an estate near Inverness in Scotland.]
A loose-fitting overcoat with a small, rounded collar, typically having raglan sleeves.

bal masqué /bal maske/ *noun phr.* Pl. ***bals masqués*** (pronounced same). M18.
[ORIGIN French.]
A masked ball.

balm-cricket /ˈbɑːmkrɪkɪt/ *noun*. Also †**baum-**. M17.
[ORIGIN Partial translation of German *Baumgrille* lit. 'tree cricket', alt. after BALM *noun*¹.]
A cicada.

Balmer /ˈbɑːmə/ *noun*. L19.
[ORIGIN J. J. *Balmer* (1825–98), Swiss physicist.]
PHYSICS. Used *attrib.* & (now *rare*) in *possess.* to designate (the mathematical formula describing) a series of lines in the visible and ultraviolet spectrum of atomic hydrogen, between 656 and 365 nanometres.

balmoral /balˈmɒr(ə)l/ *noun*. Also **B-**. M19.
[ORIGIN from *Balmoral* Castle, a royal residence in NE Scotland.]
1 In full ***Balmoral boot***. A stout front-lacing ankle boot. M19.
2 *hist.* In full ***Balmoral petticoat***. A stiff woollen or horsehair underpetticoat. M19.
3 A round flat cap worn by some Scottish regiments. L19.

bal musette /bal myzɛt/ *noun phr.* Pl. ***bals musettes*** (pronounced same). E20.
[ORIGIN French.]
In France, a popular dancehall (with an accordion band).

balmy /ˈbɑːmi/ *adjective*¹. LME.
[ORIGIN from BALM *noun*¹ + -Y¹.]
1 Fragrant, aromatic, or soothing like balm. LME.

> M. R. MITFORD Under the shade of those balmy firs. E. IRVING The cure for a disease, is to send . . balmy medicines.

2 Deliciously soft and soothing; pleasant. E17.

> E. YOUNG Tir'd Nature's sweet restorer, balmy Sleep! G. CLARE Those happy and balmy days for fathers, when they and their wishes were immediately obeyed.

3 Of the weather, air, etc.: mild and fragrant. E17.

> G. SANTAYANA The next spring was singularly balmy. Crocuses and snowball blossoms were out in April. C. SAGAN A time . . of balmy temperatures, soft nights.

4 Yielding or producing balm. M17.
■ **balmily** *adverb* M19. **balminess** *noun* M18.

balmy *adjective*² var. of BARMY.

balneal /ˈbalnɪəl/ *adjective*. M17.
[ORIGIN from Latin *balneum* bath + -AL¹.]
Of or pertaining to a (warm) bath or bathing.

B

B

balneary /ˈbalnɪəri/ *noun & adjective*. M17.
[ORIGIN Latin *balnearium* bathing place, use as noun of neut. of *balnearius* adjective, from *balneum* bath: see -ARY¹.]
▸ **A** *noun*. A bath or bathing place; a medicinal spring. M17.
▸ **B** *adjective*. Of or pertaining to baths or bathing. L19.

balneo- /ˈbalnɪəʊ/ *combining form* of Latin *balneum* bath: see -O-.
■ **balneo'logical** *adjective* of or pertaining to balneology L19. **balne'ologist** *noun* an expert in or student of balneology L19. **balne'ology** *noun* the branch of knowledge that deals with the medicinal effects of bathing and mineral springs M19. **balneo'therapy** *noun* the treatment of disease by bathing, esp. in mineral springs L19.

Baloch, Balochi *nouns & adjectives* see BALUCHI.

baloney /bəˈləʊni/ *noun*. *colloq*. Also **bol-**. E20.
[ORIGIN from BOLOGNA.]
1 A Bologna sausage. *N. Amer.* E20.
2 Humbug; nonsense. Also as *interjection*. E20.

baloo /bəˈluː/ *noun & interjection*. *obsolete* exc. *dial.* Also **balow** /bəˈləʊ/. E17.
[ORIGIN App. a children's word of unknown origin.]
A lullaby. As *interjection*, used to lull a child to sleep.

BALPA /ˈbalpə/ *abbreviation*.
British Air Line Pilots Association.

balsa /ˈbɒlsə/ *noun*. E17.
[ORIGIN Spanish = raft.]
1 A raft or fishing boat, used chiefly on the Pacific coasts of S. America. E17.
2 A tropical American tree, *Ochroma pyramidale* (more fully ***balsa tree***); its strong, very light wood, used for rafts, floats, etc. (more fully ***balsa wood***). M19.

balsam /ˈbɔːlsəm, ˈbɒl-/ *noun*. OE.
[ORIGIN from Latin *balsamum* from Greek *balsamon*, perh. of Semitic origin (cf. Arabic *balasān*).]
1 A resinous exudation from various trees, *esp.* = BALM *noun*¹ 1. OE. ▸**b** *spec. CHEMISTRY*. A resinous product which is insoluble in water and is a source of benzoic or cinnamic acid. L17.
Canada balsam: see CANADA 1.
2 A tree yielding balsam; = BALM *noun*¹ 5. OE.
3 An aromatic ointment or other resinous medicinal preparation; *esp.* one of various substances dissolved in oil or turpentine. L16. ▸**b** *fig.* A healing or soothing agency. E17.

> **b** TENNYSON Was not the people's blessing . . a balsam to thy blood?

FRIAR's balsam. ***TOLU balsam***.
†**4** *ALCHEMY*. A healthful preservative essence considered by Paracelsus to exist in all organic bodies. M17–M18.
†**5** = BALM *noun*¹ 2; *fig.* a preservative. M17–M18.
6 Any plant of the genus *Impatiens* (see IMPATIENS), *esp.* (*a*) (more fully ***garden balsam***) *Impatiens balsamina*, native to southern and eastern Asia and cultivated for its showy pink flowers; (*b*) (in full ***Himalaya balsam***) *I. glandulifera*, a large Himalayan plant with purplish-pink flowers now widely naturalized along streams in Europe and N. America (also called ***policeman's helmet***). M18.
– COMB.: **balsam apple** (the fruit of) the tropical gourd *Momordica balsamina*; **balsam fir** a common N. American fir, *Abies balsamea*, yielding Canada balsam; **balsam pear** (the pear-shaped fruit of) the tropical gourd *Momordica charantia*; **balsam poplar** any of several N. American poplars, esp. *Populus balsamifera*, whose buds exude a fragrant gum.
■ **balsa'miferous** *adjective* yielding balsam L17. †**balsamine** *noun* (*a*) = ***balsam-apple*** above; (*b*) = ***garden balsam*** (sense 6 above): L16–M19. **balsamy** *adjective* like balsam in fragrance, balmy L17.

balsam /ˈbɔːlsəm, ˈbɒl-/ *verb trans*. M17.
[ORIGIN from the noun.]
Anoint or impregnate with balsam.

balsamic /bɔːlˈsamɪk, bɒl-/ *adjective & noun*. E17.
[ORIGIN from BALSAM *noun* + -IC.]
▸ **A** *adjective*. Of the nature of or yielding balsam; fragrant; soothing. E17.
balsamic vinegar a dark, sweet Italian red-wine vinegar from the Modena region, matured in wooden casks.
▸ **B** *noun*. A soothing medicine. E18.

†**balsamum** *noun*. OE–M17.
[ORIGIN Latin: see BALSAM *noun*.]
Balm; balsam.

bals costumés, bals masqués, bals musettes *noun phrs.* pls. of BAL COSTUMÉ etc.

Balt /bɔːlt, bɒlt/ *noun*. L19.
[ORIGIN Late Latin *Balthae* pl.]
A native or (esp. German) inhabitant of one of the Baltic states.

balter /ˈbɒltə/ *verb*¹ *intrans*. *obsolete* exc. *dial.* LME.
[ORIGIN Prob. from Old Norse: cf. Danish *baltre*, *boltre* wallow, welter, tumble.]
Tumble about; walk unsteadily.

balter /ˈbɒltə/ *verb*². *obsolete* exc. *dial.* Also **bolter**. E17.
[ORIGIN Perh. frequentative of BALL *verb*¹.]
1 *verb trans*. Clot, clog; tangle (the hair). E17.
2 *verb intrans*. Become tangled; form into lumps or balls. E17.

Balthazar /balˈθazə, ˈbalθəzɑː/ *noun*. Also **-sar**, **Belshazzar** /bɛlˈʃazə/. M20.
[ORIGIN The King of Babylon who 'made a great feast . . and drank wine before the thousand' (*Daniel* 5:1).]
A very large wine bottle, usually holding the quantity of sixteen regular bottles.

balti /ˈbɔːlti, ˈbalti/ *noun*¹. Pl. **-s**. L20.
[ORIGIN Uncertain; perh. a use of BALTI *adjective & noun*², or from Punjabi *bāṭṭī* deep brass dish.]
A type of Pakistani cuisine in which the food is cooked and served in a small two-handled pan known as a karahi and accompanied by nan bread; a dish prepared in this way.

Balti /ˈbalti/ *adjective & noun*². M19.
[ORIGIN Balti.]
▸ **A** *adjective*. Of or relating to Baltistan, a Himalayan region of Kashmir (now in northern Pakistan), its inhabitants, or their language. M19.
▸ **B** *noun*. **1** The Tibetan language of Baltistan. M19.
2 (Pl. **-is**.) A native or inhabitant of Baltistan. L19.

Baltic /ˈbɔːltɪk, ˈbɒlt-/ *adjective & noun*. L16.
[ORIGIN medieval Latin *Balticus*, formed as BALT: see -IC.]
▸ **A** *adjective*. **1** Designating, of, or pertaining to an almost landlocked sea separating Scandinavia from the rest of Europe. L16.
the Baltic states Lithuania, Latvia, and Estonia, which border the Baltic Sea between Poland and Russia.
2 Designating a branch of the Indo-European languages comprising Lithuanian, Latvian, and Old Prussian, usu. classified with the Slavonic group (see BALTO-). L19.
▸ **B** *noun*. *The* Baltic Sea; *the* lands bordering on it. E18.

Baltimore /ˈbɔːltɪmɔː, ˈbɒlt-/ *noun*. M17.
[ORIGIN Lord *Baltimore* (*c* 1580–1632), English proprietary of Maryland, the bird's colours being those of his coat of arms.]
In full ***Baltimore oriole***, ***Baltimore bird***. A N. American oriole, *Icterus galbula galbula*, coloured bright orange and black.

Baltimorean /bɒltɪˈmɔːrɪən/ *noun*. E19.
[ORIGIN from *Baltimore* (see below) + -AN.]
A native or inhabitant of the city of Baltimore in Maryland, USA.

Balto- /ˈbɔːltəʊ, ˈbɒltəʊ/ *combining form*.
[ORIGIN from BALTIC + -O-.]
Forming combs. in the sense 'Baltic and —'.
■ **Balto-Sla'vonic** *adjective & noun* (designating, of, or pertaining to) the group of Indo-European languages which comprises the Baltic branch and the Slavonic branch. E20.

Baluchi /bəˈluːtʃi/ *noun & adjective*. Also **-lochi** /-ˈləʊtʃi/; **-ch**. E17.
[ORIGIN Persian *Balūčī*.]
▸ **A** *noun*. Pl. same, **-s**. A native or inhabitant of Baluchistan, a region lying between the lower Indus and SE Iran; the Iranian language of Baluchistan. E17.
▸ **B** *adjective*. Of or pertaining to the people or language of Baluchistan. M19.

Baluchistan /bəˈluːtʃɪstɑːn/ *adjective*. E20.
[ORIGIN A province of SW Pakistan.]
1 Of or designating a type of rug, made largely by Baluchi people, characterized by its dark colours. E20.
2 = BALUCHI *adjective*. E20.

balun /ˈbalʌn/ *noun*. M20.
[ORIGIN Short for *balance to unbalance* (*transformer*).]
ELECTRICITY. A type of transformer used to connect a balanced circuit (i.e. one whose two terminals are equal and opposite with respect to ground) to an unbalanced one.

baluster /ˈbaləstə/ *noun*. E17.
[ORIGIN French *balustre* from Italian *balaustro*; so named from Italian *balausta*, *balaustra* blossom of the wild pomegranate (Latin *balaustium*, Greek *balaustion*), which a baluster resembles in shape.]
1 A short pillar or column of circular section and with a curving outline, usu. one of a series called a balustrade. Also, a similar pillar used in a window. E17.
2 A slender upright post helping to support a rail. M17. ▸**b** Usu. in *pl.* = BANISTER. M18.
3 *collect. sing.* = BALUSTRADE. *arch.* M17.

balustrade /baləˈstreɪd/ *noun*. M17.
[ORIGIN French after Italian *balaustrata*, Spanish *balaustrada*: see BALUSTER, -ADE.]
A row of balusters surmounted by a rail or a coping as an ornamental parapet to a terrace, balcony, etc.
■ **balustraded** *adjective* having a balustrade L18. **balustrading** *noun* balustrade-work L19.

Balzacian /balˈzakɪən/ *adjective & noun*. L19.
[ORIGIN from *Balzac* (see below) + -IAN.]
▸ **A** *adjective*. Pertaining to or characteristic of the French novelist Honoré de Balzac (1799–1850) or his works. L19.
▸ **B** *noun*. An admirer or student of Balzac or his writing. E20.

bam /bam/ *verb & noun*. *slang & dial.* E18.
[ORIGIN Rel. to BAMBOOZLE: either an abbreviation of it or the source of its 1st syll. Sense B.2 and the compounds may be unrelated to this.]
▸ **A** *verb trans. & intrans*. Infl. **-mm-**. = BAMBOOZLE *verb* 1. E18.
▸ **B** *noun*. **1** A hoax, a trick. E18.
2 A foolish or silly person. *Scot.* M20.

> I. PATTISON Ya ungrateful bam! I just saved your poxy life!

– COMB.: **bampot**, **bamstick** *Scot.* = sense B.2 above.

bam /bam/ *interjection*. E20.
[ORIGIN Imit.]
Repr. the sound of a hard blow. Also *gen.* introducing a sudden action or occurrence.

> B. HOLIDAY Then bam, they'd be drafted and end up right back in some camp in the South. M. FRENCH 'All of a sudden, bam!' She put her hand on her head. 'The lump's as big as a marble!'

bambino /bamˈbiːnəʊ, -əʊ/ *noun*. Pl. ***-ni*** /-ni/, ***-nos***. E18.
[ORIGIN Italian, dim. of *bambo* silly.]
A young child or baby (in Italy); *spec.* an image of the infant Jesus in swaddling clothes.

bamboo /bamˈbuː/ *noun & verb*. Also (earlier) †**-bos**, †**-b(o)us**. L16.
[ORIGIN Dutch *bamboes*, mod. Latin *bambusa*, ult. from Malay *mamby*. Forms in *-s* later taken as pl.]
▸ **A** *noun*. **1** Any of numerous, mainly tropical, giant grasses belonging to the genus *Bambusa* and various related genera; the hollow stem of such a plant, used as a stick or as material. L16.
2 Cane-coloured biscuit porcelain. L18.
3 A light yellowish brown. M19.
– COMB.: **bamboo curtain** [after *iron curtain*] a political and economic barrier between China and non-Communist countries; **bamboo fish** a small fish, *Sarpa salpa*, of the family Sparidae, found in the eastern Atlantic and the Mediterranean; **bamboo shoot** a young shoot of bamboo, eaten as a vegetable.
▸ **B** *verb trans*. Beat with a bamboo; provide with bamboo. E19.

bamboozle /bamˈbuːz(ə)l/ *verb & noun*. *slang*. E18.
[ORIGIN Prob. of cant origin: cf. BAM *verb & noun*.]
▸ **A** *verb*. **1** *verb trans*. Hoax, deceive, trick, cheat. E18.

> N. ROWE You intend to bamboozle me out of a Beef Stake. P. ROTH She had allowed herself to be bamboozled . . into eating lobster Newburg.

2 *verb trans*. Mystify, perplex. E18.

> E. GASKELL He fairly bamboozles me. He is two chaps.

▸ **B** *noun*. = BAMBOOZLEMENT. *rare*. E18.
■ **bamboozlement** *noun* hoaxing; cheating; tricky deception; mystification: M19. **bamboozler** *noun* E18.

†**bambos** *noun* see BAMBOO.

bamboula /bamˈbuːlə/ *noun*. M19.
[ORIGIN Louisiana creole.]
A dance of black American origin to tambourine accompaniment.

†**bamb(o)us** *nouns* see BAMBOO.

bamia /ˈbamɪə/ *noun*. M19.
[ORIGIN Arabic *bāmiya* okra.]
A variety of okra; a dish prepared using okra.

bammie /ˈbami/ *noun*. *Jamaican*. M20.
[ORIGIN Gã-Adangme (a W. African lang.) *bami*.]
More fully ***bammie cake***. A type of bread or cake made from cassava meal.

ban /ban/ *noun*¹. See also BANNS. ME.
[ORIGIN In branch I, partly aphet. from Middle English *iban*, Old English *ġebann* (cf. Old High German *ban*, Old Norse *bann*), partly from Old French *ban* from Germanic base of BAN *verb*, whence late Latin *bannus*, *bannum*. In branch II, strictly a separate word, from BAN *verb*.]
▸ **I 1** A public proclamation or edict; a summons (esp. to arms); *spec.* the gathering of the (French) King's vassals for war, or the body of vassals so assembled (orig. = ARRIÈRE-BAN). Now *arch. & hist.* ME.
2 A section of an army; *esp.* formerly in France, the younger part of the population liable to serve in the militia, as distinct from the arrière-ban of reserves. E19.
▸ **II 3** A formal ecclesiastical denunciation, an interdict, an excommunication; *gen.* a curse supposed to have supernatural sanction. L15. ▸**b** The invoking or utterance of a curse; an angry execration. *arch.* L16.
4 A formal or authoritative prohibition (*on* or *against* something), an interdict. M17. ▸**b** A proclamation issued against a person by the civil power; a sentence of outlawry. L17.

> *Daily Mail* A complete ban on smoking.

test ban etc.

ban /ban/ *noun*². E17.
[ORIGIN Persian *bān* lord, master, introduced by the Avars who ruled in Slavonic countries subject to Hungary.]
hist. A viceroy and military commander of certain districts in Hungary, Slavonia, and Croatia.

ban /bɑːn/ *noun*³. Pl. **bani** /ˈbɑːni/. L19.
[ORIGIN Romanian.]
A monetary unit of Romania, equal to one-hundredth of a leu.

ban /ban/ *verb*. Infl. **-nn-**.
[ORIGIN Old English *bannan* = Old Frisian *banna*, Middle Low German, Middle Dutch *bannen*, Old High German *bannan*, Old Norse *banna*, from Germanic base repr. also by Greek *phanai*, Latin *fari* speak. Cf. BAN *noun*¹.]

†**1** *verb trans.* Summon by proclamation (esp. to arms). OE–LME.
2 *verb trans.* Curse or damn. *arch.* ME. ▸**b** *spec.* Pronounce an ecclesiastical curse upon. *arch.* ME.

W. MORRIS Ever she blessed the old and banned the new.

3 *verb intrans.* Utter curses. *arch.* ME.

BYRON Yet harsh and haughty, as he lay he bann'd.

4 *verb trans. & intrans.* Chide, speak angrily (to). *dial.* ME.
5 *verb trans.* Exclude or proscribe (a person, esp. *from* something); interdict or formally prohibit. LME.

W. STORY He banned them from the city. A. J. P. TAYLOR The American government banned virtually all trade with Japan. E. LONGFORD His wife tried to ban his friends in the misguided belief that she was protecting her hero.

■ **bannable** *adjective* E20.

banal /bəˈnɑːl, -ˈnal; ˈbeɪn(ə)l/ *adjective*. M18.
[ORIGIN Old French & mod. French, from *ban*: see BAN *noun*¹, -AL¹.]
1 *hist.* Of or belonging to compulsory feudal service. M18.
2 Commonplace, trite, trivial. M19.
■ **banalize** *verb trans.* M20. **banally** *adverb* M20.

banality /bəˈnalɪti/ *noun*. M19.
[ORIGIN French *banalité*: see BANAL, -ITY.]
A trite or trivial thing, a commonplace; commonplace character, triviality.

banana /bəˈnɑːnə/ *noun*. L16.
[ORIGIN Spanish & Portuguese, from Mande.]
1 The edible finger-shaped pulpy fruit of any of various tropical and subtropical plants of the genus *Musa* (family Musaceae), borne in clusters and yellow-skinned when ripe. L16.
2 The treelike herbaceous plant bearing this fruit, which has a stem of overlapping leaf sheaths. L17.
3 In ***top banana***, ***second banana***. The most important, second most important, person in an organization, activity, etc. Orig. *theatrical slang*, with ref. to comedians in a variety show. *colloq.* (orig. *US*). M20.
– PHRASES: **go bananas** *slang* become crazy or angry.
– COMB.: **banana belt** a region in which bananas are grown, or which is warm enough for bananas to be grown; **banana bird** any of various fruit-eating birds; *esp.* = ***bananaquit*** below; **Bananaland** *Austral. colloq.* Queensland; **Bananalander** *Austral. colloq.* a Queenslander; **banana plug** ELECTRONICS a single-pole connector with a curved strip of metal forming a spring along its tip; **bananaquit** [QUIT *noun*¹] a tropical American passerine bird, *Coereba flaveola*; **banana republic** (usu. *derog.*) a small tropical (usu. Central or S. American) country that is economically dependent on its fruit-exporting or similar trade; **banana skin** *fig.* a cause of upset or humiliation; **banana split** a dessert of ice cream and a split banana.

banate *noun* var. of BANNAT.

banausic /bəˈnɔːsɪk/ *adjective*. *derog.* M19.
[ORIGIN Greek *banausikos* of or for artisans: see -IC.]
Suitable for artisans; uncultivated; materialistic.

Banbury /ˈbanb(ə)ri/ *noun*. M20.
[ORIGIN Fernley H. *Banbury*, English-born US inventor.]
In full ***Banbury mixer***. (Proprietary name for) a type of mixing machine used in the manufacture of rubber and plastics.

Banbury cake /ˈbanb(ə)rɪ keɪk/ *noun phr.* L16.
[ORIGIN *Banbury* in Oxfordshire, where orig. made.]
A cake of pastry filled with a currant mixture.

bancassurance /ˈbaŋkəˌʃɔːrəns/ *noun*. Also **bank-assurance**. L20.
[ORIGIN Blend of BANK *noun*³ and ASSURANCE, perh. from French.]
The selling of insurance products and services, esp. life assurance, by banking institutions.
■ **bancassurer** *noun* L20.

bancha /banˈtʃɑː/ *noun*. E20.
[ORIGIN Japanese, from *ban* vigil, watch (because the tea is sometimes used to promote wakefulness during meditation) + *cha* tea.]
A type of green tea produced in Japan, containing old or inferior leaves and stalks.

banco /ˈbaŋkəʊ/ *interjection*. L18.
[ORIGIN French from Italian: see BANK *noun*³.]
In baccarat etc.: expr. a player's willingness to meet single-handed the banker's whole stake. Cf. VA BANQUE.

band /band/ *noun*¹. *arch.* exc. as identified with BAND *noun*². LOE.
[ORIGIN Old Norse *band* = Old Frisian, Old Saxon *band*, Old High German *bant* (Dutch *band*, German *Band*), from Germanic, from base of BIND *verb*. Cf. BAND *noun*², BEND *noun*¹, BOND *noun*².]
▸ **I** *lit.* **1** A thing with which a person is bound in restraint of personal liberty; a shackle, a chain. LOE.
2 A string with which some loose thing (esp. straw) is bound. LOE. ▸**b** BOOKBINDING. Each of the cords or straps crossing the back of a book, to which the sheets are attached; the raised part on the spine formed by this. M18.
3 A connecting piece that holds together the parts of something. LOE.
4 A strap, chain, etc., used as a lead for a child or animal. LOE.
5 A hinge. LME.
▸ **II** *fig.* **6** The restraint on freedom of action regarded as imposed by sin, convention, sleep, etc. LOE.
7 An obligation or circumstance which restricts action or binds persons reciprocally; a tie, a restraint; a binding agreement or promise; a force effecting or maintaining union. LOE. ▸**b** Security given; a legally executed deed. *arch.* E16.
8 A covenant, a league. *Scot. obsolete* exc. *hist.* LME.
†**9** Binding quality or power. Only in E17.
■ **bandster** *noun* (*dial.*) a person who binds sheaves L18.

band /band/ *noun*². LME.
[ORIGIN Old French & mod. French *bande*, earlier *bende* (cf. BEND *noun*²) = Provençal, Spanish, Italian, medieval Latin *benda*, from Germanic, from base of BIND *verb*. Cf. BAND *noun*¹.]
1 A hoop; a ring of metal etc., now *esp.* one round a bird's leg to identify it. LME.

H. ALLEN The rather ponderous wedding ring . . had just below it a narrow, worn, gold band.

2 A flat strip of thin flexible material to contain or bind (cf. BAND *noun*¹ 2, 3) or (in later use) to identify or label; (freq. with specifying word) a fabric strip round or forming part of a dress, hat, etc. L15. ▸**b** *spec.* The neckband or collar of a shirt, a collar, a ruff, (now *arch.* or *hist.*); (now in *pl.*) the development of this into two strips hanging down in front in clerical, legal, or academic dress. M16. ▸**c** A strip of linen etc. wrapped round (part of) the body; a bandage. *arch.* L16.

AV *Ecclus* 6:30 Her bands are purple lace. W. J. LOCKE He selected a cigar, . . removed the band and clipped the point. Q. D. LEAVIS An enterprising publisher will reissue the novel with a band or new dust-jacket exhibiting the caption. M. LASKI There was a black band round the sleeve of his jacket. H. E. BATES Many pound notes, neatly folded and packed tight inside the hat, under the greasy leather band. **b** G. CRABBE Careless was he of surplice, hood, and band. J. ARCHER The official dress of the Vice-Chancellor, bands, collar, white tie and all.

armband, ***hairband***, ***hatband***, ***headband***, ***neckband***, ***waistband***, etc. ***Alice band***: see ALICE 2b. **elastic band**, **rubber band** a band of rubber to hold papers etc. together. **c *swaddling band(s)***: see SWADDLING *verbal noun* 2.

3 A stripe distinguished by colour or aspect from the surface which it crosses; a particular portion of a certain breadth crossing a surface. L15. ▸**b** A ring or stripe around an object. M19. ▸**c** *fig.* A range of values within a series; a scale extending between certain limits. E20. ▸**d** A section of a disc, tape, etc., containing a specified sequence of recorded material. M20.

GEO. ELIOT The . . sunshine . . came . . through the windows in slanting bands of brightness. S. BECKETT It seemed to have a red band or stripe running down its side. **b** G. K. CHESTERTON There seemed to be . . a continuous band round the earth . . a thing like the ring of Saturn.

4 An endless belt or strap transmitting motion between two wheels, pulleys, etc. E18.
5 A narrow stratum of coal or rock. M19.
6 PHYSICS etc. A broad feature in a spectrum; a range of wavelengths, energies, etc., between well-defined limits. M19.

R. V. JONES All we needed to do was to listen in the right frequency band.

Citizens' Band: see CITIZEN *noun*. ***narrowband***: see NARROW *adjective*. ***S-band***: see S, S 9.
– COMB.: **bandfish** any of several elongated bottom-dwelling marine fishes of the family Cepolidae, with long continuous fins; **band gap** PHYSICS the difference in energy between the valence and conduction bands of a semiconductor, consisting of a range of energy values forbidden to electrons; **band-limited** *adjective* (ELECTRONICS) (of a signal) restricted to a particular range of frequencies; **bandpass** the band of frequencies transmitted by a filter; **bandsaw** an endless saw, consisting of a steel belt with a serrated edge running over wheels; **bandwidth** the extent of a band of frequencies, esp. of one used in telecommunications.
■ **bandlet** *noun* = BANDELET M18. **bandlike** *adjective* M19.

band /band/ *noun*³. L15.
[ORIGIN Old French & mod. French *bande* = Provençal, Spanish, Italian, medieval Latin *banda*, prob. of Germanic origin and assoc. with medieval Latin *banda* scarf, *bandum* banner (cf. Gothic *bandwa* sign), also company, crowd.]
1 An organized company of people having a common purpose; *spec.* a troop of armed men, robbers, etc. L15.

BYRON The 'black bands' who still Ravage the frontier. S. GIBBONS Mr. Mybug and Rennet joined the band of watchers. F. FITZGERALD The enemy in the south consisted of little more than a band of guerrillas.

Band of Hope an association of young people pledged to total abstinence from intoxicating liquors. ***sacred band***: see SACRED *adjective*.

2 A company of people or animals in movement. E17. ▸**b** A herd, a flock. *N. Amer.* E19.

AV *Gen.* 32:7 Hee diuided the . . camels into two bands. J. R. GREEN The little band of fugitives.

3 A body of musicians, now *esp.* those playing brass or wind instruments; (a section of) an orchestra. Now also, a rock or pop group. M17.

P. KAVANAGH I joined the Sinn Fein Pipers' Band that was started. P. SCOTT She felt and heard the thrum and drum of the band.

big band, ***brass band***, ***German band***, ***jazz band***, ***marching band***, ***military band***, ***silver band***, ***wind band***, etc. **beat the band** *fig.* (*slang*) surpass everything. ***Schrammel band***: see SCHRAMMEL 2. **when the band begins to play** *fig.* when matters become serious.
– COMB.: **bandmaster** the leader or conductor of a band of musicians; **bandmate** a fellow musician in a band (chiefly a pop or rock one). **bandshell** a bandstand in the form of a large concave shell with special acoustic properties; **bandsman** a member of a band of musicians; **bandstand** a covered outdoor platform on which a band plays; **bandwagon** (orig. *US*) a large wagon used by a band in a parade etc.; *fig.* as of one carrying a group of successful (political) leaders, esp. in ***climb on the bandwagon***, ***jump on the bandwagon***, seek to join the party or group that is likely to succeed.

band /band/ *noun*⁴. E16.
[ORIGIN Unknown.]
A ridge of a hill; in the Lake District of northern England, a long hill resembling a ridge, or a narrow sloping offshoot from a higher hill or mountain.

band /band/ *verb*¹. L15.
[ORIGIN Old French & mod. French *bander*, formed as BAND *noun*². Perh. partly from the English nouns.]
1 *verb trans.* Bind or fasten with a band or bands. L15.
2 *verb trans.* Provide or cover with a band. *rare* in *gen.* sense. M16. ▸**b** *spec.* Provide (a bird) with an identifying band. E20.
3 *verb trans.* (chiefly *refl.*) & *intrans.* Join or form into a band or company; unite. M16.

MILTON What multitudes Were banded to oppose his high Decree. R. ELLISON We have banded together in brotherhood so as to do something about it. I. COLEGATE People banding themselves together in order to work for a better world.

4 *verb trans.* Mark with a band or stripe, or with bands or stripes. Freq. as ***banded*** *ppl adjective*. M18.

E. K. KANE An opalescent purple, that banded the entire horizon. D. ATTENBOROUGH Waving tentacles of the most delicate colours, banded, striped and patterned in many shades.

banded rudder-fish: see RUDDER *noun*.

5 *verb trans.* Divide into bands or ranges based on a numerical characteristic, with a view to treating the bands differently; EDUCATION group or allocate (pupils) on the basis of ability. L20.

Financial Times Making the community charge more fair by banding the rate of charge in proportion to ability to pay.

†**band** *verb*². L16–L17.
[ORIGIN Abbreviation of BANDY *verb*.]
= BANDY *verb*.

bandage /ˈbandɪdʒ/ *noun & verb*. L16.
[ORIGIN French, formed as BAND *noun*² + -AGE.]
▸ **A** *noun*. **1** A strip of woven material used to bind up a wound or to protect an injured part of the body. L16.
2 A strip of material used for binding or covering up, esp. for blindfolding the eyes. E18.
3 A strip or band of stone, iron, etc., used to bind together and strengthen any structure. *arch.* M18.
▸ **B** *verb trans.* Tie or bind up with a bandage. L18.
■ **bandaging** *noun* the applying of bandages; material for bandages: E19.

Band-Aid /ˈbandeɪd/ *noun, adjective, & verb*. Also **band-aid**. E20.
[ORIGIN from BAND *noun*² + AID *noun*.]
▸ **A** *noun*. **1** (Proprietary name for) a type of sticking plaster with a gauze pad; a strip of this. E20.
2 *fig.* A makeshift or temporary solution to a problem etc.; a palliative. M20.
▸ **B** *adjective*. Makeshift, temporary; palliative. L20.
▸ **C** *verb trans.* Apply a makeshift or temporary solution to (a problem etc.). L20.

bandanna /banˈdanə/ *noun*. Also **-ana**. M18.
[ORIGIN Prob. from Portuguese from Hindi (*bādhnū* method of tie-dyeing, spotted cloth, from *bādhnā* to tie).]
A coloured silk or cotton handkerchief or headscarf with white or yellow spots.

bandar /ˈbʌndə/ *noun*. Also **-der**. L19.
[ORIGIN Hindi *bādar* from Sanskrit *vānara*.]
In the Indian subcontinent: the rhesus monkey.
– COMB.: **bandar-log** /-ləʊg/ [Hindi *log* people from Sanskrit *loka*] the monkeys collectively; a body of irresponsible chatterers.

B & B *abbreviation*.
Bed and breakfast.

bandbox /ˈbandbɒks/ *noun & adjective*. M17.
[ORIGIN from BAND *noun*² + BOX *noun*².]
▸ **A** *noun*. A lightweight paper-covered box for millinery (orig. for neckbands). M17.
look as if one came out of a bandbox & vars., look extremely smart.
▸ **B** *attrib.* or as *adjective*. Resembling a bandbox; providing little space; fragile, flimsy; conspicuously neat and smart. L18.

N. SHUTE It had come through the Grand Prix unscratched, in bandbox condition.

■ **bandˈboxical** *adjective* resembling a bandbox, esp. in providing little space L18. **bandboxy** *adjective* = BANDBOX *adjective* M19.

bandeau /ˈbandəʊ, *foreign* bɑ̃do/ *noun*. Pl. **-eaux** /-əʊz, *foreign* -o/. **E18.**
[ORIGIN French from Old French *bandel* dim. of *bande*: see BAND *noun*², -EL².]
1 A band or strip of material, *esp*. one used for binding a woman's hair. **E18.**
2 A woman's strapless top formed from a band of fabric fitting around the bust. **E20.**

bandelet /ˈband(ə)lɪt/ *noun*. Also †**-ette**. **M17.**
[ORIGIN French *bandelette* dim. of Old French *bandele* fem. of *bandel*: see BANDEAU.]
A small band, streak, or fillet; ARCHITECTURE a small flat moulding, encompassing a column.

bander /ˈbandə/ *noun*¹. *arch*. **M16.**
[ORIGIN from BAND *verb*¹ + -ER¹.]
A member of a league, a confederate.

bander *noun*² var. of BANDAR.

banderilla /bandeˈriʎa, bandəˈrɪljə/ *noun*. Pl. ***-as*** /-as, -əz/. **L18.**
[ORIGIN Spanish, dim of *bandera* banner.]
A decorated dart thrust into a bull's neck or shoulders during a bullfight.

banderillero /ˌbanderiˈʎero, ˌbandərɪˈljɛːrəʊ/ *noun*. Pl. **-os** /-ɔs, -əʊz/. **L18.**
[ORIGIN formed as BANDERILLA + *-ero* agent-suff.]
A bullfighter who uses banderillas.

banderole /ˈbandərəʊl/ *noun*. Also **-ol** /-əʊl, -(ə)l/; (esp. in sense 2, the earlier form) **bannerol** /ˈbanərəʊl, -(ə)l/. **M16.**
[ORIGIN French *ban(n)erole*, later *banderole*, from Italian *banderuola* dim. of *bandiera* BANNER *noun*¹: see -OLE¹.]
1 A long narrow flag with a cleft end, flown from the masthead of a ship. **M16.**
2 A rectangular banner borne at the funerals of public figures and placed over the tomb. **M16.**
3 An ornamental streamer of the kind attached to a knight's lance. **L16.**
4 = BANNER *noun*¹ 4. *rare*. **L16.**
5 A ribbon-like scroll bearing a device or inscription. **E17.**

bandersnatch /ˈbandəsnatʃ/ *noun*. **L19.**
[ORIGIN Invented by Lewis Carroll; presumably a portmanteau word.]
A fabulous creature of dangerous propensities, immune to bribery and too fast to flee from; *allus*. any creature with such qualities.
C. S. LEWIS No one ever influenced Tolkien—you might as well try to influence a bandersnatch.

bandh /bʌːnd/ *noun*. **M20.**
[ORIGIN Hindi, Urdu *bāndh* from Sanskrit *bāndh* tie, fetter, from *bāndhnā* to bind, tie, shut, close, stop.]
In India: a stoppage of work as a form of protest; *spec*. a general strike.

bandicoot /ˈbandɪkuːt/ *noun*. **L18.**
[ORIGIN Alt. of Telugu *pandikokku* lit. 'pig-rat'.]
1 A large destructive southern Asian rat, *Bandicota indica*. Also ***bandicoot rat***. **L18.**
2 Any of various mainly insectivorous marsupials of the family Peramelidae, found in Australia and New Guinea. **L18.**

bandit /ˈbandɪt/ *noun*. Pl. **bandits**, (now chiefly *hist*.) **banditti** /banˈdɪti/. **L16.**
[ORIGIN Italian *bandito*, pl. *-ti*, use as noun of pa. pple of *bandire* ban = medieval Latin *bannire* proclaim, proscribe, banish.]
1 An outlaw; a lawless robber or marauder; a gangster. **L16.** ▸**b** In *pl*. **banditti** as *collect. sing*. A company of bandits. *arch*. **E18.**
J. R. GREEN The routed soldiery turned into free companies of bandits. W. H. AUDEN The bandit who is good to his mother. P. THEROUX Bandits stop this train and rob the passengers. **b** SIR W. SCOTT Deer-stealers . . are ever a desperate banditti.
one-arm bandit, **one-armed bandit** *colloq*. a fruit machine or the like operated by pulling down an armlike handle.
2 An enemy aircraft in action. *military slang*. **M20.**
T. CLANCY Sounds like forty to fifty bandits, sir.
■ **banditism** *noun* the practices of bandits **L19**. **banditry** *noun* = BANDITISM **E20.**

bandobast *noun* var. of BUNDOBUST.

bandog /ˈbandɒg/ *noun*. **ME.**
[ORIGIN from BAND *noun*¹ + DOG *noun*.]
Orig., a (fierce) dog kept on a chain; a mastiff, a bloodhound. Now usu. *spec*., a dog specially bred for fighting by crossing aggressive breeds.

bandoleer *noun* var. of BANDOLIER.

bandolero /bandəˈlɛːrəʊ/ *noun*. Pl. **-os**. **M17.**
[ORIGIN Spanish.]
A Spanish bandit.

bandolier /bandəˈlɪə/ *noun*. Also **-eer**. **L16.**
[ORIGIN French *bandoulière* perh. from Spanish *bandolera*, from *banda* sash or from Catalan *bandolera*, from *bandoler* bandit.]
†**1** A shoulder belt for carrying a wallet. **L16–M18.**
2 A shoulder belt for holding ammunition, (*hist*.) with small cases each containing a charge for a musket, (now) with small loops or pockets for carrying cartridges. **L16.** ▸**b** Any of the cases containing a charge for a musket. Now *arch*. or *hist*. **E17.**
■ **bandoliered** *adjective* wearing a bandolier **E20.**

bandoline /ˈbandəliːn/ *noun & verb*. Now *arch*. or *hist*. **M19.**
[ORIGIN French, formed as BANDEAU + Latin *linere* bedaub, anoint.]
▸ **A** *noun*. A gummy preparation for setting hair. **M19.**
▸ **B** *verb trans*. Set (hair) with this. **M19.**

bandoneon /banˈdəʊnɪən/ *noun*. Also **-ion**. **E20.**
[ORIGIN (Spanish *bandoneón* from) German *Bandonion*, from Heinrich *Band* its inventor, a 19th-cent. German musician + *-on-* as in *harmonika* harmonica + *-ion* as in *akkordion* accordion.]
A type of concertina used esp. in S. America.

bandora /banˈdɔːrə/ *noun*. Also **bandore** /banˈdɔː/. **M16.**
[ORIGIN Uncertain: cf. Dutch *bandoor*, Spanish *bandurria*, Italian *pandora*, *-ura* from Latin *pandura* from Greek *pandoura* PANDORA *noun*. Cf. BANJO, VANDOLA.]
A bass stringed instrument of the cittern family, having a long neck and a scallop-shaped body.

†**bandore** *noun*. **L17–E18.**
[ORIGIN Alt. of French BANDEAU.]
A widow's headdress.

bandulu /banˈduːluː/ *noun*. *W. Indian*. **L20.**
[ORIGIN Perh. W. African.]
Crime or fraudulent dealings.

bandura /banˈduːrə/ *noun*. **M20.**
[ORIGIN Ukrainian, Russian *bandúra*, perh. from Polish from Italian *pandura*, *pandora*: cf. BANDORA.]
A Ukrainian stringed instrument resembling a large asymmetrical lute with thirty or more strings, held vertically and plucked like a zither.

bandurria /banˈdʊərɪə, *foreign* banˈdurria/ *noun*. **M19.**
[ORIGIN Spanish.]
A Spanish stringed instrument of the lute type.

b. & w. *abbreviation*.
Black and white (television etc.).

bandy /ˈbandi/ *noun*¹. **L16.**
[ORIGIN Obscurely rel. to BANDY *verb*.]
†**1** A (now unknown) way of playing tennis. **L16–E17.**
†**2** A stroke with a racket; a ball, esp. a return, struck at tennis. **L16–M17.**
3 (A bent or curved stick used in) a form of hockey. **E17.**

bandy /ˈbandi/ *noun*². **L18.**
[ORIGIN Telugu *baṇḍi*, Tamil *vaṇṭi*.]
In the Indian subcontinent: a carriage, a buggy, a cart.

bandy /ˈbandi/ *adjective*. **L17.**
[ORIGIN Perh. attrib. use of BANDY *noun*¹ 3.]
Of legs: curved so as to be wide apart at the knees. Of a person: bandy-legged.
■ **bandiness** *noun* **M19.**

bandy /ˈbandi/ *verb*. **L16.**
[ORIGIN Perh. from French *bander* take sides at tennis, formed as BAND *noun*³. Cf. Italian *bandare*, Spanish *bandear*.]
1 *verb trans*. Throw, pass, strike (a ball) to and fro (as in tennis etc.). Chiefly *fig*. **L16.**
TENNYSON To be the ball of Time, Bandied by the hands of fools.
†**2** *verb trans*. Cast away or aside; *fig*. dismiss or reject. **L16–M17.**
C. MARLOWE The Cardinal, would bandy me away from Spain.
3 *verb trans*. Toss from side to side, from one to another, or *about*; esp. *fig*., pass (words, stories, etc.) around in a circle or group, discuss in this way. **L16.** ▸**b** Give and take (blows, words, etc.); exchange (conversation, compliments, etc.) *with* a person. **L16.**
G. ANSON Thus was this unhappy vessel bandied about within a few leagues of her intended harbour. DICKENS The stories they invent . . and bandy from mouth to mouth! H. READ The poet must use words which are bandied about in the daily give-and-take of conversation. W. IRVING Your name is . . frequently bandied at table among us. **b** J. L. MOTLEY Bandying blows in the thickest of the fight. N. MITFORD She bandied repartee with the various Rorys and Rolys.
†**4** *verb trans*. (esp. *refl*.) & *intrans*. Band together, confederate. **L16–E19.**
G. HERBERT Joyntly bandying, They drive them soon away. SIR W. SCOTT Here is his son already bandying and making a faction.
†**5** *verb intrans*. Contend, fight. **L16–E18.**
MILTON Neither did the People of Rome bandy with their Senate while any of the Tarquins liv'd.

bandy-bandy /ˈbandɪˌbandi/ *noun*. **E20.**
[ORIGIN Uncertain: perh. from Kattang (an Australian Aboriginal language of New South Wales) *bandi-bandi*.]
A nocturnal Australian snake, *Vermicella annulata*, marked with black and white bands.

bane /beɪn/ *noun & verb*.
[ORIGIN Old English *bana* = Old Frisian *bona*, Old Saxon, Old High German *bano*, Old Norse *bani*, from Germanic: ult. connections unkn.]
▸ **A** *noun*. **1** A slayer, a murderer. Long *arch*. *rare*. **OE.**
2 A thing which causes death or destroys life, *esp*. poison. Long *arch*. exc. in *comb*., as ***henbane***, ***wolf's bane***, etc. **OE.**
TOLKIEN The Ring gleamed and flickered as he held it up . . . 'Behold Isildur's Bane!' said Elrond.
†**3** Murder, death, destruction. **ME–M17.**
SHAKES. *Macb*. I will not be afraid of death and bane Till Birnam Forest come to Dunsinane.
4 Ruin, woe. Chiefly *poet*. **LME.**
R. GREENE That sweet boy that wrought bright Venus bane.
5 A cause of ruin, harm, or trouble. **L16.**
BURKE Theoretic plans of constitution have been the bane of France. C. BRONTË She who had been the bane of his life. M. M. KAYE His attentions soon became the bane of the boy's existence.
– COMB.: **baneberry** any of several Eurasian and N. American plants of the genus *Actaea*, of the buttercup family; the bitter poisonous fruit of these plants; **banewort** *dial*. any of various, mainly poisonous, plants, *esp*. lesser spearwort, *Ranunculus flammula*.
▸ **B** *verb trans*. **1** Hurt, harm, poison. *arch*. **LME.**
†**2** Esp. of poison: kill. Only in **L16.**
■ **baneful** *adjective* lethal; poisonous; pernicious: **L16.**

†**banes** *noun pl*. see BANNS.

bang /baŋ/ *noun*¹. **M16.**
[ORIGIN from BANG *verb*¹.]
1 A heavy resounding blow; a thump. **M16.**
Suffolk bang: see SUFFOLK 1.
2 A sudden loud sharp noise, as the report of a gun; the sound of an explosion. **M19.**
B. KINGSOLVER The door flew open with a bang.
bang for the buck, **bang for one's buck** *N. Amer. colloq*. value for money (orig. of military weapons spending), return on investment. ***Big Bang***: see BIG *adjective*. ***sonic bang***: see SONIC 2. **with a bang** *fig*. successfully; impressively, spectacularly; ***go out with a bang***, make a dramatic exit, perform a final startling or memorable act.
3 An injection of a drug. Cf. BHANG. *US slang*. **E20.**
4 Excitement, pleasure; a thrill. *N. Amer. slang*. **M20.**
5 An act of sexual intercourse. *slang*. **M20.**
gang-bang: see GANG *noun*.

bang /baŋ/ *noun*². Chiefly *N. Amer*. **L19.**
[ORIGIN from BANG *adverb*: cf. BANGTAIL.]
A fringe of hair cut straight across the forehead.

†**bang** *noun*³ var. of BHANG.

bang /baŋ/ *verb*¹. **M16.**
[ORIGIN Imit., perh. of Scandinavian origin (cf. Old Norse *bang* hammering, *banga* hammer): Low German has *bange(l)n* beat.]
1 *verb trans*. Strike or shut noisily; cause to make the sound of a blow or explosion. **M16.**
TENNYSON Like an iron-clanging anvil banged With hammers. A. KOESTLER It was the sound of Sonia banging the bathroom-door behind her that woke him.
bang out produce (a tune on a piano, etc.) noisily and roughly.
2 *verb intrans*. Move impetuously, dash, jump. *dial*. **L16.**
3 *verb trans*. Knock about, damage, (*N. Amer*. also foll. by *up*); drub, defeat (*lit. & fig*.). **E17.**
M. EDGEWORTH English Clay . . banged down to Clay-hall. SHAKES. *Oth*. The desperate tempest hath so bang'd the Turk That their designment halts.
banged to rights: see RIGHT *noun*¹.
4 *verb intrans*. Strike or shut violently or noisily, thump; make a sudden loud noise. **E18.**
WILKIE COLLINS Taking great pains not to let the doors bang. C. JACKSON She had only to bang on the small painted drum.
bang heads together reprimand people severely, esp. in an attempt to stop them arguing. ***bang one's head against a brick wall***: see WALL *noun*¹.
5 *verb trans*. Surpass. Chiefly *dial*. **L18.**
DICKENS The next Pickwick will bang all the others.
6 *verb trans*. STOCK EXCHANGE. Depress (share prices, the market). *arch*. **L19.**
7 *verb trans. & intrans*. Copulate (with). *slang*. **L19.**
8 *verb intrans*. ***bang away***, continue in or *at* an action persistently or repetitively. **L19.**
G. JOSIPOVICI Genius is . . poor old Sartre banging away at his trilogy.
9 *verb intrans*. ***bang on***, talk tediously and at length *about* something. *colloq*. **L20.**
■ **banging** *adjective* (*slang*) (of dance music) having a loud relentless beat; *fig*. lively, excellent: **L20.**

bang /baŋ/ *verb*² *trans*. Orig. *US*. **L19.**
[ORIGIN from BANG *noun*².]
Cut (hair) in a fringe straight across the forehead.

bang /baŋ/ *adverb*. **L18.**
[ORIGIN from BANG *verb*¹.]
1 With sudden impact; abruptly; explosively (as the conventional imitation of a shot or explosion, *lit. & fig*.). Freq. in ***go bang***. **L18.**
O. W. HOLMES Bang went the magazine! T. STOPPARD Bang goes your credit at the off-licence.

B

2 Completely; exactly. Also as a mere intensive. *colloq.* E19.

Times Lit. Suppl. Bang-up-to-date neutron know-how. E. CRISPIN Gobbo certainly did leave here that evening bang on time.

bang off *slang* immediately. **bang on** *slang* exactly right, excellent. ***bang to rights***: see RIGHT *noun*[1]. **bang-up** *adjective* (*N. Amer. slang*) first-class, splendid.

Bangalore torpedo /baŋɡəˈlɔː tɔːˈpiːdəʊ/ *noun phr.* Pl. **Bangalore torpedoes**. E20.
[ORIGIN from *Bangalore*, a city in southern India.]
MILITARY. A tube containing explosive used by infantry for blowing up wire entanglements etc.

bangalow /ˈbaŋɡələʊ/ *noun*. E19.
[ORIGIN Dharawal (an Australian Aboriginal language of New South Wales) *bangala*.]
Either of two Australian palms of the genus *Archontophoenix*, having feathery leaves. Also ***bangalow palm***.

bangarang /ˈbaŋəraŋ/ *noun*. *W. Indian*. M20.
[ORIGIN Prob. imit., perh. influenced by Portuguese *banguelê* riot, disorder.]
An uproar or disturbance.

bang-bang /baŋˈbaŋ/ *noun & adjective*. Orig. *US*. M20.
[ORIGIN Redupl. of BANG *noun*[1].]
▸ **A** *noun*. (Repeated) gunfire or explosions; armed combat. M20.
▸ **B** *attrib.* or as *adjective*. Characterized by gunfire or explosions, or *transf.* by any rapid and thrilling sequence of events (*spec.* in BASEBALL, the near-simultaneous arrival of a runner and the ball at a base). M20.

banger /ˈbaŋə/ *noun*[1]. Chiefly *colloq.* M17.
[ORIGIN from BANG *verb*[1] + -ER[1].]
Something which makes a bang or is noisily conspicuous; *spec.* (**a**) a blatant lie; (**b**) a firework which goes off with a bang; (**c**) an enthusiastic kiss; (**d**) a sausage; (**e**) a dilapidated old car.

†**banger** *noun*[2] var. of BANJO.

banghy *noun* var. of BANGY.

Bangla /ˈbʌŋlɑː/ *noun & adjective*. M20.
[ORIGIN Bengali *bāṅglā*.]
(Of or pertaining to) the Bengali language.

Bangladeshi /baŋɡləˈdɛʃi, bʌŋɡ-/ *noun & adjective*. Pl. of noun same, **-s**. L20.
[ORIGIN from *Bangladesh* (see below) + -I[2].]
(A native or inhabitant) of the People's Republic of Bangladesh in the north-east of the Indian subcontinent (formerly East Pakistan).

bangle /ˈbaŋɡ(ə)l/ *noun*. L18.
[ORIGIN Hindi *baṅglī* (orig.) coloured glass bracelet.]
A rigid ring as a bracelet or anklet.
slave bangle: see SLAVE *noun*[1] & *adjective*[1].
■ **bangled** *adjective* wearing or adorned with bangles M19.

bangle /ˈbaŋɡ(ə)l/ *verb*. *obsolete* exc. *dial.* M16.
[ORIGIN Unknown.]
1 *verb intrans.* Flap, hang loosely; waste time, mess about. M16.
2 *verb trans.* Fritter *away*, squander. E17.

bango /ˈbaŋɡəʊ/ *interjection*. *US*. E20.
[ORIGIN from BANG *noun*[1] + -O.]
Suddenly, all of a sudden, that instant.

C. BUCKLEY Finally we're getting some cooperation and then bango, the top law enforcement officer goes.

Bangorian /baŋˈɡɔːrɪən/ *adjective*. E18.
[ORIGIN from *Bangor*, a town in N. Wales + -IAN.]
Of or pertaining to Bangor; *spec.* (*hist.*) designating a religious controversy raised by a sermon directed against nonjurors preached before George I by the then Bishop of Bangor.

bangster /ˈbaŋstə/ *noun*. *Scot.* M16.
[ORIGIN from BANG *verb*[1] + -STER.]
A bully, a thug; a victor in fights.
■ **bangstry** *noun* violence to person or property L16.

bangtail /ˈbaŋteɪl/ *noun*. L19.
[ORIGIN from BANG *verb*[1] + TAIL *noun*[1].]
(A horse etc. with) a tail cut straight across.
– COMB.: **bangtail muster** *Austral.* a counting of cattle by cutting across the tuft of each animal's tail.
■ **bangtailed** *adjective* M19.

bangy /ˈbʌŋɡi/ *noun*. Also **-ghy**. L18.
[ORIGIN Hindi *bahaṅgī*, Marathi *baṅgī* (Sanskrit *vihaṅgikā*).]
In the Indian subcontinent: a shoulder yoke with containers for carrying loads.

bani *noun* pl. of BAN *noun*[3].

bania /ˈbʌnɪə/ *noun*. L18.
[ORIGIN Hindi *baniyā* from Sanskrit *vāṇija*: see BANYAN.]
A Hindu trader or merchant.

banian *noun* var. of BANYAN.

banish /ˈbanɪʃ/ *verb trans.* LME.
[ORIGIN Old French *baniss-* lengthened stem of *banir* (mod. *bannir*) from Proto-Romance from Germanic, from base of BAN *noun*[1]: see -ISH[2].]
†**1** Proclaim (a person) an outlaw. LME–E17.
2 Condemn to removal esp. to another country; exile. LME.

SHAKES. *Temp.* This damn'd witch Sycorax . . from Argier . . was banish'd. J. MORSE He that shall be convicted there of is to be banished the kingdom.

3 *gen.* Dismiss from one's presence or mind; expel. LME.

DISRAELI Who had they dared to imitate him . . would have been banished society. E. M. FORSTER He was . . a stimulus, and banished morbidity. R. LOWELL Old lumber banished from the Temple. W. TREVOR He tried to think of something else, to banish away the face of the man who had been rude.

†**4** Clear out, empty. L15–L16.
■ **banisher** *noun* LME. **banishment** *noun* the action of banishing; a state of exile or enforced absence; dismissal: L15.

banister /ˈbanɪstə/ *noun*. Also **-nn-**, (earlier) †**barrister**. M17.
[ORIGIN Alt. of BALUSTER, partly by assoc. with BAR *noun*[1].]
Any of the upright pillars supporting the handrail of a staircase; the whole structure of rail and uprights. Usu. in *pl.*

banjax /ˈbandʒaks/ *verb trans.* *Irish*. M20.
[ORIGIN Unknown.]
Ruin, destroy; incapacitate.

banjo /ˈbandʒəʊ/ *noun*. Pl. **-o(e)s**. Also †**-ore**, †**banger**. M18.
[ORIGIN Black American alt. of BANDORA.]
1 A stringed musical instrument of the guitar family, with a round open-backed soundbox of parchment stretched over a metal hoop. M18.
2 Any of various appliances resembling this instrument in shape; *Austral. & NZ slang* a shovel. M19.
■ **banjoist** *noun* a person who plays the banjo L19.

banjolele *noun* var. of BANJULELE.

banjolin /ˈbandʒəlɪn/ *noun*. Also **-ine**. L19.
[ORIGIN from BANJO + MANDOLIN.]
A four-stringed instrument, combining characteristics of the banjo and the mandolin.

†**banjore** *noun* var. of BANJO.

banjulele /bandʒəˈleɪli/ *noun*. Also **-jo-**. E20.
[ORIGIN from BANJO + UKULELE.]
A simplified banjo tuned as a ukulele.

bank /baŋk/ *noun*[1]. ME.
[ORIGIN Old Norse *bakki* ridge, bank (Old Danish *banke*; Swedish *backe*, Danish *bakke* hillock, ascent) from Germanic; rel. to BENCH *noun*.]
1 The sloping margin of a river, stream, etc.; ground at the side of a river etc. Also, the edge of a hollow place such as a mine shaft, ditch, etc. ME.

SHAKES. *Jul. Caes.* Tiber trembled underneath her banks. W. WOLLASTON Daisies on the banks of the road.

burst its banks: see BURST *verb* 8. **left bank**, **right bank** (of a river): respectively to left or right of someone looking down stream. ***South Bank***: see SOUTH.
2 A ridge or shelf of ground with (steeply) sloping sides; a slope of such a ridge etc. ME.

SHAKES. *Mids. N. D.* I know a bank where the wild thyme blows. E. WAUGH I . . organized lines of men to pass the stores from hand to hand down the steep bank.

3 A hill, a hillside (*dial.*); a railway incline. LME.

J. A. H. MURRAY Thomas, lying on Huntley Banks, sees the lady riding by.

4 The seashore. *obsolete* exc. *dial.* LME.
5 A shelving elevation in the seabed or a riverbed. L16.

Scottish Daily Express The Albert had been fishing in the Belgian banks of the North Sea. *fig.*: SHAKES. *Macb.* But here upon this bank and shoal of time—We'd jump the life to come.

6 A long flat-topped mass (of cloud, fog, snow, etc.). E17.
7 An anthill. *obsolete* exc. *dial.* M17.
8 The lateral inclination of an aircraft when turning in flight; a lateral inclination given to a road at a curve. E20.
– COMB.: **bank barn** *N. Amer.* a barn built on a slope; **bank-full** *adjective* full to the bank or brink; **bank martin** a sand martin; **bankside** (**a**) the sloping side of a bank; (**b**) the margin of a lake, river, etc.; **banksman** MINING a pithead overseer; **bank swallow** = ***bank martin*** above; ***bank vole***: see VOLE *noun*[2].
■ **bankless** *adjective* without banks or borders E17. **banky** *adjective* full of banks, hilly; like a bank, inclined: E17.

bank /baŋk/ *noun*[2]. ME.
[ORIGIN Old French & mod. French *banc* (= Provençal *banc*, Spanish, Italian *banco*), from Proto-Romance deriv. of Germanic: see BANK *noun*[1], BENCH *noun*.]
†**1** A bench; a platform. (Cf. ***mountebank***.) ME–L17.
†**2** A seat of justice. ME–L19.
3 A bench or table used in various trades, esp. in printing to receive the printed sheets. *obsolete* exc. *hist.* M16.
4 The bench occupied by the rowers of each oar in a galley; a line of oars set at the same height, esp. on either side of a galley. L16.
5 A set of similar pieces of equipment grouped together, esp. in rows or tiers. L19.

T. C. BOYLE A bank of booming speakers.

bank /baŋk/ *noun*[3]. L15.
[ORIGIN French *banque* or its source Italian *banca* (also *banco*), from medieval Latin *bancus*, *banca*, from Germanic: cf. BANK *noun*[1], *noun*[2].]
†**1** The place of business of a money-dealer; the table on which such business is conducted. L15–M19.
2 An accumulated sum of money; a joint stock, esp. contributed for charitable purposes. *obsolete* exc. as in sense 4 below. E16.
3 An establishment for the custody, deposit, loan, exchange, or issue of money, which it pays out on the customer's order; a building occupied by such an establishment. E17.

G. STEIN She would not let Lena touch her wages, but put it in the bank for her. G. GREENE Drawing a cheque is not nearly so simple an operation in an American bank as in an English one.

bank of issue, **bank of circulation**: one that issues its own notes. **central bank** a national (not commercial) bank. CLEARING ***bank***. **cry all the way to the bank** *colloq. iron.* receive ample financial compensation or reward. ***Federal Reserve Bank***: see FEDERAL. **in bank**, **in the bank** *fig.* to one's credit, in reserve. ***joint-stock bank***: see JOINT *adjective*. ***merchant bank***: see MERCHANT *adjective*. **private bank**: one with not more than twenty unincorporated partners. ***reserve bank***: see RESERVE *noun & adjective*. ***savings bank***: see SAVING *noun*. ***Swiss bank***. **the Bank (of England)** the central bank of the UK, which acts as the Government's banker, manages the public debt, and issues legal tender.
4 In gaming, the amount of money, chips, etc., which the keeper of the table, or one player playing against all the others, has before him or her; the proprietor as controlling this. E18.
break the bank: see BREAK *verb*.
5 A small enclosed receptacle for money. Chiefly in ***piggy bank*** s.v. PIGGY *noun*. M20.
6 A reserve of something (e.g. blood, data) stored for future use; a place holding this. M20.

I. ASIMOV The time would come when unfertilised ova could be stored in banks at liquid-air temperatures and utilised for artificial insemination. *Times* We must be prepared for the day when 'banks' of different organs . . will be integral parts of all major hospitals.

bottle bank, ***paper bank***, etc.
– COMB.: **bank balance** the net amount held by a depositor in a bank, *loosely* a person's wealth; **bank bill** (**a**) a bill drawn by one bank on another; (**b**) *N. Amer.* a banknote; **bank book** a book supplied by a bank to a customer to provide a record of sums deposited or withdrawn; **bank card** a cheque card; **bank charge** commission charged by a bank for transactions and services; **bank holiday** a weekday on which banks are legally closed, in Britain usu. kept as a general holiday; **bank manager** the person in charge of a local branch of a bank; **banknote** a banker's promissory note, esp. from a central bank, payable to the bearer on demand, and serving as money; **bank rate** (**a**) *hist.* the minimum rate at which the Bank of England would agree to discount approved bills of exchange; (**b**) a bank's base rate; **bankroll** *noun & verb* (orig. *N. Amer.*) (**a**) *noun* a roll of banknotes; funds; (**b**) *verb trans.* (*colloq.*) finance, remunerate; **bank statement** a statement showing the balance of a bank account together with amounts paid in or withdrawn.

bank /baŋk/ *verb*[1]. LME.
[ORIGIN from BANK *noun*[1].]
1 *verb trans.* Confine or contain within a bank or banks; border, edge, surround. LME.

R. GREENE A silent streame . . Banckt about with choyce of flowers. SOUTHEY A ridge of rocks that bank'd its side. M. MCCARTHY The altar was completely banked with flowers.

2 *verb trans.* Heap or pile (*up*) into banks; build (a fire) up or *up* with tightly packed fuel so that it burns slowly. M16.

H. MARTINEAU They had banked up the snow. J. KOSINSKI Before retiring for the night women would bank up ashes to make certain that the embers would keep glowing until morning. D. BAGLEY Consoles of telemetering devices were banked fore and aft.

†**3** *verb trans.* Coast, skirt. *rare* (Shakes.). Only in L16.
4 *verb trans. & intrans.* WATCHMAKING. Limit the movement of (the escapement) in a watch; (of a watch or its escapement) impinge against its limits of movement. M18.
5 *verb intrans.* Rise or pile up or *up* into banks; build *up*. L18.
6 *verb trans.* Assist (a train) to ascend an incline by pushing at the rear. E20.
7 a *verb trans.* Tilt (an aeroplane, road vehicle, etc.) sideways in making a turn; build (a road etc.) higher at one side than the other to assist fast cornering. E20. ▸**b** *verb intrans.* Tilt in this way. E20.

a R. V. JONES Cecil, with all his old bomber pilot's reactions, banked us sharply into a turn heading directly at the fighter. **b** C. A. LINDBERGH I banked around in an attempt to get back to the field.

bank /baŋk/ *verb*[2]. M17.
[ORIGIN from BANK *noun*[3].]
1 *verb intrans.* Keep a bank; trade in money. M17.
2 *verb intrans.* In gaming: act as banker. E19. ▸**b** Put one's money *on* or *upon*; base one's hopes (*up*)*on*; count or rely (*up*)*on*. L19.
3 *verb intrans.* Keep money *at* or *with* (a particular bank etc.). M19.
4 *verb trans.* Deposit (money etc.) in a bank. M19.
5 *verb trans.* Store (blood, tissue, etc.) for future use. M20.

B

■ **banka'bility** *noun* the quality or condition of being bankable **L20.** **bankable** *adjective* receivable at a bank; profitable, commercially feasible: **E19.**

bankassurance *noun* var. of **BANCASSURANCE.**

banker /ˈbaŋkə/ *noun*[1]. Long *arch.* & *dial.* **ME.**
[**ORIGIN** Anglo-Norman *bankeur* = Old Northern French *bankier, banquier*, from *banc*: see **BANK** *noun*[2], **-ER**[2].]
A covering for a bench or chair.

banker /ˈbaŋkə/ *noun*[2]. **M16.**
[**ORIGIN** Old French & mod. French *banquier* (cf. Italian *banchiere*, Anglo-Latin *bancarius*), from *banque*: see **BANK** *noun*[3], **-ER**[2].]
1 A person who keeps or manages a bank (see **BANK** *noun*[3] 1, 3); in *pl.* also, a banking company. **M16.**
merchant banker: see **MERCHANT** *adjective*. ***Swiss banker***.
2 In gaming, a person who keeps the bank; the dealer in some games of chance. **E19.** ▸**b** A particular gambling game of cards. **L19.**
3 In a football pool: a result which one forecasts identically in a series of entries; *gen.* a match etc. for which a specified outcome is confidently predicted. **M20.**
– **COMB.**: **banker's card** a cheque card; ***banker's order***: see **ORDER** *noun*; ***bankers' ramp***: see **RAMP** *noun*[3].
■ **bankerish** *adjective* bankerly **M20.** **bankerly** *adjective* characteristic of or appropriate to a banker **L20.**

banker /ˈbaŋkə/ *noun*[3]. **M17.**
[**ORIGIN** from **BANK** *noun*[1] or *verb*[1] + **-ER**[1].]
1 A ship or fisherman employed in cod-fishing on the Newfoundland banks. **M17.**
2 A labourer who makes banks of earth etc. *dial.* **E18.**
3 A river flooded to the top of its banks. *Austral.* & *NZ.* **M19.**
4 A locomotive used for banking (see **BANK** *verb*[1] 6). **E20.**

banker /ˈbaŋkə/ *noun*[4]. **L17.**
[**ORIGIN** from **BANK** *noun*[2]; perh. alt. of Italian *banco* (a statuary's) bench.]
A wooden or stone bench on which bricks are dressed or stone is worked.

banket /baŋˈkɛt, ˈbaŋkɪt/ *noun*. Orig. *S. Afr.* **L19.**
[**ORIGIN** Afrikaans = almond toffee.]
GEOLOGY. Compact gold-bearing conglomerate.

banking /ˈbaŋkɪŋ/ *noun*. **E17.**
[**ORIGIN** from **BANK** *nouns* & *verbs* + **-ING**[1].]
1 The construction of banks or embankments. **E17.** ▸**b** An embankment or artificial bank. **M18.**
2 The business of a banker (**BANKER** *noun*[2]). **M18.**
merchant banking: see **MERCHANT** *adjective*.
3 Sea-fishing on a bank, esp. on the Newfoundland banks. **L18.**
4 *WATCHMAKING.* Limitation of the motion of the balance, usu. by special pins. **E19.**
5 The raising of the outer side of a road etc. on a bend to facilitate cornering. **E20.**
– **COMB.**: **banking house** a mercantile firm engaged in banking.

bankrupt /ˈbaŋkrʌpt/ *noun*, *adjective*, & *verb*. Also †**-rout**. **M16.**
[**ORIGIN** Italian *banca rotta* lit. 'bench (or table) broken', infl. by French *banqueroute* and assim. to Latin *ruptus* broken.]
▸ **A** *noun*. †**1** = **BANKRUPTCY** 1. **M16–E18.**
2 An insolvent debtor, a person who is hopelessly in debt; *spec.* an insolvent person (orig., a trader or merchant) whose estate is administered and distributed for the benefit of all his or her creditors by a court of law. **M16.**
▸ **B** *adjective*. **1** Insolvent; undergoing legal process of bankruptcy. **M16.**
2 *fig.* At the end of one's resources; destitute or bereft *of* (a quality etc.). **L16.**
▸ **C** *verb*. †**1** *verb intrans.* Become bankrupt; fail financially. **M16–L17.**
2 *verb trans.* Make bankrupt, reduce to insolvency; *fig.* exhaust the resources of, beggar. **L16.**

bankruptcy /ˈbaŋkrʌptsi/ *noun*. **E18.**
[**ORIGIN** from **BANKRUPT** *adjective* + **-CY**.]
1 The state of being, or fact of becoming, bankrupt. **E18.**

ADAM SMITH Bankruptcies are most frequent in the most hazardous trades. H. CECIL They would be put into bankruptcy and their affairs investigated.

bankruptcy order *ENGLISH LAW* a court order declaring a person bankrupt and placing his or her property under the control of a receiver or trustee.
2 *fig.* Total loss (of a quality etc.); ruin. **M18.**

BURKE A general bankruptcy of reputation in both parties.

bankshall /ˈbaŋkʃɔːl/ *noun*. **E17.**
[**ORIGIN** Malay *bangsal* shed, perh. from Sanskrit *vaṇikśālā* merchants' hall.]
In the Indian subcontinent and SE Asia: a warehouse; the office of a harbour master etc.

banksia /ˈbaŋksɪə/ *noun*. **L18.**
[**ORIGIN** mod. Latin, from Sir Joseph *Banks* (1743–1820), English naturalist, or (sense 2) his wife Dorothea: see **-IA**[1].]
1 Any of various evergreen flowering shrubs of the proteaceous genus *Banksia*, native to Australia. **L18.**
2 ***banksia rose***, a climbing rose, *Rosa banksiae*, native to China. **L19.**
■ **banksian** *adjective* (**a**) ***Banksian cockatoo***, a largely black Australian cockatoo, *Calyptorhynchus banksii*; (**b**) ***banksian rose*** = ***BANKSIA rose***; (**c**) ***banksian pine***, the jack pine, *Pinus banksiana*: **L18.**

bannat /ˈbanət/ *noun*. Also **banate**. **E19.**
[**ORIGIN** Serbian and Croatian, formed as **BAN** *noun*[2] + **-ATE**[1].]
hist. The district under the jurisdiction of a ban.

banner /ˈbanə/ *noun*[1] & *adjective*. **ME.**
[**ORIGIN** Anglo-Norman *banere*, Old French *baniere* (mod. *bannière*) ult. from medieval Latin *bandum*: see **BAND** *noun*[3].]
▸ **A** *noun*. **1** A piece of cloth attached by one side to the upper part of a pole, and used as the standard of a king, knight, army, etc.; a national flag, esp. as inspiring emotional attachment; *HERALDRY* a flag displaying a person's arms. **ME.** ▸†**b** The company ranged under a particular banner. *rare*. **ME–E19.** ▸†**c** A fringed flag hanging on a trumpet. *rare* (Shakes.). Only in **L16** ▸**d** A flag awarded as a distinction. *US.* **M19.**
follow the banner of, **join the banner of** *fig.* adhere to the cause of. ***red banner***: see **RED** *adjective*. ***Star-Spangled Banner***: see **STAR** *noun*[1] & *adjective*.
2 A flag or standard with a symbolic device as the emblem of a guild, company, or other group; a long strip of cloth bearing a slogan or design, carried in a demonstration or procession or hung in a public place. **ME.** ▸**b** *fig.* Something used as a symbol of principles. **E19.**

b *World Monitor* Socialist, democratic, and liberal parties, unified under the banner of a 'democratic Russia'.

3 *hist.* Any of the principal divisions of the Manchu army, each with a distinguishing flag or banner. Also, a military subdivision of Mongolian tribes. **M19.**
4 An advertisement on a website in the form of bar, column, or box. **L20.**
– **COMB.**: **banner-cry** *arch.* a cry summoning men to join a banner, a slogan; **bannerman** (**a**) *Scot. arch.* a standard-bearer; (**b**) *hist.* a soldier of one of the banners of the Manchu army.
▸ **B** *attrib.* or as *adjective*. **1** Entitled to a banner of distinction; pre-eminent, supreme. *US.* **M19.**
2 Conspicuous. **E20.**

V. GOLLANCZ The *Daily Herald* came out with a huge banner headline, in letters half an inch high, on its opening page.

■ **bannerer** *noun* (*obsolete* exc. *hist.*) a standard-bearer **LME.**

banner /ˈbanə/ *noun*[2]. **LME.**
[**ORIGIN** from **BAN** *verb* + **-ER**[1].]
A person who bans something or someone.

banner /ˈbanə/ *verb*. **L16.**
[**ORIGIN** from **BANNER** *noun*[1].]
†**1** *verb intrans.* Raise a banner or standard *against*. *rare*. Only in **L16.**
2 *verb trans.* Provide with a banner or banners. Chiefly as ***bannered*** *ppl adjective*. **M17.**
3 *verb trans.* Bear or blazon on a banner. Chiefly as ***bannered*** *ppl adjective*. **L18.**
4 *verb trans.* Announce in a banner headline. **M20.**

banneret /ˈbanərɪt/ *noun*[1]. Also (as a title) **B-**. **ME.**
[**ORIGIN** Old French *banerez*, (later) *-et*, ult. formed as **BANNER** *noun*[1].]
hist. **1** (Also ***knight banneret***) Orig., (the title of) a knight able and entitled to bring vassals into the field under his own banner (esp. a French rank). Later, (the title of) a person on whom a knighthood was conferred on the field for valour in the king's presence; hence as a rank or order of knighthood. **ME.**
2 = **BANNERER. LME.**
3 A title borne by certain officers in some of the Swiss cantons and Italian republics. **L17.**

banneret /ˈbanərɪt/ *noun*[2]. Also **bannerette** /banəˈrɛt/. **ME.**
[**ORIGIN** Old French *banerete* dim. of *baniere*: see **BANNER** *noun*[1], **-ETTE**.]
A small banner.

bannerol *noun* see **BANDEROLE.**

bannister *noun* var. of **BANISTER.**

†**bannition** *noun*. **M17–M18.**
[**ORIGIN** medieval Latin *bannitio(n-)*, from *bannit-* pa. ppl stem of *bannire* from Proto-Romance base also of **BANISH**: see **-ION**.]
Banishment, expulsion, esp. from university.

bannock /ˈbanək/ *noun*. *Scot.* & *N. English*.
[**ORIGIN** Old English *bannuc* (recorded once), orig. from a British word repr. by Welsh *ban*, Breton *bannac'h*, *banne*, Cornish *banna* drop.]
A round, flat, fairly thick girdle cake, usu. made of oatmeal, barley, pease, or flour (local usage varies).

banns /banz/ *noun pl.* Also (with unexpl. lengthening of the vowel) †**banes**. **ME.**
[**ORIGIN** Pl. of **BAN** *noun*[1], after medieval Latin pl. *banna*.]
1 Notice given in church etc. of an intended marriage, read on three Sundays to give an opportunity for objections to be made. **ME.**
ask the banns, †***bid the banns***, ***publish the banns***. **forbid the banns** make a formal objection to an intended marriage.
2 Proclamation of a performance of a play; a prologue. Long *obsolete* exc. *hist.* **LME.**

banoffi pie /bəˈnɒfi pʌɪ/ *noun phr.* Also **banoffee pie**. **L20.**
[**ORIGIN** Blend of **BANANA** and (alt. of) **TOFFEE**.]
A dessert made with toffee (derived from condensed milk), bananas, and cream, and typically with a base or flan of shortcrust pastry.

banquet /ˈbaŋkwɪt/ *noun*. **L15.**
[**ORIGIN** Old French & mod. French, dim. of *banc* bench, **BANK** *noun*[2].]
1 A sumptuous entertainment of food and drink; (now usu.) an elaborate dinner with speeches in celebration of something or to further a cause. **L15.**
†**2** A slight meal or snack between meals. Also ***running banquet***. **E16–M17.**
3 A course of sweets, fruit, and wine; a dessert. Long *obsolete* exc. *Scot.* & *N. English*. **E16.** ▸†**b** A sweet confection; *collect.* sweets, confectionery foods for dessert. **M16–L17.**
†**4** A wine-drinking carousal. **M16–E18.**

banquet /ˈbaŋkwɪt/ *verb*. **L15.**
[**ORIGIN** French *banqueter*, formed as **BANQUET** *noun*.]
1 *verb intrans.* Take part in a banquet or banquets; feast, carouse. **L15.**
2 *verb trans.* Entertain at a banquet or banquets; feast, regale. **E16.**
†**3** *verb intrans.* Take a snack, take dessert, (see **BANQUET** *noun* 2, 3). **M16–E19.**
■ **banque'teer** *noun* = **BANQUETER** (b) **E19.** **banqueter** *noun* †(**a**) the giver of a banquet; (**b**) a guest at a banquet; a feaster, a reveller: **M16.**

banquette /baŋˈkɛt/ *noun*. **E17.**
[**ORIGIN** French from Italian *banchetta* dim. of *banca* bench, shelf: see **-ETTE**.]
1 A raised step or way running along the inside of a rampart, at the bottom of a trench, etc., on which soldiers stand to fire at the enemy. **E17.**
2 A raised footway or sidewalk. *arch. rare*. **L18.**
3 A long upholstered seat along a wall. **M19.**

banshee /banˈʃiː, ˈbanʃiː/ *noun*. **L17.**
[**ORIGIN** Irish *bean sídhe*, Old Irish *ben síde*, from *ben* woman + *síde* of the fairy world.]
In Irish and Scottish folklore: a female spirit whose wail portends death in a house.

bantam /ˈbantəm/ *noun*. **M18.**
[**ORIGIN** App. from *Bantam*, a district of NW Java, but the fowls are not native there.]
1 A small kind of domestic fowl, of which the cock is a spirited fighter. **M18.**
2 *fig.* A small but spirited person. **L18.**
– **COMB.**: **bantamweight** (of) a weight at which boxing etc. matches are made, intermediate between featherweight and flyweight, in the amateur boxing scale now being between 51 and 54 kg, though differing for professionals, wrestlers, and weightlifters, and according to time and place; (a boxer etc.) of this weight.

banteng /ˈbantɛŋ/ *noun*. **E19.**
[**ORIGIN** Malay.]
An ox, *Bos banteng*, of SE Asia.

banter /ˈbantə/ *verb* & *noun*. **L17.**
[**ORIGIN** Unknown.]
▸ **A** *verb*. **1** *verb trans.* Make fun of (a person), tease good-humouredly. **L17.**
2 *verb trans.* Impose upon (a person), orig. in jest; delude, cheat, bamboozle. *arch.* **L17.**
3 *verb intrans.* Indulge in banter; talk jestingly. **L17.**
4 *verb trans.* Challenge or defy to a race, match, etc. *arch. US.* **L18.**
▸ **B** *noun*. **1** Nonsense talked to ridicule a subject or person; humorous ridicule; good-natured personal remarks. **L17.**

S. VICKERS Some banter ensued concerning the amount of time the bridegroom had been spending in bed.

2 An instance of such humorous ridicule. *arch.* **E18.**
3 A challenge to a race, match, etc. *arch. US.* **M19.**
■ **banterer** *noun* **L17.** **banteringly** *adverb* in a bantering manner, jestingly **M19.**

Banting /ˈbantɪŋ/ *noun*. *arch.* Also **b-**. **M19.**
[**ORIGIN** W. *Banting* (d. 1878), English dietitian.]
The treatment of obesity by abstinence from sugar, starch, and fat.
■ **Bantingism** *noun* **M19.**

bantling /ˈbantlɪŋ/ *noun*. **L16.**
[**ORIGIN** Perh. from German *Bänkling* bastard, from *Bank* bench, **BANK** *noun*[2]: see **-LING**[1] and cf. **BASTARD**.]
A young child, a brat. Formerly also, an illegitimate child, a bastard.

fig.: BYRON The interest you have taken in me and my poetical bantlings.

Bantu /banˈtuː, ˈbantuː/ *adjective* & *noun*. **M19.**
[**ORIGIN** In certain Bantu langs., pl. of *-ntu* person.]
(Designating, of or pertaining to) a group of Niger-Congo languages spoken extensively in equatorial and southern Africa. Also (now *offensive*), (of or pertaining to, a member of) the family of peoples speaking these languages.
– **NOTE**: A strongly offensive term under the apartheid regime in South Africa, esp. when used to refer to a single individual. Outside South Africa the word is still used as a neutral 'scientific' term for the group of languages and their speakers collectively.
■ **Bantustan** /-ˈstɑːn, -ˈstan/ *noun* (*S. Afr. hist.*) [*-stan* as in *Hindustan* etc.] a partially self-governing area set aside during the period of apartheid for a particular indigenous African people, a 'homeland'. **M20.**

banxring /ˈbaŋksrɪŋ/ *noun*. **E19**.
[ORIGIN Javanese *bangsring*.]
In Java and adjacent islands: a tree shrew.

banyan /ˈbanɪən, -njən/ *noun*. Also **banian**. **L16**.
[ORIGIN Portuguese from Gujarati *vāṇiyo* man of the trading caste, from Sanskrit *vāṇija* merchant.]
▸ **I 1** = BANIA. **L16**.
2 An Indian broker or steward attached to a firm or individual; a sircar. **M17**.
3 In full ***banyan shirt*** etc. A loose flannel shirt or jacket. **E18**.
▸ **II** [Orig. applied by Europeans to a particular tree under which traders had built a pagoda.]
4 In full ***banyan tree***. An Indian fig tree, *Ficus benghalensis*, the branches of which root themselves over a wide area. **M17**.
– COMB.: **banyan-day** *arch.* (chiefly NAUTICAL): on which no meat is served; ***banyan shirt***: see sense 3 above; ***banyan tree***: see sense 4 above.

banzai /banˈzʌɪ/ *interjection & adjective*. **L19**.
[ORIGIN Japanese, lit. 'ten thousand years of life to you', from *ban* ten thousand + *sai* years (of life to you).]
▸ **A** *interjection*. A form of acclamation used by the Japanese esp. to their Emperor, a cheer used in battle etc. **L19**.
▸ **B** *attrib.* or as *adjective*. (As if) shouting 'banzai'; uproarious; (of an attack by Japanese) reckless. *slang*. **E20**.

banzuke /banˈzuːki/ *noun*. **L20**.
[ORIGIN Japanese, from *ban* number, ranking + *zuke* stuck up (on display).]
The ranking list of sumo wrestlers.

baobab /ˈbeɪəbab/ *noun*. **M17**.
[ORIGIN Prob. from a central African lang.: first mentioned (in Ethiopia) in Latin by Prosper Alpinus (1592).]
An African tree, *Adansonia digitata* (family Bombacaceae), having an enormously thick trunk and large edible pulpy fruit that hangs down on stalks; *Austral.* = ***goutystem*** s.v. GOUTY 2. Also ***baobab tree***.

BAOR *abbreviation*.
British Army of the Rhine.

bap /bap/ *noun*. **L16**.
[ORIGIN Unknown.]
1 A large soft bread roll. **L16**.
2 In *pl.* A woman's breasts. *slang*. **L20**.

Baphometic /bafəˈmɛtɪk/ *adjective*. **M19**.
[ORIGIN from French *baphomet* from medieval Latin (for *Mahomet*), + -IC.]
hist. Of or pertaining to (the worship of) Baphomet, the alleged idol of the Knights Templar.

baptise *verb* var. of BAPTIZE.

baptism /ˈbaptɪz(ə)m/ *noun*. **ME**.
[ORIGIN Old French *ba(p)te(s)me* (now *baptême*) from ecclesiastical Latin *baptismus*, *-um* (also *-a*) from ecclesiastical Greek *baptismos* ceremonial washing, *baptisma* baptism, from *baptizein* BAPTIZE. Refashioned after Latin & Greek.]
1 The application of water to a person by immersion, pouring, or sprinkling, as a religious rite, symbolical of purification or regeneration, and, with Christians, betokening initiation into the Church, often accompanied by naming. **ME**.
fig.: **baptism of blood** martyrdom of the unbaptized. **baptism of fire** a soldier's first battle.
2 The naming of church bells and of ships. **L16**.

baptismal /bapˈtɪzm(ə)l/ *adjective*. **M17**.
[ORIGIN medieval Latin *baptismalis*, from *baptismus* etc.: see BAPTISM, -AL[1].]
Of, pertaining to, or connected with baptism.
baptismal name the personal or Christian name given at baptism. ***baptismal vows***: see VOW *noun*.
▪ **baptismally** *adverb* **M19**.

baptist /ˈbaptɪst/ *noun & adjective*. Also (as a specific epithet and of the religious body) **B-**. **ME**.
[ORIGIN Old French & mod. French *baptiste* from ecclesiastical Latin *baptista* from ecclesiastical Greek *baptistēs*, from *baptizein* BAPTIZE: see -IST.]
▸ **A** *noun*. **1** A person who baptizes; *spec.* John, the forerunner of Christ (St John the Baptist). **ME**.
2 A member of a Protestant Christian religious body practising baptism only of believers (not infants) and by immersion (cf. ANABAPTIST 2). **L16**.
Free Will Baptist: see FREE WILL. ***Particular Baptist***: see PARTICULAR *adjective*. ***Primitive Baptist***: see PRIMITIVE *adjective & noun*. ***Southern Baptist***: see SOUTHERN *adjective*.
▸ **B** *attrib.* or as *adjective*. Of or pertaining to the religious body of the Baptists; being a Baptist. **E18**.

baptistery /ˈbaptɪst(ə)ri/ *noun*. Also **-try** /-tri/. **ME**.
[ORIGIN Old French *ba(p)tistere*, *-erie* (mod. *baptistère*) from ecclesiastical Latin *baptisterium* from ecclesiastical Greek *baptistērion*, from *baptizein* (see BAPTIZE).]
1 That part of a church (or, formerly, a separate building adjacent to a church) used for baptism. **ME**.
2 In a Baptist chapel, a receptacle containing water for baptism by immersion. **M19**.

baptize /bapˈtʌɪz/ *verb*. Also **-ise**. **ME**.
[ORIGIN Old French & mod. French *baptiser* from ecclesiastical Latin *baptizare* from Greek *baptizein* dip, immerse, (eccl.) baptize.]
1 *verb trans.* Administer baptism to. **ME**. ▸**b** *verb intrans.* Administer baptism. **ME**.
2 *verb trans.* Name (as in baptism), denominate, nickname. **LME**.
▪ **baptizable** *adjective* capable of or fit for baptism **M17**. †**baptization** *noun* = BAPTISM **LME–E18**. **baptizer** *noun* **L15**.

bapu /ˈbʌpuː/ *noun*. *Indian*. **M20**.
[ORIGIN Gujarati, from Sanskrit *vapra*.]
Father.

bar /bɑː/ *noun*[1]. **ME**.
[ORIGIN Old French & mod. French *barre* from Proto-Romance, of unknown origin.]
▸ **I 1** *gen.* A straight piece of wood, metal, or other rigid material, long in proportion to its thickness. **ME**.
parallel bars: see PARALLEL *adjective*. ***T-bar***: see T, T 2. **lower the bar**, **raise the bar** lower or raise standards, esp. for qualification.
2 *spec.* ▸**a** A rod or pole made to fasten, confine, or obstruct. **ME**. ▸**b** A thick rod thrown in a trial of strength. **L15**. ▸**c** = BARRE 2. **L19**. ▸**d** *The* crossbar of a football goal. **L19**. ▸**e** A heating element of an electric fire. **E20**.
a behind bars in prison. CROSSBAR *noun*
†**3** An ornamental (esp. transverse) band or boss. **ME–M16**.
4 A straight stripe, a broad band of colour etc. on a surface. **LME**.
Stars and Bars: see STAR *noun*[1] *& adjective*.
5 HERALDRY. A narrow horizontal stripe equal to or less than one fifth of the width of the field. Cf. BARRULET. **LME**.
bar sinister (erron. for) a bend or baton sinister, a supposed sign of bastardy.
6 An oblong piece of metal or something manufactured (as soap, chocolate, etc.). **L16**. ▸**b** One pound sterling. *slang*. **E20**.
7 In *pl.* The transverse ridged divisions of a horse's palate. **E17**.
8 A strip of silver below the clasp of a medal signifying an additional distinction; a distinction so signified. **M19**.
▸ **II 9** A material structure of any shape, forming a barrier. **ME**.
10 *hist. spec.* ▸**a** A barrier or gate closing the entrance into a city. **ME**. ▸**b** A toll house gate or barrier. **M16**.
11 In *pl.* Prisoner's base (see BASE *noun*[2]) or a similar children's game. Cf. ***prison bars*** s.v. PRISON, ***prisoners' bars*** s.v. PRISONER. **ME**.
12 LAW. A plea or objection of force sufficient to block an action or claim. **LME**.
in bar of as a sufficient reason or plea against to prevent. ***personal bar***: see PERSONAL *adjective*.
13 *fig.* An obstruction, an obstacle; a restriction. **M16**.

> BURKE Thereby fixing a permanent bar against any relief. L. A. G. STRONG Disparity in years . . is not invariably a bar to harmony.

14 A bank of sand, silt, etc., across the mouth of a river or harbour, obstructing navigation. **L16**.
15 MUSIC. Any of successive vertical lines across the staff dividing a composition into metrical groupings, often of equal time value, and placed before the initial accent of each grouping; a section between two such lines, a measure. **M17**.
double bar: see DOUBLE *adjective & adverb*.
▸ **III** Specialized uses in courts of law, legislative assemblies, etc.
16 In a court of law, the barrier or rail at which a prisoner stands. In the Inns of Court, formerly, a barrier or partition separating the seats of the benchers from the rest of the hall, to which students, after they had reached a certain standing, were 'called' (long popularly understood to refer to that in a court of justice, beyond which the King's or Queen's Counsel (and Serjeants-at-Law) have place, but not ordinary barristers). **ME**. ▸**b** A tribunal (*lit. & fig.*); a (particular) court of law. **LME**.

> **b** CARLYLE The Judgment-bar of the Most High God. H. P. BROUGHAM I have practised at the bar of the House of Lords. *New Republic* The United States may be called to account before the bar of world opinion . . for its Latin-American policy.

at the bar, (*arch.*) **at bar** in court, in open court. **be called to the Bar** be admitted as a barrister. **be called within the Bar** be appointed King's or Queen's Counsel. **call to the Bar** admission as a barrister. ***go to the Bar***: see GO *verb*. ***inner Bar***: see INNER *adjective*. PRISONER ***at the bar***.
17 ***the Bar***: ▸**a** The whole body of barristers or (*US*) lawyers; ***the outer Bar***, barristers not King's or Queen's Counsel. **LME**. ▸**b** The profession of barrister; occupation as counsel in a court of justice. **M17**.
18 A rail dividing off a space in a legislative assembly etc. to which non-members may be admitted on business. **L16**.
▸ **IV** Any other barrier or rail acquiring technical significance from its use.
19 A counter in a public house, hotel, etc., across which alcoholic refreshments are served; the space behind such a counter; the room or premises containing such a counter. **L15**.

> J. HELLER He went to the bar for more bourbon. P. NORMAN Although Jack worked in a bar, it did not seem to make him tired of bars.

lounge bar, ***public bar***, etc. ***prop up the bar***: see PROP *verb* 2. ***wet bar***: see WET *adjective*.
20 With specifying word: a place where something is served or offered across a counter; a specialized department in a large shop. **M20**.
coffee bar, ***food bar***, ***snack bar***, ***suchi bar***, ***tapas bar***, etc. ***heel bar***, ***stocking bar***, etc.
– COMB.: **barbell** an iron bar with a heavy ball at each end used in exercising; **bar billiards** a game (popular in public houses) using a small table similar to a billiard table but with holes of different score values on the bed of the table, into which the balls have to be directed; **bar chart** a chart using bars to represent quantities; **bar code** a code of lines and numbers printed in a band on wrappings, packages, etc., and interpretable by an optical scanner; **bar-coding** the practice or process of marking goods etc. with bar codes; **barfly** *colloq.* (**a**) a person who frequents the bars of public houses etc.; (**b**) (more fully ***barfly jumping***) the practice of taking a running jump at a specially coated hanging surface with the aim of sticking to it on impact; **bar girl** *US* a woman employed to encourage customers to buy drinks at a bar; **barhop** *verb intrans.* spend time drinking in a series of bars, staying in each one for only a short while; ***bar-keel***: see KEEL *noun*[1]; **barkeep** *N. Amer.* = ***bartender*** below; **bar line** MUSIC a line across a stave marking metrical accent (see sense 15 above); ***bar magnet***: see MAGNET 2; **barmaid**, **barman** a female, male, bartender; **bar-room** a room with a bar selling alcoholic refreshments; **bar soap** soap made up into bars (rather than cakes or tablets); **bartend** *verb* serve alcoholic refreshments at a bar; **bartender** a person serving alcoholic refreshments at a bar; ***bar tracery***: **barwing** an Asian bird of the genus *Actinodura*, of the babbler family, having barred feathers on the wings and tail.
▪ †**barful** *adjective* (*rare*, Shakes.) full of hindrances: only in **E17**.

bar /bɑː/ *noun*[2]. **E18**.
[ORIGIN French *bar(s)* from Dutch *baars*: see BARSE, & cf. BASS *noun*[1].]
= MEAGRE *noun*[1].

bar /bɑː/ *noun*[3]. *US*. **E19**.
[ORIGIN Louisiana French *boire*.]
In full ***mosquito bar***. A type of mosquito netting.

bar /bɑː/ *noun*[4]. **E20**.
[ORIGIN Greek *baros* weight.]
Chiefly METEOROLOGY. A unit of pressure equal to 10^5 pascal (about 0.9870 atmosphere).

bar /bɑː/ *verb trans.* Infl. **-rr-**. **ME**.
[ORIGIN Old French & mod. French *barrer*, formed as BAR *noun*[1].]
▸ **I** Make fast with a bar or bars.
1 Make fast (a door etc.) with a bar or bars; fasten up (a place) with a bar or bars; provide with a bar or bars. **ME**.
2 Fasten in, shut up, or confine securely (a person or thing) with a bar or bars; keep or shut *in* or *out*. **LME**.
3 LAW. Block (a person, an action or claim) by objection. **LME**.
bar an entail LAW (now chiefly *hist.*) convert an entail into an absolute interest in the land. ***statute-barred***: see STATUTE *noun*. ***time-barred***: see TIME *noun*.
4 Hinder, prevent, or prohibit (a person) *from*; deprive or debar *of*. Also foll. by (*arch.*) 2nd obj., †*to do*. **LME**.

> N. HARPSFIELD Is there anything here that barreth those that be under the patriarch of Alexandria . . to appeal to the see apostolic? SHAKES. *2 Hen. IV* I will bar no honest man my house. R. L'ESTRANGE A Disease . . barrs us of some Pleasures, but procures us others. TENNYSON Last from her own home-circle . . They barr'd her.

5 Stop, hinder, prevent, prohibit, (an action or event). **M16**.

> P. G. WODEHOUSE Games with nothing barred except biting and bottles. F. RAPHAEL Its sale was barred on station bookstalls.

no holds barred, ***with no holds barred***: see HOLD *noun*[1] 2b.
6 Exclude from consideration, set aside, (cf. BAR, BARRING *prepositions*). **L16**.

> R. HERRICK When next thou do'st invite, barre state, And give me meate.

7 Obstruct (a way of approach, a person's progress). **L16**.
8 Take exception to, object to. Now *slang*. **E17**.
▸ **II 9** Mark with bars or stripes; divide or make into bars. Chiefly as ***barred ppl adjective***. **LME**.

> KEATS Eyed like a peacock, and all crimson barr'd.

bar /bɑː/ *preposition*. **E18**.
[ORIGIN Imper. of BAR *verb*, prob. after *except*, *save*, etc.: cf. BARRING *preposition*.]
Except; excluding from consideration; but for.
all over bar the shouting. **bar none** with no exceptions. **bar two**, **bar three**, etc. (in stating the odds in RACING) except the two, three, etc., horses already named; also *ellipt.* with the number omitted.

bara brith /ˌbarə ˈbriːθ/ *noun phr.* Also **barabrith**. Pl. same. **M20**.
[ORIGIN Welsh, lit. 'speckled bread', from *bara* bread, loaf + *brith* mottled, spotted.]
A traditional Welsh tea bread, typically made with raisins, currants, and candied peel.

baracan *noun* var. of BARRACAN.

B

barack /ˈbaratsk, ˈbarak/ *noun*. M20.
[ORIGIN Shortened from Hungarian *barackpálinka* apricot brandy, from *barack* apricot + *pálinka* brandy, schnapps.]
A type of apricot brandy originating in Hungary.

baragouin /baragwɛ̃, barəˈgwɪn/ *noun*. E17.
[ORIGIN French.]
Gibberish; unintelligible jargon.

baraka /bəˈrakə/ *noun*. E20.
[ORIGIN Arabic.]
ISLAM. Divine blessing; a quality of grace derived from Allah.

Baralipton /barəˈlɪpt(ə)n/ *noun*. L16.
[ORIGIN A mnemonic of scholastic philosophers, first used in medieval Latin, A indicating a universal affirmative proposition and I a particular affirmative proposition.]
LOGIC. The first indirect mood of the first syllogistic figure, in which a particular affirmative conclusion is drawn from two universal affirmative premisses.

barasingha /barəˈsɪŋgə/ *noun*. M19.
[ORIGIN Hindi *bārah-siṅgā* lit. 'twelve-tined'.]
= ***swamp deer*** s.v. SWAMP *noun*.

barathea /barəˈθiːə/ *noun & adjective*. M19.
[ORIGIN Unknown.]
(Of) a fine-textured twill cloth, made of wool or a man-made fibre, often with an admixture of silk, cotton, or other lighter fibre.

barathrum /ˈbarəθrəm/ *noun*. *obsolete* or *hist*. Pl. **-thra** /-θrə/, **-thrums**. E16.
[ORIGIN Latin from Greek *barathron* pit, gulf.]
†**1** Hell. E16–M18.
†**2** An insatiable extortioner or glutton. E–M17.
3 *hist*. A pit in Athens into which condemned criminals were thrown. M19.

baraza /bəˈrɑːzə/ *noun*. L19.
[ORIGIN Kiswahili.]
In E. Africa: a place of public audience or reception; a meeting, a reception.

barb /bɑːb/ *noun*¹. In sense 1 also **barbe**. ME.
[ORIGIN Old French & mod. French *barbe* from Latin *barba* beard.]
1 A piece of vertically pleated linen cloth worn over or under the chin, as by nuns. ME.
2 †**a** A man's beard. *rare*. LME–L17. ▸**b** An appendage in an animal resembling a beard; *esp*. = BARBEL 2. L15.
3 A secondary backward-projecting point of an arrow, fish hook, etc., making its extraction difficult. LME. ▸**b** *fig*. A wounding quality or remark. L18.
4 *VETERINARY MEDICINE*. Usu. in *pl*. Any of the folds of the mucous membrane which protect the submaxillary glands of cattle and horses; (in *pl*.) inflammation of these folds. E16.
5 *HERALDRY*. A sepal (in *pl*. the calyx) of a flower. Also, the head of an arrow. L16.
6 Any of the lateral processes from the shaft of a feather. M19.
7 A sciaenid fish of the genus *Menticirrhus*, found on the N. American Atlantic and Gulf coasts; also called ***kingfish***. Also, a brightly coloured tropical fish of the genus *Barbus*. L19.
– COMB.: **barbwire** (chiefly *US*) = ***barbed wire*** s.v. BARBED *adjective*¹ 2.

†**barb** *noun*². M16–M17.
[ORIGIN Alt. of BARD *noun*².]
Usu. in *pl*. = BARD *noun*² 1.

> SPENSER His loftie steed with . . goodly gorgeous barbes.

barb /bɑːb/ *noun*³. M17.
[ORIGIN French *barbe* from Italian *barbero* of Barbary: see BARBARY 1.]
1 (An animal of) a breed of horse from Barbary. M17.
2 (A bird of) a breed of pigeon from Barbary. E18.
3 A black kelpie dog. *Austral*. L19.

barb /bɑːb/ *noun*⁴. *slang*. M20.
[ORIGIN Abbreviation.]
A barbiturate (tablet).

barb /bɑːb/ *verb trans*. LME.
[ORIGIN French †*barber*, formed as BARB *noun*¹.]
1 Clip or trim (a fleece, cloth, coin, etc.). Long *rare*. LME.
2 Shave or trim the beard of. Long *rare*. L16.
3 Provide (an arrow, hook, etc.) with a barb or barbs. E17.

> *fig*.: R. H. TAWNEY The needlessly sharp censures with which he barbed the fine imposed upon an enclosing landlord.

Barbadian /bɑːˈbeɪdɪən/ *noun & adjective*. E18.
[ORIGIN from BARBADOS, †(*the*) *Barbadoes* + -IAN.]
(A native or inhabitant) of Barbados in the W. Indies. Cf. BADIAN.

†**Barbadoes** *noun* var. of BARBADOS.

†**Barbadoes** *verb trans*. M17–M19.
[ORIGIN from (*the*) *Barbadoes*: see BARBADOS.]
Transport to Barbados.

Barbados /bɑːˈbeɪdɒs/ *noun*. Also †**-oes**. L17.
[ORIGIN An island in the W. Indies, formerly (*the*) *Barbadoes*.]
Used ***attrib***. to designate things from or characteristic of Barbados, esp. plants.
Barbados cherry (the edible fruit of) a neotropical tree, *Malpighia glabra* (family Malpighiaceae). ***Barbados*** GOOSEBERRY. **Barbados lily** = HIPPEASTRUM. **Barbados pride** a W. Indian leguminous shrub, *Caesalpinia pulcherrima*, bearing red flowers with yellow petal margins.

barbal /ˈbɑːb(ə)l/ *adjective*. *rare*. M17.
[ORIGIN from Latin *barba* beard + -AL¹.]
Of or pertaining to the beard.

†**barbar** *noun & adjective*. LME.
[ORIGIN formed as BARBAROUS.]
▸ **A** *noun*. = BARBARIAN *noun*. LME–E18.
▸ **B** *adjective*. = BARBAROUS. LME–E18.

Barbara /ˈbɑːbərə/ *noun*. M16.
[ORIGIN Latin = barbarous things, taken as a mnemonic for its three *a*'s, A indicating a universal affirmative proposition.]
LOGIC. The first mood of the first syllogistic figure, in which both premisses and the conclusion are universal affirmatives.

Barbaresco /bɑːbəˈrɛskəʊ/ *noun*. M20.
[ORIGIN The name of a village in Piedmont, NW Italy.]
A variety of red wine produced from the Nebbiolo grape in the vicinity of Barbaresco.

Barbaresque /bɑːbəˈrɛsk/ *adjective & noun*. In sense A.2 **b-**. E19.
[ORIGIN French *barbaresque* from Italian *barbaresco* from *Barbaria* Barbary: see BARBARY 1, -ESQUE.]
▸ **A** *adjective*. **1** Of or pertaining to Barbary (see BARBARY 1). Now *arch*. or *hist*. E19.
2 Barbarous in (esp. artistic) style. E19.
▸ **B** *noun*. A native or inhabitant of Barbary. Now *arch*. or *hist*. E19.

barbarian /bɑːˈbɛːrɪən/ *adjective & noun*. ME.
[ORIGIN French †*barbarien* or Latin, extended (after *chrétien* etc. CHRISTIAN *adjective*, *noun*) from Old French & mod. French *barbare* formed as BARBAR: see -IAN.]
▸ **A** *adjective*. **1** Foreign; *spec*. non-Hellenic, (*esp*.) non-Roman; also, pagan, non-Christian. Usu. *derog*. Now *arch*. or *hist*. ME.

> SHAKES. *Tr. & Cr.* Thou art here but to thrash Trojans, and thou art bought and sold . . like a barbarian slave. POPE Barbarian blindness, Christian zeal conspire. H. T. COLEBROOKE Several other terms . . are not Sanscrit, but, apparently, barbarian. H. HALLAM Establishment of the barbarian nations on the ruins of the Roman Empire.

2 Uncivilized, savage. L16.

> A. PATON A barbarian people, who not long since plundered and slaughtered . . under the most terrible chief of all.

†**3** Of or pertaining to Barbary (see BARBARY 1). L16–L17.
▸ **B** *noun* **I 1** A foreigner; a person with a different language or different customs; *spec*. a non-Hellene, a non-Roman; also, a pagan, a non-Christian. Usu. *derog*. Now *arch*. or *hist*. LME.

> SHAKES. *Coriol.* I would they were barbarians . . not Romans. HOBBES The Athenians . . expecting the coming of the Barbarian. J. CLAVELL Even that would not have mattered . . if he still had the barbarian in his power . . ; he would simply have handed over the foreigner.

2 A savage, wild, or uncivilized person. L15.

> DRYDEN Skins of Beasts, the rude Barbarians wear. K. CLARK Into that chaos came real barbarians like the Huns, who were totally illiterate and destructively hostile to what they couldn't understand.

3 An uncultured person; a person without sympathy for literary or artistic culture. M18.

> D. HUME Cromwell, though himself a barbarian, was not insensible to literary merit.

▸ †**II 4** A native or inhabitant of Barbary (see BARBARY 1). LME–E18.

barbaric /bɑːˈbarɪk/ *noun & adjective*. LME.
[ORIGIN French †*barbarique* or Latin *barbaricus* from Greek *barbarikos*, from *barbaros* foreign: see -IC.]
▸ †**A** *noun*. = BARBARIAN *noun* 1. Only in LME.
▸ **B** *adjective*. **1** Uncivilized, uncultured; savage; savagely cruel. L15.

> H. J. LASKI The noble savage, on investigation, turns out to be a barbaric creature with a club and scalping knife.

2 Of or pertaining to barbarians; characteristic of the artistic taste or style of barbarians; unrestrained. M17.

> MILTON Barbaric pearl and gold. R. LEHMANN Like one moving in a barbaric rite of dedication towards some altar.

3 = BARBARIAN *adjective* 1. *arch*. M19.

> G. GROTE Sending envoys to the Persian King and not to other barbaric powers.

■ **barbarically** *adverb* M19.

†**Barbarin** *noun* var. of BERBERINE.

†**barbarious** *adjective*. L15–M18.
[ORIGIN from (the same root as) BARBARY + -OUS.]
= BARBAROUS.

barbarise *verb* var. of BARBARIZE.

barbarism /ˈbɑːbərɪz(ə)m/ *noun*. LME.
[ORIGIN Old French & mod. French *barbarisme* from Latin *barbarismus* from Greek *barbarismos*, from *barbarizein* behave or speak like a foreigner: see -ISM.]
1 Uncivilized nature or condition; uncultured ignorance; absence of culture; barbaric style (in art etc.), unrestrainedness. LME. ▸**b** A trait or characteristic of such uncivilized condition. M17.

> A. P. STANLEY The imperceptible boundary between civilisation and barbarism. K. CLARK Its sculpture is miserably crude, without even the vitality of barbarism. **b** J. HOWELL Plundering and other barbarismes that reign now abroad.

2 The use of words and idioms not in accordance with the (supposed) normal standard language, esp. of those of foreign origin; absence of cultivation in language. M16. ▸**b** A foreign, non-classical, or non-standard word or idiom. L16.
†**3** = BARBARITY 3. E–M17.

barbarity /bɑːˈbarɪti/ *noun*. M16.
[ORIGIN from Latin *barbarus* (see BARBAROUS) + -ITY.]
†**1** = BARBARISM 2. M16–L18.
2 Absence of culture and civilization; barbarism. L16.
3 Savage cruelty; harsh unkindness. L17. ▸**b** An act of savage cruelty. E18.

barbarize /ˈbɑːbərʌɪz/ *verb*. Also **-ise**. LME.
[ORIGIN Late Latin *barbarizare* from Greek *barbarizein* (see BARBARISM) or formed as BARBAROUS + -IZE.]
1 *verb intrans*. Use barbarisms in speech or writing; violate classical grammatical rules. LME.
2 *verb trans*. Make (esp. language) barbarous. E17.
3 *verb intrans*. Become barbarous. E19.
■ **barbariˈzation** *noun* E19.

barbarous /ˈbɑːbərəs/ *adjective*. Also occas. in Latin form †**-rus**. LME.
[ORIGIN from Latin *barbarus* (from Greek *barbaros* non-Greek, foreign, esp. of speech) + -OUS.]
1 Uncultured; uncivilized; rough; rude; coarse. LME.

> SHAKES. *Twel. N.* Ungracious wretch, Fit for the mountains and the barbarous caves, Where manners ne'er were preach'd! CARLYLE An uncultured semi-barbarous son of Nature. J. HAWKES Most of them [villas] were built by romanized Britons, sometimes even on the foundations of their old barbarous homes of wood and wattle.

2 *spec*. Of language: not Greek; not Greek or Latin; not classical or standard; having many barbarisms. M16.

> W. COWPER The Carians, people of a barbarous speech. D. BAGLEY Formulating his phrases carefully in the barbarous French these people used.

3 Of a person: = BARBARIAN *adjective* 1. *arch*. M16.
4 Cruelly savage; harshly unkind. M16.

> HENRY FIELDING It would be barbarous to part Tom and the girl. G. B. SHAW England was a civilized Power and would not stand these barbarous lashings and vindictive hangings.

5 Harsh-sounding; coarsely noisy. M17.

> YEATS The barbarous clangour of a gong.

†**6** = BARBARIC *adjective* 2. *rare*. Only in E18.

> DRYDEN The trappings of his horse emboss'd with barbarous gold.

■ **barbarously** *adverb* M16. **barbarousness** *noun* M16.

Barbary /ˈbɑːbəri/ *noun*. In sense 2 also **b-**. ME.
[ORIGIN Sense 1 ult. from Arabic *barbar* (cf. BERBER); sense 2 from Old French *barbarie* or Latin *barbaria*, *-ies* land of barbarians, formed as BARBAROUS: see -Y³.]
1 (An old name for) the western part of N. Africa. ME.
†**2** Foreign nationality; paganism; barbarity; barbarism; foreign or non-Christian lands. LME–M17.
– COMB.: **Barbary ape** a macaque, *Macaca sylvana*, of N. Africa and Gibraltar; **Barbary coast** (an old name for) the Mediterranean coast of N. Africa; **Barbary falcon** a falcon, *Falco pelegrinoides*, of N. Africa and the Middle East; **Barbary partridge** a N. African partridge, *Alectoris barbara*; **Barbary sheep** = AOUDAD.

barbasco /bɑːˈbaskəʊ/ *noun*. Pl. **-os**. M19.
[ORIGIN Amer. Spanish, app. from Spanish *verbasco* from Latin *verbascum* mullein.]
(A poison obtained from the roots of) any of various S. American plants; *esp*. = CUBE *noun*².

barbastelle /bɑːbəˈstɛl, ˈbɑːbəstɛl/ *noun*. L18.
[ORIGIN French from Italian *barbastello*.]
Either of two bats of the genus *Barbastella*; esp. *B. barbastellus*, found in southern Britain.

barbate /ˈbɑːbeɪt/ *adjective*. M18.
[ORIGIN Latin *barbatus* bearded, from *barba* beard: see -ATE².]
Bearded; having a small hairy tuft or tufts.

barbe *noun* see BARB *noun*¹.

barbecue /ˈbɑːbɪkjuː/ *noun*. M17.
[ORIGIN Spanish *barbacoa* perh. from Arawak *barbacoa* raised wooden framework of sticks.]
▸ †**I 1** A wooden framework for storage, sleeping on, etc. M–L17.
▸ **II 2** An animal broiled or roasted whole, esp. out of doors; meat etc. cooked out of doors on a frame over an open fire. E18.

3 An outdoor entertainment at which meat is cooked on a frame over an open fire. **M18.**
4 A wooden or (now esp.) metal frame for cooking, smoking, or drying meat over an open fire; a (usu. portable) fireplace containing such a frame. **L19.**
▸ **III 5** An open floor on which coffee beans etc. may be spread out to dry. **M18.**
– COMB.: **barbecue sauce** a highly seasoned sauce used esp. with grilled or roasted meat.

barbecue /ˈbɑːbɪkjuː/ *verb trans.* **M17.**
[ORIGIN from (the same root as) BARBECUE *noun*.]
Cook, smoke, or dry (meat) on a frame over an open fire, esp. out of doors.

barbed /bɑːbd/ *adjective*[1]. **LME.**
[ORIGIN from BARB *noun*[1], *verb*: see -ED[2], -ED[1].]
†**1** Wearing a barb (see BARB *noun*[1] 1). **LME–E17.**
2 Having a barb or barbs (see BARB *noun*[1] 3, BARB *verb* 3). **E17.**
barbed wire wire of twisted strands with short pointed pieces inserted at intervals, used for fences and as an obstruction in war.
3 HERALDRY. Of a flower: having a calyx of a specified tincture. **E17.**

barbed /bɑːbd, *poet.* ˈbɑːbɪd/ *adjective*[2]. Long *arch.* **E16.**
[ORIGIN from BARB *noun*[2] + -ED[2].]
Barded (see BARD *verb* 1).

barbel /ˈbɑːb(ə)l/ *noun.* **LME.**
[ORIGIN Old French from late Latin *barbellus* dim. of *barbus*, from *barba* beard.]
1 A large European freshwater fish of the genus *Barbus*, having a number of fleshy filaments hanging from its mouth. **LME.**
2 A fleshy filament hanging from the mouth of any fish. **E17.**

barber /ˈbɑːbə/ *noun & verb.* **ME.**
[ORIGIN Anglo-Norman *barber*, *-our*, Old French *barbier*, from Old French & mod. French *barbe* beard: see BARB *noun*[1], -ER[2].]
▸ **A** *noun.* **1** A person who cuts and dresses men's hair and shaves or trims beards; a men's hairdresser; *hist.* such a person also acting as a surgeon and dentist. **ME.**
spud barber: see SPUD *noun*.
2 A cutting cold wind. *colloq.* (chiefly *Canad. & NZ*). **M19.**
– COMB.: **barber shop** (*a*) (now chiefly *N. Amer.*) a shop where a barber works; (*b*) *attrib.* designating (an ensemble, esp. a male quartet, singing) close harmony music; **barber's itch**, **barber's rash** ringworm of the face or neck communicated by unsterilized shaving apparatus; **barber's pole** a pole spirally painted in red and white, used as a barber's sign; ***barber's rash***: see ***barber's itch*** above.
▸ **B** *verb.* **1** *verb trans.* Cut or trim the hair or beard of; cut (grass etc.) short. **E17.**
2 *verb intrans.* Work as a barber. Chiefly as ***barbering*** *verbal noun.* **M17.**
■ **barbery** *noun* (now *rare*) the art or craft of a barber **LME.**

barberry /ˈbɑːbəri/ *noun.* Also **ber-** /ˈbɑː-/. **LME.**
[ORIGIN Old French BERBERIS, assim. to BERRY *noun*[1].]
1 Any of numerous shrubs of the genus *Berberis* (family Berberidaceae), usu. thorny and with yellow wood; esp. *B. vulgaris*, bearing racemes of yellow flowers succeeded by red oblong berries. **LME.**
2 The berry of such a shrub. **M16.**

barbet /ˈbɑːbɪt/ *noun.* **L16.**
[ORIGIN French, from *barbe* beard: see -ET[1].]
†**1** A poodle. **L16–E19.**
2 Any of numerous brightly coloured fruit-eating tropical birds of the family Capitonidae, which have tufts of bristles at the base of the bill. **E19.**

barbette /bɑːˈbɛt/ *noun.* **L18.**
[ORIGIN French, formed as BARBET: see -ETTE.]
A platform in a fort or ship from which guns fire over a parapet etc. and not through an embrasure.

barbican /ˈbɑːbɪk(ə)n/ *noun.* **ME.**
[ORIGIN Old French & mod. French *barbacane* = medieval Latin *barbacana*, *barbi-*, prob. ult. from Arabic]
An outer defence to a city or castle, *esp.* a double tower erected over a gate or bridge.

barbicel /ˈbɑːbɪs(ə)l/ *noun.* **M19.**
[ORIGIN Italian & mod. Latin *barbicella* dim. of *barba* beard.]
Any of the minute hooked filaments which interlock the barbules of a bird's feathers.

barbie /ˈbɑːbi/ *noun. colloq.* (chiefly *Austral.*). **L20.**
[ORIGIN Abbreviation: see -IE.]
= BARBECUE *noun* 3, 4.

Barbie doll /ˈbɑːbɪ dɒl/ *noun phr.* **M20.**
[ORIGIN from dim. of female personal name *Barbara* + DOLL *noun*[1].]
(Proprietary name for) a doll representing a slim, fashionably dressed, conventionally attractive young woman; *transf.* a pretty but passive or characterless woman.

barbiers /ˈbɑːbɪəz/ *noun. arch.* **L17.**
[ORIGIN French, alt. of BERIBERI.]
A paralytic disease occurring in the Indian subcontinent.

barbital /ˈbɑːbɪt(ə)l/ *noun. US.* **E20.**
[ORIGIN formed as BARBITURIC + -AL[2].]
= BARBITONE.

barbiton *noun* var. of BARBITOS.

barbitone /ˈbɑːbɪtəʊn/ *noun.* **E20.**
[ORIGIN formed as BARBITURIC + -ONE.]
5,5-Diethylbarbituric acid, or its sodium salt (usu. ***barbitone sodium***), used as a hypnotic drug. Also called ***veronal***.

barbitos /ˈbɑːbɪtəs/ *noun.* Pl. **-toi** /-tɔɪ/. Also **-ton** /-tən/. **M16.**
[ORIGIN Latin from Greek.]
An ancient musical instrument with many strings, prob. a type of lute or lyre.

barbiturate /bɑːˈbɪtjʊrət/ *noun.* **L19.**
[ORIGIN from BARBITURIC + -ATE[1].]
A salt of barbituric acid; any of the large class of hypnotic and sedative drugs derived from barbituric acid.

barbituric /bɑːbɪˈtjʊərɪk/ *adjective.* **M19.**
[ORIGIN French *barbiturique* from German *Barbitur(säure* acid), from *Barbara* a woman's name: see URIC.]
CHEMISTRY. ***barbituric acid***, malonyl urea, $C_4H_4O_3N_2$, a synthetic cyclic dibasic acid from which many hypnotic and sedative drugs are derived.

Barbizon /ˈbɑːbɪzɒn, *foreign* barbizɔ̃/ *noun.* **L19.**
[ORIGIN A village near the forest of Fontainebleau, France.]
Used ***attrib.*** to designate (a member of) a mid-19th cent. school of naturalistic painters.

barbola /bɑːˈbəʊlə/ *noun.* **E20.**
[ORIGIN Arbitrary formation from BARBOTINE.]
In full ***barbola work***. Decorative work on small articles consisting of coloured models of flowers, fruit, etc., made from a plastic paste.

barbotine /ˈbɑːbətɪn, -tiːn/ *noun.* **M19.**
[ORIGIN French.]
(Pottery ornamented with) a slip of kaolin clay.

Barbour /ˈbɑːbə/ *noun.* **L20.**
[ORIGIN John *Barbour* (d. 1918), a draper in NE England who sold weatherproof clothing.]
In full ***Barbour coat***, ***Barbour jacket***. (Proprietary name for) a type of weatherproof garment manufactured by J. Barbour and Sons, Ltd.

bar-b-q /ˈbɑːbɪkjuː/ *noun. colloq.* **M20.**
[ORIGIN Respelling of BARBECUE *noun*.]
A barbecue; used esp. in advertisements for, or names of, restaurants serving barbecue food.

Barbudan /bɑːˈbuːd(ə)n/ *noun & adjective.* **L20.**
[ORIGIN from *Barbuda* (see below) + -AN.]
(A native or inhabitant) of the W. Indian island of Barbuda, part of the country Antigua and Barbuda.

barbule /ˈbɑːbjuːl/ *noun.* **M19.**
[ORIGIN Latin *barbula* dim. of *barba* beard: see -ULE.]
1 = BARBEL 2. Now *rare* or *obsolete*. **M19.**
2 A filament branching from a barb of a feather as the barb from the shaft. **M19.**

BarcaLounger /ˈbɑːkəˌlaʊndʒə/ *noun. US.* **L20.**
[ORIGIN from *Barca* (of unknown origin) + LOUNGER.]
(Proprietary name for) any of various models of reclining easy chair.

barcarole /ˈbɑːkərəʊl, bɑːkəˈrəʊl/ *noun.* Also **-rolle** /-rɒl/. **L18.**
[ORIGIN French *barcarolle* from Venetian Italian *barcarola* rel. to *barcarolo* gondolier, from *barca* BARK *noun*[3].]
A song sung by Venetian gondoliers; a piece of music in imitation of such songs or suggestive of the rocking motion of a boat.

Barcelona /bɑːsɪˈləʊnə/ *noun.* **M18.**
[ORIGIN A city in Spain.]
†**1** In full ***Barcelona handkerchief***, ***Barcelona neckerchief***. A handkerchief or neckerchief of soft twilled silk. **M18–M19.**
2 In full ***Barcelona nut***. A hazelnut imported from Spain or an adjacent country. **M19.**

barchan /ˈbɑːk(ə)n/ *noun.* Also **-ane**. **L19.**
[ORIGIN Turkic *barkhan*.]
A shifting crescent-shaped sand dune, concave on the leeward side.

Barcoo /bɑːˈkuː/ *noun. Austral. slang.* **L19.**
[ORIGIN A river in western Queensland.]
1 ***Barcoo grass***, a Queensland pasture grass. **L19.**
2 ***Barcoo rot***, chronic ulceration of the skin. **L19.**
3 ***Barcoo spew***, ***Barcoo vomit***, etc., illness accompanied by acts of vomiting. **L19.**
4 A violent storm. Also ***Barcoo buster***. **M20.**

bard /bɑːd/ *noun*[1]. **ME.**
[ORIGIN Gaelic *bàrd*, Irish *bard*, Welsh *bardd*, from Celtic (whence Greek *bardos*, Latin *bardus*). First used in Scotland and as a term of contempt, but idealized by Sir Walter Scott.]
1 Any of an ancient Celtic order of minstrel-poets, who composed and sang (usu. to the harp) verses celebrating the achievements of chiefs and warriors, recording historical events, traditional lore, etc. In Wales *spec.* a poet honoured at an eisteddfod. **ME.** ▸**b** A strolling musician or minstrel. *Scot. arch.* **LME.** ▸**c** A minstrel or poet of any other oral tradition, as an Anglo-Saxon scop, a Scandinavian scald, etc. **M18.**
2 Any poet; *esp.* a lyric or epic poet. *literary.* **M17.**
the Bard (**of Avon**) Shakespeare.
■ **bardic** *adjective* of, pertaining to, or characteristic of a bard **L18.** **bardish** *adjective* (somewhat *derog.*) = BARDIC **E17.** **bardism** *noun* the art or practice of bards **E18.** **bardling** *noun* a young or inexperienced poet, a poetaster **M18.** **bardship** *noun* the office, dignity, or character of a bard **L18.**

bard /bɑːd/ *noun*[2]. **L15.**
[ORIGIN Old French & mod. French *barde* ult. from Arabic *barḏa'a* saddlecloth, stuffed saddle.]
1 *hist.* Usu. in *pl.* A covering of armour for the breast and flanks of a warhorse; occas. an ornamental covering of velvet or the like. **L15.** ▸†**b** Armour for men-at-arms composed of metal plates. **M16–E17.**
2 COOKERY. A thin slice of bacon used in covering a fowl etc. **E18.**

bard /bɑːd/ *verb trans.* **E16.**
[ORIGIN French *barder*, formed as BARD *noun*[2].]
1 *hist.* Arm or caparison with bards. Freq. as ***barded*** *ppl adjective.* **E16.**
2 Cover (a fowl etc.) with slices of bacon. **M17.**

†**bardash** *noun.* **M16–L19.**
[ORIGIN French *bardache* from Italian *bardascia*, perh. from Arabic *bardaj* slave.]
A catamite.

Bardfield oxlip /ˈbɑːdfiːld ˈɒkslɪp/ *noun phr.* **M19.**
[ORIGIN *Bardfield*, a village in Essex, England.]
The true oxlip, *Primula elatior*.

bardi /ˈbɑːdi/ *noun. Austral.* Also **-dee**, **-die**. **M19.**
[ORIGIN Nyungar.]
The edible wood-boring grub of a beetle or moth. Also ***bardi grub***.

bardo /ˈbɑːdəʊ/ *noun.* **M19.**
[ORIGIN Tibetan *bár-do*, from *bar* intermediate space, interval + *do* two.]
In Tibetan Buddhism: a state of existence between death and rebirth, varying in length according to a person's conduct in life and manner of, or age at, death.

bardolatry /bɑːˈdɒlətri/ *noun.* **E20.**
[ORIGIN from BARD *noun*[1] + -O- + -LATRY.]
Excessive admiration of a poet, *spec.* of Shakespeare, 'the Bard of Avon'.
■ **bardolater** *noun* a worshipper of the Bard **E20.** **bardolatrous** *adjective* **E20.**

Bardolino /bɑːdəˈliːnəʊ/ *noun.* **M20.**
[ORIGIN The name of a village in northern Italy in the region of which the wine is produced.]
A light, dry, red wine produced in northern Italy.

Bardolphian /bɑːˈdɒlfɪən/ *adjective.* **M18.**
[ORIGIN from *Bardolph* (see below) + -IAN.]
Resembling or characteristic of Bardolph, a character in Shakespeare's *Henry IV*, *Henry V*, and *Merry Wives of Windsor*, noted for his red nose.

bare /bɛː/ *adjective, adverb, & noun.*
[ORIGIN Old English *bær* = Old Frisian, Old Saxon, Old & mod. High German *bar*, Middle Dutch *baer* (Dutch *baar*), Old Norse *berr*, from Germanic from Indo-European.]
▸ **A** *adjective.* **1** Of the body or its parts: unclothed, naked. **OE.** ▸**b** With the head uncovered; hatless. *arch.* **LME.**
2 *fig.* Open to view, unconcealed. **OE.**

MILTON Bare in thy guilt how foul must thou appear! J. A. FROUDE His mind was . . in contact with the bare facts of life.

3 Of things: without the natural covering which they have at other times; lacking vegetation, foliage, etc. **OE.**

AV *Joel* 1:7 He hath . . barked my figge tree: he hath made it cleane bare. A. P. STANLEY Hills which are now bare were then covered with forest. R. LEHMANN Every branch was bare at last.

4 Deprived of hair, wool, flesh, etc.; bald. **ME.**
5 Lacking appropriate covering; unfurnished; undecorated. **ME.** ▸**b** Of weapons: unsheathed. Esp. of the hands: unarmed. **ME.**

EDWARD THOMAS No one left and no one came On the bare platform. I. MURDOCH Laid down as a covering upon the bare floorboards. S. KING The two bare, dangling light bulbs.

under bare poles: see POLE *noun*[1] 1c.
6 Without addition; mere, simple; scant, slight. **ME.**

ADDISON Nature indeed furnishes us with the bare Necessaries of Life. H. P. BROUGHAM A bare majority of seven to five. G. MURRAY I know only the barest outline of what took place. G. GREENE It was hard for me to show even bare politeness.

bare bones: see BONE *noun*.
†**7** Unprotected, deserted; laid waste, desolate. **ME–M17.**
8 Destitute, empty, short, *of*; lacking *in*. **ME.**
9 *absol.* **a** Of a person: destitute, needy. *arch.* **ME.** ▸**b** Empty; without contents. **LME.**
10 Spare, meagre. Chiefly of literary style etc.: plain, unelaborate. **ME.**
†**11** Poor in quality; paltry. **LME–L16.**

SHAKES. *Ven. & Ad.* What bare excuses mak'st thou to be gone!

▸ **B** *adverb.* (With numeral adjectives.) = BARELY. *arch.* **ME.**
▸ **C** *noun.* †**1** A naked part of the body; a bare space or place. **ME–E18.**
2 The bare skin. **LME.**

– COMB.: **bareback** *adjective & adverb* (of a horse or rider) without a saddle; **bare-backed** *adjective & adverb* with the back bare, esp. = *bareback* above; **barebacking** *slang* the practice of having anal sex without the protection of a condom; **bareboat** *noun & verb* (*a*) *noun* a vessel chartered under an arrangement by which the charterer is responsible for manning the vessel and operating costs; (*b*) *verb intrans.* charter or sail a bareboat; **barefaced** *adjective* with the face uncovered or clean-shaven; *fig.* undisguised, impudent, shameless; **barefacedly** *adverb* in a barefaced manner; **barefacedness** the quality of being barefaced; **barefoot** *adjective & adverb* = *barefooted* below (**barefoot doctor**, (in rural China) a paramedical worker with basic training; ***dance barefoot***: see DANCE *verb*); **barefooted** *adjective & adverb* without shoes or stockings, with naked feet; **barehand** *verb trans.* (BASEBALL) field (a ball) with one's bare hand; **barehanded** *adjective & adverb* having nothing in or covering the hands, *esp.* carrying no weapon; **barehead** *adjective & adverb* (*arch.*) = *bareheaded* below; **bareheaded** *adjective & adverb* with the head uncovered, esp. as a sign of respect.
■ **bareness** *noun* LME. **barish**, **bareish** *adjective* M17.

bare /bɛː/ *verb*[1] *trans.*
[ORIGIN Old English *barian* (formed as BARE *adjective, adverb, & noun*) = Old Frisian *baria*, Old High German *gibarōn*, Old Norse *bera*.]
1 Make bare, uncover; expose to view; unsheathe (a weapon). OE.
J. R. GREEN Earl Warrenne bared a rusty sword. TENNYSON He bows, he bares his head. J. KIRKUP Scalpel bares a creamy rib. N. GORDIMER Sometimes . . she bares her teeth without smiling, a mannerism like a pleased snarl.
2 *fig.* Make manifest, reveal. ME.
D. PARKER The intimate places of your heart . . you bared to me, as in confession.
3 Strip, divest, denude, (*of*). LME.
D. LIVINGSTONE He quite bared his garden in feeding us.

bare *verb*[2] arch. pa. t. of BEAR *verb*[1].

bareca /bəˈreɪkə/ *noun*. L18.
[ORIGIN Spanish: cf. BARRICO.]
A small cask or keg; = BREAKER *noun*[2].

barège /barɛːʒ/ *noun & adjective*. E19.
[ORIGIN French, from *Barèges* a village in SW France.]
▸ **A** *noun*. Pl. pronounced same. (A garment made of) a gauzelike fabric of silk and wool. E19.
▸ **B** *adjective*. Made of *barège*. M19.

barely /ˈbɛːli/ *adverb*. OE.
[ORIGIN from BARE *adjective* + -LY[2].]
1 Without concealment or disguise; nakedly; plainly, explicitly. *arch.* OE.
J. HACKET Here is the Resurrection of our Saviour barely and positively affirmed.
2 Merely, simply. *arch.* LME.
JAS. MILL The only objection . . might have been easily removed, by barely prescribing what sort of evidence they ought to receive.
3 Scarcely, hardly; only just. L15.
J. GALSWORTHY How much older he looked than on that day, barely two months ago, when she first saw him. A. HALEY George began singing one of Miss Malizy's songs, barely audibly, as if just for himself. C. FREEMAN At first he didn't even recognize her because he could barely see.
4 Scantily, poorly. *arch.* M16.
G. CRABBE Thy coat is thin; . . thou'rt barely drest.

baresark *noun & adjective* var. of BERSERK.

barf /bɑːf/ *verb & noun*. *slang* (chiefly *N. Amer.*). M20.
[ORIGIN Prob. imit.]
▸ **A** *verb intrans. & trans.* Vomit. M20.
▸ **B** *noun*. An act of vomiting; vomited food etc. Also as *interjection*. L20.

barfam /ˈbɑːf(ə)m/ *noun*. *dial.* Also †**bargham**, **barkum** /ˈbɑːk(ə)m/, BRECHAM, & other vars. ME.
[ORIGIN from stem of Old English *be(o)rgan* protect + HAME *noun*[1].]
A collar for a draught horse.

barfi *noun* var. of BURFI.

bargain /ˈbɑːgɪn/ *noun*. ME.
[ORIGIN Old French *barga(i)gne*, *-g(u)igne*: see BARGAIN *verb*.]
†**1 a** Discussion between two parties over terms; haggling. ME–L16. ▸**b** Contention, struggle, fight. *Scot. & N. English*. LME–L19.
2 An agreement on the terms of a transaction, a compact. With specifying word, as *good*, *bad*, etc.: a good, bad, etc., agreement from the point of view of one of the parties. ME.
bargain and sale LAW (a contract for) a sale followed by the payment of the agreed price, *esp.* (*hist.*) referring to the sale of an estate etc. without deeds. ***drive a hard bargain***: see DRIVE *verb*. ***Dutch bargain***: see DUTCH *adjective*. **into the bargain**, (*US*) **in the bargain** over and above what is agreed; besides. **make a bargain**, **strike a bargain** come to terms over a transaction. ***make the best of a bad bargain***: see BEST *adjective & adverb*. ***Smithfield bargain***: see SMITHFIELD *noun*[1]. ***strike a bargain***: see *make a bargain* above.
3 A thing acquired by bargaining; any purchase, esp. regarded according to whether or not one obtained value for money; *spec.* an advantageous purchase. LME. ▸**b** An article offered at a reduced or allegedly reduced price, esp. in a special sale. L19.
I. GERSHWIN It's very nice! It's a bargain at double the price! **b** *attrib.*: *New York Times* For a bargain $13 you can sample a bit of dozens of dishes.
– COMB.: **bargain basement**, **bargain counter**: where bargains are offered for sale; **bargain-hunter** a person who shops for bargains; **bargain-hunting** shopping for bargains; **bargain price** a low or (allegedly) reduced price.

bargain /ˈbɑːgɪn/ *verb*. LME.
[ORIGIN Old French *bargaignier* trade, dispute, hesitate (mod. *barguigner* hesitate) = Provençal *barganhar*, Italian *bargagnare*, medieval Latin *barcaniare*, prob. from Germanic, whence Old High German *borgēn* look after, Middle High German, German *borgen* borrow: the *-a-* of the 1st syll. is unexpl.]
1 *verb intrans.* Discuss the terms of a transaction, negotiate; seek to secure the most favourable terms, haggle. LME.
H. ALLEN They were congratulating him; already beginning to chaffer and bargain. R. P. JHABVALA He had to bargain quite hard in order to be quoted a reasonable price. J. M. KEYNES A system of free wage-bargaining.
bargaining counter, **bargaining chip** a potential concession etc. which can be used to advantage in negotiations. ***plea bargaining***: see PLEA *noun*.
†**2** *verb intrans.* Contend, struggle, fight. *Scot. & N. English*. LME–L19.
3 *verb intrans.* Arrange or agree terms; strike a bargain. Foll. by *with* a person, *for* a thing, *that*, *to do*. L15.
SHAKES. *Tam. Shr.* 'Tis bargain'd 'twixt us twain . . That she shall still be curst in company. ADDISON A merchant . . bargained for it, and carried it off. M. W. MONTAGU The marble was bespoke and the sculptor bargained with.
4 *verb trans.* Agree to buy and sell; contract for; *obsolete* exc. (LAW) in ***bargain and sell***. L15.
5 *verb trans.* Foll. by *away*: part with in a bargain; sell cheaply. M19.
GEO. ELIOT The heir . . had somehow bargained away the estate. M. L. KING Fathers and mothers were sold from their children and children were bargained away from their parents.
– WITH PREPOSITIONS IN SPECIALIZED SENSES: **bargain for** expect, be prepared for (usu. with neg. or *more than*). **bargain on** *colloq.* (*a*) = *bargain for* above; (*b*) count on.
■ **bargaiˈnee** *noun* the purchaser in an agreement of bargain and sale L16. **bargainer** *noun* a person who bargains LME. **bargaiˈnor** *noun* the seller in an agreement of bargain and sale E17.

bargander *noun* var. of BERGANDER.

barge /bɑːdʒ/ *noun & verb*. ME.
[ORIGIN Old French & mod. French *barge*, medieval Latin *bargia*, perh. ult. from Greek *baris* Egyptian boat: cf. BARK *noun*[3].]
▸ **A** *noun*. **1** A small seagoing vessel with sails; *spec.* one next in size above a balinger. *obsolete* exc. *hist.* ME.
schooner barge: see SCHOONER *noun*[1].
2 A flat-bottomed freight boat or lighter, for canals, rivers, and harbours. LME.
3 A ceremonial vessel of state, usu. one propelled by oars; an ornamental houseboat. LME.
4 A small boat; now *spec.* a warship's boat for the conveyance of senior officers. LME.
5 A large carriage. *US*. L19.
– COMB.: **bargeman** a person who has charge of, or works on, a barge; **bargemaster** the master or owner of a barge; **bargepole** a long pole used on a barge for fending; ***would not touch with a bargepole*** (colloq.), would refuse to have anything to do with.
▸ **B** *verb* **1** †**a** *verb trans.* with *it*. Travel by barge. Only in L16. ▸**b** *verb intrans.* Travel by barge. E20.
2 *verb trans.* Carry by barge. M17.
3 *verb intrans.* Lurch or rush heavily (*into*, *against*, *about*, etc.). L19. ▸**b** *verb trans.* Make *one's way* thus. E20.
K. MANSFIELD Why should he come barging over to this exact spot? B. HINES He . . barged into the kitchen door, and bounced back when it wouldn't open. M. RICHLER The moment Joshua barged into the room, Uncle Oscar slapped the book shut.
barge in butt in, intrude.
4 *verb trans.* Push or collide with heavily; cause to move thus. E20.
W. J. LOCKE By degrees he edged (or barged) his huge frame to the front rank. *Western Mail (Cardiff)* Uncle Owen was barged from behind, spilling his beer over the second tenor.

barge- /bɑːdʒ/ *combining form*.
[ORIGIN Cf. medieval Latin *bargus* a kind of gallows (= classical Latin *furca*).]
Forming terms in ARCHITECTURE relating to the gable of a building.
■ **bargeboard** *noun* a board or ornamental screen along the edge of a gable M19. **barge-couple** *noun* a strong pair of rafters at a gable end M16. **barge-course** *noun* coping or tiles overhanging the wall of a house at a gable end M17.

bargee /bɑːˈdʒiː/ *noun*. M17.
[ORIGIN from BARGE *noun* + -EE[1] (used irreg.).]
A bargeman.

Bargello /bɑːˈdʒɛləʊ/ *noun & adjective*. M20.
[ORIGIN The *Bargello* Palace in Florence, Italy.]
(Designating) a kind of embroidery worked on canvas in stitch patterns suggestive of flames.

†**bargeret** *noun* var. of BERGERETTE.

†**bargham** *noun* var. of BARFAM.

barghest /ˈbɑːgɛst/ *noun*. M18.
[ORIGIN Unknown.]
A goblin in the shape of a large dog, fabled to portend death or misfortune.

†**barghmaster** *noun* var. of BARMASTER.

†**barghmote** *noun* var. of BARMOTE.

bar-goose /ˈbɑːguːs/ *noun*. *dial.* Pl. **bar-geese**. L16.
[ORIGIN *bar* app. abbreviation of BARNACLE *noun*[1] or as in *bargander* var. of BERGANDER.]
A barnacle goose; a shelduck.

bariatrics /barɪˈatrɪks/ *noun pl.* M20.
[ORIGIN from BARO- + IATRIC + -S.]
The branch of medicine concerned with obesity and weight control.
■ **bariatric** *adjective* L20. **bariaˈtrician** *noun* a doctor who specializes in obesity and weight control M20.

barilla /bəˈrɪlə/ *noun*. E17.
[ORIGIN Spanish *barrilla* dim. of *barra* bar.]
1 The alkali plant, *Salsola soda*. E17.
2 Impure alkali made in Spain and neighbouring regions by burning dried plants, esp. of this species. E17.

Barisal guns /barɪˈsɑːl gʌnz/ *noun phr.* L19.
[ORIGIN from *Barisal*, a town in Bangladesh.]
Booming sounds of unknown origin.

barista /baˈriːstə/ *noun*. L20.
[ORIGIN Italian = barman.]
A person who serves in a coffee bar.

barite /ˈbarʌɪt, ˈbɛː-/ *noun*. Also **-yte**. M19.
[ORIGIN from BARIUM *noun* + -ITE[1].]
MINERALOGY. = BARYTES 2.

baritone /ˈbarɪtəʊn/ *noun & adjective*. Also †**barytone**; (sense A.2) **baryton** /ˈbarɪtɒn/. E17.
[ORIGIN Italian *baritono* from Greek *barutonos* deep-sounding, from *barus* deep + *tonos* pitch: cf. BARYTONE *noun*[1] & *adjective*[1].]
▸ **A** *noun*. **1** The male voice between tenor and bass, ranging typically from lower A in the bass clef to lower F in the treble clef; a singer having such a voice; a part written for such a voice. E17.
2 A kind of bass viol. M17.
3 The member of a family of similar instruments pitched between tenor and bass, *esp.* a tenor saxhorn in B flat or C. L19.
▸ **B** *adjective*. **1** Of the voice: having a compass intermediate between bass and tenor. Hence, suited for or possessing such a voice. E18.
2 Of an instrument: pitched between tenor and bass varieties (cf. sense A.3). L19.
baritone horn, ***baritone oboe***, ***baritone saxophone***, etc.
■ **bariˈtonal** *adjective* L20.

barium /ˈbɛːrɪəm/ *noun*. E19.
[ORIGIN from BARYTA + -IUM.]
A reactive white chemical element, atomic no. 56, which is one of the alkaline earth metals (symbol Ba).
– COMB.: **barium meal** a radio-opaque mixture containing barium sulphate, taken before radiological examination of the alimentary tract.

bark /bɑːk/ *noun*[1].
[ORIGIN Old English *(ge)beorc*: later from BARK *verb*[1].]
1 The sharp explosive cry of a dog, fox, squirrel, etc. OE.
one's bark (opp. ***one's bite***) one's words as opp. to one's actions.
2 Any harsh, abrupt noise, as of a cannon, cough, shouted command, etc. L19.
■ **barkless** *adjective*[1] (of a dog) having no bark M20.

bark /bɑːk/ *noun*[2]. ME.
[ORIGIN Old Norse *bark-*, *bǫrkr* (Swedish, Danish *bark*), perh. rel. to BIRCH *noun*: the Old English word is RIND *noun*[1].]
1 The layer of tissue lying outside the vascular cambium in the stem of a tree or woody plant, consisting of phloem, cortex, and periderm; *esp.* the corky outer layer of this. ME. ▸**b** *spec.* That used in dyeing, tanning, etc., or its bruised residue. LME. ▸**c** *spec.* That of certain trees used medicinally, *esp.* cinchona. LME.
bitter bark: see BITTER *adjective*. ***Peruvian bark***: see PERUVIAN *noun & adjective*. ***red bark***: see RED *adjective*. ***SLIPPERY elm bark***. ***sweetwood bark***: see SWEET *adjective & adverb*.
2 *gen.* or *fig.* An outer covering; a rind, a husk; the skin. Now *dial.* or *obsolete*. LME.
– COMB.: **bark beetle** a wood-boring beetle of the family Scolytidae (***typographer bark beetle***: see TYPOGRAPHER 3); **barkcloth** cloth made from the inner bark of the paper mulberry or similar tree; **bark-tree** a cinchona.
■ **barken** *adjective* (chiefly *poet.*) made or consisting of bark M18. **barkless** *adjective*[2] devoid of bark E17. **barky** *adjective* covered with or of the nature of bark L16.

bark /bɑːk/ *noun*[3]. Also (esp. sense 3) **barque**. LME.
[ORIGIN Old French & mod. French, prob. from Provençal *barca* from late Latin: cf. BARGE *noun*.]
1 Any small sailing vessel. Now only *poet.* LME.
2 A (large) rowing boat. Now only *poet.* L16.
3 An ocean-going sailing vessel of particular rig; *spec.* one with the aftermost mast fore-and-aft rigged and the other masts square-rigged. E17.

■ **barkey** *noun* (*colloq.*) a little bark; a ship: **E18**.

bark /bɑːk/ *verb*[1].
[**ORIGIN** Old English *beorcan* from Germanic, perh. ult. metath. alt. of **BREAK** *verb*.]
1 *verb intrans.* Of a dog, fox, etc.: utter a sharp explosive cry. **OE**.
barking bird the black-throated huet-huet, *Pteroptochos tarnii*, of S. America. **barking deer** = **MUNTJAC**. **barking squirrel** = *prairie dog* s.v. **PRAIRIE**.
2 *verb intrans.* Speak or cry out aggressively, petulantly, or imperiously. **ME**.
H. **LATIMER** It is the scripture and not the translation, that ye bark against.
3 *verb trans.* Utter as a bark; ejaculate with a bark. **LME**.
SPENSER Cerberus, whose many mouthes doo bay And barke out flames. J. **CLARE** The dog bark'd a welcome. L. **URIS** Bill Fry stood on his bridge barking orders through a megaphone. S. **BRILL** He popped a few mints into his mouth, looked up and barked, 'Let's get started.'
4 *verb trans.* Drive *away*, *back*, *off*, by barking. **E19**.
5 *verb intrans.* Of a firearm etc.: emit a harsh explosive sound. **M19**.
S. E. **WHITE** The Colt's forty-five barked once, and then again.
6 *verb intrans.* & *trans.* Call out to attract custom (for); tout. *US*. **E20**.
– **PHRASES**: **bark against the moon**, **bark at the moon** clamour to no effect. **bark up the wrong tree** make an effort in the wrong direction, be on the wrong track.

bark /bɑːk/ *verb*[2] *trans.* **LME**.
[**ORIGIN** from **BARK** *noun*[2].]
1 Steep in an infusion of bark; tan. **LME**.
2 a Strip the bark from (a tree). **M16**. ▸**b** Abrade skin from (a shin, knuckle, etc.). **E19**.
3 Enclose (as) with bark; encrust. **M17**.

barkentine *noun* var. of **BARQUENTINE**.

barker /ˈbɑːkə/ *noun*[1]. **ME**.
[**ORIGIN** from **BARK** *verb*[2] + **-ER**[1].]
1 A tanner. Now *rare* or *obsolete*. **ME**.
2 A person who barks trees. **E17**.

barker /ˈbɑːkə/ *noun*[2]. **LME**.
[**ORIGIN** from **BARK** *verb*[1] + **-ER**[1].]
1 A person who or thing which barks; *spec.* a dog. **LME**.
2 A noisy assailant or protester. **LME**.
3 Any of various wading birds with harsh cries, *esp.* a spotted redshank, avocet, or godwit. *dial.* **M17**.
4 A tout at an auction room, sideshow, etc. Chiefly *N. Amer.* **L17**.
5 A pistol; a cannon. *arch. slang.* **E19**.

barkevikite /ˈbɑːkəvɪkʌɪt/ *noun*. **L19**.
[**ORIGIN** from *Barkevik*, a place in Norway + **-ITE**[1].]
MINERALOGY. An iron-rich sodium and potassium amphibole occurring as dark brown or black monoclinic crystals.

barkle /ˈbɑːk(ə)l/ *verb trans. dial.* **E19**.
[**ORIGIN** from **BARK** *verb*[2] + **-LE**[3].]
Cake, encrust, (with dirt etc.).

barkum *noun* see **BARFAM**.

barley /ˈbɑːli/ *noun*.
[**ORIGIN** Old English *bærlīc* adjective, formed as **BERE** *noun*[1] + **-LY**[1]: cf. Old Norse *barr* barley, Gothic *barizeins* of barley.]
(The grain of) a hardy awned cereal of the genus *Hordeum*, used as food and in making malt liquors and spirits.
four-rowed barley, ***pearl barley***, ***sea barley***, ***sprat-barley***, etc.
– **COMB.**: **barley-bird** *dial.* any of various birds which appear at the time of barley-sowing in spring, e.g. a wryneck, yellow wagtail, or nightingale; **barley-bree**, **barley-broth** strong ale; **barley-hood** (now *rare* or *obsolete*) a fit of drunkenness or of bad temper brought on by drinking; **barleymow** a stack of barley; **barley sugar** a confection of boiled sugar, usu. in twisted sticks; **barley sugar** *adjective* (of columns etc.) twisted like barley sugar; **barley water** a decoction of pearl barley for invalids etc. or (esp. with some further flavouring) drunk for refreshment; **barley wine** a wine or ale prepared from barley; *spec.* a strong English ale.

barley /ˈbɑːli/ *interjection*. *Scot.* & *N. English*. **LME**.
[**ORIGIN** Perh. alt. of French *parlez* **PARLEY**.]
In children's games: parley, truce.

barley-break /ˈbɑːlɪbreɪk/ *noun*. **M16**.
[**ORIGIN** Perh. from **BARLEY** *noun* or *interjection* + **BREAK** *verb*.]
An old country catching game, resembling prisoner's base, played by three couples, one of which had to catch the others, who were allowed to 'break' and change partners when hard-pressed.

barleycorn /ˈbɑːlɪkɔːn/ *noun*. **LME**.
[**ORIGIN** from **BARLEY** *noun* + **CORN** *noun*[1].]
1 = **BARLEY** *noun*. **LME**. ▸**b** Personified as ***John Barleycorn***, esp. as the source of malt liquors. **E17**.
2 *hist.* The length of a grain of barley as a measure, usu. ⅓ inch. **LME**.

†**barling** *noun*. **ME–M18**.
[**ORIGIN** Old Norse: cf. Swedish *bärling* pole, from *bära* to bear.]
A pole, *esp.* one on or used with a boat.

barlow /ˈbɑːləʊ/ *noun*. *US*. **L18**.
[**ORIGIN** Russell *Barlow*, 18th-cent. English inventor.]
In full ***barlow knife***. A large single-bladed pocket knife.

barm /bɑːm/ *noun*[1]. Long *obsolete* exc. *dial.* in comb.
[**ORIGIN** Old English *barm*, *bearm* = Old Frisian, Old Saxon, Old High German *barm*, Old Norse *barmr*, Gothic *barms*, from Germanic, rel. to **BEAR** *verb*[1].]
A bosom, a lap.
Abraham's barm: see **ABRAHAM** 1.
– **COMB.**: **barm cloth** an apron; **barm-skin** a leather apron.

barm /bɑːm/ *noun*[2] & *verb*. Also **balm**.
[**ORIGIN** Old English *beorma* prob. from Low German: cf. Old Frisian *berme*, *barm*, Danish *bärme*, Swedish *bärma*, German *Bärme*.]
▸ **A** *noun*. The froth on the top of fermenting malt liquors, used to leaven bread and to ferment other liquors; yeast, leaven. **OE**.
▸ **B** *verb trans.* & *intrans.* Mix with yeast, leaven; rise in froth or fermentation. **LME**.

barmaster /ˈbɑːmɑːstə/ *noun*. Also †**bargh-**. **M16**.
[**ORIGIN** German *Bergmeister* from *Berg-* mining: see **MASTER** *noun*[1].]
hist. An officer of a barmote.

barmbrack /ˈbɑːmbrak/ *noun*. *Irish*. Also **barn-** /ˈbɑːn-/. **M19**.
[**ORIGIN** Irish *bairín breac* speckled cake.]
A currant bun.

Barmecide /ˈbɑːmɪsʌɪd/ *noun* & *adjective*. **E18**.
[**ORIGIN** Arabic *barmakī*, the patronymic of a prince in the *Arabian Nights' Entertainments* who feasted a beggar on a succession of empty dishes to test his humour.]
▸ **A** *noun*. A person who offers imaginary food or illusory benefits. **E18**.
▸ **B** *attrib.* or as *adjective*. Illusory, unreal; offering imaginary food or illusory benefits. **M19**.
■ **Barmeˈcidal** *adjective* illusory, unreal **M19**.

bar mitzvah /bɑː ˈmɪtsvə/ *noun* & *verb phr.* Also **B-**. **M19**.
[**ORIGIN** Hebrew *bar miṣwāh* son of commandment.]
▸ **A** *noun phr.* (A religious initiation ceremony for) a Jewish boy aged thirteen, regarded as liable to observe the religious precepts and eligible to take part in public worship. **M19**.
▸ **B** *verb trans.* In *pass.* Be confirmed in the Jewish faith at a bar mitzvah ceremony. **M20**.

barmkin /ˈbɑːmkɪn/ *noun*. *N. English*. Now *arch.* or *hist.* **LME**.
[**ORIGIN** Perh. alt. of **BARBICAN**.]
(The battlement of) the outer fortification or barbican of a castle; a turret or tower on this.

barmote /ˈbɑːməʊt/ *noun*. Also †**bargh-**. **M16**.
[**ORIGIN** formed as **BARMASTER** + *mote* var. of **MOOT** *noun*[1].]
hist. A local court with jurisdiction as to lead-mining rights and related matters.

barmy /ˈbɑːmi/ *adjective*. Also **balmy**. **L15**.
[**ORIGIN** from **BARM** *noun*[2] + **-Y**[1].]
1 Of, full of, or covered with barm; frothy. **L15**.
2 *fig.* Excitedly active; empty-headed, daft, crazy. Now *slang*. **L16**.
barmy in the crumpet, ***barmy on the crumpet***: see **CRUMPET** 3.

barn /bɑːn/ *noun*[1] & *verb*.
[**ORIGIN** Old English *ber(e)n*, earlier *berern*, formed as **BERE** *noun*[1] + *ærn*, *ern* a place.]
▸ **A** *noun*. **1** A covered building for the storage of grain, hay, straw, flax, etc. **OE**.
Dutch barn: see **DUTCH** *adjective*. ***ROBIN HOOD's barn***.
2 A building for housing livestock, vehicles, etc. *N. Amer.* **L18**.
receiving barn: see **RECEIVING** *adjective*.
3 A large unduly plain building or room. **M20**.
4 *PHYSICS.* A unit of area equal to 10^{-28} sq. metre, used in expressing nuclear cross-sections. **M20**.
– **COMB.**: **barn-ball** *US* a children's game involving bouncing a ball off the gable of a building; **barn-burner** *N. Amer. colloq.* an excellent, rousing, or remarkable person or event; **barn dance** (***a***) an informal social occasion for country dancing (orig. one held in a barn); (***b***) a dance for a number of couples forming a line or circle, with the couples moving along it in turn; **barn door** the large door of a barn; *fig.* a target etc. too large to be missed; ***nail to the barn door***: see **NAIL** *verb*; **barn-gallon** *hist.* a measure of two imperial gallons; **barnlot** *US* the ground upon or around which a barn stands; **barn owl** an owl of the genus *Tyto*; esp. *T. alba*, which usu. has a white face and underside and frequently nests in farm buildings; **barnstorm** *verb intrans.* [back-form. from *barnstormer*] tour etc. as a barnstormer (chiefly as ***barnstorming*** *verbal noun* or *ppl adjective*); **barnstormer** (orig. & chiefly *N. Amer.*) (***a***) an itinerant actor; (***b***) a politician making a rapid electioneering tour; (***c***) an aviator who tours the country giving aerobatic displays, an adventurous pilot; **barn swallow** *N. Amer.* the common swallow, *Hirundo rustica*.
▸ **B** *verb trans.* House in a barn; garner. **LME**.

barn *noun*[2] var. of **BAIRN**.

Barnabite /ˈbɑːnəbʌɪt/ *noun*. **E18**.
[**ORIGIN** from *Barnabas* the apostle + **-ITE**[1].]
A member of a small religious order founded in 1530, named from its church of St Barnabas in Milan.

Barnaby /ˈbɑːnəbi/ *noun*. **L16**.
[**ORIGIN** By-form of *Barnabas* (see **BARNABITE**): cf. French *Barnabé*.]
1 ***Barnaby bright***, ***Barnaby-day***, ***long Barnaby***, St Barnabas' day, 11 June, the longest day of the year, Old Style. **L16**.
2 ***Barnaby thistle***, ***Barnaby's thistle***, ***St Barnaby's thistle***, the yellow star-thistle, *Centaurea solstitialis*, flowering on or near St Barnabas' day. **L16**.

barnacle /ˈbɑːnək(ə)l/ *noun*[1]. **ME**.
[**ORIGIN** medieval Latin *bernaca*, of unknown origin.]
1 A black, white, and grey goose, *Branta leucopsis*, breeding in the Arctic and visiting Britain in winter. Now usu. ***barnacle goose***. **ME**.
2 A marine crustacean of the subclass Cirripedia, which attach themselves directly or by a fleshy footstalk to rocks, ships' bottoms, or other objects. **L16**.
3 *fig.* A companion or follower who is difficult to shake off. **E17**.
– **NOTE**: The geese, whose breeding grounds were long unknown, were formerly fabled to grow from the shells of the crustaceans, or else from a tree or its fruit.
■ **barnacled** *adjective*[1] covered with barnacles (**BARNACLE** *noun*[1] 2); *fig.* encrusted: **L17**.

barnacle /ˈbɑːnək(ə)l/ *noun*[2]. **LME**.
[**ORIGIN** Alt. of Anglo-Norman *bernac*, of unknown origin.]
1 A kind of bit or twitch for restraining a horse or ass; *spec.* an instrument of two branches joined by a hinge, placed on the nose of the animal. Usu. in *pl.* **LME**.
2 In *pl.* Spectacles. *arch.* & *dial.* **L16**.
3 An instrument of torture fashioned and applied like a barnacle (sense 1 above). Usu. in *pl. obsolete* exc. *hist.* **E17**.
■ **barnacled** *adjective*[2] (*arch.* or *dial.*) wearing spectacles **E18**.

Barnardo /bəˈnɑːdəʊ/ *noun*. **E20**.
[**ORIGIN** See below.]
Used ***attrib.*** and in ***possess.*** to designate an orphan or destitute child brought up in one of the homes founded by the British philanthropist Dr Thomas John Barnardo (1845–1905).
P. **HOBSON** She was a Barnardo baby . . she was illegitimate. M. **HARDWICK** I was a Barnardo's girl . . . They found me in a slum in Walsall.

barnbrack *noun* var. of **BARMBRACK**.

barnet /ˈbɑːnɪt/ *noun*. *rhyming slang*. **M19**.
[**ORIGIN** *Barnet*, now a borough of Greater London.]
In full ***barnet fair***. The hair; the head.

barney /ˈbɑːni/ *noun* & *verb*. *colloq.* **M19**.
[**ORIGIN** Unknown.]
▸ **A** *noun*. A noisy altercation; an argument, a quarrel. **M19**.
▸ **B** *verb intrans.* Quarrel, argue. **M19**.

barngun /ˈbɑːngʌn/ *noun*. *dial.* **M18**.
[**ORIGIN** from var. of **BURN** *verb* + var. of **GOUND**.]
An eruption of the skin; shingles.

Barnum /ˈbɑːnəm/ *noun*. **M19**.
[**ORIGIN** Phineas T. *Barnum* (1810–91), US showman.]
Humbug; empty showmanship.
– **COMB.**: **Barnum effect** *PSYCHOLOGY* the tendency of individuals to accept types of information such as character assessments or horoscopes as being particularly true of themselves, even when the information is so vague as to be worthless.
■ **Barnuˈmese** *noun* inflated or sensational language **L19**.

barnyard /ˈbɑːnjɑːd/ *noun* & *adjective*. **LME**.
[**ORIGIN** from **BARN** *noun*[1] + **YARD** *noun*[1].]
▸ **A** *noun*. The enclosure round a barn, a farmyard. **LME**.
– **COMB.**: **barnyard grass** = ***COCKSPUR grass***.
▸ **B** *attrib.* or as *adjective*. Typical of a barnyard; *fig.* earthy, coarse, scatological. *colloq.* **M20**.

baro- /ˈbarəʊ/ *combining form* of Greek *baros* weight, usu. with the sense 'pressure': see **-O-**.
■ **barogram** *noun* the record made by a barograph **L19**. **barograph** *noun* a self-recording barometer **M19**. **barophile** *noun* a barophilic organism **M20**. **baroˈphilic** *adjective* (of an organism, esp. a bacterium) growing optimally under high pressures (as in the deep ocean), or requiring such conditions to survive **M20**. **baroreˈceptor** *noun* (*PHYSIOLOGY*) a receptor sensitive to changes in pressure **M20**. **baroˈreflex** *noun* (*PHYSIOLOGY*) a reflex mechanism whereby blood pressure in the arteries is sensed by baroreceptors, and controlled by various feedback processes **M20**. **barostat** *noun* an automatic device for regulating pressure **M20**. **baroˈthermograph** *noun* an instrument which records pressure and temperature simultaneously **L19**. **baroˈtolerance** *noun* the behaviour of a barotolerant organism **L20**. **baroˈtolerant** *adjective* (of an organism, esp. a bacterium) capable of growing in conditions of very high pressure although growing optimally at or near atmospheric pressure **M20**. **barotrauma** *noun* (*MEDICINE*) ear injury due to change in ambient pressure **M20**.

barocco /bəˈrɒkəʊ/ *adjective* & *noun*. Pl. of noun **-os**. **L19**.
[**ORIGIN** Italian.]
= **BAROQUE**.

baroclinic /barəˈklɪnɪk/ *adjective*. **E20**.
[**ORIGIN** from **BARO-** + Greek *klinein* to bend, slope + **-IC**.]
METEOROLOGY. Characterized by or associated with an atmospheric condition in which surfaces of constant pressure intersect surfaces of constant density.
■ **baroclinically** *adverb* **M20**. **baroclinicity** /-ˈnɪsɪti/, **baroclinity** *nouns* **M20**.

Baroco /bəˈrəʊkəʊ/ *noun*. Also **-oko**. Pl. **-os**. **M16**.
[**ORIGIN** A mnemonic of scholastic philosophers, first used in medieval Latin, A indicating a universal affirmative proposition and O a particular negative proposition.]
LOGIC. The fourth mood of the second syllogistic figure, in which a particular negative conclusion is drawn from a universal affirmative major premiss and a particular negative minor.

B

Barolo /bəˈrəʊləʊ/ *noun*. L19.
[ORIGIN A region of Piedmont, Italy.]
A full-bodied red Italian wine from Barolo.

barometer /bəˈrɒmɪtə/ *noun*. M17.
[ORIGIN from BARO- + -METER.]
An instrument for measuring the pressure of the atmosphere, freq. also giving a forecast of change in the weather.
fig.: H. W. VAN LOON The arts are an even better barometer of what is happening in our world than the stock market or the debates in Congress.

barometric /barəˈmɛtrɪk/ *adjective*. E19.
[ORIGIN from BARO- + -METRIC.]
Of, pertaining to, or indicated by a barometer.
■ **barometrical** *adjective* = BAROMETRIC M17. **barometrically** *adverb* L18.

barometry /bəˈrɒmɪtri/ *noun*. E18.
[ORIGIN from BAROMETER: see -METRY.]
The art or science of barometric observation.

barometz /ˈbarəmɛts/ *noun*. E17.
[ORIGIN Russian *baranets* dim. of *baran* ram.]
A fabulous Russian creature, half plant and half sheep; the inverted woolly caudex etc. of the tree fern *Cibotium barometz*, which was used to create the illusion of such a creature.

baron /ˈbar(ə)n/ *noun*. ME.
[ORIGIN Anglo-Norman *barun*, Old French & mod. French *baron*, accus. of *ber* = Provençal *bar*, accus. *baron*, from medieval Latin *baro*, *-on-* man, male, warrior, prob. of Frankish origin.]
▸ **I 1** *hist.* A person who derived a title, by military or other honourable service, from the king or other superior; a noble, a peer, *esp.* any of those summoned to attend Parliament; *Scot.* a holder of a barony (sense 3). ME.
2 A member of the lowest order of the British or Irish nobility. ME. ▸**b** A holder of a similar foreign title. L19.
3 Applied to Christ and the saints, or to any man out of respect. *rare*. ME.
4 *hist.* A freeman of London, York, or certain other cities; a freeman or a burgess of the Cinque Ports. LME.
5 *hist.* A judge of the Court of Exchequer. LME.
6 LAW (now *hist.*) & HERALDRY. Husband (conjoined with *fem(m)e*). LME.
7 A magnate in industry, finance, etc. (usu. with specifying word, as ***beef baron***, ***press baron***); *gen.* a powerful or influential person. Orig. *US*. E19.
▸ **II 8** ***baron of beef***, a joint consisting of two sirloins left joined at the backbone. M18.
– COMB.: **baron-bailie** SCOTTISH HISTORY a deputy appointed by a baron to exercise the latter's jurisdiction in a court; **baron court** *hist.* = COURT BARON.
■ †**baronry** *noun* = BARONY LME–M18.

baronage /ˈbar(ə)nɪdʒ/ *noun*. ME.
[ORIGIN Old French *barnage*, medieval Latin *bar(o)nagium*: see BARON, -AGE.]
1 The body of barons or nobles collectively. ME.
†**2** = BARONY. ME–M17.
3 An annotated list of barons or peers. L19.

baroness /ˈbar(ə)nɪs/ *noun*. LME.
[ORIGIN Old French *bar(o)nesse* (Anglo-Latin *baronissa*, *-essa*): see BARON, -ESS[1].]
The wife or widow of a baron; a woman holding the rank of baron in her own right.

baronet /ˈbar(ə)nɪt/ *noun & verb*. LME.
[ORIGIN Anglo-Latin *baronettus*: see BARON, -ET[1].]
▸ **A** *noun*. †**1** A lesser baron; *esp.* a gentleman, not a baron by tenure from the king, who was summoned to Parliament. LME–M17.
2 A member of the lowest hereditary titled British order, with the status of a commoner but able to use the prefix 'Sir'. E17.
▸ **B** *verb trans.* Infl. **-t-**, ***-tt-**. Raise to the rank of a baronet. M18.
■ **baronetage** *noun* the rank of baronet; baronets collectively; an annotated list of baronets: E18. **baronetcy** *noun* a baronet's rank or patent E19. **baronetess** *noun* (*rare*) the wife of a baronet M17. **baronetize** *verb trans.* confer a baronetcy on M19.

baronial /bəˈrəʊnɪəl/ *adjective*. M18.
[ORIGIN from BARONY + -IAL.]
1 Of or pertaining to a baron or barons; befitting the rank of baron. M18.
2 ARCHITECTURE. Of or in the turreted style characteristic of Scottish country houses. Usu. ***Scottish baronial***, ***Scotch baronial***. L19.

barony /ˈbar(ə)ni/ *noun*. ME.
[ORIGIN Old French *baronie* (mod. *-nn-*), medieval Latin *baronia*: see BARON, -Y[3].]
1 The domain of a baron. ME. ▸**b** SCOTTISH HISTORY. An estate held under barony (see sense 3 below). LME. ▸**c** IRISH HISTORY. A division of a county. L16.
†**2** The barons collectively. ME–L16.
3 The tenure of a baron from the Crown; *spec.* in SCOTTISH HISTORY, the freehold of a chief tenant of a single unit of lands (not necessarily contiguous) with defined rights of civil and criminal jurisdiction. LME.
4 The rank or dignity of baron. L18.

■ **baronian** /bəˈrəʊnɪən/ *adjective* (*rare*) = BARONIAL M17.

baroque /bəˈrɒk, -ˈrəʊk/ *adjective & noun*. Orig. *derog.* Also **B-**. M18.
[ORIGIN French (in earliest use, of pearls) from Portuguese *barroco*, Spanish *barrueco*, (of architecture) Italian BAROCCO: ult. origin unknown.]
▸ **A** *adjective*. **1** Of, pertaining to, or characterized by an exuberant and ornate style prevalent in the arts (esp. in architecture and music) of the 17th and early 18th cents. M18.
H. READ Michelangelo has been called the father of Baroque art. *Observer* Poetically crumbling baroque churches.
2 *gen.* Elaborately or grotesquely ornate; whimsical, bizarre. M19.
S. SPENDER The baroque extravagance, the ribbons and trimmings, of Tony's conversation.
3 Of a pearl: irregularly shaped. L19.
▸ **B** *noun*. (The style, music, or architecture of) the 17th and early 18th cents.; baroque ornamentation. L19.
J. N. SUMMERSON At Blenheim the English Baroque culminates.

barosaurus /barəˈsɔːrəs/ *noun*. E20.
[ORIGIN mod. Latin (see below), from Greek *baros* heavy, weight + *sauros* lizard.]
A very large herbivorous sauropod dinosaur of the upper Jurassic genus *Barosaurus*, with a long neck and tail.

barotitis /barəˈtʌɪtɪs/ *noun*. L20.
[ORIGIN from BARO- + OTITIS.]
MEDICINE. Discomfort and inflammation in the ear caused by the changes of pressure occurring during air travel.

barotropic /barəˈtrəʊpɪk, -ˈtrɒpɪk/ *adjective*. E20.
[ORIGIN from BARO- + -TROPIC.]
METEOROLOGY. Characterized by or associated with an atmospheric condition in which surfaces of equal pressure coincide with surfaces of equal density.
■ **barotropically** *adverb* M20. **baˈrotropy** *noun* E20.

Barotse /bəˈrɒtsi/ *noun & adjective*. *arch.* Pl. of noun same. M19.
[ORIGIN Bantu.]
= LOZI.

barouche /bəˈruːʃ/ *noun*. E19.
[ORIGIN German dial. *Barutsche* from Italian *baroccio* (Spanish *barrocho*) two-wheeled ult. from Latin *birotus*, from BI- + *rota* wheel.]
Chiefly *hist.* A four-wheeled horse-drawn carriage with a collapsible half hood, a seat in front for the driver, and seats facing each other for passengers.
■ **barouchette**, **-et** *noun* a kind of light barouche E19.

barque *noun* var. of BARK *noun*[3].

barquentine /ˈbɑːkəntiːn/ *noun*. Also **bark-**. L17.
[ORIGIN from *barque* BARK *noun*[3] after *brigantine*.]
A three-masted vessel with foremast square-rigged and main and mizzen masts rigged fore and aft.

barquette /bɑːˈkɛt/ *noun*. L19.
[ORIGIN French, lit. 'little boat', from *barque* (see BARK *noun*[3], -ETTE).]
A small, boat-shaped pastry shell with a sweet or savoury filling.

barrable /ˈbɑːrəb(ə)l/ *adjective*. L15.
[ORIGIN from BAR *verb* + -ABLE.]
Able to be legally excluded or stayed.

barracan /ˈbarək(ə)n/ *noun*. Also **bara-**. M17.
[ORIGIN French *barracan*, *bouracan* from Arabic *burrukān*, *barrakān* cloak of camlet: cf. BARRAGON.]
1 A coarsely woven fabric of wool, silk, and goat's hair. M17.
2 In Eastern countries, a cloak or mantle made of this or another fabric. E19.

barrace /ˈbarəs/ *noun*. *obsolete* exc. *hist.* LME.
[ORIGIN Old French pl. of *barre* BAR *noun*[1].]
†**1** A barrier or outwork in front of a fortress. LME–L15.
2 The scene of knightly contests; the lists. LME.
†**3** Contention, strife. L15–E17.

barrack /ˈbarək/ *noun*[1]. L17.
[ORIGIN French *baraque* from Italian *baracca* or Spanish *barraca* soldier's tent: ult. origin unknown.]
1 A temporary hut or cabin. *obsolete* exc. *N. English*. L17.
GIBBON He lodged in a miserable hut or barrack.
2 *sing.* & (usu.) in *pl.* (also treated as *sing.*) A set of buildings used as a residence for soldiers. L17. ▸**b** *transf.* A large building or range of buildings in which a number of people are housed; any large, austere building suggestive of a military barracks. E19. ▸**c** The regular quarters of the Salvation Army. *obsolete* exc. *hist.* L19.
DISRAELI His own idea of a profession being limited to a barrack in a London park. **b** E. GASKELL We went to . . her old town house, . . an immense barrack of an old half-fortified house. JOYCE I don't like being alone in this big barracks of a place.
– COMB.: **barrack-room lawyer** a would-be knowledgeable, pompously argumentative person; **barrack square** a drill ground near a barracks.

barrack /ˈbarək/ *noun*[2]. *Austral. & NZ*. L19.
[ORIGIN from BARRACK *verb*[2].]
An act, or the action, of barracking a person, team, etc.

barrack /ˈbarək/ *verb*[1] *trans.* E18.
[ORIGIN from BARRACK *noun*[1].]
Provide barracks for, locate in barracks.

barrack /ˈbarək/ *verb*[2] *intrans. & trans.* Orig. *Austral. & NZ*. L19.
[ORIGIN Prob. from N. Irish dial.]
Of spectators at games etc.: shout vociferously (*for*), jeer (at).
■ **barracker** *noun* L19.

barracoon /barəˈkuːn/ *noun*. M19.
[ORIGIN Spanish *barracón* augm. of *barraca*: see BARRACK *noun*[1], -OON.]
hist. An enclosure in which black slaves were confined for a limited period.

barracouta /barəˈkuːtə/ *noun*. Pl. same, **-s**. L17.
[ORIGIN Alt. of BARRACUDA.]
▸ †**I 1** See BARRACUDA. L17.
▸ **II 2** A long slender food fish, *Thyrsites atun* (family Gempylidae), of southern oceans; = SNOEK *noun*. L18.
3 A small narrow loaf of bread. *NZ*. E20.

barracuda /barəˈkuːdə/ *noun*. Also †**-couta**. See also BARRACOUTA. Pl. same, **-s**. L17.
[ORIGIN Unknown.]
1 Any of various fishes of the family Sphyraenidae, comprising predatory perciform fishes of tropical and temperate seas. L17.
great barracuda a large tropical barracuda, *Sphyraena barracuda*, of the western Atlantic which is readily provoked to attack humans and is valued as a game fish; also called ***picuda***.
2 See BARRACOUTA.

barracudina /ˌbarəkuːˈdiːnə/ *noun*. L20.
[ORIGIN Amer. Spanish, dimin. of BARRACUDA.]
Any of various predatory ocean fishes of the family Paralepididae, which have a slender body with a long head.

barragan *noun* var. of BARRAGON.

barrage /ˈbarɑːʒ/ *noun & verb*. M19.
[ORIGIN French, formed as BAR *verb*: see -AGE.]
▸ **A** *noun*. **1** A barrier constructed in a river (esp. the Nile) to increase the depth of water. M19.
2 An intensive artillery or machine-gun bombardment, employed to check an enemy, or protect one's own soldiers, in advancing or retreating. E20. ▸**b** A rapid succession of questions, utterances, etc. E20.
S. SASSOON My only idea was to collect all available ammunition and then renew the attack while the Stokes-gun officer put up an enthusiastic barrage. H. KISSINGER The North Vietnamese attacked with the heaviest artillery barrage of the war and large numbers of tanks. **b** C. S. FORESTER They shielded Curzon . . by grouping themselves round him and surrounding him with a protective barrage of professional explanation. S. KING There was a moment's gaping pause . . and then the barrage of questions came again, everything mixed together into a meaningless stew of voices.
CREEPING ***barrage***.
3 A heat or deciding event in fencing, showjumping, etc. M20.
– COMB.: **barrage balloon** a large captive balloon supporting a steel cable forming part of an anti-aircraft barrier.
▸ **B** *verb trans.* **1** Subject to a barrier of continuous fire. E20.
2 Bombard with questions, exclamations, etc. M20.

barragon /ˈbarəg(ə)n/ *noun*. Also **-gan**. M17.
[ORIGIN Spanish *barragán* from Arabic: see BARRACAN.]
A coarsely woven cloth; a kind of fustian.

barramundi /barəˈmʌndi/ *noun*. L19.
[ORIGIN Uncertain: prob. from an Australian Aboriginal language of Queensland.]
Any of various Australian freshwater food fishes; *spec.* the percoid fish *Lates calcarifer*, of estuaries and coastal waters.

barranca /bəˈraŋkə/ *noun*. Also **-co** /-kəʊ/, pl. **-os**. L17.
[ORIGIN Spanish.]
A narrow, winding river gorge.

barras /ˈbarəs/ *noun*. Now *dial.* Also **burras** /ˈbʌrəs/. L15.
[ORIGIN French *bourras*.]
A coarse linen or hessian cloth; canvas.

barrator /ˈbarətə/ *noun*. Also **-er**. LME.
[ORIGIN Anglo-Norman *baratour*, Old French *barateor* cheat, trickster, from *barater* from Proto-Romance from Greek *prattein* do, perform, manage, practise (sometimes dishonestly); perh. infl. by Old Norse *barátta* contest, fighting.]
1 A person who buys or sells ecclesiastical preferment or offices of state or accepts money to influence judicial proceedings. Now *rare* exc. *hist.* LME.
†**2** A person who indulges in riotous or violent behaviour, esp. for money; a hired bully. LME–L18.
3 A malicious raiser of discord; a troublemaker; *spec.* a vexatious litigant (now *hist.*). LME.

barratry /ˈbarətri/ *noun*. LME.
[ORIGIN Old French & mod. French *baraterie* deceit, from Old French *barat(e)* deceit, fraud, trouble, etc., from *barater*: see BARRATOR, -ERY.]

B

1 *hist.* The purchase or sale of ecclesiastical or state preferments or of judicial influence. LME.
2 The malicious incitement of discord; *spec.* (now *hist.*) the persistent practice of vexatious litigation. L16.
3 MARITIME LAW. Fraud or gross or criminal negligence prejudicial to a ship's owner(s) or underwriters on the part of the master or crew. E17.
■ **barratrous** *adjective* (MARITIME LAW) of or pertaining to barratry M19. **barratrously** *adverb* M19.

†**barratta** *noun* see BALATA.

Barr body /bɑː ˈbɒdi/ *noun phr.* M20.
[ORIGIN from M. L. *Barr* (1908–95), Canad. anatomist.]
GENETICS. A strongly heterochromatic body just inside the membrane of non-dividing cell nuclei in females, representing a condensed, inactive X chromosome and diagnostic of genetic femaleness.

barre /bɑː/ *noun.* E20.
[ORIGIN French: see BAR *noun*[1].]
1 MUSIC. (A finger used as) a capotasto. E20.
2 A waist-level horizontal bar to help dancers keep their balance during some exercises. M20.

barré /bare/ *adjective & noun.* Pl. of noun pronounced same. L19.
[ORIGIN French, pa. pple of *barrer* BAR *verb*.]
MUSIC. (A chord) played with strings stopped by a capotasto or finger.

barred /bɑːd/ *adjective.* LME.
[ORIGIN from BAR *noun*[1], *verb*: see -ED[2], -ED[1].]
1 Marked or ornamented with bars; striped; streaked. LME.
2 Secured or shut with a bar or bars. E16.
3 Of a harbour: obstructed by a sandbank. M16.
4 Having a bar or bars (BAR *noun*[1] 1). L16.
5 MUSIC. Marked off by bars. L19.

barrel /ˈbar(ə)l/ *noun.* ME.
[ORIGIN from Old French & mod. French *baril* from medieval Latin *barriclus* a small cask.]
1 A wooden vessel of cylindrical form, usu. bulging in the middle, made of curved staves bound together by hoops, with flat ends; a similar vessel made of metal, plastic, etc. Cf. CASK *noun* 1. ME.
over a barrel (chiefly *N. Amer.*) helpless. **scrape the barrel** be obliged to use the last available resources.
2 Such a vessel and its contents; the capacity of such a vessel as a measure for both liquid and dry goods, varying with the commodity; *spec.* a unit of capacity for oil and oil products equal to 35 imperial or 42 US gallons (about 159 litres). LME.
a barrel of fun, **a barrel of laughs** *colloq.* (a source of) much amusement. ***a barrel of monkeys***: see MONKEY *noun*.
3 A revolving cylinder around which a chain or rope is wound as in a capstan, watch, and other machines. LME.
†**4** Brand, quality, sort. M16–L18.
5 The cylindrical body or trunk of an object, as a pump, a fountain pen, etc. M17.
6 The metal tube of a gun, through which the shot is discharged. In ***double-barrel***, ***single-barrel***, etc., also, a gun with the specified number of barrels. M17.
lock, stock, and barrel: see LOCK *noun*[2].
7 The trunk of a horse etc. E18.
8 Money for use in a political campaign, esp. for corrupt purposes. *US slang* (now *hist.*). L19.
– COMB.: **barrel-chested** *adjective* having a large rounded chest; **barrel distortion** a type of defect in optical or electronic images in which vertical or horizontal straight lines appear as convex curves; **barrelfish** a large stromateoid fish, *Hyperoglyphe perciforme*, of the western Atlantic, often seen near floating wreckage or following vessels; **barrelhead** the flat top of a barrel; ***on the barrelhead*** (*N. Amer.*), (esp. of payment) without delay, immediately; **barrelhouse** (***a***) a low-class drinking saloon; (***b***) a kind of forceful unrestrained jazz music; **barrel organ** a musical instrument in which a handle-turned pin-studded cylinder opens pipes to act upon the keys or strikes metal tongues; **barrel vault** a vault with a roof of uniform concave structure.
■ **barrelage** *noun* the total amount of any commodity, esp. beer, as measured by barrels (during a specified period) L19.

barrel /ˈbar(ə)l/ *verb.* Infl. **-ll-**, ***-l-**. LME.
[ORIGIN from the noun.]
1 *verb trans.* Place or store in a barrel or barrels. LME. ▸**b** Store *up*. L16.

> **b** MILTON All benefit and use of Scripture, as to public prayer, should be deny'd us, except what was barreld up in a Common-praier Book.

2 *verb intrans.* Drive fast; proceed with force and speed. Freq. foll. by *along*. *N. Amer. slang.* M20.

> K. ATKINSON Wooden carts barrel across the cobblestones.

barren /ˈbar(ə)n/ *adjective & noun.* ME.
[ORIGIN Anglo-Norman *barai(g)ne* from Old French *bar(a)haine*, *brehai(g)ne* (mod. *bréhaigne*), of unknown origin.]
▸ **A** *adjective.* (Foll. by *of*.)
1 Of a woman: incapable of bearing children; infertile. *arch.* ME.
2 Of an animal: not pregnant at the usual season. ME.
3 Of a tree or plant: not producing fruit or seed. LME.
barren strawberry: see STRAWBERRY 2.
4 Of land: producing little vegetation; unproductive; infertile. LME.

> I. SINCLAIR Barren and blasted tundra.

5 Lacking interest or attraction; arid; dull. LME.
6 Producing no result; fruitless; unprofitable. M16.
7 Of a person: unresponsive; dull. L16.
– COMB.: **barrenwort** a low rhizomatous herb of the barberry family, *Epimedium alpinum*, once thought to cause sterility.
▸ **B** *noun.* **1** A barren woman or animal. Long *dial. rare.* ME.
2 A tract of barren land, esp. (freq. in *pl.* and with specifying word) in N. America. M17.
oak barrens, ***pine barrens***, etc.
■ **barrenly** *adverb* M16. **barrenness** /-n-n-/ *noun* ME.

†**barren** *verb trans.* L16–E18.
[ORIGIN from the adjective.]
Make barren or unfruitful; render unproductive.

barrera /baˈrrera/ *noun.* E20.
[ORIGIN Spanish = BARRIER.]
(The row of seats nearest to) the barrier encircling a bull-ring.

barret /ˈbarɪt/ *noun.* E19.
[ORIGIN French *barette* from Italian †*bar(r)etta*: see BIRETTA.]
A small flat cap, *esp.* a biretta.

barrette /baˈrɛt/ *noun.* E20.
[ORIGIN French, dim. of BARRE: see -ETTE.]
A bar-shaped clip or ornament for a woman's or girl's hair; a hairslide.

barretter /bəˈrɛtə/ *noun.* E20.
[ORIGIN App. from BARRATOR with the idea of exchange.]
ELECTRICITY. A device consisting essentially of a fine wire with a high temperature coefficient of resistance, used esp. for current stabilization.

barricade /barɪˈkeɪd/ *noun.* L16.
[ORIGIN French, from *barrique* from Spanish *barrica* cask, from stem of *barril* BARREL *noun*: see -ADE. Cf. BARRICADO.]
1 A rampart constructed of barrels, stones, furniture, etc., set up across a street, esp. during revolutionary fighting or some other such civil disturbance; freq. (esp. in *pl.*) used allusively of the site of the final defences of a cause, movement, etc. L16.

> *fig.*: E. GLASGOW Would die upon the literary barricade of defending the noble proportions of 'War and Peace'.

man the barricades, **go to the barricades** oppose strongly or protest against a government or other institution or its policy.
2 Any barrier or defensive construction impeding passage. L16.
3 NAUTICAL (now *hist.*). A wooden fence built across the quarterdeck of a sailing man-of-war, barricaded to provide protection for those stationed there during an action. M18.

barricade /barɪˈkeɪd/ *verb trans.* L16.
[ORIGIN from the noun after French *barricader*.]
1 Block (a street etc.) with a barricade, obstruct, render impassable. L16.
2 Defend (a place, a person) as with a barricade. M17.
■ **barricading** *noun* (***a***) the action of the verb; (***b***) (the materials of) a barricade: L17.

barricado /barɪˈkeɪdəʊ/ *noun & verb. arch.* L16.
[ORIGIN formed as BARRICADE *noun*: see -ADO.]
▸ **A** *noun.* Pl. **-o(e)s**. = BARRICADE *noun*. L16.
▸ **B** *verb trans.* = BARRICADE *verb*. L16.

barrico /bəˈriːkəʊ/ *noun.* Pl. **-oes**. M16.
[ORIGIN Spanish *barrica* cask: see BARRICADE *noun* and cf. BARECA.]
A keg, a small barrel.

barrier /ˈbarɪə/ *noun & verb.* LME.
[ORIGIN Anglo-Norman *barrere*, Old French *barriere* from Proto-Romance formed as BAR *noun*[1]: see -IER.]
▸ **A** *noun.* **1** A palisade or stockade erected to defend a gate, passage, etc.; a fortification commanding an entrance. Now chiefly *hist.* LME.
2 *gen.* Any fence or railing barring advance or preventing access; a physical obstacle placed in the way. LME. ▸**b** The starting gate of a racecourse. E17. ▸**c** The point of access to a railway platform at which tickets must be shown. M20.

> **b** SHERWOOD ANDERSON Then when the barrier goes up he is off like his name, Sunstreak.

vapour barrier: see VAPOUR *noun*.
3 In *pl.* The martial exercise of sword-fighting across the central railing dividing a tournament ground (freq. in ***to fight at barriers***). Also, the palisades enclosing a tourney ground, the lists. *obsolete* exc. *hist.* L15.
4 Any physical, esp. natural, obstacle which prevents access or separates; *spec.* the mass of ice fringing the Antarctic coast. E18.
ISOLATING ***barrier***.
5 Anything abstract that obstructs, prevents communication, or separates. E18. ▸**b** PHYSICS. A state, region, or level of high potential energy which must be surmounted (or tunnelled through) for a given physical change to occur. E20.

> **b** J. A. WHEELER Odd nuclei have a higher barrier against fission than corresponding even nuclei.

sonic barrier, ***sound barrier***, ***thermal barrier***, etc. **b** SCHOTTKY ***barrier***.
– COMB.: **barrier cream** a cream to protect the skin from damage, infection, etc.; **barrier method** a method of contraception using a device or preparation which prevents live sperm from reaching an ovum; **barrier reef** a coral reef separated by a broad deep channel from the adjacent land.
▸ **B** *verb trans.* Close or shut with a barrier. M18.

barring /ˈbɑːrɪŋ/ *verbal noun.* LME.
[ORIGIN BAR *verb* + -ING[1].]
The action of BAR *verb*; marking with or dividing into bars.
– COMB.: **barring-out** (*obsolete* exc. *hist.*) a form of schoolboy rebellion in which a master was shut out of a classroom or school by his pupils.

barring /ˈbɑːrɪŋ/ *preposition.* L15.
[ORIGIN Use of pres. pple of BAR *verb* 6: see -ING[2]. Cf. BAR *preposition*.]
Excluding from consideration, except.

barrio /ˈbarɪəʊ/ *noun.* Pl. **-os**. M19.
[ORIGIN Spanish, perh. from Arabic]
A ward or quarter of a town or city in Spain and Spanish-speaking countries; a Spanish-speaking quarter of a US town or city.

barrique /bəˈriːk, *foreign* barik (*pl. same*)/ *noun.* L18.
[ORIGIN French = barrel, cask.]
A wine barrel; *spec.* a small cask of new oak in which Bordeaux and other wines are aged.

barrister /ˈbarɪstə/ *noun*[1]. LME.
[ORIGIN from BAR *noun*[1], perh. after LEGISTER or MINISTER *noun*.]
A lawyer who has been called to the bar, and has the right of representing clients in the higher courts (more fully ***barrister-at-law***); *US* any lawyer.
■ **barristerial** /barɪˈstɪərɪəl/ *adjective* of or pertaining to a barrister M19.

†**barrister** *noun*[2] see BANISTER.

barrow /ˈbarəʊ/ *noun*[1]. See also BERRY *noun*[2], BURROW *noun*[3]
[ORIGIN Old English *beorg* = Old Frisian, Old Saxon, Old High German (Dutch, German) *berg*, from Germanic. Cf. Old Norse *berg*, *bjarg* rock, precipice, Gothic *bairgahei* hill country.]
1 A mountain, a hill. *obsolete* exc. as forming a place name element. OE.
2 ARCHAEOLOGY. A grave mound or tumulus. OE.
round barrow: see ROUND *adjective*.
– COMB.: **barrow-wight** *pseudo-arch.* a guardian spirit believed to inhabit a grave mound.

barrow /ˈbarəʊ/ *noun*[2]. *obsolete* exc. *dial.*
[ORIGIN Old English *b(e)arg* = Old Frisian, Middle Dutch *barch* (Dutch *barg*), Old Saxon, Old High German *bar(u)g* (German dial. *Barch*), Old Norse *bǫrgr* from Germanic.]
A castrated boar.

barrow /ˈbarəʊ/ *noun*[3] & *verb*[1].
[ORIGIN Old English *bearwe* from Germanic, from base of BEAR *verb*[1]. Cf. BIER.]
▸ **A** *noun.* **1** A frame for loads etc. carried by two people; a stretcher, a bier. Now usu. more fully ***hand-barrow***. OE.
2 A shallow open box with shafts for pushing by hand and a wheel or wheels, for the transportation of loads; *spec.* (***a***) = WHEELBARROW *noun* 1; (***b***) a two-wheeled handcart used by a costermonger; (***c***) a metal frame with two wheels for transporting luggage etc. ME.
3 The quantity carried by a barrow; the contents of a barrow. LME.
– COMB.: **barrow boy** a costermonger.
▸ **B** *verb trans.* Wheel or transport in a barrow. *rare.* M16.
■ **barrowful** *noun* = BARROW *noun*[3] 3 L15.

barrow /ˈbarəʊ/ *verb*[2] *intrans. Austral. & NZ.* M20.
[ORIGIN Uncertain: cf. Irish, Gaelic *bearradh* shearing, clipping.]
Of a novice shearer or shedhand: complete the shearing of or partly shear a sheep for a shearer.

Barrowist /ˈbarəʊɪst/ *noun.* L16.
[ORIGIN from *Barrowe* (see below) + -IST.]
hist. A follower of (the beliefs of) Henry Barrowe, one of the founders of Congregationalism, executed in 1593 for nonconformity.

barrulet /ˈbarjʊlɪt/ *noun.* M16.
[ORIGIN Dim. of assumed Anglo-Norman dim. of French BARRE: see -ULE, -LET.]
HERALDRY. A narrow horizontal stripe, equal to the fourth part of a bar (see BAR *noun*[1] 5).

barruly /ˈbarjʊli/ *adjective.* M16.
[ORIGIN Anglo-Norman *barrulé*: see BARRULET, -Y[5].]
HERALDRY. Of a field: crossed by ten or more bars.

barry /ˈbɑːri/ *adjective.* L15.
[ORIGIN French *barré* barred, striped, from *barrer* BAR *verb*: see -Y[5].]
HERALDRY. Of a field: divided horizontally into equal parts by eight or fewer bars of alternating tinctures. (Foll. by *of* the number of parts.)

Barsac /ˈbɑːsak/ *noun.* E18.
[ORIGIN French (see below).]
A sweet white wine from the district of Barsac, department of Gironde, France.

B

barse /bɑːs/ *noun*. Long *dial*.
[ORIGIN Old English *bærs*, *bears* = Old Saxon *bars*, Middle Dutch *ba(e)rse*, Dutch *baars*, Middle High German *bars*, German *Barsch*: cf. BAR *noun*², BASS *noun*¹.]
A kind of fish, *esp*. a perch.

Bart /bɑːt/ *noun*. Also (esp. when following a name) **Bart.** (point). L18.
[ORIGIN Abbreviation.]
= BARONET.
– NOTE: *Baronet* is preferably abbreviated *Bt*.

†**Bartelemy** *noun* var. of BARTHOLOMEW.

barter /ˈbɑːtə/ *noun*. LME.
[ORIGIN from the verb.]
1 Traffic by exchange of goods. LME.
2 Goods to be bartered. M18.
3 *fig*. Exchange, interchange, (of blows, insults, talk, etc.). E19.

barter /ˈbɑːtə/ *verb*. LME.
[ORIGIN Prob. from Old French *barater*: see BARRATOR.]
1 *verb trans*. Exchange (goods or something intangible, *for* other goods etc.). LME. ▸**b** Foll. by *away*. Dispose of by barter, part with for a (usu. mercenary or unworthy) consideration. M17.

YEATS Barter gaze for gaze. L. VAN DER POST He . . replaced it with what he could buy, or barter, from Somalis. C. V. WEDGWOOD The Scots bartered him to the English Parliament in return for payment for their troops.

2 *verb intrans*. Trade by exchange. L15.

F. QUARLES With thy bastard bullion thou hast barter'd for wares of price. D. LIVINGSTONE We did not see much evidence of a wish to barter.

■ **barterable** *adjective* M19. **barterer** *noun* E17.

Barthian /ˈbɑːtɪən/ *adjective* & *noun*. E20.
[ORIGIN from *Barth* (see below) + -IAN.]
▸ **A** *adjective*. Of, pertaining to, or characteristic of the Swiss theologian Karl Barth (1886–1968) or his writings. E20.
▸ **B** *noun*. A follower of Barth. M20.

Bartholomew /bɑːˈθɒləmjuː/ *noun*. Also †**Bart(e)lemy**. LME.
[ORIGIN Name of the apostle, from ecclesiastical Latin *Bartholomaeus*, Greek *Bartholomaios* partly through French *Barthélemy*.]
1 ***Bartholomew-day***, ***Bartholomew-tide***, St Bartholomew's day, 24 August. *arch*. LME.
2 ***Bartholomew Fair***, a fair held at West Smithfield annually from 1133 to 1855 around St Bartholomew's day. ***Bartholomew pig*** etc., a pig etc. sold at this fair. *obsolete* exc. *hist*. L16.

bartizan /bɑːtɪˈzan/ *noun*. *obsolete* exc. *hist*. Also **-san**. M16.
[ORIGIN Scot. form of BRATTICING found esp. in 17 and reinterpreted E19 by Sir Walter Scott.]
A battlemented parapet at the top of a castle or church; *esp*. a battlemented turret projecting from an angle at the top of a tower.
■ **bartizaned** *adjective* having a bartizan or bartizans E19.

†**Bartlemy** *noun* var. of BARTHOLOMEW.

Bartlett /ˈbɑːtlɪt/ *noun*. Chiefly *N. Amer*. M19.
[ORIGIN Enoch *Bartlett* (1779–1860), US merchant who first distributed the pear in the US.]
More fully ***Bartlett pear***. = WILLIAMS *noun*¹.

barton /ˈbɑːt(ə)n/ *noun*.
[ORIGIN Old English *bere-tūn*, formed as BERE *noun*¹ + TOWN *noun*. Cf. BARN *noun*¹.]
†1 A threshing floor. Only in OE.
2 *hist*. A demesne farm; land on a manor not let to tenants but retained for the owner's use. ME.
3 A farmyard. *arch*. M16.
†4 A pen for poultry. M16–L18.

bartonellosis /bɑːtənɛˈləʊsɪs/ *noun*. Pl. **-loses** /-ˈləʊsiːz/. E20.
[ORIGIN from mod. Latin *Bartonella* (see below), from Alberto L. *Barton* (1871–1950), Peruvian physician: see -OSIS.]
MEDICINE. Infection with the micro-organism *Bartonella bacilliformis*, endemic in parts of S. America and manifested either as an acute febrile anaemia (also called ***Oroya fever***) or in wartlike eruptions of the skin (also called ***verruga peruana***). Cf. CARRION'S DISEASE.

bartsia /ˈbɑːtsɪə/ *noun*. M18.
[ORIGIN mod. Latin *Bartsia*, from Johann *Bartsch* (1709–38), Prussian physician and botanist: see -IA¹.]
A plant of the genus *Bartsia*, of the figwort family, or formerly included in this genus; *esp*. (more fully ***red bartsia***) *Odontites verna*, a common wayside weed bearing racemes of purplish-red flowers.

barwood /ˈbɑːwʊd/ *noun*. L18.
[ORIGIN Prob. from BAR *noun*¹ + WOOD *noun*¹.]
A hard red African wood, orig. that of the tree *Baphia nitida*, but now usu. padouk.

barycentric /barɪˈsɛntrɪk/ *adjective*. L19.
[ORIGIN from Greek *barus* heavy + -CENTRIC.]
Of or pertaining to the centre of gravity.
■ ˈ**barycentre** *noun* the centre of gravity E20.

baryon /ˈbarɪɒn/ *noun*. M20.
[ORIGIN formed as BARYCENTRIC + -ON.]
PARTICLE PHYSICS. Any of the heavier elementary particles (proton, neutron, and hyperons), which have half-integral spins and take part in the strong interaction.
■ **baryˈonic** *adjective* M20.

barysphere /ˈbarɪsfɪə/ *noun*. E20.
[ORIGIN formed as BARYCENTRIC + -SPHERE.]
The dense interior of the earth, under the lithosphere.

baryta /bəˈrʌɪtə/ *noun*. E19.
[ORIGIN from BARYTES after *soda* etc.]
Barium oxide or hydroxide.

baryte *noun* var. of BARITE.

barytes /bəˈrʌɪtiːz/ *noun*. Also **baryte**. L18.
[ORIGIN from Greek *barus* heavy + *-itēs* -ITE¹.]
†1 = BARYTA. L18–M19.
2 Native barium sulphate, occurring usu. as white or colourless tabular crystals; heavy spar. L18.
■ **barytic** /-ˈrɪ-/ *adjective* of, pertaining to, or containing baryta or barium L18.

baryton *noun* see BARITONE *noun* 2.

barytone /ˈbarɪtəʊn/ *noun*¹ & *adjective*¹. M17.
[ORIGIN Late Latin *barytonos* from Greek *barutonos* not oxytone: cf. BARITONE.]
GREEK GRAMMAR. (A word) not having the acute accent on the last syllable.

†**barytone** *noun*² & *adjective*² var. of BARITONE *noun* & *adjective*.

basal /ˈbeɪs(ə)l/ *adjective* & *noun*. E17.
[ORIGIN from BASE *noun*¹ + -AL¹.]
▸ **A** *adjective*. 1 Of, pertaining to, situated at, or forming a base. E17.
basal body a kinetosome. **basal cell** BIOLOGY & MEDICINE a cell located at or near the base of an organ or other structure; *spec*. any of the relatively undifferentiated cells that form the lowest layer of the epithelium, and from which more specialized cells are generated; ***basal-cell carcinoma***, a common type of skin cancer that originates in the basal cells of the epithelium or hair follicles. **basal ganglion** ANATOMY any of the ganglia situated at the base of the cerebrum, i.e. the lentiform, caudate, and amygdaloid nuclei. **basal metabolism**: of an organism completely at rest. **basal pinacoid plane**, **basal plane** CRYSTALLOGRAPHY a pinacoid intersecting the vertical axis.
2 *fig*. Fundamental. M19.
▸ **B** *noun*. Something pertaining to, forming part of, or situated at the base. E17.

basalt /ˈbasɔːlt, -(ə)lt; bəˈsɔːlt, -ˈsɒlt/ *noun*. Orig. in Latin form †**basaltes**. E17.
[ORIGIN Latin *basaltes* var. of *basanites* from Greek *basanitēs* (*lithos* stone), from *basanos* touchstone.]
GEOLOGY. A dark, fine-grained igneous rock, often displaying columnar structure and usu. composed largely of plagioclase with pyroxene and olivine.
■ **basaltic** /bəˈsɔːltɪk, -ˈsɒlt-/ *adjective* of, pertaining to, or consisting of basalt; of the nature of basalt: L18. **baˈsaltiform** *adjective* having the form of basalt L18.

basan /ˈbaz(ə)n/ *noun*. Also **bazan**. See also BASIL *noun*³. L15.
[ORIGIN Old French & mod. French *basane* from Provençal *bazana* from Spanish *badana* (cf. medieval Latin *bedana*, Anglo-Latin *basana*) from Arabic *biṭāna* (dressed sheepskin used as) lining.]
Sheepskin tanned in bark.

basanite /ˈbasənʌɪt/ *noun*. L18.
[ORIGIN Latin *basanites*: see BASALT, -ITE¹.]
A black form of jasper or quartzite, formerly used as a touchstone; GEOLOGY any basaltic rock consisting of calcic plagioclase, augite, olivine, and a feldspathoid.

bas bleu /bɑ blø/ *noun phr*. Pl. ***bas bleus*** (pronounced same). L18.
[ORIGIN French, translating from English.]
A bluestocking.

bascinet *noun* var. of BASINET.

bascule /ˈbaskjuːl/ *noun*. L17.
[ORIGIN French (earlier *bacule*) = see-saw, from stem of *battre* to beat + *cul* buttocks.]
A lever apparatus of which one end is raised when the other is lowered.
– COMB.: **bascule bridge** a type of bridge raised or lowered with a counterpoise.

base /beɪs/ *noun*¹. ME.
[ORIGIN Old French & mod. French, or directly from Latin BASIS.]
▸ **I** 1 The part of a column between the shaft and the pedestal or pavement; the pedestal of a statue. ME.

Nation They toppled the statue of Mussolini . . and inscribed a motto on its base.

2 *gen*. Something on which a thing stands or by which it is supported. LME. ▸**b** GEOMETRY. The line or surface of a plane or solid figure on which it is regarded as standing. L16. ▸**c** HERALDRY. The lower part of a shield. E17. ▸**d** BOTANY & ZOOLOGY. The extremity of a part or organ by which it is attached to the trunk or main part. M18. ▸**e** SURVEYING. A known line used as a geometrical basis for trigonometry. M19.

A. WILSON They passed the magnolia tree, around whose base lay the last fallen petals. J. IRVING There was a flat shelf at the base of the slope.

3 *fig*. A fundamental principle; a foundation. L15.

R. L. STEVENSON A man who has a few friends . . cannot forget on how precarious a base his happiness reposes. G. MURRAY That is my feeling, and there must be some base for it.

4 The principal ingredient, the fundamental element. L15.

J. C. OATES He brewed a special concoction of poison, with an arsenic base.

5 A starting point, goal line, or station in certain games; *esp*. in BASEBALL, each of the four stations that must be reached in turn when scoring a run. L17.

G. GREENE It was like that child's game when you . . are sent back to base to start again. C. POTOK Mr Galanter always began a ball game by putting me at second base.

6 CHEMISTRY. Any substance which is capable of combining with an acid to form a salt (including, but wider than, *alkali*). Also, in mod. use, any species capable of donating pairs of electrons or of accepting protons. E19. ▸**b** *spec*. in BIOCHEMISTRY. Any of the purine or pyrimidine groups present in nucleotides and nucleic acids. M20.
7 MATH. The number from whose various powers a system of counting, logarithms, etc., proceeds. E19.

T. LEHRER Base eight is just like base ten really—if you're missing two fingers.

8 A town, camp, harbour, airfield, etc., from which (esp. military) operations are conducted and where stores and supporting facilities are concentrated; a centre of operations, a headquarters. M19.

S. SASSOON He had been two years with a fighting battalion and was now down at the Base for good. N. MONSARRAT Malta was a base for bombers as well. M. ARNOLD-FORSTER Halsey's immediate objective was the Japanese air base at Munda. E. HEATH The YMCA hostel . . provided us with a base for the next few days.

9 GRAMMAR. A root or stem as the origin of a word or as the element from which a derivative is formed by affixation etc. M19.
10 The middle part of a transistor, between collector and emitter. M20.
11 A notional structure or entity conceived of as underlying some system of activity or operations; the resources etc. on which something draws or depends for its operation. Usu. with specifying word. M20.

Economist After its customer base, IBM's biggest asset is that $1 billion annual R&D budget.

database: see DATA.
▸ **II** 12 *sing*. & (usu.) in *pl*. A pleated skirt appended to a doublet, reaching from the waist to the knee; an imitation of this in mailed armour for man or horse. Also, the skirt of a woman's outer petticoat or robe. *obsolete* exc. *hist*. LME.
– PHRASES: **base on balls** BASEBALL a batter's advance to the first base when the pitcher has delivered four balls outside specified limits (see BALL *noun*¹ 2c). ***conjugate base***: see CONJUGATE *adjective*. **get to first base** *N. Amer. slang* achieve the first step towards one's objective. NAVAL ***base***. **off base** *N. Amer. slang* (**a**) mistaken; (**b**) unprepared, unawares. **off one's base** *US slang* mistaken. ***power base***: see POWER *noun*. ***Schiff base***, ***Schiff's base***: see SCHIFF. SEMIDINE ***base***. ***touch base***: see TOUCH *verb*.
– COMB.: **baseband** the waveband occupied by the modulating signals of a carrier wave, or of signals transmitted without a carrier wave; **baseboard** a board forming a base; *spec*. (*N. Amer.*) a skirting board; **base hit** BASEBALL a hit enabling the batter to reach a base safely; **base level** GEOLOGY a level representing a lower limit of erosion; **baseline** a starting line, a reference line; *esp*. (**a**) TYPOGRAPHY the imaginary straight line through the feet of most letters in a line of type; (**b**) the back line at each end of the court in tennis, badminton, etc.; (**c**) BASEBALL the line between bases which a runner must stay close to when running; **base load** the permanent minimum load that a power supply system is required to deliver; **baseman** BASEBALL a fielder stationed near the specified (*first*, *second*, or *third*) base; **base pair** BIOCHEMISTRY a pair of complementary bases, one in each strand of double-stranded nucleic acid, held together by a hydrogen bond; **base pay** = *basic pay* s.v. BASIC *adjective* 1b; **base rate** a standard minimum rate, esp. of interest charged or allowed by a bank (generally, or *US* in particular circumstances); **base-runner** BASEBALL a member of the batting team at a base or running between bases; **base-running** BASEBALL running between bases; **bases-loaded** *adjective* (BASEBALL) made or occurring with runners occupying the first, second, and third bases; **base station** (**a**) a relay located at the centre of any of the cells of a cellular telephone system; (**b**) a short-range transceiver which connects a cordless phone to the main telephone network; **base-stealer** BASEBALL a base-runner who advances to the next base when no hit or error has been made; **base-stealing** BASEBALL advancing to the next base when no hit or error has been made.

base /beɪs/ *noun*². LME.
[ORIGIN Prob. alt. of *bars*: see BAR *noun*¹ 11.]
More fully ***prisoner's base***. A chasing game played by two sides occupying distinct areas, the object being to catch and make prisoner any player from the other side running from his or her home area.
†**bid a person base** challenge a person to a chase in this game; *gen*. challenge.

†**base** *noun*³ var. of BASS *noun*².

†**base** *noun*[4] var. of **BASS** *noun*[1].

base /beɪs/ *adjective.* **LME.**
[**ORIGIN** Old French & mod. French *bas* from medieval Latin *bassus*, found in classical Latin as a cognomen.]
1 Low; of small height. *arch.* **LME.** ▸**b** In plant names: of low growth. **L16.**
2 Low-lying, esp. topographically or geographically. Now *rare* or *obsolete.* **LME.**
3 Of a sound: low, not loud; deep, bass. Now *rare* or *obsolete.* **LME.**
4 Of inferior quality, of little value; mean, poor, shabby, worthless; (of language) debased, not classical. **LME.** ▸**b** Of coin etc.: alloyed, counterfeit. **E16.**
5 *LAW.* Of feudal service, tenure, etc.: involving villeinage etc. rather than military service (*hist.*); later (of tenure etc.), held in fee simple subject to some qualification or limitation. **LME.**
6 Low in the social scale, plebeian; menial, degrading. *arch.* **L15.**
7 Reprehensibly cowardly, selfish, or mean; despicable. **M16.**

W. RALEIGH A most base piece of flatterie. H. BELLOC A few base contemporaries no older than ourselves, but cads. B. RUSSELL He has thoughts and feelings and impulses which may be wise or foolish, noble or base. J. BRAINE Underneath the rough exterior their hearts were as base as anyone's.

8 Low in the natural scale. *arch.* **M16.**

SHAKES. *A.Y.L.* Civet is of a baser birth than tar—the very uncleanly flux of a cat.

9 Illegitimate. *obsolete* exc. in ***baseborn*** below. **L16.**
– **SPECIAL COLLOCATIONS & COMB.:** **baseborn** *adjective* of low birth or (*arch.*) origin; illegitimate. **base metal**: not classified as noble or precious. **base-minded** *adjective* having a base mind, mean, despicable. ***base relief***: see **BAS-RELIEF.**
■ **basely** *adverb* **L15.** **baseness** *noun* **LME.**

base /beɪs/ *verb trans.* **L16.**
[**ORIGIN** from **BASE** *noun*[1].]
1 Make or act as a foundation for. *rare.* **L16.**

G. MACDONALD Great roots based the tree-columns.

2 Found, build, or construct (*up*)*on* a given base, build up *around* a base, (chiefly *fig.*); provide with a base; establish securely. Freq. in *pass.* **M19.**

F. RAPHAEL His pools forecasts were based entirely on what the experts said. E. J. HOWARD A whole set of false assumptions, based on sentiment, lust and . . nostalgia. *Scientific American* The roads were always carefully based and drained. *Listener* I doubt whether ten years from now this 'science-based' or technological university will be very different from any other. *Classic CD* The famous second movement . . is based around a *Ländler*.

3 Station or deploy *at* a particular place as centre of operations or headquarters, or *on* land, the sea, etc. Freq. in *pass.* **E20.**

E. F. NORTON No. 1 party was to . . remain based there for the purpose of getting the next camp on to the North Col. *New Scientist* United States bases in the Pacific were warned to expect a carrier-based air strike. D. FRASER The British Eastern fleet was based at Kalindini on the Kenyan coast.

baseball /ˈbeɪsbɔːl/ *noun.* **E19.**
[**ORIGIN** from **BASE** *noun*[1] + **BALL** *noun*[1].]
A team game played with a bat and ball, in which runs are scored by reaching a number of bases in turn; now *spec.* an American field game played by two teams of nine players, the object of which is for each batter to hit the ball delivered by the opponent's pitcher and then traverse a diamond-shaped circuit of four bases to score a run; a ball used in this game.
– **COMB.:** **baseball cap** a cotton cap of a kind originally worn by baseball players, with a large peak and an adjustable strap at the back.

base-court /ˈbeɪskɔːt/ *noun.* **L15.**
[**ORIGIN** French †*basse-court* (now *basse-cour*): see **BASE** *adjective* 2, **COURT** *noun*[1].]
hist. The lower or outer court of a castle, mansion, etc., usu. occupied by servants.

†**base dance** *noun phr.* see **BASSE DANSE.**

base jump /ˈbeɪs dʒʌmp/ *noun & verb phr.* Also **BASE jump.** **L20.**
[**ORIGIN** *base* from building, antenna-tower, span, earth (denoting the types of starting point used).]
▸ **A** *noun phr.* A parachute jump from a fixed point, typically a high building or promontory, rather than an aircraft.
▸ **B** *verb intrans.* Perform a base jump.
■ **base jumper** *noun* **L20.** **base jumping** *noun* **L20.**

baselard /ˈbasɪlɑːd/ *noun. obsolete* exc. *hist.* **LME.**
[**ORIGIN** Old French *baselard(e)* (more commonly *bazelaire, bad-*) = medieval Latin *baselardus, basi-*, etc., of unknown origin.]
A dagger or hanger, worn at the girdle.

baseless /ˈbeɪslɪs/ *adjective.* **E17.**
[**ORIGIN** from **BASE** *noun*[1] + **-LESS.**]
Without a base; groundless, unfounded.
■ **baselessly** *adverb* **E20.** **baselessness** *noun* **M19.**

basement /ˈbeɪsm(ə)nt/ *noun.* **M18.**
[**ORIGIN** Prob. from Dutch †*basement* foundation, in Western Flemish *bazement*, perh. from Italian *basamento* base of a column etc., from *basare* to base: see **-MENT.** Cf. Old French & mod. French *soubassement.*]
1 A storey of a building wholly or partially below ground level. **M18.**

attrib.: T. S. ELIOT They are rattling breakfast plates in basement kitchens. J. G. BENNETT My wife and I had found a small basement flat in Bayswater.

bargain basement: see **BARGAIN** *noun.*
2 The lowest or fundamental part of a structure; an underlying layer. **L18.** ▸**b** *GEOLOGY.* The oldest rocks underlying a given area; *spec.* an Archaean formation underlying identifiable strata. Freq. *attrib.* **M19.**

F. HOYLE When a glacier or ice sheet rests on a flat, slippery basement, such as sand or water, the ice can move more quickly at its base than at its surface.

– **COMB.:** **basement membrane** *ANATOMY* the thin delicate membrane separating the epithelium from underlying tissue.

basenji /bəˈsɛndʒi/ *noun.* **M20.**
[**ORIGIN** Bantu.]
A smallish hunting dog of a central African breed, which rarely barks.

base relief *noun* var. of **BAS-RELIEF.**

bases *nouns* pls. of **BASE** *noun*[1], **BASIS.**

bash /baʃ/ *noun.* **E19.**
[**ORIGIN** from **BASH** *verb*[2].]
1 A heavy blow. Orig. *Scot.* **E19.**

M. GEE Peg's injunction to 'give 'im a bash'.

2 A party, an entertainment; a drinking bout, a binge. *slang.* **E20.**

K. MILLETT We were invited to the big bash for Marjory Strider's opening. N. THORNBURG A party there . . a cocktail bash for the energy conference delegates.

3 An attempt, a go. *slang.* **M20.**

Times Tried some anti-rust oil? Worth a bash.

– **PHRASES:** **have a bash at** *slang* (**a**) strike a blow at; (**b**) make an attempt at. **on the bash** *slang* on a drinking bout.

bash /baʃ/ *verb*[1]. Long *obsolete* exc. *dial.* **LME.**
[**ORIGIN** Aphet. from **ABASH.**]
1 *verb trans.* Disconcert, dismay, abash. **LME.**
2 *verb intrans.* Be daunted; be abashed. **LME.**

bash /baʃ/ *verb*[2]. **M17.**
[**ORIGIN** Ult. imit.: perh. blend of *bang* and ending of *dash, smash*, etc.]
1 *verb trans.* Strike heavily; beat soundly (also foll. by *up*); smash *down* etc. with a heavy blow; injure by striking; *fig.* act or speak to the detriment of, criticize heavily. **M17.** ▸**b** Subject to some prolonged arduous activity. Usu. as verbal noun as 2nd elem. of a comb. with specifying word, as ***earbashing***, ***spud-bashing***, ***square-bashing***. *slang.* **M20.**

D. LESSING London's full of students rushing about bashing policemen. J. HERRIOT He had lifted a stone from the pasture and was bashing something with it. *fig.*: *Times* Voices in the Conservative Party arguing moderation rather than 'union bashing' in its approach to the closed shop.

2 *verb intrans.* Strike *at* heavily and repeatedly; work *at* crudely and persistently. **M19.**

J. B. PRIESTLEY It wasn't my kind of painting, and I just bashed away at it. J. RABAN Men were bashing at pavements with pickaxes and sledgehammers.

3 *verb intrans.* Carry *on* unheedingly. **M20.**
■ **basher** *noun* **L19.** **bashing** *noun* the action of the verb; an instance of this, a heavy beating: **M18.**

basha /ˈbaʃə/ *noun.* **E20.**
[**ORIGIN** Bengali.]
In SE Asia: a bamboo hut with a thatched roof.

†**bashalik** *noun* see **PASHALIC.**

bashaw /bəˈʃɔː/ *noun. arch.* **L15.**
[**ORIGIN** Var. of **PASHA.**]
1 = **PASHA.** **L15.**
2 *fig.* A grandee; a haughty imperious man. **L16.**
■ **bashawship** *noun* **L17.**

bashert /baˈʃəːt/ *noun.* **L20.**
[**ORIGIN** Yiddish = fate, destiny.]
In Jewish use: a person's soulmate or ideal marriage partner.

bashful /ˈbaʃfʊl, -f(ə)l/ *adjective.* **L15.**
[**ORIGIN** from **BASH** *verb*[1] + **-FUL.**]
†**1** Lacking self-possession; daunted. **L15–E18.**
2 Shy, diffident, modest; shamefaced, sheepish. **M16.**
■ **bashfully** *adverb* **M16.** **bashfulness** *noun* **M16.**

bashi-bazouk /ˌbaʃɪbəˈzuːk/ *noun.* **M19.**
[**ORIGIN** Turkish *başı bozuk* lit. 'wrong-headed', from *baş* head + *bozuk* out of order.]
hist. A mercenary of the Turkish irregulars, notorious for pillage and brutality.

Bashkir /baʃˈkɪə/ *noun & adjective.* **E19.**
[**ORIGIN** Russian from Turkic *Başkurt.*]
▸ **A** *noun.* Pl. **-s**, same.
1 A member of a Muslim people living in the southern Urals. **E19.**
2 The language of this people. **L19.**
▸ **B** *adjective.* Of or pertaining to the Bashkirs or their language. **M19.**

bashlik /ˈbaʃlɪk/ *noun.* **L19.**
[**ORIGIN** Russian *bashlyk* from Turkic.]
A kind of hood with long side pieces, worn orig. by Russians as protection against the weather.

bashment /ˈbaʃmənt/ *noun.* **L20.**
[**ORIGIN** Prob. from **BASH** *noun* + **-MENT.**]
1 *W. Indian.* A large party or dance. **L20.**
2 An uptempo style of popular music derived from dancehall and ragga. **L20.**

basho /ˈbaʃəʊ/ *noun.* Pl. same, **-os.** **L20.**
[**ORIGIN** Japanese.]
A sumo wrestling tournament.

basi- /ˈbeɪsi/ *combining form* of **BASE** *noun*[1], **BASIS** *noun*: see **-I-.**
■ **basiˈbranchial** *adjective* (*ZOOLOGY*) of, pertaining to, or forming, the base of the branchial arch (in fishes) **L19.** **basiˈcranial** *adjective* (*ANATOMY*) of, pertaining to, or forming, the base of the cranium **M19.** **basifixed** *adjective* (*BOTANY*) (of an anther) attached to its filament by the base **L19.** **basifugal** /beɪˈsɪfjʊg(ə)l/ *adjective* (*BOTANY*) tending away from the base **L19.** **baˈsifugally** *adverb* (*BOTANY*) in a basifugal manner, away from the base **L19.** **basilect** /ˈbasɪlɛkt, ˈbeɪsɪ-/ *noun* [**-LECT**] *LINGUISTICS* the dialect or variety of any language with the lowest prestige **M20.** **basilectal** /basɪˈlɛkt(ə)l, beɪsɪ-/ *adjective* (*LINGUISTICS*) of, pertaining to, or characteristic of the basilect **L20.** **basiocˈcipital** *adjective* (*ANATOMY*) of, pertaining to, or forming, the base of the occiput **M19.** **basipetal** /beɪˈsɪpɪt(ə)l/ *adjective* (*BOTANY*) developing from the apex towards the base **M19.** **baˈsipetally** *adverb* (*BOTANY*) in a basipetal manner, from the apex towards the base **M20.** **basiˈsphenoid** *adjective & noun* (*ANATOMY & ZOOLOGY*) (forming or pertaining to) a bone of the floor of the cranium (in the human skull, the hind part of the sphenoid bone) **M19.**

BASIC /ˈbeɪsɪk/ *noun*[1]. Also **Basic.** **M20.**
[**ORIGIN** Acronym, from Beginners' All-purpose Symbolic Instruction Code, after **BASIC** *adjective.*]
The name of a high-level programming language designed for easy learning.

basic /ˈbeɪsɪk/ *adjective & noun*[2]. **M19.**
[**ORIGIN** from **BASE** *noun*[1] + **-IC.**]
▸ **A** *adjective.* **1** Of, pertaining to, or forming a base; fundamental, essential. **M19.** ▸**b** Constituting a minimum, esp. in a standardized scale (of wages, prices, etc.); at the lowest acceptable level. **E20.**

A. J. CRONIN In his complete severance from tradition he has lost sight of the basic principles of proportion. E. ROOSEVELT The basic food of the people is rice for every meal. J. IRVING He felt a need, almost as basic as survival, to find something he could finish. **b** *New York Times* Most offer basic accommodations (many don't have electricity or hot water).

Basic English a simplified form of English with a select vocabulary of 850 words, for international use. **basic industry** an industry of great economic importance. **b basic pay** a standard rate of pay exclusive of extra payments, overtime, and allowances.
2 a *CHEMISTRY.* Having the properties of a base; derived from or characteristic of a base. **M19.** ▸**b** *GEOLOGY.* Of an igneous rock: having a relatively low silica content. **L19.** ▸**c** *METALLURGY.* Pertaining to, resulting from, or designating steel-making processes involving lime-rich refractories and slags. **L19.**
basic dye a dye which is a salt of a coloured organic base. **basic salt** a salt formed by incomplete neutralization of a base. **basic slag** phosphate-rich slag from basic steel-making, freq. used as a fertilizer. **c basic oxygen process** a steel-making process in which a jet of oxygen is delivered on to molten iron in a retort lined with a heat-resistant substance, burning away excess carbon and producing enough heat to keep the iron molten while oxidized impurities are removed as gases or slag.
▸ **B** *noun.* Something basic, esp. basic pay; (**B-**) Basic English; in *pl.*, essentials, fundamental aspects. **M20.**

A. HACKNEY There's a job in Stores and Packing. Hundred and eighty-nine shillings basic. *Times* The Commission should ignore the grander politics and concentrate on the basics.

back to basics (a catchphrase calling for) a return to fundamental principles, esp. in education.
– **NOTE:** In techn. senses opp. **ACID** *adjective.*
■ **basically** *adverb* (**a**) fundamentally, essentially, in sum; (**b**) (esp. modifying a sentence) actually, in fact: **E20.**

basicity /beɪˈsɪsɪti/ *noun.* **M19.**
[**ORIGIN** from **BASIC** *adjective* + **-ITY.**]
Chiefly *CHEMISTRY.* **1** The number of hydrogen atoms replaceable by a base in a particular acid. **M19.**
2 Basic character or condition. **L19.**

basidiomycete /bəˌsɪdɪəˈmʌɪsiːt/ *noun.* Orig. only in pl. **-mycetes** /-ˈmʌɪsiːts, -mʌɪˈsiːtiːz/. **L19.**
[**ORIGIN** Anglicized sing. of mod. Latin *Basidiomycetes* (see below), formed as **BASIDIUM** + **-O-** + Greek *mukētes* pl. of *mukēs* fungus.]
MYCOLOGY. A fungus of the subdivision Basidiomycotina (formerly the class Basidiomycetes), which includes the agarics.
■ **basidiomyˈcetous** *adjective* **L19.**

B

basidium /bəˈsɪdɪəm/ *noun*. Pl. **-dia** /-dɪə/. **M19**.
[ORIGIN mod. Latin, from Greek BASIS: see -IDIUM.]
BOTANY. A club-shaped spore-bearing structure produced by a basidiomycete.
■ **basidiocarp** *noun* a fruiting body which bears basidia **M20**. **basidiospore** *noun* a spore produced by a basidium. **M19**.

basil /ˈbaz(ə)l, -zɪl/ *noun*[1]. **LME**.
[ORIGIN Old French *basile* from medieval Latin *basilicum* from Greek *basilikon*: see BASILICON.]
1 A shrubby aromatic labiate herb of the genus *Ocimum*; esp. *O. basilicum* (more fully ***sweet basil***) and *O. minimum* (more fully ***bush basil***), having culinary use; (in the Indian subcontinent) *O. sanctum* (more fully ***holy basil***), sacred to Hindus. Also, the dried leaves of such a herb, used as flavouring. **LME**.
2 In full ***wild basil***. An aromatic labiate herb, *Clinopodium vulgare*, of hedges and scrub. **M16**.
– COMB.: **basil thyme** a small aromatic labiate herb, *Clinopodium acinos*, of dry arable land.

basil /ˈbaz(ə)l, -zɪl/ *noun*[2]. Now *rare* or *obsolete*. **M16**.
[ORIGIN Old French *basile* basilisk.]
†**1** = BASILISK 2. Only in **M16**.
2 A prisoner's ankle iron. **L16**.

basil /ˈbaz(ə)l, -zɪl/ *noun*[3]. Also **bazil**. **E17**.
[ORIGIN App. var. of BASAN.]
= BASAN.

basil *noun*[4] *& verb* var. of BEZEL.

basilar /ˈbasɪlə/ *adjective*. **M16**.
[ORIGIN mod. Latin *basilaris*, irreg. from Latin BASIS: see -AR[1].]
Of, pertaining to, or situated at the base, esp. of the skull.
basilar membrane a membrane in the cochlea of the ear, bearing sensory cells.
■ **basilary** *adjective* = BASILAR **E19**.

Basilian /bəˈzɪlɪən/ *adjective*. **L18**.
[ORIGIN from Latin *Basilius* Basil (see below) + -AN.]
Of or pertaining to St Basil the Great (*c* 330–79), Bishop of Caesarea, or the order of monks and nuns following his monastic rule.

basilic /bəˈsɪlɪk/ *noun*. **E18**.
[ORIGIN French *basilique* or its source Latin BASILICA.]
†**1** = BASILICA 1, 2. **E18–M19**.
2 In *pl.* = BASILICA 4. **M18**.

basilic /bəˈsɪlɪk/ *adjective*. **LME**.
[ORIGIN Old French & mod. French *basilique* or its source Latin *basilicus* from Greek *basilikos* royal: see -IC.]
1 *ANATOMY*. ***basilic vein***, the large superficial vein of either arm. **LME**.
2 Kingly, royal. *rare*. **E17**.
■ **basilical** *adjective*[1] †(*a*) = BASILIC *adjective* 1; (*b*) = BASILIC *adjective* 2: **M17**.

basilica /bəˈsɪlɪkə, -ˈzɪl-/ *noun*. **M16**.
[ORIGIN Latin: branch I lit. 'royal palace' from Greek *basilikē* use as noun of fem. of *basilikos* royal, from *basileus* king; branch II from Greek *basilika* neut. pl. of *basilikos*.]
► **I** *sing.* (pl. **-cas**, (*rare*) **-cae** /-kiː/).
1 *hist.* A large oblong hall or building, with double colonnades and a semicircular apse, used for courts of law and public assemblies. **M16**.
2 A building of this form used as a Christian church. Also, used as the title of certain churches granted privileges by the Pope. **M16**.
†**3** *ANATOMY*. The basilic vein (see BASILIC *adjective* 1). **L16–M18**.
► **II** *pl.* **4** *hist.* (**B-**.) *The* 9th-cent. Byzantine legal code initiated by the emperor Basil I. **M17**.
■ **basilical** *adjective*[2] = BASILICAN **E17**. **basilican** *adjective* of, pertaining to, or resembling a basilica **L18**.

†**basilicon** *noun*. Also **-cum**. **LME**.
[ORIGIN Latin *basilicum* or Greek *basilikon* use as noun of neut. of *basilikos*: see BASILICA.]
1 = BASIL *noun*[1]. **LME–L15**.
2 Any of several ointments supposed to possess sovereign virtues. **LME–L18**.

Basilidian /basɪˈlɪdɪən/ *noun & adjective*. *hist.* **L16**.
[ORIGIN from Latin *Basilides* (see below), Greek *Basileidēs* + -IAN.]
► **A** *noun*. A disciple or follower of Basilides, a 2nd-cent. Alexandrian Gnostic. **L16**.
► **B** *adjective*. Of or pertaining to Basilides or his followers. **L19**.

basilisk /ˈbazɪlɪsk/ *noun & adjective*. **LME**.
[ORIGIN Latin *basiliscus* from Greek *basiliskos* kinglet, kind of serpent, goldcrest, dim. of *basileus* king.]
► **A** *noun*. Also (after Spanish) †**-lisco**, (after Latin) †**-liscus**.
1 A fabulous reptile, whose gaze or breath is fatal, hatched by a serpent from a cock's egg (= COCKATRICE 1); *HERALDRY* = COCKATRICE 1b. **LME**.
2 *fig.* A person who casts a malicious look; a person or thing with a destructive influence. **L15**.

C. BURNEY Satire . . becomes a basilisk in the hands of a man . . who employs it to blast the reputation of another.

3 A large brass cannon. **E16**.
4 A small tropical American iguanid lizard of the genus *Basiliscus*, having a prominent crest. **E19**.
► **B** *attrib.* or as *adjective*. Of a glance, eye, etc.: malicious, casting an evil influence. **L15**.

G. W. KNIGHT Fixed by the basilisk eye of a nameless terror.

basin /ˈbeɪs(ə)n/ *noun*. Also (*arch.*) **bason**. **ME**.
[ORIGIN Old French *bacin* (mod. *bassin*) from medieval Latin *ba(s)cinus*, from *bacca* water-container, perh. from Gaulish.]
1 A circular vessel of greater width than depth, esp. for holding water, a bowl, a dish; a fixed shallow open container for water for washing etc. **ME**. ▸**b** The quantity held by a basin; a basinful. **LME**.

E. HEMINGWAY They were all eating, holding their chins close over the basin. J. CHEEVER The noise of the fountains whose basins were disfigured and cracked. **b** H. ALLEN He set the example by pouring himself a large basin of tea.

washbasin: see WASH *verb*.
†**2** A cymbal or other metal dish struck or clashed to produce sound. **ME–E17**.
†**3** *ANATOMY*. = PELVIS 1, 2. Only in **18**.
4 A hollow depression containing water; a landlocked harbour or bay; a large submarine depression. **E18**.

WORDSWORTH And in a basin black and small Receives a lofty waterfall. H. D. THOREAU The harbour of Quebec . . a basin two miles across. R. K. NARAYAN The villagers had made an artificial basin in sand and . . fetched water from distant wells and filled it. N. CALDER The ocean basins were known to be very deep and to constitute huge depressions in the Earth.

5 A dock with floodgates to maintain the water level; a widened part of a canal or river with wharves. **E18**.
tidal basin: see TIDAL *adjective*.
6 A circular or oval valley or natural depression; *spec.* (*a*) the tract of country drained by a river, or which drains into a lake or sea; (*b*) a circumscribed geological formation in which the strata dip inwards to the centre. **E19**.

A. P. STANLEY The traveller finds himself in a wide basin encircled by hills. L. D. STAMP The Thames breaks into the basin . . by . . Goring Gap. *Encycl. Brit.* The Amazon . . is . . the largest river in the world in volume and in area of its drainage basin.

■ **basinful** *noun* as much as a basin will hold; the contents of a basin; *colloq.* an excessive amount, a lot: **L18**.

basinet /ˈbasɪnɪt/ *noun*. Also **bascinet**, **basnet** /ˈbasnɪt/. **ME**.
[ORIGIN Old French *bacinet* dim. of *bacin* BASIN: see -ET[1].]
hist. A light steel helmet usu. with a visor.

basis /ˈbeɪsɪs/ *noun*. Pl. **bases** /ˈbeɪsiːz/. **L16**.
[ORIGIN Latin from Greek = stepping. Cf. BASE *noun*[1].]
1 The base or bottom of something material; the foundation; a pedestal. *arch.* **L16**. ▸**b** *BOTANY & ZOOLOGY*. = BASE *noun*[1] 2d. **E17**.

SHAKES. *Temp.* To th' shore, that o'er his wave-worn basis bowed, As stooping to relieve him. ADDISON Observing an English inscription upon the basis.

†**2** *GEOMETRY*. = BASE *noun*[1] 2b. **L16–M18**.
3 The main constituent. **E17**.

JABEZ HOGG Colouring-solutions should be always prepared with glycerine . . as a basis.

4 A thing by or on which anything abstract is supported or sustained. **E17**.

SHAKES. *Macb.* Great tyranny, lay thou thy basis sure. J. TYNDALL This speculation . . rested upon a basis of conjecture.

5 A thing on which anything is constructed and by which its constitution or operation is determined; a footing (of a specified kind); a determining principle; a set of underlying or agreed principles. **E17**.

JOHN BRIGHT It is necessary therefore to have a basis for our discussion. J. GALSWORTHY She believed . . in putting things on a commercial basis.

on the basis of using as a criterion or a principle of action; taking account of.
6 = BASE *noun*[1] 8. *arch.* **M19**.
– COMB.: **basis point** *FINANCE* the smallest unit in which a rate or value (esp. an interest rate) is expressed (usu. equal to one-hundredth of one per cent).

bask /bɑːsk/ *adjective*. *dial.* **ME**.
[ORIGIN Old Norse *beisk*.]
Bitter, acrid.

bask /bɑːsk/ *verb & noun*. **LME**.
[ORIGIN Uncertain, perh. from Old Norse precursor of *baðast* refl. of *baða* BATHE *verb*.]
► **A** *verb*. †**1** *verb intrans.* & *refl.* Bathe; *fig.* swim in blood. **LME–M16**.
2 *verb trans.* (usu. *refl.*). Expose to a flood of warmth, esp. sunshine. **E17**.

MILTON The lubbar fiend . . Basks at the fire his hairy strength. R. DAHL Do you like to swim and to bask yourself in the sun?

3 *verb intrans.* Disport oneself or revel in warmth and light, esp. of the sun, a fire, or *fig.* of love, favour, pleasant feelings. **M17**.

J. GALSWORTHY The sun now only reached the wall at the end, whereon basked a crouching cat. *fig.*: E. A. FREEMAN Traitors basking in the royal smiles. D. HALBERSTAM Everyone wanted to talk to him, to sit next to him at dinner, to bask in the excitement and originality of his mind. P. P. READ He basked in the confident feeling that should he want them they were his for the taking.

basking shark a very large plankton-eating shark, *Cetorhinus maximus*, which habitually lies near the sea surface.
► **B** *noun*. A spell of basking; radiance etc. in which one basks. **M18**.

Baskerville /ˈbaskəvɪl/ *noun*. **E19**.
[ORIGIN See below.]
TYPOGRAPHY. A typeface modelled on that designed by John Baskerville (1706–75), English type founder and printer; a book printed by Baskerville.

basket /ˈbɑːskɪt/ *noun*. **ME**.
[ORIGIN In Anglo-Latin *baskettum*, Anglo-Norman & Old French *basket*, of unknown origin.]
1 A container made of plaited or interwoven osiers, cane, rushes, wire, etc. **ME**. ▸**b** *spec.* Such a container regarded as the model of daily or charitable provisions; alms. **M16**.
bread basket, ***clothes basket***, ***fruit basket***, ***wastebasket***, ***work basket***, etc. ***hanging basket***: see HANGING *adjective*. **in the basket** (of a dish of (esp. fried) food) served in a small basket lined with paper etc., not on a plate. ***waste-paper basket***: see WASTE *noun*.
2 A basketful. **LME**.
3 Chiefly *hist.* The overhanging back compartment on the outside of a stagecoach. **L18**.
4 A structure suspended from the envelope of a balloon for carrying crew, ballast, etc. **L18**.
5 A net fixed on a ring (or orig. a basket) used as a goal in basketball; a goal scored in basketball. **L19**.
6 *fig.* A group, category; a range. **E20**.

HUGH WALPOLE Semyonov at this time flung Nikitin, Andrew Vassilievitch, Trenchard and myself into one basket. We were all 'crazy romantics'. *Times* Sterling's effective devaluation against a basket of other currencies rose to 43.6 per cent.

7 *euphem.* = BASTARD *noun*. *colloq.* **M20**.

N. COWARD Come on, Johnnie—don't argue with the poor little basket.

– COMB.: **basket-boat** a boat of basketwork; **basket case** *colloq.* (*offensive*) a person who has lost both arms and both legs; *fig.* a completely helpless person, a nervous wreck, a bankrupt country; **basket chair** a wickerwork chair; **basket clause**: of a comprehensive nature; **basket fish** a brittlestar having branched arms; **basket hilt** a sword hilt with a guard resembling basketwork; **basket-hilted** *adjective* having a basket hilt; **basket maker** a person who makes baskets; *spec.* in *ARCHAEOLOGY* (with cap. initials) used *attrib.* to designate an ancient culture in the south-western US characterized by basketwork; **basket meal**: served 'in the basket' (see sense 1 above); **basket star** = ***basket fish*** above; **basket weave** a style of weave whose pattern resembles basketwork; **basket-woman**: carrying goods for sale in a basket; **basketwork** (the art of making) a structure of interwoven osiers etc.
■ **basketful** *noun* the content of a basket **ME**. **basketing** *noun* basketwork **E17**. **basketry** *noun* basketwork **M19**.

basket /ˈbɑːskɪt/ *verb trans.* **L16**.
[ORIGIN from the noun.]
1 Put into, or hang up in, a basket. **L16**.
2 Throw into the waste-paper basket; discard, reject. **E19**.

basketball /ˈbɑːskɪtbɔːl/ *noun*. **L19**.
[ORIGIN from BASKET *noun* + BALL *noun*[1].]
A game for two teams of five players, the object of which is to toss a large inflated ball through the opponent's goal, a net fixed on a ring mounted on a board ten feet above the ground at either end of the court of play, and in which players may throw the ball to each other or advance bouncing it but not run or walk with the ball in their hands; the ball used in this.

Baskish *noun & adjective* var. of BASQUISH.

basmati /basˈmɑːti, -z-/ *noun*. **M19**.
[ORIGIN Hindi *bāsmatī* lit. 'fragrant'.]
More fully ***basmati rice***. A kind of rice with very long thin grains and a delicate fragrance.

basnet *noun* var. of BASINET.

bason /ˈbeɪs(ə)n/ *noun*[1] *& verb*. **E18**.
[ORIGIN Unknown.]
HAT-MAKING (chiefly *hist.*).
► **A** *noun*. A bench with a hot plate, on which to harden felt. **E18**.
► **B** *verb trans.* Harden the felt of (a hat) on a bason. **E18**.

bason *noun*[2] see BASIN.

basophil /ˈbeɪsəfɪl/ *adjective & noun*. Also **-phile** /-fʌɪl/. **L19**.
[ORIGIN from Greek BASIS + -O- + -PHIL.]
BIOLOGY. ► **A** *adjective*. Readily stained by basic dyes; esp. in ***basophil cell***, a kind of granulocyte having this property. **L19**.
► **B** *noun*. A basophil cell. **E20**.
■ **basoˈphilia** *noun* affinity for basic dyes; the presence of abnormally large numbers of basophil cells in the blood: **E20**. **basoˈphilic** *adjective* basophil; pertaining to or displaying basophilia: **L19**.

Basotho /bəˈsuːtuː/ *noun & adjective*. Also (earlier, now *arch.* or *hist.*) **Basuto**. **M19**.
[ORIGIN Sesotho, from *ba-* pl. prefix + SOTHO.]
► **A** *noun*. **1** (*erron.*) *sing.* Pl. **-os**. A member of the Sotho people, (*sing.*) a Mosotho. **M19**.
2 *pl.* (Members of) the Sotho people. **L19**.
► **B** *attrib.* or as *adjective*. = SOTHO *adjective*. **M19**.

Basque /bask, bɑːsk/ *adjective & noun.* In sense B.3 usu. **b-**. **E19.**
[ORIGIN French from Latin *Vasco*: cf. GASCON.]
▸ **A** *adjective.* Of or pertaining to an ancient people inhabiting both slopes of the western Pyrenees, adjacent to the Bay of Biscay, or their non-Indo-European language. **E19.**
Basque beret, **Basque cap** a beret as traditionally worn by Basque peasants. ***Saut Basque***: see SAUT 1.
▸ **B** *noun.* **1** A native or inhabitant of the Pyrenees area adjacent to the Bay of Biscay; a member of the Basque people. **M19.**
2 The Basque language. **M19.**
PAS de basque.
3 A short continuation of a doublet, waistcoat or bodice below the waist; a bodice having this. **M19.**
■ **basqued** *adjective* having a basque (sense 3) **L19.**

basquine /baˈskiːn, bɑː-/ *noun.* Also **-ina** /-iːnə/, **-iña** /-iːnjə/. **E19.**
[ORIGIN (French, from) Spanish *basquiña*, from *basco* Basque.]
1 An ornamented outer skirt worn by Basque and Spanish women. **E19.**
2 A type of jacket having a basque. **M19.**

Basquish /ˈbaskɪʃ, ˈbɑːsk-/ *noun & adjective.* Also **Baskish**. **E17.**
[ORIGIN formed as BASQUE + -ISH[1].]
(Of or pertaining to) the Basque language.

bas-relief /ˈbasrɪliːf, ˈbɑː(s)-/ *noun.* Also **bass-relief**, †**base relief**. **E17.**
[ORIGIN Italian *basso-rilievo* (see BASSO-RELIEVO), assim. to French.]
(A sculpture, moulding, carving, etc., in) low relief (see RELIEF *noun*[2]).

bass /bas/ *noun*[1]. Also **basse**, †**base**. Pl. **-es** /-ɪz/, (usu.) same. **LME.**
[ORIGIN Alt. of BARSE.]
The common perch; any of numerous spiny-finned freshwater and marine percoid fishes related to or resembling the common perch; *esp.* a European marine fish, *Dicentrarchus labrax*.
black bass, largemouth bass, striped bass, white bass, etc.

bass /beɪs/ *noun*[2]. Also †**base**. **LME.**
[ORIGIN from BASE *adjective*, BASS *adjective*.]
1 The lowest part in harmonized musical composition; the deepest male voice, or the lowest tones of an instrument or group of similar instruments, which sound this part. **LME.**
figured bass = THOROUGH BASS. ***fundamental bass***: see FUNDAMENTAL *adjective*. ***ground bass***: see GROUND *noun*. THOROUGH BASS. ***walking bass***: see WALKING *ppl adjective*.
2 An instrument, string, etc., having such a part or compass; *spec.* a double bass or bass guitar. **M16.**
DOUBLE BASS.
3 A singer having a bass voice; a bass player. **L16.**
4 The low-frequency component of transmitted or reproduced sound. **M20.**

attrib.: *Which?* Treble and bass controls are good enough, but you can also get a graphic equaliser.

– COMB.: **bass-bar** a strip of wood glued inside the table of a stringed instrument along the line of the lowest string, to support the left foot of the bridge; **bassman** (chiefly JAZZ) = BASSIST (b). (See also combs. of BASS *adjective*, with which attrib. uses of the noun sometimes merge.)
■ **bassist** *noun* (*a*) *rare* a bass singer; (*b*) a person who plays a bass instrument, esp. a double bass or bass guitar: **L19.**

†**bass** *noun*[3]. **LME–L16.**
[ORIGIN Prob. from BASS *verb*[1] (though recorded earlier). Cf. BUSS *noun*[2].]
A kiss.

bass /bas/ *noun*[4]. **L17.**
[ORIGIN Alt. of BAST *noun*.]
1 A fibre obtained from certain palm trees or (orig.) from the inner bark of the lime or linden. **L17.**
2 An article made of this. **E18.**
– COMB.: **basswood** (the wood of) the American lime or linden, *Tilia americana*.

bass /bas/ *noun*[5]. **L17.**
[ORIGIN Perh. for *bas-* or *base-coal*, as in *base coin* (BASE *adjective* 4b).]
MINING. Carbonaceous shale.

bass /beɪs/ *adjective.* **LME.**
[ORIGIN from BASE *adjective*, assim. to Italian BASSO.]
†**1** Low in sound, soft. **LME–E16.**
2 Deep-sounding, low in the musical scale; of, pertaining to, or suited to the bass (BASS *noun*[2]); lowest-pitched (in a series of similar instruments or strings). **E16.**
– COMB. (partly attrib. uses of BASS *noun*[2]): **bass-baritone** *noun & adjective* (designating) a voice higher than bass, yet of bass and not tenor quality; a singer having such a voice; **bass clef**: placing F below middle C on the second highest line of the stave; **bass drum** a large drum of indefinite low pitch; **bass-horn** an early instrument made in the shape of a bassoon but much deeper in its tones; **bass viol** (*a*) a viola da gamba for playing the bass part in older concerted music; (*b*) US a double bass.

†**bass** *verb*[1] *trans. & intrans.* **L15–L16.**
[ORIGIN Prob. from Old French & mod. French *baiser* from Latin *basiare*.]
Kiss.

†**bass** *verb*[2] *trans. rare* (Shakes.). Only in **E17.**
[ORIGIN from BASS *noun*[2].]
Utter with bass sound.

bass-ackwards /basˈakwədz/ *adverb & adjective. N. Amer. slang. joc.* Also **bass-ackward**. **M20.**
[ORIGIN Alt.]
=ASS-BACKWARDS.

bassarid /ˈbasərɪd/ *noun.* **M19.**
[ORIGIN Latin *Bassarid-*, *-aris*, from Greek *Bassaris* Thracian bacchanal, lit. 'fox' (prob. from the dress of fox-skins).]
A Thracian bacchanal; a Bacchante.

basse *noun* var. of BASS *noun*[1].

basse dance *noun phr.* see BASSE DANSE.

basse danse /bas dɑ̃ːs/ *noun phr.* Pl. **-s -s** (pronounced same). Also **basse dance**. Orig. fully anglicized as †**base dance**. **E16.**
[ORIGIN French = low dance.]
hist. A slow stately dance; *spec.* a court dance in duple or triple time which originated in France in the 15th cent.

basset /ˈbasɪt/ *noun*[1]. **M16.**
[ORIGIN Unknown.]
The edge of a geological stratum exposed at the surface; an outcrop. Freq. *attrib.*

basset /ˈbasɪt/ *noun*[2]. **E17.**
[ORIGIN French, from *bas* low: see -ET[1].]
A short-legged, long-bodied hound with long drooping ears, used for hunting hares. Also ***basset hound***.

basset /ˈbasɪt/ *noun*[3]. *obsolete* exc. *hist.* Also **-ette**. **M17.**
[ORIGIN French *bassette* from Italian *bassetta* fem. of BASSETTO.]
A card game from which faro originated.

basset /ˈbasɪt/ *verb intrans.* **L17.**
[ORIGIN from BASSET *noun*[1].]
Of the edge of a geological stratum: be exposed at the surface, crop out.

basse-taille /bastɑːj/ *noun.* **L19.**
[ORIGIN French, from *basse* fem. of *bas* low (see BASE *adjective*) + *taille* cut.]
A technique of applying translucent enamels to metal reliefs so that the shade of the enamel is darkest where the relief is most deeply cut.

basset-horn /ˈbasɪthɔːn/ *noun.* **M19.**
[ORIGIN German, partial translation of French *cor de basset* from Italian *corno di bassetto* (*corno* horn, *di* of, BASSETTO.]
A tenor clarinet with extended compass.

bassette *noun* var. of BASSET *noun*[3].

bassetto /bəˈsɛtəʊ/ *noun.* Pl. **-os**. **E18.**
[ORIGIN Italian, dim. of BASSO.]
A violoncello.

bassi *noun* pl. of BASSO, BASSUS *nouns*.

bassinet /basɪˈnɛt/ *noun.* Also **-ette**. **L16.**
[ORIGIN French, dim. of *bassin* BASIN: see -ET[1].]
†**1** A marsh marigold; a geranium, a ranunculus. **L16–E18.**
2 A hooded wicker cradle or pram. **M19.**

basso /ˈbasəʊ/ *noun & adjective.* Pl. **bassos**, **bassi** /ˈbasi/. **E18.**
[ORIGIN Italian = low from Latin *bassus*: see BASE *adjective*. Earlier in English in BASSO-RELIEVO.]
MUSIC. = BASS *noun*[2] (esp. sense 3), *adjective*.
– COMB. & SPECIAL COLLOCATIONS: **basso buffo** /ˈbʊfəʊ/, pl. **bassi buffi** /-fi/, **basso buffos**, [BUFFO] a bass singer who takes comic parts in opera; **basso cantante** /kanˈtanteɪ/, pl. **bassi cantanti** /-ti/, [lit. 'singing'] (a singer with) a voice in the upper register of the bass range; **basso continuo** /kənˈtɪnjʊəʊ/, pl. **basso continuos**, [CONTINUO] a figured bass, a thorough bass; **basso ostinato** /ɒstɪˈnɑːtəʊ/, pl. **basso ostinatos**, [OSTINATO] = ***ground bass*** s.v. GROUND *noun*; **basso profundo** /prəˈfʌndəʊ/ (occas. **basso profondo** /-ˈfɒnd-/), pl. **bassi profundi** /-di/, **basso profundos**, [lit. 'deep'] (a singer with) a very deep and rich voice.

bassoon /bəˈsuːn/ *noun.* **E18.**
[ORIGIN French *basson* from Italian *bassone* augm. of BASSO: see -OON.]
1 (A player of) a bass instrument of the oboe family. **E18.**
double bassoon: larger and longer than the normal bassoon and an octave lower in pitch.
2 An organ or harmonium stop similar in tone to this instrument. **L19.**
■ **bassoonist** *noun* a bassoon player **E19.**

basso-relievo /ˌbasəʊrɪˈliːvəʊ/ *noun.* Also **-rilievo** /-rɪˈljeɪvəʊ/. Pl. **-os**. **M17.**
[ORIGIN Italian *basso-rilievo*: see BASSO, RILIEVO.]
= BAS-RELIEF.

bass-relief *noun* var. of BAS-RELIEF.

bassus /ˈbasʌs/ *noun & adjective.* Pl. of noun **-ssi** /-sʌɪ, -siː/. **L16.**
[ORIGIN Latin: see BASE *adjective*.]
EARLY MUSIC. = BASS *noun*[2], *adjective*.

bast /bast/ *noun.*
[ORIGIN Old English *bæst*, corresp. to Middle Dutch & mod. Dutch, Old & mod. High German, Old Norse *bast* from Germanic, of unknown origin.]
Fibrous material from the phloem of certain plants, as hemp, jute, or (orig.) the lime tree. Also (BOTANY), the phloem or vascular tissue of a plant.
■ **basten** *adjective* (now *rare* or *obsolete*) made of bast **OE.**

basta /ˈbasta/ *interjection.* **L16.**
[ORIGIN Italian.]
Enough! No matter!

bastard /ˈbɑːstəd, ˈbast-/ *noun & adjective.* Also *S. Afr.* (senses A.4, B.6) **bastaard**, **baster** /ˈbɑːstə/. **ME.**
[ORIGIN Old French *bastart* (mod. *bâtard*) = Provençal *bastard*, Italian, Spanish, Portuguese *bastardo*, from medieval Latin *bastardus*, prob. from *bastum* packsaddle: see BAT *noun*[2], -ARD.]
▸ **A** *noun.* **1** A person conceived and born out of wedlock; an illegitimate child. Now *arch.* or *derog.* **ME.**

fig.: T. FULLER Fame being a bastard or *filia populi*, 'tis very hard to find her father.

2 A sweet Spanish wine, resembling muscatel; any sweetened wine. *obsolete* exc. *hist.* **LME.**

SHAKES. *Meas. for M.* We shall have all the world drink brown and white bastard.

3 Something of unusual make, shape, or proportion, or of inferior quality; *esp.* (*a*) a kind of culverin; (*b*) a size of paper. **L15.**
4 A person of mixed Nama and European ancestry; a Griqua, a Rehobother. *S. Afr.* **L18.**
5 An unpleasant or unfortunate person or thing; (in weakened sense) a chap, a fellow. *colloq.* **M19.**

H. G. WELLS Serve the cocky little bastard right. T. RATTIGAN Johnny, you old bastard! Are you all right? J. MACLAREN-ROSS This bastard of a bump on the back of my head. M. SHADBOLT At first Ned and Nick had to milk in the open, which was a bastard when it rained.

6 Bastarda script. **E20.**
▸ **B** *adjective.* **1** Born out of wedlock. Now *arch.* or *derog.* **ME.**
2 Hybrid; not genuine; spurious, corrupt. **LME.**

DISRAELI That bastard, but picturesque style of architecture, called the Italian Gothic. J. CHEEVER It was not Italian . . it was a bastard language of a little Spanish and a little something that Clementina had never heard before.

3 Of unusual shape or size (applied e.g. to a file intermediate between coarse and fine, to a font of type, etc.). **LME.**
4 Irregular, unauthorized, unrecognized. **M16.**

BACON Usurie . . is the Bastard use of Money.

5 Having the appearance of; of an inferior kind; *esp.* (in names of animals, plants, etc.) closely resembling (the species etc. whose name follows). **M16.**

R. I. MURCHISON A bastard limestone charged with encrinites.

bastard balm, bastard pellitory, bastard saffron, bastard toadflax, etc.
6 Designating, of or pertaining to, a person of mixed Nama and European race. *S. Afr.* **L18.**
7 Bastarda. **L19.**
– SPECIAL COLLOCATIONS & COMB.: **bastard hartebeest** = TSESSEBI. **bastard mahogany** any of several Australian eucalypts, esp. *Eucalyptus botryoides*. **bastard sandalwood** = NAIO. **bastard title** a half-title. **bastard-trench** *verb trans.* (HORTICULTURE) dig (ground) by digging over the lower soil with the topsoil temporarily removed. **bastard trout** *US* the silver sea trout, *Cynoscion nothus*. **bastard wing** ORNITHOLOGY a group of small quill feathers borne by the first digit of a bird's wing.
■ †**bastardism** *noun* = BASTARDY **L16–M18.** †**bastardly** *adjective* = BASTARD *adjective* **M16–L18.**

bastarda /baˈstɑːdə/ *noun & adjective.* **M20.**
[ORIGIN Italian *bastardo*: see BASTARD.]
(Designating, of or pertaining to) a cursive Gothic script for vernacular use, originating in France and used in Germany and the Low Countries in the 14th and 15th cents.

bastardize /ˈbɑːstədʌɪz, ˈbast-/ *verb.* Also **-ise**. **L16.**
[ORIGIN from BASTARD *noun* + -IZE.]
1 *verb trans. & intrans.* (Cause to) deteriorate. **L16.**
†**2** *verb trans.* Beget as a bastard. *rare* (Shakes.). Only in **E17.**
3 *verb trans.* Declare or stigmatize as illegitimate. **E17.**
■ **bastardiˈzation** *noun* **E19.**

bastardy /ˈbɑːstədi, ˈbas-/ *noun.* **LME.**
[ORIGIN Anglo-Norman, Old French *bastardie* (medieval Latin *bastardia*): see BASTARD *noun*, -Y[3].]
1 The condition of being a bastard; illegitimate birth. **LME.**
2 Begetting of bastards, fornication. *arch.* **L16.**
– COMB.: **bastardy order** (now *arch.* or *hist.*) = ***AFFILIATION order***.

baste /beɪst/ *verb*[1] *trans.* **LME.**
[ORIGIN Old French *bastir* tack, prepare, from Frankish equiv. of Old High German, Middle High German *besten* lace, sew, from Germanic: rel. to BAST.]
Sew loosely together; *esp.* tack together temporarily with long loose stitches.

fig.: SIR W. SCOTT You have . . basted up your first story very hastily and clumsily.

baste /beɪst/ *verb*[2] *trans.* **L15.**
[ORIGIN Unknown.]
1 Moisten (roasting meat) with gravy or melted fat to prevent drying. **L15.**
†**2** Cover with a liquid or viscous substance. **L16–M18.**

baste /beɪst/ *verb*³ *trans. arch. slang.* **M16.**
[ORIGIN Perh. a fig. use of BASTE *verb*².]
Beat soundly, cudgel, thrash.

bastel-house /ˈbast(ə)lhaʊs/ *noun.* Also **bastle-**. **M16.**
[ORIGIN from var. of BASTILLE *noun* + HOUSE *noun*¹.]
A fortified house.

baster *noun & adjective* see BASTARD.

bastide /baˈstiːd/ *noun.* **E16.**
[ORIGIN Old French from Provençal *bastida* (medieval Latin *bastida*): see BASTILLE *noun*.]
1 *hist.* A fortlet; a fortified village or town. **E16.**
2 A country house in southern France. **E18.**

bastile *noun, verb* var. of BASTILLE *noun, verb.*

bastille /baˈstiːl/ *noun.* Also **-ile**. **LME.**
[ORIGIN Old French & mod. French, refashioning of contemp. *bastide* from Provençal *bastida* use as noun of fem. pa. pple of *bastir* build.]
1 *hist.* A tower or bastion of a castle; a small fortress. **LME.**
2 In siege operations, a wooden tower on wheels, or an entrenched protective hut used by the besiegers. **LME.**
3 a (**B-**.) *The* prison fortress built in Paris in the 14th cent., and destroyed in 1789. **M16.** ▸**b** A prison. **E18.**
– COMB.: **Bastille Day** 14 July, the date of the storming of the Bastille in 1789, celebrated as a national holiday in France.

bastille /baˈstiːl/ *verb trans. arch.* Also **-ile**. **L15.**
[ORIGIN Sense 1 from Old French *bastiller*, formed as BASTILLE *noun*; sense 2 from BASTILLE *noun*.]
†**1** Fortify (a building). **L15–E16.**
2 Confine in a bastille; imprison. **M18.**

bastillion /baˈstɪljən/ *noun.* **M16.**
[ORIGIN Old French *bastillon* dim. of BASTILLE *noun*.]
hist. A small fortress or castle; a fortified tower.

bastinade /bastɪˈneɪd/ *noun & verb trans. arch.* Also **-onade** /-əˈneɪd/. **E17.**
[ORIGIN Refashioning of BASTINADO after French *bastonnade*: see -ADE.]
= BASTINADO.

bastinado /bastɪˈneɪdəʊ/ *noun & verb.* **L16.**
[ORIGIN Spanish *bastonada*, from *bastón* stick, cudgel: see BATON *noun*, -ADO.]
▸ **A** *noun.* Pl. **-o(e)s**.
1 A blow with a stick or cudgel, *esp.* one on the soles of the feet. *arch.* **L16.**
2 a A beating with a stick, a cudgelling. *arch.* **L16.** ▸**b** *spec.* (Punishment or torture involving) a caning on the soles of the feet. **E18.**
3 A stick, staff, truncheon, or similar instrument. **L16.**
▸ **B** *verb trans.* **1** Beat with a stick; thrash. *arch.* **E17.**
2 *spec.* Beat or cane on the soles of the feet. **L17.**

bastion /ˈbastɪən/ *noun.* **M16.**
[ORIGIN French from Italian *bastione*, from *bastire* to build.]
1 A fortified outwork often in the form of an irregular pentagon, projecting from the main works so as to allow defensive fire in several directions. **M16.** ▸**b** A similar natural rock formation. **M19.**
2 *fig.* An institution, person, principle, etc., serving as a defence. **L17.**

> A. KOESTLER We have made our country a bastion of the new era. G. GREENE We are the true bastion against the communists.

■ **bastioned** *adjective* defended by a bastion **E19.**

bastite /ˈbastʌɪt/ *noun.* **M19.**
[ORIGIN from *Baste* in the Harz Mountains in Germany: see -ITE¹.]
MINERALOGY. A greenish or brownish kind of serpentine occurring as foliated masses and having a characteristic schiller. Also called ***schiller spar***.

bastle-house *noun* var. of BASTEL-HOUSE.

bastnäsite /ˈbastnɛsʌɪt/ *noun.* Also **-naes-**. **L19.**
[ORIGIN from *Bastnäs*, a locality in Västmanland, Sweden, + -ITE¹.]
MINERALOGY. A yellow to brown hexagonal fluorocarbonate of cerium and other rare earth metals.

basto /ˈbɑːstəʊ, ˈbast-/ *noun.* **L17.**
[ORIGIN Spanish (*el*) *basto* (the ace of) clubs.]
In ombre, quadrille, and related card games, the ace of clubs in its fixed capacity as third highest trump.

baston /ˈbast(ə)n/ *noun.* **ME.**
[ORIGIN Old French: see BATON *noun*.]
1 A staff or stick used as a weapon or a symbol of office. *arch. & dial.* **ME.**
†**2** HERALDRY. = BATON *noun* 3 **L16–M17.**

bastonade *noun & verb* var. of BASTINADE.

basuco /bəˈsuːkəʊ/ *noun.* Also **-z-**. **L20.**
[ORIGIN Colombian Spanish, perh. rel. to Spanish *bazucar* shake violently.]
Impure cocaine mixed with coca paste and other substances, often including tobacco and marijuana (a highly addictive preparation when smoked); *gen.* impure or low-grade cocaine.

Basuto *noun & adjective* see BASOTHO.

bat /bat/ *noun*¹. In sense 9 also **batt**. **LOE.**
[ORIGIN Perh. partly from Old French & mod. French *batte*, from *batre*: see BATTER *verb*¹; sense 6 from BAT *verb*². Branch III of unknown origin.]
▸ **I 1** A club, a cudgel; a stick or staff for support or defence. Now *arch. & dial.* **LOE.**

> SPENSER A handsome bat he held, On which he leaned. SIR W. SCOTT I have given up . . my bat for a sword.

2 An implement with a rounded (usu. wooden) handle and a solid head, for striking a ball in cricket, rounders, baseball, table tennis, etc. **E17.** ▸**b** An object like a table-tennis bat used to guide taxiing aircraft. Usu. in *pl.* **M20.**
at bat BASEBALL taking one's turn at batting (see also AT-BAT). ***beat the bat***: see BEAT *verb*¹ 5. **carry one's bat**, **carry the bat** CRICKET be not out at the end of a side's completed innings (esp. after having batted throughout the innings). ***dead bat***: see DEAD *adjective & adverb*. ***hang one's bat out to dry***: see HANG *verb*. **off one's own bat** *fig.* unaided, on one's own initiative. **right off the bat** *fig.* (*N. Amer.*) immediately.
3 A person who uses a bat in cricket etc.; a batter, a batsman. **M18.**

> E. LINKLATER He was an accomplished bat and . . fielded boldly at cover-point.

▸ **II 4** A firm blow as with a staff, club, etc. **LME.**
5 Rate of stroke or step; pace, speed. *dial. & slang.* **E19.**

> J. WELCOME We turned on to the main . . road and started going a hell of a bat across the Cotswolds.

6 A movement of the eyelids, a blink. **M20.**

> C. FRY We were at the boy in the bat of an eye.

▸ **III 7 a** A lump, a piece. Long *obsolete* in *gen.* sense exc. in ***bits and bats*** (see BIT *noun*²). **LME.** ▸**b** *spec.* A piece of brick with one end entire. *obsolete* exc. in ***brickbat*** (see BRICK *noun*). **E16.** ▸**c** POTTERY. A small piece of baked ware separating pieces of biscuit ware in the kiln; a flattened-out piece of unfired clay. **E19.**
8 Shale interstratified between seams of coal, iron ore, etc. **L17.**
9 HAT-MAKING. A felted mass. **M19.**
– COMB.: **batboy** BASEBALL a boy or youth who looks after the bats of a team etc.; †**bat-fowling** catching birds by night using lights to dazzle them.

bat /bat/ *noun*². *obsolete* exc. *hist.* Also **bât** /bɑː/. **LME.**
[ORIGIN Old French *bat*, earlier *bast*, (mod. *bât*), from Provençal *bast* from medieval Latin *bastum* packsaddle.]
A packsaddle. Only in *comb.* as below.
bat-horse: carrying the baggage of military officers during a campaign. BATMAN *noun*². **bat-money** an allowance for carrying baggage in the field. **bat-mule**: used as a pack animal in a military campaign. †**bat-needle** a packing needle.

bat /bat/ *noun*³. **L16.**
[ORIGIN Alt. (perh. by assoc. with medieval Latin *b(l)atta*, *blacta*) of forms with /-k/ from a Scandinavian word repr. in Middle Swedish *aftanbakka*, *natbakka* night bat, Middle Danish *nat(h)bakke*.]
1 A member of the order Chiroptera of mainly nocturnal flying mammals which have forelimbs modified to support membranous wings extending to the tail. **L16.**
2 A large moth or butterfly. Chiefly *W. Indian.* **L16.**
– PHRASES: **blind as a bat** completely blind. **have bats in the belfry** *colloq.* be crazy or eccentric. **like a bat out of hell** *colloq.* very quickly, at top speed. ***serotine bat***: see SEROTINE *noun*¹. ***vampire bat***: see VAMPIRE *noun* 3.
– COMB.: **batfish** a marine fish of the family Ogcocephalidae, related to and resembling the anglerfishes; **batwing sleeve** a sleeve with a deep armhole and a tight cuff.

bat /bat/ *noun*⁴. *slang.* **M19.**
[ORIGIN Unknown: cf. BATTER *noun*⁴.]
A drinking bout, a binge.

bat /bat/ *noun*⁵. *arch. slang.* **L19.**
[ORIGIN Hindi *bāt* speech, language, word.]
The colloquial language of a foreign country.
sling the bat speak the local language abroad.

†**bat** *noun*⁶ var. of BATH *noun*².

†**bat** *noun*⁷ see BATZ.

bat /bat/ *verb*¹. Infl. **-tt-**. **LME.**
[ORIGIN from BAT *noun*¹ or formed as BATTER *verb*¹.]
1 *verb trans.* Strike with or as with a bat; cudgel; beat. **LME.**

> W. BARNES Well here . . 'S a ball for you if you can bat it. B. HINES He batted him twice about the ears.

2 *verb intrans.* Use a bat; have an innings at cricket, baseball, etc. **M18.**

> H. DE SÉLINCOURT Padded and gloved, and rather nervously waiting his turn to bat.

3 *verb intrans.* Move, esp. in a casual or aimless fashion (*about, along, around*, etc.). *dial. & slang.* **L19.**
– PHRASES: **bat around** (*a*) discuss (an idea) idly or casually; (*b*) *N. Amer. colloq.* travel widely, frequently, or casually. **bat a thousand** *US colloq.* be very successful.

bat /bat/ *verb*². Infl. **-tt-**. **E17.**
[ORIGIN Var. of BATE *verb*¹, *verb*².]
1 *verb intrans.* = BATE *verb*¹ 2. **E17.**
2 *verb trans.* Blink; flutter (one's eyelashes), esp. in a flirtatious manner. **E19.**
not bat an eye(lid) (*a*) not sleep a wink; (*b*) betray no emotion.

Batak /ˈbatək/ *noun*¹ *& adjective.* **E19.**
[ORIGIN Batak (Indonesian): cf. BATTA *noun*³ *& adjective*.]
▸ **A** *noun.* Pl. same, **-s**. A member of a people of the northern part of Sumatra; the Indonesian language of this people. **E19.**
▸ **B** *attrib.* or as *adjective.* Of or pertaining to the Batak or their language. **L19.**

Batak /bəˈtɑːk/ *noun*² *& adjective.* Pl. of noun same, **-s**. **E20.**
[ORIGIN Batak (Austronesian).]
A member of, of or pertaining to, a people on the island of Palawan, Philippines; (of) the Austronesian language of this people.

batardeau /batardo/ *noun.* Pl. ***-eaux*** /-o/. **M18.**
[ORIGIN French, earlier *bastardeau* dim. of Old French *bastard* of unknown origin.]
A cofferdam. Also, a wall built across the moat or ditch surrounding a fortification.

batata /bəˈtɑːtə/ *noun.* **M16.**
[ORIGIN Spanish from Taino.]
= ***sweet potato*** s.v. POTATO *noun* 1.

Batavian /bəˈteɪvɪən/ *noun & adjective.* Now *arch.* or *hist.* **M16.**
[ORIGIN from Latin *Batavia*, from *Batavi* the people of Betawe (see below), + -AN.]
▸ **A** *noun.* **1** A member of an ancient people who inhabited the island of Betawe between the Rhine and the Waal (now part of the Netherlands). **M16.**
2 A Dutch person. **M18.**
▸ **B** *adjective.* Of or pertaining to the ancient people of Betawe or the people of the Netherlands. **L18.**
Batavian endive: see ENDIVE 2.

batch /batʃ/ *noun*¹ *& verb*¹. **L15.**
[ORIGIN from base of BAKE *verb* (cf. *watch, wake*). Repr. an Old English word: cf. Old English *ġebæċ* baking, thing baked.]
▸ **A** *noun.* †**1** The process of baking. **L15–M16.**
2 A baking; the quantity of bread produced at one baking. Also = ***batch loaf*** below. **L15.**
3 The quantity of flour or dough used for one baking. Long *arch.* **M16.**

> COVERDALE A lytle leauen sowreth the whole batche, wherwith it is myngled.

†**4** The sort or lot to which a thing belongs by origin. **L16–E18.**

> MILTON This worthy Motto, No Bishop, no King is of the same batch, and infanted out of the same feares.

5 A quantity produced at one operation. **E18.**

> M. E. BRADDON That last batch of soup was excellent.

6 A number of things or persons coming at once and treated as a set; (less commonly) a quantity of a thing coming at one time, an instalment. **L18.**

> T. HOOD I am not going to favour you with a batch of politics. SAKI Several packages, evidently an early batch of Christmas presents. G. GORER Most of the questions were arranged in batches of 4 or 5 dealing with the same subject. A. SCHLEE The next batch of tourists was arriving at the head of the path.

– COMB.: **batch loaf** a loaf baked close to others in a batch (and so not completely crusted at the sides); **batchmate** *Indian* a classmate; **batch process**: treating materials in batches, not continuously; **batch processing** (*a*) the processing of raw materials in batches in an industrial process; (*b*) COMPUTING the processing of previously collected batches of data, jobs, etc., esp. offline without user intervention; **batch production** = ***batch process*** above.
▸ **B** *verb trans.* Treat or arrange in batches. **L19.**

batch *noun*² *& verb*² var. of BACH *noun*¹ *& verb.*

†**batchelor** *noun* var. of BACHELOR.

batchy /ˈbatʃi/ *adjective. slang.* **L19.**
[ORIGIN Uncertain: cf. BATTY.]
Crazy, dotty; = BATTY 2.

†**bate** *noun*¹. Long *dial.* exc. in MAKEBATE. **LME–L19.**
[ORIGIN Aphet. from DEBATE *noun*, or from BATE *verb*¹.]
Contention, strife; an argument.

bate /beɪt/ *noun*². Long *dial.* **LME.**
[ORIGIN from BATE *verb*².]
Deduction; diminution; discount.

bate /beɪt/ *noun*³. Long *dial.* **M17.**
[ORIGIN Unknown.]
The grain of wood or stone.

bate /beɪt/ *noun*⁴. *slang.* Also **bait**. **M19.**
[ORIGIN from BAIT *verb*¹.]
Esp. among children: a rage, a temper.

bate /beɪt/ *verb*¹. Also **bait**. **ME.**
[ORIGIN Old French *batre*: see BATTER *verb*¹.]
†**1** *verb intrans. & (rare) refl.* Fight, contend, with blows or arguments. (Foll. by *on*.) *dial.* **ME–M19.**
†**2** *verb trans.* Beat, flutter, (wings etc.). *rare.* **ME–M17.**
3 *verb intrans.* FALCONRY. Beat the wings impatiently and flutter away from the fist or perch. **LME.** ▸†**b** *fig.* Struggle; be restless or impatient. **L16–L17.**

> **b** DRYDEN You are eager, and baiting to be gone.

bate /beɪt/ *verb*². **ME.**
[ORIGIN Aphet. from ABATE *verb*¹.]
†**1** = ABATE *verb*¹ 1. Only in **ME.**
2 *verb trans. & (rare) intrans.* = ABATE *verb*¹ 4. Now chiefly in ***bate one's breath***, restrain one's breathing through anxiety, suspense, etc. **ME.**

R. L. STEVENSON The pirates no longer ran separate and shouting . . , but kept side by side and spoke with bated breath.

†**3** *verb trans.* Lower, let down; humble, depress. Cf. ABATE *verb*[1] 2. LME–M19. ▸†**b** = ABATE *verb*[1] 2b. LME–E19.
4 *verb trans.* = ABATE *verb*[1] 5. *arch.* LME. ▸**b** = ABATE *verb*[1] 5b. *obsolete* exc. as BATING *preposition*. E17.

ADDISON They offered . . to bate him the article of bread and butter in the tea-table account. W. IRVING I do not bate one nail's breadth of the honest truth. E. GASKELL Take the bated wage, and be thankful.

†**5** *verb trans. & intrans.* = ABATE *verb*[1] 3. L15–L17.
6 *verb trans.* Blunt (*lit.* & *fig.*). Cf. ABATE *verb*[1] 7. Long *rare*. M16.
■ **bateless** *adjective* (*rare*) †(**a**) that cannot be blunted; (**b**) unabating: L16.

bateau /batəʊ, *foreign* bato/ *noun*. Pl. **-eaux** /-əʊz, *foreign* -o/. Also †**battoe**. E18.
[ORIGIN French = boat.]
A light riverboat, esp. of a flat-bottomed kind used in Canada.
bateau-mouche /batomuʃ/, pl. ***bateaux-mouches*** (pronounced same), a boat which takes sightseers on the Seine in Paris.

bateleur /ˈbat(ə)ləː/ *noun*. M19.
[ORIGIN French, lit. 'juggler, mountebank'.]
A short-tailed African eagle, *Terathopius ecaudatus*. Also ***bateleur eagle***.

batement /ˈbeɪtm(ə)nt/ *noun*. LME.
[ORIGIN Aphet. from ABATEMENT *noun*[1].]
1 ***batement light***, in Gothic architecture, an upper window or opening with a sloping or curved sill (i.e. cut off at the low end to accommodate the curve of an arch etc.). LME.
†**2** Reduction, diminution. L15–L17.

Bates /beɪts/ *noun*. E20.
[ORIGIN W. H. *Bates* (1860–1931), Amer. ophthalmologist.]
Bates method, a technique of alternative medicine intended to improve eyesight using eye exercises rather than lenses or surgery.

Batesian /ˈbeɪtsɪən/ *adjective*. Also **b-**. L19.
[ORIGIN from H. W. *Bates* (1825–92), English naturalist + -IAN.]
ZOOLOGY. Designating or characterized by a form of mimicry in which an edible species is protected by its resemblance to one avoided by predators.

batey /ˈbeɪti/ *adjective*. *slang*. Also **baity**. E20.
[ORIGIN from BATE *noun*[4] + -Y[1].]
In a rage; bad-tempered.

bath /bɑːθ/ *noun*[1]. Pl. **baths** /bɑːðz/. In branch II **B-**.
[ORIGIN Old English *bæþ* = Old Frisian *beth*, Old Saxon *bad*, Old & mod. High German *bad*, Old Norse *bað*, from Germanic.]
▸ **I 1** An immersion in liquid for cleansing or therapy. Also (with specifying word), an immersion in or copious application of any medium to produce analogous effects. OE.
have a bath, ***take a bath***, ***cold bath***, ***hot bath***, etc. ***dust bath***, ***mud-bath***, ***shower bath***, ***sunbath***, ***Turkish bath***, ***vaporous bath***, etc. ***bloodbath***: see BLOOD *noun*. **Order of the Bath** an order of knighthood, named from the bath which preceded the knight's installation. ***warm bath***: see WARM *adjective*.
2 A quantity of water or other liquid for bathing or taking a bath in. OE.

STEELE To rise the next Morning and plunge into the Cold Bath. C. KINGSLEY Countess, your bath is ready.

†**3** A spring of water suitable for bathing in, *esp.* one that is hot or contains minerals. OE–E18.
4 A place for bathing for cleansing or therapeutic purposes; a town with mineral springs or other facilities for therapeutic bathing etc., a spa; (chiefly *N. Amer.* & in advertisements) a bathroom; *sing.* & (usu.) in *pl.*, a building for bathing or swimming in. ME.
municipal baths, ***swimming baths***, etc. ***Russian bath***, ***steam bath***, ***Turkish bath***, etc.
5 A medicinal or disinfectant wash or lotion; a vessel for containing or applying such a wash etc. LME.
6 The state of being suffused with a liquid, esp. perspiration. Now *rare*. L16.
7 a (A vessel containing) a medium such as water, oil, sand, ice, or steam, in which chemical or other apparatus can be placed and subjected to a steady high or low temperature. L16. ▸**b** (A vessel containing) a chemical in which objects can be immersed, as film for developing, etc. L18.
b ***nitrate bath***, ***silver bath***, etc.
8 A receptacle for liquid, usu. water, for bathing or taking a bath in. E17.
bird bath, ***hip bath***, etc.
▸ **II 9** (**B-**.) A town in SW England named from its hot springs. Also †***the Bath***. OE.
– COMB.: **Bath brick** a preparation for cleaning polished metal; **Bath bun** a type of round spiced bun with currants and icing; **Bath chair** a wheeled chair for an invalid; **Bath chap** a type of pickled pig's chap; **bath cube**: of a preparation which crumbles and dissolves to soften or perfume bathwater; **bath essence** a concentrated liquid to soften or perfume bathwater; **bath mat**: on which one stands after getting out of a bath; **Bath metal** a silvery-white alloy of zinc and copper, formerly used for tableware; **Bath Oliver** an unsweetened biscuit invented by Dr William Oliver (1695–1764) of Bath; **bathrobe** a dressing gown, esp. of towelling; **bathroom** a room containing a bath and often other toilet facilities; *euphem.* a water closet, a lavatory; **bath salts**: that dissolve to soften or perfume bathwater; **Bath stone** oolite from the formation near Bath, used as building stone; **bath towel** a large towel; **bathtub** = sense 8 above; **bathwater** water in a bath (***throw out the baby with the bathwater***: see BABY *noun* 1); **Bath white** a white butterfly, *Pontia daplidice*, with greenish mottling on the underwings, which is a rare migrant to Britain.

bath /baθ/ *noun*[2]. Also †**bat(us)**. LME.
[ORIGIN Hebrew *baṯ*; late Latin (Vulgate) *batus*.]
An ancient Hebrew liquid measure equivalent to about 40 litres, or 9 gallons.

bath /bɑːθ/ *verb trans. & intrans.* L15.
[ORIGIN from BATH *noun*[1]. In early instances perh. only a variant spelling of *bathe*.]
Wash (a child, invalid, animal, etc., or oneself) in a bath; take a bath.

bathe /beɪð/ *noun*. M19.
[ORIGIN from BATHE *verb* 4.]
An immersion in liquid, esp. in the sea, a river, a swimming pool, etc., for recreation.

bathe /beɪð/ *verb*.
[ORIGIN Old English *baþian* = Dutch *baden*, Old High German *badōn* (German *baden*), Old Norse *baða*, from Germanic, from base of BATH *noun*[1].]
▸ **I** *verb trans.* **1** Immerse in liquid for cleansing or therapy. Also, immerse in any other medium for analogous effects. OE.

F. W. ROBERTSON The later martyr bathes his fingers in the flames.

2 Wash; wet or moisten all over; apply liquid to. OE.

J. HERVEY The laborer, bathed in sweat, drops the scythe. GIBBON The river bathed the foot of the walls. B. T. WASHINGTON Rarely was there any place provided . . where one could bathe even the face and hands. K. GRAHAME He . . bathed the Mole's shin with warm water.

3 Envelop, suffuse, encompass. E16.

COVERDALE *Isa.* 63:6 And thus have I troden downe the people in my wrath, and bathed them in my displeasure. J. AGATE Changes of lighting bathe the audience in a glow of tender dawn warming to wanton sunset. P. G. WODEHOUSE If when I have finished you are not bathed in shame and remorse, you must be dead to all human feeling. S. J. PERELMAN The room was bathed in dense shadow. D. ATTENBOROUGH This mixture allowed ultraviolet rays from the sun to bathe the earth's surface with an intensity that would be lethal to modern animal life.

▸ **II** *verb intrans.* **4** Immerse oneself in water, esp. in the sea, a river, a swimming pool, etc., for recreation. (Cf. BATH *verb*.) OE.
bathing beauty, **bathing belle** an attractive woman in a swimsuit.
5 *transf.* & *fig.* Bask; wallow; immerse oneself in any medium. LME.

C. MARLOWE Now lie the Christians bathing in their bloods. J. TRAPP Shall Christians be bathing in their beds on their Lord's day?

sun-bathe: see SUN *noun*[1].
■ **bather** *noun* †(**a**) an attendant at a bath; (**b**) a person who bathes; (**c**) in *pl.* (esp. *Austral.*), swimming trunks, a swimming costume: M17.

bathetic /bəˈθɛtɪk/ *adjective*. L18.
[ORIGIN from BATHOS after *pathos*, *pathetic*.]
Marked by bathos.

bathing /ˈbeɪðɪŋ/ *noun*. LME.
[ORIGIN from BATHE *verb* + -ING[1].]
1 The action of BATHE *verb*; immersion in or exposure to water or some other medium; application of liquid, wetting, moistening. LME.
sea bathing etc. MIXED ***bathing***.
2 The conditions for bathers at a particular resort etc. M19.
– ATTRIB. & COMB.: Designating garments worn when bathing, as ***bathing costume***, ***bathing suit***, etc. Special combs., as **bathing machine** *hist.* a wheeled dressing box drawn into the sea for bathing from.

bathochromic /baθəˈkrəʊmɪk/ *adjective*. L19.
[ORIGIN from Greek BATHOS + *khrōma* colour + -IC.]
Causing or characterized by a shift of the absorption spectrum towards longer wavelengths.

batholith /ˈbaθəlɪθ/ *noun*. E20.
[ORIGIN from Greek BATHOS + -LITH.]
GEOLOGY. A large dome-shaped mass of igneous intrusive rock extending to unknown depth.
■ **bathoˈlithic** *adjective* L19.

bathometer /bəˈθɒmɪtə/ *noun*. L19.
[ORIGIN from Greek BATHOS + -OMETER.]
An instrument for ascertaining the depth of water.
■ **bathoˈmetric** *adjective* = BATHYMETRIC L20. **bathometry** *noun* = BATHYMETRY M20.

Bathonian /bəˈθəʊnɪən/ *adjective & noun*. M18.
[ORIGIN from *Bathonia* Latinized form of *Bath* (see BATH *noun*[1] II) + -AN.]
1 (A native or inhabitant) of the town of Bath. M18.
2 GEOLOGY. (Denoting or pertaining to) a subdivision of the Jurassic typified by formations at Bath. M19.

bathorhodopsin /baθərəˈdɒpsɪn/ *noun*. L20.
[ORIGIN formed as BATHOS + RHODOPSIN.]
BIOCHEMISTRY. = PRELUMIRHODOPSIN.

bathos /ˈbeɪθɒs/ *noun*. M17.
[ORIGIN Greek = depth. In purely English sense 2 introduced by Pope.]
1 Depth, lowest phase, bottom. *rare*. M17.

S. JOHNSON Declining . . to the very bathos of insipidity.

2 RHETORIC. Ludicrous descent from the elevated to the commonplace; anticlimax. E18.
3 A comedown; an anticlimax; a performance absurdly unequal to the occasion. E19.

F. MARRYAT It was rather a bathos . . to sink from a gentleman's son to an under usher. L. A. G. STRONG The rest of their married life will be one hideous bathos after the glory of its start.

bathotic /bəˈθɒtɪk/ *adjective*. M19.
[ORIGIN Irreg. from BATHOS after *chaos*, *chaotic*.]
= BATHETIC.

Bathurst bur /ˈbaθəːst bəː/ *noun phr. Austral.* M19.
[ORIGIN from *Bathurst*, a town in New South Wales + BUR *noun*[1].]
(A bur from) the spiny cocklebur, *Xanthium spinosum*, naturalized in Australia.

bathy- /ˈbaθi/ *combining form* of Greek *bathus* deep.
■ **bathypeˈlagic** *adjective* pertaining to or inhabiting the depths of the sea, *spec.* below the level to which light penetrates L19. **bathysphere** *noun* a large strong submersible sphere for deep-sea observation M20. **bathyˈthermograph** *noun* an automatic instrument for recording water temperature at various depths M20.

bathyal /ˈbaθɪəl/ *adjective*. E20.
[ORIGIN from BATHY- + -AL[1].]
Of or pertaining to the zone of the sea between the continental shelf and the abyssal zone.

bathybius /bəˈθɪbɪəs/ *noun*. M19.
[ORIGIN mod. Latin, formed as BATHY- + Greek *bios* living.]
(A name given by Thomas Huxley to) a gelatinous inorganic substance obtained from the bed of the Atlantic Ocean, and at first supposed to be a formless mass of living protoplasm.

bathymetry /bəˈθɪmɪtri/ *noun*. M19.
[ORIGIN from BATHY- + -METRY.]
The measurement of depths in oceans, seas, or lakes.
■ **bathyˈmetric**, **bathyˈmetrical** *adjectives* pertaining to or connected with bathymetry M19. **bathyˈmetrically** *adverb* L19.

bathyscaphe /ˈbaθɪskaf/ *noun*. Also **-scaph**. M20.
[ORIGIN French, formed as BATHY- + Greek *skaphos* ship.]
A navigable manned submersible vessel for deep-sea diving and observation.

batik /ˈbatɪk, bəˈtiːk/ *noun & adjective*. L19
[ORIGIN Javanese, lit. 'painted'.]
▸ **A** *noun*. A method (orig. used in Java) of making coloured designs on textiles by waxing the parts not to be dyed; (a garment made of) a fabric dyed by this method. L19.
▸ **B** *attrib.* or as *adjective*. Executed or ornamented by this method. E20.

bating /ˈbeɪtɪŋ/ *preposition*. *arch.* M17.
[ORIGIN Absol. use of pres. pple of BATE *verb*[2] 4b.]
Excepting, leaving out of account.

batiste /bəˈtiːst/ *noun & adjective*. E19.
[ORIGIN French (earlier *batiche*), perh. from base of *battre*: see BATTER *verb*[1].]
(Of) a fine light cotton or linen fabric like cambric.

†**batler** *noun*. *rare* (Shakes. First Folio). Only in E17.
[ORIGIN Perh. taken as from BATTLE *verb*[3] + -ER[1].]
= BATLET.

†**batlet** *noun*. *dial.* M17–L19.
[ORIGIN from BAT *noun*[1] + -LET.]
A wooden stick for beating and stirring clothes during washing, etc.
– NOTE: Substituted in the second (and subsequent) folios of Shakes. for the first folio's BATLER (*A.Y.L.* II) and preferred in many mod. editions.

batman /ˈbatmən/ *noun*[1]. L16.
[ORIGIN Turkish *batmān*, *batman* (whence also Russian *batman*).]
hist. A weight in Turkey, Persia, etc., varying according to the locality.

batman /ˈbatmən/ *noun*[2]. Pl. **-men**. M18.
[ORIGIN from BAT *noun*[2] + MAN *noun*.]
MILITARY. Formerly, a man in charge of a bat-horse and its load. Now, an officer's personal servant, an orderly.
■ **batwoman** *noun* M20.

bat mitzvah /bɑːt ˈmɪtsvə/ *noun phr.* Also **B-**. M20.
[ORIGIN Hebrew *baṯ miṣwāh* daughter of commandment, after BAR MITZVAH.]
(A religious initiation ceremony for) a Jewish girl aged twelve years and one day, regarded as the age of religious maturity.

batologist /bəˈtɒlədʒɪst/ *noun*. L19.
[ORIGIN from Greek *batos* bramble + -OLOGIST.]
A botanist who specializes in the genus *Rubus*, and esp. in the microspecies of bramble (*R. fruticosus* aggregate).

B

baton /ˈbat(ə)n; *in senses 4 and 6 also foreign* batɔ̃ (*pl. same*)/ *noun*. E16.
[ORIGIN French *bâton* (earlier *baston*) = Provençal, Spanish *baston*, Italian *bastone*, from Proto-Romance from late Latin *bastum* stick.]
1 A staff or stick used as a weapon; a cudgel, a club. *obsolete* in *gen.* sense. E16. ▸**b** In *pl.* One of the four suits (represented by cudgels or batons) in packs of playing cards in Italy, Spain, and Spanish-speaking countries, and in some tarot packs. Cf. CLUB *noun* 4. M19. ▸**c** *spec.* A police constable's truncheon, *esp.* a relatively long one. L19.
2 A staff etc. carried as a symbol of office, *esp.* that of a field marshal. L16.
3 HERALDRY. A narrow truncated bend. M18.
baton sinister a supposed sign of bastardy.
4 MUSIC. A conductor's wand for beating time etc.; a drum major's stick. L18.
under the baton of conducted by.
5 A staff or stick used in walking. Now *rare*. E19.
6 A long loaf or stick of bread. M19.
7 A short tube or stick carried in a relay race and passed from one participant to the next. E20.
– COMB.: **baton charge** a charge by police constables with drawn truncheons; **baton-charge** *verb intrans. & trans.* make a baton charge (at); **baton round** a rubber or plastic bullet.

baton /ˈbat(ə)n/ *verb trans.* E17.
[ORIGIN from the noun.]
Strike with a baton.

batoon /bəˈtuːn/ *noun & verb. arch.* M16.
[ORIGIN formed as BATON *noun*: see -OON.]
▸**A** *noun.* **1** = BATON *noun* 1. M16.
2 = BATON *noun* 2. M16.
†**3** = BATON *noun* 3. M16–E18.
▸**B** *verb trans.* = BATON *verb*. L16.

batrachian /bəˈtreɪkɪən/ *adjective & noun.* M19.
[ORIGIN from mod. Latin *Batrachia* former name of the order Anura, from Greek *batrakheia* neut. pl. (sc. *zōa* animals) of adjective from *batrakhos* frog: see -AN.]
(Pertaining to, of the nature or characteristic of) a frog or toad; = ANURAN.

batracho- /ˈbatrəkəʊ/ *combining form* of Greek *batrakhos* frog: see -O-.
▪ **batracho'toxin** *noun* an extremely toxic alkaloid secreted by the Colombian frog *Phyllobates aurotaenia* M20.

bats /bats/ *adjective* (usu. *pred.*). *colloq.* E20.
[ORIGIN from ***have bats in the belfry*** s.v. BAT *noun*³.]
Crazy, dotty; = BATTY *adjective* 2.

J. COE Poor Aunty Tabs has been driven completely bats by the news.

batsman /ˈbatsmən/ *noun*. Pl. **-men**. M18.
[ORIGIN from BAT *noun*¹ + -'S¹ + MAN *noun*.]
1 A user of a cricket, baseball, etc., bat. M18.
batsman's wicket a cricket pitch favouring batsmen.
2 A signaller using bats to guide an aircraft. M20.
▪ **batsmanship** *noun* the art of batting at cricket etc.; batting performance: E20.

Batswana /bəˈtswɑːnə/ *noun & adjective*. Also (earlier, now *arch.* or *hist.*) **Bechuana**, **-wana**, /bɛtʃʊˈɑːnə, bɛˈtʃwɑːnə/. E19.
[ORIGIN Setswana, from *ba-* pl. prefix + TSWANA.]
▸**A** *noun.* **1** (*erron.*) *sing.* Pl. **-s**. A member of the Tswana people, (*sing.*) a Motswana. E19.
2 *pl.* (Members of) the Tswana people. L19.
▸**B** *attrib.* or as *adjective*. = TSWANA *adjective*. E19.

batt *noun* see BAT *noun*¹.

batta /ˈbatə/ *noun*¹. *obsolete* exc. *hist.* E17.
[ORIGIN Urdu *baṭṭā*.]
In the Indian subcontinent: agio; discount on coins not current or of short weight.

batta /ˈbatə/ *noun*². *Indian. obsolete* exc. *hist.* L17.
[ORIGIN Portuguese (of the Indian subcontinent) *bata* = Kannada *bhatta* rice from Sanskrit *bhakta* food.]
Allowance for subsistence; extra pay; *spec.* that given to officers serving in India.

Batta /ˈbatə/ *noun*³ *& adjective*. L18.
[ORIGIN Batak (Indonesian).]
= BATAK *noun*¹ *& adjective*.

battailous /ˈbat(ə)ləs/ *adjective*. *arch.* LME.
[ORIGIN Old French *bataillos*, *-eus*, formed as BATTLE *noun*: see -OUS.]
Fond of fighting; ready for battle.

battalia /bəˈtɑːlɪə/ *noun*. *arch.* L16.
[ORIGIN Italian *battaglia* BATTLE *noun*.]
†**1** = BATTALION 1. L16–E19.
2 Order of battle; battle array. Esp. in ***in battalia***, ***into battalia***. E17.

battalia pie /bəˈtɑːlɪə pʌɪ/ *noun phr. arch.* Orig. †**beatille pie** & other vars. M17.
[ORIGIN French *béatilles*, medieval Latin *beatillae* small blessed articles (as samplers worked by nuns, etc.), dim. of *beatus* blessed: popular assim. to BATTALIA.]
A pie of titbits such as sweetbreads, cocks' combs, etc.

battalion /bəˈtalɪən/ *noun & verb*. L16.
[ORIGIN French *bataillon* from Italian *battaglione* augm. of *battaglia* BATTLE *noun*.]
▸**A** *noun*. **I** MILITARY.
1 *gen.* A large body of men in battle array; each of the large divisions of an army. L16.
2 *spec.* A unit of infantry composed of several companies and forming part of a brigade or regiment. E18.
▸**II** *transf. & fig.* **3** A large well-ordered group; an array; a large group of people with similar tasks etc. E17.
▸**B** *verb trans.* Form into a battalion or battalions. *rare*. E19.

battel /ˈbat(ə)l/ *verb* †*trans. & intrans. arch.* Also **battle**. L16.
[ORIGIN Cf. BATTLE *verb*².]
At Oxford University: charge (one's provisions etc.) to a college account.
▪ **batteler**, **battler** *noun* (*obsolete* exc. *hist.*, at Oxford University) a person who boards and lodges in college; *spec.* a member of an order of students below commoners: E17.

battels /ˈbat(ə)lz/ *noun pl.* L16.
[ORIGIN Perh. from BATTLE *verb*².]
At Oxford University (formerly also elsewhere): a college account for board and provisions supplied, or for all college expenses.

battement /batmɑ̃ (*pl. same*); ˈbatmɒ̃/ *noun*. M19.
[ORIGIN French = beating.]
DANCING. Any of a number of beating leg movements.
grand battement: see GRAND *adjective*². ***petit battement***: see PETIT *adjective*².

batten /ˈbat(ə)n/ *noun*¹. L15.
[ORIGIN Old French *batant* use as noun of pres. pple of *batre*: see BATTER *verb*¹, -ANT¹.]
1 A long narrow piece of squared timber. L15.
2 A strip of wood used for clamping the boards of a door etc. M17.
3 NAUTICAL. A strip of wood or metal for securing tarpaulin over a hatchway or for preventing chafing of masts and spars. M18.
4 A strip of wood etc. carrying electric (or formerly gas) lamps. M19.

batten /ˈbat(ə)n/ *noun*². M19.
[ORIGIN French *battant*.]
A movable bar in a loom which closes the weft.

batten /ˈbat(ə)n/ *verb*¹. L15.
[ORIGIN from BATTEN *noun*¹.]
1 *verb trans.* Strengthen or secure with battens. L15.

K. DOUGLAS We dried our clothes on the exhaust . . and battened ourselves into the turret. F. WELDON Boarded up by means of a row of assorted doors battened together with railway sleepers. I. MCEWAN A kiosk, shuttered and battened for the night.

2 *verb trans. & intrans.* NAUTICAL. Fasten *down* (the hatches etc.) against bad weather. M17.
▪ **battening** *noun* the application or addition of battens; strengthening or securing with battens; a structure formed with battens: L18.

batten /ˈbat(ə)n/ *verb*². L16.
[ORIGIN Old Norse *batna* improve, get better (for base cf. Old English *ġebatian* get better): see -EN⁵. Cf. BATTLE *verb*⁴.]
1 *verb intrans.* Improve in condition; *esp.* (of an animal) grow fat. L16.

JONSON It makes her fat you see. Shee battens with it.

2 *verb intrans.* Feed gluttonously *on* or *upon*. E17.

E. B. BROWNING The strong carnivorous eagle shall . . batten deep Upon thy dusky liver.

3 *verb intrans. fig.* Thrive, prosper, esp. at the expense of another. (Foll. by *on*.) E17.

D. LESSING There are some unscrupulous firms . . which batten on the ignorance of Africans about legal matters.

†**4** *verb trans.* Feed to advantage, fatten up. M17–L18.

MILTON Battening our flocks with the fresh dews of night.

Battenberg /ˈbat(ə)nbəːg/ *noun*. Also **-burg**. E20.
[ORIGIN A town in Germany.]
In full ***Battenberg cake***. A marzipan-covered oblong sponge cake whose slices show four squares in two colours.

batter /ˈbatə/ *noun*¹. LME.
[ORIGIN Anglo-Norman *bat(t)ure* = Old French *bateüre* (mod. *batture*) action of beating, from *batre*: see BATTER *verb*¹, -ER².]
▸**I 1** A runny mixture of flour and eggs or the like beaten up with milk or water, for cooking. LME.
†**2** A cement or paste of flour and water. Chiefly *Scot.* LME–M19.
3 A thick paste of any kind. E17.
▸**II 4** PRINTING. A damaged area of metal type or blocks. E19.

batter /ˈbatə/ *noun*². M18.
[ORIGIN from BATTER *verb*².]
A receding slope from the ground upwards.

batter /ˈbatə/ *noun*³. L18.
[ORIGIN from BAT *verb*¹ + -ER¹.]
A player using a bat.

batter /ˈbatə/ *noun*⁴. *slang*. M19.
[ORIGIN Unknown: cf. BAT *noun*⁴.]
A period of unrestrained drinking or enjoyment, a binge.
on the batter (*a*) on a binge; (*b*) engaged in prostitution.

batter /ˈbatə/ *verb*¹. ME.
[ORIGIN Old French *batre* (mod. *battre*) to strike, beat, fight, from Proto-Romance devel. of Latin *bat(t)uere* beat: ending after verbs in -ER⁵. Cf. BATTLE *noun*.]
1 *verb trans. & intrans.* Strike repeatedly so as to bruise, shatter, or break; beat continuously or violently. Now often *spec.*, subject (one's spouse, partner, or child) to repeated violence and assault. ME. ▸**b** *fig.* Subject (a person, opinion, etc.) to heavy or persistent attack. L16.

SHAKES. *Temp.* With a log Batter his skull. J. REED A number of huge packing cases stood about, and upon these the Red Guards and soldiers fell furiously, battering them open with the butts of their rifles. R. GRAVES The door was battered down and in came the Palace guard. G. MAXWELL The hail roars and batters on the windows. D. LESSING I unroll the veal that I remembered to batter out flat this morning.

battered baby a baby with signs of repeated violence by adults. **battered wife** a woman subjected to repeated violence by her husband.
2 *verb trans.* Operate against (walls, fortifications, etc.) with artillery or (formerly) with a battering ram. L16.

W. S. CHURCHILL For six hours these two ironclads battered each other with hardly any injury or loss on either side. F. WARNER City now utterly destroyed, her walls, Her sanctuary battered down.

3 *verb trans.* Beat out of shape; indent; damage by blows or other rough usage. L16.

DICKENS The sexton's spade gets worn and battered. J. RHYS Some of the flowers were battered.

▪ **batterer** *noun* E17.

batter /ˈbatə/ *verb*² *intrans.* M16.
[ORIGIN Unknown.]
Of a wall etc.: incline from the perpendicular; have a receding slope from the ground upwards.

†**batter** *verb*³ *trans.* L16.
[ORIGIN from BATTER *noun*¹.]
1 Mix into a paste or batter. L16–E17.
2 Paste, fix as with paste; cover with things stuck on. *Scot.* E17–L19.

batterie /batri/ *noun*. Pl. pronounced same. E18.
[ORIGIN French: see BATTERY *noun*.]
1 DANCING. A movement in which the feet or calves are beaten together during a leap. E18.
2 ***batterie de cuisine*** /də kɥizin/ [French = for cookery], apparatus or utensils for serving or preparing a meal. L18.
3 = BATTERY 16. M20.

battering /ˈbatərɪŋ/ *noun*. ME.
[ORIGIN from BATTER *verb*¹ + -ING¹.]
1 The action of BATTER *verb*¹; a prolonged or violent assault. ME.
2 The result of BATTER *verb*¹; a bruise, indentation, or other mark of damage from continuous or violent beating etc. L16.
– COMB.: **battering engine** MILITARY HISTORY = ***battering ram*** (a); **battering ram** (*a*) MILITARY HISTORY a swinging beam used for breaching walls, sometimes with a ram's-head end; (*b*) a similar object used by firemen etc. to break down doors; **battering train** MILITARY HISTORY a number of cannon intended for siege purposes.

Battersea enamel /ˈbatəsɪ ɪˈnam(ə)l/ *noun phr.* M19.
[ORIGIN from *Battersea* a district of London + ENAMEL *noun*.]
Decorative enamel work produced at York House, Battersea, London, in the 18th cent.

battery /ˈbatəri/ *noun*. ME.
[ORIGIN Old French *baterie* (mod. *batterie*), from *batre*: see BATTER *verb*¹, -ERY.]
▸**I 1** (Articles of) metal, esp. (of) brass or copper, wrought by hammering. *arch.* ME.
▸**II** MILITARY uses.
2 A number of pieces of artillery combining in action; an artillery unit of guns and men and vehicles. LME.

N. MONSARRAT The Turks put batteries of their largest cannon . . on Tigré Point. A. EDEN Marjorie advocated the Royal Horse Artillery . . as that battery was already on active service. *fig.*: SMOLLETT The fellow who accused him has had his own battery turned upon himself.

†**3** A succession of heavy blows inflicted on the walls of a city or fortress by means of artillery; a bombardment. M16–M19.

MILTON By Batterie, Scale, and Mine, Assaulting.

4 An emplacement for artillery on land or on a ship. L16.

WELLINGTON The batteries and works erecting at Cadiz. F. MARRYAT She continued her destructive fire . . from the main-deck battery.

▸**III** Physical beating of a person.
5 The action of assailing with blows; LAW the infliction of any menacing touch to the clothes or person. M16.
assault and battery: see ASSAULT *noun*3.
†**6** A mark of beating; a bruise. L16–M17.

SHAKES. *Ven. & Ad.* For where a heart is hard they make no batt'ry.

▸**IV** Uses rel. to or devel. from branch II.

†**7** A number of Leyden jars connected together so as to act simultaneously. **M18–M19.**
8 A device, consisting of one or more cells, in which chemical energy is converted into electricity. **E19.**

E. J. HOWARD The battery was low in the torch and it can't have been very strong to see. J. BARNES We couldn't start the car: the heater had run the battery flat. *attrib.*: M. MCLUHAN The Bedouin with his battery radio.

solar battery: see SOLAR *adjective*[1]. **recharge one's batteries** *fig.* have a period of rest and recuperation. *voltaic battery*: see VOLTAIC *adjective*[1].
9 = *batterie de cuisine* s.v. BATTERIE 2. **E19.**
10 *MINING.* A set of stamps that work in one mortar of a stamp mill. **M19.**
11 A submerged box or boat used in wildfowl shooting. *US.* **M19.**
12 *BASEBALL.* The pitcher and catcher (orig. the pitcher alone). **M19.**
13 *gen.* A set of connected similar units of equipment; an extensive series, sequence, or range, (*of*). **L19.**

Times Adults were interviewed and asked a battery of questions. A. TOFFLER Lectures must inevitably give way to a whole battery of teaching techniques. F. HOYLE It would be necessary to use a battery of the largest and fastest computers.

14 *PSYCHOLOGY.* A series of tests. **E20.**
15 A series of cages etc. in which hens are confined for intensive laying or in which poultry or cattle are reared and fattened. **M20.**
battery hen, *battery system*, etc.
▸**V 16** *MUSIC.* The percussion section of an orchestra or band. **E20.**

batting /ˈbatɪŋ/ *noun.* **E17.**
[ORIGIN from BAT *verb*[1] + -ING[1].]
1 The action of BAT *verb*[1]. **E17.**
2 Cotton fibre prepared in sheets for quilts etc. **E19.**

battle /ˈbat(ə)l/ *noun.* **ME.**
[ORIGIN Old French & mod. French *bataille* battle (also, fortifying tower) from Proto-Romance devel. of late Latin *battualia* military or gladiatorial exercises, from *bat(t)uere* to beat: cf. BATTER *verb*[1].]
▸**I** A fight; fighting.
1 A fight between (esp. large organized) opposing forces. **ME.**
2 A fight between two people; a single combat, a duel. **ME.** ▸**b** A fight between two animals, esp. as providing sport. **E17.**

JOYCE It was a historic and a hefty battle when Myler and Percy were scheduled to don the gloves.

3 Fighting; conflict between enemies; war. **ME.**
4 *fig.* A contest; conflict. **ME.**

COVERDALE *Ps.* 55:21 Yet have they batell in their mynde. E. O'NEILL A perpetual battle of wits with his elder son. K. MILLETT That imposition of male authority euphemistically referred to as 'the battle of the sexes'.

†**5** A war. **LME–M16.**
6 The victory in a fight or other contest. **LME.**

AV *Eccles.* 9:11 The race is not to the swift nor the battle to the strong.

▸**II** (The disposition of) a body of troops.
7 = BATTALION 1. Long *arch.* **ME.**

SIR W. SCOTT In battles four beneath their eye, The forces of King Robert lie.

†**8** The main body of an army or navy force. **M16–M19.**
†**9** = BATTALIA 1. Only in **L16.**
– PHRASES: *battle of the giants*: see GIANT *noun*. **battle royal** a battle in which several combatants or all available engage; a free fight; a general argument. **do battle** fight. **give battle** attack, engage in combat. **half the battle** a large contributory factor in success; the main effort. **join battle** enter into a combat. **line of battle** (the disposition of) troops or warships arranged for battle; *line-of-battle ship*, a ship of sufficient size to take part in a main attack, a battleship. *losing battle*: see LOSING *ppl adjective*. **order of battle** the disposition of sections of an army or navy force; now *spec.* (the discovery of, a tabular record of) the organization, movements, weaponry, etc., of an enemy force. *pitched battle*: see PITCHED *adjective*[1]. *running battle*: see RUNNING *ppl adjective*. *set battle*: see SET *adjective*. **trial by battle** *hist.* the legal decision of a dispute by the issue of a single combat. *wager of battle*: see WAGER *noun* 5b.
– COMB.: **battle array** the disposition of troops etc. arranged for battle; **battleaxe** (*a*) a type of broad-bladed axe used as a weapon, esp. in medieval or prehistoric times and in Africa; (*b*) *colloq.* a formidable or domineering (esp. middle-aged) woman; **battlebus** a bus or coach used as a mobile operational centre during an election campaign; **battlecruiser** a heavy-gunned warship of higher speed and lighter armour than a battleship; **battle cry** a war cry, a slogan; **battledress** a soldier's or airman's everyday khaki uniform of a tunic and trousers; **battle fatigue** mental illness due to stress in wartime combat (= *combat fatigue*); **battlefield** a field or ground on which a battle is fought (*lit.* & *fig.*); **battlefront** the region or line where opposing armies engage in combat. **battleground** a battlefield. **battleship** [from *line-of-battle ship* above] a warship of the most heavily armed and armoured class, of sufficient size to take part in a main attack; *battleship grey*, a slightly bluish grey (often used for warships as reducing their visibility); **battlewagon** *slang* a battleship; an armed or armoured vehicle.
■ **battleworthy** *adjective* fit for use in battle **L19.**

battle /ˈbat(ə)l/ *adjective. obsolete* exc. *dial.* Also (*Scot.*) **baittle** /ˈbeɪt(ə)l/. **E16.**
[ORIGIN Prob. from base also of BATTEN *verb*[2]: see -LE[1]. Cf. BATTLE *verb*[4].]
1 Of grass or pasture: improving to sheep and cattle, fattening. **E16.**
2 Of soil or land: rich, fertile, productive. **M16.**

battle /ˈbat(ə)l/ *verb*[1]. **ME.**
[ORIGIN Old French & mod. French *bataillier*, formed as BATTLE *noun*.]
1 *verb intrans.* **a** Fight; engage in war. Now *rare* in *lit.* sense. **ME.** ▸**b** *fig.* Contend; struggle (*against*, *for* an end etc., *through* a hostile environment etc., *with*, etc.); carry *on* struggling. **LME.**

b J. R. GREEN Walpole battled stubbornly against the cry of war. D. BAGLEY A series of bloody civil wars engendered by ruthless men battling for power. H. FAST To battle through the storm and cold waves. A. MCCOWEN My little auntie Peggy battling with a complicated menu in the kitchen. A. BRINK I was just battling on blindly, not really knowing what was happening.

†**2** *verb trans.* Arrange for battle; dispose in battalions. Only in **ME.**
3 *verb trans.* Fight or struggle against. Now chiefly *N. Amer.* **LME.**

Times Lit. Suppl. Battling the anarchy of fragmenting cultures.

4 *verb trans.* with *it*. Fight, struggle **E18.**

BYRON They battle it beyond the wall.

battle it out fight to a conclusion.
5 *verb trans.* Make *one's way* fighting or struggling. **L18.**

battle /ˈbat(ə)l/ *verb*[2] *trans. arch.* **ME.**
[ORIGIN Later Old French *bataillier*: see BATTLE *verb*[1].]
Fortify or provide with battlements. Chiefly as ***battled*** *ppl adjective.*

TENNYSON The valleys of grape-loaded vines that glow Beneath the battled tower.

†**battle** *verb*[3] *trans. dial.* **E16–L19.**
[ORIGIN Frequentative of BAT *verb*[1]: see -LE[3].]
Beat (clothes) with a wooden stick (see BATTLEDORE 1).

†**battle** *verb*[4]. Long *dial.* **M16.**
[ORIGIN App. from BATTLE *adjective*. Cf. BATTEN *verb*[2].]
1 *verb trans.* Nourish (as a rich pasture does); render (soil etc.) fertile and productive. **M16–M19.**
2 *verb intrans.* Grow fat, thrive; become fertile and productive. **L16–E18.**

battle *verb*[5] var. of BATTEL.

battledore /ˈbat(ə)ldɔː/ *noun.* **LME.**
[ORIGIN Perh. from Provençal *batedor* beater, from *batre* to beat (see BATTER *verb*[1]): cf. BATTLE *verb*[3].]
1 A wooden usu. paddle-shaped instrument used in washing for beating, stirring, or smoothing clothes; a similarly shaped utensil for inserting objects into an oven, kiln, etc. Now chiefly *hist.* **LME.**
†**2** More fully ***battledore book***. A hornbook, an ABC, a child's primer. (So called from its usual shape.) **M17–L19.**
3 A small racket used with a shuttlecock. Also (more fully ***battledore and shuttlecock***) the game played with these, a forerunner of badminton. **L17.**
– PHRASES: **not know a B from a battledore** *arch.* be completely illiterate or ignorant.

battlement /ˈbat(ə)lm(ə)nt/ *noun.* **LME.**
[ORIGIN from Old French *bataillier* (see BATTLE *verb*[1], *verb*[2]) + -MENT.]
Usu. in *pl.* **1** An alternately high and low parapet at the top of a wall, for the defence of a building. **LME.**
2 A roof enclosed by this. **L16.**
■ **battlemented** *adjective* surrounded by battlements **E17.**

battler /ˈbatlə/ *noun*[1]. **ME.**
[ORIGIN Orig. from Old French *batailleor*, -*ier* warrior, formed as BATTLE *verb*[1]; in mod. use from BATTLE *verb*[1] + -ER[1].]
1 A person who battles (usu. *fig.*); *colloq.* a person who fights against the odds or does not give up easily. **ME.**
2 A swagman. *Austral.* **L19.**

battler *noun*[2] var. of BATTELER.

†**battoe** *noun* var. of BATEAU.

battology /bəˈtɒlədʒi/ *noun.* **L16.**
[ORIGIN mod. Latin *battologia* from Greek, from *battos* stammerer: see -LOGY.]
A needless and tiresome repetition in speaking or writing.
■ **battologize** *verb trans.* & *intrans.* repeat (a word or phrase, words or phrases, etc.) needlessly **M17.**

battue /bəˈt(j)uː; *foreign* baty (*pl. same*)/ *noun.* **E19.**
[ORIGIN French, use as noun of fem. pa. pple of *battre*: see BATTER *verb*[1].]
1 A driving of game towards the guns by beaters; a shooting party on this plan. **E19.**
2 *transf.* **a** A thorough search. **M19.** ▸**b** A wholesale slaughter. **M19.**

batture /bəˈtjʊə/ *noun. N. Amer.* **E19.**
[ORIGIN French.]
1 A stretch of river shore, usu. formed by deposition, between the natural embankment and the low-water mark. **E19.**
2 *Canad.* A sandbar in a river. **E19.**

battuta /bəˈtuːtə/ *noun.* **E18.**
[ORIGIN Italian, from *battere* to beat.]
MUSIC. The beating of time; a strong beat; the regular beat.
a battuta a direction: return to the strict tempo.

batty /ˈbati/ *noun. W. Indian & black English colloq.* **M20.**
[ORIGIN from BOTTY (hypocoristic form of BOTTOM *noun*).]
The buttocks, the backside.
– COMB.: **batty boy**, **batty man** *derog.* a homosexual man.

batty /ˈbati/ *adjective.* **L16.**
[ORIGIN from BAT *noun*[3] + -Y[1]; for sense 2 cf. BATS.]
1 Of, pertaining to, or characteristic of a bat or bats. **L16.**
2 Crazy, dotty. *colloq.* **E20.**

†**batus** *noun* see BATH *noun*[2].

Batwa *noun pl.* see TWA *noun*[1].

batz /bats/ *noun. obsolete* exc. *hist.* Pl. **-en** /-ən/, **-es**. Also †**bat**. **L16.**
[ORIGIN German †*Batze* (now *Batzen*); English *bat* by mistaking for a pl.]
A small coin of Switzerland and South Germany, worth four kreutzers.

bauble /ˈbɔːb(ə)l/ *noun.* **ME.**
[ORIGIN Old French *ba(u)bel* child's toy, plaything, perh. ult. from redupl. of *bel* beautiful: cf. BIBELOT.]
1 A showy trinket; a piece of vulgar or ostentatious jewellery. **ME.**

SHAKES. *Tam. Shr.* It is a paltry cap, . . a bauble, a silken pie. LYTTON The knight's baubles become the alderman's badges. J. CAREY Women dripping with baubles.

2 *hist.* A baton surmounted by a fantastically carved head with asses' ears, carried by a jester as a rod of office. **LME.**
3 **a** A plaything, a toy. *obsolete* exc. as passing into other senses. **LME.** ▸**b** A coloured glass ball or similar ornament hung for decoration on a Christmas tree. **M20.**
4 A childish or trivial matter; something of no importance. **M16.**

LD MACAULAY The Right Honourable before my name is a bauble.

■ †**baubling** *adjective* trifling, paltry **E17–M19.**

bauch /bɑːx, bɔːx/ *adjective. Scot.* **E16.**
[ORIGIN Perh. from Old Norse *bágr* uneasy: cf. Icelandic *bágur* difficult, hard, (*eiga*) *bágt* (be) poor, hard up.]
Weak, poor, spineless.

bauchle /ˈbɑːx(ə)l, ˈbɔː-/ *noun. Scot.* **E17.**
[ORIGIN Uncertain: cf. BAUCHLE *verb*.]
1 A spoiled or distorted thing; *spec.* an old shoe worn down at the heel. **E17.**
2 A ne'er-do-well. **E19.**

bauchle /ˈbɑːx(ə)l, ˈbɔː-/ *verb trans. Scot.* Long *dial. rare.* **L15.**
[ORIGIN Uncertain: perh. from BAUCH.]
Subject to disgrace or ignominy, vilify; = BAFFLE *verb* 1.

baud /bəʊd, bɔːd/ *noun.* Pl. **-s**, same. **M20.**
[ORIGIN from J. M. E. *Baudot* (1845–1903), French engineer.]
TELECOMMUNICATIONS & COMPUTING. A unit of signal transmission speed equal to one information unit per second; *loosely* a unit of data transmission speed of one bit per second.

baudekin /ˈbɔːdɪkɪn/ *noun. obsolete* exc. *hist.* Also **baudkin** /ˈbɔːdkɪn/, & other vars. **ME.**
[ORIGIN Old French from medieval Latin *baldachinus* formed as BALDACHIN.]
= BALDACHIN 1.

Baudelairean /bəʊdəˈlɛːrɪən/ *adjective & noun.* Also **-ian**. **L19.**
[ORIGIN from *Baudelaire* (see below) + -EAN.]
▸**A** *adjective.* Of, pertaining to, or characteristic of the French poet and critic Charles Baudelaire (1821–67) or his works. **L19.**
▸**B** *noun.* An admirer or student of Baudelaire or his writing. **E20.**

baudkin *noun* var. of BAUDEKIN.

baudrons /ˈbɔːdrənz/ *noun. Scot.* **L15.**
[ORIGIN Unknown: cf. BAWD *noun*[2].]
(A name for) the cat.

SIR W. SCOTT He had a beard too, and whiskers . . as long as baudrons'.

bauera /ˈbaʊərə/ *noun.* **E19.**
[ORIGIN mod. Latin, from Franz (1758–1840) and Ferdinand (1760–1826) *Bauer*, Austrian botanical draughtsmen: see -A[1].]
A small Australian evergreen shrub of the genus *Bauera*, bearing rose-coloured or purple flowers.

Bauhaus /ˈbaʊhaʊs/ *noun.* **E20.**
[ORIGIN German, from *Bau* building + *Haus* house.]
(The principles of) a German school of architecture and design founded by Walter Gropius in 1919 and closed in 1933.

bauhinia /bəʊˈhɪnɪə/ *noun.* **L18.**
[ORIGIN mod. Latin, from Jean (1541–1613) and Gaspard (1560–1624) *Bauhin*, Swiss botanists: see -IA[1].]
A leguminous plant of the tropical genus *Bauhinia*, of which there are many species.

B

baulk /bɔːlk, bɔːk/ *noun*. Also **balk**. LOE.
[ORIGIN Old Norse *bálkr* partition, from Germanic; rel. to Old Frisian *balca*, Old Saxon, Old High German *balco* (Dutch *balk*, German *Balken*), Old Norse *bjálki*, from a Germanic base meaning 'beam'.]
▸ **I** †**1** A ridge, a mound, *esp.* a grave mound; a dividing ridge of land. LOE–M17.
2 A ridge left in ploughing, either intentionally (esp. as a boundary line between sections) or unintentionally. LOE.
make a baulk of good ground waste an opportunity.
†**3** A mistake, a blunder; an omission. LME–L19.
†**4** A ridge in one's way; a stumbling block, an obstacle. LME–M18.
5 *fig.* A hindrance, a check; a disappointment. M17.

DEFOE This was a balk to them and put a damp to their new projects. D. LESSING The balk, the disappointment, is felt as a promise that has been broken.

6 BILLIARDS & SNOOKER etc. A marked-off area on the table from which play begins and which governs play in certain situations varying according to the game being played (for example, protecting a ball from a direct stroke); the area between the baulk line and the bottom cushion. Also (in some games), a play bringing one's own and the red ball within this area. L18.
baulk-cushion, *baulk-end*, *baulk-pocket*, etc. *give a miss-in-baulk*: see MISS *noun*[1].
7 BASEBALL. An illegal action by a pitcher. M19.
▸ **II 8** A beam of timber; a tie beam of a house (now chiefly *N. English*). ME.

J. MASTERS Each man carried a stave—a big balk of wood, rather.

9 The beam of a balance. *obsolete* exc. *dial.* LME.
– COMB.: **baulk line** a line drawn on a billiard or snooker table parallel to the face of the bottom cushion at a distance one-fifth of the length of the playing area.

baulk /bɔːlk, bɔːk/ *verb*. Also **balk**. LME.
[ORIGIN from the noun.]
†**1** *verb trans. & intrans.* Make baulks in (land) in ploughing. LME–E17. ▸**b** *verb trans. fig.* Heap up in ridges. *rare*. Only in L16.
2 *verb trans.* Shirk or ignore; pass over (a topic, opportunity, etc.); avoid or refuse (a duty, thing offered, etc.). LME.

SHAKES. *Twel. N.* This was look'd for at your hand, and this was baulk'd. S. JOHNSON I never . . balked an invitation out to dinner. D. H. LAWRENCE It's got to be done, so why balk it?

†**3** *verb trans.* Pass by (a place); avoid, shun. L15–L18.
4 *verb intrans.* Stop short as at an obstacle; jib or shy (*lit. & fig.*). L16.

C. J. LEVER Burke . . suddenly swerved his horse round, and affecting to baulk, cantered back. B. SPOCK A baby may first balk at the transition from bottle to weaning cup. W. GOLDING Steam could lift a weight that an elephant would baulk at.

†**5** *verb trans.* Miss by error or inadvertence. L16–E18.

SPENSER They . . balk the right way, and strayen abroad.

6 *verb trans.* Place a baulk in the way of (a person); hinder, thwart, disappoint, frustrate. L16.

POPE Balk'd of his prey, the yelling monster flies. DEFOE An enemy who is baulked and defeated, but not overcome. SWIFT The most effectual Way to baulk Their Malice, is—to let them talk. H. MARTINEAU My home affections . . all the stronger for having been repressed and baulked. H. READ A personal will to dominate material and form which refuses to be balked by any conventions.

†**7** *verb intrans. & trans.* Quibble; argue; chop (logic). L16–M17.
■ **baulkiness** *noun* the quality of being baulky L19. **baulky** *adjective* liable to baulk (BAULK *verb* 4); reluctant to proceed; perverse: M19.

†**baum-cricket** *noun* var. of BALM-CRICKET.

Baumé /ˈbəʊmeɪ/ *noun*. Also **Beaumé**. M19.
[ORIGIN See below.]
1 Used *attrib.* and in *possess.* to denote a kind of hydrometer invented by Antoine Baumé (1728–1804), French chemist, and an associated arbitrary scale of relative density. M19.
2 *degree Baumé*, a unit on this scale. L19.

baum marten /baʊm ˈmɑːtɪn/ *noun phr.* L19.
[ORIGIN Partial translation of German *Baummarder* lit. 'tree marten'.]
The pine marten; the fur of this animal.

bauson /ˈbɔːs(ə)n/ *noun*. *arch. & dial.* Also **baw-**. LME.
[ORIGIN from BAUSOND.]
1 = BADGER *noun*[2]. LME.
2 A fat or obstinate person. E18.

bausond /ˈbɔːs(ə)nd/ *adjective*. *dial.* Also **baw-**. ME.
[ORIGIN Old French *bausant* piebald = Provençal *bausan* (Italian *balzano*, whence mod. French *balzan*), from Proto-Romance adjective (= belted, striped), from Latin *balteus* belt.]
Of an animal: having white spots on a black or bay ground; *esp.* having a white patch on the forehead, or a white stripe down the face.

bauxite /ˈbɔːksʌɪt/ *noun*. Also †**beaux-**. M19.
[ORIGIN French, orig. *beauxite*, from *Les B(e)aux*, locality near Arles, France: see -ITE[1].]
The major commercial source of aluminium, an earthy rock consisting of hydrated alumina with variable proportions of iron oxides and other impurities.
■ **bauxitic** /bɔːkˈsɪtɪk/ *adjective* L19.

bavardage /bavardaːʒ/ *noun*. E19.
[ORIGIN French, from *bavarder* to chatter, from *bavard* talkative, from *bave* saliva, drivel.]
Idle gossip, chit-chat.

Bavarian /bəˈvɛːrɪən/ *adjective & noun*. E17.
[ORIGIN from *Bavaria* (German *Bayern*) (see below) + -AN.]
▸ **A** *adjective*. Of or pertaining to Bavaria, formerly a kingdom of the German Empire, now a state in Germany, its natives or inhabitants, or their dialect. E17.
Bavarian cream = BAVAROISE.
▸ **B** *noun*. A native or inhabitant of Bavaria; the dialect of German used there. L18.

bavaroise /bavəˈwɑːz, *foreign* bavarwaːz/ *noun*. Also **-ois** /-ˈwɑː, *foreign* -wa/. M19.
[ORIGIN French, use as noun of fem. adjective, = BAVARIAN.]
A dessert containing gelatin and whipped cream, served cold.

bavaroy /ˈbavərɔɪ/ *noun*. *obsolete* exc. *hist.* E18.
[ORIGIN Prob. from French *bavarois* BAVARIAN.]
A type of greatcoat or cloak for men.

baviaan /bavɪˈɑːn/ *noun*. *S. Afr.* M18.
[ORIGIN Dutch.]
= BABOON 2, 3.

bavin /ˈbavɪn/ *noun*. ME.
[ORIGIN Unknown.]
(A bundle of) brushwood, firewood.

baw /bɔː/ *interjection*. *arch.* LME.
[ORIGIN Imit.: cf. BAH.]
Expr. contempt or aversion.

bawbee /ˈbɔːbiː/ *noun*. Chiefly *Scot.* M16.
[ORIGIN from the laird of Sille*bawby*, mint-master under James V.]
Orig., a silver coin worth three, later six, Scottish pennies. Now, a coin of low value.

bawcock /ˈbɔːkɒk/ *noun*. *arch. colloq.* L16.
[ORIGIN French *beau coq* fine cock.]
A good fellow.

bawd /bɔːd/ *noun*[1]. LME.
[ORIGIN Shortened from BAWDSTROT.]
A procurer, now only a female one, a woman who obtains women for prostitution.

bawd /bɔːd/ *noun*[2]. *dial.* L15.
[ORIGIN Perh. from BAUDRONS: cf. the English use of *puss* and Scot. of *malkin* for both hare and cat.]
A hare.

†**bawd** *verb intrans.* M17–E18.
[ORIGIN from BAWD *noun*[1].]
Pander.

bawdry /ˈbɔːdri/ *noun*. LME.
[ORIGIN from BAWD *noun*[1] + -RY.]
†**1** The practice of a bawd; procuring. LME–E18.
†**2** Immorality, fornication. LME–M17.
3 Obscenity in speech or writing. L16.

†**bawdstrot** *noun*. ME–L15.
[ORIGIN Old French *baudetrot*, *baudestroyt*, from *baut*, *baude* lively, gay, shameless (from Germanic, = BOLD *adjective*) + base of Anglo-Norman *trote* TROT *noun*[2].]
= BAWD *noun*[1].

†**bawdy** *adjective*[1]. LME–E17.
[ORIGIN Origin unkn., but cf. Welsh *bawaidd* dirty, vile, from *baw* dirt.]
Soiled, dirty.
■ †**bawdiness** *noun*[1] M16–M18.

bawdy /ˈbɔːdi/ *adjective*[2] *& noun*. E16.
[ORIGIN from BAWD *noun*[1] + -Y[1]: prob. assoc. with BAWDY *adjective*[1].]
▸ **A** *adjective*. Of or befitting a bawd, *esp.* (of language) humorously indecent. E16.
bawdy-house *arch.* a brothel.
▸ **B** *noun*. Humorously indecent language or talk (esp. in *talk bawdy*); licentiousness. M17.
■ **bawdily** *adverb* E17. **bawdiness** *noun*[2] M18.

bawl /bɔːl/ *verb & noun*. LME.
[ORIGIN Imit.: cf. medieval Latin *baulare* bark, Icelandic *baula* (Swedish *böla*) low, as an ox.]
▸ **A** *verb*. **1** *verb intrans.* Bark, howl, etc., as an animal. *obsolete* exc. *dial.* LME.

ROBERT BURTON A barking dog that alwayes bawls, but seldome bites.

2 *verb intrans.* Shout, howl, etc., at the top of one's voice; weep or wail loudly. L15.

W. COWPER And ev'ry soul cried out, well done, As loud as he could bawl. P. G. WODEHOUSE Her Uncle George was bawling to somebody to fetch a policeman. T. CAPOTE He started to cry. Sat down and bawled like a kid.

3 *verb trans.* Utter with bawling, shout loudly. (Freq. foll. by *out*.) L16.

SHAKES. *2 Hen. IV* Those that bawl out the ruins of thy linen shall inherit his kingdom. THACKERAY 'I will fling you out of window' . . bawled out Mr. Pen. E. BUSHEN They all rose and bawled the final hymn.

4 *verb trans.* Foll. by *out*. Reprove or reprimand severely. *colloq.* (orig. *US*). E20.

L. A. G. STRONG He bawled him out. Gave him such a tongue-lashing. M. GEE They bawled each other out in the street.

▸ **B** *noun*. A shout at the top of one's voice; a loud prolonged cry. L18.
■ **bawler** *noun* L16.

bawley /ˈbɔːli/ *noun*. L19.
[ORIGIN Unknown.]
A fishing smack used on the coasts of Essex and Kent.

bawn /bɔːn/ *noun*. M16.
[ORIGIN Irish *badún*, perh. from *ba* cows + *dún* fortress.]
1 *hist.* A fortified enclosure; the fortified court or outwork of a castle. M16.
2 A fold for cattle. *dial.* M19.
3 An expanse of rocks, a meadow, etc., on which salted cod are spread out to dry. *Canad. dial.* L19.

bawneen /ˈbɔːniːn/ *noun*. Also in Irish form **báinín** (pronounced same). E20.
[ORIGIN Irish *báinín* dim. of *bán* white.]
Undyed off-white yarn used in Ireland for knitting (esp. in Aran wear) and weaving; a garment made of this.

bawson *noun*, **bawsond** *adjective*, vars. of BAUSON, BAUSOND.

baxter /ˈbakstə/ *noun*. Long *dial.* (esp. *Scot.*).
[ORIGIN Old English *bæcestre* fem. of *bæcere* BAKER: see -STER.]
A baker.

bay /beɪ/ *noun*[1]. ME.
[ORIGIN Old French *bai* or aphet. from ABAY from Old French *abai* (mod. *aboi*), from *(a)baiier* BAY *verb*[1].]
1 The deep bark of a large dog or of hounds in pursuit; *esp.* the chorus raised on drawing close to the hunted quarry. ME.

C. BRONTË Formidable-looking dogs . . all bristle and bay.

2 The position or action of a hunted animal when, unable to flee further, it turns and defends itself at close quarters. Freq. *fig.* Only in *at bay*, *to bay*, †*at a bay*, †*to a bay*. ME.

SHAKES. *Ven. & Ad.* The hounds are at a bay. T. H. WHITE The boar was not at bay any more, but charging Master Twyti. *fig.*: SHAKES. *Rich. II* To rouse his wrongs and chase them to the bay. D. H. LAWRENCE Gerald seemed always to be at bay against everybody.

bring to bay come close to (the quarry). **hold at bay**, **keep at bay** keep at a distance, resist, hold off. **stand at bay** turn against one's assailants.

bay /beɪ/ *noun*[2]. LME.
[ORIGIN Old French & mod. French *baie* from Latin *baca* berry.]
†**1** A berry, esp. of the laurel. LME–M19.
2 In full *bay tree*. An evergreen tree of the laurel family, *Laurus nobilis*, with dark green aromatic leaves. Also (*US*), any of various similarly aromatic trees and shrubs, esp. of the genera *Magnolia* and *Myrica*. M16.
red bay: see RED *adjective*. *sweet bay*: see SWEET *adjective & adverb*.
3 *sing.* & (usu.) in *pl.* Leaves or twigs of bay, esp. as a wreath for a conqueror or poet; *fig.* fame. M16.
4 In the coastal states of south-eastern US: a tract of low marshy wooded ground with numerous bay trees. L18.
– COMB.: *bay laurel*: see LAUREL *noun* 1; **bay leaf** a dried leaf of sweet bay, used as flavouring; **bay rum** perfume (esp. for the hair) distilled from rum and leaves of the bayberry *Pimenta acris*.

bay /beɪ/ *noun*[3]. LME.
[ORIGIN Old French & mod. French *baie* from Old Spanish & mod. Spanish *bahia*, perh. of Iberian origin.]
1 (A part of the sea filling) a broad, large indentation in a coastline. LME.

SHAKES. *A.Y.L.* My affection hath an unknown bottom, like the Bay of Portugal. N. CALDER Around the bay are sunken ruins of other seaports.

2 An indentation or recess in a range of hills etc. M19.

L. VAN DER POST Each bay cut in a cliff of green was ardent with white and blue lilies' hearts.

– COMB.: **bayman** *N. Amer.* a person resident beside a (usu. specified) bay; *Canad.* a backwoodsman, a rustic; **bay salt**: obtained as large crystals by slow evaporation (orig. by the sun from seawater); **bayside** *adjective* on or near the shore of a bay; **Bay State** *US* Massachusetts; **bay-whaler** *Austral. & NZ hist.* a boat used or person engaged in bay whaling; **bay whaling** *Austral. & NZ hist.* whaling from land-based stations, practised when whales came into shallow inshore waters to calve; **baywood** [*Bay* of Campeche, Mexico] mahogany from the Central American tree *Swietenia macrophylla*.

bay /beɪ/ *noun*[4]. LME.
[ORIGIN Old French & mod. French *baie*, from *bayer* (earlier *baer*, *beer*) stand open, gape from medieval Latin *batare*, of unknown origin.]
1 A division (of a wall) of a room between columns, bookcases, etc. LME.

F. R. WILSON The last two bays of the nave . . are unoccupied. J. HILTON A very delightful library . . containing a multitude of books so retiringly housed in bays and alcoves.

2 (In full *bay window*, a window across) an internal recess formed by the outward projection of a wall beyond the general line. Cf. ***bow window*** s.v. BOW *noun*[1]. LME.

E. WALFORD A substantial brick house, the front diversified by two bays. H. FAST A slanted bay looked out over a greenery-choked backyard.

3 A recess, a compartment; a partitioned or marked area forming a unit. Freq. with specification of purpose, as ***bomb bay***, ***loading bay***, ***sickbay***. L16.

C. RYAN From the bays of the B-24s.. supplies began to fall haphazardly. E. CRISPIN A single-lane carriageway lined on either side with V-shaped bays in which pedestrians could take refuge.

4 A railway line at a station, having a closed end and acting as a terminus for a sideline; a platform adjoining this. Usu. *attrib.* E20.

A. CHRISTIE A train.. came slowly puffing in and deposited itself in a modest bay.

– COMB.: ***bay window***: see sense 2 above; **bay-windowed** *adjective* having a bay window.
■ **bayed** *adjective* (of a window) having or set in a bay E19.

bay /beɪ/ *noun*[5]. LME.
[ORIGIN Unknown.]
An embankment, a dam.

bay /beɪ/ *noun*[6]. M16.
[ORIGIN from BAY *adjective*.]
1 A bay horse. M16.
2 *hist.* ***The Bays***, ***The Queen's Bays***, the 2nd Dragoon Guards (now incorporated in the 1st Queen's Dragoon Guards), who orig. rode bay horses. M19.

bay /beɪ/ *noun*[7]. *obsolete* exc. *hist.* L16.
[ORIGIN Old French & mod. French *baie* or Dutch *baai*, from *bai* BAY *adjective*: see BAIZE.]
Baize. Freq. in *pl.* (whence BAIZE, the mod. form).

bay /beɪ/ *noun*[8]. M19.
[ORIGIN Abbreviation of BEZ-ANTLER.]
The second branch of a stag's horn, above the brow antler. Also ***bay-antler***.

bay /beɪ/ *adjective*. ME.
[ORIGIN Old French & mod. French *bai* from Latin *badius* chestnut-coloured (only of horses), rel. to Old Irish *buide* yellow.]
Usu. of a horse: reddish-brown and (of a horse) with black mane and tail.

bay /beɪ/ *verb*[1]. LME.
[ORIGIN Old French *(a)baiier* (mod. *aboyer*) = Italian *(ab)baiare* from an imit. base: infl. by BAY *noun*[1].]
1 *verb intrans.* Esp. of a large dog: bark, howl. Freq. foll. by *at*. LME.

fig.: P. GALLICO For twenty years they have been baying at your heels in Washington. B. MALAMUD The wind bayed at the window like starving wolves.

2 *verb trans.* Bark at, assail with barking. LME.

SHAKES. *Jul. Caes.* I had rather be a dog and bay the moon Than such a Roman. *fig.*: COLERIDGE Superstition and her wolfish brood Bay his mild radiance.

3 *verb trans.* Utter by baying, shout. L16.

E. K. KANE These.. servants.. bayed their full-mouth welcome.

4 *verb trans.* Pursue with barking like a pack of hounds. L16.

SHAKES. *2 Hen. IV* The French and Welsh Baying him at the heels. C. DARWIN The jaguar is killed by the aid of dogs baying and driving him up a tree.

5 *verb trans.* Bring to bay, hold at bay. L16.

SHAKES. *Jul. Caes.* We are at the stake, And bay'd about with many enemies.

bay /beɪ/ *verb*[2] *trans.* L16.
[ORIGIN Conn. with BAY *noun*[5], either as source or (prob.) as deriv.]
Obstruct, dam (water). Usu. foll. by *back*, *up*.

†**bay** *verb*[3] *trans. rare* (Spenser). Only in L16.
[ORIGIN App. pseudo-arch. alt. of BATHE *verb*. Cf. EMBAY *verb*[2].]
Bathe, immerse.

bay /beɪ/ *verb*[4] *intrans. & trans. rare.* M17.
[ORIGIN from BAY *noun*[1].]
Stand at bay (against).

bayadère /beɪjəˈdɛː, -ˈdɪə/ *noun*. L16.
[ORIGIN French from Portuguese *bailadeira*, from *bailar* to dance, rel. to medieval Latin *ballare* to dance.]
1 A Hindu dancing girl (esp. at a southern Indian temple). L16.
2 A striped textile fabric. M19.

bayard /ˈbeɪɑːd/ *adjective & noun. arch.* ME.
[ORIGIN Old French *baiart*, *-ard*, from *bai* BAY *adjective*: see -ARD. Sense B.2 alludes to the name of the magic steed given (in medieval romance) by Charlemagne to Renaud de Montauban, which was celebrated as a type of blind recklessness.]
▸ **A** *adjective*. Bay-coloured. ME.
▸ **B** *noun*. **1** A bay horse. LME.
†**2** A person blind to his or her own ignorance, a self-confident fool. E16–L17.

bayberry /ˈbeɪbɛri/ *noun*. E16.
[ORIGIN from BAY *noun*[2] + BERRY *noun*[1].]
1 The fruit of the bay tree. E16.
2 A N. American shrub or small tree, *Myrica cerifera*, allied to the bog myrtle (also called ***wax myrtle***); the fruit of this tree, which yields a wax made into candles. L17.
3 (The fruit of) a fragrant oil-bearing W. Indian tree, *Pimenta acris*. M18.

Bayes' theorem /ˈbeɪz ˌθɪərəm/ *noun phr.* M19.
[ORIGIN The Revd Thomas *Bayes* (1702–61), English mathematician.]
MATH. A theorem expressing the probability of each of a number of mutually exclusive events, given some other event *E*, in terms of the probabilities of those events independently of *E* and the probabilities of *E* given each of those events in turn.
■ **Bayesian** *adjective & noun* (**a**) *adjective* pertaining to or employing concepts arising out of Bayes' work on calculations of probability; *esp.* designating methods of statistical inference in which use is made of prior information on the distributions of parameters; (**b**) *noun* a person who uses or advocates Bayesian methods: M20. **Bayesianism** *noun* advocacy or use of Bayesian methods L20.

bayonet /ˈbeɪənɪt/ *noun & verb.* L17.
[ORIGIN French *baïonnette*, from *Bayonne*, France, the orig. place of manufacture: see -ET[1].]
▸ **A** *noun*. †**1** A short flat dagger. L17–E18.
2 A swordlike stabbing blade which may be fixed to a rifle muzzle for use in hand-to-hand fighting. E18. ▸**b** A soldier armed with a bayonet; military force. L18.
Spanish bayonet: see SPANISH *adjective*.
3 A pin, plug, etc., which engages in a hole or socket by a push-and-twist action (orig. merely by pushing). Usu. *attrib.*, designating electrical fittings designed to engage in this way. L18.
▸ **B** *verb trans.* **1** Stab with a bayonet. L17.
2 Coerce by means of bayonets. L18.
– COMB.: **bayonet-grass** *NZ* = SPANIARD *noun* 3.

bayou /ˈbʌɪuː/ *noun. US.* M18.
[ORIGIN Amer. French from Choctaw *bayuk*.]
In the southern states: a marshy offshoot of a river, lake, etc.

bazaar /bəˈzɑː/ *noun*. L16.
[ORIGIN Italian *bazarro* from Turkish from Persian *bāzār* market.]
1 An Eastern market. L16.
2 A large shop, or arcade of shops, selling fancy goods, bric-a-brac, etc. E19.
3 A sale of miscellaneous (usu. second-hand) goods in aid of charity. E19.

bazan *noun* var. of BASAN.

baze /beɪz/ *verb trans.* Long *obsolete* exc. *dial.* E17.
[ORIGIN Unknown: cf. Dutch *bazen*.]
Stupefy; frighten.

bazil *noun* var. of BASIL *noun*[3].

bazillion /bəˈzɪljən/ *noun. colloq.* (orig. & chiefly *N. Amer.*). L20.
[ORIGIN Prob. alt. of BILLION after *gazillion*.]
A very large (but indefinite) number or quantity.

K. KELLY Take ten designs.. and do the tenth one up in a bazillion variations.

bazoo /bəˈzuː/ *noun. US slang.* L19.
[ORIGIN Unknown: cf. Dutch *bazuin* trombone, trumpet.]
1 = KAZOO. L19.
2 The mouth. E20.

bazooka /bəˈzuːkə/ *noun*. M20.
[ORIGIN App. from BAZOO.]
1 A crude musical instrument resembling a trombone. *US*. M20.
2 A portable tubular anti-tank rocket launcher. M20.

bazoom /bəˈzuːm/ *noun. slang.* M20.
[ORIGIN Prob. alt. of BOSOM *noun*.]
A woman's breast. Usu. in *pl.*

bazuco *noun* var. of BASUCO.

BB *abbreviation*.
double-black (of pencil lead).

b-ball /ˈbiːbɔːl/ *noun. N. Amer. slang.* L20.
[ORIGIN Abbreviation.]
Basketball.

BBB *abbreviation*.
treble-black (of pencil lead).

BBC *abbreviation*.
British Broadcasting Corporation.
BBC English a form of standard English regarded as characteristic of BBC announcers.

bbl. *abbreviation*.
Barrels (esp. of oil).

b-boy /ˈbiːbɔɪ/ *noun. US slang.* L20.
[ORIGIN *b-* prob. from BEAT *noun*[1] or BREAK-DANCING.]
A young man involved with hip hop culture.

BBQ *abbreviation*.
Barbecue.

BBS *abbreviation*.
COMPUTING. Bulletin board system.

BC *abbreviation*.
1 Before Christ.
2 British Columbia.
– NOTE: In sense 1 usu. written in small capitals and placed after the numerals, as in 72 BC.

bcc *abbreviation*.
Blind carbon copy.

BCD *abbreviation*.
Binary coded decimal.

BCE *abbreviation*.
Before the Common Era.

BCF *abbreviation*.
British Cycling Federation.

BCG *abbreviation*.
Bacillus of Calmette and Guérin (anti-tuberculosis vaccine), developed by Albert Calmette (1863–1933) and Camille Guérin (1872–1961), French bacteriologists.

BD *abbreviation*.
Bachelor of Divinity.

BDD *abbreviation*.
Body dysmorphic disorder.

Bde *abbreviation*.
Brigade.

bdellium /ˈdɛlɪəm/ *noun*. LME.
[ORIGIN Latin from Greek *bdellion*, of Semitic origin: cf. Hebrew *bᵉdōlah*.]
A tree, esp. of the genus *Commiphora*, yielding a fragrant gum resin; the resin itself.

bdelloid /ˈdɛlɔɪd/ *adjective*. E20.
[ORIGIN from Greek *bdella* leech + -OID.]
ZOOLOGY. ***bdelloid rotifer***, a rotifer of the order Bdelloidea, resembling a leech.

Bdr *abbreviation*.
Bombardier.

BDS *abbreviation*.
Bachelor of Dental Surgery.

BDSM *abbreviation*.
Bondage, domination, sadism, masochism.

BE *abbreviation*.
1 Bachelor of Education.
2 Bachelor of Engineering.
3 Bill of exchange.

Be *symbol*.
CHEMISTRY. Beryllium.

be /biː, *unstressed* bɪ/ *verb*. Pres. indic.: 1 **am** /am, əm/; 2 & *pl.* **are** /ɑː, ə/; 3, (*dial.*) 1, 2, & *pl.* **is** /ɪz/; 2 (*arch.*) **art** /ɑːt, ət/; 2 & *pl.* (*arch. & dial.*) **be**. Past indic.: 1 & 3 **was** /wɒz, wəz/; 2 & *pl.* **were** /wəː, wɛː, wə/, (*dial.*) **was**; 2 (*arch.*) **wast** /wɒst, wəst/ or **wert** /wəːt, wət/. Pres. subjunct. (now often repl. by indic. forms): **be**; 2 *sing.* also †**beest**. Past subjunct.: **were**; 1 & 3 *sing.* (*colloq.*), & 2 & *pl.* (*arch. & dial.*) also **was**; 2 *sing.* also (*arch.*) **wert**. Imper.: **be**. Pres. pple **being** /ˈbiːɪŋ/. Pa. pple **been** /biːn, bɪn/. Informal abbreviated forms: **'m** = *am*; **'s** = *is*, **'re** = *are*; **aren't** /ɑːnt/ = *are not*, (interrog.) *am not*; **isn't** /ˈɪz(ə)nt/ = *is not*; **i'nt** /ɪnt/ (*non-standard*) = *is not*; **wasn't** /ˈwɒz(ə)nt/, (now *dial.*, chiefly *US*) **wa'n't** /wɑːnt/ = *was not*; **weren't** /wəːnt, wɛːnt/ = *were not*; **ain't** /eɪnt/, (*arch.*) **an't** /ɑːnt/ (*colloq.*) = *am not*, (*slang & joc.*) = *is not*, *are not*. OE.
[ORIGIN An irreg. and defective verb, the full set of forms of which is made up of the surviving inflections of four bases: (i) the Indo-European verb with stem base also of Sanskrit *as-*, Greek *es-*, Latin *es-*, *'s-*; (ii) the Indo-European verb with stem base also of Sanskrit *vas-*, Gothic *wisan* to remain; (iii) the Indo-European verb with stem base also of Sanskrit *bhū-*, Greek *phu-*, Latin *fu-*, Old English *bēon* become; (iv) the Germanic perfect formation, base of *are*, of unknown origin.]
▸ **I** As full verb.
1 Have place in the realm of fact; exist, live. OE.

AV *Gen.* 5:24 Enoch walked with God: and hee was not, for God tooke him. DRYDEN Troy is no more. POPE Some nymphs there are, too conscious of their face. R. HEBER Cherubim and seraphim falling down before Thee, Which wert, and art, and evermore shall be. DICKENS There ain't anything the matter.

2 Come into existence, come about; happen, occur, take place. OE.

R. B. SHERIDAN Your husband that shall be. OED The flower-show was last week.

3 (With adverbs and preposition phrs.) Have or occupy a given position; exist in a stated circumstance, condition, or relation; occupy oneself in a given way, hold a given opinion, etc. OE. ▸**b** Take or direct oneself; go, come; (often with infinitive expr. purpose); (in *pa. pple*) called, visited. M17.

SHAKES. *Rich. III* Where is thy husband now? Where be thy brothers? EVELYN There was not his equal in the whole world. R. BURNS Oh, were I on Parnassus' Hill! W. S. GILBERT Peter's been at the old brown sherry. J. GALSWORTHY I thought that you . . might . . ascertain what the fellow is about. DYLAN THOMAS The House is 5 minutes from the station. R. KENNEDY One fifth of the people are against everything all the time. J. I. M. STEWART I do have two daughters. They're still at school. **b** C. BURNEY Fanny . . had been to enquire after him 2 days ago. A. E. HOUSMAN Oh I have been to Ludlow fair.

4 Go on in its existing condition; remain, continue; take or last (a specified time). **ME.**

SHAKES. *All's Well* Nay, I'll fit you, And not be all day neither. V. MCNABB St. Malachy was some months in reaching Clairvaux.

5 Be the case or the fact; obtain. **ME.**

SHAKES. *2 Hen. IV* You loiter here too long, being you are to take soldiers up in counties as you go. ALDOUS HUXLEY It may be that, later on, I shall take your advice after all.

6 Befall, pertain (*un*)*to*; (now only in exclams. and wishes). **ME.**

SHAKES. *Lear* To thine and Albany's issues Be this perpetual.

▸ **II** As copular verb.

7 (With noun, adjective, or (passing into sense 3) adjectival phr.) Have the state or quality expressed by the predicate. **OE.**

SHAKES. *Ant. & Cl.* Be'est thou sad or merry, The violence of either thee becomes. J. GRAINGER What is fame? an empty bubble. SIR W. SCOTT Be of good courage. GEO. ELIOT I'm a stranger in Florence. E. WAUGH Aunt Julia . . lived to be eighty-eight. P. GALLICO He was an honest man, was Patrick. P. LARKIN Some must employ the scythe . . That the walks be smooth For the feet of the angel.

8 (With noun.) Coincide with, be identical to; form the essential constituent of, act the part of. **OE.** ▸**b** Amount to, mean; cost. **ME.**

J. AUSTEN We have got a play . . and I am to be Count Cassel. G. STEIN Rose is a rose is a rose is a rose. A. J. P. TAYLOR The overriding problem was where to land. *Listener* For us during thirty years Kingsley Martin . . *was* the *New Statesman*. J. BRONOWSKI The gas was oxygen. **b** AV *Lam.* 1:12 Is it nothing to you, all ye that passe by? T. HARDY A genial and pleasant gentleman, whom to meet . . was to know, to know was to drink with, and to drink with was, unfortunately, to pay for. D. L. SAYERS Yours is one-and-a-penny and mine's ninepence.

▸ **III** As auxiliary verb.

9 With pa. pple of verb trans., forming the pass. voice. **OE.** ▸**b** With pa. pple of verb intrans., forming perfect tenses. *arch.* (now usu. repl. by *have*). **OE.**

SHAKES. *Com. Err.* Ill deeds is doubled with an evil word. G. WHITE The manor of Selborne, was it strictly looked after . . would swarm with game. C. M. YONGE His parents were grown old. D. PARKER If all the girls attending it were laid end to end, I wouldn't be at all surprised. **b** MILTON Therefore I am returned. GOLDSMITH Silence is become his mother tongue.

10 With pres. pple forming progressive act. tenses. **OE.** ▸**b** With pres. pple, or more usu. with *being* + pa. pple, forming progressive pass. tenses. **M16.**

BUNYAN He was talking of thee. DYLAN THOMAS I'll be ringing you in August. **b** C. LAMB A man who is being strangled. OED We stayed there while our house was building.

11 With infinitive, expr. duty or obligation (often repl. by *have*), intention, possibility, destiny, or hypothesis. **ME.**

S. RICHARDSON I am to thank you . . for your kind Letter. DICKENS You was to come to him at six o'clock. E. A. FREEMAN Normandy was to be invaded on each side. J. CONRAD He was nowhere to be seen. R. A. KNOX It wasn't for him to mix himself up in political quarrels.

– PHRASES ETC.: BE-ALL. **be at** be doing, aim at, intend. **be away** leave (at once), depart, set out. **been and —**, **been and gone and —**: colloq. amplification of pa. pple expr. surprise or annoyance. **be for** be bound for, be on the side of, agree with, want. **being that**, **being as** *arch.* & *dial.* it being the case that, since. ***be me***: see ME *pers. pronoun*. **be off** = ***be away*** (freq. as command). ***be that as it may***: see MAY *verb*[1]. **bride-to-be** etc., a future bride etc. **for the time being** for the present, just now. HAS-BEEN. **I were better**, **I were as good**, etc. (& similar constructions) *arch.* I had better etc., it would be (or have been) better etc. for me. ***let be***: see LET *verb*[1]. **(Miss X) that was**: her maiden name being (X). ***powers-that-be***: see POWER *noun*. ***so being***: see SO *adverb, conjunction, & adjective*. ***such as it is***, ***such as they are***, etc.: see SUCH *demonstr. adjective & pronoun*. ***tell it like it is***: see TELL *verb*. ***thanks be***: see THANK *noun*. ***that is as may be***: see MAY *verb*[1]. ***THAT was***. ***THERE it is***. ***THERE you are***. ***time was***: see TIME *noun*. TO-BE.

be- /bɪ/ *prefix*.

[ORIGIN Old English *be-*, weak form of *bi-*, *big* BY *preposition & adverb*.]

A freely productive prefix forming verbs and adjectives.

1 Forming verbs from verbs, with the sense 'around, all over, throughout', as ***beset***, ***besmear***, etc.; with intensive force 'thoroughly, excessively', as ***begrudge***, ***belabour***, etc.; or (no longer productive) with the privative sense 'off, away', as ***bereave*** etc.

2 Forming trans. verbs from intrans. verbs by adding a prepositional relation, as ***bemoan***, ***bespeak***, ***bestride***, etc.

3 Forming trans. verbs from adjectives and nouns, with the sense 'make —', as ***befoul***, ***besot***, etc., or 'call, dub', as ***bemadam*** etc.

4 Forming trans. verbs from nouns, with the sense 'surround or cover with, affect with, treat in the manner of', as ***becloud***, ***bedew***, ***befriend***, ***benight***, etc., or (no longer productive) 'deprive of', as ***behead*** etc.

5 Forming adjectives from nouns + -ED[2], with the sense 'having, covered with' (often excessively or conspicuously), as ***bejewelled***, ***bespectacled***, ***bewhiskered***, etc.

BEA *abbreviation*.

1 British Epilepsy Association.

2 *hist.* British European Airways.

beach /biːtʃ/ *noun*. **M16.**

[ORIGIN Uncertain: perh. identical with Old English *bæce*, *bece* brook, stream (cf. BECK *noun*[2]), with transf. meaning '(pebbly) river valley', surviving in many place names as Sand*bach*, Wis*bech*.]

1 The water-worn pebbles of the seashore; sand and shingle. *arch.* **M16.**

2 The sandy or pebbly shore of the sea, a lake, or a large river; *esp.* that part lying between high- and low-water marks. **L16.**

on the beach (orig. NAUTICAL) ashore, retired, unemployed. **raised beach** GEOLOGY a beach now situated above water level owing to changes since its formation. ***the only pebble on the beach***: see PEBBLE *noun*.

– COMB.: **beach ball** a large inflatable ball for games on a beach; **beach buggy** a motor vehicle with large tyres for use on beaches; **beach bum** *slang* a loafer on or around a beach; **beach front** (chiefly *N. Amer.*) the seafront beside a beach; **beach grass** marram, *Ammophila arenaria*; **beachhead** [after *bridgehead*] the first position established on a beach by the landing of troops; **beach master** an officer supervising the landing of troops; **beach plum** (the edible fruit of) a straggling N. American maritime shrub, *Prunus maritima*; **beach rock** a conglomerate consisting of beach sand cemented by calcium carbonate; **beachwear** clothes for wearing on a beach.

■ **beached** *adjective* (*rare*) having a beach, covered with shingle or sand **L16.** **beachward(s)** *adverb* towards the beach **M19.** **beachy** *adjective* covered with sand and shingle **L16.**

beach /biːtʃ/ *verb trans.* **M19.**

[ORIGIN from the noun.]

1 Haul or run up (a ship, whale, etc.) on the beach; freq. *refl.*, drive itself on to the beach, become stranded. **M19.**

2 *fig.* As ***beached ppl adjective*** = ***on the beach*** s.v. BEACH *noun* 2. **E20.**

beachcomber /ˈbiːtʃkəʊmə/ *noun*. **M19.**

[ORIGIN from BEACH *noun* + COMBER *noun*[1].]

1 A white person in the Pacific islands etc. living by collecting jetsam; a longshore vagrant. **M19.**

2 A long wave rolling in from the sea. **M19.**

■ **beachcombing** *noun* the activity of a beachcomber, searching the beach for jetsam **M19.**

beach-la-mar /biːtʃlə'mɑː/ *noun*. **E19.**

[ORIGIN Alt. of Portuguese *bicho do mar*: see BÊCHE-DE-MER. Cf. BISLAMA.]

†**1** = BÊCHE-DE-MER 1. Only in **E19.**

2 (Also **B-**.) An English-based pidgin formerly used as a trade language and contact vernacular in the SW Pacific. Also = BISLAMA. **L19.**

beacon /ˈbiːk(ə)n/ *noun & verb*.

[ORIGIN Old English *bēacn* = Old Frisian *bēcen*, *bācen*, Old Saxon *bōkan*, Old High German *bouhhan*, from West Germanic (cf. BECKON *verb*), of unknown origin.]

▸ **A** *noun*. †**1** A sign, a portent; an ensign, a standard. **OE–L15.**

2 A signal fire lighted on a pole, a hill, or other high place. **ME.**

3 A signal station, a watchtower. **LME.**

4 Any light or other object serving as a signal, warning, or guide, esp. at sea (a lighthouse etc.) or on an airfield. **LME.** ▸**b** A radio transmitter whose signal helps to determine the position of a ship, aircraft, or spacecraft. **E20.**

M. LOWRY The mariner who, sighting the faint beacon of Start Point after a long voyage, knows that he will soon embrace his wife. M. M. KAYE With the lights of the camp providing a beacon that could be seen for miles across the plains. *fig.*: SHAKES. *Tr. & Cr.* Modest doubt is call'd The beacon of the wise.

BELISHA BEACON.

5 A conspicuous hill suitable for the site of a signal fire. Freq. in names, as ***Brecon Beacons***, ***Dunkery Beacon***, etc. **L16.**

▸ **B** *verb*. †**1** *verb trans.* Foll. by *up*: kindle as a beacon. Only in **M17.**

2 *verb trans.* Provide or indicate with a beacon or beacons. **L18.**

3 *verb trans.* Illuminate, lead, or guide in the manner of a beacon. **E19.**

4 *verb intrans.* Shine like a beacon. **E19.**

■ **beaconage** *noun* (*a*) a toll paid for the maintenance of beacons; (*b*) a system of beacons: **E17.**

bead /biːd/ *noun*. **OE.**

[ORIGIN Partly aphet. from *gebed* prayer, partly generalized from *bedhus* house of prayer: rel. to Old Frisian *bede*, Old Saxon *beda* (Dutch *bede*), *gibed*, Old High German *beta*, *gibet* (German *Gebet*), Gothic *bida*, from Germanic. Cf. BID *verb*.]

1 *sing.* & (usu.) in *pl.* Prayer; devotions, latterly *spec.* using a rosary. *arch.* **OE.**

JOYCE Confession will be heard all the afternoon after beads.

bid a bead, **say one's beads** offer a prayer.

2 Each of a string of small perforated balls forming the rosary or paternoster, used for keeping count of the prayers said. **LME.**

tell one's beads, **count one's beads** say one's prayers.

3 A small rounded perforated piece of glass, metal, wood, etc., used ornamentally, either threaded with others on string or wire or sewn on fabric; (in *pl.*) a necklace of such beads. **LME.**

4 a A drop of liquid, or of molten metal etc. **L16.** ▸**b** A bubble, esp. in sparkling wine, spirits, etc. **M18.** ▸**c** A small knob forming the front sight of a gun. **M19.**

C. P. SNOW In the warm evening, beads of sweat were standing out. R. P. WARREN The leaves and the grass . . were wet, and beads of water hung here and there, glistening in the clear light.

c draw a bead on *N. Amer.* take aim at.

5 a An ornamental moulding resembling a string of beads; an individual ornament in this. **L18.** ▸**b** A narrow moulding of semicircular section. **E19.**

6 The thickened inner edge of a pneumatic tyre, gripping the rim of the wheel. **E20.**

– COMB.: **bead-folk** *arch.* people who pray for a benefactor, almsfolk; **bead-house** a chapel; an almshouse; **bead-plant** a small creeping plant of the madder family, *Nertera granatensis*, of the southern hemisphere, bearing round orange fruits and sometimes grown for ornament; **bead-rim** a thickened, rounded rim; **bead-roll** a (long) list of names (orig. of persons to be prayed for); **bead sedge** the bur-reed, *Sparganium erectum*; **bead-tree** = AZEDARAC; **beadwork** (*a*) ornamental work with beads, beading; (*b*) open-mesh canework in furniture.

■ **beadily** *adverb* in a beady manner **M20.** **beadiness** *noun* beady quality **L19.** **beadlet** *noun* a small bead; *spec.* a type of sea anemone: **M19.** **beadlike** *adjective* resembling (that of) a bead **M19.** **beady** *adjective* (*a*) beadlike, (of eyes) small, round, and glittering; (*b*) covered or decorated with beads: **E19.**

bead /biːd/ *verb*. **L16.**

[ORIGIN from the noun.]

1 *verb trans.* Provide or ornament with beads or beading. **L16.**

2 *verb trans.* Make into beads; string together like beads. **L16.**

3 *verb intrans.* Form or grow into a bead or beads. **L19.**

■ **beading** *noun* (*a*) the action of the verb; (*b*) decoration in the form of or resembling beads, esp. lacelike looped edging; (*c*) bead moulding; the bead of a tyre: **M19.**

beadle /ˈbiːd(ə)l/ *noun*. Also (now only in sense 3) **bedel(l)**.

[ORIGIN Old English *bydel* = Old High German *butil* (German *Büttel*) from Germanic base of Old English *bēodan* (see BID *verb*), superseded by forms from Old French *bedel* (mod. *bedeau*) from Proto-Romance from Germanic.]

†**1** A person who makes a proclamation; a court usher; a town crier. **OE–L17.**

†**2** A messenger or under-officer of justice. **OE–E18.**

3 A ceremonial usher, a mace-bearer, *spec.* in certain universities, city companies, etc. (sometimes conventionally spelled *bedel*, *-ell*); in University College London, a porter. **ME.**

4 a *hist.* A parish officer appointed by the vestry to keep order in church, punish petty offenders, etc. **L16.** ▸**b** In Scotland, a church official attending on the minister. **M19.**

■ **beadledom** *noun* (*arch.*) stupid officiousness **M19.** **beadleship** *noun* the office or jurisdiction of a beadle **M16.**

beadsman /ˈbiːdzmən/ *noun*. Orig. †**beadman**; also (*arch.*) **bedesman**. Pl. **-men**. **ME.**

[ORIGIN from BEAD *noun* + MAN *noun*: prob. altered after *almsman*.]

hist. **1** A person who prays for the soul of another. **ME.**

†**your beadsman**: used as a conventional form when writing to a superior or patron.

2 A person paid to pray for others; a pensioner bound to pray for his benefactors, an almsman; (in Scotland) a public almsman, a licensed beggar. **LME.**

3 A petitioner. **LME.**

beagle /ˈbiːg(ə)l/ *noun & verb*. **L15.**

[ORIGIN Perh. from Old French *beegueule* having the mouth open, from *beer* open wide (cf. BAY *noun*[4]) + *gueule* throat (see GULES).]

▸ **A** *noun*. **1** (An animal of) a breed of usu. small hound, used for hare-hunting when the field follows on foot. **L15.**

legal beagle: see LEGAL *adjective*.

2 *fig.* A spy, an informer; a constable. **M16.**

▸ **B** *verb intrans.* Hunt with beagles. Freq. as ***beagling verbal noun***. **E19.**

■ **beagler** *noun* **M19.**

beak /biːk/ *noun*[1]. **ME.**

[ORIGIN Old French & mod. French *bec* from late Latin *beccus*, of Celtic origin.]

1 The horny projecting termination of the jaws of a bird, esp. when strong and hooked as in a bird of prey (cf. BILL *noun*[2]). **ME.** ▸**b** The elongated head, proboscis, or sucker mouth of certain insects, e.g. a weevil. **M17.** ▸**c** The (freq. horny) extremities of the mandibles of some other animals, e.g. a turtle or a squid. **E19.**

2 A sharp point or projection, a peak. **LME.** ▸**b** BOTANY & ZOOLOGY. A projecting tip; e.g. that of a carpel in a cranesbill etc., or an umbo of a shell or valve. **E19.**

3 A human nose, esp. when hooked. *joc.* **LME.**

4 = ***beakhead*** (a) below. **M16.**

5 The tapered spout of a retort, still, etc. **M17.**

– COMB.: **beakhead** (*a*) an (ornamented) projection at the prow of an ancient warship; (*b*) the space before the forecastle of a sailing ship (in men-of-war used as a latrine); (*c*) an ornament in Norman architecture resembling a head with a beak; ***beak-iron***: see BICKERN; **beak-sedge** a sedge of the genus *Rhynchospora*, in which the persistent base of the style forms a beak to the fruit; *esp.* (more fully ***white beak-sedge***) *R. alba* of wet heaths and moors in Europe and N. America.
■ **beakful** *noun* as much as can be held in a bird's beak M17. **beakless** *adjective* L16. **beaklike** *adjective* resembling (that of) a beak M19. **beaky** *adjective* having a beak, beaklike E18.

beak /biːk/ *noun*[2]. *slang*. L18.
[ORIGIN Prob. orig. thieves' cant; cf. HARMAN 2.]
1 A magistrate. L18.
2 A schoolmaster. L19.

beak /biːk/ *verb*. ME.
[ORIGIN Old French *bequ(i)er* peck, formed as BEAK *noun*[1].]
1 *verb trans. & intrans.* Strike or seize with the beak; push the beak into. ME.
2 *verb intrans.* Project with or as with a beak. *rare*. ME.

beaked /biːkt/ *adjective*. LME.
[ORIGIN from BEAK *noun*[1] + -ED[2].]
1 Pointed or hooked. LME.
2 HERALDRY. Having the beak a different tincture from the body. E16.
beaked parsley [from the beaked fruit] any of several plants of the genus *Anthriscus*, *esp.* cow parsley, *A. sylvestris*.
3 Provided with a beak. E16. ▸**b** BOTANY & ZOOLOGY. Having a beaklike projection or proboscis; rostrate. Freq. in names, as ***beaked whale***. E19.

beaker /ˈbiːkə/ *noun*. ME.
[ORIGIN Old Norse *bikarr* = Old Saxon *bikeri*, Middle Dutch & mod. Dutch *bēker*, Old High German *behhari* (German *Becher*), from popular Latin, perh. from Greek *bikos* drinking bowl: cf. PITCHER *noun*[1].]
1 A large drinking vessel with a wide mouth and no handles, a goblet. *arch.* or *literary* in *gen.* sense. ME. ▸**b** A tumbler-shaped metal or (usu.) plastic drinking vessel; a metal or plastic mug. E20. ▸**c** ARCHAEOLOGY. A type of pottery drinking vessel without a handle, characteristic of the early Bronze Age in western Europe. Cf. ***funnel beaker*** s.v. FUNNEL *noun*. E20.
2 The contents of a beaker. E19.
3 A lipped cylindrical glass vessel used for scientific experiments. M19.
– COMB.: **Beaker Culture**, (*arch.*) **Beaker folk**, a people believed to have been the sole makers of beakers (sense 1c).

beak-iron *noun* see BICKERN.

beal /ˈbɪəl/ *noun & verb*. *obsolete* exc. *dial.* LME.
[ORIGIN App. alt. of BOIL *noun*[1].]
▸ **A** *noun*. A pustule, a boil. LME.
▸ **B** *verb intrans.* Suppurate, fester. E16.

bealach /ˈbɛlax/ *noun*. *Scot.* L18.
[ORIGIN Gaelic, from Middle Irish *belach* pass, road.]
A narrow mountain pass.

be-all /ˈbiːɔːl/ *noun*. E17.
[ORIGIN from BE *verb* + ALL *pronoun*.]
The whole being or essence (*of*). Chiefly in ***the be-all and end-all*** (after Shakes.).

SHAKES. *Mach.* That but this blow Might be the be-all and the end-all here.

beam /biːm/ *noun*.
[ORIGIN Old English *bēam* = Old Frisian *bām*, Old Saxon *bām*, *boom*, Middle Dutch & mod. Dutch *boom* (see BOOM *noun*[2]), Old High German *boum* (German *Baum*), from West Germanic; obscurely rel. to Gothic *bagms*, Old Norse *baðmr* tree.]
1 A tree. *obsolete* since Old English exc. in ***hornbeam***, ***whitebeam***, etc. OE.
†**2** The rood tree, the Cross (cf. *Acts* 5:30). OE–E18.
3 A long piece of squared timber, metal, or reinforced concrete, used in building and construction esp. as a horizontal load-bearing member. (See also sense 10.) OE.

AV *2 Kings* 6:2 Let vs . . take thence euery man a beame, and let vs make vs a place there where we may dwell. H. ALLEN The shafts . . also formed the beams of the wagon platform. M. LASKI Everything in splendid confusion was tacked to the walls, to the platform, to the beams in the ceiling. J. BRONOWSKI If we picture a beam lying across two columns, then . . the stresses in the beam increase as we move the columns farther apart.

cross-beam, ***hammer beam***, ***stretching beam***, ***summer beam***, etc.
4 A wooden cylinder in a loom, on which the warp or cloth is wound. OE.
5 a The chief timber of a plough. OE. ▸†**b** The pole or shaft of a chariot. Only in 17.
6 A ray or pencil of light; a set of parallel light rays. OE. ▸**b** A ray or pencil of radiation of any kind; a narrow directed flow of particles. M19. ▸**c** A strongly directional radio transmission, esp. as used to guide aircraft, missiles, etc. E20.

D. LODGE The rain swept in great folds across the beam of the headlights. A. GRAY A beam of early morning summer sunlight shone on it and on me. **c** S. SPENDER He . . landed on a beam when all but the last drop of petrol was exhausted. K. KESEY Carrying the [TV] set every place the cord will reach, in search of a good beam.

7 The transverse bar of a balance; the balance itself. LME.
8 The main stem of a stag's horn, bearing the antlers. LME.
9 Radiance; a gleam, a bright glance, *esp.* a radiant or good-natured smile. L16.

BYRON Her cheek all purple with the beam of youth. S. GIBBONS She found her hand taken into a friendly clasp and met the beam of a wind-reddened, open, boyish countenance. S. O'FAOLÁIN Then he began to smile, slowly expanding his mouth into a wide beam of relief.

10 a A horizontal timber stretching from side to side of a ship. E17. ▸**b** The greatest breadth of a ship. E17. ▸**c** Either side of a ship; a sideways direction from a ship. E17. ▸**d** *transf.* (The width of) a person's hips or buttocks. *colloq.* E20.

c F. MARRYAT Land on the lee beam! **d** HUGH WALPOLE He stood watching disgustedly Bigges' broad beam.

11 In a steam engine etc.: an oscillating pivoted shaft through which the piston movement is transmitted to the crank. M18.
12 GYMNASTICS. A raised horizontal bar, 10 cm in width, on which exercises are performed while balancing; a competitive event using this apparatus. L19.
– PHRASES ETC.: **abaft the beam** to one side and behind an imaginary line drawn across the centre of a ship. **beam in one's eye** *fig.* a fault great compared to another's (*Matthew* 7:3). **before the beam** to one side and ahead of an imaginary line drawn across the centre of a ship. **kick the beam** be greatly outweighed in the balance. ***main beam***: see MAIN *adjective*. **off beam**, **off the beam** *colloq.* not on the right track, mistaken. **on the beam** *colloq.* on the right track, right. ***post-and-beam***: see POST *noun*[1]. RETRICK ***one's beams***. ***split beam***: see SPLIT *ppl adjective*. **strike the beam** = ***kick the beam*** above.
– COMB.: **beam compass(es)**: with the legs connected by a beam with sliding sockets, for drawing large circles; **beam ends** the ends of a ship's beams; ***on her beam ends***, (of a ship) on its side, almost capsizing; ***on one's beam ends*** (fig.), at the end of one's resources; **beam engine** a steam engine having a beam (sense 11 above); **beam sea**: one rolling against a ship's side; **beam-splitter** a device for dividing a beam of radiation into two (or more) separate beams; **beam-tree** whitebeam.
■ **beamed** *adjective* (*a*) having or emitting beams of light (usu. of a specified quality); (*b*) (of a stag) having a horn of the fourth year; (*c*) built with a beam or beams: OE. **beamish** *adjective* (*arch.*) shining brightly, radiant M16. **beamless** *adjective* L17.

beam /biːm/ *verb*. LME.
[ORIGIN from the noun.]
1 *verb trans.* Emit in beams; radiate (light, affection, etc.). LME. ▸**b** Direct (radio signals etc.) to a specific area; transmit. E20. ▸**c** SCIENCE FICTION. Foll. by *up*: transport (a person) to a spaceship by a directed flow of energy. M20.

W. SHENSTONE The genial sun . . Beams forth ungentle influences. **b** M. L. KING Television beamed the image of this extraordinary gathering across the border oceans. C. SAGAN A search for signals beamed in our general direction by civilizations interested in communicating with us.

2 *verb trans.* Stretch (cloth, hide, etc.) over a beam. E17.
3 *verb intrans.* Shine brightly. M17.

G. M. HOPKINS Their harness beams like scythes in morning grass. JOYCE The young May moon, she's beaming, love.

4 *verb intrans.* Smile broadly or radiantly. L19.

J. M. BARRIE Her face beamed with astonishment and mirth. T. DREISER She beamed upon him in a melting and sensuous way.

■ **beamer** *noun* (*a*) a person who beams; (*b*) a person who arranges yarn on the beam of a loom; (*c*) CRICKET a full toss aimed at the batsman's head: M19. **beamingly** *adverb* radiantly M17.

beamy /ˈbiːmi/ *adjective*. LME.
[ORIGIN from BEAM *noun* + -Y[1].]
1 Emitting beams, radiant. LME.
2 Massive as a (weaver's) beam. M17.
3 Possessing full-grown antlers. L17.
4 Of a ship: broad in the beam. L19.
■ **beaminess** *noun* radiance M18.

bean /biːn/ *noun*.
[ORIGIN Old English *bēan* = Middle Dutch *bōne* (Dutch *boon*), Old High German *bōna* (German *Bohne*), Old Norse *baun*, from Germanic.]
1 a The smooth kidney-shaped edible seed, borne in long pods, of the leguminous plant *Vicia faba*; the plant itself. Also more fully ***broad bean***. OE. ▸**b** (The seed of) any of various related plants, *esp.* the French bean, *Phaseolus vulgaris*. M16.
b ***black bean***, ***French bean***, ***haricot bean***, ***kidney bean***, ***Lima bean***, ***navy bean***, ***runner bean***, ***vanilla bean***, ***velvet bean***, ***yellow bean***, etc.
2 A seed resembling the broad bean in shape, produced by any of several other plants, e.g. coffee, cocoa. LME.
3 Something resembling a bean in shape and size. M16. ▸**b** The head. *slang* (orig. *US*). E20.
4 A coin, a small sum of money. Usu. in neg. contexts. *slang*. E19.

E. NEWBY English kings and queens never have a bean on them.

– PHRASES: BAKED ***beans***. **full of beans** full of energy, in high spirits. **give (a person) beans** deal severely with, scold. **hill of beans** (chiefly *N. Amer.*) a thing of little value (freq. in ***not worth a hill of beans***, worthless). ***jelly bean***: see JELLY *noun*[1] & *verb*. **know how many beans make five** be intelligent. **not a bean** *slang* no money whatever. ***old bean***: see OLD *adjective*. ***spill the beans***: see SPILL *verb* 12.
– COMB.: **beanbag** a small closed bag filled with beans, used esp. in children's games; ***beanbag chair***, a chair consisting of a large bag filled with loose plastic granules, which takes the shape of the sitter; **bean ball** BASEBALL *slang* a ball pitched at the batter's head; **bean caper** a plant of the genus *Zygophyllum*, esp. the Mediterranean *Z. fabago*, with flower buds used as capers; **bean counter** (*colloq.*, usu. *derog.*) an accountant, esp. one who compiles statistical records; someone overly concerned with accounts or figures; **bean curd** a paste made from soya beans; **beanfeast** (*a*) an annual dinner given to employees by their employer(s) (at which beans and bacon used to be regarded as an indispensable dish); (*b*) a festival, a celebration, a merry time; **bean goose** a grey goose, *Anser fabalis*, breeding in the Arctic and visiting Britain in small numbers in winter; **bean-meal** meal made by grinding beans; **beanpole** (*a*) a pole for beans to twine round; (*b*) *fig.* a tall thin person; **bean sprouts** the sprouts of a legume, esp. the mung bean, used esp. in Chinese cookery; **beanstalk** the stem of a bean plant; **bean trefoil** a poisonous leguminous shrub, *Anagyris foetida*, of the Mediterranean region; **bean tree** any of various trees bearing podded seeds, *esp.* laburnum.
■ **beanery** *noun* (*N. Amer. slang*) a cheap restaurant L19.

bean /biːn/ *verb trans.* *slang* (chiefly *N. Amer.*). E20.
[ORIGIN from the noun.]
Hit on the head.

beanie /ˈbiːni/ *noun*. Orig. *US*. E20.
[ORIGIN Prob. from BEAN *noun* 3b + -IE.]
A hat; *spec.* (*a*) a small close-fitting hat worn at the back of the head; (*b*) a small round woollen hat worn on top of the head.

beano /ˈbiːnəʊ/ *noun*. *slang*. Pl. **-os**. L19.
[ORIGIN from BEAN *noun* + -O.]
= ***beanfeast*** s.v. BEAN *noun*.

bear /bɛː/ *noun*[1].
[ORIGIN Old English *bera* = Middle Dutch *bere* (Dutch *beer*), Old High German *bero* (German *Bär*), from West Germanic: rel. to Old Norse *bjǫrn*.]
1 Any of several large heavily built mammals constituting the family Ursidae (order Carnivora), with thick fur and a plantigrade gait. OE. ▸**b** With specifying word: an animal resembling or likened to a bear. E17. ▸**c** ***the Bear***, Russia, the former USSR. E19. ▸**d** A figure of a bear made as a child's toy. Cf. TEDDY. E20.

c W. S. CHURCHILL The left paw of the Bear bars Germany from the Black Sea.

black bear either of two bears, (*a*) (more fully ***American black bear***) *Ursus americanus*, of N. American forests; (*b*) (more fully ***Asian black bear***) *Selenarctos thibetanus*, a small, mainly herbivorous bear of SE Asia. **brown bear** a bear, *Ursus arctos*, of western N. America and parts of Eurasia that is the world's largest carnivore (cf. GRIZZLY *adjective*[1] 2, KODIAK). ***polar bear***, ***sloth bear***, ***spectacled bear***, etc. **b** ***koala bear***, ***sea-bear***, ***skunk bear***, etc.
2 ASTRONOMY. ***the Bear*** (more fully ***the Great Bear***) = URSA ***Major***; ***the Lesser Bear***, ***the Little Bear*** = URSA ***Minor***. LME.
3 *fig.* A rough, unmannerly, or uncouth person. Also, a large, heavy, cumbersome man. L16.

LD MACAULAY This great soldier . . was no better than a Low Dutch bear.

4 STOCK EXCHANGE etc. [Perh. with ref. to expression 'selling the bear's skin before killing the bear'.] Orig., stock contracted to be sold at a set price at a future date, in the seller's expectation of lower market prices then. Now, a person who sells such stock, a speculator for a fall. Cf. BULL *noun*[1] 4. E18.
5 A rough or shaggy mat, *esp.* a block covered with matting for scrubbing the deck of a vessel. L18.
6 [Ellipt. for *Smokey Bear* s.v. SMOKY.] A police officer; (*collect.*) *the* police. *slang* (orig. *US*). L20.
sky bear: see SKY *noun*.
– PHRASES: **like a bear with a sore head** *colloq.* angry, bad-tempered. **loaded for bear** *US colloq.* fully prepared. **play the bear with** treat rudely and roughly. ***Smokey Bear***: see SMOKY *adjective*.
– COMB.: **bear animalcule** = TARDIGRADE *noun* 2; **bear-baiting** *hist.* setting dogs to attack a captive bear, for sport; **bearberry** (the fruit of) an evergreen shrub or small tree of the chiefly N. American genus *Arctostaphylos*, of the heath family, with white or pinkish flowers, esp. *A. uva-ursi* (more fully ***red bearberry***), a trailing moorland plant with bright red astringent berries; **bearcat** (*a*) the red panda; (*b*) the binturong; (*c*) *N. Amer. colloq.* an aggressive or forceful person; a person of great energy or ability; **bear claw** *US* a semi-circular almond-flavoured pastry often containing raisins; **bear-covering** STOCK EXCHANGE the action of a bear in buying stock which he has previously contracted to sell; **bear garden** (*a*) a place set apart for bear-baiting or similar sports; (*b*) *fig.* a scene of tumult; **beargrass** *N. Amer.* any of various plants with long, coarse, grasslike leaves, *esp.* yucca or a related plant; **bearherd** *hist.* the keeper of a bear; one who leads a bear for show; **bear hug** a powerful embrace; **bearleader** *fig.* a rich young man's travelling tutor; **bear market** STOCK EXCHANGE: in which prices are falling; **bear pit** a sunken enclosure in which bears are kept; **bear's breech** = ACANTHUS 1; **bear's ear** = AURICULA 1; **bear's foot** stinking hellebore, *Helleborus foetidus*; **bear's garlic** ramsons, *Allium ursinum*; **bear's grease** *arch.* pomade; **bearskin** (*a*) a wrap etc. made of bear's skin; (*b*) a tall furry cap worn by Guards in the British army; **bearskinned** *adjective* wearing a bearskin; **Bear State** *US* Arkansas; **bearward** = ***bear-herd*** above.
■ **bearlike** *adverb* & *adjective* (*a*) *adverb* in the manner of a bear, roughly; (*b*) *adjective* resembling (that of) a bear: E17.

B

†**bear** *noun*², *noun*³ vars. of BERE *noun*¹, *noun*².

bear /bɛː/ *verb*¹. Pa. t. **bore** /bɔː/, (*arch.*) **bare** /bɛː/. Pa. pple & ppl adjective **borne** /bɔːn/, BORN. See also YBORN.
[ORIGIN Old English *beran* = Old Saxon, Old High German *beran*, Old Norse *bera*, Gothic *bairan*, from Germanic from Indo-European base also of Sanskrit *bharati*, Armenian *berem*, Greek *pherein*, Latin *ferre*.]
▸ **I** *verb trans.* Carry, hold, possess.
1 Carry (esp. something weighty), transport; bring or take by carrying; *fig.* have, possess. Now *literary* or *formal.* OE. ▸**b** BACKGAMMON. Remove (a piece) from the board at the end of a game. Also foll. by *off.* M16. ▸†**c** Take along as a companion; carry as a consequence. L16–E17.

CHAUCER On his bak he bar . . Anchises. R. HOLINSHED This pope Leo . . bare but seauen and thirtie yeeres of age. SHAKES. *Macb.* I bear a charmed life, which must not yield To one of woman born. E. WAUGH Music was borne in from the next room. T. BLACKBURN I met a child beside a river, Who asked if I would bear him over. K. LAFFAN We all have our crosses to bear. *absol.*: SHAKES. *Rich. II* Forgiveness, horse! Why do I rail on thee, Since thou . . Wast born to bear?

2 Carry about with or upon one, esp. visibly; show, display; be known or recognized by (a name, device, etc.); have (a character, reputation, value, etc.) attached to or associated with one. OE. ▸†**b** Wear (clothes, ornaments). OE–L16.

SHAKES. *Wint. T.* If I Had servants true about me that bare eyes To see alike mine honour as their profits. STEELE Falshood . . shall hereafter bear a blacker Aspect. W. H. PRESCOTT Four beautiful girls, bearing the names of the principal goddesses. A. P. STANLEY The staff like that still borne by Arab chiefs. R. GRAVES Postumus . . now bore the rank of regimental commander. S. BRETT The old comedian's face bore a smile of unambiguous cynicism.

3 *refl.* Carry or conduct oneself; behave or acquit oneself. ME.

W. S. CHURCHILL Let us . . so bear ourselves that if the British Empire and its Commonwealth last for a thousand years men will still say, 'This was their finest hour'.

4 Wield, exercise, (power etc.); hold (an office). *arch.* ME.

COVERDALE 1 *Chron.* 27:6 Sonnes . . which bare rule in the house of their fathers. R. ASCHAM To beare some office in the common wealth.

5 Entertain, harbour, (a feeling etc. towards someone or something; foll. by indirect obj., *for, towards*). ME.

SWIFT The contempt they bear for practical geometry.

6 Hold or possess (a relation etc.) *to* something else. ME.

J. LOCKE Nothing finite bears any proportion to infinite. G. GREENE I thought I could believe in some kind of a God that bore no relation to ourselves.

▸ **II** Support, sustain, endure.
7 *verb trans.* Sustain, support (a weight, strain, or burden). OE. ▸**b** *verb trans.* Sustain successfully, withstand; admit of, be fit for. E16. ▸**c** *verb intrans.* Support a load. L17.

J. SMEATON Proportionate . . to the stress it was likely to bear. *fig.*: AV *Gen.* 13:6 The land was not able to beare them, that they might dwell together. E. F. SCHUMACHER A large part of the costs of private enterprise has been borne by the public authorities. C. PRIEST This, alone of all my problems, was one . . for which I bore some responsibility. **b** SHAKES. *Lear* Thy great employment Will not bear question. J. RUSKIN It is not less the boast of some styles that they can bear ornament. J. RABAN Only the great families of the Italian Renaissance could seriously bear comparison with the Gulf emirs. **c** G. WASHINGTON Attempted to go into the Neck on the Ice, but it wd. not bear.

8 *verb trans.* Sustain (something painful); (usu. in neg. or interrog. contexts) endure, tolerate, reconcile oneself to, bring oneself *to do* something. OE. ▸**b** *verb intrans.* Foll. by *with*: be patient or put up with, make allowance for. M16.

AV *Gen.* 4:13 My punishment is greater then I can beare. SMOLLETT With an intrepid heart . . he bears the brunt of their whole artillery. R. L. STEVENSON Though I could, perhaps, bear to die, I could not bear to look upon my fate as it approached. W. CATHER It will take more courage to bear your going than everything that has happened before. N. COWARD *Sibyl*: I don't believe you like mother. *Elyot*: Like her! I can't bear her. V. S. PRITCHETT Father could not bear a drip of oil or grease on his own hands. **b** E. A. FREEMAN A foreign King had to be borne with. F. KING Sometimes he would wonder if she really liked him at all or merely bore with him out of her kindness and tolerance.

9 **a** *verb trans.* Hold, keep, or lift *up*; prevent from falling or sinking; hold aloft, hold in position on the top etc. ME. ▸**b** *verb trans.* Keep going (the refrain or a part of a song). *arch.* LME. ▸**c** *verb intrans.* Keep one's spirits or courage *up*; cheer *up*. M17.

a R. KNOLLES The Spaniards bearing themselves upon their wealth, were too proud. AV *Judg.* 16:29 The two middle pillars . . on which it was borne vp. O. CROMWELL To bear up our honour at sea. P. SHAFFER A small Queen Anne table bearing a fine opaline lamp. **c** BURKE Bearing up against those vicissitudes of fortune. E. B. BROWNING He bears up, and talks philosophy.

10 *verb trans.* Have written, inscribed, etc., on it; (in *pass.*) be registered or enrolled in a book etc. thus. ME.

STEELE A long Letter bearing Date the fourth Instant. JOHN PHILLIPS Coins, bearing the effigy of the Horse. H. COX All persons borne on the books of Queen's ships in commission.

11 *verb trans.* Have or convey the meaning *that*, purport *to be*. *arch.* ME.

LEIGH HUNT A portrait . . bearing to be the likeness of a certain Erasmus Smith, Esq.

▸ **III** *verb trans.* Produce, give birth to.
12 Bring forth, produce, yield (fruit, crops, minerals, etc.). OE.

SHAKES. *Timon* The oaks bear mast, the briars scarlet hips. DRYDEN India, black Ebon and white Ivory bears. ANNE STEVENSON Some beds bear nearly a thousand petunias.

13 Of a woman or (less commonly) any female mammal: give birth to (a child, children, young); provide (offspring, with the father as indirect obj. or with *to*). See also BORN *pple & adjective*. OE.

I. MURDOCH Fanny had lived, she had married a distinguished man, she had borne children. NEB *Luke* 23:29 Happy are the barren, the wombs that never bore a child. TOLKIEN Aredhel bore to Eöl a son in the shadows of Nan Elmoth.

▸ **IV** Push, move, apply.
14 *verb trans.* Move onward by pressure; force, drive. ME.

SOUTHEY Borne backward Talbot turns.

†**15** *verb trans.* Pierce, stab (*through*). ME–L15.
16 **a** *verb intrans.* Press or come (*up*)*on* or †*at* with (esp. downward) force; exert or transmit mechanical pressure (*up*)*on* or *against*; apply weight, thrust. LME. ▸**b** *verb trans.* Bring *down* or tend to force *down* with pressure. L17.

a L. T. C. ROLT The frame was . . moved forward . . by horizontal jacks bearing against the newly completed brickwork behind. *fig.*: SOUTHEY While she pray'd the load of care Less heavily bore on her heart. **b** TENNYSON The dead weight . . bore it down. N. SHUTE He bore his weight down on the plate with her and the boat lifted sodden sails out of the water.

17 *verb intrans.* (Try to) move in a certain direction, esp. deliberately or persistently; diverge, turn; (of a vessel) sail in a given direction. Freq. with adverbs. L16. ▸**b** Extend or stretch away in a given direction. E17.

SHAKES. *Jul. Caes.* Stand back. Room! Bear back. J. SMEATON The wind being now fair for that port, we bore away for it. H. I. JENKINSON On arriving at the top of the crag, bear a little to the right. TOLKIEN They turned north and then bore to the north-west.

18 *verb intrans.* Lie off or be situated in a certain direction from a given point. Cf. BEARING 5. L16.

SHAKES. *Tam. Shr.* This is Lucentio's house; My father's bears more toward the market-place. P. O'BRIAN Dawn on the seventeenth instant, the Dry Salvages bearing SSE two leagues.

19 *verb intrans.* Foll. by (*up*)*on*: exert a practical effect on; have relevance to. L17.

J. MASTERS We've been able to get a little information bearing . . on the accident.

20 *verb intrans.* Of a gun: have the intended target in its line of fire, be aimed at the target. L17.

H. NELSON Our after guns ceased to bear. CARLYLE Finck had no artillery to bear on Daun's transit through the Pass.

▸ **V** Special uses of **borne** *pa. pple & ppl adjective*.
21 As 2nd elem. of a comb.: carried or transported by, as ***airborne*** etc. E17.

– PHRASES, & WITH ADVERBS IN SPECIALIZED SENSES: ***as much as the traffic will bear***: see TRAFFIC *noun*. ***bear a bob***: see BOB *noun*¹. ***bear a great stroke***: see STROKE *noun*¹. **bear a hand** assist, help. **bear and forbear** be patient and tolerant. **bear a part** (*a*) take part, share, (*in*); (*b*) play a part as actor or actress. ***bear arms***: see ARM *noun*². ***bear a stroke***: see STROKE *noun*¹. **bear away** carry away, win as a prize (***bear away the bell***: see BELL *noun*¹). **bear company** accompany (a person). **bear date** be dated (as specified). **bear down** (*a*) push to the ground, overthrow, prevail against; (*b*) see sense 16b above; (*c*) exert downward force, press down *on*; (*d*) ***bear down on***, ***bear down upon*** (NAUTICAL), sail with the wind towards; *gen.* move rapidly and purposefully towards. **bear fruit** *fig.* yield results, be productive. ***bear great state***: see STATE *noun*. **bear hard** (*a*) *arch.* take badly, resent; (*b*) ***bear hard on***, ***bear hard upon***, oppress, affect adversely or harmfully. **bear heavily** †(*a*) = ***bear hard*** (a) above; (*b*) = ***bear hard*** (b) above. †**bear in hand** profess falsely; delude, deceive. **bear in mind** not forget, keep in one's thoughts. **bear off** †(*a*) repel, ward off; (*b*) carry off, win as a prize; see also sense 1b above. **bear out** (*a*) *arch.* support, back up, (a person); (*b*) corroborate, tend to confirm or justify (a statement, a person making a statement). †**bear over** = ***bear down*** (a) above. ***bear state***: see STATE *noun*. ***bear suspicion***: see SUSPICION *noun*. ***bear tack***: see TACK *noun*¹. **bear testimony** testify (*to*). ***bear the bell***: see BELL *noun*¹. ***bear the stroke***: see STROKE *noun*¹. **bear up** NAUTICAL bring the vessel before the wind, sail to leeward; (see also senses 9a, c above). **bear witness** testify (*to*). **be borne in upon one** be impressed upon one, become one's conviction (*that*). **bring to bear** bring into effective operation, begin using, aim (a gun etc.), (***bring pressure to bear***: see PRESSURE *noun*). ***grin and bear it***: see GRIN *verb*².

– NOTE: The pple *born* is now used only in sense 13, and there only in the pass. when not followed by *by* and the mother. In all other cases *borne* is usual.

bear /bɛː/ *verb*². M19.
[ORIGIN from BEAR *noun*¹ 4.]
STOCK EXCHANGE etc.
1 *verb intrans.* Speculate for a fall. M19.
2 *verb trans.* Produce a fall in the price of (stocks etc.). M19.

bearable /ˈbɛːrəb(ə)l/ *adjective*. LME.
[ORIGIN from BEAR *verb*¹ + -ABLE.]
Able to be borne; endurable, tolerable.
■ **bearableness** *noun* (earlier in UNBEARABLENESS) M19. **bearably** *adverb* (earlier in UNBEARABLY) L19.

bearance /ˈbɛːr(ə)ns/ *noun*. E18.
[ORIGIN from BEAR *verb*¹ + -ANCE.]
1 Endurance, toleration. E18.
2 = BEARING 6. *rare*. E19.

bearbind /ˈbɛːbʌɪnd/ *noun*. *dial.* Also **-bine** /-bʌɪn/. LME.
[ORIGIN from *bear* var. of BERE *noun*¹ + BIND *verb*.]
Convolvulus or a similar twining plant.

beard /bɪəd/ *noun*.
[ORIGIN Old English *beard* = Old Frisian *berd*, Middle Dutch *baert* (Dutch *baard*), Old High German *bart*, German *Bart*, from West Germanic, rel. to Old Church Slavonic *brada*, Latin *barba*.]
1 A mass of hair growing on the chin and lower face of a man (excluding the moustache and whiskers); such hair collectively. OE.

P. BARKER Men with white beards and wing collars. *Independent* I cut a week's beard away from my face..

2 The hair of the face or chin of any animal, e.g. a lion or goat. ME. ▸**b** Chiefly ZOOLOGY. Any of various animal growths suggestive of or resembling beards; *esp.* the gills of an oyster; the byssus of a mollusc; the beak bristles of certain birds. LME.
3 BOTANY. A tuft of hairs or bristles on a plant; *esp.* the awn of a grass. LME.
4 A protruding part, esp. †(*a*) the barb of an arrow, fish hook, etc.; (*b*) TYPOGRAPHY the part of the type above and below the letter. E17.
5 The tail of a comet. *obsolete* exc. *hist.* M17.
6 *slang* (orig. *US*). ▸**a** A person who completes a bet or other transaction on behalf of another in order to conceal the identity of the principal; a frontman. M20. ▸**b** A woman who accompanies a homosexual man as an escort to a social occasion, in order to help him conceal his homosexuality. L20.

– PHRASES & COMB.: ***beards wag***: see WAG *verb*. **beardtongue** = PENTSTEMON. ***Jupiter's beard***: see JUPITER. ***old man's beard***: see OLD MAN. ***Spanish beard***: see SPANISH *adjective*. ***torpedo beard***: see TORPEDO *noun*. ***Vandyke beard***: see VANDYKE *noun* 4.
■ **beardless** *adjective* having no beard; *fig.* youthful, immature: ME. **beardlet** *noun* a small beard or awn L19. **beardlike** *adjective* M19. **beardy** *adjective* bearded L16.

beard /bɪəd/ *verb*. ME.
[ORIGIN from the noun.]
1 *verb trans.* Cut off the beard of; seize the beard of. ME. ▸**b** *fig.* Oppose openly, defy; attack audaciously. E16.
beard the lion in his den, **beard the lion in his lair** attack someone on his or her own ground or subject.
2 *verb trans.* Provide with a beard. Usu. in *pass.* LME.
†**3** *verb intrans.* Grow a beard. L15–L17.

bearded /ˈbɪədɪd/ *adjective*. ME.
[ORIGIN from BEARD *noun*, *verb*: see -ED², -ED¹.]
1 Having a beard, awn, or similar growth. ME.
2 Of a comet etc.: having a tail. *obsolete* exc. *hist.* LME.
†**3** Barbed or jagged. E17–E19.

– SPECIAL COLLOCATIONS: **bearded collie**: of a shaggy breed with long hair on the face. **bearded iris** any of several cultivated irises with beards on the falls. ***bearded*** REEDLING. **bearded seal** an Arctic seal, *Erignathus barbatus*, of the Arctic Ocean. **bearded tit** = REEDLING 2. **bearded vulture** = LAMMERGEIER.
■ **beardedness** *noun* L19.

beardie /ˈbɪədi/ *noun*. Also **-dy**. E19.
[ORIGIN from BEARD *noun* + -IE.]
1 (A nickname for) a bearded man. E19.
2 A loach; a stickleback. *Scot.* E19. ▸**b** The red-brown gadoid fish *Lotella callarias* of S. Australian coasts. Also called ***ling***. L19.
3 A bearded collie. E20.

bearer /ˈbɛːrə/ *noun*. ME.
[ORIGIN from BEAR *verb*¹ + -ER¹.]
1 A person who or (less commonly) thing which carries or helps to carry; a porter. ME. ▸**b** *spec.* A person who helps to carry a coffin at a funeral; a pallbearer. M17. ▸**c** *spec.* A palanquin carrier (*hist.*). Also, a personal servant. *Indian*. M18.

AV 2 *Chron.* 2:18 To be bearers of burdens. W. MORRIS Fleeces . . In their own bearer's blood were dyed. J. HILTON They travelled in bamboo sedan-chairs, swinging perilously over precipices while their bearers . . picked a way nonchalantly down the steep track. W. STEVENS Lantern without a bearer, you drift.

cupbearer: see CUP *noun*. ***pallbearer***: see PALL *noun*¹. ***standard-bearer***: see STANDARD *noun*. ***stretcher-bearer***: see STRETCHER. ***train-bearer***: see TRAIN *noun*¹. ***c sardar-bearer***: see SARDAR 2.
2 A person who brings letters, a message, news, etc.; a messenger. ME.
3 †**a** A person who supports a burden (*lit.* & *fig.*); an upholder. LME–M18. ▸**b** Something which supports or sustains a burden or takes off pressure. L17.
4 A person who or thing which brings forth or produces (fruit, offspring, etc.). LME.
good bearer, **poor bearer**, etc., a plant that produces well etc.
5 The holder of an office or rank; the possessor of a name, quality, etc. L16.

SHAKES. 2 *Hen. IV* O majesty! When thou dost pinch thy bearer [etc.]. JOYCE The gallant young Oxonian (the bearer . . of one of the most timehonoured names in Albion's history).

office-bearer: see OFFICE *noun*.

6 *HERALDRY*. A person who bears heraldic arms. L16.

7 The holder or presenter of a cheque, draft, etc.; the holder of shares in a company etc. L17.

bearing /ˈbɛːrɪŋ/ *noun*. ME.
[ORIGIN from BEAR *verb*[1] + -ING[1].]
1 The action of BEAR *verb*[1]: carrying, bringing; supporting, sustaining, enduring; giving birth, producing; thrusting, pressing. ME.
2 Manner of carrying oneself, bodily attitude; demeanour. ME.

W. BLACK The . . courtesy of his bearing towards women. J. R. ACKERLEY Upon the platform . . was a tall, handsome, elegantly tailored young man, of military bearing.

3 A material support; a supporting surface. ME.

J. SMEATON Each floor . . lying upon the horizontal bearings furnished by these ledges.

4 A heraldic charge or device: in *pl.*, that which is depicted on a coat of arms; a heraldic achievement, a coat of arms. M16.

TENNYSON A gateway she discerns With armorial bearings stately.

5 The direction in which a place, object, etc., lies; direction of movement, orientation; in *pl.*, (knowledge of) relative position. M17.

L. GARFIELD On went the old gentleman, confident now in his bearings, deeper and deeper into the . . Town. H. WOUK The RAF could measure the range and bearing of a ship down to a hundred yards or less. *fig.*: DAY LEWIS A child first begins to get his bearings and realise its identity by seeing itself reflected from two opposite sides—its father and its mother.

lose one's bearings, ***take one's bearings***, etc.

6 *sing.* & (freq.) in *pl.* Part of a machine which bears friction, esp. between a rotating part and its housing. L18.
ball bearing: see BALL *noun*[1]. *FOOTSTEP* ***bearing***. ***roller bearing***: see ROLLER *noun*[1]. ***split bearing***: see SPLIT *adjective*.
7 Practical relation or effect (*up*)*on*; influence, relevance. L18.

CONAN DOYLE We seem to be faced by a long series of inexplicable incidents with no bearing upon each other. D. M. THOMAS She could not think of any unpleasant episode which might have had a bearing on her illness.

– COMB.: **bearing metal**: used for antifriction linings of bearings. **bearing rein** a fixed rein passing from the bit to the harness pad, serving to keep the horse's head up and its neck arched.

bearish /ˈbɛːrɪʃ/ *adjective*. M18.
[ORIGIN from BEAR *noun*[1] + -ISH[1].]
1 Like a bear, esp. in manner; rough, surly. M18.
2 *STOCK EXCHANGE* etc. Pertaining to, showing, or tending to produce a fall in prices; *gen.* pessimistic. L19.
■ **bearishly** *adverb* M19. **bearishness** *noun* M19.

Béarnaise /beɪəˈneɪz, *foreign* bearnɛːz/ *adjective*. L19.
[ORIGIN French, fem. of *béarnais* of Béarn, a region of SW France.]
Béarnaise sauce (also †***sauce Béarnaise***), a rich white sauce flavoured with tarragon.

beast /biːst/ *noun*. ME.
[ORIGIN Old French *beste* (mod. *bête*) from popular Latin *besta* from Latin *bestia*.]
1 *gen.* An animal (orig. including, now as distinct from, man); a creature. Now *dial.* & *joc.* exc. as explicitly contrasted with *man*. ME. ▸**b** *The* animal nature in humans. M17.

AV *Rev.* 13:1 I . . saw a beast rise vp out of the sea, hauing seuen heads, and ten hornes. OED There's a little beast crawling up your back! C. HAMPTON No help at all to man or beast.

2 A quadruped mammal, as distinct from birds, reptiles, fish, insects, etc.; *esp.* a wild animal, or one hunted as game. ME.

AV 1 *Kings* 4:33 Hee spake also of beasts, and of foule, and of creeping things, and of fishes. G. B. SHAW There are wild beasts in this wood: lions, they say.

3 A domesticated animal; *esp.* (***a***) a bovine farm animal; (***b***) a draught animal. ME.

LD MACAULAY Travellers . . compelled to alight and lead their beasts. D. HOLLIDAY That year the farmers prospered, beasts were fat.

4 A brutal, savage, or loathsome person; someone one detests or dislikes (freq. in a weakened sense). ME. ▸**b** Something loathsome; an abominable or unpleasant example *of*. M19.

SHAKES. *Meas. for M.* O you beast! O faithless coward! O dishonest wretch! STEELE Morn' sends stagg'ring Home a Drunken Beast. E. WAUGH He's in an amorous stupor, poor beast, and doesn't quite know where he is. **b** W. S. GILBERT It's a beast of a name. H. C. BUNNER I've got to stay and finish my grind. It's a beast.

5 *CARDS*. An obsolete game resembling nap; a penalty at this game, or at ombre or quadrille. M17.
– PHRASES: **beast of burden** a draught animal. **beast of prey** an animal that kills and feeds on the flesh of other animals. ***blond beast***: see BLOND *adjective*. **the Beast** Antichrist (***the mark of the Beast***, a sign of heresy or evil nature). **the beast with two backs**, **two-backed beast** a man and woman copulating. ***the nature of the beast***: see NATURE *noun*.
– NOTE: Orig. used to translate Latin *animal* (in which it replaced Old English *dēor* DEER), and in turn largely supplanted by ANIMAL itself in senses 1–3.
■ **beastie** *noun* (*Scot.* or *joc.*) a small animal; an insect: L18. **beastish** *adjective* (now *rare*) beastly, brutish LME. **beastlike** *adjective* like a beast in nature or manner E16.

beast /biːst/ *verb trans*. M17.
[ORIGIN from the noun.]
1 Make a beast of; treat or regard as a beast. *rare*. M17.
2 ***be beasted***, fail to win the game, incur a penalty, at ombre. M17.

beastings *noun pl.* var. of BEESTINGS.

beastly /ˈbiːstli/ *adjective*. ME.
[ORIGIN from BEAST *noun* + -LY[1].]
†**1** Unthinking, unintelligent, irrational. ME–E18.

R. RECORDE To bring the people from beastly rage to manly reason.

2 Obeying animal instincts, sensual. ME.

SWIFT The beastly vice of drinking to excess.

3 Of, pertaining to, or of the nature of a beast; animal, natural. *arch.* LME.

J. RUSKIN The 'breeding' of a man is what he gets from the Centaur Chiron; the 'beastly' part of him in a good sense.

4 Abominable, foul; disgusting, offensive; *colloq.* unpleasant, ill-natured, undesirable, detestable. L16.

DISRAELI The steam packet is a beastly conveyance. N. COWARD It was beastly of you to laugh like that, I felt so humiliated. STEVIE SMITH There goes the beastly bell Tolling us to lessons. J. JOHNSTON You must stop biting your nails. It's a beastly habit.

■ **beastliness** *noun* beastly quality or behaviour LME.

beastly /ˈbiːstli/ *adverb*. LME.
[ORIGIN from BEAST *noun* + -LY[2].]
†**1** In a beastly manner, like a beast. LME–E17.
2 (W. adjectives.) Abominably, offensively, brutally; now usu. in weakened sense: regrettably, very. M16.

beat /biːt/ *noun*[1]. ME.
[ORIGIN from BEAT *verb*[1]. Branch III perh. a different word.]
▸ **I** †**1** Beating, whipping. Only in ME.
2 A blow, a stroke in beating. ME. ▸**b** *FENCING*. A blow struck upon the opponent's weapon. ME. ▸**c** *BALLET*. = BATTEMENT. E20.
3 A stroke upon or the striking of a drum; the sound or a signal so produced. L17.
4 (The sound produced by) any recurring stroke, or a regular sequence of strokes, e.g. of the heart, the pulse, a clock, etc. E18.

E. GASKELL The measured beat of the waters against the sides of the boat. W. FAULKNER The dry, dust-laden air vibrated steadily to the rapid beat of the engine. J. MASTERS One of the telegraphs was ringing the call-attention beat. S. KING Her heart slowed a little and then made speed for a dozen beats or so.

5 A pulsation or periodic variation of amplitude produced by the combination of two sounds or other oscillations (e.g. radio waves) of slightly different frequencies. M18.
6 *MUSIC*. **a** A grace note or ornament. *obsolete* exc. *hist.* E19. ▸**b** (The movement of a conductor's baton indicating) the principal recurring accent of a piece of music; a unit of measurement of greater or lesser rhythmic accentuation (expressed as a certain number of beats *to* or *in the bar*). L19. ▸**c** The strongly marked rhythm of jazz or popular music. M20.

b M. KENNEDY In 12/8 time there are 12 beats to a bar. A. SCHLEE Charlotte heard his foot tap restlessly to the beat of the new waltz. **c** L. ARMSTRONG Anything played with beat and soul is jazz. *Crescendo* The jazz Messengers were . . a beat group!

b OFFBEAT.
7 *US*. ▸**a** Something which surpasses, excels, or outdoes something else. E19. ▸**b** A journalistic scoop. L19.

a O. HENRY I never saw the beat of him for elegance.

8 An act or spell of beating to rouse game. L19.
▸ **II** **9** The course or area regularly patrolled by a police officer, sentinel, etc.; *gen.* a person's habitual round, territory, or ambit. E18.

DICKENS The costermongers repaired to their ordinary 'beats' in the suburbs. W. C. WILLIAMS The cop on the beat yelled at him to halt.

10 A tract of country traversed by a hunter in search of game; a stretch of water fished by an angler. M19.
▸ **III** **11** A distance sailed, or a spell of sailing, to windward. L19.
– COMB.: **beatbox** (***a***) a type of synthesizer producing percussion sounds; (***b***) a CD player, radio, etc. used to play loud music, esp. rap; (**c**) music, esp. rap music, with a largely percussive backing; **beatboxing** the action or practice of imitating the sounds of an electronic drum machine with the voice; **beatdown** *US* a physical beating or assault; a defeat; **beat frequency** the number of beats per second, equal to the difference in the frequencies of the two interacting tones or oscillations.
■ **beaty** *adjective* (of popular music) having a strongly marked beat M20.

beat /biːt; *dial. also* beɪt/ *noun*[2]. Also **beet**. LME.
[ORIGIN Perh. from BEAT *verb*[1].]
A bundle of flax or hemp.

beat /biːt; *dial. also* beɪt/ *noun*[3]. E17.
[ORIGIN Unknown: cf. BEAT *verb*[2].]
The rough sod or matted growth of waste or fallow land.

beat /biːt/ *adjective* & *noun*[4]. LME.
[ORIGIN Shortened from BEATEN.]
▸ **A** *adjective*. **1** = BEATEN. *arch.* & *dial.* exc. as below. LME.
2 Overcome with hard work or difficulty, worn out, exhausted. Cf. DEAD BEAT *adjective*. M18.

P. FRANKAU I was too beat and hazy to take anything in.

3 ***beat-up***, (***a***) = sense 2 above; (***b***) worn out, shabby, damaged by overuse. E20.

Daily Express We were all beat up after few days of the hardest soldiering you ever dreamt of. W. R. BURNETT The girl was sitting . . in the beat-up leather chair.

4 Belonging or pertaining to the beat generation. M20.

A. TATE For the Beat poets, antiquity ends at about 1956.

▸ **B** *noun*. **1** An idle or worthless man, a vagrant. Cf. DEAD BEAT *noun*. *US*. M19.
2 A member of the beat generation (see below). M20.
– COMB.: **the beat generation** a movement of young people in the 1950s and early 1960s who rejected conventional society, valuing free self-expression and favouring modern jazz.

beat /biːt/ *verb*[1]. Pa. t. **beat**; pa. pple **beaten** /ˈbiːt(ə)n/, (*arch. colloq.*) **beat** (esp. in sense 5).
[ORIGIN Old English *bēatan* = Old High German *bōzan*, Old Norse *bauta* from Germanic.]
▸ **I** Strike repeatedly, thrash, defeat.
1 *verb trans.* Strike with repeated blows. OE.

S. JOHNSON At what hour they may beat the door of an acquaintance. J. RHYS Then I beat my fist on a stone, forcing myself to speak calmly.

beat one's breast: in woe or mourning. **beat the air** strive in vain. ***beat the meat***: see MEAT *noun*. **beat the wind** = ***beat the air*** above.
2 *verb trans.* Inflict blows on with fist(s) or a weapon, thrash; punish, assault, or injure in this way. OE.

J. RUSKIN My brothers would beat me to death, Sir. DAY LEWIS He never beat me, even for major crimes. A. HAILEY The businessman . . attacked the company serviceman with a pipe wrench and beat him badly.

beat into fits, ***beat to fits***: see FIT *noun*[2].
3 *verb trans.* Strike (the ground etc.) in walking, tramp; make (a path) by trampling; make (one's way). OE.
beat it *slang* go away, clear off.
4 Of natural agents or forces: ▸**a** *verb trans.* Dash against, impinge upon, assail. OE. ▸**b** *verb intrans.* Impinge, fall, come violently or relentlessly (*against*, *at*, (*up*)*on*, etc.); freq. (esp. of the sun's rays) foll. by *down*. OE.

a WORDSWORTH Some island which the wild waves beat. **b** AV *Mark* 4:37 The waues beat into the ship. SOUTHEY We heard the rain beat hard. R. MACAULAY That place where the hot sun beat down on the fig trees.

5 *verb trans.* Overcome, conquer; defeat esp. in games or other competition; get the better of, baffle; outdo, surpass; be quicker than. (See also BEAT *adjective*.) ME. ▸**b** *verb intrans.* Gain the victory, win. *arch.* L18.

STEELE He had beat the Romans in a pitched battle. C. BRONTË I have heard of love at first sight, but this beats all! W. DE LA MARE Why you should have taken so much trouble about it simply beats me. E. BOWEN You can't beat the military swagger. J. FOWLES We played chess and he let me beat him.

beat all to sticks: see STICK *noun*[1]. ***beat a person at his or her own game***: see GAME *noun*. ***beat creation***: see CREATION 4. ***beat the band***: see BAND *noun*[3] 3. **beat the bat** *CRICKET* make the batsman play and miss. ***beat the clock***: see CLOCK *noun*[1]. **beat the gun**, **beat the pistol** = ***jump the gun*** s.v. GUN *noun*. ***beat the rap***: see RAP *noun*[1]. **beat to it**, **beat to the punch** get there before, anticipate, (a person). **can you beat it?** *slang*: expr. surprise or amazement.
6 *verb intrans.* Strike repeated blows, knock *against*, *at*, (*up*)*on*. ME.

SHAKES. *Lear* O Lear, Lear, Lear! Beat at this gate that let thy folly in. TOLKIEN Gandalf stood before the door of Orthanc and beat on it with his staff.

7 *verb intrans.* Of the heart, pulse, etc.: throb, pulsate rhythmically; *gen.* pulsate, make rhythmic strokes or sounds. (Cf. sense 17 below.) ME. ▸**b** Produce a beat (BEAT *noun*[1] 5). E19.

fig.: DRYDEN Such Rage of Honey in their Bosom beats.

†**8** *verb trans.* Assail with sound or voice. LME–L17.

WYCLIF *Ecclus* 43:18 The vois of his thunder schal beten the erthe.

†**9** *verb trans.* Batter with missiles, bombard. LME–M17.
10 *verb trans.* & *intrans.* **a** Flap (the wings) forcefully; move the wings up and down rapidly. LME. ▸†**b** Strike (the eyelids or teeth) together. LME–E17.

SHAKES. *Tam. Shr.* These kites That bate and beat, and will not be obedient. TOLKIEN The great beast beat its hideous wings, and the wind of them was foul.

B

†**11** *verb trans. & intrans.* Hammer at (a subject); thrash out, discuss; insist repeatedly (*up*)*on*. **L15–M17.**
▸ **II** Shape, alter, move, etc., by striking.
12 *verb trans.* Pulverize with repeated blows, pound. **OE.** ▸**b** Mix or stir vigorously, whip (eggs, cream, etc.). **LME.**

b R. WEST She heated the fruit and . . the sugar and beat them up together for half an hour.

13 *verb trans.* Work, shape, deform, by repeated blows; hammer, forge. **LME.**

AV *Isa.* 2:4 They shall beate their swords into plow-shares.

14 *verb trans.* Impel or force (a thing) to move by blows; drive (a person, army, etc.) by force *away, back, off, out of* (a place), etc. **LME.**

DEFOE The blow . . beat the breath . . quite out of my body. W. FAULKNER A Cossack sergeant beat his brains out with the shod hooves of a horse. *fig.*: LEIGH HUNT The classics were beaten into their heads at school.

beat hell out of: see HELL *noun*. ***beat the PANTS off***. ***beat the shit out of***: see SHIT *noun*. ***beat the STUFFING out of***. ***beat the tar out of***: see TAR *noun*[1] 1.
15 *verb trans.* Strike (cover of any kind) in order to rouse or drive out game; range over in hunting; *fig.* work over roughly, search unceremoniously. **LME.** ▸**b** *verb intrans.* Cover an area thus; go *over* or *about* an area thus. **L16.** ▸†**c** *verb intrans.* Of the brain: think hard. **E–M17.**
beat about the bush *fig.* approach a subject indirectly, not come to the point. ***beat one's brains***: see BRAIN *noun*. **beat the bounds** trace out the boundaries of a parish, striking certain points with rods.
16 *verb intrans. & trans.* Of game: move here and there in an attempt to escape; take to (a stream etc.) to elude pursuit. **LME.**
17 a *verb trans.* Strike (a drum or other instrument) so as to make a rhythmical sound; make or express (a signal, rhythm, etc.) by striking or sounding (often of the heart, a clock, etc.: cf. sense 7 above). **LME.** ▸**b** *verb intrans.* Of a drum etc.: sound when struck. Of a signal: be sounded upon a drum. **M17.**

a N. MASKELYNE A pendulum clock beating half seconds. LD MACAULAY The drums of Limerick beat a parley.

a beat a retreat *fig.* retreat, abandon an undertaking. **beat time** mark or follow the time of music with the feet, a baton, etc. **beat to quarters** *NAUTICAL* summon the crew to action stations.
18 *verb trans.* Break, smash, or bring down by hard knocks. **L16.**

H. NELSON The man who may have his Ship beat to pieces.

19 *verb trans.* Bring down (a price) by haggling; cause (the seller) to reduce his price. Now only foll. by *down*. **L16.**
20 *verb trans.* Strike (a carpet, a tree, etc.) repeatedly so as to loosen or shake out dust, fruit, etc.; strike repeatedly so as to put out a fire. **E17.**

AV *Deut.* 4:20 When thou beatest thine olive trees, thou shalt not go over the boughs again. J. HERSEY Mr. Tanimoto . . told others to beat the burning underbrush with their clothes.

▸ **III 21** *verb intrans. & (rare) trans.* *NAUTICAL.* Sail to windward, make way against the wind. Freq. foll. by *up*. **L17.**

POPE The toss'd navies beat the heaving main. W. S. MAUGHAM A big schooner . . was beating up against the breeze towards the harbour. J. CLAVELL To beat to windward . . or to run before the wind.

— WITH ADVERBS & PREPOSITIONS IN SPECIALIZED SENSES: **beat down** (*a*) *verb phr. trans.* force or drive down, demolish, or overthrow by beating; (see also sense 19); (*b*) *verb phr. intrans.* see sense 4b. **beat in** drive or smash in, or crush, with heavy blows. **beat off** drive back; overcome (a challenge etc.). **beat out** (*a*) forge, make, or remove by hammering; (*b*) extinguish (a fire) by beating; (*c*) sound (a rhythm) by beating; (*d*) *N. Amer.* defeat in a competition. **beat up** (*a*) *verb phr. trans.* thrash (a person) severely, assault with blows; (*b*) *verb phr. trans.* collect or attract (recruits etc.); (*c*) *verb phr. trans.* pass very closely in an aeroplane; (*d*) *verb phr. intrans.*: see sense 21; (*e*) *verb phr. refl.* (*colloq.*) reproach or criticize oneself excessively.
■ **beatable** *adjective* that can be beaten **E17.**

beat /biːt; *dial. also* beɪt/ *verb*[2] *trans.* **M16.**
[**ORIGIN** Unknown: cf. BEAT *noun*[3].]
Slice off the rough turf from (uncultivated or fallow land).

beaten /ˈbiːt(ə)n/ *ppl adjective.* **ME.**
[**ORIGIN** pa. pple of BEAT *verb*[1].]
▸ **I** *gen.* **1** That has been beaten. **ME.**
▸ **II** *spec.* **2** Shaped by hammering; *esp.* (of metal) hammered into foil. **ME.**
3 Trodden, worn by repeated use. **L15.** ▸†**b** *fig.* Trite, hackneyed. **M16–M18.**
beaten-up = *beat-up* (b) s.v. BEAT *adjective* 3. **the beaten track** the ordinary or usual way, the well-frequented route, well-known territory, (*lit. & fig.*); freq. in ***off the beaten track***.
4 Whipped to a uniform consistency; pulverized, pounded. **M16.**
5 Conquered, defeated; overcome, baffled, dejected. **M16.**
6 *MILITARY.* Of a zone: covered by gunfire. **E20.**

beatenest /ˈbiːt(ə)nɪst/ *adjective. US dial.* **M19.**
[**ORIGIN** from BEATEN or *beating* pres. pple of BEAT *verb*[1] + -EST[1].]
Best, finest; most unusual.

beater /ˈbiːtə/ *noun.* **ME.**
[**ORIGIN** from BEAT *verb*[1] + -ER[1].]
1 An implement or device for beating something. **ME.** ▸**b** *spec.* A machine for preparing wet pulp for the making of paper. **E19.**
carpet-beater, ***egg beater***, etc.
2 A person who beats something or someone. **LME.** ▸**b** *spec.* A person engaged to rouse and drive game. **E19.**
panel beater: see PANEL *noun*[1]. ***world-beater***: see WORLD *noun*.

beath /biːð/ *verb trans.* Long *obsolete* exc. *dial.*
[**ORIGIN** Old English *beþian* from Germanic: rel. to BATHE *verb*.]
†**1** Bathe, foment. **OE–ME.**
2 Heat (unseasoned wood) in order to straighten it. **LME.**

beatific /biːəˈtɪfɪk/ *adjective.* **M17.**
[**ORIGIN** French *béatifique* or Latin *beatificus*, from *beatus* blessed: see -FIC.]
Making blessed, imparting supreme happiness; *colloq.* (of a smile etc.) blissful, serenely happy.
beatific vision *CHRISTIAN THEOLOGY* the first sight of the glories of heaven; the direct experience of God by those in heaven.
■ **beatifical** *adjective* (now *rare*) **E17.** **beatifically** *adverb* **E17.**

beatification /bɪˌatɪfɪˈkeɪʃ(ə)n/ *noun.* **E16.**
[**ORIGIN** Old French & mod. French *béatification* or ecclesiastical Latin *beatificatio(n-)*, from *beatificat-* pa. ppl stem of *beatificare*: see BEATIFY, -ATION.]
1 The action of making or being made blessed. **E16.**
2 *ROMAN CATHOLIC CHURCH.* A declaration by the Pope that a deceased person is in a state of bliss, constituting a first step towards canonization and permitting public veneration. **E17.**

beatify /bɪˈatɪfʌɪ/ *verb trans.* **M16.**
[**ORIGIN** Old French & mod. French *béatifier* or ecclesiastical Latin *beatificare*, from Latin *beatus* blessed: see -FY.]
1 Make blessed or supremely happy. **M16.**
2 *ROMAN CATHOLIC CHURCH.* Announce the beatification of; declare blessed. **E17.**

†**beatille pie** *noun phr.* see BATTALIA PIE.

beating /ˈbiːtɪŋ/ *verbal noun.* **ME.**
[**ORIGIN** from BEAT *verb*[1] + -ING[1].]
▸ **I** *gen.* **1** The action of BEAT *verb*[1]. **ME.**
▸ **II** *spec.* **2** A punishment or assault in which the victim is hit repeatedly, a thrashing. **ME.**
beating-up a violent assault on a person.
3 A pulsation or throbbing, esp. of the heart. **LME.**
4 A defeat; defeating, surpassing. **L19.**
have the beating of be able to defeat. **take a lot of beating**, **take some beating** be hard to defeat or surpass.

beatitude /bɪˈatɪtjuːd/ *noun.* **LME.**
[**ORIGIN** Old French & mod. French *béatitude* or Latin *beatitudo*, from *beatus* blessed: see -TUDE.]
1 Supreme blessedness; bliss. **LME.**
2 A declaration of blessedness, a blessing; *spec.* (in *pl.*) those made by Jesus in the Sermon on the Mount (*Matthew* 5:3–11). **E16.**
3 ***his Beatitude***, ***your Beatitude***: an honorific patriarchal title in the Orthodox Church. **M17.**
4 = BEATIFICATION 2. **M19.**

Beatle /ˈbiːt(ə)l/ *noun.* **M20.**
[**ORIGIN** from 'The Beatles', the name of a pop and rock group from Liverpool, active in the 1960s.]
Used *attrib.* to designate the pudding-basin hairstyle or other characteristics of the Beatles or of their imitators.
■ **Beatleˈmania** *noun* enthusiastic or frenzied admiration for the Beatles or their music **M20.** **Beatleˈmaniac** *noun* **M20.** **Beatlˈesque** *adjective* **L20.**

beatnik /ˈbiːtnɪk/ *noun.* **M20.**
[**ORIGIN** from BEAT *adjective* & *noun*[4] + -NIK.]
A member of the beat generation.

Beatrician /bɪəˈtrɪʃ(ə)n/ *adjective.* **M20.**
[**ORIGIN** from *Beatrice* (see below) + -IAN.]
Of, pertaining to, or resembling (the vision of) Beatrice in Dante's *Vita Nuova* and *Divina Commedia*; of or concerning a revelatory or transcendental vision, experience, etc.

beatster /ˈbiːtstə/ *noun*[1]. Also **beet-**. **L16.**
[**ORIGIN** from BEET *verb* + -STER.]
A mender or mounter of fishing nets.

beatster /ˈbiːtstə/ *noun*[2]. **M20.**
[**ORIGIN** from BEAT *adjective* & *noun*[4] + -STER.]
A member of the beat generation.

beau /bəʊ/ *noun.* Pl. **beaux** /bəʊz/, **beaus**. **L17.**
[**ORIGIN** French, use as noun of adjective, ult. from Latin *bellus* fine, beautiful.]
1 A fashionable man, a ladies' man; a fop, a dandy. **L17.**
2 A lady's male companion, a suitor; a boyfriend, a lover. Now chiefly *N. Amer.* **E18.**
■ **beauish** *adjective* foppish, dandified **L17.**

beaucoup /bəʊˈkuː/ *adjective, noun, & adverb. colloq.* (chiefly *N. Amer.*). **M19.**
[**ORIGIN** French.]
▸ **A** *adjective.* Much; many. **M19.**

T. ROBBINS Jesse James robbed beaucoup banks and near as many trains.

▸ **B** *noun.* An abundance, a large amount. **E20.**
▸ **C** *adverb.* In abundance. **E20.**

beaufin *noun* see BIFFIN.

Beaufort scale /ˈbəʊfət skeɪl/ *noun phr.* **M19.**
[**ORIGIN** Sir Francis *Beaufort* (1774–1857), English admiral.]
A scale of whole numbers denoting ranges of wind speed, from 0 for 0–0.2 metres per second (calm) to 12 for over 32.6 metres per second (hurricane).

beau geste /bo ʒɛst/ *noun phr.* Pl. ***beaux gestes*** (pronounced same). **E20.**
[**ORIGIN** French = splendid gesture.]
A display of magnanimity; a generous act.

beau gregory /bəʊ ˈgrɛg(ə)ri/ *noun phr.* **M19.**
[**ORIGIN** Unknown.]
A blue and yellow percoid fish, *Eupomacentrus leucostictus* (family Pomacentridae), of the W. Indies and Florida.

beau idéal /bəʊ ʌɪˈdɪəl/ *noun phr.* **E19.**
[**ORIGIN** French = ideal beauty (now often misunderstood as = beautiful ideal): see BEAU, IDEAL.]
One's highest or ideal type of excellence or beauty; the perfect model.

Beaujolais /ˈbəʊʒəleɪ, *foreign* boʒɔlɛ/ *noun.* **M19.**
[**ORIGIN** See below.]
A red or (less commonly) white light burgundy wine produced in the Beaujolais district of France.
Beaujolais nouveau /nuːˈvəʊ, *foreign* nuvo/ [= new]: of the latest vintage.

Beaumé *noun* var. of BAUMÉ.

beau monde /bəʊ ˈmɒnd, *foreign* bo mɔ̃ːd/ *noun phr.* **L17.**
[**ORIGIN** French = fine world.]
(The world of) fashionable society.

beaumontage /bəʊmɒnˈtɑːʒ/ *noun.* Also **Beaumont('s) egg** /ˌbəʊmɒnt(s) ˈɛg/ & other vars. **L19.**
[**ORIGIN** Unknown.]
A composition used to conceal cracks and holes in metal, wood, etc.

Beaune /bəʊn, *foreign* boːn/ *noun.* **E19.**
[**ORIGIN** A town in the department of Côte d'Or, France.]
A red burgundy wine produced in the district around Beaune.

beau-pot /ˈbəʊpɒt/ *noun.* **M18.**
[**ORIGIN** Alt. of ***bough-pot*** s.v. BOUGH *noun*.]
(A large vase containing) a display of cut flowers.

beau rôle /bo roːl/ *noun phr.* Pl. ***beaux rôles*** (pronounced same). **L19.**
[**ORIGIN** French = fine role.]
A fine acting part; the leading part.

beau sabreur /bo sabrœːr/ *noun phr.* Pl. ***beaux sabreurs*** (pronounced same). **M19.**
[**ORIGIN** French = fine (or handsome) swordsman: orig. a sobriquet of Joachim Murat (1767–1815), French cavalry officer and brother-in-law of Napoleon.]
A gallant warrior, a handsome or dashing adventurer.

beaut /bjuːt/ *noun & adjective. slang.* Chiefly *N. Amer., Austral., & NZ.* **M19.**
[**ORIGIN** Abbreviation of BEAUTY.]
▸ **A** *noun.* A beautiful or outstanding person or thing. **M19.**
▸ **B** *adjective.* Beautiful, first-rate. **M20.**

beauté du diable /bote dy djɑːbl/ *noun phr.* **M19.**
[**ORIGIN** French = devil's beauty.]
Superficial attractiveness; captivating charm.

beauteous /ˈbjuːtɪəs/ *adjective. literary.* **LME.**
[**ORIGIN** from BEAUTY after *bounteous*, *plenteous*.]
Beautiful.
■ **beauteously** *adverb* **L15.** **beauteousness** *noun* **M17.**

beautician /bjuːˈtɪʃ(ə)n/ *noun.* **E20.**
[**ORIGIN** from BEAUTY + -ICIAN.]
A person who runs a beauty parlour; a specialist in beauty treatment.

beautification /ˌbjuːtɪfɪˈkeɪʃ(ə)n/ *noun.* **M17.**
[**ORIGIN** from BEAUTIFY: see -FICATION.]
The action or an act of beautifying; (an) adornment.

beautiful /ˈbjuːtɪfʊl, -f(ə)l/ *adjective & noun.* **LME.**
[**ORIGIN** from BEAUTY + -FUL.]
▸ **A** *adjective.* **1** Full of beauty, delightful to the eye or ear, or to any faculty or taste. **LME.**

AV *Ps.* 48:2 Beautifull for situation, the ioy of the whole earth is mount Sion. N. HAWTHORNE It had been the beautifullest of weather all day. E. ST V. MILLAY Sweet sounds, oh, beautiful music, do not cease! G. B. SHAW Her lover, a beautiful youth of eighteen. E. O'NEILL Your mother was one of the most beautiful girls you could ever see. DAY LEWIS It is . . a face which might be beautiful one day and plain another, but never uninteresting.

beautiful letters *US* = BELLES-LETTRES. **beautiful people** *colloq.* (*a*) hippies, *esp.* flower people; (*b*) the fashionable rich. **the — beautiful** the — in its ideal form, esp. as a cult. **the beautiful game** [perh. after Brazilian Portuguese *o jogo bonito*] Association football, soccer.
2 Morally or intellectually impressive or satisfying; *colloq.* very good, excellent; pleasing, delightful. **L16.**

D. HUME Another argument . . which seems to me very strong and beautiful. ALDOUS HUXLEY A very nice fellow and a beautiful pianist.

▸ **B** *absol.* as *noun*. **1** Beautiful one. Used chiefly as a form of address. M16.

2 That which is beautiful; *the* qualities constituting beauty. M18.

▪ **beautifully** *adverb* in a beautiful manner, delightfully; *colloq.* very well, excellently: M16. **beautifulness** *noun* E16.

beautify /ˈbjuːtɪfʌɪ/ *verb trans.* E16.
[ORIGIN from BEAUTY + -FY.]
Make beautiful; adorn, embellish.
▪ **beautifier** *noun* L16.

beauty /ˈbjuːti/ *noun & verb.* ME.
[ORIGIN Anglo-Norman *beuté*, Old French *belte*, *beaute* (mod. *beauté*) from Proto-Romance, from Latin *bellus*: see BEAU, -TY¹.]

▸ **A** *noun*. **1** That quality or combination of qualities which delights the senses or mental faculties; *esp.* that combination of shape, colour, and proportion which is pleasing to the eye. ME. ▸**b** (B-.) This quality personified. LME.

KEATS A thing of beauty is a joy for ever; Its loveliness increases: it will never Pass into nothingness. TENNYSON There sat . . All beauty compass'd in a female form, The Princess. T. E. LAWRENCE That trumpet call had an almost liquid beauty. M. DRABBLE Her gawky, bony clumsiness had suddenly transformed itself into dazzling beauty.

line of beauty: see LINE *noun*².

2 A beautiful feature, a charm, an embellishment; a particular point giving pleasure or satisfaction. ME. ▸**b** In *pl.* (In titles) choice examples of the work of a writer etc. *arch.* M18.

S. RICHARDSON That's the beauty of it; to offend and make up at pleasure. LD MACAULAY The one beauty of the resolution is its inconsistency.

3 A beautiful person, *esp.* a beautiful woman. LME. ▸**b** Beautiful persons collectively. E17.

P. S. BUCK It is better to be first with an ugly woman than the hundredth with a beauty. **b** BYRON Belgium's capital had gather'd then Her Beauty and her Chivalry.

bathing beauty: see BATHE *verb* 5. ***sleeping beauty***: see SLEEPING *ppl adjective*.

4 A beautiful thing; a particularly good specimen of something. M18.

P. G. WODEHOUSE She . . swung her right and plugged Slingsby a perfect beauty in the eye.

In names of butterflies and moths: ***brindled beauty***, ***Camberwell beauty***, ***oak beauty***, ***painted beauty***, etc.

5 PARTICLE PHYSICS. A quark flavour associated with a charge of −⅓. Also called **bottom**. (Symbol *b*.) L20.

– COMB.: **beauty contest**, (*N. Amer.*) **beauty pageant** a competition for a prize given to the woman judged the most beautiful; **beauty mark** *N. Amer.* = ***beauty spot*** (a) below; **beauty parlour** an establishment in which beauty treatment is practised professionally; **beauty queen** a winner of a beauty contest; **beauty salon**, (*US*) **beauty shop** = ***beauty parlour*** above; **beauty sleep**: before midnight; **beauty spot** (*a*) a small patch placed on a woman's face as a foil to her complexion; (*b*) a beautiful locality; **beauty treatment** the use of cosmetics, manicuring, hairdressing, etc., to enhance personal appearance.

▸ **B** *verb trans.* Beautify, adorn. *arch.* LME.
▪ **beautiless** *adjective* L16.

beaux *noun pl.* see BEAU.

beaux arts /boz ɑːr/ *noun & adjectival phr.* Also ***beaux-arts***. E19.
[ORIGIN French *beaux-arts*.]

▸ **A** *noun phr. pl.* Fine arts. Also *ellipt.*, the *École des Beaux-Arts* in Paris. E19.

▸ **B** *adjectival phr.* Of or pertaining to the classical decorative style maintained by the *École des Beaux-Arts* esp. in the 19th cent. E20.

beaux esprits, ***beaux gestes*** *noun phrs.* pls. of BEL ESPRIT, BEAU GESTE.

†**beauxite** *noun* var. of BAUXITE.

beaux rôles, ***beaux sabreurs*** *noun phrs.* pls. of BEAU RÔLE, BEAU SABREUR.

beaux yeux /boz jø/ *noun phr.* E19.
[ORIGIN French.]
Beautiful eyes; admiring glances; favourable regard.

beaver /ˈbiːvə/ *noun*¹ & *adjective.*
[ORIGIN Old English *beofor*, *befor* = Middle & mod. Low German, Middle Dutch & mod. Dutch *bever*, Old High German *bibar* (German *Biber*), Old Norse *bjórr* from Germanic, ult. from Indo-European base meaning 'brown'.]

▸ **A** *noun*. **1** Pl. same, **-s**. A semi-aquatic rodent (of which there are two species, the Eurasian *Castor fiber* and the N. American *C. canadensis*), which has a broad flat paddle-like tail and soft fur, and is notable for its habit of making dams to maintain a supply of water, and its ability to gnaw down trees. OE.

eager beaver *colloq.* a zealous or overzealous person. MOUNTAIN *beaver*. **work like a beaver** be very industrious, work hard.

2 The fur of the beaver. LME.

3 A hat made of beaver's fur. E16.

4 A heavy woollen cloth resembling beaver's fur. M18.

5 A shade of brown like the colour of beaver's fur. L19.

6 (B-.) A member of a group of six- to eight-year-old boys affiliated to the Scout Association. L20.

▸ **B** *attrib.* or as *adjective*. Made of beaver's fur; coloured like beaver's fur. LME.

– COMB.: **Beaverboard** *N. Amer.* (proprietary name for) a type of wood-fibre building board; **beaver cloth** = sense 4 above; ***beaver dam***: see DAM *noun*¹ 1b; **beaver lamb** lambskin cut and dyed to resemble beaver's fur; ***beaver meadow***: see MEADOW *noun* 3; **beaver-tail** a tapering wedge-shaped end.

beaver /ˈbiːvə/ *noun*². *obsolete* exc. *hist.* L15.
[ORIGIN Old French *baviere* orig. child's bib, from *baver* slaver, from Proto-Romance.]
The lower face guard of a helmet.

Beaver /ˈbiːvə/ *noun*³. Pl. **-s**, same. L18.
[ORIGIN from BEAVER *noun*¹, translating Chipewyan *Tsa-ttine* dwellers among beavers.]
A member of a group of Athabaskan peoples of northern Alberta, Canada; the language of this group.

beaver /ˈbiːvə/ *noun*⁴. *slang.* E20.
[ORIGIN Unknown.]

1 A bearded man; a beard. E20.

2 The female genitals; a woman or girl (*offensive*). Chiefly *N. Amer.* M20.

split beaver: see SPLIT *adjective*.

beaver *noun*⁵ see BEVER *noun*.

beaver /ˈbiːvə/ *verb intrans.* M20.
[ORIGIN from BEAVER *noun*¹.]
beaver away, work very hard or persistently (*at*).

beavered /ˈbiːvəd/ *adjective*. E17.
[ORIGIN from BEAVER *noun*¹, *noun*², *noun*⁴ + -ED².]
Wearing a beaver hat; bearded; (of a helmet etc.) equipped with a beaver.

bebeeru /bɪˈbɪəruː/ *noun*. Also **bibira** /bɪˈbɪərə/ & other vars. M19.
[ORIGIN Spanish *bibirú* from Carib.]
(The timber of) the greenheart tree, *Ocotea rodiaei*, of northern S. America.

bebleed /bɪˈbliːd/ *verb trans.* Long *arch.* Pa. t. & pple **-bled** /-ˈblɛd/. ME.
[ORIGIN from BE- 2 + BLEED *verb*.]
Soak or stain with blood; make bloody.

†**bebless** *verb trans.* Pa. t. & pple **-blessed**, **-blest**. L16–L18.
[ORIGIN from BE- 1 + BLESS *verb*¹.]
Cover with blessings; bless profusely.

beblister /bɪˈblɪstə/ *verb trans.* L16.
[ORIGIN from BE- 1 + BLISTER *verb*.]
Blister (skin etc.) badly; cover with blisters.

beblood /bɪˈblʌd/ *verb trans.* Long *arch.* L16.
[ORIGIN from BE- 4 + BLOOD *noun*.]
= BEBLEED.

beblubber /bɪˈblʌbə/ *verb trans.* M16.
[ORIGIN from BE- 1 + BLUBBER *verb*.]
Smear over or suffuse with tears; disfigure with weeping. Chiefly as ***beblubbered*** *ppl adjective*.

bebop /ˈbiːbɒp/ *noun*. Orig. *US.* M20.
[ORIGIN Imit. of a typical musical phrase.]
A kind of modern jazz characterized by complex harmony and rhythm.
▪ **bebopper** *noun* a performer or adherent of bebop M20.

Bebung /ˈbeːbʊŋ/ *noun*. L19.
[ORIGIN German = trembling.]
MUSIC. A pulsating or trembling effect given to a sustained note; *spec.* such an effect produced on the clavichord by rocking the fingertip.

becall /bɪˈkɔːl/ *verb trans.* ME.
[ORIGIN from BE- 1 + CALL *verb*.]

†**1** Accuse *of*. Only in ME.

†**2** Call upon, summon, challenge. LME–L15.

3 Miscall, abuse; rail at. Long *dial.* L17.

becalm /bɪˈkɑːm/ *verb trans.* M16.
[ORIGIN from BE- 1, 4 + CALM *verb*.]

1 NAUTICAL. Deprive (a ship) of wind. Usu. in *pass.* M16.

LD MACAULAY The fleet was becalmed off the Goodwin Sands.

2 Make calm or still, soothe, assuage. E17.

POPE What power becalms the innavigable seas?

became *verb pa. t.* of BECOME *verb*.

becard /ˈbeɪkɑːd/ *noun*. M19.
[ORIGIN French *bécarde*, from *bec* beak.]
Any of numerous tyrant flycatchers of the genus *Pachyramphus*, of Central and S. America.

because /bɪˈkɒz/ *adverb & conjunction.* ME.
[ORIGIN Orig. two words, formed as BY *preposition* + CAUSE *noun*, after Old French *par cause de* by reason of.]

▸ **A** *adverb*. **1** For the reason *that* (also foll. by †*why*). *arch.* ME.

BYRON I abhor death, because that thou must die.

2 By reason *of*, on account *of*. LME.

A. LURIE Clark doesn't support me because of my writing, but in spite of it.

3 ***because why?*** why? Chiefly *dial.* L19.

D. H. LAWRENCE The painters try to paint her . . in vain. Because why?

▸ **B** *conjunction*. **1** For the reason that, inasmuch as, since. LME. ▸**b** Used ellipt. in answer to a question, implying that a fuller reply has been withheld. M18.

R. KIPLING I buy them because they are pretty. **b** M. CARROLL 'Why didn't you leave the bottle?' 'Because!' I said shortly. I wasn't going to explain my feelings on the matter.

†**2** In order that, with the purpose that. L15–M17.

ROBERT BURTON Anointing the doors and hinges with oyl, because they should not creak.

– PHRASES: †**for because** = senses A.1, 2, B.1 above.

beccafico /bɛkəˈfiːkəʊ/ *noun*. Pl. **-os**. E17.
[ORIGIN Italian, from *beccare* to peck + *fico* FIG *noun*¹.]
Any of a number of warblers esteemed as a delicacy in the Mediterranean region.

béchamel /ˈbeɪʃəmɛl, *foreign* beʃamɛl/ *noun*. M18.
[ORIGIN from the Marquis de *Béchamel*, steward of Louis XIV.]
COOKERY. More fully ***béchamel sauce***. A fine savoury white sauce, freq. made with added cream or milk.

bechance /bɪˈtʃɑːns/ *verb*. E16.
[ORIGIN from BE- + CHANCE *verb*.]

1 *verb intrans.* Happen, fall out; occur by chance. E16.

2 *verb trans.* Befall. M16.

becharm /bɪˈtʃɑːm/ *verb trans.* ME.
[ORIGIN from BE- 1 + CHARM *verb*¹.]
Charm, fascinate; subject to an enchantment.

bêche-de-mer /bɛʃdəˈmɛː/ *noun*. Pl. same, **bêches-** /bɛʃ-/. L18.
[ORIGIN Pseudo-Fr. from Portuguese *bicho do mar* lit. 'worm of the sea'. Cf. BEACH-LA-MAR, BISLAMA.]

1 A sea cucumber eaten as a Chinese or Japanese delicacy. L18.

2 = BEACH-LA-MAR 2. Also ***bêche-de-mer English***. L19.

Bechuana, **Bechwana** *nouns & adjectives* see BATSWANA.

beck /bɛk/ *noun*¹. Long *dial. rare.*
[ORIGIN Old English *becca*, perh. ult. from Celtic: cf. Welsh *bach* hook.]
An agricultural implement with two hooks, a mattock.

beck /bɛk/ *noun*². Long *N. English.* ME.
[ORIGIN Old Norse *bekkr* from Germanic; rel. to German *Bach*.]
A brook, a rivulet; *spec.* a mountain, hill, or moorland stream.

beck /bɛk/ *noun*³. ME.
[ORIGIN from BECK *verb*.]

1 A bow, a curtsy, a gesture of acknowledgement. ME.

A. WILSON He equally ignored all Rose Lorimer's flustered bobs, becks and smiles.

2 A significant gesture indicating agreement, command, etc. ME.

DEFOE With a beck of the head or hand, as we beckon to servants.

at the beck and call of subservient to, at the absolute command of.

beck /bɛk/ *verb. arch.* ME.
[ORIGIN Shortened from BECKON *verb*.]

1 *verb intrans.* = BECKON *verb* 1. ME.

2 *verb trans.* = BECKON *verb* 2. L15.

3 *verb intrans.* Make a sign of acknowledgement; bow, curtsy. Chiefly *Scot.* M16.

becket /ˈbɛkɪt/ *noun*¹. *obsolete* exc. *dial.* LME.
[ORIGIN Prob. from obsolete var. of BEAK *noun*¹ + -ET¹.]
Any protruding or overhanging structure, as a corbel, a mantelpiece, etc.

becket /ˈbɛkɪt/ *noun*². E18.
[ORIGIN Unknown.]
NAUTICAL. A contrivance of rope, hook, bracket, etc., used to secure loose ropes, tackle, or spars.

becket /ˈbɛkɪt/ *noun*³. *dial.* M18.
[ORIGIN from BECK *noun*¹ + -ET¹.]
A spade used in cutting peat or turf.

beckon /ˈbɛk(ə)n/ *verb & noun.*
[ORIGIN Old English *bēcnan* (*biecnan*) = Old Saxon *bōknian*, Old High German *bouhnen*, from West Germanic, formed as BEACON *noun*.]

▸ **A** *verb*. **1** *verb intrans.* Signal with a gesture of head, hand, or finger, esp. to indicate that someone should approach. OE.

JOYCE The old woman, seeing that I hesitated to enter, began to beckon to me again repeatedly with her hand. *fig.*: S. BRETT The West End then beckoned, and he appeared as a solid juvenile in . . light comedies.

2 *verb trans.* (orig. with dat. obj.). Gesture to (a person) to approach, by a movement of head, hand, or finger; summon by such a signal. OE.

SHAKES. *Oth.* Iago beckons me; now he begins the story.

▸ **B** *noun*. A significant gesture, esp. one indicating assent or command. *rare.* E18.

beclad *verb* see BECLOTHE *verb*.

beclip /bɪˈklɪp/ *verb trans. arch.* Infl. **-pp-**.
[ORIGIN Old English *beclyppan*, formed as BE- 1 + CLIP *verb*¹.]

†**1** Embrace, fold in the arms. OE–M17.

2 Enclose or wrap round; encircle. *arch.* OE.

†**3** Lay hold of, grip; overtake. LME–M16.

beclog /bɪˈklɒɡ/ *verb trans. arch.* Infl. **-gg-**. LME.
[ORIGIN from BE- 1 + CLOG *verb*.]
Encumber with a sticky substance; daub liberally with clotted matter. Usu. in *pass.*

beclothe /bɪˈkləʊð/ *verb trans.* Pa. t. & pple **-clothed**, **-clad** /-ˈklad/. LME.
[ORIGIN from BE- 1 + CLOTHE *verb*.]
Clothe round, dress. Usu. in *pass.*

becloud /bɪˈklaʊd/ *verb trans.* L16.
[ORIGIN from BE- 4 + CLOUD *noun*.]
Cover or darken with clouds or murk; make obscure or gloomy.

become /bɪˈkʌm/ *verb.* Pa. t. **became** /bɪˈkeɪm/; pa. pple **become**.
[ORIGIN Old English *becuman* = Old Frisian *bicuma*, Middle Low German, Middle Dutch & mod. Dutch *bekomen*, Old High German *biqueman* (German *bekommen*) obtain, receive, Gothic *biqiman*, from Germanic: see BE-, COME *verb*.]
▸ **I** Come —.
†**1** *verb intrans.* Come to a place, arrive; travel, go. OE–M18.

> BACON Houses so full of Glasse, that one cannot tell, where to become, to be out of the Sunne.

†**2** *verb intrans.* **a** Come in the course of time (*to be* or *do*). OE–E19. ▸**b** Foll. by *of*: come from, originate from. ME–E17.

> **a** SYD. SMITH It becomes to be loved on its own account.

†**3** *verb intrans.* with dat. or *to*, later *verb trans.* Happen, befall. OE–M17.
4 As *copula* with noun or adjective compl. or †*verb intrans.* with (*in*)*to*. Come to be, begin to be. ME.

> EVELYN The Church of God, being now become, from a private family . . to a great and numerous nation. LD MACAULAY When first they became known to the Tyrian mariners. E. M. FORSTER Their pleasantry and their piety show cracks, their wit becomes cynicism, their unselfishness hypocrisy. S. BELLOW Depressives tended to form frantic dependencies and to become hysterical when cut off. R. K. NARAYAN After college, the question was whether I should become a dancer or do something else. C. MILNE You can keep tadpoles until they become frogs or toads.

5 *verb trans.* Foll. by *of*: (formerly) result from; (now) happen to, befall. Only with *what* as subj. M16.

> SHAKES. *Twel. N.* What will become of this? . . My state is desperate. J. CONRAD I haven't seen him for a week. What has become of him?

6 *verb intrans.* Come into being. *rare.* L16.
▸ **II** Befit.
7 *verb trans.* (orig. with dat. obj.). Accord with, be appropriate to, befit. Also *impers.* in **(*it*) *becomes*** etc. ME.

> DISRAELI He had that public spirit which became his station. SIR W. SCOTT I thought it became me to make public how far I was concerned.

†**8** *verb intrans. impers.* in ***it becomes***, be appropriate or fitting (*to*, *for*, *that*). (Replaced by ***is becoming***.) ME–L16.
9 *verb trans.* Of a property, attribute, quality, etc.: suit, look well on or with, (its owner or subject). ME.

> SHAKES. *Macb.* Nothing in his life Became him, like the leaving it. J. K. JEROME This hat fits me sufficiently well, but . . do you consider that it becomes me?

10 Of a person: grace (a place, position, etc.); look well in (a dress etc.). *arch.* L16.

> STEELE A graceful man . . who became the dignity of his function. A. HELPS She with her dark hair did most become that yellow gown.

■ †**becomed** *ppl adjective* (*rare*, Shakes.) befitting: only in L16. †**becomely** *adjective* fitting ME–L15.

becoming /bɪˈkʌmɪŋ/ *verbal noun.* E17.
[ORIGIN from BECOME + -ING[1].]
1 [BECOME II.] The action of befitting or gracing; something becoming. *rare.* E17.
2 [BECOME 4.] The action of coming to be something or passing into a state. M19.

becoming /bɪˈkʌmɪŋ/ *adjective.* L15.
[ORIGIN formed as BECOMING *noun* + -ING[2].]
Fitting, suitable; characterized by grace or decorum; tending to show the wearer etc. to advantage, attractive-looking.

> L. M. MONTGOMERY We are so much older . . that it isn't becoming to talk of childish matters. W. C. WILLIAMS In their crisp and becoming uniforms, they appear as beautiful young women. I. MURDOCH Her hair is permanently waved in whatever fashion is declared to be the most becoming. N. PEVSNER Wren's sense of becoming conformity in putting Tom Tower on Cardinal Wolsey's gatehouse at Christ Church. *absol.*: LD MACAULAY Self-command and a fine sense of the becoming.

■ **becomingly** *adverb* E17. **becomingness** *noun* M17.

becquerel /ˈbɛkərɛl/ *noun.* In sense 1 **B-**. L19.
[ORIGIN A. H. *Becquerel* (1852–1908), French physicist, discoverer of radioactivity.]
PHYSICS. **1** ***Becquerel rays***, ***Becquerel's rays***, radiation from radioactive substances. *obsolete* exc. *hist.* L19.
2 The SI unit of radioactivity, equal to one disintegration per second. (Symbol Bq.) L20.

becripple /bɪˈkrɪp(ə)l/ *verb trans.* M17.
[ORIGIN from BE- 1 + CRIPPLE *verb*.]
Make lame, cripple.

becross /bɪˈkrɒs/ *verb trans.* M16.
[ORIGIN from BE- 1, 4 + CROSS *verb* or *noun*.]
Mark with the sign of the cross; decorate with crosses. Chiefly as ***becrossed*** *ppl adjective.*

becrown /bɪˈkraʊn/ *verb trans.* L16.
[ORIGIN from BE- 1 + CROWN *verb*[1].]
Surround as a crown, crown.

becudgel /bɪˈkʌdʒ(ə)l/ *verb trans.* Infl. **-ll-**, *-l-. L16.
[ORIGIN from BE- 1 + CUDGEL *verb*.]
Cudgel soundly.

becurl /bɪˈkɜːl/ *verb trans.* E17.
[ORIGIN from BE- 1, 4 + CURL *verb* or *noun*.]
Form into curls; cover or deck with curls.

bed /bɛd/ *noun.*
[ORIGIN Old English *bed*(*d*) = Old Frisian *bed*(*d*), Old Saxon *bed*, *beddi*, Middle Dutch *bedde* (Dutch *bed*), Old High German *betti* (German *Bett*), Gothic *badi*, from Germanic.]
▸ **I** The sleeping place of people or animals.
1 A permanent structure for sleeping or resting on, *esp.* a framework equipped with mattress and covers; also, a mattress. (In preposition phrs. usu. without article or possessive.) OE. ▸**b** (The place of) conjugal union, sexual intimacy, or (*arch.*) procreation and childbirth. ME. ▸**c** The use of a bed; being in bed; the time to go to bed. L15. ▸**d** A bed and associated facilities in a hospital; a place for a patient in hospital. L19. ▸**e** *spec.* Uninflected *pl.* after a numeral or quantifier: bedrooms. (Chiefly an advertising term.) E20.

> CAXTON He was in his bed and a slepe on a fethyr bedde. M. W. MONTAGU I carried my own bed with me. J. CARLYLE My great comfortable four-posted bed. **b** STEELE He betrays the Honour and Bed of his Neighbour. G. CRABBE And hoped, when wed, For loves fair favours, and a fruitful bed. J. I. M. STEWART I don't believe . . that Lawrence was any good in bed. **c** S. PEPYS We began both to be angry, and so continued till bed. R. FORD The traveller should immediately on arriving secure his bed. M. PATTISON Bed, with its warmth and recumbent posture, he found favourable to composition. **d** *Times* Twenty beds have been closed at the 52-bed post-operative Courtaulds Hospital. **e** P. G. WODEHOUSE A joyous suburban villa equipped with main drainage, . . four bed, . . and the usual domestic offices.

bunk bed, ***camp bed***, ***double bed***, ***single bed***, ***twin bed***, etc. ***deathbed***, ***hospital bed***, ***marriage bed***, ***sickbed***, etc.
2 Any sleeping place; an extemporized resting place for the night. ME.

> SHAKES. *Mids. N. D.* Find you out a bed For I upon this bank will rest my head.

3 (Usu. with specifying adjective or contextual indication.) The grave. Freq. in ***narrow bed***. ME.

> R. BURNS Welcome to your gory bed, Or to victorie. F. O'CONNOR The desolate edges of the bog that was to be their last earthly bed.

4 The resting place of an animal. L17.

> DRYDEN The Water-Snake . . lyes poyson'd in his Bed.

▸ **II** Other uses.
5 A garden plot (to be) filled with plants; a place where osiers, willows, etc., are grown. OE.

> L. A. G. STRONG A small, neat front garden, with . . a circular bed containing four standard rose-trees. G. HEYER The narrow paths which separated various beds filled with vegetables and currant bushes.

flower bed, ***onion bed***, etc.
6 The bottom of a sea, lake, river, or other watercourse. L16.
7 A level surface or other base upon which something rests or in which something is embedded; an extended substructure providing a support or foundation. L16. ▸**b** The surface of a stone or brick that is embedded in the mortar; the underside of a slate. L17. ▸**c** The body of a cart, wagon, or truck. *dial.* & *N. Amer.* E18. ▸**d** The foundation of a road or railway. L19. ▸**e** The slates or other flat surface below the cloth cover of a billiard table. L19.

> WELLINGTON The mortar beds and howitzer carriages. ARNOLD BENNETT There was another cracking sound . . beneath the bed of the machine. M. LASKI A diamond ring, . . on its cream velvet bed. V. STRAUSS The bed of the press . . is a flat, even surface on which the form is placed for printing. O. DOPPING An acoustic coupler contains a 'bed' upon which a telephone receiver is laid.

8 A layer, *esp.* one of several; a horizontal course. E17. ▸**b** A layer of small animals congregated in a particular spot; *esp.* a layer of oysters etc. E17. ▸**c** A geological stratum. L17.

> *New Yorker* Scallops on a bed of spinach sautéed in butter.

9 A division of the marked surface in hopscotch, shovel-board, etc.; in *pl.* (*local*), hopscotch. E19.
– PHRASES ETC.: **bed and board** (hospitality with) food and lodging; *arch.* full connubial relations with a husband. **bed and breakfast** overnight accommodation and breakfast next morning as offered by hotels etc.; *fig.* (*attrib.*) designating financial transactions in which shares are sold and then bought back the next morning. **bed-and-breakfast** *verb trans.* sell (shares) and then buy back the next morning. **bed of justice** FRENCH HISTORY the throne of the king in the parliament of Paris; a sitting of this parliament in the presence of the king, *esp.* one to enforce the registration of one of his own decrees. **bed of nails** (*a*) a board studded with protruding nails, lain upon for self-mortification or as a display of self-control or skill; (*b*) *fig.* a hazardous or uncomfortable situation brought upon or chosen by oneself. **bed of roses** a position of ease and luxury. **bed of sickness** the state of being an invalid. **brought to bed** *arch.* delivered of (or *of*) a child. ***die in one's bed***: see DIE *verb*[1]. **get out of bed on the wrong side** (usu. in pa. t.), **have got out of bed on the wrong side** behave bad-temperedly during the day. **go to bed** retire for the night; have sexual intercourse *with*; of a newspaper: go to press. **in bed**, **into bed** between the lower and upper bedclothes. ***hop into bed***: see HOP *verb*[1]. ***hotbed***: see HOT *adjective*. **keep one's bed** remain in bed because of illness etc. **lie in the bed one has made** accept the natural consequences of one's acts. **make a bed** put a bed in order after it has been used. **make up a bed** (*a*) put bedclothes on a bed; (*b*) prepare an extemporized resting place for the night. MIXED ***bed***. **out of bed** from between the lower and upper bedclothes, up and about away from one's bed. **put to bed** prepare (a person) for rest in bed; send (a newspaper) to press. ***Reading beds***: see READING *adjective*[2] 1. ***red beds***: see RED *adjective*. **take to bed**, **take to one's bed** retire to bed because of illness, often for a prolonged period of time. ***test bed***: see TEST *noun*[1].
– COMB.: **bed-blocking** the long-term occupation of hospital beds by the elderly due to a shortage of places in residential homes; **bed-bottle** a bottle for urination for the use of male invalids in bed; **bedbug** a bloodsucking hemipteran insect of the genus *Cimex* (esp. *C. lectularius*), which infests beds; **bedchamber** a bedroom (*arch.* exc. in the titles of attendants of the monarch, as ***lady of the bedchamber***, ***lord of the bedchamber***, ***gentleman of the bedchamber***, etc.); **bedclothes** the sheets, blankets, covers, etc., which are put on a bed; ***bedcover***: see COVER *noun*[1] 2b; **bedfast** *Scot.* & *N. English* confined to bed; **bedfellow** a person who shares a bed with another; a companion, an associate (*lit.* & *fig.*); **bedgown** *arch.* (*a*) a nightgown, a nightdress; (*b*) *N. English* a kind of jacket formerly worn (usu. over a petticoat) by working women; **bedhead** the upper end of a bed; **bed-hop** *verb intrans.* (*colloq.*) engage in successive casual sexual affairs; **bedjacket** a short jacket worn, esp. by women, when sitting up in bed; **bedlinen** sheets and pillowcases; **bedload** the sediment transported by a river in the form of particles too heavy to be in suspension; **bedmaker** a person who puts beds in order after use; *spec.* a person who attends to the bedrooms and other living accommodation in a college, hotel, etc.; **bedmate** a person, esp. a sexual partner, with whom one shares a bed; **bed-moulding** ARCHITECTURE: under a projection, as a cornice; **bedpan** †(*a*) a warming pan; (*b*) an invalid's utensil for urination or defecation when in bed; **bedplate** a metal plate forming the base of a machine; **bedpost** one of the upright supports of the framework of a bed (***between you and me and the bedpost***: see BETWEEN *preposition* 3); **bed rest** (*a*) a support for a person in bed; (*b*) the confinement of a sick person to bed; **bedrock** solid rock underlying alluvial deposits etc.; *fig.* the ultimate facts or principles of a belief, character, etc.; **bedroll** *N. Amer., Austral.,* & *NZ* an item or set of bedding rolled into a bundle for carrying; **bedsettee** a settee that can be converted into a bed; **bedsit** (*colloq.*), **bedsitter** (*colloq.*), **bed-sitting room** a room serving as both a bedroom and a sitting room; **bedsock** a warm sock worn in bed; **bedsore** an ulceration of the buttocks, heels, etc., developed by the constant pressure of the mattress on an invalid's skin; **bedspread** (orig. *US*) a cloth or sheet to cover a bed when not in use; †**bedstaff** a staff from a bed, used as a cudgel; **bedstead** †(*a*) the place occupied by a bed; (*b*) the framework of a bed (***French bedstead***: see FRENCH *adjective*); **bedstock** (*obsolete* exc. *dial.*) one of the upright parts of the framework of a bed; a bedstead; **bedtable** a small tray or table for the use of a person sitting up in bed; **bedtick** a flat four-sided case or cover filled with feathers, straw, or other material to form a bed; **bed-warmer** a device for warming a bed; **bedwetter** a person, esp. a child, given to bedwetting; **bedwetting** urinary incontinence while in bed.
■ **beddy** *adjective* (of stone) having natural cleavages, with a tendency to split E18. **beddy-bye(s)** /ˈbɛdɪbʌɪ(z)/ *noun* a child's word for bed or sleep E20. **bedward(s)** *adverb* [orig. *to bedward*] †(*a*) towards bedtime; (*b*) towards bed: LME. **bedworthy** *adjective* (*colloq.*) sexually attractive E20.

bed /bɛd/ *verb.* Infl. **-dd-**.
[ORIGIN Old English *beddian*, formed as BED *noun*.]
▸ **I** Uses connected with a bed for sleeping.
†**1** *verb intrans.* & *trans.* with cognate obj. Prepare (a bed). OE–LME.
2 *verb trans.* Put to bed; put (an animal) to rest for the night; provide with a bed or bedding. Also foll. by *down*. Freq. as ***bedded*** *pa. pple.* ME.

> W. WHATELEY To see a stranger bedded with him instead of his owne Spouse. J. WESLEY See . . that your horse be rubbed, fed, and bedded. DYLAN THOMAS Young girls lie bedded soft.

3 *verb intrans.* Go to bed (*with*). Now usu. foll. by *down*. ME.

> H. CAREY O then we'll wed, and then we'll bed. N. MARSH She meant to come back and bed down with Garcia. T. STURGE MOORE They bedded on the downs.

4 *verb trans.* Take (a woman) to bed; have sexual intercourse with. M16.

> SHAKES. *Tam. Shr.* Him . . that would thoroughly woo her, wed her, and bed her. P. COHEN Rodolphe, her previous lover who was only interested in bedding her.

▸ **II** Other uses.
5 *verb trans.* Plant (*out*) in or as in a garden bed. LME.
6 *verb trans.* Lay (bricks, stones, etc.) in position in cement or mortar. LME.
7 *verb trans.* Embed. M16.

R. HOOKER A place where the ships lie bedded. I. WALTON Many of them [eels] together bed themselves, and live without feeding on anything. MRS H. WOOD The bullet . . must have bedded itself in the wall.

8 *verb trans.* Lay or strew in a layer; stratify in beds. Chiefly as ***bedded*** *ppl adjective.* E17.
9 *verb intrans.* Form a compact layer. E17.
10 *verb intrans.* Rest *on*, lie *on* for support. M19.
■ **beddable** *adjective* sexually attractive M20.

B.Ed. *abbreviation.*
Bachelor of Education.

bedabble /bɪˈdab(ə)l/ *verb trans. arch.* L16.
[ORIGIN from BE- 1 + DABBLE *verb.*]
Sprinkle over or stain with dirty liquid. Chiefly as ***bedabbled*** *ppl adjective.*

bedad /bɪˈdad/ *interjection. Irish. arch.* E18.
[ORIGIN Alt. of *by God!*: cf. BEGAD etc.]
Expr. amazement or emphasis.

bedaff /bɪˈdaf/ *verb trans.* Long *obsolete* exc. *dial.* LME.
[ORIGIN from BE- 3 + DAFF *noun*[1].]
Make a fool of, bewilder.

bedangled /bɪˈdaŋg(ə)ld/ *adjective. rare.* E17.
[ORIGIN from BE- 1 + DANGLE *verb* + -ED[1].]
Adorned or hung about with dangling objects.

bedark /bɪˈdɑːk/ *verb trans. rare.* LME.
[ORIGIN from BE- 1 + DARK *verb.*]
Cover with darkness.

bedarken /bɪˈdɑːk(ə)n/ *verb trans.* L16.
[ORIGIN from BE- 1 + DARKEN *verb.*]
Make dark; overshadow; obscure.

bedash /bɪˈdaʃ/ *verb trans.* LME.
[ORIGIN from BE- 1 + DASH *verb*[1].]
1 Beat about; dash down. LME.
2 Cover with dashes of colour etc. L15.

bedaub /bɪˈdɔːb/ *verb trans.* M16.
[ORIGIN from BE- 1 + DAUB *verb.*]
1 Besmear; *fig.* vilify. M16.

T. OTWAY The names of Honest Men bedawb'd. P. H. GOSSE With a painter's brush had bedaubed the trunks of several large trees.

2 Overload with ornamentation. L16.

MARVELL Set off, and bedawb'd with Rhetorick. M. W. MONTAGU All bedaubed with diamonds.

bedaze /bɪˈdeɪz/ *verb trans.* LME.
[ORIGIN from BE- 1 + DAZE *verb.*]
Daze; bewilder; stupefy. Chiefly as ***bedazed*** *ppl adjective.*
■ **bedazement** *noun* L19.

bedazzle /bɪˈdaz(ə)l/ *verb trans.* L16.
[ORIGIN from BE- 1 + DAZZLE *verb.*]
Dazzle completely or thoroughly; confuse by excess of brilliance.
■ **bedazzlement** *noun* E19.

bedder /ˈbɛdə/ *noun*[1]. LME.
[ORIGIN from BED *noun* + -ER[1].]
▸ **I 1** A manufacturer of beds; an upholsterer. *obsolete* exc. *dial.* LME.
2 A college bedmaker. *colloq.* L19.
3 ***early bedder***, ***early go-to-bedder***, a person who habitually goes to bed early; ***late bedder***, ***late go-to-bedder***, a person who habitually goes to bed late. E20.
▸ **II 4** A bedding-out plant. M19.

bedder /ˈbɛdə/ *noun*[2]. *slang.* L19.
[ORIGIN from BED *noun* + -ER[6].]
A bedroom.

bedding /ˈbɛdɪŋ/ *noun.* OE.
[ORIGIN from BED *noun* or *verb* + -ING[1].]
1 *collect. sing.* or †*pl.* The articles which compose a bed, as mattress, bedclothes, etc.; materials provided for sleeping or resting on. OE. ▸†**b** Sleeping accommodation. LME–L17.

JONSON He hath sold my hangings, and my beddings! DRYDEN Spread with Straw, the bedding of thy Fold. C. V. WEDGWOOD Fairfax . . ordered the citizens to provide bedding so that every two soldiers could share a mattress, a bolster and a pair of sheets and blankets. **b** SPENSER The ground . . which useth to be his bedding.

2 A putting to bed, esp. of a bride; (an act of) sexual intercourse. L16.

SIR W. SCOTT A . . description of the wedding, bedding, and throwing the stocking. V. S. PRITCHETT Their private sexual comedy, in momentary beddings in the backs of cars.

3 A bottom layer, a foundation. E17.
4 GEOLOGY. Layering or stratification of rocks. M19.
5 The process of planting flowers (*out*) in beds. M19.
– COMB.: **bedding plant**, **bedding-out plant** a plant suitable for setting out in a garden bed; **bedding plane** a plane forming the junction between two layers or strata of rock.

bedeck /bɪˈdɛk/ *verb trans.* M16.
[ORIGIN from BE- 1 + DECK *verb.*]
Deck round, adorn, (*with*).

bedeguar /ˈbɛdɪgɑː/ *noun.* LME.
[ORIGIN French *bédégar* from Persian *bād-āwar(d* lit. 'wind-brought'.]
A mosslike gall on a rose bush caused by the gall wasp *Diplolepis rosae.*

bedel(l) *nouns* see BEADLE.

bedene /bɪˈdiːn/ *adverb. obsolete* exc. *dial.* ME.
[ORIGIN from unkn. 1st elem. + Old English *ǣne* once, at once, in one, together.]
= ANON *adverb*; occas. a mere expletive or rhyme word.

bedesman *noun* see BEADSMAN.

bedevil /bɪˈdɛv(ə)l/ *verb trans.* Infl. **-ll-**, ***-l-**. L16.
[ORIGIN from BE- 3, 4 + DEVIL *noun.*]
1 Possess (*as*) with a devil. Chiefly as ***bedevilled*** *ppl adjective.* L16.

CARLYLE One age, he is hagridden, bewitched; the next, priestridden, befooled; in all ages, bedevilled.

2 Transform mischievously; corrupt, spoil. L17.

DISRAELI So bedevil a bottle of Geisenheim . . you wouldn't know it from the greenest Tokay.

3 Treat with diabolical violence or abuse; drive frantic; plague, afflict. M18.

BYRON My poor . . Muse . . they have . . so be-deviled with their . . ribaldry. S. RUSHDIE Confused thinking was to bedevil much of his career.

■ **bedevilment** *noun* E19.

bedew /bɪˈdjuː/ *verb trans.* ME.
[ORIGIN from BE- 4 + DEW *noun.*]
Cover or soak with dew or drops of moisture; bathe, suffuse.

Bedford cord /ˌbɛdfəd ˈkɔːd/ *noun phr.* L19.
[ORIGIN *Bedford*, a town in central England + CORD *noun*[1].]
A woven fabric with prominent cords running in the direction of the warp. In *pl.*, trousers made of this.

Bedfordshire /ˈbɛdfədʃə/ *noun. joc.* M17.
[ORIGIN An English county.]
= BED *noun* 1 in prepositional phrases.

bediasite /bɪˈdʌɪəsʌɪt/ *noun.* M20.
[ORIGIN from *Bedias* a locality in Texas + -ITE[1].]
GEOLOGY. A tektite from the strewn field in Texas.

bedight /bɪˈdʌɪt/ *verb trans. arch.* Pa. t. **bedight**; pa. pple **bedight(ed)**. LME.
[ORIGIN from BE- 1 + DIGHT *verb.*]
Equip, apparel, bedeck.

bedim /bɪˈdɪm/ *verb trans. arch.* Infl. **-mm-**. M16.
[ORIGIN from BE- 1 + DIM *verb.*]
Make dim, cloud, obscure.

bedip /bɪˈdɪp/ *verb trans. arch.* Infl. **-pp-**.
[ORIGIN Old English *bedyppan*: see BE- 1, DIP *verb.*]
Dip, immerse.

†**bedirt** *verb trans.* E16–E18.
[ORIGIN from BE- 4 + DIRT *noun.*]
Make dirty, throw filth at, defile.

bedizen /bɪˈdʌɪz(ə)n, -ˈdɪz-/ *verb trans.* M17.
[ORIGIN from BE- 1 + DIZEN *verb.*]
Deck or ornament, esp. overlavishly; trick out.
■ **bedizenment** *noun* M19.

bedlam /ˈbɛdləm/ *adjective & noun.* In senses A.1, 2, & occas. others **B-**. LME.
[ORIGIN Form of *Bethlehem* (see below).]
▸ **A** *noun.* †**1** The town of Bethlehem in Judaea. LME–E17.
2 The Hospital of St Mary of Bethlehem (Bethlem Royal Hospital in London), used as an asylum for the insane. *arch.* LME.
Tom o' Bedlam, **Jack o' Bedlam** *arch.* a person who is mentally ill.
†**3** A person who was mentally ill; *spec.* a discharged but not fully cured patient of the Hospital of St Mary of Bethlehem, licensed to beg. E16–E18.

SWIFT She roar'd like a Bedlam.

4 An asylum. *arch.* M17.

R. GRAVES Declared him a lunatic and shut him up in a Bedlam.

5 (A scene of) mad confusion; a wild uproar. M17.

QUILLER-COUCH Hearkenin' to the bedlam outside: for 'twas the big storm in 'Seventy. M. MITCHELL Amid a bedlam of hounds barking and small black children shouting. J. P. DONLEAVY I'm a man for bedlam . . Did you ever relish the broken dish or twisted chandelier?

▸ **B** *adjective.* Belonging to or fit for an asylum; lunatic; foolish. L16.

MILTON This which followes is plaine bedlam stuff.

■ **Bedlamite** *noun* an inmate of Bedlam or a madhouse, a mentally ill person L16.

bedlar /ˈbɛdlə/ *adjective & noun. obsolete* exc. *Scot.* LME.
[ORIGIN from BED *noun* + Old Norse *lag* lying + -ER[1].]
(A person who is) bedridden.

Bedlington /ˈbɛdlɪŋt(ə)n/ *noun.* M19.
[ORIGIN A village in Northumberland, N. England.]
In full ***Bedlington terrier***. A narrow-headed sporting terrier with fairly long legs and curly grey hair.

Bedouin /ˈbɛdʊɪn/ *noun & adjective.* Also **Beduin**, **b-**. LME.
[ORIGIN Old French *beduin* (mod. *bédouin*) ult. (through medieval Latin *beduini* pl.) from Arabic *badawī*, pl. *badawīn* (from *badw* desert, nomadic desert tribes): see -INE[1]. Cf. BEDU.]
▸ **A** *noun.* **1** An Arab of the desert. LME.
2 A person living a nomadic life; a Gypsy. M19.
▸ **B** *adjective.* Of the desert or Bedouins; nomadic, wandering. M19.

bedrabble /bɪˈdrab(ə)l/ *verb trans. arch.* LME.
[ORIGIN from BE- 1 + DRABBLE *verb.*]
Make wet or dirty with rain or mud. Chiefly as ***bedrabbled*** *ppl adjective.*

bedraggle /bɪˈdrag(ə)l/ *verb trans.* E18.
[ORIGIN from BE- 1 + DRAGGLE *verb.*]
Wet (an article of clothing etc.) so that it hangs limp; make (a person) wet and untidy or dishevelled (chiefly as ***bedraggled*** *ppl adjective*).

bedral /ˈbɛdr(ə)l/ *noun*[1]. *Scot.* E16.
[ORIGIN App. alt. of BEADLE, perh. under infl. of BEDRAL *adjective & noun*[2].]
A minor church officer, often acting as clerk, sexton, and bell-ringer. Also, a gravedigger.

bedral /ˈbɛdr(ə)l/ *adjective & noun*[2]. *Scot.* Also **-rel**. E16.
[ORIGIN Prob. metath. alt. of BEDLAR.]
▸ †**A** *adjective.* Bedridden. E16–E17.
▸ **B** *noun.* A bedridden person. E16.

bedrench /bɪˈdrɛn(t)ʃ/ *verb trans.* LME.
[ORIGIN from BE- 1 + DRENCH *verb.*]
Drench completely; soak.

bedrid /ˈbɛdrɪd/ *noun & adjective. arch.*
[ORIGIN Old English *bedreda*, *-rida*, formed as BED *noun* + short base of RIDE *verb.*]
▸ †**A** *noun.* A bedridden person. OE–ME.
▸ **B** *adjective.* = BEDRIDDEN. OE.

bedridden /ˈbɛdrɪd(ə)n/ *adjective.* ME.
[ORIGIN Irreg. from BEDRID + -EN[4].]
Confined to bed through sickness or infirmity; *fig.* worn-out, decrepit.

bedroom /ˈbɛdruːm, -rʊm/ *noun.* L15.
[ORIGIN from BED *noun* + ROOM *noun*[1].]
1 Space in a bed. *rare.* L15.

SHAKES. *Mids. N. D.* Then by your side, no bedroom me deny.

2 A room intended to house a bed; a sleeping apartment. E17. ▸**b** Used *attrib.* to designate a town or suburb inhabited largely by people who work in a nearby larger urban area. *N. Amer.* M20.
– COMB.: **bedroom eyes** eyes holding an expression of sensual invitation; **bedroom farce** a play depicting an absurd situation deriving from one or more (esp. extramarital) sexual adventures; **bedroom slipper** a soft indoor shoe intended to be worn when one is not fully dressed.

bedrop /bɪˈdrɒp/ *verb trans. arch.* Infl. **-pp-**. Pa. t. & pple **-dropped**, **-dropt**. LME.
[ORIGIN from BE- 2, 4 + DROP *verb, noun.*]
Drop upon; sprinkle with or (chiefly as *pa. ppl adjective*) as with drops.

Beds. *abbreviation.*
Bedfordshire.

bedside /ˈbɛdsʌɪd/ *noun.* ME.
[ORIGIN Contr. of *bed's side*: see BED *noun*, -'S[1], SIDE *noun.*]
The place or position at the side of a bed.
bedside lamp, ***bedside table***, etc.
– COMB.: **bedside book** a book for reading in bed; **bedside manner** the manner of a doctor when attending a patient (freq. with specifying adjective, as *good*).

bedstraw /ˈbɛdstrɔː/ *noun.* LME.
[ORIGIN from BED *noun* + STRAW *noun.*]
†**1** Straw used for bedding. LME–M17.
2 Any of numerous straggling plants of the genus *Galium*, belonging to the madder family and bearing many tiny flowers; *esp.* (in full ***lady's bedstraw***) a yellow-flowered European plant, *Galium verum*, of dry grassland. E16.

bedtime /ˈbɛdtʌɪm/ *noun.* ME.
[ORIGIN from BED *noun* + TIME *noun.*]
The hour at which a person habitually goes to bed.
bedtime story a story told to a child at bedtime.

Bedu /ˈbɛduː/ *noun & adjective.* Pl. of noun same. E20.
[ORIGIN Arabic *badw*: see BEDOUIN.]
(Of) a Bedouin; *collect.* (of) Bedouins.

Beduin *noun & adjective* var. of BEDOUIN.

bedull /bɪˈdʌl/ *verb trans.* L16.
[ORIGIN from BE- 1 + DULL *verb.*]
Make dull.

bedust /bɪˈdʌst/ *verb trans. arch.* LME.
[ORIGIN from BE- 4 + DUST *noun.*]
Cover with dust. Chiefly as ***bedusted*** *ppl adjective.*

B

bedye /bɪˈdʌɪ/ *verb trans.* Pa. t. & pple **bedyed**; pres. pple & verbal noun **bedyeing**. E16.
[ORIGIN from BE- 1 + DYE *verb*.]
Stain (as) with dye. Chiefly as ***bedyed** ppl adjective*.

bee /biː/ *noun*[1].
[ORIGIN Old English *bēo* = Old Frisian *bē*, Middle Low German, Middle Dutch *bie* (Dutch *bij*), Old High German *bia* (German dial. *Beie*), Old Norse *bý*, from Germanic.]
1 A stinging hymenopterous social insect of the genus *Apis*, which collects nectar and pollen and produces wax and honey: a colony consists of one perfect female or 'queen', several males or 'drones', and very many sterile females or 'workers'. OE. ▸**b** Any of numerous other insects, including both social and solitary species, constituting the superfamily Apoidea. Freq. with specifying word. OE.
b *bumblebee*, *carpenter bee*, *mason bee*, *mining bee*, etc.
2 A busy worker. Also (now *rare* or *obsolete*), a pleasing writer. M18.
3 A gathering for combined work or amusement. Usu. with word specifying its purpose. Orig. *US*. M18.

W. IRVING Now were instituted quilting bees and husking bees and other rural assemblages. J. GALT I made a bee; that is, I collected . . the settlers to assist at the raising.

SPELLING *bee*.
4 A lump of yeast which rises and falls in a brew as bubbles of carbon dioxide are produced. E20.
– PHRASES: **as busy as a bee** very busy or industrious. **bees and honey** *rhyming slang* money. ***goat and bee jug***: see GOAT. **have a bee in one's bonnet** be obsessed on some point. **put the bee on** (*slang*, chiefly *US*) (*a*) put an end to; beat; (*b*) ask for a loan, borrow money, from (cf. STING *verb*). **the bee's knees** *slang* something or someone outstandingly good.
– COMB.: **bee balm** the plant Oswego tea, *Monarda didyma*; **bee-bird** any of various birds, *esp.* a spotted flycatcher; **bee-biter** *dial.* the great tit; **bee bread** †(*a*) a honey-containing honeycomb; (*b*) a compound of honey and pollen used as food by bees in the nest; **bee-eater** a brightly coloured insectivorous bird of the family Meropidae; esp. *Merops apiaster*, a rare visitor to Britain (***wattled bee-eater***: see WATTLED 2); **bee fly** a parasitic fly of the family Bombyliidae, resembling a bee; **bee-glue** propolis; **bee-gum** *US* a hollow gum tree acting as or fashioned into a beehive; **bee-keeper** a person who keeps bees; **beeline** a straight line or course between two places (***make a beeline for***, hurry towards, go straight up to); **bee man**, **bee-master** a man who keeps bees; **bee martin** *US* a kingbird (*Tyrannus*); **bee-moth** = ***wax moth*** s.v. WAX *noun*[1]; **bee orchid** an orchid, *Ophrys apifera*, with a flower in part resembling a bee; **bee plant** any plant visited by bees for nectar; *esp.* (more fully ***Rocky Mountain bee plant***) a N. American cleome, *Cleome serrulata*, formerly grown by bee-keepers; **bee-stung** *adjective* (orig. & chiefly *US*) (of lips) full, red, and pouting.

bee /biː/ *noun*[2].
[ORIGIN Old English *bēag*, *bēah* = Old Norse *baugr*, Old High German *bouc*, from Germanic; rel. to BOW *verb*[1].]
1 A ring or torque of metal, usu. for the arm or neck. Long *obsolete* exc. *Scot.* OE.
2 In full ***bee block***. A wooden block bolted to the side of a bowsprit, occas. with metal sheaves to reeve the fore-topmast stays through. L15.

Beeb /biːb/ *noun*. *colloq.* M20.
[ORIGIN Abbreviation.]
The BBC.

beebee *noun* var. of BIBI.

beech /biːtʃ/ *noun*.
[ORIGIN Old English *bēce* = Middle Low German *bōke*, *bȫke* (weak fem.) from Germanic base rel. to that of Old English *bōc* (see BUCKWHEAT): cogn. with Latin *fagus* beech, Greek *phagos*, *phēgos* edible oak.]
1 A forest tree of the genus *Fagus*, having thin, smooth bark and glossy oval leaves, and bearing nuts; *esp.* the European *F. sylvatica*. Also (usu. with specifying word), any of various similar trees, esp. (in the southern hemisphere) of the genus *Nothofagus*. Also ***beech tree***. OE.
copper beech: see COPPER *noun*[1]. ***red beech***: see RED *adjective*. ***silver beech***: see SILVER *noun & adjective*. **southern beech** = NOTHOFAGUS.
2 The wood of this tree. ME.
– COMB.: **beech-drops** *N. Amer.* a broomrape, *Epifagus virginiana*, parasitic on beech roots; **beech fern** a fern of damp rocky woods, *Phegopteris connectilis*; **beech marten** the stone marten, *Martes foina*; **beechmast** the fruit of the beech, beechnuts; **beechnut** the small triangular brown fruit of the beech, pairs of which are enclosed in a prickly case; **beech oil** an oil extracted from beechmast; ***beech tree***: see sense 1 above; **beechwood** (*a*) = sense 2 above. (*b*) a wood of beech trees.
■ **beechen** *adjective* (*arch.* & *poet.*) (*a*) of, pertaining to, or derived from the beech; (*b*) made of the wood of the beech: OE. **beechy** *adjective* of, characterized by, or having many beeches E17.

beedi *noun* var. of BIDI.

beef /biːf/ *noun*. Pl. **beefs**, in sense 2 also **beeves** /biːvz/. ME.
[ORIGIN Anglo-Norman, Old French *boef*, *buef* (mod. *bœuf*) from Latin *bov-*, *bos* ox: cf. COW *noun*[1].]
1 The flesh of an ox, bull, or cow, used as food. ME. ▸**b** *fig.* Muscle, flesh; strength, size, power. M19.

b P. V. WHITE As from his cattle, the beef had dwindled from the man, but he was still large. R. M. PATTERSON We . . were . . putting all the beef we could behind it.

beef olive, ***beef stew***, etc. ***baby beef***: see BABY *adjective*. ***beef* STROGANOFF**. ***corned beef***: see CORNED *adjective*[2] 2. ***sour beef***: see SOUR *adjective*. **b beef to the heel(s)** *slang* (of a person) massive, brawny.
2 An ox or similar beast, *esp.* a fattened one or its carcass. Exc. *US* usu. in *pl.* ME. ▸**b** *collect.* Cattle. *US*. E18.

CLARENDON One half in Money, and the other half in good Beefs. **b** S. E. WHITE Drivin' some beef up to the troops.

3 A complaint, a grievance. *colloq.* (orig. *US*). L19. ▸**b** A criminal charge. *US colloq.* E20.

D. RUNYON A beef from her over keeping the baby out in the night air.

– COMB.: **beefburger** a hamburger; **beefcake** *slang* (the display of) sturdy masculine physique; **beef cattle**: raised for beef; **beefeater** (*a*) an eater of beef; †(*b*) *colloq.* a well-fed menial; (*c*) *colloq.* a Yeoman of the Guard, a Yeoman Warder in the Tower of London; **beefsteak** a thick slice of beef, usu. cut from the hindquarters, for frying or grilling (***beefsteak fungus***, a red bracket fungus, *Fistulina hepatica*, resembling raw meat in appearance; ***beefsteak tomato*** (*N. Amer.*) = ***beef tomato*** below); **beef tea** stewed-beef juice used as food for invalids; **beef tomato** an exceptionally large and firm variety of tomato; **beef-witted** *adjective* stupid; **beefwood** (the timber of) any of various Australian and W. Indian trees with red wood, esp. (*Austral.*) casuarina.
■ **beefer** *noun* an animal bred for beef M17.

beef /biːf/ *verb*. M19.
[ORIGIN from the noun.]
1 *verb trans.* Slaughter for beef; *fig.* (*US slang*) knock down. M19.
2 *verb trans.* Put muscle into, strengthen, reinforce; add power or importance to. Usu. foll. by *up*. *slang* (orig. *US*). M19.

D. ACHESON The Defense Department required no persuasion that the defense of Europe needed, in their phrase, 'beefing up'. I. BANKS I'd brought a half bottle of whisky . . which we used to beef up the coffee.

3 *verb intrans.* Complain, grumble, protest. *slang* (orig. *US*). L19.

STEVIE SMITH Not beefing about being solitary Or the sparseness of the fare.

beefalo /ˈbiːfələʊ/ *noun*. Pl. **-oes**, same. L20.
[ORIGIN from BEEF *noun* + BUFFALO.]
(An animal of) a breed of bovine that is ⅝ buffalo and ⅜ domestic cow.

beefing *noun* see BIFFIN.

beefy /ˈbiːfi/ *adjective*. M18.
[ORIGIN from BEEF *noun* + -Y[1].]
Resembling beef; containing much beef; muscular, solid.

J. K. ROWLING He was a big, beefy man with hardly any neck.

■ **beefiness** *noun* M19.

beehive /ˈbiːhʌɪv/ *noun*. ME.
[ORIGIN from BEE *noun*[1] + HIVE *noun*.]
1 An artificial habitation for bees, traditionally of thick straw work in the shape of a dome, but now usu. a wooden box containing the combs on wooden slides. ME. ▸**b** *fig.* A busy place etc. E17.
2 ***the Beehive***, (the name of) a star cluster in the constellation Cancer. Also called ***Praesepe***. M19.
3 A hat or hairstyle having the shape of a traditional beehive. E20.
– COMB.: **beehive hat** a hat shaped like a traditional beehive; **beehive tomb** a dome-shaped tomb cut into a hillside, distinctive of Mycenaean Greece.

Beelzebub /bɪˈɛlzɪbʌb/ *noun*. OE.
[ORIGIN Late Latin *Beëlzebub* (Vulgate), translating (i) Hebrew *baʿal zᵉḇūḇ* Lord of Flies, a Philistine god (*2 Kings* 1:2) and (ii) Greek *Beelzeboul* (*Matthew* 12:24).]
The Devil; a devil.

been *verb pa. pple* of BE *verb*.

been-to /ˈbiːntuː/ *noun*. M20.
[ORIGIN from BEEN + TO *preposition*.]
In Africa and Asia, a person who has been to Britain, esp. for education.

beep /biːp/ *noun & verb*. E20.
[ORIGIN Imit.]
▸ **A** *noun*. The sound of a car horn; a short high-pitched sound emitted by any device (e.g. an echo sounder). E20.
▸ **B** *verb trans. & intrans.* (Cause to) emit a beep or beeps. M20.
■ **beeper** *noun* a device that emits beeps M20.

beer /bɪə/ *noun*[1].
[ORIGIN Old English *bēor* = Old Frisian *biār*, *bier*, Middle Low German, Middle Dutch *bēr* (Dutch *bier*), Old High German *bior* (German *Bier*), from a West Germanic word from monastic Latin *biber* drink, from *bibere* to drink.]
1 Alcoholic liquor produced by fermentation of malt etc. and flavoured with hops or other bitters, *esp.* the lighter kind of liquor so produced; a type of this; a drink of this. Cf. ALE, PORTER *noun*[2]. OE.
bitter beer, ***keg beer***, ***lager beer***, ***mild beer***, etc. ***all beer and skittles***: see SKITTLE *noun*. **on the beer** on a bout of drinking. ***porter's beer***: see PORTER *noun*[2] 3. ***single beer***: see SINGLE *adjective & adverb*. **small beer** weak beer, or a small measure of beer (usu. half a pint); *fig.* small matters, something of little importance (***think no small beer of***, have a high opinion of).
2 A similar drink made from other ingredients. Usu. with specifying word. OE.
birch beer, ***ginger beer***, ***nettle beer***, ***root beer***, ***spruce beer***, etc.
– COMB.: **beer belly** *slang* = ***beer gut*** below; **beer-boy** (now *arch.* or *hist.*) a pot-boy; **beer cellar** a cellar for storing beer; a bar etc. selling beer in a cellar or basement; **beer engine** = ***beer pump*** below; **beer garden** a garden where beer is served; **beer glass** a glass for beer or similar long drinks; **beer gut** *slang* a protruding abdomen (regarded as) due to drinking large quantities of beer; **beer hall** a hall where beer is served; **beerhouse** a public house licensed for the sale of beer, but not spirits; **beer mat** a small table mat for a beer glass; **beer money** (*a*) *hist.* an allowance of money to servants, instead of beer; (*b*) a small amount of money allowed or earned; **beer-off** *slang* an off-licence; **beer parlour** *Canad.* a room in a hotel or tavern where beer is served; **beer pump** a machine for drawing beer up from barrels in the cellar to the bar; **beer-swilling** *adjective* (*derog.*) that drinks a lot of beer; disreputable, rowdy; **beer-up** a drinking bout or party.
■ **beerage** *noun* (*slang*) brewers collectively, *esp.* those who have been created peers; *derog.* the British peerage: L19. **beerless** *adjective* M19.

beer /ˈbiːə/ *noun*[2]. *rare*. Also **be-er**. LME.
[ORIGIN from BE *verb* + -ER[1].]
Someone who is or exists, esp. *the* Self-existent, God.

beer /bɪə/ *noun*[3]. E18.
[ORIGIN Alt. of BIER.]
In weaving, a (variable) number of ends in a warp.

beer *noun*[4] var. of BERE *noun*[2].

beeregar /ˈbɪərɪɡə/ *noun*. L15.
[ORIGIN from BEER *noun*[1] after VINEGAR.]
= ALEGAR.

Beerenauslese /ˈbeːrənˌaʊsleːzə/ *noun*. Pl. **-sen** /-zən/, **-ses**. E20.
[ORIGIN German, from *Beeren* berries, grapes + as AUSLESE.]
A white wine made (esp. in Germany) from selected individual grapes picked later than the general harvest.

Beersheba *noun* see DAN *noun*[3].

beery /ˈbɪəri/ *adjective*. M19.
[ORIGIN from BEER *noun*[1] + -Y[1].]
Pertaining to or containing beer; resembling beer; showing the influence of beer.
■ **beerily** *adverb* L19. **beeriness** *noun* L19.

†beest *noun*. OE–L18.
[ORIGIN Old English *bēost* = Northern Frisian *bjast*, *bjüst*, Middle Dutch & mod. Dutch *biest*, Old High German *biost* (German *Biest*, as in *Biestmilch*), from West Germanic: ult. origin unknown.]
= BEESTINGS.

†beest *verb* see BE *verb*.

beestings /ˈbiːstɪŋz/ *noun pl.* Also **beast-**. OE.
[ORIGIN Rel. to BEEST *noun*.]
The first milk drawn, esp. from a cow, after parturition.

beesty *noun* var. of BHISTI.

beeswax /ˈbiːzwaks/ *noun & verb*. L17.
[ORIGIN from BEE *noun*[1] + -'S[1] + WAX *noun*[1].]
▸ **A** *noun*. **1** Wax secreted by bees as material for their combs, used as a polish etc. L17.
2 A person's concern or business. *N. Amer. colloq.* M20.

L. COLWIN It's none of your beeswax.

▸ **B** *verb trans.* Rub or polish with beeswax. M19.

beeswing /ˈbiːzwɪŋ/ *noun*. E19.
[ORIGIN from BEE *noun*[1] + -'S[1] + WING *noun*.]
A filmy second crust of tartar formed in port and other wines after long keeping; an old wine.

beet /biːt/ *noun*[1].
[ORIGIN Old English *bēte* = Middle Low German *bēte* (Low German *beete*, whence German *Bete*), Middle Dutch *bēte* (Dutch *beet*), Old High German *bieza*, from early West Germanic from Latin *beta*, perh. of Celtic origin.]
A plant, *Beta vulgaris*, of the goosefoot family, having a red or white succulent root; numerous varieties are cultivated as garden vegetables, as cattle food, and as a source of sugar. Also = BEETROOT *noun*.
seakale beet, ***silver beet***, ***spinach beet***, ***sugar beet***, etc.
– COMB.: BEETROOT *noun*; **beet sugar** sugar from beets.

beet *noun*[2] var. of BEAT *noun*[2].

beet /biːt/ *verb trans.* *obsolete* exc. *dial.*
[ORIGIN Old English *bētan*, older *bœ̄tan* = Old Saxon *bōtian* (Middle Low German *bōten*, Middle Dutch *boeten*), Old High German *buozen* (German *büßen*), Old Norse *bœta*, Gothic *botjan* from Germanic, from base of BOOT *noun*[1].]
1 Make good; mend or repair; relieve or supply (a want). OE.
2 Make, kindle, mend, or feed (a fire). OE.

Beethovenian /beɪthəʊˈviːnɪən/ *adjective & noun*. L19.
[ORIGIN from *Beethoven* (see below) + -IAN.]
▸ **A** *adjective*. Of or pertaining to the German composer Ludwig van Beethoven (1770–1827), his music, or his theories of musical composition. L19.
▸ **B** *noun*. An interpreter, student, or admirer of Beethoven or his music. M20.
■ ˈ**Beethovenish** *adjective* resembling or suggestive of Beethoven or his music, characteristic of Beethoven L19.

beetle /ˈbiːt(ə)l/ *noun*[1].
[ORIGIN Old English *bētel*, (West Saxon) *bīetel* from Germanic, from base of BEAT *verb*[1]: see -LE[1].]
1 A tool with heavy head and handle for ramming, crushing, driving wedges, etc. OE.
(as) deaf as a beetle *arch.* completely deaf or unresponsive. **(as) dumb as a beetle** *arch.* insensitive, dumb.
2 A machine for beetling cloth. L19.
– COMB.: **beetle-brain** = *beetle-head* (a) below; **beetle-head** (*a*) a blockhead; (*b*) the monkey of a pile-driving engine.

beetle /ˈbiːt(ə)l/ *noun*[2].
[ORIGIN Old English *bitula*, *bitela*, from short base of *bītan* BITE *verb*: see -LE[1].]
1 An insect of the order Coleoptera, having the forewings converted to hard, opaque wing cases closing over the hindwings; in popular use extended to other (esp. black) insects of similar appearance, such as the cockroach. OE.
black beetle, *diving beetle*, *shard-born beetle*, *skipjack beetle*, etc. **blind as a beetle** short-sighted; devoid of moral etc. sense.
2 *fig.* A person who is (esp. intellectually) short-sighted. L16.

A. TUCKER A blockhead, yea a numbskull, not to say a beetle.

3 A dice game with the object of drawing or assembling a figure resembling a beetle. M20.
– COMB.: **beetle back** a back shaped like the closed wing cases on the back of a beetle; **beetle-backed** *adjective* having a beetle back; **beetle-crusher** *colloq.* a heavy boot or foot; **beetle drive** a social gathering at which beetle is played.

beetle /ˈbiːt(ə)l/ *adjective*. LME.
[ORIGIN Unknown.]
1 ***beetle-browed***, having prominent or bushy eyebrows; scowling. LME.

R. H. BARHAM A beetle-browed hag.

2 ***beetle brow(s)***, prominent or bushy eyebrows; a scowling expression. M16.

fig.: P. SIDNEY A pleasant valley of either side of which high hills lifted up their beetle-browis.

■ **beetled** *adjective* = *beetle-browed* above E16.

beetle /ˈbiːt(ə)l/ *verb*[1] *intrans.* E17.
[ORIGIN from BEETLE *adjective*.]
Project, overhang; *fig.* hang threateningly.

SHAKES. *Haml.* The dreadful summit of the cliff That beetles o'er his base into the sea. DICKENS His beetling brow almost obscured his eyes.

– NOTE: First recorded in Shakes.

beetle /ˈbiːt(ə)l/ *verb*[2] *trans.* E17.
[ORIGIN from BEETLE *noun*[1].]
Beat with a beetle in order to crush, flatten, etc.; emboss or heighten the lustre of (cloth) by pressure from rollers.

beetle /ˈbiːt(ə)l/ *verb*[3] *intrans. colloq.* E20.
[ORIGIN from BEETLE *noun*[2].]
Move or fly (like a beetle), make one's way; go, take oneself *off*.

P. G. WODEHOUSE 'What are you doing about two weeks from now?'.. 'Nothing in particular. Just beetling around.' N. COWARD There was.. a terrible scene.. and Freda beetled off to America.

beetroot /ˈbiːtruːt/ *noun & adjective*. L16.
[ORIGIN from BEET *noun*[1] + ROOT *noun*[1].]
▸ **A** *noun*. A root of beet, *esp.* the deep crimson form eaten as a vegetable. L16.
▸ **B** *attrib.* or as *adjective*. Deep red, crimson; red-faced esp. from embarrassment. *colloq.* E20.

beetster *noun* var. of BEATSTER *noun*[1].

beeve /biːv/ *noun*. M19.
[ORIGIN Back-form. from BEEVES.]
An ox; = BEEF *noun* 2.

beeves *noun* see BEEF *noun*.

beezer /ˈbiːzə/ *noun & adjective*. *slang*. E20.
[ORIGIN Unknown: senses perh. different words.]
▸ **A** *noun*. **1** A (smart) person; a chap, a fellow. Orig. *Scot.* E20.
2 The nose. E20.
3 Something which is a particularly impressive or large example of its kind. E20.
▸ **B** *adjective*. Excellent, fantastic; of the highest quality. M20.

J. BURCHILL So finally Matt's got a beezer set of twenty-four of these babies.

BEF *abbreviation*.
British Expeditionary Force, the British army on the Western Front, August–November 1914 and 1939–40.

Befa /biːˈfɑː/ *noun*. *obsolete* exc. *hist.* Also **B fa**. LME.
[ORIGIN from *B* as a pitch letter + *fa* designating a tone in the solmization of Guido d'Arezzo (*c* 990–1050).]
MEDIEVAL MUSIC. The note B flat in Guido d'Arezzo's 3rd and 6th hexachords, where it was sung to the syllable *fa*. Cf. ALAMIRE, BEMI, CEFAUT, etc.

befall /bɪˈfɔːl/ *verb*. Pa. t. **befell** /bɪˈfɛl/; pa. pple **befallen** /bɪˈfɔːl(ə)n/.
[ORIGIN Old English *befeallan* = Old Frisian *befalla*, Old Saxon, Old High German *bifallan*: see BE-, FALL *verb*.]
†**1** *verb intrans.* Fall. Chiefly *fig.* OE–M17.
2 *verb intrans.* Fall *to*; pertain, belong, be fitting. *arch.* ME.

J. M. NEALE Giving to the dearer ones What to each befalleth.

3 a *verb intrans.* Take place, happen; *arch.* foll. by (*un*)*to*, *upon* (a person etc.). ME. ▸**b** *verb trans.* (orig. with dat. obj.). Happen to. ME.

a THACKERAY Ethel's birthday befel in the Spring. C. KINGSLEY And so it befell that they often quarrelled. **b** MILTON Thus it shall befall Him who.. Lets her Will rule. C. CHAPLIN Only when ill-fortune befell her did she seek relief. D. JACOBSON The most significant events that befell the kingdom and its people during David's reign.

†**4** *verb intrans.* Become *of*. LME–L16.

SHAKES. *Com. Err.* Do me the favour to dilate at full What have befall'n of them and thee till now.

■ **befalling** *noun* (*a*) the action of the verb; (*b*) an occurrence, an event: LME.

befile /bɪˈfʌɪl/ *verb trans.* Long *rare*. OE.
[ORIGIN from BE- 1 + FILE *verb*[1].]
Befoul, defile.

befit /bɪˈfɪt/ *verb trans.* Infl. **-tt-**. L16.
[ORIGIN from BE- 1 + FIT *verb*[1].]
1 Be fitted or appropriate for, suit. L16. ▸**b** Be morally right for. E17.

SHAKES. *Temp.* Any business that We say befits the hour. E. L. DOCTOROW His son now had a desk, as befitted all young students. B. TRAPIDO We're giving you the guest room, as befits your station as.. senior guest. **b** SHAKES. *Haml.* It us befitted To bear our hearts in grief.

†**2** Equip *with*. L16–M18.

L. STERNE He had.. befitted him with just such a bridle and saddle.

■ **befitting** *adjective* suitable, fitting, appropriate, due M16. **befittingly** *adverb* M17.

beflower /bɪˈflaʊə/ *verb trans.* L16.
[ORIGIN from BE- 4 + FLOWER *noun*.]
Cover or deck (as) with flowers.

befoam /bɪˈfəʊm/ *verb trans.* E17.
[ORIGIN from BE- 4 + FOAM *noun*.]
Cover (as) with foam.

befog /bɪˈfɒɡ/ *verb trans.* Infl. **-gg-**. E17.
[ORIGIN from BE- 4 + FOG *noun*[2].]
Envelop in fog; obscure, confuse.

befool /bɪˈfuːl/ *verb trans.* LME.
[ORIGIN from BE- 3, 4 + FOOL *noun*[1].]
Make a fool of, dupe, delude; treat as or call a fool.

before /bɪˈfɔː/ *adverb, preposition, & conjunction*.
[ORIGIN Old English *beforan* = Old Frisian *befora*, Old Saxon *biforan*, Old High German *bifora* (German *bevor*), from Germanic: see BY *adverb & preposition*, FORE *adverb & preposition*.]
▸ **A** *adverb*. **1** In front in place or order; ahead, at or on the front. OE.

SHAKES. *Mids. N. D.* I am sent with broom before, To sweep the dust behind the door. SHAKES. *Macb.* Had he his hurts before? .. Ay, on the front. S. BARING-GOULD Onward, Christian soldiers, Marching as to war, With the Cross of Jesus Going on before.

2 Earlier in time; previously, beforehand, in the past. ME. ▸**b** *spec.* Contrasted with ***after*** (see AFTER *adverb* 2b): preceding an event or (esp.) the use of a remedy, cosmetic, or other product. M18.

LD MACAULAY Charles the First, eighteen years before, withdrew from his capital. ARNOLD BENNETT He had never spoken to Tom Orgreave before. C. CAUSLEY He felt younger than he had for some time before. D. BOGARDE He would come back one day and it would all be as before. **b** *Punch* A 'before and after' racket for a hair-renewer advertisement.

have been THERE before. ***have seen it all before***: see SEE *verb*. ***the mixture as before***: see MIXTURE 1C.
▸ **B** *preposition*. **I** Of motion or position.
1 Of motion: ahead of, in advance of. OE. ▸**b** Driven in front of, under the impulse of. M16.

LD MACAULAY Behind him march the halbardiers; before him sound the drums. **b** SHAKES. *2 Hen. VI* Our enemies shall fall before us. A. SILLITOE Running before the wrath of cop or farmer. A. J. P. TAYLOR The anti-waste campaign.. swept all before it.

2 Of position or direction: in front of. OE.

TENNYSON Once more before my face I see the moulder'd Abbey-walls. T. S. ELIOT Each man fixed his eyes before his feet. A. SILLITOE Emerging to scrub himself dry.. before the fire. M. BRAGG His back to the fells, before him the plain and the sea.

3 In the sight or presence of; under the notice of. OE.

STEELE As ill an Action as any that comes before the Magistrate. J. M. BARRIE Is it to be before the ladies, Mr. Ernest, or in the privacy of the wood? TOLKIEN The song of Lúthien before Mandos was the song most fair that ever in words was woven.

4 In the view or opinion of. *arch.* OE.

P. STUBBES Though this be not theft before the world.

5 Open to the knowledge of; claiming the attention of. LME.

H. T. BUCKLE The accusations.. are before the world. T. HARDY Such was the argument that Oak set outwardly before him.

6 In prospect for, open to; awaiting. (Merging with branch II, of time.) LME.

MILTON The World was all before them, where to choose, Their place of rest. B. WEBB Sidney and I have plenty of work before us—Sidney in the Labour Party and I on Government Committees.

▸ **II** Of time.
7 Preceding in order of time. OE.

BYRON Brave men were living before Agamemnon. J. D. WATSON With luck, Francis's coiled coils would get into print as soon as if not before Pauling's.

8 Previous to, earlier than (an event, point of time, etc.). ME. ▸**b** Earlier than the end of (a future period of time). M19.

S. JOHNSON It was written before the Conquest of Granada. A. J. P. TAYLOR Singapore had been neglected before the war and still more during it. **b** A. TROLLOPE This grief.. may be cured some day before long.

▸ **III** Of order or rank.
9 In advance of in development; further on than. ME.

HOBBES Atrides is before you in command. LD MACAULAY The nation which was so far before its neighbours in science.

10 In preference to, rather than. ME.

AV *2 Sam.* 6:21 The Lord.. chose me before thy father, & before all his house.

11 In comparison with. E18.

ADDISON The Women were of such an enormous Stature, that we appeared as Grashoppers before them.

– PHRASES: **before Christ** (of a date) reckoned backwards from the birth of Jesus. **before God** as God sees me (usu. as solemn oath). ***before one's time***: see TIME *noun*. ***before the beam***: see BEAM *noun*. ***before the mast***: see MAST *noun*[1] 1. ***before the secular worlds***: see SECULAR *adjective* 5. **before the wind** helped or driven on by the force of the wind. ***leg before wicket***: see LEG *noun*. ***not before time***: see TIME *noun*. ***walk before one can run***: see WALK *verb*[1].
▸ **C** *conjunction*. **1** Previous to the time when. Also (*arch.*) ***before that***. ME.

AV *John* 1:48 Before that Philip called thee.. I saw thee. E. HEMINGWAY I woke for good long before it was light. D. LODGE His hair is the texture and colour of Brillo pads before they've been used.

2 Of preference: sooner than that, rather than that. L16.

SHAKES. *Merch. V.* Treble that, Before a friend.. Shall lose a hair through Bassanio's fault. OED I will die before I submit.

beforehand /bɪˈfɔːhand/ *adverb & pred. adjective*. Orig. two words. ME.
[ORIGIN from BEFORE *preposition* + HAND *noun*: cf. Anglo-Norman, Old French *avant main*.]
In advance; in anticipation; in readiness, esp. (*arch.*) financially.

AV *Mark* 13:11 Take no thought before hand what ye shall speake. STEELE Having little or nothing before-hand, and living from Hand to Mouth. K. AMIS Do you write all this stuff out beforehand and learn it off, or.. [do] you make it up as you go along?

be beforehand with anticipate, forestall.

†**beforesaid** *adjective*. Orig. two words. ME–M18.
[ORIGIN from BEFORE *adverb* + SAID *ppl adjective*.]
Previously mentioned, aforesaid.

beforetime /bɪˈfɔːtʌɪm/ *adverb*. Orig. two words. ME.
[ORIGIN from BEFORE *preposition* + TIME *noun*.]
Formerly, previously.

befortune /bɪˈfɔːtʃuːn/ *verb trans. & intrans. rare*. L16.
[ORIGIN from BE- 1 + FORTUNE *verb*.]
Befall.

befoul /bɪˈfaʊl/ *verb trans.* ME.
[ORIGIN from BE- 1 + FOUL *verb*.]
Make foul (*lit.* & *fig.*), cover with filth.
■ **befoulment** *noun* M19.

befriend /bɪˈfrɛnd/ *verb trans.* M16.
[ORIGIN from BE- 3 + FRIEND *noun*.]
Act as a friend to; help, favour.
■ **befriender** *noun* M19.

befringe /bɪˈfrɪn(d)ʒ/ *verb trans.* E17.
[ORIGIN from BE- 1 + FRINGE *verb*.]
Border, provide, or adorn (as) with a fringe.

befrog /bɪˈfrɒɡ/ *verb trans.* Infl. **-gg-**. M19.
[ORIGIN from BE- 4 + FROG *noun*[3].]
Decorate with frogging.

befuddle /bɪˈfʌd(ə)l/ *verb trans.* L19.
[ORIGIN from BE- 1 + FUDDLE *verb*.]
Make stupid through drink etc.; confuse, bewilder.
■ **befuddlement** *noun* E20.

befur /bɪˈfəː/ *verb trans.* Infl. **-rr-**. L15.
[ORIGIN from BE- 1, 4 + FUR *verb*, *noun*[1].]
Cover (as) with a fur or furs; deck out with furs. Chiefly as ***befurred*** *ppl adjective*.

beg /bɛg/ *noun*[1]. L16.
[ORIGIN Turkish: cf. BEGUM, BEY.]
hist. = BEY.

beg /bɛg/ *verb* & *noun*[2]. ME.
[ORIGIN Prob. from Old English *bedecian*, from Germanic base of BID *verb*: cf. Gothic *bidagwa* beggar.]
▸ **A** *verb*. Infl. **-gg-**.
1 a *verb trans.* Ask for (food, money, etc.) as a charitable gift. ME. ▸**b** *verb intrans.* Ask for (or *for*) a charitable gift of food, money, etc.; live by asking for such gifts. (Foll. by *of*, *from*, †*at* a person.) ME.

a C. S. LEWIS Father's ruin was approaching, that we should all soon beg our bread in the streets. S. BECKETT I went to the house and begged a glass of milk and a slice of bread and butter. **b** G. ORWELL A fat man eating quails while children are begging for bread is a disgusting sight. P. S. BUCK Holding up a bowl and begging of any one who passed. C. HAMPTON A hunchback . . who used to sit on the pavement and beg. P. SCOTT If the hippie was there, and came begging at the coffee shop, Ibrahim threw him a few paise.

a beg, borrow, or steal acquire by any means at all. **b go a-begging, go begging** *fig.* (of an opportunity etc.) find no taker; (of a thing) be unwanted.

2 *verb trans.* & *intrans.* Ask someone earnestly or humbly for a thing desired. As obj. the person asked, the thing asked (which may take the form of a noun or pronoun, a clause introduced by *that*, or an inf. phr.), or both. (Also foll. by †*at*, *of*, *from* the person asked, *for* the thing desired.) E16.

TINDALE *Matt.* 27:58 Ioseph . . went to Pilate and begged the body of Iesus. SHAKES. *L.L.L.* How I would make him fawn, and beg, and seek. EVELYN Our prisoners . . beg at us, as a mercy, to knock them on the head. HOR. WALPOLE I have three favours to beg of you. TENNYSON I will beg of him to take thee back. LD MACAULAY Shrewsbury begged that . . he might be appointed. C. STEAD She also begged them for money so that she could take home presents to all the children. A. KOESTLER I beg you to take note that I am not moralising. J. BALDWIN Of them all she would have begged forgiveness, had they come with ears to hear. D. LODGE He turned up again yesterday evening to beg a rather odd favour. J. UPDIKE Did they die ignobly, begging and cackling for mercy?

3 *verb trans.* Ask (pardon, leave, etc.) formally or politely. L16. ▸**b** *ellipt.* Ask or take leave *to do* something. M18. ▸**c** *ellipt.* As an epistolary formula: offer, wish to send (compliments etc.). *arch.* M18.

ADDISON I must however beg Leave to dissent from so great an Authority. **b** OED I beg to enclose my price list. D. L. SAYERS Here Sir Impey Biggs interposed and begged with submission to suggest that his lordship should remind the jury of the evidence given by Mr. Challoner. **c** DICKENS Begging my best remembrances to Mrs. Thomson.

beg a person's pardon (*a*) express polite apology or disagreement; (*b*) request a remark to be repeated. **beg yours** *Austral.* & *NZ colloq.* I beg your pardon.

4 *verb trans.* Take (a disputed matter) for granted without warrant. Chiefly in ***beg the question*** below. L16.

H. ROGERS Many say it is begging the point in dispute.

beg the question (*a*) assume the truth of an argument or proposition to be proved, without arguing it; (*b*) raise a point that has not been dealt with, invite an obvious question.

5 *verb trans.* & *intrans.* Foll. by *off*: get (a person) excused a penalty etc.; decline to take part etc. M18.

S. RICHARDSON Is the Creature begging me off from Insult? J. RATHBONE I was a little drunk and very tired and begged off.

6 *verb trans.* & *intrans.* CARDS. Of the elder hand in all fours (seven-up): ask for (a point, or three additional cards and a new trump). L18.
7 *verb intrans.* Of a (trained) dog: sit up with forepaws raised expectantly. Freq. in *imper.* as a command. E19.
– COMB.: **begging letter**: asking for a charitable gift to be sent; **beg-pardon** *Austral.* & *NZ colloq.* an apology.
▸ **B** *noun*. An act of begging. E19.
■ **beggingly** *adverb* in the manner of a person who begs. L16.

begad /bɪˈgad/ *interjection*. L16.
[ORIGIN Alt. of *by God!*: cf. EGAD etc.]
Expr. amazement or emphasis.

begah *noun* var. of BIGHA.

began *verb pa. t.* of BEGIN.

begat *verb* see BEGET.

begem /bɪˈdʒɛm/ *verb trans.* Infl. **-mm-**. M18.
[ORIGIN from BE- 4 + GEM *noun*.]
Set about or stud with gems.

beget /bɪˈgɛt/ *verb trans.* Pa. t. **begot** /bɪˈgɒt/, (*arch.*) **begat** /bɪˈgat/; pres. pple **begetting**; pa. pple **begotten** /bɪˈgɒt(ə)n/.
[ORIGIN Old English *begietan*, corresp. to Old Saxon *bigetan* seize, Old High German *bigezzan* receive = Gothic *bigetan* find: see BE-, GET *verb*.]
†**1** Get, acquire, esp. by effort. OE–E17.
2 Procreate (usu. said of the father, occas. of both parents). ME. ▸†**b** Get *with child*. LME–E17.

SHAKES. *1 Hen. VI* Richard, Edward's son, The first-begotten and the lawful heir. V. WOOLF Begetting one son . . by Lady Bradshaw. A. STORR It is unproven that the strongest males necessarily beget the strongest offspring. *fig.*: *Book of Common Prayer* The Son is of the Father alone: not made, nor created, but begotten.

3 *fig.* Call into being, occasion; give rise to. L16.

CONAN DOYLE As usual, familiarity begat contempt.

■ **begetter** *noun* a person who begets; a procreator, an originator: LME.

beggar /ˈbɛgə/ *noun*. ME.
[ORIGIN from BEG *verb* + -AR[3].]
1 A person who begs; *esp.* a person who lives by begging. ME.

Proverb: Beggars cannot be choosers.

sturdy beggar: see STURDY *adjective*. ***valiant beggar***: see VALIANT *adjective* 1.

2 A person in needy circumstances; a poor person. ME.

COVERDALE *Ecclus* 37:30 Some man . . can geve . . prudent councell . . and contynueth a begger.

3 A mean or low fellow; *joc.* a person, a chap. Now also *euphem.* for BUGGER *noun*[1] 3. ME.

E. LANGLEY At last, the poor little beggars did their dialogue to a thunder of well-fed applause. *Fortune* The plane starts taxiing in from the runway, and look: the beggars are already standing up, ready to jump off.

†**4** A person who begs a favour; a suppliant. LME–E17.
†**5** A person who begs the question. L16–E19.
– COMB.: **beggar's purse** *N. Amer.* an appetizer consisting of a crêpe stuffed with a savoury filling, orig. caviar and crème fraiche; **beggarticks** (the prickly fruits of) any of several N. American bur-marigolds, esp. *Bidens frondosa*.
■ **beggarhood** *noun* (people in) the condition of a beggar ME. **beggarism** *noun* (now *rare*) practice characteristic of a beggar, beggary M17.

beggar /ˈbɛgə/ *verb trans.* LME.
[ORIGIN from the noun.]
1 Make a beggar of; impoverish. LME.

M. MITCHELL The Cause which had taken their friends, lovers, husbands and beggared their families. M. NA GOPALEEN He also beggared nine weak-minded relatives.

beggar-my-neighbour a card game in which one seeks to capture one's opponent's cards; *fig.* a policy of advancement at the expense of one's neighbours.

2 Exhaust the resources of; go beyond, outdo. E17.

SHAKES. *Ant. & Cl.* For her own person, It beggar'd all description. C. PRIEST It beggared belief that she should twice interrupt me at precisely the same place.

beggarly /ˈbɛgəli/ *adjective*. E16.
[ORIGIN from BEGGAR *noun* + -LY[1].]
1 In the condition of or befitting a beggar; poverty-stricken; *fig.* intellectually poor, valueless. E16.
2 Mean, sordid. L16.
■ **beggarliness** *noun* M16.

beggarly /ˈbɛgəli/ *adverb*. *arch.* LME.
[ORIGIN from BEGGAR *noun* + -LY[2].]
As a beggar; indigently, humbly.

beggary /ˈbɛgəri/ *noun*. LME.
[ORIGIN from BEGGAR *noun* + -Y[3].]
1 The condition of a beggar; extreme poverty. LME.

SWIFT This coin . . will reduce the kingdom to beggary.

2 The action or habit of begging. LME.

X. HERBERT Perhaps he would abandon beggary when there was no poor fool about to beg from.

†**3** Contemptible stuff, rubbish. M16–M17.

J. FOXE Your Ceremonies in the Church be beggary and poyson.

4 Beggars collectively. *arch.* M16.
†**5** Contemptible meanness. Only in E17.

SHAKES. *Cymb.* Not I . . pronounce the beggary of his change.

beghard /ˈbɛgəd/ *noun*. M16.
[ORIGIN medieval Latin *Beghardus* from Old French *Bégard*, *-art*, Middle Dutch *Beggaert*, Middle High German *Beghart*, from stem of *Beguina* etc.: see BEGUINE *noun*[1], -ARD.]
A member of one of the lay brotherhoods which arose in the Low Countries in the 13th cent. in imitation of the female beguines.

begift /bɪˈgɪft/ *verb trans.* LME.
[ORIGIN from BE- 4 + GIFT *noun*.]
†**1** Entrust. Only in LME.
2 Present with gifts. L16.

begild /bɪˈgɪld/ *verb trans.* Pa. pple **begilded**, **begilt** /bɪˈgɪlt/. L16.
[ORIGIN from BE- 1 + GILD *verb*[1].]
Cover with, or as with, gold.

begin /bɪˈgɪn/ *verb*. Pa. t. **began** /bɪˈgan/, †**begun**. Pres. pple **beginning** /bɪˈgɪnɪŋ/. Pa. pple **begun** /bɪˈgʌn/.
[ORIGIN Old English *beginnan* = Old Frisian *biginna*, Old Saxon, Old High German *biginnan* (Dutch, German *beginnen*), from West Germanic, formed as BE- + Germanic base of unknown origin, found in various compounds meaning 'begin'.]
1 *verb intrans.* Take the first step in some action or process; commence, start. (Foll. by inf.) OE.

AV *Gen.* 4:26 Then began men to call upon the Name of the Lord. BYRON My way is to begin with the beginning. E. O'NEILL During dinner I began to get a headache. DAY LEWIS The night I began to be born. G. VIDAL He paused and then he began to speak carefully but casually.

2 *verb intrans.* Come into being, start occurring, arise; have its commencement or nearest boundary (at some place or time). OE.

AV *Num.* 16:46 There is wrath gone out from the Lord; the plague is begun. J. BRYCE The greatness of the Prussian monarchy begins with Frederick II. OED The paragraph begins about the middle of the page. L. DURRELL He had already given the signal for dinner to begin.

3 *verb trans.* Set about doing, start upon; perform the first part of. OE.

CHESTERFIELD The Spaniards began their conquests . . by the islands of St. Domingo and Cuba. EARL OF CHATHAM I rejoice to hear you have begun Homer's Iliad. J. B. PRIESTLEY They begin work at half-past seven and end at five. R. GRAVES The senior Consul called for order and began reading the letter.

4 *verb trans.* Start (a thing) on its course, bring into being, initiate; be the first to do. ME.

POPE Proud Nimrod first the savage chace began. J. M. BARRIE Watch whether Crichton begins any of his answers to my questions with 'The fact is'. R. H. TAWNEY The events which seemed to aristocratic Parliamentarians to close the revolution seemed to the left wing of the victorious army only to begin it.

5 *verb intrans.* & *trans.* Start speaking (with the words). LME.

MILTON To whom th' Arch-Enemy . . Breaking the horrid silence, thus began: [etc.]. SCOTT FITZGERALD 'You ought to live in California—' began Miss Baker, but Tom interrupted her.

6 *verb intrans.* (Usu. with preceding neg.) Come anywhere near, show any attempt or likelihood *to do* something; *ellipt.* (*US*) compare in any degree (*with*). *colloq.* M19.

M. TWAIN There ain't a book that begins with it. N. MAILER The American hipsters' writings cannot begin to compare with the work of the arch-hipsters of modern European literature, Celine and Genet. LADY BIRD JOHNSON I cannot begin to say how impressed I am with Mrs. Rose Kennedy.

– PHRASES ETC.: **begin at** start from. **begin on** set to work at. **begin school** attend school for the first time. ***begin the dance***: see DANCE *noun*. **begin the world** start in life. **begin upon** = *begin on* above. **begin with** take first or as one's starting point. **to begin with** at the outset; as a first point.
■ **beginning** *adjective* that begins; EDUCATION (*N. Amer.*) elementary: L16.

beginner /bɪˈgɪnə/ *noun*. LME.
[ORIGIN from BEGIN + -ER[1].]
1 A person who begins; an originator. LME.
2 A person just beginning to learn a skill etc.; a novice, an inexperienced person. LME.
beginner's luck good luck supposed to attend a beginner at games etc.

beginning /bɪˈgɪnɪŋ/ *noun*. ME.
[ORIGIN formed as BEGINNER + -ING[1].]
1 Entering upon existence or action; bringing into existence; commencing, origination. ME.
2 The point at which anything begins; *spec.* the time when the universe began to be. ME.

COVERDALE *Hab.* 1:12 Thou o Lorde . . art from the begynnynge. B. SPOCK If you miss, you must penalize yourself, go back to the beginning, and start again. P. DAVIES The vexed question of whether it is possible . . for time to have a beginning or ending has been debated by philosophers for over two thousand years.

3 An origin or source. ME. ▸†**b** A first cause, a first principle. LME–L16.

CARLYLE Thy true . . Beginning and Father is in Heaven.

4 The first part (of a period of time, of a book, journey, etc.); the earliest stage of development (freq. in *pl.*). ME.

Book of Common Prayer Who hast safely brought us to the beginning of this day. ADAM SMITH Great fortunes acquired from small beginnings. J. R. GREEN The beginnings of physical science were more slow and timid there. G. B. SHAW You have made a slip at the very beginning of your fairy tale. ISAIAH BERLIN All movements have origins, forerunners, imperceptible beginnings. DAY LEWIS Looking at that photograph of our house in the Queen's County, and blindly reaching out across fifty-four years to my beginnings.

the beginning of the end the first clear sign of the end of something.
■ **beginningless** *adjective* without a beginning, uncreated L16.

begird /bɪˈgəːd/ *verb trans.* Now *literary*. Pa. t. & pple **begirt** /bɪˈgəːt/.
[ORIGIN Old English *begyrdan*: see BE- 1, GIRD *verb*[1].]
1 Gird about or around. OE.
2 Encompass, encircle *with*. OE.
†**3** Besiege. L16–L18.

begirdle /bɪˈgəːd(ə)l/ *verb trans.* M19.
[ORIGIN from BE- 1 + GIRDLE *verb*.]
Encompass like a girdle.

begirt /bɪˈgəːt/ *verb*[1] *trans.* Pa. t. & pple **begirt**. E17.
[ORIGIN from BE- 1 + GIRT *verb*[1].]
Surround, encircle.

begirt *verb*[2] *pa. t. & pple* of BEGIRD.

beglamour /bɪˈglamə/ *verb trans.* Also ***-or**. M19.
[ORIGIN from BE- 4 + GLAMOUR *noun*.]
Glamorize; invest with (deceptive) glamour.

beglerbeg /ˈbɛgləbɛg/ *noun*. Also **-bey** /-beɪ/. M16.
[ORIGIN Turkish = bey of beys, from BEG *noun*[1], pl. *begler*.]
hist. The governor of a province of the Ottoman Empire, in rank next to the grand vizier.

begloom /bɪˈgluːm/ *verb trans.* L18.
[ORIGIN from BE- 4 + GLOOM *noun*[1].]
Make gloomy.

begnaw /bɪˈnɔː/ *verb trans.* Pa. pple **-gnawed**, **-gnawn** /-ˈnɔːn/.
[ORIGIN Old English *begnagan*: see BE- 1, GNAW *verb*.]
Gnaw at, nibble, corrode.

bego /bɪˈgəʊ/ *verb trans.* Long *obsolete* exc. as pa. pple **begone** /bɪˈgɒn/, now only in WOEBEGONE.
[ORIGIN Old English *begān*, Old Saxon *bigangan*, Old High German *bigān*, Gothic *bigaggan*: see BE- 2, GO *verb*.]
Go round or about; surround, overrun; beset, afflict; adorn, clothe.

begob /bɪˈgɒb/ *interjection*. *Irish*. L19.
[ORIGIN Alt. of *by God!*: cf. BEGAD etc.]
Expr. amazement or emphasis.

begone /bɪˈgɒn/ *verb*[1] *intrans.* Only in *imper.* & *inf.* LME.
[ORIGIN Imper. & inf. *be gone* (see GO *verb* 30) treated as one word; cf. BEWARE.]
Go away immediately.

CARLYLE Kaiser's Ambassador . . is angrily ordered to begone. W. DE LA MARE Sweet sounds, begone.

begone *verb*[2] see BEGO.

begonia /bɪˈgəʊnɪə/ *noun*. M18.
[ORIGIN mod. Latin (see below), from Michel *Bégon* (1638–1710), French patron of science: see -IA[1].]
A plant of the genus *Begonia*, having a coloured perianth but no petals, and often brilliant foliage.

begorra /bɪˈgɒrə/ *interjection*. *Irish*. Also **-ah**. M19.
[ORIGIN Alt. of *by God!*: cf. BEGAD etc.]
Expr. amazement or emphasis.

begot, **begotten** *verbs* see BEGET.

begrace /bɪˈgreɪs/ *verb trans.* E16.
[ORIGIN from BE- 3 + GRACE *noun*.]
Address as 'your grace'.

begrease /bɪˈgriːs/ *verb trans.* M16.
[ORIGIN from BE- 1 + GREASE *verb*.]
Besmear with grease.

begrime /bɪˈgrʌɪm/ *verb trans.* M16.
[ORIGIN from BE- 4 + GRIME *noun*.]
Blacken with grime; make grimy.

begrudge /bɪˈgrʌdʒ/ *verb trans.* LME.
[ORIGIN from BE- 1 + GRUDGE *verb*.]
Feel or show dissatisfaction at (a thing); resentfully envy (a person) the possession of; give reluctantly.

S. UNWIN No time spent by parents on their children during that period should be begrudged. D. LODGE I didn't really begrudge him the food, since he was obviously starved of decent home cooking.

■ **begrudger** *noun* L19. **begrudgery** *noun* (chiefly *Irish*) a begrudging attitude, envy L20. **begrudging** *adjective* given or done in a grudging manner or spirit M19. **begrudgingly** *adverb* M19.

begrutten /bɪˈgrʌt(ə)n/ *adjective*. *Scot.* E17.
[ORIGIN from BE- + *grutten* pa. pple of GREET *verb*[2].]
Swollen in the face with much weeping.

beguile /bɪˈgʌɪl/ *noun*. *arch.* Long *obsolete* exc. *Scot.* LME.
[ORIGIN from the verb.]
Deception.

beguile /bɪˈgʌɪl/ *verb trans.* ME.
[ORIGIN from BE- 1 + GUILE *verb*: cf. Middle Dutch *begilen*, Anglo-Norman *degiler*.]
1 Deceive, delude. ME.
2 Deprive *of* by fraud; cheat (*out*) *of* (something) or *into* (doing). ME.
†**3** Cheat (hopes etc., or a person in them); disappoint, foil. L15–M17.
4 Divert or distract (a person); charm, amuse. L16.

H. I. JENKINSON The charms of this stream will beguile the tourist.

5 Divert one's attention pleasantly from (time passing, something tedious or unpleasant); while away (time). L16.

S. LEWIS Thus in the Vale of Arcady nymphs and satyrs beguiled the hours.

■ **beguilement** *noun* E19. **beguiler** *noun* LME. **beguiling** *ppl adjective* that beguiles; *esp.* charming, fascinating: L16. **beguilingly** *adverb* M19.

béguin /begɛ̃/ *noun*. Pl. pronounced same. E20.
[ORIGIN Colloq. French.]
An infatuation, a fancy.

beguine /beɪˈgiːn/ *noun*[1]. Also **bé-**. LME.
[ORIGIN Old French & mod. French *béguine* (Middle Dutch, Middle High German *begīne*), medieval Latin *Beguina*, perh. ult. from Middle Dutch verb = mutter (prayers): see -INE[3].]
A member of a lay sisterhood in the Low Countries, formed in the 12th cent. and not bound by vows.
■ **beguinage** /ˈbeɪgɪnɪdʒ, -nɑːʒ/ *noun* an establishment of, or house for, beguines L17.

beguine /bɪˈgiːn/ *noun*[2]. E20.
[ORIGIN Amer. French from French BÉGUIN.]
(The distinctive rhythm of) a dance of W. Indian origin.

begum /ˈbeɪgəm/ *noun*. M17.
[ORIGIN Urdu *begam* from Eastern Turkic *begim*, formed as BEG *noun*[1] + *-im* 1st person sing. possess. suffix.]
In the Indian subcontinent: a Muslim noblewoman or lady of high rank. Also (**B-**), a title given to a married Muslim woman (= Mrs).

begun *verb* see BEGIN.

begunk /bɪˈgʌŋk/ *noun* & *verb*. *Scot.* E18.
[ORIGIN Unknown.]
▸ **A** *noun*. A piece of deception, a trick. E18.
▸ **B** *verb trans.* Play a trick on, take in. E19.

behalf /bɪˈhɑːf/ *noun*. ME.
[ORIGIN from combination of earlier phrs. *on his halve* and *bi halve him*, both meaning 'on his side': see BY *preposition*, HALF *noun*.]
1 *on behalf of*, (now chiefly N. Amer.) *in behalf of*: ▸**a** As the agent or representative of (another); in the name of. ME. ▸**b** On the part of, proceeding from. (Long *rare* or *obsolete* but revived L20.) LME. ▸**c** In the interest or for the benefit of (another person, a cause, etc.); for the sake of. L16.
2 *in this behalf*, *in that behalf*, †*on this behalf*, †*on that behalf*, in respect of or concerning a particular matter. *arch.* LME.

behang /bɪˈhaŋ/ *verb trans.* *obsolete* exc. as pa. pple **behung** /bɪˈhʊŋ/.
[ORIGIN Old English *behōn*: see BE- 1, HANG *verb*.]
Drape or hang (a thing) about *with*.

†**behappen** *verb trans.* & *intrans.* LME–M17.
[ORIGIN from BE- 1, 2 + HAPPEN *verb*.]
Befall.

Behari *adjective* & *noun* var. of BIHARI.

behave /bɪˈheɪv/ *verb*. LME.
[ORIGIN from BE- 1 + HAVE *verb* (with early stressed pronunc.).]
1 *verb refl.* & (now usu.) *intrans.* Conduct or bear oneself in a specified manner. LME.

New Statesman Younger siblings tend to behave better with an older brother on hand.

ill-behaved: see ILL *adverb*. *well-behaved*: see WELL *adverb*.
†**2** *verb trans.* Handle, manage, regulate. E16–M17.
3 *verb refl.* & *intrans.* Esp. to or of a child: conduct oneself well or with propriety; show good manners. L17.

C. HIGSON You've got to promise me you'll behave.

4 *verb intrans.* Of a thing: function, act, or react in a specified manner. M19.

S. HAWKING We consider matter to behave according to quantum theory.

behavior *noun*, **behavioral** *adjective*, **behaviorism** *noun* see BEHAVIOUR etc.

behaviour /bɪˈheɪvjə/ *noun*. Also ***-or**. LME.
[ORIGIN from BEHAVE after HAVIOUR.]
1 Manner of bearing oneself; demeanour, manners; observable actions; treatment shown *to* or *towards* another or others. LME. ▸†**b** *spec.* Good manners, elegant deportment. L16–E18.
be on one's best behaviour, **be on one's good behaviour** take care to behave well (when being observed or tested).
2 (As a count noun) An instance or way of behaving. Now usu. of animals or people as objects of study: an observable pattern of actions, a response to a stimulus. M16.
3 The way in which an object, device, substance, etc., acts or works. L17.
– COMB.: **behaviour pattern** a set of actions which occur characteristically in a given situation and are regarded as a unified whole; **behaviour therapy** treatment of a psychological disorder by gradual training of the patient to react normally.

behavioural /bɪˈheɪvjər(ə)l/ *adjective*. Also ***-ior-**. E20.
[ORIGIN from BEHAVIOUR + -AL[1].]
Of, pertaining to, or forming part of behaviour.
behavioural science the science of animal (and human) behaviour.
■ **behaviouralism** *noun* behavioural science esp. as applied to politics M20. **behaviouralist** *noun* & *adjective* (*a*) *noun* a practitioner of behaviouralism; (*b*) *adjective* of or pertaining to behaviouralism or behaviouralists: M20. **behaviourally** *adverb* as regards behaviour M20.

behaviourism /bɪˈheɪvjərɪz(ə)m/ *noun*. Also ***-ior-**. E20.
[ORIGIN formed as BEHAVIOURAL + -ISM.]
PSYCHOLOGY. The doctrine that objective investigation of stimuli and responses is the only valid psychological method; psychological analysis in terms of stimulus and response.
■ **behaviourist** *noun* an adherent or practitioner of behaviourism E20. **behaviouˈristic** *adjective* E20. **behaviouˈristically** *adverb* E20.

behead /bɪˈhɛd/ *verb trans.*
[ORIGIN Old English *behēafdian*: see BE- 4, HEAD *noun*.]
Cut off the head or top part of; kill in this way.
■ **beheadal** *noun* M19.

beheld *verb pa. t.* & *pple* of BEHOLD.

behemoth /bɪˈhiːmɒθ, ˈbiːhɪməʊθ/ *noun*. LME.
[ORIGIN Hebrew *bĕhēmōṯ* intensive pl. of *bĕhēmāh* beast.]
An enormous creature (in *Job* 40:15 prob. a hippopotamus or a crocodile); *fig.* something vast.

S. B. FLEXNER The *Great Eastern* . . , an iron behemoth designed for the England-to-India run.

■ **behemothian** /biːhɪˈməʊθɪən/ *adjective* (*literary*) of a behemoth; monstrously huge: E20.

behest /bɪˈhɛst/ *noun*.
[ORIGIN Old English *behǣs* (+ parasitic *t*) from Germanic base meaning 'bid, call': see BE-, HEST, HIGHT *verb*.]
†**1** A vow, a promise. OE–L16.
2 A command; bidding, instigation. Now chiefly in ***at the behest of***. ME.

behight /bɪˈhʌɪt/ *verb trans.* Long *obsolete* exc. *dial.* (*rare*). Pa. t. & pple **behight**, (later) **-ed**.
[ORIGIN Old English *behātan*, *bi-* = Old High German *biheizzan*: see BE-, HIGHT *verb*.]
▸ **I** Proper uses.
1 Vow, promise; hold out hope of; warrant. OE.
▸ **II** Improper uses introduced by Spenser.
†**2** Grant, deliver; command, ordain. Only in L16.
3 Call, name. L16.

behind /bɪˈhʌɪnd/ *adverb*, *preposition*, & *noun*.
[ORIGIN Old English *behindan*, *bi-* = Old Saxon *bihindan*, from *bi* BY *preposition* + *hindan* from behind (= Old High German *hintana* (German *hinten*) behind, Gothic *hindana* beyond, etc.: cf. HIND *adjective*.]
▸ **A** *adverb*. **1** Remaining after the departure of oneself or others; in a place, position, state, etc., from which others or other things have gone or been removed. OE. ▸**b** In reserve, still to come. *arch.* ME. ▸**c** In the past. LME.

DONNE To leave this world behinde, is death. T. H. HUXLEY The salt is left entirely behind, and nothing but pure water evaporated. A. J. P. TAYLOR Conditions for those who remained behind were also bad. P. JAY I left the table behind In the attic. **b** LD MACAULAY But stronger evidence is behind. **c** SHAKES. *Sonn.* My grief lies onward and my joy behind.

2 At the back of something stationary, in the rear; on the far side of something, hidden. OE. ▸**b** *spec.* Behind the scenes in a theatre. E19.

SHAKES. *Jul. Caes.* Damned Casca, like a cur, behind Struck Cæsar on the neck. T. S. ELIOT Shall I part my hair behind? J. SQUIRE A place Of dingy yards with towering buildings behind. *Daily Telegraph* To be caught behind off the last ball of an over.

stop behind: see STOP *verb* 22c.
3 In the rear of something moving; following, trailing; at a less advanced stage of progress, rank, attainment, etc. ME. ▸**b** Less advanced than one should be; in arrears (*with* payments etc.). LME.

JAS. MILL The opponents were not behind in violence. W. S. CHURCHILL In a poll of about 23,000 votes . . I was 1,300 behind and Mr. Mawdsley about 30 lower. B. ENGLAND Now Lt Truly hobbles on from the right, far behind, limping. **b** W. MAXWELL His father gets behind in his spring plowing because of the rains. E. FIGES A bit rushed, having somehow got behind with everything.

come from behind win after lagging.
4 Late; slow in coming forward. Long *obsolete* exc. *dial.* ME.
5 Towards or into the rear; backwards. LME.

WORDSWORTH O'er rough and smooth she trips along, And never looks behind.

▸ **B** *preposition* (in Old English also with dat. obj.).
1 In a place, position, state, etc. left by (a person who or thing which has gone); existing from or belonging to the earlier life of (a person still alive or now dead). (Usu. with pronoun.) OE.

SHAKES. *Twel. N.* He left behind him myself and a sister. G. B. SHAW I had left the follies . . of the old days behind me for ever. K. AMIS The last two and a half years freelancing . . , with even a book behind him. S. HILL The gate clicked shut behind Doctor Sparrow.

2 At the rear or back of (someone or something stationary); on the further side of (esp. so as to be concealed), beyond. OE. ▸**b** *fig.* At the back of as a supporter or as a cause or instigator. M19.

S. JOHNSON They wondered how a youth of spirit could spend the prime of life behind a counter. G. EWART I know that behind her spectacles she/ has the most beautiful eyes. J. LE CARRÉ He lives in Chelsea, just behind Sloane Square. **b** J. MARTINEAU Behind every phenomenon we must assume a power. S. HILL She liked flowers, liked even more the thought behind them. B. ENGLAND At least it would have the sanction of proper authority behind it.

behind bars: see BAR *noun*[1] 2a. ***behind* CLOSED *doors***. ***behind one's back***: see BACK *noun*[1]. ***behind the curtain***: see CURTAIN *noun* 4. ***behind the scenes***: see SCENE. ***behind the veil***: see VEIL *noun* 3. ***hide***

B

behind a person's skirts: see SKIRT *noun* 1. †**behind the hand** = BEHINDHAND.

3 Towards the back or further side of; backwards from; into a position at the rear of. ME. ▸**b** *fig.* Out of one's attention or thought. M19.

AV *Matt.* 26:23 Get thee behind mee, Satan. S. JOHNSON Venturing to look behind him. OED The sun has sunk behind the mountains. L. URIS She walked up behind him and touched his shoulder.

b put behind one refuse to consider.

4 In the rear of; after, following; inferior to in progress, rank, attainment, etc. LME.

R. HOOKER Beasts, though otherwise behind men, may . . in actions of sense and fancy go beyond them. SIR W. SCOTT Behind him rode two gallant squires. E. WAUGH Of the University he said: 'No, I was never here. It just means you start life three years behind the other fellow'. J. LE CARRÉ Peters was three or four behind him in the queue.

behind the curve: see *ahead of the curve* s.v. AHEAD *adverb*. *behind the times*: see TIME *noun*.

5 Later than (a set time). L16.

SHAKES. *A.Y.L.* If you . . come one minute behind your hour, I will think you the most pathetical break-promise.

behind schedule, **behind time** unpunctual, late.

▸**C** *noun*. **1** The buttocks. *colloq.* L18.

2 *AUSTRAL. RULES FOOTBALL.* A kick etc. scoring one point. L19.

behindhand /bɪˈhʌɪndhand/ *adverb & pred. adjective*. M16.
[ORIGIN from BEHIND *preposition* + HAND *noun*, after BEFOREHAND.]

1 In arrears with regard to payments or other obligations. M16.

2 Less advanced than others or than one should be; lacking *in* (a quality etc.). M16.

3 Behind time, late; out of date. E18.

behither /bɪˈhɪðə/ *preposition & adverb*. *obsolete* exc. *dial.* E16.
[ORIGIN from BE- + HITHER: cf. BEHIND etc.]
On this side (of).

Behmenism *noun* var. of BOEHMENISM.

behold /bɪˈhəʊld/ *verb*. *literary* or *arch.* Pa. t. **beheld** /-ˈhɛld/; pa. pple **beheld**, †**beholden** (cf. next).
[ORIGIN Old English *bihaldan* = Old Frisian *bihalda*, Old Saxon *bihaldan*, (Dutch *behouden*), Old High German *bihaltan* (German *behalten*): see BE-, HOLD *verb*.]

†**1** *verb trans.* Hold, retain. OE–E16.

†**2** *verb trans. & intrans.* Concern, relate to; pertain *to*. OE–LME.

†**3** *verb trans. & intrans.* Regard, consider; have regard (*un*)*to*. OE–LME.

4 *verb trans.* See, become aware of by sight; hold in view, watch. OE.

T. MO The pyrotechnical displays . . are really quite something to behold.

5 *verb intrans.* Look. Now only *imper.*, used to call or direct attention: Look! Lo! *arch.* or *literary*. ME.

C. BEATON Behold! A golden door behind him burned in that fair sunlight.

lo and behold: see LO *interjection*[1].

†**6** *verb trans.* Of buildings, land, etc.: look towards, face. LME–L17.

■ **beholder** *noun* a person who beholds, a watcher: LME. **beholding** *noun* seeing, sight; a thing beheld, a vision: ME. **beholding** *adjective* (**a**) looking, watching; (**b**) (*obsolete* exc. *dial.*: orig. an error for *beholden*) under an obligation, dependent: L15.

beholden /bɪˈhəʊld(ə)n/ *pred. adjective*. LME.
[ORIGIN Orig. pa. pple of BEHOLD, which is not otherwise attested in these senses.]

1 Under an obligation (*to*); indebted. LME.

2 Duty-bound. Now *rare* or *obsolete*. LME.

behoof /bɪˈhuːf/ *noun*. *arch.*
[ORIGIN Old English *behōf* = Old Frisian *bihōf*, Middle Dutch & mod. Dutch *behoef*, Middle High German *behuof* (German *behuf*), from West Germanic, formed as BE- + var. of base of HEAVE *verb*.]
Benefit, advantage. Chiefly in ***for behoof of***, ***for the behoof of***, ***on behoof of***, ***on the behoof of***, ***to behoof of***, ***to the behoof of***.

behove /bɪˈhəʊv/ *verb*. Also *__behoove__ /bɪˈhuːv/.
[ORIGIN Old English *behōfian* = Old Frisian *bihōvia*, Middle Low German *behōven*, Middle Dutch *behoeven*, from BEHOOF.]

†**1** *verb trans.* Have need of, require. OE–M17.

†**2** *verb trans. & intrans.* Be physically of use or needful (to). OE–M17.

3 *verb trans.* Be morally required of (a person), be incumbent upon; befit. Now usu. *impers.* in ***behoves to do***, (usu.) ***it behoves to do***, etc. *arch.* OE.

W. IRVING It behoved him to keep on good terms with his pupils.

4 *verb intrans.* Be proper or due, be suited. Now usu. *impers.* in (***it***) ***behoves*** etc. (Foll. by *to*; impers. *to do, that*.) *arch.* OE.

5 *verb intrans.* (with pers. subj.) Be under obligation *to do*. Long *obsolete* exc. *Scot.* LME.

■ **behovely** *adjective* (long *rare*) = BEHOVEFUL OE.

behoveful /bɪˈhəʊvfʊl, -f(ə)l/ *adjective*. *arch.* LME.
[ORIGIN from BEHOOF + -FUL.]
Advantageous, expedient; necessary, fitting.

behung *verb pa. t. & pple* of BEHANG.

beige /beɪʒ, beɪdʒ/ *noun & adjective*. M19.
[ORIGIN French.]

▸**A** *noun*. **1** A fine woollen fabric, usu. undyed and unbleached. M19.

2 A yellowish-grey colour like that of undyed and unbleached wool. L19.

▸**B** *adjective*. Esp. of fabrics: of a yellowish-grey colour. L19.

beigel *noun* var. of BAGEL.

beignet /ˈbɛnjeɪ, bɛnˈjɛ; *foreign* bɛɲɛ (*pl. same*)/ *noun*. Chiefly *N. Amer.* M19.
[ORIGIN French.]
A fritter; *spec.* a square of fried dough eaten hot sprinkled with icing sugar. Usu. in *pl.*

bein /biːn/ *adjective & adverb*. Long *obsolete* exc. *dial.* (chiefly *Scot.*). Also **bien**. ME.
[ORIGIN Unknown.]

▸**A** *adjective*. **1** Pleasant, kindly; nice, good. ME.

2 Comfortable, well-furnished. M16.

3 Comfortably off, well-to-do. M16.

▸**B** *adverb*. Pleasantly, nicely. LME.

being /ˈbiːɪŋ/ *noun*. ME.
[ORIGIN from BE + -ING[1].]

1 Existence, material or abstract; life. ME. ▸**b** Existence in some specified condition, circumstance, etc. E16.

TINDALE *Acts* 17:28 In him we lyve, move & have oure beynge. S. JOHNSON Good humour . . is the balm of being. E. A. FREEMAN The house had no corporate being. TOLKIEN The Light of the Trees I brought into being. **b** COVERDALE *Luke* 9:33 Master here is good beynge for vs. G. BURNET What he has acquired during his being a Bishop. W. FAULKNER Evil is a part of man, . . the same as repentance and being brave.

being-for-itself *PHILOSOPHY* conscious being, being as actuality. **being-in-itself** *PHILOSOPHY* being that lacks conscious awareness, being as potentiality. ***call into being***: see CALL *verb*. ***fleet in being***: see FLEET *noun*[1]. **in being** existing, in existence.

†**2** Condition; standing, position; livelihood. ME–E19.

STEELE Such . . as want help towards getting into some being in the world.

3 Substance, constitution; nature, essence; person. ME.

TREVISA The comparyson bitwene a poynte and a lyne in beynge. M. DE LA ROCHE He awoke with a start, excited in all his being. B. BETTELHEIM Man's innermost being . . —man's soul.

4 That which exists or is conceived as existing; *esp.* a person or other intelligent creature or entity. LME.

BARONESS ORCZY A surging, seething, murmuring crowd, of beings that are human only in name. I. MURDOCH A separate being with troubles and desires of her own. C. SAGAN The probability that we are frequently visited by extraterrestrial beings.

human being: see HUMAN *adjective*. **the Supreme Being** God.

■ **beingness** *noun* M17.

being *verb pres. pple* of BE.

beisa /ˈbeɪsə/ *noun*. M19.
[ORIGIN Amharic.]
A gemsbok of the E. African race, *Oryx gazella beisa*. Also ***beisa oryx***.

Beja /ˈbɛdʒə/ *noun & adjective*. E19.
[ORIGIN African name.]

▸**A** *noun*. Pl. same. A member of a nomadic Cushitic people living between the Nile and the Red Sea; the Cushitic language of this people. E19.

▸**B** *adjective*. Of or pertaining to the Beja. M20.

bejabers /bɪˈdʒeɪbəz/ *interjection*. *Irish*. Also **-jabb-** /-ˈdʒab-/, †**-jap(p)-**. E19.
[ORIGIN Alt. of *by Jesus!*: cf. BEJESUS.]
Expr. amazement or emphasis.

bejant /ˈbiːdʒ(ə)nt/ *noun*. *Scot.* Also †**-jan**. M17.
[ORIGIN French *béjaune*, from *bec jaune* yellow beak, i.e. fledgling, with parasitic *t*.]
A first-year undergraduate, orig. at any Scottish university but now only at St Andrews.

†**bejap(p)ers** *interjection* vars. of BEJABERS.

bejasus *interjection* var. of BEJESUS.

bejel /ˈbeɪdʒ(ə)l, ˈbɛdʒ-/ *noun*. E20.
[ORIGIN Iraqi Arabic]
MEDICINE. A non-venereal form of syphilis formerly endemic in N. Africa and the Middle East.

bejesuit /bɪˈdʒɛzjʊɪt/ *verb trans.* M17.
[ORIGIN from BE- 3, 4 + JESUIT.]
Initiate into Jesuitism; subject to the influence of Jesuits.

bejesus /bɪˈdʒiːzəs/ *interjection*. Also (esp. *Irish*) **bejasus** /bɪˈdʒeɪzəs/. E20.
[ORIGIN Alt. of *by Jesus!*: cf. BEJABERS.]
Expr. amazement or emphasis.

bejewel /bɪˈdʒuːəl/ *verb trans.* Infl. **-ll-**, *__-l-__. M16.
[ORIGIN from BE- 4 + JEWEL *noun*.]
Deck or adorn (as) with jewels; spangle.

bekiss /bɪˈkɪs/ *verb trans.* L16.
[ORIGIN from BE- 1 + KISS *verb*.]
Kiss excessively; cover with kisses.

beknave /bɪˈneɪv/ *verb trans.* E16.
[ORIGIN from BE- 3 + KNAVE *noun*.]
Treat as or call a knave.

beknow /bɪˈnəʊ/ *verb trans.* Long *arch.* & *dial.* Pa. t. **beknew** /bɪˈnjuː/; pa. pple **beknown** /bɪˈnəʊn/. ME.
[ORIGIN from BE- 1 + KNOW *verb*.]
Be or become acquainted with; recognize, acknowledge, know.
be beknown of be aware of, avow, acknowledge.

bel /bɛl/ *noun*[1]. E20.
[ORIGIN from Alexander Graham *Bell* (1847–1922), inventor of the telephone.]
A logarithmic unit used in comparing electrical power levels, intensities of sounds, etc., corresponding to a power ratio of 10 to 1. Cf. DECIBEL.

bel *noun*[2] var. of BAEL.

†**bel** *adjective*. ME–L17.
[ORIGIN Old French (fem. *bele*) from Latin *bellus*, fem. *bella*.]
Fair, fine, beautiful.

belabour /bɪˈleɪbə/ *verb trans.* Also *__-or__. LME.
[ORIGIN from BE- 1, 2 + LABOUR *verb*.]

†**1** Cultivate, till. Only in LME.

2 Buffet, thrash, assail. LME.

†**3** Labour at, ply. Only in 17.

4 Labour (a point etc.); treat at excessive length, overuse. E20.

†**bel-accoil** *noun*. ME–L16.
[ORIGIN Old French *bel acoil* fair welcome.]
Kindly greeting, welcome.

belah /ˈbiːlə/ *noun*. *Austral.* Also **-ar**. M19.
[ORIGIN Wiradhuri *bilaarr*.]
(The timber of) any of various trees of the genus *Casuarina*.

†**belamour** *noun*. L16–E17.
[ORIGIN French, formed as BEL *adjective* + AMOUR.]
A loved one, a sweetheart.

†**belamy** *noun*. ME–L17.
[ORIGIN Old French *bel ami*.]
Fair friend (esp. as a form of address).

belap /bɪˈlap/ *verb trans.* Long *rare*. Infl. **-pp-**. ME.
[ORIGIN from BE- 1 + LAP *verb*[2].]
Lap about, enfold, surround.

belar *noun* var. of BELAH.

Belarusian /ˌbɛlə(ʊ)ˈrʌʃ(ə)n, ˌbɛlə(ʊ)ˈruːsɪən/ *adjective & noun*. Also **Belarussian**. L20.
[ORIGIN from *Belarus* (see below) + -IAN.]

▸**A** *noun*. A native or inhabitant of Belarus, a country in eastern Europe, formerly a republic of the USSR; the Slavonic language of Belarus. L20.

▸**B** *adjective*. Of or pertaining to Belarus, its people, or their language. L20.

belate /bɪˈleɪt/ *verb trans.* Earliest & now only as BELATED. E17.
[ORIGIN from BE- 3 + LATE *adjective*.]
Make late, delay.

belated /bɪˈleɪtɪd/ *adjective*. E17.
[ORIGIN from BELATE + -ED[1].]

1 Overtaken by darkness. *arch.* E17.

G. WHITE Belated shepherd swains See the cowl'd spectre.

2 Delayed; tardy; coming (too) late. M17.

S. T. WARNER I have been shamelessly belated in writing to thank you. D. BAGLEY He . . realized with belated terror that he had nearly been shot.

■ **belatedly** *adverb* L19. **belatedness** *noun* M17.

Belauan *noun & adjective* var. of PALAUAN.

belaud /bɪˈlɔːd/ *verb trans.* M19.
[ORIGIN from BE- 1 + LAUD *verb*.]
Load with praise.

belay /bɪˈleɪ, *in MOUNTAINEERING also* ˈbiːleɪ/ *verb & noun*.
[ORIGIN Old English *belecgan* = Old Frisian *bilega*, Dutch *beleggen*, Old High German *bileggen* (German *belegen*); branch II is app. a re-formation on the Dutch: see BE-, LAY *verb*[1].]

▸**A** *verb* †**I 1** *verb trans.* Surround, enclose, adorn, etc., *with*; beset, beleaguer; waylay. OE–M18.

SPENSER A woodmans iacket . . Of Lincolne greene, belayd with silver lace. DRYDEN The speedy Horse all passages belay.

▸**II 2** *verb trans. & intrans.* *NAUTICAL.* Fix (a rope) round a cleat, pin, etc., to secure it; secure (something) thus. M16. ▸**b** In *imper.*, freq. foll. by *there*: stop! enough! no more of (something)! *slang*. E19.
belaying pin a heavy wooden or iron pin which can be fixed in position for belaying on.

3 *transf.* **a** *verb trans. gen.* Make fast, tie, secure. M18. ▸**b** *verb trans. & intrans.* *MOUNTAINEERING.* Fix (a rope) round a rock, piton, etc.; secure (a climber, oneself) in this way. E20.

▸ **B** *noun. MOUNTAINEERING.* An act of belaying; the point where this is done. **E20.**
running belay, thread belay, etc.

bel canto /bɛl ˈkantəʊ/ *noun phr.* **L19.**
[ORIGIN Italian = fine song.]
(A style of) singing characterized by full rich broad tone, legato phrasing, and accomplished technique.

belch /bɛltʃ/ *verb & noun.* Also (long *obsolete* exc. *dial.*) **belk** /bɛlk/. See also BOLK.
[ORIGIN Old English: forms in /k/ repr. *bælcan*, forms in /tʃ/ repr. either a related form or a shortening of *belċettan*, *beal-*.]
▸ **A** *verb.* **1** *verb intrans.* Emit wind noisily from the stomach through the mouth. **OE.**
2 *verb trans.* Emit by belching; utter forcibly, give vent to. Usu. foll. by *out.* **OE.**
3 *verb trans.* †**a** *lit.* Vomit. **M16–L18.** ▸**b** Eject, send *forth* or *out*; expel violently. **L16.**
4 *verb intrans.* Gush out; flow in gulps. **L16.**
▸ **B** *noun.* **1** An act of belching. **E16.**
2 Poor beer; malt liquor. *arch. slang.* **L17.**

belcher /ˈbɛltʃə/ *noun. arch.* **E19.**
[ORIGIN Jem *Belcher* (d. 1811), English boxer.]
A neckerchief with white spots on a blue ground.

beldam /ˈbɛldəm/ *noun. arch.* Also **-dame. LME.**
[ORIGIN from BEL *adjective* + DAM *noun*[2].]
†**1** A grandmother; any remote ancestress. **LME–M19.**
2 An old woman; a hag, a virago. **L16.**

beleaguer /bɪˈliːgə/ *verb trans.* **L16.**
[ORIGIN Dutch *belegeren*, formed as BE- + LEAGUER *noun*[1] or *verb*.]
Besiege (*lit.* or *fig.*).
■ **beleaguerer** *noun* (*rare*) **E17.**

belee /bɪˈliː/ *verb trans. rare.* Pa. t. & pple **beleed. E17.**
[ORIGIN from BE- 4 + LEE *noun*[1].]
Cut off from the wind, becalm.

belemnite /ˈbɛləmnʌɪt/ *noun.* **E17.**
[ORIGIN mod. Latin *belemnites*, from Greek *belemnon* dart: see -ITE[1].]
PALAEONTOLOGY. A tapering sharp-pointed fossil from the internal shell of an extinct cephalopod of the order Belemnoidea, most abundant in Jurassic and Cretaceous deposits; the animal itself.
■ **belemnitic** /-ˈnɪtɪk/ *adjective* pertaining to or yielding belemnites **M19. belemnoid** *adjective & noun* (a cephalopod) belonging to Belemnoidea; pertaining to or resembling an animal of this order: **L19.**

bel esprit /bɛl ɛspri/ *noun phr.* Pl. ***beaux esprits*** /boz ɛspri/. **M17.**
[ORIGIN French = fine mind.]
A brilliant or witty person.

Belfast sink /ˈbɛlfɑːst sɪŋk/ *noun phr.* **M20.**
[ORIGIN from *Belfast*, a city in Northern Ireland + SINK *noun*.]
A type of deep rectangular kitchen sink, traditionally made of glazed white porcelain.

belfry /ˈbɛlfri/ *noun.* **ME.**
[ORIGIN Old French *berfrei*, later *belfrei*, *be(l)froi* (mod. *beffroi*), in medieval Latin *bel-*, *berfridus*, etc., from Frankish (= Middle High German *ber(c)vrit*), prob. from verb meaning 'protect' + base of FRITH *noun*[1]: forms with *l* reinforced by assoc. with *bell*.]
1 A (movable) wooden tower employed as a siege engine. Long *obsolete* exc. *hist.* **ME.**
2 A bell tower, usu. attached to a church etc., but sometimes standing separate. **ME.** ▸**b** A chamber or storey in which bells are hung. **M16.** ▸**c** A chamber or space where bell-ringers stand. **M16.**
b ***have bats in the belfry***: see BAT *noun*[3].
3 A shed for cattle, carts, etc. *dial.* **M16.**
4 A housing or canopy for a ship's bell, often highly decorated. **M18.**
5 The head. *slang.* **E20.**

Belgae /ˈbɛldʒiː/ *noun pl.* **E17.**
[ORIGIN Latin.]
An ancient people of N. Gaul and S. Britain.

†**belgard** *noun.* **L16–E19.**
[ORIGIN Italian *bel guardo*.]
A kind or loving look.

Belgian /ˈbɛldʒ(ə)n/ *noun & adjective.* **E17.**
[ORIGIN from *Belgium* (see below) + -AN.]
(A native or inhabitant) of Belgium, orig. the whole Continental territory of the Belgae or the Low Countries generally, since 1830 an independent country on the south shore of the North Sea and English Channel.
– SPECIAL COLLOCATIONS: **Belgian block** *US* a type of stone paving block; **Belgian hare** a dark-red slender long-eared breed of domestic rabbit.

Belgic /ˈbɛldʒɪk/ *adjective.* **L16.**
[ORIGIN from Latin *Belgicus*, from BELGAE: see -IC.]
1 Of or pertaining to the Belgae. **L16.**
2 Of the Low Countries. **E17.**

Belgie /ˈbɛldʒi/ *noun.* Now *derog.* **E17.**
[ORIGIN from BELGIAN + -IE.]
A Belgian.

Belgravian /bɛlˈgreɪvɪən/ *noun & adjective.* **M19.**
[ORIGIN from *Belgravia* (see below), from *Belgrave* Square in this district: see -IA[1], -AN.]
(A resident) of Belgravia, a fashionable part of London south of Knightsbridge.

Belial /ˈbiːlɪəl/ *noun.* **ME.**
[ORIGIN Hebrew *bĕliyya'al* worthlessness.]
The Devil, Satan.

belibel /bɪˈlʌɪb(ə)l/ *verb trans.* Infl. **-ll-**, ***-l-. E17.**
[ORIGIN from BE- 1 + LIBEL *verb*.]
Assail with libels; traduce, slander.

belie /bɪˈlʌɪ/ *verb trans.* Pa. t. **belied** /bɪˈlʌɪd/; pres. pple & verbal noun **belying** /bɪˈlʌɪɪŋ/.
[ORIGIN Old English *belēogan* = Old Frisian *biliuga*, Old High German *biliugan* (German *belügen*): see BE-, LIE *verb*[2].]
▸ **I** †**1** Deceive by lying. Only in **OE.**
2 Tell lies about (someone); slander. **ME.** ▸†**b** Tell lies about (*the truth*, something). **LME–M17.**

> D. HUME It was rendered criminal to belie the subjects of the king.

†**3** Give the lie to, contradict; reject as false **L16–M17.**

> AV *Jer.* 5:12 They haue belyed the Lord, and said; It is not he.

4 Misrepresent; give a false notion of. **E17.** ▸**b** Disguise, mask. **E18.**

> MILTON He a declar'd Papist, If his own letter to the Pope belye him not. G. GREENE Her face didn't belie her nature, for she was the kindest woman I knew. **b** L. DEIGHTON The grimy condition of the coasters was belied by the fresh rain that had glossed their decks and given their hulls the polish of old jackboots.

5 Act or speak at variance with, be false or faithless to; show to be false, fail to corroborate or justify. **L17.**

> W. COWPER Novels . . Belie their name, and offer nothing new. M. BEERBOHM Only in that he forgot there was nothing to pay did he belie his calm. M. BRAGG There was a silence after he stepped into the cottage, one so marked that it belied the existence of the querulous voice which had bidden him in. H. CLURMAN The actor who merely 'imitates' the surface impression that we might gather from a perusal of the play's text . . belies the art of the theatre. J. C. OATES That Veronica had a dainty appetite was bluntly belied by her full, comfortable figure.

▸ †**II 6** Fill with lies. *rare* (Shakes.). Only in **E17.**
■ **belier** *noun* a person who belies **M16.**

belief /bɪˈliːf/ *noun.* **ME.**
[ORIGIN Alt. of Old English *ġelēafa*: cf. BELIEVE.]
1 Trust, confidence; faith. (Foll. by *in*, †*of* a person or thing.) **ME.** ▸**b** *spec.* Trust in God; religious faith; acceptance of any received theology (passing into sense 2). **ME.**

> TENNYSON Beyond mine old belief in womanhood. A. J. P. TAYLOR He had no belief in the administrative capacity of the Unionists. **b** CARLYLE That war of the Puritans . . the war of Belief against Unbelief. C. P. SNOW He went to church out of propriety more than belief.

2 Mental acceptance of a statement, fact, doctrine, thing, etc., as true or existing. (Foll. by *in* a thing, *in* or *of* a statement etc., *that* something is the case.) **ME.**

> P. SIDNEY My only defence shal be beleefe of nothing. OED His statements are unworthy of belief. ARNOLD BENNETT He had been brought up in the belief that the Dragon was a place of sin. R. D. LAING Many people are prepared to have faith in the sense of scientifically indefensible belief in an untested hypothesis.

beyond belief: see BEYOND *preposition* 6. ***to the best of one's belief***: see BEST *adjective* etc.
3 The thing believed; a proposition or set of propositions held to be true; a religion; an opinion or persuasion. **ME.**

> M. W. MONTAGU It is my belief you will not be at all the richer. J. GALSWORTHY If he had a political belief, it was a tax on wheat. C. S. FORESTER Some of his beliefs and convictions had been almost shaken lately.

4 ***the Belief***, †***one's Belief***, the Apostles' Creed. *arch.* **ME.**

believe /bɪˈliːv/ *verb.*
[ORIGIN Late Old English *belȳfan*, *belēfan*, replacing, by prefix-substitution, earlier *ġelēfan*, (West Saxon) *ġelīefan* = Old Frisian *gelēva*, Old Saxon *gilōban* (Dutch *gelooven*), Old High German *gilouben* (German *glauben*), Gothic *galaubjan*, from Germanic, formed as Y- + LIEF.]
▸ **I** *verb intrans.* **1** Have confidence or faith *in* or (*arch.*) *on* (a person, God, etc.). **LOE.**

> AV *John* 3:16 For God . . gave his only begotten Sonne: that whosoever beleeveth in him, should not perish, but have eternall life. G. B. SHAW I am going to be frank with you. I don't believe in doctors. G. BOYCOTT Be positive and believe in yourself, otherwise you will start to doubt your own ability.

2 Put one's trust or have confidence *in* (or †*on*) the truth of (a proposition, doctrine, etc.), the efficacy or advisability of (a principle, institution, practice, etc.), the existence of (a person or thing), the occurrence of (an event). **LOE.**

> M. W. MONTAGU I find that I have . . a strong disposition to believe in miracles. J. B. PRIESTLEY It is only up here that you can believe in such people as Heathcliffe. G. VIDAL Sullivan believed in exercise. A. J. P. TAYLOR Protection was carried by the Conservatives who claimed to believe in free enterprise.

3 *absol.* Exercise (esp. religious) faith; *gen.* hold an opinion, think. **LME.**

> HENRY FIELDING I will not believe so meanly of you. G. B. SHAW The right to think and believe according to our conscience. B. RUBENS How long ago, Norman thought, had he truly believed, and when and at what precise moment, had he lost his faith.

†**4** Give credence *to* (a person, statement, etc.). **LME–M17.**
▸ **II** *verb trans.* **5** Accept the truth or reality of (a proposition etc.). **ME.**

> J. TYNDALL The Guide Chef evidently did not believe a word of it. E. O'NEILL The bartender cannot believe his luck for a moment.

6 Hold as true, be of the opinion, *that*; (with adverbial obj.) think *so* etc.; *ellipt.* (passing into *verb intrans.*, parenthetically) think that it is, was, etc. **ME.**

> DEFOE He believed there were more wolves a coming. B. JOWETT Some one—Critias, I believe—went on to say [etc.]. E. WAUGH There's another sister too, I believe, in the schoolroom. G. ORWELL How easy it was, thought Winston, . . to believe that the physical type set up by the Party as an ideal . . existed and even predominated.

7 Give credence to (someone making statements etc.). **LME.**

> SHAKES. *Sonn.* When my love swears that she is made of truth, I do believe her.

†**8** Hold as true the existence of. **L15–M18.**

> G. BERKELEY Shall we believe a God?

9 Think or suppose (someone or something) to be or *to be*. **E16.**

> MILTON Our Conqu'ror whom I now Of force believe Almighty. B. LOVELL Anaximander believed our world to be only one of many.

– PHRASES: **believe it or not** *colloq.* it is surprising though true. ***believe me***: see ***believe you me*** below. **believe one's ear(s)**, **believe one's eyes**, etc., accept that what one apparently perceives is true (usu. in neg. contexts). **believe you me**, **believe me** *colloq.* it really is so. ***make believe***: see MAKE *verb*. **would you believe it?** *colloq.*: emphasizing the truth of a surprising fact etc. ***you'd better believe (it)***: see BETTER *adjective* etc.
■ **believaˈbility** *noun* ability to be believed; credibility: **M19. believable** *adjective* able to be believed; credible: **LME. believer** *noun* a person who believes, *esp.* in a particular religion (***Old Believer***: see OLD *adjective*) **LME. believingly** *adverb* with belief or faith **M17.**

belike /bɪˈlʌɪk/ *adverb & adjective. arch.* **M16.**
[ORIGIN from BY *preposition* + LIKE *adjective* or *noun*[2].]
▸ **A** *adverb.* Probably; perhaps. Freq. *iron.* **M16.**
▸ †**B** *adjective.* Like, likely (*to do* something). **M16–E19.**

Belisha beacon /bɪˈliːʃə ˈbiːk(ə)n/ *noun phr.* **M20.**
[ORIGIN Leslie Hore-*Belisha* (1893–1957), Brit. politician, Minister of Transport 1931–7.]
A black and white post topped by an amber-coloured globe (now usu. containing a flashing light), erected on the pavement at each end of a pedestrian crossing.

belittle /bɪˈlɪt(ə)l/ *verb trans.* Orig. *US.* **L18.**
[ORIGIN from BE- 3 + LITTLE *adjective*.]
1 Make small; diminish in size. **L18.**
2 Depreciate, decry. **L18.**
3 Cause to appear small; dwarf. **M19.**
■ **belittlement** *noun* **L19. belittlingly** *adverb* in a belittling manner, depreciatingly **L20.**

belive /bɪˈlʌɪv/ *adverb. obsolete* exc. *Scot.* **ME.**
[ORIGIN from BY *preposition* + oblique form of LIFE *noun*: cf. ALIVE.]
Quickly, speedily; before long, soon.

Belizean /bɛˈliːzɪən/ *noun & adjective.* Also **-ian. M20.**
[ORIGIN from *Belize* (see below) + -AN, -IAN.]
(A native or inhabitant) of Belize, a country on the Caribbean coast of Central America, formerly British Honduras.

belk *verb & noun* see BELCH.

bell /bɛl/ *noun*[1].
[ORIGIN Old English *belle* = Middle Low German, Middle Dutch *belle* (Dutch *bel*): perh. rel. to BELL *verb*[1].]
1 A hollow body formed to emit a sound when struck, typically of cast metal in a deep cup shape widening at the lip, and emitting a clear musical note when struck by a clapper or hammer usu. suspended within it; any instrument or device designed to emit a similar sound for calling attention etc. Also, the sounding of such an instrument or device for summoning worshippers to church, schoolchildren to classes, warning of a fire or other hazard, etc. **OE.**
alarm bell, church bell, dinner bell, doorbell, electric bell, fire bell, handbell, school bell, sleigh bell, wedding bells, etc.
2 *spec.* ▸**a** A bell rung to tell the hours; the bell of a clock. **LME.** ▸**b** *NAUTICAL.* The bell which is struck on board ship every half-hour, indicating by the number of strokes the number of half-hours elapsed in a watch; a period thus indicated. **E19.** ▸**c** In boxing etc., the bell rung to mark the start or end of a round. **M20.** ▸**d** A telephone call. *colloq.* **L20.**

> **b** R. H. DANA At seven bells in the morning all hands were called aft.

3 Any object or part shaped like a bell; *spec.*: ▸**a** A bell-shaped corolla of a flower; the female flowering cone of the hop. Also in the names of plants with bell-shaped flowers. **L16.** ▸**b** A bell-shaped vessel. **M17.** ▸**c** *ARCHITECTURE.* The part of a Corinthian or composite capital around which the foliage and volutes are arranged. **M17.** ▸**d** *MUSIC.* The flared open end of a wind instrument. **E19.**

a bluebell, Canterbury bells, Coventry bells, harebell, etc.

– **PHRASES:** *(as)* ***clear as a bell***: see **CLEAR** *adjective.* **bear away the bell**, **bear the bell** take first place, win. **bell, book, and candle**: a formula for cursing (alluding to the rite of excommunication). **bells and whistles** *COMPUTING (colloq.)* speciously attractive but superfluous facilities. **bells of Ireland** the shell flower, *Moluccella laevis.* ***cap and bells***: see **CAP** *noun*[1]. ***diving bell***: see **DIVING** *verbal noun.* ***hell's bells***: see **HELL** *noun.* **ring a bell** *colloq.* awaken a memory. **ring the bell** *colloq.* be the best of the lot (in allusion to a fairground strength-testing machine). ***ring the bells backward(s)***: see **BACKWARD** *adverb* 8. **saved by the bell** in boxing, saved by the end of a round from being counted out; *fig.* saved (from an unpleasant occurrence) in the nick of time. ***slow bell***: see **SLOW** *adjective & adverb.* **sound as a bell** very sound, in good order or health. ***tubular bells***: see **TUBULAR** *adjective* 1. ***warm the bell***: see **WARM** *verb.*

– **COMB.:** **bell-animal**, **bell-animalcule** = **VORTICELLA**; **bellbird** any of various S. American or Australasian birds with a clear ringing call, *esp.* a cotinga of the genus *Procnias*; **bell-bottomed** *adjective* (of trousers) flared below the knee; **bell-bottoms** bell-bottomed trousers; **bellboy** *N. Amer.* a pageboy in a hotel or club; **bell buoy** a buoy with a warning bell rung by wave motion; **bell captain** *N. Amer.* a supervisor of a group of bellboys; **bell-cord** a cord that is pulled to ring a bell; **bell-cot(e)** a shelter protecting a bell; **bell-crater** *GREEK ANTIQUITIES* a large wine-mixing bowl shaped like an inverted bell; **bell curve** a graph of a normal (Gaussian) distribution; **bellflower** a campanula (***ivy-leaved bellflower***: see **IVY** *noun*); **bell-founder**, **bell-founding**, **bell-foundry** a caster, the casting, a manufactory, of large bells; **bell glass** a bell-shaped glass cover for plants; **bell-hanger** a person who installs bells; **bell heather** *Erica cinerea*, a common heath with bell-shaped flowers; also called ***fine-leaved heath***; **bellhop** *N. Amer.* = ***bellboy*** above; **bellhouse** *arch.* a belfry; **bell jar** a bell-shaped glass esp. for covering instruments or containing gas in a laboratory; **bell lyra** = ***lyra glockenspiel*** s.v. **GLOCKENSPIEL** 2; **bellman** *hist.* a town crier; **bell metal** an alloy of copper and tin (with more tin than in bronze), used for casting bells; **bell miner** an Australian honeyeater, *Manorina melanophrys*, noted for its bell-like call; **bell pepper** a large bell-shaped variety of capsicum; **bell pull** a cord or handle attached to a bell wire, by which a bell is rung; **bell punch** a punch which perforates a ticket and rings a bell at the same time; **bell push** a button that is pushed to ring an electric bell; **bell-ringer** a practitioner of bell-ringing; **bell-ringing** the ringing of church etc. bells with changes, freq. as a hobby; **bell rope** a rope by which a bell is rung, esp. in a church; **bell-shaped** *adjective* shaped like a bell, *esp.* having the shape of an inverted cup widening at the lip; **bell skirt** a skirt flared widely from a narrow waist; **bell sleeve** a long sleeve flared at the lower edge; **bell string** = ***bell rope*** above; **bell tent** a conical tent with a central pole; **bell-topper** a top hat, esp. one with a bell-shaped crown. **bellwether** (***a***) the leading sheep of a flock, on whose neck a bell is hung; (***b***) a ringleader; (***c***) a clamorous person; (***d***) something which sets a standard or leads a trend; **bell wire** a wire pulled to ring a bell, esp. at a door; **bellwort** *N. Amer.* a plant of the genus *Uvularia* of the lily family, bearing yellow bell-like flowers.

■ **bell-like** /-l-l-/ *adjective* resembling (that of) a bell, bell-shaped, having a clear musical note **M18.**

bell /bɛl/ *noun*[2]. Now chiefly *Scot.* **L15.**
[**ORIGIN** Unknown: cf. synon. Dutch *bel*, Middle Dutch *bellen* bubble up; corresp. to **BELL** *verb*[4].]
A bubble.

bell /bɛl/ *noun*[3]. **E16.**
[**ORIGIN** from **BELL** *verb*[1].]
The cry of a stag or buck at rutting time.

Bell /bɛl/ *noun*[4]. *US.* **M20.**
[**ORIGIN** The name of the N. Amer. *Bell* System or Telephone Company (from the surname of Alexander Graham *Bell* (1847–1922), Scots-born Amer. inventor of the telephone), part of AT&T and before divestiture in 1984 the major US telephone company.]
1 ***Ma Bell***, a familiar name for the Bell System. **M20.**
2 ***Baby Bell***, any of the subsidiary regional US telephone companies after divestiture. **L20.**

bell /bɛl/ *verb*[1].
[**ORIGIN** Old English *bellan*, corresp. to Old High German *bellan* (German *bellen*) bark, bray: cf. Old Norse *belja* and **BELLOW** *verb.*]
1 *verb intrans.* Bellow, roar (*spec.* of a stag or buck at rutting time). **OE.**
2 *verb trans.* Shout, bellow forth. **L16.**

bell /bɛl/ *verb*[2] *intrans. obsolete* exc. *Scot.* Pa. pple **bollen** /ˈbɒlən/. **ME.**
[**ORIGIN** Perh. from Old English *belgan*, pa. pple *bolgen* swell.]
Swell up, be puffed out.

bell /bɛl/ *verb*[3]. **LME.**
[**ORIGIN** from **BELL** *noun*[1].]
1 *verb trans.* Provide or equip with a bell. **LME.**
bell the cat take the danger of a shared enterprise upon oneself (in allusion to the fable in which mice proposed hanging a bell around a cat's neck so as to be warned of its approach).
2 *verb intrans.* Of hops: be or begin to be in flower (the female flowers being in bell-shaped cones). **L16.**
3 *verb trans. & intrans.* (Cause to) spread or flare *out* like the lip of a bell. **L19.**

bell /bɛl/ *verb*[4] *intrans. obsolete* exc. *dial.* **L16.**
[**ORIGIN** from **BELL** *noun*[2].]
Bubble.

belladonna /bɛləˈdɒnə/ *noun.* **M18.**
[**ORIGIN** mod. Latin from Italian *bella donna* lit. 'fair lady'.]
1 ***belladonna lily***, a southern African amaryllis, *Amaryllis belladonna*, with red or white flowers. **M18.**
2 a A therapeutic preparation of the leaves and root of deadly nightshade, of which the active principle is atropine. **L18.** ▸**b** Deadly nightshade, *Atropa belladonna.* **M19.**

bellarmine /ˈbɛləmiːn/ *noun.* **M17.**
[**ORIGIN** St Robert F. R. *Bellarmine* (1542–1621), Jesuit cardinal and theologian.]
hist. A large glazed drinking jug in the form of a pot-bellied burlesque likeness of Cardinal Bellarmine.

belle /bɛl/ *noun.* **E17.**
[**ORIGIN** French, fem. of *bel*, **BEAU**, from Latin *bella* fem. of *bellus* pretty.]
A beautiful woman; *the* reigning beauty *of* a place etc.

J. GRENFELL I'd like a great big . . party And the belle of the ball is me. E. MCBAIN A Southern belle waiting to be asked for a dance.

bathing belle: see **BATHE** *verb* 5. ***yellow belle***: see **YELLOW** *adjective.*

belled /bɛld/ *adjective.* **M18.**
[**ORIGIN** from **BELL** *noun*[1], *verb*[3]: see **-ED**[2], **-ED**[1].]
1 (With flowers) shaped like a bell. **M18.**
2 Having a bell or bells. **M19.**

Belleek /bɛˈliːk/ *noun.* **M19.**
[**ORIGIN** A town in Fermanagh, N. Ireland.]
In full ***Belleek ware*** etc. A light, fragile kind of porcelain pottery produced in Belleek.

belle époque /bɛl eɪˈpɒk/ *noun phr.* Pl. **belles époques** /bɛlz eɪˈpɒk/. **M20.**
[**ORIGIN** French = fine period.]
A period of settled comfort and prosperity, spec. *the* period in France from the late 19th cent. to the First World War.

belle laide /bɛl lɛd/ *noun phr.* Pl. **-s -s** (pronounced same). **E20.**
[**ORIGIN** French, from *belle* beautiful + *laide* ugly (fem. adjectives).]
An attractive though ugly woman.

belleric /bɪˈlɛrɪk/ *noun.* Now *rare* or *obsolete.* **M17.**
[**ORIGIN** French *belléric* ult. from medieval Arab. *balīlaj* from Persian *balīla.*]
The fruit of the Indian tree *Terminalia bellirica*, a source of tannin. Also ***belleric myrobalan.***

belles laides *noun phr.* pl. of **BELLE LAIDE.**

belles-lettres /bɛllɛtr/ *noun pl.* (occas. treated as *sing.*). **M17.**
[**ORIGIN** French, lit. 'fine letters'.]
Studies or writings of a purely literary character, *esp.* essays, criticism, etc. Orig. more widely, literature generally, the humanities.

belletrist /bɛlˈlɛtrɪst/ *noun.* Also †**belles-lettreist.** **E19.**
[**ORIGIN** from **BELLES-LETTRES** + **-IST.**]
A devotee or practitioner of *belles-lettres.*
■ **belletrism** *noun* the study or composition of *belles-lettres* **M20.** **belleˈtristic** *adjective* of or pertaining to *belles-lettres* **E19.** **belleˈtristical** *adjective* = **BELLETRISTIC** **L18.**

bellicose /ˈbɛlɪkəʊs/ *adjective.* **LME.**
[**ORIGIN** Latin *bellicosus*, from *bellicus* warlike, from *bellum* war: see **-IC**, **-OSE**[1].]
Inclined to war or fighting; warlike.

D. MORTMAN Her fingers curled into a bellicose fist. T. KIZZIA For the government to take away native hunting rights . . would be a bellicose act by an outside power.

■ **bellicosity** /bɛlɪˈkɒsɪti/ *noun* warlike inclination **M19.**

bellied /ˈbɛlɪd/ *adjective.* **L15.**
[**ORIGIN** from **BELLY** *noun*, *verb*: see **-ED**[2], **-ED**[1].]
1 Having a belly (usu. of a specified size or form). **L15.** ▸**b** Big-bellied, corpulent; *fig.* bombastic. **M16.**
2 Made large and full; blown or puffed out. **L16.**

belligerence /bɪˈlɪdʒ(ə)r(ə)ns/ *noun.* **E19.**
[**ORIGIN** from **BELLIGERENT** + **-ENCE.**]
The carrying on of hostilities; pugnacious behaviour; the position or status of a belligerent.
■ **belligerency** *noun* = **BELLIGERENCE** **M19.**

belligerent /bɪˈlɪdʒ(ə)r(ə)nt/ *adjective & noun.* Also †**-ant.** **L16.**
[**ORIGIN** Latin *belligerant-* pres. ppl stem of *belligerare* wage war, from *belliger* waging war, from *bellum* war: later irreg. assim. to *gerent-* pres. ppl stem of *gerere* bear, carry, carry on; see **-GEROUS**, **-ENT.**]
▸ **A** *adjective.* **1** Waging regular war as recognized by the law of nations; pugnacious, aggressively hostile. **L16.**
2 Of or pertaining to a belligerent. **M19.**
▸ **B** *noun.* A nation, party, or person engaged in conflict. **E19.**
■ **belligerently** *adverb* **M19.**

†**belligerous** *adjective.* **M16–L18.**
[**ORIGIN** from Latin *belliger*: see **BELLIGERENT**, **-GEROUS.**]
Waging war, belligerent.

Bellini /bɛˈliːni/ *noun.* **M20.**
[**ORIGIN** Named after Giovanni *Bellini* (c 1430/40–1516), Venetian painter (the cocktail is said to have been invented in Venice).]
A cocktail consisting of peach juice mixed with champagne.

bellipotent /bɪˈlɪpət(ə)nt/ *adjective.* Now *rare* or *obsolete.* **M17.**
[**ORIGIN** Latin *bellipotent-*, *-ens*, from *bellum* war + *potens* mighty, **POTENT** *adjective*[2].]
Mighty or powerful in war.

Bellona /bɛˈləʊnə/ *noun.* **L16.**
[**ORIGIN** Latin, the Roman goddess of war, from *bellum* war.]
A war goddess; a spirited woman of commanding presence.

bellow /ˈbɛləʊ/ *verb & noun.* **ME.**
[**ORIGIN** Perh. from late Old English *bylgan* rel. to **BELL** *verb*[1].]
▸ **A** *verb.* **1** *verb intrans.* Of a bull or excited cow: roar. Of another animal or a human: roar like a bull; cry in a loud deep voice, shout; roar with pain. Of a thing: make a loud roaring noise. **ME.**

MILTON Not fit for that liberty which they . . bellowed for. WORDSWORTH And Ocean bellow from his rocky shore.

2 *verb trans.* Utter or proclaim loudly and usu. angrily; give forth with loud noise. Freq. foll. by *out*, *forth.* **L16.**

A. RANSOME He put his hand like a trumpet to his mouth and bellowed one word. K. VONNEGUT Everything that any one of us said . . was bellowed out at the crowd through . . horns.

▸ **B** *noun.* A bellowing sound; a roar. **L18.**
■ **bellower** *noun* a person who or thing which bellows **M17.**

bellows /ˈbɛləʊz/ *noun pl.* (occas. treated as *sing.*). **ME.**
[**ORIGIN** Prob. repr. Old English *belga*, *belgum* pl. of *bel(i)ġ*, *bæl(i)ġ* **BELLY** *noun*, abbreviation of *blǣstbel(i)ġ* 'blowing bag' = Old Norse *blástrbelgr*: cf. German *Blasebalg.*]
1 A portable or fixed contrivance for producing a blast of air, esp. for fanning a fire or for supplying an organ, harmonium, etc. (The simplest form consists of two boards connected by flexible sides and enclosing a cavity of alterable volume so that air may be drawn in and then expelled through an attached nozzle.) **ME.** ▸**b** *fig.* That which blows up or fans the fires of passion etc. **LME.** ▸**c** *fig.* The lungs. **E17.**

b KEATS My voice is not a bellows unto ire.

pair of bellows a two-handled bellows used to blow a fire. **c bellows to mend** *colloq.* short wind.

2 A flexible sleeve connecting the lens to the body of a camera. **L19.**

– **COMB.:** **bellows-blower** a person who works the bellows of an organ etc.; **bellows-fish** the snipefish, *Macrorhamphosus scolopax*; **bellows pocket** a patch pocket with side folds allowing it to expand or lie flat.

†**bellows** *verb trans.* **E17–M18.**
[**ORIGIN** from **BELLOWS** *noun.*]
Blow (with bellows); gather *up* (wind).

Bell's inequality /bɛlz ɪnɪˈkwɒlɪti/ *noun phr.* **L20.**
[**ORIGIN** John S. *Bell* (1928–90), Brit. physicist.]
The statement (serving as a test of the validity of quantum theory) that the number of pairs of particles measured as having positive spin in one pair out of three directions is less than the total number of pairs measured as having positive spin in the other two pairs of directions.

Bell's palsy /bɛlz ˈpɔːlzi/ *noun phr.* **M19.**
[**ORIGIN** Sir Charles *Bell* (1774–1842), Scot. anatomist.]
MEDICINE. Paralysis of the facial nerve causing muscular weakness in one side of the face with drooping of the corner of the mouth and inability to close the eye.

†**belluine** *adjective.* **E17–M18.**
[**ORIGIN** Latin *belluinus*, from *bellua* beast: see **-INE**[1].]
Pertaining to or characteristic of beasts; brutal.

bellum /ˈbɛləm/ *noun.* **E20.**
[**ORIGIN** Iraqi Arabic *belem.*]
A small wooden boat used to carry passengers for short distances along the coasts of the Persian Gulf.

belly /ˈbɛli/ *noun.*
[**ORIGIN** Old English *belġ* var. of *bæl(i)ġ* (West Saxon) *biel(i)ġ*, *byl(i)ġ* = Middle Dutch *balch*, Old High German *balg*, Old Norse *belgr*, Gothic *balgs* from Germanic (= bag), from a base meaning 'be inflated, swell'.]
▸ †**I 1** A bag, a purse. Only in **OE.**
▸ **II** Of humans (increasingly regarded as colloq. or coarse) and animals.
2 The cavity of the human body from the diaphragm to the groin, containing the stomach, bowels, etc.; the abdomen; the front surface of the body from waist to groin. **ME.** ▸**b** The part of a garment covering the belly. **L16.**
3 The corresponding part or surface of the body of an animal. **LME.** ▸**b** In full ***belly-wool.*** The inferior wool from a sheep's belly. *Austral. & NZ.* **M19.** ▸**c** In full ***belly of pork.*** A cut of pork from the underside between the legs. **L19.**

MILTON A monstrous Serpent on his Belly prone. C. A. JOHNS The Common Curlew . . belly white, with longitudinal dusky spots.

4 The stomach; the body as needing food; appetite; gluttony. **LME.** ▸†**b** The bowels. **LME–L17.**

S. JOHNSON He who does not mind his belly, will hardly mind any thing else.

5 The womb. LME.

SHAKES. *L.L.L.* She's quick; the child brags in her belly already.

†**6** The internal cavity of the body. L15–M17.

R. BERNARD It made my heart cold in my belly.

▸ **III** Of things.

7 The internal cavity or interior of anything, whether material or abstract. M16.

J. POTTER Ships of Burden . . having large and capacious Bellies. J. A. FROUDE A . . candle lighted in the belly of a dark dead past.

8 The bulging part of anything, e.g. of a pot or bottle, a vein of ore, etc.; a concave surface; the front, inner, or lower surface of anything. L16.

SPENSER Leaning on the belly of a pot. R. H. DANA To fall from aloft and be caught in the belly of a sail. G. JONES Put the belly of your hand here on my heart and swear it.

9 *spec.* ▸**a** The surface of a violin etc. across which the strings pass. L16. ▸**b** The thicker part of a muscle. E17. ▸**c** The soundboard of a piano. M19. ▸**d** The under part of the fuselage of an aircraft. E20.

– COMB.: **bellyache** *noun & verb* (*a*) *noun* pain or discomfort in the abdomen, colic; *slang* a querulous complaint; (*b*) *verb intrans.* (*slang*) complain whiningly, grumble; **bellyband** a band around a horse's belly for holding carriage shafts etc. in place; *slang* a wide belt or corset; **belly button** *colloq.* the navel; **belly dance** a Middle Eastern solo dance by a woman, involving the rippling of her abdominal muscles; **belly dancer** a woman who performs belly dances; **bellyflop** *noun & verb* (*colloq.*) (make) a dive landing flat on the belly; **belly-god** (*arch.* exc. *Jamaican*) a glutton; **belly landing** the crash-landing of an aircraft on its belly without the use of the undercarriage; **belly laugh** *colloq.* a deep unrestrained laugh; **belly-timber** (*obsolete* exc. *dial.*) food, provisions; **belly-up** *adverb & adjective* in or into a position with the belly uppermost, esp. (of a fish) in or into such a position as a result of death; *fig.* (of businesses, projects, etc.) in or into a state of bankruptcy; ***belly-wool***: see sense 3b above.

belly /ˈbɛli/ *verb.* E17.
[ORIGIN from the noun.]
1 *verb trans. & intrans.* (Cause to) swell out (usu. of sails). E17.
†**2** *verb intrans.* Become corpulent. M17–L18.

bellyful /ˈbɛlɪfʊl, -f(ə)l/ *noun.* M16.
[ORIGIN from BELLY *noun* + -FUL.]
As much as the belly will hold; a sufficiency of food; *slang* as much as or more than one wants of anything.

SMOLLETT I never once had my belly-full, even of dry bread. S. BECKETT Will you stop whining! I've had about my bellyful of your lamentations.

†**belock** *verb trans. rare* (Shakes.). Only in E17.
[ORIGIN from BE- 1 + LOCK *verb*[1].]
Lock firmly, clasp.

belomancy /ˈbɛləʊmansi/ *noun.* M17.
[ORIGIN from Greek *belos* dart + -MANCY.]
Divination by means of arrows.

belong /bɪˈlɒŋ/ *verb intrans.* ME.
[ORIGIN Prob. intensive of LONG *verb*[2]: see BE- 1.]
▸ **I** Foll. by *to*, †*unto*.

1 Be rightly assigned or appropriate to as an adjunct, function, duty, etc. ME.

AV *Dan.* 9:9 To the Lord our God belong mercies. GEO. ELIOT He . . works with all the zest that belongs to fresh ideas.

2 Pertain or relate to. *arch.* ME.

AV *1 Cor.* 7:22 He that is unmarried careth for the things that belong to the Lord.

3 Be the property or rightful possession of. LME. ▸**b** Be a property or an attribute of. M17.

M. MCCARTHY Around one tan wrist was a gold bracelet that had belonged to her grandmother. **b** J. LOCKE This way of containing all things can by no means belong to God.

4 Be connected with as a member, part, inhabitant, dependency, etc. LME.

ADDISON The great Yard that belongs to my Friend's Country-House. O. SITWELL Its flat spread dome belongs to an exceedingly primitive type. L. HELLMAN I belonged, on my mother's side, to a banking, storekeeping family from Alabama. JAN MORRIS Every undergraduate [in Oxford] belongs to a college.

▸ **II** *absol.* & with other constructions.

5 Be right or appropriate *to do*, *be*. Usu. *impers.* in (*it*) ***belongs*** etc. *arch.* M17.

KEATS Here . . it doth not well belong To speak. C. CAUSLEY And a Cornish man with a Cornish maid is how it belongs to be.

6 (With other prepositions and with adverbs.) Be related or connected; be naturally or rightly placed; be classified. Orig. *US.* E19.

W. WHITMAN He was not a closet man, belonged out-of-doors. P. G. WODEHOUSE I looked as if I belonged in Whipsnade. J. AGEE He had lost their contempt and could belong among them if he wanted to. J. HELLER A woman belongs with her husband always.

7 *absol.* Be a member; fit a specified environment, not be out of place. E20.

D. H. LAWRENCE He belonged [to the choir] just because he had a tenor voice, and enjoyed singing. M. MCCARTHY It was the Moscow trials that made him know . . that he did not really 'belong'.

belonging /bɪˈlɒŋɪŋ/ *noun.* E17.
[ORIGIN from BELONG + -ING[1]; pl. perh. from pres. pple, = 'things belonging'.]
▸ **I** In *pl.* (*sing.* rare).

1 Circumstances or relations connected with a person or thing. *arch.* E17.

BROWNING All my belongings, what is summed in life, I have submitted wholly . . to your rule.

2 Possessions, goods, effects. E19.

W. S. CHURCHILL It struck me as rather grim to see the intimate belongings of one's comrade of the day before . . thus unceremoniously distributed among strangers.

3 One's family or relatives. *colloq.* M19.

DICKENS I have been trouble enough to my belongings in my day.

▸ **II 4** The fact of appertaining or being a part; relationship; *esp.* an individual's membership of, and acceptance by, a group or society. L19.

W. PLOMER He had little sense of belonging.

■ **belongingness** *noun* †(*a*) the state of having properties appropriate to something; (*b*) the state or condition of belonging: M17.

belord /bɪˈlɔːd/ *verb trans.* L16.
[ORIGIN from BE- 3 + LORD *noun.*]
Call 'lord', address as 'lord'.

Belorussian /bɛləʊˈrʌʃ(ə)n/ *adjective & noun.* Also **Byelo-** /bjɛləʊ-/. M20.
[ORIGIN from *Belorussia* (see below) from Russian *Belorossiya*, from *belyĭ* white + *Rossiya* Russia, + -AN.]
▸ **A** *adjective.* Of or pertaining to Belorussia (now Belarus), a country in eastern Europe, its people, or their Slavonic language; Belarusian. Formerly also called WHITE RUSSIAN. M20.
▸ **B** *noun.* A native or inhabitant of Belarus; their language. M20.

belote /bəˈlɒt/ *noun*[1]. Also **belotte**. M20.
[ORIGIN French, perh. from F. *Belot*, a Frenchman said to have developed the game.]
A card game like pinochle, played with a 32-card pack, popular in France; the combination of king and queen of trumps in this game.

belove /bɪˈlʌv/ *verb.* ME.
[ORIGIN from BE- 1 + LOVE *verb.*]
†**1** *verb intrans.* Please, be pleasing. Only in ME.
2 *verb trans.* Love. Now only in *pass.* (foll. by *by*, *of*). LME.

SHAKES. *Mids. N. D.* I am belov'd of beauteous Hermia. BYRON I loved, and was beloved again. G. B. SHAW The master beloved by masters, Mozart.

beloved /bɪˈlʌvɪd, *less usu.* -ˈlʌvd/ *ppl adjective & noun.* LME.
[ORIGIN from BELOVE + -ED[1].]
▸ **A** *ppl adjective.* Dearly loved. LME.

SHAKES. *Lear* Sorrow would be a rarity most beloved If all could so become it. LD MACAULAY Impatient to be once more in his beloved country.

▸ **B** *noun.* A beloved person, a sweetheart. LME.

below /bɪˈləʊ/ *adverb & preposition.* LME.
[ORIGIN from *be* BY *preposition* + LOW *adjective.*]
▸ **A** *adverb.* **1** *gen.* At or to a lower position relative to another; lower down. LME. ▸**b** Lower down a slope or the course of a river, downstream. M17. ▸**c** Lower on a sheet or page; at the foot of the page; later in a book or article. L17.

GOLDSMITH The child . . leaped from her arms into the flood below. TENNYSON From below Sweet gales, as from deep gardens, blow. K. AMIS The slamming of the car doors below made them both jump.

2 a Under heaven; on earth (often preceded by *here*). *arch.* or *poet.* L16. ▸**b** Under the earth; *rhet.* in hell. E17.

a KEATS Finer spirits cannot breathe below In human climes. **b** SHAKES. *Temp.* Night kept chain'd below. SOUTHEY The fiends below were ringing his knell.

3 On or to a lower floor; downstairs; *esp.* (NAUTICAL) below deck. L16.

SHAKES. *Merry W.* There's one Master Brook below would fain speak with you. R. H. DANA It being the turn of our watch to go below.

4 *fig.* In or to a lower rank, position, station, etc. E17.

D. M. WALKER The result of an appeal may be to affirm, modify, or reverse the decision of the court below.

5 Lower than the zero of a temperature scale. L18.

P. THEROUX This is the worst winter I've ever seen. Ten below in Chicago.

▸ **B** *preposition.* **1** *gen.* Lower in position than, at less elevation than. L16. ▸**b** Lower down a slope than; downstream from; further south than. E17. ▸**c** Lower down a page than; later in a work than. M18.

SIR W. SCOTT He never counted him a man Would strike below the knee. T. S. ELIOT At dawn we came down to a temperate valley, Wet, below the snowline. **b** SHAKES. *Meas. for M.* Meet me at the consecrated fount, A league below the city. *Publishers Weekly* In the desperately poor South, the country below Naples.

2 Directly beneath; covered by, underneath; deeper than. E17.

TENNYSON Some dolorous message knit below The wild pulsation of her wings. LD KELVIN The necessity for study below the surface seems to have been earliest recognised in anatomy. A. S. J. TESSIMOND The still green light below tall trees.

3 Lower in rank, position, etc., than. E17. ▸**b** Lower in some quality than; inferior to. E18. ▸**c** Lower in amount, value, weight, temperature, etc., than. E18.

STEELE He . . gives his orders . . to the Servants below him. J. HELLER In marrying your father, I married very far below my station. **b** LD MACAULAY How far my performance is below excellence.

4 Unworthy of, unbefitting to, lowering to (more freq. expressed by *beneath*). M17.

STEELE It was below a Gentlewoman to wrangle. R. A. PROCTOR Too far below contempt to be worth castigating.

– PHRASES (of adverb & preposition): ***below deck(s)***: see DECK *noun*[1] 2. ***below ground***: see GROUND *noun.* ***below one's breath***: see BREATH *noun.* ***below par***: see PAR *noun*[1]. ***below stairs***: see STAIR 1. ***below the belt***: see BELT *noun.* ***below the gangway***: see GANGWAY 3b. **below there!**: warning to beware of a falling object. ***below the salt***: see SALT *noun*[1]. **from below** from a lower place. ***watch below***: see WATCH *noun.*

Bel Paese /bɛl pɑːˈeɪzi, *foreign* bɛl paˈeːze/ *noun phr.* E20.
[ORIGIN Italian, lit. 'beautiful country'.]
(Proprietary name for) a rich, white, creamy cheese of mild flavour orig. made in Italy.

Belshazzar *noun* see BALTHAZAR.

†**belswagger** *noun.* L16–L18.
[ORIGIN Perh. a contr. of *belly-swagger* 'one who swags his belly': see SWAG *verb*, -ER[1].]
A swaggering bully; a pimp.

belt /bɛlt/ *noun.*
[ORIGIN Old English *belt*, corresp. to Old High German *balz*, Old Norse *belti* (Swedish *bälte*, Danish *bælte*), from Germanic from Latin *balteus* girdle, of Etruscan origin. In branch II from the verb.]
▸ **I 1** A flat encircling strip of cloth, leather, etc., worn around the waist or from the shoulder to the opposite hip to support clothes, weapons, etc., or as a decorative accessory. OE. ▸**b** *spec.* Such a belt worn as a mark of rank or distinction by an earl, knight, boxing champion, etc. LME. ▸**c** *spec.* Such a belt used to support the figure; a suspender belt; a corset. L19. ▸**d** (W. specifying colour.) Such a belt indicating by its colour the wearer's level of proficiency in judo or karate; a person entitled to wear this. E20.

C. BOUTELL The sword . . hung from a belt that passed over the shoulder. A. POWELL He wore a loosely made camel's-hair overcoat, the unfastened belt of which trailed behind him. J. STEINBECK His jeans were held up by a wide harness-leather belt with a big square brass buckle. *fig.*: SHAKES. *Macb.* He cannot buckle his distemper'd cause Within the belt of rule. **b** THACKERAY They fight each other for the champion's belt and two hundred pounds a side. **c** R. LEHMANN Etty wears . . just her belt and knickers.

chastity belt, ***suspender belt***, etc. **d** ***black belt***, ***red belt***, ***white belt***, etc.

2 A broad strip or stripe of any kind, or a continuous series of objects, encircling something. M17.

SOUTHEY A level belt of ice which bound . . The waters of the sleeping Ocean round. R. W. EMERSON A belt of mirrors round a taper's flame. P. MOORE Through a small telescope Jupiter shows as a yellowish, flattened disk, crossed by the streaks which we term belts.

3 A broad flexible strap. L17. ▸**b** A flexible strip for feeding a machine gun with ammunition. L19.

conveyor belt, ***safety belt***, ***seat belt***, etc.

4 An endless strap passing around wheels, rollers, etc., for communicating motion or for conveying articles or material. L18.

C. S. FORESTER The belt bore the peas steadily along to the farther drum. *Reader's Digest* Automobiles leaving the belt as finished products.

5 A broad band or stripe crossing a surface (esp. that of the earth) from which it is differentiated in some way; a zone or region of distinct character or occupancy. E19.

A. B. HART Illinois is divided into a wheat belt, a corn belt, and the city of Chicago. TOLKIEN A belt of tall and very ancient oaks. U. LE GUIN The Green Mountains where it rained up to forty inches a year, the rain belt.

BIBLE Belt. ***green belt***: see GREEN *adjective.*

▸ **II 6** The wool sheared from the hindquarters of a sheep. Now *rare* or *obsolete.* M17.
7 A heavy blow or stroke. L19.

– PHRASES: **belt and braces** *fig.* a policy of twofold security. ***hit below the belt***: see HIT *verb.* ***SAM BROWNE belt***. **tighten one's belt** *fig.* (*a*) bear hunger philosophically; (*b*) introduce economies. **under one's belt** (*a*) (of food) eaten or otherwise absorbed; (*b*) securely acquired. VAN ALLEN BELT.

– COMB.: **belt conveyor** a conveyor belt; **belt drive** a driving mechanism powered by a flexible endless belt; **belt line** *US* a railway or tramline that encircles a city or metropolitan area; **belt sander** a sander with a motorized continuous belt of abrasive material running over rollers; **belt-tightening** *fig.* the introduction of rigorous economies; **beltway** *N. Amer.* a highway that encircles a city or metropolitan area, esp. (*Beltway*) that around Washington DC; (freq. *attrib.*) Washington as the seat of the US government.
■ **beltless** *adjective* LME.

belt /bɛlt/ *verb*. ME.
[ORIGIN from the noun.]
1 *verb trans.* Put a belt on or around; invest with a distinctive belt (esp. of knighthood). ME. ▸**b** Fasten on with a belt. E16.

SIR W. SCOTT Allen-a-Dale was ne'er belted a knight. **b** T. PENNANT An enormous shield . . is belted to his body.

2 *verb trans.* Thrash with a belt. L15. ▸**b** Hit; attack; give a thrashing to. M19.

b J. GALSWORTHY Megan'll get his mates to belt him.

b belt the bottle *slang* drink heavily.
3 *verb trans.* Shear the hindquarters of (a sheep). Now *rare* or *obsolete*. E16.
4 *verb trans.* Encircle with a band of colour etc.; surround; mark with bands or stripes. M16.

WORDSWORTH They belt him round with hearts undaunted. J. N. LOCKYER The meteors belted the sky like the meridians on a terrestrial globe.

5 *verb intrans.* Hurry, rush. *colloq.* L19.

T. MANGOLD There can be no errors when the equivalent of five million tons of TNT is belting towards Washington at 18,000 miles an hour.

– WITH ADVERBS IN SPECIALIZED SENSES: **belt down** *colloq.* of the sun's rays etc.: beat down (see BEAT *verb*¹ 4b). **belt out** *verb phr. trans.* (*colloq.*) sing, play, utter, etc., vigorously. **belt up** *colloq.* (*a*) be quiet, shut up; (*b*) fasten a seat belt, wear a seat belt.

Beltane /ˈbɛlteɪn/ *noun*. LME.
[ORIGIN Gaelic *bealltainn*, *-tuin* (= Old Irish *bel(l)taine*, Manx *boaltinn*, *boaldyn*).]
1 The first day of May, Old Style, one of the ancient Scottish quarter days. LME.
2 An ancient Scottish and Irish festival celebrated on May Day, at which great bonfires were lit. M18.

belted /ˈbɛltɪd/ *adjective*. L15.
[ORIGIN from BELT *noun*, *verb*: see -ED², -ED¹.]
1 Wearing or fastened by a belt; *esp.* (usu. *rhet.*) wearing the distinctive cincture of an earl etc. L15.
2 Marked by a band or bands of colour etc. L16.
belted GALLOWAY.

belter /ˈbɛltə/ *noun*. E19.
[ORIGIN from BELT *noun* or *verb* + -ER¹.]
1 A heavy blow; a beating. *Scot. & N. English*. E19.
2 An impressive performer; an outstanding person or thing; a person who sings or speaks loudly and forcibly. *slang*. L20.

belting /ˈbɛltɪŋ/ *noun*. M16.
[ORIGIN from BELT *noun* or *verb* + -ING¹.]
1 Belts collectively, material for belts; a belt. M16.
2 The action of BELT *verb*; *esp.* a beating, a thrashing. M19.

belting /ˈbɛltɪŋ/ *adjective*. M19.
[ORIGIN from BELT *verb* + -ING².]
1 Girdling, encircling, surrounding. M19.
2 Of a song: sung or composed to be sung vigorously and powerfully; (of a voice) loud, strong. L20.

beluga /bɪˈluːɡə/ *noun*. L16.
[ORIGIN Russian (sense 1) *beluga*, (sense 2) *belukha*, from *belyĭ* white + *-uga*, *-ukha* formative suffixes.]
1 (Caviar from) the great sturgeon or hausen, *Huso huso*, of the Caspian and Black Seas. L16.
2 A small white toothed whale, *Delphinapterus leucas*, of coastal waters in the Arctic. L18.

belvedere /ˈbɛlvɪdɪə/ *noun*. L16.
[ORIGIN Italian = fair sight, from *bel*, *bello* beautiful + *vedere* see.]
1 A raised turret or summer house commanding a fine view. L16.
2 The summer cypress, *Bassia scoparia*. L16.

belying *verb pres. pple & verbal noun* of BELIE.

BEM *abbreviation*.
1 British Empire Medal.
2 Bug-eyed monster.

bema /ˈbiːmə/ *noun*. Pl. **-mas**, **-mata** /-mətə/. L17.
[ORIGIN Greek *bēma* a step, a raised place to speak from.]
1 CHRISTIAN CHURCH. The altar part or sanctuary in ancient and Orthodox churches; the chancel. L17.
2 GREEK ANTIQUITIES. The platform from which Athenian orators spoke. E19.

bemad /bɪˈmad/ *verb trans*. Infl. **-dd-**. E17.
[ORIGIN from BE- 1 + MAD *verb*.]
Make mad.

SHAKES. *Lear* Unnatural and bemadding sorrow.

bemata *noun pl.* see BEMA.

bemaul /bɪˈmɔːl/ *verb trans*. E17.
[ORIGIN from BE- 1 + MAUL *verb*.]
Maul thoroughly.

bemazed /bɪˈmeɪzd/ *adjective*. *arch.* ME.
[ORIGIN from BE- + *mazed* pa. pple of MAZE *verb*.]
Stupefied, bewildered.

Bemba /ˈbɛmbə/ *noun*. Pl. same. M20.
[ORIGIN Bantu.]
A member of a people in Zambia and the Congo; the Bantu language of this people.

Bembo /ˈbɛmbəʊ/ *noun*. M20.
[ORIGIN Pietro *Bembo* (1470–1547), Italian cardinal and scholar.]
A typeface modelled on that used in the Aldine edition of Bembo's tract *De Aetna*.

bemean /bɪˈmiːn/ *verb trans*. M17.
[ORIGIN from BE- 3 + MEAN *adjective*¹, prob. after DEMEAN *verb*².]
Render mean, abase.

†**bemeet** *verb trans. & intrans.* Pa. t. & pple **-met**. E–M17.
[ORIGIN from BE- 1 + MEET *verb*.]
Meet (*with*).

SHAKES. *Lear* Our very loving sister, well bemet.

†**bemete** *verb trans. rare* (Shakes.). Only in L16.
[ORIGIN from BE- 1 + METE *verb* 1.]
Measure.

Bemi /biːˈmiː/ *noun*. *obsolete* exc. *hist.* Also **B mi**. LME.
[ORIGIN from B as a pitch letter + *mi* designating a tone in the solmization of Guido d'Arezzo (*c* 990–1050).]
MEDIEVAL MUSIC. The note B in Guido d'Arezzo's 1st, 4th, and 7th hexachords, where it was sung to the syllable *mi*. Cf. ALAMIRE, BEFA, CEFAUT, etc.

bemire /bɪˈmʌɪə/ *verb trans*. M16.
[ORIGIN from BE- 4 + MIRE *noun*¹.]
Befoul with or plunge in mire; (in *pass.*) sink in the mire, be stuck in mud.

SWIFT I was filthily bemired. *fig.*: J. WESLEY Doubt . . bemires the soul.

bemist /bɪˈmɪst/ *verb trans*. L16.
[ORIGIN from BE- 4 + MIST *noun*¹.]
Cover or surround (as) with mist; confuse, obscure.

bemoan /bɪˈməʊn/ *verb trans. & intrans.*
[ORIGIN Old English *bemǣnan*, formed as BE- + MEAN *verb*², alt. (16) after MOAN *verb*.]
Lament; weep or express sorrow (for or over); *refl.* bewail one's lot.

AV *Job* 42:11 They bemoned him, and comforted him. BACON Politique persons . . are euer bemoaning themselves, what a Life they lead. C. LAMB I do not know whether I ought to bemoan or rejoice that my old friend is departed. J. M. BARRIE Foreign words in the text annoyed her and made her bemoan her want of a classical education.

bemock /bɪˈmɒk/ *verb trans*. E17.
[ORIGIN from BE- 1 + MOCK *verb*.]
Flout; delude mockingly.

SHAKES. *Coriol.* Nay, but his taunts! . . Bemock the modest moon.

bemoil /bɪˈmɔɪl/ *verb trans. obsolete* exc. *dial.* L16.
[ORIGIN from BE- 1 + MOIL *verb*.]
Bemire.

bemoisten /bɪˈmɔɪs(ə)n/ *verb trans*. L16.
[ORIGIN from BE- 1 + MOISTEN *verb*.]
Make moist.

bemonster /bɪˈmɒnstə/ *verb trans*. E17.
[ORIGIN from BE- 3 + MONSTER *noun*.]
1 Make monstrous, deform. E17.
2 Regard as or call a monster. L17.

bemuse /bɪˈmjuːz/ *verb trans*. M18.
[ORIGIN from BE- 2 + MUSE *verb*².]
Make utterly muddled, as with drink; stupefy. Chiefly as *bemused ppl adjective*.
■ **bemusedly** /-zɪdli/ *adverb* L19.

ben /bɛn/ *noun*¹. M16.
[ORIGIN Repr. N. African pronunc. of Arabic *bān* ben tree.]
The seeds of Asian and N. African trees of the genus *Moringa* (family Moringaceae), esp. *M. oleifera*, which yield a valuable oil. Usu. in *comb.*, as *ben nut*, *ben oil*, *ben tree*.

ben /bɛn/ *noun*². L18.
[ORIGIN Gaelic, Irish *beann* = Old Irish *benn*, Welsh *ban* prominence, peak, height.]
A Scottish or Irish mountain peak. Chiefly in names, as *Ben Nevis*, *Ben Bulben*.

ben /bɛn/ *adverb, preposition, adjective, & noun*³. *Scot. & N. English*. LME.
[ORIGIN Repr. Old English *binnan* (= Old Frisian *binna*, Middle & mod. Low German, Middle Dutch & mod. Dutch, Middle & mod. High German *binnen*), formed as BY *preposition* etc. + IN *adverb*.]
▸ **A** *adverb*. Within, towards the inner part; *spec.* in or into the inner part of a house (orig. the parlour of a two-roomed house with only one outer door, opening into the kitchen). Cf. BUT *adverb* 1. LME.
▸ **B** *preposition*. In or into the inner part of (a house). L17.
▸ **C** *adjective*. Inner, interior. L18.
▸ **D** *noun*. The inner room of a two-roomed house. Cf. BUT *noun* 2. L18.
– PHRASES: *but and ben*: see BUT *noun* 2.

benab /ˈbɛnab/ *noun*. M19.
[ORIGIN Arawak (*u*)*bannabuhu*.]
In Guyana: a shelter made of a framework of poles, covered with branches and leaves.

†**bename** *verb trans.* Pa. t. & pple **benamed**, **benempt(ed)**.
[ORIGIN Old English *benemnan*, formed as BE- + NAME *verb*.]
1 Declare solemnly or on oath. OE–E17.
2 Name; describe as. L16–M19.

bench /bɛn(t)ʃ/ *noun*. See also BINK.
[ORIGIN Old English *benć* = Old Frisian *benk*, Old Saxon *banc* (Dutch *bank*), Old High German *bank* (German *Bank*), (cf. also Old Norse *bekkr*, Icelandic *bekkur*), from Germanic: rel. to BANK *noun*¹, *noun*².]
1 A long seat, usually of wood or stone, with or without a back. OE. ▸**b** A seat or thwart in a boat. M16.

COVERDALE *Esther* 1:6 The benches were of golde and siluer. M. SPARK The small girls took their lessons seated on three benches arranged about the elm.

2 A bank or shelf of ground; a level ledge in earthwork, masonry, etc.; an outcropping level stratum; *US* a river terrace. ME.
3 The seat on which the judge or judges sit in court; the office or status of a judge. ME. ▸**b** A place where justice is administered; a court of law. ME. ▸**c** The judge or magistrate; the judges or magistrates collectively. L16.

D. JACOBSON He was in due course promoted to the bench, on which he served to the end of his days. **c** DISRAELI Now, prisoner, the bench is ready to hear your confession.

on the bench serving as a judge or magistrate. **b King's Bench Division of the High Court**, **Queen's Bench Division of the High Court**, (*hist.*) **King's Bench**, **Queen's Bench** one of the divisions of the High Court (formerly a court at which the monarch presided).
4 A seat where a number of people sit side by side in some official capacity; *esp.* one occupied by a group in the British Parliament. ME. ▸**b** The people collectively who occupy such a seat; their status or dignity. E17.

W. SHENSTONE A little bench of heedless bishops And there a chancellor in embryo. W. S. CHURCHILL I invite former colleagues on the opposite Bench to share the credit.

back bench, *cross bench*, *front bench*, *Treasury bench*, etc.
5 Formerly, a merchant's table; a banker's counter. Now, a worktop used by a carpenter etc., or in a laboratory. LME.

J. S. HUXLEY Between days of hard work at my bench I explored the exciting neighbourhood.

optical bench: see OPTICAL *adjective*.
6 LAW (now *hist.*). ***free bench*** [Anglo-Latin *bancus francus*], a widow's dower out of copyholds to which she was entitled by the customs of some manors. L17.
7 A ledge or floor upon which retorts stand; a set of retorts. M19.
8 A collection of dogs as exhibited at a show on benches or platforms. L19.
9 A seat used by officials and players when not participating in a game; the persons collectively who occupy such a seat. E20.
– COMB.: **bench-end** the end of a seat in a church, freq. ornamented; †**bench-hole** a privy, a lavatory; **bench-hook** a board with stops fitted at each end on opposite faces, used on a carpenter's bench to secure a workpiece; **benchland** *N. Amer.* a relatively narrow, naturally occurring terrace often backed by a steep slope; **bench press** a body-building and weightlifting exercise in which a lifter lies on a bench with feet on the floor and raises a weight with both arms; **bench-press** *verb trans. & intrans.* raise (a weight) in a bench press; **bench-screw** a vice attached to a carpenter's bench; **bench seat** a seat across the whole width of a car etc.; **bench-stop**, **bench-strip** a pillar or strip which projects above the surface of a carpenter's bench, used to secure a workpiece; **bench table** (*a*) a low stone seat on the inside of walls or round the bases of pillars, in churches, cloisters, etc.; (*b*) *hist.* an official body of benchers at the Inner Temple; **bench test** a test of a motor engine carried out in a workshop before it is fitted to a motor body; **bench-test** *verb trans.* subject to a bench test, test in conditions simulating real use; **bench-warmer** *colloq.* a sports player who does not get selected to play, a substitute; **bench-warrant** a warrant issued by a judge in court for the arrest of a person who fails to appear, as opp. to a justice's or magistrate's warrant.
■ **benchlet** *noun* a little bench; a stool: M19.

bench /bɛn(t)ʃ/ *verb*. LME.
[ORIGIN from the noun.]
1 *verb trans.* Equip with benches. LME.
2 *verb trans. & intrans.* Seat (oneself) on a bench. L16. ▸**b** *verb trans.* Put (a dog) on a show bench for exhibition; exhibit at a dog show. L19.
3 *verb trans.* Remove or retire (a player) to the bench for non-participants. *N. Amer.* E20.

bencher /ˈbɛn(t)ʃə/ *noun*. ME.
[ORIGIN formed as BENCH *verb* + -ER¹.]
1 A person who sits on a bench, *esp.* a magistrate, judge, etc. ME.

backbencher: see BACK-. CROSS-BENCHER. ***frontbencher***: see FRONT *noun & adjective*.

2 Each of the senior members of an Inn of Court. L16.

■ **benchership** *noun* the position of a bencher in an Inn of Court E19.

benchmark /ˈbɛn(t)ʃmɑːk/ *noun, adjective, & verb*. M19.
[ORIGIN from BENCH *noun* + MARK *noun*[1].]
▸ **A** *noun*. **1** A surveyor's mark consisting of a broad arrow with a horizontal bar through its apex, cut in rock etc. to indicate a point whose position and height have been surveyed. M19.
2 *fig.* A point of reference, a criterion. L19.
▸ **B** *attrib.* or as *adjective*. Serving or used as a benchmark. M20.

Intercity Magazine Bass Draught is a benchmark bitter, with an excellent balance of ingredients.

▸ **C** *verb trans.* Test or check by comparison with a benchmark. (Foll. by *to*.) L20.

bend /bɛnd/ *noun*[1].
[ORIGIN Old English *bend* = Gothic *bandi*, from Germanic, from base of BIND *verb*: later infl. by Old French *bende* BAND *noun*[2]. Replaced by *band* or *bond* exc. in nautical use.]
†**1** A band, a fetter; in *pl.*, bonds, imprisonment. OE–LME.
†**2** A clamp; a connecting piece. ME–L16.
3 NAUTICAL. Any of various kinds of knot, as ***cable bend***, ***fisherman's bend***, etc. E18.

bend /bɛnd/ *noun*[2]. OE.
[ORIGIN App. orig. a sense of BEND *noun*[1]. Later identified with Old French *bende* (mod. *bande*): see BAND *noun*[2].]
1 A thin flat strip used to bind round; a ribbon, fillet, etc.; a scroll etc. in decorative work. *obsolete* exc. *dial.* OE.
2 HERALDRY. An ordinary drawn from the dexter chief to the sinister base of the shield, with breadth one fifth or, if charged, one third part of the field. LME.
bend sinister a bend drawn from sinister chief to dexter base (a supposed mark of bastardy). **in bend** placed in a diagonal line. **party per bend** divided diagonally. **sinister bend** = ***bend sinister*** above.
3 A shape or size in which hides are tanned into leather, forming half of a butt (BUTT *noun*[4] 4). L16.
– COMB.: **bend-leather** the leather of a bend, i.e. the stoutest kind; sole leather.
■ **bendlet** *noun* (HERALDRY) a bend with half the normal width L16. **bendwise** *adverb* (HERALDRY) at the angle of a bend E17.

bend /bɛnd/ *noun*[3]. LME.
[ORIGIN from BEND *verb*.]
1 The action or an act of bending. LME.

N. HAWTHORNE A wave just on the bend, and about to break over. K. VONNEGUT He . . did a deep-knee bend.

†**2** Inclination of the eye in any direction; glance. *rare* (Shakes.). Only in L16.
†**3** Turn of mind, inclination, bent. L16–E19.

H. FUSELI The prevalent bend of the reigning taste.

4 A thing of bent shape; a curved part of a thing; a curve of a road, river, etc. L16.

R. MACAULAY Aunt Dot was a clever, impetuous driver, taking the sharpest bends with the greatest intrepidity. P. MATTHIESSEN The river curves in a broad bend of . . gravel bars.

U-bend, ***Z-bend***, etc.
5 NAUTICAL. A ship's wale. Usu. in *pl.* E17.
6 In *pl.*, usu. with *the*. Pain (esp. in the joints) which is a symptom of decompression sickness. Also, the illness itself. *colloq.* L19.
– PHRASES: **above one's bend** *US* beyond one's powers. ***Grecian bend***: see GRECIAN *adjective*. **on a bend**, **on the bend** *slang* on a binge (cf. BENDER). **round the bend** *colloq.* crazy, insane.

bend /bɛnd/ *verb*. Pa. t. & pple **bended** (*arch.* exc. in **bended knee(s)**: see below), **bent** /bɛnt/.
[ORIGIN Old English *bendan* = Old Norse *benda*, from Germanic, from base of BAND *noun*[1].]
▸ **I** Constrain; bow, curve.
†**1** *verb trans.* Put in bonds. Only in OE.
2 *verb trans.* Bring (a bow etc.) into tension by a string; *fig.* tighten, wind up, brace. Freq. foll. by *up*. OE. ▸**b** NAUTICAL. Tie, fasten on, make fast. LME.

SHAKES. *Hen. V* Hold hard the breath, and bend up every spirit To his full height. SIR W. SCOTT Her whole mind apparently bent up to the solemn interview. **b** R. L. STEVENSON He had with his own hand bent and run up the colours.

3 *verb trans.* Force (a thing having some rigidity) out of straightness or normal form; bow, curve, crook, inflect. ME.

J. GERARD Branches . . so easie to be bent or bowed, that hereof they make Hoops. DICKENS His form is bent by age. A. RANSOME He stooped and bent his long legs and worked his way through the tunnel. HARPER LEE Mrs Crenshaw took some chicken wire and bent it into the shape of a cured ham. T. E. HULME To bend the steel out of its own curve and into the exact curve you want.

4 *verb intrans.* Assume or receive a curved or angled form; curve over from an erect position. LME.

DRYDEN The waving Harvest bends beneath his blast. F. O'BRIEN He . . roosted on its slender perch till it bowed beneath him and bent till it slammed him to the ground.

5 *verb intrans. spec.* Of a person: incline the body, stoop; bow, esp. in submission; *fig.* yield (*to*), be pliant or subservient. LME.

MILTON Who hate the Lord should then be fain To bow to him and bend. LYTTON He bent down and kissed her cheek. C. MACKENZIE His thin body bending over the table like a tall black note of interrogation. C. FREEMAN She missed Jacob terribly and berated herself for not being able to bend to his will.

6 *verb trans.* Cause (a person, the will, etc.) to bow, stoop, incline, or relent. LME.

LD MACAULAY The spirit of the rustic gentry was not to be bent. J. W. KRUTCH He has learned her [Nature's] laws and can bend her to his will, making her serve *his* purposes, not hers.

7 *verb trans.* Turn away from the straight line; deflect, turn. E16.

J. BRONOWSKI Blue [light] is bent or refracted more than red.

8 *verb trans.* Pervert, make illicit or dishonest (now *slang*); modify or interpret (rules etc.) to suit oneself. (*rare* before M19.) M16.

Observer There are honest landladies . . who let a flat to someone they think is an ordinary girl, who then proceeds to 'bend' it: uses it for prostitution. *Times* Trying to get other members of the European Community to 'bend the rules' so that exports can be resumed.

†**9** *verb trans. & intrans.* Incline in mind. M16–M18.
10 *verb intrans.* Have a direction away from the straight line; incline, trend. L16.

LONGFELLOW And now the land . . Bent southward suddenly.

▸ **II** Direct, aim.
11 *verb intrans.* (*arch.*) & *trans.* Direct or turn (one's way, steps, etc.). LME.

SHAKES. *All's Well* For thence we came And . . Thither we bend again. MILTON Thither his course he bends Through the calm Firmament.

12 *verb trans.* Apply or bring to bear (one's mind, energies, etc.) *on* or *upon*. E16. ▸**b** *verb refl. & intrans.* Apply oneself *to* or *to do*. *arch.* L16.

A. J. CRONIN Immobilized suddenly, his attention bent upon the sheet before him. D. J. ENRIGHT He bends his strength against the flood. H. J. LASKI Yet it was a great work to which they bent their effort. **b** BUNYAN If any shall . . bend themselves to disappoint the designs of the Eternal God. E. K. KANE Bending to our oars.

†**13** *verb trans.* Aim or level (weapons, forces, etc.; *against* or *at*). M16–E19.

SPENSER So bent his speare and spurd his horse. O. CROMWELL They bent their guns at the frigate.

14 *verb trans.* Direct or turn (one's eyes, *on* something seen; one's ears, *to* something heard). L16.

MILTON And to my cries . . Thine ear with favor bend. SOUTHEY Every eye on her was bent.

15 *verb trans. fig. & gen.* Direct or turn (*against*, *on*, *to*(*wards*), etc.). L16.

WILLIAM COLLINS To Britain bend his iron Car. E. WELTY [He] bent on her his benign smile.

– PHRASES: **bend one's elbow** *slang* = ***crook one's elbow*** s.v. CROOK *verb* 1. **bend over** put oneself into position to be thrashed on the buttocks. ***bend over backward(s)***: see BACKWARD *adverb* 1. **bend someone's ear** importune someone with persistent talk; have a word with someone. **bend the brow(s)** †(*a*) arch the eyebrows; (*b*) knit the brow; scowl. **bend the head**, †**bend the face** bow the head. ***bend the rules***; see RULE *noun*. **catch a person bending** *colloq.* catch a person at a disadvantage. **on bended knee(s)** kneeling, esp. in reverence, supplication, or submission.
■ **bendable** *adjective* E17.

benday process /ˈbɛndeɪ ˌprəʊsɛs/ *noun phr. obsolete* exc. *hist.* Also **Ben Day process**. E20.
[ORIGIN *Benjamin Day* (1838–1916), US printer.]
A method of tint production in lithography and photo-engraving by transferring lines or dots from gelatin sheets.

bender /ˈbɛndə/ *noun*. L15.
[ORIGIN from BEND *verb* + -ER[1].]
1 An instrument for bending; a pair of pliers. L15.
2 A person who bends. L16.
3 †**a** A hard drinker. *Scot.* E18–E19. ▸**b** A bout of drinking; a riotous party. *colloq.* M19.

b *New Yorker* He went on a ten-day bender.

4 A sixpence. Cf. CRIPPLE *noun* 2a. *slang.* E19.
5 A leg or knee. *slang.* Orig. *US*. M19.
6 A male homosexual. *slang. derog.* L20.
7 A shelter made by covering a framework of bent branches with canvas or tarpaulin. *colloq.* L20.

bendy /ˈbɛndi/ *adjective*[1]. L15.
[ORIGIN Old French *bendé* (mod. *bandé*): see BEND *noun*[2], -Y[5].]
HERALDRY. Of a field: divided into an even number of bends, coloured alternately.

bendy /ˈbɛndi/ *adjective*[2]. E20.
[ORIGIN from BEND *verb* + -Y[1].]
1 Capable of bending; soft and flexible. E20.
2 Of a road, track, etc.: that has many bends. L20.

bene /biːn/ *noun*. Long *arch.*
[ORIGIN Old English *bēn* = Old Norse *bœn* from Germanic base of BOON *noun*[1].]
Prayer, petition.

B

beneaped /bɪˈniːpt/ *adjective*. L17.
[ORIGIN from BE- 5 + NEAP *verb* + -ED[2].]
Left aground by a neaping spring tide.

beneath /bɪˈniːθ/ *adverb, preposition, & adjective*.
[ORIGIN Old English *biniþan*, *bineoþan*, from *bi* BY *preposition* etc. + *niþan*, *neoþan* below, down, (orig.) from below, from Germanic base of NETHER.]
▸ **A** *adverb*. **1** *gen.* In a lower position; = BELOW *adverb* 1. OE. ▸**b** *fig.* Lower in rank, position, quality, etc. *arch.* OE.

SOUTHEY Pure water in a font beneath reflects The many-colour'd rays.

2 **a** Under heaven; on earth. *arch.* ME. ▸**b** Under the earth; in hell. *arch.* ME.
3 Directly below; underneath. ME.

DRYDEN Spread with Straw, the bedding of thy Fold; With Fern beneath. D. DU MAURIER It was a gold chain for my keys, with a disk upon it bearing our initials, . . and the date beneath.

▸ **B** *preposition*. **1** *gen.* In a position lower than (= BELOW *preposition* 1); downhill or downstream from. Now *rare* or *obsolete*. OE.
2 *fig.* Lower than in rank, position, quality, etc. OE.

ADDISON Beings above and beneath us have probably no Opinions at all. J. MCCOSH The copies ever fall beneath the original.

3 Unbefitting the dignity of; unworthy of. OE.

SHAKES. *Twel. N.* So far beneath your soft and tender breeding. S. BELLOW I shut the door with a crash, already aware, under my anger, that this was beneath me and altogether out of proportion to the provocation.

4 Directly down from; overhung by; at the foot of. ME.

DRYDEN Lands that lye beneath another Sun. W. H. AUDEN We see you sitting / in a wide-brimmed hat beneath a monkey-puzzle. W. TREVOR In the far distance, a speck on the beach beneath the cliffs, Commander Abigail ran towards the sea.

5 Under, as overwhelmed by pressure; under the weight of. Often *fig.* ME.

SHAKES. *Macb.* Our country sinks beneath the yoke. R. BLOOMFIELD Brisk goes the work beneath each busy hand.

6 Immediately under; covered or concealed by. E17.

DAY LEWIS A scoop of sandy earth beneath a boulder. B. BAINBRIDGE The underground spring that ran beneath the sloping street overflowed from time to time. *fig.*: A. HAILEY Beneath his outward reaction, Nim was startled and shocked.

– PHRASES: **beneath contempt** not worth despising. ***beneath one's dignity***: see DIGNITY 2. ***beneath the sun***: see SUN *noun*[1].
▸ †**C** *adjective*. Lower. *rare* (Shakes.). Only in E17.

benedicite /bɛnɪˈdʌɪsɪti/ *interjection & noun*. ME.
[ORIGIN Latin, 2nd person pl. imper. of *benedicere* wish well to, bless, from *bene* well + *dicere* say.]
▸ **A** *interjection*. **1** Expr. a wish: God bless you! ME.
2 Expr. astonishment: Good gracious! ME.
▸ **B** *noun*. **1** An invocation of a blessing; *esp.* a grace at table. ME.
2 CHRISTIAN CHURCH. ***the Benedicite***, the canticle beginning *Benedicite, omnia opera* 'O all ye works [of the Lord], bless ye [the Lord]', known also as 'The Song of the Three Children', which is an alternative to the *Te Deum* at matins in the *Book of Common Prayer*. M17.

Benedick /ˈbɛnɪdɪk/ *noun*. Also **-dict** /-dɪkt/. E19.
[ORIGIN A character in Shakespeare's *Much Ado*.]
A newly married man; *esp.* an apparently confirmed bachelor who marries.

Benedict /ˈbɛnɪdɪkt/ *noun*. E20.
[ORIGIN Stanley R. *Benedict* (1884–1936), Amer. chemist.]
Benedict's reagent, ***Benedict's solution***, an aqueous solution of sodium or potassium citrate, sodium carbonate, and copper sulphate, which is blue in colour but yields a red, orange, or yellow precipitate in the presence of reducing sugars such as glucose, and hence is used clinically to test urine for evidence of diabetes.

Benedictine /bɛnɪˈdɪktɪn/ *noun*[1] *& adjective*. E17.
[ORIGIN French *bénédictin* or mod. Latin *benedictinus*, from *Benedictus* of Nursia (St Benedict), *c* 480–*c* 550, abbot of Monte Cassino: see -INE[1].]
▸ **A** *noun*. A member of a community of monks (also known, from their dress, as 'Black Monks'), following the rule established by St Benedict *c* 529. E17.
▸ **B** *adjective*. Of or belonging to St Benedict or the order following his rule. M17.

Benedictine /bɛnɪˈdɪktiːn/ *noun*[2]. Also **b-**. L19.
[ORIGIN French *Bénédictine*, fem. of *bénédictin* (see BENEDICTINE *noun*[1] *& adjective*).]
(Proprietary name for) a liqueur of brandy and herbs, made orig. by Benedictine monks.

benediction /bɛnɪˈdɪkʃ(ə)n/ *noun*. LME.
[ORIGIN (Old French & mod. French *bénédiction* from) Latin *benedictio(n-)*, from *benedict-* pa. ppl stem of *benedicere*: see BENEDICITE, -ION.]

1 The utterance of a blessing; devout or formal invocation of blessedness, prosperity, etc., esp. at the conclusion of a church service, at the consecration of an abbot, or as a grace at table. LME. ▸**b** A chiefly Roman Catholic service in which the congregation is blessed with the Blessed Sacrament. E19.

> J. A. FROUDE Amidst the benedictions of tens of thousands of people.

2 Blessedness, favour. L15.

> SHAKES. *Wint. T.* As if my trinkets . . brought a benediction to the buyer. F. NORRIS A sense of benediction brooded low—a divine kindliness manifesting itself in beauty, in peace, in absolute repose.

▪ **benedictional** *noun* a book of forms of benediction M18. **benedictionary** *noun* = BENEDICTIONAL L18. **benedictory** *adjective* of or pertaining to the utterance of benediction E18.

benedictive /bɛnɪˈdɪktɪv/ *adjective*. M17.
[ORIGIN from Latin *benedict-* (see BENEDICTION) + -IVE.]
Tending to bless.

Benedictus /bɛnɪˈdɪktəs/ *noun*. M16.
[ORIGIN Latin, pa. pple of *benedicere* bless: see BENEDICITE.]
1 The canticle beginning *Benedictus Dominus Deus* 'Blessed be the Lord God' from the hymn of Zacharias (*Luke* 1:68). M16.
2 The fifth section of the ordinary of the Mass, beginning *Benedictus qui venit* 'Blessed is he who comes'; a musical setting of this. L19.

benedight /bɛnɪˈdʌɪt/ *adjective*. Long *arch*. ME.
[ORIGIN from Latin *benedictus* (see BENEDICTUS), with assim. to DIGHT.]
Blessed.

bene esse /ˈbɛnɪ ɛsi/ *noun phr*. E17.
[ORIGIN mod. Latin.]
Well-being, welfare, esp. opp. ESSE.

benefact /ˈbɛnɪfakt/ *verb*. L16.
[ORIGIN Back-form. from BENEFACTOR.]
†**1** *verb intrans.* Act as a benefactor. *rare*. Only in L16.
2 *verb trans.* Help or endow as a benefactor. L19.

benefaction /bɛnɪˈfakʃ(ə)n/ *noun*. M17.
[ORIGIN Late Latin *benefactio(n-)*, from *bene facere* do good (to), pa. ppl stem *fact-*: see -FACTION.]
1 A doing good, beneficence; a benefit or blessing. M17.
2 *esp.* The bestowal of money for a charitable purpose; a gift, an endowment. L17.

benefactive /bɛnɪˈfaktɪv/ *adjective & noun*. M20.
[ORIGIN from Latin *benefactus* capable of giving (formed as BENEFACTION) + -IVE.]
GRAMMAR. (An affix, phrase, or verbal aspect) indicating that someone is benefited.

benefactor /ˈbɛnɪfaktə/ *noun*. LME.
[ORIGIN Latin, from *bene facere*: see BENEFACTION, -OR.]
1 A person who gives friendly aid; a patron of or donor to a cause or charitable institution. LME.

> J. LE CARRÉ You cannot imagine that some kindly benefactor . . would ever concern himself with putting you on your feet. K. M. E. MURRAY As a benefactor of Keble College he was influential in Oxford circles.

2 A person who does good. *rare*. E17.

> SHAKES. *Meas. for M.* Well—what benefactors are they? Are they not malefactors?

▪ **benefactory** *adjective* of or pertaining to a benefactor; beneficial: M18. **benefactress** *noun* a female benefactor E18. †**benefactrice** *noun* = BENEFACTRESS LME–E18. **benefactrix** *noun* = BENEFACTRESS E17.

benefic /bɪˈnɛfɪk/ *adjective*. E17.
[ORIGIN Latin *beneficus* formed as BENEFACTOR: see -FIC.]
1 ASTROLOGY. Of favourable influence. E17.
2 *gen.* Beneficent, kindly. M17.

benefice /ˈbɛnɪfɪs/ *noun & verb*. ME.
[ORIGIN Old French (mod. *bénéfice* profit, perquisite) from Latin *beneficium* favour, support, from (after *beneficus* BENEFIC) *bene* well + *fic-* var. of *fac-* in *facere* do, make. In sense A.2 translating Latin.]
▸ **A** *noun* **I 1** An ecclesiastical living; property held by a rector, vicar, or other church officer. ME.
2 *hist.* Land granted in feudal tenure, a fief. L15.
▸ **II** †**3** A kindness or favour; an indulgence. LME–L17.
4 Favourable influence or operation; advantage, protection. *obsolete* exc. *hist.* LME.
†**5** Beneficial property or action (as of natural causes). LME–M17.
▸ **B** *verb trans.* Endow or invest with a church living. Chiefly as ***beneficed*** *ppl adjective*. LME.

beneficence /bɪˈnɛfɪs(ə)ns/ *noun*. LME.
[ORIGIN Latin *beneficentia*, from *beneficus*: see BENEFIC, -ENCE.]
1 Doing good, active kindness. LME.

> A. S. NEILL A child is born neither good nor bad, but with tendencies toward both beneficence and criminality.

2 A benefaction; a gift; a good deed. M17.

> CARLYLE Sterling now . . zealously forwarded schools and beneficences. R. NIEBUHR The universal beneficences of nature.

▪ **beneficency** *noun* (now *rare*) = BENEFICENCE 1 L16.

beneficent /bɪˈnɛfɪs(ə)nt/ *adjective*. E17.
[ORIGIN Latin *beneficent-* stem of *beneficentior* compar. of *beneficus* BENEFIC: cf. MAGNIFICENT.]
Doing good; actively kind; showing or expressive of active kindness; beneficial (*to*).

> POPE Gentle of speech, beneficent of mind. H. J. LASKI A revolution which, beneficent to the masses, would be fatal to themselves. W. STYRON His face is illumined by a beneficent smile.

▪ **beneficential** /-ˈsɛnʃ(ə)l/ *adjective* of or pertaining to beneficence M19. **beneficently** *adverb* E18.

beneficiaire /ˌbɛnɪfɪʃɪˈɛː/ *noun*. M19.
[ORIGIN French *bénéficiaire*, from *bénéfice* BENEFICE + *-aire* -AR².]
The recipient of the proceeds from a benefit performance etc.

beneficial /bɛnɪˈfɪʃ(ə)l/ *adjective*. LME.
[ORIGIN Old French & mod. French *bénéficial* or late Latin *beneficialis*, from *beneficium*: see BENEFICE, -AL¹.]
1 Of benefit, advantageous, (*to*). LME. ▸†**b** Lucrative, bringing pecuniary profit. E16–M19.

> *New Scientist* The beneficial effects of a diet that includes soya beans. *Decanter* A moderate daily intake is beneficial to health.

†**2** Actively kind. E16–M17.
†**3** Of or pertaining to a church benefice; beneficed. M16–M19.
4 LAW. Of, pertaining to, or having the use or benefit of property; (of a trust) in which legal entitlement to property is vested in a trustee, who is obliged to hold the property for the benefit of the person or persons entitled under the trust. M19.
▪ **beneficially** *adverb* M16. **beneficialness** *noun* E16.

beneficiary /bɛnɪˈfɪʃ(ə)ri/ *adjective & noun*. E17.
[ORIGIN Latin *beneficiarius*, from *beneficium*: see BENEFICE, -ARY¹.]
▸ **A** *adjective*. Holding, held as, or pertaining to the holding of, a benefice; *spec.* (*hist.*) feudatory. E17.
▸ **B** *noun*. **1** *hist.* The holder of a fief; a feudatory. E17.
2 The holder of a church living. M17.
3 A person who receives or is entitled to receive a favour or benefit, esp. under a trust or will or life insurance policy. M17.

beneficiate /bɛnɪˈfɪʃɪeɪt/ *verb trans*. L19.
[ORIGIN from Spanish *beneficiar*, from *beneficio* benefit: see -ATE³.]
Treat (ore, raw material, etc.) to improve its properties.
▪ **benefici'ation** *noun* L19.

benefit /ˈbɛnɪfɪt/ *noun*. LME.
[ORIGIN Anglo-Norman *benfet*, Old French *bienfet*, *-fait* ult. from Latin *benefactum* good deed, from *bene facere*: see BENEFACTION.]
†**1** A thing well done; a good deed. LME–E19.
2 A kind deed; a favour, gift; a benefaction. *arch.* LME.

> SHAKES. *A.Y.L.* [Fortune's] benefits are mightily misplaced.

3 LAW (now *hist.*). The advantage of belonging to a privileged order exempted from the jurisdiction or sentence of ordinary courts of law. L15.
4 *gen.* (An) advantage, (a) good. E16. ▸†**b** A natural advantage or gift. *rare* (Shakes.). L16–E17. ▸**c** Pecuniary profit. L16.

> S. JOHNSON Having long laboured for the benefit of mankind. J. F. KENNEDY We have, however, one great advantage over the English. We have the benefit of their experience. B. PLAIN The . . fancy decorated birthday cake was for the children's benefit. B. BETTELHEIM Whatever practical benefits may be derived from psychoanalysis, they are only incidental to its cultural achievements. **b** SHAKES. *A.Y.L.* Disable all the benefits of your own country. **c** STEELE My Estate is seven hundred Pounds a Year, besides the Benefit of Tin-Mines.

5 = BENEFICE *noun* 1. *obsolete* exc. *dial.* M16.
6 A theatrical performance, concert, sporting event, etc., the proceeds of which go to a player or other particular person or group; also, the proceeds from such a performance etc. E18.

> C. CHAPLIN Three months before I left the troupe we appeared at a benefit for my father. R. K. NARAYAN It was a benefit show for building a maternity home.

benefit match, ***benefit performance***, etc.
7 The allowance to which a person is entitled under a social security or insurance scheme or as the member of a benefit club or society. L19.
maternity benefit, ***retirement benefit***, ***sickness benefit***, ***supplementary benefit***, ***unemployment benefit***, etc.
– PHRASES: ***benefit of*** CLERGY. **benefit of the doubt** assumption of a person's innocence, rightness, etc., rather than the contrary in the absence of proof. ***fringe benefit***: see FRINGE *noun & adjective*. **on benefit** supported by social security etc. payments. ***social benefit***: see SOCIAL *adjective*.
– COMB.: **benefit club**, **benefit society**: whose members, by the regular payment of small sums, are entitled to pecuniary help in time of distress; **benefit tourist** *colloq.* a person who travels to or within Britain in order to live off social security payments while untruthfully claiming to be seeking work.

benefit /ˈbɛnɪfɪt/ *verb*. Infl. **-t-**, ***-tt-**. L15.
[ORIGIN from the noun.]
1 *verb trans.* Do good to, be of advantage to; improve. L15.

> J. GALSWORTHY It had long been her pet plan that her uncles should benefit themselves and Bosinney by building country homes. H. KISSINGER The lessons we learned benefited our handling of later crises.

2 *verb intrans.* Receive benefit; profit. (Foll. by *by*, *from*.) E17.

> N. MITFORD The younger ones were now benefiting from the fact that Louisa and Linda were married women. E. LONGFORD Lord Castlereagh was no financial wizard and it was through Wellington's labours that the world at large benefited.

Benelux /ˈbɛnɪlʌks/ *noun*. M20.
[ORIGIN Acronym, from *Belgium*, *Netherlands*, *Luxemburg*.]
Belgium, the Netherlands, and Luxembourg collectively; *esp.* these countries in association as a regional economic group.

benempt(ed) *verb* see BENAME.

benet /ˈbɛnɪt/ *noun*. LME.
[ORIGIN Anglo-Norman *benet*, Old French *beneëit* from Latin *benedictus* blessed: see BENEDICTUS.]
ECCLESIASTICAL HISTORY. = EXORCIST 1b.

benet /bɪˈnɛt/ *verb trans*. Infl. **-tt-**. ME.
[ORIGIN from BE- 1, 4 + NET *verb*¹ or *noun*¹.]
Cover as with, or catch in, a net. Chiefly *fig.*

Beneventan /bɛnɪˈvɛnt(ə)n/ *adjective*. E20.
[ORIGIN Italian *beneventano* from medieval Latin *Beneventanus*, from *Beneventum* Benevento, a province of Italy + -AN.]
Designating or pertaining to a medieval script principally of southern Italy.
▪ Also **Beneventine** *adjective* (now *rare* or *obsolete*) L19.

benevolence /bɪˈnɛvəl(ə)ns/ *noun*. ME.
[ORIGIN Old French & mod. French *bénévolence* (Old French also *beni-*) from Latin *benevolentia*, from *benevolent-*: see BENEVOLENT, -ENCE.]
1 Disposition to do good; kindness, generosity, charitable feeling (towards humankind at large). ME.
†**2** Affection, goodwill (towards a particular person or on a particular occasion). LME–E19.
do one's benevolence lend one's friendly offices.
3 An act of kindness; a gift of money, a charitable contribution. LME.
4 *hist.* A forced loan or contribution levied by certain English monarchs without the consent of Parliament (first demanded by Edward IV in 1473 as a token of goodwill). L15.

†**benevolency** *noun*. M16–M18.
[ORIGIN formed as BENEVOLENCE: see -ENCY.]
The quality of being benevolent; a gift of money.

benevolent /bɪˈnɛv(ə)l(ə)nt/ *adjective*. LME.
[ORIGIN Old French *benivolent* from Latin *benevolent-* pres. ppl stem of *bene velle* wish well: see -ENT.]
1 Desirous of the good of others; of a kindly disposition; charitable. LME.

> POPE Beloved old man! benevolent as wise. J. GALSWORTHY Her plan met with more opposition from Providence than so benevolent a scheme deserved.

2 Well-disposed (*to* another). L15.

> MILTON Raphael now . . Benevolent and facil thus repli'd.

▪ **benevolently** *adverb* M16.

Benford's law /ˈbenfədz lɔː/ *noun phr*. M20.
[ORIGIN Frank *Benford* (1887–1948), American physicist and electrical engineer.]
A statistical law to the effect that, in lists of numerical data with a smooth distribution and a spread of at least an order of magnitude, the figure 1 is the leading digit in around 30 per cent of instances, and the frequency of occurrence as a leading digit decreases from 1 to 9.

B.Eng. *abbreviation*.
Bachelor of Engineering.

benga /ˈbɛŋgə/ *noun*. L20.
[ORIGIN Luo.]
A style of popular music originating in Kenya, characterized by a fusion of traditional Kenyan music and a lively arrangement of guitars, bass, and vocals.

Bengal /bɛŋˈgɔːl/ *noun & adjective*. L17.
[ORIGIN A former Indian province: see BENGALI.]
▸ **A** *noun*. †**1** In *pl.* Fabrics or clothing, esp. silks, imported from Bengal. L17–M19.
2 ***royal Bengal***, = ***Bengal tiger*** below. L19.
▸ **B** *attrib.* or as *adjective*. Of or pertaining to Bengal. E18.
Bengal light a firework producing a steady and vivid blue light. **Bengal quince** = BAEL. **Bengal tiger**, **royal Bengal tiger** a tiger of a variety found in the Indian subcontinent, distinguished by unbroken stripes.

Bengalese /bɛŋgəˈliːz/ *adjective & noun*. Pl. of noun same. L18.
[ORIGIN from BENGAL + -ESE.]
= BENGALI.

Bengali /bɛŋˈgɔːli/ *adjective & noun*. Also †**-lee**. L18.
[ORIGIN from Hindi *baṅgālī*.]
▸ **A** *adjective*. Of or pertaining to Bengal, a former Indian province, now constituting Bangladesh and the Indian state of West Bengal, its people, or their language. L18.
▸ **B** *noun*. A native or inhabitant of Bengal, or of Bangladesh or West Bengal; the Indo-Aryan language of Bengal, the national language of Bangladesh and the official language of West Bengal. E19.

bengaline /ˈbɛŋɡəliːn/ *noun*. L19.
[ORIGIN French, so named because of the similarity to *Bengals* (see BENGAL *noun* 1).]
A strong ribbed fabric made of a mixture of silk and either cotton or wool.

benight /bɪˈnʌɪt/ *verb trans*. LME.
[ORIGIN from BE- 4 + NIGHT *noun*.]
1 Cover, hide, or involve in the darkness of night. Usu. (and *arch.* exc.) in *pass.* LME.
DE QUINCEY The tourists were benighted in a forest.
2 *fig.* Involve in intellectual or moral darkness; darken, cloud. Freq. in *pass.* E17.
W. DAVENANT Now jealousie no more benights her face. J. WILSON What men.. call Religion, now benighting half the earth. ISAIAH BERLIN The mass of the proletarians themselves were too benighted to grasp the role which history had called on them to play.
■ **benightedness** *noun* the state of being benighted M19. **benightment** *noun* (*rare*) M17.

benign /bɪˈnʌɪn/ *adjective*. ME.
[ORIGIN Old French & mod. French *bénigne* from Latin *benignus* prob. for *benigenus*, from *bene* well + *-genus* born; for the formation cf. MALIGN *adjective*, for the sense Latin *gentilis* GENTLE *adjective*.]
1 Of a kindly disposition, gracious. ME.
R. D. LAING Assurance that during sleep he is being watched over by benign presences (parents, good fairies, angels).
2 Manifesting kindly feeling; bland, gentle, mild. LME.
R. MACAULAY He nodded and was benign, but anyone could see he did not agree. J. HELLER Sid was regarding the assault upon Gold with a smiling and benign countenance.
benign neglect lack of attention reflecting confidence in or a favourable disposition towards a person or thing; well-intentioned or beneficial neglect.
3 Of a thing: favourable, propitious, salutary. LME.
C. BRONTË On whose birth benign planets have certainly smiled. A. J. P. TAYLOR The weather was uniformly benign. E. F. SCHUMACHER We were very rapidly using up a certain kind of irreplaceable capital asset, namely the *tolerance margins* which benign nature always provides.
4 MEDICINE. †**a** Of a medicine: mild in action. M17–M18. ▸**b** Of a disease or tumour: not malignant. M18.
■ **benignly** *adverb* LME.

benignant /bɪˈnɪɡnənt/ *adjective*. L18.
[ORIGIN from BENIGN or Latin *benignus*, after *malignant*: see -ANT¹.]
1 Kind or gracious to inferiors or dependants; (esp. condescendingly) benevolent. L18.
2 Of things: favourable, beneficial. L18.
3 MEDICINE. = BENIGN 4b. L19.
■ **benignancy** *noun* L19. **benignantly** *adverb* L18.

benignity /bɪˈnɪɡnɪti/ *noun*. LME.
[ORIGIN Old French & mod. French *bénignité* or Latin *benignitas*, from *benignus*: see BENIGN, -ITY.]
1 Kindly feeling; kindness of disposition or of manner (esp. towards inferiors or juniors). LME. ▸**b** A kindly or generous deed. M16.
2 Of things: benign quality. *arch.* E17.

Benin /bɛˈniːn/ *noun pl. & adjective*. L19.
[ORIGIN Unknown.]
(Of or pertaining to) a people of southern Nigeria, noted for their production of fine bronzes and carved ivories.
■ **Beniˈnese** *noun*, pl. same, a member of the Benin people L19.

Benioff /ˈbɛnɪɒf/ *noun*. M20.
[ORIGIN V. Hugo *Benioff* (1899–1968), US seismologist.]
GEOLOGY. **1** ***Benioff seismograph***, ***Benioff seismometer***, an instrument of a kind invented by Benioff in which movement of a horizontal rod induces an electrical voltage. M20.
2 ***Benioff zone***, an inclined zone of high seismicity underlying island-arc systems at the overlap of oceanic and continental crust. M20.

benison /ˈbɛnɪz(ə)n, -s-/ *noun*. ME.
[ORIGIN Old French *beneiçon*, (later) *benisson* from Latin *benedictio(n-)* BENEDICTION.]
A blessing, benediction; blessedness, beatitude.
JER. TAYLOR The most glorious issues of Divine Benison upon this Kingdome. SIR W. SCOTT I have slept sound under such a benison. P. NORMAN The benison of that smile, bestowed on well-eaten dinner or an unusual Dinky car.

bénitier /benitje/ *noun*. Pl. pronounced same. M19.
[ORIGIN French, from *bénit(e* blessed + *-ier* -ER².]
A vessel for holy water.

benitoite /bəˈniːtəʊʌɪt/ *noun*. E20.
[ORIGIN from San *Benito* County, California + -ITE¹.]
MINERALOGY. A sapphire-blue hexagonal barium titanium silicate, sometimes of gem quality.

benjamin /ˈbɛndʒəmɪn/ *noun*¹. M16.
[ORIGIN Alt. of *benjoin* var. of BENZOIN, by assoc. with male forename *Benjamin*.]
= BENZOIN 1.
– COMB.: **benjamin bush** = ***benjamin-tree*** (b) below; **benjamin-tree** (*a*) a tree yielding benzoin; (*b*) a spicebush.

benjamin /ˈbɛndʒəmɪn/ *noun*². *arch.* E19.
[ORIGIN Perh. the name of a tailor.]
A type of overcoat for men.

Benjamin /ˈbɛndʒəmɪn/ *noun*³. M19.
[ORIGIN The youngest son of the patriarch Jacob (*Genesis* 43 etc.).]
The youngest (and favourite) child.
Benjamin's portion the largest share.

†**benjoin** *noun* var. of BENZOIN.

benne *noun* var. of BENNI.

bennet /ˈbɛnɪt/ *noun*¹. LME.
[ORIGIN Old French *herbe benëite*, medieval Latin *herba benedicta* lit. 'blessed plant' (said to put the Devil to flight).]
Usu. (now only) in full ***herb bennet***. Wood avens, *Geum urbanum*. Formerly also, any of several other plants, *esp.* hemlock.

bennet *noun*² see BENT *noun*¹.

benni /ˈbɛni/ *noun*. Also **benne**. M18.
[ORIGIN Mande.]
The sesame plant, *Sesamum orientale*. Usu. in *comb.*, as ***benniseed***.

benny /ˈbɛni/ *noun*¹. *US slang*. E20.
[ORIGIN App. abbreviation of BENJAMIN *noun*²: see -Y⁶.]
A sack coat; an overcoat.

benny /ˈbɛni/ *noun*². *slang* (orig. *US*). M20.
[ORIGIN from BEN(ZEDRINE + -Y⁶.]
(A tablet of) Benzedrine.

benomyl /ˈbɛnəmɪl/ *noun*. M20.
[ORIGIN from BEN(Z)O- + M(ETH)YL.]
An imidazole derivative used as a systemic fungicide on fruit and vegetable crops.

benorth /bɪˈnɔːθ/ *adverb & preposition*. Long *obsolete* exc. *Scot.*
[ORIGIN Old English *be norþan*, from BY *preposition* + *norþan* (adverb) from the north: cf. BEFORE.]
To the north (of).

Bensonian /bɛnˈsəʊnɪən/ *adjective & noun*. *hist.* E20.
[ORIGIN from *Benson* (see below) + -IAN.]
▸**A** *adjective*. Of or pertaining to the actor-manager Sir F. R. Benson (1858–1939) or his Shakespearean company. E20.
▸**B** *noun*. A member of this company. E20.

bent /bɛnt/ *noun*¹. Also (now *dial.*) **bennet** /ˈbɛnɪt/. ME.
[ORIGIN Repr. Old English *beonet* in place names, e.g. *Beonetlēah* (Bentley), perh. 'meadow of stiff grass': corresp. to Old Saxon *binet*, Old High German *binuz* (German *Binse*), from West Germanic, of unknown origin.]
1 A place covered with grass, an open field; unenclosed pasture, heath; *arch.* a field of battle. ME.
take the bent escape to open country.
2 A stiff-stemmed reedy or rushlike grass; such grass collectively; BOTANY any grass of the genus *Agrostis*. Also ***bent grass***. LME.
R. HERRICK Sweet bents wode bow, to give my love the day.
creeping bent = FIORIN.
3 The stiff flower stalk of grasses. L16.
■ **benting** *noun* (now *dial.*) feeding on bents (by birds) L17. **benty** *adjective* of the nature of or pertaining to bent; covered with bent: M16.

bent /bɛnt/ *noun*². LME.
[ORIGIN Prob. from BEND *verb* on the analogy of pairs like *descend* and *descent*, *extend* and *extent*.]
1 The condition of being deflected in some direction; a twist, inclination, cast; chiefly *fig.*, mental inclination, disposition, bias, tendency. LME.
SHAKES. *Tr. & Cr.* But gives all gaze and bent of amorous view On the fair Cressid. MILTON The whole bent of their actions was against the King. SHELLEY I sit—and smile or sigh as is my bent. J. GROSS If he showed a special bent, it was towards mathematics.
2 A curved position, form, or piece; curvature. Now *rare*. M16.
T. ELYOT In the fourme of a bowe, that hath a great bente. I. WALTON Make these fast at the bent of the hook.
†**3** An act of bending, bowing, or stooping. M16–E18.
†**4** Aim, purpose. L16–L18.
T. R. MALTHUS The principal bent of this work.
†**5** Impetus, elan. L16–M18.
E. YOUNG False joys, indeed, are born from want of thought; From thought's full bent, and energy, the true.
6 Degree of tension (of a bow etc.); degree of endurance; limit of capacity. Now only in ***to the top of one's bent*** (after Shakes. *Haml.*), to one's heart's content. L16.
M. DRAYTON Beyond the bent of his unknowing Sight.
7 A section of a framework or framed building. E19.

bent /bɛnt/ *adjective*. ME.
[ORIGIN pa. pple of BEND *verb*.]
†**1** Wound up or braced for action; levelled as a weapon. ME–L17.
2 Constrained into a curve, bowed, crooked; deflected from a straight line. LME.
J. G. COZZENS A man in a worn grey felt hat and a shabby brown suit stepped, bent, into the rain. P. DAVIES In a bent spacetime, it is no surprise if the paths of light rays are bent.
bent brow *arch.* a wrinkled or knit brow. **bentwood** wood artificially curved for making furniture.
3 Determined, resolved, set. Now only *pred.* Foll. by *on*, *upon*, (arch.) *to do*. LME.
R. ASCHAM The bent enemie against God and good order. W. MORRIS Like my fathers, bent to gather fame. L. M. MONTGOMERY As you're evidently bent on talking you might as well talk to some purpose. G. CHARLES I was still bent.. on a career in journalism.
4 *fig.* Dishonest, criminal; illicit, stolen; perverted, homosexual. Cf. CROOKED *adjective* 3, 4. *slang*. E20.
P. LAURIE They could go bent on us—I hope most policemen would laugh at £500, but they might not. G. F. NEWMAN The two rooms held nothing bent. Q. CRISP I used to tell the audience that I was about to deliver a straight talk from a bent speaker.

bent *verb pa. t. & pple*: see BEND *verb*.

Benthamism /ˈbɛntəmɪz(ə)m, ˈbɛnθ-/ *noun*. L18.
[ORIGIN from *Bentham* (see below) + -ISM.]
1 An act characteristic of Bentham (see sense 2). *rare*. L18.
2 The utilitarian philosophical system of Jeremy Bentham (1748–1832), English jurist and writer, in which the pursuit of the greatest happiness of the greatest number is the highest moral goal. E19.
■ **Benthamic** /-ˈtamɪk, -θ-/ *adjective* = BENTHAMITE *adjective* M19. **Benthamite** *noun & adjective* (*a*) *noun* an adherent of Benthamism; (*b*) *adjective* of or pertaining to Bentham or Benthamism: E19.

benthos /ˈbɛnθɒs/ *noun*. L19.
[ORIGIN Greek = depth of the sea.]
The flora and fauna of the bottom of the sea (or a lake).
■ **benthic** *adjective* of or pertaining to the benthos E20. **benˈthonic** *adjective* = BENTHIC L19.

bentincks /ˈbɛntɪŋks/ *noun pl.* M19.
[ORIGIN Capt. J. A. *Bentinck* (1737–75), their inventor.]
NAUTICAL (now *hist.*). Triangular sails for use on the lowest yards of square-rigged vessels.

bento /ˈbɛntəʊ/ *noun*. E17.
[ORIGIN Japanese = lunch, lunch box.]
A Japanese lunch box, traditionally made from wood and lacquered or highly decorated; a Japanese-style packed lunch, typically containing rice, vegetables, sashimi, etc.

bentonite /ˈbɛntənʌɪt/ *noun*. L19.
[ORIGIN from Fort *Benton*, Montana, US + -ITE¹.]
A highly colloidal, plastic, absorbent kind of clay having numerous uses esp. as an absorbent or filler.
■ **bentonitic** /-ˈnɪtɪk/ *adjective* M20.

ben trovato /ben troˈvaːto/ *adjectival phr.* L19.
[ORIGIN Italian, lit. 'well found'.]
Of a story etc.: happily invented; appropriate though untrue.

benumb /bɪˈnʌm/ *verb trans.* L15.
[ORIGIN from strong pa. pple of Old English *beniman* deprive, formed as BE- 1 + NIM *verb*: cf. NUMB *adjective*.]
Make insensible, torpid, or powerless (esp. of cold); deaden, stupefy; paralyse (the mind or will, action, etc.).

benz- /bɛnz/ *combining form* of BENZENE or BENZOIC. Cf. BENZO-.
■ **benˈzaldehyde** *noun* a colourless liquid aromatic aldehyde, C_6H_5CHO, which has the odour of bitter almonds and is used esp. in the manufacture of dyes and perfumes M19. **benzˈhydrol** *noun* diphenyl carbinol, $(C_6H_5)_2CHOH$, forming colourless crystals M20. **benzidine** *noun* biphenyl-4,4′-diamine $(C_6H_5NH_2)_2$, a colourless basic solid used in dye manufacture L19. **benzil** *noun* the compound 1,2-diphenylethanedione, $C_6H_5{\cdot}CO{\cdot}CO{\cdot}C_6H_5$, a yellow crystalline diketone formed by oxidation of benzoin with nitric acid M19. **benzilic** /-ˈzɪlɪk/ *adjective*: ***benzilic acid***, a colourless solid, $(C_6H_5)_2C(OH)COOH$, formed when benzil rearranges in the presence of alkali M19. **benzˈpyrene** *noun* a polycyclic aromatic hydrocarbon, $C_{20}H_{12}$, found in coal tar and considered to be the major carcinogen of tobacco smoke E20. **benzyl** *noun* the radical $C_6H_5CH_2{\cdot}$, also called ***phenylmethyl*** M19. **benˈzylic** *adjective* of, pertaining to, or of the nature of benzyl M19.

Benzedrine /ˈbɛnzɪdriːn/ *noun*. M20.
[ORIGIN from BENZ- + EPH)EDRINE.]
(Proprietary name for) amphetamine; a tablet of this.

benzene /ˈbɛnziːn/ *noun*. M19.
[ORIGIN from BENZOIC + -ENE.]
CHEMISTRY. A colourless liquid cyclic hydrocarbon, C_6H_6, obtained from coal and petroleum and used esp. as a solvent, as a fuel, and in chemical manufacture.
– COMB.: **benzene ring** the conjugated ring of six carbon atoms present in benzene and most aromatic compounds.
■ **benzenoid** *adjective* derived from, related to, or pertaining to benzene L19.

benzine /ˈbɛnziːn/ *noun*. Also †**-in**. M19.
[ORIGIN formed as BENZENE + -INE⁵.]
1 = BENZENE. Now *rare* or *obsolete*. M19.
2 A mixture of paraffins distilled from petroleum, used as a solvent and fuel. L19.

benzo- /ˈbɛnzəʊ/ *combining form* of BENZENE or BENZOIC: see -O-. Cf. BENZ-.
■ **benzocaine** *noun* [*-caine*, after COCAINE] a white crystalline powder, ethyl para-aminobenzoate $(NH_2{\cdot}C_6H_4{\cdot}COOC_2H_5)$, used

mainly as a local anaesthetic E20. **benzodiazepine** /ˌbɛnzəʊdʌɪˈeɪzɪpiːn, -ˈazəpiːn/ *noun* [DIAZO- + -EPINE] any of a class of heterocyclic compounds used as tranquillizers, including Librium and Valium M20. **benzophenone** *noun* a white crystalline ketone, $C_6H_5{\cdot}CO{\cdot}C_6H_5$, used in perfume, sunscreen, and as a flavouring agent L19. **benzoˈquinone** *noun* the simplest quinone, $C_6H_4O_2$ M20. **benzoyl** /-zəʊʌɪl, -zəʊɪl/ *noun* the radical $C_6H_5COO{\cdot}$, benzenecarbonyl M19.

benzoic /bɛnˈzəʊɪk/ *adjective*. L18.
[ORIGIN from BENZOIN + -IC.]
CHEMISTRY. ***benzoic acid***, a colourless crystalline aromatic acid, C_6H_5COOH, present in gum benzoin and many other resins.
■ ˈ**benzoate** *noun* a salt or ester of benzoic acid L18.

benzoin /ˈbɛnzəʊɪn/ *noun*. Also †**benjoin**. M16.
[ORIGIN French *benjoin* = Spanish *benjuí*, Portuguese *benjoim*, Italian *benzoi*, from Proto-Romance from Arabic *lubānjāwī* incense from Sumatra (the Proto-Romance reflex of *lu-* being taken for the def. article).]
1 A fragrant aromatic resin obtained from eastern Asian trees of the genus *Styrax*. Also ***gum benzoin***. Cf. BENJAMIN *noun*[1]. M16.
2 The spicebush, *Lindera benzoin*. (Formerly a genus name.) M18.
3 CHEMISTRY. A colourless crystalline ketone that is present in gum benzoin; 2-hydroxy-1,2-diphenylethanone, $C_6H_5{\cdot}CHOH{\cdot}CO{\cdot}C_6H_5$. M19.

benzol /ˈbɛnzɒl/ *noun*. Also **-ole** /-əʊl/. M19.
[ORIGIN from BENZOIC *adjective* + -OL.]
Benzene, esp. in impure commercial forms used as fuel.

Beothuk /bɪˈɒθək/ *noun & adjective*. Pl. **-s**, same. E19.
[ORIGIN Prob. from Beothuk.]
A member of, of or pertaining to, an extinct N. American Indian people of Newfoundland; (of) the language of this people.

bepaint /bɪˈpeɪnt/ *verb trans*. L15.
[ORIGIN from BE- 1 + PAINT *verb*.]
Paint over; paint obtrusively; colour.

bepatched /bɪˈpatʃt/ *adjective*. E17.
[ORIGIN from BE- + PATCH *verb* + -ED[1].]
Mended with patches; wearing patches.

bepearled /bɪˈpəːld/ *adjective*. M17.
[ORIGIN from BE- 5 + PEARL *noun*[1] + -ED[2].]
Covered (as) with pearls.

bepelt /bɪˈpɛlt/ *verb trans*. E17.
[ORIGIN from BE- 1 + PELT *verb*[1].]
Pelt thoroughly (with missiles etc.).

bepity /bɪˈpɪti/ *verb trans. arch*. L16.
[ORIGIN from BE- 1 + PITY *verb*.]
Pity exceedingly.

beplaster /bɪˈplɑːstə/ *verb trans*. E17.
[ORIGIN from BE- 1 + PLASTER *verb*.]
Plaster over or about; smear thickly (*with*).

beplumed /bɪˈpluːmd/ *adjective*. L16.
[ORIGIN from BE- 5 + PLUME *noun* + -ED[2].]
Adorned with feathers.

bepommel /bɪˈpɒm(ə)l/ *verb trans*. Infl. **-ll-**, ***-l-**. L16.
[ORIGIN from BE- 1 + POMMEL *verb*.]
Pommel soundly, drub.

bepowder /bɪˈpaʊdə/ *verb trans*. L16.
[ORIGIN from BE- 1 + POWDER *verb*[1].]
Powder over.

bepraise /bɪˈpreɪz/ *verb trans*. M17.
[ORIGIN from BE- 1 + PRAISE *verb*.]
Praise greatly or to excess.

bepuff /bɪˈpʌf/ *verb trans*. M19.
[ORIGIN from BE- 1 + PUFF *verb*.]
Puff out; *fig.* puff up, praise greatly.

bepuzzle /bɪˈpʌz(ə)l/ *verb trans*. L16.
[ORIGIN from BE- 1 + PUZZLE *verb*.]
Puzzle utterly.
■ **bepuzzlement** *noun* E19.

bequeath /bɪˈkwiːð/ *verb trans*. OE.
[ORIGIN from BE- + QUETHE.]
†**1** Say, declare; express, mean. OE–ME.
2 Leave (an estate or piece of property) *to* a person by will. Also with the inheritor as indirect obj. Cf. DEVISE *verb* 7. OE. ▸†**b** Transfer (property) *to* a person with immediate effect. ME–E17. ▸**c** *fig.* Transmit (an example, quality, etc.) to posterity. E17.

> **b** SHAKES. *John* Wilt thou forsake thy fortune, Bequeath thy land to him and follow me? **c** S. JOHNSON This narrative he has bequeathed to future generations. A. SCHLEE Her beautiful hair was scarcely faded from the deep coppery colour she had bequeathed to her daughter.

†**3** Commit *to*, *unto*; entrust, bestow, yield. ME–E19.

> EVELYN Gentlemen . . who generally so bequeath themselves to this service. N. FAIRFAX That which bequeaths it this slow pace. POPE We to flames our slaughtered friends bequeath.

■ **bequeathable** *adjective* M17. **bequeathal** *noun* the action of bequeathing M17. **bequeather** *noun* E16. **bequeathment** *noun* the action of bequeathing, a bequest E17.

bequest /bɪˈkwɛst/ *noun*. ME.
[ORIGIN from (after BEQUEATH) BE- + Middle English †*quiste* repr. Old English *-cwiss* (in comb.), repl. *cwide* saying, testament: for the parasitic *t* cf. BEHEST.]
1 The action of bequeathing; gift by will. Cf. DEVISE *noun* 2. ME.
2 A thing bequeathed; a legacy. LME.

ber /bəː/ *noun*. M19.
[ORIGIN Hindi.]
In the Indian subcontinent: a jujube tree, *Ziziphus jujuba*; its edible fruit.

berate /bɪˈreɪt/ *verb trans*. M16.
[ORIGIN from BE- 1 + RATE *verb*[2].]
Scold, rebuke.

berattle /bɪˈrat(ə)l/ *verb trans*. *rare* (usu. after Shakes.). M16.
[ORIGIN from BE- 1 + RATTLE *verb*[1].]
Rattle away upon or at; fill with din.

> SHAKES. *Haml.* These . . so berattle the common stages . . that many wearing rapiers . . dare scarce come thither.

beray /bɪˈreɪ/ *verb trans*. Now *rare* or *obsolete*. Also **bewray**. M16.
[ORIGIN from BE- 1 + RAY *verb*[1].]
Disfigure, defile, befoul; *fig.* besmirch, slander.

Berber /ˈbəːbə/ *noun & adjective*. M18.
[ORIGIN from Arabic *barbar*: cf. BARBARY.]
▸ **A** *noun*. Pl. **-s**, same. A member of any of the indigenous Caucasian peoples of N. Africa; their Hamito-Semitic language (of which there are several local forms). M18.
▸ **B** *attrib.* or as *adjective*. Of or pertaining to the Berbers or their language. E19.

Berberine /bəːbəˈriːn/ *noun*[1]. Also †**Barbarin**. E19.
[ORIGIN from BERBER, perh. after ALGERINE, TANGERINE.]
A Berber.

berberine /ˈbəːbəriːn/ *noun*[2]. M19.
[ORIGIN from BERBERIS + -INE[5].]
A bitter yellow alkaloid obtained from barberry and other plants.

berberis /ˈbəːbərɪs/ *noun*. L16.
[ORIGIN mod. Latin or Old French from medieval Latin *barbaris*.]
Any shrub of the genus *Berberis* (see BARBERRY); *esp.* one grown for ornament.

berberry *noun* var. of BARBERRY.

berceau /bɛrso/ *noun*. Pl. ***-eaux*** /-o/. L17.
[ORIGIN French, lit. 'cradle'.]
An arbour, a bower; a shaded or leafy walk.

berceuse /bɛrsøːz, bɛːˈsəːz/ *noun*. Pl. pronounced same. L19.
[ORIGIN French, from *bercer* to rock + fem. agent-suffix *-euse*.]
MUSIC. A lullaby; an instrumental piece with a gently rocking rhythm.

berdache /bəˈdaʃ/ *noun*. Also **-dash**. E19.
[ORIGIN French *bardache* BARDASH.]
Among N. American Indians: a transvestite.

bere /bɪə/ *noun*[1]. Chiefly *Scot.* Also †**bear**.
[ORIGIN Old English *bære*, *bere*, 1st elem. of BARLEY *noun*.]
Barley; *spec.* six-rowed barley, *Hordeum vulgare*, or its reputedly hardier four-rowed variety (cf. BIG *noun*[2]).

bere /bɪə/ *noun*[2]. *obsolete* exc. *dial.* Also **bear**, **beer**. LME.
[ORIGIN Uncertain: connection with Low German *büre* (German *Bühre*) has been proposed.]
A pillowcase. Usu. more fully ***pillow-bere***.

bereave /bɪˈriːv/ *verb trans*. Pa. t. & pple **-d**, **bereft** /bɪˈrɛft/, (*arch.*) **bereaven** /-v(ə)n/.
[ORIGIN Old English *berēafian* = Old Frisian *birāvia*, Old Saxon *birōƀon* (Dutch *beroven*), Old High German *biroubōn* (German *berauben*), Gothic *biraubōn* from Germanic: see BE-, REAVE *verb*[1].]
1 Orig., deprive or dispossess *of* a possession. Now usu., deprive *of* a relative or loved one by death; leave orphaned or widowed. Freq. as ***bereaved ppl adjective***. See also BEREFT. OE. ▸**b** With double obj.: deprive of. *arch.* ME.

> SHAKES. *Merch. V.* Madam, you have bereft me of all words. J. R. ACKERLEY He was lately bereaved of his wife. *Daily Telegraph* A bereaved husband killed himself hours after his wife died from cancer. *fig.*: P. USTINOV Laughter would be bereaved if snobbery died. **b** MILTON Bereaue me not . . thy gentle looks, thy aid.

†**2** Snatch away, remove by violence. ME–E18.

> SHAKES. *Lucr.* If . . thine honour lay in me, From me by strong assault it is bereft.

– NOTE: The more usual form of ppl adjective is *bereaved* in the case of loss by death, and *bereft* with reference to the loss of things.
■ **bereavement** *noun* the state or an instance of being bereaved (now only of a relative etc. by death) M18.

bereft *adjective*. L16.
[ORIGIN pa. t. & pple of BEREAVE.]
1 Deprived of or lacking something, esp. a non-material asset. L16.

> L. P. HARTLEY His hands dropped to his sides, and he looked as bereft of dignity as any human being could.

2 Of a person: lonely and abandoned, esp. through someone's death or departure. E19.

> G. MACDONALD I cry to thee . . Because I am bereft.

Berenice's Hair /bɛrɪˈnʌɪsiːz hɛː/ *noun phr*. M16.
[ORIGIN translating Latin COMA BERENICES.]
= COMA BERENICES.

beret /ˈbɛreɪ, -ri/ *noun*. E19.
[ORIGIN French *béret* from SW French dial. & Old Provençal *berret*: see BIRETTA.]
A round felt or cloth cap that lies flat on the head, covering it closely (as traditionally worn by Basque peasantry); such a cap forming part of military uniform.
Basque beret: see BASQUE *adjective*. ***Green Beret***: see GREEN *adjective*.

beretta *noun* var. of BIRETTA.

berg /bəːg/ *noun*[1]. E19.
[ORIGIN Abbreviation of ICEBERG.]
A very large floating mass (of ice); an iceberg.
tabular berg: see TABULAR 1.
■ **bergy** *adjective* having many icebergs; of the nature of an iceberg: M19.

berg /bəːg, *foreign* bɛrx/ *noun*[2]. *S. Afr.* E19.
[ORIGIN Afrikaans from Dutch = Old English *beorg* etc. BARROW *noun*[1].]
A mountain.
– COMB.: **berg adder** an adder, *Bitis atropos*, found in highland areas of southern Africa; ***Berg* DAMARA**; **berg wind** a hot dry northerly wind blowing from the interior to coastal districts.

Bergamasque /ˈbəːgəmɑːsk/ *adjective & noun*. Also †**-mask**; in sense B.1 **b-**. L16.
[ORIGIN (French from) Italian *Bergamasco* of Bergamo (see below).]
▸ **A** *adjective*. Of or pertaining to the northern Italian city and province of Bergamo. L16.
▸ **B** *noun*. **1** A dance resembling a tarantella. L16.
2 A native or inhabitant of Bergamo. E17.

bergamot /ˈbəːgəmɒt/ *noun*[1]. E17.
[ORIGIN French *bergamotte* from Italian *bergamotta* from Turkish *begarmudu*, from *beg* prince, BEG *noun*[1] + *armud* pear + *-u* possess. suffix.]
A variety of fine pear.

bergamot /ˈbəːgəmɒt/ *noun*[2]. L17.
[ORIGIN from *Bergamo*, a city & province in northern Italy.]
1 A citrus tree, *Citrus aurantium* subsp. *bergamia*, bearing fruit similar to an orange, from the rind of which a fragrant essence is prepared. L17.
bergamot orange, ***bergamot tree***.
2 †**a** Snuff scented with this essence. Only in 18. ▸**b** The essence itself. M18.
3 Any of several labiate plants smelling like bergamot, *esp.* (**a**) (more fully ***bergamot mint***) a mint, *Mentha* × *piperita* var. *citrata*, grown for its fragrance; (**b**) *northern Amer.* (more fully ***wild bergamot***) = MONARDA. M19.

Bergan *noun* var. of BERGEN.

bergander /bəˈgandə/ *noun*. *dial.* Also **bar-** /bɑː-/. M16.
[ORIGIN Perh. from Old Norse *ber* berry (from the red horn on the beak of the male) + GANDER *noun*.]
A shelduck.

Bergen /ˈbəːgən/ *noun*. Also **-gan**, **b-**. E20.
[ORIGIN Unknown.]
In full ***Bergen pack***, ***Bergen rucksack***, etc. A type of rucksack supported by a frame.

bergenia /bəˈgiːnɪə/ *noun*. M19.
[ORIGIN mod. Latin, from K. A. von *Bergen* (1704–60), German physician & botanist: see -IA[1].]
Any of various perennial plants of the genus *Bergenia*, of the saxifrage family, having large, thick leaves and usu. pink, red, or purple flowers.

bergère /bɛrʒɛːr/ *noun*. Pl. pronounced same. M18.
[ORIGIN French = shepherdess.]
A long-seated upholstered armchair fashionable in the 18th cent. Also, a chair with canework seat, back, and sides.

bergerette /bəːʒəˈrɛt/ *noun*. Also †**bargeret**. LME.
[ORIGIN French, from *berger* shepherd: see -ETTE.]
A pastoral or rustic song about shepherds, for dancing to.

berghaan /ˈbəːghɑːn, *foreign* ˈbɛrx-/ *noun*. *S. Afr.* M19.
[ORIGIN Afrikaans, from BERG *noun*[2] + *haan* cock.]
An eagle, *esp.* a bateleur.

bergschrund /ˈbəːgʃrʊnd, *foreign* ˈbɛrkʃrʊnt/ *noun*. Pl. **-ds** /-dz/, **-de** /-də/. M19.
[ORIGIN German, from *Berg* mountain (see BARROW *noun*[1]) + SCHRUND.]
A crevasse or gap at the junction of a glacier or snowfield with a steep upper slope.

Bergsonian /bəːgˈsəʊnɪən/ *adjective & noun*. E20.
[ORIGIN from *Bergson* (see below) + -IAN.]
▸ **A** *adjective*. Of, pertaining to, or characteristic of the French philosopher Henri Bergson (1859–1941). E20.
▸ **B** *noun*. A follower or adherent of Bergson. E20.

bergylt /ˈbəːgɪlt/ *noun*. L18.
[ORIGIN from Old Norse *berg* rock + *gyltr* sow, GILT *noun*[1].]
1 The ballan wrasse. *Shetland*. L18.
2 The Norway haddock. M19.

berhyme /bɪˈrʌɪm/ *verb trans.* Also **berime**. L16.
[ORIGIN from BE- 2, 4 + RHYME *verb* or *noun*.]
Compose rhymes about; lampoon in rhyme.

beriberi /bɛrɪˈbɛri/ *noun*. E18.
[ORIGIN Sinhalese = weakness.]
A disease due to vitamin B_1 deficiency, which is characterized by polyneuritis and freq. oedema and cardiac disorder, and is mainly associated with rice-based diets.

berime *verb* var. of BERHYME.

berk /bəːk/ *noun*. *slang*. Also **birk**, **burk(e)**. M20.
[ORIGIN Abbreviation of BERKELEY HUNT.]
A foolish person.
JACQUELINE WILSON Mark looked a right berk in his trunks.

Berkeleian /bɑːˈkliːən/ *noun & adjective*. E19.
[ORIGIN from *Berkeley* (see below) + -AN.]
(A follower or adherent) of the Irish philosopher Bishop George Berkeley (1685–1753) or of his philosophy, in which the objective existence of matter was denied.
■ **Berkeleianism** *noun* the philosophical opinions held by Berkeley and his followers E19. **ˈBerkeleyism** *noun* = BERKELEIANISM M19.

Berkeley hunt /ˈbəːkli hʌnt, ˈbɑː-/ *noun phr.* *rhyming slang*. M20.
[ORIGIN A hunt in Gloucestershire.]
= CUNT (esp. sense 2).

berkelium /bəːˈkiːlɪəm, ˈbəːklɪəm/ *noun*. M20.
[ORIGIN from *Berkeley*, California, where first made + -IUM.]
A radioactive metallic chemical element of the actinide series, atomic no. 97, which is produced artificially (symbol Bk).

Berks. *abbreviation*.
Berkshire.

Berkshire /ˈbɑːkʃə/ *noun*. E19.
[ORIGIN A county in England.]
In full *Berkshire pig* etc. (An animal of) a breed of black pig.

Berlin /bəːˈlɪn/ *noun*[1]. In sense 1 usu. **b-**, & also (after French) **-line** /-ˈliːn/. L17.
[ORIGIN A city in northern Germany.]
1 Chiefly *hist.* A four-wheeled covered carriage with a hooded seat behind. L17.
2 *attrib.* Designating things associated with Berlin. L18.
Berlin black a black varnish used on metal ware. **Berlin blue** Prussian blue. **Berlin glove** a strong glove of washable cotton. **Berlin pattern** a pattern in Berlin work. **Berlin wool** a fine dyed merino wool used for knitting or embroidery. **Berlin work** worsted embroidery on canvas.
■ **Berliner** *noun* a native or inhabitant of Berlin M19.

berlin *noun*[2], **berling** *noun* vars. of BIRLING.

Berliozian /bɛːlɪˈəʊzɪən/ *adjective & noun*. E20.
[ORIGIN from *Berlioz* (see below) + -IAN.]
▸ **A** *adjective*. Of, pertaining to, resembling, or characteristic of the French composer Hector Berlioz (1803–69) or his music. E20.
▸ **B** *noun*. An interpreter, student, or admirer of Berlioz or his music. M20.

berm /bəːm/ *noun*. E18.
[ORIGIN French *berme* from Dutch *berm*, prob. rel. to Old Norse *barmr* brim.]
1 A narrow space or ledge; *esp.* in fortification, the space between a ditch and the base of a parapet. E18.
2 A flat strip of land, raised bank, or terrace bordering a river etc.; a path or grass strip beside a road. L19.

Bermuda /bəˈmjuːdə/ *noun*. M17.
[ORIGIN A group of islands in the W. Atlantic.]
▸ **I 1** A variety of cigar or rolled tobacco. Now *rare* or *obsolete*. M17.
2 In *pl.* Bermuda shorts. M20.
▸ **II 3** *attrib.* Also (earlier) †**-as**. Designating things from or associated with Bermuda. M18.
Bermuda buttercup a bulbous yellow-flowered southern African oxalis, *Oxalis pes-caprae*, widespread as a weed in warmer parts of the world. **Bermuda cedar**, †**Bermudas cedar** a juniper, *Juniperus bermudiana*, native to Bermuda. **Bermuda grass** *N. Amer.* = DOG'S TOOTH 2. **Bermuda rig** a yachting rig with a high tapering mainsail. **Bermuda shorts** knee-length shorts. **Bermuda Triangle** an area of the W. Atlantic Ocean where a disproportionately large number of ships and aeroplanes are said to have been mysteriously lost.
■ **Bermudan** *adjective* = BERMUDIAN *adjective* L19.

Bermudian /bəˈmjuːdɪən/ *noun & adjective*. L18.
[ORIGIN from BERMUDA + -IAN.]
▸ **A** *noun*. A native or inhabitant of Bermuda; a vessel from Bermuda; a ship with a Bermuda rig. L18.
▸ **B** *adjective*. Of or pertaining to Bermuda or its inhabitants. E19.
Bermudian mainsail a high tapering mainsail. **Bermudian rig** = *BERMUDA rig*.

Bernardine /ˈbəːnədɪn/ *noun & adjective*. M16.
[ORIGIN mod. Latin *Bernardinus*, from St *Bernard* (1091–1153), abbot of Clairvaux in France and a pioneer of the Cistercian order: see -INE[1].]
= CISTERCIAN.

Bernese /bəːˈniːz/ *noun & adjective*. L17.
[ORIGIN from *Bern(e)* (see below) + -ESE.]
▸ **A** *noun*. Pl. same. A native or inhabitant of Berne (Bern), a city and canton of Switzerland. L17.
▸ **B** *adjective*. Of or pertaining to Berne. E19.
■ Also †**Bernois** *noun* L17–M19.

Bernician /bəːˈnɪʃ(ə)n/ *noun & adjective*. E19.
[ORIGIN from medieval Latin *Bernicia* (see below) + -AN: cf. Old English *Beornice* inhabitants of Bernicia.]
▸ **A** *noun*. A native or inhabitant of Bernicia, an Anglian kingdom founded in the 6th cent., later forming part of Northumbria. E19.
▸ **B** *adjective*. Of or pertaining to Bernicia or its inhabitants; GEOLOGY designating the Lower Carboniferous rocks of Northumberland and its borders. M19.

Bernoulli /bəːˈnuːi, -ˈnuːli/ *noun*. M18.
[ORIGIN Name of a Swiss family: sense 1 from Jacques (1654–1705), sense 2 from Daniel (1700–82), mathematicians.]
1 a ***Bernoulli numbers***, ***Bernoulli series***, ***Bernoulli's numbers***, ***Bernoulli's series***, a series of rational numbers arising in formulae for the sums of powers of integers. M18. ▸**b** ***Bernoulli law***, = ***law of large numbers*** s.v. LARGE *adjective*. M19.
2 ***Bernoulli's theorem***, ***Bernoulli's principle***, a statement of the inverse relation between pressure and the square of velocity in a steadily moving incompressible fluid. M19.
■ **Bernoullian** *adjective* (esp. with ref. to Bernoulli numbers): L19.

berob /bɪˈrɒb/ *verb trans.* Infl. **-bb-**. ME.
[ORIGIN from BE- 1 + ROB *verb*.]
Rob.

beroe /ˈbɛrəʊi/ *noun*. M18.
[ORIGIN Latin *Beroë* from Greek *Beroē* a daughter of Oceanus.]
A bell-shaped ctenophore of the genus *Beroe*, lacking tentacles. Now only as mod. Latin genus name.

berry /ˈbɛri/ *noun*[1].
[ORIGIN Old English *beri(ġ)e*, cogn. with Old Saxon *beri*, Middle Dutch *bēre*, Middle Dutch & mod. Dutch *bezie* (Dutch *bes*), Old High German *beri* (German *Beere*), Old Norse *ber*, Gothic *basi*, from Germanic.]
1 Any small globular or ovate juicy fruit, not having a stone. In early use *esp.* a grape. OE. ▸**b** BOTANY. A fruit with seeds enclosed in pulp, as grape, gooseberry, tomato, etc. E19.
2 An egg of a fish or lobster. M18.
3 A dollar; a pound. Usu. in *pl.* *slang*. E20.
4 ***the berries***, an outstandingly good person or thing. *slang*. E20.
■ **berried** *adjective* (*a*) = BACCATE *adjective*; (*b*) bearing eggs: M18. **berry-like** *adjective* resembling a berry, esp. in size and shape M19.

berry /ˈbɛri/ *noun*[2]. Long *obsolete* exc. *dial.* ME.
[ORIGIN Repr. Old English *beorge* dat. of *beorg* hill: see BARROW *noun*[1].]
A mound, hillock, or barrow.

berry /ˈbɛri/ *noun*[3]. Long *obsolete* exc. *dial.* LME.
[ORIGIN Var. of BURROW *noun*[2].]
A (rabbit's) burrow.

berry /ˈbɛri/ *verb intrans.* M19.
[ORIGIN from BERRY *noun*[1].]
1 Come into berry. M19.
2 Go gathering berries. M19.

bersaglieri /bersaʎˈʎɛːri, ˌbɛːsɑːlɪˈɛːriː/ *noun pl.* M19.
[ORIGIN Italian, from *bersaglio* target.]
Highly trained Italian infantry, orig. riflemen or sharpshooters.

berserk /bəˈsəːk, -z-/ *noun & adjective*. Also (*arch.*) **baresark** /ˈbɛːsɑːk/, **bersark** /bəˈsɑːk/; (chiefly as noun) **berserker**, **-kar** /bəˈsəːkə/. E19.
[ORIGIN Old Norse *berserkr*, accus. *berserk* (Icelandic *berserkur*), prob. from *birn-*, *bjǫrn* BEAR *noun*[1] + *serkr* coat, SARK *noun*, but also explained as from BARE *adjective*.]
▸ **A** *noun*. A wild Norse warrior who fought with frenzied fury. E19.
▸ **B** *adjective*. Wild, frenzied. Esp. in ***go berserk***. M19.
■ **berserkly** *adverb* M20.

berth /bəːθ/ *noun & verb*[1]. Orig. NAUTICAL. Also †**birth**. E17.
[ORIGIN from BEAR *verb*[1] (sense 17) + -TH[1].]
▸ **A** *noun*. **1** NAUTICAL. ▸**a** Sea room (to avoid hazards, swing at anchor, etc.). Usu. with specifying adjective etc.; (simply) adequate sea room. E17. ▸**b** A place where a ship lies at anchor; a ship's place at a wharf. M18.
a J. SMEATON Giving the Lighthouse a clear birth of 50 fathoms to the southward. **b** N. SHUTE Peter Holmes walked down to the berth occupied by H.M.A.S. Sydney.
a give a wide berth to NAUTICAL & *gen.* not go too near, steer clear of, avoid.
2 a NAUTICAL. The space allotted to a ship's company for storage of belongings, eating, sleeping, etc. E18. ▸**b** *transf.* The proper place for something; an allotted place in a barracks, conveyance, etc. M18.
a F. MARRYAT The first day in which he had entered the midshipmen's berth, and was made acquainted with his messmates. **b** SIR W. SCOTT The first comer hastens to secure the best berth in the coach.
3 a NAUTICAL. A situation or office on board ship or elsewhere. E18. ▸**b** *transf.* A paid position of employment; a situation, an appointment, esp. a comfortable or easy one. M18.
a J. DOS PASSOS He had taken a berth as donkey-engineman on a freighter bound for South America. **b** M. MCCARTHY Her background was perfect for a berth in publishing. *Sunday Telegraph* In ministerial quarters there are plenty of plushy berths to be filled.
4 a NAUTICAL. A sleeping place in a ship; a long box or shelf on the side of the cabin for sleeping. L18. ▸**b** *transf.* A similar sleeping place or bunk in a railway carriage, caravan, etc. E19.
a BYRON Passengers their berths are clapt in. **b** Z. M. PIKE We returned to the chief's lodge, and found a birth provided for each of us. J. DOS PASSOS He lay awake all night in the upper berth in the sleeper for Pittsburgh.
▸ **B** *verb*. **1** *verb trans.* Moor (a ship) in a suitable place. M17.
B. ENGLAND A small jetty . . where a boat sat sluggishly berthed.
2 *verb intrans.* Of a ship: come to mooring. M19.
J. B. MORTON She will not berth like other liners, but will turn round outside the harbour.
3 *verb trans.* Provide (a person) with a berth. M19.
4 *verb intrans.* Of a person: occupy a berth or berths. L19.
H. WOUK He was berthing below with the refugees.
■ **berthage** *noun* position in a berth; accommodation for mooring vessels; the dues payable for such accommodation: M19. **berthing** *noun*[1] (*a*) the action of the verb; (*b*) mooring position; accommodation in berths: E19.

berth /bəːθ/ *verb*[2] *trans. & intrans.* L16.
[ORIGIN Perh. from Icelandic *byrða*, from Old Norse *byrði* board (side) of a ship.]
SHIPBUILDING. Construct or cover (the side etc. of a ship) with planks. Also foll. by *up*.
■ **berthing** *noun*[2] (*a*) the action of the verb; (*b*) the upright planking of the sides etc. of a ship, *esp.* that above the sheer strake: E18.

bertha /ˈbəːθə/ *noun*[1]. Also **berthe** /bəːθ/. M19.
[ORIGIN *Bertha* (French *Berthe*) female forename.]
A deep falling collar or small cape on a dress.

Bertha /ˈbəːθə/ *noun*[2]. *military slang*. E20.
[ORIGIN Frau *Bertha* Krupp von Bohlen und Halbach, owner of the Krupp steel works in Germany 1903–43.]
A German gun or mortar of large bore, used in the First World War. Freq. ***Big Bertha***.

bertillonage /bɛrtijɔnaʒ/ *noun*. L19.
[ORIGIN French *bertillonnage*, from *Bertillon* (see below) + -AGE.]
The system of identification of criminals by anthropometric measurements, fingerprints, etc., invented by the French criminologist Alphonse Bertillon (1853–1914).

bertrandite /ˈbəːtrəndʌɪt/ *noun*. L19.
[ORIGIN from Émile *Bertrand*, 19th-cent. French mineralogist + -ITE[1].]
MINERALOGY. An orthorhombic basic silicate of beryllium, occurring as small tabular colourless or pale yellow crystals.

beryl /ˈbɛrɪl/ *noun & adjective*. ME.
[ORIGIN Old French *beril* (mod. *béryl*) from Latin *beryllus* from Greek *bērullos*, prob. of foreign origin.]
▸ **A** *noun*. **1** A transparent precious stone of a pale green colour passing into light blue, yellow, and white, distinguished only by colour from emerald and including aquamarine. Also ***beryl-stone***. ME.
†**2** Crystal; a piece of cut crystal. LME–E17.
3 MINERALOGY. A hexagonal silicate of beryllium and aluminium, of which beryl (sense 1), emerald, morganite, etc., are varieties. M19.
4 The colour of beryl (sense 1). M19.
▸ **B** *attrib.* or as *adjective*. Of beryl; composed of or resembling beryl. L15.

beryllium /bəˈrɪlɪəm/ *noun*. M19.
[ORIGIN from BERYL + -IUM.]
A chemical element, atomic no. 4, which is the lightest of the alkaline earth metals and of which the mineral beryl is the major source (symbol Be). Orig. called ***glucinum***.
■ **beryllia** *noun* beryllium oxide, BeO, a white heat-resistant solid L19. **berylliˈosis** *noun*, pl. **-oses** /-ˈəʊsiːz/, MEDICINE poisoning caused by exposure to beryllium compounds, *esp.* a severe pneumoconiosis due to their inhalation M20.

beryllonite /bəˈrɪlənʌɪt/ *noun*. L19.
[ORIGIN from BERYLLIUM + *-on* + -ITE[1].]
MINERALOGY. A monoclinic phosphate of beryllium and sodium, occurring as colourless or pale yellow prisms.

besaiel /bɪˈseɪ(ə)l/ *noun*. Long *obsolete* exc. *hist.* Also **-aile**, **-ayle**. LME.
[ORIGIN Old French *besaiuel*, *besaiol* (mod. *bisaïeul*), from *bes* from Latin *bis* twice + *as* AIEL.]
LAW. A great-grandfather.

B

writ of besaiel *LAW* an action by a party based on the seisin of a great-grandfather for the recovery of land of which that party had been dispossessed.

besaint /bɪˈseɪnt/ *verb trans. arch.* E17.
[ORIGIN from BE- 3 + SAINT *noun*.]
Make a saint of, canonize.

besang *verb* see BESING.

besaw *verb pa. t.*: see BESEE.

besayle *noun* var. of BESAIEL.

bescatter /bɪˈskatə/ *verb trans.* L16.
[ORIGIN from BE- 1 + SCATTER *verb*.]
Sprinkle (*with*); scatter about.

bescratch /bɪˈskratʃ/ *verb trans.* M16.
[ORIGIN from BE- 1 + SCRATCH *verb*.]
Cover with scratches.

bescrawl /bɪˈskrɔːl/ *verb trans.* M16.
[ORIGIN from BE- 1 + SCRAWL *verb*².]
Scribble over; cover with scrawl.

bescreen /bɪˈskriːn/ *verb trans.* L16.
[ORIGIN from BE- 1 + SCREEN *verb*.]
Screen from view; obscure, overshadow.

bescribble /bɪˈskrɪb(ə)l/ *verb trans.* L16.
[ORIGIN from BE- 1 + SCRIBBLE *verb*¹.]
Write untidily; scribble about; scribble on.

besee /bɪˈsiː/ *verb*. Long *arch.* Infl. as SEE *verb*; pa. t. usu. **-saw** /-ˈsɔː/, pa. pple usu. **-seen** /-ˈsiːn/.
[ORIGIN Old English *besēon*, *bi-* = Old Saxon, Old High German *bisehan*, Gothic *bisaihwan*, formed as BE- + SEE *verb*.]
▸ †**I 1** *verb intrans.* Look; see *to*, attend *to*. OE–ME.
2 *verb trans.* Look at; see to, attend to; ordain, determine. OE–L16.
▸ **II 3** As pa. pple ***beseen***. Seen or viewed, having an appearance; provided with, appointed. LME.

SPENSER I late was wont to . . maske in mirth with Graces well beseene. W. MORRIS The dukes . . well beseen in purple dye and gold.

†**beseech** *noun*. Only in E17.
[ORIGIN from the verb.]
(An) entreaty.

SHAKES. *Tr. & Cr.* Therefore this maxim out of love I teach: Achievement is command; ungain'd, beseech.

beseech /bɪˈsiːtʃ/ *verb*. Pa. t. & pple **-ed**, **besought** /bɪˈsɔːt/. ME.
[ORIGIN formed as BE- + SEEK *verb*: *seech* would be the normal reflex of Old English *sēċan*.]
†**1** *verb trans.* Search for, try to obtain. Only in ME.
2 *verb trans.* Ask earnestly for (a thing; also foll. by *that*, †*to do*). ME.
3 *verb trans.* Entreat, implore, (a person; a person *to do*, *for* or †*of* a thing, *that* (arch.), †a thing). ME.
4 *verb intrans.* Make an earnest request (*for* or †*of* a thing; †*(un)to* a person). *arch.* ME.
▪ **beseecher** *noun* LME. **beseeching** *noun* (*a*) the action of the verb; (*b*) an earnest request, an entreaty: ME. **beseechingly** *adverb* M19. **beseechment** *noun* (*rare*) L17.

beseem /bɪˈsiːm/ *verb*. *arch.* ME.
[ORIGIN from BE- 1 + SEEM *verb*.]
†**1** *verb intrans.* Seem, look. ME–L19.
2 *verb trans.* & *intrans.* (now usu. *impers.* in (*it*) ***beseems*** etc.). ▸**a** With qualification: appear or look *well*, *ill*, etc., for (a person) to wear, have, do, etc. ME. ▸**b** Without qualification: be fitting (for), be creditable (to). LME.
▪ **beseemingly** *adverb* E17. **beseemingness** *noun* M17. **beseemliness** *noun* the quality of being beseemly M17. **beseemly** *adjective* becoming, befitting M18.

beseen *verb pa. pple* of BESEE.

beset /bɪˈsɛt/ *verb trans.* Infl. **-tt-**. Pa. t. & pple **beset**.
[ORIGIN Old English *besettan* = Old Frisian *bisetta*, Old Saxon *bisettian* (Dutch *bezetten*), Old High German *bisezzan* (German *besetzen*), Gothic *bisatjan*, from Germanic, formed as BE- + SET *verb*¹.]
▸ **I 1** Set about or surround *with* (esp. appendages or accessories). Now only as pa. pple. *arch.* OE.

DE QUINCEY A tiara beset with pearls.

2 Surround with hostile intent, besiege, assail on all sides. Freq. *fig.* of temptations, doubts, difficulties, etc. OE.

POPE The lioness . . beset by men and hounds. H. KELLER As I began to teach her, I was beset by difficulties. W. S. CHURCHILL There were no more half-rations . . to give to the soldiers, and they were beset on three sides. A. MOOREHEAD They were so beset by flies and dust they wore goggles and veils. C. CHAPLIN A spell of melancholy beset me.

besetting sin a temptation to which a person is especially subject; a characteristic weakness.

3 Occupy and make impassable (a gate, road, etc.). ME.

J. R. MCCULLOCH The mob . . beset all the avenues to the House of Commons.

4 *gen.* Close round, hem in. M16.

N. HAWTHORNE The mountains which beset it round.

▸ †**II 5** Place, set, bestow. OE–E17.
6 Arrange, ordain. LME–L15.

▪ **besetment** *noun* the act of besetting; the condition of being beset; a besetting sin etc.: E19.

beshade /bɪˈʃeɪd/ *verb trans.*
[ORIGIN Old English *besċeadian*, formed as BE- 1 + SHADE *verb*¹.]
Cover with shade, obscure.

beshadow /bɪˈʃadəʊ/ *verb trans.* ME.
[ORIGIN from BE- 1 + SHADOW *verb*.]
Cast a shadow on; screen from light.

beshine /bɪˈʃʌɪn/ *verb trans. arch.* Infl. as SHINE *verb*; pa. t. & pple usu. **-shone** /-ˈʃɒn/.
[ORIGIN Old English *besċīnan*, *bi-*, formed as BE- 1 + SHINE *verb*.]
Illumine; shine about or upon.

beshrew /bɪˈʃruː/ *verb trans. arch.* ME.
[ORIGIN from BE- 1 + SHREW *verb*.]
†**1** Make wicked; deprave. ME–M16.
2 Invoke evil upon; curse; blame for a misfortune. Now chiefly in imprecations: the Devil take —, curse —. LME.

SHAKES. *Oth.* Beshrew me, if I would do such a wrong for the whole world. G. SWIFT We agreed with her, beshrewed 'other people', and enjoyed ourselves in our own way.

beside /bɪˈsʌɪd/ *adverb & preposition*.
[ORIGIN Old English *be sīdan*, formed as BY *preposition* etc. + SIDE *noun*. First found as one word in Middle English.]
▸ **A** *adverb*. (*arch.*: largely superseded by BESIDES.)
1 By the side, by one's side; close by, near. OE.

SOUTHEY Mervyn beside, Hangs over his dear mistress. J. P. DONLEAVY Massive horses galloping beside.

2 = BESIDES *adverb* 2. ME.

CARLYLE It was by stealth if he read or wrote any thing beside. BROWNING Beside, when he found speech, you guess the speech.

†**3** = ASIDE *adverb* 1. LME–E17.
†**4** By the side so as to miss, past. LME–L16.

SHAKES. *Ven. & Ad.* Yet sometimes falls an orient drop beside Which her cheek melts.

5 = BESIDES *adverb* 3. L16.

J. WILSON We talk'd Of thee and none beside.

▸ **B** *preposition*. **1** By the side of, close by, next to. ME. ▸**b** Compared with; on a level with. E16.

AV *S. of S.* 1:8 Feede thy kiddes beside the shepheards tent. DAY LEWIS I stood beside her, manipulating the stops of the harmonium. **b** J. RUSKIN Gainsborough's power of colour . . is capable of taking rank beside that of Rubens.

2 = BESIDES *preposition* 3. ME.

G. H. LEWES Other men beside ourselves.

3 Outside of, out of, wide of, away from. Now only *fig.* LME.

S. BUTLER Vagabonds . . are ne'er beside their way. M. W. MONTAGU This question almost put him beside his gravity. S. JOHNSON At Durham, beside all expectation, I met an old friend. J. A. FROUDE The point on which the battle was being fought lay beside the real issue.

beside the mark, ***beside the point***, ***beside the question***, etc. **beside oneself** distraught (*with* or *for* an emotion). ***beside the saddle***: see SADDLE *noun*.

4 = BESIDES *preposition* 2. LME.

R. DAHL The only one beside myself who had come alone.

besides /bɪˈsʌɪdz/ *adverb & preposition*. ME.
[ORIGIN from BESIDE + -S³.]
▸ **A** *adverb*. †**1** = BESIDE *adverb* 1. Only in ME.
2 In addition, as well; moreover. M16.

ARNOLD BENNETT Besides, the letter would be more effective. V. S. NAIPAUL Ramlogan had . . come to regard Ganesh as a total loss and a crook besides.

3 Other than that mentioned, else. L16.

I. ASIMOV Military potential, standard of living, happiness, and all besides.

†**4** = BESIDE *adverb* 4. E–M17.
▸ **B** *preposition*. †**1** = BESIDE *preposition* 1. ME–L17.
2 Other than, else than, except, excluding. LME.

ADDISON No living Creature ever walks in it besides the Chaplain.

3 Over and above, in addition to, as well as. E16.

R. FRY Mankind is so constituted as to desire much besides pleasure.

†**4** = BESIDE *preposition* 3. E16–E18.

besiege /bɪˈsiːdʒ/ *verb trans.* ME.
[ORIGIN from ASSIEGE by substitution of BE-.]
1 Place armed forces before or around (a town etc.) in order to capture it; lay siege to. ME.
2 *transf.* & *fig.* Assail, crowd round, beset. E17.

SHAKES. *Sonn.* When forty winters shall besiege thy brow. W. GERHARDIE He was besieged with notes requesting private interviews.

▪ **besieger** *noun* M16.

besilver /bɪˈsɪlvə/ *verb trans.* E17.
[ORIGIN from BE- 1 + SILVER *verb*.]
Cover over or adorn with silver.

besing /bɪˈsɪŋ/ *verb trans. arch.* Infl. as SING *verb*¹; pa. t. usu. **-sang** /-ˈsaŋ/, pa. pple **-sung** /-ˈsʌŋ/. M16.
[ORIGIN from BE- 2 + SING *verb*¹.]
Sing to or about; celebrate in song.

beslave /bɪˈsleɪv/ *verb trans.* E17.
[ORIGIN from BE- 3 + SLAVE *noun*.]
Make a slave of, enslave; treat or address as a slave.

beslaver /bɪˈslavə, -ˈsleɪv-/ *verb trans.* L16.
[ORIGIN from BE- 2 + SLAVER *verb*.]
Slaver or dribble over.

beslobber /bɪˈslɒbə/ *verb trans.* LME.
[ORIGIN from BE- 1, 2 + SLOBBER *verb*.]
Slaver or slobber over.

beslubber /bɪˈslʌbə/ *verb trans.* LME.
[ORIGIN from BE- 1 + SLUBBER *verb*.]
Smear or daub over with liquid or sticky matter.

besmear /bɪˈsmɪə/ *verb trans.*
[ORIGIN Old English *bismierwan*, formed as BE- + SMEAR *verb*.]
Smear over; cover or soil with a greasy or sticky substance; *fig.* sully (reputation etc.), defame.

besmirch /bɪˈsməːtʃ/ *verb trans.* L16.
[ORIGIN from BE- 1 + SMIRCH *verb*.]
Dull or discolour, as with smoke or mud; dim the brightness of; *fig.* sully (reputation etc.).

besmoke /bɪˈsməʊk/ *verb trans.* LME.
[ORIGIN from BE- 2 + SMOKE *verb*.]
Subject to or suffuse with smoke; fumigate; make smoky.

besmut /bɪˈsmʌt/ *verb trans.* Infl. **-tt-**. E17.
[ORIGIN from BE- 1 + SMUT *verb*.]
Blacken (as) with soot; *fig.* defame.

besmutch /bɪˈsmʌtʃ/ *verb trans.* M19.
[ORIGIN from BE- 1 + SMUTCH *verb*.]
= BESMIRCH.

besnow /bɪˈsnəʊ/ *verb trans.*
[ORIGIN Old English *bisniwian*, formed as BE- + SNOW *verb*.]
Cover (as) with snow.

†**besognio** *noun*. Also **besonio**, **bisogn(i)o**. Pl. **-os**. L16–E19.
[ORIGIN Italian *bisogno* lit. 'need, want'.]
A raw recruit, esp. one poorly equipped. Also, a needy or worthless fellow. Cf. BEZONIAN.

besoil /bɪˈsɔɪl/ *verb trans.* ME.
[ORIGIN from BE- 1 + SOIL *verb*¹.]
Soil, sully; defile.

besom /ˈbiːz(ə)m, ˈbɪz-/ *noun & verb*.
[ORIGIN Old English *bes(e)ma* = Old Frisian *besma*, Old Saxon *besmo* (Dutch *bezem*), Old High German *besamo* (German *Besen*), from West Germanic.]
▸ **A** *noun*. †**1** A bundle of rods or twigs used for flogging. OE–ME.
2 An implement for sweeping; *spec.* a brush consisting of a bunch of birch or other twigs tied to one end of a stick. OE.

fig.: T. FULLER The riuer Kishon, God's besom to sweep away Sisera's great army.

3 A woman or girl. *joc.* or *derog.* Chiefly *Scot. & dial.* L18.

J. AGATE In comparison with Rosalind's pure flame Juliet is a man-struck little besom.

▸ **B** *verb*. †**1** *verb intrans.* Sweep with force. Only in LME.
2 *verb trans.* Sweep (*away*, *out*, etc.). L18.

†**besonio** *noun* var. of BESOGNIO.

†**besort** *verb & noun*. *rare* (Shakes.). Only in E17.
[ORIGIN from BE- 2 + SORT *verb*.]
▸ **A** *verb trans.* Befit, match. E17.
▸ **B** *noun*. Suitable company. E17.

besot /bɪˈsɒt/ *verb trans.* Infl. **-tt-**. L16.
[ORIGIN from BE- 1, 3 + SOT *verb* or *noun*, after ASSOT.]
1 Make foolishly affectionate; infatuate *with*. Now chiefly as ***besotted*** *ppl adjective*. L16.
2 Stupefy mentally or morally; intoxicate. L16.
▪ **besottedly** *adverb* E17. **besottedness** *noun* E17.

besought *verb pa. t. & pple* of BESEECH *verb*.

besouth /bɪˈsaʊθ/ *preposition*. Long *obsolete* exc. *Scot.* LME.
[ORIGIN from BE- + SOUTH.]
On the south side of; to the south of.

bespake *verb* see BESPEAK *verb*.

bespangle /bɪˈspaŋg(ə)l/ *verb trans.* L16.
[ORIGIN from BE- 4 + SPANGLE *noun*.]
Decorate or adorn (as) with spangles.

bespatter /bɪˈspatə/ *verb trans.* M17.
[ORIGIN from BE- 1 + SPATTER *verb*.]
Spatter (liquid etc.) over or about; shower *with* abuse, flattery, etc.; vilify, defame.

bespeak /bɪˈspiːk/ *noun*. L18.
[ORIGIN from the verb.]
THEATRICAL. A benefit night with a specially chosen play.

bespeak /bɪˈspiːk/ *verb*. Pa. t. **bespoke** /bɪˈspəʊk/, (*arch.*) **bespake** /bɪˈspeɪk/. Pa. pple **bespoken** /bɪˈspəʊk(ə)n/,

(less commonly) **bespoke**. Pa. ppl adjective BESPOKE *adjective*, (less commonly) **bespoken**.
[ORIGIN Old English *bisprecan* = Old Frisian *bispreka*, Old Saxon *besprekan* (Dutch *bespreken*), Old High German *bisprehhan* (German *besprechen*): see BE-, SPEAK *verb*.]

†**1** *verb intrans. & trans.* Speak up or out; exclaim (*that*); (later simply) speak. OE–L18.

MILTON Until their Lord himself bespake, and bid them go.

†**2** *verb trans.* Speak against, oppose. OE–ME.

†**3** *verb trans.* Speak about; discuss; determine upon or *to do*. ME–M17.

4 *verb trans.* Arrange for, engage beforehand; order (goods), commission to be made; ask for (a favour etc.). L16. ▸†**b** Request or engage (a person) *to do*. L16–M18.

STEELE She bespoke the Play of Alexander the Great, to be acted by the Company of Strollers. E. BOWEN The taxi bespoken by Cousin Francis to drive him back. L. GARFIELD The good offices of a certain gentleman were not yet bespoke.

5 *verb trans.* Speak to (a person); address. Chiefly *poet.* L16.

POPE Medon first th' assembled chiefs bespoke.

6 *verb trans.* Indicate; give evidence of; augur. E17.

N. HAWTHORNE Circumstances that bespeak war and danger. D. LODGE His handsomely bound old missal bespeaks wealth and taste.

bespeck /bɪˈspɛk/ *verb trans.* M16.
[ORIGIN from BE- 1 + SPECK *verb*.]
Mark with spots or specks. Usu. in *pass.*

bespeckle /bɪˈspɛk(ə)l/ *verb trans.* E17.
[ORIGIN from BE- 1 + SPECKLE *verb*.]
Speckle over; cover with dots or flecks.

bespectacled /bɪˈspɛktək(ə)ld/ *adjective.* M18.
[ORIGIN from BE- 5 + SPECTACLE *noun*[1] + -ED[2].]
Wearing spectacles.

bespell /bɪˈspɛl/ *verb trans.* L19.
[ORIGIN from BE- 4 + SPELL *noun*[1].]
Cast a spell on; bewitch, enchant.

bespoke /bɪˈspəʊk/ *adjective & noun.* M18.
[ORIGIN See BESPEAK *verb*.]
▸ **A** *adjective.* That has been bespoken; *spec.* of goods: commissioned, made to order, (opp. ***ready-made***); of a person: making or selling such goods. M18.
▸ **B** *noun.* A bespoke article. E20.

bespoke *verb* see BESPEAK *verb*.

bespoken *verb* see BESPEAK *verb*.

besport /bɪˈspɔːt/ *verb trans. & intrans.* M19.
[ORIGIN Alt. of DISPORT *verb* by substitution of BE-.]
Disport (*oneself*).

bespot /bɪˈspɒt/ *verb trans.* Infl. **-tt-**. ME.
[ORIGIN from BE- 1 + SPOT *verb*.]
Mark or cover with spots or with blemishes.

bespout /bɪˈspaʊt/ *verb trans.* L16.
[ORIGIN from BE- 1 + SPOUT *verb*.]
Spout out or over; utter or address in a declamatory manner.

bespread /bɪˈsprɛd/ *verb trans.* Pa. t. & pple **bespread**. ME.
[ORIGIN from BE- 1, 2 + SPREAD *verb*.]
1 Spread *with*. ME.
2 Cover by spreading over. M16.
3 Spread out. M16.

besprenge /bɪˈsprɛndʒ/ *verb trans.* Long *obsolete* exc. as pa. pple & ppl adjective. (*arch.*) **besprent** /bɪˈsprɛnt/.
[ORIGIN Old English *besprengan*, formed as BE- + SPRENGE *verb*.]
1 Sprinkle all over *with* (pa. ppl adjective also in *comb.*). OE.

MILTON Knot-grass dew-besprent.

2 Sprinkle about, strew. E16.

W. MORRIS The flowers besprent about.

besprent *verb & ppl adjective* see BESPRENGE

besprinkle /bɪˈsprɪŋk(ə)l/ *verb trans.* M16.
[ORIGIN from BE- 1, 2 + SPRINKLE *verb*.]
1 Sprinkle all over *with*; dot *with*; sprinkle (liquid etc.) *over*. M16.

GIBBON The walls were besprinkled with holy water. DICKENS Sloping banks besprinkled with pretty villas.

2 Of a liquid etc.: be sprinkled on. M18.

Bessarabian /bɛsəˈreɪbɪən/ *adjective & noun.* M19.
[ORIGIN from *Bessarabia* (see below) + -AN.]
(A native or inhabitant) of Bessarabia, a region in eastern Europe, now divided between Moldova and Ukraine.

Bessel function /ˈbɛs(ə)l ˌfʌŋ(k)ʃ(ə)n/ *noun phr.* L19.
[ORIGIN Friedrich W. *Bessel* (1784–1846), German astronomer.]
A solution of a certain differential equation, which occurs in many problems in mathematical physics.

Bessemer /ˈbɛsɪmə/ *noun.* M19.
[ORIGIN Sir Henry *Bessemer* (1813–98), English engineer.]
Bessemer process, a steel-making process (now obsolete) in which carbon, silicon, etc. are removed from molten pig iron by an air blast in a special retort; ***Bessemer converter***, such a retort; ***Bessemer steel***, ***Bessemer iron***, etc., the products of this process.
■ **bessemerize** *verb trans.* treat by the Bessemer process L19.

best /bɛst/ *adjective, noun, & adverb.*
[ORIGIN Old English *betest*, adverb *betost*, *betst* = Old Frisian, Old Saxon (Dutch) *best*, Old High German *bezzist-o* (German *best*), Old Norse *beztr*, *baztr*, Gothic *batist-s*, from Germanic superl.: cf. BET *adverb & pred. adjective*, BETTER *adjective* etc., & see -EST[1].]
▸ **A** *adjective.* Superl. of GOOD *adjective*.
1 Excelling all others in quality (inherently or relative to some standard); outstanding. OE.

HENRY FIELDING I will fight the best man of you all for twenty pound. J. AUSTEN The little Table . . has most conveniently taken itself off into the best bedroom. LD MACAULAY The best Roman Catholic families in England.

2 Most appropriate, advantageous, or desirable; of a person also: kindest. OE.

SHAKES. *Macb.* In best time We will require her welcome. J. N. LOCKYER The best way to obtain a knowledge of the various constellations. S. BEDFORD It would be best if we had something from old Felden himself.

3 Greatest in size or quantity; largest, most. M16.

M. MEYER He was to continue his voluntary exile for the best part of two decades.

▸ **B** *absol.* as *noun.* **I** *absol.* **1** pl. *The* best people, things, circumstances, etc. OE.
2 *The* chief advantage, merit, etc. ME.
3 *One's* best (possible) achievement, condition, clothes, etc. ME.
▸ **II** Individualized, as a count noun.
4 That which is best; *esp.* in SPORT, a best performance recorded to date. L16.

SHAKES. *Sonn.* These particulars are not my measure: All these I better in one general best.

▸ **C** *adverb.* (Superl. of WELL *adverb*.) In the best manner; to the greatest degree; most usefully. (With (ppl) adjectives & in comb. freq. with hyphen.) OE.

R. BURNS The best-laid schemes o' mice an' men Gang aft agley. COLERIDGE He prayeth best, who loveth best All things both great and small. ARNOLD BENNETT The best-dressed woman in the place.

– SPECIAL COLLOCATIONS, PHRASES, & COMB.: **all the best**: an expression of goodwill, used as a toast or a valediction. **as best one can**, **as best one may** as well as one is able to do under the circumstances. **at best** on the most hopeful view. **at its best**, **at one's best** in the best state or condition possible. **at the best of times** even in the most favourable circumstances. ***be on one's best*** BEHAVIOUR. **best before date**: marked on food to show the date after which it can be expected to deteriorate. ***best bib and tucker***: see BIB *noun*. ***best bower***: see BOWER *noun*[3]. **best boy** the assistant to the chief electrician of a film crew. ***best buy***: see BUY *noun*. **best end** the rib end of a neck of lamb etc. for cooking. **best friend** one's favourite friend (***best friends*** (colloq.) mutually favourite friends (*with*)). **best girl** (orig. *US*) a man's favourite female companion. **best man** *spec.* a bridegroom's chief attendant at a wedding. **best-of** a list or collection comprising the best examples of something. **best of breed** (***a***) the animal in a competitive show judged to be the best representative of its breed; (***b***) *fig.* any item or product considered to be the best of its kind. **best-seller** (orig. *US*) (the author of) a book having a large sale. **best-selling** *adjective* that is a best-seller. ***do one's best***: see DO *verb*. **for the best** aiming at or tending to the best result. **get the best of it**, **have the best of it** win a fight, argument, etc.; come out on top. **give best to** admit the superiority of, give way to. ***have the best of it***: see ***get the best of it*** above. **make the best of a bad bargain**, **make the best of a bad job**, etc., achieve the best available resolution of difficult circumstances. **make the best of it**, **make the best of things** accept adverse conditions with equanimity. **make the best of one's way** *arch.* go by the quickest route, go with the greatest possible speed. ***make the best of things***: see ***make the best of it*** above. **one had best do**, †**one were best do**, †**one were best to do** orig. impers. with oblique case (= for one), later pers. (with nom.) one would find it most advisable or advantageous to do. **one of the best** an excellent person. ***one's level best***: see LEVEL *adjective*. **one's Sunday best** one's smartest or most formal clothes. **put one's best foot forward** make the greatest effort of which one is capable. **six of the best** a caning, a beating, (also with other specified numbers of strokes). ***the best club in London***: see CLUB *noun*. **the best of** (an odd number): one more than half of. ***the best of both worlds***: see WORLD *noun*. ***the best of British*** (***luck***): see BRITISH *adjective* 2. ***the best thing since sliced bread***: see SLICED 1b. **to the best of one's ability**, **to the best of one's belief**, **to the best of one's knowledge**, **to the best of one's power**, etc., to the furthest extent of one's ability etc.; so far as one can do, judge, etc. **with the best (of them)** as well as anyone.
■ **bestest** *adjective, noun, & adverb* (*dial.* & *joc.*) very best M19. **bestness** *noun* M16.

best /bɛst/ *verb trans. colloq.* M19.
[ORIGIN from BEST *adjective, noun, & adverb*: cf. WORST *verb*.]
Get the better of; take advantage of; defeat, outwit.
■ **bester** *noun* a person who gets the better of another; a cheat: M19.

†**bestad** *pa. pple & ppl adjective* var. of BESTED.

bestain /bɪˈsteɪn/ *verb trans.* M16.
[ORIGIN from BE- 1 + STAIN *verb*.]
Mark with stains.

bestar /bɪˈstɑː/ *verb trans.* Infl. **-rr-**. E17.
[ORIGIN from BE- 4 + STAR *noun*[1].]
Spangle or decorate (as) with stars. Chiefly as ***bestarred*** *ppl adjective*.

bestead *pa. pple & ppl adjective* var. of BESTED.

bestead /bɪˈstɛd/ *verb trans. & intrans. arch.* Pa. t. **besteaded**; pa. pple **bestead**. L16.
[ORIGIN from BE- 1 + STEAD *verb*.]
Help; avail.

bested /bɪˈstɛd/ *pa. pple & ppl adjective. arch.* Also **bestead**, †**bestad**. ME.
[ORIGIN from BE- 1 + Old Norse *staddr* pa. pple of *steðja* to place, with later assim. to native *ste(a)d*.]
1 With adverbs, esp. *ill*, *hard*, *sore*, etc.: circumstanced, situated. ME. ▸†**b** Without adverb: badly circumstanced. LME–L16.
2 Beset *by* or †*with* enemies, *with* dangers etc. ME.
†**3** Located; settled. Only in ME.
– NOTE: Spenser also uses *bestad* as a pa. t.

bestial /ˈbɛstɪəl/ *noun.* Long *obsolete* exc. *Scot.* ME.
[ORIGIN Partly from Old French *bestial* from medieval Latin *bestiale* use as noun of neut. sing. of late Latin *bestialis* (see BESTIAL *adjective*); partly (Middle English forms) from Old French *bestaille* from medieval Latin *bestialia* neut. pl. of *bestialis*.]
1 *collect.* Farm and domestic animals; cattle. ME.
2 A single beast. LME.

bestial /ˈbɛstɪəl/ *adjective.* LME.
[ORIGIN Old French from late Latin *bestialis*, from Latin *bestia* BEAST *noun*: see -IAL.]
1 Of or pertaining to the lower animals, esp. quadrupeds. LME.
2 Like a beast or beasts; brutish, irrational; cruel, savage; depraved, lustful, obscene. LME.
■ **bestialize** *verb trans.* change into the form or nature of a beast; debase: L17. **bestially** *adverb* LME.

bestiality /bɛstɪˈalɪti/ *noun.* LME.
[ORIGIN Old French & mod. French *bestialité*, formed as BESTIAL *adjective*: see -ITY.]
1 The state or quality of being bestial. LME.
2 Copulation between a person and an animal. E17.
3 A disgusting vice, a beastly practice. Now *rare*. M17.

bestiary /ˈbɛstɪəri/ *noun.* M19.
[ORIGIN medieval Latin *bestiarium*, from Latin *bestia* BEAST *verb*: see -ARY[1].]
A medieval moralizing treatise on beasts.

bestick /bɪˈstɪk/ *verb trans.* Pa. t. & pple **bestuck** /bɪˈstʌk/. E17.
[ORIGIN from BE- 1, 2 + STICK *verb*[1].]
Stick all over, bedeck; *arch.* pierce through, transfix. Usu. in *pass.*

bestill /bɪˈstɪl/ *verb trans.* L18.
[ORIGIN from BE- 1 + STILL *verb*[1].]
Make still or quiet.

bestir /bɪˈstəː/ *verb.* Infl. **-rr-**. ME.
[ORIGIN from BE- 1 + STIR *verb*.]
1 *verb trans.* Stir up; exert or busy *oneself*; rouse to action. ME.
2 *verb intrans.* Exert oneself, move quickly. *rare* (Shakes.). E17.

bestorm /bɪˈstɔːm/ *verb trans.* M17.
[ORIGIN from BE- 1 + STORM *verb*.]
Storm; assail on all sides.

bestow /bɪˈstəʊ/ *verb trans.* ME.
[ORIGIN from BE- 4 + STOW *verb*[1].]
1 Apply, employ (time, effort, etc., *in* an occupation). *arch.* ME. ▸†**b** *spec.* Spend, lay out, (money). LME–M17. ▸†**c** *refl.* Acquit oneself. L16–E17.

I. WALTON Bestow one day with me and my friends in hunting the otter.

2 Place, locate, put; store, stow away; lodge, put up. *arch.* LME.

TINDALE *Luke* 12:17 I have noo roume where to bestowe my frutes. BYRON See that the women are bestow'd in safety In the remote apartments. V. SACKVILLE-WEST Stooping . . to bestow the presents into eager hands. L. A. G. STRONG She received his hat and his Malacca cane, and bestowed them safely.

3 Settle or give in marriage. *arch.* LME.

H. ALLEN A widower . . anxious to see his only child well and securely bestowed.

4 Confer as a gift (*on*, *upon*, †*of* a person; †*to* a purpose). M16.

L. EDEL The hope that ultimately she will bestow upon him more than sweet words and a smile. F. TUOHY The Rudowskis had . . bestowed on him a name that could not be anglicized. E. REVELEY The impulse to bestow trinkets.

■ **bestowal** *noun* the action of bestowing L18. **bestower** *noun* M16. **bestowment** *noun* (***a***) bestowal; (***b***) *rare* a gift: M18.

†**bestraught** *adjective.* M16–M18.
[ORIGIN from DISTRAUGHT *adjective* by substitution of BE-.]
Distracted, distraught.

B

bestreak /bɪˈstriːk/ *verb trans.* L16.
[ORIGIN from BE- 1 + STREAK *verb*[2].]
Mark or decorate with streaks.

bestrew /bɪˈstruː/ *verb trans.* Also **bestrow** /bɪˈstrəʊ/. Pa. pple **bestrewed**, **bestrewn** /bɪˈstruːn/; **bestrown** /bɪˈstrəʊn/.
[ORIGIN Old English *bestrēowian*, formed as BE- + STREW *verb*.]
1 Strew (a surface) *with*. OE.
2 Scatter (things) about. M17.
3 Lie scattered over. E18.

bestride /bɪˈstrʌɪd/ *verb trans.* Pa. t. **bestrode** /bɪˈstrəʊd/, †**bestrid**; pa. pple **bestridden** /bɪˈstrɪd(ə)n/, **bestrode**, †**bestrid**.
[ORIGIN Old English *bestrīdan*, formed as BE- + STRIDE *verb*.]
1 Get or sit upon (orig. and esp. a horse) with legs astride. OE.

SHAKES. *Rich. II* That horse that thou so often hast bestrid. T. GRAY Sisters, hence with spurs of speed, . . Each bestride her sable steed. *fig.*: W. COWPER Through the pressed nostrils, spectacle-bestrid.

2 Stand astride over (a place, person, etc.), esp. as a victor over the fallen or to defend a fallen man; straddle; span. E16.

SHAKES. *Jul. Caes.* He doth bestride the narrow world Like a Colossus. E. YOUNG How I bestride your prostrate conqueror! TENNYSON As he bestrode my Grandsire, when he fell, And all else fled.

3 Step or stride across. E17.

SHAKES. *Coriol.* When I first my wedded mistress saw Bestride my threshold.

†**bestrip** *verb trans.* Infl. **-pp-**. OE–E17.
[ORIGIN Old English *bestrȳpan*, formed as BE- + STRIP *verb*[1]: cf. Middle High German *bestroufen*.]
Despoil (*of*).

bestrode *verb pa. t.*: see BESTRIDE.

bestrow(n) *verb* see BESTREW.

bestuck *verb pa. t. & pple* of BESTICK.

bestud /bɪˈstʌd/ *verb trans.* Infl. **-dd-**. E17.
[ORIGIN from BE- 1 + STUD *verb*.]
Decorate (as) with studs.

besuited /bɪˈsuːtɪd/ *adjective*. M20.
[ORIGIN from BE- + SUITED.]
Of a man: wearing a suit.

R. T. DAVIES Ordinarily, he's a quiet, besuited deputy bank manager.

besung *verb* see BESING.

bet /bɛt/ *noun*. L16.
[ORIGIN Uncertain: perh. aphet. from ABET *noun*, but see BET *verb*.]
1 The staking of money etc. on the outcome of a doubtful issue; a wager; the sum of money etc. staked. L16. ▸**b** *fig.* *One's* guess or opinion. *colloq.* M20.

A. SILLITOE A bet on Fair Glory in the two-thirty won him twelve pounds. **b** J. B. PRIESTLEY My bet is there's been a fair amount of swift dirty work round here.

2 With qualifying adjective, esp. *good* or *best*: a person, event, etc., on which to bet, a choice, a course of action. *colloq.* E20.

P. G. WODEHOUSE Thinks I'm not a good bet? L. A. G. STRONG Keep that up . . . It's our best bet.

– PHRASES: ***safe bet***: see SAFE *adjective*. ***Yankee bet***: see YANKEE *adjective*.

bet /bɛt/ *verb trans. & intrans.* Infl. **-tt-**. Pa. t. & pple **bet**, **betted**. L16.
[ORIGIN Perh. from the noun, but the verb & noun are contemporaneous.]
1 Stake (an amount of money etc.) against another's in support of an affirmation or on the outcome of a doubtful event; risk an amount of money etc. against (a person) by agreeing to forfeit it if the truth or outcome is not as specified. (Foll. by *on* or *against* an outcome or competitor, *that* something is or will be so, *against* a person who disagrees.) L16.

SHAKES. *2 Hen. IV* 'A [he] shot a fine shoot. John a Gaunt . . betted much money on his head. THACKERAY I don't bet on horses I don't know. J. GALSWORTHY Offering to bet the driver half a crown he didn't do it in the three-quarters of an hour. C. P. SNOW Humphrey would have betted that . . Briers would take on more drink that evening. C. ISHERWOOD You could bet thousands of dollars against this happening.

2 In hyperbolical assertions & absol.: (be able to) feel sure (*that*). *colloq.* M19.

J. K. JEROME If Harris's eyes fill with tears, you can bet it is because Harris has been eating raw onions. J. GRENFELL And I bet I look a million years old and he won't ever recognise me. I. SHAW 'You're ruining my sex life,' he said. 'I bet,' she said.

– PHRASES: ***bet like the Watsons***: see WATSON *noun*[2]. ***bet one's bottom dollar***: see BOTTOM *adjective*. ***bet one's shirt***: see SHIRT *noun*. ***bet the farm***: see FARM *noun* 4. **you bet (you)**, **you bet your boots**, **you bet your life** you can be certain (*that*) (cf. BETCHER).

†**bet** *adverb & pred. adjective*. OE–M17.
[ORIGIN Old English *bet* = Old Frisian *bet*, Old Saxon *bat*, *bet*, Old High German *baz* (German *bass*), Old Norse *betr*, from Germanic adverb: cf. BEST *adjective* etc., BETTER *adjective* etc.]
Better.

beta /ˈbiːtə/ *noun*. ME.
[ORIGIN Latin from Greek.]
1 The second letter (Β, β) of the Greek alphabet. ME.
2 Denoting the second in a numerical sequence: ▸**a** *attrib.* SCIENCE. Freq. written β: (***a***) ASTRONOMY (preceding the genitive of the Latin name of the constellation) designating the second brightest star in a constellation; (***b***) CHEMISTRY designating the second of a number of isomeric forms of a compound, or of allotropes of an element, etc.; (***c***) PHYSICS designating a negatively charged particle now known to be an electron, which is one of the three main types of decay product emitted by radioactive substances; also designating decay, emission, radiation, etc., associated with such a particle; (***d***) ***beta rhythm***, ***beta waves***, rapid low-amplitude electrical activity of the conscious brain, consisting of oscillations with a frequency of 18 to 25 hertz; (***e***) MEDICINE. ***beta receptor***, one of two kinds of adrenergic receptor in the sympathetic nervous system, stimulation of which results esp. in increased cardiac activity; ***beta-adrenergic adjective***, pertaining to or involving beta receptors; ***beta blocker***, a drug preventing stimulation of beta receptors; (***f***) ***beta test***, a test of machinery, software, etc., in the final stages of development, carried out by a party unconnected with its development; ***beta-test*** *verb trans.*, perform a beta test on. L17. ▸**b** A second-class mark in an examination etc. E20.
a beta GLOBULIN. **b beta plus**, **beta minus** rather better, worse, than the average second class.

betaine /ˈbiːtəiːn, ˈbiːteɪn/ *noun*. M19.
[ORIGIN Irreg. from Latin *beta* BEET *noun*[1] + -INE[5]: the first was isolated from sugar beet.]
CHEMISTRY. A zwitterionic *N*-trialkyl derivative of an amino acid; *spec.* that derived from glycine, $(CH_3)_3N^+ \cdot CH_2CO_2^-$, a crystalline base found in many plant juices.

betake /bɪˈteɪk/ *verb*. Pa. t. **betook** /bɪˈtʊk/; pa. pple **betaken** /bɪˈteɪk(ə)n/. ME.
[ORIGIN from BE- 1 + TAKE *verb*.]
†**1** *verb trans.* = BETEACH. Long *dial.* ME–L19.

EVELYN To God Almighty I betake it for support and speedy good success.

2 a *verb refl.* & (long *rare*) *intrans.* Have recourse *to*; go (*to*). L16. ▸**b** *verb trans.* with (part of) the body as obj. = sense 2a above. M19.

a SPENSER Then to her yron wagon she betakes. BUNYAN They betook themselves to a short debate. G. F. KENNAN Ambassador Francis . . betook himself . . to the provincial town of Vologda. **b** J. AGATE The kind of place to which . . Evelyn Waugh's characters would have betaken their vile bodies.

betatron /ˈbiːtətrɒn/ *noun*. M20.
[ORIGIN from BETA + -TRON.]
PHYSICS. An apparatus for accelerating electrons electromagnetically in a circular path.

†**betaught** *verb pa. t. & pple* of BETEACH.

betcher /ˈbɛtʃə/ *verb* (*pres.*). *colloq.* Also **betcha**. E20.
[ORIGIN Repr. an informal pronunc.]
Bet you, bet your (life).

†**beteach** *verb trans.* Pa. t. & pple **betaught**. OE–M18.
[ORIGIN Old English *betǣcan*, formed as BE- + TEACH *verb*.]
Hand over; entrust *to*; commit or commend *to*.

betel /ˈbiːt(ə)l/ *noun*. M16.
[ORIGIN Portuguese from Malayalam *veṟṟila*.]
The leaf of a climbing evergreen shrub, *Piper betle*, of the pepper family, which is chewed in the East with areca-nut parings and a little lime. Also (more fully ***betel pepper***), the plant itself.
– COMB.: **betel nut** the nut of the areca palm; **betel palm**, **betel tree** the areca palm, *Areca catechu*.

bête noire /beɪt ˈnwɑː, *foreign* bɛt nwaːr/ *noun phr.* Pl. **-s -s** (pronounced same). M19.
[ORIGIN French, lit. 'black beast'.]
The bane of someone's life; an insufferable person or thing; an object of aversion.

Beth Din /beɪt ˈdiːn/ *noun phr.* L18.
[ORIGIN Hebrew *bēṯ dīn* house of judgement.]
A Jewish court of law composed of three rabbinic judges, responsible for matters of Jewish religious law and the settlement of civil disputes between Jews.

bethel /ˈbɛθ(ə)l/ *noun*. E17.
[ORIGIN Hebrew *bēṯ-'ēl*, from *bēṯ* house of + *'ēl* god.]
1 A place where God is worshipped (see *Genesis* 28:17–19). E17.
2 *transf.* A Nonconformist chapel; a seamen's church. E19.

Bethesda /bɛˈθɛzdə/ *noun*. *arch.* M19.
[ORIGIN A place mentioned in *John* 5:2–4: given as a name to some Nonconformist chapels etc.]
A Nonconformist chapel.

Beth Hamidrash /beɪt hamɪˈdrɑːʃ, beɪt haˈmɪdrɑːʃ/ *noun phr.* L19.
[ORIGIN Hebrew *bēṯ ham-midrāš* lit. 'the house of study'.]
A place where Jews gather to study and pray.

bethink /bɪˈθɪŋk/ *verb*. Pa. t. & pple **bethought** /bɪˈθɔːt/.
[ORIGIN Old English *biþenćan* = Old Frisian *bithanka*, *bithenzia*, Old Saxon *biþenkian*, Old High German *bidenken* (Dutch, German *bedenken*), Gothic *biþagkjan*, from Germanic, formed as BE- + THINK *verb*[2].]
▸ **I** *verb trans.* **1** Bear in mind; recall, recollect. Now only (*arch.*) with obj. clause. OE.
†**2** Think over; plan, arrange. ME–M17.
†**3** ***be bethought*** = branch II. ME–E17.
▸ **II** *verb refl.* †**4** Collect one's thoughts; take thought. OE–M17.
5 Reflect, stop to think, remind oneself. (Foll. by obj. clause (esp. indirect interrog.), as *how*; *of*, †(*up*)*on*, †*to do*.) ME.

W. IRVING Rip bethought himself a moment. A. HELPS To bethink themselves how little they may owe to their own merit. L. P. HARTLEY She bethought her of her duties as a hostess.

6 Resolve. (Foll. by *of*, *that*, †*to do*.) *arch.* LME.

SHAKES. *Jul. Caes.* It may be I shall otherwise bethink me. J. GALSWORTHY He bethought him that he would go to the opera.

▸ **III** *verb intrans.* **7** Consider, think. (Formerly foll. by *of*, (*up*)*on*.) *arch.* ME.

BYRON Bethink ere thou dismiss us, ask again.

†**bethrall** *verb trans.* *rare* (Spenser). Only in L16.
[ORIGIN from BE- 3 + THRALL *noun*.]
Enthral, enslave.

bethumb /bɪˈθʌm/ *verb trans.* M17.
[ORIGIN from BE- 1 + THUMB *verb*.]
Take hold of or mark with the thumb.

bethump /bɪˈθʌmp/ *verb trans.* L16.
[ORIGIN from BE- 1 + THUMP *verb*.]
Thump soundly.

bethwack /bɪˈθwak/ *verb trans.* M16.
[ORIGIN from BE- 1 + THWACK *verb*.]
Thrash or cudgel soundly.

bethwine /ˈbɛθwʌɪn/ *noun*. *dial.* E17.
[ORIGIN Unknown.]
Any of various twining plants, e.g. bindweed, traveller's joy.

betide /bɪˈtʌɪd/ *verb*. Pa. pple **-tided**, **-tid** /-ˈtɪd/. ME.
[ORIGIN from BE- 1 + TIDE *verb*[1].]
1 *verb intrans. & trans.* (orig. with dat. obj.). Happen (to or (*un*)*to*), befall. Only in inf. & 3rd person (now pres. subjunct.). ME.

SHELLEY Took that child so fair From his weak arms, that ill might not betide him Or her. E. DICKINSON I hope I'm ready for 'the worst'—Whatever prank betides!

woe betide (a person): orig. a curse, now usu. a warning.
2 *verb trans.* Bode, betoken. *rare*. L18.

W. COWPER Awaking, how could I but muse At what such a dream should betide?

†**betime** *adverb*. ME–M17.
[ORIGIN formed as BY *preposition* + TIME *noun*.]
In good time; early; at an early hour.

SHAKES. *Ant. & Cl.* To business that we love we rise betime.

betimes /bɪˈtʌɪmz/ *adverb*. ME.
[ORIGIN from BETIME + -S[3].]
1 At an early time, period, or season. ME.
2 *spec.* Early in the morning. LME.
3 In good time; before it is too late. LME.
4 Soon; speedily. LME.

bêtise /beˈtiːz, beɪˈtiːz/ *noun*. Pl. pronounced same. E19.
[ORIGIN French = stupidity, from *bête* foolish from Old French *beste* BEAST *noun*.]
A foolish, ill-timed remark or action; a piece of folly.

betitle /bɪˈtʌɪt(ə)l/ *verb trans.* M17.
[ORIGIN from BE- 3 + TITLE *noun*.]
Give a name or title to; entitle.

†**betoil** *verb trans.* M17–M19.
[ORIGIN from BE- 2, 4 + TOIL *verb*[1] or *noun*[1].]
Worry or preoccupy with toil.

betoken /bɪˈtəʊk(ə)n/ *verb trans.*
[ORIGIN Old English *betācnian* = Old Frisian *bitēknia*, Dutch *betekenen*, Old High German *bizeihhanōn* (German *bezeichnen*): see BE-, TOKEN *verb*.]
†**1** Signify; express in words. OE–E17.
†**2** Typify; symbolize. ME–M17.

MILTON In the Cloud a Bow . . Betok'ning peace from God and Cov'nant new.

3 Be a sign or omen of; augur, presage. ME.

SHAKES. *Ven. & Ad.* Like a red morn, that ever yet betoken'd Wreck to the seaman, tempest to the field.

4 Give evidence of, indicate, suggest. L15.

L. M. MONTGOMERY He had the buggy and the sorrel mare, which betokened that he was going a considerable distance. I. COLEGATE That rather ironical, rather penetrating look which not everyone knew betokened affection.

betony /ˈbɛtəni/ *noun*. ME.
[ORIGIN Old French & mod. French *bétoine* from popular Latin var. of Latin *betonica* from *Vettonica* (Pliny), perh. from name of an Iberian tribe.]
1 A purple-flowered labiate plant, *Stachys officinalis*. ME.
2 Any of various similar plants. ME.
Paul's betony, ***water betony***, etc.

betook *verb pa. t.* of BETAKE.

†**betorn** *ppl adjective*. ME–L18.
[ORIGIN from BE- 1 + *torn* pa. pple of TEAR *verb*.]
Torn, tattered.

betrap /bɪˈtrap/ *verb trans. arch.* Infl. **-pp-**.
[ORIGIN Old English *betreppan*, *-træppan*: see BE-, TRAP *verb*[2].]
Entrap, enclose.

betray /bɪˈtreɪ/ *verb*. ME.
[ORIGIN from BE- 1 + TRAY *verb*.]
▸ **I** *verb trans.* **1** Give up treacherously (a person or thing, *to* an enemy, †*to* punishment). ME.
2 Be or prove false to; be disloyal to; disappoint the expectations of. ME.

E. M. FORSTER I will never forgive Eleanor. She has betrayed my confidence. R. MACAULAY I had betrayed David, broken my promise.

3 Lead astray, deceive. ME.

E. B. PUSEY Pride and self-confidence betray man to his fall. C. ISHERWOOD The poor betrayed girl who gets abandoned by her lover.

4 Reveal treacherously or involuntarily. L16.

A. RANSOME Looking for a hat, a hand, a leg, no matter what, that betray their hiding place. J. C. RANSOM This speech may have betrayed a fluttery private apprehension which should not have been made public. S. BRETT A tremble of her features betrayed the truth.

5 Show incidentally; constitute evidence or a symptom of. L17.

H. ADAMS A figure also called a king, but so charmingly delicate in expression that the robes alone betray his sex.

▸ **II** *verb intrans.* **6** Act treacherously; deceive. E17.

GOLDSMITH When lovely Woman stoops to folly, And finds too late that men betray.

■ **betrayal** *noun* the act of betraying; a treacherous or disloyal act; a disclosure: E19. **betrayer** *noun* L15. **betrayment** *noun* (*rare*) M16.

betrim /bɪˈtrɪm/ *verb trans.* Infl. **-mm-**. E17.
[ORIGIN from BE- 1 + TRIM *verb*.]
Trim, decorate.

betroth /bɪˈtrəʊð, -θ/ *verb trans.* ME.
[ORIGIN formed as BE- + TRUTH *noun*, later assim. to TROTH.]
1 Enter into an engagement to marry (a woman). *arch.* ME.
2 Bind (two people; one person, esp. a woman, *to* another) in an engagement to marry. Usu. in *pass.* M16.
†**3** *gen.* Engage; pledge (oneself) *to*; pledge oneself to. M16–L17.
■ **betrothal** *noun* the act of betrothing; the fact of being betrothed; an engagement to marry: M19. **betrothed** *noun* the person to whom one is betrothed, one's fiancé(e) L16. **betrothment** *noun* = BETROTHAL M16.

†**betrust** *verb trans.* LME–M18.
[ORIGIN from BE- 1 + TRUST *verb*.]
Trust; entrust.

Betsy /ˈbɛtsi/ *noun. slang & dial.* (chiefly *US*). Also **b-**. M19.
[ORIGIN Female forename, a familiar abbreviation of *Elizabeth*: cf. BETTY.]
(A name given to) a gun or pistol, *esp.* a favourite one. Also ***old Betsy***.

better /ˈbɛtə/ *noun*[1]. E17.
[ORIGIN from BET *verb* + -ER[1].]
A person who bets; = BETTOR.

better /ˈbɛtə/ *adjective, noun*[2], *& adverb*.
[ORIGIN Old English *betera* (masc. adjective) = Old Frisian *betera*, Old Saxon *betiro* (Dutch *beter*), Old High German *bezziro* (German *besser*), Old Norse *betri*, Gothic *batiza*, from Germanic compar.: cf. BEST *adjective* etc., BET *adverb & pred. adjective*, & see -ER[3].]
▸ **A** *adjective*. Compar. of GOOD *adjective*. (In pred. & ellipt. uses merging with the adverb.)
1 Of superior quality; more outstanding. OE.

G. B. SHAW The grey mare is the better horse here. V. WOOLF Andrew would be a better man than he had been. ALDOUS HUXLEY Better planes, better explosives, better guns and gases—every improvement increases the sum of fear and hatred.

2 More appropriate, advantageous, or desirable; of a person also: kinder. ME.

MILTON Better to reign in Hell than serve in Heav'n. L. STERNE I can give no better advice. W. STEVENS It would have been better for his hands To be convulsed.

3 Greater in size or quantity; larger; more. ME.

WORDSWORTH For the better part Of two delightful hours we strolled along.

4 Improved in health; partly or fully recovered from illness. LME.

S. JOHNSON Dr. Taylor is better, and is gone out in the chaise.

▸ **B** *absol.* as *noun*. **1** *One's* superior in some personal quality or attainment or (now only in *pl.*) in social status. OE.

SHAKES. *2 Hen. VI* Ambitious Warwick, let thy betters speak.

2 Something better. OE.

J. USSHER The Iberians had the better of it. G. B. SHAW The change from burning to hanging or shooting may strike us as a change for the better.

3 More. ME.

New Yorker Since the members of the select Committee . . voted by better than two to one to release the report.

4 *The* superiority or mastery. Now chiefly in ***get the better of***, defeat, outwit. LME.
▸ **C** *adverb*. [Superseding earlier BET *adverb*.] (Compar. of WELL *adverb*. In pred. uses after *be* & ellipt. merging with the adjective.) In a better manner; to a greater degree; more usefully. (With (ppl) adjectives & in comb. freq. with hyphen.) ME.

SYD. SMITH His awe of better-dressed men and better-taught men. V. WOOLF Without knowing why she felt that he liked her better than he had ever done before. F. SWINNERTON I could run any paper in England . . better than it's ever been run before.

– PHRASES ETC.: ***against one's better judgement***. ***be better than one's word***: see WORD *noun*. ***better days***: see DAY *noun*. **better feelings** conscience. ***better late than never***: see LATE *adverb*. **better off** better situated as regards money or other personal circumstances; ***the better off*** (absol.), those so situated. **better-to-do** above the well-to-do in social condition and material wealth; ***the better-to-do***, those above the well-to-do. **for better, for worse**, **for better or for worse** whatever changes may take place, whatever happens. ***get better***: see GET *verb*. **go one better (than)**, (*N. Amer.*) **go a person one better** outbid etc. by one unit, outdo. ***go to a better place***, ***go to a better world***: see GO *verb*. ***have seen better days***: see SEE *verb*. **know better**, **know better than that**, **know better than to do** be too wise or well-informed (to believe that), be too experienced or well-mannered (to do), etc. **no better than** practically, merely. **no better than one should be**, **no better than one ought to be** of doubtful moral character, (usu.) of easy virtue. **one had better do**, †**one were better do**, †**one were better to do** orig. impers. with oblique case (= for one), later pers. (with nom.) one would find it more advisable or advantageous to do; (also *colloq.* with ellipsis of *had*). **one's better half** (now chiefly *joc.*) a person very close to one; one's husband or (*esp.*) one's wife. ***one's better nature***: see NATURE *noun*. ***one's better self***: see SELF *noun* 3a. ***streets better (than)***: see STREET *noun*. ***think all the better of***, ***think better of***, ***think the better of***: see THINK *verb*[2]. **you'd better believe (it)** *colloq.* you may be assured.
■ **betterness** *noun* the quality of being better; *spec.* fineness of precious metals above the standard: LME.

better /ˈbɛtə/ *verb*. LME.
[ORIGIN from BETTER *adjective* etc.]
1 *verb trans.* Amend; improve; *refl.* improve one's financial or social condition. LME.

F. MARRYAT She left to better herself, and obtained the situation of nurse. W. C. WILLIAMS Their speech and dress were bettered while she kept them in her charge. L. DURRELL I lack the will-power to do anything with my life, to better my position by hard work.

2 *verb trans.* Surpass. M16.

L. DEIGHTON His Hamlet had been compared with Gielgud's, and his Othello bettered only by Olivier.

3 *verb intrans.* Grow better, improve. M17.

CARLYLE The general condition of the poor must be bettering instead of worsening.

betterment /ˈbɛtəm(ə)nt/ *noun*. L16.
[ORIGIN from BETTER *verb* + -MENT.]
1 Improvement, amendment. L16.
2 A local improvement to property; an improved property. *US*. L18.
3 Enhanced value (of real property) through local improvements. Orig. *US*. L19.

betting /ˈbɛtɪŋ/ *noun*. L16.
[ORIGIN from BET *verb* + -ING[1].]
1 The action of BET *verb*. L16.
2 The odds offered. E20.
– COMB.: **betting office**, (*colloq.*) **betting shop** an establishment licensed to handle bets (on horse races, dog races, etc.); **betting slip** a slip of paper on which a bet is entered.

bettong /ˈbɛtɒŋ/ *noun. Austral.* E19.
[ORIGIN Dharuk *bidung*]
A short-nosed rat-kangaroo of the genus *Bettongia*.

bettor /ˈbɛtə/ *noun*. M17.
[ORIGIN from BET *verb* + -OR.]
A person who bets; = BETTER *noun*[1].

Betty /ˈbɛti/ *noun*. Also **b-**. M17.
[ORIGIN Female forename, a familiar abbreviation of *Elizabeth*: cf. BETSY.]
1 A crowbar used by burglars. *slang*. Long *arch.* M17.
2 ***Betty lamp***, a type of hanging lamp used in America. *hist.* L19.

betulin /ˈbɛtjʊlɪn/ *noun*. M19.
[ORIGIN from Latin *betula* birch + -IN[1].]
CHEMISTRY. A solid terpenoid alcohol, $C_{30}H_{50}O_2$, present in birch bark.

†**betumble** *verb trans. rare* (Shakes.). Only in L16.
[ORIGIN from BE- 1 + TUMBLE *verb*.]
Disorder.

between /bɪˈtwiːn/ *preposition, adverb, & noun*.
[ORIGIN Old English *betwēonum* (beside *betwēon* and *betwēonan*), formed as BY *preposition* etc. + Germanic formation with *-n*-suffix (cf. Old Frisian *twine*, Gothic *tweihnai* two each) from base of Old English *twēo*, Old Saxon *tweho*, Old High German *zweho* doubt, difference, ult. rel. to TWO.]
▸ **A** *preposition*. **1** Expr. reciprocal action or relation involving two or more agents individually; reciprocally on the part of. OE.

W. CATHER I thought that day there was some kind of feeling, something unusual, between them. A. BEVAN The unbridgeable antagonism between private wealth, poverty and political democracy. M. AMIS A brilliant argument was taking place between Sir Herbert and Willie, all about youth.

2 Expr. motion or communication from each of two or more bodies, places, etc., to the other or others; to and from. OE.

STEELE Two Letters which passed between a Mother and Son lately. A. RANSOME Titty and Dorothea raced backwards and forwards between the camp and the well.

3 Expr. confinement or restriction to two or more parties. OE.
between ourselves, **between you and me** (**and the bedpost** or **gatepost**) in confidence.
4 In the interval separating (two points of time, events, etc.); intermediate to (two quantities etc.); partaking of the nature of (two qualities etc.). (The separate times, quantities, etc., joined by *and* or (colloq.) *to*.) OE.

K. MANSFIELD She looked fascinating in her black suit, something between a Bishop and a Fly. C. MORGAN When he was between boy and man, he had often driven these waggons himself. J. BETJEMAN To travel by the Underground all day Between the rush hours. *Listener* Panels can be built up . . to form screen sizes of between 5.3 to 17.6 feet.

5 In or through the space, line, or route (*lit. & fig.*) separating (two points, objects, etc.) or bounded by (more than two points etc. considered individually). OE.

MILTON Jehovah . . thron'd Between the Cherubim. HOR. WALPOLE To hold the balance between liberty and prerogative. TENNYSON By thirty hills I hurry down Or slip between the ridges. S. HEANEY Between my finger and my thumb The squat pen rests. F. SWINNERTON Anna . . had been delayed by traffic between Broadcasting House and the River.

be torn between: see TEAR *verb*[1]. ***between a rock and a hard place***: see ROCK *noun*[1]. ***between cup and lip***: see CUP *noun* 1. ***between the devil and the deep (blue) sea***: see DEVIL *noun*. ***between wind and water***: see WIND *noun*[1]. **come between**, **stand between**: *esp.* as a mediator, as a protector, or to keep from or destroy union. ***fall between two stools***: see STOOL *noun* 2b. ***stand between***: see ***come between*** above.
6 Occupying the space bounded by (two points etc.); dividing, separating; connecting, uniting. ME.

R. BURNS The lang Scots miles That lie between us and our hame. W. PALEY There is no comparison between a fortune which a man acquires by well-applied industry, and one . . received from another. DICKENS The lines of demarcation between the two colours. LD MACAULAY A coalition was formed between the Royalists and a large body of Presbyterians. J. FRAME The unmade road between Maheno and Waipori.

7 By the joint action of; (to be) shared by (collectively or distributively); in portions to each of. ME.

OED They had it between them. G. B. SHAW Our Prime Ministers . . divide their time between the golf course and the Treasury Bench. R. DAVIES I think between us we'll do something extraordinary with this film.

8 So as to separate, select from, or discriminate one from another of; in or involving selection from. ME.

R. HOOKER To judge rightly between truth and error. LD MACAULAY A complete separation between the naval and military services. OED The choice lies between the two last-named applicants.

9 In alternation of; by the combined effect of. E17.

ROBERT BURTON Thus between hope and fear, suspicions, angers . . we bangle away our best days. S. JOHNSON I . . hope, that, between publick business, improving studies, and domestick pleasures, neither melancholy nor caprice will find any place for entrance.

▸ **B** *adverb*. (Mostly the preposition with obj. understood.)
1 In or into an intermediate position or course (*lit. & fig.*); intermediately in amount, order, etc.; occupying intermediate space, intervening. OE.

POPE He hangs between, in doubt to act or rest. SOUTHEY The man . . That instant rush'd between. T. HARDY And I am here, and you are there, And a hundred miles between!

BETWIXT ***and between***. ***far between***: see FAR *adverb*. ***few and far between***. ***in between***: see IN *adverb*.
2 In the interval; at intervals. ME.

TENNYSON They would pelt me with starry spangles and shells, Laughing and clapping their hands between.

3 To and fro as a mediator. Long *obsolete* exc. in GO-BETWEEN. ME.

SHAKES. *Tr. & Cr.* I have . . gone between and between, but small thanks for my labour.

– COMB. (of preposition & adverb): **between-decks** *adverb & noun* (in) the space(s) between the decks of a ship; **between-lens shutter** *PHOTOGRAPHY* a type of shutter fitted between the components of a compound lens close to the diaphragm; **between-maid** a servant assisting two others, as the cook and the housemaid; **between-time** an intervening time, an interval; **between times**, **between whiles** *adverbs* in the interval between other actions, occasionally.

▸ **C** *noun.* An interval (also ***in between*** s.v. IN *adverb*); something intermediate. *rare.* E17.

■ **betweenity** *noun* [after *extremity* etc.] intermediateness of kind, quality, or condition; anything intermediate: M18. **betweenness** /-n-n-/ *noun* L19.

betwixt /bɪˈtwɪkst/ *preposition & adverb.* Now *poet., arch., & dial.*
[ORIGIN Old English *betwēohs*, *betweox*, *betwyx* corresp. to Old Frisian *bituischa*, *bituiskum*, formed as BY *preposition* etc. + Germanic base repr. also by Old Frisian *twiska*, Old Saxon *twisc*, Old High German *zwiski* two each, twofold, formed as TWO + -ISH[1].]
= BETWEEN *preposition & adverb*.
betwixt and between *colloq.* intermediate(ly), neither one thing nor the other. ***betwixt cup and lip***: see CUP *noun* 1.

beudantite /ˈbjuːdəntʌɪt/ *noun.* E19.
[ORIGIN from François *Beudant* (1787–1850), French mineralogist + -ITE[1].]
MINERALOGY. A hexagonal basic sulphate of lead and ferric iron, occurring as black, dark green, or brown rhombohedra.

beurre /bœːr/ *noun.* M19.
[ORIGIN French = butter.]
1 ***beurre noir*** /nwaːr/ [= black], a sauce made by heating butter until it is brown, usu. mixing it with vinegar. M19.
2 ***beurre manié*** /manje/ [= handled], a mixture of flour and butter used for thickening sauces or soups. M20.
3 ***beurre blanc*** /blɑ̃/ [= white], a creamy sauce made with butter, onions, and vinegar or lemon juice, typically served with seafood dishes. M20.

beurré /ˈbjʊəri, *foreign* bœːre/ *noun.* E18.
[ORIGIN French, lit. 'buttered, buttery'.]
A mellow variety of pear.

BeV *abbreviation.*
Billion (10^9) electronvolts.

bevel /ˈbɛv(ə)l/ *adjective & noun.* Also (now *rare*) **bevil**. L16.
[ORIGIN from Old French dim. of *baif* open-mouthed (mod. *béveau*), from *baer* to gape: see BAY *noun*[4]: cf. Old French *bever* give bias to. Cf. earlier BEVILLY.]
▸ **A** *adjective.* Oblique; at more than a right angle; sloping. L16.

L. MACNEICE The blue and bevel hills of Uig.

▸ **B** *noun.* **1** A joiner's and mason's tool consisting of a flat rule with a movable tongue stiffly jointed to one end, for adjusting angles. E17.
2 An obtuse angle; a slope from the horizontal or vertical; a sloping surface. L17.
– COMB.: **bevel gear** a gear working one shaft from another at an angle to it by bevel wheels; **bevel wheel** a toothed wheel whose working face is oblique to the axis.

bevel /ˈbɛv(ə)l/ *verb.* Also **bevil**. Infl. **-ll-**, ***-l-**. L17.
[ORIGIN from the noun.]
1 *verb trans.* Impart a bevel to; cut away (a square edge) to a more obtuse angle. L17.
2 *verb intrans.* Slope, slant. L17.
■ **bevelled** *adjective* (**a**) made with a bevel; (**b**) *HERALDRY* = BEVILLY: M18. **beveller** *noun* L19. **bevelling** *noun* (**a**) the action of the verb; (**b**) an angle or slant produced by bevelling, bevelled work, a bevelled portion or surface: M18. **bevelment** *noun* the process of bevelling E19.

bever /ˈbiːvə/ *noun.* Also **beaver**. LME.
[ORIGIN Anglo-Norman *bever*, Old French *beivre* (later *boivre*) drinking, drink, use as noun of verb *beivre* (mod. *boire*) from Latin *bibere* to drink.]
†**1** A drink, potation; a time for drinking. LME–E17.
2 Light refreshment between meals; a snack. Now chiefly *colloq. & dial.* E16.

beverage /ˈbɛv(ə)rɪdʒ/ *noun.* ME.
[ORIGIN Old French *be(u)vrage* (mod. *breuvage*) from Proto-Romance, from Latin *bibere* to drink: see BEVER, -AGE.]
1 A liquid for drinking; drink. In early use also *spec.* a drink to seal a bargain, *transf.* a bargain sealed by a drink. Now *formal* or *joc.* ME. ▸**b** A specific drink, as lemonade, cider, etc., according to locality. *dial.* E17.
†**2** Drinking; a draught of liquid; *fig.* suffering, a bitter experience. ME–L17.

bevil *adjective & noun, verb* see BEVEL *adjective & noun, verb*.

bevilly /ˈbɛvɪli/ *adjective.* M16.
[ORIGIN formed as BEVEL *adjective*.]
HERALDRY. Of a line: having a break formed from alternate right and left turns at equal acute angles (and resembling a bevel).

Bevin boy /ˈbɛvɪn bɔɪ/ *noun phr.* M20.
[ORIGIN Ernest *Bevin* (1881–1951), Minister of Labour and National Service 1940–5.]
During the Second World War, a young man of age for National Service selected by lot to work as a miner.

bévue /bevy/ *noun.* Pl. pronounced same. L17.
[ORIGIN French, from *bé-*, *bes-* pejorative + *vue* VIEW *noun*.]
An error of inadvertence; a blunder.

bevvy /ˈbɛvi/ *noun & verb intrans. slang.* Also **bevy**. L19.
[ORIGIN from BEV(ERAGE + -Y[6].]
▸ **A** *noun.* (A) drink, esp. (of) beer or other alcoholic liquor. L19.

S. MACKAY I'd had a few bevvies at a party, as you do. J. KELMAN I was on the bevy last night.

▸ **B** *verb.* **1** *verb intrans.* Drink, esp. beer or other alcoholic liquor. M20.
2 *verb trans.* Make drunk. Chiefly as ***bevvied*** *ppl adjective.* M20.

bevy /ˈbɛvi/ *noun*[1]. LME.
[ORIGIN Unknown.]
1 A company of ladies, roes, quails, or larks. LME.
2 A group or company of any kind. E17.

bevy *noun*[2] *& verb* var. of BEVVY.

bewail /bɪˈweɪl/ *verb.* ME.
[ORIGIN from BE- 2 + WAIL *verb*.]
1 *verb trans.* Wail over (esp. the dead). ME.
2 *verb trans.* Express great sorrow or regret for; mourn. LME.
3 *verb intrans.* Lament, mourn. LME.
■ **bewailable** *adjective* E17. **bewailer** *noun* E17. **bewailment** *noun* (*rare*) E17.

beware /bɪˈwɛː/ *verb.* Orig. & now again only in *imper. & inf.* ME.
[ORIGIN Imper. & inf. *be ware* treated as one word: cf. BEGONE *verb*[1].]
1 *verb intrans. & trans.* Be cautious; take heed (of or *of* a danger etc.; *lest*, *how*, *that* . . *not*). ME.

SHAKES. *Macb.* Macbeth! Macbeth! Beware Macduff. MILTON I had bewar'd if I had foreseen. W. MORRIS Beware lest . . Thou tell'st the story of thy love unseen. H. ALLEN Someone who . . he felt was an enemy; a being to beware of.

†**2** *verb intrans. & trans.* Take care (of or *of*, *that*, *to do*); take notice *of*. LME–M19.

SHAKES. *1 Hen. VI* Priest, beware your beard; I mean to tug it. AV *Exod.* 23:21 Behold, I send an Angel before thee . . . Beware of him, and obey his voice. R. W. EMERSON We beware to ask only for high things.

†**3** *verb intrans.* Take warning *by*. E16–E17.

W. CAMDEN It is good to beware by other mens harmes.

†**4** *verb trans.* Make cautious. L16–E18.

DRYDEN Once warn'd is well bewar'd.

†**bewed** *verb trans.* Infl. **-dd-**. Pa. t. & pple **bewedded**, **bewed**. OE–E18.
[ORIGIN Old English *beweddian*, formed as BE- + WED *verb*.]
Marry; unite closely *to*.

beweep /bɪˈwiːp/ *verb. arch.* Pa. t. & pple **bewept** /bɪˈwɛpt/.
[ORIGIN Old English *bewēpan*, formed as BE- + WEEP *verb*.]
1 *verb trans.* Weep for or over; deplore; lament. OE.
2 *verb trans.* Wet or moisten (as) with tears. LME.
†**3** *verb intrans.* Weep. Only in LME.

bewest /bɪˈwɛst/ *adverb & preposition.* Long *obsolete* exc. *Scot.*
[ORIGIN Old English *be westan*, formed as BE- + *westan* (adverb) from the west.]
▸ †**A** *adverb.* On or to the west. OE–L15.
▸ **B** *preposition.* To the west of. OE.

bewet /ˈbjuːɪt/ *noun.* Also **bewit**. L15.
[ORIGIN App. from an unrecorded Anglo-Norman or Old French dim. of Old French *buie* collar, bond, fetter, from popular Latin var. of Latin *boiae* (pl.) collar for the neck.]
FALCONRY. A ring or slip of leather for attaching a bell to a hawk's leg.

†**bewet** *verb trans.* Infl. **-tt-**. LME–L18.
[ORIGIN BE- 1 + WET *verb*.]
Wet profusely.

†**bewhore** *verb trans.* E–M17.
[ORIGIN from BE- 3 + WHORE *noun*.]
Call whore; make a whore of.

SHAKES. *Oth.* My lord hath so bewhor'd her, Thrown such . . heavy terms upon her.

Bewick /ˈbjuːɪk/ *noun.* M19.
[ORIGIN Thomas *Bewick* (1753–1828), English engraver and naturalist.]
Bewick's swan, ***Bewick swan***, a Eurasian race of the tundra swan, *Cygnus columbianus*, which breeds in Arctic regions of Siberia and winters in northern Europe and central Asia.

bewig /bɪˈwɪɡ/ *verb trans.* Infl. **-gg-**. L18.
[ORIGIN from BE- 4 + WIG *noun*[3].]
Provide or cover with a wig. Chiefly as ***bewigged*** *ppl adjective.*

bewilder /bɪˈwɪldə/ *verb trans.* L17.
[ORIGIN from BE- 1 + WILDER *verb*.]
Lead astray, cause to lose the way; perplex; confuse; puzzle.
■ **bewildered** *adjective* (**a**) led astray, perplexed, puzzled; (**b**) *transf.* pathless, confusingly tangled: L17. **bewilderingly** *adverb* in a bewildering manner, so as to bewilder M19. **bewilderment** *noun* (**a**) the condition of being led astray, perplexity, puzzlement; (**b**) *rare* a tangled confusion, an inextricable medley: E19.

bewit *noun* var. of BEWET *noun*.

bewitch /bɪˈwɪtʃ/ *verb trans.* ME.
[ORIGIN from BE- 1 + WITCH *verb*[1].]
Subject to the (esp. malefic) influence of magic or witchcraft; cast a spell over; enchant, fascinate; charm.
■ **bewitcher** *noun* M16. **bewitchery** *noun* (*arch.*) bewitching influence or charm; bewitchment: M17. **bewitchingly** *adverb* charmingly, in a bewitching manner L17. **bewitchment** *noun* the act of bewitching; the ability to charm; the state of being bewitched: E17.

bewrap /bɪˈrap/ *verb trans.* Long *rare.* Infl. **-pp-**. ME.
[ORIGIN from BE- 1 + WRAP *verb*.]
Wrap up, envelop, conceal.

bewray /bɪˈreɪ/ *verb*[1] *trans.* Long *arch.* ME.
[ORIGIN from BE- 1 + WRAY *verb*.]
†**1** Accuse, malign. Only in ME.
†**2** Expose (a person) by divulging his or her secrets etc.; reveal as the unknown doer of an act. ME–E17.
3 Divulge or reveal (a secret) prejudicially. LME.
†**4** *gen.* Make known, show, reveal. LME–E17.
†**5** Expose or betray (a fugitive *to* enemies or justice). M16–E17.
6 Reveal unintentionally, esp. the existence, presence, or true character of (a person or thing). M16.
†**7** = BETRAY 5. L16–M18.
■ **bewrayer** *noun* LME.

bewray *verb*[2] see BERAY.

bewritten /bɪˈrɪt(ə)n/ *ppl adjective.* L19.
[ORIGIN Orig. pa. pple: see BE-, WRITE *verb*.]
Written about.

bey /beɪ/ *noun.* L16.
[ORIGIN Turkish, mod. form of BEG *noun*[1].]
The governor of a district or province in the Ottoman Empire. Also formerly used in Turkey and Egypt as a courtesy title.
■ **beylik**, **-lic** /ˈbeɪlɪk/ *noun* [Turkish *beylik*] the (area of) jurisdiction of a bey M18.

beyond /bɪˈjɒnd/ *adverb, preposition, & noun.*
[ORIGIN Old English *beg(e)ondan*, from *be* BY *preposition* etc. + *g(e)ondan* from Germanic base of YOND *preposition & adverb*.]
▸ **A** *adverb.* At or to the further side; further away. OE.
▸ **B** *preposition.* **1** At or on the further side of, at a more distant point than. OE.

MILTON Both here and beyond the seas. J. RUSKIN Out of which rise the soft rounded slopes of mightier mountains, surge beyond surge.

2 To the further side of, so as to leave behind, further than. OE.

KEATS His spirit pass'd beyond its golden bourn Into the noisy world. G. GREENE The water rose beyond my waist. M. FRAYN He felt unable to look beyond the prospect of small pleasures in the immediate future.

3 In addition to, besides, over and above; (in neg. contexts) apart from. LME.

W. H. DIXON Beyond his labours as a preacher, he composed . . twenty-six books of controversy. S. RAVEN Beyond writing to his uncle about money he had made no effort to communicate with Baron's Lodge.

4 Later than, past. LME.

C. BRONTË We arrived . . about an hour and a half beyond our time.

5 Surpassing or exceeding in quality or quantity; superior to; more than. L15.

MILTON Beyond the bliss of dreams. JOYCE The meal was prolonged beyond an hour and still my uncle did not come.

6 Outside the limit of; out of the reach, comprehension, or range of; not subject to. E16.

GOLDSMITH It was beyond one man's strength to remove it. E. O'NEILL Why Gordon should take such a fancy to that old sissy is beyond me. M. KEANE Complicated conversations requiring answers far beyond Mrs. Brock's limited knowledge of the language. W. BRONK Beyond the slightest doubt I find you right.

– PHRASES: **beyond a joke** outside the limits of what can be considered funny; serious. **beyond belief** unbelievable, incredible. ***beyond measure***: see MEASURE *noun*. ***beyond one's grasp***: see GRASP *noun*. ***beyond price***: see PRICE *noun*. ***beyond question***: see QUESTION *noun*. ***beyond reproach***: see REPROACH *noun*. ***beyond sea(s)***: see SEA *noun*. ***beyond the black stump***: see STUMP *noun*[1]. ***beyond the sea(s)***: see SEA *noun*. ***beyond the veil***: see VEIL *noun* 3. **beyond words** (modifying an adjective) to an inexpressible degree, in the extreme. †**go beyond** *fig.* circumvent. †**look beyond** *fig.* (*rare*, Shakes.) misconstrue, misunderstand.
▸ **C** *noun.* Anywhere distant, distant places; a remote place or experience; *the* future life, *the* unknown. L16.
the back of beyond a very remote or out-of-the-way place.

bezant /ˈbɛz(ə)nt/ *noun*. Also **byzant** /bɪˈzant/. ME.
[ORIGIN Old French *besant*, nom. *besanz*, from Latin *Byzantius* (sc. *nummus* coin) adjective: see BYZANTIAN.]
1 *hist.* A gold or silver coin, orig. minted at Byzantium (later Constantinople, the modern Istanbul), widely used in the currency of medieval Europe. ME.
2 *HERALDRY.* A gold roundel representing such a coin. L15.

bezantee *adjective* var. of BEZANTY.

bez-antler /ˈbeɪantlə, ˈbeɪz-/ *noun*. L16.
[ORIGIN Old French *besantoillier*, from *bes-* twice + *antoillier* ANTLER.]
= BAY *noun*[8].
■ Also **bez tine** *noun* M19.

bezanty /bɪˈzanti/ *adjective*. Also **bezantee**. E17.
[ORIGIN Old French *besanté*: see BEZANT, -Y[5].]
HERALDRY. Charged with bezants.

bezel /ˈbɛz(ə)l/ *noun & verb*. Also (esp. in sense A.1) **basil** /ˈbaz(ə)l, -zɪl/. L16.
[ORIGIN Old French (mod. *biseau*, *béseau*), of unknown origin.]
▸ **A** *noun*. **1** The groove and projecting lip holding a gem, watch glass, etc.; the rim holding a cover of glass etc. L16.
2 The sloped edge of a chisel or other cutting tool. E17.
3 The oblique sides or faces of a cut gem. E19.
▸ **B** *verb*. Infl. **-ll-**, *-**l**-. Grind or cut to a sloping edge; bevel. Now *rare*. L17.

bezesteen /ˈbɛzɪstiːn/ *noun*. M17.
[ORIGIN (Ult., perh. through French or Italian, from) Turkish *bezesten* (now *bedesten*) covered market for fine cloth and valuables, from Persian *bazistān*, from *baz* (Turkish *bez*) from Arabic *bazz* cloth + *-istān* suffix of place.]
An exchange, bazaar, or marketplace in the Middle East.

bezique /bɪˈziːk/ *noun*. M19.
[ORIGIN French *bésigue*, also *bésy*, perh. from Persian *bāzīgar* acrobat, *bāzī* game.]
A card game for two like pinochle, played usu. with a double pack of sixty-four cards (from seven up to ace only); the combination in this game of queen of spades and jack of diamonds.

bezoar /ˈbiːzɔː, ˈbɛzəʊɑː/ *noun*. L15.
[ORIGIN French *bézoard* (earlier *bezar*, *bezahar(d)*), Spanish *bezar*, mod. Latin *beza(h)ar*, ult. from Arabic *bādizahr*, *bāzahr* from Persian *pādzahr* antidote, from *pād* protecting (from) + *zahr* poison.]
†**1** A stone, a concretion. L15–M17.
2 A concretion with a hard nucleus found in the stomach or intestines of certain animals (chiefly ruminants), formerly believed to be antidotal. L16.
†**3** An antidote. Passing into fig. use of sense 2. L16–M18.
†**4** More fully ***bezoar goat***, ***bezoar antelope***. The wild goat of Persia (the best-known source of the concretion of sense 2). E17–L18.
■ **bezoardic** /bɛzəʊˈɑːdɪk/, †**-tic** *adjective & noun* (*arch.*) [mod. Latin *bezoardicus*, *-ticus*] (**a**) *adjective* of or pertaining to a bezoar, antidotal; (**b**) an antidote: E17.

†**bezonian** *noun*. L16–M19.
[ORIGIN Italian *bisogno*, Spanish *bisoño* need + -AN, -IAN: see BESOGNIO.]
= BESOGNIO.

bezzle /ˈbɛz(ə)l/ *verb*. Long *obsolete* exc. *dial.* LME.
[ORIGIN Anglo-Norman *besiler*, *beseler*, Old French *besillier*, Provençal *besillar* maltreat, ravage, of unknown origin: see EMBEZZLE.]
†**1** *verb trans.* Plunder or spoil; make away with (the property of another). LME–E18.
2 *verb intrans. & trans.* Consume (drink) to excess; guzzle; 'booze'. E17.

b.f. *abbreviation*.
1 Bloody fool. *colloq.*
2 Boldface (of type). *US.*
3 Brought forward.

BFI *abbreviation*.
British Film Institute.

BFPO *abbreviation*.
British Forces Post Office.

Bh *symbol*.
CHEMISTRY. Bohrium.

bhadralok /ˈbʌdrəlɒk/ *noun*. *Indian*. Also **bhadralog** /ˈbʌdrəlɒg/. L19.
[ORIGIN Hindi, Bengali, from Sanskrit *bhadrá* worthy, respectable + *loká* folk, people.]
Prosperous, well-educated people, esp. Bengalis, regarded as members of a social class. Also, a member of this class.

Bhagwan /bʌgˈwɑːn/ *noun*. L19.
[ORIGIN Hindi *bhagvān* from Sanskrit *bhagavan*, *bhagavat* divine or adorable one (esp. the name of Vishnu-Krishna or Shiva), (as *adjective*) divine, holy, from *bhaj* to honour, revere, adore.]
HINDUISM. **1** A supreme being, a god. L19.
2 A spiritual leader, a guru (esp. as a title or term of address). M20.

bhajan /ˈbʌdʒ(ə)n/ *noun*. E20.
[ORIGIN Sanskrit *bhajana*.]
HINDUISM. A devotional song.

bhaji /ˈbɑːdʒi/ *noun*. Also **bhajia**. Pl. **-s**, **bhajia**. E19.
[ORIGIN Hindi *bhājī* fried vegetables, from Sanskrit *bhrajj* to fry.]
An Indian dish of fried vegetables; a small cake or ball of vegetables deep-fried in batter.

bhakta /ˈbʌktə/ *noun*. E19.
[ORIGIN Sanskrit.]
HINDUISM. A religious devotee; a worshipper, a believer.

bhakti /ˈbʌkti/ *noun*. M19.
[ORIGIN Sanskrit.]
HINDUISM. Religious devotion or piety as a means of salvation.
bhakti-marga /-mɑːgə/ [*mārga* path] the way to salvation through religious devotion or faith.

B'ham *abbreviation*.
Birmingham.

bhang /baŋ/ *noun*. Also †**bang**. L16.
[ORIGIN (Portuguese *bangue* from) Persian & Urdu *bang*, later assim. to Hindi *bhāṅ* from Sanskrit *bhaṅgā*.]
The drug cannabis. Also (now *rare*), the cannabis plant, Indian hemp.

bhangra /ˈbɑːŋgrə/ *noun*. M20.
[ORIGIN Punjabi *bhāṅgrā*.]
1 A type of Punjabi folk dance for men. M20.
2 A style of popular (esp. dance) music combining Punjabi folk music with rock or dance music. L20.

bharal /ˈbʌr(ə)l/ *noun*. Also **burhel**. M19.
[ORIGIN Hindi.]
The wild or blue sheep of the Himalayas and Tibet, *Pseudois nayaur*.

Bharatiya Janata Party /ˌbɑːrɑːtiːjə ˈdʒʌnəːtɑː ˈpɑːti/ *noun phr.* L20.
[ORIGIN from Hindi *bhāratīya* Indian + *jantā* people + PARTY *noun*.]
In India, a Hindu nationalist political party. Abbreviation *BJP*.

BHC *abbreviation*.
Benzene hexachloride.

Bheel *noun* var. of BHIL.

bheesty *noun* var. of BHISTI.

bhelpuri /ˈbeɪlpuːri/ *noun*. L20.
[ORIGIN from Hindi *bhel* mixture + *pūrī* deep-fried bread.]
An Indian dish of puffed rice, onions, spices, and hot chutney.

bhikkhu /ˈbɪkuː/ *noun*. Also ***bhikku***. M19.
[ORIGIN Pali *bhikkhu* formed as BHIKSHU.]
A Buddhist mendicant or religious devotee. Cf. BHIKSHU.

bhikshu /ˈbɪkʃuː/ *noun*. Pl. **-s**, same. E19.
[ORIGIN Sanskrit *bhikṣu* beggar, from *bhikṣ* beg.]
A brahminical or Buddhist mendicant or religious devotee. Cf. BHIKKHU.

Bhil /biːl/ *noun & adjective*. Also **Bheel**. E19.
[ORIGIN Hindi *Bhīl* from Sanskrit *Bhilla*.]
A member of, of or pertaining to, a central Indian people.

bhisti /ˈbiːsti/ *noun*. Also **b(h)eesty**. L18.
[ORIGIN Urdu *bhīstī* from Persian *bihištī* a person of paradise.]
In the Indian subcontinent: a servant who supplies an establishment with water.

bhoodan /buːˈdɑːn/ *noun*. M20.
[ORIGIN Sanskrit *bhūdana*, from *bhū* earth, land + *dāna* gift.]
In India, the giving by landowners of land to the poor.

bhoona *noun* var. of BHUNA.

bhoosa /ˈbuːsə/ *noun*. Also **bhoos**, **bhusa**. E19.
[ORIGIN Hindi *bhūs*, *bhūsā*.]
In the Indian subcontinent: husks and broken straw, used as food for cattle.

Bhora *noun* var. of BORA *noun*[1].

†**Bhotanese** *noun & adjective* var. of BHUTANESE.

Bhotia /ˈbəʊtɪə/ *noun & adjective*. Also **Bhutia** /ˈbuːtɪə/ & other vars. E19.
[ORIGIN Sanskrit *Bhoṭiya* Tibetan, from *Bhoṭa* Tibet.]
(A native or inhabitant) of the region including Tibet and Bhutan; (of) the language of this region.

bhoy /bəˈhɔɪ/ *noun*. *colloq.* Also **b'hoy**. M19.
[ORIGIN Repr. a supposed Irish pronunc. of BOY *noun*.]
A lively or spirited fellow.

b.h.p. *abbreviation*.
Brake horsepower.

bhuna /ˈbuːnə/ *noun*. Also **bhoona**. M20.
[ORIGIN from Bengali, Urdu *bhunnā* to be fried, ult. from Sanskrit *bhrajj* to fry, parch, roast.]
A medium-hot, dry curry (esp. of meat) originating in Bengal, prepared by frying the ingredients with spices at a high temperature.

bhusa *noun* var. of BHOOSA.

bhut /buːt/ *noun*. Also ***bhuta*** /ˈbuːtə/. L18.
[ORIGIN Sanskrit *bhūt(a)* lit. 'a being'.]
In the Indian subcontinent: a spirit; a demon, a goblin.

Bhutanese /buːtəˈniːz/ *noun & adjective*. Also †**Bhot-**. Pl. of noun same. M19.
[ORIGIN from *Bhutan* (see below) + -ESE.]
(A native or inhabitant) of Bhutan, a country in the SE Himalayas.

Bhutia *noun & adjective* var. of BHOTIA.

Bi *symbol*.
CHEMISTRY. Bismuth.

bi /bʌɪ/ *adjective & noun*. *slang*. M20.
[ORIGIN Abbreviation.]
= BISEXUAL.

bi- /bʌɪ/ *prefix*. Often **bin-** /bɪn/ before a vowel (cf. BIS-).
[ORIGIN Latin (earlier *dui-*, cogn. with Greek DI-[2], Sanskrit *dvi-*) = twice, doubly, having two, two-.]
Used in words adopted from Latin and in English formations modelled on these, and as a productive prefix, forming (*a*) adjectives (and corresp. adverbs etc.) from adjectives or adverbs, with the senses 'having or involving two', as ***bicoloured***, ***bilateral***, ***bimanual***, ***binaural***, 'doubly, in two ways', as ***biconcave***, ***bipyramidal***, (*BOTANY & ZOOLOGY*) 'twice over, divided into similarly divided parts', as ***bipinnate***, 'lasting for two, appearing every two', or (with resulting ambiguity) 'appearing twice in', as ***biannual***, ***biennial***, ***bimonthly***, and 'joining two', as ***biparietal***; (*b*) nouns from nouns with the sense 'double, thing having two', as ***bilayer***, ***biplane***; in *CHEMISTRY* forming names of salts having a doubled proportion of acid to base radicals, as ***bicarbonate***, ***binoxalate***, ***bisulphate***, or of molecules formed from two identical radicals, as ***biphenyl***.

BIA *abbreviation*.
Bureau of Indian Affairs, a US government office responsible for the administration of matters concerning American Indians.

Biafran /bɪˈafrən, bʌɪ-/ *adjective & noun*. M20.
[ORIGIN from *Biafra* (see below) + -AN.]
(A native or inhabitant) of Biafra, an ancient region of W. Africa, which seceded from federal Nigeria from 1967 to 1970.

bialy /bɪˈɑːli/ *noun*. Pl. **-s**. M20.
[ORIGIN Yiddish, from *Białystok* in N.E. Poland, where such bread was originally made.]
A flat, semi-hard bread roll topped with onion flakes.

bi-amping /ˈbʌɪampɪŋ/ *noun*. L20.
[ORIGIN from BI- + AMP(LIFIER + -ING[1].]
AUDIO. The use of two amplifiers for high- and low-frequency ranges in an audio circuit.

bianco sopra bianco /ˈbjaŋko ˌsopra ˈbjaŋko/ *noun phr.* L19.
[ORIGIN Italian, lit. 'white upon white'.]
A form of white decoration upon white porcelain. Cf. earlier SOPRA BIANCO.

biannual /bʌɪˈanjʊəl/ *adjective & noun*. L19.
[ORIGIN from BI- + ANNUAL.]
▸ **A** *adjective*. Appearing, occurring, etc., twice a year. L19.
▸ **B** *noun*. = BIENNIAL. L19.
■ **biannually** *adverb* L19.

bias /ˈbʌɪəs/ *adjective, noun, & adverb*. M16.
[ORIGIN Old French & mod. French *biais* from Provençal, perh. irreg. from Greek *epikarsios* oblique, athwart.]
▸ **A** *adjective* †**1** **a** Slanting, oblique. M16–L17. ▸**b** *DRESSMAKING* etc. Cut obliquely across the warp. E19.
†**2** Bulging like the bias fashioned into a bowl. *rare* (Shakes.). Only in E17.
▸ **B** *noun*. **1** An oblique or slanting line. *obsolete* exc. *DRESSMAKING* etc., an edge cut obliquely across the warp. M16.
cut on the bias cut obliquely across the warp.
2 *BOWLS.* The eccentric form given to a bowl; the swerving course in which this makes it run; the type of impetus effecting such a course. L16.

SHAKES. *Tam. Shr.* Well, forward, forward! thus the bowl should run, And not unluckily against the bias. HAZLITT The skittle-player bends his body to give a bias to the bowl he has already delivered from his hand. A. W. HARE Just as a bowl with a bias, if you try to send it straight, the longer it rolls, the further it will swerve.

3 An inclination, a propensity, a predisposition, (*towards*); prejudice. L16.

C. S. FORESTER Choosing his words with the greatest possible care, . . so that they could be read . . without conveying an impression of bias. W. J. ONG Made up . . of images (with a bias towards visual images). J. BARTH Republicans with a pronounced anti-liberal bias.

†**4** A set course. L16–L18.

D. HUME Superstition, which throws the Government off its bias.

5 A directing influence. L16.

GLADSTONE He could not possibly be under any bias.

†**6** *CRICKET.* The turning of the course of a ball from leg to off side after pitching. M19–E20.
7 *STATISTICS.* (A) systematic distortion of a result, arising from a neglected factor. E20.
8 A steady voltage, magnetic field, etc., applied to an electronic system or device to establish its operation over a particular range, esp. used for minimizing distortion in tape recording. E20.
▸ **C** *adverb*. **1** Obliquely. *obsolete* exc. *DRESSMAKING* etc., obliquely across the warp. L16.

B

†**2** *fig.* Off the straight, awry. **E–M17.**
– **COMB.**: **bias binding** *DRESSMAKING* etc., a narrow strip of cloth cut on the bias and used for binding.
■ **biaswise** *adverb* (now *rare*) obliquely **M16.**

bias /ˈbʌɪəs/ *verb.* Infl. **-s-**, **-ss-**. **E17.**
[**ORIGIN** from **BIAS** *adjective, noun, & adverb.*]
1 *verb trans.* Give a bias to (a bowl etc.); cause to swerve from a course (*lit. & fig.*); influence (usu. unfairly), inspire with prejudice. **E17.**
†**2** *verb intrans.* Incline to one side, swerve from the right course. Only in **17.**
3 *verb trans.* Apply a steady voltage, magnetic field, etc., to: see **BIAS** *noun* 8. **E20.**
■ **biased**, **biassed** *adjective* having a bias; influenced, prejudiced: **E17.**

biathlon /bʌɪˈaθlɒn, -lən/ *noun.* **M20.**
[**ORIGIN** from **BI-** + Greek *athlon* contest, after **PENTATHLON.**]
An athletic or sporting contest in which competitors engage in two events, skiing and shooting.
■ **biathlete** *noun* a competitor in a biathlon **L20.**

biauricular /bʌɪɔːˈrɪkjʊlə/ *adjective.* **M19.**
[**ORIGIN** from **BI-** + **AURICULAR** *adjective.*]
Having two auricles; pertaining to both auricles (of the ears).

biaxial /bʌɪˈaksɪəl/ *adjective.* **M19.**
[**ORIGIN** from **BI-** + **AXIAL.**]
Having or pertaining to two axes; *esp.* of crystals: having two optic axes.
■ **biaxially** *adverb* **L19.**

bib /bɪb/ *noun.* **L16.**
[**ORIGIN** Prob. from the verb.]
1 A cloth etc. placed under a child's chin to keep his or her clothing clean; the top front part of an apron, overall, etc. **L16.** ▸**b** A patch resembling a bib under the bill of a bird. **M19.**
best bib and tucker best clothes.
2 An edible marine fish, *Trisopterus luscus*, of the cod family, having a distensible membrane able to cover its head. Also called ***pout***, ***pouting***. **L17.**

bib /bɪb/ *verb trans. & intrans. arch.* Infl. **-bb-**. **LME.**
[**ORIGIN** Prob. from Latin *bibere* to drink.]
Drink much or often; tipple.
■ **biˈbation** *noun* tippling; a drinking bout: **M19.** **bibber** *noun* a tippler (freq. as 2nd elem. of comb., as ***wine-bibber***) **M16.**

bibacious /bɪˈbeɪʃəs/ *adjective.* **L17.**
[**ORIGIN** from Latin *bibax, -acis* + **-OUS**: see **-ACIOUS.**]
Given to drinking, bibulous.
■ **bibacity** /bɪˈbasɪti/ *noun* addiction to drinking, tippling **L16.**

bibasic /bʌɪˈbeɪsɪk/ *adjective.* **M19.**
[**ORIGIN** from **BI-** + **BASIC** *adjective.*]
CHEMISTRY. Dibasic.

bibb /bɪb/ *noun*[1]. **L18.**
[**ORIGIN** Var. of **BIB** *noun.*]
NAUTICAL. A bracket under the trestletree of a mast.

bibb /bɪb/ *noun*[2]. **L19.**
[**ORIGIN** Named after Jack *Bibb* (1789–1884), US horticulturist, who developed it.]
An American variety of lettuce that has crisp, glossy, dark green leaves.

bibble /ˈbɪb(ə)l/ *verb.* **E16.**
[**ORIGIN** from **BIB** *verb* + **-LE**[3].]
1 *verb intrans. & trans.* Keep drinking; drink, tipple. **E16.**
2 *verb intrans.* Dabble with the bill as a duck. **M16.**
■ **bibbler** *noun* a tippler **M16.**

bibble-babble /ˈbɪb(ə)lbab(ə)l/ *noun.* **M16.**
[**ORIGIN** Redupl. of **BABBLE** *noun*: cf. *tittle-tattle* etc.]
Idle talk, prating.

bib cock /ˈbɪbkɒk/ *noun.* **L18.**
[**ORIGIN** Perh. from **BIB** *noun* + **COCK** *noun*[1].]
A tap with a bent nozzle fixed at the end of a pipe.

bibelot /ˈbɪbələʊ; *foreign* biblo (*pl. same*)/ *noun.* **L19.**
[**ORIGIN** French, from redupl. of *bel* beautiful: cf. **BAUBLE.**]
A small curio or artistic trinket.

biberon /bibrɔ̃/ *noun.* Pl. pronounced same. **M19.**
[**ORIGIN** French.]
A drinking vessel with elongated spout, formerly used by travellers, invalids, and children.

bibi /ˈbiːbiː/ *noun.* Also **beebee**. **E19.**
[**ORIGIN** Urdu *bībī* from Persian.]
In the Indian subcontinent: a mistress of a household; a non-European female consort.

bibira *noun* var. of **BEBEERU.**

bibition /bɪˈbɪʃ(ə)n/ *noun.* **L15.**
[**ORIGIN** Late Latin *bibitio(n-)*, from *bibere* to drink: see **-ITION.**]
(A bout of) drinking.

Bible /ˈbʌɪb(ə)l/ *noun.* Also **b-**. **ME.**
[**ORIGIN** Old French & mod. French *bible* = Provençal *bibla*, Spanish *biblia*, Italian *bibbia*, from ecclesiastical Latin *biblia* neut. pl. (taken as fem. sing.), from Greek (*ta*) *biblia* 'the books'. The Greek sing. *biblion*, dim. of *biblos*, *bublos* papyrus, scroll, etc. (of Semitic origin) lost its dim. sense and became the ordinary word for 'book' before its application to the Judaeo-Christian sacred writings.]
1 *The* Scriptures; *spec.* (**a**) *the* Christian sacred writings collected as the Old and New Testaments (formerly & *dial.* also occas. the Old Testament alone); a copy of these; (with specifying word or contextually) (a copy of) a particular edition of these; (**b**) the Hebrew Scriptures; a copy of these. **ME.**
Bishops' Bible: see **BISHOP** *noun.* ***Breeches Bible***: see **BREECH** *noun.* ***Great Bible***: see **GREAT** *adjective.* ***Printers' Bible***: see **PRINTER.** ***Vinegar Bible***: see **VINEGAR.** ***Wicked Bible***: see **WICKED** *adjective*[1] 1.
2 The sacred writings of some other religion. **LME.**
3 A large or lengthy book; a tome. Now *rare.* **LME.**
4 (**b-**.) An authoritative textbook or indispensable work. **E19.**

Daily Telegraph The US Schwann catalogue, bible of record collectors.

– **COMB.**: **Bible-banger**, **Bible-basher**, **Bible-pounder**, **Bible-puncher**, **Bible-thumper** *colloq.* a person who expounds or follows the Bible in an aggressive way, *esp.* an evangelical member of the clergy; **Bible-banging**, **Bible-bashing**, **Bible-pounding**, **Bible-punching**, **Bible-thumping** *verbal nouns & ppl adjectives* (*colloq.*) aggressively expounding or following the Bible; **Bible Belt** an area of the central and southern US noted for its puritanical and fundamentalist Christian beliefs; **Bible-box** a large flat-lidded box, esp. of the 17th cent., able to hold a family Bible; **Bible class** a class for the study of the Bible; **Bible clerk** a student of the Bible; *spec.* a student at some of the colleges at Oxford having the duty of reading the lessons in chapel and saying grace in Hall; **Bible Christian** (**a**) a Christian according to scriptural standard; (**b**) *hist.* a member of a 19th-cent. Methodist sect founded in SW England by William O. Bryan; **Bible oath** a solemn oath taken on the Bible; ***Bible-pounder***, ***Bible-pounding***, etc.: see ***Bible-banger***, ***Bible-banging*** above.
■ **biblist** /ˈbɪblɪst/ *noun* a person who makes the Bible the sole rule of faith; a biblical student: **M16.**

biblical /ˈbɪblɪk(ə)l/ *adjective.* **L18.**
[**ORIGIN** from medieval Latin *biblicus*, from *biblia* (see **BIBLE**) + **-AL**[1].]
Of, pertaining to, or contained in the Bible; resembling the language of the Bible.
■ **biblic** *adjective* (now *rare*) = **BIBLICAL** **L17.** **biblically** *adverb* **M19.**

Biblicist /ˈbɪblɪsɪst/ *noun.* **M19.**
[**ORIGIN** from **BIBLIC** + **-IST.**]
A person who interprets the Bible literally. Freq. *attrib.*
■ **Biblicism** *noun* **M19.**

biblio- /ˈbɪblɪəʊ/ *combining form.*
[**ORIGIN** Greek stem & combining form of *biblion* book: see **-O-.**]
Used in words adopted from Greek and in English formations modelled on these, with the sense 'of or relating to books or a book'.
■ **biblioklept** /-klɛpt/ *noun* [Greek *kleptēs* thief] a book-thief **L19.** **bibliˈolatry** *noun* extravagant admiration of a book or for books **M18.** **bibliˈology** *noun* the branch of knowledge that deals with books, book-lore; bibliography: **E19.** **bibliomancy** *noun* divination by books; *spec.* divination by verses of the Bible: **M18.** **bibliomane** *noun* = **BIBLIOMANIAC** *noun* **E19.** **biblioˈmania** *noun* a passion for the collecting and possessing of books **M18.** **biblioˈmaniac** *noun & adjective* (a person) affected with or given to bibliomania **E19.** **bibliomaˈniacal** *adjective* (of a) bibliomaniac **E19.** **biblioˈmetric** *adjective* of or pertaining to bibliometrics **L20.** **biblioˈmetrics** *noun* statistics as applied in bibliography; statistical analysis of books, articles, or other publications: **M20.** **bibliopegy** /-ˈpɒpɛdʒi/ *noun* [Greek *-pēgia*, from *pēgnunai* fix] bookbinding as a fine art **L19.** **biblioˈtherapy** *noun* the use of reading matter for therapeutic purposes **E20.** **biblioˈthetic** *adjective* relating to the placing and arrangement of books on the shelves of a library **L19.**

bibliograph /ˈbɪblɪəgrɑːf/ *noun. rare.* **E19.**
[**ORIGIN** Prob. from French *bibliographe*, from Greek *bibliographos*: see **BIBLIOGRAPHER.**]
A bibliographer.

bibliograph /ˈbɪblɪəgrɑːf/ *verb trans.* **M20.**
[**ORIGIN** Back-form. from **BIBLIOGRAPHY.**]
Compile a bibliography of; provide (a scholarly work) with a bibliography.

bibliographer /bɪblɪˈɒgrəfə/ *noun.* **M17.**
[**ORIGIN** from Greek *bibliographos* (formed as **BIBLIO-** + **-GRAPH**) + **-ER**[1].]
†**1** A writer of books; a copyist. **M17–M18.**
2 A practitioner of bibliography. **L18.**

bibliography /bɪblɪˈɒgrəfi/ *noun.* **L17.**
[**ORIGIN** French *bibliographie* or mod. Latin *bibliographia* from Greek: see **BIBLIO-**, **-GRAPHY.**]
†**1** The writing of books. Only in **L17.**
2 The history or systematic description of books, their authorship, printing, publication, editions, etc. **E19.** ▸**b** A book containing such details, esp. of the books on a particular subject. **E19.**
3 A list of books of a particular author, printer, country, etc.; a list of works consulted in a scholarly work; a reading list. **E19.**
■ **biblioˈgraphic** *adjective* of or pertaining to bibliography **E19.** **biblioˈgraphical** *adjective* = **BIBLIOGRAPHIC** **L17.** **biblioˈgraphically** *adverb* **E19.** **bibliographize** *verb trans.* compile a bibliography of **E19.**

bibliophile /ˈbɪblɪəfʌɪl/ *noun.* Also **-phil** /-fɪl/. **E19.**
[**ORIGIN** French: see **BIBLIO-**, **-PHILE.**]
A lover of books; a book collector.
■ **bibliophilic** /-ˈfɪlɪk/ *adjective* of or pertaining to bibliophiles or bibliophily **L19.** **bibliˈophily** *noun* love of books **L19.**

bibliopole /ˈbɪblɪəpəʊl/ *noun.* **L18.**
[**ORIGIN** Latin *bibliopola* from Greek *bibliopōlēs*, from *biblion* book + *pōlēs* seller.]
A dealer in (esp. rare) books.
■ **biblioˈpolic** *adjective* **E19.** **bibliˈopolist** *noun* = **BIBLIOPOLE** **M16.** **bibliˈopoly** *noun* bookselling **M19.**

bibliotheca /bɪblɪəˈθiːkə/ *noun.* **OE.**
[**ORIGIN** Latin from Greek *bibliothēkē* library, from *biblion* book + *thēkē* repository.]
†**1** The Bible. Only in **OE.**
2 A collection of books or treatises; a library; a bibliographer's catalogue. **E19.**
■ **bibliˈothec** *noun & adjective* (**a**) *noun* a librarian; (**b**) *adjective* belonging to a library or librarian: **M17.** **biblioˈthecal** *adjective* belonging to a library **E19.**

bibliothecary /bɪblɪˈɒθɪk(ə)ri/ *noun & adjective.* **L16.**
[**ORIGIN** Latin *bibliothecarius, -um*, formed as **BIBLIOTHECA** + **-ARY**[1].]
▸ **A** *noun.* †**1** A library. Only in **L16.**
2 A librarian. **E17.**
▸ **B** *adjective.* Of or belonging to a library or librarian. **E19.**
■ **bibliotheˈcarial** *adjective* = **BIBLIOTHECARY** *adjective* **L19.** **bibliotheˈcarian** *adjective & noun* = **BIBLIOTHECARY** **L17.**

bibliothèque /bibliɔtɛk/ *noun.* Pl. pronounced same. **M16.**
[**ORIGIN** French formed as **BIBLIOTHECA.**]
A library.
– **NOTE**: Formerly naturalized, but now treated as French.

biblus /ˈbɪbləs/ *noun.* Also **-os**. **M17.**
[**ORIGIN** (Latin from) Greek *biblos.*]
(The inner bark of) the papyrus.

bibulous /ˈbɪbjʊləs/ *adjective.* **L17.**
[**ORIGIN** from Latin *bibulus* freely or readily drinking, from *bibere* to drink: see **-ULOUS.**]
1 Absorbent of moisture. **L17.**
2 Relating to drink. **E19.**
3 Given to drinking alcoholic liquors. **M19.**
■ **bibuˈlosity** *noun* (fondness for) tippling **E20.** **bibulously** *adverb* **M19.** **bibulousness** *noun* **M19.**

bicameral /bʌɪˈkam(ə)r(ə)l/ *adjective.* **M19.**
[**ORIGIN** from **BI-** + Latin **CAMERA** chamber + **-AL**[1].]
Having two (legislative) chambers; having two compartments.
■ **bicameralism** *noun* advocacy or adoption of a bicameral system **M20.**

bicarb /bʌɪˈkɑːb/ *noun. colloq.* **E20.**
[**ORIGIN** Abbreviation of **BICARBONATE.**]
Sodium bicarbonate (see **BICARBONATE**).

bicarbonate /bʌɪˈkɑːbəneɪt/ *noun.* **E19.**
[**ORIGIN** from **BI-** + **CARBONATE** *noun.*]
In *CHEMISTRY*, a salt containing the anion HCO_3^-, i.e. containing double the proportion of carbon dioxide present in a carbonate; *popularly* (in full ***sodium bicarbonate***, ***bicarbonate of soda***) the sodium salt $NaHCO_3$, used as an antacid and in baking powder.

bice /bʌɪs/ *adjective & noun.* **ME.**
[**ORIGIN** Old French & mod. French *bis* dark grey = Provençal *bis*, Italian *bigio*, of unknown origin.]
▸ †**A** *adjective.* Brownish grey, dark grey. Only in **ME.**
▸ **B** *noun.* **1** More fully ***blue bice***. A shade of blue duller than ultramarine or azure. **LME.**
2 A pigment of this colour made from basic copper carbonate or smalt; (more fully ***green bice***) a green pigment similarly made. **M16.**

bicentenary /bʌɪsɛnˈtiːnəri, -ˈtɛn-, bʌɪˈsɛntɪn-/ *adjective & noun.* **M19.**
[**ORIGIN** from **BI-** + **CENTENARY.**]
(The occasion or a celebration) of a two-hundredth anniversary.

bicentennial /bʌɪsɛnˈtɛnɪəl/ *adjective & noun.* **L19.**
[**ORIGIN** from **BI-** + **CENTENNIAL.**]
▸ **A** *adjective.* Lasting or occurring every two hundred years; of or pertaining to a two-hundredth anniversary. **L19.**
▸ **B** *noun.* = **BICENTENARY** *noun.* **L19.**

bicephalous /bʌɪˈsɛf(ə)ləs, -ˈkɛf-/ *adjective.* **E19.**
[**ORIGIN** from **BI-** + Greek *kephalē* head + **-OUS.**]
Two-headed.

biceps /ˈbʌɪsɛps/ *adjective & noun.* **M17.**
[**ORIGIN** Latin, from **BI-** + *-ceps*, *caput* head.]
▸ **A** *adjective.* Having two heads or summits. Now only *spec.* of a muscle: having two heads or points of attachments at one end. **M17.**
▸ **B** *noun.* Pl. same. A biceps muscle; *esp.* a flexor muscle of the front of the upper arm (often taken as the type of physical strength) or of the thigh. **M17.**
■ **bicep** *noun* (*non-standard*) = **BICEPS** *noun* **M20.**

bichir /ˈbɪʃɪə/ *noun.* **L19.**
[**ORIGIN** French, from dial. Arabic *ʻabu šīr.*]
Any of various elongated African freshwater fishes of the genus *Polypterus* (family Polypteridae), having an armour of hard shiny scales and a series of separate fins along the back.

Bichon /ˈbiːʃ(ə)n/ *noun*. M20.
[ORIGIN from French *barbichon* little water spaniel, from *barbet* water spaniel from *barbe* beard, in ref. to the dog's coat.]
A breed of small dog, esp. (in full ***Bichon Frise*** /friːz/ [French *frisé* curly-haired]) one originating in the Canary Islands with a fine, curly white coat; a dog of this breed.

bichromate /bʌɪˈkrəʊmeɪt/ *noun*. M19.
[ORIGIN from BI- + CHROMATE.]
CHEMISTRY. = DICHROMATE *noun*[1].

bichrome /ˈbʌɪkrəʊm/ *noun & adjective*. E20.
[ORIGIN from BI- + Greek *khrōma* colour.]
(A design etc.) having two colours.

bicipital /bʌɪˈsɪpɪt(ə)l/ *adjective*. M17.
[ORIGIN from Latin *bicipit-*, BICEPS + -AL[1].]
1 = BICEPS *adjective*. M17.
2 Of or pertaining to a biceps muscle. M19.

bick /bɪk/ *noun*. L19.
[ORIGIN Abbreviation of BICKERN or its var. *bick-iron*.]
= BICKERN.

bicker /ˈbɪkə/ *noun*[1]. ME.
[ORIGIN Unknown: cf. BICKER *verb*.]
1 Skirmishing; a skirmish; an encounter with missiles. *obsolete* exc. *Scot.*, a street or school fight with stones etc. ME.
2 A quarrel; an angry altercation. ME.
3 A short rapid run (cf. BICKER *verb* 5b). *Scot.* L18.
4 The sound of fighting or conflict. L19.

bicker /ˈbɪkə/ *noun*[2]. *Scot.* LME.
[ORIGIN Var. of BEAKER.]
A (wooden) bowl or dish for containing liquor; formerly a drinking cup.

bicker /ˈbɪkə/ *verb*. ME.
[ORIGIN Unknown: cf. BICKER *noun*[1].]
1 *verb intrans.* Skirmish, fight. ME.
> C. KINGSLEY Slaughtered bickering for some petty town.

2 *verb trans.* Attack with repeated strokes. Long *obsolete* exc. *dial.* ME.
3 *verb intrans.* Quarrel, wrangle, squabble. L15.
> E. M. FORSTER He had . . squabbled with his sister, and bickered with his mother.

4 *verb intrans.* Flash, gleam, quiver, glisten. *poet.* M17.
> SHELLEY The restless wheels . . Whose flashing spokes Bicker and burn.

5 *verb intrans.* Make any repeated noisy action, as the showering of blows, the flowing of a stream over a stony channel, the pattering of rain, etc. M18. ▸**b** Make a short rapid run (describing the pounding of the feet). *Scot.* L18.
> COLERIDGE Against the glass The rain did beat and bicker. TENNYSON And sparkle out among the fern, To bicker down a valley.

■ **bickering** *noun* the action of the verb; a skirmish; a quarrel, a squabble: ME. **bickerment** *noun* bickering L16.

bickern /ˈbɪkən/ *noun*. Also (by false etym.) **beak-iron** /ˈbiːkʌɪən/, **bick-iron** /ˈbɪkʌɪən/. M17.
[ORIGIN Alt. of BICORN *noun* 1, or from its source French *bigorne*.]
An anvil with two projecting taper ends; one such taper end of an anvil.

bicky /ˈbɪki/ *noun*. Also **bikky**. E20.
[ORIGIN Dim. of BISCUIT: see -Y[6].]
A child's word for a biscuit.

bicoastal /bʌɪˈkəʊst(ə)l/ *adjective & noun*. *US*. L20.
[ORIGIN from BI- + COASTAL.]
▸ **A** *adjective*. Situated, taking place on, or involving both the Atlantic and Pacific coasts of the US; (of a person) having a home on, or commuting frequently between, both coasts.
▸ **B** *noun*. A bicoastal person.

bicolour /ˈbʌɪkʌlə/ *adjective & noun*. Also *-color. L19.
[ORIGIN Latin *bicolor* or French *bicolore* adjective: see BI-, COLOUR *noun*.]
(A blossom or animal) of two colours.

bicoloured /ˈbʌɪkʌləd/ *adjective*. Also *-color-. M19.
[ORIGIN from BI- + COLOURED *adjective*.]
Of two colours.

biconcave /bʌɪˈkɒnkeɪv/ *adjective*. M19.
[ORIGIN from BI- + CONCAVE *adjective*.]
Concave on both sides.

biconditional /bʌɪkənˈdɪʃ(ə)n(ə)l/ *noun*. M20.
[ORIGIN from BI- + CONDITIONAL *adjective*.]
LOGIC. The relation between two propositions when one is true only if the other is true, and false if the other is false, represented by the logical operator 'if and only if'.

bicone /ˈbʌɪkəʊn/ *noun*. E20.
[ORIGIN from BI- + CONE *noun*.]
An object, esp. a bead, of the form of two cones placed base to base.

biconical /bʌɪˈkɒnɪk(ə)l/ *adjective*. L19.
[ORIGIN from BI- + CONICAL.]
Of the shape of a bicone.

biconvex /bʌɪˈkɒnvɛks/ *adjective*. M19.
[ORIGIN from BI- + CONVEX *adjective*.]
Convex on both sides.

bicorn /ˈbʌɪkɔːn/ *noun & adjective*. LME.
[ORIGIN (French *bigorne* (in sense A.1) from Provençal *bigorna* from) Latin *bicornis* two-horned, two-pronged, from BI- + *cornu* horn.]
▸ **A** *noun*. †**1** = BICKERN. LME–M18.
2 An animal with two horns. LME.
▸ **B** *adjective*. Having two horns or hornlike processes. M19.
■ **bicorned** *adjective* = BICORN *adjective* E17. **biˈcornous** *adjective* = BICORN *adjective* M17.

bicultural /bʌɪˈkʌltʃ(ə)r(ə)l/ *adjective*. M20.
[ORIGIN from BI- + CULTURAL.]
Having or combining two cultures.
■ **biculturalism** *noun* M20.

bicuspid /bʌɪˈkʌspɪd/ *adjective & noun*. M19.
[ORIGIN from BI- + Latin *cuspid-*, *-is* CUSP: see -ID[2].]
▸ **A** *adjective*. Having two cusps or points. M19.
bicuspid valve the mitral valve of the heart.
▸ **B** *noun*. A human premolar tooth. M19.

bicycle /ˈbʌɪsɪk(ə)l/ *noun & verb*. M19.
[ORIGIN from BI- + Greek *kuklos* circle, wheel, CYCLE *noun*.]
▸ **A** *noun*. A vehicle having two wheels turned by pedalling, typically with handlebars at the front and a seat or saddle for the rider. M19.
exercise bicycle: see EXERCISE *noun*. *motor bicycle*: see MOTOR *noun* & *adjective*. *safety bicycle*: see SAFETY *noun* & *adjective*. *stationary bicycle*: see STATIONARY *adjective*.
– COMB.: **bicycle chain** a chain which transmits the driving power from the pedals of a bicycle to its rear wheel (also used as a weapon in street fighting); **bicycle clip** a clip used to confine a cyclist's trouser leg at the ankle; **bicycle lizard** = RACEHORSE *lizard*; **bicycle motocross** bicycle racing on a dirt track (abbreviation *BMX*); **bicycle pump** a portable pump for inflating the tyres of bicycles; **bicycle rickshaw** a rickshaw pulled by a person on a bicycle.
▸ **B** *verb intrans.* Ride on a bicycle. M19.
■ **bicycler** *noun* = BICYCLIST M19. **bicyclist** *noun* a person who rides a bicycle, a cyclist L19.

bicyclic /bʌɪˈsʌɪklɪk, -ˈsɪk-/ *adjective*. L19.
[ORIGIN from BI- + Greek *kuklos* circle + -IC.]
Having two circles or rings; *esp.* in *CHEMISTRY*, (composed of molecules) with two usu. fused rings of atoms.

bid /bɪd/ *noun*. L18.
[ORIGIN from the verb.]
1 The offer of a price, esp. at an auction; an offer made at a stated price, a tender. L18.
2 *CARDS*. A proposal to win a specified minimum number of tricks (in bridge, the number in excess of six) or points, usu. with a specified trump suit or in no trumps; a player's turn to bid. L19.
3 An attempt to obtain something; a try, an effort. L19.
> *Punch* Britain's Bid for War-Plane Supremacy. J. VAN DRUTEN That's not a bid for pity, it's just telling you why I feel this way.

make a bid for try to secure.
– COMB.: **bid price** the price at which a market-maker or institution, esp. a unit trust, will buy back shares or units (cf. *offer price* s.v. OFFER *noun*).

bid /bɪd/ *verb*. Pa. t. & pple **bid**; pres. pple **bidding**; alternative forms (*obsolete* in sense 7, not used in sense 8): pa. t. **bade** /bad, beɪd/, †**bad**; pa. pple **bidden** /ˈbɪd(ə)n/. OE.
[ORIGIN Combining two verbs: (i) Old English *biddan* (pa. t. *bæd*, *bǣdon*, pa. pple *beden*) ask, entreat, demand = Old Frisian *bidda*, *bidia*, Old Saxon *biddian*, Middle Dutch *bidden*, Old High German, German *bitten*, Old Norse *biðja*, Gothic *bidjan* from Germanic, from base repr. by Old English *ġebed* prayer, BEAD *noun*; (ii) Old English *bēodan* (pa. t. *bēad*, *budon*, pa. pple *boden*) offer, proclaim, announce, command, decree = Old Frisian *biada*, Old Saxon *biodan*, Middle Dutch & mod. Dutch *bieden*, Old High German *biotan* (German *bieten*), Old Norse *bjóða*, Gothic *biudan* from Indo-European.]
▸ **I** Senses chiefly from Old English *biddan*.
1 *verb trans. & intrans.* Ask pressingly, beg, entreat, pray. Long *obsolete* exc. in ***bid a bead*** (see BEAD *noun* 1), ***bidding prayer*** (see BIDDING *noun*), etc. (which are now usu. understood in other senses of the verb). OE.
2 *verb trans.* Command, enjoin, order, tell. (Foll. by inf., †cl.) Now *dial.* & *literary*. OE.
> E. A. FREEMAN The two Earls were . . bidden to be diligent. L. M. MONTGOMERY Just you go and do as I bid you. W. H. AUDEN Good Captain, bid the drums be silent.

3 *verb trans.* Ask to come, invite. *arch.* & *dial.* ME.
> J. BARET I was bidde to an other place to dinner. AV *Zeph.* 1:7 He hath bid his ghests. TENNYSON I made a feast; I bad him come.

4 *verb trans.* Say, express, *welcome*, *farewell*, *good morning*, etc., (to). (Orig. with some sense of invocation or wishing.) ME.
▸ **II** Senses chiefly from Old English *bēodan*.
5 *verb trans.* Proclaim, declare, announce. *arch.* OE.
> POPE The herald . . To bid the banquet interrupts their play. SOUTHEY At this late hour, When even I shall bid a truce to thought.

6 *verb trans.* Offer (esp. as a challenge). *obsolete* exc. in ***bid defiance*** and in spec. senses. OE. ▸**b** *verb intrans.* ***bid fair***, offer a reasonable prospect (*for*), seem likely (*to do*). M17.
> T. FULLER Whom he bade battle, and got the day.

bid a person base: see BASE *noun*[2].
7 *verb trans.* Offer (a certain price, *for*). ME. ▸**b** *verb intrans.* Offer a price (*for*); make an offer at a stated price, make a tender; *fig.* try (*for*, *to do*). E17.
> S. JOHNSON [They] bade her half the price she asked. OED Who bids five shillings for this lot? **b** G. B. SHAW We all bid for admiration without the least intention of earning it. J. MCGAHERN He caused a stir in the mart by turning up to bid for several cattle.

b bid against compete with in bidding. **bid up** raise in price by successive bids.
8 *CARDS*. **a** *verb intrans.* Make a bid. L19. ▸**b** *verb trans.* Make a bid of (a specified number), in (a specified suit), or as the holder of (a given hand). L19.
> R. DAHL The girl badly overestimated her partner's hand and bid six spades. *fig.*: A. J. P. TAYLOR In trying to remain a World Power in all spheres, the British people . . were bidding above their strength.

– COMB.: †**bid-ale** an entertainment or celebration to which a general invitation was given; †**bidstand** a highwayman.

bidarka /bʌɪˈdɑːkə/ *noun*. E19.
[ORIGIN Russian *baĭdarka*, pl. *-ki*, dim. of *baĭdara* an umiak.]
In Alaska and adjacent regions: a portable canoe for one or more persons; a kayak.

biddable /ˈbɪdəb(ə)l/ *adjective*. L18.
[ORIGIN from BID *verb* + -ABLE.]
1 Ready to do what is bidden; obedient, docile. L18.
2 *CARDS*. Of a hand: strong enough to warrant a bid. Of (cards held in) a suit: strong enough to warrant a bid in that suit. Of a contract: that can be the result of normal bidding. L19.
■ **biddaˈbility** *noun* obedience M20.

biddance /ˈbɪd(ə)ns/ *noun*. E19.
[ORIGIN from BID *verb* + -ANCE.]
Bidding, invitation.

bidden *verb* see BID *verb*.

bidder /ˈbɪdə/ *noun*. ME.
[ORIGIN from BID *verb* + -ER[1].]
A person who bids, esp. at an auction or at cards.

biddery *noun* var. of BIDRI.

bidding /ˈbɪdɪŋ/ *noun*. ME.
[ORIGIN from BID *verb* + -ING[1].]
1 *gen.* The action of BID *verb*. ME.
2 The offering or an offer of a price for an article; *collect.* the offers at an auction. ME.
3 A command, an order. Usu. ***the bidding of*** or ***someone's bidding***. ME.
> T. E. LAWRENCE Heedfully they hastened to do his bidding.

4 An invitation, a summons. E19.
5 *CARDS*. The act or process of making a bid or bids; the bid or bids made. L19.
– PHRASES: †**bidding of prayers** praying of prayers; (later understood as) directing or enjoining of prayers. ***force the bidding***: see FORCE *verb*[1].
– COMB.: **bidding prayer** a prayer inviting the congregation to join in, now usu. a group of intercessionary prayers.

biddy /ˈbɪdi/ *noun*[1]. E17.
[ORIGIN Unknown: cf. CHICKABIDDY. Sense 2 prob. infl. by BIDDY *noun*[2]; sense 3 perh. a different word.]
1 A chicken; a fowl. *obsolete* exc. *dial.* E17.
2 A woman. Usu. somewhat *derog.* L18.
3 In full ***red biddy***. A drink consisting of methylated spirits and cheap red wine; inferior red wine. E20.

biddy /ˈbɪdi/ *noun*[2]. Chiefly *US*. M19.
[ORIGIN from *Biddy* familiar form of female forename *Bridget*.]
An Irish maidservant.

biddy-bid /ˈbɪdɪbɪd/ *noun*. *NZ*. Also **biddy-biddy**, **bidibidi**, /-bɪdi/. M19.
[ORIGIN Alt. of Maori PIRIPIRI.]
(The bur of) the piripiri.

bide /bʌɪd/ *verb*. Exc. as in sense 5 now *arch.* & *dial.*
[ORIGIN Old English *bīdan* = Old Saxon *bīdan*, Old High German *bītan*, Old Norse *bíða*, Gothic *beidan*, from Germanic.]
▸ **I** *verb intrans.* **1** Remain in expectation; wait. OE.
2 Remain or continue *in* some state or action. OE.
bide by stand firm by, adhere to.
3 Stay, esp. when others go. Of a thing: remain, be left. OE.
> J. KESSON If it promises rain, we'd maybe better bide at home.

4 Remain in residence; dwell. ME.
▸ **II** *verb trans.* **5** Wait for, await. *obsolete* exc. in ***bide one's time***, await one's opportunity. OE.
> E. B. WHITE They bide their time until the morning has advanced a good long way.

6 Await in resistance, face, encounter; = ABIDE 6. ME.
†7 Endure, suffer, bear; = ABIDE 7. ME–E19.
8 Tolerate, put up with; = ABIDE 9. ME.

bident /ˈbʌɪd(ə)nt/ *noun*. L17.
[ORIGIN Latin *bident-*, *-dens* having two teeth, two-pronged, formed as BI- + *dent-*, *dens* tooth.]
1 An instrument or weapon with two prongs. L17.
2 A two-year-old sheep. *rare.* M19.

bidental /bʌɪˈdɛnt(ə)l/ *noun*. **E17.**
[ORIGIN from Latin *bident-*: see BIDENT, -AL[1].]
ROMAN ANTIQUITIES. A place struck by lightning, consecrated, and enclosed.

bidentate /bʌɪˈdɛnteɪt/ *adjective*. **E19.**
[ORIGIN from BI- + -DENTATE.]
1 ZOOLOGY. Having two teeth or toothlike projections. **E19.**
2 CHEMISTRY. Of a ligand: forming two bonds, usu. with the same central atom. Of a molecule or complex: formed by such a ligand. **M20.**

bidet /ˈbiːdeɪ/ *noun*. **M17.**
[ORIGIN French = pony, ass, from *bider* to trot, of unknown origin.]
1 A small horse. **M17.**
2 A shallow oval basin used for washing esp. the genital and anal regions. **L18.**

bidi /ˈbiːdi/ *noun*. Also **beedi**, **biri** /ˈbiːri/. **L19.**
[ORIGIN Hindi *bīḍī* betel plug, cigar, from Sanskrit *vīṭikā*.]
In the Indian subcontinent: a cigarette or cigar of unprocessed tobacco rolled in leaves.

bidialectal /ˌbʌɪdʌɪəˈlɛkt(ə)l/ *adjective*. **M20.**
[ORIGIN from BI- + DIALECTAL.]
Fluent in the use of two dialects of the same language, involving the use of two dialects, esp. a standard and a non-standard variety.
■ **bidialectalism**, **bidialectism** *nouns* facility in using two dialects of the same language, the use of two dialects, esp. a standard and a non-standard variety **M20.**

bidibidi *noun* var. of BIDDY-BID.

bidie-in /ˌbʌɪdɪˈɪn/ *noun*. *Scot.* **E20.**
[ORIGIN from BIDE + IN *adverb*; see -IE.]
A person who lives with another in a relationship outside marriage, a cohabitee.

bidimensional /bʌɪdɪˈmɛnʃ(ə)n(ə)l, -dʌɪ-/ *adjective*. **E20.**
[ORIGIN from BI- + DIMENSIONAL.]
Having, or perceived in, two dimensions.

biding /ˈbʌɪdɪŋ/ *noun*. **ME.**
[ORIGIN from BIDE + -ING[1].]
1 The action of BIDE *verb*; awaiting, remaining, dwelling. **ME.**
†**2** A dwelling, an abode. Only in **17.**

SHAKES. *Lear* I'll lead you to some biding.

– COMB.: **biding place** place of abode.

bidirectional /bʌɪdɪˈrɛkʃ(ə)n(ə)l, -dʌɪ-/ *adjective*. **M20.**
[ORIGIN from BI- + DIRECTIONAL.]
Functioning in two directions.
■ **bidirectionally** *adverb* **M20.**

bidon /bidɔ̃/ *noun*. Pl. pronounced same. **M19.**
[ORIGIN French.]
A container for liquids; a canteen for water etc.; an oil drum or petrol tin.

bidonville /ˈbɪd(ə)nvɪl; *foreign* bidɔ̃vil (*pl. same*)/ *noun*. **M20.**
[ORIGIN French, from BIDON + *ville* town.]
A shanty town built of oil drums etc., esp. on the outskirts of a French or N. African city.

bidri /ˈbɪdri/ *noun*. Also **biddery** /ˈbɪd(ə)ri/, **bidry**. **L18.**
[ORIGIN Urdu *bidrī*, from *Bidar* or *Bedar* a town in India.]
An alloy of copper, lead, tin, and zinc, used as a ground for inlaying with gold and silver, in ***bidri-ware***.

Biedermeier /ˈbiːdəmʌɪə/ *adjective* (*attrib.*). *derog.* Also **-maier**, **-meyer**. **E20.**
[ORIGIN Gottlieb *Biedermaier*, fictitious German poet created by L. Eichrodt in 1854.]
Designating, pertaining to, or characteristic of the styles of interior decoration, esp. of furniture, fashionable in Germany in the period 1815–48; *transf.* conventional, bourgeois.

bield /biːld/ *noun*. *obsolete* exc. *dial.*
[ORIGIN Old English *beldu*, (West Saxon) *bieldu* = Old High German *baldī*, Gothic *balþei* boldness, from Germanic, formed as BOLD *adjective*: cf. BIELD *verb*.]
†**1** Boldness. **OE–L15.**
†**2** (A means or provider of) help or succour. **ME–E19.**
3 (A place of) refuge or shelter. *Scot. & N. English.* **LME.**
■ **bieldy** *adjective* (*Scot.*) affording shelter **M18.**

bield /biːld/ *verb*. *obsolete* exc. *dial.* Pa. t. **bield(ed)**; pa. pple **bield**.
[ORIGIN Old English *beldan*, (West Saxon) *bieldan* = Old Saxon *beldian*, Old High German *belden*, Gothic *balþjan*, from Germanic, formed as BOLD *adjective*.]
†**1** *verb trans. & intrans.* Make, grow or be, bold. **OE–L15.**
2 *verb trans.* Defend, protect, shelter. *Scot. & N. English.* **ME.**
▸†**b** *verb intrans.* Find protection or shelter. Only in **LME.**

Bielid /ˈbiːlɪd/ *noun*. **L19.**
[ORIGIN from Wilhelm von *Biela* (1782–1856), Austrian astronomer, discoverer of a comet of which the Andromedid meteor swarm is believed to be the remnant, + -ID[3].]
ASTRONOMY. = ANDROMEDID.

bien *adjective & adverb* var. of BEIN.

bien entendu /bjɛ̃n ɑ̃tɑ̃dy/ *adverbial phr.* **M19.**
[ORIGIN French, from *bien* well + *entendu* pa. pple of *entendre* hear, understand.]
Of course; that goes without saying.

bien-être /bjɛ̃nɛːtr/ *noun*. **M19.**
[ORIGIN French, from *bien* well + *être* be.]
A state of well-being.

biennale /biːɛˈnɑːli/ *noun*. **M20.**
[ORIGIN Italian, formed as BIENNIAL.]
A large (esp. biennial) art exhibition or music festival, orig. *spec.* (**B-**) that held biennially in Venice, Italy.

biennia *noun pl.* see BIENNIUM.

biennial /bʌɪˈɛnɪəl/ *adjective & noun*. **E17.**
[ORIGIN from Latin *biennis* of two years, or BIENNIUM: see BI-, -AL[1], and cf. ANNUAL.]
▸ **A** *adjective*. **1** Existing or lasting for two years; *esp.* (BOTANY) that is a biennial. **E17.**
2 Occurring every two years. **M18.**
▸ **B** *noun*. **1** BOTANY. A plant which springs from seed and vegetates one year, and flowers, fructifies, and perishes the next. **L18.**
2 An event taking place biennially. Chiefly *US*. **M19.**
■ **biennially** *adverb* every two years **L18.**

biennium /bʌɪˈɛnɪəm/ *noun*. Pl. **-iums**, **-ia** /-ɪə/. **E20.**
[ORIGIN Latin, formed as BI- + *annus* year.]
A period of two years.

bien pensant /bjɛ̃ pɑ̃sɑ̃/ *adjectival & noun phr.* As noun ***bien-pensant*** (pl. pronounced same). **E20.**
[ORIGIN French, *bien* well, *pensant* pres. pple of *penser* think.]
(A person who is) right-thinking, orthodox, conservative.

bienséance /bjɛ̃seɑ̃ːs/ *noun*. **L17.**
[ORIGIN French, from *bien* well + *séant*, from *seoir* befit.]
Decorum.

†**bienvenue** *noun*. **LME.**
[ORIGIN French, from *bien* well + *venue* coming.]
1 Welcome. **LME–M17.**
2 A fee exacted from a new workman. **L17–L18.**

bier /bɪə/ *noun*.
[ORIGIN Old English *bēr*, (West Saxon) *bǣr* = Old Frisian *bēre*, Old Saxon, Old High German *bāra* (German *Bahre*), from West Germanic, from Germanic base of BEAR *verb*[1].]
1 A framework for carrying; a barrow; a litter. Long *obsolete* exc. *hist.* **OE.**
2 A movable frame on which a coffin or corpse is placed before burial or cremation; a support on which a coffin or corpse is carried to the grave. **OE.**
3 *transf.* A tomb; a sepulchre. **LME.**
– COMB.: †**bier-baulk** a baulk in a field where there is a right of way for funerals; †**bier-right** an ordeal in which those accused of murder were required to approach the corpse and clear themselves on oath.

bierhaus /ˈbiːrhaʊs/ *noun*. Pl. ***-häuser*** /-hɔyzər/. **M20.**
[ORIGIN German, from *Bier* beer + *Haus* house.]
A public house or alehouse in a German-speaking country.

Bierstube /ˈbiːrʃtuːbə, -st-/ *noun*. Pl. ***-ben*** /-bən/, ***-bes***. **E20.**
[ORIGIN German, from *Bier* beer + *Stube* room.]
A German tavern, taproom, or bar. Cf. WEINSTUBE.

biface /ˈbʌɪfeɪs/ *noun*. **M20.**
[ORIGIN BI- + FACE *noun*.]
ARCHAEOLOGY. A type of prehistoric stone implement flaked on both faces.

bifacial /bʌɪˈfeɪʃ(ə)l/ *adjective*. **L19.**
[ORIGIN from BI- + FACIAL *adjective*.]
Having two faces; *spec.* (**a**) BOTANY having distinct dorsal and ventral surfaces; (**b**) ARCHAEOLOGY (of a flint etc.) worked on both faces.
■ **bifacially** *adverb* **M20.**

bifarious /bʌɪˈfɛːrɪəs/ *adjective*. **M17.**
[ORIGIN from Latin *bifarius* twofold, double (formed as BI-) + -OUS.]
†**1** Twofold; ambiguous. **M17–L18.**
2 BOTANY. Ranged in two rows. **L18.**
■ **bifariously** *adverb* **M17.**

biff /bɪf/ *interjection, verb, & noun*. *colloq.* (orig. *US*). As interjection also **bif**. **M19.**
[ORIGIN Imit.]
▸ **A** *interjection*. Repr. the sound of a smart blow. **M19.**
▸ **B** *verb*. *slang*.
1 *verb trans.* Hit, strike. **L19.**

E. WAUGH I'd like to hear less about denying things to the enemy and more about biffing him. *Club Tennis* She was not put on this earth to biff balls over nets.

2 *verb intrans.* Go; proceed. **E20.**

P. G. WODEHOUSE To biff down to Twing and rally round young Bingo.

3 *verb trans. & intrans.* Throw. *Austral. & NZ*. **M20.**
▸ **C** *noun*. A blow; a whack. **L19.**

biffin /ˈbɪfɪn/ *noun*. Also **beefing** /ˈbiːfɪŋ/, (by false etym.) **beaufin** /ˈbəʊfɪn/. **L18.**
[ORIGIN Repr. dial. pronunc. of *beefing*, from BEEF *noun* (with ref. to the colour) + -ING[3].]
1 A deep-red cooking apple cultivated esp. in Norfolk. **L18.**
2 A baked apple flattened in the form of a cake. **E19.**

biffy /ˈbɪfi/ *noun*. *N. Amer. slang*. **M20.**
[ORIGIN Perh. from a child's pronunciation of *bathroom* or *privy*.]
A toilet, a lavatory.

bifid /ˈbʌɪfɪd/ *adjective*. **M17.**
[ORIGIN Latin *bifidus*, formed as BI- + base of *findere* split. Cf. *trifid*.]
Divided into two parts by a deep cleft or notch.
■ **biˈfidity** *noun* **L19.** **bifidly** *adverb* **M19.**

bifilar /bʌɪˈfʌɪlə/ *adjective*. **M19.**
[ORIGIN from BI- + Latin *filum* thread + -AR[1].]
Consisting of or involving two threads or wires.
■ **bifilarly** *adverb* **L19.**

bifocal /bʌɪˈfəʊk(ə)l/ *adjective & noun*. **E19.**
[ORIGIN from BI- + FOCAL.]
▸ **A** *adjective*. Having two foci; *esp.* designating a lens having two parts each with a different focal length, one for distant vision and one for near vision. **E19.**
▸ **B** *noun*. In *pl.* A pair of glasses with bifocal lenses. **L19.**
■ **bifocalled** *adjective* wearing bifocals **M20.**

bifold /ˈbʌɪfəʊld/ *adjective*. **E17.**
[ORIGIN from BI- + -FOLD.]
Double, twofold.

bifolium /bʌɪˈfəʊlɪəm/ *noun*. Pl. **-ia** /-ɪə/. **M20.**
[ORIGIN from BI- + Latin *folium* leaf.]
PALAEOGRAPHY. A pair of conjoint leaves.

biforked /ˈbʌɪfɔːkt/ *adjective*. **L16.**
[ORIGIN from BI- + FORKED.]
Having two forks, branches, or peaks.

biform /ˈbʌɪfɔːm/ *adjective*. **E19.**
[ORIGIN Latin *biformis* from BI- + *forma* shape, FORM *noun*.]
Having or partaking of two forms.
■ **biformed** *adjective* = BIFORM **L16.** **biˈformity** *noun* **E17.**

bifront /ˈbʌɪfrʌnt/ *adjective*. **L16.**
[ORIGIN Latin *bifrons*, *-front-*, from BI- + *frons* forehead, face.]
Having two faces or aspects; double.
■ **biˈfrontal** *adjective* = BIFRONT **M19.** **biˈfronted** *adjective* = BIFRONT **L16.**

biftek /biftɛk/ *noun*. Pl. pronounced same. **M19.**
[ORIGIN French, from *beefsteak* (see BEEF *noun*).]
(A) beefsteak.

bifunctional /bʌɪˈfʌŋ(k)ʃ(ə)n(ə)l/ *adjective*. **E20.**
[ORIGIN from BI- + FUNCTIONAL *adjective*.]
1 Having two functions. **E20.**
2 CHEMISTRY. Having two highly reactive binding sites in each molecule. **E20.**

bifurcate /bʌɪˈfəːkət/ *adjective*. **M19.**
[ORIGIN medieval Latin *bifurcatus*, formed as BIFURCATE *verb*: see -ATE[2].]
Having two forks, branches, or peaks.

bifurcate /ˈbʌɪfəkeɪt/ *verb trans. & intrans.* **E17.**
[ORIGIN medieval Latin *bifurcat-* pa. ppl stem of *bifurcare*, from Latin *bifurcus* two-forked, from BI- + *furca* FORK *noun*: see -ATE[3].]
Divide into two forks, branches, or peaks.
■ **bifurˈcation** *noun* division into two forks or branches; the point of such division; either or both of two such forks or branches: **E17.**

big /bɪg/ *noun*[1]. *obsolete* exc. *dial.* Also **bigg**. **LME.**
[ORIGIN Unknown.]
A teat.

big /bɪg/ *noun*[2]. *Scot. & dial.* Also **bigg**. **LME.**
[ORIGIN Old Norse *bygg* barley (Danish *byg*, Swedish *bjug*), corresp. to Old English *bēow* grain, Old Saxon *beo*, *bewod* harvest.]
The four-rowed barley, an inferior but hardy variety of six-rowed or winter barley.

big /bɪg/ *adjective & adverb*. Compar. & superl. **-gg-**. **ME.**
[ORIGIN Unknown.]
▸ **A** *adjective*. †**1** Of a living being: great in strength; mighty. **ME–L16.**
2 Of a thing: strong; stiff; violent; vehement. Long *obsolete* exc. *dial.* **LME.**

SHAKES. *Oth.* Farewell the plumed troops, and the big wars That makes ambition virtue.

3 Of considerable size, amount, extent, intensity, etc. (less formal than *large* and usu. without the emotional implications of *great*). (In comparisons, neutral as to absolute size.) **LME.** ▸**b** *esp.* Grown large(r) or tall(er); (more) grown up; elder. **LME.** ▸**c** Of a letter: capital, upper case. **L19.**

MILTON Seeming bigger than they are through the mist and vapour. TENNYSON Apt at arms and big of bone. I. MURDOCH How very big Peter was, plump and burly, broad-shouldered. A. BURGESS It's all big words nowadays in whatever you read. J. HERRIOT He wasn't a big eater but he did love his breakfast. **b** ARNOLD BENNETT Your big sister isn't out of school yet? **c** *Times* An attempt to impose Culture, with a big 'C', on the . . people.

4 Far advanced in pregnancy; filled to bursting, distended. Usu. foll. by *with*. **M16.**

BURKE The mind of this political preacher . . big with some extraordinary design. A. HALEY One man's wife, big with child, had died on the road.

5 Full in voice, loud. **L16.**

6 Of a high position; important; influential; momentous. L16.

C. ISHERWOOD James L. Schraube, he explained, was a very big man in Chicago. A. HALEY Virgil sent L'il Kizzy racing from the field to tell . . that something big must have happened.

7 Haughty; pretentious; boastful. L16.
8 Generous, magnanimous. Usu. *iron. colloq.* (orig. *US*). M20.

N. COWARD That's big of her I must say.

9 Keen *on*. *colloq.* M20.

– PHRASES: **be a big boy (now)**, **be a big girl (now)** be old enough to take responsibility for one's own actions, no longer need protection or supervision. ***big girl's blouse***: see GIRL *noun*. ***go big***: see GO *verb*. ***go for the big spit***: see SPIT *noun*². ***great big***: see GREAT *adjective*. ***heap big***: see HEAP *noun*. **in a big way** on a large scale; *colloq.* with great enthusiasm or display. ***the Big Apple***: see APPLE *noun*. ***the big bird***: see BIRD *noun*. **the big C** *colloq.* cancer. ***the Big Drink***: see DRINK *noun*. ***the big IDEA***. ***the big pond***: see POND *noun* 2. ***the big screen***: see SCREEN *noun*¹. ***the big smoke***: see SMOKE *noun*. **the Big Three**, **the Big Four**, etc., the dominant group of three etc. **too big for one's boots**, **too big for one's breeches** *colloq.* conceited.

– SPECIAL COLLOCATIONS & COMB.: **big air** a high jump in skateboarding, BMX riding, etc. ***big ask***: see ASK *noun*¹. **big band** a large band of musicians playing jazz, dance music, etc. **Big Bang** (*a*) (ASTRONOMY) *the* violent expansion of all matter from a state of high density and temperature, postulated as the origin of the universe; (*b*) (STOCK EXCHANGE, *colloq.*) *the* deregulation of the London Stock Exchange in 1986. **Big Ben**, the great bell, or *loosely* the clock or tower, of the Palace of Westminster in London. ***Big Bertha***: see BERTHA *noun*². **Big Board** *US colloq. the* New York Stock Exchange. **big bore** *US* a rifle of large calibre. **big box** *N. Amer. colloq.* a very large store which sells goods at discount prices. **Big Brother** [from the head of State in George Orwell's novel *Nineteen Eighty-Four* (1949)] an apparently benevolent but ruthlessly omnipotent dictator. **big bud** a plant disease caused by gall mites. **big bug** *colloq.* an important person. **big business** (orig. *US*) (those involved in) large mercantile organizations or transactions (freq. with sinister implications). **big cat** any of the larger carnivores of the cat family, Felidae, such as a lion, leopard, or cheetah. ***big cheese***: see CHEESE *noun*² 2. ***big chief***: see CHIEF *noun*. **big crunch** ASTRONOMY a contraction of the universe to a state of extremely high density and temperature (a hypothetical opposite to the big bang). **Big Daddy** a paternal, dominating, or influential person. **big deal** *colloq.* a cause of concern or excitement (chiefly in neg. contexts). ***big dipper***, ***Big Dipper***: see DIPPER 5. **big end** the end of the connecting rod that encircles the crankpin. **bigeye** (*a*) a large-eyed reddish fish, *Priacanthus arenatus*, which lives in moderately deep waters of the tropical Atlantic and the western Indian Ocean; (*b*) (***bigeye tuna***) a large migratory tuna, *Thunnus obesus*, found in warm seas. **Bigfoot** a large hairy apelike creature supposedly inhabiting north-west America (cf. SASQUATCH). **big game** large animals as lions, elephants, etc., hunted as game. **big gun** *colloq.* an important person. **big hair** *colloq.* a bouffant hairstyle, esp. one that has been teased, sprayed, or permed to create volume. **big-head** (*a*) a disease of sheep or other livestock in which there is swelling of the head; (*b*) *US & Austral.*, any of various large-headed fishes; (*c*) *colloq.* conceit, arrogance; a conceited or arrogant person. **big-headed** *adjective* (*a*) large-headed; (*b*) *colloq.* conceited, arrogant. **big-headedness** *colloq.* conceit, arrogance. **big-hearted** *adjective* generous. **big-heartedness** generosity. **bighorn** the Rocky Mountain sheep, *Ovis canadensis*. **big house** (*a*) the principal house of an estate, village, etc.; (*b*) *slang* a prison. **big league** a major baseball league; *transf.* a top group. **big-league** *attrib. adjective* top-class. **big leaguer** a player in or member of a big league. **big money** (orig. *US*) much money, esp. as pay or profit. **big mouth** (orig. *US*) a very talkative or boastful person; loquacity, boastfulness. **big-mouthed** *adjective* loquacious, boastful. **big name** (orig. *US*) a famous person, esp. in the field of entertainment. **big noise** *colloq.* an important person. **big-note**, **big-note oneself** *verb Austral. & NZ colloq.* boastfully exaggerate one's own wealth or importance. **big pot**, **big shot** *colloq.* an important person. ***big show***: see SHOW *noun*¹. **big stick** (orig. *US*) (a display of) force or power. ***big stiff***: see STIFF *noun*. ***big talk***: see TALK *noun*¹. **big tent** a political party which seeks to be inclusive by permitting or encouraging a broad-spectrum of views among its members. **big-ticket** *attrib. adjective* constituting a major expense (freq. in ***big-ticket item***). **big time** *slang* (orig. *US*) the highest rank (among entertainers etc.). **big-timer** a top-ranker. **big toe** either of the innermost and largest toes. **big top** (the main tent of) a circus. **big tree** *US* the wellingtonia, *Sequoiadendron giganteum*. **big wheel** (*a*) a Ferris wheel; (*b*) *colloq.* an important person. ***big white chief***: see CHIEF *noun*. **bigwig** *colloq.* [with allus. to the large wigs formerly worn by men of importance] an important person.

► **B** *adverb*. In a big manner. Chiefly in phrs. below. M16.

come over big, **go over big**: with great effect, successfully. **look big**: haughtily. **talk big**: boastfully, confidently. **think big**: ambitiously.

■ **biggie** *noun* (*a*) *slang* someone or something big, an important person or event; (*b*) in *pl.* (*euphem.*), excrement: M20. **biggish** *adjective* rather big E17. **biggity** /ˈbɪgɪti/ *adjective* (chiefly *US dial.*) [perh. after *bigoted* or *uppity*] conceited, boastful, assertive L19. **bigly** *adverb* †(*a*) violently, firmly; (*b*) loudly, boastfully, haughtily: LME. **bigness** *noun* large size; (in comparisons) size; pompousness: L15.

big /bɪg/ *verb*. *obsolete* exc. *Scot. & N. English*. Infl. **-gg-**. ME.
[ORIGIN Old Norse *byggja*.]
†**1** *verb intrans. & trans.* Dwell (in); place *oneself*. ME–L15.
2 *verb trans.* Build; erect, pile up. ME.
■ **bigging** *noun* (*a*) the action of the verb; †(*b*) a dwelling place; (*c*) a building, an outbuilding: ME. **bigly** *adjective* habitable, pleasant LME.

biga /ˈbʌɪgə/ *noun*. Pl. **-gae** /-giː/. E17.
[ORIGIN Latin.]
ROMAN ANTIQUITIES. A two-horsed chariot.

bigamy /ˈbɪgəmi/ *noun*. ME.
[ORIGIN Old French & mod. French *bigamie*, from *bigame* from late Latin *bigamus*, from Latin BI- + Greek *-gamos* married.]
1 The crime of going through a form of marriage while a previous marriage is still in existence; having two wives or husbands at once. ME.
2 ECCLESIASTICAL LAW. Remarriage after the death of a spouse; marriage with a widow or widower. *obsolete* exc. *hist.* LME.
■ **bigamist** *noun* a person who commits or lives in bigamy M17. **bigamous** *adjective* living in or involving bigamy M19. **bigamously** *adverb* L19.

bigarade /bɪgəˈrɑːd; *foreign* bigarad (*pl. same*)/ *noun*. E18.
[ORIGIN French from Provençal *bigarrado*.]
The Spanish bitter orange.

bigarreau /ˈbɪgərəʊ/ *noun*. Pl. **-s**, **-x** (pronounced same). E17.
[ORIGIN French, from *bigarré* variegated.]
In full ***bigarreau cherry***. A variety of sweet cherry, usu. heart-shaped and with firm flesh.

bigeminal /bʌɪˈdʒɛmɪn(ə)l/ *adjective*. M19.
[ORIGIN from BI- + Latin *geminus* twin + -AL¹.]
Existing or arranged in pairs.
■ **bigeminy** *noun* (MEDICINE) the occurrence of double pulse beats E20.

bigeminate /bʌɪˈdʒɛmɪnət/ *adjective*. M18.
[ORIGIN from BI- + GEMINATE *adjective*.]
= BIGEMINAL.

bigener /ˈbʌɪdʒɪnə/ *noun*. M19.
[ORIGIN Latin, from BI- + *gener-*, GENUS.]
BOTANY. A hybrid between two genera.
■ **bigeˈneric** *adjective* L19.

bigg *noun* var. of BIG *noun*¹, *noun*².

biggen /ˈbɪgən/ *verb trans. & intrans. obsolete* exc. *dial.* M17.
[ORIGIN from BIG *adjective* + -EN⁵.]
Make or become big; increase.

biggin /ˈbɪgɪn/ *noun*¹. Now *arch.* or *hist.* L15.
[ORIGIN French *béguin*, formed as BEGUINE *noun*¹.]
1 A child's cap; ***the biggin*** (fig.), infancy. L15.
2 A hood for the head; the coif of a serjeant-at-law. L15.

biggin /ˈbɪgɪn/ *noun*². L18.
[ORIGIN App. from a Mr *Biggin* of Manchester (fl. late 18th cent.), its inventor.]
A type of coffee pot containing a strainer preventing the grounds from mixing with the infusion.

biggonet /ˈbɪgənɪt/ *noun*. *Scot.* Now *arch.* or *hist.* M17.
[ORIGIN Dim. of BIGGIN *noun*¹; cf. Old French *beguinet*.]
A woman's cap or headdress.

bigha /ˈbiːgə/ *noun*. Also **begah** & other vars. M18.
[ORIGIN Hindi *bighā*.]
In the Indian subcontinent: a measure of land area varying locally from ⅓ to 1 acre (⅛ to ⅖ hectare).

bight /bʌɪt/ *noun*.
[ORIGIN Old English *byht* from Germanic: cf. Middle Low German *bucht* (whence Dutch *bocht*, German *Bucht*, Swedish, Danish *bugt*); rel. to BOW *verb*¹.]
1 A bending, a bend; an angle, a hollow, a fork. Now *rare* in *gen.* sense. OE.
2 A bend or curve as a geographical feature; an indentation in a coastline, body of ice, etc.; a bend in a river; *spec.* a bay, esp. in names as ***Bight of Benin***, ***Australian Bight***. L15.
3 The loop of a rope (as distinct from its ends). E17.

bignonia /bɪgˈnəʊnɪə/ *noun*. L18.
[ORIGIN mod. Latin, from Abbé J. P. *Bignon* (1662–1743), librarian to Louis XIV: see -IA¹.]
A plant of the chiefly tropical genus *Bignonia*, with showy trumpet-shaped flowers.

bigot /ˈbɪgət/ *noun*. L16.
[ORIGIN French, of unknown origin.]
†**1** A hypocritical or superstitious adherent of religion. L16–M17.
2 An obstinate and unreasonable adherent of a religious or other opinion; an intolerant and narrow-minded person. M17.
■ **bigoted** *adjective* unreasonably intolerant M17.

bigotry /ˈbɪgətri/ *noun*. L17.
[ORIGIN from BIGOT + -RY; partly through French *bigoterie*.]
Obstinate and unreasonable adherence to a religious or other opinion; narrow-minded intolerance; an instance of this.

biguanide /bʌɪˈgwɑːnʌɪd/ *noun*. L19.
[ORIGIN from BI- + GUANIDINE + -IDE.]
CHEMISTRY. A crystalline base, $NH(C(NH)(NH_2))_2$, formed by condensation of two guanidine molecules; any substituted derivative of this.

Bihari /bɪˈhɑːri/ *adjective & noun*. Also **Be-**. L19.
[ORIGIN Hindi *bihārī*, from *Bihār* (see below).]
(A native or inhabitant) of Bihar, a state of NE India; (of) a group of Indo-Aryan dialects of NE India.

bijection /bʌɪˈdʒɛkʃ(ə)n/ *noun*. M20.
[ORIGIN from BI- after *injection*.]
MATH. A mapping that is both one-to-one and onto.
■ **bijective** *adjective* of the nature of or pertaining to a bijection M20.

B

bijou /ˈbiːʒuː, *foreign* biʒu/ *noun & adjective*. M17.
[ORIGIN French from Breton *bizoù* finger ring, from *biz* finger.]
► **A** *noun*. Pl. **-oux** /-uː(z), *foreign* -u/. A jewel, a trinket. M17.
► **B** *adjective*. Small and elegant. M19.
■ ***bijouterie*** /biʒutri/ *noun* [French: see -ERY] jewellery, trinkets, etc. E19.

bijugate /bʌɪˈdʒuːgət/ *adjective*. E18.
[ORIGIN from BI- + Latin *jugatus* pa. pple of *jugare* join together: see -ATE².]
1 Of a coin: bearing two overlapping side-facing heads. E18.
2 BOTANY. Having two pairs of leaflets. M19.

bike /bʌɪk/ *noun*¹. *Scot. & N. English*. ME.
[ORIGIN Unknown.]
1 A nest of wasps, hornets, or wild bees; a swarm. ME.
2 *fig.* A well-provisioned storehouse or dwelling. L15.
3 *fig.* A swarm of people, a crowd. M16.

bike /bʌɪk/ *noun*² *& verb*. *colloq.* L19.
[ORIGIN Abbreviation of BICYCLE.]
► **A** *noun*. A bicycle; a motorcycle. L19.
exercise bike: see EXERCISE *noun*. **get off one's bike** *Austral. & NZ colloq.* become annoyed. **get on your bike**, **on your bike** *slang* go away (and do something useful). ***motor bike***: see MOTOR *noun & adjective*. ***pushbike***: see PUSH-. ***scrambler bike***: see SCRAMBLER 2. ***stationary bike***: see STATIONARY *adjective*.
– COMB.: **bike boy** *colloq.* a motorcyclist, a biker; **bikeway** a path or lane for the (usu. exclusive) use of bicycles.
► **B** *verb*. **1** *verb intrans.* Ride on a bike. L19.
2 *verb trans.* Cause (a letter or package) to be delivered by bicycle or motorcycle. L20.

M. AMIS He seriously considered typing this out and biking it in.

■ **biker** *noun* a cyclist; a motorcyclist, *esp.* one who is a member of a gang: L19. **bikie** *noun* (*Austral. & NZ colloq.*) = BIKER M20.

bikini /bɪˈkiːni/ *noun*. M20.
[ORIGIN *Bikini*, an atoll in the Marshall Islands, where an atomic bomb test was carried out in 1946.]
A scanty two-piece beach garment worn by women and girls.
– COMB.: **bikini briefs** women's briefs resembling those of a bikini.

bikky *noun* var. of BICKY.

Bikram yoga /ˈbɪkram/ *noun*. L20.
[ORIGIN named after *Bikram* Choudhury (b. 1946), Indian yoga teacher, who developed it.]
(Proprietary name for) a type of hatha yoga performed in a room heated to around 100° F.

bilabial /bʌɪˈleɪbɪəl/ *adjective & noun*. M19.
[ORIGIN from BI- + LABIAL *adjective*.]
► **A** *adjective*. **1** = BILABIATE. *rare*. M19.
2 PHONETICS. Of certain consonants (e.g. /p/, /b/, /m/, /w/): produced by the juncture or apposition of the lips. L19.
► **B** *noun*. PHONETICS. A bilabial consonant. L19.

bilabiate /bʌɪˈleɪbɪət/ *adjective*. M18.
[ORIGIN from BI- + LABIATE *adjective*.]
Chiefly BOTANY. = ***two-lipped*** s.v. TWO *adjective*.

bilal /bɪˈlɑːl/ *noun*. M19.
[ORIGIN Malay, from Arabic *Bilal*, the forename of an Abyssinian slave appointed as the first muezzin following Muhammad's pilgrimage to Mecca in 629.]
In Malaysia: a muezzin.

bilander /ˈbɪləndə, ˈbʌɪ-/ *noun*. Also **-ll-**, **by-**. M17.
[ORIGIN Dutch *bijlander* (Flemish *billander*), from *bij* BY *preposition* + *land* LAND *noun*¹: see -ER¹.]
hist. A small Dutch or Flemish merchant ship with a lateen mainsail and square foresail, used esp. for coastal traffic.

bilateral /bʌɪˈlat(ə)r(ə)l/ *adjective*. L18.
[ORIGIN from BI- + LATERAL *adjective*.]
1 Of, on, or with, two sides. L18.
bilateral symmetry symmetry about a plane.
2 Orig. (LAW), made or entered on by two parties. Later more widely, involving two states as parties to an agreement, esp. in respect of trade and finance. E19.
■ **bilateralism** *noun* = BILATERALITY M19. **bilateˈrality** *noun* bilateral nature or condition L19. **bilaterally** *adverb* M19.

bilayer /ˈbʌɪleɪə/ *noun*. M20.
[ORIGIN from BI- + LAYER *noun*.]
BIOCHEMISTRY. A film two molecules thick (formed e.g. by lipids), in which each molecule is arranged with its hydrophobic end directed inwards towards the opposite side of the film and its hydrophilic end directed outwards.

bilbergia *noun* var. of BILLBERGIA.

bilberry /ˈbɪlb(ə)ri/ *noun*. Also †**bill-**. L16.
[ORIGIN Prob. of Norse origin: cf. Danish *bøllebær*, from *bølle* bilberry + *bær* BERRY *noun*¹.]
1 (The small blue-black fruit of) a dwarf hardy northern European shrub, *Vaccinium myrtillus*, growing on heaths,

B

moors, and in mountain woods. Also called ***whortleberry***, ***blaeberry***. L16.
2 Any of certain related plants or their fruit. M17.
■ **bilberrying** *verbal noun* collecting bilberries M19.

bilbo /ˈbɪlbəʊ/ *noun*. Pl. **-o(e)s**. M16.
[ORIGIN from †*Bilboa*, Bilbao in Spain.]
hist. A slender sword having a blade of notable temper and elasticity.

†**bilbocatch** *noun* see BILBOQUET.

bilboes /ˈbɪlbəʊz/ *noun pl.* M16.
[ORIGIN Unknown.]
hist. An iron bar with sliding shackles for confining the ankles of prisoners.

bilboquet /bɪlbəʊˈkɛt/ *noun*. In sense 2 also †**-catch**. E17.
[ORIGIN French (*bille boucquet* in Rabelais), of uncertain origin.]
†**1** A cord with sticks fastened to it, for measuring or laying out garden beds. Only in 17.
2 (The game and plaything) cup-and-ball. M18.

bilby /ˈbɪlbi/ *noun*. *Austral.* L19.
[ORIGIN Yuwaalaraay (an Australian Aboriginal language of New South Wales) *bilbi*.]
The rabbit bandicoot.

Bildungsroman /ˈbɪldʊŋzroˌmaːn/ *noun*. Pl. **-e** /-ə/. E20.
[ORIGIN German, from *Bildung* education + *Roman* novel.]
A novel dealing with one person's formative years or spiritual education.

bile /bʌɪl/ *noun*[1]. M16.
[ORIGIN French from Latin *bilis*.]
1 a A bitter yellow, brown, or green fluid secreted by the liver, stored in the gall bladder, and passed into the duodenum to assist in the digestion of fats; formerly regarded as one of the four humours of the body (cf. CHOLER). M16. ▸**b** Excess or derangement of the bile. E19.
a black bile = *choler adust* s.v. CHOLER.
2 *fig.* Anger, peevishness. M19.
– COMB.: **bile duct** a duct conveying bile from the liver to the intestine; **bile pigment** any of a number of coloured compounds formed by the breakdown of haemoglobin and excreted in the bile.

†**bile** *noun*[2] var. of BOIL *noun*[1].

bilge /bɪldʒ/ *noun & verb*. Also †**billage**. L15.
[ORIGIN Prob. var. of BULGE *noun*.]
▸ **A** *noun*. **1** The nearly horizontal part of a ship's bottom; the lowest internal portion of the hull. L15.
round bilge: see ROUND *adjective*.
2 The belly or widest part of the circumference of a barrel or similar vessel. E16.
3 In full ***bilge water***. The filth, stale water, etc., which collects inside the bilge of a ship. E17. ▸**b** Nonsense, rubbish, rot. *slang*. L19.
– COMB.: **bilge keel** a timber or plate fastened under the bilge of a ship to prevent rolling or to support the ship's weight in dry dock; **bilge pump** a pump to draw off bilge water; ***bilge water***: see sense 3 above.
▸ **B** *verb*. **1** *verb trans*. Stave in the bilge of (a ship). M16.
2 *verb intrans*. Spring a leak in the bilge. E18.
3 *verb intrans*. Bulge, swell out. E19.
■ **bilgy** *adjective* L19.

bilharzia /bɪlˈhɑːtsɪə/ *noun*. M19.
[ORIGIN mod. Latin, former name of the genus *Schistosoma*, from Theodor *Bilharz* (1825–62), German physician: see -IA[1].]
MEDICINE. A schistosome; also, schistosomiasis.
■ **bilharzial** *adjective* L19. **bilharˈziasis** *noun*, pl. **-ases** /-əsiːz/, schistosomiasis E20. **bilharziˈosis** *noun*, pl. **-oses** /-ˈəʊsiːz/, schistosomiasis E20.

bili- /ˈbɪli/ *combining form* of Latin *bilis* BILE *noun*[1]: see -I-.
■ **bilifiˈcation** *noun* the production of bile; making into bile: L17. **biliˈrubin** *noun* [Latin *ruber* red] one of the two major bile pigments, an orange compound containing four pyrrole nuclei M19. **bilirubiˈnaemia** *noun* (MEDICINE) the presence of excess bilirubin in the blood, causing jaundice if sufficiently great E20. **biliˈverdin** *noun* [French *vert* green] one of the two major bile pigments, a green oxidized precursor of bilirubin M19.

biliary /ˈbɪlɪəri/ *adjective*. M18.
[ORIGIN French *biliaire*, formed as BILE *noun*[1] + *-aire* -ARY[2].]
1 Of or pertaining to the bile. M18.
2 Bilious. Now *rare* or *obsolete*. M19.

bilimbi /bɪˈlɪmbi/ *noun*. Also **blimbing** /ˈblɪmbɪŋ/. L18.
[ORIGIN Malay *bilimbing*.]
(The edible astringent fruit of) a tropical Asian evergreen tree, *Averrhoa bilimbi*, of the oxalis family. Also called ***cucumber tree***.

biliment /ˈbɪlɪm(ə)nt/ *noun*. *obsolete* exc. *hist.* Also **-ll-**. M16.
[ORIGIN Aphet. from HABILIMENT.]
An ornamental article of women's dress, esp. for the head or headdress.

bilinear /bʌɪˈlɪnɪə/ *adjective*. M19.
[ORIGIN from BI- + LINEAR.]
MATH. **1** Of, pertaining to, or contained by two straight lines. M19.
2 Linear and homogeneous in two (sets of) variables. L19.
■ **bilineˈarity** *noun* (in sense 2) M20.

bilingual /bʌɪˈlɪŋgw(ə)l/ *adjective & noun*. M19.
[ORIGIN from Latin *bilinguis*, from BI- + *lingua* tongue, + -AL[1].]
▸ **A** *adjective*. **1** Having two languages; speaking two languages fluently; *loosely* bidialectal. M19.
2 Of an inscription etc.: written or inscribed in two languages. M19.
▸ **B** *noun*. **1** A bilingual inscription. L19.
2 A bilingual person. M20.
■ **bilingualism** *noun* facility in using two languages or (*loosely*) dialects L19. **bilinguˈality** *noun* = BILINGUALISM M20. **bilingually** *adverb* L19.

bilious /ˈbɪlɪəs/ *adjective*. M16.
[ORIGIN Latin *biliosus*, from *bilis* BILE *noun*[1]: see -OUS.]
†**1** = BILIARY 1. M16–L17.
2 *fig.* Bad-tempered. M16.
3 Orig., affected by or arising from excess or derangement of the bile. Now usu., affected by or associated with nausea or vomiting; nauseated, nauseous. M17.
4 Of the colour of bile; (esp. of a person's complexion) having an unhealthy greenish or yellowish hue.

> *www.fictionpress.com* The fluorescent lighting cast a bilious pigment on my skin.

■ **biliously** *adverb* M19. **biliousness** *noun* E19.

biliteral /bʌɪˈlɪt(ə)r(ə)l/ *adjective*. L18.
[ORIGIN from BI- + LITERAL *adjective*.]
Consisting of two letters.

-bility /ˈbɪlɪti/ *suffix*.
[ORIGIN French *-bilité*, Latin *-bilitatem*.]
Forming abstract nouns from adjectives in -BLE.

bilk /bɪlk/ *noun & verb*. M17.
[ORIGIN Uncertain: perh. alt. of BAULK *noun*, *verb*.]
▸ **A** *noun*. †**1** A meaningless or worthless statement. M17–M18.
2 A hoax, a deception; also, a person who cheats or bilks. *arch.* M17.
†**3** CRIBBAGE. A balking or spoiling of the opponent's score in his or her crib. L18–E19.
▸ **B** *verb trans*. †**1** CRIBBAGE. Balk or spoil the score of (an opponent, an opponent's crib). M17–M19.
2 Balk (expectation etc.); cheat (*of*); evade payment of (a creditor, a bill); give the slip to. L17.
■ **bilker** *noun* E18.

bill /bɪl/ *noun*[1].
[ORIGIN Old English *bil* = Old Saxon *bil*, Old High German *bill* (Middle High German *bil*, German *Bille* axe), from West Germanic.]
1 *hist.* Any of various bladed or pointed hand weapons, as a kind of broadsword mentioned in Old English poetry, a weapon like a halberd with a hook instead of a blade, a similar long-handled weapon carried by constables of the watch. OE.
2 An implement with a long concave-edged blade often (in this form also called ***billhook***) ending in a sharp hook, used for pruning, lopping trees, etc. OE.
3 *hist.* More fully ***bill-man***. A soldier, watchman, etc., armed with a bill. L15.

bill /bɪl/ *noun*[2].
[ORIGIN Old English *bile*, of unknown origin.]
1 A bird's beak, esp. when slender, flattened, or weak, and in pigeons and web-footed birds. OE. ▸**b** The muzzle of a platypus. M19.
2 A beaklike projection; *spec.* a narrow promontory, as in ***Portland Bill***. LME.
3 NAUTICAL. The point of an anchor fluke. M18.
– COMB.: **billfish** (**a**) any of various large marine game fishes of the family Istiophoridae, with long spearlike upper jaws, comprising the sailfish, marlins, and spearfishes; (**b**) = GARFISH; (**c**) = SAURY.
■ **billed** *adjective* having a bill (usu. as 2nd elem. of combs., as ***broad-billed***, ***soft-billed***, etc.) LME.

bill /bɪl/ *noun*[3]. ME.
[ORIGIN Anglo-Norman *bille* or Anglo-Latin *billa*, prob. alt. of Old French *bulle*, medieval Latin *bulla* BULL *noun*[2].]
1 A written list or catalogue; an inventory. Long *obsolete* exc. with specifying word or phr. & in some techn. & spec. uses, as: (**a**) at certain public schools, a list of pupils; hence, roll-call; (**b**) NAUTICAL a list of people appointed to duties; (**c**) PRINTING a list of the quantities of each letter required for a font. ME. ▸†**b** MEDICINE. A prescription. E16–M18.
2 A document (orig. sealed); a formal statement in writing, a memorandum. *obsolete* exc. with specifying phr. in legal and commercial use (see below). LME. ▸†**b** A lampoon. LME–L16.
†**3** A written supplication; a petition. LME–E18.
4 A draft of proposed legislation. LME.
5 LAW. A written statement of a case, esp. that of a plaintiff. *obsolete* exc. in ***true bill*** below. LME.
6 A note of charges for goods supplied or services rendered; the amount thus owed. LME.

> *Which?* Pay the bills yourself, and then seek compensation. *New Scientist* A massive August phone bill for £358.08.

†**7** A label. *rare*. L15–E17.
8 A written or printed advertisement, a poster, a placard, an announcement. L15. ▸**b** (A list of) the items of entertainment on a theatre etc. programme. M19.
9 More fully ***bill of exchange***. A written order to pay a specified sum of money on a certain date to a drawer or to a named payee; a promissory note. L16. ▸**b** A banknote. Chiefly *N. Amer.* L17.
– PHRASES: ***accommodation bill***. **bill of costs** a solicitor's account of charges and expenses incurred on a client's business. ***bill of exchange***: see sense 9 above. **bill of fare** a menu; *fig.* a programme. **bill of goods** (chiefly *N. Amer.*) a consignment of merchandise (***sell a bill of goods***, persuade (a person) to accept something undesirable, swindle). **bill of health** a certificate relating to the incidence of infectious disease on ship or in port at time of sailing; ***clean bill of health***, certification of freedom from such infection, freq. *fig.* of a person or thing examined and found in good condition. ***bill of indictment***. **bill of lading** a shipmaster's detailed receipt to a consignor of goods for carriage by sea. **bill of mortality** *hist.* a weekly statement of deaths in and near London. ***bill of privilege***: see PRIVILEGE *noun*. **bill of quantities** a detailed statement of work, prices, dimensions, etc., for the erection of a building by contract. ***Bill of Rights***: see RIGHT *noun*[1]. **bill of sale** a certificate of transfer of personal property, *esp.* a borrower's certificate that a chattel is pledged as security. ***bill of sufferance***: see SUFFERANCE 5b. ***butcher's bill***: see BUTCHER *noun*. ***double bill***: see DOUBLE *adjective & adverb*. **fill the bill**, **fit the bill** fulfil the necessary requirements; come up to the requisite standard. ***public bill***: see PUBLIC *adjective & noun*. ***send a bill upstairs***: see UPSTAIRS *adverb* 2a. ***short bill***: see SHORT *adjective*. ***Treasury bill***: see TREASURY 5. ***true bill***: see TRUE *adjective*.
– COMB.: **billboard** a large outdoor board or hoarding for advertisements; **bill-clerk** *US* a clerk who deals with bills at a hotel; **billfold** *US* a wallet for banknotes; **billhead** a printed account form with the issuer's name etc. at the head; **billposter**, **billsticker** a person who pastes up placards.

Bill /bɪl/ *noun*[4]. *slang*. M20.
[ORIGIN From the cartoon character *Old Bill*, a First World War soldier with a walrus moustache.]
The police; a police officer. Also ***Old Bill***.

bill /bɪl/ *verb*[1] *intrans*. ME.
[ORIGIN from BILL *noun*[2].]
†**1** Peck. ME–L17.
2 Of doves: stroke bill with bill. L16. ▸**b** *transf.* Exchange caresses. Esp. in ***bill and coo***. E17.

bill /bɪl/ *verb*[2] *trans*. ME.
[ORIGIN from BILL *noun*[3].]
†**1** Enter in a catalogue, book, account, etc. ME–M17.
2 Enter the name of in a list, enrol, enlist. *arch.* LME.

> J. MASEFIELD Send out your press. Bill every able-bodied man. Bill the women if the men won't come.

3 Announce by bill; place in a programme; advertise *as*. L17.

> A. E. STEVENSON The conference had been billed as an effort to define the relationship of the federal government to education. A. S. BYATT The Father was billed to speak on Openings for the Ambitious. *fig.*: E. BOWEN She was billed, it appeared, for yet another confession.

4 Plaster over with bills. E19.
5 Send a bill or account to; charge. M19.

> N. SHUTE If there's a scratch on it, I'll bill you for it.

6 Book as passenger or freight. *US*. M19.
■ **billable** *adjective* †(**a**) indictable; (**b**) liable to be charged for: L16.

bill /bɪl/ *verb*[3] *trans*. LME.
[ORIGIN from BILL *noun*[1].]
Hack, lop, or chop (as) with a bill.

billabong /ˈbɪləbɒŋ/ *noun*. *Austral.* M19.
[ORIGIN Wiradhuri *bilabang*.]
A branch of a river, forming a blind channel, backwater, or stagnant pool.

†**billage** *noun & verb* var. of BILGE.

billander *noun* var. of BILANDER.

billard /ˈbɪləd/ *noun*. *obsolete* exc. *dial.* Also **billet** /ˈbɪlɪt/. M17.
[ORIGIN Unknown.]
A saithe, *esp.* a young one.

billbergia /bɪlˈbəːgɪə/ *noun*. Also **bilb-**. E19.
[ORIGIN mod. Latin, from Gustaf *Billberg* (1772–1844), Swedish botanist: see -IA[1].]
A tropical American epiphyte of the genus *Billbergia*, which belongs to the bromelia family and includes several ornamental species.

†**billberry** *noun* var. of BILBERRY.

billet /ˈbɪlɪt/ *noun*[1]. LME.
[ORIGIN Anglo-Norman *billette* or Anglo-Latin *billetta* dim. of *billa* BILL *noun*[3]: see -ET[1].]
1 A short written document, a small notice. Long *obsolete* in *gen.* sense. LME.
2 A short informal letter, a note. *arch.* L16.

> LD MACAULAY Carrying billets backward and forward between his patron and the.. maids of honour.

†**3** A ballot paper. E17–L18.
4 An order requisitioning lodging for military personnel, civilian evacuees, etc.; a lodging for troops etc.; a place to stay; a destination; an appointment, a situation. M17.

> J. WESLEY He never received one wound. So true is the odd saying of King William, that 'every bullet has its billet'. P. G. WODEHOUSE George took up his abode.. in the plainly-furnished but not uncomfortable cottage... He might have found a worse billet. A. SILLITOE We were allotted to four different houses, and taken by car to our separate billets.

5 An admission ticket, a pass. *arch.* L17.

E. DOWSON Tell me whether you will come, as otherwise I will give Johnson your billet.

billet /ˈbɪlɪt/ *noun*[2]. LME.
[ORIGIN Old French *billette* and *billot*, dims. of *bille* tree trunk, length of round timber, from medieval Latin *billa*, *billus* branch, trunk, prob. of Celtic origin (cf. Old Irish & mod. Irish *bile* sacred tree, large tree): see -ET[1].]
▸ **I 1** A thick length of wood, *esp.* one cut for firewood. LME. ▸†**b** Firewood. LME–M17.

G. ANSON Some of our men . . were employed in cutting down trees, and splitting them into billets.

2 A small bar of metal. E17.

A. G. GARDINER Billets of steel that scorch you as they pass from the furnace to the steam-press.

3 *ARCHITECTURE.* A decorative short cylindrical piece inserted at intervals in a moulding. M19.
▸ **II 4** *HERALDRY.* A charge in the form of an upright rectangle. LME.
5 *SADDLERY.* A strap which enters a buckle; a loop which receives a buckled strap. L15.

billet *noun*[3] var. of BILLARD.

billet /ˈbɪlɪt/ *verb.* L16.
[ORIGIN from BILLET *noun*[1].]
1 *verb trans.* Quarter (troops etc., *on* or *with* a person, *on*, *in*, or *at* a place); assign accommodation to, place. L16. ▸**b** Of a householder etc.: provide (a soldier etc.) with board and lodging, lodge. M17.
2 *verb intrans.* Have quarters. *rare.* E17.
†**3** *verb trans.* Enter in a list, enrol. Only in E17.
■ **bille'tee** *noun* a person who is billeted M20. **billeter** *noun* one who billets M17.

billet-doux /bɪlɪˈduː/ *noun.* Now chiefly *joc.* Pl. **billets-doux** /bɪlɪˈduːz/. L17.
[ORIGIN French, lit. 'sweet note'.]
A love letter.

billeté /ˈbɪləti/ *adjective.* Also **-etté**, **-etty**. L16.
[ORIGIN French *billeté* from *billette*: see BILLET *noun*[2] 4, -Y[2].]
HERALDRY. Charged with billets.

billiards /ˈbɪljədz/ *noun* (orig. *pl.*, but soon treated as *sing.*). Sing. form used only in comb. L16.
[ORIGIN French *billard* the game and the cue, from *bille*: see BILLET *noun*[2], -ARD.]
A game played with cues and balls on an oblong smooth cloth-covered table: in the standard form played with three balls on a table with six pockets at the corners and sides into which the balls are struck.
bar billiards: see BAR *noun*[1]. ***pocket billiards***: see POCKET *noun* & *adjective*.
– COMB.: ***billiard ball***, ***billiard cue***, ***billiard hall***, ***billiard player***, ***billiard room***, ***billiard table***, etc.; **billiard marker** a person or apparatus whose function is to record the score in billiards.
■ **billiardist** *noun* a person who plays billiards M19.

billie *noun* var. of BILLY *noun*[1].

billiken /ˈbɪlɪkɪn/ *noun.* Also **-kin**. E20.
[ORIGIN Prob. from BILLY *noun*[2] + -KIN.]
A small, squat, smiling figure used as a mascot.

billiment *noun* var. of BILIMENT.

billingsgate /ˈbɪlɪŋzɡeɪt/ *noun.* Also **B-**. M17.
[ORIGIN *Billingsgate* market, a fish market in London noted for vituperative language.]
1 Scurrilous abuse, violent invective. M17.
†**2** A foul-mouthed person, a scold. M17–L18.

billion /ˈbɪljən/ *noun* & *adjective.* L17.
[ORIGIN French, formed as MILLION by substitution of BI-.]
▸ **A** *noun.* Pl. same with specified number, **-s** when indefinite.
1 A million million, 10^{12}. Cf. TRILLION. (Now only in British popular use.) L17.
2 A thousand million, 10^9; in *pl.* (without specifying word), several billions, very large numbers. M19.
▸ **B** *adjective.* After an article, possessive, etc.: a million times a million (now only in British popular use); a thousand times a million; *hyperbol.* a very great many. After a numeral or quantifier: multiples of a billion. M20.
■ **billio'naire** *noun* [after MILLIONAIRE] a person possessing a thousand million dollars etc. M19. **billionth** *adjective* & *noun* (*a*) *adjective* one thousand (or million) millionth; (*b*) *noun* a billionth part; the billionth person or thing: L18.

billitonite /ˈbɪlɪtənʌɪt/ *noun.* E20.
[ORIGIN from *Billiton* (see below) + -ITE[1].]
GEOLOGY. A tektite from Belitung (formerly Billiton) Island, Indonesia.

billon /ˈbɪlən/ *noun.* E18.
[ORIGIN Old French & mod. French, (orig.) ingot, (now) bronze or copper money, from *bille*: see BILLET *noun*[2], -OON.]
An alloy of gold or silver with a predominating amount of base metal.

billow /ˈbɪləʊ/ *noun* & *verb.* M16.
[ORIGIN Old Norse *bylgja* (Swedish *bölja*, Danish *bølge*), from Germanic base rel. to that of BELLY *noun*.]
▸ **A** *noun.* **1** A great wave (of a stretch of water, esp. the sea, or *transf.* of flame, smoke, sound, moving bodies, etc.); *poet.* (*sing.* & in *pl.*) *the* sea. M16.
†**2** A swell on the sea. M16–E17.
▸ **B** *verb intrans.* Rise in billows; surge, swell; undulate. L16.

H. VAUGHAN When his waters billow thus, Dark storms and wind Incite them. T. ROETHKE Their skirts billowing out wide into tents. A. MACLEAN Black smoke billowing into the night sky.

■ **billowy** *adjective* of, pertaining to, characterized by, or of the nature of billows E17.

billy /ˈbɪli/ *noun*[1]. *Scot.* & *N. English.* Also **billie**. E16.
[ORIGIN Unknown.]
A comrade or close friend; a companion; a brother.

billy /ˈbɪli/ *noun*[2]. L18.
[ORIGIN from *Billy*, pet form of male forename *William*.]
1 A slubbing machine. L18.
2 A bludgeon; *spec.* (*US*, more fully ***billy club***) a police officer's truncheon. M19.
3 More fully ***billy goat***. A male goat. M19.

billy /ˈbɪli/ *noun*[3]. *Austral.* & *NZ.* M19.
[ORIGIN Scots *billy-pot* cooking utensil.]
A cylindrical tin etc. or enamelled container used as kettle, cooking pot, food carrier, etc. Also ***billycan***.

F. KIDMAN A beam across Ming's shoulder supported the tea billy.

boil the billy: see BOIL *verb*.

billycock /ˈbɪlɪkɒk/ *noun.* M19.
[ORIGIN Said to be from the name of *William Coke*, nephew of Thomas William Coke, Earl of Leicester (1752–1842).]
hist. A kind of bowler hat.

billy-o /ˈbɪlɪəʊ/ *noun. colloq.* Also **-oh**. L19.
[ORIGIN Unknown.]
like billy-o, intensely, vigorously, etc.
fight like billy-o, ***rain like billy-o***, ***run like billy-o***, etc.

bilobate /bʌɪˈləʊbeɪt/ *adjective.* L18.
[ORIGIN from BI- + LOBATE.]
Having two lobes.

bilobed /bʌɪˈləʊbd/ *adjective.* M18.
[ORIGIN from BI- + LOBED *adjective*.]
= BILOBATE.

bilocation /bʌɪləˈkeɪʃ(ə)n/ *noun.* M17.
[ORIGIN from BI- + LOCATION.]
The fact or power of being in two places simultaneously.

bilocular /bʌɪˈlɒkjʊlə/ *adjective.* L18.
[ORIGIN formed as BI- + LOCULAR.]
Having or divided into two cavities or compartments.

bilophodont /bʌɪˈlɒfədɒnt/ *adjective.* M19.
[ORIGIN from BI- + LOPHO- + -ODONT.]
ZOOLOGY. Of molar teeth: having two transverse ridges on the grinding surface.

biltong /ˈbɪltɒŋ/ *noun. S. Afr.* E19.
[ORIGIN Afrikaans, from Dutch *bil* buttock + *tong* tongue.]
Lean meat cut into strips and dried.

BIM *abbreviation.*
British Institute of Management.

Bim /bɪm/ *noun*[1]. *colloq.* M19.
[ORIGIN Unknown.]
A native or inhabitant of Barbados in the W. Indies.

bim /bɪm/ *noun*[2]. *N. Amer. slang.* E20.
[ORIGIN Abbreviation.]
= BIMBO 2.

bimah /ˈbiːmə/ *noun.* Also **bima**. M19.
[ORIGIN Hebrew *bīmah* from Greek *bēma* step, platform (see BEMA).]
JUDAISM. A raised platform in a synagogue from which the Torah is read.

bimanous /ˈbʌɪmənəs/ *adjective.* M19.
[ORIGIN from mod. Latin *bimana* neut. pl., two-handed animals (in Cuvier's obsolete classification), from Latin BI- + *manus* hand, + -OUS.]
Having two hands.
■ Also **bimanal** *adjective* M19.

bimanual /bʌɪˈmanjʊəl/ *adjective.* L19.
[ORIGIN from BI- + MANUAL *adjective*.]
Performed with both hands.
■ **bimanually** *adverb* L19.

bimbashi /bɪmˈbɑːʃi/ *noun.* E19.
[ORIGIN Turkish *binbaşı* = 'a person who is head of a thousand', from *bin* thousand + *baş* head + -ı possess. suffix. Cf. YUZBASHI.]
A Turkish major, naval commander, or squadron leader. Also formerly in Egypt, a British officer in the service of the Khedive.

bimbo /ˈbɪmbəʊ/ *noun. slang* (usu. *derog.*). Pl. **-o(e)s**. E20.
[ORIGIN Italian = little child, baby.]
1 A fellow, a chap. E20.
2 A woman, *esp.* a sexually attractive or provocative but empty-headed or unintelligent one. E20.
■ **bim'bette** *noun* a young (female) bimbo L19.

bimeby /ˈbʌɪmbʌɪ/ *adverb. dial.* E18.
[ORIGIN Reduced form.]
By and by.

bimestrial /bʌɪˈmɛstrɪəl/ *adjective.* M19.
[ORIGIN from Latin *bimestris*, from BI- + *mensis* month, + -AL[1].]
Lasting two months; occurring every two months.

bimetallic /bʌɪmɪˈtalɪk/ *adjective.* L19.
[ORIGIN French *bimétallique*, from BI- + *métallique* METALLIC *adjective*.]
1 Using gold and silver as legal tender to any amount at a fixed ratio to each other. L19.
2 *gen.* Made of or using two metals. E20.
bimetallic strip a temperature-sensitive device (used in thermostats etc.), made of two bands of different metals, one of which expands more than the other on heating, causing the strip to bend.
■ **'bimetal** *noun* & *adjective* (*a*) *noun* a bimetallic object or material; (*b*) *adjective* bimetallic: M20. **bi'metallism** *noun* the system of bimetallic currency L19. **bi'metallist** *noun* an advocate of bimetallism L19.

bimillenary /bʌɪmɪˈlɛnəri, -ˈliːn-; bʌɪˈmɪlənəri/ *adjective* & *noun.* M19.
[ORIGIN from BI- + MILLENARY.]
(A period) of two thousand years; (a celebration) of the two thousandth anniversary.

bimodal /bʌɪˈməʊd(ə)l/ *adjective.* E20.
[ORIGIN from BI- + MODAL *adjective*.]
Chiefly *STATISTICS.* Having two modes.
■ **bimo'dality** *noun* E20.

bimolecular /bʌɪməˈlɛkjʊlə/ *adjective.* L19.
[ORIGIN from BI- + MOLECULAR.]
CHEMISTRY. Involving two molecules; of a reaction: having a molecularity of two.

bimonthly /bʌɪˈmʌnθli/ *adverb, adjective,* & *noun.* M19.
[ORIGIN from BI- + MONTHLY *adverb, adjective* & *noun*.]
▸ **A** *adverb.* Every two months or twice a month. M19.
▸ **B** *adjective* & *noun.* (A periodical) appearing or occurring bimonthly. M19.

bimorphemic /bʌɪmɔːˈfiːmɪk/ *adjective.* M20.
[ORIGIN from BI- + MORPHEMIC.]
LINGUISTICS. Consisting of or pertaining to two morphemes.

bin /bɪn/ *noun* & *verb.*
[ORIGIN Old English *bin(n)*, *binne* from Brittonic base of Welsh *ben* cart or from Gaulish (recorded in medieval Latin as *benna*) whence French *banne*, Italian dial. *benna* hamper, Dutch *ben*, German *Benne* body of a cart.]
▸ **A** *noun* **I 1** *gen.* A receptacle (orig. of wickerwork or basketwork). OE.
▸ **II** *spec.* **2** A receptacle for animal feed in a stable; a manger. Long *obsolete* exc. *dial.* OE.
3 (Freq. with specifying word.) ▸**a** A receptacle for storing grain, bread, or other foodstuffs. OE. ▸**b** A receptacle for storing coal etc. M19. ▸**c** A receptacle for litter, household rubbish, etc. M19.
4 A canvas receptacle used in hop-picking. M18.
5 A partitioned stand for storing wine in bottles; *transf.* wine from a particular bin. M18.
6 Any of a number of open compartments in a woolshed where wool is stowed by classes after sorting. *Austral.* & *NZ.* M19.
7 In full ***loony bin***. A mental home or hospital. *colloq.* E20.
8 Each of a series of ranges of numerical value into which data are sorted in statistical analysis. M20.
– COMB.: **bin bag** a (usu. plastic) bag for holding rubbish; **bin-end** one of the last bottles of wine from a particular bin; **bin liner** a strong bag put inside a litter or rubbish bin and removed along with the contents when the bin is full; **binman** (*a*) a man in charge of a bin during hop-picking; (*b*) *Scot., Irish,* & *N. English* a dustman.
▸ **B** *verb trans.* Infl. **-nn-**.
1 Place in a bin; throw away, discard. M19.
2 Group together (data) in bins. L20.

bin- *prefix* see BI-.

binal /ˈbʌɪn(ə)l/ *adjective.* M17.
[ORIGIN medieval Latin *binalis* twin, from Latin *bini* two together: see -AL[1].]
Twin, double, twofold.

binant /ˈbʌɪnənt/ *noun.* E20.
[ORIGIN from BIN- after QUADRANT *noun*[1].]
A half of a circle or circular body.

binary /ˈbʌɪnəri/ *noun* & *adjective.* LME.
[ORIGIN Late Latin *binarius*, from *bini* two together: see -ARY[1].]
▸ **A** *noun.* **1** A combination of two things; a pair; a duality. LME.
2 *ASTRONOMY.* A binary star. M19.
visual binary: see VISUAL *adjective*.
3 *MATH.* The binary scale; binary arithmetic. M20.
4 A binary weapon. L20.
▸ **B** *adjective.* Of, pertaining to, characterized by, or compounded of, two; of or involving pairs; dual. L16.
binary arithmetic: employing the binary scale. **binary coded decimal** (designating) a number in which each digit of a decimal number is represented by its binary equivalent. **binary compound** *CHEMISTRY* a compound of two elements or radicals. **binary digit** either of two digits (usu. 0 and 1) used to express numbers in the binary scale. **binary fission** *BIOLOGY* the division of

a cell or organism into two parts. **binary form** *MUSIC*: of a movement in two complementary sections. **binary measure** *MUSIC*: of two beats in a bar. **binary scale** a scale of numerical notation in which the base is two (successive places denoting units, twos, fours, etc.). **binary star** a system of two stars revolving round each other. **binary tree** *COMPUTING* a tree in which each node has no more than two subtrees or pointers. **binary weapon** a poison gas which is stored and handled in the form of two separate harmless precursors.

binate /ˈbʌɪneɪt/ *adjective*. E19.
[ORIGIN mod. Latin *binatus*, from Latin *bini* two together: see -ATE².]
BOTANY. Composed of two equal parts; growing in pairs.

binational /bʌɪˈnaʃ(ə)n(ə)l/ *adjective*. L19.
[ORIGIN from BI- + NATIONAL *adjective*.]
Concerning or consisting of two nations.

binaural /bɪˈnɔːr(ə)l, bʌɪ-/ *adjective*. M19.
[ORIGIN from BIN- + AURAL *adjective*¹.]
1 Of, pertaining to, or used with both ears. M19.
2 Of sound reproduction: employing two separate microphones, with the recordings usu. transmitted separately to the two ears of the hearer; of, pertaining to, or produced by such a system. M20.
■ **binaurally** *adverb* M20.

bind /bʌɪnd/ *noun*. See also BINE. OE.
[ORIGIN from the verb.]
1 Something used to bind; a band, a tie. OE. ▸**b** *MUSIC*. A (usu. curved) line above or below notes of the same pitch indicating that they are to be joined as a continuous sound; a tie. L19.
2 a = BINE. LME. ▸**b** = BINDWEED (now only sense 1). LME.
3 A quantitative measure of salmons and eels. *obsolete* exc. *dial*. L15.
4 Capacity, limit. *Scot*. E16.
5 Indurated clay. L18.
6 A bore, a nuisance. *colloq*. M20.

M. GAYLE Work is a bit of a bind.

7 A position that prevents free action. *colloq*. M20.
double bind: see DOUBLE *adjective & adverb*. **in a bind** *N. Amer.* in difficulty.

bind /bʌɪnd/ *verb*. Pa. t. **bound** /baʊnd/; pa. pple **bound**, (*arch.*) **bounden** /ˈbaʊnd(ə)n/. See also BOUND *adjective*², BOUNDED *adjective*², BOUNDEN *adjective*, YBOUND.
[ORIGIN Old English *bindan* strong = Old Frisian *binda*, Old Saxon *bindan*, Middle Dutch & mod. Dutch *binden*, Old High German *bintan* (German *binden*), Old Norse *binda*, Gothic *bindan*, from Indo-European base repr. also by Sanskrit *bandh-*.]
▸ **I** *verb trans*. **1** Tie, fasten, attach, (*lit. & fig.*). (Foll. by *to*, (*up*)*on*, *together*.) OE.

AV *Deut.* 6:8 Thou shalt bind them for a seal upon thine hand. BURKE The way in which you take up my affairs binds me to you. N. MITFORD A community of . . people, bound together by shared intellectual tastes. R. BRADBURY The pair of . . bicycle clips that bound his thin pants to his bony ankles.

2 Put in bonds; restrain; confine; obstruct (esp. in pass. combs. as ***fogbound***, ***snowbound***, etc.). OE.

B. JOWETT My father bound him hand and foot and threw him into a ditch. J. JOSEPH I knew That grief has uses—that a father dead Could bind the bully's fist a week or two.

3 Fasten round, encircle, (something); bandage (the body, a part of it). (Foll. by *with*.) OE. ▸**b** Put dressings and bandages on (a wound). Usu. foll. by *up*. ME. ▸**c** Fasten, wreathe, (something) *about*, (*a*)*round*, *on*. LME.

POPE A belt her waist, a fillet binds her hair. A. WILSON The icy tightness of the bandage as she began to bind his ankle. **c** TENNYSON I, maiden, round thee, maiden, bind my belt.

4 Fasten or hold together; unite in marriage. OE.

MILTON Her bow'r she leaves, With Thestylis to bind the sheaves. G. CRABBE To bind in law, the couple bound by love.

bound up closely associated *with*; concerned *in* to a degree that excludes other considerations.
5 (Now esp. in *COOKERY*.) Cause to cohere. OE. ▸**b** Hold by chemical bonding; combine with. E20.

SMOLLETT When Lybian sands are bound in frost. W. STYRON The blood, which we saved to bind stews.

6 Edge with a strengthening material, as a garment with braid, a box or jewel with metal, etc. ME.
7 Conclude (a bargain, an agreement; †a story); ratify, secure (a contract). ME.
8 Oblige by covenant, promise, etc., or by legal authority, (*to* or *from* an action, *to do*, *that*); (freq. foll. by *over*) subject to a legal obligation (*to*, *to do*; absol. *spec.* to keep the peace). ME. ▸**b** In *pass.* Be compelled or obliged (*to do*); be certain (*to be*, *do*) (also *impers.* in ***there is bound***, ***there was bound***, etc., there is or was certain *to be* etc.); *N. Amer.* be resolved. ME.

DICKENS The Mayor . . declared he would . . bind them over to keep the peace. F. O'BRIEN I bind you that . . you will come to me each evening. K. AMIS Whether he was going to bind them to silence. **b** BACON Princes are not bound to communicate all matters. J. CARY After a really serious crisis . . there is bound to be an enquiry. HARPER LEE He was bound and determined they wouldn't get away with it.

b I'll be bound I guarantee the truth of (a statement), I feel certain. ***in honour bound***: see HONOUR *noun*.

9 Make constipated. LME.
10 Fasten together the sheets of (a book), fasten (the sheets of a book, issues of a periodical, etc.), into a (usu. stiff) cover. LME.
11 Indenture as an apprentice (or *apprentice*). (Foll. by *out*, *over*.) E16.

THACKERAY Rebecca . . was bound-over as an articled-pupil. J. DOS PASSOS His mother bound him out to a farmer. J. MORTIMER They sent me away when I was your age . . . Bound as a stable lad.

12 Bore, weary. *slang*. E20.
▸ **II** *verb intrans*. **13** Of a hawk or hawks: grapple (*with* or with each other). L16.
14 Cohere in a mass. L17.
15 Form a chemical bond *to* a substance; combine chemically *with*. M20.
16 Complain. *slang*. M20.

bindaas /ˈbɪndɑːs/ *adjective*. *Indian colloq*. L20.
[ORIGIN Gujarati *bin-dās*, lit. 'without servitude', from Sanskrit *vinā* + *dāsya*.]
Carefree, fashionable, and independent-minded.

India Today Bollywood's most bindaas babe.

binder /ˈbʌɪndə/ *noun*. OE.
[ORIGIN from BIND *verb* + -ER¹.]
1 *gen*. A person who binds. OE.
2 *spec*. ▸**a** A bookbinder. LME. ▸**b** A person who binds sheaves. M16.
†**3** A substance that causes constipation. E16–L17.
4 A bandage, a band; a headband. E17.
5 A connecting piece, as a tie beam, a bondstone in a wall, etc. M17.
6 A cementing substance. L17.
7 A machine for (reaping and) binding grain into sheaves. M19.
8 A detachable cover for unbound magazines, papers, etc. M19.
9 A large quantity, esp. of food; a satisfying meal. *dial. & NZ colloq*. L19.
10 A last (alcoholic) drink. *slang*. L19.
■ **bindery** *noun* a bookbinder's workshop E19.

bindi /ˈbɪndiː/ *noun*. Pl. **-s**. E20.
[ORIGIN Hindi *bindī*.]
A decorative mark or jewel worn in the middle of the forehead by Indian women, esp. traditionally by married Hindu women.

bindi-eye /ˈbɪndɪʌɪ/ *noun*. *Austral*. L19.
[ORIGIN Kamilaroi and Yuwaalaraay (an Australian Aboriginal language of New South Wales) *bindayaa*.]
A small plant, *Calotis cuneifolia*, with fruits resembling burs.

binding /ˈbʌɪndɪŋ/ *noun*. ME.
[ORIGIN from BIND *verb* + -ING¹.]
1 The action of BIND *verb*; the state of being bound. ME.
2 Something with which a thing is bound; a fastening. ME.
3 *spec*. ▸**a** (A) tape, braid, etc., for protecting raw edges. L16. ▸**b** A band of masonry and brickwork; a connecting timber etc. E17. ▸**c** The strong covering of a book holding the sheets together. M17.
c ***perfect binding***, ***unsewn binding***, etc.

binding /ˈbʌɪndɪŋ/ *ppl adjective*. LME.
[ORIGIN formed as BINDING *noun* + -ING².]
1 That binds physically; causing or tending to cohere; astringent, styptic. LME.
binding energy *PHYSICS* the mass defect (see MASS *noun*²) of a nucleus, expressed as energy; also, the energy required to remove a given particle from a nucleus. **binding post** *ELECTRONICS* a connector consisting of a threaded screw to which bare wires are attached and held in place by a nut. **binding site** *BIOCHEMISTRY* a location on a macromolecule or cellular structure at which chemical interaction with a specific active substance takes place.
2 *fig*. Obligatory (*on*), coercive. E17.

bindle /ˈbɪnd(ə)l/ *noun*. *N. Amer. slang*. E20.
[ORIGIN Prob. alt. of BUNDLE *noun*.]
A bundle or package; *esp*. a tramp's bundle of bedding etc.
– COMB.: **bindlestiff** a tramp carrying a bundle of bedding etc.

bindweed /ˈbʌɪndwiːd/ *noun*. M16.
[ORIGIN from BIND *verb* + WEED *noun*¹.]
1 Any of various twining plants of the family Convolvulaceae, with funnel-shaped corollas; *esp*. (*a*) (more fully ***hedge bindweed***) *Calystegia sepium*, a hedge plant with large white flowers; (***b***) (more fully ***field bindweed***) *Convolvulus arvensis*, a cornfield weed with smaller white or pink flowers. M16.
sea bindweed: see SEA *noun*.
2 Any of various other climbing plants, e.g. honeysuckle. L16.
black bindweed a twining weed of the knotgrass family, *Fallopia convolvulus*, with heart-shaped leaves and small white flowers.

bine /bʌɪn/ *noun*. E19.
[ORIGIN Var. of BIND *noun*.]
A flexible shoot; a stem of a climbing plant, esp. of the hop.

Binet /ˈbiːneɪ/ *noun*. Also **Binet–Simon** /-ˌsiːmɒ̃/. E20.
[ORIGIN Alfred *Binet* (1857–1911) & Théodore *Simon* (1873–1961), French psychologists.]
Binet scale, ***Binet test***, (a scale of intelligence associated with) a form of intelligence test developed by Binet and Simon.

bing /bɪŋ/ *noun*¹. ME.
[ORIGIN With sense 1 cf. Danish *bing* bin; sense 2 from Old Norse *bingr* heap (Swedish *binge*).]
1 = BIN *noun*. Now *dial*. ME.
2 A heap or pile, esp. of metallic ore or of waste from a mine. Now chiefly *Scot*. E16.

bing /bɪŋ/ *noun*² *& interjection*. L19.
[ORIGIN Imit.]
▸ **A** *noun*. A sudden bang; a thump. *dial*. L19.
▸ **B** *interjection*. Indicating a sudden action or event. E20.

binge /bɪn(d)ʒ/ *noun*¹. *Scot*. L15.
[ORIGIN from BINGE *verb*¹.]
A servile bow.

binge /bɪn(d)ʒ/ *noun*². M19.
[ORIGIN from BINGE *verb*².]
1 A soaking. *dial*. M19.
2 A bout of heavy drinking or unrestrained enjoyment. *slang*. M19.

binge /bɪn(d)ʒ/ *verb*¹ *intrans*. *Scot*. Pres. pple & verbal noun **bingeing**, **binging**. L15.
[ORIGIN App. after *bow*, *bend*, etc., and *cringe* etc.]
Make a servile bow; curtsy; fawn.

binge /bɪn(d)ʒ/ *verb*². Pres. pple & verbal noun **bingeing**, **binging**. E19.
[ORIGIN Unknown.]
1 *verb trans*. Soak. *dial*. E19.
2 *verb refl. & intrans*. Have a bout of heavy drinking or unrestrained enjoyment. *slang*. M19.
3 *verb trans*. Liven *up*, ginger *up*. *slang*. L19.

bingee *noun* var. of BINGY.

binghi /ˈbɪŋgɪ/ *noun*. *Austral. slang* (usu. *derog.*). M19.
[ORIGIN Awabakal *bingay* elder brother.]
An Aborigine.

bingle /ˈbɪŋg(ə)l/ *noun & verb*. E20.
[ORIGIN from BOB *noun*¹ + SHINGLE *noun*¹.]
▸ **A** *noun*. A short hairstyle for women, between a bob and a shingle. E20.
▸ **B** *verb trans*. Cut (hair) in this style. E20.

bingo /ˈbɪŋgəʊ/ *noun*¹. *arch. slang*. L17.
[ORIGIN Prob. from initial *b-* of *brandy* + ST)INGO.]
Brandy.

bingo /ˈbɪŋgəʊ/ *noun*². M20.
[ORIGIN Perh. from the winner's exclamation: cf. BINGO *interjection*.]
A popular gambling game like lotto, played esp. in public halls, with cards divided into numbered squares, in which the first player to cover all or a specified set of numbers on the card wins a prize.

bingo /ˈbɪŋgəʊ/ *interjection*. E20.
[ORIGIN Imit.: cf. BING *interjection*.]
Indicating a sudden action or event (= BING *interjection*), esp. the winning of a game of bingo.

bingy /ˈbɪn(d)ʒi/ *noun*. *Austral. slang*. Also **bingee**. L18.
[ORIGIN Dharuk *bindhi*.]
The stomach, the belly.

biniou /ˈbɪnɪuː/ *noun*. M19.
[ORIGIN Breton *bin(r)iou*, pl. of *benveg* tool, (musical) instrument.]
A Breton bagpipe.

binit /ˈbɪnɪt/ *noun*. M20.
[ORIGIN Abbreviation.]
A binary digit.

Binitarian /bʌɪnɪˈtɛːrɪən/ *noun & adjective*. Also **b-**. E20.
[ORIGIN from Latin *bini* two together, after TRINITARIAN.]
A believer in, of or pertaining to, the doctrine of a Godhead of two persons only.
■ **Binitarianism** *noun* E20.

bink /bɪŋk/ *noun*. *Scot. & N. English*. LME.
[ORIGIN Var. of BENCH *noun*.]
A bench; a shelf; a plate rack, a dresser.

binnacle /ˈbɪnək(ə)l/ *noun*. Orig. †**bittacle** & similar forms. L15.
[ORIGIN Spanish *bitácula*, *bitácora* or Portuguese *bitacola*, corresp. to Provençal *abitacle*, Italian *abitacolo*, French *habitacle*, from Latin *habitaculum* HABITACLE.]
A receptacle for a ship's compass, usu. on the navigation bridge or, in small sailing vessels, a box on the deck near the helm.

binocle /ˈbɪnək(ə)l/ *noun*. *arch*. L17.
[ORIGIN French, formed as BINOCULAR.]
= BINOCULAR *noun*.

binocs /bɪˈnɒks/ *noun pl*. *colloq*. M20.
[ORIGIN Abbreviation.]
A pair or pairs of binoculars.

binocular /bɪˈnɒkjʊlə/ *adjective & noun*. E18.
[ORIGIN from Latin *bini* two together + *oculus* eye + -AR¹, after OCULAR.]
▸ **A** *adjective*. †**1** Having two eyes. *rare*. Only in E18.

2 Adapted to or using two eyes; also, stereoscopic. M18.
▸ **B** *noun sing.* & (usu.) in *pl.* A field glass or opera glass for use with both eyes. L19.
■ **binocu'larity** *noun* binocular quality; simultaneous employment of both eyes: M19. **binocularly** *adverb* L19.

binomial /bʌɪˈnəʊmɪəl/ *noun & adjective*. M16.
[ORIGIN from French *binôme* or mod. Latin *binomium*, from BI- + Greek *nomos* part, portion + -AL[1].]
▸ **A** *noun*. **1** MATH. An expression which contains the sum or difference of two terms. M16.
2 A name having two parts, esp. of a plant or animal (cf. sense B.2 below). E20.
▸ **B** *adjective*. **1** MATH. Consisting of two terms; of or pertaining to a binomial or the binomial theorem (see below). L16.
binomial theorem a formula for the expansion of any power of a binomial.
2 Having or using two names, esp. those of genus and species in scientific nomenclature of living organisms. M17.
■ **binomially** *adverb* L19.

binominal /bʌɪˈnɒmɪn(ə)l/ *adjective*. M19.
[ORIGIN from Latin *binominis*, from BI- + *nomin-*, *nomen* name, + -AL[1].]
= BINOMIAL *adjective* 2.

binormal /bʌɪˈnɔːm(ə)l/ *noun*. M19.
[ORIGIN from BI- + NORMAL *noun*.]
MATH. A normal at right angles to the plane containing the tangent at a given point on a curve.

binoxalate /bɪˈnɒksəleɪt/ *noun*. E19.
[ORIGIN from BIN- + OXALATE.]
CHEMISTRY. An acid salt of oxalic acid.

bins /bɪnz/ *noun pl. colloq.* M20.
[ORIGIN Abbreviation.]
Binoculars. Also, spectacles.

bint /bɪnt/ *noun*. *colloq.* (orig. *military slang*), usu. *derog.* M19.
[ORIGIN Arabic = daughter, girl.]
A girl or woman.

binturong /ˈbɪntjʊrɒŋ/ *noun*. E19.
[ORIGIN Malay.]
A large prehensile-tailed civet, *Arctictis binturong*, of southern Asia.

binucleate /bʌɪˈnjuːklɪət/ *adjective*. L19.
[ORIGIN from BI- + NUCLEATE *adjective*.]
BIOLOGY. Having two nuclei.

bio /ˈbʌɪəʊ/ *noun*[1]. *colloq.* Pl. **-os**. M20.
[ORIGIN Abbreviation.]
A biography.

bio /ˈbʌɪəʊ/ *noun*[2]. *colloq.* M20.
[ORIGIN Abbreviation.]
Biology.

bio- /ˈbʌɪəʊ/ *combining form* of Greek *bios* life, course or way of living (opp. *zōē* animal life, organic life) in scientific words usu. with the senses 'of living organisms', 'biological': see -O-.
■ **bioa'ccumulate** *verb intrans.* (of a toxic chemical) become concentrated inside the bodies of living organisms L20. **bioaccumu'lation** *noun* the build-up of a toxic chemical in the bodies of living organisms M20. **bioa'coustics** *noun* the branch of acoustics concerned with sounds produced by or affecting living organisms, esp. as relating to communication M20. **bio'active** *adjective* having an effect on or interacting with living tissue M20. **bioac'tivity** *noun* the quality or condition of being bioactive M20. **bioa'ssay** *noun* measurement of the concentration or strength of a substance by means of its effect on a living organism E20. **bioavaila'bility** *noun* the rate at which a drug etc. is absorbed by the body or exerts an effect after absorption L20. **biobiblio'graphical** *adjective* of or pertaining to biobibliography E19. **biobibli'ography** *noun* a bibliography containing biographical information about the author(s) E20. **bio'centric** *adjective* centring in life; regarding or treating life as a central fact: L19. **bio'centrism** *noun* the view or belief that all life is important L20. **biochip** *noun* a device analogous to a conventional chip but made of proteins or other organic material L20. **bio'cidal** *adjective* that acts as a biocide M20. **biocide** *noun* (*a*) the destruction of life; (*b*) a poisonous substance, *esp.* a pesticide: M20. **biocircuit** *noun* = BIOCHIP L20. **biocli'matic** *adjective* of or pertaining to the interrelation of climate and the activities and distribution of living organisms E20. **bioclima'tology** *noun* biology in relation to climate E20. **biocompati'bility** *noun* the property of being biocompatible L20. **biocom'patible** *adjective* not harmful or toxic to living tissue L20. **biocom'puter** *noun* (*a*) a human being or the human brain regarded as a computer; (*b*) a computer envisioned as being based on circuits and components formed from biological molecules or structures: M20. **biocontrol** *noun* = BIOLOGICAL *control* M20. **biocon'version** *noun* the conversion of one substance, or one form of energy, into another by living organisms M20. **biodata** *noun sing.* & *pl.* (esp. in the Indian subcontinent) a curriculum vitae; biographical details M20. **biodiesel** *noun* a biofuel intended as a substitute for diesel L20. **biodi'versity** *noun* diversity of plant and animal life L20. **bioelec'tronics** *noun* the branch of science concerned with the application of biological materials and processes in electronics, and the use of electronic devices in living systems M20. **bioener'getic** *adjective* of or pertaining to bio-energetics M20. **bioener'getics** *noun* (the branch of science that deals with) the transformation of energy in living organisms M20. **bioengi'neer** *noun* a person engaged in bioengineering M20. **bioengi'neering** *noun* the application of engineering and the physical sciences to biological processes; the industrial use of biological processes: M20. **bio'feedback** *noun* the use of electronic monitoring of a normally automatic bodily function in order to train a person to acquire voluntary control of that function L20. **bio'flavonoid** *noun* any of the citrin flavonoids (see CITRIN) M20. **biofouler** *noun* an organism that causes biofouling L20. **biofouling** *noun* the fouling of underwater pipes and other surfaces by organisms such as barnacles and algae L20. **biofuel** *noun* a fuel derived immediately from living matter L20. **biogas** *noun* gaseous fuel (usu. methane) produced by fermentation of organic matter, esp. in apparatus designed for this purpose L20. **biogeo'chemical** *adjective* of or pertaining to biogeochemistry M20. **biogeo'chemistry** *noun* the science of the interaction of living organisms with the chemistry of the environment M20. **biohazard** *noun* a risk to humans or the environment associated with biological work, *esp.* with harmful micro-organisms; something constituting such a risk: M20. **bio'hazardous** *adjective* of the nature of a biohazard L20. **bioherm** *noun* [Greek *herma* sunken rock, reef] GEOLOGY a circumscribed body of sedimentary rock consisting of the remains of living organisms E20. **bio'hermal** *adjective* (of the nature) of a bioherm M20. **bioindicator** *noun* an organism used as an indicator of the quality of an ecosystem M20. **biolumi'nescence** *noun* the biochemical production of light; light so emitted: E20. **biolumi'nescent** *adjective* exhibiting bioluminescence E20. **biomarker** *noun* a naturally occurring molecule, gene, or characteristic by which a particular pathological or physiological process, disease, etc. can be identified L20. **biomass** *noun* (*a*) the total weight of living organisms in a given area or of a given species; (*b*) organic matter consisting of or recently derived from living organisms (esp. regarded as fuel): M20. **biomaterial** *noun* (*a*) biological material, spec. in applications in which inorganic or synthetic substances have hitherto been used; (*b*) synthetic material used in place of natural tissue etc.: M20. **biomathe'matics** *noun* the science of the application of mathematics to biology E20. **biome** *noun* [-OME] ECOLOGY (the distinct major habitat occupied by) a community of plants and animals, e.g. in a prehistoric period E20. **bio'medical** *adjective* of or pertaining to both biology and medicine M20. **biomedicine** *noun* biology and medicine considered together E20. **biometeo'rology** *noun* the study of the relationship between living organisms and weather M20. **biomi'metic** *adjective* mimicking a biochemical process, involving biomimicry L20. **biomi'metics**, **bio'mimicry** *nouns* the design and production of materials, structures, and systems that are modelled on biological entities and processes L20. **biomolecule** *noun* a molecule involved in the maintenance and metabolic processes of living organisms E20. **biomorph** *noun* a decorative form representing a living object L19. **bio'morphic** *adjective* of the nature of a biomorph L19. **bio-or'ganic** *adjective* pertaining to or designating the organic chemistry of living organisms M20. **bio'piracy** *noun* the exploitation of naturally occurring biochemical or genetic material for commercial profit while failing to pay fair compensation to the country or community from which it originates L20. **biopharma'ceutical** (*a*) *adjective* of or pertaining to biopharmaceutics; (*b*) *noun* a biological macromolecule or cellular component used as a pharmaceutical: M20. **biopharma'ceutics** *noun* the study of the chemical and physical properties of drugs and the biological effects produced by them M20. **biopoesis** /-pəʊˈiːsɪs/ *noun* [Greek *poiēsis* making] the hypothetical origination of life from replicating inanimate matter M20. **bio'polymer** *noun* a polymeric biochemical M20. **biopros'pecting** *noun* the action or process of searching for plant and animal species that may yield commercially valuable biochemicals or genetic material L20. **bioprospector** *noun* a person engaged in bioprospecting L20. **biopsy'chology** *noun* the branch of psychology concerned with its biological and physiological aspects M20. **bioreactor** *noun* an apparatus or structure in which a biological reaction or process is carried out, esp. on a commercial scale M20. **bioremedi'ation** *noun* the use of either naturally occurring or deliberately introduced micro-organisms to consume and break down environmental pollutants L20. **bioscience** *noun* (any of) the life sciences M20. **bioscientist** *noun* a life scientist M20. **bioscope** *noun* †(*a*) a view or survey of life; (*b*) an early form of cinematograph; (*c*) *S. Afr.* a cinema, a moving picture: E19. **biose'curity** *noun* protection of the human population against harmful biological agents L20. **biosensor** *noun* a thing for detecting chemicals by the use of a living organism or a product of one; an organism used for this purpose: L20. **bio'social** *adjective* of or pertaining to the interaction of biological and social factors E20. **biosocio'logical** *adjective* of or pertaining to biology and sociology E20. **biosolids** *noun* organic matter recycled from sewage, especially for use in agriculture L20. **biosphere** *noun* (*a*) the regions of the earth's crust and atmosphere occupied by living organisms; (*b*) an artificial structure enclosing a self-contained ecosystem or ecosystems: L19. **bio'spheric** *adjective* of or pertaining to the biosphere E20. **biostrome** /-strəʊm/ *noun* [Greek *strōma* mattress, bed] GEOLOGY a bedded stratum of sedimentary rock consisting of the remains of living organisms M20. **biosurgery** *noun* the medical use of maggots to clean infected wounds L20. **bioterrorism** *noun* the use of infectious agents or other harmful biological or biochemical substances as weapons of terrorism L20. **bioterrorist** *noun* a person who engages in bioterrorism L20. **biotherapy** *noun* a biologically based therapy, *esp.*: (*a*) a form of cancer treatment which aims to modify the body's biological response to cancer; (*b*) the use of living organisms in the treatment of disease: L20. **biotope** *noun* (ECOLOGY) the region of a habitat associated with a particular ecological community E20. **biotransfor'mation** *noun* the alteration of a substance, esp. a drug, within the body M20. **biotur'bated** *adjective* (GEOLOGY) affected by bioturbation M20. **biotur'bation** *noun* (GEOLOGY) the disturbance of sedimentary deposits by living organisms M20. **biotype** *noun* a group of organisms having an identical genetic constitution E20. **biowarfare** *noun* = BIOLOGICAL *warfare* M20. **bioweapon** *noun* a harmful biological agent used as a weapon of war L20.

biocenosis *noun* see BIOCOENOSIS.

biochemical /bʌɪə(ʊ)ˈkɛmɪk(ə)l/ *adjective & noun*. M19.
[ORIGIN from BIO- + CHEMICAL *adjective*.]
▸ **A** *adjective*. Of or pertaining to biochemistry. M19.
▸ **B** *noun*. A substance involved in biochemical processes. M20.
■ **bio'chemic** *adjective* biochemical L19. **biochemically** *adverb* L19.

biochemistry /bʌɪə(ʊ)ˈkɛmɪstri/ *noun*. L19.
[ORIGIN from BIO- + CHEMISTRY.]
(The branch of science that deals with) the chemical and physico-chemical processes which occur in living organisms.
■ **biochemist** *noun* an expert in or student of biochemistry L19.

bioclast /ˈbʌɪə(ʊ)klast/ *noun*. M20.
[ORIGIN from BIO- + CLAST (see CLASTIC).]
GEOLOGY. A fragment of a shell or fossil forming part of a sedimentary rock.
■ **bio'clastic** *adjective* M20.

biocoenosis /ˌbʌɪə(ʊ)sɪˈnəʊsɪs/ *noun*. Also ***-cen-**. Pl. **-noses** /-ˈnəʊsiːz/. L19.
[ORIGIN mod. Latin, from BIO- + Greek *koinōsis* sharing, from *koinos* common.]
ECOLOGY. An association of organisms forming a closely integrated community; the relationship existing between these organisms.
■ **biocoenology** *noun* the branch of science that deals with biocoenoses M20. **biocoenotic** /-ˈnɒtɪk/ *adjective* of, pertaining to, or of the nature of a biocoenosis E20.

biodegradable /ˌbʌɪə(ʊ)dɪˈɡreɪdəb(ə)l/ *adjective*. M20.
[ORIGIN from BIO- + DEGRADE *verb* + -ABLE.]
Able to be decomposed by bacteria or other organisms.
■ **biodegrada'bility** *noun* M20. **biodegra'dation** *noun* decomposition brought about by living organisms M20. **biodegrade** *verb intrans.* & *trans.* (cause to) undergo biodegradation L20.

biodynamic /ˌbʌɪə(ʊ)dʌɪˈnamɪk/ *adjective*. L19.
[ORIGIN from BIO- + DYNAMIC *adjective*.]
Of or pertaining to dynamic effects brought about or experienced by living organisms; (of farming) using only organic fertilizers etc.

biodynamics /ˌbʌɪə(ʊ)dʌɪˈnamɪks/ *noun*. M20.
[ORIGIN from BIO- + DYNAMICS.]
(The study or application of) biodynamic effects collectively.

bioelectricity /ˌbʌɪəʊɪlɛkˈtrɪsɪti/ *noun*. M20.
[ORIGIN from BIO- + ELECTRICITY.]
Electricity or electrical phenomena produced within living organisms.
■ **bioe'lectric** *adjective* E20. **bioe'lectrical** *adjective* M20.

bioethics /bʌɪəʊˈɛθɪks/ *noun*. L20.
[ORIGIN from BIO- + *ethics*: see ETHIC *noun* 4.]
The ethics of biological research, esp. of medical techniques such as organ transplantation.
■ **bioethical** *adjective* L20. **bioethicist** /-sɪst/ *noun* an expert in or student of bioethics L20.

biofilm /ˈbʌɪəʊfɪlm/ *noun*. L20.
[ORIGIN from BIO- + FILM *noun*.]
A thin but robust layer of mucilage adhering to a solid surface and containing a community of bacteria and other micro-organisms.

biog /ˈbʌɪɒɡ/ *noun*. *colloq.* M20.
[ORIGIN Abbreviation.]
A biography.

biogenesis /bʌɪə(ʊ)ˈdʒɛnɪsɪs/ *noun*. L19.
[ORIGIN from BIO- + -GENESIS.]
1 The hypothesis that living matter arises only from other living matter. L19.
2 The synthesis of a substance by living organisms. M20.
3 The hypothetical development of living matter from complex inanimate substances. M20.
■ **biogenesist** *noun* (*hist.*) an advocate of the hypothesis of biogenesis (sense 1) L19. **biogenetic** /-dʒɪˈnɛtɪk/ *adjective* of, pertaining to, or produced by biogenesis, in any sense L19. **biogenetically** /-dʒɪˈnɛtɪk(ə)li/ *adverb* M20.

biogenic /bʌɪə(ʊ)ˈdʒɛnɪk/ *adjective*. E20.
[ORIGIN from BIO- + -GENIC.]
1 = BIOGENETIC *adjective*. E20.
2 Produced or brought about by living organisms. (The predominant sense.) E20.
■ **biogenically** *adverb* M20.

biogenous /bʌɪˈɒdʒɪnəs/ *adjective*. M20.
[ORIGIN from BIO- + -GENESIS + -OUS.]
= BIOGENIC.

biogeography /ˌbʌɪəʊdʒɪˈɒɡrəfi, -ˈdʒɒɡ-/ *noun*. L19.
[ORIGIN from BIO- + GEOGRAPHY.]
The science of the geographical distribution of living organisms.
■ **biogeographer** *noun* E20. **biogeo'graphic** *adjective* L19. **biogeo'graphical** *adjective* E20. **biogeo'graphically** *adverb* E20.

biography /bʌɪˈɒɡrəfi/ *noun & verb*. L17.
[ORIGIN French *biographie* or mod. Latin *biographia*, medieval Greek *biographia*: see BIO-, -GRAPHY.]
▸ **A** *noun*. **1** The history of the lives of individuals, as a branch of literature. L17.
2 A written life of a person. L18.
3 The life course of a living (esp. human) being. M19.
▸ **B** *verb trans.* Write the life of; make the subject of a biography. M19.
■ **biogra'phee** *noun* a person who is the subject of a biography M19. **biographer** *noun* a writer of biographies or the life of a person E18. **bio'graphic** *adjective* of or pertaining to (a) biography L18. **bio'graphical** *adjective* = BIOGRAPHIC *adjective* M18.

bio'graphically *adverb* M18. **biographist** *noun* = BIOGRAPHER M17. **biographize** *verb trans. & intrans.* write a biography (of) E19.

bioinformatics /ˌbʌɪə(ʊ)ɪnfəˈmatɪks/ *noun pl.* L20.
[ORIGIN from BIO- + INFORMATICS.]
The science of collecting and analysing complex biological data such as genetic codes.

biolistics /bʌɪə(ʊ)ˈlɪstɪks/ *noun pl.* L20.
[ORIGIN Blend of BIOLOGICAL and BALLISTICS.]
A technique in genetic engineering for introducing DNA into cells, in which the DNA is delivered on the surface of microscopic metal (usu. gold) particles, which are fired through the cell wall.
■ **biolistic** *adjective* L20.

biological /bʌɪə(ʊ)ˈlɒdʒɪk(ə)l/ *adjective & noun.* M19.
[ORIGIN from BIOLOGY *noun* + -ICAL.]
▸ **A** *adjective.* Of, pertaining to, or of the nature of biology or the phenomena of living organisms. M19.
biological clock an innate mechanism controlling rhythmic activity of an organism. **biological control** the control of a pest by the introduction of a natural enemy of it. **biological mother, biological father, biological parent**: who procreated the child in question (esp. as opp. to the one(s) who nursed or brought up the child). **biological science** = ***life science*** s.v. LIFE *noun.* **biological warfare** the use of harmful micro-organisms or biological products as weapons.
▸ **B** *noun.* A biological product, esp. one used therapeutically. E20.
■ **biologic** *adjective* = BIOLOGICAL *adjective* M19. **biologically** *adverb* L19.

biologise *verb* var. of BIOLOGIZE.

biologism /bʌɪˈɒlədʒɪz(ə)m/ *noun.* M19.
[ORIGIN from BIOLOGY *noun* + -ISM.]
†**1** = ELECTROBIOLOGY (b). *rare.* Only in M19.
2 The interpretation of human life from a strictly biological point of view. E20.
■ **biolo'gistic** *adjective* M20.

biologist /bʌɪˈɒlədʒɪst/ *noun.* E19.
[ORIGIN from BIOLOGY *noun* + -IST.]
A person who studies biology.

biologize /bʌɪˈɒlədʒʌɪz/ *verb.* Also **-ise**. M19.
[ORIGIN from BIOLOGY + -IZE.]
†**1** *verb trans.* Mesmerize. M–L19.
2 *verb intrans. & trans.* Practise biology or biologism; treat or interpret biologically. L19.

biology /bʌɪˈɒlədʒi/ *noun.* E19.
[ORIGIN French *biologie* from German (as BIO-, -LOGY).]
The science of life, dealing with the morphology, physiology, anatomy, behaviour, origin, and distribution of living organisms; occas. = PHYSIOLOGY. Also, life processes and phenomena collectively.
MOLECULAR biology.

biomagnetism /bʌɪə(ʊ)ˈmagnɪtɪz(ə)m/ *noun.* L19.
[ORIGIN from BIO- + MAGNETISM.]
†**1** Animal magnetism. Only in L19.
2 The interaction of living organisms with magnetic fields. M20.
■ **biomag'netic** *adjective* L19.

biomechanics /ˌbʌɪə(ʊ)məˈkanɪks/ *noun pl.* (usu. treated as *sing.*). E20.
[ORIGIN from BIO- + MECHANICS.]
The mechanics of the structures and movements of living organisms.
■ **biomechanical** *adjective* M20. **biomechanically** *adverb* M20. **bio'mechanist** *noun* M20.

biometric /bʌɪə(ʊ)ˈmɛtrɪk/ *adjective.* E20.
[ORIGIN from BIO- + -METRIC.]
Of or pertaining to biometry.
– SPECIAL COLLOCATIONS: **biometric signature** the unique pattern of a bodily feature such as the retina, iris, voice, etc., encoded on an identity card and used for recognition.
■ **biometrical** *adjective* E20. **biometrically** *adverb* E20.

biometrics /bʌɪə(ʊ)ˈmɛtrɪks/ *noun.* E20.
[ORIGIN from BIOMETRIC: see -ICS.]
= BIOMETRY *noun* 2.
■ **biome'trician** *noun* E20.

biometry /bʌɪˈɒmɪtri/ *noun.* M19.
[ORIGIN from BIO- + -METRY.]
†**1** The measurement and study of the duration of human life. M–L19.
2 The application of statistical methods to biological investigation. E20.

bionic /bʌɪˈɒnɪk/ *adjective.* E20.
[ORIGIN from BIO- + ELECTRONIC.]
Of or relating to bionics; having mechanical body parts, or superhuman powers resulting from these. Also in trivial use: powerful, energetic.

bionics /bʌɪˈɒnɪks/ *noun.* M20.
[ORIGIN from BIONIC: see -ICS.]
The study and construction of mechanical systems that function like (parts of) living beings.

bionomic /bʌɪə(ʊ)ˈnɒmɪk/ *adjective.* L19.
[ORIGIN from BIO- + ECONOMIC.]
Of or pertaining to bionomics; ecological.
■ Also **bionomical** *adjective* E20.

bionomics /bʌɪə(ʊ)ˈnɒmɪks/ *noun.* L19.
[ORIGIN from BIO- + ECONOMICS.]
The branch of biology that deals with organisms' behaviour and modes of life in their natural environment; ecology.

-biont /ˈbʌɪɒnt/ *suffix.*
[ORIGIN Extracted from SYMBIONT.]
BIOLOGY. Forming nouns denoting kinds of living organism, esp. with ref. to particular modes of life, as ***halobiont, parabiont, trophobiont***, freq. after adjectives in *-biotic*.

biophilia /bʌɪə(ʊ)ˈfɪlɪə/ *noun.* M20.
[ORIGIN from BIO- + -PHILIA, after *necrophilia*.]
1 *PSYCHOANALYSIS.* (In the writings of Erich Fromm) a love of life or self-love enabling normal emotional and social development. M20.
2 A love of or empathy with the natural world, seen as a human instinct. L20.

biophysics /bʌɪə(ʊ)ˈfɪzɪks/ *noun.* L19.
[ORIGIN from BIO- + PHYSICS.]
The science of the application of the laws of physics to biological phenomena.
■ **biophysical** *adjective* E20. **biophysically** *adverb* L20. **biophysicist** *noun* an expert in or student of biophysics E20.

biopic /ˈbʌɪəʊpɪk/ *noun. colloq.* M20.
[ORIGIN from BIO(GRAPHICAL + PIC *noun*[3].]
A biographical film.

biopsy /ˈbʌɪɒpsi/ *noun & verb.* L19.
[ORIGIN from BIO- + Greek *opsis* sight, after *necropsy*.]
▸ **A** *noun.* Examination of tissue taken from the human body for diagnostic purposes; the removal of such tissue. L19.
▸ **B** *verb trans.* Subject to biopsy. M20.

bioregion /ˈbʌɪəʊriːdʒən/ *noun.* L20.
[ORIGIN from BIO- + REGION.]
A geographical area whose limits are defined by characteristics of the natural environment rather than by imposed political or administrative boundaries.
■ **bio'regional** *adjective* L20. **bio'regionalism** *noun* an ecological philosophy which promotes bioregions as the basis for social organization L20. **bio'regionalist** *noun* L20.

biorhythm /ˈbʌɪə(ʊ)rɪð(ə)m/ *noun.* M20.
[ORIGIN from BIO- + RHYTHM *noun*.]
Any recurring cycle in the physiology of an organism; *spec.* a cyclic pattern of physical, emotional, or mental activity said to occur in the life of a person.
■ **bio'rhythmic** *adjective* pertaining to or of the nature of biorhythm M20. **bio'rhythmically** *adverb* with regard to biorhythms or biorhythmics L20. **bio'rhythmicist** *noun* an advocate or student of biorhythmics L20. **bio'rhythmics** *noun* the branch of science that deals with biorhythms, esp. one's own M20.

BIOS *abbreviation.*
COMPUTING. Basic input/output system.

biospeleology /ˌbʌɪə(ʊ)spiːlɪˈɒlədʒi/ *noun.* Also **-laeo-**. M20.
[ORIGIN French *biospéléologie*: see BIO-, SPELEOLOGY.]
The branch of science that deals with the fauna and flora of caves.
■ **biospeleo'logical** *adjective* M20. **biospeleologist** *noun* M20.

biostatistics /ˌbʌɪə(ʊ)stəˈtɪstɪks/ *noun.* Orig. *US.* L19.
[ORIGIN from BIO- + STATISTICS.]
The branch of statistics that deals with data relating to life; vital statistics.
■ **biostatistical** *adjective* M20. **biostati'stician** *noun* M20.

biostratigraphy /ˌbʌɪə(ʊ)strəˈtɪgrəfi/ *noun.* E20.
[ORIGIN from BIO- + STRATIGRAPHY.]
The branch of stratigraphy that deals with life in the geological past; stratigraphy based on fossils.
■ **biostratigrapher** *noun* M20. **biostrati'graphic** *adjective* E20. **biostrati'graphical** *adjective* M20. **biostrati'graphically** *adverb* M20.

biosynthesis /bʌɪə(ʊ)ˈsɪnθɪsɪs/ *noun.* M20.
[ORIGIN from BIO- + SYNTHESIS.]
Synthesis (of a chemical substance) by a living organism.
■ **biosynthesize** *verb trans.* produce by biosynthesis M20. **biosyn'thetic** *adjective* of, pertaining to, or produced by biosynthesis M20. **biosyn'thetically** *adverb* M20.

biosystematics /ˌbʌɪə(ʊ)sɪstəˈmatɪks/ *noun.* M20.
[ORIGIN from BIO- + *systematics*: see SYSTEMATIC *noun* 2.]
Taxonomy based on the study of the genetic evolution of plant and animal populations.
■ **biosystematic** *adjective* of or pertaining to biosystematics M20. **biosystematically** *adverb* M20. **biosy'stematist** *noun* M20.

biota /bʌɪˈəʊtə/ *noun.* E20.
[ORIGIN mod. Latin from Greek *biotē* life.]
The animal and plant life of a region.

biotech /ˈbʌɪəʊtɛk/ *noun. colloq.* L20.
[ORIGIN Abbreviation.]
= BIOTECHNOLOGY.

biotechnology /ˌbʌɪə(ʊ)tɛkˈnɒlədʒi/ *noun.* M20.
[ORIGIN from BIO- + TECHNOLOGY.]
Orig., the branch of technology that dealt with the actions and requirements of human beings. Now, the industrial application of biological processes.
■ **biotechno'logical** *adjective* M20. **biotechnologist** *noun* L20.

biotecture /ˈbʌɪəʊtɛktʃə/ *noun.* L20.
[ORIGIN from BIO- + ARCHI)TECTURE.]
The use of living plants as an integral part of the design of buildings.

biotic /bʌɪˈɒtɪk/ *adjective.* E17.
[ORIGIN Late Latin *bioticus* from Greek *biōtikos*, from *bios* life: see -IC. In mod. use from French *biotique*.]
†**1** Of or pertaining to (secular) life. *rare.* Only in E17.
2 Of, pertaining to, or resulting from living organisms, esp. in their ecological relations. L19.
■ **biotical** *adjective* (*rare*) = BIOTIC 2 M19. **biotically** *adverb* M20.

biotin /ˈbʌɪətɪn/ *noun.* M20.
[ORIGIN from Greek *biotos* life + -IN[1].]
BIOCHEMISTRY. A vitamin of the B complex which is found widely in nature, esp. in yeast, liver, and egg yolk, and is essential for the metabolism of fats in particular. Also (chiefly *US*) called ***vitamin H***.

biotite /ˈbʌɪətʌɪt/ *noun.* M19.
[ORIGIN from J.-B. *Biot* (1774–1862), French physicist + -ITE[1].]
MINERALOGY. A dark brown, green, or black ferromagnesian mica which is a constituent of many igneous and metamorphic rocks.

biparental /bʌɪpəˈrɛnt(ə)l/ *adjective.* E20.
[ORIGIN from BI- + PARENTAL.]
BIOLOGY. Of, pertaining to, or derived from two parents.

biparietal /bʌɪpəˈrʌɪɪt(ə)l/ *adjective.* M19.
[ORIGIN from BI- + PARIETAL *adjective*.]
ANATOMY. Joining or involving the two parietal bones of the skull.

biparous /ˈbɪpərəs/ *adjective.* M18.
[ORIGIN from BI- + -PAROUS.]
1 Producing two offspring at once. M18.
2 *BOTANY.* Of a cyme: having two branches at every node; forming a dichasium. L19.

biparted /bʌɪˈpɑːtɪd/ *adjective.* L16.
[ORIGIN from BI- + PARTED *adjective*[1].]
= BIPARTITE.

bipartisan /ˌbʌɪpɑːtɪˈzan/ *adjective.* E20.
[ORIGIN from BI- + PARTISAN *adjective*.]
Of, representing, or composed of members of two (political etc.) parties.

bipartite /bʌɪˈpɑːtʌɪt/ *adjective.* LME.
[ORIGIN Latin *bipartitus* pa. pple of *bipartire*, formed as BI- + PARTITE.]
1 Divided into or consisting of two parts. LME.
2 Of a treaty, contract, etc.: drawn up in two corresponding parts. E16.
3 Shared by or involving two parties. E17.
4 *MATH.* Of a curve, graph, etc.: consisting of two distinct sets of points. M19.
■ **bipartitely** *adverb* M17. **bipar'tition** *noun* M17.

biped /ˈbʌɪpɛd/ *noun & adjective.* M17.
[ORIGIN Latin *biped-*, *-pes*, from BI- + *ped-*, *pes* foot.]
▸ **A** *noun.* A two-footed animal. M17.
▸ **B** *adjective.* Having two feet. L18.

bipedal /bʌɪˈpiːd(ə)l/ *adjective.* LME.
[ORIGIN Latin *bipedalis*, formed as BIPED + -AL[1]; in mod. use from BIPED + -AL[1].]
†**1** Two feet long. Only in LME.
2 Having two feet; *spec.* using the hind limbs for locomotion. E17.
3 Of, pertaining to, or caused by a biped. E19.
■ **bipedalism** *noun* E20. **bipe'dality** *noun* M19. **bipedally** *adverb* L19.

biphasic /bʌɪˈfeɪzɪk/ *adjective.* E20.
[ORIGIN from BI- + PHASE *noun* + -IC.]
Having two phases.

biphenyl /bʌɪˈfiːnʌɪl, -ˈfɛnɪl/ *noun.* L19.
[ORIGIN from BI- + PHENYL.]
CHEMISTRY. A crystalline aromatic hydrocarbon, $(C_6H_5)_2$, formed by pyrolysis of benzene and containing two benzene rings; any substituted derivative of this.
POLYBROMINATED ***biphenyl***. *POLYCHLORINATED* ***biphenyl***.

bipinnate /bʌɪˈpɪneɪt/ *adjective.* M18.
[ORIGIN from BI- + PINNATE.]
1 *BOTANY.* Of a compound leaf: pinnately divided, with the leaflets themselves pinnate. M18.
2 *ZOOLOGY.* Having feathery appendages in opposed pairs. M19.

bipinnatifid /bʌɪpɪˈnatɪfɪd/ *adjective.* E19.
[ORIGIN from BI- + PINNATIFID.]
BOTANY. Of leaves: pinnatifid, with the pinnae themselves similarly divided.
■ Also **bipinnatisect** *adjective* L19.

biplane /ˈbʌɪpleɪn/ *noun.* **L19.**
[ORIGIN from BI- + PLANE *noun*³, *noun*⁴.]
†**1** *MATH.* Either of two planes tangential to a surface at the same point. **L19–E20.**
2 An aeroplane having two sets of wings, one above the other. **L19.**
■ **biˈplanar** *adjective* (*MATH.*) situated in two tangent planes **M19.**

bipolar /bʌɪˈpəʊlə/ *adjective.* **E19.**
[ORIGIN from BI- + POLAR *adjective*.]
1 Having two poles or opposite extremities. **E19.**
2 *spec.* ▸**a** Of a nerve cell: having two axons, one either side of the cell body. **M19.** ▸**b** Of psychiatric illness: characterized by both manic and depressive episodes, or manic ones only (in individual or family history). **M20.**
b bipolar disorder = *manic depression* s.v. MANIC.
3 Of or occurring in both polar regions. **L19.**
■ **bipoˈlarity** *noun* (**a**) the state of having two poles; (**b**) the occurrence of the same species in each of the polar regions: **M19.**

bippy /ˈbɪpi/ *noun. US slang.* **M20.**
[ORIGIN Unknown.]
The buttocks.

biprism /ˈbʌɪprɪz(ə)m/ *noun.* **L19.**
[ORIGIN from BI- + PRISM.]
PHYSICS. A combination of two long narrow prisms joined by the base, or an equivalent single prism, used to produce interference effects. Also ***Fresnel biprism***.

bipyramidal /bʌɪpɪˈramɪd(ə)l/ *adjective.* **M19.**
[ORIGIN from BI- + PYRAMIDAL.]
Having the form of two like pyramids joined base to base.
■ **biˈpyramid** *noun* a bipyramidal object or structure **E20.**

biquadratic /bʌɪkwɒˈdratɪk/ *adjective & noun.* **M17.**
[ORIGIN from BI- + QUADRATIC.]
MATH. ▸**A** *adjective.* Of, pertaining to, or containing the fourth power (or root) of a number. **M17.**
▸**B** *noun.* A biquadratic equation. Formerly also, the fourth power of a number. **M17.**
■ Also †**biquadrate** *adjective & noun* **L17–E19.**

†**biquaternion** *noun.* **M19–E20.**
[ORIGIN from BI- + QUATERNION.]
MATH. A quaternion with complex coefficients. Also, a combination of two quaternions obeying certain conditions.

biracial /bʌɪˈreɪʃ(ə)l/ *adjective.* **E20.**
[ORIGIN from BI- + RACIAL.]
Concerning or containing (members of) two racial groups.

biramous /bʌɪˈreɪməs/ *adjective.* **L19.**
[ORIGIN from BI- + RAMUS + -OUS.]
ZOOLOGY. Distally forked (esp. of crustacean limbs and antennae).
■ Also **biramose** *adjective* **L19.**

birational /bʌɪˈraʃ(ə)n(ə)l/ *adjective.* **L19.**
[ORIGIN from BI- + RATIONAL *adjective*.]
MATH. Of a transformation: relating two sets of variables of which each set is expressed rationally in terms of the other.
■ **birationally** *adverb* **E20.**

birch /bəːtʃ/ *noun.* Also (*N. English*) **birk** /bəːk/.
[ORIGIN Old English *birċe*, *bierċe* = Middle Low German *berke*, Old High German *birihha*, *birka* (German *Birke*) from Germanic.]
1 Any of various hardy northern trees or shrubs of the genus *Betula* (family Betulaceae), having smooth, tough bark and slender branches; *esp.* (in Europe) *B. pendula* (more fully ***silver birch***) and *B. pubescens* (more fully ***downy birch***), and (in N. America) *B. papyrifera* (more fully ***paper birch***). Also ***birch tree***. **OE.**
black birch, ***canoe birch***, ***river birch***, etc.
2 The wood of the birch. **LME.**
3 A bundle of birch twigs used for flogging. **M17.**
4 In *pl.* in form *birks*. A grove of birches. *N. English.* **E18.**
5 A canoe made of the bark of *Betula papyrifera*. *N. Amer.* **M19.**
– COMB.: **birchbark** *N. Amer.* (a canoe made of) the bark of *Betula papyrifera*; **birch beer** *N. Amer.* a fermented drink flavoured with oil extracted from the birch; a soft drink resembling this; **birch partridge** *N. Amer.* the ruffed grouse, *Bonasa umbellus*; **birch rod** = sense 3 above; ***birch tree***: see sense 1 above; **birch water** the sap obtained from the birch in spring; **birch wine** wine prepared from birch water; **birchwood** (**a**) a wood of birch trees; (**b**) = sense 2 above.
■ **birchen** *adjective* of or pertaining to (the) birch; composed of birch: **ME.**

birch /bəːtʃ/ *verb trans.* **M19.**
[ORIGIN from the noun.]
Flog with a birch.
■ **birching** *noun* the action of the verb; a flogging with a birch: **M19.**

bircher /ˈbəːtʃə/ *noun*¹. **L19.**
[ORIGIN from BIRCH *verb* + -ER¹.]
A person who flogs somebody with a birch; an advocate of birching.

Bircher /ˈbəːtʃə/ *noun*². **M20.**
[ORIGIN John *Birch*, a USAF officer killed by Chinese Communists in 1945, 'the first casualty of the Cold War' + -ER¹.]
A member or supporter of the John Birch Society, an extreme right-wing and anti-Communist American organization founded in 1958.

bird /bəːd/ *noun.*
[ORIGIN Old English *brid*, (late Northumbrian) *bird*, of unknown origin and without cognates.]
1 A nestling, a fledgling; a chick. Long *obsolete* exc. *N. English.* **OE.**
2 A feathered, warm-blooded, amniote animal of the vertebrate class Aves, characterized by modification of the forelimbs as wings for flight, oviparous reproduction, and care for the young. **ME.** ▸**b** *SPORT.* A game bird; *spec.* a partridge; *fig.* prey. **LME.**
game bird: see GAME *noun*.
3 A maiden, a girl; a young woman. (Orig. a var. of BURD, later taken as *fig.* use of sense 1 or 2.) Now *slang* (freq. *derog.*). **ME.**
4 A person (freq. with specifying adjective). *colloq.* **M19.**
5 A first-rate person, animal, or thing. *US slang.* **M19.**
6 [Abbreviation of BIRDLIME *noun* 2.] A prison sentence; prison. *slang.* **E20.**
7 An aircraft; a missile, rocket, satellite, spacecraft, etc. *slang.* **M20.**
8 In badminton: a shuttlecock. **L20.**
– PHRASES: **a bird in the hand** something certain. **a little bird** an unnamed informant. ***ARABIAN bird***. **Bird of Freedom** *US* the emblematic bald eagle of the US. **bird of Jove** the eagle. **bird of Juno** the peacock. **bird of paradise** (**a**) any of the family Paradisaeidae of passerine birds, mostly native to New Guinea, which are remarkable for the beauty and brilliance of their plumage; (**b**) (***the Bird of Paradise***) = APUS; (**c**) ***bird-of-paradise flower*** = STRELITZIA. ***bird of passage***: see PASSAGE *noun*. **bird of prey** a bird that kills and feeds on the flesh of other animals; *spec.* one belonging to the orders Cathartiformes, Accipitriformes, or Falconiformes (or sometimes Strigiformes). **birds of a feather** those of like character. ***box of birds***: see BOX *noun*². **for the birds** = ***strictly for the birds*** below. ***hear a bird sing***: see SING *verb*¹. **kill two birds with one stone** achieve two aims at once. **like a bird** swiftly; easily; without resistance or hesitation. ***old bird***: see OLD *adjective*. ***rare bird***: see RARE *adjective*¹. ***singing bird***: see SINGING *ppl adjective*. ***soldier bird***: see SOLDIER *noun*. ***stinking bird***: see STINKING *adjective*. **strictly for the birds** trivial; appealing only to the gullible. **the bird**, **the big bird** *slang* (orig. *THEATRICAL*) hissing and booing; dismissal, the sack; (esp. in ***get the bird***, ***give the big bird***, etc.). **the bird has flown** the prisoner etc. has escaped. †**the bird in the bosom** one's own secret or pledge, one's conscience. **the birds and the bees** *euphem.* (*colloq.*) details of human sexual functions. **the early bird** one who rises early or acts promptly.
– COMB.: **bird banding** = *bird-ringing* below; **bird bath** a basin in a garden etc. with water for birds to bathe in; †**bird-bolt** a blunt-headed arrow used for shooting birds; **birdbrain** *colloq.* a bird-brained person; **birdbrained** *adjective* (*colloq.*) stupid, flighty; **birdcage** a (usu. wire) cage for a bird or birds; an object of similar design; *slang* a paddock at a racecourse; **bird call** the natural call of a bird; an instrument imitating this; **bird cherry** a Eurasian wild cherry, *Prunus padus* (in Britain mostly northern), which bears its flowers in long racemes; **bird dog** *N. Amer.* a gun dog trained to retrieve birds; also, a tout; **bird-eating spider** any of various large tropical spiders which occasionally trap small birds; **bird-fancier** a person who knows about, collects, breeds, or deals in, birds; ***bird-fancier's lung***, a respiratory disease caused by inhaling dust consisting of feathers, droppings, and other organic matter from birds; **bird flu** a severe form of influenza that affects birds, esp. poultry, and can also spread to humans; **birdlife** = AVIFAUNA; **birdman** (**a**) a man who catches, sells, etc. birds; *colloq.* an ornithologist; (**b**) *colloq.* an airman; †**bird-mouthed** *adjective* unwilling to speak out; **bird pepper** a tropical American capsicum pepper, *Capsicum annuum* var. *glabriusculum* or *C. frutescens* var. *typicum*, thought to be the ancestor of both sweet and chilli peppers; **bird ringing** the fixing of an identifying band to a bird's leg; **bird sanctuary** an area where birds are protected and encouraged to breed; **bird's-beak moulding** a moulding which in cross-section forms an ovolo or ogee with or without a fillet under it, followed by a hollow; **birdseed** special seeds given as food to caged birds; **bird's-eye** (**a**) any of various plants with small round bright flowers, *esp.* a primrose, *Primula farinosa* (usu. ***bird's-eye primrose***), having yellow-centred purple flowers, and germander speedwell, *Veronica chamaedrys*; (**b**) manufactured tobacco with the ribs of the leaves cut along with the fibre; (**c**) (a fabric woven in) a design consisting in a small diamond with a centre dot; (**d**) *attrib.* of or pertaining to a bird's eye; marked as with bird's eyes, spotted; ***bird's eye view***, a view from overhead *of* a landscape etc., such as a bird might have, *fig.* a résumé or overview *of* a subject; **bird's-foot** (**a**) any of various objects, esp. plants, resembling a bird's foot; *spec.* a vetch, *Ornithopus perpusillus*, having claw-shaped seed pods; (**b**) *attrib.*: ***bird's-foot delta***, a delta built out from a coastline by deposition along a number of channels; ***bird's-foot fenugreek***, a small white-flowered clover, *Trifolium ornithopodioides*, sometimes classified with the fenugreeks (*Trigonella*); ***bird's-foot fern***, a small fern, *Pellaea mucronata*, native to the south-western US; ***bird's-foot trefoil***, a superficially trifoliate leguminous plant of the genus *Lotus*, esp. *L. corniculatus*, with yellow flowers streaked with red and pods that spread like a bird's claw; ***bird's-foot violet***, a violet, *Viola pedata*, of the eastern US; **bird shot** the smallest size of shot (for sporting rifles etc.); **bird's nest** (**a**) the nest of a bird; ***bird's-nest soup***, soup made from the edible nests of SE Asian swifts of the genus *Aerodramus*; (**b**) (usu. with hyphen) any of various plants, *esp.* the wild carrot and either of two saprophytic plants, *Neottia nidus-avis* (usu. called ***bird's-nest orchid***) and *Monotropa hypopitys* (usu. called ***yellow bird's-nest***); **bird's-nest** *verb intrans.* search for birds' nests, usu. to take the eggs; **bird's-nesting** (**a**) the action or occupation of searching for birds' nests; (**b**) the furring of a passage, *spec.* of a boiler tube; **birdsong** the musical call or sound made by a bird or birds; **bird strike** a collision between an aircraft and a bird or birds; **bird table** a raised platform on which food for birds is placed; **birdwatcher** one who observes birds in their natural surroundings; **birdwatching** the occupation of a birdwatcher; **bird-witted** *adjective* (*colloq.*) lacking the faculty of attention.
■ **birdless** *adjective* **E16.** **birdlike** *adjective* **L16.**

bird /bəːd/ *verb intrans.* **M16.**
[ORIGIN from the noun.]
Engage in fowling or birdwatching. Freq. as ***birding verbal noun***.

birder /ˈbəːdə/ *noun.* **ME.**
[ORIGIN from BIRD *noun* + -ER¹.]
†**1** A fowler. **ME–M17.**
†**2** A wild cat. *dial.* **E18–M19.**
3 A breeder of birds. **E19.**
4 A birdwatcher. **M20.**

birdie /ˈbəːdi/ *noun & verb.* **L18.**
[ORIGIN from BIRD *noun* + -IE.]
▸**A** *noun.* **1** A small bird. Also, a little girl, a young woman. (Used affectionately.) **L18.**
2 *GOLF.* A hole played in one stroke under par or bogey. **E20.**
▸**B** *verb trans. GOLF.* Play (a hole) in one stroke under par or bogey. **M20.**

birdlime /ˈbəːdlʌɪm/ *noun & verb.* **LME.**
[ORIGIN from BIRD *noun* + LIME *noun*¹.]
▸**A** *noun.* **1** A glutinous substance spread on twigs to catch birds. **LME.**
2 Time; *spec.* a term of imprisonment. *rhyming slang.* **M19.**
▸**B** *verb trans.* Smear or catch (as) with birdlime. **L16.**

birefringence /bʌɪrɪˈfrɪndʒ(ə)ns/ *noun.* **L19.**
[ORIGIN from BI- + REFRINGENT *adjective* + -ENCE.]
Double refraction.
■ **birefringent** *adjective* having double refraction **L19.**

bireme /ˈbʌɪriːm/ *noun & adjective.* **L16.**
[ORIGIN Latin *biremis*, from BI- + *remus* oar.]
hist. (A galley) having two banks of oars.

biretta /bɪˈrɛtə/ *noun.* Also **ber-**, **birr-**. **L16.**
[ORIGIN Italian *berretta* or Spanish *birreta*, fem. dims. corresp. to Old Provençal *berret* BERET, based on late Latin *birrus*, *-um* hooded cape or cloak, perh. of Celtic origin.]
A square cap worn by Roman Catholic ecclesiastics (black by priests, purple by bishops, red by cardinals) or by other clergymen.

biri *noun* var. of BIDI.

biriani *noun* var. of BIRYANI.

birk *noun*¹ var. of BERK.

birk *noun*² see BIRCH *noun*.

Birkenstock /ˈbəːk(ə)nstɒk/ *noun.* **L20.**
[ORIGIN from the name of the manufacturer.]
(Proprietary name for) a type of shoe or sandal with a contoured cork-filled sole and a thick leather upper.

birkie /ˈbəːki/ *noun & adjective. Scot.* Also **-k(e)y**. **E18.**
[ORIGIN Unknown.]
▸**A** *noun.* **1** A fellow; an opinionated or arrogant man. **E18.**
2 The card game beggar-my-neighbour (see BEGGAR *verb* 1). **L18.**
▸**B** *adjective.* Mettlesome. **E19.**

birl /bəːl/ *noun.* In sense 3 also **burl** /bəːl/. **M19.**
[ORIGIN Imit.: cf. BIRL *verb*.]
1 A twist, a spin, a whirl. *Scot. & N. English.* **M19.**
2 A rattling or whirring sound. *Scot. & N. English.* **L19.**
3 A try, an attempt. Esp. in ***give it a birl***. *Austral. & NZ colloq.* **E20.**

birl /bəːl/ *verb.* Orig. & chiefly *Scot.* **E18.**
[ORIGIN Imit.: cf. BIRL *noun*.]
1 *verb trans.* Cause to rotate rapidly; spin (a coin); toss (a coin) on the table as one's contribution to a joint fund, contribute. **E18.**
2 *verb intrans.* Revolve or rotate rapidly (often with a rattling or whirring sound). **L18.**

birle /bəːl/ *verb.* Long *obsolete* exc. *dial.*
[ORIGIN Old English *byrelian*, Old Norse *byrla* from *byrele* cup-bearer, perh. rel. to BEAR *verb*¹.]
1 *verb trans.* Draw or pour out (drink, *to* or *for* a person). **OE.**
2 *verb trans.* Supply or ply *with* drink. **ME.**
3 *verb intrans. & trans.* Carouse; drink and pass (the cup). **L16.**

birley, **birlie** *nouns* see BYRLAW.

birling /ˈbəːlɪŋ, ˈbɪə-/ *noun.* Also **berlin(g)**, **birlinn**. **L16.**
[ORIGIN Gaelic *birlinn*, *beirlinn*.]
A large rowing boat or barge, formerly used in the Western Islands of Scotland.

Birman /ˈbəːmən/ *noun.* **L20.**
[ORIGIN var. of BURMAN.]
A cat of a long-haired breed, typically with a cream body, dark head, tail, and legs, and white paws.

Birmingham /ˈbəːmɪŋəm/ *noun & adjective.* Also †**Brummagem** & other local vars. **L17.**
[ORIGIN A town (now a city) in central England, with ref. to the counterfeit coins etc. once made there.]
ENGLISH HISTORY. (Designating) a supporter of the 1680 Exclusion Bill, (a) Whig. Cf. ANTI-BIRMINGHAM.

biro /ˈbʌɪrəʊ/ *noun*. Pl. **-os**. M20.
[ORIGIN László József *Biró* (1899–1985), Hungarian inventor.]
(Proprietary name for) a ballpoint pen.

birr /bəː/ *noun*^{1}. ME.
[ORIGIN Branch I from Old Norse *byrr* favouring wind; branch II prob. imit.]
▸ **I** Long chiefly *Scot. & N. English*.
1 A strong wind. ME.
2 Momentum, impetus; might; also, a thrust. ME. ▸**b** Force of enunciation. E19.
▸ **II 3** An energetic whirring sound. M19.

birr /bəː/ *noun*^{2}. Pl. same, **-s**. L20.
[ORIGIN Amharic.]
The basic monetary unit of Ethiopia, equal to 100 cents.

birr /bəː/ *verb intrans.* Chiefly *Scot.* E16.
[ORIGIN from BIRR *noun*^{1}.]
Emit a whirring noise; move with a whirring noise.

birretta *noun* var. of BIRETTA.

birse /bəːs/ *noun*. Long only *Scot.*
[ORIGIN Old English *byrst* = Old Saxon *brusta*, Old High German *burst* (German *Borste*), Old Norse *burst(i)*.]
= BRISTLE *noun*.

birsle /ˈbəːs(ə)l/ *verb trans. Scot. & N. English.* LME.
[ORIGIN Unknown: cf. BRISTLE *verb*^{2}.]
Scorch, parch, toast hard.

birth /bəːθ/ *noun*^{1}. ME.
[ORIGIN Old Norse *byrð* = Gothic *gabaurþs* from East Germanic (corresp. to Old English *gebyrd*, Old Saxon *giburd*, Old High German *giburt* (German *Geburt*) from West Germanic), from base of BEAR *verb*^{1}: see -TH^{1}.]
1 The emergence of young from the body of the mother (viewed as an act of the mother or as a fact pertaining to the offspring). ME.

HENRY FIELDING The birth of an heir by his beloved sister. TENNYSON Mine by right, from birth till death.

give birth to bring (offspring) into the world (*lit. & fig.*). **new birth** THEOLOGY spiritual regeneration. ***virgin birth***: see VIRGIN *adjective*.
2 Of things: ▸†**a** Rising of the sun or a star. Only in ME. ▸**b** Coming into existence; origin, beginning. E17.

b J. BENTHAM Offences which owe their birth to the joint influence of indolence and pecuniary interest.

3 †**a** That which is borne in the womb. ME–M17. ▸**b** That which is born into the world; offspring; product, creation. *arch.* LME.

b ADDISON Others hatch their Eggs and tend the Birth, 'till it is able to shift for it self.

4 Parentage, descent, inherited position; conditions or relations involved in birth; *spec.* noble lineage. ME.

D. HUME Birth, titles, & place, must be honoured above industry & riches. J. GALSWORTHY Political by birth rather than by nature. J. DOS PASSOS My own sister by birth and blood. P. WARNER The arrow took no account of rank or birth.

†**5** Natural character; kind. ME–L16.

SHAKES. *Rom. & Jul.* Nor aught so good but, strain'd from that fair use, Revolts from true birth.

†**6** Fortune as influenced by the planets at the moment of birth. Only in L16.

SHAKES. *2 Hen. VI* A cunning man did calculate my birth And told me that by water I should die.

– COMB.: **birth certificate** an official document giving the date and place of a person's birth; **birth control** (the practice of) methods of preventing unwanted pregnancy or limiting births; **birthdate** the date on which a person is born; **birth father** a biological (as opp. to an adoptive etc.) father; **birthmark** an unusual mark, esp. a blotch of brown or dark red skin, on the body at or from birth; **birth mother** a biological (as opp. to an adoptive etc.) mother; **birthnight** (the anniversary of) the night of one's birth; **birth parent** a biological (as opp. to an adoptive etc.) parent; **birth pill** a contraceptive pill; **birthplace** place of birth, origin, or commencement; **birth rate** the ratio of the number of births to the population, usu. calculated per thousand of population per year; **birthright** the rights, privileges, or possessions belonging to one by birth, as an eldest son, as being born in a certain status or country, or as a human being; **birthroot** any of various trilliums, *esp.* the purple or red trillium, *T. erectum*; **birth sign** the astrological sign under which one is born; **birthstone** a gemstone associated with the month of one's birth; **birthweight** weight at birth; **birthwort** = ARISTOLOCHIA.

†**birth** *noun*^{2} var. of BERTH *noun*.

birth /bəːθ/ *verb*^{1}. ME.
[ORIGIN from BIRTH *noun*^{1}.]
1 *verb intrans.* Have birth, be born. *rare.* ME.
2 *verb intrans.* Give birth. Chiefly as ***birthing*** *verbal noun*. E20.
3 *verb trans.* Give birth to. *dial.* (esp. *US*) & *W. Indian*. E20.

E. BRODBER Asking her what she was going to do about the one pickney she birth.

– COMB.: **birthing pool** a large bath for women to give birth in.

†**birth** *verb*^{2} var. of BERTH *verb*^{1}.

birthday /ˈbəːθdeɪ/ *noun*. ME.
[ORIGIN from BIRTH *noun*^{1} + DAY *noun*.]
(The anniversary of) the day of one's birth; the day of origin or commencement.
official birthday: see OFFICIAL *adjective*.
– COMB.: **birthday book** a book in diary form for recording birthdays; **birthday boy**, **birthday girl** *colloq.* the person present or otherwise known whose birthday it is; **birthday card** a greetings card marking the anniversary of a person's birthday; ***birthday girl***: see ***birthday boy*** above; **birthday honours** the titles of honour conferred by the British monarch on each anniversary of his or her official birthday; **birthday party**, **birthday present**: given to mark the anniversary of a person's birthday; **birthday suit** (***a***) *hist.* a dress worn on the monarch's birthday; (***b***) *joc.* the bare skin.

biryani /bɪrɪˈɑːni/ *noun*. Also **biriani** & other vars. M20.
[ORIGIN Urdu from Persian *biryānī*, from *biryān* fried, grilled.]
A dish of the Indian subcontinent consisting of spiced meat or vegetables and cooked rice.

bis /bɪs/ *adverb*. E17.
[ORIGIN French & Italian, from Latin *bis* twice.]
Encore; again; twice; *spec.* as a direction in a musical score indicating that a passage is to be repeated.

bis- /bɪs/ *prefix*.
Var. of BI- used occas. before *s*, *c*, or a vowel, and in CHEMISTRY to form the names of compounds containing two groups identically substituted or coordinated, as ***bis(2-chloroethyl) ether*** (cf. TETRAKIS-, TRIS-).

biscacha *noun* var. of VISCACHA.

Biscayan /ˈbɪskeɪən/ *noun & adjective*. Now *arch.* or *hist.* L16.
[ORIGIN from *Biscay* in NW Spain (Spanish *Vizcaya*, now a province of the region of Vascongadas y Navarra) + -AN: cf. BASQUE.]
(A native or inhabitant) of Biscay or the Basque Country.

†**biscotin** *noun*. E18–E19.
[ORIGIN French from Italian *biscottino* dim. of *biscotto* corresp. to French BISCUIT.]
A kind of sweet biscuit.

biscotti /bɪsˈkɒti/ *noun pl.* M20.
[ORIGIN Italian = biscuits.]
Long, thin, hard Italian biscuits containing nuts, typically served with a hot drink into which they are dipped.

biscuit /ˈbɪskɪt/ *noun & adjective*. Also †**bisket**. ME.
[ORIGIN Old French *bescuit*, *besquit* (mod. *biscuit*), ult. from Latin *bis* twice + *coctus* pa. pple of *coquere* to cook.]
▸ **A** *noun*. **1** A piece of usu. unleavened cake or bread of various ingredients, usu. crisp, dry, and hard, and in a small flat thin shape. ME. ▸**b** A small round cake like a scone. *N. Amer.* E19.
Bourbon biscuit, ***dog biscuit***, ***garibaldi biscuit***, ***Savoy biscuit***, etc. ***take the biscuit***: see TAKE *verb*.
2 Porcelain or other ware which has undergone firing but no further treatment. L18.
3 A light-brown colour regarded as characteristic of biscuits. L19.
4 Each of the three square sections of a soldier's mattress. E20.
5 CARPENTRY. A small round or oval piece of wood, a row of which are glued or wedged into semicircular slots in each of two pieces of wood in order to join them together. M20.
– COMB.: **biscuit barrel** a barrel or barrel-shaped container for biscuits.
▸ **B** *attrib.* or as *adjective*. Of the colour of biscuit, light brown. L19.
■ **biscuit-like** *adjective* M19. **biscuity** *adjective* resembling a biscuit in texture, flavour, colour, etc. L19.

bise /biːz/ *noun*. ME.
[ORIGIN French, of unknown origin.]
A keen dry north wind prevalent in Switzerland, southern France, etc.

bisect /bʌɪˈsɛkt/ *verb trans.* M17.
[ORIGIN from BI- + Latin *sect-* pa. ppl stem of *secare* to cut.]
Cut or divide into two (orig. equal) parts.
■ **bisection** *noun* division into two (equal) parts M17.

biserial /bʌɪˈsɪərɪəl/ *adjective*. E19.
[ORIGIN from BI- + SERIAL.]
BOTANY & ZOOLOGY. Arranged in or consisting of two series or rows.

bisexual /bʌɪˈsɛkʃʊəl/ *adjective & noun*. E19.
[ORIGIN from BI- + SEXUAL.]
▸ **A** *adjective*. Of two sexes; having both sexes in one individual; (of a person) sexually attracted to individuals of both sexes. E19.
▸ **B** *noun*. A bisexual person. E20.
■ **bisexuˈality** *noun* M19.

bish /bɪʃ/ *noun*^{1}. *joc.* E20.
[ORIGIN Abbreviation.]
= BISHOP *noun*.

bish /bɪʃ/ *noun*^{2}. *slang.* M20.
[ORIGIN Unknown.]
A mistake, a blunder.

bish /bɪʃ/ *verb*^{1} *trans. arch. joc.* L19.
[ORIGIN Abbreviation.]
= BISHOP *verb*^{1}.

bish /bɪʃ/ *verb*^{2} *trans. Austral. & NZ slang.* M20.
[ORIGIN Imit.]
Throw.

bishop /ˈbɪʃəp/ *noun*. Also (esp. in titles) **B-**.
[ORIGIN Old English *biscop* = Old Frisian, Old Saxon *biskop*, Middle Dutch & mod. Dutch *bisschop*, Old High German *biscof* (German *Bischof*), Old Norse *biskop* from popular var. of ecclesiastical Latin *episcopus* from Greek *episkopos* overseer, from EPI- + *-skopos* looking (see -SCOPE).]
1 CHRISTIAN CHURCH. **a** In episcopal Churches, a member of the clergy consecrated as the governor of a diocese, possessing the powers to confirm, institute, and ordain, ranking next below an archbishop (where these exist) and above priests, deacons, etc. OE. ▸**b** In some versions of the New Testament, an officer or overseer of the early Church (translating Greek *episkopos*, used both as a descriptive term and as a title). Also (as a descriptive term only) a pastor or chief elder of a non-episcopal Church. LME.
a cardinal bishop, ***metropolitan bishop***, ***suffragan bishop***, ***titular bishop***, etc. ***Lord Bishop***: see LORD *noun*.
2 A chief priest of any religion. Now *rare* or *obsolete*. OE.
3 CHESS. Each of the four pieces that move diagonally and have the upper part shaped like a mitre. Cf. ARCHER 3, ALFIN. E16.
4 a A ladybird; a moth. *dial.* L16. ▸**b** Any of several African weaver birds of the genus *Euplectes*. Also ***bishop bird***. L19.
b red bishop: see RED *adjective*.
5 Mulled and spiced wine (esp. port). M18.
6 Any of various articles of clothing; *spec.* (***a***) *US* (*hist.*) a bustle; (***b***) *dial.* a smock or all-round pinafore. L18.
– COMB.: ***bishop bird***: see sense 4b above; **Bishops' Bible** a version of the Bible published in 1568; **bishop's cap** mitrewort (genus *Mitella*); **bishop sleeve** a full sleeve gathered at the wrist; **bishopstool** (now *arch.* or *hist.*) the throne or see of a bishop; ***bishop suffragan***: see SUFFRAGAN *noun* 1; **bishop's weed** ground elder, *Aegopodium podagraria*; **bishop's wort** betony.
■ **bishopdom** *noun* †(***a***) = BISHOPHOOD; (***b***) episcopal order, bishops collectively: OE. **bishopess** *noun* (chiefly *joc.*) (***a***) the wife of a bishop; (***b***) a female bishop: L17. **bishophood** *noun* the rank or office of a bishop OE. **bishoplike** *adjective & adverb* (***a***) *adjective* resembling a bishop; formerly also, episcopal; (***b***) *adverb* in the manner of a bishop: M16. **bishoply** *adjective* (now *rare*) episcopal OE. **bishopric** *noun* [Old English *rīce* realm, rule] the diocese or jurisdiction of a bishop; the rank or office of a bishop: OE.

bishop /ˈbɪʃəp/ *verb*^{1} *trans. arch.*
[ORIGIN Old English *biscēopian*, from BISHOP *noun*.]
1 Administer the rite of confirmation to; confirm. Now *rare* or *obsolete*. OE.
2 Appoint to the office of bishop. M16.

bishop /ˈbɪʃəp/ *verb*^{2} *trans.* E18.
[ORIGIN from *Bishop*, a surname.]
File and tamper with the teeth of (a horse) to deceive as to age.

bisk *noun* var. of BISQUE *noun*^{3}.

bisket *noun* obsolete var. of BISCUIT.

Bislama /ˈbɪʃləmɑː/ *noun*. L20.
[ORIGIN Alt. of BEACH-LA-MAR.]
An English-based pidgin used as a lingua franca in Fiji and esp. in Vanuatu (formerly New Hebrides).

Bismarck /ˈbɪzmɑːk/ *noun*. Also **b-**; (in sense 4) **-mark**. L19.
[ORIGIN formed as BISMARCKIAN; sense 4 perh. a different word.]
1 In full ***Bismarck brown***. = VESUVIN. L19.
2 A drink consisting of a mixture of champagne and stout. Cf. ***black velvet*** s.v. BLACK *adjective*. E20.
3 In full ***Bismarck herring***. A marinaded herring served cold. M20.
4 A jam-filled doughnut. *US*. M20.

Bismarckian /bɪzˈmɑːkɪən/ *adjective*. L19.
[ORIGIN from *Bismarck* (see below) + -IAN.]
Of, pertaining to, or characteristic of the German statesman Prince Otto von Bismarck (1815–98) or his policies.
■ **Bismarckianism** *noun* L19.

Bismark *noun* see BISMARCK.

bismillah /bɪsˈmɪlə/ *interjection & noun*. L18.
[ORIGIN Arabic *bi-smi-llāh(i)*, the first word of the Koran.]
(The exclamation) in the name of God: used by Muslims at the beginning of any undertaking.

bismite /ˈbɪzmʌɪt/ *noun*. M19.
[ORIGIN from BISMUTH + -ITE^{1}.]
MINERALOGY. Monoclinic bismuth trioxide, occurring usu. as greyish-green to yellow granular or earthy masses.

bismuth /ˈbɪzməθ/ *noun*. Also †**wismuth**. M17.
[ORIGIN mod. Latin *bisemutum* from German *Wismut*, of unknown origin.]
A reddish-white easily fusible metallic chemical element, atomic no. 83 (symbol Bi). Also, a compound of this used medicinally.
– COMB.: **bismuth glance** = BISMUTHINITE; **bismuth ochre** = BISMITE.
■ **bismuthate** *noun* a salt formed (as) by reaction of bismuth trioxide with an alkali M19. **bismuthic** /-ˈmjuː-/ *adjective* of or containing bismuth L18. **bismuthyl** *noun* the radical ·BiO; the cation BiO^{+}: L19.

bismuthine /ˈbɪzm(j)ʊθiːn/ *noun*. M19.
[ORIGIN from BISMUTH + -INE[5].]
1 MINERALOGY. = BISMUTHINITE. Now *rare* or *obsolete*. M19.
2 CHEMISTRY. A very unstable gas, BiH_3. Also, any substituted derivative of this. L19.

bismuthinite /bɪzˈm(j)ʊθɪnʌɪt/ *noun*. M19.
[ORIGIN from BISMUTHINE + -ITE[1].]
MINERALOGY. Orthorhombic bismuth trisulphide occurring usu. as grey or white metallic needles or foliated masses.

bismutite /ˈbɪzm(j)ʊtʌɪt/ *noun*. Also **-thite** /-θʌɪt/. M19.
[ORIGIN German *Bismutit*, from mod. Latin *bisemutum* BISMUTH: see -ITE[1].]
MINERALOGY. A tetragonal bismuthyl carbonate, which usu. occurs as dull yellow or grey earthy masses.

†**bisogn(i)o** *nouns* vars. of BESOGNIO.

bison /ˈbʌɪs(ə)n/ *noun*. Pl. same. LME.
[ORIGIN Latin, ult. from Germanic base also of WISENT.]
1 Either of two heavily built wild oxen of the genus *Bison*, with a high shoulder hump, long shaggy hair on the shoulders and forequarters, and a large head with short horns: (*a*) (more fully ***European bison***) *B. bonasus*, exterminated in the wild but re-established in Poland and the Caucasus (also called ***wisent***), (*b*) (more fully ***American bison***) *B. bison*, surviving in small numbers on the N. American plains (also called ***buffalo***). LME.
2 More fully ***Indian bison*** = GAUR. L19.
■ **biˈsontine** *adjective* [Latin *bisont-*] pertaining to or resembling the bison L19.

bisphenol /ˈbɪsfiːnɒl/ *noun*. M20.
[ORIGIN from BIS- + PHENOL.]
CHEMISTRY. A compound containing two identically substituted phenol groups; esp. (more fully ***bisphenol-A***) a synthetic crystalline compound, $HOC_6H_4C(CH_3)_2C_6H_4OH$, used as a monomer in the manufacture of epoxy resins and polycarbonates.

bisque /bɪsk/ *noun*[1]. M17.
[ORIGIN French, of unknown origin.]
In various games, esp. tennis, croquet, and golf, (the allowing of) a point or stroke to be scored or taken when desired as a handicapping advantage.

bisque /bɪsk/ *noun*[2]. M17.
[ORIGIN from BISCUIT.]
A variety of unglazed white porcelain used for statuettes etc. Also = BISCUIT 2.

bisque /bɪsk, biːsk/ *noun*[3]. Also **bisk** /bɪsk/. M17.
[ORIGIN French = crayfish soup.]
A rich soup usu. made from shellfish but also from birds etc.

bissextile /bɪˈsɛkstʌɪl/ *adjective* & *noun*. L16.
[ORIGIN Late Latin *bi(s)sextilis* (*annus*) (year) containing the *bis sextus dies*, the doubled sixth day before the calends of March, i.e. 24 February.]
▸ **A** *adjective*. Containing the extra day the Julian calendar inserts in a leap year. L16.
▸ **B** *noun*. A leap year. L16.

†**bisson** *adjective*.
[ORIGIN Old English (late Northumbrian) *bisene* of unknown origin.]
1 Blind; purblind. OE–L19.
2 Blinding. *rare* (Shakes.). Only in E17.

SHAKES. *Haml.* Threat'ning the flames With bisson rheum.

bistable /bʌɪˈsteɪb(ə)l/ *adjective*. M20.
[ORIGIN from BI- + STABLE *adjective*.]
Having two stable states.

bister *noun* var. of BISTRE.

bistort /ˈbɪstɔːt/ *noun*. E16.
[ORIGIN French *bistorte* or medieval Latin *bistorta*, from *bis* twice + *torta* fem. pa. pple of *torquere* twist.]
Any of certain polygonums with twisted roots; *spec*. the species *Persicaria bistorta*, which bears cylindrical spikes of pink flowers and has an astringent root.

bistoury /ˈbɪstʊri/ *noun*. M18.
[ORIGIN French *bistouri*, earlier *bistorie* dagger, of unknown origin.]
A surgeon's knife with a straight or curved narrow blade.

bistre /ˈbɪstə/ *noun*. Also **bister**. E18.
[ORIGIN French, of unknown origin.]
(The colour of) a brown pigment prepared from soot.
■ **bistred** *adjective* stained with bistre L19.

bistro /ˈbiːstrəʊ, ˈbɪs-/ *noun*. Pl. **-os**. Also **-ot**. E20.
[ORIGIN French.]
A small bar or restaurant.

bisulphate /bʌɪˈsʌlfeɪt/ *noun*. Also (US & CHEMISTRY) **-sulf-**. E19.
[ORIGIN from BI- + SULPHATE *noun*.]
CHEMISTRY. A salt of the anion HSO_4^-, i.e. containing double the proportion of the acid radical present in a sulphate.

bisulphite /bʌɪˈsʌlfʌɪt/ *noun*. Also (US & CHEMISTRY) **-sulf-**. M19.
[ORIGIN from BI- + SULPHITE.]
CHEMISTRY. A sulphite containing two sulphite anions in the molecule.

bit /bɪt/ *noun*[1].
[ORIGIN Old English *bite* = Old Frisian *bit(e)*, Old Saxon *biti* (Middle Dutch *bēte*, Dutch *beet*), Old High German *biz* (German *Biss*), Old Norse *bit* (Swedish *bett*, Danish *bid*), from Germanic, from base also of BITE *verb*.]
▸ **I** Biting; what one bites.
†**1** The act or action of biting; = BITE *noun* 1. OE–M17.
2 Food to bite; victuals. Chiefly *dial.* E18.
a bit and a sup, ***bit and sup***: see SUP *noun*[1].
▸ **II** The biting or gripping part of something.
†**3 a** The cutting blade or edge of an edged tool, axe, etc. ME–M18. ▸**b** The biting or cutting end or part of a tool, as the movable boring piece of a drill, the cutting head of a (machine) lathe, the nipping part of pincers, etc. L16.
4 The part of a key that engages with the lock lever. M17.
5 The metal head of a soldering iron. L19.
▸ **III 6** The mouthpiece of a horse's bridle. LME.
bridle bit, ***snaffle bit***, ***tongue bit***, etc. ***champing at the bit***: see CHAMP *verb* 1. **off the bit** on a loose rein. **on the bit** on a tight rein. **take the bit between one's teeth**, †**take the bit in one's teeth** escape from control. **up to the bit** to the highest speed allowed by the restraint applied.
■ **bitless** *adjective* not having a bridle bit E17.

bit /bɪt/ *noun*[2] & *adjective*.
[ORIGIN Old English *bita* = Old Frisian *bita*, Old High German *bizzo* (Middle High German *bizze*, German *Bissen*), Old Norse *biti*, from Germanic, from base of BITE *verb*.]
▸ **A** *noun*. †**1** A bite or mouthful. OE–M17.
2 A morsel or small piece of food. ME.
3 A small piece, a fragment (of something); a small portion or quantity, a little. Freq. foll. by *of*. L16. ▸**b** A small item in a popular periodical. *arch.* L19. ▸**c** More fully ***bit part***. A small acting role in a play or film. E20.

SHAKES. *Tr. & Cr.* The fragments, scraps, the bits, and greasy relics Of her o'er-eaten faith. B. STOKER A most noble ruin . . full of beautiful and romantic bits. D. H. LAWRENCE He's lost every bit of shame—every bit—if ever he had any—which I doubt very much. L. URIS By 1900 there were fifty thousand Jews in Palestine and a bit more social life for Jossi.

4 a A sum of money. *arch. slang.* E17. ▸**b** An obsolete silver coin of the southern states of America, the W. Indies, etc., having a value equal to some fraction of the Spanish dollar; the value of this coin. Still *US*, a unit of value equivalent to one-eighth of a dollar, the amount of 12½ cents, (used almost exclusively in even multiples). L17. ▸**c** A small coin. *colloq.* E19.

b J. W. SCHULTZ Whisky dropped to the price of 'two bits' per drink.

c threepenny bit etc.
5 a A moment; *a* short time. *colloq.* M17. ▸**b** *The* nick of time. *Scot.* L18. ▸**c** A prison sentence. *slang.* M19.

a K. AMIS He couldn't be expected to get on with his play for a bit. **c** E. R. HAGEMANN Away he went to the Minnesota big house for a ten-year bit.

6 In full ***bit of fluff***, ***bit of goods***, (arch.) ***bit of muslin***, ***bit of skirt***, ***bit of stuff***, etc. A (young) woman. *slang* (usu. *derog.*). E19.

M. GEE Mr. Tatlock . . went and married some young bit half his age.

7 An action or display of attitude, an adopted role. Esp. in ***the — bit***, ***one's — bit*** (the specified action etc. being well known or characteristic). *slang* (orig. *US*). M20.

F. ASTAIRE We were in Detroit—stranded—and that is where Mother did the pawning-of-the-jewels bit.

8 In *pl.* A person's genitals. *colloq.* L20.

Loaded Airing your bits in public . . has remained taboo.

— PHRASES: **a bit** — *colloq.* somewhat —. **a bit much** rather excessive, annoying. **a bit of** *colloq.* (*a*) rather; (*b*) a small quantity of; (*c*) a fair quantity of. **a bit of a —** a small or unimportant example of, a mild case of. ***a bit of all right***: see ALL RIGHT *noun phr.* ***a bit of crumpet***: see CRUMPET 5. ***a bit of no good***: see GOOD *noun.* ***a bit thick***: see THICK *adjective.* ***a wee bit***: see WEE *adjective.* **bit by bit** gradually. ***bit of fluff***, ***bit of goods***, ***bit of muslin***: see sense 6 above. ***bit of rough***: see ROUGH *noun.* ***bit of skirt***: see sense 6 above. ***bit of spare***: see SPARE *noun*[1] 3. ***bit of stuff***: see sense 6 above. **bits and bats**, **bits and bobs**, **bits and pieces** *colloq.* odds and ends. **do one's bit** *colloq.* contribute service or money to a cause. **every bit as** *colloq.* quite as. ***give a bit of one's mind to***: see MIND *noun*[1]. **go to bits** *colloq.* go to pieces. **not a bit (of it)** *colloq.* not at all. ***one's — bit***: see sense 7 above. **take a bit of doing** *colloq.* require all one's efforts, be difficult to do. ***tear off a bit***: see TEAR *verb*[1]. ***the — bit***: see sense 7 above. **to bits** *colloq.* into small fragments. TWIDDLY ***bit***.
— COMB.: ***bit part***: see sense 3c above; **bit-player** an actor of bit parts.
▸ **B** *attrib.* or as *adjective*. Little, small. *Scot.* L18.

bit /bɪt/ *noun*[3]. M20.
[ORIGIN Abbreviation of *binary digit* (see BINARY *adjective*), after BIT *noun*[2] & *adjective*.]
Chiefly COMPUTING. A unit of information expressed as a choice between two equally probable alternatives (represented by the values 0 and 1).
parity bit: see PARITY *noun*[1] 3c.
— COMB.: **bitmap** *noun & verb* (*a*) *noun* a representation in which each item is shown by one or more bits of information; *esp.* a display of the contents of a memory store; (*b*) *verb trans.* provide with or represent by a bitmap; **bit rate** the number of bits per second that can be transmitted along a digital network; **bitstream** (*a*) a stream of data in binary form; (*b*) (**Bitstream**) (proprietary name for) a system of digital-to-analogue signal conversion used in some audio CD players, in which the signal from the CD is digitally processed to give a signal at a higher frequency before being converted to an analogue signal; **bit string** a sequence of bits representing a character.
■ **bitwise** *adjective* designating an operator in a programming language which manipulates the individual bits in a byte or word L20.

bit /bɪt/ *verb*[1] *trans.* Infl. **-tt-**. L16.
[ORIGIN from BIT *noun*[1].]
Provide with or accustom to a bit; *fig.* curb, restrain.

bit *verb*[2] var. of BUDE.

bit *verb*[3] *pa. t.* & *pple* of BITE *verb*.

bitch /bɪtʃ/ *noun* & *adjective*.
[ORIGIN Old English *biċċe* rel. to Old Norse *bikkja*.]
▸ **A** *noun*. **1** A female dog. OE. ▸**b** A female fox, otter, wolf, or (occas.) similar animal. LME.
2 A man. Latterly *derog.* Now *rare*. ME. ▸**b** An effeminate man; a passive homosexual. *derog. slang.* E20.
3 A woman, esp. (formerly) a promiscuous one or (now) a malicious or treacherous one. *derog.* LME. ▸**b** Any woman (used in a non-derogatory sense). *black slang.* L20.

Company Does saying 'no' to people make you feel like a bitch?

4 Something difficult or unpleasant. *colloq.* M18.

Quarterly The night-shift . . is such a bitch.

5 A simple lamp made by placing a wick in bacon fat. *Canad.* E20.
6 a A complaint. M20. ▸**b** A person who makes malicious or spitefully critical comments. M20.
▸ **B** *attrib.* or as *adjective*. (Of an animal) female; like a bitch. LME.
— PHRASES ETC.: **bitch goddess** (material or worldly) success. **bitch-slap** *US colloq.* deliver a stinging blow to. ***son of a bitch***: see SON *noun*[1].
■ **bitchery** *noun* bitchy behaviour M16.

bitch /bɪtʃ/ *verb*. L17.
[ORIGIN from the noun.]
†**1** *verb intrans.* Frequent the company of prostitutes; call someone 'bitch'. L17–E18.
2 *verb trans.* Spoil, botch. Freq. foll. by *up*. *colloq.* E19.
3 *verb trans.* & *intrans.* Behave bitchily (towards); be spiteful, malicious, or unfair (to). *colloq.* M20.

ROSEMARY HARRIS I'm sorry I bitched you. *Sunday Telegraph* They gossip and bitch about other colleagues.

4 *verb intrans.* Complain, grumble. *colloq.* M20.

H. N. SCHWARZKOPF The officers and enlisted men bitched nonstop about the cold.

■ **bitching** *adjective* (*slang*, chiefly *US*) (*a*) expressive of contempt, derision, dislike, or anger; (*b*) great, excellent, wonderful: E20.

bitchy /ˈbɪtʃi/ *adjective*. E20.
[ORIGIN from BITCH *noun* + -Y[1].]
1 Sexually provocative; malicious, catty. E20.
2 Of a male dog: resembling a bitch. M20.
■ **bitchily** *adverb* M20. **bitchiness** *noun* M20.

bite /bʌɪt/ *noun*. L15.
[ORIGIN from the verb.]
1 The action or an act of biting. L15. ▸**b** The bringing together of the teeth in occlusion; the imprint of this in a plastic material. M19. ▸**c** The corrosive action of acid on a metal in etching. L19. ▸**d** The action of a machine indenting metal etc. L19. ▸**e** The keen cutting effect of a harsh wind. L19. ▸**f** *fig.* Incisiveness; point or cogency of style, language, etc. L19.
2 a A piece bitten off; a mouthful; a morsel of food; a small meal, a snack. Now freq. explicitly ***a bite to eat***. M16. ▸**b** Food to eat. *arch.* M16.

a TOLKIEN I haven't had a bite since breakfast. C. ISHERWOOD Taking a huge bite out of his sandwich. T. SHARPE He'd . . have a bite to eat in a pub. M. GEE Grandpa never ate more than a bite and the rest sat on his plate. **b** M. E. BRADDON He had lain . . for fourteen days without either bite or sup.

3 ANGLING. The seizure of bait by a fish. L16.

W. S. MAUGHAM Occasionally he got a bite, now and then a fish.

4 A wound inflicted by biting. E17.

R. LEHMANN Rat bites can be very poisonous. W. BOYD The tiny black flies that raised florin sized bites.

5 PRINTING (now *hist.*). A blank due to the accidental covering of part of the forme by the frisket. L17.
†**6** An imposition, a deception; a person who or thing which swindles or deceives. *slang.* E18–M19.
7 Grip, hold, (*lit.* & *fig.*). M19.
8 A share of profits etc. *N. Amer. slang.* E20.
— PHRASES: ***a bite and a sup***: see SUP *noun*[1]. ***a second bite at the cherry***: see CHERRY *noun*. ***bite and sup***: see SUP *noun*[1]. **one's bite** (opp. ***one's bark***) one's actions as opp. to one's words. ***open bite***: see OPEN *adjective*. **put the bite on** *slang* (orig. *US*) ask for a loan, extort money from, threaten, blackmail. ***two bites at the cherry***: see CHERRY *noun*.
— COMB.: **bite-size**, **bite-sized** *adjectives* small enough to be eaten in one bite; very small or short.

B

bite /bʌɪt/ *verb*. Pa. t. **bit** /bɪt/; pa. pple **bitten** /ˈbɪt(ə)n/, (now *arch. & non-standard*) **bit**.
[ORIGIN Old English *bītan* = Old Frisian *bīta*, Old Saxon *bītan* (Dutch *bijten*), Old High German *bīzan* (German *beissen*), Old Norse *bíta*, Gothic *beitan*, from Germanic.]
1 *verb trans. & intrans.* Cut (into), pierce, nip, or wound with the teeth (*verb intrans.* habitually); take a bite (from); (with adverbial compl.) remove or sever by biting. OE.
I. WATTS Let dogs delight to bark and bite. DAY LEWIS I bite into my chocolate. S. BECKETT Takes carrot from coat pocket, bites off a piece. W. MAXWELL My grandfather. . was bitten on the ear by a rat or a ferret and died . . of blood poisoning. D. M. THOMAS She was . . nibbling a cucumber sandwich (he glimpsed her small, pearly, even teeth as she bit).
2 *verb trans. & intrans.* Of something sharp or with a sharp edge: cut (into), penetrate. OE.
TENNYSON Who heaved his blade aloft, And crack'd the helmet thro', and bit the bone. B. ENGLAND The razor bit deeply in and the blood spouted startlingly. P. MATTHIESSEN The thin straps bite at my shoulders.
3 *verb trans. & intrans.* Wound with mouthparts, the jaw, pincers, etc.; *loosely* (of a living creature) sting. ME.
AV *Prov.* 23:32 At the last it biteth like a serpent. G. B. SHAW He put his handkerchief round my neck because a gnat bit me.
†**4** *verb trans. & intrans.* Nibble, eat. ME–M17.
5 *verb trans. & intrans.* Cause a sharp (esp. smarting) pain (to). ME.
J. LYLY These medecines bite hot.
†**6** *verb trans. & intrans.* Speak sharply or deprecatingly (against); carp (at). ME–L17.
7 *verb trans. & intrans.* Engage (sympathy, interest, etc.); impress. *arch.* LME.
8 *verb trans. & intrans.* Of an implement, part of a mechanism, etc.: grip or take hold of (a surface etc.). E16. ▸**b** *verb intrans. spec.* in CRICKET. Of the ball: get a grip of the surface of the ground on pitching. M19.
9 *verb trans. & intrans.* Affect painfully or harmfully with intense cold. Cf. ***frost-bitten***. M16.
10 *verb trans. & intrans.* Corrode, as an acid or alkali; act as a mordant (upon). E17.
J. BETJEMAN The chemicals from various factories Have bitten deep into the Portland stone.
11 *verb intrans.* Of a fish & *fig.*: take or be caught by bait; snap *at* bait. M17.
I. WALTON He thought that Trout bit not for hunger but wantonness. T. JEFFERSON Do not bite at the bait of pleasure till you know there is no hook beneath it. M. PUZO 'It's a good story, you'll like it.' And she saw me bite.
12 *verb trans.* Deceive, swindle. Now only in *pass. colloq.* E18.
13 *verb intrans.* Have an (esp. adverse) effect; make an impression. E20.
14 *verb trans.* Borrow from (a person), esp. without intention or likelihood of repayment. (Foll. by *for* the thing borrowed.) *Austral. & NZ slang.* E20.
15 *verb trans.* Excite; worry, perturb. Esp. in ***what's biting you?*** *colloq.* (orig. *US*). E20.
– PHRASES: **bite a person's head off**, †**bite a person's nose off** respond curtly or angrily. **bite back** restrain (speech) by an effort. ***bite by the nose***: see NOSE *noun*. **bite off more than one can chew** (orig. *US*) undertake too much, be too ambitious. ***bite one's lip***: see LIP *noun*. ***bite one's nails***: see NAIL *noun*. ***bite on granite***: see GRANITE *noun*. **bite on the bullet**, **bite the bullet** behave stoically, avoid showing fear or distress. **bite the dust**, **bite the ground** *joc. & rhet.* fall and die, come to an unfortunate end. **bite the hand that feeds one** injure a benefactor, act ungratefully. ***bite the thumb at***: see THUMB *noun*. **bitten with** infected by (enthusiasm etc.). **something to bite on** *fig.* a problem to work on or think seriously about. **the biter bit** the deceiver deceived in turn.

biter /ˈbʌɪtə/ *noun*. ME.
[ORIGIN from BITE *verb* + -ER[1].]
1 *gen.* A person who or thing which bites. ME.
2 *spec.* A deceiver, a swindler. *obsolete* exc. in ***the biter bit*** (cf. BITE *verb*). L17.

biternate /bʌɪˈtəːneɪt/ *adjective*. L18.
[ORIGIN from BI- + TERNATE.]
BOTANY. Of a compound leaf: ternate with the primary divisions themselves being ternate.

biting /ˈbʌɪtɪŋ/ *adjective*. ME.
[ORIGIN from BITE *verb* + -ING[2].]
1 That bites. ME.
2 *spec.* That causes sharp physical or mental pain; pungent, stinging; sarcastic. ME.
– SPECIAL COLLOCATIONS: ***biting lice***: see LOUSE *noun* 1. ***biting*** MIDGE. ***biting stonecrop***: see STONE *noun, adjective, & adverb*.
■ **bitingly** *adverb* LME.

bitonality /bʌɪtəʊˈnalɪti/ *noun*. E20.
[ORIGIN from BI- + TONALITY.]
MUSIC. The simultaneous use of two keys in a composition.
■ **bi'tonal** *adjective* characterized by bitonality M20.

Bitrex /ˈbɪtrɛks/ *noun*. M20.
[ORIGIN Invented name.]
(Proprietary name for) a bitter-tasting synthetic organic compound (denatonium benzoate, $C_{28}H_{34}N_2O_3$) added to cleaning fluids or other products to make them unpalatable.

bitsy /ˈbɪtsi/ *adjective*. *colloq.* E20.
[ORIGIN from BIT *noun*[2] or BITTY *adjective* + -SY.]
Tiny, (charmingly) small. Cf. ITSY-BITSY.

bitt /bɪt/ *noun & verb*. ME.
[ORIGIN Prob. orig. a Low German sea term: cf. Low German, Dutch *beting*.]
▸ **A** *noun*. Any of the posts fixed in pairs on the deck of a ship, for fastening cables, belaying ropes, etc. Usu. in *pl.* ME.
▸ **B** *verb trans.* Coil or fasten upon the bitts. M18.

†**bittacle** *noun* see BINNACLE.

bitten *verb pa. pple* of BITE *verb*.

bitter /ˈbɪtə/ *noun*[1]. OE.
[ORIGIN from the adjective.]
1 That which is bitter; bitterness. OE.
TENNYSON All words . . Failing to give the bitter of the sweet. E. JONG Woman is a Mixture of Sweets and Bitters.
2 A bitter medicinal substance; now *esp.* a liquor flavoured with gentian, wormwood, orange peel, etc., used to promote appetite or digestion or as a flavouring. Now usu. in *pl.* E18.
J. DOS PASSOS Gin with a dash of bitters in it . . helped her over the last few days of the crossing.
3 (A drink of) bitter beer. M19.
Westminster Gazette A bitter having been bought, he quaffed it to his second's health. D. L. SAYERS He ordered a tankard of bitter.

bitter /ˈbɪtə/ *noun*[2]. E17.
[ORIGIN from BITT *noun* + -ER[1].]
NAUTICAL. A turn of the anchor cable around the bitts.
– COMB.: **bitter end** (*a*) a part of the anchor cable attached to the bitts, remaining on board when the ship is at anchor; (*b*) (see BITTER *adjective*).

†**bitter** *noun*[3] see BITTERN *noun*[1].

bitter /ˈbɪtə/ *adjective & adverb*.
[ORIGIN Old English *biter* = Old Saxon, Old High German *bittar* (Dutch, German *bitter*), Old Norse *bitr*, Gothic *baitrs*, prob. from Germanic base of BITE *verb*.]
▸ **A** *adjective*. **1** Having a sharp pungent taste, as of wormwood, quinine, etc. Opp. ***sweet***. OE. ▸**b** *fig.* Unpalatable; unpleasant; hard to swallow or admit. E19.
BURKE All men are agreed to call vinegar sour, honey sweet, and aloes bitter. M. MITCHELL Without sugar or cream it was bitter as gall. ANTHONY HUXLEY Bitter and very toxic leaves which even goats will not sample. **b** COLERIDGE Some bitter truths, respecting our military arrangements.
a bitter taste in the mouth: see TASTE *noun*[1].
2 Attended by severe pain or suffering; grievous; full of affliction. OE.
W. S. CHURCHILL The same bitter struggle with nature. E. M. FORSTER I know by bitter experience.
†**3** Causing pain or suffering; cruel, harmful, severe. OE–M17.
SHAKES. *1 Hen. IV* Those blessed feet Which fourteen hundred years ago were nail'd For our advantage on the bitter cross.
4 Characterized by intense animosity; virulent. OE.
DAY LEWIS She was . . capable of bitter resistance against domestic bullying. C. HILL Renegades against whom Cromwell was particularly bitter.
5 Of words or their utterer: stinging, cutting, harsh, cruelly reproachful. ME.
P. G. WODEHOUSE It was a good exit speech—mordant—bitter, satirical.
6 Of wind: sharp, keen, severe. Of weather: bitingly cold. ME.
J. C. POWYS The bitter east wind made the girl pull her black woollen scarf tightly round her neck. J. CARY It had been a bitter winter—Fred and I came into the . . kitchen quite perished.
7 Expressing or betokening intense grief or affliction of spirit. ME.
C. KINGSLEY Bursting into bitter tears.
8 Mournful; full of affliction L15.
WORDSWORTH Concealing In solitude her bitter feeling.
– COMB. & SPECIAL COLLOCATIONS: **bitter-apple** = COLOCYNTH; **bitter bark** any of various shrubs and trees yielding a bitter principle from the bark; **bitter beer**: much flavoured with hops (opp. *mild*); ***bitter cassava***: see CASSAVA 1; **bitter-cress** any cruciferous plant of the genus *Cardamine*; **bitter-cucumber** = ***bitter-gourd*** below; **bitter end** *the* last extremity [but perh. from ***bitter end*** (a) s.v. BITTER *noun*[2]]; **bitter-ender** *colloq.* a person who fights or holds out to the bitter end, a person who refuses to yield or compromise; **bitter-gourd** (*a*) = COLOCYNTH; (*b*) = KARELA; **bitter lemon** a carbonated semi-sweet soft drink flavoured with lemons; **bitter-nut** *N. Amer.* swamp hickory, *Carya amara*; **bitter orange** the Seville orange; ***bitter*** PECAN; **bitter pill** *fig.* a hard thing to take, an unpalatable truth etc.; **bitter pit** a disease of apples, characterized by sunken brown spots; **bitter root** any of various plants with bitter roots; esp. (*N. Amer.*) *Lewisia rediviva*, of the purslane family, with edible roots and red or white flowers; **bitter sage** = ***wood sage*** s.v. WOOD *noun*[1] & *adjective*[1]; **bitter-vetch** any of certain vetches and vetchlings, esp. *Lathyrus linifolius* and *Vicia orobus*; **bitter-weed** any of various bitter plants, esp. (*N. Amer.*) of the family Compositae; **bitter-wood** (the wood of) a W. Indian tree, *Picrasma excelsa* (family Simaroubaceae). See also BITTERSWEET.
▸ **B** *adverb*. Bitterly. *arch., poet., & dial.* OE.
T. CAMPBELL How bitter she wept o'er the victim of war! S. BEDFORD It was bitter cold.
■ **bitterish** *adjective* L16. **bitterly** *adverb* in a bitter manner, with bitterness OE. **bitterness** *noun* the quality or state of being bitter; bitter taste; grievousness to the mind; acrimony, animosity; intensity of frost or cold; an instance or feeling of bitterness: OE.

bitter /ˈbɪtə/ *verb*.
[ORIGIN Old English *biterian*, formed as BITTER *adjective*.]
†**1** *verb intrans.* Be or become bitter. Only in OE.
2 *verb trans.* Make bitter. ME.

bitterling /ˈbɪtəlɪŋ/ *noun*. L19.
[ORIGIN German, formed as BITTER *adjective* (translating Latin *amarus*) + -LING[1].]
A small central European freshwater fish, *Rhodeus amarus*, of the carp family.

bittern /ˈbɪtən/ *noun*[1]. Orig. †-**r**. See also BLITTER. LME.
[ORIGIN Old French *butor* from Proto-Romance, from Latin *butio* bittern + *taurus* bull. Forms with -*n* (16) are perh. due to assoc. with *hern* HERON.]
Any of several marsh birds of the heron family, generally smaller than herons; *esp.* the European *Botaurus stellaris* and the American *B. lentiginosus*, which have brown and buff striated plumage and are noted for the deep booming call of the male in the breeding season.
little bittern a small bittern of the genus *Ixobrychus*, esp. *I. minutus*, a vagrant to Britain. ***sunbittern***: see SUN *noun*[1].

bittern /ˈbɪtən/ *noun*[2]. L17.
[ORIGIN Obscurely from BITTER *adjective*.]
1 The lye which remains after the crystallization of salt from seawater etc. L17.
2 A mixture of quassia and other bitter substances formerly used in adulterating beer. L18.

bittersweet /ˈbɪtəswiːt/ *noun & adjective*. LME.
[ORIGIN from BITTER *adjective* + SWEET *noun, adjective*.]
▸ **A** *noun*. **1** A bittersweet thing; sweetness or pleasure alloyed with bitterness. LME.
2 A variety of apple with a bittersweet taste. LME.
3 = ***woody*** NIGHTSHADE. M16.
4 Any of several climbing shrubs of the genus *Celastrus* (family Celastraceae), *esp.* (more fully ***climbing bittersweet***, ***false bittersweet***, ***American bittersweet***) *C. scandens* of N. America (also called ***staff vine***). E19.
▸ **B** *adjective*. Sweet with an admixture or aftertaste of bitterness; *fig.* agreeable or pleasant with an alloy of pain or bitterness. E17.
Bookseller A bittersweet tale of a 12-year-old American boy.
bittersweet chocolate *N. Amer.* plain chocolate.
■ †**bitter-sweeting** *noun* (*rare*, Shakes.) = BITTERSWEET *noun* 2: only in L16.

bittock /ˈbɪtək/ *noun*. *Scot. & N. English*. E19.
[ORIGIN from BIT *noun*[2] + -OCK.]
A small piece or portion.

bitty /ˈbɪti/ *adjective*. L19.
[ORIGIN from BIT *noun*[2] + -Y[1].]
1 Made up of unrelated bits, scrappy. L19.
2 Covered with bits of some material. E20.
3 = BITSY. *N. Amer. colloq.* E20.
■ **bittiness** *noun* M20.

Bitumastic /bɪtjʊˈmastɪk/ *noun*. L19.
[ORIGIN from BITUMEN + MASTIC *noun*.]
(Proprietary name for) any of various asphaltic compositions used as protective coatings etc.

†**bitume** *noun & verb*. E17.
[ORIGIN French & Italian, formed as BITUMEN.]
▸ **A** *noun*. = BITUMEN. E–M17.
▸ **B** *verb trans.* Smear or spread with bitumen. *rare* (Shakes.). Only in E17.

bitumen /ˈbɪtjʊmən/ *noun*. LME.
[ORIGIN Latin *bitumen*, *-min-*.]
1 Naturally occurring asphalt from the Middle East, used as mortar etc. LME.
2 Any natural or artificial black or brown solid or viscous liquid consisting largely of hydrocarbons. E17.
3 A pigment made from asphalt. M19.
4 *The* tarred road. *Austral. & NZ colloq.* M20.
■ †**bituminate** *verb trans.* cement with bitumen; convert into or impregnate with bitumen: E17–L18. **bitumi'niferous** *adjective* yielding bitumen L18.

bituminize /bɪˈtjuːmɪnʌɪz/ *verb trans.* Also **-ise**. M18.
[ORIGIN formed as BITUMEN + -IZE.]
Convert into bitumen; impregnate or cover with bitumen.
■ **bitumini'zation** *noun* E19.

bituminous /bɪˈtjuːmɪnəs/ *adjective*. M16.
[ORIGIN French *bitumineux* from Latin *bituminosus*, formed as BITUMEN: see -OUS.]
Of or containing bitumen; of the nature of bitumen.
bituminous coal black coal which has a relatively high volatile content and burns with a bright smoky flame.

biunique /bʌɪjuːˈniːk/ *adjective.* **M20.**
[**ORIGIN** from **BI-** + **UNIQUE.**]
Designating or having a one-to-one correspondence between members of two sets.
■ **biuniqueness** *noun* **M20.**

biuret /ˈbʌɪjʊrɛt/ *noun.* **M19.**
[**ORIGIN** German, formed as **BI-**, **UREA**, **-URET.**]
CHEMISTRY. A crystalline compound, $NH_2CONHCONH_2$, formed when urea is heated.
– **COMB.:** **biuret reaction** the formation of a violet colour when compounds containing the group ·CONH· are treated with copper sulphate solution in the presence of alkali; **biuret test** this reaction used as a test esp. for proteins.

bivalence /*esp. CHEMISTRY* bʌɪˈveɪl(ə)ns, *esp. CYTOLOGY* ˈbɪv(ə)l(ə)ns/ *noun.* **L19.**
[**ORIGIN** from **BI-** + **VALENCE** *noun*[1].]
1 *CHEMISTRY & CYTOLOGY.* The quality of being divalent. **L19.**
2 *LOGIC.* The existence of only two truth values; *spec.* in ***principle of bivalence***: that every proposition is either true or false. **M20.**
■ **bivalency** *noun* **L19.**

bivalent /*esp. CHEMISTRY* bʌɪˈveɪl(ə)nt, *esp. CYTOLOGY* ˈbɪv(ə)l(ə)nt/ *adjective & noun.* **M19.**
[**ORIGIN** from **BI-** + **-VALENT.**]
▸ **A** *adjective.* **1** *CHEMISTRY.* Having a valency of two; divalent. **M19.**
2 *CYTOLOGY.* Of, pertaining to, or forming a bivalent (see below). **L19.**
▸ **B** *noun. CYTOLOGY.* A pair of homologous or partly homologous chromosomes united during meiosis. **M20.**

bivallate /bʌɪˈvalət/ *adjective.* **M20.**
[**ORIGIN** from **BI-** + **VALLATE** *adjective.*]
Having two encircling ramparts.

bivalve /ˈbʌɪvalv/ *adjective & noun.* **M17.**
[**ORIGIN** from **BI-** + **VALVE** *noun.*]
▸ **A** *adjective.* **1** Chiefly *ZOOLOGY.* Having two folding parts; *spec.* (of a mollusc) having a shell of two parts hinged together by a ligament. **M17.**
2 *BOTANY.* Of a seed capsule: having two valves. **M18.**
▸ **B** *noun. ZOOLOGY.* A member of the class Bivalvia; a bivalve mollusc. **L17.**

bivariate /bʌɪˈvɛːrɪət/ *adjective.* **E20.**
[**ORIGIN** from **BI-** + **VARIATE** *noun.*]
STATISTICS. Involving or depending on two variates.

biventral /bʌɪˈvɛntr(ə)l/ *adjective.* **E18.**
[**ORIGIN** from **BI-** + **VENTRAL** *adjective.*]
ANATOMY. = **DIGASTRIC** *adjective.*
■ †**biventer** *noun* = **DIGASTRIC** *noun* **E18–M19.**

bivious /ˈbɪvɪəs/ *adjective.* **M17.**
[**ORIGIN** from Latin *bivius*, from **BI-** + *via* way, + **-OUS.**]
Having or offering two ways.

bivium /ˈbɪvɪəm/ *noun.* **L19.**
[**ORIGIN** Latin = place where two ways meet, formed as **BI-** + *via* way: see **-IUM.**]
ZOOLOGY. The two posterior ambulacra of an echinoderm (dorsal in a holothurian). Cf. **TRIVIUM** 2.

bivoltine /bʌɪˈvɒltʌɪn/ *adjective.* **L19.**
[**ORIGIN** French *bivoltin*, from Italian *volta* time: see **BI-**, **-INE**[1].]
Of an insect (esp. a silkworm moth): producing two broods in a year.

bivouac /ˈbɪvʊak, ˈbɪvwak/ *noun & verb.* **E18.**
[**ORIGIN** French, prob. from Swiss German *Bîwacht* lit. 'extra watch' (see **BY** *adjective*, **WATCH** *noun*), said to have been used in Aargau and Zürich to denote a patrol of citizens to assist the ordinary town watch.]
▸ **A** *noun.* Orig., a night watch by a whole army. Later, a temporary encampment, usu. for the night, without tents; the place of such an encampment. **E18.**
▸ **B** *verb intrans. & trans.* in *pass.* Infl. **-ck-**. Remain in the open air (esp. during the night) without tents etc. **E19.**

bivvy /ˈbɪvi/ *noun & verb intrans. slang.* **E20.**
[**ORIGIN** Abbreviation of **BIVOUAC.**]
▸ **A** *noun.* A shelter; a small tent. **E20.**
bivvy bag, **bivvy sac(k)** a person-sized waterproof bag in which one may sleep when out of doors.
▸ **B** *verb intrans.* Spend the night in the open air without a tent, esp. in a bivvy bag; encamp with little or no shelter. **M20.**

biweekly /bʌɪˈwiːkli/ *adverb, adjective, & noun.* **M19.**
[**ORIGIN** from **BI-** + **WEEKLY** *adverb, adjective & noun.*]
▸ **A** *adverb.* Every two weeks or twice a week. **M19.**
▸ **B** *adjective & noun.* (A periodical) appearing or occurring biweekly. **L19.**

bixbyite /ˈbɪksbɪʌɪt/ *noun.* **L19.**
[**ORIGIN** from Maynard *Bixby*, late 19th-cent. US mineralogist + **-ITE**[1].]
MINERALOGY. A rare mixed oxide of manganese and ferric iron occurring as black metallic cubic crystals.

bixin /ˈbɪksɪn/ *noun.* **M19.**
[**ORIGIN** from mod. Latin *Bixa* (*orellana*), the tree yielding annatto (from Carib *bija* red) + **-IN**[1].]
CHEMISTRY. A carotenoid which is the principal pigment of annatto.

biyearly /bʌɪˈjɪəli, -ˈjəː-/ *adjective & adverb.* **L19.**
[**ORIGIN** from **BI-** + **YEARLY** *adjective.*]
(Appearing or occurring) every two years or twice a year.

biz /bɪz/ *noun. colloq.* (orig. *US*). **M19.**
[**ORIGIN** Abbreviation.]
Business. Freq. in ***showbiz*** s.v. **SHOW** *noun*[1].

bizarre /bɪˈzɑː/ *adjective & noun.* **M17.**
[**ORIGIN** French from Italian *bizzarro* angry, of unknown origin. Cf. Spanish & Portuguese *bizarro* handsome, brave.]
▸ **A** *adjective.* **1** Eccentric, fantastic, grotesque. **M17.**
2 Designating variegated forms of garden flowers, as carnations, tulips, etc. **M18.**
▸ **B** *noun.* **1** A bizarre carnation, tulip, etc. **L18.**
2 *absol. The* bizarre quality of things; bizarre things. **M19.**
■ **bizarrely** *adverb* **L19.** **bizarreness** *noun* **E20.** **bizarrerie** /bɪˈzɑːrəriː/ *noun* [French: see **-ERY**] (a) bizarre quality **M18.**

bizarro /bɪˈzɑːrəʊ/ *adjective. colloq.* (chiefly *US*). **L20.**
[**ORIGIN** Italian; orig. in ***mondo bizarro*** (see **MONDO** *adverb*).]
Bizarre, strange.

> G. Cox Her mind wasn't expanding fast enough to keep up with all these bizarro concepts.

†**bizcacha** *noun* var. of **VISCACHA.**

BJP *abbreviation.*
Bharatiya Janata Party.

bk *abbreviation.*
Book.

Bk *symbol.*
CHEMISTRY. Berkelium.

BL *abbreviation.*
1 Bachelor of Law.
2 Bill of lading.
3 *hist.* British Leyland.
4 British Library.

bl. *abbreviation.*
1 Barrel.
2 Black.

blab /blab/ *noun*[1]. **ME.**
[**ORIGIN** Prob. ult. from imit. Germanic base: cf. Old High German *blabbizōn* (Middle High German *blepzen*), Icelandic *blabbra* (Danish *blabbre*).]
1 A person who gossips or chatters; a babbler; a telltale. **ME.**
2 Loose talk or chatter; gossip. **LME.**

blab /blab/ *noun*[2]. Long *obsolete* exc. *dial.* **M17.**
[**ORIGIN** Var. of **BLEB** *noun*, **BLOB** *noun.*]
A bubble; a blister.

blab /blab/ *verb*[1]. Infl. **-bb-**. **LME.**
[**ORIGIN** from **BLAB** *noun*[1].]
1 *verb intrans.* Chatter, babble. Now *spec.* talk foolishly or indiscreetly, reveal secrets. **LME.**

> C. Morgan An honest blackmailer who never blabbed without reason.

2 *verb trans.* Babble. Now *spec.* tell foolishly or indiscreetly, reveal (a secret). Freq. foll. by *out.* **M16.**

> W. H. Dixon He blabbed out the secret to his priest. T. E. Lawrence I begin to blab . . what I feel, just like any other chap. *transf.*: Shakes. *2 Hen. VI* Beaufort's red sparkling eyes blab his heart's malice.

– **COMB.:** **blab-mouth** *slang* = **BLAB** *noun*[1] 1.

blab /blab/ *verb*[2] *trans. obsolete* exc. *Scot.* Infl. **-bb-**. **E17.**
[**ORIGIN** Cf. **BLAB** *noun*[2].]
Make swollen (the cheeks) with weeping etc.; bedaub.

blabber /ˈblabə/ *noun.* **ME.**
[**ORIGIN** from **BLAB** *verb*[1] + **-ER**[1].]
= **BLAB** *noun*[1] 1.

†**blabber** *adjective* see **BLUBBER** *adjective.*

blabber /ˈblabə/ *verb.* Now *Scot. & N. Amer.* **LME.**
[**ORIGIN** formed as **BLAB** *noun*[1]: see **-ER**[5].]
†**1** *verb intrans.* Speak inarticulately, mumble, babble. **LME–L18.**
2 *verb intrans.* Chatter, blab. **LME.**

> A. J. Cronin Get ahead wi' it now and don't blabber so much.

†**3** *verb trans.* = **BLAB** *verb*[1] 2. **E16–E17.**
†**4** *verb intrans.* Move the tongue between the lips in mockery. **M16–E17.**
– **COMB.:** **blabbermouth** *slang* = **BLAB** *noun*[1] 1.

black /blak/ *noun.* **OE.**
[**ORIGIN** The adjective used ellipt. or absol.]
1 Black substance; *spec.* †(***a***) ink; (***b***) black pigment, dye, or varnish (freq. with specifying word); (***c***) *dial.* soot. **OE.** ▸**b** *The* credit side of an account. Cf. **RED** *noun* 1d. **E20.**
carbon black, ***ivory black***, ***lampblack***, etc.
b in the black solvent, in credit.
2 Black colour; a shade of this; blackness, darkness. **ME.**

> W. M. Craig We must take black and white into our list, as colours with the painter though not with the optician. J. Cheever The cold black of 6 A.M.

in black and white (***a***) recorded in writing or print; (***b***) in monochrome film. †**under black and white** = *in black and white* (***a***) above.
3 A black speck or particle; *spec.* (***a***) in *pl.*, fungus or smut attacking wheat etc.; (***b***) a flake of soot, a smut. **ME.**
†**4** *The* pupil of the eye. **LME–M17.**
5 Black clothing or fabric, in *pl.* black clothes or (*arch.*) hangings, esp. as a sign of mourning. **LME.**

> L. Strachey The widowed lady, in her voluminous blacks. Dylan Thomas The Reverend Eli Jenkins . . gropes out of bed into his preacher's black.

All Black: see **ALL** *adverb* 1.
6 A member of a dark-skinned people, esp. one of African or Australian Aboriginal ancestry. **E17.**
7 A member of a party, faction, etc., adopting black as its colour. Cf. **WHITE** *noun* 14. **L17.**
8 *ellipt.* Anything distinguished by black colour, as the black divisions in roulette and rouge-et-noir, the black ball in snooker, a black postage stamp, a black horse, a black pigeon or duck, etc.; (usu. **B-**) the player of the black pieces in chess or draughts. **M19.**
Egyptian black: see **EGYPTIAN** *adjective.* **men in black** dark-clothed men of unknown identity who supposedly visit those who have seen a UFO or reported an alien encounter, in order to prevent them publicizing their experience. ***Welsh Black***: see **WELSH** *adjective.*
9 = **BLACKMAIL** *noun* 1b. *slang.* **E20.**
put the black on blackmail (a person).
10 A serious mistake or blunder (cf. ***black mark*** s.v. **BLACK** *adjective*). *slang.* **M20.**
put up a black make a serious error.
– **COMB.:** **black spot** the spot on which the black ball is placed in snooker.

black /blak/ *adjective.*
[**ORIGIN** Old English *blæc*, *blac-* corresp. to Old Saxon *blac* ink, Old High German *blah-*, *blach-*; cf. Old Norse *blakkr* dusky, black, dun: ult. origin unknown.]
▸ **I** *lit.* **1** Opposite to white; colourless from the absence or complete absorption of light. Also, so near this as to have no distinguishable colour, very dark. **OE.** ▸**b** *CARDS.* Belonging to spades or clubs. **L17.** ▸**c** Of coffee or (occas.) tea: served without milk, cream, etc. **L18.**

> AV *Matt.* 5:36 Thou canst not make one haire white or blacke. Pope The priest himself . . Pours the black wine. J. Rhys Her eyes . . were the blackest I had ever seen.

2 a Dark-skinned or dark-haired; swarthy. *obsolete* in *gen.* sense. **OE.** ▸**b** Of or pertaining to any human group having dark-coloured skin, esp. of African or Australian Aboriginal ancestry. **LME.**

> **b** T. Keneally 'Are there even any black ministers of religion?' 'The Benedictine priests . . did—I believe—ordain three aboriginal priests.' N. Gordimer Whites are not allowed to go into black townships without a permit. *New Statesman* A black section . . as an internal training-ground and pressure group.

3 Wearing black clothing. **ME.**
4 Deeply stained with dirt, soiled, filthy. **ME.**

> M. Drabble It was vaulted and filthy, black with the grime of decades.

5 Characterized by the absence of light; dusky, gloomy; overcast. **LME.**

> Byron The blackest sky Foretells the heaviest tempest. D. Bagley The sun had set and it was pitchy black.

▸ **II** *fig.* **6** Foreboding or threatening; angry, sulky; dismal; melancholy. **LME.**

> V. Brittain The black apprehension of the previous year, with its fear of bread riots and revolutions. S. King The depression had lifted . . , but he remembered how black it had been.

7 Foul, atrocious; wicked; hateful. **M16.**

> P. J. Bailey Die with the black lie flapping on your lips.

8 a Malignant, deadly; sinister. **L16.** ▸**b** Macabre; presenting tragedy or bitter reality in comic terms. **M20.**

> Hor. Walpole The throne . . usurped by the Queen's black enemy, Philip. **b** *Listener* His recent group of Swiftean black comedies.

9 Disgraceful, deserving censure, illegal. **E17.**
10 a Of work, goods, etc.: not (to be) undertaken or handled, because of an industrial dispute. **E20.** ▸**b** Of or performed by blacklegs during a strike. **M20.**
11 Contravening economic regulations. **M20.**
– **PHRASES:** **black and blue** discoloured with bruises. **black and tan** (***a***) (a terrier) with a black back and tan markings on face, flanks, and legs; (***b***) a drink composed of porter (or stout) and ale. **Black and Tans** *colloq.* an irregular force recruited in 1920 to fight Irish nationalist forces, so called from their wearing a mixture of black constabulary and khaki military uniforms. **black and white** (***a***) written, printed, etc., in black ink on white paper; (***b***) of a building: painted white with black timbers; (***c***) of film: not colour, monochrome; (***d***) *fig.* comprising only opposite extremes. **black in the face** purple in the face through strangulation, passion, or exertion. ***little black dress***: see **LITTLE** *adjective.* **not so black as one is painted** better than one's reputation. ***paint a person black***: see **PAINT** *verb.*
– **SPECIAL COLLOCATIONS & COMB.:** **Black Africa** Africa south of the Sahara inhabited predominantly by black people (as opp. to Arabs) or governed by black people (as opp. to white people). ***black alder***: see **ALDER** *noun* 1b. **black ant** any of various ants which are black in colour; *esp.* the small *Lasius niger*, which is abundant in Eurasia and N. America. ***black antimony***: see **ANTIMONY.** **black arches** = **NUN** *noun*[1] 3. **black art** [prob. after Low German *swarte*

B

kunst, German *schwarze Kunst*; cf. Latin *niger* black, (fig.) wicked, and medieval Latin var. *nigromantia* of *necromantia* NECROMANCY] magic, necromancy. **black ash** (the wood of) a N. American ash, *Fraxinus nigra*. **blackback** = *black-backed gull* below. **black-backed** *adjective* having a black back; ***black-backed gull***, any of several gulls with black backs and wings, *esp.* (more fully ***greater black-backed gull***) *Larus marinus* and (more fully ***lesser black-backed gull***) *L. fuscus*, both of the N. Atlantic. **black ball** (*a*) a ball placed in a ballot box etc. to record an adverse vote; (*b*) a hard black or black and white sweet; (*c*) ***black ball game***, a game of snooker the outcome of which depends on the final potting of the black ball. **blackball** *verb trans.* record an adverse vote against (a candidate) by placing a black ball in a ballot box etc.; *loosely* reject, ostracize. **black-band** (a deposit of) an earthy ironstone or siderite containing carbonaceous matter. **black bass** either of two freshwater fishes of the percoid family Centrarchidae, native to N. America and widely introduced elsewhere, the large-mouth *Micropterus salmoides* and the small-mouth *M. dolomieui*. **black bean** (*a*) (the black seed of) any of certain plants of the genus *Phaseolus*; (*b*) (the timber of) an Australian hardwood tree, *Castanospermum australe*. ***black bear***: see BEAR *noun*[1] 1. **black beetle** the cockroach. **black belt** (*a*) a region of the southern US in which black people predominate; (*b*) (the holder of) a belt marking the attainment of a certain high degree of proficiency in judo or karate. **black bent** a bent grass, *Agrostis gigantea*. ***black bindweed***: see BINDWEED 2. **black birch** (the wood of) either of two N. American birches, *Betula lenta* and *B. nigra*. **blackboard** a board with a dark (usu. black) surface used in schools etc. for writing or drawing on with chalk. **black body** PHYSICS a hypothetical perfect absorber and radiator of electromagnetic radiation. **black book** (*a*) *hist.* the distinctive name of various official books (usu. bound in black) of public significance; (*b*) (a book containing) a record of the names of people liable to censure or punishment (***in someone's black books***, in disfavour with someone); (*c*) a record of valuable, esp. confidential, information. **black bottom** (*a*) *US* a low-lying area inhabited by a black population; (*b*) a popular dance of the 1920s. **black box** any apparatus of unspecified or unknown internal design, *esp.* a flight recorder in an aircraft (not black in colour). **blackboy** (*a*) a young black man, a black manservant (now *offensive*); (*b*) an Australian grass tree of the genus *Xanthorrhoea*, esp. *X. preissii*. **black bread** coarse rye bread. **black-browed** *adjective* dark-browed, dark-faced; frowning; scowling. ***black bryony***: see BRYONY 2. **blackbuck** an Indian gazelle, *Antilope cervicapra*. **black bun** (*a*) rich fruit cake in a pastry case, traditionally eaten in Scotland at New Year. **blackbutt** (the timber of) an Australian eucalyptus, *Eucalyptus pilularis*. **black butter** = ***BEURRE noir***. **black cap**, **blackcap** (*a*) (***black cap***) *hist.* a cap worn by a judge when passing a sentence of death; (*b*) (***blackcap***) any of various birds having the top of the head black; *spec.* a warbler, *Sylvia atricapilla*; (*c*) a halved apple baked with the flat side downwards and topped with (caramelized) sugar; (*d*) *N. Amer.* = ***black RASPBERRY***. ***black CATTLE***. ***black chameleon***: see CHAMELEON *noun* 2. ***black cherry***: see CHERRY *noun*. **black coal** †(*a*) charcoal; (*b*) coal of a black colour, *esp.* bituminous coal. **black-coat (worker)** a person in a clerical or professional as distinguished from an industrial or commercial occupation. **blackcock** the male of the black grouse, *Tetrao tetrix*. ***black coffee***: see COFFEE *noun*. ***black COHOSH***. **Black Country** areas of the West Midlands of England supposedly blackened by the coal and iron trades. ***black cumin***: see CUMIN 2. ***black CURASSOW***. **black damp** = *choke-damp* s.v. CHOKE *verb*. **Black Death** the great epidemic of plague in Europe in the 14th cent. ***black diamond***: see DIAMOND *noun*. **black disc** a black vinyl gramophone record (opp. ***compact disc***). **black disease** (of sheep) necrotic hepatitis accompanying liver-fluke infestation. **black dog** †(*a*) *slang* a base silver coin; (*b*) melancholy or depression; ***have the black dog on one's back***, be in the sulks. ***black draught***: see DRAUGHT *noun* 3c. **black drop** †(*a*) a dark-coloured preparation containing opium; (*b*) a drop-shaped appearance of the disc of a planet (esp. Venus) at the beginning and end of solar transit. **black earth** dark soil, *spec.* = CHERNOZEM. **black economy** financial transactions etc. not officially declared or recorded. **black English** the form(s) of English used by black people, esp. in the US. **black eye** (*a*) an eye with a very dark-coloured iris; (*b*) an eye around which the skin is bruised and discoloured; (*c*) *fig.* a severe rebuff; a snub; (*d*) ***black-eye pea***, = ***black-eyed pea*** below. **black-eyed** *adjective* having black eyes; ***black-eyed Susan***, any of various plants having light-coloured flowers with dark centres, esp. the yellow *Rudbeckia hirta* of N. America; ***black-eyed bean***, ***black-eyed pea***, a kind of cowpea having white seeds with a black hilum; the (freq. dried) seed of this plant, eaten as a pulse. **blackface** (*a*) an animal, esp. a sheep, with a dark face (***Scottish blackface***: see SCOTTISH *adjective*); (*b*) make-up for the role of a black person; ***blackface minstrel*** (chiefly *hist.*), a member of a troupe of entertainers, usu. white men who blacken their faces, performing songs and dances associated with plantation life in the southern US. **black-faced** *adjective* having a dark face; *fig.* threatening, foreboding. **blackfellow** *Austral.* (*arch.* or *hist.*, *offensive*) an Aborigine. **black-figure** *adjective* (ARCHAEOLOGY) designating a type of Greek pottery ornamented with figures in black silhouette. **blackfish** (*a*) a salmon just after spawning; (*b*) a small whale, *esp.* a pilot whale; also, a killer whale; (*c*) any of several dark-coloured fishes, e.g. the marine fish *Centrolophus niger*, the tautog (*N. Amer.*), and the Australian freshwater fish *Gadopsis marmoratus*. ***black flag***: see FLAG *noun*[4]. **blackfly** any of various dark-coloured insects, *esp.* (*a*) certain thrips and aphids infesting plants; (*b*) a biting fly of the family Simuliidae; = SIMULIUM. **blackfoot** *Scot.* (pl. **-feet**) a lovers' go-between. **Blackfoot** *noun* & *adjective* (*a*) *noun* (pl. **-feet**, same) a member of a N. American Indian confederacy comprising the Siksika, the Bloods, and the Peigan; the Algonquian language of these people; (*b*) *adjective* of or pertaining to these people or their language. **Black Forest cake**, **Black Forest gateau** [translating German *Schwarzwald*, a forest area in SW Germany] a rich chocolate cake or gateau with black cherries. **black fox** a dark colour phase of the N. American red fox. **Black Friar** [from the colour of the order's habit] a Dominican friar. **Black Friday** (*a*) *US* STOCK EXCHANGE. Friday 24 Sept. 1869, a day of financial panic on Wall Street precipitated by the introduction into the market of a large quantity of government gold; (*b*) *US* the day after Thanksgiving, which traditionally marks the start of the Christmas shopping season. ***black frost***: see FROST *noun*. **black game** the black grouse. **black gold** (*colloq.*, chiefly *N. Amer.*) oil. **black grape**: that is purple or blue-black when ripe. **black grouse** a large Eurasian grouse, *Tetrao tetrix*, the male of which has glossy blue-black plumage and a lyre-shaped tail (cf. ***blackcock*** above, ***greyhen*** s.v. GREY *adjective*); also called ***black game***. **black gum** *N. Amer.* (the wood of) a deciduous tree of the south-eastern US, *Nyssa sylvatica*; also called ***sour gum***. **blackhead** (*a*) any of various black-headed birds, *esp.* the scaup, *Aythya marila*, or the black-headed gull, *Larus ridibundus*; (*b*) a black-tipped plug of sebaceous matter in a hair follicle; (*c*) an infectious disease of turkeys producing discoloration of the head, caused by a protozoon. **black-headed** *adjective* having a black head; ***black-headed gull***, any of several gulls with black heads, esp. *Larus ridibundus*, common in many parts of the Old World. **black-heart** (*a*) a dark reddish-black variety of sweet cherry; (*b*) malleable cast iron with a core of graphite. **black heat** a temperature just below visible red. **black hole** (*a*) MILITARY HISTORY the punishment cell of a barracks; *loosely* any place of confinement; ***Black Hole of Calcutta***, a dungeon in which over 100 English prisoners were confined overnight in 1756, only 23 surviving. (*b*) ASTRONOMY a region where gravitation is so powerful that no matter or electromagnetic radiation can escape (***Schwarzschild black hole***: see SCHWARZSCHILD 2). ***black HOREHOUND***. **black house** *Scot.* (*a*) a turf house; (*b*) a house built of unmortared stone, found esp. in NW Scotland and the Hebrides. **black ice** a thin, hard, transparent ice, esp. as forming on roads. **black Irish** Irish people of Mediterranean appearance. **black Italian poplar** a commonly planted hybrid poplar that resembles the black poplar but has upcurved branches. ***black ivory***: see IVORY *noun*. **blackjack**, **black jack** †(*a*) *Scot.* a black leather jerkin; (*b*) *hist.* a large tar-coated leather jug for beer; (*c*) zinc blende; (*d*) *N. Amer.* (the wood of) a shrubby oak, *Quercus marilandica*; also ***blackjack oak***; (*e*) a small black beetle or caterpillar; *esp.* the larva of the turnip sawfly, *Athalia spinarum*; (*f*) *hist.* a pirate's black ensign; (*g*) (chiefly *S. Afr.*) a S. American bur-marigold, *Bidens pilosa*, introduced elsewhere; the hooked seed of this plant; (*h*) a flexible loaded bludgeon; (*i*) = VINGT-ET-UN. ***Black Jew***: see JEW *noun*. **black kite** a dark brown kite, *Milvus migrans*, of southern Europe, Africa, Asia, and Australia. **black knight** STOCK EXCHANGE a person or company making an unwelcome takeover bid for another company (cf. ***WHITE knight***). **blacklead** *noun* & *verb* (*a*) *noun* graphite, esp. as used in pencils or as a domestic polish; (*b*) *verb trans.* polish with graphite. ***black LEOPARD***. **black letter** (printing in) a heavy early style of type. **black level** TELEVISION the level of the picture signal that corresponds to black in the transmitted image. **black light** invisible ultraviolet or infrared radiation. **blacklist** *noun* & *verb* (*a*) *noun* a list of the names of those who have incurred suspicion, censure, or punishment; (*b*) *verb trans.* enter the name of (a person) on a blacklist. ***black locust***: see LOCUST *noun* 3(c). **black lung** (chiefly *US*) = ANTHRACOSIS. ***black magic***: see MAGIC *noun*. ***black MAMBA***. **black man** (*a*) a man having dark skin; (*b*) *colloq.* & *dial.* an evil spirit, devil, or bogeyman. ***black MANGROVE***. **Black Maria** (*a*) *colloq.* a van for the conveyance of prisoners; (*b*) (a card game having) the queen of spades as a penalty card. **black mark** a mark of discredit against a person's name (*lit.* & *fig.*). **black market** (a place of) illegitimate traffic in officially controlled goods or currencies or in commodities in short supply. **black marketeer** a person engaged in dealing in the black market. **black marketeering** dealing in the black market. **black mass** (*a*) a mass for the dead at which vestments and drapings are black; a requiem mass; (*b*) a travesty of the Mass said to be used in satanism. ***Black MONDAY***. **black money** †(*a*) copper coins; (*b*) money not declared for tax. **Black Monk** [from the colour of the order's habit] a Benedictine monk. ***black Moor***: see BLACKAMOOR. **black-mouth** †(*a*) one having a black mouth; *fig.* a slanderer; (*b*) *dial.* a saithe. **black Muslim** a member of a sect of black US Muslims, formerly advocating separation of black and white people. ***black mustard***: see MUSTARD *noun*. **black neb** (*a*) a crow or other black-billed bird; (*b*) SCOTTISH HISTORY a sympathizer with the French Revolution. ***black NIGHTSHADE***. **black oak** (the wood of) any of various trees with dark bark or foliage; *spec.* the quercitron, *Quercus velutina*. **black oil** any of various dark-coloured oils; *spec.* heavy crude oil used for lubrication. ***black olive***: see OLIVE *noun*[1] 1b. **black operations**, (*colloq.*) **black ops** clandestine (and usu. illegal) military operations carried out by government agents; **black panther** (*a*) = ***black LEOPARD***; (*b*) (with cap. initials) a member of an extremist organization in the US fighting for black rights. ***black pepper***: see PEPPER *noun*. **black pine** any of several conifers, *esp.* the Austrian pine, the matai, and the matsu. **black plate** thin sheets of iron not coated with tin. **blackpoll (warbler)** an American warbler, *Dendroica striata*, streaked grey and white with a black crown. ***Black Pope***: see POPE *noun*[1]. **black poplar** a Eurasian poplar, *Populus nigra*, with a blackish-brown trunk and arching lower branches; also = ***black Italian poplar*** above. **black-pot** a beer mug; a toper. **black powder** gunpowder. **Black Power** (a slogan used by) a movement in support of black civil rights. **Black Prince** (a name given to) the eldest son of Edward III of England. **black pudding** a sausage-shaped pudding made with blood and suet. **black quarter** = BLACKLEG *noun* 1a. ***black RASPBERRY***. ***black rat***: see RAT *noun*[1]. ***black REDSTART***. ***black RHINOCEROS***. **blackrobe** CANAD. HISTORY (an Indians' name for) a Christian priest. **Black Rod** (the office of) the chief gentleman usher to the Lord Chamberlain's department, usher to the House of Lords, etc. **black rubric** (an inaccurate term for) the declaration explanatory of the rubric concerning kneeling at the reception of Holy Communion, first inserted at the end of the Communion service in the *Book of Common Prayer* of 1552. **black rust** = ***stem rust*** s.v. STEM *noun*[1]. ***black sage***: see SAGE *noun*[1] 1b. ***black SALSIFY***. ***black SALTWORT***. **black sand** an alluvial or beach sand, esp. in Australia and New Zealand, consisting predominantly of grains of heavy dark minerals or rocks. **black scoter** a scoter, *Melanitta nigra*, of Arctic and north temperate regions. **black sheep** a disreputable or unsatisfactory member (*of* a family etc.). **blackshirt** a member of the Italian Fascist Party, *gen.* a Fascist. **black-shouldered kite** either of two small Old World kites of the genus *Elanus*, with pale grey and white plumage and black shoulder patches. **black-snake** (*a*) any of various dark-coloured snakes; *esp.* an Australian snake, *Pseudechis porphyriacus*, and a N. American racer, *Coluber constrictor*; (*b*) *US* (more fully ***black-snake whip***) a long whiplash. **blacksnake** *verb trans.* flog with a black-snake whip. ***black snakeroot***: see SNAKE *noun*. **black soil** = ***black earth*** above. ***black SPAULD***. **black spleenwort** a small fern of rocks and walls, *Asplenium adiantum-nigrum*, with a triangular frond. **black spot**, **blackspot** (*a*) any of various diseases of plants, esp. of roses, producing black spots; (*b*) a place of anxiety or danger, *esp.* a section of a road noted for accidents. ***black squall***: see SQUALL *noun*[1] 1. ***black stinkwood***: see STINK *noun*. **Black Stone** the sacred reddish-black stone built into the outside wall of the Kaaba. **blackstrap** †(*a*) an inferior kind of port wine; also, a drink consisting of a mixture of rum and treacle; (*b*) dark viscous molasses used esp. in industrial processes and as cattle feed. ***black stump***: see STUMP *noun*[1]. ***black swallower***: see SWALLOWER (b). ***black swallowwort***: see SWALLOWWORT 1. **black swan** (*a*) an Australian and New Zealand swan, *Cygnus atratus*, having all black plumage with a red beak; (*b*) an extremely rare thing. **blacktail** (*a*) any of various fishes, *esp.* (*S. Afr.*) = DASSIE 2; (*b*) the mule deer, *Odocoileus hemionus*, of western N. America. ***black tang***: see TANG *noun*[2]. ***black tar***: see TAR *noun*[1] 1d. **black tea** tea fully fermented before drying (cf. ***green tea*** s.v. GREEN *adjective*); (see also sense 1c above). **black tern** an Old World migratory tern, *Chlidonias niger*, with a dark head and underparts. **black tie** *spec.* a man's black bow tie worn with a dinner jacket; *ellipt.* evening dress including a black tie. ***black TIL***. ***black tin***: see TIN *noun* 1. ***black titi***: see TITI *noun*[2]. **blacktop** *US* a type of blackish road surfacing, asphalt, tarmacadam; a road etc. surfaced with this. **black tracker** *Austral.* an Aborigine employed by the police to track down fugitives or persons lost in the bush. ***black treacle***: see TREACLE *noun* 4. **black tripe** unbleached tripe. ***black truffle***: see TRUFFLE *noun* 1. ***black TURNSTONE***. **black velvet** (*a*) a drink consisting of a mixture of champagne and stout (cf. BISMARCK 2); (*b*) *Austral. slang* (*offensive*) an Aboriginal woman; Aboriginal women collectively. **black vomit** yellow fever; dark material (containing blood) vomited during this. **black vulture** (*a*) a vulture, *Aegypius monachus*, found from Spain to central Asia; (*b*) a vulture, *Coragyps atratus*, of N. and S. America. ***black walnut***: see WALNUT 3. ***black wash***: see WASH *noun*. **Black Watch** the Royal Highland Regiment (distinguished by their dark-coloured tartan). **black water**, **blackwater** (*a*) a stream stained brown by peat; (*b*) a disease of animals, esp. a form of babesiasis, in which dark urine is passed; (*c*) (a term used by Indians, esp. Hindus, for) the sea; (*d*) ***blackwater fever***, a form of malignant tertian malaria in which haemoglobin is present in the urine owing to massive red-cell destruction. **black widow** a venomous black N. American spider of the genus *Latrodectus*, esp. *L. mactans*, the female of which usu. devours its mate. **blackwood** (the dark timber of) any of various hardwood trees, esp. of the tropical genus *Dalbergia*, and *Acacia melanoxylon* of Australia and South Africa. **blackwork** a type of embroidery done in black thread on white cloth, popular esp. in Tudor times.

■ **blackish** *adjective* tending to black L15. **blackly** *adverb* in a black or gloomy manner M16. **blackness** *noun* ME. **blacky** *adjective* somewhat black, blackish L16. **blacky** *noun* (*a*) *colloq.* (*offensive*) a black person; (*b*) *dial.* & *colloq.* a blackbird: E19.

black /blak/ *verb*. ME.

[ORIGIN from the adjective.]

†**1** *verb intrans.* Be or become black. Long *dial. rare*. ME–M19.

2 *verb trans.* Make black; put black colour on. ME. ▸**b** *spec.* Polish with blacking. M16. ▸**c** *spec.* Bruise or discolour (a person's eye). E20.

3 *verb trans.* Defame, speak evil of. LME.

4 *verb trans.* Blackmail. *slang*. E20.

5 *verb trans.* Declare (goods etc.) black in an industrial dispute. M20.

– WITH ADVERBS IN SPECIALIZED SENSES: **black out** (*a*) *verb phr. trans.* obliterate or obscure (as) with black; extinguish all lights in, extinguish or obscure (lights), esp. during a stage performance or in anticipation of air raids; (*b*) *verb phr. intrans.* be obscured or extinguished, undergo a blackout of lighting; (*c*) *verb phr. intrans.* suffer temporary loss of consciousness, loss of memory, or blindness. **black up** *verb phr. refl.* & *intrans.* (THEATRICAL) colour one's face to play the role of a black person.

■ **blacker** *noun* M17.

blackamoor /ˈblakəmʊə, -mɔː/ *noun*. *arch.* Also †**black Moor**. E16.

[ORIGIN from BLACK *adjective* + MOOR *noun*[2]: connecting *-a-* unexpl.]

A black African; a very dark-skinned person.

blackavised /ˈblakəvʌɪzd, -st/ *adjective*. *arch.* (chiefly *N. English*). M18.

[ORIGIN from BLACK *adjective* + French *vis* face (perh. orig. *black-à-vis* or *black o'vis*) + -ED[2].]

Dark-complexioned.

blackberry /ˈblakb(ə)ri/ *noun*. OE.

[ORIGIN from BLACK *adjective* + BERRY *noun*[1].]

1 a The fruit of the bramble shrub. OE. ▸**b** The shrub itself. L16.

as plentiful as blackberries as plentiful as can be.

2 The blackcurrant; the bilberry. *N. English*. M16.

■ **blackberrying** *noun* gathering blackberries L18.

blackbird /ˈblakbəːd/ *noun*. ME.

[ORIGIN from BLACK *adjective* + BIRD *noun*.]

1 A common European thrush, *Turdus merula*, the male of which is black with an orange beak, and the female brown. ME.

2 Any of various N. American birds, esp. grackles, with black plumage. E17.

3 *hist.* A kidnapped black or Polynesian person on a slave ship. M19.

■ **blackbirder** *noun* (*hist.*) a man or a vessel engaged in blackbirding L19. **blackbirding** *noun* (*hist.*) the capture and transportation of black or Polynesian slaves L19.

Blackburnian /blakˈbəːnɪən/ *adjective* & *noun*. *N. Amer.* L18.

[ORIGIN from Mrs Hugh *Blackburn* (fl. 18th cent.) + -IAN.]

(Designating) a N. American warbler, *Dendroica fusca*, distinguished by orange or yellow throat markings.

blackcurrant /blak'kʌr(ə)nt/ *noun*. Also **black currant**. E17.
[ORIGIN from BLACK *adjective* + CURRANT.]
The small round edible black berry of the shrub *Ribes nigrum*, of the gooseberry family, borne in loose hanging clusters; this shrub, much grown for its fruit.
attrib.: ***blackcurrant jam***, ***blackcurrant jelly***, etc.

blacken /'blak(ə)n/ *verb*. ME.
[ORIGIN from BLACK *adjective* + -EN⁵.]
1 *verb intrans.* Become or grow black(er); darken. ME.
2 *verb trans.* Make black(er) or dark(er); defame, speak evil of. LME.
■ **blackener** *noun* M17.

blackguard /'blagɑːd, -gəd/ *noun & adjective*. Orig. two words. E16.
[ORIGIN from BLACK *adjective* + GUARD *noun*: orig. significance unkn.]
▸ **A** *noun*. †**1** A guard, attendant, or group of attendants black in person, dress, or character. E16–M18.
†**2** ***the blackguard***: ▸**a** The lowest menials of a household; the scullions; an army's camp followers. M16–E18. ▸**b** Criminals or vagrants as a group or class. L17–M18.
†**3** A vagrant child. Only in 18.
4 A worthless or contemptible man, a villain. *arch.* M18.
5 More fully ***Irish blackguard***. A kind of snuff. L18–L19.
▸ **B** *adjective*. †**1** Pertaining to vagrants. L17–E19.
2 Dishonourable, villainous; scurrilous. L18.
■ **blackguardism** *noun* blackguardly language or behaviour L18. **blackguardly** *adverb & adjective* (*a*) *adverb* (*rare*) in the manner of a blackguard; (*b*) *adjective* characteristic of a blackguard, worthless, scurrilous: E19.

blackguard /'blagɑːd, -gəd/ *verb*. L18.
[ORIGIN from the noun.]
†**1** *verb intrans.* Behave like a blackguard. *rare*. Only in L18.
2 *verb trans.* Treat as a blackguard; abuse scurrilously, revile. E19.

blacking /'blakɪŋ/ *noun*. L16.
[ORIGIN from BLACK *verb* + -ING¹.]
1 A preparation for making something black; *spec.* a paste or liquid for blacking or polishing boots etc. L16.
2 The action of BLACK *verb*. E17.

blackleg /'blaklɛg/ *noun & adjective*. E18.
[ORIGIN from BLACK *adjective* + LEG *noun*.]
▸ **A** *noun*. **1** *sing.* & in *pl.* **a** An acute infectious bacterial disease of cattle and sheep, causing necrosis in one or more legs. E18. ▸**b** Any of various diseases of vegetables. L19.
2 A swindler, *esp.* a swindling bookmaker. L18.
3 A person who continues to work despite a ban or strike by a trade union etc.; a person who takes a striker's place. M19.
▸ **B** *attrib.* or as *adjective*. That is a blackleg during a strike etc.; of or pertaining to blacklegs. L19.

blackleg /'blaklɛg/ *verb*. Infl. **-gg-**. L18.
[ORIGIN from the noun.]
1 *verb intrans.* Act as a blackleg. L18.
2 *verb trans.* Replace, injure, or betray as a blackleg. L19.

blackmail /'blakmeɪl/ *noun & verb*. Orig. two words. M16.
[ORIGIN from BLACK *adjective* + MAIL *noun*¹.]
▸ **A** *noun* **1** **a** *hist.* A tribute levied by freebooting Scottish chiefs in return for protection or immunity from plunder. M16. ▸**b** *transf.* Any payment or other benefit extorted by threats or pressure, esp. by threatening to reveal a discreditable secret; the criminal action of seeking to extort such a payment or benefit; the use of threats or moral pressure. E19.
2 LAW (now *hist.*). Rent payable in cattle, labour, or coin other than silver. E17.
▸ **B** *verb trans.* Extort money from by blackmail, use threats or moral pressure against. L19.
■ **blackmailer** *noun* M19.

†**black Moor** *noun* var. of BLACKAMOOR.

blackout /'blakaʊt/ *noun*. E20.
[ORIGIN from ***black out*** s.v. BLACK *verb*.]
1 An act of blacking out or the state of being blacked out; *spec.* (*a*) the darkening of a theatre stage for a performance; (*b*) the extinguishing or obscuring of lights in anticipation of air raids; (*c*) a temporary complete failure of memory or loss of consciousness; an aviator's temporary blindness etc. resulting esp. from centrifugal force when a sudden turn is made; (*d*) the loss of radio reception through fading or jamming; (*e*) the suppression of information or news. E20.
2 A period during which lights must be extinguished or obscured. M20.

blacksmith /'blaksmɪθ/ *noun*. L15.
[ORIGIN from BLACK *adjective* + SMITH *noun*.]
A smith who works in iron.
■ **black'smithery** *noun* (*a*) *US* a smithy; (*b*) (orig. *US*) blacksmith's work: M19. **blacksmithing** *noun* performing blacksmith's work M19.

blackthorn /'blakθɔːn/ *noun*. ME.
[ORIGIN from BLACK *adjective* + THORN *noun*.]
1 **a** A thorny European shrub, *Prunus spinosa*, of the rose family, bearing white flowers before the leaves and fruit (sloes) like small dark plums. ME. ▸**b** A stick or cudgel of the wood of this shrub. M19.
2 Any of certain other shrubs; *esp.* a N. American hawthorn, *Crataegus calpodendron*. M18.
– COMB.: **blackthorn winter** a period of cold weather with north-east winds at the time of the blackthorn's flowering in early spring.

Blackwood /'blakwʊd/ *noun*. M20.
[ORIGIN E. F. *Blackwood* (1903–92), Amer. bridge player, inventor of the system.]
BRIDGE. A system of bidding four no trumps so that the partner's response can show the number of aces held.

blad /blad/ *verb & noun*. *Scot.* Also **blaud** /blɔːd/. E16.
[ORIGIN Prob. imit.: the senses of the noun perh. not all the same word.]
▸ **A** *verb trans.* Infl. **-dd-**. Slap heavily. E16.
▸ **B** *noun*. **1** A fragment, a large portion; a selection, a specimen. E16.
†**2** A bodily injury; an illness. Usu. in *pl.* M16–M19.
3 A heavy slap; a stroke, a blow. E18.
4 A blast (of wind); a downpour. E19.

bladder /'bladə/ *noun*.
[ORIGIN Old English *blǣdre*, later *blæddre* = Old Saxon *blādara*, Middle Low German, Middle Dutch *blāder* (Dutch *blaar*), Old High German *blātara* (German *Blatter*), Old Norse *blāðra*, from Germanic, from base of BLOW *verb*¹ + instr. suffix corresp. to Latin *-trum*, Greek. *-tra*, *-tron*, Sanskrit *-tram*.]
1 **a** The muscular membranous bag in the human or other animal body which serves as the receptacle for urine from the kidneys. Also ***urinary bladder***. OE. ▸**b** Any of various similar organs. Usu. with specifying word. ME.
b ***gall-bladder***: see GALL *noun*¹. ***swim bladder***: see SWIM *noun*.
2 A morbid vesicle containing fluid; a boil, a blister. OE.
3 The prepared bladder of an animal used for various purposes, as a container, inflated as a float, etc. ME.
bladder of lard *slang* a bald-headed or fat person.
4 A bubble. L15.
5 *fig.* Anything inflated and hollow; a pompous person, a windbag; *slang* a newspaper, esp. a poor one. L16.
6 BOTANY. An inflated pericarp; a hollow vesicle, as in many seaweeds. L16.
– COMB.: **bladder-campion** a common white campion, *Silene vulgaris*, with an inflated calyx; **bladder-fern** a fern of the genus *Cystopteris*, having bladder-like indusia; **bladder nut** any of various north temperate shrubs and small trees of the genus *Staphylea* (family Staphyleaceae) with white flowers and inflated capsules; *esp.* the central European *S. pinnata*; **bladder senna** a leguminous shrub, *Colutea arborescens*, with inflated pods; **bladder worm** a tapeworm larva in its encysted state, or in the intermediate or first host; **bladderwort** any of various chiefly aquatic plants constituting the genus *Utricularia* (family Lentibulariaceae), which have capillary leaves bearing bladders in which insects are trapped; **bladderwrack** a seaweed with air vesicles in its fronds, esp. *Fucus vesiculosus*.
■ **bladdered** *adjective* (*colloq.*) drunk, intoxicated L20. **bladder-like** *adjective* resembling (that of) a bladder: E17. **bladdery** *adjective* L18.

blade /bleɪd/ *noun & verb*.
[ORIGIN Old English *blæd*, pl. *bladu*, = Old Frisian *bled*, Old Saxon (Dutch) *blad*, Old High German *blat* (German *Blatt*), Old Norse *blað* leaf, blade of rudder, knife, etc., from Germanic, perh. pa. ppl formation on the base of BLOW *verb*².]
▸ **A** *noun* **1** **a** The leaf of a herb or plant. Now *poet.* & *dial.* in *gen.* sense. OE. ▸**b** *spec.* A flat spear-shaped leaf, esp. of grass or a cereal crop; the whole of such plants before the ear appears. LME.
b in the blade with only the blade (not yet the ear) showing; *fig.* in the early stage, immature.
2 The broad, flattened part of any instrument or utensil, as an oar, spade, bat, paddle wheel, turbine, propeller, etc. OE.
3 A broad flat bone; *esp.* that of the shoulder of humans or other large animals (of some also as a joint of meat). ME.
shoulder blade: see SHOULDER *noun*.
4 The thin cutting part of a sword, chisel, knife, etc. ME. ▸**b** An edged weapon; a sword. Chiefly *literary*. LME. ▸**c** In full ***razor blade***. A flat piece of metal with usu. two sharp edges, used in a safety razor. M19. ▸**d** In *pl.* Hand shears. *Austral.* & *NZ*. E20.
switchblade: see SWITCH *noun*.
5 A dashing or energetic young man. *colloq.* L16.

> S. PEPYS The present fashion among the blades. S. JOHNSON When we meet we will be jolly blades. G. CLARE Father was neither a young blade nor a rake.

6 A thin piece *of* something (esp. mace). M17.
7 BOTANY. The broad thin part of a leaf or petal, excluding the petiole. E19.
8 Esp. PHONETICS. The flat part of the tongue behind the tip. L19.
9 ARCHAEOLOGY. A long narrow flake. E20.
– COMB.: **blade bone** = sense 3 above; **blade-consonant** PHONETICS a consonant (e.g. /s/, /n/) formed with the blade of the tongue; **bladework** control of the blade of an oar in rowing.
▸ **B** *verb*. **1** *verb trans.* Remove the (esp. outside) leaves from. *dial.* LME.
2 *verb trans.* Provide with a (cutting) blade. LME.
3 *verb intrans.* Put out blades or leaves, sprout. M16.
4 *verb intrans.* Skate on Rollerblades. L20.
■ **bladed** *adjective* (*a*) having blades or a blade (freq. as 2nd elem. of comb., of a specified kind); (*b*) having been bladed; †(*c*) having put out leaves: L16. **bladeless** *adjective* M19. **bladelike** *adjective* resembling a blade M19. **blader** *noun* L20.

blady /'bleɪdi/ *adjective*. E17.
[ORIGIN from BLADE *noun* + -Y¹.]
Like a blade; characterized by blades.
blady grass a coarse grass, *Imperata arundinacea*, of Australia and parts of SE Asia.

blae /bleɪ/ *adjective & noun*. *Scot. & N. English*. ME.
[ORIGIN Old Norse *blár* (whence also BLO): see BLUE *adjective*.]
▸ **A** *adjective*. **1** Blackish-blue; livid; lead-coloured. ME.
2 Bleak, sunless. E16.
▸ **B** *noun*. A kind of bluish-grey soft slate. M17.

blaeberry /'bleɪb(ə)ri/ *noun*. *Scot. & N. English*. ME.
[ORIGIN from BLAE *adjective* + BERRY *noun*¹.]
= BILBERRY.

blag /blag/ *noun*¹ *& verb*¹. *slang*. L19.
[ORIGIN Unknown.]
▸ **A** *noun*. A (violent) robbery. L19.

> C. HIGSON He had millions stashed away after some blag.

▸ **B** *verb intrans. & trans.* Infl. **-gg-**. Rob, esp. with violence; steal. M20.
■ **blagger** *noun*¹ M20.

blag /blag/ *verb*² *& noun*². *colloq.* M20.
[ORIGIN from BLAGUE; perh. also a weakening of BLAG *noun*¹.]
▸ **A** *verb trans. & intrans.* Infl. **-gg-**. Coax or persuade (someone) by pretence, deceitful talk, etc.; scrounge (something). M20.

> JAYNE MILLER I'll . . see what companies I like the look of and blag my way in. S. STEWART Have you blagged a job then?

▸ **B** *noun*. A tall story, bluff, or pretence; a hoax or con. M20.
■ **blagger** *noun*² M20.

blague /blag/ *noun*. M19.
[ORIGIN French.]
Humbug, claptrap.
sans blague: see SANS *preposition*.

blagueur /blagœːr/ *noun*. Pl. pronounced same. L19.
[ORIGIN French, formed as BLAGUE + *-eur* -OR.]
A pretentious talker; a joker, a teller of tall stories.

blah /blɑː/ *noun, verb, & adjective*. *colloq.* Also redupl. **blah-blah**. E20.
[ORIGIN Imit.]
▸ **A** *noun*. Meaningless, nonsensical, insincere, or pretentious talk or writing. E20.
▸ **B** *verb intrans.* Utter or write nonsense; be insincere or pretentious. E20.
▸ **C** *adjective*. **1** Mad. E20.
2 Dull, unexciting; pretentious. M20.

blahs /blɑːz/ *noun pl.* *colloq.* (orig. *US*). M20.
[ORIGIN Repr. a dial. pronunc. of *blues*.]
The blues (see BLUES), depression.

blain /bleɪn/ *noun & verb*.
[ORIGIN Old English *blegen* = Middle Dutch *bleine* (Dutch *blein*), Low German *bleien*, from West Germanic.]
▸ **A** *noun*. An inflamed swelling or sore on the skin. See also CHILBLAIN. OE.
▸ **B** *verb trans.* Affect with blains. LME.

Blairism /'blɛːrɪz(ə)m/ *noun*. L20.
[ORIGIN from *Blair* (see below) + -ISM.]
The political policies and outlook of the British Labour politician Anthony Charles Lynton ('Tony') *Blair* (b. 1953), Prime Minister 1997–2007, characterized by a combination of traditional Labour Party concern for social issues and an acceptance of many aspects of market-based economics.
■ **Blairite** *adjective & noun* L20.

Blakeian /'bleɪkɪən/ *adjective*. E20.
[ORIGIN from *Blake* (see below) + -IAN.]
Of, pertaining to, or characteristic of the poet and painter William Blake (1757–1827) or his work, esp. in its visionary aspects.

blamable *adjective* var. of BLAMEABLE.

blame /bleɪm/ *noun*. ME.
[ORIGIN Old French, formed as BLAME *verb, adverb, & adjective*.]
1 The action of blaming, censure. ME.

> G. GREENE No one can please me much with praise or hurt me with blame. W. TREVOR The poor nurse will get the blame for negligence.

2 Responsibility for a bad result or something wrong. ME.
bear the blame (for); ***lay the blame on***, ***put the blame on***, etc.
†**3** An accusation. ME–L16.
4 Blameworthiness; fault. *arch.* ME.

> SHAKES. *1 Hen. VI* And shall my youth be guilty of such blame?

– COMB.: **blame game** *colloq.* a situation in which one party blames others rather than attempting to seek a solution.
■ **blameful** *adjective* (*a*) imputing or conveying blame; (*b*) deserving blame: LME. **blameless** *adjective* †(*a*) exempt from blame;

B

(*b*) guiltless: LME. **blamelessly** *adverb* E17. **blamelessness** *noun* L17. **blameworthiness** *noun* the quality or state of being blameworthy L16. **blameworthy** *adjective* deserving blame LME.

blame /bleɪm/ *verb, adverb, & adjective*. ME.
[ORIGIN Old French *bla(s)mer* (mod. *blâmer*) from popular Latin *blastemare* for ecclesiastical Latin *blasphemare* revile, reproach, from Greek *blasphēmein* (dial. *blast-*) BLASPHEME.]
▸ **A** *verb trans.* **1** Find fault with (*for* an offence etc.). ME.
†**2** Rebuke, scold. ME–M16.
†**3** Accuse (*of*). ME–M17.
4 a Fix the responsibility on, hold answerable. ME. ▸**b** Fix the responsibility for (a bad result etc.) *on*. *colloq.* M19.
†**5** Bring into disrepute. L16–E17.
6 *imper.* & in *pass.* = DAMN *verb* 3. *dial.* & *N. Amer.* M19.

M. TWAIN Blame it, I ain't going to stir him much. R. KIPLING Blame that boy! H. R. MARTIN I'm blamed if I dare adwise you.

– PHRASES: **be to blame** deserve censure, be responsible, (*for*).
▸ **B** *adverb & adjective*. = BLAMED. *dial.* & *N. Amer.* M19.
■ **blamed** *adjective & adverb* (*dial.* & *N. Amer.*) confounded(ly), damned M19. **blamer** *noun* LME.

blameable /ˈbleɪməb(ə)l/ *adjective*. Also **blamable**. LME.
[ORIGIN from BLAME *verb* + -ABLE.]
Deserving blame, culpable.
■ **blameably** *adverb* (earlier in UNBLAMEABLY) E18.

blanc /blɑ̃/ *noun & adjective*. M18.
[ORIGIN French = white: see BLANK *adjective*.]
▸ **A** *noun*. Pl. pronounced same.
▸ **I** Used without qualification.
1 White paint, esp. for the face. Now *arch.* or *hist.* M18.
2 A type of light-coloured stock or gravy. M19.
▸ **II** In phrases.
3 ***blanc fixe*** /fiks/, barium sulphate, esp. as used in paints. M19.
4 ***blanc de chine*** /də ʃin/, a white glazed Chinese porcelain, esp. of the Ming period, = DEHUA. L19.
5 ***blanc de perle*** /də pɛrl/, pearl-white. L19.
6 ***blanc de blanc(s)*** /də blɑ̃/, a (usu. sparkling) white wine made from white grapes only. M20.
▸ **B** *adjective*. Of French wine: white. L18.

blancbec /blɑ̃bɛk/ *noun*. Pl. pronounced same. M19.
[ORIGIN French, lit. 'white beak'.]
A raw youngster, a greenhorn.

blanch /blɑːn(t)ʃ/ *adjective, noun, & adverb*. Now *arch.* or *hist.* Also (*Scot.*) **blench** /blɛn(t)ʃ/. ME.
[ORIGIN Old French & mod. French *blanche* fem. of *blanc* white: see BLANK *adjective*.]
▸ **A** *adjective*. **1** White, pale. Long *arch.* ME.
2 *hist.* = BLANCHFARM *adjective*. M16.
▸ **B** *noun*. *hist.* = BLANCHFARM *noun*. M16.
▸ **C** *adverb*. *hist.* = BLANCHFARM *adverb*. M16.

blanch /blɑːn(t)ʃ/ *verb*[1]. Also (by assoc. with BLENCH *verb*[1]) **blench** /blɛn(t)ʃ/. ME.
[ORIGIN Old French & mod. French *blanchir*, formed as BLANCH *adjective, noun, & adverb*.]
1 *verb trans.* Make white, esp. by withdrawing colour; bleach. ME.

KEATS Blanched linen, smooth and lavendered. T. S. ELIOT The hedgerow Is blanched . . with transitory blossom Of snow.

2 *verb trans.* Peel (almonds etc.), esp. by scalding. Now also, cook (vegetables or meat) lightly in boiling water. LME.
3 *verb trans.* Palliate by misrepresentation. (Foll. by *over*.) Long *rare*. M16.

MILTON To blanch and varnish her deformities.

4 *verb trans.* Make pale with cold, fear, hunger, etc. E17.
5 *verb trans.* Whiten (plants) by depriving them of light. M17.
6 *verb intrans.* Turn white; bleach; pale. M18.

blanch *verb*[2] see BLENCH *verb*[1].

blanchfarm /ˈblɑːn(t)ʃfɑːm/ *noun, adverb, & adjective*. *obsolete* exc. *hist.* Chiefly *Scot.* Also **blench-** /ˈblɛn(t)ʃ-/. LME.
[ORIGIN Old French *blanche ferme* white rent.]
▸ **A** *noun*. Rent paid in silver; any nominal quit-rent. LME.
in blanchfarm as one's property for payment of a blanchfarm.
▸ **B** *adverb*. = ***in blanchfarm*** above. L15.
▸ **C** *adjective*. Held in or paid as blanchfarm. L15.

blancmange /bləˈmɒnʒ, -ˈmɑːnʒ/ *noun*. Also (earlier) †**-manger**. LME.
[ORIGIN Old French *blanc mangier* (mod. *blancmanger*), from *blanc* white + *mang(i)er* food, use as noun of *mang(i)er* eat. Shortened in 18.]
†**1** A dish of white meat or fish in a cream sauce. LME–L15.
2 An opaque jelly made with isinglass or gelatin and milk or (now usu.) cornflour and milk, often flavoured and sweetened. M16.

blanco /ˈblaŋkəʊ/ *noun & verb trans.* L19.
[ORIGIN from French *blanc* white (see BLANK *adjective*) + -O.]
MILITARY. (Treat with) a white preparation for whitening belts etc., or a similar coloured substance.

bland /bland/ *noun*. E17.
[ORIGIN Old Norse *blanda* mixture of fluids: see BLEND *verb*[2].]
In Orkney and Shetland: a drink made of buttermilk and water.

bland /bland/ *adjective*. LME.
[ORIGIN from Latin *blandus* soft, smooth.]
1 Gentle or suave in manner. LME.
2 Of things: mild, soothing; not irritating, not stimulating. M17.
■ **blandly** *adverb* E19. **blandness** *noun* M19.

blandander /blanˈdandə/ *verb trans.* *colloq.* L19.
[ORIGIN Cf. Irish *blanndar* dissimulation, flattery.]
Tempt by blandishment (*into*); cajole.

blandish /ˈblandɪʃ/ *verb*. ME.
[ORIGIN from Old French *blandiss-* lengthened stem of *blandir* from Latin *blandiri*, formed as BLAND *adjective*: see -ISH[2].]
1 *verb trans.* Flatter gently, coax; cajole. ME.
2 *verb intrans.* Use blandishments. ME.
■ **blandishment** *noun* (usu. in *pl.*) flattery, cajolery, *fig.* (an) allurement L16.

blank /blaŋk/ *noun*. LME.
[ORIGIN The adjective used absol. or ellipt.]
†**1** A small French coin, orig. of silver, later of copper. Also, a silver coin of Henry V's reign, current in the parts of France then held by the English. LME–M19.
2 The 1⁄230400 part of a grain weight. M16.
3 a A blank space left to be filled up in a document. M16. ▸**b** A document with a blank space or blank spaces to be filled up. M16.
in blank [after French *en blanc*] with blank spaces for the filling in of details.
4 A lottery ticket which does not gain a prize. M16.
draw a blank: see DRAW *verb* 8.
5 The white spot in the centre of a target; *fig.* something aimed at. Also, the range of an aim (*lit.* & *fig.*), *esp.* point-blank range. L16.
6 Blank verse. L16.
7 A piece of metal, wood, glass, wax, etc., intended for further fabrication; *esp.* in coinage, the disc of metal before stamping. L16.
8 A vacant space, place, or period. E17.

SLOAN WILSON He had . . tried hard to think of nothing, to make his mind a complete blank. D. PIPER Those two years before he entered the Inns of Court in 1592 are virtually a blank.

9 Anything insignificant; nothing at all. L17.

SIR W. SCOTT His debts amount to blank—his losses to blank—his funds to blank—leaving a balance of blank in his favour.

10 Used as a substitute for an omitted letter, name, or (esp. abusive or profane) noun or in reading a printed or written dash so used. L18.

B. HARTE What in blank are you waiting for? *Listener* Anecdotes . . about Lord Blank's personality and foolish views.

11 A domino without pips on one or (also ***double blank***) both of its halves. E19.
12 A zero score in a game. *N. Amer.* M19.
13 A blank cartridge. L19.
14 (A substance employed in) a control test done without a specimen. E20.
15 A blank leaf in a printed book or a manuscript. M20.

blank /blaŋk/ *adjective & adverb*. ME.
[ORIGIN Old French & mod. French *blanc* white from Proto-Romance from Germanic base of Old High German *blanc* white, shining, Old English *blanca* white steed, Old Norse *blakkr* pale (horse).]
▸ **A** *adjective*. †**1** White; pale, colourless. ME–E19.

MILTON The blanc Moone.

2 Of paper, (a part of) a piece of paper, etc.: left white, not written or printed on, to be filled in. Of a document: with a space or spaces left for a signature or details. LME.

SHAKES. *Merry W.* I warrant he hath a thousand of these letters, writ with blank space for different names. LD MACAULAY A blank safe conduct in the largest terms. J. G. COZZENS Each article and report began with a big inset blank square which was to be filled by an illuminated initial.

3 Void of interest, incident, result, or expression. M16. ▸**b** Disconcerted, nonplussed, puzzled. M16.

D. LESSING Molly's voice had gone blank, empty even of condemnation. J. RHYS Trying to protect herself with silence and a blank face. A. GRAY Every life has its blank moments when . . there's nothing to do but think. **b** MILTON Adam . . amaz'd, Astonied stood and Blank.

4 Of emotions: stark, unrelieved; *gen.* pure, sheer, absolute (with negative or privative force). M17.

W. DE LA MARE His deadliest danger now was blank despair. T. BENN Pressure for full disclosure is likely to be met by a blank refusal.

5 *gen.* Empty, without contents. M18.

W. OWEN The stark, blank sky. L. WOOLF One of those people whose minds go blank the moment they are faced by the slightest crisis.

6 Used as a substitute for an (esp. abusive or profane) adjective or in reading a printed or written dash so used. M19.

M. DIVER Colonel Stanham Buckley . . inquired . . when . . this blankety blank train was supposed to start.

7 CARDS. Lacking in support from other cards of the same suit. L19.

– SPECIAL COLLOCATIONS & COMB.: **blank-book** a book of clean writing paper; **blank cartridge**: without a bullet, to make a sound only; **blank charter** a document given to the agents of the crown in Richard II's reign, with power to fill it up as they pleased; *transf.* & *fig.* = CARTE BLANCHE; **blank cheque** a cheque which is not made out; a cheque which is made out except for the amount, which the payee is to decide and fill in; *transf.* & *fig.* = CARTE BLANCHE; **blank flange** a disc used to block off the end of a pipe; **blank test** a control test done without a specimen; **blank verse** verse without rhyme; *esp.* the iambic pentameter or unrhymed heroic; **blank wall** (**a**) a wall without an opening in it; (**b**) an apparently impenetrable obstacle; **blank window** an imitation window.
▸ **B** *adverb*. Used as a substitute for an (esp. abusive or profane) adverb or in reading a printed or written dash so used. L19.
■ **blankety**, **blanky** *adjectives & adverbs* = BLANK *adjective* 6, *adverb* L19. **blankly** *adverb* E19. **blankness** *noun* M19.

blank /blaŋk/ *verb*. L15.
[ORIGIN from the noun.]
†**1** = BLANCH *verb*[1] 1. L15–M17.
2 *verb trans.* Put out of countenance; disconcert. *arch.* M16.
3 *verb trans.* Frustrate; make void; invalidate. *arch.* M16.
4 *verb trans.* Veil from sight; make invisible or undetectable. Also foll. by *out*. M18.
5 a *verb trans.* Substitute a dash for, indicate by a dash. *rare*. L18. ▸**b** *verb trans.* & *intrans.* Used as a substitute for an (esp. abusive or profane) verb or in reading a printed or written dash so used. L19.

b C. READE Blank him! that is just like him.

6 *verb trans.* CARDS. Leave (a card) unsupported by another card of the same suit. L19.
7 *verb trans.* Dismiss (a sports team) without a score; prevent from scoring. *N. Amer.* L19.
8 *verb trans.* Seal, render inoperative. Foll. by *off*, *up*. E20.
9 *verb trans.* & *intrans.* Cut or prepare (as) a blank for fabrication. Freq. foll. by *out*. E20.
10 *verb intrans.* Become blank or empty. Also foll. by *out*. M20.

R. LOWELL My mind always blanked . . when Mother asked prying questions.

11 *verb trans.* Cold-shoulder, ignore (a person). *slang*. L20.
■ **blanked** *ppl adjective & adverb* (**a**) *adjective* that has been blanked; (**b**) *adjective & adverb* = DAMNED *adjective* 4, *adverb*: E16.

blanket /ˈblaŋkɪt/ *noun & adjective*. ME.
[ORIGIN Old Northern French *blanquet*, *blanket*, Old French *blanchet* (Anglo-Latin *blanchettum*, *-ketum*, *-chetta*), from *blanc*, *blanche* white: see BLANK *adjective*, BLANCH *adjective*, -ET[1].]
▸ **A** *noun*. †**1** An undyed woollen stuff used for clothing. Only in ME.
2 A large piece of woollen etc. material used for warmth, esp. as a bed covering, simple garment, etc. ME.
3 *fig.* A thick covering mass or layer (*of*). E17.

A. E. STEVENSON America was covered with a blanket of trees. A. SILLITOE A blanket of dark cloud lay low over the city as if, were God to pull a lever, it would release a six-foot blanket of snow.

4 PRINTING. A woollen etc. cloth used to equalize the impression of the platen or cylinder or intaglio plate; in offset printing, a rubber-surfaced sheet transferring the impression from plate to paper etc. L17.
5 In full ***blanket-piece***. A layer of blubber in whales. M19.
– PHRASES: **born on the wrong side of the blanket** illegitimate. **electric blanket** a blanket that can be connected to the mains and heated by means of internal wiring. ***pig in a blanket***: see PIG *noun*[1]. ***receiving blanket***: see RECEIVING *adjective*. ***stroud blanket***: see STROUD 1. ***Wagga blanket***. ***wet blanket***: see WET *adjective*.
– COMB.: **blanket bath** the washing of a patient in bed; **blanket bog** an extensive peat bog existing as a consequence of high rainfall or humidity rather than of local water sources; **blanket coat** *N. Amer.* a coat made from a blanket; **blanket finish** a very close finish in a race (such that the contestants could be covered with a blanket); **blanket flower** = GAILLARDIA; ***blanket-piece***: see sense 5 above; **blanket roll** *US* a soldier's blanket and kit made into a roll for use on active service; **blanket stiff** *slang* a tramp; **blanket stitch** a buttonhole stitch worked on the edge of blankets or other material too thick to be hemmed; **blanket weed** a common green freshwater alga of the genus *Spirogyra*, which forms long unbranched filaments and can spread uncontrollably in over-enriched water and garden ponds.
▸ **B** *adjective*. Covering all or many cases or classes, inclusive, general rather than individual, indiscriminate. L19.

T. HEGGEN The blanket prescription of aspirin tablets for all complaints. J. GLASSCO His blanket condemnation of almost everything.

■ **blankeˈteer** *noun* (*obsolete* exc. *hist.*) a person who uses a blanket; *spec.* in *pl.*, a body of hand-loom weavers who met at Manchester in 1817, provided with blankets etc., in order to march to London and call attention to their grievances: M18.

blanket /ˈblaŋkɪt/ *verb trans.* E17.
[ORIGIN from the noun.]
1 Cover (as) with a blanket; stifle, keep quiet, (a scandal, question, etc.). E17.
2 Toss in a blanket (as a punishment). *obsolete* exc. *hist.* E17.
3 Supply with blankets. L19.
4 SAILING. Take the wind from the sails of (another craft) by passing to windward. L19.
5 Exclude (a radio signal) from reception by the use of a stronger signal. (Foll. by *out*.) M20.

blanketing /ˈblaŋkɪtɪŋ/ *noun*. **L16**.
[**ORIGIN** from **BLANKET** *verb* or *noun* + **-ING**¹.]
1 The action or an instance of tossing a person in a blanket (as a punishment). *obsolete* exc. *hist.* **L16**.
2 Material for blankets; supply of blankets. **L17**.
3 The action of covering (as) with a blanket. **L19**.

blanquette /blɑ̃kɛt/ *noun*. Pl. pronounced same. **M18**.
[**ORIGIN** French, formed as **BLANKET** *noun*.]
A dish of light meat, esp. veal, cooked in a white sauce.

Blanquism /ˈblɑ̃ːkɪz(ə)m/ *noun*. **E20**.
[**ORIGIN** from *Blanqui* (see below) + **-ISM**.]
The doctrine that socialist revolution must be initiated by a small conspiratorial group, advocated by the French revolutionary communist Louis Auguste Blanqui (1805–81).
■ **Blanquist** *noun* **L19**.

blare /blɛː/ *noun*. **E19**.
[**ORIGIN** from the verb.]
1 A strident sound; the sound of a trumpet etc.; *dial.* the sound of weeping, bellowing, etc. **E19**.
2 Brightness and conspicuousness of colour; a bright conspicuous colour. **L19**.

blare /blɛː/ *verb*. **LME**.
[**ORIGIN** Middle Dutch & mod. Dutch *bleren*, Middle Low German, Middle Dutch *blaren*: of imit. origin.]
1 *verb intrans.* Roar with prolonged sound in weeping, as a child; bellow, as a calf. Now chiefly *dial.* **LME**.

W. GOLDING The shattering call of a rutting stag blared just under the tree.

2 *verb intrans.* Of a trumpet etc.: sound out. Of a broadcasting apparatus etc.: sound stridently. **L18**.
3 *verb trans.* Utter or sound stridently. Also foll. by *out*. **M19**.

TENNYSON A tongue To blare its own interpretation. E. HUXLEY A radio blares out pop music at full blast. B. PLAIN Traffic . . blared furious horns.

blarney /ˈblɑːni/ *noun* & *verb*. **L18**.
[**ORIGIN** *Blarney*, a village and castle near Cork in the Republic of Ireland, with a stone said to confer a cajoling tongue on whoever kisses it.]
▸ **A** *noun*. Smoothly flattering or cajoling talk; nonsense. **L18**.
▸ **B** *verb*. **1** *verb intrans.* Use blarney. **E19**.
2 *verb trans.* Subject to blarney. **M19**.

blart /blɑːt/ *verb intrans. dial.* **E19**.
[**ORIGIN** Prob. a form of **BLEAT** *verb*.]
1 Bleat, low. **E19**.
2 Cry, howl, whimper. **L19**.

blasé /ˈblɑːzeɪ/ *adjective*. **E19**.
[**ORIGIN** French.]
Cloyed with or tired of pleasure; bored or unimpressed by things from having seen or experienced them too often.

blaspheme /blasˈfiːm/ *verb*. **ME**.
[**ORIGIN** Old French *blasfemer* (mod. *blasphémer*) from ecclesiastical Latin *blasphemare* revile, reproach from Greek *blasphēmein*, from *blasphēmos*: see **BLASPHEMOUS**. Cf. **BLAME** *verb*.]
1 *verb intrans.* Talk profanely. **ME**.
2 *verb trans.* Speak irreverently of (something supposed to be sacred). **LME**.
3 *verb trans.* Speak evil of; calumniate; abuse. **LME**.
■ **blasphemer** *noun* **LME**.

blasphemous /ˈblasfəməs/ *adjective*. **LME**.
[**ORIGIN** from ecclesiastical Latin *blasphemus* (from Greek *blasphēmos* evil-speaking) + **-OUS**.]
1 Uttering profanity; impiously irreverent. **LME**.
†**2** Abusive; slanderous; defamatory. Only in **E17**.
■ **blasphemously** *adverb* **M16**. **blasphemousness** *noun* **M19**.

blasphemy /ˈblasfəmi/ *noun*. **ME**.
[**ORIGIN** Old French *blasfemie* from ecclesiastical Latin *blasphemia* from Greek *blasphēmia* slander, blasphemy: see **-Y**³.]
Profane talk of something supposed to be sacred; impious irreverence.

blast /blɑːst/ *noun*¹.
[**ORIGIN** Old English *blǣst* = Old High German *blāst*, Old Norse *blástr* (perh. the immediate source in Middle English) from Germanic, from base also of **BLAZE** *verb*².]
1 A blowing or strong gust of air or wind. **OE**.
2 A puff of air through the mouth or nostrils; a breath. *arch.* **ME**.
3 A blow on a trumpet or other wind instrument or on a whistle; a sounding of a car horn, siren, etc.; the sound of a trumpet, whistle, car horn, etc. **ME**.
4 A sudden infection destructive to vegetable or animal life; blight; a blasting, withering, or pernicious influence; a curse. *arch.* **M16**.
5 A strong current of air produced artificially, *spec.* one used in smelting etc. **E17**. ▸**b** A severe reprimand, a violent outburst. *colloq.* **L19**.
†**6** A stroke of lightning; a thunderbolt. **M17–M18**.
7 An explosion. **M17**. ▸**b** A destructive wave of highly compressed air spreading outwards from an explosion. **M19**. ▸**c** The quantity of explosive used in a blasting operation. **L19**.
8 A party; a good time; an enjoyable experience. *slang.* **M20**.

B. ELTON 'You should have a reunion,' he said smiling. 'You'd have a blast.'

– PHRASES: **at full blast** at maximum speed or capacity, at full pitch, very loudly. †**at one blast** [Latin *uno flatu*] at the same time. **full blast**, †**in full blast** = *at full blast* above. **out of blast** not at work; stopped.
– COMB.: **blast bomb**: depending for its effect on the blast of air spreading outwards from the explosion (see sense 7b above); **blast-freezing** refrigeration (of meat etc.) in rapidly circulating cold air; **blast furnace** a smelting furnace in which a blast of air is used, *esp.* one for iron-smelting using a compressed hot air blast; **blast hole** a hole for an explosive charge in blasting; **blast pipe** (*a*) a pipe through which air is passed into a blast furnace; (*b*) in a steam locomotive, a pipe conveying the steam from the cylinders into the funnel and so increasing the draught.
■ **blasty** *adjective* characterized by gusts of wind **L15**.

blast /blast/ *noun*². **E20**.
[**ORIGIN** Greek *blastos*: see **-BLAST**.]
BIOLOGY. An immature proliferative differentiated cell of an organism. Also ***blast cell***.

blast /blɑːst/ *verb*. **ME**.
[**ORIGIN** from **BLAST** *noun*¹.]
▸ **I** *gen.* **1** *verb intrans.* Blow; puff violently, pant. Long *obsolete* exc. *Scot.* **ME**.
†**2** **a** *verb intrans.* & *trans.* Blow (a trumpet etc.). **LME–M16**. ▸**b** *verb trans.* Assail with trumpeting etc. **E17–M19**.
3 *verb trans.* Fill (*up*) with air etc., swell (*up*). Long *dial.* **L16**.
4 *verb trans.* Blow up (rocks etc.) by explosion; create *out of* or *from* rocks etc. by explosion. **M18**.
blasting gelatin. **blasting powder** a mixture like gunpowder but with sodium nitrate instead of potassium nitrate, used for blasting.
5 *verb intrans.* Of a rocket, spacecraft, etc.: take *off* from the launching site. **M20**.
▸ **II** To ill effect.
6 *verb trans.* Of a wind etc.: blow or breathe balefully or perniciously on; wither, shrivel, (a plant, limb, etc.). **M16**.
7 *verb trans. transf.* & *fig.* ▸**a** Blight, ruin, (plans, prosperity, etc.); bring infamy upon (character, reputation, etc.). **L16**. ▸**b** Strike (the eyes or vision) with dimness or horror. *arch.* **L18**.
†**8** *verb intrans.* Wither or fall under a blight. **L16–M19**.
9 *verb trans.* Curse, strike with the wrath of heaven. Freq. in imprecations in imper. or optative form (for ***God blast*** — etc.). **M17**. ▸**b** *verb intrans.* Curse, use profane language. **M18**. ▸**c** *verb intrans.* as *interjection* = **DAMN** *verb* 3b. **E20**.

LD MACAULAY Calling on their Maker to curse them . . blast them, and damn them. W. OWEN O blast this pencil. 'Ere, Bill, lend's a knife. **b** B. BEHAN He . . never damned or blasted. **c** E. F. BENSON 'There's an extra confirmation class this evening.' . . 'Oh, blast!'

■ **blaster** *noun* a person who or thing which blasts; *fig.* a heavy lofted golf club for playing from bunkers: **L16**.

-blast /blast/ *suffix*.
[**ORIGIN** Greek *blastos* sprout, germ.]
Forming nouns denoting embryonic cells (as ***erythroblast***: cf. **-CYTE**) or germ tissue (***epiblast***).

blasted /ˈblɑːstɪd/ *adjective* & *adverb*. **M16**.
[**ORIGIN** from **BLAST** *verb* + **-ED**¹.]
▸ **A** *adjective*. **1** *gen.* That has been blasted. **M16**.
2 Cursed, damnable, bloody. *colloq.* **L17**.
3 Intoxicated. *slang.* **L20**.
▸ **B** *adverb*. Cursedly, damnably, bloody. *colloq.* **M19**.

blastema /blaˈstiːmə/ *noun*. Pl. **-mas**, **-mata** /-mətə/. **M19**.
[**ORIGIN** Greek *blastēma* sprout.]
BIOLOGY. A mass of undifferentiated cells from which a part develops or is regenerated.
■ **blastemal** *adjective* **M19**. **blasteˈmatic** *adjective* **M19**.

blasto- /ˈblastəʊ/ *combining form* of Greek *blastos* sprout, germ: see **-O-**. Used chiefly in *BIOLOGY* with the sense 'germ', 'bud'.
■ **blastocoel(e)** /ˈblastə(ʊ)siːl/ *noun* [Greek *koilos* hollow] the central cavity of a blastula **L19**. **blastoˈcoelic** *adjective* of or pertaining to a blastocoele **L19**. **blastocyst** *noun* a mammalian blastula in which some differentiation of cells has occurred **L19**. **blastoderm** *noun* a blastula having the form of a disc of cells on top of the yolk **M19**. **blastodisc** *noun* = **BLASTODERM L19**. **blastoˈgenesis** *noun* reproduction by budding or gemmation **L19**. **blastoˈgenic** *adjective* of, pertaining to, or formed by blastogenesis **L19**. **blastomere** *noun* each of the cells formed by cleavage of a fertilized ovum **L19**. **blastomyˈcosis** *noun* a disease caused by infection with parasitic fungi of the genus *Blastomyces*, affecting the skin or the internal organs **E20**. **blastoˈmylonite** *noun* (*PETROGRAPHY*) recrystallized mylonite retaining traces of cataclastic structure **M20**. **blastoˈporal** *adjective* of or pertaining to a blastopore **L19**. **blastopore** *noun* an opening formed by invagination of the surface of a blastula **L19**. **blastospore** *noun* a fungal spore formed by budding **M20**.

blast-off /ˈblɑːstɒf/ *noun*. **M20**.
[**ORIGIN** from *blast off*: see **BLAST** *verb* 5.]
(The initial thrust for) the launching of a rocket, spacecraft, etc.

blastoid /ˈblastɔɪd/ *noun* & *adjective*. **L19**.
[**ORIGIN** from mod. Latin *Blastoidea* (see below): see **BLASTO-**, **-OID**.]
PALAEONTOLOGY. ▸**A** *noun*. An extinct echinoderm of the class Blastoidea. **L19**.
▸ **B** *adjective*. Of or pertaining to this class. **L19**.

blastula /ˈblastjʊlə/ *noun*. Pl. **-lae** /-liː/, **-las**. **L19**.
[**ORIGIN** mod. Latin, from Greek *blastos*: see **BLASTO-**, **-ULE**.]
BIOLOGY. A structure, freq. a hollow sphere, formed by the cells of an embryo after cleavage of the ovum and before gastrulation. Cf. **BLASTOCYST**.
■ **blastular** *adjective* **E20**. **blastuˈlation** *noun* formation of a blastula **L19**.

blat /blat/ *noun*¹. *slang*. Also **-tt**. **M20**.
[**ORIGIN** German *Blatt*.]
A newspaper.

blat /blat/ *verb* & *noun*². Chiefly *US*. **M19**.
[**ORIGIN** Imit.]
▸ **A** *verb*. Infl. **-tt-**.
1 *verb intrans.* Bleat, make a sound like a bleat; make a loud harsh noise; talk garrulously or impulsively. **M19**.
2 *verb trans.* Blurt *out*; blast out. **L19**.
▸ **B** *noun*. A bleat or similar cry; a loud harsh noise. **E20**.

blatant /ˈbleɪt(ə)nt/ *adjective*. Also †**-tt-**. **L16**.
[**ORIGIN** Perh. alt. of Scot. *blatand* bleating, assoc. with **BLATTER**.]
1 ***the blatant beast***, the thousand-tongued monster produced by Cerberus and Chimaera, symbolizing calumny. **L16**.
2 Orig., noisy, clamorous, noticeably loud. Now usu., obtrusive, lacking in subtlety, obvious; (of bad behaviour) openly and unashamed. **M17**.
3 Bleating. *poet.* **L18**.

Earth Matters The Government's blatant disregard of its own legislation. *Independent* Blatant sex appeal is sacrificed for style.

– NOTE: First recorded in Spenser.
■ **blatancy** *noun* blatant quality **E17**. **blatantly** *adverb* **M19**.

blate /bleɪt/ *adjective*. *Scot.* & *N. English*. **LME**.
[**ORIGIN** Uncertain: corresp. phonet. but not in sense to Old English *blāt* pale, ghastly.]
1 Spiritless, timid, bashful. **LME**.
2 Dull, stupid. **E16**.

blateration /blatəˈreɪʃ(ə)n/ *noun*. *rare*. **M17**.
[**ORIGIN** Late Latin *blateratio(n-)*, from *blaterat-* pa. ppl stem of *blaterare*: see **BLATTER**, **-ATION**.]
Babbling chatter.

blather /ˈblaðə/ *verb* & *noun*. Orig. *Scot.* & *N. English*. Also **blether** /ˈblɛðə/. See also **BLITHER**. **LME**.
[**ORIGIN** Old Norse *blaðra*, from *blaðr* nonsense.]
▸ **A** *verb*. **1** *verb intrans.* Talk loquacious nonsense. **LME**.
2 *verb trans.* Utter loquaciously. **E19**.
3 *verb intrans.* Cry loudly, blubber. *dial.* **M19**.
▸ **B** *noun*. **1** Loquacious nonsense. **E18**.
2 An idle chatterer. **E19**.

blatherskite /ˈblaðəskʌɪt/ *noun*. *dial.* & *US colloq.* Also **bletherskate** /ˈblɛðəskeɪt/. **M17**.
[**ORIGIN** from **BLATHER** + **SKATE** *noun*³.]
A foolish and voluble talker, a blathering person. Also, foolish talk, nonsense.

blatt *noun* var. of **BLAT** *noun*¹.

blatta /ˈblatə/ *noun*. Pl. †**-ttae**. **E17**.
[**ORIGIN** Latin.]
A nocturnal insect; *spec.* a cockroach. Now only as mod. Latin genus name.

†**blattant** *adjective* var. of **BLATANT**.

blatter /ˈblatə/ *verb* & *noun*. **M16**.
[**ORIGIN** Partly from Latin *blaterare* babble, partly imit.]
▸ **A** *verb*. **1** *verb intrans.* & *trans.* Prate volubly. **M16**.
2 *verb intrans.* Move with a clatter; strike repeatedly. Chiefly *Scot.* **E18**.
▸ **B** *noun*. A volley of clattering words; a sound of rapid motion. Chiefly *Scot.* **E19**.
■ **blatterer** *noun* a voluble prater **E17**.

blaud *verb* & *noun* var. of **BLAD**.

blawort /ˈblɑːwəːt/ *noun*. *Scot.* **E18**.
[**ORIGIN** from **BLAE** + **WORT** *noun*¹.]
A harebell; a cornflower.

blaxploitation /ˌblakspl ɔɪˈteɪʃ(ə)n/ *noun*. *US colloq.* **L20**.
[**ORIGIN** Blend of *Blacks* pl. (see **BLACK** *noun* 6) and **EXPLOITATION**.]
The exploitation of black people, esp. in films.

blay /bleɪ/ *noun*. Also **bley**.
[**ORIGIN** Old English *blǣge* = Middle Low German, Middle Dutch *bleie* (Dutch *blei*), German *Blei(h)e*, from West Germanic, of unknown origin.]
= **BLEAK** *noun*.

blaze /bleɪz/ *noun*¹.
[**ORIGIN** Old English *blæse*, *blase* from Germanic; cf. Middle High German *blas* torch, rel., through the gen. sense 'shining', to **BLAZE** *noun*².]
†**1** A torch. **OE–M16**.
2 A bright flame or fire. **OE**. ▸**b** In *pl.* Hell. *slang.* **E19**.

b DICKENS How the blazes you can stand the head-work you do, is a mystery to me. DAY LEWIS What the blue blazes is all this?

in a blaze in flames, on fire. **b** ***ballyhoo of blazes***: see **BALLYHOO** *noun*¹. **go to blazes** be ruined or destroyed; (as *interjection*) go away. **like blazes** furiously, with great energy.
3 A brilliant display; a glow of bright colour; brilliance; clear or full light (*lit.* & *fig.*). **LME**.

B

MILTON O dark, dark, dark, amid the blaze of noon. LD MACAULAY The theatres were . . one blaze of orange ribands. W. E. H. LECKY The blaze of publicity. J. B. PRIESTLEY The hall was now a blaze of light.

4 A violent outburst (*of* passion etc.). L16.
5 *POKER.* A hand containing court cards only. L19.

blaze /bleɪz/ *noun*². M17.
[ORIGIN Uncertain. Identical in meaning with Old Norse *blesi*, Middle Dutch *blesse* (Dutch *bles*), German *Blässe*, *Blesse*: cf. synon. Old High German *blassa* (Middle High German *blasse*) and Old High German *blas/ros*, Middle Low German *blasenhengst* horse with a blaze; also Middle High German *blas* bald, German *blass* pale, and parallel formations with *r*, as Middle Low German *blare*, Dutch *blaar* cow with a blaze, Middle Dutch *blaer* bald.]
1 A white spot or streak on the face of a horse, ox, etc. M17.
2 A mark made on a tree by chipping off bark, to indicate a route, record a reference number, etc. M18.
■ **blazed** *adjective* having a blaze L17.

blaze /bleɪz/ *verb*¹. ME.
[ORIGIN from BLAZE *noun*¹: no corresp. verb in other Germanic langs.]
1 *verb intrans.* Burn with a bright flame. ME. ▸**b** Be lit by a blaze. L19.

b J. R. GREEN The streets of London blazed with bonfires.

2 *verb intrans.* Show intense passion, anger, excitement, etc. ME.

I. HAMILTON If one disagreed with him, he would begin to blaze.

3 *verb intrans.* Shine like fire; show bright colours; emit bright light; be conspicuously brilliant (*lit.* & *fig.*). LME.

G. ORWELL The sun blazed on them. J. UPDIKE The white woman's eyes blazed.

4 *verb trans.* Cause to burn with a flame. L15. ▸**b** *verb trans.* & *intrans.* Light (a pipe or cigarette of marijuana); smoke (marijuana). *slang.* L20.
– WITH ADVERBS IN SPECIALIZED SENSES: **blaze away** fire continuously with a rifle etc. (*at*), work enthusiastically at anything. **blaze out** *arch.* exhaust in passion or excess. **blaze up** burst into flame, burst out in anger.

blaze /bleɪz/ *verb*². LME.
[ORIGIN Middle Low German, Middle Dutch *blāzen* blow = Old High German *blāsen* (German *blasen*), Old Norse *blása*, Gothic *uf*]*blesan* puff up, from Germanic extension (whence also BLAST *noun*¹) of base of BLOW *verb*¹.]
†**1** *verb trans.* Blow *out* on a trumpet etc. Only in LME.
†**2** *verb trans.* Adorn with heraldic devices etc.; emblazon. *rare.* LME–E19.
†**3** *verb trans.* = BLAZON *verb* 1. LME–E17.
†**4** *verb intrans.* Blow, puff. L15–M16.
5 *verb trans.* Proclaim (as with a trumpet), make known. Freq. foll. by *abroad.* M16.
†**6** *verb trans.* = BLAZON *verb* 2. M16–M17.

blaze /bleɪz/ *verb*³ *trans.* M18.
[ORIGIN from BLAZE *noun*².]
Mark (a tree, a path, etc.) by chipping off bark.
blaze the trail, **blaze the way**, etc., show the way for others to follow (*lit.* & *fig.*).

blazer /ˈbleɪzə/ *noun*¹. Now *rare* or *obsolete*. LME.
[ORIGIN from BLAZE *verb*² + -ER¹.]
= BLAZONER.

blazer /ˈbleɪzə/ *noun*². M17.
[ORIGIN from BLAZE *verb*¹ + -ER¹.]
1 A thing which blazes or shines. *rare* in *gen.* sense. M17.
2 A person who or thing which attracts attention. Chiefly *US.* M19.
3 A small cooking apparatus. L19.
4 A lightweight unlined jacket worn by schoolchildren, sportsmen, etc.; a man's plain or striped jacket not worn with matching trousers. L19.
■ **blazered** *adjective* wearing a blazer M20.

blazing /ˈbleɪzɪŋ/ *adjective.* LME.
[ORIGIN from BLAZE *verb*¹ + -ING².]
1 That blazes. LME.
blazing star †(**a**) a comet; (**b**) *arch.* a centre of attraction or admiration; (**c**) *N. Amer.* any of various plants with star-shaped flowers; spec. *Aletris farinosa*, a member of the lily family, with yellow or white flowers; also = ***devil's bit*** (b) s.v. DEVIL *noun*; also = LIATRIS.
2 Used as a substitute for an abusive or profane adjective. L19.
■ **blazingly** *adverb* M19.

blazon /ˈbleɪz(ə)n/ *noun.* ME.
[ORIGIN Old French & mod. French *blason* (orig.) shield (whence Spanish *blasón*, Portuguese *brasão*, Italian *blasone*) = Provençal *blezon*, *blizon*; of unknown origin.]
1 A shield, orig. as armour, long *spec.* as bearing a heraldic device; a coat of arms; armorial bearings; a banner bearing arms. ME.
2 A correct description of armorial bearings etc.; a record or description, esp. of virtues etc. L16.
3 Divulgation, publication. *rare.* E17.

blazon /ˈbleɪz(ə)n/ *verb trans.* LME.
[ORIGIN from BLAZON *noun* and BLAZE *verb*².]
1 Describe heraldically in a correct manner. LME.
2 Describe fitly or vividly; depict; celebrate. L15.
3 Announce boastfully. M16.
4 Proclaim; = BLAZE *verb*² 5. Also foll. by *out*. Freq. *derog.* L16.
5 Depict or paint heraldically. L16.
6 Paint or depict in colours; illuminate. L17.
7 Inscribe with (or *with*) arms, names, etc., in colours or ornamentally. E19.
■ **blazoner** *noun* (**a**) a person who blazons arms, a herald; (**b**) a recorder or proclaimer (*of*): L16. **blazonment** *noun* proclamation, making known L19.

blazonry /ˈbleɪz(ə)nri/ *noun.* E17.
[ORIGIN from BLAZON *verb* + -RY.]
1 (The correct description or depicting of) heraldic devices or armorial bearings. E17.
2 Brightly coloured display. E19.

-ble /b(ə)l/ *suffix.*
[ORIGIN Old French & mod. French from Latin *-bilem*, nom. *-bilis* forming act. or pass. verbal adjectives from verbs or pa. ppl stems.]
See -ABLE, -IBLE, -UBLE.

bleach /bliːtʃ/ *noun.*
[ORIGIN Old English *blǣće*, from *blǣć* pale. Branch II from BLEACH *verb.*]
▸ **I 1** Whiteness, paleness. Long *rare.* OE.
†**2** Leprosy; a skin disease. OE–E17.
▸ **II 3 a** *attrib.* [partly repr. the verb.] Designating locations of industrial bleaching, as ***bleachfield***, ***bleachworks***, etc. E18. ▸**b** An act of bleaching; a bleached condition. L19.
4 (A) bleaching substance, *spec.* a solution of sodium hypochlorite or hydrogen peroxide used for sterilizing drains, sinks, etc. L19.

bleach /bliːtʃ/ *verb.*
[ORIGIN Old English *blǣćan* = Old Norse *bleikja* from Germanic, from a base meaning 'shining, white, pale' (whence also BLEAK *adjective*).]
1 *verb trans.* Blanch, make white; deprive of colour; *spec.* whiten (linen etc.) by washing and exposure to sunlight or by a chemical process. OE. ▸**b** *PHOTOGRAPHY.* Remove the silver image from (a negative or print) after development. L19.

W. HOLTBY Hair . . bleached flax-white by sun and weather. J. RABAN The wood . . had been bleached to a pale whisky colour.

2 *verb intrans.* Become white, pale, or colourless; whiten. Also foll. by *out*. E17.

SHAKES. *Wint. T.* The white sheet bleaching on the hedge. A. BRINK Where one could shrivel up and bleach out like a dried bone in the sun.

■ **bleachery** *noun* a place where bleaching is carried out E18.

bleacher /ˈbliːtʃə/ *noun.* ME.
[ORIGIN from BLEACH *verb* + -ER¹.]
1 A person who bleaches (esp. textiles). ME.
2 A vessel or chemical used in bleaching. L19.
3 An outdoor uncovered bench for spectators at a sports ground. Usu. in *pl.* exc. *attrib.* Chiefly *N. Amer.* L19.

bleak /bliːk/ *noun.* L15.
[ORIGIN Prob. from Old Norse *bleikja* = Old High German *bleicha*, from Germanic, formed as BLEAK *adjective*.]
A small silvery river fish, *Alburnus alburnus*, of the carp family. Also, any of certain related fishes. Cf. earlier BLAY.

bleak /bliːk/ *adjective.*
[ORIGIN Old English *blāc* = Old Norse *bleikr* shining, white, from Germanic, from base also of BLEACH *verb*; later directly from Old Norse.]
†**1** Shining, white. OE–L15.
2 Pale, pallid, wan; of a sickly hue; drained of colour. Long *obsolete* exc. *dial.* OE. ▸**b** Yellow. *N. English.* L16.
3 Bare of vegetation; exposed. M16.

R. L. STEVENSON Toano, a little station on a bleak, high-lying plateau in Nevada.

4 Cold, chilly. L16.

WORDSWORTH In bleak December, I retraced this way.

5 *fig.* Cheerless, dreary; unpromising; inhospitable. E18.

P. G. WODEHOUSE He looked into the future. It had a grey and bleak aspect. A. MACLEAN The room was bleak, monastic, linoleum-covered.

■ **bleakish** *adjective* L16. **bleakly** *adverb* M16. **bleakness** *noun* E17. **bleaky** *adjective* (*poet.*) tending to bleakness, somewhat bleak L17.

blear /blɪə/ *verb*, *adjective*, & *noun.* ME.
[ORIGIN Unknown: cf. Middle High German *blerre* blurred vision, Low German *blarroged*, *blerr-* bleary-eyed.]
▸ **A** *verb.* **1** *verb intrans.* Have watery or inflamed eyes, be bleary-eyed. Long *rare.* ME.
2 *verb trans.* Dim (the eyes) with tears, rheum, sleep, etc. ME.
blear the eye of, **blear the eyes of** *arch.* hoodwink, deceive.
3 *verb trans.* Blur (the face etc.) with tears, rheum, etc.; make bleary-eyed. LME.
▸ **B** *adjective.* **1** Of the eyes: bleary. Chiefly in ***blear-eyed*** below. LME.
2 *gen.* Dim, misty, indistinct. M17.
– COMB.: **blear-eyed** *adjective* = ***BLEARY-eyed***; **blear-eyedness** = ***BLEARY-eyedness***.
▸ **C** *noun.* †**1** In *pl.* Bleary eyes. *rare.* Only in E17.
2 The state or condition of being bleared. *rare.* M19.
■ **blearedness** *noun* LME. **blearness** *noun* M16.

bleary /ˈblɪəri/ *adjective.* LME.
[ORIGIN from BLEAR *adjective* + -Y¹.]
(Of the eyes) dim, dull, filmy, full of sleep; *gen.* dim, misty, indistinct.
– COMB.: **bleary-eyed** *adjective* having bleary eyes; half asleep; *fig.* dull of perception, short-sighted; **bleary-eyedness** the state or condition of being bleary-eyed.
■ **blearily** *adverb* E20. **bleariness** *noun* LME.

bleat /bliːt/ *verb* & *noun.*
[ORIGIN Old English *blǣtan* = Old High German *blāzen*, Dutch *blaten*, of imit. origin.]
▸ **A** *verb.* **1** *verb intrans.* Of a sheep, goat, or calf: give its natural tremulous cry. OE.
2 *verb intrans.* Speak, cry, etc., in a feeble manner, foolishly, or plaintively. M16.
3 *verb trans.* Say, cry, etc., (as) with a bleat. Also foll. by *out*. L17.
▸ **B** *noun.* †**1** = BLEATER. Only in LME.
2 The natural tremulous cry of a sheep, goat, or calf; any similar cry, *esp.* a querulous or feeble one. E16.
3 A feebly expressed complaint or grievance. *colloq.* E20.
■ **bleater** *noun* an animal that bleats M16. **bleatingly** *adverb* in a bleating manner, plaintively M20.

bleb /blɛb/ *noun* & *verb.* E17.
[ORIGIN Var. of earlier BLOB *noun*.]
▸ **A** *noun.* **1** A small swelling on the skin; a similar swelling on plants. E17.
2 A bubble in water, glass, or other substances previously fluid. M17.
3 A vesicular body. L18.
4 *CYTOLOGY.* A swelling due to injury on the surface of a cell. M20.
▸ **B** *verb.* Infl. **-bb-**.
1 *verb trans.* Provide with blebs. *rare.* E19.
2 *verb intrans.* Form or develop a bleb or blebs. M20.
■ **blebby** *adjective* full of blebs M18.

bleck /blɛk/ *noun* & *verb. obsolete* exc. *Scot.* & *dial.* ME.
[ORIGIN Old Norse *blek* (Swedish *bläck*, Danish *blæk*) ink, from base of BLACK *adjective*.]
▸ **A** *noun.* **1** A black fluid substance; *spec.* (**a**) ink; (**b**) a preparation used for blacking leather; (**c**) black grease for axles etc. ME.
2 Soot; a particle of soot. L16.
▸ **B** *verb trans.* **1** Make black; blacken with ink etc. LME.
2 *fig.* Blacken morally; defile. LME.
3 Enter with ink; write. LME.

bled /bled/ *noun.* M20.
[ORIGIN French from Algerian Arab., corresp. to classical Arab. *balad* vast stretch of country, *bilād* land, country.]
In NW Africa: uncultivated land behind a fertile populated area.

bled *verb pa. t.* & *pple* of BLEED *verb.*

blee /bliː/ *noun.* Long *arch.*
[ORIGIN Old English *blēo(h)*, *blīo(h)* = Old Frisian, Old Saxon *blī*, Northern Frisian *blåy*.]
1 Colour. OE.
2 Complexion; visage. ME.

bleed /bliːd/ *noun.* L16.
[ORIGIN from the verb.]
1 The action or an instance of bleeding. L16.
nosebleed: see NOSE *noun*.
2 A page printed or trimmed so as to leave no margin (cf. BLEED *verb* 8, 14). M20.

bleed /bliːd/ *verb.* Pa. t. & pple **bled** /blɛd/.
[ORIGIN Old English *blēdan* = Old Frisian *blēda*, Middle Low German *blōden*, Old Norse *blœða*, from Germanic, from base of BLOOD *noun*.]
▸ **I** *verb intrans.* **1** Emit, discharge, or lose blood. OE.
bleed like a pig, ***bleed like a stuck pig***: see PIG *noun*¹. **one's heart bleeds**, **the heart bleeds** (freq. *iron.*) one feels sorry (*for*).
2 Lose blood from severe wounds; be severely wounded; die by bloodshed. ME.

SHAKES. *Jul. Caes.* O that we then could come by Caesar's spirit, And not dismember Caesar! But, alas, Caesar must bleed for it!

3 Drop, flow, ooze. ME.

SHAKES. *John* But a quantity of life, Which bleeds away. POPE For me the balm shall bleed, and amber flow.

4 ***bleed well***, (of corn etc.) give a large yield. *N. English.* M17.
5 Part with money; pay lavishly (*for*); have money extorted. *colloq.* M17.
6 Of a plant: emit sap. L17.
7 Of a dye: come out in water. M19.
8 *TYPOGRAPHY.* Be cut into when pages are trimmed. M19.
9 Be as red as blood. M19.

D. WEVILL I watch the blue-veined snowfields bleed with sunrise.

▸ **II** *verb trans.* **10** Emit (blood or any other fluid) as from a wound. ME.

DRYDEN Roapy Gore, he from his Nostrils bleeds. B. TAYLOR Thy tawny hills shall bleed their purple wine.

11 Draw or let blood from, *spec.* (chiefly *hist.*) as a method of treatment in medicine. LME.
12 Draw or extort money from. *colloq.* L17.

D. STOREY It bled us, you know, educating you.

bleed white drain completely of resources.
13 Allow (a fluid) to drain or escape from a closed system through a valve etc.; treat (a system) thus. L19.
14 TYPOGRAPHY. Extend (usu. an illustration) to the edge of a page when trimming; cut into the printed area of (a book etc.) when trimming. E20.

bleeder /ˈbliːdə/ *noun*. ME.
[ORIGIN from BLEED *verb* + -ER[1].]
1 Chiefly *hist.* A person who draws blood, esp. surgically; a phlebotomist. ME.
2 A person who loses or sheds blood; *spec.* one inclined to bleed excessively from a slight wound, a haemophiliac. LME.
3 A stupid, unpleasant, or contemptible person or thing. *slang*. L19.

bleeding /ˈbliːdɪŋ/ *adjective & adverb*. ME.
[ORIGIN from BLEED *verb* + -ING[2].]
▸**A** *adjective*. **1** Losing or emitting blood; *rare* running or suffused with blood. ME. ▸**b** *fig.* Full of anguish from suffering, compassion, etc.; devastated by war or other catastrophe. L16.
2 Cursed, damnable, bloody. *colloq.* M19.

T. ROBBINS You come along on your bleeding errand, oblivious, unmindful.

– PHRASES: **bleeding edge** *colloq.* [after *leading edge*], the very forefront of technological innovation, extremely new technological advances or theories. **bleeding heart** (*a*) any of various plants; *esp.* a member of the genus *Dicentra*, of the fumitory family, with arching stems of red flowers; (*b*) *colloq.* a person who is too soft-hearted or sentimental.
▸**B** *adverb*. †**1** Conspicuously, completely. *rare* (Shakes., modifying *new*). Only in E17.
2 Cursedly, damnably, bloody. *colloq.* L19.

Times Why don't you bleeding do something about it?

bleep /bliːp/ *noun & verb*. M20.
[ORIGIN Imit.: cf. BLIP.]
▸**A** *noun*. An intermittent high-pitched sound, esp. as a radio signal or to replace censored words in broadcasting. Also (the word itself), used as a substitute for a censored word or phrase in reading aloud. M20.
▸**B** *verb*. **1** *verb intrans.* Emit a bleep or bleeps. M20.
2 *verb trans.* Substitute a bleep or bleeps for. Also foll. by *out*. L20.
3 *verb trans.* Alert or summon by a bleep or bleeps. L20.
■ **bleeper** *noun* a miniature radio receiver that emits bleeps M20. **bleeping** *adjective* (*a*) that bleeps; (*b*) *slang* = BLEEDING *adjective* 5: M20.

blellum /ˈblɛləm/ *noun*. *Scot.* L18.
[ORIGIN Perh. blend of BLAB *noun*[1], BLABBER *noun* and *skellum* var. of SKELM.]
A blab, an idle chatterer.

blemish /ˈblɛmɪʃ/ *noun*. E16.
[ORIGIN from the verb.]
A physical or moral defect; a stain; a flaw.
■ **blemishless** *adjective* L16.

blemish /ˈblɛmɪʃ/ *verb trans.* LME.
[ORIGIN Old French *ble(s)miss-* lengthened stem of *ble(s)mir* render pale, injure, prob. of Germanic origin: see -ISH[2].]
†**1** Hurt, damage, deface. LME–E17.
2 Injure the working of. LME.
3 Impair the beauty, brightness, or perfection of; sully, stain. LME. ▸†**b** Defame. LME–M18.
■ **blemisher** *noun* LME. **blemishment** *noun* L16.

†**blench** *noun*[1]. Also (*Scot. & N. English*) **blenk**. ME.
[ORIGIN from BLENCH *verb*[1]; later infl. by BLINK *noun*.]
1 (As *blench*.) A trick. Only in ME.
2 (As *blenk*.) A sudden gleam of light. ME–E16.
3 (Both forms.) A (usu. bright or cheerful) glance; a side glance. LME–L16.

blench *adjective, noun*[2], *& adverb* see BLANCH *adjective, noun, & adverb*.

blench /blɛn(t)ʃ/ *verb*[1]. Also (by assoc. with BLANCH *verb*[1]) **blanch** /blɑːn(t)ʃ/; (chiefly *Scot. & N. English*) †**blenk**.
[ORIGIN Old English *blenćan* = Old Norse *blekkja* impose upon, from Germanic; later infl. by BLINK *verb*.]
▸**I** All forms.
†**1** *verb trans.* Deceive, cheat. OE–E17.
2 *verb intrans.* Start aside, shy, flinch, shrink; of the eyes: lose firmness of glance, quail. ME.
3 *verb trans.* Elude, avoid; flinch from; ignore. ME.
4 *verb trans.* Turn (esp. deer) aside; *fig.* disconcert. L15.
▸†**II** Chiefly *Scot. & N. English*, as *blenk*.
5 *verb intrans.* Glitter, gleam. ME–E17.
6 *verb intrans.* Glance. LME–E17.
■ **blencher** *noun* †(*a*) a person who or thing which frightens away or turns (esp. deer) aside; (*b*) a person who flinches (*at*): M16.

blench *verb*[2] see BLANCH *verb*[1].

blenchfarm *noun* var. of BLANCHFARM.

blend /blɛnd/ *noun*. L19.
[ORIGIN from BLEND *verb*[2].]
1 A blending; a mixture formed by blending various sorts or grades (of spirits, tea, tobacco, wool, etc.) or personal or abstract qualities. L19.

DAY LEWIS That strange Anglo-Irish blend of reticence and emotionalism.

2 A portmanteau word. E20.

†**blend** *verb*[1] *trans.* Pa. t. & pple **blended**, **blent**. See also YBLENT *pa. pple & ppl adjective*[1].
[ORIGIN Old English *blendan* = Old Frisian *blenda*, Middle Low German *blenden*, Old High German *blenten* (German *blenden*), from Germanic causative formed as BLIND *adjective*.]
1 = BLIND *verb* 1. OE–E17.
2 *fig.* Blind the understanding, judgement, or moral sense of. ME–L16.

blend /blɛnd/ *verb*[2]. Pa. t. & pple **blended**, (*poet. & rhet.*) **blent** /blɛnt/. See also YBLENT *pa. pple & ppl adjective*[2]. ME.
[ORIGIN Prob. of Scandinavian origin, from *blend-* pres. stem, *blĕnd-* pa. stem of Old Norse *blanda* mix = Old English, Old Saxon, Gothic *blandan*, Old High German *blantan* mix: cf. BLAND *noun*.]
▸**I** *verb trans.* **1 a** Mix or mingle together. *obsolete* in *gen.* sense. ME. ▸**b** Mix (sorts or grades of spirits, tea, tobacco, etc.) so as to produce a certain quality; produce by so mixing. LME. ▸**c** Mix (components) intimately or harmoniously so that they are inseparable and their individuality is obscured; produce by so mixing. E17.

c CONAN DOYLE A cry in which joy and surprise seemed to be blended. TOLKIEN Evil dreams and evil waking were blended into a long tunnel of misery. D. LESSING Ant-heap earth . . has . . been blended by the jaws of a myriad workers.

b blended whisky: whisky made of blended malt and grain whiskies.
†**2** Stir up; trouble, agitate, disturb. ME–L16.

SPENSER These stormes, which now his beauty blend, Shall turn to calmes.

3 Mix or mingle intimately or closely *with*; mix thoroughly *in* (*with*) or *into*. L16.

WORDSWORTH Never to blend our pleasure or our pride With sorrow of the meanest thing that feels. R. CARRIER Blend in egg yolks until the mixture is a smooth homogeneous mass.

▸**II** *verb intrans.* **4** Mix or mingle together; unite intimately so as to form a uniform or harmonious mixture; (esp. of colours) pass imperceptibly into each other. LME.

B. PLAIN The air was full of sounds, blending into one long hum of afternoon. M. MOORCOCK The town and country met and blended in almost perfect harmony.

5 Mix or mingle intimately or closely *with*; mix harmoniously or thoroughly *in* (*with*); pass imperceptibly *into*. LME.

P. G. WODEHOUSE Pleasant Spring scents . . to blend with the robuster aroma of coffee and fried bacon. J. MCPHEE His fur blends so well into the tundra colors that sometimes it is hard to see him.

■ **blender** *noun* a person who blends (esp. spirits, tea, tobacco, etc.); an implement for blending, *esp.* a (usu. electric) device for blending foods (***Waring blender***: see WARING *noun*[2]): M19.

blende /blɛnd/ *noun*. L17.
[ORIGIN German, from *blenden* deceive (see BLEND *verb*[1]): so called from its resembling galena but yielding no lead.]
Native zinc sulphide, sphalerite.

Blenheim /ˈblɛnɪm/ *noun*. M19.
[ORIGIN *Blenheim* Palace, the name of the Duke of Marlborough's seat, at Woodstock, Oxfordshire, named after his victory (1704) at Blenheim in Bavaria.]
1 In full ***Blenheim spaniel***. A white variety of spaniel with chestnut markings. M19.
2 A golden-coloured late-ripening variety of apple. Also more fully ***Blenheim Orange***, ***Blenheim Pippin***. M19.

†**blenk** *noun, verb* see BLENCH *noun*[1], *verb*[1].

blenniid /ˈblɛnɪɪd/ *adjective & noun*. L19.
[ORIGIN from BLENNY + -ID[3].]
(A blenny) of the family Blenniidae.

blenno- /ˈblɛnəʊ/ *combining form* of Greek *blennos*, *blenna* mucus: see -O-.
■ **blennoˈrrhagia**, **blennoˈrrhoea** *nouns* a copious discharge of mucus, esp. from the urethra in gonorrhoea E19.

blenny /ˈblɛni/ *noun*. M18.
[ORIGIN from Latin *blennius* from Greek *blennos* slime (with ref. to the mucous coating of the scales).]
Any of various small spiny-finned marine fishes belonging to the Blenniidae or a related family, most of which are bottom-dwelling fishes of intertidal and shallow inshore waters.
BUTTERFLY ***blenny***. ***smooth blenny***: see SMOOTH *adjective & adverb*. ***viviparous blenny***: see VIVIPAROUS 1.

blent *verb* see BLEND *verb*[1], *verb*[2].

blepharitis /blɛfəˈrʌɪtɪs/ *noun*. M19.
[ORIGIN formed as BLEPHARO- + -ITIS.]
MEDICINE. Inflammation of an eyelid.

blepharo- /ˈblɛf(ə)rəʊ/ *combining form* of Greek *blepharon* eyelid: see -O-.
■ **blepharoconjunctiˈvitis** *noun* inflammation of the eyelid and conjunctiva L19. **blepharoplast** *noun* (BIOLOGY) an organelle from which a flagellum or cilium develops L19. **blepharoˈplastic** *adjective* of or pertaining to blepharoplasty M19. **blepharoplasty** *noun* (an instance of) the surgical repair or reconstruction of an eyelid M19. **blepharospasm** *noun* involuntary tight closure of the eyelids L19.

blerry /ˈblɛri/ *adjective & adverb*. *S. Afr. slang*. Also **blirry** /ˈblɪri/. E20.
[ORIGIN Alt. of BLOODY *adjective & adverb*.]
Bloody, damn, cursed(ly).

blesbok /ˈblɛsbɒk/ *noun*. Also **-buck** /-bʌk/. E19.
[ORIGIN Afrikaans, from Dutch *bles* BLAZE *noun*[2] + *bok* BUCK *noun*[1].]
A white-faced southern African antelope, *Damaliscus dorcas*.

bless /blɛs/ *verb*[1] *trans.* Pa. t. & pple **blessed** /blɛst, *arch. & poet.* ˈblɛsɪd/, (*arch.*) **blest** /blɛst/. See also BLESSED.
[ORIGIN Old English *blētsian*, *blēdsian*, *blœ̄dsian*, formed as BLOOD *noun*. No corresp. verb in other Germanic langs.]
1 Consecrate by a religious rite, a spoken formula, a prayer, etc.; invoke divine favour upon. OE. ▸**b** *spec.* Sanctify by the sign of the cross. *arch.* OE.

SOUTHEY The bishop had blest the meat. **b** M. W. MONTAGU I fancy I see you bless yourself at this terrible relation.

2 Call holy, adore, praise, (God); give thanks to for especial goodness or beneficence; attribute one's good fortune to (esp. one's stars). OE.

SHAKES. *Tam. Shr.* Then, God be bless'd, it is the blessed sun.

3 (Pronounce words to) confer or invoke divine favour upon; load with devout good wishes. OE.

STEELE The Fatherless . . and the Stranger bless his unseen Hand in their Prayers.

4 Confer well-being upon, make happy, cause to prosper; endow *with*. OE.

BYRON I have possess'd, And come what may, I have been blest.

†**5** Protect, guard, (another, oneself, a thing) *from* evil or danger. ME–M19.

MILTON The bellmans drowsy charm To bless the doors from nightly harm. SMOLLETT He blessed himself from such customers.

6 *refl.* Account oneself supremely happy or fortunate (*in*, *that*, *with*). *arch.* E17.

AV *Jer.* 4:2 The Lord liveth . . ; and the nations shall bless themselves in him.

7 *iron.* Pronounce an imprecation upon; curse; damn. *colloq.* E19.

DICKENS Blessed if I don't think he's got a main in his head as is always turned on.

– PHRASES: **bless her heart**, **bless his heart**, etc.: expr. pleasure in a person. **bless me**: expr. surprise, pleasure, or indignation. **bless my heart**: expr. surprise. **bless my soul**: expr. surprise, pleasure, or indignation. **God bless** (*sc.* you): expr. well-wishing. **God bless me**, **God bless my soul**, **Lord bless me**, **Lord bless my soul**: expr. surprise, pleasure, or indignation. **Lord bless you**: expr. surprise. **not have a penny to bless oneself with** be impoverished (with ref. to the cross on the silver penny).
– NOTE: 'Mark or consecrate with blood' was prob. the original meaning (for this type of rite cf. *Exodus* 12:23). During the Christianizing of Britain, however, the word was used to render Latin *benedicere* 'praise, (from Hebrew) bend the knee, worship'. Later also assoc. with BLISS *noun*.
■ **blesser** *noun* L16.

†**bless** *verb*[2] *trans. & intrans.* ME.
[ORIGIN Anglo-Norman *blechier*, Old French *blecier* (mod. *blesser*) injure, wound; sense 2 perh. a different word.]
1 Inflict injury or damage (on); thrash. ME–E17.
2 Wave about, brandish; make a flourish round (*with*). L16–E17.

blessed /ˈblɛsɪd, *esp. pred.* blɛst/ *adjective, noun, & adverb*. Also (now chiefly *poet.*) **blest** /blɛst/. ME.
[ORIGIN from BLESS *verb*[1] + -ED[1].]
▸**A** *adjective*. **1** Enjoying supreme felicity; fortunate; happily endowed *with*; ROMAN CATHOLIC CHURCH beatified. ME.

R. BURNS Kings may be blest, but Tam was glorious. C. CHAPLIN Mrs Jackson was not blessed with abundant good looks.

2 Consecrated, made holy. ME.
the Blessed Sacrament: see SACRAMENT *noun*.
3 Worthy to be reverenced; adorable. ME.
Blessed Virgin (Mary): see VIRGIN *noun*. ***the Blessed Holy Virgin***: see VIRGIN *noun*.
4 Pleasurable; bringing happiness; blissful. LME. ▸**b** Of plants and herbs: endowed with healing virtues. Now chiefly in plant names. M16.

F. A. KEMBLE The blessed unconsciousness and ignorance of childhood.

b *blessed thistle*: see CARDUUS.
5 *iron.* Wretched; cursed, damnable, bloody. *colloq.* M18.

W. WINDHAM One of the happy consequences of our blessed system of printing debates. S. O'CASEY A letter that I got today . . I'm blessed if I know where I put it.

▸**B** *absol.* as *noun*. *The* souls in paradise; (ROMAN CATHOLIC CHURCH) *the* beatified saints. ME.
▸**C** *adverb*. Blessedly; *esp.* cursedly, extremely. E17.
■ **blessedly**, (*arch.*) **blestly** *adverb* in a blessed manner; *colloq.* cursedly, extremely: LME. **blessedness** *noun* the state of being blessed, esp. with divine favour (***single blessedness***, orig.

(Shakes. *Mids. N. D.*) the state of a life consecrated to chastity, now *joc.* the state of being unmarried) ME.

blessing /ˈblɛsɪŋ/ *noun*. OE.
[ORIGIN from BLESS *verb*[1] + -ING[1].]
1 The bestowal, declaration, or invocation of (esp. divine) favour and prospering influence; a benediction. OE.

SHAKES. *Temp.* All the blessings Of a glad father compass thee about. J. M. SYNGE The blessing of God and the holy angels on your head, young fellow. M. RICHLER In the synagogue, Joshua stumbled through the blessings he was obliged to pronounce.

ask a blessing say grace before or after food. ***second blessing***: see SECOND *adjective*.
†**2** Consecration, hallowing; *spec.* making the sign of the cross. OE–M16.
3 A gift of God, nature, etc.; anything of which one is glad. ME. ▸†**b** A favour, a present. LME–E17.

SHAKES. *Hen. VIII* Eminence, wealth, sovereignty.. are blessings. K. AMIS What a blessing to be in such good hands.

blessing in disguise an apparent misfortune that eventually does good, an unwelcome but salutary experience. **count one's blessings** not forget the things one should be glad of. ***MIXED blessing***. ***UNMIXED blessing***.

blest *verb, adjective, noun, & adverb*: see BLESS *verb*[1], BLESSED.

blether *verb & noun*, **bletherskate** *noun* vars. of BLATHER, BLATHERSKITE.

bleu /blɜː, *foreign* blø (*pl. same*)/ *noun & adjective*. *Canad.* L19.
[ORIGIN French = blue.]
In French Canadian politics: (a) conservative.

bleu celeste /blɜː sɪˈlɛst/ *noun & adjectival phr.* L20.
[ORIGIN French = celestial blue.]
HERALDRY. (Of) the tincture sky-blue.

bleu-du-roi /blødyrwa/ *noun & adjective*. Also **-de-** /-də-/. M19.
[ORIGIN French = king's blue.]
(Of) the ultramarine blue of Sèvres porcelain.

†**blew** *noun, adjective, verb*[1] see BLUE *noun, adjective, verb*[1].

blew *verb*[2], *verb*[3] *pa. t.* of BLOW *verb*[1], *verb*[2].

†**blewish** *adjective* var. of BLUISH.

blewits /ˈbluːɪts/ *noun*. Pl. same. E19.
[ORIGIN Prob. from BLUE *adjective*.]
A late edible mushroom of the genus *Lepista*, with a lilac stem.

bley *noun* var. of BLAY.

blight /blʌɪt/ *noun*. M16.
[ORIGIN Uncertain: perh. ult. rel. to BLEACH *noun*.]
1 (An) inflammation or eruption of the skin. M16.
2 (The state resulting from) an atmospheric or other influence that suddenly blasts, nips, withers, or destroys plants or affects them with disease; *spec.* a plant disease caused by fungoid parasites, as mildew, rust, smut, etc. L16. ▸**b** *collect.* Destructive aphids. L19.
late blight: see LATE *adjective*. ***ray blight***: see RAY *noun*[1].
3 Any (esp. obscure) malignant influence or effect. M17. ▸**b** *spec.* More fully ***urban blight***. (The development or existence of) derelict or unsightly areas in a town or city. M20.

S. BELLOW The insidious blight of nostalgia. C. MCCULLOUGH The rabbits were as much of a blight as ever.

– COMB.: **blight-bird** *Austral. & NZ* the white-eye (noted for feeding on insect pests).

blight /blʌɪt/ *verb trans.* M17.
[ORIGIN from the noun.]
Affect with blight; exert a malignant influence on; frustrate; wither, mar.
■ **blighted** *ppl adjective* (***a***) that has been blighted; (***b***) *slang* = BLASTED 2: M17. **blighter** *noun* (***a***) a blighting agent or influence; (***b***) *slang* a (usu. contemptible or annoying) person: E19.

Blighty /ˈblʌɪti/ *noun & adjective*. *military slang*. Also **b-**. E20.
[ORIGIN Urdu *b'lāytī*, colloq. form of *bilāyatī*, *wilāyatī* foreign, (esp.) European, from Arabic *wilāya(t)* dominion, district. Cf. VILAYET.]
▸ **A** *noun*. **1** England, home, after foreign service. E20.
2 A wound securing return to England or home. E20.
▸ **B** *attrib.* or as *adjective*. Of or pertaining to England or home; securing return to England or home. E20.

blik /blɪk/ *noun*. M20.
[ORIGIN Arbitrary.]
PHILOSOPHY. A personal slant on something; a conviction, *esp.* a religious one.

blimbing *noun* var. of BILIMBI.

blimey /ˈblʌɪmi/ *interjection*. *coarse slang*. L19.
[ORIGIN Alt. of *blind me!* or *blame me!*: see BLIND *verb*, BLAME *verb* 6.]
Expr. surprise, contempt, etc. Freq. in ***cor blimey!*** (see COR *interjection* and cf. GORBLIMEY).

blimp /blɪmp/ *noun*. E20.
[ORIGIN Unknown.]
1 A small non-rigid airship; a barrage balloon. E20.
2 A soundproof cover for a cine camera. E20.
3 (Also **B-**.) More fully ***Colonel Blimp*** [from a character invented by the cartoonist David Low (1891–1963)]. (A name given to the type of) an obese reactionary ex-officer, a pompous elderly diehard. M20.
■ **blimpery** *noun* behaviour or speech characteristic of a blimp M20. **blimpish** *adjective* typical of a blimp M20.

blin /blɪn/ *noun*. Pl. **blini**, **-y** /ˈblɪni/, **blinis** /ˈblɪnɪz/. L19.
[ORIGIN Russian.]
A kind of pancake, freq. stuffed. Cf. BLINTZE.

†**blin** *verb intrans. & trans.* Infl. **-nn-**. OE–M18.
[ORIGIN Old English *blinnan*, formed as BE- + LIN *verb*.]
Leave off, stop, cease (from).

blind /blʌɪnd/ *noun*. OE.
[ORIGIN from BLIND *adjective* or *verb*.]
▸ **I** The adjective used *absol.*
1 A blind person. Long only *collect. pl.*, *the* class of blind people. OE.

AV *Matt.* 15:14 If the blind lead the blind, both shall fall into the ditch.

2 A blind baggage car. *US*. L19.
ride the blind(s): see RIDE *verb*.
▸ **II** **3** A screen or other protective structure in fortification etc. E17.
4 A place of concealment; *spec.* (*US*) a hide or screen for a hunter or naturalist. M17.
5 *fig.* A thing or action intended to conceal one's real design; a pretence, a pretext; a legitimate business concealing an illegitimate one. M17.

SWIFT These verses were only a blind to conceal the most dangerous designs of the party.

double-blind: see DOUBLE *adjective & adverb*.
6 A thing which obstructs the light or sight; *spec.* (***a***) a screen for a window, *esp.* one mounted on a roller; an awning over a shop window; (***b***) *US* a blinker for a horse etc. E18.
Venetian blind: see VENETIAN *adjective*.
7 *POKER.* A stake put up by a player before seeing his or her cards. M19.
8 A drunken bout or orgy. *slang*. E20.
■ **blindage** *noun* = BLIND *noun* 3 E19. **blindless** *adjective* M19.

blind /blʌɪnd/ *adjective & adverb*.
[ORIGIN Old English *blind* = Old Frisian, Old Saxon *blind*, Old High German *blint* (German *blind*), Old Norse *blindr*, Gothic *blinds*, from Germanic.]
▸ **A** *adjective*. **1** Not having the sense of sight. OE. ▸**b** *AERONAUTICS.* Without direct observation, using instruments only. E20.
blind as a bat, ***blind as a beetle***, etc. ***colour-blind***, ***green-blind***, etc.
2 Enveloped in darkness. *arch.* OE. ▸†**b** Having its light extinguished. LME–E18.

S. PEPYS The little blind bed-chamber.

3 Lacking discernment or foresight; deficient in intellectual or moral perception. OE.

H. ROBBINS Men were sometimes such blind fools.

4 Reckless, heedless; not ruled by purpose. ME.

HARPER LEE He just broke into a blind raving charge at the fence.

5 Covered or concealed from sight; out of the way; secret, obscure; (of a way or path) confusing, intricate, uncertain. ME. ▸**b** Of a corner or other feature of a road: round or to the other side of which one cannot see. E20.

MILTON In the blind mazes of this tangled wood. S. PEPYS A blind place where Mr. Goldsborough was to meet me. J. MORSE Blind rocks, sunk a few feet below the water.

6 Dim, indistinct; faintly marked. *arch.* LME.

N. HAWTHORNE Written in such a queer, blind.. hand.

†**7** False, deceitful. LME–M16.
8 Having no openings for light or passage; walled or boarded up; that cannot be seen through. E16.

POPE Some huntsman.. From the blind thicket wounds a stately deer. J. H. PARKER The clerestory window has a smaller blind arch on each side of it.

9 Closed at one end; (of a geographical feature) terminating abruptly. M17.
10 Drunk, thoroughly intoxicated. *colloq.* M17.
11 Of a plant: without buds or eyes, or without a terminal flower. M19.
12 Without complete information; (of a test or experiment) in which information which might bias results is withheld from the tester or the subject or both. M20.
double-blind: see DOUBLE *adjective & adverb*.
13 *attrib.* Slight(est), single. Esp. in ***a blind bit of***, the slightest, the least. Usu. in neg. contexts. *colloq.* M20.

C. CAUSLEY Maloney never said a blind word to contradict him.

– PHRASES: **blind to** incapable of appreciating or recognizing. ***steal a person blind***: see STEAL *verb*. ***strike me blind***: see STRIKE *verb*. **turn a blind eye (to)** pretend not to notice.
– SPECIAL COLLOCATIONS & COMB.: **blind alley** †(***a***) an out-of-the-way or secret alley; (***b***) a cul-de-sac; *fig.* an unprofitable or useless course of action; also *attrib.* designating a job etc. with no prospect of advancement. **blind baggage car** *US* a railroad car without end doors, for baggage. **blind coal** anthracite (from its burning without a bright flame). **blind date** *colloq.* a social engagement with a view to a personal relationship between two people (usu. of the opposite sex) who have not met before; a person with whom such a date is arranged. **blind fish** any of various fishes with eyes vestigial or absent, living in subterranean waters. **blind god** Eros or Cupid (associated with love). **blind gut** the caecum. ***blind HOOKEY***. **blind man's buff**, (*N. Amer.*) **blind man's bluff** a game in which a blindfold player tries to catch other players, who push him or her about. **blind-man's holiday** the time just before lamps are lit. **blind nettle** a dead-nettle or similar plant. **blind pig** *N. Amer. colloq.* a place where liquor is illicitly sold. **blind side** (***a***) the unguarded, weak, or assailable side of a person or thing; †(***b***) the unsightly or unpresentable side. **blind-side** *verb trans.* (*N. Amer.*) attack on the blind side, take advantage of, take unawares. **blindsight** *MEDICINE* the ability to respond to visual stimuli without consciously perceiving them, a condition which can occur after certain types of brain damage. **blind snake** any of various small burrowing snakes of the infraorder Scolecophidia, with reduced eyes, esp. of the family Typhlopidae. **blind spot** (***a***) a part of the retina insensitive to light, at the point of entry of the optic nerve; (***b***) *CRICKET* that spot of ground in front of the batsman where a ball pitched by the bowler leaves the batsman in doubt whether to play forward or back; (***c***) *RADIO* a point of unusually weak reception; (***d***) *transf. & fig.* an area where vision or understanding is lacking. **blind-stitch** *noun & verb* (***a***) *noun* a sewing stitch visible on one side only; (***b***) *verb trans. & intrans.* sew thus. **blind stamping**, **blind tooling** *BOOKBINDING* ornamentation by impression without the use of colour or gold leaf. **blind tiger** *US colloq.* = ***blind pig*** above. **blind trust** a trust independently administering the private business interests of a person in public office to prevent conflict of interest. **blindworm** (***a***) the slow-worm (from its small eyes); (***b***) any of various legless skinks of the genus *Typhlosaurus*.
▸ **B** *adverb*. Blindly. L18.
bake blind bake (a pastry or flan case etc.) without a filling. **blind drunk** insensible through drink. **go blind** *POKER* put up a stake before seeing one's cards. **go it blind** *colloq.* act recklessly or without proper consideration. **swear blind** swear vehemently (*that*).
■ **blindish** *adjective* E17. **blindling** *noun* (long *rare*) a blind person M16. **blindling(s)** *adverb* (*Scot. & N. English*) blindly, recklessly ME. **blindly** *adverb* OE. **blindness** *noun* (***a***) the state or condition of being blind; †(***b***) (*rare*, Shakes.) concealment: OE.

blind /blʌɪnd/ *verb*. ME.
[ORIGIN from BLIND *adjective & adverb*, repl. BLEND *verb*[1].]
▸ **I** *verb trans.* **1** Make unable to see, permanently or temporarily. ME.
blind me!, **blind him!**, etc.: used as an imprecation. ***eff and blind***: see EFF 2.
2 Rob of understanding, judgement, or moral sense, deceive, (with regard *to*). ME.

R. B. SHERIDAN How jealousy blinds people! W. S. MAUGHAM The glamour of their resounding titles blinded him to their faults.

blind with SCIENCE.
3 Conceal, obscure. *arch.* ME.

KEATS Wherefore did you blind Yourself from his quick eyes.

4 Deprive of light, darken; eclipse. *arch.* L15.

DRYDEN Such darkness blinds the sky. TENNYSON [Aurora's] sweet eyes.. blind the stars.

5 [from BLIND *noun*.] ▸**a** Draw a blind over (a window etc.). E18. ▸**b** Provide with protective structures. M19.
▸ **II** *verb intrans.* **6** Become blind. *rare*. ME.
7 Go blindly or heedlessly, esp. in a motor vehicle. *slang*. E20.
■ **blinding** *adjective* (***a***) that blinds; very bright; (***b***) (of a headache) very severe; (***c***) *colloq.* remarkably skilful: L18. **blindingly** *adverb* (***a***) in a blinding manner; (***b***) very, completely: M19.

blinder /ˈblʌɪndə/ *noun*. L16.
[ORIGIN from BLIND *verb* + -ER[1].]
1 *gen.* A person who or thing which blinds. L16.
2 A blinker for a horse etc.; a shade for a person's eye. Chiefly *US*. E19.
3 An excellent performance in a game; something very good. *colloq.* M20.

†**blindfell** *verb trans.* OE–M16.
[ORIGIN Old English *ġeblindfellian*, formed as BLIND *adjective & adverb* + FELL *verb*[1].]
Strike blind; blindfold.
■ †**blindfeld** *adjective & adverb* blindfold LME–L16.

blindfold /ˈblʌɪn(d)fəʊld/ *noun*. M17.
[ORIGIN from BLINDFOLD *adjective & adverb*.]
†**1** Blindfolding. *rare*. Only in M17.
2 A bandage to prevent a person from seeing; *fig.* an obstruction to perception or judgement. L19.

blindfold /ˈblʌɪn(d)fəʊld/ *adjective & adverb*. M16.
[ORIGIN from BLINDFELD, as BLINDFOLD *verb*.]
With eyes bandaged to prevent vision; *CHESS* without sight of board or pieces; *fig.* without circumspection, heedless(ly).

blindfold /ˈblʌɪn(d)fəʊld/ *verb trans.* E16.
[ORIGIN from pa. t. & pple of BLINDFELL, by assoc. with FOLD *verb*[1].]
1 Deprive (the eyes, a person) of sight with a bandage. E16.
2 *fig.* Obscure the understanding or judgement of. L16.
■ **blindfolder** *noun* M17.

bling /blɪŋ/ *noun, adjective, & verb*. Also **bling-bling** /blɪŋˈblɪŋ/. *slang* (orig. *US*). L20.
[ORIGIN Redupl. of *bling*, perh. imit. of light reflecting off jewellery, or of jewellery clashing together.]
▸ **A** *noun*. (The wearing of) expensive designer clothing and flashy jewellery. L20.

Time Out New York It don't mean a thing if she ain't got that bling.

▸ **B** *adjective*. Flashy, ostentatious. **E21**.

I. KNIGHT Resplendent in yellow track suit and bling-bling jewellery.

▸ **C** *verb intrans*. Adopt a flamboyant or ostentatious lifestyle or appearance. **E21**.

Washington Post I'm blinging for the troops, so they can feel good.

blini(s) *noun pl*. see BLIN *noun*.

blink /blɪŋk/ *noun*. **ME**.
[ORIGIN from BLINK *verb*: cf. BLENCH *noun*¹.]
†**1** A trick; in *pl*. boughs thrown to turn aside deer. **ME–E17**.
2 A glimmer, a spark, a sudden brief gleam of light. **ME**.
on the blink *colloq*. in a bad state, going wrong.
3 A (usu. bright or cheerful) glance; a brief glimpse. Chiefly *Scot*. **L16**.
4 In *pl*. A fleshy plant of the purslane family, *Montia fontana*, with tiny white flowers, of damp and wet habitats in temperate regions worldwide. Also ***water blinks***. **L17**.
5 **a** More fully ***iceblink***. A luminous appearance on the horizon, caused by the reflection from ice. **L18**. ▸**b** *loosely*. A large mass or pack of ice. **M19**.
6 An instant. Chiefly *Scot*. **E19**.
7 The action or an act of blinking. **E20**.

blink /blɪŋk/ *adjective*. **E19**.
[ORIGIN Afrikaans = shining.]
Bright. Only in ***blink klip*** s.v. KLIP 1, 3.

blink /blɪŋk/ *verb*. **ME**.
[ORIGIN Partly from †*blenk* var. of BLENCH *verb*¹, partly from Middle Dutch & mod. Dutch *blinken* shine, glitter: cf. Danish *blinke*, Swedish *blinka* wink, twinkle.]
1 *verb trans*. Deceive, cheat. *dial*. (now *Scot*.). **ME**.
†**2** *verb intrans*. = BLENCH *verb*¹ 2. *rare*. Only in **ME**.
†**3** *verb intrans*. Open the eyes from sleep. *rare*. Only in **ME**.
4 *verb intrans*. Glance, (now) look with the eyes opening and shutting; move the eyelids up and down; shut the eyes for a moment, esp. involuntarily. **M16**. ▸**b** *verb trans*. Shut (one's eyes) momentarily. **M19**. ▸**c** *verb trans*. Send (tears) *away*, *back*, by blinking. **E20**.

SHAKES. *Mids. N. D.* Show me thy chink, to blink through with mine eyne. S. J. PERELMAN A fat orange tabby blinks before the fire. P. LIVELY Other eyes have blinked in the light from that window.

†**5** *verb trans. & intrans*. Turn sour. **E17–M18**.
6 *verb trans*. Shut the eyes to; ignore; avoid consideration of. Now *rare*. **M18**.

A. TATE There is no use blinking these facts.

7 *verb intrans*. Cast a sudden gleam of light; shine intermittently or fitfully. **L18**.

G. SWIFT The lighthouse beacon blinking in the dusk.

8 *verb trans*. Look on with the evil eye, bewitch. *Scot. & Irish*. **L19**.
9 *verb intrans*. Back down from a confrontation. **L20**.

H. N. SCHWARZKOPF The Iraqis had blinked and . . the likelihood of an immediate invasion had decreased.

– COMB.: **blink-eyed** *adjective* given to blinking.
■ **blinking** *adjective & adverb* (*a*) *adjective* that blinks; (*b*) *adjective & adverb* (*colloq*.) cursed(ly), bloody: **M16**.

blinkard /ˈblɪŋkəd/ *noun & adjective*. *arch*. **E16**.
[ORIGIN from BLINK *noun* + -ARD.]
▸ **A** *noun*. **1** A person who blinks or has imperfect sight. **E16**.
2 A person who lacks intellectual perception. **E16**.
▸ **B** *adjective*. Of or pertaining to a blinkard; dull; heedless. **E16**.

blinker /ˈblɪŋkə/ *noun & verb*. **E17**.
[ORIGIN formed as BLINKARD + -ER¹.]
▸ **A** *noun*. **1** A person who blinks; a purblind person. **E17**.
2 In *pl*. Corrective or protective spectacles; goggles. Now *rare* or *obsolete*. **E18**.
3 Either of a pair of usu. leather screens fitted to a bridle to prevent a horse etc. from seeing sideways. Usu. in *pl*. **L18**.
4 A sporting dog that refuses to see and mark the position of the game. **E19**.
5 More fully ***blinker-light***. An intermittent flashlight. **E20**.
▸ **B** *verb trans*. Put blinkers on; *fig*. hoodwink, deceive. **M19**.
■ **blinkered** *ppl adjective* provided with blinkers; *fig*. having a limited range of outlook: **M19**.

blintze /blɪn(t)s/ *noun*. **E20**.
[ORIGIN Yiddish *blintse* from Russian *blinets* dim. of BLIN *noun*.]
= BLIN *noun*.

bliny *noun pl*. see BLIN *noun*.

blip /blɪp/ *noun & verb*. **L19**.
[ORIGIN Imit.: cf. BLEEP.]
▸ **A** *noun*. **1** A sudden rap or tap; a twitch. **L19**.
2 A quick popping sound; a short bleep. **M20**.
3 A small image of an object on a radar screen etc. **M20**.
4 A temporary and insignificant movement or fluctuation; a sudden small change, esp. for the worse. **L20**.

Economist The present slump, claims Boeing, is little more than a blip.

▸ **B** *verb*. Infl. **-pp-**.
1 *verb trans*. Rap or tap suddenly; press (an accelerator etc.) briefly; open (the throttle of a motor vehicle) momentarily. **E20**.
2 *verb intrans*. Switch an engine on and off in rapid succession; of an engine: switch on and off. **E20**.
3 **a** *verb intrans*. Make a quick popping sound or short bleep. **M20**. ▸**b** *verb trans*. Substitute a short bleep for (words) in broadcasting. **M20**.
4 *verb intrans*. Of a figure, price, etc.: rise, esp. in short sporadic bursts. Also foll. by *up*. **L20**.

blipvert /ˈblɪpvəːt/ *noun*. **L20**.
[ORIGIN Blend of BLIP *noun* and ADVERT.]
A short, information-packed advertisement or other broadcast. Also, a subliminal image projected very briefly during a music video.

blirry *adjective & adverb* var. of BLERRY.

blirt /bləːt/ *noun & verb*. *Scot. & N. English*. **E17**.
[ORIGIN Imit.: cf. BLURT.]
▸ **A** *noun*. †**1** = BLURT *noun* 1. Only in **E17**.
2 An outburst of tears, a sudden fit of weeping. **L18**.
3 A gust of wind and rain; a squall. **E19**.
▸ **B** *verb intrans*. Burst into tears, weep violently. **E18**.
■ **blirty**, **-ie** *adjective* squally **E19**.

bliss /blɪs/ *noun*.
[ORIGIN Old English *bliss*, *bliþs* = Old Saxon *blīzza*, *blīdsea*, *blītzea*, from Germanic, from base of BLITHE.]
†**1** Blitheness of aspect, kindness of manner. Only in **OE**.
2 Gladness, enjoyment, perfect joy or happiness; blessedness; the state of being in heaven; paradise. **OE**.
3 A cause of perfect joy or happiness. Now *poet*. **OE**.
■ **blissful** *adjective* (*a*) full of bliss; perfectly joyous or happy; happily oblivious; †(*b*) beatified, sacred: **ME**. **blissfully** *adverb* **ME**. **blissfulness** *noun* **LME**. **blissless** *adjective* **L16**.

bliss /blɪs/ *verb*.
[ORIGIN Old English *blissian*, *bliþsian* = Old Saxon *blīdsean*, *blizzen*, formed as BLISS *noun*.]
†**1** *verb intrans*. Be glad, rejoice. **OE–LME**.
†**2** *verb trans*. Give joy to, gladden. **OE–M17**.
3 *verb trans*. Foll. by *out*: cause to reach ecstasy. Freq. as ***blissed-out*** *ppl adjective*. *N. Amer. slang*. **L20**.
– COMB.: **blissout** *N. Amer. slang* a state of ecstasy.

blister /ˈblɪstə/ *noun*. **ME**.
[ORIGIN Perh. from Old French *blest(r)e*, *blo(u)stre* swelling, pimple.]
1 A thin vesicle on the skin filled with serum, caused by friction, a burn, other injury, or disease. **ME**.
2 MEDICINE. An application to raise a blister. Now chiefly *hist*. **M16**.
3 A swelling (filled with air or fluid) on the surface of a plant, cloth, cooled metal, painted wood, etc. **L16**.
4 An offensive or troublesome person; a worthless fellow. *slang*. **E19**.
5 A disease of peach trees caused by the fungus *Taphrina deformans*, which produces a distortion of the leaves. **M19**.
6 NAUTICAL. An underwater outer covering fitted to a vessel. **E20**.
7 A summons. *slang*. **E20**.
8 A rounded compartment protruding from the body of an aeroplane. **M20**.
– COMB.: **blister beetle**, **blister fly** any of various beetles of the family Meloidae, exuding a vesicant when disturbed, esp. *Lytta vesicatoria* (also called ***Spanish fly***); **blister blight** a fungal disease of tea plants, producing blistered leaves; **blister copper** impure copper with a blistered appearance, obtained during smelting; ***blister fly***: see ***blister beetle*** above; **blister gas** poison gas causing blisters on the skin; **blister pack**, **blister packaging**: consisting of a transparent moulded cover sealed to a card etc.; **blister pearl** an irregular pearly excrescence on an oyster shell; **blister steel** carbon steel made by cementation, freq. with a blistered surface.
■ **blistery** *adjective* characterized by blisters **LME**.

blister /ˈblɪstə/ *verb*. **LME**.
[ORIGIN from the noun.]
1 *verb intrans*. Be or become covered with blisters. **LME**.
2 *verb trans*. Cover with blisters; raise blisters on. **LME**.
3 *verb intrans*. Cause blisters. **LME**.
■ **blistering** *adjective* that causes blisters; *colloq*. (contextually) extremely hot, fast, severe, etc.: **LME**. **blisteringly** *adverb* **L19**.

blite /blʌɪt/ *noun*. **LME**.
[ORIGIN Latin *blitum* from Greek *bliton*.]
Any of various plants of the goosefoot family formerly eaten as vegetables; *esp*. Good King Henry, *Chenopodium bonus-henricus*.
sea-blite: see SEA *noun*. STRAWBERRY ***blite***.

blithe /blʌɪð/ *adjective & adverb*.
[ORIGIN Old English *bliþe* = Old Frisian *blī(d-)*, Old Saxon *blīþi* (Dutch *blijde*, *blij*), Old High German *blīdi* cheerful, friendly, Old Norse *blíðr*, Gothic *bleiþs*: from Germanic. Cf. BLISS *noun*.]
▸ **A** *adjective*. **1** Kindly, clement, gentle. Long *obsolete* exc. *Scot. dial*. **OE**.
2 Joyous, merry; glad, happy, well pleased. Now chiefly *poet*. **OE**.

MILTON A daughter fair, So buxom, blithe, and debonair. SIR W. SCOTT A blithe salute The minstrels well might sound.

3 Heedless, careless. **E20**.

A. MCCOWEN Their complacency, and their blithe intolerance of most of the outside world.

▸ **B** *adverb*. In a blithe manner. Now chiefly *poet*. **OE**.
■ **blitheful** *adjective* †(*a*) kindly, friendly; (*b*) joyous, merry: **OE**. **blithefully** *adverb* **M19**. **blithely** *adverb* in a blithe manner; heedlessly, carelessly: **OE**. **blitheness** *noun* **OE**. **blithesome** *adjective* cheerful **E18**. **blithesomely** *adverb* **M19**.

blither /ˈblɪðə/ *verb & noun*. *colloq*. **M19**.
[ORIGIN Var. of BLATHER.]
▸ **A** *verb intrans. & trans*. = BLATHER *verb* 1, 2. **M19**.
▸ **B** *noun*. = BLATHER *noun* 1. **M19**.
■ **blithering** *adjective* senselessly discursive or talkative; (as an intensive) consummate, utter, hopeless; contemptible: **L19**.

B.Litt. *abbreviation*.
Latin *Baccalaureus Litterarum* Bachelor of Letters.

blitter /ˈblɪtə/ *noun*. *dial*. **L18**.
[ORIGIN Var.]
= BITTERN *noun*¹.
bog-blitter: see BOG *noun*¹.

blitz /blɪts/ *noun & verb*. **M20**.
[ORIGIN Abbreviation of BLITZKRIEG.]
▸ **A** *noun*. **1** A sudden or intensive (esp. aerial) attack with the object of immediate destruction or reduction of defences; spec. *the* air raids on London in 1940. **M20**.
2 *transf. & fig*. **a** *gen*. A period of sudden or intense activity. **M20**. ▸**b** AMER. FOOTBALL. A charge by one or more defensive backs into the offensive backfield to anticipate a pass. **M20**.

a *Guardian* The women did only the bare essentials of housework during the week, with a 'blitz' at weekends.

▸ **B** *verb*. **1** *verb intrans*. Make a sudden or intensive (esp. aerial) attack. **M20**.
2 *verb trans*. Attack, damage, or destroy by a blitz. **M20**.
3 *verb intrans*. AMER. FOOTBALL. Charge into the offensive backfield. **M20**.

blitzkrieg /ˈblɪtskriːg/ *noun*. Also **B-**. **M20**.
[ORIGIN German, from *Blitz* lightning + *Krieg* war.]
A violent campaign intended to bring about speedy victory.

blivit /ˈblɪvɪt/ *noun*. *US slang*. Also **-et**. **M20**.
[ORIGIN Unknown.]
Something pointless, useless, or impossible; a nuisance. Also, a gadget.

blizzard /ˈblɪzəd/ *noun*. Orig. *US*. **E19**.
[ORIGIN Uncertain: perh. imit.]
1 A sharp blow or knock; a shot. *US*. **E19**.
2 A severe snowstorm. **L19**.
3 *fig*. A large or overwhelming amount *of* something, typically arriving suddenly. **M20**.

L. ERDRICH A blizzard of legal forms.

■ **blizzardy** *adjective* **L19**.

BLM *abbreviation*.
Bureau of Land Management, a US government office responsible for the administration of public lands.

†**blo** *adjective*. *dial*. **ME–L18**.
[ORIGIN formed as BLAE.]
= BLAE *adjective* 1.

bloat /bləʊt/ *noun*. **M19**.
[ORIGIN from BLOAT *adjective*².]
1 A conceited or contemptible person. *US slang*. **M19**.
2 **a** A disease of livestock characterized by an accumulation of gas in the stomach. **L19**. ▸**b** *gen*. Bloatedness. **E20**.

†**bloat** *adjective*¹. **ME**.
[ORIGIN Perh. from an Old Norse word parallel to *blautr* soaked: with sense 2 cf. Old Norse *blautr fiskr* soft fish. Relation to BLOAT *adjective*² obscure.]
1 Soft and wet. *rare*. Only in **ME**.
2 ***bloat herring***, a bloater. **L16–M17**.

bloat /bləʊt/ *adjective*². *arch*. **ME**.
[ORIGIN Old Norse *blautr* soft, infl. by BLOAT *adjective*¹ The spelling *bloat* is recorded from **M17** although it is not the regular representative of Middle English *blout*, and has been used for the *blowt* of quartos of Shakes. *Haml*. III. iv. 182 from **M18**.]
†**1** Soft, pliable. Only in **ME**.
2 Swollen, puffy, esp. with overindulgence. **E17**.
– NOTE: Now only in echoes of Shakes.

bloat /bləʊt/ *verb*¹ *trans*. **L16**.
[ORIGIN App. from BLOAT *adjective*¹.]
Cure (herring etc.) by salting and smoking slightly.

OED *Bloated* herrings are opposed to *dried* or *red* herrings.

bloat /bləʊt/ *verb*². **L17**.
[ORIGIN App. from BLOAT *adjective*².]
1 *verb trans*. Blow out, inflate, make turgid. **L17**.
2 *verb intrans*. Swell, become turgid. **M18**.
■ **bloated** *adjective* swollen, puffy, esp. through overindulgence; of excessive size; swollen with pride, pampered: **M17**. **bloatedness** *noun* **M17**.

bloater /ˈbləʊtə/ *noun*. M19.
[ORIGIN from BLOAT *verb*[1] + -ER[1].]
A herring cured by bloating.
YARMOUTH bloater.

bloatware /ˈbləʊtwɛː/ *noun*. *colloq*. L20.
[ORIGIN from BLOAT *noun* + WARE *noun*[2].]
COMPUTING. Software whose usefulness is reduced because of the excessive memory it requires.

blob /blɒb/ *noun & verb*. See also BLEB. LME.
[ORIGIN Imit.: cf. BLUBBER *noun*, *verb*, BUBBLE *noun*, *verb*.]
▸ **A** *noun*. **1** A bubble. *obsolete* exc. *N. English*. LME.
†**2** A pimple, a pustule. *Scot. & N. English*. LME–E17.
3 A drop or globule of liquid or viscous substance. E18.
4 A small roundish mass of colour or a viscous substance. M19.

A. WARNER A flat, grey blob of chewed gum.

5 A batsman's score of no runs (o) at cricket. *slang*. L19.
6 A blunder, a senseless error; a fool, an idiot, a useless person. *slang*. E20.
▸ **B** *verb trans*. Infl. **-bb-**. Mark with a blob of ink, colour, etc.; blot. LME.
■ **blobby** *adjective* LME.

†**blobber** *adjective* see BLUBBER *adjective*.

bloc /blɒk/ *noun*. E20.
[ORIGIN French: see BLOCK *noun*.]
A combination of states, parties, groups, or people, formed to promote a particular interest. See also earlier EN BLOC.
– COMB.: **bloc vote** = *block vote* s.v. BLOCK *noun*.

block /blɒk/ *noun*. ME.
[ORIGIN Old French & mod. French *bloc* from Middle Dutch *blok*, Middle & mod. Low German *block*, of unknown origin.]
▸ **I** A solid piece or mass.
1 A log; a tree stump. ME.
chip off the old block, **chip of the old block**, a child resembling a parent or ancestor, esp. in character. **on the block** *N. Amer.* for sale at auction.
2 A large piece of wood on which chopping, hammering, etc., is done. LME. ▸**b** *spec. hist.* The piece of wood on which the condemned were beheaded. L15. ▸**c** A piece of wood on which something can be moulded or shaped; *esp.* a mould for a hat; *fig.* (*arch.*) a style or fashion of hat. L16. ▸**d** A stump etc. from which to mount a horse. E17. ▸**e** In full ***starting block***. A shaped rigid piece for bracing the foot of a runner at the start of a race. M20.
Chinese block: see CHINESE *adjective*.
3 A pulley or system of pulleys mounted in a case, used to direct or increase the lifting power of the rope(s) running through it. LME.
block and tackle: see TACKLE *noun* 5a.
4 *gen.* Any bulky or massive piece of matter; a large amount or body of anything treated as a whole. LME. ▸**b** *spec.* An unhewn lump of rock; a piece of stone or other material prepared for building; one of a set of wooden or plastic cubes etc. that fit together, as a child's toy. M19. ▸**c** A compact set of sheets of drawing paper etc. fastened together at one edge. M19. ▸**d** A body of rock (often of large extent) bounded by faults. L19. ▸**e** = BLOC. E20. ▸**f** A square unit in a patchwork design. E20.

J. TYNDALL The more solid blocks of ice shoot forward in advance of the lighter debris. J. G. HOLLAND The combination began by selling large blocks of the Stock for future delivery. O. DOPPING The information on the tape is concentrated into blocks, separated by empty gaps.

b ***erratic block***: see ERRATIC *adjective*.
5 A lump of stone, wood, or other material that bars one's way; an obstacle. Now chiefly in ***stumbling block*** s.v. STUMBLE *verb*. L15. ▸**b** A chock. M20.
6 *fig.* **a** A stupid person, a blockhead; a stolid or hard-hearted person. M16. ▸**b** The head. *slang*. E17.
b do one's block, **lose one's block** (chiefly *Austral. & NZ*) become angry or agitated. **knock someone's block off** *slang* strike someone about the head, thrash someone. **off one's block** *slang* crazy, angry.
7 A piece of wood or metal engraved for printing on paper or fabric. M18.
8 a A compact mass of buildings bounded by (usu. four) streets; (chiefly *N. Amer.*) any urban or suburban area so bounded, the length of such an area. L18. ▸**b** A large area of land or seabed sold or allocated to one person or organization for settlement, development, etc. M19. ▸**c** A large single building, *esp.* one divided into offices or flats. M19.

a A. MILLER There's not a person on the block who doesn't know the truth. S. KAUFFMANN He had walked six blocks to the nearest subway station. J. T. STORY She cruised round the block twice.

b ***backblocks***: see BACK-. **c** ***tower block***: see TOWER *noun*[1] 3h.
▸ **II** Senses from the verb.
†**9** A bargain, an exchange; a scheme. *Scot.* E16–L18.
10 An act or instance of blocking; a stoppage, an obstruction. E19. ▸**b** An interruption of physiological function, esp. in the passage of nerve impulses. L19. ▸**c** *PSYCHOLOGY*. A sudden and temporary inability to continue a thought process or mental link. In popular use usu. more fully ***mental block***, ***psychological block***. M20. ▸**d** *AMER. FOOTBALL*. Obstruction of an opponent with the body, as a legal move. M20.

J. GALSWORTHY Swithin was so long over this course . . that he caused a block in the progress of the dinner. P. G. WODEHOUSE One of those blocks in the traffic which are inevitable in so congested a system as that of London. J. T. STORY We were stopped by a two-car police block at the junction with the Huntingdon Road. **c** M. STEWART He's been going through a bad period, a more or less complete block since he got *Tiger Tiger* off his desk.

roadblock: see ROAD *noun*. **b** ***heart block***: see HEART *noun*. ***spinal block***: see SPINAL *adjective*.
11 *CRICKET*. The spot on which the batsman rests the toe of the bat when facing the bowling. M19.
12 *CHESS*. A problem position in which Black is not under threat but must become exposed to a threat if obliged to move. E20.
– COMB.: **blockboard** a plywood board with a core of thin wooden strips; **block-book**: printed from woodcut blocks; **block booking** the booking of a large number of seats etc. as a unit; **blockbuster** *slang* (**a**) a heavy aerial bomb; (**b**) a thing of great power or size, *esp.* an epic best-selling book or successful film; **block capitals** capital block letters; **block delete** *COMPUTING* the deletion of a block of text or data in a single operation; **block diagram**: in which squares and other conventional symbols show the general arrangement of parts of an apparatus; **block-faulting** *GEOLOGY* faulting which divides a region into blocks having different elevations; **block grant** an inclusive grant made for a particular purpose; **blockhead** †(**a**) a wooden block for hats or wigs; a wooden head (*lit. & fig.*); (**b**) *colloq.* a stupid person; **blockheaded**, **blockheadish** *adjectives* (*colloq.*) stupid, dull, obtuse; **blockheadism** *colloq.* blockheaded behaviour, stupidity; **block heater** a storage heater; **blockhole** *CRICKET* (**a**) = sense 11 above; (**b**) an indentation marking this; **blockhouse** [Middle Dutch & mod. Dutch *blokhuis*] (**a**) a detached fortified defensive building with loopholes, usu. of timber or concrete; (**b**) a house of squared logs; (**c**) a concrete shelter; **block letters** (esp. capital) letters written without serifs and separate from each other; **block mountain** a mountain formed by block-faulting; **block move** *COMPUTING* the process or an act of moving a block of text or data as a whole; **block party** *US* a (usu. outdoor) party for all the residents of a block or neighbourhood; **block plane** a plane with a blade set at an acute angle, used esp. for planing end grain; **block release** release of a person from his employment for the whole of a stated period to attend a course of study; **blockship** a ship moored or grounded in order to block a channel; **block signalling**, **block system** a system of railway signalling which divides the track into sections and allows no train to enter a section that is not wholly clear; **block tin** refined tin cast in ingots; **block vote** (a vote by) a method of voting whereby a delegate's vote has influence according to the number of members he or she represents.
■ **blockish** *adjective* of the nature of a block; like a block in form or character; obtuse, stupid, clumsy: M16. **blockishly** *adverb* M16. **blockishness** *noun* M16. **blocky** *adjective* of the nature of or resembling a block or blocks L19.

block /blɒk/ *verb*. LME.
[ORIGIN from the noun or from French *bloquer*, formed as BLOC.]
▸ **I** Obstruct, hinder.
1 *verb trans.* Obstruct, close, seal, or confine with obstacles; put obstacles in the way of, hinder the progress of, prevent. Freq. foll. by *up*, *in*, or *off*. LME.

W. PRYNNE Blocking vp their hearts against the Lord. E. K. KANE Our little harbor was completely blocked in by heavy masses [of ice]. T. WILLIAMS Mitch has started towards the bedroom. Stanley crosses to block him. G. GREENE The passage was nearly blocked by dustbins. E. J. HOWARD Cressy had tried to talk to him, but he had courteously blocked conversation.

2 *verb trans. spec.* Blockade, besiege. L16.
3 *verb trans. & intrans. CRICKET*. Stop (a ball) with the bat, with no attempt to score runs. L18.
4 *verb trans.* Obstruct or prevent (a physiological or mental function or effect, esp. the passage of nerve impulses); interrupt the action of (a nerve, organ, etc.). L19.
5 *verb trans. CARDS*. Prevent (cards, esp. in a particular suit) from being played as winners. L19.
6 *verb trans. & intrans. AMER. FOOTBALL*. Obstruct (an opponent) with the body, as a legal move. L19.
7 *verb trans.* Restrict the use or conversion of (currency or other assets). M20.
▸ **II** In constructive senses.
8 *verb intrans.* Make a bargain or an exchange. *Scot.* L16.
9 *verb trans.* Shape, mould, or smooth on a block. L16. ▸**b** Emboss or impress a design on (a book cover) by means of a block. M19.
10 *verb trans.* Sketch or mark *out* or *in* roughly; lay out, plan. L16.

J. G. LOCKHART The latter Cantos having . . been merely blocked out when the first went to press. P. MCGERR Wednesday Warren finished blocking the first act.

11 *verb trans.* Make into blocks; provide or support with blocks. M19.
blocked letters: designed so as to appear three-dimensional.
■ **blockage** *noun* a blocked(-up) state; an obstruction: L19. **blocking** *noun* (**a**) the action of the verb; (**b**) railway signalling by the block system; (**c**) a wooden block; blocks collectively: L16.

blockade /blɒˈkeɪd/ *noun & verb*. L17.
[ORIGIN from BLOCK *verb* + -ADE, prob. after *ambuscade*.]
▸ **A** *noun*. **1** The surrounding of a place, blocking of a harbour, patrolling of a coast, etc., by hostile forces in order to prevent supplies or forces from entering or leaving it. L17.
raise a blockade, **raise the blockade** (compel to) withdraw the blockading forces. **run a blockade**, **run the blockade** (attempt to) evade the blockading force.
2 *transf. & fig.* A stoppage or obstruction, esp. (*N. Amer.*) of a road or railway by snow etc. M18. ▸**b** Obstruction or prevention of a physiological or mental function. M20.
– COMB.: **blockade-man** *hist.* a coastguard active against smuggling; **blockade-runner** a ship or a person attempting to run a blockade.
▸ **B** *verb trans.* Subject to blockade; block up, obstruct. L17.
■ **blockader** *noun* a person or a ship engaged in a blockade M19.

blocker /ˈblɒkə/ *noun*. ME.
[ORIGIN from BLOCK *noun* or *verb* + -ER[1].]
1 A person who uses a block (in various trades). ME.
2 A person who or thing which blocks or obstructs; *spec.* (**a**) *CRICKET* a habitually defensive batsman; (**b**) *AMER. FOOTBALL* a player whose task is to block opponents; (**c**) a substance which prevents or inhibits a given physiological function. M19.
beta blocker: see BETA 2a(e).
3 A person who occupies or farms a block of land. Chiefly in ***backblocker*** s.v. BACK-. L19.
4 A bowler hat. *slang*. M20.

blodge /blɒdʒ/ *noun*. M20.
[ORIGIN Imit.: cf. *blotch*, *splodge*, *splotch*, etc.]
A splotch, a blotch.

blog /blɒg/ *noun & verb*. L20.
[ORIGIN Shortened from WEBLOG.]
COMPUTING. ▸**A** *noun*. A weblog. L20.

Guardian Since finding his blog by accident, I have followed every posting with gratitude.

▸ **B** *verb intrans.* Infl. **-gg-**. Maintain a weblog. L20.
■ **blogger** *noun* L20. **blogosphere** *noun* personal websites and weblogs collectively L20. **blogroll** *noun* (on a weblog) a list of hyperlinks to other weblogs E21.

bloke /bləʊk/ *noun*. *colloq*. M19.
[ORIGIN Shelta.]
A man, a fellow.
■ **blokey** *adjective* = BLOKEISH M20.

blokeish /ˈbləʊkɪʃ/ *adjective*. Also **blokish**. M20.
[ORIGIN from BLOKE + -ISH.]
Of, relating to, or characteristic of a bloke or ordinary man; stereotypically masculine.

Grace Some blokeish task, like waxing the car or mowing the lawn. *Independent on Sunday* He is not blokeish: he is serious, fastidious and moral.

■ **blokeishly** *adverb* L20. **blokeishness** *noun* L20.

blonde /blɒnd/ *adjective & noun*. Also **blond** (see note below). L15.
[ORIGIN Old French & mod. French from medieval Latin *blundus*, *blondus* yellow, perh. of Germanic origin: fem. form introduced from French in 17.]
▸ **A** *adjective*. (Esp. of the hair) of a light golden-brown colour, flaxen, fair; (of the complexion) light-coloured with fair hair. L15.
ash blonde, ***platinum blonde***, ***silver blonde***, ***strawberry blonde***, etc. **blond beast** [translating German *blonde Bestie*] a man of the Nordic type. ***blonde bombshell***: see ***bombshell*** s.v. BOMB *noun*. **blonde lace** silk lace (orig. unbleached) of two threads, twisted and formed in hexagonal meshes. **blonde ray** a pale brown ray, *Raja brachyura*, of SW European coastal waters.
▸ **B** *noun*. **1** A person (esp. a woman) with blonde hair and complexion. M18.

F. EXLEY She discovered that the poet was quite contentedly married to a bleached blonde. I. EDWARDS-JONES I've donned . . wigs to see if blondes really do have more fun.

dumb blonde: see DUMB *adjective & noun*. ***peroxide blonde***: see PEROXIDE *noun* 2.
2 (**blonde**) = ***blonde lace*** above. M18.
– NOTE: The spellings *blonde* and *blond* correspond to the feminine and masculine forms in French, but in English the distinction is not always made. However, the word is more commonly used of women, and as a noun the spelling is usu. *blonde*.
■ **blondish** *adjective* somewhat blonde or light-coloured M20. **blondness**, **blondeness** *noun* L19.

Blondin /ˈblɒndɪn/ *noun*. Also **b-**. M19.
[ORIGIN Professional name of J. F. Gravelet (1824–97), French tightrope walker.]
A tightrope walker; a tightrope, a cableway.

blondine /blɒnˈdiːn/ *noun & verb*. *US*. L19.
[ORIGIN from BLONDE *adjective* + -INE[4].]
▸ **A** *noun*. A bleach for the hair. L19.
▸ **B** *verb trans.* Bleach with blondine. L19.

blood /blʌd/ *noun*.
[ORIGIN Old English *blōd* = Old Frisian, Old Saxon *blōd* (Dutch *bloed*), Old High German *bluot* (German *Blut*), Old Norse *blóð*, Gothic *blōþ* (Crimean Gothic *plut*), from Germanic, of unknown origin.]
1 A complex fluid, red when oxygenated and containing various suspended cells, circulating in the arteries and veins of the higher animals; the corresponding fluid in other multicellular organisms. OE. ▸**b** A liquid or juice resembling blood (always with conscious ref. to the primary sense). LME.

b SHAKES. *Timon* Go, suck the subtle blood o' th' grape.

2 a Blood that is shed, in theological writings esp. in sacrifice, as that of Christ; the taking of life. **OE.** ▸**b** The guilt of bloodshed. **OE.** ▸**c** A blood-and-thunder story. Freq. in ***penny blood***. Usu. in *pl. arch.* **L19.**

a R. HOOKER Either my blood or banishment shall sign it. ADDISON An Affront that nothing but Blood can expiate. **b** C. V. WEDGWOOD The blood of Strafford lay heavy on his conscience because he had consented to his death in the knowledge that he was innocent.

†**3** Vital fluid; the vital principle; life. **ME–M18.**

4 a The blood as the supposed seat of emotion; passion, temperament, mettle. **ME.** ▸**b** The blood as the supposed seat of animal or sensual appetite; sexual desire. **ME.**

a SHAKES. *Merch. V.* The brain may devise laws for the blood, but a hot temper leaps o'er a cold decree.

5 a The blood as the vehicle of hereditary characteristics or relationship; consanguinity; parentage, lineage; family, race, nationality. **ME.** ▸**b** Persons of any specified blood or family collectively; kindred. **ME.** ▸**c** Good parentage or stock. **LME.** ▸**d** One's offspring; a near relative. *arch.* **LME.** ▸**e** A fellow black person. *US black English.* **M20.**

a POPE Your antient but ignoble blood Has crept thro' Scoundrels ever since the Flood. L. VAN DER POST They had clear traces of Bushman blood. *Proverb*: Blood is thicker than water. **b** SHAKES. *John* Father, to arms! . . Against the blood that thou hast married? **c** R. W. EMERSON The obstinate prejudice in favour of blood, which lies at the base of the feudal and monarchical fabrics of the old world. **d** DRYDEN Thou art my blood where Jonson has no part. HOR. WALPOLE So many cousins, and uncles, and aunts and bloods.

†**6** A living being. Only in **ME.**

†**7** A disease in sheep or swine. **E16–L18.**

8 a A fashionable and dashing young man. Now *arch.* or *hist.* **M16.** ▸**b** A leader of fashion, esp. at a public school or university. *slang.* **L19.**

9 (**B-.**) Pl. **-s**, same. A member of a N. American Indian people belonging to the Blackfoot confederacy. Pl. same. **L18.**

– PHRASES: **bad blood** ill feeling. **blood and iron** [translating German *Blut und Eisen*] military force as distinguished from diplomacy, esp. as associated with Bismarck (see BISMARCKIAN). ***blue blood***: see BLUE *adjective*. ***corruption of blood***. **first blood** the first shedding of blood (in BOXING or *fig.*). ***flesh and blood***: see FLESH *noun*. ***freeze someone's blood***: see FREEZE *verb*. **fresh blood** = *new blood* below. ***full-blood***: see FULL *adjective*. **get blood from a stone**, **get blood from a turnip**, **get blood out of a stone**, **get blood out of a turnip** achieve the impossible, *esp.* obtain pity from the hard-hearted or money from the impecunious or avaricious. †**God's blood!** an oath or forcible exclamation; abbreviation **'SBLOOD**. ***half blood***: see HALF-. **ill blood** = *bad blood* above. **in blood** HUNTING (of an animal) full of life, vigorous. **in cold blood** without passion, deliberately. **in one's blood** characteristic of one's family etc., fundamental in one's character. **let (a person) blood** (now *arch.* or *hist.*) bleed (a person) as medical treatment, *transf.* shed the blood of, kill, (a person) (freq. in indirect pass. as ***be let blood***). MIXED ***blood***. **new blood** a new member or new members admitted to a family, society, etc. ***one's blood boils***: see BOIL *verb*. **one's blood is up** one is in fighting mood. **one's blood runs cold** one is horrified. **out for a person's blood** determined to defeat him or her. **out of blood** HUNTING (of an animal) lifeless, not vigorous. **restore in blood**, **restore to blood** *hist.* readmit (a person under sentence of 'corruption of blood') to forfeited privileges. ***seal one's testimony with blood***: see TESTIMONY *noun* 3. ***shed the blood of***: see SHED *verb*[1] 6. ***spit blood***: see SPIT *verb*[2]. ***suck the blood of***: see SUCK *verb*. ***sweat blood***: see SWEAT *verb* 2b. **taste blood** *fig.* be stimulated by early success. **the blood (royal)** the royal lineage or family (***of the blood***, royal). **young blood** (*a*) *arch.* a young rowdy or dandy; (*b*) a young member of a party etc.

– COMB.: **blood-ally** a white toy marble marked with red spiral lines; **blood-and-soil** *adjective* [from Nazi catchphrase *Blut und Boden*] of or pertaining to Nazism; **blood-and-thunder** *adjective* designating a book etc. describing bloodshed and violence; **blood bank** a place where a supply of blood for transfusion is stored; **bloodbath** a massacre; †**blood-boltered** *adjective* (esp. of hair) clotted with blood; **blood–brain barrier** ANATOMY a semi-permeable membrane separating the blood from the cerebrospinal fluid; **blood brother** (*a*) a brother by birth; (*b*) a person who has been bound to another in solemn friendship by a ceremonial mingling of blood; **blood cell**, **blood corpuscle** any of the kinds of cell normally circulating in the blood; **blood count** (a determination of) the number of corpuscles in a definite volume of blood; **blood-curdling** *adjective* so horrific as to seem to curdle the blood; **blood donor** a person who gives blood for transfusion; **blood doping** the injection of oxygenated blood into an athlete before an event in an (illegal) attempt to enhance athletic performance; **blood eagle** [Old Norse *blóð-ọrn*] *hist.* a Viking method of killing someone, usu. the slayer of a man's father, by cutting out the ribs in the shape of an eagle; **blood feud** a feud between families of which one has killed or injured a member or members of the other; **blood-flower** (*a*) = *blood-lily* below; (*b*) a tropical American plant, *Asclepias curassavica*, with deep red flowers; **blood group** any of the types into which human blood may be divided according to its compatibility in transfusion; *esp.* each of the four types based on the A and B antigens; **blood-grouping** the determination of the blood group of a person or sample of blood; **blood guilt**, **blood-guiltiness** responsibility for bloodshed; **blood-guilty** *adjective* responsible for bloodshed; **blood heat** the ordinary temperature of human blood in health, approx. 37°C (98°F); **blood horse** (chiefly *N. Amer.*) a thoroughbred horse; **bloodhound** a large keen-scented dog, formerly used to track cattle, criminals, etc.; *fig.* a detective; **blood knot** a knot tied in a rope used as a whip, in order to draw blood; **blood-letter** a person who or thing which lets blood; **blood-letting** surgical removal of some of a patient's blood; *joc.* bloodshed; **blood-lily** a haemanthus, *esp.* one grown for ornament; **bloodline** descent, pedigree, esp. as transmitting characteristics in an animal; **bloodlust** lust for the shedding of blood; **blood meal** [German *Blutmehl*] dried blood used for feeding animals and as a fertilizer; **blood money** (*a*) a reward for bringing about the death of another, as a reward paid to a witness for securing a capital sentence; (*b*) a fine paid to the next of kin for the slaughter of a relative; **blood orange** a variety of orange with red-streaked pulp; **blood plasma** the straw-coloured liquid fraction of the blood, in which the cells and platelets are suspended; ***blood platelet***; **blood poisoning** the presence of pathogenic bacteria or bacterial toxins in the blood; **blood pressure** the pressure of circulating blood on the walls of the arteries; *colloq.* hypertension; **blood pudding** (a) black pudding; **blood-red** red as blood; **blood relation**, **blood relative** a person related to another or others by blood, not marriage; **bloodroot** any of various plants; esp. a N. American plant, *Sanguinaria canadensis*, of the poppy family, with white flowers and red sap; **blood sausage** (a) black pudding; **bloodshedder** a slaughterer, a murderer; **bloodshedding** (*a*) = BLOODSHED *noun* 1; †(*b*) = BLOODSHED *noun* 2; ***blood spavin***: see SPAVIN *noun*[1]; **blood sports** sports involving the killing of animals, *esp.* hunting; **bloodstain** a stain made by blood; **bloodstained** *adjective* stained with blood, *fig.* disgraced by bloodshed; **bloodstock** thoroughbred or pedigree horses collectively; **bloodstone** a precious stone, esp. a green chalcedony, that is streaked or spotted with red; †**blood-strange** [origin unknown.] the plant mousetail, *Myosurus minimus*; **bloodstream** the circulating blood; **blood sugar** (the concentration of) glucose contained in the blood; **blood test** a test performed on a sample of blood esp. for diagnosis; **blood-test** *verb trans.* test the blood of (a person or animal); **bloodthirst** eagerness for bloodshed; ***blood transfusion***: see TRANSFUSION 2; **blood-tub** *slang* a theatre presenting lurid melodrama; **blood-vein (moth)** a geometrid moth, *Timandra griseata*, with a red line across its wings; **blood vessel** a vein, artery, or capillary, conveying blood; **blood wagon** *slang* an ambulance; **bloodwite**, **-wit** [WITE *noun*[2]] (*a*) *hist.* in Anglo-Saxon England, a fine for shedding blood paid to an alderman or king (cf. WERGELD); (*b*) *gen.* a penalty for murder; **bloodwood** (the red wood of) any of various trees, esp. certain Australian eucalypts; **bloodworm** a bright red worm or worm-like creature, *esp.* (*a*) a worm of the genus *Arenicola* or *Tubifex*; (*b*) the aquatic larva of a midge of the genus *Chironomus*; **blood-wort** a plant with red roots or leaves, *esp.* red-veined dock, *Rumex sanguineus*.

■ †**blooding** *noun* a black pudding **LME–L18.** **bloodlike** *adjective* resembling blood **LME.**

blood /blʌd/ *verb trans.* **M16.**
[ORIGIN from the noun.]

1 Bleed, esp. surgically. **M16.**
2 Wet or smear with blood. Now *rare* in *gen.* sense. **L16.**
†**3** Arouse the hostile feelings of (esp. soldiers) *against* an enemy. Only in **17.**
4 Give a first taste of blood to (a hound); smear the face of (a novice at hunting) with the blood of the kill; initiate. **L18.**

blooded /ˈblʌdɪd/ *adjective.* **ME.**
[ORIGIN from BLOOD *noun*, *verb*: see -ED[2], -ED[1].]

†**1** Stained with blood. **ME–M17.**
2 As 2nd elem. of comb.: having blood of the specified kind. **L16.**
cold-blooded, ***full-blooded***, ***warm-blooded***, etc.
3 Of a horse: of good breed, thoroughbred. **L18.**

bloodless /ˈblʌdlɪs/ *adjective.* **ME.**
[ORIGIN from BLOOD *noun* + -LESS.]

1 Without blood, lifeless; pale, pallid; unemotional. **ME.**
2 Without bloodshed. **E17.**
■ **bloodlessly** *adverb* **E19.** **bloodlessness** *noun* **M19.**

bloodshed /ˈblʌdʃɛd/ *noun & adjective.* **LME.**
[ORIGIN from *shed blood*.]

▸ **A** *noun.* **1** The spilling of the blood of another or others; slaughter. **LME.**

STEELE He took the French Lines without Bloodshed.

†**2** The shedding of one's own blood (orig. & chiefly with ref. to Jesus). **L15–M19.**
†**3** An act of spilling blood. **L16–L17.**
†**4** = BLOODSHOT *noun*. **L17–M18.**
▸ **B** *adjective.* = BLOODSHOT *adjective* 2. Long *obsolete* exc. *Scot.* **E17.**

bloodshot /ˈblʌdʃɒt/ *adjective & noun.* **M16.**
[ORIGIN from BLOOD *noun* + SHOT *ppl adjective*.]

▸ **A** *adjective.* †**1** Of a person: with eyeballs tinged with blood. Only in **M16.**
2 Of the eyeball: tinged with blood. **E17.**
▸ †**B** *noun.* An effusion of blood affecting the eyeball. **L16–L17.**
■ Also **bloodshotten** *adjective* (*arch.*) **LME.**

bloodsucker /ˈblʌdsʌkə/ *noun.* **LME.**
[ORIGIN from BLOOD *noun* + SUCKER *noun*.]

1 An animal which sucks blood; *esp.* (*a*) the leech; (*b*) any of various Asian and Australian lizards, *esp.* an Australian crested lizard of the genus *Amphibolurus*. **LME.**
†**2** A bloodthirsty or blood-guilty person. **M16–M17.**
3 An extortioner; a sponger. **E17.**
■ **bloodsucking** *adjective & noun* **L16.**

bloodthirsty /ˈblʌdθəːsti/ *adjective.* **M16.**
[ORIGIN from BLOOD *noun* + THIRSTY, after Luther's *blutdürstig*.]
Eager for bloodshed.
■ **bloodthirstily** *adverb* **L19.** **bloodthirstiness** *noun* **M17.**

bloody /ˈblʌdi/ *adjective & adverb.*
[ORIGIN Old English *blōdig* = Old Frisian *blōdich*, Old Saxon *blōdig* (Dutch *bloedig*), Old High German *bluotag* (German *blutig*), Old Norse *blóðigr* from Germanic: see BLOOD *noun*, -Y[1].]

▸ **A** *adjective.* **1** Of the nature of, composed of, resembling, or pertaining to blood. **OE.**
2 Covered, smeared, or stained with blood. **OE.**

YEATS Their throats torn and bloody.

3 Accompanied by or involving bloodshed. **ME.**

D. BAGLEY Serrurier . . took power in bloody revolution and kept it by equally bloody government.

4 Of thoughts, words, etc.: concerned with, portending, or decreeing bloodshed. **ME.**
†**5** Of animal bodies: containing blood. **LME–E19.**

E. TOPSELL A Serpent [is] . . a Bloudy Beast without feet.

6 Bloodthirsty, blood-guilty. **M16.**

AV *Ps.* 5:6 The Lord will abhorre the bloodie and deceitfull man.

7 Blood-red. **L16.**

G. M. HOPKINS Tender pinks with bloody Tyrian dye.

8 (See comment at sense B.2.) ▸**a** Used vaguely as a strong imprecation or intensive; confounded, damnable, cursed. **M17.** ▸**b** Unpleasant, deplorable; perverse. **M20.**

OED Not a bloody *one*. S. L. ELLIOTT The Army must be payin' you more than the bloody Colonel. E. BLISHEN That bloody boy! Wait till I get you home. **b** C. CONNOLLY Oxford is just bloody. R. LEHMANN He made me so mean and bloody.

call a spade a bloody shovel: see SPADE *noun*[1].

▸ **B** *adverb.* †**1** Bloodily. Only in **ME.**
2 Used vaguely as a strong imprecation or intensive; exceedingly, very; confoundedly, damnably. Also inserted within words (tmesis). (In general colloq. use until **M18**; later regarded as on a par with obscene or profane language, hence numerous euphemistic alternatives as *blasted*, *blinking*, *blooming*, etc.; now usu. regarded as strong but not deeply offensive.) **L17.**

DRYDEN The doughty Bullies enter bloody drunk. HENRY FIELDING This is a bloody positive old fellow. G. B. SHAW Walk! Not bloody likely. L. W. MEYNELL Remember the *News Chronicle*? . . On sale one day. Amalga-bloody-mated the next. R. RENDELL The furthest bloody abroad I'm going ever again will be the Isle of Wight.

– COMB. & SPECIAL COLLOCATIONS: **bloody flux**, †**bloody flix** dysentery; **bloody grave** the grave of one who has been murdered; **bloody hand**: the armorial device of some baronets; **Bloody Mary** (*a*) Mary Tudor; (*b*) a mixed drink of vodka and tomato juice; **bloody-minded** *adjective* (*a*) inclined to bloodshed, bloodthirsty, cruel; (*b*) perverse, cantankerous, stubbornly intransigent; **bloody-mindedly** *adverb* in a bloody-minded manner; **bloody-mindedness** the state or quality of being bloody-minded; ***Bloody Monday***: see MONDAY *noun*; **bloody-nosed beetle** a large black beetle, *Timarcha tenebricosa*, which exudes a red liquid from its mouth when handled; ***bloody shirt***: see SHIRT *noun*; **bloody sweat** an exudation of blood mixed with sweat; ***bloody warrior***: see WARRIOR *noun* 2; ***raw head and bloody bones***: see RAW *adjective*.
■ **bloodily** *adverb* in a bloody manner; with blood, with bloodshed: **M16.** **bloodiness** *noun* **L16.**

bloody /ˈblʌdi/ *verb trans.* **E16.**
[ORIGIN from the adjective.]
Make bloody; stain with blood.

blooey /ˈbluːi/ *adjective & adverb.* *US slang.* **E20.**
[ORIGIN Unknown.]
(Gone) awry, amiss.

bloom /bluːm/ *noun*[1]. **ME.**
[ORIGIN Old Norse *blóm* flower, blossom; *blómi* prosperity, pl. flowers, = Old Saxon *blōmo*, Middle Dutch *bloeme* (Dutch *bloem*), Old High German *bluomo*, *-ma* (German *Blume*), Gothic *blōma* from Germanic, from base of BLOW *verb*[2].]

1 A blossom or flower of a plant, *esp.* one which is grown or admired chiefly for this; *collect.* blossom, flowers. **ME.**

MILTON Sight of vernal bloom. L. M. MONTGOMERY 'June bells', those shyest and sweetest of woodland blooms. *fig.*: R. ELLIS A chosen array, rare bloom of valorous Argos.

2 Flowering; *fig.* the state or season of greatest beauty; prime; perfection. **ME.**

ADDISON While her Beauty was yet in all its Height and Bloom.

3 The delicate powdery deposit on grapes, plums, etc.; a similar deposit or appearance; a cloudiness on a shiny surface. **M17.** ▸**b** Freshness; delicate beauty. **L18.** ▸**c** In full ***water bloom***. (A scum formed by) the rapid proliferation of microscopic algae on water. **E20.**

H. E. BATES Covered with a white bloom of chalk dust. N. GORDIMER The blur of frost: a cold bloom formed on the outside of a glass.

4 The crimson tint of the cheek; flush; glow. **M18.**

HENRY FIELDING Miss Bath had not only recovered her health but her bloom.

– PHRASES: **in bloom** in flower, flowering. **take the bloom off** deprive (a thing) of its first freshness or beauty.
■ **bloomless** *adjective* **L16.** **bloomy** *adjective* (chiefly *poet.*) (*a*) full of blooms, flowery; (*b*) in the bloom of youth; (*c*) covered with or resembling a powdery bloom: **L16.**

B

bloom /bluːm/ *noun*[2].
[ORIGIN Old English *blōma*, identical in form with BLOOM *noun*[1], but prob. a different word.]
A mass of iron, steel, or other metal rolled or hammered into a thick bar for further working. Also *loosely*, an unworked mass of puddled iron.
■ **bloomery**, **-ary** *noun* a forge or mill where blooms (esp. of wrought iron) are rolled or hammered L16.

bloom /bluːm/ *verb*[1]. ME.
[ORIGIN from BLOOM *noun*[1].]
▸ **I** *verb intrans.* **1** Bear flowers, come into flower. ME.
2 Come into or be in full beauty or vigour; flourish; culminate. ME.

B. JOWETT Your beauty is fading away, just as your true self is beginning to bloom.

3 Glow with warm colour. M19.

J. TYNDALL Heaps of snow.. bloomed with a rosy light.

▸ **II** *verb trans.* **4** Bring into bloom; cause to flourish. *arch.* L16.

R. GREENE Each fair thing that summer bloomed.

5 Colour with a soft warm tint. E19.

KEATS While barred clouds bloom the soft-dying day.

6 Cloud (a shiny surface). M19.
7 PHOTOGRAPHY. Coat (a lens) so as to reduce reflection from its surfaces. M20.
■ **blooming** *adjective & adverb* (*a*) *adjective* that blooms; (*b*) *adjective & adverb* (*colloq.*) cursed(ly), bloody: LME. **bloomingly** *adverb* M19.

bloom /bluːm/ *verb*[2] *trans.* E19.
[ORIGIN from BLOOM *noun*[2].]
Make (iron etc.) into blooms. Chiefly as ***blooming*** *verbal noun.*

bloomed /bluːmd, *poet.* ˈbluːmɪd/ *adjective.* E16.
[ORIGIN from BLOOM *noun*[1], *verb*[1]: see -ED[2], -ED[1].]
1 In bloom; bearing blooms. Chiefly *poet.* E16.
2 That has been bloomed (esp. in sense 7 of BLOOM *verb*[1]). M20.

bloomer /ˈbluːmə/ *noun*[1]. M18.
[ORIGIN from BLOOM *verb*[1] + -ER[1].]
1 A plant that blooms (esp. in a specified manner). M18.
2 A floriated letter. L19.
3 [= *blooming error*.] A great mistake, a blunder. *slang.* L19.

bloomer /ˈbluːmə/ *noun*[2]. M19.
[ORIGIN Amelia Jenks *Bloomer* (1818–94) of New York, who advocated such dress.]
▸ **I** *sing. hist.*
1 In full ***bloomer costume***, ***bloomer dress***, = sense 4 below. M19.
2 ***bloomer trousers***, = sense 5 below. M19.
3 A woman who wears a bloomer costume. M19.
▸ **II** In *pl.*
4 *hist.* A woman's costume with loose trousers gathered at the ankle or knee. M19.
5 *hist.* Knee-length trousers or knickerbockers, esp. as worn by women for active pursuits as cycling etc. L19.
6 A woman's or girl's loose knee-length knickers; *colloq.* knickers of any style. E20.
■ **bloomered** *adjective* wearing bloomers L19. **bloomerism** *noun* (*hist.*) the principles of A. J. Bloomer as to female dress M19.

bloomer /ˈbluːmə/ *noun*[3]. M20.
[ORIGIN Unknown.]
A large loaf with a rounded diagonally slashed top.

Bloomfieldian /bluːmˈfiːldɪən/ *noun & adjective.* M20.
[ORIGIN from *Bloomfield* (see below) + -IAN.]
▸ **A** *noun.* An adherent or student of the (largely structuralist) linguistic theories of the American scholar Leonard Bloomfield (1887–1949). M20.
▸ **B** *adjective.* Of, pertaining to, or characteristic of Bloomfield or his theories or adherents. M20.

Bloomsbury /ˈbluːmzb(ə)ri/ *adjective & noun.* E20.
[ORIGIN A district in west central London.]
▸ **A** *adjective.* Designating, characteristic of, or pertaining to a group of writers and aesthetes living in or associated with Bloomsbury in the early 20th cent.; intellectual, highbrow. E20.
▸ **B** *noun.* The Bloomsbury group; (also *joc.* **Bloomsberry**) a member of this. E20.
■ **Bloomsburyite** *noun* a member of the Bloomsbury group M20.

bloop /bluːp/ *verb, noun, & adjective.* E20.
[ORIGIN Imit.]
▸ **A** *verb.* **1** *verb intrans.* (Cause a radio set to) emit a howling noise. E20.
2 *verb trans.* Patch or treat (a splice on a soundtrack) so as to prevent an intrusive noise during projection. M20.
3 *verb trans.* BASEBALL. Hit (a ball) weakly or make (a hit) that lands just beyond the reach of the infielders. L20.
▸ **B** *noun.* A howling or popping sound. M20.
▸ **C** *adjective.* BASEBALL. Of a run: scored by hitting a ball just beyond the reach of the infielders. M20.
■ **blooper** *noun* (*colloq.*, chiefly *N. Amer.*) (*a*) a radio set that causes others to bloop; (*b*) an embarrassing error, a blunder (*c*) BASEBALL a weakly hit fly ball landing just beyond the reach of the infielders: E20.

blooter /ˈbluːtə, *Scot.* ˈblutər/ *noun & verb.* *colloq.* (orig. & chiefly *Scot.*). E17.
[ORIGIN Unknown.]
▸ **A** *noun.* **1** A stupid, clumsy, noisy, or babbling person; an oaf, a blunderer. E17.
2 A hard and (usu.) wild kick; a ball kicked in this way. L20.
▸ **B** *verb.* †**1** *verb intrans.* Cry shrilly. L18.
2 *verb intrans.* Bungle, blunder; talk foolishly, babble. M19.
3 *verb trans.* Kick (a ball) hard and (usu.) wildly. L20.
4 *verb trans.* Hit hard; beat up; smash. L20.
■ **blootered** *adjective* very drunk E19. **blootering** *adjective* stupid; clumsy; babbling M19.

blooth *noun* see BLOWTH.

blore /blɔː/ *noun.* Long *arch.* LME.
[ORIGIN Prob. imit.: cf. *blow*, *blast*.]
A violent blowing.

blossom /ˈblɒs(ə)m/ *noun.*
[ORIGIN Old English *blōstm*, *blōs(t)ma* = West Frisian *blossum*, Middle Dutch & mod. Dutch *bloesem*, Middle Low German *blōs(s)em* (cf. also Old Norse *blómstr*), gen. referred to the same base as BLOOM *noun*[1].]
1 A flower, esp. as promising fruit; *collect.* the mass of flowers on a fruit tree etc. OE.

DAY LEWIS The white blossom streaming away on a gale. W. BRONK Tulips or other big blossoms. *fig.*: W. H. PRESCOTT The first blossoms of that literature which was to ripen into so rich a harvest.

2 The state or season of blossoming (*lit. & fig.*); an early stage of growth; promise. ME.

SHAKES. *Haml.* Thus was I.. cut off even in the blossoms of my sin.

3 A person who is lovely and full of promise. LME.

SHAKES. *1 Hen. VI* And there died, my Icarus, my blossom, in his pride.

4 (Minerals forming) the decomposed outcrop of an ore or coal deposit. E19.
– PHRASES: **in blossom** in flower, blossoming.
■ **blossomed** *adjective* covered with blossoms; in blossom: LME. **blossomless** *adjective* M19. **blossomy** *adjective* covered or adorned with blossoms LME.

blossom /ˈblɒs(ə)m/ *verb intrans.*
[ORIGIN Old English *blōstmian*, formed as BLOSSOM *noun*.]
Bear blossom; open into flower (*lit. & fig.*); develop desirably or advantageously (*into*).

POPE Now hawthorns blossom. M. L. KING [Neither] expected this quiet beginning to blossom into a large-scale operation. D. STOREY Mrs. Reagan, in adversity, appeared to blossom. S. KING This thought suddenly blossomed in his mind.

blot /blɒt/ *noun*[1]. LME.
[ORIGIN Prob. of Scandinavian origin; cf. Old Norse *blettr* (Icelandic *blettur*) blot, stain, Danish dial. *blat* spot, blot.]
1 A spot or stain of ink, mud, etc.; any black or dark patch; a blemish, a disfigurement. LME. ▸**b** *spec.* An obliteration by way of correction. E18.

N. MITFORD It looked.. like an ordinary ink blot. *Listener* Charabancs and monstrous hordes of hikers are blots upon the landscape.

a blot on one's ESCUTCHEON.
2 **a** A moral stain; a disgraceful act or quality in a good character; a defect. LME. ▸**b** Imputation of disgrace; defamation. L16. ▸**c** A person who is in disgrace. *colloq.* E20.

J. R. GREEN The execution of Wallace was the one blot on Edward's clemency.

3 BIOLOGY & MEDICINE. The distribution of proteins etc. on a medium on to which they have been blotted. L20.
Northern blot: see NORTHERN *adjective*. SOUTHERN BLOT. ***Western blot***: see WESTERN *adjective*.
■ **blotless** *adjective* LME. **blotty** *adjective* M19.

blot /blɒt/ *noun*[2]. L16.
[ORIGIN Prob. from Dutch *bloot* naked, exposed, but as noun only in English.]
1 BACKGAMMON. An exposed piece liable to be taken; the action of exposing a piece. L16.
2 An exposed point in one's procedure; a mark, a butt. M17.

blot /blɒt/ *verb.* Infl. **-tt-**. LME.
[ORIGIN from BLOT *noun*[1].]
▸ **I** *verb trans.* **1** Spot or stain with ink, tears, etc.; blur, smudge. LME.
blot one's copybook *colloq.* spoil one's character or record, commit an indiscretion.
†**2** Cover (paper) with worthless writing. LME–M17.
3 Disgrace; tarnish, sully, (good qualities or reputation). *arch.* LME. ▸†**b** Stigmatize, calumniate. LME–E17.

N. ROWE Blot not thy innocence with guiltless blood.

4 Obliterate (writing); efface; obscure (a view etc.); exterminate, destroy. Usu. foll. by *out*. LME.

SHAKES. *Rich. II* My name be blotted from the book of life. C. S. FORESTER The German trenches were blotted out by the smoke and debris. E. FIGES My arrival has been blotted out: I cannot remember it. A. PRICE Any chance of a reply.. was blotted out by the roar of another big jet.

5 Dry with blotting paper. M19.
6 BIOLOGY & MEDICINE. Transfer from a medium used for electrophoretic or chromatographic separation to an immobilizing medium where the constituents can be identified. L20.
▸ **II** *verb intrans.* **7** Of a pen, ink, etc.: make blots. LME.
†**8** Sully a reputation etc. *rare* (Shakes.). Only in L16.
9 Become blotted, smudge. M19.

blotch /blɒtʃ/ *noun.* M17.
[ORIGIN Partly alt. of PLOTCH *noun* after BLOT *noun*[1], partly blend of BLOT *noun*[1] and BOTCH *noun*[1].]
1 A discoloured patch on the skin; a pustule, a boil. M17. ▸**b** A plant disease characterized by areas of discoloration. E20.
b ***leaf blotch***: see LEAF *noun*[1]. ***sooty blotch***: see SOOTY *adjective*.
2 A large irregular spot or blot of ink, colour, etc. M18.
■ **blotchiness** *noun* E20. **blotchy** *adjective* E19.

blotch /blɒtʃ/ *verb trans.* E17.
[ORIGIN from the noun.]
Mark with a blotch or blotches.

blotter /ˈblɒtə/ *noun.* L16.
[ORIGIN from BLOT *verb* + -ER[1].]
1 A person who or thing which blots or blots out (or *out*); *spec.* (*a*) an inferior writer, a scribbler; (*b*) something used for drying ink marks, as a blotting pad. L16.
2 A temporary recording book, as a police charge sheet. *N. Amer.* L17.

blottesque /blɒˈtɛsk/ *adjective.* M19.
[ORIGIN from BLOT *verb* + -ESQUE, after *grotesque* etc.]
Of painting: characterized by blotted touches heavily laid on.

blotting /ˈblɒtɪŋ/ *noun.* LME.
[ORIGIN from BLOT *verb* + -ING[1].]
1 The action of BLOT *verb*; an instance of this; a blot, smear, obliteration. Also foll. by *out*. LME.
2 (Material for) blotting paper. L19.
– COMB.: **blotting pad** a pad of blotting paper; **blotting paper** absorbent unsized paper for drying wet ink.

blotto /ˈblɒtəʊ/ *adjective.* *slang.* E20.
[ORIGIN from BLOT *noun*[1] or *verb* + -O.]
Very drunk, intoxicated.

blouse /blaʊz/ *noun & verb.* E19.
[ORIGIN French, of unknown origin.]
▸ **A** *noun.* **1** A loose linen or cotton garment resembling a shirt, usu. belted at the waist, worn by workmen or peasants, esp. in France. E19. ▸**b** *transf.* A French workman. M19.
2 A jacket as part of US military uniform; the upper part of a soldier's or airman's battledress. M19.
3 A woman's loose upper garment usu. worn tucked into a skirt or trousers at the waist. L19.
– PHRASES: ***(big) girl's blouse*** see GIRL *noun*.
▸ **B** *verb.* **1** *verb intrans.* Swell out or hang loosely like a blouse. E20.
2 *verb trans.* Make (a bodice etc.) loose like a blouse. M20.

blouson /ˈbluːzɒn; *foreign* bluzɔ̃ (*pl. same*)/ *noun.* E20.
[ORIGIN French.]
A short jacket shaped like a blouse.

bloviate /ˈbləʊvɪeɪt/ *verb intrans.* *US.* M19.
[ORIGIN perh. from BLOW *verb*[1] + *-viate* as in DEVIATE *verb*.]
Talk at length, esp. in an inflated or empty way.

W. DEVERELL Bloviating to the press about all manner of nonsense.

■ **bloviation** *noun* the action or process of bloviating, inflated or empty speech M19. **bloviator** *noun* M19.

blow /bləʊ/ *noun*[1]. LME.
[ORIGIN Unknown.]
1 A (usu. hard) stroke with the fist, an implement, etc. LME. ▸**b** A stroke of the shears in shearing sheep. *Austral. & NZ.* L19. ▸**c** An outcrop of mineral. *Austral. & NZ.* L19.

D. H. LAWRENCE Catching him a light blow.. with the back of her hand. R. DAHL It was too late to check the blow and the axe blade struck the tree. *fig.*: SHAKES. *Lear* A most poor man, made tame to fortune's blows.

at one blow at a single stroke, in one operation. ***a word and a blow***: see WORD *noun*. ***break a blow***: see BREAK *verb*. **come to blows**, (*arch.*) **fall to blows** begin fighting. **exchange blows** fight. **strike a blow** take action (foll. by *for*, on behalf of, *against*, in opposition to). **strike the first blow** take the first action, begin a process. **without striking a blow** without a struggle, putting up no opposition. **b** ***long blow***: see LONG *adjective*[1].
2 *fig.* A sudden disaster, a shock, a setback. L17.

C. CHAPLIN Dicky died at the age of nineteen, a sad and terrible blow from which she never recovered.

– COMB.: **blow-by-blow** *adjective* (of a description etc.) giving all details in sequence.

blow /bləʊ/ *noun*[2]. L15.
[ORIGIN from BLOW *verb*[1].]
1 A blowing; a blast of air; a gust of wind; *colloq.* a breath of fresh air; a blowing of one's nose; a blowing of a wind instrument; *slang* a jazz session. L15. ▸**b** (The quantity of metal dealt with in) a single operation of a steel-making retort using an oxygen or air blast. L19.

2 A fly's egg deposited in meat etc. (Earlier in FLYBLOW *noun*.) E17.
3 A boast; boastfulness; a boaster. Chiefly *US*. L17.

blow /bləʊ/ *noun*³. *arch*. E18.
[ORIGIN from BLOW *verb*².]
1 A display of blossoms; a brilliant display. E18.
2 Blossoming; bloom. M18.
3 (A) blossom. L18.

blow /bləʊ/ *verb*¹. Pa. t. **blew** /bluː/; pa. pple **blown** /bləʊn/, (senses 12d, 19, & *non-standard*) **blowed**.
[ORIGIN Old English *blāwan*, pa. t. *blēow*, pa. pple *blāwen* = Old High German *blā(h)an*, repl. by weak Old High German *blājan* (German *blähen* blow up, swell), from Indo-European base repr. also by Latin *flare*.]
▸ **I** Senses connected with the production of an air current.
1 *verb intrans*. Of wind, air, etc., or *impers*. with *it*: move along, act as an air current. Freq. with the type or strength of wind as compl. OE.

I. WALTON Heark how it rains and blows. OED It blew a gale. J. STEINBECK The wind blew fierce and strong.

2 *verb intrans*. Send a directed air current from the mouth; (of a bellows etc.) produce an air current. OE. ▸†**b** Hiss; whistle. ME–M16. ▸**c** Of a whale: eject water and air, spout. L17.
3 *verb trans*. Send out by breathing; emit or pass (air); drive, carry, or move by an air current; *fig*. proclaim, publish. Usu. with adverbs & prepositions of direction. ME.

DRYDEN Winnow'd Chaff by Western Winds is blown. SIR W. SCOTT As soon as Richard's return is blown abroad. P. SAVAGE The winds . . blow the dead leaves down. J. HERRIOT He blew smoke pleasurably from his nostrils. A. PRICE He . . blew the dust from it.

4 *verb intrans*. Breathe hard, puff, pant; *dial*. (simply) breathe. LME.

POPE Each spent courser at the chariot blow.

5 *verb intrans*. Bluster; boast, brag. Chiefly *dial*. or *US*, *Austral*., & *NZ colloq*. LME. ▸†**b** *verb trans*. Utter, esp. boastfully, angrily, or maliciously. Also foll. by *out*. LME–L19.
6 *verb trans*. Work (bellows); work the bellows of (an organ etc.). LME.
7 *verb trans*. Cause to pant, exhaust of breath. Usu. in *pass*. M17.

Blackwood's Magazine The Russians . . were . . pretty well blown in the pursuit.

8 *verb intrans*. Be driven, carried, or moved by the wind or other air current. Freq. with adverbs & prepositions of direction. M17. ▸**b** *verb intrans*. & *trans*. Depart suddenly (from). *slang*. E20.

TENNYSON Her cap blew off, her gown blew up. W. CATHER Her skirts blowing in the wind. **b** E. LINKLATER He's blown. He's gone up north. R. MACDONALD I'm blowing this town tonight.

▸ **II** Senses connected with the application of an air current.
9 *verb trans*. Make (a wind instrument) sound; *slang* play jazz on (any instrument). Also, sound (a note, a signal) on (or *on*, *upon*, *with*) a wind instrument. Of a wind instrument: sound (a note, a signal). OE.

TENNYSON The belted hunter blew His wreathed bugle-horn. N. SHUTE The siren blew five blasts.

10 *verb intrans*. Of a wind instrument, its blower, or the note etc. produced: sound. Also (*slang*) play jazz (on any instrument). ME.

TENNYSON Let the mournful martial music blow. R. KIPLING The bugles blew for dinner. J. KEROUAC Everybody in Frisco blew. R. BOLT A pilot's whistle, upon which he will blow.

11 *verb trans*. Direct an air current at so as to cool, warm, dry, etc. (also with the effect as compl.) or (with a fire as obj.) to make burn more brightly (also foll. by *up*). ME. ▸†**b** *fig*. Inflame, arouse, (feeling). Usu. foll. by *up*. ME–L18.

SHAKES. *Ven. & Ad*. To . . blow them dry again. F. MARRYAT The winter was cold . . and he blew his fingers.

12 *verb trans*. Swell by an air current; make or shape (a bubble, glass, etc.) by blowing into it. (Foll. by *up*, *out*.) LME. ▸†**b** Inflate (a person) with pride or vanity. Usu. foll. by *up*. LME–E18. ▸**c** Enlarge, magnify; exaggerate. Usu. & now only foll. by *up*. M16. ▸**d** Cause (the stomach of an animal) to swell. L18. ▸**e** In *pass*. Of a food tin etc.: be swollen by internal gas pressure. L19.

J. DICKEY I blew up the air mattresses with a hand pump. **c** *Punch* I blew up the two faces on an epidiascope.

13 *verb trans*. Clear (the nose, a pipe, an egg, etc.) by an air current. M16.
14 *verb trans*. Scatter, destroy, or send flying by an explosion etc. (freq. with adverbs, esp. *up*, or with the result as compl.); break into (a safe etc.) with explosives; *fig*. (*colloq*.) bungle. Foll. by *up* also †(**a**) destroy, ruin; (**b**) *colloq*. reprove, scold. L16. ▸**b** *verb intrans*. Be shattered etc. by an explosion, explode, (usu. foll. by *up*); *fig*. foll. by *up*, lose one's temper. L17. ▸**c** *verb trans*. Produce (a hole etc.) by an explosion etc. L19.

STEELE One of our Bombs fell into a Magazine . . and blew it up. R. CONQUEST The bridge attributed to Belisarius Is blown. J. BETJEMAN When mankind Has blown himself to pieces. **b** C. KINGSLEY The mountain had blown up like a barrel of gunpowder. J. CLAVELL When the magazine blew.

15 *verb trans*. Expose, reveal; inform on. (Foll. by †*up*.) Now *slang*. L16. ▸**b** *verb intrans*. Act as an informer, reveal a secret. *slang*. M19.
16 *verb intrans*. & *trans*. Of an electric filament or fuse: melt when overloaded. Also, cause (an electric filament etc.) to melt on overload. Also foll. by *out*. L19.

J. RABAN Every light bulb blows when you switch it on.

17 *verb trans*. Fellate. *coarse slang*. M20.
▸ **III** Other senses.
18 *verb trans*. Of a fly etc.: deposit eggs on or in; = FLYBLOW *verb* 1. L16. ▸†**b** *verb trans*. & *intrans*. Deposit (eggs). E17–L18.

A. BURGESS The flies blew the cold beef on the kitchen table.

19 *verb trans*. Curse, confound, damn, (freq. in *pass*.). Foll. by *if* with 1st person expr. surprise or as a disclaimer (also foll. by †*up*). *slang*. L18. ▸**b** *verb intrans*. in *imper*. Damn! E20.

P. EGAN Blow me tight if ever I saw such a thing in my life before. DICKENS One blowed thing and another.

20 *verb trans*. Squander, spend (money) recklessly. Also (chiefly *US*) foll. by *in*. (Cf. BLUE *verb*².) *slang*. L19.
21 *verb trans*. Treat (a person *to*). *US slang*. L19.
– PHRASES: **blow a cloud** *colloq*. smoke a pipe. *blow a fuse*: see FUSE *noun*². *blow a gasket*: see GASKET *noun*. **blow a kiss** kiss one's fingers and wave or pretend to blow something from them to a (distant) person. **blow a person's brains out** shoot a person through the head. **blow a person's mind** *slang* cause a person to have drug-induced hallucinations or a similar experience. **blow great guns** (of wind) blow violently. **blow high, blow low** *US* whatever may happen. **blow hot and cold** vacillate, be inconsistent. **blow one's cool** *slang* lose one's composure, become angry or agitated. **blow one's own trumpet** praise oneself. **blow one's top**, (*N. Amer*.) **blow one's stack** *colloq*. show great anger. *blow sky-high*: see SKY *noun*. *blow that for a game of soldiers*: see SOLDIER *noun*. *blow the gaff*: see GAFF *noun*³. **blow the whistle on** draw attention to (something illicit or undesirable), bring to a sharp conclusion, inform on. *blow trade*: see TRADE *noun*.
– WITH ADVERBS & PREPOSITIONS IN SPECIALIZED SENSES: **blow away** *slang* kill, destroy, defeat. **blow in** (**a**) *verb phr. trans*. (METALLURGY) set (a blast furnace) in operation; (**b**) *verb phr. intrans*. (*colloq*.) come in unexpectedly; (see also sense 20 above). **blow off** *verb phr. trans*. allow (steam etc.) to escape forcibly; *fig*. get rid of (superfluous energy etc.) in a noisy way. **blow on —**, **blow upon —** discredit, defame, make stale; (see also sense 9 above). **blow out** (**a**) *verb phr. trans*. & *intrans*. extinguish or be extinguished by blowing; (**b**) *verb phr. trans*. (METALLURGY) take (a blast furnace) out of operation; (**c**) *verb phr. intrans*. (of a pneumatic tyre) burst; (see also senses 5b, 12, 16 above). **blow over** pass off without threatened consequences. **blow up** *verb phr. intrans*. (of a wind) increase in force; arise, come to notice; (see also senses 11, 12, 14, 15, 19 above). *blow upon*: see *blow on* above.
– COMB.: **blow-away** *adjective* likely to be blown away by the wind etc.; **blow-back** the action or process of blowing back, esp. (**a**) of pressure in a boiler or internal-combustion engine; (**b**) of gunpowder that has not burned completely; (**c**) of the slide or breechblock of some firearms; (**d**) (chiefly *US*) the unintended adverse results of a political action or situation; **blow-ball** the globular seed head of a dandelion etc.; **blowdown** (**a**) a gust of wind down a chimney; (**b**) *N. Amer*. a tree blown down by the wind; the blowing down of trees by the wind; (**c**) the removal of solids or liquids from a container or pipe using pressure; **blow-drier** a blower used in blow-drying; **blow-dry** *verb & noun* (**a**) *verb trans*. arrange (hair) while drying it with a hand-held blower; (**b**) *noun* an act or instance of blow-drying hair; **blowfish** (a popular name for) any of several fishes which inflate their bodies when frightened etc.; **blowfly** any of various flies of the family Calliphoridae, which deposit their eggs on meat and carcasses; a bluebottle, a meat fly; **blowhard** *adjective & noun* (*colloq*.) (a person who is) boastful; **blowhole** (**a**) a hole for breathing through; the nostril of a whale etc.; (**b**) a hole formed by escaping air, steam, etc.; (**c**) a vent in a tunnel etc. for the escape of steam, gas, etc.; **blowjob** *coarse slang* an act or instance of fellatio or cunnilingus; **blowlamp** a lamp or torch for directing a very hot flame on a selected spot; **blow-off** *adjective & noun* (of or pertaining to) the removal of water or sediment from a boiler by the force of steam; *fig*. an outburst; **blowout** (**a**) *colloq*. a large meal; (**b**) *dial*. & *US* an outbreak of rage, a row; (**c**) (orig. *US*) an isolated hill with a crater-like top created by the wind; a hollow eroded by the wind; (**d**) a bursting of a pneumatic tyre; (**e**) a rapid uncontrolled uprush of fluid from an oil well; *blowout preventer*: see PREVENTER 3; **blowpipe** (**a**) a tube for heating flame by blowing air or other gas into it; (**b**) a tube used in glass-blowing; (**c**) a tube for propelling arrows or darts by blowing; **blowtorch** = *blowlamp* above; **blow-up** (**a**) an explosion; *fig*. an outburst of anger, a row; (**b**) the vessel in which raw sugar is dissolved; (**c**) *colloq*. a photographic enlargement.

blow /bləʊ/ *verb*². *arch*. Pa. t. **blew** /bluː/; pa. pple **blown** /bləʊn/.
[ORIGIN Old English *blōwan* strong, corresp. to weak verbs Old Frisian *blōia*, Old Saxon *blōjan* (Middle Dutch & mod. Dutch *bloeien*), Old High German *bluojan*, *bluoen* (German *blühen*), from Germanic base also of BLOOM *noun*¹, BLOSSOM *noun* & perh. BLADE.]
1 *verb intrans*. Blossom, flower; *fig*. flourish, bloom. OE.
†**2** *verb trans*. Cause to bloom. M17–E19.

blowed *verb* see BLOW *verb*¹.

blowen /ˈbləʊən/ *noun*. *arch*. *slang*. Also **blowing** /ˈbləʊɪŋ/. L17.
[ORIGIN Unknown.]
A prostitute.

blower /ˈbləʊə/ *noun*¹. OE.
[ORIGIN from BLOW *verb*¹ + -ER¹.]
1 *gen*. A person who or thing which blows. (Foll. by *of*.) OE.
2 A boaster, a blusterer. Chiefly *dial*. or *US* & *Austral*. *colloq*. L16.
3 An apparatus that produces or increases an air current, as a sheet of iron across a fireplace to increase a fire's draught, a fan heater, etc. L18.
4 An escape of gas through a fissure in a coalmine etc.; a fissure through which gas escapes. E19.
5 A telephone or (formerly) a speaking tube. *colloq*. E20.

J. SIMPSON I'll get onto the blower to him right away.

blower /ˈbləʊə/ *noun*². *rare*. M18.
[ORIGIN from BLOW *verb*² + -ER¹.]
A plant that blooms *early*, *late*, etc.

blowing *noun* var. of BLOWEN.

blown /bləʊn/ *adjective*. *colloq*. M20.
[ORIGIN Pa. pple of BLOW *verb*¹.]
Of a vehicle's engine: provided with a turbocharger.

blown *verb*¹, *verb*² *pa. pple* of BLOW *verb*¹, *verb*².

blowse *noun* & *verb*, **blowsy** *adjective* vars. of BLOWZE, BLOWSY.

blowsy /ˈblaʊzi/ *adjective*. Also **blowzy**. E17.
[ORIGIN from BLOWZE + -Y¹.]
Of a woman: coarse and red-faced; unkempt, dishevelled.
■ **blowsily** *adverb* E20. **blowsiness** *noun* M19.

blowth /bləʊθ/ *noun*. Long *obsolete* exc. *dial*. Also (*dial*.) **blooth** /bluːθ/. E17.
[ORIGIN from BLOW *verb*² + -TH¹.]
Blossoming; (a) bloom.

blowy /ˈbləʊɪ/ *adjective*. E19.
[ORIGIN from BLOW *verb*¹ + -Y¹.]
Windy.

blowze /blaʊz/ *noun* & *verb*. Also **blowse**. L16.
[ORIGIN Unknown.]
▸ **A** *noun*. †**1** A beggar's female companion. L16–E18.
2 A coarse red-faced woman. Long *obsolete* exc. *dial*. L16.
▸ **B** *verb*. **1** *verb trans*. Make red-faced; dishevel. Chiefly as ***blowzed*** *ppl adjective*. M18.
†**2** *verb intrans*. Tend to be blowsy. Chiefly as ***blowzing*** *ppl adjective*. M18–M19.

blowzy *adjective* var. of BLOWSY.

BLT *abbreviation*.
Bacon, lettuce, and tomato (sandwich).

blub /blʌb/ *verb* & *noun*. *colloq*. E19.
[ORIGIN Abbreviation of BLUBBER *verb*.]
▸ **A** *verb*. Infl. **-bb-**.
1 *verb trans*. Wet or disfigure with weeping. E19.
2 *verb intrans*. Shed tears, weep. M19.
▸ **B** *noun*. A fit or spell of weeping. L19.

blubber /ˈblʌbə/ *noun*. LME.
[ORIGIN Prob. imit.: cf. Low German *blubbern* bubble, German *blubbern* bubble, splutter.]
†**1** The foaming of the sea. Only in LME.
2 A bubble on water. *obsolete* exc. *dial*. LME.
3 The fat of whales, seals, etc. LME.
4 More fully ***sea blubber***. A jellyfish. E17.
5 The action of blubbering. M17.
■ **blubbery** *adjective* L18.

blubber /ˈblʌbə/ *adjective*. Also (the earliest form) †**blab-**; †**blob-**. L15.
[ORIGIN Prob. imit.: cf. BLEB, BLOB, BUBBLE *noun* & *adjective*.]
Esp. of the lips or cheeks: swollen, protruding.

blubber /ˈblʌbə/ *verb*. LME.
[ORIGIN from BLUBBER *noun*.]
1 *verb intrans*. Bubble (up); make a bubbling sound. LME.
2 *verb intrans*. Weep noisily; weep and sob unrestrainedly. LME.

BRENDAN CLEARY Her mouth agape and blubbering she fled into the kitchen.

3 *verb trans*. Utter with crying and sobbing. (Foll. by *out*, arch. *forth*.) L16.
4 *verb trans*. Wet, disfigure, or swell (the face) with weeping. L16.
■ **blubberer** *noun* L18. **blubberingly** *adverb* with noisy weeping M19.

blucher /ˈbluːkə, *foreign* ˈblyçər/ *noun*. Also **B-**. E19.
[ORIGIN G. L. von *Blücher* (1742–1819), Prussian general.]
hist. **1** A kind of horse-drawn cart or coach. Also more fully ***Blucher coach***. E19.
2 A strong laced leather half-boot or high shoe. Also ***blucher boot***. Usu. in *pl*. M19.

bludge /blʌdʒ/ *verb* & *noun*. *slang* (chiefly *Austral*. & *NZ*). L19.
[ORIGIN Back-form. from BLUDGER.]
▸ **A** *verb*. **1** *verb intrans*. **a** Shirk responsibility or hard work. L19. ▸**b** Impose *on*. E20. ▸**c** Pimp. Now *rare*. E20.

B

2 *verb trans.* Cadge, scrounge. M20.
▸ **B** *noun.* An easy job or assignment. M20.

bludgeon /ˈblʌdʒ(ə)n/ *noun & verb.* M18.
[ORIGIN Unknown.]
▸ **A** *noun.* A heavy-headed stick or club. M18.
▸ **B** *verb trans.* Strike repeatedly or fell with a bludgeon; coerce. M19.

A. BURGESS I did not wish to give up my freedom. I was bludgeoned into marriage.

■ **bludgeoner** *noun* a person who is armed with or uses a bludgeon M19.

bludger /ˈblʌdʒə/ *noun. slang.* M19.
[ORIGIN Abbreviation of BLUDGEONER.]
1 A man who works with prostitutes to rob their clients; a pimp. Now *rare.* M19.
2 A loafer, a shirker; a sponger, a scrounger. *Austral. & NZ.* E20.

blue /bluː/ *noun.* Also †**blew**. ME.
[ORIGIN The adjective used ellipt. or absol.]
1 Blue colour; a shade of this. ME. ▸**b** A pigment of a blue colour (freq. with specifying word); a blue substance; *spec.* a blue powder used as a whitener in laundering. L15.

J. RUSKIN The blue of distance, however intense, is not the blue of a bright blue flower. **b** S. ROWLANDS Set her to starch a band . . She euer spoyles the same with too much blew.

cobalt blue, electric blue, navy blue, Prussian blue, royal blue, etc. **b** ***French blue***: see FRENCH *adjective.* ***scratch blue***: see SCRATCH *verb.* SCRATCHED ***blue***. VERDIGRIS ***blue***.

2 Blue clothing, dress, or uniform; blue fabric. ME. ▸**b** *spec.* The uniform of the Union troops in the American Civil War. *US.* M19.
men in blue, **boys in blue**, etc., policemen; the Royal Navy; US Federal troops.
3 *ellipt.* Anything distinguished by blue colour, as the blue ball in snooker, a blue butterfly (*spec.* one of the family Lycaenidae), etc. L16.
Admiral of the Blue *hist.*: of the Blue squadron (one of three divisions of the Royal Navy made between the 17th and 19th cents.). ***Danish blue***: see DANISH *adjective.* ***RUSSIAN Blue***. See also BLUES.
4 The clear sky; the sea; the desert; the indefinite distance, the unknown. M17.

GEO. ELIOT Where one may float between blue and blue. J. T. STORY I am not . . one of those people who can vanish into the blue never to be heard of again. N. MACCAIG The weather doodles a faint cloud / on the blue / then pensively washes it out.

bolt from the blue, bolt out of the blue: see BOLT *noun*[1]. **out of the blue** without warning, unexpectedly.

5 As the colour adopted by a party, faction, etc. (cf. BLUE *adjective* 5); *transf.* a member of such a group. M17. ▸**b** = BLUESTOCKING *noun. arch.* L18. ▸**c** (Also **B-**.) A person who has represented Oxford University or Cambridge University at a particular sport in a match between the two universities; such a distinction. L19.
dark blue, **light blue**: adopted by the Universities of Oxford and Cambridge respectively. **c get one's blue**, **win one's blue**, etc., represent one's university etc. in a sporting contest.
6 A soldier, police officer, etc., in blue uniform. Usu. in *pl.* M18.
the Blues (in the British army) the Royal Horse Guards, later merged with the 1st Dragoons as ***the Blues and Royals***.
7 An argument, a fight or brawl; a mistake, a blunder. *Austral. & NZ slang.* M20.

K. TENNANT Every time Rene comes round there's some kind of a blue. N. SHUTE I put up a blue right away by ordering a pink gin.

8 A nickname for a red-headed person. *Austral. & NZ colloq.* M20.
– COMB.: **blue bag** a bag containing laundry blue, used also in the treatment of insect bites and stings; **blue on blue** [from the use of blue to indicate friendly forces in military exercises] designating an attack made by one's own side that accidentally harms one's own forces; **blue spot** the spot on which the blue ball is placed in snooker.

blue /bluː/ *adjective.* Also †**blew**. ME.
[ORIGIN Old French & mod. French *bleu* from Proto-Romance from Germanic (whence also Old English *blǣ-hǣwen, blǣwen* blue, Old Norse *blár* dark-blue, livid, BLAE).]
1 Of the colour of the sky and the deep sea, between green and violet in the spectrum; of a hue resembling this. ME. ▸**b** Livid, leaden-coloured (esp. of the skin as a result of cold, fear, etc.). ME. ▸**c** Of a flame or flash: without red glare. L16.

SHAKES. *Ant. & Cl.* My bluest veins to kiss. SCOTT FITZGERALD The blue smoke of brittle leaves. C. MACKENZIE Eyes as blue as the kingfisher's wing. L. VAN DER POST A great plain between blue hills. I. MCEWAN 'Can I borrow a blue pencil?' 'Blue for the sea or blue for the sky?' **b** MILTON Blue meagre hag. T. C. WOLFE His lips chattered and turned blue. **c** DEFOE When the candles burn blue the Devil is in the room.

between the devil and the deep blue sea: see DEVIL *noun.* **b** ***black and blue***: see BLACK *adjective.* **blue in the face** livid with effort, excitement, etc. (used *hyperbol.*).

2 **a** Taken as the colour of constancy. LME. ▸**b** Taken as the colour of sorrow or anguish (see also sense 3). LME. ▸**c** Taken as the colour of plagues and things hurtful. E16.

b V. NABOKOV A combination of blue sulks and rosy mirth. **c** E. YOUNG Riot, pride, perfidy, blue vapours breathe.

3 *fig.* Depressed, low-spirited; dismayed, downcast; (of circumstances) dismal, unpromising. M16. ▸**b** Intoxicated. *slang* (chiefly *US*). E19. ▸**c** *MUSIC.* Pertaining to or characteristic of the blues. E20.

R. BOLDREWOOD It seemed a rather blue look-out. G. STEIN She wondered . . how she could go on living when she was so blue.

4 Dressed in blue; wearing blue. L16.
thin blue line: see THIN *adjective.*
5 Belonging to a party or group that has chosen blue for its colour; *spec.* (***a***) the Scottish Presbyterian or Whig party in the 17th cent.; (***b***) the Conservative Party in the UK. M17.

G. B. SHAW The bluest of Tories.

6 Of a woman: learned, pedantic (cf. BLUESTOCKING). *arch. derog.* L18.

M. EDGEWORTH They are all so wise, and so learned, so blue.

7 Obscene, indecent; profane. *colloq.* M19.

P. G. WODEHOUSE A jocund little tale, slightly blue in spots. R. LOWELL What blue movie is worth a seat at the keyhole.

– SPECIAL COLLOCATIONS & COMB.: **blue asbestos** crocidolite. **blue baby** a baby with congenital cyanosis. **blueback** (chiefly *N. Amer.*) a bird or fish, esp. a trout or a sockeye salmon, having a bluish back. **blue bag** a barrister's (orig. a solicitor's) brief bag of blue material; (see also BLUE *noun*). **blue beat (music)** = SKA. **blueberry** any of certain N. American shrubs of the genus *Vaccinium*, of the heath family, allied to the bilberry but bearing their fruits in clusters; the sweet edible blue or blackish fruit of such a plant. **bluebill** *N. Amer. & dial.* = SCAUP. **bluebird** (***a***) a small N. American bird of the genus *Sialia*, related to the thrushes, and having sky-blue upperparts; *esp.* the eastern bluebird, *S. sialis*; (***b***) *fig.* happiness. **blue-black** *adjective & noun* (of) a black colour with a tinge of blue. **blue blood** [translating Spanish *sangre azul*, claimed by certain families of Castile, as having no Moorish, Jewish, or other admixture] a sign of high birth. **blue-blooded** *adjective* aristocratic. **blue bonnet** (***a***) a peasant or soldier wearing a broad round flat woollen cap, formerly in general use in Scotland; (***b***) any of various blue flowers and blue-headed birds; *esp.* (*N. Amer.*) either of two lupins, *Lupinus subcarnosus* and *L. texensis*, native to Texas. **blue book** a book bound in blue, *spec.* (***a***) a parliamentary or Privy Council report, issued in a blue cover; (***b***) *US* a printed book giving personal details of government officials. **bluebottle** (***a***) a cornflower or occas. another blue-flowered plant; (***b***) a nickname for a beadle (*arch.*) or a police officer; (***c***) a large dark-blue fly of the genus *Calliphora*; (***d***) *Austral., NZ, & S. Afr.*, a Portuguese man-of-war. ***bluebunch wheatgrass***: see WHEAT *noun.* **blue-bush** any of various shrubs with bluish foliage or blue flowers, *esp.* (*Austral.*) a bluish-leaved shrub of the genus *Bassia*. **bluecap** †(***a***) a Scotsman; (***b***) *dial.* a salmon in its first year (so called because of a blue spot on its head); a cornflower; a blue tit. **blue-cheeked** *adjective* having blue cheeks; ***blue-cheeked bee-eater***, an African and Asian bee-eater, *Merops superciliosus*, which has mainly green plumage with a black eyestripe bordered by pale blue. **blue cheese** cheese marked with veins of blue mould (***Danish blue cheese***: see DANISH *adjective*). **blue chip** (orig. *US*) a high-value poker counter; *transf.* a stock exchange investment considered to be fairly reliable, though not entirely without risk. **blue-chip** *adjective* of the highest quality; (of an investment) fairly reliable. **blue coat** a person who wears a blue coat, e.g. a police officer, a sailor, a scholar at a charity school (esp. Christ's Hospital), (formerly) an almsman, a beadle. ***blue* COHOSH**. **blue-collar** *adjective* designating a manual or industrial worker, as opp. to a 'white-collar' (office) worker. ***blue* COPPERAS**. **blue corn** *N. Amer.* a variety of maize with bluish grains. **blue crab** a large edible crab, *Callinectes sapidus*, of the N. American Atlantic coast. ***blue crane***: see CRANE *noun*[1] 1b. **blue dahlia** something rare or unheard of. **blue devil** (***a***) a baleful demon; (***b***) in *pl.*, depression of spirits; delirium tremens (cf. BLUES 1). **blue-domer** *colloq.* one who does not go to church, preferring to worship beneath the 'blue dome' of heaven. **blue duck** a grey-blue duck, *Hymenolaimus malacorhynchos*, of mountain streams in New Zealand; also called ***mountain duck***, ***whio***. ***blue ensign***: see ENSIGN *noun.* **blue eye** (***a***) an eye of which the iris is blue; †(***b***) = ***black eye*** (b) s.v. BLACK *adjective*; (***c***) a blueness round the eye from weeping etc. **blue-eyed** *adjective* having a blue eye or blue eyes; ***blue-eyed boy*** (colloq.) a favourite, a pet; ***blue-eyed grass***, any of several plants of the genus *Sisyrinchium*, bearing blue flowers; ***blue-eyed Mary***, a blue-flowered ornamental plant, *Omphalodes verna*, of the borage family. **bluefin (tuna)** *N. Amer.* the common tuna, *Thunnus thynnus*. **bluefish** any of various fishes of a blue colour; *esp.* (***a***) (chiefly *N. Amer.*) *Pomatomus saltatrix* (family Pomatomidae), a large edible blue-backed percoid marine fish; (***b***) (*Austral. & NZ*) *Girella cyanea* (family Kyphosidae), a bright blue edible percoid marine fish. **blue flag** (***a***) a European award for beaches based on cleanliness and safety; (***b***) *MOTOR RACING* a blue flag used to indicate to a driver that there is another driver trying to lap him. **blue fly** a bluebottle. **blue funk** *slang* a state of extreme nervousness. **bluegill (sunfish)** a small fish, *Lepomis macrochirus*, of lakes and ponds in central and south-eastern US. **blue gown** *hist.* in Scotland, (the dress of) a king's bedesman or licensed beggar. **bluegrass** (***a***) any of various grasses with bluish flowers; spec. *Poa pratensis*, characteristic of Kentucky and Virginia, or other grasses of the same genus; (***b***) the state of Kentucky; (***c***) a type of folk music associated with Kentucky and Virginia. **blue-green (alga)** a primitive prokaryotic alga containing blue and green photosynthetic pigments; also called ***cyanobacterium***. **blue-grey** a breed of cattle, a cross between Aberdeen Angus and shorthorn. ***blue groper***: see GROPER *noun*[2] 2. **blue ground** dark greyish-blue brecciated kimberlite in which diamonds may be found. **bluegum** any of several Australian eucalypts with bluish bark or leaves. **blue hare** = ***MOUNTAIN hare***. **blue hawk** any of various bluish-grey birds of prey; *esp.* the male hen harrier. **blue heeler** *Austral. & NZ* a cattle dog with a dark speckled body. **blue helmet** a member of a United Nations peacekeeping force. **bluejacket** a sailor, esp. as opp. to a marine. **blue jay** (***a***) a crested jay, *Cyanocitta cristata*, largely blue with white underparts, native to eastern N. America; (***b***) = ROLLER *noun*[2]. **Blue John** (***a***) a blue or purple variety of fluorite found in Derbyshire, England; †(***b***) = ***after-wort*** s.v. AFTER-. **blue-joint** *US* a grass of the genus *Calamagrostis* or a related genus, with bluish stems. **blue laws** *US* severe puritanical laws, orig. those alleged to have been in force among early colonists of New England. **blue line**: *spec.* marking off an area of play in a game, as in *ICE HOCKEY* either of the two lines midway between the centre of the rink and each goal. **blue ling** either of two small lings, *Molva macrophthalma* and *M. dypterygia*. ***blue* MARGUERITE**. **Bluemantle** one of four pursuivants of the English College of Arms. **blue metal** bluish argillaceous shale, used in road-making. **blue monkey** the samango monkey, *Cercopithecus mitis*. **blue moon** *colloq.* a rarely recurring period (esp. in ***once in a blue moon***). **blue mould** a fungus in food, esp. in certain cheeses when mature. **Blue Mountain (coffee)** a type of Jamaican coffee. **blue-mouth** a spiny deep-water scorpaenid fish of the N. Atlantic, *Helicolenus dactylopterus*, with a reddish body and a blue mouth; also called ***red bream***. **blue murder** *slang* an extravagant outcry, a loud or alarming noise. **bluenose** (chiefly *N. Amer.*) (***a***) (**B-**) a person or thing from Nova Scotia; (***b***) a priggish or puritanical person. **blue-nosed** *adjective* (chiefly *N. Amer. colloq.*) priggish, puritanical; contemptible. **blue note** *MUSIC* a minor interval where a major would be expected; an off-pitch note. ***blue* PEAFOWL**. **blue pencil** a pencil with a blue lead, used in marking corrections, etc. **blue-pencil** *verb trans.* score through or obliterate with a blue pencil, make cuts in, censor. **Blue Peter** a blue flag with a white square in the centre, hoisted by a ship as a signal of immediate sailing. **blue pill** (chiefly *hist.*) a mercurial antibilious pill. ***blue* PINCUSHION**. **blue-plate** *adjective* (*N. Amer.*) designating a restaurant meal in which the main course is served as a single menu item. ***blue* POINTER**. **blueprint** *noun & verb* (***a***) *noun* a photographic print composed of white lines on a blue ground or vice versa, used for making copies of plans and designs; *fig.* a plan, scheme; (***b***) *verb trans.* plan, project. **blue riband**, **blue ribbon** (***a***) a ribbon of blue silk, worn as a badge of honour; *esp.* that of the Order of the Garter; (***b***) the greatest distinction, the first place or prize; *attrib.* of first quality, carefully chosen; (***c***) a small strip of blue ribbon worn as a sign of teetotalism. **blue-ribbon** *adjective* (*N. Amer.*) (***a***) of the highest quality, first-class; (***b***) (of a jury or committee) specially selected. **blue rinse** (an elderly woman with) a bluish tint for grey or white hair. **blue-rinsed** *adjective* having a blue rinse. ***blue roan***: see ROAN *adjective & noun*[2]. ***blue rock***: see ROCK *noun*[1]. **blue rod** an official of the order of St Michael and St George. **blue ruin** *slang* gin, esp. of poor quality. ***blue runner***: see RUNNER 5c. **blue-screen** *adjective* designating or employing a special-effects technique in which scenes filmed against a blue background are superimposed on other scenes. **blue shark** a large shark, *Prionace glauca*, having a dark-blue back. **blue shift** displacement of spectral lines towards shorter wavelengths or the blue end of the spectrum (opp. REDSHIFT *noun*). **blue-sky** *adjective* (***a***) *N. Amer.*, designating dealing in worthless securities or legislation to prevent their sale; (***b***) creative or visionary and unconstrained by practicalities. ***blue sowthistle***: see ***sowthistle*** s.v. SOW *noun*[1]. **blue state** *US colloq.* [from the typical colour used to represent the Democratic Party on maps during elections] a US state that predominantly votes for or supports the Democratic Party (cf. *red state* s.v. RED *adjective*). **blue stone** (***a***) copper sulphate; (***b***) a bluish-grey stone used for building, esp. *US* a sandstone from near the Hudson River, *Austral. & NZ* a basalt; (***c***) any of the dolerite stones forming the inner parts of Stonehenge, believed to be from the Preseli Hills, S. Wales. **blue streak** *colloq.* (chiefly *N. Amer.*) a fast-moving thing or person; a constant stream of words. ***blue tangle***: see TANGLE *noun*[2] 3. **bluethroat** a Eurasian bird, *Luscinia svecica*, related to the robin, having a blue throat with a chestnut or white spot. **blue tit** a common European tit, *Parus caeruleus*, having blue upperparts. **bluetongue** (***a***) (orig. *S. Afr.*) an insect-borne viral disease of sheep (transmissible with less serious effects to cattle and goats), characterized by fever, lameness, and a blue, swollen mouth and tongue; also occas. a comparable disease of horses; (***b***) *Austral.* a lizard of the genus *Tiliqua*. ***blue* TULP**. **blue vinny (cheese)**, **blue vinney (cheese)** a blue-mould skimmed-milk cheese; also called ***Dorset cheese***. ***blue* VITRIOL**. **blue water** the open sea. **blue whale** a baleen whale, *Balaenoptera musculus*, the largest of all animals. **blue whiting** a small blue-backed oceanic whiting, *Micromesistius poutassou*, common in the eastern Atlantic. **blue-wing** the blue-winged teal, *Anas discors*, of N. America.
■ **bluely** *adverb* (***a***) with a blue colour or tinge; †(***b***) badly (only in ***come off bluely***): M17. **blueness** *noun* L15.

blue /bluː/ *verb*[1] *trans.* Pres. pple **blueing**, **bluing**. Also †**blew** (cf. BLUE *adjective*). E17.
[ORIGIN from the adjective.]
1 Make blue. E17.
2 Treat (laundry) with blue. L18.
■ **blueing**, **bluing** *noun* (***a***) the action of the verb; (***b***) laundry blue: M17.

blue /bluː/ *verb*[2] *trans. slang.* Pres. pple & verbal noun **blueing**, **bluing**. M19.
[ORIGIN Perh. from past tense of BLOW *verb*[1] 20.]
Spend extravagantly, squander.

Bluebeard /ˈbluːbɪəd/ *noun.* E19.
[ORIGIN A character in a fairy tale told in French (*Barbe-bleue*) by Perrault.]
A man who has murdered several wives and concealed their bodies, or has other mysterious or horrible things to conceal.

bluebell /ˈbluːbɛl/ *noun.* L16.
[ORIGIN from BLUE *adjective* + BELL *noun*[1].]
1 The harebell, *Campanula rotundifolia*. Chiefly *Scot. & N. English.* L16.
2 A bulbous-rooted woodland plant, *Hyacinthoides non-scripta*, bearing racemes of narrow bell-like blue flowers in spring; a flowering stem of this plant. L18.

Spanish bluebell: see SPANISH *adjective*. ***Virginia bluebell***: see VIRGINIA 1.

blueish *adjective* var. of BLUISH.

blueism /ˈbluːɪz(ə)m/ *noun. arch.* Also **bluism**. L18.
[ORIGIN from BLUE *adjective* + -ISM.]
The characteristics or behaviour of a bluestocking; feminine learning.

blues /bluːz/ *noun*. M18.
[ORIGIN Ellipt. for *blue devils*: see BLUE *adjective*.]
1 *pl.* ***the blues***, depression of spirits, melancholy. M18.
S. BELLOW He realized he had not spoken three words to a living soul and the blues descended on him.
2 *pl.* & (sometimes) *sing.* A (type of) haunting melody or melancholy song, freq. in a twelve-bar sequence using blue notes, originating among southern black Americans. E20.
J. BALDWIN Frank sang the blues. R. D. LAING Martyn's electronic version of the Skip James blues 'I'd Rather Be The Devil'.
bluesman a male performer of blues music. ***RHYTHM and blues***.
■ **bluesy** *adjective* of, pertaining to, or characteristic of blues music M20.

bluestocking /ˈbluːstɒkɪŋ/ *adjective* & *noun. derog.* L17.
[ORIGIN from BLUE *adjective* + STOCKING *noun*².]
▸**A** *adjective*. **1** Wearing blue worsted stockings; in homely dress. *arch.* L17.
2 Designating or pertaining to (those frequenting) assemblies for literary conversation etc. held at Montagu House in London about 1750 (where some of the men wore the blue stockings of ordinary daytime dress). L18.
3 Of a woman: having or affecting literary tastes, learned. E19.
▸**B** *noun*. A female supporter of bluestocking assemblies; a learned woman. L18.
■ **bluestockingism** *noun* E19.

bluet /ˈbluːɪt/ *noun*. Chiefly *US*. E18.
[ORIGIN French *bl(e)uet* dim. of *bleu* BLUE *adjective*: see -ET¹.]
Any of various blue-flowered plants; *esp.* (**a**) the cornflower, *Centaurea cyanus*; (**b**) the plant *Hedyotis caerulea*, of the madder family. Also called ***innocence***, ***quaker-lady***. Freq. in *pl.*

Bluetooth /ˈbluːtuːθ/ *noun*. L20.
[ORIGIN Said to be named after King Harald *Bluetooth* (910–85), credited with uniting Denmark and Norway.]
A standard for the short-range wireless interconnection of mobile phones, computers, and other electronic devices; (proprietary name for) devices conforming to this standard.

bluey /ˈbluːi/ *adjective, adverb, & noun*. E19.
[ORIGIN from BLUE *adjective* + -Y¹.]
▸**A** *adjective & adverb*. More or less blue; with a blue tinge. E19.
▸**B** *noun*. **1** Lead. *slang*. Now *rare* or *obsolete*. M19.
2 a A bushman's bundle (often wrapped in a blue blanket); a swag. *Austral. & NZ colloq.* L19. ▸**b** A rough outer garment; the material from which such garments are made. *Austral. colloq.* L19.
hump bluey travel with a swag, hit the trail.
3 A summons (on blue paper) to appear in court. *Austral. & NZ colloq.* E20.
4 A blue cattle dog. *Austral. colloq.* M20.
5 A nickname for a red-headed person. *Austral. & NZ colloq.* M20.

bluff /blʌf/ *noun*¹. Orig. *N. Amer.* M17.
[ORIGIN from the adjective.]
1 A cliff or headland with a broad precipitous face; a high steep bank, esp. by a river or shore. M17.
2 A grove or clump of trees. *Canad.* M18.

bluff /blʌf/ *noun*². L18.
[ORIGIN Prob. from the verb, to which it is certainly related, but perh. earlier.]
1 A blinker for a horse. Now *obsolete* or *dial.* L18.
2 The game of poker; the action or an act of bluffing, orig. in poker; threatening or confident language or behaviour adopted without basis, in order to intimidate or mislead an opponent. Orig. *US*. M19.
C. CONNOLLY I learnt that sulking, crying, moping, and malingering were bluffs that paid. A. WILSON There's a lot of bluff goes with this act; he knows nothing about brandy.
call someone's bluff challenge or invite a showdown with someone believed to be bluffing. ***double bluff***: see DOUBLE *adjective & adverb*.

bluff /blʌf/ *adjective*. E17.
[ORIGIN Orig. nautical, perh. of Low Dutch origin.]
1 Presenting a broad, flattened front; (of a ship's bows) broad and with little or no rake. E17.
2 *fig.* **a** Rough or surly in manner; abrupt, curt. E18. ▸**b** Good-naturedly blunt; frank, hearty. E19.
a SWIFT I maul'd you when you look'd so bluff. LYTTON Finally wound up with a bluff 'Go, or let alone'. B. PLAIN You're so blunt and bluff lately, so outspoken! **b** R. L. STEVENSON He had a bluff, rough-and-ready face. W. FAULKNER He would correct them . . with a bluff, hearty amiability, making a joke of it.
■ **bluffly** *adverb* L18. **bluffness** *noun* M19.

bluff /blʌf/ *verb*. L17.
[ORIGIN Dutch *bluffen* brag, boast, or *bluf* bragging, boasting.]
1 *verb trans.* Blindfold, hoodwink. Now *obsolete* or *dial.* L17.
2 *verb trans. & intrans.* (Attempt to) deceive or intimidate by a pretence of strength (orig. in the game of poker). Orig. *US*. M19.
CONAN DOYLE I bluffed him by giving him the impression that I was absolutely certain. J. F. KENNEDY There was considerable feeling . . that Hitler and Mussolini were just bluffing. Show strength and they will back down.
bluff it out seek to avoid trouble by bluffing. **bluff off** frighten off by bluffing.
■ **bluffer** *noun* L19.

bluggy /ˈblʌgi/ *adjective*. L19.
[ORIGIN Repr. a supposed infantile pronunc. of BLOODY *adjective*.]
Bloody; *spec.* bloodthirsty, blood-and-thunder.

bluing *verb & noun* see BLUE *verb*¹, *verb*².

bluish /ˈbluːɪʃ/ *adjective*. Also **blueish**, †**blewish**. LME.
[ORIGIN from BLUE *adjective* + -ISH¹.]
Somewhat blue; with a blue tinge.
■ **bluishness** *noun* E17.

bluism *noun* var. of BLUEISM.

blunder /ˈblʌndə/ *noun*. LME.
[ORIGIN App. from the verb.]
†**1** Confusion; clamour. LME–L18.
2 A stupid or careless mistake. E18.

blunder /ˈblʌndə/ *verb*. ME.
[ORIGIN Prob. of Scandinavian origin: cf. Middle Swedish *blundra*, Norwegian *blundre* shut the eyes, frequentative of Old Norse, Swedish *blunda*, Old Danish *blunde*, rel. to BLIND *adjective*.]
1 *verb intrans.* Move blindly; flounder, stumble. ME.
J. B. PRIESTLEY He felt as if he had blundered into a party given by a complete stranger. B. BAINBRIDGE Someone behind him, blundering through the undergrowth.
blunder upon find through a stupid or careless mistake.
2 *verb trans.* Orig., treat clumsily, damage. Later, mingle; make turbid; mix up (*lit.* & *fig.*). *arch.* & *dial.* ME.
3 *verb trans.* Utter thoughtlessly; blurt *out*. L15.
4 *verb intrans.* Make a stupid or careless mistake. E18.
TENNYSON The soldier knew Someone had blunder'd.
5 *verb trans.* Mismanage, make a blunder in. E19.
SIR W. SCOTT The banker's clerk, who was directed to sum my cash-account, blundered it three times.
blunder away waste or lose by mismanagement.
■ **blunderer** *noun* LME. **blunderingly** *adverb* in a blundering manner E19.

blunderbuss /ˈblʌndəbʌs/ *noun*. M17.
[ORIGIN Alt. (by assoc. with *blunder*) of Dutch *donderbus*, from *donder* thunder + *bus* gun (orig. box, tube; cf. German *Büchse*).]
1 *hist.* A short gun with a large bore, firing many balls or slugs at once. M17.
2 A talkative or blundering person. L17.

blunderhead /ˈblʌndəhɛd/ *noun*. L17.
[ORIGIN Prob. alt. of DUNDERHEAD.]
A blundering dunderheaded person.
■ **blunderheaded** *adjective* M18.

blunge /blʌn(d)ʒ/ *verb trans.* E19.
[ORIGIN Combining *plunge* with words in *bl-* as *blend*.]
POTTERY. Mix (clay, bone, flint powder, etc.) with water in a revolving apparatus.
■ **blunger** *noun* an apparatus for blunging E19.

†**blunket** *adjective & noun*. LME–L18.
[ORIGIN Unknown: unlikely to be rel. to BLANKET *noun & adjective*.]
(Fabric of) greyish blue.

blunt /blʌnt/ *adjective & noun*. ME.
[ORIGIN Perh. from Scandinavian neut. formation (cf. *scant*, *thwart*) on base of Old Norse *blundr* dozing, sleep, *blunda* shut the eyes (Norwegian *blunde* doze): cf. BLUNDER *verb*.]
▸**A** *adjective*. **1** Of sight, the perceptions generally, the intellect: dull, insensitive. ME.
2 Without a sharp edge or point; (of an angle, point, etc.) not sharp, obtuse. LME.
AV *Eccles.* 10:10 If the yron be blunt, and he doe not whet the edge, then must he put to more strength. G. GREENE The man's moving fingers . . were short, blunt and thick.
blunt instrument *fig.* a crude means to an end.
3 Rude, unpolished, without refinement. Now *rare* or *obsolete*. LME.
POPE Tho' not in phrase refin'd; Tho' blunt my tale.
†**4** Barren, bare. M–L16.
5 Abrupt in speech or manner; unceremonious; outspoken; uncompromising. L16.
A. RADCLIFFE Be pretty blunt with them if they want to come in here. W. S. CHURCHILL In his blunt way he declared . . that the militia was useless. K. CROSSLEY-HOLLAND Good, blunt words with Anglo-Saxon roots.
▸**B** *noun*. †**1** A blunt sword for fencing. E17–E19.
2 Ready money. *arch. slang*. E19.
3 A type of needle used for heavy stitching work. M19.
4 [from *(Phillies) Blunt*, proprietary name for a brand of cigar.] A cigar whose wrapper has been emptied of tobacco and stuffed with marijuana. L20.
■ **bluntish** *adjective* M16. **bluntly** *adverb* LME. **bluntness** *noun* LME.

blunt /blʌnt/ *verb*. LME.
[ORIGIN from the adjective.]
▸**I** *verb trans.* **1** Dull or make less sharp (an edge, point, etc.). LME.
C. MCCULLOUGH Eucalyptus wood blunted the sharpest axe in no time at all. *fig.*: H. ARENDT It blunts the impact of one of the basic totalitarian tenets.
2 Make dull (the feelings or faculties). L16.
I. MURDOCH My appetite for Hugo's conversation was not blunted. J. HELLER Twenty-nine months in the service had not blunted his genius for ineptitude.
3 Weaken the sharpness of (anything acid etc.); neutralize partly; dilute. M18.
▸**II** *verb intrans.* **4** Become dull or less sharp. L17.
M. MITCHELL Her weapons of scorn, coldness and abuse blunted in her hands.

blur /bləː/ *noun*. M16.
[ORIGIN Perh. rel. to BLEAR.]
1 A smear which partially obscures; *fig.* a moral stain or blemish. M16.
F. QUARLES He that clenses a blot with blotted fingers makes a greater blurre. MILTON These blurs are too apparent in his life.
2 An indistinct, unfocused, or dim image, sound, or apprehension; confused dimness. M19.
S. GIBBONS A confused blur of voices and boots in the yard outside. I. MURDOCH The farther roses merged into a multi-coloured blur.
■ **blurriness** *noun* blurry condition M20. **blurry** *adjective* full of blurs, indistinct L19.

blur /bləː/ *verb*. Infl. **-rr-**. M16.
[ORIGIN formed as BLUR *noun*.]
▸**I** *verb trans.* **1** Smear (clear writing etc.) with ink etc. M16.
2 *fig.* Sully, disfigure, defile. L16.
SHAKES. *Haml.* Such an act That blurs the grace and blush of modesty.
3 Make indistinct. E17.
TENNYSON One low light . . Blurr'd by the creeping mist. N. GORDIMER Reception was blurred by static interference. R. HAYMAN A narrative style which helps to blur distinctions between mental events and external reality.
4 Dim or make undiscriminating (the senses, judgement, etc.). E17.
H. WOUK The alcohol hadn't blurred his brain.
▸**II** *verb intrans.* **5** Become smeared or indistinct. E17.
6 Make blurs in writing. E17.
– WITH ADVERBS IN SPECIALIZED SENSES: **blur out** efface, blot out. **blur over** obscure by a blur, make indistinct.

Blu-ray /ˈbluːreɪ/ *noun*. E21.
[ORIGIN from *blu* (respelling of BLUE *adjective*) + RAY *noun*¹.]
A format of DVD designed for the storage of high-definition video and data.

blurb /bləːb/ *noun*. *slang* (orig. *US*). E20.
[ORIGIN Fanciful form by US humorist Gelett Burgess.]
A publisher's brief, usu. eulogistic, description of a book, printed on its jacket or in advertisements; descriptive or commendatory matter.

blurt /bləːt/ *verb & noun*. L16.
[ORIGIN Prob. imit.: cf. BLIRT.]
▸**A** *verb*. **1** *verb trans.* Utter abruptly or injudiciously; burst *out* with. L16.
Q. BELL She told secrets, not realising they would be blurted out in company. W. STYRON 'I'm going to miss you, Sophie,' I blurted.
†**2** *verb intrans.* Make a contemptuous puffing gesture with the lips. L16–M17.
▸**B** *noun*. †**1** An (esp. contemptuous) eruptive emission of breath. L16–E17.
2 An abrupt or injudicious utterance. *rare*. M19.

blush /blʌʃ/ *noun & adjective*. LME.
[ORIGIN from the verb.]
▸**A** *noun*. **1** A gleam; a blink; a glance, glimpse. *obsolete* exc. as below. LME.
at first blush, **at the first blush**, **on first blush**, **on the first blush** on the first glance or impression.
2 A reddening, redness, of the face caused by embarrassment, shame, modesty, etc. L16.
WORDSWORTH Her blushes are joy-flushes. W. BOYD The hot blush had left his face but he felt his ears were still glowing.
put to the blush put to shame. **spare a person's blushes** not embarrass a person by praise.
3 A flush of light or colour; *spec.* a rosy colour or glow as of dawn. L16.
4 A blush wine. L20.
▸**B** *adjective*. Delicate pink; of the colour of a blush. L16.
blush wine a wine with a slight pink tint, made in the manner of a white wine but with a red grape variety.

B

■ **blushful** *adjective* given to blushing; rosy, ruddy: **E17**. **blushless** *adjective* **M16**. **blushy** *adjective* **E17**.

blush /blʌʃ/ *verb*. Pa. t. & pple **-ed**, (*arch.*) **-t**.
[**ORIGIN** Old English *blyscan* corresp. to Middle Low German *bloschen*, Low German *blüsken*; rel. to Middle Dutch *blözen*, *blözen* (Dutch *blozen*) blush. Cf. Old English *āblysian* blush, etc.]
1 *verb intrans.* Glow red; be or become roseate. **OE**.

SHAKES. *Rich. II* The blushing discontented sun.

†**2** *verb intrans.* Shine forth; glance. Only in **LME**.
3 *verb intrans.* Become red in the face because of embarrassment, shame, modesty, etc. **LME**.

J. BRAINE She blushed and turned away. D. M. THOMAS She blushed scarlet and was full of apologies.

4 *verb intrans.* Be ashamed *at*, *for*, *to do*. **M16**.
5 *verb trans.* Make red or roseate. **L16**.

SHAKES. *2 Hen. VI* To blush and beautify the cheek.

■ **blushingly** *adverb* with blushing, as if ashamed **L16**.

blusher /ˈblʌʃə/ *noun*. **M17**.
[**ORIGIN** from **BLUSH** *verb* + **-ER**[1].]
1 Something red or roseate. *rare*. **M17**.
2 A person who blushes with embarrassment etc. **L19**.
3 The edible mushroom *Amanita rubescens*, the flesh of which reddens when bruised. **L19**.
4 A cosmetic used to give colour to the face. **M20**.

blusht *verb* see **BLUSH** *verb*.

bluster /ˈblʌstə/ *noun*. **L16**.
[**ORIGIN** from the verb.]
1 Boisterous blowing; a rough and stormy blast; *fig.* the storm or tempest of the passions; a noisy commotion. **L16**.
2 (A sound like) the blast of a wind instrument. *rare*. **E18**.
3 Noisy, inflated talk; violent but empty self-assertion, menace, etc. **E18**.
■ **blusterous** *adjective* rough, stormy; truculent, given to blustering: **M16**. **blusterously** *adverb* **M16**. **blustery** *adjective* stormy, windy; noisily self-assertive: **M18**.

bluster /ˈblʌstə/ *verb*. **LME**.
[**ORIGIN** Ult. imit.: cf. Low German *blustern*, *blistern* flutter. Sense 1 may be another word.]
†**1** *verb intrans.* Wander or stray blindly. Only in **LME**.
2 *verb intrans.* Of the wind, waves, or other elements: blow or beat violently. **LME**.

J. K. BAXTER Waves bluster up the bay. J. T. STORY The rain . . was blustering against the window.

3 *verb intrans.* Of a person: storm or rage boisterously; talk with exaggerated violence; utter loud empty menaces, protests, etc. **LME**.

A. WILSON Ron began to bluster and expostulate.

4 *verb trans.* Utter with stormy violence. Usu. foll. by *out*. **LME**.
5 *verb trans.* Force *into* (an action) by violent or hectoring talk. **M17**.
■ **blusterer** *noun* **L16**. **blustering** *ppl adjective* stormy, tempestuous; noisily self-assertive: **E16**. **blusteringly** *adverb* **M16**.

Blu-tack /ˈbluːtak/ *noun & verb*. **L20**.
[**ORIGIN** from *Blu-* (alt. of **BLUE** *adjective*) + **TACK** *noun*[1].]
▸ **A** *noun*. (Proprietary name for) a blue sticky material used to attach paper to walls.
▸ **B** *verb trans.* Attach using Blu-tack.

blutwurst /ˈbluːtwəːst/ *noun*. **M19**.
[**ORIGIN** German, from *Blut* blood + *Wurst* sausage.]
(A) black pudding.

BM *abbreviation*.
1 Bachelor of Medicine.
2 British Museum.

BMA *abbreviation*.
British Medical Association.

BMI *abbreviation*.
MEDICINE. Body mass index.

B mi *noun* var. of **BEMI** *noun*.

BMR *abbreviation*.
BIOLOGY. Basal metabolic rate.

B.Mus. *abbreviation*.
Bachelor of Music.

BMX *abbreviation*.
Bicycle motocross.

Bn *abbreviation*[1].
Battalion.

bn *abbreviation*[2].
Billion.

BNF *abbreviation*.
COMPUTING. Backus–Naur form (see **BACKUS**).

BNP *abbreviation*.
British National Party.

BO *abbreviation*. *colloq.*
Body odour.

bo /bəʊ/ *noun*[1]. *slang* (chiefly *US*). **E19**.
[**ORIGIN** Perh. a shortening of *boy*.]
(As a form of address) mate, old chap.

bo /bəʊ/ *interjection & noun*[2]. Now *rare* or *obsolete*. Also **boh**. **LME**.
[**ORIGIN** Imit.: cf. **BOO** *noun*[1] *& interjection*.]
An exclamation intended to startle.

boa /ˈbəʊə/ *noun*. **LME**.
[**ORIGIN** Latin (Pliny), of unknown origin.]
1 Any of numerous constricting snakes of the family Boidae, *esp.* any of the larger New World examples; *loosely* any constricting snake, a python. **LME**.
rainbow boa, *sand boa*, *tree boa*, *yellow boa*, etc.
2 A long coil of fur or feathers worn around a woman's neck. **M19**.
– **COMB.**: **boa constrictor** a very large boa, *Constrictor constrictor*, of South and Central America; *loosely* = sense 1 above.

BOAC *abbreviation*.
hist. British Overseas Airways Corporation.

Boal *noun* var. of **BUAL**.

Boanerges /bəʊəˈnəːdʒiːz/ *noun pl.* (also used as *sing.*). **E17**.
[**ORIGIN** Greek, prob. ult. from Aramaic (= sons of thunder), repr. the name given by Jesus to the two sons of Zebedee (*Mark* 3:17).]
Loud vociferous speakers or preachers; (as *sing.*) one such person.

boar /bɔː/ *noun*.
[**ORIGIN** Old English *bār* = Old Saxon *bēr-swin*, Middle Dutch & mod. Dutch *beer*, Old High German *bēr* (arch. German *Bär* boar), from West Germanic.]
1 An uncastrated male pig. Also, the (full-grown) male of certain other animals, esp. the badger, guinea pig, and hedgehog. **OE**. ▸**b** *wild boar*, the wild pig, *Sus scrofa*, of Europe, Asia, and Africa. **ME**.
2 The flesh of the animal. **ME**.
– **COMB.**: **boarfish** a marine fish, *Capros aper*, related to the dory.
■ **boarish** *adjective* pertaining to or resembling a boar; sensual, cruel; (cf. **BOORISH**): **M16**.

board /bɔːd/ *noun*. See also **BORD**.
[**ORIGIN** Old English *bord*, combining two Germanic words with meanings 'board, plank' and 'border, ship's side': reinforced in Middle English by cognate Old French *bort*, French *bord*, edge, rim, ship's side, and Old Norse *borð* board, table.]
▸ **I** A piece of wood etc.
1 A long thin usu. narrow piece of sawn timber, a thin plank, often *spec.* as used for floors or other purposes in building; such timber collectively. **OE**.

SOUTHEY They carried her upon a board In the clothes in which she died. TENNYSON Pattering over the boards, she comes and goes at her will. J. STEINBECK Grass grew up through the porch boards. W. VAN T. CLARK The buildings were log or unpainted board.

floorboard, *skirting board*, *tread board*, etc.
2 A thin rigid usu. rectangular piece of any substance, used esp. for display or support; *spec.* a blackboard; a noticeboard; a scoreboard. Also, a surface or structure likened to this. **ME**. ▸**b** *spec.* The surface or frame on which some games are played, as chess, backgammon, Monopoly, etc. Also, the target in darts. **LME**. ▸**c** A surfboard. **L18**.

Times They had 84 on the board for eight wickets. A. BRINK When I come into my classroom, I find insults scrawled all over the board. **b** C. S. LEWIS All over the board my pieces were in the most disadvantageous positions.

billboard, *blackboard*, *circuit board*, *headboard*, *ironing board*, *mortarboard*, *noticeboard*, *pegboard*, *sandwich board*, *scoreboard*, *skateboard*, *surfboard*, *switchboard*, *weatherboard*, etc. **b** *chessboard*, *dartboard*, *draughtboard*, *shovelboard*, etc.
3 In *pl.* Rectangular pieces of strong card etc. used for the cover of a hardback book. **L15**.
4 Material of various kinds, esp. compressed wood fibres, made into stiff sheets. **M17**.
cardboard, *chipboard*, *hardboard*, *pasteboard*, *strawboard*, etc.
▸ **II** A table.
5 *gen.* A table. *obsolete* exc. as below. **OE**. ▸**b** A piece of furniture like a table. Now chiefly in *sideboard*. **LME**.
stall-board. **ABOVE-BOARD**.
6 A table used for meals or spread for a meal. **ME**. ▸**b** Food served at a table; the provision of daily meals (and often also lodging), esp. at an agreed price or in return for services. **ME**. ▸**c** The condition of boarding at a house etc. **LME**.

G. M. TREVELYAN The labourer . . ate at the board of the farmer. **b** J. HEATH-STUBBS He'd be glad of a share of your board, Or a place by the fire. J. C. OATES To work at the castle for no salary, only for room and board? **c** J. CLEVELAND An expensive Lord, That . . lives at board.

7 A table at which meetings are held; the meeting of a council etc. round a table; a committee, a body of examiners, interviewers, etc.; *spec.* the body of directors of a company. **M16**.

LD MACAULAY How little he was pleased with what had passed at the board. A. J. P. TAYLOR The poor law was administered by local boards of guardians. H. FAST The second vice president of the Seldon Bank . . delivered the formal sentiments of the board.

Board of Customs and Excise, *Board of Inland Revenue*, *Federal Reserve Board*, *medical board*, etc.
▸ †**III 8** A shield. **OE–M16**.
▸ **IV** A side, an edge.
9 A border, an edge; a coast. Long *obsolete* exc. in **SEABOARD**. **OE**.
10 The side of a ship. Now only in distinct phrases and combs. (often used in non-nautical contexts). **OE**.
larboard, *overboard*, *starboard*, etc.
11 NAUTICAL. A distance covered in one tack. **M16**.

CAPT. COOK We passed the night in making short boards.

12 MINING. = **BORD**. **E18**.
– **PHRASES**: **across the board** all-embracing(ly), general(ly). *bed and board*: see **BED** *noun*. **board and board** (**a**) (of ships) close alongside, side by side; (**b**) (sailing) by a succession of short tacks. **board and lodging** provision of accommodation and meals. **board of control** a supervisory body; *spec.* (*hist.*) a board of six members established by Pitt in 1784 to govern British India. **board of trade** (**a**) *US* a Chamber of Commerce; (**b**) (*Board of Trade*) a (now nominal) British government department concerned with commerce and industry (*Board of Trade Unit* (*hist.*), a kilowatt-hour). *full board*: see **FULL** *adjective*. **go by the board** (of a mast etc.) fall overboard; *fig.* be entirely neglected, go for good and all. *half board*: see **HALF-**. **on board** = **ABOARD** *adverb & preposition*. *red board*: see **RED** *adjective*. *sweep the board*: see **SWEEP** *verb*. **take on board** *fig.* (**a**) drink, consume, swallow; (**b**) accept (an idea etc.), come to terms with. **the board** *Austral. & NZ* the part of the floor of a shearing shed where the shearers work, the shearers working there. **the boards** *spec.* those forming the stage of a theatre or music hall; *fig.* the actor's profession. *tread the boards*: see **TREAD** *verb*. **within board**, **without board** NAUTICAL within, outside of, the ship.
– **COMB.**: **board foot** a unit of volume (for timber) equal to 144 cu. in.; **board game** a game played on a special board; **boardroom** (the meeting place of) the directors of a company; **boardsailing** windsurfing; **board school** *hist.* an elementary school under the management of a School Board, established in Britain by the Education Act of 1870; **board shorts** long shorts of a kind originally worn by surfers; **board-wages** *arch.* wages allowed to servants for food; **boardwalk** (chiefly *N. Amer.*) a footway (of a type originally) made of boards; **board-work** wig-making.

board /bɔːd/ *verb*. **LME**.
[**ORIGIN** from the noun: cf. **ABORD** *verb*, French *border*.]
▸ **I** Rel. to *board* = side.
1 *verb trans. & intrans.* Orig., come close up to or alongside (a ship), usu. for the purpose of attacking (†*verb intrans.* foll. by *with* the ship). Now, force one's way on board (a ship). **LME**.

M. ARNOLD To decide the battle by boarding.

2 *verb trans. fig.* Approach, assail; make advances to. *arch.* **M16**.

J. VANBRUGH What . . do you expect from boarding a woman . . engag'd to another?

3 *verb trans. & intrans.* Go on board of, embark on (a ship), esp. in a hostile manner. **L16**. ▸**b** Enter (a train, vehicle, aircraft, etc.); *be boarding*, (of an aircraft) be ready for passengers to get on. **M19**.

b I. WELSH We boarded the train at Edinburgh.

†**4** *verb trans. & intrans.* Border (*on*); approach; lie close *by*. **L16–M17**.
5 *verb intrans. & trans.* (with *it*). Of a ship: tack. **E17**.
▸ **II** Rel. to *board* = thin plank, table.
6 *verb trans.* Cover or provide with boards; close *up* with boards. **LME**.

W. D. HOWELLS The floors were roughly boarded over.
W. HAVIGHURST Many people boarded their houses tight.
L. HELLMAN I went down to the corner store. It was boarded up and nobody answered the bell.

7 *verb trans.* Provide with daily meals and usu. also lodging, esp. at a fixed rate. **M16**. ▸**b** Put up and feed (an animal). **L19**.

SHAKES. *Hen. V* We cannot lodge and board a dozen or fourteen gentlewomen.

8 *verb intrans.* Receive daily meals and usu. also lodging; live *with* for an agreed price. **M16**.

W. IRVING He had engaged to board with the family.
C. MCCULLOUGH They were sent to the convent . . to board, for there was no school closer.

9 *verb trans.* Place in lodgings etc. Freq. foll. by *out*. **M17**.

E. FIGES My brother . . had been boarded out with the family of a schoolfriend.

10 *verb trans.* Bring (a candidate) before a board of interviewers. **E20**.

New Society Of the 715 candidates boarded, 104 were selected.

■ **boarder** *noun* (**a**) a person who boards at a house etc.; *spec.* a pupil who boards at a school; (**b**) a sailor who boards an enemy ship: **M16**. **boarding** *noun* (**a**) the action of the verb; an instance of this; *boarding house* a house offering board and lodging for paying guests; *boarding school* a school at which most or all pupils board; (**b**) material for boards, boards collectively: **L15**.

boardly *adjective* var. of **BUIRDLY**.

boart *noun* var. of BORT.

boast /bəʊst/ *noun*[1]. ME.
[ORIGIN Unknown: cf. BOAST *verb*[1].]
1 Loud speech, outcry, clamour; menacing speech, threats. Long *obsolete* exc. *dial.* ME.
2 Proud or vainglorious speech, bragging; an excessively proud statement. ME.

SHAKES. *Cymb.* The swell'd boast Of him that best could speak. E. A. FREEMAN They soon found such a boast was vain indeed.

3 An occasion or cause of pride. L16.

T. E. LAWRENCE Some make a boast of vice, to cover innocence. M. SPARK One of Joyce Emily's boasts was that her brother . . had gone to fight in the Spanish Civil War.

■ **boastful** *adjective* full of or given to boasting ME. **boastfully** *adverb* LME. **boastfulness** *noun* E19.

boast /bəʊst/ *noun*[2]. L19.
[ORIGIN Perh. from French *bosse* a projection of the wall in a French tennis court.]
REAL TENNIS & RACKETS. A stroke which causes the ball to strike either of the side walls before hitting the end wall.

boast /bəʊst/ *verb*[1]. LME.
[ORIGIN Unknown: cf. BOAST *noun*[1].]
1 *verb trans. & intrans.* Threaten, speak menacingly (to). Long *obsolete* exc. *dial.* LME.
2 *verb intrans.* & †*refl.* Praise oneself, make boasts; brag *of*, *about*. LME.
3 *verb trans.* Speak of with (excessive) pride, claim proudly (*that*). Chiefly with obj. clause. LME. ▸**b** Display ostentatiously, show off. *arch.* L16.

T. E. LAWRENCE She boasted that she had spent one night clasped in Zeus' own encircling arms.

4 *verb trans.* Possess as a source of pride, have to show. L17.

Ships Monthly The workers . . boast 112 years of flag-making experience between them.

■ **boaster** *noun*[1] a person who boasts ME. **boastingly** *adverb* in a boasting manner LME.

boast /bəʊst/ *verb*[2] *trans.* E19.
[ORIGIN Unknown.]
Shape or model (stone, wood, etc., or a design in these) roughly with a chisel.
■ **boaster** *noun*[2] a heavy chisel used on masonry etc. (cf. BOLSTER *noun*[2]) L19.

boast /bəʊst/ *verb*[3] *trans. & intrans.* L19.
[ORIGIN Cf. BOAST *noun*[2].]
REAL TENNIS & RACKETS. Play a boast; make (a stroke) into a boast.

boat /bəʊt/ *noun.*
[ORIGIN Old English *bāt* rel. to Old Norse *beit*, from Germanic: Dutch *boot*, German *Boot*, French *bateau*, have come from English or Scandinavian.]
1 A small open vessel propelled by oars, engine, or sail. Also (*colloq.*, esp. among submariners) a submarine. OE. ▸**b** Any small or distinctive kind of vessel, *esp.* a fishing vessel, mail packet, ferry, or small steamer. Also (chiefly *US*) a large seagoing vessel. L16.
cockboat, ***ferryboat***, ***gunboat***, ***houseboat***, ***lifeboat***, ***longboat***, ***motor boat***, ***narrowboat***, ***rowing boat***, ***showboat***, ***speedboat***, ***stake boat***, ***steamboat***, ***tugboat***, ***U-boat***, ***whaleboat***, etc. ***bridge of boats***: see BRIDGE *noun*[1] 1. ***burn one's boats***: see BURN *verb* 8. ***dreamboat***: see DREAM *noun*[2]. **in the same boat** *fig.* in the same predicament, facing like risks etc. ***miss the boat***: see MISS *verb*[1]. **push the boat out** *colloq.* celebrate. ***rock the boat***: see ROCK *verb*[1]. **ship's boat** a small boat carried on board a ship. ***swingboat***: see SWING *verb*. **take boat** embark in a boat. **take to the boats** escape from a sinking ship using the ship's boats; *fig.* abandon an undertaking precipitously. ***the man in the boat***: see MAN *noun*.
2 A boat-shaped utensil for holding gravy, sauce, incense, etc. L17.
gravy boat, ***sauce boat***, etc.
– COMB.: **boat-axe** ARCHAEOLOGY. [Swedish *båtyx*] a boat-shaped battle-axe of the Neolithic period in northern Europe; **boatbill** a neotropical heron, *Cochlearius cochlearius*, with a broad, flat bill; **boat-cloak**: orig. for use by officers on duty at sea, now worn mainly on social occasions; **boat deck** the deck from which a ship's boats are launched; **boat-drill** exercise in the launching and manning of a ship's boats; **boat-fly** a water boatman; **boat hook** a long pole bearing a hook and spike, for fending off or pulling a boat; **boat-house** a shed at the water's edge for keeping a boat or boats; **boatlift** [after ***airlift*** s.v. AIR *noun*[1]] the transportation of people by boat; **boatload** as many or as much as a boat will hold; **boatman** (*a*) a man who hires out a boat or boats, or who provides transport by boat; (*b*) (in full ***water boatman***) an aquatic bug of the family Notonectidae, which swims on its back; **boatmanship** (skill in) managing a boat; **boat neck**, **boat neckline** a wide neckline passing below the collarbone; **boat people** (*a*) people who live on boats; (*b*) refugees fleeing a country by boat; **boat race** (*a*) a race between rowing crews; *spec.* that between Oxford and Cambridge Universities, held annually on the River Thames from Putney to Mortlake; (*b*) *rhyming slang* the face; **boat-shaped** *adjective* resembling a boat in shape; *spec.* shaped like the outline of the hull of a boat; **boat-tail** a N. American grackle, *Quiscalus major*, with a boat-shaped tail; **boat train** a train scheduled to connect with the arrival or departure of a boat; **boatwoman** a woman who rows or manages a boat; **boatyard**: in which boats are built and stored.
■ **boatful** *noun*, pl. **boatfuls**, †**boatsful**, as much or as many as a boat will hold LME. **boatie** *noun* (*colloq.*, chiefly *Austral. & NZ*) a boating enthusiast L20.

boat /bəʊt/ *verb.* E16.
[ORIGIN from the noun.]
1 *verb trans.* Place or carry in a boat. E16.
boat the oars lift the oars out of the rowlocks and lay them inside the boat.
2 *verb intrans.* Take boat, embark. *Scot.* M16.
3 *verb intrans. & trans.* (with *it*). Go in a boat; row, sail, esp. for pleasure. Chiefly as ***boating*** *verbal noun.* L17.
4 *verb trans.* Go in boats upon or across, navigate. L17.
■ **boatable** *adjective* navigable by boat L17. **boatage** *noun* (a charge paid for) carriage by boat E17.

boatel *noun* var. of BOTEL.

boater /ˈbəʊtə/ *noun.* ME.
[ORIGIN from BOAT *noun* or *verb* + -ER[1].]
1 A person who rows or manages a boat; a person who goes boating. *rare.* ME.
2 A hard flat straw hat (orig. assoc. with boating). L19.

boatswain /ˈbəʊs(ə)n/ *noun.* Also BOSUN.
[ORIGIN Late Old English *bātswegen*, formed as BOAT *noun* + SWAIN.]
1 A ship's petty officer or warrant officer who has charge of sails, rigging, etc., and is responsible for summoning men to duty. LOE.
2 The Arctic skua, *Stercorarius parasiticus*. L18.
– COMB.: **boatswain bird** a tropicbird; **boatswain's chair** a wooden seat suspended from ropes for work on the side of a ship or building; **boatswain's mate** a boatswain's deputy or assistant.

bob /bɒb/ *noun*[1]. LME.
[ORIGIN Unknown: cf. BOB *verb*[4].]
▸ **I 1** A bunch, a cluster. *Scot. & N. English.* LME.
†**2** The grub of a beetle used as a bait for fish. Also, a beetle (usu. in *comb.*). L16–L18.
3 A rounded mass at the end of a rod etc.; a knob. L16. ▸**b** *spec.* The weight on a pendulum, a plumb line, etc. L17.
4 An ornamental pendant; a pendent earring. M17.
5 A bunch of lobworms threaded together as bait for eels. M17.
6 A knot or bunch of hair; a short bunch, a curl resembling a tassel. L17. ▸**b** In full ***bob-periwig***, ***bob-peruke***, ***bob-wig***. A wig having the bottom locks turned up into bobs or short curls. L17.
7 A horse's tail docked short; a short knoblike tail. E18. ▸**b** A style of cutting the hair short and even all round; hair cut in this way. E20.
8 A knob, knot, or bunch of coloured ribbons; a weight on the tail of a kite. M18.
9 A short sleigh runner. *N. Amer.* M19. ▸**b** In full ***bobsled***, ***bobsleigh***. Either of two types of sledge, (*a*) *US* (either of) two short sledges coupled and used for tobogganing and drawing logs; (*b*) a mechanically braked and steered sledge used in Alpine sport. M19.
▸ **II 10** The refrain or burden of a song. *arch.* E17. ▸**b** The short line at the end of the stanza in some old forms of versification. Cf. WHEEL *noun.* M19.
– PHRASES: **bear a bob** *arch.* join in a chorus. ***bits and bobs***: see BIT *noun*[2]. ***odds and bobs***: see ODDS *noun pl.*
– COMB.: **bobcat** a short-tailed N. American lynx, *Felis rufus*; ***bob-periwig***, ***bob-peruke***: see sense 6b above; **bobskate** *Canad.* an adjustable skate for a child's foot, consisting of two sections of double runners; ***bobsled***: see sense 9b above; **bobsledding** riding in a bobsled, esp. as a sport; ***bobsleigh***: see sense 9b above; **bobsleighing** = ***bobsledding*** above; ***bob-wig***: see sense 6b above.
■ **boblet** *noun* a bobsled for two people E20.

bob /bɒb/ *noun*[2]. M16.
[ORIGIN from BOB *verb*[3].]
1 An act of bobbing or suddenly jerking up and down; *Scot.* any of various dances. M16.
2 A curtsy. E19.

bob /bɒb/ *noun*[3]. *obsolete* exc. *dial.* L16.
[ORIGIN from BOB *verb*[2].]
1 A blow with the fist. L16.
2 A sharp rebuke; a taunt, a bitter jibe. L16.

bob /bɒb/ *noun*[4]. L17.
[ORIGIN Perh. connected with BOB *noun*[3].]
BELL-RINGING. One of several kinds of change in long peals.
plain bob: see PLAIN *adjective*[1] & *adverb*.

bob /bɒb/ *noun*[5]. E18.
[ORIGIN Pet form of male forename *Robert*.]
1 With certain specifying adjectives (see below): a man, a boy. E18.
2 = BOBWHITE. L19.
– COMB. & PHRASES: ***Bob's-a-dying***: see BOBSY-DIE. **Bob's your uncle**, **bob's your uncle** *slang* everything is all right, the thing needed is done. **dry-bob**, **wet-bob** (at Eton College) a boy who is involved in land or water sports respectively, esp. in the summer term. **light-bob** a soldier of the light infantry.

bob /bɒb/ *noun*[6]. *slang.* Pl. same. L18.
[ORIGIN Unknown.]
A shilling (now *hist.*); five decimal pence, a five pence piece.
bob a job: the former slogan of the Scout Association's annual fund-raising effort during which odd jobs are done for a nominal charge (orig. a shilling). **bob a nob** a payment of a shilling a head.

bob /bɒb/ *adjective.* M17.
[ORIGIN Sense 1 *bob* in BOBTAIL used as a separate word; sense 2 perh. from BOB *verb*[3].]
1 Cut short (as a horse's tail). M17.
2 Lively; agreeable. *arch. slang.* E18.

bob /bɒb/ *verb*[1] *trans. obsolete* exc. *dial.* Infl. **-bb-**. ME.
[ORIGIN Old French *bober* befool (cf. *bobu* stupid, and Spanish *bobo* fool): see BOOBY *noun*[1].]
1 Make a fool of; deceive; cheat. ME.
bob of, **bob out of** cheat out of.
†**2** Take by deception; filch. *rare* (Shakes.). Only in E17.

bob /bɒb/ *verb*[2] *trans.* Infl. **-bb-**. ME.
[ORIGIN Prob. imit.]
†**1** Strike with the fist; buffet. ME–E17.
2 Cause to rap or bounce *against*, *at*, etc. (Merging into BOB *verb*[3] 2.) E17.
3 Rap, tap. M18.

bob /bɒb/ *verb*[3]. Infl. **-bb-**. LME.
[ORIGIN Prob. same word as BOB *verb*[2].]
1 *verb intrans.* Make a quick short movement up and down; rebound; dance; curtsy; come or go *in*, *into*, *up*, etc., quickly or briefly. LME.
bob and weave make quick bodily movements up and down and from side to side (as a boxer evading punches, etc.). **bob for** try to catch (floating or hanging fruit) with the mouth, as a game.
2 *verb trans.* Move (a thing) up and down with a slight jerk. (Merging into BOB *verb*[2] 2.) L17.
3 *verb trans.* Move up and down quickly or briefly in (a curtsy). L19.
– COMB.: **bob-apple**, **bob-cherry** a game in which the players bob for apples or cherries respectively; **bob-fly** ANGLING a dry fly that bobs on the water, to indicate the position of the tail fly.

bob /bɒb/ *verb*[4]. Infl. **-bb-**. E17.
[ORIGIN Unknown: cf. BOB *noun*[1]. Prob. earlier in BOBTAIL.]
1 *verb intrans.* Fish with a bob (*for* eels). E17.
2 *verb trans.* Provide with a bob; *esp.* dock, cut short, (a horse's tail etc.). M17. ▸**b** Cut (a person's hair) short and even all round. E20.
3 *verb intrans.* Ride on a bobsleigh. Chiefly as ***bobbing*** *verbal noun.* L19.

bobac /ˈbəʊbak/ *noun.* Also **-ak**. L17.
[ORIGIN Polish *bobak*.]
A marmot, *Marmota bobak*, of the east European and Asian steppes.

bobachee /ˈbɒbətʃiː/ *noun. arch.* Also **-archee**; **-jee** /-dʒiː/. E19.
[ORIGIN Urdu *bābarchī* from Persian *bāwarch*.]
In the Indian subcontinent: a male cook.

Bobadil /ˈbɒbədɪl/ *noun.* L18.
[ORIGIN A character in Jonson's *Every Man in His Humour*.]
A braggart who pretends to prowess.

bobajee *noun* var. of BOBACHEE.

bobak *noun* var. of BOBAC.

bobance /ˈbɒb(ə)ns/ *noun.* Long *arch.* or *hist.* ME.
[ORIGIN Old French.]
Boasting; pomp.

bobarchee *noun* var. of BOBACHEE.

bobber /ˈbɒbə/ *noun*[1]. L18.
[ORIGIN from BOB *verb*[3] + -ER[1].]
A person who or thing which bobs up and down; *spec.* in ANGLING (*a*) a type of float; (*b*) a bob-fly.

bobber /ˈbɒbə/ *noun*[2]. L19.
[ORIGIN from BOB *verb*[4] + -ER[1].]
1 A person who bobs for eels. L19.
2 A bobsleigh rider. E20.

bobber /ˈbɒbə/ *noun*[3]. E20.
[ORIGIN Perh. from BOB *noun*[6], as an hourly rate of pay.]
A workman who unloads fish from trawlers and drifters.

bobbery /ˈbɒb(ə)ri/ *noun & adjective.* Chiefly *Indian.* E19.
[ORIGIN Alt. of Hindi *Bāp re* O father! an exclam. of surprise or grief.]
▸ **A** *noun.* A noisy disturbance; a row. E19.
▸ **B** *adjective.* (Of a pack of hounds) miscellaneous in breed or quality; *loosely* poor in quality, made from what is available. L19.

bobbin /ˈbɒbɪn/ *noun.* M16.
[ORIGIN French *bobine*, †*bobin*, of unknown origin.]
1 A small cylinder or similar article round which thread or yarn is wound, in order to be wound off again as required, for use in weaving, sewing, etc.; a reel round which wire etc. is coiled; a spool. M16.
2 A fine cord or narrow braid in haberdashery. L16.
3 A rounded piece of wood attached to a string for raising a door latch. E18.
4 In *pl.* Nonsense, rubbish. *N. English.* L20.
– COMB.: **bobbin lace** lace made by hand with threads wound on bobbins and worked over a pillow.

bobbinet /ˈbɒbɪnɛt/ *noun.* Also **bobbin-net**. M19.
[ORIGIN from BOBBIN + NET *noun*[1].]
A machine-made cotton or silk net, orig. imitating bobbin lace.

B

bobbish /ˈbɒbɪʃ/ *adjective. dial. & slang.* L18.
[ORIGIN from BOB *adjective* or *verb*[3] + -ISH[1].]
Well; in good spirits.
■ **bobbishly** *adverb* E19.

bobble /ˈbɒb(ə)l/ *noun*[1]. E20.
[ORIGIN from BOB *noun*[1] + -LE[1].]
A small woolly ball used as an ornament or trimming.
■ **bobbled** *adjective* ornamented with bobbles M20.

bobble /ˈbɒb(ə)l/ *verb & noun*[2]. *colloq.* E19.
[ORIGIN from BOB *verb*[3] + -LE[3].]
▸ **A** *verb.* **1** *verb intrans. & refl.* Move with continual bobbing. E19.
2 *verb intrans. & trans.* SPORT. Fumble (a catch), mishandle (a ball). *US.* M20.
▸ **B** *noun.* **1** Bobbling motion; choppiness of water. L19.
2 SPORT. A fumbling of a catch, a mishandling of a ball. *US.* E20.
■ **bobbly** *adjective* uneven, knobbly E20.

bobby /ˈbɒbi/ *noun*[1]. *colloq.* Also **B-**. M19.
[ORIGIN Pet form of male forename *Robert*, after Sir Robert Peel (1788–1850), who founded the Irish constabulary and introduced the new Police Act in Britain in 1828. Cf. PEELER *noun*[2].]
A (British) policeman.

bobby /ˈbɒbi/ *attrib. adjective & noun*[2]. L19.
[ORIGIN Prob. from BOB *noun*[1] + -Y[1].]
▸ **A** *adjective.* In various collocations (see below), usu. with the sense 'small, short'. L19.
bobby calf an unweaned calf slaughtered soon after birth. **bobby pin** *N. Amer.* a kind of sprung hairpin or small clip, orig. for use with bobbed hair. **bobby socks**, **bobby sox** (orig. *US*) socks reaching just above the ankle, *esp.* those worn by girls. **bobby-soxer** (usu. *derog.*) an adolescent girl wearing bobby socks. **bobby wren** *dial.* the wren.
▸ **B** *noun.* = *bobby calf* above. E20.

bobby-dazzler /bɒbɪˈdazlə/ *noun. dial. & slang.* M19.
[ORIGIN from obscure 1st elem. + DAZZLER.]
A remarkable or excellent thing or person; a strikingly dressed person.

Bobo /ˈbəʊbəʊ/ *noun.* Pl. **-os**. *colloq.* L20.
[ORIGIN Abbreviation.]
A bourgeois bohemian, a person having both the values of the counterculture of the 1960s and the materialism of the 1980s.

bobolink /ˈbɒbəlɪŋk/ *noun.* Also (earlier) **bob(-o')-lincoln** /bɒb(ə)ˈlɪŋkən/ & other vars. L18.
[ORIGIN App. imit. of the bird's call.]
A N. American songbird, *Dolichonyx oryzivorus* (family Icteridae), the male of which is black with yellow and white markings, and the female yellowish buff. Also called ***meadow bird***.

bobotie /bəˈbʊəti/ *noun. S. Afr.* L19.
[ORIGIN Afrikaans, prob. from Malay *bobotok*.]
A dish of curried minced meat with a variety of additional ingredients.

bobstay /ˈbɒbsteɪ/ *noun.* M18.
[ORIGIN from BOB (uncertain in what sense) + STAY *noun*[1].]
NAUTICAL. A rope used to hold down the bowsprit of a ship and keep it steady.

bobsy-die /bɒbzɪˈdʌɪ/ *noun. dial.* or *Austral. & NZ colloq.* Also (earlier) **Bob's-a-dying** /bɒbzəˈdʌɪɪŋ/. E19.
[ORIGIN See BOB *noun*[5].]
A great fuss, pandemonium.

bobtail /ˈbɒbteɪl/ *noun & verb.* M16.
[ORIGIN Prob. from BOB *verb*[4] (though recorded earlier) + TAIL *noun*[1].]
▸ **A** *noun.* †**1** A broad-headed arrow. Only in M16.
2 (A horse or dog with) a docked tail. E17.
3 †**a** A contemptible person. Only in E17. ▸**b** *collect.* in ***ragtag and bobtail***, ***rag, tag, and bobtail***, earlier *tagrag* ***and bobtail***, ***tag, rag, and bobtail***. The rabble, the common herd. M17.
4 In full ***bobtail discharge***. A dishonourable discharge. *US.* L19.
5 In full ***bobtail flush***, ***bobtail straight***. A hand needing one card to make a flush or a straight in draw poker. *US.* L19.
▸ **B** *verb trans.* Dock the tail of; *fig.* curtail. L16.
■ **bobtailed** *adjective* with tail cut short, short-tailed M17.

bobwhite /ˈbɒbwʌɪt/ *noun.* E19.
[ORIGIN Imit. of the bird's call.]
Any of several quails constituting the American genus *Colinus*, esp. *C. virginianus*. Also ***bobwhite quail***.

bob-wire /ˈbɒbwʌɪə/ *noun. N. Amer. colloq.* E20.
[ORIGIN Alt. of *barb wire*.]
Barbed wire.

bocage /bəˈkɑːʒ, *foreign* bɔkaːʒ (*pl. same*)/ *noun.* L16.
[ORIGIN French: see BOSCAGE.]
1 Wooded country interspersed with pasture (in France); a thicket, a wood. L16.
2 (A, the) representation of sylvan scenery in ceramics. Freq. *attrib.* E20.

Bocardo /bəˈkɑːdəʊ/ *noun.* E16.
[ORIGIN A mnemonic of scholastic philosophers first used in medieval Latin, O indicating a particular negative proposition and A a universal affirmative proposition.]
1 LOGIC. The fifth mood of the third syllogistic figure, in which a particular negative conclusion is drawn from a particular negative major premiss and a universal affirmative minor. E16.
2 **a** *hist.* The prison in the old North Gate of the city of Oxford, pulled down in 1771. M16. ▸†**b** (**b-**.) Pl. **-os**. A prison, a dungeon. M16–E18.

bocasin /ˈbɒkəsɪn/ *noun.* LME.
[ORIGIN Spanish *bocací(n)* cotton stuff used for lining (so French *boucassin*, †*boccasin*) from Turkish *boğası*.]
A fine buckram.

bocca /ˈbɒkə/ *noun.* L18.
[ORIGIN Italian = mouth.]
1 A circular opening in a glass furnace through which the pots can be inserted and withdrawn. L18.
2 A volcanic vent from which lava emerges. L19.

boccaro /ˈbɒkərəʊ/ *noun.* Also **bucc-** /ˈbʌk-/. Pl. **-os**. L19.
[ORIGIN Prob. from Spanish *búcaro* from Portuguese *púcaro* clay cup, ult. from Latin *poculum* cup.]
A scented red unglazed earthenware of a type orig. made by the Portuguese.

bocce /ˈbɒtʃeɪ/ *noun.* Also **boccia** /ˈbɒtʃɪə/. M19.
[ORIGIN Italian, pl. of *boccia* ball.]
An Italian game similar to bowls but played on a shorter, narrower green.

bocconcino /bɒkɒnˈtʃiːnəʊ/ *noun.* Pl. **-cini** /-ˈtʃiːni/. L20.
[ORIGIN Italian.]
A small ball of mozzarella cheese.

bocconia /bəˈkəʊnɪə/ *noun.* E19.
[ORIGIN mod. Latin, from Paolo *Boccone* (1633–1704), Sicilian botanist: see -IA[1].]
A plant or shrub of the genus *Bocconia*, of the poppy family, or one formerly included in this genus; esp. *Macleaya cordata*, which bears cream-coloured flowers.

Boche /bɒʃ/ *noun & adjective. slang. derog.* E20.
[ORIGIN French slang, = rascal, (from the First World War) German.]
▸ **A** *noun.* A German (soldier); *the* Germans collectively. E20.
▸ **B** *adjective.* German. E20.

bock /bɒk/ *noun.* M19.
[ORIGIN French from German, abbreviation of (*Eim*)*bockbier* = *Einbecker bier*, from *Einbeck*, a town in Lower Saxony.]
A strong dark variety of German beer; a glass or drink of this or other beer.

bockety /ˈbɒkɪti/ *adjective. Irish.* L19.
[ORIGIN from Irish *bacach* lame.]
Unsteady, wobbly.

bocking /ˈbɒkɪŋ/ *noun.* M18.
[ORIGIN *Bocking*, a village in Essex, England.]
A coarse woollen drugget or baize made in or near Bocking.

BOD *abbreviation.*
Biochemical oxygen demand.

bod /bɒd/ *noun. colloq.*, orig. *Scot.* L18.
[ORIGIN Abbreviation of BODY *noun*; in Scot. use perh. from BODACH.]
A body. Also, a person.

J. COE We all know that you Labour bods are in cahoots with CND. *www.cinescene.com* The film's approach .. inescapably focuses on her gorgeous bod.

odd bod: see ODD *adjective*.

bodach /ˈbəʊdɑːx/ *noun. Scot. & Irish.* E19.
[ORIGIN Gaelic & Irish.]
A male peasant. Also (*Scot.*), a spectre.

bodacious /bəˈdeɪʃəs/ *adjective & adverb. US dial.* M19.
[ORIGIN Perh. var. of BOLDACIOUS.]
Complete(ly), utter(ly), downright.
■ **bodaciously** *adverb* M19.

bode /bəʊd/ *noun*[1]. Long *obsolete* exc. *hist.*
[ORIGIN Old English *boda* = Old Frisian *boda*, Old Saxon *bodo*, Old High German *boto* (German *Bote*), Old Norse *boði*, from Germanic, from weak grade of base of BID *verb*.]
A herald, a messenger.

bode /bəʊd/ *noun*[2]. *arch. & dial.*
[ORIGIN Old English *bod* (chiefly north. for *gebod*) = Old Frisian *bod*, Old Saxon *gibod*, Old High German *gibot* (German *Gebot*), Old Norse *boð*, from Germanic, from base also of BODE *noun*[1].]
†**1** A command; behest. OE–ME.
†**2** A message, tidings. ME–M17.
3 A bid. Long *obsolete* exc. *Scot. & N. English.* ME.
4 A premonition, an omen; a foreboding. *arch.* LME.
– COMB.: **bodeword** (*Scot. & N. English*) †(**a**) a command; †(**b**) a message; (**c**) a premonition.

bode /bəʊd/ *verb*[1].
[ORIGIN Old English *bodian* = Old Frisian *bodia*, formed as BODE *noun*[1].]
†**1** *verb trans.* Announce, proclaim. OE–ME. ▸**b** *verb intrans.* Preach the gospel. OE–ME.
2 *verb trans.* Of a person: foretell, presage, have a presentiment of (esp. evil). OE.

B. FRANKLIN There are croakers in every country, always boding its ruin.

3 *verb trans., & intrans.* with *well*, *ill*. Of a thing: betoken, portend, promise. ME.

J. TYNDALL That lingering rosy hue which bodes good weather. A. SILLITOE Winnie laughed, an expression of mirth that boded no good for her husband.

†**4** *verb trans.* Command (a person) *that*. Only in ME.
■ **bodement** *noun* an augury, omen; a presentiment; a prophecy, a prediction: E17. **boder** *noun* OE. **boding** *noun* (**a**) the action of the verb; (**b**) = BODEMENT: OE. **bodingly** *adverb* ominously; with a presentiment: E19.

bode *verb*[2] var. of BUDE.

bodeful /ˈbəʊdfʊl, -f(ə)l/ *adjective.* E19.
[ORIGIN from BODE *noun*[2] + -FUL.]
Ominous, presageful.

bodega /bəˈdiːɡə, *foreign* boˈdeɡa/ *noun.* M19.
[ORIGIN Spanish from Latin *apotheca*: see BOUTIQUE.]
(Orig. in Spain) a shop selling wine.

bodegón /bodeˈɡɒn/ *noun.* Pl. ***bodegones*** /bodeˈɡɒnes/. M19.
[ORIGIN Spanish, from BODEGA, as orig. representing a bodega scene.]
A Spanish picture representing still life or a genre subject.

boden /ˈbəʊdɪn, ˈbɒd-/ *adjective. Scot. arch.* Also **-in**. LME.
[ORIGIN Unknown.]
†**1** Accoutred, armed. LME–E19.
2 (Esp. *well*, *ill*) provided, prepared, dressed. LME.

Bode's law /ˈbəʊdz lɔː, ˈbəʊdəz/ *noun phr.* M19.
[ORIGIN Johann E. *Bode* (1747–1826), German astronomer, who drew attention to the law; it had been discovered earlier by another German, Johann D. Titius (1729–96).]
ASTRONOMY. An empirical formula giving the approximate distances of several planets from the sun as a geometric progression in powers of 2, starting at the orbit of Mercury.

bodge /bɒdʒ/ *verb & noun.* M16.
[ORIGIN Alt. of BOTCH *verb* (cf. *grudge* from *grutch*).]
▸ **A** *verb trans.* = BOTCH *verb.* M16.
▸ **B** *noun.* = BOTCH *noun*[2]. L16.

bodger /ˈbɒdʒə/ *noun*[1]. Now *dial.* M16.
[ORIGIN from BODGE *verb* + -ER[1].]
= BOTCHER *noun*[1].

bodger /ˈbɒdʒə/ *noun*[2]. *dial.* M18.
[ORIGIN Perh. var. of BADGER *noun*[1].]
A pedlar, a dealer.

bodger /ˈbɒdʒə/ *adjective. Austral. slang.* M20.
[ORIGIN Prob. from BODGE *verb*.]
Inferior, worthless; (of a name) false, assumed.

bodgie /ˈbɒdʒi/ *noun. Austral. & NZ.* Now *hist.* M20.
[ORIGIN Perh. from BODGER *adjective* + -IE.]
A young lout, a larrikin; a Teddy boy.

Bodhisattva /bɒdɪˈsɑːtvə/ *noun.* E19.
[ORIGIN Sanskrit = a person whose essence is perfect knowledge, from *bodhi* perfect knowledge (from *budh-* know: see BUDDHA) + *sattva* being, reality.]
BUDDHISM. In Mahayana Buddhism, a person who is near to attaining nirvana but delays doing so because of compassion for human suffering. In Theravada Buddhism, the future Buddha.

bodhrán /ˈbaʊrɑːn, baʊˈrɑːn/ *noun.* E20.
[ORIGIN Irish Gaelic, from *bodhar* dull (of sound).]
A shallow one-sided Irish drum, typically played using a short stick with knobbed ends.

bodice /ˈbɒdɪs/ *noun.* Orig. †**bodies** pl. M16.
[ORIGIN Pl. of BODY *noun*, retaining earlier unvoiced sound of -S[1] (cf. DICE *noun*).]
1 The upper part of a woman's or girl's dress down to the waist; *spec.* the part covering the upper body (excluding sleeves); a (usu. sleeveless) undergarment for the upper body. M16.
liberty bodice, ***petticoat bodice***, ***Watteau bodice***, ***Zouave bodice***, etc.
2 *hist. pl.* More fully ***pair of bodice***. A whalebone corset for the upper body. E17.
– COMB.: **bodice-ripper** *colloq.* a sexually explicit romantic (esp. historical) novel or film with seduction of the heroine.

bodied /ˈbɒdɪd/ *adjective.* LME.
[ORIGIN from BODY *noun* + -ED[2]: cf. BODY *verb*.]
1 As 2nd elem. of comb.: having a body of the specified kind. LME.

SHAKES. *Com. Err.* Ill-fac'd, worse bodied, shapeless everywhere.

able-bodied, ***big-bodied***, ***full-bodied***, ***wide-bodied***, etc.
2 Having material form, corporeal, embodied. *rare.* M17.

BROWNING Like the bodied heaven in clearness Shone the stone.

bodikin /ˈbɒdɪkɪn/ *noun. arch.* L16.
[ORIGIN Dim. of BODY *noun*: see -KIN.]
1 ***God's bodikins!***, ***ods bodikins!*** & vars., God's dear body!: an oath. See also 'SBODIKINS. L16.
†**2** A small body; a minute particle of matter. M17–L18.

bodiless /ˈbɒdɪlɪs/ *adjective*. LME.
[ORIGIN from BODY *noun* + -LESS.]
Having no body; incorporeal; insubstantial.

bodily /ˈbɒdɪli/ *adjective*. ME.
[ORIGIN from BODY *noun* + -LY[1].]
1 Corporeal, physical, (opp. spiritual); real, actual. Now *rare*. ME.

R. G. COLLINGWOOD Something bodily and perceptible, a painted canvass, a carved stone, . . and so forth.

2 Of, belonging to, or affecting the human body or physical nature. LME.

T. REID My memory is not limited by any bodily organ. F. SWINNERTON A return of bodily discomforts and melancholy thoughts.

grievous bodily harm: see GRIEVOUS *adjective*.
†**3** Solid; of or pertaining to a solid. M16–E17.
■ **bodiliness** *noun* (*rare*) corporeality, substance L16.

bodily /ˈbɒdɪli/ *adverb*. ME.
[ORIGIN from BODILY *adjective*: see -LY[2].]
†**1** Corporeally, unspiritually. ME–L17.
2 In body, in person. LME.

SOUTHEY This is our father Francisco, Among us bodily.

3 With the whole bulk or body; as a whole, completely. L18.

E. B. BROWNING As if that . . Bodily the wind did carry The great altar. J. CONRAD To hurl himself bodily against the panels.

bodin *adjective* var. of BODEN.

bodkin /ˈbɒdkɪn/ *noun*. ME.
[ORIGIN Uncertain; perh. dim. from Celtic (cf. Irish *bod*, Welsh *bidog*, Gaelic *biodag* dagger).]
†**1** A dagger, a stiletto. ME–M17.
2 A small pointed instrument for piercing cloth etc. LME.
3 A long pin used to fasten up the hair. L16.
4 A person squeezed between two others. *arch*. M17.
ride bodkin, **sit bodkin**, etc., ride etc. squeezed between two others.
5 PRINTING. An instrument for removing pieces of type for correction etc. L17.
6 A blunt thick needle with a large eye for drawing tape etc. through material. E18.

bodle /ˈbɒd(ə)l/ *noun*. M17.
[ORIGIN Perh. from a mint-master named *Bothwell*: cf. BAWBEE.]
hist. A Scottish copper coin equivalent to one-sixth of an English (old) penny; the smallest coin. Also called ***turner***.

SIR W. SCOTT Not that I cared a brass bodle for his benison.

Bodleian /ˈbɒdlɪən, *esp. as adjective* bɒdˈliːən/ *noun & adjective*. M17.
[ORIGIN from Sir Thomas *Bodley* (1545–1613), English diplomat, who re-founded the library in 1603, + -AN.]
(Designating, of, or pertaining to) *the* Library of Oxford University.
■ Also **Bodley** *noun* (*colloq.*) M17.

Bodoni /bəˈdəʊni/ *noun & adjective*. L19.
[ORIGIN See below.]
(A book or edition) printed by the Italian printer Giambattista Bodoni (1740–1813); (in) a typeface based on that of Bodoni.

†**bodrag** *noun*. M–L16.
[ORIGIN Prob. from Irish: cf. *buaidhreadh* molestation, disturbance, tumult, Old Irish *búdraise* excitement.]
A hostile incursion, a raid.
■ Also †**bodraging** *noun*: only in L16.

body /ˈbɒdi/ *noun*.
[ORIGIN Old English *bodiġ* corresp. to Old High German *botah* corpse (Middle High German *botich*, mod. German Bavarian dial. *Bottech* body of a chemise), ult. origin unknown.]
▸ **I** The material frame of people or animals.
1 The physical frame of a human or an animal; the whole material organism. OE. ▸**b** The corporeal nature of a human; flesh as opp. to soul or spirit. ME.

J. STEINBECK Then down from the car the weary people climbed, and stretched stiff bodies. D. ATTENBOROUGH Elongated animals with segmented bodies. **b** POPE All are but parts of one stupendous whole, Whose body Nature is, and God the soul. SIR W. SCOTT While we are yet in the body.

2 A corpse. ME.

SHAKES. *John* At Worcester must his body be interr'd. TENNYSON In the ghastly pit . . a body was found.

3 CHRISTIAN CHURCH. The consecrated bread used in the Eucharist. ME.
4 An individual, a person. Now chiefly *colloq*. ME.

SHAKES. *Merry W.* 'Tis a great charge to come under one body's hand. F. WELDON She was a plump, busy little body, with a husband two years dead.

anybody, ***everybody***, ***nobody***, ***somebody***.
5 The material being of a human; the person. LME.

Book of Common Prayer With this Ring I thee wed . . with my body I thee worship.

▸ **II** The main portion.
6 The main part of the human or animal frame, apart from the head and limbs; the trunk. OE. ▸**b** The main stem of a tree, plant, etc. ME.

SHAKES. *3 Hen. VI* But when the fox hath once got in his nose, He'll soon find means to make the body follow.

7 The main portion of something as distinct from subordinate parts or appendages, as the nave of a church, hull of a ship, load-bearing part of a vehicle, central text of a document, etc. (Foll. by *of*.) OE.

C. COTTON The body of the Emblem was a figure of the Duke himself. A. TROLLOPE The body of the will was in the handwriting of the widow, as was also the codicil. E. BLISHEN Once inside we hurled ourselves into the body of the cinema.

8 The majority, the larger part of anything. (Foll. by *of*.) LME.

LD MACAULAY The great body of the people leaned to the royalists.

9 a The part of a dress down to the waist, or the portion of the dress that covers the body as distinct from the arms. See also BODICE. *arch*. M16. ▸**b** A woman's usu. close-fitting stretch garment for the upper body, fastening at the crotch. L20.
†**10** A chemical retort. M16–E19.
11 TYPOGRAPHY. (The breadth of) a shank of metal type from head to tail; the nominal depth of photocomposed type. L17.
▸ **III** An aggregate of individuals.
12 An artificial person created by legal authority; a corporation; an officially constituted organization, an assembly, an institution, a society. ME.

B. T. WASHINGTON The Alabama Legislature was in session . . . This body passed a resolution to adjourn. JAN MORRIS The Thames Water Authority, the managing body of the river.

13 A force of fighting men; *gen*. an assemblage of persons or things characterized by a common purpose or attribute; a collective mass. L16.

W. ROBERTSON Escorted by a body of horse. J. P. MAHAFFY This large and respectable body of opinion. H. J. LASKI The State must live with other States, both as regards its individual members, and as a collective body.

14 A collection of the details of any subject; a collection of information; *arch*. a textbook. M17.

ADDISON I could wish our Royal Society would compile a Body of Natural History.

▸ **IV** A portion of matter; substance.
15 A separate piece of matter, a material thing. LME. ▸**b** GEOMETRY. A figure of three dimensions, a solid. *arch*. M16. ▸**c** ANATOMY & MEDICINE. With specifying word: a distinguishable component of structure. M19.

S. JOHNSON All attraction is increased by the approach of the attracting body. F. HOYLE All bodies collapse in one way or another when the forces inside them become large enough.

16 Substance as opp. to representation; reality. LME.

W. VAN T. CLARK Sparks had given a kind of body . . to an ideal.

17 A distinct form or kind of matter: ▸†**a** Each of the seven metals, gold, silver, iron, mercury, lead, tin, and copper, answering to the seven heavenly bodies (see below). Only in LME. ▸**b** CHEMISTRY & MINERALOGY. Any kind of (solid, liquid, or gaseous) substance. *arch*. M16. ▸**c** Paste or clay (of a particular kind) used in porcelain manufacture. L18.

b D. BREWSTER Crystallised bodies, such as nitre and arragonite.

18 METAPHYSICS etc. A thing which has existence and occupies space; that which is perceptible to the senses, matter. L16.

J. S. MILL A body . . may be defined, the external cause to which we ascribe our sensations. F. BOWEN We cannot think of body without extension.

19 A compact quantity, an amount, a bulk; *spec*. a deposit of metalliferous ore. M17.

R. I. MURCHISON Another body of igneous rock lies subjacent. C. FRANCIS The oceans and seas of the world form one continuous body of salt water.

20 Comparative solidity or fullness; substantial character or flavour in a material, wine, colour, etc. M17.

R. DAHL It [a wine] is far too light in the body to be from either St Emilion or Graves. J. C. OATES Her hair . . was dull and lusterless, and lacked body.

– PHRASES: ***astral body***: see ASTRAL *adjective* 3. ***black body***: see BLACK *adjective*. **body corporate** a corporation. **body of Christ** (*a*) the community of the Christian Church, of which Christ is held to be the head; (*b*) = sense 3 above. **body politic** the state; organized society. **celestial body** the sun, the moon, a planet, a star, etc. **dead body** a corpse; ***over my dead body***, ***over his dead body***, etc. (hyperbol.), entirely without my etc. consent, with the strongest opposition from me etc. ***fruiting body***: see FRUIT *verb*. ***governing body***: see GOVERN *verb*. **heavenly body** the sun, the moon, a planet, a star, etc. (***the seven heavenly bodies***, (in medieval astrology etc.) the sun, the moon, Mars, Mercury, Saturn, Jupiter, and Venus). ***heir of one's body***, ***heir of the body***: see HEIR *noun*. **in a body** all together, as one. **keep body and soul together** manage to remain alive. PITUITARY ***body***. ***Platonic body***: see PLATONIC *adjective* 1. ***polar body***: see POLAR *adjective*. ***soul and body lashing***: see SOUL *noun*. ***squire of the body***: see SQUIRE *noun*[1] 1c.
– COMB.: **body art** (*a*) items of jewellery or clothing worn on the body and regarded as art; (*b*) the practice of decorating the body by means of tattooing, piercing, etc.; (*c*) an artistic genre, originating in the 1970s, in which the actual body of the artist or model is integral to the work; **body bag** (*a*) a sleeping bag; (*b*) a bag for carrying a corpse from the scene of warfare, an accident, a crime, etc.; **body blow** a blow to the body in boxing etc.; *fig*. a crushing setback; **bodyboard** a short, light type of surfboard ridden in a prone position; **bodyboarder** a person who surfs on a bodyboard; **body-builder** (*a*) a person who builds vehicle bodies; (*b*) a person who develops the muscles of the body by systematic exercise; **body-building** (*a*) the building of vehicle bodies; (*b*) development of the muscles of the body by systematic exercise; **body-centred** *adjective* (of a crystal structure) in which an atom or ion occurs at each vertex and at the centre of the unit cell; **body-check** *noun & verb* (*a*) *noun* (in various sports) the placing of one's body in the way of an opponent in order to impede him; (*b*) *verb trans*. impede thus; **body clock** the biological clock of the human body; **body colour** an opaque pigment; **body count** *colloq*. a list or total of casualties; **body double** a stand-in for a film actor during stunts or nude scenes; **body dysmorphic disorder** a psychiatric disorder in which a person becomes preoccupied with an imagined defect in their appearance; **bodyguard** (a member of) an escort or personal guard of a dignitary etc.; **body language** gestures and movements by which a person unconsciously conveys meaning; **body-line** (**bowling**) CRICKET fast short-pitched bowling on the leg side, threatening the batsman's body; **body louse** a human louse infesting the body rather than the head; **body mass index** MEDICINE an approximate measure of whether a person is over- or underweight, calculated by dividing his or her weight in kilograms by the square of their height in metres; abbreviation *BMI*; **body odour** the (esp. unpleasant) smell of the body; **body-piercing** the piercing of parts of the body (other than the ear) in order to insert rings, studs, or other ornaments; **body-popping** (orig. *US*) a kind of dancing with jerky movements of the joints; **body scanner** a scanner designed to screen the whole body for the presence of cancer etc.; **body search** a search of a person's body and clothing for a hidden weapon, concealed drugs, etc.; **body-servant** a valet; **bodyshell** the metal frame of a motor or railway vehicle, to which the metal panels are attached; **body shop** a workshop where vehicle bodies are repaired; **bodysnatcher** *hist*. an illicit exhumer of corpses for dissection; **body-snatching** *hist*. illicit exhumation of corpses for dissection; **body stocking** a (woman's) one-piece undergarment covering the trunk and legs; **bodysuit** a close-fitting one-piece stretch garment, esp. worn by women for sporting activities; **bodysurf** *verb intrans*. ride a breaking wave without using a surfboard; **body type**: used for printing the main text of a book; **body wave** an artificial wave in the hair to give it fullness; **body whorl** CONCHOLOGY the last-formed and usu. largest whorl of a spiral shell, containing the animal itself when alive; **bodywork** (*a*) the structure of a vehicle body; (*b*) therapies in complementary medicine which involve touching or manipulating the body; **bodyworker** a practitioner of a therapy that involves bodywork.
■ **bodyhood** *noun* (*rare*) the quality of having or being a body L17.

body /ˈbɒdi/ *verb trans*. LME.
[ORIGIN from the noun.]
1 Provide with a body; embody; give substance to; reinforce. *arch*. LME.
2 Foll. by *forth*: give mental shape to; exhibit in outward form; typify. L16.

Boehm /bəːm, *foreign* bøːm/ *noun*. M19.
[ORIGIN Theobald *Böhm* (1794–1881), German musician.]
Applied ***attrib***. to a system of keys and fingering which Böhm invented, and to woodwind instruments (esp. flutes) which use this system.

Boehmenism /ˈbəːmənɪz(ə)m/ *noun*. Also **Beh-** /ˈbeɪ-/. M17.
[ORIGIN from Jacob *Böhme* or *Boehme* (see below), known in Britain also as *Behmen*, + -ISM.]
The mystical and theosophical doctrines of the German mystic Böhme (1575–1624).
■ **Boehmenist** *noun & adjective* M17. **Boehmist** *noun & adjective* M18.

boehmite /ˈbəːmʌɪt/ *noun*. E20.
[ORIGIN from Johann *Böhm* (1895–1952), German chemist + -ITE[1].]
MINERALOGY. An orthorhombic basic aluminium oxide occurring esp. as a major constituent of bauxite.

Boeotarch /bɪˈəʊtɑːk/ *noun*. E19.
[ORIGIN Greek *Boiōtarkhēs*, from *Boiōtia* Boeotia (see BOEOTIAN) + *-arkhēs* -ARCH.]
ANCIENT HISTORY. A chief magistrate of the Boeotian league.

Boeotian /bɪˈəʊʃ(ə)n/ *noun & adjective*. L15.
[ORIGIN from *Boeotia* (see below) + -AN.]
▸ **A** *noun*. A native of Boeotia, a district of ancient Greece proverbial for the stupidity of its inhabitants; a stupid person. L15.
▸ **B** *adjective*. Of Boeotia; dull, stupid. L16.
■ **Boeotic** /bɪˈɒtɪk/ *adjective* = BOEOTIAN *adjective* M17.

Boer /bɔː, ˈbəʊə, bʊə/ *noun & adjective*. M19.
[ORIGIN Dutch *boer* farmer: cf. BOOR.]
▸ **A** *noun*. A South African of Dutch descent, an Afrikaner; *hist*. an early Dutch inhabitant of the Cape. Cf. BOOR 1b. M19.
▸ **B** *attrib*. or as *adjective*. Of or pertaining to Boers. L19.
Boer War: between Britain and the Boer Republics in South Africa 1880–1 and (esp.) 1899–1902.

boerewors /ˈbuːrəvɔːs, ˈbʊə-/ *noun*. *S. Afr*. M20.
[ORIGIN Afrikaans, from *boere* Afrikaner, farmer's + *wors* sausage.]
A type of traditional sausage containing coarsely ground beef and pork.

boeuf /bœf/ *noun*. E20.
[ORIGIN French = beef.]
COOKERY. Used in the names of various beef dishes.
boeuf bourguignon /burgiɲɔ̃/ [= of Burgundy] beef stewed in red wine. ***boeuf*** STROGANOFF.

boff /bɒf/ *noun & verb*. *US slang*. L19.
[ORIGIN Imit.]
▸ **A** *noun*. **1** A blow or punch; *fig.* a buzz, a thrill. L19.
2 A resoundingly successful theatrical production, song, etc., a hit. M20.
3 A joke intended to produce a belly laugh. M20.
4 (An instance of) sexual intercourse; a person (esp. a woman) regarded as the object of intercourse. M20.
▸ **B** *verb*. **1** *verb trans.* Hit or strike (a person); handle roughly. M20.

D. RUNYON You cannot find out if he can take a punch . . until you see him boffed around good in the ring.

2 *verb trans. & intrans.* Have sexual intercourse (with); copulate. M20.

T. CLANCY Those kind will start boffing every girl that crosses their path.

▪ **boffing** *noun* M20.

boffin /ˈbɒfɪn/ *noun*. *slang*. M20.
[ORIGIN Unknown.]
1 An elderly naval officer. M20.
2 A person engaged in scientific or technical research, a technical expert. Now also, an intellectual or academic. M20.
▪ **boffinry**, **-ery** *noun* boffins (sense 2) collectively; the activity of a boffin: M20.

boffo /ˈbɒfəʊ/ *adjective*. *N. Amer. slang*. M20.
[ORIGIN Abbreviation of BOFFOLA.]
1 (Of a review of a theatrical production etc.) wholeheartedly commendatory; resoundingly successful; extraordinarily good. M20.
2 (Of a laugh) deep and unrestrained, loud, raucous; boisterously funny. M20.

boffola /bɒˈfəʊlə/ *noun*. *US slang*. M20.
[ORIGIN Extension of BOFF: cf. -OLA.]
= BOFF.

Bofors /ˈbəʊfəz/ *noun*. Pl. same. M20.
[ORIGIN Site of a munition works in Sweden.]
In full ***Bofors gun*** etc. A type of light anti-aircraft gun with single or twin 40-mm (approx. 1.6-inch) barrels.

bog /bɒg/ *noun*¹. ME.
[ORIGIN Gaelic (& Irish) *bogach*, from *bog* soft.]
(A tract of) wet, spongy ground too soft to support any heavy body; ECOLOGY wet land with acid, peaty soil (cf. ***fen***). RAISED ***bog***. SERBONIAN ***bog***.
– COMB.: ***bog asphodel***: see ASPHODEL 2; **bog-bean** = BUCKBEAN; **bog berry** cranberry; **bog-blitter**, **bog-bumper** *dial.* the bittern; **bog-butter** butter of medieval or earlier origin found buried in peat bogs; **bog fir**, **bog oak**, **bog pine**: preserved as ancient timber in a blackened state in peat bogs; **bog garden** a piece of land laid out and irrigated to grow plants which prefer a damp habitat; **bog-hole** a natural hole in the ground with a swampy bottom; **bog iron (ore)** soft, spongy limonite deposited in bogs; **bogland** marshy land; *joc.* Ireland; ***bog*** LEMMING; **bogman** *Irish derog.* a person from a rural area; **bog moss** sphagnum; **bog myrtle** a fragrant shrub, *Myrica gale*, which grows in moist ground; = GALE *noun*¹; ***bog oak***: see ***bog fir*** above; ***bog onion***: see ONION *noun* 1b; **bog orchid** a small orchid, *Hammarbya paludosa*, with tiny yellow-green flowers; **bog ore** = ***bog iron ore*** above; ***bog*** PIMPERNEL; ***bog pine***: see ***bog fir*** above; **bog rosemary** = ANDROMEDA 2; **bog-rush** (**a**) a densely tufted sedge of the genus *Schoenus*; esp. *S. nigricans* of Eurasia and N. Africa; (**b**) *N. Amer.* a rush of the genus *Juncus*; ***bog spavin***: see SPAVIN *noun*¹; **bog-trot** *verb intrans.* trot over, live among, bogs; **bog-trotter** *offensive* an Irishman; **bog violet** (**a**) butterwort; (**b**) = ***marsh violet*** s.v. MARSH *noun*¹.
▪ **bogginess** *noun* boggy quality M17. **boggy** *adjective* of the nature of, or characterized by, bog L16.

bog /bɒg/ *noun*². *colloq.* M17.
[ORIGIN Uncertain: perh. same word as BOG *noun*¹.]
A privy, a lavatory. Orig. as ***bog-house*** (now *arch.*).

bog /bɒg/ *verb trans. & intrans.* Infl. **-gg-**. E17.
[ORIGIN from BOG *noun*¹.]
Sink or submerge in a bog (*lit. & fig.*). Freq. in *pass.* and foll. by *down*.

P. V. WHITE He would proceed awkwardly across the mud, but soon became bogged. A. MOOREHEAD They . . bogged most fearfully in the waterholes. A. POWELL He gets bogged down in self-pity about the difficulties of a writer's life.

bog off *slang* go away (usu. in *imper.*).

bogart /ˈbəʊgɑːt/ *verb*. *slang* (orig. & chiefly *US*). M20.
[ORIGIN from Humphrey *Bogart* (1899–1957), US film actor who specialized in tough-guy roles.]
1 *verb intrans. & trans.* Act or treat like a tough guy; bully (someone). M20.
2 *verb trans.* Selfishly appropriate (something); take an unduly large share of (something, esp. a cannabis joint). M20.

A. GARLAND Don't bogart that joint, my friend.

bogey /ˈbəʊgi/ *noun*¹. Also **bogy**. M19.
[ORIGIN Prob. rel. to BOGLE etc., BUG *noun*¹.]
1 (As a proper name, **B-**.) The Devil. M19. ▸**b** An evil spirit, now *esp.* one used to frighten children. Also ***bogeyman***. M19. ▸**c** A source of fear or alarm, a bugbear. M19.

c R. SHILTS We tell ourselves that pestilence is a mere bogey of the mind.

2 A detective or police officer. *slang*. E20.
3 A piece of nasal mucus. *colloq.* M20.
4 An unidentified enemy aircraft. *US military slang*. L20.

bogey /ˈbəʊgi/ *noun*². *Austral. colloq.* Also **bogie**, **bogy**. M19.
[ORIGIN from BOGEY *verb*¹.]
A swim, a bathe; a bath.

bogey /ˈbəʊgi/ *noun*³. L19.
[ORIGIN Prob. from BOGEY *noun*¹ as an imaginary opponent.]
GOLF. Orig., the number of strokes a scratch player should need for the course or for a hole. Now, a score of one over par for a hole.
double bogey: see DOUBLE *adjective & adverb*.

bogey /ˈbəʊgi/ *verb*¹ *intrans. Austral. colloq.* Also **bogie**, **bogy**. L18.
[ORIGIN Dharuk *bugi*.]
Swim, bathe.

bogey /ˈbəʊgi/ *verb*² *trans. & intrans.* M20.
[ORIGIN from BOGEY *noun*³.]
GOLF. Complete (a hole) in one stroke over par.

boggard /ˈbɒgəd/ *noun*. *dial.* Also **-art** /-ɑːt/. L16.
[ORIGIN Rel. to BOGGLE *verb & noun*², BOGLE, etc.]
1 = BOGLE. L16.
†**2** An object at which a horse boggles. E17–E18.

boggle *noun*¹ var. of BOGLE.

boggle /ˈbɒg(ə)l/ *verb & noun*². L16.
[ORIGIN Prob. of dial. origin & rel. to BOGLE, BOGGARD, etc.]
▸ **A** *verb*. **1** *verb intrans.* Start with fright, shy as a startled horse. L16.
2 *verb intrans.* Equivocate, quibble. E17.
3 *verb intrans.* Hesitate, demur *at*, *about*, etc.; (of the mind) be overwhelmed or baffled. M17.
4 *verb trans.* Cause to hesitate or demur; baffle, overwhelm mentally. (*rare* before M20.) M17.
mind-boggling: see MIND *noun*¹.
▸ **B** *noun*. **1** The act of shying or taking alarm. *dial.* M17.
2 Scruple, demur. Chiefly in ***make a boggle***. M17.
3 A bungle. M19.
▪ **boggler** *noun* a person who boggles or hesitates E17.

bogie /ˈbəʊgi/ *noun*¹. E19.
[ORIGIN Unknown.]
1 A low truck on four small wheels; a trolley. *N. English*. E19.
2 An undercarriage with two or more wheel pairs, pivoted below the end of a railway vehicle. M19.

bogie *noun*², *verb* var. of BOGEY *noun*², *verb*¹.

bogle /ˈbəʊg(ə)l/ *noun*. *Scot. & N. English*. Also (*N. English*) **boggle** /ˈbɒg(ə)l/. E16.
[ORIGIN Prob. rel. to BOGEY.]
1 A phantom; a goblin; an undefined creature conjured up by superstitious dread. E16.
2 A bugbear; a scarecrow. M17.

BOGOF /ˈbɒgɒf/ *abbreviation*.
Buy one, get one free.

Bogomil /ˈbəʊgəmɪl, ˈbɒg-/ *noun*. Also **-mile** /-mʌɪl/. M19.
[ORIGIN medieval Greek *Bogomilos* from *Bogomil*, the first propagator of the heresy, lit. 'beloved of God', from Old Church Slavonic *Bogŭ* god + *milŭ* dear.]
ECCLESIASTICAL HISTORY. A member of a heretical medieval Balkan sect professing a modified Manichaeism.
▪ **Bogoˈmilian** *adjective & noun* M19. **Bogomilism** *noun* L19.

bogong /ˈbəʊgɒŋ/ *noun*. *Austral.* Also **bug-** /ˈbuːg-/. M19.
[ORIGIN Ngarigo (an Australian Aboriginal language of southern New South Wales and northern Victoria) *bugung*.]
A large dark noctuid moth, *Agrotis infusa*, prized as food by Aborigines.

bog-standard /ˈbɒgˌstandəd/ *adjective*. *colloq.* M20.
[ORIGIN Prob. alt. of *box-standard* = unmodified, as in its original packaging.]
Ordinary, basic; unexceptional or uninspired.

Independent The day of the bog-standard comprehensive is over.

bogue /bəʊg/ *noun*. M19.
[ORIGIN French from Old Provençal *boga* from medieval Latin *boca*, Latin, Greek *bōx*, from *boax* a grunting fish.]
A sea bream, *Boops boops*, found mainly in the Mediterranean.

bogus /ˈbəʊgəs/ *noun & adjective*. Orig. *US*. L18.
[ORIGIN Unknown.]
▸ †**A** *noun*. An apparatus for making counterfeit coins; a counterfeit coin. L18–M19.
▸ **B** *adjective*. **1** Spurious, sham, fictitious. M19. **2** Very displeasing or inferior, bad. *US slang*. L20.
▪ **bogusly** *adverb* M19. **bogusness** *noun* E20.

bogy *noun*¹, *noun*², *verb* vars. of BOGEY *noun*¹, *noun*², *verb*¹.

boh *interjection & noun* var. of BO *interjection & noun*².

Bohairic /bəˈhʌɪrɪk/ *noun & adjective*. Also **Bahiric**. M19.
[ORIGIN from *Bohairah* etc., a province of Lower Egypt, from Arabic *buḥayra* lake: see -IC.]
(Of) the standard form of Coptic formerly spoken in Alexandria and the NW Nile Delta, and used in the Bible of the Coptic Church.

bohea /bəʊˈhiː/ *adjective & noun*. E18.
[ORIGIN Chinese dial. *Bu-yi* var. of *Wu-yi* (see below).]
▸ **A** *adjective*. Of the Wuyi hills in Fukien province, SE China, whence black tea first came to Britain. Also, designating black tea grown elsewhere. E18.
▸ **B** *noun*. (An infusion of) black tea, orig. of the finest, now of the lowest, quality. E18.

Bohemia /bəʊˈhiːmɪə/ *noun*. M19.
[ORIGIN formed as BOHEMIAN in transf. uses.]
The world of social bohemians.

Bohemian /bəʊˈhiːmɪən/ *noun & adjective*. In senses A.3, B.3 also **b-**. LME.
[ORIGIN from *Bohemia* (see below) + -AN; senses A.2, 3, B.2, 3 from French *bohémien*.]
▸ **A** *noun*. **1** A native or inhabitant of Bohemia, formerly a central European kingdom, now forming the western part of the Czech Republic. LME.
2 A Gypsy. L17.
3 A socially unconventional person, esp. an artist or writer, of free-and-easy habits, manners, and sometimes morals. M19.
▸ **B** *adjective*. **1** Of or pertaining to Bohemia; *loosely*. Czech. E17.
Bohemian WAXWING.
2 Of or pertaining to Gypsies. M18.
3 Of, or characteristic of, social Bohemians. M19.
▪ **Bohemianism** *noun* the conduct and manners of a social Bohemian M19.

bohereen *noun* var. of BOREEN.

boho /ˈbəʊhəʊ/ *noun & adjective*. *colloq.* E20.
[ORIGIN Abbreviation of BOHEMIAN.]
▸ **A** *noun*. **1** A person from Bohemia, a Czech, *spec.* one who is resident in the US. *rare*. E20.
2 A person who has an unconventional or bohemian way of life. Also, such a lifestyle, or the subculture associated with it. M20.

Ticket Hippies and bohos gather to freak-out to the rockier end of acid jazz.

▸ **B** *adjective*. Of or pertaining to bohos or their lifestyle; unconventional, decadent; artistic, fashionable. M20.

Atlantic The romance of the boho artist for whom no social rules apply.

Bohora *noun* var. of BORA *noun*¹.

Bohr /bɔː/ *noun*. E20.
[ORIGIN Niels *Bohr* (1885–1962), Danish physicist.]
PHYSICS. Used *attrib.* with ref. to a simple theory of atomic structure in which the nucleus is surrounded by planetary electrons in quantized orbits.

bohrium /ˈbɔːrɪəm/ *noun*. L20.
[ORIGIN from BOHR + -IUM.]
A radioactive transuranic chemical element, atomic no. 107, produced artificially by high-energy atomic collisions (symbol Bh). Orig. called ***Nielsbohrium***.

bohunk /ˈbəʊhʌŋk/ *noun*. *N. Amer. slang* (*derog.*). E20.
[ORIGIN App. from BOHEMIAN + *-hunk* alt. of HUNG(ARIAN. Cf. HUNK *noun*³.]
An immigrant from central or SE Europe.

boier *noun* var. of BOYER.

boil /bɔɪl/ *noun*¹. Also †**bile**.
[ORIGIN Old English *bȳl*, *bȳle* = Old Frisian *bēle*, *beil*, Old Saxon *būla* (Dutch *buil*), Old High German *būlla* bladder (German *Beule*), from West Germanic (cf. Gothic *uf*)*bauljan* puff up, Old Norse *beyla* hump).]
An inflamed suppurating swelling of the skin, caused usu. by infection of a hair follicle.

boil /bɔɪl/ *noun*². LME.
[ORIGIN from BOIL *verb*.]
1 An act of boiling. LME. ▸**b** *spec.* An act of making tea, esp. outdoors. M20.
rolling boil: see ROLLING *adjective*.
2 Something boiled, a boiling preparation. M18.
3 (The state of being at) the boiling point. E19.
off the boil *fig.* no longer at its most active or urgent. **on the boil**, **at the boil** at boiling point (*lit. & fig.*). **to the boil** to boiling point (*lit. & fig.*).
4 A swirling upheaval of water in a river etc.; a whirlpool. *N. Amer.* E19.
5 ANGLING. A sudden rise of a fish at a fly. L19.
– COMB.: **boil-off** the evaporative loss from liquefied gases; **boil-up** an act of boiling, esp. of water for making tea.

boil /bɔɪl/ *verb*. ME.
[ORIGIN Old French *boillir* (earlier *bolir*, mod. *bouillir*) from Latin *bullire* bubble, boil, from *bulla* a bubble.]
▸ **I** *verb intrans.* **1** Of liquid: be at or reach the temperature at which it becomes a vapour; bubble up, undulate. Also predicated of the containing vessel or of any substance in the heated liquid (for cooking etc.). ME.

P. FLETCHER Boyling in sulphur, and hot-bubbling pitch. EDMUND SMITH [Pierce] the oranges as they are boiling. B. JOWETT Putting in anything that we like while the pot is boiling. J. CHEEVER He puts some water on to boil.

2 Move with agitation like boiling water; seethe. ME.

POPE The storm thickens, and the billows boil. G. SANTAYANA A torrent romantically boiled among the wildest of rocks and bushes.

3 *fig.* Of passions, persons, etc.: be stirred up or inflamed. LME.

D. HUME Resentment was boiling in his sullen, unsociable mind. C. S. FORESTER Curzon boiled with contempt for Phelps at that moment.

▸ **II** *verb trans.* **4** Subject to the heat of boiling liquid; *esp.* cook in boiling water. ME. ▸**b** *hist.* Execute (a person) by boiling. M16.

AV *Ezek.* 46:20 The place where the Priests shall boyle the trespasse offring.

5 Bring (liquid, the vessel containing it, a substance in it) to or keep at the boiling point; cause to bubble with heat; manufacture (soap etc.) by boiling. LME. ▸†**b** *fig.* Agitate or inflame (a person, feelings, etc.); make fervent. LME–E18.

H. GLASSE When you boil a leg of pork . . save the liquor. A. SIMON Add cream, but do not boil mixture again. B. PYM She never really used the kitchen except to boil a kettle or make a piece of toast.

– PHRASES: ***boil a wallop***: see WALLOP *noun* 2. **boil the kettle**, (*Austral. & NZ*) **boil the billy** *colloq.* make tea. ***boil the pot***, ***keep the pot boiling***: see POT *noun*[1]. **one's blood boils** one is in a state of extreme anger or indignation.

– WITH ADVERBS IN SPECIALIZED SENSES: **boil away** *verb phr. intrans. & trans.* (cause to) evaporate in boiling. **boil down** (***a***) *verb phr. trans.* reduce by boiling; *fig.* condense, epitomize; (***b***) *verb phr. intrans.* with *to* (*fig.*) amount to, signify basically. **boil off** *verb phr. trans.* cause to evaporate in boiling. **boil over** *verb phr. intrans.* overflow by boiling; *fig.* (of passions etc.) get out of control, (of a person) lose one's temper. **boil up** *verb phr. intrans.* (***a***) reach boiling point; (***b***) *colloq.* boil water, make tea.

boiled /bɔɪld/ *adjective & noun.* LME.
[ORIGIN from BOIL *verb* + -ED[1].]
▸ **A** *adjective.* **1** Brought to boiling point; subjected to boiling. LME.
boiled lobster: see LOBSTER *noun*[1] 2. **boiled oil** a preparation of linseed oil used as a drying oil. **boiled shirt** a dress shirt with a starched front. **boiled sweet** a sweet made of boiled sugar. ***hard-boiled***: see HARD *adjective, adverb, & noun*. ***soft-boiled***: see SOFT *adjective*.
2 Intoxicated. *slang.* L19.
▸ **B** *noun.* Boiled beef, mutton, etc. *arch. colloq.* E19.

boiler /ˈbɔɪlə/ *noun.* ME.
[ORIGIN from BOIL *verb* + -ER[1].]
1 A person who or thing which boils something. ME.
potboiler: see POT *noun*[1].
2 A vessel in which water or other liquid is boiled; *esp.* a strong vessel for generating steam under pressure in a locomotive, ship, etc.; a tank in which water is heated for central heating etc.; a metal tub for boiling laundry. E18.
Cornish boiler, ***double boiler***, ***Lancashire boiler***, ***Scotch boiler***, etc.
3 An article of food best cooked by boiling. E19.
4 An unattractive or unpleasant woman, esp. one who is middle-aged or elderly. Freq. in ***old boiler***. *colloq., derog.* M20.
– COMB.: **boilermaker** a person who makes boilers, a metal-worker in heavy industry; **boilerplate** (a piece of) rolled steel for making boilers; *fig.* (*US*) stereotyped writing esp. as syndicated for newspapers; MOUNTAINEERING (in *pl.*) smooth, overlapping, and undercut slabs of rock; **boiler suit** a one-piece garment combining overalls and shirt; **boiler tube** each of the tubes by which heat is diffused through the water in a boiler.

boilery /ˈbɔɪləri/ *noun.* E17.
[ORIGIN French *bouillerie* distillery, from *bouillir* BOIL *verb*: see -ERY.]
A place where boiling (of salt, sugar, etc.) is carried on. Freq. in *comb.*
sugar-boilery etc.

boilie /ˈbɔɪli/ *noun.* L20.
[ORIGIN Perh. from BOIL *verb* + -IE.]
A type of flavoured fishing bait, spherical in shape with a hard outer layer, used chiefly to catch carp.

boiling /ˈbɔɪlɪŋ/ *noun.* LME.
[ORIGIN from BOIL *verb* + -ING[1].]
1 The action of bubbling up under the influence of heat; the action of bringing to or keeping at the boiling point. LME.
2 *fig.* Violent agitation; raging. LME.
3 A substance or quantity of liquid subjected to boiling; a decoction. L17.
the whole boiling *slang* the whole lot.
– COMB.: **boiling point** the temperature at which a liquid (esp. water) boils; *fig.* a state of high excitement or extreme agitation.

boiling /ˈbɔɪlɪŋ/ *adjective & adverb.* ME.
[ORIGIN from BOIL *verb* + -ING[2].]
▸ **A** *adjective.* **1** (Bubbling up) at the boiling point. ME.
2 Violently agitated; raging. LME.
3 Very hot. *colloq.* M20.
▸ **B** *adverb.* ***boiling hot***, very hot. *colloq.* E17.
■ **boilingly** *adverb* (*rare*) E19.

boina /boˈina/ *noun.* E20.
[ORIGIN Spanish from Basque.]
A flat cap worn in northern Spain.

boing /bɔɪŋ/ *interjection.* Also redupl. **boing boing**. M20.
[ORIGIN Imit.]
Repr. the noise of a compressed spring suddenly released, or a reverberating sound.

bois brûlé /bwa bryle/ *noun phr. N. Amer.* Pl. ***bois brûlés*** (pronounced same). E19.
[ORIGIN French = burnt wood.]
An American Indian half-breed, *esp.* one of French and Indian descent.

bois d'arc /bwa dark/ *noun phr. N. Amer.* E19.
[ORIGIN French = bow-wood.]
The wood of the maclura (Osage orange), used by American Indians for making bows.

boiserie /bwazri/ *noun.* M19.
[ORIGIN French.]
Wainscoting, wooden panelling.

boist /bɔɪst/ *noun. obsolete* or *dial.* ME.
[ORIGIN Old French *boiste* (mod. *boîte*) from medieval Latin *buxida* from late Greek *puxid-, -is* box.]
†**1** A box, a casket. ME–M17.
2 A temporary bed or lodging place. *dial.* M19.

†**boisteous** *adjective* var. of BOISTOUS.

boisterous /ˈbɔɪst(ə)rəs/ *adjective.* LME.
[ORIGIN Alt. of BOISTOUS, through var. of *-eous*.]
†**1** Coarse in texture; rank; stiff, unyielding. LME–E18.
†**2** Of a thing: violent in action or properties. M16–L17.
3 Rough and turbulent in behaviour and speech; (now *esp.*) exuberant, noisily cheerful. M16. ▸†**b** Savage, truculent. L16–L18. ▸**c** Of wind, weather, etc.: rough, stormy, wild. L16.

Harper's Magazine The sounds of song and boisterous revelry.

†**4** Rough in effect or operation. L16–E17.
†**5** Massive, bulky, cumbrous. L16–M17.
■ **boisterously** *adverb* LME. **boisterousness** *noun* LME.

boistous /ˈbɔɪstəs/ *adjective.* Long *obsolete* exc. *dial.* Also **bustious** /ˈbʌstɪəs/; †**-eous**, †**-uous**. ME.
[ORIGIN Unknown.]
†**1** Of a person: rustic, coarse, unpolished. ME–M16.
2 Massive, bulky. Now only of a person: corpulent. ME.
†**3** Fierce, powerful, rough. LME–E19.
†**4** Coarse in texture. LME–L16.
■ †**boistously** *adverb* LME–L16. †**boistousness** *noun* LME–L16.

boîte /bwat/ *noun.* Pl. pronounced same. E20.
[ORIGIN French = box.]
A small (French) restaurant or nightclub.

bokay /bəʊˈkeɪ/ *noun. non-standard.* M19.
[ORIGIN Repr. a pronunc.]
= BOUQUET.

bok choy *noun* see PAK CHOI.

†**boke** *noun*[1] var. of BOKO.

boke /bəʊk/ *verb*[1] *trans. obsolete* exc. *dial.* M16.
[ORIGIN App. var. of POKE *verb*[1].]
Prod, butt.

boke *verb*[2] *& noun*[2] var. of BOLK.

Bok globule *noun phr.* see GLOBULE 3.

Bokhara /bəˈkɑːrə/ *noun.* E20.
[ORIGIN *Bukhara*, a town and district in Uzbekistan, central Asia.]
A Turkoman rug or carpet (most commonly having red as the main colour).

bokken /ˈbɒk(ə)n/ *noun.* M20.
[ORIGIN Japanese.]
A wooden sword used as a practice weapon in kendo.

Bokmaal *noun* var. of BOKMÅL.

bokmakierie /bɒkməˈkɪəri/ *noun. S. Afr.* M19.
[ORIGIN Afrikaans, imit. of the bird's call.]
A yellow, green, and black shrike, *Telophorus zeylonus*, of southern Africa.

Bokmål /ˈboːkmɔːl/ *noun.* Also ***Bokmaal***. M20.
[ORIGIN Norwegian, from *bok* BOOK *noun* + *mål* language.]
The Danish language as modified and used in Norway after its separation from Denmark. Cf. LANDSMÅL, RIKSMÅL.

boko /ˈbəʊkəʊ/ *noun. slang.* Pl. **-os**. Also †**boke**. M19.
[ORIGIN Unknown.]
The nose.

bola *noun* see BOLAS.

bolar /ˈbəʊlə/ *adjective.* L17.
[ORIGIN from BOLE *noun*[2] + -AR[1].]
Consisting or of the nature of bole clay.
■ Also †**bolary** *adjective* (*rare*): only in M17.

bolas /ˈbəʊləs/ *noun sing.* (with pl. **bolases**) or *pl.* Also (*sing.*) **bola** /ˈbəʊlə/. E19.
[ORIGIN Spanish, Portuguese, pl. of *bola* ball.]
A missile (chiefly S. American) consisting of balls connected by a strong cord, which is thrown to entangle the legs of a quarry.

bold /bəʊld/ *adjective, adverb, & noun.*
[ORIGIN Old English *bald*, (West Saxon) *beald* = Old Saxon *bald* (Dutch *boud*), Old High German *bald* (Middle High German *balt*, surviving in German adverb *bald* soon), Old Norse *ballr* dangerous, fatal, from Germanic.]
▸ **A** *adjective.* **1** Courageous, enterprising, confident, stout-hearted; daring, brave. OE.

MILTON The bold design Pleas'd highly those infernal States. R. GRAVES Nobody could be found bold enough to take their places. W. S. MAUGHAM Though attered, he put on a bold front.

2 Presumptuous, forward, immodest. ME.

K. A. PORTER The girl . . had fine eyes, but her bold, airy manner spoiled her looks.

3 Strong, big. Now *dial.* or *obsolete*. ME.

ALLAN RAMSAY Boreas with his blasts sae bauld.

†**4** Certain, sure (*of*), trusting (*in*). ME–E17.

SHAKES. *Cymb.* I would I were so sure To win the King as I am bold her honour Will remain hers.

5 Of a cliff, coast, etc.: steep, projecting, bluff. Also (NAUTICAL), used of water close to a steeply shelved shore. E17.
6 Striking, well marked, clear; free or vigorous in conception etc. M17. ▸**b** TYPOGRAPHY. Of type: having a heavy and conspicuous appearance. L19.

S. JOHNSON I do not think Gray a first-rate poet. He has not a bold imagination.

– PHRASES: ***as bold as brass***: see BRASS *noun*. **make bold** (**as**), **make so bold** (**as**), **be so bold** (**as**) venture, presume, (*to do*). †**make bold with** take liberties with. ***put a bold face on***: see FACE *noun*.
– COMB.: **boldface** *noun & adjective* (***a***) (a person who is) impudent; (***b***) TYPOGRAPHY bold (type); **boldfaced** *adjective* (***a***) that looks bold, impudent; (***b***) TYPOGRAPHY = sense 6b above.
▸ **B** *adverb.* In a bold manner. Now *rare*. ME.
▸ **C** *absol.* as *noun.* **1** A bold person. Now only as collect. pl. ***the bold***. ME.
2 TYPOGRAPHY. Bold type. L19.
■ **boldly** *adverb* OE. **boldness** *noun* ME.

bold /bəʊld/ *verb.* Long *obsolete* exc. *Scot. & N. English.*
[ORIGIN Old English *baldian* = Old High German *baldēn*, from BOLD *adjective, adverb, & noun*.]
†**1** *verb intrans.* Be or appear bold; grow strong. OE–E18.
†**2** *verb trans.* Embolden, encourage. ME–E17.
3 *verb trans.* Kindle (glowing coals); blow up (a fire). LME.

boldacious /bəʊlˈdeɪʃəs/ *adjective. dial.* L19.
[ORIGIN from BOLD *adjective* + AUDACIOUS.]
Impudent, brazen.

bolden /ˈbəʊld(ə)n/ *verb trans. obsolete* exc. *dial.* E16.
[ORIGIN from BOLD *adjective* + -EN[5].]
Embolden.

boldo /ˈbɒldəʊ/ *noun.* Pl. **-os**. E18.
[ORIGIN Amer. Spanish from Mapuche *voldo*.]
A Chilean evergreen tree, *Peumus boldus*. Also, a medicinal preparation of its leaves, formerly used as a tonic.

bole /bəʊl/ *noun*[1]. ME.
[ORIGIN Old Norse *bolr*: cf. Middle High German *bole* (German *Bohle*) plank. Perh. rel. to BAULK *noun*.]
The stem or trunk of a tree.

bole /bəʊl/ *noun*[2]. ME.
[ORIGIN Late Latin BOLUS.]
1 Any of various kinds of fine, compact, earthy clay, usu. coloured by the presence of iron oxide. ME.
Armenian bole, †**bole Armeniac** an astringent earth from Armenia, formerly used as an antidote and styptic.
†**2** = BOLUS *noun* 1a. E17–E18.

bole /bəʊl/ *noun*[3]. *Scot.* Also (earlier) †**bowall**, **-ell**. E16.
[ORIGIN Unknown.]
1 A small recess in a wall for holding articles; a small cupboard. E16.
2 An unglazed (usu. shuttered) aperture in a wall for admitting air or light. E19.

†**bole** *noun*[4]. L17–M19.
[ORIGIN Anglo-Latin *bola*, of unknown origin.]
A place or furnace where lead ores were anciently smelted.

bolection /bəˈlɛkʃ(ə)n/ *adjective & noun.* Also **ba-**. M17.
[ORIGIN Unknown.]
(Designating) a decorative moulding above or around a panel etc.

bolero /bəˈlɛːrəʊ, *in sense 2 also* ˈbɒlərəʊ/ *noun.* Pl. **-os**. L18.
[ORIGIN Spanish.]
1 A lively Spanish dance; a piece of music for this dance. L18.
2 A short jacket just reaching the waist, worn by men in Spain; a woman's short open jacket, with or without sleeves. L19.

B

B

boletus /bəˈliːtəs/ *noun*. Pl. **-ti** /-tʌɪ/, **-tuses**, same. Also anglicized as **bolet** /bəˈlɛt/, **-lete** /-ˈliːt/. E16.
[ORIGIN Latin, from Greek *bōlitēs*, perh. from *bōlos* lump.]
A mushroom or toadstool of the large genus *Boletus*, having the undersurface of the cap full of pores.

bolide /ˈbəʊlʌɪd/ *noun*. E19.
[ORIGIN French from Latin *bolid-*, *bolis*, from Greek *bolis* missile.]
A large meteor, a fireball.

bolivar /bɒlɪˈvɑː, bɒˈliːvɑː/ *noun*. L19.
[ORIGIN from *Bolívar*: see BOLIVIAN.]
The basic monetary unit of Venezuela, equal to 100 céntimos.

Bolivian /bəˈlɪvɪən/ *adjective & noun*. M19.
[ORIGIN from *Bolivia* (see below), from Simón *Bolívar* (1783–1830), S. Amer. soldier and statesman: see -AN.]
(A native or inhabitant) of Bolivia, a republic in S. America.

boliviano /bəlɪvɪˈɑːnəʊ/ *noun*. Pl. **-os**. L19.
[ORIGIN Spanish, formed as BOLIVIAN.]
The basic monetary unit of Bolivia (1863–1962 and since 1987), equal to 100 centavos or cents.

bolk /bəʊk/ *verb & noun*. *dial*. Also **boke**. ME.
[ORIGIN Var. of BELCH *verb*.]
► **A** *verb intrans. & trans.* Belch, vomit, retch. ME.
► **B** *noun*. A belch, a vomiting. LME.

boll /bəʊl/ *noun*[1]. ME.
[ORIGIN Middle Dutch *bolle*, Dutch *bol* round object: corresp. to Old English *bolla* BOWL *noun*[1].]
†**1** A bubble. Only in ME.
2 A rounded seed vessel or pod, esp. of flax or cotton. LME.
– COMB.: **boll weevil** a weevil, *Anthonomus grandis*, which is a pest of cotton plants in N. America; **bollworm** (chiefly *US*) an insect pest of cotton, *esp*. (**a**) the boll weevil or its larva; (**b**) = ***corn earworm*** s.v. CORN *noun*[1]; (**c**) = ***pink bollworm*** s.v. PINK *adjective*[2].
■ †**bolled** *adjective* having bolls M16–M17.

boll /bəʊl/ *noun*[2]. ME.
[ORIGIN Old Norse *bolli* (cf. *blótbolli* sacrificial bowl) = Old English *bolla* BOWL *noun*[1]: cf. BOLL *noun*[1].]
A dry measure for grain etc., most commonly equivalent to six bushels.

†**boll** *noun*[3] var. of BOWL *noun*[1].

Bollandist /ˈbɒləndɪst/ *noun*. M18.
[ORIGIN from *Bolland* (see below) + -IST.]
Any of the Jesuit writers who continued *Acta Sanctorum*, first published by the Flemish Jesuit John Bolland (1595–1665).

bollard /ˈbɒlɑːd, -ləd/ *noun*. ME.
[ORIGIN Perh. from Old Norse *bolr* BOLE *noun*[1] + -ARD.]
1 A post on a ship, quay, etc., for securing ropes to. ME.
2 A post on a traffic island. M20.
– NOTE: After an isolated ME use not recorded again until 19.

bollen *verb pa. pple* of BELL *verb*[2].

bollito misto /bɒˌliːtəʊ ˈmɪstəʊ/ *noun phr.* Pl. **bolliti misti** /bɒˌliːti ˈmɪsti/. L20.
[ORIGIN Italian = boiled mixed (meat).]
An Italian dish of mixed meats, as chicken, veal, and sausage, boiled with vegetables in broth.

bollix /ˈbɒlɪks/ *verb & noun pl.* *coarse slang*. Also **-lux** /-ləks/. M20.
[ORIGIN Alt. of *bollocks*, pl. of BOLLOCK *noun*.]
► **A** *verb trans.* Bungle, confuse; mess *up*. M20.
► **B** *noun*. **1** A mess, a state of confusion. M20.
2 A foolish or contemptible man. *Irish*. M20.

bollock /ˈbɒlək/ *noun*. *coarse slang*. Pl. **-s**, BOLLIX. M18.
[ORIGIN Var. of BALLOCK *noun*.]
1 A testicle. Usu. in *pl*. M18.
2 *fig*. In *pl*. (treated as *sing*.). Nonsense; a mess, a muddle. Also as *interjection*. E20.

bollock /ˈbɒlək/ *verb trans.* *coarse slang*. Also **ballock**. M20.
[ORIGIN from the noun.]
Reprimand severely. Freq. as ***bollocking*** *verbal noun*

R. TREMAIN He doesn't bollock me or threaten me with expulsion. I. RANKIN Is he in for a bollocking?

bollux *verb & noun pl.* var. of BOLLIX.

Bollywood /ˈbɒlɪwʊd/ *noun*. *colloq*. L20.
[ORIGIN Blend of *Bombay* and HOLLYWOOD.]
The Indian popular film industry, based in the city of Bombay (Mumbai).

attrib.: S. RUSHDIE Why must everything I say end up sounding like . . a goddam cheap Bollywood song?

bolo /ˈbəʊləʊ/ *noun*[1]. Also **B-**. Pl. **-os**. E20.
[ORIGIN Paul *Bolo*, a Frenchman executed in 1918 for pro-German activities: later reinforced by association with BOLSHEVIK.]
A Bolshevik, a Communist.

bolo /ˈbəʊləʊ/ *noun*[2]. *US*. Pl. **-os**. M20.
[ORIGIN Unknown.]
BOXING. An uppercut.

bolo /ˈbəʊləʊ/ *noun*[3]. *N. Amer.* Pl. **-os**. M20.
[ORIGIN Alt. of *bola* (see BOLAS).]
In full ***bolo tie***. A type of tie consisting of a cord worn around the neck with a large ornamental fastening at the throat.

Bologna /bəˈləʊnjə, -ˈlɒn-/ *noun*. M19.
[ORIGIN A city in Italy.]
1 (Also **b-**.) In full ***Bologna sausage***. A large sausage made of bacon, veal, pork suet, etc. and usu. sold ready for eating cold. M19.
2 ***Bologna spar***, ***Bologna stone***, native barium sulphate from near Bologna, exhibiting phosphorescence when calcined. L19.
■ **Bolognian** *adjective* of or pertaining to Bologna L16.

Bolognese /bɒləˈn(j)eɪz, *foreign* boloˈɲeːze/ *noun & adjective*. M18.
[ORIGIN Italian: see BOLOGNA, -ESE.]
► **A** *noun*. Pl. same.
1 *hist.*. *The* territory of Bologna, in Italy. M18.
2 A native or inhabitant of Bologna. E19.
3 The Italian dialect of Bologna. M19.
► **B** *adjective*. Of or pertaining to Bologna. E19.
SPAGHETTI ***Bolognese***.

bolometer /bəˈlɒmɪtə/ *noun*. L19.
[ORIGIN from Greek *bolē* ray of light + -OMETER.]
PHYSICS. An instrument for measuring the intensity of electromagnetic radiation (esp. infrared and microwaves) electrically.
■ **boloˈmetric** *adjective* of, pertaining to, employing, or measured by a bolometer; ***bolometric magnitude*** (*ASTRONOMY*), a measure of the total energy emitted (e.g. by a star) over all wavelengths: L19. **boloˈmetrically** *adverb* M20. **bolometry** *noun* E20.

boloney *noun* var. of BALONEY.

Bolshevik /ˈbɒlʃɪvɪk/ *noun & adjective*. E20.
[ORIGIN Russian *bol'shevik* = member of the majority, from *bol'she* greater from *bol'shoĭ* big.]
► **A** *noun*. **1** *hist.* A member of the majority faction of the Russian Social Democratic Party, which in 1903 favoured extreme measures; an advocate of proletarian dictatorship in Russia by soviets; a Russian Communist. Cf. MENSHEVIK *noun*. E20.
2 *gen*. A socialist revolutionary. E20.
► **B** *adjective*. Of or pertaining to Bolsheviks or Bolshevism. E20.
■ **Bolshevism** *noun* the doctrine and practices of the Bolsheviks; revolutionary communism: E20. **Bolshevist** *noun & adjective* = BOLSHEVIK E20. **Bolshevize** *verb trans.* make Bolshevik; convert (a country etc.) to Bolshevik government: E20.

Bolshie /ˈbɒlʃi/ *noun & adjective*. *slang*. Also **-shy**, **b-**. E20.
[ORIGIN from BOLSHEVIK + -Y[6].]
► **A** *noun*. = BOLSHEVIK *noun*. E20.
► **B** *adjective*. = BOLSHEVIK *adjective*; left-wing; uncooperative, recalcitrant. E20.
■ **bolshiness** *noun* L20.

bolson /ˈbəʊls(ə)n/ *noun*. Orig. *US*. M19.
[ORIGIN Spanish *bolsón* augm. of *bolsa* purse.]
A basin-shaped depression surrounded by mountains, esp. in the southern US and Mexico.

bolster /ˈbəʊlstə/ *noun*[1].
[ORIGIN Old English *bolster* = Middle Dutch & mod. Dutch *bolster*, Old High German *bolstar* (German *Polster*), Old Norse *bolstr*, from Germanic, perh. from base meaning 'swell': cf. BELLY *noun*.]
1 A long pillow or cushion for the head of a resting or sleeping person; now *esp*. a long thick pillow placed under other pillows for support. OE.
2 Any of various kinds of padding or support, esp. in a machine or instrument; *NAUTICAL* a piece of wood fitted to prevent chafing. E16. ►†**b** A surgical compress. M16–E19.

bolster /ˈbəʊlstə/ *noun*[2]. E20.
[ORIGIN Prob. alt. of BOASTER *noun*[2].]
A heavy chisel used to cut bricks etc.

bolster /ˈbəʊlstə/ *verb*. E16.
[ORIGIN from BOLSTER *noun*[1].]
1 *verb trans.* Support with a bolster; *fig.* prop up, aid, strengthen; uphold, aid and abet (evil, wrongdoers, etc.). Freq. foll. by *up*. E16.

WELLINGTON I have done every thing in my power to bolster up the credit of the government. M. DRABBLE Inseparable friends, who bolstered each other by their mutual devotion. *Daedalus* The Inquisitors had bolstered their principal accusation with . . vague secondary charges.

2 *verb trans.* Pad; stuff out with padding. M16. ►†**b** Equip with a surgical compress. E17–M19.
†**3** *verb intrans.* Share the same pillow. *rare* (Shakes.). Only in E17.
4 *verb trans.* Belabour with bolsters. M19.
■ **bolstering** *noun* (**a**) the action of the verb; (**b**) padding, support: M16.

bolt /bəʊlt/ *noun*[1].
[ORIGIN Old English *bolt* = Middle Low German *bolte(n)* bolt, fetter, Middle Dutch & mod. Dutch *bout*, Old High German *bolz* (German *Bolzen*) arrow, bolt for a door: of unknown origin.]
► **I** A projectile.
1 An arrow, *esp*. a short heavy one for a crossbow. OE.
have shot one's bolt *fig.* have done all one can.
2 A discharge of lightning with a clap of thunder. (Earlier in THUNDERBOLT.) L16.
bolt from the blue, **bolt out of the blue** *fig.* something completely unexpected.
► **II 3** A stout pin for fastening; a door fastening comprising a sliding bar and a socket on a jamb, lintel, or threshold; a metal pin with a head for holding things together, usu. secured with a nut or riveted. ME.
expansion bolt, ***joint bolt***, ***safety bolt***, ***screw bolt***, ***toggle bolt***, etc. ***nuts and bolts***: see NUT *noun*.
†**4** A fetter. L15–L17.
5 The sliding piece of the breech mechanism of a rifle. M19.
► **III 6** A measure of rolled fabric. ME.
7 A bundle of osiers etc. of a certain size. ME.
– COMB.: **bolt head** (**a**) the head of a bolt; (**b**) *arch.* a long-necked globular flask used in distillation; **bolt rope** a rope sewn round the edge of a sail to prevent tearing.
■ **boltless** *adjective* M19.

bolt /bəʊlt/ *noun*[2]. Also **boult**. LME.
[ORIGIN from BOLT *verb*[1].]
1 A flour sieve. Long *dial*. LME.
2 *hist.* A hypothetical law case privately propounded and argued for practice by students of the Inns of Court. M16.

bolt /bəʊlt/ *noun*[3]. M16.
[ORIGIN from BOLT *verb*[2].]
1 A sudden start. M16.
2 An act of breaking away or fleeing. Freq. in ***make a bolt***. M19.

bolt /bəʊlt/ *verb*[1] *trans.* Also **boult**. ME.
[ORIGIN Old French *bulter* (mod. *bluter*), earlier *buleter* = Italian *burattare*, ult. origin unknown: the spelling *bolt* has arisen by assoc. with BOLT *noun*[1].]
Sift, pass through a sieve; *fig.* investigate, find out.
■ **bolter** *noun*[1] (**a**) a person who sifts flour etc.; (**b**) a sieve, a piece of cloth, etc., for sifting: LME. **bolting** *noun*[1] (**a**) the action of the verb; (**b**) in *pl*., coarse matter separated by sifting: ME.

bolt /bəʊlt/ *verb*[2]. ME.
[ORIGIN from BOLT *noun*[1].]
► **I** Move suddenly.
†**1** *verb intrans.* Spring or start (*up*, *upright*); fall back, recoil. ME–E19.

SIR W. SCOTT Screaming with agony and fright, He bolted twenty feet upright.

2 *verb trans.* Discharge like a bolt; shoot, expel. LME. ►**b** Cause (an animal) to leave its hole or burrow. L16.
3 *verb intrans.* Move suddenly, dart, rush, (*away*, *forth*, *off*); flee, escape; spring, bound, (*into*, †*upon*). E16. ►**b** Of a rabbit, fox, etc.: escape from its burrow or earth. Of a horse: escape from control. L16.

N. HAWTHORNE The landlord . . keeping his eye on a man who he suspected of an intention to bolt. D. LODGE They seemed to avoid him, bolting into their offices just as he emerged from his own.

4 *verb trans.* Ejaculate, blurt (*out*, *forth*). L16.
5 *verb trans.* Gulp down or *down* hastily without chewing. *colloq.* L18.

L. LEE I sprinkled some sugar on a slice of bread and bolted it down.

6 *verb trans. & intrans.* Break away from, refuse to support further, (a political party etc.). *US colloq.* E19.
7 *verb intrans.* Of a plant: run to seed. L19.
► **II** Make fast.
†**8** *verb trans.* Fetter, shackle. LME–E17.
9 *verb trans.* Secure (a door etc.) with a bolt; shut *in*, *out*, *up*, etc., thus. L16.

R. HAYMAN It is useless to bolt the door against him: he breaks it down with an axe.

10 *verb trans.* Fasten (together) with bolts. E18.

J. BRAINE My feet seemed bolted to the floor.

11 *verb intrans.* Of a door etc.: be secured with a bolt (in a particular manner). E20.
– COMB.: **bolt-hole** a hole by which to escape; **bolt-on** *adjective* (of car parts etc.) able to be fixed by bolts; *fig.* able to be added when required.
■ **bolter** *noun*[2] a person who or thing which bolts, *esp.* (**a**) a horse etc. liable to bolt; (**b**) *AUSTRAL. HISTORY* a fugitive: L17. **bolting** *noun*[2] (**a**) the action of the verb (***bolting hole*** = ***bolt-hole*** above); (**b**) a sudden flight etc.: L17.

bolt /bəʊlt/ *adverb*. ME.
[ORIGIN from BOLT *noun*[1], *verb*[2].]
1 ***bolt upright***, †***bolt up***, rigidly erect (like a bolt). ME.
2 With sudden rapid motion. E19.

T. HOOD Bolt up the stairs they ran.

■ **bolt-ˈuprightness** *noun* E18.

boltel /ˈbəʊlt(ə)l/ *noun*. Also **bowtell** /ˈbaʊt(ə)l/. LME.
[ORIGIN Unknown.]
ARCHITECTURE. A plain round moulding; a shaft of a clustered pillar.

bolter *noun*[1], *noun*[2] see BOLT *verb*[1], *verb*[2].

bolter *noun*[3] var. of BOULTER.

bolter *verb* var. of BALTER *verb*[2].

Boltzmann /ˈbəʊltsmən/ *noun*. L19.
[ORIGIN Ludwig *Boltzmann* (1844–1906), Austrian physicist.]
PHYSICS. Used *attrib.* and in *possess.* to designate various concepts, esp. relating to the statistical description of large systems of molecules obeying classical mechanics.
Boltzmann constant: see ***Boltzmann's constant*** below. **Boltzmann distribution** (a formula describing) the statistical distribution of particles in a system among different energy levels, proportional to exp. $(-E/kT)$, where E is the level energy, k is Boltzmann's constant, and T is the absolute temperature. **Boltzmann's constant**, **Boltzmann constant** the gas constant per molecule, equal to 1.381×10^{-23} joule per kelvin. STEFAN-BOLTZMANN.

bolus /ˈbəʊləs/ *noun & verb*. M16.
[ORIGIN Late Latin from Greek *bōlos* clod, lump of earth.]
▸ **A** *noun* **1 a** A large pill of medicine. Often *derog. arch.* exc. VETERINARY MEDICINE (cf. sense 1c below). M16. ▸**b** A small rounded mass of anything, esp. of masticated food at the moment of swallowing. L18. ▸**c** MEDICINE. A single dose of a pharmaceutical preparation given intravenously. M20.
2 = BOLE *noun*[2] 1. Now *rare* or *obsolete*. L16.
▸ **B** *verb trans.* Dose with a bolus or boluses. M18.

boma /ˈbəʊmə/ *noun*. *E. Afr.* L19.
[ORIGIN Kiswahili.]
A defensible enclosure, esp. for animals; a police or military post; a magistrate's office.

bomb /bɒm/ *noun*. L16.
[ORIGIN French *bombe* from Italian *bomba* prob. from Latin *bombus* from Greek *bombos* booming, humming, of imit. origin.]
†**1** ***bomb of fire*** [translating Spanish *bomba de fuego*], a fireball (weapon). Only in L16.
2 Orig., an explosive projectile fired from a mortar. Now, a container filled with high explosive or incendiary material, smoke, poison gas, etc., or a body of high explosive etc., which may be dropped from an aircraft, fired from a gun, thrown, or deposited manually, and is exploded in various ways. L17.
atomic bomb, ***buzz bomb***, ***hydrogen bomb***, ***incendiary bomb***, ***Mills bomb***, ***nuclear bomb***, ***plastic bomb***, ***smoke bomb***, ***Stokes bomb***, ***time bomb***, etc.
3 *hist.* In full ***bomb-ketch***, ***bomb-vessel***, etc. A small naval vessel equipped with one or more mortars for throwing bombs. L17.
4 More fully ***volcanic bomb***, ***lava bomb***. A rounded mass of lava thrown out of a volcano. L18.
5 An airtight vessel used to conduct scientific experiments under pressure. E20.
6 A large sum of money. *colloq.* M20.

> M. FRAYN It must have cost a bomb.

7 An old road vehicle. *Austral. & NZ slang.* M20.
8 A marijuana cigarette. *slang.* M20.
9 AMER. FOOTBALL. A long pass or kick. M20.
– PHRASES: **go down a bomb** *colloq.* be a great success. **like a bomb** *colloq.* at great speed; very successfully. **the bomb** the atomic or hydrogen bomb as the supreme weapon.
– COMB.: **bomb bay** a compartment in an aircraft for holding bombs; **bomb calorimeter** a thick-walled steel container used in experiments to determine the energy contained in a substance by measuring the heat generated during its combustion; **bomb disposal** the defusing, or removal and detonation, of unexploded and delayed-action bombs; **bomb factory** a factory or other place where bombs are made, esp. illegally by terrorists; **bomb-happy** *adjective* (*colloq.*) shell-shocked; ***bomb-ketch***: see sense 3 above; **bombproof** *adjective & noun* (**a**) *adjective* able to resist attack by bombs; *US* not exposed to the dangers of war; (**b**) *noun* a bombproof shelter; *US* = ***bombproofer*** below; **bombproofer** *US* a person who avoids exposure to the dangers of war; **bombshell** an artillery shell; *fig.* a devastating or shattering act, event, etc. (***blonde bombshell***, a fair-haired person, esp. a woman, regarded as having a startling physique or good looks); **bombsight** a device used in an aircraft for aiming bombs; **bomb site** an area where buildings have been destroyed by bombing; **bomb squad** a division of a police force appointed to investigate the planting and exploding of terrorist bombs; ***bomb-vessel***: see sense 3 above.
■ **bomblet** *noun* a small bomb M20.

bomb /bɒm/ *verb*. L17.
[ORIGIN from the noun.]
1 *verb trans. & intrans.* Attack with a bomb or bombs; throw or drop a bomb or bombs (on). L17. ▸**b** *verb trans.* Drive *out* of a building etc. by bombing. E20.

> I. B. SINGER The building where both of them lived was bombed.

2 *verb trans.* Foll. by *up*: load (an aircraft) with bombs. M20.
3 *verb intrans.* Fail, flop. *colloq.* (orig. *US*). M20.

> M. MEDVED The movie promptly bombed at the box office.

4 *verb intrans.* Move or travel quickly. Usu. with adverb or adverbial phr. *colloq.* M20.

> N. COHN At weekends, they bombed up and down the coastline in their hotrods.

■ **bombing** *verbal noun* L17.

†**bombace** *noun*. See also BOMBAST *noun*. M16–M17.
[ORIGIN Old French from medieval Latin *bombax*, *-acis*, alt. of BOMBYX. Cf. BOMBAZINE.]
Raw cotton; cotton fibre for padding etc.

bombachas /bɒmˈbatʃəz/ *noun pl.* M20.
[ORIGIN S. Amer. Spanish, from *bombacho* loose-fitting, wide.]
Baggy trousers worn in some S. American countries.

bombard /ˈbɒmbɑːd/ *noun*. In sense 2 also **-de**. LME.
[ORIGIN Old French & mod. French *bombarde*, medieval Latin *bombarda*, prob. from Latin *bombus*: see BOMB *noun*.]
1 *hist.* A cannon of the earliest type, usu. firing stone cannonballs. LME.
2 MUSIC. A low-pitched shawm. LME. ▸**b** A bombardon stop in an organ. L19.
3 A leather jug or bottle for liquor. *obsolete* exc. *hist.* L16.
†**4** = BOMB *noun* 3. L18–M19.

bombard /bɒmˈbɑːd/ *verb*. L16.
[ORIGIN French *bombarder*, formed as BOMBARD *noun*.]
1 *verb trans. &* †*intrans.* Fire heavy guns at, batter with shot and shell, assault with artillery. L16.
2 *verb trans. transf. & fig.* Assail forcefully (*with* arguments, questions, abuse, etc.); subject to a hail of missiles. M18. ▸**b** PHYSICS. Subject (a substance) to a stream of high-energy particles. E20.
3 *verb trans.* Stuff (a fillet of veal). Now *rare* or *obsolete*. M18.
■ **bombarder** *noun* L16. **bombardment** *noun* E18.

bombardier /bɒmbəˈdɪə/ *noun*. M16.
[ORIGIN French: see BOMBARD *noun*, -IER.]
1 A soldier in charge of a bombard, an artilleryman; a master gunner's man employed with mortars and howitzers. Now *arch.* or *hist.* M16.
2 In the British army, a non-commissioned officer in the artillery. M19.
3 A person who aims and releases bombs from an aircraft. *N. Amer.* M20.
– COMB.: **bombardier beetle** any of various carabid beetles able to eject audibly an irritant vapour when alarmed; spec. *Brachinus crepitans*, found in Britain.

bombardon /ˈbɒmbɑːd(ə)n/ *noun*. Also **-done** /-ˈdəʊni/. M19.
[ORIGIN Italian *bombardone* augm. of *bombardo* BOMBARD *noun*.]
MUSIC. A low-pitched brass instrument of the tuba family; an organ reed stop imitating this.

†**bombase** *verb trans.* See also BOMBAST *adjective*. M–L16.
[ORIGIN from BOMBACE.]
Stuff (with cotton wool), pad.

bombasine *noun* var. of BOMBAZINE.

bombast /ˈbɒmbast/ *noun*. M16.
[ORIGIN Var. of BOMBACE.]
1 Raw cotton; cotton wool, esp. as padding. *obsolete* exc. *hist.* M16.
2 *fig.* Inflated, turgid, or high-sounding language; empty rhetoric. L16.
■ **bomˈbastic** *adjective* of the nature of bombast; given to inflated language: E18. **bomˈbastical** *adjective* (*arch.*) = BOMBASTIC M17. **bomˈbastically** *adverb* E19.

bombast /ˈbɒmbast/ *adjective*. M16.
[ORIGIN Orig. pa. pple of BOMBASE *verb*; later = the noun used attrib.]
†**1** Stuffed, padded. M16–M17.
2 *fig.* Puffed, empty, inflated; grandiloquent, bombastic. E17.

bombast /bɒmˈbast, ˈbɒmbast/ *verb trans. arch.* M16.
[ORIGIN from the noun.]
†**1** Stuff or pad with cotton wool or the like. M16–E19.
2 *fig.* Stuff, swell out, inflate. M16.

bombax /ˈbɒmbaks/ *noun*[1]. M19.
[ORIGIN mod. Latin from Latin BOMBYX.]
Any deciduous tropical tree of the genus *Bombax*, bearing fruit containing seeds surrounded by a silky fibre; *esp.* the Indian silk-cotton tree, *B. ceiba*.

†**bombax** *noun*[2] var. of BOMBYX.

Bombay duck /ˌbɒmbeɪ ˈdʌk, bɒmˌbeɪ/ *noun phr.* M19.
[ORIGIN Alt. of *bombil* (see BUMMALO), infl. by *Bombay* (now Mumbai), a city in India.]
Bummalo, esp. dried as a relish.

Bombay mix /ˌbɒmbeɪ ˈmɪks, bɒmˌbeɪ/ *noun phr.* L20.
[ORIGIN from *Bombay* (see BOMBAY DUCK) + MIX *noun*.]
An Indian snack consisting of lentils, peanuts, sev, and spices.

bombazine /ˈbɒmbəziːn/ *noun*. Also **-sine**. M16.
[ORIGIN Old French & mod. French *bombasin* from medieval Latin *bombacinum* from *bombycinum* neut. of *bombycinus* silken, from BOMBYX: see -INE[1].]
†**1** = BOMBACE. M–L16.
2 A twilled dress material of worsted with or without silk or cotton; *esp.* a black kind formerly much used in mourning. L16.

bombe /bɒmb, *foreign* bɔ̃ːb (*pl. same*)/ *noun*. L19.
[ORIGIN French = BOMB *noun*.]
A conical or cup-shaped confection, freq. frozen.

bombé /bɔ̃be/ *adjective*. E20.
[ORIGIN French, pa. pple of *bomber* swell out: cf. BOMBED *adjective*[1].]
Esp. of furniture: rounded, convex.

bombed /bɒmd, *poet.* ˈbɒmbɪd/ *adjective*[1]. *rare*. L19.
[ORIGIN formed as BOMBÉ + -ED[1].]
Rounded, convex.

bombed /bɒmd/ *adjective*[2]. M20.
[ORIGIN from BOMB *verb* + -ED[1]]
1 Subjected to bombing; ***bombed-out***, driven out by bombing, rendered uninhabitable by bombing. M20.
2 Intoxicated by drink or drugs. Also ***bombed-out***. M20.

bomber /ˈbɒmə/ *noun*. E20.
[ORIGIN from BOMB *verb* + -ER[1].]
1 A person who throws, plants, activates, or is otherwise involved in the use of, bombs, esp. as a terrorist. E20.
2 An aircraft used for dropping bombs. E20.
3 A large rolled cigarette containing marijuana, cannabis resin, etc. Also, a barbiturate drug. *slang*. M20.
– COMB.: **bomber jacket** a short zipped jacket tightly gathered at the waist and cuffs.

bombilate /ˈbɒmbɪleɪt/ *verb intrans. literary*. L19.
[ORIGIN medieval Latin *bombilat-* pa. ppl stem of *bombilare* buzz, from Latin *bombus*: see BOMB *noun*, -ATE[3]. Cf. BOMBINATE.]
Buzz, hum.
■ **bombiˈlation** *noun* M17.

bombilla /bɒmˈbɪljə/ *noun*. M19.
[ORIGIN Amer. Spanish, dim. of Spanish *bomba* strainer.]
A tube with a strainer at the end, from which maté is drunk in S. America.

bombinate /ˈbɒmbɪneɪt/ *verb intrans. literary*. L19.
[ORIGIN medieval Latin *bombinat-* pa. ppl stem of *bombinare* buzz, from Latin *bombus*: see BOMB *noun*, -ATE[3]. Cf. BOMBILATE.]
Buzz, hum.
■ **bombiˈnation** *noun* E19.

bombo /ˈbɒmbəʊ/ *noun*. Pl. **-os**. L20.
[ORIGIN Spanish, from Latin *bombus*: see BOMB *noun*.]
A large, deep bass drum, used in traditional Portuguese, Spanish, and S. American music.

bombora /bɒmˈbɔːrə/ *noun*. *Austral.* L19.
[ORIGIN Perh. from Dharuk *bumbora*.]
A dangerous stretch of water where waves break over a submerged reef.

bombyx /ˈbɒmbɪks/ *noun*. Also †**-ax**. LME.
[ORIGIN Latin from Greek *bombux*.]
A silkworm or silkworm moth.
■ **bombykol** *noun* a pheromone secreted by the female of the silkworm moth *Bombyx mori* M20.

bon /bɔ̃/ *adjective*. L16.
[ORIGIN French: see BOON *adjective*.]
The French (masc.) for 'good', occurring in various phrases used in English
■ ***bon appétit*** /bɔn apeti/ [lit. 'good appetite']: used as a salutation to a person about to eat M19. ***bon chrétien*** /kretjɛ̃/, pl. ***-s -s*** (pronounced same), [lit. 'good Christian'] any of several varieties of pear L16. ***bon enfant*** /bɔn ɑ̃fɑ̃/ [lit. 'good child'] good company M19. ***bon gré mal gré*** /gre mal gre/ [lit. 'good will, ill will'] (whether) willingly or unwillingly E19. ***bon jour*** /ʒuːr/, ***bonjour*** *interjection* good day, hello L16. ***bon mot*** /mo/, pl. ***-s -s*** (pronounced same), [lit. 'good word'] a clever or witty remark, a witticism M18. ***bon ton*** /tɔ̃/ [lit. 'good tone'] the fashionable world, *arch.* good breeding M18. ***bon vivant*** /vivɑ̃/, pl. ***-s -s*** (pronounced same), [lit. 'who lives well'] a gourmand, an epicure L17. ***bon viveur*** /vivœːr/, pl. ***-s -s*** (pronounced same), [pseudo-French after *bon vivant*, from *viveur* a living person] a person who lives luxuriously M19. ***bon voyage*** /vwajaːʒ/ [lit. 'pleasant journey']: used as a salutation to a person about to travel L17. (See also ***no bon*** s.v. NO *adjective*.)

bona fide /ˌbəʊnə ˈfʌɪdi/ *adverbial & adjectival phr.* M16.
[ORIGIN Latin = with good faith (abl. of BONA FIDES).]
(Acting or done) in good faith; sincere(ly), genuine(ly).

bona fides /ˌbəʊnə ˈfʌɪdiːz/ *noun phr.* L18.
[ORIGIN Latin = good faith.]
1 Good faith, freedom from intent to deceive. L18.
2 (Erron. treated as pl.) Guarantees of good faith, credentials. M20.

bonaght /bəˈnɔːt/ *noun*. M16.
[ORIGIN Irish.]
IRISH HISTORY. A tax or tribute levied by Irish chiefs for the maintenance of soldiers.

bonallie /bɒˈnali/ *noun*. *Scot. arch.* Also **bonnail(lie)** /bɒˈneɪl(i)/. L15.
[ORIGIN from Old French & mod. French BON + *aller* go.]
(A wish for) a good journey, farewell.
Esp. in ***drink a person's bonallie***.

bonanza /bəˈnanzə/ *noun & adjective*. Orig. *US*. E19.
[ORIGIN Spanish = fair weather, prosperity, from Latin *bonus* good.]
▸ **A** *noun*. A run of good luck, an unexpected success (orig. esp. in mining); prosperity; a source of great wealth or good fortune. E19.
▸ **B** *adjective*. Greatly prospering or productive. L19.

Bonapartist /ˈbəʊnəpɑːtɪst/ *noun & adjective*. *hist.* Also **Buon-**. E19.
[ORIGIN from *Bonaparte* (see below) + -IST.]
▸**A** *noun*. An adherent of the government and dynasty of Napoleon Bonaparte (1769–1821), Emperor of France. E19.
▸ **B** *adjective*. Of or adhering to Bonaparte or Bonapartism. E19.
■ **Bonapartism** *noun* attachment to or advocacy of the government and dynasty of Napoleon E19.

B

bona-roba /bəʊnəˈrəʊbə/ *noun*. Now *rare* or *obsolete*. L16.
[ORIGIN Italian *buonaroba*, from *buona* good + *roba* dress.]
A prostitute or disreputable woman.

bonasus /bəˈnasəs/ *noun*. Now *rare* or *obsolete*. Pl. **-nasi** /-ˈnasʌɪ, -ˈnasiː/. L16.
[ORIGIN Latin from Greek *bonasos*.]
The European bison.

bona vacantia /ˌbəʊnə vəˈkantɪə/ *noun phr*. M18.
[ORIGIN Latin = ownerless goods (*vacare* be ownerless).]
LAW. Goods without any apparent owner, and to which the Crown has right.

bonaventure /bɒnəˈvɛntʃə/ *noun*. *obsolete* exc. *hist*. L15.
[ORIGIN Italian *bonaventura* lit. 'good fortune', from †*bona* (now *buona*) good + *ventura* fortune.]
NAUTICAL. A lateen sail carried on an extra mizzenmast; a mast with such a sail (freq. more fully ***bonaventure mast***, ***bonaventure mizzen***).

bonavist /ˈbɒnəvɪst/ *noun*. M17.
[ORIGIN Perh. from *Bona Vista* var. of Boa Vista, Cape Verde islands.]
= LABLAB. Also ***bonavist bean***.

bonbon /ˈbɒnbɒn/ *noun*. L18.
[ORIGIN French, lit. 'good-good': see BON.]
A piece of confectionery, a sweet.
■ **bonbonnière** /bɔ̃bɔnjɛːr (*pl. same*)/ *noun* a fancy box for holding sweets E19.

bonce /bɒns/ *noun*. M19.
[ORIGIN Unknown.]
1 (A game played with) a large marble. M19.
2 The head. *slang*. L19.

bond /bɒnd/ *noun*[1] & *adjective*. LOE.
[ORIGIN Old Norse *bóndi* occupier and tiller of the soil (cf. HUSBAND *noun*) from *bóandi* use as noun of pres. pple of *bóa* var. of *búa* dwell, from Germanic base also of BOOTH.]
▸ **A** *noun*. †**1** A householder, a husband. Only in LOE.
†**2** A peasant. Only in ME.
3 A serf, a base vassal; a slave. *obsolete* exc. *hist*. ME.
▸ **B** *adjective*. **1** In a state of slavery; in bondage; tied *to*. *arch*. ME.
†**2** Servile, slavish. LME–M16.
– COMB.: **bond-land** *hist*. land held by bondage; **bondmaid**, **bondmaiden** a slave girl; **bondman** (now *arch*. or *hist*.) a peasant; a serf, a slave; a villein; **bondmanship** the state or condition of a bondman; **bondservice** slavery; **bondslave** a slave; a person in a state of utter servitude; **bondwoman** a female slave.

bond /bɒnd/ *noun*[2]. ME.
[ORIGIN Alt. of BAND *noun*[1], preserving more the connection with *bind*, *bound*.]
▸ **I** *lit*. **1** Something with which a person is bound; a shackle; a fetter; confinement, imprisonment, custody. Now usu. in *pl*. ME.

MILTON To endure Exile, or ignominy, or bonds, or pain.

2 Something with which a thing is tied, fastened to another, or made to cohere. ME.

L. T. C. ROLT Bags of clay laced with hazel rods to form a bond.

†**3** A bandage. LME–L17.
▸ **II** *fig*. **4** A restricting or imprisoning circumstance; a constraining force, a tie. ME. ▸†**b** Obligation, duty. LME–M17.

F. M. FORD To enjoy a woman's favours made him feel that she had a bond on him for life. D. H. LAWRENCE Breaking the bonds of authority.

5 A binding engagement, an agreement. ME.

R. C. SHERRIFF An honourable man whose word was his bond.

6 A uniting or cementing force or influence; adhesion, union. LME.

J. LOCKE Speech being the great Bond that holds Society together. J. GALSWORTHY Attached to the dead by the bond of kinship. W. H. AUDEN Siblings can live in a bond / as close as wedlock.

▸ **III** Legal & techn. uses.
7 A deed by which one person binds himself or herself to pay another; a (government's) documentary promise to repay borrowed money, usu. with interest; a debenture; an insurance policy; a financial guarantee against the collapse of a company, esp. a tour operator etc. L16.
8 Surety; *spec*. security for a released prisoner's return for trial, bail. *arch*. exc. *US*. M17.
9 The jointing or fastening of masonry, timber, etc.; *esp*. any of various methods of holding a wall together by making bricks overlap. L17.
English bond *BRICKLAYING*: with alternate courses of headers and stretchers. **Flemish bond** *BRICKLAYING*: with courses of alternate headers and stretchers. **monk bond** *BRICKLAYING*: with courses alternating with pairs of stretchers.
10 Storage of goods in special warehouses under the charge of Customs pending the payment of duty by the importer. Chiefly in ***in bond***, ***out of bond***, etc. M19.
11 *CHEMISTRY*. A linkage between atoms in a molecule; *esp*. = ***covalent bond*** s.v. COVALENT *adjective*. M19.
double bond: see DOUBLE *adjective* & *adverb*. ***metallic bond***: see METALLIC *adjective*. ***sigma bond***: see SIGMA 2a.
12 *ELECTRICITY*. A conductor connecting metal parts, esp. for the purpose of earthing. M19.
13 In full ***bond paper***. Writing paper of high quality suitable for bonds etc. L19.
– COMB.: **bondholder** a person holding a bond granted by a private person or company; ***bond paper***: see sense 13 above; **bondstone** a stone or brick running through a wall to bind or strengthen it; **bond-washing** dividend-stripping.

bond /bɔ̃nt/ *noun*[3]. *S. Afr*. L19.
[ORIGIN Afrikaans from Dutch (= German *Bund*), from *binden* bind.]
An Afrikaner league or association.

bond /bɒnd/ *verb*. L16.
[ORIGIN from BOND *noun*[2].]
▸ **I** *verb trans*. **1** Pledge or confirm by a bond. L16. ▸**b** In *pass*. Of a travel agency, tour operator, etc.: be bound by an agreement limiting loss and inconvenience to customers if the company should cease trading. L20.
2 Reinforce or make solid by a bond or bonds; bind (bricks etc.) together by making them overlap; cement or clamp together; hold together by embedding in a solid. L16.
3 Connect by overlapping or by a bond *to*. L18.
4 Put (goods) into bond. E19.
bonded warehouse: where goods are kept in bond.
5 Subject to bondage. M19.
6 Connect by means of an electrical bond. L19.
7 *CHEMISTRY*. Join or hold by a chemical bond. Freq. in *pass*. E20.
8 Join or hold by an emotional or psychological bond. M20.
▸ **II** *verb intrans*. **9** Hold together; adhere. M19.
10 Form an emotional or psychological bond (*with*). L20.

A. TYLER She and her husband need to bond with the baby.

■ **bonding** *noun* (*a*) the action of the verb; (*b*) the manner in which bricks, atoms, etc., are bonded, bonds collectively: L17.

bondage /ˈbɒndɪdʒ/ *noun* & *verb*. ME.
[ORIGIN Anglo-Latin *bondagium*, from BOND *noun*[1]: see -AGE. Infl. in sense by BOND *noun*[2].]
▸ **A** *noun*. **1** Serfdom, slavery; *hist*. tenure in villeinage, services due from a tenant to a proprietor. ME.
2 The condition of being bound or tied; *fig*. subjection to authority, constraining force, or obligation. LME. ▸**b** *spec*. Sadomasochism involving binding, handcuffing, etc. M20.
3 That which binds; obligation. *rare*. E17.
▸ **B** *verb trans*. Reduce to bondage, enslave. *arch*. E17.
■ **bondager** *noun* (*hist*.) a person who performs services as a condition of feudal tenure; in S. Scotland and NE England, a female outworker supplied to a proprietor by a tenant: M19.

bonder /ˈbɒndə/ *noun*[1]. *rare*. M19.
[ORIGIN from BOND *verb* + -ER[1].]
1 *BUILDING*. A binding stone or brick. M19.
2 A person who puts goods into bond or owns goods in bond. L19.

bonder /ˈbɒndə/ *noun*[2]. M19.
[ORIGIN Erron. from Norwegian *bonde*, pl. *bönder*.]
hist. A Norwegian peasant farmer or petty freeholder.

bondieuserie /bɔ̃djøzri/ *noun*. Pl. pronounced same. M20.
[ORIGIN French, from *bon* good + *Dieu* God.]
A church ornament or devotional object, *esp*. one of little artistic merit; such objects collectively.

bondsman /ˈbɒn(d)zmən/ *noun*. Pl. **-men**. E18.
[ORIGIN from BOND *noun*[1], *noun*[2] + -'S[1] + MAN *noun*.]
1 A person who stands surety for a bond. E18.
2 A person in bondage, a slave; = ***bondman*** s.v. BOND *noun*[1]. M18.

bonduc /ˈbɒndʌk/ *noun*. L17.
[ORIGIN French from Arabic *bunduq* hazelnuts, ult. from Greek *pontikon* marine (*karuon* nut).]
= ***nicker tree*** s.v. NICKER *noun*[4].

bone /bəʊn/ *noun*.
[ORIGIN Old English *bān* = Old Frisian, Old Saxon *bēn* (Middle Dutch, Low German *been*), Old High German, German *bein*, Old Norse *bein*, from Germanic.]
1 Any of the pieces of hard tissue that make up the skeleton of a vertebrate animal, and consist largely of calcium phosphate or carbonate in a matrix of collagen fibres. OE. ▸**b** (Part of) a bone to which some meat adheres, providing possible sustenance. LME. ▸**c** *spec*. A bone used by Australian Aborigines in spells to cause death or sickness. L19.
backbone, ***breastbone***, ***cheekbone***, ***collarbone***, ***frontal bone***, ***funny bone***, ***jawbone***, ***knuckle bone***, ***marrowbone***, ***shin bone***, ***thigh bone***, ***wishbone***, etc.
2 In *pl*. The skeleton; the body; the mortal remains; *fig*. the essential framework of anything. OE.

P. LARKIN The plain bones of the matter is just this: if you're prepared to work . . we shall get on splendidly. W. GOLDING Here the bones of the land showed, lumps of smooth grey rock.

3 The bony structure of the body; the body's hard, solid, or essential part. OE.

DICKENS An immense brown horse displaying great symmetry of bone.

4 The material or tissue of the bones; any similar animal substance, as ivory, dentine, etc. OE.
whalebone etc.
5 An article orig. or usu. made from bone or ivory, *esp*. a domino, (in *pl*.) dice, castanets. LME. ▸**b** *spec*. A strip of whalebone or other stiffening material in a corset etc. L16.
6 A dollar. *US slang*. L19.
– PHRASES: **a bone in her mouth** *NAUTICAL* (*arch*.) water foaming before a ship's bows. **a bone in one's leg**, **a bone in one's head** *colloq*. a (feigned) reason for idleness. **a bone to pick with someone** a dispute or problem to resolve with someone. ***bag of bones***: see BAG *noun*. **bare bones** the mere essentials. ***be skin and bone***: see SKIN *noun*. **bone of contention** a subject of dispute. ***bred in the bone***: see BRED *ppl adjective*. **close to the bone** = *near the bone* below. ***dog and bone***: see DOG *noun*. **feel in one's bones**, **know in one's bones**, etc.: instinctively, in one's innermost being. ***lay one's bones***: see LAY *verb*[1]. ***long bone***: see LONG *adjective*[1]. **make no bones about** not hesitate or scruple about. **make old bones** live to an old age. NAPIER'S BONES. **near the bone** (*a*) destitute; (*b*) near the permitted limit (esp. of decency). **point the bone**: in an Australian Aboriginal ritual intended to bring about a person's death or sickness. ***rack of bones***: see RACK *noun*[4]. ***roll the bones***: see ROLL *verb*. ***skin and bone***: see SKIN *noun*. **to the bone** *fig*. to the bare minimum; penetratingly. **work one's fingers to the bone** work very hard.
– COMB.: **bone-ache** *arch*. pain in the bones, *spec*. as a symptom of venereal disease; **bone ash** the mineral residue of calcined bones; **bone-black** a mixture of bone ash and charcoal obtained by carbonizing bones; **bone breccia** breccia containing fossil bones; **bone charcoal** = *bone black* above; **bone china** chinaware made of clay mixed with bone ash; **bone-dry** *adjective* completely dry; **bone earth** = *bone ash* above; ***bonefire***: see BONFIRE; **bonefish** (chiefly *N. Amer*.) a fish with many small bones, spec. *Albula vulpes*, a silvery marine game fish; **bonehead** *slang* a stupid person; **boneheaded** *adjective* (*slang*) thick-headed, stupid; **bone idle** *adjective* utterly idle; **bone-lace** bobbin lace of a type orig. made with bone bobbins; **bone lazy** *adjective* utterly lazy; ***bone marrow***: see MARROW *noun*[1] 1; **bonemeal** crushed or ground bones used esp. as fertilizer; **bone-oil** dark, fetid oil obtained in the carbonizing of bones; **bone-seed** a chiefly southern African plant of the genus *Osteospermum*, of the composite family; **bone-seeking** *adjective* (of a substance) tending to be deposited in the bones; **bone-setter** a person who sets broken or dislocated bones, esp. without being a qualified surgeon; **boneshaker** *colloq*. a jolting vehicle; *hist*. a bicycle without rubber tyres; ***bone spavin***: see SPAVIN *noun*[1]; **bone-tired** *adjective* utterly tired; ***bone turquoise***: see TURQUOISE *noun* 2; **bone-weary** *adjective* utterly weary; †**bone-wort** any of various plants held to be of use in healing bone, e.g. the daisy and the violet; **boneyard** a place where the bones of dead animals are deposited; *slang* a cemetery.
■ **boned** *adjective* having bones (of a specified kind) ME. **boneless** *adjective* without bones; *fig*. lacking backbone or willpower; ***boneless wonder***: see WONDER *noun*: OE. **boner** *noun* (*slang*, orig. *US*) (*a*) a stupid mistake; (*b*) an erection of the penis: E20.

bone /bəʊn/ *verb*[1]. L15.
[ORIGIN from the noun: sense 3 is perh. a different word.]
1 *verb trans*. Remove the bones from (meat, fish, etc.). L15.
2 *verb trans*. Treat or equip with bone, esp. as stiffening or strengthening. L17.
3 *verb intrans*. Apply oneself diligently; study intensively. Usu. foll. by *up*, study hurriedly. (Foll. by *on* the object of study etc.) *slang* (orig. *US*). M19.
4 *verb trans*. Point a bone at (a person) as part of an Australian Aboriginal ritual intended to bring about death or sickness. E20.

bone /bəʊn/ *verb*[2] *trans*. *slang*. L18.
[ORIGIN Unknown.]
Seize; snatch, steal.

boneen /bəˈniːn/ *noun*. *Irish*. Pl. **-s**, same. M19.
[ORIGIN Irish *bainbhín*, from *banbh* sucking pig + *-in* dim. suffix.]
A young pig.

†**bonefire** *noun* & *verb* var. of BONFIRE.

boneset /ˈbəʊnsɛt/ *noun*. L17.
[ORIGIN Prob. from BONE *noun* + SET *verb*[1], on account of medicinal use.]
†**1** Comfrey. Only in L17.
2 A plant of the composite family, *Eupatorium perfoliatum*, bearing white flowers; = THOROUGHWORT 2. *N. Amer*. E19.

boneta *noun* var. of BONITO.

bonfire /ˈbɒnfʌɪə/ *noun* & *verb*. Also †**bonefire**. LME.
[ORIGIN from BONE *noun* + FIRE *noun*.]
▸ **A** *noun*. Orig., a large open-air fire in which bones were burnt; also, a fire in which heretics, proscribed books, etc., were burnt. Now, any large open-air fire kindled for the disposal of waste material, brushwood, garden refuse, etc., or in celebration of some event or occasion (as was often the case with 'bone-fires'), or for other purposes. LME.

W. RALEIGH Celebrate the victorie with bonefiers in euerie town.

make a bonfire of destroy.
– COMB.: **Bonfire Night** 5 November, the anniversary of the Gunpowder Plot (1605), on which large fires are built and effigies of the conspirator Guy Fawkes are burnt.
▸ **B** *verb trans*. & *intrans*. Light bonfires (in). E17.

bong /bɒŋ/ *noun*[1] & *verb intrans*. Orig. *US*. E20.
[ORIGIN Imit.]
(Emit) a low-pitched sound as of a bell.

bong /bɒŋ/ *noun*[2]. M20.
[ORIGIN Prob. imit.]
MOUNTAINEERING. A large piton.

B

bong /bɒŋ/ *noun*³. L20.
[ORIGIN Thai *baung* cylindrical wooden tube.]
A kind of water pipe used for smoking marijuana or other drugs.

bongo /ˈbɒŋgəʊ/ *noun*¹. Pl. same, -**s**. M19.
[ORIGIN Kikongo.]
A large striped antelope, *Tragelaphus euryceros*, of central Africa.

bongo /ˈbɒŋgəʊ/ *noun*². Pl. -**o(e)s**. E20.
[ORIGIN Amer. Spanish *bongó*.]
Either of a pair of small drums, usu. held between the knees and played with the fingers.

bongrace /ˈbɒngreɪs/ *noun*. M16.
[ORIGIN French *bonnegrace* lit. 'good grace': see BON, GRACE *noun*.]
1 A shade worn on the front of a woman's bonnet to protect the complexion. *obsolete* exc. *hist.* M16.
2 A broad-brimmed hat. *arch. & dial.* L16.

bonham /ˈbɒnəm/ *noun*. *Irish*. L19.
[ORIGIN Irish *banbh*.]
A young pig, a piglet.

bonheur du jour /bɒnœːr dy ʒuːr/ *noun phr.* Pl. ***bonheurs du jour*** (pronounced same). L19.
[ORIGIN French, lit. 'happiness of the day'.]
A small writing table, usu. fitted to hold toilet accessories, popular in 18th-cent. France.

bonhomie /ˈbɒnəmiː/ *noun*. Also †-**hommie**. L18.
[ORIGIN French, from BONHOMME + -*ie* -Y³.]
Good-natured friendliness, geniality.
■ **bonhomous** *adjective* showing bonhomie E20.

bonhomme /ˈbɒnɒm, *foreign* bɔnɔm (*pl. same*)/ *noun*. E16.
[ORIGIN French, lit. 'good man, good fellow': in medieval Latin *bonus homo*.]
hist. A member of an order of mendicant friars who arrived in England in the 13th cent.

†**bonhommie** *noun* var. of BONHOMIE.

Boniface /ˈbɒnɪfeɪs/ *noun*. *arch.* E19.
[ORIGIN A character in G. Farquhar's *The Beaux' Stratagem*.]
(A name for) an innkeeper.

boniform /ˈbɒnɪfɔːm/ *adjective*. L17.
[ORIGIN mod. Latin *boniformis* (Henry More) translating Greek *agathoeidēs* (Plato): see -FORM.]
Cognizant of moral goodness; having the form of good.

bonify /ˈbɒnɪfʌɪ/ *verb trans.* E17.
[ORIGIN French *bonifier* improve, formed as BON + -*fier* -FY.]
†**1** Benefit. Only in E17.
2 Make good; turn into good. L17.

boning /ˈbəʊnɪŋ/ *noun*. L18.
[ORIGIN Unknown.]
SURVEYING etc. The process of judging the straightness of a surface or line by eye, as by looking along the tops of two straight edges, or along a line of poles. Freq. *attrib.*

bonism /ˈbɒnɪz(ə)m/ *noun*. L19.
[ORIGIN from Latin *bonus* good + -ISM.]
The doctrine that the world is good, but not the best possible.
■ **bonist** *noun* L19.

bonitary /ˈbɒnɪt(ə)ri/ *adjective*. M19.
[ORIGIN from late Latin *bonitarius* from Latin *bonitas* goodness + -*arius* -ARY¹.]
ROMAN LAW. Beneficial; having beneficial possession without formal legal title.
■ Also **boniˈtarian** *adjective* M19.

bonito /bəˈniːtəʊ/ *noun*. Pl. -**os**. Also **boneta** /bəˈniːtə/. L16.
[ORIGIN Spanish.]
Any of various small tuna with stripes on the back, esp. *Sarda sarda* of the Atlantic and Mediterranean.

†**bonity** *noun*. L16–L18.
[ORIGIN Latin *bonitas* goodness, BOUNTY: see -ITY.]
Goodness.

bonjour *interjection* see BON.

bonk /bɒŋk/ *noun*. *slang*. M20.
[ORIGIN Imit.]
1 An abrupt heavy sound of impact; a bump. M20.
2 A level of exhaustion that makes a cyclist or runner unable to go further. M20.
3 An act of sexual intercourse. L20.
– COMB.: **bonkbuster** [after BLOCKBUSTER] a type of popular novel characterized by frequent explicit sexual encounters.

bonk /bɒŋk/ *verb trans. & intrans. slang*. E20.
[ORIGIN Imit.]
1 Hit resoundingly; bang, bump. E20.
2 Have sexual intercourse (with). L20.

bonkers /ˈbɒŋkəz/ *adjective*. *slang*. M20.
[ORIGIN Unknown: see -ER⁶.]
Crazy; insane.

bonnail, **bonnaillie** *nouns* vars. of BONALLIE.

bonne /bɔn/ *adjective & noun*. E16.
[ORIGIN French, fem. of BON.]
▶ **A** *adjective*. Good. Long restricted to certain phrs. adopted from French (see below). E16.
à la bonne femme, ***bonne femme*** /(a la) bɔn fam/ [lit. 'in the manner of a good housewife'] applied esp. postpositively to designate particular dishes of food. ***bonne bouche*** /buʃ/, pl. -**s** -**s** (pronounced same), [French = mouth] a dainty morsel, a titbit, esp. to end a meal. ***bonne fortune*** /bɔn fɔrtyn/, pl. -**s** -**s** (pronounced same), a lady's favours, as a source of pride for the recipient.
▶ **B** *noun*. Pl. pronounced same.
†**1** A good girl. Only in E16.
2 A (French) nursemaid. L18.

bonnet /ˈbɒnɪt/ *noun*. LME.
[ORIGIN Old French *bonet* from medieval Latin *abonnis* headgear.]
1 **a** A headdress of men and boys, usu. soft and brimless; a round brimless Scotch cap. LME. ▸**b** An outdoor headdress of women or children, usu. with no brim at the back, and tied with strings. L15. ▸**c** The ceremonial headdress of an American Indian. Usu. more fully ***war-bonnet***. M19. ▸**d** HERALDRY. The velvet cap within a coronet. L19.
a fill a person's bonnet fill a person's place. ***have a bee in one's bonnet***: see BEE *noun*¹. ***poke bonnet***: see POKE *noun*³. ***Scotch bonnets***: see SCOTCH *adjective*. ***vail bonnet***, ***vail one's bonnet***, ***vail the bonnet***: see VAIL *verb*² 2.
2 NAUTICAL. An additional strip of canvas laced to the foot of a sail to catch more wind. LME.
3 A raised portion of a fortification at a salient angle, serving to protect from enfilade fire etc. L17.
4 The reticulum or second stomach of a ruminant. L18.
5 A thing or person used to put a good face on underhand proceedings. *arch. slang*. E19.
6 A protective cover or cap, *esp.* a hood over the engine of a car, a cowl on a chimney, etc. M19.
– COMB.: **bonnethead** a hammerhead shark, *Sphyrna tiburo*, with a relatively narrow head; **bonnet laird** *arch.* a petty Scottish landowner wearing a bonnet like the humbler classes; **bonnet monkey** an Indian macaque, *Macaca radiata*, having a tuft of hair on top of the head; **bonnet-piece** a gold coin of James V of Scotland, on which the king is represented wearing a bonnet; ***bonnet rouge*** /bɔnɛ ruːʒ/, pl. -**s** -**s** (pronounced same), [French = red] the red cap of the French sans-culottes of 1793, taken as a symbol of the revolutionary spirit.

bonnet /ˈbɒnɪt/ *verb*. E17.
[ORIGIN from the noun.]
†**1** *verb intrans.* Take off the bonnet in token of respect. *rare* (Shakes.). Only in E17.
2 *verb trans.* Put a bonnet on. E19.
3 *verb trans.* Crush down the hat of (a person) over the eyes. M19.

bonnibel /ˈbɒnɪbɛl/ *noun*. *arch.* L16.
[ORIGIN Perh. from French *bonne et belle* 'good and fair'.]
A fair maid.

bonny /ˈbɒni/ *adjective*. *dial. & colloq.* L15.
[ORIGIN Uncertain: perh. to be referred to Old French BON (fem. *bone*) good.]
1 Pleasing to the sight; comely; expressing homely beauty. *Scot. & N. English*. L15.
2 Nice, good, fine. Often *iron. Scot. & N. English*. M16.
†**3** Smiling; bright. L16–E19.
4 Of fine size, big. Now usu. (healthily) plump, looking well. L16.
■ **bonnily** *adverb* L16. **bonniness** *noun* E17.

bonny-clabber /ˈbɒnɪklabə/ *noun*. *Irish*. E17.
[ORIGIN Irish *bainne clabair* thick milk for churning, from *bainne* milk, *clabar* dasher of a churn.]
Milk naturally clotted on souring.

bonobo /ˈbɒnəbəʊ/ *noun*. Pl. -**os**. M20.
[ORIGIN African name.]
The pygmy chimpanzee, *Pan paniscus*, of the Congo.

bonsai /ˈbɒnsʌɪ/ *noun*. Pl. same. E20.
[ORIGIN Japanese, from *bon* tray + *sai* planting.]
The (Japanese) practice of cultivating artificially dwarfed potted plants or small trees; a plant or tree cultivated by this method.

bonsense /ˈbɒns(ə)ns/ *noun*. L17.
[ORIGIN from French BON good, after *nonsense*.]
Good sense.

bonspiel /ˈbɒnspiːl/ *noun*. *Scot.* M16.
[ORIGIN Prob. of Low German origin: cf. Western Flemish *bonespel* a children's game.]
A sporting contest, a match. Now *spec.* a major curling match.

bontebok /ˈbɒntəbɒk/ *noun*. Also -**tb**- /-tb-/. Pl. same. L18.
[ORIGIN Afrikaans, from Dutch *bont* pied + *bok* BUCK *noun*¹.]
A reddish white-faced southern African antelope (usu. regarded as conspecific with the blesbok *Damaliscus dorcas*).

bonus /ˈbəʊnəs/ *noun*. L18.
[ORIGIN Prob. joc. or ignorant use of Latin *bonus* (masc.) for *bonum* (neut.) good thing: prob. orig. Stock Exchange slang.]
1 Something, esp. money, over and above that which is normally expected; something to the good or into the bargain. Occas., a douceur, a bribe. L18.
2 *spec.* An extra dividend paid to shareholders of a company; a portion of profits allowed to the holder of an insurance policy; a gratuity to employees beyond their normal pay. E19.
no-claim bonus, ***no-claims bonus***: see NO *adjective*.
– COMB.: **bonus issue** = ***scrip issue*** s.v. SCRIP *noun*³.

bonxie /ˈbɒŋksi/ *noun*. Orig. *Shetland*. L18.
[ORIGIN Norwegian *bunksi*, from *bunke* dumpy body from Old Norse *bunki* heap (cf. Norwegian *bunke* fat woman).]
The great skua.

bony /ˈbəʊni/ *adjective*. LME.
[ORIGIN from BONE *noun* + -Y¹.]
1 Of, pertaining to, or of the nature of bone or bones; consisting or made of bone or bones. LME.
2 Having many bones; having large or prominent bones, esp. with little flesh. LME.
– SPECIAL COLLOCATIONS: **bony fish** (*a*) a fish with bones rather than a cartilaginous skeleton, i.e. a member of the class Pisces (or Osteichthyes), to which the majority of living fishes belong; (*b*) *N. Amer.* the menhaden, *Brevoortia tyrannus*. **bony labyrinth** ANATOMY the system of bony canals and chambers surrounding the membranous labyrinth of the inner ear.
■ **boniness** *noun* L19.

bonze /bɒnz/ *noun*. L16.
[ORIGIN French *bonze* or Portuguese *bonzo* (prob. from Japanese *bonzō*, *bonsō* priest).]
A Japanese or Chinese Buddhist religious teacher.
■ **bonˈzess** *noun* (*rare*) a female bonze M19.

bonzer /ˈbɒnzə/ *adjective*. *Austral. & NZ slang*. E20.
[ORIGIN Perh. alt. of BONANZA.]
Excellent, first-rate.

boo /buː/ *noun*¹, *interjection*, & *verb*. E19.
[ORIGIN Imit.: cf. BO *interjection & noun*².]
▶ **A** *noun & interjection*. A prolonged sound expressing derision or disapproval, or an exclamation intended to startle. Occas., a sound (as) of cattle lowing. E19.
can't say boo to a goose is very timid or shy.
▶ **B** *verb trans. & intrans.* Make such a sound (at); jeer (a person, an action, etc.). E19.
■ **booer** *noun* E20.

boo /buː/ *noun*². *slang*. M20.
[ORIGIN Unknown.]
Marijuana.

boo /buː/ *noun*³. *US slang*. L20.
[ORIGIN Uncertain; prob. alt. of French *beau* BEAU.]
A person's boyfriend or girlfriend.

booay /ˈbuːʌɪ/ *noun*. *NZ colloq.* Also **boo(h)ai**. M20.
[ORIGIN Perh. from place name *Puhoi*, N. Auckland, NZ.]
The remote rural districts.
up the booay completely wrong or astray.

boob /buːb/ *noun*¹ & *verb*. *slang* (orig. *US*). E20.
[ORIGIN Abbreviation of BOOBY *noun*¹.]
▶ **A** *noun*. **1** = BOOBY *noun*¹ 1. E20.
2 A lock-up, a cell. E20.
3 A foolish mistake. M20.
– COMB.: **boob tube** *noun*¹ *the* or a television.
▶ **B** *verb intrans.* Make a foolish mistake. M20.

boob /buːb/ *noun*². *slang* (orig. *US*). M20.
[ORIGIN from BUB *noun*³ or abbreviation of BOOBY *noun*².]
A woman's breast. Usu. in *pl.*
– COMB.: **boob tube** *noun*² a woman's low-cut close-fitting strapless top.

boobialla *noun* var. of BOOBYALLA.

booboisie /buːbwɑːˈziː/ *noun*. *US slang*. E20.
[ORIGIN Joc. from BOOB *noun*¹ after *bourgeoisie*.]
Boobs as a class, stupid people.

boo-boo /ˈbuːbuː/ *noun*. *slang* (orig. *US*). E20.
[ORIGIN Prob. redupl. of BOOB *noun*¹.]
1 A prank, a trick. E20.
2 = BOOB *noun*¹ 3. E20.

boobook /ˈbuːbʊk/ *noun*. E19.
[ORIGIN Dharuk *bubug*, imit. of the bird's call.]
In full ***boobook owl***. A small brown spotted owl, *Ninox novaeseelandiae*, native to Australasia. Also called ***mopoke***, ***morepork***.

booby /ˈbuːbi/ *noun*¹. E17.
[ORIGIN Prob. from Spanish *bobo* (in both senses), from Latin *balbus* stammering, stuttering: see -Y⁶.]
1 A silly, stupid, or childish person. E17.
2 Any of various seabirds of the genus *Sula*, closely related to the gannet. M17.
– COMB.: **booby hatch** (*a*) NAUTICAL a small companion or hatch cover; (*b*) *US slang* a lock-up, a cell; an asylum; **booby prize**: awarded in fun or ridicule to the last competitor, lowest scorer, etc.; **booby trap** (*a*) something designed as a practical joke to catch the unwary, *esp.* an object placed on top of a door so as to fall on the first opener; (*b*) an apparently harmless device concealing an explosive charge designed to go off when tampered with; **booby-trap** *verb trans.* place one or more booby traps in or on.
■ **boobyish** *adjective* awkward and silly L18.

booby /ˈbuːbi/ *noun*². *slang* (orig. *US*). M20.
[ORIGIN Alt. of BUBBY *noun*¹.]
= BOOB *noun*². Usu. in *pl.*

boobyalla /buːbɪˈalə/ *noun*. *Austral.* Also **boobi-**. M19.
[ORIGIN Aboriginal language of south-east Tasmania *bubiala*.]
Any of various coastal trees and shrubs, *esp.* a wattle, *Acacia longifolia*, or a shrub of the genus *Myoporum*.

B

boodie /ˈbuːdi/ *noun. Austral.* M19.
[ORIGIN Nyungar *burdi*.]
A rat-kangaroo, *Bettongia lesueuri*. Also **boodie-rat**.

boodle /ˈbuːd(ə)l/ *noun & verb. slang* (chiefly *US*). E17.
[ORIGIN Dutch *boedel*, *boel* possessions, disorderly mass, = Old Frisian *bōdel* movable goods, Low German *bōdel*.]
▶ **A** *noun*. **1** Crowd, pack, lot; = CABOODLE. E17.
2 Money; *spec.* money acquired or spent illegally or improperly; proceeds of corruption. M19.
▶ **B** *verb trans. & intrans.* Bribe; give or take bribes. L19.
■ **boodler** *noun* L19.

boogaloo /buːɡəˈluː/ *noun & verb intrans.* Chiefly *US*. M20.
[ORIGIN Perh. alt. of BOOGIE-WOOGIE after *hullabaloo* etc.]
(Perform) a dance with swivelling and shuffling movements.

booger /ˈbʊɡə, ˈbuːɡə/ *noun. N. Amer. slang.* L19.
[ORIGIN Perh. alt. of BUGGER *noun*¹ or BOGEY *noun*¹.]
A piece of nasal mucus.

boogie /ˈbuːɡi/ *noun*¹. *US slang. offensive.* E20.
[ORIGIN Perh. alt. of BOGEY *noun*¹.]
A black person.

boogie /ˈbuːɡi/ *noun*² & *verb*. E20.
[ORIGIN Unknown.]
▶ **A** *noun*. **1** A party, *esp.* a rent party. *US slang.* E20.
2 = BOOGIE-WOOGIE. Also, a dance to pop or rock music. M20.
▶ **B** *verb intrans.* Pres. pple & verbal noun **boogieing**. Dance (orig. to boogie-woogie music). M20.
– COMB.: **boogie board** = BODYBOARD.

boogie-woogie /buːɡɪˈwuːɡi/ *noun*. E20.
[ORIGIN Prob. redupl. of BOOGIE *noun*².]
A percussive style of playing blues, esp. on piano, with a repetitive bass figure.

boohai *noun* var. of BOOAY.

boohoo /buːˈhuː/ *interjection, noun, & verb intrans.* M19.
[ORIGIN Imit.]
(Make) a sound of loud esp. childish weeping, or occas. laughter or derision.

boojum /ˈbuːdʒəm/ *noun*. L19.
[ORIGIN Nonsense word invented by Lewis Carroll.]
An imaginary dangerous animal.

book /bʊk/ *noun*.
[ORIGIN Old English *bōc* = Old Frisian, Old Saxon *bōk* (Dutch *boek*), Old High German *buoh* (German *Buch*), Old Norse *bók* (cf. Gothic *bōka* letter of the alphabet), from a Germanic base usu. taken to be rel. to BEECH, as the wood of rune tablets.]
1 A writing, a written document; a charter, a deed. Long *obsolete* exc. *hist.* OE.

AV *Jer.* 32:12 The witnesses, that subscribed the booke of the purchase.

†**2** A narrative, a record, a list. OE–L17.

AV *Gen.* 5:1 The booke of the generations of Adam.

3 A collection of sheets of paper or other material, blank, written, or printed, fastened together so as to form a material whole; *esp.* one with sheets pasted or sewn together at the edge, with protective covers; a literary composition of any kind long enough to fill one or more such volumes. OE.

G. GISSING She must read the best books that had been written on the training of children's minds. ALDOUS HUXLEY Life became safe, things assumed meaning, only when they had been translated into words and confined between the covers of a book. R. HOGGART Of another author's books more than six million copies are said to have been sold in three years. K. A. PORTER She sits in her deep chair with an open book on her knees.

commonplace book, ***daybook***, ***guidebook***, ***handbook***, ***hymn book***, ***log book***, ***notebook***, ***picture book***, ***prompt book***, ***scrapbook***, ***service book***, ***textbook***, ***wordbook***, etc.

4 *spec.* ▸**a** *The* Bible. Formerly also, a copy of the Bible. ME. ▸**b** A volume of blank sheets in which financial transactions, minutes, notes, etc., are entered; in *pl.*, accounts, annals, records. LME. ▸**c** The script of a play, film, etc.; the libretto of an opera, oratorio, etc. L16. ▸**d** A magazine. Now *colloq.* E19. ▸**e** A record of bets made with several different people on a particular race etc. E19. ▸**f** *The* telephone directory. E20.

b J. MORLEY The books show that the nett profits . . had exceeded £23,000 for the year. B. HINES Just tell him to put it in t' book and I'll pay him at t' week-end. **e** P. G. WODEHOUSE I am still willing to make a little book from time to time to entertain sportsmen and gentlemen.

5 A main subdivision of a literary composition; any of the component works forming the Bible. ME.

SHAKES. *Hen. V* In the book of Numbers is it writ. J. GROSS As a child, Mill [had] . . an entire book of *The Faerie Queene* read aloud to him.

6 Book learning, study, scholarship. Now only in *pl.*, passing into sense 3. ME. ▸†**b** Benefit of clergy. E17–E18.

SHAKES. *Merry W.* My son profits nothing in the world at his book.

7 *fig.* Anything from which one may learn or be instructed; an imaginary narrative, record, etc. LME.

SHAKES. *Wint. T.* My name put in the book of virtue! J. G. STRUTT That great poet to whom the book of Nature . . seemed . . laid open.

8 A set of things bound or collected together to resemble a book, e.g. sheets of gold leaf, tickets, matches, stamps, six tricks at cards, etc.; an aggregate of laminar crystals. L15.

– PHRASES: ***bell, book, and candle***: see BELL *noun*¹. ***black book***: see BLACK *adjective*. ***blue book***: see BLUE *adjective*. **book of fate** the future as being predetermined. **book of life** THEOLOGY the record of those achieving salvation. ***book of reference***: see REFERENCE *noun* 7. **book of words** a libretto; a set of rules etc. **bring to book** call to account. **by the book** according to the rules; in set phrases. **closed book** a thing of which one has no understanding. **close the books** make no further entries, cease business etc. ***comic book***: see COMIC *adjective*. **Good Book** *the* Bible. ***have one's nose in a book***: see NOSE *noun*. ***in someone's bad books***, ***in someone's black books*** in disfavour with someone. **in someone's good books** in favour with someone. **in my book** as I see the matter. **know someone like a book** have a thorough knowledge of someone's character. ***make a book***: see MAKE *verb*. **not in the book** not allowed, irregular. ***one for the book***, ***one for the end book***: see ONE *adjective, noun, & pronoun*. **on the books**, **upon the books** listed as a member etc., on the staff. ***open book***: see OPEN *adjective*. **People of the Book** people adhering to a book of divine revelation, *spec.* the Jews and Christians as regarded by Muslims. **read someone like a book** understand someone's motives or intentions fully. ***red book***: see RED *adjective*. ***SEALED book***. ***Sibylline books***: see SIBYLLINE *adjective*. **speak like a book**: with full or correct information. **suit one's book** be convenient to one. ***symbolical books***: see SYMBOLICAL 4. ***take a leaf out of a person's book***: see LEAF *noun*¹. ***talking book***: see TALKING *ppl adjective*. **throw the book at** make all possible charges against. ***upon the books***: see ***on the books*** above. **without book** from memory; without authority.

– COMB.: **bookbinder** a person whose trade is bookbinding; **bookbindery** a bookbinding establishment; **bookbinding** the binding of books; **bookcase** a case containing shelves for books; **book club** (*a*) a society whose members can buy selected books on special terms; (*b*) a group that meets regularly to discuss books; **book-craft** *arch.* scholarship; authorship; **bookend** either of a pair of often ornamental props for keeping a row of books upright; **book-fell** *hist.* a skin prepared for writing on; a vellum or parchment manuscript; **book group** a group that meets regularly to discuss books; **book hand** *hist.* a formal style of handwriting used by professional transcribers of books before the invention of printing; **bookkeep** *verb intrans.* [back-form.] do bookkeeping; **bookkeeper** a person responsible for keeping the accounts of a trader, public office, etc.; **bookkeeping** (the art of) keeping accounts; **bookland** *hist.* land granted by charter into private ownership; **book-Latin** Latin; scholarly language; **book-learned** *adjective* knowing books (but lacking practical experience); **book learning**, **book-lore** knowledge gained from books, mere theory; **booklouse** a minute insect of the order Psocoptera, harmful to old books; **book lung** a lamellate respiratory organ of an arachnid; **bookmaker** (*a*) a professional betting person; a person who manages a betting shop; (*b*) (usu. *derog.*) a compiler of books; †(*c*) a printer and bookbinder; **bookmaking** the trade or action of a bookmaker; **bookman** (*a*) a scholar; (*b*) an author or publisher, a literary man; **bookmobile** *N. Amer.* a mobile library; **book-muslin** fine muslin (folded like a book when sold in the piece); **book name** a name for a plant or animal (other than its scientific name) not widely used except in books; **book page** (*a*) a page of a book; (*b*) a page of a newspaper etc. devoted to reviews of books; **bookplate** a label affixed to a book as a mark of ownership; **book-post** the transmission of books by post at special lower rates; **bookrest** an adjustable support for an open book on a table etc.; **book-scorpion** a small pseudoscorpion, *Chelifer cancroides*, found in houses; **bookseller** a dealer in books; **bookselling** the selling of books, esp. as a trade; **bookshop** a shop where books are sold; **book-shy** *adjective* reluctant or unwilling to read books; ***bookstack***: see STACK *noun* 1c; **bookstall** a stall for the sale of books out of doors or in a station etc.; **bookstore** *N. Amer.* a bookshop; **book token** a voucher exchangeable for books costing up to a specified amount of money; **book trough** a V-shaped rack for displaying books on a table etc. to show their titles; **book value** value as entered in a book, as opp. to market value; **book-wise** *adjective* = ***book-learned*** above; **bookwork** the studying of textbooks, as opp. to practical work; **bookworm** (*a*) the larva of a wood-boring beetle which feeds on books; (*b*) *fig.* a person devoted to reading.

■ **bookful** *noun* the entire contents of a book; as much as fills a book: L16. **bookless** *adjective* lacking books; *poet.* unscholarly, uneducated: L16. **booklet** *noun* a small book, esp. if paper-covered M19. **booklike** *adverb & adjective* (*a*) *adverb* in the manner of a book; (*b*) *adjective* resembling (that of) a book: M19. **bookling** *noun* (now *rare*) a tiny book E19. **booky** *adjective* (*colloq.*) bookish M19.

book /bʊk/ *verb*. OE.
[ORIGIN from the noun.]
1 *verb trans.* Grant or assign (land) by charter. *obsolete* exc. *hist.* OE.
2 *verb trans.* Enter in a book or list; record, register, enrol. ME. ▸**b** *spec.* Of a police officer, referee, etc.: make an entry of or against the name of (a person) for an (alleged) offence; *slang* apprehend, catch. M19. ▸**c** *verb trans. & intrans.* Register the arrival or departure of (a guest at a hotel, an employee, etc.), or of oneself. Usu. foll. by *in*, *out*, or *off*. E20.
3 *verb trans. & intrans.* Engage (one or more seats, tickets, etc.) for oneself or others, usu. in advance; reserve. E19. ▸**b** *verb trans.* Engage seats, rooms, transport, etc., for; issue a travel ticket to. E19.
4 *verb trans.* Engage (a person) as a guest, performer, etc. L19.
■ **bookable** *adjective* (*a*) able to be booked or reserved; (*b*) FOOTBALL (of an offence) serious enough for the offending player to be cautioned by the referee: E20.

booker /ˈbʊkə/ *noun*. OE.
[ORIGIN from BOOK *noun* + -ER¹: later re-formed on BOOK *verb*.]
†**1** A writer of books. OE–ME.
2 A person who makes entries in a book etc., a bookkeeper. M19.

bookie /ˈbʊki/ *noun. colloq.* L19.
[ORIGIN Abbreviation: see -IE.]
= ***bookmaker*** (a) s.v. BOOK *noun*.

booking /ˈbʊkɪŋ/ *noun*. L16.
[ORIGIN from BOOK *verb* + -ING¹.]
1 The action of BOOK *verb*; an instance of this. L16.
2 *spec.* ▸**a** A reservation of a seat, room, ticket, etc. L19. ▸**b** The issue of a ticket for travel. L19. ▸**c** The recording of a person's name for an (alleged) offence. M20.
b ***booking clerk***, ***booking hall***, ***booking office***, etc.

bookish /ˈbʊkɪʃ/ *adjective*. M16.
[ORIGIN from BOOK *noun* + -ISH¹.]
1 Of or pertaining to a book or books; (of language) literary rather than colloquial. M16.
2 Studious, addicted to reading books; getting knowledge only from books. L16.
■ **bookishly** *adverb* M17. **bookishness** *noun* L16.

bookmark /ˈbʊkmɑːk/ *noun & verb*. M19.
[ORIGIN from BOOK *noun* + MARK *noun*¹.]
▶ **A** *noun*. **1** A strip of leather, paper, etc., for marking one's place in a book. M19.
2 COMPUTING. A tag or marker placed in an electronic file at a particular location so that it can be rapidly accessed; *esp.* a record of an Internet address, stored in browser software. L20.
▶ **B** *verb trans.* COMPUTING. Identify (a particular location, file, etc.) with a bookmark. L20.
■ **bookmarker** *noun* = sense A.1 above M19.

booksy /ˈbʊksi/ *adjective. colloq.* M20.
[ORIGIN from BOOK *noun* + -SY.]
Having literary or bookish pretensions.

bool *noun* var. of BOUL.

Boolean /ˈbuːlɪən/ *adjective*. Also **-ian**. M19.
[ORIGIN from George *Boole* (1815–64), English mathematician + -AN.]
Of, pertaining to, or described by an abstract system of postulates and symbols applicable to logical problems.

boom /buːm/ *noun*¹. L15.
[ORIGIN from BOOM *verb*¹.]
A loud deep resonant sound as of a distant explosion, breaking surf, a bass drum, etc.; a hum or buzz; the cry of the bittern.
sonic boom: see SONIC 2.
– COMB.: **boom box** *slang* a portable radio and cassette recorder.
■ **boomy** *adjective*¹ having a loud, deep, resonant sound E19.

boom /buːm/ *noun*². M16.
[ORIGIN Dutch = BEAM *noun*, tree, pole.]
†**1** *gen.* A beam, a pole. Only in M16.
†**2** A pole set up to mark a channel etc. in water. L16–M18.
3 A bar or barrier stretched across a river etc. to obstruct navigation. E17. ▸**b** A line of floating timber stretched across a river etc. to retain or guide floating logs. *N. Amer.* L17.
4 A long spar or pole hinged at one end, securing the bottom of a ship's sail. E17. ▸**b** In *pl.* Part of a sailing ship's deck where the spare spars are stowed. M18.
5 A movable arm supporting a camera, microphone, etc. M20.
– PHRASES: ***lower the boom***: see LOWER *verb*¹.

boom /buːm/ *noun*³. Orig. *US*. L19.
[ORIGIN Prob. from BOOM *verb*¹.]
A sudden increase or development esp. in business or economic activity; a rapid rise in the price of a commodity, in profits, etc.

attrib.: R. LOWELL The risk—a small one in those boom years—of resigning from the Navy.

boom and bust (a cycle of) great prosperity followed by economic slump.
– COMB.: **boom town** a town owing its origin, growth, or prosperity to a boom in some commodity or activity.
■ **boomlet** *noun* a small boom, esp. on a stock exchange L19. **boomy** *adjective*² of or pertaining to a boom in business etc. L19.

boom /buːm/ *verb*¹. LME.
[ORIGIN Ult. imit.: perh. from Dutch *bommen* hum, buzz.]
1 *verb intrans.* Make a loud, deep, resonant sound; hum or buzz like a bee etc.; speak loudly and with deep resonance. Of the (male) bittern: utter its characteristic resonant call. LME.
2 *verb intrans.* Rush violently along. M16.
3 *verb trans.* Give forth or utter with a booming sound. Usu. foll. by *out*. M19.
■ **booming** *noun* (*a*) the action of the verb; (*b*) a deep resonant sound: M16. **boomingly** *adverb* with a booming sound M19.

boom /buːm/ *verb*² *trans.* E17.
[ORIGIN from BOOM *noun*².]
Provide with a boom or booms; extend (a sail) with a boom (usu. foll. by *out*).

boom /buːm/ *verb*³. Orig. *US*. L19.
[ORIGIN from BOOM *noun*³.]
1 *verb intrans.* Burst into sudden economic activity; prosper. L19.

K. M. E. MURRAY Trade for him never boomed and he earned only about twelve shillings a week.

2 *verb trans.* Force upon the attention of the public, promote. L19.

S. LEACOCK We're doing all we can . . to boom Toronto as a Whisky Centre.

■ **booming** *adjective* L19.

boomer /ˈbuːmə/ *noun*. M19.
[ORIGIN Prob. from BOOM *verb*¹ + -ER¹. In branch II ellipt.]
▸ **I 1** A large male kangaroo. *Austral.* M19.
2 Something large or notable of its kind. *Austral. & NZ slang.* M19.
▸ **II 3** = ***baby boomer*** s.v. BABY *noun*. M19. *colloq.* (chiefly *N. Amer.*) L20.

boomerang /ˈbuːməraŋ/ *noun & verb*. L18.
[ORIGIN Dharuk *bumariny*.]
▸ **A** *noun*. **1** A thin curved hardwood missile (of a kind) traditionally used by Australian Aborigines as a hunting weapon, *esp.* one that can be thrown so as to return to the thrower. L18.
2 *fig.* A scheme etc. that recoils on its originator. M19.
▸ **B** *verb intrans.* Act as a boomerang; *fig.* recoil on the originator. L19.

boomslang /ˈbuːmslaŋ/ *noun*. L18.
[ORIGIN Afrikaans, from Dutch *boom* tree + *slang* snake.]
A highly venomous southern African tree snake, *Dispholidus typus*.

boon /buːn/ *noun*¹. ME.
[ORIGIN Old Norse *bón* (Swedish, Danish *bön*, *bøn*) from Germanic base also of BENE.]
†**1** A prayer, a petition; the asking of a favour. ME–E17.
†**2** A request made with authority; a command couched as a request. ME–L16.
3 The matter prayed for or asked; a thing asked as a favour. *arch.* ME.

J. MASEFIELD You in my life for always is the boon I ask from life.

4 Something, now esp. an abstract thing, freely given whether in response to asking or not; a gift, a gratuity. *arch.* LME.

R. C. TRENCH The gods had no better boon for him than an early death. F. HOYLE Our expected lifetime (granted the boon of indefinite good health) would be a few thousand years.

5 *hist.* An unpaid service due by a tenant to the landlord. L16.
6 A gift considered with reference to its value to the recipient; a blessing, an advantage. M18.

H. KELLER It is an unspeakable boon to me to be able to speak in winged words that need no interpretation. B. RUSSELL Enjoying more of what makes life a boon and not a curse.

– COMB.: **boon service**, **boon work** *hist.* unpaid service due by a tenant to the landlord.

boon /buːn/ *noun*². LME.
[ORIGIN Unknown: cf. BUN *noun*¹.]
The stalk of flax or hemp after the fibre has been removed.

boon /buːn/ *adjective*. LME.
[ORIGIN Old French & mod. French *bon* from Latin *bonus* good.]
†**1** Good, goodly. LME–L17.
†**2** Advantageous, fortunate, favourable. LME–M17.
3 Convivial, jolly, genial. Orig. & chiefly in ***boon companion***. M16.
4 Gracious, bounteous, benign. *poet.* E17.

boon /buːn/ *verb*. ME.
[ORIGIN from BOON *noun*¹.]
†**1** *verb trans.* Pray for, ask as a boon. Only in ME.
2 *verb intrans. hist.* Do boon service. *rare.* L17.
3 *verb trans.* Repair (public roads). *obsolete* exc. *dial.* L18.

boondock /ˈbuːndɒk/ *noun*. *N. Amer. slang*. M20.
[ORIGIN Tagalog *bundok* mountain.]
sing. & (usu.) in *pl.* Rough or isolated country; remote parts.

boondoggle /ˈbuːndɒɡ(ə)l/ *noun & verb*. *N. Amer. slang*. M20.
[ORIGIN Unknown.]
▸ **A** *noun*. A trivial, useless, or unnecessary undertaking. Also, a dishonest undertaking, a fraud. M20.
▸ **B** *verb intrans.* Engage in such an undertaking. M20.

boong /buːŋ/ *noun*. *Austral. slang. offensive.* E20.
[ORIGIN Uncertain: perh. from Indonesian (Jakarta dialect) *bung* elder brother.]
An Aborigine; a member of an indigenous New Guinean people; any non-white person.

boongary /buːnˈɡɛːri/ *noun*. *Austral.* L19.
[ORIGIN Warrgamay (an Australian Aboriginal language of northern Queensland) *bulnggarri*.]
A tree kangaroo, *Dendrolagus lumholtzi*, of northern Queensland.

boonies /ˈbuːniz/ *noun pl.* *N. Amer. colloq.* L20.
[ORIGIN Abbreviation.]
The boondocks; remote or wild areas.

J. ELLROY Shortell took off for a vacation in the Montana boonies.

boor /bʊə/ *noun*. M16.
[ORIGIN Low German *būr* or Dutch *boer*: repr. earlier by Old English *gebūr*. Cf. BOER, NEIGHBOUR *noun*.]
1 A husbandman, a peasant; *esp.* a Dutch, German, or other foreign peasant. Now *rare* or *obsolete*. M16. ▸†**b** *spec.* (**B-**.) = BOER *noun*. L18–M19.
boor's mustard [rendering German *Bauernsenfe* 'peasant's mustard'] field pennycress, *Thlaspi arvense*.
2 A rustic, a yokel; a clumsy or unrefined person; a rude, ill-mannered, inconsiderate person. L16.
■ **boorish** *adjective* of, pertaining to, or characteristic of boors; rude, ill-mannered; coarse, uncultured: M16. **boorishly** *adverb* E17. **boorishness** *noun* L18.

boosa *noun* var. of BOZA.

boost /buːst/ *noun & verb*¹. Orig. *US*. E19.
[ORIGIN Unknown.]
▸ **A** *noun*. **1** A push from below, a lift; a help; a scheme of advertisement, a promotion; an increase (in value, reputation, etc.); a reinforcement of self-confidence or morale; encouragement, assistance, increase. *colloq.* E19.

SEBA SMITH I got a pretty good boost in Boston, by the editors giving me recommendations. *Listener* The recording needs treble boost, but is otherwise excellent. A. STORR The patient's dependency on him is providing him with a boost to his own self-esteem.

2 (The action of) a booster; a supercharger, supercharging. M20.
▸ **B** *verb*. **1** *verb trans.* Push from below; assist; raise; increase the reputation, value, etc., of by praise, advertising, etc. *colloq.* E19.
2 *verb trans.* Amplify (an electrical signal); raise (voltage etc.); *gen.* equip or augment with a booster. E20.
3 *verb intrans. & trans.* Steal, shoplift; rob. *US slang.* E20.

boost /buːst/ *verb*² (orig. *3 sing. pres. indic.*). *Scot.* (formerly also *N. English*). Also **buist** /byst/, †**bus**, & other vars. ME.
[ORIGIN Contr. of *behoves*: -*t* perh. by assoc. with *must*. Cf. BUDE.]
†**1** *impers.* in *(it)* **boosts** etc., (it) behoves. ME–L15.
2 Must, ought. L18.

booster /ˈbuːstə/ *noun*. Orig. *US*. L19.
[ORIGIN from BOOST *verb*¹ + -ER¹.]
1 A person who boosts. *colloq.* L19. ▸**b** A shoplifter, a thief. *US slang.* E20.
2 An apparatus for providing an increase or temporary assistance; *esp.* (***a***) a device for increasing electrical voltage, signal strength, etc., an amplifier; (***b***) an auxiliary engine or rocket for giving an initial acceleration. Freq. *attrib.* L19.
booster rocket, ***booster seat***, etc.
3 MEDICINE. A dose of a vaccine etc. increasing or renewing the effect of an earlier one. M20.
■ **boosterism** *noun* (*colloq.*) the tendency to praise, advertise, or promote oneself or one's own (town, country, product, etc.) E20.

boosy /ˈbuːzi/ *noun*. *dial.*
[ORIGIN Old English *bōsig*.]
A stall for an ox or cow; a manger.

boot /buːt/ *noun*¹. In *hist.* use chiefly **bot(e)** /bəʊt/.
[ORIGIN Old English *bōt* = Old Frisian *bōte*, Old Saxon *bōta*, Middle Dutch & mod. Dutch *boete*, Old High German *buoza* (German *Busse*), Old Norse *bót*, Gothic *bōta*, from Germanic, from base also of BETTER, BEST *adjectives* etc.]
▸ **I** Good, advantage.
1 ***to boot***, besides, as well, additionally. OE.
†**2** Advantage, profit, use. ME–L17.
3 A premium, compensation. *obsolete* exc. *Scot. dial.* L15.
▸ **II** Making good or mending; amends.
4 (A contribution levied for) the repair of decaying structures. Long *obsolete* exc. *hist.* OE. ▸**b** The right of a tenant to take timber etc. for necessary purposes such as repair. Usu. with specifying word. E16.
b fire-boot, ***housebote***, etc.
†**5** A medicinal cure or remedy. OE–M16.
6 Help or deliverance from evil or peril; relief, rescue. *arch.* OE. ▸†**b** A way of mending matters, a better alternative. ME–L16.
7 A payment or compensation for injury etc. Usu. with specifying word. Long *obsolete* exc. *hist.* OE.
manbote etc.
8 Expiation of sin, an offering by way of atonement. Long *obsolete* exc. *hist.* OE.

boot /buːt/ *noun*². See also BOOTS. ME.
[ORIGIN Old Norse *bóti* or its source Old French *bote* (mod. *botte*), prob. rel. to *bot* blunt, stumpy, & ult. to BUTT *noun*¹.]
1 An outer foot covering, usu. of leather, extending above the ankle. ME. ▸†**b** A greave. LME–E17. ▸**c** A covering for the lower part of a horse's leg. E19.
Chelsea boot, ***Cossack boot***, ***cowboy boot***, ***hiking boot***, ***riding boot***, etc.
2 A former instrument of torture in Scotland, which encased the foot while wedges were driven between it and the foot. M16.
3 A cover of leather, rubber, etc., which fits over an object in the manner of a boot on the foot. L16.
4 †**a** An uncovered space on or by the step on a coach where attendants sat; the step itself; a low outside compartment before or behind the body of the vehicle. L16–E19. ▸**b** A receptacle for luggage etc. in a coach under the seat of the guard or coachman (chiefly *hist.*); the luggage compartment of a motor vehicle, usu. situated at the rear. L18.

b R. PILCHER They had made their way back to her car, dumped their purchases in the boot.

5 The feathered leg of a bird; ORNITHOLOGY an undivided tarsal envelope characteristic of the legs of some birds. M19.
6 *US slang*. ▸**a** A navy or marines recruit under basic training. E20. ▸**b** A person; *spec.* (***a***) a black person; (***b***) a woman, *esp.* an unattractive one (see also ***old boot*** s.v. OLD *adjective*). *derog.* M20.
7 A (heavy) kick. *colloq.* E20.
– PHRASES: **boot and saddle** [alt. of French *boute-selle* place saddle]: a cavalry signal to mount. **boots and all** *Austral. & NZ colloq.* with no holds barred, wholeheartedly. **fill one's boots** *colloq.* have as much of something as one wants. **get the boot**, **get the order of the boot** be dismissed from employment etc. **give the boot**, **give the order of the boot** dismiss (a person) from employment etc. ***hang up one's boots***: see HANG *verb*. ***have one's heart in one's boots***: see HEART *noun*. ***lick a person's boots***: see LICK *verb*. **like old boots** *slang* vigorously, tremendously. ***old boot***: see OLD *adjective*. **put the boot in** kick brutally, take decisive action. ***seven-league boots***: see SEVEN *noun*. **the boot is on the other foot**, **the boot is on the other leg** the position is reversed, the advantage etc. is the other way round. ***too big for one's boots***: see BIG *adjective*. ***tough as old boots***: see TOUGH *adjective*. ***you bet your boots***: see BET *verb* 2.
– COMB.: **bootblack** *N. Amer.* a person who blacks boots and shoes; **bootblacking** (blacking for) polishing shoes etc.; **bootboy** (***a***) a boy employed to clean shoes etc.; (***b***) *slang* a hooligan (wearing heavy boots); **boot camp** *N. Amer. slang* a centre for the initial training of marine or naval recruits; **boot-cut** (of jeans or trousers) cut with a leg that is flared very slightly from the knee to the ankle, so as to be worn comfortably over boots; **boot-faced** *adjective* grim, expressionless; **Boot Hill** *US* (*joc.*) the cemetery in a frontier town; **boot-hose** = ***boot-stocking*** below; **bootjack** an appliance for pulling boots off; **bootlace** a cord or leather strip for lacing boots; a thin strip of anything resembling this; **bootlick** *verb & noun* (***a***) *verb trans. & intrans.* curry favour (with), toady (to); (***b***) *noun* = ***bootlicker*** below; **bootlicker** a toady, a sycophant; **bootmaker** a maker or manufacturer of boots; **boot-stocking** a stocking which covers the leg like a jackboot; BOOTSTRAP; **boot-top** *noun & verb* (***a***) *noun* the upper part of a boot; NAUTICAL = ***boot-topping*** below; (***b***) *verb trans.* apply protective boot-topping to; **boot-topping** NAUTICAL part of the hull of a vessel between the light and load lines; any protective film or treatment applied to this; **boot tree** a mould for keeping a boot in shape.
■ **bootery** *noun* (*US*) a shop selling boots and shoes E20.

boot /buːt/ *noun*³. *arch.* L16.
[ORIGIN App. from BOOT *noun*¹, infl. by BOOTY.]
Booty, spoil, plunder.
Esp. in ***make boot of***.

boot /buːt/ *noun*⁴. L20.
[ORIGIN formed as BOOT *verb*³.]
COMPUTING. The operation or procedure of booting a computer or an operating system; a bootstrapping routine.
warm boot: see WARM *adjective*.

boot /buːt/ *verb*¹. ME.
[ORIGIN from BOOT *noun*¹: repl. BEET *verb*.]
†**1** *verb trans.* Make better; make good (a deficiency etc.). ME–M16.
2 *verb trans. & intrans. impers.*, usu. with subj. *it*. Profit, avail; matter to or *to*. Usu. in neg. & interrog. contexts. *arch.* LME.

A. COWLEY With Fate what boots it to contend? BROWNING Little boots Our sympathy with fiction!

†**3** *verb trans.* Benefit, enrich. *rare* (Shakes.). Only in E17.

boot /buːt/ *verb*². LME.
[ORIGIN from BOOT *noun*².]
1 *verb trans. & intrans.* Put boots on (oneself or another); put on one's boots. LME.
2 *verb trans. hist.* Torture with the boot. L16.
3 *verb trans.* Kick hard. *colloq.* L19.
4 *verb trans.* Eject, dismiss (a person). Freq. foll. by *out* (*of* one's house, job, etc.). *colloq.* L19.

Independent His wife booted him out when she found out about me.

boot /buːt/ *verb*³. L20.
[ORIGIN Abbreviation of BOOTSTRAP.]
COMPUTING. **1** *verb trans.* Prepare (a computer) for operation by causing an operating system to be loaded into its memory; cause (an operating system) to be loaded in this way; load a routine on (a disk) into a computer's memory. Freq. foll. by *up*. L20.

2 *verb intrans.* Undergo booting; (of an operating system) be loaded into a computer's memory; (of a computer) have an operating system loaded into it. L20.
■ **boota'bility** *noun* the facility or property of being bootable L20. **bootable** *adjective* able to be booted; containing the software required for booting a computer: L20.

bootakin *noun* var. of BOOTIKIN.

booted /ˈbuːtɪd/ *adjective.* M16.
[ORIGIN from BOOT *noun*[2], *verb*[2]: see -ED[2], -ED[1].]
1 Having boots on, equipped with boots. M16.
2 Of a bird: having feathered legs; having an undivided tarsal envelope. L18.

bootee /buːˈtiː/ *noun.* L18.
[ORIGIN from BOOT *noun*[2] + -EE[2].]
A woman's short lined boot; an infant's boot of wool etc.

Boötes /bəʊˈəʊtiːz/ *noun.* M16.
[ORIGIN Latin from Greek *boōtēs* ploughman, Boötes, from *bous* ox + *ōthein* to push.]
(The name of) a constellation of the northern hemisphere between Draco and Virgo; the Herdsman.

booth /buːð, buːθ/ *noun.* ME.
[ORIGIN Old Norse var. of *búð* (Swedish, Danish *bod* stall, shop), from *bóa*: see BOND *noun*[1].]
1 A temporary dwelling or shelter of branches, canvas, etc. ME.
2 A covered place where business is transacted, as (**a**) a market stall; (**b**) a refreshment tent at a fair; (**c**) a boxlike office at which tickets etc. are sold. ME.
ticket booth, token booth, tollbooth, etc.
3 A partly or completely enclosed area for voting, telephoning, sitting in a restaurant, etc. M19.
polling booth, telephone booth, etc.

bootikin /ˈbuːtɪkɪn/ *noun.* Also **-tak-** /-tək-/. E18.
[ORIGIN Dim. of BOOT *noun*[2]: cf. MANNIKIN.]
1 *hist.* = BOOT *noun*[2] 2. E18.
2 †**a** A soft boot or mitten worn as a cure for gout. M–L18. ▸**b** = BOOTEE. M19.

bootleg /ˈbuːtlɛg/ *adjective, noun, & verb.* Orig. *US.* E20.
[ORIGIN from BOOT *noun*[2] + LEG *noun*.]
▸ **A** *adjective.* **1** (Of goods, esp. liquor) smuggled, sold illicitly; (of musical recordings) pirated. E20.
2 AMER. FOOTBALL. Designating or pertaining to a play in which a player carrying the ball feigns a pass to another then continues with the ball concealed near his hip. M20.
▸ **B** *noun.* **1** Smuggled or illicit liquor. E20.
2 AMER. FOOTBALL. A bootleg play. M20.
▸ **C** *verb.* Infl. **-gg-**.
1 *verb trans. & intrans.* Smuggle, sell (esp. liquor) illicitly; pirate (musical recordings). E20.
2 *verb intrans.* AMER. FOOTBALL. Make a bootleg play. M20.
■ **bootlegger** *noun* a smuggler of liquor, a trafficker in illicit goods or pirated recordings L19.

bootless /ˈbuːtlɪs/ *adjective*[1] & *adverb.* OE.
[ORIGIN from BOOT *noun*[1] + -LESS.]
▸ **A** *adjective.* **1** Of an injury: unable to be compensated by payment etc. Long *obsolete* exc. *hist.* OE.
†**2** Incurable, remediless. ME–M17.
3 Unavailing, to no purpose. LME.
▸ **B** *adverb.* Bootlessly. Chiefly *poet.* LME.
■ **bootlessly** *adverb* unavailingly, unsuccessfully E17.

bootless /ˈbuːtlɪs/ *adjective*[2]. LME.
[ORIGIN from BOOT *noun*[2] + -LESS.]
Without boots.

boots /buːts/ *noun.* E17.
[ORIGIN Pl. of BOOT *noun*[2], used as sing.]
1 As 2nd elem. of combs. with the sense 'person, fellow', in familiar or joc. appellations, as ***bossyboots, slyboots***, etc. E17.
2 (A name for) a hotel servant who cleans boots and shoes, carries luggage, etc. L18.

bootstrap /ˈbuːtstrap/ *noun & verb.* L19.
[ORIGIN from BOOT *noun*[2] + STRAP *noun*.]
▸ **A** *noun.* **1** A strap attached to a boot for pulling it on, or for holding down a woman's riding habit; a bootlace. L19.
pull oneself up by one's own bootstraps, **lift oneself up by one's own bootstraps**, etc.: by one's own unaided efforts.
2 Chiefly COMPUTING. The action of bootstrapping; a bootstrapping procedure or routine. Usu. *attrib.* M20.
▸ **B** *verb trans.* Infl. **-pp-**.
1 Make (one's way) or get (oneself) *into* a new state using existing resources; modify or improve by making use of what is already present. Usu. *refl.* M20.

> R. M. PIRSIG Some valuable Aristotelian technique of bootstrapping oneself into new areas of knowledge.

2 COMPUTING. = BOOT *verb*[3] 1. Freq. as ***bootstrapping*** *verbal noun.* M20.

> D. R. HOFSTADTER Once a certain minimal core of compiler had been written, then that . . could translate bigger compilers into machine language—which in turn could translate yet bigger compilers . . . This process is affectionately known as 'bootstrapping'.

booty /ˈbuːti/ *noun*[1]. LME.
[ORIGIN Middle Low German *bûte*, *buite* exchange, distribution (whence German *Beute*) rel. to Old Norse *býta* deal out, exchange, of unknown origin.]
1 Orig., plunder, spoil, etc., acquired in common and destined to be divided. Now, anything gained by plunder etc. whether common property or not; spoil. LME.
2 A thing taken by force, a prize. Usu. in *pl.* Now *rare* or *obsolete.* M16.
– PHRASES: **play booty** *arch.* (in games) combine against another player; play or act falsely for gain, lose intentionally.

booty /ˈbuːti/ *noun*[2]. *N. Amer. slang.* L20.
[ORIGIN Prob. alt. of BOTTY.]
The buttocks, the backside.

> E. CURRIE I was gonna . . try to work my booty off!

– COMB.: **booty call** a sexual invitation or rendezvous.

bootylicious /ˌbuːtɪˈlɪʃəs/ *adjective. slang* (chiefly *US*). L20.
[ORIGIN from BOOTY *noun*[2] + -LICIOUS.]
Of a woman: sexually attractive.

> *Heat* Catch the bootylicious trio wowing the UK's biggest arenas this week.

booza *noun* var. of BOZA.

booze /buːz/ *verb & noun. colloq.* Also **bouse**, **bowse** /baʊz/. ME.
[ORIGIN Middle Dutch *būsen* (Dutch *buizen*) drink to excess.]
▸ **A** *verb intrans.* & (now *rare*) *trans.* Drink for company and enjoyment; drink (alcoholic liquor) habitually or excessively. ME.
▸ **B** *noun.* **1** Drink, *esp.* alcoholic drink. ME.

> C. SHIELDS Dorrie got worried about all the booze he was soaking up.

hit the booze: see HIT *verb*.
2 A drinking bout. L18.
on the booze on a heavy drinking session.
– COMB.: **booze-up** a drinking bout.
■ **boozed** *adjective* intoxicated, drunk, (also foll. by *up*) M19. **boozer** *noun* (**a**) a person who boozes; (**b**) *slang* a public house: E17. **booze'roo** *noun* (*NZ slang*) a drinking bout M20. **boozily** *adverb* in a boozy manner L19. **booziness** *noun* the quality of being boozy M19. **boozy** *adjective* showing the effects of alcoholic drink; characterized by or given up to boozing: E16.

BOP *abbreviation.*
hist. Boy's Own Paper.

bop /bɒp/ *noun*[1]. *colloq.* M20.
[ORIGIN Imit.]
A popping sound. Also, a blow with a fist, club, etc.

bop /bɒp/ *noun*[2]. *colloq.* M20.
[ORIGIN Abbreviation.]
1 = BEBOP. Orig. *US.* M20.
2 A dance to pop music; a social occasion for such dancing. M20.
■ **bopster** *noun* = BEBOPPER M20.

bop /bɒp/ *verb*[1]. Infl. **-pp-**. L19.
[ORIGIN Imit.]
1 *verb trans.* **a** Throw down with a resounding noise. *dial. rare.* L19. ▸**b** Hit, strike, punch. *colloq.* (orig. *US*). M20.
2 *verb intrans.* Fight. *US colloq.* M20.

bop /bɒp/ *verb*[2] *intrans. colloq.* (orig. *US*). Infl. **-pp-**. M20.
[ORIGIN from BOP *noun*[2].]
Play or sing bebop; dance, jive.
■ **bopper** *noun* = BEBOPPER (see also TEENY-BOPPER) M20.

bo-peep /bəʊˈpiːp/ *noun.* E16.
[ORIGIN from BO *interjection* + PEEP *verb*[2].]
1 = PEEKABOO *noun.* E16.
2 A peep, a look. *Austral. & NZ colloq.* M20.

Bora /bɒˈrɑː, ˈbɔːrə/ *noun*[1]. Also **Bhora**, **Borah**, **Bohora** /bɒˈhɔːrə/. L17.
[ORIGIN Hindi *bohrā*.]
A member of a Shiite Muslim sect found mainly in western India. Formerly also, a Muslim Indian trader.

bora /ˈbɔːrə/ *noun*[2]. M19.
[ORIGIN Dial. var. of Italian *borea* from Latin *boreas* north wind.]
A strong northerly squally wind which blows in the northern Adriatic.

bora /ˈbɔːrə/ *noun*[3]. Also **borah**. M19.
[ORIGIN Kamilaroi *buuru*.]
A rite among the Aborigines of eastern Australia signifying admission to manhood.

†**borachio** *noun.* Pl. **-os**. L16.
[ORIGIN Spanish *borracha* leather bag for wine, *borracho* drunkard.]
1 In Spain: a goatskin bag used for wine or other liquors. L16–L18.
2 A drunkard. E17–E18.

boracic /bəˈrasɪk/ *adjective.* L18.
[ORIGIN from medieval Latin *borac-*, BORAX *noun*[1] + -IC.]
1 Of, containing, or derived from borax. L18.
boracic acid = *BORIC acid*.
2 [from *boracic lint*, rhyming slang for 'skint'.] Having no money, penniless. *slang.* M20.

boracite /ˈbɔːrəsʌɪt/ *noun.* L18.
[ORIGIN formed as BORACIC + -ITE[1].]
MINERALOGY. A chloroborate of magnesium usu. occurring as greyish-white cubic crystals.

borage /ˈbɒrɪdʒ/ *noun.* ME.
[ORIGIN Old French & mod. French *bourrache* from medieval Latin *bor(r)ago*, *-agin-*, perh. from Arabic *'abū ḥurāš* father of roughness, with ref. to the leaves.]
A plant of the genus *Borago* (family Boraginaceae); *esp.* the plant *B. officinalis*, which has hairy leaves and bright blue flowers, and is sometimes used in salads, cordials, etc.
■ **boragi'naceous** *adjective* (BOTANY) of or pertaining to the family Boraginaceae M19.

Borah, **borah** *nouns* vars. of BORA *noun*[1], BORA *noun*[3].

borak /ˈbɔːrak/ *noun. Austral. & NZ colloq.* Also **borax** /-ks/. M19.
[ORIGIN Wathawurung *burag*, lit. 'no, not'.]
Nonsense; banter. Freq. in ***poke borak***, poke fun (*at*).

borane /ˈbɔːreɪn/ *noun.* E20.
[ORIGIN from BORON + -ANE.]
CHEMISTRY. Any of the series of binary compounds of boron and hydrogen, or a substituted derivative of such a compound.

†**boras** *noun* var. of BORAX *noun*[1].

borasco /bəˈraskəʊ/ *noun.* Now *rare.* Pl. **-os**. Also **-ca** /-kə/, **-asque** /-ask/. E17.
[ORIGIN French *bourrasque*, Italian *burrasca*, Spanish *borrasca*, from Latin *boreas*: see BORA *noun*[2].]
A violent squall of wind.

borassus /bəˈrasəs/ *noun.* L18.
[ORIGIN mod. Latin from Greek *borassos* palm tree fruit.]
A palm of the genus *Borassus*; *esp.* the palmyra, *B. flabellifer*. Also ***borassus palm***.

borate /ˈbɔːreɪt/ *noun.* L18.
[ORIGIN from BORAX *noun*[1] + -ATE[1].]
CHEMISTRY. A salt or ester of boric acid; any salt with an oxyanion containing boron.

borax /ˈbɔːraks/ *noun*[1]. Also †**boras**. LME.
[ORIGIN medieval Latin from colloq. Arabic *būrāq* from Pahlavi *būrak* (Persian *būra*).]
1 A hydrated sodium borate, $Na_2B_4O_7{\cdot}10H_2O$, which is a white efflorescent crystalline solid found as a native deposit or prepared from other minerals. LME.
2 Cheap, inferior, or ostentatious goods or design (after a borax soap producer who gave away cheap furniture as a premium). *colloq.* M20.

borax *noun*[2] var. of BORAK.

Borazon /ˈbɔːrəzɒn/ *noun.* M20.
[ORIGIN from BORON with insertion of AZO-.]
(Proprietary name for) a form of boron nitride, used as an abrasive.

borborygm /ˈbɔːbərɪgəm/ *noun.* Also in mod. Latin form **borborygmus** /bɔːbəˈrɪgməs/, pl. **-mi** /-mʌɪ/. E18.
[ORIGIN Greek *borborugmos*.]
A rumbling in the bowels.
■ **borbo'rygmic** *adjective* characterized by borborygms or rumblings E20.

bord /bɔːd/ *noun.* M19.
[ORIGIN Var. of BOARD *noun*.]
Any of a series of parallel workings in a coal seam.
bord and pillar a system of working with pillars of coal left at intervals.

bordage /ˈbɔːdɪdʒ/ *noun.* ME.
[ORIGIN Old French & mod. French (= medieval Latin *bordagium*), from *borde* small farm, cottage, from Proto-Gallo-Romance from Frankish (= BOARD *noun*): see -AGE.]
hist. **1** More fully ***bordage tenure***. The tenure of a bordar. ME.
2 The services due from a bordar. ME.

bordar /ˈbɔːdə/ *noun.* ME.
[ORIGIN Anglo-Latin *bordarius* (= Old French & mod. French *bordier*), from *borda* from Old French & mod. French *borde*: see BORDAGE, -ER[2].]
hist. A villein of the lowest rank, who rendered menial service for a cottage held at the will of his lord.

Bordeaux /bɔːˈdəʊ/ *noun.* Pl. same /-z/. M16.
[ORIGIN A city in SW France.]
1 A red (claret) or white wine from the district of Bordeaux. M16.
2 ***Bordeaux mixture***, copper sulphate and lime used as a fungicide. L19.

bordel /bɔːˈdɛl/ *noun.* Now chiefly *US.* ME.
[ORIGIN Old French & mod. French (= medieval Latin *bordellum*, *-us*) dim. of *borde*: see BORDAGE, -EL[2].]
= BORDELLO.

bordelaise /bɔːdəˈleɪz, *foreign* bɔrdəlɛz/ *adjective.* M19.
[ORIGIN French, fem. of *bordelais* of BORDEAUX.]
Designating or served with a sauce of red wine and onions.

bordello /bɔːˈdɛləʊ/ *noun*. Now chiefly *N. Amer.* Pl. **-os**. L16.
[ORIGIN Italian, formed as BORDEL.]
A brothel.

border /ˈbɔːdə/ *noun*. Also (*arch. rare* exc. in branch II, where now usual) **-ure** /-jʊə/. LME.
[ORIGIN Old French *bordeüre* (mod. *bordure*) from Proto-Romance, ult. from one of the Germanic bases of BOARD *noun*: see -ER².]
▸ **I** Mod. *border*.
1 A side, an edge, a brink, a margin; a limit, a boundary (*lit.* & *fig.*); the part lying along the boundary or outline. LME.
HOR. WALPOLE He affected an impartiality that by turns led him to the borders of insincerity and contradiction.
2 a *sing.* & (now usu.) in *pl.* A frontier district of a country or territory. LME. ▸**b** The frontier line which separates one country from another. M16.
a the Border (*a*) *sing.* & (freq.) in *pl.*, the boundary and adjoining districts between England and Scotland; (*b*) the boundary between Northern Ireland and the Republic of Ireland, or between the US and Mexico.
3 A continuous bed which forms a fringe round a garden area. LME.
MIXED border.
4 A distinct edging for strength, ornament, or definition round anything. LME.
OED The newspapers appeared with black borders in sign of mourning. L. M. MONTGOMERY It was an old-fashioned oval . . surrounded by a border of very fine amethysts. J. MASTERS Har Singh stitched a border on to one of the plain white saris.
TRAC border.
†**5** A plait or braid of hair worn round the forehead or temples. E17–M19.
6 *sing.* & (usu.) in *pl.* A strip of cloth masking the top of a theatre stage as seen from the auditorium. E19.
▸ **II** Mod. *bordure*.
7 HERALDRY. A bearing of uniform width around the edge of a shield. LME.
– COMB.: **Border ballad**: celebrating a raid in the Borders; **border collie** a medium-sized sheepdog of a breed originating near the border between England and Scotland; **borderland** land or district on or near a border; *fig.* an intermediate condition, debatable ground; **Border Leicester** (an animal of) a breed of sheep originating as a cross between the Cheviot and the Leicester; **borderline** *noun* & *adjective* (*a*) *noun* a strip of land forming a boundary; a line of demarcation; (*b*) *adjective* on the borderline, marginal; **border print** printed cotton fabric with a design running parallel to the edge; **Border terrier** (an animal of) a breed of small rough-haired terrier originating in the Cheviot Hills.

border /ˈbɔːdə/ *verb*. Also †**-ure**. LME.
[ORIGIN from the noun.]
▸ **I** *verb trans.* **1** Put or form a border, edging, or boundary to. LME. ▸†**b** Keep within bounds; confine. *rare* (Shakes.). Only in E17.
SWIFT His night-cap border'd round with lace. H. WILLIAMSON Trimmed quickthorn hedges bordering the road.
bordered pit: see PIT *noun*¹.
†**2** Cut up (a pasty). E16–M19.
3 Lie on the borders of; adjoin. M17.
C. LYELL Lands bordering the Mediterranean.
▸ **II** *verb intrans.* **4** Foll. by *on*, *upon*: lie on the border of, be contiguous to; *fig.* approach in character, verge on. M16.
M. ELPHINSTONE Hill tribes, bordering on cultivated countries. B. MAGEE A sense of persecution which bordered on paranoia.

bordereau /bɔːdəˈrəʊ, *foreign* bɔrdəro/ *noun*. Pl. **-eaux** /-əʊz, *foreign* -o/. L19.
[ORIGIN French, dim. of *bord* BOARD *noun*.]
A memorandum of contents, a schedule, a docket.

borderer /ˈbɔːdərə/ *noun*. LME.
[ORIGIN from BORDER *verb* or *noun* + -ER¹.]
1 A person who lives near a border, esp. that of England and Scotland. Also (**B-**), a member of a regiment from the Welsh or Scottish borders. LME.
2 A person who or (*rare*) thing which borders (*on*, *upon*); a nearest neighbour. M16.

bord-land /ˈbɔːdland/ *noun*. ME.
[ORIGIN formed as BORDAGE OF BORDAR + LAND *noun*¹.]
hist. Land held in bordage tenure.

bordure *noun*, *verb* see BORDER *noun*, *verb*.

bore /bɔː/ *noun*¹. ME.
[ORIGIN Partly from BORE *verb*¹, partly from Old Norse *bora* borehole = Old High German *boro* auger: cf. Old English *bor* gimlet, Old Norse *borr* borer, from Germanic base also of BORE *verb*¹.]
1 A hole made by boring, a perforation, an aperture. *obsolete* or *arch.* exc. as below. ME.
R. BURNS Frighted rattons . . seek the benmost bore.
2 The hollow of a gun barrel, tube, cylinder, etc. L16. ▸**b** The internal diameter of this; calibre. L16.
H. WILLIAMSON Owing to the cordite in the cartridges . . remaining in the bore, flashes occurred during re-loading.
3 A deep narrow hole made in the earth, esp. to find water, oil, etc. Also (*Austral.*), an artificial waterhole for animals. L17.
– COMB.: **borehole** = sense 3 above; **borescope** an instrument used in engineering etc. to inspect the inside of a structure through a small hole.

bore /bɔː/ *noun*². ME.
[ORIGIN Perh. from Old Norse *bára* wave.]
†**1** A wave, a billow. Only in ME.
2 More fully ***tidal bore***. A steep-fronted wave caused by the meeting of two tides or by the constriction of a tide as it passes up a narrowing estuary. E17.

bore /bɔː/ *noun*³. M18.
[ORIGIN Unknown: early sources suggest French derivation.]
†**1** Boredom, ennui; a dull time. M18–M19.
2 A thing which bores; a tedious nuisance or annoyance. L18.
3 A tiresome or tediously dull person. L18.
■ **boredom** *noun* (*a*) the state of being bored; tedium, ennui; (*b*) (now *rare*) the behaviour of a bore, bores collectively: M19. **boresome** *adjective* tending to be a bore, boring L19. **boresomeness** *noun* M19.

bore /bɔː/ *verb*¹.
[ORIGIN Old English *borian* = Middle Low German, Middle Dutch *boren*, Old High German *borōn* (German *bohren*), Old Norse *bora* from Germanic base also of BORE *noun*¹; sense 4 may be a different word.]
1 *verb trans.* Pierce, make a hole in or through, esp. (as) with an auger etc. OE. ▸**b** Pierce with a cylindrical cavity; hollow out (a gun barrel, tube, etc.). M18.
2 *verb intrans.* Make a hole or perforation (*in*, *into*, *through*); sink a borehole. ME.
3 *verb trans.* Make (a hole, tunnel, one's way, etc.) by boring, excavation, pressure, etc. E16. ▸**b** *verb trans.* & *intrans.* Of a horse: push (another horse etc.) out of the way; thrust the head straight forward. L17.
†**4** *verb trans.* Trick, cheat. Only in E17.
■ **borer** *noun* (*a*) a person who bores; a horse which bores; (*b*) any of various worms, molluscs, insects, or other creatures which bore holes; (*c*) an instrument for boring: L15. **boring** *noun* (*a*) the action of the verb; (*b*) a borehole: LME.

bore /bɔː/ *verb*² *trans.* M18.
[ORIGIN from (the same root as) BORE *noun*³.]
Cause (a person) to feel weary and uninterested by tedious talk or monotony.
E. M. FORSTER Perhaps Italy bores him; you ought to try the Alps or the Lakes. D. DABYDEEN Although largely bored by his stories, I affected an interest.
bore rigid: see RIGID *adjective*. ***bore stiff***: see STIFF *adjective*. ***bore the PANTS off***. ***bore to tears***: see TEAR *noun*¹.
■ **bored** *adjective* wearied by dullness or monotony (foll. by *with*, (*non-standard*) *of*) E19. **boredly** *adverb* E20. **boring** *adjective* tediously dull, wearisome: M19. **boringly** *adverb* M19. **boringness** *noun* L19. **borish** *adjective* (now *rare*) boring M18.

bore *verb*³ *pa. t.* of BEAR *verb*¹.

boreal /ˈbɔːrɪəl/ *adjective* & *noun*. LME.
[ORIGIN Old French & mod. French *boréal* or late Latin *borealis*, formed as BOREAS: see -AL¹.]
▸ **A** *adjective*. **1** Northern; of the North or the Arctic; of the north wind. LME.
2 a Designating or characteristic of a biogeographical zone south of the Arctic, esp. the cold temperate region dominated by taiga and forests of birch, poplar, and conifers. M19. ▸**b** (**B-**.) Designating or pertaining to a relatively warm dry climatic period in post-glacial northern Europe between the Preboreal and Atlantic periods, marked by the spread of hardwood forests. L19.
▸ **B** *noun*. *The* Boreal period. M20.

Boreas /ˈbɔːrɪəs/ *noun*. *literary*. LME.
[ORIGIN Latin from Greek.]
The north wind, esp. personified; the god of the north wind.
■ **borean** *adjective* (*rare*) = BOREAL 1 M17.

borecole /ˈbɔːkəʊl/ *noun*. E18.
[ORIGIN Dutch *boerenkool* lit. 'peasant's cabbage', from *boer* BOOR + *kool* COLE *noun*¹.]
= KALE 1.

bore da /ˈbɒrɛ ˌdɑː/ *interjection*. *Welsh*. M20.
[ORIGIN Welsh, from *bore* morning + *da* good.]
Good morning!

boree /ˈbɔːriː/ *noun*¹. *Austral.* M19.
[ORIGIN Wiradhuri and Kamilaroi *burrii*.]
The weeping myall, *Acacia pendula*.

†**boree** *noun*² var. of BOURRÉE.

boreen /bɔːˈriːn/ *noun*. *Irish*. Also **bohereen**. M19.
[ORIGIN Irish *bóithrín* dim. of *bóthar* road: see -EEN².]
A narrow country road, a lane.

borek /bɔːˈrɛk/ *noun*. M19.
[ORIGIN Turkish = pie.]
An envelope of thin pastry filled with cheese, spinach, or minced meat and baked or fried.

borel *adjective* var. of BORREL.

borgata /bɔːˈɡɑːtə/ *noun*. E20.
[ORIGIN from Italian *borgatà* district, village, from *borgo* small centre of habitation, from Latin *burgus* castle, fort, rel. to BOROUGH.]
1 In Italy: a district of poor-quality housing; a slum. E20.
2 An organized branch of the Mafia. *US*. M20.

Borgesian /bɔːˈxɛsɪən/ *adjective*. L20.
[ORIGIN from the name of Jorge Luis *Borges* (1899–1986), Argentinian writer of short stories and poetry + -IAN.]
Characteristic or reminiscent of the work of Borges, esp. his use of techniques of magic realism in the creation of labyrinthine fictional worlds.

boric /ˈbɔːrɪk/ *adjective*. M19.
[ORIGIN from BORON + -IC.]
CHEMISTRY. Of boron; ***boric acid***, a weakly acidic crystalline solid, $B(OH)_3$, which is derived from borax and is used as an antiseptic.

boride /ˈbɔːrʌɪd/ *noun*. M19.
[ORIGIN from BORON + -IDE.]
CHEMISTRY. A binary compound of boron with a metallic element.

bork /bɔːk/ *verb trans.* *US*. L20.
[ORIGIN from the name of Robert *Bork* (b. 1927), a judge whose nomination to the US Supreme Court in 1987 was rejected following unfavourable publicity for his allegedly illiberal and extreme views.]
Defame or vilify (a person) systematically, esp. with the aim of making it difficult for him or her to hold public office.

borlotti /bɔːˈlɒti/ *noun pl.* L20.
[ORIGIN Italian = kidney beans.]
In full ***borlotti beans***. Kidney beans of a variety with a pink speckled skin that turns brown when cooked.

born /bɔːn/ *ppl adjective* (orig. *pple*).
[ORIGIN Old English *boren* pa. pple of BEAR *verb*¹: long distinct from *borne*.]
▸ **I** *pred.* **1** Brought forth by birth as offspring; *fig.* brought into existence, started in life; destined; innately suited. OE.
SHAKES. *Temp.* If he be not born to be hang'd, our case is miserable. TENNYSON Some sudden turn of anger born Of your misfaith. N. MITFORD She was born a Miss Perrotte. M. H. ABRAMS Poets who are born and poets who are made. L. HELLMAN An old, very black lady who had been born into slavery. J. G. FARRELL The other infant, a girl born to Mrs Wright . . , survived. D. FRASER His eldest child . . had just been born.
firstborn, ***freeborn***, ***high-born***, ***low-born***, etc.
▸ **II** *attrib.* **2** That has been born; of (specified) birth; *fig.* destined by birth or inherent qualities; naturally gifted; (in unfavourable sense) utter, hopeless. ME.
DRYDEN Authors nobly born will bear their part. S. RICHARDSON I, a poor helpless Girl . . shall put on Lady-airs to a Gentlewoman born. E. A. FREEMAN The Danish-born Bernard. G. B. SHAW An ignorant dupe and a born fool into the bargain. K. M. E. MURRAY He was himself a born teacher, never . . able to resist passing on information.
3 Of a quality: innate, inherited. M18.
– PHRASES & COMB.: **born-again** *adjective* (*a*) regenerate, revitalized, *esp.* claiming spiritual rebirth as a Christian; (*b*) full of enthusiastic zeal for a cause. ***born and bred***: see BRED *ppl adjective*. ***born in the purple***: see PURPLE *adjective* & *noun*. ***born with a silver spoon in one's mouth***: see SPOON *noun*. ***not born YESTERDAY***. **one's born days** one's life hitherto. ***to the manner born***: see MANNER *noun*¹.
– NOTE: Until 18 *borne* and *born* were simply vars. of the pa. pple of BEAR *verb*¹, used interchangeably with no distinction in meaning. By around 1775, however, the present distinction in use had become established.

born /bɔːn/ *verb*. *US*. M20.
[ORIGIN Irreg. from BORN *adjective*.]
1 *verb trans.* Cause to be born; bring into the world. *rare*. M20.
2 *verb intrans.* Be born; come to birth or into existence. Chiefly as **borning** *ppl adjective* & *verbal noun* (cf. ABORNING). M20.

Borna disease /ˈbɔːnə dɪˌziːz/ *noun phr.* E20.
[ORIGIN *Borna*, a town and district near Leipzig in Germany where an outbreak occurred.]
An infectious neurological disease affecting horses and other mammals and birds, caused by an RNA virus.

borne *verb* & *ppl adjective* see BEAR *verb*¹.

borné /bɔrne/ *adjective*. L18.
[ORIGIN French, pa. pple of *borner* limit.]
Limited in scope, intellect, outlook, etc.

Bornean /ˈbɔːnɪən/ *adjective* & *noun*. E19.
[ORIGIN from *Borneo* (see below) + -AN.]
▸ **A** *adjective*. Of or pertaining to the E. Indian island of Borneo. E19.
▸ **B** *noun*. A native or inhabitant of Borneo. M19.

borneol /ˈbɔːnɪɒl/ *noun*. M19.
[ORIGIN formed as BORNEAN + -OL.]
CHEMISTRY. A crystalline terpenoid alcohol, $C_{10}H_{18}O$, present in many essential oils; *esp.* that of the Borneo camphor tree *Dryobalanops aromatica*.

Bornholm disease /ˈbɔːnhəʊm dɪˌziːz/ *noun phr.* M20.
[ORIGIN *Bornholm*, a Danish island in the Baltic.]
An epidemic viral disease causing severe pain in the intercostal muscles and the diaphragm.

B

B

bornite /ˈbɔːnʌɪt/ *noun*. E19.
[ORIGIN from Ignatius von *Born* (1742–91), Austrian mineralogist + -ITE[1].]
MINERALOGY. A brittle reddish-brown sulphide of copper and iron, occurring usu. as cubic or dodecahedral crystals.

boro- /ˈbɔːrəʊ/ *combining form* of next: see -O-.
■ **boro'hydride** *noun* a compound of the anion BH_4^- M20. **boro'silicate** *noun* a substance derived from or containing both silica and boric oxide (B_2O_3), *esp.* a kind of glass E19.

boron /ˈbɔːrɒn/ *noun*. E19.
[ORIGIN from BORAX *noun*[1] after *carbon*, which it resembles in certain respects.]
A relatively inert non-metallic chemical element, atomic no. 5, occurring as a dark brown amorphous powder and as black crystals (symbol B).

boronia /bəˈrəʊnɪə/ *noun*. L18.
[ORIGIN mod. Latin, from Francesco *Borone* (1769–94), Italian botanist: see -IA[1].]
A fragrant Australian shrub of the genus *Boronia*, of the rue family.

borough /ˈbʌrə/ *noun*. Sense 1 *hist.* also **burh**. See also BURGH, BURROW *noun*[2]
[ORIGIN Old English *burg*, *burh* = Old Frisian *burch*, Old Saxon *burg* (Middle Dutch *burch*, Dutch *burg*), Old High German *burug* (German *Burg*), Old Norse *borg*, Gothic *baurgs*, from Germanic; rel. to Old English *beorgan*: see BORROW *verb*[1].]
1 A fortress, a castle, a citadel; a court, a manor house. Long *obsolete* exc. *hist.* as *burh*. OE.
2 Orig., a fortified town. Later, a town, district, large village, etc., with some form of municipal organization. In Britain, long *obsolete* or *hist.* exc. as below. OE. ▸**b** *spec.* An administrative division of London or of New York City. L19. ▸**c** *spec.* In Alaska, a territorial division corresponding to a county. M20.
3 A town (as distinct from a city) with a corporation and privileges granted by royal charter; *hist.* a town sending representatives to Parliament. LME.
close borough, **pocket borough** *hist.* a borough where elections were controlled by a wealthy private person or family. **rotten borough** *hist.* a borough represented in Parliament although no longer having a real constituency. **the Borough**: *esp.* that of Southwark, London.
4 *hist.* A property held by burgage tenure. E18.
– COMB.: **borough council** a council which conducts the affairs of a borough; **borough-English** *hist.* tenure whereby the youngest son inherited all lands and tenements; †**borough-master** = BURGOMASTER; **boroughmonger** *hist.* a person who traded in parliamentary seats for boroughs; **boroughmongering** *ppl adjective & verbal noun* (*hist.*) (involved in) trading in parliamentary seats for boroughs; **boroughmongery** *hist.* the practice of boroughmongering; **borough-reeve** †(*a*) the governor of a town or city; (*b*) *hist.* the chief municipal officer of certain English towns; **borough-town** *arch.* a town which is a borough.

borrel /ˈbɒr(ə)l/ *adjective*. *arch.* Also **borel**. LME.
[ORIGIN Perh. orig. an attrib. use of BUREL with ref. to coarse clothing.]
1 Belonging to the laity. LME.
2 Unlearned, rude; rough. L15.

Borrovian /bɒˈrəʊvɪən/ *noun & adjective*. L19.
[ORIGIN from *Borrow* (see below) + -IAN, after *Harrovian* etc.]
▸ **A** *noun*. An admirer or student of the English writer George Borrow (1803–81) or his work; the diction characteristic of Borrow's writing. L19.
▸ **B** *adjective*. Of, pertaining to, or characteristic of Borrow or his writing. E20.

borrow /ˈbɒrəʊ/ *noun*.
[ORIGIN Old English *borg* = Old Frisian *borg*, Middle High German *borc* pledge, from Germanic; rel. to Old English *beorgan* (see BORROW *verb*[1]). Sense 4 from BORROW *verb*[1].]
1 A pledge; a guarantee, bail; a ransom. Long *arch.* exc. *SCOTS LAW*. OE.
law-borrow(s): see LAW *noun*[1].
2 A surety; a person who stands bail. Long *arch.* OE.
3 *hist.* A frank-pledge, a tithing. L16.
4 A borrowing. *rare* in *gen.* sense. E17. ▸**b** *GOLF*. A borrowing to allow for the slope of the green etc.; the amount borrowed. M19.
– COMB.: **borrow-head** = BORSHOLDER; **borrow-hole**, **borrow-pit**: made by removing material for use in embanking etc.

borrow /ˈbɒrəʊ/ *verb*[1].
[ORIGIN Old English *borgian* = Old Frisian *borgia*, Middle Low German, Middle Dutch *borgen*, Old High German *borgēn* (German *borgen*), from Germanic, rel. to Old English *beorgan* = Old Saxon, Old High German *bergan* (Dutch, German *bergen*), Old Norse *bjarga*, Gothic *bairgan*, from Germanic base meaning 'protect, shelter', whence also BURY *verb*.]
1 *verb trans. & intrans.* Orig., take (a thing) on security given for its safe return. Now, get temporary use of (money or property to be returned later); take on loan. (Foll. by *from*, *of* a person etc.) OE. ▸**b** *MATH.* In subtraction, transfer (a unit of the next higher denomination) in the number being subtracted from, compensating for this at the next step. L16.

COVERDALE 2 *Esd.* 5:3 Let vs borowe money of the kinge vpon vsury. G. B. SHAW I will not borrow from my friends. W. STYRON He had managed once again to borrow Larry's car for the weekend.

2 *verb trans. fig.* Adopt, use without being the true owner or inventor; derive from another; import from an alien source. ME.

SHAKES. *John* Inferior eyes, That borrow their behaviours from the great. B. JOWETT No man can be happy who, to borrow Plato's illustration, is leading the life of an oyster.

3 *verb trans.* Be surety for; ransom. Long *arch.* ME.
4 *verb trans. MUSIC.* Derive (an organ stop) from the pipe of another stop; equip (an organ) with such stops. Chiefly as ***borrowed*** *ppl adjective*. M19.
5 *verb trans. & intrans. GOLF.* Allow (a certain distance) for sideways motion due to wind or slope, when putting. L19.
– PHRASES: ***beg, borrow, or steal***: see BEG *verb*. **borrowed days** *hist.* in Scotland, the last three days of March (Old Style), said to have been borrowed from April and to be particularly stormy. **borrowed light** (*a*) reflected light; (*b*) a window in an internal wall designed to admit light. **borrowed plumage**, **borrowed plumes** a pretentious display not of one's own making. **borrowed time** an unexpected extension of time, esp. of life (chiefly in ***living on borrowed time***). **borrow trouble** *N. Amer. colloq.* go out of one's way to find trouble.
■ **borrower** *noun* LME. **borrowing** *noun* (*a*) the action of the verb (***borrowing days*** = ***borrowed days*** above); (*b*) that which is borrowed: LME.

borrow /ˈbɒrəʊ/ *verb*[2] *intrans.* L16.
[ORIGIN Perh. var. of BURROW *verb*.]
NAUTICAL. Approach closely to land or wind.

Borsalino /bɔːsəˈliːnəʊ/ *noun*. Also **b-**. Pl. **-os**. E20.
[ORIGIN Name of the manufacturer.]
(Proprietary name for) a man's wide-brimmed felt hat.

borscht /bɔːʃt/ *noun*. Also **borsch**, **borshch**, /bɔːʃ/, **bortsch** /bɔːtʃ/. E19.
[ORIGIN Russian *borshch*.]
A Russian, Polish, or Ukrainian soup of various ingredients including beetroot.
– COMB.: **Borscht Belt** *US* a humorous term for a resort area in the Catskill mountains, in the state of New York, frequented chiefly by Jewish people of Eastern European origin.

borsholder /ˈbɔːshəʊldə/ *noun*. ME.
[ORIGIN Anglo-Latin *borgesalder* (Anglo-Norman *burghaldre*), from Middle English *borȝes* genit. sing. of BORROW *noun* + *alder*, Old English *aldor* chief (see ALDERMAN).]
hist. The chief of a frank-pledge. Later, a petty constable.

Borstal /ˈbɔːst(ə)l/ *noun*. Also **b-**. E20.
[ORIGIN A village in Kent, England, site of the first such institution.]
In full ***Borstal institution***. A custodial institution to which young offenders may be sent for reformative training.

borstch *noun* var. of BORSCHT.

bort /bɔːt/ *noun*. Also **boart**. E17.
[ORIGIN Dutch *boort*.]
Coarse diamonds of poor quality; diamond fragments esp. used as an abrasive.

Borussian /bəʊˈrʌʃ(ə)n/ *adjective & noun*. *arch.* E17.
[ORIGIN from medieval Latin *Borussi* pl., *Borussia*, alt. of *Prussi*, *Prussia* as if from Slavonic *po* by, alongside, + *Russi*, *Russia*: see PRUSSIAN, RUSSIAN, -IAN.]
(A) Prussian.

borzoi /ˈbɔːzɔɪ/ *noun*. L19.
[ORIGIN Russian *borzoĭ* adjective, *borzaya* noun, from *borzyĭ* swift.]
(An animal of) a Russian breed of large wolfhound, with a usu. white silky coat.

bosa *noun* var. of BOZA.

bosbok /ˈbɒsbɒk/ *noun*. *S. Afr.* Also †**bosch-**. L18.
[ORIGIN Afrikaans, from Dutch *bosch* BUSH *noun*[1] + *bok* BUCK *noun*[1].]
= ***bushbuck*** s.v. BUSH *noun*[1].

boscage /ˈbɒskɪdʒ/ *noun*. Also **-sk-**. LME.
[ORIGIN Old French (mod. BOCAGE) from Proto-Gallo-Romance, ult. from base of BUSH *noun*[1]: see -AGE.]
1 A mass of trees or shrubs, a thicket; wooded scenery. LME.
†**2** A representation of wooded landscape, foliage, etc. Only in 17.

†**boschbok** *noun* var. of BOSBOK.

bose /bəʊs/ *verb trans.* E20.
[ORIGIN Perh. alt. of BOSS *verb*[1].]
Test (ground) for the presence of buried structures by noting the sound of percussion from a weighted object. Chiefly as ***bosing*** *verbal noun*
■ **boser** *noun* an instrument used for bosing ground M20.

Bose–Einstein statistics /bəʊzˈʌɪnstʌɪn stəˌtɪstɪks/ *noun phr.* E20.
[ORIGIN S. N. *Bose* (see BOSON) + A. *Einstein* (see EINSTEINIAN).]
PHYSICS. A type of quantum statistics used to describe systems of identical particles to which the exclusion principle does not apply.

bosey *noun* var. of BOSIE.

bosh /bɒʃ/ *noun*[1]. L17.
[ORIGIN Unknown.]
1 In *pl.*, the inwardly sloping sides of a blast furnace, extending downwards from the belly to the hearth. Later also *sing.*, this lower part of the furnace. L17.
2 A trough or sink, esp. for cooling metal in water. *dial.* L19.

bosh /bɒʃ/ *noun*[2]. *slang*. M19.
[ORIGIN Turkish *boş* empty, worthless.]
Nonsense, foolish talk. Also as *interjection*.
■ **bosher** *noun* a person who talks bosh E20. **boshy** *adjective* worthless; nonsensical: M19.

bosie /ˈbəʊzi/ *noun*. *Austral.* Also **-sey**. E20.
[ORIGIN from B. J. T. *Bos(anquet)* (1877–1936), English cricketer + -IE.]
= GOOGLY *noun*.

bosk /bɒsk/ *noun*. ME.
[ORIGIN Var. of BUSH *noun*[1]: in mod. literary use back-form. from BOSKY.]
1 A bush. Long *obsolete* exc. *dial.* ME.
2 A thicket of bushes etc.; a small wood. E19.

boskage *noun* var. of BOSCAGE.

bosker /ˈbɒskə/ *adjective*. *Austral. & NZ slang*. Now *rare*. E20.
[ORIGIN Unknown.]
Good, excellent, first-rate.

bosket /ˈbɒskɪt/ *noun*. Also **-squ-**. M18.
[ORIGIN French *bosquet* from Italian *boschetto* dim. of *bosco* wood. Cf. BOUQUET.]
A plantation of small trees in a garden, park, etc.; a thicket.

bosky /ˈbɒski/ *adjective*. L16.
[ORIGIN from BOSK + -Y[1]: sense 2 may be a different word.]
1 Full of bushes or thickets; bushy. L16.
2 Fuddled by drink, tipsy. *dial. & slang*. M18.

Bosman /ˈbɒzmən/ *noun*. L20.
[ORIGIN Jean-Marc *Bosman* (b. 1964), Belgian footballer, who brought a legal case in 1995 which resulted in the ruling.]
1 Used attrib. with ref. to a European Court ruling which obliges professional football or other sports clubs to allow players over the age of 25 to move freely between clubs once their contracts have expired, without the new club being required to pay a transfer fee. L20.
2 (A player available on) a free transfer under this ruling. L20.

bo's'n *noun* var. of BOSUN.

Bosnian /ˈbɒznɪən/ *noun & adjective*. L18.
[ORIGIN from *Bosnia* (see below) + -IAN.]
▸ **A** *noun*. A native or inhabitant of Bosnia, a region in the Balkans now a part of Bosnia-Herzegovina. L18.
▸ **B** *adjective*. Of or pertaining to Bosnia. M19.
■ Also **Bosniak**, **Bosniac** *noun* M19.

bosom /ˈbʊz(ə)m/ *noun & adjective*.
[ORIGIN Old English *bōsm* = Old Frisian *bōsm*, Old Saxon *bōsom* (Dutch *boezem*), Old High German *buosam* (German *Busen*), from West Germanic, perh. ult. from base of BOUGH.]
▸ **A** *noun*. **1** The breast of a human being, esp. of a woman; *poet.* the breast of a bird etc. Also (*colloq.*, chiefly *US*) in *pl.*, a woman's breasts. OE.
2 *fig.* The surface *of* the sea, a river, the ground, etc. OE.
3 The part of the dress which covers the breast; the space between the dress and the breast, esp. considered as a receptacle for money, letters, etc. OE. ▸**b** A shirt front. *US*. M19.
4 A concavity, a recess, a hollow interior. OE.
5 The enclosure formed by the breast and the arms. ME.
6 The breast considered as the seat of emotions, desires, secret thoughts, etc. ME.

SHAKES. *Oth.* I will bestow you where you shall have time To speak your bosom freely.

friend of one's bosom, ***wife of one's bosom*** (with rhet. emphasis).
7 *fig.* The interior, the midst; the enfolding relationship *of* one's family, the Church, etc. LME.

GEO. ELIOT Deep in the bosom of the hills.

†**8** *transf.* A person. Cf. ***hand***, ***head***, etc. L16–M18.
9 = ***bosom friend*** below. *colloq.* E20.
– PHRASES: ***Abraham's bosom***: see ABRAHAM *noun* 1. **take to one's bosom** *arch.* marry. ***the bird in the bosom***: see BIRD *noun*.
▸ **B** *attrib.* or as *adjective*. Intimate, confidential. Chiefly in ***bosom friend*** below. L16.
bosom friend [cf. German *Busenfreund*] a specially intimate or dear friend.
■ **bosomy** *adjective* (*a*) full of sheltered hollows; (*b*) (of a woman) with a prominent bosom: E17.

bosom /ˈbʊz(ə)m/ *verb*. LME.
[ORIGIN from the noun.]
1 *verb intrans.* Swell out. Now *rare* or *obsolete*. LME.
2 *verb trans.* Put into or carry in the bosom; embrace, take to the bosom; *fig.* receive into intimate companionship; keep in mind (a secret thought etc.). *arch.* L16.

bosomed /ˈbʊz(ə)md/ *adjective*. E17.
[ORIGIN from BOSOM *noun*, *verb*: see -ED[2], -ED[1].]
1 Having a bosom (of a specified kind); shaped like a bosom, swelled out. E17.
2 Confined in the bosom; enclosed, hidden, (of the breath) bated. M17.

boson /ˈbəʊzɒn/ *noun*. M20.
[ORIGIN from S. N. *Bose* (1894–1974), Indian physicist, who with Einstein stated the statistical relations describing the behaviour of such particles: see -ON.]

PHYSICS. A particle that has a symmetric wave function, and hence integer spin, and can be described by Bose–Einstein statistics. Cf. FERMION.

bosquet *noun* var. of BOSKET.

BOSS *abbreviation.*
S. AFR. HISTORY. Bureau of (properly for) State Security.

boss /bɒs/ *noun*[1]. ME.
[ORIGIN Old French *boce* (mod. *bosse*) from Proto-Romance, of unknown origin.]
1 A protuberance on the body of an animal or plant; a convex or knoblike excrescent portion of an organ or structure. ME.

S. BECKETT Cascades of light . . fell on the hairless domes and bosses of his skull. P. V. WHITE He stood in the entrance to the cave . . resting his forehead against a boss of cold rock.

2 A round knob in sculptured or carved work; an ornamental projection at an intersection in vaulting; a metal stud on a book, bridle, shield, etc. LME. ▸**b** An enlarged or projecting mechanical part, e.g. of a shaft, sternpost, etc.; the central part of a propeller. M19.
3 A rocky outcrop or knoll; GEOLOGY a mass of rock protruding through other strata, *esp.* an igneous intrusion of rounded form. L15.
4 A soft pad used in ceramics and glass manufacture for smoothing colours and for cleaning. M19.
■ **bosset** *noun* a small protuberance or knob M19.

boss /bɒs/ *noun*[2]. M16.
[ORIGIN Perh. from Middle Dutch *bosse, busse*, Dutch *bos, bus* box.]
A plasterer's tray; a hod.

boss /bɒs/ *noun*[3]. Now *dial.* L17.
[ORIGIN Perh. alt. of BASS *noun*[3], but cf. Dutch *bos* bundle of straw.]
A seat of straw; a hassock.

boss /bɒs/ *noun*[4] *& adjective. colloq.* (orig. *US*). E19.
[ORIGIN Dutch *baas* master.]
▸ **A** *noun.* **1** The master; a person in authority, an overseer, a business manager. Freq. as a form of address. E19.
2 A manager of a political organization. *US.* M19.
▸ **B** *attrib.* or as *adjective.* (Of a person) master, chief; (of a thing) most excellent; *US slang* excellent, wonderful. M19.
– SPECIAL COLLOCATIONS & COMB.: **boss-cocky** *Austral. & NZ slang* a farmer who shares the work with employees; a person in authority. **boss-man** a man in charge, the master.
■ **bossism** *noun* (*US*) the system in which political parties are controlled by bosses L19. **boss-ship** *noun* the rule or position of a boss or bosses, esp. in politics L19.

boss /bɒs/ *noun*[5]. *dial. & US.* E19.
[ORIGIN Unknown.]
A cow; a bovine animal. Chiefly as a form of address.

boss /bɒs/ *noun*[6]. *dial. & slang.* L19.
[ORIGIN Rel. to BOSS *verb*[3].]
In full ***boss shot***. A bad shot or aim; an unsuccessful attempt.

boss /bɒs/ *verb*[1]. LME.
[ORIGIN from BOSS *noun*[1].]
†**1** *verb trans. & intrans.* (Cause to) project; swell or round out. LME–M17.
2 *verb trans.* Shape in relief; beat or press *out* into a raised ornament; emboss. LME.
3 *verb trans.* Provide or ornament with bosses. M16.
4 *verb trans.* Smooth (a ceramic surface) by means of a boss. M19.
5 *verb trans. & intrans.* Bang. *dial.* L19.

boss /bɒs/ *verb*[2] *trans. colloq.* (orig. *US*). M19.
[ORIGIN from BOSS *noun*[4].]
Be the master or manager of; give orders to, direct.
boss about continually give peremptory orders to.

boss /bɒs/ *verb*[3] *trans. & intrans. dial. & slang.* L19.
[ORIGIN Rel. to BOSS-EYED.]
Miss or bungle (a shot); make a mess (of).

bossage /ˈbɒsɪdʒ/ *noun.* E18.
[ORIGIN French, from *bosse* BOSS *noun*[1]: see -AGE.]
ARCHITECTURE. Projecting stonework, bosses; *esp.* a type of rustic work.

bossa nova /bɒsə ˈnəʊvə/ *noun phr.* M20.
[ORIGIN Portuguese *bossa* tendency, *nova* fem. sing. of *novo* new.]
A style of Brazilian music related to the samba; a dance to this music.

bosselated /ˈbɒsɪleɪtɪd/ *adjective.* M19.
[ORIGIN French *bosselé* pa. pple of *bosseler*, from *bosse* BOSS *noun*[1]: see -ATE[3], -ED[1].]
Formed into small protuberances.

boss-eyed /ˈbɒsʌɪd/ *adjective. colloq.* M19.
[ORIGIN Unknown: cf. BOSS *noun*[6], *verb*[3].]
Having only one good eye; squint-eyed, cross-eyed; *fig.* crooked.

bossy /ˈbɒsi/ *noun. dial. & US.* M19.
[ORIGIN from BOSS *noun*[5] + -Y[6].]
A cow, a calf.

bossy /ˈbɒsi/ *adjective*[1]. M16.
[ORIGIN from BOSS *noun*[1] + -Y[1].]
Swelling in or projecting like a boss; having bosses.
■ **bossiness** *noun*[1] L19.

bossy /ˈbɒsi/ *adjective*[2]. *colloq.* (orig. *US*). L19.
[ORIGIN from BOSS *noun*[4] + -Y[1].]
Given to acting like a boss; domineering.
– COMB.: **bossyboots** an unwarrantedly bossy person.
■ **bossiness** *noun*[2] E20.

bostangi /bɒsˈtandʒi/ *noun. obsolete* exc. *hist.* L17.
[ORIGIN Turkish *bostancı* lit. 'gardener'.]
A soldier of the Turkish palace guard.

bosthoon /bɒsˈtuːn/ *noun. Irish.* M19.
[ORIGIN Irish *bastún*]
An ignorant lout; a tactless, insensitive person.

bosting /ˈbɒstɪŋ/ *adjective. dial.* Also **bostin** /ˈbɒstɪn/. L20.
[ORIGIN Prob. dial. pronunc. of *bursting* ppl adjective of BURST *verb* or *busting* ppl adjective of BUST *verb.*]
Very good, excellent.

J. HAWES A decent, cheap pint at last! Bostin!

Boston /ˈbɒst(ə)n/ *noun & verb.* E19.
[ORIGIN A city in Massachusetts, USA: sense A.1 is through French.]
▸ **A** *noun.* **1** A card game resembling solo whist. E19.
2 ***Boston baked beans***, a dish of baked beans with salt pork and molasses. M19.
3 A variation of the waltz or of the two-step. L19.
4 In full ***Boston bull terrier***, ***Boston terrier***. (A dog of) a breed of small smooth-coated terrier originating in Massachusetts from a crossing of the bulldog and terrier. L19.
5 ***Boston ivy***, a Virginia creeper, *Parthenocissus tricuspidata*. L19.
6 ***Boston crab***, a wrestling hold in which a wrestler sits astride a prone opponent and pulls upwards on the opponent's legs. M20.
▸ **B** *verb intrans.* Dance the Boston. E20.
■ **Bostoˈnese** *noun* (*a*) *collect.* Bostonians; (*b*) the method of speech or the manners said to be affected by Bostonians: L18. **Bosˈtonian** *noun & adjective* (*a*) *noun* a native or inhabitant of Boston; (*b*) *adjective* belonging or native to Boston: L17.

bostryx /ˈbɒstrɪks/ *noun.* L19.
[ORIGIN Greek *bostrux* curl of hair.]
BOTANY. A helicoid cyme.

bosun /ˈbəʊs(ə)n/ *noun.* Also **bo's'n**, **bo'sun**. M17.
[ORIGIN Repr. pronunc. of BOATSWAIN.]
= BOATSWAIN.

Boswell /ˈbɒzwɛl/ *noun.* M19.
[ORIGIN James *Boswell* (1740–95), companion and biographer of Samuel Johnson.]
A person who, as a constant companion or attendant, witnesses and records the life of another.
■ **Bosˈwellian, -ean** *adjective & noun* (*a*) *adjective* resembling Boswell as a biographer; (*b*) an admirer or student of Boswell or his writing: M19. **Boswellism** *noun* the manner or style of Boswell as a biographer E19. **Boswellize** *verb trans. & intrans.* write (of) in the manner of Boswell M19.

bot /bɒt/ *noun*[1]. Also **-tt**. E16.
[ORIGIN Prob. of Low Dutch origin: cf. Dutch *bot*, West Frisian *botten* (pl.), Western Flemish *botse*, Northern Frisian *galboten* liver-worm, West Frisian *botgalle* disease caused by bots.]
1 A parasitic worm or maggot infesting livestock; *spec.* the larva of a fly (called ***botfly***) of the genus *Oestrus*, which affects esp. the digestive organs; ***the bots*** (as *sing.*), the disease caused by these parasites. E16.
2 A cadger; a useless person; a hanger-on. *Austral. & NZ slang.* E20.

bot /bɒt/ *noun*[2]. Also **-tt**. E20.
[ORIGIN Abbreviation of BOTTOM *noun*: cf. BOTTY.]
A child's word for the buttocks.

bot *noun*[3] see BOOT *noun*[1].

bot /bɒt/ *noun*[4]. M20.
[ORIGIN Short for ROBOT.]
1 A robot. M20.
2 COMPUTING. An autonomous program on the Internet or other network which can interact with computer systems or users. L20.
cancelbot, ***chatterbot***, ***knowbot***, etc.

bot /bɒt/ *verb. Austral. & NZ slang.* Infl. **-tt-**. E20.
[ORIGIN from BOT *noun*[1].]
1 *verb trans.* Cadge. E20.
2 *verb intrans.* Foll. by *on*: impose on, cadge from. M20.

bot. *abbreviation.*
1 Botanic(al), botany.
2 Bottle.
3 Bought.

botanic /bəˈtanɪk/ *adjective & noun.* M17.
[ORIGIN French *botanique* or its source late Latin *botanicus* from Greek *botanikos*, from *botanē* plant: see -IC.]
▸ **A** *adjective.* Of or pertaining to botany; *arch.* exc. in names of institutions etc., as ***botanic gardens***. M17.
▸ **B** *noun.* †**1** A botanist. M17–E18.
2 In *pl.* Botany. Now *rare.* L17.

botanical /bəˈtanɪk(ə)l/ *adjective.* M17.
[ORIGIN formed as BOTANIC + -AL[1].]
Of, pertaining to, or concerned with botany.
■ **botanically** *adverb* M18.

botanise *verb* var. of BOTANIZE.

botanist /ˈbɒtənɪst/ *noun.* M17.
[ORIGIN French *botaniste*, formed as BOTANIC + *-iste* -IST.]
An expert in or student of botany.

botanize /ˈbɒtənʌɪz/ *verb.* Also **-ise**. M18.
[ORIGIN mod. Latin *botanizare* from Greek *botanizein* gather plants, from *botanē* plant: see -IZE.]
1 *verb intrans.* Seek plants for botanical purposes; study plants, esp. where they are growing. M18.
2 *verb trans.* Explore or examine botanically. M19.
■ **botanizer** *noun* E19.

botano- /ˈbɒtənəʊ/ *combining form* of Greek *botanē* plant: see -O-.
■ **botaˈnographer** *noun* (*rare*) a person who describes plants L17. †**botanographist** *noun* = BOTANOGRAPHER M17–E18. †**botanology** *noun* botany M17–E18. **botanomancy** *noun* (*rare*) divination by means of plants E17.

botany /ˈbɒtəni/ *noun.* L17.
[ORIGIN from BOTANIC + -Y[3].]
1 The science of the structure, physiology, classification, and distribution of plants. L17.
2 *a* ***Botany Bay*** (*hist.*) [in New South Wales, Australia, named from its varied flora and formerly the site of a convict settlement], the destination of a transported convict, transportation. E19. ▸**b** In full ***Botany wool***. Merino wool, esp. from Australia. L19.

botch /bɒtʃ/ *noun*[1]. LME.
[ORIGIN Old Northern French *boche* var. of Old French *boce* BOSS *noun*[1].]
†**1** A hump, a swelling, a tumour. LME–E16.
2 A boil, an ulcer, a pimple. Now *dial.* LME.
†**3** An eruptive disease or plague. Chiefly in ***botch of Egypt***. LME–M19.
■ †**botchy** *adjective*[1] pertaining to, or of the nature of, a botch; covered with botches: LME–M18.

botch /bɒtʃ/ *noun*[2]. E17.
[ORIGIN from BOTCH *verb.*]
1 A botched place or part; a blemish arising from unskilful workmanship, a clumsy patch. E17.
2 A bungled piece of work. M17.

S. LAWRENCE He had made such a botch of washing his clothes.

3 = BOTCHER *noun*[1]. *dial. & colloq.* E19.
■ **botchy** *adjective*[2] full of bungling work L19.

botch /bɒtʃ/ *verb.* LME.
[ORIGIN Uncertain: perh. transf. use of BOTCH *noun*[1]. Cf. BODGE *verb.*]
1 *verb trans.* (freq. foll. by *up*) & *intrans.* Patch, mend, repair (now only clumsily or imperfectly). LME.
2 *verb trans.* Spoil by unskilful work; bungle. M16.

S. KING The job had been botched somehow.

3 *verb trans.* Put or stitch together clumsily; construct or compose in a bungling manner. Freq. foll. by *up*, *together*. M16.

P. O'BRIAN Even now I cannot congratulate her on that botched-together bowsprit.

botcher /ˈbɒtʃə/ *noun*[1]. LME.
[ORIGIN from BOTCH *verb* + -ER[1].]
1 An unskilful worker; a bungler. LME.
2 A mender, a patcher; *esp.* a cobbler or tailor who does repairs. L15.
■ **botchery** *noun* a botcher's work E17.

botcher /ˈbɒtʃə/ *noun*[2]. E17.
[ORIGIN Unknown.]
A young salmon; a grilse.

bote *noun* see BOOT *noun*[1].

botel /bəʊˈtɛl/ *noun.* Orig. *US.* Also **boatel**. M20.
[ORIGIN Blend of BOAT *noun* and HOTEL.]
1 A hotel catering for boat-owners. M20.
2 A ship with the facilities of a hotel. M20.

boteroll /ˈbəʊtərɒl/ *noun.* M19.
[ORIGIN French *bouterolle* tip of a scabbard etc.]
HERALDRY. A charge resembling the tip of a scabbard.

both /bəʊθ/ *adjective & pronoun* (in mod. usage also classed as a *determiner*), *pronoun*, *& adverb.* ME.
[ORIGIN Old Norse *báðir* masc., *báðar* fem., *báði*, *bæði* neut. = Old Frisian *be(i)the*, *be(i)de*, Old Saxon *bēþia*, Old High German *bēde* (German *beide*): extended form of the base found in Old English *bēgen* masc., *bā*, *bū* fem. and neut., Gothic *bai* masc., *ba* neut., and in Latin *ambo*.]
▸ **A** *adjective.* The one and the other; the two (and not just one). (Within the noun phr.: preceding a pl. noun and any determiners (demonstratives, possessives, etc.); †between a determiner and a pl. noun; following a pl. pronoun or (with emphasis, esp. with the subject of a sentence) noun. Outside the noun phr.: following *be* or (*rare*) *become*, *seem*, etc., or an auxiliary verb.) ME.

G. CHAPMAN To plate the both horns round about with gold. TENNYSON Both thy brethren are in Arthur's hall. DICKENS We are both men of the world. OED The brothers might both have come. E. HEMINGWAY I held on to the timber with both hands. R. MACAULAY We both keep a kind of daily journal. J. JOHNSTON One heart seemed to beat in both their bodies.

both ways RACING = ***EACH way***. ***cut both ways***: see CUT *verb*. ***have it both ways***: see HAVE *verb*. ***play both sides of the street***: see STREET

B

noun. ***swing both ways***: see SWING *verb*. ***the best of both worlds***: see WORLD *noun*.

▸ **B** *pronoun*. **1** The one and the other (and not just one). ME.

S. JOHNSON The old gentlewoman considered herself wiser than both. LD MACAULAY Both were Tories: both were men of hot temper and strong prejudices.

2 Each, the two, *of* (two persons, things, etc.). Also (*colloq.*) ***the both of***. Usu. followed by a pronoun L16.

AV *Gen.* 22:8 They went both of them together. B. JOWETT Both of us often talk to the lads. J. P. DONLEAVY I'll make a nice pot of tea for the both of us.

▸ **C** *adverb*. With equal truth in either of two (or *arch.* more) cases. (Preceding (or, for reasons of style or emphasis, following) two words or phrs. of the same kind coupled by *and*, *both* adds emphasis by means of an implied contrast.) ME.

SHAKES. 1 *Hen. VI* I will rule both her, the King, and realm. GOLDSMITH A masterpiece both for argument and style. R. HODGSON See an old unhappy bull, Sick in soul and body both. J. IRVING There were a million images from the film on his mind, both real and imagined. A. MCCOWEN The actor is both pimp and prostitute.

bother /ˈbɒðə/ *noun & verb*. L17.
[ORIGIN Of Anglo-Irish origin: prob. rel. to Irish *bodhaire* deafness, noise, *bodhraim* deafen, annoy.]

▸ **A** *noun*. **1** Noise; prating, chatter. *dial.* L17.

2 (A cause of) worry, fuss, minor trouble; a worried state. L18.

J. GALSWORTHY One had better save oneself the bother of thinking too. G. GREENE. It's no bother. It's the 'short times' that are the bother. B. PYM It was a bother to cook anything.

▸ **B** *verb*. **1** *verb trans.* Bewilder with noise; confuse, fluster. *dial.* E18.

2 *verb trans.* Give trouble to; pester, annoy, worry. M18. ▸**b** *verb trans. & intrans.* In *imper.* (expr. impatience). Curse, confound, damn. M19.

J. DOS PASSOS All the boys bothered their parents to buy them Rough Rider suits. E. ALBEE Why don't you go back to your necking and stop bothering me? I want to read. M. DRABBLE Oh, I'm not bothered, it's all the same to me. M. MOORCOCK I had begun to develop one of the headaches which have since bothered me all my life. **b** DICKENS To this amorous address Miss Brass briefly responded 'Bother!' L. O'FLAHERTY Bother the mugs. We can drink outa the neck.

can't be bothered will not make the required effort. ***hot and bothered***: see HOT *adjective*.

3 *verb intrans.* Worry or trouble oneself, make a fuss; make the required effort; be concerned (*with*, *about*). L18.

CARLYLE Make money; and don't bother about the Universe. L. M. MONTGOMERY I'd always be too tired at night to bother saying prayers. E. M. FORSTER You despise my mother . . because she's conventional and bothers over puddings. J. CHEEVER It was quite dark, but no one had bothered to turn on a light.

■ **botheˈration** *noun* the act of bothering; freq. as *interjection*, bother!: L18. **bothersome** *adjective* causing bother, mildly troublesome or annoying M20.

bothy /ˈbɒθi/ *noun*. *Scot.* Also **-ie**. L18.
[ORIGIN Obscurely rel. to Irish, Gaelic *both*, *bothán*, perh. cogn. with BOOTH.]
A hut, a cottage; a one-roomed building in which labourers are lodged.

botling /ˈbɒtlɪŋ/ *noun*. Now *rare* or *obsolete*. E17.
[ORIGIN Perh. rel. to Dutch *bot* stumpy.]
The chub.

boto /ˈbəʊtəʊ/ *noun*. Pl. **-os**. Also **boutu** /ˈbəʊtuː/ M19.
[ORIGIN Local name.]
A grey and pink river dolphin, *Inia geoffrensis*, found in the Amazon and Orinoco River systems in S. America.

botony /ˈbɒtəni/ *adjective*. Also **bott-**. L16.
[ORIGIN Old French *botoné* (mod. *boutonné* covered with buds): see BUTTON *noun*, -Y[5].]
HERALDRY. Of a cross: having the end of each limb ornamented with three projections like buds.

Botox /ˈbəʊtɒks/ *noun*. L20.
[ORIGIN Shortened from BOTULINUM TOXIN.]
(Proprietary name for) a drug prepared from botulin, used medically to treat certain muscular conditions and cosmetically to remove wrinkles by temporarily paralysing facial muscles.
■ **Botoxed** *adjective* treated with Botox L20.

bo tree /ˈbəʊtriː/ *noun*. M19.
[ORIGIN Repr. Sinhalese *bōgaha*, from *bō* (from Pali, Sanskrit *bodhi* perfect knowledge) + *gaha* tree.]
A fig tree, *Ficus religiosa*, of India and SE Asia, regarded as sacred by Buddhists (because the Buddha received enlightenment under one). Also called ***peepul***, ***pipal***.

botryoidal /ˈbɒtrɪɔɪd(ə)l/ *adjective*. L18.
[ORIGIN from Greek *botruoeidēs*, from *botrus*: see BOTRYTIS, -OID, -AL[1].]
Chiefly MINERALOGY. Resembling a cluster of grapes in shape.
■ Also **botryoid** *adjective* M18.

botrytis /bəˈtrʌɪtɪs/ *noun*. L19.
[ORIGIN mod. Latin, from Greek *botrus* cluster of grapes.]
A fungus of the genus *Botrytis*; plant disease caused by such a fungus.

Botswanan /bɒtˈswɑːnən/ *noun & adjective*. M20.
[ORIGIN from *Botswana* (see below) + -AN.]
A native or inhabitant of, of or pertaining to, Botswana, an inland country of southern Africa (formerly Bechuanaland).

bott *noun* var. of BOT *noun*[1], *noun*[2].

bottarga /bəʊˈtɑːɡə/ *noun*. Also **botargo** /bəˈtɑːɡəʊ/. L16.
[ORIGIN Italian, from Arabic *butarkhah*, from Coptic *outarakhon*, from Coptic *ou-* (indef. article) + Greek *tarikhion* pickle.]
A relish made of salted and dried tuna or grey mullet roe.

Botticellian /bɒtɪˈtʃɛlɪən/ *adjective*. L19.
[ORIGIN from *Botticelli* (see below) + -AN.]
Characteristic of or resembling the work of the Florentine painter Sandro Botticelli (1444–1510).

bottine /ˈbɒtiːn/ *noun*. Now *rare* or *obsolete*. E16.
[ORIGIN French, dim. of *botte* BOOT *noun*[2]: see -INE[4].]
A buskin or half-boot.

bottle /ˈbɒt(ə)l/ *noun*[1]. LME.
[ORIGIN Old French *boteille* (mod. *bouteille*) from medieval Latin *butticula* dim. of late Latin *buttis* BUTT *noun*[3].]

1 A narrow-necked vessel, orig. of leather, now usu. of glass or plastic, for storing liquids. LME. ▸**b** *spec.* An infant's feeding bottle. M19. ▸**c** A hot-water bottle. M19. ▸**d** A metal cylinder for liquefied or compressed gas. E20.
beer bottle, ***feeding bottle***, ***hot-water bottle***, ***ink bottle***, ***milk bottle***, ***water bottle***, ***wine bottle***, etc.

2 The quantity (esp. of liquor) held by a bottle. L17.

3 The act or habit of drinking alcoholic liquor. E18.

4 A collection or share of money. *slang*. L19.

5 In full ***bottle and glass***. = ARSE *noun*. *rhyming slang*. M20.

6 Courage, nerve, guts. *colloq.* M20.

New Musical Express I just didn't have the bottle to end it.

– PHRASES: ***hit the bottle***: see HIT *verb*. **lose one's bottle** *slang* lose one's nerve. ***magnetic bottle***: see MAGNETIC *adjective*. ***new wine in old bottles***: see WINE *noun*. **no bottle**, **not much bottle** *slang* no good, useless. **on the bottle** drinking heavily, addicted to alcohol. **over a bottle** while drinking. ***ship in a bottle***: see SHIP *noun* 1.

– COMB.: **bottle age** time spent by a wine etc. maturing in the bottle; **bottle-arsed** *adjective* (of type) wider at one end than the other; **bottle bank** a receptacle for used bottles to be left for recycling of glass; **bottle blonde** (of a woman's hair) of a shade of blonde that looks as though it has been artificially lightened or bleached; **bottlebrush** (*a*) a cylindrical brush for cleaning the insides of bottles; (*b*) a plant suggestive of this, *esp.* an Australian shrub (e.g. banksia or callistemon) with brushlike flowers; **bottle-fed** *adjective*, **bottle-feed** *verb trans. & intrans.*, **bottle-feeding**: with milk from a feeding bottle rather than from a woman's breast; **bottle-glass** coarse dark-green glass; ***bottle gourd***: see GOURD 1; **bottle green** *adjective & noun* dark green; **bottle-head** (now *rare* or *obsolete*) (*a*) a stupid person; (*b*) = ***bottlenose*** (c) below; **bottle-holder** a person who holds a bottle, *esp.* (*arch.*) a boxer's second; **bottleneck** (*a*) the neck of a bottle; *spec.* one used over a guitarist's finger to produce sliding effects on the strings; any implement so used; guitar playing with sliding effects; (*b*) a narrow place where road traffic etc. readily becomes congested; an obstruction to the even flow of production etc.; **bottlenose** (*a*) a swollen nose or snout; (*b*) *dial.* a puffin; (*c*) (more fully ***bottlenose whale***) a whale of the genus *Hyperoodon*, or a dolphin of the genus *Tursiops*, with a long snout; **bottle-nosed** *adjective* having a swollen nose or snout; **bottle-opener** a device for removing the caps from bottles of beer etc.; **bottle party** a drinking party; a party to which each guest brings a bottle of wine etc.; **bottle-tit** *dial.* the long-tailed tit, *Aegithalos caudatus* (so called from the form of its nest); **bottle tree** an Australian tree of the genus *Brachychiton*, of the sterculia family, with a swollen bottle-shaped trunk; **bottle-washer** *colloq.* a menial, a factotum, an underling.
■ **bottle-o(h)** *noun* (*Austral. & NZ colloq.*) a collector of empty bottles L19.

bottle /ˈbɒt(ə)l/ *noun*[2]. Now *dial.* or *obsolete* exc. in phr. below. LME.
[ORIGIN Old French *botel* dim. of *botte* bundle, from Middle Low German, Middle Dutch *bote* bundle of flax, prob. from Germanic base of BUTT *verb*[1].]
A bundle of hay or straw.
look for a needle in a bottle of hay: see NEEDLE *noun*.

bottle /ˈbɒt(ə)l/ *noun*[3]. M16.
[ORIGIN Alt. of BUDDLE *noun*[1]: infl. by BOTTLE *noun*[1].]
A flower or insect, usu. of a distinctive colour. Now only as 2nd elem. of comb. forming distinct names, as ***bluebottle***, ***greenbottle***, etc.

bottle /ˈbɒt(ə)l/ *verb*. E17.
[ORIGIN from BOTTLE *noun*[1].]

1 *verb trans.* Put into a bottle or bottles for keeping; preserve (fruit etc.) in bottles; *fig.* (usu. foll. by *up*) conceal, restrain (feelings etc.) for a time; entrap or keep entrapped. E17.

2 *verb intrans.* Foll. by *out*: fail to act, back out through cowardice etc. *colloq.* L20.

bottled /ˈbɒt(ə)ld/ *adjective*. L16.
[ORIGIN from BOTTLE *noun*[1], *verb*: see -ED[2], -ED[1].]

1 Bottle-shaped; protuberant, swollen. Now *rare*. L16.

2 Stored or kept in a bottle or bottles; *fig.* (usu. foll. by *up*) pent up, kept under restraint. M17.

bottled gas liquefied butane.

3 Drunk. *slang*. E20.

bottler /ˈbɒtlə/ *noun*. LME.
[ORIGIN formed as BOTTLED + -ER[1].]

†**1** A bottle-maker. LME–L15.

2 A person who bottles liquor. L19.

3 Someone or something excellent. *Austral. & NZ slang*. L19.

bottom /ˈbɒtəm/ *noun & adjective*.
[ORIGIN Old English *botm* (*boþm*) = Old Saxon *bodom* (Dutch *bodem*), corresp. with variation of suffix (cf. Old English *bytme*, *byþme*, *byþne* bottom, keel) to Old Norse *botn*, and parallel to Old English *bodan*, corresp. to Old High German *Bodam* (German *Boden* ground, earth), from Germanic, rel. to Latin *fundus*: sense 2 is infl. by Dutch.]

▸ **A** *noun*. **I** The lowest part or surface.

1 The lowest part of a material thing; the surface of an object upon which the object rests; the undersurface, the base. OE. ▸**b** The buttocks. Also, the seat of a chair. L18.

LD MACAULAY Barrels with the bottoms knocked out served the purpose of chimneys. J. STEINBECK His stiff jeans, with the bottoms turned up eight inches to show his heeled boots. **b** D. DU MAURIER He sent my nurse packing . . because she smacked my bottom with a hair-brush.

2 The keel or (horizontal part of) the hull of a ship; a ship or other vessel, esp. considered as a cargo-carrier. OE.

BYRON He transferr'd his lading . . to another bottom.

3 The ground under the water of the sea, a lake, a river, etc. OE.

G. BENNETT Two salvoes sent the *Cöln* to the bottom, with Admiral Maass . . and all but one of her crew.

†**4** A deep place, an abyss. OE–M18.

AV *Wisd.* 17:14 The same sleepe . . came vpon them out of the bottomes of ineuitable hell.

5 The lowest part of a valley; a low-lying alluvial plain; a dell, a hollow. ME.

6 The lowest part of anything considered as a position in space, as the foot of a hill or slope, etc. ME. ▸**b** The last place in a list etc.; the lowest place in point of honour, rank, etc.; the person occupying such a place. M17. ▸**c** *sing.* & (freq.) in *pl.* The lowest workings in a mine. L18.

C. KINGSLEY At the bottom of a hill they came to a spring. S. BECKETT In the other direction, I mean from top to bottom, it was the same. J. LE CARRÉ It was his signature all right . . . She'd seen it at the bottom of roneoed notices masses of times. **b** M. MCCARTHY That was like starting from the bottom in a factory. E. BLISHEN You came bottom in geography, didn't you, Hutchings?

7 The furthest, most remote, or inmost part. E17.

DAY LEWIS At the bottom of the garden lay the lily ponds. P. O'BRIAN At the bottom of the bay [lay] the village of Trégonnec.

8 *sing.* & (usu.) in *pl.* Matter remaining at the bottom of a liquid; dregs, sediment. M17.

▸ **II** Something which underlies or supports.

9 A thing upon which something is built or rests. Now only *fig.*, foundation, basis, footing. LME. ▸**b** A core on which to wind thread; a skein or ball of thread. Long *dial.* LME.

HENRY MORE All the stately works and monuments Built on this bottome. W. PENN If we could not all meet upon a Religious Bottom, at least we might upon a Civil One.

10 The fundamental character, essence, reality. L16.

G. ANSON If this matter was examined to the bottom.

11 Physical resources, staying power; substance, stability. L18.

A. BOYLE I personally prefer Trevor-Roper's thesis to Angleton's; it has more 'bottom' and better perspective. S. CRAIG Whatever his faults, C. P. Snow possesses . . that old-fashioned English upper-class quality *bottom*.

12 PARTICLE PHYSICS. = BEAUTY *noun* 5. L20.

– PHRASES: **at bottom** in reality, essentially, basically. **be at the bottom of** cause, underlie. ***black bottom***: see BLACK *adjective*. ***bottom of the heap***: see HEAP *noun*. **bottoms up!**: a call to drain one's glass. **bottom up** upside down. ***from the bottom of one's heart***: see HEART *noun*. ***from top to bottom***: see TOP *noun*[1]. **get to the bottom of** fully investigate and explain, find out the truth about. ***knock the bottom out of***: see KNOCK *verb*. ***second bottom***: see SECOND *adjective*. **stand on one's own bottom** *arch.* be independent, act for oneself. **the bottom drops out of**, **the bottom falls out of** there is a collapse of. **touch bottom** (*a*) reach the bottom of the water (esp. with the feet); reach the lowest or worst point; (*b*) be in possession of the full facts.

▸ **B** *adjective*. **1** Lowest, last; at or forming the bottom. M16.

I. FLEMING The captain was sitting at the wheel, a light aluminium affair consisting only of the bottom half of a circle. S. HILL He put his foot on the bottom rung of the loft ladder. O. SCHELL Golden carp and common carp . . are bottom fish.

2 PARTICLE PHYSICS. Designating a *b* quark. L20.

– SPECIAL COLLOCATIONS & COMB.: **bottom dog** = UNDERDOG. **bottom dollar** (one's) last dollar (***bet one's bottom dollar***, stake all, be very confident). **bottom drawer** *fig.* a woman's store of clothes etc. kept in preparation for marriage. **bottom-dwelling** *adjective* (of an aquatic organism) dwelling on or near the bed of the sea, a lake, etc. ***bottom edge***: see EDGE *noun* 4. **bottom feeder** (*a*) any marine organism that lives on or near the bed of

the sea and feeds by scavenging; (*b*) *N. Amer. colloq.* a member of a group of very low social status who survives by any means possible. **bottom fermentation** BREWING a process in which the yeast falls to the bottom during fermentation, as in the making of lager beers. **bottom-fermented** *adjective* (BREWING) (of beer) made by bottom fermentation. **bottom gear** a vehicle's lowest gear. **bottomland** *US* low-lying land, esp. by a river. **bottom line** the final total of an account, balance sheet, etc.; *fig.* the underlying reality, the final position. **bottom yeast** a yeast that falls to the bottom during fermentation.
■ **bottomless** *adjective* without bottom; baseless; inexhaustible; immeasurably deep (***the bottomless pit***, hell): LME. **bottommost** *adjective* at the very bottom, lowest M19.

bottom /ˈbɒtəm/ *verb*. E16.
[ORIGIN from the noun.]
1 *verb trans.* Put a bottom to, provide with a bottom; *fig.* base, ground, (*up*)*on*. E16.
OED Send this saucepan to be new bottomed.
†**2** *verb trans.* Wind (as a skein). L16–E17.
†**3** *verb intrans.* Be based or grounded. M17–L18.
4 *verb trans.* Reach or touch the bottom of; find the extent or real nature of; drain, empty (a glass etc.). L18.
COLERIDGE Openly declaiming on subjects . . which they had never bottomed.
5 *verb intrans.* Reach or touch bottom; reach its lowest level (freq. foll. by *out*). L19. ▸**b** *spec.* Strike gold etc. Also foll. by *on* (gold etc.). *Austral. & NZ.* L19.
Glasgow Herald Others with shallower purses are content to wait until prices have bottomed.
■ **bottomer** *noun* a person who provides or fits bottoms (esp. for chairs) E18.

bottomed /ˈbɒtəmd/ *adjective*. M16.
[ORIGIN from BOTTOM *noun*, *verb*: see -ED[2], -ED[1].]
Having a bottom, provided with a bottom or foundation (of specified form or nature).

bottomry /ˈbɒtəmri/ *noun & verb*. L16.
[ORIGIN from BOTTOM *noun* + -RY, after Dutch *bodemerij*.]
▸ **A** *noun*. The system of lending money to the owner or master of a ship on the security of the ship for the purpose of completing a voyage, the lender losing the money if the ship is lost. L16.
▸ **B** *verb trans.* Pledge (a ship) thus. M18.

bottony *adjective* var. of BOTONY.

botty /ˈbɒti/ *noun*. L19.
[ORIGIN from BOTTOM *noun* + -Y[6]: cf. BOT *noun*[2].]
A child's word for the buttocks.

botulism /ˈbɒtjʊlɪz(ə)m/ *noun*. L19.
[ORIGIN German *Botulismus* orig. 'sausage-poisoning', from Latin *botulus* sausage: see -ISM.]
Food poisoning due to the bacillus *Clostridium botulinum*, found esp. in improperly sterilized tinned meats and other preserved foods.
■ **botulin** *noun* the bacterial toxin involved in botulism E20. **botulinum toxin** /bɒtjʊˈlʌɪnəm ˈtɒksɪn/, **botulinus toxin** /-əs/ *noun phrs.* = BOTULIN E20.

boubou /ˈbuːbuː/ *noun*. E19.
[ORIGIN French, from Malinke *bubu*.]
1 An African bush shrike noted for the duet of bell-like calls produced by the male and female together. E19.
2 A long loose-fitting garment worn by both sexes in parts of Africa. M20.

boucan /ˈbuːk(ə)n/ *noun*. Also **buccan** /ˈbʌk(ə)n/. E17.
[ORIGIN French from Tupi *mukem*, *mocaém*.]
1 In S. America: a wooden frame for cooking, smoking, or drying meat over an open fire. Cf. BARBECUE *noun* 4. E17.
2 Meat cooked or cured on such a frame. Cf. BARBECUE *noun* 2. M19.
3 = BARBECUE *noun* 5. M19.

boucan /ˈbuːk(ə)n/ *verb trans.* Also **buccan** /ˈbʌk(ə)n/. E17.
[ORIGIN French *boucaner*, formed as BOUCAN *noun*.]
Cook, smoke, or dry (meat etc.) on a boucan. Cf. BARBECUE *verb*.

bouchée /buʃe/ *noun*. Pl. pronounced same. M19.
[ORIGIN French = mouthful, from *bouche* mouth.]
A small baked confection. Usu. in *pl.*

bouclé /ˈbuːkleɪ/ *adjective & noun*. L19.
[ORIGIN French = buckled, curled.]
(Fabric) woven with a knotted and curled appearance; (yarn) of looped or curled ply.

boudin /*in sense 2 only* ˈbuːdɪn; *foreign* budɛ̃ (*pl. same*)/ *noun*. M19.
[ORIGIN French.]
1 (Not naturalized.) A black pudding; forcemeat shaped like a sausage. M19.
2 GEOLOGY. Any of a number of roughly parallel elongated sections resulting from the fracturing of a rock stratum during folding. E20.
■ **boudinage** /buːdɪˈnɑːʒ/ *noun* (GEOLOGY) (the formation of) a structure containing a number of boudins E20.

boudoir /ˈbuːdwɑː/ *noun*. L18.
[ORIGIN French, lit. 'place to sulk in', from *bouder* pout, sulk.]
A (woman's) small private room.

bouffant /ˈbuːfɑ̃/ *noun & adjective*. E19.
[ORIGIN French, pres. pple of *bouffer* swell: see -ANT[1].]
▸ **A** *noun*. A puffed-out part of a dress etc.; a puffed-out hairstyle. E19.
▸ **B** *adjective*. Of a dress, hairstyle, etc.: puffed out. L19.

bougainvillea /buːɡ(ə)nˈvɪlɪə/ *noun*. Also **-llaea**, **-llia**. M19.
[ORIGIN mod. Latin, from L. A. de *Bougainville* (1729–1811), French navigator: see -A[1], -IA[1].]
A tropical S. American plant of the genus *Bougainvillea*, with large brightly coloured bracts almost concealing the flowers.

bouge /buːdʒ/ *noun & verb*. *obsolete* exc. *dial.* See also BUDGE *noun*[2]. LME.
[ORIGIN Old French & mod. French: see BUDGET *noun*, BULGE *noun & verb*.]
▸ **A** *noun*. †**1** = BULGE *noun* 1. LME–E17.
†**2** A swelling, a hump. LME–L15.
3 The bilge of a cask. M18.
▸ **B** *verb*. **1** *verb intrans.* Swell out, bulge. LME.
†**2** *verb trans.* Stave in (a ship's bottom, etc.), bilge. L15–E17.

bouget /ˈbuːdʒɪt/ *noun*. L16.
[ORIGIN Var. of BUDGET *noun*.]
HERALDRY. An ancient water vessel consisting of a yoke with two leather pouches or skins attached.

bough /baʊ/ *noun & verb*.
[ORIGIN Old English *bōg*, *bōh* = Middle Low German *boch*, *būch* (Low German *boog*), Middle Dutch *boech* (Dutch *boeg* shoulders, chest of a horse, bows of a ship), Old High German *buog* shoulder, forearm (German *Bug* horse's hock or point of shoulder, bow of a ship), Old Norse *bógr* shoulder, from Germanic, rel. to Greek *pēkhus* forearm, cubit.]
▸ **A** *noun*. †**1** The shoulder of an animal. OE–LME.
2 Any of the larger limbs or offshoots of a tree; a (main) branch. OE.
3 A limb, a leg. *Scot.* M16.
4 The gallows. *arch.* L16.
– COMB.: **bough-house** (*a*) *US* a temporary structure made of boughs; (*b*) *dial.* (now *hist.*) a house opened only during a fair for the sale of liquor; **bough-pot** (*arch. & dial.*) = BEAU-POT.
▸ **B** *verb trans.* Strip of boughs. *rare.* E16.
■ **boughed** /baʊd/ *adjective* having boughs; stripped of boughs: LME.

bought /baʊt/ *noun*[1] & *verb*[1]. Long *arch. & dial.* LME.
[ORIGIN Prob. Low German *bucht* (see BIGHT): cf. BOUT *noun*.]
▸ **A** *noun*. **1** A bend, a curve. LME.
2 A loop or turn of a rope etc.; a coil. LME.
▸ **B** *verb trans. & intrans.* Bend, wind, fold. LME.

bought /baʊxt, bʌxt/ *noun*[2] & *verb*[2]. *Scot.* Also **bught**. LME.
[ORIGIN Unknown.]
▸ **A** *noun*. A sheepfold. LME.
▸ **B** *verb trans.* Pen or fold (sheep); fence in. E18.

bought *verb pa. t. & pple* of BUY *verb*.

boughten /ˈbɔːt(ə)n/ *ppl adjective*. *N. Amer., dial., & poet.* L18.
[ORIGIN from BOUGHTEN *verb*: see -EN[6].]
Bought; purchased at a shop as opp. to home-made.

boughten *verb pa. pple*: see BUY *verb*.

bougie /ˈbuːʒi/ *noun*. M18.
[ORIGIN French from *Bougie* (repr. colloq. pronunc. of Arabic *Bijāya*) a town in Algeria which carried on a trade in wax.]
1 A wax candle. M18.
2 MEDICINE. A rod or tube for exploring or dilating the passages of the body. M18.
■ **bougienage** /buːʒɪˈnɑːʒ/ *noun* (MEDICINE) dilatation by means of a bougie E20.

bouillabaisse /buːjəˈbeɪs, *foreign* bujabɛs/ *noun*. M19.
[ORIGIN French from mod. Provençal *bouiabaisso*.]
A Provençal dish of fish stewed in water or white wine.

bouilli /ˈbuːji, *foreign* buji/ *noun*. E17.
[ORIGIN French, use as noun of pa. pple of *bouillir* BOIL *verb*: cf. BULLY *noun*[2].]
Boiled or stewed meat, esp. beef.

bouillon /ˈbuːjɔ̃, *foreign* bujɔ̃/ *noun*. M17.
[ORIGIN French, from *bouillir* BOIL *verb*.]
Broth, thin soup. See also COURT BOUILLON.
– COMB.: **bouillon cube** a stock cube.

bouk /buːk/ *noun*. Now *Scot. & dial.*
[ORIGIN Old English *būc* = Old Frisian, Middle Low German *būk*, Old High German *būh* (German *Bauch*), Old Norse *búkr*, from Germanic.]
†**1** The belly. OE–L15.
2 The trunk; the body of a person or animal. ME.
3 Bulk, volume, size. L17.

boul /buːl/ *noun*. *obsolete* exc. *Scot. & N. English*. Also **bool**. L15.
[ORIGIN Perh. from Middle Dutch *böghel* (Dutch *beugel*, German *Bügel*) rel. to Germanic base of BOW *verb*[1]: see -EL[1].]
Something bent into a curve; *esp.* the curved handle of a pail, kettle, etc.

boulangerite /bʊˈlandʒərʌɪt/ *noun*. M19.
[ORIGIN from C. L. *Boulanger* (1810–49), French mining engineer + -ITE[1].]
MINERALOGY. A monoclinic sulphide of antimony and lead, usu. occurring as elongated or fibrous grey metallic crystals.

Boulangist /buːˈlandʒɪst/ *noun & adjective*. L19.
[ORIGIN from *Boulanger* (see below) + -IST.]
hist. (A member) of a French political party formed by General Georges E. J. M. Boulanger (1837–91), advocating a policy of anti-German militarism.
■ **Boulangism** *noun* L19.

boulder /ˈbəʊldə/ *noun & verb*. Also ***bowlder**. LME.
[ORIGIN Shortened from BOULDERSTONE.]
▸ **A** *noun*. A large rock, *esp.* one that has been worn smooth by water or weather. LME.
– COMB.: **boulder clay** GEOLOGY clay containing many large stones and boulders, formed by deposition from melting glaciers and ice sheets.
▸ **B** *verb*. **1** *verb trans.* Make into boulders. *rare.* M19.
2 *verb intrans.* Climb large boulders. Chiefly as ***bouldering*** *verbal noun*. E20.
■ **bouldery** *adjective* M19.

boulderstone /ˈbəʊldəstəʊn/ *noun*. ME.
[ORIGIN Of Scandinavian origin: cf. Swedish dial. *bullersten*, *buldurstajn*, perh. rel. to Swedish *bullra* rumble.]
A boulder.

boule /ˈbuːli/ *noun*[1]. M19.
[ORIGIN Greek *boulē* senate.]
A legislative body of ancient or modern Greece.

boule /buːl, *foreign* bul/ *noun*[2]. Pl. **boules** /*in sense 2* buːl, *in sense 3* buːlz, *foreign* bul/. E20.
[ORIGIN French = BOWL *noun*[2].]
1 A form of roulette. E20.
2 *sing.* & in *pl.* A French form of bowls played on rough ground, usu. with metal bowls. E20.
3 A small pear-shaped mass of synthetic sapphire, ruby, etc., made by fusing suitably tinted alumina. M20.

boule *noun*[3] var. of BUHL.

boulevard /ˈbuːləvɑːd/ *noun*. M18.
[ORIGIN French, formed as BULWARK: in French orig. = rampart, (later) a promenade on the site of this.]
1 A broad street (esp. in France) with rows of trees planted along it. M18.
2 A dual carriageway; a broad main urban road. *N. Amer.* E20.
– COMB.: **boulevard strip** *N. Amer.* a grassy strip between a road and a pavement.
■ **boulevarded** *adjective* provided with boulevards L19.

boulevardier /ˌbuːləvɑːˈdjeɪ, *foreign* bulvardje/ *noun*. Pl. pronounced same. L19.
[ORIGIN French, formed as BOULEVARD + *-ier* -ER[1].]
A person who frequents (French) boulevards.

bouleverse /buːlˈvəːs/ *verb trans.* L17.
[ORIGIN French *bouleverser* turn as a ball, formed as BOULE *noun*[2] + *verser* turn.]
Overturn, upset.

bouleversement /bulvɛrsəmɑ̃/ *noun*. Pl. pronounced same. L18.
[ORIGIN French, formed as BOULEVERSE: see -MENT.]
An inversion, *esp.* a violent one; an upset, an upheaval.

boulle *noun* var. of BUHL.

boult *noun*, *verb* vars. of BOLT *noun*[2], *verb*[1].

boulter /ˈbəʊltə/ *noun*. Also **bolter**. L16.
[ORIGIN Unknown.]
A long fishing line with many hooks.

†**boun** *adjective* var. of BOUND *adjective*[1].

boun /baʊn/ *verb*. Long *arch. & dial.* ME.
[ORIGIN from †*boun* var. of BOUND *ppl adjective*[1].]
1 *verb trans.* (usu. *refl.*) & *intrans.* Prepare (oneself); make ready; dress. ME.
2 *verb intrans.* Set out, go *to*. ME.

bounce /baʊns/ *noun*[1]. E16.
[ORIGIN from the verb.]
1 A resounding knock; a heavy blow, a thump; an explosion, the report of a gun. Now *rare* or *obsolete*. E16.
2 A leap, a bound; *esp.* the rebound of a ball etc. from a hard surface. E16.
on the bounce (*a*) in continual spasmodic motion; (*b*) in the act of rebounding.
3 Orig., a swaggering boast, a boastful falsehood. Now, swagger, exaggeration; rebounding power, vitality, exuberance. E18. ▸**b** A buoyant musical rhythm. *colloq.* (orig. *US*). M20.
DE QUINCEY The whole story is a bounce of his own. L. P. HARTLEY All the glow and bounce and boyishness had gone out of him.
4 An act of ejection or dismissal. *slang* (orig. *US*). L19.
– COMB.: **bounce flash** (a device for giving) reflected photographic flashlight.
■ **bouncy** *adjective* that bounces, boisterous, buoyant; resilient, springy (***bouncy castle***: see CASTLE *noun*[1] 1b): E20.

bounce /baʊns/ *noun*[2]. E18.
[ORIGIN Unknown.]
The nurse hound, *Scyliorhinus stellaris*.

bounce /baʊns/ *verb*. ME.
[ORIGIN Uncertain: perh. from Low Dutch (cf. Low German *bunsen* beat, thump, Dutch *bons* a thump), or of independent imit. origin.]
▸ **I** †**1** *verb trans.* Beat, thump; slam (a door etc.). ME–E19.

†2 *verb intrans.* Make an explosive or banging noise; knock loudly at a door etc. (Cf. earlier BOUNCE *interjection* 1.) M16–E18.
3 *verb trans. & intrans.* Talk big, bluster (at); hector; swagger; hustle by bluff etc. *into* or *out of* something. E17. ▸b Blurt *out*; come *out with*. M17.
▸ II Of movement.
4 *verb intrans.* & †*trans.* with *it*. Move back away from a surface after hitting it; rebound. E16. ▸b *verb trans.* Cause to rebound. L19. ▸c *verb intrans.* Foll. by *back*: recover well after a setback or problem. M20.

> *Times* His chip over Keller bounced off the post. **b** *Sun* Andrew Magee. . bounced his ball off another player's putter for an incredible 333-yard hole-in-one. **c** D. HART-DAVIS A year later, after an operation and chemotherapy, she bounced back.

5 *verb intrans.* Come or go *in*, *into*, *out*, etc., energetically or noisily; move *about* vigorously or unceremoniously; jump *up*. L17.

> S. FRY He bounced springily along the corridor.

6 *verb intrans. & trans.* Of a cheque: be returned by a bank when there are no funds to meet it. Of a bank: return (such a cheque). *colloq.* E20. ▸b Of an email: be returned to its sender after failing to reach its destination. Also, return such an email. L20.

> *Which?* You won't face the embarrassment of having your cheques bounced. **b** *www.corante.com* When my email bounced, I contacted AOL.

7 *verb trans.* CRICKET. Bowl a bouncer or bouncers at (a batsman). M20.
8 *verb trans.* Eject summarily; dismiss, sack. *colloq.* (orig. *US*). L19.
■ **bouncing** *adjective* that bounces; boisterous; big of its kind, (of a baby) big and healthy; ***bouncing Bet***, the soapwort *Saponaria officinalis*; ***bouncing castle***: see CASTLE *noun*[1] 1b: E16. **bouncingly** *adverb* E16.

bounce /baʊns/ *interjection & adverb*. E16.
[ORIGIN Imit. or from the verb.]
▸ A *interjection*. †1 Repr. the sound of a gun or a heavy blow: bang! E16–E17.
2 Repr. a bouncing movement. M19.
▸ B *adverb*. With a bounce. E17.

bouncebackability /ˌbaʊnsbakəˈbɪlɪti/ *noun*. *colloq.* M20.
[ORIGIN from *bounce back* + -ABILITY.]
Esp. in sport: the capacity to recover quickly from a setback.

> *Daily Record* We then showed some true bouncebackability when we equalised with a fine header from Christie.

bouncer /ˈbaʊnsə/ *noun*. L16.
[ORIGIN from BOUNCE *verb* + -ER[1].]
1 A large specimen of its kind; *spec.* a gross or flagrant lie. *arch.* L16.
2 A person who blusters or talks big; a boaster, a liar. *arch.* M18.
3 A person employed to eject troublesome persons from a dancehall, nightclub, etc. *colloq.* M19.
4 CRICKET. A fast short-pitched ball that rises sharply. E20.

bound /baʊnd/ *noun*[1]. ME.
[ORIGIN Anglo-Norman *bunde*, Old French *bodne*, later *bo(u)sne*, *bo(u)ne*, *bonde*, etc. (mod. *borne*), from medieval Latin *bodina*, earlier *butina*, of unknown origin: cf. BOURN *noun*[2].]
†1 a A landmark. Only in ME. ▸b A territorial limit, a boundary line. Usu. in *pl.* LME.
beat the bounds: see BEAT *verb*[1] 15. **out of bounds** beyond set limits, esp. those set by the rules of a school, military regulations, etc.; forbidden, inaccessible.
2 *sing.* & (usu.) in *pl.* Territory situated near a boundary; borderland; land within set limits. ME. ▸b A tract of ground taken in by a tin-miner. L17.
3 *fig.* A limitation or restriction upon feeling, action, duration, etc. Usu. in *pl.* LME. ▸b A limiting value. Chiefly in ***upper bound***, ***lower bound***. E20.

bound /baʊnd/ *noun*[2]. E16.
[ORIGIN Old French & mod. French *bond*, formed as BOUND *verb*[2].]
A springy movement upward or forward, a leap; a bounce or recoil (of a ball etc.).
by leaps and bounds: see LEAP *noun*[1].

bound /baʊnd/ *adjective*[1]. Orig. †**boun**. ME.
[ORIGIN Old Norse *búinn* pa. pple of *búa* prepare, *-d* partly euphonic, partly infl. by BOUND *adjective*[2]: cf. BOUN *verb*.]
†1 Ready, prepared; attired. ME–M19.

> SIR W. SCOTT A band of war Has for two days been ready boune.

2 Ready to start or having set out (*for*, *on*, †*to*); moving in a specified direction. LME.

> J. F. W. HERSCHEL Bound on we know not what errand. C. A. LINDBERGH My grandfather. . embarked on a ship bound for America.

homeward-bound, ***northbound***, ***outward-bound***, ***southbound***, etc.
3 About *to do*, going *to do*. *N. English*. M19.

bound /baʊnd/ *adjective*[2]. LME.
[ORIGIN pa. pple of BIND *verb*, abbreviation of BOUNDEN *adjective*. Earlier in UNBOUND *adjective*[1].]
1 That has been bound: see BIND *verb* I. LME.
2 LINGUISTICS. Of a grammatical element: occurring only in combination with another form. E20.

bound /baʊnd/ *verb*[1]. LME.
[ORIGIN from BOUND *noun*[1].]
1 *verb trans.* Set bounds to, limit, restrict. Now only *fig.* LME.

> MILTON He shall. . bound his Reign With earth's wide bounds. A. B. JAMESON His views were not bounded by any narrow ideas of expediency.

2 *verb intrans.* Abut *on* a territory etc.; share a boundary (*with*). *arch.* M16.
3 *verb trans.* Form the boundary of; enclose. L16.

> H. BELLOC Some wood which bounded our horizon.

■ **bounding** *noun*[1] (*a*) the action of the verb; †(*b*) a boundary: M16.

bound /baʊnd/ *verb*[2]. L16.
[ORIGIN Old French & mod. French *bondir* resound, (later) rebound, from Proto-Romance var. of late Latin *bombitare* var. of *bombilare*: see BOMBILATE.]
1 *verb intrans.* Spring, leap; advance lightly and buoyantly. L16.
2 *verb intrans.* Recoil, rebound; bounce. L16.
†3 *verb trans.* Cause (a horse) to leap. Only in L16.
■ **bounding** *verbal noun*[2] (*a*) the action of the verb; (*b*) a leap, a bound: E17.

bound /baʊnd/ *verb*[3] *intrans. & refl. rare*. L16.
[ORIGIN Var. of BOUN *verb*.]
Direct one's course, go.

bound *verb*[4] *pa. t. & pple* of BIND *verb*.

boundary /ˈbaʊnd(ə)ri/ *noun*. E17.
[ORIGIN Alt. of BOUNDER *noun*[1], perh. after *limitary*.]
1 A thing which serves to mark the limits of something; the limit itself, a dividing line. E17.
2 *spec.* The limit of a cricket field; a hit to this, scoring four or six runs. M19.
– COMB.: **boundary condition** MATH. a condition that is required to be satisfied at all or part of the boundary of a region in which a set of differential conditions is to be solved; **boundary layer** the layer of a fluid adjacent to a body in it when the two are in relative motion; **boundary rider** *Austral. & NZ* a stockman employed to ride round a sheep or cattle station mending fences etc; **boundary value** MATH. a value specified by a boundary condition.

bounded /ˈbaʊndɪd/ *adjective*[1]. L16.
[ORIGIN from BOUND *verb*[1] + -ED[1].]
Subject to bounds or limits; *fig.* circumscribed, restricted.
■ **boundedness** *noun* bounded quality; limited range: L17.

†**bounded** *adjective*[2]. L16–E19.
[ORIGIN from BOUND *adjective*[2] + -ED[1].]
= BOUND *adjective*[2] 1.

bounden /ˈbaʊnd(ə)n/ *adjective*. ME.
[ORIGIN pa. pple of BIND *verb*.]
1 = BOUND *adjective*[2] 1. *arch.* ME.
2 Of duty etc.: obligatory. M16.

bounden *verb pa. pple*: see BIND *verb*.

bounder /ˈbaʊndə/ *noun*[1]. E16.
[ORIGIN from BOUND *verb*[1] + -ER[1].]
1 A limit, a boundary; a landmark. Long *arch. & dial.* E16.
2 A person who occupies a boundary area; *spec.* the holder of a bound of tin-ore ground. Now *rare*. M16.
3 A person who sets or marks bounds or limits. L16.

bounder /ˈbaʊndə/ *noun*[2]. *slang*. M19.
[ORIGIN from BOUND *verb*[2] + -ER[1].]
†1 A four-wheeled cab or trap. Only in M19.
2 An ill-bred person, a cad. L19.

boundless /ˈbaʊndlɪs/ *adjective*. L16.
[ORIGIN from BOUND *noun*[1] + -LESS.]
Without bounds or limits; unrestricted, infinite.
■ **boundlessly** *adverb* E17. **boundlessness** *noun* E17.

bounteous /ˈbaʊntɪəs/ *adjective*. Now chiefly *rhet.* LME.
[ORIGIN from Old French *bontif*, *-ive* benevolent (from *bonté* BOUNTY) after PLENTEOUS.]
1 Full of goodness (to others); generous, munificent. LME.
2 Of things: generously bestowed; ample, abundant. M16.
■ **bounteously** *adverb* M16. **bounteousness** *noun* liberality, munificence LME.

bountiful /ˈbaʊntɪfʊl, -f(ə)l/ *adjective*. E16.
[ORIGIN from BOUNTY + -FUL.]
= BOUNTEOUS.
Lady Bountiful: see LADY *adjective & noun*.
■ **bountifully** *adverb* L16. **bountifulness** *noun* L15.

bountihead /ˈbaʊntɪhɛd/ *noun*. *rare* (chiefly Spenser). L16.
[ORIGIN from BOUNTY + -HEAD[1].]
Bounteousness.

bountith /ˈbaʊntɪθ, ˈbʌn-/ *noun*. *Scot. & N. English*. *arch.* LME.
[ORIGIN App. from Old French *bontet*, *buntet* earlier form of *bonté*: see BOUNTY.]
A gratuity; a reward.

bounty /ˈbaʊnti/ *noun*. ME.
[ORIGIN Old French & mod. French *bonté* from Latin *bonitas*, from *bonus* good: see -TY[1].]
†1 Goodness in general, worth, excellence; high estate; in *pl.*, virtues. ME–E17. ▸†b Valour, prowess. ME–M16.
†2 (An act of) kindness. ME–M17.
3 Goodness shown in giving, munificence, liberality. ME.

> J. A. FROUDE Many of these people. . were dependent on his bounty.

4 An act of generosity; a gift, a gratuity. ME. ▸b *spec.* A monetary reward or premium paid by the state, Crown, etc., e.g. (*a*) to recruits on enlistment, (*b*) for promoting trade in particular ways, (*c*) for the killing of dangerous animals etc. E18.
King's bounty, **Queen's bounty** *hist.* a grant paid to the mother of three or more children born at once. **Queen Anne's bounty** *hist.* a fund for augmenting poor benefices.
– COMB.: **bounty hunter** a person who tracks and captures outlaws or kills dangerous animals etc. for the reward offered; **bounty-jumper** US HISTORY a recruit who enlisted for the bounty and promptly deserted (to enlist again).

bouquet /bʊˈkeɪ, bəʊˈkeɪ, ˈbʊkeɪ/ *noun*. See also BOKAY. E18.
[ORIGIN French (earlier = clump of trees), from dial. var. of Old French *bos*, *bois* wood. Cf. BUSH *noun*[1], -ET[1].]
1 A bunch of flowers, *esp.* a large attractive one for use at a ceremony. E18. ▸b *fig.* A compliment. E20.
2 The perfume of wine etc. M19.
3 ***bouquet garni*** /ˈɡɑːni/ [French, lit. 'garnished bouquet'], a bunch of herbs for flavouring. M19.
4 A number of rockets etc. fired together. L19.
■ **bouquetier** /bʊkəˈtɪə, *foreign* buktje (*pl. same*)/ *noun* a small holder for a bunch of flowers L18.

bouquetin /ˈbuːkətɪn/ *noun*. L18.
[ORIGIN French from Old French *boc estaign*, from Middle High German STEINBOCK.]
The Alpine ibex.

Bourbon /ˈbʊəbən/ *noun*[1] & *adjective*. M18.
[ORIGIN French (see below), from *Bourbon* (*l'Archambault*), a town in central France.]
▸ A *noun*. 1 *hist.* A member of the House of Bourbon, a former royal dynasty holding sovereignty in France, Naples, and Spain. M18.
2 [from the former name (Isle de *Bourbon*) of the island of Réunion.] A hybrid rose, *Rosa* × *borboniana*, of a group descended from *Rosa chinensis* and *R. damascena*. Also ***Bourbon rose***. E19.
3 A political reactionary. *US*. M19.
▸ B *attrib.* or as *adjective*. Of or pertaining to the House of Bourbon; *US* reactionary in politics. M18.
Bourbon biscuit a chocolate-flavoured biscuit with a chocolate-cream filling.
■ **Bourbonism** *noun* adherence to the Bourbon dynasty or (*US*) to reactionary policies L19. **Bourbonist** *noun* a supporter of the Bourbon dynasty E19.

bourbon /ˈbəːbən, ˈbʊə-/ *noun*[2]. Also **B-**. M19.
[ORIGIN *Bourbon* County, Kentucky.]
(A drink of) an American whiskey distilled from maize and rye.

bourd /bʊəd/ *noun & verb*. *obsolete* exc. *Scot.* ME.
[ORIGIN Old French & mod. French *bourde* lie, cheating = Provençal *borda*, of unknown origin.]
▸ A *noun*. An amusing tale, a jest; joking, banter, fun. ME.
▸ B *verb*. 1 *verb intrans. & trans.* Say things in jest; make fun (of), mock. ME.
†2 *verb intrans.* Play games. LME–M16.
■ **bourder** *noun* (*obsolete* exc. *hist.*) a jester; a mocker: ME.

bourdon /ˈbʊəd(ə)n/ *noun*. Also **burdoun**. ME.
[ORIGIN Old French & mod. French = drone, from Proto-Romance, of imit. origin.]
1 = BURDEN *noun* 6 (with which early merged). Now *rare* or *obsolete*. ME.
2 A low-pitched stop in an organ or harmonium; the drone pipe of a bagpipe. M19.
3 The lowest-pitched in a peal of bells. E20.

bourdonné /bʊəˈdɒneɪ, *foreign* burdɔne/ *adjective*. E17.
[ORIGIN French, from *bourdon* (pilgrim's knobbed) staff.]
HERALDRY. Terminating in knobs or balls.

bourg /bʊəɡ/ *noun*. LME.
[ORIGIN Old French & mod. French from Latin *burgus* BOROUGH.]
A town or village under the shadow of a castle (*hist.*); a Continental town.

bourgade /burɡad/ *noun*. Pl. pronounced same. E17.
[ORIGIN French, formed as BOURG + -ADE.]
A (Continental) large village or straggling unwalled town.

bourgeois /ˈbʊəʒwɑː, *foreign* burʒwa/ *adjective & noun*[1]. M16.
[ORIGIN French: see BURGESS.]
▸ A *adjective*. 1 Of, pertaining to, characteristic of, or resembling, the bourgeois (see sense B. below); middle-class; conventionally respectable and unimaginative, humdrum; selfishly materialistic; capitalistic, reactionary. M16.
2 Of French wine: next in quality to wines classified as the best. E20.
▸ B *noun*. Pl. same.
1 Orig., a (French) citizen or freeman of a city or burgh, as distinct from a peasant or a gentleman. Now, any member of the middle class. L17.

2 In Communist or socialist writing: a capitalist, an exploiter of the proletariat. *derog.* L19.
3 A socially or aesthetically conventional person, a philistine. *derog.* M20.
■ **bourgeoisdom** *noun* (the political ascendancy of) the bourgeoisie L19. **bourgeoisification** /bʊəˌʒwɑːzɪfɪˈkeɪʃ(ə)n/ *noun* the action of bourgeoisifying a community etc. M20. **bourgeoisify** /bʊəˈʒwɑːzɪfʌɪ/ *verb trans.* convert to a bourgeois outlook or way of life M20.

bourgeois /bəːˈdʒɔɪs/ *noun*². E19.
[ORIGIN Conjectured to be from the name of a printer; but perh. referring to its intermediate size.]
A former size of type between long primer and brevier.

bourgeoise /ˈbʊəʒwɑːz, burʒwaz/ *noun & adjective fem.* Pl. of noun pronounced same. L18.
[ORIGIN French, fem. of BOURGEOIS *adjective & noun*¹.]
▸ **A** *noun.* A female bourgeois. L18.
▸ **B** *adjective.* Of a female: bourgeois. M20.

bourgeoisie /bʊəʒwɑːˈziː, *foreign* burʒwazi/ *noun.* E18.
[ORIGIN French, from BOURGEOIS *adjective & noun*¹: see -Y³.]
The bourgeois collectively; the middle class.
HAUTE BOURGEOISIE. PETITE BOURGEOISIE. ***petty bourgeoisie***: see PETTY *adjective.*

bourn /bɔːn, bʊən/ *noun*¹. Also **bourne**. ME.
[ORIGIN S. English var. of BURN *noun*¹.]
A small stream, a brook.

bourn /bɔːn, bʊən/ *noun*². Also **bourne**. E16.
[ORIGIN French *borne*: see BOUND *noun*¹.]
†**1** A boundary between fields etc.; a frontier. E16–L18.
2 A bound, a limit. *arch.* E17.

J. THOMSON From the far bourne Of utmost Saturn.

3 Destination; a goal. *arch.* E19.

WORDSWORTH The selected bourne Was now an Island.

4 Realm, domain. *poet. rare.* E19.

KEATS In water, fiery realm, and airy bourne.

– NOTE: Senses 3 & 4 both arise from interpretations of Shakes. *Haml.* ('Something after death—The undiscover'd country, from whose bourn No traveller returns'), which prob. belongs with sense 1.

bourne *noun* var. of BOURN *noun*¹, *noun*².

bournonite /ˈbʊənənʌɪt/ *noun.* E19.
[ORIGIN from Count J. L. de *Bournon* (1751–1825), French mineralogist + -ITE¹.]
MINERALOGY. An orthorhombic sulphide of lead, copper, and antimony, usu. occurring as steel-grey prisms.

bourock /ˈbuːrək/ *noun. Scot.* M18.
[ORIGIN Perh. rel. to BOWER *noun*¹ or to BOROUGH: see -OCK.]
1 A mound; a heap; a mass. M18.
2 A little cot or hut. L18.
3 A group; a crowd. E19.

bourrée /ˈbʊəreɪ; *foreign* bure (*pl. same*)/ *noun.* Also †**boree**. L17.
[ORIGIN French.]
A lively dance of French origin, resembling the gavotte; a piece of music for this dance or in its rhythm, *esp.* one which forms a movement of a suite.
– COMB.: **bourrée step** a sideways step in dancing in which one foot crosses behind or in front of the other.

bourse /bʊəs/ *noun.* M19.
[ORIGIN French: see BURSE.]
A money market; an exchange; *esp.* (**B-**) the Paris stock exchange. Cf. BURSE 2.

Boursin /ˈbʊəsã, *foreign* bursɛ̃/ *noun.* M20.
[ORIGIN French.]
(Proprietary name for) a kind of soft cheese from France, often flavoured with herbs, garlic, or pepper.

bourtree /ˈbʊətriː/ *noun. Scot. & N. English.* LME.
[ORIGIN Unknown.]
The elder, *Sambucus nigra.*

bouse *noun & verb*¹ var. of BOOZE.

bouse /baʊz/ *verb*² *trans.* Also **bowse**. L16.
[ORIGIN Unknown.]
Chiefly NAUTICAL. Haul with tackle.

boustrophedon /baʊstrəˈfiːd(ə)n, buː-/ *adverb & adjective.* E17.
[ORIGIN Greek = as the ox turns in ploughing, from *bous* ox + *-strophos* STROPHE + *-don* adverbial suffix.]
(Written) from right to left and from left to right in alternate lines.
■ **boustropheˈdonic** *adjective* E19.

bout /baʊt/ *noun & verb.* M16.
[ORIGIN var. of BOUGHT *noun*¹: assoc. with BOUT *preposition*.]
▸ **A** *noun.* **1** A bending, a curve; = BOUGHT *noun*¹ 1; *esp.* a curve of the side of a violin etc. M16.
2 †**a** A circuit, a roundabout way. M16–M17. ▸**b** The going of a plough along two adjacent furrows. E17.
3 A spell of or a turn at work or exercise. L16. ▸**b** A spell of drinking. L17. **this bout, that bout** (now *dial.*) this, that, occasion or time.
4 A boxing or wrestling match; a fight, a contest of strength. L16.
5 An attack of illness etc. L19.

C. BEATON This nervous stress brings on another bout of asthma.

▸ **B** *verb trans.* Plough in bouts. M18.

bout /baʊt/ *preposition & (rare) adverb. colloq. & dial.* ME.
[ORIGIN Aphet.]
= ABOUT.

boutade /buːˈtɑːd/ *noun.* E17.
[ORIGIN French, from *bouter* thrust: see -ADE.]
A sudden outburst or outbreak.

†**boutefeu** *noun.* L16–M19.
[ORIGIN French, from *bouter* put + *feu* fire.]
A person who kindles strife, a firebrand.

boutique /buːˈtiːk/ *noun.* M18.
[ORIGIN French from Old Provençal *botica* (Italian *bottega*) from Latin *apotheca* from Greek *apothēkē* storehouse: cf. BODEGA.]
A small shop. Now usu. *spec.* a shop, or department in a store, selling fashionable clothes or accessories.
– COMB.: **boutique hotel** a stylish small hotel situated in a fashionable urban location.

bouton /ˈbuːtɒn/ *noun.* M19.
[ORIGIN French = button.]
1 In full ***bouton pearl***. A round pearl with a flat back. M19.
2 ANATOMY. An enlarged part of a nerve fibre or cell, esp. an axon, where it forms a synapse. M20.

boutonnière /buːtɒnˈjɛː; *foreign* butɔnjɛːr (*pl. same*)/ *noun.* L19.
[ORIGIN French.]
= BUTTONHOLE *noun* 3.

bouts rimés /buː riːˈmeɪ/ *noun phr. pl.* E18.
[ORIGIN French = rhymed endings.]
Rhyming words upon which verses are (to be) composed.

boutu *noun* var. of BOTO.

bouvardia /bʊˈvɑːdɪə/ *noun.* L18.
[ORIGIN mod. Latin, from Charles *Bouvard* (1572–1658), superintendent of the Jardin du Roi, Paris: see -IA¹.]
A Central American plant of the genus *Bouvardia*, of the madder family, bearing handsome red, yellow, or white flowers.

Bouvier /ˈbuːvɪeɪ/ *noun.* M20.
[ORIGIN French = cowherd.]
A large, powerful dog of a rough-coated breed originating in Belgium.

bouzouki /bʊˈzuːki/ *noun.* M20.
[ORIGIN Greek *mpouzouki*: cf. Turkish *bozuk* spoilt, with ref. to roughly made instruments.]
A Greek form of long-necked lute.

bovarism /ˈbəʊvərɪz(ə)m/ *noun.* E20.
[ORIGIN French *bovarysme*, from the principal character in Flaubert's novel *Madame Bovary*: see -ISM.]
(Domination by) a romantic or unreal conception of oneself.
■ **bovarize** *verb intrans. & refl.* view oneself in a romantic or unreal light E20.

bovate /ˈbəʊveɪt/ *noun.* L17.
[ORIGIN medieval Latin *bovata*, from Latin *bov-*, *bos* ox: see -ATE¹.]
hist. An oxgang of land.

bove /bʌv/ *adverb & preposition.* Now *poet.* Now also **'b-**.
[ORIGIN Old English *bufan*, from *bi* BY *preposition* + *ufan* above (ult. formed as UP *adverb*¹ etc.); later aphet. from ABOVE.]
= ABOVE.

Bovey coal /ˈbʌvɪ kəʊl/ *noun phr.* M18.
[ORIGIN from *Bovey*, a parish in Devonshire.]
A form of lignite found in SW England.

bovid /ˈbəʊvɪd/ *adjective & noun.* L19.
[ORIGIN from Latin *bov-*, *bos* ox + -ID³.]
ZOOLOGY. ▸**A** *adjective.* Of, pertaining to, or designating the family Bovidae of ruminants, including cattle, antelope, sheep, and goats. L19.
▸ **B** *noun.* An animal of this family. L19.

bovine /ˈbəʊvʌɪn/ *adjective & noun.* E19.
[ORIGIN Late Latin *bovinus*, formed as BOVID: see -INE¹.]
▸ **A** *adjective.* **1** Pertaining to or characteristic of an ox or similar animal; belonging to the ox tribe. E19.
bovine somatotrophin a growth hormone occurring naturally in cows that has been added to cattle feed to increase milk production; abbreviation ***BST***. **bovine spongiform encephalopathy** a usually fatal virus disease of cattle involving the central nervous system and causing extreme agitation; abbreviation ***BSE***.
2 *fig.* Sluggish; stupid. M19.
▸ **B** *noun.* A bovine animal. M19.
■ **bovinely** *adverb* E20.

Bovril /ˈbɒvrɪl/ *noun.* Also **b-**. L19.
[ORIGIN from Latin *bov-*, *bos* ox; perh. based on VRIL.]
(Proprietary name for) a concentrated essence of beef; a drink of this.
■ **bovrilize** *verb trans.* (*arch. colloq.*) condense, epitomize E20.

bovver /ˈbɒvə/ *noun. slang.* M20.
[ORIGIN Repr. a cockney pronunc. of BOTHER *noun*.]
Deliberate troublemaking.
– COMB.: **bovver boot** a heavy boot; **bovver boy** a violent hooligan.

B

bow /bəʊ/ *noun*¹.
[ORIGIN Old English *boga* = Old Frisian *boga*, Old Saxon *bogo* (Dutch *boog*), Old High German *bogo* (German *Bogen*), Old Norse *bogi*, from Germanic: cf. BOW *verb*¹.]
1 A thing bent or curved; a bend, a bent line; *esp.* (chiefly *poet.*) a rainbow. OE. ▸†**b** An arc of a circle. M16–L17.

MILTON A dewie Cloud, and in the Cloud a bow. P. GALLICO The grim line of her mouth unfroze and altered, down-drawn into a bow of pain.

bow of promise: see PROMISE *noun*. ***saddle-bow***: see SADDLE *noun*. ***secondary bow***: see SECONDARY *adjective*.
2 An arch (of masonry). *obsolete* exc. *dial.* OE.
3 A weapon for shooting arrows, consisting of a cord joining the ends of a curved piece of elastic wood etc. OE. ▸**b** In *pl.* Archers. L15.
Cupid's bow: see CUPID. ***have two strings to one's bow, have many strings to one's bow, second string to one's bow***: see STRING *noun*. See also CROSSBOW, ***longbow*** s.v. LONG *adjective*¹
4 A yoke for oxen. Cf. OXBOW. LME.
5 A knot with a single or double loop; a necktie, ribbon, etc., so tied. M16.
6 MUSIC. A rod with horsehair etc. stretched along it for playing a stringed instrument; a single passage of this across the strings. L16.
musical bow: see MUSICAL *adjective*. ***Tourte bow***: see TOURTE *noun*².
7 A ring or hoop forming a handle; = BAIL *noun*⁴. E17. ▸**b** A side piece or lens frame of a pair of spectacles. Chiefly *US*. E18.
8 ARCHITECTURE. A curved part of a building projecting from a straight wall; *esp.* = ***bow window*** (a) below. E18.
9 CALLIGRAPHY. A curved stroke forming part of a letter. E20.
– COMB.: **bow-arm**, **bow-hand**: holding the bow (in archery or music); **bow-backed** *adjective* (*arch.*) [perh. partly from BOW *verb*¹] hunchbacked, having an arched back; **bow-bearer** a person who carries a bow; *esp.* (*hist.*) a forester who dealt with trespasses affecting vert and venison; **bow compass(es)** a pair of compasses with jointed legs; †**bow-draught** = ***bowshot*** below; **bowfin** a large voracious holostean fish, *Amia calva*, of still fresh waters in eastern N. America; ***bow-hand***: see ***bow-arm*** above; **bowhead (whale)** the Greenland right whale, *Balaena mysticetus*; **bowhunt** *verb trans. & intrans.* hunt (animals) with a bow rather than a firearm; **bowhunter** a person who bowhunts; **bowknot** a double-looped ornamental knot in a ribbon, tie, etc.; **bow-legged** *adjective* having outwardly bent legs, bandy-legged; **bow legs** bandy legs; **bowman** *noun*¹ an archer; **bow net** a cylinder of wickerwork closed at one end and having a narrow funnel-shaped entrance at the other, used to trap lobsters etc.; **bow saw** having a narrow blade stretched like a bowstring on a light frame. **bowshot** the distance an arrow can be shot from a bow; †**bowstaff**, pl. **-staves**, a stick to be made into a bow; **bow tie** a necktie (to be) tied in the manner of a bow; **bow window** (**a**) a curved bay window; (**b**) *slang* a big belly.
■ **bowless** *adjective* M19.

bow /buː, baʊ/ *noun*². Long *obsolete* exc. *Scot. dial. & hist.* ME.
[ORIGIN Old Norse *bú* farming, farm, farm stock, corresp. to Old English, Old Saxon *bū* dwelling, habitation, Old High German *bū* dwelling, building, tillage (Middle High German *bū*, *bou*, German *Bau*, Dutch *bouw* tillage, building), from Germanic word rel. to Latin *colere* cultivate.]
The stock of cattle on a farm; a herd.

bow /baʊ/ *noun*³. LME.
[ORIGIN Low German *boog*, Dutch *boeg* (whence Swedish *bog*, Danish *boug*): see BOUGH. Pronunc. infl. by popular assoc. with BOW *verb*¹.]
1 *sing.* & (freq.) in *pl.* The fore-end of a boat or ship from where it begins to curve inwards to the stem. LME.
on the bow within 45° of the point right ahead. **shot across the bows** a warning salvo (freq. *fig.*).
2 = ***bowman*** below. M19.
– COMB.: **bow-chaser** a forward-firing gun in the bow of a ship; **bow-fast** a mooring rope etc. at the bow; **bow line** the line of a ship's forebody in vertical section (see also BOWLINE); **bowman** *noun*² the oarsman who sits nearest to the bow of a boat; **bow oar** (the rower of) the oar nearest the bow; **bow-on**, **bows-on** *adverbs* with the bow turned towards the object considered; **bow wave** a wave set up at the bow of a vessel under way or in front of any object moving through a fluid.

bow /baʊ/ *noun*⁴. M17.
[ORIGIN from BOW *verb*¹.]
A forward bending of the head or upper body in salutation, assent, etc.
make one's bow make a formal entrance or exit. **take a bow** acknowledge applause.

Bow /bəʊ/ *noun*⁵. M18.
[ORIGIN Stratford-le-*Bow*, a village in Essex (now a district in London).]
In full ***Bow china***, ***Bow porcelain***. Fine porcelain of a kind orig. manufactured at Stratford-le-Bow.

bow /baʊ/ *verb*¹.
[ORIGIN Old English *būgan* corresp. to Middle Low German *būgen*, Middle Dutch *būghen*, Old High German *biogan* (German *biegen*), Gothic *biugan*, from Germanic: cf. BOW *noun*¹.]
▸ **I** *verb intrans. & †refl.* **1** Assume a bent or crooked shape or attitude; bend; stoop. *arch. & dial.* OE.

B

SHAKES. *Meas. for M.* Like an ass whose back with ingots bows. AV *Eccles.* 12:3 When.. the strong men shall bowe themselves. TENNYSON She bow'd down And wept in secret.

†**2** Turn aside, off, or away; swerve; make one's way, go. OE–L16.
†**3** Have a curved direction, be bent; tend. OE–M18.
4 Bend the neck (as if) beneath a yoke. Now chiefly *fig.*, be subject (*to*), submit, yield. OE.

DRYDEN Under Iron Yokes make Indians Bow. A. P. STANLEY He at last bows to the inevitable course of events.

5 Bend or kneel (*down*) in token of reverence, respect, or submission. (Foll. by *to*, *before*.) OE.

GIBBON An hundred princes bowed before his throne.

bow in the house of Rimmon: see HOUSE *noun*[1].
6 Incline the head or body (*to*) in recognition or assent; make a bow. E17.
bow and scrape behave obsequiously. **bowing acquaintance** a slight degree of acquaintance.
▸ **II** *verb trans.* **7** Cause to bend, curve; cause to stoop, crush (as) with a load. ME.

SHAKES. *Hen. VIII* A threepence bow'd would hire me. MILTON With sickness and disease thou bow'st them down. F. ORMSBY This late guest bowed with winter offerings.

†**8** Turn, direct. ME–E18.
9 Bend downwards, lower, incline. ME.

E. A. FREEMAN Lanfranc refused to bow his shoulders to such a burden. DAY LEWIS The worshippers bowed their heads to the gale.

bow the knee: see KNEE *noun*.
†**10** Obey. Only in ME.
11 Express with a bow; usher *in* or *out* by bowing. E17.
– WITH ADVERBS IN SPECIALIZED SENSES: **bow out** take one's leave, esp. with formality; retreat, withdraw.
■ **bowing** *noun*[1] (*a*) the action of the verb; (*b*) (*obsolete* exc. *dial.*) a curved or bent part: LME.

bow /bəʊ/ *verb*[2] *intrans. & trans.* M19.
[ORIGIN from BOW *noun*[1].]
Use the bow on (a violin etc.); play with the bow.
■ **bowing** *noun*[2] (the manner of) playing a violin etc. with a bow M19.

†**bowall** *noun* var. of BOLE *noun*[3].

bowdlerize /ˈbaʊdlərʌɪz/ *verb trans.* Also **B-**, **-ise**. M19.
[ORIGIN from Thomas *Bowdler* (1754–1825), English editor, who published an expurgated edition of Shakespeare: see -IZE.]
Expurgate (a book etc.) by removing or altering material considered improper or offensive; emasculate.
■ **bowdlerism** *noun* textual expurgation M19. **bowdleriˈzation** *noun* the act of bowdlerizing L19.

bowel /ˈbaʊəl/ *noun & verb*. ME.
[ORIGIN Anglo-Norman *buel*, Old French *boël*, *bouel* (mod. *boyau*), from Latin *botellus* pudding, sausage (Martial), small intestine, dim. of *botulus* sausage: see -EL[2] 1.]
▸ **A** *noun*. **1** The part of the alimentary canal below the stomach; the intestine; the gut. Exc. in medical use now usu. in *pl.*, the intestines, the entrails. ME. ▸†**b** Any internal organ of the body. LME–L18.
2 In *pl.* The interior of the body. Chiefly *fig.*, (the innermost source of) pity or sympathetic feeling. *arch.* LME.

CARLYLE Had idle readers any bowels for him.

bowels of compassion, *bowels of mercy*, etc.
3 In *pl.* The innermost parts *of* anything. E16.

S. RUSHDIE He lived somewhere in the insanitary bowels of the old wooden-house quarter.

bowels of the earth the depths of the earth.
†**4** In *pl.* Offspring. E16–L17.

SHAKES. *Meas. for M.* Thine own bowels which do call thee sire.

▸ **B** *verb trans.* Infl. **-ll-**, *-**l-**. Disembowel. *arch.* ME.
■ **bowelled** *adjective* (*a*) having bowels or recesses; (*b*) disembowelled: L16. **bowelless** /-l-l-/ *adjective* (*arch.*) without mercy, pitiless M17.

†**bowell** *noun* var. of BOLE *noun*[3].

bowenite /ˈbəʊənʌɪt/ *noun*. M19.
[ORIGIN from George T. *Bowen* (1803–28), US mineralogist + -ITE[1].]
MINERALOGY. A hard, compact, translucent form of serpentine, resembling nephrite.

bower /ˈbaʊə/ *noun*[1].
[ORIGIN Old English *būr* corresp. to Old Saxon *būr* (Low German *buur*), Old High German *būr* (German *Bauer* birdcage), Old Norse *bur*, from Germanic, from base meaning 'dwell' (also of BUILD *verb*): for mod. spelling cf. FLOWER *noun*, TOWER *noun*[1].]
1 A dwelling, a habitation; *esp.* an ideal abode. Now chiefly *poet.* OE.
2 An inner apartment; a bedroom. *arch. & dial.* OE. ▸**b** A lady's private apartment; a boudoir. Now *poet.* OE.
3 A place closed in with foliage; an arbour; a summer house. L15.
4 A structure raised by a bowerbird. M19.
– COMB. & PHRASES: **bowerbird** (*a*) any of various passerine birds of the family Ptilonorhynchidae, native to Australia and New Guinea, which construct elaborate runs adorned with feathers, shells, etc., during courtship; (*b*) *Austral. slang* a collector of trivia or odds and ends; **bower-maiden**, **bower-woman** *arch.* a lady-in-waiting, a chambermaid; *virgin's bower*: see VIRGIN *noun*.

bower /ˈbaʊə/ *noun*[2]. ME.
[ORIGIN from BOW *noun*[1] + -ER[1].]
†**1** = BOWYER 1. ME–M18.
2 A person who plays with a bow on a violin etc. *rare*. L17.

bower /ˈbaʊə/ *noun*[3]. L15.
[ORIGIN from BOW *noun*[3] + -ER[1].]
Either of two anchors carried at a ship's bow (more fully ***bower anchor***). Also (usu. more fully ***bower cable***), the cable of such an anchor.
best bower, **small bower** the starboard, port, bower anchor (or cable).

bower /ˈbaʊə/ *noun*[4]. L16.
[ORIGIN from BOW *verb*[1] + -ER[1].]
A person who bows or bends; a thing which causes bending.

bower /ˈbaʊə/ *noun*[5]. L19.
[ORIGIN German *Bauer* lit. 'husbandman, peasant, rustic': see BOOR.]
Either of the two highest cards in euchre, the jack of trumps (***right bower***) and the jack of the same colour (***left bower***).

bower /ˈbaʊə/ *verb*. L16.
[ORIGIN from BOWER *noun*[1].]
1 *verb trans.* Embower, shade, enclose (*lit. & fig.*). L16.
†**2** *verb intrans.* Lodge, shelter. *rare* (Spenser). Only in L16.

bowery /ˈbaʊəri/ *noun & adjective*. *US*. M17.
[ORIGIN Dutch *bouwerij* husbandry, farm, from *bouwen* cultivate: cf. BOOR & see -ERY.]
▸ **A** *noun*. A (former) farm or plantation in Dutch colonial America; *spec.* (***the Bowery***) a street in New York City (on the site of a former governor's bowery) notorious as a resort of prostitutes, drunks, derelicts, etc. M17.
▸ **B** *attrib.* or as *adjective*. (**B-**.) Of, pertaining to, or characteristic of the Bowery in New York City; disreputable, rough, rowdy. M19.

bowery /ˈbaʊəri/ *adjective*. E18.
[ORIGIN from BOWER *noun*[1] + -Y[1].]
Embowering; leafy, shady.

bowet /ˈbaʊɪt, ˈbuːɪt/ *noun*. *Scot. obsolete* exc. *hist.* LME.
[ORIGIN App. from medieval Latin *boeta* box or pyx as housing for a candle: cf. BOIST.]
A small lantern.

bowie /ˈbaʊi, ˈbəʊi/ *noun*[1]. *Scot.* M16.
[ORIGIN Perh. dim. of Scot. form of BOLL *noun*[1]: see -Y[6].]
A shallow tub; a wooden milk bowl.

Bowie /ˈbəʊi/ *noun*[2]. Also **b-**. M19.
[ORIGIN James *Bowie* (1799–1836), Amer. soldier.]
More fully ***Bowie knife***. A long knife with a blade double-edged at the point, used as a weapon by American pioneers.

bowl /bəʊl/ *noun*[1]. Also (earlier) †**boll**.
[ORIGIN Old English *bolla*, *bolle* corresp. to Old Saxon *bollo* cup (Dutch *bol* round object, BOLL *noun*[1]), Old High German *bolla* bud, round pod, globular vessel, from Germanic base meaning 'swell'.]
1 A vessel, usu. hemispherical or nearly so, to hold liquids or food; a basin. OE. ▸**b** *esp.* Such a vessel for holding drink. *arch.* OE. ▸**c** The contents of a bowl; a bowlful. M16.
finger bowl, *goldfish bowl*, *punchbowl*, *salad bowl*, *soup bowl*, *sugar bowl*, *wash-bowl*, etc. **b** *hanging bowl*: see HANGING *adjective*. **the bowl** drinking; conviviality.
2 A more or less bowl-shaped part, as of a cup, tobacco pipe, spoon, balance, etc. OE.
†**3** NAUTICAL. A round space at the masthead for men to stand in. E17–E19.
4 A bowl-shaped natural basin; a (bowl-shaped) stadium (freq. in the names of American football stadiums), an amphitheatre. M19. ▸**b** A sporting occasion held in a football stadium, featuring a football game; *spec.* = ***bowl game*** below. *US*. M20.

P. THEROUX San Salvador.. lies in a bowl, surrounded by mountains.

dust bowl: see DUST *noun*.
– COMB.: **bowl-barrow** a prehistoric grave mound in the shape of an inverted bowl; **bowl game** *US* an established American football fixture after the main season, usu. at a stadium with 'bowl' in its name.
■ **bowlful** *noun* the contents of a bowl, the quantity held by a bowl E17.

bowl /bəʊl/ *noun*[2]. LME.
[ORIGIN Old French & mod. French *boule* from Latin BULLA.]
1 A sphere, a globe, a ball. Long *obsolete* exc. *dial.* in *gen.* sense. LME.
2 *spec.* A ball of wood, hard rubber, etc., rolled in various games; in the game of bowls itself (see sense 3 below) now made slightly out of spherical shape to make it run in a curved course; in skittles, ninepins, etc., made either flattened or spherical. LME.
3 In *pl.* (usu. treated as *sing.*). A game played with bowls, on a green or in an alley; *spec.* a game in which players aim bowls at a target ball (the jack). L15.
4 a A delivery of the ball in cricket (now usu. *ball*); a spell of bowling. M19. ▸**b** A turn in bowls, skittles, etc.; a delivery of the ball in bowls etc. L19.
5 A roller or antifriction wheel, esp. for moving or pressing fabrics. L19.

bowl /bəʊl/ *verb*. LME.
[ORIGIN from BOWL *noun*[2].]
1 *verb intrans.* Play at bowls or skittles etc.; roll a bowl, hoop, etc., along the ground. LME.
2 *verb trans.* Cause to roll; send rolling. L16. ▸**b** Convey on wheels (in a carriage etc.). E19.

MOLLIE HARRIS Some of the boys had large iron hoops..; for miles and miles they bowled them.

3 *verb intrans.* Move by revolution; move on wheels. E17.

S. JOHNSON A fashionable lady.. bowling about in her own coach.

4 *verb intrans. & trans.* CRICKET. Propel towards the batsman (the ball, an over, etc.), orig. underarm; dismiss (a batsman) by the ball thus propelled breaking the wicket; get (a side, a batsman) *out*. M18. ▸**b** *verb trans.* Use (a player) to bowl. M19.

E. BLISHEN He took the ball and prepared to bowl the first over. N. CARDUS I have.. not been able to find out if Trumble bowled over or round the wicket. **b** ALAN ROSS Hutton bowled Tyson and Statham for an hour.

– WITH ADVERBS IN SPECIALIZED SENSES: **bowl along** go fast and smoothly. **bowl over** knock down; *fig.* disconcert, render helpless, impress greatly.

bowlder *noun & verb* var. of BOULDER.

bowler /ˈbəʊlə/ *noun*[1]. E16.
[ORIGIN from BOWL *verb* + -ER[1].]
1 A person who plays at bowls. E16.
2 A player who bowls at cricket. E18.
fast bowler, *medium-pace bowler*, *slow bowler*, etc. **bowler's wicket** a cricket pitch favouring bowlers.

bowler /ˈbəʊlə/ *noun*[2]. M19.
[ORIGIN William *Bowler*, English hatter who designed it in 1850.]
In full ***bowler hat***. A hard felt hat with a rounded crown and a narrow curled brim.
be given one's bowler (hat), **get one's bowler (hat)** *slang* be retired to civilian life, be demobilized.
– COMB.: **bowler-hatted** *adjective* (*a*) wearing a bowler; (*b*) *slang* civilian, retired from the forces.

bowline /ˈbəʊlɪn/ *noun*. ME.
[ORIGIN Middle Low German *bōline*, Middle Dutch *boechlijne* from *boeg* BOW *noun*[3] + *lijne* LINE *noun*[2]. See also ***bow line*** s.v. BOW *noun*[3].]
1 A rope passing from the weather edge of a square sail to the port or starboard bow, for the purpose of holding the sail closer to the wind. ME.
on a bowline close-hauled.
2 In full ***bowline knot***. A simple knot for forming a non-slipping loop at the end of a rope. E17.
running bowline: see RUNNING *adjective*. *Spanish bowline*: see SPANISH *adjective*.

bowling /ˈbəʊlɪŋ/ *noun*. E16.
[ORIGIN from BOWL *verb* + -ING[1].]
1 Playing at bowls; the action of rolling a ball etc. E16.
tenpin bowling: see *tenpin* s.v. TEN *noun*.
2 CRICKET. The action of delivering the ball. M18. ▸**b** The strength or resources of the bowlers in a cricket team. M19.
fast bowling, *medium-pace bowling*, *slow bowling*, etc.
– COMB.: **bowling alley** (a building containing) an alley for playing at bowls or skittles; *bowling analysis*: see ANALYSIS 2; **bowling crease** in cricket, the line from behind which the bowler delivers the ball; **bowling green** a smooth green upon which to play bowls.

Bowman's capsule /bəʊmənz ˈkapsjuːl, -jʊl/ *noun phr.* L19.
[ORIGIN Sir William *Bowman* (1816–92), English surgeon.]
ANATOMY & ZOOLOGY. A cup-shaped dilatation of the end of a uriniferous tubule, surrounding each glomerulus in the vertebrate kidney.

bowse *verb*[1] *& noun* var. of BOOZE.

bowse *verb*[2] var. of BOUSE *verb*[2].

bowser /ˈbaʊzə/ *noun*. Also **B-**. E20.
[ORIGIN Unknown.]
A tanker used for fuelling aircraft, tanks, etc., or for supplying water; (chiefly *Austral. & NZ*, proprietary name for) a petrol pump.

bowsie /ˈbaʊziː/ *noun*. *Irish*. E19.
[ORIGIN Unknown.]
A low-class or unruly person.

bowsprit /ˈbəʊsprɪt/ *noun*. ME.
[ORIGIN Middle & mod. Low German *bōgsprēt*, Middle Dutch *boechspriet*, formed as BOW *noun*[3], SPRIT *noun*[1].]
A large spar or boom running out from the stem of a vessel, to which the forestays are fastened.

Bow Street /bəʊ striːt/ *noun phr.* E19.
[ORIGIN Site of the principal metropolitan magistrates' court in London.]
hist. ***Bow Street officer***, ***Bow Street runner***, a (London) detective, *spec.* of the early 19th cent.

bowstring /ˈbəʊstrɪŋ/ *noun & verb*. OE.
[ORIGIN from BOW *noun*[1] + STRING *noun*.]
▸ **A** *noun*. The cord of a bow; *spec.* (*hist.*) this used in Turkey for strangling offenders. OE.

– COMB.: **bowstring bridge** a girder bridge consisting of an arch and a horizontal tie; **bowstring hemp** = SANSEVIERIA.
▸ **B** *verb trans.* Pa. t. & pple **-stringed**, **-strung** /-strʌŋ/. Chiefly *hist.* Strangle with a bowstring. E19.

bowtell *noun* var. of BOLTEL.

bow-wow /*interjection & verb* baʊˈwaʊ; *noun* ˈbaʊwaʊ/ *interjection, noun, & verb. nursery & joc.* L16.
[ORIGIN Imit.]
▸ **A** *interjection.* Repr. the sound of a dog barking, or a similar sound. L16.
▸ **B** *noun.* **1** The bark of a dog. L18.
2 A dog. L18.
▸ **C** *verb intrans.* Bark. M19.

bowyang /ˈbəʊjaŋ/ *noun. Austral. & NZ* & (sense 1) *dial.* Sense 1 **bow-yanky** /ˈbəʊjaŋki/ & other vars. M19.
[ORIGIN Unknown.]
1 In *pl.* Leather leggings. M19.
2 A band or strap worn over the trousers below the knee, esp. by labourers. L19.

bowyer /ˈbəʊjə/ *noun.* ME.
[ORIGIN from BOW *noun*¹ + -YER: cf. BOWER *noun*².]
1 A person who makes or trades in bows. ME.
2 An archer. LME.

box /bɒks/ *noun*¹. OE.
[ORIGIN Latin *buxus* from Greek *puxos*.]
1 More fully ***box tree***. A small evergreen tree or shrub of the genus *Buxus* (family Buxaceae); esp. *Buxus sempervirens*, with dark leathery leaves, often planted in garden borders. OE. ▸**b** Any of various Australasian eucalypts and other trees with wood like that of *Buxus*. E19.
b grey box, ***white box***, etc.
2 The hard, heavy, close-grained wood of the box, or of certain other trees, much used by turners and engravers. LME.
– COMB.: **box elder** a pinnate-leaved N. American elder, *Acer negundo*; **box-gum** = sense 1b above; **boxthorn** a shrub of the genus *Lycium*, of the nightshade family, bearing red berries, some species of which are used for hedging; esp. *L. barbarum*, naturalized in Britain; ***box tree***: see sense 1 above; **boxwood** = sense 2 above; also, the tree itself.
■ **boxen** *adjective* (*arch.*) of or pertaining to box; made of or like boxwood: M16.

box /bɒks/ *noun*². LOE.
[ORIGIN Prob. from late Latin *buxis*, *-id-* var. of Latin PYXIS box of boxwood.]
1 A case or receptacle, usu. rectangular or cylindrical and with a lid, of wood, metal, card, etc. (Freq. with function, type, etc., specified or understood contextually.) LOE. ▸**b** A numbered receptacle at a post office in which letters for a subscriber are kept until called for, or at a newspaper office for replies to an advertisement. M19. ▸**c** A coffin. *slang.* E20. ▸**d** ***the box***, television. *slang.* M20. ▸**e** The female genitals. *N. Amer. slang.* M20.

S. JOHNSON My landlady . . took the opportunity of my absence to search my boxes. E. BOWEN Who, seeing the house shuttered, would have dropped a letter in at the box? **b** P. G. WODEHOUSE My address will be Box 341, *London Morning News*.

ballot box, ***Christmas box***, ***dispatch box***, ***jukebox***, ***letterbox***, ***mailbox***, ***matchbox***, ***money box***, ***musical box***, ***pillarbox***, ***pillbox***, ***postbox***, ***snuffbox***, ***soapbox***, ***soundbox***, ***strongbox***, ***tuck box***, ***window box***, etc. ***chatterbox***: see CHATTER *noun*.
2 A box and its contents; the quantity contained in a box, a boxful. ME. ▸**b** *spec.* A money box and its contents; a fund. LME. ▸**c** A Christmas box. L16.

B. JOWETT He who is to be a workman should have his box of tools when he is a child. R. MAUGHAM Munching her way through a large box of chocolates. **b** SHAKES. *Timon* Nothing but an empty box . . which . . I come to entreat your honour to supply.

3 A protective case or covering for a piece of mechanism, such as a compass; a cylinder in which the journal of an axle etc. revolves. L15. ▸**b** CRICKET. A light protective shield worn over the genitals. M20.
gearbox etc.
4 (A box under) the coachman's seat on a carriage. E17.
5 A separate compartment, esp. in court for a witness or jury or one with seats at a theatre, restaurant, stadium, etc. E17. ▸**b** *transf.* In *pl. The* occupants of the boxes at a theatre etc. (orig. for ladies). L17. ▸**c** A separate stall for a horse in a stable or vehicle; a closed vehicle for transporting one or more horses. M19. ▸**d** The confessional. E20.
jury box, ***witness box***, etc.
6 A simple shelter or building; *esp.* one for a sentry, railway signals, or a telephone. E18.

T. HOOD The Watchman in his box was dosing.

call box, ***prompt box***, ***sentry box***, ***signal box***, ***telephone box***, etc.
7 A small country house, *esp.* one for temporary use while hunting etc. E18.
8 An excavation in the trunk of a tree for sap to collect. E18.
9 A confined area; a space enclosed by (esp. printed) lines; the area occupied by the batter or pitcher in baseball; (*colloq.*) *the* penalty area of a soccer pitch. L19.

A. S. BYATT He filled the little boxes, date of birth, places of education, parentage, nationality.

10 A mixing up of different flocks of sheep. *Austral. & NZ.* L19.
11 A close formation of aircraft, pattern of bombs, etc. M20.
– PHRASES: **a box of birds** *Austral. & NZ colloq.* excellent, very well, fine. ***black box***: see BLACK *adjective*. ***Chinese box***: see CHINESE *adjective*. **in the same box** in a similar predicament. **in the wrong box** unsuitably or awkwardly placed; in a difficulty, at a disadvantage. ***loose box***: see LOOSE *adjective*. **one out of the box** *Austral. & NZ colloq.* an excellent person or thing. ***red box***: see RED *adjective*. ***Skinner box***: see SKINNER *noun*². SOLANDER box
– COMB.: **box barrage**: directed to all sides of an area, to prevent escape; **boxboard** a type of stiff cardboard used to make boxes; **box camera** a simple box-shaped hand camera; **box canyon** a narrow canyon with a flat bottom and vertical walls; **boxcar** *N. Amer.* an enclosed railway goods wagon; **box-cloth** thick coarse cloth used esp. for riding garments; **box coat** a heavy caped overcoat for a coachman etc.; **boxfish** = ***trunkfish*** s.v. TRUNK *noun*; **box girder** a hollow girder that is square or rectangular in cross-section; **box junction** a road junction with a central yellow-striped area which a vehicle must not enter unless it can leave immediately, except when turning right with only oncoming traffic preventing exit; **box kite** a tailless kite with a light rectangular frame at each end; **box number**: identifying a box in a post office or newspaper office (sense 1b above); **box office** an office for booking seats at a theatre etc.; *fig.* entertainment etc. likely to attract audiences; **box pew**: enclosed like a box; **box pleat**: with two parallel contrary pleats forming a raised band; **box plot** STATISTICS a statistical plot in which a rectangle is drawn to represent the second and third quartiles, usually with a vertical line inside to indicate the median value, the lower and upper quartiles being shown as horizontal lines either side of the rectangle; **box room** a room in which boxes, trunks, etc., are stored; **box score** the tabulated results of a baseball game etc.; **box seat** the driver's seat on a carriage; **box set** = ***boxed set*** s.v. BOX *verb*¹. **box spanner** a cylindrical spanner with a socket head fitting over the nut; **box spring** each of a set of vertical springs in a mattress; **box tortoise**, **box turtle** a N. American land turtle of the genus *Terrapene*, able by means of a hinged lower carapace to close itself up completely; **box-wallah** (in the Indian subcontinent) a dealer, a pedlar.
■ **boxful** *noun* as much or as many as a box will hold E18. **boxlike** *adjective* resembling (that of) a box M19. **boxy** *adjective* resembling, comparable to, or suggesting a box; (of recorded sound) restricted in tone: M19.

box /bɒks/ *noun*³. LME.
[ORIGIN Unknown.]
1 A blow. *obsolete* in *gen.* sense. LME.
2 *spec.* A slap on the ear or the side of the head. LME.

box /bɒks/ *verb*¹ *trans.* LME.
[ORIGIN from BOX *noun*².]
1 Provide or fit with a box; put into a box, enclose in a box or casing; fit compactly as in a box; *fig.* confine and restrict the movement of, confine uncomfortably. Freq. foll. by *in*, *up*. LME. ▸**b** Print within a border of rules. E20.
boxed set a set of related items, esp. books or recordings, sold or packaged together in a box;
†**2** Bleed by cupping. LME–E17.
3 Make an excavation in the trunk of (a tree) for sap to collect. E18.
4 Mix *up*, muddle, (esp. different flocks of sheep). Chiefly *Austral. & NZ.* M19.

box /bɒks/ *verb*². E16.
[ORIGIN from BOX *noun*³.]
1 *verb trans.* Beat, strike. Now *spec.* slap (the ear or the side of the head), cuff. E16.

N. MITFORD She was so furious she . . rushed at Polly and boxed her ears.

2 *verb trans. & intrans.* Fight (a person) with the fists, now usu. in padded gloves as a sport, with set rules. M16.

C. MCCULLOUGH A lightweight under orders to keep Frank at a distance and find out if he could box as well as he could punch.

box clever *slang* use one's wits.

box /bɒks/ *verb*³. M18.
[ORIGIN Perh. from Spanish *bojar* (*boxar*) sail round, from Middle Low German *bōgen* bend, bow, from base of BOW *noun*¹, *verb*¹.]
NAUTICAL. **1** *verb trans.* ***box the compass***, (be able to) recite the compass points in correct order; *fig.* make a complete turn, go round and end where one began. M18.
2 *verb trans. & intrans.* Turn (a ship), *spec.* by hauling the head sheets to windward and laying the head yards aback. Also = BOX-HAUL. Usu. foll. by *off*. M18.

Box and Cox /bɒks (ə)nd ˈkɒks/ *noun phr. & verb.* L19.
[ORIGIN Title of a play by J. M. Morton (1811–91), in which two people unknowingly become tenants of the same room.]
▸ **A** *noun.* Two people who are never together or never at home at the same time; two people sharing office facilities etc. and using them at different times; two people who take turns in a part etc. Chiefly in ***play Box and Cox***.
▸ **B** *verb.* Share accommodation, office facilities, etc., by a strictly timed arrangement. L20.

boxcalf /ˈbɒkskɑːf/ *noun.* E20.
[ORIGIN from Joseph *Box*, late-19th-cent. London bootmaker + CALF *noun*¹.]
Chrome-tanned calfskin with a hatched grain.

boxer /ˈbɒksə/ *noun*¹. *rare.* M16.
[ORIGIN from BOX *verb*¹ + -ER¹.]
A person who puts things in boxes.

boxer /ˈbɒksə/ *noun*². L17.
[ORIGIN from BOX *verb*² + -ER¹.]
1 A person who boxes; a pugilist. L17.
2 *hist.* (**B-**.) [Repr. Chinese *yì hé quán* lit. 'righteous harmonious fists'.] A member of a Chinese nationalist secret society responsible for a rising in 1900. E20.
3 A dog of a smooth-coated square-built breed of the bulldog type, originating in Germany. E20.
– COMB.: **boxer shorts**, **boxers** men's loose shorts or underpants.

Boxercise /ˈbɒksəsʌɪz/ *noun.* L20.
[ORIGIN Blend of BOXER *noun*² and *exercise*.]
(Proprietary name for) a form of exercise based on boxing training and using boxing equipment.

box-haul /ˈbɒkshɔːl/ *verb trans.* M18.
[ORIGIN from BOX *verb*³ + HAUL *verb*.]
NAUTICAL. Veer (a ship) round on its stern.

boxiana /bɒksɪˈɑːnə/ *noun pl.* E19.
[ORIGIN from BOXING *noun*² + -IANA.]
Publications or other items concerning or associated with boxing and boxers.

boxing /ˈbɒksɪŋ/ *noun*¹. E16.
[ORIGIN from BOX *verb*¹ + -ING¹.]
The action of BOX *verb*¹. Also, boxes, casing.
Boxing Day the first day (strictly, the first weekday) after Christmas Day (on which Christmas boxes were traditionally given).

boxing /ˈbɒksɪŋ/ *noun*². E18.
[ORIGIN from BOX *verb*² + -ING¹.]
The action of fighting with fists, *spec.* as a sport, using padded gloves.
– COMB.: **boxing glove** a thick padded glove used in boxing; **boxing ring** an enclosure, now usu. a raised square with surrounding ropes, for boxing; **boxing weight** any of a series of weight ranges at which boxers are officially matched (as *bantamweight*, *flyweight*, *heavyweight*, etc.).

boxty /ˈbɒksti/ *noun.* L19.
[ORIGIN Irish *bacstaí*.]
A type of bread made using grated raw potatoes and flour, originally made in Ireland. Also ***boxty bread***.

boy /bɔɪ/ *noun.* ME.
[ORIGIN Perh. rel. to Old English *Bōia*, *Bōja*, Old High German *Buobo* male personal names, Middle High German *buobe* boy; cf. also Frisian *boi* boy.]
1 A male child; a youth. Also, a grown-up son. ME.

BYRON Ah! happy years! once more who would not be a boy? ARNOLD BENNETT Edwin had left school; and, if he was not a man, he was certainly not a boy. E. WAUGH That . . was Lord Sebastian Flyte . . . The Marquis of Marchmain's second boy.

2 A man, *esp.* a young or relatively young one; a man belonging to some specified or understood group (as one's habitual companions, a team, a gang, the army, etc.). Freq. as a familiar form of address. ME. ▸**b** A familiar form of address to a male dog, horse, or other animal. LME. ▸**c** A man of any age. *dial.* (esp. *Irish*). M18.

SHAKES. *Much Ado* If thou kill'st me, boy, thou shalt kill a man. *Spectator* The public relations boys could really go to town. J. LE CARRÉ It was just like old times . . : the boys together and the night their oyster. I. F. ELLIS 'That's all right, my boy', said the officer.

†**3** A male person of lowly status; a worthless or contemptible man. ME–E17.

SHAKES. *Coriol.* Name not the god, thou boy of tears . . no more.

4 A male servant, an underling, *esp.* a young one; a helper, a messenger. *obsolete* exc. as in sense 4b or when a boy in sense 1. LME. ▸**b** A servant or labourer from an indigenous people in Africa, Asia, etc. Now *offensive*. E17.

COVERDALE *1 Sam.* 2:13 The prestes boye came, whyle the flesh was seething. P. LOVESEY Newspaper-boys . . bawled their wares.

button boy, ***pageboy***, ***shop boy***, etc.
5 As *interjection*. An exclamation of surprise, excitement, relief, etc. Freq. ***oh boy!*** Orig. *US.* E20.

M. HODGE Boy! They don't wear a damned thing! N. SHUTE Boy! was I glad to be on the ground!

– PHRASES: ***backroom boy***: see BACK-. ***be a big boy (now)***: see BIG *adjective* 3b. ***best boy***: see BEST *adjective* etc. **Boys' Brigade** a boys' organization resembling the Scouts, connected with Presbyterian and Nonconformist churches. ***boys in blue***: see BLUE *noun* 2. ***BROTH of a boy***. ***home boy***: see HOME *adjective*. **jobs for the boys** preferment for one's supporters or favourites. *man and boy*: see MAN *noun*. ***mother's boy***: see MOTHER *noun*¹. ***naked boys***: see NAKED *adjective*. ***old boy***: see OLD *adjective*. **one of the boys** a man who conforms to the behaviour of his companions, a good fellow. ***principal boy***: see PRINCIPAL *adjective*. SKOLLY boy. ***sort out the men from the boys***: see MAN *noun*. **the boy** *arch. slang* champagne. ***the boy next door***: see NEXT *adjective*. ***white-headed boy***: see WHITE *adjective*. ***wide boy***: see WIDE *adjective*.
– COMB.: **boy band**, **girl band** a pop group composed of attractive young men (or young women), aimed primarily at a young teenage audience; **boyfriend** a person's (esp. a young woman's) usual or preferred male companion or sexual partner; **boy-meets-girl** a conventional or ideal romance (freq. *attrib.*); **boy racer** a young man who is fond of driving fast and aggressively in high-powered cars; ***Boy Scout***: see SCOUT *noun*³ 2c; **boy's-love** southernwood, *Artemisia abrotanum*; **boys' play** *arch.* amusement

B

for boys, child's play; **boy toy** *colloq., derog.* (*a*) a young woman considered sexually attractive to young men; (*b*) a young man considered sexually attractive to women; **boy wonder** an exceptionally talented young man or boy.
■ **boyhood** *noun* (*a*) the state of being a boy; the time when one is a boy; (*b*) boys collectively: M18. **boyish** *adjective* of or pertaining to boys or boyhood; boylike, high-spirited: M16. **boyishly** *adverb* L16. **boyishness** *noun* M16. **boyism** *noun* (now *rare*) a boyish characteristic; boyish character: E18. **boykin(s)** *noun* (*arch.*) a small boy (esp. as an affectionate form of address) M16. **boylike** *adverb & adjective* characteristic(ally) of a boy or boys M19.

boy /bɔɪ/ *verb. rare.* M16.
[ORIGIN from the noun.]
1 *verb intrans.* Act like a boy. M16.
2 *verb trans.* Represent on stage by a boy actor; call 'boy'. L16.

boyar /bəʊˈjɑː/ *noun.* Also †**-ard**. L16.
[ORIGIN Russian *boyarin* grandee.]
hist. A member of an order of Russian aristocracy (abolished by Peter the Great), next in rank to a prince.

boycott /ˈbɔɪkɒt/ *verb & noun.* Also †**B-**. L19.
[ORIGIN Capt. C. C. *Boycott* (1832–97), land agent in Ireland who was so treated in 1880.]
▸ **A** *verb trans.* Combine to coerce or punish (a person, group, nation, etc.) by a systematic refusal of normal commercial or social relations; refuse to handle or buy (goods), refuse to attend (a meeting, lecture, etc.), with this aim. L19.
▸ **B** *noun.* Such a course of action. L19.
■ **boycotter** *noun* L19.

boyer /ˈbɔɪə/ *noun.* Also **boier**. M16.
[ORIGIN Dutch *boeier* smack.]
A single-masted Dutch vessel, orig. a seagoing sloop but now a bluff-ended craft used on inland waterways.

Boyle's law /ˈbɔɪlz lɔː/ *noun phr.* M19.
[ORIGIN Robert *Boyle* (1627–91), English scientist.]
CHEMISTRY. A law stating that the pressure and volume of a gas are in inverse proportion to each other at constant temperature.

boyo /ˈbɔɪəʊ/ *noun. Welsh & Irish colloq.* Pl. **-os**. L19.
[ORIGIN from BOY *noun* + -O.]
Boy, lad, fellow. Chiefly as a familiar form of address.

boysenberry /ˈbɔɪz(ə)nbɛri, -s-/ *noun.* M20.
[ORIGIN from Robert *Boysen*, 20th-cent. US horticulturist + BERRY *noun*[1].]
A cultivar of the loganberry, with larger fruit; the fruit of this plant.

boza /ˈbəʊzə/ *noun.* Also **bosa**, **boo-** /ˈbuː-/. M17.
[ORIGIN Turkish from Persian.]
A fermented drink made in Turkey and the Middle East; *spec.* an infusion of millet seed.

bozo /ˈbəʊzəʊ/ *noun. slang* (chiefly *N. Amer.*). Pl. **-os**. E20.
[ORIGIN Unknown.]
A stupid, despised, or insignificant person.

T. ROBBINS This bozo might be capable of understanding art, after all.

BP *abbreviation*[1].
1 Before the present (counting backwards from 1800).
2 Blood pressure.
3 Boiling point.
4 British Petroleum.
5 British Pharmacopoeia.

Bp *abbreviation*[2].
Bishop.

bp *abbreviation*[3].
BIOCHEMISTRY. Base pair(s).

b.p. *abbreviation.*
Boiling point.

BPC *abbreviation.*
British Pharmaceutical Codex.

BPH *abbreviation.*
MEDICINE. Benign prostatic hyperplasia (or hypertrophy).

B.Phil. *abbreviation.*
Bachelor of Philosophy.

bpi *abbreviation.*
COMPUTING. Bits per inch.

bpm *abbreviation.*
Beats per minute.

bps *abbreviation.*
COMPUTING. Bits per second.

Bq *abbreviation.*
PHYSICS. Becquerel(s).

BR *abbreviation.*
hist. British Rail (earlier, Railways).

Br *symbol.*
CHEMISTRY. Bromine.

Br. *abbreviation.*
1 British.
2 Brother.

bra /brɑː/ *noun*[1]. M20.
[ORIGIN Abbreviation of BRASSIERE.]
1 A woman's undergarment worn to support the breasts, a brassiere. M20.
2 More fully ***auto bra***, ***car bra***. A carbon-based cover that fits over the front bumper of a car, absorbing the microwaves used in police radar equipment to minimize the risk of detection for the speeding motorist. *N. Amer.* L20.
■ **braless** *adjective* M20. **bralessness** *noun* L20.

bra /brɑː/ *noun*[2]. M20.
[ORIGIN from BRA(CKET *noun*: cf. KET *noun*[2].]
QUANTUM MECHANICS. A vector in Hilbert space that is the complex conjugate of a ket and is symbolized by ⟨|. Freq. ***bra vector***.

braai /ˈbrɑːɪ/ *noun & verb. S. Afr.* M20.
[ORIGIN Abbreviation of BRAAIVLEIS.]
▸ **A** *noun.* = BRAAIVLEIS. M20.
▸ **B** *verb trans. & intrans.* Grill (meat) over an open fire. M20.

braaivleis /ˈbrɑːɪfleɪs/ *noun. S. Afr.* M20.
[ORIGIN Afrikaans = grilled meat, from *braai* to grill + *vleis* meat.]
Meat grilled over an open fire; a picnic, barbecue, etc., at which meat is cooked in this way.

brab /brab/ *noun.* L17.
[ORIGIN Portuguese (*palmeira*) *braba* wild (palm tree).]
The palmyra, *Borassus flabellifer*.

brabble /ˈbrab(ə)l/ *verb & noun.* Now *arch. & dial.* E16.
[ORIGIN Prob. ult. imit., but perh. from Middle Dutch & mod. Dutch *brabbelen* jabber, or a blend of BRAWL *verb* and BABBLE *verb*.]
▸ **A** *verb intrans.* †**1** Dispute obstinately. E16–E17.
2 Quarrel about trifles; quarrel noisily, squabble. M16.
▸ **B** *noun.* **1** A paltry altercation, a noisy quarrel. M16. ▸†**b** A brawl, a skirmish. L16–E17.
†**2** A quibble; *spec.* a frivolous legal action. L16–L17.
3 Discordant babble. M19.
■ **brabblement** *noun* (an) altercation, (a) contentious uproar M16. **brabbler** *noun* †(*a*) a quibbler; (*b*) a brawler: M16.

braccio /ˈbratʃəʊ/ *noun.* Pl. **-ccia** /-tʃə/. M18.
[ORIGIN Italian = arm.]
A former Italian measure of length, about 60 centimetres.

brace /breɪs/ *noun*[1]. LME.
[ORIGIN Old French = two arms, the distance between the fingertips with arms extended (mod. *brasse* fathom) from Latin *bracchia* pl. of *bracchium* arm (whence French *bras*) from Greek *brakhiōn*. Some senses from BRACE *verb*[1].]
▸ **I** A pair of arms.
†**1** A portion of a suit of armour covering the arms. LME–E17. ▸†**b** A suit of armour; armed state. *rare* (Shakes.). Only in E17.
†**2** A measure of length, orig. the distance between fingertips with arms extended. LME–M18.
3 A tool in carpentry having a crank handle and a socket etc. to hold a bit for boring. M16.
▸ **II** A thing which clasps.
4 A clasp, buckle, or other fastener. LME. ▸**b** DENTISTRY. A wire device for straightening the teeth. M20.
French brace: see FRENCH *adjective*.
5 A leather thong which slides up and down the cord of a drum, regulating the tension of the skins, and hence the pitch of any note produced. L16.
6 The sign } (or {) used in printing etc. for the purpose of uniting two or more lines, words, staves of music, etc. or in pairs as a form of brackets; *loosely* in *pl.*, square brackets [ ]. M17.
7 Either of a pair of straps of elastic, leather, etc., used to support trousers etc. Usu. in *pl.* L18.
belt and braces: see BELT *noun*.
8 NAUTICAL. A metal strap secured to the sternpost and bottom planks for supporting the rudder. M19.
▸ **III** Pl. usu. same (preceded by a numeral or quantifier).
9 A pair, a couple, esp. of dogs, game, pistols, *derog.* persons, CRICKET ducks. LME.
in a brace of shakes: see SHAKE *noun*.
▸ **IV** A thing which imparts rigidity.
10 A length of wood or metal fixed (usu. diagonally) to a wall, theatrical flat, or other structure to keep it from distorting out of shape. LME.
11 A metal band used as a support, e.g. in mounting church bells. M18.

brace /breɪs/ *noun*[2]. LME.
[ORIGIN French *bras* (*de vergue*) lit. '(yard-)arm', assim. to BRACE *noun*[1].]
NAUTICAL. A rope attached to the yard of a square-rigged vessel for the purpose of trimming the sail.
main brace: see MAIN *adjective*.

brace /breɪs/ *verb*[1]. ME.
[ORIGIN Old French *bracier* embrace, formed as BRACE *noun*[1]: later senses directly from BRACE *noun*[1].]
▸ **I** *verb trans.* **1** Clasp, fasten up tight. ME.

POPE The adverse winds in leathern bags he brac'd.

†**2** Embrace. LME–L16.
3 Encompass, surround, encircle. LME.

T. AIRD A flowing wood the middle mountain braced.

4 Make tight or tense. LME.

SHAKES. *John* Even at hand a drum is ready brac'd That shall reverberate all as loud as thine.

5 Tense or give firmness or tone to (nerves, sinews, oneself, etc.); invigorate; *fig.* prepare mentally for a task, unwelcome intelligence, etc. (Foll. by *up*.) L15.

C. THIRLWALL Nothing now remained but to brace every nerve for the battle. W. GOLDING He braced his hands, stiffening the muscles of his arms. D. LODGE Mentally, you brace yourself for the ending of a novel. K. M. E. MURRAY A few days change . . would brace him up.

6 Fix, render firm, steady, set rigidly or firmly down (esp. by tightly binding); support. L18.

G. J. WHYTE-MELVILLE He braced his foot in the stirrup to afford a purchase for her ascent.

▸ **II** *verb intrans.* **7** Foll. by *up*: brace oneself; pull oneself together for an effort; take a drink for this purpose. Orig. *US.* E19.
■ **bracing** *noun* (*a*) the action of the verb; (*b*) an appliance or arrangement that braces: LME. **bracing** *ppl adjective* that braces; *esp.* (of air, climate, etc.) invigorating: M18.

brace /breɪs/ *verb*[2] *trans. & intrans.* M17.
[ORIGIN from BRACE *noun*[2]: cf. French *brasser*.]
NAUTICAL. Swing (a yard) round by means of braces. Freq. with adverbs, as *aback*, *about*, *in*, *to*, etc.

bracelet /ˈbreɪslɪt/ *noun.* LME.
[ORIGIN Old French & mod. French, from *bras* arm: see -EL[2], -ET[1].]
1 An ornamental ring or band worn on the arm or wrist. LME.
2 *hist.* A piece of armour covering the arm. L16.
3 A fetter for the wrists; *slang* a handcuff. Usu. in *pl.* E17.
■ **braceleted** *adjective* M17.

bracer /ˈbreɪsə/ *noun*[1]. LME.
[ORIGIN Old French *braciere*, from *bras* arm.]
A portion of a suit of armour covering the arm (now *hist.*); a sort of wrist guard used in archery etc.

bracer /ˈbreɪsə/ *noun*[2]. M16.
[ORIGIN from BRACE *verb*[1] + -ER[1].]
1 A thing which clamps or binds, a brace. M16.
2 A tonic or medicine for bracing the nerves. Now chiefly (*colloq.*) a drink taken to brace one up, a pick-me-up. M18.

bracero /brəˈsɪərəʊ, *foreign* braˈθero, -ˈsero/ *noun.* Pl. **-os**. E20.
[ORIGIN Spanish, lit. 'labourer', from *brazo* arm from Latin *bracchium*.]
A Mexican labourer allowed into the United States for a limited time as a seasonal agricultural worker.

brach /bratʃ/ *noun. arch.* LME.
[ORIGIN Orig. in pl. from Old French *brachez* pl. of *brachet* dim. of Provençal *brac* from Proto-Romance from Frankish (whence also Old High German *brakko*, German *Bracke*).]
A kind of hound which hunts by scent. In later use *gen.* and always fem.: a bitch hound.
■ Also **brachet** *noun* LME.

brachia *noun* pl. of BRACHIUM.

brachial /ˈbreɪkɪəl/ *noun & adjective.* LME.
[ORIGIN Latin *brachialis* adjective, from *brachium* arm: see -AL[1].]
▸ **A** *noun.* †**1** A vestment or a piece of armour for the arm. LME–M16.
2 *ellipt.* A brachial vein, bone, etc. M19.
▸ **B** *adjective.* Chiefly ANATOMY & ZOOLOGY.
1 Of the arm. L16.
2 Of the nature of or resembling an arm. M19.
■ **brachialis** /-ˈeɪlɪs/ *noun* (ANATOMY) a muscle in the upper arm, serving to flex the forearm L19.

brachiate /ˈbrakɪət, ˈbreɪk-/ *adjective.* Now *rare* or *obsolete*. M18.
[ORIGIN Latin *brachiatus* with boughs or branches, formed as BRACHIAL: see -ATE[2].]
BOTANY. Having long decussate branches.

brachiate /ˈbrakɪeɪt/ *verb intrans.* M20.
[ORIGIN Back-form. from BRACHIATOR: see -ATE[3].]
Move as a brachiator does.
■ **brachiˈation** *noun* L19.

brachiator /ˈbrakɪeɪtə/ *noun.* M19.
[ORIGIN from Latin *brachium* arm + -ATOR.]
ZOOLOGY. An ape which moves by using the arms to swing from branch to branch.

brachiocephalic /ˌbrakɪəʊsɪˈfalɪk, -kɛˈfalɪk/ *adjective.* M19.
[ORIGIN mod. Latin *brachiocephalicus*, from Greek *brakhiōn* arm: see -CEPHALIC.]
ANATOMY. Pertaining to both arm and head; *esp.* designating the innominate veins and artery.

brachiopod /ˈbrakɪəpɒd/ *noun.* M19.
[ORIGIN mod. Latin *brachiopoda* pl., from Greek *brakhiōn* arm + -POD.]
ZOOLOGY. A marine invertebrate of the phylum Brachiopoda (esp. a fossil one), with a two-valved chalky shell and a ciliated feeding arm (lophophore); a lamp shell.

brachiosaurus /brakɪəˈsɔːrəs/ *noun*. Pl. **-ruses**, **-ri** /-rʌɪ/. E20.
[ORIGIN mod. Latin, from Greek *brakhiōn* arm + *sauros* -SAUR.]
A huge sauropod dinosaur of the genus *Brachiosaurus*, with the forelegs longer than the hind legs, found fossilized in Jurassic strata.

brachistochrone /brəˈkɪstəkrəʊn/ *noun*. L18.
[ORIGIN from Greek *brakhistos* superl. of *brakhus* short (see -O-) + *khronos* time.]
A curve joining two points such that a body travelling along it (e.g. under gravity) takes a shorter time than is possible along any other curve between the points.

brachium /ˈbreɪkɪəm, ˈbrak-/ *noun*. Pl. **-chia** /-kɪə/. M18.
[ORIGIN Latin.]
ANATOMY & ZOOLOGY. The arm; *spec.* the upper arm from shoulder to elbow.

brachy- /ˈbraki/ *combining form* of Greek *brakhus* short. (Cf. DOLICHO-, PLATY-.)
■ **brachycataˈlectic** *adjective & noun* (PROSODY) (a verse) lacking one foot or two syllables E17. **brachyˈdactylous** *adjective* having abnormally short fingers and toes L19. **brachyˈdactyly** *noun* brachydactylous condition L19. **brachyodont** *adjective* characterized by or designating teeth with low crowns and well-developed roots L19. **brachyˈpellic** *adjective* [Greek *pella* bowl] having or designating a pelvis whose anteroposterior diameter is much greater than its transverse diameter M20. **braˈchypterous** *adjective* short-winged M19.

brachycephalic /ˌbrakɪsɪˈfalɪk, -kɛˈfalɪk/ *adjective*. Also †**-keph-**. M19.
[ORIGIN from BRACHY- + -CEPHALIC.]
Short-headed; *spec.* having a cranial index between 80 and 85.
■ **brachycephal** /brakɪˈsɛf(ə)l, ˈbrakɪsɛf(ə)l; -kɛf-/ *noun* [back-form. from mod. Latin *brachycephales* pl.] a brachycephalic person E20. **brachycephales** /-liːz/, **-cephali** /-lʌɪ, -liː/ *nouns pl.* (now *rare* or *obsolete*) [mod. Latin] brachycephals M19. **brachyˈcephalism** *noun* brachycephalic condition M19. **brachyˈcephalous** *adjective* brachycephalic L19. **brachyˈcephaly** *noun* brachycephalism M19.

brachygraphy /brəˈkɪɡrəfi/ *noun*. *obsolete* exc. *hist.* L16.
[ORIGIN French *brachygraphie*: see BRACHY-, -GRAPHY.]
= STENOGRAPHY.

brachylogy /brəˈkɪlədʒi/ *noun*. Also (earlier) in Latin form †**-logia**. M16.
[ORIGIN Late Latin *brachylogia* from Greek *brakhulogia*: see BRACHY-, -LOGY.]
Concise speech; a concise expression.

brachytherapy /brakɪˈθɛrəpi/ *noun*. L20.
[ORIGIN from BRACHY- + THERAPY.]
The treatment of cancer (esp. prostate cancer) by the insertion of radioactive implants directly into the tissue.

brachyurous /brakɪˈjʊərəs/ *adjective*. E19.
[ORIGIN from BRACHY- + Greek *oura* tail + -OUS.]
ZOOLOGY. Of a decapod crustacean: having a relatively short abdomen.
■ **brachyuran** *noun & adjective* (*a*) *noun* a crustacean (e.g. many crabs) belonging to the section Brachyura which includes most brachyurous kinds; (*b*) *adjective* of or pertaining to the Brachyura: L19.

brack /brak/ *noun*[1]. ME.
[ORIGIN In branch I from Old Norse *brak* = Old English *ġebræc*, Old Saxon *gibrak* creaking noise, from Germanic base of BREAK *verb*. In branch II parallel to BREAK *noun*[1].]
▸ †**I 1** Noise, outcry. ME–E16.
▸ **II** †**2** A breach, rupture; a quarrel; a broken piece, a fragment. M16–E19.
3 A flaw (in cloth). Now chiefly *dial.* M16.

brack /brak/ *noun*[2] & *verb trans.* Now *rare* or *obsolete*. M18.
[ORIGIN German *Bracke* noun, *bracken* verb.]
(Sort or examine by) a system of inspection at Baltic ports.
■ **bracker** *noun* an official carrying out this system M18.

brack /brak/ *noun*[3]. *Irish*. M19.
[ORIGIN from (the same root as) BARMBRACK.]
= BARMBRACK.

brack /brak/ *adjective & noun*[4]. *obsolete* exc. *dial.* E16.
[ORIGIN Middle Low German, Middle Dutch *brac* (Low German, Dutch *brak*), of unknown origin.]
▸ **A** *adjective*. Salt, brackish. E16.
▸ **B** *noun*. Salt water, the sea. L16.
■ **bracky** *adjective* brackish L16.

bracken /ˈbrak(ə)n/ *noun*[1]. ME.
[ORIGIN Old Norse (Swedish *bräken*, Danish *bregne*).]
1 A large fern, *Pteridium aquilinum*, common on hillsides, heaths, etc.; any of various other ferns of the genus *Pteridium*; *collect.* a mass of such ferns. ME.
2 A shade of brown. E20.
– COMB.: **bracken-clock** a common chafer (beetle), *Phyllopertha horticola*.
■ **brackened** *adjective* overgrown with bracken L19. **brackeny** *adjective* = BRACKENED M19.

†**bracken** *noun*[2]. Also **brochan**. M16–L19.
[ORIGIN Gaelic *breacan*, Irish *breacán* from *breac* chequered.]
A tartan plaid.

bracket /ˈbrakɪt/ *noun*. Orig. †**-g(g)-**. L16.
[ORIGIN French *braguette* codpiece, or Spanish *bragueta* codpiece, bracket, corbel, dim. of French *brague* mortise, (in pl.) breeches, lashing, from Provençal *braga* (pl.) breeches, ult. from Latin *braca*, pl. *bracae* breeches.]
1 A flat-topped, usu. decorated, projection from a wall, serving as a support to a statue, arch, etc. L16. ▸**b** A small (ornamental) shelf with a slanting underprop for fixing to a wall. M17.
2 A wooden or metal angular support; a support for a lamp, projecting from a wall. E17.
3 Either of the two side pieces of a gun carriage. M18.
4 A mark used, usu. in pairs ( ), [ ], { }, ⟨ ⟩, for enclosing a word or words, figures, etc., so as to separate them from the context; *spec.* (TYPOGRAPHY) a square bracket. M18.
angle bracket, ***round bracket***, ***square bracket***, etc.
5 MILITARY. (The distance between) shots fired short of and over the target in rangefinding. L19.
6 A group (of people) classed together as similar or as falling between certain limits (of income etc.). L19.

> M. INNES They were both from the same social bracket.
> J. K. GALBRAITH Tax reductions affecting the upper surtax brackets.

7 SKATING. A series of turns resembling a bracket { L19.
– COMB.: **bracket clock**: designed to stand on a wall bracket; **bracket fungus**: forming shelflike projections on tree trunks etc.

bracket /ˈbrakɪt/ *verb*. M19.
[ORIGIN from the noun.]
1 *verb trans.* Link or couple (lines, names, etc.) by means of a brace; *fig.* imply connection or equality of. (Foll. by *together*, *with* another.) M19.
2 *verb trans.* Provide with brackets; enclose in brackets as parenthetic, spurious, etc., or (MATH.) to indicate some special relation to what precedes or follows. M19.
3 *verb intrans. & trans.* MILITARY. Find the range for artillery by means of a bracket; fire or land short of and over (the target). E20.
■ **bracketing** *noun* (*a*) framework etc. used as a support for moulding etc. on a wall; (*b*) the action of the verb: E19.

Brackett series /ˈbrakɪt sɪəriːz/ *noun phr.* M20.
[ORIGIN Frederick Sumner *Brackett* (1896–1972), US physicist.]
A series of lines in the infrared spectrum of atomic hydrogen, between 4.04 and 1.46 micrometres.

brackish /ˈbrakɪʃ/ *adjective*. M16.
[ORIGIN from BRACK *adjective* + -ISH[1].]
1 Of water: slightly salt. M16.
2 Spoilt by mixture. E17.
■ **brackishness** *noun* L16.

brackmard /ˈbrakmɑːd/ *noun*. *obsolete* exc. *hist.* E16.
[ORIGIN French *braquemart*.]
A short broad-bladed sword, a cutlass.

braconid /ˈbrakənɪd/ *noun & adjective*. L19.
[ORIGIN mod. Latin *Braconidae* (see below), from *Bracon* genus name (irreg. from Greek *brakhus* short) + -ID[3].]
▸ **A** *noun*. Any insect of the family Braconidae of hymenopterous insects similar to ichneumon flies. L19.
▸ **B** *adjective*. Of, pertaining to, or designating this family. L19.

bract /brakt/ *noun*. Orig. also in Latin form †**bractea**, pl. **-eae**. L18.
[ORIGIN Latin *bractea* var. of *brattea* thin plate of metal, gold leaf.]
BOTANY. A leaf or scale, usu. small, growing below the calyx of a plant.
■ **bractlet** *noun* = BRACTEOLE M19.

bracteate /ˈbraktɪət/ *adjective & noun*. E19.
[ORIGIN Latin *bracteatus*, formed as BRACT: see -ATE[2].]
▸ **A** *adjective*. **1** BOTANY. Having or bearing bracts. E19.
2 Made of metal beaten thin. M19.
▸ **B** *noun*. A coin or ornament of thinly beaten metal. M19.
■ **bracteated** *adjective* = BRACTEATE *adjective* 1 E19.

bracteole /ˈbraktɪəʊl/ *noun*. E19.
[ORIGIN Latin *bracteola* dim. of *bractea* BRACT: see -OLE[1].]
BOTANY. A small bract.
■ **bracteolate** *adjective* having bracteoles E19.

brad /brad/ *noun*. LME.
[ORIGIN Var. of BROD *noun*.]
A thin, flat, small-headed nail.

bradawl /ˈbradɔːl/ *noun*. E19.
[ORIGIN from BRAD + AWL.]
A small boring tool with a non-spiral blade.

Bradbury /ˈbradb(ə)ri/ *noun*. *colloq.* (now *hist.*). E20.
[ORIGIN John S. *Bradbury*, Brit. Secretary to the Treasury 1913–19.]
A one-pound note.

bradoon *noun* var. of BRIDOON.

Bradshaw /ˈbradʃɔː/ *noun*. M19.
[ORIGIN Named after George *Bradshaw* (1801–53), the first publisher of the guide.]
In full ***Bradshaw's Railway Guide***. A timetable of all passenger trains in Britain, issued 1839–1961.

brady- /ˈbradi/ *combining form* of Greek *bradus* slow.
■ **bradyˈcardia** *noun* abnormal slowness of heart action L19. **bradymetaˈbolic** *adjective* (ZOOLOGY) pertaining to or characterized by bradymetabolism L20. **bradymeˈtabolism** *noun* (ZOOLOGY) the low level of metabolism characteristic of cold-blooded vertebrates; poikilothermy: L20. **bradypepsy** *noun* (now *rare* or *obsolete*) [Greek *bradupepsia*] slowness of digestion L16.

bradykinin /bradɪˈkʌɪnɪn/ *noun*. M20.
[ORIGIN from BRADY- + Greek *kinēsis* motion + -IN[1].]
BIOCHEMISTRY. Any of a class of naturally occurring peptides which cause contraction of smooth muscle. Cf. KININ.

bradyseism /ˈbradɪsʌɪz(ə)m/ *noun*. L19.
[ORIGIN from BRADY- + Greek *seismos* earthquake.]
A slow rise or fall of the earth's crust.
■ **bradyˈseismic** *adjective* L19.

brae /breɪ/ *noun*. *Scot. & N. English*. ME.
[ORIGIN Old Norse *brá* eyelash = Old English *brǣw* eyelid, Old Frisian *brē*, Old Saxon, Old High German *brāwa* (German *Braue*) eyebrow: the sense-development is parallel to that of BROW *noun*[1].]
A steep bank beside a river valley; a hillside, a slope.

Braeburn /ˈbreɪbəːn/ *noun*. M20.
[ORIGIN *Braeburn* Orchards, NZ, where it was first grown commercially.]
A dessert apple of a variety with crisp flesh.

brag /braɡ/ *noun*. LME.
[ORIGIN Unknown: cf. BRAG *adjective & adverb*, BRAG *verb*.]
1 Arrogant or boastful language; boasting; a boast. LME.

> SHAKES. *A.Y.L.* Caesar's . . brag of 'I came, saw, and overcame'.
> MILTON Beauty is nature's brag.

†**2** Show; pompous demeanour. LME–M17.
†**3** The bray of a trumpet. L15–E16.
4 A braggart. L17.
5 A card game resembling poker. M18.
– COMB.: **brag book** *N. Amer. colloq.* an album of photographs intended to show the subjects (esp. one's family) to advantage.

brag /braɡ/ *adjective & adverb*. ME.
[ORIGIN Unknown: cf. BRAG *noun*, BRAG *verb*.]
▸ **A** *adjective*. †**1** Mettlesome, spirited, lively. ME–E17.
†**2** Boastful (*of*). ME–M17.
3 First-rate, surpassingly good. *US*. M19.
▸ †**B** *adverb*. Boastfully. LME–L16.
■ †**bragly** *adverb* M16–E18.

brag /braɡ/ *verb*. Infl. **-gg-**. LME.
[ORIGIN Unknown: cf. BRAG *adjective & adverb*, BRAG *noun*.]
†**1** *verb intrans. & trans.* Sound (a trumpet) loudly. Only in LME.
2 *verb intrans. & trans.* Boast (of). LME. ▸†**b** *verb intrans.* Swagger, show off. M–L16.
3 *verb trans.* Challenge; bully, overawe by boasting. Chiefly *dial.* M16.
■ **bragger** *noun* a boaster, a braggart LME. **braggery** *noun* (*a*) bragging; †(*b*) *the* rabble: M16.

†**braget** *noun* var. of BRACKET *noun*.

Bragg /braɡ/ *noun*. E20.
[ORIGIN Sir William Henry (1862–1942) and his son Sir William Lawrence (1890–1971) *Bragg*, English physicists.]
PHYSICS. ***Bragg law***, ***Bragg's law***, a relation giving the conditions for maximum reflection of electromagnetic waves (esp. X-rays) or particles by planes of atoms in a crystal. Hence ***Bragg angle***, an angle of incidence at which maximum reflection occurs for a given wavelength.

braggadocio /braɡəˈdəʊtʃɪəʊ/ *noun*. Pl. **-os**. L16.
[ORIGIN Pseudo-Italian personal name (Spenser), from *brag* or *braggart* + *-occio* Italian augm. suffix.]
1 An empty idle boaster. L16.
2 Empty boasting, bluster. M18.
■ †**braggadocian** *adjective* L16–E18.

braggart /ˈbraɡət, -ɑːt/ *noun & adjective*. L16.
[ORIGIN French †*bragard*, from †*braguer* vaunt: see -ART.]
▸ **A** *noun*. A person given to bragging, a boaster. L16.
▸ **B** *adjective*. Given to bragging, boastful. E17.
■ **braggartism** *noun* L16.

bragget /ˈbraɡət/ *noun*[1]. LME.
[ORIGIN Early Welsh *brac(h)aut* (mod. *bragod*) = Irish *brogóid*, from Celtic, from base repr. by Latin *brace*, Gaulish *bracis* kind of grain.]
A drink made of honey, or (latterly) sugar and spices, and ale fermented together.

†**bragget** *noun*[2] var. of BRACKET *noun*.

†**brahm** *noun* var. of BRAHMAN *noun*[1].

Brahma /ˈbrɑːmə/ *noun*[1]. Also **Brahman**. L17.
[ORIGIN Sanskrit *brahmā* (nom. of *brahmán*) priest.]
In Hinduism: the creator, one of the three supreme personal deities. In Hindu and Buddhist thought: the highest god.

Brahma /ˈbrɑːmə/ *noun*[2]. L19.
[ORIGIN Abbreviation.]
= BRAHMAPUTRA.

brahma *noun*[3] var. of BRAHMAN *noun*[1].

brahmacharya /brɑːməˈtʃɑːrɪə/ *noun*. E20.
[ORIGIN Sanskrit *brahmacarya*, from *bráhman* prayer, worship + *carya* conduct.]
Purity of life, esp. regarding sexual matters (freq. used with reference to the life and teachings of M. K. Gandhi).
■ ***brahmachari*** *noun* a person who practises brahmacharya L18.

B

brahman /ˈbrɑːmən/ *noun*[1]. Also **brahma** /ˈbrɑːmə/, †**brahm**, **B-**. L18.
[ORIGIN Sanskrit *brāhman* sacred utterance.]
In Hindu philosophy: the ultimate reality underlying all phenomena.

Brahman *noun*[2] var. of BRAHMA *noun*[1].

brahman *noun*[3] var. of BRAHMIN.

Brahmaputra /brɑːməˈpuːtrə/ *noun*. Also **b-**, †**-pootra**. M19.
[ORIGIN *Brahmaputra*, a river in Bangladesh and West Bengal.]
A variety of domestic fowl originating in the Indian subcontinent.

Brahmi /ˈbrɑːmi/ *noun*. L19.
[ORIGIN Sanskrit *brāhmī*.]
One of the two oldest alphabets of the Indian subcontinent, of Semitic origin. Cf. KHAROSHTI.

brahmic /ˈbrɑːmɪk/ *adjective*. M19.
[ORIGIN from Sanskrit *brāhma* (see BRAHMO) + -IC.]
Pertaining to the Hindu movement Brahmo Sabha or Samaj (cf. BRAHMO).

brahmin /ˈbrɑːmɪn/ *noun*. Also **-man** /-mən/, **B-**. ME.
[ORIGIN Sanskrit *brāhmaṇa* one of the brahmin caste, from *brahman* (nom. *brahmā*) priest.]
1 A member of the highest or priestly Hindu caste. ME.
2 *transf.* (Usu. **B-**.) A highly cultured or intellectually aloof person; *spec.* a member of the upper classes of Boston, Massachusetts, USA. M19.
3 (Usu. **B-**.) In full ***Brahmin bull***, ***Brahmin ox***, etc. A zebu ox, or an animal of a breed of beef cattle developed from this. M19.
■ **brahˈminic**, **brahˈmanic** /-ˈman-/ *adjective* of or pertaining to the brahmins M19. **brahˈminical**, **brahˈmanical** /-ˈman-/ *adjective* = BRAHMINIC L16. **brahminism**, **brahmanism** *noun* the principles and practice of brahmins E19.

brahminy /ˈbrɑːmɪni/ *adjective*. Also *arch.* **-nee**, **B-**. E19.
[ORIGIN from BRAHMIN on the analogy of native Indian words like BENGALI.]
Pertaining to the brahmin caste; appropriated to the brahmins. Now chiefly as below.
Brahminy bull = BRAHMIN 3. **Brahminy duck** the ruddy shelduck, *Tadorna ferruginea*. **Brahminy kite** a white-headed kite of southern Asia and Australia, *Haliastur indus*.

Brahmo /ˈbrɑːməʊ/ *noun & adjective*. Pl. of noun **-os**. L19.
[ORIGIN Bengali from Sanskrit *brāhma* a person who knows brahman.]
(An adherent) of the Hindu reform movement Brahmo Sabha (or Brahmo Samaj) 'society of worshippers of Brahma'.
■ **Brahmoism**, †**Brahmism** *noun* the doctrines of the Brahmo movement M19.

Brahms and Liszt /ˌbrɑːmz (ə)nd ˈlɪst/ *adjectival phr. rhyming slang*. L20.
[ORIGIN from *Brahms*, *Liszt*: see BRAHMSIAN, LISZTIAN.]
Drunk, intoxicated.

Brahmsian /ˈbrɑːmzɪən/ *adjective & noun*. L19.
[ORIGIN from *Brahms* (see below) + -IAN.]
▸ **A** *adjective*. Of, pertaining to, or characteristic of the German composer Johannes Brahms (1833–97) or his music. L19.
▸ **B** *noun*. An interpreter, student, or admirer of Brahms or his music. E20.

Brahui /brəˈhuːɪ/ *noun & adjective*. E19.
[ORIGIN Brahui.]
▸ **A** *noun*. Pl. **-s**, same. A member of a pastoral people of Baluchistan; their Dravidian language. E19.
▸ **B** *attrib.* or as *adjective*. Of or pertaining to the Brahuis or their language. M19.

braid /breɪd/ *noun*. See also BREDE *noun*[2]. OE.
[ORIGIN from BRAID *verb*[1].]
†**1** An adroit turn; a trick, a subtlety. OE–L16.
†**2** A sudden or brisk movement. ME–E19.
3 A blow, an attack, an outburst. Long *obsolete* exc. *dial.* ME.
4 A thing plaited or interwoven, *esp.* a plait of hair. M16. ▸**b** A string or band confining or entwined in the hair. L16.
5 A woven band made of thread of silk, gold, silver, etc., used for trimming or binding garments. L16.
Hercules braid, ***military braid***, ***soutache braid***, etc.

†**braid** *adjective*[1]. *rare* (Shakes.). Only in E17.
[ORIGIN Of uncertain meaning and origin: cf. BRAID *noun* 1.]
Deceitful.

braid *adjective*[2], *adverb* see BROAD *adjective*, *adverb*.

braid /breɪd/ *verb*[1]. Pa. pple & ppl adjective **braided**, BROWDEN. See also BREDE *verb*[2].
[ORIGIN Old English *bregdan* = Old Frisian *breida*, *brīda*, Old Saxon *bregdan* (Dutch *breien*), Old High German *brettan*, Old Norse *bregða*, from Germanic, of unknown origin. In senses 5, 6 from BRAID *noun*.]
▸ **I** †**1** *verb trans.* Make a sudden movement with (the hand, foot, etc.); brandish (a spear), draw (a sword etc.); jerk, fling, etc., with a sudden effort. OE–E17.
†**2** *verb intrans.* Change suddenly or abruptly. OE–LME.
3 *verb intrans.* Start, usu. out of sleep; burst into motion, speech, etc. *arch.* ME.
▸ **II 4** *verb trans.* Twist in and out, interweave; embroider; make (a cord, garment, etc.) by plaiting; arrange (the hair) in braids. OE.
5 *verb trans.* Bind (the hair) with a braid, ribbon, etc. L18.
6 *verb trans.* Ornament or trim with braid; outline (a design for point-lace work) by means of braid. M19.
– WITH PREPOSITIONS IN SPECIALIZED SENSES: **braid of** *dial.* take after, resemble.
■ **braider** *noun* a person who or thing which makes or applies braids M19. **braiding** *noun* (**a**) the action of the verb; (**b**) braids collectively; braided work: LME.

†**braid** *verb*[2] *trans.* LME–E17.
[ORIGIN Aphet. from UPBRAID *verb*.]
Upbraid; reproach.

brail /breɪl/ *noun & verb*. LME.
[ORIGIN Old French *braiel*, *braël* from medieval Latin *bracale* waist belt, from *braca*: see BRACKET *noun*.]
▸ **A** *noun*. **1** In *pl.* Small ropes fastened to the leech of fore-and-aft sails to truss them up before furling. LME.
2 In *pl.* The rump of an animal; *spec.* the feathers about a hawk's rump. Now *rare* or *obsolete*. LME.
3 A girdle used to confine a hawk's wings. E19.
▸ **B** *verb trans.* **1** Haul *up* (sails) by means of brails. E17.
2 Confine (a hawk's wings) with a girdle. M17.

Braille /breɪl/ *noun & verb*. M19.
[ORIGIN from Louis *Braille* (1809–52), French teacher of the blind, who invented the system.]
▸ **A** *noun*. A system of printing or writing for blind people, in which the characters are represented by arrangements of raised points. M19.
▸ **B** *verb trans.* Print or transcribe in Braille characters. M20.

brain /breɪn/ *noun*.
[ORIGIN Old English *brægen* = Middle Low German *bragen*, *bregen*, Middle Dutch & mod. Dutch *brein* from West Germanic.]
1 The mass of substance contained in the skull of humans and other vertebrates; *sing.* & (usu.) in *pl.* cerebral substance. Orig. *spec.* the cerebrum, now the entire organ; *transf.* an analogous organ of an invertebrate. OE.
2 This organ as the seat of sensation, motion, or human speech, the organ of thought, memory, or imagination; *sing.* & (freq.) in *pl.* intellectual power, intellect; thought, sense, imagination. ME. ▸**b** *sing.* & (freq.) in *pl.* A clever person; *the* cleverest person in a group etc., *the* mastermind. *colloq.* M19.

W. STUBBS Was that plan the conception of any one brain? V. BRITTAIN Men of all ages who . . hadn't the brains of an earwig. **b** C. KINGSLEY The accomplished Mysseri . . was in fact the brain of our corps. *Times* Admiral . . Wynter, 'the brains' of the victory.

3 An electronic device comparable in function to a brain; a computer. Usu. more fully ***electronic brain***. M20.
– PHRASES: **beat one's brains**, **cudgel one's brains**, **rack one's brains** search for ideas, think very hard. ***blow a person's brains out***: see BLOW *verb*[1]. ***cells of the brain***: see CELL *noun*[1] 7b. ***cudgel one's brains***: see ***beat one's brains*** above. **get on the brain**, **have on the brain** be constantly thinking of, be obsessed by. ***pick a person's brains***: see PICK *verb*[1]. ***rack one's brains***: see ***beat one's brains*** above. SOFTENING ***of the brain***. ***turn a person's brain***: see TURN *verb*. VISCERAL ***brain***. ***wash one's brain***: see WASH *verb*. ***water on the brain***: see WATER *noun*.
– COMB.: **brainbox** (**a**) the cranium; (**b**) *colloq.* the mind, the intellect; a clever person; **braincase** *colloq.* the cranium; **brain cell** any of the cells forming the brain tissue; **brainchild** *colloq.* the product of thought; an invention; **brain coral** coral forming a compact mass with a surface resembling the convolutions of the brain; **brain damage** injury to the brain (permanently) impairing its functions; **brain-damaged** *adjective* having suffered brain damage; **brain-dead** *adjective* (**a**) having suffered brain death; (**b**) *colloq.* extremely stupid; (**c**) *colloq.* thoroughly exhausted; **brain death** permanent cessation of the functions of the brainstem that control respiration etc.; **brain drain** *colloq.* the loss of highly trained or qualified people by emigration; **brain-fag** *colloq.* mental exhaustion; **brain fever** inflammation or other malaise affecting the brain; ***brain-fever bird***, an Indian hawk-cuckoo, *Cuculus varius*, having a maddeningly persistent call; **brain fungus** a soft yellow gelatinous fungus, *Tremella mesenterica*, with a lobed and folded surface, living on dead wood; **brainpan** *colloq.* the cranium; **brainpower** mental ability or intelligence; **brain-sand** minute calcareous particles deposited in the pineal gland; **brain scan** a diagnostic radiographic scan of the brain; **brain scanner** an apparatus for performing a brain scan; **brainsick** *adjective* diseased in the mind, mad; proceeding from a diseased mind; **brainsickly** *adverb* (*rare*) in a brainsick manner; **brainstem** the medulla oblongata, pons, and midbrain; **brain-stone** = ***brain coral*** above; **brainstorm** (**a**) a succession of sudden and severe phenomena, due to some cerebral disturbance; (**b**) = ***brainwave*** (c) below; (**c**) (orig. *US*) a brainstorming session; **brainstorming** (orig. *US*) attack on a problem by spontaneous discussion in search of new ideas; **brains trust**, **brain trust** (**a**) (usu. ***brains trust***) a group of people assembled to give impromptu views on topics of interest; (**b**) a group of experts appointed to give advice or guidance to a government etc.; **brain-teaser** a difficult problem or puzzle; ***brain trust***: see ***brains trust*** above; **brain-twister** = ***brain-teaser*** above; **brainwash** *verb trans.* systematically and often forcibly replace established ideas in the mind of (a person) by new (usu. political) ideas; **brainwave** (**a**) a hypothetical telepathic vibration; (**b**) *sing.* & (usu.) in *pl.*, a measurable electrical impulse in the brain; (**c**) *colloq.* a sudden inspiration or bright idea; **brainwork** mental activity.
■ **brained** *adjective* having a brain or brains (of a specified kind) LME. **brainish** *adjective* (*arch.*) passionate, headstrong M16. **brainless** *adjective* (**a**) devoid of brain; (**b**) foolish; wanting intelligence: LME. **brainlessly** *adverb* E17. **brainlessness** *noun* L19.

brain /breɪn/ *verb trans.* LME.
[ORIGIN from the noun.]
1 Dash out the brains of; kill with a heavy blow to the head. LME.
†**2** Conceive in the brain. *rare* (Shakes.). Only in E17.

brainiac /ˈbreɪnɪak/ *noun*. *N. Amer. colloq.* L20.
[ORIGIN from the name of a superintelligent alien character of the Superman comic strip; a blend of *brain* and *maniac*.]
An exceptionally intelligent person; an expert.

P. BRONSON It might be a . . mistake to turn our culture over to a gang of brainiacs.

brainy /ˈbreɪni/ *adjective*. M19.
[ORIGIN from BRAIN *noun* + -Y[1].]
Having plenty of brains; acute, clever.
■ **brainily** *adverb* E20. **braininess** *noun* E20.

braird /brɛːd/ *noun & verb*. Orig. & chiefly *Scot.* L15.
[ORIGIN Alt. of BRERD.]
▸ **A** *noun*. The first shoots of grass, corn, or other crop. L15.
▸ **B** *verb intrans.* Sprout; appear above the ground. L15.

braise /breɪz/ *verb & noun*. M18.
[ORIGIN French *braiser*, from *braise* live coals: cf. BRAZIER *noun*[2].]
▸ **A** *verb trans.* Cook slowly with a little liquid in a tightly closed vessel. M18.
▸ **B** *noun*. Braised meat; the materials for braising meat etc. with. M18.

brak /brak/ *adjective & noun*. *S. Afr.* L18.
[ORIGIN Afrikaans from Dutch: see BRACK *adjective & noun*[4].]
▸ **A** *adjective*. Brackish; alkaline. L18.
▸ **B** *noun*. Brackishness; alkalinity of soil or water. L19.

brake /breɪk/ *noun*[1].
[ORIGIN Old English *bracu* (recorded in genit. pl. *fearnbraca* beds of fern), corresp. to Middle Low German *brake* branch, twig, tree stump; perh. reinforced in Middle English from Low German.]
1 ***fernbrake***, a bed or thicket of ferns. OE.
2 *gen.* A clump of bushes, brushwood, or briars; a thicket. LME.

brake /breɪk/ *noun*[2]. ME.
[ORIGIN Perh. shortening of BRACKEN *noun*[1], the latter being interpreted as pl.]
A fern; bracken.

brake /breɪk/ *noun*[3]. LME.
[ORIGIN Corresp. to Middle Low German *brake* or ODu. *braeke*, Dutch *braak* flax-brake, from Dutch *breken* BREAK *verb*.]
1 A toothed instrument for braking flax or hemp. LME.
2 A baker's kneading machine. LME.
3 In full ***brake harrow***. A heavy harrow for crushing clods. M17.
4 An instrument for peeling the bark from willows for basket making. E19.

brake /breɪk/ *noun*[4]. LME.
[ORIGIN Uncertain: perh. rel. to French *braquer* point (a cannon), turn (the rudder).]
†**1** The winch of a crossbow; a crossbow, ballista, or similar engine. LME–M19.
2 The handle of a pump. E17.

†**brake** *noun*[5]. LME–M18.
[ORIGIN Perh. from ODu. *braeke* (see BRAKE *noun*[3]) in sense 'a nose ring for a draught ox'.]
A bridle, a curb.

brake /breɪk/ *noun*[6]. In branch II also **break**. E16.
[ORIGIN Unknown: the two branches may represent different words.]
▸ **I** †**1** A cage, a trap; a snare, a difficulty. E16–M17.
†**2** An instrument of torture; a rack. M16–M19.
3 A framework intended to hold something steady; a frame in which a horse's foot is placed when being shod. E17.
▸ **II 4** A carriage frame without a body, for breaking in young horses. M19.
5 A large wagonette; an estate car. M19.
shooting brake an estate car.

brake /breɪk/ *noun*[7]. Also **break**. L18.
[ORIGIN Prob. from BRAKE *noun*[4] or *noun*[5].]
An apparatus for checking (usu. rotary) motion; *fig.* a retarding agency.
apply the brakes, **put on the brakes** *fig.* moderate one's enthusiasm.
– COMB.: **brake block** (**a**) the block which holds a brake shoe; (**b**) a block (usu. made of hardened rubber) which is applied to a bicycle wheel as a brake; **brake-cylinder** the cylinder in which the piston of an air or hydraulic brake works; **brake drum** a cylinder attached to a wheel or hub, upon which the brake shoe presses; **brake fluid** specially formulated liquid for use in hydraulic brakes; **brake horsepower** the power available at the shaft of an engine, measurable by means of a brake; **brake light** a red light at the back of a vehicle that is automatically illuminated when the brakes are applied; **brake lining** a layer of material attached to the face of a brake shoe to increase friction and provide a renewable surface; **brakeman** a man in charge of a brake or brakes, esp. on a train; **brake parachute** a parachute attached to the tail of an aeroplane and opened to serve as a brake; **brake-pipe** the pipe of an air-, vacuum-, or hydraulic

brake, conveying the working medium to the brakes of a train, motor vehicle, etc.; **brake shoe** that part of a brake which comes in contact with the object whose motion is to be checked; **brakesman** = ***brakeman*** above; **brake van** a compartment, carriage, or wagon in a train which contains braking apparatus operated by the guard.

brake /breɪk/ *verb*[1] *trans.* LME.
[ORIGIN from BRAKE *noun*[3].]
1 Beat and crush (flax, hemp, etc.). LME.
2 Break (clods) with a harrow. E19.
3 Knead (dough). M19.

†**brake** *verb*[2] *trans. & intrans.* LME–M18.
[ORIGIN Perh. rel. to Old English *bræc* phlegm, mucus, saliva, = Middle Low German *brēke*: cf. Old Dutch *bracken*, Middle Low German, Dutch *braken* vomit, rel. to BREAK *verb*.]
Spew, vomit.

brake /breɪk/ *verb*[3]. M19.
[ORIGIN from BRAKE *noun*[7].]
1 *verb trans.* Apply a brake to; retard or stop by means of a brake or brakes. M19.
2 *verb intrans.* Apply or be checked by the brake(s). L19.
– COMB.: **braking distance** the distance covered by a vehicle etc. before coming to rest following application of the brakes (usu. in specified conditions).

brake *verb*[4] see BREAK *verb*.

braky /ˈbreɪki/ *adjective*. M17.
[ORIGIN from BRAKE *noun*[1] or *noun*[2] + -Y[1].]
Overgrown with brushwood or fern.

Bramantip /ˈbram(ə)ntɪp/ *noun*. M19.
[ORIGIN A mnemonic of scholastic philosophers, A indicating a universal affirmative proposition, I a particular affirmative proposition.]
LOGIC. The first mood of the fourth syllogistic figure, in which two universal affirmative premisses yield a particular affirmative conclusion.

bramble /ˈbramb(ə)l/ *noun*.
[ORIGIN Old English *bræmbel*, earlier *brǣmel*, *brēmel*, from Germanic base also of BROOM: see -LE[1].]
1 A rough prickly shrub of the genus *Rubus*, with long trailing shoots; *esp.* any member of the aggregate species *R. fruticosus*, with purplish-black fruit; a blackberry bush. OE.
2 A blackberry. Chiefly *Scot. & N. English*. E19.
– COMB.: **bramble-berry** the fruit of the bramble; a blackberry; **bramble-rose** a white trailing dogrose.
■ **brambly** *adjective* covered or overgrown with brambles L16.

bramble /ˈbramb(ə)l/ *verb*. E17.
[ORIGIN from the noun.]
1 *verb trans.* Cover or make overgrown with brambles. Chiefly as ***brambled*** *ppl adjective*. E17.
2 *verb intrans.* Gather blackberries. Chiefly as ***brambling*** *verbal noun*. Chiefly *Scot. & N. English*. M19.

brambling /ˈbramblɪŋ/ *noun*. M16.
[ORIGIN Uncertain: cf. BRANDLING 2, German †*Brämling*.]
A brightly coloured finch, *Fringilla montifringilla*, which is a winter visitor to Britain.

†**brame** *noun*. *rare* (Spenser). Only in L16.
[ORIGIN Prob. from Italian *brama* strong desire.]
Longing.

Bramley /ˈbramli/ *noun*. E20.
[ORIGIN from Matthew *Bramley*, a Nottinghamshire butcher, in whose garden it is said to have been first grown c 1850.]
In full ***Bramley seedling***, ***Bramley's seedling***. A large green variety of cooking apple.

bran /bran/ *noun*. ME.
[ORIGIN Old French & mod. French *bran*, †*bren* (formerly) bran, (now) excrement, muck, filth, = Provençal, Old Spanish, Italian dial. *bren*, of unknown origin (adopted in Celtic langs. from French and English).]
1 Husks of grain separated from flour after grinding. ME.
†**2** Dandruff. LME–L16.
– COMB.: **bran pie**, **bran tub** a tub filled with bran or other material in which prizes are hidden, to be drawn out at random by children.
■ **branlike** *adjective* L19. **branny** *adjective* LME.

branch /brɑːn(t)ʃ/ *noun*. ME.
[ORIGIN Old French & mod. French *branche* = Provençal, Spanish *branca* claw, Italian *branca* claw, paw, Romanian *brîncă* hand, paw, from late Latin *branca* (in *branca ursina* bear's foot, acanthus), of unknown origin.]
1 A limb of a tree or shrub springing from the trunk or stem, or from a bough. ME.
OLIVE BRANCH. ***root and branch***: see ROOT *noun*[1].
2 A lateral extension or subdivision of a main body, e.g. of a mountain range, river, railway, road, artery, deer's horn, candelabrum, etc. ME. ▸†**b** A candelabrum or chandelier, esp. in a church. LME–L18. ▸†**c** A human arm (or hand). *rare* (Shakes.). Only in L16. ▸**d** A small stream. *US*. M17.

W. WHISTON A Branch or Bay of the Great Ocean. J. BARNES The Metropolitan Line (by which the purist naturally meant the Watford, Chesham and Amersham branches).

private branch exchange: see PRIVATE *adjective*.
3 (Conn. with ***family tree***.) A division of a family or race according to the differing lines of descent from the common ancestor. ME. ▸**b** A descendant, a child. Now only *joc.* ME.
Red Branch: see RED *adjective*.
4 A (sub)division of a subject, pursuit, philosophy, detailed proposition, etc. E16.

W. CRUISE The express declaration of the testator in almost every branch of his will. R. MACAULAY May one ask what branch of art you have been practising this evening? Drawing in charcoal? A. J. P. TAYLOR Coal entered into every branch of industrial life.

5 A component part of an organization or system such as a government, police force, church, etc. L17.

J. REED Others were dispatched to provincial cities, to form branches of the Committee for Salvation. E. CRISPIN Graveney was the Inspector in charge of Glazebridge's uniform branch. I. HAMILTON The army medical corps or some similar non-combatant branch of the forces.

Special Branch: see SPECIAL *adjective*.
6 A subordinate establishment of a library, bank, or other business, serving a particular area. E19.
7 The nozzle of a fire hose. L19.
– COMB.: **branch library** a library other than the main one in an area; **branch line** a secondary railway line running from a main line to a terminus; **branch officer** the equivalent, in the Royal Navy, of a warrant officer; **branch water** *US* ordinary water, especially when added to alcoholic drinks; **branch-work** ornamental figured patterns.
■ **branchery** *noun* (*a*) branches in the mass; †(*b*) the ramifications of the endocarp in a fruit: L17. **branchless** *adjective* E17. **branchlet** *noun* a little branch M18.

branch /brɑːn(t)ʃ/ *verb*. LME.
[ORIGIN from the noun.]
1 *verb intrans.* Bear branches; put branches *forth*, *out*. LME.
2 *verb intrans.* Spring or spread out in the manner of branches from a tree; deviate, diverge, divide. Chiefly with adverbs LME.

MAX-MÜLLER Speech from which these dialects branched off. E. A. FREEMAN The Foss Way . . branched off from the Eastern gate. L. MACNEICE In one chapter of this book . . he branches out into a very much wider field. T. COLLINS The track branches there.

3 *verb trans.* Adorn or embroider with work representing flowers and foliage. E16.
4 *verb trans.* Divide into or spread out as branches; arrange in branches. *arch.* E17.

J. BENTHAM The whole system of offences . . is branched out into five classes. TENNYSON Gold that branch'd itself Fine as ice-ferns.

■ **branching** *adjective* (*a*) that branches; (*b*) *poet.* antlered: LME.

branched /brɑːn(t)ʃt/ *adjective*. LME.
[ORIGIN from BRANCH *noun*, *verb*: see -ED[2], -ED[1].]
1 Having branches (of a specified kind or number). LME.
2 Embroidered, chased, etc., with figured work. E16.

brancher /ˈbrɑːn(t)ʃə/ *noun*. LME.
[ORIGIN Anglo-Norman var. of Old French & mod. French *branchier* (orig. adjective), formed as BRANCH *noun* + -ER[2].]
A young hawk etc. when it first leaves the nest and takes to the branches.

branchia /ˈbraŋkɪə/ *noun*. Pl. **-iae** /-ɪiː/, same. L17.
[ORIGIN Latin, pl. *-iae*, from Greek *bragkhia* pl.: see -A[3], -AE.]
A respiratory organ of fishes etc.; a gill. Also, a vestigial gill cleft present in mammalian embryos. Usu. in *pl.*
■ **branchiate** *adjective* having gills L19. **branchiated** *adjective* = BRANCHIATE M19.

branchial /ˈbraŋkɪəl/ *adjective*. L18.
[ORIGIN formed as BRANCHIA + -AL[1].]
Of or pertaining to branchiae; of the nature of or resembling gills.
branchial arch = ***gill arch*** s.v. GILL *noun*[1]. **branchial cleft** = ***gill slit*** s.v. GILL *noun*[1]. ***branchial tuft***: see TUFT *noun* 1a.

branchio- /ˈbraŋkɪəʊ/ *combining form* of Greek *bragkhia* gills: see -O-.
■ **branchiobdellid** /ˌbraŋkɪə(ʊ)ˈdɛlɪd/ *noun & adjective* [Greek *bdella* leech] (*a*) *noun* an oligochaete worm of the family Branchiobdellidae, members of which resemble leeches and commonly live among the gills of crayfish; (*b*) *adjective* of or pertaining to the Branchiobdellidae: M20. **branchioˈmeric** *adjective* (esp. of the visceral muscles of fishes) displaying branchiomerism E20. **branchiˈomerism** *noun* arrangement into a number of segments each containing a gill arch or cleft L19. **branchiˈostegal** *adjective* [Greek *stegein* to cover] pertaining to the protection of the gills; covering or protecting the gills: M18. **branchiˈostegite** *noun* a membrane covering the gills (of crustaceans) L19. **branchiˈostegous** *adjective* (*a*) having gill covers; (*b*) = BRANCHIOSTEGAL: M18.

branchiopod /ˈbraŋkɪə(ʊ)pɒd/ *adjective & noun*. E19.
[ORIGIN from mod. Latin *Branchiopoda* (see below), formed as BRANCHIO- + -POD + -A[3].]
ZOOLOGY. Of or pertaining to, a crustacean of, the subclass Branchiopoda, having gills upon the feet.

branchy /ˈbrɑːn(t)ʃi/ *adjective*. LME.
[ORIGIN from BRANCH *noun* + -Y[1].]
Bearing or consisting of branches; putting forth offshoots, ramifying; antlered.
■ **branchiness** *noun* E17.

brand /brand/ *noun*.
[ORIGIN Old English *brand* = Old Frisian, Middle Dutch & mod. Dutch *brand*, Old High German *brant* (German *Brand*), Old Norse *brandr*, from Germanic, from base also of BURN *verb*.]
†**1** Burning. OE–ME.
2 A burning or charred log or stick; *poet.* a torch. OE.
brand from the burning *fig.* a rescued person, a convert.
3 A sword, a blade. *poet.* or *arch.* OE.
4 A permanent mark made by burning with a hot iron, usu. deliberately. M16. ▸**b** *fig.* A mark, usu. of infamy; a stigma. L16. ▸**c** *spec.* A mark of ownership impressed on cattle, horses, etc., by branding. M17.

DEFOE My comrade, having the brand of an old offender, was executed. **b** R. HOOKER To mark that age with the brand of error and superstition.

b brand of Cain blood guilt.
5 A kind of blight in which leaves etc. look burnt. M17.
6 An iron stamp for burning in a mark. E19.
7 (A make or kind of goods bearing) a trademark; *fig.* a kind, a sort. E19.

D. LESSING A brand of Marxist Socialism peculiar to himself.

– COMB.: **brand image** the assumed impression of a product in the minds of potential consumers; *fig.* the general or popular conception of some person or thing; BRANDIRON; **brand leader** the best-selling or best-known product of its type; **brand mark** (*a*) the mark left by a hot iron stamp; (*b*) a trademark; **brand name** a trade or proprietary name; BRAND-NEW.

brand /brand/ *verb trans.* LME.
[ORIGIN from the noun.]
1 Burn and mark permanently with a hot iron, usu. a sign of ownership (of cattle etc.) or to distinguish criminals, slaves, etc.; *gen.* mark indelibly for such purpose. LME.
branding iron a metal implement which is heated and used to brand livestock or (esp. formerly) criminals or slaves.
2 Stigmatize. E17.
3 Apply as a brand, denote by means of a brand; *fig.* impress indelibly on the memory etc. L17.

C. KINGSLEY To brand upon your thoughts How she was once a woman. E. F. BENSON It was an evening branded into her memory.

4 Label with a trademark. L19.

brandade /brɑ̃dad/ *noun*. E19.
[ORIGIN French from mod. Provençal *brandado* lit. 'thing which has been moved or shaken'.]
A Provençal dish made from salt cod.

branded /ˈbrandɪd/ *adjective*. *obsolete* exc. *dial.* LME.
[ORIGIN North. var. of BRINDED.]
Brindled.

brandenburgs /ˈbrand(ə)nbəːgz/ *noun pl.* M18.
[ORIGIN from *Brandenburg*, town and former principality in NE Germany, prob. because worn in the Elector's army.]
Ornamental facings to the breast of an officer's coat. Also, froggings on a woman's coat etc.

brander /ˈbrandə/ *noun & verb*. *Scot. & N. English*. LME.
[ORIGIN Alt. of BRANDIRON.]
▸ **A** *noun*. A gridiron. LME.
▸ **B** *verb trans. & intrans.* Cook on a gridiron; grill. L18.
■ **brandering** *noun* the covering of joists with battens for plastering M19.

brandiron /ˈbrandʌɪən/ *noun*. *obsolete* exc. *dial.* LME.
[ORIGIN from BRAND *noun* + IRON *noun*. See also BRANDER.]
1 A gridiron; a trivet. LME.
†**2** A sword. L16–E17.

brandise /ˈbrandɪs/ *noun*. *dial.*
[ORIGIN Old English *brandisen*, from BRAND *noun* + *īsen* IRON *noun*: cf. BRANDIRON.]
A gridiron; a trivet; (= BRANDIRON 1).
– NOTE: Not recorded between OE and 19: intervening history uncertain.

brandish /ˈbrandɪʃ/ *verb & noun*. ME.
[ORIGIN Old French & mod. French *brandiss-* lengthened stem (see -ISH[2]) of *brandir* from Proto-Romance, from Germanic base of BRAND *noun*: see -ISH[2].]
▸ **A** *verb*. **1** *verb trans.* Flourish (a weapon) by way of threat or display; wave or flaunt as if a weapon. ME.

MILTON Lawes which they so impotently brandish against others. A. HALEY Flailing their arms, brandishing their fists. P. ACKROYD His wife brandished a copy of a women's magazine.

†**2** *verb intrans. & trans.* Scatter (rays of light), glitter, flash. M16–M17.
3 *verb intrans.* Of a sword etc.: be flourished. *rare*. M17.
▸ **B** *noun*. An act of brandishing. L16.
■ **brandisher** *noun* E17.

brandling /ˈbrandlɪŋ/ *noun*. *dial.* M17.
[ORIGIN from BRAND *noun* + -LING[1].]
1 A red worm with rings of brighter colour, used as bait by anglers. Also ***brandling worm***. M17.
2 = BRAMBLING. *rare*. L17.
3 A salmon parr. E18.

B

brand-new /bran(d)ˈnjuː/ *adjective*. Also (now *non-standard*) **bran-new** /branˈnjuː/. L16.
[ORIGIN from BRAND *noun* + NEW *adjective* (as if glowing from the furnace).]
Conspicuously or completely new.

brandreth /ˈbrandrɪθ/ *noun*. *dial*. LME.
[ORIGIN Old Norse *brandreið* grate, from *brandr* BRAND *noun* + *reið* carriage, vehicle.]
1 A gridiron; a trivet. LME.
2 A wooden framework as a container, support, etc. LME.

brandy /ˈbrandi/ *noun* & *verb*. E17.
[ORIGIN Dutch *brandewijn* (German *Branntwein*), from *branden* burn, distil + *wijn* WINE *noun*.]
▸ **A** *noun*. Earlier †*brandy-wine*.
1 A strong spirit distilled from wine, or from fermented fruit juice (as ***apple brandy***, ***cherry brandy***, ***peach brandy***, etc.). E17.
2 A drink of this. L19.
– COMB.: **brandy-ball** a kind of sweet flavoured with brandy; **brandy-bottle** (*a*) a bottle (for) containing brandy; (*b*) *dial*. the yellow water lily, *Nuphar luteum*; ***brandy butter***: see BUTTER *noun*[1] 1; **brandy-cherry** (*a*) a cherry preserved in brandy; †(*b*) cherry brandy; **brandy snap** a rolled gingerbread wafer; ***brandy-wine***: see above.
▸ **B** *verb trans*. †**1** ***brandy it***, drink brandy in excess. *rare*. Only in E19.
2 Mix or treat with brandy; refresh with brandy. M19.

brane /breɪn/ *noun*. L20.
[ORIGIN Shortened from MEMBRANE.]
PHYSICS. An extended object with any given number of dimensions, of which the strings of string theory are examples with one dimension.

brangle /ˈbraŋɡ(ə)l/ *verb* & *noun*. *obsolete* exc. *dial*. E16.
[ORIGIN French *branler* shake: infl. by WRANGLE *verb*.]
▸ **A** *verb*. **1** *verb trans*. & *intrans*. Shake, (cause to) totter, (*lit*. & *fig*.). E16.
2 *verb intrans*. Wrangle, squabble. E16.
▸ **B** *noun*. A brawl, a wrangle. M16.
■ **branglement** *noun* (a) disorderly dispute E17. **brangler** *noun* a brawler, a wrangler E17.

brank /braŋk/ *noun*[1]. *obsolete* exc. *dial*. L16.
[ORIGIN Unknown.]
Buckwheat.

brank *noun*[2] see BRANKS.

brank /braŋk/ *verb*[1] *intrans*. *Scot*. & *dial*. LME.
[ORIGIN Unknown.]
Of a horse: prance. Of a person: strut, prance.

brank /braŋk/ *verb*[2] *trans*. *Scot*. M16.
[ORIGIN App. from sing. of BRANKS.]
Bridle, restrain.

branks /braŋks/ *noun pl*. Chiefly *Scot*. Also (*rare*) in sing. **brank**. M16.
[ORIGIN Uncertain: cf. BARNACLE *noun*[2], German *Pranger* the pillory, a barnacle for a horse, Dutch *prang* a fetter.]
1 *hist*. An instrument of punishment for a scolding woman, consisting of an iron framework for the head and a sharp metal gag for restraining the tongue. M16.
2 A type of wooden muzzle used as a bridle. M16.
3 The mumps. L18.

brank-ursine /braŋkˈəːsɪn/ *noun*. LME.
[ORIGIN French *branche* (dial. *branque*) *ursine* or medieval Latin *branca ursina*, lit. 'bear's claw': see BRANCH *noun*, URSINE *adjective*.]
Bear's breech, acanthus.

branle /ˈbran(ə)l/ *noun*. Also †**bransle**. L16.
[ORIGIN French, from *branler* shake.]
†**1** Wavering, agitation. Only in L16.
2 Chiefly *hist*. A rustic ring dance of French origin. Cf. BRAWL *noun*[2] 2. L16.

bran-new *adjective* see BRAND-NEW.

†**bransle** *noun* var. of BRANLE.

brant *noun* var. of BRENT *noun*.

brant /brant/ *adjective* & *adverb*. *Scot*. & *N. English*. Also **brent** /brɛnt/.
[ORIGIN Old English *brant* corresp. to Old Norse *brattr* (Swedish *brant*, Danish *brat*).]
▸ **A** *adjective*. Lofty, steep, sheer. OE.
▸ **B** *adverb*. Straight (up); steeply. LME.

†**brantle** *noun*. M17–M19.
[ORIGIN formed as BRANLE: cf. Old French *brandeler* shake.]
= BRANLE 2.

brasero /braˈsero/ *noun*. Pl. **-os** /-ɔs/. M17.
[ORIGIN Spanish.]
= BRAZIER *noun*[2].

brash /braʃ/ *noun*[1]. Chiefly *Scot*. & *dial*. LME.
[ORIGIN Perh. imit.]
1 Orig., a crash, a blow. Later, an assault, an attack, a bout. LME.
2 A slight attack of illness. E17.
3 An eruption of fluid; a shower. E19.
water-brash a painful regurgitation of acid gastric juice.
■ **brashy** *adjective*[1] (*Scot*.) showery E19.

brash /braʃ/ *noun*[2]. L18.
[ORIGIN Unknown.]
Loose broken rock or ice, rubble; hedge refuse, clippings, twigs.
■ **brashy** *adjective*[2] of the nature of brash; broken, crumbly: E18.

brash /braʃ/ *adjective*[1]. Now chiefly *US*. M16.
[ORIGIN Perh. imit.]
Fragile, brittle.

brash /braʃ/ *adjective*[2]. Orig. *dial*. E19.
[ORIGIN Perh. expressive form of *rash*.]
1 Rash, impetuous; cheeky; vulgarly self-assertive. E19.

> A. S. BYATT Orange had never been a colour he liked, seeming brash and violent. D. HALBERSTAM He was cocky and brash and self-mocking.

2 Rough, harsh; active, lively. *US*. M19.
■ **brashly** *adverb* M19. **brashness** *noun* M19.

brash /braʃ/ *verb*[1] *trans*. *Scot*. L16.
[ORIGIN from BRASH *noun*[1].]
Assault, batter, breach.

brash /braʃ/ *verb*[2] *trans*. M20.
[ORIGIN from BRASH *noun*[2].]
Remove the lower branches from (a tree, plantation, etc.).

†**Brasil** *noun* var. of BRAZIL *noun*[1].

†**Brasilian** *adjective* & *noun* var. of BRAZILIAN.

brasque /brɑːsk/ *noun* & *verb*. Now *rare* or *obsolete*. M19.
[ORIGIN French from Italian dial. *brasca* coal-ash.]
▸ **A** *noun*. An inert lining material for furnaces and crucibles, consisting of clay and charcoal. M19.
▸ **B** *verb trans*. Line with brasque. L19.

brass /brɑːs/ *noun* & *adjective*.
[ORIGIN Old English *bræs* = Old Frisian *bres*, Middle Low German *bras* metal, of unknown origin.]
▸ **A** *noun*. **1** Orig., any alloy of copper with tin or zinc or occas. other metals. Now, a yellow alloy of copper and zinc only (cf. BRONZE *noun*). OE. ▸**b** Brass taken as a type of hardness or insensitivity; impudence, effrontery, nerve. LME.

> **b** SHAKES. *Hen. VIII* Men's evil manners live in brass: their virtues We write in water. T. T. LYNCH An empty, vaunting person, who has brass enough to face the world.

Corinthian brass: see CORINTHIAN *adjective* 1. NAVAL ***brass***. ***white brass***: see WHITE *adjective*. **b as bold as brass** very bold(ly), impudent(ly); brazen-faced(ly).
2 A brass object; such objects collectively, brassware; *spec*. wind instruments of brass, the section of an orchestra or band comprising these. LME. ▸**b** A monumental or sepulchral tablet of brass, bearing figures, inscriptions, etc., laid in the floor or set into the wall of a church. M16. ▸**c** A bearing or block for a shaft. M16. ▸**d** In full ***horse brass***. A brass ornament worn by a draught horse. E20. ▸**e** A brass block or die used to impress a design etc. on a book cover. M20.

> D. L. SAYERS Her manner is unpolished, but I have observed that her brass is not.

3 Orig., copper or bronze coin. Now (*colloq*.), money generally, cash. LME.
4 High-ranking officers in the armed forces (cf. ***brass hat*** below); *gen*. leaders, bosses. Also ***top brass***. *slang* (orig. *US*). L19.
5 *ellipt*. = ***brass nail*** below. *slang*. M20.
– COMB.: **brass-bound** *adjective* (*fig*.) adhering inflexibly to tradition; **brass rubbing** the process of reproducing the design on a monumental brass by rubbing paper laid upon it with heelball etc.; an impression so produced.
▸ **B** *attrib*. or as *adjective*. (Made) of brass, brazen. LME.
brass band a group of musicians with brass (and percussion) instruments. **brass farthing** the least possible amount (usu. in neg. contexts). **brass hat** *slang* an officer of high rank (having gold braid on the cap). **brass-monkey(s)** [cf. MONKEY *noun*] *slang* (of weather etc.) bitterly cold. **brass nail** [rhyming slang for *tail*] *slang* a prostitute. **brass plate** an engraved plate with the name, trade, etc., of its owner displayed outside the owner's home or place of business. **brass rags** sailors' cleaning cloths; ***part brass rags*** cease friendship (*with*). ***brass rule***: see RULE *noun*. **brass tacks** *slang* actual details, real business (chiefly in ***get down to brass tacks***). **brassware** utensils etc. made of brass.

brass /brɑːs/ *verb*. M19.
[ORIGIN from BRASS *noun* & *adjective*.]
1 *verb trans*. Coat with brass; *fig*. cover with effrontery. M19.
2 *verb intrans*. Pay *up*. L19.
3 *verb trans*. & *intrans*. Foll. by *off*: grumble; tell off. *slang*. E20.

brassage /ˈbrasɪdʒ/ *noun*. L18.
[ORIGIN French, from *brasser* to mix, brew, from popular Latin, from Latin *brace*: see BRAGGET *noun*[1], -AGE.]
A charge to cover the cost of coining money.

brassard /ˈbrasɑːd/ *noun*. L16.
[ORIGIN French, from *bras* arm: see -ARD.]
1 *hist*. A piece of armour for the upper arm. L16.
2 A badge worn on the arm; an armlet. L19.

brassed /brɑːst/ *adjective*. ME.
[ORIGIN from BRASS *noun*, *verb*: see -ED[2], -ED[1].]
1 Made of or overlaid with brass. ME.
2 ***brassed off***, fed up, disgruntled. *slang*. M20.

brasserie /ˈbrasəri/ *noun*. M19.
[ORIGIN French (orig. = brewery), from *brasser* to brew.]
A (French) saloon selling beer and usu. food; *gen*. an informal restaurant.

brassey *noun* var. of BRASSIE.

brassic /ˈbrasɪk/ *adjective*. *slang*. L20.
[ORIGIN Contr. of BORACIC.]
In full ***brassic lint***. Penniless, having no money.

brassica /ˈbrasɪkə/ *noun*. Pl. **-cas**, **-cae** /-kiː/. E19.
[ORIGIN Latin = cabbage.]
A cruciferous plant of the genus *Brassica* (family Brassicaceae or Cruciferae), which includes cabbage, turnip, rape, etc.
■ **brassiˈcaceous** *adjective* of or pertaining to the family Brassicaceae (Cruciferae), cruciferous M19.

brassie /ˈbrasi, ˈbrɑːsi/ *noun*. Now *rare*. Also **brass(e)y**. L19.
[ORIGIN from BRASS *noun* + -IE.]
A wooden golf club shod with brass; a shot played with such a club.

brassiere /ˈbrasɪə, -z-/ *noun*. Also **-ière**. E20.
[ORIGIN French *brassière* = child's reins, camisole, etc.]
A woman's undergarment worn to support the breasts, a bra.

brassil *noun* var. of BRAZIL *noun*[2].

brassy *noun* var. of BRASSIE.

brassy /ˈbrɑːsi/ *adjective*. L16.
[ORIGIN from BRASS *noun* + -Y[1].]
1 Consisting of or covered in brass. L16.

> L. ELLMANN She added a thick brassy bracelet to the general effect.

2 *fig*. **a** Pitiless, unfeeling. L16. ▸**b** Impudently confident. L16. ▸**c** Pretentious. L16.

> **b** B. ELTON This tawdry, brassy, blousey woman waggling her tongue at him across the table.

3 a Tasting like brass. L18. ▸**b** Looking like brass. E19. ▸**c** Sounding like brass instruments, harsh-toned. M19.
■ **brassily** *adverb* L19. **brassiness** *noun* M18.

brast *verb* see BURST *verb*.

brastle *verb* var. of BRUSTLE *verb*[1].

brat /brat/ *noun*[1]. Now *dial*.
[ORIGIN Old English (late Northumbrian) *bratt* from Old Irish *bratt* (Irish, Gaelic *brat*) mantle.]
1 Orig., a cloak. In later *dial*. use, a pinafore, an apron; *derog*. a rag, a scrap (of clothing). OE.
2 The tough skin which forms on porridge etc. *Scot*. L17.

brat /brat/ *noun*[2]. Usu. *derog*. M16.
[ORIGIN Perh. abbreviation of BRATCHET, or same word as BRAT *noun*[1].]
A child. Now *esp*. an ill-behaved child.

> O. CROMWELL I should be glad to hear how the little brat doth. I. MURDOCH Your loathsome idle spineless ill-mannered brat of an offspring.

■ **bratling** *noun* a little brat M17. **brattery** *noun* a nursery, a collection of brats L18. **bratty** *adjective* of, pertaining to, or characteristic of a brat M20.

brat /brat/ *noun*[3]. M18.
[ORIGIN Var. of BRET.]
The turbot.

bratchet /ˈbratʃɪt/ *noun*. *Scot*. Usu. *derog*. L16.
[ORIGIN App. same word as BRACHET.]
A little brat, an infant.

brattice /ˈbratɪs/ *noun* & *verb*. Also (*dial*.) **-ish** /-ɪʃ/. ME.
[ORIGIN Anglo-Norman, Old French *bretesche* (mod. French *bretèche*) from medieval Latin *brittisca* from Old English *brittisc* BRITISH.]
▸ **A** *noun*. **1** A temporary breastwork, parapet, or gallery of wood, for use during a siege. *obsolete* exc. *hist*. ME.
2 A wooden partition or shaft-lining in a mine. M19.
▸ **B** *verb trans*. †**1** Fortify with a brattice. Only in LME.
2 Foll. by *up*: line (a shaft etc.) with a brattice. M19.

bratticing /ˈbratɪsɪŋ/ *noun*. Also (*dial*. in branch I, the usual spelling in branch II) **-ishing** /-ɪʃɪŋ/. See also BARTIZAN. LME.
[ORIGIN from BRATTICE + -ING[1].]
▸ **I** †**1** (The erection of) a temporary breastwork, parapet, etc.: see BRATTICE *noun* 1. LME–M17.
2 Partitioning or shaft-lining in a mine. M19.
▸ **II 3** ARCHITECTURE. A cresting of open carved work on a screen or shrine. M16.

brattish *noun* & *verb* see BRATTICE.

brattishing *noun* see BRATTICING.

brattle /ˈbrat(ə)l/ *noun* & *verb*. Chiefly *Scot*. E16.
[ORIGIN Prob. imit., by assoc. with *break*, *rattle*.]
▸ **A** *noun*. A sharp rattling sound, esp. of something breaking, of blows, of scampering feet, etc. E16.

▸ **B** *verb intrans.* Produce a rattling noise; rush with a rattling noise; scamper. E16.

bratwurst /ˈbratvəːst, *foreign* ˈbratvʊrst/ *noun*. Pl. **-wursts**, **-würste** /-vyrstə/. E20.
[ORIGIN German, from *Brat* a spit (*braten* roast etc.) + *Wurst* sausage.]
(A) mild-flavoured German pork sausage.

braunite /ˈbraʊnʌɪt/ *noun*. E19.
[ORIGIN from A.E. *Braun*, 19th-cent. German treasury official and mineralogist + -ITE¹.]
MINERALOGY. A tetragonal oxide and silicate of manganese, usu. with some iron, which occurs as dark brownish-black pyramidal crystals or granular masses.

brava /ˈbrɑːvə/ *noun & interjection*. E19.
[ORIGIN Italian, fem. of *bravo*: see BRAVO *interjection & noun*².]
(A cry addressed to a woman or girl meaning) excellent, well done!

†**bravade** *noun & verb*. L16.
[ORIGIN French from Italian *bravata*, from *bravo*: see BRAVE *adjective* etc., -ADE.]
▸ **A** *noun*. = BRAVADO *noun* 1. L16–M19.
▸ **B** *verb intrans. & trans.* Assume a bold or brazen manner (towards); swagger; defy. L16–E19.

bravado /brəˈvɑːdəʊ/ *noun & verb*. L16.
[ORIGIN Spanish *bravada*, from *bravo* BRAVO *noun*¹ with alt. of suffix: see -ADO.]
▸ **A** *noun*. Pl. **-o(e)s**.
1 Boastful or threatening behaviour (freq. to conceal timidity etc.); ostentatious boldness or defiance; (now *rare*) an instance of this, a show of daring. L16.
†**2** An arrogant, swaggering man. M17–M19.
▸ **B** *verb intrans.* Show bravado. Now *rare* or *obsolete*. L16.

Bravais lattice /ˈbraveɪ ˈlatɪs/ *noun phr.* M20.
[ORIGIN Auguste *Bravais* (1811–63), French physicist.]
CRYSTALLOGRAPHY. A lattice in which every point has exactly the same environment (as regards the distances and directions of other points of the lattice); *spec.* any of the fourteen different lattices of this kind in three dimensions.

brave /breɪv/ *adjective, adverb, & noun*. See also BRAW. L15.
[ORIGIN French from Italian *bravo* bold or Spanish *bravo* courageous, savage, from Proto-Romance from Latin *barbarus* BARBAROUS.]
▸ **A** *adjective*. **1** Courageous, daring; intrepid; able to face and withstand danger or pain. L15.
> MILTON High hopes of living to be brave men, and worthy Patriots. S. HILL It is a brave act of valour to condemn death.

2 Splendid; spectacular; showy; handsome. Now *literary*. M16.
> SIR W. SCOTT Now might you see the tartans brave.

3 Of excellent quality, admirable; fine, highly pleasing. Freq. as an exclam. of approval. Now *arch. & dial.* L16.
> W. PENN Many brave Families have been ruin'd by a Gamester.

brave new world [title of a satirical novel by Aldous Huxley (1932), after Shakes. *Temp.*] a Utopia produced by technological and social advance (usu. *iron.*).
▸ **B** *adverb*. Bravely. *poet.* L16.
▸ **C** *noun*. **1** A boast, a threat; a bravado. Now *rare* or *obsolete*. L16.
†**2** A bravo, a hired bully. L16–M19.
3 *absol.* Now only as *pl.* *The* brave men; *the* brave people. L17.
> W. COWPER Toll for the brave! The brave that are no more.

4 A fighting man; *esp.* a N. American Indian warrior. M18.
■ **bravely** *adverb* E16. **braveness** *noun* (now *rare*) M16.

brave /breɪv/ *verb trans.* M16.
[ORIGIN French *braver*, formed as BRAVE *adjective, adverb, & noun*, after Italian *bravare*.]
1 Treat with bravado; challenge; dare. *arch.* M16.
†**2** With *it*. Swagger; make a splendid show. M16–M19.
†**3** Deck out, adorn. L16–E17.
4 Endure or face (danger or unpleasant conditions) without showing fear; defy. L18.
> I. WELSH We braved the elements and struggled up Morrison Street to the pub.

brave it out defy suspicion or blame.
■ **braver** *noun* L16.

bravery /ˈbreɪv(ə)ri/ *noun*. M16.
[ORIGIN French *braverie* or Italian *braveria*, formed as BRAVE *adjective* etc. + -ERY.]
†**1** (An act of) bravado; ostentatious defiance, swaggering. M16–E19.
2 Display; show, ostentation; splendour. Now *literary*. M16. ▸**b** Finery; an embellishment; an ornament. *arch.* M16. ▸†**c** A thing to exhibit; a thing to be proud of. L16–M17.
3 Brave conduct or nature; daring; fortitude, valour. L16.
†**4** A gallant, a beau; gallants etc. collectively. E–M17.

bravo /ˈbrɑːvəʊ/ *noun*¹. Pl. **-o(e)s**. L16.
[ORIGIN Italian: see BRAVE *adjective* etc.]
1 A thug or hired assassin; a desperado. L16.
†**2** = BRAVADO *noun* 1. *rare*. E17–E18.

bravo /brɑːˈvəʊ, ˈbrɑːvəʊ/ *interjection & noun*². M18.
[ORIGIN French formed as BRAVO *noun*¹: cf. BRAVA.]
▸ **A** *interjection*. Excellent, well done! M18.
▸ **B** *noun*. Pl. **-os**. A cry of 'bravo!', a cheer. M19.

bravura /brəˈv(j)ʊərə/ *noun & adjective*. M18.
[ORIGIN Italian, from *bravo* BRAVE *adjective*: see -URE.]
1 (A passage or style of music, esp. singing) requiring exceptional powers of execution. M18.
2 (A performance that is) brilliant or ambitious; (a display that is) daring, dash(ing). E19.

braw /brɔː/ *adjective & noun*. *Scot.* L16.
[ORIGIN Var. of BRAVE *adjective* etc.]
▸ **A** *adjective*. **1** Worthy; capital; fine, good. L16.
2 Handsome; splendid, showy. E18.
▸ **B** *noun*. In *pl.* Fine clothes, adornments. E18.
■ **brawly** *adverb* well, excellently M17.

brawl /brɔːl/ *noun*¹. LME.
[ORIGIN from BRAWL *verb*.]
1 A noisy quarrel; a rowdy fight. LME.
†**2** A noisy exclamation; a clamour. M16–E17.

†**brawl** *noun*². E16.
[ORIGIN French BRANLE.]
1 A certain pace or movement in dancing. E–M16.
2 A French dance resembling a cotillion; a piece of music for this dance. M16–M19.

brawl /brɔːl/ *verb*. LME.
[ORIGIN Perh. ult. imit. Cf. Dutch & Low German *brallen* brag; Old Provençal *braul(h)ar*, *bralhar*, etc. (Old French & mod. French *brailler*) rel. to BRAY *verb*¹.]
1 *verb intrans.* Quarrel or fight noisily; wrangle. LME.
2 *verb intrans.* **a** Make a clamour or disturbance. Now *rare* or *obsolete*. LME. ▸**b** Of a stream: run noisily. L16.
3 *verb trans.* Revile, scold. *obsolete* exc. *dial.* L15.
4 *verb trans.* Drive or force *down*, *out*, etc., by clamouring, quarrelling, etc. L16.
■ **brawler** *noun* a quarrelsome or blustering person LME.

brawn /brɔːn/ *noun & verb*. ME.
[ORIGIN Anglo-Norman *braun*, Old French *braon* fleshy part esp. of the hind leg, from Germanic (Old High German *brāto*, German *Braten* roast flesh; cf. synon. Old English *brǣde*, and *brǣdan* to roast).]
▸ **A** *noun*. **1** Muscle, lean flesh, esp. of the arm, leg, or thumb; *loosely* muscularity, physical strength. ME. ▸†**b** The arm, calf, or buttock. LME–M19.
2 Boar's flesh as food. Now usu. *spec.*, pig's head etc. boiled, chopped, and moulded. LME.
shield of brawn: see SHIELD *noun*¹ 4a.
†**3** The flesh of other animals as food. LME–M17.
4 A boar fattened for the table. *obsolete* exc. *dial.* LME.
†**5** Calloused skin. M16–M17.
▸ **B** *verb*. †**1** *verb trans.* Harden, make callous. L16–M17.
2 *verb trans. & intrans.* Fatten (a boar), (of a boar) grow fat, for the table. Now *rare* or *obsolete*. L16.
■ **brawner** *noun* (*obsolete* exc. *dial.*) a boar fattened for the table M17.

brawny /ˈbrɔːni/ *adjective*. LME.
[ORIGIN from BRAWN *noun* + -Y¹.]
1 Characterized by brawn; strong, muscular. LME.
2 Calloused, hardened. Now *rare* or *obsolete*. L16.
■ **brawniness** *noun* M17.

Braxton Hicks /ˈbrakstən ˌhɪks/ *noun*. E20.
[ORIGIN John *Braxton Hicks* (1823–97), English gynaecologist.]
MEDICINE. ***Braxton Hicks contractions***, ***Braxton Hicks sign***, intermittent weak contractions of the uterus occurring during pregnancy.

braxy /ˈbraksi/ *noun & adjective*. Orig. *Scot.* L18.
[ORIGIN Uncertain: perh. from BRACK *noun*¹.]
▸ **A** *noun*. **1** A fatal clostridial infection of sheep, esp. in upland areas; *spec.* infection by *Clostridium septicum*. L18.
2 Meat from a diseased or otherwise naturally dead sheep. L18.
▸ **B** *attrib.* or as *adjective*. Of meat: from a diseased or otherwise naturally dead sheep. E19.

bray /breɪ/ *noun*. ME.
[ORIGIN from BRAY *verb*¹ or Old French *brai(t)* a cry, formed as BRAY *verb*¹.]
†**1** Outcry; a yell, a shriek. ME–L16.
2 (A sound like) the sound of a harshly played trumpet. L16.
3 (A sound like) the cry of an ass; a harsh whine. M17.

bray /breɪ/ *verb*¹. ME.
[ORIGIN Old French & mod. French *braire* to cry, from Proto-Romance, perh. of Celtic origin.]
†**1** *verb intrans.* Cry out, shriek. ME–E17.
2 *verb intrans.* Of wind, a wind instrument, etc.: produce a harsh jarring sound. ME.
3 *verb intrans.* Of an animal (now chiefly a donkey): utter a harsh cry. LME. ▸**b** Of a person or voice: speak loudly without thought or meaning. M17.
4 *verb trans.* Utter (a harsh cry); utter or say with a bray. LME.
> *Church Times* Sloane Square is full of people braying 'Caroline!' and 'Arabella!'

■ **brayer** *noun*¹ a person who or thing which brays, esp. an ass L16.

bray /breɪ/ *verb*² *trans.* LME.
[ORIGIN Anglo-Norman *braier*, Old French *breier* (mod. *broyer*), from Germanic base of BREAK *verb*.]
1 Pound or crush into small pieces, esp. with a pestle and mortar. LME.
2 Beat, thrash. *dial.* E19.
■ **brayer** *noun*² (PRINTING, now *hist.*) a wooden pestle employed to rub out ink L17.

bray /breɪ/ *verb*³ *trans.* *S. Afr.* Also **brei**, **brey**. M19.
[ORIGIN Afrikaans *brei*, from Dutch *breien* BRAID *verb*¹.]
Prepare for use, dress, (the skin of an animal).

braze /breɪz/ *verb*¹ *trans.* Now *rare*.
[ORIGIN Old English *brasian*, from BRASS *noun*: reinforced by analogy of GLASS *noun*, GLAZE *verb*¹.]
Make of or like brass; ornament with brass; *fig.* harden, inure.

braze /breɪz/ *verb*² *& noun*. M16.
[ORIGIN Partly from Old French *braser* burn, partly from French *braser* solder, ult. from Germanic.]
▸ **A** *verb trans.* †**1** Expose to the action of fire. M–L16.
2 Solder with an alloy of copper and zinc. L17.
▸ **B** *noun*. The process of brazing; a brazed joint. M20.
■ **brazeless** *adjective* made without or not involving brazing L19.

brazen /ˈbreɪz(ə)n/ *adjective*.
[ORIGIN Old English *bræ sen*, from BRASS *noun & adjective*: see -EN⁴.]
1 Made of brass; strong as brass. OE.
brazen age a mythological age of humankind, said to come between the silver and the iron age.
2 Hardened in effrontery; shameless; impudent. L16.
> J. BALDWIN She offended him because she was so brazen in her sins.

3 Of a brassy colour or sound; burnished; strident; harsh. L16.
> P. S. BUCK This brazen, glittering sunshine.

– COMB.: **brazen-face** *arch.* an impudent or shameless person; **brazen-faced** *adjective* impudent, shameless; **brazen-facedly** *adverb* in a brazen-faced manner.
■ **brazenly** *adverb* E18. **brazenness** /-n-n-/ *noun* M18.

brazen /ˈbreɪz(ə)n/ *verb trans.* M16.
[ORIGIN from the adjective.]
1 Foll. by *out*: face or undergo without shame or impudently. M16.
> R. B. SHERIDAN I am resolved to brazen the brunt of the business out.

brazen it out act as if unashamed of one's (mis)behaviour, show no remorse.
2 Harden; render brazen in appearance; make uncaring or careless. E19.
> HUGH WALPOLE Do not believe novelists are pleased with their efforts. They only brazen their faces before the world.

brazier /ˈbreɪzjə, -ʒə/ *noun*¹. *arch.* ME.
[ORIGIN Prob. from BRASS *noun* + -IER, on the analogy of GLASS *noun*, GLAZIER.]
A worker in brass.
■ **braziery** *noun* a brazier's work L18.

brazier /ˈbreɪzjə, -ʒə/ *noun*². L17.
[ORIGIN French *brasier*, from *braise* live coals: cf. BRAISE.]
A pan or stand for holding lighted coals as a portable heater.

Brazil /brəˈzɪl/ *noun*¹. Also **b-**, †**-s-**. ME.
[ORIGIN from medieval Latin *brasilium*, of uncertain origin; in sense 3, name of the S. Amer. country (Portuguese *Brasil*), which derived its name from the wood.]
1 The hard red wood of various tropical trees, esp. of the genus *Caesalpinia*. Now usu. ***Brazil wood***. ME.
†**2** A red dye obtained from this wood. LME–E19.
3 In full ***Brazil nut***. The large three-sided nut of the S. American tree *Bertholletia excelsa*. M19.
– NOTE: In sense 1 formerly taken as a type of hardness, and as such often confused with BRAZIL *noun*², with corresp. pronunc.

brazil /ˈbraz(ə)l/ *noun*². *dial.* Also **brassil**. E18.
[ORIGIN Prob. from BRASS *noun*.]
Iron pyrites; coal containing this.

brazilletto /brazɪˈlɛtəʊ/ *noun*. M17.
[ORIGIN Spanish, Portuguese *brasilete*, Portuguese *brasileto*, dim. of *brasil* Brazil wood.]
Any of various mainly W. Indian dyewoods, related (but inferior) to Brazil wood.

Brazilian /brəˈzɪlɪən/ *adjective & noun*. Also †**-s-**. E17.
[ORIGIN from *Brazil* the country (see BRAZIL *noun*¹) + -IAN.]
▸ **A** *adjective*. Of or pertaining to the S. American country of Brazil. E17.
Brazilian nutmeg: see NUTMEG *noun*. **Brazilian rosewood** = PALISANDER. **Brazilian tapir** a dark brown tapir, *Tapirus terrestris*, found widely in tropical S. America east of the Andes.
▸ **B** *noun*. **1** A native or inhabitant of Brazil. Also, Brazilian coffee. E17.
2 A style of waxing a woman's pubic hair in which only a very small central strip is left. *colloq.* L20.

B

brazilin /ˈbrazɪlɪn/ *noun*. M19.
[ORIGIN from BRAZIL *noun*[1] + -IN[1].]
CHEMISTRY. A yellow crystalline polycyclic alcohol, $C_{16}H_{14}O_5$, which is isolated from Brazil wood and is a reduced form of the red colouring matter of the wood.

BRCS *abbreviation*.
British Red Cross Society.

breach /briːtʃ/ *noun & verb*. ME.
[ORIGIN Old French & mod. French *brèche* = Provençal *breca* from Proto-Gallo-Romance from Frankish from Germanic base of BREAK *verb*. Superseded Old English *bryce* (ult. related), with which there is no continuity.]
▸ **A** *noun*. **I** The action of breaking.
†**1** The physical act of breaking; fracture; breakage. ME–L17.
2 The breaking or neglect of (or *of*) a legal or moral bond or obligation; the infraction of (or *of*) someone's privileged rights. LME.

SHAKES. *L.L.L.* Receive such welcome . . As honour, without breach of honour, may Make tender of to thy true worthiness. C. S. FORESTER To call out in that fashion was a grave breach of discipline. F. RAPHAEL His manager's breach of the rationing laws.

breach of confidence, *breach of contract*, *breach of trust*, etc. *breach of faith*: see FAITH *noun*. **breach of promise** the breaking of one's word, esp. of a promise to marry. **breach of the peace** public disturbance, or conduct likely to provoke one. **in breach of** so as to infringe or contravene.
†**3** An inroad *into*, an infringement *upon*. L16–M18.
4 A breaking of relations of (or *of*) union, continuity, etc.; *esp.* a separation, an estrangement, a quarrel. L16.

SHAKES. *Oth.* There's fall'n between him and my lord An unkind breach. W. BLACKSTONE By the breach and dissolution of . . the relation itself.

5 The breaking of waves over a vessel or on a coast. E17.
6 The leaping of a whale clear out of the water. M19.
▸ **II** The product of breaking.
7 A portion of land broken up by the plough. *obsolete* exc. *dial.* ME.
8 A break or fissure; *esp.* a gap in a fortification made by artillery. LME.

S. JOHNSON The crew implore the liberty of repairing their breaches. M. RENAULT A great breach blasted in the walls of heaven.

stand in the breach bear the brunt of an attack. **step into the breach** fill someone's place or give help, esp. in a crisis.
†**9** Surf; a breaker. Usu. in *pl.* E16–E18.
†**10** An interval; a division marked by breaks or intervals. Only in L16.
†**11** A bay, a harbour. *rare*. Only in E17.
12 A state of severed relations or disagreement. L17.

R. GRAVES The breach with the Pope had been healed.

▸ **B** *verb*. **1** *verb trans.* Break through, make a gap in; *fig.* contravene, violate. M16.

W. S. CHURCHILL He breached the ramparts with his cannon. I. WALLACE I should not have breached security by leaving my briefcase unlocked.

†**2** *verb intrans.* Cause or make a breach; separate. L16–M17.
3 *verb intrans.* Of a whale: leap clear out of the water. M19.
■ **breachy** *adjective* (chiefly *US*) (of cattle) apt to break fences and get out of enclosures L18.

bread /brɛd/ *noun*[1].
[ORIGIN Old English *brēad* = Old Frisian *brād*, Old Saxon, Middle & mod. Low German *brōd*, Old High German *brōt* (German *Brot*), Old Norse *brauð*, from Germanic, of unknown origin.]
†**1** A piece or morsel of food. Only in OE.
2 Flour moistened, kneaded, and baked, usu. with leaven. OE. ▸**b** A loaf, a roll; a piece of bread. Now *rare*. LME. ▸**c** *hist.* Ship's biscuit. M17.
3 Essential food. ME.

K. SMITH The field is clear, its straw / lined and ordered: it will be bread and bedding for safe cattle.

4 The means of subsistence; one's livelihood. E18.

C. ISHERWOOD I wish to leave school and begin to learn something useful, that I can win my bread.

5 Money. *slang*. M20.
– PHRASES ETC.: *baker's bread*: see BAKER. *bee bread*: see BEE *noun*[1]. *black bread*: see BLACK *adjective*. **bread and butter** (*a*) slices of bread spread with butter; necessary food; (*b*) *fig.* one's livelihood, routine work to provide an income (*quarrel with one's bread and butter*: see QUARREL *verb*). **bread-and-butter** *adjective* (*a*) *arch.*, of an age when bread and butter is staple fare, boyish or girlish; (*b*) commonplace, humdrum; (*c*) *bread-and-butter letter*, a guest's written thanks for hospitality; (*d*) *bread-and-butter pudding*, a dessert consisting of slices of bread and butter layered with dried fruit and sugar and baked with a mixture of milk and egg. *bread and circuses*: see CIRCUS 7. **bread and milk** pieces of bread in hot boiled milk. **bread and scrape** bread scantily buttered. **bread and water**: the plainest possible diet. **bread and wine** CHRISTIAN CHURCH the Eucharist. **bread of idleness** food not worked for. *bread of trete*: see TREAT *noun*[1] 1. **break bread** *arch.* take food, share a meal *with* someone. **breaking of bread** CHRISTIAN CHURCH the Eucharist. *brown bread*: see BROWN *adjective*. *cast one's bread upon the waters*: see WATER *noun*. **daily bread** a livelihood. **eat the bread of** be subjected to (affliction etc.). *French bread*: see FRENCH *adjective*. **have one's bread buttered on both sides**, **want one's bread buttered on both sides** have etc. a state of easy prosperity. **know which side one's bread is buttered** know where one's advantage lies. *light bread*: see LIGHT *adjective*[1]. *loaf of bread*, *loaf o' bread*: see LOAF *noun*[1]. *quick bread*: see QUICK *adjective & adverb*. *sour bread*: see SOUR *adjective*. *sourdough bread*: see SOURDOUGH 1b. *sweet bread*: see SWEET *adjective & adverb*. **take the bread out of a person's mouth** deprive a person of his or her living, esp. by competition. *the best thing since sliced bread*, *the greatest thing since sliced bread*: see SLICED 1b. *want one's bread buttered on both sides*: see *have one's bread buttered on both sides* above. *wastel-bread*: see WASTEL 1. *white bread*: see WHITE *adjective*.
– COMB.: **bread basket** (*a*) a basket for bread; (*b*) *slang* the stomach; (*c*) (a region etc. which is) a producer of cereals for bread, a source of staple food; **bread bin** a container for loaves; **breadboard** a strong flat board for cutting bread on; *colloq.* a board on which an electric circuit etc. can be set out; **bread-corn** grain for making bread; **breadcrumb** *noun & verb* (*a*) *noun* a crumb of bread, *esp.* (in *pl.*) such crumbs used in cooking, e.g. as a coating for fried or grilled food; the soft inner part of bread; (*b*) *verb trans.* coat with breadcrumbs; **breadfruit** any of various tropical fruits with edible breadlike pulp; *spec.* that of the tree *Artocarpus altilis* of the Pacific islands; **bread-kind** *W. Indian* food like bread, e.g. yams, sweet potatoes; **breadhead** *colloq.* a person who is motivated by, or obsessed with, making money; **bread knife** a long knife, usu. with a serrated edge, for slicing bread; **breadline** (orig. *US*) a queue of poor people waiting to receive food; (fig.) *the* subsistence level; *bread roll*: see ROLL *noun*[1]; **bread-root** (the edible root of) a N. American leguminous plant, *Psoralea esculenta*; also called *prairie turnip*; **bread sauce** a milk sauce thickened with breadcrumbs; **bread stick** a long thin roll of crisp bread; **breadstuffs** (*a*) grain flour; (*b*) articles of bread; **bread tree** a tree yielding breadfruit or other breadlike food; *bread wheat*: see WHEAT *noun* 1; **breadwinner** the person whose work supports a family.
■ **breaden** *adjective* (*arch.*) made of bread L16. **breadless** *adjective* without bread; without food: LME. **breadlike** *adjective* L17.

†**bread** *noun*[2] var. of BREDE *noun*[2].

bread /brɛd/ *verb*[1] *trans.* E17.
[ORIGIN from BREAD *noun*[1].]
Dress with breadcrumbs; treat or provide with bread. Chiefly as ***breaded*** *ppl adjective*.

†**bread** *verb*[2] var. of BREDE *verb*[2].

breadth /brɛdθ, -t-/. *noun*. E16.
[ORIGIN from BREDE *noun*[1] + -TH[1], after LENGTH.]
1 Measure or distance from side to side; broadness, width. E16.

F. R. WILSON The breadth, across the transepts, is 54 feet.

hair's breadth: see HAIR *noun*. *thumb's breadth*: see THUMB *noun* 2.
2 A piece (of cloth etc.) of full breadth, a width. L16.
3 Extent, distance; full extent. L16.

Folk Roots Travelling the length and breadth of Britain.

4 ART. A broad effect; unity achieved by disregarding unnecessary detail. L18.
5 Largeness, freedom from limitations (esp. *of* mind or view); liberality, catholicity; toleration. M19.

Vanity Fair This book . . seems to be a work of astonishing breadth and depth.

■ **breadthen** *verb intrans.* (*rare*) increase in breadth E19. **breadthless** *adjective* M17. **breadthways** *adverb* in the direction of the breadth L17. **breadthwise** *adverb* = BREADTHWAYS M18.

break /breɪk/ *noun*[1]. ME.
[ORIGIN from the verb.]
1 An act of breaking or separation; fracture, breakage, severance. ME. ▸**b** The act of breaking electrical contact; the position or condition in which contact is broken. L19.
tiebreak: see TIE-.
2 A broken place, a gap, an opening. ME.

E. HEMINGWAY The last of the sun came through in the breaks between the strips of matting. D. ATTENBOROUGH We cannot hear a break between sounds of less than one tenth of a second. J. CHEEVER He noticed . . a break in the wall of buildings.

3 An interruption of continuity or uniformity; a change of direction etc. L15. ▸**b** A mark indicating an abrupt pause in print or writing. E18. ▸**c** A short spell of recreation or refreshment in a period of work etc. M19. ▸**d** A sudden or sharp fall in share prices etc. L19. ▸**e** A short solo or instrumental passage in jazz or popular music. E20.

R. H. DANA Foster went as far as the break of the deck. S. HILL We were strafed for about three hours without a break. **c** S. UNWIN A short break for a sandwich lunch. F. RAPHAEL The children spilled out for their break like mice. S. RAVEN Perhaps Georgy and Bessie would like a little trip abroad. We all need a bit of a break.

clean break: see CLEAN *adjective*. **c** *coffee-break*, *tea break*, etc.
4 The first appearance of light, onset. Chiefly in ***break of day***, dawn. L16.
5 A tract of ground of distinct appearance, *esp.* an area broken up for cultivation, or (*US*) an area of rough broken country. L17.
6 A surplus piece of metal remaining on the shank of a newly cast type. L17.
7 A quantity or amount; a large number. Chiefly *dial.* L18.
8 An act of breaking out or away; a sudden dash; an escape from prison etc. M19. ▸**b** A bud or shoot sprouting from a stem. M20.

T. ROOSEVELT The slightest attempt at a break would result in their being shot down.

9 CRICKET etc. The deviation of a ball on pitching. M19.
leg break: see LEG *noun*.
10 BILLIARDS & SNOOKER etc. (The points scored in) a consecutive series of successful shots. M19.
11 a A mistake, a blunder. *colloq.* L19. ▸**b** An opportunity, a (fair) chance; a piece of (good) luck. *colloq.* E20.

a P. G. WODEHOUSE Fear he was going to make a break of some kind. **b** G. GREENE We had a lucky break. B. SCHULBERG Learn to give the other fellow a break and we'll *all* live longer.

b bad break (*a*) an unfortunate remark or ill-judged action; (*b*) a piece of bad luck. **even break** a fair chance.

break *noun*[2] see BRAKE *noun*[6].

break *noun*[3] var. of BRAKE *noun*[7].

break /breɪk/ *verb*. Pa. t. **broke** /brəʊk/, (*arch.*) **brake** /breɪk/. Pa. pple **broken** /ˈbrəʊkən/, (chiefly *arch.*) **broke** /brəʊk/ (see also BROKE, BROKEN *adjectives*).
[ORIGIN Old English *brecan* = Old Frisian *breka*, Old Saxon *brekan* (Dutch *breken*), Old High German *brehhan* (German *brechen*), Gothic *brikan* from Germanic, from Indo-European base also of Latin *frangere* break.]
▸ **I** Sever, fracture, part; shatter, crush, destroy.
1 *verb trans.* Divide into distinct parts by force (by accident or design), other than by cutting or tearing; part by violence, fracture; shatter, smash. OE. ▸**b** Rend, tear, (cloth etc.). *obsolete* exc. *dial.* OE. ▸**c** Cut up, tear in pieces, (an animal's body). ME. ▸†**d** Wreck (a ship). ME–E17. ▸**e** Make (a whole) incomplete; divide, take away a part from; spend partially, change (a banknote etc.) for currency of smaller denominations. M18. ▸**f** PHONOLOGY. Subject (a vowel) to breaking. M19. ▸**g** Open (a gun) at the hinge between the stock and the barrel. L19.

STEELE A natural Inclination to break Windows. SIR W. SCOTT I've broke my trusty battle-axe. N. COWARD Once I broke four gramophone records over his head. *Daily Telegraph* Break the three eggs into a mixing bowl. **c** SIR W. SCOTT Raven . . watching while the deer is broke.

2 *verb trans.* Fracture, undergo fracture of, the bones of (a limb etc., a person's body); dislocate the bones of (the back, the neck). OE.

R. L. STEVENSON Anderson's ball . . had broken his shoulder-blade and touched the lung. B. JAMES Caldow broke a leg.

3 *verb trans.* Lay open the surface of; rupture, burst, crack; graze. ME.

SHAKES. *Com. Err.* Back, slave, or I will break thy pate across. A. PRICE He couldn't break the skin on a rice pudding.

4 *verb trans.* Destroy, make useless, ruin; defeat, foil. ME. ▸†**b** Disband; dissolve. L16–L18. ▸**c** Nullify (a will) by legal process. *arch.* L19. ▸**d** Better (a record, score, etc.). L19. ▸**e** Defeat the object of (a strike), esp. by engaging other workers. E20. ▸**f** TENNIS. Win a game against (an opponent's service, the server). M20. ▸**g** Disprove (an alibi). M20.

HENRY MORE Each laboureth to breake that the other maketh. E. A. FREEMAN Their moral force was utterly broken.

5 a *verb trans.* Cause (a formation of troops etc.) to part or disperse in confusion. ME. ▸**b** *verb intrans.* Of a formation of troops etc.: be parted, disperse in confusion. L16. ▸**c** *verb intrans.* Of clouds etc.: show a gap, disperse. E19. ▸**d** *verb trans. & intrans.* BILLIARDS & SNOOKER etc. Of a player: aim to strike (the ball(s)) with the cue ball, *spec.* as the first stroke of a game. Of the balls: separate on being struck. M19.

TENNYSON The foeman's line is broke.

6 *verb trans.* Separate or remove by parting or snapping. ME.

AV *Gen.* 27:40 Thou shalt breake his yoke from off thy necke. OED Great boughs broken from the trees.

7 *verb trans.* Disrupt, loosen, (a tie or band, a confining or restricting force); disconnect (electrical contact etc.), opp. ***make***. ME.

LD MACAULAY The spell which bound his followers to him was not altogether broken. E. F. BENSON Real friendships . . must not be lightly broken.

8 *verb intrans.* Undergo fracture, severance by force, shattering, rupture, etc.; part, dissolve, fail. ME. ▸**b** Of waves etc.: curl over and disintegrate in foam, beat as surf. LME. ▸**c** Of the voice: change tone with emotion or at (male) puberty. M17. ▸**d** Of a lake etc.: display water bloom. L19. ▸**e** Of boxers etc.: separate after a clinch, esp. on the order of the referee. E20. ▸**f** BRIDGE. Of a suit: be distributed between two hands (in a specified way or *absol.* evenly). M20.

SHAKES. *Ven. & Ad.* The berry breaks before it staineth. G. O. TREVELYAN His health was breaking fast. J. TYNDALL The glacier was evidently breaking beneath our feet. I. MURDOCH The clasp had broken and Tallis had said he'd mend it.

9 *verb trans.* Crush in strength, spirit, or resistance; weary, exhaust; discourage, intimidate. L15. ▸**b** Reduce to obedience or discipline, tame; subject or habituate *to*. L15.

MILTON An Iron Rod to bruise and breake Thy disobedience. D. HUME A person . . easily broken by affliction. N. MONSARRAT No desperate assault ever broke their spirit.

10 a *verb intrans.* Become bankrupt, fail financially. Now *rare*. L16. ▸**b** *verb trans.* Ruin financially, make bankrupt. E17. ▸**c** *verb trans.* Wreck the career of; cashier, strip of rank. L17.

▸**II** Violate, transgress; disrupt or be disrupted in continuance or uniformity.

11 *verb trans.* Fail to keep (a law, promise, treaty, etc.), act contrary to. OE.

COVERDALE *Luke* 16:18 Who so ever putteth awaye his wife and marieth another breaketh matrimony. G. K. CHESTERTON There is something wrong with a man if he does not want to break the Ten Commandments.

12 *verb trans.* Cut short, stop; suspend, interrupt; add variation to; become no longer subject to (a habit). ME.

G. K. CHESTERTON His meditations were broken by a sudden and jarring stoppage. H. HENDERSON Breaking a jeep journey at Capuzzo. J. BARTH I was breaking a thirteen-year-old habit of not seeing doctors. H. KISSINGER Once the deadlock was broken, the tension all but vanished. I. MCEWAN High, dark walls, broken at irregular intervals by deeply recessed doorways.

13 *verb intrans.* Interrupt or pause in one's activities; be interrupted or stopped; *esp.* (of weather) change suddenly after a long settled period. LME. ▸**b** Of prices etc.: fall suddenly or sharply. L19.

G. VIDAL Ice clattered and the silence broke. C. PRIEST The drought had at last broken, and it had been raining . . for the past week. E. FIGES It would soon be time to break for a bite to eat.

14 *verb intrans. & trans.* (Cause to) change direction or course; change *into* a different way of proceeding. LME. ▸**b** *verb trans. & intrans.* HORTICULTURE. (Cause to) become striped or variegated under cultivation. E18. ▸**c** *verb intrans. & trans.* CRICKET etc. Of a ball: change direction on pitching. Of a bowler: cause (a ball) to do this. M19. ▸**d** *verb intrans.* Of a horse: change gait. M19.

▸**III** Penetrate, enter or leave forcibly; issue, escape, begin, release.

15 *verb trans.* Burst (a barrier) so as to force a way through. Usu. with adverbs OE. ▸**b** Make (a hole, a passage, a trail, a way, etc.) by force, by separating obstacles, etc. ME. ▸**c** Solve (a code etc.). E20.

SHAKES. *Coriol.* They . . sigh'd forth proverbs—That hunger broke stone walls. GIBBON The doors were instantly broke open.

16 *verb trans.* Enter (a house etc.) by force or illegally. Now chiefly in ***break and enter***, ***housebreaking***, and related phrs. OE.

17 *verb trans. & intrans.* Escape (from) or leave by force or without permission; escape from restraint; emerge from hiding etc. suddenly, flee. OE. ▸**b** *verb intrans.* Of an athlete: get off the mark prematurely. L19.

BURKE Am I to congratulate an highwayman . . who has broke prison, upon the recovery of his natural rights? OED Scholars gated for a week for breaking bounds. DAY LEWIS My struggle to break free. B. MALAMUD He wanted to break and run but didn't dare.

18 *verb intrans.* Issue forth, emerge; come suddenly to notice; (of a storm etc.) begin violently; (of news etc.) be made known. ME. ▸**b** Of plants, buds, etc.: sprout into bloom. ME. ▸**c** Begin to give light, emerge out of darkness. M16. ▸**d** Happen, occur, turn out (favourably). *slang*. E20.

J. AGATE A terrific thunderstorm broke. Great crashes and a lot of lightning. E. WAUGH A big story is going to break. O. MANNING At that moment a voice broke shrilly from the loud-speaker. F. TUOHY Tears of laughter broke from his eyes. I. WALLACE Dilman's immediate reaction of concern broke across his features.

19 *verb trans.* Deliver, reveal, publish, disclose, (news, thoughts, etc.). LME. ▸†**b** *verb intrans.* Speak *with* (or *to*) someone concerning news etc. LME–E17. ▸**c** *verb trans.* Utter, display; crack (a joke etc.). L16. ▸**d** *verb trans.* Free and shake out (a flag, sail, etc.). Freq. foll. by *out*. L19.

M. M. ATWATER Are you breaking the story in the morning papers? A. BRINK Will you please tell Dad? But break it gently. **b** SHAKES. *Two Gent.* I am to break with thee of some affairs That touch me near. **c** SOUTHEY He brake a sullen smile. H. MACDIARMID The hawthorn tree Which in early Spring breaks Fresh emerald.

20 *verb trans.* Impinge upon, penetrate; relieve (a state, mood, etc.). L16.

C. THIRLWALL Only one ray of hope broke the gloom of her prospects. W. SANSOM Only the trotting jingle of our sleigh-bell broke the air.

▸**IV 21** *verb intrans.* Perform break-dancing. L20.

– PHRASES: **break a blow**, **break a fall**: weaken its effect. ***break a** BUTTERFLY **on a wheel***. ***break a close***: see CLOSE *noun*[1] 1. ***break a fall***: see ***break a blow*** above. **break a horse (to the rein)** accustom a horse to being controlled by reins. **break a lance** enter into competition (*with*). **break a leg** *imper.* (*theatrical slang*) do well, good luck, (as it is considered unlucky to wish good luck directly). **break and enter** force one's way into (a house etc.) illegally, commit burglary. **break a set** sell the parts of a set separately. ***break bread***: see BREAD *noun*[1]. ***break bulk***: see BULK *noun*[1]. **break cover** (of game etc.) emerge into the open. **break even** have balancing gains and losses, make no net profit or loss. ***break for tall timber***, ***break for the tall timber***: see TALL *adjective*. **break ground** = ***break the ground*** below. ***break in shivers***, ***break into shivers***: see SHIVER *noun*[1] 1. **break new ground** do pioneering work. **break of**: make (someone) no longer have (a habit etc.). **break one's duck** CRICKET score one's first run. ***break one's fast***: see FAST *noun*[1]. **break one's head**: graze or bruise it. ***break one's heart***: see HEART *noun*. ***break one's silence***: see SILENCE *noun*. †**break one's wind** exhaust oneself. ***break one's word***: see WORD *noun*. **break on the wheel** (chiefly *hist.*) fracture the bones of or dislocate on a wheel as a form of punishment or torture (cf. ***break a** BUTTERFLY **on a wheel***). ***break rank(s)***: see RANK *noun*. ***break shins***: see SHIN *noun*[1]. **break ship** fail to rejoin a ship after absence on leave. ***break short (off)***: see SHORT *adverb*. ***break silence***: see SILENCE *noun*. ***break someone's heart***: see HEART *noun*. ***break step***: see STEP *noun*[1]. ***break the back of***: see BACK *noun*[1]. **break the bank** (in gaming) exhaust the bank's resources or limit of payment, win spectacularly. **break the ground** begin digging, plough for the first time; do pioneering or preparatory work (*for*). ***break the habit***: see HABIT *noun*. ***break the ice***: see ICE *noun*. ***break the mould***: see MOULD *noun*[3]. **break the pack** SNOOKER disturb the triangle of red balls. ***break the record***: see RECORD *noun*. ***break the sound barrier***: see SOUND *noun*[2]. **break the wicket** CRICKET dislodge the bails in stumping or running out a batsman. †**break time** MUSIC fail to keep time. **break water** (*a*) appear at the surface; (*b*) HUNTING (of a stag etc.) wade a river etc. **break wind** void wind from the stomach or bowels. ***make or break***: see MAKE *verb*. ***one's heart breaks***: see HEART *noun*. ***the last straw that breaks the camel's back***: see STRAW *noun*.

– WITH ADVERBS & PREPOSITIONS IN SPECIALIZED SENSES: **break away** make or become separate or free, secede. **break down** (*a*) *verb phr. intrans.* collapse, fail, cease to function, be decomposed, lose self-control; (*b*) *verb phr. trans.* demolish, decompose, analyse (*into* components), overcome (resistance etc.). **break forth** burst out, suddenly emerge. **break in** (*a*) *verb phr. intrans.* intrude forcibly, esp. as a thief; interrupt (foll. by (*up*)*on* a person or action interrupted); (*b*) *verb phr. trans.* tame, subject (an animal) to discipline, accustom to habit or use etc., wear until comfortable; *Austral. & NZ* bring (land) under cultivation. **break into** enter forcibly, begin to utter (laughter etc.), *colloq.* manage to become involved in (an activity or occupation); (see also sense 14 above). **break off** (*a*) *verb phr. intrans.* become detached, detach oneself, cease; (*b*) *verb phr. trans.* detach by breaking, discontinue, bring to an end; (*c*) *verb phr. intrans.* play the first stroke in billiards, snooker, etc. **break out** (*a*) *verb phr. intrans.* begin suddenly or violently, burst from restraint or concealment, exclaim, become covered *in* (a rash etc.); *Austral. & NZ* (of a goldfield) come into operation; (*b*) *verb phr. trans.* open up (a container) and begin to remove its contents, get from out of storage; (see also sense 19d above). **break through** *verb phr. trans. & intrans.* penetrate, force one's way through, make sudden rapid progress. **break up** (*a*) *verb phr. trans. & intrans.* break into small pieces, disintegrate; (esp. of school at end of term) disband, disperse; stop; disconcert; terminate a personal, esp. sexual, relationship (*with*); (*b*) *verb phr. intrans.* become feeble or convulsed (*with* laughter etc.), (of weather) = sense 13 above; (*c*) *verb phr. intrans.* (of a radio or telephone signal) be interrupted by interference. **break with** quarrel or cease relations with; (see also sense 19b above).

■ **breakable** *adjective & noun* (*a*) *adjective* able to be broken; (*b*) *noun* in *pl.*, breakable things: L16. **breakage** *noun* the action or fact or an instance of breaking; loss or damage caused by breaking: L18.

break- /breɪk/ *combining form*. ME.

[ORIGIN Repr. BREAK *verb* or (occas.) *noun*[1].]

Prefixed esp. to nouns and adverbs to form nouns and adjectives usu. with the sense '(a thing) which breaks, an act or state of breaking'.

break-back *adjective & noun* (*a*) *adjective* that breaks the back, crushing, very heavy; (*b*) *noun* (CRICKET) a ball which turns sharply from the off side on pitching. **break-bone (fever)** dengue. **break-crop**: grown to avoid the repeated growing of cereals. **break-dance** *verb intrans.* perform break-dancing. **break-dancer** a person who performs break-dancing. **break-dancing** (orig. *US*) an energetic kind of (usu. solo) dancing, freq. involving spinning on the floor on the back or head. **break-even** *adjective & noun* (designating or pertaining to) the point or state at which one breaks even. **break-fall** (in martial arts) a controlled fall in which most of the impact is absorbed by the arms or legs. **break-front** *adjective & noun* (a piece of furniture) having the line of its front broken by a curve or angle. **break-line** TYPOGRAPHY the last line of a paragraph (usu. not of full length). **breakneck** *adjective & noun* (*a*) *adjective* endangering the neck, headlong, dangerously fast; †(*b*) *noun* a headlong fall, destruction. **break-point** (*a*) a point at which an interruption or change is made; a turning point; (*b*) = BREAKING ***point***; (*c*) TENNIS a situation in which the receiving player(s) can break the opponent's service at the next point; a point at which the service is or can be broken. **breakstone** (now *rare* or *obsolete*) a saxifrage; also, parsley piert. **breakwater** a structure which provides protection against the force of waves, *esp.* a mole or groyne. **breakwind** (chiefly *Austral.*) a windbreak.

breakaway /ˈbreɪkəweɪ/ *noun & adjective*. L19.

[ORIGIN from BREAK- + AWAY *adverb*.]

▸**A** *noun*. **1** The action of breaking away; severance, secession. L19.

2 SPORT. A sudden attack or forward movement; a false start to a race. L19.

3 A stampede. *Austral. & NZ*. L19.

4 A person who or thing which breaks away. L19. ▸**b** RUGBY. An outside back-row forward. M20.

▸**B** *attrib.* or as *adjective*. That breaks away or has broken away. E20.

breakbeat *noun*. L20.

[ORIGIN from BREAK *noun*[1] + BEAT *noun*[1].]

A sample of a syncopated drum beat, usually repeated to form a rhythm used as a basis for dance music.

breakdown /ˈbreɪkdaʊn/ *noun*. E19.

[ORIGIN from BREAK- + DOWN *adverb*.]

1 A boisterous country dance. *US*. E19.

2 Collapse, failure; (a stoppage due to) mechanical malfunction; failure of health or (esp.) mental powers. M19. ▸**b** Failure of electrical insulation; the sudden passage of current through an insulator. E20. ▸**c** Chemical or physical decomposition. E20.

NERVOUS breakdown.

3 An analysis or classification (of statistics etc.). M20.

breaker /ˈbreɪkə/ *noun*[1]. ME.

[ORIGIN from BREAK *verb* + -ER[1].]

1 A person who or thing which breaks (in any sense), crushes, or destroys. ME.

circuit-breaker, ***housebreaker***, ***record-breaker***, ***ship-breaker***, etc.

2 *spec.* A person who violates or transgresses a law, oath, promise, etc. LME.

3 A person who subdues, tames, or trains (horses etc.). Also ***breaker-in***. M16.

4 A heavy ocean wave breaking on the coast or on a reef etc. L17.

5 A person who interrupts the conversation of others on Citizens' Band radio; any user of Citizens' Band radio. *slang*. M20.

6 A break-dancer. L20.

breaker /ˈbreɪkə/ *noun*[2]. M19.

[ORIGIN from Spanish *bareca*, *barrica*: see BARRICO.]

NAUTICAL. A small keg, esp. for drinking water.

breakfast /ˈbrɛkfəst/ *noun & verb*. LME.

[ORIGIN from BREAK- + FAST *noun*[1].]

▸**A** *noun*. The first meal of the day. Occas., any meal. LME.

SHAKES. *Two Gent.* I would have been a breakfast to the beast Rather than have false Proteus rescue me.

bed and breakfast: see BED *noun*. ***continental breakfast***: see CONTINENTAL *adjective*. ***dog's breakfast***: see DOG *noun*. ***English breakfast***: see ENGLISH *adjective*. **have for breakfast** *fig.* (*slang*) easily defeat (a person). ***second breakfast***: see SECOND *adjective*. ***WEDDING breakfast***.

– COMB.: **breakfast service** a matching set of cups, saucers, plates, etc., for serving breakfast.

▸**B** *verb*. **1** *verb intrans.* Have breakfast. M17.

2 *verb trans.* Provide with breakfast. M17.

■ **breakfasting** *verbal noun* (*a*) the action of the verb; (*b*) *arch.* a taking of breakfast: M18. **breakfastless** *adjective* L18.

break-in /ˈbreɪkɪn/ *noun*. M19.

[ORIGIN from BREAK- + IN *adverb*.]

1 An interruption. *rare*. M19.

2 A collapse inwards. *rare*. E20.

3 A forcible entry; an incursion; *spec.* an illegal entry into a house etc., a burglary. M20.

breaking /ˈbreɪkɪŋ/ *noun*. OE.

[ORIGIN from BREAK *verb* + -ING[1].]

1 The action of BREAK *verb*. OE. ▸**b** PHONOLOGY. The development of a diphthong from a simple vowel owing to the influence of an adjacent sound, esp. a following consonant; a diphthong so formed. L19. ▸**c** Break-dancing. L20.

breaking of bread: see BREAD *noun*[1].

2 A piece of land newly ploughed for the first time. *US*. M19.

– COMB.: **breaking ball** BASEBALL a pitch that changes direction, *esp.* a curve ball or slider; **breaking point** the point at which a thing or person gives way under stress; **breaking strength** the maximum stress that a thing can withstand without breaking.

break-off /ˈbreɪkɒf/ *noun*. E19.

[ORIGIN from BREAK- + OFF *adverb*.]

1 A part of the stock of a musket or rifle into which the barrel fits. E19.

2 Discontinuance; a severing of relations. M19.

breakout /ˈbreɪkaʊt/ *noun & adjective*. E19.

[ORIGIN from BREAK- + OUT *adverb*.]

▸**A** *noun*. **1** A bursting from confinement etc.; an escape, esp. of several people. E19.

2 An outbreak. L19.

▸**B** *adjective*. *colloq.*

1 Suddenly and extremely popular or successful. L20.

2 Denoting or relating to groups which break away from a conference or other large gathering for discussion. *US*. L20.

breakthrough /ˈbreɪkθruː/ *noun*. E20.

[ORIGIN from BREAK- + THROUGH *adverb*.]

An act of breaking through an obstacle, barrier, etc.; a major advance in knowledge etc.

– COMB.: **breakthrough bleeding** bleeding from the uterus occurring between menstrual periods (a side effect of some oral contraceptives).

break-up /ˈbreɪkʌp/ *noun*. L18.

[ORIGIN from BREAK *verb* + UP *adverb*[1].]

The action of breaking up; an act or instance of breaking up; *esp.* (*a*) a dissolution or disruption of a meeting, government, etc.; (*b*) the end of term at a school etc.; (*c*) a termination of a personal, esp. sexual, relationship; (*d*) a

B

winding up and dispersal of the assets of a company etc.; (*e*) *Canad.* the breaking up of thawing ice, or the melting of snow and unfreezing of the ground, in spring.

B

bream /briːm/ *noun.* Pl. same. Also (*N. Amer. & Austral.*) **brim** /brɪm/. LME.
[ORIGIN Old French *bre(s)me* (mod. *brème*) from Frankish (= Old Saxon *bressemo*, Old High German *brahsema* (German *Brachsen*, *Brassen*)).]
1 A deep-bodied freshwater fish of the carp family, *Abramis brama*, of northern Europe and parts of Asia. Also, any of certain related fishes, *esp.* (more fully ***silver bream***, ***white bream***), a European freshwater fish, *Blicca bjoerkna*, similar to *Abramis brama*. LME.
2 Any of various similar percoid marine fishes, *esp.* (*a*) = ***SEA bream***; (*b*) = POMFRET 2. LME.
RAY'S BREAM. ***red bream***: see RED *adjective*.
3 A freshwater sunfish of the genus *Lepomis* (family Centrarchidae). *N. Amer.* M17.

bream /briːm/ *verb trans.* L15.
[ORIGIN Prob. of Low German origin and rel. to BROOM *noun* (cf. Dutch *brem* broom, furze).]
hist. Clear (a ship's bottom, or the vessel itself) of accumulated weed, shells, etc., by burning and scraping.

breast /brɛst/ *noun.*
[ORIGIN Old English *brēost* = Old Frisian *briast*, Old Saxon *briost*, Old Norse *brjóst*, from Germanic.]
1 Either of two soft protuberant organs situated on the front of a woman's thorax, secreting milk for a period after childbirth; the analogous rudimentary organ in men; *the* organs as a source of milk; *fig.* a source of nourishment. OE.

SHAKES. *Macb.* Come to my woman's breasts, And take my milk for gall, you murd'ring ministers. STEELE One Country Milch-Wench, to whom I was . . put to the Breast.

2 The front of the human thorax, the chest. OE. ▸**b** Part of a garment, piece of armour, etc., covering this. LME.

F. NORRIS A gray flannel shirt, open at the throat, showed his breast.

beat one's breast: see BEAT *verb*[1] 1.
3 The seat of the affections, emotions, etc.; the heart; one's private thoughts or feelings. OE.

P. PULLMAN She felt a strange exultation welling slowly in her breast.

make a clean breast of confess fully.
4 The thorax of an animal. ME. ▸**b** A joint of meat or portion of poultry cut from the breast. LME.

O. WILDE The Nightingale flew to the Rose-tree, and set her breast against the thorn.

†**5** The whole of the upper torso. LME–M18.
†**6** Breath, voice in singing. LME–E18.

J. FLETCHER Let's hear him sing, he has a fine breast.

†**7** A broad even front of a moving company. Cf. ABREAST. LME–E19.
8 Any surface, part of a thing, etc., analogous in shape or position to the human breast; a broad or bulging forward part. M16.
chimney breast the projecting wall enclosing the flues of a chimney within a room.
– COMB.: **breast-board** the mould board of a plough; **breastbone** = STERNUM; **breast collar** a part of harness across a draught animal's breast through which the power of drawing is directly exerted; **breast drill** a drill on which pressure is brought to bear by the operator's chest; **breastfeed** *verb trans. & intrans.* feed (a baby) with milk from a woman's breasts rather than from a feeding bottle; **breast-high** *adjective & adverb* high as the breast; (submerged) to the breast; **breast-pin** a jewelled or other ornamental pin worn in the tie; **breastplate** a vestment or piece of armour worn over the chest; the lower shell of a tortoise, turtle, etc.; an inscription plate on a coffin; **breast-plough** a type of plough pushed by the breast; **breast pocket** a pocket over the breast of a garment; **breast pump** an instrument for drawing milk from the breasts by suction; **breast shell** a shallow receptacle that fits over the nipple of a lactating woman to catch any milk that flows; **breaststroke** a stroke made while swimming on the breast by extending the arms in front and sweeping them back; BREASTSUMMER; **breast-wall** a retaining wall, *esp.* one supporting a bank of earth; **breast-wheel** a water wheel in which the water is admitted near the axle; **breastwork** a breast-high fieldwork thrown up for defence; a parapet.
■ **breasted** *adjective* having a breast (of specified form) ME. **breastwise** *adverb* side by side, abreast E17. **breasty** *adjective* (*colloq.*) (of a woman) with prominent breasts M20.

breast /brɛst/ *verb.* M16.
[ORIGIN from the noun.]
1 *verb trans.* Protect with a breastwork. Now *rare* or *obsolete.* M16.
2 *verb trans.* Apply or oppose the breast to, push with the breast; meet in full opposition, contend with, face. L16.

KEATS As swift As bird on wing to breast its eggs again. J. BUCHAN A baker's van breasted the hill. B. BAINBRIDGE Like a swimmer breasting a wave.

breast the tape: see TAPE *noun* 1C.
3 *verb intrans.* Press forward, climb; leap forward. *Scot.* L18.
■ **breasting** *noun* (*a*) the action of the verb; (*b*) a breastplate; a breastwork: L16.

breastsummer /ˈbrɛstsʌmə/ *noun.* Also **bressumer** /ˈbrɛsʌmə/. E17.
[ORIGIN from BREAST *noun* + SUMMER *noun*[2].]
A beam spanning a wide opening and supporting a superstructure.

breath /brɛθ/ *noun.*
[ORIGIN Old English *brǣþ* from Germanic from Indo-European, from base meaning 'burn, heat'. In sense 3 etc. replaced Old English *æþm*, *anda*.]
1 An odour, a smell, a scent. Long *obsolete* exc. *dial.* OE.
2 †**a** A vapour given off by heated objects etc.; reek; steam. ME–M17. ▸**b** Air exhaled from anything, or impregnated with its exhalations (cf. sense 7 below). E17.

b R. KIPLING A land-breeze . . Milk-warm wi' breath of spice an' bloom. G. ORWELL The heat rolled from the earth like the breath of an oven.

3 Air exhaled from the lungs (as made manifest by smell or sight); *gen.* air inspired or expired in respiration. ME. ▸**b** The air blown into or out of a musical instrument. *poet.* E17. ▸**c** PHONETICS. Voiceless expiration of air. M19.

G. B. SHAW Mrs Dudgeon, greatly relieved, exhales the pent up breath and sits at her ease again. W. TREVOR He could see her breath on the icy air. **b** DRYDEN Before the Breath Of brazen Trumpets rung the Peals of Death.

4 The faculty or action of breathing; existence, spirit, life. ME.

T. HOOD I often wish the night Had borne my breath away. TENNYSON And so the Word had breath.

5 An act of breathing, a single inspiration. ME.

SIR W. SCOTT To cry for assistance and almost in the same breath to whimper for mercy. W. S. MAUGHAM Almost in a breath they touched upon the latest play, the latest dressmaker, the latest portrait painter. M. M. KAYE His first breath had been a lungful of the cold air that blew down from the far rampart of the mountains.

6 A whisper; an utterance, a speech; spoken judgement or will. ME.

I. MCEWAN The faintest sound, barely more than a breath, left her lips. *fig.*: J. GALSWORTHY Every breath of the old scandal had been carefully kept from her.

7 A gentle blowing (*of* wind etc.), a puff; *fig.* the enlivening or favourable influence (*of*); (passing into sense 2b), a whiff, a trace. LME.

H. R. REYNOLDS Forced into new attitudes by the changing breath of human appreciation. J. RHYS There was no breeze, not a breath of air. J. CLAVELL A few days here, half a year there, like a butterfly on the summer's breath.

8 The power of breathing; free or easy breathing. L16.

SIR W. SCOTT Two dogs . . Unmatched for courage, breath, and speed.

9 An opportunity or time for breathing. Cf. BREATHER 4. L16.

SHAKES. *Rich. III* Give me some little breath, some pause, dear lord, Before I positively speak in this.

– PHRASES: ***bate one's breath***: see BATE *verb*[2] 2. **below one's breath**, **under one's breath** in a whisper. **breath of fresh air** *fig.* someone or something refreshing, a pleasant change. **catch one's breath** stop breathing for a moment in fear, anticipation, etc. **draw breath** breathe, live. **hold one's breath** stop breathing for a short time. **keep one's breath to cool one's porridge** abstain from useless talk. **out of breath** unable to breathe quickly enough after exertion. **save one's breath** (**to cool one's porridge**) = ***keep one's breath to cool one's porridge*** above. ***SHORTNESS of breath***. ***stop the breath of***: see STOP *verb.* **take breath** pause to recover free or easy breathing. **take a person's breath away** make a person breathless with delight, surprise, etc. **the breath of life** *fig.* a necessity. ***under one's breath***: see ***below one's breath*** above. **waste breath** talk in vain. ***yield one's breath***, ***yield up one's breath***: see YIELD *verb.*
– COMB.: **breath consonant** PHONETICS a voiceless (esp. continuant) consonant; **breathtaking** *adjective* that takes one's breath away, surprising, astonishing; **breathtakingly** *adverb* in a breathtaking manner, to a breathtaking extent; **breath test** a test administered to determine the level of alcohol in the breath; **breath-test** *verb trans.* administer a breath test to.
■ **breathed** *adjective* having breath (of a specified kind); ***long-breathed***, long-winded, long-lived: M16. **breathful** *adjective* (now *rare* or *obsolete*) full of breath; having breath, alive; redolent: L16.

breathalyser /ˈbrɛθəlʌɪzə/ *noun.* Also *-**zer**, (proprietary) **Breathalyzer**. M20.
[ORIGIN from BREATH *noun* + ANALYSER.]
An instrument for determining the level of alcohol in the breath. Cf. DRUNKOMETER.
■ **breathalyse** *verb trans.* carry out a test on (a person) using a breathalyser M20.

breatharian /brɛθˈɛːrɪən/ *noun.* L20.
[ORIGIN from BREATH + -ARIAN after *vegetarian*, *fruitarian*, etc.]
A person who believes that it is possible, through meditation, to reach a level of consciousness where one requires no nutrients but those absorbed from the air or sunlight.

breathe /briːð/ *verb.* ME.
[ORIGIN from BREATH.]
▸ **I** *verb intrans.* †**1** Exhale, steam, evaporate. ME–L17.

SHAKES. *Per.* A warmth Breathes out of her.

2 Emit odour, smell. Now only *fig.*, be redolent *of.* LME.

TENNYSON Francis just alighted from the boat, And breathing of the sea.

3 a Exhale air from the lungs. LME. ▸**b** Exhale and inhale, respire. LME.

a YEATS Breathe on the burnished mirror of the world. **b** TENNYSON And answer made King Arthur, breathing hard. *Scientific American* An ostrich breathes about six times a minute.

4 Live, exist. LME.

SHAKES. *Rich. III* Clarence still breathes; Edward still lives and reigns. DISRAELI Within five minutes you will breathe a beggar and an outcast.

5 Take breath; *fig.* pause, take rest. L16.

J. OZELL Orders to give Antony no Time to Breathe, but to pursue him forthwith. TENNYSON Twice they fought, and twice they breathed.

6 Give forth audible breath; speak, sing, be sounded. L16.

MILTON As I wake, sweet music breathes.

7 Of wind etc.: blow softly. E17.

POPE Where cooling vapours breathe along the mead.

8 Of wine, the skin, etc.: have or be affected by contact with air. Of material: admit air or moisture. M20.

A. E. LINDOP I opened a bottle of wine and left it to 'breathe'. N. GOULD Rubber soles . . do not 'breathe'. *Daily Telegraph* We go jogging in trainers which don't allow the feet to breathe.

▸ **II** *verb trans.* **9** Exhale; send *out* as breath; (of a thing) emit; *fig.* infuse *into*, communicate. LME.

W. COWPER Place me where Winter breathes his keenest air. J. MORLEY He breathed new life into them. I. MCEWAN He inhaled . . and breathed smoke across the pots of geraniums.

10 Exercise briskly. Now *spec.* put out of breath, tire. LME.

J. F. COOPER The warriors who had breathed themselves so freely in the preceding struggle.

11 a Utter passionately or vehemently. Also, utter quietly; whisper. M16. ▸**b** Display, evince. M17.

a SPENSER Two knights . . breathing vengeaunce. J. CONRAD Those red lips that almost without moving could breathe enchanting sounds into the world. R. DAVIES 'Looking so alive it is,' Ivor breathed in admiration. **b** A. P. STANLEY The whole period breathes a primitive simplicity.

12 Allow to breathe, rest. L16.

W. S. CHURCHILL Having breathed my horse, for I did not wish to arrive in a flurry.

13 Respire; *esp.* inhale. L16.

L. DEIGHTON Breathing long grassy lungfuls of the wet night air.

14 Let blood from (a vein). *obsolete* exc. *hist.* M17.
15 Give breath to, blow (a wind instrument). E18.
– PHRASES, & WITH ADVERBS & PREPOSITIONS IN SPECIALIZED SENSES: **breathe again** *fig.* recover from fear etc., be at ease after a crisis. **breathe down a person's neck** be close behind a person, esp. in mistrust or pursuit. **breathe freely** *fig.* be at ease. **breathe in** inhale. **breathe one's last** die. **breathe out** exhale. ***breathe short***: see SHORT *adverb.* †**breathe to** aspire to. **breathe upon** *fig.* infect, contaminate, tarnish. **not breathe a word of** keep quite secret.
■ **breathability** *noun* the quality of being breathable M20. **breathable** *adjective* (*a*) fit or agreeable to breathe; (*b*) through which the skin or body can breathe: M18.

breather /ˈbriːðə/ *noun.* LME.
[ORIGIN from BREATHE + -ER[1].]
1 A person who breathes, a living being; a person who speaks or utters. LME.
†**2** A person who or thing which supplies breath; an inspirer. E17–E18.
3 A spell of exercise. Now *rare.* M19.
4 A short rest, a break from exercise etc. E20.

C. DEXTER Strange took a breather, gulped down the last of his coffee.

5 More fully ***breather-pipe*** etc. A vent allowing release of pressure e.g. from the crankcase of an internal-combustion engine. E20.

breathing /ˈbriːðɪŋ/ *noun.* LME.
[ORIGIN from BREATHE + -ING[1].]
1 The action of BREATHE; an instance of this; respiration; a breath. LME.
deep breathing: see DEEP *adjective.*
†**2** Ventilation; a vent. LME–L17.
†**3** Time to rest; respite. L16–L17.
4 = BREATHER 3. Now *rare.* M18.
5 An aspiration, an aspirate; *spec.* (GREEK GRAMMAR) ***rough breathing***, ***smooth breathing***, the signs ʽ and ʼ respectively indicating the presence or absence of aspiration on an initial vowel, diphthong, or rho. M18.
– COMB.: **breathing room**, **breathing space** time or space to breathe, a rest, a period of inactivity.

breathless /ˈbrɛθlɪs/ *adjective*. LME.
[ORIGIN from BREATH + -LESS.]
1 Not breathing; lifeless, dead. LME.
2 Out of breath, panting, breathing with difficulty. (The usual sense.) LME.

J. BANVILLE I was shaky and breathless and my legs felt wobbly.

3 Holding the breath through excitement etc. E19.
4 Unstirred by wind. E19.
■ **breathlessly** *adverb* M19. **breathlessness** *noun* E17.

breathy /ˈbrɛθi/ *adjective*. E16.
[ORIGIN from BREATH + -Y[1].]
1 Of, pertaining to, or of the nature of breath. E16.
2 Of the (singing) voice: having an admixture of the sound of breathing. L19.
■ **breathiness** *noun* L19.

breccia /ˈbrɛtʃə, -tʃɪə/ *noun*. L18.
[ORIGIN Italian = gravel, rubble, cogn. with Old French & mod. French *brèche*, from Germanic base of BREAK *verb*.]
GEOLOGY. Rock consisting of angular fragments cemented together e.g. by lime; an example of this.

brecciate /ˈbrɛtʃɪeɪt/ *verb trans.* L18.
[ORIGIN from BRECCIA + -ATE[3].]
Form into breccia. Chiefly as ***brecciated*** *ppl adjective*.
■ **brecciˈation** *noun* L19.

brecham /ˈbrɛxəm/ *noun*. *Scot.* E16.
[ORIGIN Metath. formed as BARFAM.]
A collar for a draught horse.

Brechtian /ˈbrɛxtɪən, -kt-/ *adjective & noun*. M20.
[ORIGIN from *Brecht* (see below) + -IAN.]
► **A** *adjective*. Of, pertaining to, or characteristic of, the German playwright and poet Bertolt Brecht (1898–1956) or his plays or dramatic technique. M20.
► **B** *noun*. An admirer or student of Brecht or his writing. M20.

breck /brɛk/ *noun*. ME.
[ORIGIN Parallel to BREAK *noun*[1] or directly from BREAK *verb*.]
1 A breach, a tear, a fracture; a blemish. Long *dial.* ME.
2 = BREAK *noun*[1] 5; *spec.* (in *pl.* or as ***Breckland***) the region of heathland around Thetford in Norfolk, England. L18.

bred /brɛd/ *noun*. Long *dial.*
[ORIGIN Old English *bred* = Old High German *bret* (German *Brett*) from Germanic var. of BOARD *noun*.]
A board; a tablet.

bred /brɛd/ *adjective*. ME.
[ORIGIN pa. pple of BREED *verb*.]
1 That has been bred; reared, brought up, trained, esp. in a specified way. ME.

W. GURNALL Paul was a bred scholar.

born and bred, (less commonly) **bred and born**, by birth and upbringing. **bred in the bone** hereditary. ***country-bred***, ***ill-bred***, ***well-bred***, etc.
2 Esp. of an animal: of good breed, of (specified) purity of breed. E18.
half-bred, ***thoroughbred***, etc.

bred *verb pa. t. & pple* of BREED *verb*.

brede /briːd/ *noun*[1]. Now *N. English*.
[ORIGIN Old English *brǣdu* = Old Frisian *brēde*, Old High German *breitī* (German *Breite*), Old Norse *breidd*, Gothic *braidei* from Germanic base of BROAD *adjective*.]
1 Breadth, width. OE.
2 A standard width of fabric; a piece of stuff of the full breadth. LME.

brede /briːd/ *noun*[2]. *arch.* Also †**bread**. M17.
[ORIGIN Var. of BRAID *noun*.]
= BRAID *noun* 4.

brede /briːd/ *verb*[1] *trans. & intrans.* Long *dial.*
[ORIGIN Old English *brǣdan* = Old Saxon *brēdian*, Old High German, German *breiten*, Old Norse *breiða*, Gothic *braidjan*, from Germanic (as BREDE *noun*[1]).]
Broaden; spread out, extend.

†**brede** *verb*[2] *trans.* Also **bread**. LME–L17.
[ORIGIN Var. of BRAID *verb*[1].]
Intertwine, plait, wreathe, twist.

bree /briː/ *noun*[1]. Long *obsolete* exc. *Scot. & N. English*.
[ORIGIN Old English *brǣw* eyelid, Old Frisian *brē*, Old Saxon, Old High German *brāwa* (German *Braue*) eyebrow, Old Norse *brá* eyelash: cf. BRAE. Not allied to BROW *noun*[1].]
†**1** The eyelid. OE–ME.
2 The eyebrow. ME.
†**3** An eyelash. LME–M17.

bree /briː/ *noun*[2]. Long *obsolete* exc. *Scot.*
[ORIGIN Old English *briw*, *brīġ* = Middle Low German, Middle Dutch *brī* (Dutch *brij*), Old High German *brīo* (German *Brei*) from Germanic.]
†**1** A thick pottage made of meal etc. OE–ME.
2 Liquor in which anything has been steeped or boiled, or which flows from it; broth, juice. LME.

breech /briːtʃ/ *noun*. In sense 2c also **britch** /ˈbrɪtʃ/. In sense 1b pl. also pronounced /ˈbrɪtʃɪz/. See also BREEK.
[ORIGIN Old English *brōc*, pl. *brēc*, corresp. to Old Frisian *brōk*, pl. *brēk*, Old Saxon *brōk* (Dutch *broek*), Old High German *bruoh* (German †*Bruch*), Old Norse *brók*, pl. *brœkr*, from Germanic.]
1 †**a** A garment covering the loins and thighs. OE–M17. ►**b** In *pl.* & †*sing.* Short trousers, *esp.* those fastened below the knee, now used esp. for riding or in court costume etc.; knickerbockers; *dial. & colloq.* trousers. Also ***pair of breeches***. ME.
b leather breeches: see LEATHER *noun & adjective*. ***too big for one's breeches***: see BIG *adjective* 3. ***wear the breeches***: see WEAR *verb*[1].
2 The buttocks. *arch.* in *gen.* sense. M16. ►**b** *spec.* The buttocks of a baby at or before birth. Also, a breech presentation or birth. L17. ►**c** The hindquarters of an animal or its skin or fleece. E18.
3 The hinder part of anything; *spec.* the back part of a rifle or gun barrel, the part of a cannon behind the bore. L16.
4 The roe of the cod. Long *dial.* L17.
5 *NAUTICAL*. The external angle of a ship's knee timber etc. M19.
– COMB.: **breech action** the mechanism at the breech of a gun; **breech baby** a baby born in a breech presentation; **breech birth**, **breech delivery**, **breech presentation**, etc.: in which the baby is so positioned in the uterus that its buttocks (or feet) are delivered first; **breechblock** the block in a breech-loading firearm which closes the rear of the bore against the force of the charge; ***breech delivery***: see ***breech birth*** above; **Breeches Bible** the Geneva Bible of 1560 (so named on account of the rendering of *Genesis* 3:7 with *breeches* for *aprons*, although this occurred already in Wyclif); **breeches buoy** a lifebuoy on a rope with a canvas support resembling breeches; **breeches part** a theatrical role in which a woman dresses as a man; **breech-loader**, **breech-loading** *adjective* (a firearm) that is loaded at the breech and not through the muzzle; ***breech presentation***: see ***breech birth*** above.
■ **breechless** *adjective* without breeches, having bare buttocks LME.

breech /briːtʃ, brɪtʃ/ *verb trans.* LME.
[ORIGIN from the noun.]
1 Cover or clothe with, or as with, breeches; *arch.* put (a boy) into breeches instead of petticoats. LME.

R. L. STEVENSON Before he was breeched, he might have clambered on the boxes. *fig.*: SHAKES. *Macb.* Their daggers Unmannerly breech'd with gore.

†**2** Flog. L16–E19.
3 *NAUTICAL*. Secure (a cannon etc.) by a breeching. L16.

breeching /ˈbriːtʃɪŋ, ˈbrɪtʃ-/ *noun*. E16.
[ORIGIN from BREECH *noun*, *verb* + -ING[1].]
1 A strong leather strap passing round the hindquarters of a shaft horse, enabling the horse to push backwards. E16.
†**2** A flogging. E16–E17.
3 *NAUTICAL*. A thick rope used to secure the carriages of cannon etc. and to absorb the force of the recoil. E17.
4 = ***breech action*** s.v. BREECH *noun*. E19.
– COMB.: †**breeching boy**, †**breeching scholar** a young scholar still subject to the birch.

breed /briːd/ *noun*. LME.
[ORIGIN from the verb.]
†**1** Growth. Only in LME.
2 Breeding, birth; lineage; extraction. L15.

G. HERBERT Nothing useth fire, But man alone, to show his heavenly breed. CONAN DOYLE He has breed in him, a real aristocrat of crime.

3 A stock, a strain, a race; a line of descendants perpetuating particular hereditary qualities, *esp.* a stock of animals of a particular species, developed by deliberate selection. M16. ►**b** *gen.* A kind, a species, a set. L16.

SIR W. SCOTT Two dogs of black Saint Hubert's breed. JOHN BROOKE The Hanoverians were a tough breed. **b** D. HALBERSTAM He was of the old breed of reporters, he liked action stories.

lesser breed: see LESSER *adjective*.
4 Offspring; a litter, a brood. Now *dial.* L16.

SHAKES. *Sonn.* Nothing 'gainst Time's scythe can make defence Save breed.

5 A person of mixed descent, a half-breed. Chiefly *N. Amer.* L19.

breed /briːd/ *verb*. Pa. t. & pple **bred** /brɛd/.
[ORIGIN Old English *brēdan* = Old High German *bruotan* (German *brüten*), from West Germanic, from Germanic base of BROOD *noun*.]
1 *verb trans.* Bring (offspring) forward from conception to birth; hatch (young) from the egg; bear, generate, (off-spring). OE.
2 *verb intrans.* **a** Of an animal species: produce young, reproduce. ME. ►**b** Of a woman: be pregnant. E17.
3 *verb trans.* Give rise to; be the source of; engender, develop; produce. ME. ►**b** Produce (fissile material) within a nuclear reactor. Cf. BREEDER 2. M20.

J. BARET Rotten timber breedeth wormes. J. BUCHAN I couldn't leave any clues to breed suspicions. T. S. ELIOT April is the cruellest month, breeding Lilacs out of the dead land. M. L. KING Poverty and ignorance breed crime.

4 *verb intrans.* Come into being or existence; be produced; arise, originate. ME.

BACON Fleas breed principally of Straw or Mats, where there hath been a little moisture. JAS. MILL [He] allowed . . discontents & jealousies to breed in the army.

5 *verb trans.* Promote or control the propagation of, raise, (animals, plants, etc.); develop (a particular breed or kind of animal or plant). LME. ►**b** Put (an animal) *to* another for mating. L19.

J. RAY The manner of breeding Canary-birds. ANTHONY HUXLEY Breeding short-stemmed cereals for ease of combine harvesting.

6 *verb trans.* Bring up from childhood, raise (as); bring up *in* a faith etc., train up *to* a profession, status, etc.; (now *arch. rare*) train, educate (as). Also foll. by *up*. LME.

T. FULLER Sir John Mason was . . bred in All Souls in Oxford. DEFOE Thou talkest as if thou hadst been bred a heathen. SOUTHEY He did not determine upon breeding him either to the Church or the Law. H. T. BUCKLE The old traditions in which they had been bred. D. H. LAWRENCE She was demeaning herself shamefully . . . After all, she had been bred up differently from that.

†**7** *verb trans.* Begin to exhibit naturally (teeth, wings, etc.). M16–M18.
– WITH ADVERBS & PREPOSITIONS IN SPECIALIZED SENSES: **breed in** (usually) mate with or marry near relatives. **breed in and in**: within a limited stock. **breed out** eliminate (a characteristic) by (controlled) breeding.
– COMB.: †**breed-bate** a mischief-maker.
■ **breedy** *adjective* breeding readily, prolific M18.

breeder /ˈbriːdə/ *noun*. M16.
[ORIGIN from BREED *verb* + -ER[1].]
1 A thing which or person who breeds or produces; a person who rears animals etc. M16.
2 A nuclear reactor which can create more fissile material than it uses in the chain reaction. Also ***breeder reactor***. M20.
fast-breeder (reactor): see FAST *adjective*.

breeding /ˈbriːdɪŋ/ *noun*. ME.
[ORIGIN formed as BREEDER + -ING[1].]
1 Bringing to birth; hatching; the production of young, reproduction. ME. ►†**b** Extraction; parentage. L16–E17.
attrib.: ***breeding plumage***, ***breeding season***, etc.
2 Origination; production; development. M16. ►**b** *spec.* The production of fissile material. M20.
3 The rearing and training of the young (formerly *spec.*, education). L16.

S. LEWIS He knew himself to be of a breeding altogether more esthetic and sensitive than Thompson's.

4 The results of training as shown in (good) manners and behaviour. L16.

DISRAELI Her ignorance of all breeding is amusing. C. BLACKWOOD A couple of rough young men with no breeding at all.

good breeding: see GOOD *adjective*. ***ill breeding***: see ILL *adjective & adverb*.
– COMB.: **breeding ground** (*a*) an area of land where an animal, esp. a bird, habitually breeds; (*b*) a thing that favours the development or occurrence of something, esp. something unpleasant (foll. by *for*).

breek /briːk/ *noun*. *dial.* ME.
[ORIGIN Var. of BREECH *noun*.]
Usu. in *pl.* (*sing.* long *rare*). Trousers, breeches.

breeze /briːz/ *noun*[1].
[ORIGIN Old English *briosa*, of unknown origin.]
A gadfly or similar insect. Also ***breeze-fly***.

breeze /briːz/ *noun*[2]. M16.
[ORIGIN Prob. from Old Spanish, Portuguese *briza* (Spanish *brisa*) north-east wind (cf. Italian *brezza*, dial. *brisa* cold wind).]
†**1** A north or north-east wind. M16–E18.
2 The cool onshore wind that blows by day on warm coasts. Also, the offshore wind that blows by night. Now chiefly as ***sea breeze***, ***land breeze*** respectively. E17.
3 Any gentle or light wind; on the Beaufort scale, a wind of 6–50 kph; *NAUTICAL* any wind. E17.
4 *fig. slang.* **a** A disturbance; a row. L18. ►**b** A breath of news; a whisper, a rumour. L19. ►**c** Something that is easy to achieve, handle, etc. Orig. *US*. E20.

c *What Personal Computer* The camera itself is a breeze to use.

– PHRASES: **get the breeze up** *colloq.* = ***get the wind up*** s.v. WIND *noun*[1]. **have the breeze up** *colloq.* = ***have the wind up*** s.v. WIND *noun*[1]. **hit the breeze** *slang* depart. **put the breeze up** *colloq.* = ***put the wind up*** s.v. WIND *noun*[1]. ***shoot the breeze***: see SHOOT *verb*. **split the breeze**, **take the breeze** *slang* = ***hit the breeze*** above.
– COMB.: **breezeway** (chiefly *N. Amer.*) a roofed outdoor passage.
■ **breezeless** *adjective* M18.

breeze /briːz/ *noun*[3]. L16.
[ORIGIN French *braise*, earlier *brese*, burning charcoal, hot embers, etc.]
Small cinders, coke dust, etc., often used with sand and cement to make lightweight building blocks (***breeze blocks***).

breeze /briːz/ *verb intrans.* L17.
[ORIGIN from BREEZE *noun*[2].]
1 Blow gently, as a breeze. *rare*. L17.
2 Move *along*, come *in*, etc., in a lively or offhand manner. *colloq.* (orig. *US*). E20.
– WITH ADVERBS IN SPECIALIZED SENSES: **breeze up** (*a*) *NAUTICAL* (of a wind) freshen; (*b*) (of a noise) rise on the breeze.

B

breezy /ˈbriːzi/ *adjective*. E18.
[ORIGIN from BREEZE *noun*² + -Y¹.]
1 Exposed to breezes, windswept. E18.
2 Attended by breezes; (pleasantly) windy. Also *fig.*, fresh, airy, spirited, jovial; careless. M18.
■ **breezily** *adverb* M19. **breeziness** *noun* M19.

bregma /ˈbrɛgmə/ *noun*. Pl. **-mas**, **-mata** /-mətə/. L16.
[ORIGIN Greek = front of the head.]
ANATOMY. The region of the skull where the frontal and the two parietal bones join.
■ **bregmatic** /brɛgˈmatɪk/ *adjective* M19.

Breguet /ˈbrʌgeɪ/ *noun & adjective*. E19.
[ORIGIN A. L. *Breguet* (1747–1823), French watchmaker.]
(Designating, a timepiece with) a hairspring ending in an overcoil.

Brehon /ˈbriːhən/ *noun*. M16.
[ORIGIN Irish *breitheamhan* genit. pl. of *breitheamh* (in Old Irish *brithem*), from *breith* judgement.]
A judge in ancient Ireland.
– COMB.: **Brehon law** the code of law which prevailed in Ireland before its occupation by the English.

brei /brʌɪ/ *noun*. M20.
[ORIGIN German = pulp, mush, jelly.]
BIOLOGY. A homogenized pulp of organic tissue prepared for experimental work.

brei *verb* var. of BRAY *verb*³.

breithauptite /ˈbrʌɪthaʊptʌɪt/ *noun*. M19.
[ORIGIN from Johann F. A. *Breithaupt* (1791–1873), German mineralogist + -ITE¹.]
MINERALOGY. Nickel antimonide, a hexagonal copper-red mineral with a metallic appearance, usu. occurring in massive form in veins.

breitschwanz /ˈbrʌɪtʃvɑːnts/ *noun*. E20.
[ORIGIN German = broad tail.]
The lustrous pelt of a young karakul lamb.

brekekekex /brɛkəkəˈkɛks/ *noun & interjection*. E17.
[ORIGIN Greek, imit., used by Aristophanes.]
(Repr.) the croaking of frogs (usu. with *coax coax* /kəʊˈaks/).

brekker /ˈbrɛkə/ *noun*. *colloq.* (orig. *Univ. slang*). L19.
[ORIGIN from BREAK(FAST *noun* + -ER⁶.]
Breakfast.

brekkie /ˈbrɛki/ *noun*. *slang*. Also **-y**. E20.
[ORIGIN from BREAK(FAST *noun* + -Y⁶.]
Breakfast.

breloque /brəˈləʊk/ *noun*. M19.
[ORIGIN French.]
A small ornament fastened to a watch chain; a trinket.

breme /briːm/ *adjective*. Now *arch.* & *dial.* Also **brim** /brɪm/. ME.
[ORIGIN Unknown.]
1 Fierce, stern, raging, furious. Long *obsolete* in *gen.* sense. ME.
2 *spec.* Of the sea, wind, etc.: rough, stormy, raging, severe. ME.

bremsstrahlung /ˈbrɛmzʃtrɑːlʊŋ/ *noun*. M20.
[ORIGIN German, from *bremsen* to brake + *Strahlung* radiation.]
PHYSICS. Electromagnetic radiation emitted by a charged particle upon retardation by an electric field (esp. by that of a nucleus).
thermal bremsstrahlung: see THERMAL *adjective*.

Bren /brɛn/ *noun*. M20.
[ORIGIN from *Brno* in the Czech Republic (where orig. made) + *Enfield* (see ENFIELD where later made).]
In full *Bren gun*. A kind of light quick-firing machine gun.

brennage /ˈbrɛnɪdʒ/ *noun*. M18.
[ORIGIN Old French *brenage*, from *bren* BRAN + -AGE, or medieval Latin *brennagium*.]
hist. A payment in, or in lieu of, bran, made by tenants to feed their lord's hounds.

brent /brɛnt/ *noun*. Also ***brant** /brant/. LME.
[ORIGIN Unknown.]
In full ***brent goose***. A small black, grey, and white goose, *Branta bernicla*, which breeds in the Arctic and visits Britain in winter.
– NOTE: By early writers often confused with the barnacle goose.

brent *adjective & adverb* var. of BRANT *adjective & adverb*.

brent *verb pa. t. & pple*: see BURN *verb*.

brer /brɛː, brəː/ *noun*. *colloq.* (orig. *US*). L19.
[ORIGIN Repr. a Black or southern US pronunc. of BROTHER *noun*.]
Brother.

brerd /brəːd/ *noun*. Long *obsolete* exc. *dial.* See also BRAIRD.
[ORIGIN Old English *brerd*: cf. Old High German *brort*, *brord* prow, margin, lip.]
The topmost surface or edge; the brim.

bresaola /brɛˈsaʊlə/ *noun*. M20.
[ORIGIN Italian, from *bresada* past part. of *brasare*, from French *braiser* BRAISE.]
An Italian dish of raw beef cured by salting and air-drying, usu. served with an olive oil, lemon juice, and pepper dressing.

bressumer *noun* var. of BREASTSUMMER.

bret /brɛt/ *noun*. See also BRAT *noun*³. LME.
[ORIGIN Unknown.]
†1 A brill, a turbot. LME–M19.
2 = BRIT *noun*². E18.

bretelle /brəˈtɛl/ *noun*. M19.
[ORIGIN French = strap, sling, (in pl.) trouser braces.]
Each of a pair of ornamental straps extending over the shoulders from the belt on the front of a dress to the belt on the back. Usu. in *pl.*

bretessy /ˈbrɛtəsi/ *adjective*. L16.
[ORIGIN French *bretessé* bratticed: see -Y⁵.]
HERALDRY. Embattled on both sides with the battlements at the same points on each edge. Cf. COUNTER-EMBATTLED.
■ Also **bretessed** *adjective* E19.

brethren *noun pl.* see BROTHER *noun*.

Breton /ˈbrɛt(ə)n/ *noun & adjective*. LME.
[ORIGIN Old French: see BRITON.]
▸ **A** *noun*. A native or inhabitant of Brittany in NW France; the Celtic language of Brittany. LME.
▸ **B** *attrib.* or as *adjective*. Belonging to, or characteristic of Brittany, its inhabitants, or their language. L15.
Breton hat a type of hat with a round crown and an upward-curved brim. ***Breton lai***: see LAI *noun*¹. †**Breton tackle** = BURTON *noun*¹ 1.

Brett *noun* var. of BRIT *noun*¹ & *adjective*¹.

Bretwalda /brɛtˈwɔːldə/ *noun*.
[ORIGIN Old English *Bretwalda*, varying with *Brytenwalda*, from *Brettas* (see BRIT *noun*¹ & *adjective*¹), *Bryten* (see BRITAIN *noun*¹) + Germanic base of WIELD *verb*.]
Lord of the Britons, lord of Britain: a title given in the Anglo-Saxon Chronicle to King Egbert, and (retrospectively) to some earlier Anglo-Saxon kings, and occas. assumed by later ones.

bretzel *noun* see PRETZEL.

breve /briːv/ *noun*. ME.
[ORIGIN Var. of BRIEF *noun*¹.]
1 *hist.* An authoritative letter, esp. from a pope or monarch. ME.
2 MUSIC. A note of the value of two semibreves (now rarely used). LME.
†3 GRAMMAR. A short syllable. *rare*. M16–M18.
4 The mark ˘ written or printed over a short or unstressed vowel, or as a diacritic over various letters in certain languages. L19.

brevet /ˈbrɛvɪt/ *noun & verb*. LME.
[ORIGIN Old French & mod. French, formed as BRIEF *noun*¹ + -ET¹.]
▸ **A** *noun*. †1 An official letter; *esp.* a papal indulgence. LME–M18.
2 A document from a monarch or government conferring privileges; *spec.* one conferring nominal military rank without corresponding pay. Freq. *attrib.* L17.
– COMB.: **brevet captain**, **brevet colonel**, etc., **brevet rank** a nominal rank (of captain, colonel, etc.) conferred by a brevet.
▸ **B** *verb trans.* Confer a brevet rank on. M19.

breviary /ˈbriːvɪəri/ *noun*. LME.
[ORIGIN Latin *breviarium* summary, abridgement, from *breviare*: see ABBREVIATE *verb*, -ARY¹.]
1 CHRISTIAN CHURCH. A book containing the service for each day, to be recited by those in orders. In early use also, an abridged version of the psalms. LME.
matter of breviary an accepted truth.
†2 *gen.* A brief statement, a summary. M16–E19.

†**breviate** *noun & ppl adjective*. LME.
[ORIGIN Latin *breviatus* pa. pple of *breviare*: see ABBREVIATE *verb*, -ATE².]
▸ **A** *noun*. 1 A letter, a short note. LME–M18.
2 A summary, an abridgement. E16–M19.
3 A lawyer's brief. L16–M18.
▸ **B** *ppl adjective*. Shortened, abbreviated. E16–M17.

†**breviator** *noun*. M16–M18.
[ORIGIN Latin *breviator*, from *breviare*: see ABBREVIATE *verb*, -ATOR.]
= ABBREVIATOR.

brevier /brɪˈvɪə/ *noun*. L16.
[ORIGIN Dutch or German, from medieval Latin use of Latin *breviarium* BREVIARY (perhaps from its use in the printing of breviaries).]
A former size of type between bourgeois and minion.

breviloquence /brɪˈvɪləkw(ə)ns/ *noun*. *rare*. M17.
[ORIGIN Latin *breviloquentia*, from *brevis* BRIEF *adjective*, short, + *loquentia* speaking.]
Brevity of speech.

brevi manu /ˌbrɛvɪ ˈmɑːnuː/ *adverbial phr.* E19.
[ORIGIN Latin, lit. 'with short hand'.]
LAW. Summarily; without due process.

brevit /ˈbrɛvɪt/ *verb intrans.* Long *obsolete* exc. *dial.* E17.
[ORIGIN Unknown.]
Forage; beat about for game; hunt; search.

brevity /ˈbrɛvɪti/ *noun*. L15.
[ORIGIN Old French *br(i)eveté* (earlier *br(i)eté*) from Latin *brevitat-*, from *brevis* (forms with *-i-* after Old French *brief*): see BRIEF *adjective* & *adverb*, -ITY.]
1 Compact written or spoken expression; conciseness; an instance of this. L15.
2 Short span, esp. of time, life, etc. M16.

brew /bruː/ *noun*¹. E16.
[ORIGIN from the verb.]
The process or result of brewing; the amount brewed at one time; (the quality of) what is brewed; an infusion, a concoction.

brew *noun*² var. of BUROO.

brew /bruː/ *verb*.
[ORIGIN Old English *brēowan* = Old Saxon *breuwan* (Dutch *brouwen*), Old High German *briuwan*, *brūwan* (German *brauen*), Old Norse *brugga*, from Germanic.]
1 *verb trans.* **a** Make (beer etc., a quantity of beer etc.) by infusion, boiling, and fermentation. OE. ▸**b** Make (tea etc., a quantity of tea etc.) by infusion or mixture. Also foll. by *up*. E17.
2 *verb intrans.* **a** Make beer etc. ME. ▸**b** Foll. by *up*: make tea. *colloq.* E20.
3 *verb trans.* Concoct, contrive, bring about, set in train, (usu. evil or mischief). ME.

> TOLKIEN We saw a cloud of smoke and steam . . . We feared that Saruman was brewing some new devilry for us.

4 *verb intrans.* Undergo infusion, fermentation, etc.; be in the course of preparation; (esp. of evil or mischief) mature, fester, gather force. ME.

> A. UTTLEY He knew when a storm was brewing. J. MASTERS So this strike is brewing, and I'm trying to find out what is known about it here.

5 *verb trans.* Convert (malt etc., a quantity of malt etc.) into fermented liquor. Now *arch.* & *dial.* LME.
†6 *verb trans.* Mix (liquors); dilute. E16–M17.
– COMB.: **brewhouse** a brewery; **brewmaster** a person who supervises the brewing process in a brewery; **brewpub** a public house, typically including a restaurant, selling beer brewed on the premises; **brew-up** *colloq.* (a pause for) the making of tea.
■ **brewing** *noun* (**a**) the action of the verb; (**b**) the amount of liquor brewed at one time: ME.

brewage /ˈbruːɪdʒ/ *noun*. M16.
[ORIGIN from BREW *verb* + -AGE, prob. after French *breuvage* BEVERAGE.]
The process of brewing; a brew, a decoction; a concocted drink.

brewer /ˈbruːə/ *noun*. ME.
[ORIGIN from BREW *verb* + -ER¹.]
1 A person who brews; *spec.* a person whose trade is the brewing of beer etc. ME.
brewer's yeast a yeast, *Saccharomyces cerevisiae*, which is used in the brewing of top-fermenting beer and is also eaten as a source of vitamin B.
2 *fig.* A concocter or contriver *of*. M16.

brewery /ˈbrʊəri/ *noun*. M17.
[ORIGIN formed as BREWER + -ERY, prob. after Dutch *brouwerij*.]
1 A place or establishment for brewing. M17.
†2 The process or trade of brewing. Only in 18.

brewis /ˈbruːɪs/ *noun*. *obsolete* exc. *dial.* Also **browis** /ˈbraʊɪs/. See also BROSE. ME.
[ORIGIN Old French *bro(u)ez*, *-ets* pl., *bro(u)et* sing. (mod. *brouet*), from *breu* = Provençal *bro*, from Proto-Romance from Germanic (= BROTH).]
1 Bread soaked in fat or dripping. ME.
2 A kind of broth, freq. thickened with bread or meal. E16.
3 = BROSE. *rare*. M19.

brewski /ˈbruːski/ *noun*. Pl. **-is**, **-ies**. *N. Amer. colloq.* L20.
[ORIGIN Fanciful formation from BREW *noun*¹ + *-ski* final elem. in many Slavonic names.]
A beer.

> S. TUROW He has . . a wife to set him straight whenever he's had a brewski too many.

brewster /ˈbruːstə/ *noun*¹. Chiefly *Scot.* & *N. English*. Also †**browster**. ME.
[ORIGIN from BREW *verb* + -STER: cf. BAXTER.]
A brewer, orig. *spec.* a female brewer.
– COMB.: **Brewster Sessions** magistrates' sessions for the issue of licences to permit trade in alcoholic liquors.

Brewster /ˈbruːstə/ *noun*². L19.
[ORIGIN Sir David *Brewster* (1781–1868), Scot. physicist.]
Used **attrib.** and in **possess.** with ref. to Brewster's discoveries in optics.
Brewster angle, **Brewster's angle** the angle of incidence at the surface of a dielectric for which a wave polarized in the plane of incidence is not reflected at all, and an unpolarized wave is reflected as a plane-polarized wave. **Brewster's law**: that the tangent of the Brewster angle for a given medium is equal to the refractive index of that medium, or (at any interface) equals the ratio of the refractive indices of the media on either side.

brewsterite /ˈbruːstərʌɪt/ *noun*. M19.
[ORIGIN formed as BREWSTER *noun*² + -ITE¹.]
MINERALOGY. A naturally occurring zeolite which is a hydrated silicate of aluminium, barium, and strontium.

brey *verb* var. of BRAY *verb*³.

briar /ˈbrʌɪə/ *noun*[1]. Also **brier**.
[ORIGIN Old English (Anglian) *brēr*, (West Saxon) *brǣr*, of unknown origin.]
1 A prickly bush, esp. of a wild rose. OE.
Austrian briar an orange-yellow rose, *Rosa foetida*, with an unpleasant scent. **green briar** a vine of the genus *Smilax* of the lily family, esp. *S. rotundifolia*. **sensitive briar** an ornamental leguminous plant of the genus *Schrankia*, with pink or purple flowers and sensitive leaves. **sweet briar** any of several roses with fragrant-smelling leaves; esp. *Rosa rubiginosa*, a rose with deep pink flowers that is often cultivated; also called ***eglantine***.
2 A branch or twig of a wild rose etc. ME.
3 Prickly bushes collectively. LME.
4 *fig.* In *pl.* Troubles, vexations. *arch.* E16.
– COMB.: **briar rose** a dogrose.
■ **briared** *adjective* covered or overgrown with briars; entangled in briars: M16. **briary** *adjective* full of or consisting of thorns or briars; thorny; vexatious: ME.

briar /ˈbrʌɪə/ *noun*[2]. Also **brier**. M19.
[ORIGIN French *bruyère* heath, ult. from Gaulish: assim. to BRIAR *noun*[1].]
1 A southern European shrub or small tree, *Erica arborea*, whose root is used for making tobacco pipes. Also called ***tree heath***. M19.
2 A pipe made of the wood of the briar. L19.

Briard /brɪˈɑːd, *foreign* briaːr (*pl. same*)/ *noun*. M20.
[ORIGIN French (adjective), from BRIE: see -ARD.]
A sheepdog of a French breed.

Briareus /brʌɪˈɛːrɪəs/ *noun*. *literary*. E17.
[ORIGIN Greek *Briareōs*, one of three mythological giants who aided Zeus against the Titans.]
A hundred-armed giant.
■ **Briarean** *adjective & noun* (belonging to or characteristic of) a Briareus: L16.

bribable /ˈbrʌɪbəb(ə)l/ *adjective*. Also **bribeable**. E19.
[ORIGIN from BRIBE *verb* + -ABLE. Earlier in UNBRIBABLE.]
Able to be bribed, corrupt.
■ **bribaˈbility** *noun* M19.

bribe /brʌɪb/ *noun*. LME.
[ORIGIN from the verb.]
†**1** A stolen article; theft; plunder. LME–E16.
2 A sum of money or another reward offered or demanded in order to procure an (often illegal or dishonest) action or decision in favour of the giver. LME.

bribe /brʌɪb/ *verb*. LME.
[ORIGIN Old French *briber*, *brimber* beg, of unknown origin.]
▸ **I** *verb trans.* †**1** Take dishonestly; purloin; rob; extort. LME–M17.
2 Offer or give a bribe to; persuade by means of a bribe (*to do something*); win over by some inducement. E16.
B. MALAMUD He had money, bribed the guards for favours. C. ISHERWOOD I am bribed with fruit not to be tiresome about the English language.
3 Purchase or obtain by bribery. *arch.* E18.
SWIFT To bribe the judge's vote.
▸ **II** *verb intrans.* †**4** Steal; extort. LME–M16.
5 Practise bribery. M17.
LD MACAULAY He fawned, bullied, and bribed indefatigably.
■ **briˈbee** *noun* the recipient of a bribe M19.

bribeable *adjective* var. of BRIBABLE.

briber /ˈbrʌɪbə/ *noun*. LME.
[ORIGIN Partly from Anglo-Norman *bribour*, Old French *bribeur*, *brimbeur* beggar, vagabond, formed as BRIBE *verb*; partly from BRIBE *verb*: see -ER[1].]
†**1** A thief; an extortioner; a person who takes or exacts bribes. LME–E17.
†**2** A beggar or vagrant; a wretch. LME–L16.
3 A person who offers or gives a bribe. L16.
†**4** A bribe, a price paid. *rare* (Shakes.). Only in E17.

bribery /ˈbrʌɪb(ə)ri/ *noun*. LME.
[ORIGIN Old French *briberie*, *brimberie* mendicancy, formed as BRIBE *verb*: see -ERY.]
†**1** Theft, robbery; taking by force, extortion. LME–L16.
2 The exaction or acceptance of a bribe. *arch.* M16.
3 The giving or offering of a bribe. L16.

bric-a-brac /ˈbrɪkəbrak/ *noun*. Also **bric-à-brac**. M19.
[ORIGIN French *bric-à-brac*, from †*à bric et à brac* at random.]
Miscellaneous old ornaments, trinkets, small pieces of furniture, etc; antiquarian knick-knacks.

brick /brɪk/ *noun & adjective*. LME.
[ORIGIN Middle Low German, Middle Dutch *bricke*, *brike*, Dutch dial. *brik*, Western Flemish *brijke*; prob. reinforced by Old French & mod. French *brique*, from same source: ult. origin unknown.]
▸ **A** *noun*. **1** Clay kneaded, moulded, and baked or sun-dried, used as a building material. LME.
GIBBON He had found his capital of brick, and . . left it of marble.
2 A small usu. rectangular block of this substance. Also, a similarly shaped block of concrete or other building material. E16. ▸**b** A child's toy building block. M19.
P. S. BUCK The kitchen was made of earthen bricks . . , great squares of earth dug from their own fields.
3 A loaf, block of tea, or other food item formed like a brick. Now *esp.* an ice-cream block. M18.
4 A stalwart, loyal, or generous person. *colloq.* M19.
W. H. AUDEN When he is well She gives him hell, But she's a brick When he is sick.
5 A dull orange-red colour characteristic of brick. L19.
– PHRASES ETC.: **bricks and mortar** (*a*) buildings, esp. houses as property; (*b*) used to designate a business that operates conventionally rather than (or as well as) over the Internet. **drop a brick** *slang* say something indiscreet. ***gold brick***: see GOLD *noun*[1] & *adjective*. ***hit the bricks***: see HIT *verb*. ***like a cat on hot bricks***: see HOT *adjective*. **like a load of bricks**, **like a ton of bricks** *slang* with crushing weight or force. ***make bricks without straw***: see STRAW *noun*. ***redbrick***: see RED *noun*. ***shit a brick***, ***shit bricks***: see SHIT *verb*.
– COMB.: **brickbat** a piece of brick, *esp.* one used as a missile; *fig.* an uncomplimentary remark; **brick dust** (the colour of) powdered brick; **brick-earth** clay used for making bricks; **brick field** a piece of ground in which bricks are made; **brickfielder** *Austral.* a hot dry northerly wind (orig. as raising dust); **brick kiln**: for baking bricks; **bricklayer** a worker building with bricks; **bricklaying** the craft or occupation of building with bricks; **brickmaker** a person whose trade is the making of bricks; ***brick-nogging***: see NOGGING 1; **brick red** *adjective & noun* (of) a dull orange-red colour; **brick-stitch** EMBROIDERY couching in which the laid threads are secured by cross stitches arranged like the vertical joints of brickwork; **brickwork** (*a*) builder's work in brick; (*b*) in *pl.*, a factory making bricks; **brickyard** a place where bricks are made.
▸ **B** *attrib.* or as *adjective*. Built of brick. Also, brick-red. LME.
bang one's head against a brick wall, ***knock one's head against a brick wall***, ***run one's head against a brick wall***, ***see through a brick wall***, ***talk to a brick wall***: see WALL *noun*[1].
■ **brickish** *adjective* resembling a brick in appearance or colour, bricky; *colloq.* stalwart, loyal, generous: M19.

brick /brɪk/ *verb*. L16.
[ORIGIN from the noun.]
1 *verb trans.* Cover or seal (a window, opening, etc.) *up* or *over* with bricks; close *in* with bricks. L16.
2 *verb trans.* Make, line, or face with brick; give the appearance of brickwork to. L17.
3 *verb intrans.* Work with or make bricks. L18.

brickie /ˈbrɪki/ *noun*. *colloq.* Also **bricky**. L19.
[ORIGIN from BRICK *noun* + -IE, -Y[6].]
A bricklayer.

brickle *adjective* see BRUCKLE.

bricky *noun* var. of BRICKIE.

bricky /ˈbrɪki/ *adjective*. L16.
[ORIGIN from BRICK *noun* + -Y[1].]
Made of or having many bricks. Also, brick-red.

bricolage /brɪkəˈlɑːʒ; *foreign* brikɔlaːʒ (*pl. same*)/ *noun*. M20.
[ORIGIN French, from *bricoler* do odd jobs, repair, formed as BRICOLE: see -AGE.]
Construction or creation from whatever is immediately available for use; something constructed or created in this way, an assemblage of haphazard or incongruous elements.

bricole /ˈbrɪk(ə)l, brɪˈkəʊl/ *noun*. E16.
[ORIGIN Old French & mod. French from Provençal *bricola* or Italian *briccola*, of unknown origin.]
1 An engine or catapult for discharging stones or bolts. *obsolete* exc. *hist.* E16.
2 A rebound of the ball from a side wall or cushion in real tennis, billiards, etc. L16.

bricoleur /brɪkəˈləː; *foreign* brikɔlœːr (*pl. same*)/ *noun*. M20.
[ORIGIN French = handyman, from *bricoler* (see BRICOLAGE) + -*eur* -OR.]
A person who engages in bricolage; a constructor or creator of bricolages.

bridal /ˈbrʌɪd(ə)l/ *noun & adjective*.
[ORIGIN Old English *brȳd-ealu*, formed as BRIDE *noun*[1] + ALE: use and pronunc. strongly infl. by assoc. with adjectives in -AL[1].]
▸ **A** *noun sing.* & in *pl.* A wedding; a nuptial feast. *arch.* OE.
▸ **B** *adjective*. Of, pertaining to, or appropriate to a wedding or a bride. LME.
bridal suite in a hotel, a suite of rooms esp. for the use of a newly married couple. **bridal wreath** any of certain white-flowered ornamental plants; *esp.* a Chilean pink- or white-flowered plant, *Francoa sonchifolia*, of the saxifrage family (also called ***maiden's wreath***).
■ **bridally** *adverb* M19. **bridalty** *noun* (*rare*) a wedding M17.

bride /brʌɪd/ *noun*[1].
[ORIGIN Old English *brȳd* = Old Frisian *brēd*, *breid*, Old Saxon *brūd* (Dutch *bruid*), Old High German *brūt* (German *Braut*), Old Norse *brúðr*, Gothic *brūþs*, from Germanic, of unknown origin.]
1 A woman about to be married or very recently married. OE.
mourning bride: see MOURNING *adjective*.
2 A bridegroom. Long *obsolete* exc. *Jamaican*. LME.
– COMB. (orig. with the sense 'wedding'): **bride-ale** [the analytical form of BRIDAL *noun*] *hist.* a wedding celebration with drinking of ale, a wedding feast; **bride-bed** *arch.* the marriage bed; **bride-cake** (*a*) wedding cake; **bride-chamber** *arch.* the room in which a wedding is celebrated; **bride-cup** (*a*) a bowl or cup handed round at a wedding; (*b*) a spiced drink prepared at night for a newly wedded pair; **bride-lace** (*obsolete* exc. *hist.*) a coloured ribbon worn at a wedding; **bridemaid** (now *rare* or *obsolete*) = BRIDESMAID; **brideman** †(*a*) = BRIDEGROOM; (*b*) (*obsolete* exc. *dial.*) = BRIDESMAN; **bride price** ANTHROPOLOGY a payment of money or goods made to a bride or her parents by the bridegroom or his parents.

bride /brʌɪd/ *noun*[2]. ME.
[ORIGIN Old French & mod. French = bridle, bonnet string, ult. from Germanic base also of BRIDLE *noun*.]
†**1** A bridle, a rein. Only in ME.
2 A link in the network which connects the patterns in lace. Also, a bonnet string. Usu. in *pl.* M19.

bride /brʌɪd/ *verb*. M16.
[ORIGIN from BRIDE *noun*[1].]
†**1** *verb intrans. & trans.* (with *it*). Act the bride. M16–M17.
2 *verb trans.* Wed, marry. *obsolete* exc. *dial.* L16.

bridegroom /ˈbrʌɪdgruːm/ *noun*.
[ORIGIN Old English *brȳdguma* = Old Saxon *brudigomo* (Dutch *bruidegom*), Old High German *brūtigomo* (German *Bräutigam*), Old Norse *brúðgumi*: the 2nd elem. Old English *guma* man, assim. to GROOM *noun*[1].]
A man about to be married or very recently married.

bridesmaid /ˈbrʌɪdzmeɪd/ *noun*. L18.
[ORIGIN Alt. of earlier ***bridemaid*** s.v. BRIDE *noun*[1].]
A girl or unmarried woman (usu. one of several) attending the bride at a wedding.

bridesman /ˈbrʌɪdzmən/ *noun*. Pl. **-men**. E19.
[ORIGIN Alt. of earlier ***brideman*** s.v. BRIDE *noun*[1].]
The best man (the usual term) at a wedding, a groomsman.

bridewell /ˈbrʌɪdw(ə)l/ *noun*. *arch.* Also **B-**. M16.
[ORIGIN from (St) *Bride's Well* in the City of London, near which such a building stood.]
A prison, a reformatory.

bridge /brɪdʒ/ *noun*[1]. Also (*Scot. & N. English*) **brig** /brɪg/.
[ORIGIN Old English *brycg* = Old Frisian *brigge*, *bregge*, Old Saxon *bruggia*, Middle Dutch *brugghe* (Dutch *brug*), Old High German *brucca* (German *Brücke*), Old Norse *bryggja* (whence north. dial. *brig*), from Germanic.]
1 A structure carrying a road, path, railway, etc., across a stream, river, ravine, road, railway, etc. OE.
Bailey bridge, ***bascule bridge***, ***cantilever bridge***, ***drawbridge***, ***footbridge***, ***humpback bridge***, ***overbridge***, ***suspension bridge***, ***swing bridge***, ***toll bridge***, ***transporter bridge***, ***underbridge***, etc. ***asses' bridge***: see ASS *noun*[1] 2. **bridge-and-tunnel** *adjective* (*US colloq.*) (of a person) living in the suburbs and perceived as unsophisticated. **bridge of boats**: formed by boats moored abreast over a body of water. **a bridge too far** [title of a film (1977) about the World War Two Arnhem operation, from a contemporary warning about the operation] a step or act that is perceived as being too drastic. ***burn one's bridges***: see BURN *verb* 8. **cross a bridge when one comes to it** deal with a problem when and if it arises. **gold bridge**, **silver bridge** an easy and attractive escape route for an enemy. ***water under the bridge***: see WATER *noun*. ***weighbridge***: see WEIGH *verb*.
2 A gangway for a boat; a landing stage, a jetty, a pier. *obsolete* exc. *dial.* ME.
3 The upper bony part of the nose; the central part of a pair of spectacles, fitting over this. LME.
4 The upright piece over which the strings of a violin etc. are stretched. LME.
5 A ridge of rock, sand, or shingle, projecting into or crossing a body of water. (See also ***land bridge*** s.v. LAND *noun*[1].) Chiefly *dial.* or in names, as ***Filey Brig***. E19.
6 The raised platform or compartment, usu. amidships, from which a ship is directed. M19.
7 BILLIARDS & SNOOKER etc. The support for the cue formed by the hand or at the end of a rest; occas., a rest. L19.
8 An electric circuit for measuring resistance or another property by equalizing the potential at two points. L19.
post-office bridge, ***Wheatstone bridge***, etc.
9 DENTISTRY. A partial denture supported by natural teeth on either side. L19.
– COMB.: **bridge-bote** *hist.* a tax for the repair of bridges; **bridge-building** *fig.* the promotion of friendly relations, esp. between countries; **bridge circuit** = sense 8 above; **bridge-deck** = sense 6 above; **bridgehead** a position held on the opposite side of a river etc. in advance of one's main forces; *fig.* an initial position established beyond some dividing feature, as a basis for further advance. **bridge-house** *hist.* a house connected with a bridge; *spec.* the establishment formerly concerned with the care and repair of London Bridge; **bridge-man**, **bridgemaster** an officer having control of a bridge (formerly, in some boroughs, a member of the corporation); **bridge passage** a transitional passage in a musical or literary composition; **bridgeward** *hist.* the keeper or warden of a bridge; **bridgework** (the insertion of) a dental bridge.
■ **bridgeless** *adjective* E19.

bridge /brɪdʒ/ *noun*[2]. L19.
[ORIGIN Prob. of eastern Mediterranean origin.]
A card game derived from whist, in which one player's cards are exposed at a certain point and are thereafter played by his or her partner; now usu. = ***contract bridge*** below.
auction bridge: in which the players bid for the right to name trumps, and all tricks won count towards game whether contracted for or not. **contract bridge**: in which the players bid for the right to name trumps, and tricks won count towards game only if contracted for. ***duplicate bridge***: see DUPLICATE *adjective*.
– COMB.: **bridge roll** a small soft bread roll.

bridge /brɪdʒ/ *verb trans.*
[ORIGIN Old English *brycgian*, from BRIDGE *noun*[1].]
1 Be or make a bridge over. OE. ▸**b** Span as with a bridge. M19.

B

P. MATTHIESSEN A canal bridged here and there by ten-foot granite slabs. **b** M. TWAIN A speculator bridged a couple of barrels with a board. *fig.*: B. C. BRODIE To bridge over the space which separates the known from the unknown.

b *bridge a gap*: see GAP *noun*.

2 Form (a way) by means of a bridge. *rare*. **M17.**

■ **bridgeable** *adjective* **M19.** **bridging** *verbal noun* (*a*) the action of the verb; (*b*) MOUNTAINEERING a method of climbing chimneys etc. with legs astride: **LME.** **bridging** *ppl adjective* that bridges something; *bridging loan*, a loan made to cover the short interval between buying a house etc. and selling another: **E19.**

Bridgettine /ˈbrɪdʒətɪn/ *noun & adjective*. **M16.**
[ORIGIN medieval Latin *Brigittinus* adjective, from *Brigitta* of Sweden (St Bridget), 1303–73: see -INE[1].]
(A member, usu. a nun) of a religious order founded by St Bridget.

bridie /ˈbrʌɪdi/ *noun*. *Scot*. **L19.**
[ORIGIN Perh. from obsolete *bride's pie*, a large pie traditionally baked by a bride's family or friends for wedding guests.]
A pasty filled with mince and onions in gravy.

bridle /ˈbrʌɪd(ə)l/ *noun*.
[ORIGIN Old English *bridel* = Old Frisian *bridel*, Middle Dutch & mod. Dutch *breidel*, Old High German *brittil*, from West Germanic, from Germanic base of BRAID *verb*[1]: see -LE[1].]
1 The gear by which a horse etc. is controlled and guided, comprising headstall, bit, and rein. **OE.**
double bridle, *draw bridle*, *snaffle bridle*, etc. *turn bridle*: see TURN *verb*.
2 *fig.* A restraint, a curb. **ME.**

BACON The reverence of a mans self is, next religion, the chiefest Bridle of all Vices. J. A. FROUDE He kept his tongue under a bridle.

3 A securing rope or cord etc. Chiefly NAUTICAL: (*a*) a loop of rope etc. attached to a spar etc., by which a line can be attached; (*b*) the end part of a fixed mooring, which can be secured to a vessel. **ME.**
4 = BRANKS 1. Also *scold's bridle*. **E17.**
5 A ligament or membrane restricting the motion of a bodily part. **L17.**
6 The action or gesture of bridling (BRIDLE *verb* 2). **M18.**
– COMB.: **bridle-hand** the hand which holds the bridle in riding; **bridle path**, **bridle road**, **bridleway**: a thoroughfare fit for riders but not vehicles; **bridle rein** a rein attached to the bit of a bridle; **bridle-wise** *adjective* (*US*) (of a horse) readily guided by a touch of the bridle.
■ **bridleless** /-l-l-/ *adjective* **LME.**

bridle /ˈbrʌɪd(ə)l/ *verb*.
[ORIGIN Old English *bridlian*, from BRIDLE *noun*.]
1 *verb trans.* Put a bridle on, equip with a bridle; *fig.* curb, check, restrain, hold *in*. **OE.**

D. HUME Forts were erected in order to bridle Rochelle. F. M. FORD A sudden explosion of the passion that had been bridled all his life.

2 a *verb intrans.* Express offence, wounded pride, etc., by throwing up the head and drawing in the chin; assume a dignified or offended manner. Also foll. by *up*. **LME.** ▸†**b** *verb trans.* Move (the head etc., oneself) thus. **L15–M19.**

a DICKENS Everybody bridled up at this remark. B. CHATWIN If she saw him bridling with annoyance, she would change the subject.

■ **bridler** *noun* **L16.**

bridoon /brɪˈduːn/ *noun*. Also **bradoon** /brəˈduːn/. **M18.**
[ORIGIN French *bridon*, formed as BRIDE *noun*[2]: see -OON.]
The snaffle in a double bridle.

Brie /briː/ *noun*. Also **b-**. **M19.**
[ORIGIN An agricultural district in northern France.]
A soft creamy cheese with a white mould skin, orig. and esp. made in Brie.

brief /briːf/ *noun*[1]. See also BREVE, BRIEVE. **ME.**
[ORIGIN Anglo-Norman *bref*, Old French *brief*, from late Latin *breve* dispatch, note, use as noun of neut. of Latin *brevis*: see BRIEF *adjective & adverb*.]
1 *hist.* An official or legal letter of authority; a royal mandate; a writ, a summons. **ME.** ▸**b** Letters patent issued by the British monarch as Governor of the Church of England, licensing a collection in churches for a specific object of charity. **L16.**
2 A disciplinary letter from the Pope to an individual or community (less formal than a *bull*). **LME.**
†**3** *gen.* A letter, a dispatch, a note; writing, something written. **LME–L18.**
†**4** MUSIC. A short note; a breve. **LME–M17.**
5 A short account or summary, a synopsis. Now *US* (exc. as below). **M16.**
6 A list, a catalogue, etc. *arch.* **L16.**
7 LAW. A summary of the facts and legal points in a case, drawn up for a barrister to argue in court and usu. stating the fee payable; a piece of work for a barrister; *US* LAW a written statement of the arguments for a case. **M17.** ▸**b** *gen.* A set or summary of instructions etc.; an appointed task; *esp.* a set of instructions for carrying out a military operation. **M19.** ▸**c** A legal representative; a lawyer, solicitor, or barrister. *colloq.* **M20.**

b D. JACOBSON My special brief was to take care of the political prisoners. *Times* [He] rounds on the . . Authority for exceeding its brief. JO GRIMOND A minister opening a debate must speak from a prepared brief.

dock brief: see DOCK *noun*[4]. **hold a brief for** be retained as counsel for; *fig.* wish or be obliged to argue in favour of (usu. in neg. contexts). **take a brief** accept the conduct of a case. *watching brief*: see WATCH *verb*.
– COMB.: **brief-bag** a bag in which a barrister carries briefs; **briefcase** a rectangular case for carrying papers, documents, etc.
■ **briefless** *adjective* without a brief, (of a barrister etc.) unemployed **E19.**

brief /briːf/ *noun*[2]. **LME.**
[ORIGIN from the adjective.]
1 *in brief*, in short, briefly. **LME.**
†**2** *The* little that need be said etc. **L16–E17.**
3 In *pl.* Short underpants or knickers. **M20.**

brief /briːf/ *adjective & adverb*. **ME.**
[ORIGIN Anglo-Norman *bref*, Old French *brief* (mod. *bref*), from Latin *brevis* short, brief. The origin of sense A.4 is obscure.]
▸ **A** *adjective*. **1** Of short duration, quickly passing. **ME.** ▸†**b** Hasty, expeditious. **LME–E17.**

TOLKIEN In his living face they caught a brief vision of the power and majesty of the kings of stone. W. S. CHURCHILL Their freedom was brief. The British refused to recognise the republic.

2 Short in (spatial) extent; curtailed, limited. **ME.**

SIR W. SCOTT Wearing the briefest petticoat of any nymph of St. Ronan's.

3 Consisting of or employing few words; concise in expression. **LME.**

S. KAUFFMANN A brief note simply to say that they had arrived safely. J. D. SALINGER As brief as a gatekeeper at a Trappist monastery.

be brief speak in few words.
4 Rife, prevalent, epidemic. *dial.* **E18.**
▸ **B** *adverb*. Briefly; in brief. Now *rare*. **M16.**
■ **briefly** *adverb* shortly, in a few words **LME.** **briefness** *noun* (*a*) brevity, conciseness; †(*b*) quickness: **LME.**

brief /briːf/ *verb trans.* **M19.**
[ORIGIN from BRIEF *noun*[1].]
1 Reduce to the form of a legal brief; put into a brief. **M19.**
2 Give a brief to (a barrister), instruct by brief; retain as counsel in a suit. **M19.**
3 Instruct or inform thoroughly; give precise instructions to, esp. with regard to a military operation etc. **M19.**
■ **briefer** *noun* **E20.** **briefing** *noun* (*a*) the action of the verb; (*b*) a meeting for this: **M19.**

brier *noun*[1], *noun*[2] vars. of BRIAR *noun*[1], *noun*[2].

brieve /briːv/ *noun*. **E17.**
[ORIGIN Var. of BRIEF *noun*[1].]
SCOTS LAW (now *hist.*). A Chancery writ directing trial by jury of a specified question.

brig /brɪg/ *noun*[1]. **E18.**
[ORIGIN Shortened from BRIGANTINE *noun*[1].]
1 Orig., = BRIGANTINE *noun*[1] 1. Now, a two-masted square-rigged vessel with an additional lower fore-and-aft sail on a gaff and boom to the mainmast. **E18.**
hermaphrodite brig = BRIGANTINE *noun*[1] 3.
2 A place of detention, orig. on board a ship; a naval or military prison. *slang* (orig. *US*). **M19.**

brig *noun*[2] see BRIDGE *noun*[1].

Brig. *abbreviation*.
Brigadier.

brigade /brɪˈgeɪd/ *noun & verb*. **M17.**
[ORIGIN French from Italian *brigata* troop, company, from *brigare* contend, be busy with, from *briga* strife, contention: see -ADE.]
▸ **A** *noun*. †**1** A company or set of people. Only in **M17.**
2 A large body of troops; *spec.* a subdivision of an army. In the British army: an infantry unit consisting of usu. three battalions and forming part of a division; a corresponding armoured unit. **M17.**
3 A uniformed or organized band of workers etc. **E19.**
– PHRASES: *Boys' Brigade*: see BOY *noun*. *fire brigade*: see FIRE *noun*. *International Brigade*: see INTERNATIONAL *adjective*. NAVAL *brigade*. *Red Brigade(s)*: see RED *adjective*.
– COMB.: **brigade major** a staff officer attached to a brigade to assist the brigadier in command.
▸ **B** *verb trans.* Form into a brigade. **E19.**

brigadier /brɪgəˈdɪə/ *noun*. Also (esp. in titles) **B-**. **L17.**
[ORIGIN French, formed as BRIGADE + -IER.]
An officer commanding a brigade; (a titular rank granted to) a staff officer of similar standing, above colonel and below major-general. Formerly also *brigadier-general*.
– COMB.: **brigadier-general** (*a*) *hist.* see above; (*b*) an officer ranking above a colonel and below a major-general in the US Army, Air Force, and Marine Corps; **brigadier wig** *hist.* a full wig tied back in two curls.

Brigadoon /brɪgəˈduːn/ *noun*. **L20.**
[ORIGIN Title of a musical by A. J. Lerner and F. Loewe (1947), set in the fictional Highland village of *Brigadoon*.]
(Name of a place representing) an idealized or romanticized representation of Scotland.

attrib.: P. THEROUX A fleeting Brigadoon embodiment of a dreamland.

brigalow /ˈbrɪgələʊ/ *noun*. *Austral.* **M19.**
[ORIGIN Perh. from Kamilaroi *burriigal*.]
Any of various acacias forming thick scrub.

brigand /ˈbrɪg(ə)nd/ *noun & verb*. **LME.**
[ORIGIN French from Italian *brigante*, orig. = foot soldier, use as noun of pres. pple of *brigare*: see BRIGADE.]
▸ **A** *noun*. †**1** A lightly armed irregular foot soldier. **LME–L18.**
2 A bandit or robber, *esp.* one of a band living by pillage and ransom. **LME.**
▸ **B** *verb trans.* In *pass.* Be attacked by brigands. *rare*. **L19.**
■ **brigandage** *noun* the practice of brigands, banditry, pillage; brigands collectively: **E17.** **brigandish** *adjective* **L19.** **brigandism** *noun* the life of brigands, brigandage **M19.** **brigandry** *noun* = BRIGANDISM **E20.**

brigandine /ˈbrɪg(ə)ndiːn/ *noun*. Also **-tine** /-tiːn/. **LME.**
[ORIGIN French, or its source Italian *brigantina*, formed as BRIGAND: see -INE[4].]
A coat of mail, esp. one made of iron rings or plates attached to canvas etc.

brigantine /ˈbrɪg(ə)ntiːn/ *noun*[1]. **E16.**
[ORIGIN Old French *brigandine* (mod. *brigantin*) or its source Italian *brigantino*, from *brigante*: see BRIGAND, -INE[4].]
1 A small vessel equipped for both sailing and rowing, employed for espionage, piracy, etc. *obsolete* exc. *hist.* **E16.**
2 *loosely*. A foreign vessel, as a galleon etc. **M16.**
3 A two-masted vessel with a square-rigged foremast and fore-and-aft rigged mainmast. **L16.**

brigantine *noun*[2] var. of BRIGANDINE.

bright /brʌɪt/ *adjective & noun*.
[ORIGIN Old English *beorht*, (Anglian) *berht*, (Northumbrian) *breht* = Old Saxon *ber(a)ht*, Old High German *beraht*, *-eht*, Old Norse *bjartr*, Gothic *bairhts*, from Germanic.]
▸ **A** *adjective*. **1** Emitting or reflecting much light, shining; pervaded by light, sunlit; (of wine etc.) clear, translucent. **OE.** ▸**b** *fig.* Lit up with happiness, gladness, hope, etc.; hopeful, encouraging, cheering. **M18.**

TINDALE *Rev.* 22:16 The bright mornynge starre. J. BETJEMAN The church is bright with candlelight. E. BIRNEY Dusty September orchards . . bright with apples. B. PLAIN Even on the brightest afternoon, the bulb . . had to be lit. **b** I. MURDOCH A sad eclipse of all their bright hopes.

bright lights urban places of entertainment. **brightwork** polished metalwork on ships etc. **b bright-eyed** (*a*) having shining eyes; (*b*) alert and lively; *bright-eyed and bushy-tailed*: see BUSHY *adjective*. *honour bright*: see HONOUR *noun*. **look on the bright side** *colloq.* be optimistic or cheerful.
†**2** Clear or luminous to mental perception. **OE–M18.**
3 Of sound: clear; shrill, giving (undue) prominence to high frequencies. **OE.**
4 Illustrious, glorious, splendid. **OE.**

SHAKES. *Lucr.* Troy had been bright with fame, and not with fire.

5 Of a person: beautiful, handsome. *arch.* **ME.**

COLERIDGE A bright lady, surpassingly fair.

6 Vividly or brilliantly coloured. Of a colour: intense, vivid. **ME.** ▸**b** Of tobacco: having a light shade or colour. Orig. *US*. **M18.**

HUGH WALPOLE Light grey flannel trousers . . showing bright purple socks. J. RHYS She had a bright patchwork counterpane.

bright-line brown-eye = *tomato moth* s.v. TOMATO *noun*. *paint in bright colours*: see COLOUR *noun*.
7 Of a person, a face etc.: cheerful, animated, vivacious. **E17.**

SHAKES. *Macb.* Be bright and jovial among your guests to-night. S. LEACOCK The bright smiling faces of working people.

bright young thing a fashionable member of the younger generation (esp. in the 1920s and 1930s) noted for exuberant and outrageous behaviour.
8 Of thought, conversation, writing, etc.: witty, clever, imaginative, sparkling. **E18.**

A. G. GARDINER I thought of a bright thing to say now and then.

9 Displaying great intelligence; quick-witted; talented. **M18.**

JILLY COOPER They're also quite bright: you can't get in unless you have five O's and three A-levels. G. F. NEWMAN It wasn't very bright threatening to break Evans's arms. *iron.*: J. M. KEYNES The bright idea of reducing Economics to a mathematical application of the hedonistic calculus of Bentham!

▸ **B** *noun*. Brightness, light. *arch.* **ME.**
■ **brightish** *adjective* **L16.** **brightly** *adverb* in a bright manner, with brightness **OE.** **brightness** *noun* **OE.** **brightsome** *adjective* (*arch.*) showing brightness, brightish **M16.** **brightsomeness** *noun* (*arch.*) **M16.**

bright /brʌɪt/ *verb*. *arch.*
[ORIGIN Old English *beorhtian*, from BRIGHT *adjective*.]
†**1** *verb intrans.* Be bright, shine. **OE–ME.**
2 *verb trans.* Make bright. **OE.**

bright /brʌɪt/ *adverb*.
[ORIGIN Old English *beorhte*, from the adjective.]
Brightly.
bright and early very early in the morning.

brighten /ˈbrʌɪt(ə)n/ *verb trans. & intrans.*
[ORIGIN Old English *(ge)beorhtnan verb intrans.*, *-ian verb trans.*, formed as BRIGHT *adjective*. Later from BRIGHT *adjective*: see -EN[5].]
Make or become bright(er). Often *fig.*, make or become more cheerful, lively, hopeful, etc. Freq. foll. by *up*.
■ **brightener** *noun* L18.

Bright's disease /ˈbrʌɪts dɪˌziːz/ *noun phr.* M19.
[ORIGIN Richard *Bright* (1789–1858), English physician.]
MEDICINE. Kidney disease associated with albuminuria; *esp.* glomerulonephritis.

brigue /briːɡ/ *noun*. Now *rare* or *obsolete*. LME.
[ORIGIN Old French & mod. French from Italian *briga*: see BRIGADE.]
†**1** Strife, contention. LME–L17.
2 Intrigue, faction; a faction. M17.

†**brigue** *verb*. LME.
[ORIGIN from BRIGUE *noun* or French *briguer*: sense 1 may repr. a different word.]
1 *verb trans.* Ensnare. Only in LME.
2 *verb intrans.* Intrigue; solicit. Chiefly *Scot.* L16–M19.

brill /brɪl/ *noun*. Pl. same. L15.
[ORIGIN Unknown.]
A flatfish, *Scophthalmus rhombus*, resembling the turbot.

brill /brɪl/ *adjective*. *slang*. L20.
[ORIGIN Abbreviation of BRILLIANT *adjective*.]
Excellent, outstanding.

†**brillant** *noun, adjective* var. of BRILLIANT *noun, adjective*.

brillante /brɪˈlɑːnteɪ/ *adverb & adjective*. M18.
[ORIGIN Italian.]
MUSIC. (A direction:) in a showy or sparkling style.

brilliance /ˈbrɪlj(ə)ns/ *noun*. M18.
[ORIGIN from BRILLIANT *adjective*: see -ANCE.]
1 Brilliant quality; intense or sparkling brightness, radiance, or splendour; an instance of this. M18.

C. FREMLIN The low autumn sun was blazing with uncanny brilliance right into my eyes.

2 Exceptional talent, skill, or intelligence. L18.

New York Times Flashes of genuine brilliance alternate with appalling ineptitude.

■ Also **brilliancy** *noun* M18.

brilliant /ˈbrɪlj(ə)nt/ *noun*. Also †**brillant**. L17.
[ORIGIN French *brillant*, formed as BRILLIANT *adjective*.]
†**1** Brilliance. Only in L17.
2 A diamond of the finest cut and brilliance; *spec.* one cut with horizontal upper and lower faces joined by facets. L17.
3 A former very small size of type equal to about 3½ points. L19.

brilliant /ˈbrɪlj(ə)nt/ *adjective*. Also †**brillant**. L17.
[ORIGIN French *brillant* pres. pple of *briller* shine, from Italian *brillare*, prob. ult. from Latin *beryllus* BERYL.]
1 Brightly shining; glittering, sparkling, lustrous. L17.

P. PULLMAN It was a place of brilliant sunlight.

2 Exceptionally clever, talented, or skilful; outstanding, celebrated. M18. ▸**b** Excellent. *colloq.* L20.

ARNOLD BENNETT Edwin's own suggestions never seemed very brilliant, . . but they were never silly. C. POTOK This boy . . was brilliant, literally a genius. **b** S. TOWNSEND I allowed Pandora to visit me in my darkened bedroom. We had a brilliant kissing session.

■ **brilliantly** *adverb* E19.

brilliant /ˈbrɪlj(ə)nt/ *verb trans. rare*. M18.
[ORIGIN from the noun.]
Cut (a diamond) as a brilliant.

brilliantine /ˈbrɪlj(ə)ntiːn/ *noun*. L19.
[ORIGIN French *brillantine*, from *brillant* BRILLIANT *adjective*.]
1 A cosmetic for imparting a gloss to the hair. L19.
2 A shiny fabric for dresses etc. *N. Amer.* L19.
■ **brilliantined** *adjective* made glossy with brilliantine E20.

Brillo pad /ˈbrɪləʊ pad/ *noun phr.* M20.
[ORIGIN Uncertain: perh. from *brill-* (in BRILLIANT *adjective*) + -O.]
1 (Proprietary name for) a pad made of steel wool impregnated with soap, used for scouring pans. M20.
2 (A mass of) wiry or tightly curled hair. *colloq.* M20.

Daily Telegraph Bruce Forsyth's sideburns and Brillo pad combover were a joy to behold.

brim /brɪm/ *noun*[1]. ME.
[ORIGIN Uncertain: corresp. in sense to Middle High German *brem* (German *Bräme*, *Brähme*), Old Norse *barmr* edge.]
1 The border, margin, edge, brink, etc., of the sea or any piece of water, or *gen.* of other things. Now *obsolete* or *dial.* exc. as transf. use of sense 2. ME.

SPENSER Upon the brim of his brode-plated shield. JER. TAYLOR He . . is at the margin and brim of that state of finall reprobation.

2 The edge, margin, or lip of a cup, bowl, basin, or anything of similar shape, artificial or natural. LME.

AV *2 Chron.* 4:2 He made a molten Sea of ten cubites, from brim to brim. *fig.*: SHAKES. *Ant. & Cl.* He will fill thy wishes to the brim With principalities.

pelvic brim the rim between the upper and lower parts of the pelvis.

3 The upper surface of water. *arch.* M16.

SIR W. SCOTT Not lighter does the swallow skim Along the smooth lake's level brim.

4 The projecting edge of a hat. L16.
– COMB.: **brim-full**, (*arch.*) **brimful** *adjective* full to the brim, on the point of overflowing.
■ **brimless** *adjective* E17. **brimmed** *adjective* (of a hat etc.) having a brim (of a specified kind) E17. **brimmy** *adjective* (of a hat) having a wide brim; broad-brimmed: L19.

brim *noun*[2] see BREAM *noun*.

brim *adjective* var. of BREME.

brim /brɪm/ *verb*. Infl. **-mm-**. E17.
[ORIGIN from BRIM *noun*[1].]
1 *verb trans.* Fill to the brim. E17.
2 *verb intrans.* Be or become full to the brim (*with*). E19.
brim over overflow.
■ **brimming** *ppl adjective* (**a**) that rises to the brim of its vessel, basin, bed, etc.; (**b**) (of a container) full to overflowing: M17.

brimborion /brɪmˈbɔːrɪən/ *noun*. Also **-rium** /-rɪəm/. M17.
[ORIGIN French, earlier *breborion*, alt. of medieval Latin *breviarium* BREVIARY.]
A thing without use or value; trash, nonsense.

brimmer /ˈbrɪmə/ *noun*. Now *arch. & dial.* M17.
[ORIGIN from BRIM *noun*[1], *verb* + -ER[1].]
1 A brimming cup or goblet. M17.
2 A hat (*spec.* a straw hat) with a brim. M17.

brimstone /ˈbrɪmst(ə)n, -stəʊn/ *noun*.
[ORIGIN Late Old English *brynstān*, prob. from *bryne* (= Old Norse *bruni*) burning (formed as BURN *verb*) + STONE *noun*.]
1 Sulphur; *esp.* (otherwise *arch.*) burning sulphur, (the fuel of) hellfire. LOE. ▸**b** *fig.* Fire, passion. E17.
fire and brimstone: see FIRE *noun*.
†**2** A spirited or nagging woman. L17–E19.
3 In full ***brimstone butterfly***. A pierid butterfly, *Gonepteryx rhamni*, with sulphur-yellow wings. L17.
– COMB.: ***brimstone butterfly***: see sense 3 above; **brimstone moth** a geometrid moth, *Opisthograptis luteolata*, with yellow wings; **brimstone-wort** a yellow-flowered umbellifer of the genus *Peucedanum*, sulphurwort.
■ **brimstony** *adjective* of, pertaining to, or resembling brimstone; sulphureous, fiery: LME.

brinded /ˈbrɪndɪd/ *adjective*. *arch.* See also BRANDED. ME.
[ORIGIN Prob. of Scandinavian origin: cf. Old Norse *brǫndóttr* brindled, from *brandr* burning, and *brandkrossóttr* brindled, having a white cross on the forehead.]
= BRINDLED.

brindle /ˈbrɪnd(ə)l/ *adjective & noun*. L17.
[ORIGIN Back-form. from BRINDLED.]
▸ **A** *adjective*. = BRINDLED. L17.
▸ **B** *noun*. (A dog etc. of) brindled colour. L17.

brindled /ˈbrɪnd(ə)ld/ *adjective*. L17.
[ORIGIN Alt. of BRINDED, prob. by assoc. with *grizzled*, *speckled*, etc.]
Of a tawny or brownish colour with (esp. indistinct) streaks or spots of a different hue; *gen.* streaked, spotted, (*with*).
brindled beauty a European geometrid moth, *Lycia hirtaria*, with grey-brown banded wings.

brine /brʌɪn/ *noun & verb*.
[ORIGIN Old English *brīne* = Middle Dutch *brīne* (Dutch *brijn*), of unknown origin.]
▸ **A** *noun*. **1** Water saturated or strongly impregnated with salt; salt water. OE.
2 (The water of) the sea. Usu. *poet.* L16.
3 (Salty) tears. *poet.* L16.
– COMB.: **brine pan** (**a**) a shallow iron vessel in which salt is evaporated; (**b**) a salt pan; **brine shrimp** any of various branchiopods of the genus *Artemia*, inhabiting salt lakes, brine pans, etc.
▸ **B** *verb trans.* Steep in or saturate with brine. M16.
■ **brinish** *adjective* of or like brine, briny L16.

Brinell /brɪˈnɛl/ *noun*. E20.
[ORIGIN J. A. *Brinell* (1849–1925), Swedish engineer.]
Used *attrib.* with ref. to a test for hardness in which a steel ball is pressed into the material and the diameter of the indentation measured.

bring /brɪŋ/ *verb trans.* Pa. t. & pple **brought** /brɔːt/, (*dial.*) **brung** /brʌŋ/.
[ORIGIN Old English *bringan* (pa. t. *brōhte*, pple *brōht*) = Old Frisian *bringa*, Old Saxon, Old High German *bringan* (Dutch *brengen*, German *bringen*), Gothic *briggan*, from Germanic.]
1 Cause to come, come with, or convey, by carrying, leading, impelling, attracting, etc. OE. ▸**b** Escort, accompany on his or her way. *obsolete* exc. *dial.* LME.

DRYDEN I . . shall in Triumph come From conquer'd Greece, and bring her Trophies home. THACKERAY Those lines . . brought tears into the Duchess's eyes. TENNYSON She brought strange news. J. T. STORY Finally I brought both fists down together and he fell like an axed pig. I. MCEWAN The narrow passage-way had brought them on to a large . . square.

bring-and-buy sale, **bring-and-buy stall**, etc.: at which customers bring things for sale and buy what others have brought. ***bring home the bacon***: see BACON *noun* 1. ***bring into line***: see LINE *noun*[2]. ***bring to bay***: see BAY *noun*[1] 2. ***bring to light***: see LIGHT *noun*. **bring to mind** (cause oneself to) remember. ***brought to bed***: see BED *noun*.

2 Prefer (a charge); initiate (legal action); advance (an argument etc.). OE.

M. EDGEWORTH Arguments . . brought by his companions in their . . master's justification.

3 Produce as a consequence, cause to have, result in; be sold for (a price). OE.

TENNYSON The loss that brought us pain. J. UPDIKE Gifts bring men, men bring bullets, bullets bring oppression.

4 Bear (young, fruit, etc.), yield, produce; = ***bring forth*** below. ME.

COVERDALE *Hab.* 3:17 The londe shall bringe no corne.

5 Cause to come *from*, *into*, *out of*, *to*, etc., a state or condition, *to* an action; cause to become; cause, induce, persuade (usu. a reluctant person) *to be* or *to do*. ME.

COVERDALE *Judg.* 3:30 Thus were the Moabites broughte vnder the hande of the children of Israel. J. BUTLER Persons . . by a course of vice, bring themselves into new difficulties. C. THIRLWALL The prosecutors brought Demosthenes to trial first. D. W. JERROLD A woman may be brought to forgive bigamy, but not a joke. D. LODGE Some kind of physical malformation which the man could not even bring himself to describe.

bring a person to his or her senses: see SENSE *noun*. ***bring home to***: see HOME *adverb*. **bring into being** cause to exist. ***bring into play***: see PLAY *noun*. **bring into the world** give birth to, (of a midwife etc.) deliver. ***bring to a head***: see HEAD *noun* 28. ***bring to bear***: see BEAR *verb*[1]. ***bring to book***: see BOOK *noun*. ***bring to*** GRIEF. ***bring to life***: see LIFE *noun*. ***bring to pass***: see PASS *noun*[2]. **bring to the party**, **bring to the table** contribute (something of value) to a discussion, project, etc. ***bring to utterance***: see UTTERANCE *noun*[2].

†**6** Deduce, infer, derive. L16–E18.

SHAKES. *1 Hen. VI* He From John of Gaunt doth bring his pedigree.

7 NAUTICAL. Cause to come or go into a certain position or direction. L17.

DEFOE Her main-mast and fore-mast were brought by the board.

bring the port tacks aboard, ***bring the starboard tacks aboard***, ***bring the tacks aboard***: see TACK *noun*[1].
– WITH ADVERBS IN SPECIALIZED SENSES: **bring about** (**a**) cause to happen, accomplish; †(**b**) complete by a revolving; (**c**) turn round; reverse (a ship); convert. **bring back** cause to return, recall, bring to mind. **bring down** (**a**) cause to fall or collapse (***bring down the house***, ***bring the house down*** (THEATRICAL), get loud applause); (**b**) cause (a flying bird, an aircraft, etc.) to fall to the ground; cause (a penalty etc.) to fall *on*; kill, wound; overthrow; abase; (**c**) lower (a price etc.); (**d**) continue (a record etc.) *to* a point in time. **bring forth** (**a**) produce, yield, give birth to, cause; †(**b**) utter; advance as an argument etc.; †(**c**) bring to light, expose to public view. **bring forward** (**a**) draw attention to; (**b**) move to an earlier date or time, transfer from a previous page or account. **bring in** (**a**) introduce (a custom, fashion, topic, legislation, etc., †a person), adduce; produce as profit or increase; (**b**) pronounce (a verdict; a person *guilty* etc.). **bring off** (**a**) rescue (*arch.* in *gen.* sense), *spec.* conduct away from a ship, wreck, etc.; (**b**) conduct successfully, succeed in, achieve. **bring on** (**a**) introduce (a topic for discussion etc.), cause, bring into action; (**b**) advance the progress of. **bring out** †(**a**) produce, yield; (**b**) express, publish, make known, exhibit clearly, make prominent; (**c**) introduce (a girl) to society. **bring over** win over, convert; **bring round** (**a**) restore to consciousness; (**b**) win over. **bring through** treat or tend successfully through illness etc. **bring to** (**a**) *verb phr. trans. & intrans.* check the motion of; come to a stop; (**b**) *verb phr. trans.* restore to consciousness. **bring under** subdue. **bring up** (**a**) *verb phr. trans.* supervise the training of (a child) in habits, manners, etc.; be responsible for or care for to the point of maturity; in *pass.* also, grow up, esp. in a particular place or manner; (**b**) *verb phr. trans.* call attention to; (re)introduce (a topic etc.); cause to appear in court etc.; (**c**) *verb phr. trans.* vomit; (**d**) *verb phr. trans. & intrans.* (orig. NAUTICAL) (cause to) come to a stop, pull up; (**e**) ***bring up short***: see SHORT *adverb*; (***f***) ***bring up the rear***: see REAR *noun*; (***g***) ***bring up with a round turn***: see ROUND *adjective*. **bring up to date** provide with what is needed to cover the most recent developments.
– COMB.: **bringdown** *US colloq.* a depressing or disappointing person or experience.
■ **bringer** *noun* ME.

†**brinie** *noun* var. of BYRNIE.

brinjal /ˈbrɪndʒɔːl/ *noun*. E17.
[ORIGIN Ult. from Portuguese *berinjela*, formed as AUBERGINE.]
Esp. in the Indian subcontinent: an aubergine.

brinjarry /brɪnˈdʒɑːri/ *noun*. *arch.* Also **bunjara** /bʌnˈdʒɑːrə/. M17.
[ORIGIN Alt. of Deccan Urdu *banjāra* from Hindi, ult. from Sanskrit *vaṇijā* trade.]
A travelling grain and salt merchant of the Deccan in southern India.

brink /brɪŋk/ *noun*. ME.
[ORIGIN Old Norse *brekka* slope corresp. to Middle Low German *brink* edge of a field, (brow of) a hill (whence German dial. *Brink* hill), Middle Dutch *brinc* (Dutch *brink* grassland), of unknown origin.]
1 The margin or bank of a body of water; *gen.* an edge, a margin, a border. (Now usu. only when steep, passing into sense 3.) ME.

BYRON All these are coop'd within one Quarto's brink.
J. MASEFIELD To halt at the chattering brook, in the tall green fern at the brink.

2 *fig.* The verge *of* some state, event, action, time, etc.; the point *of being*, *doing*, etc. ME.

DICKENS She is on the brink of being sold into wretchedness for life. W. CATHER Hard times that brought everyone . . to the brink of despair. D. ACHESON The United States hesitated on the brink of action.

B

teeter on the brink: see TEETER *verb* 1b. **the brink** the verge of (esp. nuclear) war.

3 The edge, margin, or border of a steep place, such as a precipice, chasm, etc. LME.

MILTON The warie fiend Stood on the brink of Hell and look'd a while. T. H. HUXLEY The church . . is now on the very brink of the cliff. TOLKIEN The places behind where there was a black brink and an empty fall into nothingness.

4 The brim of a vessel. *obsolete* exc. *dial.* LME.

■ **brinkmanship** *noun* [-MANSHIP] a policy or the art of advancing to the very brink of some action (esp. war) but not engaging in it M20.

briny /ˈbrʌɪni/ *adjective & noun*. L16.
[ORIGIN from BRINE *noun* + -Y¹.]
▶ **A** *adjective*. Of or pertaining to brine or the sea; saturated with salt. L16.
▶ **B** *noun*. *The* sea, *the* ocean. *slang*. M19.

brio /ˈbriːəʊ/ *noun*. M18.
[ORIGIN Italian.]
Vivacity, liveliness, verve. See also CON BRIO.

brioche /briːˈɒʃ, ˈbriːɒʃ/ *noun*. E19.
[ORIGIN French.]
A small usu. round sweet cake made with light yeast dough.

briony *noun* var. of BRYONY.

briquet /brike/ *noun*¹. Pl. pronounced same. E19.
[ORIGIN French.]
A steel for striking light from a flint; a representation of this, esp. as a heraldic ornament.

briquet *noun*² var. of next.

briquette /brɪˈkɛt/ *noun & verb*. Also **-et**. L19.
[ORIGIN French, dim. of *brique* BRICK *noun*: see -ETTE.]
▶ **A** *noun*. A small block or slab, esp. of compressed coal dust for use as fuel. L19.
▶ **B** *verb trans*. Form into briquettes. L19.

bris /brɪs/ *noun*. Also **brith** /brɪt, brɪθ/. E20.
[ORIGIN Hebrew *bĕrīṯ*, short for *bĕrīṯ mīlah* covenant of circumcision (with ref. to *Genesis* 17:9–10).]
In full ***bris milah*** /ˈmiːlə/. The Jewish ceremony of circumcision.

brisé /brize/ *noun*. Pl. pronounced same. L18.
[ORIGIN French, pa. pple of *briser* break.]
BALLET. A movement in which the feet or legs are lightly beaten together in the air.

brise-soleil /brizsɔlɛːj, briːzsɒˈleɪ/ *noun*. Pl. pronounced same. M20.
[ORIGIN French, lit. 'sun-breaker'.]
A device (as a perforated screen, louvre, etc.) for shutting out direct or excessive sunlight.

brish /brɪʃ/ *verb trans. & intrans. dial.* M17.
[ORIGIN Var. of BRUSH *verb*².]
= BRUSH *verb*² 3. Chiefly as ***brishing*** *verbal noun*.

brisk /brɪsk/ *adjective & verb*. L16.
[ORIGIN Prob. from French BRUSQUE.]
▶ **A** *adjective*. **1** Quick, smart, or efficient in movement or action; lively, rapid, active. L16. ▸**b** In an unfavourable sense: curt, brusque, peremptory. Also (now *rare* or *obsolete*) transient; fast-living; hasty. E17.

P. KAVANAGH Demand for all sorts of cattle was brisk. D. DU MAURIER He whipped the horses to a brisker pace. P. H. JOHNSON This brisk and officer-like behaviour. W. TREVOR She wished she was grown-up, brisk and able to cope. **b** SHAKES. *Twel. N.* These most brisk and giddy-paced times. C. CIBBER The briskest loose Liver or intemperate Man. C. ISHERWOOD Her tone was peremptory and brisk.

2 Agreeably sharp to the taste, effervescent. Also, (of the air etc.) fresh, keen. L16.

SHAKES. *2 Hen. IV* A cup of wine that's brisk and fine. L. DURRELL It is brisk weather, clear as waterglass.

†**3** Spruce, smartly dressed. L16–E17.
▶ **B** *verb trans. & intrans.* †**1** Smarten (*up*), dress smartly. L16–M19.
2 Make or become (more) brisk or lively; quicken, enliven; move or behave briskly. Freq. foll. by *up*. E17.

R. L. STEVENSON Modestine brisked up her pace. H. L. WILSON As I brisked out of bed the following morning. T. ROETHKE A flicker of fire brisked by a dusty wind.

■ **brisken** *verb intrans. & trans.* become or make brisk (also foll. by *up*), = BRISK *verb* 2 M18. **briskly** *adverb* L16. **briskness** *noun* M17. **brisky** *adjective* brisk, lively, smart L16.

brisket /ˈbrɪskɪt/ *noun*. ME.
[ORIGIN Perh. from Old Norse *brjósk* (Norwegian, Danish *brusk*) cartilage, gristle + -ET¹.]
1 The breast of an animal, esp. as a joint of meat. ME.
2 The human breast. *Scot. colloq.* L18.

brisling /ˈbrɪslɪŋ, ˈbrɪz-/ *noun*. Also **bristling**. Pl. same, **-s**. E20.
[ORIGIN Norwegian, Danish.]
The sprat, *Sprattus sprattus*.

bristle /ˈbrɪs(ə)l/ *noun*. ME.
[ORIGIN formed as BIRSE + -EL¹. Prob. in Old English: cf. Middle Dutch & mod. Dutch *borstel*.]
1 Any of the stiff hairs that grow on the back and sides of the pig, esp. as used in brushes etc. ME.
2 *gen.* Any short stiff hair or filament, e.g. of a man's short-cropped beard; a filament of a brush, of whatever material; a seta; bristles collectively. ME.

R. CHANDLER A black brush with a few blond hairs in its black bristles. J. FULLER Patches of unshaven bristle on his jowls.

– COMB.: **bristlebird** an Australian reed warbler of the genus *Dasyornis*; **bristlecone pine** a very slow-growing, shrubby pine, *Pinus aristata*, of western N. America, important for dendrochronology; **bristle fern** any of various chiefly tropical ferns of the genus *Trichomanes*, with a hairlike receptacle protruding from the indusium; **bristle grass** a grass of the genus *Setaria*; **bristletail** an apterygote insect of the orders Thysanura (including the silverfish and firebrat, more fully ***three-pronged bristletail***) or Diplura (more fully ***two-pronged bristletail***); **bristle worm** a polychaete.

■ **bristle-like** *adjective* M19. **bristly** *adjective* covered or set with bristles; of the nature of or like bristles: LME.

bristle /ˈbrɪs(ə)l/ *verb*¹. See also BRUSTLE *verb*². ME.
[ORIGIN from the noun.]
▶ **I** *verb trans.* **1** Cover, set, or tip with bristles; make prickly or bristly; *fig.* set thickly as with bristles. ME.

HOBBES The brissled Ranks Of th' armed Greeks. LYTTON He would bristle all the land with castles. K. KESEY His arms . . are sunburned and bristled with curly orange hairs.

2 Erect (hair etc.) stiffly like bristles; *fig.* cause to show anger or hostility. Also foll. by *up*. L16.

SHAKES. *John* Now . . Doth dogged war bristle his angry crest. C. KINGSLEY He would . . bristle up his feathers, just as a cock-robin would.

▶ **II** *verb intrans.* **3** Become or stand stiff like bristles. L15.

G. ORWELL White moustaches that bristled forward like those of a prawn. W. S. CHURCHILL Solid squares with eighteen foot pikes bristling in every direction. J. BRAINE There was something about its tone which . . made the hairs on the nape of my neck bristle.

4 Raise the bristles as a sign of anger or excitement; *fig.* be roused to temper or hostility. Also foll. by *up*. M16.

THOMAS HUGHES There now! don't bristle up like a hedgehog. J. FENTON My dog had halted, Its skin bristling.

5 Be or become bristly; be thickly set (as) with bristles; chiefly *fig.*, be covered, teem, abound *with*. E17.

CARLYLE All France to the utmost borders bristles with bayonets. C. I. LEWIS Treatises . . bristling with . . difficulties. K. A. PORTER Faded dry hair bristling with wire hairpins. U. LE GUIN He had left the chin bristling to match his short, iron-grey head hair.

bristle /ˈbrɪs(ə)l/ *verb*² *trans. & intrans. obsolete* exc. *dial.* L15.
[ORIGIN Unknown: cf. BIRSLE.]
Make or become crisp with heat.

bristling *noun* var. of BRISLING.

Bristol /ˈbrɪst(ə)l/ *noun*. In sense 2 usu. **b-**. M16.
[ORIGIN A city and port in the west of England.]
▶ **I 1** Used *attrib.* to designate things from or associated with Bristol. M16.
Bristol board a kind of fine pasteboard with a smooth surface. **Bristol cream** (proprietary name for) a kind of sweet sherry. **Bristol fashion**, **shipshape and Bristol fashion** (orig. NAUTICAL) with all in good order. **Bristol glass** opaque (esp. blue) glass manufactured in Bristol. ***Bristol milk***: see MILK *noun*. **Bristol porcelain** a kind of porcelain resembling delftware, manufactured in Bristol. **Bristol stone** etc., rock crystal from the Bristol area.
▶ **II 2** In *pl.*, or in full ***Bristol cities*** (= titties). The breasts. *rhyming slang*. M20.

brisure /ˈbriːʒə/ *noun*. E17.
[ORIGIN French = fracture.]
HERALDRY. A variation of or addition to a coat of arms serving as a distinguishing mark.

Brit /brɪt/ *noun*¹ & *adjective*¹. Long *obsolete* exc. *hist.* Also **Brett** /brɛt/.
[ORIGIN Old English *Bret* (pl. *Brettas*), based on Latin *Britto* (pl. *Brittones*) or its Celtic equiv. Cf. BRIT *noun*³ & *adjective*².]
▶ **A** *noun*. An ancient Briton (the ordinary name in the Anglo-Saxon Chronicle). OE.
▶ **B** *adjective*. British. *rare*. M16.

brit /brɪt/ *noun*². *dial.* Also **-tt**. E17.
[ORIGIN Unknown.]
A young herring or sprat; *gen.* small fry.

Brit /brɪt/ *noun*³ & *adjective*². *colloq.* Often *derog.* E20.
[ORIGIN Abbreviation of BRITON, BRITISH, or BRITISHER. Cf. BRIT *noun*¹ & *adjective*¹.]
▶ **A** *noun*. A British person. E20.
▶ **B** *adjective*. British. M20.

Brit. *abbreviation*.
1 Britain.
2 British.

Britain /ˈbrɪt(ə)n/ *noun*¹.
[ORIGIN Old English *Breoten*, *Breten*, *Bryten* from Latin *Brittones* (see BRITON); later forms from Old French *Bretaigne* (mod. *-agne*), from Latin *Brittan(n)ia* from *Brit(t)anni*, corresp. to Greek *Bret(t)anoi*, *Pret(t)anoi*.]
More fully (esp. as a political term) ***Great Britain***. As a geographical and political term: (the main island and smaller offshore islands making up) England, Scotland, and Wales, sometimes with the Isle of Man. Also (as a political term) the United Kingdom, Britain and its dependencies, (formerly) the British Empire.
Middle Britain: see MIDDLE *adjective*. ***North Britain***: see NORTH *adjective*.
– NOTE: *Britain*, after the Old English period, was for long used only as a historical term, but in 1604 James I & VI was proclaimed 'King of Great Britain' and this name was adopted at the Union in 1707.
■ †**Britainer** *noun* = BRITON *noun* L16–E19.

Britain /ˈbrɪt(ə)n/ *noun*² & *adjective*. M16.
[ORIGIN Latin *Brit(t)annus*, *Brittanus* Briton, British: cf. BRITAIN *noun*¹.]
▶ †**A** *noun*. An ancient Briton. M16–M18.
▶ **B** *adjective*. †**1** = BRITISH *adjective* 1. L16–M17.
2 = BRITISH *adjective* 2. Now only in ***Britain crown***, a gold coin struck in the reign of James I & VI, orig. valued at 5*s*., afterwards at 5*s*. 6*d*. E17.

Britannia /brɪˈtanjə/ *noun*. OE.
[ORIGIN Latin *Brit(t)annia*, *Brittania* (Bede), corresp. to Greek *Brettania* (Diodorus Siculus): see BRITAIN *noun*¹.]
1 The Latin name of Britain; Britain personified as a female; the figure emblematic of Britain, a woman with a shield, helmet, and trident, shown on coins etc. OE.
2 In full ***Britannia metal***. An alloy of tin with small proportions of antimony and copper, resembling silver. E19.
– COMB.: ***Britannia metal***: see sense 2 above; **Britannia silver** hall-marked silver of at least 95.8 per cent purity.
■ **Britannian** *adjective* (now *rare*) = BRITISH *adjective* 2 L16. †**Britany** *noun* Britain LME–M17.

Britannic /brɪˈtanɪk/ *adjective*. M17.
[ORIGIN Latin *Britannicus*, formed as BRITANNIA: see -IC.]
Of Britain; British. Chiefly in ***Her Britannic Majesty***, ***His Britannic Majesty***.
■ **Britannically** *adverb* (now *rare*) in British fashion; in reference to Great Britain: E18. **Britannicize** /-sʌɪz/ *verb trans.* make British in form or character L19.

britch *noun* see BREECH *noun*.

britchel *adjective* see BRUCKLE.

brith *noun* var. of BRIS.

Briticisation *noun* var. of BRITICIZATION.

Briticism /ˈbrɪtɪsɪz(ə)m/ *noun*. M19.
[ORIGIN from BRITISH after *Gallicism*, *Scotticism*, etc.]
A word, phrase, or idiom characteristic of the English of Great Britain as opp. to the US etc.

Briticization /ˌbrɪtɪsʌɪˈzeɪʃ(ə)n/ *noun*. Also **-isation**. M20.
[ORIGIN formed as BRITICISM + -IZATION, after *anglicization* etc.]
The process of making British (esp. by the ancient Britons); the result of this.

British /ˈbrɪtɪʃ/ *adjective & noun*.
[ORIGIN Old English *Brettisc*, *Brittisc*, *Bryttisc*, formed as BRIT *noun*¹ & *adjective*¹ + -ISH¹.]
▶ **A** *adjective*. **1** Of or pertaining to the ancient Britons or their Celtic language (cf. BRITTONIC *adjective*); *loosely*. Welsh, (occas.) Cornish. OE.
2 Of or pertaining to Great Britain or its inhabitants. LME.
British BULLDOG. ***British Commonwealth***: see COMMONWEALTH. **British crown** a gold crown (coin) struck in the reign of Charles I. **British disease** a problem or failing supposed to be characteristically British, *esp.* proneness to industrial unrest. **British Empire** *hist.* the empire consisting of Great Britain and the other British possessions, dominions, and dependencies. **British English** the English language as spoken or written in the British Isles, esp. as contrasted with those forms of English characteristic of the US or other English-speaking countries. **British Isles** Britain, Ireland, and the Isle of Man, and sometimes also the Channel Islands. ***British Lion***: see LION *noun* 3b, c. ***British*** RAJ. **British Restaurant** *hist.* a government-subsidized restaurant opened in Britain during and after the Second World War. ***British Service warm***: see WARM *noun*. **British Sign Language** a form of sign language developed in the UK for the use of deaf people. **British Standard** (a document containing) the specification of recommended procedure, terminology, etc., in a particular field, drawn up and published by the British Standards Institution. **British Standard Time** *hist.* the time system used in Britain from 1968 to 1971, which was the same as Central European Time and was equivalent to the British Summer Time throughout the year. ***British Summer Time***: see SUMMERTIME 2. ***British storm petrel***: see STORM PETREL 1. **British thermal unit** the quantity of heat necessary to heat one pound of water at its maximum density by one degree Fahrenheit; = 1055 joule. ***British warm***: see WARM *noun*. ***Great British Public***: see GREAT *adjective*. **the best of British (luck)**: an expression of encouragement, often with the iron. implication that good luck will not be forthcoming.
▶ **B** *noun*. **1** The Celtic language of the ancient Britons (formerly also ***Old British***; cf. BRITTONIC *noun*); *loosely*. Welsh, (occas.) Cornish. M16.
2 *collect. pl. The* British people; British soldiers etc. M17.
■ **Britisher** *noun* a British subject (usu. as distinct from an American) E19. **Britishism** *noun* (any of) the characteristic qualities of the British; a British peculiarity, a Briticism: L19. **Britishly** *adverb* †(**a**) *rare* in the British language; (**b**) after the manner of the British; in British fashion: M17. **Britishness** *noun* †(**a**) *rare* the conditions of life of the ancient Britons; (**b**) the quality or character of the British: L17.

B

Brito- /ˈbrɪtəʊ/ *combining form.*
[ORIGIN Latin, from *Brit(t)o* BRITON.]
Forming adjectives & nouns with the sense 'British (or ancient British) and —', as ***Brito-Roman***.
■ **Brito'centric** *adjective* having Britain as the centre E20.

Briton /ˈbrɪt(ə)n/ *noun & adjective.* ME.
[ORIGIN Old French & mod. French *Breton* from Latin *Britto*, *-on-* or its Celtic equiv. (whence Welsh *Brython*).]
▸ **A** *noun.* **1** A native or inhabitant of (Great) Britain; (now *rare* exc. *hist.* of the British Empire) a British subject. ME. ***North Briton***: see NORTH *adjective*.
2 *spec.* (now more fully ***ancient Briton***). A member of the (Celtic) people living in S. Britain at the time of the Roman conquest. ME.
▸ †**B** *adjective.* = BRITISH *adjective*. M16–E17.
■ **Britoness** *noun* (*rare*) a female Briton L16.

Britonic *adjective & noun* var. of BRITTONIC.

Britpop /ˈbrɪtpɒp/ *noun.* L20.
[ORIGIN Blend of BRITISH and POP *noun*[6].]
Pop music by British groups, *spec.* that of the mid 1990s which was seen as influenced by the Beatles and other British groups of the 1960s.

britt *noun* var. of BRIT *noun*[2].

brittle /ˈbrɪt(ə)l/ *adjective.* LME.
[ORIGIN from base of Old English *gebryttan* break in pieces, ult. from Germanic base also of Old English *brēotan* break up = Old Norse *brjóta*: see -LE[1].]
1 Hard but liable to break easily. LME.
N. S. MOMADAY There were drifts of hard and brittle snow about the fenceposts and the stones.
brittle fracture: occurring in a metal without appreciable prior plastic deformation. **brittlestar** a starfish-like echinoderm of the class Ophiuroidea, with long thin brittle arms.
†**2** Liable to destruction; perishable, mortal. LME–L18.
3 *fig.* Frail, weak; insecure, unstable; showing signs of instability or nervousness. M16.
J. COE There was still something brittle and mannered about the way they kissed each other on the cheek.
■ **brittlely** *adverb* L16. **brittleness** *noun* L15. **brittly** *adverb* L17.

Brittonic /brɪˈtɒnɪk/ *adjective & noun.* Also **Britonic**. E20.
[ORIGIN from Latin *Britto(n-)* BRITON + -IC.]
▸ **A** *adjective.* Of or pertaining to the ancient Britons; *spec.* designating or pertaining to Brittonic (see sense B. below). E20.
▸ **B** *noun.* The language group comprising Welsh, Cornish, and Breton; = ***P-Celtic*** s.v. CELTIC *noun*. Cf. BRITISH *noun* 1, BRYTHONIC *noun*. M20.

britzka /ˈbrɪtskə/ *noun.* Also **britzska** & other vars. E19.
[ORIGIN Polish *bryczka*.]
Chiefly *hist.* An open carriage with calash top and space for reclining.

Brix /brɪks/ *noun.* L19.
[ORIGIN from the name of A. F. W. *Brix* (1798–1890), German scientist.]
Used *attrib.* of a hydrometer calibrated according to the ***Brix scale***, a scale for the measurement of the specific gravity of a sugar solution.

bro /brəʊ/ *noun. colloq.* Pl. **bros**, **Bros** /brɒs, brɒz/. M17.
[ORIGIN Abbreviation of BROTHER *noun*.]
A brother. In pl. (***Bros***) freq. in names of firms.

bro. *abbreviation.*
Brother.

broach /brəʊtʃ/ *noun*[1]. Also †**broche**, BROOCH. ME.
[ORIGIN Branch I from Old French & mod. French *broche* spit, from Proto-Romance use as noun of fem. of Latin *brocc(h)us* in *brocci dentes* projecting teeth; branch II from BROACH *verb*[1].]
▸ **I 1** A pointed rod; a lance; a bodkin, an awl, a skewer, etc.; *esp.* a roasting spit. *arch. & dial.* ME.
2 a A spindle. *obsolete* exc. *Scot.* LME. ▸**b** A shuttle used in weaving tapestry. L18.
3 A pointed, pliant rod of wood, used in thatching to fix work. LME.
4 A (church) spire; now *spec.* the base of an octagonal spire rising from a square tower without a parapet. E16.
5 The sharply pointed growth of a young stag's first antlers. L16.
6 A tapered bit used for smoothing or enlarging holes. M18.
▸ **II 7** An incision made by piercing or boring; a perforation. E16.
on broach (now *rare*) = ABROACH.
– COMB.: **broach spire** etc.: supported by a broach.

broach /brəʊtʃ/ *noun*[2]. E17.
[ORIGIN *Broach* (now *Bharuch*), a city and district of Gujarat State, India.]
Surat cotton from the Bharuch district.

broach /brəʊtʃ/ *verb*[1] *trans.* Also †**broche**. ME.
[ORIGIN Old French & mod. French *brochier* (now *brocher*), from Proto-Romance deriv. of base of BROACH *noun*[1].]
†**1** Spur, prick with spurs. ME–M16.
2 Stab, pierce through; pin. LME. ▸**b** Incise (stone) with a narrow-pointed chisel. M16.
†**3** Transfix (meat etc.) with a spit; stick *on* a spit or pointed weapon. LME–E18.
4 Pierce (a cask) to draw off liquor, tap; release (liquid) by this means; *loosely* open and begin to use the contents of (a box etc.); make a start on, set in train. LME.
R. L. STEVENSON A barrel of apples standing broached . . , for any one to help himself. R. HUGHES They ransacked the vessel . . broaching rum-casks and breaking the necks off wine-bottles.
5 Begin a discussion of (a subject); make public; air; raise. L16.
E. F. BENSON It was the fulfilment of . . ideas which he had broached to her before marriage. E. HEATH Rather tentatively over coffee and cognac I broached the question.
6 Enlarge or finish (a drilled hole) with a boring bit. Freq. foll. by *out*. M19.
■ **broacher** *noun* (***a***) a person who broaches something; †(***b***) a spit: L16.

broach /brəʊtʃ/ *verb*[2] *intrans. & trans.* E18.
[ORIGIN Unknown.]
Veer or cause (a ship) to veer and present a side to wind and waves. Also foll. by *to*.
R. H. DANA They hove the wheel up just in time to save her from broaching to. *fig.*: T. H. WHITE Its lovely ruined walls . . standing broached to the sun and wind.

broad /brɔːd/ *noun.* ME.
[ORIGIN from the adjective.]
†**1** ***on broad***, = ABROAD *adverb*. Only in ME.
2 (Usu. **B-**.) A large extent of fresh water formed by the widening of a river, *spec.* (usu. **B-**) any of several in East Anglia. M17.
3 *hist.* = ***broad-piece*** s.v. BROAD *adjective*. E18.
4 The broad part (*of* the back etc.). M18.
5 In *pl.* Playing cards. *slang.* L18.
6 A woman (usu. *derog.*); a prostitute. *slang* (chiefly *N. Amer.*). E20.
E. HEMINGWAY There were a couple of broads sitting at the next table.

broad /brɔːd/ *adjective.* Also (*Scot. & N. English*) **braid** /breɪd/.
[ORIGIN Old English *brād* = Old Frisian, Old Saxon *brēd* (Dutch *breed*), Old High German, German *breit*, Old Norse *breiðr*, Gothic *braiþs*, from Germanic.]
1 Extended in direction from side to side, large across, wide, not narrow; (a specified extent) in breadth. OE. ▸**b** Designating or pertaining to certain fabrics (orig.) distinguished by their width, esp. ***broadcloth*** below. LME.
EVELYN A Leaf no broader than a Three-pence. C. DAY A bed . . so broad that it could have easily held several guests. D. MURPHY Shoulders too broad for feminine grace.
as broad as it is long *fig.* (*colloq.*) the same either way.
2 Less definitely: of great extent, spacious, ample. OE.
MILTON In ample space under the broadest shade.
land of the broad acres, **the broad acres** Yorkshire, NE England.
†**3** Large in amount. OE–LME.
4 Wide open; fully developed or expanded. OE.
C. ACHEBE He broke into a broad smile showing smoke- and kola-stained teeth. A. BRINK When I woke up it was broad daylight and the birds were singing.
5 Plain, clear, explicit; most apparent, main. LME.
R. BENTLEY Surely this is a hint broad enough.
6 Of language, a speaker, etc.: outspoken, unreserved, trenchant; vulgar, somewhat coarse or indecent. L15.
H. HALLAM The broadest and most repulsive declaration of all the Calvinistic tenets. S. MIDDLETON Hollies dropped no sexual hint; the broad tongue of the dining room he'd discarded for a politer approach.
7 Of speech, pronunciation, etc.: markedly dialectal, distinctive of a region or class. Cf. BROAD *adverb* 3. L16.
T. GUNN One of my contemporaries arrived at Cambridge with a broad Yorkshire accent.
8 Unrestrained, going to full lengths. E17.
W. IRVING She was the picture of broad, honest, vulgar enjoyment.
9 Tolerant, liberal, catholic, widely inclusive. M19.
New Society The Broad Left—ie, Labour plus Communists.
10 Bold in effect or style; MUSIC slow and expressive. M19.
G. GROTE A portrait . . drawn in colours broad and glaring.
11 Widely applicable, far-ranging; inclusive; general. L19.
J. MORLEY Intellectual education in the broadest sense. N. CHOMSKY The effects of the American invasion were far broader. *Times* In broad outline, the bill dissolves all registered trade unions.
12 Designating a phonetic transcription that distinguishes phonemes but not allophones. L19.
– SPECIAL COLLOCATIONS & COMB.: **broad arrow** a mark resembling a broad arrowhead, distinguishing British government stores, esp. (formerly) prison clothing. **broad-axe** an axe with a broad head. ***broad bean***: see BEAN *noun* 1a. **broadbill** any of certain birds with broad bills; *esp.* (***a***) a shoveler, a scaup; (***b***) a tropical passerine of the Old World family Eurylaimidae. **broad-brim** a hat with a broad brim; *arch.* a member of the Society of Friends (wearing such a hat). **broad-brow** *colloq.* a person with broad interests. **broad-brush** *adjective* general, generalized, incomplete, lacking detail. **Broad Church** Anglican clergy favouring comprehensiveness over an exclusivity of doctrine; *transf.* any group allowing its members a wide range of opinion. **broadcloth** [phr. in Act of Parliament of 1482 specifying width retained, as designation of high quality] cloth of fine twilled woollen or worsted, or of plain-woven cotton. **broad gauge** a railway gauge wider than the standard one (in Great Britain 1.435 metres); *spec.* (*hist.*) the 7-foot (2.1 m) gauge of the Great Western Railway, abolished in 1892. **broadjump** (now *N. Amer.*) = ***long jump*** s.v. LONG *adjective*[1]. **broadleaf** (***a***) any of certain trees or other plants with broad leaves, *esp.* a Jamaican tree, *Terminalia latifolia*, or (*NZ*) the papauma, *Griselinia littoralis*; (***b***) a non-coniferous tree. **broadleaved** *adjective* having broad leaves; *spec.* (of trees) having relatively broad flat leaves rather than needles, i.e. non-coniferous; (of woodland) composed of such trees. **broad ligament** ANATOMY either of the folds of peritoneal tissue that support the uterus, ovaries, and Fallopian tubes. **broadloom** (a carpet) woven in broad width. **broad money** ECONOMICS money in any form including bank or other deposits as well as notes and coins. ***broad pennant***: see PENNANT *noun*[1]. **broad-piece** *hist.* a twenty-shilling piece of the reigns of James I and Charles I (broader and thinner than succeeding coinage). **broad reach** *noun & verb* (SAILING) (***a***) *noun* a point of sailing in which the wind blows over a boat's quarter, between the beam and the stern; (***b***) *verb intrans.* (***broad-reach***) sail with the wind in this position. **broadscale** *adjective* on a broad scale, extensive. **broad seal** (chiefly *hist.*) the Great Seal of England. **broadsheet** (***a***) a large sheet of paper carrying information etc. printed on one side only; (***b***) a newspaper with a large format. **broad-spectrum** *adjective* (of a drug) effective against a wide range of pathogens. **broadsword** a sword with a broad blade. **broadtail** = BREITSCHWANZ. **broadwalk** a broad street or footpath. **broadway** (***a***) a wide road; (***b***) (**B-**) [a street in New York City famous for its theatres] the main commercial part of New York theatre life.
■ **broaden** *verb trans. & intrans.* make or become broader; widen (*out*), dilate. E18. **broadish** *adjective* LME. †**broadling(s)** *adverb* = BROADWAYS ME–E18. **broadly** *adverb* in a broad manner; widely, generally, fully: L16. **broadness** *noun* (***a***) (now *rare*) breadth; (***b***) coarseness, indelicacy: LME. **broadways**, †**-way** *adverb* in the direction of the breadth, laterally L16. **broadwise** *adverb* = BROADWAYS L17.

broad /brɔːd/ *adverb.* Also (*Scot. & N. English*) **braid** /breɪd/.
[ORIGIN Old English *brāde*, formed as BROAD *adjective*.]
1 Broadly, in an extensive way; widely; fully. OE.
J. WESLEY Being in bed, but broad awake.
2 Outspokenly, plainly. LME.
3 With a broad pronunciation etc. M16.
4 NAUTICAL. At a distance to one side. Foll. by *on* the bow etc. M19.

broadcast /ˈbrɔːdkɑːst/ *adjective, noun, & adverb.* M18.
[ORIGIN from BROAD *adverb* + pa. pple of CAST *verb*.]
▸ **A** *adjective.* **1** Of seed, sowing, etc.: sown or performed by scattering widely rather than by placing in drills or rows. Also *gen.* (chiefly *fig.*), widely disseminated or scattered abroad. M18.
2 Disseminated by means of radio or television. E20.
▸ **B** *noun.* **1** Broadcast sowing of seed. M18.
2 (An act of) broadcasting by radio or television; a radio or television transmission or programme. E20.
outside broadcast: see OUTSIDE *adjective*.
▸ **C** *adverb.* (Sown etc.) in a broadcast manner. M19.

broadcast /ˈbrɔːdkɑːst/ *verb.* Pa. t. & pple **-cast**, (occas.) **-casted**. L18.
[ORIGIN from BROAD *adverb* + CAST *verb*.]
1 *verb trans.* Sow (seed) in a broadcast manner; *gen.* (chiefly *fig.*) spread widely. L18.
2 a *verb trans.* Disseminate (news, music, etc.) by radio or television. E20. ▸**b** *verb intrans.* Speak, sing, play, etc., for radio or television transmission; put out a radio or television transmission. E20.
■ **broadcaster** *noun* (***a***) a person whose speech, performance, etc., is (esp. habitually) broadcast on radio or television; a person, company, etc., that puts out broadcasts; (***b***) an instrument for broadcasting seed etc.: E20.

broad-minded /brɔːdˈmʌɪndɪd/ *adjective.* L19.
[ORIGIN from BROAD *adjective* + MINDED.]
Tolerant or liberal in thought or opinion.
■ **broad-mindedness** *noun* L19.

broadside /ˈbrɔːdsʌɪd/ *noun, adverb, & verb.* Orig. two words. E16.
[ORIGIN from BROAD *adjective* + SIDE *noun*.]
▸ **A** *noun.* **1** The part of a ship's side above the water between the bow and the quarter. E16.
2 (A discharge of) all the guns situated or able to fire on one side of a ship; *fig.* a verbal onslaught. L16.
3 A broadsheet. L16.
▸ **B** *adverb.* With the side turned to or *to* a given point or object; *loosely* set sideways. L19.
broadside on with the side turned towards a given object etc.
▸ **C** *verb intrans.* Of a motorcycle, motorcyclist, etc.: perform a controlled skid as part of a deliberate manoeuvre. M20.

broast /brəʊst/ *verb trans. N. Amer.* L20.
[ORIGIN Blend of BROIL *verb*[1] and ROAST *verb*.]
Prepare (food) using a cooking process that combines broiling and roasting. Freq. as ***broasted*** *ppl adjective.*

Brobdingnagian /brɒbdɪŋˈnagɪən/ *noun & adjective*. **E18.**
[ORIGIN from *Brobdingnag*, a land in Swift's *Gulliver's Travels* where everything is on a gigantic scale, + -IAN.]
▸ **A** *noun*. An inhabitant of Brobdingnag; a giant, a huge person. **E18.**
▸ **B** *adjective*. Gigantic, colossal. **E18.**
■ Also **Brobdingnag** *adjective* **E19.**

Broca /ˈbrəʊkə/ *noun*. **L19.**
[ORIGIN P. Paul *Broca* (1824–80), French surgeon and anthropologist.]
Used in *possess.* to denote things studied by Broca.
Broca's aphasia aphasia with severe impairment or loss of speech. **Broca's area** the region of the frontal cortex of the brain concerned with the production of speech.

brocade /brəˈkeɪd/ *noun & verb*. Orig. †**-a(r)do** (pl. of noun **-os**). **L16.**
[ORIGIN Spanish, Portuguese *brocado*, with blending of French *brocart* from Italian *broccato* = embossed fabric, from *brocco* twisted thread: see -ADE.]
▸ **A** *noun*. A rich fabric woven with raised patterns, orig. with added gold or silver threads. **L16.**
▸ **B** *verb trans.* Work with a raised pattern. Chiefly as ***brocaded*** *ppl adjective*. **M17.**

†**brocage** *noun* var. of BROKAGE.

brocard /ˈbrəʊkəd, *foreign* brɔkaːr (*pl. same*)/ *noun*. **M16.**
[ORIGIN French, or medieval Latin *brocardus*, appellative use of the Latinized form of *Burchart*, 11th-cent. bishop of Worms and compiler of volumes of ecclesiastical rules.]
1 A cutting speech, a jibe. *rare*. **M16.**
2 An elementary legal principle or maxim. **E17.**

†**brocardo** *noun* see BROCADE *noun*.

brocatelle /brɒkəˈtɛl/ *noun*. **M17.**
[ORIGIN French (earlier *brocatel*) from Italian *broccatello* gold tinsel, dim. of *broccato*: see BROCADE.]
An inferior type of brocade, usu. of silk or wool.

brocatello /brɒkəˈtɛləʊ/ *noun*. **M18.**
[ORIGIN Italian *brocatello di Siena*, so called from its colouring: see BROCATELLE.]
A kind of variegated marble, clouded and veined chiefly with yellow.

broccoli /ˈbrɒkəli/ *noun*. Also †**brocoli**. **M17.**
[ORIGIN Italian pl. of *broccolo* cabbage sprout or head, dim. of *brocco* shoot, BROACH *noun*[1].]
A hardy variety of cauliflower; *esp.* (often more fully ***sprouting broccoli***) a form of this producing many small heads.

broch /brɒk, brɒx/ *noun*. In senses 1 & 2 *Scot. & N. English*. Also **brough**, **brugh**, /brʌx, brʌf/. **L15.**
[ORIGIN Metath. alt. of BURGH: cf. Old Norse *borg* enclosure, castle.]
1 = BURGH. **L15.**
2 A luminous ring round the moon etc.; a halo. **L15.**
3 (In ARCHAEOLOGY usu. ***broch.***) A prehistoric round stone tower in N. Scotland and adjacent islands. **M17.**

brochan /ˈbrɒxən/ *noun*[1]. *Scot.* **E18.**
[ORIGIN Gaelic.]
Gruel; thin porridge.

†**brochan** *noun*[2] var. of BRACKEN *noun*[2].

brochantite /ˈbrɒʃ(ə)ntʌɪt/ *noun*. **E19.**
[ORIGIN from A. J. M. *Brochant* de Villiers (1772–1840), French geologist + -ITE[1].]
MINERALOGY. A bluish-green monoclinic basic copper sulphate usu. occurring as prismatic or elongated crystals or as crystal aggregates.

†**broche** *noun*, *verb*[1] see BROACH *noun*[1], *verb*[1], BROOCH.

†**broche** *verb*[2] *trans.* **L15–M19.**
[ORIGIN from French *brocher* to stitch, brocade: see BROACH *verb*[1].]
Stitch or work with raised figures.

broché /ˈbrəʊʃeɪ, *foreign* brɔʃe/ *adjective & noun*. **L19.**
[ORIGIN French, pa. pple of *brocher*: see BROCHE *verb*[2].]
(A material, esp. silk) woven with a pattern on the surface.

brochette /brɒˈʃɛt/ *noun*. **L15.**
[ORIGIN French, dim. of *broche* BROACH *noun*[1]: see -ETTE.]
1 A small broach, skewer, or spit; *spec.* a skewer on which chunks of meat are cooked. **L15.**
À LA ***brochette***.
2 A pin or bar used to fasten medals, orders, etc., to clothing; a set of decorations worn in this way. **M19.**

brochure /ˈbrəʊʃə, brɒˈʃʊə/ *noun*. **M18.**
[ORIGIN French, lit. 'stitching, stitched work', formed as BROCHE *verb*[1] + -URE.]
A booklet or pamphlet, esp. giving information about the amenities of a place etc.

brock /brɒk/ *noun*[1].
[ORIGIN Old English *broc(c)* from Celtic base of Welsh, Cornish *broch*, Breton *broc'h*, Irish, Gaelic *broc*, Old Irish *brocc*.]
1 A badger (often qualified as *stinking*). **OE.**
2 A disreputable or dirty man. **E17.**

brock /brɒk/ *noun*[2]. Now *rare* or *obsolete*. **E16.**
[ORIGIN Abbreviation.]
= BROCKET 1.

brock *noun*[3] see BROKE *noun*.

brocked *adjective* var. of BROCKIT.

Brocken /ˈbrɒk(ə)n/ *noun*. **E19.**
[ORIGIN The highest of the Harz Mountains in Germany, where particularly observed.]
Brocken spectre, ***spectre of the Brocken***, a magnified shadow on a bank of cloud in high mountains, often with a coloured halo.

brocket /ˈbrɒkɪt/ *noun*. **LME.**
[ORIGIN Anglo-Norman *broquet* dim. (see -ET[1]) of *broque* dial. var. of *broche* BROACH *noun*[1]: cf. French *brocard* young roe, brocket.]
1 A red deer stag in its second year, with straight horns. **LME.**
2 A small Central or S. American deer of the genus *Mazama*. **M19.**

brockit /ˈbrɒkɪt/ *adjective*. *Scot.* Also **brocked**. **L16.**
[ORIGIN Perh. from BROCK *noun*[1] + -ED[2], but cf. Norwegian *broket*, Danish *broget*.]
Of mixed colour, esp. black and white; with black and white spots or stripes.

Brock's benefit /brɒks ˈbɛnɪfɪt/ *noun phr.* **E20.**
[ORIGIN Name of the public fireworks display held annually at the Crystal Palace, London, from 1865 to 1936, from C. T. *Brock*, firework manufacturer.]
A spectacular display of pyrotechnics. Freq. *fig.*

†**brocoli** *noun* var. of BROCCOLI.

brod /brɒd/ *noun & verb*. Long *obsolete* exc. *dial.* See also BRAD. **ME.**
[ORIGIN App. from Old Norse *broddr* = Old English *brord* spike: cf. BROG *noun*, PROD *noun*[1].]
▸ **A** *noun*. †**1** A shoot. Only in **ME.**
2 = BRAD. **ME.**
3 (A prick from) a goad. **LME.**
▸ **B** *verb*. Infl. **-dd-**.
†**1** *verb intrans.* Sprout. Only in **ME.**
2 *verb trans.* Goad, prod. *Scot. & N. English*. **LME.**
■ **brodder** *noun* (*Scot. & N. English*) a person who uses a brod **L19.**

brodekin /ˈbrɒdɪkɪn/ *noun*. Also **-quin**, **brodkin** /ˈbrɒdkɪn/. **L15.**
[ORIGIN French *brodequin*: see BUSKIN.]
hist. A buskin.

broderer /ˈbrəʊdərə/ *noun*. *arch.* **LME.**
[ORIGIN Var. of BROIDERER.]
An embroiderer. (Now only used as a guild-name.)

broderie anglaise /ˌbrəʊd(ə)rɪ ɒŋˈɡleɪz/ *noun phr.* **M19.**
[ORIGIN French = English embroidery.]
Open embroidery on linen, cambric, etc.; fabric so embroidered.

brodkin *noun* var. of BRODEKIN.

Broeder /ˈbruːdə, *foreign* ˈbrudər/ *noun*. *S. Afr.* **M20.**
[ORIGIN Afrikaans from Dutch: see BROTHER *noun*.]
A member of the Broederbond, a largely secret society open only to male Protestant Afrikaners.

brog /brɒg/ *noun & verb*. *Scot. & N. English*. **L15.**
[ORIGIN Unknown: cf. BROD.]
▸ **A** *noun*. **1** A pricking or boring instrument, a bradawl. Also, a prick with this. **L15.**
2 A short stick, esp. to stand in the ground. **L18.**
▸ **B** *verb*. Infl. **-gg-**.
1 *verb intrans.* = BROGGLE. **L17.**
2 *verb trans.* Prick, prod; pierce with a brog. **L18.**

brogan /ˈbrəʊg(ə)n/ *noun*. **M19.**
[ORIGIN Irish *brógán*, Gaelic *brógan* dim. of *bróg* BROGUE *noun*[2].]
A coarse stout leather shoe reaching to the ankle.

†**brogger** *noun*. **LME–E18.**
[ORIGIN Var. of BROKER: thus Anglo-Norman *brogour* beside *brocour*.]
A broker; *esp.* a corrupt jobber of offices.

broggle /ˈbrɒg(ə)l/ *verb intrans.* *N. English*. **M17.**
[ORIGIN Frequentative of BROG *verb*: see -LE[3].]
Fish for eels with a baited stick, sniggle.

brogue /brəʊg/ *noun*[1]. Long *obsolete* exc. *Scot.* **M16.**
[ORIGIN Unknown.]
An escheat; a fraud, a trick.

brogue /brəʊg/ *noun*[2]. **L16.**
[ORIGIN Irish, Gaelic *bróg* (Old Irish *bróc*) from Old Norse *brók*: see BREECH *noun*.]
1 a A rough shoe of untanned hide worn (esp. formerly) in the wilder parts of Ireland and the Scottish Highlands. **L16.** ▸**b** A strong outdoor shoe with ornamental perforated bands. **E20.**
†**2** In *pl.* Hose, trousers; waterproof leggings with feet, used in angling. **E17–L19.**
■ **brogued** *adjective* (**a**) made with a strong vamp like a brogue; (**b**) *rare* wearing brogues: **E19.**

brogue /brəʊg/ *noun*[3] & *verb*. **E18.**
[ORIGIN Perh. same word as BROGUE *noun*[2].]
▸ **A** *noun*. A strongly marked dialectal (esp. Irish) accent. **E18.**
▸ **B** *verb trans. & intrans.* Speak or utter with a brogue. *rare*. **E19.**

†**broid** *verb trans.* **ME–E17.**
[ORIGIN Alt. of BRAID *verb*[1] after pa. pple *broiden*: see BROWDEN.]
Plait, interweave.

†**broiden** *ppl adjective* var. of BROWDEN.

broider /ˈbrɔɪdə/ *verb trans. & intrans.* *arch.* **LME.**
[ORIGIN Old French *brosder*, *brou(s)der* (mod. *broder*) with inf. ending retained; alt. by assoc. with BROID.]
Embroider; adorn (as) with embroidery.
■ **broiderer** *noun* (*arch.*) an embroiderer **LME.** **broidery** *noun* (*poet.*) embroidery **LME.**

broil /brɔɪl/ *noun*[1]. **E16.**
[ORIGIN from BROIL *verb*[2].]
A tumult; a quarrel.

broil /brɔɪl/ *noun*[2]. **L16.**
[ORIGIN from BROIL *verb*[1].]
1 A broiling; great heat. **L16.**
2 (A piece of) broiled meat. **E19.**
LONDON ***broil***.

broil /brɔɪl/ *verb*[1]. **LME.**
[ORIGIN Old French *bruler*, *bruller*, earlier *brusler* (mod. *brûler*) burn, from Proto-Romance, perh. from Germanic base of BURN *verb* + Latin *ustulare* burn up.]
†**1** *verb trans.* Burn; char. **LME–M16.**
2 *verb trans.* Cook (meat) by placing it over a fire on a gridiron etc.; grill. **LME.**
3 *verb intrans.* Be subjected to heat; become very hot, esp. *fig.* with excitement, anger, etc. **M16.**
4 *verb trans.* Scorch, make very hot. **M17.**

broil /brɔɪl/ *verb*[2]. **LME.**
[ORIGIN Anglo-Norman *broiller*, Old French *bröoillier* (mod. *brouiller*), from Proto-Romance, from base of Old French *breu*: see BREWIS.]
†**1** *verb trans.* Mix confusedly. **LME–M17.**
2 *verb intrans.* Engage in a broil, wrangle. **LME.**
3 *verb trans.* Involve in confusion, discompose; embroil. Now *rare* or *obsolete*. **E16.**

broiler /ˈbrɔɪlə/ *noun*[1]. **ME.**
[ORIGIN from BROIL *verb*[1] + -ER[1].]
1 A person who or thing which broils meat etc. **ME.** ▸**b** *spec.* A gridiron or other apparatus used in broiling. **LME.** ▸**c** A very hot day. *colloq.* **E19.**
2 A chicken reared for broiling. **M19.**
– COMB.: **broiler chicken**, **broiler fowl** = sense 2 above; **broiler house** a building for rearing broiler chickens in close confinement.

broiler /ˈbrɔɪlə/ *noun*[2]. *rare*. **M17.**
[ORIGIN from BROIL *verb*[2] + -ER[1].]
A person who stirs up or engages in broils.

†**brokage** *noun*. Also **brocage**. **LME–M18.**
[ORIGIN Anglo-Norman *brocage*, Anglo-Latin *brocagium*: see BROKER, -AGE.]
Brokerage; usu. in an unfavourable sense: corrupt dealing, bribery, pimping, etc.

broke /brəʊk/ *noun*. Also (now *dial.*) **brock** /brɒk/.
[ORIGIN Old English *broc* (sense 1), *gebroc* (sense 2), formed as BREAK *verb*.]
†**1** Affliction, misery. Only in **OE.**
2 A fragment. Long *obsolete* exc. *dial.* **OE.**
†**3** A wound, a rupture. **LME–M16.**
4 In *pl.* Short pieces of wool esp. from the edge of a fleece. **L19.**

broke /brəʊk/ *adjective*. **ME.**
[ORIGIN pa. pple (now arch.) of BREAK *verb*.]
1 = BROKEN. Long *arch.* in *gen.* sense. **ME.**
2 *pred.* Without money, penniless; ruined, bankrupt. *colloq.* **E18.**
With intensive: ***dead broke***, ***flat broke***, ***stony broke***, ***broke to the wide***, etc. **go broke** go bankrupt. **go for broke** (orig. *US*) give one's all, make strenuous efforts.
3 Of a horse: broken to harness. Chiefly *US*. **E19.**

broke /brəʊk/ *verb*[1] *intrans.* & (*rare*) *trans.* **LME.**
[ORIGIN Back-form. from BROKER.]
Bargain, negotiate; traffic (in). Now *spec.* in commercial matters: act as a broker or agent (*in*, *for*).

broke *verb*[2] *pa. t.* of BREAK *verb*.

broken /ˈbrəʊk(ə)n/ *adjective*. **ME.**
[ORIGIN pa. pple of BREAK *verb*.]
▸ **I** *gen.* **1** In the senses of BREAK *verb*: separated forcibly into parts, in fragments, fractured, shattered, burst, split, not intact or in working order, damaged; produced by breaking, fragmentary. **ME.**

AV *Ps.* 31:12 I am like a broken vessell. J. TYNDALL Broken fragments of rock. T. PYNCHON The table littered with broken-spined books.

▸ **II** *spec.* **2** Of a limb etc.: having the bone fractured. Of the back or neck: suffering fracture or dislocation of bones. Of the head: grazed, laid open. **LME.**
3 Not continuous or uniform; uneven, interrupted, disjointed, disconnected. **LME.** ▸**b** Of language: imperfectly spoken, with incomplete syntax. **L16.**

LD MACAULAY His rest that night was broken. BOSW. SMITH The Carthaginian cavalry and elephants extricated themselves . . from the broken ground. J. MCPHEE The skies are broken, and around the gray clouds are wide bays of blue. **b** A. POWELL A Viennese . . who talked Comic Opera broken English.

4 Crushed in health, strength, feelings, etc.; exhausted, enfeebled; subdued, humbled. **L15.** ▸**b** Chiefly of

animals: trained to obedience or discipline; tamed. Freq. foll. by *in*. E19.
5 Financially ruined, bankrupt. L16.
6 Violated, transgressed, not kept. E17.

A. LEWIS A mirror cracked by broken vows.

7 Of water: foaming, turbulent; choppy, rough. L18.
8 Dispersed in confusion, routed. E19.

SIR W. SCOTT Now leader of a broken host.

9 *MUSIC*. Of an octave or other chord: of which the notes are played in succession rather than together. L19.
– SPECIAL COLLOCATIONS & COMB.: **broken-backed** *adjective* †(*a*) hunch-backed; (*b*) having a broken back; *NAUTICAL* (of a ship) drooping at both ends through damage to the frame. **broken colour**: mixed or juxtaposed closely with another. **broken-down** worn out, dilapidated, decayed, ruined, having ceased to function. **broken field** *AMER. FOOTBALL* the area beyond the line of scrimmage where the defenders are relatively scattered (giving opportunities for the opposing players to run with the ball). **broken-field** *adverb* (*N. Amer. colloq.*) in the manner of a footballer running in the broken field. **broken heart** a spirit crushed by grief etc. **broken home**: that of a family lacking one parent, usu. through divorce or separation. **broken line**: made up of dashes. **broken man** (*a*) a man reduced to despair; (*b*) *SCOTTISH HISTORY* an outlaw. ***broken reed***: see REED *noun*[1]. **broken tea** tea siftings. **broken time** (working) time reduced by interruptions. **broken wind** a chronic disabling condition of horses due to rupture of air cells in the lungs. **broken-winded** *adjective* suffering from broken wind (often *fig.*).
■ **brokenly** *adverb* L16. **brokenness** /-n-n-/ *noun* E17.

broken-hearted /brəʊk(ə)nˈhɑːtɪd/ *adjective*. E16.
[ORIGIN from BROKEN + HEARTED.]
Having a broken heart; crushed by grief etc.
■ **broken-heartedly** *adverb* L17. **broken-heartedness** *noun* L18.

broker /ˈbrəʊkə/ *noun & verb*. ME.
[ORIGIN Anglo-Norman *brocour*, *brogour* = Anglo-Latin *brocator*, Provençal *abrocador*, of unknown origin.]
▸ **A** *noun* †**1 a** A retailer; *derog*. a pedlar, a petty dealer. ME–M18. ▸**b** A dealer in second-hand furniture, clothing, etc.; a pawnbroker. L16.
2 A middleman in business, *esp*. a stockbroker; an agent, a commissioner; *gen*. an intermediary. ME.
honest broker: see HONEST *adjective*.
†**3** A go-between in love affairs, a matchmaker; a pimp, a bawd. LME–L17.
4 A person licensed to sell or appraise distrained goods. E19.
– COMB.: **broker-dealer** a person combining the former functions of a broker and jobber on the Stock Exchange.
▸ **B** *verb*. **1** *verb intrans*. Act as a broker. Chiefly as ***brokering*** *verbal noun & ppl adjective*. *rare*. M17.
2 *verb trans*. Act as a broker with respect to, arrange as a broker. M20.
■ **brokerage** *noun* (*a*) = BROKING 1; (*b*) a broker's fee or commission: LME. **brokeress** *noun* (now *rare* or *obsolete*) a female broker L16. †**brokery** *noun* (*a*) = BROKING 1; (*b*) a broker's wares: L16–M18.

broking /ˈbrəʊkɪŋ/ *noun*. M16.
[ORIGIN from BROKE *verb*[1] + -ING[1].]
1 The trade of a broker, acting as a broker. M16.
†**2** Dishonest or disreputable dealing. L16–E17.

brolga /ˈbrɒlɡə/ *noun*. L19.
[ORIGIN Kamilaroi *burralga*.]
An Australian crane, *Grus rubicunda*. Also called ***native companion***.

brolly /ˈbrɒli/ *noun*. L19.
[ORIGIN Alt. of UMBRELLA.]
1 An umbrella. *colloq*. L19.
2 A parachute. *slang*. M20.

brom- *combining form* see BROMO-.

bromate /ˈbrəʊmeɪt/ *noun*. M19.
[ORIGIN from BROMIC + -ATE[1].]
CHEMISTRY. A salt or ester of bromic acid.

bromatology /brəʊməˈtɒlədʒi/ *noun*. *rare*. E19.
[ORIGIN from Greek *brōmat-*, *brōma* food + -OLOGY.]
The science of food; a treatise on this.

brome /brəʊm/ *noun*. M18.
[ORIGIN mod. Latin *Bromus* (see below) from Latin *bromos*, from Greek *bromos*, *brōmos* oats.]
Any of several grasses of the genus *Bromus* and related genera, usu. having spikelets in loose panicles and with long-awned lemmas. Also ***brome-grass***.
false brome any of several grasses resembling bromes, of the genus *Brachypodium*, esp. *B. sylvaticum*, common in woods and hedges. ***soft brome***: see SOFT *adjective*.

bromelia /brəˈmiːlɪə/ *noun*. E19.
[ORIGIN mod. Latin, from Olaf *Bromel* (1639–1705), Swedish botanist: see -IA[1].]
A plant of the New World family Bromeliaceae (and esp. of the genus *Bromelia*), having short stems and lance-shaped spiny leaves, e.g. pineapple.
■ **bromeliˈaceous** *adjective* of or pertaining to the family Bromeliaceae L19. **bromeliad** *noun* a plant of the family Bromeliaceae M19.

bromelin /ˈbrəʊmɪlɪn/ *noun*. L19.
[ORIGIN from BROMELIA + -IN[1].]
A proteolytic enzyme present in the juice of the pineapple.

bromic /ˈbrəʊmɪk/ *adjective*. E19.
[ORIGIN from BROMINE + -IC.]
CHEMISTRY. Of or containing bromine; ***bromic acid***, a strongly oxidizing acid, $HBrO_3$, known only as an aqueous solution.

bromide /ˈbrəʊmʌɪd/ *noun*. M19.
[ORIGIN from BROMINE + -IDE.]
1 *CHEMISTRY*. A compound of bromine with a less electronegative element or radical; a salt or ester of hydrobromic acid. M19.
2 a (A dose of) potassium or sodium bromide taken as a sedative. L19. ▸**b** *fig*. Something or someone boring, commonplace, or conventional; *esp*. a soothing platitude or trite remark. Orig. *US*. E20.
3 A reproduction on bromide paper. L20.
– COMB.: **bromide paper** photographic printing paper coated with silver bromide emulsion.
■ **bromidic** /brə(ʊ)ˈmɪdɪk/ *adjective* of the nature of a bromide; commonplace, trite: E20.

bromidrosis /brəʊmɪˈdrəʊsɪs/ *noun*. M19.
[ORIGIN from Greek *brōmos* stink + *hidrōs* sweat + -OSIS.]
MEDICINE. Offensively odorous perspiration due to bacterial breakdown of sweat.

brominate /ˈbrəʊmɪneɪt/ *verb trans*. M19.
[ORIGIN from BROMINE + -ATE[3].]
Treat with bromine; *CHEMISTRY* introduce one or more bromine atoms into (a compound or molecule) usu. in place of hydrogen. Freq. as ***brominated*** *ppl adjective*.
■ **bromiˈnation** *noun* M19.

bromine /ˈbrəʊmiːn/ *noun*. E19.
[ORIGIN from French *brome* bromine, from Greek *brōmos* stink: see -INE[5].]
A rank-smelling, highly toxic, dark red volatile liquid which is a chemical element of the halogen group, atomic no. 35 (symbol Br).
■ **bromize** *verb trans*. (now *rare* or *obsolete*) treat, compound, or impregnate with bromine or its compounds M19.

bromism /ˈbrəʊmɪz(ə)m/ *noun*. M19.
[ORIGIN from BROMINE + -ISM.]
MEDICINE. A condition of torpor and weakness caused by excessive intake of bromides.

bromo /ˈbrəʊməʊ/ *noun*. *colloq*. Pl. **-os**. E20.
[ORIGIN from BROMIDE + -O.]
A bromide (BROMIDE 2a, b), bromides. Also, toilet paper.

bromo- /ˈbrəʊməʊ/ *combining form* of BROMINE: see -O-. Before a vowel also **brom-** /brəʊm/.
■ **bromargyrite** /brəˈmɑːdʒɪrʌɪt/ *noun* (*MINERALOGY*) native silver bromide, a mineral crystallizing in the cubic system and usu. occurring as colourless, grey, pale yellow, or green crystals M19. **bromoform** *noun* (*CHEMISTRY*) a colourless liquid, $CHBr_3$, analogous to chloroform and formerly having some germicidal use M19. **Bromo-ˈSeltzer** *noun* (proprietary name for) an analgesic preparation containing sodium bromide L19. †**bromuret** *noun* = BROMIDE 1 M–L19. **bromyrite** /ˈbrəʊmɪrʌɪt/ *noun* = BROMARGYRITE M19.

bromocriptine /brəʊməʊˈkrɪptiːn/ *noun*. L20.
[ORIGIN from BROMO- + ERGO)CRYPTINE.]
PHARMACOLOGY. A synthetic derivative of the alkaloid ergocryptine that stimulates the dopaminergic receptors of the brain, inhibiting the release of prolactin, and is used in the treatment of Parkinsonism, galactorrhoea, and other conditions.

Brompton /ˈbrɒm(p)t(ə)n/ *noun*. E18.
[ORIGIN A district of London in the borough of Kensington and Chelsea.]
1 *HORTICULTURE*. In full ***Brompton stock***. A biennial variety of stock developed at Brompton Park Nursery. E18.
2 ***Brompton cocktail***, a powerful painkiller and sedative consisting of vodka or other liquor laced with morphine and sometimes also cocaine, supposedly invented at Brompton Hospital for the use of cancer patients. L20.

bronc /brɒŋk/ *noun*. *colloq*. L19.
[ORIGIN Abbreviation.]
A bronco.

bronchi *noun* pl. of BRONCHUS.

bronchia /ˈbrɒŋkɪə/ *noun pl*. Now *rare* or *obsolete*. Formerly also treated as *sing*. with pl. **-chiae** /-kɪiː/. L17.
[ORIGIN Late Latin from Greek *brogkhia*, from *brogkhos* windpipe.]
The ramifications of the two main bronchi in the lungs. Cf. BRONCHUS.

bronchial /ˈbrɒŋkɪəl/ *adjective*. L17.
[ORIGIN from BRONCHIA + -AL[1].]
Of or pertaining to the bronchi or their branches.
■ **bronchially** *adverb* L19.

bronchiectasis /brɒŋkɪˈɛktəsɪs/ *noun*. L19.
[ORIGIN from BRONCHIA + Greek *ektasis* dilatation.]
MEDICINE. Widening of the bronchi or their branches.

bronchio- *combining form* see BRONCHO-.

bronchiole /ˈbrɒŋkɪəʊl/ *noun*. M19.
[ORIGIN mod. Latin *bronchiolus*, *-um* dims. of BRONCHIA: see -OLE[1].]
ANATOMY. Any of the smallest branches of a bronchus, without mucous glands or cartilage.
■ **bronchiolar** /brɒŋkɪˈəʊlə/ *adjective* E20. **bronchiolitis** /ˌbrɒŋkɪəˈlʌɪtɪs/ *noun* inflammation of the bronchioles L19.

bronchitic /brɒŋˈkɪtɪk/ *adjective & noun*. M19.
[ORIGIN from BRONCHITIS + -IC.]
▸ **A** *adjective*. Of, or pertaining to bronchitis; suffering from bronchitis. M19.
▸ **B** *noun*. A sufferer from bronchitis. L19.

bronchitis /brɒŋˈkʌɪtɪs/ *noun*. E19.
[ORIGIN from BRONCHUS + -ITIS.]
Inflammation of the mucous membranes of the bronchi.
verminous bronchitis: see VERMINOUS 3a.

broncho *noun & adjective* var. of BRONCO.

broncho- /ˈbrɒŋkəʊ/ *combining form*. Also (occas.) **bronchio-** /ˈbrɒŋkɪəʊ/.
[ORIGIN Greek *brogkho-*, from *brogkhos* BRONCHUS; forms with *-io-* from BRONCHIA: see -O-.]
Forming nouns and adjectives with the sense 'of the bronchi, windpipe, or lungs'.
■ **bronchocele** *noun* [Greek *brogkhokēlē*: see -CELE] (*a*) (a) localized widening of a bronchus; (*b*) (now *rare* or *obsolete*) goitre: M17. **bronchoconˈstriction** *noun* narrowing of the bronchi E20. **bronchoconˈstrictor** *noun* a substance which causes bronchoconstriction E20. **bronchodiˈlator** *noun* a substance which causes widening of the bronchi E20. **bronchogenic** /-ˈdʒɛnɪk/ *adjective* of bronchial origin E20. **bronchogram** *noun* an X-ray image of the bronchi produced by partially filling them with a radio-opaque material M20. **bronchography** /brɒŋˈkɒɡrəfi/ *noun* X-ray examination of the bronchi M20. **bronchophonic** /-ˈfɒnɪk/ *adjective* of or pertaining to bronchophony M19. **bronchophony** /brɒŋˈkɒfəni/ *noun* abnormally loud vocal resonance audible stethoscopically in consolidating lung disease M19. **bronchopneuˈmonia** *noun* infection of the pulmonary alveoli spreading by the bronchi and bronchioles M19. **bronchoˈpulmonary** *adjective* pertaining to or affecting the bronchi and lungs M19. **bronchoˈrrhoea** *noun* persistently excessive bronchial secretion of mucus M19. **bronchoscope** *noun* an instrument for internal inspection of the bronchi L19. **bronchoscopic** /-ˈskɒpɪk/ *adjective* of or pertaining to the bronchoscope or bronchoscopy E20. **bronchoscopy** /brɒŋˈkɒskəpi/ *noun* the use of a bronchoscope E20. **bronchospasm** *noun* spasm of bronchial smooth muscle producing narrowing of the bronchi E20. **bronchotomy** /brɒŋˈkɒtəmi/ *noun* (now *rare* or *obsolete*) tracheotomy E18.

bronchus /ˈbrɒŋkəs/ *noun*. Usu. in pl. **bronchi** /ˈbrɒŋkʌɪ/. L17.
[ORIGIN Late Latin from Greek *brogkhos* windpipe.]
ANATOMY. Orig., either of the two branches into which the windpipe divides. Now also, any of the ramifying system of cartilage-lined passages between the windpipe and the bronchioles. Cf. BRONCHIA, BRONCHIOLE.

bronco /ˈbrɒŋkəʊ/ *noun & adjective*. Also **-cho**. M19.
[ORIGIN Spanish = rough, rude.]
▸ **A** *noun*. Pl. **-os**. A wild or half-tamed horse, esp. of the western US. M19.
– COMB.: **broncobuster** *slang* a breaker-in of broncos.
▸ **B** *adjective*. Wild, uncontrollable, rough. *US colloq*. M19.

bronto- /ˈbrɒntəʊ/ *combining form* of Greek *brontē* thunder: see -O-.
■ **brontology** /brɒnˈtɒlədʒi/ *noun* (*rare*) the branch of knowledge that deals with thunder M18. **brontoˈphobia** *noun* irrational fear of thunderstorms E20. **brontothere** *noun* a titanothere, esp. of the genus *Brontotherium* L19.

brontosaurus /brɒntəˈsɔːrəs/ *noun*. Pl. **-ruses**, **-ri** /-rʌɪ/. L19.
[ORIGIN mod. Latin, formed as BRONTO- + Greek *sauros* -SAUR.]
A large herbivorous sauropod dinosaur of the genus *Brontosaurus* (or *Apatosaurus*), known as fossils of the Jurassic and Cretaceous periods.
■ **ˈbrontosaur** *noun* a large dinosaur of the group which includes the brontosaurus; *spec*. = BRONTOSAURUS: L19. **brontosaurian** *adjective* of or like a brontosaurus; chiefly *fig*., ponderous, clumsy: E20.

Bronx /brɒŋks/ *noun*. *US*. E20.
[ORIGIN A borough of New York City.]
1 In full ***Bronx cocktail***. A cocktail of gin, vermouth, and orange juice. E20.
2 ***Bronx cheer***, a sound of derision or contempt made by blowing through closed lips with the tongue between; = RASPBERRY 3a. E20.

bronze /brɒnz/ *noun & adjective*. E18.
[ORIGIN French from Italian *bronzo*, prob. from Persian *birinj* brass.]
▸ **A** *noun*. **1** A brown alloy of copper with up to one-third tin, often with small amounts of other metals; (with specifying word) such an alloy with a particular composition or constituent. Cf. BRASS *noun*. E18. ▸**b** Bronze taken as a type of hardness or insensitivity; impudence, effrontery, nerve. Now *rare*. E18. ▸**c** = ***bronze medal*** below. M20.
ALUMINIUM ***bronze***. ***Corinthian bronze***: see CORINTHIAN *adjective* 1. *MANGANESE* ***bronze***. *PHOSPHOR* ***bronze***. ***plastic bronze***: see PLASTIC *adjective & noun*[3]. ***white bronze***: see WHITE *adjective*.
2 A statue or other work of art made of bronze. E18.
3 A brown metallic powder used in painting etc. M18.
4 The colour of bronze. E19.
▸ **B** *attrib*. or as *adjective*. Made of bronze; of the colour of bronze. M19.
– SPECIAL COLLOCATIONS & COMB.: **Bronze Age** the period when weapons and tools were predominantly made of copper and its

B

alloys. **bronze diabetes** = HAEMOCHROMATOSIS. **bronze medal**: awarded for a third place in the modern Olympic Games etc. **bronze powder** = sense A.3 above. **bronzewing** any of a number of Australasian pigeons, esp. *Phaps chalcoptera*.
■ **bronzy** *adjective* tinged with bronze colour; like bronze: M19.

bronze /brɒnz/ *verb*. M17.
[ORIGIN from the noun or French *bronzer*.]
1 *verb trans.* Give a surface of bronze or resembling bronze to. M17. ▸**b** *fig.* Make unfeeling or shameless, harden. Now *rare* or *obsolete*. E18.
2 *verb trans. & intrans.* Make or become like bronze in colour; brown, suntan. L18.
bronzed diabetes = HAEMOCHROMATOSIS.
■ **bronzer** *noun* (**a**) one who gives objects a surface or appearance of bronze; (**b**) a cosmetic liquid or powder applied to the skin to give it colour or shine (usu. to give the appearance of a suntan): M19.

bronzite /ˈbrɒnzʌɪt/ *noun*. E19.
[ORIGIN from BRONZE *noun* + -ITE¹.]
MINERALOGY. A bronze-coloured iron-containing variety of enstatite.

broo /bruː/ *noun*¹. *Scot.* LME.
[ORIGIN Old French *breu*: see BREWIS.]
= BREE *noun*² 2.

broo *noun*² var. of BUROO.

brooch /brəʊtʃ/ *noun & verb*. Also †**broche**. ME.
[ORIGIN Var. of BROACH *noun*¹.]
▸ **A** *noun*. **1** An ornament with a hinged pin and catch, usu. worn fastened to a woman's clothing or as a badge etc. ME.
spray brooch: see SPRAY *noun*¹ 2C. ***stomacher brooch***: see STOMACHER *noun*¹ 2.
†**2** Any jewelled ornament; a trinket. ME–L17.
▸ **B** *verb trans.* Adorn as with a brooch. *rare*. E17.

brood /bruːd/ *noun*.
[ORIGIN Old English *brōd*, corresp. to Middle Dutch *broet* (Dutch *broed*), Old High German *bruot* (German *Brut*), from Germanic, from base meaning 'warm, heat'.]
1 Progeny or offspring of animals that lay eggs; a family of young from one hatching; *spec.* (**a**) bee or wasp larvae; (**b**) the spat of oysters in its second year. OE. ▸**b** Of human beings: a family, children. Now *derog.* or *joc.* ME. ▸**c** *fig.* The products or results of circumstances, actions, etc. L16.

AV *Luke* 13:34 As a henne doeth gather her brood vnder her wings. **b** SHAKES. *Temp.* She will become thy bed . . And bring thee forth brave brood. **c** MILTON The brood of Folly without father bred. GEO. ELIOT A brood of guilty wishes.

2 The fostering of the fetus in egg or womb; hatching, breeding. *arch.* exc. in *comb.* below. ME. ▸†**b** Parentage, descent. ME–L16.

b SPENSER The virgin borne of heauenly brood.

sit on brood sit as a hen on her eggs, sit brooding (cf. ABROOD).
3 A race, a kind; a group of men, things, etc., having common qualities. Usu. *derog.* LME.

ADDISON Its tainted air and all its broods of poisons. E. A. FREEMAN A brood of petty despots.

4 A state or period of contemplative brooding. L19.

W. GOLDING I drifted off into a dreary brood.

– COMB.: **brood cell**, **brood comb** a cell in, the part of, a comb used for the rearing of bee larvae; **brood hen**, **brood mare**, etc.: kept for breeding; **brood patch** a denuded area of a bird's ventral surface, facilitating the transfer of heat from the parent to the egg(s); **brood pouch** a saclike structure for the protection of developing eggs or young, found in various vertebrate and invertebrate animals; **brood queen** = QUEEN *noun* 6.

brood /bruːd/ *verb*. LME.
[ORIGIN from the noun.]
▸ **I** *verb trans.* **1** Sit on (eggs) so as to hatch them, incubate. LME. ▸**b** *fig.* Breed, hatch, (products, projects). E17.

b SOUTHEY There brood the pestilence and let The earthquake loose.

2 Cherish (young) under the wings, as a hen. L16. ▸**b** *fig.* Cherish in the mind etc.; contemplate, nurse (wrath etc.). Now *rare* (cf. sense 5 below). L16.

b DRYDEN You'll sit and brood your Sorrows on a throne.

▸ **II** *verb intrans.* **3** Incubate eggs; sit as a hen on eggs. L16.
4 *fig.* Of night, silence, etc.: hang or hover close *over*, *(up)on*, etc. M17.

DRYDEN Perpetual Night . . In silence brooding on th' unhappy ground. LD MACAULAY Mists and storms brood over it [Glencoe] through the greater part of the finest Summer.

5 Meditate (*on*, *upon*, *over*, *about*), esp. moodily or resentfully. L17.

R. MACAULAY She brooded darkly for a while. A. BRINK Ben was in no mood to talk, brooding over his own thoughts.

6 Lie as a cherished nestling, thought, etc. L17.

N. HAWTHORNE The themes that were brooding deepest in their hearts.

■ **brooder** *noun* (**a**) a hen etc. that broods or hatches eggs; (**b**) a person who broods over things; (**c**) a heated house or a device providing heat for chicks, piglets, etc.: L16. **broodingly** *adverb* in a brooding manner M19.

broody /ˈbruːdi/ *adjective & noun*. E16.
[ORIGIN from BROOD *noun* + -Y¹.]
▸ **A** *adjective*. **1** Apt or inclined to breed; prolific. *obsolete* exc. *dial.* E16.
2 Of a hen: wishing or inclined to incubate eggs. Of a woman (*joc.*): wishing to be pregnant. E16.
3 Inclined to meditate resentfully; feeling depressed. M19.
▸ **B** *noun*. A broody hen. E20.
■ **broodiness** *noun* L19.

brook /brʊk/ *noun*.
[ORIGIN Old English *brōc*, corresp. to Low German & High German words meaning 'marsh, bog', Middle Low German *brōk*, Middle Dutch & mod. Dutch *brock*, Old High German *bruoh* (German *Bruch*): of unknown origin.]
A small stream; orig., a torrent.
babbling brook: see BABBLE *verb* 2.
– COMB.: **brook char** = ***brook trout*** (b) below; **brooklime** [Old English *hleomoce*, name of the plant] a speedwell common in wet places, esp. *Veronica beccabunga*; **brook trout** †(**a**) the brown trout, *Salmo trutta*; (**b**) a migratory char, *Salvelinus fontinalis*, native to north-eastern N. America; also called ***brown char***; **brookweed** a small white-flowered plant, *Samolus valerandi*, of the primrose family, found in wet places; also called ***water pimpernel***.
■ **brooklet** *noun* a little brook E19.

brook /brʊk/ *verb trans.*
[ORIGIN Old English *brūcan* = Old Frisian *brūka*, Old Saxon *brūkan* (Dutch *bruiken*), Old High German *brūhhan* (German *brauchen*), Gothic *brūkjan*, from Germanic base meaning 'to use', from Indo-European (whence Latin *frui* enjoy).]
1 Enjoy the use of, profit by; possess, hold. *arch.* exc. *Scot.* OE.
†**2** Make use of (food); digest. OE–L16.
3 Put up with, tolerate; admit of. Usu. with neg. Now *literary*. M16.

M. MUGGERIDGE A son-in-law who was an elementary school supply teacher was not to be brooked. E. REVELEY Her mother's frenzy brooked no delay.

■ **brookable** *adjective* (chiefly *Scot.*) endurable, tolerable (earlier in UNBROOKABLE) E19.

brookite /ˈbrʊkʌɪt/ *noun*. E19.
[ORIGIN from Henry J. *Brooke* (1771–1857), English mineralogist + -ITE¹.]
MINERALOGY. The orthorhombic form of titanium dioxide, usu. occurring as dark brown or black prisms.

Brooklynese /brʊklɪˈniːz/ *noun*. E20.
[ORIGIN from *Brooklyn* (see below) + -ESE.]
An uncultivated form of New York speech associated esp. with the borough of Brooklyn.

Brooklynite /ˈbrʊklɪnʌɪt/ *noun*. M19.
[ORIGIN from *Brooklyn* (see BROOKLYNESE) + -ITE¹.]
A native or inhabitant of Brooklyn.

brool /bruːl/ *noun*. M19.
[ORIGIN German *Brüll* (poet. for *Gebrüll*), from *brüllen* to roar.]
A low humming sound; a murmur.

broom /bruːm/ *noun & verb*.
[ORIGIN Old English *brōm*, corresp. to Middle Low German *brām*, Middle Dutch *brāme* (Dutch *braam*), Old High German *brāmo*, *brāma*, from Germanic base also of BRAMBLE *noun*.]
▸ **A** *noun*. **1** Any of various chiefly yellow-flowered leguminous shrubs of the genera *Cytisus* and *Genista*, esp. the common species *C. scoparius* of western Eurasia. Also (with specifying word), any of certain other plants similar to these in use or appearance. OE.
butcher's broom, ***Spanish broom***, ***sweet broom***, etc.
2 A sweeping implement, usu. on a long handle, orig. one made of twigs of broom, heather, etc. ME.
new broom *fig.* a newly appointed person eager to make changes. ***shovel and broom***: see SHOVEL *noun* 1.
– COMB.: **broomball** (orig. *Canad.*) a team game similar to ice hockey in which participants score by pushing a ball into the opponents' goal using brooms; **broom corn** *N. Amer.* a variety of sorghum whose dried inflorescences are used for brooms; **broom grass** *N. Amer.* = ***broom sedge*** below; **broom hickory** a kind of hickory, *Carya glabra*, once used for making brooms; also called **pignut**; **broomrape** [Latin *rapum* tuber] a brown leafless plant belonging to the genus *Orobanche* or a related genus, and growing on the roots of other plants; **broom sedge** *N. Amer.* any of various coarse grasses, esp. of the genus *Andropogon*, occas. used for brooms or thatch; **broomstaff**, pl. **-staffs**, **-staves**, a broomstick; **broomstick** the handle of a broom (allegedly ridden through the air by witches); ***marry over the broomstick***, go through a sham marriage ceremony in which the parties jump over a broom.
▸ **B** *verb trans.* **1** = BREAM *verb*. Only in Dicts. E17.
2 Sweep with a broom. E19.
■ **broomie** *noun* (*Austral. & NZ colloq.*) a person who sweeps the floor in a shearing shed L19. **broomy** *adjective* covered with or having much broom M17.

broose /bruːz/ *noun*. *Scot.* M17.
[ORIGIN Unknown.]
A traditional race by young men present at country weddings in Scotland, the course being from the bride's former home to the bridegroom's house.

Bros *noun pl.* see BRO.

brose /brəʊz/ *noun*. Chiefly *Scot.* M17.
[ORIGIN Var. of BREWIS.]
A dish of oatmeal with boiling water or milk poured on it.
ATHOLE BROSE. ***PEASE-brose***.

broth /brɒθ/ *noun*.
[ORIGIN Old English *broþ* = Old High German *brod*, Old Norse *broð*, from Germanic, from base of BREW *verb*.]
1 Unclarified meat or fish stock; a thin soup made from this and vegetables. OE.
broth of a boy (chiefly *Irish*) a good fellow. ***Scotch broth***: see SCOTCH *adjective*.
2 Stock etc. used as a culture medium for bacteria. L19.
■ **brothy** *adjective* (*rare*) of, or of the nature of, broth M17.

brothel /ˈbrɒθ(ə)l/ *noun*. LME.
[ORIGIN Ult. from Old English *brēoþan* deteriorate, degenerate, of unknown origin. In sense 3 abbreviation of *brothel-house*, infl. by and superseding BORDEL.]
†**1** A worthless wretch, a good-for-nothing. LME–L16.
†**2** A prostitute. LME–E17.
3 A house where prostitutes work. L16.
– COMB.: **brothel creepers** *slang* soft-soled (usu. suede) shoes; **brothel-house** *arch.* = sense 3 above.
■ †**brotheller** *noun* a whoremonger E17–E19. **brothelly** *adjective* (*rare*) whorish E17. **brothelry** *noun* (**a**) *arch.* lechery, sexual immorality; †(**b**) a brothel: M16.

brother /ˈbrʌðə/ *noun & adjective*. Pl. **brothers**, (chiefly in senses 2b & 3) **brethren** /ˈbrɛðr(ə)n/.
[ORIGIN Old English *brōþor* = Old Frisian *brōther*, *brōder*, Old Saxon *brōþar*, Middle Dutch & mod. Dutch *broeder*, Middle & mod. Low German *brōder*, Old High German *bruodar* (German *Bruder*), Old Norse *brōðir*, Gothic *brōþar*, from Germanic from Indo-European, whence Latin *frater*, Greek *phratēr*, Sanskrit *bhrātṛ*.]
▸ **A** *noun*. **1** A male related to one or more other persons (male or female) by having the same parents or by having one parent in common. OE. ▸**b** Chiefly in biblical translations (a Hebraism): a kinsman, as uncle, nephew, or cousin. ME.

AV *Prov.* 18:24 A friend that sticketh closer than a brother. TENNYSON Here two brothers . . had met And fought.

adoptive brother, ***foster-brother***, ***full brother***, ***half-brother***, ***stepbrother***, etc.
2 (With possible inclusion of a minority of females in pl., if not considered significant. Also used before a name and as a form of address or reference.) ▸**a** A man who is a close friend; a (male) fellow citizen or fellow countryman; an associate, an equal; a person of the same race, colour, or class; a fellow creature. OE. ▸**b** A (male) fellow Christian, a co-religionist, a (male) fellow member of a religious society or sect. In *pl.* (**Brethren**) *spec.* members of the Plymouth Brethren (see below). OE. ▸**c** *ROMAN CATHOLIC CHURCH*. A member of a men's religious congregation or order. ME. ▸**d** A (male) fellow member of a guild, trade union, society, regiment, profession, etc.; an official of certain companies etc. LME. ▸**e** Used as a familiar form of address to a man. Also as *interjection* expr. surprise, annoyance, etc. Chiefly *N. Amer.* E20.

a TENNYSON My friend, the brother of my love, My Arthur! C. G. SELIGMAN The extinct Guanches of the Canary Islands showed as least as much racial mixture as their brethren of the mainland. *Black Scholar* This Black Studies Class will help open the eyes of our so many sleeping brothers. A. STORR Faced with a common enemy . . we become brothers in a way which never obtains in ordinary life. **b** J. MORLEY The Protestants . . found warm hospitality among their northern brethren. W. G. SIMMS Call me not Mr., I pray thee . . . If thou wilt call me Brother Cross, my heart shall acknowledge the bonds between us. **c** B. MOORE Behind Brother Martin, gazing at the shiny tonsure. **d** A. H. QUINN He was a member of Kappa Phi, and . . he had a right to anything his brothers could give him.

3 *fig.* An identical or similar thing, a counterpart. LME.

POPE Grove nods at grove, each Alley has a brother.

– PHRASES: ***a man and a brother***: see MAN *noun*. ***Big Brother***: see BIG *adjective*. **brother consanguineous**, **consanguineous brother** (esp. *ROMAN LAW*): having the same father only. **brother german**: having the same parents. **brother uterine**, **uterine brother**: having the same mother only. **Christian Brethren** *the* Plymouth Brethren; members of the Plymouth Brethren. ***consanguineous brother***: see ***brother consanguineous*** above. ***Elder Brother***: see ELDER *adjective*. **Exclusive Brethren** *the* more exclusive section of the Plymouth Brethren; members of the Exclusive Brethren. ***lay brother***: see LAY *adjective*. **Open Brethren** *the* less exclusive section of the Plymouth Brethren; members of the Open Brethren. **Plymouth Brethren** *the* Calvinistic religious body formed at Plymouth *c* 1830 with no formal creed and no official order of ministers; members of the Plymouth Brethren. **the Brethren** (**a**) in the New Testament, the members of the early Christian Churches; (**b**) the Plymouth Brethren. ***United Brethren***: see UNITED *adjective*. ***uterine brother***: see ***brother uterine*** above.
▸ **B** *attrib.* or as *adjective*. (Freq. with hyphen.) That is a brother; belonging to the same group; close as a brother; fellow-. LME.

POPE Two brother-heroes shall from thee be born. R. BURNS Land o' Cakes and brither Scots. J. RABAN One of his brother officers wandered into the mess.

– SPECIAL COLLOCATIONS & COMB.: **brother-in-arms** a fighter in the same cause. **brother-in-law**, pl. **brothers-in-law**, the brother of one's husband or wife, or the husband of one's sister(-in-law). ***Brother JONATHAN***.
■ **brothership** *noun* (a) brotherhood OE.

brother /ˈbrʌðə/ *verb trans.* LME.
[ORIGIN from the noun.]
Make a brother of; admit to brotherhood; treat or address as brother.

brotherhood /ˈbrʌðəhʊd/ *noun.* Also †**-head**. ME.
[ORIGIN Prob. from BROTHERRED with assim. to -HEAD[1], -HOOD.]
1 The (freq. spiritual) relation of a brother or of brothers mutually. ME.
2 Brotherliness, companionship, friendly alliance. ME.

N. HAWTHORNE We live in great harmony and brotherhood.

3 Orig., Christian fellowship. Now *gen.*, community of feeling, fellowship, unity. LME.

R. W. DALE There is a brotherhood between Christ and all believers. JOYCE Three cheers for universal brotherhood! G. MURRAY A scholar . . draws the strength that comes from communion or brotherhood.

4 The members of a fellowship etc. collectively; an association of equals for mutual help; a fraternity, a guild, etc. LME. ▸**b** *spec.* (*a*) A trade union, esp. of railwaymen; (*b*) a profession. *N. Amer.* L19.

SOUTHEY The grey brotherhood Chaunted the solemn mass. SHELLEY And make the earth One brotherhood. P. H. GIBBS A new brotherhood of peoples turning their backs on blood and ruin.

†**5** The rank of brother in a corporation etc. M16–E17.
6 *fig.* A group of related or similar things. E18.

brotherly /ˈbrʌðəli/ *adjective & adverb.*
[ORIGIN Old English *brōþorlīc* adjective, formed as BROTHER *noun* + -LY[1].]
▸ **A** *adjective.* Of or befitting a brother; kind, affectionate. OE.
▸ **B** *adverb.* In the manner of a brother. Now *rare.* E16.
■ **brotherliness** *noun* the quality of being brotherly, brotherly feeling. M16.

†**brotherred** *noun.* OE–M16.
[ORIGIN from BROTHER *noun* + -RED.]
A brotherhood.

brotulid /ˈbrɒtjʊlɪd/ *noun & adjective.* L19.
[ORIGIN from mod. Latin *Brotula* genus name, prob. from Amer. Spanish *brótula*, + -ID[3].]
(A fish) of a numerous group of predominantly deep-sea or cave-dwelling fishes belonging to the cusk-eel family Ophidiidae.

brough *noun* var. of BROCH.

brougham /ˈbruː(ə)m/ *noun.* M19.
[ORIGIN Henry Peter, Lord *Brougham* (1778–1868).]
Chiefly *hist.* A one-horse closed carriage. Also, a similar electric vehicle, or a car with the driver's seat outside.

brought *verb pa. t. & pple* of BRING *verb.*

brouhaha /ˈbruːhɑːhɑː/ *noun.* L19.
[ORIGIN French.]
A commotion, a sensation; uproar, hubbub.

brouillon /brujɔ̃/ *noun.* Pl. pronounced same. L17.
[ORIGIN French.]
A rough draft.

brow /braʊ/ *noun*[1].
[ORIGIN Old English *brū* from Germanic from Indo-European, whence Greek *ophrus*, Sanskrit *bhrū*.]
†**1** In *pl.* The eyelashes. Only in OE.
2 An arch of hair growing in a ridge over the eye; an eyebrow. Usu. in *pl.* OE. ▸**b** In *pl.* The prominences of the forehead above the eyes. Now *poet.* = sense 3. L16.

b SHAKES. *Jul. Caes.* Did not they Put on my brows this wreath of victory?

knit one's brows frown.
3 The whole part of the face above the eyes, the forehead, *poet.* esp. as expressing emotion; hence (*arch.*) expression of countenance, confronting aspect. ME. ▸†**b** Composure, confidence, effrontery. M17–E18. ▸**c** [from *highbrow* etc.] Level of intellectual attainment or interest. *colloq.* E20.

SIR W. SCOTT The old man, who had . . resisted the brow of military and civil tyranny. LD MACAULAY That brow of hate, that mouth of scorn. SIAN EVANS His hair . . hung in tags over a flat red brow.

by the sweat of one's brow: see SWEAT *noun.* **have no brow of** *Scot.* not be impressed by.
4 The top or projecting edge of a cliff, hill, etc., standing over a precipice or slope; the top of a hill in a road. LME.
– COMB.: **brow antler** = *brow tine* below; **brow-band** a band worn across the brow; *spec.* the band of a bridle etc. which passes in front of a horse's forehead; **brow ridge** a superciliary ridge; **brow tine** the lowest tine of a stag's horn.
■ **browed** *adjective* having a brow or brows (of a specified kind) LME. **browless** *adjective* †(*a*) without shame, unabashed; (*b*) without eyebrows: E17.

brow /braʊ/ *noun*[2]. M19.
[ORIGIN Prob. from Norwegian *bru*, Old Norse *brú* bridge.]
NAUTICAL. A gangway from ship to shore. Also, the hinged part of the bow or stern of a landing craft or ferry, which is lowered to form a landing platform or ramp.

brow /braʊ/ *verb trans. rare.* M17.
[ORIGIN from BROW *noun*[1].]
Form a brow to; be on the brow of.

browallia /brəʊˈwɔːlɪə/ *noun.* L18.
[ORIGIN mod. Latin, from Johann *Browall* (1707–55), Swedish botanist: see -IA[1].]
A tropical American plant of the genus *Browallia*, of the nightshade family, with violet, blue, or white flowers.

browbeat /ˈbraʊbiːt/ *verb trans. & intrans.* Infl. as BEAT *verb*[1]; pa. t. **-beat**, pa. pple usu. **-beaten** /-biːt(ə)n/. L16.
[ORIGIN from BROW *noun*[1] + BEAT *verb*[1].]
Intimidate or discourage with stern, arrogant, or insolent looks or words; bully.
■ **browbeater** *noun* L17.

browden /ˈbraʊd(ə)n/ *adjective.* Long *obsolete* exc. *Scot.* Also †**broiden**.
[ORIGIN Old English (*ge*)*brogden* pa. pple of *bregdan* BRAID *verb*[1].]
†**1** Plaited, interwoven. OE–LME.
†**2** Embroidered; adorned. LME–M19.
3 Enamoured, fond. L16.
4 Impudent, bold. M19.

browis *noun* var. of BREWIS.

brown /braʊn/ *noun.* ME.
[ORIGIN The adjective used ellipt. or absol.]
1 Brown colour; a shade of this; a pigment of a brown colour. ME.
chocolate-brown, ***clove-brown***, ***saddle brown***, ***Spanish brown***, ***toffee-brown***, ***Vandyke brown***, etc. **fire into the brown** (**of them**) fire into the brown mass of a flock of game birds instead of singling out one; *transf.* let fly at random into a mass.
2 A thing distinguished by brown colour, as the brown ball in snooker, a brown butterfly (*spec.* one of the family Satyridae), brown ale, brown clothing, etc. ME. ▸**b** A copper coin. *slang.* E19. ▸**c** A person of mixed race. M19.
wall brown: see WALL *noun*[1] 9.
– COMB.: **brown spot** the spot on which the brown ball is placed in snooker.

brown /braʊn/ *adjective.*
[ORIGIN Old English *brūn* = Old Frisian, Old Saxon *brūn* (Dutch *bruin*), Old High German *brūn* (German *braun*), Old Norse *brúnn*, from Germanic (whence French, Provençal *brun*, Italian *bruno*). Reinforced in Middle English by Old French & mod. French *brun*.]
1 Dusky, dark. Now only *poet.* OE.

POPE Ere brown ev'ning spreads her chilly shade.

2 Of a person: having the skin of a dark or dusky colour as a racial characteristic; also, dark-complexioned, tanned. OE.

P. FRANKAU He was too fair to turn brown at once.

3 Of or denoting a composite colour produced by a mixture of red, yellow, and black. ME.
†**4** Of steel etc.: burnished. ME–L18.
– PHRASES: ***bright-line brown-eye***: see BRIGHT *adjective* 6. **do brown** *slang* deceive, cheat.
– SPECIAL COLLOCATIONS & COMB.: **brown alga** an alga of the division Phaeophyta, members of which contain xanthophyll in addition to chlorophyll and include many seaweeds. ***brown argus***: see ARGUS 2. **brown bag** (chiefly *N. Amer.*) a plain paper bag, esp. for carrying food and drink, often used to conceal the nature of its contents. **brown-bag** *verb trans.* (chiefly *N. Amer.*) carry (esp. food and drink) in a plain paper bag, esp. to conceal the contents. **brown-bagger** (chiefly *N. Amer.*) a person who carries a brown bag, esp. containing food or drink. ***brown bear***: see BEAR *noun*[1] 1. **brown belt** (the holder of) a belt marking the attainment of a certain degree of proficiency in judo or karate. **Brown Bess** *colloq.* (*hist.*) the old British army flintlock musket, with brown walnut stock. **Brown Betty** (chiefly *N. Amer.*) a baked pudding containing apples and breadcrumbs. **brown-bill** *hist.* a kind of halberd used by foot soldiers and watchmen. **brown bread** any bread of a darker colour than white bread; *spec.* bread made of unbolted flour or wholemeal. **brown coal** lignite. **brown creeper** (chiefly *N. Amer.*) the common treecreeper, *Certhia familiaris.* **brown dwarf** ASTRONOMY a celestial object intermediate in size between a giant planet and a small star, believed to emit mainly infrared radiation. **brown earth** a type of soil having a brown humus-rich surface layer. **brown eye**: with a brown iris. **brown-eyed** *adjective* having brown eyes. **brownfield** *adjective* (of an urban site for potential building development) having had previous development on it. ***brown* GEORGE. brown goods** household furniture such as television sets and audio equipment (opp. ***white goods***). **brown hare** a common Eurasian hare, *Lepus europaeus* (esp. as distinct from the blue or Arctic hare). ***brown* HAEMATITE. brown holland** an unbleached linen fabric. ***brown* HYENA. brown job** *slang* a soldier; *collect.* the Army. ***brown loaf***: see LOAF *noun*[1]. **brown malt**: roasted to a dark brown colour. ***brown mustard***: see MUSTARD *noun* 2. **brown-nose**, **brown-noser** *slang* (chiefly *N. Amer.*) a sycophant. **brown owl** (*a*) the tawny owl; (*b*) (with cap. initials) the adult leader of a Brownie pack. **brown paper** a coarse stout kind of paper made of unbleached materials, used chiefly for wrapping. ***brown rat***: see RAT *noun*[1] 1a. **brown rice** unpolished rice with only the husk of the grain removed. **brown rot** (**disease**) a fungal disease of various plants, esp. of the rose family, causing mummification of the fruit. **brown sauce** a savoury sauce made with browned fat or gravy; any brown-coloured savoury sauce. **Brownshirt** *hist.* a Nazi; *spec.* a member of the *Sturmabteilung* (SA) in Nazi Germany. **brown snake** a poisonous Australian snake of the genus *Pseudonaja.* **brown spar** any hexagonal carbonate mineral coloured brown by the presence of iron, e.g. siderite, ankerite. **brownstone** *noun & adjective* (*US*) (*a*) *noun* a kind of reddish-brown sandstone used for building (esp. in front elevation); a house faced with this; (*b*) *adjective* affluent, well-to-do. **brown study** a state of mental abstraction or musing; *esp.* an idle reverie. **brown sugar** unrefined or partially refined sugar. **brown-tail** a white European moth, *Euproctis chrysorrhoea* (family Lymantriidae), which has a brown tip to the abdomen and the larvae of which have irritating hairs. ***brown thrasher***: see THRASHER *noun*[2]. **brown top** any of various pasture grasses of Australia or New Zealand. **brown trout** the trout, *Salmo trutta*; *spec.* a small dark non-migratory form occurring in smaller rivers and pools. **brownwort** water figwort, *Scrophularia auriculata.*
■ **brownish** *adjective* LME. **brownly** *adverb* with a brown colour E19. **brownness** /-n-n-/ *noun* LME. **browny** *adjective* inclining to brown L16.

brown /braʊn/ *verb.* ME.
[ORIGIN from the adjective or (sense 3) noun.]
1 *verb intrans.* Become brown. ME.
2 *verb trans.* Make brown; roast brown; give a dull brown lustre to (gun barrels etc.). L16.
browned off *slang* bored, fed up, discontented.
3 *verb trans.* Fire indiscriminately at (a covey of birds, a mass of men, etc.) L19.
– COMB.: **brown-out** (chiefly *N. Amer.* & *Austral.*) a partial blackout.

Brownian /ˈbraʊnɪən/ *adjective.* L19.
[ORIGIN from Robert *Brown* (1773–1858), English botanist + -IAN.]
Brownian motion, ***Brownian movement***, the irregular oscillations of microscopic particles suspended in a fluid.

brownie /ˈbraʊni/ *noun.* In sense 4 also **B-**. E16.
[ORIGIN from BROWN *adjective* + -IE.]
1 A benevolent goblin, supposed to haunt old houses (esp. farmhouses in Scotland) and occas. to do household work secretly. E16.
2 a A sweet currant bread. *Austral. & NZ.* L19. ▸**b** A small square of rich (usu. chocolate) cake containing nuts. *N. Amer.* L19.
3 (An angler's name for) a trout. E20.
4 A member of the junior branch of the Guides. E20.
– COMB.: **brownie point** a credit for an achievement.

browning /ˈbraʊnɪŋ/ *noun*[1]. M18.
[ORIGIN from BROWN *verb* + -ING[1].]
1 A preparation for giving a brown colour to gravy etc. M18.
2 The action of BROWN *verb.* L18.

Browning /ˈbraʊnɪŋ/ *noun*[2]. E20.
[ORIGIN John M. *Browning* (1855–1926), US designer.]
A type of esp. automatic firearm.

Browningesque /braʊnɪŋˈɛsk/ *adjective.* L19.
[ORIGIN from *Browning* (see below) + -ESQUE.]
Of, pertaining to, or characteristic of the English poet Robert Browning (1812–89) or his style.

Brownism /ˈbraʊnɪz(ə)m/ *noun.* E17.
[ORIGIN from *Brown* (see below) + -ISM.]
The system of church government advocated by the Puritan Robert Brown (*c* 1550–*c* 1633), and adopted by the Independents.
■ **Brownist** *noun* an adherent or student of the ecclesiastical principles of Robert Brown L16. **Brow'nistical** *adjective* M17.

browse /braʊz/ *noun*[1]. Also †**-ze**. E16.
[ORIGIN Old French *brost*, later *broust* (mod. *brout*) bud, young shoot, prob. of Germanic origin.]
1 Young shoots and twigs of shrubs, trees, etc., used as food by animals; something that is or can be browsed. E16.
2 The action of browsing. E19.

browse /braʊz/ *noun*[2]. M19.
[ORIGIN Unknown.]
A mixture of partly reduced ore and fuel, produced during smelting of lead.

browse /braʊz/ *verb.* Also †**-ze**. LME.
[ORIGIN Old French *broster* (mod. *brouter*) to crop, formed as BROWSE *noun*[1].]
1 *verb intrans.* Of an animal: feed on or *on* the leaves and shoots of trees and bushes. LME.

G. ORWELL The great shining horses browse and meditate.

2 *verb trans.* Crop and eat (leaves, twigs, etc.). LME.

New York Times The elk have also browsed aspen and willows to the verge of disappearance.

3 *verb trans.* Feed (an animal) *on* twigs etc. M16.
4 *verb intrans. & trans.* Look through (books etc.) casually; read desultorily. L19. ▸**b** Read or survey (data files, Internet sites, etc.), typically via a network. L20.

R. PILCHER Lucilla and Jeff wanted to . . browse around the famous street market. **b** *Japan Times* The PC won't be the only way to browse the Internet.

■ **browser** *noun* †(*a*) a person who feeds deer (in wintertime); (*b*) an animal which browses; a person who browses among books etc.; (*c*) COMPUTING a program used to locate and display particular items in a given data collection; *spec.* a program used to navigate the Internet by connecting to a Web server, allowing the user to locate, access, and display hypertext documents: M16. **browsing** *noun* (*a*) the action of the verb; (*b*) shoots and leaves; browsing ground: LME. **browsy** *adjective* †(*a*) (of vegetation) scanty, twiggy; (*b*) characterized by or suitable for browsing or casual reading: M18.

browst /braʊst/ *noun. Scot.* E16.
[ORIGIN from base of BREW *verb.*]
A brewing; a brew.

†**browster** *noun* var. of BREWSTER *noun*[1].

B

†**browze** *noun, verb* var. of BROWSE *noun*[1], *verb*.

brrr /br-r-r/ *interjection*. L19.
[ORIGIN Imit.]
Expr. shivering.

BRS *abbreviation*.
British Road Services.

brucellosis /bruːsəˈləʊsɪs/ *noun*. Pl. **-loses** /-ˈləʊsiːz/. M20.
[ORIGIN from mod. Latin *Brucella* (see below), from Sir David *Bruce* (1855–1931), Scot. physician + -ELLA: see -OSIS.]
Infection with bacteria of the genus *Brucella*, which produces contagious abortion in cattle and other livestock, and undulant fever in humans.

bruchid /ˈbruːkɪd/ *noun & adjective*. L19.
[ORIGIN mod. Latin *Bruchidae* (see below), from *Bruchus* genus name from Latin *bruchus* from Greek *broukhos* wingless locust: see -ID[3].]
▸ **A** *noun*. Any beetle of the family Bruchidae, which includes many species resembling weevils and destructive to leguminous crops. L19.
▸ **B** *adjective*. Of, pertaining to, or designating this family. L19.

brucine /ˈbruːsiːn/ *noun*. E19.
[ORIGIN from mod. Latin *Brucea* genus name of a tree formerly thought to be the source of false angostura bark, from James *Bruce* (1730–94), Scot. traveller: see -INE[5].]
CHEMISTRY. A highly toxic alkaloid present in false angostura bark and nux vomica.
■ **brucia** *noun* (now *rare* or *obsolete*) = BRUCINE E19.

brucite /ˈbruːsʌɪt/ *noun*. E19.
[ORIGIN from Archibald *Bruce* (1777–1818), US mineralogist + -ITE[1].]
MINERALOGY. Native magnesium hydroxide, which usu. occurs as white, grey, or light green hexagonal tabular crystals or in massive form.

bruckle /ˈbrʌk(ə)l/ *adjective*. Long *dial*. Also **brickle** /ˈbrɪk(ə)l/, **britchel** /ˈbrɪtʃ(ə)l/.
[ORIGIN Old English *-brucol*, *-bryċel* ult. from Germanic base of BREAK *verb*. For vars. cf. *mickle*, *muckle*, *much*.]
†**1** As 2nd elem. of comb. Liable to cause breakage of, that breaks. Only in OE.
2 Liable to break; fragile, brittle; frail, delicate, uncertain. ME.

brugh *noun* var. of BROCH.

bruilzie *noun* var. of BRULZIE.

Bruin /ˈbruːɪn/ *noun*. Also **b-**. L15.
[ORIGIN Dutch = brown, a name for the bear in *Reynard the Fox*.]
(A personal name for) a bear.

bruise /bruːz/ *noun*. LME.
[ORIGIN from the verb.]
†**1** A breaking, a breach. LME–M16.
2 A hurt or injury to the body manifested as a discoloration of the skin, caused by an impact or blow. M16. ▸**b** A discoloration of the surface of a plant, fruit, etc. L17.

bruise /bruːz/ *verb*.
[ORIGIN Old English *brȳsan* reinforced in Middle English by Anglo-Norman *bruser*, Old French *bruisier* (mod. *briser*) break, smash, of unknown origin.]
1 *verb trans*. Injure or damage with a heavy blow or weight. Now usu. *spec.*, injure by a blow which discolours the skin but does not lacerate it or break any bones. OE. ▸**b** Produce a similar lesion in (a plant, fruit, etc.). LME.
†**2** *verb trans*. [After French.] Break, smash. ME–E17.
3 *verb trans*. *fig*. Crush, wound, disable; hurt (pride etc.). ME.

> MILTON An Iron Rod to bruise and breake Thy disobedience. J. HELLER She was bruising his most vulnerable feelings.

4 *verb trans*. Beat small, crush, grind down. LME.

> DRYDEN Some scatt'ring Pot-herbs . . bruis'd with Vervain.

5 *verb trans*. Crush by pressure, jam, squeeze. *obsolete* exc. *Scot*. E17.
6 *verb intrans*. Esp. of fruit: become bruised. E20.
■ **bruiser** *noun* (*a*) a person who bruises; (*b*) a prizefighter, a brawny muscular man; (*c*) a machine or implement for crushing or grinding: L16. **bruising** *noun* (*a*) the action of the verb; (*b*) injury so caused; (*c*) prizefighting: LME.

bruisewort /ˈbruːzwɜːt/ *noun*. OE.
[ORIGIN from BRUISE *noun* or *verb* + WORT *noun*[1].]
Any of various plants supposed to heal bruises, *esp.* the daisy.

bruit /bruːt; *in sense 4 foreign* brɥi (*pl. same*)/ *noun*. *arch*. LME.
[ORIGIN Old French & mod. French, use as noun of pa. pple of *bruire* roar from Proto-Romance alt. of Latin *rugire* roar by assoc. with source of BRAY *verb*[1].]
1 Noise, clamour. LME.
2 Rumour, report. LME.
†**3** Fame, reputation. L15–E17.
4 MEDICINE. Any sound (esp. an abnormal one) heard in auscultation. M19.

bruit /bruːt/ *verb*. *arch*. exc. *US*. L15.
[ORIGIN from the noun.]
1 *verb trans*. Spread (a report etc.) *abroad* or *about*, rumour. L15.

> SHAKES. *1 Hen. VI* I find thou art no less than fame hath bruited. LYTTON They do bruit it that he sees visions. J. I. M. STEWART For a fortnight . . nothing about it could be bruited abroad.

2 *verb trans*. Speak of, make famous. E16.

> MILTON A man so much bruited for learning.

3 *verb intrans*. Make noise. *rare*. E19.

> KEATS Bronze clarions . . faintly bruit, Where long ago a giant battle was.

brulzie /ˈbruːli, -lji/ *noun*. *Scot*. Also **bruil-**. M16.
[ORIGIN formed as BROIL *noun*[1].]
A disturbance, a squabble.

Brum /brʌm/ *noun*. *slang*. M19.
[ORIGIN Shortened from BRUMMAGEM.]
(A nickname for) the town (now a city) of Birmingham, England.

Brumaire /bruːˈmɛː, *foreign* brymɛːr (*pl. same*)/ *noun*. E19.
[ORIGIN French, formed as BRUME + *-aire* -ARY[1].]
The second month of the French Republican calendar (introduced 1793), extending from 22 October to 20 November.

brumal /ˈbruːm(ə)l/ *adjective*. *literary*. E16.
[ORIGIN Latin *brumalis*, from *bruma* winter: see -AL[1].]
Like winter, wintry.

brumby /ˈbrʌmbi/ *noun & adjective*. *Austral. & NZ*. L19.
[ORIGIN Unknown.]
(Designating) a wild or unbroken horse.

brume /bruːm/ *noun*. *literary*. E18.
[ORIGIN French = fog, from Latin *bruma* winter.]
Fog, mist, vapour.

Brummagem /ˈbrʌmədʒ(ə)m/ *adjective & noun*. *arch*. M17.
[ORIGIN Dial. form of BIRMINGHAM.]
▸ **A** *adjective*. **1** Of the quality of coins and some other goods made in Birmingham, England; counterfeit, sham, tawdry. M17.
†**2** See BIRMINGHAM.
▸ **B** *noun*. †**1** See BIRMINGHAM.
2 (An article of) counterfeit or cheap and showy ware. M19.

Brummie /ˈbrʌmi/ *noun & adjective*. *colloq*. Also **-y**. M20.
[ORIGIN formed as BRUMMAGEM: see -IE.]
(A native or inhabitant) of Birmingham, England.

brumous /ˈbruːməs/ *adjective*. *literary*. M19.
[ORIGIN French *brumeux* from late Latin *brumosus*, from *bruma* winter: see -OUS.]
Foggy; wintry.

brunch /brʌn(t)ʃ/ *noun & verb*. *colloq*. L19.
[ORIGIN Blend of BREAKFAST *noun* and LUNCH *noun*.]
▸ **A** *noun*. A single meal intended to combine breakfast and lunch. L19.
– COMB.: **brunch coat** *Austral. & NZ* a woman's short housecoat.
▸ **B** *verb intrans*. Eat brunch. M20.
■ **bruncher** *noun* L20.

brunette /bruːˈnɛt, ˌbrʊ-/ *noun & adjective*. Also (now chiefly *US*) **brunet**. M16.
[ORIGIN French *brunet* masc., *-ette* fem., dim. of *brun* brown: see -ET[1], -ETTE.]
(A white person, now esp. a woman or girl) with a dark complexion or (now usu.) brown hair.

> A. CARTER She was a brunette at her wedding, but had gone blonde with age.

brung *verb* see BRING.

Brünnich's guillemot /ˈbruːnɪtʃɪz ˌɡɪlɪmɒt/ *noun phr*. L19.
[ORIGIN M. T. *Brünnich* (1737–1827), Danish naturalist.]
A guillemot, *Uria lomvia*, with a shorter beak than the common guillemot and restricted to latitudes north of the British Isles.

brunoise /bruːnˈwɑːz/ *noun*. L19.
[ORIGIN French, from *brun* brown.]
A mixture of finely diced vegetables fried in butter and used to flavour soups and sauces.

Brunswick /ˈbrʌnzwɪk/ *noun*. L15.
[ORIGIN In branch I from *Brunswick*, a city and province of northern Germany, Low German *Brunswik*, German *Braunschweig*; in branch II, from a county named after this in Virginia, US.]
▸ **I 1** A fabric or garment from Brunswick; *esp.* (in full ***Brunswick gown***) a long-sleeved gown with a train from the shoulders. *obsolete* exc. *hist*. L15.
2 ***Brunswick green***, a dark green pigment orig. made of a basic chloride of copper; this shade of green. E19.
▸ **II 3** ***Brunswick stew***, a stew of squirrel, now also of game or chicken, with onions and sometimes other vegetables. *US*. M19.

brunt /brʌnt/ *noun*. LME.
[ORIGIN Unknown.]
†**1** A blow. LME–E17.
†**2** A sudden movement or effort. LME–L17.
†**3** An assault, an attack, (*lit.* of an army etc. or *fig.* of sickness, temptation, etc.). LME–E19.
4 Shock, violence, force, (*of* an attack etc.). Now *rare* in *gen.* sense. LME.
5 The chief stress, violence, or burden (*of*). Chiefly in ***bear the brunt of***. M18.

> *Time* Crumple zones help absorb the brunt of an impact. *Gay Times* Rick has had to bear the brunt of a lot of snide jokes and comments.

brunt /brʌnt/ *verb*. *rare*. LME.
[ORIGIN from the noun.]
†**1** *verb intrans*. Make an assault or attack. LME–L17.
2 *verb trans*. Bear the brunt of. LME.

bruschetta /brʊˈskɛtə/ *noun*. M20.
[ORIGIN Italian, fem. of *bruschetto*, from *brusco* past part. of *bruscare* to burn, heat in a fire + *-etto* -ET[1].]
Toasted Italian bread drenched in olive oil, seasoned, and rubbed with garlic, served typically with chopped tomatoes as a starter or side dish.

brush /brʌʃ/ *noun*[1]. ME.
[ORIGIN Anglo-Norman *bruce*, Old French *broce* (mod. *brousse*), perh. ult. from Latin *bruscum* excrescence on the maple.]
1 Loppings of trees or hedges; *US* cut brushwood; a faggot of this. ME.
2 Undergrowth, thicket, small trees and shrubs; land covered in such growth; *Austral.* forest. Now chiefly *N. Amer., Austral., & NZ*. ME.
3 Stubble. *obsolete* exc. *dial*. L17.
– COMB.: **brushfire** *noun & adjective* (*a*) *noun* a fire in brush or scrub; (*b*) *adjective* (of a war etc.) small-scale, localized; **brush kangaroo** = ***brush wallaby*** below; **brush-turkey** any of several Australasian megapodes which build mounds for incubating their eggs, esp. *Alectura lathami* of E. Australia; **brush wallaby** any of various wallabies found esp. in coastal brush; **brushwood** undergrowth, thicket; cut or broken twigs etc.
■ **brushed** *adjective* covered or overgrown with brush M17.

brush /brʌʃ/ *noun*[2]. ME.
[ORIGIN Old French *broisse*, (also mod.) *brosse*, perh. ult. = BRUSH *noun*[1] Branch III & perh. branch I from BRUSH *verb*[1]. Branch IV perh. a different word.]
▸ **I 1** A hostile collision or encounter. Now usu. a short, sharp encounter, a skirmish (*with*). ME.

> SHAKES. *Tr. & Cr.* Tempt not yet the brushes of the war. J. A. MICHENER Three ugly brushes with the law over charges he could not understand.

at first brush, **after first brush** at, after, the first meeting.
2 A rapid race; a contest of speed. Chiefly *US*. M19.
▸ **II 3** An implement consisting of bristles of hair, wire, plastic, or similar material, set in wood etc. and used for scrubbing, sweeping, etc. LME.
bottlebrush, ***clothes brush***, ***hairbrush***, ***nail brush***, ***scrubbing brush***, ***toothbrush***, ***wire brush***, etc. **daft as a brush**, **soft as a brush** *colloq.* (of a person or animal) very daft or soft-hearted. **live over the brush** *colloq.* (of a man and a woman) live together unmarried.
4 An instrument consisting of a bunch of hairs etc. attached to a straight handle, quill, etc., for applying paint, ink, glue, etc. L15. ▸**b** The painter's art or skill. L17.

> **b** BYRON A young American brother of the brush.

paintbrush, ***paste brush***, ***shaving brush***, etc. ***airbrush***: see AIR *noun*[1]. ***painter's brush***: see PAINTER *noun*[1].
5 Any brushlike tuft or bunch; *esp.* the bushy tail of a fox. L16. ▸**b** A brushlike organ on the leg of a bee, used to carry pollen. E19.

> G. DURRELL A Brush-tailed Porcupine . . about the size of a cat. K. A. PORTER White-blond hair clipped in a brush over his . . forehead.

6 a More fully ***brush discharge***. A brushlike electrical discharge of sparks. L18. ▸**b** A brushlike figure seen when crystals etc. are examined with polarized light. E19.
7 A piece of carbon or metal, ending in wires or strips, securing electrical contact between a fixed and a moving part; a movable strip of conducting material for making and breaking connection. L19.
8 Either of a pair of thin sticks with long wire bristles for striking a drum, cymbal, etc. E20.
▸ **III 9** An application of a brush; a brushing. Also, a graze. E18.

> C. CAUSLEY Tenderly kisses his wife's cheek—The brush of a child's lips. J. OSBORNE His hair is . . thick and silky from its vigorous daily brush.

wash and brush-up: see WASH *noun* 1.
▸ **IV 10** A girl, a young woman; *collect.* girls, young women. *Austral. & NZ slang*. M20.
– COMB.: ***brush discharge***: see sense 6a above; **brushstroke** a mark made by a paintbrush drawn across a surface; **brushtail (possum)** any of several Australian possums of the genus *Trichosurus*, having a bushy tail, pointed snout, and prominent ears; *esp.* the common *T. vulpecula*, which has a commercially valuable pelt; **brushware** brushes of various kinds; **brushwork** a painter's (style of) manipulation of the brush.
■ **brushless** *adjective* (*a*) without a brush; (*b*) (of shaving cream) made for use without a brush: M19. **brushlike** *adjective* resembling (that of) a brush M19.

brush /brʌʃ/ *verb*[1]. LME.
[ORIGIN Perh. Old French & mod. French *brosser* sweep from *brosse* BRUSH *noun*[2]. In mod. use infl. by BRUSH *verb*[2].]
†**1** *verb intrans*. Rush with force or speed, usu. into a collision. LME–M17.
2 *verb trans*. Force on, drive with a rush; drive hard. *obsolete* exc. *US*. L15.
3 *verb intrans*. Burst away with a rush, move off abruptly, make off. *arch*. L17.

4 *verb intrans.* Move *by, through, against*, etc., so as to make brief contact in passing. Cf. BRUSH *verb*[2] 5. L17.

J. CLARE Often brushing through the dripping grass. V. WOOLF The friction of people brushing past her was evidently painful. F. HERBERT Do not brush against a bush lest you leave a thread to show our passage.

brush /brʌʃ/ *verb*[2]. See also BRISH. LME.
[ORIGIN from BRUSH *noun*[2].]
1 *verb trans.* Pass a brush across (a surface); sweep or scrub clean, put in order, with a brush; treat (a surface) with a brush to change its nature or appearance. LME. ▸**b** *verb intrans.* Use a brush. E19.
2 *verb trans.* Remove with a brush; sweep away (as) with a brush. L15.

J. B. PRIESTLEY The other [hand] trying to brush the cigar ash off his lapels.

3 *verb trans.* Trim (a hedge). Cf. BRISH. E16.
4 *verb trans.* Rub or touch lightly in passing. M17.

J. HEATH-STUBBS Hope, the butterfly, but seldom brushes my page With her mazarine wing. G. BOYCOTT The ball brushed his thigh-pad just hard enough to take the pace off it.

5 *verb intrans.* Come lightly *against*, pass lightly *over*, as with a brush. Cf. BRUSH *verb*[1] 4. M17.

J. SELDEN His Feathers brushed against the Kings Crown. M. SHADBOLT Pale green tree ferns . . brushed lightly over his face.

6 *verb trans.* Injure (a horse etc.) by a grazing blow. L17.
7 *verb trans.* Paint or put in, apply with the brush. Freq. foll. by *in*. L19.
– WITH ADVERBS IN SPECIALIZED SENSES: **brush aside** push out of the way in passing; *fig.* dismiss or dispose of curtly or lightly. **brush off** remove by brushing; *fig.* dismiss, rebuff. **brush over** paint lightly with a brush; (see also sense 5 above). **brush up** (*a*) refurbish by brushing; (*b*) *fig.* refresh one's acquaintance with (a subject etc.); also foll. by *on* the subject etc.
– COMB.: **brushback** *adjective & noun* (BASEBALL) (designating) a pitch thrown close to the batter's body in an attempt to force him to step back from the plate; **brush-off** a dismissal, a rebuff; **brush-up** the action of brushing up; an instance of this.
■ **brushed** *ppl adjective* (*a*) swept or smoothed with a brush; (*b*) (of fabric) having a raised nap; (*c*) **brushed aluminium**: treated so as to be lustreless: L15. **brusher** *noun* a person who uses a brush L16.

brushite /ˈbrʌʃʌɪt/ *noun*. M19.
[ORIGIN from George J. *Brush* (1831–1912), US mineralogist + -ITE[1].]
MINERALOGY. A monoclinic acid phosphate of calcium, usu. occurring on phosphate deposits as efflorescences and crusts of minute colourless crystals.

brushy /ˈbrʌʃi/ *adjective*. L16.
[ORIGIN from BRUSH *noun*[1] or *noun*[2] + -Y[1].]
1 Bushy, shaggy. L16.
2 Covered with brushwood. M17.

brusk /brʊsk/ *noun & adjective*[1]. *arch.* L15.
[ORIGIN Unknown.]
HERALDRY. (Of) the colour tenné.

†**brusk** *adjective*[2] var. of next.

brusque /brʊsk, bruːsk/ *adjective & verb*. Also †**brusk**. E17.
[ORIGIN French = lively, fierce, harsh, from Italian *brusco* sour, tart, use as adjective of noun = Spanish, Portuguese *brusco* butcher's broom (a spiny bush) from Proto-Romance.]
▸ **A** *adjective*. †**1** Tart. Only in E17.
2 Rough or rude in manner or speech; blunt, offhand, abrupt. M17.
▸ **B** *verb trans.* Treat in an offhand manner. Now *rare*. L18.
■ **brusquely** *adverb* L17. **brusqueness** *noun* M19. **brusquerie** /ˈbrʊsk(ə)riː, bruː-; *foreign* bryskəri/ *noun* [French: see -ERY] bluntness or abruptness of manner M18.

Brussels /ˈbrʌs(ə)lz/ *noun*. Also (in sense 3) **Brussel**. M18.
[ORIGIN The capital of Belgium.]
1 ***Brussels lace***, a rich type of pillow lace or needle lace. M18.
2 In full ***Brussels carpet***. A kind of carpet with a woollen pile and a stout linen back. L18.
3 In full ***Brussels sprout***. A variety of cabbage producing many small cabbage-like buds; one of these buds eaten as a vegetable. Usu. in *pl.* L18.
4 The Commission of the European Union, with headquarters in Brussels. M20.

Investors Chronicle From 1993, Brussels will set common financial and technical standards.

brustle /ˈbrʌs(ə)l/ *verb*[1] *intrans.* Also **brastle** /ˈbras(ə)l/.
[ORIGIN Old English *brastlian*, of imit. origin.]
†**1** Crackle, rustle. OE–M18.
2 Bustle, go hastily. *obsolete* exc. *Scot.* M17.

†**brustle** *verb*[2] *intrans.* E17–E18.
[ORIGIN Var. of BRISTLE *verb*[1].]
= BRISTLE *verb*[1] 4.

Brut /bruːt/ *noun*. *obsolete* exc. *hist.* ME.
[ORIGIN Welsh = chronicle, transf. use of *Brut* = *Brutus* (see below).]
A chronicle of British history from the time of Brutus, the legendary founder of the British race.

brut /bruːt, *foreign* bryt/ *adjective*. L19.
[ORIGIN French.]
Of wine: unsweetened, very dry.

brut /brʌt/ *verb intrans. & trans. obsolete* exc. *dial.* Infl. **-tt-**. L16.
[ORIGIN Perh. from French *brouter* (see BROWSE *verb*) or from Old English *brēotan* (see BRITTLE).]
Browse upon trees etc.; break *off* (by browsing).

bruta fulmina *noun phr.* pl. of BRUTUM FULMEN.

brutal /ˈbruːt(ə)l/ *adjective*. L15.
[ORIGIN Old French & mod. French, or medieval Latin *brutalis*, formed as BRUTE + -AL[1].]
†**1** = BRUTE *adjective* 1. Also, belonging to the (lower) animals. L15–M19.

G. S. FABER The angel . . daily infuses them into human and brutal bodies.

2 = BRUTISH 3. Now *rare*. E16.

SMOLLETT The slaves of brutal appetite. DISRAELI The students affected a sort of brutal surprise.

3 Inhuman, savagely cruel; merciless. M17.

G. K. CHESTERTON Our ordinary treatment of the poor criminal was a pretty brutal business. *Arena* The film opens with the brutal murder of a bunch of happy party-goers.

4 Crude, coarse; harsh, unrefined; direct and without attempting to disguise unpleasantness. E18. ▸**b** Very bad. *N. Amer. slang*. L20.

LD MACAULAY His brutal manners made him unfit to represent the . . crown. J. CHEEVER The forthright and sometimes brutal language that came from the loudspeaker.

■ **brutalism** *noun* brutal state, brutality; *spec.* a style of art, architecture, etc., characterized by a deliberate crudity of design: E19. **brutalist** *noun & adjective* (*a*) *noun* an exponent of brutalism, esp. in art, architecture, or literature; (*b*) *adjective* pertaining to or marked by brutalism: M20. **brutally** *adverb* M18.

brutalise *verb* var. of BRUTALIZE.

brutality /bruːˈtalɪti/ *noun*. M16.
[ORIGIN from BRUTAL + -ITY: cf. French *brutalité*.]
†**1** A state of brutish ignorance. Only in M16.
2 Brutal quality or condition, inhumanity, savage cruelty; sensuality. M17.
3 A brutal action. L19.
■ **brutaliˈtarian** *noun & adjective* [after *humanitarian*] (*a*) *noun* a person who practises or advocates brutality; (*b*) *adjective* pertaining to or characteristic of brutalitarians: E20.

brutalize /ˈbruːt(ə)lʌɪz/ *verb*. Also **-ise**. E18.
[ORIGIN formed as BRUTALITY + -IZE: cf. French *brutaliser*.]
1 *verb trans.* Render brutal or inhuman. E18.
2 *verb intrans.* Live in the fashion of a brute; become brutal. E18.
3 *verb trans.* Treat (a person) as a brute; treat brutally. L19.

P. CORNWELL Their wives . . had been brutalized and murdered.

■ **brutaliˈzation** *noun* L18.

brute /bruːt/ *adjective & noun*. LME.
[ORIGIN French *brut*, *brute* = Spanish, Italian *bruto*, from Latin *brutus* heavy, stupid, dull.]
▸ **A** *adjective*. **1** Of animals: not possessing the capacity of reason or understanding. LME.

G. BERKELEY To degrade human-kind to a level with brute beasts.

2 Of people or their actions etc.: unthinking, unreasoning; senseless, stupid; bestial, cruel; sensual, passionate. M16. ▸**b** Crude, unrefined; = BRUTAL 4. Now *rare*. M16.

J. SYLVESTER Man (alas!) is bruter than a Brute. Y. MENUHIN Imposing the only order the Soviets know, which is brute order.

3 Of things: unconscious, impersonal, merely material. M16.

M. FRAYN The brute glare of the noonday sun.

4 Of surfaces etc.: rugged, unpolished. *rare*. E17.

SOUTHEY The value of the brute diamond.

– SPECIAL COLLOCATIONS: **brute creation** *the* animals (as opp. to humans). **brute fact** a simple inescapable or unexplained fact; *loosely* (often in *pl.*) the plain truth. **brute force** irrational force; the simple or unthinking exertion of strength.
▸ **B** *noun*. **1** Any of the lower animals, as distinguished from humans; a large or powerful animal. E17.

POPE Man . . the middle Link between Angels and Brutes. W. HOLTBY The big black brute that Carne rode.

the brute animal nature in humans.
2 A person of brutish or animal tendencies; a person lacking in sensibility; (*colloq.*) a disliked or despised person. L17. ▸**b** *transf.* A large, awkward, or unpleasant thing. *colloq.* L19.

G. STEIN What could you expect when Melanctha had such a brute of a . . father. E. LANGLEY She's often asked him to bring us down to see her; but the brute wouldn't. **b** GEO. ELIOT The brute of a cigar required relighting.

■ **brutedom** *noun* brutish nature L19. **brutehood** *noun* M19. **brutely** *adverb* (now *rare*) in a brutal or brutish manner L16. **bruteness** *noun* M16.

brutify /ˈbruːtɪfʌɪ/ *verb trans. & intrans.* L16.
[ORIGIN from BRUTE + -FY.]
Make or become brutish; brutalize.
■ **brutifiˈcation** *noun* L17.

brutish /ˈbruːtɪʃ/ *adjective*. L15.
[ORIGIN from BRUTE *noun* + -ISH[1].]
†**1** Rough; savage, brutal. L15–L18.
2 Of or pertaining to the lower animals, as opp. to humans. M16.
3 Resembling or characteristic of an animal, esp. in unreasoning or sensual nature; irrational; stupid. M16.

HOBBES The life of man, solitary, poor, nasty, brutish, and short. *Times* Displaying brutish callousness.

■ **brutishly** *adverb* L16. **brutishness** *noun* M16.

brutism /ˈbruːtɪz(ə)m/ *noun*. L17.
[ORIGIN from BRUTE *noun* + -ISM.]
The behaviour or condition of a brute.

brutum fulmen /ˌbruːtəm ˈfʌlmən/ *noun phr.* Pl. ***bruta fulmina*** /ˌbruːtə ˈfʌlmɪnə/. E17.
[ORIGIN Latin, lit. 'unfeeling thunderbolt' (Pliny).]
A mere noise; an ineffective act, an empty threat.

Brutus /ˈbruːtəs/ *adjective & noun*. L18.
[ORIGIN Marcus Junius *Brutus* (85–42 BC).]
(Designating) a head or wig of short roughly cropped hair, fashionable in the 18th cent.

bruvver /ˈbrʌvə/ *noun*. *dial. & slang*. L19.
[ORIGIN Repr. a cockney pronunc.]
= BROTHER *noun*.

bruxism /ˈbrʌksɪz(ə)m/ *noun*. M20.
[ORIGIN from Greek *brukhein* gnash the teeth + -ISM.]
MEDICINE. Involuntary or habitual grinding or clenching of the teeth.

bryology /brʌɪˈɒlədʒi/ *noun*. M19.
[ORIGIN from Greek *bruon* moss + -OLOGY.]
The branch of botany that deals with mosses and liverworts.
■ **bryoˈlogical** *adjective* L19. **bryoˈlogically** *adverb* L19. **bryologist** *noun* M19.

bryony /ˈbrʌɪəni/ *noun*. Also **bri-** & (in medicinal contexts) in Latin form **bryonia** /brʌɪˈəʊnɪə/. OE.
[ORIGIN Latin *bryonia* from Greek *bruōnia*.]
1 A climbing plant of the genus *Bryonia*, of the gourd family; *esp.* (more fully ***white bryony***) *Bryonia dioica*, which bears greenish-white flowers and red berries. OE.
2 More fully ***black bryony*** (from the colour of its tubers). A similar but unrelated plant, *Tamus communis*, of the yam family. L16.

bryophyte /ˈbrʌɪəfʌɪt/ *noun*. L19.
[ORIGIN mod. Latin *Bryophyta* pl., from Greek *bruon* moss: see -PHYTE.]
Any plant of the group Bryophyta of small primitive cryptogams, comprising the liverworts and mosses.
■ **bryophytic** /-ˈfɪtɪk/ *adjective* E20.

bryozoan /brʌɪəˈzəʊən/ *noun & adjective*. L19.
[ORIGIN from mod. Latin *Bryozoa* (see below), from Greek *bruon* moss + *zōia* pl. of *zōion* animal: see -AN.]
ZOOLOGY. ▸**A** *noun*. A member of the group Bryozoa (now regarded as comprising the phyla Ectoprocta and Entoprocta) of lophophorates, which form colonies often suggesting mossy growths. Also *spec.* = ECTOPROCTAN *noun*. L19.
▸ **B** *adjective*. Of or pertaining to the group Bryozoa. L19.
■ **bryozoˈologist** *noun* an expert in or student of bryozoology M20. **bryozoˈology** *noun* the branch of zoology that deals with bryozoans M20. **bryozoon** *noun*, pl. **-zoa**, = BRYOZOAN *noun* (usu. in *pl.*) M19.

Brythonic /brɪˈθɒnɪk/ *adjective & noun*. L19.
[ORIGIN from Welsh *Brython* (see BRITON) + -IC.]
= BRITTONIC.

BS *abbreviation*.
1 Bachelor of Science. *US*.
2 Bachelor of Surgery.
3 Blessed Sacrament.
4 British Standard.
5 Bullshit.

B.Sc. *abbreviation*.
Bachelor of Science.

BSE *abbreviation*.
Bovine spongiform encephalopathy.

BSI *abbreviation*.
British Standards Institution.

BSL *abbreviation*.
British Sign Language.

BST *abbreviation*.
1 Bovine somatotrophin.
2 British Standard Time (1968–71).
3 British Summer Time.

BT *abbreviation*.
British Telecom.

Bt. *abbreviation*.
Baronet.

B

B.th.u. *abbreviation.*
hist. British thermal unit.

B2B *abbreviation.*
Business-to-business, designating trade conducted via the Internet between businesses.

B2C *abbreviation.*
Business-to-consumer, denoting trade conducted via the Internet between businesses and consumers.

B-tree /ˈbiːtriː/ *noun.* **M20.**
[ORIGIN from *B* repr. *balanced* or *binary* + TREE *noun*.]
COMPUTING. A tree in which all the terminal nodes are at the same distance from the root and all the non-terminal nodes have between *n* and *2n* subtrees or pointers, where *n* is a positive integer.

BTU *abbreviation.*
hist. **1** Board of Trade Unit.
2 (Also **B.t.u.**) British thermal unit.

BTW *abbreviation.*
By the way.

bu. *abbreviation.*
Bushel(s).

Bual /ˈbuːal/ *noun.* Also **Boal**, **b-**. **L19.**
[ORIGIN Portuguese *boal*.]
A variety of wine-making grape grown esp. in Madeira; (a drink of) medium sweet Madeira made from this.

BUAV *abbreviation.*
British Union for the Abolition of Vivisection.

bub /bʌb/ *noun*[1]. **L17.**
[ORIGIN Perh. imit.]
1 Alcoholic liquor; *esp.* strong beer. *arch. slang.* **L17.**
2 A mixture of meal and yeast with warm wort and water, used to promote fermentation. **M19.**

bub /bʌb/ *noun*[2]. *N. Amer. colloq.* **M19.**
[ORIGIN Abbreviation of BUBBY *noun*[2].]
Boy, man, brother: used chiefly as a familiar form of address.

bub /bʌb/ *noun*[3]. *colloq.* **M19.**
[ORIGIN Abbreviation of BUBBY *noun*[1].]
A woman's breast. Usu. in *pl.*

bubal /ˈbjuːb(ə)l/ *noun.* Also **-ale**. **L18.**
[ORIGIN French *bubale* from Latin *bubalus*: see BUFFALO.]
A hartebeest; *spec.* one of the N. African race, now extinct. Also ***bubal hartebeest***.

bubaline /ˈbjuːbəlʌɪn/ *adjective.* **E19.**
[ORIGIN from mod. Latin *Bubalus* genus name from Latin *bubalus* BUFFALO: see -INE[1].]
Of or pertaining to buffaloes.

bubba /ˈbʌbə/ *noun. N. Amer. colloq.* **L19.**
[ORIGIN Alt. of BROTHER; cf. BUB *noun*[2].]
1 Brother: used chiefly as a familiar form of address. **L19.**

> L. R. BANKS Don't lie to me, bubba.

2 An uneducated conservative white male of the southern US. *derog.* **L20.**

> J. HYNES Tight-jeaned, potbellied bubbas in their pickups.

bubbie /ˈbʌbi/ *noun.* Also **bubbe** /ˈbʊbə/. **L19.**
[ORIGIN Yiddish *bube*.]
In Jewish use: one's grandmother; an old woman.

bubble /ˈbʌb(ə)l/ *noun & adjective.* **ME.**
[ORIGIN Partly imit. (as Dutch *bobbel*, German dial. *Bobbel*, *Bubbel*), partly alt. of BURBLE *noun*.]
▸ **A** *noun.* **1** A gas-filled cavity in liquid or in solidified liquid (as glass, amber, paint, etc.); a spherical envelope of liquid enclosing air etc. **ME.**
2 *fig.* An unsubstantial or visionary (esp. commercial or financial) project, enterprise, etc. **L16.**
South Sea bubble: see SOUTH *adverb, adjective*, etc.
†**3** A person who is cheated or duped. **M17–E19.**
4 The process, sound, or appearance of bubbling; an agitated or bubbling motion. **M19.**
bubble and squeak (*a*) cold meat or (now usu.) potatoes fried with cabbage or other vegetables; (*b*) *rhyming slang* (a) Greek.
5 A car. Also *ellipt.*, a bubble car. *colloq.* **E20.**
6 A transparent domed canopy covering the cockpit of an aeroplane. *slang.* **M20.**
7 A small mobile domain of reverse magnetization in a crystalline material, *esp.* one forming a unit of stored information in a computer memory. Also ***magnetic bubble***. **M20.**
– COMB.: **bubble bath** (a bath in water to which has been added) a usu. perfumed toilet preparation which causes water to foam; **bubble car** a small usu. three-wheeled car with a transparent dome; **bubble chamber** PHYSICS a container of superheated liquid used to detect charged particles by the trails of bubbles which they produce; **bubble economy** an economy undergoing an unsustainable boom; *spec.* that of Japan in the late 1980s, brought about by artificially adjusted interest rates; **bubblegum** (*a*) chewing gum that can be blown into bubbles; (*b*) (in full ***bubblegum music***) pop music with simple trivial words; **bubblehead** *slang* a foolish, unintelligent, or empty-headed person; **bubblejet** COMPUTING a system of inkjet printing in which the ink is heated, producing bubbles which force droplets of ink on to the paper (usu. *attrib.*, esp. in ***bubblejet printer***); **bubble memory** COMPUTING a type of memory which stores data as a pattern of magnetic bubbles in a thin layer of magnetic material; **bubble pack** a small package enclosing goods in a transparent case on a flat backing; **bubble shell** any of various opisthobranchs with thin, more or less cylindrical, external shells; **bubble tea** an East Asian drink of tea or coffee with tapioca pearls, shaken to a froth and usu. served cold; **bubble wrap**, (US proprietary name for) a protective packaging material formed from plastic sheeting incorporating small pockets of air.
▸ **B** *attrib.* or as *adjective.* Of a project, enterprise, etc.: unsubstantial, delusive, fraudulent. Now *arch.* or *hist.* **M17.**

> E. LINKLATER In 1837 he lost some money by speculating in one of the many bubble companies of that year.

bubble /ˈbʌb(ə)l/ *verb.* **LME.**
[ORIGIN Partly imit. (as Dutch *bobbelen*, German dial. *bobbeln*, *bubbeln*, Swedish *bubla*, Danish *boble*), partly alt. of BURBLE *verb*.]
1 *verb intrans.* Form or rise in or like bubbles; well *up*, *out*, etc., in or like bubbles; boil or brim *over* (lit.) in bubbles or (fig.) *with* merriment, anger, excitement, etc.; make the sound of bubbles. **LME.**

> TENNYSON Yon swoll'n brook that bubbles fast. C. KINGSLEY Wild thoughts bubbled within her. P. G. WODEHOUSE The silver bubbling of a thrush. J. MASEFIELD A spring comes bubbling up there.

2 *verb trans.* Send out in or like bubbles. **E17.**
3 *verb trans.* Delude, dupe, cheat, esp. in a commercial or financial enterprise. Now *rare.* **L17.**
4 *verb intrans.* Weep, lament. *Scot. & N. English.* **E18.**
5 *verb trans.* Cause (a baby) to bring up wind. *US colloq.* **M20.**
■ **bubblement** *noun* (now *rare*) effervescence **L19.** **bubbler** *noun* a person who or thing which bubbles; *esp.* (*arch.*) a swindler, a cheat: **E18.**

bubbly /ˈbʌbli/ *adjective & noun.* **M16.**
[ORIGIN from BUBBLE *noun* + -Y[1].]
▸ **A** *adjective.* Full of bubbles, frothy. Of a person: vivacious; full of high spirits. **M16.**
▸ **B** *noun.* Champagne. *slang.* **E20.**

bubbly-jock /ˈbʌblɪdʒɒk/ *noun. Scot.* **E19.**
[ORIGIN from *bubbly* imit. of the bird's call + male forename *Jock*.]
A turkeycock.

bubby /ˈbʌbi/ *noun*[1]. Now *dial.* **L17.**
[ORIGIN Cf. German dial. *Bübbi* teat.]
A woman's breast. Usu. in *pl.*

bubby /ˈbʌbi/ *noun*[2]. *US colloq.* **M19.**
[ORIGIN Childish form of BROTHER *noun* or from German *Bube* boy.]
= BUB *noun*[2].

bubinga /bjuːˈbɪŋgə/ *noun.* **L20.**
[ORIGIN African name.]
(The reddish-brown timber of) any of several tropical African trees of the genus *Guibourtia* (family Leguminosae), having wood used chiefly for inlay work and as a veneer.

bubo /ˈbjuːbəʊ/ *noun.* Pl. **-oes**. **LME.**
[ORIGIN Latin from Greek *boubōn* groin, swelling in the groin.]
A swollen inflamed lymph node esp. in the groin or armpit.

bubonic /bjuːˈbɒnɪk/ *adjective.* **L19.**
[ORIGIN from Latin *bubon-*, BUBO + -IC.]
Characterized by the presence of buboes.
bubonic plague a highly contagious bacterial disease in which buboes appear.

bubonocele /bjuːˈbɒnəsiːl/ *noun.* Now *rare* or *obsolete.* **E17.**
[ORIGIN mod. Latin from Greek *boubōnokēlē*, formed as BUBO: see -CELE.]
MEDICINE. Hernia of the groin.

bucatini /bʊkəˈtiːni/ *noun pl.* **L20.**
[ORIGIN Italian, from *bucato* perforated, hollow.]
Long, narrow tubes of pasta.

buccal /ˈbʌk(ə)l/ *adjective.* **E19.**
[ORIGIN from Latin *bucca* cheek + -AL[1].]
Of the cheek; of or in the mouth.
■ **buccally** *adverb* towards the cheek **M20.**

buccan *noun, verb* var. of BOUCAN *noun, verb.*

buccaneer /bʌkəˈnɪə/ *noun & verb.* **M17.**
[ORIGIN French *boucanier*, formed as BOUCAN *verb*: see -EER.]
▸ **A** *adjective.* †**1** A person, esp. a hunter, who cooks or cures meat on a boucan. **M17–M18.**
2 A pirate, orig. of the Spanish-American coasts; an unscrupulous adventurer. **L17.**
▸ **B** *verb.* **1** *verb intrans.* Be or act as a pirate or adventurer. **E18.**
2 *verb trans.* = BOUCAN *verb.* Now *rare.* **L18.**
■ **buccaneerish** *adjective* **E19.**

buccaro *noun* var. of BOCCARO.

buccinator /ˈbʌksɪneɪtə/ *noun.* **L17.**
[ORIGIN Latin, from *buccinare* blow the trumpet, from *buccina* kind of trumpet: see -ATOR.]
ANATOMY. A flat thin muscle in the wall of the cheek.
■ **buccinatory** *adjective* of or pertaining to a trumpet or trumpeter (***buccinatory muscle*** = BUCCINATOR) **M18.**

buccinum /ˈbʌksɪnəm/ *noun.* **E17.**
[ORIGIN Latin, from *buccina*: see BUCCINATOR.]
A whelk; *spec.* one of the genus *Buccinum*.
■ **buccinoid** *adjective* resembling a buccinum **M19.**

bucco- /ˈbʌkəʊ/ *combining form* of Latin *bucca* cheek: see -O-.
■ **bucco'lingual** *adjective* of or pertaining to the cheeks and tongue; (of direction) passing through both tongue and cheek: **E20.** **bucco'lingually** *adverb* in the buccolingual direction **E20.**

buccra *noun* var. of BUCKRA.

bucellas /bjuːˈsɛləs/ *noun.* **E19.**
[ORIGIN A village near Lisbon.]
A Portuguese white wine; a drink of this.

Bucentaur /bjuːˈsɛntɔː/ *noun.* Also †**Bucentoro**. **M16.**
[ORIGIN French *bucentaure* from (after *centaure* CENTAUR) Italian *bucentoro*, perh. from Venetian Italian, lit. 'barge in gold'.]
hist. The state barge used by the Doge of Venice for the Ascension Day festival of marrying the Adriatic.

Bucephalus /bjuːˈsɛfələs/ *noun.* Chiefly *joc.* **M17.**
[ORIGIN Latin from Greek *Boukefalos*, Alexander the Great's charger, from *bous* ox + *kephalē* head.]
A horse for riding, a mount.

Buchmanism /ˈbʊkmənɪz(ə)m, ˈbuːk-/ *noun.* Usu. *derog.* **E20.**
[ORIGIN from Frank *Buchman* (1878–1961) Amer. evangelist + -ISM.]
The theories or practice of the Oxford Group Movement.
■ **Buchmanite** *noun & adjective* (*a*) *noun* an adherent of Buchmanism; (*b*) *adjective* of or pertaining to Buchmanites or Buchmanism: **E20.**

buchu /ˈbʌkuː, ˈbʊxʊ/ *noun.* **M18.**
[ORIGIN Afrikaans from Nama.]
Any of various South African shrubs of the rue family (esp. *Agathosma betulina* and *A. crenulata*) whose leaves yield a diuretic drug; the powdered dried leaves of such a shrub.

buck /bʌk/ *noun*[1] *& adjective.* **OE.**
[ORIGIN Partly Old English *buc* male deer = Middle Dutch *boc* (Dutch *bok*), Old High German *boc* (German *Bock*), Old Norse *bukkr*, *bokkr*, partly Old English *bucca* he-goat = Old Norse *bokki* my good fellow, old buck, both from Germanic.]
▸ **A** *noun.* **I** The male of various animals. (The corresponding female animal is usu. called ***doe***.)
†**1** A male goat (cf. GOAT 1). **OE–M16.**
2 A male deer, *spec.* the fallow deer and roe deer. **OE.**
3 The male of certain other kinds of deer, as the reindeer; the male of certain other horned mammals, as the antelope; *US* a ram. **L17.**
4 A male hare, rabbit, ferret, or rat. **M18.**
5 An adult male kangaroo. *Austral.* **M19.**
▸ **II** *transf.* **6** A man. *rare* exc. as below. **ME.**
7 A fashionable and spirited young man. *arch.* **E18.**
8 A male American Indian; a black male; a male Australian Aborigine. *offensive.* Chiefly *US & Austral.* **E19.**
– COMB.: **buckbrush** *N. Amer.* brush on which deer browse; any of various shrubs of this sort; **buckbush** buckbrush; also, any of various Australian shrubs; **buck fever** *US* nervousness when called on to take action; **buckhorn** (*a*) (the material of) a male deer's horn; (*b*) *dial.* dried whiting or other fish; **buckhound** a small variety of staghound; **buckjump** *noun, verb intrans.* = BUCK *noun*[4] 2, BUCK *verb*[2] 2a; **buckjumper** (*a*) a horse that bucks; (*b*) one who rides bucking horses in rodeos etc.; **buck naked** *N. Amer. colloq.* [perh. alt. of *butt naked*] completely naked; **buck rarebit** Welsh rarebit with poached egg; **buck's horn** any of various plants resembling a male deer's horn, esp. a plantain, *Plantago coronopus* (usu. more fully ***buck's horn plantain***); **buckshot** coarse lead shot used in shotgun shells; **buckskin** (*a*) (leather of) the skin of a male deer or similar skin; in *pl.*, breeches made of this; (*b*) a strong smooth cotton, woollen, or twilled cloth; **buckstall** *hist.* a large net for catching deer; **buck tooth** a tooth that projects.
▸ **B** *attrib.* or as *adjective.* **1** Of an animal or *derog.* a black man etc.: male. **E17.**
2 Of the lowest grade of a specific military rank. *US slang.* **E20.**
■ **buckish** *adjective* **LME.** †**buckism** *noun* foppish behaviour **M18–E19.**

buck /bʌk/ *noun*[2]. *obsolete* exc. *hist.* **M16.**
[ORIGIN from BUCK *verb*[1].]
1 Alkaline lye in which linen, yarn, etc., was steeped or boiled in buck-washing (see below) or bleaching. **M16.**
buck-washing washing very dirty linen by boiling it in an alkaline lye and afterwards beating and rinsing it in clear water.
2 A quantity of clothes etc. (to be) steeped or boiled in buck. **M16.**
drive a buck (of clothes): see DRIVE *verb.*

†**buck** *noun*[3]. **L16–E19.**
[ORIGIN Abbreviation.]
= BUCKWHEAT.

buck /bʌk/ *noun*[4]. **L16.**
[ORIGIN from BUCK *verb*[2].]
†**1** An act of copulation by a male rabbit, hare, etc. **L16–E17.**
2 A vertical jump by a horse etc. with the back arched and feet drawn together. **L19.**
3 A try, an attempt. *Austral. & NZ slang.* **E20.**
– COMB.: **buck-and-wing** *noun & adjective* (*US*) (designating) a lively solo dance usu. performed in wooden-soled shoes; **buck dance** *US* a buck-and-wing dance.

buck /bʌk/ *noun*[5]. L17.
[ORIGIN Perh. var. of BOUK.]
The body of a cart.
– COMB.: **buckboard** *US* (a vehicle with) a body formed by a plank on wheels.

buck /bʌk/ *noun*[6]. L17.
[ORIGIN Unknown.]
(Esp. on the River Thames) a wooden framework at a weir supporting baskets for trapping eels; a basket for trapping eels.

buck /bʌk/ *noun*[7]. E19.
[ORIGIN Dutch *(zaag-)bok* (German *(Säge)bock*), formed as SAW *noun*[1] + BUCK *noun*[1]: cf. French *chèvre*.]
1 A frame supporting wood for sawing. *N. Amer.* E19.
2 A short vaulting horse. M20.
– COMB.: **buck saw** *N. Amer.* a heavy frame saw used with a buck.

buck /bʌk/ *noun*[8]. *N. Amer. & Austral. slang.* M19.
[ORIGIN Unknown.]
A dollar.
a fast buck, **a quick buck** easy money.

buck /bʌk/ *noun*[9]. M19.
[ORIGIN Unknown.]
An article placed as a reminder before a player whose turn it is to deal at poker.
the buck stops here *colloq.* the responsibility for something cannot or should not be passed to someone else. **pass the buck** *fig.* (*colloq.*) shift responsibility (*to* another).
– COMB.: **buck-passing** *colloq.* shifting of responsibility to another.

buck /bʌk/ *noun*[10]. *slang.* L19.
[ORIGIN Hindi *bak*.]
Conversation; boastful talk.

buck /bʌk/ *verb*[1] *trans. obsolete* exc. *hist.* LME.
[ORIGIN Corresp. to Middle High German *büchen* (German *beuchen*), Low German *büken*, Swedish *byka*, Danish *byge*, from Germanic: prob. in Old English.]
1 Steep or boil in an alkaline lye in buck-washing or bleaching. LME.
†**2** Drench, soak. L15–E17.
■ **bucking** *noun* (*a*) the action of the verb; (*b*) = BUCK *noun*[2]: L15.

buck /bʌk/ *verb*[2]. M16.
[ORIGIN from BUCK *noun*[1].]
†**1** *verb intrans. & trans.* Of a male rabbit, hare, etc.: copulate (with). M16–M18.
2 **a** *verb intrans.* Of a horse etc.: jump vertically with the back arched and feet drawn together. M19. ▸**b** *verb trans.* Throw (a rider or burden) by so jumping. Also foll. by *off*. L19.
3 *verb intrans. & trans.* Foll. by *up*: ▸**a** Dress up. *arch. & dial.* M19. ▸**b** Cheer up; become or make more vigorous or lively; hurry up, make an effort. *colloq.* M19.
■ **bucked** *adjective* (*colloq.*) encouraged, elated E20. **bucker** *noun*[1] a horse etc. that bucks M19.

buck /bʌk/ *verb*[3] *trans.* L17.
[ORIGIN Cf. Dutch *boken*, *boocken* beat or strike.]
MINING. Break (ore) into small pieces with a special hammer.
■ **bucker** *noun*[2] (MINING) a hammer for bucking ore M17.

buck /bʌk/ *verb*[4]. M18.
[ORIGIN Perh. alt. of BUTT *verb*[1] by assoc. with BUCK *noun*[1].]
1 *verb trans.* Push with the head; butt into or against; *fig.* come up against, oppose, resist, get the better of (cf. BUCK *verb*[2] 2b). Chiefly *dial.* (in *lit.* sense) & *N. Amer.* M18.

F. CHICHESTER I . . kept swimming, not trying to buck the flood. K. KESEY Some mornings . . I hide and try to buck the schedule.

buck the tiger: see TIGER *noun*.
2 *verb intrans.* Foll. by *against*, *at*: oppose, resist. Chiefly *N. Amer.* M19.

G. BONNER There's no good bucking against bad luck.

buck /bʌk/ *verb*[5] *trans. N. Amer.* L19.
[ORIGIN from BUCK *noun*[7].]
Cut (wood) with a buck saw.
■ **bucker** *noun*[3] a person who saws trees into logs E20.

buck /bʌk/ *verb*[6] *intrans. slang.* L19.
[ORIGIN Cf. BUCK *noun*[10].]
Swagger, brag.

buckaroo /bʌkəˈruː/ *noun. US. arch.* E19.
[ORIGIN Alt. of VAQUERO.]
A cowboy.

buckbean /ˈbʌkbiːn/ *noun.* L16.
[ORIGIN Flemish *bocks boonen* goat's beans.]
A common marsh plant, *Menyanthes trifoliata*, bearing racemes of white or pinkish flowers. Also called ***marsh trefoil***.

buckeen /bʌˈkiːn/ *noun. Irish.* L18.
[ORIGIN from BUCK *noun*[1] + -EEN[2].]
hist. A young (impecunious) man from inferior Irish gentry.

bucket /ˈbʌkɪt/ *noun*[1]. ME.
[ORIGIN Anglo-Norman *buket*, *buquet* tub, pail (Anglo-Latin *bokettum*, *bu-*), perh. from Old English *būc* belly, pitcher: see -ET[1].]
1 A (usu. round) open vessel with a handle, for use when drawing water etc. or for holding or carrying liquids or other substances or objects (orig. of leather or wood, now also of metal, plastic, and other materials). Also, a bucketful. ME.
a drop in the bucket: see DROP *noun* 3.
2 The piston of a lift pump. M17.
3 Each of the compartments on the circumference of a water wheel; each of the scoops of a dredger, grain elevator, etc. M18.
4 A (usu. leather) socket or rest for a whip, carbine, or lance. M19.
5 ROWING. A hurried or jerky forward movement of the body. L19.
– COMB.: **bucketload** (*a*) the amount contained in a bucket; (*b*) a large quantity of something; **bucket seat** a seat with a rounded back to fit one person; **bucket shop** an unauthorized office for gambling in stocks, speculating on markets, dealing in discounted airline tickets, etc.; **bucket wheel** a contrivance for raising water, comprising buckets fixed round the rim of a wheel, which fill at the bottom and empty themselves at the top.
■ **bucketful** *noun* the amount contained in a bucket; in *pl.*, large quantities of rain, tears, etc.: M16.

bucket /ˈbʌkɪt/ *noun*[2]. Long *obsolete* exc. as below. L16.
[ORIGIN Perh. from Old French *buquet* balance.]
A beam or yoke on which anything may be hung.
kick the bucket [perh., & now usu. interpreted as, BUCKET *noun*[1]] *slang* die.

bucket /ˈbʌkɪt/ *verb.* L16.
[ORIGIN from BUCKET *noun*[1].]
1 *verb intrans.* Use a bucket (of water). Chiefly as ***bucketing*** *verbal noun.* L16.
2 *verb trans.* Pour buckets of water over. E17.
3 *verb trans.* Lift or carry in buckets. M17.
4 **a** *verb trans.* Ride (a horse) hard; drive or move (a vehicle etc.) jerkily or bumpily. M19. ▸**b** *verb intrans.* Of a vehicle etc.: jerk or bounce up and down, move roughly. E20.
5 *verb intrans. & trans.* ROWING. Hurry the forward swing of (the body); hurry (recovery of position). L19.
6 *verb intrans. & trans.* with *it*. Of rain etc.: pour down (or *down*) heavily. *colloq.* E20.
■ **bucketing** *ppl adjective* (ROWING) hurried, jerky M19.

buckeye /ˈbʌkʌɪ/ *noun & adjective.* Exc. sense A.1 *US.* M18.
[ORIGIN from BUCK *noun*[1] + EYE *noun.*]
▸ **A** *noun.* **1** (The nut or fruit of) a tree or shrub of the genus *Aesculus*; an American horse chestnut. M18.
2 A backwoodsman; a native of Ohio. E19.
3 An inferior person or thing; a shop selling inferior goods. M19.
– COMB.: **Buckeye State** *US* Ohio, where buckeye trees are abundant.
▸ **B** *attrib.* or as *adjective.* **1** Of Ohio. M19.
2 Inferior; showy but not impressive. E20.

buckie /ˈbʌki/ *noun. Scot.* E16.
[ORIGIN Sense 1 of unknown origin (cf. BUCCINUM); sense 2 app. from BUCK *noun*[1] + -IE.]
1 A whorled mollusc's shell. E16.
2 A perverse or refractory person. E18.

buckle /ˈbʌk(ə)l/ *noun.* ME.
[ORIGIN Anglo-Norman *bucle*, Old French *bocle* (mod. *boucle*) from Latin *buccula* cheek-strap of a helmet, dim. of *bucca* cheek.]
1 A flat frame with a hinged pin, for securing a strap, belt, etc.; a similarly shaped ornament on a shoe etc. ME.
†**2** The state of hair when crisped and curled; a kink or curl in hair. E18–E19.

buckle /ˈbʌk(ə)l/ *verb.* LME.
[ORIGIN Branch I from the noun; branch II from French *boucler* bulge.]
▸ **I** **1** *verb trans.* Fasten with a buckle. (Foll. by *up*, *on*, etc.) LME. ▸**b** *verb intrans.* Foll. by *up*: fasten a seat belt, wear a seat belt. *N. Amer.* L20.
2 *verb intrans.* Grapple, engage, *with*. Now *dial.* M16.

SIR W. SCOTT Would . . interrupt you just when you were buckling with your labours.

3 *verb intrans. & †refl.* Equip oneself, prepare, for battle, an expedition, etc. Now only *fig.* foll. by *to* (preposition & adverb), *down* (*to*): prepare for or set about (work etc.), apply oneself vigorously (to). M16.

BURKE I have shook off idleness, and begun to buckle to. T. F. DIBDIN Now buckles himself to the uninterrupted perusal of the . . text. B. HARTE Chiquita Buckled right down to her work. E. REVELEY You'll really have to buckle down and cram for those exams.

4 *verb intrans. & trans.* Marry. *dial. & joc.* L17.
†**5** *verb trans.* Fix (hair) in curl. E18–M19.
▸ **II** **6** *verb trans. & intrans.* (Cause to) give way or crumple up, esp. under longitudinal pressure. E16.

A. POWELL One of the legs buckled, but the chair did not break. D. ATTENBOROUGH The . . rocks . . are twisted and buckled. T. BERGER Her knees threatened to buckle.

7 *verb intrans. fig.* Submit, cringe. *obsolete* exc. *dial.* M17.
– COMB.: †**buckle-beggar** *Scot.* a clergyman who performed irregular marriages.

buckler /ˈbʌklə/ *noun & verb.* ME.
[ORIGIN Anglo-Norman *bucler*, Old French *bocler* (mod. *bouclier*), orig. adjective in *escu bocler* shield having a boss, from *bocle* boss, BUCKLE *noun*: see -ER[2].]
▸ **A** *noun.* **1** *hist.* A small round shield usu. held by a handle. ME.
2 *fig.* A means of defence. LME.
3 A shieldlike part of the protective covering of an animal. E19.
– COMB.: **buckler-fern** any of certain ferns of the genus *Dryopteris*, with kidney-shaped indusia.
▸ **B** *verb trans.* **1** Act as a buckler to, shield. L16.
†**2** Ward or catch (blows). *rare* (Shakes.). Only in L16.
■ **bucklered** *adjective* armed with a buckler M19.

Buckley's /ˈbʌklɪz/ *noun. Austral. & NZ colloq.* L19.
[ORIGIN Unknown.]
In full ***Buckley's chance***. Little or no chance.

buckling /ˈbʌklɪŋ/ *noun.* E20.
[ORIGIN German *Bückling* bloater.]
A smoked herring.

buckminsterfullerene /ˌbʌkmɪnstəˈfʊləriːn/ *noun.* L20.
[ORIGIN from R. *Buckminster Fuller* (1895–1983), US engineer and architect who invented the geodesic dome + -ENE.]
CHEMISTRY. A form of carbon in which 60 carbon atoms are joined together as a hollow polyhedron of 12 pentagons and 20 hexagons.

bucko /ˈbʌkəʊ/ *adjective & noun. nautical slang.* Pl. of noun **-o(e)s**. L19.
[ORIGIN from BUCK *noun*[1] + -O.]
(A person who is) swaggering or domineering.
– COMB.: **bucko mate** an officer who drives the crew by bullying methods.

buckra /ˈbʌkrə/ *noun. W. Indian & Southern US.* Freq. *derog.* Also **buccra** & other vars. M18.
[ORIGIN Ibibio & Efik *(m)bakara* European, master.]
(A black person's name for) a white man, a master.

buckram /ˈbʌkrəm/ *noun, adjective, & verb.* ME.
[ORIGIN Anglo-Norman *bukeran*, Old French *boquerant* (mod. *bougran*), corresp. to Provençal *bocaran*, Spanish *bucaran*, Italian *bucherame*, perh. obscurely from *Bukhara*, a town in central Asia, west of Samarkand: for the change of final *n* to *m* cf. *grogram*, *megrim*, *vellum*.]
▸ **A** *noun.* **1** A kind of fine linen or cotton fabric. Long *obsolete* exc. *hist.* ME.
2 A coarse linen or other cloth stiffened with gum or paste. LME.
men in buckram non-existent persons, figments (in allusion to Shakes. *1 Hen. IV*).
3 *fig.* Stiffness of manner. L17.
▸ **B** *attrib.* or as *adjective.* Of or like buckram; *fig.* stiff in manner. M16.
▸ **C** *verb trans.* Pad or stiffen with buckram; *fig.* give a starched pomposity or illusory strength to. L18.

Bucks *abbreviation.*
Buckinghamshire.

Buck's Fizz /bʌks ˈfɪz/ *noun phr.* M20.
[ORIGIN from *Buck's* Club, London + FIZZ *noun.*]
Champagne or sparkling white wine mixed with orange juice; a drink of this.

buckshee /bʌkˈʃiː, *esp. attrib.* ˈbʌkʃiː/ *adjective* /ˈbʌkʃiː/ *noun*[1], *adjective, & adverb. slang.* E20.
[ORIGIN Alt. of BAKSHEESH.]
▸ **A** *noun.* Something in addition to the usual allowance; something extra or free. E20.
▸ **B** *adjective & adverb.* Free of charge, gratuitous(ly). E20.

buckshee *noun*[2] var. of BUKSHI.

buckthorn /ˈbʌkθɔːn/ *noun.* L16.
[ORIGIN from BUCK *noun*[1] + THORN *noun*, translating mod. Latin *cervi spina* stag's thorn.]
A shrub or small tree of the genus *Rhamnus* (family Rhamnaceae); *esp.* (more fully ***purging buckthorn***) the shrub *R. cathartica*, whose berries yield sap green and are strongly cathartic.
ALDER **buckthorn**. SEA **buckthorn**.

buckwheat /ˈbʌkwiːt/ *noun.* M16.
[ORIGIN Middle Dutch *boecweite* or Middle Low German *bōkwēte* lit. 'beech wheat', its grains resembling beechmast.]
1 A cereal plant of the genus *Fagopyrum* (family Polygonaceae), esp. *F. esculentum*, the seed of which is used for horse and poultry food, and in N. America is milled for making breakfast pancakes. M16.
2 A buckwheat cake. *N. Amer.* M19.

buckyball /ˈbʌkɪbɔːl/ *noun.* CHEMISTRY, *colloq.* L20.
[ORIGIN from BUCK(MINSTERFULLERENE + -Y[6] + BALL *noun*[1].]
A fullerene molecule.

bucolic /bjuːˈkɒlɪk/ *noun.* E16.
[ORIGIN Latin *bucolica*, Greek *boukolika* (both pl.), formed as BUCOLIC *adjective*.]
1 A pastoral poem, e.g. Virgil's eclogues. Usu. in *pl.* E16.
2 A pastoral poet; *joc.* a rustic. *rare.* L18.

bucolic /bjuːˈkɒlɪk/ *adjective.* E17.
[ORIGIN Latin *bucolicus* from Greek *boukolikos*, from *boukolos* herdsman, from *bous* ox: see -IC.]
Of shepherds, pastoral; rustic, rural.
■ **bucolical** *adjective* (now *rare*) bucolic E16. **bucolically** *adverb* L19.

B

bud /bʌd/ *noun*¹. LME.
[ORIGIN Unknown.]
1 a A rudiment of a shoot, flower, or foliage; a leaf or flower not yet fully open. LME. ▸**b** *ZOOLOGY*. A growth which later separates to form a new individual asexually. M19.
a in bud putting forth buds. **nip in the bud** *fig.* destroy at an early stage of development. ***red bud***: see RED *adjective*.
2 Anything resembling a bud, esp. in respect of shape or of immature state of development; *spec.* (***a***) a child, a youngster; (***b***) *dial.* a yearling calf; (***c***) *colloq.* (chiefly *US*) a debutante; (***d***) the rudiment of a horn or of an insect's leg or other appendage when it begins to sprout; (***e***) a small wad of cotton wool etc. on a stick. L16.
– COMB.: **budworm** a grub or caterpillar destructive to buds.
▪ **budless** *adjective* M19. **budlet** *noun* a small or secondary bud M19.

bud /bʌd/ *noun*². *N. Amer. colloq.* M19.
[ORIGIN Abbreviation.]
= BUDDY *noun*.

bud /bʌd/ *verb*. Infl. **-dd-**. LME.
[ORIGIN from BUD *noun*¹.]
1 *verb intrans.* Send out buds, sprout; come or push *out* as a bud. LME.
2 *verb intrans. fig.* Begin to grow or develop. M16.
E. WAUGH Two daughters just budding into womanhood.
3 *verb trans. & intrans. ZOOLOGY*. Form (as) a bud. L16.
D. MORRIS It must divide and bud off a lower, second cell.
D. ATTENBOROUGH The polyps bud in a different way and produce miniature medusae which detach themselves and wriggle away.
4 *verb trans.* Bring into bud, cause to bud. E17.
5 *verb trans. HORTICULTURE*. Graft a bud of (a plant) on to another plant. M17.

budda /ˈbʌdə/ *noun*. *Austral.* Also **-ah**. L19.
[ORIGIN Wiradhuri and Yuwaalaraay (an Australian Aboriginal language of New South Wales) *budaa*.]
An E. Australian tree, *Eremophila mitchelli*, with aromatic timber resembling sandalwood.

Buddha /ˈbʊdə/ *noun*. L17.
[ORIGIN Sanskrit = enlightened, pa. pple of *budh-* awake, know, perceive.]
The title of the successive teachers, past and future, of Buddhism (see BUDDHISM), esp. of its founder, the Indian religious teacher Gautama (fl. 5th cent. BC); any of the numerous and often massive carved figures of the Buddha.
▪ **Buddhahood** *noun* the condition of a Buddha M19.

Buddhism /ˈbʊdɪz(ə)m/ *noun*. E19.
[ORIGIN from BUDDHA + -ISM.]
The religious and philosophical system founded by the Buddha Gautama (see BUDDHA), teaching that all human sorrows arise from desire and can be eradicated by following the disciplines of his eightfold path.
▪ **Buddhist** *adjective & noun* (***a***) *adjective* relating to or connected with Buddhism; (***b***) *noun* an adherent of Buddhism: E19. **Buˈddhistic**, **Buˈddhistical** *adjectives* = BUDDHIST *adjective* M19.

budding /ˈbʌdɪŋ/ *adjective*. L16.
[ORIGIN from BUD *verb* + -ING².]
1 That forms buds. L16.
2 *fig.* Beginning to develop to maturity. L16.
G. MACDONALD This gave a great help to his budding confidence. L. T. C. ROLT Budding engineers who bombarded the Company with impracticable schemes.

buddle /ˈbʌd(ə)l/ *noun*¹. *dial.* LME.
[ORIGIN Unknown.]
The corn marigold.

buddle /ˈbʌd(ə)l/ *noun*² *& verb*. M16.
[ORIGIN Unknown.]
MINING. ▸**A** *noun*. A shallow inclined vat in which ore is washed. M16.
▸**B** *verb trans.* Wash (ore) in a buddle. L17.

buddleia /ˈbʌdlɪə/ *noun*. Also **-lea**. L18.
[ORIGIN mod. Latin, from Adam *Buddle* (d. 1715), English botanist: see -IA¹.]
A shrub or tree of the genus *Buddleja*, native to America, Asia, and southern Africa; esp. *B. davidii*, a large ornamental shrub bearing panicles of fragrant lilac flowers which attract butterflies. Also called ***butterfly bush***.

buddy /ˈbʌdi/ *noun & verb*. *colloq.* (orig. *US*). M19.
[ORIGIN Alt. of BROTHER *noun* or var. of BUTTY *noun*¹.]
▸**A** *noun*. **1** Brother, companion, friend (freq. as a familiar form of address). M19.
2 A working companion with whom close cooperation is required. E20. ▸**b** A person who befriends and gives special help to another with an incapacitating disease, esp. Aids. L20.
– COMB.: **buddy-buddy** *adjective* (*N. Amer. colloq.*) exceptionally close or friendly; **buddy film**, **buddy movie** a film featuring friendship between two individuals, esp. men; **buddy system** (***a***) organized cooperation of individuals for mutual help or safety; (***b***) the practice of appointing friends or allies to positions of influence.
▸**B** *verb intrans.* Become friendly. Usu. foll. by *up*. M20.

buddy /ˈbʌdi/ *adjective*. *rare*. L16.
[ORIGIN from BUD *noun*¹ + -Y¹.]
Full of buds; like a bud.

bude /buːd, byd/ *verb* (orig. 3rd person sing. pa. indic., later other persons, pres., pa. pple, & inf.). *Scot.* (formerly also *N. English*). Also **bit** /bɪt/, **bode** /bəʊd/, **buit** /byt/, & other vars. ME.
[ORIGIN Contr. of *behoved*: cf. BOOST *verb*².]
Behoved, behoves, behove (see above); must, ought.

budge /bʌdʒ/ *noun*¹ *& adjective*. *obsolete* exc. *hist.* LME.
[ORIGIN Origin unkn. (orig. disyllabic, = Anglo-Latin *buggetum*).]
▸**A** *noun*. A fur of lamb's skin with the wool dressed outwards. LME.
▸†**B** *attrib.* or as *adjective*. Made of budge; wearing budge. Hence, solemn in demeanour, pompous, formal. LME–L18.

budge /bʌdʒ/ *noun*². *rare* exc. as below. E17.
[ORIGIN Var. of BOUGE *noun*.]
= BOUGE *noun* 1.
– COMB.: **budge-barrel** *hist.* a small powder barrel having a leather cover with a long neck.

†**budge** *noun*³. *slang*. L17–M18.
[ORIGIN Unknown.]
A sneak thief.

budge /bʌdʒ/ *verb*. L16.
[ORIGIN French *bouger* = Provençal *bolegar* disturb oneself, Italian *bulicare* bubble up, from Proto-Romance frequentative of Latin *bullire*, from BULLA.]
1 *verb intrans.* Stir, move from one's or its place; change opinion. (Almost always in neg. contexts.) L16. ▸†**b** Wince, flinch, shirk. L16–M17.
R. L. STEVENSON We'll have to budge, mates. A. CARTER The old car stuck fast in a rut, wouldn't budge an inch. S. BRETT I've argued with him about this, but he won't budge.
2 *verb trans.* Stir or move (a heavy thing). L16.
▪ **budger** *noun* (*rare*) E17.

budgeree /ˈbʌdʒəri/ *adjective*. *Austral. colloq.* L18.
[ORIGIN Dharuk *bujiri*.]
Good, excellent.

budgerigar /ˈbʌdʒ(ə)rɪɡɑː/ *noun*. M19.
[ORIGIN Prob. alt. of Kamilaroi *gijirrigaa*.]
A small Australian parakeet, *Melopsittacus undulatus*, a popular cage bird, green in the wild state, although captive birds are bred in a variety of colours.

budgerow /ˈbʌdʒərəʊ/ *noun*. *Indian*. *obsolete* exc. *hist.* E18.
[ORIGIN Hindi, Bengali *bajrā*.]
A type of barge formerly much used on the Ganges.

budget /ˈbʌdʒɪt/ *noun & adjective*. See also BOUGET. LME.
[ORIGIN Old French *bougette* dim. of *bouge* leather bag from Latin *bulga*: see BULGE, -ET¹.]
▸**A** *noun*. **1** A pouch or wallet. *obsolete* exc. *dial.* LME. ▸†**b** *spec.* A leather container, *esp.* a leather or skin bottle. L16–M19.
open one's budget speak one's mind.
2 The contents of a bag or wallet; a bundle, a collection, a stock. *arch.* L16. ▸**b** *spec.* A long letter full of news. E19.
SWIFT I read.. the whole budget of papers you sent. *fig.*: HAZLITT His budget of general knowledge. **b** DAY LEWIS I had a budget from her last week.
3 A periodic (esp. annual) estimate of the revenue and expenditure of a country or organization; an account or statement of this, *esp.* one made by the Chancellor of the Exchequer in the House of Commons; a similar estimate for a private individual or family. Also, the amount of money needed or available for spending. M18.
J. K. GALBRAITH The balanced budget.. has been the *sine qua non* of sound and sensible management of the public purse. B. CASTLE The Chancellor must be free to have a later budget next year. P. DAVIES Most 'pure' scientists work in large laboratory teams.. and annual budgets run into hundreds of millions of dollars.
on a budget with a restricted amount of money.
– COMB.: **budget buster** (chiefly *US*) a person, policy, or measure proposing or effecting expenditure in excess of an agreed budget.
▸**B** *attrib.* or as *adjective*. Designed or suitable for someone of limited means; cheap. M20.
Woman's Own Budget meals for the family.
budget account: see ACCOUNT *noun*.
▪ **budgetary** *adjective* of or pertaining to a budget L19. **budgeˈteer** *noun* a person who makes up or supports a budget M19.

budget /ˈbʌdʒɪt/ *verb*. E17.
[ORIGIN from the noun.]
†**1** *verb trans.* Put in a budget or wallet; store *up*. Only in E17.
2 *verb intrans.* Draw up or prepare a budget, esp. *for* a certain supply, establishment, or a particular financial result. L19. ▸**b** *verb trans.* Arrange (for) in a budget. L19.

budgie /ˈbʌdʒi/ *noun*. *colloq.* E20.
[ORIGIN Abbreviation: see -IE.]
A budgerigar.

budo /ˈbuːdəʊ/ *noun*. E20.
[ORIGIN Japanese *budō*, from *bu-* military + *dō* way.]
The code on which Japanese martial arts are all based. Also (treated as *sing.* or *pl.*), Japanese martial arts collectively.

buer /ˈbjʊə/ *noun*. *N. English & slang*. Usu. *derog.* (or considered to be so). E19.
[ORIGIN Unknown.]
A sexually attractive or available woman.

buff /bʌf/ *noun*¹. LME.
[ORIGIN Old French *bufe* BUFFET *noun*¹.]
A blow, a stroke, a buffet. Now chiefly in ***blind man's buff*** s.v. BLIND *adjective*.
stand buff *arch.* stand firm, not flinch.

buff /bʌf/ *noun*² *& adjective*. M16.
[ORIGIN Prob. formed as BUFFLE. In recent use in sense A.1 repr. an abbreviation of BUFFALO.]
▸**A** *noun*. **1** A buffalo. Now *colloq.* M16.
2 Stout dressed ox leather of a dull-yellow colour and velvety surface. L16. ▸**b** Military attire (for which buff was formerly much used). *arch.* L16.
b SIR W. SCOTT In buff and bandoleer for King Charles.
3 *The* bare skin, *the* nude. *colloq.* E17.
G. MCINNES Undressing down to the buff.
4 *MEDICINE*. = ***buffy coat*** s.v. BUFFY *adjective*¹. M18.
5 *hist.* ***the Buffs***, ***the Old Buffs***, the 3rd regiment of the line, later the East Kent Regiment (so called from their buff facings). M18.
steady the Buffs: see STEADY *adjective, adverb, & interjection*.
6 The colour of buff; pale dull yellow. L18.
7 A stick or wheel covered with buff or a similar material, used for polishing. M19.
8 Orig., an enthusiast for watching fires (so called from the buff uniforms of volunteer firemen in New York City). Now, an enthusiast or expert in any (specified) subject or activity. *colloq.* (orig. *US*). E20.
E. REVELEY Though no wine buff, even he could tell that this must have been one of Felix's finest hocks.
▸**B** *attrib.* or as *adjective*. Made of buff; like buff; of the colour of buff, pale dull yellow. L16.
buff arches: see ARCH *noun*¹ 6. **buff coat** a coat of buff; *transf.* (*arch.*) a soldier. **buff leather** = sense A.2 above. **buff-stick**, **buff-wheel** = sense A.7 above.
▪ **buffed** *adjective* clad in or covered with buff M17. **buffish** *adjective* E19.

†**buff** *noun*³. *colloq.* E–M18.
[ORIGIN Cf. BUFFER *noun*¹.]
= BUFFER *noun*¹ 2.

buff /bʌf/ *verb*¹. *obsolete* exc. *dial.* ME.
[ORIGIN Prob. imit.: cf. *puff*, BUFF *noun*¹.]
1 *verb intrans.* Stutter, splutter; burst *out* into laughter etc. ME.
2 *verb intrans. & trans.* Make a sound as a soft inflated object does when struck; strike so as to cause such a sound. M16.

buff /bʌf/ *verb*² *trans.* M19.
[ORIGIN from BUFF *noun*².]
1 Polish, *spec.* with a buff. M19.
K. KESEY Get them to work buffing the floor. F. KING Fingernails buffed to an opalescent pink.
2 Impart a velvety surface to (leather). L19.

buffalo /ˈbʌfələʊ/ *noun*¹ *& verb*. M16.
[ORIGIN Prob. immed. from Portuguese *bufalo* (now *bufaro*) = Italian *bufalo*, Spanish *búbalo*, *búfalo*, from late Latin *bufalus* from Latin *bubalus* from Greek *boubalos* wild ox, antelope. Cf. BUFF *noun*², BUFFLE.]
▸**A** *noun*. Pl. **-oes**, same.
1 a Any of several wild Asiatic oxen of the genus *Bubalus*, with long curved horns, esp. *B. arnee* (more fully ***water buffalo***), which has been domesticated. M16. ▸**b** A similar wild African ox, *Syncerus caffer* (more fully ***Cape buffalo***). L17.
2 = ***American bison*** s.v. BISON 1. Chiefly *N. Amer.* M17.
3 A large river fish of the genus *Ictiobus*, of the sucker family. *N. Amer.* L18.
4 In full ***buffalo robe***. A rug or cloak made of lined trimmed buffalo hide. *N. Amer.* E19.
5 (**B-**.) A member of the Royal Antediluvian Order of Buffaloes, a social club and benevolent society. M19.
6 An amphibious tank. M20.
– COMB.: **buffalo berry** (the edible fruit of) a tree or shrub of the N. American genus *Shepherdia*, of the oleaster family, esp. *S. canadensis* and *S. argentea*; **buffalo bird** (***a***) an oxpecker; (***b***) a cowbird; **buffalo chips** dried buffalo dung used as fuel; **buffalo clover** a native N. American clover, *Trifolium stoloniferum*, found on the prairies; **buffalo fish** *N. Amer.* = sense 3 above; **buffalo fly**, **buffalo gnat** = ***blackfly*** (b) s.v. BLACK *adjective*; **buffalo grass** any of various grasses, *esp.* (*N. Amer.*) *Buchloe dactyloides*, (*Austral. & NZ*) *Stenotaphrum secundatum*; **buffalo-nut** (the oily nut of) a parasitic N. American shrub, *Pyrularia pubera*, of the sandalwood family; ***buffalo robe***: see sense 4 above; **buffalo runner** *N. AMER. HISTORY* a swift horse for hunting buffalo.

▸ **B** *verb trans.* Overawe, bemuse, baffle, outwit. *N. Amer. slang.* **E20.**

M. PUZO He could still command a hefty advance for a book, he still had critics buffaloed.

Buffalo /ˈbʌfələʊ/ *noun*². **M20.**
[ORIGIN A city in New York state, USA, where the recipe was developed.]
Buffalo (chicken) wing, a chicken wing coated in a spicy sauce and deep fried, typically served with blue cheese dressing.

buffe /bʊf/ *noun.* **L16.**
[ORIGIN Italian *buffa*.]
†**1** A breathing hole of a helmet. Only in **L16.**
2 *hist.* A piece of armour for the chin, pierced with breathing holes. **E17.**

buffel *noun* var. of BUFFLE.

buffer /ˈbʌfə/ *noun*¹ *& verb.* **LME.**
[ORIGIN Prob. from BUFF *verb*¹ + -ER¹.]
▸ **A** *noun* **I** †**1** A stammerer. Only in **LME.**
2 A fellow; *esp.* an old-fashioned or incompetent fellow. Freq. in ***old buffer***. *slang.* **M18.** ▸**b** NAUTICAL. A boatswain's mate; a petty officer. **M19.**
▸ **II 3** An apparatus for deadening impact; *spec.* either of a pair of projecting shock absorbers fitted to a cross-beam at the end of a railway vehicle or on a fixed mounting across the end of a railway line (usu. in *pl.*). Also *fig.*, a protective intermediary. **M19.**

B. TRAPIDO She has a tendency to answer questions for him as if he needed her as a buffer between himself and a hostile world.

4 CHEMISTRY. A substance or mixture of substances (usu. a weak acid or base with one of its salts) which tends to stabilize the pH of a solution; a solution containing this. **E20.**
5 COMPUTING. An intermediate memory for the temporary storage of information during data transfers, *esp.* one that accepts data at one rate and delivers them at another. **M20.**
– COMB.: **buffer area** (*lit.* & *fig.*): separating potential belligerents; **buffer solution** CHEMISTRY a solution containing a buffer; **buffer state** a small country lying between two possible belligerents, diminishing the chance of hostilities; **buffer stock** a stock of a commodity held in reserve so as to offset price fluctuations; **buffer stop** a pair of buffers fixed at the end of a railway line; **buffer zone**: separating potential belligerents.
▸ **B** *verb trans.* **1** Act as a buffer to (chiefly *fig.*); lessen the impact of. **L19.**
2 CHEMISTRY. Treat with a buffer; stabilize by means of a buffer. **E20.**

buffer /ˈbʌfə/ *noun*². *arch.* **E19.**
[ORIGIN Prob. imit.]
A dog.

buffer /ˈbʌfə/ *noun*³. **M19.**
[ORIGIN from BUFF *verb*² + -ER¹.]
A person who polishes with a buff; a device for buffing.

buffet /ˈbʌfɪt/ *noun*¹. **ME.**
[ORIGIN Old French *buf(f)et* dim. of *bufe* BUFF *noun*¹: see -ET¹.]
1 A blow, esp. with the hand; a knock, an impact. **ME.**

A. P. HERBERT Mr. Walker gave him a buffet in the ribs with his fist. S. T. WARNER Calamities go on having a buffet at us.

2 AERONAUTICS. = BUFFETING (c). **M20.**

buffet /ˈbʌfɪt/ *noun*². Now *dial.* **LME.**
[ORIGIN Old French *buf(f)et*, of unknown origin.]
1 A low stool; a footstool. Also ***buffet-stool***. **LME.**
2 A hassock. **L19.**

buffet /ˈbʊfeɪ; *in sense 1 also* ˈbʌfɪt/ *noun*³. **E18.**
[ORIGIN French, formed as BUFFET *noun*².]
1 A sideboard or recessed cupboard for china, plate, etc. **E18.**
2 (A place offering) a service of food from a sideboard or counter where guests or customers can help themselves; *esp.* (***a***) a refreshment room in a station or other public building; (***b***) (in full ***buffet car***) a railway carriage serving light refreshments. **L18.**
– COMB.: ***buffet car***: see sense 2 above; **buffet meal**, **buffet party**, etc.: at which food is served from a sideboard etc.

buffet /ˈbʌfɪt/ *verb.* **ME.**
[ORIGIN Old French & mod. French *buffeter*, formed as BUFFET *noun*¹.]
1 *verb trans.* Beat, strike, thump, knock about, (*lit.* & *fig.*). **ME.** ▸**b** Beat back, contend with (waves, wind, etc.). **L16.**

O. MANNING As the crowd pressed past him, he was buffeted mercilessly from side to side. B. BAINBRIDGE The train, buffeted by wind, was swaying over the steel lattice of a bridge. **b** SHAKES. *Jul. Caes.* The torrent roar'd, and we did buffet it With lusty sinews.

2 *verb intrans.* Deal blows, fight, struggle. **L16.**

fig.: TENNYSON I heard . . the great echo flap And buffet round the hills.

3 *verb trans.* Drive, force, or produce by buffeting. **L17.**

F. PARKMAN He buffeted his way to riches and fame.

■ **buffeting** *noun* (***a***) the action of the verb; (***b***) a beating, a thumping; (***c***) AERONAUTICS irregular oscillation of a part of an aircraft owing to turbulence, esp. near sonic speed: **ME.**

†**buffin** *noun.* **L16–E18.**
[ORIGIN Unknown.]
(A gown of) a kind of coarse cloth.

buffle /ˈbʌf(ə)l/ *noun.* Long *obsolete* exc. in comb. Also **-el**. **E16.**
[ORIGIN Old French & mod. French from Italian *bufalo*: see BUFFALO.]
1 A buffalo. **E16.**
2 A fool, a fathead. **M17.**
– COMB.: **bufflehead** (***a***) = sense 2 above; (***b***) a black and white N. American diving duck, *Bucephala albeola*, with a relatively large head; **buffle-headed** *adjective* †(***a***) having a head like a buffalo's; (***b***) large-headed; fat-headed, foolish, stupid.

buffo /ˈbʊfəʊ/ *noun & adjective.* **M18.**
[ORIGIN Italian = puff of wind, buffoon, from *buffare*: see BUFFOON.]
▸ **A** *noun.* Pl. **-os**. A comic actor, a singer in comic opera. **M18.**
primo buffo: see PRIMO *adjective*.
▸ **B** *adjective.* Comic, burlesque. **L18.**
BASSO ***buffo***.

buffoon /bəˈfuːn/ *noun, adjective, & verb.* **M16.**
[ORIGIN French *bouffon* from Italian *buffone*, from medieval Latin *buffo* clown, from Proto-Romance verb meaning 'puff', of imit. origin: see -OON.]
▸ **A** *noun.* †**1** A pantomine dance. *Scot. rare.* Only in **M16.**
2 A (professional) jester, a clown. *arch.* **L16.**
3 A (vulgar or ludicrous) joker, a wag, a mocker. Usu. *derog.* **L16.**
▸ **B** *attrib.* or as *adjective.* Belonging to or characteristic of a buffoon; vulgarly jocular. *arch.* **E17.**
▸ **C** *verb.* **1** *verb trans.* Ridicule, burlesque. *arch.* **M17.**
2 *verb intrans.* Play the buffoon. **L17.**
■ **buffoonery** *noun* the actions or an act of a buffoon; silliness, farce: **E17.** **buffoonish** *adjective* like or characteristic of a buffoon; silly, ridiculous: **L17.**

buffy /ˈbʌfi/ *adjective*¹. **L18.**
[ORIGIN from BUFF *noun*² or *adjective* + -Y¹.]
Resembling buff in colour or appearance.
buffy coat MEDICINE a thin pale layer of white cells which forms on clotted blood, or between the red cells and plasma when blood is centrifuged.

buffy /ˈbʌfi/ *adjective*². *slang.* **M19.**
[ORIGIN Unknown.]
Tipsy, moderately drunk.

†**bufonite** *noun.* **M17–M19.**
[ORIGIN from Latin *bufon-*, *bufo* toad + -ITE¹.]
= TOADSTONE *noun*¹.

bufotenine /bjʊfəˈtɛniːn/ *noun.* **E20.**
[ORIGIN French *bufoténine*, from Latin *bufo* toad + (prob.) *tenere* hold (because of an ability to cause paralysis): see -INE⁵.]
CHEMISTRY. An alkaloid which occurs in various amphibian secretions, mushrooms, and tropical plants, and has hallucinogenic, hypertensive, and vasoconstrictive actions.

†**bug** *noun*¹. **LME–L19.**
[ORIGIN Rel. to BOGGARD, BOGLE, etc. Connection with Welsh *bwg*, *bwgan* (ghost, hobgoblin), *bygwl* (fear, threat) uncertain. Cf. BUGBEAR.]
An (imaginary) object of terror; a bugbear, a bogey; a scarecrow.
– COMB.: **bug-word** a word meant to frighten.

bug /bʌg/ *noun*². **E17.**
[ORIGIN Uncertain. Perh. from Old English *-budda*, as in *scearnbudda* dung beetle, or rel. to BUG *noun*¹.]
1 a A hemipteran insect; orig. *spec.* a bedbug (see BED *noun*). **E17.** ▸**b** *gen.* Any insect, *esp.* a small beetle or grub. Freq. with specifying word, as ***harvest bug***, ***ladybug***, etc. (absol. chiefly *N. Amer.*). *colloq.* **M17.**
big bug: see BIG *adjective*.
2 A person obsessed by an idea; an enthusiast. Also, an obsession, a craze. *slang.* **M19.**

Which? A boy bitten by the railway bug.

firebug, ***jitterbug***, etc.
3 A defect or fault in a machine, plan, etc.; *spec.* a mistake or malfunction in a computer program or system. *colloq.* **L19.**
4 A (school)boy, usu. of specified age or status. *slang.* **E20.**

S. MACKAY You've probably been here for yonks and I'm only the new bug.

new bug: see NEW *adjective*.
5 A micro-organism, *esp.* a virus; a disease caused by this. *colloq.* **E20.**

Health Now A change in foods or drinking water can cause tummy bugs.

6 A burglar-alarm system. *US slang.* **E20.**
7 A concealed microphone. **M20.**
– COMB.: **bugbane**, **bugwort** any of various tall plants of the genus *Cimicifuga* of the buttercup family, bearing small white flowers (*C. foetida* was formerly used to drive away bedbugs).

bug /bʌg/ *adjective.* Long *obsolete* exc. *dial.* **M16.**
[ORIGIN Unknown.]
Pompous; conceited; fine.

bug /bʌg/ *verb*¹ *trans.* Infl. **-gg-**. **M19.**
[ORIGIN from BUG *noun*².]
1 Clear (plants etc.) of insects. **M19.**
2 Equip with an alarm system or a concealed microphone; listen to by means of a concealed microphone. **E20.**
3 Annoy, bother. *colloq.* **M20.**

bug /bʌg/ *verb*² *intrans. N. Amer. colloq.* Infl. **-gg-**. **L19.**
[ORIGIN Unknown.]
Of the eyes: bulge *out*.
– COMB.: **bug-eyed** *adjective* having bulging eyes (***bug-eyed monster***, an extraterrestrial monster (with bulging eyes)).

bug /bʌg/ *verb*³ *intrans. slang* (chiefly *US*). Infl. **-gg-**. **M20.**
[ORIGIN Origin of sense 1 uncertain. In sense 2 abbreviation of BUGGER *verb*.]
1 Get *out*, leave quickly. **M20.**
2 Foll. by *off*: go away. **L20.**

bugaboo /ˈbʌgəbuː/ *noun.* **M18.**
[ORIGIN Cf. Welsh *bwci bo* bogey, Cornish *bucca*.]
1 A bogey; a bugbear. **M18.**
2 Loud or empty talk; nonsense, rubbish. **L19.**

bugaku /ˈbʊgakuː/ *noun.* **L19.**
[ORIGIN Japanese, from *bu* dancing + *gaku* music.]
A Japanese classical dance in which pure dance form and symmetry are emphasized, and masks are used.

bugbear /ˈbʌgbɛː/ *noun & adjective.* **L16.**
[ORIGIN Prob. from BUG *noun*¹ + BEAR *noun*¹.]
▸ **A** *noun.* **1** A sort of hobgoblin (perhaps in the shape of a bear) supposed to devour naughty children; *gen.* any imaginary being invoked to frighten children. **L16.**
2 *transf.* An object of (needless) dread; an imaginary terror; an annoyance. **L16.**
▸ **B** *attrib.* or as *adjective.* Needlessly alarming or annoying. **E17.**

bugger /ˈbʌgə/ *noun*¹. **ME.**
[ORIGIN (Middle Dutch from) Old French & mod. French *bougre* †heretic, sodomite (arch.), person (colloq.), from medieval Latin *Bulgarus* Bulgarian (esp. as adhering to the Orthodox Church), heretic, Albigensian: see BULGAR *noun*¹.]
▸ **I** †**1** (**B-**.) A heretic; *spec.* an Albigensian. **ME–M18.**
2 A person who commits buggery. *coarse slang* exc. LAW. **M16.**
▸ **II** Extended uses: all *coarse slang*.
3 An unpleasant or undesirable person or thing; (in weakened sense) a person, a chap. Cf. BEGGAR *noun* 3. **E18.**

F. MANNING There are two poor buggers dead. G. ORWELL This business of class-breaking is a bugger.

play silly buggers fool about, mess around.
4 A negligible amount. **E20.**
not care a bugger, ***not give a bugger***. ***bugger all***: see ALL *pronoun* & *noun* 3.

bugger /ˈbʌgə/ *noun*². **M20.**
[ORIGIN from BUG *verb*¹ + -ER¹.]
A person who installs a concealed microphone.

bugger /ˈbʌgə/ *verb.* **L16.**
[ORIGIN from BUGGER *noun*¹.]
▸ **I 1** *verb trans. & intrans.* Commit buggery (with). **L16.**
▸ **II** Extended uses: all *coarse slang*.
2 *verb trans.* Curse, damn. Freq. in imprecations in imper. or in optative form (for ***God bugger*** — etc.). **L18.** ▸**b** *verb intrans.* Curse. As *interjection*: damn! **M19.**

S. BECKETT Bugger these buttons! C. P. SNOW I'm buggered if I vote for Crawford.

3 a *verb trans.* Ruin, spoil; mess *up*; mess *about* or *around* (with); tire, exhaust, (chiefly as ***buggered*** *ppl adjective*). **E20.** ▸**b** *verb intrans.* Mess or potter *about*, *around*. **M20.**
4 *verb intrans.* Foll. by *off*: go away. **E20.**
■ **buggeˈration** *interjection* (*coarse slang*) expr. annoyance, frustration, etc. **L20.**

buggery /ˈbʌgəri/ *noun.* **ME.**
[ORIGIN Middle Dutch *buggerie*, Old French *bougrerie*, *bouguerie*, formed as BUGGER *noun*¹: see -Y³.]
†**1** Abominable heresy. Only in **ME.**
2 Sodomy, anal intercourse. Also (formerly in LAW), bestiality. **E16.**
3 ***to buggery***, to hell, to the devil, to damnation. *coarse slang.* **E20.**

E. LINDALL 'Go to buggery,' Minogue snarled.

†**Buggess** *noun.* **L17–E19.**
[ORIGIN formed as BUGIS.]
A SE Asian soldier in European service.

Buggins' turn /ˈbʌgɪnz tɜːn/ *noun phr.* **E20.**
[ORIGIN from *Buggins*, a 'typical' surname used generically + TURN *noun*.]
Appointment in rotation rather than by merit.

buggy /ˈbʌgi/ *noun.* **M18.**
[ORIGIN Unknown.]
1 A light horse-drawn vehicle for one or two people, with two or (in N. America) four wheels. **M18.**
horse-and-buggy: see HORSE *noun*.
2 *transf.* **a** A pram. More fully ***baby buggy***. *N. Amer.* **L19.** ▸**b** A motor vehicle; *esp.* a small sturdy vehicle (freq. with specified use). **E20.**
b ***beach buggy***, ***dune buggy***, etc.

B

– COMB.: **buggy-ride** (chiefly *N. Amer.*) a ride in a buggy (***thanks for the buggy-ride*** (colloq.): an expression of thanks for help given).

buggy /ˈbʌgi/ *adjective*. E18.
[ORIGIN from BUG *noun*² + -Y¹.]
1 Infested with bugs; like a bug. E18.
2 COMPUTING. Of computer software: containing mistakes and so malfunctioning; having many bugs. L20.

bughouse /ˈbʌghaʊs/ *adjective & noun*. *slang*. L19.
[ORIGIN from BUG *noun*² + HOUSE *noun*¹.]
▸ **A** *adjective*. Crazy; very eccentric. Chiefly *US*. L19.
▸ **B** *noun*. **1** A psychiatric hospital. Orig. *US*. E20.
2 A theatre or cinema. *derog*. M20.

bught *noun & verb* var. of BOUGHT *noun*² & *verb*².

Bugis /ˈbuːgɪs/ *noun & adjective*. Also **Bugi** /ˈbuːgi/. E18.
[ORIGIN Malay.]
▸ **A** *noun*. Pl. **-i(s)**. A member of a people of southern Sulawesi, Indonesia; the language of this people. E18.
▸ **B** *attrib*. or as *adjective*. Of or pertaining to the Bugis or their language. E19.
■ Also **Bugiˈnese** *noun & adjective* (pl. of noun same) E20.

bugle /ˈbjuːg(ə)l/ *noun*¹. ME.
[ORIGIN Old French from Latin *buculus* dim. of *bos* ox.]
†**1 a** A buffalo or wild ox. ME–L17. ▸**b** A young bull. *dial*. L19.
2 In full ***bugle-horn***. Orig., a horn of a wild ox etc. used to give signals in hunting. Now, a brass instrument like a small trumpet similarly used or for giving military signals, or (*US*) in marching bands. ME.
key-bugle: see KEY *noun*¹.
■ **bugler** *noun* a person who plays a bugle; *spec*. a soldier who signals orders on a bugle: M19. **buglet** *noun* a small bugle E19.

bugle /ˈbjuːg(ə)l/ *noun*². ME.
[ORIGIN Late Latin *bugula*.]
A creeping plant of the genus *Ajuga*, of the mint family; esp. *A. reptans*, which bears blue flowers.
– COMB.: **bugleweed** *N. Amer.* (**a**) = sense above; (**b**) a related plant, *Lycopus virginicus*, found in wet soil.

bugle /ˈbjuːg(ə)l/ *noun*³. L16.
[ORIGIN Unknown.]
A tube-shaped bead, usu. black, sewn on a dress etc. as ornament.

> *attrib*.: SHAKES. *A.Y.L.* Your inky brows, your black silk hair, your bugle eyeballs.

bugle /bjuːg(ə)l/ *verb*. M19.
[ORIGIN from BUGLE *noun*¹.]
1 *verb trans*. Give forth (a sound) like a bugle; sound (a call) on a bugle. M19.
2 *verb intrans*. Sound a bugle; make a sound like a bugle. L19.

bugloss /ˈbjuːglɒs/ *noun*. LME.
[ORIGIN Old French & mod. French *buglosse* or Latin *buglossus* from Greek *bouglōssus* 'ox-tongued', from *bous* ox + *glōssa* tongue.]
Any of various plants of the borage family, *esp*. (**a**) a Eurasian weed of arable land, *Anchusa arvensis*, bearing blue flowers; (**b**) *US* a kind of alkanet, *Anchusa officinalis*.
viper's bugloss: see VIPER *noun*.

bugology /bʌˈgɒlədʒi/ *noun*. *joc*. Chiefly *US*. M19.
[ORIGIN from BUG *noun*² + -OLOGY.]
Entomology.
■ **bugologist** *noun* L19.

bugong *noun* var. of BOGONG.

buhl /buːl/ *noun & adjective*. Also **boul(l)e**, **B-**. E19.
[ORIGIN German *buhl*, French *boule*, from André Charles *Boulle* (1642–1732), French cabinetmaker.]
(Of) brass, tortoiseshell, etc., worked into ornamental patterns for inlaying; (work) inlaid thus.

buhr *noun* see BURR *noun*⁴.

build /bɪld/ *noun*. LME.
[ORIGIN from the verb: cf. BUILT *noun*.]
†**1** A building. Only in LME.
2 Style of construction, make; proportions of the human body, physique. M17.

> S. PEPYS The difference in the build of ships now and heretofore. M. MUGGERIDGE A tall man, rather the build of Bernard Shaw.

build /bɪld/ *verb*. Pa. t. & pple **built** /bɪlt/, (*arch. & poet*.) **builded**. See also BUILT *ppl adjective*.
[ORIGIN Old English *byldan* (cf. *bylda* builder), from *bold*, *botl* dwelling, house = Old Frisian *bōdel*, Old Saxon *bodl*, Old Norse *ból*, from Germanic, from base meaning 'dwell' (also of BOWER *noun*¹).]
1 *verb trans*. Construct (a house, church, factory, etc.) as a dwelling or for occupation; construct (a vehicle, road, or other large or complex structure) by putting parts or material together. OE. ▸**b** *verb intrans*. Be built. Only in ***be building***. L17.
2 *verb trans*. Give form to, create; establish or accumulate gradually; improve. ME.
3 *verb trans*. Put together (parts, material) *into* a structure; join *together* to form a structure; lay, insert, or incorporate *in* or *into* as an integral part of a larger unit. LME.
4 *verb trans. & intrans*. Found (an argument, hope, confidence, progress, etc.) *on* a basis; rely *on*. E16.
– PHRASES: ***build a sconce***: see SCONCE *noun*² 2. ***build castles in the air***, ***build in the air***: see AIR *noun*¹ 3.
– WITH ADVERBS IN SPECIALIZED SENSES: **build down** reduce or destroy gradually or in a planned way. **build in** surround with houses etc., block up, enclose by building; (see also sense 4 above). **build round** surround with houses etc. **build up** (**a**) *verb phr. trans. & intrans*. increase in size, mass, or strength; accumulate; establish (itself) gradually; (**b**) *verb phr. trans*. surround with houses etc., block up; (**c**) *verb phr. trans*. boost, praise.
– COMB.: **build-down** a systematic reduction or destruction. **build-out** *US* (**a**) completion of a project; (**b**) exhaustion of space available for continued expansion; (**c**) growth, development, or expansion of something.
■ **buildable** *adjective* able to be built (on) E20.

builder /ˈbɪldə/ *noun*. ME.
[ORIGIN from BUILD *verb* + -ER¹.]
1 A person who builds; *esp*. a contractor for building houses. ME.
builders' merchant a supplier of materials to builders. ***speculative builder***: see SPECULATIVE 4.
2 A substance added to soap or to a detergent to increase its efficiency. M20.

building /ˈbɪldɪŋ/ *noun*. ME.
[ORIGIN formed as BUILDER + -ING¹.]
1 A thing which is built; a structure, an edifice; a permanent fixed thing built for occupation, as a house, school, factory, stable, church, etc. ME.
2 The action of BUILD *verb*. LME.
3 A company (of rooks); a rookery. *rare*. LME.
– COMB.: **building block** (**a**) = BLOCK *noun* 4b; (**b**) one of the temporary supports for a ship's keel while the ship is being built; **building brick** = BRICK *noun* 2, 2b; **building lease** a lease of land upon which to build; **building line** a prescribed limit beyond which a building must not extend; **building society**: accepting investments at interest, and lending to persons building or buying houses etc.; **building term** the duration of a building lease.

build-up /ˈbɪldʌp/ *noun*. E20.
[ORIGIN from BUILD *verb* + UP *adverb*¹.]
1 A period of preparation and often excitement before a significant event. E20. ▸**b** The gradual development of a theme, work of art, etc. M20.

> *Croydon Guardian (online ed.)* Does the build-up to Christmas start too early? **b** *www.cinescene.com* The film's social observation and build-up of tension is quite compelling.

2 A gradual accumulation or increase, esp. of troops or of something negative. M20.

> *New Republic* The relentless and ominous build-up of Syria's missile forces.

†**built** *noun*. E17–L18.
[ORIGIN from BUILD *verb*.]
Style of construction; build.

built /bɪlt/ *ppl adjective*. L16.
[ORIGIN pa. pple of BUILD *verb*.]
Constructed or constituted, esp. in a specified way; having a specified build; *spec*. composed of separately prepared parts (= ***built-up*** (b) below).

> M. PRIOR With well-built Verse to keep his Fame alive. J. RUSKIN The built and tower-like shaft. L. URIS Ari Ben Canaan was . . built like his father.

built-in (esp. of the fittings of a house) constructed to form an integral part of a larger unit; *fig*. inherent, integral, innate. ***built on sand***: see SAND *noun*. **built-up** (**a**) increased in height etc. by addition of parts; (**b**) composed of separately prepared parts; (**c**) (of a locality) fully occupied by houses etc. ***clinker-built***: see CLINKER *noun*¹.

built *verb pa. t. & pple* of BUILD *verb*.

buirdly /ˈbyrdli/ *adjective*. *Scot*. Also **boardly** /ˈbɔːdli/. L18.
[ORIGIN Var. of BURLY *adjective* with *-d-* perh. after forms of BOARD *noun*.]
Large and well made, stately; sturdy.

buist *verb* var. of BOOST *verb*².

buit *verb* var. of BUDE.

bukshi /ˈbʌkʃiː/ *noun*. *Indian*. *obsolete* exc. *hist*. Also **bu(c)kshee**. E17.
[ORIGIN Persian *bakšī* giver, from *bakšīdan* give: cf. BAKSHEESH.]
A paymaster general; an army paymaster.

bulb /bʌlb/ *noun & verb*. LME.
[ORIGIN Latin *bulbus* from Greek *bolbos* onion, bulbous root.]
▸ **A** *noun*. **1** The globular underground organ of an onion, lily, or similar plant, which contains the following year's bud and scale leaves that serve as food reserves. Also, a plant growing from a bulb. LME. ▸†**b** *spec*. An onion. M16–E18.
2 ANATOMY. A spheroidal dilatation of the end of an organ or other structure, e.g. of the spinal cord (the medulla oblongata) or of a hair root. E18.
3 a A dilated part of a glass tube, e.g. forming the reservoir of a thermometer. E19. ▸**b** (The glass envelope of) an electric lamp. M19. ▸**c** A compressible rubber device for the pneumatic operation of a syringe etc. L19.
▸ **B** *verb intrans*. Form a root shaped like a bulb; swell into a form like a bulb or rounded. L17.
■ **bulbed** *adjective* shaped like a bulb; having a bulb or bulbs: L16. **bulbiferous** /bʌlˈbɪf(ə)rəs/ *adjective* bearing a bulb, producing bulbs L17. **bulbiform** *adjective* shaped like a bulb M19. **bulblet** *noun* a bulbil M19. **bulblike** *adjective* resembling (that of) a bulb M19.

bulbar /ˈbʌlbə/ *adjective*. L19.
[ORIGIN from BULB *noun* + -AR¹.]
Chiefly ANATOMY. Of or pertaining to a bulb, esp. to the medulla oblongata (see BULB *noun* 2).

†**bulbel** *noun* var. of BULBIL.

bulberry *noun* see BULL *noun*¹.

bulbil /ˈbʌlbɪl/ *noun*. Also †**-el**. M19.
[ORIGIN mod. Latin *bulbillus* dim. of *bulbus* BULB.]
A small aerial bulb borne in a leaf axil or an inflorescence, which can develop into an independent plant when detached. Also, a small bulb formed at the side of an ordinary bulb.

bulbo- /ˈbʌlbəʊ/ *combining form* of Latin *bulbus* BULB *noun*, used chiefly in ANATOMY: see -O-.
■ **bulbo-uˈrethral** *adjective* of or pertaining to the urethra and the bulb (proximal region) of the penis; ***bulbo-urethral gland***, either of a pair of small glands which open into the urethra at the base of the penis and secrete a constituent of seminal fluid (also called ***Cowper's gland***): M19.

bulbous /ˈbʌlbəs/ *adjective*. L16.
[ORIGIN from Latin *bulbosus* or directly from BULB *noun* + -OUS.]
1 Of, pertaining to, or of the nature of a bulb. L16.
2 Growing from a bulb; having roots like bulbs. L16.
3 Shaped like a bulb; rounded, swollen. L18.

> W. GOLDING The bulbous legs of a grand piano. R. GRAVES The bulbous nose, the sunken chin.

■ **bulbose** *adjective* (*rare*) bulbous L16. **bulbosity** /bʌlˈbɒsɪti/ *noun* bulbous condition or quality E20.

bulbul /ˈbʊlbʊl/ *noun*. M17.
[ORIGIN Persian, of imit. origin.]
Any of various Asian or African songbirds of the large family Pycnonotidae; *spec*. an Iranian bird admired for its song. Also *fig*., a singer, a poet.

†**bulchin** *noun* var. of BULKIN.

bulerias /bʊləˈrɪəs/ *noun*. E20.
[ORIGIN Spanish *bulerías*, from *bulería* mockery, fun or *bullería* racket, shouting.]
A type of fast-paced flamenco dance; a piece of music for this dance, usu. played on the guitar and accompanied by singing.

bulfinch *noun* see BULLFINCH.

Bulgar /ˈbʌlgɑː/ *noun*¹. LME.
[ORIGIN medieval Latin *Bulgarus* from Old Church Slavonic *Blŭgary* pl. Bulgarian *Bălgari* pl.).]
A member of an ancient Turkic people who settled in the region of Bulgaria in the 7th cent. Also, a native or inhabitant of Bulgaria, a Bulgarian.
– NOTE: Rare before M18.
■ **Bulgarize** *verb trans*. make Bulgarian in character M19.

bulgar /ˈbʌlgə/ *noun*². Also **bulgur**, **-gh-**. M20.
[ORIGIN Turkish *bulgur* = Persian *bulgūr* bruised grain.]
Wholewheat partially boiled and then dried; a dish made from this. Also ***bulgar wheat***.

Bulgarian /bʌlˈgɛːrɪən/ *noun & adjective*. M16.
[ORIGIN from (medieval Latin) *Bulgaria* (see below), formed as BULGAR *noun*¹, + -AN.]
▸ **A** *noun*. A native or inhabitant of Bulgaria, a country in the Eastern Balkans. Also, the Slavonic language of Bulgaria. M16.
▸ **B** *adjective*. Of or pertaining to Bulgaria, its people, or their language. L18.

bulge /bʌldʒ/ *noun & verb*. ME.
[ORIGIN Old French *bou(l)ge* from Latin *bulga* leather sack, bag, of Gaulish origin.]
▸ **A** *noun*. †**1** A wallet or bag, esp. of hide. ME–E17.
2 = BILGE *noun* 1. Now *rare* or *obsolete*. E17.
3 A convex part or irregular swelling on an otherwise flat(ter) surface or line. M18. ▸**b** *spec*. A protuberance added to a ship's hull for protection or increased stability. E20. ▸**c** MILITARY. A salient. E20.

> L. DEIGHTON He didn't want to . . stuff it into his pocket for it would make bulges in his newly pressed uniform jacket. W. BOYD His palm cautiously inched up the slack bulge of her breast.

4 *fig*. **a** An advantage, a lead. Chiefly in ***have the bulge on***, ***get the bulge on***, get an advantage over (a person). *slang* (chiefly *N. Amer*.). M19. ▸**b** A temporary increase or rise in volume, numbers, etc. *colloq*. L19.

> **b** *Lancet* The number of births will increase . . when the people born in the 'bulge' of the 1950's start to reproduce.

▸ **B** *verb*. †**1** *verb trans*. = BILGE *verb* 1. LME–E19.
†**2** *verb intrans*. = BILGE *verb* 2. Also, strike (*on*, *against*) so as to damage the bilge. E17–E19.
3 *verb intrans*. Protrude, swell out; be swollen, esp. by being full. L17.

> E. NESBIT Boxes . . with more Indian things bulging out of them. I. FLEMING The muscles bulged under the exquisitely cut sharkskin jacket. A. C. BOULT His pockets bulging with £20 notes.

4 *verb trans*. Make protuberant, cause to swell, esp. by filling. M19.

S. PLATH A snug corset affair that curved her in at the middle and bulged her out again spectacularly above and below. J. HERRIOT Her plump figure bulged her uniform tightly.

5 *verb intrans.* Rush *in*; make a dash *for*. *US colloq.* M19.

■ **bulgy** *adjective* swollen, that bulges M19.

bulimarexia /bjʊˌlɪməˈrɛksɪə, ˌbʊ-/ *noun.* L20.
[ORIGIN from BULIMIA + ANOREXIA.]
MEDICINE. Bulimia nervosa (see BULIMIA).
■ **bulimarexic** *adjective & noun* L20.

bulimia /bjʊˈlɪmɪə, ˌbʊ-/ *noun.* Also (earlier) anglicized as †**bulimy**. LME.
[ORIGIN medieval Latin *bolismus* or mod. Latin *bulimia* from Greek *boulimia* ravenous hunger, from *bou-* huge (from *bous* ox) + *limos* hunger: see -IA[1].]
MEDICINE. Abnormal craving for food; *esp.* (in full ***bulimia nervosa*** /nəːˈvəʊsə/) gross overeating alternating with self-induced vomiting or evacuation of the food eaten.
■ **bulimic** *adjective & noun* (**a**) *adjective* of, pertaining to, or exhibiting bulimia; (**b**) *noun* a person with bulimia (nervosa): M19.

bulk /bʌlk/ *noun[1] & adjective.* ME.
[ORIGIN Senses 1, 2 from Old Norse *búlki* cargo; other senses perh. alt. of BOUK.]
▸**A** *noun.* **1** A ship's cargo, esp. as a whole; the whole amount (of a commodity). ME.

OED The bulk is not equal to sample.

break bulk begin unloading.
2 A heap, a pile (now *rare* in *lit.* use); a large quantity. LME. **in bulk** loose, not packaged; in large quantities.
3 The hull or hold of a ship. Long *obsolete* exc. *dial.* LME.
4 The body, the trunk; now *spec.* a bodily frame of large proportions. LME.

F. NORRIS His arms moved, and his head, but the great bulk of the man remained immobile in its place. E. FIGES He shifted his bulk in the creaking chair.

5 Bodily magnitude; volume, size, weight. LME. ▸**b** *spec.* Considerable volume etc. E17. ▸**c** Roughage in food. M20.

T. H. HUXLEY Sea water is denser . . . bulk for bulk, than fresh water. J. A. MICHENER Those [bones] that were higher in her body were of successively lighter bulk. **b** LD MACAULAY The facility and assiduity with which he wrote are proved by the bulk . . of his works.

6 A (large) mass or shape. L16.

TENNYSON A Tudor-chimnied bulk Of mellow brickwork.

7 *The* greater part or number *of*. E18.

R. L. STEVENSON The bulk of the time I spent in repeating as much French poetry as I could remember.

▸**B** *attrib.* or as *adjective.* In bulk. L17.
– COMB.: **bulk-buying** (**a**) buying in large amounts at a discount; (**b**) the purchase by one buyer of all or most of a producer's output; **bulk carrier** a ship that carries cargo in bulk; **bulk modulus** the relative change in volume of a body produced by unit compressive or tensile stress acting uniformly over its surface.
■ **bulked** *adjective* having bulk, bulky LME. **bulker** *noun* a bulk carrier L20.

bulk /bʌlk/ *noun[2].* M16.
[ORIGIN Prob. from BAULK *noun* or (its source) Old Norse *bálkr*.]
A framework projecting from the front of a shop; a stall.

bulk /bʌlk/ *verb.* M16.
[ORIGIN from BULK *noun*[1].]
1 *verb intrans.* Be of bulk; appear large or weighty; seem *large* etc. in respect of size or importance. M16.

G. GORER Some qualities which bulk very high for one sex, drop to practical insignificance for the other.

bulk up swell, rise in bulk or mass.
2 *verb trans.* Pile in heaps. E17.
3 *verb trans.* Combine (consignments of a commodity) together. L19.
4 *verb trans.* Make (paper, yarn, etc.) appear thicker by suitable treatment. M20.

bulkhead /ˈbʌlkhɛd/ *noun.* L15.
[ORIGIN formed as BULK *noun*[2] + HEAD *noun*.]
1 A (substantial) upright partition separating compartments in a ship, aircraft, etc. L15.
2 (The roof of) a projecting stall. E18.
■ **bulkheaded** *adjective* E19.

bulkin /ˈbʊlkɪn/ *noun. obsolete* exc. *Jamaican.* Also †**bulchin**. ME.
[ORIGIN Middle Dutch *bul(le)tjen*, *bul(le)kin* bull calf & *boeletjen*, *boelekijn* darling: see BULL *noun*[1], BULLY *noun*[1], -KIN.]
A bull calf. Also used as a term of endearment, or of contempt.

bulky /ˈbʌlki/ *adjective.* LME.
[ORIGIN from BULK *noun*[1] + -Y[1].]
Of large bulk, voluminous, massive; of too great size, unwieldy.

T. C. BOYLE A new purchase that was too bulky to bring up the back stairway. B. BRYSON You ought to be wearing a bulky Arran sweater and a captain's cap.

■ **bulkily** *adverb* L19. **bulkiness** *noun* L17.

bull /bʊl/ *noun[1] & adjective.*
[ORIGIN Late Old English *bula* (only in place names) from Old Norse *boli*, corresp. to Middle Low German *bulle*, Middle Dutch *bulle*, *bolle* (Dutch *bul*).]
▸**A** *noun.* **1** The uncastrated male of the ox or other bovine animal. LOE.
a story of a cock and a bull: see COCK *noun*[1]. **bull in a china shop** a reckless or clumsy destroyer. ***cock and bull story***: see COCK *noun*[1]. ***full as a bull***: see FULL *adjective*. **like a bull at a gate** with direct or impetuous attack. ***red rag to a bull***: see RED RAG 3. **take the bull by the horns** meet a difficulty boldly. ***talk of a cock and a bull***: see COCK *noun*[1].
2 The male of various other large animals, e.g. the elephant, rhinoceros, whale, and seal. LME.
3 (Usu. **B-**.) *The* constellation and zodiacal sign Taurus. LME.
4 *STOCK EXCHANGE* etc. Orig., stock bought in the hope of selling for a higher price later. Now, a person who buys such stock, a speculator for a rise. Cf. BEAR *noun*[1] 4. E18.
5 A police officer. *US slang.* L19.
▸**B** *attrib.* or as *adjective.* Of an animal: male. Also, like (that of) a bull; large, coarse. ME.

W. P. KELLER A mature bull elk bugling his mating call. R. WEST A bull neck almost the same size round as his head.

– COMB. & SPECIAL COLLOCATIONS: **bull-and-cow** *rhyming slang* = ROW *noun*[3]; **bull ant** *Austral.* = BULLDOG *noun* 4b; **bull-at-a-gate** *adjective* directly or impetuously attacking; **bull-baiting** *hist.* baiting a captive bull with dogs, for sport; **bullbar** (orig. & chiefly *Austral.*) a metal bar or framework fitted to the front of a vehicle, orig. or ostensibly to provide protection in the event of a collision with an animal; **bull-bat** *US* the common nighthawk, *Chordeiles minor*; †**bull-beggar** [perh. from a different word] a scarecrow; a bogey, a bugbear; **bullberry**, **bulberry** = ***buffalo berry*** s.v. BUFFALO *noun*; **bulldust** *Austral. & NZ* (**a**) fine dust; (**b**) *slang* rubbish, nonsense; **bull fiddle** *US colloq.* a double bass; **bullfight**, **bullfighter**, **bullfighting** (an event, a participant, in) a chiefly Spanish sport in which a bull is first baited by armed fighters on horseback and on foot, and finally killed by a matador; BULLFINCH; **bullfrog** any of several large frogs with bellowing calls; *esp.* the largest N. American frog, *Rana catesbeiana*; **bullhead** (**a**) any of certain small freshwater fishes with large heads; *spec.* the miller's thumb, *Cottus gobio*, or (*N. Amer.*) a catfish of the genus *Ictalurus* (esp. the horned pout, *I. nebulosus*); (**b**) *dial.* a tadpole; (**c**) a blockhead; **bull-headed** *adjective* obstinate, impetuous, blundering; **bullhorn** a megaphone; ***bull huss***: see HUSS *noun*; **bull-kelp** a large kelp found in Pacific and Antarctic waters; **bull market** (*STOCK EXCHANGE* etc.): with rising prices; **bull mastiff** (a dog of) a crossbreed of bulldog and mastiff; **bull neck** a short thick neck; **bull-necked** *adjective* having a bull neck; **bull nose** *noun & adjective* (having) a nose or other projection with a rounded end; **bull-nosed** *adjective* having a bull nose; **bull-of-the-bog** the bittern; **bullpen** (chiefly *N. Amer.*) (**a**) a pen or enclosure for bulls; *transf.* any enclosure, a lock-up; (**b**) an exercise area for baseball pitchers, esp. relief pitchers; *transf.* the relief pitchers; **bull-pine** *N. Amer.* the ponderosa pine; **bull point** *colloq.* a point of superiority; **bull-puncher** *Austral.* a bullock driver; **bull-pup** a bulldog pup; **bullring** (**a**) an arena for bullfighting; (**b**) *hist.* a place where bulls were baited; **bullroarer** a flat strip of wood tied to a string, making a roaring sound when whirled round, esp. as used in religious rites by Australian Aborigines; **bullrout** *Austral.* an E. Australian estuarine and freshwater fish, *Notesthes robusta*, with poisonous spines; **bullshit** *noun & verb* (*coarse slang*) (**a**) *noun* = BULL *noun*[4] 3, 4; (**b**) *verb trans. & intrans.* talk nonsense (to), mislead, bluff; **bullshitter** *coarse slang* a person who talks nonsense, a boaster, a pretentious person; **bullshot** a cocktail made with vodka, beef bouillon or consommé, and Worcestershire sauce; **bull snake** a large N. American constricting snake of the genus *Pituophis*; **bull's wool** (**a**) *Austral.* the inner bark of the stringybark tree; (**b**) *Austral. & NZ slang* rubbish, nonsense; **bull terrier** a (breed of) stocky short-haired dog that is a cross between bulldog and terrier (***pit bull terrier***, ***Staffordshire bull terrier***, etc.); ***bull thatch***: see THATCH *noun* 2b; **bull trout** any of various large migratory trout, *esp.* the sea trout and lake trout; *US* the trout *Salvelinus confluentus* of the west coast of the US; **bull-weed** [perh. from BOLL *noun*[1]] knapweed; **bull-whacker** *US* a cattle driver; **bullwhip** *noun & verb* (chiefly *N. Amer.*) (**a**) *noun* a whip with a long heavy lash; (**b**) *verb trans.* thrash with such a whip; **bullwort** a large European umbelliferous plant, *Ammi majus*.

bull /bʊl/ *noun[2].* ME.
[ORIGIN Old French & mod. French *bulle* from Latin BULLA (in medieval Latin) seal, sealed document.]
†**1** A seal attached to an official document, *esp.* the leaden seal of a papal edict. ME–M18.
2 An edict or mandate; *spec.* a papal edict. ME.

bull /bʊl/ *noun[3].* E16.
[ORIGIN Unknown.]
Each of the main bars of a harrow.

bull /bʊl/ *noun[4].* E17.
[ORIGIN Unknown. In senses 3, 4 usu. assoc. with synonymous ***bullshit*** s.v. BULL *noun*[1]: cf. BULL *verb*[3].]
1 An expression containing a contradiction in terms or implying a ludicrous inconsistency. Often more fully ***Irish bull***. E17.

R. L. STEVENSON The only weak brother I am willing to consider is (to make a bull for once), my wife.

2 A bad blunder. *US slang.* M19.
3 Trivial, insincere, or worthless talk or writing; nonsense. *slang.* E20.

P. G. WODEHOUSE You threw a lot of bull about being the brains of the concern.

4 Unnecessary routine tasks or ceremonial; pointlessly excessive discipline; red tape. *slang* (orig. *MILITARY*). M20.

A. BARON Them turning out the guard for us, us marching past eyes right, all that sort of bull.

– COMB.: **bull session** *N. Amer.* an informal group discussion.

bull /bʊl/ *noun[5].* E19.
[ORIGIN Abbreviation.]
= BULLDOG *noun* 1.

bull /bʊl/ *noun[6].* E19.
[ORIGIN Unknown.]
A drink made of water flavoured by being put in an empty spirits cask; *AUSTRAL. HISTORY* a sweet or alcoholic drink consumed esp. by Aborigines.

bull /bʊl/ *noun[7].* M19.
[ORIGIN Unknown.]
A game in which small flat sandbags are thrown on an inclined board marked with numbered squares.

bull /bʊl/ *noun[8].* E20.
[ORIGIN Abbreviation.]
= BULL'S-EYE 6.

bull /bʊl/ *verb[1] trans. & intrans.* ME.
[ORIGIN from BULL *noun*[1].]
1 Serve (a cow) with the bull. Of a cow: take or seek the bull. ME.
2 *STOCK EXCHANGE* etc. Speculate for a rise; produce a rise in the price of (stocks etc.). M19.
3 Behave or move like a bull; act or treat violently. M19.

bull /bʊl/ *verb[2] trans.* Now *rare* or *obsolete.* ME.
[ORIGIN from BULL *noun*[2].]
Publish as a (papal) bull; deal with in a papal bull.

bull /bʊl/ *verb[3].* M16.
[ORIGIN Old French *boler*, *bouler* deceive: later assoc. with BULL *noun*[4].]
1 *verb trans.* Make a fool of; cheat, deceive. Now *slang.* M16.
2 *verb intrans.* Talk emptily or boastfully. *slang.* M19.
3 *verb trans.* Polish (equipment etc.) in order to meet excessive standards of neatness. *military slang.* M20.

bulla /ˈbʊlə/ *noun.* Pl. **bullae** /ˈbʊliː/. E19.
[ORIGIN Latin = bubble.]
1 *MEDICINE.* A large blister on the skin containing watery fluid. Also, a thin-walled air cavity in the lung due to emphysema or of congenital origin. E19.
2 *ZOOLOGY.* An opisthobranch of the genus *Bulla*. M19.
3 *ANATOMY.* A rounded bony prominence, *esp.* that of the ethmoid bone. L19.

bullace /ˈbʊlɪs/ *noun.* ME.
[ORIGIN Old French *buloce*, *beloce* sloe, from Proto-Romance, perh. of Gaulish origin.]
A wild or semi-cultivated plum from the tree *Prunus domestica* subsp. *insititia*; the tree itself (also ***bullace tree***).

bullamacow /ˈbʊləməkaʊ/ *noun.* L19.
[ORIGIN Fijian English, comb. of BULL *noun*[1] and COW *noun*[1].]
In Polynesia etc.: cattle; corned beef.

bullary /ˈbʊləri/ *noun.* Also in Latin form **bullarium** /bʊˈlɛːrɪəm/. L17.
[ORIGIN medieval Latin *bullarium*, from *bulla* BULL *noun*[2]: see -ARY[1].]
A collection of papal bulls.

bullate /ˈbʊleɪt/ *adjective.* M18.
[ORIGIN medieval Latin *bullatus*, formed as BULLA + -ATE[2].]
Chiefly *BOTANY.* Having blisters or swellings resembling blisters.
■ **bullated** *adjective* blistered, bullate L17.

bulldog /ˈbʊldɒg/ *noun & verb.* E16.
[ORIGIN from BULL *noun*[1] + DOG *noun*.]
▸**A** *noun.* **1** (An animal of) a thickset, large-headed, and smooth-haired breed of dog, renowned for power and boldness. E16. ▸**b** *fig.* A tenacious and courageous person. M19.
2 Orig., a sheriff's officer. Now, a proctor's attendant at Oxford and Cambridge Universities. *colloq.* L17.
3 A gun; a cannon; a revolver. *colloq.* (now *rare* or *obsolete*). E18.
4 a A large biting fly of the genus *Tabanus*. *N. Amer.* L18. ▸**b** A large ant with a vicious sting. *Austral.* M19.
5 A short briar pipe. L19.
6 More fully ***British bulldog***. A children's game in which players have to cross an open space without being intercepted and seized by an opponent in the middle. M20.
– COMB.: **bulldog ant** = sense 4b above; **bulldog bond** a sterling bond issued by an overseas borrower; **bulldog breed** Englishmen regarded as having the qualities of dogged courage; **Bulldog clip** (proprietary name for) a clip with a powerful closure.
▸**B** *verb trans.* Infl. **-gg-**. Attack like a bulldog, wrestle with; treat roughly. Chiefly *US.* M19.

bulldoze /ˈbʊldəʊz/ *verb trans. colloq.* (orig. *US*). L19.
[ORIGIN Perh. from BULL *noun*[1] + alt. of DOSE *noun*.]
1 Coerce by violence or threats; intimidate, force. (Increasingly infl. by sense 2.) L19.

C. P. SNOW She was not going to be bulldozed into a conviction she did not feel.

2 Clear, level, move, etc., with a bulldozer; force (one's way) thus. M20.

B

ANTHONY HUXLEY This vigorous growth has been bulldozed . . to make room for the replanting of coconuts. *fig.*: B. CASTLE He and Harold have got the whole government machine with which to bulldoze their views through.

bulldozer /ˈbʊldəʊzə/ *noun*. L19.
[ORIGIN from BULLDOZE + -ER¹.]
1 A person who bulldozes (BULLDOZE *verb* 1). Chiefly *US*. L19.
2 A powerful tractor with a broad upright blade at the front, used for clearing or levelling ground. M20.

bull-dyke /ˈbʊldʌɪk/ *noun*. *slang*. *derog*. Also **bull-dike**. M20.
[ORIGIN from BULL *noun*¹ + *dike* var. of DYKE *noun*².]
A masculine lesbian.
■ Also **bull-dyker** *noun* E20.

bullen-bullen *noun* var. of BULN-BULN.

buller /ˈbʊlə/ *noun*¹. *Scot*. L15.
[ORIGIN Prob. imit.: cf. Swedish *buller* noise, roar, Danish *bulder* tumbling noise, Middle High German, German *bollern* make a noise.]
A roaring noise of waves etc.; a boiling up or tumult of water.

buller /ˈbʊlə/ *noun*². *slang*. E20.
[ORIGIN from BULLDOG + -ER⁶.]
A proctor's attendant at Oxford and Cambridge Universities.

bullet /ˈbʊlɪt/ *noun*. E16.
[ORIGIN French *boulet*, *-ette* dim. of *boule* BALL *noun*¹: see -ET¹.]
1 A ball for a cannon or other piece of ordnance. *obsolete* exc. *hist*. E16.
2 A projectile of lead etc. for a rifle, revolver, machine gun, etc. (orig. round but now usu. cylindrical and pointed). M16. ▸**b** *fig*. Notice to quit, *the* sack. *slang*. M19.
bite on the bullet, ***bite the bullet***: see BITE *verb*. ***magic bullet***: see MAGIC *adjective*. ***plastic bullet***: see PLASTIC *adjective & noun*³.
†**3** A missile from a sling. L16–M19.
4 A small ball of any material. L16. ▸**b** In *pl*. Peas or beans. *slang*. E20.
5 An ace in poker etc. *US slang*. E19.
6 PRINTING. A small circle used to identify items in a list, draw attention to a line, etc. Freq. as ***bullet point***. M20.
– COMB.: **bullet-head** a round head; **bullet-headed** *adjective* round-headed; *fig*. (*US*) obstinate; **bulletproof** *adjective & verb* (*a*) *adjective* impenetrable by bullets; (*b*) *verb trans*. make bulletproof: **bullet train** a high-speed passenger train, *esp*. a Shinkansen (in Japan).

bulletin /ˈbʊlɪtɪn/ *noun & verb*. M17.
[ORIGIN French from Italian *bullettino*, *boll-*, from *bulletta* passport, dim. of *bulla* BULL *noun*²: sense 1 directly from Italian.]
▸ **A** *noun*. **1** In Italy, France, etc.: an official warrant or certificate. Now *rare*. M17.
2 A short official account, statement, or broadcast report of a public event, news, weather conditions, a prominent invalid's health, etc. M18.
– COMB.: **bulletin board** (*a*) *N. Amer*. a noticeboard; (*b*) a computer system, usu. dedicated to one topic, by which users can read or download files supplied by others and add their own files.
▸ **B** *verb trans*. Make known by or describe in a bulletin. E19.

bullet-tree *noun* var. of BULLY-TREE.

bullfinch /ˈbʊlfɪn(t)ʃ/ *noun*. In sense 1 also **bulfinch**. L16.
[ORIGIN from BULL *noun*¹ + FINCH *noun*. In sense 2 perh. alt. of *bull fence*.]
1 Any of a number of Eurasian finches of the genus *Pyrrhula*; spec. *P. pyrrhula*, a sturdy grey, black, and white finch the male of which has a rose-pink throat and breast. L16.
2 A quickset hedge with a ditch. M19.

bullgine /ˈbʊldʒʌɪn/ *noun*. *colloq*. (chiefly *N. Amer*.). M19.
[ORIGIN from BULL *noun*¹ after ENGINE *noun*.]
A locomotive or steam engine.

Bulli /ˈbʊli/ *noun*. *Austral*. E20.
[ORIGIN A town in New South Wales, Australia.]
In full ***Bulli earth***, ***Bulli soil***. A kind of soil used esp. for cricket pitches.

bullimong /ˈbʊlɪmʌŋ/ *noun*. ME.
[ORIGIN Perh. from BULL *noun*¹ + *-imong* from Old English *gemang*, *gemong* mixture.]
A mixture of grains sown together for feeding cattle.

bullion /ˈbʊlj(ə)n/ *noun*¹. ME.
[ORIGIN Anglo-Norman, app. = mint, var. of Old French & mod. French *bouillon* from Proto-Romance, from Latin *bullire* to boil: see -ION.]
†**1** A melting house, a mint; a place of exchange. ME–E18.
2 Metal, esp. gold or silver, in lump form before coining or manufacture, or valued simply as raw metal. LME. ▸**b** Solid gold or silver as opp. to superficial imitations. L16.
†**3** Impure gold or silver; base metal. L16–E19.
■ **bullionist** *noun* (*hist*.) an advocate of a currency based on gold or silver E19.

bullion /ˈbʊlj(ə)n/ *noun*². LME.
[ORIGIN App. from French *boulon* (spelt *bouillon* in Cotgrave), formed as BOULE *noun*²: see -OON.]
†**1** A knob or boss, usu. of metal; a convex ornament on a book, harness, etc. LME–M19.
2 = BULL'S-EYE 5. M19.
3 A small round pane of glass. L19.

bullion /ˈbʊlj(ə)n/ *noun*³. M16.
[ORIGIN French *bouillon*: see BULLION *noun*¹ (with which the word is now often associated).]
†**1** Trunk-hose, puffed out at the upper part in several folds. M16–M17.
2 An ornamental fringe made of twists of gold or silver thread; material for this. M17.

bullish /ˈbʊlɪʃ/ *adjective*. M16.
[ORIGIN from BULL *noun*¹ + -ISH¹.]
1 Like a bull, esp. in nature; impetuous, aggressive. M16.
2 STOCK EXCHANGE etc. Pertaining to, showing, or tending to produce a rise in prices; *gen*. optimistic. L19.
■ **bullishly** *adverb* E19. **bullishness** *noun* L19.

†**bullition** *noun*. E17–L18.
[ORIGIN Late Latin *bullitio(n-)*, from *bullit-* pa. ppl stem of *bullire* to boil: see -ION.]
Bubbling, boiling.

bullock /ˈbʊlək/ *noun*.
[ORIGIN Late Old English *bulluc* dim. of BULL *noun*¹: see -OCK.]
Orig., a young bull. Now, a bull after castration. Also *loosely*, any bovine animal, an ox.
– COMB.: **bullock cart** a cart drawn by one or more bullocks; **bullock-puncher** *Austral. & NZ* a cattle driver; **bullock's heart** (the fruit of) a W. Indian custard apple, *Annona reticulata*; †**bullock's lungwort** great mullein, *Verbascum thapsus*.
■ **bullocky** *noun* (*a*) *Austral. slang* beef; (*b*) *Austral. & NZ* a cattle driver: M19. **bullocky** *adjective* like a bullock; having to do with bullocks: L19.

bullock /ˈbʊlək/ *verb*. E18.
[ORIGIN from the noun, or alt. of BULLY *verb*¹.]
1 *verb trans. & intrans*. = BULLY *verb*¹. *obsolete* exc. *dial*. E18.
2 *verb intrans*. Work strenuously without intermission. *Austral. & NZ colloq*. L19.
3 *verb trans*. Force (one's way) heavily. E20.

T. WINTON Scully gathered up their gear and bullocked a path toward the exit.

bullous /ˈbʊləs/ *adjective*. M19.
[ORIGIN from BULLA + -OUS.]
MEDICINE. Characterized by bullae of the skin; resembling a bulla.

bullrush *noun* var. of BULRUSH.

bull's-eye /ˈbʊlzʌɪ/ *noun*. *transf. & fig*. M18.
[ORIGIN from BULL *noun*¹ + -'S¹ + EYE *noun*.]
1 NAUTICAL. A block of wood with a central hole for a rope to pass through, and a groove around the rim for a second rope. M18.
2 A large round peppermint sweet. E19.
3 A hemispherical piece or thick disc of glass used as a light esp. in a ship's deck or side. Also, any small circular window or opening. E19.
4 (A lantern with) a hemispherical lens. M19.
5 A boss of glass formed at the centre of a blown glass sheet. M19.
6 (A shot, dart, etc., that hits) the centre of a target; *fig*. an accurate remark or guess. M19.
7 Any of various large-eyed Australian fishes; *esp*. the edible red *Priacanthus macracanthus*. L19.

bullsh /bʊlʃ/ *noun*. *coarse slang*. E20.
[ORIGIN Abbreviation.]
= ***bullshit*** *noun* s.v. BULL *noun*¹ *& adjective*.

bully /ˈbʊli/ *noun*¹. M16.
[ORIGIN Prob. from Middle Dutch *boele* lover (Middle High German *buole*, German *Buhle*): cf. BULCHIN.]
1 Orig. sweetheart, darling. Later only of a man: good friend, mate. (Usu. as a term of endearment or familiarity.) Now *arch. & dial*. M16.
2 A person who uses strength or power to coerce or intimidate weaker persons. L17. ▸**b** A hired thug. Now usu. more fully ***bully boy***. M18.
3 A pimp. *arch*. E18.
– COMB.: **bully boy** (*a*) a young bully, *spec*. a hired thug; (*b*) *arch*. a fine fellow, a gallant; **bully pulpit** *US colloq*. a prominent position in public life allowing the promulgation of personal (esp. moralistic) views; †**bully-rock**, **-rook** [origin unknown.] = senses 1, 2 above.

bully /ˈbʊli/ *noun*². M18.
[ORIGIN Alt. of BOUILLI.]
In full ***bully beef***. Boiled or (usu.) corned beef, esp. as part of army rations etc.

bully /ˈbʊli/ *noun*³. M19.
[ORIGIN Perh. from BULLY *noun*¹.]
1 A scrimmage in the Eton College wall game. M19.
2 HOCKEY. A procedure for putting the ball in play, beginning with the threefold striking of two opposing players' sticks. Also ***bully-off***. L19.

bully /ˈbʊli/ *noun*⁴. M19.
[ORIGIN Perh. from **bullhead** s.v. BULL *noun*¹.]
A small fish; *esp*. (*NZ*) = COCKABULLY.

bully /ˈbʊli/ *adjective & interjection*. L16.
[ORIGIN Attrib. use of BULLY *noun*¹.]
▸ **A** *adjective*. **1** Of a person: worthy, gallant, fine, jolly. *arch*. L16.

SHAKES. *Mids. N. D.* What sayest thou, bully Bottom?

2 Resembling or characteristic of a bully or thug. Now *rare*. E18.

SWIFT Those bully Greeks, who . . Instead of paying chairmen, run them through.

3 Very good, capital, first-rate. *slang* (chiefly *N. Amer*.). M19.

H. L. WILSON It sounded just the thing to call him. It sounded bully.

▸ **B** *interjection*. Bravo! Chiefly in ***bully for you!***, ***bully for them!***, etc. Freq. *iron*. M19.

bully /ˈbʊli/ *verb*¹. E18.
[ORIGIN from BULLY *noun*¹.]
1 *verb trans. & intrans*. Act the bully (towards); persecute, intimidate, oppress (physically or morally) by threats or superior force. E18.

DICKENS Mr. Bumble . . had a decided propensity for bullying . . and, consequently, was (it is needless to say) a coward. W. PLOMER He bullies her dreadfully, keeps her in her place, orders her about.

2 *verb trans*. Drive or force by threats or superior force *into*, *out of*, etc. E18.

DEFOE What ails you, to bully away our customers so? JOHN BRIGHT I have no belief that Russia . . would have been bullied into any change of policy. R. HAYMAN Kafka needed a friend who would bully him to write, and to publish.

bully /ˈbʊli/ *verb*². L19.
[ORIGIN from BULLY *noun*³.]
HOCKEY. **1** *verb trans*. Put (the ball) into play with a bully. *rare*. L19.
2 *verb intrans*. Start play with a bully. Usu. foll. by *off*. E20.

bullyrag /ˈbʊlɪrag/ *verb*. *dial. & slang*. Also **bally-** /ˈbalɪ-/. Infl. **-gg-**. L18.
[ORIGIN Unknown.]
1 *verb trans*. Overawe; intimidate; maltreat by jeering at or playing practical jokes on. L18.
2 *verb intrans*. Jeer; indulge in horseplay or practical jokes. E19.

bully-tree /ˈbʊlɪtriː/ *noun*. Also **bullet-tree** /ˈbʊlɪtˌtriː/. M17.
[ORIGIN Alt. of BALATA.]
= BALATA.

buln-buln /ˈbʊlnbʊln/ *noun*. Also **bullen-bullen** /ˈbʊlənbʊlən/. *Austral*. M19.
[ORIGIN Wuywurung *bulen-bulen*, imit. of the bird's call.]
The lyrebird.

bulrush /ˈbʊlrʌʃ/ *noun*. Also **bull-**. LME.
[ORIGIN Prob. from BULL *noun*¹ *& adjective*, with the sense 'large, coarse' (cf. *bullfrog*, *bullfinch*), + RUSH *noun*¹.]
Any of various tall water plants resembling rushes, *esp*. (*a*) the clubrush *Schoenoplectus lacustris*; (*b*) a reed mace of the genus *Typha*; (*c*) (in the Bible) a papyrus plant.

AV *Exod*. 2:3 She tooke for him an arke of bul-rushes. M. WEBB Tall bulrushes with their stout heads of brown plush.

seek a knot in a bulrush: see KNOT *noun*¹.
– COMB.: **bulrush millet** a millet, *Pennisetum americanum*, with a long spike of flowers.

†**bulse** *noun*. E18–M19.
[ORIGIN Portuguese *bolsa* from medieval Latin *bursa* BURSE.]
A package of diamonds, gold dust, etc.

bult /bʌlt, *foreign* bœlt/ *noun*. *S. Afr*. M19.
[ORIGIN Afrikaans from Dutch = hump, unch.]
A ridge, a rise.

bulwark /ˈbʊlwək/ *noun & verb*. LME.
[ORIGIN Middle Low German, Middle Dutch *bolwerk* (= Middle High German *bol(e)werk*, German *Bollwerk*), ult. formed as BOLE *noun*¹ + WORK *noun*.]
▸ **A** *noun*. **1** A substantial defensive work; a rampart, a fortification. LME. ▸**b** A mole, a breakwater. E16.
2 *fig*. A person or principle etc. that acts as a defence or shelter. LME.

POPE He stood, the bulwark of the Grecian band. H. HALLAM Preserving human learning as a bulwark to theology. I. MURDOCH Rupert's strong, full reassuring presence, a completely effective bulwark against anxiety of any kind.

3 The part of a ship's side above the level of the deck. Usu. in *pl*. E19.
▸ **B** *verb trans*. Provide with bulwarks; serve as a bulwark to, defend, protect, shelter. LME.

bum /bʌm/ *noun*¹. LME.
[ORIGIN Unknown.]
1 (The region of) the buttocks. LME.
2 A lazy or worthless person. Now identified with BUM *noun*². M16.
3 *hist*. In full ***bum-bailiff***. [So called as approaching from behind.] A bailiff employed in arrests. E17.
– COMB.: **bumbag** a small bag or pouch worn on a belt around the waist; ***bum-bailiff***: see sense 3 above; **bumbaste** *verb trans*. (*obsolete* exc. *dial*.) beat on the buttocks, flog; **bum-boat** †(*a*) a scavenger's boat removing refuse and filth from ships moored in the River Thames (and also bearing provisions); (*b*) a boat bearing fresh provisions etc. to ships; **bumboy** *slang* a young male homosexual, *esp*. a prostitute; a catamite; **bum-fluff** *slang* the sparse, downy hair of an adolescent boy's beard and moustache; **bum-fodder** *slang* = BUMF; **bum-freezer**, **bum-perisher**, **bum-**

shaver *slang* a short jacket, coat, etc.; **bum-suck** *verb intrans.* (*slang*) toady, suck up; **bum-sucker** (*slang*) a sycophant.

bum /bʌm/ *noun*[2] & *adjective*. *slang* (orig. & chiefly *N. Amer.*). **M19.**
[ORIGIN Prob. from BUMMER: cf. BUM *noun*[1] 2.]
▸ **A** *noun*. **1** A habitual loafer or tramp; a lazy dissolute person. **M19.**
the bum's rush forcible ejection. **bum-rush** *verb trans.* (*US colloq.*) force or barge one's way into.
2 ***on the bum***, vagrant, begging; also, in a disordered state. **L19.**
▸ **B** *adjective*. Of poor quality, worthless, useless. **M19.**
bum rap imprisonment on a false charge. ***bum steer***: see STEER *noun*[3].

bum /bʌm/ *verb*[1] *intrans.* *obsolete* exc. *dial.* Infl. **-mm-**. **LME.**
[ORIGIN Var. of BOOM *verb*[1].]
Hum loudly; boom.
– COMB.: **bum-bee** *Scot.* a bumblebee; **bum-clock** *Scot. & N. English* a cockchafer or similar beetle.

bum /bʌm/ *verb*[2] *trans.* Long *rare*. Infl. **-mm-**. **L16.**
[ORIGIN Perh. from BUM *noun*[1].]
Strike, beat, thump.

bum /bʌm/ *verb*[3]. *slang* (orig. *US*). Infl. **-mm-**. **M19.**
[ORIGIN Perh. from German *bummeln*: see BUMMER and cf. BUM *noun*[2].]
1 *verb intrans.* Wander aimlessly *around*, travel *around* as a tramp; loaf, be lazy and dissolute. **M19.**
2 *verb trans.* Cadge, scrounge. **M19.**

bumbaze /bʌmˈbeɪz/ *verb trans.* Chiefly *Scot.* **M17.**
[ORIGIN App. from BAZE with *bum-* as a meaningless intensive or redupl. prefix.]
Confound, bamboozle.

†**bumbelo** *noun* see BUMMALO.

bumbershoot /ˈbʌmbəʃuːt/ *noun*. *US colloq.* **L19.**
[ORIGIN from alt. of UMBRELLA + PARA)CHUTE.]
An umbrella.

bumble /ˈbʌmb(ə)l/ *noun*. **M17.**
[ORIGIN Imit.: in sense 3 from the name of the beadle in Dickens's *Oliver Twist*.]
1 A confusion, a jumble. **M17.**
2 A blunderer; an idler. **L18.**
3 A self-important official. **M19.**
– COMB.: **bumblefoot** (*a*) a club foot; (*b*) a condition in which birds' feet become inflamed and ulcerated.
▪ **bumbledom** *noun* stupid officiousness and pomposity, esp. by petty officials **M19.**

bumble /ˈbʌmb(ə)l/ *verb*. **LME.**
[ORIGIN Partly from BOOM *verb*[1], BUM *verb*[1] + -LE[3]; partly from BUMBLE *noun*.]
1 *verb intrans.* Hum, buzz, drone; ramble *on* in speaking; move or act ineptly or flounderingly. **LME.**
†**2** *verb trans.* Grumble at, blame, take to task. **L17–L18.**
▪ **bumbler** *noun* (*a*) a blunderer; (*b*) a bumblebee: **L16.**

bumblebee /ˈbʌmb(ə)lbiː/ *noun*. **M16.**
[ORIGIN from BUMBLE *verb* + BEE *noun*[1].]
A large loud-humming bee of the genus *Bombus*; a humble-bee.

bumble-puppy /ˈbʌmb(ə)lpʌpi/ *noun*. **E19.**
[ORIGIN Unknown.]
1 = ***nine-holes*** (a) s.v. NINE *adjective & noun*. *obsolete* exc. *hist.* **E19.**
2 Whist, bridge, etc., played disregarding or reversing rules. **M19.**
3 A game in which a tennis ball attached by string to a post is struck with a racket by each player with the object of winding the string entirely around the post. **E20.**

bumbo /ˈbʌmbəʊ/ *noun*. Now *arch.* or *hist.* **M18.**
[ORIGIN Perh. from Italian *bombo* child's word for a drink.]
A drink composed of rum, sugar, water, and nutmeg; any similar drink.

bumf /bʌmf/ *noun*. *slang*. Also **bumph**. **L19.**
[ORIGIN Abbreviation of *bum-fodder* s.v. BUM *noun*[1].]
Toilet paper; worthless literature; (usu. *derog.*) documents, official papers.

bumiputra /buːmɪˈpuːtrə/ *noun & adjective*. **M20.**
[ORIGIN Malay from Sanskrit, lit. 'son of the soil'.]
▸ **A** *noun*. Pl. **-s**, same. A Malaysian of indigenous Malay origin. **M20.**
▸ **B** *attrib.* or as *adjective*. Of or pertaining to the bumiputras; indigenous Malay. **L20.**
▪ **bumiputraiˈzation** *noun* the policy or practice of giving precedence to indigenous Malays (rather than Chinese) in business, education, etc. **L20.**

bumkin /ˈbʌmkɪn/ *noun*. Also **bump-** /ˈbʌmp-/. **M17.**
[ORIGIN Dutch *boomken* (also *boompje*), from *boom* tree, boom + *-ken* -KIN.]
NAUTICAL. A short boom, esp. on the stern to sheet the mizzensail.

bummalo /ˈbʌmələʊ/ *noun*. Also (earlier) †**bumbelo**. Pl. same. **L17.**
[ORIGIN Perh. from Marathi *bombil*.]
A small edible fish, *Harpodon nehereus*, of southern Asian coasts. Also called ***Bombay duck***.

bummaree /bʌməˈriː/ *noun*. **L18.**
[ORIGIN Unknown.]
1 *hist.* A middleman at Billingsgate fish market, London. **L18.**
2 A self-employed licensed porter at Smithfield meat market, London. **M20.**

bummel /ˈbʌm(ə)l, ˈbʊm-/ *noun & verb*. **E20.**
[ORIGIN German *Bummel* a stroll, *bummeln* to stroll, loaf about. Cf. BUMMER.]
▸ **A** *noun*. A leisurely stroll or journey. **E20.**
▸ **B** *verb intrans.* Infl. **-l(l)-**. Stroll or wander in a leisurely fashion. **E20.**

bummer /ˈbʌmə/ *noun*. Orig. & chiefly *N. Amer. slang*. **M19.**
[ORIGIN Perh. from German *bummler*, from *bummeln*: see BUMMEL.]
1 An idler, a loafer. **M19.**
2 An unpleasant occurrence or experience; a mistake; a failure. **M20.**

†**bummery** *noun*. **M17–M19.**
[ORIGIN Dutch *bommerye*, *bodmerij*: see BOTTOMRY.]
= BOTTOMRY *noun*.

bump /bʌmp/ *noun*[1]. **L16.**
[ORIGIN Imit., perh. of Scandinavian origin: cf. Middle Danish *bumpe* strike with the fist.]
1 **a** A swelling caused by a blow or collision; an irregular prominence on a road, cricket pitch, etc. **L16.** ▸**b** *PHRENOLOGY*. One of the prominences of the cranium associated with various mental capacities; a faculty indicated by such a prominence. **E19.** ▸**c** The protruding abdomen of a pregnant woman. *colloq.* **L20.**
2 A dull-sounding blow, knock, or collision. **E17.** ▸**b** In a race where boats start at fixed intervals (chiefly at the Universities of Oxford and Cambridge): an overtaking (and touching) of a boat by the next in line, entitling the latter to start before the former in the next race. **M19.**
3 A sudden (esp. upwards) movement (whether or not accompanied by noise); *spec.* (*a*) (a rising air current causing) an irregularity in an aircraft's motion; (*b*) *slang* a dancer's forward thrust of the abdomen. **L19.**
– PHRASES: **bump of locality** (a phrenological bump indicating) a supposed faculty of recognizing places and finding one's way. ***musical bumps***: see MUSICAL *adjective*. **with a bump** *fig.* abruptly, with a shock.
– COMB.: **bump-ball** *CRICKET* a ball hit hard on to the ground close to the bat and coming to a fielder like a possible catch; **bump-out** *US* an extension built on to a house; **bump supper** (chiefly in the Universities of Oxford and Cambridge) a dinner held to celebrate a college's achievements in the bumping races.

bump /bʌmp/ *noun*[2]. **E16.**
[ORIGIN from BUMP *verb*[2].]
The cry of the bittern.

bump /bʌmp/ *verb*[1] & *adverb*. **M16.**
[ORIGIN formed as BUMP *noun*[1].]
▸ **A** *verb* †**1** **a** *verb intrans.* Bulge out; be big. **M16–E18.** ▸**b** *verb trans.* Cause to swell *up*. **M17–E18.**
2 *verb trans.* Push, thump, knock heavily, (usu. *against*, *on*); hurt (one's head etc.) by striking it (*against*, *on*). **E17.**

> J. HILTON Bumping his head against the roof. J. L. WATEN Arms folded, each endeavoured to bump the other to the ground.

3 *verb trans. & intrans.* Overtake and touch (the next boat) in a bumping race (see BUMPING *verbal noun* below). **E19.**
4 *verb intrans.* Strike solidly (*against*, *into*); come with a bump or jolt *against*; go (*along*) with repeated bumps. **M19.** ▸**b** *CRICKET*. Of a ball: rise abruptly to an unusual height. **M19.** ▸**c** Boil explosively. **L19.**

> J. D. SALINGER Careful not to bump into anything and make a racket. C. ISHERWOOD Jostling, bumping against each other's bodies.

5 *verb trans.* Displace; move from position by a bump; oust, dismiss; *spec.* transfer to another airline flight because of overbooking etc.; *slang* murder. Chiefly *N. Amer.* **E20.**
– PHRASES ETC.: **bump and run** *AMER. FOOTBALL* (of a cornerback) deliberately bump into the receiver and run with him to block a pass. **bump into** *fig.* (*colloq.*) meet by chance. **bump off** *slang* (orig. *US*) kill, murder. **bump up** *colloq.* increase or raise suddenly.
▸ **B** *adverb*. With a bump; suddenly, violently. **E19.**
▪ **bumpety**, **-ity** *adverb* with a bump (usu. redupl. *bumpety-bump*) **M19.** **bumping** *noun* the action of the verb; a bump; ***bumping race***, a boat race in which places are determined by bumps (see BUMP *noun*[1] 2b): **M19.** **bumping** *ppl adjective* (*a*) *arch. colloq.* huge, great; (*b*) that bumps: **M16.**

bump /bʌmp/ *verb*[2]. **M17.**
[ORIGIN Imit.]
Of the bittern: make its characteristic cry.

bumper /ˈbʌmpə/ *noun*[1]. **L17.**
[ORIGIN from BUMP *verb*[1] (branch I as BUMPING *ppl adjective* (a)) + -ER[1].]
▸ **I** **1** A cup or glass of wine etc. filled to the brim, esp. for a toast. **L17.**
2 Anything unusually large, abundant, or excellent. Usu. *attrib.* **M18.**

> LYNDON B. JOHNSON A bumper crop, the largest in India's history.

3 *spec.* A crowded house at the theatre. *slang*. **L18.**
▸ **II** **4** A railway buffer. *US*. **M19.**
5 A shock-absorbing attachment on a ship, vehicle, etc.; *spec.* a metal, rubber, or plastic bar attached to (usu. the front or back) of a motor vehicle etc. to reduce damage in collisions or as a trim. **M19.**
6 *CRICKET*. A short-pitched ball that rises high after pitching. **M19.**
7 *gen.* A person who or thing which bumps. **L19.**
– COMB.: **bumper car** = DODGEM; **bumper sticker** a sticker with a slogan, advertisement, etc., to be displayed on a vehicle's bumper; **bumper-to-bumper** (travelling) very close together.

bumper /ˈbʌmpə/ *noun*[2]. *Austral. & NZ slang*. **L19.**
[ORIGIN Blend of BUTT *noun*[4] and STUMP *noun*[1] + -ER[1].]
A cigarette end.

bumper /ˈbʌmpə/ *verb*. *arch.* **L17.**
[ORIGIN from BUMPER *noun*[1].]
1 *verb trans.* with *it* & *intrans.* Drink bumpers. **L17.**
2 *verb trans.* Fill to the brim. **L18.**
3 *verb trans.* Toast in a bumper. **E19.**

bumph *noun* var. of BUMF.

bumpkin /ˈbʌm(p)kɪn/ *noun*[1]. **L16.**
[ORIGIN Perh. from Dutch *boomken* little tree, or Middle Dutch *bommekijn* little barrel, used fig. for 'squat figure'.]
A rustic or awkward person.
▪ **bumpkinet** *noun* (*rare*) a little bumpkin **L18.** **bumpkinish** *adjective* **L18.** **bumpkinly** *adjective* (*rare*) **L17.**

bumpkin *noun*[2] var. of BUMKIN.

bumpology /bʌmˈpɒlədʒi/ *noun*. *joc.* **E19.**
[ORIGIN from BUMP *noun*[1] + -OLOGY.]
Phrenology.
▪ **bumpologist** *noun* a phrenologist **E19.**

bumptious /ˈbʌm(p)ʃəs/ *adjective*. **E19.**
[ORIGIN Joc. from BUMP *verb*[1] after FRACTIOUS.]
Self-assertive, offensively conceited.
▪ **bumptiously** *adverb* **L19.** **bumptiousness** *noun* **M19.**

bumpy /ˈbʌmpi/ *adjective*. **M19.**
[ORIGIN from BUMP *noun*[1] or *verb*[1] + -Y[1].]
Full of bumps; causing bumps, uneven.
▪ **bumpiness** *noun* **E19.**

bumsters /ˈbʌmstəz/ *noun pl.* **L20.**
[ORIGIN from BUM *noun*[1] + -STER as in *hipsters*.]
Trousers that are cut very low on the hips.

bun /bʌn/ *noun*[1]. Long *obsolete* exc. *dial.*
[ORIGIN Old English *bune*, of unknown origin.]
1 A hollow stem, esp. of an umbelliferous plant. **OE.**
2 The stalk or stalky part of flax or hemp. **LME.**

bun /bʌn/ *noun*[2]. **LME.**
[ORIGIN Unknown.]
1 A small soft round sweet bread or cake with currants etc.; *Scot.* a rich fruit cake or currant bread. **LME.**
black bun: see BLACK *adjective*. ***bun in the oven***: see OVEN *noun*. ***cross bun***, ***hot cross bun***: see CROSS-. ***Kitchener bun***: see KITCHENER *noun*[2] & *adjective*. ***saffron bun***: see SAFFRON *adjective*. ***take the bun***: see TAKE *verb*.
2 (A hairstyle with) hair in a coil at the back of the head. **L19.**
– COMB.: **bun fight** *slang* a tea party.

bun /bʌn/ *noun*[3]. **E16.**
[ORIGIN Unknown.]
1 *sing.* & (*N. Amer.*) in *pl.* The buttocks. *Scot. & N. Amer. slang*. **E16.**
2 A hare's or rabbit's tail. *Scot. & N. English*. **E18.**

bun /bʌn/ *noun*[4]. Chiefly *dial.* **L16.**
[ORIGIN Unknown. Cf. BUNNY *noun*[2].]
A squirrel; a rabbit. Also used as a term of endearment to a person.

Buna /ˈbjuːnə/ *noun*. Also **b-**. **M20.**
[ORIGIN German, formed as BUTADIENE + *Natrium* sodium.]
Synthetic rubber made by polymerization of butadiene.
Buna N *hist.* = PERBUNAN.

Bunbury /ˈbʌnb(ə)ri/ *noun*. **L19.**
[ORIGIN An imaginary person (so used in Oscar Wilde's *The Importance of Being Earnest*).]
A fictitious excuse for making a visit or avoiding an obligation.

bunce /bʌns/ *noun*. *slang*. **E18.**
[ORIGIN Unknown.]
Money; profit.

bunch /bʌn(t)ʃ/ *noun*. **LME.**
[ORIGIN Unknown.]
1 A protuberance, a hump; a goitre. Now *rare*. **LME.**
2 A cluster of things growing or fastened together; (less commonly) a quantity of a substance brought together; a collection, the lot; *slang* a gang, a group. **LME.**

> TENNYSON Grapes with bunches red as blood. A. G. GARDINER A bunch of wood to boil our kettle. V. BRITTAIN A large bunch of the year's first Parma violets. E. F. BENSON The younger son of an impecunious baronet . . was the best of the bunch. G. ORWELL A bunch of nerves at the back of the neck. R. LARDNER I'm not going to have a bunch of cheap reporters make a fool of me.

bunch of fives: see FIVE *noun*. ***mixed bunch***.
– COMB.: **bunchberry** *N. Amer.* (the fruit of) a dwarf cornel, *Cornus canadensis*; **bunchflower** *N. Amer.* a plant of the lily family,

B

Melanthium virginicum, with greenish-yellow flowers; **bunch grass** *N. Amer.* any of various kinds of grass growing in clumps.

bunch /bʌn(t)ʃ/ *verb*[1] *trans.* Long *obsolete* exc. *dial.* ME.
[ORIGIN Unknown: perh. imit.]
Strike, thump; bruise; kick.

bunch /bʌn(t)ʃ/ *verb*[2]. LME.
[ORIGIN from BUNCH *noun*.]
†**1** *verb intrans.* Bulge, protrude, stick *out*. LME–E18.
2 *verb intrans.* Form a bunch or bunches; crowd together in a body. E17.

G. GORDON There's queues of other kids bunching up behind her.

3 *verb trans.* Make into a bunch or bunches; gather (material) into close folds. L19.
4 *verb trans.* Present (a person) with a bunch of flowers. Now *rare*. E20.

buncher /ˈbʌn(t)ʃə/ *noun*. L19.
[ORIGIN from BUNCH *noun* or *verb*[2] + -ER[1].]
1 A person who or thing which bunches; *spec.* a machine for forming bunches or collecting things in bunches. L19.
2 PHYSICS. A device that modulates a beam of charged particles and causes them to collect in groups. M20.

bunchy /ˈbʌn(t)ʃi/ *adjective*. LME.
[ORIGIN from BUNCH *noun* + -Y[1].]
1 Bulging, protuberant; full of protuberances or swellings. LME.
2 Like a bunch; having bunches; gathered into close folds. E19.
bunchy top a viral disease of plants (esp. bananas), causing crowded growth of leaves at the tip of the stem.

bunco /ˈbʌŋkəʊ/ *noun & verb*. *US slang*. Also **bunko**. L19.
[ORIGIN Perh. from Spanish *banca* a card game.]
▸ **A** *noun*. Pl. **-os**. A swindle, esp. by card sharping or a confidence trick. L19.
– COMB.: **bunco-steerer** a swindler.
▸ **B** *verb trans.* Swindle. L19.

buncombe *noun* var. of BUNKUM.

bund /bʌnd/ *noun*[1] *& verb*. Chiefly *techn.* or *Indian*. E19.
[ORIGIN Urdu *band* from Persian.]
▸ **A** *noun*. An embankment or causeway. Also *spec.*, a wall surrounding an industrial fuel tank; the area enclosed by such a wall. E19.
▸ **B** *verb trans.* Embank. L19.

bund /bʊnd, *foreign* bʊnt/ *noun*[2]. Pl. **bunds**, ***bunde*** /ˈbʊndə/. M19.
[ORIGIN German *Bund* something joined, union: rel. to BAND *noun*[2], BIND *verb*.]
A German league, confederacy, or association.

bunder /ˈbʌndə/ *noun*. E17.
[ORIGIN Urdu *bandar* from Persian.]
In the Indian subcontinent: a landing place, a quay, a harbour.
– COMB.: **bunder-boat**: used for coastal and harbour work.

Bundesrat /ˈbʊndəzrɑːt/ *noun*. Also †**-rath**. L19.
[ORIGIN German, from genit. of BUND *noun*[2] + *Rat(h)* council.]
A federal council in Germany and German-speaking countries; *spec.* the Upper House of Parliament in Germany and in Austria.

Bundestag /ˈbʊndəztɑːg/ *noun*. L19.
[ORIGIN German, formed as BUNDESRAT + *tagen* confer.]
A representative assembly in Germany and German-speaking countries; *spec.* the Lower House of Parliament in Germany.

bundle /ˈbʌnd(ə)l/ *noun*. ME.
[ORIGIN Orig. perh. repr. Old English *byndelle* binding, taken in concr. sense, = Old Saxon *bundilin* (Dutch *bundel* bundle), Old High German *gibuntili* (German *Bündel*), but reinforced later by (if not wholly due to) Low German, Dutch *bundel*.]
1 A collection of things fastened together, esp. loosely (now esp. clothes, papers, or odds and ends in a large handkerchief or paper); (freq. *derog.*) a collection, a lot. ME.

P. GRACE I picked up the bundle of sticks for the morning fire. *Entertainment Weekly* A Manhattan nerd who's a quivering bundle of anxieties and phobias.

2 A collection of fibres (esp. nerves), vessels, or the like, running parallel in an animal body or plant. M18.
3 A woman, *esp.* a fat woman. *dial. & slang. derog.* M19.
4 A large amount of money. *slang* (orig. *US*). E20.
5 A fight, a scrap. *slang*. M20.
– PHRASES: **bundle of joy** *joc.* a newly born baby. ***bundle of nerves***: see NERVE *noun*. CONCENTRIC ***bundle***. **drop one's bundle** *Austral. & NZ slang* lose self-control, panic. **go a bundle on** *slang* (orig. *US*) (*a*) bet much money on; (*b*) *fig.* be very fond of. VASCULAR ***bundle***.
– COMB.: **bundle-sheath** the layer of cells surrounding the vascular bundle of a leaf.
■ **bundly** *adjective* (*rare*) like a bundle L19.

bundle /ˈbʌnd(ə)l/ *verb*. L16.
[ORIGIN from the noun.]
1 *verb trans.* Tie in a bundle; make *up* into a bundle; wrap (*up*) warmly or cumbersomely (usu. in *pass.*). L16. ▸**b** *fig.* Collect or group *together* without distinction. E17.

C. M. YONGE She . . bundled up her hair as best she might. W. STYRON Men and women bundled against the cold. **b** A. STORR Are dreams, day-dreams and works of art all to be bundled together in the same category?

2 *verb intrans.* Pack for a journey; leave with one's luggage etc.; move or go hurriedly or unceremoniously. (Foll. by *in*, *off*, *out*.) L18.

R. BURNS Bundle and go! D. ABSE Leo bundled out of the train. C. CHAPLIN We bundled into Mr Sennett's . . racing car.

3 *verb intrans.* Sleep in one's clothes *with* another person (esp. as a former local custom during courtship). Also foll. by *up*. L18.
4 *verb trans.* Put or send (esp. a person) hurriedly or unceremoniously *out*, *off*, *away*, etc.; throw confusedly *into* a receptacle. E19.

D. WELCH I tried . . to bundle my guest through the dining-room. W. S. MAUGHAM I . . bundled my things into my rucksack. W. TREVOR They came briefly, as moments rapidly hurrying, one bundled away by the next.

bundobust /ˈbʌndəbʌst/ *noun*. Also **bandobast**. L18.
[ORIGIN Urdu from Persian *band-o-bast* tying and binding.]
In the Indian subcontinent: arrangements, organization.

bundook /ˈbʌnduːk/ *noun*. L19.
[ORIGIN Urdu *bandūq* from Persian *bundūq* firearm; rel. to BONDUC.]
In the Indian subcontinent: a musket or similar firearm.

Bundt /bʌnt/ *noun*. E20.
[ORIGIN German *Bund* (see BUND *noun*[2]).]
More fully ***Bundt cake***. (Proprietary name for) a type of ring-shaped cake of Austrian or German origin.

bundu /ˈbʊnduː/ *noun*. *S. Afr.* M20.
[ORIGIN Prob. from Shona *bundo* grasslands.]
Uncivilized rural country; *the* wilds.

bung /bʌŋ/ *noun*[1]. LME.
[ORIGIN Middle Dutch *bonghe*, of unknown origin.]
1 A stopper, *esp.* a large cork for stopping the hole in a cask. LME.
2 *transf.* = ***bunghole*** below. *obsolete* exc. *dial.* L16.
3 A brewer; a publican. M19.
– COMB.: **bung-ho** *interjection* an exclamation at parting or as a toast; **bunghole** a hole in a cask for filling and emptying it.

†**bung** *noun*[2]. *slang*. M16.
[ORIGIN Unknown.]
1 A purse. M16–E18.
2 A pickpocket. *rare* (Shakes.). Only in L16.

bung /bʌŋ/ *noun*[3]. *slang*. M20.
[ORIGIN Unknown: cf. BUNG *verb*[3].]
A bribe; a tip.

bung /bʌŋ/ *adjective*. *Austral. & NZ slang*. M19.
[ORIGIN Prob. ult. from Yagara (an Australian Aboriginal language of SE Queensland).]
Ruined, useless, broken; bankrupt. Formerly also, dead. Freq. in ***go bung***, break down, fail or go bankrupt; die.

I. WYNER We had a sort of society before that, but it went bung.

bung /bʌŋ/ *verb*[1] *trans.* M16.
[ORIGIN from BUNG *noun*[1].]
Stop (with a bung); shut *up*, block, close.

bung /bʌŋ/ *verb*[2] *& adverb*. *dial. & slang*. E19.
[ORIGIN Imit.]
▸ **A** *verb trans.* Throw, toss; put forcibly or unceremoniously. E19.

C. MACKENZIE Let's bung these sticks into the sea. B. TRAPIDO We're giving you the guest room . . and bunging Katherine in with the children.

▸ **B** *adverb*. Abruptly, unceremoniously; exactly. Cf. BANG *adverb*. L19.

bung /bʌŋ/ *verb*[3] *trans.* *slang*. M20.
[ORIGIN Unknown: cf. BUNG *noun*[3].]
Bribe; tip.

G. F. NEWMAN Having been picked up by the CID . . he had bunged the DI and pulled himself clear.

bungalow /ˈbʌŋgələʊ/ *noun*. L17.
[ORIGIN Hindi *baṅglā* belonging to Bengal.]
A one-storeyed house.
■ **bungaloid** *adjective* (usu. *derog.*) resembling a bungalow, consisting of bungalows E20.

bungarotoxin /bʌŋgərə(ʊ)ˈtɒksɪn/ *noun*. M20.
[ORIGIN from mod. Latin *Bungarus*, genus name (perh. from Sanskrit *bhaṅgura* bent) + -O- + TOXIN.]
BIOCHEMISTRY. Each of three neurotoxins from the venom of a krait, *Bungarus multicinctus*, which bind to acetylcholine receptors with a high degree of specificity.

bungarra /bʌŋˈgarə/ *noun*. L19.
[ORIGIN Nhanta (an Australian Aboriginal language of Western Australia) *bangarra*.]
= ***sand goanna*** s.v. SAND *noun*.

bungee /ˈbʌndʒi/ *noun*. Also **bungie**, **bungy**. E20.
[ORIGIN Unknown.]
1 A rubber, an eraser. *slang*. E20.
2 Strong elasticated cord or cable; a piece of this, usu. with a hook at each end and used esp. for securing baggage in transit. Also ***bungee cord***, ***bungee rope***. M20.
– COMB.: ***bungee cord***: see sense 2 above; **bungee jumping** jumping from a height, as from a bridge, while attached to an elasticated rope, as a sport or recreation; ***bungee rope***: see sense 2 above.

bungle /ˈbʌŋg(ə)l/ *noun*. M17.
[ORIGIN from the verb.]
A botch, a blunder; muddle, failure.

E. LONGFORD Through some bungle the courier . . had missed them on the road. N. GORDIMER Care to avoid bungle by haste and lack of strategy.

bungle /ˈbʌŋg(ə)l/ *verb*. M16.
[ORIGIN Imit.: cf. BUMBLE *verb*.]
1 *verb trans.* Do or make clumsily or unskilfully; spoil by clumsiness or lack of skill; fail to accomplish (a task). M16.
2 *verb intrans.* Be or act clumsily or unskilfully, blunder. M16.
■ **bunglesome** *adjective* (*US*) bungling and troublesome L19. **bungler** *noun* M16. **bungling** *ppl adjective* (*a*) that bungles; (*b*) showing clumsiness or lack of skill: L16. **bunglingly** *adverb* E17.

bungy *noun* var. of BUNGEE.

bunion /ˈbʌnj(ə)n/ *noun*. E18.
[ORIGIN Perh. extension of BUNNY *noun*[1], or ult. from Old French *buignon*, from *buigne* (mod. *bigne*) bump on the head, perh. of Germanic origin (cf. Middle High German *bunge* lump): see -OON.]
An inflamed swelling on the foot, esp. of the bursa of the first joint of the big toe.

bunjara *noun* var. of BRINJARRY.

bunk /bʌŋk/ *noun*[1]. M18.
[ORIGIN Uncertain: perh. rel. to BUNKER.]
A sleeping berth, *esp.* one of two or more arranged one on top of the other.
– COMB.: **bunk bed** (a bunk in) a piece of furniture comprising two bunks; **bunkhouse** a house where workmen etc. are lodged.
■ **bunkie** *noun* (*US colloq.*) a person who shares a bunk with another M19.

bunk /bʌŋk/ *noun*[2]. *slang*. L19.
[ORIGIN Unknown: cf. BUNK *verb*[2].]
do a bunk, make off, vanish.

bunk /bʌŋk/ *noun*[3]. *slang*. E20.
[ORIGIN Abbreviation of BUNKUM.]
Nonsense, humbug.

bunk /bʌŋk/ *verb*[1] *intrans.* M19.
[ORIGIN from BUNK *noun*[1].]
Sleep in or lie *down* on a bunk or improvised bed.

bunk /bʌŋk/ *verb*[2]. *slang*. M19.
[ORIGIN Unknown: cf. BUNK *noun*[2].]
1 *verb intrans.* Be off, vanish. Also foll. by *off*. M19.

N. HORNBY The other kids in the class might have worked out that he was bunking off.

2 *verb trans.* Expel from school. L19.

bunker /ˈbʌŋkə/ *noun & verb*. M16.
[ORIGIN Unknown.]
▸ **A** *noun*. **1** A seat or bench. *Scot.* M16.
2 An earthen seat or bank in the fields. *dial.* E19.
3 GOLF. A pit containing sand etc. and constituting a hazard. E19.
4 A (large) container for fuel. M19.
5 A reinforced underground shelter. M20.
▸ **B** *verb* **1 a** *verb trans.* Fill the bunkers of (a ship etc.). L19. ▸**b** *verb intrans.* Of a ship: take in a supply of coal or oil. L19.
2 *verb trans.* GOLF. Trap (a ball, *transf.* a player, a shot) in a bunker. Usu. in *pass.* L19. ▸**b** *fig.* Bring into difficulties. L19.

bunko *noun & verb* var. of BUNCO.

bunkum /ˈbʌŋkəm/ *noun*. Also **buncombe**. M19.
[ORIGIN from *Buncombe* County, N. Carolina, USA, whose member made an irrelevant speech in Congress *c* 1820 simply to impress his constituents.]
Nonsense; ostentatious talking.

bunk-up /ˈbʌŋkʌp/ *noun*. *dial. & slang*. E20.
[ORIGIN Unknown.]
A push or pull up.

†**bunny** *noun*[1]. LME–L19.
[ORIGIN Old French *buigne*: see BUNION.]
A swelling, esp. on an animal's joint.

bunny /ˈbʌni/ *noun*[2]. E17.
[ORIGIN from BUN *noun*[4] + -Y[6].]
1 Used as a term of endearment to a person. E17.
2 (A pet name for) a rabbit. L17. ▸**b** More fully ***bunny girl***. A club hostess wearing a brief costume suggestive of a rabbit. M20.
3 A person of a specified kind. *colloq.* M20.

Arena He likes to keep in shape . . but he's no gym bunny. *Star* Jason . . has just got out of prison and he's not a happy bunny.

– COMB.: **bunny-boiler** [with ref. to the film *Fatal Attraction*, in which a jilted mistress boils her lover's pet rabbit] *colloq.* a woman who is vindictive after having been spurned by her lover; ***bunny girl***: see sense 2b above; **bunny-hug** a dance in ragtime rhythm with close contact between partners; **bunny-hugger** (*a*) a person who dances the bunny-hug; (**b**) *colloq., derog.* an animal lover; a conservationist; **bunny slope** SKIING, US a gentle slope suitable for beginners, a nursery slope.

bunny-hop /ˈbʌni hɒp/ *noun & verb.* M20.
[ORIGIN from BUNNY *noun*² + HOP *noun*² & *verb*¹.]
▶ **A** *noun.* **1** An informal dance in which participants form a line and perform jumping and kicking movements. Orig. *US.* M20.
2 Any leaping movement reminiscent of that made by a rabbit, *spec.* ▸**a** a jump made in a crouched position; ▸**b** a movement in figure skating consisting of a leap made from one foot to the toe of the other whilst gliding forwards, followed immediately by a return to the original foot. M20.
3 CYCLING. A manoeuvre in which the bicycle is lifted from the ground with a jumping motion, esp. in order to clear an obstruction. L20.
▶ **B** *verb.* **1** *verb intrans.* Perform a bunny-hop; dance the bunny-hop. L20.
2 *verb trans.* Avoid (an obstacle) by jumping over it. L20.

bunodont /ˈbjuːnədɒnt/ *adjective.* L19.
[ORIGIN from Greek *bounos* mound + -ODONT.]
Characterized by molar teeth whose crowns have a number of rounded cusps. Of molar teeth: having this form.

Bunraku /ˈbʊnrakʊ, *foreign* ˈbunraku/ *noun & adjective.* E20.
[ORIGIN Uemura *Bunrakuken* (d. 1810), Japanese puppet master.]
(Of, pertaining to, or characteristic of) Japanese puppet drama, *spec.* as practised by the Bunraku-za company.

Bunsen /ˈbʌns(ə)n/ *noun.* L19.
[ORIGIN Robert W. *Bunsen* (1811–99), German chemist.]
In full ***Bunsen burner***. A small gas and air burner used esp. in chemical laboratories to heat substances.

bunt /bʌnt/ *noun*¹. L16.
[ORIGIN Unknown.]
1 NAUTICAL. The middle part of a sail. L16.
2 The cavity or baggy part of a fishing net etc. E17.
– COMB.: **buntline** a rope confining the bunt of a sail and preventing it from bellying when being furled.

bunt /bʌnt/ *noun*². E17.
[ORIGIN Unknown.]
1 A puffball fungus. Now *rare* or *obsolete*. E17.
2 A smut fungus of the genus *Tilletia*, attacking wheat; disease caused by this. L18.
■ **bunty** *adjective* infested with bunt M19.

bunt /bʌnt/ *noun*³. M18.
[ORIGIN Cf. BUTT *verb*¹, *noun*⁹, BUNT *verb*².]
1 A push with the head or horns, a butt. Chiefly *N. Amer.* & *dial.* M18.
2 BASEBALL. An act of letting the ball rebound from the bat without swinging. L19.

bunt /bʌnt/ *verb*¹. NAUTICAL. E17.
[ORIGIN from BUNT *noun*¹.]
1 *verb trans.* Haul up the middle part of (a sail) in furling. E17.
2 *verb intrans.* Of a sail: belly. L17.

bunt /bʌnt/ *verb*² *trans. & intrans. US & dial.* E19.
[ORIGIN from (the same root as) BUNT *noun*³.]
1 Push with the head or horns, butt. E19.
2 BASEBALL. Let (the ball) rebound from the bat without swinging. L19.

buntal /ˈbʌnt(ə)l/ *noun.* E20.
[ORIGIN Tagalog.]
Straw made from the talipot palm. Cf. BALIBUNTAL.

bunter /ˈbʌntə/ *noun*¹. *obsolete* exc. *dial.* E18.
[ORIGIN Unknown.]
A woman who gathers rags and bones in the streets; a disreputable woman.

Bunter /ˈbʌntə/ *noun*² & *adjective.* Also **b-**. M19.
[ORIGIN German *bunter* (*Sandstein* sandstone), from *bunt* variegated.]
GEOLOGY. (Designating or pertaining to, the sandstones and conglomerates of) the Lower Triassic in Europe, esp. Germany.

bunting /ˈbʌntɪŋ/ *noun*¹. ME.
[ORIGIN Unknown.]
1 Any of numerous mainly seed-eating birds of the subfamily Emberizinae, related to the finches. ME.
cirl bunting, ***corn bunting***, ***reed bunting***, ***snow bunting***, ***yellow bunting***, etc.
2 Used as a term of endearment (infl. by BUNTING *adjective*). M16. ▸**b** Also ***bunting bag***. A snug, hooded sleeping bag for infants. *N. Amer.* E20.

> *Nursery rhyme*: Bye baby bunting, Daddy's gone a hunting.

3 A kind of shrimp or prawn. *dial.* Now *rare* or *obsolete*. M18.

bunting /ˈbʌntɪŋ/ *noun*². E18.
[ORIGIN Unknown.]
(A loosely woven fabric used for) flags and festive decorations.

bunting /ˈbʌntɪŋ/ *adjective. dial.* L16.
[ORIGIN from BUNT *verb*¹ + -ING².]
Swelling; plump.

bunton /ˈbʌntən/ *noun.* M17.
[ORIGIN Unknown.]
1 A piece of squared timber. Long *obsolete* in *gen.* sense. M17.
2 Any of a series of strong baulks of timber placed crosswise in a mine shaft. Usu. in *pl.* M19.

bunya-bunya /ˈbʌnjəbʌnjə/ *noun. Austral.* Also **bunya**. M19.
[ORIGIN Yagara (an Australian Aboriginal language of SE Queensland).]
A tall Australian tree, *Araucaria bidwillii*, bearing large cones with an edible pulp.

Bunyanesque /bʌnjəˈnɛsk/ *adjective.* L19.
[ORIGIN from *Bunyan* (see below) + -ESQUE.]
1 Of, pertaining to, or characteristic of the English author John Bunyan (1628–88). L19.
2 Of, pertaining to, or characteristic of the legendary American hero Paul Bunyan. M20.

bunyip /ˈbʌnjɪp/ *noun. Austral.* M19.
[ORIGIN Wemba-wemba *banib*.]
A fabulous monster of swamps and lagoons.

Buonapartist *noun & adjective* var. of BONAPARTIST.

buoy /bɔɪ/ *noun.* ME.
[ORIGIN Prob. from Middle Dutch *bo(e)ye, boeie* (Dutch *boei*) from Germanic base meaning 'signal', whence also French *bouée*, Spanish *boya*.]
1 A floating object fastened in a particular place to point out the position of shoals, rocks, anchors, etc. under the water, or the course for ships etc., or to float a cable in a rocky anchorage. ME. ▸**b** In full ***lifebuoy***. A device, usu. a ring, used to keep a person afloat. E19.
stream the buoy: see STREAM *verb*.
2 *fig.* Something which marks out a course, indicates danger, or keeps one afloat. E17.
■ **buoyage** *noun* providing of or with buoys; buoys collectively; a series of buoys which mark out a channel: E19.

buoy /bɔɪ/ *verb.* L16.
[ORIGIN Branch I from Spanish *boyar* (see BUOYANT); branch II from BUOY *noun*.]
▶ **I** †**1** *verb intrans.* Rise to or float on the surface of a liquid; rise, swell (as the sea). L16–L17.

> SHAKES. *Lear* The sea . . would have buoy'd up and quench'd the stelled fires.

2 a Foll. by *up*: raise to the surface of a liquid; bring afloat (a sunken ship etc.). E17. ▸**b** Keep from sinking, keep afloat. Usu. foll. by *up*. M17.
3 *verb trans. fig.* Sustain (a person, courage, etc.); raise (the spirits etc.), uplift, encourage. Usu. foll. by *up*. M17.

> D. CECIL Belonging to a famous and venerated institution, and buoyed up by its confident corporate spirit.

▶ **II 4** *verb trans.* Provide or mark (as) with a buoy or buoys. L16.

buoyancy /ˈbɔɪənsi/ *noun.* E18.
[ORIGIN from BUOYANT: see -ANCY.]
1 Power of floating on liquid or in air; tendency to float; power of supporting a floating body. E18. ▸**b** The vertical upward force of a fluid on a floating or immersed body, which is equal to the weight of fluid displaced by the body. L18.
2 *fig.* Elasticity of spirit, resilience, recuperative power; cheerfulness. Also, tendency to rise (in stock market prices, revenue, etc.). E19.

> DAY LEWIS Children . . can ride such disasters with extraordinary buoyancy. *Observer* On the strength of this buoyancy, the group launched a . . £55 million rights issue.

– COMB.: **buoyancy aid** a jerkin of a buoyant material, worn for sailing and other water sports.

buoyant /ˈbɔɪənt/ *adjective.* L16.
[ORIGIN Old French *bouyant* or Spanish *boyante* light-sailing, pres. pple of *boyar* float, from *boya* BUOY *noun*: see -ANT¹.]
1 Able to float; tending to float or rise; floating; lightly elastic; resilient, able to recover, light-hearted. L16.

> A. BRIGGS Trade remained buoyant and agriculture improved. X. J. KENNEDY The springer spaniel and the buoyant hare Seem half at home reclining in mid-air. U. BENTLEY He was buoyant, childishly happy.

2 Able to keep things up or afloat. L17.
■ **buoyantly** *adverb* M19. **buoyantness** *noun* (*rare*) M17.

BUPA /ˈbuːpə/ *abbreviation.*
British United Provident Association.

buphthalmos /bʊfˈθalmɒs/ *noun.* E19.
[ORIGIN Greek *bouphthalmon* ox-eye, from *bous* ox + *ophthalmos* eye.]
OPHTHALMOLOGY. Gross enlargement of the eyeball owing to increased intra-ocular pressure; now *spec.* (as a sign of) congenital glaucoma.
■ **buphthalmic** *adjective* characterized by or displaying buphthalmos L19.

bupkis /ˈbʌpkɪs/ *noun. US slang.* L20.
[ORIGIN Yiddish.]
Nothing at all.

buppie /ˈbʌpi/ *noun. colloq.* (chiefly *US*). L20.
[ORIGIN Blend of BLACK *adjective* and YUPPIE *noun*, or acronym from black urban professional + -IE.]
A young black professional working in a city, a black yuppie.

bupropion /bjuːˈprəʊpɪən/ *noun.* L20.
[ORIGIN from BU(TANE + PROPIO(NIC + -*n* (perh. from -ONE).]
PHARMACOLOGY. An antidepressant drug, $C_{13}H_{18}ClNO$, which is also given to relieve the symptoms of nicotine withdrawal. Proprietary name ***Zyban***.

bur /bəː/ *noun*¹. Also **burr** (for other senses see BURR *noun*⁴). ME.
[ORIGIN Senses 1, 2 perh. of Scandinavian origin: cf. Danish *burre* bur, burdock, Swedish *kard-borre* burdock. Senses 3–5 perh. from French: cf. BURL *noun*¹, *bourre* vine bud.]
1 A rough or prickly seed vessel or flower head of a plant, *esp.* the flower head of the burdock; also, the husk of the chestnut. ME. ▸**b** *fig.* Something which clings like a bur; a person who is hard to shake off. L16.
bur in the throat a thing that appears to stick in the throat.
2 A plant which produces burs. L15.
3 The rounded knob forming the base of a deer's horn. L16.
4 a A knob or knot in a tree. E18. ▸**b** An ornamental (esp. walnut) veneer, containing knots. L19.
5 The female catkin of the hop before fertilization. E19.
– COMB.: **bur-marigold** any of several plants constituting the genus *Bidens*, of the composite family, with flat yellow flower heads; **bur oak** (the wood of) a N. American oak, *Quercus macrocarpa*, with large fringed acorn cups; **bur-parsley** either of two umbelliferous plants, *Caucalis platycarpos* and *Turgenia latifolia*, with bristly fruits; **bur-reed** any of several aquatic plants constituting the genus *Sparganium*, with globose flower heads; **bur walnut** walnut wood containing knots, used as a veneer; **bur-weed** = *cocklebur* s.v. COCKLE *noun*¹.

bur *noun*² var. of BURR *noun*¹.

bur *noun*³ var. of BURR *noun*⁴.

buran /ˈbuːrɑːn/ *noun.* M19.
[ORIGIN Russian from Turkic *boran*.]
In the steppes, a snowstorm, *esp.* one accompanied by high winds; a blizzard.

burb /bəːb/ *noun.* Also **'burb**. *colloq.* (orig. *US*). L20.
[ORIGIN Abbreviation.]
A suburb or suburban area. Freq. in ***the burbs***.

> D. GAINES Being different was a problem in the 'burbs to begin with.

burble /ˈbəːb(ə)l/ *noun.* ME.
[ORIGIN from the verb.]
1 A bubble; bubbling. Long *obsolete* exc. *Scot.* ME.
2 A pimple, a boil. Long *obsolete* exc. *dial.* LME.
3 A murmurous flow of words. L19.

burble /ˈbəːb(ə)l/ *verb.* ME.
[ORIGIN Imit.: cf. Spanish *borbollar* bubble, gush, *barbullar* talk loud and fast, Italian *borbugliare*.]
1 *verb intrans.* Bubble. Long *obsolete* exc. *Scot.* ME.
2 *verb intrans. & trans.* Speak or say murmurously or in a rambling manner; make a murmuring noise. L19.
3 *verb intrans.* AERONAUTICS. Of an airflow: break up into turbulence. Chiefly as ***burbling*** *verbal noun.* E20.
– COMB.: **burble point**: at which the smooth flow of air over an aerofoil is broken up.

burbot /ˈbəːbət/ *noun.* ME.
[ORIGIN Old French *borbete* (mod. *bourbotte*), prob. from Old French *borbe* mud, slime.]
A freshwater fish, *Lota lota*, of the cod family, with a broad head and barbels.

Burchell's zebra /bəːtʃ(ə)lz ˈziːbrə, ˈzɛbrə/ *noun phr.* M20.
[ORIGIN from William John *Burchell* (1782–1863), English naturalist.]
The common zebra, *Equus burchellii*, which has broad stripes and a striped belly, and is abundant on the E. African savannah.

burd /bəːd/ *noun.* Long *obsolete* exc. *poet.* ME.
[ORIGIN Unknown.]
A woman, a lady, a maiden.

burden /ˈbəːd(ə)n/ *noun.* Also (*arch.*) **burthen** /ˈbəːð(ə)n/.
[ORIGIN Old English *byrþen* = Old Saxon *burþinnia*, from West Germanic, from base of BIRTH *noun*¹: see -EN². In senses 6–8 conf. with BOURDON.]
1 That which is borne; a load (*lit.*, or *fig.* of labour, duty, sorrow, etc.). OE. ▸**b** An obligatory expense. M17.

> E. M. FORSTER Carrying a burden of acorns. E. GLASGOW I'd rather die . . than be a burden. E. ROOSEVELT The burden of training a family.

burden of proof the obligation to prove a controversial assertion, falling upon the person who makes it; LAW onus probandi.
the White man's burden: see WHITE *adjective*.
2 The bearing of loads. Chiefly in phrs. below. ME.
beast of burden: see BEAST *noun*. ***ship of burden*** a merchant ship.
3 A load, as a measure of quantity. Now only the carrying capacity of a ship, as a measure of weight; tonnage. LME.
4 In biblical translations translating Hebrew *maśśā'* (*Zech.* 12:1 etc.): an oracle, an oracular judgement. (Understood as) a burdensome or heavy lot or fate. *arch.* LME.

†**5 a** That which is borne in the womb; a child. L15–M17. ▸**b** That which is borne by the soil; produce, crop. E16–M19.
6 The bass or undersong of a melody; the drone of a bagpipe. Now *rare* or *obsolete*. L16.
7 The refrain or chorus of a song. L16.
8 *fig.* The chief theme or gist of a poem, book, speech, etc. M17.
■ †**burdened** *adjective* (*rare*, Shakes.) imposed as a burden: only in L16. †**burdenous** *adjective* (*a*) burdensome; (*b*) oppressed: E16–E19. **burdensome** *adjective* (*a*) of the nature of a burden, oppressive, wearisome; †(*b*) *US* capable of carrying a good burden: M16. **burdensomely** *adverb* (*rare*) E17. **burdensomeness** *noun* L16.

burden /ˈbəːd(ə)n/ *verb trans.* Also (*arch.*) **burthen** /ˈbəːð(ə)n/. M16.
[ORIGIN from the noun.]
1 Lay a burden on, load, (*lit.* & *fig.*); encumber, oppress. M16.
†**2** Charge (a person) *with* (an accusation); lay as a charge *upon*. M16–L18.

burdock /ˈbəːdɒk/ *noun*. L16.
[ORIGIN from BUR *noun*¹ + DOCK *noun*¹.]
Any of several coarse plants constituting the genus *Arctium*, of the composite family, with purplish-red flower heads, prickly fruits, and large leaves like those of the dock.

burdoun *noun* var. of BOURDON.

bure /bjʊə/ *noun*. L16.
[ORIGIN French: see BUREAU.]
A coarse woollen stuff.

bureau /ˈbjʊərəʊ/ *noun*. Pl. **-x** /-z/, **-s**. L17.
[ORIGIN French (Old French *burel*), orig. = woollen stuff, baize (used for covering writing desks), prob. from *bure* var. of *buire* dark brown from Proto-Romance alt. of Latin *burrus* fiery red from Greek *purros* red.]
1 A writing desk with drawers for papers etc. L17. ▸**b** A chest of drawers. *N. Amer.* E19.
2 An office, esp. for the transaction of public business; a department of public administration. L17. ▸**b** An office or business with a specified function; an agency for the coordination of related activities, the distribution of information, etc. E20.
b *information bureau*, *marriage bureau*, etc. **bureau de change** /byro də ʃɑ̃ʒ, ˌbjʊərəʊ də ˈʃɒʒ/ [French, lit. 'office of exchange'] an establishment at which customers can exchange foreign money.

bureaucracy /bjʊ(ə)ˈrɒkrəsi/ *noun*. Also †**-cratie**. E19.
[ORIGIN French *bureaucratie*: see BUREAU, -CRACY.]
(Government by) a central administrative group, esp. one not accountable to the public etc.; officials of such a group collectively; excessive official routine.

bureaucrat /ˈbjʊərəkrat/ *noun*. M19.
[ORIGIN French *bureaucrate*: see BUREAU, -CRAT.]
An official, esp. an unimaginative or doctrinaire one, in a bureaucracy; a person who endeavours to centralize administrative power.
■ **bureaucratˈese** *noun* the language or jargon of bureaucrats or bureaucracy L20. **bureauˈcratic** *adjective* of or pertaining to bureaucracy; excessively concerned with official routine: M19. **bureauˈcratically** *adverb* M19. **buˌreaucratiˈzation** *noun* transformation into a bureaucracy; making bureaucratic: E20. **bureaucratize** *verb trans.* transform into a bureaucracy; make bureaucratic: L19.

†**bureaucratie** *noun* var. of BUREAUCRACY.

†**burel** *noun*. ME–E18.
[ORIGIN Old French: see BUREAU.]
A coarse woollen cloth, frieze; a garment of this; plain clothing.

burette /bjʊˈrɛt/ *noun*. Also *-**et**. M19.
[ORIGIN French.]
A graduated glass tube with tap, used for measuring small quantities of liquid in chemical analysis.

burfi /ˈbəːfiː/ *noun*. Also **barfi** /ˈbʌrfiː/. M19.
[ORIGIN Urdu, from Persian *barfī* icy, snowy, also denoting a kind of sweet decorated with silver leaf.]
An Indian sweet made from boiled milk solids and sugar and typically flavoured with cardamom or nuts.

burg /bəːg/ *noun*. M18.
[ORIGIN Sense 1 from Latin *burgus* (see BURGESS); sense 2 from German *Burg* (see BOROUGH).]
1 *hist.* An ancient or medieval fortress or walled town. M18.
2 A town, a city. *N. Amer. colloq.* M19.

burgage /ˈbəːgɪdʒ/ *noun*. *obsolete* exc. *hist.* LME.
[ORIGIN medieval Latin *burgagium*, from Latin *burgus*: see BURGESS, -AGE.]
1 LAW. More fully ***burgage tenure***. A tenure by which lands, tenements, etc., in towns or cities were held from the lord for an annual rent or service. LME.
2 A freehold property in a borough; a house etc. held by burgage tenure. LME.

burgee /bəːˈdʒiː/ *noun*. M18.
[ORIGIN Uncertain: perh. from French *bourgeois* (see BURGESS) = master, owner.]
A triangular or swallow-tailed flag flown by yachts etc., usu. bearing distinguishing colours or the emblem of a yacht club or sailing club.

burgeon /ˈbəːdʒ(ə)n/ *noun*. Now *literary*. ME.
[ORIGIN Old French *borjon*, *bur-* (mod. *bourgeon*), from Proto-Romance from late Latin *burra* wool.]
A young shoot or bud; a new growth.

burgeon /ˈbəːdʒ(ə)n/ *verb*. Now *literary*. ME.
[ORIGIN Old French & mod. French *bourgeonner*, from *bourgeon*: see BURGEON *noun*.]
1 *verb intrans.* Put out shoots or buds; spring forth as a young shoot or shoots; *fig.* begin to develop rapidly. ME.
> G. PEELE The watery flowers burgen all in ranks. SIR W. SCOTT A hydra whose heads burgeoned . . as fast as they were cut off. P. USTINOV A burgeoning country, in the grip of an industrial revolution.

2 *verb trans.* Put out as a young shoot or shoots; develop rapidly. Long *rare*. LME.

burger /ˈbəːgə/ *noun*. *colloq.* (orig. *US*). M20.
[ORIGIN Abbreviation.]
A hamburger. Also as 2nd elem. of combs. with specification of ingredients, as ***beefburger***, ***cheeseburger***, ***nutburger***, etc.

burgess /ˈbəːdʒɪs/ *noun*. ME.
[ORIGIN Anglo-Norman *burgeis*, Old French *borjois* (mod. *bourgeois*) from Proto-Romance, from Latin *burgus* castle, fort (in medieval Latin fortified town, BOROUGH) + *-ensis* (see -ESE).]
1 An inhabitant of a borough having full municipal rights; a citizen. ME. ▸**b** *hist.* A Member of Parliament for a borough, corporate town, or university. L15.
2 A magistrate or member of the governing body of a town. *hist.* exc. *US*. ME.
– COMB.: **burgess oath** *hist.*: taken by a burgess, swearing acceptance of the authorized religion of the realm.
■ **burgessdom** *noun* (*rare*) the body of burgesses M17. **burgessship** *noun* the status and privileges of a burgess LME.

burggrave *noun* var. of BURGRAVE.

burgh /ˈbʌrə/ *noun*. *Scot.* or *hist.* See also BROCH. LME.
[ORIGIN Var. of BOROUGH.]
A borough, a chartered town.
royal burgh: see ROYAL *adjective*.
– COMB.: **burgh-bote** *hist.* a tax for the repair of fortifications; **burghmote** *hist.* the judicial assembly of a borough.
■ **burghal** /ˈbəːg(ə)l/ *adjective* of or pertaining to a burgh L16.

burgher /ˈbəːgə/ *noun*. ME.
[ORIGIN from BURGH + -ER¹, partly from German or Dutch *burger*, from *burg* BOROUGH.]
1 An inhabitant of a borough or chartered town (now *arch.* or *joc.*); a freeman or citizen of a foreign town. ME.
> P. LARKIN Not the sort of thing the sturdy burghers of Manchester would wish to read.

2 *hist.* (**B-**.) A member of the section of the Secession Church in Scotland which upheld the legality of the burgess oath. Cf. ANTIBURGHER. M18.
3 *S. AFR. HISTORY.* A citizen of the Cape not employed by the Dutch East India Company; a citizen of a Boer republic. M18.
4 In Sri Lanka: a descendant of a Dutch or Portuguese colonist. E19.
– COMB.: **burghermaster** (*rare*) = BURGOMASTER.
■ **burgherly** *adjective* of or characteristic of a burgher M18. **burghership** *noun* the rights and privileges of a burgher M16.

burghul /bəːˈguːl/ *noun*. Also **-gul**. E20.
[ORIGIN Arabic *burġul* from Persian *burġūl* var. of *bulġūr*: see BULGAR *noun*².]
= BULGAR *noun*².

burglar /ˈbəːglə/ *noun* & *verb*. M16.
[ORIGIN Law French †*burgler* (cf. Anglo-Norman *burgur*), Anglo-Latin *burg(u)lator*, app. from base meaning 'pillage'.]
▸ **A** *noun*. A person who is guilty of burglary. M16.
cat burglar: see CAT *noun*¹.
– COMB.: **burglar alarm** (a device with) an alarm that sounds if a house etc. is broken into.
▸ **B** *verb trans.* & *intrans.* = BURGLE *verb*. Now *rare*. L19.
■ **burglarize** *verb trans.* & *intrans.* = BURGLE *verb* L19.

burglarious /bəːˈglɛːrɪəs/ *adjective*. M18.
[ORIGIN from BURGLARY + -OUS: cf. *felonious*.]
Of or pertaining to burglary; like a burglar.
■ **burglariously** *adverb* E19.

burglary /ˈbəːgləri/ *noun*. E16.
[ORIGIN Law French †*burglarie* (cf. Anglo-Norman *b(o)urgerie*, Anglo-Latin *burgaria*), formed as BURGLAR: see -Y³.]
LAW. **1** The crime of entering a building (in English law formerly by night only) with intent to commit an arrestable offence. Cf. HOUSEBREAKING. E16.
2 An act of so entering a building. E17.
– NOTE: In English law before 1968, burglary was a crime under statute and in common law; since 1968 it has been a statutory crime only.

burgle /ˈbəːg(ə)l/ *verb* & *noun*. Orig. *joc.* & *colloq.* L19.
[ORIGIN Back-form. from BURGLAR.]
▸ **A** *verb*. **1** *verb intrans.* Commit burglary. L19.
2 *verb trans.* Rob (a place or person) by burglary; steal (goods) by burglary. L19.
▸ **B** *noun*. A burglary. *rare*. L19.

burgomaster /ˈbəːgəmɑːstə/ *noun*. L16.
[ORIGIN Dutch *burgemeester* (both senses), from *burg* (see BOROUGH) + *meester*, assim. to MASTER *noun*¹.]
1 The mayor of a Dutch or Flemish town. L16.
2 The glaucous gull, *Larus hyperboreus*. L17.

burgonet /ˈbəːgənɛt/ *noun*. L16.
[ORIGIN French *bourguignotte*, perh. fem. of *bourgignot* Burgundian, with assim. to -ET¹.]
hist. A visored helmet that can be fitted or attached to the gorget or neck-piece. Also, a pikeman's light steel cap.

†**Burgonian** *noun* & *adjective*. M16–E17.
[ORIGIN from French *Bourgogne* (see BURGUNDY) + -IAN.]
= BURGUNDIAN *noun* & *adjective*.

burgoo /bəːˈguː/ *noun*. L17.
[ORIGIN formed as BURGHUL.]
1 A thick porridge. *nautical slang*. L17.
2 Soup or stew for an outdoor meal. *N. Amer.* M18.

burgrave /ˈbəːgreɪv/ *noun*. Also **-gg-**. M16.
[ORIGIN German *Burggraf*, from *Burg* BOROUGH + *Graf* GRAVE *noun*².]
hist. The governor or (*esp.*) hereditary ruler of a German town or castle.

burgul *noun* var. of BURGHUL.

Burgund /ˈbəːgʌnd/ *noun*.
[ORIGIN Old English *Burgendan*, *-as* pl. from late Latin *Burgundii*, *-iones* pl.: ult. origin unknown.]
hist. A member of the Germanic Burgundians. Usu. in *pl.*

Burgundian /bəːˈgʌndɪən/ *noun* & *adjective*. E17.
[ORIGIN from *Burgundy* (see BURGUNDY) + -AN; partly from late Latin *Burgundii* (see BURGUND). Cf. earlier BURGONIAN.]
▸ **A** *noun*. A native or inhabitant of Burgundy, France. Also *hist.*, a member of a Germanic people who inhabited a region from the Main to the Vistula and who entered Gaul and established the kingdom of Burgundy in the 5th cent. AD. E17.
▸ **B** *adjective*. Of or pertaining to Burgundy or the Burgundians. M17.

burgundy /ˈbəːgəndi/ *noun* & *adjective*. In sense A.1 also **B-**. L17.
[ORIGIN *Burgundy* (French *Bourgogne*) a region of eastern France (formerly a duchy, earlier a kingdom) from medieval Latin *Burgundia*, from late Latin *Burgundii*: see BURGUND.]
▸ **A** *noun*. **1** A wine made in Burgundy (without specification usu. red wine). Also, similar wine from other countries. L17.
2 The red colour of this wine. L19.
– COMB.: **Burgundy pitch** resin from the Norway spruce.
▸ **B** *adjective*. Of the red colour of burgundy. L19.

burh *noun* see BOROUGH.

burhel *noun* var. of BHARAL.

buriable /ˈbɛrɪəb(ə)l/ *adjective*. L16.
[ORIGIN from BURY + -ABLE.]
Able to be buried.

burial /ˈbɛrɪəl/ *noun*. Also (earlier) †**buriels**.
[ORIGIN Old English *byrġels* = Old Saxon *burgisli* from Germanic, formed as BURY: see -LE¹. Early (Middle English) taken erron. as pl.]
1 A burying place, a grave, a tomb. *obsolete* exc. ARCHAEOLOGY. OE.
2 The action of burying something, esp. a dead body; an interment; a funeral. ME.
> BURKE Every Minister shall keep a register of births, burials and marriages.

– PHRASES: ***crouched burial***: see CROUCH *verb* 1. ***secondary burial***: see SECONDARY *adjective*.
– COMB.: **burial ground** a cemetery; **burial service** a religious service held at a funeral.

Buriat *noun* & *adjective* var. of BURYAT.

†**buriels** *noun* see BURIAL.

burier /ˈbɛrɪə/ *noun*. OE.
[ORIGIN from BURY + -ER¹.]
A person who or thing which buries something or someone. Formerly also, a gravedigger.

burin /ˈbjʊərɪn/ *noun*. M17.
[ORIGIN French, rel. to Italian *burino* (*bulino*), perh. connected with Old High German *bora* boring tool: see BORE *verb*¹.]
A tool for engraving on copper or wood.

burk *noun* var. of BERK.

burka /ˈbəːkə, ˈbʊrkɑː/ *noun*¹. Also **burkha**, **burqa**. M19.
[ORIGIN Urdu (Persian) *burqa'* from Arabic *burqu'*.]
A long loose garment covering the whole body from head to feet, worn in public by women in some Muslim countries.

burka /ˈbʊəkə/ *noun*². L19.
[ORIGIN Russian.]
A long Caucasian cloak of felt or goat's hair.

burke *noun* var. of BERK.

burke /bəːk/ *verb trans.* E19.
[ORIGIN William *Burke*, executed at Edinburgh in 1829 for murdering by suffocation or strangulation to sell bodies for dissection.]
1 Kill (a person) to sell the body for dissection; suffocate or strangle secretly. *arch.* E19.
2 *fig.* Stifle, smother (publicity or inquiry); hush up, suppress (rumour); avoid (a problem). M19.

Burkinan /bəːˈkiːnən/ *adjective* & *noun*. L20.
[ORIGIN from *Burkina* (see below) + -AN.]
(A native or inhabitant) of Burkina Faso, an inland country of W. Africa. Cf. UPPER VOLTAN.

Burkitt /ˈbəːkɪt/ *noun*. **M20**.
[**ORIGIN** D. P. *Burkitt* (1911–93), Brit. surgeon.]
MEDICINE. ***Burkitt's lymphoma***, ***Burkitt tumour***, a malignant tumour of the lymphatic system occurring esp. in the jaw and viscera, and mostly affecting young children in tropical Africa.

burkundaz /bəːk(ə)nˈdɑːz/ *noun*. **L18**.
[**ORIGIN** Urdu *barqandāz* musketeer, from Persian, from Arabic *barq* lightning + Persian *andāz* thrower.]
hist. In the Indian subcontinent: an armed guard, a constable.

burl /bəːl/ *noun*[1] & *verb*. **LME**.
[**ORIGIN** Old French *bourle* tuft of wool, dim. of Old French & mod. French *bourre*, Spanish, Portuguese *borra* coarse wool, from late Latin *burra* wool: cf. **BUR** *noun*[1].]
▸ **A** *noun*. **1** A knot in wool or cloth. **LME**.
†**2** A pimple. **E–M17**.
3 A knot or excrescence in wood. *N. Amer*. **L19**.
▸ **B** *verb trans. & intrans*. Dress (cloth), esp. by removing knots or lumps. Now *rare*. **L15**.
■ **burler** *noun* **ME**.

burl *noun*[2] see **BIRL** *noun*.

burlap /ˈbəːlap/ *noun & adjective*. Orig. †**-ps**. **L17**.
[**ORIGIN** Unknown.]
(Made of) a coarse canvas esp. of jute for sacking etc.; (made of) a similar (finer) material for dress or furnishing.

burlesque /bəːˈlɛsk/ *adjective, noun, & verb*. **M17**.
[**ORIGIN** French from Italian *burlesco*, from *burla* ridicule, joke, fun, of unknown origin: see **-ESQUE**.]
▸ **A** *adjective*. †**1** Jocular, odd, grotesque. **M17–M19**.
2 Derisively or amusingly imitative; mock-heroic or mock-pathetic; bombastic. (Now chiefly of literary composition or dramatic representation.) **M17**.
▸ **B** *noun*. **1** Derisively or amusingly imitative literary or dramatic composition, bombast; mock-seriousness; an instance or example of this; (a) parody; (a) caricature. **M17**.
2 a *hist*. The concluding portion of a blackface minstrel entertainment, containing dialogue and sketches. *US*. **M19**. ▸**b** A kind of variety show, usu. featuring striptease. Orig. & chiefly *US*. **L19**.
▸ **C** *verb trans*. Imitate to deride or amuse; parody; caricature. **L17**.
■ **burlesquely** *adverb* **E19**. **burlesquer** *noun* (*a*) a person who burlesques; (*b*) an actor in burlesque drama: **M17**.

burletta /bəːˈlɛtə/ *noun*. *obsolete* exc. *hist*. **M18**.
[**ORIGIN** Italian, dim. of *burla*: see **BURLESQUE**, cf. **-ETTE**.]
A musical farce.

Burley /ˈbəːli/ *noun*[1]. Also **b-**. **L19**.
[**ORIGIN** Unknown.]
A variety of tobacco, pale or dark, grown mainly in Kentucky, USA.

burley *noun*[2], **burlie** *noun* see **BYRLAW**.

burly /ˈbəːli/ *adjective*. **ME**.
[**ORIGIN** Prob. formed as **BOWER** *noun*[1] + **-LY**[1]; perh. already in Old English: cf. Old High German *burlīh* exalted, stately.]
†**1** Stately, dignified, imposing. **ME–M17**. ▸**b** Of a thing: goodly, excellent. **LME–L19**.
2 Sturdy; big and strong; massively built. **LME**.

> E. B. **BROWNING** Burly oaks projecting from the line. R. **HAYMAN** The big, burly, bull-necked, . . successful business man.

3 Domineering; forceful; bluff, forthright. **L16**.

> J. H. **NEWMAN** As generous as they are hasty and burly. **GEOFFREY HILL** Against the burly air I strode.

■ **burlily** *adverb* **M19**. **burliness** *noun* **E17**.

Burman /ˈbəːmən/ *noun & adjective*. **E19**.
[**ORIGIN** formed as **BURMESE** + **-AN**.]
= **BURMESE**.

Burmese /bəːˈmiːz/ *adjective & noun*. **E19**.
[**ORIGIN** from *Burma* (see below) + **-ESE**.]
▸ **A** *adjective*. Of or pertaining to Burma (Myanmar), a country in SE Asia, its inhabitants, or their language. **E19**.
Burmese cat a breed of short-coated domestic cat. ***Burmese*** **ROSEWOOD**.
▸ **B** *noun*. Pl. same.
1 A native or inhabitant of Burma; *spec*. a member of the majority ethnic group of Burma. **E19**.
2 The Sino-Tibetan language of the Burmese people. **M19**.
3 = ***Burmese cat*** above. **M20**.

burn /bəːn/ *noun*[1]. Now *Scot. & N. English*.
[**ORIGIN** Old English *burna*, *burne*, *burn*, corresp. to Old Frisian *burna*, Middle Low German *borne*, *born*, Middle Dutch *borne* (Low German, Dutch *born*), repr. metath. var. of Germanic base of Old Saxon, Old High German *brunno* (Dutch *bron*, German *Brunnen*), Old Norse *brunnr*, Gothic *brunna*: cf. **BOURN** *noun*[1].]
A stream, a brook, a spring.

burn /bəːn/ *noun*[2]. **E16**.
[**ORIGIN** from the verb.]
1 The act or effect of burning; a mark or injury made by burning. **E16**.
slow burn *colloq*. (a state of) slowly mounting annoyance or anger.
2 The clearing of vegetation by burning; an area so cleared. *N. Amer., Austral., & NZ*. **L18**.
3 A smoke, a cigarette. *slang*. **M20**.
4 A spell of operation by a spacecraft's engine. **M20**.
5 A car race, a fast drive. *slang*. **M20**.
– **COMB.**: **burn-bag**, **burn-basket** *US*: for classified (esp. incriminating) material which is to be destroyed by burning.

burn /bəːn/ *verb*. Pa. t. **burned**, **burnt** /bəːnt/, †**brent**; pa. pple **burned**, **burnt**, (*dial*.) **brent** /brɛnt/. See also **BURNT** *ppl adjective*, **YBRENT**.
[**ORIGIN** Old English *birnan* var. of *brinnan* (branch I) = Old Saxon, Old High German, Gothic *brinnan*; Old English *bærnan* (branch II) = Old Saxon, Old High German *brennan* (German *brennen*), Old Norse *brenna*, Gothic *brannjan*: both from same Germanic base.]
▸ **I** *verb intrans*. **1** Of fire, a furnace, etc.: be in the state of activity characteristic of fire, be in combustion. **OE**. ▸**b** Of a spacecraft's engine: provide thrust. **M20**.

> A. **SILLITOE** A bright fire burned in the modernised grate. J. **RHYS** The flames burned straight.

2 Be on fire, be consumed by flames; undergo combustion; undergo oxidation with evolution of heat. **OE**. ▸**b** Undergo nuclear reactions producing energy. **M20**.

> **SHAKES.** *Rich. II* That hand shall burn in never-quenching fire That staggers thus my person. A. J. P. **TAYLOR** They were medieval towns, full of wooden houses, and burnt well. F. **HOYLE** All the oxygen would have been quickly consumed, since biomaterial burns very easily.

3 *fig*. Be passionate, rage; be consumed with emotion, longing, etc. **OE**.

> AV *Gen*. 44:18 Let not thine anger burne against thy seruant. R. L. **STEVENSON** I burn to see you on the gallows. G. **EWART** I burned with desire to distress you.

4 Be or become very hot; feel a sensation of heat, be inflamed. **OE**. ▸**b** *fig*. Be very close to the object sought (in games etc.). Cf. **HOT** *adjective* 8b. **E19**.
one's ears burn one feels (rightly or wrongly) that one is being talked about.
5 Give light by combustion or heat; glow, shine, appear as if on fire. **OE**.

> **SHAKES.** *Jul. Caes*. How ill this taper burns! E. **O'NEILL** One bulb burning doesn't cost much. B. **SPENCER** Snow on pine gorges can burn blue like Persian cats.

6 Suffer the effects of combustion, heat, the sun's rays, acid, extreme cold, etc.; be scorched, blackened, parched, or tanned; be charred by overcooking. **ME**. ▸**b** Cause injury or pain by the action of fire, heat, extreme cold, etc.; (of acid etc.) eat its way *into* by burning. **M17**.

> V. **WOOLF** Bones bleach and burn far away in Indian sands. T. **FRISBY** Would you like to make sure that nothing burns in the kitchen? **b** J. H. **NEWMAN** Ice which blisters may be said to burn.

7 Suffer death by fire. *arch*. **ME**.

> T. **FORREST** Here . . women often . . burn with their deceased husbands.

▸ **II** *verb trans*. **8** Of fire: consume, destroy. Of a person etc.: cause to be alight, or to be destroyed or consumed by fire. **OE**. ▸**b** Make a burnt offering of; sacrifice or execute by burning. **ME**. ▸**c** Consume as fuel for heat or light; oxidize with evolution of heat; use the nuclear energy of. **L16**. ▸**d** *fig*. Spend or use freely. *slang*. **L19**. ▸**e** Smoke (tobacco). *slang*. **E20**.

> **SPENSER** The fire which them to ashes brent. P. **SHAFFER** It's fantastically dangerous to burn a naked flame in this room! A. S. **BYATT** The pierced dustbin in which he burned garden rubbish. **b** **SHAKES.** *1 Hen. VI* O, burn her, burn her! Hanging is too good. **MILTON** One [altar] of Syrian mode whereon to burn His odious offerings. **c** O. **LODGE** Burning 1,000 tons of coal. *Lancet* The thesis . . that muscles could burn sugar only.

burn alive kill by burning. **burn one's boats**, **burn one's bridges**, **burn one's ships** commit oneself irrevocably to a course of action. **have to burn** have (money etc.) in great abundance. ***pare and burn***: see **PARE** *verb*. **b burn daylight** *arch*. use artificial light in daytime; waste day(light). **c** ***burn the candle at both ends***: see **CANDLE** *noun*. ***burn midnight oil***, ***burn the midnight oil***: see **OIL** *noun*.
9 Produce the effects of fire or heat upon, expose to fire or heat; scorch, blacken; char or cause to adhere by overcooking; calcine, bake. **OE**. ▸**b** Make by burning. **ME**.

> T. **D'URFEY** 'Till Pudding and Dumpling are burnt to Pot. M. **DRABBLE** It was burned black on the outside and raw in the middle. J. G. **FARRELL** No clay or shale that you can burn into bricks. **b** **DEFOE** These [earthen vessels] I burnt in the fire.

burn to a chip, ***burn to a cinder***, ***burn to a crisp***, ***burn to a frazzle***, etc. **b burn a hole in one's pocket** (esp. of money) make one wish to spend or dispose of it.
10 Injure or cause pain to by the action of fire or heat. **ME**. ▸**b** Cauterize; brand. **ME**. ▸†**c** Infect with (esp. venereal) sores. **E16–M18**. ▸**d** *fig*. Swindle, cheat. *slang*. **M17**.

> S. **HILL** You cannot manage it without burning your mouth. B. **ENGLAND** MacConnachie's wrist, where the rope had burned it, was suppurating a little.

burn one's fingers *fig*. suffer, esp. financially, for meddling or rashness.
11 *fig*. Inflame or consume with emotion etc.; *slang* annoy, rile. **ME**.

> **DRYDEN** With two fair Eyes his Mistress burns his Breast.

12 Produce an effect on like that of fire or heat, e.g. by corrosive substances, extreme cold, sunlight, etc.; injure or hurt thus; corrode, wither, parch, tan. **ME**.

> **DRYDEN** Goats . . graze the Field, and burn it bare. W. S. **MAUGHAM** His face and neck burnt brown by the hot sun.

13 Copy or record sound, data, etc., on to (a compact disc). **L20**.
– **WITH ADVERBS IN SPECIALIZED SENSES**: **burn away** diminish to nothing by burning. **burn down** (*a*) burn less vigorously as fuel fails; (*b*) destroy (a building etc.) by burning. **burn in** (*a*) imprint by burning (*lit. & fig*.); (*b*) *PHOTOGRAPHY* darken selected areas of a photographic print by allowing additional exposure during the printing process; (*c*) test a device for defects by operating it continuously (sometimes at an elevated temperature) for a fixed period of time; (*d*) mark a video tape with captions or timing information. **burn low** nearly go out. **burn off** (*a*) (cause to) evaporate, disappear, etc., under the action of heat; (*b*) *N. Amer., Austral., & NZ* clear (land) for cultivation by burning vegetation; burn (vegetation) to clear land. **burn out** (*a*) burn away, (make) fail by burning; consume the contents of by burning, *fig*. exhaust the powers of; (*b*) make homeless by burning a dwelling, drive out *of* by burning a place. **burn up** (*a*) get rid of, consume completely, by fire; (*b*) flash into a blaze; (*c*) *N. Amer. slang* be or make furious; (*d*) *colloq*. traverse at high speed.
– **COMB.**: ***burning glass***: see **GLASS** *noun*; **burn-in** (*a*) a continuous period of operation undergone by an electronic device (sometimes at an elevated temperature), to check for defects; (*b*) the formation of a permanent mark on a television or computer screen which occurs when a very bright image has been displayed for too long; (*c*) a video recording feature which enables captions or timing information to be incorporated on to a tape; **burn-off** *N. Amer., Austral., & NZ* the clearing of land for cultivation by burning vegetation; **burn-out** destruction by fire; failure of an electrical component etc. through overheating; exhaustion, disillusion, or depression associated with occupational stress; **burn rate** the rate at which a new company spends its initial capital until it starts earning a return on investment; **burn-up** (*a*) consumption of fuel; (*b*) *slang* a very fast drive or motorcycle ride etc.
■ **burnable** *adjective* able to be burnt or consumed by fire **E17**.

burned *ppl adjective* var. of **BURNT**.

burner /ˈbəːnə/ *noun*. **LME**.
[**ORIGIN** from **BURN** *verb* + **-ER**[1].]
1 A person who burns or consumes with fire. **LME**. ▸**b** With specifying adjective: a substance, esp. a fuel, that burns in the specified manner. **L20**.
2 A person who produces charcoal etc. by burning. **LME**.
3 An appliance which provides a flame for heating, lighting, etc.; the part of a lamp, cooker, etc., that emits a flame; *N. Amer*. the heating element of an electric cooker. **L18**.
Argand burner, ***Bunsen burner***, ***fishtail burner***, ***oil burner***, etc. **on the back burner** *slang* receiving little attention, having a low priority. **on the front burner** *slang* receiving much attention, having a high priority.
4 A device for producing a compact disc or DVD by copying from an original or master copy. **L20**.

burnet /ˈbəːnɪt/ *adjective & noun*. **ME**.
[**ORIGIN** Old French *brunet* adjective (see **BRUNETTE**), *brunete*, *burnete* nouns = brown cloth, brown-flowered plant, dims. of *brun* **BROWN** *adjective*: see **-ET**[1].]
▸ †**A** *adjective*. Of a dark brown colour. **ME–E17**.
▸ **B** *noun*. †**1** A superior wool cloth, orig. of dark brown colour. Only in **ME**.
2 A plant of the genus *Sanguisorba*, of the rose family, with pinnate leaves and globular heads of apetalous flowers; *esp*. either of two Eurasian plants, *S. officinalis* (more fully ***great burnet***) of damp meadows, with ovate leaflets, and *S. minor* (more fully ***salad burnet***) of calcareous grassland, with roundish leaflets tasting of cucumber. **LME**.
3 A day-flying moth of the genus *Zygaena*, typically dark green with crimson-spotted wings. Also ***burnet moth***. **L18**.
– **COMB.**: ***burnet moth***: see sense B.3 above; **burnet rose** a small wild rose, *Rosa pimpinellifolia*, with white flowers and leaves like those of salad burnet; **burnet saxifrage** an umbellifer of the genus *Pimpinella*; *esp*. the Eurasian species *P. saxifraga* of dry grassland, with rosette leaves freq. like those of salad burnet.

Burnham /ˈbəːnəm/ *noun*. **E20**.
[**ORIGIN** Viscount *Burnham* (1862–1933), first chairman of the committee.]
Burnham scale, a national salary scale for teachers in maintained schools in England and Wales, recommended by a standing committee (***Burnham committee***) of Local Education Authorities' and teachers' representatives (established 1919).

burning /ˈbəːnɪŋ/ *adjective*. **OE**.
[**ORIGIN** from **BURN** *verb* + **-ING**[2].]
1 *lit*. That burns; that is on fire or very hot. **OE**.
burning bush [with allus. to *Exodus* 3] (*a*) any of various shrubs with red fruits or red autumn foliage; (*b*) = **FRAXINELLA** (because of its production of flammable volatile essences). **burning mountain** *arch*. a volcano.
2 *fig*. Ardent, passionate; flagrant; exciting, hotly discussed, controversial. **ME**.

> **STEELE** It is really a burning shame this Man should be tolerated. **SOUTHEY** With copious tears Of burning anger. A. J. P. **TAYLOR** There was no burning question to excite the passions of the electors. M. **GEE** Moira Penny had one burning ambition.

■ **burningly** *adverb* **ME**.

burnish /ˈbəːnɪʃ/ *verb*[1] & *noun*. ME.
[ORIGIN Old French *burniss-* lengthened stem of *burnir* var. of *brunir* make brown, from *brun* BROWN *adjective*: see -ISH[2].]
▸ **A** *verb*. **1** *verb trans.* Polish (esp. metal) by rubbing. ME. ▸**b** Of a stag: rub the dead velvet from (the antlers or head). LME.

> WORDSWORTH The whole wide lake . . like a burnished mirror glows.

2 *verb trans.* Make bright or glossy in any way; spread with lustre. LME.

> MILTON Fruit burnisht with Golden Rind, Hung amiable. D. LESSING The autumn green of the trees was gilded and burnished with the low sunlight.

3 *verb intrans.* Become bright or glossy; shine, gleam. E17.

> SWIFT I've seen a snake . . Burnish, and make a gaudy show.

▸ **B** *noun*. A polish by rubbing; burnished appearance, lustre. *rare*. M17.
■ **burnisher** *noun* a person who or thing which burnishes something; a tool for burnishing: ME.

burnish /ˈbəːnɪʃ/ *verb*[2] *intrans. obsolete* exc. *dial.* LME.
[ORIGIN Unknown.]
Grow plump or stout; increase in girth.

burnous /bəːˈnuːs/ *noun*. Also **-oose** & other vars. L16.
[ORIGIN French from Arabic *burnus*, *-ūs*.]
An Arab or Moorish hooded cloak; a fashion garment resembling this.

Burnsian /ˈbəːnzɪən/ *adjective* & *noun*. E20.
[ORIGIN from *Burns* (see below) + -IAN.]
▸ **A** *adjective*. Of or pertaining to the Scottish poet Robert Burns (1759–96); characteristic of Burns or his style. E20.
▸ **B** *noun*. An admirer or student of Burns or his works. E20.
■ **Burnsiˈana** *noun pl.* [-ANA] publications or other items concerning or associated with Burns L19.

burnside /ˈbəːnsʌɪd/ *noun*. *US. arch.* L19.
[ORIGIN General Ambrose *Burnside* (1824–81), US army officer.]
sing. & (freq.) in *pl.* Moustache and whiskers with no beard on the chin.

burnt /bəːnt/ *ppl adjective*. Also **burned** /bəːnt, bəːnd/. ME.
[ORIGIN pa. pple of BURN *verb*.]
Consumed by fire; affected, damaged, or injured by fire or extreme heat; charred, scorched.
burnt almond an almond enclosed in caramelized sugar. **burnt cork** charred cork used esp. to blacken the face, hands, etc. **burnt cream** = *crème brûlée* s.v. CRÈME 1. **burnt ochre**, **burnt sienna**, **burnt umber**, etc.: having a deeper colour obtained by calcination. **burnt offering** a religious sacrifice offered by burning. **burnt-out** *adjective* (*a*) gutted or driven out by fire; exhausted, spent; (*b*) cured of leprosy (esp. in *burnt-out case*); also *fig.* passing into sense (a). ***burnt sienna***: see ***burnt ochre*** above. **burnt taste**: like that of food that has been charred. ***burnt umber***: see ***burnt ochre*** above.

buroo /bəˈruː/ *noun*. *colloq.* (orig. & chiefly *Scot.*). Also **brew**, **broo**, /bruː/. M20.
[ORIGIN Alt. of BUREAU.]
A social security office, a labour exchange.
on the buroo receiving unemployment benefit.

burp /bəːp/ *noun* & *verb*. *colloq.* (orig. *US*). M20.
[ORIGIN Imit.]
▸ **A** *noun*. A belch. M20.
– COMB.: **burp gun** *US* an automatic pistol.
▸ **B** *verb intrans.* & *trans.* (Cause to) belch. M20.

burpee /ˈbəːpiː/ *noun*. Also **-ie** /-ɪ/. M20.
[ORIGIN R. H. *Burpee* (b. 1897), US psychologist.]
A physical exercise with a squat thrust between standing positions.

burqa *noun* var. of BURKA *noun*[1].

burr /bəː/ *noun*[1]. Also **bur**. LME.
[ORIGIN Abbreviation of BURROW: cf. BROCH.]
1 A circle. *rare* in *gen.* sense. LME.
†**2** A broad iron ring on a tilting spear. L15–E17.
3 A washer placed on the small end of a rivet before the end is swaged down. E17.
4 A luminous ring round the moon etc., a halo. M17.
– COMB.: **burr-pump** NAUTICAL a bilge pump with the piston so made as not to require a valve.

burr /bəː/ *noun*[2]. L16.
[ORIGIN Unknown.]
A sweetbread.

burr /bəː/ *noun*[3]. L16.
[ORIGIN Unknown.]
The external meatus of the ear; the opening leading to the tympanum.

burr /bəː/ *noun*[4]. Also **bur** (for other senses see BUR *noun*[1]). In branch II also **buhr**. E17.
[ORIGIN Var. of BUR *noun*[1].]
▸**I 1** A rough edge left on cut or punched metal, paper, etc. E17.
2 In full ***burr-drill***. A dentist's or surgeon's tool for producing a smooth cavity. M19.
▸ **II** More fully (esp. in sense 3) ***burr-stone***.
3 A hard siliceous rock used for millstones, whetstones, etc.; a piece of this; a millstone or whetstone of this. M17.
4 A kind of limestone used for building, containing hard siliceous inclusions. *dial.* E19.
5 A mass of vitrified brick; a clinker. E19.

burr /bəː/ *noun*[5] & *verb*. M18.
[ORIGIN Prob. imit., but perh. transf. use of BURR *noun*[4].]
▸ **A** *noun*. **1** A rough sounding of the phoneme /r/ (repr. by the letter r); *spec.* the uvular trill characteristic of Northumberland. M18. ▸**b** *loosely*. A rough or dialectal pronunciation. M19.
2 A whirr; a vibratory, buzzing, or rushing noise. E19.
▸ **B** *verb*. **1** *verb intrans.* Make a buzzing or whirring noise. L18.
2 *verb intrans.* Use a uvular trill; use a rough or dialectal pronunciation; speak indistinctly. E19.
3 *verb trans.* Pronounce with a burr. M19.

burr *noun*[6] var. of BUR *noun*[1].

burra /ˈbʌrə/ *adjective*. E19.
[ORIGIN Hindi *barā*, *barā* great, greatest.]
In the Indian subcontinent: prominent, high-ranking, great. Only in ***burra sahib***, ***burra memsahib***, and similar phrases used as modes of reference to important people.

burras *noun* var. of BARRAS.

burrawang /ˈbʌrəwaŋ/ *noun*. Also **-wong** /-wɒŋ/. *Austral.* E19.
[ORIGIN Dharuk *buruwan*.]
A cycad of the genus *Macrozamia*; a seed of such a tree.

burrel-fly /ˈbʌrəlflʌɪ/ *noun*. M17.
[ORIGIN Unknown.]
The gadfly.

burrito /bʌˈriːtəʊ/ *noun*. Pl. **-os**. M20.
[ORIGIN Amer. Spanish, dim. of BURRO.]
A tortilla rolled round a filling of spiced beef and other ingredients.

burro /ˈbʌrəʊ/ *noun*. Chiefly *N. Amer.* Pl. **-os**. E19.
[ORIGIN Spanish.]
A small donkey used as a pack animal.

burrow /ˈbʌrəʊ/ *noun*[1]. Long *obsolete* exc. *dial.*
[ORIGIN Old English *beorg*, *beorh*, from *beorgan*: see BORROW *verb*[1].]
(A) shelter.

burrow /ˈbʌrəʊ/ *noun*[2]. ME.
[ORIGIN Var. of BOROUGH. Cf. BERRY *noun*[3].]
1 A hole or excavation in earth made by a rabbit, a fox, etc., as a place of shelter. ME. ▸**b** *transf.* & *fig.* Any secluded or small dwelling place or retreat. M17.
village burrow: see VILLAGE 3.
2 In *pl.* exc. *attrib.* Boroughs, towns; burgesses collectively. *Scot. arch.* LME.
– COMB.: **burrow-duck** *dial.* the shelduck; **burrows-town** *Scot. arch.* = ***BOROUGH-town***.

burrow /ˈbʌrəʊ/ *noun*[3]. *dial.* & *techn.* L15.
[ORIGIN Var. of BARROW *noun*[1].]
A heap or mound, esp. of mining refuse.

burrow /ˈbʌrəʊ/ *verb*. E17.
[ORIGIN from BURROW *noun*[2].]
1 *verb intrans.* Make a burrow; live in a burrow; hide oneself in or as in a burrow. E17.
burrowing owl a small American owl, *Speotyto cunicularia*, nesting in burrows.
2 *verb trans.* Hide in or as in a burrow (usu. in *pass.* of oneself); push *in* or *into* as in(to) a burrow. E17.

> G. CRABBE An infant . . Left by neglect, and burrowed in that bed. J. BUCHAN He . . burrowed a drowsy head into the cushions.

3 *verb intrans.* Bore or make one's way under the surface. E19.

> N. HAWTHORNE We were burrowing through its bewildering passages. B. ENGLAND He . . burrowed deep into the thick scrub.

burrow into *fig.* investigate the mysteries etc. of.
4 *verb trans.* Make (a hole etc., one's way) by excavating. M19.
■ **burrower** *noun* M19.

burru /ˈbʌruː/ *noun*. Also **buru**. E20.
[ORIGIN Perh. from Twi *búru* filthiness, sluttishness or Yoruba *buru* wicked.]
A Jamaican dance with provocative posturing; music or drumming to accompany this.

burry /ˈbəːri/ *adjective*. LME.
[ORIGIN from BUR *noun*[1] + -Y[1].]
Full of burs; rough, prickly.

bursa /ˈbəːsə/ *noun*. Pl. **-sae** /-siː/. E19.
[ORIGIN medieval Latin = bag, PURSE *noun*.]
ANATOMY. A fluid-filled sac of fibrous tissue, *esp.* one serving to lessen friction between moving parts, e.g. at a joint, or formed in response to unusual friction. Also, a pouch of the peritoneum.
bursa of Fabricius /fəˈbrɪʃəs/ [Latinized form of the name of Girolamo *Fabrici* (1533–1619), Italian anatomist] ORNITHOLOGY a glandular sac which opens into a bird's cloaca and is involved in the development of the bird's immune system.
■ **bursal** *adjective* of, pertaining to, or of the nature of a bursa M18.

bursar /ˈbəːsə/ *noun*. LME.
[ORIGIN Sense 1 from Old French & mod. French *boursier* or medieval Latin *bursarius*: see BURSARY, -AR[2], -ER[2]. Sense 2 from French *boursier*.]
1 A treasurer; a person in charge of the funds or other property of a college etc. LME.
domestic bursar: see DOMESTIC *adjective* 1. ***estates bursar***: see ESTATE *noun*.
2 A student who holds a bursary. Orig. *Scot.* M16.
■ **bursarship** *noun* (*a*) the position of a bursar; (*b*) a bursary for a student: E17.

bursarial /bəːˈsɛːrɪəl/ *adjective*. M19.
[ORIGIN from BURSAR + -IAL or BURSARY + -AL[1].]
Of or pertaining to a bursar or bursary.

bursary /ˈbəːsəri/ *noun*. LME.
[ORIGIN Sense 1 from medieval Latin *bursarius*, senses 2 & 3 from medieval Latin *bursaria* bursar's office (cf. Old French *bourserie* money coffer): see BURSA, -ARY[1].]
†**1** = BURSAR 1. LME–M16.
2 A treasury; the bursar's room at a college etc. L17.
3 An endowment given to a student. Orig. *Scot.* M18.

burse /bəːs/ *noun*. LME.
[ORIGIN Old French & mod. French *bourse* or medieval Latin BURSA; in sense 2 cf. BOURSE.]
1 A purse, *esp.* as the designation of one of the official insignia of the Lord Chancellor. LME. ▸**b** ECCLESIASTICAL. A receptacle for the corporal or linen cloth used to cover the elements in the Eucharist. M19.
2 A money market, an exchange, (= BOURSE). *obsolete* exc. *hist.* as below. M16.
the Burse *hist.* the Royal Exchange in Cornhill, London.
3 = BURSARY 3. M16. ▸†**b** A fund to provide bursaries. L17–M18.
4 A German college or academic hall. L16.

bursectomy /bəːˈsɛktəmi/ *noun*. E20.
[ORIGIN from BURSA: see -ECTOMY.]
Surgical removal or (hormonal) destruction of a bird's bursa of Fabricius, esp. in immunological research; an instance of this.
■ **burˈsectomize** *verb trans.* perform bursectomy on E20.

bursiform /ˈbəːsɪfɔːm/ *adjective*. M19.
[ORIGIN from BURSA + -I- + -FORM.]
Purse-shaped.

bursitis /bəːˈsʌɪtɪs/ *noun*. M19.
[ORIGIN from BURSA + -ITIS.]
Inflammation of a bursa.

burst /bəːst/ *noun*. See also BUST *noun*[2].
[ORIGIN Old English *byrst* = Old High German *brust* from Germanic base of BURST *verb*; branch II directly from the verb.]
▸†**I 1** Damage, injury, harm. OE–LME.
▸ **II 2** An act or the result of bursting open or splitting. ME.

> G. MEREDITH When beech-buds were near the burst.

3 A sudden and violent issuing out (of flame, light, gunfire, etc.); a vehement outbreak (of emotion, laughter, etc.); an explosion, an eruption; a pulse (of radiation etc.). LME. ▸**b** A sudden opening on the view. L18.

> SOUTHEY Burst after burst the innocuous thunders brake. P. G. WODEHOUSE She flung her arms round his neck in a burst of remorseful affection. W. BOYD A loud and prolonged burst of applause. **b** J. AUSTEN Here is a fine burst of country.

4 A spell of increased activity; a display of energy, a spurt; a hard gallop. L18.

> THACKERAY A burst over the Downs after a hare. M. ARNOLD The burst of creative activity in our literature. *Sports Illustrated* Short bursts of speed are more important than long-term stamina.

5 A binge, a drinking bout; a large meal. *colloq.* M19.
■ **bursty** *adjective* occurring or existing in bursts; *spec.* in COMPUTING, pertaining to or designating the transmission of data in short bursts of signals: L20.

burst /bəːst/ *verb*. Pa. t. & pple **burst**; (*dial.*) **-ed**, **-en** /-(ə)n/. Also (*arch.* & *dial.*) **brast** /brast/. See also BUST *verb*.
[ORIGIN Old English *berstan* = Old Frisian *bersta*, Old Saxon, Old High German *brestan* (Dutch *bersten*, *barsten*), Old Norse *bresta*, from Germanic.]
▸ **I** *verb intrans.* †**1** Break suddenly, snap, crack. OE–E19.
2 Fly apart or into pieces or break open with expansion of contents or release of pressure; split; explode; (of a cloud etc.) release rain with sudden force; (of a door) fly *open* suddenly. OE.

> SPENSER Poyson . . Made him to swell, that nigh his bowells brust. S. SASSOON A bomb burst in the water. DAY LEWIS A gigantic wave had just burst on the fo'c'sle. J. BOWEN Bubbles on a tarred roof, which grew, and burst, and grew again. P. F. BOLLER There was a loud ripping sound; the seam of his trousers had burst.

bursting at the seams: see SEAM *noun*[1]. **bursting point** the internal pressure at which a container will burst (usu. *transf.*). ***burst in shivers***, ***burst into shivers***: see SHIVER *noun*[1] 1.
3 Issue suddenly (as if) by breaking restraint or overcoming resistance; break out suddenly or forcibly. OE. ▸**b** Of thoughts, emotions, etc.: find (sudden) utterance or manifestation. M16.

> BUNYAN What sighs and groans brast from Christians heart. TENNYSON A river . . Ready to burst and fill the world with foam.

4 Force one's way *through*, *out*, *into*, etc., come or appear suddenly, intrude. ME.

> S. O'FAOLÁIN The weeds bursting through the gravel. V. BRITTAIN Winifred Holtby burst suddenly in upon this morose atmosphere of ruminant lethargy.

5 Be full to overflowing (*with*); be unable to contain oneself; have an overwhelming desire or urgent need *to do* something; (of the heart) break. ME.

AV *Prov.* 3:10 Thy presses shall burst out with new wine. G. B. SHAW It was something that was just bursting to be said. DAY LEWIS Plums bursting with ripeness. S. HILL She was bursting . . to talk now.

6 Break out into sudden activity or expression of feelings; exclaim, begin suddenly. Usu. with *into, out.* LME.

SPENSER The wisard . . brusting forth in laughter, to her sayd. B. JOWETT The crew of his own trireme also burst out laughing. T. H. HUXLEY The taper will burst again into full flame. J. CARY She burst into tears and called for her mama. K. AMIS Bowen burst into song.

▸ **II** *verb trans.* **7** Cause to fly apart or into pieces, disrupt with internal pressure, rupture, cause to split; suffer rupture of. ME. ▸**b** *spec.* Separate (esp. computer printout paper) along perforated edges, esp. automatically. M20.

C. KINGSLEY He . . played leap-frog . . till he burst his buttons. G. B. SHAW Morell bursts open the cover of a copy of The Church Reformer. *Daily Express* The force of the explosion burst the water tanks. C. FRY One day I shall burst my bud Of calm, and blossom into hysteria.

burst one's sides: see SIDE *noun.*

8 Open (a door etc.) forcibly, force one's way through, break free from (bonds etc.). LME.

SHAKES. *1 Hen. VI* Open the gates unto the Lord Protector, Or we'll burst them open. A. F. DOUGLAS-HOME A . . crowd . . burst the barriers and swarmed across the route.

burst its banks (of a river etc.) break through or overflow its banks and cause flooding.

9 *gen.* Break suddenly, snap, shatter; interrupt. Now *rare* or *obsolete.* LME.

C. MARLOWE Whose chariot-wheels have burst the Assyrians' bones. TENNYSON Many a . . heel against the pavement echoing burst their drowse.

10 Cause (the body) to swell to bursting point (usu. *hyperbol.*, as an imagined result of overeating or exertion); fill to overflowing; break (the heart). LME.

MILTON Cramm'd and gorged, right burst With suck'd and glutted offal. DRYDEN That Crop . . bursts the crowded Barns. DEFOE Water, with which . . he would have burst himself.

burster /ˈbəːstə/ *noun.* E17.
[ORIGIN from BURST *verb* + -ER[1].]

1 A person or thing which bursts. E17. ▸**b** *spec.* A machine for separating continuous stationery into its constituent sheets. M20.
2 = BUSTER 3. *Austral. & NZ.* M19.
3 ASTRONOMY. A cosmic source of powerful short-lived bursts of X-rays or other radiation. L20.

burthen *noun, verb* see BURDEN *noun, verb.*

burton /ˈbəːt(ə)n/ *noun*[1]. E18.
[ORIGIN Alt. of BRETON (*tackle*).]

NAUTICAL. **1** More fully ***burton-tackle***. A light handy two-block tackle. E18.
Spanish burton: see SPANISH *adjective.*
2 Athwartship stowage of casks etc. Also ***a-burton*** *adverb* [A-[2]]. M19.

burton /ˈbəːt(ə)n/ *noun*[2]. *colloq.* (orig. *RAF slang*). Also **B-**. M20.
[ORIGIN Uncertain: perh. from *Burton* ale from *Burton* upon Trent, a town in Staffordshire, England.]
go for a burton, be killed, destroyed, ruined, or lost.

buru *noun* var. of BURRU.

bury /ˈbɛri/ *verb trans.*
[ORIGIN Old English *byrġan* from West Germanic, from base also of Old English *beorgan*: see BORROW *verb*[1].]

1 Deposit (a corpse, human remains) in the earth, in a tomb, in the ocean, etc., with funeral rites; lose (a relative etc.) by death. OE. ▸**b** Put under the ground in sign of final abandonment or abrogation; dispose of thus. M16.

STEELE My elder Sister buried her Husband about Six Months ago. B. CHATWIN There were snowdrops in the graveyard when they buried her. **b** SHAKES. *Temp.* I'll break my staff, Bury it certain fathoms in the earth.

dead and buried: see DEAD *adjective.* **b *bury the hatchet***: see HATCHET *noun.* ***bury the tomahawk***: see TOMAHAWK *noun.*

2 *fig.* Consign to oblivion, abandon and forget; renounce; consign to obscurity or inaccessibility. ME.

SIR W. SCOTT To retire from the world and bury herself in the recesses of the cloister. A. B. ELLIS The natives . . had buried their own differences and united to repel the invaders.

3 *gen.* Cover up with earth; conceal in the ground. ME.

E. W. LANE I . . buried 3000 pieces of gold. T. A. COWARD One habit [of the jay] . . is that of burying nuts, acorns, or even inedible objects.

burying beetle = SEXTON *beetle.* ***bury one's head in the sand***: see SAND *noun.*

4 Plunge deeply *in(to)* so as to remove from sight; immerse, hide; *fig.* profoundly absorb or engross (oneself) *in* (freq. in *pass.*). LME.

BYRON Bury your steel in the bosoms of Gath. S. LEACOCK So buried in his own thoughts that he was oblivious of our approach. J. CHEEVER He buried his nose in the paper.

5 Of inanimate agents: cover up or over with material, submerge. M18.

O. SITWELL Vesuvius has doubtless in its time buried town after town. R. P. JHABVALA Some of the older houses would collapse and bury the people inside.

■ **burying** *verbal noun* (*a*) the action of the verb (***burying ground***, ***burying place***, a cemetery); (*b*) (now *dial.*) a burial, a funeral: ME.

Buryat /ˈbuːrɪət/ *noun & adjective.* Also **Buriat.** M19.
[ORIGIN Mongolian *Buriyad.*]

▸ **A** *noun.* **1** A member of a Mongolian people inhabiting the borders of Lake Baikal, Siberia. M19.
2 The Mongolic language of this people. L19.

▸ **B** *attrib.* or as *adjective.* Of or pertaining to the Buryats or their language; designating or pertaining to the territory of the Buryats. E20.

bus /bʌs/ *noun.* Also (now *rare*) **'bus**; (sense 4) **buss.** Pl. **buses**, ***busses.** E19.
[ORIGIN Abbreviation of OMNIBUS.]

1 A large passenger road vehicle running on a fixed route. E19.
miss the bus: see MISS *verb*[1].
2 Any conveyance, as a car, aeroplane, etc. *colloq.* L19.
3 A hand-pushed trolley used esp. for carrying dishes etc. in a cafeteria. *N. Amer.* M20.
4 COMPUTING. = HIGHWAY 1C. M20.

– COMB.: **busbar** an electrical conductor serving as a common connection between several circuits, esp. in a generating station; **busboy** *N. Amer.* a waiter's assistant who clears tables etc.; a person who pushes a trolley carrying dishes etc. in a cafeteria; **bus conductor** (*a*) the conductor of a bus; (*b*) = *busbar* above; **bus conductress** a female bus conductor; **bus lane** a traffic lane mainly for the use of buses; **busload** as many people as a bus will hold; **busman** a driver of a bus (***busman's holiday***, a period of leisure time spent in the same kind of occupation as one's regular work); **bus shelter** a roadside shelter affording protection from the weather to passengers awaiting buses; ***bus station***: see STATION *noun*; **bus stop** a place at which a bus regularly stops; **busway** a bus lane, *spec.* one with means to guide the movement of buses.

bus /bʌs/ *verb*[1]. Infl. **-s-**, ***-ss-**. M19.
[ORIGIN from the noun.]

1 *verb intrans. & trans.* with *it.* Go by bus. M19.
2 *verb trans.* Transport by bus, *spec.* (*US*) to a school in a different area in order to counteract racial segregation. Chiefly *N. Amer.* M20. ▸**b** Carry or remove (dishes etc.) in a cafeteria etc., clear from tables; clear (a table in a cafeteria etc.) of dishes etc. *US.* M20.

†**bus** *verb*[2] var. of BOOST *verb*[2].

busby /ˈbʌzbi/ *noun.* M18.
[ORIGIN Unknown.]

†**1** A large bushy wig. M18–L19.
2 A tall fur hat forming part of the dress uniform of hussars, artillerymen, and guardsmen. E19.
■ **busbied** *adjective* wearing a busby E20.

buscarl /ˈbʌskɑːl/ *noun.* Long *obsolete* exc. *hist.* Also **butsecarl** /ˈbʌtsɪkɑːl/. OE.
[ORIGIN Old Norse *búzukarl.*]
A seaman, a sailor.

bush /bʊʃ/ *noun*[1]. Also (*dial.*) **busk** /bʌsk/. See also BOSK. ME.
[ORIGIN Partly from Old French *bos, bosc* vars. of *bois* wood, partly from Old Norse *buski*, from Germanic base repr. also by Old Saxon *busc* (Dutch *bos, bosch*), Old High German *busc* (German *Busch*) (corresp. form prob. in Old English but not recorded). Sense 7 prob. directly from Dutch *bosch.*]

1 A shrub or clump of shrubs with stems of moderate length. ME. ▸**b** A subshrub; a clump of dwarf shrubs or herbaceous plants. *Scot. & N. English.* E16.
beat about the bush: see BEAT *verb*[1] 15. ***burning bush***: see BURNING 1. ***caustic bush***: see CAUSTIC *adjective* 1. ***stag bush***: see STAG *noun.* ***take the rag off the bush***: see RAG *noun*[1].
2 Thicket; bushy ground. *obsolete* exc. as coinciding with sense 7. ME.
3 A bunch of ivy anciently used as a vintner's sign. LME.

Proverb: Good wine needs no bush.

4 A luxuriant growth of hair. E16. ▸**b** Pubic hair, esp. of a woman. *slang.* E20.
†**5** A bushy mass of foliage, feathers, etc. E16–M17.
†**6** A bushy tail; a fox's brush. L16–E17.
7 (An area of) woodland, forest, uncultivated land, *the* remote rural areas, esp. in Australia, New Zealand, or Africa. M17.
go bush *Austral. & NZ colloq.* leave one's usual surroundings (for the country), run wild. ***native bush***: see NATIVE *adjective.* ***Sydney or the bush***: see SYDNEY 2.

– COMB.: **bushbaby** a small tree-dwelling African primate of the subfamily Galaginae (family Lorisidae); ***bush basil***: see BASIL *noun*[1] 1; **bush-bean** *N. Amer.* the kidney bean; **bushbuck** a small African antelope, *Tragelaphus scriptus*, red-brown with white chest band and spots; **bush burn** *NZ* the burning of bush on cultivable land, land so cleared; **bush canary** *Austral. & NZ* any of various songbirds; **bush carpenter** *Austral. & NZ* an untrained or unskilled carpenter; **bush-cat** the serval; **bush clover** = LESPEDEZA; **bush cow** (*a*) a wild cow of the bush; (*b*) a tapir; **bushcraft** skill in living in the bush; ***bush cranberry***: see CRANBERRY 2; ***bush cricket***: see CRICKET *noun*[1]; **bush-eel** *dial.* a snake, esp. as food; **bush fire** a fire in the bush (sense 7); **bush-fly** a pestiferous Australian fly, esp. *Musca vestusissima*; **bush-harrow** *noun & verb trans.* (*hist.*) (harrow etc. with) an agricultural implement underneath which bushes are interwoven, for harrowing grassland or covering in seed; **bush hen** *NZ* the weka; **bush jacket** a belted cotton jacket; **bush lawyer** (*a*) *NZ* the New Zealand bramble, *Rubus australis*; (*b*) *Austral.* the lawyer cane or lawyer vine; (*c*) a layman pretending to legal knowledge; an argumentative person; **bush league** *N. Amer.* a minor league of a professional sport, orig. *spec.* baseball; **bush-league** *adjective* (*N. Amer. colloq.*) inferior, minor, unsophisticated; **bush-leaguer** *N. Amer.* a player in a bush league; **bushline** the altitude above which bush does not grow; **bushmaster** a large venomous viper, *Lachesis muta*, of tropical America; also called ***surucucu***; **bushmeat** (in parts of Africa) the meat of wild animals as food; **bush pig** (*a*) a long-haired southern African wild hog, *Potamochoerus porcus*; (*b*) *NZ* a wild pig; **bush poppy** *N. Amer.* a yellow-flowered shrub of the poppy family, *Dendromecon rigida*, native to California and NW Mexico; **bushranger** *Austral. & NZ hist.* a brigand living in the bush; **bush-ranging** *hist.* living as a bushranger; **bush-rat** any of various small rodents; **bush-rope** a tropical vine or creeper; **bush shrike** any African shrike of the subfamily Malaconotinae; **bush shirt** = ***bush jacket*** above; **bush-sick** *adjective* (chiefly *NZ*) suffering from bush sickness; **bush sickness** (chiefly *NZ*) disease of animals due to cobalt deficiency in soil; **bush tea**: made from the dried leaves of certain shrubs and used medicinally in southern Africa; **bush telegraph** a rapid informal spreading of information, rumour, etc.; **bushtit** a N. American tit of the genus *Psaltriparus*; **bushveld** *S. Afr.* veld composed largely of bush; a wooded region in Transvaal; **bush vetch** a climbing purple-flowered vetch, *Vicia sepium*; **bush walk** *Austral.* a tramp or camping expedition in the bush; **bush-walk** *verb intrans.* (*Austral.*) go tramping or camping in the bush;
■ **busher** *noun* (*N. Amer. colloq.*) = ***bush-leaguer*** above E20. **bushless** *adjective* M19.

bush /bʊʃ/ *noun*[2]. L15.
[ORIGIN Middle Dutch *busse* (Dutch *bus*). Cf. German *Büchse.*]
A metal lining for an axle hole or other circular orifice; a perforated plug; a box or bearing in which a shaft revolves; ELECTRICITY an insulating sleeve.
■ **bushing** *noun* a bush, esp. of an electrically insulating material L19.

bush /bʊʃ/ *verb*[1]. ME.
[ORIGIN from BUSH *noun*[1].]

†**1** *verb trans.* Conceal in a bush. Usu. in *pass.* (of oneself). ME–E17.
2 *verb trans. & intrans.* (Cause to) grow thick like a bush; (cause to) grow or stick *out* like a bush. L15.
3 *verb trans.* Protect or support with bushes. E17.
4 *verb trans.* with *it* & *intrans.* Camp in the bush. *Austral. & NZ.* E19.

bush /bʊʃ/ *verb*[2] *intrans. obsolete* exc. *dial.* LME.
[ORIGIN Perh. from Old French *buschier* knock, beat or from Middle Dutch *buuschen* (= Middle High German *biuschen*) in same sense.]
Butt, push.

bush /bʊʃ/ *verb*[3] *trans.* M16.
[ORIGIN from BUSH *noun*[2].]
Provide with a bush.

bushed /bʊʃt/ *adjective. colloq.* M19.
[ORIGIN from BUSH *noun*[1] + -ED[2].]

1 Lost in the bush; bewildered. *Austral. & NZ.* M19.
2 Tired, exhausted. Orig. *N. Amer.* L19.

bushel /ˈbʊʃ(ə)l/ *noun & verb*[1]. ME.
[ORIGIN Old French *boisel* (mod. *boisseau*) = Provençal *boissel*, perh. of Gaulish origin.]

▸ **A** *noun.* **1** A British unit of dry and liquid measure equal to 8 gallons or 32 quarts (approx. 36.4 litres); a US unit of dry measure equal to 4 pecks or 32 quarts (approx. 35.2 litres). ME.
Winchester bushel: see WINCHESTER 1.
2 *loosely.* A very large number or quantity. LME.
3 A vessel used as a measure of a bushel. *arch.* exc. as below. LME.
hide one's light under a bushel conceal one's merits.

▸ **B** *verb trans.* Infl. **-l(l)-**. Hide (a light etc.) under a bushel (*fig.*): see sense A.3 above. *rare.* M17.
■ **bushelful** *noun* as much as a bushel will hold; a large quantity: LME.

bushel /ˈbʊʃ(ə)l/ *verb*[2] *trans. & intrans. US.* M19.
[ORIGIN Perh. from German *bosseln* do odd jobs.]
Mend or alter (clothes).
– COMB.: **bushelman**, **bushelwoman**: employed to mend or alter clothes.

bushido /ˈbuːʃɪdəʊ, bʊˈʃiːdəʊ/ *noun.* L19.
[ORIGIN Japanese, from *bushi* warrior + *dō* way.]
The code of honour and morals evolved by the samurai.

bushie *noun* var. of BUSHY *noun.*

Bushman /ˈbʊʃmən/ *noun & adjective.* L18.
[ORIGIN from BUSH *noun*[1] + MAN *noun*; sense A.1 after Dutch *boschjesman.*]

▸ **A** *noun.* Pl. **-men.**
1 a A member of any of various aboriginal southern African peoples. L18. ▸**b** (Any of) the group of languages of these peoples, = SAN *noun*[2] 2. M19.
2 (**b-**.) A dweller, farmer, or (esp. skilled) traveller in the bush of Australia or New Zealand. Also, a person who fells timber. E19.

▸ **B** *attrib.* or as *adjective.* Of or pertaining to the Bushmen or their language. M19.
Bushman grass *S. Afr.* = TWAA-GRASS.
■ **Bushmanoid** *adjective* (ANTHROPOLOGY) resembling Bushmen in physical type M20. **bushmanship** *noun* bushcraft M19.

B

bushment /ˈbʊʃm(ə)nt/ *noun*. *arch.* LME.
[ORIGIN Sense 1 aphet. from AMBUSHMENT; sense 2 app. from BUSH noun[1] + -MENT.]
1 = AMBUSHMENT. LME.
2 A mass of bushes. L16.

bushwa /ˈbʊʃwɑː/ *noun*. *N. Amer. slang*. Also **-wah**. E20.
[ORIGIN App. euphem. for *bullshit* noun s.v. BULL noun[1] & adjective.]
Rubbish, nonsense.

bushwhack *verb*. M19.
[ORIGIN from BUSH noun[1] + WHACK verb.]
1 *verb intrans.* Live or travel in wild or uncultivated country. *N. Amer.* M19. ▸**b** Cut or push one's way through dense vegetation. *N. Amer. & NZ.* M19. ▸**c** Work clearing scrub and felling trees in the country. *Austral. & NZ.* E20.

> **b** *New York Review of Books* He . . was discouraged by the difficulty of bushwhacking through dense brush.

2 *verb trans.* Surprise (someone) by attacking them from a hidden place; ambush. *N. Amer.* M19.

> D. HAMMETT If I get there first I can bushwhack him.

■ **bushwhacked** *adjective* (*N. Amer. colloq.*) worn out, exhausted; drunk: M20. **bushwhacker** (*a*) *N. Amer.* a backwoodsman; (*b*) *US HISTORY* a deserter, a guerrilla; (*c*) *Austral. & NZ* a person who clears land of bush, a timber worker: E19.

bushy /ˈbʊʃi/ *noun*. *Austral. & NZ colloq.* Also **bushie**. L19.
[ORIGIN from BUSH noun[1] + -Y[6].]
= BUSHMAN 2.

bushy /ˈbʊʃi/ *adjective*. LME.
[ORIGIN from BUSH noun[1] + -Y[1].]
1 Having many bushes; covered with bush. LME.
2 Growing thickly; like a bush. M16.
– COMB.: **bushy-tailed** *adjective* with a bushy tail; *fig.* alert, lively (freq. in ***bright-eyed and bushy-tailed***).

busily /ˈbɪzɪli/ *adverb*. ME.
[ORIGIN from BUSY adjective + -LY[2].]
In a busy manner.

business /ˈbɪznɪs/ *noun*.
[ORIGIN Old English *bisignis*, formed as BUSY adjective + -NESS.]
▸ †**I** The state of being busy (cf. BUSYNESS).
1 Anxiety; distress, uneasiness. OE–L16.
2 The state of being busily engaged; activity; application, industry; diligent labour. ME–E18.
3 Eagerness; importunity; officiousness. LME–L16.
4 Attention, care; observance. LME–M16.
5 Trouble, difficulty; ado; commotion. LME–L17.
▸ **II** The object of concern or activity.
†6 The object of serious effort; an aim. LME–M16.
7 An appointed task; a duty, a province; *spec.* a particular errand, a cause of coming. LME.

> BUNYAN What is your business here so late to Night? W. S. CHURCHILL The Prime Minister . . believed that the primary business of government was to administer the existing order.

8 Action demanding time and labour; serious work. LME.

> *Proverb*: Business comes before pleasure.

9 A habitual occupation, a profession, a trade. L15.

> CARLYLE I wished to be a fisherman, and tried that business for a time.

10 A thing that concerns one; a matter in which one may take part. E16.

> M. LEITCH What went on in between was their business, none of hers.

11 A particular matter requiring attention; a piece of work; a job; an agenda. M16. ▸†**b** A topic, a subject. Only in 17. ▸**c** A difficult matter. *colloq.* M19.

> POPE What I act, survey, And learn from thence the business of the day. **c** CARLYLE If he had known what a business it was to govern the Abbey.

12 *gen.* An affair; a concern, a process; a matter; a structure; *slang* all that is available. Usu. *derog.* E17.

> C. STEAD The difficult . . and dangerous business of climbing on the roof. D. CUSACK That nasty business in Second Year . . . They lampooned the Staff in their class paper.

13 Dealings, intercourse, (*with*). E17.
14 THEATRICAL. Action on stage (as opp. to dialogue). L17.
15 Trade; commercial transactions or engagements; total bookings, receipts, etc. E18.
16 A commercial house, a firm. L19.
– PHRASES ETC.: **any other business** matters not specifically listed on the agenda for a meeting. ***bad business***: see BAD adjective. ***big business***: see BIG adjective. **business as usual** normal trading, proceedings, etc., despite disturbances. **do one's business** *colloq.* urinate or (*esp.*) defecate. **do the business** *colloq.* do what is required or expected, achieve the desired result. ***funny business***: see FUNNY adjective. **get down to business** begin serious work, begin in earnest. **go about one's business** stop interfering in another's affairs, go away, (freq. in *imper.*). **in business** habitually occupied in trade or commerce; *fig.* able to begin operations, operational. **in the business of** engaged or involved in, concerned with, (usu. in neg. contexts). ***line of business***: see LINE noun[2]. **make it one's business to** make a particular effort to, undertake to. **mean business** be in earnest. **mind one's own business** refrain from interfering in another's affairs (freq. in *imper.*). ***mind-your-own-business***: see MIND verb. ***monkey business***: see MONKEY noun. **nobody's business** *colloq.* something extraordinary (***like nobody's business***, to an extraordinary degree). **on business** with a definite purpose, esp. one relating to one's trade or profession. **send about his or her business** send (a person) packing, dismiss (a person). ***way of business***: see WAY noun.
– COMB.: **business card**: with one's name and information about one's firm etc.; **business cycle** the trade cycle; **business end** *colloq.* the working end of a tool etc.; **business hours**: in which business is regularly transacted, during which shops or offices are open; **business lunch**: at which commercial transactions are discussed; **businessman**: engaged in trade or commerce (***the TIRED businessman***); **business studies** the analysis of commercial activities as an academic subject; **business suit** a lounge suit; **businesswoman**: engaged in trade or commerce.
– NOTE: Orig. trisyllabic (cf. BUSYNESS). The disyllabic pronunc. has been promoted through loss of direct assoc. with BUSY adjective.
■ **businesslike** *adjective* efficient, practical, systematic L18.

busk /bʌsk/ *noun*[1]. L16.
[ORIGIN French *busc* from Italian *busco* splinter, rel. to Old French *busche* (mod. *bûche*) log, from Germanic.]
hist. A strip of wood, whalebone, steel, etc. used for stiffening the front of a corset; a corset.

busk *noun*[2] see BUSH *noun*[1].

busk /bʌsk/ *verb*[1]. Now *Scot. & N. English*. ME.
[ORIGIN Old Norse *búask* refl. of *búa* prepare: cf. BOUND adjective[1].]
1 *verb intrans. & refl.* Get oneself ready; get dressed. ME.
2 *verb trans.* Prepare, fit out; adorn, attire. Also foll. by *up*. ME.
3 *verb intrans. & trans.* Hurry, hasten; betake *oneself*. ME.
■ **busker** *noun*[1] M16.

busk /bʌsk/ *verb*[2] *intrans.* *obsolete* exc. *dial.* M16.
[ORIGIN Unknown.]
Of a bird: move or shift about; nestle.

busk /bʌsk/ *verb*[3]. M17.
[ORIGIN French †*busquer* seek, hunt for, from Italian *buscare* or Spanish *buscar*, from Germanic.]
1 *verb intrans.* NAUTICAL. Cruise about, tack. Now *rare* or *obsolete*. M17.
2 *verb intrans.* Look *for*, seek *after*. *rare*. M18.
3 *verb intrans.* Play music, or otherwise entertain, for money in public places. Formerly also, peddle goods. Chiefly as ***busking*** *verbal noun*. M19.
4 *verb trans. & intrans.* Improvise. *slang*. M20.

> D. ADAMS He had no idea what he was going to find. He would just have to busk it.

■ **busker** *noun*[2] an itinerant musician or actor, *esp.* one performing in the street M19.

buskin /ˈbʌskɪn/ *noun & adjective*. Now *hist.* or *arch.* E16.
[ORIGIN Prob. from Old French *bousequin* var. of *brousequin* (mod. *brodequin*) prob. from Middle Dutch *broseken*, corresp. to Catalan, Spanish *borcegui*, Provençal *borzeguim*, Italian *borzacchino*, of unknown origin.]
▸ **A** *noun*. **1** A half-boot. E16.
2 A kind of thick-soled boot worn by tragic actors in the ancient Athenian theatre; *fig.* tragic drama, tragedy. L16.

> BYRON He was a critic upon operas, too, And knew all niceties of the sock and buskin.

put on the buskin(s) assume a tragic style, write tragedy. ***sock and buskin***: see SOCK noun[1].
▸ **B** *attrib.* or as *adjective*. Of or pertaining to tragic drama. E17.
■ **buskined** *adjective* shod with buskins; *fig.* concerned with tragedy, elevated, lofty: L16.

†**buskle** *verb intrans. & trans.* M16–M17.
[ORIGIN from BUSK verb[1] + -LE[3].]
= BUSK verb[1].

busky /ˈbʌski/ *adjective*. Now *arch. & dial.* L16.
[ORIGIN from BUSK noun[2] + -Y[1].]
Full of bushes or thickets, bushy, (= BOSKY 1).

buss /bʌs/ *noun*[1]. ME.
[ORIGIN Old French *buce*, (later) *busse*, infl. by Middle Dutch *buisse* (mod. *buis*): ult. origin unknown.]
hist. **1** A ship for carrying loads. ME.
2 A two- or three-masted vessel of various sizes, used esp. in the North Sea herring fishery. L15.

buss /bʌs/ *noun*[2] & *verb trans. & intrans.* Now *arch., dial., & N. Amer. colloq.* L16.
[ORIGIN Prob. alt. of BASS noun[3], verb[1].]
(A) kiss.

buss *noun*[3] see BUS *noun*.

bussu /bəˈsuː/ *noun*. M19.
[ORIGIN Portuguese from Tupi *ubu-ussu*, from *ubu* leaf + *ussu* big.]
A palm of tidal swamps in Central and S. America, *Manicaria saccifera*, with immense leaves that are used for thatching.

bust /bʌst/ *noun*[1]. M17.
[ORIGIN (French *buste* from) Italian *busto* from Latin *bustum* funeral pyre, tomb, sepulchral monument.]
†**1** The upper part or torso of a larger sculpture. *rare*. Only in M17.
2 A piece of sculpture representing a person's head, shoulders, and chest. L17. ▸**b** (Such a piece as) a sepulchral monument. *poet.* M18.
3 The upper front of the body; the bosom, esp. of a woman. E18. ▸**b** The circumference of a woman's body at the level of her bust. Also ***bustline***. L19.

> *Sunday Telegraph* Barbie's waist has thickened and her bust has shrunk.

■ **busty** *adjective* (*colloq.*) (of a woman) having a prominent bust M20.

bust /bʌst/ *noun*[2]. *colloq.* (orig. *US*). M18.
[ORIGIN Var. of BURST noun.]
1 = BURST noun 2. *rare*. M18.
2 A binge, a drinking bout (= BURST noun 5). M19.

> A. POWELL He . . would celebrate with some sort of bust in the way of food and drink.

3 A sudden failure or collapse of trade etc. M19.

> H. A. WALLACE We cannot afford either a speculative boom or its inevitable bust.

4 A burglary. M19.
5 A worthless thing or person; *spec.* a bad hand at cards. E20.

> P. G. WODEHOUSE At the age of ten I was a social bust.

6 A blow with the fist. E20.

> J. F. POWERS How'd you like a bust in the nose?

7 A police raid, an arrest. M20.

bust /bʌst/ *verb*. *colloq.* (orig. *US*). Pa. t. & pple **bust**, **busted**. E19.
[ORIGIN Var. of BURST verb.]
▸ **I** *verb trans.* **1** Burst; break; beat or smash *up*. E19.

> L. SHORTEN We go to this house and take this hockey stick and bust the window. C. BATEMAN He busted a hand the week before in a . . scrap.

bust a gut: see GUT noun 2.
2 Reduce to insolvency. E19.
go bust become bankrupt.
3 Break into (a house etc.). M19.
4 Break in (a horse). L19.
5 Dismiss; demote; arrest; catch in possession of illegal drugs; jail. Usu. in *pass.* E20.

> K. LETTE One got busted for heroin and got both her children taken off her.

6 Strike with the fist etc. E20.
▸ **II** *verb intrans.* **7** Burst, explode. M19.
8 Go bankrupt. M19.
– COMB.: **bust-head** *US slang* cheap strong liquor; **bust-up** an explosion (*lit. & fig.*); a violent severance; a quarrel.

bustard /ˈbʌstəd/ *noun*. L15.
[ORIGIN Perh. from Anglo-Norman blending of Old French *bistarde*, *oustarde*, both from Latin *avis tarda* 'slow bird', the inappropriate adjective being unexpl.]
1 Any of various large swift-running birds of the family Otididae, allied to the cranes and rails. L15.
RUFFED bustard. ***STANLEY bustard***.
2 = BUZZARD noun[2]. *dial.* M19.

bustee /ˈbʌstiː/ *noun*. L19.
[ORIGIN Hindi *bastī* dwelling, settlement.]
A group of huts in a shanty town or slum in the Indian subcontinent.

busteous *adjective* see BOISTOUS.

buster /ˈbʌstə/ *noun*. Chiefly *colloq.* M19.
[ORIGIN Var. of BURSTER or from BUST verb + -ER[1].]
1 = BURSTER 1. Chiefly as 2nd elem. of comb.: a person who or thing which breaks, beats, masters, prevents, or eliminates (the 1st elem.). M19.
ball-buster, ***chartbuster***, ***dambuster***, etc.
2 **a** An impressive or startling person or event; a person who or thing which provokes admiration. M19. ▸**b** A mate, a fellow, a chap. Usu. as a familiar or disrespectful form of address. E20.
3 A violent gale. M19.
Barcoo buster.
4 A horsebreaker. *N. Amer.* L19.
broncobuster.
5 A heavy fall. *Austral. & NZ.* L19.

†**bustian** *noun*. LME–E18.
[ORIGIN Perh. alt. of Old French *bustan(n)e* kind of fabric made at Valenciennes, after FUSTIAN.]
A cotton fabric of foreign manufacture.

bustier /ˈbʌstɪeɪ, ˈbʊst-; *foreign* bystje (*pl. same*)/ *noun*. L20.
[ORIGIN French, from *buste*: see BUST noun[1].]
A close-fitting usu. strapless bodice or top worn by women.

bustious *adjective* see BOISTOUS.

bustle /ˈbʌs(ə)l/ *noun*[1]. E17.
[ORIGIN from the verb.]
1 Conflict; a struggle; a scuffle. *arch.* E17.
2 Excited activity; fuss; a state of busy haste. M17. ▸**b** Movement during fermentation. *arch.* L17.
3 Money. *criminals' slang*. Now *rare* or *obsolete*. M18.

bustle /ˈbʌs(ə)l/ *noun*[2]. L18.
[ORIGIN Unknown.]
hist. A pad or frame worn to puff out the top of a woman's skirt at the back.

bustle /ˈbʌs(ə)l/ *verb*. LME.
[ORIGIN Perh. var. of BUSKLE.]
1 *verb intrans.* Be fussily or noisily active; move *about* in an energetic and busy manner; make a show of activity. LME. ▸**b** Of a place: be teeming *with*. L19.

2 *verb trans.* Bestir, rouse, (oneself or another); hurry in a fussy manner. Also foll. by *up*. Now *rare*. M16.
†**3** *verb intrans.* Struggle, scuffle; contend. E17–E18.
■ **bustler** *noun* L17. **bustlingly** *adverb* in a bustling manner E19.

†**busto** *noun*. Pl. **-o(e)s**. E17–M19.
[ORIGIN Italian: see BUST *noun*[1].]
= BUST *noun*[1] 2.

bustuous *adjective* see BOISTOUS.

busy /ˈbɪzi/ *noun*. *slang*. E20.
[ORIGIN from the adjective.]
A detective; a police officer.

busy /ˈbɪzi/ *adjective*.
[ORIGIN Old English *bisig* = Middle Low German, Middle Dutch *besich* (Dutch *bezig*), of unknown origin.]
1 Occupied, actively engaged or employed, with attention concentrated. (Foll. by *in*, *with*, *at*, *doing*, (arch.) *about*.) OE. ▸**b** Of a telephone line: engaged. L19.

> OED Don't interrupt me, I'm busy. D. H. LAWRENCE She was busy washing a garment in the bowl. J. B. PRIESTLEY Their fingers would be busy with the sewing machines or irons, but their minds could be far away. C. PRIEST The other people seemed unaware of me, busy in their own lives.

2 Constantly active or in motion; unresting; habitually employed. ME.

> S. HILL Miss Cress is a busy woman, I am astonished she would waste a whole afternoon in such a way.

†**3** Solicitous, careful. Only in ME.
4 Fussy, meddlesome; prying; officious, importunate. LME.

> COLERIDGE A busy and inquisitorial tyranny.

†**5** Of a thing: involving much work; elaborate; intricate. LME–E17.
6 Of an action, employment, etc.: requiring or carried on with energy; keenly pursued. M16.

> POPE On every side the busy combat grows.

7 Indicating activity or business. M17.

> M. W. MONTAGU People, with . . busy faces.

8 Of a time or place: full of business and stir; bustling. L17.

> E. HEMINGWAY The hospital was quite busy . . and that kept her occupied.

9 Full of detail. E20.
– PHRASES & COMB.: *as busy as a bee*: see BEE *noun*[1]. *busy Lizzie*: see LIZZIE 4. **busywork** work that keeps a person busy but has little value in itself.
■ **busyness** *noun* the state of being busy (cf. BUSINESS I) E19.

busy /ˈbɪzi/ *verb*.
[ORIGIN Old English *bisgian*, *bysgian*, from BUSY *adjective*.]
1 *verb trans.* Occupy (esp. oneself, one's hands, etc.); keep busy. (Foll. by *with*, *in*, *at*, *about*, *doing*.) OE.

> S. BRETT In the kitchen Carole busied herself finding corkscrew and glasses.

†**2** *verb trans.* Trouble; afflict; disturb. OE–L16.
3 *verb intrans.* Be busy; occupy oneself; take trouble. (Foll. by *with*, *about*, etc.) Now *rare*. LME.

busybody /ˈbɪzɪbɒdi/ *noun & verb*. E16.
[ORIGIN from BUSY *adjective* + BODY *noun*.]
▸**A** *noun*. **1** A meddlesome, prying person; a mischief-maker. E16.
2 A mirror set at the side of a building to reflect a view of the street etc. *US*. L19.
▸**B** *verb intrans.* Meddle; pry; interfere; behave as a busybody. M19.
■ **busybodied** *adjective* (now *rare*) meddlesome, prying L18. **busybodyness** *noun* (*rare*) meddlesomeness, desire to interfere M17.

but /bʌt/ *noun*. L16.
[ORIGIN formed as BUT *verb*.]
1 The conjunction 'but'; a statement beginning with 'but', an objection. L16.
but me no buts: see BUT *verb* 2. **ifs and buts** uncertainties, doubtful factors, qualifications.
2 The outer room of a two-roomed house. Cf. BEN *noun*[3]. *Scot. & N. English*. E18.
but and ben a two-roomed cottage, a small or humble home.

but /bʌt/ *verb*. Infl. **-tt-**. M16.
[ORIGIN from BUT *preposition, adverb, conjunction, & pronoun*.]
1 *verb intrans.* Make a statement beginning with 'but'; raise an objection. *rare*. M16.
2 *verb trans.* **but me no buts**, do not raise objections. E18.

but /bʌt/ *preposition, adverb, conjunction, & rel. pronoun*.
[ORIGIN Old English *būtan* (*beūtan*, *būton*, *būta*) = Old Saxon *biūtan*, *būtan*, Old High German *biūzan* (Middle High German *būzen*), from West Germanic, formed as BY *preposition & adverb* + OUT *adverb*.]
▸**A** *preposition*. **1** Outside of; without, lacking. Long *obsolete* exc. *Scot. & N. English*. OE.

> OED Gang but the house and see who is there.

2 Leaving out, barring, with the exception of. (No longer clearly distinguishable from the conjunction: see below.) OE.
▸**B** *adverb*. (Not always distinguishable from the conjunction.)
1 Without, outside; *spec.* in or into the outer part of a house (orig. the kitchen of a two-roomed house, into which the only outer door opened). Cf. BEN *adverb*. Long *obsolete* exc. *Scot. & N. English*. OE.
2 Only, no more than. ME.

> F. NORRIS They agreed to charge but two-fifty, and they've got to stick to it. L. LERNER Those airs But fascinate the sight; No true delight is hers. P. REDGROVE Is there but one spider in all this spacious room?

▸**C** *conjunction & neg. rel. pronoun*. **1** In a simple sentence, introducing a word, phr., or (rarely) clause: without, with the exception of, except, save; if not, unless; *ellipt.* anything else than, other(wise) than. OE.

> SHAKES. *Temp.* I should sin To think but nobly of my grandmother. STEELE There needed no more but to advance one step. M. EDGEWORTH He wants nothing but a little common sense. T. JEFFERSON I cannot but be gratified by the assurance. F. D. HEMANS The boy stood on the burning deck, Whence all but he had fled. W. C. SMITH You have no choice but marry Doris now. OED Why have they come but to annoy us? WILL ROGERS I got all my feet through but one. R. LOWELL Who but my girlfriend set the town on fire?

2 In a complex sentence, introducing a subord. clause (also (arch.) *but that*): ▸**a** Except that, if it were not that, short of the condition that. OE. ▸**b** If not, unless, except; rather than . . shall prove untrue; even though the preceding were necessary. OE. ▸**c** (With neg. & interrog.) That . . not; *ellipt.* not to say that . . not; without; *arch.* that, before, than. Also (colloq.) *but what*. LME.

> **a** SOUTHEY I too should be content to dwell in peace . . But that my country calls. H. MATTHEWS Nothing would please him but I must try on his mitres. **b** DEFOE I'd burn the house down but I'd find it. C. M. YONGE Ten to one but the police have got them. **c** ROBERT BURTON How is it possible but that we should be discontent? HENRY FIELDING No sooner acquainted my brother, but he immediately wanted to propose it. A. TROLLOPE Nor am I yet so old but what I can rough it still. J. RUSKIN I do not doubt but that you are surprised. OED Not but that I should have gone if I had had the chance. J. FREEMAN There's not a bird singing upon this bough But sings the sweeter in our English ears. *Proverb*: It never rains but it pours.

3 In a compound sentence, connecting the two parts (the second of which may be greatly contracted), or introducing a separate but related sentence: ▸**a** On the contrary. OE. ▸**b** Nevertheless, yet, however; on the other hand, despite this; moreover. ME. ▸**c** As an intensive, freq. after an exclamation, or introducing an emphatic repetition. M19.

> **a** J. HEALEY Monkeyes, and Babiounes, were not men but beasts. M. HAMBURGER He must not sleep, but leans against the boards. D. ATTENBOROUGH You might be excused for thinking . . that the lamprey is a true fish. But it is not. **b** G. PUTTENHAM It is not only allowable, but also necessary. J. WILSON Fare ye well. But list! sweet youths . . beware. B. JOWETT They not only tell lies but bad lies. N. COWARD Had she my talent for organisation? . . No, but she hadn't your mother either. H. NEMEROV He cries a little but is brave. A. PRICE 'Did you have a brilliant idea?' . . 'Not exactly brilliant, but an idea.' **c** OED Excuse me! but your coat is dusty. M. CORELLI 'I believe you would do it if I asked you!' . . 'But, of course!' D. H. LAWRENCE And about *everything* I talked to her: but everything. I. FLEMING I'm goin' fix that man, but good.

– PHRASES: *anything but*: see ANYTHING *pronoun*. **but and** (*obsolete* exc. *Scot.*) and also. **but for** except for, were it not for. **but one**, **but two**, etc., if one, two, etc., were excluded from the count (with ordinals etc.). *but that*, *but what*: see sense C.2 above. *but then*: see THEN *adverb* etc. **but too** — only too —.

butadiene /bjuːtəˈdʌɪiːn/ *noun*. E20.
[ORIGIN from BUTANE + DI-[2] + -ENE.]
CHEMISTRY. A gaseous unsaturated hydrocarbon, C_4H_6, of which there are two isomers; *esp.* the isomer $CH_2{=}CH{\cdot}CH{=}CH_2$ (*buta*-1,3-*diene*), used in making synthetic rubber.

butane /ˈbjuːteɪn/ *noun*. L19.
[ORIGIN from BUTYL + -ANE.]
CHEMISTRY. A gaseous alkane, C_4H_{10} (of which there are two isomers), used esp. in liquefied form as a fuel.
■ **butaˈnoic** *adjective* = BUTYRIC M20. **butanol** *noun* each of four isomeric liquid alcohols, C_4H_9OH; butyl alcohol: L19. **butanone** *noun* a liquid ketone, $C_2H_5COCH_3$; methyl ethyl ketone: E20.

Butazolidin /bjuːtəˈzɒlɪdɪn/ *noun*. Also **b-**, **-ine**. M20.
[ORIGIN from BUTYL + PYRAZOLE + -IDINE.]
PHARMACOLOGY. (Proprietary name for) the drug phenylbutazone.

butch /bʊtʃ/ *noun*[1]. *colloq.* (chiefly *N. Amer.*). E20.
[ORIGIN Abbreviation.]
A butcher; *esp.* = BUTCHER *noun* 4.
news butch: see NEWS *noun*.

butch /bʊtʃ/ *noun*[2] *& adjective*. *slang*. M20.
[ORIGIN Uncertain: perh. from BUTCHER *noun*.]
▸**A** *noun*. A tough youth or man; a mannish woman; a homosexual (esp. female) of masculine behaviour or appearance. M20.
▸**B** *adjective*. Toughly masculine, mannish (freq. of homosexuals). M20.
butch haircut *N. Amer.* a crew cut.

butch /bʊtʃ/ *verb trans. & intrans.* *dial.* L18.
[ORIGIN Back-form. from BUTCHER *noun*.]
Follow the trade of a butcher; cut up, hack.

butcher /ˈbʊtʃə/ *noun*. ME.
[ORIGIN Anglo-Norman var. of Old French *bo(u)chier* (mod. *boucher*), from Old French *boc* he-goat (mod. *bouc*), prob. from Celtic formed as BUCK *noun*[1]: see -ER[2].]
1 A person whose trade is to slaughter animals for food, or simply (now the predominant sense) to sell the flesh of animals for food; a trader in meat. ME.
2 *fig.* A person responsible for the slaughter of people; a person who kills needlessly or wantonly; a brutal murderer. ME.

> *Vanity Fair* The man who has been called the Butcher of the Balkans, the father of 'ethnic cleansing'.

3 A kind of artificial angling fly. M19.
4 A seller of refreshments, newspapers, etc. in a train, theatre, etc. *N. Amer. colloq.* L19.
5 *butcher's*, *butchers*, = *butcher's hook* below. *slang*. M20.

> *Company* Just take a butcher's at this page every month.

– PHRASES & COMB.: **butcher-bird** a shrike of the family Laniidae or (*Austral.*) Cracticidae. **butcher block** *N. Amer.* a material used to make kitchen worktops and tables, consisting of strips of wood glued together. **butcher blue** a dark blue like that often used for butchers' aprons. **butcher-boots** high boots without tops. **butcher's bill** *colloq.* the list of casualties in a battle. **butcher's broom** a low evergreen shrub of the chiefly Mediterranean genus *Ruscus*, of the lily family; esp. *R. aculeatus*, which has stiff flat spine-tipped leaflike shoots. **butcher's hook** *noun & adjective* (*rhyming slang*) (*a*) *noun* a look; (*b*) *adjective* (*Austral. & NZ*) [from CROOK *adjective* 3] angry. **butcher's knife** a meat knife; any large strong-bladed knife. **butcher meat**, **butcher's meat**: excluding poultry, fish, game, and cured meats. FAMILY *butcher*. *news butcher*: see NEWS *noun*. **the butcher, the baker, the candlestick-maker** people of all trades.
■ **butcherly** *adjective* like a butcher; brutal: E16.

butcher /ˈbʊtʃə/ *verb*. M16.
[ORIGIN from the noun.]
1 *verb trans.* Slaughter in the manner of a butcher; kill needlessly, wantonly, or brutally. M16. ▸**b** *fig.* Ruin by clumsiness or ineptitude. M17.
2 *verb trans. & intrans.* Cut up and divide (meat) as a butcher does; carry on the trade of a butcher. L18.
■ **butcherer** *noun* M17.

butchery /ˈbʊtʃəri/ *noun*. ME.
[ORIGIN Old French & mod. French *boucherie* formed as BUTCHER *noun* + -Y[3].]
1 A butcher's establishment (usu. public), a slaughterhouse or meat market. ME.
2 The trade of a butcher. Now usu. *attrib.* LME.
3 Cruel or wanton slaughter, carnage. M16.

bute /bjuːt/ *noun*. *colloq.* M20.
[ORIGIN Abbreviation; cf. BUTAZOLIDIN.]
The drug phenylbutazone.

butea /ˈbjuːtɪə/ *noun*. L18.
[ORIGIN mod. Latin, from John Stuart, Earl of *Bute* (1713–92): see -A[1].]
A leguminous tree or climbing plant of the genus *Butea*, native to tropical Asia; *esp.* the dhak tree, *B. monosperma*.

butene /ˈbjuːtiːn/ *noun*. L19.
[ORIGIN from BUTYL + -ENE.]
CHEMISTRY. A gaseous alkene, C_4H_8, of which there are three isomers. Also called *butylene*.
■ **butenyl** *noun* a radical, $C_4H_7{\cdot}$, derived from any of these isomers L19.

buteo /ˈbjuːtɪəʊ/ *noun*. Pl. **-os**. L19.
[ORIGIN Latin, = buzzard, hawk.]
Any of the broad-winged birds of prey belonging to the genus *Buteo*, typified by the Eurasian common buzzard and the American red-tailed hawk.

buteonine /bjʊˈtiːənʌɪn/ *adjective*. M19.
[ORIGIN from Latin *buteo(n-)* hawk, buzzard + -INE[1]: see BUZZARD *noun*[1].]
Of the nature of or resembling a buzzard.

Buteyko /buːˈteɪkəʊ/ *noun*. L20.
[ORIGIN Konstantin Pavlovich *Buteyko* (1923–), Russian physiologist, who devised the method.]
Used *attrib.* to designate a method of breathing which aims to control hyperventilation, increasing the level of carbon dioxide in the lungs, and appears in some cases to alleviate the symptoms of asthma, as *Buteyko method*.

†**butine** *noun* var. of BUTYNE.

butler /ˈbʌtlə/ *noun & verb*. ME.
[ORIGIN Anglo-Norman *buteler*, Old French & mod. French *bouteillier* cup-bearer, from *bouteille* BOTTLE *noun*[1]: see -ER[2].]
▸**A** *noun*. **1** A servant who has charge of a household's or other establishment's wine cellar and plate etc.; a principal manservant. ME.
2 *hist.* An officer of high rank (nominally) in charge of wine for the royal table. ME.
▸**B** *verb trans. & intrans.* Act as a butler (to); deal with as a butler. M18.
■ **butlerage** *noun* (*a*) *hist.* a duty on imported wine payable to the king's butler; (*b*) the office of butler, a butler's department: L15. **butleress** *noun* (*rare*) a female butler E17. **butlership** *noun* the office of butler M16. **butlery** *noun* a butler's room or pantry; a buttery: ME.

butment /ˈbʌtm(ə)nt/ *noun*. E17.
[ORIGIN from BUTT *verb*[2] + -MENT.]
An abutment; an abutting piece of ground etc.

B

butobarbitone /bjuːtəʊˈbɑːbɪtəʊn/ *noun*. **M20**.
[ORIGIN from BUT(YL + -O- + BARBIT(URIC + -ONE.]
PHARMACOLOGY. A sedative and hypnotic drug, 5-butyl-5-ethylbarbituric acid, $C_{10}H_{16}N_2O_3$. Proprietary name *Soneryl*.

butoh /ˈbuːtəʊ/ *noun*. **L20**.
[ORIGIN Japanese = dance.]
A style of Japanese modern dance featuring dancers covered in white body paint.

butoxide /bjuːˈtɒksʌɪd/ *noun*. **M20**.
[ORIGIN from BUTYL + OXIDE.]
CHEMISTRY. A compound of the radical $C_4H_9O\cdot$.

butsecarl *noun* var. of BUSCARL.

Butskellism /ˈbʌtskəlɪz(ə)m/ *noun*. **M20**.
[ORIGIN Blend of R. A. *Butler* (Conservative Chancellor of the Exchequer 1951–5) and H. T. N. *Gaitskell* (Labour Chancellor of the Exchequer 1950–1 and subsequently Shadow Chancellor) + -ISM.]
POLITICS. The adoption of economic policies broadly acceptable to both main British political parties.
■ **Butskellite** *adjective & noun* (an adherent) of Butskellism **M20**.

butt /bʌt/ *noun*^{1}. Long *dial*. **ME**.
[ORIGIN Middle Low German *but*, Middle Dutch *but(te)*, *bot(te)*, prob. rel. to Low German *but*, Middle Dutch *bot* stumpy: cf. BUTT *noun*^{4}.]
A flatfish, *esp*. a sole, plaice, or turbot. Cf. HALIBUT.

butt /bʌt/ *noun*^{2}. **ME**.
[ORIGIN Old French & mod. French *but*, of unknown origin: perh. infl. by French *butte* rising ground, knoll, (also) target (cf. BUTT *noun*^{10}).]
1 A mound upon which a target is set up for archery or shooting practice; a target; in *pl*., a range for target practice. **ME**. ▸**b** The length of a shooting range. Now *rare* or *obsolete*. **M16**. ▸**c** A concealed stand for grouse-shooting, screened by a low wall of turf or stone. **L19**.
2 A terminal point, a boundary mark. Now *dial*. & *N. Amer.* **LME**.
3 A thing towards which one's efforts are directed; an end, an aim, a goal. **L16**.

SHAKES. *Hen. V* To which is fixed as an aim or butt Obedience.

4 An object of (or *of*) teasing, ridicule, abuse, etc. **E17**.

P. MORTIMER Poor man, the butt of everyone's anger. K. M. E. MURRAY He was the butt of the bigger boys because of his inability to pronounce 'ch'. P. F. BOLLER As Truman's popularity . . dropped . . he became the butt of bad jokes and nasty quips.

butt /bʌt/ *noun*^{3}. **LME**.
[ORIGIN Anglo-Norman *but*, Old French *bot*, *bout* (mod. *botte*), from late Latin *buttis*. In Anglo-Latin *butta*, *bota*.]
A cask or barrel, esp. for wine or ale; this as a former measure of capacity, usu. equal to two hogsheads.

SIR T. MORE Hastely drouned in a Butte of Malmesey. J. MASEFIELD Only the water . . gurgled through the rain-pipe to the butt.

SCUTTLEBUTT. *SCUTTLED butt*.

butt /bʌt/ *noun*^{4}. **LME**.
[ORIGIN App. rel. to Middle Dutch & mod. Dutch *bot* stumpy (cf. BUTT *noun*^{1}) and to base of BUTTOCK (cf. BUTT *noun*^{5}).]
1 The thicker end of anything, esp. of a tool or weapon, or of the handle of a gun, fishing rod, etc. **LME**.
2 The end of a plank (in a ship's side) which meets a similar plank end on. **LME**.
3 The buttocks. *dial*. & *N. Amer.* **LME**.
4 (Leather made from) the thicker or hinder end of a hide. **M16**.
5 The trunk of a tree, *esp*. the part just above the ground. **E17**. ▸**b** The foot of a branch or leaf stalk. **L17**.
6 The stub of a cigarette or cigar. **M19**.
– COMB.: **butt end** a butt (chiefly senses 2 and 6 above); **butt-head** = sense 2 above; **butt joint**, **butt weld**: in which pieces are joined end to end; **butt naked** *adjective* (*colloq*.) completely naked.

butt /bʌt/ *noun*^{5}. **LME**.
[ORIGIN Prob. from base of BUTTOCK; rel. to Low German *butt*, Middle Dutch *botte*, Middle High German *butze*, Old Norse *butr*, Old English *bytt* small piece of land. Perh. already in Old English (cf. Anglo-Latin *butta*, *buttes*).]
A ridge of ploughed land, esp. a short one at the edge of a field; *sing*. & (usu.) in *pl*., a small piece of land.

butt /bʌt/ *noun*^{6}. **LME**.
[ORIGIN French *botte* from Middle Low German *bōte*: cf. BOTTLE *noun*^{2}.]
A bundle (of cloth etc.); *dial*. a hassock.

butt /bʌt/ *noun*^{7}. *dial*. **M16**.
[ORIGIN Unknown.]
A basket used for catching fish.

butt /bʌt/ *noun*^{8}. **L16**.
[ORIGIN Perh. from BUTT *verb*^{1}.]
A promontory, a headland. *obsolete* exc. in proper names, as *Butt of Lewis*.

butt /bʌt/ *noun*^{9}. **M17**.
[ORIGIN from BUTT *verb*^{1}.]
A push or thrust with the head or horns.
full butt with violent collision, head-on, full tilt.

butt /bʌt/ *noun*^{10}. *obsolete* exc. *dial*. **L17**.
[ORIGIN Old French & mod. French BUTTE.]
A hillock, a mound.

butt /bʌt/ *verb*^{1}. **ME**.
[ORIGIN Anglo-Norman *buter*, Old French *bo(u)ter* from Germanic (repr. by Middle Dutch *botten* strike, sprout).]
1 *verb trans*. & *intrans*. Strike, thrust, shove, usu. with the head or horns; thrust (the head) forward thus; drive or push thus. **ME**.

J. DORAN A couple of rams butting at each other. J. B. MORTON The ridiculous speed with which big boats butt through the waves. A. HIGGINS A heifer was butting its skull against the bars of a gate. P. ROTH With a sharp upward snap of the skull, she butted me on the underside of the jaw. P. THEROUX Most people merely put their heads down and butted their way into the next car.

butt in intrude; intervene, meddle. **butt out** *slang* stop intruding, intervening, or meddling.
2 *verb intrans*. Project, jut (*out*). **LME**.

T. CORYAT A little square gallery butting out from the Tower.

butt /bʌt/ *verb*^{2}. **ME**.
[ORIGIN Partly from BUTT *noun*^{2}; partly aphet. from ABUT.]
1 *verb intrans*. & *trans*. (Cause to) touch with an end, abut, or adjoin; *spec*. lie or place with one end flat *against*, *on*, etc., meet or join end to end. **ME**.
2 *verb trans*. Fix or mark (*out*) the limits of lengthwise; terminate, limit, bound. Usu. in *pass*. Now *rare* or *obsolete*. **E16**.

butte /bjuːt/ *noun*. **M19**.
[ORIGIN French: see BUTT *noun*^{2}.]
PHYSICAL GEOGRAPHY & *N. Amer.* An isolated hill with steep sides and a flat top, similar to but narrower than a mesa.

butter /ˈbʌtə/ *noun*^{1}.
[ORIGIN Old English *butere*, corresp. to Old Frisian, Old High German *butera* (Dutch *boter*, German *Butter*), from West Germanic from Latin *butyrum* from Greek *bouturon*.]
1 The fatty substance obtained from cream by churning, used to spread on bread etc., and in cookery. **OE**. ▸**b** *fig*. Unctuous flattery. *colloq*. **E19**.
black butter: see BLACK *adjective*. **brandy butter**, **rum butter**, etc., a hard sauce containing brandy, rum, etc., and butter. *bread and butter*: see BREAD *noun*^{1}. **look as if butter would not melt in one's mouth** seem demure. **melted butter** (*a*) butter that has been melted; (*b*) a sauce of butter, flour, etc.
2 *transf*. Any substance resembling butter in appearance or consistency. **LME**. ▸**b** *CHEMISTRY*. The anhydrous chloride *of* antimony, arsenic, etc. *arch*. **M17**.
butter of almonds a preparation of cream, whites of eggs, and blanched almonds. *cocoa butter*: see COCOA *noun*^{1}. *PEANUT butter*. *SHEA butter*. **vegetable butter** any edible fatty substance similar to butter, obtained from plants.
– COMB.: **butter-and-egg man** *US slang* a wealthy but unsophisticated man who spends money freely; **butter-and-eggs** a plant whose flower has two shades of yellow, esp. toadflax; **butterball** (*a*) a piece of butter moulded into a ball; (*b*) *N. Amer.* [because very fat in autumn] = *bufflehead* (b) s.v. BUFFLE; **butter bean** (*a*) a variety of French bean with yellow pods; (*b*) a dried white Lima bean; **butter-box** (*a*) a box for holding butter; a vessel or vehicle resembling this; (*b*) *derog*. a Dutchman; a Dutch ship; (*c*) *US* = *butterball* (b) above; **butterbur** a streamside plant of the composite family, *Petasites hybridus*, bearing spikes of pale purple flowers and with large soft leaves formerly used for wrapping butter; also (with specifying word), any of several related plants; **butter-bush** *Austral*. a small tree, *Pittosporum phylliraeoides*, of which the wood is used for turnery and the leaves for fodder; **butter cloth** a thin loosely woven cloth with a fine mesh, orig. used primarily as a wrapping for butter; **butter-cooler** a vessel for keeping butter cool when on the table; **buttercream** a mixture of butter, sugar, etc., as a filling or a topping for a cake; **butterfat** the essential fats of pure butter; **butter-fingered** *adjective* apt to let things fall or slip; **butter-fingers** a butter-fingered person; *esp*. one who fails to hold a catch; **butterfish** any of various slippery mucus-coated fishes, *esp*. the gunnel, or (*N. Amer.*) an edible marine fish of the family Stromateidae; **butter knife** a blunt knife for cutting butter at table; **buttermilk** the acidulous milk which remains after the butter has been churned out; **butter muslin** = *butter cloth* above; **butternut** (*a*) any of certain trees or bushes yielding oily nuts; *esp*. the N. American white walnut, *Juglans cinerea*; also, its timber or fruit; (*b*) *N. Amer.* a brownish-grey colour; **butternut squash**, a popular winter squash of a pear-shaped variety with light yellowish-brown rind and orange flesh; **butter pat** (*a*) a pat of butter; (*b*) a wooden implement for working butter into shape; **butter-print** a stamp for marking butter pats; an impression from this; **butterscotch** a kind of toffee made chiefly with butter and sugar; **butter-tree** an African or Indian tree yielding vegetable butter, *esp*. the shea; †**butter-weight** 18 or more ounces to the pound; good measure; **butterwort** any of various insectivorous plants of peat bogs, of the genus *Pinguicula* of the bladderwort family, with purple flowers and yellowish-green greasy leaves.
■ **butterless** *adjective* **M19**.

†**butter** *noun*^{2}. **L15–E17**.
[ORIGIN Old French & mod. French *boutoir*, from *bo(u)ter* BUTT *verb*^{1}.]
= BUTTERIS.

butter /ˈbʌtə/ *noun*^{3}. **E17**.
[ORIGIN from BUTT *verb*^{1} + -ER^1.]
An animal that butts.

butter /ˈbʌtə/ *verb trans*. **LME**.
[ORIGIN from BUTTER *noun*^{1}.]
1 Spread with butter; cook or dish up with butter. **LME**.

Proverb: Fine words butter no parsnips.

have one's bread buttered on both sides, *want one's bread buttered on both sides*, *know which side one's bread is buttered*: see BREAD *noun*^{1}.
2 *fig*. Flatter lavishly. Now usu. foll. by *up*. **E18**.

M. MITCHELL Buttering them up with smiles and kind words was the surest way to get their business for her mill.

butter-bump /ˈbʌtəbʌmp/ *noun*. *dial*. **L17**.
[ORIGIN from var. of BITTERN *noun*^{1} + BUMP *verb*^{2}.]
The bittern.

buttercup /ˈbʌtəkʌp/ *noun*. In sense 2 orig. †**-cups**. **E16**.
[ORIGIN from BUTTER *noun*^{1} + CUP *noun*.]
†**1** A cup for holding butter. **E–M16**.
2 Any of various plants of the genus *Ranunculus* (family Ranunculaceae), bearing bright yellow cup-shaped flowers; a flowering stem of such a plant. **L18**.
creeping buttercup, *meadow buttercup*, *turban buttercup*, etc.
– PHRASES: *Bermuda buttercup*: see BERMUDA 3.
■ **buttercupped**, **buttercuppy** *adjectives* having many buttercups, covered with buttercups **L19**.

butterfly /ˈbʌtəflʌɪ/ *noun*. **OE**.
[ORIGIN from BUTTER *noun*^{1} + FLY *noun*^{1}, perh. with ref. to the yellow or creamy-white colour of familiar species such as the brimstone.]
1 Any of a large group of insects which together with moths constitute the order Lepidoptera and are distinguished from moths (in most instances) by diurnal activity, clubbed or dilated antennae, thin bodies, the usu. erect position of the wings when at rest, and brighter colouring. **OE**.
break a butterfly on a wheel use unnecessary force in destroying something fragile. *brimstone butterfly*, *comma butterfly*, *monarch butterfly*, *peacock butterfly*, *tortoiseshell butterfly*, etc.
2 *fig*. **a** A showy or frivolous person. **L16**. ▸**b** A person whose period of work or occupation of a place is transitory or seasonal. **L19**.
a social butterfly: see SOCIAL *adjective*.
3 Usu. in *pl*. Fluttering sensations felt before any formidable venture. Esp. in *butterflies in the stomach* etc. **E20**.

Sunday Times I always have butterflies when I open Parliament.

4 In full *butterfly stroke*. A swimming stroke in which both arms are lifted out of the water at the same time. **M20**.
– COMB.: **butterfly blenny** a blenny, *Blennius ocellaris*, having a broad, ocellated dorsal fin; **butterfly bow** a bow made up or tied with the loop and end on each side spread apart like the expanded wings of a butterfly; **butterfly bush** a buddleia, *esp*. the species *Buddleja davidii*; **butterfly cake** a small sponge cake with the top cut off and divided into two pieces, which are then fixed to the cake with buttercream at an angle to resemble a butterfly's wings; **butterfly effect** [expressed as 'Does the flap of a butterfly's wings in Brazil set off a tornado in Texas?' (title of a paper by Edward N. Lorenz, 1979)] (with ref. to chaos theory) the phenomenon whereby a minute localized change in a complex system can eventually lead to a large effect elsewhere; **butterfly fish** any of various fishes suggesting a butterfly in shape or coloration, esp. (*a*) = *butterfly blenny* above; (*b*) = CHAETODON; **butterfly flower** (*a*) a papilionaceous flower; (*b*) = SCHIZANTHUS; **butterfly kiss** a fluttering of the eyelashes against the cheek; **butterfly knife** a long, broad knife used in pairs in some forms of kung fu; **butterfly net**: for catching butterflies; **butterfly nose** a dog's nose when spotted or mottled; **butterfly nut** a wing nut; **butterfly orchid** any of various orchids with flowers resembling a butterfly in shape; *esp*. either of two widely distributed European orchids, *Platanthera chlorantha* and *P. bifolia*, with whitish or greenish-white flowers; **butterfly pea** a S. American leguminous plant (esp. of the genus *Clitoria*), with papilionaceous flowers; *butterfly stroke*: see sense 4 above; **butterfly valve** a valve with hinged semicircular plates; **butterfly weed** *N. Amer.* a milkweed, esp. the orange-flowered *Asclepias tuberosa*.

butteris /ˈbʌt(ə)rɪs/ *noun*. **L16**.
[ORIGIN Unexpl. alt. of BUTTER *noun*^{2}.]
A farrier's tool for paring a horse's hoof.

buttery /ˈbʌt(ə)ri/ *noun*. **ME**.
[ORIGIN Anglo-Norman *boterie*, perh. from *but* BUTT *noun*^{3} or rel. to Old French *botelerie* BUTLERY: see -ERY.]
A place where provisions (orig. liquor) are kept and supplied, *esp*. one in a college or other establishment.
– COMB.: **buttery bar** a board or ledge on a buttery hatch, on which to rest tankards etc.; **buttery hatch** a half-door over which provisions from a buttery are served.

buttery /ˈbʌt(ə)ri/ *adjective*. **LME**.
[ORIGIN from BUTTER *noun*^{1} + -Y^1.]
1 Of the nature of or containing butter; smeared with butter. **LME**.
2 Like butter in consistency. **LME**.
■ **butteriness** *noun* **E16**.

buttie *noun* var. of BUTTY *noun*^{2}.

buttinsky /bʌˈtɪnski/ *noun*. *slang* (orig. *US*). **E20**.
[ORIGIN from *butt in* (see BUTT *verb*^{1}) + *-sky* final elem. in many Slavonic names.]
A person who (habitually) butts in; an intruder, a meddler.

buttle /ˈbʌt(ə)l/ *verb trans*. & *intrans*. *joc*. **M19**.
[ORIGIN Back-form. from BUTLER.]
Serve out (drink); do a butler's work.

buttock /ˈbʌtək/ *noun* & *verb*.
[ORIGIN Old English *buttuc*: see BUTT *noun*^{5}, -OCK.]
▸ **A** *noun*. †**1** = BUTT *noun*^{5}. Only in **OE**.
2 Either of the two fleshy protuberances on the lower rear part of the human body; a corresponding part of an animal. Usu. in *pl*. **ME**.

T. HARDY Sheep . . stood with their buttocks to the winds. M. BRADBURY Plastic chairs, their seats moulded to the shape of some average universal buttock.

3 *NAUTICAL*. The breadth of a ship where the hull rounds down to the stern. **E17**.
4 *WRESTLING*. A throw using the buttocks or hip. **L17**.
5 *MINING*. A break in the line of a coalface, from which coal is being broken out. **L19**.
▸ **B** *verb trans.* †**1** Overtake (a horse) in a race. Only in **E17**.
2 *WRESTLING*. Throw by a manoeuvre using the buttocks or hip. **L19**.
■ **buttocked** *adjective* having buttocks (of a specified kind) **LME**.

button /ˈbʌt(ə)n/ *noun*. **ME**.
[**ORIGIN** Old French & mod. French *bouton* from Proto-Romance from Germanic (rel. to BUTT *verb*[1]).]
1 A small knob, stud, or disc attached to any object; *esp.* one sewn to a garment to fasten it by passing through an opening (a buttonhole), or for ornament, or attached as a badge. **ME**. ▸**b** A button as a type of anything of little value. **ME**. ▸**c** In *pl.* (treated as *sing.*). (A name for) a boy servant in livery, a page. *colloq.* **M19**.
F. RAPHAEL His privilege was to wear the top two buttons of his jacket undone. **b** J. CLAVELL Cheap . . they hardly cost a button a week.
2 A bud, or other similarly shaped part of a plant; *esp.* = ***button mushroom*** below. **ME**. ▸**b** In names of plants: having button-like flowers, seed vessels, etc. Usu. in *pl.* **M16**.
3 A small rounded lesion, esp. of leishmaniasis. **L16**.
4 Any small rounded body, as a knob fixed on the point of a fencing foil (to make it harmless), a globule of metal remaining in a crucible after fusion, etc. **E17**. ▸**b** The point of the chin. *US slang*. **E20**.
5 A knob etc. which is pressed or turned to fasten a door, operate a mechanism, complete an electric circuit, etc. **E17**.
A. MACLEAN Schaffer pressed the 'start' button and a generator whined into life.
– PHRASES: **a button short** *colloq.* of low intelligence, not very bright. ***bachelor's button(s)***: see BACHELOR. ***be dollars to buttons***: see DOLLAR. ***belly button***: see BELLY *noun*. ***olive button***: see OLIVE *noun*[1] & *adjective*. **on the button** (chiefly *N. Amer.*) on the point of the chin; exactly on the target; precise(ly), on the dot. ***pink button***: see PINK *adjective*[2]. **press the button** *fig.* initiate an action or train of events, esp. nuclear war. **take by the button** = BUTTONHOLE *verb* 2.
– COMB.: **buttonball** = *buttonwood* (a) below; **button-boy** a page; **buttonbush** *N. Amer.* a shrub of the madder family, *Cephalanthus occidentalis*, having globular flower heads; **button chrysanthemum** *US* a variety of chrysanthemum with many small round flower heads; **button day** *Austral.* a day on which money is raised for a cause by the sale of badges which are worn as evidence of support; **button ear** a dog's ear which laps over and hides the inside; **button grass** *Austral.* any of various sedges and grasses with rounded or compact inflorescences; †**button-hold** *verb trans.* [back-form. from *button-holder*] = BUTTONHOLE *verb* 2; **button-holder** †(*a*) a person who buttonholes another; (*b*) a case for holding buttons; **buttonhook** (*a*) a hook for drawing small buttons into place; (*b*) *AMER. FOOTBALL* a type of pass for the receiver running straight downfield and then doubling back a few steps to receive it; **button-mould** a disc of wood etc. to be covered with cloth to form a button; **button mushroom** a young unopened mushroom; **button-nosed** *adjective* having a small roundish nose; **button-quail** a bird of the family Turnicidae, resembling a quail but related to the crakes and rails; **button spider** a highly venomous African spider of the genus *Latrodectus*, a close relative of the American black widow; **button-stick** an appliance used to protect the cloth around a button during polishing; **button-tree** a tropical tree or shrub of the genus *Conocarpus*, found in mangrove swamps; **buttonwood** (*a*) the N. American plane, *Platanus occidentalis*; (*b*) its timber; (*c*) = *button-tree* above.
■ **buttonless** *adjective* **M17**. **button-like** *adjective* resembling a button, small and round **M19**. **buttony** *adjective* **L16**.

button /ˈbʌt(ə)n/ *verb*. **LME**.
[**ORIGIN** from the noun. Earlier in UNBUTTON.]
▸ **I** Corresp. to BUTTON *noun* 1.
1 *verb trans.* Provide or adorn with a button or buttons. **LME**.
2 *verb trans.* Fasten or secure with buttons; fasten the clothing of (a person, esp. oneself) with buttons. Freq. foll. by *up*. **LME**. ▸**b** *verb trans. fig.* Close (*up*) tightly, fasten, confine. **L16**. ▸**c** *verb intrans.* Fasten one's buttons *up*. **M19**.
R. L. STEVENSON I buttoned myself into my coat. **b** CARLYLE Thoughts—which he must button close up.
b button one's lip, **button one's face** *slang* be silent, stop talking.
3 *verb intrans.* Of a garment: be (able to be) fastened (*up*) with buttons. **L18**.
▸ **II** Corresp. to BUTTON *noun* 2.
4 *verb intrans.* Of (a part of) a plant: bud; assume a globular shape. **LME**.
– COMB.: **button-down** *adjective* (orig. *US*) (of a collar) having the points buttoned to the shirt; **button-through** *adjective* (of a dress etc.) fastening by buttons over its whole length; **button-up** *adjective* that buttons up.
■ **buttoning** *noun* (*a*) the action of the verb; (*b*) (now *rare*) a button fastening, a button: **L16**.

buttoned /ˈbʌt(ə)nd/ *adjective*. **M16**.
[**ORIGIN** from BUTTON *noun*, *verb*: see -ED[2], -ED[1].]
1 Having buttons (of specified kind or number); adorned with buttons. **M16**.
2 Fastened with buttons; with one's clothes fastened with buttons. **E19**.
buttoned up *fig.* (*a*) (of a person) reserved, uncommunicative; (*b*) *slang* (of a plan etc.) successfully arranged.

buttonhole /ˈbʌt(ə)nhəʊl/ *noun* & *verb*. **M16**.
[**ORIGIN** from BUTTON *noun* + HOLE *noun*[1]. In sense B.2 app. alt. of *button-hold* s.v. BUTTON *noun*.]
▸ **A** *noun*. **1** An opening made in a garment in order to receive a button for fastening; a similar opening made for ornamentation in the lapel of a coat etc. **M16**.
take a buttonhole lower, **take down a buttonhole** humiliate.
2 *transf.* A slit or other opening resembling a buttonhole. **L16**.
3 A flower or bouquet worn in a lapel buttonhole. **L19**.
– COMB.: **buttonhole stitch** a looped stitch used for edging buttonholes.
▸ **B** *verb*. **1** *verb intrans.* Sew buttonholes. **E19**. ▸**b** *verb trans.* Make buttonhole openings in; sew with buttonhole stitch. **E20**.
2 *verb trans.* Take hold of (as) by a coat or waistcoat button; detain (a listener) willy-nilly. **M19**.
J. GALSWORTHY It was his salutary custom to buttonhole a director afterwards, and ask him whether he thought the coming year would be good or bad.
■ **buttonholer** *noun* (*a*) a person who makes buttonholes; (*b*) an appliance for making buttonholes; (*c*) a person who buttonholes another: **L19**.

buttress /ˈbʌtrɪs/ *noun* & *verb*. **ME**.
[**ORIGIN** Old French (*ars*) *bo(u)terez* thrusting arch, from *bo(u)ter* BUTT *verb*[1].]
▸ **A** *noun*. **1** A structure of wood, stone, or brick built against a wall to strengthen or support it. **ME**.
H. ADAMS At this corner the architect had to provide a heavy buttress against a double strain. *fig.*: T. FULLER His title . . had strong buttresses.
flying buttress: see FLYING *ppl adjective*.
2 *loosely*. A prop, a pier, an abutment. **LME**.
W. H. PRESCOTT An aqueduct . . carried . . on huge buttresses of masonry.
3 A similarly projecting portion of a hill or mountain. **L17**.
P. MATTHIESSEN A series of ridges that terminate in buttresses . . where the mountain falls away into Black River.
– COMB.: **buttress root** a tree root whose upper parts project from the trunk like a buttress.
▸ **B** *verb trans.* Provide, sustain, or strengthen with a buttress (freq. *fig.*). Occas. foll. by *up*. **LME**.
E. LINKLATER Their tenuous blood-relationship was buttressed firmly by friendship. L. VAN DER POST Traps . . woven out of reeds and buttressed with young karee wood.

butty /ˈbʌti/ *noun*[1]. *dial.* **L18**.
[**ORIGIN** Prob. from *play* BOOTY.]
1 A confederate; a mate. **L18**.
2 *MINING*. A middleman who contracts to raise coal or ore. *obsolete* exc. *hist.* **M19**.
3 In full ***butty boat***. A second barge or freight boat in tow by a first. **E20**.
– COMB.: **butty gang** a gang of men jointly undertaking a large job and sharing the profits equally.

butty /ˈbʌti/ *noun*[2]. Also **buttie**. *N. English*. **M19**.
[**ORIGIN** from BUTTER *noun*[1] + -Y[6].]
A slice of bread and butter; a sandwich.
I. RANKIN The canteen did a fine bacon buttie.

butut /ˈbuːtuːt/ *noun*. Pl. **-s**, same. **L20**.
[**ORIGIN** W. African.]
A monetary unit of (The) Gambia, equal to one-hundredth of a dalasi.

butyl /ˈbjuːtʌɪl, -tɪl/ *noun*. **M19**.
[**ORIGIN** from BUTYRIC + -YL.]
CHEMISTRY. **1** A radical, C_4H_9·, derived from a butane. Usu. in *comb.* Also called ***tetryl***. **M19**.
2 In full ***butyl rubber***. Synthetic rubber made by polymerizing isobutylene (2-methylpropene). **M20**.
■ **butylate** *verb trans.* introduce a butyl substituent into (a compound) **M20**. **butylene** *noun* = BUTENE **M19**.

butyne /ˈbjuːtʌɪn/ *noun*. Orig. †**-ine**. **L19**.
[**ORIGIN** from BUTYL + -YNE.]
CHEMISTRY. A gaseous alkyne, C_4H_6, of which there are two isomers.

butyraceous /bjuːtɪˈreɪʃəs/ *adjective*. **M17**.
[**ORIGIN** formed as BUTYRATE + -ACEOUS.]
1 Of the nature of butter; buttery. **M17**.
2 Producing or containing butter. **M19**.

butyrate /ˈbjuːtɪreɪt/ *noun*. **M19**.
[**ORIGIN** from BUTYRIC + -ATE[1].]
CHEMISTRY. A salt or ester of butyric acid.

butyric /bjuːˈtɪrɪk/ *adjective*. **E19**.
[**ORIGIN** from Latin *butyrum* BUTTER *noun*[1] + -IC.]
Of or pertaining to butter (*rare* in *gen.* sense); ***butyric acid*** (*CHEMISTRY*), a syrupy fatty acid, C_3H_7COOH, present in rancid butter (also called ***butanoic acid***).

butyrometer /bjuːtɪˈrɒmɪtə/ *noun*. **L19**.
[**ORIGIN** formed as BUTYRIC + -OMETER.]
A refractometer used for measuring the amount of butterfat in milk.

butyrophenone /ˌbjuːtɪrəʊfɪˈnəʊn, -ˈfɛnəʊn/ *noun*. **E20**.
[**ORIGIN** formed as BUTYRIC + -PHENONE.]
CHEMISTRY & PHARMACOLOGY. A liquid ketone, $C_6H_5{\cdot}CO(CH_2)_2CH_3$, *n*-propyl phenyl ketone. Also, any of a class of piperidine derivatives of this used as antipsychotic drugs.

B

butyrous /ˈbjuːtɪrəs/ *adjective*. Now *rare* or *obsolete*. **M17**.
[**ORIGIN** formed as BUTYRIC + -OUS.]
= BUTYRACEOUS.

buvette /bjuːˈvɛt, *foreign* byvɛt (*pl. same*)/ *noun*. **M18**.
[**ORIGIN** French.]
A tavern; a small inn; a refreshment bar or room.

buxarry /ˈbʌksəri/ *noun*. *obsolete* exc. *hist.* **M18**.
[**ORIGIN** Hindi *baksārī* person from *Baksar* (Buxar), a town in Bihar, India.]
In the Indian subcontinent: a soldier with a matchlock.

buxom /ˈbʌksəm/ *adjective*. **ME**.
[**ORIGIN** from stem of Old English (*ge*)*būgan* bend, BOW *verb*[1] + -SOME[1].]
†**1** Compliant (*to*); meek; gracious, obliging, kindly; easily moved, prone (*to do*). **ME–M19**.
†**2** Physically pliable, flexible, unresisting. **L16–L17**.
MILTON Wing silently the buxom air.
3 Bright, lively, cheerful. *arch.* **L16**.
R. HEBER Freedom's buxom blast.
4 Chiefly of a woman: full of health, vigour, and good temper; plump and comely. **L16**.
CONAN DOYLE An elderly, motherly woman of the buxom land-lady type. *Economist* Her jolly, kindly personality and her buxom charm.
■ **buxomness** *noun* **ME**.

buy /bʌɪ/ *noun*. Orig. *US*. **L19**.
[**ORIGIN** from the verb.]
A purchase; a thing bought or considered for buying.
best buy: that giving the best value for money. **good buy** a favourable bargain, a thing cheaply bought.

buy /bʌɪ/ *verb*. Pa. t. **bought** /bɔːt/; pa. pple **bought**, (*dial.*) **boughten** /ˈbɔːt(ə)n/.
[**ORIGIN** Old English *byċġan* = Old Saxon *buggian*, Old Norse *byggja* let out, lend, Gothic *bugjan*, from Germanic.]
▸ **I** *verb trans.* **1** Get possession of by giving an equivalent, usu. in money; obtain by paying a price; purchase. Also with indirect obj., obtain for (oneself, another) thus. **OE**. ▸**b** Of things: be an equivalent price for; be the means of procuring, be the payment for. **L16**.
SHAKES. *2 Hen. IV* He's gone into Smithfield to buy your worship a horse. J. STEINBECK Water grew scarce, water was to be bought, five cents, ten cents, fifteen cents a gallon.
be bought and sold *fig.* (*arch.*) be betrayed for a bribe. **bought deal**: in which a securities firm buys a complete issue of shares and then resells them at a prearranged price. ***buy a pig in a poke***: see PIG *noun*[1]. ***buy a pup***: see PUP *noun*. ***buy GAPE-SEED***. **buy money** *slang* bet heavily on a favourite at short odds. ***buy the rabbit***: see RABBIT *noun*.
2 *fig.* Obtain in exchange for something else, or by making some sacrifice; *arch.* redeem, ransom. **ME**.
MILTON Oh dearly bought revenge, yet glorious! *Times* The preservation of Jordan last month has bought time. I. WATTS God the Son . . who bought us with his blood. C. V. WEDGWOOD He had been expected . . to buy his life by incriminating the King.
†**3** = ABY *verb* 2. **ME–E17**.
G. CHAPMAN Not long . . Before thou buy this curious skill with tears.
4 Win over, hire, engage. Usu. in a bad sense: win the favour of by money, influence, etc., bribe. **M17**.
DRYDEN Nor is [he] with Pray'rs, or Bribes, or Flatt'ry bought.
5 Suffer (some mishap); *esp.* (with *it*) be wounded, killed, or destroyed. *slang*. **E19**.
R. LEHMANN The whole street . . had bought it in the blitz.
6 Believe; accept; approve. *slang*. **E20**.
I. WALLACE Part of a conspiracy to overthrow the government—I don't think anyone will buy that.
▸ **II** *verb intrans.* **7** Make a purchase or purchases. **OE**.
R. P. JHABVALA People are buying from the hawkers.
bring-and-buy sale, ***bring-and-buy stall***: see BRING *verb* 1. **buy into** purchase a commission in; obtain a share in by payment; subscribe to (an idea, proposal, etc.).
– WITH ADVERBS IN SPECIALIZED SENSES: **buy in** (*a*) *verb phr. trans.* & *intrans.* collect a stock of (commodities) by purchase; (*b*) *verb phr. trans.* buy back for the owner, e.g. at an auction when the bids are too low; (*c*) *verb phr. trans.* & *intrans.* obtain (entry, a share, etc.) by purchase; purchase (a commission etc.). **buy off** pay to get rid of; induce (a person) to forgo a claim, opposition, etc., by a payment of money. **buy out** (*a*) pay (a person) to give up property, a share, a post, etc.; (*b*) obtain release for (oneself) by payment; (*c*) get rid of (liability) by payment; †(*d*) ransom, redeem. **buy over** win over by a payment, bribe. **buy up** purchase (a stock or the whole of any commodity) with a view to controlling the supply; buy as much as possible of; absorb (a firm etc.) by purchase.
– COMB.: **buy-back** buying a thing after having sold it; **buy-in** (*a*) *US STOCK EXCHANGE* a procedure whereby a broker buys replacement stock for stock not received as contracted, losses being chargeable to the party failing to deliver; (*b*) a buying back of a company's own shares; (*c*) *fig.* agreement with, or acceptance of,

a policy, suggestion, etc.; **buyout** the purchase of the controlling share in a company. **buy side** *US* STOCK EXCHANGE retail brokers and analysts that buy securities (opp. ***sell side*** s.v. SELL *noun*²).
■ **buyable** *adjective* L15.

buyer /ˈbʌɪə/ *noun*. ME.
[ORIGIN from BUY *verb* + -ER¹.]
1 A person who buys. ME.
buyer's market, **buyers' market** conditions in which goods are plentiful and cheap. FIRST-*time buyer*. *special buyer*: see SPECIAL *adjective*.
2 *spec.* An agent who selects and buys stock for a large shop etc. L19.

†**buz** *noun*, *verb* vars. of BUZZ *noun*¹, *verb*¹.

buzz /bʌz/ *noun*¹. Also †**buz**. E17.
[ORIGIN from BUZZ *verb*¹.]
1 A sibilant hum, as that of bees, flies, and other insects. E17. ▸**b** The buzzing sound made by a telephone, electric bell, etc.; *slang* a telephone call. E20.
2 A confused sound made by many people talking or busily occupied; a stir, a ferment; general movement. E17.

ADDISON I found the whole . . Room in a Buz of Politicks. C. MACKENZIE There was a buzz of agreement.

†**3** A groundless fancy; a whim. E–M17.
4 A busy rumour, news. L18.
5 A feeling of excitement or euphoria, *esp.* one induced by narcotic drugs. *slang*. M20.
– COMB.: **buzz bomb** *colloq.* a flying bomb esp. in the Second World War; **buzz cut** a very short haircut in which the hair is clipped close to the head with a razor; **buzzkill** *N. Amer. slang* a person who or thing which dampens enthusiasm or enjoyment; **buzz saw** (orig. *US*) a circular saw; **buzzword** a catchword, a slogan, a pretentious word of little exact meaning.
■ **buzzy** *adjective*¹ (*a*) making a buzz; full of buzzing; (*b*) *colloq.* lively and exciting: L19.

buzz /bʌz/ *noun*². E17.
[ORIGIN Perh. imit.: cf. FUZZ *noun*¹.]
1 A bur. E17.
2 A chafer or similar beetle used as bait; an imitation of this. M18.
– COMB.: **buzzwig** [perh. rel. to BUSBY] a large bushy wig; a person wearing such a wig, a bigwig.
■ **buzzy** *adjective*² hairy, fuzzy M19.

buzz /bʌz/ *verb*¹. Also †**buz** (infl. **-zz-**). LME.
[ORIGIN Imit.]
1 *verb intrans.* Make a humming sibilant sound like that of bees etc.; fly *in*, *out*, etc., with such a sound. LME. ▸**b** *fig.* Flutter or hover (*about*, *over*, etc.) like a buzzing insect; move about busily. M17. ▸**c** Go (quickly). Chiefly in ***buzz off***. *slang*. E20.

b SWIFT Boys and wenches buzzing about the cake-shops like flies.

2 *verb intrans.* **a** Mutter; murmur busily. Usu. *derog. arch.* M16. ▸**b** Make the hum produced by many people talking; be filled with (or *with*) activity. M19.

b Q. BELL Cambridge was . . a place buzzing with ideas.

3 *verb trans.* Tell in a low murmur; whisper busily. *arch.* L16.

F. W. FARRAR Buzzing their envenomed slanders into the ears of these country people.

4 *verb trans.* Spread as a rumour with whispering or busy talk. E17.

GEO. ELIOT Stories . . beginning to be buzzed about.

5 *verb trans.* Assail by buzzing. Now *spec.* fly an aircraft fast and close to (another etc.). L17.
6 *verb trans.* Utter with, or express by, buzzing. M18.

THACKERAY The professional gentlemen hummed and buzzed a sincere applause.

7 *verb trans.* Cause to make a buzz. E19.
8 *verb trans.* Throw swiftly or forcibly. *colloq.* L19.
9 *verb trans.* Signal or telephone by a buzzer; telephone. E20.

buzz /bʌz/ *verb*² *trans. colloq.* L18.
[ORIGIN Unknown.]
Finish to the last drop in the bottle.

†**buzz** *interjection*. E17.
[ORIGIN Unknown.]
1 Expr. impatience. Only in E17.
2 (Used by conjurors and jugglers.) Expr. command. M17–M19.

buzzard /ˈbʌzəd/ *noun*¹. LME.
[ORIGIN Old French *busard*, *buson* from Latin *buteo(n-)* falcon: see -ARD.]
1 A bird of prey of the genus *Buteo* (family Accipitridae), with broad wings and rounded tail; *esp.* one of the common Eurasian species *Buteo buteo*. Also used (esp. formerly) in names of other raptors regarded as unsuitable for falconry. LME. ▸**b** A New World vulture, a condor; *esp.* (also ***turkey buzzard***) the turkey vulture. *N. Amer.* E19.
between hawk and buzzard *arch.* between good and bad of the same kind. *honey buzzard*: see HONEY *noun*. *rough-legged buzzard*: see ROUGH *adjective*.
2 An ignorant or stupid person. Now usu. with weakened sense, fellow, chap, (esp. in ***old buzzard***). *colloq.* LME.

buzzard /ˈbʌzəd/ *noun*². *dial.* M17.
[ORIGIN from BUZZ *verb*¹ + -ARD.]
A moth, cockchafer, or other insect flying at night.

buzzer /ˈbʌzə/ *noun*. E17.
[ORIGIN from BUZZ *verb*¹ + -ER¹.]
1 An insect that buzzes. E17.
†**2** A person who whispers tales. *rare* (Shakes.). Only in E17.
3 An apparatus for making a buzzing noise as a signal; a whistle, a hooter; an electric bell. L19.

BVI *abbreviation*.
British Virgin Islands.

BVM *abbreviation*.
Blessed Virgin Mary.

b/w *abbreviation*.
Black and white (television etc.).

bwana /ˈbwɑːnə/ *noun*. L19.
[ORIGIN Kiswahili.]
In Africa: master, sir. Freq. (formerly) as a term of respectful address.

BWI *abbreviation*.
hist. British West Indies.

BWR *abbreviation*.
Boiling-water (nuclear) reactor.

by /bʌɪ/ *noun*¹. Pl. **bys**. OE.
[ORIGIN Old Norse *bœr*, *býr* (Swedish, Danish *by*), from *búa* dwell: a common elem. in place names, as *Grimsby*.]
hist. A place of habitation, village, or town (of orig. Scandinavian settlement); *gen.* a place whose name ends in *-by*.

by *noun*², *adjective* vars. of BYE *noun*, *adjective*.

by /bʌɪ, unstressed preposition bɪ/ *preposition & adverb*.
[ORIGIN Old English *bī*, unstressed *bi*, *be* = Old Frisian, Old Saxon, Old High German *bī*, *bi* (Dutch *bij*, German *bei*), Gothic *bi*, from Germanic, prob. identical with the 2nd syll. of Greek *amphi-*, Latin *ambi-*, Old English *ymb(e)-* around.]
▸ **A** *preposition*. **1** Of position in space. ▸**a** At the side or edge of; near, close to, beside; in the company of; about the person or in the possession of. OE. ▸**b** In the region or general direction of, towards; slightly inclining to. OE. ▸**c** In the domain of, (vaguely) on, in. Chiefly in ***by land***, etc. (passing into sense 5). ME. ▸**d** In addition to, beside. *Scot. & N. English*. ME. ▸**e** Beyond; against, in spite of. *obsolete* exc. *Scot.* LME.

a COVERDALE *Acts* 9:43 He taried . . at Joppa by one Simon. DICKENS Down by the Docks they 'board seamen' at the eating houses. R. JARRELL A cat sits on the pavement by the house. **b** J. STALLWORTHY Greatcoats, lined By the right, marched from their pegs. **c** C. KINGSLEY I never saw one yet, by flood or field. **d** SIR W. SCOTT Few folks ken o' this place . . there's just twa living by mysell. **e** OED That's by belief.

2 Of motion. ▸**a** Alongside of, along; in passing along; through, via (passing into sense 5); so as to pass, past; outstripping; avoiding. OE. ▸**b** Near to, into the presence of. ME. ▸**c** At, to, or within the distance of; *gen.* expr. the amount of excess or increase, inferiority or diminution. ME.

a LD BERNERS To goo by the stretes as vacabundes. R. BURNS They gang as saucy by poor folk, As I wad by a stinking brock. E. BOWEN The ducks went . . out by the window again. M. INNES The best connexion was by Leeds. H. MACDIARMID The ladder he has come up by. C. SAGAN *Pioneer 10* passed by Jupiter in early December, 1973. **b** OED Come close by me, and tell me what is the matter. **c** CAXTON There is nother castell nor towne by xx myles nyghe aboute it. JONSON He is taller than either of you by the head. G. GREEN Blackpool were in the lead by two goals to one.

3 Of time. ▸**a** In the course of, at, in, on; during, for. Now only in ***by day***, ***by night***. OE. ▸**b** On or before, not later than. ME.

a AV *Acts* 20:31 By the space of three yeeres, I ceased not to warne euery one. **b** MILTON Had Judah that day joined . . They had by this possessed the towers of Gath. D. ABSE He'll be back by now. I. MURDOCH Pinn . . was usually home by five.

4 Of relationship. ▸**a** In forms of swearing or adjuration: as surely as one believes in, in the name of; (app. orig. with some sense of touching or presence). OE. ▸**b** With respect to, as regards, concerning. Now chiefly with ref. to actions or (*colloq.*) indicating agreement or acquiescence. OE. ▸**c** In accordance or conformity with. OE. ▸**d** According to (a quantity or rate). OE. ▸**e** Indicating succession of groups, quantities, etc., of the same kind, multiplication (esp. as expressing area), or division. ME.

a R. W. EMERSON By God, it is in me, and must go forth of me. L. URIS He swore by the beard of Allah that the Jews would be thrown into the sea. **b** HENRY FIELDING I always love to speak by people as I find. GOLDSMITH He murdered Hiempsal . . and attempted the same by Adherbal. J. AUSTEN He will consider it a right thing by Mrs. Grant, as well as by Fanny. N. SHUTE If it pleases you to think like that, it's O.K. by me. G. CHARLES A musician by profession. **c** LD MACAULAY The right by which freeholders chose knights of the shire. C. KINGSLEY They had timed their journey by the tides. R. HARDY The families of settlers met by arrangement. **d** J. P. DONLEAVY We sell butter usually by the weight—half pound or a pound. **e** E. A. FREEMAN By twenties, by hundreds, by thousands, the force gathered. I. C. SMITH Stone by stone the castles crumble. W. BRONK The garden grew more tangled year by year.

5 Indicating agency, means, cause, attendant circumstance, conditions, manner, effects. OE. ▸**b** *spec.* Indicating the partner in begetting offspring or the sire of a colt, filly, etc. OE. ▸**c** *spec.* (In accounts etc.) indicating means or amount of payment. L17.

H. LATIMER Christe . . draweth soules unto hym by his bloudy sacrifice. SHAKES. *3 Hen. VI* Warwick's brother, and by that our foe. AV *Matt.* 4:4 Man shall not live by bread alone. C. THIRLWALL He began by banishing 700 families. J. B. YEATS By ambition the rebel angels fell. M. TWAIN No gas to read by. W. OWEN By his dead smile I knew we stood in Hell. DAY LEWIS A brisk walk, which by a tremendous effort I prevent from degenerating into a trot. D. J. ENRIGHT How did he get there . . ? By lift? By helicopter? A. WHITE I like being admired, flattered, . . and listened to by men. J. BRONOWSKI Spiritual and carnal love are inseparable. A poem by John Donne says that. A. MCCOWEN We were joined by Lapkah and the bearers. **b** J. AUSTEN By a former marriage, Dashwood had one son. W. HOLTBY A grand animal, by Albert the Good out of Sweet Sophia. **c** *Which?* You are protected if you pay by credit card.

– PHRASES: (Of the many phrs. in which *by* governs a noun or forms an elem. in a phrasal verb, few are listed here: see the nouns and verbs.) **by oneself** etc., alone, unaided, without prompting. ***by seeming***: see SEEMING *noun*. ***by the bye***: see BYE *noun*. **by the head** NAUTICAL deeper in the water at the head. ***by themselves***, ***by then*** (***that***): see THEN *adverb* etc. **by the stern** NAUTICAL deeper in the water at the stern. ***by the way***: see WAY *noun*. ***by the yard***: see YARD *noun*². ***by turns***, ***by turn***: see TURN *noun*. ***by water***: see WATER *noun*. ***by your leave***: see LEAVE *noun*¹. **north by east** etc., one point east of north, i.e. between N and NNE, etc. ***two by two***: see TWO *noun* 1.
▸ **B** *adverb*. (Earlier as BY-.)
1 Near, close at hand, in another's presence or vicinity. ME.

P. MASSINGER My brother being not by now to protect her. D. IGNATOW To forgo love . . is to set bread upon the table and a knife discreetly by.

2 Aside, out of the way; out of use or consideration; in reserve. LME.

GOLDSMITH Vile things that nature designed should be thrown by into her lumber room. W. WINDHAM Laying something by for a rainy day.

3 Past a certain point or time, beyond. LME.

JONSON They marched by in pairs. DISRAELI The days are gone by for senates to have their beards plucked in the forum.

†**4** In addition, besides, also. LME–E19.
5 Over, finished, past; done for, dead. *Scot. & N. English*. L18.

R. L. STEVENSON You're by with it, James More. You can never show your face again.

– PHRASES: (For *by* adverb as an element in phrasal verbs see the verbs.) BY AND BY. **by and large** (*a*) NAUTICAL to the wind and off it; (*b*) on the whole, everything considered. **full and by** NAUTICAL close-hauled to the wind.

by- /bʌɪ/ *combining form*. Also **bye-**. OE.
[ORIGIN Repr. BY *adverb*. See also BYE *adjective*.]
Forming combs. (chiefly with nouns) in adverbial or adjectival relation, with the senses 'beside, past' (***bygone***, ***bypass***, ***bystander***), 'at or to one side, aside' (***by-blow***, ***by-room***), 'subsidiary, subordinate' (***byname***, ***byplay***), 'unfrequented, devious' (***byroad***, ***byway***), 'incidental, casual, extra' (***by-election***, ***by-product***), 'underhand, private' (***by-end***).

-by /bɪ/ *suffix*. *arch.*
[ORIGIN After place names and surnames in *-by*: see BY *noun*¹.]
Forming (joc. or derog.) descriptive nouns, as ***rudesby***, ***sneaksby***, ***wigsby***, etc.

by and by /bʌɪ (ə)nd ˈbʌɪ/ *adverbial & noun phr.* ME.
[ORIGIN See BY *adverb*, AND *conjunction*¹.]
▸ **A** *adverbial phr.* †**1** One by one, successively. Only in ME.
†**2** Continuously. ME–E17.
3 Before long; presently; soon; shortly. E16.
†**4** Therefore, as a consequence. M16–E17.
†**5** Directly; immediately. L16–L17.
▸ **B** *noun phr.* Procrastination; a delay; the (or *the*) future. L16.

by-blow /ˈbʌɪbləʊ/ *noun*. L16.
[ORIGIN from BY- + BLOW *noun*¹.]
1 A blow aimed at a person who is not a main opponent; a sidestroke. L16.
2 An illegitimate child. L16.

bycoket /bɪˈkɒkɪt/ *noun*. Long *obsolete* exc. *hist.* LME.
[ORIGIN Old French *bicoquet* ornate military headdress etc., of unknown origin.]
A kind of medieval cap or headdress, peaked at front and back.

by-corner /ˈbʌɪkɔːnə/ *noun*. *arch.* M16.
[ORIGIN from BY- + CORNER *noun*.]
An out-of-the-way corner; a nook.

bye /bʌɪ/ *noun*. Also (in sense 1) **by**. M16.
[ORIGIN Ellipt. use of BY- or BYE *adjective*.]
1 A secondary object or undertaking, a side issue, an incidental matter. Now chiefly in ***by the bye***, parenthetically, incidentally. M16.
the Bye *hist.* = ***the Bye Plot*** s.v. BYE *adjective*.
2 A (sporting) match not listed in the programme; a side event. E18.
3 CRICKET. A run made from a ball that passes the batsman without being struck. M18.
leg bye a bye from a ball that touches the batsman.

B

4 *GOLF.* A hole or holes remaining to be played when a match is decided. **L19.**
5 (The position of) a competitor against whom no opponent has been drawn, and who proceeds to the next round of a sporting competition without a contest. **L19.**

bye /bʌɪ/ *adjective.* Also **by.** **M17.**
[ORIGIN Independent use of BY-: see below.]
Situated to one side, out of the way; *fig.* subsidiary, incidental, secondary; clandestine.

S. RICHARDSON Nothing can be more bye and unfrequented.

the Bye Plot *hist.* the less important of two plots against the government of James I (opp. ***the Main Plot***).

bye /bʌɪ/ *interjection. colloq.* **E18.**
[ORIGIN Abbreviation.]
Goodbye.

bye- *combining form* var. of BY-.

bye-bye /ˈbʌɪbʌɪ/ *noun.* Also **-byes** /-bʌɪz/. **M19.**
[ORIGIN from a refrain or sound used in lullabies.]
(A child's word for) sleep, bed.

bye-bye /bʌɪˈbʌɪ/ *interjection. colloq.* **E18.**
[ORIGIN Child's var. of GOODBYE.]
Goodbye.

bye-byes *noun* var. of BYE-BYE *noun.*

by-effect /ˈbʌɪɪfɛkt/ *noun.* **E19.**
[ORIGIN from BY- + EFFECT *noun.*]
A side effect.

bye-law *noun* var. of BY-LAW.

by-election /ˈbʌɪɪlɛkʃ(ə)n/ *noun.* **L19.**
[ORIGIN from BY- + ELECTION.]
The election of a Member of Parliament etc. held at a time other than that of a general election.

bye-line *noun* see BYLINE.

Byelorussian *adjective & noun* var. of BELORUSSIAN.

by-end /ˈbʌɪɛnd/ *noun.* **E17.**
[ORIGIN from BY- + END *noun.*]
A secondary or subordinate aim or object, *esp.* one with a covert purpose of personal advantage.

by-form /ˈbʌɪfɔːm/ *noun.* **L19.**
[ORIGIN from BY- + FORM *noun.*]
A secondary form of a word etc.

bygoing /ˈbʌɪɡəʊɪŋ/ *verbal noun.* Chiefly *Scot.* Also (*Scot.*) **byganging** /ˈbʌɪɡaŋɪŋ/. **E17.**
[ORIGIN from BY- + GOING *noun.*]
The action of passing by.
in the bygoing by the way, incidentally.

bygone /ˈbʌɪɡɒn/ *adjective & noun.* **LME.**
[ORIGIN from BY- + GONE *adjective.*]
► **A** *adjective.* **1** That has gone by in time, past, former. **LME.**
2 No longer living. **E16.**
3 Antiquated. **M19.**
► **B** *noun.* **1** In *pl.* Past events; *esp.* past offences. Now chiefly as below. **M16.**
let bygones be bygones forgive and forget.
2 In *pl.* Overdue payments, arrears. Chiefly *Scot.* **L16.**
3 A person or thing of the past; *spec.* an obsolete domestic object or other artefact (usu. in *pl.*). **M19.**

bylander *noun* var. of BILANDER.

by-lane /ˈbʌɪleɪn/ *noun.* **L16.**
[ORIGIN from BY- + LANE *noun*[1].]
A side lane; a side passage in a mine.

by-law /ˈbʌɪlɔː/ *noun.* Also **bye-**. **ME.**
[ORIGIN Prob. from BYRLAW, but assoc. with BY-, LAW *noun*[1].]
1 = BYRLAW; *spec.* an ordinance made by common consent in a court leet or court baron. Long *obsolete* exc. *hist.* **ME.**
2 A regulation made by a local authority or corporation; a regulation of a company etc. **LME.**
3 A secondary, subordinate, or accessory law. **M16.**
– COMB.: **bylawman** *hist.* = ***byrlawman*** s.v. BYRLAW.

bylina /bəˈliːnə/ *noun.* Pl. ***-ny*** /-ni/, ***-nas***. **L19.**
[ORIGIN Russian.]
A Russian traditional heroic poem.

byline /ˈbʌɪlʌɪn/ *noun & verb.* In sense A.2 also **bye-**. **E20.**
[ORIGIN from BY *preposition*, BY- + LINE *noun*[2].]
► **A** *noun.* **1** A line in a newspaper etc. naming the writer of an article. **E20.**
2 The goal line in soccer etc. **M20.**
► **B** *verb trans.* Print with a byline. **M20.**
■ **byliner** *noun* a journalist etc. whose work is bylined **M20.**

byliny *noun* pl. of BYLINA.

byname /ˈbʌɪneɪm/ *noun & verb.* **L16.**
[ORIGIN from BY- + NAME *noun.*]
► **A** *noun.* A subsidiary name; a sobriquet; a nickname. **L16.**
► **B** *verb trans.* Give a specified name to; nickname. Long *rare.* **L16.**

BYO *abbreviation.*
Bring your own (on a party invitation etc.); also, a restaurant etc. to which customers may bring their own alcoholic drinks.

BYOB *abbreviation.*
Bring your own bottle, booze, etc.

BYOG *abbreviation. Austral. & NZ.*
Bring your own grog.

bypass /ˈbʌɪpɑːs/ *noun & verb.* **M19.**
[ORIGIN from BY- + PASS *noun*[1].]
► **A** *noun.* **1** A secondary channel permitting the free flow of gas, electricity, blood, etc., when a main passage is blocked. **M19.**
2 A road passing round (the centre of) a town, providing an alternative route for through traffic. **E20.**
3 *transf. & fig.* An alternative route or means. **E20.**
► **B** *verb trans.* **1** Provide with a bypass. **L19.**

Times A By-passed village in Kent.

2 Take an indirect route around; avoid. **E20.**

LYNDON B. JOHNSON A President must be willing to bypass the Congress to take the issue to the people. F. WELDON Pulling out the gas cooker to adjust the pipe so that the supply would bypass the meter.

3 Conduct (gas, liquid, etc.) by means of a bypass. **E20.**

by-passer /ˈbʌɪpɑːsə/ *noun. arch.* **M16.**
[ORIGIN from BY- + PASSER.]
A passer-by.

bypast /ˈbʌɪpɑːst/ *adjective. arch.* **LME.**
[ORIGIN from BY- + PAST *adjective.*]
Bygone.

bypath /ˈbʌɪpɑːθ/ *noun.* **LME.**
[ORIGIN from BY- + PATH *noun*[1].]
A side path; a secluded way; *fig.* a minor branch of a subject etc.

by-place /ˈbʌɪpleɪs/ *noun. arch.* **L16.**
[ORIGIN from BY- + PLACE *noun*[1].]
An out-of-the-way place; an odd corner.

byplay /ˈbʌɪpleɪ/ *noun.* **E19.**
[ORIGIN from BY- + PLAY *noun.*]
Subsidiary action, esp. on stage; incidental play.

by-product /ˈbʌɪprɒdəkt, -dʌkt/ *noun.* **M19.**
[ORIGIN from BY- + PRODUCT *noun.*]
An incidental or secondary product of manufacture etc.; a side effect.

byre /ˈbʌɪə/ *noun.*
[ORIGIN Old English *bȳre*, perh. cogn. with BOWER *noun*[1].]
A cowshed.

byrlaw /ˈbəːlɔː/ *noun. obsolete* exc. *hist.* In comb. also **birley, burley, -ie**, /ˈbəːli/. See also BY-LAW. **ME.**
[ORIGIN from Old Norse *býjar* genit. sing. of *býr* (see BY *noun*[1]) + *lagu* LAW *noun*[1].]
The local custom or law of a manor, district, etc., whereby disputes over boundaries, trespass, etc., were settled without recourse to the public courts of law.
– COMB.: **byrlaw-court**: to settle local disputes etc.; **byrlawman** an officer appointed to administer the byrlaw.

byrnie /ˈbəːni/ *noun. obsolete* exc. *hist.* Also (earlier) †**brinie**. **ME.**
[ORIGIN Old Norse *brynja*. Metathetic var. orig. Scot.]
A coat of mail.

byroad /ˈbʌɪrəʊd/ *noun.* **M16.**
[ORIGIN from BY- + ROAD *noun.*]
A side or minor road; a little-frequented road.

Byronic /bʌɪˈrɒnɪk/ *adjective & noun.* **E19.**
[ORIGIN from *Byron* (see below) + -IC.]
► **A** *adjective.* Of, pertaining to, or characteristic of the poet George Gordon, Lord Byron (1788–1824) or his writings. **E19.**
► **B** *noun.* In *pl.* Byronic utterances or behaviour. **M19.**
■ **Byronically** *adverb* in a Byronic manner **M19.**

Byronism /ˈbʌɪərənɪz(ə)m/ *noun.* **E19.**
[ORIGIN formed as BYRONIC + -ISM.]
The characteristics of Byron or his poetry; imitation of Byron.

by-room /ˈbʌɪruːm, -rʊm/ *noun.* Now *rare.* **L16.**
[ORIGIN from BY- + ROOM *noun*[1].]
A side room; a small or private room.

byssi *noun* pl. of BYSSUS.

byssine /ˈbɪsɪn/ *noun & adjective.* **LME.**
[ORIGIN Latin *byssinus* (*byssinum* noun) from Greek *bussinos*, from *bussos*: see BYSSUS, -INE[1].]
hist. (Made of) byssus or fine linen.

byssinosis /bɪsɪˈnəʊsɪs/ *noun.* Pl. **-noses** /-ˈnəʊsiːz/. **L19.**
[ORIGIN formed as BYSSINE + -OSIS.]
MEDICINE. Chronic lung disease due to inhalation of fine particles of textile fibres.
■ **byssinotic** /-ˈnɒtɪk/ *adjective* **M20.**

byssus /ˈbɪsəs/ *noun.* Pl. (*rare*) **byssi** /ˈbɪsʌɪ/, **byssuses**. **LME.**
[ORIGIN Latin from Greek *bussos*, of Semitic origin.]
1 *hist.* A fine textile fibre and fabric, orig. of flax. **LME.**
†**2** (A) filamentous fungoid growth. **M18–M19.**
3 *ZOOLOGY.* A tuft of fine filaments by which some bivalve molluscs adhere to rocks. **M19.**
■ **byssal** *adjective* (*ZOOLOGY*) of, pertaining to, or of the nature of a byssus **L19.**

bystander /ˈbʌɪstandə/ *noun.* **M16.**
[ORIGIN from BY- + STANDER.]
A person who is standing by; a passive witness; a spectator.

bystanding /ˈbʌɪstandɪŋ/ *adjective.* **E17.**
[ORIGIN from BY- + STANDING *adjective.*]
Standing by or near.

by-street /ˈbʌɪstriːt/ *noun.* **L17.**
[ORIGIN from BY- + STREET *noun.*]
A side street; a little-used street.

by-talk /ˈbʌɪtɔːk/ *noun. arch.* **M16.**
[ORIGIN from BY- + TALK *noun*[1].]
Incidental talk; small talk; gossip.

byte /bʌɪt/ *noun.* **M20.**
[ORIGIN Arbitrary, based on BIT *noun*[3] and BITE *noun.*]
COMPUTING. A group of binary digits (usu. eight) operated on as a unit.

by-thing /ˈbʌɪθɪŋ/ *noun. arch.* **E18.**
[ORIGIN from BY- + THING *noun*[1].]
A minor matter; a side issue.

by-time /ˈbʌɪtʌɪm/ *noun.* **E17.**
[ORIGIN from BY- + TIME *noun.*]
Time not occupied by one's main work or pursuits; spare time; odd hours.

bytownite /ˈbʌɪtaʊnʌɪt/ *noun.* **M19.**
[ORIGIN from *Bytown*, former name of Ottawa, Canada + -ITE[1].]
MINERALOGY. A calcic plagioclase feldspar occurring in many basic igneous rocks.

†**by-view** *noun.* **M18–E19.**
[ORIGIN from BY- + VIEW *noun.*]
An unavowed or self-interested aim.

by-walk /ˈbʌɪwɔːk/ *noun.* **M16.**
[ORIGIN from BY- + WALK *noun.*]
A private or secluded walk; a by-path (*lit. & fig.*).

bywater /ˈbʌɪwɔːtə/ *noun.* **L19.**
[ORIGIN from BY- + WATER *noun.*]
A diamond of inferior water, *esp.* one that is yellowish.

byway /ˈbʌɪweɪ/ *noun.* **ME.**
[ORIGIN from BY- + WAY *noun.*]
A byroad, a bypath.

bywoner /ˈbʌɪwəʊnə, ˈbeɪvəʊnə/ *noun. S. Afr.* **L19.**
[ORIGIN Afrikaans, from *by* with + *woon* live + *-er* -ER[1].]
A farmer holding land under a *métayage* system.

byword /ˈbʌɪwəːd/ *noun.*
[ORIGIN Old English *biwyrde* = Old High German *biwurti*, rendering Latin *proverbium* PROVERB: see BY-, WORD *noun.*]
1 A proverb; a proverbial saying. **OE.**
2 A person etc. taken as typical of a (usu. bad) quality; a quality in a person etc. that is widely recognized. **M16.** ▸**b** A (usu. scornful or mocking) nickname. Now *rare.* **L16.**

J. A. FROUDE The Church courts were a byword for iniquity. L. DEIGHTON Blessing's efficiency was a byword. P. ACKROYD I would rather be a byword of infamy . . than an object of gross ridicule. **b** R. L. STEVENSON They are . . known by a generic byword, as Poor Whites.

†**3** A casual word; a hint; an aside. **M16–M17.**
†**4** A word or phrase frequently used, esp. by an individual. **M16–E18.**

by-work /ˈbʌɪwəːk/ *noun.* **L16.**
[ORIGIN from BY- + WORK *noun.*]
Incidental work; work performed in spare time or odd hours. Also, work with an unavowed or self-interested aim.

byzant *noun* var. of BEZANT.

Byzantian /bɪˈzantɪən, bʌɪ-, -ʃ(ə)n/ *noun & adjective.* **E17.**
[ORIGIN from Latin *Byzantius*, from *Byzantium* (see BYZANTINE), + -AN.]
= BYZANTINE *noun* 2, *adjective* 1.

Byzantine /bɪˈzantʌɪn, bʌɪ-/ *noun & adjective.* **L16.**
[ORIGIN French *byzantin* or Latin *Byzantinus*, from *Byzantium* from Greek *Buzantion* Byzantium, the city later called Constantinople, now Istanbul: see -INE[1].]
► **A** *noun.* **1** (**b-**.) *hist.* = BEZANT. **L16.**
2 A native or inhabitant of Byzantium or the Eastern Roman Empire. **M17.**
► **B** *adjective.* **1** Of or pertaining to Byzantium, the Eastern Roman Empire, or the Orthodox Church. **L18.**
2 *spec.* Characteristic of the artistic (esp. architectural) style developed in the Eastern Roman Empire. **M19.**
3 Like Byzantine politics; complicated; inflexible; underhand. **M20.**
■ **Byzantinism** /-tɪn-/ *noun* the style and methods of architecture etc. developed in the Eastern Roman Empire **M19.** **Byzantinist** /-tɪn-/ *noun* an expert in or student of Byzantine matters **L19.**

Cc

C

C, c /siː/.
The third letter of the modern English alphabet and of the ancient Roman one, orig. corresp. to Greek *gamma*, Semitic *gimel*. In early Latin the letter represented both the voiced /g/ and voiceless /k/ velar plosive consonants; subsequently it stood only for the latter. When the Roman alphabet was introduced into Britain, C had only the /k/ sound, and this remains the case in the Celtic langs. As a result of developments both in Britain and in Continental Europe in the Old English and Middle English periods, C in mod. English has a number of values according to the following general rules. (i) C has the 'hard' sound /k/ before *a, o, u*, before a consonant exc. *h*, and when final. Final *c* is largely avoided exc. in mod. words adopted from or modelled on Latin or Greek (***disc***, ***sac***, ***italic***), the /k/ sound being usu. expressed by *k* or *ck*. When hard *c* is followed in inflection by *e* or *i*, it is usu. changed to *ck* (***frolicking***, ***picnicker***). (ii) C has the 'soft' sound /s/ before *e, i, y*. Where the /s/ sound is final, it is written *ce*, and this *e* is retained in composition before *a, o, u*. (iii) *ci* (rarely *ce*) preceding another vowel has freq. the sound /ʃ/, esp. in the endings *-cious, -cial, -cion* (cf. **T**, **T**). (iv) *ch* is in effect a separate consonant: see before the beginning of the *ch-* words. (v) In adoptions from other langs. C may retain the foreign pronunciation (***ceilidh***, ***cello***). Pl. **cees**, **C's**, **Cs**.
▸ **I 1** The letter and its sound.
2 The shape of the letter.
C-shaped *adjective* having a shape or cross-section like the letter C. **C-spring** a C-shaped spring, used to support the body of a carriage.
▸ **II** Symbolical uses.
3 Used to denote serial order; applied e.g. to the third group or section, sheet of a book, etc.
C-DNA *BIOCHEMISTRY* a form of double-stranded DNA adopted in the presence of certain solvents, more tightly coiled than B-DNA.
4 *MUSIC*. (Cap. C.) The first note of the natural major scale (C major), often defined as having a frequency of 256 Hz. Also, the scale of a composition with C as its keynote.
C clef the soprano, alto, or tenor clef. ***middle C***: see MIDDLE *adjective*.
5 The third hypothetical person or example.
6 *MATH*. (Usu. italic *c*.) The third known quantity; a constant; *spec.* (*PHYSICS*) denoting the velocity of light in a vacuum.
7 (Usu. cap. C.) Designating the third-highest class (of academic marks, population as regards affluence, etc.).
C Special *hist.* a member of an unpaid occasional police force in Northern Ireland. **C3** /siː ˈθriː/ the lowest grade of medical fitness in the First World War; *colloq.* unfit, worthless.
8 The roman numeral for 100.
9 (Cap. C.) Designating a range of international standard paper sizes with a fixed shape and twice the area of the next size, as ***C0***, ***C1***, ***C2***, ***C3***, ***C4***, etc.
10 (Cap. C.) A computer programming language originally developed for implementing the Unix operating system.
▸ **III 11** Abbrevs.: **C.** = Cape; Catholic; Command Paper (second series, 1870–99); Conservative. **C** = cancer (in ***the big C*** s.v. BIG *adjective*); (*ELECTRICITY*) capacitance; (*CHEMISTRY*) carbon; cargo (in designations of US aircraft types); Celsius, centigrade; Channel (as in ***C4***, a television channel); (*PARTICLE PHYSICS*) charge conjugation; cocaine; (*MUSIC*) common time; (*PHYSICS*) coulomb(s); (*BIOCHEMISTRY*) Cytosine. **c.** = (*CRICKET*) caught by; cent(s); centuries; century; chapter; (*METEOROLOGY*) cloudy; cold; colt; cubic. **c.** = [Latin] *circa* about (also *ca.*). **c** = (as *prefix*) centi-; (*PARTICLE PHYSICS*) = CHARM *noun*[1] 4. **c/-** (*Austral. & NZ*) = care of. © = copyright.

CA *abbreviation*.
1 California.
2 Chartered accountant. *Scot. & Canad.*

Ca *symbol*.
CHEMISTRY. Calcium.

ca' *noun, verb* see CALL *noun, verb*.

ca. *abbreviation*.
Latin *circa* about. (Freq. italicized.)

CAA *abbreviation*.
Civil Aviation Authority.

Caaba *noun* var. of KAABA.

caa'ing whale *noun phr.* var. of CA'ING WHALE.

caatinga /ˈkɑːtɪŋɡə/ *noun*. M19.
[ORIGIN Portuguese from Tupi, from *caá* natural vegetation, forest + *tinga* white.]
In Brazil, a forest consisting of thorny shrubs and stunted trees.

CAB *abbreviation*.
1 Citizens' Advice Bureau.
2 Civil Aeronautics Board. *US*.

cab /kab/ *noun*[1]. E19.
[ORIGIN Abbreviation of CABRIOLET.]
1 a *hist.* A hackney carriage. E19. ▸**b** A taxi. Also ***taxicab***. L19.
2 A driver of a cab. M19.
3 A shelter or compartment for the driver of a train, lorry, crane, etc. M19.
spy in the cab: see SPY *noun*.
– COMB.: **cabman** a man who drives a cab; **cab rank**, **cab stand** a place where cabs are authorized to wait.

†**cab** *noun*[2] see KAB.

cab /kab/ *verb intrans. & trans.* (with *it*). Infl. **-bb-**. M19.
[ORIGIN from CAB *noun*[1].]
Travel in or drive a cab.

caba /kəˈbɑː/ *noun*. Chiefly *US*. Also **cabas** /kəˈbɑːs/. M19.
[ORIGIN French *cabas* basket, pannier.]
A small satchel or handbag.

†**cabaia** *noun* see KEBAYA.

cabal /kəˈbal/ *noun & verb*. L16.
[ORIGIN French *cabale* from medieval Latin *cab(b)ala* (Italian, Spanish *cabala*): see KABBALAH.]
▸ **A** *noun*. †**1** = KABBALAH. L16–M18.
2 A secret intrigue, a conspiracy; petty plotting. *arch.* E17.

BURKE Centres of cabal. W. IRVING Cabals breaking out in the company.

3 A secret meeting (of intriguers). *arch.* M17.

MARVELL Is he in caball in his cabinett sett.

4 A political clique, a faction; *spec.* (**C-**) a committee of five ministers under Charles II whose surnames happened to begin with C, A, B, A, and L (Clifford, Arlington, Buckingham, Ashley, and Lauderdale). M17.

G. B. SHAW The radical cabal in the cabinet which pursues my family with rancorous class hatred.

▸ **B** *verb intrans.* Infl. **-ll-**. Combine (*together*) for some private end (usu. *derog.*); intrigue (*against*). L17.
■ **caballer** *noun* a person who cabals, an intriguer L17.

Cabala *noun* var. of KABBALAH.

cabaletta /kabəˈlɛtə/ *noun*. M19.
[ORIGIN Italian, var. of *coboletta* dim. of *cob(b)ola* stanza, couplet from Old Provençal *cobla* from Latin COPULA.]
MUSIC. A simple aria with a repetitive rhythm; the uniformly quick final section of an aria.

caballada /kabəˈljɑːdə/ *noun*. *US*. M19.
[ORIGIN Spanish, from *caballo* horse. See also CAVAYARD.]
A drove of horses or mules.

caballero /kabəˈljɛːrəʊ/ *noun*. Pl. **-os**. M19.
[ORIGIN Spanish = French *chevalier*, Italian *cavaliere*: see CAVALIER *noun*.]
A Spanish gentleman.

caballine /ˈkabəlʌɪn/ *adjective*. LME.
[ORIGIN Latin *caballinus*, from *caballus* horse: see -INE[1].]
Equine.
caballine fountain [Latin *fons caballinus*] the fountain Hippocrene (see HIPPOCRENE).

caban /kəˈbɑːn/ *noun*. L17.
[ORIGIN (Persian from) Arabic *qabā'*.]
A type of coat or tunic worn esp. by Arab men.

cabana /kəˈbɑːnə/ *noun*. Chiefly *US*. Also **-ña** /-njə/. L19.
[ORIGIN Spanish *cabaña* from late Latin *capanna*, *cav-* CABIN.]
A cabin; *spec.* a shelter at a beach or swimming pool.

cabane /kəˈbɑːn/ *noun*. M19.
[ORIGIN French: see CABIN.]
1 A hut, a cabin. *Canad. dial.* M19.
2 A pyramidal structure supporting the wings of an aircraft. E20.

cabaret /ˈkabəreɪ; *in sense 1 also foreign* kabarɛ (*pl. same*)/ *noun*. M17.
[ORIGIN Old French & mod. French, orig. Walloon & Picard, from Middle Dutch var. of *camaret*, *cambret* from Old Picard *camberet* little room.]
1 A public house in France etc. M17.
2 An entertainment provided in a restaurant etc. while customers are at table; a restaurant, nightclub, etc., providing such entertainment. E20.

cabas *noun* var. of CABA.

cabbage /ˈkabɪdʒ/ *noun*[1]. LME.
[ORIGIN Old French (Picard) *caboche* head, var. of Old French *caboce*, of unknown origin.]
1 The compact round head or heart formed by the leaves of a cultivated variety of the cruciferous plant *Brassica oleracea*, used as a green culinary vegetable; a plant of this species. Also (with specifying word), any of various related or otherwise similar plants. LME.
Chinese cabbage, ***Kerguelen cabbage***, ***red cabbage***, ***Savoy cabbage***, etc. **my cabbage** [translating French *mon chou*] my dear, my darling.
2 The edible terminal bud of a cabbage palm or other palm. M17.
3 A brainless person; someone utterly lacking interests or ambition, or reduced by illness to inactivity, a 'vegetable'. *colloq.* L19.

Guardian I stayed at home for nearly a year. It was awful. I became a cabbage.

4 Money. *slang* (chiefly *N. Amer.*). E20.
– COMB.: **cabbage-bark** (the bark or timber of) the angelin, *Andira inermis*; **cabbage butterfly** = ***cabbage white*** below; **cabbage-head** *fig.* a stupid person; ***cabbage-looking***: see ***be not so green as one is cabbage-looking*** s.v. GREEN *adjective*; **cabbage lettuce** a variety of lettuce with broad rounded leaves forming a more or less globular head close to the ground; **cabbage moth** a noctuid moth, *Mamestra brassicae*, whose larvae are pests of cabbages; **cabbage palm** any of various palms having edible terminal buds or other similarities to the cabbage, *esp.* (***a***) either of two tall W. Indian palms, *Roystonea oleracea* and *Sabal palmetto*, with edible buds; (***b***) an Australian palm, *Livistona australis*, with large leaves used to make hats, etc.; **cabbage roll** *N. Amer.* a boiled cabbage leaf formed into a roll with a stuffing of rice and minced meat and baked; **cabbage rose** an old double garden rose, *Rosa centifolia*, with a large round compact flower; **cabbage tree** any of various tropical trees suggesting cabbages, *esp.* = ***cabbage palm*** above, or (*NZ*) a tree of the agave family, *Cordyline australis*, with narrow leaves crowded at the top of the stem; **cabbage white** a white pierid butterfly whose larvae feed on cabbage leaves, esp. the large white, *Pieris brassicae*.
■ **cabbage-like** *adjective* resembling (that of) a cabbage M19. **cabbagy** *adjective* M19.

cabbage /ˈkabɪdʒ/ *noun*[2]. M17.
[ORIGIN Unknown.]
1 Shreds (or larger pieces) of cloth appropriated by tailors in cutting out clothes. M17.
†**2** A tailor. *slang*. L17–E18.

cabbage /ˈkabɪdʒ/ *verb*[1]. Sense 1 also †**caboche**. LME.
[ORIGIN French *cabocher*, from *caboche* (see CABBAGE *noun*[1]) or directly from CABBAGE *noun*[1].]
1 *verb trans.* Cut off (a deer's head) close behind the horns; cut off the head of (a deer) so. LME.
†**2** *verb intrans.* Of the horns of a deer: grow to a head. Only in E16.
3 *verb trans.* In *pass.* Be formed into a head like a cabbage. L16.
4 *verb intrans.* Of a cabbage, lettuce, etc.: form a head. E17.

cabbage /ˈkabɪdʒ/ *verb*[2] *trans. & intrans.* E18.
[ORIGIN from CABBAGE *noun*[2]: cf. Old French *cabas* deceit, theft, Dutch *kabassen* pilfer.]
Pilfer (orig. pieces of cloth), appropriate surreptitiously.

H. L. MENCKEN The quacks . . in all probability cabbaged most of their victims' property.

Cabbala *noun* var. of KABBALAH.

cabby /ˈkabi/ *noun*. *colloq.* M19.
[ORIGIN from CAB *noun*[1] + -Y[6].]
A driver of a cab.

caber /ˈkeɪbə/ *noun*. *Scot.* E16.
[ORIGIN Gaelic, Irish *cabar*.]
A roughly trimmed tree trunk, *esp.* one with a slightly tapered end used in Highland Games.
tossing the caber the sport of throwing such a tree trunk.

Cabernet /ˈkabəneɪ, *foreign* kabɛrnɛ/ *noun*. M19.
[ORIGIN French.]
(Any of several vines yielding) a black grape used in wine-making; red wine made from these grapes.
Cabernet Franc /frɒ̃, frɑ̃/, **Cabernet Sauvignon** /ˈsəʊvɪnjɒn, sovinjɔ̃/: two of the chief varieties.

cabezon /ˈkabɪzɒn/ *noun*. M20.
[ORIGIN Spanish *cabezón* big-headed.]
A sculpin (fish), *Scorpaenichthys marmoratus*, with a broad tentacle above each eye and a green-brown body with white patches, found on the west coast of North America.

cabildo /ka'bildo, kə'bɪldəʊ/ *noun*. Pl. **-os** /-ɒs, -əʊz/. E19.
[ORIGIN Spanish from late Latin *capitulum* chapter house: see CHAPTER *noun*.]
A town hall or town council in Spain and Spanish-speaking countries.

cabin /'kabɪn/ *noun & verb*. ME.
[ORIGIN Old French & mod. French *cabane* from Provençal *cabana* = Italian *capanna* from late Latin *capanna*, *cavanna*.]
▸ **A** *noun*. **1** A room or compartment in a ship, aircraft, spacecraft, etc., for housing passengers, crew (in an aircraft), or cargo. ME. ▸†**b** A berth in a ship. L16–M18.
ladies' cabin: see LADY *noun & adjective*. ***outside cabin***: see OUTSIDE *adjective*. ***pressure cabin***: see PRESSURE *noun*.
†**2** A temporary shelter; a booth. LME–M19.
3 A permanent habitation of rough or rudimentary construction; a poor dwelling. LME.
†**4** A small room; a cell. LME–E17.
†**5** A natural cave or grotto; an animal's den. LME–L18.
†**6** A litter for carrying a person. L16–M17.
†**7** A political cabinet. Usu. *attrib.* M–L17.
8 A driver's cab; the enclosed compartment of a crane, lorry, etc. M20.
– COMB.: **cabin boy**: attending to officers or passengers on a ship; **cabin class** an intermediate class of accommodation on a passenger ship; **cabin crew**: attending to passengers and cargo on an aircraft; **cabin cruiser** a power-driven vessel equipped with a cabin and living accommodation; **cabin fever** *N. Amer. colloq.* lassitude, irritability, etc., resulting from long confinement or isolation in one's home etc. during the winter.
▸ **B** *verb*. **1** *verb intrans. & trans.* Dwell or lodge (as) in a cabin; take or give shelter (as) in a cabin. L16.
2 *verb trans.* Confine in a small space; cramp. Chiefly as ***cabined*** *ppl adjective*. E17.

cabinet /'kabɪnɪt/ *noun & verb*. M16.
[ORIGIN from CABIN + -ET[1], infl. by French *cabinet* from Italian *gabinetto* closet, press, chest of drawers.]
▸ **A** *noun*. **I** *gen.* †**1** A secret receptacle, a repository. Chiefly *fig.* M16–L17.
2 A case or cupboard with drawers, shelves, etc., for storing or displaying objects. M16. ▸**b** A piece of furniture containing a radio or television receiver etc. M20.
3 A small chamber; a private room. *arch.* M16.
†**4** A small cabin; a tent; a rustic lodging; an animal's den. L16–M17.
†**5** A summer house; a bower. L16–M18.
†**6** A room devoted to the display of works of art; a gallery. L17–L18.
▸ **II** POLITICS (from sense 3). (Usu. **C-**.)
7 *The* council chamber in which the inner circle of a Government meet; *the* world of politics. *arch.* E17.
8 A committee of senior ministers responsible for determining Government policy. M17. ▸†**b** A meeting of a Cabinet. E18–E19.

Times She will remain in the Cabinet until the election.

inner cabinet: see INNER *adjective*.
– COMB.: **Cabinet Council** *arch.* = senses 8, 8b above; **cabinetmaker** a person who makes cabinets, a skilled joiner; **cabinetmaking** the activity or occupation of a cabinetmaker; **Cabinet minister** a member of the Cabinet; **cabinet organ** (*a*) a reed organ in a case resembling that of an upright piano; (*b*) a chamber or portative organ; **cabinet photograph**: measuring approximately 6 by 4 inches; **cabinet piano** a small upright piano; **cabinet pudding** a steamed pudding made with dried fruit; ***cabinet scraper***: see SCRAPER 3; **cabinetwork** fine furniture, skilled joinery.
▸ **B** *verb trans.* Infl. **-t-**, ***-tt-**. Enclose (as) in a cabinet. M17.

Cabistan *noun & adjective* var. of KABISTAN.

cable /'keɪb(ə)l/ *noun*. ME.
[ORIGIN Anglo-Norman, Old Northern French var. of Old French *chable* (mod. *câble* from Provençal *cable*) from late Latin *cap(u)lum* halter, assoc. with Latin *capere* seize, hold; reinforced by Middle & mod. Low German, Middle Dutch & mod. Dutch *kabel* from Proto-Romance.]
1 A strong thick rope of hemp or wire. ME.
2 NAUTICAL. A strong rope or studded link chain attached to an anchor. LME. ▸**b** More fully ***cable length***. A unit of length of 200 yards. M16.
slip one's cable: see SLIP *verb*[1].
3 (A length of) material in the form of an insulated wire or wires sheathed in a protective casing (orig. of wire strands, now also of plastic etc.), and used for carrying electric signals and electric power. M19. ▸**b** A cablegram. L19. ▸**c** In full ***cable television***, ***cable TV***. The system of transmitting television signals by cable, usu. to the receiving sets of individual subscribers. M20.
cable's end: see END *noun* 7b. COAXIAL ***cable***. CONCENTRIC ***cable***. ***jumper cable***: see JUMPER *noun*[1]. ***paper cable***: see PAPER *noun & adjective*. ***pilot cable***: see PILOT *noun* 5. ***standard cable***: see STANDARD *adjective*.
4 ARCHITECTURE. More fully ***cable moulding***. An ornamental moulding that looks like rope. M19.
5 In full ***cable pattern***, ***cable stitch***. A pattern or stitching in knitting or embroidery that looks like twisted rope. L19.
– COMB.: **cable car**: moved by an endless cable; **cable-knit** *adjective* (of a garment) knitted using cable stitch; **cable-laid** *adjective* (of rope) having three triple strands; ***cable length***: see sense 2b above; ***cable moulding***: see sense 4 above; ***cable pattern***: see sense 5 above; **cable railway**: with cars or carriages drawn along an endless cable moved by a fixed engine; **cable-stayed bridge**: in which the weight of the deck is supported by a number of cables running directly to one or more towers; ***cable stitch***: see sense 5 above; ***cable television***, ***cable TV***: see sense 3c above; **cablevision** cable television (see sense 3c above); **cableway** a transporting system with a (usu. elevated) cable.
■ **cablegram** *noun* a message by telegraphic cable M19. **cable-'ese**, **cab'lese** *noun* the contracted or cryptic style of expression used in cablegrams M20. **cablet** /'keɪblɪt/ *noun* a small cable or cable-laid rope, *spec.* one of less than ten inches in circumference L15.

cable /'keɪb(ə)l/ *verb*. E16.
[ORIGIN from the noun.]
1 *verb trans.* Provide or equip with a cable or cables; fasten (as) with a cable, tie *up*. E16.
2 *verb trans.* ARCHITECTURE. Ornament with cable moulding. M17.
3 *verb trans. & intrans.* Transmit (a message) or transmit a message to (a person) by telegraphic cable. L19.
4 *verb trans.* Provide with or equip for cable television. L20.
■ **cabler** *noun* L19.

cabob *noun* see KEBAB.

caboceer /kabə'sɪə/ *noun*. E18.
[ORIGIN Portuguese *caboceiro*, from *cabo* head: cf. -EER.]
A headman of a W. African village or tribe.

†**caboche** *verb* see CABBAGE *verb*[1].

caboched *adjective* var. of CABOSHED.

cabochon /'kabəʃɒn/ *adjective & noun*. M16.
[ORIGIN Old French & mod. French, dim. of *caboche*: see CABBAGE *noun*[1], -OON.]
(A gem) polished but not faceted. See also EN CABOCHON.

Caboclo /kə'bəʊkləʊ/ *noun*. Pl. **-os**. E19.
[ORIGIN Brazilian Portuguese, perh. from Tupi *Kaa-boc* one who has the colour of copper.]
In Brazil: an American Indian. Also, a Brazilian of mixed white and Indian or Indian and black ancestry.

caboodle /kə'buːd(ə)l/ *noun*. *slang* (orig. *US*). Also **k-**. M19.
[ORIGIN Perh. from *kit and boodle*: see KIT *noun*[1], BOODLE *noun* 1.]
the whole caboodle, ***the whole kit and caboodle***, the whole set or lot, everything, everyone.

caboose /kə'buːs/ *noun*. Also (now *rare*) **camb-** /kam'buːs/. M18.
[ORIGIN Dutch *cabuse*, *combuse*, now *kabuis*, *kombuis*, = Middle & mod. Low German *kabūse*, of unknown origin.]
1 A small kitchen on the deck of a ship. M18. ▸**b** An oven or fireplace erected on land. E19.
2 A hut, a cabin; a poor dwelling. Chiefly *N. Amer.* E19. ▸**b** A prison, a lock-up. *slang* (orig. *US*). M19. ▸**c** A mobile hut or bunkhouse. *Canad.* E20.
3 A guard's van on a train; a car for workmen etc. on a goods train. *N. Amer.* M19.
4 A person's buttocks. *US slang*. E20.

caboshed /kə'bɒʃt/ *adjective*. Also **caboched**, **cabossed** /kə'bɒst/. L16.
[ORIGIN from French *caboché* pa. pple of *cabocher*: see CABBAGE *verb*[1], -ED[1].]
HERALDRY. Of the head of a stag, bull, etc.: shown full-faced and cut off close behind the ears.

cabotage /'kabətɑːʒ, -ɪdʒ/ *noun*. M19.
[ORIGIN French, from *caboter* coast along (a place), perh. ult. from Spanish *cabo* CAPE *noun*[1]: see -AGE.]
1 Coastal trade. M19.
2 The right to operate sea, air, etc. services within a particular territory. Also, reservation to a country of (esp. air) traffic operation within its territory. M20.

cabotin /kabɔtɛ̃/ *noun*. Fem. **-tine** /-tin/. Pl. pronounced same. E20.
[ORIGIN French = strolling player, perh. formed as CABOTAGE from resemblance to vessels travelling from port to port.]
A third-rate or low-class actor.
■ ***cabotinage*** /kabɔtinɑːʒ/ *noun* the life and behaviour supposedly characteristic of third-rate actors. L19.

cabri /'kabri, kə'briː/ *noun*. *Canad.* L18.
[ORIGIN Prob. French = kid from Latin *capra* goat, but perh. repr. an Indian word.]
= ***pronghorn*** s.v. PRONG *noun*.

cabrio /'kabrɪəʊ/ *noun*. Pl. **-os**. L20.
[ORIGIN Abbreviation.]
= CABRIOLET *noun* 3.

cabriole /kabrɪ'əʊl; *foreign* kabri(j)ɔl (*pl. same*)/ *noun*. L18.
[ORIGIN French, from *cabrioler*, earlier *caprioler*, from Italian *capriolare*: see CAPRIOLE.]
1 A springing dance step in which one leg is extended and the other brought up to it. L18.
2 *hist.* More fully ***cabriole chair***. A kind of small armchair. L18.
3 Chiefly *hist.* = CABRIOLET 1. L18.
4 A kind of curved leg characteristic of Chippendale and Queen Anne furniture. L19.

cabriolet /'kabrɪəleɪ/ *noun*. M18.
[ORIGIN French, formed as CABRIOLE + -ET[1].]
1 Chiefly *hist.* A light two-wheeled hooded one-horse chaise. M18.
2 A bonnet or hat shaped like a cabriolet. L18.
3 A car with a folding top. E20.

†**Cabuli** *adjective & noun* var. of KABULI.

cac- *combining form* see CACO-.

ca-ca /'kaka/ *noun*. *slang* (chiefly *N. Amer.*). L19.
[ORIGIN Spanish, French *caca*, from Latin *cacare* defecate.]
Excrement. Also, rubbish, nonsense.

ca'canny /kɑː'kani, *Scot.* -'kɒni/ *noun*. L19.
[ORIGIN from *ca'* var. of CALL *verb* (sense 9) + CANNY *adverb*.]
Moderation, caution; the policy of going slow or limiting output at work.

cacao /kə'kɑːəʊ, -'keɪəʊ/ *noun*. Pl. **-os**. See also COCOA *noun*[1]. M16.
[ORIGIN Spanish from Nahuatl *cacauatl*, from *uatl* tree.]
1 The seed of the tree *Theobroma cacao*, native to tropical America, from which cocoa and chocolate are made. M16.
†**2** = COCOA *noun*[1] 2. Only in M17.
3 The tree itself. M18.
– COMB.: **cacao bean** = sense 1 above; **cacao butter** fat extracted from the seeds of cacao or related trees, used esp. in confectionery manufacture; **cacao tree** = sense 2 above.

†**cacaroch** *noun* var. of COCKROACH.

cacciatore /katʃə'tɔːreɪ, -ri/ *adjective*. Also **-ora** /-rə/. M20.
[ORIGIN Italian = hunter (so named because of the use of ingredients that a hunter might have to hand).]
(Of chicken) prepared in a spicy tomato sauce with mushrooms and herbs. Usu. *postpositive*.

cachaca /kə'ʃɑːkə/ *noun*. M19.
[ORIGIN Brazilian Portuguese, from Portuguese *cacaça* rum, white rum.]
A Brazilian white rum made from sugar cane.

cachalot /'kaʃəlɒt/ *noun*. M18.
[ORIGIN French, from Spanish, Portuguese *cachalote*, from *cachola* big head.]
= SPERM WHALE 1.

cache /kaʃ/ *noun & verb*. L18.
[ORIGIN French, from *cacher* to hide.]
▸ **A** *noun*. **1** A hiding place for goods, provisions, ammunition, treasure, etc. L18.
2 A hidden store of provisions etc. M19.
3 An auxiliary computer memory from which high-speed retrieval is possible. Also ***cache memory***. M20.
▸ **B** *verb trans.* Place or store in a cache. E19.

cachectic /kə'kɛktɪk/ *adjective*. E17.
[ORIGIN French *cachectique* or Latin *cachecticus*, from Greek *kakhektikos*: see CACHEXIA, -IC.]
Of or pertaining to cachexia; characterized by or affected with cachexia.
■ Also **cachectical** *adjective* (now *rare* or *obsolete*) E17.

cache-peigne /kaʃpɛɲ/ *noun*. Pl. pronounced same. L19.
[ORIGIN French, from *cacher* to hide + *peigne* comb.]
A bow or other trimming for a hat, usu. worn at the back.

cache-pot /kaʃpo (*pl. same*), 'kaʃpɒt/ *noun*. L19.
[ORIGIN French, formed as CACHE-PEIGNE + *pot* POT *noun*[1].]
An ornamental holder for a flowerpot.

cache-sexe /kaʃsɛks (*pl. same*), 'kaʃsɛks/ *noun*. E20.
[ORIGIN French, formed as CACHE-PEIGNE + *sexe* SEX *noun*.]
A covering for the genitals, esp. as worn by erotic dancers or tribal peoples.

cachet /'kaʃeɪ/ *noun*. E17.
[ORIGIN French, from *cacher* (in sense 'press', repr. now in *écacher* crush) from Proto-Romance alt. of Latin *coactare* constrain.]
1 A seal for letters, documents, etc. Now *rare* or *obsolete*. E17.
LETTRE ***de cachet***.
2 A characteristic or distinguishing mark; a characteristic feature or quality conferring prestige or distinction; high status. M19.
3 A small digestible case enclosing a dose of medicine. L19.

cachexia /kə'kɛksɪə/ *noun*. Also anglicized as **cachexy** /-'kɛksi/. M16.
[ORIGIN French *cachexie* or late Latin *cachexia* from Greek *kakhexia*, from *kakos* bad + *hexis* habit: see -IA[1].]
1 MEDICINE. A condition of weakness and wasting due to severe chronic illness. M16.
2 A bad mental condition; a state of depravity. M17.

cachinnate /'kakɪneɪt/ *verb intrans.* E19.
[ORIGIN Latin *cachinnat-* pa. ppl stem of *cachinnare*, of imit. origin: see -ATE[3].]
Laugh loudly or immoderately.
■ **cachin'natory** *adjective* of or connected with loud laughter E19.

cachinnation /kakɪ'neɪʃ(ə)n/ *noun*. E17.
[ORIGIN Latin *cachinnatio(n-)*, formed as CACHINNATE: see -ATION.]
(A burst of) loud or immoderate laughter.

cacholong /'kaʃəlɒŋ/ *noun*. L18.
[ORIGIN French from Mongolian *kas chilagun* precious stone.]
An opaque variety of opal.

cachou /ˈkaʃuː, kəˈʃuː/ *noun*. **L16**.
[ORIGIN French from Portuguese *cachu* from Malay *kacu*.]
1 = CATECHU. **L16**.
2 A lozenge taken to sweeten the breath. **E18**.

cachucha /kəˈtʃuːtʃə/ *noun*. **M19**.
[ORIGIN Spanish.]
A lively Spanish solo dance with castanets.

cacique /kəˈsiːk/ *noun*. **M16**.
[ORIGIN Spanish or French, from Taino.]
1 A W. Indian or S. American Indian native chief. **M16**. ▸**b** A political boss in Spain or Latin America. **L19**.
2 A gregarious tropical American blackbird of the genus *Cacius*, marked with patches of red or yellow. **E19**.
■ **caciquism** *noun* government by caciques **E20**.

cack /kak/ *noun*. Now *dial.* or *slang*.
[ORIGIN Old English *cac-* in *cachūs* (*hūs* house), rel. to CACK *verb*.]
1 Excrement, dung; filth. **OE**.
2 *fig.* Rubbish; nonsense. **M20**.
■ **cacky** *adjective* **L19**.

cack /kak/ *verb*. Now *dial.* **LME**.
[ORIGIN Middle Low German, Middle Dutch *cacken* (Dutch *kakken*) from Latin *cacare*.]
1 *verb intrans.* Defecate. **LME**.
2 *verb trans.* Void as excrement. **L15**.

cack-handed /kakˈhandɪd/ *adjective*. *colloq.* **M19**.
[ORIGIN from CACK *noun* + HAND *noun* + -ED[2].]
Left-handed; clumsy.

cackle /ˈkak(ə)l/ *verb & noun*. **ME**.
[ORIGIN Prob. from Middle & mod. Low German, Middle Dutch *kākelen*, partly of imit. origin, partly from *kāke* jaw, cheek.]
▸ **A** *verb*. **1** *verb intrans.* Of a hen: make the clucking noise characteristically made after laying an egg. Of a goose: make its similar characteristic noise, gaggle. **ME**. ▸†**b** Of a jackdaw, magpie, starling, etc.: chatter. **ME–L17**.
2 *verb intrans.* Of a person: be full of noisy chatter; laugh spasmodically or in a loud and silly manner. **ME**.
3 *verb trans.* Utter with or express by cackling. **ME**.
▸ **B** *noun*. **1** The cackling of a hen or goose. **ME**.
2 Idle chattering; noisy inconsequential talk. **L17**.
cut the cackle *colloq.* (stop talking and) come to the point.
3 A spasmodic or loud and silly laugh. **M19**.
■ **cackler** *noun* **LME**.

caco- /ˈkakəʊ/ *combining form*. Before a vowel also **cac-**.
[ORIGIN Repr. Greek *kako-*, from *kakos* bad: see -O-.]
In words from Greek and in English words modelled on these, with the sense 'bad, evil'.
■ †**cacochymic** *adjective* pertaining to or suffering from an unhealthy state of the bodily humours **LME–M19**. †**cacochymical** *adjective* = CACOCHYMIC **E17–M19**. †**cacochymy** *noun* [Greek *kakokhumia*] an unhealthy state of the bodily humours **LME–M19**. **caˈcodorous** *adjective* ill-smelling, malodorous **M19**. **cacoˈdoxical** *adjective* (*rare*) of or pertaining to wrong opinion, heterodox **L17**. **cacodoxy** *noun* (*rare*) [Greek *kakodoxia*] a wrong doctrine, heterodoxy **M19**. **caco-magician** *noun* an evil sorcerer **M17**. **caconym** *noun* an example of bad (scientific) nomenclature or terminology **L19**.

cacodemon /kakəˈdiːmən/ *noun*. Also **-daemon**. **L16**.
[ORIGIN Greek *kakodaimōn* evil genius, formed as CACO- + *daimōn*: see DEMON *noun*[1].]
1 An evil spirit. **L16**.
2 A malignant or deprecated person. **E18**.

cacodyl /ˈkakədʌɪl, -dɪl/ *noun*. **M19**.
[ORIGIN from Greek *kakōdēs* stinking + -YL.]
CHEMISTRY. A malodorous, toxic, spontaneously flammable liquid, tetramethyldiarsine, $((CH_3)_2As)_2$. Also, the radical $(CH_3)_2As\cdot$, dimethylarsenic (freq. *comb.*).
■ **cacoˈdylic** *adjective* of cacodyl; ***cacodylic acid***, dimethylarsinic acid, $(CH_3)_2AsO(OH)$: **M19**. **cacoˈdylate** *noun* a salt or ester of cacodylic acid **M19**.

cacoepy /kaˈkəʊɪpi, ˈkakəʊ-/ *noun*. **L19**.
[ORIGIN Greek *kak(o)epia*, formed as CACO- + *epos* word: see -Y[3].]
Bad pronunciation (opp. ***orthoepy***).

cacoethes /kakəʊˈiːθiːz/ *noun*. **M16**.
[ORIGIN Latin from Greek *kakoēthes* use as noun of adjective *kakoēthes* ill-disposed, formed as CACO- + ETHOS.]
An evil habit; a passion or 'itch' for doing something inadvisable.
cacoethes scribendi /skrɪˈbɛndiː/ an irresistible desire to write.

cacography /kəˈkɒɡrəfi/ *noun*. **L16**.
[ORIGIN from CACO- + -GRAPHY, after *orthography*.]
1 Incorrect spelling; a bad system of spelling. **L16**.
2 Bad handwriting; bad writing. **M17**.
■ **cacographer** *noun* **L19**. **cacoˈgraphical** *adjective* **M19**.

cacology /kəˈkɒlədʒi/ *noun*. **E17**.
[ORIGIN Greek *kakologia* vituperation, formed as CACO- + -LOGY.]
†**1** Evil report. Only in Dicts. Only in **17**.
2 Bad choice of words; bad pronunciation. **L18**.

cacomistle /ˈkakəmɪs(ə)l/ *noun*. **M19**.
[ORIGIN Amer. Spanish *cacomixtle* from Nahuatl *tlacomiztli*.]
A small raccoon of Central America, Mexico, and the south-western US, belonging to the genus *Bassariscus*.

cacophonous /kəˈkɒf(ə)nəs/ *adjective*. **L18**.
[ORIGIN from Greek *kakophōnos* ill-sounding, formed as CACO- + *phōnē* sound: see -OUS.]
Discordant in sound; ill-sounding.
■ **cacophonously** *adverb* **M19**.

cacophony /kəˈkɒf(ə)ni/ *noun*. **M17**.
[ORIGIN French *cacophonie* from Greek *kakophōnia*, formed as CACOPHONOUS: see -PHONY.]
Discordant sound; an instance of this.
■ **cacoˈphonic**, **cacoˈphonical** *adjectives* = CACOPHONOUS **M19**.

cactus /ˈkaktəs/ *noun*. Pl. **cacti** /ˈkaktʌɪ/, **-uses**. **E17**.
[ORIGIN Latin from Greek *kaktos* cardoon.]
†**1** = CARDOON. **E17–E19**.
2 A succulent plant of the family Cactaceae, with thick fleshy stems, usu. spiny and without leaves, and often brilliantly coloured flowers. **M18**.
– COMB.: **cactus dahlia** a variety of dahlia with rolled-back flower rays resembling a cactus flower.
■ **cactaceous** /kakˈteɪʃəs/ *adjective* of or pertaining to the family Cactaceae **M19**.

cacuminal /kəˈkjuːmɪn(ə)l/ *adjective*. **M19**.
[ORIGIN from Latin *cacuminare* make pointed (from *cacumin-*, *-men* top, summit) + -AL[1].]
PHONETICS. Pronounced with the tip of the tongue curled up towards the hard palate.

CAD *abbreviation*.
Computer-aided (or -assisted) design.

cad /kad/ *noun*. **L18**.
[ORIGIN Abbreviation of CADDIE *noun* or CADET *noun*[1].]
†**1** An unbooked passenger taken up by a coach driver for his own profit. Only in **L18**.
2 The person who takes the fare of or attends to the passengers of a coach; the conductor of a coach or bus. *obsolete* exc. *hist.* **E19**.
3 = CADDIE *noun* 2. *arch.* **M19**.
4 A man who behaves in a dishonourable or ungentlemanly way, esp. towards a woman. *arch. colloq.* **M19**.

B. BRYSON She found out that her husband was a philanderer, the beastly cad.

cadastral /kəˈdastr(ə)l/ *adjective*. **M19**.
[ORIGIN French, formed as CADASTRE + -AL[1].]
Of or according to a cadastre; having reference to the extent, value, and ownership of land, *spec.* for taxation; *loosely*, showing the extent and measurement of every plot of land.

cadastre /kəˈdastə/ *noun*. **L18**.
[ORIGIN French from mod. Provençal *cadastro* from Italian *catast(r)o* earlier *catastico* from late Greek *katastikhon* list, register, from *kata stikhon* line by line.]
A register of property showing the extent, value, and ownership, of land for taxation.

cadaver /kəˈdɑːvə, -ˈdeɪ-/ *noun*. **LME**.
[ORIGIN Latin, from *cadere* to fall.]
Now chiefly *MEDICINE*. A dead body, a corpse.

cadaveric /kəˈdav(ə)rɪk/ *adjective*. **M19**.
[ORIGIN French *cadavérique* or from CADAVER + -IC.]
Of, pertaining to, or characteristic of a corpse.

cadaverine /kəˈdav(ə)riːn/ *noun*. **L19**.
[ORIGIN formed as CADAVER + -INE[5].]
CHEMISTRY. A toxic liquid base, 1,5-diaminopentane, $H_2N(CH_2)_5NH_2$, formed by the putrefaction of proteins.

cadaverous /kəˈdav(ə)rəs/ *adjective*. **LME**.
[ORIGIN Latin *cadaverosus*, formed as CADAVER: see -OUS.]
Of, pertaining to, or resembling a corpse; *esp.* deathly pale.
■ **cadaverously** *adverb* **M19**. **cadaverousness** *noun* **M17**.

cad-bait /ˈkadbeɪt/ *noun*. Now *dial.* Also (earlier) **cod-**. **E17**.
[ORIGIN formed as CAD-WORM: see BAIT *noun*[1].]
= CADDIS *noun*[2] 1.

caddice *noun* var. of CADDIS *noun*[2].

caddie /ˈkadi/ *noun*. Orig. *Scot.* Also **caddy**, CADEE, †**cadie**. **M17**.
[ORIGIN French CADET *noun*[1].]
†**1** = CADET *noun*[1] 2. **M17–E19**.
2 A boy or man on the lookout for odd jobs. **M18**.
3 A young fellow, a lad. *Scot. joc.* **L18**.
4 A golfer's assistant for carrying clubs etc. **L18**.
– COMB.: **caddie-car**, **caddie-cart** a light two-wheeled trolley for transporting golf clubs during a game.

caddie /ˈkadi/ *verb intrans.* Also **caddy**. **E20**.
[ORIGIN from the noun.]
Act as caddie (*for* a golfer).

caddis /ˈkadɪs/ *noun*[1]. *obsolete* exc. *Scot.* **ME**.
[ORIGIN Sense 1 from Old French *cadas*, *-z*, sense 2 from Old French & mod. French *cadis* from Provençal, both of unknown origin.]
1 Cotton wool; floss silk; fluff; surgical lint. **ME**.
†**2** (A tape or binding of) worsted yarn, crewel; worsted material; coarse serge. **M16–L19**.

caddis /ˈkadɪs/ *noun*[2]. Also **-ice**. **E17**.
[ORIGIN Unknown: cf. CAD-BAIT, CADEW, CAD-WORM.]
1 More fully ***caddis bait***, ***caddis worm***. The aquatic larva of a caddis fly (see sense 2 below), which often makes cylindrical protective cases of debris and is commonly used as fishing bait. **E17**.
2 ***caddis fly***, a feeble-flying usu. nocturnal insect of the order Trichoptera, living near water. **M17**.

caddish /ˈkadɪʃ/ *adjective*. *arch. colloq.* **M19**.
[ORIGIN from CAD *noun* + -ISH[1].]
Of the nature of or characteristic of a cad; dishonourable, ungentlemanly.
■ **caddishly** *adverb* **L19**. **caddishness** *noun* **M19**.

caddle /ˈkad(ə)l/ *verb & noun*. *dial.* **L18**.
[ORIGIN Unknown.]
▸ **A** *verb trans.* Trouble, disturb. **L18**.
▸ **B** *noun*. Disorder, confusion; trouble. **E19**.

caddow /ˈkadəʊ/ *noun*[1]. *obsolete* exc. *dial.* **LME**.
[ORIGIN Prob. formed as CAW + DAW *noun*: cf. KAE *noun*.]
A jackdaw.

caddow /ˈkadəʊ/ *noun*[2]. Long *obsolete* exc. *dial.* **L16**.
[ORIGIN Cf. CADDIS *noun*[1] 2.]
A rough woollen covering.

caddy /ˈkadi/ *noun*[1]. **L18**.
[ORIGIN Alt. of CATTY *noun*.]
1 More fully ***tea caddy***. A small box for holding tea. **L18**.
2 A container, sometimes with divisions, for other substances or small objects ready for use. **L19**.

caddy *noun*[2], *verb* var. of CADDIE *noun*, *verb*.

†**cade** *noun*[1]. **ME–L19**.
[ORIGIN Latin *cadus* wine-jar, measure for liquids from Greek *kados* cask, jar, of Semitic origin (cf. Hebrew *kad* pitcher).]
A cask, a barrel, *esp.* of herrings.

cade /keɪd/ *noun*[2] *& adjective*. **LME**.
[ORIGIN Unknown.]
(A lamb, foal, etc.) brought up by hand as a pet.

cade /keɪd/ *noun*[3]. **L16**.
[ORIGIN French from Provençal from medieval Latin *catanus*, perh. from Gaulish.]
cade oil, ***oil of cade***, a bitter dark oil, having some medicinal use, distilled from the wood of a juniper, *Juniperus oxycedrus*.

cadeau /kado/ *noun*. Pl. ***-eaux*** /-o/. **L18**.
[ORIGIN French.]
A gift.

†**cadee** *noun*. **M17–L18**.
[ORIGIN French CADET *noun*[1]: cf. CADDIE *noun*.]
= CADET *noun*[1] 2.

cadelle /kəˈdɛl/ *noun*. **M19**.
[ORIGIN French from Latin *catella*, *catellus* young (of an animal), little dog.]
A small dark beetle, *Tenebroides mauritanicus*, frequently found in food stores where it scavenges and preys on other insects.

cadence /ˈkeɪd(ə)ns/ *noun & verb*. **LME**.
[ORIGIN Old French from Italian *cadenza* from popular Latin, from Latin *cadent-* pres. ppl stem of *cadere* fall: see -ENCE.]
▸ **A** *noun*. **1** (A) rhythm; (a) metrical or musical beat; (a) measured movement, esp. of sounds. **LME**.

SHAKES. *L.L.L.* The elegancy, facility, and golden cadence of poesy. F. NORRIS Listening to the one-two-three, one-two-three cadence of the musicians. *Scientific American* A bicyclist confronting a head wind . . tries to maintain his customary . . pedaling cadence by shifting gears.

2 a (A pattern of) falling intonation or pitch of voice, esp. at the end of a sentence etc. **L16**. ▸**b** *gen.* Intonation; an intonation pattern; (a) modulation of the voice; (a) national or local accent. **E18**.

a L. STERNE A low voice, with a . . sweet cadence at the end of it. **b** G. MURRAY The accent, the cadences, the expression, with which the words were originally spoken. J. BERGER The cadence of their voices is like that of a couple talking in bed.

3 The close of a musical phrase; a sequence of notes resolving discord or establishing arrival in a key. Also, a flourish at the close of a movement, a cadenza. **L16**.
imperfect cadence: see IMPERFECT *adjective*. ***medial cadence***: see MEDIAL *adjective*. ***perfect cadence***: see PERFECT *adjective*. ***PLAGAL cadence***.
†**4** Sinking or falling down. **E–M17**.

MILTON Now was the Sun in Western cadence low.

5 The sound of the rising and (esp.) falling of a storm, the sea, etc. *arch.* **M17**.
– COMB.: **cadence braking** repeated rhythmic application of the brakes of a motor vehicle.
▸ **B** *verb*. **1** *verb trans.* Compose metrically. *rare*. **M18**.
2 *verb intrans.* Flow in rhythm; resolve discord or establish a key with a cadence. **E20**.
■ **cadenced** *adjective* characterized by cadence, rhythmical, measured **L18**.

cadency /ˈkeɪd(ə)nsi/ *noun*. **E17**.
[ORIGIN formed as CADENCE: see -ENCY.]
1 = CADENCE *noun* 1. Now *rare*. **E17**.
2 The status of a younger branch of a family. **E18**.

cadent /ˈkeɪd(ə)nt/ *adjective & noun*. **L16**.
[ORIGIN Latin *cadent-*: see CADENCE.]
▸ **A** *adjective*. **1** *ASTROLOGY.* Designating or pertaining to each of the four mundane houses (the 3rd, 6th, 9th, and 12th of the twelve divisions of the heavens) next clockwise from the angles (ANGLE *noun*[3] 3). Cf. SUCCEDENT *adjective* 2. **L16**.

2 Falling in intonation or pitch; rhythmical; modulated. *arch.* E17.
3 *gen.* Falling. Long *arch.* E17.
▸ **B** *noun.* ASTROLOGY. A cadent house (see A.1 above). *obsolete* exc. *hist.* L16.

cadential /kəˈdɛnʃ(ə)l/ *adjective.* M19.
[ORIGIN from CADENCE, after *essence, essential*, etc.: see -IAL.]
Of or pertaining to a cadence or cadenza.

cadenza /kəˈdɛnzə/ *noun.* M18.
[ORIGIN Italian: see CADENCE.]
MUSIC. A (sometimes improvised) flourish or passage for a solo instrument or voice, usu. near the close or between the divisions of a movement; *spec.* such a passage in a concerto in which the main themes of the movement (usu. the first or last) are developed.

cadet /kəˈdɛt/ *noun*[1]. E17.
[ORIGIN French, earlier *capdet* from Gascon dial. (= Provençal *capdel*) from Proto-Romance dim. of Latin *caput, -it-* head: see -ET[1].]
1 A younger son or brother; also occas. (a member of) a younger branch of a family. *formal* or *arch.* E17. ▸**b** The youngest son or brother. M17.
2 *hist.* A gentleman who entered the army without a commission, to learn the profession. M17.
3 A student in a naval, military, or air force college. L18. ▸**b** A member of a corps receiving elementary military or police training. L19.
4 A young man learning sheep-farming. *NZ.* M19.
■ **cadetship** *noun* a place as a cadet; the status of a cadet: E19.

Cadet /kəˈdɛt/ *noun*[2]. Also **K-**. E20.
[ORIGIN Russian *Kadet*, from *Ka de*, pronunc. of the initials of *Konstitutsionnyĭ demokrat* Constitutional Democrat, with ending assimilated to that of CADET *noun*[1].]
RUSSIAN HISTORY. A member of the Constitutional Democratic Party.

cadew /ˈkadjuː/ *noun.* Now *rare* or *obsolete.* M17.
[ORIGIN Rel. to CAD-BAIT, CADDIS *noun*[2], CAD-WORM.]
= CADDIS *noun*[2] 1.

cadge /kadʒ/ *noun*[1]. E17.
[ORIGIN App. alt. of CAGE *noun*, perh. conf. with CADGE *verb* 2.]
FALCONRY. A (usu. wooden) framework on which hawks are carried.

cadge /kadʒ/ *verb & noun*[2]. LME.
[ORIGIN Unknown. Exc. in sense A.1 (which may be a different word) perh. back-form. from CADGER *noun*[1].]
▸ **A** *verb.* **1** *verb trans.* Fasten, tie, bind, knot. *obsolete* exc. *dial.* LME.

T. ROETHKE So caged and cadged.

2 *verb trans.* Carry about. *obsolete* exc. *dial.* E17.
3 *verb trans.* Load, stuff, (the stomach). *dial.* L17.
4 *verb trans.* Hawk, peddle (*Scot.*); get by begging or scrounging. E18.

R. HOGGART Those who can cadge a few coppers from their mothers. E. REVELEY I'm cadging a lift home with you people.

5 *verb intrans.* Go about begging or scrounging. E19.

J. BUCHAN I cadged . . for invitations to tea.

▸ **B** *noun.* †**1** A circuit for begging. *Scot.* Only in L17.
2 The action of cadging. *colloq.* E19.

cadger /ˈkadʒə/ *noun*[1]. L15.
[ORIGIN Unknown: cf. CADGE *verb & noun*[2].]
1 A carrier; an itinerant dealer, esp. travelling between town and country; a hawker. *arch.* Chiefly *Scot. & N. English.* L15.
2 A person who scrounges or begs habitually; a sponger. M19.

cadger /ˈkadʒə/ *noun*[2]. M19.
[ORIGIN Prob. from CADGE *noun*[1] + -ER[1]: cf. Old French *cagier.*]
FALCONRY. A man who carries hawks.

cadgy /ˈkadʒi/ *adjective. Scot. & N. English.* E18.
[ORIGIN Unknown.]
1 Amorous; wanton. E18.
2 Cheerful, merry. E18.
■ **cadgily** *adverb* E18. **cadginess** *noun* L19.

cadi /ˈkɑːdi, ˈkeɪdi/ *noun.* Also **k-**, **q-**. L16.
[ORIGIN Arabic *(al-)qāḍī*. See also KAZI.]
A civil judge in a Muslim country.

†**cadie** *noun* var. of CADDIE *noun.*

cadilesker /kɑːdɪˈlɛskə/ *noun.* L16.
[ORIGIN Turkish *cadilaskar* from Arabic *qāḍī (a)l-ʿaskar* judge of the army.]
A chief judge in the Ottoman Empire, whose jurisdiction originally included the army.

†**cadjan** *noun & adjective* see KAJANG.

Cadmean /kadˈmiːən/ *adjective.* Also **-aean**. E17.
[ORIGIN from Latin *Cadmeus* from Greek *Kadmeios*, from *Kadmos* Cadmus (see below) + -AN.]
Pertaining to Cadmus, the legendary founder of Thebes; Theban; *spec.* designating a victory gained at too great a cost.

cadmium /ˈkadmɪəm/ *noun.* E19.
[ORIGIN from Latin *cadmia* (see CALAMINE) + -IUM.]
A bluish-white metallic chemical element, atomic no. 48, which occurs in small amounts in zinc ores and resembles zinc chemically (symbol Cd).
– COMB.: **cadmium cell** a voltaic cell with cadmium amalgam and mercury electrodes and saturated cadmium sulphate electrolyte, used as a standard of electromotive force; **cadmium yellow** an intense yellow pigment containing cadmium sulphide.
■ **cadˈmiferous** *adjective* yielding cadmium E19.

†**cadouk** *adjective & noun.* Chiefly *Scot.* As noun also **caduac**. LME.
[ORIGIN French *caduc*: see CADUCITY.]
▸ **A** *adjective.* Liable to fall; perishable; transitory; frail. LME–L17.
▸ **B** *noun.* An incidental payment; a windfall. M17–E19.

cadre /ˈkɑːdə, ˈkɑːdr(ə), ˈkadri/ *noun.* M19.
[ORIGIN French from Italian *quadro* from Latin *quadrus* square.]
1 A frame, a framework; a plan. *rare.* M19.
2 MILITARY. **a** A permanent establishment of trained personnel forming a nucleus for expansion at need. M19. ▸**b** (A list of) the complement of the officers of a regiment etc. M19.
3 (A member of) a group of workers acting to promote the aims and interests of the Communist Party. M20. ▸**b** In the People's Republic of China, an office-holder in a Party, governmental, or military organization. M20.

†**caduac** *noun* var. of CADOUK *noun.*

caduceus /kəˈdjuːsɪəs/ *noun.* Pl. **-cei** /-sɪʌɪ/. L16.
[ORIGIN Latin *caduceus, -um* from Doric Greek *karuk(e)ion* = Attic *kērukeion* neut. adjective used as noun, from *kērux, -uk-* herald.]
In CLASSICAL HISTORY, a Greek or Roman herald's wand; *spec.* (also **C-**) the wand carried by the messenger god Hermes or Mercury, usu. represented with two serpents twined round it.
■ **caducean** *adjective* M17.

caduciary /kəˈdjuːsjəri/ *adjective.* Now *rare.* M18.
[ORIGIN Late Latin *caducarius*, from *caducus* (in *bona caduca* lapsed possessions): see CADUCITY, -ARY[1].]
LAW. (Of a bequest, esp. of an estate) subject to reversion; pertaining to reversion of a bequest.

caducity /kəˈdjuːsɪti/ *noun.* M18.
[ORIGIN French *caducité*, from *caduc* from Latin *caducus* liable to fall, perishable, from *cadere* to fall: see -ITY.]
1 The infirmity of old age, senility. M18.
2 *gen.* Tendency to fall; transitoriness; frailty. L18.
3 LAW. The lapse of a testamentary gift. L19.

caducous /kəˈdjuːkəs/ *adjective.* L17.
[ORIGIN from Latin *caducus* (see CADUCITY) + -OUS.]
†**1** Epileptic. Only in L17.
2 BOTANY & ZOOLOGY. Of an organ or part: that falls off naturally after serving its purpose. Opp. PERSISTENT 1. M18.
3 LAW. Of a bequest: subject to reversion. L19.

cad-worm /ˈkadwəːm/ *noun.* Now *dial.* Also (earlier) †**cod-**. LME.
[ORIGIN Origin of 1st elem. unkn.: cf. CAD-BAIT, CADDIS *noun*[2], CADEW. See WORM *noun.*]
= CADDIS *noun*[2] 1.

cady /ˈkeɪdi/ *noun. dial. & slang.* M19.
[ORIGIN Unknown.]
A hat, a cap.

Caecias /ˈsiːsɪəs/ *noun. literary.* E17.
[ORIGIN Latin from Greek *kaikios.*]
The north-east wind, esp. personified.

caecilian /sɪˈsɪlɪən/ *noun.* Also **coe-**. L19.
[ORIGIN from mod. Latin *Caecilia* genus name from Latin *caecilia* slow-worm: see -AN.]
A legless, superficially snakelike, burrowing amphibian of the order Gymnophiona, with poorly developed eyes; = APODAN.

caecum /ˈsiːkəm/ *noun.* Also ***cecum**. Pl. **-ca** /-kə/. LME.
[ORIGIN Latin *(intestinum) caecum* blind gut, translating Greek *tuphlon enteron.*]
ANATOMY. **1** The blind prolongation of the large intestine beyond the junction with the small intestine, bearing the vermiform appendix; the blind gut. LME.
2 Any blind-ended tube or vessel. M18.
■ **caecal** *adjective* of, pertaining to, or resembling the caecum E19. **caecitis** /siːˈsʌɪtɪs/ *noun* inflammation of the caecum M19. **caecostomy** /siːˈkɒstəmi/ *noun* (an instance of) the surgical formation of an opening in the caecum through which intestinal contents may be removed L19.

Caelum /ˈsiːləm/ *noun.* M19.
[ORIGIN Latin *caelum* chisel.]
A minor constellation of the southern hemisphere, next to Eridanus; the Chisel.

caenogenesis /siːnəˈdʒɛnɪsɪs/ *noun.* Also **keno-** /ˈkiːnə/, ***ceno-**; **caino-**, **kaino-** /ˈkʌɪnə-/. L19.
[ORIGIN from Greek *kainos* new, recent + -GENESIS.]
BIOLOGY. Orig., the development of features in ontogenesis which are the result of environmental adaptation (opp. ***palingenesis*** or ***recapitulation***). Now *spec.*, the development in embryonic or larval forms of functional adaptations not present in the adult.
■ **caenogeˈnetic** *adjective* L19.

Caenozoic *adjective & noun* var. of CENOZOIC.

Caen stone /ˈkeɪn stəʊn/ *noun phr.* LME.
[ORIGIN from *Caen*, a town in Normandy.]
A lightish-yellow building stone found near Caen.

Caerphilly /kɛːˈfɪli, kɑː-, kə-/ *noun.* E20.
[ORIGIN A town in S. Wales.]
More fully ***Caerphilly cheese***. A kind of mild white cheese, orig. marketed in Caerphilly.

caerulean *adjective & noun* var. of CERULEAN.

Caesar /ˈsiːzə/ *noun.*
[ORIGIN Old English *cāsere*, Old Frisian *kaiser, keiser*, Old Saxon *kēsar*, Old High German *keisar*, Old Norse *keisari*, Gothic *kaisar*, from Germanic from Latin family name of Gaius Julius *Caesar*, Roman statesman d. 44 BC: cf. KAISER, TSAR.]
1 A Roman emperor, *esp.* one of those from Augustus to Hadrian. OE. ▸†**b** (The heir of) the Emperor of the Holy Roman Empire. M16–E18.
appeal to Caesar: to the highest possible authority. **Caesar's wife** a person required to be above suspicion.
2 *transf. & fig.* **a** An absolute monarch; an autocrat. ME. ▸**b** A temporal ruler; the civil power. E17.
3 MEDICINE. (A case of or baby delivered by) Caesarean section. Now *slang.* M16.
– COMB.: **Caesar baby** MEDICINE, *slang*: delivered by Caesarean section. **Caesar salad** [named after *Caesar* Cardini, the Mexican restaurateur who invented it in 1924]: consisting of cos lettuce and croutons served with a dressing of olive oil, lemon juice, raw egg, Worcester sauce, and seasoning.
■ **Caesarism** *noun* the principle of absolute government; imperialism: M19. **Caesarist** *noun* †(**a**) *rare* a monarch, an emperor; (**b**) an adherent of Caesarism: L16. **Caesaro-ˈpapism** *noun* the supremacy of the civil power in ecclesiastical affairs L19.

Caesarean /sɪˈzɛːrɪən/ *noun & adjective.* Also ***Ces-**, **-ian**. E16.
[ORIGIN from Latin *Caesarianus* or *Caesareus*, from *Caesar*: see CAESAR, -EAN, -IAN.]
▸ **A** *noun.* **1** A follower or adherent of Caesar; a person in favour of autocracy or imperialism. E16.
2 *ellipt.* (A) Caesarean section; a Caesarean birth. E20.
▸ **B** *adjective.* **1** [From the story that Julius Caesar was so delivered.] ***Caesarean section***, ***Caesarean operation***, the surgical operation of cutting the walls of the abdomen to deliver a child. Hence ***Caesarean birth***, ***Caesarean delivery***, etc. E17.
2 Of or pertaining to Caesar or the Caesars; imperial. M17.

caesious /ˈsiːzɪəs/ *adjective.* E19.
[ORIGIN from Latin *caesius* + -OUS.]
Greyish-blue or -green.

caesium /ˈsiːzɪəm/ *noun.* Also ***ces-**. M19.
[ORIGIN formed as CAESIOUS + -IUM: named from having characteristic lines in the blue part of the spectrum.]
A soft highly reactive chemical element of the alkali metal group, atomic no. 55 (symbol Cs).
– COMB.: **caesium clock** an atomic clock that uses the vibrations of caesium atoms as a time standard.

caespititious /sɛspɪˈtɪʃəs/ *adjective.* Also ***ces-**. L18.
[ORIGIN Latin *caespiticius*, formed as CAESPITOSE: see -ITIOUS[2].]
Made of turf.

caespitose /ˈsɛspɪtəʊs/ *adjective.* Also ***ces-**. M18.
[ORIGIN from Latin *caespit-, -es* sod, turf + -OSE[1].]
Chiefly BOTANY. Growing in tufts or clumps.

caesura /sɪˈzjʊərə/ *noun.* M16.
[ORIGIN Latin *caesura*, from *caes-* pa. ppl stem of *caedere* cut: see -URE.]
1 PROSODY. A break or pause between words within a metrical foot in classical prosody or near the middle of a line in English etc. prosody. M16.
2 *gen.* A break, a stop, an interruption. L16.
■ **caesural** *adjective* M18.

CAF *abbreviation. US.*
Cost and freight.

caf *noun* var. of CAFF.

cafard /kaˈfɑː, *foreign* kafaːr/ *noun.* M16.
[ORIGIN French = cockroach, hypocrite, prob. from late Latin *caphardum*: see CAFFA.]
†**1** A hypocrite. M16–M17.
2 Melancholia. E20.

cafe /ˈkafeɪ, -fi/ *noun.* Also **café**. E19.
[ORIGIN French *café* coffee, coffee house.]
1 A coffee house; a tea shop; an informal restaurant; *US* a bar. E19.
2 A small shop selling confectionery, tobacco, newspapers, etc. *S. Afr.* M20.
– COMB.: **cafe curtain** a curtain covering only the lower half of a window; **cafe society** regular patrons of fashionable cafes and nightspots.

café /kafe/ *noun.* Pl. pronounced same. M18.
[ORIGIN See CAFE.]
The French for 'coffee' or 'coffee house', occurring in various phrases used in English
■ ***café au lait*** /o lɛ/ coffee with milk; (of) the light brown colour of this: M18. ***café chantant*** /ʃɑ̃tɑ̃/ [lit. 'singing cafe'], pl. **-s -s** (pronounced same), a cafe with live musical entertainment M19. ***café noir*** /nwaːr/ black coffee M19.

C

C

cafeteria /kafɪˈtɪərɪə/ *noun*. Orig. *US*. M19.
[ORIGIN Amer. Spanish *cafetería*, from *café* coffee.]
1 A coffee house or restaurant; now *esp.* a self-service restaurant. M19.
2 *attrib.* a Designating a court in which a perpetrator of a minor motoring offence may pay a fixed fine without having to stand trial. *US LAW*. M20. ▸b Designating any system in which people may choose for themselves from a number of available options, esp. one in which an employee may select a personal package of company benefits. *N. Amer.* M20.

cafetière /kaf(ə)ˈtjɛː(r)/ *noun*. M19.
[ORIGIN French, formed as CAFE.]
A coffee pot, *spec.* one with a plunger.

caff /kaf/ *noun*. *slang*. Also **caf**. M20.
[ORIGIN Abbreviation.]
A cafe or cafeteria.

†**caffa** *noun*. L15.
[ORIGIN Old French from late Latin *caphardum* university gown, of unknown origin.]
1 A rich silk cloth. L15–M17.
2 A kind of painted cotton cloth made in India. M18–E19.

caffè /ˈkaffɛ, ˈkafeɪ/ *noun*. M19.
[ORIGIN Italian = coffee, cafe.]
1 An Italian coffee shop or cafe. M19.
2 (A drink of) coffee. M19.
caffè latte /ˌkafeɪ ˈlateɪ, ˌkaffɛ ˈlatte/ [Italian = milk coffee], a drink made by adding a shot of espresso coffee to a glass or cup of frothy steamed milk. **caffè macchiato** /ˌkafeɪ makɪˈɑːtəʊ/ [Italian = stained coffee], a drink made by adding a dash of frothy steamed milk to an espresso coffee.

caffeine /ˈkafiːn/ *noun*. M19.
[ORIGIN French *caféine*, formed as CAFE + -INE[5].]
CHEMISTRY. A crystalline alkaloid, $C_8H_{10}N_4O_2$, which is found esp. in tea and coffee plants and is a central nervous system stimulant; 1,3,7-trimethylxanthine.
■ **caffeinated** *adjective* (*a*) (of coffee or tea) containing natural caffeine, or with caffeine added; (*b*) stimulated (as if) with caffeine: L20. **caffeinism** *noun* headache, sleeplessness, and palpitations caused by excessive intake of caffeine L19.

caffle /ˈkaf(ə)l/ *verb intrans. dial.* M19.
[ORIGIN Var. of CAVIL *verb*.]
Argue; prevaricate.

Caffrarian *adjective* see KAFFRARIAN.

Caffre *noun* see KAFFIR.

cafila /ˈkɑːfɪlə/ *noun*. L16.
[ORIGIN Arabic *qāfila*: cf. COFFLE.]
A company of travellers in the Middle East, a caravan.

caftan *noun* var. of KAFTAN.

cafuffle *noun* var. of KERFUFFLE.

cag /kag/ *noun*. *obsolete* exc. *Scot.* & *US dial.* See also KEG. LME.
[ORIGIN Old Norse *kaggi*.]
A small cask, a keg.

cage /keɪdʒ/ *noun* & *verb*. ME.
[ORIGIN Old French & mod. French from Latin *cavea* stall, cage, coop, etc.]
▸ **A** *noun*. **1** A box or place of confinement for birds, animals, etc., made wholly or partly of wire, or bars of metal, wood, etc., so as to admit air and light. ME.
GILDED ***cage***.
2 A prison, a lock-up. ME. ▸b An enclosure for prisoners of war. E20.
3 *fig.* That which confines or imprisons. ME.

W. BEVERIDGE The Cage of Flesh, Wherein the Soul is penned.

4 A structure resembling a cage for birds etc.; an open framework of various kinds; *spec.* (*a*) a frame for hoisting men, wagons, etc., in a mine; (*b*) a compartment for passengers etc. in a lift. LME.
RIBCAGE. *THORACIC* ***cage***.
– COMB.: **cage bird**: (of a kind customarily) kept in a cage; **cagework** (*a*) openwork like the bars of a cage; †(*b*) the upper works of a ship.
▸ **B** *verb trans.* Confine in or as in a cage. L16.
■ **cageling** *noun* a bird kept in a cage M19. **cager** *noun* (*N. Amer. colloq.*) a basketball player E20.

cagey /ˈkeɪdʒi/ *adjective*. *colloq.* (orig. *US*). Also **cagy**. E20.
[ORIGIN Unknown.]
Shrewd; wary; secretive; uncommunicative.
■ **cageyness**, **caginess** *noun* M20. **cagily** *adverb* E20.

cagmag /ˈkagmag/ *noun* & *verb*. *dial.* M18.
[ORIGIN Unknown.]
▸ **A** *noun*. A tough old goose; unwholesome meat; offal. M18.
▸ **B** *verb intrans.* & *trans.* Infl. **-gg-**. Quarrel; nag. L19.

cagnotte /kaɲɔt/ *noun*. L19.
[ORIGIN French.]
Money reserved from the stakes for the bank at certain gambling games.

cagot /kago/ *noun*. Pl. pronounced same. M16.
[ORIGIN French.]
†1 An affectedly pious person. *Scot.* Only in M16.
2 A member of an outcast group in southern France (*hist.*); an outcast, a pariah. E19.

cagoulard /kagulaːr/ *noun*. Pl. pronounced same. M20.
[ORIGIN French, formed as CAGOULE: see -ARD.]
A member of a secret French right-wing organization in the 1930s.

cagoule /kəˈguːl/ *noun*. Also **k-**. M20.
[ORIGIN French, lit. 'cowl'.]
A hooded thin waterproof garment pulled on over the head.

cagy *adjective* var. of CAGEY.

cahier /kaje/ *noun*. Pl. pronounced same. L18.
[ORIGIN French: see QUIRE *noun*[1].]
1 In *pl.* The instructions prepared by each of the three representative bodies as a guide for their policy at the French National Assembly of 1789. L18.
2 An exercise book; a pamphlet, a fascicle. M19.

cahoot /kəˈhuːt/ *noun*. *slang* (orig. *US*). E19.
[ORIGIN Unknown.]
sing. & (now usu.) in *pl.* Company, partnership; collusion. Chiefly in ***in cahoots with***.

cahoun *noun* var. of COHUNE.

cahow /kəˈhaʊ/ *noun*. E17.
[ORIGIN Imit.]
A large rare petrel, *Pterodroma cahow*, which breeds in Bermuda.

CAI *abbreviation*.
Computer-aided (or -assisted) instruction.

caid *noun* see KAID.

cailleach /ˈkɛljʌx/ *noun*. *Scot.* Also **-iach**. E19.
[ORIGIN Gaelic = old woman.]
An old (Highland) woman, a crone.

†**caimacam** *noun* var. of KAIMAKAM.

caiman /ˈkeɪmən/ *noun*. Also **cay-**. L16.
[ORIGIN Spanish *caimán*, Portuguese *caimão*, from Carib *acayuman*.]
Any of a number of crocodilians closely related to the alligator and native to S. and Central America; *loosely* any New World crocodilian.
spectacled caiman: see SPECTACLED 2.

cain /keɪn/ *noun*[1]. *Scot.* & *Irish*. Also **k-**. ME.
[ORIGIN Irish & Gaelic *cáin*.]
A rent paid in kind.

Cain /keɪn/ *noun*[2]. ME.
[ORIGIN The eldest son of Adam, who murdered his brother Abel (*Genesis* 4).]
1 A murderer, a fratricide. ME.
2 ***raise Cain***, make a disturbance, create trouble. *colloq.* M19.
■ **Cainite** *noun* (*ECCLESIASTICAL HISTORY*) a member of a gnostic sect which exalted everyone and everything reviled by God in the Old Testament M17.

-caine /keɪn/ *suffix*. Also **-cain**.
[ORIGIN from COCAINE.]
PHARMACOLOGY. Forming nouns denoting drugs, esp. ones with anaesthetic properties, as ***lignocaine***, ***Novocaine***.

ca'ing whale /ˈkɑːɪŋ weɪl/ *noun phr.* Also **caa'ing whale**. M20.
[ORIGIN Scot. *ca'ing* calling (see CALL *verb* 9).]
The pilot whale, *Globicephala melaena*.

cainogenesis *noun* var. of CAENOGENESIS.

Cainozoic *adjective* & *noun* var. of CENOZOIC.

caipirinha /kʌɪpɪˈrɪnjə/ *noun*. L20.
[ORIGIN Brazilian Portuguese, from *caipira* yokel.]
A Brazilian cocktail made with cachaca, lime or lemon juice, sugar, and crushed ice.

caique /kʌɪˈiːk, kə-/ *noun*[1]. E17.
[ORIGIN French *caïque* from Italian *caicco* from Turkish *kayık*.]
1 A light rowing boat or skiff used on the Bosporus. E17.
2 An eastern Mediterranean sailing vessel. M17.

caique /kʌɪˈiːkə, -keɪ/ *noun*[2]. M20.
[ORIGIN Spanish or Portuguese.]
Either of two small tropical S. American parrots of the genus *Pionites*, mainly green, yellow, and black in colour. Cf. SACKIE.

caird /kɛːd/ *noun*. *Scot.* LME.
[ORIGIN Gaelic *ceard* artificer in metal = Irish *ceard*, Old Irish *cerd* craftsman.]
A travelling tinker; a Gypsy.

Cairene /ˈkʌɪriːn, kʌɪˈriːn/ *noun* & *adjective*. M19.
[ORIGIN from *Cairo* (see below) + *-ene*, after *Nazarene* etc.]
▸ **A** *noun*. A native or inhabitant of the Egyptian city of Cairo. M19.
▸ **B** *adjective*. Of or pertaining to Cairo or its inhabitants. M19.

cairn /kɛːn/ *noun* & *verb*. LME.
[ORIGIN Gaelic *carn* corresp. to Old Irish, Welsh *carn*.]
▸ **A** *noun*. **1** A pyramid of rough stones raised as a memorial or to mark a path etc. LME.
horned cairn: see HORNED *adjective*. ***stalled cairn***: see STALL *verb*[1].
2 In full ***cairn terrier***. A small terrier with short legs, a longish body, and a shaggy coat. E20.
▸ **B** *verb trans.* Provide or mark with a cairn or cairns; pile as a cairn. Chiefly as ***cairned*** *ppl adjective*. M16.

cairngorm /ˈkɛːngɔːm/ *noun*. L18.
[ORIGIN A mountain in northern Scotland, = Gaelic *carn gorm* blue cairn.]
(A piece of) smoky quartz, esp. as found in parts of Scotland. Also ***cairngorm stone***.

caisson /ˈkeɪs(ə)n, kəˈsuːn/ *noun*. L17.
[ORIGIN French = large chest, from Italian *cassone* with assim. to *caisse* CASE *noun*[2]: see -OON.]
1 A large watertight chamber open at the bottom, from which the water is kept out by air pressure, used in laying foundations under water. L17. ▸b A floating vessel used as a dock gate. M19.
2 An ammunition chest; an ammunition wagon. E18.
– COMB.: **caisson disease** illness of workers in compressed air, resulting from too rapid decompression; the 'bends'.

caitiff /ˈkeɪtɪf/ *noun* & *adjective*. *arch.* ME.
[ORIGIN Old French *caitif* captive, var. of *chaitif* (mod. *chétif* wretched) from Proto-Romance alt. of Latin *captivus* CAPTIVE *adjective*.]
▸ **A** *noun* †**1 a** A captive, a prisoner. ME–E17. ▸b A wretched or miserable person, a poor wretch. LME–L17.
2 A base, despicable wretch; a villain; a coward. ME.
▸ **B** *adjective*. †**1** Wretched, miserable. ME–L16.
2 Vile, base, wicked; worthless; cowardly. ME.

cajan /ˈkeɪdʒ(ə)n, ˈkɑː-/ *noun*. L17.
[ORIGIN Malay *kacang*.]
A tropical leguminous shrub of the genus *Cajanus*, esp. *C. cajan*, cultivated for its edible pulses.

cajang *noun* & *adjective* see KAJANG.

cajeput *noun* var. of CAJUPUT.

cajole /kəˈdʒəʊl/ *verb*. M17.
[ORIGIN French *cajoler*.]
1 *verb trans.* Persuade or prevail upon (a person) by delusive flattery, specious promises, etc. (Foll. by *into*, *out of*, *to do*.) M17. ▸b Coax (something) *out of* a person. M18.

W. IRVING The populace . . are not to be cajoled out of a ghost story by any of these plausible explanations. V. WOOLF We tried to cajole him to write with £10 p. 1,000 for bait. T. DREISER She cajoled him into getting things for her and then would not even let him kiss her.

2 *verb intrans.* Use cajolery. M17.

S. KING Herb talked to her, then cajoled, finally demanded.

■ **cajolement** *noun* E19. **cajoler** *noun* L17.

cajolery /kəˈdʒəʊləri/ *noun*. M17.
[ORIGIN French *cajolerie*, formed as CAJOLE: see -ERY.]
The action or an instance of cajoling; persuasion by flattery, deceit, etc.

Cajun /ˈkeɪdʒ(ə)n/ *noun* & *adjective*. *N. Amer. colloq.* M19.
[ORIGIN Alt. of ACADIAN.]
▸ **A** *noun*. A French-speaking descendant of early settlers in Acadia, living esp. in Louisiana and Maine; *gen.* an Acadian. M19.
▸ **B** *adjective*. Of or pertaining to the Cajuns; *gen.* Acadian. L19.

cajuput /ˈkadʒəpʌt/ *noun*. Also **caje-**. L18.
[ORIGIN Malay *kayuputih*, name of the tree, from *kayu* tree + *puteh* white.]
More fully ***cajuput oil***, ***oil of cajuput***. An aromatic medicinal oil obtained from certain E. Indian trees of the genus *Melaleuca*, of the myrtle family.

cake /keɪk/ *noun*. ME.
[ORIGIN Of Scandinavian origin: cf. Icelandic, Swedish *kaka*, Danish *kage*, rel. to German *Kuchen*.]
1 (A quantity of) bread baked in smallish flattened rounds or other regular shapes, usu. turned in baking and so hard on both sides. Now chiefly *hist.* ME.
2 (A quantity of) thin oaten bread. Cf. ***oatcake*** s.v. OAT *noun*. *Scot.* & *N. English*. LME.
3 (A quantity of) sweet usu. unleavened bread with other ingredients besides flour, e.g. currants, spice, butter, eggs, sugar, usu. baked in a round or other ornamental shape. LME.
birthday cake, ***chocolate cake***, ***cupcake***, ***seed cake***, ***shortcake***, ***sponge cake***, ***teacake***, etc. ***cheesecake***: see CHEESE *noun*[1]. ***wastel cake***: see WASTEL 1.
4 A flattish compact mass of other food or of any compressed substance. LME.
cake of soap, etc. ***cattle cake***, ***cotton cake***, ***fishcake***, ***linseed cake***, ***mint cake***, ***oilcake***, ***potato cake***, etc. ***beefcake***: see BEEF *noun*.
– PHRASES: **cakes and ale** merrymaking, good things. ***hot cake***: see HOT *adjective*. **have one's cake and eat it**, **eat one's cake and have it** enjoy both alternatives. **land of cakes** (sense 2) Scotland. ***one's cake is dough***: see DOUGH *noun*. **piece of cake** *colloq.* something easy or pleasant. **the cake** *fig.* assets etc. to be shared out (***slice of the cake***, a share in benefits etc.). ***take the cake***: see TAKE *verb*.
– COMB.: **cake-bread** (now *rare*) (*a*) bread of the fine texture of cake; (*b*) bread made in flattened cakes; †**cake-house**: where cakes are sold; **cakehole** *slang* a person's mouth;
■ **cakelet** *noun* a small cake M19. **cakey** *adjective* like (a) cake M16.

cake /keɪk/ *verb*. E17.
[ORIGIN from the noun.]
1 *verb trans.* & *intrans.* Form into a compact mass. E17.

SHAKES. *Timon* Their blood is cak'd, 'tis cold, it seldom flows. H. G. WELLS Black mud.. had caked in hard ridges.

2 *verb trans.* Cover *with* a hardened mass. M20.

P. L. FERMOR Hair caked with snow.

cakewalk /ˈkeɪkwɔːk/ *noun & verb.* Orig. *US.* M19.
[ORIGIN from CAKE *noun* + WALK *noun.*]
▸ **A** *noun.* **1** (A dance developed from) a black Americans' contest in graceful walking with a cake as the prize. M19.
2 A moving platform on which people walk, as a fairground entertainment. E20.
3 An easy task. E20.
▸ **B** *verb intrans.* Walk as in a cakewalk; dance the cakewalk. L19.

CAL *abbreviation*[1].
Computer-aided (or -assisted) learning.

Cal *abbreviation*[2].
(Large) calorie.

cal *abbreviation*[3].
(Small) calorie.

Cal. *abbreviation.*
California.

calabar *noun* var. of CALABER.

Calabar bean /ˈkaləbɑː biːn/ *noun phr.* L19.
[ORIGIN from *Calabar* a town and province in Nigeria + BEAN *noun.*]
The poisonous seed of a leguminous climbing plant, *Physostigma venenosum*, which contains physostigmine and is used in W. Africa in trials of witchcraft; = ORDEAL *bean.*

calabash /ˈkaləbaʃ/ *noun.* M17.
[ORIGIN French *calebasse* formed as CALABAZA.]
1 a A gourd or similar large fruit that can be used as a container for liquid; *esp.* the fruit of the bottle gourd or (*N. Amer.*) that of the tree *Crescentia cujete* (family Bignoniaceae). M17. ▸**b** A tree yielding such a fruit, *esp.* (**a**) a tree of the genus *Crescentia*; (**b**) the baobab. Also ***calabash tree.*** M17.
2 A vessel or other utensil (as a pipe) made from or having a resemblance to such a fruit; such a vessel full *of* a substance. M17.
†**3** The head. *US slang.* E18–M19.
– COMB.: ***calabash nutmeg***: see NUTMEG *noun* 1; ***calabash tree***: see sense 1b above.

calabaza /kaləˈbɑːzə/ *noun.* L16.
[ORIGIN Spanish, perh. ult. from Persian *ḵarbuz* melon.]
= CALABASH 1.

calaber /ˈkaləbə/ *noun.* Also **-bar**. LME.
[ORIGIN medieval Latin *calabris*, *-ebrum*, app. from *Calabria*: see CALABRIAN.]
Squirrel fur; now *spec.* the fur of grey varieties of the common Eurasian squirrel *Sciurus vulgaris.*

calaboose /kaləˈbuːs/ *noun. US.* L18.
[ORIGIN Southern US black French *calabouse* from Spanish *calabozo* dungeon.]
A prison, a lock-up.

calabrese /ˈkaləbriːs, kaləˈbriːs, kaləˈbreɪsi/ *noun.* M20.
[ORIGIN Italian = Calabrian.]
A variety of sprouting broccoli.

Calabrian /kəˈlabrɪən/ *adjective & noun.* L16.
[ORIGIN from *Calabria* (see below) + -AN.]
(A native or inhabitant) of Calabria, a region of southern Italy.

caladium /kəˈleɪdɪəm/ *noun.* M19.
[ORIGIN mod. Latin, from Malay *keladi*: see -IUM.]
A plant of the tropical American genus *Caladium*, of the arum family, with starchy tubers.

calalu *noun* var. of CALLALOO.

calamanco /kaləˈmaŋkəʊ/ *noun & adjective.* Pl. of noun **-oes**. L16.
[ORIGIN Unknown: cf. Dutch *kal(a)mink*, German *kalmank*, French *calmande.*]
hist. (Of) a glossy worsted material.

calamander /ˈkaləmandə/ *noun.* E19.
[ORIGIN Sinhalese *kalumädiriya*, perh. from English COROMANDEL *ebony*, assim. to Sinhalese *kaḷu* black.]
A fine-grained red-brown ebony, streaked with black, from the southern Asian tree *Diospyros quaesita*. Also, the tree itself.

calamary /ˈkaləməri/ *noun.* Pl. **-ies**, in mod. culinary use **calamari** /kaləˈmɑːri/, **calamares** /kaləˈmɑːreɪz/. M16.
[ORIGIN medieval Latin *calamarium* pen case, use as noun of neut. of Latin *calamarius* adjective, from *calamus* from Greek *kalamos* pen: see -ARY[1]. Mod. culinary use from Italian.]
A squid, *esp.* one of the common genus *Loligo*; in *pl.*, squid served as food.

calambac /ˈkal(ə)mbak/ *noun.* L16.
[ORIGIN French, Spanish, or Portuguese, from Malay *kelembak.*]
= ***aloes wood*** s.v. ALOE.

calamine /ˈkaləmʌɪn/ *noun.* LME.
[ORIGIN Old French & mod. French from medieval Latin *calamina* alt. of Latin *cadmia* from Greek *kadm(e)ia* (*gē*) Cadmean (earth), from *Kadmos*: see CADMEAN.]
An ore of zinc, *spec.* the carbonate (smithsonite), or less commonly the basic silicate (hemimorphite). Also, a pink preparation of powdered zinc carbonate or oxide used in lotions, ointments, etc.

calamint /ˈkaləmɪnt/ *noun.* ME.
[ORIGIN Old French *calament* from medieval Latin *calamentum* from late Latin *calaminthe* from Greek *kalaminthē.*]
An aromatic herb or shrub of the genus *Clinopodium* (formerly *Calamintha*), of the mint family.

calamistrum /kaləˈmɪstrəm/ *noun.* Pl. **-stra** /-strə/. M19.
[ORIGIN Latin = curling iron.]
ZOOLOGY. A comblike structure on the fourth pair of legs of certain spiders, serving to 'card' the silk as it is secreted.

calamite /ˈkaləmʌɪt/ *noun.* M19.
[ORIGIN mod. Latin *Calamites* genus name, formed as CALAMUS: see -ITE[1].]
PALAEONTOLOGY. A reedlike plant of an extinct group related to the horsetails, found as fossils chiefly of Carboniferous age.
▪ **calaˈmitean** *adjective* L19.

calamitous /kəˈlamɪtəs/ *adjective.* M16.
[ORIGIN French *calamiteux* or Latin *calamitosus*, formed as CALAMITY: see -OUS.]
1 Disastrous, deeply distressing. M16.
†**2** In deep distress; grievously afflicted. M17–M18.
▪ **calamitously** *adverb* L18. **calamitousness** *noun* (*rare*) M17.

calamity /kəˈlamɪti/ *noun.* LME.
[ORIGIN Old French & mod. French *calamité* from Latin *calamitas*: see -ITY.]
1 Adversity; deep distress. LME.

S. JOHNSON So full is the world of calamity, that every source of pleasure is polluted.

2 A grievous disaster. M16.

E. WILSON And all the kinds of calamities befell them: fires and typhoid epidemics.

– COMB.: **calamity-howler**, **Calamity Jane** *N. Amer.* a prophet of disaster.

calamondin /kaləˈmɒndɪn/ *noun.* E20.
[ORIGIN Tagalog *kalamunding.*]
More fully ***calamondin orange***. A small hybrid citrus plant, × *Citrofortunella microcarpa*, which bears fragrant white flowers followed by small orange-yellow fruit, native to the Philippines and widely grown as a house plant.

calamus /ˈkaləməs/ *noun.* LME.
[ORIGIN Latin from Greek *kalamos.*]
†**1** A reed; a cane. LME–E18.
2 More fully ***sweet calamus***: ▸**a** An Eastern aromatic plant mentioned in the Bible (e.g. *Exodus* 30:23). LME. ▸**b** The sweet flag, *Acorus calamus*. M17.
3 A rattan palm of the genus *Calamus*. M19.
4 The hollow lower part of the shaft of a feather, which lacks barbs. L19.

†**calander** *noun* see CALANDRA.

calando /kəˈlandəʊ, *foreign* kaˈlando/ *adverb.* E19.
[ORIGIN Italian = slackening.]
MUSIC. Gradually decreasing in speed and volume.

calandra /kəˈlandrə/ *noun.* Orig. †**-der**. L16.
[ORIGIN Old French & mod. French *calandre* from medieval Latin *calandrus* from Greek *kalandros.*]
More fully ***calandra lark***. A lark, *Melanocorypha calandra*, native to southern Europe, N. Africa, and the Middle East.

calandria /kəˈlandrɪə/ *noun.* E20.
[ORIGIN Spanish, from Greek *kylindros* CYLINDER.]
A closed cylindrical vessel with a number of tubes passing through it, serving as a heat-exchanger etc.

calanoid /ˈkalənɔɪd/ *noun & adjective.* M20.
[ORIGIN from mod. Latin *Calanus* genus name + -OID.]
ZOOLOGY. (Designating or pertaining to) a planktonic copepod of the order Calanoida.

calash /kəˈlaʃ/ *noun.* Also **calèche**, **-eche**, /kəˈlɛʃ/, †**galeche**. M17.
[ORIGIN French *calèche*, †*g-* from German *Kalesche* from Polish *kołasa* (or Czech *kolesa*), from *koło* (*kolo*) wheel.]
Chiefly *hist.* **1** A light low-wheeled carriage with a removable folding hood. M17.
2 In Canada, a two-wheeled one-horse vehicle with a seat for the driver on the splashboard. M18.
3 A woman's large and folding hooped hood. L18.
4 A folding hood on a vehicle. M19.

calathea /kaləˈθɪə/ *noun.* M19.
[ORIGIN mod. Latin (see below), from Greek *kalathos* basket.]
Any plant of the tropical American genus *Calathea* (family Marantaceae), typically with variegated leaves and including several species grown as greenhouse or indoor plants.

calathus /ˈkaləθəs/ *noun.* Pl. **-thi** /-θʌɪ/. M18.
[ORIGIN Latin from Greek *kalathos.*]
CLASSICAL ANTIQUITIES. A basket, as depicted in sculpture etc.

calavance /ˈkaləvans/ *noun. obsolete* exc. *Canad. dial.* Earlier †**cara-**. E17.
[ORIGIN Ult. from Spanish *garbanzo* chickpea.]
Any of certain kinds of pulse; a small bean.

calaverite /kaləˈvɛːrʌɪt/ *noun.* M19.
[ORIGIN from *Calaveras* County, California + -ITE[1].]
MINERALOGY. A monoclinic gold telluride, usu. occurring as elongated bronze-yellow or silvery-white metallic crystals, or as granular or massive deposits.

calc- /kalk/ *combining form.*
[ORIGIN German *kalk* lime, alt. after Latin *calc-* CALX: cf. CALCI-.]
Forming words chiefly GEOLOGY & MINERALOGY with the sense 'lime'.
▪ **calˈcalkaline** *adjective* (PETROGRAPHY) relatively rich in both calcium and alkali metals E20. **calc-sinter** *noun* a crystalline calcareous deposit from mineral springs; travertine: E19. **calc-spar** *noun* calcite E19. **calc-tuff** *noun* a porous calcareous deposit from mineral springs E19.

calcaneo- /kalˈkeɪnɪəʊ/ *combining form* of next: see -O-.
▪ **calcaneoˈcuboid** *adjective* of or pertaining to both calcaneum and cuboid bone M19.

calcaneum /kalˈkeɪnɪəm/ *noun.* Pl. **-ea** /-ɪə/. Also **-eus** /-ɪəs/, pl. **-ei** /-ɪʌɪ/. M18.
[ORIGIN Latin.]
ANATOMY. The large bone of the heel.
▪ **calcaneal** *adjective* M19. **calcanean** *adjective* L19. †**calcany** *noun* (*rare*) = CALCANEUM: only in L16.

calcar /ˈkalkə/ *noun*[1]. Now *rare* or *obsolete*. M17.
[ORIGIN Italian *calcara*: cf. late Latin *calcaria* limekiln.]
A small calcining furnace used in glass-making.

calcar /ˈkalkə/ *noun*[2]. M18.
[ORIGIN Latin = spur.]
BOTANY & ZOOLOGY. A spurlike projection on a petal, bone, etc.
▪ **calcarate** *adjective* having a calcar or spur E19.

calcarenite /kalkəˈriːnʌɪt/ *noun.* E20.
[ORIGIN from CALC- + Latin (*h*)*arena* sand + -ITE[1].]
GEOLOGY. A limestone built up from particles similar in size to sand grains.

calcareous /kalˈkɛːrɪəs/ *adjective.* Also **-ious**. L17.
[ORIGIN from Latin *calcarius* of lime (see CALX, -ARY[1]) + -OUS.]
Of or containing calcium carbonate or other, usu. insoluble, calcium salt; of the nature of calcium carbonate.

calcarine /ˈkalkərʌɪn/ *adjective.* L19.
[ORIGIN from Latin CALCAR *noun*[2] + -INE[1].]
ANATOMY. Spurlike: esp. designating a small fissure of the occipital lobes of the cerebrum.

calcarious *adjective* var. of CALCAREOUS.

calcedony *noun* var. of CHALCEDONY.

calceolaria /kalsɪəˈlɛːrɪə/ *noun.* L18.
[ORIGIN mod. Latin, from Latin *calceolus* dim. of *calceus* shoe + *-aria*: see -ARY[1].]
A S. American plant of the genus *Calceolaria*, of the figwort family, bearing slipper-shaped flowers.

calceolate /ˈkalsɪəleɪt/ *adjective.* M19.
[ORIGIN from Latin *calceolus* (see CALCEOLARIA) + -ATE[2].]
BOTANY. Shaped like a slipper.

calces *noun pl.* see CALX.

calci- /ˈkalsi/ *combining form* of Latin *calc-*, CALX lime, usu. with the sense 'calcium carbonate': see -I-. Cf. CALC-.
▪ **calcicole** *adjective & noun* [Latin *colere* inhabit] BOTANY (a plant) growing best in calcareous soil L19. **calˈcicolous** *adjective* = CALCICOLE *adjective* L19. **calˈcigerous** *adjective* containing lime M19. **calcifuge** *adjective & noun* (BOTANY) (a plant) not suited by calcareous soil M19. **calciˈtonin** *noun* a polypeptide hormone secreted by the thyroid, having the effect of lowering blood calcium; also called ***thyrocalcitonin***: M20.

calcic /ˈkalsɪk/ *adjective.* M19.
[ORIGIN from CALCIUM + -IC.]
Of or containing calcium; relatively rich in calcium.

calciferol /kalˈsɪfərɒl/ *noun.* M20.
[ORIGIN from CALCIFEROUS + -OL: so called because of its activity in promoting bone calcification.]
BIOCHEMISTRY. A sterol which is formed when its isomer ergosterol is exposed to ultraviolet light, and is essential for the deposition of calcium in bones and the prevention of rickets and osteomalacia. Also called ***vitamin D_2***, ***ergocalciferol***.

calciferous /kalˈsɪf(ə)rəs/ *adjective.* L18.
[ORIGIN from CALCI- + -FEROUS.]
Yielding calcium carbonate.

calcify /ˈkalsɪfʌɪ/ *verb.* M19.
[ORIGIN from CALCI- + -FY.]
1 *verb trans.* Convert into calcium carbonate or other insoluble calcium compounds; harden by deposition of such compounds; petrify. Freq. as ***calcified*** *ppl adjective.* M19.

fig.: P. GALLICO The humanity in her had been calcified by the pursuit of money.

2 *verb intrans.* Undergo or become hardened by such deposition. M19.
▪ **calˈcific** *adjective* of or pertaining to calcification M19. **calcifiˈcation** *noun* the process of becoming calcified; a calcified structure: M19.

C

calcimine /ˈkalsɪmʌɪn/ *noun & verb*. M19.
[ORIGIN Alt., after Latin *calc-*, CALX lime.]
= KALSOMINE.

calcination /kalsɪˈneɪʃ(ə)n/ *noun*. LME.
[ORIGIN Old French & mod. French, or medieval Latin *calcinatio(n-)*, from *calcinat-* pa. ppl stem of *calcinare*: see CALCINE, -ATION.]
1 The action or process of reducing to a friable substance by heat; calcining. LME. ▸†**b** Oxidation. E17–E19.
2 *gen.* Burning to ashes, roasting; complete combustion. E17.

calcine /ˈkalsʌɪn, -sɪn/ *verb*. LME.
[ORIGIN Old French *calciner* or medieval Latin *calcinare*, from late Latin *calcina* lime, from Latin *calc-*, CALX.]
1 *verb trans.* **a** Reduce by roasting or burning to quicklime or a similar friable substance or powder. LME. ▸**b** *gen.* Burn to ashes, consume by fire; roast. E17. ▸†**c** *fig.* Consume or purify as if by fire. M17–E18.
2 *verb intrans.* Undergo any of these processes. E18.

> V. S. NAIPAUL In the dry season the earth baked, cracked, and calcined.

■ **calˈcinable** *adjective* M17. **calˈciner** *noun* (*a*) *rare* a person who calcines; (*b*) a kiln or other apparatus for calcining: M17.

calcio- /ˈkalsɪəʊ/ *combining form*.
[ORIGIN from CALCIUM + -O-.]
Used with the sense 'calcium', esp. to form mineral names.

calcite /ˈkalsʌɪt/ *noun*. M19.
[ORIGIN from Latin *calc-*, CALX + -ITE[1].]
MINERALOGY. Trigonal calcium carbonate, which occurs widely in a variety of forms, e.g. as prismatic crystals of Iceland spar etc., or in limestone, marble, and other rocks, and is colourless or white when pure.
■ **calcitic** /kalˈsɪtɪk/ *adjective* of, pertaining to, or of the nature of calcite L19.

calcitrate /ˈkalsɪtreɪt/ *verb trans. & intrans.* E17.
[ORIGIN Latin *calcitrat-* pa. ppl stem of *calcitrare* kick out with the heels, from *calx* heel: see -ATE[3].]
Kick.
■ **calciˈtration** *noun* M17.

calcium /ˈkalsɪəm/ *noun*. E19.
[ORIGIN from Latin *calc-*, CALX + -IUM.]
A greyish-white chemical element, atomic no. 20, which is one of the alkaline earth metals and occurs abundantly in nature, esp. as its carbonate (limestone etc.) (symbol Ca).
– COMB.: **calcium antagonist** MEDICINE any substance that reduces the influx of calcium into the cells of cardiac and smooth muscle, weakening contractions and tending to lower blood pressure; **calcium carbonate** a white insoluble solid, $CaCO_3$, occurring naturally as chalk, limestone, marble, and calcite, and forming mollusc shells and stony corals; **calcium hydroxide** a soluble white crystalline solid, $Ca(OH)_2$, commonly produced in the form of slaked lime; **calcium oxide** a white caustic alkaline solid, CaO, commonly produced in the form of quicklime.

calcrete /ˈkalkriːt/ *noun*. E20.
[ORIGIN from CALC- + CON)CRETE *noun*.]
A breccia or conglomerate cemented together by calcareous material; a calcareous duricrust.

calculable /ˈkalkjʊləb(ə)l/ *adjective*. M18.
[ORIGIN from CALCULATE + -ABLE.]
Able to be calculated. Of a person: predictable.
■ **calculaˈbility** *noun* L19.

calculate /ˈkalkjʊleɪt/ *verb*. LME.
[ORIGIN Late Latin *calculat-* pa. ppl stem of *calculare*, formed as CALCULUS: see -ATE[3].]
1 *verb trans.* Estimate or determine by arithmetical or mathematical reckoning; estimate or determine by practical judgement or on the basis of experience. LME.

> S. BELLOW He could calculate percentages mentally at high speed. I. MURDOCH She was now calculating how soon she could decently rise to go.

2 *verb trans.* Ascertain esp. beforehand the time or circumstances of (an event etc.) by exact reckoning. LME.

> SHAKES. *2 Hen. VI* A cunning man did calculate my birth And told me that by water I should die.

3 *verb intrans.* Perform a calculation or calculations; make an estimate; form a judgement about the future. E17.
4 *verb trans.* Plan deliberately; think out, frame. M17.

> R. W. EMERSON The English did not calculate the conquest of the Indies.

5 *verb trans.* Arrange, design, adjust, adapt; be intended. Foll. by *for* a purpose, *to do*. Now always pass. in meaning and usu. in form (see CALCULATED 1). M17.

> T. S. ELIOT His manners and appearance did not calculate to please.

6 *verb intrans.* Rely, reckon, count, *on*, *upon*. E19.

> H. B. TRISTRAM We had calculated on a quiet Sunday.

7 *verb trans.* Suppose, believe, (*that*); intend (*that*, *to do*). *US colloq.* E19.
■ **calculative** *adjective* of or pertaining to calculation; given to calculating: M18. **calculatory** *adjective* (now *rare*) of or pertaining to calculation E17.

calculated /ˈkalkjʊleɪtɪd/ *ppl adjective*. E18.
[ORIGIN from CALCULATE + -ED[1].]
1 Intended *to do*; fitted, suited, apt, *to do*. E18.

> S. J. PERELMAN A scene of activity calculated to inspire even the most torpid.

2 Reckoned, estimated; considered; with consequences etc. known. M19.

> GEO. ELIOT When he did speak it was with a calculated caution. *Listener* Obviously, the Soviet Union is taking a calculated risk.

■ **calculatedly** *adverb* L19.

calculating /ˈkalkjʊleɪtɪŋ/ *ppl adjective*. E19.
[ORIGIN formed as CALCULATED + -ING[2].]
That calculates; *esp.* shrewdly or selfishly reckoning the chances of gain or advantage, acting self-interestedly.
■ **calculatingly** *adverb* M19.

calculation /kalkjʊˈleɪʃ(ə)n/ *noun*. LME.
[ORIGIN Old French & mod. French from late Latin *calculatio(n-)*, formed as CALCULATE: see -ATION.]
1 Arithmetical or mathematical reckoning; computation; estimation of outcome or probability; shrewd or selfish reckoning of the chances of gain or advantage. LME. ▸**b** An act or instance of so reckoning or estimating. LME.

> M. KLINE Calculation was done on various forms of the abacus. J. GROSS The impression which remains longest is one of artfulness and calculation. **b** E. J. HOWARD She did some . . calculations then, and said thirty-eight.

2 A form in which reckoning is made; a product or result of calculating; a forecast. LME.

> J. AUSTEN If the first calculation is wrong, we make a second better.

■ **calculational** *adjective* L19.

calculator /ˈkalkjʊleɪtə/ *noun*. LME.
[ORIGIN Latin *calculator*, formed as CALCULATE: see -OR. In mod. use from CALCULATE + -OR.]
1 A person who calculates; a reckoner. LME.
2 A set of tables to facilitate calculations; a machine to carry out calculations. L18. ▸**b** A programmed electronic device for carrying out calculations, *esp.* (also ***pocket calculator***) a small flat one with a keyboard and visual display. M20.

†**calcule** *noun*. L16–M18.
[ORIGIN French *calcul* from Latin CALCULUS.]
= CALCULATION.

calculiform /ˈkalkjʊlɪfɔːm/ *adjective*. E20.
[ORIGIN from Latin CALCULUS + -I- + -FORM.]
Pebble-shaped.

calculous /ˈkalkjʊləs/ *adjective*. E17.
[ORIGIN from Latin *calculosus*, formed as CALCULUS: see -ULOUS.]
MEDICINE. Of, pertaining to, or of the nature of a calculus; affected with calculi.

calculus /ˈkalkjʊləs/ *noun*. Pl. **-li** /-lʌɪ, -liː/, **-luses**. M17.
[ORIGIN Latin = small stone (used in reckoning with an abacus).]
1 a A particular method or system of calculation or reasoning; *esp.* (MATH.) infinitesimal calculus (see below). M17. ▸†**b** *gen.* Computation; calculation. L17–E19.
calculus of variations: see VARIATION. **differential calculus** the part of infinitesimal calculus that deals with derivatives and differentiation. **infinitesimal calculus** the branch of mathematics that deals with the finding and properties of derivatives and integrals of functions, by methods orig. based on the summation of infinitesimal differences. **integral calculus** the part of infinitesimal calculus that deals with integrals and integration. ***predicate calculus***: see PREDICATE *noun*. ***PROPOSITIONAL calculus***.
2 MEDICINE. A stone. M18.

caldarium /kalˈdɛːrɪəm/ *noun*. Pl. **-ria** /-rɪə/. M18.
[ORIGIN Latin.]
An ancient Roman hot bath or bathroom.

caldera /kɒlˈdɛːrə, -ˈdɪərə/ *noun*. L17.
[ORIGIN Spanish from late Latin *caldaria* pot for boiling.]
A volcanic crater of great size; *spec.* one whose breadth greatly exceeds that of the vent(s) within it.

caldron *noun* var. of CAULDRON.

calean /ˈkalɪɑːn/ *noun*. M18.
[ORIGIN Persian *ḡilyān*, *qalyān* from Arabic *ḡilyān* for *ḡalayān* bubbling up, boiling: cf. KALIAN.]
A hookah.

calèche, **caleche** *nouns* vars. of CALASH.

Caledonian /kalɪˈdəʊnɪən/ *adjective & noun*. E17.
[ORIGIN from Latin *Caledonia* Caledonia, Roman name of part of northern Britain, later applied to Scotland or the Scottish Highlands, + -AN.]
▸ **A** *adjective*. **1** Of or pertaining to ancient Caledonia; Scottish, of the Scottish Highlands, (now *joc.* or *literary* exc. in names of existing institutions etc.). E17.
2 GEOLOGY. Designating or pertaining to an episode of mountain-building in NW Europe in the Palaeozoic era. E20.
▸ **B** *noun*. A native or inhabitant of ancient Caledonia; a Scotsman, a Scottish Highlander, (now *joc.* or *literary*). M18.

caledonite /ˈkalɪdənʌɪt/ *noun*. M19.
[ORIGIN formed as CALEDONIAN + -ITE[1].]
MINERALOGY. An orthorhombic basic sulphate and carbonate of copper and lead, usu. occurring as blue or blue-green prisms.

calefacient /kalɪˈfeɪʃ(ə)nt/ *noun & adjective*. M17.
[ORIGIN Latin, pres. ppl stem of *calefacere*, from *calere* be warm: see -FACIENT.]
MEDICINE. (A substance) producing a sense of warmth.

calefaction /kalɪˈfakʃ(ə)n/ *noun*. Now *rare*. LME.
[ORIGIN Old French & mod. French *caléfaction* or late Latin *calefactio(n-)*, from *calefact-* pa. ppl stem of *calefacere*: see CALEFACIENT, -FACTION.]
1 (A) heated condition of the body. LME.
2 The action of making something warm (*lit.* & *fig.*); heating. E16.

calefactive /kalɪˈfaktɪv/ *adjective*. Now *rare*. LME.
[ORIGIN from Latin *calefact-* (see CALEFACTION) + -IVE.]
Having the tendency to warm; warming.

calefactory /kalɪˈfakt(ə)ri/ *noun & adjective*. LME.
[ORIGIN Late Latin *calefactorius* adjective, medieval Latin *-torium* noun, formed as CALEFACTIVE: see -ORY[1].]
▸ **A** *noun*. †**1** MEDICINE. = CALEFACIENT *noun*. LME–M17.
2 *hist.* A vessel providing heat; *spec.* a metal ball containing hot water on which a priest could warm his hands before administering the Eucharist. M16.
3 A warm room in a monastery. L17.
▸ **B** *adjective*. Adapted to warming; producing warmth. E18.

calembour /kalɑ̃buːr/ *noun*. Also **-bourg** /-buːr/. Pl. pronounced same. E19.
[ORIGIN French.]
A pun.

calendar /ˈkalɪndə/ *noun*. Also (now *rare*) **k-**. ME.
[ORIGIN Anglo-Norman *calender*, Old French *calendier* (mod. *calendrier*) from Latin *kalendarium*, *c-* account book, from *kalendae* (the day on which accounts were due): see CALENDS, -AR[2].]
1 The system by which the beginning, duration, and subdivisions of a year are fixed. ME.
Gregorian calendar: see GREGORIAN *adjective*. ***Julian calendar***: see JULIAN *adjective*. ***Liberian calendar***: see LIBERIAN *adjective*[1].
2 A table or set of tables displaying the months, weeks, festivals, etc., of a given year, or with dates important to a particular pursuit or occupation. LME. ▸**b** A contrivance for reckoning days, months, etc.; an adjustable device showing the day's date etc. E18.
gardener's calendar, ***racing calendar***, etc. ***perpetual calendar***: see PERPETUAL *adjective*.
†**3** *fig.* A guide; an example; a model. LME–E17.
4 A list, a register, *spec.* (***a***) of canonized saints, (***b***) of cases for trial, (***c***) of documents arranged chronologically with summaries, (***d***) *US* of matters for debate. LME.
Newgate Calendar: see NEWGATE *noun*.
– COMB.: **calendar month** any of the (usu. twelve) portions into which a year is divided; the period between the same dates in successive months; ***calendar year***: see YEAR *noun*[1] 2.
■ **calenˈdarial** *adjective* of, pertaining to, or according to a calendar E19. **calendary** *noun & adjective* †(*a*) *noun* = CALENDAR *noun*; (*b*) *adjective* = CALENDARIAL: LME. **caˈlendric** *adjective* of the nature of a calendar L19. **caˈlendrical** *adjective* = CALENDRIC *adjective* M19.

calendar /ˈkalɪndə/ *verb trans*. L15.
[ORIGIN from the noun.]
1 Register or enter in a calendar, esp. of saints or saints' days. L15.
2 Arrange, analyse, and index (documents). M19.
■ **calendarer** *noun* M19.

calender /ˈkalɪndə/ *noun*[1]. E16.
[ORIGIN Old French & mod. French *calandre*, formed as CALENDER *verb*.]
†**1** = CALENDERER. E16–L18.
2 A machine in which cloth, paper, etc. is pressed by rollers to glaze or smooth it. E17.

calender /ˈkalɪndə/ *noun*[2]. L16.
[ORIGIN Persian *qalandar*.]
A mendicant dervish.

calender /ˈkalɪndə/ *verb trans*. L15.
[ORIGIN Old French & mod. French *calandrer*, of unknown origin.]
Press (cloth, paper, etc.) in a calender.
■ **calenderer** *noun* a person who calenders cloth etc. L15.

calends /ˈkalɪndz/ *noun pl*. Also **k-** & †in *sing*. OE.
[ORIGIN (Old French & mod. French *calendes* from) Latin *kalendae*, *c-* (pl.) first day of the month, when the order of days was proclaimed, from base of Latin *calare*, Greek *kalein* call, proclaim.]
†**1** In *sing.* A month; an appointed time. Only in OE.
†**2** The Jewish festival of the new moon. LME–E17.
3 The first day of the month in the ancient Roman calendar. LME.
on the Greek Calends, **at the Greek Calends** never. **till the Greek Calends** for ever.
†**4** A prelude, a beginning. LME–E17.
5 A calendar, a record. *rare*. LME.

calendula /kəˈlɛndjʊlə/ *noun*. L16.
[ORIGIN mod. Latin, dim. of *calendae* (see CALENDS), perh. because it flowers for most of the year.]
A marigold of the genus *Calendula*, with large yellow or orange flowers.

calenture /ˈkal(ə)ntjʊə/ *noun*. **L16.**
[**ORIGIN** French from Spanish *calentura*, from *calentar* be hot from Proto-Romance from Latin *calere* be warm.]
1 A form of delirium formerly supposed to afflict sailors in the tropics, in which the sea is mistaken for green fields; a fever, sunstroke. **L16.**
2 *fig.* A burning passion, ardour, zeal. **L16.**

calescence /kəˈlɛs(ə)ns/ *noun*. *rare*. **M19.**
[**ORIGIN** from Latin *calescent-* pres. ppl stem of *calescere* grow warm, from *calere* be warm: see **-ESCENCE.**]
Increasing warmth or heat.
■ **calescent** *adjective* **E19.**

calf /kɑːf/ *noun*[1]. Pl. **calves** /kɑːvz/.
[**ORIGIN** Old English *cælf*, *ċealf* = Old Saxon *calf* (Dutch *kalf*), Old High German *kalb* neut. (German *Kalb*), *kalba* fem., Old Norse *kálfr*, Gothic *kalbō*, from Germanic. In sense 4 from Old Norse.]
1 A young bovine animal, esp. the domestic cow, *spec.* in its first year. **OE.** ▸**b** A stupid or inoffensive person. **M16.**
2 The young of some other large mammals, as the elephant, deer, whale, etc. **LME.**
3 *sea-calf*, the common seal. **LME.**
4 A small island lying close to a larger one. *rare* exc. in ***the Calf of Man*** (off the Isle of Man). **L17.**
5 Leather made from the hide or skin of a calf, used esp. in shoemaking and bookbinding. **E18.**
MOTTLED ***calf***. ***rough calf***: see **ROUGH** *adjective*.
6 A floating piece of ice detached from an iceberg. **E19.**
– **PHRASES:** *GOLDEN* ***calf***. **in calf** (of a cow etc.) pregnant. ***kill the fatted calf***: see **FAT** *verb*. **with calf** (of a cow etc.) pregnant.
– **COMB.:** **calf love** romantic affection felt by a young person; **calf's foot** (*a*) the foot of a calf, esp. as food; †(*b*) wild arum, cuckoo pint; **calfskin** = sense 5 above; **calf's snout** the plant weasel's snout, *Misopates orontium*.
■ **calfhood** *noun* **L19.** **calfless** *adjective*[1] **LME.**

calf /kɑːf/ *noun*[2]. Pl. **calves** /kɑːvz/. **ME.**
[**ORIGIN** Old Norse *kálfi*, of unknown origin.]
The fleshy hinder part of the leg below the knee; *transf.* the corresponding part of a stocking, trouser leg, etc.
– **COMB.:** **calf-length** *adjective* (of a garment, boots, etc.) reaching to the calf.
■ **calfless** *adjective*[2] **E16.**

calfish /ˈkɑːfɪʃ/ *adjective*. Also **calvish** /ˈkɑːvɪʃ/. **L16.**
[**ORIGIN** from **CALF** *noun*[1] + **-ISH**[1].]
Like a calf; stupid; untrained, immature.

Caliban /ˈkalɪban, -bən/ *noun*. **L17.**
[**ORIGIN** A character in Shakes. *Temp.*]
A man of a degraded bestial nature.

caliber *noun* see **CALIBRE.**

calibogus /kalɪˈbəʊgəs/ *noun*. *US*. **M18.**
[**ORIGIN** Unknown.]
A mixture of rum and spruce beer.

calibrate /ˈkalɪbreɪt/ *verb trans*. **M19.**
[**ORIGIN** from **CALIBRE** + **-ATE**[3].]
Measure the calibre of; measure the irregularities of (a tube, gauge, etc.) before graduating it; graduate (a tube, etc.) with allowance for irregularities; determine the correct value, position, capacity, etc. of; correlate the readings of (an instrument) with a standard.
■ **calibrator** *noun* an instrument or device used in calibrating **E20.**

calibration /kalɪˈbreɪʃ(ə)n/ *noun*. **L19.**
[**ORIGIN** from **CALIBRATE**: see **-ATION.**]
The action or process of calibrating an instrument, gauge, etc. Also, (one of) a set of graduations on an instrument, etc.

calibre /ˈkalɪbə, kəˈliːbə/ *noun*. Also ***-ber**. **M16.**
[**ORIGIN** Old French & mod. French from Italian *calibro* or Spanish *calibre*, perh. from Arabic *qālib* mould from *qālab* ult. from Greek *kalapous* shoemaker's last.]
1 (Orig. social) standing, rank, importance; ability, personal capacity, weight of character; worth. **M16.**

> B. **MAGEE** Works of this calibre, complexity and depth take a lot of getting to know. D. **PIPER** Two of the three most impressive sculptors who flourished in England in his lifetime were of considerable calibre.

2 The diameter of a projectile; the bore or internal diameter of a gun. **L16.** ▸**b** *transf.* The diameter of any body of circular section, esp. a tube, as an artery etc. **E18.**

> **b** H. **ALLEN** The gross calibre of the white linen socks ending in small, black, varnished shoes.

■ **calibred** *adjective* having a calibre (of a specified kind) **L19.**

calice *noun* var. of **CALIX.**

caliche /kəˈliːtʃi/ *noun*. **M19.**
[**ORIGIN** Amer. Spanish.]
A mineral deposit found in arid areas of N. or S. America, *esp.* Chile nitre.

caliciform /ˈkalɪsɪfɔːm/ *adjective*. **M19.**
[**ORIGIN** from Latin **CALIX**, *-ic-* + **-I-** + **-FORM.**]
Cup-shaped; resembling a calyx.

calicivirus /ˈkeɪlɪsɪˌvʌɪrəs/ *noun*. **M20.**
[**ORIGIN** mod. Latin *Calicivirus*, from *calici-* in **CALICIFORM** + **VIRUS.**]
Any of a group (originally the genus *Calicivirus*, now the family Caliciviridae) of viruses which are pathogens of humans, swine, cats, and various other animals.

calicle /ˈkalɪk(ə)l/ *noun*. **M19.**
[**ORIGIN** Latin *caliculus* dim. of **CALIX**, *-ic-*: see **-CLE.**]
ZOOLOGY. A small cup-shaped structure.
■ **calicular** /kəˈlɪkjʊlə/ *adjective* of or pertaining to a calicle, cuplike **M19.**

calico /ˈkalɪkəʊ/ *noun & adjective*. Orig. also †**-cut**. **M16.**
[**ORIGIN** Alt. of *Calicut*, a town in India.]
▸ **A** *noun*. Pl. **-oes**, ***-os**.
1 a Orig. ***calico cloth***. Cotton cloth, orig. as imported from the East; fabric resembling this. Now *esp.* (*a*) plain white unprinted bleached or unbleached cotton cloth; (*b*) *N. Amer.* printed cotton cloth. **M16.** ▸**b** A piece or example of such cloth. **L16.**
2 A piebald horse. *US*. **M19.**
– **COMB.:** **calico-bush** *N. Amer.* the mountain laurel, *Kalmia latifolia*; **calico-printer**, **calico-printing** (a person engaged in) the production of printed patterns on calico.
▸ **B** *adjective*. **1** Of calico. **L16.**
2 Suggestive of printed calico; multicoloured; piebald. *N. Amer.* **E19.**
calico cat a cat with black, ginger, and white patches.

calid /ˈkalɪd/ *adjective*. *arch.* **LME.**
[**ORIGIN** Latin *calidus*.]
Warm, tepid; hot.

caliduct /ˈkalɪdʌkt/ *noun*. **M17.**
[**ORIGIN** formed as **CALID**, after *aqueduct*.]
A pipe for conveying heat.

calif, **califate** *nouns* vars. of **CALIPH**, **CALIPHATE.**

Calif. *abbreviation*.
California.

Californian /kalɪˈfɔːnɪən/ *adjective & noun*. **E18.**
[**ORIGIN** from *California* (see below) + **-AN.**]
▸ **A** *adjective*. Of or belonging to, native or peculiar to, California, a state on the Pacific coast of N. America. **E18.**
Californian *CONDOR*. **Californian holly** the toyon, *Heteromeles arbutifolia*. ***Californian jack***: see **JACK** *noun*[1]. **Californian poppy** (*a*) an eschscholtzia, *Eschscholtzia californica*; (*b*) = **ROMNEYA.** ***Californian sea lion***: see **SEA LION** 3.
▸ **B** *noun*. A native or inhabitant of California. **L18.**

californite /kalɪˈfɔːnʌɪt/ *noun*. **E20.**
[**ORIGIN** formed as **CALIFORNIAN** + **-ITE**[1].]
MINERALOGY. A green variety of vesuvianite resembling jade.

californium /kalɪˈfɔːnɪəm/ *noun*. **M20.**
[**ORIGIN** from *California* University, where first made + **-IUM.**]
A radioactive metallic chemical element of the actinide series, atomic no. 98, which is produced artificially (symbol Cf).

caliginous /kəˈlɪdʒɪnəs/ *adjective*. *arch.* **M16.**
[**ORIGIN** Latin *caliginosus*, from *caligo*, *-in-* mistiness: see **-OUS.**]
Misty, dim; obscure, dark.
■ **caligiˈnosity** *noun* (*arch.*) dimness of sight **M17.**

calinda /kəˈlɪndə/ *noun*. **M18.**
[**ORIGIN** Amer. Spanish.]
A black American dance found in Latin America and the southern US.

calipash /ˈkalɪpaʃ/ *noun*. **L17.**
[**ORIGIN** Perh. W. Indian or alt. of Spanish *carapacho* **CARAPACE.**]
Orig. the upper shell or carapace of the turtle. Now, that part next to this, containing a dull green gelatinous substance; also, this substance, which is regarded as a delicacy. Cf. **CALIPEE.**

calipee /ˈkalɪpiː/ *noun*. **M17.**
[**ORIGIN** Perh. W. Indian: cf. **CALIPASH.**]
Orig., the lower shell or plastron of the turtle. Now, that part next to this, containing a light yellowish gelatinous substance; also, this substance, which is regarded as a delicacy. Cf. **CALIPASH.**

caliper /ˈkalɪpə/ *noun & verb*. Also **calli-**. **L16.**
[**ORIGIN** App. alt. of **CALIBRE.**]
▸ **A** *noun*. **1** ***caliper compasses***, ***calipers***, ***pair of calipers***, compasses with bowed legs for measuring the diameter of convex bodies, or with out-turned points for measuring cavities. **L16.**
2 A metal support for the leg. Also ***caliper splint***. **L19.**
▸ **B** *verb trans*. Measure with calipers. **L19.**

caliph /ˈkeɪlɪf, ˈka-/ *noun*. Also **calif**, **khalif**. **LME.**
[**ORIGIN** Old French & mod. French *caliphe* (medieval Latin *calipha*, *-es*) from Arabic *ḵalīfa* deputy (of God), from title *ḵalīfat Allāh*, or successor (of Muhammad), from title *ḵalīfat rasūl Allāh* of the Messenger of God, from *ḵalafa* succeed. See also **KHALIFA.**]
Chiefly *hist.* The chief civil and religious ruler of the Muslim community.
■ **caliphal** *adjective* **L19.**

caliphate /ˈkalɪfeɪt/ *noun*. Also **-f-**, **khalif-**. **E17.**
[**ORIGIN** from **CALIPH** + **-ATE**[1]: cf. French *caliphat*.]
Chiefly *hist.* **1** A country governed by a caliph. **E17.**
2 The reign or term of office of a caliph. **M18.**
3 The rank or dignity of a caliph. **M18.**

Calippic *adjective* var. of **CALLIPPIC.**

calisthenic *adjective & noun* var. of **CALLISTHENIC.**

caliver /ˈkalɪvə/ *noun*. *obsolete* exc. *hist.* **M16.**
[**ORIGIN** Var. of **CALIBRE**, prob. first in French *arquebuse, pièce de calibre*.]
A light kind of harquebus fired without a rest.

calix /ˈkeɪlɪks/ *noun*. Also **-ice** /-ɪs/. Pl. **-ices** /-ɪsiːz/. **E18.**
[**ORIGIN** Latin *calix*, *-ic-* cup: cf. **CALYX.**]
Chiefly *ANATOMY*. A cuplike cavity or structure; *esp.* one of the divisions of the renal pelvis.

Calixtine /ˈkalɪkstɪn/ *noun*. **E18.**
[**ORIGIN** medieval Latin *Calixtini* pl., formed as **CALIX.** Cf. French *calixtin*.]
ECCLESIASTICAL HISTORY. A member of a section of the Hussites who maintained that both the cup and the bread should be administered to the laity during the Eucharist.

calk /kɔːk/ *noun*. Also ***cork**. **L16.**
[**ORIGIN** App. ult. from Latin *calc-*, *calcaneum* heel, or *calcar* spur: see **CALKIN.**]
1 = **CALKIN.** **L16.**
2 A piece of iron projecting from the heel of a boot etc. to prevent slipping. *US*. **E19.**

calk /kɔːk/ *verb*[1] *trans*. Also ***cork**. **E17.**
[**ORIGIN** from the noun.]
Provide (a horseshoe, a boot, etc.) with a calk or calkin.
■ **calker** *noun* (chiefly *Scot.*) = **CALKIN** **L18.**

calk /kɔːk/ *verb*[2] *trans*. **M17.**
[**ORIGIN** French *calquer* to copy, trace from Italian *calcare* from Latin *calcare* to tread.]
Copy (a design etc.) by colouring the back and following its lines so as to trace them on to a surface placed beneath.

calk *verb*[3] see **CAULK** *verb*[1].

calkin /ˈkɔːkɪn, ˈkalkɪn/ *noun*. **LME.**
[**ORIGIN** Middle Dutch *kalkoen* or its source Old French *calcain*, from Latin *calcaneum* heel, from *calx*, *calc-* heel.]
1 The turned-down ends of a horseshoe; a turned edge under the front of a horseshoe. **LME.**
2 The irons nailed on the heels and soles of shoes or clogs to make them last. **M19.**

call /kɔːl/ *noun*. Also (*Scot.*) **ca'** /kɑː/ (the usual form in sense 10). **ME.**
[**ORIGIN** from the verb.]
▸ **I 1** A loud vocal utterance; a cry, a shout. **ME.** ▸**b** The reading aloud of a list of names; a roll-call. **E17.**

> **BUNYAN** They gave but a call, and in came their Master.

roll-call: see **ROLL** *noun*[1].
2 The cry of an animal, esp. a bird. Also, an imitation of this, or an instrument imitating this, esp. as used to attract birds. **M16.** ▸†**b** A decoy bird. **L16–E18.**

> J. **STEINBECK** The twittering call of a raccoon.

3 A signal, summons, or short theme sounded on an instrument; a whistle etc. used for this. **L16.**

> J. **MASTERS** Two buglers . . blew a short loud call.

▸ **II** With less emphasis on the actual sound.
4 A summons, an invitation; exhortation, bidding. **ME.** ▸**b** *spec.* An invitation or summons to undertake the office of pastor, from God, one's conscience, or a congregation. **M17.** ▸**c** A summons for an actor etc. to appear on stage to receive applause, begin a performance, etc. **L18.** ▸**d** *CARDS*. A bid, pass, double, or redouble; a player's right or turn to bid. **M19.** ▸**e** *CRICKET*. A shouted direction by a batsman to his or her partner to run or to remain in the crease; the responsibility to do this in a particular case. **M19.** ▸**f** A direction in a square dance given by the caller. **M19.** ▸**g** A shout or call by an umpire or referee indicating that the ball has gone out of play or that a fault or foul has been committed; the decision or ruling indicated. **L19.**

> P. **BROOK** Alienation is a call to halt: alienation is . . holding something up to the light, making us look again. E. **LONGFORD** The call had come. He was to be Prime Minister. *Times* An official TUC call not to take part in the protest.

c ***curtain call***: see **CURTAIN** *noun* 5a. **g** ***bad call***, ***late call***, etc.
5 A demand, a requisition, a claim. **ME.** ▸**b** Chiefly *STOCK EXCHANGE*. A demand for the payment of lent or unpaid capital. Also, an option of buying stock at a fixed price at a given date. **E18.**

> S. **JOHNSON** The call for novelty is never satisfied. **CONAN DOYLE** The busy medical man, with calls on him every hour.

6 Divine, spiritual, or inner prompting; a vocation, calling. **M16.**
7 Requirement, need; occasion. **L17.**

> K. **AMIS** A girl like you's got no call to be depressed about anything. L. **GARFIELD** He was inclined to show courage when there was no call for it.

8 A short visit; a stop en route. **L18.**

> A. **TROLLOPE** She had . . made a morning call on Martha Biggs.

C

9 A communication by telephone, radio, etc.; a telephone conversation. **L19.**

> L. DEIGHTON I heard the operator asking Charlie if he'd accept a reversed charge call.

▸ **III 10** Driving; a place where cattle etc. are driven; exertion, hard breathing. *Scot.* **M18.**

– PHRASES: **at call**, **on call** ready or available when wanted; (of money lent) repayable on demand; ***at the beck and call of***: see BECK *noun*³ 2. ***call of nature***: see NATURE *noun*. ***call to the Bar***: see BAR *noun*¹ 16. ***close call***: see CLOSE *adjective & adverb*. **get one's call**, **get the call** *dial.* die, be about to die. **good call!** used to express approval of a person's decision or suggestion. [with ref. to decisions made by referees or umpires.] ***house of call***: see HOUSE *noun*¹. ***hurry call***: see HURRY *noun*. ***local call***: see LOCAL *adjective*. ***moderate a call***, ***moderate in a call***: see MODERATE *verb*. ***on call***: see ***at call*** above. **pay a call** make a visit (***pay a call on a person***, ***pay a person a call***); *colloq.* go to the lavatory. **port of call** a place at which a ship etc. calls. ***sick call***: see SICK *adjective*. **within call** near enough to be summoned by calling.

– COMB.: **call box** a public telephone kiosk; **call boy** (*a*) a messenger boy; *spec.* a prompter's attendant employed to summon the actors; (*b*) a male prostitute accepting appointments by telephone; **call centre** an office in which large numbers of telephone calls are handled, esp. one providing the customer services functions of a large organization; **call changes** *BELL-RINGING* changes rung in response to oral instructions; **call-day**, **call-night**: on which law students are called to the bar; **call girl** a prostitute accepting appointments by telephone; **call money** money loaned by a bank or other institution which is repayable on demand; **call note** a bird's characteristic call; **call sign**, **call signal** a conventional signal indicating the identity of a radio transmitter; **call waiting** a service whereby someone making a telephone call is notified of an incoming call on the line that he or she is already using, esp. one that allows the first call to be placed on hold while the second is answered.

call /kɔːl/ *verb*. Also (*Scot.*) **ca'** /kɑː/ (the usual form in sense 9), pa. t. **ca'(e)d**. **LOE.**

[ORIGIN Old Norse *kalla* cry, summon loudly = Middle Low German, Middle Dutch & mod. Dutch *kallen*, Old High German *kallōn* talk, chatter, from Germanic.]

▸ **I** Shout, utter loudly; summon.

1 *verb intrans.* Cry, shout, (*out*); speak loudly or distinctly, in order to engage attention. (Foll. by *after*, *to* a person.) **LOE.** ▸**b** Of an animal: make its characteristic note. **L15.** ▸**c** Rhythmically shout or chant (the steps or figures) to people performing a barn dance. **M19.**

> SHAKES. *Tam. Shr.* Sometimes you would call out for Cicely Hacket. T. ELLWOOD He calling earnestly after me. S. T. WARNER He called softly. *fig.*: TENNYSON To the billow the fountain calls. **b** J. GRENFELL The little owls that call by night.

2 *verb trans.* Utter loudly or distinctly, shout (*out*), proclaim; read out (a list of names, etc.). **ME.** ▸**b** *verb trans. & intrans. CARDS.* Make a demand for (a card, show of hands, etc.); name (a suit, contract) in bidding. **L17.** ▸**c** *verb trans. & intrans.* Name (heads or tails) in the tossing of a coin. **E19.** ▸**d** *verb trans. CRICKET.* Of an umpire: declare (a bowler) to have bowled a no-ball; declare (a delivery) illegal. **M19.**

> THACKERAY The word we used at school when names were called. LD MACAULAY His duties were to call the odds when the Court played at hazard. R. GRAVES Gratus called out, 'Hey, Sergeant! Look whom we have here!' J. L. WATEN I continued to call my wares as though at the market.

3 *verb trans.* Summon by calling; demand the presence or attention of. **ME.** ▸**b** *verb trans. spec.* Summon to another world; take by death. **E16.** ▸**c** *verb trans.* Rouse from sleep, summon to get up. **E17.** ▸**d** *verb trans. & intrans.* Make a telephone call (to); communicate (with) by radio. **L19.** ▸**e** *COMPUTING.* Cause the execution of (a subroutine, procedure, etc.); invoke (a program). **M20.**

> COVERDALE *Mark* 15:16 The soudyers . . called the whole multitude together. P. MORTIMER My mother called the doctor in. C. ISHERWOOD George calls the bartender—very loudly, so he can't pretend not to have heard. T. STOPPARD What witnesses do you want to call? B. MASON A long blast on a whistle called her home.

4 *verb trans.* Convene, fix a time for, (a meeting etc.); announce as ensuing. **ME.**

> LD MACAULAY It might be necessary to call a Parliament. *Daily Telegraph* The strike was called because we want to ensure that any future owners . . will take notice of what we say.

5 *verb trans.* Nominate by a personal summons, inspire with a vocation; of duty, God, etc.: bid, enjoin, urge, *to do* something. **ME.** ▸**b** Invite formally to a pastorate. **M16.**

> SHAKES. *1 Hen. VI* Is my Lord of Winchester . . call'd unto a cardinal's degree? AV *Acts* 13:7 Separate me Barnabas and Saul for the work whereunto I have called them. J. WESLEY I am called to preach the Gospel both by God and man.

6 *verb intrans.* Make or pay a visit (orig. with the notion of a summons at the door); of a vessel, train, etc.: make a brief visit. (Foll. by *on*, *upon* someone, *at* a place). **L16.**

> W. COWPER A young gentleman called here yesterday who came six miles out of his way to see me. G. F. FIENNES The Fishguard boat train called at Challow to pick up commuters. I. COLEGATE Her friend . . simply detested being called on before 4 o'clock in the afternoon.

▸ **II** Name, describe as.

7 *verb trans.* Give as name or title to; name; style, designate, or address as; reckon, consider. **ME.**

> COVERDALE *Matt.* 1:25 He . . called his name Iesus. DONNE You can cal it pleasure to be beguil'd in troubles. G. BERKELEY To call things by their right names. SOUTHEY Her parents mock at her and call her crazed. TOLKIEN Nobody else calls us hobbits; we call ourselves that. H. WILLIAMSON A shame, I calls it, Mr. Maddyzun. C. HILL His mother, his wife and his favourite daughter were all called Elizabeth. ANNE STEVENSON The aunts . . called everybody 'sugar'.

8 *verb trans.* Apply rude or abusive names to, vilify. *dial.* **E19.**

▸ **III 9** *verb trans. & intrans.* Drive, urge forward; be driven. *Scot.* **LME.**

> R. BURNS Ca' the yowes to the knowes.

– PHRASES, & WITH ADVERBS & PREPOSITIONS IN SPECIALIZED SENSES: ***be called to the Bar***, ***be called within the Bar***: see BAR *noun*¹ 16. ***ca' canny***: see CANNY *adverb*. **call a halt (to)** demand or order a stop (to). ***call all to naught***: see NAUGHT *pronoun & noun* 1. **call a person names** abuse someone in speech. ***call a spade a bloody shovel***, ***call a spade a shovel***, ***call a spade a spade***: see SPADE *noun*¹. ***call a truce***: see TRUCE *noun*. **call attention to** direct notice to, point out. **call away** divert, distract. **call back** (*a*) *verb phr. trans.* summon to return, recall, retract; (*b*) *verb phr. intrans. & trans.* return to pay a short visit; repeat or return a telephone call or radio communication (to). **call cousin(s)** *arch.* address each other as cousin, claim kinship *with*. **call down** (*a*) invoke from above; (*b*) *colloq.* reprimand, reprove. **call for** (*a*) ask for, order, demand; need, require; (*b*) go to or stop briefly at a place in order to get. **call forth** elicit, summon up. ***call home***: see HOME *adverb*. **call in** (*a*) *verb phr. trans.* withdraw from circulation, recall to oneself, require repayment of; seek advice or help from; (*b*) *verb phr. intrans.* pay a short visit, esp. in passing. ***call in evidence***: see EVIDENCE *noun*. **calling hare** a pika. **call in question**, **call into question** cast doubt on, dispute. **call into being**, **call into existence** create. ***call into play***: see PLAY *noun*. ***call into question***: see ***call in question*** above. ***call it a day***: see DAY *noun*. ***call it quits***: see QUITS *adjective*. **call off** (*a*) cancel (an engagement etc.); (*b*) order (a pursuer etc.) to desist, divert. **call on**, **call upon** (*a*) invoke, appeal to; request or require *to do* etc.; †(*b*) impeach, challenge; (*c*) pay a short visit to (someone). **call one's own** claim ownership of, possess. ***call one's shot***: see SHOT *noun*¹. ***call one's soul one's own***: see SOUL *noun*. **call out** summon out esp. to active service (as troops to aid civil authorities); elicit; challenge to a duel; summon (workers) to strike; (see also senses 1, 2 above). **call out of one's name** *arch.* address by a name other than the true one. **call over** (*a*) read aloud (a list etc.); (*b*) ***call over the coals***: see COAL *noun*. ***call quits***: see QUITS *adjective*. ***call someone's bluff***: see BLUFF *noun*² 2. ***call the roll***: see ROLL *noun*¹. ***call the shots***: see SHOT *noun*¹. ***call the tune***: see TUNE *noun*. ***call the turn***: see TURN *noun*. **call to account** summon to answer for his or her conduct, bring to justice. **call to mind** recollect. **call to order** request to be orderly, declare (a meeting) open. ***call truce***: see TRUCE *noun*. **call up** (*a*) summon from below, summon up; recollect; (*b*) call to action; conscript for military service; (*c*) call on the telephone. ***call upon***: see ***call on*** above. ***pay the piper and call the tune***: see PAY *verb*¹.

– COMB.: **call-down** *N. Amer.* a rebuke, an abusive tirade; **call-in** *N. Amer.* a radio or television programme which members of the public participate in by phoning the studio, a phone-in; **call-over** a roll-call; the reading aloud of a list of betting prices; **call-up** a summons to action or service; *spec.* conscription.

■ **callable** *adjective* **E19**. **callee** *noun* a person who is called or called on **L19**.

calla /ˈkalə/ *noun*. **E19.**

[ORIGIN mod. Latin: cf. Italian *calla* arum lily.]

An aquatic plant of the arum family, *Calla palustris*. Also, an arum lily (*Zantedeschia*) or similar plant. Also ***calla lily***.

callaloo /kaləˈluː/ *noun*. Also **calalu**. **M18.**

[ORIGIN Amer. Spanish *calalú*.]

Any of various tropical American plants, esp. of the aroid genus *Xanthosoma*, cultivated for their edible leaves; soup or stew made with these.

Callanetics /kaləˈnɛtɪks/ *noun*. Also **c-**. **L20.**

[ORIGIN from *Callan* Pinckney (b. 1939), US deviser of the system, perh. after *athletics*.]

(Proprietary name for) a system of physical exercises based on small repeated movements.

callant /ˈkɑːl(ə)nt/ *noun*. *Scot. & N. English*. **E16.**

[ORIGIN Flemish *kalant* from northern French dial. *caland*, earlier *calland*, var. of *chaland* customer, chap, from *chaloir* be warm from Latin *calere*.]

†**1** A customer. **E16–M17.**

2 A boy, a youth; a (young) fellow. **L16.**

callback /ˈkɔːlbak/ *noun*. **M20.**

[ORIGIN from ***call back*** s.v. CALL *verb*.]

1 An instance of returning to a customer to repair a previously sold product, esp. when this is covered by a guarantee. **M20.**

2 A telephone call made to return one that someone has received. **M20.**

3 An invitation to return for a second audition or interview. Chiefly *N. Amer.* **M20.**

4 A security feature used by some computer systems accessed by telephone, in which a user must log on from a previously registered phone number, to which the system then places a return call. **L20.**

caller /ˈkɔːlə/ *noun*. **LME.**

[ORIGIN from CALL *verb* + -ER¹.]

1 One who or that which calls aloud. **LME.** ▸**b** *spec.* One who announces the directions in a square dance, or calls out the numbers in bingo etc. **L19.** ▸**c** One who makes a telephone call. **L19.** ▸**d** One employed to knock up workers for duty. **L19.**

2 A driver. *Scot.* **LME.**

3 One who pays a (short) visit. **L18.**

caller /ˈkɑːlə/ *adjective*. *Scot. & N. English*. **LME.**

[ORIGIN Alt. of CALVER *adjective*: cf. *siller*, *silver*.]

1 Esp. of fish: fresh, not decaying. **LME.**

2 Of air etc.: fresh and cool. **E16.**

callet /ˈkalɪt/ *noun & verb*. *obsolete* exc. *dial.* **LME.**

[ORIGIN Old French & mod. French *caillette* dim. of *caille* QUAIL *noun*: see -ET¹.]

▸ **A** *noun*. A prostitute or promiscuous woman. Also, a hag, a scold. **LME.**

▸ **B** *verb intrans.* Scold, rail. **L17.**

calliard /ˈkalɪɑːd/ *noun*. *dial.* **L18.**

[ORIGIN Unknown.]

A hard smooth flinty gritstone.

callidity /kəˈlɪdɪti/ *noun*. Now *rare* or *obsolete*. **LME.**

[ORIGIN French *callidité* or Latin *calliditas*, from *callidus* skilful, cunning: see -ITY.]

Craftiness, cunning.

calligraph /ˈkalɪɡrɑːf/ *noun & verb*. **M19.**

[ORIGIN French *calligraphe* from medieval Latin *calligraphus* from Greek *kalligraphos*: see CALLIGRAPHY. Sense A.2 and verb after *autograph* etc.]

▸ **A** *noun*. **1** A person who writes beautifully, a calligrapher. **M19.**

2 An example of calligraphy. **L19.**

▸ **B** *verb trans.* Write beautifully or ornamentally. **L19.**

calligrapher /kəˈlɪɡrəfə/ *noun*. **M18.**

[ORIGIN formed as CALLIGRAPHY + -ER¹.]

A person who writes beautifully; *spec.* a professional transcriber of manuscripts.

calligraphy /kəˈlɪɡrəfi/ *noun*. **E17.**

[ORIGIN Greek *kalligraphia*, from *kalligraphos* fair writer, from *kalli-*, *kallos* beauty: see -GRAPHY.]

1 Beautiful handwriting; elegant penmanship. **E17.**

2 Style of handwriting, penmanship generally. **M17.**

3 In painting etc.: beauty of line; (elegant) brushwork. **E20.**

■ **calliˈgraphic** *adjective* of or pertaining to calligraphers or calligraphy; having beauty of style or line: **L18**. †**calligraphical** *adjective* = CALLIGRAPHIC: only in **M17**. **calliˈgraphically** *adverb* **L19**. **calligraphist** *noun* = CALLIGRAPHER **E19**.

calling /ˈkɔːlɪŋ/ *noun*. **ME.**

[ORIGIN from CALL *verb* + -ING¹.]

▸ **I 1** The action of CALL *verb*. **ME.**

▸ **II 2** (An inward conviction of) divine prompting to salvation or to serve God (with ref. to the Christian ministry with mixture of sense 4); a strong impulse towards a course of action as the right thing to do; (a) vocation. **ME.**

> F. NIGHTINGALE What is it to feel a calling for any thing? M. L. KING I am a preacher by calling.

†**3** Station in life; rank. **M16–L17.**

4 An occupation, a profession, a trade. **M16.**

> J. BUCHAN Business is now accepted as a calling for those who have received a liberal education. MOLLIE HARRIS Men who were known by their calling—Carter Temple, Shepherd Spindlow, . . Cowman Godfrey.

– COMB.: **calling card** (chiefly *N. Amer.*) a visiting card; *esp.* (*fig.*) a distinctive mark left behind by someone.

calliope /kəˈlʌɪəpi/ *noun*. *N. Amer.* **M19.**

[ORIGIN Greek *Kalliopē* (lit. 'beautiful-voiced') the Muse of epic poetry.]

A set of steam whistles producing musical notes, played by a keyboard like that of an organ. Also ***steam calliope***.

Callippic /kəˈlɪpɪk/ *adjective*. Also **Calippic**. **L17.**

[ORIGIN from *Callippus* Greek astronomer of the 4th cent. BC + -IC.]

ASTRONOMY (now *hist.*). Designating a period of 76 years, equal to four Metonic cycles, at the end of which, by omission of one day, the phases of the moon recur at the same day and hour.

callipygian /kalɪˈpɪdʒɪən/ *adjective*. **L18.**

[ORIGIN from Greek *kallipūgos* (epithet of a statue of Venus), from *kalli-*, *kallos* beauty + *pūgē* buttocks: see -IAN.]

Pertaining to or having well-shaped buttocks.

■ Also **callipygous** /-ˈpɪdʒəs, -ˈpʌɪɡəs/ *adjective* **E20**.

callistemon /kalɪˈstiːmən/ *noun*. **M19.**

[ORIGIN mod. Latin, from Greek *kalli-*, *kallos* beauty + *stēmōn* thread, STAMEN.]

An evergreen myrtaceous shrub or small tree of the Australian genus *Callistemon*, bearing flowers (resembling a bottlebrush) with many long red or yellow stamens.

callisthenic /kalɪsˈθɛnɪk/ *adjective & noun*. Also **cali-**. **E19.**

[ORIGIN from Greek *kalli-*, *kallos* beauty + *sthenos* strength + -IC.]

▸ **A** *adjective*. Suitable for producing strength and grace; of or pertaining to callisthenics. **E19.**

▸ **B** *noun*. In *pl.* Gymnastic exercises designed to promote bodily health and grace of movement. **E19.**

callithrix /ˈkalɪθrɪks/ *noun*. Also **-trix** /-trɪks/. **E17.**

[ORIGIN mod. Latin from Latin = a kind of Ethiopian monkey, from Greek *kallitrikhos* beautiful-haired.]

A marmoset. Now only as mod. Latin genus name.

callithumpian /kalɪˈθʌmpɪən/ *noun & adjective*. *US colloq.* M19.
[ORIGIN Fanciful: cf. GALLITHUMPIAN.]
▸ **A** *noun*. A member of a band of discordant instruments. M19.
▸ **B** *adjective*. Designating, pertaining to, or resembling such a band. M19.

callitriche /kəˈlɪtrɪki/ *noun*. L18.
[ORIGIN mod. Latin genus name from Greek *kallitrikhos*: see CALLITHRIX.]
A water starwort (see STARWORT 1).

callitrix *noun* var. of CALLITHRIX.

calloo /kəˈluː/ *noun*. *Scot.* L18.
[ORIGIN Imit. of the duck's call.]
The long-tailed duck, *Clangula hyemalis*.

callop /ˈkaləp/ *noun*. *Austral.* E20.
[ORIGIN Perh. from an Australian Aboriginal language of South Australia.]
= ***golden perch*** s.v. GOLDEN *adjective*.

callosal /kəˈləʊs(ə)l/ *adjective*. M19.
[ORIGIN formed as CALLOSE + -AL[1].]
ANATOMY. Of or pertaining to the corpus callosum of the brain.

callose /kəˈləʊs/ *adjective*. M19.
[ORIGIN Latin *callosus*: see CALLOUS, -OSE[1].]
BOTANY. Having callosities.

callosity /kəˈlɒsɪti/ *noun*. LME.
[ORIGIN French *callosité* or Latin *callositas*, formed as CALLOSE: see -ITY.]
1 Abnormal hardness and thickness of the skin or other tissue. LME.
2 A callus; a hardened insensitive part of the skin etc. LME.
3 *fig.* A hardened state of mind; callousness. M17.

callous /ˈkaləs/ *adjective, noun, & verb*. LME.
[ORIGIN (French *calleux* from) Latin *callosus*, from *callum*, *-us* hardened skin: see -OUS.]
▸ **A** *adjective*. **1** Chiefly of the skin or other tissue: hardened, indurated, esp. by continual friction; naturally hard. LME.

W. CONGREVE With labouring callous hands.

2 *fig.* Hardened in feeling etc.; insensitive, unfeeling. L17.

ARNOLD BENNETT He had shown a singular, callous disregard for the progress of the rest of the house. H. T. LANE Hardened in wrongdoing and callous to all good influence.

▸ **B** *noun*. = CALLUS 1. M17.
▸ **C** *verb trans.* Make callous, harden. Chiefly ***calloused*** *ppl adjective*. Cf. CALLUS *verb*. M19.
■ **callously** *adverb* L19. **callousness** *noun* (**a**) callous quality or condition; *esp.* callous behaviour, insensitivity; (**b**) a callosity: M17.

callow /ˈkaləʊ/ *adjective & noun*.
[ORIGIN Old English *calu* = Middle Low German *kale*, Middle Dutch *kale* (Dutch *kaal*), Old High German *kalo* (German *kahl*) from West Germanic, prob. from Latin *calvus* bald.]
▸ **A** *adjective*. †**1** Bald. OE–LME.
2 Unfledged; downy, downlike; chiefly *fig.*: inexperienced, raw, youthful. L16.

DRYDEN The callow Down began to cloath my Chin. C. LAMB The first callow flights in authorship. N. MITFORD The callow young world of my acquaintance.

3 Of land: bare; *Irish* low-lying and liable to flooding. L17.
▸ **B** *noun*. †**1** A bald person. Only in ME.
†**2** A callow nestling; a raw youth. M–L17.
3 Topsoil, overburden. *dial.* M19.
4 A low-lying meadow liable to flooding. *Irish*. M19.
■ **callowly** *adverb* L20. **callowness** *noun* M19.

calluna /kəˈluːnə/ *noun*. E19.
[ORIGIN mod. Latin, from Greek *kallunein* beautify, sweep clean, from *kallos* beauty.]
Common heather or ling, *Calluna vulgaris*.

callus /ˈkaləs/ *noun & verb*. M16.
[ORIGIN Latin (more commonly *callum*).]
▸ **A** *noun*. **1** A thickened and hardened part of the skin or soft tissue, a callosity. M16.

E. LINKLATER Their noses were unremarkable, being small and without sufficient callus to give them a definite shape. *fig.*: O. W. HOLMES Editors have . . to develop enormous calluses at every point of contact with authorship.

2 *MEDICINE.* The bony healing tissue which forms around the ends of broken bone. L17.
3 *BOTANY.* A hard formation of tissue; new tissue formed over a wound. L19.
▸ **B** *verb intrans.* Form a callus, become hardened (*over*). Cf. CALLOUS *verb*. M19.
■ Also †**callum** *noun* LME–L18.

calm /kɑːm/ *noun*[1]. LME.
[ORIGIN Perh. from popular Latin alt. (cf. medieval Latin *calmus* adjective, *calmacio(n-)*) of late Latin *cauma* from Greek *kauma* heat (of the day or sun), by assoc. with Latin *calere* be warm.]
1 Stillness, tranquillity, quiet, serenity, (of the weather, air, or sea, of (esp. social or political) conditions or circumstances, of the mind or behaviour). LME.
2 An absence of wind; a period of stillness or tranquillity. E16.

calm /kɑːm, kɔːm, *in sense 2 also* keɪm/ *noun*[2]. Sense 2 also **came** /keɪm/. E16.
[ORIGIN Unknown.]
1 A mould in which metal objects are cast. *Scot.* E16.
2 An enclosing frame for a pane of glass etc.; *spec.* a grooved slip of lead used for framing the glass in lattice windows (usu. in *pl.*). L16.

calm /kɑːm/ *adjective*. LME.
[ORIGIN medieval Latin *calmus*, formed as CALM *noun*[1].]
1 Of the weather, air, or sea, of the mind or behaviour, of conditions or circumstances: still, tranquil, quiet, serene. LME.
2 Self-confident; impudent. *colloq.* M20.
– PHRASES: ***keep a calm sough***: see SOUGH *noun*[1].
■ **calmly** *adverb* L16. **calmness** *noun* E16. **calmy** *adjective* (*literary*, now *rare*) tranquil, peaceful L16.

calm /kɑːm/ *verb*. LME.
[ORIGIN from the adjective.]
1 *verb intrans.* Become calm. Now only foll. by *down*. LME.

L. URIS Let's stop yelling at each other . . . Let's calm down.

2 *verb trans.* Make calm. Also foll. by *down*. M16.

G. GREENE It calms the nerves and soothes the emotions.

†**3** *verb trans.* Becalm (a ship). L16–M18.
■ **calmant** /ˈkɑːm(ə)nt, ˈkal-/ *noun* [French] a calmative, a sedative E19. **calmer** *noun* a person who or thing which calms M17. **calmingly** *adverb* in a calming manner E20.

calmative /ˈkɑːmətɪv, ˈkal-/ *adjective & noun*. L19.
[ORIGIN from CALM *verb* + -ATIVE.]
MEDICINE. (An agent) that has a calming effect, (a) sedative.

calmodulin /kalˈmɒdjʊlɪn/ *noun*. L20.
[ORIGIN from CAL(CIUM + MODUL(ATE + -IN[1].]
BIOCHEMISTRY. A calcium-binding protein in eukaryotic cells which is involved in regulating a variety of cellular activities.

†**calmstone** *noun* see CAMSTONE.

calomel /ˈkaləmɛl/ *noun*. L17.
[ORIGIN mod. Latin, perh. from Greek *kalos* beautiful + *melas* black.]
Mercury(I) chloride, Hg_2Cl_2, a white powder formerly much used as a purgative.

Calor /ˈkalə/ *noun*. M20.
[ORIGIN Latin *calor* heat.]
In full ***Calor gas***. (Proprietary name for) liquefied gas (chiefly butane) supplied under pressure in containers for use as domestic fuel.

caloric /kəˈlɒrɪk, ˈkalərɪk/ *noun & adjective*. L18.
[ORIGIN French *calorique*, from Latin *calor* heat: see -IC.]
▸ **A** *noun*. **1** *hist.* A hypothetical fluid formerly thought to be responsible for the phenomena of heat. L18.
2 Heat. *arch.* L18.
▸ **B** *adjective*. Of or pertaining to heat; expressed in calories. M19.
■ **calorically** /kəˈlɒrɪk(ə)li/ *adverb* as or in the manner of heat; as regards heat: M19.

calorie /ˈkaləri/ *noun*. Also **calory**. M19.
[ORIGIN French, from Latin *calor* heat + French *-ie* -Y[3].]
A unit of heat or energy; *spec.* (**a**) the quantity of heat required to raise the temperature of one kilogram of water by one degree centigrade (also called ***kilocalorie***, ***large calorie***, ***great calorie***), freq. used as a measure of the energy value of foods (abbreviation ***Cal***); (**b**) the quantity of heat required to raise the temperature of one gram of water by one degree centigrade, equal to approximately 4.19 joule (also called ***small calorie***, abbreviation ***cal***).
empty calories: see EMPTY *adjective*.

calorific /kaləˈrɪfɪk/ *adjective*. L17.
[ORIGIN Latin *calorificus*, from *calori-*, *calor* heat: see -FIC.]
1 Producing heat; *loosely* of or pertaining to heat. L17.
calorific value the energy contained in a fuel or food, determined by measuring the heat produced by the complete combustion of a specified quantity of it.
2 Relating to the number of calories contained in food; (of food) containing many calories and so likely to be fattening. L20.

H. H. TAN I got the most calorific dishes possible—roast pork rice, . . fried carrot cake.

calorimeter /kaləˈrɪmɪtə/ *noun*. L18.
[ORIGIN from Latin *calori-*, *calor* heat + -METER.]
An apparatus for measuring the amount of heat involved in a chemical reaction or other process.
■ **calorimetric** /kalərɪˈmɛtrɪk/ *adjective* of, pertaining to, or by means of calorimeters or calorimetry M19. **caloriˈmetrical** *adjective* = CALORIMETRIC L19. **caloriˈmetrically** *adverb* L19. **calorimetry** *noun* the measurement of quantities of heat M19.

calory *noun* var. of CALORIE.

calotte /kəˈlɒt/ *noun*. M17.
[ORIGIN French, perh. rel. to *cale* CAUL *noun*[1].]
1 A skullcap, esp. as worn by Roman Catholic priests. M17.
2 A snowcap, an ice cap. L19.

calotype /ˈkalətʌɪp/ *noun & verb*. *hist.* M19.
[ORIGIN from Greek *kalos* beautiful + -TYPE.]
▸ **A** *noun*. A photographic process in which negatives were made using paper coated with silver iodide. M19.
▸ **B** *verb trans.* Photograph by this process. M19.

caloyer /ˈkalɔɪə, *foreign* kalɔje (*pl. same*)/ *noun*. L16.
[ORIGIN French from Italian *caloiero* from ecclesiastical Greek *kalogēros*, from *kalos* beautiful + *gēros*, *-as* old age.]
A Greek monk, esp. of the order of St Basil.

calpac /ˈkalpak/ *noun*. Also **-pack**, **kalpa(c)k**. L16.
[ORIGIN Turkish *kalpak*.]
An oriental cap; *spec.* a tall felt or sheepskin cap worn in east central Asia.

calque /kalk/ *noun & verb*. M20.
[ORIGIN French = copy, tracing, formed as CALK *verb*[2].]
▸ **A** *noun*. A loan translation (*of*, *on*). M20.
▸ **B** *verb trans.* Form as a calque. Usu. in *pass.* (foll. by *on*). M20.

caltha /ˈkalθə/ *noun*. L16.
[ORIGIN mod. Latin *Caltha* genus name from Latin.]
A marsh marigold.

caltrop /ˈkaltrəp/ *noun*. Also **-trap**.
[ORIGIN Old English *calcatrippe* from medieval Latin *calcatrippa*, *-trappa*; senses 2 & 3 from (ult. identical) Old French *kauketrape* dial. var. of *cauchetrape*, *chauche-* (mod. *chaussetrape*), from *chauchier* tread + *trappe* trap.]
1 Orig., a plant which tended to catch or entangle the feet. Later, a plant with a flower head suggestive of the military instrument (sense 3 below); *spec.* (**a**) a water chestnut, *Trapa natans* (also ***water caltrop(s)***); (**b**) a member of the genus *Tribulus*. OE.
†**2** A trap or snare for the feet. ME–M19.
3 *hist.* An iron ball with four spikes placed so that one is always projecting upwards, thrown on the ground to impede cavalry horses. Also, a heraldic representation of this. LME.

calumba /kəˈlʌmbə/ *noun*. E19.
[ORIGIN Perh. from *Colombo*, Sri Lanka, erron. regarded as the source.]
The dried root of the tree *Jateorhiza palmata*, native to E. Africa and Madagascar, used as a bitter tonic. Also ***calumba root***.

calumet /ˈkaljʊmɛt/ *noun*. L17.
[ORIGIN French, dial. var. of *chalumeau* from late Latin *calamellus* dim. of CALAMUS reed.]
An American Indian tobacco pipe with a clay bowl and reed stem, smoked esp. as a sign of peace; *transf.* & *fig.* a symbol of peace.

calumniate /kəˈlʌmnɪeɪt/ *verb*. M16.
[ORIGIN Latin *calumniat-* pa. ppl stem of *calumniari*, formed as CALUMNY *noun*: see -ATE[3].]
1 *verb trans.* Slander, defame, make false charges against. M16.
†**2** *verb intrans.* Utter calumnies. E17–E18.
■ **calumniˈation** *noun* (**a**) the action of calumniating; (**b**) a calumny: M16. **calumniator** *noun* a slanderer, a false accuser M16. **calumniatory** *adjective* slanderous E17.

calumnious /kəˈlʌmnɪəs/ *adjective*. L15.
[ORIGIN Old French & mod. French *calomnieux* or Latin *calumniosus*, formed as CALUMNY *noun*: see -OUS.]
Of the nature of a calumny; slanderous; defamatory.
■ **calumniously** *adverb* M16.

calumny /ˈkaləmni/ *noun*. LME.
[ORIGIN Latin *calumnia*.]
Malicious misrepresentation, slander, libel; a false charge, a slanderous or libellous statement or report.

calumny /ˈkaləmni/ *verb*. M16.
[ORIGIN (French *calomnier* from) late Latin *calumniare* for *calumniari* (see CALUMNIATE). In mod. use from the noun.]
†**1** *verb trans.* Utter calumnies. Only in M16.
†**2** *verb trans.* Declare calumniously. Only in M16.
3 *verb trans.* Calumniate, slander. E19.
■ †**calumnize** *verb trans.* calumniate E17–E18.

calutron /kəˈluːtrɒn/ *noun*. M20.
[ORIGIN from *California University cyclotron*.]
A device that uses large electromagnets to separate uranium isotopes from uranium ore, in order to produce highly enriched weapons-grade uranium.

Calvados /ˈkalvədɒs/ *noun*. E20.
[ORIGIN Name of a department in Normandy, France.]
Apple brandy, traditionally made in the Calvados region; a drink of this.

calvaria /kalˈvɛːrɪə/ *noun*. Pl. **-iae** /-ɪiː/. Also **-ium** /-ɪəm/, pl. **-ia** /-ɪə/. LME.
[ORIGIN Latin *calvaria*: see CALVARY.]
ANATOMY. The vault of the skull.

Calvary /ˈkalv(ə)ri/ *noun*. Also **c-**. L17.
[ORIGIN The site of the Crucifixion of Jesus, from Latin *calvaria* skull (from *calva* scalp, *calvus* bald), translating Greek GOLGOTHA.]
1 *HERALDRY.* ***Calvary cross***, ***cross Calvary***: with the upper and side limbs of equal length and the lower limb considerably longer, mounted on a pyramid of three grises or steps. L17.

C

2 *ROMAN CATHOLIC CHURCH.* A sculptured or pictorial representation of the Crucifixion. **E18.**
3 A place of crucifixion (*lit. & fig.*). **L19.**

calve /kɑːv/ *verb*[1].
[**ORIGIN** Old English *calfian, ċealfian*, from **CALF** *noun*[1].]
1 *verb intrans.* Give birth to a calf. **OE.**
2 *verb trans.* Give birth to (a calf). Usu. in *pass.* **LME.**
3 *verb trans. & intrans.* Of an iceberg etc.: split to produce (a detached part). **E19.**
■ **calver** *noun* a cow that calves **L18.**

calve *verb*[2] see **CAVE** *verb*[3].

calved /kɑːvd/ *adjective.* **L16.**
[**ORIGIN** from **CALF** *noun*[2]: see **-ED**[2].]
Having calves (of a given description etc.).

calver /ˈkɑːvə/ *adjective & verb.* Long *obsolete* exc. *hist.* **ME.**
[**ORIGIN** Perh. rel. to Middle Low German *keller* & from Germanic base meaning 'be cold'.]
▶ **A** *adjective.* Of fish, esp. salmon: fresh; prepared in a now unknown way while alive or newly dead. Cf. **CALLER** *adjective.* **ME.**
▶ **B** *verb.* **1** *verb trans.* Prepare (fish) when fresh in a now unknown way. Chiefly as ***calvered*** *ppl adjective.* **E17.**
†**2** *verb intrans.* Behave as a 'calver' fish when cooked. **M17–M18.**

calves *noun* pl. of **CALF** *noun*[1].

Calvinian /kalˈvɪnɪən/ *adjective & noun.* **M16.**
[**ORIGIN** from *Calvin* (see **CALVINISM**) + **-IAN.**]
▶ **A** *adjective.* Of or pertaining to Calvin; Calvinistic. **M16.**
▶ †**B** *noun.* A Calvinist. **M16–M18.**

Calvinise *verb* var. of **CALVINIZE.**

Calvinism /ˈkalvɪnɪz(ə)m/ *noun.* **L16.**
[**ORIGIN** French *calvinisme* or mod. Latin *calvinismus*, from *Calvin* (see below): see **-ISM.**]
The doctrines of the French Protestant reformer Jean Calvin (1509–64) and his followers, *esp.* those relating to grace and election to salvation; adherence to these doctrines.

Calvinist /ˈkalvɪnɪst/ *noun & adjective.* **M16.**
[**ORIGIN** formed as **CALVINISM** + **-IST.**]
▶ **A** *noun.* An adherent of Calvinism. **M16.**
▶ **B** *adjective.* Of or pertaining to Calvinists or Calvinism. **M16.**
■ **Calviˈnistic** *adjective* of, pertaining to, or following the doctrines of Calvinism **M18.** **Calviˈnistical** *adjective* = **CALVINISTIC** **L16.** **Calviˈnistically** *adverb* **L17.**

Calvinize /ˈkalvɪnʌɪz/ *verb.* Also **-ise.** **M17.**
[**ORIGIN** from *Calvin* (see **CALVINISM**) + **-IZE.**]
1 *verb intrans.* Follow Calvin; teach Calvinism. **M17.**
2 *verb trans.* Imbue with Calvinism. **E19.**

calvish *adjective* var. of **CALFISH.**

calvity /ˈkalvɪti/ *noun. rare.* **E17.**
[**ORIGIN** Latin *calvitium*, from *calvus* bald.]
Baldness.

calx /kalks/ *noun.* Pl. **calces** /ˈkalsiːz/, †**calxes.** **LME.**
[**ORIGIN** Latin *calx, calc-* lime, prob. from Greek *khalix* pebble, limestone.]
1 A powder or friable substance produced by roasting or burning a mineral or metal, formerly taken as the essence of the mineral. *arch.* **LME.**
2 Orig. more fully †***calx vive.*** Quicklime. *arch.* **LME.**
3 The area behind goal line in the Eton College wall game. **M19.**

calycanthus /kalɪˈkanθəs/ *noun.* **L18.**
[**ORIGIN** mod. Latin, formed as **CALYX** + Greek *anthos* flower.]
A shrub of the N. American genus *Calycanthus*; *esp.* Carolina allspice (**ALLSPICE** 2).

calyces *noun pl.* see **CALYX.**

calycine /ˈkalɪsʌɪn/ *adjective.* **M18.**
[**ORIGIN** from Latin *calyci-*, **CALYX** + **-INE**[1].]
Of or pertaining to the calyx; resembling a calyx.

calycle /ˈkalɪk(ə)l, ˈkeɪ-/ *noun.* Also in Latin form **calyculus** /kəˈlɪkjʊləs/, pl. **-li** /-lʌɪ, -liː/. **M18.**
[**ORIGIN** Latin *calyculus* dim. of **CALYX**, *-yc-*: see **-CLE.**]
BOTANY. A small calyx or calycine structure, esp. of bracts.
■ **calycled** *adjective* = **CALYCULATED** **L18.** **calycular** /kəˈlɪkjʊlə/ *adjective* of or pertaining to a calycle, calycine **M17.** **calyculate** /kəˈlɪkjʊlət/ *adjective* = **CALYCULATED** **M19.** **calyculated** /kəˈlɪkjʊleɪtɪd/ *adjective* enclosed in or having a calycle **L17.**

calypso /kəˈlɪpsəʊ/ *noun.* Pl. **-os.** **E20.**
[**ORIGIN** Unknown.]
A type of W. Indian (orig. Trinidadian) ballad or song, usu. with a topical theme; the kind of music to which this is sung.
■ **calypˈsonian** *noun* a composer and singer of calypsos **M20.**

calyptra /kəˈlɪptrə/ *noun.* **M18.**
[**ORIGIN** mod. Latin from Greek *kaluptra* covering, veil.]
BOTANY. A hood, a protective cover; *spec.* (***a***) a layer of parenchymatous cells protecting the tip of a growing root (also called ***root-cap***); (***b***) a structure over the capsule of a moss.

calyx /ˈkalɪks, ˈkeɪ-/ *noun.* Pl. **-yces** /-ɪsiːz/, **-yxes.** **L17.**
[**ORIGIN** Latin *calyx, -yc-* from Greek *kalux* shell, husk, pod, from base of *kaluptein* to hide.]
1 *BOTANY.* A whorl of leaves (sepals), forming the outer case of a bud or the envelope of a flower. **L17.**
2 = **CALIX.** **M19.**
– **COMB.:** ***calyx tube***: see **TUBE** *noun* 10.

calzone /kalˈzəʊneɪ/ *noun.* Pl. **-ni** /-ni/, **-nes** /-neɪz/. **M20.**
[**ORIGIN** Italian dial., prob. use of *calzone* trouser leg, with ref. to the shape of the pizza.]
A type of filled pizza that is folded in half.

cam /kam/ *noun*[1]. **L18.**
[**ORIGIN** Dutch *kam* comb, as in *kamrad* toothed wheel, cogwheel.]
A projecting part of a wheel etc. in machinery, used to impart reciprocal or variable motion to another part with which it makes sliding contact as it rotates.
– **COMB.:** **camshaft** a shaft carrying a cam or cams, esp. (in an internal-combustion engine) for operating the cylinder valves (***overhead cam***: see **OVERHEAD** *adjective* 1).

cam *noun*[2] *colloq.* **L20.**
[**ORIGIN** Abbreviation.]
A camera.

> *attrib.: Entertainment Weekly* Seven young Londoners . . gather at a beautiful country estate to shoot a video-cam horror film.

cam /kam/ *adjective & adverb.* Long *obsolete* exc. *dial.* Also †**k-.** **M16.**
[**ORIGIN** Welsh (also Irish, Gaelic, Manx) from Celtic.]
Crooked(ly), perverse(ly); awry, askew.

camaieu /kamajø/ *noun.* Pl. pronounced same. **L16.**
[**ORIGIN** French: see **CAMEO.**]
†**1** A cameo. **L16–L18.**
2 A method of monochrome painting. **E18.**

camail /ˈkameɪl/ *noun.* **L17.**
[**ORIGIN** Old French & mod. French from Provençal *capmalh*, from *cap* head + *malh, malhar* **MAIL** *noun*[1].]
hist. **1** A hood worn by the Roman Catholic clergy. Also, a blue or purple ornament worn by a bishop over his rochet. **L17.**
2 A piece of chainmail attached to the headpiece and protecting the neck and shoulders. **E19.**

Camaldolese /kəˈmaldəliːz/ *adjective & noun.* **E19.**
[**ORIGIN** from *Camaldoli* (see below) + **-ESE.**]
▶ **A** *adjective.* Designating or belonging to a religious order founded by St Romuald at Camaldoli, Italy, in the 11th cent. **E19.**
▶ **B** *noun.* Pl. same. A member of this order. **E19.**
■ **Camaldolite** *noun* = **CAMALDOLESE** *noun* **E18.**

camalote /kaməˈləʊti/ *noun.* Also **camel-.** **L19.**
[**ORIGIN** Amer. Spanish.]
A floating island of vegetation in N. or S. America; a blue-flowered aquatic plant of the genus *Pontederia*, which forms such islands.

caman /ˈkamən/ *noun.* **L19.**
[**ORIGIN** Irish *camán*, Old Irish *cammán*, from *cam* bent, crooked.]
The stick used in shinty.

camaraderie /kaməˈrɑːd(ə)ri, -riː/ *noun.* **M19.**
[**ORIGIN** French, from *camarade* **COMRADE**: see **-ERY.**]
The mutual trust and sociability of comrades.

camarilla /kaməˈrɪlə, -ljə/ *noun.* **M19.**
[**ORIGIN** Spanish, dim. of *camara* **CHAMBER.**]
A cabal, a clique.

camaron /kaməˈrəʊn, ˈkamər(ə)n/ *noun.* **L19.**
[**ORIGIN** Spanish *camarón* shrimp.]
A freshwater shrimp or prawn resembling a crayfish.

camas /kwəˈmaʃ, ˈkwɒmaʃ/ *noun.* Also **camass, quamash.** **E19.**
[**ORIGIN** Chinook Jargon *kamass*, perh. from Nootka.]
A N. American plant of the lily family, *Camassia quamash*, the bulbs of which are used as food by N. American Indians; any of various other plants of this genus, and of the related genus *Zigadenus*, having starry blue or purple flowers.

Camb. *abbreviation.*
Cambridge.

Cambazola *noun* var. of **CAMBOZOLA.**

camber /ˈkambə/ *noun.* **LME.**
[**ORIGIN** Old French *cambre*, from dial. var. of *chambre* arched from Latin *camurus* curved inwards.]
1 A harbour, a dock; a dockyard where cambering is performed. *rare.* **LME.**
2 A slight upward convexity, an arched form, esp. of a road surface or aerofoil in cross-section, a beam, deck, etc. **E17.** ▸**c** Sideways inclination of a motor vehicle's wheel. **M20.**

camber /ˈkambə/ *verb.* **LME.**
[**ORIGIN** French *cambrer*, formed as **CAMBER** *noun.*]
1 *verb intrans.* Be or become slightly convex so that the centre is higher than the ends. **LME.**
2 *verb trans.* Cause (a beam etc.) to arch upwards slightly in the middle; give camber to (a road surface, wing, etc.). **E17.**

Camberwell beauty /ˈkambəwɛl ˈbjuːti/ *noun phr.* **M18.**
[**ORIGIN** *Camberwell*, a village, now a district of SE London.]
A holarctic nymphalid butterfly, *Nymphalis antiopa*, with dark brown cream-bordered wings, which is a rare migrant to Britain from Continental Europe. Cf. ***mourning cloak*** (b) s.v. **MOURNING** *noun*[1].

cambia *noun* pl. of **CAMBIUM.**

†**cambio** *noun.* Pl. **-os.** **M16–L18.**
[**ORIGIN** Italian from medieval Latin **CAMBIUM.**]
(A place, a bill, of) exchange.

cambist /ˈkambɪst/ *noun.* Now *rare* or *obsolete.* **E19.**
[**ORIGIN** French *cambiste* from Italian *cambista*, formed as **CAMBIO**: see **-IST.**]
An expert in or a manual of financial exchange; a dealer in bills of exchange, a speculator.

cambium /ˈkambɪəm/ *noun.* Pl. **-ia** /-ɪə/. **L16.**
[**ORIGIN** medieval Latin = (ex)change.]
1 One of the alimentary humours formerly supposed to nourish the body. *obsolete* exc. *hist.* **L16.**
2 *BOTANY.* (A layer of) cellular tissue from which phloem, xylem, or cork grows by division. **L17.**
3 (A place of) exchange or barter. *rare.* **E18.**
■ **cambial** *adjective* (***a***) *BOTANY* of, pertaining to, or of the nature of cambium; †(***b***) relating to financial exchange: **M19.**

†**camblet** *noun & verb* var. of **CAMLET.**

†**cambock** *noun* var. of **CAMMOCK** *noun*[2].

Cambodian /kamˈbəʊdɪən/ *noun & adjective.* **L18.**
[**ORIGIN** from *Cambodia* (see below) + **-AN.**]
▶ **A** *noun.* **1** A native or inhabitant of Cambodia, a country in SE Asia. **L18.**
2 The language of Cambodia, Khmer. **M19.**
▶ **B** *adjective.* Of or pertaining to Cambodia, its people, or its language. **M19.**

camboose *noun* var. of **CABOOSE.**

Cambozola /ˌkambəˈzəʊlə/ *noun.* Also **Cambazola.** **L20.**
[**ORIGIN** Blend of **CAMEMBERT** and **GORGONZOLA.**]
(Proprietary name for) a type of German blue soft cheese with a rind like Camembert, produced using Gorgonzola blue mould.

cambré /kɑ̃bre/ *adjective.* **E20.**
[**ORIGIN** French, pa. pple of *cambrer* **CAMBER** *verb.*]
Curved, arched; *BALLET* (of the body) bent from the waist sideways or backwards.

cambrel /ˈkambr(ə)l/ *noun. obsolete* exc. *dial.* In sense 2 also †**ch-.** **LME.**
[**ORIGIN** Sense 1 perh. from Anglo-Norman var. of Old French *chambril* lath; sense 3 prob. rel. to Welsh *cambren* crooked tree, bent stick, swingletree, butcher's cambrel, etc., from *cam* crooked (see **CAM** *adjective & adverb*) + *pren* wood, stick. Cf. **GAMBREL.**]
†**1** A spatula. Only in **LME.**
2 The hock of a horse's hind leg. **E17.**
3 A bent piece of wood or iron used by butchers to hang carcasses on. **M17.**

Cambrian /ˈkambrɪən/ *adjective & noun.* **M17.**
[**ORIGIN** from medieval Latin *Cambria* Wales, var. (with differentiation of sense) of *Cumbria* (see **CUMBRIAN**), + **-AN.**]
▶ **A** *adjective.* **1** Of or pertaining to Wales, Welsh; a Welsh person. **M17.**
2 *GEOLOGY.* Designating or pertaining to the earliest period of the Palaeozoic era, preceding the Ordovician. **M19.**
▶ **B** *noun. GEOLOGY.* The Cambrian period; the system of rocks dating from this time. **M19.**

cambric /ˈkambrɪk, ˈkeɪm-/ *noun & adjective.* **LME.**
[**ORIGIN** Flemish *Kamerijk* Cambrai, a town in northern France, where orig. made.]
(Of) a fine white linen; (of) a similar cotton fabric.
– **COMB.:** **cambric tea** *US* a drink mainly of hot milk and water given esp. to children.

Cambridge /ˈkeɪmbrɪdʒ/ *noun.* **M19.**
[**ORIGIN** A university city and the county town of Cambridgeshire, a county in eastern England.]
1 ***Cambridge sausage***, a variety of pork sausage. **M19.**
2 ***Cambridge blue***, a light blue (adopted by Cambridge University). **L19.**

Cambridgeshire nightingale /ˈkeɪmbrɪdʒʃə ˈnʌɪtɪŋgeɪl/ *noun phr.* **M19.**
[**ORIGIN** from *Cambridgeshire* (see **CAMBRIDGE**) + **NIGHTINGALE** *noun*[1]: they were introduced into East Anglia in the 17th cent.]
= ***edible frog*** s.v. **EDIBLE** *adjective.*

Cambro- /ˈkambrəʊ/ *combining form.* **E17.**
[**ORIGIN** mod. Latin, from *Cambria* (see **CAMBRIAN**), or from **CAMBRIAN**: see **-O-.**]
Welsh (as ***Cambro-Briton***); Cambrian (as ***Cambro-Ordovician***).

Cambs. *abbreviation.*
Cambridgeshire.

camcorder /ˈkamkɔːdə/ *noun.* **L20.**
[**ORIGIN** from **CAMERA** + **RECORDER** *noun*[1].]
A portable video camera incorporating a built-in video recorder.

came *noun* see **CALM** *noun*[2].

came *verb pa. t.* of **COME** *verb.*

camel /ˈkam(ə)l/ *noun*. OE.
[ORIGIN Latin *camelus* from Greek *kamēlos* from Semitic (cf. Hebrew *gāmāl*): in Middle English reinforced by Old French *c(h)amel*, *-eil*.]
1 Either of two large hornless long-necked domesticated ruminants of the genus *Camelus*, (more fully ***Arabian camel***) the dromedary, *C. dromedarius*, with one hump, and (more fully ***Bactrian camel***) *C. ferus*, with two humps. OE.
swallow a camel (with allusion to *Matthew* 23:24) make no difficulty about something incredible or unreasonable. ***the last straw that breaks the camel's back***: see STRAW *noun*.
2 An apparatus consisting of one or more watertight chests, used to provide buoyancy for a sunken ship etc. E18.
3 A shade of fawn colour. L19.
– COMB.: **camelback** (*a*) a kind of rubber used esp. to retread tyres; (*b*) (a sofa having) a back with a hump-shaped curve; **camel hair**, **camel's hair** the hair of the camel, or (in paintbrushes) of a squirrel's tail; **camel spider** = SOLIFUGID; **camel thorn** (*a*) a Middle Eastern leguminous shrub, *Alhagi camelorum*; (*b*) a south-ern African shrub, *Acacia giraffae*.
■ **cameˈleer** *noun* a camel-driver E19. **camelid** *adjective & noun* (ZOOLOGY) (an animal) of the family Camelidae, which includes the camels and llamas: L20. **camel-like** *adjective* resembling (that of) a camel M18. **cameloid** *adjective & noun* (a) camelid; camel-like: L19. **camelry** *noun* troops mounted on camels M19.

†cameleon *noun* var. of CHAMELEON.

cameline /ˈkam(ə)lɪn/ *noun*[1]. Now *rare* or *obsolete*. ME.
[ORIGIN Old French *camelin* from medieval Latin *camelinum* use as noun of neut. of adjective *camelinus* of a camel: see CAMEL, -INE[1].]
A kind of fabric made from or supposedly made from camel's hair; a garment made of this. Cf. CAMLET.

cameline /ˈkamɪlʌɪn/ *noun*[2]. L16.
[ORIGIN French, earlier *camamine*, from late Latin *chamaemelinus* resembling camomile.]
A cruciferous plant of the genus *Camelina*; *esp.* gold of pleasure, *C. sativa*.

camellia /kəˈmiːlɪə, -ˈmɛlɪə/ *noun*. M18.
[ORIGIN mod. Latin, from Joseph Kamel or *Camellus* (1661–1706), Moravian Jesuit and botanist: see -IA[1].]
An evergreen shrub of the Far Eastern genus *Camellia*, of the tea family; esp. *C. japonica*, bearing showy red, pink, or white flowers.

camelopard /ˈkamɪlə(ʊ)pɑːd, kəˈmɛləpɑːd/ *noun*. Also (now only in sense 2) in Latin forms **-pardalis** /kəmɛləˈpɑːd(ə)lɪs/, **-pardus** /kəmɛləˈpɑːdəs/. LME.
[ORIGIN Latin *camelopardus*, *-pardalis* from Greek *kamēlopardalis*, from *kamēlos* (see CAMEL) + *pardalis* (see PARD *noun*[1]).]
1 A giraffe. *arch.* LME.
2 (C-.) A constellation of the northern hemisphere between the Pole Star and Perseus; the Giraffe. M18.

camelote *noun* var. of CAMALOTE.

Camembert /ˈkamãbɛː, ˈkaməmbɛː/ *noun*. L19.
[ORIGIN A village in Normandy, France.]
A rich soft cheese orig. made near Camembert.

Camenes /ˈkam(ə)niːz/ *noun*. M19.
[ORIGIN A mnemonic of scholastic philosophers, A indicating a universal affirmative proposition, E a universal negative proposition.]
LOGIC. The second mood of the fourth syllogistic figure, in which a universal affirmative major premiss and a universal negative minor premiss yield a universal negative conclusion.

cameo /ˈkamɪəʊ/ *noun*. Pl. **-os**. LME.
[ORIGIN Old French *came(h)u*, *camahieu* (mod. CAMAIEU): cf. medieval Latin *camahutus* etc. Later infl. by Italian *cam(m)eo*, corresp. to medieval Latin *cammaeus*.]
1 A small piece of relief-carving in onyx, agate, etc., usu. with colour layers, the lower of which serves as ground; a relief design of similar form. LME.
2 A short literary sketch or acted scene; (more fully ***cameo part***) a small character part in a play, film, etc. M19.
– COMB.: **cameo glass** a decorative glass consisting of layers of different colours, the outermost being cut away to leave a design in relief; ***cameo part***: see sense 2 above.

camera /ˈkam(ə)rə/ *noun*. L17.
[ORIGIN Latin = vault, arched chamber, from Greek *kamara* object with arched cover: cf. CHAMBER *noun*.]
1 In Italy, Spain, etc. a (council or legislative) chamber; the treasury department of the papal Curia. L17.
2 An arched or vaulted roof or chamber. Chiefly in the names of (parts of) buildings. See also IN CAMERA. E18.
3 *ellipt.* = CAMERA OBSCURA. M18.
4 A device for recording visual images in the form of photographs, movie film, or video signals. M19.
cine camera, ***digital camera***, ***movie camera***, ***television camera***, ***video camera***, ***X-ray camera***, etc. ***candid camera***: see CANDID *adjective* 6. **off camera** while not being filmed. **on camera** while being filmed.
– COMB.: **camera-eye** an eye that records detailed impressions; a person capable of unusually detailed or detached observation or memory; **cameraman**: operating a camera professionally, esp. in cinema or television; **camera phone** a mobile phone with a built-in camera; **camera-ready** *adjective* (PRINTING) (of copy) in a form suitable for photographing or electronic scanning; **camera shake** (blurring due to) unintentional movement of the camera during photography or filming; **camera-shy** *adjective* not liking to be photographed or filmed; **camerawoman**: operating a camera professionally esp. in cinema or television; **camerawork** the manner or technique of positioning and using cameras in films, television, etc.
■ **camerist** *noun* (chiefly *US*, *arch.*) a person who uses a camera M19.

†camerade *noun* see COMRADE.

cameral /ˈkam(ə)r(ə)l/ *adjective*. M18.
[ORIGIN German *kameral* from medieval Latin *cameralis*, from Latin CAMERA (in medieval Latin sense 'treasury'): see -AL[1].]
hist. Of or pertaining to the management of state finance in Germany.

cameralism /ˈkam(ə)r(ə)lɪz(ə)m/ *noun*. E20.
[ORIGIN from CAMERAL + -ISM.]
hist. The theory that economic management should be directed primarily at benefiting the treasury (prevalent in 18th-cent. Germany); advocacy of this theory.
■ **cameralist** *noun* an advocate of cameralism E20.

cameralistic /ˌkam(ə)r(ə)ˈlɪstɪk/ *adjective*. L19.
[ORIGIN from CAMERAL or CAMERALIST: see -ISTIC.]
Characteristic of cameralism or cameralists; *gen.* pertaining to or characterized by emphasis on political factors in economic management.

camera lucida /ˌkam(ə)rə ˈluːsɪdə/ *noun phr.* Pl. **camera lucidas**. M18.
[ORIGIN Latin = bright chamber.]
An instrument by which the rays of light from an object are reflected by a prism and produce an image on paper placed beneath the instrument, traceable with a pencil.

camera obscura /ˌkam(ə)rə ɒbsˈkjʊərə/ *noun phr.* Pl. **camera obscuras**. E18.
[ORIGIN Latin = dark chamber.]
A darkened box or enclosure with an aperture for projecting an image of external objects on a screen placed at the focus of the lens; a building containing such a box or enclosure.

camerate /ˈkam(ə)rət/ *adjective*. M16.
[ORIGIN Latin *cameratus* pa. pple, formed as CAMERATE *verb*: see -ATE[2].]
Divided into chambers.

camerate /ˈkam(ə)reɪt/ *verb trans.* Now *rare* or *obsolete*. E17.
[ORIGIN Latin *camerat-* pa. ppl stem of *camerare* vault or arch over, formed as CAMERA: see -ATE[3].]
Chiefly as ***camerated*** *ppl adjective*.
1 *ARCHITECTURE*. Vault, arch over. E17.
2 Divide into chambers. M19.

camerlingo /kaməˈlɪŋgəʊ/ *noun*. Also **-lengo** /-ˈlɛŋgəʊ/. Pl. **-os**. E17.
[ORIGIN Italian from Frankish: see CHAMBERLAIN.]
A chamberlain or treasurer; *spec.* (*a*) the Pope's chamberlain and financial secretary; (*b*) the treasurer of the Sacred College of cardinals.

Cameronian /kaməˈrəʊnɪən/ *noun & adjective*. *hist.* L17.
[ORIGIN from *Cameron* (see below) + -IAN.]
▶**A** *noun*. A follower of Richard Cameron (1648–80), a Scottish Covenanter; a member of the Reformed Presbyterian Church. Also, a member of the Cameronian regiment (see below). L17.
▶**B** *adjective*. Of or pertaining to Richard Cameron, his tenets, or his followers. L17.
Cameronian regiment a former infantry regiment of the British army orig. raised from Cameron's followers and other Presbyterians.

Cameroonian /kaməˈruːnɪən/ *noun & adjective*. Also **-oun-**. M20.
[ORIGIN from *Cameroon* (see below) + -IAN.]
A native or inhabitant of, of or pertaining to, Cameroon, a country on the west coast of Africa between Nigeria and Gabon.

Camestres /kəˈmɛstriːz/ *noun*. M16.
[ORIGIN A mnemonic of scholastic philosophers first used in medieval Latin, A indicating a universal affirmative proposition, E a universal negative proposition.]
LOGIC. The second mood of the second syllogistic figure, in which the major premiss is a universal affirmative, the minor premiss and the conclusion universal negatives.

Camford /ˈkamfəd/ *noun*. M19.
[ORIGIN from CAMBRIDGE + OXFORD.]
= OXBRIDGE.

camiknickers /ˈkamɪnɪkəz/ *noun pl.* E20.
[ORIGIN from CAMISOLE + KNICKERS.]
A woman's one-piece undergarment which combines camisole and knickers.

camion /ˈkamɪən/ *noun*. L19.
[ORIGIN French.]
A large dray; a lorry; a bus.

†camis *noun*. *rare* (Spenser). Also **camus**. Only in L16.
[ORIGIN Prob. Spanish, Portuguese *camisa* from late Latin *camisia*: see CHEMISE.]
A light loose dress of silk or linen.

camisado /kamɪˈsɑːdəʊ/ *noun*. Now *arch.* or *hist.* Pl. **-oes**. M16.
[ORIGIN Spanish *camisada*, from *camisa*: see CAMIS, -ADO.]
A night attack; orig. one in which the attackers wore shirts over their armour as a means of mutual recognition.

Camisard /ˈkamɪsɑː, kamɪˈsɑː/ *noun*. E18.
[ORIGIN French from Provençal *camisa* from late Latin *camisia* (see CHEMISE): see -ARD.]
Any of the French Protestant insurgents of the Cévennes who rebelled against the persecution following the revocation of the Edict of Nantes (1685).

camise *noun* see KAMEEZ.

camisole /ˈkamɪsəʊl/ *noun*. E19.
[ORIGIN French from Italian *camiciola* or Spanish *camisola*, dim. of (respectively) *camicia*, *camisa* from late Latin *camisia*: see CHEMISE, -OLE[1].]
1 *hist.* A type of sleeved short jacket worn by men. E19.
2 *hist.* A short loose jacket worn by women when dressed in négligé. M19.
3 A woman's underbodice, usu. straight with shoulder straps and embroidered or otherwise ornamentally trimmed. M19.

camlet /ˈkamlɪt/ *noun & verb*. *arch.* Also **†cham-** (earlier), **†-blet**. LME.
[ORIGIN Old French *chamelot*, *c-*, ult. from Arabic *ḵamla(t)* nap, pile of velvet: popularly assoc. with CAMEL.]
▶**A** *noun*. Orig., a costly eastern fabric. Later, a light cloth used for cloaks etc., made of various materials. Also, a garment of such a fabric. LME.
†watered camlet: having a wavy appearance.
▶**†B** *verb trans.* Mark or variegate as (watered) camlet. E17–E18.
■ **camleteen** *noun* an imitation or inferior camlet M18.

cammock /ˈkamək/ *noun*[1]. *obsolete* exc. *dial.*
[ORIGIN Old English *cammoc*, of unknown origin.]
Restharrow. Also, any of various other weeds of pasture.

cammock /ˈkamək/ *noun*[2]. *obsolete* exc. *Scot.* Also **†-bock**. LME.
[ORIGIN App. from medieval Latin *cambuca*, *-buta* curved stick, crozier, app. of Gaulish origin and rel. to CAM *adjective & adverb*, CAMAN.]
1 A crooked staff; *esp.* a hockey stick etc.; a game in which this is used. LME.
2 A crooked piece of wood; a cambrel. LME.

camo /ˈkaməʊ/ *noun*. *colloq.* L20.
[ORIGIN Abbreviation.]
= CAMOUFLAGE.

camogie /kəˈməʊgi/ *noun*. E20.
[ORIGIN from Irish *camóg* CAMMOCK *n.*[2] + -IE.]
An Irish game resembling hurling, played by women or girls.

camois *adjective & noun* var. of CAMUS *adjective & noun*[2].

camomile /ˈkaməmʌɪl/ *noun*. Also **ch-**. ME.
[ORIGIN Old French & mod. French *camomille* from late Latin *c(h)amomilla* alt. of *chamaemelon* from Greek *khamaimēlon* lit. 'earth apple': so called from the smell of the flowers.]
A creeping aromatic plant of the composite family, *Chamaemelum nobile*, with yellow-centred white-rayed flowers, formerly much grown for its fragrance. Also (with specifying word), any of various plants (mostly weeds) of the related genera *Anthemis*, *Chamomilla*, and *Matricaria*.
stinking camomile: see STINKING *adjective*.
– COMB.: **camomile tea**: an infusion of the flowers of *Chamaemelum nobile*, taken as a tonic.

camoodi *noun* var. of CAMOUDIE.

Camorra /kəˈmɔːrə, -ˈmɒrə/ *noun*. Also **c-**. M19.
[ORIGIN Italian, perh. from Spanish *camorra* dispute, quarrel.]
A secret society akin to the Mafia operating in the Neapolitan district; *gen.* any organized body engaged in extortion or other dishonest activities.

camoudie /kəˈmuːdi/ *noun*. Also **-oodi** & other vars. E19.
[ORIGIN Arawak *kamudu*.]
A boa constrictor.

camouflage /ˈkaməflɑːʒ, -mʊf-/ *noun & verb*. E20.
[ORIGIN French, from *camoufler* verb (thieves' slang) from Italian *camuffare* disguise, deceive, perh. assoc. with French *camouflet* whiff of smoke in the face: see -AGE.]
▶**A** *noun*. The disguising or concealment of guns, ships, aircraft, etc., by obscuring with splashes of various colours, foliage, netting, smokescreens, etc.; the disguise so used; *gen.* any means of disguise or evasion. E20.

> J. K. GALBRAITH An extraordinarily elaborate exercise in social camouflage has kept us from seeing what has been happening. *attrib.*: N. TINBERGEN Developed dark cross-bars (the stickleback's disruptive camouflage pattern).

▶**B** *verb trans.* Conceal by camouflage. E20.

> F. TUOHY A scarlet wool dress designed to celebrate rather than camouflage her pregnancy. ANTHONY HUXLEY Unripe fruits are green to camouflage them.

C

camouflet /ˈkamʊflɛɪ/ *noun.* **M19.**
[ORIGIN French: see CAMOUFLAGE.]
MILITARY. A countermine containing an explosive charge intended to cause the collapse of an enemy's excavation. Also, a concealed subterranean cavity caused by an explosion.

camp /kamp/ *noun*[1]. Long *obsolete* exc. *hist.*
[ORIGIN Old English *camp, comp* = Old Frisian *camp, comp*, Middle Dutch *camp* (Dutch *kamp*), Old High German *champf* (German *kampf*), Old Norse *kapp*, from Germanic from Latin *campus* CAMP *noun*[2] (in medieval Latin sense 'combat, battle').]
†**1** Combat, battle, war. **OE–LME.**
2 In full ***camp-ball***. An ancient form of football in which large numbers engaged on each side. **E17.**

camp /kamp/ *noun*[2]. **E16.**
[ORIGIN Old French & mod. French (alongside *champ*) from Italian *campo* from Latin *campus* level field, place for games or military exercises.]
1 A place where troops are lodged or trained; (the remains of) an ancient fortified site. **E16.** ▸**b** (The scene of) military service; military life in general. **E18.**
DRYDEN The Youth of Rome . . pitch their sudden Camp before the Foe. **b** J. KEBLE Through court and camp.
armed camp: see ARMED *adjective*[1] 1. ***causewayed camp***: see CAUSEWAY.
2 An encampment; the temporary quarters, often in tents or cabins, of nomads, detainees, holidaymakers, Scouts, Guides, etc. **M16.** ▸**b** An assembly place for sheep or cattle. *Austral. & NZ.* **M19.**
AV *Exod.* 16:13 At even the Quailes came vp, and couered the campe. J. STEINBECK There was no order in the camp; little gray tents, shacks, cars were scattered about at random.
concentration camp, holiday camp, motor camp, summer camp, etc. ***Siwash camp***: see SIWASH *adjective*.
3 A body of troops etc. encamping and moving together; an army on campaign; *fig.* a host. *arch.* **M16.**
S. JOHNSON Multitudes follow the camp only for want of employment.
4 A body of people encamped together; a period spent encamped. **M18.**
5 *fig.* A body of adherents of a particular doctrine, theory, or party. **L19.**
JOHN BROOKE Europe was divided into two great camps: Catholic and Protestant. M. J. LASKY One of Milton's traditionalist contemporaries in the moderate camp.
a foot in both camps connection or sympathy with two opposite groups, factions, etc.
6 [Afrikaans *kamp*.] A portion of veld fenced off for pasture. *S. Afr.* **L19.**
– COMB.: **camp bed**, **camp chair**, etc.: folding and portable; **campcraft** skill at living in camp; **campdrafting** *Austral.* a sport in which each rider selects a bullock from a herd and drives it round a set course; **camp fever** typhus; **campfire** an open-air fire in a camp etc.; ***camp fire girl*** (US), a member of a training and recreational organization; **camp follower** (now usu. *derog.*) (**a**) a non-military worker or hanger-on in a camp etc.; (**b**) a disciple of a group or theory; **camp meeting** *US* a religious open-air or tent meeting often lasting several days; **camp oven** *Austral. & NZ* a three-legged iron cooking pot with a flat top; **campsite** a place for camping; **camp stool** a light stool with collapsible legs.

camp /kamp/ *adjective & noun*[3]. **E20.**
[ORIGIN Unknown.]
▸ **A** *adjective.* Ostentatious, exaggerated, affected, theatrical; effeminate, homosexual. **E20.**
▸ **B** *noun.* Camp behaviour, mannerisms, etc. **E20.**
high camp: see HIGH *adjective*.
■ **campery** *noun* camp behaviour or manner **M20.**

camp /kamp/ *verb*[1] *intrans. obsolete* exc. *dial.* or *hist.*
[ORIGIN Old English *campian*, from CAMP *noun*[1].]
Contend, esp. at camp-ball.

camp /kamp/ *verb*[2]. **M16.**
[ORIGIN French *camper*, formed as CAMP *noun*[2].]
1 *verb intrans.* Live or stay in a camp or tent; form or pitch one's camp; encamp; *gen.* take up residence, lodge. **M16.**
camp out lodge in the open in a camp.
2 *verb trans.* Establish or place in a camp. Now usu. in *pass.* **M16.**
OED The troops would be camped along the river side.
3 *verb intrans.* Of sheep or cattle: flock together, usu. for rest or at night. *Austral. & NZ.* **M19.**
4 *verb trans. & intrans. TELEPHONY.* Reserve (a call) for connection on to or *on to* an engaged telephone as soon as it becomes free. **L20.**
– COMB.: **camp-on (busy)** *TELEPHONY* a facility allowing a call to be camped on to an engaged telephone.

camp /kamp/ *verb*[3] *trans. & intrans.* **M20.**
[ORIGIN from CAMP *adjective & noun*[3].]
Do or behave in a camp manner.
camp it up behave affectedly or with exaggeration, overact.

campagna /kamˈpɑːnjə, *foreign* kamˈpaɲɲa/ *noun.* Also †**-a(g)nia.** **L16.**
[ORIGIN Italian from late Latin *campania*: see CHAMPAIGN. Cf. CAMPAIGN.]
1 Open country; champaign. Now *rare* exc. with ref. to the Campagna di Roma. **L16.**
†**2** A military campaign. **M–L17.**

campaign /kamˈpeɪn/ *noun & verb.* **E17.**
[ORIGIN French *campagne* (alongside Old French & mod. French *champagne*) from late Latin *campania*: see CHAMPAIGN. Cf. CAMPAGNA.]
▸ **A** *noun.* **1** (A tract of) open country, as opp. to hills, woods, etc.; champaign. Now *rare* or *obsolete*. **E17.**
2 A series of military operations in a definite area or with one objective or forming the whole or a distinct part of a war. **M17.**
on campaign on military service in the field.
†**3** An expedition, an excursion; a tour. Only in **18.**
4 Any organized course of action analogous to a military campaign; *esp.* one designed to arouse public support for a party in an election, a cause, etc. **L18.**
DICKENS I am now preparing for a final reading campaign. E. ROOSEVELT President Wilson . . started out on a campaign to take the cause of the League of Nations to the American people.
plan of campaign: see PLAN *noun*.
– COMB.: **campaign trail** a route taken in the course of a political campaign, with stops for canvassing etc. (chiefly in ***on the campaign trail***); **campaign wig** *hist.* a close-fitting wig with a curled forehead, worn for travelling.
▸ **B** *verb intrans.* Serve on or conduct a campaign. **E18.**
■ **campaigner** *noun* a person who serves in a campaign; *esp.* one who has served in many campaigns (***old campaigner***, a veteran, a person skilled in adapting to circumstances): **L17.**

campana /kamˈpɑːnə/ *noun.* **E17.**
[ORIGIN Late Latin = bell.]
1 A bell; a bell-shaped flower. Now *rare* or *obsolete*. **E17.**
2 A bell-shaped vase. **E19.**

campanero /kampəˈnɛːrəʊ/ *noun.* Pl. **-os.** **E19.**
[ORIGIN Spanish, from *campana* bell.]
The S. American bellbird.

†**campania** *noun* var. of CAMPAGNA.

campaniform /kamˈpanɪfɔːm/ *adjective.* **M18.**
[ORIGIN formed as CAMPANA + -I- + -FORM.]
Bell-shaped.

campanile /kampəˈniːli/ *noun.* **M17.**
[ORIGIN Italian, from *campana* bell + *-ile* -IL, -ILE.]
A (usu. lofty and detached) bell tower, esp. in Italy.

campanist /ˈkampənɪst/ *noun.* **L19.**
[ORIGIN medieval Latin *campanista*, formed as CAMPANA: see -IST.]
A person versed in the subject of bells; a campanologist.

campanology /kampəˈnɒlədʒi/ *noun.* **M19.**
[ORIGIN mod. Latin *campanologia*, formed as CAMPANA + -OLOGY.]
The subject of bells, their founding, ringing, etc.
■ **campanologer** *noun* = CAMPANOLOGIST **E19.** **campanoˈlogical** *adjective* **M19.** **campanoˈlogically** *adverb* **L19.** **campanologist** *noun* an expert in campanology, a student of bells **M19.**

campanula /kamˈpanjʊlə/ *noun.* **E17.**
[ORIGIN mod. Latin, formed as CAMPANA: see -ULE.]
A plant of the genus *Campanula*, with usu. blue, pink, or white bell-shaped flowers; a bellflower.

campanularian /ˌkampanjʊˈlɛːrɪən/ *adjective & noun.* **M19.**
[ORIGIN from mod. Latin *Campanularia* genus name, formed as CAMPANULA + *-aria*: see -ARY[1], -AN.]
ZOOLOGY. ▸**A** *adjective.* Of, pertaining to, or characteristic of the order Calyptoblastea of hydrozoans possessing bell-shaped hydrothecae. **M19.**
▸ **B** *noun.* A member of this order. **L19.**

campanulate /kamˈpanjʊlət/ *adjective.* **M17.**
[ORIGIN formed as CAMPANULA + -ATE[2].]
Chiefly *BOTANY & ZOOLOGY.* Bell-shaped.
■ Also **campanulated** *adjective* **M18.**

Campari /kamˈpɑːri/ *noun.* **E20.**
[ORIGIN The Italian manufacturer.]
(Proprietary name for) an aperitif flavoured with bitters; a drink of this.

Campeachy /kəmˈpiːtʃi/ *noun.* Also **Campeche.** **E17.**
[ORIGIN *Campeche*, port and state of Mexico.]
In full ***Campeachy wood***. = LOGWOOD.

camper /ˈkampə/ *noun.* **M17.**
[ORIGIN from CAMP *noun*[2], *verb*[2] + -ER[1].]
†**1** A military man, a soldier; a camp follower. **M–L17.**
2 A person who takes part in a camp meeting. *US.* **E19.**
3 A person who lives or lodges in a camp or tent; a resident in a holiday camp, summer camp, etc. **M19.**
4 A trailer or (more fully ***camper van***) motor vehicle furnished with beds and other equipment for camping. Orig. *US.* **M20.**

campesino /kampeˈsino, kampəˈsiːnəʊ/ *noun.* Pl. **-os** /-ɔs, -əʊz/. **M20.**
[ORIGIN Spanish.]
In Spain and Spanish-speaking countries: a peasant farmer.

campestral /kamˈpɛstr(ə)l/ *adjective.* **E18.**
[ORIGIN from Latin *campester, -tr-*, from *campus*: see CAMP *noun*[2], -AL[1].]
Pertaining to fields or open country; growing or living in fields.
■ Also †**campestrial** *adjective*: only in **17.**

camph- /kamf/ *combining form* of CAMPHOR *noun*.
■ **camphene** *noun* (*CHEMISTRY*) a crystalline bicyclic terpene, $C_{10}H_{16}$, present in many essential oils. **M19.** **camphine** *noun* (*hist.*) an oil for lamps, distilled from turpentine **M19.**

camphor /ˈkamfə/ *noun.* **ME.**
[ORIGIN Old French *camphore* or medieval Latin *camphora* from Arabic *kāfūr* from Malay *kapur* ult. from Sanskrit *karpūra*.]
1 A colourless crystalline terpenoid ketone, $C_{10}H_{17}O$, with an aromatic smell and bitter taste, which occurs in certain essential oils and is used esp. in pharmacy and as an insect repellent. **ME.** ▸**b** ***Borneo camphor***, †***camphor of Borneo***, an essential oil consisting chiefly of borneol, obtained from the tree *Dryobalanops aromatica*. **L17.**
†**2** A tree yielding camphor (cf. ***camphor tree*** below). **L16–L17.**
– COMB.: **camphor laurel** *Austral.* any of various trees of the genus *Cinnamomum*; **camphor tree** a tree of the laurel family, *Cinnamomum camphora*, which is native to the Far East and is the major natural source of camphor; **camphor-wood** (the timber of) any of various trees with fragrant wood.
■ **camphorate** *noun* a salt or ester of camphoric acid **L18.** †**camphorate** *adjective* camphorated **LME–E18.** **camphorate** *verb trans.* impregnate or treat with camphor **M17.** **camphoric** /kamˈfɒrɪk/ *adjective* of or pertaining to camphor (***camphoric acid***, a crystalline dibasic acid, $C_{10}H_{16}O_4$, obtained by the oxidation of camphor) **L18.**

camphor /ˈkamfə/ *verb trans.* **M16.**
[ORIGIN from the noun.]
Camphorate.

campimeter /kamˈpɪmɪtə/ *noun.* **L19.**
[ORIGIN from Latin *campus* field (see CAMP *noun*[2]) + -IMETER.]
An apparatus for measuring or mapping the field of vision of the eye.
■ **campimetry** *noun* **E20.**

campion /ˈkampɪən/ *noun.* **M16.**
[ORIGIN Perh. rel. to CHAMPION *noun*[1]. Orig. used for Latin *lychnis coronaria*, Greek *lukhnis stephanōmatikē* rose campion 'used for garlands'.]
Any of various plants of the genera *Silene* and *Lychnis* of the pink family, bearing red or white flowers with notched petals. Cf. LYCHNIS, SILENE.
bladder campion, moss campion, red campion, white campion, etc.

cample /ˈkamp(ə)l/ *verb intrans. obsolete* exc. *dial.* **L15.**
[ORIGIN App. from CAMP *verb*[1] + -LE[3].]
Quarrel, dispute, wrangle.

campo /ˈkampəʊ/ *noun.* Pl. **-os.** **M19.**
[ORIGIN (Amer.) Spanish, Portuguese, Italian = field, open country, from Latin *campus*: see CAMP *noun*[2].]
1 In S. America (esp. Brazil), a grass plain with occasional stunted trees; a savannah. Freq. in *pl.* **M19.**
2 A square in an Italian or Spanish town. **L19.**

campong *noun* see KAMPONG.

campoo /kamˈpuː/ *noun.* **E19.**
[ORIGIN Hindi *kampū* from Portuguese *campo* camp.]
hist. A brigade of Maratha troops, led by a European mercenary.

campshed /ˈkampʃɛd/ *noun.* Also **-shot** /-ʃɒt/ & other vars. **L15.**
[ORIGIN Prob. from CANT *noun*[1] + SHIDE.]
A facing of piles and boarding along the bank of a river etc. or at the side of an embankment.
■ **campshedding** (also **-sheeting** & other vars.) *noun* a campshed; campsheds collectively: **E19.**

campus /ˈkampəs/ *noun.* Orig. *US.* **L18.**
[ORIGIN Latin: see CAMP *noun*[2].]
The grounds and buildings of a college, university, etc., esp. where forming a distinct area; a separate part of a university; university or college life.

campy /ˈkampɪ/ *adjective. colloq.* **M20.**
[ORIGIN from CAMP *adjective & noun*[3] + -Y[1].]
= CAMP *adjective*.
■ **campily** *adverb* **L20.** **campiness** *noun* **L20.**

campylite /ˈkampɪlʌɪt/ *noun.* **M19.**
[ORIGIN formed as CAMPYLOTROPOUS + -ITE[1].]
MINERALOGY. A variety of mimetite, occurring as small rounded orange-yellow crystals.

campylobacter /ˈkampɪləʊˌbaktə, ˌkampɪləʊˈbaktə/ *noun.* **L20.**
[ORIGIN mod. Latin (see below), formed as CAMPYLOTROPOUS + BACTER(IUM.]
A bacterium of the genus *Campylobacter*, which includes curved and spiral forms causing food poisoning in humans and abortion in some farm animals.

campylotropous /kampɪˈlɒtrəpəs/ *adjective.* **M19.**
[ORIGIN from Greek *kampulos* bent + *-tropos* turning + -OUS.]
BOTANY. Of an ovule: bent transversely across its funicle.

CAMRA /ˈkamrə/ *abbreviation.*
Campaign for Real Ale.

camstone /ˈkamstəʊn/ *noun. Scot.* Also (earlier) †**calm-.** **E16.**
[ORIGIN from unidentified 1st elem. + STONE *noun*.]
A white limestone; pipeclay used to whiten doorsteps etc.

†**camus** *noun*[1] var. of CAMIS.

camus /ˈkaməs/ *adjective & noun*[2]. Now *rare* or *obsolete*. Also **-mois**. LME.
[ORIGIN Old French & mod. French, of unknown origin.]
▸ **A** *adjective*. Of the nose: low and concave. Of a person: snub-nosed. LME.
▸ †**B** *noun*. A person or animal with a low, concave nose. L15–M18.

camwood /ˈkamwʊd/ *noun*. L17.
[ORIGIN Prob. from Temne *k'am* + WOOD *noun*[1].]
= BARWOOD.

can /kan/ *noun*.
[ORIGIN Old English *canne*, corresp. to Middle Dutch *kanne* (Dutch *kan*), Old High German *channa* (German *kanne*), Old Norse *kanna*, ult. Germanic or from late Latin *canna*.]
1 A vessel for holding liquids, now *spec.* one of metal, and usu. cylindrical with a handle over the top. Also (chiefly *N. Amer.*), any large cylindrical metal container, a bin. OE. ▸**b** A measure of capacity; about a gallon. *Scot.* E19.

WORDSWORTH I have brought thee in this can fresh water from the brook.

ashcan, *jerrycan*, *oil can*, *watering can*, etc.
2 A (usu. cylindrical) container of tin plate or aluminium in which food, drink, etc., can be hermetically sealed; (such a container and) its contents. Cf. TIN *noun* 2. M19.

J. B. PRIESTLEY We sat in the office, with a can of beer each.

3 a A chimney pot. Chiefly *Scot.* M19. ▸**b** A lavatory. *N. Amer. slang.* E20. ▸**c** *the can*, jail. *slang* (chiefly *US*). E20. ▸**d** The buttocks. *N. Amer. slang.* M20. ▸**e** A protective jacket for a nuclear fuel rod. M20. ▸**f** In *pl.* Headphones. *slang.* L20.
– PHRASES: *can of worms*: see WORM *noun*. **carry the can (back)** *slang* bear the responsibility or blame. **in the can** safely recorded on film, tape, etc., completed. **take the can (back)** *slang* = *carry the can (back)* above. *tie a can on*, *tie a can to*: see TIE *verb*[1].
– COMB.: **can bank** a collection point to which empty cans may be taken for recycling; **can-buoy** a large cone-shaped marker buoy; **can-dock** a water lily, esp. of the yellow-flowered species; **can-opener** a tool for opening cans of food etc.
■ **canful** *noun* as much or as many as a can will hold, the contents of a can E18.

can /kan, *unstressed* k(ə)n/ *verb*[1]. Pres.: **can**; 2 sing. (*arch.*) **canst** /kanst, k(ə)nst/. Pa.: **could** /kʊd, *unstressed* kəd/; 2 sing. (*arch.*) **couldst** /kʊdst, kədst/, **couldest** /ˈkʊdɪst/. Neg. **can not**, **cannot** /ˈkanət/, (*colloq.*) **can't** /kɑːnt/; **could not**, (*colloq.*) **couldn't** /ˈkʊd(ə)nt/. No other parts used. See also CON *verb*[1].
[ORIGIN Old English *cunnan* = Old Frisian *kunna*, Old Saxon *cunnan* (Dutch *kunnen*), Old High German *kunnan* (German *können*), Old Norse *kunna*, Gothic *kunnan*, ult. from Indo-European base found also in Latin *gnoscere*, Greek *gignōskein* know: a Germanic preterite-present verb with primary meaning 'have learned, come to know'.]
▸ **I** As full verb.
†**1** *verb trans.* Know; be acquainted with; have learned. OE–M19.

J. FOXE Unlearned men that can no letters. JONSON She could the Bible in the holy tongue.

2 *verb intrans.* Have knowledge, know *of*. *arch.* ME.

S. ROWLANDS I never was there (that I can of). SIR W. SCOTT Thou canst well of wood-craft.

▸ **II** As auxiliary verb (often *ellipt.* with verb understood or supplied from the context).
3 Know how to, have learned to. Now absorbed in sense 4. ME.

SPENSER Well couth hee tune his pipe.

4 Have the power or capacity to; be able to. ME.

AV *Exod.* 7:21 The Egyptians could not drinke of the water. DEFOE I will do all I can with them. OED Such language can do no good to the cause. DAY LEWIS I can remember no pain, no perturbation, no sense of parting.

5 May possibly; be enabled by circumstances etc. to. ME. ▸**b** Be allowed or given permission to; may. *colloq.* L19.

STEELE The best Sort of Companion that can be. LD MACAULAY Even if it could be believed that the court was sincere. ANTHONY SMITH Other kinds of brain-dead patients could, or should, be regarded as potential donors. **b** T. B. REED Father says you can come.

6 In pa. form (*could* etc.). Feel inclined to, would like to. M17.

ADDISON I could wish our Royal Society would compile a Body of Natural History. J. P. DONLEAVY 'Take that ten shilling note, Mr Dangerfield, and get some eggs.' 'No, I couldn't.' 'Do. Please. I insist.'

– PHRASES: *as far as I can see*: see SEE *verb*. *as far as one can tell*: see TELL *verb*. **can do** *colloq.* it is possible, I am able or willing to do it. **can-do** *colloq.* showing determination to take action and achieve results. *cannot for the life of me*: see LIFE *noun*. *cannot resist*, *could not resist*: see RESIST *verb* 2. *can skill*: see SKILL *noun*. *can you tie that*: see TIE *verb*[1]. **no can do** *colloq.* it is not possible, I am not able or willing to do it. *walk before one can run*: see WALK *verb*[1]. *who cannot want the thought?*: see WANT *verb*. *you can say that again*: see SAY *verb*[1]. *you can talk*: see TALK *verb*. *you can't lose*: see LOSE *verb*. *you can't take it with you*: see TAKE *verb*. *you can't talk*: see TALK *verb*.

can /kan/ *verb*[2] *trans.* Infl. **-nn-**. M19.
[ORIGIN from CAN *noun*.]
1 Put into a can; preserve (meat, fruit, etc.) by sealing in cans. Cf. TIN *verb* 2. M19. ▸**b** *transf.* & *fig.* Confine; preserve, esp. by recording on film, tape, etc. M19. ▸**c** Cover (a nuclear fuel rod) with a protective jacket. M20.
2 a Expel, suspend, dismiss. *N. Amer. slang.* E20. ▸**b** Desist from, leave off, cut out. *slang* (orig. *US*). E20.

a W. GOLDMAN Getting canned is always two things, shocking and painful. **b** K. LETTE 'You're not fat. You've got a lovely fig . . ' 'Can it, Debbie.'

†**can** *verb*[3] see GIN *verb*[1].

can *verb*[4] var. of CON *verb*[2].

Can. *abbreviation*.
1 Canada.
2 Canadian.

Canaan /ˈkeɪnən/ *noun*. E17.
[ORIGIN ecclesiastical Latin *Chanaan* from ecclesiastical Greek *Khanaan* from Hebrew *kĕnaʻan* ancient name of western Palestine, promised in the Old Testament and Hebrew Scriptures to the children of Israel (*Exodus* 3:17 etc.).]
A land of promise; heaven.

Canaanite /ˈkeɪnənʌɪt/ *noun*. M16.
[ORIGIN from CANAAN + -ITE[1]. In sense 2 translating Greek *Kananitēs*, from Hebrew *qannā'* zealous.]
1 A native or inhabitant of Canaan; *fig.* a heathen. M16.
2 A zealot. Now *rare* or *obsolete*. E17.
■ **Canaanitic** /-ˈnɪtɪk/ *adjective* of Canaan; of or like a Canaanite: L19. **Canaanitish** *adjective* = CANAANITIC M16.

Canada /ˈkanədə/ *noun*. L17.
[ORIGIN A Federal state (formerly a Brit. territory) in N. America.]
▸ **I** *attrib.* **1** Used *attrib.* to designate things found in or associated with Canada. L17.
Canada balsam a resin exuded from the N. American balsam fir, *Abies balsamea*, and used esp. for mounting microscope specimens. **Canada bird** *Canad.* = PEABODY. **Canada Day** 1 July, observed as a public holiday in Canada to observe the day in 1867 when four of the former colonial provinces were united under one government as the Dominion of Canada (formerly called *Dominion Day*). **Canada goose** a large grey-brown, black, and white goose, *Branta canadensis*, native to N. America and widely introduced elsewhere. **Canada jay** the N. American grey jay, *Perisoreus canadensis*. **Canada thistle** *N. Amer.* a naturalized European thistle, *Cirsium arvense*, with spreading roots.
▸ **II** *ellipt.* **2** A Canada goose. L19.

Canadian /kəˈneɪdɪən/ *noun & adjective*. M16.
[ORIGIN from CANADA + -IAN.]
▸ **A** *noun*. A native or inhabitant of Canada. M16.
▸ **B** *adjective*. Of or pertaining to Canada or its people. L17.
– PHRASES & SPECIAL COLLOCATIONS: **Canadian pondweed** = *Canadian waterweed* (b) s.v. WATER *noun*. *Canadian waterweed*: see *waterweed* s.v. WATER *noun*. *French Canadian*: see FRENCH *adjective*.
■ **Canadiˈana** *noun pl.* [-ANA] publications or other items concerning or associated with Canada M19. **Canadianism** *noun* (*a*) Canadian character or spirit; (*b*) a Canadian idiom or word: L19. **Canadianize** *verb trans.* render Canadian in character E19.

Canadien /kanadjɛ̃/ *noun & adjective*. Fem. **-ienne** /-jɛn/. Pl. pronounced same. M19.
[ORIGIN French = CANADIAN.]
(A) French Canadian.

†**canaglia** *noun*. E17–E19.
[ORIGIN Italian: see CANAILLE.]
= CANAILLE.

canaille /kanaːj/ *noun*. L16.
[ORIGIN French from Italian *canaglia* lit. 'pack of dogs', from *cane* dog.]
The rabble, *the* populace.

canakin *noun* var. of CANNIKIN.

canal /kəˈnal/ *noun*. LME.
[ORIGIN Old French & mod. French, refashioning of *chanel* CHANNEL *noun*[1] after Latin *canalis* or Italian *canale*. Cf. CANNEL *noun*[1], KENNEL *noun*[2].]
1 *gen.* A pipe or tube for conveying fluid; a faucet; a tubular cavity. Now *rare* or *obsolete*. LME.
2 A tubular duct or passage in a plant or animal body. LME. ▸**b** A groove in a mollusc's shell for protrusion of a breathing tube. M19.
ALIMENTARY **canal**. *SEMICIRCULAR* **canal**. *spinal canal*: see SPINAL *adjective*. *STENSEN'S canal*. *VALLECULAR canal*.
3 A watercourse, a channel; a strait. *obsolete* exc. as in sense 4 or (*N. Amer.*) in proper names. M16. ▸†**b** An ornamental strip of water in a garden etc. M17–E19.
4 An artificial watercourse constructed for the purpose of inland navigation or to convey water for irrigation etc. (Now the predominant sense.) L17.
junction canal: see JUNCTION *noun* 2.
5 ASTRONOMY. [translating Italian *canali* channels.] Any of a network of linear markings on Mars reported by telescopic observers. L19.
– COMB.: **canal boat** a long narrow boat designed for use on canals; **canal rays** [translating German *Kanalstrahlen* 'channel rays'] PHYSICS streams of positive ions which move towards the cathode in a high-vacuum discharge tube.

canal /kəˈnal/ *verb*. *rare*. Infl. **-ll-**, ***-l-**. E19.
[ORIGIN from the noun.]
1 *verb trans.* = CANALIZE *verb* 1. E19.
2 *verb intrans.* Construct a canal or canals; travel by canal. Chiefly as *canalling verbal noun*. M19.

canaliculus /kanəˈlɪkjʊləs/ *noun*. Pl. **-li** /-lʌɪ, -liː/. M16.
[ORIGIN Latin *canaliculus* dim. of *canalis*: see CANAL *noun*, -CULE.]
Chiefly ANATOMY. A small channel or duct.
■ **canalicular** *adjective* of or pertaining to a canaliculus; minutely tubular: L19. **canaliculate** *adjective* minutely channelled or grooved M18. **canaliculated** *adjective* = CANALICULATE M18. **caˈnalicule** *noun* = CANALICULUS M19.

C

canalize /ˈkan(ə)lʌɪz/ *verb trans.* Also **-ise**. M19.
[ORIGIN French *canaliser*: see CANAL *noun*, -IZE.]
1 Make a canal through, provide with canals; provide with locks etc. like a canal, make into a canal. M19.
2 Provide with or convey through ducts or channels. L19.
3 *fig.* Give a specific direction etc. to. E20.

J. M. KEYNES Dangerous human proclivities can be canalised into comparatively harmless channels. A. WILSON She must not allow middle-aged rancour to canalize her happiness.

■ **canaliˈzation** *noun* M19.

canapé /ˈkanəpeɪ, -pi/ *noun*. L19.
[ORIGIN French.]
1 A piece of bread, toast, etc., with a small savoury on top. L19.
2 A sofa. L19.

canard /kəˈnɑːd, ˈkanɑːd/ *noun*. M19.
[ORIGIN French, lit. 'duck'.]
1 A false report, a hoax. M19.
2 An extra surface attached to an aircraft, hydrofoil, etc., for stability or control. Also, an aircraft fitted with this. E20.

Canarese *adjective & noun* var. of KANARESE.

Canarian /kəˈnɛːrɪən/ *noun & adjective*. M17.
[ORIGIN formed as CANARY *noun* + -IAN.]
▸ **A** *noun*. A native or inhabitant of the Canary Islands. M17.
▸ **B** *adjective*. Of or pertaining to the Canary Islands off the west coast of Africa. L18.

canary /kəˈnɛːri/ *noun*. Also (esp. in senses 1 & 2) **C-**. L16.
[ORIGIN from *Canary* Islands off the west coast of Africa, from French *Canarie* from Spanish *Canaria* from Latin *Canaria* (*insula* island), from *canis* dog: one of the islands was noted in Roman times for large dogs. In sense 3 from French *canari*, †*-ie* from Spanish *canario*.]
1 *hist. sing.* & †in *pl.* A lively dance similar to the jig (perh. orig. from the Canary Islands). L16.
2 *hist. sing.* & †in *pl.* Sweet wine from the Canary Islands. L16.
3 A songbird of the finch family, *Serinus canaria*, native to the Canary Islands, Madeira, and the Azores, of which wild individuals are green and the numerous cage varieties usu. yellow. Also, any of certain other birds of this genus. L16. ▸**b** A jailbird, a convict. *slang.* L17. ▸**c** A gold coin (from its colour). L18.
4 A bright yellow. Freq. *attrib.* M19.
– COMB.: **canary-coloured** *adjective* canary yellow; **canary creeper** a yellow-flowered climbing nasturtium, *Tropaeolum peregrinum*; **canary grass** a grass, *Phalaris canariensis*, grown as a source of birdseed; also, with specifying word, any other plant of this genus (*reed canary grass*: see REED *noun*[1]); **canary seed** seed used to feed canaries, *esp.* that of canary grass; **canary yellow** *noun & adjective* (of) a bright yellow.

†**canary** *verb intrans.* L16–E19.
[ORIGIN from the noun.]
Perform the canary or other lively dance.

canasta /kəˈnastə/ *noun*. M20.
[ORIGIN Spanish = basket, ult. from Latin *canistrum* CANISTER.]
A two-pack card game of the rummy family and of Uruguayan origin, usu. played by four in two partnerships; a meld of seven or more cards in this game.

canaster /kəˈnastə/ *noun*. E19.
[ORIGIN Spanish *canastro* basket (used to pack tobacco) from medieval Latin: see CANISTER.]
A kind of tobacco made of coarsely broken dried leaves.

canaut /kəˈnɔːt/ *noun*. Now *rare*. E17.
[ORIGIN Urdu from Persian from Turkish *qanāt*.]
In the Indian subcontinent: the side wall of a tent; a canvas enclosure.

cancan /ˈkankan/ *noun*. M19.
[ORIGIN French, redupl. of *canard* duck.]
A lively dance of French origin, orig. a form of quadrille, now performed by women and involving high kicks, usu. while holding up the front of the skirts.

cancel /ˈkans(ə)l/ *noun*. E19.
[ORIGIN from the verb.]
1 PRINTING. The suppression of text by excision (of a leaf, fold, or sheet) or by pasting over it. Also (*a*) (also *cancel leaf*) a leaf so cancelled; (*b*) the new leaf substituted. Cf. CANCELLANDUM, CANCELLANS *noun*. E19.
2 *gen.* An act of cancelling; a countermand. L19.

C

3 *MUSIC.* A natural sign cancelling a preceding sharp or flat. *US.* **E20.**

cancel /ˈkans(ə)l/ *verb.* Infl. **-ll-**, **-l-*. **LME.**
[ORIGIN Old French & mod. French *canceller* from Latin *cancellare* make lattice-wise, cross out (a writing), from *cancellus*, pl. *-li* cross-bars: see CANCELLI, CHANCEL.]
▸ **I** *verb trans.* **1** Deface or obliterate (writing), by drawing or stamping lines across it, or by puncturing or tearing what it is written on; annul (a deed, a stamp, etc.) by so marking. **LME.** ▸**b** *PRINTING.* Suppress (text, a page, leaf, etc.) after it has been set up or printed off. **M18.**

T. ARNOLD In my Catholic Pamphlet . . there is one paragraph which I should now cancel. R. GRAVES A postage-stamp . . issued and cancelled by the postmaster of . . Antigua.

2 *fig.* Render void (an obligation, promise, etc.). Also foll. by *out.* **LME.**

C. THIRLWALL All debts were to be cancelled.

3 *gen.* Obliterate, abolish; countermand, revoke an order or arrangements for; put an end to. Also (*rare*) with *off.* **M16.**

MILTON Canceld from Heav'n and sacred memorie, Nameless in dark oblivion let them dwell. J. GALSWORTHY He had just cancelled their trusteeships of his will. E. HEMINGWAY It would be too wet and . . the bull-baiting . . would be cancelled.

4 *MATH.* Strike out (the same factor) from the numerator and denominator, from both sides of an equation, etc. **L16.**

5 Neutralize, counterbalance, make up for. Freq. with *out.* **M17.**

DRYDEN With publick Zeal to cancel private Crimes. J. STALLWORTHY Credit And debit columns cancelled themselves out.

6 *MUSIC.* Mark a return to natural pitch after (a sharp or flat). *US.* **M19.**

▸ **II** *verb intrans.* †**7** Become void or null. *rare.* Only in **M17.**

8 Neutralize or counterbalance each other; be equal and opposite. Freq. with *out.* **E20.**

Listener The personal preferences of your contributors are . . likely to cancel out.

■ **cancellable** *adjective* (earlier in UNCANCELLABLE) **L17.** **canceller** *noun* **E17.** **cancelment** *noun* (*rare*) cancellation **E17.**

cancelbot /ˈkansəlbɒt/ *noun.* **L20.**
[ORIGIN from CANCEL + *-bot* (from ROBOT).]
COMPUTING. A program that searches for and deletes specified mailings from Internet newsgroups.

canceleer /kansəˈlɪə/ *noun & verb.* **L16.**
[ORIGIN Old Northern French *canceler* to swerve (mod. *chanceler*), used as noun: cf. -ER[4].]
▸ **A** *noun.* The action of a hawk in canceleering. **L16.**
▸ **B** *verb intrans.* Of a hawk: turn once or twice on the wing, in order to recover before striking. **M17.**

cancellandum /kansəˈlandəm/ *noun.* Pl. **-da** /-də/. **E20.**
[ORIGIN Latin, neut. gerundive of *cancellare* CANCEL *verb.*]
PRINTING. In full ***cancellandum leaf***. A leaf for which another is substituted. Cf. CANCELLANS, CANCEL *noun* 1.

cancellans /ˈkans(ə)lanz/ *noun & adjective.* **E20.**
[ORIGIN Latin, pres. pple of *cancellare* CANCEL *verb.*]
PRINTING. ▸**A** *noun.* A leaf which replaces another. Cf. CANCELLANDUM, CANCEL *noun* 1. **E20.**
▸ **B** *adjective.* Designating a leaf, sheet, fold, etc., which replaces another, or a slip which cancels text. **M20.**

cancellarian /kansəˈlɛːrɪən/ *adjective. rare.* **M19.**
[ORIGIN from medieval Latin *cancellarius* CHANCELLOR + -AN.]
Of, or of the nature of, a chancellor.

cancellate /ˈkans(ə)lət/ *adjective.* **M17.**
[ORIGIN formed as CANCELLATION + -ATE[2].]
Chiefly *BIOLOGY.* Marked or divided (as) with cross lines; (of bone) cancellous.
■ Also **cancellated** *adjective* **L17.**

cancellation /kansəˈleɪʃ(ə)n/ *noun.* **M16.**
[ORIGIN from Latin *cancellat-* pa. ppl stem of *cancellare* CANCEL *verb* + -ION: cf. medieval Latin *cancellatio(n-)*.]
1 The action of or an instance of cancelling; a cancelling mark etc. **M16.**
2 *spec.* The action or an instance of cancelling the reservation of a seat, room, etc.; a seat, room, etc., reservation of which has been cancelled. **M20.**

cancelli /kanˈsɛlʌɪ/ *noun pl.* **M17.**
[ORIGIN Latin, dim. of *cancer*, pl. *cancri* crossing bars, grating.]
†**1** Bars of latticework; *spec.* the latticed screen between the choir and body of a church. *rare.* **M17–E18.**
2 *ANATOMY.* The latticework of spongy bone tissue; the mesh of spaces within this. **E19.**
■ **cancellous** *adjective* (of bone) containing cancelli, having a spongy appearance, porous **M19.**

cancer /ˈkansə/ *noun.* **OE.**
[ORIGIN Latin = crab, creeping ulcer, after Greek *karkinos*: cf. CANKER *noun*, CARCINOMA.]
1 (**C-**.) (The name of) an inconspicuous constellation of the northern hemisphere, on the ecliptic between Gemini and Leo; *ASTROLOGY* (the name of) the fourth zodiacal sign, usu. associated with the period 22 June to 22 July (see note s.v. ZODIAC); the Crab. **OE.** ▸**b** A person born under the sign Cancer. **M20.**

attrib.: E. KIRK The Cancer men are far more constant than the Cancer women.

tropic of Cancer: see TROPIC *noun & adjective.*

2 A malignant tumour or growth of body tissue that tends to spread and may recur if removed; disease in which such a growth occurs. Cf. CANKER *noun* 1 (the usual form until 17). **OE.** ▸**b** *fig.* An evil spreading in the manner of a cancer. **M17.**

b M. L. KING A dangerous cancer of hatred and racism in our society.

soft cancer: see SOFT *adjective.*

†**3** A crab. **E17–L18.**

– COMB.: **cancer bush** *S. Afr.* a leguminous shrub, *Sutherlandia frutescens*, cultivated for its red flowers; **cancer-root** broomrape; **cancer stick** *slang* a cigarette; †**cancer-wort** fluellen.

■ **Cancerian** /kanˈsɪərɪən/ *noun & adjective* (**a**) *noun* a person born under the sign Cancer; (**b**) *adjective* of or pertaining to the sign Cancer; (characteristic of one) born under Cancer: **E20.** **canceriˈcidal**, **canceroˈcidal** *adjectives* tending to destroy cancer cells **M20.**

cancer /ˈkansə/ *verb trans.* **L18.**
[ORIGIN from the noun.]
Affect with or as with cancer; eat into in the manner of a cancer.

GOLDSMITH The application of toads to a cancered breast. M. BRAGG This strident fanaticism which had . . cancered him with revolt.

cancerate /ˈkansəreɪt/ *verb trans. & intrans.* **L17.**
[ORIGIN Late Latin *cancerat-* pa. ppl stem of *cancerare*, formed as CANCER *noun*: see -ATE[3].]
Make or become cancerous. Chiefly as ***cancerated*** *ppl adjective.*

cancerous /ˈkans(ə)rəs/ *adjective.* **M16.**
[ORIGIN from CANCER *noun* + -OUS.]
Of the nature of or affected with cancer.

fig.: K. TYNAN This fantasy, once mild, has grown cancerous and now infects his whole world.

■ **cancerously** *adverb* **M18.** **cancerousness** *noun* **M18.**

cancrine /ˈkaŋkrʌɪn/ *adjective. rare.* **M18.**
[ORIGIN from Latin *cancr-* CANCER *noun* + -INE[1].]
1 Like or suggestive of a crab. **M18.**
2 *spec.* Of Latin verse: palindromic. **M19.**

cancrinite /ˈkaŋkrɪnʌɪt/ *noun.* **M19.**
[ORIGIN from Georg *Cancrin* (1774–1845), Russian statesman + -ITE[1].]
MINERALOGY. A hexagonal aluminosilicate and carbonate of sodium and calcium which belongs to the feldspathoid group and usu. occurs as masses of yellow-brown crystals.

cancrizans /ˈkaŋkrɪzanz/ *adjective, adverb, & noun.* **L18.**
[ORIGIN medieval Latin pres. pple of *cancrizare* walk backwards, formed as CANCROID: see -IZE.]
MUSIC. (Designating, pertaining to, in the manner of) a canon in which the theme or subject is repeated backwards in the second part.

cancroid /ˈkaŋkrɔɪd/ *adjective & noun.* **E19.**
[ORIGIN from Latin *cancr-*, CANCER *noun* + -OID.]
▸ **A** *adjective.* **1** Like a crab, esp. in structure. **E19.**
2 Resembling cancer. **M19.**
▸ **B** *noun.* **1** A crab or related crustacean. *rare.* **M19.**
2 A disease resembling cancer; a mild form of cancer. **M19.**

candareen /kandəˈriːn/ *noun.* **E17.**
[ORIGIN Malay *kenderi.*]
A former Chinese monetary unit equal to ten cash; a former Chinese unit of weight equal to about 0.4 gram (six grains).

c & b *abbreviation.*
CRICKET. Caught and bowled by.

candela /kanˈdɛlə, -ˈdiːlə, ˈkandɪlə/ *noun.* **M20.**
[ORIGIN Latin *candela*: see CANDLE *noun.*]
PHYSICS. A unit of luminous intensity, equal to 1/60 of the luminous intensity per square centimetre of the surface of a black body at the temperature of solidification of platinum.

candelabrum /kandɪˈlɑːbrəm, -ˈleɪ-/ *noun.* Pl. **-bra** /-brə/, *****-brums***. **E19.**
[ORIGIN Latin, from *candela* CANDLE *noun.*]
A large usu. branched ornamental candlestick or lampholder carrying several lights.
– COMB.: **candelabrum tree** a tropical African tree of the genus *Euphorbia*, with foliage shaped like a candelabrum.
– NOTE: The sing. form is often assumed to be *candelabra* and hence its pl. is interpreted as *candelabras.*

candelilla /kandəˈliːljə/ *noun.* **E20.**
[ORIGIN Spanish = little candle.]
A southern N. American shrub of the genus *Euphorbia*, yielding a hard wax (***candelilla wax***).

candent /ˈkand(ə)nt/ *adjective.* Now *rare.* **L15.**
[ORIGIN Latin *candent-* pres. ppl stem of *candere* be white, glow: see -ENT.]
At a white heat; glowing with heat.

candescent /kanˈdɛs(ə)nt/ *adjective. rare.* **E19.**
[ORIGIN from Latin *candere*: see CANDENT, -ESCENT.]
Glowing (as) with heat.
■ **candescence** *noun* **L19.**

candid /ˈkandɪd/ *adjective & noun.* **M17.**
[ORIGIN French *candide* or Latin *candidus*, from *candere* be white, glisten: see -ID[1].]
▸ **A** *adjective.* †**1** White. **M17–E19.**

DRYDEN The stones came candid forth, the hue of innocence.

†**2** Illustrious, fortunate. **M17–E18.**
3 Pure, clear, innocent. *arch.* **M17.**

BROWNING Where does the figment touch her candid fame?

4 Unbiased, impartial; just, fair. *arch.* **M17.**

EARL OF CHATHAM Keep your mind in a candid state of suspense.

†**5** Free from malice; kindly; favourably disposed. **M17–E19.**

POPE Laugh where we must, be candid where we can.

6 Frank, open; ingenuous; outspoken. **L17.** ▸**b** Of a photograph or photography: unposed, informal. **E20.**

J. A. FROUDE A . . very candid account of Henry's feelings. J. BARNES Previously I had . . been honest just for effect, comparatively candid.

candid camera a small camera for taking informal pictures of people, freq. without their knowledge.
▸ **B** *noun.* An informal or unposed photograph. *colloq.* **M20.**
■ **candidly** *adverb* **M17.** **candidness** *noun* **E17.**

candida /ˈkandɪdə/ *noun.* **M20.**
[ORIGIN mod. Latin (see below), fem. of Latin *candidus*: see CANDID.]
1 A yeastlike fungus of the genus *Candida*, esp. *C. albicans*. **M20.**
2 = CANDIDIASIS. **L20.**

candidacy /ˈkandɪdəsi/ *noun.* **M19.**
[ORIGIN from CANDIDATE: see -ACY.]
The position or status of a candidate; candidature.

candidate /ˈkandɪdeɪt, -dət/ *noun & verb.* **E17.**
[ORIGIN Old French & mod. French *candidat* or Latin *candidatus* clothed in white, a candidate for office (who appeared in a white toga), from *candidus*: see CANDID, -ATE[1].]
▸ **A** *noun* **I 1** A person who seeks or is nominated for (election to) an office, honour, position, etc.; *spec.* an examinee; more *gen.*, an aspirant, one who seeks something. (Foll. by *for*, †*of.*) **E17.**

S. JOHNSON A candidate for literary fame. J. BUCHAN I became the Conservative candidate for the counties of Peebles and Selkirk. DAY LEWIS The 'infant' candidate for baptism turned out to be a strapping boy of nine or ten.

2 A person or thing thought likely or worthy to gain a particular position. **M18.**

GOLDSMITH If ever there was a candidate for Tyburn, this is one. J. NARLIKAR The X-ray source Cygnus X-1 is perhaps the most promising candidate for the location of a black hole so far known.

▸ **II 3** *ROMAN HISTORY.* A member of one of four companies into which the imperial guard was divided. **M17.**
▸ **B** *verb intrans.* Stand as a candidate. Chiefly *US.* **M19.**
■ **candidateship** *noun* = CANDIDACY **L18.**

candidature /ˈkandɪdətʃə, -tʃʊə/ *noun.* **M19.**
[ORIGIN from CANDIDATE + -URE, prob. after French.]
The action of standing for election; the fact or status of being a candidate.

candidiasis /kandɪˈdʌɪəsɪs/ *noun.* Pl. **-ases** /-əsiːz/. **M20.**
[ORIGIN from CANDIDA + -IASIS.]
MEDICINE & VETERINARY MEDICINE. Infection with candida, esp. causing oral or vaginal thrush.

candied /ˈkandɪd/ *ppl adjective.* **E17.**
[ORIGIN from CANDY *verb* + -ED[1].]
1 Preserved or encrusted (as) with sugar; crystallized. **E17.**
candied peel: of citrous fruits, preserved with sugar and used in cookery.
2 *fig.* Specious, flattering. **E17.**

candiru /kandɪˈruː/ *noun.* **M19.**
[ORIGIN Portuguese from Tupi *candirú.*]
A tiny bloodsucking catfish, *Vandellia cirrhosa*, of the Amazon river system.

candle /ˈkand(ə)l/ *noun.* **OE.**
[ORIGIN Latin *candela*, earlier *candela*, from *candere* be white, glisten. In Middle English from Anglo-Norman & Old French, also from Latin.]
1 A (usu. cylindrical) body of wax, tallow, etc., enclosing a wick, for giving light by burning. **OE.** ▸**b** *fig.* A source of light, or of mental or spiritual illumination; the 'light' of life. Now *rare* or *obsolete.* **OE.**
bell, book, and candle: see BELL *noun*[1]. **burn the candle at both ends** exhaust one's strength or resources through undertaking too much. ***hold a candle to the Devil***: see HOLD *verb.* ***mould-candle***: see MOULD *noun*[3] 14. ***mutton candle***: see MUTTON 4. **not able to hold a candle to**, **not fit to hold a candle to** not to be compared with, inferior to. **not worth the candle** not worth the cost or effort (esp. in ***the game is not worth the candle***).

paschal candle: see PASCHAL *adjective*. *Roman candle*: see ROMAN *adjective*. **sell by the candle**, **sell by inch of candle** *arch.*: by auction at which the time allowed for bids is set by the burning of a candle, the last bid received during this time securing the article. *smell of the candle*: see SMELL *verb* 8a. *tallow candle*: see TALLOW *noun* 3.

2 A preparation containing aromatic etc. substances for diffusion during burning; a pastille. *obsolete* exc. *hist.* LME.

3 *PHYSICS.* A unit of luminous intensity, superseded by the candela. Also ***international candle***. Cf. ***candlepower*** below. L19.

standard candle: see STANDARD *adjective*.

4 The flower of a horse chestnut tree. E20.

in candle (of a horse-chestnut tree) in flower.

– COMB.: **candle-beam** a rood-beam; **candleberry** (the fruit of) any of various trees or shrubs whose fruit yields a wax or oil used for candles; *esp.* (*a*) (also ***candleberry myrtle***) a bayberry or related shrub; (*b*) (also ***candleberry tree***) the kukui tree; **candle end** the burnt-down end of a candle; *fig.* (*arch.*) a trifle, a scrap; **candlefish** *N. Amer.* = EULACHON; **candlelight** (*a*) the light given by a candle or candles; (*b*) dusk, twilight; **candlelit** *adjective* lit by a candle or candles; **candlenut** = KUKUI; also, its fruit; **candlepower** illuminating power expressed in candles (sense 3); ***candle-snuffer***: see SNUFFER *noun*[1]; **candlestick** a holder for a candle or (less commonly) candles (***the butcher, the baker, the candlestick-maker***: see BUTCHER *noun*); **candle-tree** (*a*) = **candleberry** (a) above; (*b*) the Central American tree *Parmentiera cerifera*, with very long cylindrical fruit; **candle-waster** *arch.* a person who studies or revels late into the night; **candlewick** (*a*) the wick of a candle; (*b*) (material with a raised usu. tufted pattern in) a thick soft cotton yarn; **candle-wood** resinous wood burning with a bright flame; a tree yielding this, esp. (*N. Amer.*) of the genus *Fouquieria*.

candle /ˈkand(ə)l/ *verb trans.* L17.

[ORIGIN from the noun.]

†**1** Cover over or rub with candle grease. *rare.* L17–E19.

2 Examine the contents of (an egg etc.) by holding it between the eye and a source of light. L19.

■ **candler** *noun* E20.

Candlemas /ˈkand(ə)lmas, -məs/ *noun.*

[ORIGIN Old English *candelmæsse*, from CANDLE *noun* + MASS *noun*[1].]

(The date, 2 February, of the celebration of) the feast of the Purification of the Virgin Mary and the presentation of Jesus in the Temple, when candles are blessed (one of the Scottish quarter days).

candomblé /kandɒmˈbleɪ/ *noun.* M20.

[ORIGIN Brazilian Portuguese.]

A Brazilian sect of the macumba cult.

candour /ˈkandə/ *noun.* Also ***-or.** LME.

[ORIGIN Latin *candor*, from base of *candidus*, *candere*: see CANDID, -OUR. Cf. French *candeur*.]

1 Whiteness; brilliance. Long *rare.* LME.

†**2** Stainless character; purity, innocence. L15–E18.

3 Freedom from bias, impartiality, fairness. Now *rare* or *obsolete.* M17.

†**4** A favourable disposition; good nature; kindness. M17–E19.

5 The quality of being open and honest; frankness, openness. M18.

J. H. NEWMAN Openness and candour are rare qualities in a statesman.

C & W *abbreviation.*

Country and western.

candy /ˈkandi/ *noun*[1]. E17.

[ORIGIN Marathi *khaṇḍī*.]

A weight formerly used in the Indian subcontinent, generally equal to 230 or 250 kg.

candy /ˈkandi/ *noun*[2]. M17.

[ORIGIN from SUGAR CANDY.]

1 Crystallized sugar, made by repeated boiling and slow evaporation. M17.

2 A sweet confection; sweets collectively. Chiefly *N. Amer.* E19.

cotton candy, *cough candy*, etc.

3 Drugs, narcotics. *N. Amer. slang.* M20.

– COMB.: **candy ass** *N. Amer. slang* a timid or cowardly person, a despicable person; **candy-assed** *adjective* (*N. Amer. slang*) timid, cowardly, despicable; **candy bar** *N. Amer.* a bar of toffee or other sweet substance, a bar of chocolate; **candy cane** *N. Amer.* a stick of striped rock with a curved end, resembling a walking stick; ***candyfloss***: see FLOSS *noun*[2] 4; **candyman** (*a*) (chiefly *hist.*) an itinerant seller of sweets etc.; (*b*) *N. Amer. slang* a pedlar or pusher of drugs; **candy store** *N. Amer.* a sweetshop; **candy stripe** a pattern, in alternate stripes of white and colour (esp. pink); **candy-striped** *adjective* having candystripes; **candy-striper** *N. Amer.* a (usu. teenage) volunteer assistant nurse in a hospital (from the striped uniform worn); **candy sugar** = SUGAR CANDY.

candy /ˈkandi/ *verb.* M16.

[ORIGIN from CANDY *noun*[2], after French *candir*, from *candi* taken as pa. pple: see SUGAR CANDY.]

1 *verb trans.* Preserve by coating and impregnating with crystallized sugar; *fig.* sweeten, render more acceptable in form or appearance. M16.

2 *verb trans.* Crystallize (sugar) by boiling; *gen.* make into crystals. L16.

3 *verb trans.* Cover or coat with a crystalline substance. E17.

4 *verb intrans.* Crystallize; become encrusted (as) with sugar. M17.

candytuft /ˈkandɪtʌft/ *noun.* E17.

[ORIGIN from *Candy* obsolete form of *Candia* the island of Crete + TUFT *noun*.]

Any of various cruciferous plants of the genus *Iberis*, with white, pink, or purple flowers in flat tufts; = IBERIS.

cane /keɪn/ *noun*[1] & *verb.* LME.

[ORIGIN Old French *can(n)e* from Latin *canna* reed, cane, tube, pipe, from Greek *kanna*, *kannē* from Semitic (cf. Assyrian *qanū*, Hebrew *qāneh* reed).]

▸ **A** *noun.* **1** The hollow jointed woody stem of certain reeds and grasses, as bamboo and sugar cane; the solid stem of slender palms, as the rattan, Malacca, etc. Also, the stem of the raspberry and its congeners. LME.

sugar cane: see SUGAR *noun*.

†**2 a** A pipe, a tube. LME–E18. ▸**b** A solid stick or rod of various substances, esp. glass. E17.

3 A length of cane used as an instrument of punishment, as a walking stick, as a support for a plant, etc.; any slender walking stick. L16. ▸†**b** A dart or lance made of a cane. L16–L17.

MALACCA cane. *WHANGEE cane*.

4 Canes collectively, esp. as material for wickerwork. L18.

– COMB.: **cane brake** *N. Amer.* (*a*) a tract of land overgrown with canes; (*b*) a tall woody grass, *Arundinaria gigantea*, forming brakes; **cane chair** a chair with a seat of woven strips of cane; **cane-coloured** *adjective* (esp. of pottery) of the colour of cane, buff, yellowish; **cane grass** (*a*) = ***cane brake*** (b) above; (*b*) a tall Australian grass, *Glyceria ramigera*; **cane juice** the juice of the sugar cane; **cane rat** an African rodent of the genus *Thryonomys*; **cane sugar** sugar obtained from the sugar cane; sucrose; **cane syrup** syrup obtained from the sugar cane; **cane toad** a very large brown toad, *Bufo marinus*, which is native to tropical and subtropical America and has been introduced elsewhere for purposes of pest control; also called ***giant toad***, ***marine toad***; **cane trash** bagasse from sugar cane; **canework** strips of cane interwoven and used to form the backs and seats of chairs and other articles of furniture; **cane-worker** a person who makes articles of cane.

▸ **B** *verb trans.* **1** Beat with a cane. M17. ▸**b** Beat (a lesson) *into* a person with a cane. M19.

2 Weave cane into (a chair etc.). L17.

3 Punish severely; defeat or criticize heavily. E18.

■ **caned** *adjective* (*a*) (of furniture) made or repaired with cane; (*b*) (*slang*) intoxicated by drink or drugs: L17. **caning** *verbal noun* (*a*) the action of the verb; (*b*) a beating with a cane. E18.

†**cane** *noun*[2] var. of KHAN *noun*[2].

†**canel** *noun*[1]. Also **-nn-**. ME–M18.

[ORIGIN Old French *canele* (mod. *cannelle*) from Provençal *canela* dim. of *cana* CANE *noun*[1]. Cf. medieval Latin CANELLA.]

Cinnamon.

†**canel** *noun*[2] var. of CANNEL *noun*[1].

canella /kəˈnɛlə/ *noun.* Also **-nn-**. L17.

[ORIGIN medieval Latin = CANEL *noun*[1].]

†**1** *gen.* Cinnamon. L17–L19.

2 = ***wild cinnamon*** s.v. CINNAMON. M18.

canephora /kəˈnɛf(ə)rə, -ˈniː-/ *noun.* Pl. **-rae** /-riː/. E17.

[ORIGIN Latin *canephora* fem., from Greek *kanēphoros* adjective, from *kaneon* basket + *-phoros* carrying.]

In ancient Greece, each of the maidens who carried on their heads baskets bearing sacred things used at certain feasts; *ARCHITECTURE* a caryatid representing or resembling such a maiden.

Canes Venatici /ˌkeɪmiːz viːˈnatɪsʌɪ/ *noun phr.* E18.

[ORIGIN Latin *canes venatici*, from *canis* dog + *venaticus* used for hunting.]

(The name of) an inconspicuous constellation of the northern hemisphere near Ursa Major; the Hunting Dogs.

canezou /ˈkɑːnzuː/ *noun.* E19.

[ORIGIN French, of unknown origin.]

hist. A woman's garment like a blouse of muslin or cambric.

Canfield /ˈkanfiːld/ *noun.* E20.

[ORIGIN R. A. *Canfield* (1855–1914), Amer. gambler.]

A card game of patience for one player, in N. America the same as British demon, in Britain the same as N. American Klondike.

cang *verb* & *noun* var. of CANGUE *verb* & *noun*.

cangia /ˈkandʒə/ *noun.* E18.

[ORIGIN Italian from Turkish *kanca* hook (in *kancabaş* boat with recurved bows) from Venetian Italian *ganzo* from Spanish *gancho* ult. from Celtic: cf. French *cange*.]

A light boat used on the Nile.

cangue /kaŋ/ *verb trans.* & *noun.* Also **cang**, (earliest) †**congo**, pl. **-oes**. L17.

[ORIGIN French from Portuguese *canga* yoke from Annamese *gong*.]

Chiefly *hist.* (Cause to wear) a heavy wooden board hung round the neck as punishment in China.

can-hooks /ˈkanhʊks/ *noun pl.* L15.

[ORIGIN from unkn. 1st elem. + HOOK *noun* + -S[1].]

Chiefly *NAUTICAL.* (Tackle consisting of) two hooks joined by a short length of chain or rope, used for hoisting casks etc.

canicular /kəˈnɪkjʊlə/ *adjective.* ME.

[ORIGIN Late Latin *canicularis*, from *canicula* Dog Star, dim. of *canis* dog.]

1 Of or pertaining to the Dog Star (Sirius); of or pertaining to the dog days. ME.

E. POUND The dry earth pants against the canicular heat.

canicular days the dog days. **canicular year** the ancient Egyptian year computed from one heliacal rising of Sirius to the next.

2 Pertaining to a dog. *joc.* L16.

■ **canicule** *noun* (*rare*) [French] the dog days E18.

C

canid /ˈkanɪd/ *noun.* L19.

[ORIGIN mod. Latin *Canidae* (see below), from Latin *canis* dog: see -ID[3].]

ZOOLOGY. An animal of the family Canidae, which includes dogs, wolves, and foxes.

canine /ˈkeɪnʌɪn, ˈka-/ *noun* & *adjective.* LME.

[ORIGIN French *canin(e)* or Latin *caninus*, *-ina*, from *canis* dog: see -INE[1].]

▸ **A** *noun.* **1** A canine tooth (see below). (*rare* before M19.) LME.

2 A dog (chiefly *joc.*); *gen.* any canid. M19.

▸ **B** *adjective.* **1** Of, pertaining to, or characteristic of a dog or dogs; having the nature or qualities of a dog; (of appetite etc.) voracious, bulimic. E17.

canine madness *arch.* rabies. ***canine*** PARVOVIRUS.

2 ***canine tooth***, a strong pointed tooth situated between the incisors and premolars (one of four in a complete human dentition). E17.

■ **caˈniniform** *adjective* (of teeth) having a shape like that of a canine tooth L19. **caninity** /kəˈnɪnɪti/ *noun* doglike nature, canine quality L18.

canions /ˈkanɪənz/ *noun pl.* L16.

[ORIGIN formed as CANYON. Cf. CANNON *noun* 2C.]

hist. Ornamental rolls on the ends of the legs of breeches.

Canis /ˈkeɪnɪs, ˈkanɪs/ *noun.* LME.

[ORIGIN Latin *canis* dog.]

1 ***Canis Major***: (the name of) a constellation of the southern hemisphere on the edge of the Milky Way, near Puppis; the Great Dog; (formerly) Sirius, its brightest star. LME.

2 ***Canis Minor***: (the name of) a constellation of the northern hemisphere on the edge of the Milky Way, near Gemini; the Little Dog; (formerly) Procyon, its brightest star. LME.

canister /ˈkanɪstə/ *noun* & *verb.* L15.

[ORIGIN Latin *canistrum* from Greek *kanastron* wicker basket, from *kanna* reed: see CANE *noun*[1].]

▸ **A** *noun.* **1** A basket (for bread, flowers, etc.). *literary.* L15.

2 A small container, usu. of metal, used for tea, shot, etc. E18.

3 *hist.* In full ***canister-shot***. Small bullets packed in cases that fit the bore of a gun. E19.

▸ **B** *verb trans.* **1** Fasten a canister to. Now *rare* or *obsolete.* E19.

2 Put in a canister. M19.

canities /kəˈnɪʃiːz/ *noun.* E19.

[ORIGIN Latin, from *canus* white.]

MEDICINE. Whitening or greying of the hair.

canker /ˈkaŋkə/ *noun.* ME.

[ORIGIN Old Northern French *cancre* (Old French CHANCRE) from Latin *cancr-*, CANCER *noun*.]

1 Orig. = CANCER *noun* 2. Later, a sore, an ulcer, ulcerous disease, (esp. of animals). ME.

2 a A caterpillar or grub that destroys buds or leaves. Cf. ***canker worm*** below. LME. ▸**b** Necrotic disease of plants, esp. fruit trees. M16.

3 Rust. *obsolete* exc. *dial.* LME.

4 *fig.* A corrupting or corrosive influence. M16.

5 In full ***canker rose***. A dogrose. *dial.* L16.

– COMB.: †**canker bloom** the flower of the dogrose; †**canker blossom** = sense 2a above; ***canker rose***: see sense 5 above; **canker worm** = sense 2a above; *spec.* (*N. Amer.*) a geometrid moth larva which destroys the foliage of trees.

■ **cankerous** *adjective* of the nature of a canker; corroding, infectious: LME. **cankery** *adjective* (*a*) cankerous; cankered; (*b*) *Scot.* cantankerous, ill-natured: LME.

canker /ˈkaŋkə/ *verb.* LME.

[ORIGIN from the noun.]

1 *verb trans.* Consume (as) with canker; infect, corrupt. LME. ▸**b** Rust, corrode, tarnish. *obsolete* exc. *dial.* LME.

2 *verb intrans.* Become consumed or infected (as) with canker; rot, fester, decay. E16.

■ **cankered** *adjective* affected with canker; *fig.* corrupt, soured, malignant, crabbed: LME.

†**cann** *verb* var. of CON *verb*[2].

canna /ˈkanə/ *noun*[1]. M18.

[ORIGIN mod. Latin *Canna* (see below) from Latin *canna* CANE *noun*[1].]

A plant of the genus *Canna*, native to tropical and subtropical America, with bright yellow, red, or orange flowers and ornamental leaves. Also ***canna lily***.

canna *noun*[2] var. of CANNACH.

cannabinoid /ˈkanəbɪnɔɪd/ *noun.* M20.

[ORIGIN formed as CANNABINOL + -OID.]

CHEMISTRY. Any of a group of closely related compounds which includes cannabinol and the active constituents of cannabis.

C

cannabinol /ˈkanəbɪnɒl, kəˈnab-/ *noun*. L19.
[ORIGIN from CANNABIS + -OL.]
CHEMISTRY. A crystalline tricyclic phenol, $C_{21}H_{26}O_2$, derivatives of which (notably a tetrahydro-derivative) are the physiologically active constituents of cannabis.

cannabis /ˈkanəbɪs/ *noun*. E18.
[ORIGIN Latin from Greek *kannabis*.]
1 A herbaceous plant with serrated leaves, *Cannabis sativa* subsp. *indica* (producing a psychotropic drug) and *sativa* (producing hemp fibre); hemp. E18.
2 A preparation of any part of this plant used as a psychotropic drug, or medicinally; marijuana. M19.
– COMB.: **cannabis resin** a sticky substance containing the active principles of cannabis, prepared esp. from the flowering tops of the female plant.

cannach /ˈkaːnəx/ *noun*. *Scot.* Also **canna** /ˈkanə/. E19.
[ORIGIN Gaelic, Irish *canach*.]
Cotton grass.

canned /kand/ *adjective*. M19.
[ORIGIN from CAN *verb*[2] + -ED[1].]
1 Preserved or contained in a can; tinned. M19.
2 *fig.* Of music etc.: artificially produced; *esp.* recorded, not live. E20.
3 Intoxicated, drunk. *slang*. E20.

†**cannel** *noun*[1]. Also **canel**. ME–M18.
[ORIGIN Old Northern French *canel* = Old French *chanel*: see CHANNEL *noun*[1]. Cf. CANAL *noun*, KENNEL *noun*[2].]
A channel, a watercourse; a gutter; a pipe, a tube, a faucet.
– COMB.: **cannel-bone** (*a*) the collarbone; (*b*) the cervical vertebrae.

cannel /ˈkan(ə)l/ *noun*[2]. Orig. *N. English*. M16.
[ORIGIN Unknown.]
In full ***cannel coal***. A bituminous coal which burns with a bright flame.

†**cannel** *noun*[3] var. of CANEL *noun*[1].

cannella *noun* var. of CANELLA.

cannellini /kanəˈliːni/ *noun pl.* M20.
[ORIGIN Italian = small tubes.]
In full ***cannellini beans***. Kidney beans of a medium-sized creamy-white variety.

cannelloni /kanəˈləʊni/ *noun pl.* M20.
[ORIGIN Italian, augm. pl. of *cannello* stalk: see -OON.]
Rolls of pasta filled with meat or cheese and seasonings; an Italian dish consisting largely of this and usu. a sauce.

cannelon /ˈkan(ə)lɒn/ *noun*. M19.
[ORIGIN Prob. formed as CANNELLONI.]
A roll of pastry with a filling.

cannelure /ˈkan(ə)ljʊə/ *noun*. M18.
[ORIGIN French, from *canneler* to groove, flute, from *canne* reed: see CANE *noun*[1], -URE.]
A groove or fluting, esp. around a bullet etc.

canner /ˈkanə/ *noun*. L19.
[ORIGIN from CAN *verb*[2] + -ER[1].]
1 A person who cans food; a machine for canning food. L19.
2 An animal whose flesh is suitable only for canned foods. Also, a fruit or vegetable suitable for canning. Chiefly *N. Amer.* L19.

cannery /ˈkanəri/ *noun*. L19.
[ORIGIN from CAN *verb*[2] + -ERY.]
A factory where foodstuffs are canned.

cannibal /ˈkanɪb(ə)l/ *noun & adjective*. M16.
[ORIGIN Spanish *Canibales* (pl.), a form (recorded by Columbus) of the name *Caribes* a people of the W. Indies: see CARIB.]
▸ **A** *noun*. **1** A person who eats human flesh; *fig.* a bloodthirsty savage. M16.
2 An animal that eats members of its own species. L18.
▸ **B** *attrib.* or as *adjective*. Cannibalistic, bloodthirsty. L16.
■ **cannibaˈlean** *adjective* (*rare*) = CANNIBALISTIC E17. **canniˈbalic** *adjective* = CANNIBALISTIC E19. **cannibalism** *noun* the practice of eating (the flesh of) members of one's own species L18. **cannibaˈlistic** *adjective* of, pertaining to, or characteristic of cannibals; practising cannibalism: M19. **cannibaˈlistically** *adverb* in the manner of a cannibal M19. **cannibally** *adverb* (*rare*) cannibalistically E17.

cannibalize /ˈkanɪb(ə)lʌɪz/ *verb trans.* Also **-ise**. M17.
[ORIGIN from CANNIBAL + -IZE.]
1 Of a human being: eat the flesh of (another human being). Of an animal: consume the flesh of (a member of the same species). (*rare* before M20.) M17.
2 Use (a machine) as a source of spare parts for another; take (a part of a machine) for use in another. M20.
3 Of a company: suffer a reduction in (sales of one of its products) as a consequence of introducing a similar product. L20.
■ **cannibaliˈzation** *noun* M20.

cannikin /ˈkanɪkɪn/ *noun*. Also **cana-** /ˈkanə-/ L16.
[ORIGIN Dutch *kanneken*: see CAN *noun*, -KIN.]
A small can or drinking vessel.

cannoli /kaˈnəʊli/ *noun*. *N. Amer.* E20.
[ORIGIN Italian, pl. of *cannolo*, from *canna* reed.]
A dessert consisting of small deep-fried pastry tubes with a creamy filling, usu. of sweetened ricotta cheese.

cannon /ˈkanən/ *noun*. LME.
[ORIGIN Old French & mod. French *canon* from Italian *cannone* augm. of *canna* tube from Latin: see CANE *noun*[1], -OON. In sense 3 alt. of CAROM.]
1 a *hist.* (Pl. usu. same.) A piece of ordnance; a gun of a size requiring it to be mounted for firing. LME. ▸**b** An automatic shell-firing gun in an aircraft. E20.
†**2 a** A tube; a cylindrical bore. L16–E18. ▸**b** In full ***cannon bit***. A smooth round bit for a horse. L16. ▸**c** *hist.* In *pl.* = CANIONS. L16. ▸**d** In full ***cannon curl***. A cylindrical curl in the hair, worn horizontally. E19. ▸**e** MECHANICS. A hollow cylinder moving independently on a shaft. L19.
3 A stroke in billiards in which the player's cue ball is made to hit both other balls; *transf.* a rebounding collision. E19.
nursery cannon: see NURSERY 6.
4 A pickpocket. *US slang*. E20.
– PHRASES: ***loose cannon***: see LOOSE *adjective*.
– COMB.: **cannonball** *hist.* a solid spherical projectile fired by a cannon; ***cannonball tree*** a S. American tree, *Couroupita guianensis*, bearing globular woody fruit; ***cannon bit***: see sense 2b above; **cannon bone** a tube-shaped bone between a horse's hock and fetlock; **cannon fodder** [translating German *Kanonenfutter*] men regarded merely as material to be consumed in war; **cannon shot** (*a*) the shooting of a cannon; (*b*) ammunition fired from a cannon, cannonballs; (*c*) the range of a cannon.
■ **cannonry** *noun* the use or discharge of cannon; artillery: L16.

cannon /ˈkanən/ *verb*. L16.
[ORIGIN from the noun.]
1 *verb trans. & intrans.* = CANNONADE *verb*. L16.
2 *verb intrans.* Strike a cannon in billiards. M19.
3 a *verb trans.* Come into collision with. *rare*. M19. ▸**b** *verb intrans.* Come into collision, strike obliquely, *against*, *into*. L19.

cannonade /kanəˈneɪd/ *noun & verb*. M16.
[ORIGIN French from Italian *cannonata*, from *cannone*: see CANNON *noun*, -ADE.]
▸ **A** *noun*. A continued discharge of cannon, continuous gunfire; an attack with cannon. M16.
▸ **B** *verb trans. & intrans.* Attack with cannon; discharge cannon (against). M17.

cannoneer /kanəˈnɪə/ *noun*. M16.
[ORIGIN French *canonnier* from Italian *cannoniere*, from *cannone*: see CANNON *noun*, -EER.]
hist. An artilleryman who lays and fires cannon.

cannot *verb* see CAN *verb*[1].

cannula /ˈkanjʊlə/ *noun*. L17.
[ORIGIN Latin, dim. of *canna* CANE *noun*[1].]
SURGERY. A small tube which can be inserted into a body cavity or vessel to allow the entry or escape of fluid.
■ **cannulate** *verb trans.* introduce a cannula into E20. **cannuˈlation** *noun* M20.

canny /ˈkani/ *adjective & adverb*. Orig. *Scot.* L16.
[ORIGIN from CAN *verb*[1] + -Y[1].]
▸ **A** *adjective*. **1** Prudent, knowing; worldly-wise, shrewd; wary, circumspect, cautious. L16.
2 Safe to meddle with; lucky, propitious, fortunate. L16.
3 Clever, skilful; cunning, wily; endowed with occult power. *arch.* M17.
4 Careful with money, thrifty, frugal. E18.

> *Guardian* Those canny business folk who run private nursery schools.

5 Agreeable, comely, nice, tidy, good. *N. English*. E18.
6 Careful in action, gentle, quiet; snug, comfortable; (of humour etc.) sly, sardonic. M18.
▸ **B** *adverb*. Cautiously, warily, quietly. Esp. in ***ca' canny***, go or act thus (see also CA'CANNY). *Scot.* E18.
■ **cannily** *adverb* L16. **canniness** *noun* M17.

canoe /kəˈnuː/ *noun*. Also (earlier) †**canow** & other vars. M16.
[ORIGIN Spanish *canoa* from Arawak from Carib *canaoua*. Present spelling due to French *canoë*.]
A narrow keelless boat propelled by paddling; *spec.* (*a*) one simply constructed from a hollowed-out tree trunk or of a wooden frame covered with skins, bark, etc.; (*b*) a lightweight recreational craft made from fibreglass or wood etc.
dugout canoe, ***log canoe***, ***woodskin canoe***, etc. ***north canoe***: see NORTH *adverb, adjective, noun, & verb*. **paddle one's own canoe** *fig.* depend on oneself alone.
– COMB.: **canoe birch** *N. Amer.* the white or paper birch, *Betula papyrifera*; **canoe wood** *N. Amer.* (the timber of) the tulip tree, *Liriodendron tulipifera*.
■ **canoeist** *noun* a person who paddles a canoe M19. **canoe-like** *adjective* resembling (that of) a canoe M19.

canoe /kəˈnuː/ *verb intrans.* M18.
[ORIGIN from the noun.]
Travel by or paddle a canoe.

canola /kəˈnəʊlə/ *noun*. L20.
[ORIGIN from CAN(ADA + -OLA (with ref. to Latin *oleum* oil).]
Any of several varieties of oilseed rape developed in Canada; (more fully ***canola oil***) the vegetable oil obtained from these.

canon /ˈkanən/ *noun*[1]. OE
[ORIGIN Latin from Greek *kanōn* rule: reinforced in Middle English by Anglo-Norman *canun*, Old French & mod. French *canon*.]
1 An ecclesiastical law or decree; *esp.* a rule laid down by an ecclesiastical council; *sing.* & (usu.) in *pl.*, canon law. OE.

> SHAKES. *All's Well* Self-love . . the most inhibited sin in the canon.

2 The part of the Mass containing the words of consecration. ME.
3 A general law, rule, or edict; a fundamental principle. LME. ▸†**b** MATH. A general rule, formula, or table. LME–L18. ▸**c** A standard of judgement; a criterion. E17.

> D. CARNEGIE I violated all the canons of courtesy, ignored everyone else. J. K. GALBRAITH The balanced budget, so long a canon of the conventional wisdom. **c** G. MURRAY We are establishing a new conventional canon of what is poetical and what not.

4 Those biblical books officially accepted by any of the Christian Churches as genuinely inspired; any collection or list of sacred works accepted as genuine. LME. ▸**b** A list or catalogue of recognized saints. E18. ▸**c** A list of the recognized genuine works of a particular author, composer, etc. L19. ▸**d** A list of literary works considered to be permanently established as being of the highest quality. E20.

> **c** D. LODGE A series of commentaries on Jane Austen which would work through the whole canon, one novel at a time. **d** F. KERMODE Authority has invented many myths for the protection of the canon.

5 MUSIC. (The style of) a composition in which different parts take up the same subject successively in strict imitation. L16.
6 LAW. A customary payment made to the Church; a quit-rent. Now *rare* or *obsolete*. M17.
7 A former size of type equal to four-line pica. L17.
8 [Prob. a different word: cf. CANNON *noun* 2.] A metal loop at the top of a bell, by which it is hung. Usu. in *pl.*, of crossed loops. L17.
9 (A period or era serving as) a basis for chronology. M19.
– PHRASES: ***MURATORIAN canon***.
– COMB.: **canon law** ecclesiastical law, esp. as laid down by papal and council pronouncements.

canon /ˈkanən/ *noun*[2]. ME.
[ORIGIN Old French *canonie* from ecclesiastical Latin *canonicus* use as noun of adjective (see CANONIC), assim. to CANON *noun*[1].]
ECCLESIASTICAL. **1** A member of an order of clergy living in a clergy house or within the precincts of a cathedral etc. in accordance with the canons of the church. ME.
canon regular, **regular canon**: living according to a rule and so renouncing private property. **secular canon**: not living according to a rule.
2 Each of the resident ecclesiastics responsible, under the dean, for a cathedral. M16.
honorary canon a titular non-residential non-stipendiary member of a cathedral chapter. **minor canon**, †**petty canon** a member of the clergy who assists in the daily service of a cathedral but is not a member of the chapter.
■ **canoness** *noun* (*a*) a member of a community of women living according to an ecclesiastical rule as opp. to having taken perpetual vows; (*b*) a woman holding a prebend or canonry: L17. **canonship** *noun* = CANONRY 1 M16.

cañon *noun & verb* var. of CANYON.

canonic /kəˈnɒnɪk/ *noun & adjective*. OE.
[ORIGIN Old French & mod. French *canonique* or Latin *canonicus* from Greek *kanonikos*, formed as CANON *noun*[1]: see -IC.]
▸ **A** *noun*. **1** = CANON *noun*[2]. *rare*. OE.
2 A system of logical rules or dialectic. M17.
▸ **B** *adjective*. = CANONICAL *adjective*. L15.

canonical /kəˈnɒnɪk(ə)l/ *adjective & noun*. LME.
[ORIGIN medieval Latin *canonicalis* from Latin *canonicus*: see CANONIC, -AL[1].]
▸ **A** *adjective*. **1** Prescribed by, in conformity with, or relating to canon law. LME.
canonical hour ECCLESIASTICAL (usu. in *pl.*) (*a*) each of the times of daily prayer appointed in the breviary; each of seven offices (matins with lauds, prime, terce, sext, nones, vespers, and compline) appointed for these times; (*b*) in the Church of England, the time (now usu. between 8 a.m. and 6 p.m.) during which a marriage may lawfully be celebrated. **canonical obedience**: owed by a member of the clergy to a bishop or other clerical superior according to canon law.
2 Of the nature of a canon or rule; authoritative; standard; accepted. M16. ▸**b** MATH. Of the nature of a general rule or standard formula; relating to or according to such an expression. M18.
canonical epistles (*rare*) = ***Catholic Epistles*** s.v. CATHOLIC *adjective*.
3 Included in the scriptural canon; relating to any (sets of) sacred books regarded as authentic. M16.
4 Of or belonging to (any member of) an ecclesiastical chapter. L16.
5 MUSIC. According to the rules of canon; in canon form. *rare*. E17.
▸ **B** *noun*. **1** A canonical epistle. *rare*. M16.
2 In *pl.* The prescribed canonical dress of the clergy. M18.
■ **canonically** *adverb* E16. **canonicalness** *noun* M17.

canonicate /kəˈnɒnɪkət/ *noun*. M17.
[ORIGIN French *canonicat* or medieval Latin *canonicatus*, from Latin *canonicus*: see CANONIC, -ATE[1].]
The office or dignity of a canon; a canonry.

canonicity /kanəˈnɪsɪti/ *noun*. **L18.**
[ORIGIN from CANONIC + -ITY.]
Canonical status; *esp.* inclusion within the scriptural canon.

canonisation *noun*, **canonise** *verb* vars. of CANONIZATION, CANONIZE.

canonist /ˈkanənɪst/ *noun*. **M16.**
[ORIGIN Old French & mod. French *canoniste* or medieval Latin *canonista*, formed as CANON *noun*[1]: see -IST.]
An expert in canon law.
■ **canoˈnistic** *adjective* pertaining to a canonist; relating to the exposition of canon law: **M17.**

canonization /ˌkanənʌɪˈzeɪʃ(ə)n/ *noun*. Also **-isation**. **LME.**
[ORIGIN medieval Latin *canonizatio(n-)*, from *canonizat-* pa. ppl stem of *canonizare*: see CANONIZE, -ATION. Cf. Old French & mod. French *canonisation*.]
The action or an act of canonizing; *esp.* formal admission to the canon of saints.

canonize /ˈkanənʌɪz/ *verb trans*. Also **-ise**. **LME.**
[ORIGIN Late Latin *canonizare* admit as authoritative, (in medieval Latin) admit to the canon of saints, formed as CANON *noun*[1] + -IZE.]
1 Admit formally to the canon of saints; regard as a saint; *fig.* idolize, glorify. **LME.** ▸†**b** Deify; apotheosize. **M16–L18.**
2 Admit to a canon of sacred writings, esp. that of any of the Christian Churches. **LME.**
3 Sanction by church authority. **LME.**
■ **canonizer** *noun* **L16.**

canonry /ˈkanənri/ *noun*. **LME.**
[ORIGIN from CANON *noun*[2] + -RY.]
1 The benefice, office, or status of a canon. **LME.**
2 An establishment of canons or canonesses. **L19.**

canoodle /kəˈnuːd(ə)l/ *verb intrans. & trans. slang* (orig. *US*). **M19.**
[ORIGIN Unknown.]
Cuddle amorously; fondle, pet.

canophilist /kəˈnɒfɪlɪst/ *noun*. Chiefly *joc.* **L19.**
[ORIGIN Irreg. from Latin *canis* dog + -PHIL + -IST.]
A lover of dogs.
■ **canoˈphilia** *noun* affection for dogs **M20.**

Canopic /kəˈnəʊpɪk/ *adjective*. Also **c-**. **L19.**
[ORIGIN Latin *Canopicus*, from *Canopus* a town in ancient Egypt: see CANOPUS, -IC.]
Designating (in ***Canopic vase***, ***Canopic jar***) a covered urn used in ancient Egyptian burials to hold the entrails and other visceral organs from an embalmed body.

Canopus /kəˈnəʊpəs/ *noun*. Sense 2 usu. **c-**. **M16.**
[ORIGIN Latin *Canopus* from Greek *Kanōpos*, (i) a star (see below), (ii) a town in ancient Egypt.]
1 The brightest star in the constellation Carina. **M16.**
2 A Canopic vase. **E18.**

canopy /ˈkanəpi/ *noun & verb*. **LME.**
[ORIGIN medieval Latin *canopeum* baldachin, alt. of Latin *conopeum*, *-ium* net over a bed, pavilion from Greek *kōnōpeion* Egyptian bed with mosquito curtains, from *kōnōps* mosquito.]
▸ **A** *noun*. **1** A covering suspended or held over a throne, bed, person, etc.; an awning. **LME.**

HOBBES The Popes are carried by Switzers under a Canopie.

2 *gen.* A covering, an overhanging shade or shelter, (often applied *fig.* to the sky). **E17.** ▸**b** The upper branches of the trees in a forest, as forming a more or less continuous layer. **E20.**

M. F. MAURY A canopy of perpetual clouds. J. MASTERS The part of the platform sheltered by the canopy was crowded with would-be passengers. C. SAGAN Thousands of stars . . peppered across the canopy of night.

3 ARCHITECTURE. A rooflike ornamental projection over a niche, door, tomb, etc. **L17.**
4 An overhead covering forming part of the upper structure of a vehicle etc.; *esp.* the cover of the cockpit of an aircraft. **L19.**
5 The expanding part of a parachute. **M20.**
▸ **B** *verb trans.* Cover (as) with a canopy. Freq. as ***canopied*** *ppl adjective*. **L16.**

canorous /kəˈnɔːrəs/ *adjective*. **M17.**
[ORIGIN from Latin *canorus*, from *canere* sing: see -OUS.]
Melodious, resonant.

canst *verb* see CAN *verb*[1].

canstick /ˈkanstɪk/ *noun*. Long *obsolete* exc. *dial.* **LME.**
[ORIGIN Contr.]
A candlestick.

cant /kant/ *noun*[1]. **ME.**
[ORIGIN In branch I from Middle Low German *kant* point, creek, border, *kante* side, edge, Middle Dutch & mod. Dutch *cant* border, side, corner, from Proto-Romance var. (repr. by Old French *cant*, French *chant*, *champ*, Spanish, Italian *canto* edge, corner, side) of Latin *cant(h)us* iron tyre. In branch II from CANT *verb*[2].]
▸ **I** †**1** An edge, brink, side. Only in **ME.**
2 A corner, an angle; a corner piece; a triangular piece. *obsolete* exc. *dial.* **E17.**
3 Each of the side pieces in the head of a cask. **E17.**
4 NAUTICAL. Each of the timbers of a ship etc. towards the bow and the stern which are sharply angled from the keel. Also, a supporting timber. **L18.**
5 The oblique line or surface which cuts off the corner of a square, cube, etc.; an oblique, inclined, or slanting face. **M19.**
▸ **II 6** A sudden movement, esp. a toss, pitch, etc., which overturns. **E18.**
7 A slope, a tilt; a deflection from the perpendicular or horizontal. **M19.**
– COMB.: **cant-line** the space between two strands on the outside of a rope, or between the bilges of two barrels side by side; **cantrail** a timber or stay supporting the roof of a railway wagon etc.

cant /kant/ *noun*[2]. Long *obsolete* exc. *dial.* **LME.**
[ORIGIN Uncertain: perh. rel. to CANT *verb*[1], CANTLE.]
A portion, a share, a division.

cant /kant/ *noun*[3]. **E16.**
[ORIGIN In branch I sporadic uses from Latin CANTUS. In branch II from CANT *verb*[3].]
▸ †**I 1** Singing; musical sound. **E16–E18.**
2 Accent; intonation. **M17–M18.**
▸ **II 3** A whining manner of speaking; a whine. Now *rare* or *obsolete*. **M17.**
4 The special phraseology of a class, sect, profession, etc.; jargon, slang. Usu. *derog.* **L17.**
5 A set form of words repeated mechanically; *esp.* a stock phrase or word temporarily in fashion. *arch.* **L17.**
6 Ephemeral catchwords; affected or insincere phraseology; *esp.* language (or occas. action) implying piety which does not exist; hypocrisy. **E18.**

G. SANTAYANA The talk about a nasty world and living pure in a nunnery was just the cant of those days. A. S. NEILL To condemn an interest in sex is sheer hypocrisy and cant.

†**7** A person who uses such language. **E18–L19.**

cant /kant/ *noun*[4]. Chiefly *Irish*. Now *rare* or *obsolete*. **L16.**
[ORIGIN from CANT *verb*[4] or aphet. from French *encant* (mod. *encan*). Cf. Irish *ceant*.]
Sale by auction.

cant /kant/ *adjective*[1]. *Scot.* (formerly) & *N. English*. **ME.**
[ORIGIN App. same word as mod. Dutch *kant* neat, clever, perh. from *kant* CANT *noun*[1]. Cf. CANTY.]
Bold, brisk, lively, hearty.

cant /kant/ *adjective*[2]. Usu. *derog.* **E18.**
[ORIGIN from CANT *noun*[3].]
Of words, phrases, speech, etc.: of the nature of cant; jargonistic; ephemerally fashionable; uttered mechanically.
■ **cantly** *adverb* in canting phraseology; in slang: **E19.**

†**cant** *verb*[1] *trans.* **LME–M16.**
[ORIGIN Uncertain: perh. rel. to CANTLE.]
Divide, apportion, share out.

cant /kant/ *verb*[2]. **M16.**
[ORIGIN from CANT *noun*[1].]
1 *verb trans.* Give an oblique or slanting edge to; bevel (*off*). **M16.**
2 *verb trans.* Throw off or empty out by tilting. **M17.**
cant off decant.
3 *verb trans.* Pitch as by the sudden lurching of a ship; toss; push or pitch sideways. **L17.**

J. SMEATON The boat took a sudden yaw . . which canted me overboard.

4 *verb intrans. & trans.* Slope, slant, tilt; turn upside down or *over*. **E18.**

S. SMILES A loose plank, which canted over. T. COLLINS The black collie was sitting . . with his head slightly canted to one side. L. DURRELL The telescope barrel had been canted downwards so that it no longer pointed at the sky.

5 *verb intrans.* NAUTICAL. Of a ship etc.: change course, swing round. **L18.**

R. D. BLACKMORE The boat canted round towards the entrance of the creek.

– COMB.: **cant dog** (**a**) a handspike with a hook; (**b**) = ***cant hook*** below; **cant hook** (an implement consisting of) an iron hook at the end of a long handle, used for rolling logs.

cant /kant/ *verb*[3]. **M16.**
[ORIGIN Prob. from Latin *cantare*: see CHANT *verb*.]
†**1** *verb intrans.* Whine; beg. **M16–M19.**
†**2** *verb intrans. & trans.* Speak; talk; say. *slang & dial.* **M16–L18.**
3 *verb intrans.* Use cant or jargon; affect fashionable or pietistic phraseology. **M16.**
4 *verb trans.* Utter with cant phraseology. Now *rare*. **M17.**
†**5** *verb trans. & intrans.* Chant; sing. **M17–E19.**
■ **canting** *adjective* (**a**) that cants, using cant; (**b**) *arch.* of the nature of cant; (**c**) HERALDRY containing an allusion to the name of the bearer: **L16.** **cantingly** *adverb* **L17.**

cant /kant/ *verb*[4] *trans.* Chiefly *Irish & N. English*. Now *rare* or *obsolete*. **L16.**
[ORIGIN Uncertain: cf. CANT *noun*[4], Latin *incantare*, *accantare* proclaim, put up to auction.]
Dispose of by auction.

Cant. *abbreviation*.
Canticles (in the Bible).

can't *verb* see CAN *verb*[1].

Cantab /ˈkantab/ *noun & adjective*. **M18.**
[ORIGIN Abbreviation of CANTABRIGIAN or (adjective) mod. Latin *Cantabrigiensis*.]
▸ **A** *noun*. A Cantabrigian. *colloq.* **M18.**
▸ **B** *adjective*. (Also **Cantab.** (point).) Of Cambridge University. **L19.**

cantabile /kanˈtɑːbɪli/ *adverb, adjective, & noun*. **E18.**
[ORIGIN Italian = that can be sung.]
MUSIC. ▸ **A** *adverb & adjective*. In a smooth flowing style, as if singing. **E18.**
▸ **B** *noun*. Cantabile style; a piece or movement in this style. **M18.**

Cantabrian /kanˈteɪbrɪən/ *noun & adjective*. **M16.**
[ORIGIN from Latin *Cantabri* pl. (the people) or *Cantabria* (see below) + -AN.]
▸ **A** *noun*. *hist.* A member of an ancient warlike people inhabiting Cantabria, a region of northern Spain. **M16.**
▸ **B** *adjective*. **1** *hist.* Of or pertaining to the Cantabrians. **M17.**
2 Of or pertaining to Cantabria. **M18.**

Cantabrigian /kantəˈbrɪdʒɪən/ *adjective & noun*. **M16.**
[ORIGIN from Latin *Cantabrigia* Cambridge (England) + -AN.]
1 (A native or inhabitant) of Cambridge, England; (a member) of Cambridge University. **M16.**
2 (A native or inhabitant) of Cambridge, Massachusetts; (a member) of Harvard University in Cambridge, Massachusetts. **L19.**

Cantal /ˈkantɑːl/ *noun*. **L19.**
[ORIGIN A department of the Auvergne, France.]
In full ***Cantal cheese***. A hard strong cheese made chiefly in the Auvergne.

cantaloupe /ˈkantəluːp/ *noun*. Also **-loup**. **L18.**
[ORIGIN French from Italian *Cantaluppi*, near Rome, where, on its introduction from Armenia, it was first grown.]
A small round ribbed variety of melon, with orange flesh. Also called ***rock melon***.

cantankerous /kanˈtaŋk(ə)rəs/ *adjective*. **M18.**
[ORIGIN Prob. blend of RANCOROUS and uncertain elem.]
Quarrelsome; perverse; bad-tempered.
■ **cantankerously** *adverb* **M19.** **cantankerousness** *noun* **L19.**

cantar *noun* var. of KANTAR.

cantarist /ˈkantərɪst/ *noun*. **E19.**
[ORIGIN medieval Latin *cantarista*, from *cantaria* CHANTRY: see -IST.]
hist. A chantry priest.

cantata /kanˈtɑːtə/ *noun*. **E18.**
[ORIGIN Italian (sc. *aria* air), fem. pa. pple of *cantare* sing.]
MUSIC. An extended composition for one or more voices with instrumental accompaniment; orig., a narrative recitative or sequence of recitatives and ariettas, for solo voice; later, a choral work resembling a short oratorio.

Cantate /kanˈtɑːteɪ, -ti/ *noun*. **M16.**
[ORIGIN Latin = sing ye, the first word of the psalm (see below).]
Psalm 98 (97 in the Vulgate) used as a canticle.

cantation /kanˈteɪʃ(ə)n/ *noun*. *rare*. **E17.**
[ORIGIN Latin *cantatio(n-)* song, (in late Latin) spell, incantation, from *cantat-* pa. ppl stem of *cantare*: see CHANT *verb*, -ION.]
†**1** Singing. **E–M17.**
2 Incantation. **M19.**

cantator /kanˈteɪtə, -ˈtɑːtə/ *noun*. *rare*. **M19.**
[ORIGIN Latin *cantator*, from *cantat-*: see CANTATION, -OR.]
A (male) singer.

cantatrice /ˈkantətriːs/ *noun*. **E19.**
[ORIGIN French & Italian, from Latin *cantatrix*: see -TRICE and cf. CANTATOR.]
A female professional singer.

canteen /kanˈtiːn/ *noun*. **M18.**
[ORIGIN French *cantine* from Italian *cantina* cellar, perh. from *canto*: see CANT *noun*[1].]
1 A provision or liquor shop in a military camp or barracks; a bar, refreshment counter, etc., at a place of public resort or at a (large) factory, school, or other institution. **M18.**
dry canteen: without liquor. **wet canteen**: chiefly for liquor.
2 A set of cooking, eating, or drinking utensils, or a water flask, for soldiers, travellers, etc. **M18.** ▸**b** A case or chest of plate or cutlery for domestic use. **L19.**
– COMB.: **canteen culture** *colloq.* a set of conservative and discriminatory attitudes said to exist within a police force or other body.

cante hondo /ˈkante ˈxondo, ˌkɑːnteɪ ˈhɒndəʊ/ *noun phr.* Also ***cante jondo***. **M20.**
[ORIGIN Spanish = deep song.]
Flamenco singing, songs, of a predominantly mournful or tragic character.

canter /ˈkantə/ *noun*[1]. **E17.**
[ORIGIN from CANT *verb*[3] + -ER[1].]
1 A person who uses the cant of thieves. Now *rare* or *obsolete*. **E17.**
2 A person who uses professional or religious cant. **M17.**

C

canter /ˈkantə/ *noun*[2]. M18.
[ORIGIN Short for *Canterbury gallop* s.v. CANTERBURY *noun*[1] 1.]
A gait between trot and gallop; an easy gallop.
win in a canter: easily.

canter /ˈkantə/ *verb*. E18.
[ORIGIN formed as CANTER *noun*[2].]
1 *verb intrans.* Of a horse etc. or rider: move at a canter. Also *transf.*, move briskly or easily. E18.
2 *verb trans.* Make (a horse etc.) go at a canter. M19.

Canterbury /ˈkantəb(ə)ri/ *noun*[1]. M16.
[ORIGIN A city in Kent, famous as the seat of the Primate of all England, and the site of the shrine of Thomas à Becket (St Thomas of Canterbury).]
▸ **I 1** Used *attrib.* to designate things associated with Canterbury, Kent, esp. as a former object of pilgrimage. M16.
Canterbury bell(s) [with ref. to the bells on pilgrims' horses], a southern European bellflower, *Campanula medium*, grown for ornament; any of several native British bellflowers. **Canterbury gallop**, **Canterbury pace**, **Canterbury trot**, etc., the pace of mounted pilgrims; a slow easy gallop (cf. CANTER *noun*[2]), trot. **Canterbury hoe**: with three prongs attached to the handle at right angles. **Canterbury tale** a story told on pilgrimage (orig. one of those in Chaucer's *Canterbury Tales*); a long tedious story.
▸ †**II 2** An easy gallop; a canter. M17–E18.
3 (Often **c-**.) A stand with partitions to hold music or books. E19.

Canterbury /ˈkantəb(ə)ri/ *noun*[2]. Now *rare*. L19.
[ORIGIN A province in the South Island, NZ.]
In full ***Canterbury lamb***. In Great Britain, formerly: lamb or mutton imported from New Zealand. In New Zealand: certain grades of lamb or mutton.

cantharis /kanˈθarɪs/ *noun*. Pl. **-rides** /-rɪdiːz/. LME.
[ORIGIN Latin from Greek *kantharis*.]
1 The Spanish fly, *Lytta vesicatoria*. Now *rare* or *obsolete*. LME.
2 In *pl.* A preparation of the dried beetles, having toxic and vesicant properties, and sometimes taken as an aphrodisiac. LME.
■ **cantha'ridean** *adjective* of the nature of or containing cantharides L18. **cantharidin** *noun* a lactone, $C_{10}H_{12}O_4$, obtained from the elytra of the insect, which is the active principle of cantharides: E19. **cantharidize** *verb trans.* (now *rare*) affect or treat with cantharides L18.

cantharus /ˈkanθ(ə)rəs/ *noun*. Pl. **-ri** /-rʌɪ/. Also **kantharos**, **c-**, pl. **-roi** /-rɔɪ/. M19.
[ORIGIN Latin from Greek *kantharos*.]
1 CLASSICAL ANTIQUITIES. A large two-handled drinking cup. M19.
2 A fountain or laver placed in the courtyard of an ancient church for the use of worshippers. M19.

canthus /ˈkanθəs/ *noun*. Pl. **-thi** /-θʌɪ/. M17.
[ORIGIN Latin from Greek *kanthos*.]
ANATOMY. The outer or inner corner of the eye, where the lids meet.

canticle /ˈkantɪk(ə)l/ *noun*. ME.
[ORIGIN Latin *canticulum* dim. of *canticum* song.]
1 A (little) song; a hymn, *spec.* one of those used in the liturgy of the Christian Church. ME.
2 *the Canticles*, the Song of Solomon. LME.
†**3** A canto of a poem. L16–M17.

canti fermi *noun phr.* pl. of CANTO FERMO.

cantikoy *noun* var. of KANTIKOY.

cantilena /kantɪˈleɪnə, -ˈliːnə/ *noun*. M18.
[ORIGIN Italian, or Latin *cantilena*.]
MUSIC. A simple or sustained vocal melody, or an instrumental passage performed in a smooth lyrical style. Also, the (highest) melodic part in a composition.

cantilever /ˈkantɪliːvə/ *noun*. M17.
[ORIGIN Unknown.]
1 A long projecting bracket supporting a balcony, cornice, etc. M17.
2 A long projecting beam or girder fixed at only one end, esp. in bridge construction. M19.
– COMB.: **cantilever bridge**: with piers each of which has two cantilevers, and long girders connecting the cantilevers of adjacent piers.
■ **cantilevered** *adjective* projecting like or supported by a cantilever E20.

cantillate /ˈkantɪleɪt/ *verb trans. & intrans.* M19.
[ORIGIN Latin *cantillat-* pa. ppl stem of *cantillare* sing low, hum, from *cantare*: see CHANT *verb*, -ATE[3].]
Chant, recite musically; *spec.* intone as in a Jewish synagogue.
■ **canti'llation** *noun* E19.

cantina /kanˈtiːnə/ *noun*. L19.
[ORIGIN Spanish & Italian.]
(In Spain, Spanish-speaking countries, and the south-western US) a bar-room, a saloon; (in Italy) a wine shop.

canting *noun* var. of TJANTING.

cantle /ˈkant(ə)l/ *noun & verb*. ME.
[ORIGIN Anglo-Norman *cantel* = Old French *chantel* (mod. *chanteau*) from medieval Latin *cantellus* dim. of Latin *cant(h)us*: see CANT *noun*[1], -EL[2].]
▸ **A** *noun*. **1** A nook, a corner; a projecting corner or angle of land. Long *rare*. ME. ▸†**b** A corner or other portion that has been cut off; a sliver. LME–E17.
2 A section or segment cut out of anything; a thick slice or cut of bread, cheese, etc. *arch.* ME. ▸**b** A segment of a circle or sphere. M16.
3 A (separate or distinct) part or portion. *arch.* ME.
4 The protuberant part at the back of a saddle. L16.
5 The crown of the head. *Scot.* E19.
▸ †**B** *verb trans.* **1** Piece together (cloth). Only in M16.
2 Cut into segments, divide; portion *out*. L16–L17.
■ **cantlet** *noun* (*arch.*) a small part or portion L17. †**cantling** *noun* = CANTLET L17–E19.

canto /ˈkantəʊ/ *noun*. Pl. **-os**. L16.
[ORIGIN Italian, lit. 'song', from Latin CANTUS.]
1 Each of the divisions of a long poem. L16.
†**2** A song, a ballad. E17–E18.
3 MUSIC. The upper part or melody in a composition. E18.

canto fermo /kantəʊ ˈfəːməʊ/ *noun phr.* Pl. **canti fermi** /-ti -mi/. L16.
[ORIGIN Italian, translating medieval Latin CANTUS FIRMUS.]
MUSIC. Orig., an unadorned melody, plainsong; later *spec.* a melody used as a basis for counterpoint. Now also, an existing melody taken as a basis for a new polyphonic composition.

canton /ˈkantən; *in sense 1 also* kanˈtɒn/ *noun*[1]. E16.
[ORIGIN Old French & mod. French from Provençal from oblique case of Proto-Romance var. of Latin *cant(h)us*: see CANT *noun*[1].]
1 A subdivision of a country; a small district; *spec.* one of the several states which form the Swiss confederation. E16. ▸**b** A division of a French *arrondissement*, containing several communes. E17.
2 A corner, an angle; a nook. Now *rare* or *obsolete*. M16.
3 HERALDRY. A square division, less than a quarter, orig. occupying one-ninth part and the upper (usu. dexter) corner of a shield. L16.
†**4** A quarter; a division of anything, a part. Only in 17.
■ **cantonal** *adjective* of, pertaining to, or of the nature of a canton M19. **cantoni'zation** *noun* division into cantons; making cantonal: M20. **cantonize** *verb trans. & intrans.* (now *rare*) divide into parts; form (into) cantons; separate: E17.

†**canton** *noun*[2]. L16–E17.
[ORIGIN Alt. of CANTO, perh. by assoc. with CANZON, CANZONE.]
= CANTO 1, 2.

canton /ˈkantən *in sense 5 also* kanˈtuːn/ *verb*. L16.
[ORIGIN Partly from CANTON *noun*[1], partly from French *cantonner* to quarter, Italian *cantonnare* to canton, quarter.]
1 *verb trans.* Quarter, divide; share *out*; subdivide (into cantons). L16.

> DEFOE He Canton'd out the Country to his Men. C. THIRLWALL They cantoned their great dioceses into Archdeaconries.

2 *verb trans.* Divide *from* or cut *out* of a whole. Now *rare* or *obsolete*. M17.

> J. LOCKE They canton out to themselves a little Goshen in the intellectual world.

3 *verb trans.* HERALDRY. Provide with a canton or cantons; place in a canton. L17.
4 *verb intrans.* Take up quarters. L17.
5 *verb trans.* Quarter (soldiers); provide with quarters. E18.
■ **cantoned** *ppl adjective* (*a*) formed or divided into cantons; (*b*) quartered in cantonments; (*c*) ARCHITECTURE having decorated angles: E17.

Cantonese /kantəˈniːz/ *adjective & noun*. L18.
[ORIGIN from *Canton* English name of the city Guangzhou + -ESE.]
▸ **A** *noun*. Pl. same. A native or inhabitant of Canton in SE China; the dialect of Chinese commonly used in Canton. L18.
▸ **B** *adjective*. Of or pertaining to Canton, its inhabitants, their dialect, cuisine, etc. M19.

cantonment /kanˈtɒnm(ə)nt, -ˈtuːn-/ *noun*. M18.
[ORIGIN French *cantonnement*, from *cantonner*: see CANTON *verb*, -MENT.]
1 The quartering of troops. M18.
2 A military encampment; quarters. In the Indian subcontinent, (the former site of) a permanent military station. M18.

Cantopop /ˈkantəʊpɒp/ *noun*. L20.
[ORIGIN Blend of CANTONESE and POP *noun*[6].]
A type of popular music combining Cantonese lyrics and Western disco music.

cantor /ˈkantɔː, -ə/ *noun*. M16.
[ORIGIN Latin = singer, from *canere*: see CHANT *verb*, -OR.]
1 a A precentor in a church. M16. ▸**b** An official who sings liturgical music and leads prayer in a synagogue, = HAZZAN. L19.
†**2** *gen.* A singer. E–M17.

cantorial /kanˈtɔːrɪəl/ *adjective*. L18.
[ORIGIN from CANTOR + -IAL.]
Of the precentor; *spec.* designating or pertaining to the north side of the choir of a church, on which the precentor usually sits (cf. DECANAL 2).

cantoris /kanˈtɔːrɪs/ *adjective*. M17.
[ORIGIN Latin, genit. of CANTOR.]
Of or belonging to the cantor or precentor; cantorial; to be sung by the cantorial side in antiphonal singing (cf. DECANI).

cantred /ˈkantrɛd/ *noun*. Also in Welsh form **-ef** /-ɛv/. ME.
[ORIGIN App. from Welsh *cantref*, (from *cant* hundred + *tref* town, settlement, farmstead) with assim. to HUNDRED.]
hist. A district of (approximately) one hundred townships, a hundred; an area consisting of two or more commots.

cantrip /ˈkantrɪp/ *noun*. *Scot.* L16.
[ORIGIN Unknown.]
A spell, a charm; a witch's trick; a playful or extravagant act.

cantus /ˈkantəs/ *noun*. Pl. ***cantus*** /ˈkantuːs, -təs/. L16.
[ORIGIN Latin = song. Cf. CANT *noun*[3], CANTO, CHANT *noun*.]
EARLY MUSIC. A song, a melody, esp. in church music. Also, the highest voice in a polyphonic song.

cantus firmus /ˌkantəs ˈfəːməs/ *noun phr.* Pl. **cantus firmi** /ˈfəːmʌɪ/. M19.
[ORIGIN medieval Latin = firm song.]
MUSIC. = CANTO FERMO.

canty /ˈkanti/ *adjective*. *Scot. & N. English*. E18.
[ORIGIN from CANT *adjective*[1] + -Y[1].]
Cheerful, lively, brisk.

Canuck /kəˈnʌk/ *noun & adjective*. *N. Amer. colloq.* M19.
[ORIGIN App. from CANADA.]
▸ **A** *noun*. **1** A Canadian, orig. *esp.* a French Canadian; a Canadian horse or pony. M19.
2 Canadian French. E20.
▸ **B** *adjective*. Canadian, orig. *esp.* French Canadian. M19.

canvas /ˈkanvəs/ *noun*[1] *& adjective*. Also **canvass**. LME.
[ORIGIN Old Northern French *canevas* var. of Old French *chanevaz* from Proto-Romance, ult. from Latin CANNABIS.]
▸ **A** *noun*. **I** As a non-count noun.
1 A strong unbleached cloth of hemp, flax, or other coarse yarn, used for sails, tents, painting on, etc.; hence, sails collectively. LME.
under canvas (*a*) in a tent or tents; (*b*) with sails spread. ***VITRY canvas***.
2 A type of this cloth woven in regular meshes and used as a basis for tapestry and embroidery. E17.
JAVA canvas. ***Penelope canvas***: see PENELOPE 3.
▸ **II** As a count noun.
3 A piece of canvas. *obsolete* exc. as below. LME.
4 A piece of canvas primed for painting; a painting, esp. in oils. E18.
5 A covering over the ends of a racing boat (orig. made of canvas); *transf.* the length between the bow and the first oarsman. L19.
win by a canvas, **lose by a canvas**, etc., (in boat-racing): by a narrow margin.
6 *The* floor of a boxing, wrestling, etc., ring, with a canvas covering. E20.
▸ **B** *attrib.* or as *adjective*. Made of canvas. LME.
– COMB.: **canvasback** (*a*) a back of a garment made of canvas; (*b*) a N. American diving duck, *Aythya valisineria*, so called from the white back of the male.

canvas *noun*[2] var. of CANVASS *noun*[1].

canvas /ˈkanvəs/ *verb trans.* Infl. **-s-**, **-ss-**. Also **canvass**. M16.
[ORIGIN from CANVAS *noun*[1].]
▸ **I** †**1** FALCONRY. Entangle or catch in a net. M16–M17.
2 Cover, line, or provide with canvas. M16.
sand and canvas: see SAND *verb*.
▸ **II** See CANVASS *verb*

canvass /ˈkanvəs/ *noun*[1]. Also **canvas**. E17.
[ORIGIN from CANVASS *verb*.]
†**1** A shaking up; a shock, an attack; a repulse. E–M17.
†**2** An examination of pros and cons. Only in 17.
3 The action or process of personally soliciting votes before an election, or of ascertaining the amount of support a candidate may count on. L17. ▸**b** A scrutiny of votes in an election. *US*. L18.
4 A solicitation of support, custom, etc. L18.

canvass *noun*[2] *& adjective* var. of CANVAS *noun*[1] *& adjective*.

canvass /ˈkanvəs/ *verb*. Also **canvas**. E16.
[ORIGIN from CANVAS *noun*[1]: the sense-development is unexpl.]
▸ **I** †**1** *verb trans.* Toss in a canvas sheet as a sport or punishment; knock about, batter. E16–M17.
2 *verb trans.* Discuss, criticize, examine fully; seek to ascertain; discuss with a view to adoption, propose (a plan etc.). M16. ▸**b** *verb intrans.* Engage in debate or discussion. M17. ▸**c** *verb trans.* Scrutinize (votes). *obsolete* exc. *US*. E18.

> DISRAELI It was canvassed and criticised sentence by sentence. J. K. GALBRAITH We canvass our public wants to see where happiness can be improved. P. G. WODEHOUSE His first act . . had been to canvass Ed. Robinson's views. **b** F. MARRYAT We sat there canvassing over the affair.

3 *verb intrans.* Solicit votes, support, goods, etc. M16.

> T. DREISER His father canvassed for a washing machine and wringer company.

4 *verb trans.* Solicit votes, support, custom, etc., from; seek to ascertain the sentiments or intentions of. L17.

> J. L. MOTLEY His most trustworthy agent . . was now actively canvassing the governments and peoples of Germany. JOYCE Mr O'Connor had been engaged by Tierney's agents to canvass one part of the ward.

▸ **II** See CANVAS *verb*.
■ **canvasser** *noun* L16.

cany /ˈkeɪni/ *adjective*. M17.
[ORIGIN from CANE *noun*[1] + -Y[1].]
Of cane; like cane.

canyon /ˈkanjən/ *noun & verb*. Also **cañon**. M19.
[ORIGIN Spanish *cañón* tube, pipe, gun barrel, etc., augm. of *caña* from Latin *canna*: see CANE *noun*[1], -OON.]
▸ **A** *noun*. A deep gorge (esp. in the US or Mexico), frequently with a stream at its bottom. M19.
▸ **B** *verb*. **1** *verb intrans*. Flow in or into a canyon. M19.
2 *verb trans*. Cut into canyons. L19.
■ **canyoning** *noun* a sport or leisure activity involving jumping into a mountain waterfall or fast-flowing stream and being swept downhill at high speed L20.

canzona /kanˈtsəʊnə, -z-/ *noun*. L19.
[ORIGIN Italian from CANZONE.]
(A musical setting of the words of) a canzone; an instrumental piece resembling a madrigal in character.

canzone /kanˈtsəʊni, -z-/ *noun*. Pl. **-ni** /-ni/. L16.
[ORIGIN Italian = song (corresp. to Old French & mod. French *chanson*) from Latin *cantio(n-)* singing, from *cant-* pa. pple of *canere* sing.]
An Italian or Provençal song or ballad; a style of lyric resembling a madrigal.
■ Also **canzon** /ˈkants(ə)n, -z-/ *noun* (long *arch. rare*) L16.

canzonet /kantsəˈnɛt, -z-/ *noun*. L16.
[ORIGIN Italian *canzonetta*, dim. of CANZONE.]
A short light song; a short canzone.
■ Also **canzonetta** *noun* E18.

Caodaism /kaʊˈdʌɪɪz(ə)m/ *noun*. M20.
[ORIGIN from Vietnamese *Cao Dai*, name of the sect, lit. 'great palace' + -ISM.]
A syncretistic religion of SE Asia.
■ **Caodaist** *noun* an adherent of Caodaism M20.

caoine /ˈkiːnə/ *noun*. E18.
[ORIGIN Irish, formed as KEEN *verb*[2].]
= KEEN *noun*.

caoutchouc /ˈkaʊtʃʊk/ *noun & adjective*. L18.
[ORIGIN French from Spanish †*cauchuc* from Quechua *kauchuk*.]
(Of) unvulcanized natural rubber.

CAP *abbreviation*.
Common Agricultural Policy (of the European Union).

cap /kap/ *noun*[1]. OE.
[ORIGIN Late Latin *cappa*, perh. from *caput* head.]
▸ **I** A covering for the head.
†**1** A hood. Only in OE.
2 A headdress for women; latterly usu. a light one of muslin etc. for indoor use, worn by a nurse, woman servant, etc. ME.
mob-cap: see MOB *noun*[2] 3.
3 Any of various kinds of brimless headdress, usu. soft and often with a peak, to be worn outdoors or for a special purpose (e.g. as part of academic or Highland dress), orig. only by men or boys. LME. ▸**b** *spec*. A helmet, a headpiece of mail. LME. ▸**c** A cardinal's biretta. L16. ▸**d** A special cap awarded as a sign of membership of a sporting team, esp. a national team in international competition; *transf*. a person awarded such a cap. L19.
cloth cap, ***dunce's cap***, ***skullcap***, ***swimming cap***, etc.
4 In full ***cap paper***: ▸**a** A kind of wrapping paper. L16. ▸**b** A size or kind of writing paper. Cf. FOOLSCAP. M19.
5 A sum of money collected in a cap, esp. at a fox hunt etc. from those who are not subscribing members. M19.
▸ **II** Something resembling this in shape, position, or use.
6 A caplike natural covering or topmost part. LME. ▸**b** *spec*. The top of a bird's head, when distinctively coloured. Also in names, as ***blackcap***. L17. ▸**c** The pileus of a mushroom or toadstool. Also in names, as ***death cap***. M18.

W. WHITMAN The tossing waves, . . the snowy, curling caps. F. O'CONNOR Her face, reddish under a cap of fox-colored hair.

ice cap, ***kneecap***, ***snowcap***, etc. WHITECAP.
7 A caplike part fitting over or forming the top or end of an object; a caplike cover or case; a device sealing the opening of a bottle etc., or protecting the lens of a camera etc. or the nib of a fountain pen. LME.

J. RAY The refining Furnace is covered with a thick cap of stone. J. STEINBECK Tom . . loosened the oil cap with a pair of pliers.

toecap: see TOE *noun*.
8 NAUTICAL. A wooden collar used to hold two masts together. E17.
9 A part laid horizontally along the top of various structures. L17.
10 In full ***percussion cap***. A metal or paper device (orig. cap-shaped) used with (real or toy) firearms and containing explosive powder which is exploded by the fall of a hammer. E19.
11 A contraceptive diaphragm. Cf. ***Dutch cap*** s.v. DUTCH *adjective*. E20.
▸ **III** Partly from the verb.
12 An imposed upper limit; an act of imposing an upper limit. L20.

– PHRASES: **cap and bells**: the insignia of the professional jester. **cap in hand** *fig*. humbly. **cap of liberty** a conical cap given to Roman slaves on emancipation, often used as a Republican symbol. **cap of maintenance** a cap or hat worn as a symbol of official dignity, or carried before a monarch etc. on ceremonial occasions. ***Dutch cap***: see DUTCH *adjective*. ***Hungarian cap***: see HUNGARIAN *adjective*. ***Kilmarnock cap***: see KILMARNOCK 1. ***legal cap***: see LEGAL *adjective*. ***Polar cap***: see POLAR *adjective*. ***pull caps***: see PULL *verb*. ***put on one's thinking cap***: see THINKING *noun* 1a. ***saffron milk-cap***: see SAFFRON *adjective*. **set one's cap at** seek to attract as a suitor. ***SHAGGY cap***. **the cap fits** *fig*. a general remark is true of the person in question. ***throw one's cap over the windmill***: see WINDMILL *noun* 1.
– COMB.: **cap-money** = sense 5 above; ***cap paper***: see sense 4 above; **cap rock** an overlying stratum of (esp. resistant) rock; **cap sleeve**: extending only a short distance from the shoulder; **capstone** a stone which caps or crowns, a coping stone.
■ **capful** *noun* the amount that a cap will contain M17. **capless** *adjective* M19. **caplike** *adjective* resembling a cap in appearance, position, or use M19.

cap /kap/ *noun*[2]. *Scot*. L16.
[ORIGIN App. var. of COP *noun*[1].]
1 A wooden bowl used as a drinking vessel. L16.
2 A measure of quantity: a quarter of a Scots peck. E17.

cap /kap/ *noun*[3]. *colloq*. Also **cap'**. M18.
[ORIGIN Abbreviation.]
= CAPTAIN *noun*.

cap /kap/ *noun*[4]. *colloq*. (chiefly *N. Amer.*). M20.
[ORIGIN Abbreviation.]
A capsule, esp. of a drug.

cap /kap/ *noun*[5]. L20.
[ORIGIN Abbreviation.]
FINANCE. Capitalization.

cap /kap/ *verb*[1]. Infl. **-pp-**. LME.
[ORIGIN from CAP *noun*[1].]
1 *verb trans*. Provide (a person, head) with a cap, put a cap on; *Scot. & NZ* confer a university degree on. LME. ▸**b** Award a cap to (a sports player) for membership of a team etc., select as a member of a national team. E20.

J. SKELTON With her clothes on her hed . . like an Egyptian capped about. **b** *Times* Baker, capped five times for England in 1959–60.

2 *verb trans. & intrans*. Take off one's cap in token of respect (to). M16.

THACKERAY He and the Proctor capped each other as they met. G. A. SALA Soon I was well known and Capped to.

3 *verb trans*. Cover or protect as with a cap; cover at the top or end; seal with a cap. L16. ▸**b** Seal (a well) to prevent or control the loss of gas or oil. L20. ▸**c** *fig*. Impose an upper limit on; limit the expenditure of. L20.

P. NICHOLSON The extremities of beams, etc., have sometimes been capped with pitch. J. CARY Sphinx-like tors with their crowns of granite capped with ermine. B. PLAIN Jessie put the remainder of the lunch into a bag and capped the Thermos.

4 *verb trans*. *fig*. ▸**a** Serve as a climax or culmination to; overtop, outdo, beat; follow (an anecdote, witticism, etc.) with a better or more apposite one. L16. ▸**b** Pass the comprehension of, puzzle. *dial*. M18.

a SHAKES. *Hen. V* I will cap that proverb with 'There is flattery in friendship'. M. BEERBOHM Katie . . uttered a loud sob. Mrs Batch capped this with a much louder one. S. UNWIN There was a Municipal Reception, a Foreign Office Reception . . a luncheon . . and finally to cap it all the members . . were invited to lunch . . with the President. *Times* The announcement . . capped a day of speculation.

a cap verses reply with a verse beginning with the last letter of the previous one.
5 *verb trans*. Form a cap or upper part to; overlie. E17.

C. LYELL The basalts . . capping the hills. B. TAYLOR One block Shall cap the pediment.

6 *verb trans. & intrans*. Give cap-money to; take cap-money. M19.
■ **capped**, †**capt** *ppl adjective* (*a*) wearing or having a (specified) cap or covering; (*b*) *dial*. puzzled, astonished: LME. **capping** *noun* (*a*) the action of the verb; (*b*) that with which anything is capped, covered, or overlaid: LME.

cap /kap/ *verb*[2] *trans*. Infl. **-pp-**. L16.
[ORIGIN Old French *caper* seize.]
1 Arrest. *obsolete* exc. *Scot*. L16.
2 Appropriate by violence, seize. *Scot*. E19.

cap. /kap/ *noun*. Also **cap** (no point). M19.
[ORIGIN Abbreviation.]
A capital letter.
small cap: see SMALL *adjective*.

capa /ˈkapa/ *noun*. L18.
[ORIGIN Spanish from late Latin *cappa*: see CAP *noun*[1].]
In Spain and Spanish-speaking countries: a cape, a cloak.

capability /keɪpəˈbɪlɪti/ *noun*. L16.
[ORIGIN from CAPABLE + -ITY.]
1 The quality of being capable; power *of* (action, *doing*); capacity *for*. L16.

B. C. BRODIE The capability of fixing the attention. H. KISSINGER Had Hanoi possessed the capability it could have inflicted . . higher casualties.

negative capability: see NEGATIVE *adjective*.
2 An undeveloped or unused faculty. Freq. in *pl*. L18.

A. W. WARD He recognised the capabilities of the character.

capable /ˈkeɪpəb(ə)l/ *adjective*. M16.
[ORIGIN French from late Latin *capabilis*, from *capere* take: see -ABLE.]
†**1 a** Able to take in (*lit. & fig.*); having sufficient room or capacity. Foll. by *of*, *to do*. (= CAPACIOUS 1.) M16–L18. ▸**b** = CAPACIOUS 2. L16–M17.

a MILTON Not capable her eare Of what was high. **b** T. FULLER That capable vessell of brass.

2 Foll. by *of*: open to, admitting of, susceptible to. L16.

SHAKES. *2 Hen. IV* You were advis'd his flesh was capable Of wounds and scars. R. BOLT Some men think the Earth is round, others think it flat; it is a matter capable of question.

3 Having the ability, power, or fitness for some specified purpose or activity; wicked or impudent enough. (Foll. by *of*, †*to do*.) L16.

O. MANNING As soon as he is capable, he will be ordered to leave. S. THEMERSON He wouldn't be capable of committing such a crime!

4 LAW. Qualified or entitled to inherit, possess, etc. (Foll. by *of*.) L16.

D. M. WALKER A person may be capable of marriage at a different age from that at which he acquires capacity to vote.

5 Having general capacity, intelligence, or ability; competent; gifted. E17.

J. S. BLACKIE A more capable . . witness could not be desired. B. TARKINGTON Lucy is so capable; she keeps house exquisitely.

■ **capableness** *noun* L16. **capably** *adverb* L19.

capable de tout /kapabl də tu/ *adjectival phr*. L19.
[ORIGIN French.]
Capable of anything; without scruple or restraint.

capacious /kəˈpeɪʃəs/ *adjective*. E17.
[ORIGIN from Latin *capac-*, *capax*, from *capere* take: see -ACIOUS.]
†**1** = CAPABLE 1a. E17–L18.

W. BRERETON A spacious harbour capacious of many thousand sail.

2 Able to hold much; roomy, spacious, wide; comprehensive. E17.

HAZLITT The capacious soul of Shakspeare. A. N. WILSON It was a large, comfortable, reassuring brick house, with capacious bow windows on three floors.

3 Disposed or adapted for the reception *of*. *arch*. L17.

M. BEERBOHM Women of her own age and kind, capacious of tragedy.

■ **capaciously** *adverb* E19. **capaciousness** *noun* M17.

capacitance /kəˈpasɪt(ə)ns/ *noun*. L19.
[ORIGIN from CAPACITY + -ANCE.]
Ability to store electrical charge; the ratio of the change in the electrostatic charge of a body to the corresponding change in its potential.

capacitate /kəˈpasɪteɪt/ *verb trans*. M17.
[ORIGIN from CAPACITY + -ATE[3].]
Endow with capacity (*for*, *to do*), make capable; make legally competent; BIOLOGY cause (a spermatozoon) to undergo changes in the female reproductive tract that enable it to penetrate and fertilize an ovum (usu. in *pass*.).
■ **capaciˈtation** *noun* M19.

capacitive /kəˈpasɪtɪv/ *adjective*. E20.
[ORIGIN from CAPACITY + -IVE.]
Of or pertaining to electrical capacitance.
■ **capacitative** *adjective* = CAPACITIVE M20. **capacitatively**, **capacitively** *adverbs* through the medium of capacitance, as regards capacitance M20.

capacitor /kəˈpasɪtə/ *noun*. E20.
[ORIGIN from CAPACITY + -OR.]
An electric circuit component which provides capacitance, usu. consisting of conducting plates separated by an insulating material; a condenser.
padder capacitor: see PADDER *noun*[2] 3.

capacity /kəˈpasɪti/ *noun & adjective*. LME.
[ORIGIN French *capacité* from Latin *capacitas*, formed as CAPACIOUS: see -ACITY.]
▸ **A** *noun*. **1** Ability to receive, contain, hold, produce, or carry; cubic content, volume (formerly also surface area, width). LME. ▸**b** = CAPACITANCE. L18. ▸**c** The maximum amount or number that can be contained, produced, etc. E20. ▸**d** The total cylinder volume that is swept by the pistons in an internal-combustion engine. M20.

SHAKES. *Ant. & Cl.* Had our great palace the capacity To camp this host, we would all sup together. A. MACLEAN His capacity for brandy was phenomenal. F. HOYLE The cranial capacity eventually grew to about 1600 cubic centimetres. **c** J. K. GALBRAITH Production is at or near capacity.

measure of capacity a measure of volume used for vessels and liquids, grain, etc. ***specific heat capacity***: see SPECIFIC *adjective*. ***specific inductive capacity***: see SPECIFIC *adjective*. ***thermal capacity***: see THERMAL *adjective*. ***vital capacity***: see VITAL *adjective*. **c to capacity** fully, completely.

2 Mental or intellectual power, as an inherent faculty or as developed; (a) talent; a mental faculty. LME.

G. BERKELEY He wants capacity to relish what true piety is. ISAIAH BERLIN The more mysterious capacities called 'insight' and 'intuition'.

3 Legal competency or qualification. LME.
legal capacity: see LEGAL *adjective*.
†4 A containing space or area; a void; a cavity. M16–M18.
5 An ability, power, or propensity for some specified purpose, activity, or experience; a susceptibility, a possibility. (Foll. by *of, for, to do*.) M17.

DEFOE To deprive them of the capacity of ever returning. S. BUTLER We are endued with Capacities of action, of happiness and misery. H. L. MENCKEN There was grave uneasiness about his physical capacity for the job. N. SHUTE It was within the capacity of his ship to execute. E. REVELEY It was not that Erv had ever laid a hand on her but the capacity was there.

6 A position, a condition, a relative character. M17.

G. K. CHESTERTON The King . . reviewed it in his capacity as literary critic. G. GREENE I was working for him . . in a secretarial capacity.

▸ **B** *attrib.* or as *adjective*. That reaches or fills maximum capacity; fully occupying. M20.

Times Lit. Suppl. Both the play and film are now drawing capacity houses in London. F. ASTAIRE Business was capacity wherever we went.

cap-à-pie /kapəˈpiː/ *adverb. arch.* E16.
[ORIGIN Old French *cap a pie* (mod. *de pied en cap*).]
From head to foot, fully (armed, ready, etc.).

caparison /kəˈparɪs(ə)n/ *noun*. Now *arch.* or *hist.* E16.
[ORIGIN French †*caparasson* (mod. *caparaçon*) from Spanish *caparazón* saddlecloth, perh. from CAPA.]
1 An ornamented covering spread over a horse's saddle or harness; (usu. in *pl.*) a horse's trappings. E16.
2 *transf.* A set of clothes or ornaments, an outfit. L16.

caparison /kəˈparɪs(ə)n/ *verb trans.* L16.
[ORIGIN French *caparassonner*, formed as CAPARISON *noun*.]
Put trappings or hangings on; deck.

capataz /kapaˈtaθ/ *noun*. Pl. **-taces** /-ˈtaθes/. E19.
[ORIGIN Spanish, irreg. from Latin *caput* head.]
In Spain or Spanish-speaking America: an overseer, a superintendent, a boss.

cape /keɪp/ *noun*[1]. LME.
[ORIGIN Old French & mod. French *cap* from Provençal (= Spanish *cabo*) from Proto-Romance from Latin *caput* head.]
▸ **I** *gen.* **1** A headland, a promontory. LME.
▸ **II** *spec.* **2** ***the Cape***, some familiar headland, *esp.* (the province containing) the Cape of Good Hope at the southern tip of Africa. M17.
3 More fully ***capeskin***. A soft leather made from South African sheepskin. E20.
– COMB.: **Cape Barren goose** [*Cape Barren*, an island in Bass Strait, Australia] a large Australian goose, *Cereopsis novaehollandiae*, which has a short black bill that is almost covered by a swollen waxy yellow cere; also called ***cereopsis*** (***goose***); **Cape brandy** *S. Afr.* brandy made from vines in the Cape; crude brandy; ***Cape buffalo***: see BUFFALO *noun* 1b; **Cape cart** *S. Afr.* a two-wheeled horse-drawn cart; **Cape chestnut** a southern African evergreen tree, *Calodendrum capense*, of the rue family; **Cape Cod** *N. Amer.* (designating) a type of rectangular house with a steeply gabled roof, characteristic of Cape Cod, Massachusetts; **Cape Coloured** *S. Afr.* a person of mixed ethnic descent living in the province of Western Cape; **Cape cowslip** = LACHENALIA; **Cape daisy** a yellow-flowered plant of the composite family, *Arctotis fastuosa*, native to southern Africa and widely introduced as an ornamental; **Cape doctor** *S. Afr.* a strong south-east wind; **Cape Dutch** *noun & adjective* (***a***) *noun* the early Dutch settlers at the Cape of Good Hope; *arch.* Afrikaans (regarded as a dialect of Dutch); (***b***) *adjective* of or pertaining to the Cape Dutch; *spec.* designating a style of architecture characterized by gables and whitewashed walls; **Cape fox** a fox, *Vulpes chama*, with a silvery-grey back, occurring in the drier areas of southern Africa; ***Cape gannet***: see GANNET 1; **Cape gooseberry** a S. American physalis or ground cherry, *Physalis peruviana*; the edible round yellow berry of this plant; ***Cape* HARTEBEEST**; **Cape hunting dog** = ***hunting dog*** (b) s.v. HUNTING *noun*; ***Cape* HYACINTH**; **Cape jasmine**, **Cape jessamine** gardenia; esp. *Gardenia jasminioides*, native to China; ***Cape leaping hare***: see LEAPING *ppl adjective*; ***Cape Malay***: see MALAY 1b; **Cape marigold** = DIMORPHOTHECA; ***Cape pigeon***: see PIGEON *noun*[1] 1; **Cape pondweed** a southern African aquatic plant, *Aponogeton distachyos*, with two spikes of fragrant white flowers; **Cape primrose** = STREPTOCARPUS; **Cape salmon** *S. Afr.* any of various fishes; *esp.* = GEELBEK; ***capeskin***: see sense 3 above; ***Cape smoke***: see SMOKE *noun* 7a; **Cape sparrow** a dark-coloured sparrow of southern Africa, *Passer melanurus*; **Cape-weed** any of various plants; *esp.* (*Austral. & NZ*) = ***Cape daisy*** above.

cape /keɪp/ *noun*[2]. M16.
[ORIGIN French from Provençal *capa* (= Old French & mod. French CHAPE) from late Latin *cappa*: see CAP *noun*[1].]
1 A short (formerly also a long) sleeveless cloak; a fixed or detachable part of a longer cloak, coat, etc., falling loosely over the shoulders from the neckband; *spec.* the red cloak used by a bullfighter. M16.
Inverness cape: see INVERNESS 1.
2 *transf.* A growth of feathers or hair suggesting a cape. L19.
■ **caped** *adjective* having a cape, wearing a cape M16. **capelet** *noun* a small cape E20.

†**cape** *verb intrans.* E16–M19.
[ORIGIN Uncertain: perh. ult. rel. to French *cap* head of the ship.]
NAUTICAL. Of a vessel or its crew: head, bear.

capeador /kapɪəˈdɔː/ *noun*. E20.
[ORIGIN Spanish, from *capear* trick a bull with a cape, from CAPA.]
A person who aids a bullfighter by distracting the bull with his cloak.

capeesh /kəˈpiːʃ/ *interjection*. *slang* (chiefly *US*). M20.
[ORIGIN Italian *capisce* 3 sing. pres. indic. of *capire* understand.]
Do you understand? Get it?

P. AUSTER Upstairs is off limits. Capeesh?

capelin /ˈkeɪplɪn, ˈkap-/ *noun*. Also **caplin**. E17.
[ORIGIN French from Provençal *capelan* CHAPLAIN.]
A smelt, *Mallotus villosus*, of northern oceans.

capeline /ˈkap(ə)lɪn/ *noun*. LME.
[ORIGIN Old French & mod. French from Provençal *capelina*, from *capel* hat (= mod. French *chapeau*).]
1 *hist.* An iron skullcap worn by medieval archers. LME.
2 A woman's hat, *esp.* one with a wide brim trimmed with feathers. Also, a light hood with an attached cape. L18.

capellane /ˈkap(ə)leɪn/ *noun*. Long *obsolete* exc. *hist.* OE.
[ORIGIN medieval Latin *cappellanus*: see CHAPLAIN.]
A chaplain; a keeper of sacred relics.

capellini /kapeˈliːni/ *noun pl.* M20.
[ORIGIN Italian = little hairs.]
A variety of pasta consisting of very thin strands.

caper /ˈkeɪpə/ *noun*[1]. LME.
[ORIGIN French *câpres* or Latin *capparis* from Greek *kapparis*: treated as pl.]
1 A trailing shrub, *Capparis spinosa*, of southern Europe. LME.
2 Usu. in *pl.* ▸**a** The flower buds of this shrub, used for pickling and served esp. in a sauce. L15. ▸**b** The seed pods of other plants, e.g. nasturtium, used similarly; any such plant. Cf. ***bean caper*** s.v. BEAN *noun*. L16.
3 A kind of scented tea. L18.
– COMB.: **caper spurge** an ornamental poisonous spurge, *Euphorbia lathyris*.

caper /ˈkeɪpə/ *noun*[2]. L16.
[ORIGIN Abbreviation of CAPRIOLE *noun*.]
1 A frisky movement, a leap, a spring; *fig.* a fantastic proceeding. L16.
cut a caper, ***cut capers***, ***cut up capers***: see CUT *verb*.
2 An activity or occupation, esp. a risky or questionable venture; a 'dodge'. *slang*. M19.

caper /ˈkeɪpə/ *noun*[3]. *obsolete* exc. *hist.* M17.
[ORIGIN Dutch *kaper*, from *kapen* take away, rob, plunder.]
(The captain of) a privateer; a corsair.

caper /ˈkapə/ *noun*[4]. *colloq.* E20.
[ORIGIN Abbreviation.]
= CAPERCAILLIE.

caper /ˈkeɪpə/ *verb intrans.* L16.
[ORIGIN formed as CAPER *noun*[2].]
Move friskily, skip, dance, (*about*).
■ **caperer** *noun* L17.

capercaillie /kapəˈkeɪli/ *noun*. Also **-lzie** /-lji, -lzi/. M16.
[ORIGIN Gaelic *capull coille* lit. 'horse of the wood': the spelling *-lz-* derives from Middle English *-ȝ-*.]
A large grouse, *Tetrao urogallus*, formerly native to and now re-established in the Scottish Highlands.

Capernaite /kəˈpəːnɪʌɪt/ *noun*. *arch. derog.* M16.
[ORIGIN from *Capernaum* in Galilee (*John* 6:26–59) + -ITE[1].]
A believer in transubstantiation.
– NOTE: Used esp. in theological controversy in 16 & 17.
■ **Caperna'itic** *adjective* L19. **Caperna'itical** *adjective* L16.

capernoited /kapəˈnɔɪtɪd/ *adjective*. *Scot. arch.* E18.
[ORIGIN Unknown.]
Irritable; peevish; muddle-headed; affected by drink.

Capetian /kəˈpiːʃ(ə)n/ *adjective & noun*. M19.
[ORIGIN French *Capétien*.]
(A member) of the dynasty of French kings founded by Hugh Capet in 987.

Caphtor /ˈkaftə/ *noun*. Pl. **-rim** /-rɪm/. LOE.
[ORIGIN Hebrew *Kaptōr*, from place name = *Caphtor*: see below. Cf. KEFTIU.]
ANCIENT HISTORY. A native or inhabitant of Caphtor, a region of the eastern Mediterranean mentioned in the Bible but not firmly located. Usu. in *pl.*

capias /ˈkeɪpɪəs, ˈkap-/ *noun*. LME.
[ORIGIN Latin = you are to seize, 2nd person sing. pres. subjunct. of *capere* take.]
LAW (now chiefly *hist.*). A writ or process commanding the arrest of the person named.
capias ad satisfaciendum /ad ˌsatɪsfasɪˈɛndəm/: after judgement, directing the imprisonment of the defendant until the plaintiff's claim is satisfied (abbreviation CA. SA.). ***capias in*** WITHERNAM. PLURIES ***capias***.

capillaceous /kapɪˈleɪʃəs/ *adjective*. E18.
[ORIGIN from Latin *capillaceus*, from *capillus* hair: see -ACEOUS.]
Hairlike, threadlike.

capillaire /kapɪˈlɛː/ *noun*. M18.
[ORIGIN French from Latin *capillaris*, late Latin *capillaris herba* maidenhair fern: see CAPILLARY.]
A syrup of maidenhair fern; a syrup flavoured with orange-flower water.

†**capillament** *noun*. L17–M19.
[ORIGIN Latin *capillamentum* the hair collectively, from *capillus* hair.]
A hairlike fibre, a filament.

capillarity /kapɪˈlarɪti/ *noun*. M19.
[ORIGIN French *capillarité*, formed as CAPILLARY + -ITY.]
Capillary attraction or repulsion; the property of exerting this.

capillary /kəˈpɪləri/ *adjective & noun*. M17.
[ORIGIN Latin *capillaris*, from *capillus* hair, after Old French & mod. French *capillaire*: see -ARY[2].]
▸ **A** *adjective*. **1** Of or pertaining to hair; hairlike, esp. in tenuity. M17.
2 Of a tube etc.: having a hairlike bore. M17.
3 Of, pertaining to, or occurring in capillaries. E19.
capillary attraction, **capillary repulsion** the tendency of liquid in a capillary tube to rise, recede, as a result of surface forces.
▸ **B** *noun*. **1** A capillary vessel; *esp.* any of the extremely narrow blood vessels which form a network between the arterioles and venules. M17.
†2 A fern, esp. the maidenhair. M17–M18.
■ Also †**capillar** *adjective* LME–L17.

capillitium /kapɪˈlɪʃɪəm/ *noun*. M19.
[ORIGIN Latin = hair collectively, from *capillus* hair.]
MYCOLOGY. Spore-containing fibrous tissue in the sporangia of certain fungi.

capital /ˈkapɪt(ə)l/ *noun*[1]. ME.
[ORIGIN Old French *capitel* (mod. *chapiteau*) from late Latin *capitellum* dim. of *caput*, *capit-* head: mod. spelling *-al* through assoc. with CAPITAL *adjective & noun*[2].]
1 The head or cornice of a pillar or column. ME.
2 The cap of a chimney, crucible, etc. E18.

capital /ˈkapɪt(ə)l/ *adjective & noun*[2]. ME.
[ORIGIN Old French & mod. French from Latin *capitalis*, from *caput*, *capit-* head: see -AL[1].]
▸ **A** *adjective*. **I** Relating to the head.
†1 Of or pertaining to the head or top. ME–L17.
2 Involving loss of the head or life; vitally harmful, fatal. LME. ▸†**b** Of an enemy, enmity: deadly, mortal. LME–M18. ▸**c** Of a crime etc.: punishable by death. E16.

CAXTON To have capytal sentence & be beheded. *fig.*: W. H. PRESCOTT In the outset, he seems to have fallen into a capital error.

▸ **II** Standing at the head (*lit.* & *fig.*).
3 Chief, principal; important, leading. LME.

W. BLACKSTONE The eldest son had the capital fee . . of his father's possessions. T. WARTON The cloister . . of some capital monastery. R. W. DALE The old traditions . . made Obedience the capital virtue of childhood.

4 Orig. (of a letter or word), standing at the head of a page, passage, etc. Now (of a letter), having the form and size used to begin a sentence, proper name, etc. LME.

W. VAN T. CLARK When Joyce spoke about Davies he said 'he' as if it had a capital H.

a — with a capital A (or similar phr.) emphatically a —, the real or quintessential a —.
5 Of funds, stock, etc.: original, serving as a basis for commercial or financial operations. E18.

ADAM SMITH The capital stock of Great Britain was not diminished even by the enormous expense of the late war.

6 Excellent, first-rate. Freq. as an exclam. of approval. *colloq.* M18.

B. JOWETT Capital, Socrates; by the gods, that is truly good. A. MOOREHEAD He is a capital officer, zealous and untiring in the performance of his duties.

▸ **B** *noun*. **1** A capital letter. LME.
small capitals: see SMALL *adjective*.
2 The stock with which a company or person enters into business; the total sum of shareholders' contributions in a joint-stock company; accumulated wealth, *esp.* as used in further production. M16. ▸**b** The holders of wealth as a class; capitalists, employers of labour. M19.

BURKE You began ill . . You set up your trade without a capital. F. RAPHAEL Lack of capital prevented Nat's buying a practice. H. MACMILLAN A widespread desire that . . economic development should be . . supported by British capital. **b** W. HOLTBY Here gallant Labour, with nothing to lose but its chains, would fight entrenched and armoured Capital.

fixed capital: invested in permanent assets such as land, buildings, machinery, etc. **make capital out of** *fig.* turn to account, turn to one's own advantage. ***organic composition of capital***: see ORGANIC *adjective*. ***refugee capital***: see REFUGEE *adjective*. **working capital**: available for the actual carrying on of business.
3 A capital town or city. M17.
– SPECIAL COLLOCATIONS & COMB.: **capital adequacy** the statutory minimum reserves of capital which a bank or other financial institution must have available. **capital gain** profit from the sale of investments or property. **capital goods** goods (to be) used in producing commodities, as opp. to consumer goods. **capital-intensive** *adjective* requiring much use of capital. **capital levy**

the appropriation by the state of a proportion of a nation's private wealth. **capital punishment** infliction of death by an authorized public authority as punishment for a crime. **capital ship** a battleship or other large warship. **capital sum** a lump sum of money, *esp.* one payable to an insured person. **capital territory**: containing the capital city of a country. **capital transfer tax**: levied on the transfer of capital by gift, bequest, etc. (in Britain 1975–86).
■ **capitalling** *noun* the providing of a word with a capital letter L17. **capitally** *adverb* in a capital manner E17.

capitalise *verb* var. of CAPITALIZE.

capitalism /ˈkapɪt(ə)lɪz(ə)m/ *noun*. M19.
[ORIGIN from CAPITAL *noun*[2] + -ISM.]
The possession of capital or wealth; a system in which private capital or wealth is used in the production or distribution of goods; the dominance of private owners of capital and of production for profit.
popular capitalism: see POPULAR *adjective*.

capitalist /ˈkapɪt(ə)lɪst/ *noun & adjective*. Freq. *derog.* L18.
[ORIGIN formed as CAPITALISM + -IST.]
▸ **A** *noun*. A person who has capital, *esp.* one who uses it in (large-scale) business enterprises. L18.
▸ **B** *adjective*. Of or pertaining to capitalists or capitalism. M19.
capitalist road: see ROAD *noun*. ***capitalist roader***: see ROADER *noun*[1] 2.
■ **capitaˈlistic** *adjective* of or pertaining to capitalists; characterized by capitalism: L19. **capitaˈlistically** *adverb* L19.

capitalize /ˈkapɪt(ə)lʌɪz/ *verb*. Also **-ise**. M18.
[ORIGIN from CAPITAL *noun*[2] + -IZE. Cf. French *capitaliser*.]
1 *verb trans.* Write or print (a letter) as a capital; begin (a word) with a capital letter; write or print in capitals. M18.
2 *verb trans.* **a** Convert into a capital sum; compute or realize the current value of; reckon the value of by setting future benefits against the cost of maintenance. M19. ▸**b** Provide with capital. Orig. *US*. L19.

> **b** *Observer* At the current price of 213p, Burmah is capitalised at a little over £300 million.

3 *verb trans. & intrans.* (foll. by *on*). Make capital out of, use to one's advantage, turn to account. M19.

> *Publishers Weekly* The publishers . . do not intend to capitalize the publicity. *Face* The boys seem well placed to capitalise on the success of their show. *Wall Street Journal* We would never capitalize on the tragedy.

■ **capitaliˈzation** *noun* M19.

capitan /ˈkapɪt(ə)n, kapɪˈtɑːn/ *noun*. M18.
[ORIGIN Spanish *capitán* CAPTAIN *noun*.]
Chiefly *hist.* A captain, a naval commander.
Capitan Pasha *hist.* the chief admiral of the Turkish fleet.

capitana /kapɪˈtɑːnə/ *noun*. L17.
[ORIGIN Italian, Spanish, & Portuguese.]
The ship of the admiral of an Italian, Spanish, etc., fleet.

capitano /kapɪˈtɑːnəʊ/ *noun*. Pl. **-os**. L16.
[ORIGIN Italian = CAPTAIN *noun*.]
In Italy or among Italian-speakers: a captain, a headman, a chief.

capitao /kapɪˈtaʊ/ *noun*. L19.
[ORIGIN Portuguese *capitão* = CAPTAIN *noun*.]
A headman, leader of a gang, etc., in E. Africa.

capita succedanea *noun phr.* pl. of CAPUT SUCCEDANEUM.

capitate /ˈkapɪteɪt/ *adjective*. M17.
[ORIGIN Latin *capitatus*, from *caput*, *capit-* head: see -ATE[2].]
1 Chiefly ANATOMY. Having a distinct head, knob-headed; *spec.* denoting the largest bone of the wrist. M17.
2 BOTANY. Having the inflorescence in a close terminal cluster. L17.
■ Also **capitated** *adjective* (now *rare* or *obsolete*) L17.

capitation /kapɪˈteɪʃ(ə)n/ *noun*. E17.
[ORIGIN French, or late Latin *capitatio(n-)*, formed as CAPITATE: see -ATION.]
1 The counting of heads or persons. E17.
2 (The levying of) a tax or fee of so much a head; a payment of so much a head. M17.
– COMB.: **capitation fee**, **capitation grant**, etc.: of so much per head subject to certain conditions.

capite /ˈkapɪti/ *noun*. E17.
[ORIGIN Latin, abl. of *caput* head.]
hist. In full ***tenure in capite***. Tenure by which land was held immediately of the Crown.

capitellum /kapɪˈtɛləm/ *noun*. Pl. **-lla** /-lə/. E17.
[ORIGIN Late Latin, dim. of Latin *capit-*, *caput* head: see -ELLUM.]
†**1** = CAPITAL *noun*[1] 1. Only in E17.
2 ANATOMY. The capitulum of the humerus. L19.

Capitol /ˈkapɪt(ə)l/ *noun*. LME.
[ORIGIN Old French *capitolie*, *-oile*, later assim. to the source, Latin *Capitolium*, from *caput*, *capit-* head.]
1 A citadel on top of a hill; esp. *the* temple of Jupiter Optimus Maximus, on the Saturnian or Tarpeian (later called Capitoline) Hill at Rome. LME.
2 *The* building occupied by the US Congress in Washington DC; in some other cities, the state legislature building. L17.
■ **Capitolian** /kapɪˈtəʊlɪən/ *adjective* = CAPITOLINE E17. **Capitoline** /kəˈpɪtəlʌɪn/ *adjective* designating or pertaining to the hill at Rome on which the Capitol stood; of or pertaining to the Capitol: E17.

capitonné /kapɪtɔne/ *adjective*. L19.
[ORIGIN French, pa. pple of *capitonner* upholster, quilt.]
Designating or characterized by a style of upholstery or embroidery in which the material is drawn in at intervals to present a quilted appearance.

capitular /kəˈpɪtjʊlə/ *adjective & noun*. E16.
[ORIGIN Late Latin *capitularis*, from Latin *capitulum*: see CHAPTER *noun*, -AR[1].]
▸ **A** *adjective*. **1** Of, pertaining to, or governed by a cathedral chapter. E16.
2 Chiefly ANATOMY. Pertaining to or of the nature of a capitulum. M19.
▸ **B** *noun*. = CAPITULARY *noun*. M17.
■ †**capitularly** *adverb* as a chapter E–M18.

capitulary /kəˈpɪtjʊləri/ *noun & adjective*. M17.
[ORIGIN Late Latin *capitularius*, formed as CAPITULAR: see -ARY[1].]
▸ **A** *noun*. **1** *hist.* A collection of ordinances, esp. of Frankish kings. M17.
2 A member of a chapter. Now *rare* or *obsolete*. L17.
3 A heading, a title. *rare*. E19.
▸ **B** *adjective*. = CAPITULAR *adjective* 1. L18.

capitulate /kəˈpɪtjʊleɪt/ *verb*. M16.
[ORIGIN medieval Latin *capitulat-*, pa. ppl stem of *capitulare* draw up under distinct heads, from late Latin *capitulum* head of a discourse: see CHAPTER *noun*, -ATE[3]. In sense 3 through French *capituler*.]
†**1** *verb intrans.* Draw up articles of agreement; treat, parley; make conditions. M16–E19. ▸**b** *verb trans.* Make terms about, negotiate. L16–M17.
†**2** *verb trans.* Draw up in chapters or under heads; enumerate. L16–L17.
3 *verb intrans.* & (less usually) *trans.* Surrender, esp. on stated conditions. L17.

> W. ROBERTSON Want of provisions quickly obliged Trevulci to capitulate. W. STYRON I knew that I was on the verge of capitulating to him, backing down.

■ **capitulator** *noun* E17. **capitulatory** *adjective* E19.

capitulation /kəpɪtjʊˈleɪʃ(ə)n/ *noun*. M16.
[ORIGIN Late Latin *capitulatio(n-)*, formed as CAPITULATE: see -ATION. In sense 3 through French *capitulation*.]
†**1** **a** The making of terms; a covenant, treaty. M16–M19. ▸**b** In *pl.* Articles of agreement, terms, conditions; *spec.* articles giving special immunities and privileges within a state to subjects of another state. Now *hist.* L16.
2 A statement of the main divisions of a subject. Cf. RECAPITULATION. L16.
3 The action of surrendering, esp. on stated conditions; an instrument containing terms of surrender. M17.

capitulum /kəˈpɪtjʊləm/ *noun*. Pl. **-la** /-lə/. E18.
[ORIGIN Latin, dim. of *caput*, *capit-* head: see -ULE.]
A small rounded head or knob; *esp.* (***a***) ANATOMY a bony protuberance articulating with another bone, *esp.* the prominence at the end of the humerus which articulates with the radius; (***b***) BOTANY a dense flat terminal cluster of sessile flowers or florets on a common receptacle, as in the composite family.

caple /ˈkeɪp(ə)l/ *noun*. Long *obsolete* exc. *dial.* Also **capul**. ME.
[ORIGIN Old Norse *kapall* from Latin *caballus*.]
A horse.

Caplet /ˈkaplɪt/ *noun*. Also **c-**. M20.
[ORIGIN from CAP(SULE *noun* & *adjective* + TAB)LET *noun*.]
PHARMACOLOGY. (Proprietary name for) a coated capsule or tablet.

caplin *noun* var. of CAPELIN.

cap'n /ˈkapm/ *noun*. *colloq.* Chiefly *N. Amer.* E19.
[ORIGIN Abbreviation.]
= CAPTAIN *noun*.

capnomancy /ˈkapnəmansi/ *noun*. *rare*. E17.
[ORIGIN from Greek *kapnos* smoke + -MANCY, perh. through French *capnomancie*.]
Divination by smoke.

capo /ˈkapəʊ/ *noun*[1]. Pl. **-os**. M20.
[ORIGIN Abbreviation.]
= CAPOTASTO.

capo /ˈkapəʊ/ *noun*[2]. Chiefly *US*. Pl. **-os**. M20.
[ORIGIN Italian from Latin *caput* head.]
The head of a crime syndicate or one of its branches.

Capo di Monte /ˌkapəʊ dɪ ˈmɒnteɪ, ˈmɒnti/ *noun phr.* Also **Capodimonte**. M19.
[ORIGIN See below.]
A type of porcelain first produced at the Capo di Monte palace near Naples in the mid 18th century, usu. in the form of tableware or figures and generally white with richly coloured rococo decoration.

capoeira /kapʊˈeɪrə/ *noun*. Also **capoiera**. M20.
[ORIGIN Portuguese.]
A martial art emphasizing leg and foot movements and performed inside a circle formed by onlookers, developed by Angolan slaves in Brazil and now widely practised both as a dance form and a competitive martial art.

capon /ˈkeɪp(ə)n/ *noun & verb*. LOE.
[ORIGIN Anglo-Norman *capun* var. of Old French & mod. French *capon*, from Proto-Romance from Latin *capo(n-)*.]
▸ **A** *noun*. **1** A castrated domestic cock (usu. one fattened for eating). Cf. POULARD. LOE.
†**2** A eunuch. ME–L17.
3 A dull-witted person. *obsolete* exc. *dial.* M16.
†**4** A billet-doux. Cf. POULET. *rare* (Shakes.). Only in L16.
5 A kind of fish, *esp.* a red herring. *dial.* M17.
Norfolk capon: see NORFOLK 1.
▸ **B** *verb trans.* Make a capon of; castrate. L16.
■ †**caponet** *noun* a small capon L16–E18. **caponize** *verb trans.* = CAPON *verb* M17.

caponata /kapə(ʊ)ˈnɑːtə/ *noun*. M20.
[ORIGIN Italian *capponata* (orig. referring to a sailor's dish containing ship's biscuit), from *cappóne* capon.]
A Sicilian dish similar to ratatouille, consisting usu. of aubergines, olives, onions, and other chopped vegetables, anchovies, and herbs in a tomato sauce, served cold as an accompaniment or starter.

caponier /kapəˈnɪə/ *noun*. L17.
[ORIGIN Spanish *caponera* (whence French *caponnière*) lit. 'capon-pen'.]
FORTIFICATION. A covered passage across a ditch.

capot /kəˈpɒt/ *noun*[1] *& verb*. M17.
[ORIGIN French, perh. from *capoter* dial. var. of *chapoter* castrate.]
PIQUET. ▸**A** *noun*. The winning of all the tricks by one player; a score awarded for this. M17.
▸ **B** *verb trans.* Infl. **-tt-**. Win all the tricks from. M17.

capot /ˈkapəʊ, kəˈpɒt; *foreign* kapo (*pl. same*)/ *noun*[2]. L17.
[ORIGIN French, masc. form of CAPOTE.]
= CAPOTE 1a.

capotasto /kapəʊˈtastəʊ/ *noun*. Pl. **-os**. Also **capo tasto**. L19.
[ORIGIN Italian, lit. 'head stop': cf. TASTO.]
MUSIC. A movable bar attached to the fingerboard of a stringed instrument to make possible the simultaneous adjustment of the pitch of all the strings.

capote /kəˈpəʊt/ *noun*. E19.
[ORIGIN French, dim. of *cape* CAPE *noun*[2].]
1 **a** A long hooded cloak worn by soldiers, travellers, etc. E19. ▸**b** A long mantle worn by women. M19.
2 A bonnet with a soft crown and stiff projecting brim. E19.

capouch *noun* var. of CAPUCHE.

cappa /ˈkapə/ *noun*. M19.
[ORIGIN Italian = CAPE *noun*[2].]
A cloak forming part of a religious habit; a cope.

Cappadocian /kapəˈdəʊʃ(ə)n/ *adjective & noun*. E17.
[ORIGIN from *Cappadocia* (see below) + -AN.]
(A native or inhabitant) of Cappadocia, an ancient kingdom of Asia Minor, now part of Turkey.

cappelletti /kapəˈlɛti/ *noun pl.* M19.
[ORIGIN Italian = little hats.]
Pieces of stuffed pasta resembling small pointed hats, filled with meat, cheese, or vegetables and served either in broth or with a sauce; this variety of pasta.

capper /ˈkapə/ *noun*. ME.
[ORIGIN from CAP *noun*[1] or *verb*[1] + -ER[1].]
1 A cap-maker. *obsolete* exc. *hist.* ME.
2 A person who or thing which provides or forms a cap. L16.
3 An accomplice, *esp.* a confederate in a gambling game. *slang* (chiefly *US*). M18.
4 A person or thing that outdoes all rivals; something surprising or puzzling. *dial.* L18.

cappuccino /kapʊˈtʃiːnəʊ/ *noun*. Pl. **-os**. M20.
[ORIGIN Italian: see CAPUCHIN.]
(A cup of) coffee with milk, esp. made with espresso coffee and topped with white foam.

Capri /ˈkapriː, kəˈpriː/ *noun*. L19.
[ORIGIN An island in the Bay of Naples.]
1 A wine from Capri. L19.
2 In *pl.*, or as ***Capri pants***. Women's close-fitting tapered trousers. M20.

capric /ˈkaprɪk/ *adjective*. M19.
[ORIGIN from Latin *caper*, *capr-* goat + -IC.]
1 CHEMISTRY. ***capric acid***, a crystalline fatty acid present in butter, coconut oil, etc.; *n*-decanoic acid, $CH_3(CH_2)_8COOH$. M19.
2 Of a goat; goatlike. L19.
■ **caprate** *noun* a salt or ester of capric acid M19.

capriccio /kəˈprɪtʃɪəʊ/ *noun*. Pl. **-os**. E17.
[ORIGIN Italian: see CAPRICE.]
†**1** = CAPRICE 1. E17–E19.
†**2** A sudden movement; a trick, a prank, a caper. M17–M19.
3 A thing or work of lively fancy in art etc.; *esp.* a lively usu. short musical composition, more or less free in form. L17.

C

C

capriccioso /kəprɪtʃɪˈəʊzəʊ/ *adverb*. **M18**.
[**ORIGIN** Italian: see **CAPRICIOUS**.]
MUSIC. A direction: in a free and impulsive style.

caprice /kəˈpriːs/ *noun*. **M17**.
[**ORIGIN** French from Italian *capriccio* (lit.) head with the hair standing on end, (hence) horror, (later, by assoc. with *capra* goat) sudden start, from *capo* head (see **CAPO** *noun*²) + *riccio* hedgehog (ult. from Latin (*h*)*ericius* **URCHIN**).]
1 An unaccountable change of mind or conduct; a whim; a freakish fancy. **M17**. ▸**b** Inclination or disposition to such changes etc.; capriciousness. **M17**.
2 = **CAPRICCIO** 3. **E18**.

capricious /kəˈprɪʃəs/ *adjective*. **E17**.
[**ORIGIN** French *capricieux* from Italian *capriccioso*, from *capriccio* (see **CAPRICE**) + *-oso* **-OUS**.]
†**1** Humorous; fantastic; characterized by far-fetched comparisons etc. **E17–E18**.
2 Guided by caprice; readily swayed by whim or fancy; inconstant. Of a thing: subject to sudden change, irregular, unpredictable. **E17**.

J. CHEEVER They cultivated tropical plants in a capricious climate.

■ **capriciously** *adverb* **E17**. **capriciousness** *noun* **L16**.

Capricorn /ˈkaprɪkɔːn/ *noun*. In sense 1 also in Latin form **Capricornus** /kaprɪˈkɔːnəs/. **OE**.
[**ORIGIN** Latin *capricornus*, from *caper*, *capr-* goat + *cornu* horn, after Greek *aigokerōs* goat-horned, (as noun) Capricorn.]
1 (The name of) a constellation of the southern hemisphere, on the ecliptic between Sagittarius and Aquarius; *ASTROLOGY* (the name of) the tenth zodiacal sign, usu. associated with the period 22 December to 19 January (see note s.v. **ZODIAC**); the Goat. **OE**. ▸**b** A person born under the sign Capricorn. **M20**.

attrib.: E. KIRK Capricorn people resent all interference.

tropic of Capricorn: see **TROPIC** *noun & adjective*.
†**2** An ibex; a chamois. **M17–M19**.
– **COMB.**: **Capricorn beetle** a longhorn beetle of the genus *Cerambyx*.
■ **Capriˈcornian** *noun & adjective* (**a**) *noun* a person born under the sign Capricorn; (**b**) *adjective* of or pertaining to Capricorn; (characteristic of one) born under Capricorn: **E20**.

caprid /ˈkaprɪd/ *adjective & noun*. **M19**.
[**ORIGIN** from Latin *caper*, *capr-* goat + **-ID**³.]
▸ **A** *adjective*. Of or pertaining to the tribe of ruminants including the goats and sheep. **M19**.
▸ **B** *noun*. A caprid animal. **L20**.

caprification /kaprɪfɪˈkeɪʃ(ə)n/ *noun*. **E17**.
[**ORIGIN** Latin *caprificatio(n-)*, from *caprificat-* pa. ppl stem of *caprificare*, from *caprificus* wild fig tree: see **-ATION**.]
1 A process of ripening figs by means of punctures produced on the fruit by the action of insects or artificially. **E17**.
2 Artificial fertilization. **M19**.

caprifoil /ˈkaprɪfɔɪl/ *noun*. Now *rare* or *obsolete*. **LME**.
[**ORIGIN** medieval Latin *caprifolium* 'goat-leaf', with spelling assim. to *trefoil* etc.]
Honeysuckle.

caprine /ˈkaprʌɪn/ *adjective*. **LME**.
[**ORIGIN** Latin *caprinus*, from *caper*, *capr-* goat: see **-INE**¹. Cf. Old French & mod. French *caprin*.]
Of or pertaining to a goat or goats; goatlike.

capriole /ˈkaprɪəʊl/ *noun & verb*. **L16**.
[**ORIGIN** French (now *cabriole*), from Italian *capriola*, from *capriolare* to leap, from *capriolo* roebuck from Latin *capreolus* dim. of *caper*, *capr-* goat: see **-OLE**¹.]
▸ **A** *noun*. **1** A leap or caper, esp. as made in dancing (cf. **CABRIOLE** 1). **L16**.
2 A trained horse's horizontal leap with the hind legs kicking vigorously. **L16**.
▸ **B** *verb intrans*. Perform a capriole; skip, leap, caper. **L16**.

capriped /ˈkaprɪpɛd/ *adjective & noun*. *rare*. Also **-pede** /-piːd/. **M18**.
[**ORIGIN** Latin *capripes*, *-ped-*, from *caper*, *capr-* goat + *pes*, *ped-* foot.]
(A person) having feet like those of a goat.

caproic /kəˈprəʊɪk/ *adjective*. **M19**.
[**ORIGIN** from Latin *capr-*, *caper* goat + **-OIC**.]
CHEMISTRY. ***caproic acid***, = ***HEXANOIC acid***.
■ **ˈcaproate** *noun* a salt or ester of this acid **M19**. **caproˈlactam** *noun* a crystalline lactam, $C_6H_{11}NO$, which is an intermediate in nylon manufacture **M20**. **caproyl** /ˈkaprəʊʌɪl, -əʊɪl/ *noun* the radical $C_5H_{11}CO\cdot$ **M19**.

capryl /ˈkaprʌɪl, -prɪl/ *noun*. **M19**.
[**ORIGIN** from **CAPRIC** + **-YL**.]
CHEMISTRY. The radical $C_9H_{19}CO\cdot$; *n*-decanoyl. Usu. in *comb.* Occas. confused with **CAPRYLYL**.

caprylic /kaˈprɪlɪk/ *adjective*. **M19**.
[**ORIGIN** from Latin *capr-*, *caper*, goat + **-YL** + **-IC**.]
CHEMISTRY. ***caprylic acid***, a liquid fatty acid present in butter and other fats; *n*-octanoic acid, $CH_3(CH_2)_6COH$.
■ **ˈcaprylate** *noun* a salt or ester of this acid **M19**. **ˈcaprylyl** *noun* the radical $CH_3(CH_2)_6\cdot$; *n*-octanoyl; (cf. **CAPRYL**): **E20**.

caps /kaps/ *noun pl.* **M19**.
[**ORIGIN** Abbreviation.]
Capital letters, capitals.

capsa /ˈkapsə/ *noun*. Pl. **capsae** /ˈkapsiː/, **capsas**. **M20**.
[**ORIGIN** Latin: see **CASE** *noun*².]
ROMAN ANTIQUITIES. A cylindrical box for holding upright rolls of documents.

capsaicin /kapˈseɪɪsɪn/ *noun*. **L19**.
[**ORIGIN** Alt. of **CAPSICINE**: see **-IN**¹.]
CHEMISTRY. A cyclic amide, $C_{18}H_{27}NO_3$, responsible for the pungency of capsicums.

Capsian /ˈkapsɪən/ *adjective & noun*. **E20**.
[**ORIGIN** French *capsien*, from Latin *Capsa* for Gafsa, central Tunisia: see **-IAN**.]
ARCHAEOLOGY. (Designating or pertaining to) a late Palaeolithic culture of N. Africa.

capsicum /ˈkapsɪkəm/ *noun*. **L16**.
[**ORIGIN** mod. Latin, perh. from Latin *capsa* **CASE** *noun*².]
Any plant of the tropical genus *Capsicum*, of the nightshade family, esp. *C. annuum*, different forms of which bear chilli peppers and sweet peppers; the fruit of such a plant, *esp.* one of the more pungent varieties.
■ **capsicine** /-siːn/ *noun* (now *rare* or *obsolete*) (*CHEMISTRY*) a substance formerly regarded as an alkaloid responsible for the pungency of capsicums **M19**.

capsid /ˈkapsɪd/ *noun*¹ *& adjective*. **L19**.
[**ORIGIN** mod. Latin *Capsidae* (see **MIRID**), from *Capsus* genus name: see **-ID**³.]
ENTOMOLOGY. = **MIRID**.

capsid /ˈkapsɪd/ *noun*². **M20**.
[**ORIGIN** from Latin *capsa* **CASE** *noun*² + **-ID**².]
MICROBIOLOGY. The protein coat or shell of certain viruses.

capsize /kapˈsʌɪz/ *verb & noun*. **L18**.
[**ORIGIN** Perh. ult. from Spanish *capuzar* sink (a ship) by the head, from *cabo* head + *chapuzar* to dive, duck.]
▸ **A** *verb*. **1** *verb trans*. Overturn, upset, (esp. a boat, people in boat). **L18**.
2 *verb intrans*. Of a boat etc.: be overturned or upset. **E19**.
▸ **B** *noun*. An act or instance of capsizing. **E19**.
■ **capsizal** *noun* = **CAPSIZE** *noun* **L19**.

capsomere /ˈkapsəʊmɪə/ *noun*. **M20**.
[**ORIGIN** French *capsomère*: see **CAPSID** *noun*², **-MER**.]
MICROBIOLOGY. Each of a number of protein subunits from which the capsid of a virus is built up.

capstan /ˈkapst(ə)n/ *noun*. Also †**capstern** & other vars. **LME**.
[**ORIGIN** Provençal *cabestan* (earlier *cabestran*), from *cabestre* halter from Latin *capistrum*, from *capere* seize.]
1 A revolving barrel on a vertical axis for winding cable etc., esp. on board ship: worked by persons walking round pushing bars fitting into the barrel, or by electricity, steam, etc. **LME**.
2 A revolving spindle on a tape recorder etc. **M20**.
– **COMB.**: **capstan lathe**: with a revolving tool-holder.

capsulate /ˈkapsjʊlət/ *adjective*. **M17**.
[**ORIGIN** from **CAPSULE** *noun & adjective* + **-ATE**².]
Chiefly *BOTANY*. Enclosed in, formed into, or having a capsule.
■ Also **capsulated** *adjective* **M17**.

capsule /ˈkapsjuːl, -sjʊl/ *noun & adjective*. Formerly also in Latin form †**-ula**, pl. **-lae**. **LME**.
[**ORIGIN** French from Latin *capsula* dim. of *capsa* **CASE** *noun*²; see **-ULE**.]
▸ **A** *noun*. **1** A small case or container; an envelope, a sheath. **LME**.

fig.: N. MAILER This is all very sketchy, but I'm trying to put seven years into a capsule.

time capsule: see **TIME** *noun*.
2 *ANATOMY*. A membranous or fibrous envelope around an organ, joint, etc.; a sac. **L17**.
Tenon's capsule: see **TENON** *noun*².
3 *BOTANY*. A dry seed case which opens when ripe by the parting of valves. **L17**.
†**4** *CHEMISTRY*. A shallow vessel for roasting or evaporating. **E18–L19**.
5 A top or cover for a bottle. **M19**.
6 A small case of gelatin etc. enclosing a dose of medicine. **L19**.
7 A detachable nose cone of a rocket, compartment of a spacecraft, etc., containing instruments or crew. **M20**.
▸ **B** *attrib.* or as *adjective*. Brief, condensed; small and compact. **M20**.

Drapers Record Designer Bella Freud has created a capsule collection for the brand.

■ **capsular** *adjective* of, pertaining to, or of the nature of a capsule **M18**. **capsulitis** /-ˈlʌɪtɪs/ *noun* (*MEDICINE*) inflammation of a capsule, esp. of a joint **M19**.

capsule /ˈkapsjuːl, -sjʊl/ *verb trans*. **M19**.
[**ORIGIN** from the noun.]
Enclose in or provide with a capsule.

capsulize /ˈkapsjʊlʌɪz/ *verb trans*. Orig. *US*. Also **-ise**. **M20**.
[**ORIGIN** from **CAPSULE** *noun* + **-IZE**.]
Compress (information etc.) into a brief and compact form.

capsulo- /ˈkapsjʊləʊ/ *combining form* of Latin *capsula* **CAPSULE** *noun*: see **-O-**.
■ **capsulotomy** /-ˈlɒtəmi/ *noun* (an instance of) surgical incision into the capsule of the lens of the eye **L19**.

Capt. *abbreviation*.
Captain.

captain /ˈkaptɪn/ *noun & verb*. **LME**.
[**ORIGIN** Late Old French *capitain* (mod. *capitaine*), superseding earlier *chevetaigne* **CHIEFTAIN** and *chataigne*, *catanie*, from late Latin *capitaneus* chief, from *caput*, *capit-* head.]
▸ **A** *noun*. **1** A chief or leader, esp. a military leader or commander. **LME**.

H. A. L. FISHER The illustrious Emperor .. the captain of Roman Christianity in the western world.

captain of industry an industrial magnate.
2 A military officer holding subordinate command. **LME**. ▸**b** *spec.* An officer in the army or (US etc.) air force, ranking below a major and above a lieutenant. **M16**. ▸**c** An officer in the Salvation Army, ranking below a major and above a lieutenant. **L19**.
b ***group captain***: see **GROUP** *noun*.
3 A naval officer commanding a warship; an officer in the navy or marines, ranking below a rear admiral and above a commander or lieutenant. Also (as a courtesy title), a commander. **M16**. ▸**b** The master or commander of a merchant ship, passenger vessel, etc. **M17**. ▸**c** The chief sailor of a group having specific duties. **E19**.
Captain of the Fleet the officer on an admiral's staff in charge of maintenance. **captain's biscuit** a hard fancy biscuit. **captain's chair** *N. Amer.* a wooden chair with a back that curves around to form armrests. ***post captain***: see **POST** *noun*⁴. **c** ***captain of the foretop***, ***captain of the hold***, etc.
4 A great soldier; an experienced commander; a strategist. **L16**.

E. A. FREEMAN How great a captain England had in her future king.

5 The head boy or girl of a school or class. **L16**.
6 The superintendent of a mine; a foreman; (chiefly *N. Amer.*) a supervisor of a group of waiters, bellboys, etc. **E17**.
7 As *voc.*: sir. *arch. slang*. **E17**.

SHAKES. *Timon* Why, how now, Captain? What do you in this wise company?

8 The leader of a sports team, sports club, etc. **E19**.
9 The pilot of a civil aircraft. **E20**.
10 In the US and elsewhere: a police officer ranking next below a chief officer. **E20**.
– **COMB.**: **captain-general** (**a**) *hist.* a commander-in-chief, a military governor; (**b**) an honorary rank esp. in the British artillery or Royal Marines; **captain-generalcy** *hist.* the office or province of a captain-general; **captain-lieutenant** *hist.* a military officer commanding a company or troop, with a captain's rank and lieutenant's pay.
▸ **B** *verb trans*. Be captain of, lead. **L16**.
■ **captainess** *noun* (now *rare*) a female captain **LME**. **captainless** *adjective* **L16**. †**captainry** *noun* captaincy; a district under a captain: **LME–L18**.

Captain Cooker /ˌkaptɪn ˈkʊkə/ *noun phr. NZ*. Also (earlier) **Captain Cook**. **L19**.
[**ORIGIN** from Capt. James *Cook* (1728–79), navigator and explorer + **-ER**¹.]
A wild boar.

captaincy /ˈkaptɪnsi/ *noun*. **E19**.
[**ORIGIN** from **CAPTAIN** *noun* + **-CY**.]
1 The position, rank, office, or authority of a captain. **E19**.
2 A captain's skill, the ability to lead. **M19**.

captainship /ˈkaptɪnʃɪp/ *noun*. **LME**.
[**ORIGIN** formed as **CAPTAINCY** + **-SHIP**. Sense 4 translating Spanish *capitania*.]
1 = **CAPTAINCY** 1. **LME**.
2 = **CAPTAINCY** 2. **E17**.
3 With possess. adjective (as ***your captainship*** etc.): a mock title of respect given to a captain. Now *rare*. **E17**.
4 *hist.* A district in S. America etc. under the rule of a captain. **L17**.

captation /kapˈteɪʃ(ə)n/ *noun*. **E16**.
[**ORIGIN** French, or Latin *captatio(n-)*, *captat-* pa. ppl stem of *captare* frequentative of *capere* seize: see **-ATION**.]
An attempt to acquire something, esp. dexterously; the making of an *ad captandum* appeal.

caption /ˈkapʃ(ə)n/ *noun & verb*. **LME**.
[**ORIGIN** Latin *captio(n-)*, from *capt-* pa. ppl stem of *capere* seize: see **-ION**.]
▸ **A** *noun* **1 a** Seizure, capture, taking. Now *rare* or *obsolete* in *gen.* sense. **LME**. ▸**b** *LAW* (orig. *Scot.*, now *hist.*). Arrest or seizure under civil process; a warrant for the civil arrest of a debtor. **L15**.
2 A petty fault-finding argument; a cavil. Now *rare*. **L16**.
3 *LAW*. A certificate attached to or written on a legal instrument detailing before whom it was made. **L17**.
4 A heading of a chapter, article, etc.; wording appended to an illustration, cartoon, etc.; a (cinema or television) subtitle. Orig. *US*. **L18**.

Listener I have seen one of these pictures used in a Chinese magazine over the caption 'US aggressor flees'.

▸ **B** *verb trans*. Provide with (as) a caption; title. **E20**.

Science An effective poem . . captioned 'The Song of the Innuit'.

captious /ˈkapʃəs/ *adjective*. LME.
[ORIGIN Old French & mod. French *captieux* or Latin *captiosus*, from *captio(n-)*: see CAPTION, -OUS.]
1 Fond of taking exception or raising objections; carping. LME.
2 Apt or intended to deceive; fallacious, misleading. *arch.* LME.
†**3** Capacious. *rare* (Shakes.). Only in E17.
■ **captiously** *adverb* M16. **captiousness** *noun* M16.

†**captivance** *noun*. *rare* (Spenser). Only in L16.
[ORIGIN from CAPTIVE *verb* + -ANCE.]
Captivity.

captivate /ˈkaptɪveɪt/ *verb trans.* E16.
[ORIGIN Late Latin *captivat-* pa. ppl stem of *captivare*: see CAPTIVE *verb*, -ATE[3].]
†**1** Subjugate (the mind, reason, etc.) *to*. E16–M19.
2 Enthral, fascinate, charm. M16.
3 Make or hold captive, capture. Now *rare* or *obsolete*. M16. ▸**b** *spec.* = CAPTURE *verb* 2. L18.
■ †**captivate** *ppl adjective* captivated M16–L17. **captivater** *noun* (now *rare*) M17. **captivatingly** *adverb* in a captivating manner M19. **captivator** *noun* M19.

captivation /kaptɪˈveɪʃ(ə)n/ *noun*. E17.
[ORIGIN Late Latin *captivatio(n-)*, formed as CAPTIVATE: see -ATION.]
The action of taking or holding captive; the state of being held captive. Now only *fig.*: fascination, enthralment.

captive /ˈkaptɪv/ *adjective & noun*. LME.
[ORIGIN Latin *captivus*, from *capt-* pa. ppl stem of *capere* seize: see -IVE. Cf. CAITIFF.]
▸ **A** *adjective*. **1** Taken prisoner; kept in confinement or under restraint; unable to escape. LME.

R. GRAVES He would bring back the whole Spartan force captive within twenty days. *fig.*: SHAKES. *All's Well* A wife . . whose words all ears took captive.

captive audience: unable to avoid being addressed etc. **captive balloon**: held by a rope from the ground. ***lead captive***: see LEAD *verb*[1].
2 Of or like a prisoner. L16.

MILTON I sorrowed at his captive state.

▸ **B** *noun*. A person or animal captured, held in confinement, or under restraint. LME.
lead captive: see LEAD *verb*[1].

captive /ˈkaptɪv, *poet. also* kapˈtʌɪv/ *verb trans. arch.* L15.
[ORIGIN Old French & mod. French *captiver* from late Latin *captivare*, from *captivus*: see CAPTIVE *adjective & noun*.]
Take captive; captivate.

captivity /kapˈtɪvɪti/ *noun*. LME.
[ORIGIN Latin *captivitas*, formed as CAPTIVE *adjective & noun*: see -ITY.]
1 The condition of a captive; the state of being held captive. LME. ▸**b** *fig.* The subjugation of the mind, reason, etc.; captivation. *arch.* M16.
the Captivity: of the Jews in Babylon, 6th cent. BC.
2 Captives collectively. Chiefly in or after biblical translations. Long *arch.* LME.

captor /ˈkaptə/ *noun*. M16.
[ORIGIN Latin, from *capt-*: see CAPTIVE *adjective & noun*, -OR.]
A person who takes by force a captive or a prize.

capture /ˈkaptʃə/ *noun*. M16.
[ORIGIN French, from Latin *captura*, from *capt-*: see CAPTIVE *adjective & noun*, -URE.]
▸ **I 1** The act of seizing or taking as a prisoner or prize; gaining possession of by force, surprise, stratagem, etc. M16. ▸**b** A thing or person captured. E18.

I. B. SINGER The capture of a mouse in a trap.

2 The capturing of a piece in chess etc. M19.
3 PHYSICAL GEOGRAPHY. The diversion of the waters of a stream into the channel of another, due to erosional encroachment by the second stream. L19.
4 ASTRONOMY. The process whereby a less massive body becomes permanently linked gravitationally to a star, planet, etc. E20.
5 PHYSICS. The absorption of an atomic or subatomic particle. E20.
M-capture: see M, M 6. RADIATIVE ***capture***.
6 In full ***data capture***. The action or process of entering data into a computer, esp. as an accompaniment to a related operation. M20.
– COMB.: **capture myopathy** VETERINARY MEDICINE a condition involving muscular wasting and partial paralysis which affects some wild animals when captured; also called ***overstraining disease***.

capture /ˈkaptʃə/ *verb trans.* L18.
[ORIGIN from the noun.]
1 Effect the capture of; take prisoner; seize or gain as a prize. L18.

fig.: J. BUCHAN A book of Norse mythology which strongly captured my fancy.

2 In CHESS etc., remove (an opponent's piece) from the board as the rules of the game allow when particular relative positions are taken up or particular moves are made. Cf. earlier CAPTIVATE 3b. E19.
3 PHYSICAL GEOGRAPHY. Of a stream etc.: divert the upper course of (another) by encroaching on its basin. E20.
4 ASTRONOMY. Of a star, planet, etc.: bring (a less massive body) permanently within its gravitational influence. E20.
5 PHYSICS. Absorb (an atomic or subatomic particle). E20.
6 Put in a relatively permanently accessible form, e.g. by portraiture or photography. M20. ▸**b** Cause (data) to be entered into a computer. L20.
■ **capturable** *adjective* M19. **capturer** *noun* a person who or thing which captures E19.

capuche /kəˈpuːʃ/ *noun*. Also **capouch**. L16.
[ORIGIN French (now *capuce*), from Italian *cappuccio*: see CAPUCHIN.]
The hood of a cloak, *esp.* that of a Capuchin.

capuchin /ˈkap(j)ʊtʃɪn/ *noun*. In sense 1 **C-**. L16.
[ORIGIN French (now *capucin*) from Italian *cappuccino*, from *cappuccio* hood, cowl, augm. of *cappa* CAPE *noun*[2].]
1 More fully ***Capuchin Friar*** etc. A Franciscan friar of the new rule of 1528 (so called from the sharp-pointed capuche adopted by the order). L16.
2 *hist.* A woman's cloak and hood resembling the dress of a Capuchin. M18.
3 In full ***capuchin pigeon***. A variety of jacobin. M18.
4 In full ***capuchin monkey***. Any of various monkeys of the genus *Cebus*, of Central and S. America, with head hair suggestive of a cowl. L18.

capul *noun* var. of CAPLE.

caput /ˈkapət/ *noun*. *obsolete* exc. *hist.* E18.
[ORIGIN Latin = head.]
The former ruling body of Cambridge University; *occas.* a member of this.

caput mortuum /ˌkapət ˈmɔːtuːəm/ *noun phr.* M17.
[ORIGIN Latin = dead head.]
†**1** A death's head, a skull. Only in M17.
2 ALCHEMY. The residue remaining after distillation or sublimation. M17.
3 Worthless residue. E18.

caput succedaneum /ˌkapət sʌksɪˈdeɪnɪəm/ *noun phr.* Pl. **capita succedanea** /ˌkapɪtə sʌksɪˈdeɪnɪə/. M19.
[ORIGIN mod. Latin, lit. 'substitute head'.]
MEDICINE. A temporary swelling of the head of an infant during childbirth resulting from compression by the birth canal.

capybara /kapɪˈbɑːrə/ *noun*. E17.
[ORIGIN Spanish *capibara* or Portuguese *capivara*, from Tupi *capiúara*, from *capí* grass + *úara* eater.]
A large tailless river-dwelling rodent, *Hydrochoerus hydrochaeris*, of Central and S. America, resembling a large guinea pig.

car /kɑː/ *noun*. LME.
[ORIGIN Anglo-Norman, Old Northern French *carre* from Proto-Romance var. of Latin *carrum* neut., *carrus* masc., from Celtic base repr. by Old Irish & mod. Irish *carr*, Welsh *car*.]
1 *gen.* A wheeled conveyance, a carriage. Without specification of type now *rare*. LME.
jaunting car: see JAUNT *verb*. ***sidecar***: see SIDE *noun*.
2 A sledge, a sleigh. Long *obsolete* exc. *Scot. & Canad. dial.* LME.
3 A chariot, esp. of war, triumph, or pageantry. *literary*. L16.

TENNYSON A reverent people behold The towering car, the sable steeds.

4 The passenger compartment of a balloon, airship, cableway, etc. L18. ▸**b** The cage of a lift. Chiefly *US*. L19.
5 A railway carriage or van; a tramway vehicle. Chiefly *N. Amer.* exc. as 2nd elem. of comb. E19. ▸**b** As many or as much as a railway car will hold; a carload. *N. Amer.* M19.
boxcar, ***buffet car***, ***dining car***, ***freight car***, ***observation car***, ***railcar***, ***sleeping car***, ***streetcar***, etc.
6 A usu. four-wheeled motorized vehicle for use on roads, able to carry a small number of people; an automobile. L19.
bubble car, ***estate car***, ***racing car***, ***rally car***, ***sports car***, etc.
– COMB.: **car bomb** a bomb concealed by terrorists under or in a (usu. parked) car; **car boot sale** an outdoor sale at which people sell unwanted possessions from the boots of their cars; ***car bra***: see BRA *noun*[1] 2; **car coat** a short coat designed esp. for motorists; **carfare** *N. Amer.* a passenger's fare to travel by streetcar, bus, etc.; **carhop** *US colloq.* a waiter at a drive-in restaurant etc.; **carload** (***a***) as many or as much as can be carried in a car; (***b***) *US* a minimum quantity of goods for which a lower rate is charged for transport; **carman** a driver of a van etc., a carrier; **car park** a space or building for parking cars; **car phone** a radio telephone for use in a car; **carpool** (chiefly *N. Amer.*) (***a***) *noun* an arrangement for sharing a car for regular travelling, a group of people with such an arrangement; (***b***) *verb intrans.* form or join a carpool, share a car for regular travelling; **carpooler** *N. Amer.* a member of a carpool; **carport** a roofed open-sided shelter for a car; **carsick** *adjective* affected with carsickness; **carsickness** nausea caused by the motion of a car; **car wash** (an establishment with) a piece of equipment for washing cars automatically.

carabao /karəˈbeɪəʊ/ *noun*. Pl. same, **-os**. L19.
[ORIGIN Spanish.]
A water buffalo.

carabid /ˈkarəbɪd/ *noun & adjective*. L19.
[ORIGIN mod. Latin *Carabidae* (see below), from Latin *carabus* a kind of crab: see -ID[3].]
(A large carnivorous beetle) of the family Carabidae.
■ **caˈrabidan** *noun* (now *rare* or *obsolete*) = CARABID *noun* M19. **caraˈbideous** *adjective* = CARABID *adjective* M19.

†**carabine** *noun* var. of CARBINE.

carabineer /karəbɪˈnɪə/ *noun*. Also **-ier**. M17.
[ORIGIN French *carabinier*, formed as CARBINE: see -EER.]
A cavalry soldier armed with a carbine.
the Carabiniers a former regiment of Dragoon Guards, now incorporated in the Royal Scots Dragoon Guards.

carabiner *noun* var. of KARABINER.

carabinero /karabiˈnero, karəbɪˈnɛːrəʊ/ *noun*. Pl. **-os** /-ɔs, -əʊz/. M19.
[ORIGIN Spanish, lit. = CARABINEER.]
A (Spanish) customs or revenue officer; a (Spanish) frontier guard.

carabinier *noun* var. of CARABINEER.

carabiniere /karabiˈnjere, karəbɪˈnjɛːri/ *noun*. Pl. **-ri** /-ri/. M19.
[ORIGIN Italian, lit. = CARABINEER.]
An Italian soldier in a corps serving as a police force.

caracal /ˈkarəkal/ *noun*. M18.
[ORIGIN French or Spanish, from Turkish *karakulak*, from *kara* black + *kulak* ear.]
A long-legged lynx-like feline, *Felis caracal*, of Africa and SW Asia.

caracara /karəˈkɑːrə/ *noun*. M19.
[ORIGIN Spanish or Portuguese *caracará*, from Tupi-Guarani, of imit. origin.]
Any of several mainly neotropical raptors of the family Falconidae that are related to the falcons but somewhat resemble vultures.
common caracara a caracara, *Polyborus plancus*, of S. America and southern N. America.

caracole /ˈkarəkəʊl/ *noun*. Also **-ol** /-ɒl/. E17.
[ORIGIN Sense 1 from French *caracol(e)* snail's shell, spiral; sense 2 formed as CARACOLE *verb*.]
†**1 a** A spiral shell. Only in E17. ▸**b** ARCHITECTURE. A helical staircase. *rare*. E18.
2 A half-turn or wheel to the right or left by a horse or rider. Formerly also, a series of such turns alternately to right and left. E17.

caracole /ˈkarəkəʊl/ *verb*. Also **-ol** /-ɒl/. M17.
[ORIGIN French *caracoler*, from *caracol(e)*: see CARACOLE *noun*.]
1 *verb intrans.* Of a horse or rider: execute a caracole; *loosely* prance about. M17.
2 *verb trans.* Make (a horse) caracole. M19.

†**caract** *noun*[1] var. of CARAT.

†**caract** *noun*[2] var. of CHARACT.

caracul *noun & adjective* var. of KARAKUL.

carafe /kəˈraf, -ˈrɑːf/ *noun*. L18.
[ORIGIN French from Italian *caraffa*, of unknown origin.]
A glass bottle for water or wine at a table, in a bedroom, etc.

caragana /karəˈgɑːnə/ *noun*. M19.
[ORIGIN mod. Latin (see below), of Turkic origin.]
Any of various leguminous shrubs and trees of the genus *Caragana*, native to central Asia and Siberia and widely planted in N. America; *esp.* the Siberian pea tree, *C. arborescens*.

†**Caraite** *noun & adjective* see KARAITE.

carama *noun* var. of SERIEMA.

caramba /kəˈrambə, *foreign* kaˈramba/ *interjection*. M19.
[ORIGIN Spanish.]
Expr. surprise or dismay.

carambola /kar(ə)mˈbəʊlə/ *noun*. L16.
[ORIGIN Portuguese, prob. from Marathi *karambal*.]
A SE Asian tree, *Averrhoa carambola*, of the oxalis family; its astringent yellow fruit (also called ***starfruit***).

carambole /ˈkar(ə)mbəʊl/ *noun & verb intrans.* L18.
[ORIGIN Spanish *carambola* (whence French *carambole* red ball in billiards), app. from *bola* ball.]
(Make) a cannon in billiards.

caramel /ˈkarəmɛl, -m(ə)l/ *noun & verb*. E18.
[ORIGIN French from Spanish *caramelo*.]
▸ **A** *noun*. **1** Burnt sugar or syrup used for colouring spirits etc.; (a) toffee made with sugar that has been melted and heated further. See also ***crème caramel*** s.v. CRÈME 1. E18.
2 A light-brown colour. Freq. *attrib.* E20.
▸ **B** *verb trans. & intrans.* = CARAMELIZE. E18.

caramelize /ˈkar(ə)məlʌɪz/ *verb trans. & intrans.* Also **-ise**. M19.
[ORIGIN French *caraméliser*, formed as CARAMEL: see -IZE.]
1 Turn into caramel. M19.
2 Cook (food) with sugar so that it becomes coated with caramel. Freq. as ***caramelized*** *ppl adjective*. L20.
■ **carameliˈzation** *noun* L19.

Carancahua *noun & adjective* var. of KARANKAWA.

carangid /kəˈrandʒɪd/ *noun & adjective*. L19.
[ORIGIN mod. Latin *Carangidae* (see below), from *Caranx* genus name: see -ID[3].]
(A percoid fish) of the large family Carangidae, which includes the scads and pompanos.
■ Also **carangoid** *noun & adjective* M19.

C

carap(a) *noun* see CRAB *noun*[3].

carapace /ˈkarəpeɪs/ *noun*. Also †**-pax**. M19.
[ORIGIN French from Spanish *carapacho*, of unknown origin.]
The upper shell of a tortoise, crustacean, etc.

fig.: N. BAWDEN I wanted to hurt you. Get through that carapace of self-regard somehow.

■ **carapaced** *adjective* having a carapace L19.

cara sposa /ˈkaːra ˈspoːza/ *noun phr.* Pl. ***care spose*** /ˈkaːre ˈspoːze/. L18.
[ORIGIN Italian.]
(One's) dear wife; a devoted wife. Cf. CARO SPOSO.

carat /ˈkarət/ *noun*. Also †**-act**, ***k-**. LME.
[ORIGIN French from Italian *carato* from Arabic *qīrāt* weight equal to one twenty-fourth of a *mithqal*, from Greek *keration* fruit of the carob, dim. of *keras* horn.]
1 A proportional measure of one twenty-fourth used in stating the purity of gold (pure gold being 24 carats). LME. ***twenty-four carat***: see TWENTY *noun*.
2 A unit of weight used for precious stones, equal to 200 milligrams. M16.
†**3** *fig.* Worth, value. L16–L17.

SHAKES. *2 Hen. IV* Therefore thou best of gold art worst of gold. Other, less fine in carat, is more precious.

caratch /kəˈratʃ, -aːtʃ/ *noun*. *obsolete* exc. *hist.* Also **ha-**. L17.
[ORIGIN Turkish from Arabic *karāj* land tax, tax.]
A tribute levied by the Ottoman Turks on their Christian subjects.

caravan /ˈkarəvan, karəˈvan/ *noun & verb*. L15.
[ORIGIN French *caravane* from Persian *kārvān*. Cf. VAN *noun*[3].]
▸ **A** *noun*. **1** A company of merchants, pilgrims, etc., travelling together, esp. across the desert in Asia or N. Africa. L15.
†**2** A fleet of Turkish or Russian (merchant) ships. L16–M18.
3 *gen.* A travelling company of people. M17.
4 Orig., a covered carriage or cart (cf. VAN *noun*[3]). Now, a vehicle equipped for living in, usu. designed to be towed; *N. Amer.* a covered motor vehicle with living accommodation. L17.
caravan: see MOTOR *noun & adjective*.
– COMB.: **caravan park**, **caravan site** a place where caravans may be parked as holiday accommodation or as more permanent dwellings.
▸ **B** *verb intrans.* Infl. **-nn-**. Travel or live in a caravan; spend a holiday in a caravan. L19.
■ **caravaˈneer** *noun* = CARAVANNER M18. **caravaˈnette** *noun* a motor vehicle furnished with beds and other domestic equipment M20. **caravanner** *noun* (**a**) a person who lives, travels, or spends holidays in a caravan; (**b**) a leader of a (travelling) caravan: E20. **caraˈvette** *noun* = CARAVANETTE M20.

†**caravance** *noun* see CALAVANCE.

caravanserai /karəˈvansərʌɪ, -ri/ *noun*. Also **-sary**, **-sery**, & other vars. L16.
[ORIGIN Persian *kārwānsarāy*, from *kārvān* (see CARAVAN) + as SERAI *noun*[1].]
An Eastern inn with a large inner court where caravans rest.

caravel /ˈkarəvɛl/ *noun*. E16.
[ORIGIN French *caravelle*: see CARVEL.]
A small light fast ship, chiefly Spanish or Portuguese, of the 15th to the 17th cents.

caraway /ˈkarəweɪ/ *noun*. ME.
[ORIGIN medieval Latin *carui* or allied Romance form from Arabic *karawiyā*, prob. ult. from Greek *karon* cumin.]
An umbelliferous European plant, *Carum carvi*; (in full ***caraway seed***) the small aromatic fruit of this, used in cakes etc. and as a source of oil.

carb /kaːb/ *noun*. *colloq.* M20.
[ORIGIN Abbreviation.]
= CARBURETTOR.

carb- *combining form* see CARBO-.

carbamazepine /kaːbəˈmeɪzɪpiːn/ *noun*. M20.
[ORIGIN from CARBAM(IDE *noun* + AZ(O- + *-epine*, suffix denoting a seven-membered ring containing nitrogen.]
PHARMACOLOGY. A tricyclic compound, $C_{15}H_{12}N_2O$, which has anticonvulsant and analgesic properties and is used to treat epilepsy, neuralgias, and manic depression.

carbamic /kaːˈbamɪk/ *adjective*. M19.
[ORIGIN formed as CARBAMIDE + -IC.]
CHEMISTRY. ***carbamic acid***, the hypothetical compound NH_2COOH, of which many salts and esters are known.
■ **ˈcarbamate** *noun* a salt or ester of carbamic acid (cf. URETHANE 1) M19.

carbamide /ˈkaːbəmʌɪd/ *noun*. M19.
[ORIGIN from CARBO- + AMIDE.]
CHEMISTRY. = UREA 1.
■ **carbamyl** *noun* the radical $NH_2CO\cdot$ E20.

carbaryl /ˈkaːbərɪl/ *noun*. M20.
[ORIGIN from CARBAMATE + -YL.]
A synthetic compound, $C_{12}H_{11}NO_2$, used as an insecticide to protect crops and to kill fleas and lice.

carbide /ˈkaːbʌɪd/ *noun*. M19.
[ORIGIN from CARBON *noun* + -IDE.]
1 CHEMISTRY. A binary compound of carbon with an element of lower or comparable electronegativity. M19. SILICON ***carbide***. ***sintered carbide***: see SINTER *verb*. TUNGSTEN ***carbide***.
2 *spec.* Calcium carbide, CaC_2, used to generate acetylene by reaction with water. L19.

carbine /ˈkaːbʌɪn/ *noun*. Also †**carabine**. E17.
[ORIGIN French *carabine*, from *carabin* mounted musketeer, of uncertain origin.]
A short rifle or smooth-bored gun orig. for use by cavalry. ***Spencer carbine***: see SPENCER *noun*[1] 4.

carbinol /ˈkaːbɪnɒl/ *noun*. M19.
[ORIGIN from CARBON *noun* + -INE[5] + -OL.]
CHEMISTRY. A monohydric alcohol; *spec.* methanol. Usu. in *comb.*
– NOTE: Chiefly in names of more complex alcohols with preceding radical name.

carbo /ˈkaːbəʊ/ *noun*. Pl. **-os**. *colloq.* L20.
[ORIGIN Shortened from CARBOHYDRATE *noun*.]
A carbohydrate, esp. as a constituent of a particular food or diet.
– COMB.: **carbo-load** *verb intrans.* (of an athlete) saturate the muscles with glycogen by exercising and dieting and then eating a large amount of carbohydrates.

carbo- /ˈkaːbəʊ/ *combining form*. Before a vowel **carb-**.
[ORIGIN from CARBON *noun*: see -O-.]
CHEMISTRY. Of or containing carbon.
■ **carbanion** /kaːˈbanʌɪən/ *noun* an organic anion in which a carbon atom bears the negative charge M20. **carbazole** *noun* a crystalline tricyclic heteroaromatic compound, $C_{12}H_9N$, present in coal tar L19. **carbene** *noun* a compound of divalent carbon, examples of which occur as intermediates in some organic reactions M20. **carboˈcyclic** *adjective* containing a ring or rings of carbon atoms only L19.

carbocation /kaːbə(ʊ)ˈkatʌɪən/ *noun*. M20.
[ORIGIN from CARBO- + CATION.]
CHEMISTRY. = CARBONIUM ION.

carbohydrate /kaːbəˈhʌɪdreɪt/ *noun*. M19.
[ORIGIN from CARBOCATION + HYDRATE *noun*.]
Any of a class of organic compounds that contain hydrogen and oxygen in the same ratio as water (2:1), and can be broken down to release energy in the animal body, e.g. sugars, starch, and other polysaccharides.

carbolic /kaːˈbɒlɪk/ *adjective & noun*. M19.
[ORIGIN from CARBO- + -OL + -IC.]
▸ **A** *adjective*. ***carbolic acid***, = PHENOL 1; ***carbolic soap***, soap containing phenol as a disinfectant. M19.
▸ **B** *noun*. Carbolic acid or soap. L19.
■ **ˈcarbolate** *verb trans.* treat or impregnate with phenol (chiefly as ***carbolated*** *ppl adjective*) L19. **ˈcarbolize** *verb trans.* = CARBOLATE L19.

carbon /ˈkaːb(ə)n/ *noun*. L18.
[ORIGIN French *carbone* from Latin *carbon-*, *carbo* coal.]
1 A non-metallic chemical element, atomic no. 6, which occurs in crystalline form as diamond and graphite, in amorphous form as coal and charcoal, and is the basis of all organic compounds (symbol C). L18.
activated carbon: see ACTIVATE *verb* 1. ***active carbon***: see ACTIVE *adjective* 5. PYROLYTIC ***carbon***. RADIOCARBON.
2 An electrode made of carbon, esp. in an arc lamp. M19.
3 A piece of carbon paper; a carbon copy. L19.
4 Carbon dioxide or other gaseous carbon compounds released into the atmosphere. L20.

attrib.: *Independent* We all know that carbon emissions are contributing to global warming.

– COMB.: **carbon black** an amorphous form of carbon suitable for use as a pigment, e.g. lampblack; **carbon copy** a copy made with carbon paper; *fig.* an exact copy; **carbon cycle** (**a**) BIOLOGY the continuous transfer of carbon in various forms from the atmosphere to living organisms by plant photosynthesis, and back to the atmosphere by respiration and decay; (**b**) ASTRONOMY a thermonuclear chain reaction postulated to occur within stars, in which carbon nuclei act as catalysts in the fusion of hydrogen to form helium; **carbon dating** = ***radiocarbon dating*** s.v. RADIOCARBON; **carbon dioxide** a colourless odourless unreactive gas, CO_2, formed by combustion of carbon and in breathing; **carbon disulphide** a colourless toxic liquid, CS_2, used as a solvent for rubber; **carbon fibre** a thin strong polycrystalline filament of carbon, freq. incorporated in plastic etc. as a strengthening material; **carbon footprint** the amount of carbon dioxide emitted due to the activities, esp. the consumption of fossil fuels, of a particular person, group, etc.; **carbon-14** a radioactive carbon isotope of mass number 14, used in isotopic dating (cf. RADIOCARBON); **carbon microphone** a microphone depending for its action on the varying electrical resistance of carbon granules; **carbon monoxide** a poisonous, colourless, odourless gas, CO, formed by the incomplete combustion of carbon; **carbon-neutral** *adjective* making no net release of carbon dioxide to the atmosphere, esp. through offsetting emissions by planting trees. **carbon paper** thin paper coated with carbon or another pigmented material, used to make copies of anything written or typed upon it; **carbon sink** a forest, ocean, or other natural environment viewed in terms of its ability to absorb carbon dioxide from the atmosphere; **carbon steel** any steel whose properties are mainly determined by its carbon content; **carbon tax** a tax on fossil fuels, esp. those used by motor vehicles, intended to reduce the emission of carbon dioxide; **carbon tetrachloride** a colourless toxic liquid, CCl_4, used as a solvent in dry cleaning etc. **carbon trading** = ***emissions trading*** s.v. EMISSION.
■ **carbonless** *adjective* M19.

carbon /ˈkaːb(ə)n/ *verb*. E20.
[ORIGIN from the noun.]
1 *verb trans.* (usu. in *pass.*) & *intrans.* Coat or become coated with carbon. E20.
2 *verb trans.* Make a carbon copy of. M20.

carbonaceous /kaːbəˈneɪʃəs/ *adjective*. L18.
[ORIGIN from CARBON *noun* + -ACEOUS.]
Of the nature of or like coal or charcoal; consisting of or containing carbon.

carbonade /kaːbəˈnaːd, -ˈneɪd/ *noun*. In sense 2 usu. **-nn-**. M17.
[ORIGIN French, formed as CARBON *noun*: see -ADE.]
1 = CARBONADO *noun*[1]. *rare*. M17.
2 A rich beef stew made with onions and beer. L19.

†**carbonade** *verb trans.* L16–M18.
[ORIGIN formed as CARBONADE *noun*.]
= CARBONADO *verb*.

carbonado /kaːbəˈneɪdəʊ/ *noun*[1] & *verb*. L16.
[ORIGIN Spanish *carbonada*, from *carbon* coal ult. from Latin *carbon-*: see CARBON *noun*, -ADO.]
▸ **A** *noun*. Pl. **-os**. A piece of meat or fish which is scored across and broiled on coals. Long *arch.* L16.
▸ **B** *verb trans.* Score across and broil (meat or fish); *transf.* cut, slash, hack. L16.

carbonado /kaːbəˈneɪdəʊ/ *noun*[2]. Pl. **-os**. M19.
[ORIGIN Portuguese.]
A dark opaque kind of diamond used as an abrasive etc.

carbonara /kaːbəˈnaːrə/ *adjective*. M20.
[ORIGIN Italian *alla carbonara*, lit. 'in a charcoal kiln'; perh. infl. by *carbonata* a dish of charcoal-grilled salt pork.]
Denoting a pasta sauce made with bacon or ham, egg, and cream. Freq. *postpositive*, as ***spaghetti carbonara***.

Carbonari /kaːbəˈnaːri/ *noun pl.* Also (*rare*) in sing. **-naro** /-ˈnaːrəʊ/. E19.
[ORIGIN Italian pl. of *carbonaro* collier, charcoal burner, from *carbone* coal ult. from Latin *carbon-* CARBON *noun*.]
The members of a secret republican association in the kingdom of Naples in the early 19th cent.
■ **Carbonarism** *noun* the political principles of the Carbonari or similar revolutionaries M19.

carbonate /ˈkaːbəneɪt/ *noun*. L18.
[ORIGIN from CARBON *noun* + -ATE[1].]
CHEMISTRY. A salt or ester of carbonic acid.
carbonate of lime: see LIME *noun*[1].

carbonate /ˈkaːbəneɪt/ *verb trans.* L18.
[ORIGIN In sense 1, from CARBON *noun* + -ATE[3]; in sense 2 from the noun.]
†**1** Carbonize; combine with carbon. Freq. as ***carbonated*** *ppl adjective*. L18–M19.
2 Convert into carbonate; impregnate with carbon dioxide, aerate. Freq. as ***carbonated*** *ppl adjective*. E19.
■ **carboˈnation** *noun* L19. **carbonator** *noun* a person who or thing which carbonates L19.

carbonatite /kaːˈbɒnətʌɪt/ *noun*. E20.
[ORIGIN from CARBONATE *noun* + -ITE[1].]
GEOLOGY. Any igneous rock composed chiefly of carbonates rather than silicates.

carbonic /kaːˈbɒnɪk/ *adjective*. L18.
[ORIGIN from CARBON *noun* + -IC.]
CHEMISTRY. Of or pertaining to carbon; ***carbonic acid***, a weak dibasic acid, H_2CO_3, formed in aqueous solutions of carbon dioxide.
carbonic acid gas *arch.* carbon dioxide. †**carbonic paper** carbon paper.

carboniferous /kaːbəˈnɪf(ə)rəs/ *adjective & noun*. In GEOLOGY usu. **C-**. L18.
[ORIGIN formed as CARBONIC + -I- + -FEROUS.]
▸ **A** *adjective*. **1** Producing or yielding coal. *rare*. L18.
2 GEOLOGY. Designating or pertaining to the fifth period of the Palaeozoic era, following the Devonian and preceding the Permian, in which many coal deposits were formed. E19.
▸ **B** *noun*. GEOLOGY. The Carboniferous period; the system of rocks dating from this time. L19.

carbonise *verb* var. of CARBONIZE.

carbonium /kaːˈbəʊnɪəm/ *noun*. E20.
[ORIGIN from CARBO- after *ammonium*.]
CHEMISTRY. In full ***carbonium ion***. An organic cation in which the positive charge is borne by a carbon atom.

carbonize /ˈkaːbənʌɪz/ *verb trans.* Also **-ise**. E19.
[ORIGIN from CARBON *noun* + -IZE.]
1 Convert into carbon; reduce to charcoal or coke; char. E19.
†**2** Carburize. Only in 19.
3 Coat (paper) with carbon for use in copying. L19.
■ **carboniˈzation** *noun* E19. **carbonizer** *noun* a person who or thing which carbonizes E20.

carbonnade *noun* see CARBONADE *noun*.

carbonyl /ˈkaːbənʌɪl, -nɪl/ *noun*. M19.
[ORIGIN from CARBON *noun* + -YL.]
CHEMISTRY. The divalent group :CO, present in ketones, aldehydes, etc.; usu. in *comb.* Also, (a complex containing) carbon monoxide bonded to a metal atom as a neutral ligand.
■ **carbonyˈlation** *noun* the introduction of a carbonyl group into a compound M20.

carborundum /kɑːbəˈrʌndəm/ *noun*. Also (US proprietary name) **C-**. L19.
[ORIGIN formed as CARBONYL + CORUNDUM.]
A very hard black solid consisting of silicon carbide, used as an abrasive.

carboxy- /kɑːˈbɒksi/ *combining form*.
[ORIGIN from CARBO- + OXY-.]
CHEMISTRY. Usu. denoting the presence of the carboxyl group.
■ **carboxyhaemoˈglobin** *noun* a compound of haemoglobin and carbon monoxide, formed in the blood when carbon monoxide is inhaled L19.

carboxyl /kɑːˈbɒksʌɪl, -sɪl/ *noun*. M19.
[ORIGIN formed as CARBOXY- + -YL.]
CHEMISTRY. The acidic radical ·COOH, present in most organic acids. Usu. in *comb*.
■ **carboxylate** *noun & verb* (**a**) a salt or ester of a carboxylic acid; (**b**) *verb trans*. introduce a carboxyl group into (a compound etc.): L19. **carboxyˈlation** *noun* the introduction of a carboxyl group into a compound E20. **carboxylic** /kɑːbɒkˈsɪlɪk/ *adjective* containing the carboxyl group L19.

carboxylase /kɑːˈbɒksɪleɪz/ *noun*. E20.
[ORIGIN from CARBOXYL + -ASE.]
BIOCHEMISTRY. An enzyme which promotes the addition of a carboxyl group to a specified substrate.

carboy /ˈkɑːbɔɪ/ *noun*. M18.
[ORIGIN Ult. from Persian *qarāba* large glass flagon.]
A large globular bottle, usu. of coloured glass and protected by a frame, used chiefly for holding acids and other corrosive liquids.

carbuncle /ˈkɑːbʌŋk(ə)l/ *noun*. ME.
[ORIGIN Old French *charbu(n)cle* etc. from Latin *carbunculus* small coal: see CARBON *noun*, -UNCLE.]
1 A red precious stone; *spec*. a garnet cut in a boss shape. ME.
2 *HERALDRY*. = ESCARBUNCLE. LME.
3 A severe abscess, esp. on the neck; a multiple boil; a red facial spot or pimple. M16.
■ **carbuncled** *adjective* †(**a**) adorned with carbuncles (sense 1); (**b**) affected with carbuncles (sense 3); †(**c**) (of earth) parched by the sun: L16. **carbuncly** *adjective* of or like a carbuncle; bearing carbuncles: L19. **carˈbuncular** *adjective* of the nature of or resembling a carbuncle (sense 3); affected with carbuncles: M18. **carˈbunculous** *adjective* = CARBUNCULAR E17.

carburation /kɑːbjʊˈreɪʃ(ə)n/ *noun*. Also ***-retion** /-ˈrɛʃ(ə)n/. L19.
[ORIGIN from CARBURET *verb* + -ATION.]
The action of a carburettor.

†**carburator** *noun* var. of CARBURETTOR.

carburet /ˈkɑːbjʊrɛt/ *noun*. *arch*. L18.
[ORIGIN from CARBO- + -URET.]
CHEMISTRY. = CARBIDE 1.

carburet /kɑːbjʊˈrɛt/ *verb trans*. Infl. **-tt-**, **-t-**. E19.
[ORIGIN from the noun.]
Charge with hydrocarbons; provide with a carburettor; *arch*. combine or charge with carbon. Chiefly as ***carburetted*** *ppl adjective*.

carburetion *noun* see CARBURATION.

carburettor /kɑːbjʊˈrɛtə, -bə-/ *noun*. Also **-etter**, ***-etor**, †**-ator**. M19.
[ORIGIN from CARBURET *verb* + -OR.]
An apparatus for charging air with a fine spray of liquid fuel for combustion, esp. in a petrol engine.
twin carburettor: see TWIN *adjective & noun*.

carburize /ˈkɑːbjʊrʌɪz/ *verb trans*. Also **-ise**. M19.
[ORIGIN formed as CARBURETTOR + -IZE.]
Chiefly *METALLURGY*. Combine with carbon; add carbon to (iron).
■ **carburiˈzation** *noun* M19.

carbylamine /kɑːˈbʌɪləmiːn/ *noun*. M19.
[ORIGIN from CARBO- + -YL + AMINE.]
CHEMISTRY. An isocyanide; *obsolete* exc. with ref. to a test for amines (the ***carbylamine test***) depending on the generation of an isocyanide.

carcajou /ˈkɑːkədʒuː, -əʒuː/ *noun*. *N. Amer*. E18.
[ORIGIN Canad. French, from Montagnais *kwa:hkwa:če:w*.]
= WOLVERINE 1.

carcake /ˈkɑːkeɪk/ *noun*. *Scot*. E19.
[ORIGIN from CARE *noun* 1 + CAKE *noun*.]
A small cake baked with eggs, eaten on Shrove Tuesday in parts of Scotland.

†**carcan** *noun*. M16.
[ORIGIN French = Provençal *carcan*, medieval Latin *carcannum*, Italian *carcome*, ult. from Germanic.]
1 An iron collar used for punishment. M16–L18.
2 = CARCANET. M16–L17.

carcanet /ˈkɑːkənɛt/ *noun*. *arch*. M16.
[ORIGIN from CARCAN + -ET[1].]
A collar or necklace, usu. of gold or jewelled.

carcass /ˈkɑːkəs/ *noun*. In branch I also **-ase**. ME.
[ORIGIN Anglo-Norman *carcois* (= Old French *charcois*) & French *carcasse*; in Anglo-Latin *carcasium*, *-osium*, *-oisum*: ult. origin unknown.]
▸ **I 1** A human corpse (now *derog*.); the dead body of an animal; *spec*. the trunk of a slaughtered animal, without the hide, head, or offal. ME.
2 Orig., the living body of a person or animal considered in its material nature. Now only *joc*. or *derog*., the human body. LME.

> W. RALEIGH His Trances proceeded through the weakness of his earthly Carcase. R. L. STEVENSON For what would they risk their carcasses but money?

3 *fig*. A shell or husk; the decaying skeleton *of* a building, ship, etc. L16.

> S. O'FAOLÁIN The carcase of the abandoned car lay damming the . . stream. A. THWAITE The carcasses of marriages of friends.

4 The skeleton or framework upon which a building, ship, piece of furniture, etc., is built up; the foundation of a motor-vehicle tyre. M17.

> R. V. JONES The extremely light carcase of the rocket was . . based on Zeppelin-type construction.

5 The bones of a cooked bird. L19.
▸ **II 6** *hist*. A spherical projectile filled with combustible material to ignite buildings etc. L17.
– COMB.: **carcass meat** raw meat as distinct from corned or tinned meat.

carcass /ˈkɑːkəs/ *verb trans*. E17.
[ORIGIN from the noun.]
1 Make a carcass of (an animal, *occas*. a person). E17.
2 Put up the carcass of (a building). L19.

carcel lamp /ˈkɑːs(ə)l lamp/ *noun phr*. M19.
[ORIGIN from *Carcel*, its French inventor.]
hist. A lamp in which oil is pumped up to the wick by clockwork.

carceral /ˈkɑːs(ə)r(ə)l/ *adjective*. L16.
[ORIGIN Late Latin *carceralis*, from *carcer* prison: see -AL[1].]
Of or belonging to a prison.

carcinogen /kɑːˈsɪnədʒ(ə)n/ *noun*. M19.
[ORIGIN from CARCINOMA + -GEN.]
A substance which is able to cause cancer (strictly, carcinoma).
– NOTE: Rare before M20.

carcinogenic /ˌkɑːs(ɪ)nəˈdʒɛnɪk/ *adjective*. E20.
[ORIGIN formed as CARCINOGEN + -GENIC.]
Able to cause cancer (strictly, carcinoma); cancer-producing.
■ **carcinogenesis** *noun* the production or origin of cancer E20. **carcinogenicity** /-ˈnɪsɪti/ *noun* M20.

carcinoid /ˈkɑːsɪnɔɪd/ *adjective & noun*. L19.
[ORIGIN from CARCINOMA + -OID.]
MEDICINE. ▸**A** *adjective*. †**1** = CANCROID *adjective* 2. Only in L19.
2 Of, pertaining to, or of the nature of a carcinoid; associated with carcinoids. E20.
▸ **B** *noun*. = ARGENTAFFINOMA. E20.

carcinology /kɑːsɪˈnɒlədʒi/ *noun*. M19.
[ORIGIN from Greek *karkinos* crab + -OLOGY.]
The zoological study of crabs and other crustaceans.
■ **carcinoˈlogical** *adjective* M19. **carcinologist** *noun* L19.

carcinoma /kɑːsɪˈnəʊmə/ *noun*. Pl. **-mas**, **-mata** /-mətə/. E18.
[ORIGIN Latin from Greek *karkinōma*, *-mat-*, formed as CARCINOLOGY + -OMA.]
MEDICINE. A cancer; now *spec*. a malignant tumour of epithelial origin.
■ **ˌcarcinomaˈtosis** *noun* widespread dissemination of carcinoma in the body E20. **carcinomatous** *adjective* of the nature of or characterized by carcinoma E18.

carcoon /kɑːˈkuːn/ *noun*. Also **karkun**. E19.
[ORIGIN Urdu *kārkun* from Persian = manager.]
In the Indian subcontinent: a clerk.

card /kɑːd/ *noun*[1]. LME.
[ORIGIN Old French & mod. French *carde* from Provençal *carda*, from *cardar* tease, comb, from popular Latin from Latin *carere* to card.]
A toothed instrument, wire brush, etc., for raising the nap on cloth or for disentangling the fibres of wool, hemp, etc., before spinning.

card /kɑːd/ *noun*[2]. LME.
[ORIGIN Old French & mod. French *carte* from Latin *charta* papyrus leaf, paper from Greek *khartēs* papyrus leaf. Cf. CHART *noun*.]
1 A flat object, typically oblong and made from layers of pasteboard pressed together, used with similar objects in a pack for playing various games, such objects being uniquely identifiable and distinguishable from one another by markings on the face (according to rank, suit, etc., in a conventional pack (see ***PLAYING card***)) but not from the back. LME. ▸**b** In *pl*. A game or games played with cards; card-playing. LME. ▸**c** *fig*. A plan or expedient of specified likelihood of success. M16.
court card, ***high card***, ***picture card***, ***tarot card***, ***trump card***, etc. **a card up one's sleeve** a plan in reserve, a hidden advantage. ***force a card***: see FORCE *verb*[1]. ***hold one's cards close to one's chest***: see CHEST *noun*. ***house of cards***: see HOUSE *noun*[1]. ***keep one's cards close to one's chest***: see CHEST *noun*. **lay all one's cards on the table**, **put all one's cards on the table** disclose all one's plans or resources. **lay one's cards on the table**, **put one's cards on the table** disclose one's plans or resources. **on the cards**, (*N. Amer*.) **in the cards** likely, possible. ***pair of cards***: see PAIR *noun*[1] 1. ***play one's cards close to one's chest***: see CHEST *noun*. **play one's cards right**, **play one's cards well**, etc., carry out a scheme successfully, act cleverly. **play the — card** introduce a specified (advantageous) usu. political factor. ***show one's cards***: see SHOW *verb*. ***stack the cards (against)***: see STACK *verb* 3. ***wild card***: see WILD *adjective*, *noun*, & *adverb*. **b** ***short cards***: see SHORT *adjective*. **c** ***doubtful card***, ***safe card***, ***sure card***, etc.
2 a A map, a plan; a chart. *obsolete* exc. *dial*. E16. ▸**b** A circular piece of stiff paper etc. bearing the thirty-two points of the compass. Also ***compass card***. L16.

> **b** *fig*.: R. HOOKER That Law . . is the Card to guide the World by.

b speak by the card *arch*. express oneself carefully, be precise.
3 A flat (usu. rectangular) piece of thick paper, thin pasteboard, etc., or now (esp. where durability is required) of plastic, blank or bearing writing, print, a picture, etc., and of various kinds for particular purposes (identified contextually or specified), as conveying an invitation, greeting, or message, displaying rules, information, etc., identifying the bearer or owner, recording membership, registration, or admission, etc. L16. ▸**b** *spec*. A programme of events at a race meeting etc. Also, a scorecard. M19. ▸**c** In full ***punched card***, ***punch card***. A piece of stiff paper etc. punched with holes in a certain pattern to represent specific information, esp. as used formerly in computing. M19. ▸**d** In *pl*. An employee's documents held by an employer. *colloq*. E20.
bank card, ***birthday card***, ***business card***, ***cheque card***, ***Christmas card***, ***cigarette card***, ***credit card***, ***identity card***, ***index card***, ***invitation card***, ***membership card***, ***party card***, ***phone card***, ***postcard***, ***scorecard***, ***showcard***, ***timecard***, ***valentine card***, ***visiting card***, ***wedding card***, etc. ***green card***: see GREEN *adjective*. ***leave a card on a person***: see LEAVE *verb*[1]. ***red card***: see RED *adjective*. ***yellow card***: see YELLOW *adjective*. **b mark a person's card** tip possible winners at a race meeting; *fig*. give prior information or advice. ***racecard***: see RACE *noun*[1]. **d ask for one's cards**, **get one's cards** resign, be dismissed from employment.
4 A published advertisement, notice, etc. *US*. M18.
5 A backing of pasteboard etc. to which several small objects, or samples of a commercial product, are fastened. M18.

> R. RENDELL Handkerchiefs, a box of tissues, a card of hairclips.

6 A person with a specified quality or specified qualities; an eccentric person, a character. *colloq*. E19.

> DICKENS Potter whose great aim it was to be considered as a 'knowing card'. ARNOLD BENNETT It would be . . a topic for years, the crown of his reputation as a card.

7 Pasteboard, cardboard. M20.
8 *ELECTRONICS*. A printed circuit board. L20.
– COMB.: **card-carrying** *adjective* having a valid (and usu. publicly known) membership of a political party or other organization; **card case** a case for visiting cards; **card game**: using playing cards; **card index**: in which each item is entered on a separate card; **card-index** *verb trans*. make a card index of; **cardmember** a holder of a particular credit or charge card; **cardphone** a public telephone operated by means of a prepaid card; **card player**, **card-playing** a person who plays, the playing of, card games; **card room** a room for playing cards; **card sharp**, **card sharper** a swindler at card games; **card swipe** an electronic reader through which a credit or charge card etc. is passed to record its number etc.; **card table** a table, usu. one which folds, designed for card-playing; **card trick** a conjuring trick using playing cards; **card vote** = ***block vote*** s.v. BLOCK *noun*.

card /kɑːd/ *verb*[1] *trans*. LME.
[ORIGIN from CARD *noun*[1].]
1 Prepare, cleanse, or comb (wool etc.) with a card; raise the nap on (cloth) with a card. LME.
carding wool short-stapled wool.
2 Lacerate (as) with a card. M16.
†**3** Stir and mix (as if) with a card. L16–M17.
■ **carder** *noun*[1] a person who or thing which cards wool etc.; ***carder bee***, any of various bumblebees which make a nest of moss or grass shreds above ground: LME.

card /kɑːd/ *verb*[2]. L15.
[ORIGIN from CARD *noun*[2].]
1 *verb intrans*. Play cards. Now *rare*. L15.
2 *verb trans*. Write or print on a card; enter in a card index. M19.
3 *verb trans*. Communicate (with) by card. L19.
4 *verb trans*. Affix to a card. L19.
■ **carder** *noun*[2] (*obsolete* exc. *dial*.) a card player LME.

Card. *abbreviation*.
Cardinal.

cardamom /ˈkɑːdəməm/ *noun*. Also **-mum**. LME.
[ORIGIN Old French & mod. French *cardamome* or Latin *cardamomum* from Greek *kardamōmon*, from *kardamon* cress + *amōmon* AMOMUM.]
A spice consisting of or made from the seed capsules of various Indo-Malayan plants, esp. *Elettaria cardamomum*; a plant yielding this.

cardan /ˈkɑːd(ə)n/ *noun*. Also **C-**. M18.
[ORIGIN from *Cardan* (Gerolamo *Cardano* (1501–76), Italian mathematician).]
Used *attrib*. and in *possess*. to designate things associated with Cardan.
cardan joint a universal joint. **Cardan's formula** *MATH*. a formula for finding the roots of a cubic equation after it has been

reduced to a form without a quadratic term. **Cardan's rule** = *Cardan's formula* above. **cardan shaft** a shaft with a universal joint at one or both ends.

cardboard /ˈkɑːdbɔːd/ *noun & adjective*. **M19.**
[**ORIGIN** from **CARD** *noun*[2] + **BOARD** *noun*.]
▶ **A** *noun*. **1** A pasteboard used esp. for cutting cards from or for making boxes etc. **M19.**
2 *fig.* Something insubstantial. **L19.**
▶ **B** *adjective*. **1** Made of cardboard. **M19.**
2 *fig.* Insubstantial, artificial. **L19.**
– **COMB.**: **cardboard city** an area where homeless people make shelters from cardboard packing cases.
■ **cardboardy** *adjective* = **CARDBOARD** *adjective* **E20.**

cardecu /ˈkɑːdɪkjuː/ *noun*. **E17.**
[**ORIGIN** French *quart d'écu* quarter of an **ÉCU**.]
hist. An old French silver coin worth a quarter of the gold *écu*.

cardi *noun* var. of **CARDIE**.

cardia /ˈkɑːdɪə/ *noun*. **L18.**
[**ORIGIN** Greek *kardia* (also = heart).]
ANATOMY. The upper opening of the stomach, where the oesophagus enters.

cardiac /ˈkɑːdɪak/ *noun & adjective*. **LME.**
[**ORIGIN** French *cardiaque* or Latin *cardiacus* adjectives, from Greek *kardiakos*, from *kardia*: see **CARDIA**, **-AC**.]
▶ **A** *noun*. †**1** A pain or ailment referred to the heart. **LME–L15.**
2 A medicine etc. affecting the heart; a cordial. Now *rare* or *obsolete*. **M18.**
3 A person with heart disease. *colloq.* **M20.**
▶ **B** *adjective*. **1** Of or pertaining to the heart. **E17.**
cardiac arrest: see **ARREST** *noun* 2b. †**cardiac passion** palpitation of the heart, heartburn. *cardiac tamponade*: see **TAMPONADE** 2.
2 Of medicines etc.: stimulating the heart; formerly, invigorating, cordial. **M17.**
cardiac glycoside any of a class of steroid glycosides which occur in plants and are heart stimulants, e.g. those present in digitalis.
3 Pertaining to or affected with heart disease. **M18.**
4 **ANATOMY.** Of or pertaining to the cardia of the stomach. **M19.**
■ **cardiacal** /kɑːˈdʌɪək(ə)l/ *adjective* (now *rare*) = **CARDIAC** *adjective* **LME.**

cardial /ˈkɑːdɪəl/ *adjective*. **M19.**
[**ORIGIN** Sense 1 formed as **CARDIA** + **-AL**[1]; sense 2 from mod. Latin *Cardium* genus name of the common cockle.]
1 = **CARDIAC** *adjective* 1. *rare*. **M19.**
2 **ARCHAEOLOGY.** Of Neolithic pottery: decorated with impressions made using cockleshells. **M20.**

cardialgy /ˈkɑːdɪaldʒi/ *noun*. Now *rare* or *obsolete*. Also in Latin form **-algia** /-ˈaldʒə/. **M17.**
[**ORIGIN** mod. Latin *cardialgia* from Greek *kardialgia*, from *kardia*: see **CARDIA**, **-ALGIA**, **-Y**[3].]
MEDICINE. Heartburn.

cardie /ˈkɑːdi/ *noun*. *colloq.* Also **-di**, **-dy**. **M20.**
[**ORIGIN** Abbreviation.]
= **CARDIGAN**.

cardigan /ˈkɑːdɪg(ə)n/ *noun*. **M19.**
[**ORIGIN** James Thomas Brudenell, seventh Earl of *Cardigan* (1797–1868), leader of the charge of the Light Brigade in the Crimean War.]
A knitted woollen etc. jacket with or without sleeves.

cardinal /ˈkɑːd(ɪ)n(ə)l/ *noun*. **OE.**
[**ORIGIN** Old French & mod. French from medieval Latin *cardinalis*: see **CARDINAL** *adjective*. Branch II from **CARDINAL** *adjective*.]
▶ **I** **1** Any of the leading dignitaries of the Roman Catholic Church who together form the sacred college which elects the Pope. **OE.** ▸**b** Either of two minor canons of St Paul's Cathedral, London. **M18.**
2 Any of a number of songbirds of the American subfamily Cardinalinae (family Emberizidae), related to the buntings; esp. the common N. American *Cardinalis cardinalis*, the male of which has scarlet plumage. **E18.**
3 *hist.* A woman's cloak, orig. of scarlet cloth with a hood. **M18.**
▶ **II** **4** In *pl.* The cardinal numerals, points, virtues, etc. **LME.**
– **COMB.**: **cardinal beetle** any of various mainly bright red beetles of the family Pyrochroidae, with feathery or comb-like antennae; **cardinal flower** a scarlet-flowered lobelia, *Lobelia cardinalis*, native to N. America; **cardinal-grosbeak** = sense 2 above; **cardinal's hat** the red hat worn by a cardinal; *fig.* the dignity or office of a cardinal; **cardinal spider** a very large spider, spec. *Tegenaria parietina*.
■ **cardinalate** *noun* the office, dignity, or rank of a cardinal **M17.** **cardinaˈlatial** *adjective* = **CARDINALITIAL** **L19.** **cardinalism** *noun* (*rare*) the institution or system of cardinals **L17.** **cardinalist** *noun* (*rare*) a supporter of a cardinal or cardinalism **M17.** **cardinalitial** /kɑːd(ɪ)nəˈlɪʃ(ə)l/ *adjective* pertaining to cardinals as a group **L17.** **cardinalize** *verb trans.* raise to the rank of cardinal **E17.** **cardinalship** *noun* the state or (tenure of) office of a cardinal **LME.**

cardinal /ˈkɑːd(ɪ)n(ə)l/ *adjective*. **LME.**
[**ORIGIN** Old French & mod. French, or Latin *cardinalis*, from *cardo*, *cardin-* hinge: see **-AL**[1]. Branch II from **CARDINAL** *noun*.]
▶ **I** **1** On which something hinges; fundamental, crucial; important; pre-eminent. **LME.**

> A. BURGESS It was a cardinal rule in the East not to show one's true feelings.

cardinal humour: see **HUMOUR** *noun*. **cardinal number**, **cardinal numeral** any of the positive whole numbers, one, two, three, etc., showing how many elements there are in a certain set (cf. *ordinal number*, *ordinal numeral* s.v. **ORDINAL** *adjective* 2); any of a series of analogous transfinite numbers. **cardinal point** any of the four main points of the compass, north, south, east, and west. **cardinal sin** (**a**) each of the seven deadly sins; (**b**) a serious error of judgement. **cardinal vein** any of a number of veins which drain the head and trunk in an embryo. **cardinal virtue** each of the four chief moral virtues (orig. of scholastic philosophy), justice, prudence, temperance, and fortitude (also called *natural virtue*); more widely, each of seven chief virtues comprising these with the three theological virtues; *gen.* an outstanding quality, a particular excellence. **cardinal vowel** each of a series of vowel sounds established by the British phonetician Daniel Jones (1881–1967), used as a standard of reference to assist in the description and classification of vowel sounds in any language. **cardinal wind**: blowing from a cardinal point.
2 **ZOOLOGY.** Of or pertaining to the hinge of a bivalve. **M19.**
▶ **II** Corresp. to **CARDINAL** *noun* 1 (merging with *attrib.* uses).
3 Belonging to the sacred college; appointed to the Roman diocese. With a title: that is also a cardinal. **M17.**
cardinal vicar the Pope's delegate acting as bishop for the diocese of Rome.
4 Of deep scarlet (as a cardinal's robe). **L19.**
■ **cardinally** *adverb* **E17.**

cardinality /kɑːdɪˈnalɪti/ *noun*. **E16.**
[**ORIGIN** from **CARDINAL** *noun*, *adjective* + **-ITY**.]
†**1** = **CARDINALATE**. **E16–E17.**
2 **MATH.** The number of elements in a set or other grouping, as a property of the set etc. **M20.**

cardines *noun* pl. of **CARDO**.

cardio- /ˈkɑːdɪəʊ/ *combining form* of Greek *kardia* heart: see **-O-**.
■ **cardiogram** *noun* a record of heart action produced by a cardiograph **L19.** **cardiomyˈopathy** *noun* (a) chronic disease of heart muscle, *esp.* one of uncertain cause **M20.** **cardioˈpulmonary** *adjective* pertaining to or involving the heart and the lungs **E20.** ˌ**cardioreˈspiratory** *adjective* relating to the action of both heart and lungs **L19.** **cardiospasm** *noun* = **ACHALASIA** **E20.** **cardiothoˈracic** *adjective* pertaining to or involving the heart and chest or lungs **M20.** **cardioˈvascular** *adjective* pertaining to or involving the heart and blood vessels **L19.**

cardiograph /ˈkɑːdɪəgrɑːf/ *noun*. **L19.**
[**ORIGIN** from **CARDIO-** + **-GRAPH**.]
An instrument which records the action of the heart.
BALLISTOCARDIOGRAPH, **ELECTROCARDIOGRAPH**, **MAGNETOCARDIOGRAPH**, etc.
■ **cardiˈographer** *noun* a person who uses a cardiograph **M20.** **cardioˈgraphic** *adjective* **L19.** **cardioˈgraphically** *adverb* **E20.** **cardiˈography** *noun* **L19.**

cardioid /ˈkɑːdɪɔɪd/ *noun & adjective*. **M18.**
[**ORIGIN** from Greek *kardioeidēs* heart-shaped, formed as **CARDIA**: see **-OID**.]
▶ **A** *noun*. **1** **MATH.** A heart-shaped curve traced by a point on the circumference of a circle as it rolls round another, identical, circle, and represented by the equation $r = a(1 + \cos \theta)$. Cf. **LIMAÇON** 2. **M18.**
2 A cardioid microphone. **M20.**
▶ **B** *adjective*. Of the form of a heart-shaped curve; *esp.* (of a microphone) having a pattern of sensitivity of this form. **M20.**

cardiology /kɑːdɪˈɒlədʒi/ *noun*. **M19.**
[**ORIGIN** from **CARDIO-** + **-LOGY**.]
The branch of knowledge that deals with the structure, action, and diseases of the heart.
■ **cardioˈlogical** *adjective* **E20.** **cardiologist** *noun* **L19.**

cardiomegaly /kɑːdɪəʊˈmɛgəli/ *noun*. **M20.**
[**ORIGIN** from **CARDIO-** + Greek *megas*, *megal-* great: see **-Y**[3].]
MEDICINE. Abnormal enlargement of the heart.

carditis /kɑːˈdʌɪtɪs/ *noun*. **L18.**
[**ORIGIN** formed as **CARDIA** + **-ITIS**.]
Inflammation of the heart.

cardo /ˈkɑːdəʊ/ *noun*. Pl. **-dines** /-dɪniːz/. **L16.**
[**ORIGIN** Latin: see **CARDINAL** *adjective*.]
†**1** **ASTROLOGY.** In *pl.* The cardinal points. **L16–M17.**
†**2** *fig.* A turning point. Only in **M17.**
3 The hinge of a bivalve. **M18.**

cardoon /kɑːˈduːn/ *noun*. **E17.**
[**ORIGIN** French *cardon*, from *carde* edible part of the artichoke, from mod. Provençal *cardo* from Proto-Romance from Latin *cardu(u)s* thistle, artichoke: see **-OON**.]
A plant of the composite family, *Cynara cardunculus*, resembling a thistle and related to the globe artichoke; the fleshy inner leaf stalks of this plant, eaten as a vegetable.

carduus /ˈkɑːdjʊəs/ *noun*. **LME.**
[**ORIGIN** Latin: see **CARDOON**.]
A thistle; *esp.* the blessed thistle, *Cnicus* (formerly *Carduus*) *benedictus*, from which a tonic was prepared. Now only as mod. Latin genus name.

cardy *noun* var. of **CARDIE**.

care /kɛː/ *noun*.
[**ORIGIN** Old English *caru* = Old Saxon *kara*, Old High German *chara* grief, lament, Old Norse *kǫr* (genit. *karar*) bed of sickness, Gothic *kara*, from Germanic.]
1 Mental suffering; sorrow, grief. *obsolete* exc. in **CARCAKE**, *Care Sunday* below. **OE.**

> POPE His words infix'd unutterable care Deep in great Hector's soul.

2 A troubled state of mind arising from fear, doubt, etc; trouble, anxiety, solicitude; an occasion for this. **OE.**

> TENNYSON Cast all your cares on God. E. MUIR Public trouble and private care Faith and hope and love can sever.

3 Serious attention, heed; caution, pains; regard, inclination, (*to*, *for*). **OE.**

> GEO. ELIOT Public spirit . . its essence is care for a common good. E. WAUGH She arranged her paints and bottles with habitual care.

4 Charge, protective oversight, guardianship. **LME.**

> J. MARQUAND It was given into my care by a friend who wishes it to be in safe hands. S. BELLOW Elena was burdened with the care of the children.

5 An object or matter of concern; a thing to be done or seen to. **L16.**

> B. JOWETT He could not himself spare the time from cares of state. S. LEACOCK My first care was to make a fire.

– **PHRASES**: **care and maintenance** the keeping of a building, ship, etc., in good condition although not in present use (freq. *attrib.*). **care in the community** = **COMMUNITY** *care*. **care of X** at X's address. **have a care** be cautious, not neglect or fail. **have the care of** be responsible for. **in care** under official guardianship. **in care of** *US* = *care of* above. **in need of care** (**and protection**) (of a destitute or dangerously circumstanced child etc.) qualifying for official guardianship. *intensive care*: see **INTENSIVE** *adjective* 2. **take care** = *have a care* above. **take care of** look after, deal with, provide for, dispose of. *tender loving care*: see **TENDER** *adjective*.
– **COMB.**: **caregiver** a person, typically either a professional or close relative, who looks after a child, elderly person, invalid, etc.; a carer; **care label**: giving advice on the cleaning of a garment or fabric; **care-laden** *adjective* laden with anxieties; **Care Sunday** the fifth Sunday in Lent; **caretake** *verb trans. & intrans.* [back-form.] act as caretaker (of); **caretaker** *noun & adjective* (**a**) *noun* a person hired to take charge, esp. of a house in its owner's absence; a person looking after a public building; (**b**) *adjective* exercising temporary control; **care worker** a person employed to provide support and supervision for vulnerable, infirm, or disadvantaged people, or those under the care of the state; **careworn** *adjective* wearied by anxieties.

care /kɛː/ *verb*.
[**ORIGIN** Old English *carian* = Old Saxon *karon*, Old High German *charōn*, *-ēn*, Gothic *karōn*, from Germanic; in later senses from the noun.]
†**1** *verb intrans.* Sorrow, grieve. **OE–M16.**
2 *verb intrans.* Feel concern or interest (*about*, *for*; *if*, *though*, *whether*; *whom*, *what*, etc.); feel deference, fondness, affection, etc. (*about*, *for*). Freq. with adverbs of degree or expletives. **OE.**

> J. GALSWORTHY I don't . . care a fig for his opinion. DYLAN THOMAS I don't care a bugger whether you won't or will. J. BRAINE I don't mean that one has to love people, but simply that one ought to care. STEVIE SMITH What care I if good God be If he be not good to me? B. TARKINGTON Don't you care enough about me to marry me?

for all I care *colloq.* as a matter of complete indifference to me. *know little and care less*, *know nothing and care less*: see **KNOW** *verb*. *not care a cent*, *not care a chip*, *not care a hang*, *not care a snap*, *not care a tinker's curse*, etc.
3 *verb intrans.* Foll. by *for*: provide for, look after, take care of. **ME.**

> R. MACAULAY A cared-for looking white skin.

4 *verb trans.* Take care of, look after, regard. Long *obsolete* exc. *dial.* **LME.**
5 *verb intrans.* Have an inclination *for*; be inclined or disposed *to*, *to do*; be agreeable or willing *to do*. **M16.**

> A. FRASER His sister . . did not care to study the art of how to please. J. FENTON Would you care for a boiled sweet?

■ **carer** *noun* a person who cares or (now esp.) takes care of another or others **L17.**

care-cloth /ˈkɛːklɒθ/ *noun*. *obsolete* exc. *hist.* **M16.**
[**ORIGIN** Unknown.]
A cloth held over or placed upon the heads of bride and bridegroom while they knelt during the marriage service.

careen /kəˈriːn/ *noun & verb*. **L16.**
[**ORIGIN** French *carène*, †*carine*, from Italian dial. *carena* from Latin *carina* keel.]
▶ **A** *noun*. The position of a ship laid or heeled over on one side; an instance of careening. **L16.**
▶ **B** *verb*. **1** *verb trans. & intrans.* Turn (a ship) over on one side for cleaning. **E17.**
2 *verb intrans.* Of a ship: incline to one side or lie over when sailing on a wind. **M18.** ▸**b** *transf.* Lean over, tilt. **L19.**
3 *verb trans.* Cause (a ship) to heel over. **M19.**
4 *verb intrans.* (Infl. by **CAREER** *verb*.) Rush headlong, hurtle unsteadily. *N. Amer.* **E20.**

■ **careenage** *noun* (the place for) the careening of a ship; the cost of this: **L18.**

career /kəˈrɪə/ *noun & adjective*. **M16.**
[ORIGIN French *carrière* from Italian *carriera* from Provençal *carreira* from Proto-Romance, from Latin *carrus* CAR.]
▸ **A** *noun*. †**1** A racecourse; the enclosure at a tournament etc.; course, road. **M16–M18.**
†**2** A short gallop of a horse at full speed; a charge, an encounter on horseback. **M16–M18.**
3 A (swift) running course; an act of careering; full speed, impetus. **M16.**

MILTON The Sun . . was hasting now with prone carreer To th' Ocean Iles. C. S. FORESTER Mr. Graham put out a huge hand that stopped a taxi in full career. Y. MENUHIN A dizzy career by jeep through the empty streets.

4 A course or progress through life or history; an occupation or profession engaged in as a life-work, a way of making a livelihood and advancing oneself. **E19.**

W. A. PERCY To the grown-ups turtle soup was simply the predestined last act of a soft-shell turtle's career. T. CAPOTE He had attempted several careers, as soldier, ranch hand, mechanic, thief. JO GRIMOND The law . . seemed a suitable career for an aspiring politician.

– COMB.: **careers master**, **careers mistress**, **careers teacher**: responsible for advising pupils on a choice of career; **career structure** the structure of an organization or profession as providing opportunities for advancement and a developing career.
▸ **B** *attrib.* or as *adjective*. Permanently employed in a particular profession; (esp. of a woman) devoted to the pursuit of a profession. **E20.**

F. J. STIMSON The career professors look somewhat askance at one who comes in from the outside world. B. FRIEDAN They are not career women . . ; they are women whose greatest ambition has been marriage and children.

■ **careerism** *noun* the practice or policy of a careerist **M20.** **careerist** *noun & adjective* (a person) mainly intent on furthering his or her own career, esp. unscrupulously **E20.**

career /kəˈrɪə/ *verb intrans.* **L16.**
[ORIGIN from the noun.]
†**1** Take a short gallop; charge; (of a horse) weave from side to side while running. **L16–L17.**
2 Go swiftly or wildly, rush headlong, hurtle. **M17.**

L. A. G. STRONG A young man on a bicycle . . careered out into the main street.

carefree /ˈkɛːfriː/ *adjective*. **L18.**
[ORIGIN from CARE *noun* + -FREE.]
Free from anxiety or responsibility.
■ **carefreeness** *noun* **E20.**

careful /ˈkɛːfʊl, -f(ə)l/ *adjective*. **OE.**
[ORIGIN from CARE *noun* + -FUL.]
†**1** Full of grief, sorrowful. **OE–E18.**
2 Full of trouble; anxious, concerned. *arch.* **OE.**
3 Full of care or concern *for*; attentive to the interests *of*; taking good care *of* or *with*. **OE.**

H. B. STOWE Be careful of the horses, Sam.

4 Applying care or attention; painstaking, circumspect. (Foll. by *to do*, *that*, *what*, etc.) **OE.** ▸**b** Done with or showing care. **M17.**

J. TYNDALL I felt just sufficient fear to render me careful. **b** LD MACAULAY Careful watch was kept all night.

5 Fraught with trouble or anxiety. Now *rare* or *obsolete*. **ME.**
†**6** On one's guard, wary. **L16–E18.**
■ **carefully** *adverb* **OE.** **carefulness** *noun* **OE.**

careless /ˈkɛːlɪs/ *adjective*. **OE.**
[ORIGIN from CARE *noun* + -LESS.]
1 Free from care, apprehension, or anxiety. Now *arch.* or *poet.* **OE.**
2 Unconcerned, taking no heed *of*; light-hearted. **OE.**
3 Inattentive, negligent (*of*), thoughtless; inaccurate. **L16.**
4 Done, caused, or said heedlessly, thoughtlessly, effortlessly, or negligently; artless, unstudied. Formerly also, uncared-for, untended. **L16.**

SHAKES. *Macb.* To throw away the dearest thing he ow'd As 'twere a careless trifle. J. OSBORNE She still looks quite smart, but in an unpremeditated, careless way. J. LE CARRÉ Careless lines of mortar hastily put on.

■ **carelessly** *adverb* **M16.** **carelessness** *noun* **OE.**

Carelian *noun & adjective* var. of KARELIAN.

care spose *noun phr.* pl. of CARA SPOSA.

caress /kəˈrɛs/ *noun*. **M17.**
[ORIGIN French *caresse* from Italian *carezza* from Proto-Romance, from Latin *carus* dear: see -ESS^{2}.]
An action of endearment, a fondling touch, a kiss; a blandishment.

caress /kəˈrɛs/ *verb trans.* **M17.**
[ORIGIN from CARESS *noun* or French *caresser*.]
Bestow a caress on; stroke or pat tenderly; fondle; treat kindly or affectionately.

fig.: J. L. WATEN The warm sun caressed our faces. H. L. MENCKEN It caresses my ego today to think of men reading me half a century after I am gone.

■ **caressable** *adjective* **M17.** **caressingly** *adverb* **M19.** **caressive** *adjective* that caresses; of the nature of a caress: **E19.** **caressively** *adverb* **E20.**

caret /ˈkarət/ *noun*. **L17.**
[ORIGIN Latin, 3rd person sing. pres. indic. of *carere* be without, lack.]
A mark (strictly ^) placed below a line of writing or printing, in a margin, etc., to show the place of an omission.

carex /ˈkɛːrɛks/ *noun*. Pl. **-rices** /-rɪsiːz/. **LME.**
[ORIGIN Latin *carex*.]
A sedge; a plant of the genus *Carex*.

carezza *noun* var. of KAREZZA.

carf /kɑːf/ *noun*. *obsolete* exc. *dial.* **LME.**
[ORIGIN Var. of KERF, infl. by CARVE. See also CURF.]
A cut, esp. in timber; a notch, a slit, an incision.

carfax /ˈkɑːfaks/ *noun*. Also (now *rare*) **-fox** /-fɒks/. **ME.**
[ORIGIN Anglo-Norman *carfuks* = Old French *carrefurcs* (mod. *carrefour*) from popular Latin, from Latin QUADRI- + *furca* FORK *noun*.]
A place where (usu. four) roads or streets meet. Now chiefly in proper names.

†**carfour** *noun* var. of CARREFOUR.

carfox *noun* see CARFAX.

carga /ˈkɑːgə/ *noun*. **E17.**
[ORIGIN Spanish: see CARGO *noun*.]
In Spain and Spanish-speaking countries: a load as a measure of weight.

cargador /kɑːgəˈdɔː/ *noun*. Pl. **-dores** /-ˈdɔːrɪz/. **E19.**
[ORIGIN Spanish, formed as CARGA.]
In Spanish-speaking parts of America: a porter.

†**cargason** *noun*. Also **-z-**. **L16–L19.**
[ORIGIN Spanish *cargazon* double augm. of *carga*.]
A (ship's) cargo.

cargo /ˈkɑːgəʊ/ *noun*. Pl. **-oes**, ***-os**. **M17.**
[ORIGIN Spanish (also *carga*), corresp. to Old French & mod. French *charge* load: see CHARGE *noun*.]
The goods carried by a ship, aircraft, lorry, etc.; a load.
– COMB.: **cargo boat**, **cargo ship**, etc.: carrying only or chiefly freight; **cargo cult** (orig. in Pacific islands) a belief in the forthcoming arrival of supernatural benefactors; **cargo pants** (orig. *US*) trousers with large, external pockets halfway up the side of each leg, typically loose-fitting and made of cotton.

cargo /ˈkɑːgəʊ/ *verb trans.* **L19.**
[ORIGIN from the noun.]
Load (*with* cargo); carry as cargo.

cargoose /ˈkɑːguːs/ *noun*. Now *rare* or *obsolete*. Pl. **-geese** /-giːs/. **L17.**
[ORIGIN App. from CARR *noun*^{2} + GOOSE *noun*.]
The great crested grebe.

cariad /ˈkarɪad/ *noun*. *Welsh*. **L19.**
[ORIGIN Welsh, lit. 'love'.]
As a form of addresss: darling, sweetheart.

cariama *noun* var. of SERIEMA.

Carian /ˈkɛːrɪən/ *noun*^{1} *& adjective*. **E17.**
[ORIGIN from Latin *Caria* (see below) from Greek *Karia*: see -AN.]
▸ **A** *noun*. A native or inhabitant, or the language, of Caria (SW Anatolia), an ancient province of Asia Minor. **E17.**
▸ **B** *adjective*. Of or pertaining to Caria or its language. **E17.**

†**Carian** *noun*^{2} see KAREN.

†**Carianer** *noun* see KAREN.

Carib /ˈkarɪb/ *noun & adjective*. **M16.**
[ORIGIN Spanish *caribe* from Haitian creole: cf. CANNIBAL.]
▸ **A** *noun*. Pl. **-s**, same.
1 Any of the aboriginal inhabitants of the southern W. Indian islands and adjacent coasts. **M16.**
2 The American Indian language of these people. **L19.**
▸ **B** *attrib.* or as *adjective*. Of or pertaining to these people or their language. **M19.**
■ Also **Cariˈbee** *noun* (now *rare* or *obsolete*) a Carib **E18.**

Caribbean /karɪˈbiːən, kəˈrɪbɪən/ *noun & adjective*. **E18.**
[ORIGIN from CARIB + -EAN.]
▸ **A** *noun*. **1** A Carib. *rare*. **E18.**
2 The region of the Atlantic between the southern W. Indian islands and Central America. **L19.**
▸ **B** *adjective*. **1** Of or pertaining to the Caribs. **L18.**
2 Designating or pertaining to the Caribbean; West Indian. **L19.**
– NOTE: The usual British English pronunc. stresses the *-be-*, while that found in the US and the Caribbean itself stresses the *-rib-*.

caribe /kəˈriːbeɪ, ˈkarɪbeɪ/ *noun*. **M19.**
[ORIGIN Spanish: see CARIB.]
= PIRANHA.

caribou /ˈkarɪbuː/ *noun*. Also **-oo**. Pl. same. **M17.**
[ORIGIN Canad. French from Micmac *γalipu* lit. 'snow-shoveller'.]
A N. American reindeer.
– COMB.: **caribou moss** reindeer moss.

†**caricatura** *noun*. **L17–E19.**
[ORIGIN Italian: see CARICATURE.]
= CARICATURE *noun*.

caricature /ˈkarɪkətjʊə/ *noun & verb*. **M18.**
[ORIGIN French from Italian *caricatura*, from *caricare* to load, exaggerate, from late Latin *car(ri)care*: see CHARGE *verb*, -URE.]
▸ **A** *noun*. **1** Grotesque or ludicrous representation by exaggeration of characteristic traits, in drawing, writing, mime, etc.; a portrait or other representation displaying this. **M18.**

E. A. FREEMAN Stories . . which . . illustrate, if only by caricature, some real feature in his character. E. WAUGH One man drew an offensive caricature of me.

2 An exaggerated or debased imitation or version (*of*), naturally or unintentionally ludicrous. **M18.**

G. SAINTSBURY *The Wanderer* is a caricature of all the very worst faults of eighteenth-century poetic diction. S. NAIPAUL He glanced at me out of the corner of his eyes, a caricature of petty crookedness.

▸ **B** *verb trans.* Portray or imitate by a grotesque or ludicrous exaggeration of characteristic traits; burlesque. **M18.**
■ **caricaˈtural** *adjective* of the nature of a caricature **L19.** **caricaturist** *noun* a person who practises caricature **L18.**

carices *noun* pl. of CAREX.

CARICOM /ˈkarɪkɒm/ *abbreviation*.
Caribbean Community and Common Market.

caries /ˈkɛːriːz/ *noun*. Pl. same. **L16.**
[ORIGIN Latin.]
Decay of a tooth or bone.

carillon /ˈkarɪljən, -lɒn, kəˈrɪljən/ *noun*. **L18.**
[ORIGIN French, alt. of Old French *car(e)ignon*, *quarregnon*, from Proto-Romance = peal of four bells.]
1 A set of bells sounded either from a keyboard or mechanically. **L18.**
2 A tune played on such bells. **L18.**

fig.: H. ACTON Nancy's laughter rose above theirs in a carillon that was almost operatic.

3 A musical instrument or part of an organ designed to imitate a peal of bells. **E19.**
■ **carilloˈnneur** *noun* [French] a person who plays a carillon **L18.**

carina /kəˈrʌɪnə, -ˈriː-/ *noun*. Pl. **-nas**, **-nae** /-niː/. **E18.**
[ORIGIN Latin = keel.]
1 BIOLOGY. A keel-like structure, a ridge; esp. (***a***) the keel of a bird's breastbone; (***b***) the cartilage at the bifurcation of the trachea to form the bronchi; (***c***) = KEEL *noun*^{1} 3C. **E18.**
2 (**C-**.) (The name of) a constellation of the southern hemisphere between Volans and the Milky Way, orig. part of Argo; the Keel. **M19.**
■ **carinal** *adjective* pertaining to or of the nature of a carina **L19.**

carinate /ˈkarɪneɪt, -ət/ *adjective*. **L18.**
[ORIGIN Latin *carinatus*, formed as CARINATE *verb*: see -ATE^{2}.]
Chiefly BIOLOGY. Having a ridge, keel, or carina; (of birds) having a keeled breastbone (opp. ***ratite***).

carinate /ˈkarɪneɪt/ *verb trans.* **L17.**
[ORIGIN Latin *carinat-* pa. ppl stem of *carinare* supply with a keel or shell, formed as CARINA: see -ATE^{3}.]
Chiefly BIOLOGY. Provide with a ridge, keel, or carina. Chiefly as ***carinated*** *ppl adjective*.
■ **cariˈnation** *noun* **L19.**

caring /ˈkɛːrɪŋ/ *noun & adjective*. **M16.**
[ORIGIN from CARE *verb* + -ING^{2}.]
▸ **A** *noun*. The action of CARE *verb*. **M16.**
▸ **B** *adjective*. Compassionate, concerned; involved in caring for others. **M20.**

E. KUZWAYO He seemed to be a caring and loving parent.

■ **caringly** *adverb* **E17.**

carioca /karɪˈəʊkə/ *noun*. **M19.**
[ORIGIN Portuguese.]
1 A native of Rio de Janeiro, Brazil. **M19.**
2 A Brazilian dance resembling a samba; a piece of music for this dance. **M20.**

cariogenic /kɛːrɪəˈdʒɛnɪk, kar-/ *adjective*. **M20.**
[ORIGIN from CARIES + -O- + -GENIC.]
Causing or promoting tooth decay.
■ **cariogenicity** /-ˈnɪsɪti/ *noun* **M20.**

cariole *noun* var. of CARRIOLE.

cariosity /kɛːrɪˈɒsɪti/ *noun*. Now *rare* or *obsolete*. **M17.**
[ORIGIN formed as CARIOUS + -ITY.]
Carious condition; a carious formation.

carious /ˈkɛːrɪəs/ *adjective*. **M16.**
[ORIGIN from Latin *cariosus*, from CARIES: see -OUS.]
Decayed, rotten; *spec.* affected with caries.

cari sposi *noun phr.* pl. of CARO SPOSO.

carissima /kaˈrissima/ *adjective*. **M19.**
[ORIGIN Italian, superl. of *cara* dear.]
A term of endearment to a woman: dearest, darling.

caritas /ˈkarɪtɑːs/ *noun*. **M19.**
[ORIGIN Latin: see CHARITY.]
= CHARITY 1.

C

C

caritive /ˈkarɪtɪv/ *adjective & noun*. **M19**.
[ORIGIN from Latin *carit-* ppl stem of *carere* lack: see -IVE.]
GRAMMAR. ▸**A** *adjective*. Designating, being in, or pertaining to a case in Caucasian and other languages expressing the lack of something. **M19**.
▸**B** *noun*. *The* caritive case; a word, form, etc., in the caritive case. **M20**.

carjacking /ˈkɑːdʒakɪŋ/ *noun*. **L20**.
[ORIGIN Blend of CAR and *hijacking* (see HIJACK).]
The stealing or commandeering of an occupied car by threatening the driver with violence.
■ **carjack** *verb & noun* **L20**. **carjacker** *noun* **L20**.

cark /kɑːk/ *noun*. Long *arch*. or *Scot*. **ME**.
[ORIGIN Anglo-Norman *karke* repr. north. var. of Old French *c(h)arche*, from *c(h)archier* from late Latin *car(ri)care*: see CHARGE *verb*.]
†**1** A load, a weight. **ME–M16**.
†**2** A charge, a burden. **ME–L16**.
3 Trouble, anxiety; labour; toil. **ME**.

LONGFELLOW The swart mechanic comes to drown his cark and care.

†**4** Care, pains; heed. **LME–E17**.

cark /kɑːk/ *verb*[1]. Long *arch*. or *Scot*. **ME**.
[ORIGIN Old Northern French *carkier* from Old French *c(h)archier*: see CARK *noun*.]
†**1** *verb trans*. Load, burden; impose as a charge on. Only in **ME**.
2 *verb trans*. Worry, harass, vex, trouble. **ME**.
3 *verb intrans*. Be anxious, be concerned; fret oneself; toil. **ME**.
†**4** *verb intrans*. Care *for*, take thought. **LME–E17**.
■ **carking** *noun* grieving, solicitude, (an) anxiety **ME**. **carking** *adjective* burdensome, wearying; toiling, anxious, niggardly: **M16**.

cark /kɑːk/ *verb*[2] *intrans*. *Austral. colloq*. **L20**.
[ORIGIN Perh. imitative of the caw of a carrion crow, or rel. to CARCASS.]
Usu. ***cark it***. Die.

E. PERKINS I realise this would be going too far, even for me. Lucinda'll probably cark it or something.

carl /kɑːl/ *noun*. Long *arch*. & *dial*. Also **carle**. **OE**.
[ORIGIN Old Norse *karl* man, male, freeman = Old High German *kar(a)l*, *charlo*, from Germanic: rel. to CHURL.]
1 A countryman, a peasant; a bondman; a villein. **OE**.
2 A low-born or rough-mannered man; a mean or grudging person. **ME**.
3 In full ***carl hemp***. The more robust kind of hemp plant (orig. considered male but later found to be the female plant). **E16**.
4 A (usu. strong or sturdy) man; a fellow. **M16**.
■ **carlish** *adjective* of or pertaining to a carl; churlish, coarse, vulgar, mean: **ME**. †**carlot** *noun* (*rare*, Shakes.) a peasant, a churl: only in **L16**.

carl /kɑːl/ *verb*[1] *intrans*. *obsolete* exc. *dial*. **E17**.
[ORIGIN Perh. from CARL *noun*.]
Speak gruffly, snarl; behave churlishly.

carl /kɑːl/ *verb*[2] *trans*. *obsolete* exc. *dial*. **E17**.
[ORIGIN Perh. back-form. from CARLING *noun*[1] taken as a ppl form.]
Prepare as carlings; parch (peas etc.).

carle *noun* var. of CARL *noun*.

Carley /ˈkɑːli/ *noun*. **E20**.
[ORIGIN Horace S. *Carley* (fl. 1900), US inventor.]
More fully ***Carley float***, ***Carley raft***. A large emergency raft carried on board ship.

carline /ˈkɑːlɪn/ *noun*[1]. Also **-ling** /-lɪŋ/. **ME**.
[ORIGIN Old Norse *karling* fem. of *karl* CARL *noun*.]
1 An (old) woman; *esp*. a witch. Chiefly *Scot*. **ME**.
2 NAUTICAL. Any of the squared timbers fitted fore and aft between the deck beams of a wooden ship to support the deck planking. **LME**.

carline /ˈkɑːlɪn/ *noun*[2]. **L16**.
[ORIGIN French from medieval Latin *carlina* perh. from *cardina* (from *cardo* thistle) by assoc. with *Carolus* Magnus (Charlemagne), to whom its medicinal qualities were reputedly revealed.]
In full ***carline thistle***. A spiny plant of the genus *Carlina* of the composite family.

†**carline** *noun*[3]. **E18–M19**.
[ORIGIN Old French & mod. French *carlin* from Italian *carlino*, from *Carlo*, name of several kings of Naples: cf. CAROLINE *noun*.]
A small silver coin formerly current in Naples and Sicily.

carling /ˈkɑːlɪŋ/ *noun*[1]. *obsolete* exc. *dial*. **M16**.
[ORIGIN Perh. from CARE *noun* in *Care Sunday*.]
Usu. in *pl*. Parched peas, traditionally eaten on ***Carling Sunday***, Care Sunday (see CARE *noun*).

carling *noun*[2] var. of CARLINE *noun*[1].

Carlism /ˈkɑːlɪz(ə)m/ *noun*. **M19**.
[ORIGIN French *carlisme* from Spanish *carlismo*, from Don *Carlos* (1788–1855), brother of King Fernando VII of Spain: see below, -ISM.]
A Spanish counter-revolutionary movement originating in support for Don Carlos and his heirs as the legitimate successors of Fernando VII, as opp. to the line of Fernando's daughter Isabella II.
■ **Carlist** *noun & adjective* (**a**) *noun* a supporter of Carlism; (**b**) *adjective* of or pertaining to Carlism or Carlists: **M19**.

Carlovingian /kɑːləˈvɪndʒɪən/ *adjective & noun*. **M18**.
[ORIGIN French *carlovingien*, from *Karl* Charles after *mérovingien* MEROVINGIAN *adjective*.]
= CAROLINGIAN.

Carlsbad plum /ˈkɑːlzbad ˈplʌm/ *noun phr*. **L19**.
[ORIGIN *Carlsbad*, a spa town formerly in Germany, now (renamed *Karlovy Vary*) in Bohemia.]
A blue-black usu. crystallized dessert plum.

Carlylism /kɑːˈlʌɪlɪz(ə)m/ *noun*. **M19**.
[ORIGIN from *Carlyle* (see below) + -ISM.]
The teachings or literary style of the Scottish-born essayist and historian Thomas Carlyle (1795–1881); a literary mannerism of Carlyle.
■ **Carlylean** *adjective* of, pertaining to, or characteristic of Carlyle or his works **E19**. **Carlyˈlese** *noun* the language or style of Carlyle **M19**.

carmagnole /karmaɲɔl/ *noun*. Pl. pronounced same. **L18**.
[ORIGIN French, orig. a style of jacket popular during the French Revolution, prob. ult. from *Carmagnola*, a town in Piedmont.]
1 A popular song and round dance of the French Revolutionary period. **L18**.
2 A French revolutionary soldier; *transf*. an author of mischief. **L18**.

Carmathian *noun & adjective* var. of KARMATHIAN.

Carmelite /ˈkɑːmɪlʌɪt/ *noun & adjective*. **LME**.
[ORIGIN French *carmélite* or medieval Latin *Carmelita* (cf. late Latin *carmelites* inhabitant of Mount *Carmel*, Palestine): see -ITE[1].]
▸**A** *noun*. **1** A member of an order of mendicant friars (also known as the White Friars), founded at Mount Carmel in the 12th cent. Also, a nun of an order modelled on the White Friars. **LME**.
2 (Also **c-**.) A fine usu. grey woollen material. **E19**.
▸**B** *adjective*. Of or pertaining to the Carmelites. **E16**.
■ Also †**Carme** *noun & adjective* **LME–L18**. †**Carmelitan** *noun & adjective* **L16–M18**.

carminative /ˈkɑːmɪnətɪv, kɑːˈmɪnətɪv/ *adjective & noun*. **LME**.
[ORIGIN Old French & mod. French *carminatif*, *-ive* or medieval Latin *carminat-* pa. ppl stem of *carminare* heal by incantation, from Latin *carmen*, *-min-*: see CHARM *noun*[1], -ATIVE.]
MEDICINE. (A medicine) having the property of relieving flatulence.

carmine /ˈkɑːmʌɪn, -mɪn/ *noun & adjective*. **E18**.
[ORIGIN Old French & mod. French *carmin* ult. from Arabic *qirmiz*: see CRIMSON.]
▸**A** *noun*. **1** A crimson pigment obtained from cochineal; = ***carminic acid*** below. **E18**.
2 The colour of this. **L18**.
▸**B** *adjective*. Of the colour of carmine; deep crimson. **M18**.
■ **carmined** *adjective* reddened with carmine **L19**. **carˈminic** *adjective* (CHEMISTRY): ***carminic acid***, a phenolic anthraquinone derivative which is the colouring matter of cochineal **M19**.

Carms. *abbreviation*.
Carmarthenshire (former Welsh county).

Carnaby Street /ˈkɑːnəbi striːt/ *noun phr*. **M20**.
[ORIGIN A street in central London.]
Used (freq. *attrib*.) as the type of what is fashionable in dress for young people, *spec*. in London in the 1960s.

carnac /ˈkɑːnak/ *noun*. *rare*. **E18**.
[ORIGIN French *cornac*, Portuguese *cornaca*, perh. from Sanskrit *karināyaka* person in charge of elephants.]
A mahout.

carnage /ˈkɑːnɪdʒ/ *noun*. **E17**.
[ORIGIN French from Italian *carnaggio* from medieval Latin *carnaticum*, from Latin *caro*, *carn-* flesh: see -AGE.]
1 The slaughter of a great number, esp. of men in battle; butchery, massacre. **E17**.
2 Carcasses collectively. Now *rare* or *obsolete*. **M17**.

carnal /ˈkɑːn(ə)l/ *adjective*. **LME**.
[ORIGIN Christian Latin *carnalis*, from Latin *caro*, *carn-* flesh: see -AL[1].]
1 Bodily, corporeal; of flesh. **LME**. ▸†**b** Related by blood. **LME–L16**.
2 Pertaining to the body as the seat of passions or appetites; fleshly, sensual; sexual. **LME**.
carnal knowledge (of) (chiefly LAW) full or partial sexual intercourse (with). ***carnal members***: see MEMBER *noun*.
3 Not spiritual; material, temporal, secular; worldly. **LME**.
†**4** Bloody, murderous. *rare* (Shakes.). Only in **L16**.
■ **carnality** /kɑːˈnalɪti/ *noun* the state of being carnal; fleshliness; sensuality; worldliness; sexual intercourse: **LME**. **carnalize** *verb trans*. make carnal **L17**. **carnally** *adverb* **LME**.

carnallite /ˈkɑːn(ə)lʌɪt/ *noun*. **M19**.
[ORIGIN from Rudolf von *Carnall* (1804–74), German mining engineer + -ITE[1].]
MINERALOGY. An orthorhombic hydrated chloride of potassium and magnesium, usu. occurring as white or reddish massive deposits.

carnaptious /kəˈnapʃəs/ *adjective*. *Scot*. & *Irish*. **M19**.
[ORIGIN Unknown.]
Bad-tempered, quarrelsome.

carnassial /kɑːˈnasɪəl/ *adjective & noun*. **M19**.
[ORIGIN from French *carnassier* carnivorous + -AL[1].]
ZOOLOGY. (A carnivore's premolar tooth) adapted for tearing.

Carnata *adjective & noun* see KARNATA.

Carnatic /kɑːˈnatɪk/ *noun & adjective*. **L18**.
[ORIGIN Anglicization of *Karnataka* in SW India: see -IC.]
▸**A** *noun*. ***the Carnatic***, the region of Karnataka in SW India when under British rule. *obsolete* exc. *hist*. **L18**.
▸**B** *adjective*. Of or pertaining to the Carnatic (*obsolete* exc. *hist*.) or the state of Karnataka; *spec*. designating or pertaining to the traditional music of southern India. **E19**.

†**carnation** *noun*[1]. **ME–E18**.
[ORIGIN Old French *carnacion*, *-tion*, app. aphet. formed as INCARNATION.]
Incarnation.

carnation /kɑːˈneɪʃ(ə)n/ *noun*[2] & *adjective*. **M16**.
[ORIGIN French from Italian *carnagione* from late Latin *carnatio(n-)* fleshiness, from Latin *caro*, *carn-* flesh: see -ATION.]
▸**A** *noun*. **1** Flesh colour; a light rosy pink; sometimes a darker crimson as in the carnation flower. **M16**.
2 In *pl*. Flesh tints; those parts of a painting representing naked skin. **E18**.
▸**B** *adjective*. Flesh-coloured. **M16**.
■ **carnationed** *adjective* (**a**) reddened; †(**b**) flesh-coloured: **M17**.

carnation /kɑːˈneɪʃ(ə)n/ *noun*[3]. **L16**.
[ORIGIN Perh. ult. from misreading of Arabic *qaranful* clove, clove pink, from Greek *karyophyllon*.]
A clove pink of a cultivated variety; a flower or flowering stem of this plant.
MALMAISON ***carnation***. ***perpetual-flowering carnation***: see PERPETUAL *adjective*.

carnauba /kɑːˈnɔːbə, -ˈnaʊbə/ *noun*. **M19**.
[ORIGIN Portuguese from Tupi.]
A Brazilian palm, *Copernicia prunifera*, whose leaves exude a yellowish wax (**carnauba wax**) used as a polish etc.

†**carnel** *noun & verb* var. of KERNEL *noun*[2] & *verb*[2].

carnelian /kɑːˈniːlɪən/ *noun*. Also **cornel-** /kɔːˈniːl-/. **LME**.
[ORIGIN Old French *corneline* (mod. *cornaline*); cf. medieval Latin *corneolus*, later *cornelius*. Var. *carn-* after Latin *carnis*, *caro* flesh, etc.]
A dull red or reddish-white kind of chalcedony.

carneous /ˈkɑːnɪəs/ *adjective*. **L16**.
[ORIGIN from late Latin *carneus*, from Latin *caro*, *carn-* flesh: see -OUS.]
1 Consisting of flesh, fleshy. **L16**.
2 Flesh-coloured. Now *rare* or *obsolete*. **L17**.

carnet /ˈkɑːneɪ, *foreign* karnɛ (*pl. same*)/ *noun*. **E19**.
[ORIGIN French.]
1 A notebook. *rare*. **E19**.
2 A permit, *spec*. one allowing a motor vehicle to be taken across a frontier for a limited period. Also, a book of tickets for use on public transport in some countries. **E20**.

carney /ˈkɑːni/ *noun*[1]. *rare*. **L17**.
[ORIGIN Unknown.]
A disease of horses in which the mouth becomes furred so that they cannot eat.

carney /ˈkɑːni/ *noun*[2], *verb*, & *adjective*. *dial*. & *slang*. Also **-ny**. **E19**.
[ORIGIN Unknown.]
▸**A** *noun*. Hypocritical or wheedling language; a smooth talker, a flatterer. **E19**.
▸**B** *verb trans*. & *intrans*. Wheedle, cajole; use flattery or persuasion. **E19**.
▸**C** *adjective*. Artful, sly. **L19**.

carney *noun*[3] var. of CARNY *noun*[1].

Carnian /ˈkɑːnɪən/ *adjective*. **E19**.
[ORIGIN formed as CARNEY *noun*[2], *verb*, & *adjective* + -IAN.]
1 = CARNIC 1. *rare*. **E19**.
2 GEOLOGY. Designating or pertaining to the lowest division of the Upper Triassic in Europe. **M20**.

Carnic /ˈkɑːnɪk/ *adjective*. **E17**.
[ORIGIN Latin *Carnicus*, from *Carni* a Celtic people of northern Italy: see -IC.]
1 ***Carnic Alps***, a range of mountains along the border of Austria and Italy. **E17**.
2 GEOLOGY. = CARNIAN 2. Now *rare*. **L19**.

carnie *noun* var. of CARNY *noun*[1].

carnifex /ˈkɑːnɪfɛks/ *noun*. *obsolete* exc. *hist*. **M16**.
[ORIGIN Latin = executioner, (in medieval Latin also) butcher.]
An executioner.

carnification /kɑːnɪfɪˈkeɪʃ(ə)n/ *noun*. **M18**.
[ORIGIN from CARNIFY: see -FICATION.]
MEDICINE. Alteration of tissue into a fleshy fibrous form, esp. in the lungs in some forms of pneumonia.

carnificial /kɑːnɪˈfɪʃ(ə)l/ *adjective*. **M17**.
[ORIGIN from Latin *carnifex*, *-fic-* + -IAL.]
Of an executioner or butcher; butcherly.

carnify /ˈkɑːnɪfʌɪ/ *verb*. **M17**.
[ORIGIN from Latin *caro*, *carn-* flesh + -FY.]
1 *verb trans*. Make or convert into flesh. Usu. in *pass*. **M17**.
†**2** *verb intrans*. Generate flesh. **M17–E19**.
3 MEDICINE. **a** *verb trans*. Bring about carnification of. **M18**. ▸**b** *verb intrans*. Undergo carnification. **M19**.

carnival /ˈkɑːnɪv(ə)l/ *noun & adjective*. **M16**.
[ORIGIN Italian *carne-*, *carnovale* (whence French *carnaval*) from medieval Latin *carnelevamen*, *-varium* Shrovetide, from Latin *caro*, *carn-* flesh + *levare* put away.]
▸ **A** *noun*. **1** In Roman Catholic countries, the week (orig. the day) before Lent, devoted to festivities; Shrovetide; the festivity of this season. **M16**.
2 Any period or occasion of riotous revelry or feasting; a festival (esp. at a regular date) usu. involving a procession. **L16**.
3 A travelling funfair; a circus. *N. Amer.* **M20**.
▸ **B** *attrib.* or as *adjective*. Of or pertaining to a carnival; resembling or characteristic of a carnival. **E17**.
▪ **carnivaˈlesque** *adjective* characteristic or of the style of a carnival **M18**. **carnivalite** *noun* a reveller at a carnival **L19**.

carnivore /ˈkɑːnɪvɔː/ *noun*. **M19**.
[ORIGIN French, from Latin *carnivorus*: see CARNIVOROUS.]
A carnivorous animal; a member of the order Carnivora of mainly carnivorous mammals (including dogs, cats, bears, seals, etc.). Also, a carnivorous plant.

carnivorous /kɑːˈnɪv(ə)rəs/ *adjective*. **L16**.
[ORIGIN Latin *carnivorus* from *caro*, *carn-* flesh: see -VOROUS.]
1 Feeding on flesh; preying on other animals; *ZOOLOGY* belonging to the order Carnivora (see CARNIVORE). **L16**.
2 Of plants: able to absorb and digest animal substances. **M19**.
▪ **carnivorously** *adverb* **M19**. **carˈnivory** *noun* carnivorous behaviour **E20**.

carnosaur /ˈkɑːnəsɔː/ *noun*. **M20**.
[ORIGIN from mod. Latin *Carnosauria* (see below), from Latin *caro*, *carn-* flesh + Greek *sauros* lizard.]
A large bipedal carnivorous dinosaur, typically with relatively small forelimbs, of a group (Carnosauria) which included tyrannosaurus, allosaurus, megalosaurus, etc.

carnose /ˈkɑːnəʊs/ *adjective*. **LME**.
[ORIGIN Latin *carnosus*, from *caro*, *carn-* flesh: see -OSE¹.]
Consisting of flesh; fleshy.

carnosity /kɑːˈnɒsɪti/ *noun*. **LME**.
[ORIGIN Old French & mod. French *carnosité* or medieval Latin *carnositas*, formed as CARNOSE: see -ITY.]
†**1** Fleshiness; pulpiness. **LME–M17**.
2 A morbid fleshy growth. **LME**.

Carnot /ˈkɑːnəʊ/ *noun*. **M19**.
[ORIGIN Sadi *Carnot* (1796–1832), French scientist.]
PHYSICS. Used ***attrib.*** and in ***possess.*** with ref. to a particular thermodynamic cycle describing the operation of an ideal heat engine.
Carnot cycle, ***Carnot's cycle***, ***Carnot theorem***, ***Carnot's theorem***, etc.

carnotite /ˈkɑːnətʌɪt/ *noun*. **L19**.
[ORIGIN from M. A. *Carnot* (1839–1920), French inspector of mines + -ITE¹.]
MINERALOGY. A monoclinic hydrated vanadate of uranium and potassium, usu. occurring as lemon-yellow microcrystalline aggregates.

carnous /ˈkɑːnəs/ *adjective*. Now *rare* or *obsolete*. **LME**.
[ORIGIN formed as CARNOSE + -OUS.]
Pulpy, fleshy.

carny /ˈkɑːni/ *noun*¹. *N. Amer. slang*. Also **carney**, **carnie**. **M20**.
[ORIGIN from CARNIVAL + -Y⁶.]
A carnival. Also, a person who works at a carnival.

carny *noun*², *verb*, & *adjective* var. of CARNEY *noun*², *verb*, & *adjective*.

carob /ˈkarəb/ *noun*. Also (after Arab.) **carouba** /kəˈrəʊbə/. **LME**.
[ORIGIN French †*car(r)obe* (mod. *caroube*) from medieval Latin *carrubia*, *-ium*, etc., from Arabic *ḵarrūb(a)*. Cf. ALGARROBA.]
1 The edible horn-shaped fleshy seed pod of an evergreen leguminous tree, *Ceratonia siliqua*, native to the Mediterranean region. Also ***carob bean***, ***carob pod***. **LME**.
2 In full ***carob tree***. The tree itself. **M16**.

caroche /kəˈrɒʃ/ *noun*. *obsolete* exc. *hist.* **L16**.
[ORIGIN French †*carroche* from Italian *carraccio*, *-ia*, augm. of *carro* chariot, CAR: cf. CAROSSE.]
A stately or luxurious carriage.

carol /ˈkar(ə)l/ *noun*. **ME**.
[ORIGIN Old French (now dial.) *carole* = Provençal *carola*, *corola* (whence Italian *carola*), of unknown origin.]
1 A ring dance accompanied by song. *obsolete* exc. *hist.* **ME**.
▸†**b** A ring, esp. of standing stones. Cf. CARREL. **ME–L15**.
2 A (joyful) song; *transf.* the song of a bird. **ME**.
3 A joyful hymn; *esp.* (in full ***Christmas carol***) one sung at Christmas. **LME**.
– COMB.: **carol service** a religious service largely devoted to the singing of Christmas carols; **carol-singer** a person who takes part in carol-singing; **carol-singing** the singing of carols, *spec.* by groups who go from door to door at Christmas with the object of raising money.

carol /ˈkar(ə)l/ *verb*. Infl. **-ll-**, ***-l-**. **ME**.
[ORIGIN Old French *caroler*, formed as CAROL *noun*.]
†**1** *verb intrans.* Sing and dance in a ring. Also, make merry, revel. **ME–M16**.
2 *verb trans.* & *intrans.* Sing (as) a carol; sing joyously; celebrate in song. **LME**.

Carolean /karəˈliːən/ *adjective & noun*. *hist.* **E20**.
[ORIGIN from medieval Latin CAROLUS + -EAN.]
▸ **A** *adjective*. Of or pertaining to Charles I (reigned 1625–49) or Charles II (reigned 1660–85), Kings of Great Britain; (characteristic) of their period. **E20**.
▸ **B** *noun*. A supporter or contemporary of either King Charles. **E20**.

caroler *noun* var. of CAROLLER.

Carolin *noun* var. of CAROLINE *noun*.

Carolina /karəˈlʌɪnə/ *noun*. **L17**.
[ORIGIN A former Brit. colony named after Charles II (see CAROLINE *adjective*), now (as *North & South Carolina*) forming two states of the USA.]
Used ***attrib.*** to designate things from or associated with Carolina.
Carolina allspice: see ALLSPICE 2. ***Carolina*** JASMINE. **Carolina pink** pinkroot, *Spigelia marilandica*. **Carolina rice** a variety of rice with a yellowish husk.

Caroline /ˈkarəlʌɪn/ *noun*. *obsolete* exc. *hist.* Also **-lin** /-lɪn/. **M16**.
[ORIGIN medieval or mod. Latin *Carolinus* (see CAROLINE *adjective*), used as noun.]
Any of various coins of different countries and values, depicting the head of a King Charles (or Karl, Carlo, etc.); *spec.* (***a***) = CARLINE *noun*³; (***b***) a gold coin of Bavaria and Württemberg. Cf. CAROLUS.

Caroline /ˈkarəlʌɪn/ *adjective*. **E17**.
[ORIGIN medieval or mod. Latin *Carolinus*, from medieval Latin CAROLUS: see -INE¹.]
Of, pertaining to, or of the period of, a (King) Charles; *spec.* (***a***) = CAROLINGIAN *adjective*; (***b***) = CAROLEAN *adjective*.

Carolingian /karəˈlɪndʒɪən/ *adjective & noun*. **L19**.
[ORIGIN Refashioning of CARLOVINGIAN after medieval Latin CAROLUS.]
▸ **A** *adjective*. **1** Of, relating, or belonging to the dynasty of Frankish kings founded by Charlemagne (d. 814). **L19**.
2 Designating or displaying a style of minuscule handwriting developed in France at the time of Charlemagne. **L19**.
▸ **B** *noun*. A member or supporter of the Carolingian dynasty. Also, Carolingian script. **L19**.

Carolinian /karəˈlɪnɪən/ *adjective & noun*. **E18**.
[ORIGIN from CAROLINA + -IAN.]
(A native or inhabitant) of (N. or S.) Carolina.

carolitic /karəˈlɪtɪk/ *adjective*. Also **-lytic**. **E19**.
[ORIGIN Alt. of French *corollitique*, from Latin COROLLA: see -IC.]
ARCHITECTURE. Of a column: having a foliated shaft.

caroller /ˈkarələ/ *noun*. Also **caroler**. **L16**.
[ORIGIN from CAROL *verb* + -ER¹.]
†**1** A reveller. Only in **L16**.
2 A person who carols; a carol-singer. **E19**.

Carolus /ˈkarələs/ *noun & adjective*. **E16**.
[ORIGIN medieval Latin = Charles, Karl.]
(Designating) a coin bearing 'Carolus' as the name of the monarch, *spec.* a gold piece of the reign of Charles I of Great Britain.

carolytic *adjective* var. of CAROLITIC.

carom /ˈkarəm/ *noun & verb*. Also **-rr-**. **L18**.
[ORIGIN Abbreviation of CARAMBOLE.]
▸ **A** *noun*. **1** A cannon in billiards. Now chiefly *N. Amer.* **L18**.
2 More fully ***carom billiards***. A game resembling billiards but played on a table without pockets and depending on cannons for scoring. **L19**.
▸ **B** *verb intrans.* Make a carom; strike and rebound (*off*). Now chiefly *N. Amer.* **M19**.

K. LETTE We caromed off the bumper of a parked car.

caroon /kəˈruːn/ *noun*. *obsolete* exc. *hist.* Also **-rr-**, **-m** /-m/. **M17**.
[ORIGIN Unknown.]
A licence from the Lord Mayor of London for keeping a cart.

caro sposo /ˈkaːro ˈspoːzo/ *noun phr.* Pl. ***cari sposi*** /ˈkaːri ˈspoːzi/. **L18**.
[ORIGIN Italian.]
(One's) dear husband; a devoted husband. Cf. CARA SPOSA.

carosse /kəˈrɒs/ *noun*. **L16**.
[ORIGIN Obsolete French (now *-rr-*) from Italian *carrozza* augm. of *carro* chariot, CAR: cf. CAROCHE.]
Chiefly *hist.* A (horse-drawn) carriage, a coach.

carotene /ˈkarətiːn/ *noun*. Also **-tin** /-tɪn/. **M19**.
[ORIGIN from Latin *carota* carrot + -ENE.]
CHEMISTRY. An orange or red hydrocarbon, $C_{40}H_{56}$, of which there are several isomers, which occurs in carrots and many other plants and is a precursor of vitamin A.
▪ **carotenoid** *noun & adjective* (***a***) *noun* any of a class of mainly yellow or red pigments of wide natural occurrence having the conjugated molecular structure typified by carotene; (***b***) *adjective* of, pertaining to, or characteristic of such a compound: **E20**.

carotic /kəˈrɒtɪk/ *adjective*. Now *rare* or *obsolete*. **M17**.
[ORIGIN Greek *karōtikos* stupefying: see CAROTID, -IC.]
1 = CAROTID *adjective*. **M17**.
2 Of the nature of stupor; in a state of stupor. **L17**.

carotid /kəˈrɒtɪd/ *adjective & noun*. **E17**.
[ORIGIN French *carotide* or mod. Latin *carotides* from Greek *karōtides* pl. of *karōtis* drowsiness from *karoun* stupefy: so named because compression of the arteries was thought to cause stupor.]
ANATOMY. ▸ **A** *adjective*. **1** ***carotid artery***, either of the two main arteries (or their major branches) which supply blood to the head and neck. **E17**.
2 Of, pertaining to, or adjoining a carotid artery. **M19**.
carotid body a small mass of receptors in the carotid artery sensitive to chemical change in the blood.
▸ **B** *noun*. A carotid artery. **E18**.

carotin *noun* var. of CAROTENE.

carouba *noun* var. of CAROB.

carousal /kəˈraʊz(ə)l/ *noun*. **E18**.
[ORIGIN from CAROUSE *verb* + -AL¹.]
A bout of carousing; a drunken revel. Formerly also identified with CAROUSEL 1.

carouse /kəˈraʊz/ *adverb*, *noun*, & *verb*. **M16**.
[ORIGIN German *gar aus (trinken)* (drink) right out, completely; as noun from the adverb taken as obj. of a verb.]
▸ †**A** *adverb*. (*Drink*, *quaff*, etc.) to the bottom of the glass etc. **M16–M17**.
▸ **B** *noun*. †**1** The act or fashion of drinking all up; a cupful drunk all up; a whole cupful, a full draught. **M16–E19**.
2 A drinking bout; carousing. **L17**.
▸ **C** *verb*. **1** *verb intrans.* Have or engage in a drinking bout; drink heavily. **M16**. ▸**b** Drink health, success, etc., *to*. Now *rare* or *obsolete*. **L16**.

N. HORNBY I came back to my flat after carousing deep into the night.

†**2** *verb trans.* Drink up, drain; drink (a health). **L16–E19**.
▪ **carouser** *noun* **L16**.

carousel /karəˈsɛl, -ˈzɛl/ *noun*. Also ***-rr-**. **M17**.
[ORIGIN French *carrousel* from Italian *carosello*, *ga-*.]
1 *hist.* A kind of tournament in which variously dressed companies of knights engaged in plays, chariot races, exercises, etc. **M17**.
2 A merry-go-round; a roundabout. Chiefly *N. Amer.* **L17**.
3 A rotating delivery or conveyor system, *esp.* one in an airport for the delivery of passengers' luggage. **M20**.
– COMB.: **carousel fraud** a fraudulent scheme involving successive moves of goods between countries in order to avoid paying VAT or to generate grants or tax refunds.

carozzi *noun* see KARROZZIN.

carp /kɑːp/ *noun*¹. **ME**.
[ORIGIN from CARP *verb*.]
†**1** Discourse. Only in **ME**.
2 A carping speech, remark, etc. **E17**.

carp /kɑːp/ *noun*². Pl. usu. same. **LME**.
[ORIGIN Old French & mod. French *carpe* from Provençal *carpa*, or the common source, late Latin *carpa*.]
A freshwater fish of the genus *Cyprinus*, esp. *C. carpio*, freq. kept in ponds. Also, any of various related fishes belonging to the family Cyprinidae.
crucian carp, ***leather carp***, ***mirror carp***, etc. ***KOI carp***. ***looking-glass carp***: see LOOKING GLASS. ***mirror carp***: see MIRROR *noun*. ***Prussian carp***: see PRUSSIAN *adjective*.
▪ **carplike** *adjective* resembling a carp **L19**.

carp /kɑːp/ *verb*. **ME**.
[ORIGIN Senses 1–3 from Old Norse *karpa* brag; later senses infl. by or from Latin *carpere* pluck, slander, calumniate.]
†**1** *verb intrans.* & *trans.* Speak, talk; say, tell. **ME–E17**.
2 *verb intrans.* Sing, recite. *obsolete* exc. *dial.* **LME**.
†**3** *verb intrans.* Prate, chatter. **LME–M16**.
4 *verb intrans.* Complain or find fault about trivial matters; cavil. (Foll. by *at*.) **LME**.

New York Times An overbearing man who constantly needled and carped at his son.

▪ **carper** *noun* **LME**. **carping** *ppl adjective* that carps, constantly finding fault **L16**.

carpaccio /kɑːˈpatʃɪəʊ/ *noun*. Pl. **-os**. **L20**.
[ORIGIN Italian, from Vittore *Carpaccio* (fl. 1490–1523), Venetian painter, who used a distinctive red colour similar to that of raw beef.]
An Italian hors d'oeuvre consisting of thin slices of raw beef or fish served with a sauce.

carpal /ˈkɑːp(ə)l/ *adjective & noun*. **M18**.
[ORIGIN from CARPUS + -AL¹.]
ANATOMY & ZOOLOGY. ▸ **A** *adjective*. Of or pertaining to the wrist or carpus. **M18**.
carpal tunnel a passage between the carpal bones and adjacent ligaments, through which pass the median nerve and the flexor tendons of the hand; ***carpal tunnel syndrome***, a condition of numbness, pain, or tingling in the hand caused by compression of the median nerve within the carpal tunnel at the wrist, esp. as the result of repetitive movements.
▸ **B** *noun*. Any of the bones of the wrist. **M19**.

Carpathian /kɑːˈpeɪθɪən/ *adjective*¹. **E17**.
[ORIGIN from *Carpathos* (see below) + -IAN.]
Of or pertaining to Carpathos (Karpathos), an island in the Aegean Sea.

C

Carpathian /kɑˈpeɪθɪən/ *adjective*[2] *& noun*. **L17**.
[**ORIGIN** Prob. from German *Karpathen* from Latin *Carpatus* from Greek *Karpatos*, + -**IAN**.]
▸ **A** *adjective*. Designating or pertaining to a range of mountains in central and eastern Europe. **L17**.
▸ **B** *noun*. In *pl.* & †*sing*. *The* Carpathian mountains. **L17**.

carpe diem /ˌkɑːpeɪ ˈdiːɛm, ˈdʌɪɛm/ *interjection*. **E19**.
[**ORIGIN** Latin, lit. 'seize the day!', a quotation from Horace (*Odes* I.xi).]
Used to urge someone to make the most of the present time and give little thought to the future.

carpel /ˈkɑːp(ə)l/ *noun*. **M19**.
[**ORIGIN** French *carpelle* or mod. Latin *carpellum*, from Greek *karpos* fruit: see -**EL**[2].]
BOTANY. The basic unit of the female reproductive part of a flower (gynoecium), consisting of ovary, stigma, and (usually) style, which occurs either singly or as one of a group.
▪ **carpellary** *adjective* of, pertaining to, or of the nature of a carpel **M19**.

carpent /ˈkɑːp(ə)nt/ *verb trans*. *rare*. **E17**.
[**ORIGIN** medieval Latin *carpentare*.]
Make by carpentry; construct, put together.

carpenter /ˈkɑːp(ə)ntə/ *noun & verb*. **ME**.
[**ORIGIN** Anglo-Norman, & Old French *carpentier*, (also mod.) *charpentier*, from late Latin *carpentarius* (*artifex*) carriage(-maker), from *carpentum* two-wheeled carriage, of Gaulish origin, rel. to **CAR**: see -**ER**[2].]
▸ **A** *noun*. A craftsman in woodwork esp. of rough solid kinds as in house- or shipbuilding (cf. **JOINER**). **ME**.
– **COMB.**: **carpenter ant**, **carpenter bee**: of a kind which bores into trees (***violet carpenter bee***: see **VIOLET** *adjective*); **carpenter trousers** loose-fitting trousers with many pockets of various sizes and loops for tools at the tops or sides of the legs; **carpenter-work** = **CARPENTRY**.
▸ **B** *verb*. **1** *verb intrans*. Do carpenter's work. **LME**.
2 *verb trans*. Make by carpentry; put together mechanically, construct (*lit. & fig.*) **LME**.

carpentry /ˈkɑːp(ə)ntri/ *noun*. **LME**.
[**ORIGIN** Anglo-Norman *carpentrie* = Old French & mod. French *charpenterie*, from *charpentier*: see **CARPENTER**, -**RY**.]
1 The work, trade, or skill of a carpenter; woodworking. **LME**.
2 Woodwork made by a carpenter. **LME**.

carpet /ˈkɑːpɪt/ *noun*. **ME**.
[**ORIGIN** Old French *carpite* or medieval Latin *carpita* from Italian †*carpita* woollen counterpane, corresp. to French *charpie* lint, use as noun of pa. pple of *charpir* from Proto-Romance var. of Latin *carpere* pluck, pull to pieces.]
1 A thick usu. woollen fabric used as a cover for beds, tables, etc.; a piece of this; a tablecloth. *obsolete* exc. in ***on the carpet*** (a) below. **ME**.
2 A piece of thick fabric, made in one piece or of lengths joined together, used for covering a floor, stairway, etc.; material for this, carpeting. Also, with specifying word, a rug, *esp*. a large oriental rug. **LME**.
Axminster carpet, ***Brussels carpet***, ***Exeter carpet***, ***kilim carpet***, ***oriental carpet***, ***Persian carpet***, etc.
3 *fig*. A smooth, soft, or bright covering or expanse, as of grass or flowers, resembling a carpet. **L16**. ▸**b** The ground. *slang*. **L19**.

Munsey's Magazine The prairie became one rolling carpet of flowers.

4 In full ***carpet moth***. Any of various geometrid moths with variegated colouring. **M19**.
– **PHRASES**: ***magic carpet***: see **MAGIC** *adjective*. **on the carpet** *fig*. (*a*) under discussion; (*b*) *colloq*. being reprimanded. ***red carpet***: see **RED** *adjective*. ***sweep a thing under the carpet***: see **SWEEP** *verb*.
– **COMB.**: **carpet bag** *noun & verb* (*a*) *noun* a travel bag, orig. made of carpet; (*b*) *verb intrans*. (*derog*., chiefly *US*) travel lightly, be a carpetbagger; **carpetbagger** (*derog*., chiefly *US*) a person seeking to achieve political success or private gain in a place with which he or she is unconnected (orig. *spec*. a northerner in the southern US after the Civil War); **carpet bed** a garden bed with dwarf plants arranged densely in a pattern; **carpet beetle** any of various dermestid beetles of the genus *Anthrenus*, whose larvae are destructive to carpets etc.; **carpet bombing** the dropping of a large number of bombs uniformly over an area; **carpet dance** an informal dance for which the carpet is not taken up; **carpet knight** *arch*. an idler, a philanderer, a ladies' man; ***carpet moth***: see sense 4 above; **carpet rod** a stair rod; **carpet shark** any of several sharks with irregular markings on the back, esp. of the genus *Orectolobus*; **carpet shell** (the shell of) any of various bivalve molluscs of the genus Venerupis (family Veneridae), with irregular coloured markings resembling tapestry; **carpet slipper** a slipper, orig. with upper made of thick material like carpet; **carpet snake** (*a*) a large variegated specimen of the Australian python *Python spilotes*; (*b*) (in the Indian subcontinent) a harmless snake which enters houses, *esp*. a wolf snake, *Lycodon aulicus*; **carpet square** a more or less small square of carpet intended to fit together with others as a floor-covering; **carpet sweeper** a household implement with a revolving brush or brushes for sweeping carpets.

carpet /ˈkɑːpɪt/ *verb trans*. **LME**.
[**ORIGIN** from the noun.]
1 Cover (as) with a carpet. **LME**.
2 Reprimand, reprove. *colloq*. **M19**.
▪ **carpeting** *noun* (*a*) the action of the verb; *esp*. a telling-off; (*b*) material for carpets, carpets collectively: **L16**.

carphology /kɑːˈfɒlədʒi/ *noun*. **M19**.
[**ORIGIN** Greek *karphologia*, from *karphos* straw + *legein* collect: see -**Y**[1].]
MEDICINE. Plucking at the bedclothes by a delirious patient.

carpincho /kɑːˈpɪntʃəʊ/ *noun*. Pl. **-os**. **M19**.
[**ORIGIN** Amer. Spanish, prob. from Tupi.]
= **CAPYBARA**.

carpo- /ˈkɑːpəʊ/ *combining form*[1] of **CARPUS**: see -**O**-.
▪ **carpoˈpedal** *adjective* relating to or involving the hands and the feet **L19**.

carpo- /ˈkɑːpəʊ/ *combining form*[2] of Greek *karpos* fruit: see -**O**-.
▪ **carpophore** *noun* (*BOTANY*) a prolongation of the axis of a flower, raising the pistil above the stamens **L19**. **carpospore** *noun* (*BOTANY*) a diploid spore produced by a carpogonium **L19**.

Carpocratian /kɑːpəʊˈkreɪʃ(ə)n/ *noun*. **L16**.
[**ORIGIN** from *Carpocrates* (see below) + -**IAN**.]
hist. A follower of Carpocrates of Alexandria, 2nd-cent. Gnostic philosopher, who asserted the mortality of Christ's body and the creation of the world by angels.

carpogonium /kɑːpə(ʊ)ˈɡəʊnɪəm/ *noun*. Pl. **-nia** /-nɪə/. **L19**.
[**ORIGIN** from **CARPO**-[2] + Greek *gonos* race + -**IUM**.]
BOTANY. The non-motile female reproductive organ of a red alga.
▪ **carpogonial** *adjective* **L19**.

carpology /kɑːˈpɒlədʒi/ *noun*. **E19**.
[**ORIGIN** from **CARPO**-[2] + -**LOGY**.]
The biology of fruits and seeds.
▪ **carpoˈlogical** *adjective* **E19**.

carpus /ˈkɑːpəs/ *noun*. Pl. **-pi** /-pʌɪ/. **LME**.
[**ORIGIN** mod. Latin from Greek *karpos* wrist.]
The part of the human skeleton between the forearm and the metacarpus, consisting of eight small bones and forming the wrist; *ZOOLOGY* the corresponding part in other tetrapods (e.g. the knee of a horse).

carr /kɑː/ *noun*[1]. *Scot. & N. English*. **OE**.
[**ORIGIN** Unknown.]
A rock; *esp*. a rocky islet off the (Scottish or Northumbrian) coast.

carr /kɑː/ *noun*[2]. **ME**.
[**ORIGIN** Old Norse *kjarr* brushwood in *kjarr-mýrr* marsh grown with brushwood (cf. Danish *kær*, *kjær*, Swedish *kärr*, Norwegian *kjær*, *kjerr*).]
1 A marsh, a fen; wet boggy ground; meadowland reclaimed from bog or marsh. **ME**.
2 A marshy copse, esp. of alders; boggy ground overgrown with shrubs. **LME**.

carrack /ˈkarək/ *noun*. *obsolete* exc. *hist*. **LME**.
[**ORIGIN** Old French & mod. French *caraque*, perh. (corresp. to Italian *caracca*) from Spanish *carraca* from Arabic, perh. from *qarāqir* pl. of *qurqūra* a type of (sometimes very large) merchant vessel.]
A large merchant ship equipped for warfare, *esp*. a Portuguese Indiaman; a galleon.

carrageen /ˈkarəɡiːn/ *noun*. Also **-gheen**. **E19**.
[**ORIGIN** Irish *carraigín*.]
In full ***carrageen moss***. An edible purple seaweed, *Chondrus crispus*, found on the coasts of northern Europe and N. America. Also called ***Irish moss***.
▪ **carraˈgeenan** *noun* a mixture of polysaccharides (galactans) extracted from various red and purple seaweeds and used as a gelling, thickening, and emulsifying agent in food products **M20**.

carrefour /karfuːr/ *noun*. Pl. pronounced same. Also †***carfour***. **L15**.
[**ORIGIN** French: see **CARFAX**.]
A crossroads, a carfax (now only in France).
– **NOTE**: Formerly naturalized.

carrel /ˈkar(ə)l/ *noun*. Also **-ll**. **L16**.
[**ORIGIN** App. rel. to **CAROL** *noun* in sense 'ring'.]
1 *hist*. A small enclosure or study in a cloister. **L16**.
2 A cubicle for a reader in a library. **E20**.

carretera /kareˈtera, kɑːrəˈtɛːrə/ *noun*. **M19**.
[**ORIGIN** Spanish.]
In Spain and Spanish-speaking countries: a main road.

carriage /ˈkarɪdʒ/ *noun*. **LME**.
[**ORIGIN** Old Northern French *cariage*, from *carier* **CARRY** *verb*: see -**AGE**.]
▸ **I** The action of carrying.
1 Conveying, transport, esp. of merchandise. **LME**.
†**2** A toll or duty payable on the transport of goods. **LME–L18**.
3 (Payment in lieu of) carrying performed by a tenant as feudal service. *obsolete* exc. *hist*. **LME**.
4 The cost of conveying goods etc.; charge so incurred. **LME**.
carriage forward with carriage to be paid by the receiver of a parcel etc. **carriage paid** with carriage paid by the sender of a parcel etc.
†**5** Ability to carry. *rare*. **L16–M18**.
6 The action of carrying out, execution; conduct, management; administration. **E17**.
7 The carrying of a motion. **L19**.
▸ **II** A thing carried; a manner of carrying.
†**8** Baggage; movable property. **LME–M18**.
9 A load, a quantity carried, a burden; *fig*. import, meaning. *obsolete* exc. *dial*. **LME**.
10 Manner of carrying, esp. of the head, body, etc.; deportment; bearing. **L16**.

J. Cary The girl was walking with her usual self-contained air . . ; the proper carriage of a school prefect and débutante. R. Gittings He seemed taller, partly because of the erect carriage of his limbs and head.

11 Demeanour; behaviour; habitual conduct. *arch*. **L16**. ▸†**b** A piece of conduct, an action. Only in **17**.

Defoe The affectionate carriage of this poor woman to her infant.

▸ **III** Means of carrying.
12 A means of conveyance; *esp*. a wheeled vehicle for conveying people. **LME**. ▸**b** *spec*. A four-wheeled private vehicle drawn by two or more horses. **M18**. ▸**c** A railway passenger vehicle. **M19**.
baby carriage, ***hackney carriage***, ***invalid carriage***, ***railway carriage***, etc. **b carriage and pair**, **carriage and four**, **carriage and six**, etc.: with the number of horses specified. *LANDAU* *carriage*. **c** ***ladies' carriage***, ***saloon carriage***, ***smoking carriage***, etc. ***train of carriages***: see **TRAIN** *noun*[1] 13.
13 A wheeled framework or support, esp. (in full ***gun carriage***) for a gun. See also **UNDERCARRIAGE**. **M16**.
14 A sliding or other moving part of a mechanism, whose function is to carry and move other parts, esp. in a typewriter. **L17**.
– **COMB.**: **carriage clock** a portable clock in a rectangular case with a handle; **carriage dog** a Dalmatian; **carriage house** *N. Amer*. a building for housing a carriage, esp. one which has been converted into a dwelling; **carriage release** the operation of allowing a typewriter to move freely, independently of the keys; a lever which makes this possible; ***carriage return***: see **RETURN** *noun* 9b; **carriage trade** (now *arch*. or *joc*.) (trade with) those of sufficient wealth or social standing to maintain a private carriage; **carriageway** (*a*) the part of a road intended for vehicular traffic (***dual carriageway***: see **DUAL** *adjective*; ***single carriageway***: see **SINGLE** *adjective*); (*b*) each of the two sides of a dual carriageway or motorway.
▪ **carriageable** *adjective* (*a*) *rare* portable; (*b*) (of a road) passable by wheeled vehicles: **L16**. **carriaged** *adjective* having a carriage or carriages (of a specified kind or number) **M17**.

carrick bend /ˈkarɪk bɛnd/ *noun phr*. **E19**.
[**ORIGIN** Perh. from alt. of **CARRACK** + **BEND** *noun*[1].]
NAUTICAL. A round knot to join ropes required to go round a capstan.

carrier /ˈkarɪə/ *noun*. **LME**.
[**ORIGIN** from **CARRY** *verb* + -**ER**[1].]
▸ **I 1** *gen*. A person who or thing which carries; a bearer, a conveyor, a porter. **LME**.
2 A person or company undertaking for hire the conveyance of goods or passengers. **LME**.

fig.: Adam Smith The Dutch were the great carriers of Europe.

common carrier: see **COMMON** *adjective*.
3 In full ***carrier pigeon***. A homing pigeon (employed to carry messages tied to its leg). **M17**.
4 A conduit or drainage channel for water. **L18**.
5 A part of a machine designed to bear or carry; *esp*. a basket, rack, etc., fixed to a bicycle for carrying luggage etc. **M19**.
6 A vessel intended or used to carry a particular kind of cargo or load; freq. *ellipt*. = **AIRCRAFT** ***carrier***. **L19**.
bulk carrier, ***ore carrier***, ***troop carrier***, etc.
7 An insoluble or inert substance used to support a pigment, catalyst, etc., or to convey a radioisotope, chromatographic sample, etc. **L19**.
8 A substance which effects a transference of an atom or other species, esp. in a biochemical process. **L19**.
9 A particle carrying an electric charge; a mobile electron or hole in a semiconductor. **E20**.
10 More fully ***carrier wave*** etc. A wave or current on which a signal can be superimposed by modulation, esp. in telecommunications. **E20**.
11 A person or animal that can transmit a disease, or an organism that can pass on a genetic characteristic to its offspring, without showing its effects. **E20**.
12 In full ***carrier bag***. A strong paper or plastic bag with handles, used for shopping. **E20**.
▸ **II 13** (**C-**.) [So called from their custom of a widow's carrying (for a period) the cremated remains of her husband in a leather bag.] A member of an Athabaskan people inhabiting British Columbia; the language of this people. Also ***Carrier Indian***. **L18**.

carriole /ˈkarɪəʊl/ *noun*. Also **cariole**. **M18**.
[**ORIGIN** French from Italian *carriuola* dim. of *carro* **CAR**: see -**OLE**[1].]
1 Chiefly *hist*. A small open carriage for one; a covered light cart. **M18**.
2 A kind of sledge used in Canada. **E19**.

carrion /ˈkarɪən/ *noun & adjective*. **ME**.
[**ORIGIN** Anglo-Norman, Old Northern French *caroi(g)ne*, Old French *charoigne* (mod. *charogne*) from Proto-Romance, from Latin *caro* flesh.]
▸ **A** *noun*. †**1** A dead body; a carcass. **ME–M18**.
2 Dead putrefying flesh. **ME**.

D. Attenborough The nautilus feeds not only on carrion but on living creatures such as crabs.

3 a Human or animal flesh regarded as no better than the dead. *obsolete* exc. as passing into sense 4. ME. ▸**b** A worthless or noxious person or beast. *obsolete* exc. *dial.* L15.
4 *fig.* Corruption, garbage, filth; something vile. LME.

J. A. FROUDE Roman fashionable society hated Cæsar, and any carrion was welcome to them which would taint his reputation.

▸ **B** *attrib.* or as *adjective.* Of or pertaining to rotting flesh or putrefaction; rotten, loathsome. LME.

G. M. HOPKINS Not, I'll not, carrion comfort, Despair, not feast on thee.

– COMB.: **carrion beetle** a beetle of the family Silphidae, feeding on carrion; ***carrion crow***: see CROW *noun*[1] 1; **carrion flower** (*a*) a plant of the African genus *Stapelia* of the milkweed family Asclepiadaceae; (*b*) a N. American plant of the lily family, *Smilax herbacea*, having fetid flowers.

Carrion's disease /karɪˈɒnz dɪˌziːz/ *noun phr.* E20.
[ORIGIN from Daniel *Carrión* (*c* 1850–86), Peruvian medical student, who died from the disease after voluntarily contracting it.]
MEDICINE. Bartonellosis; *esp.* the acute form of this (= OROYA FEVER).

carritch /ˈkarɪtʃ/ *noun. Scot.* M18.
[ORIGIN Alt. of CATECHISE *noun.*]
sing. & in *pl.* = CATECHISM.

carriwitchet /karɪˈwɪtʃɪt/ *noun. obsolete* exc. *Scot.* Also **carwitchet** /kɑːˈwɪtʃɪt/. E17.
[ORIGIN Unknown.]
A pun; a conundrum.

carrom *noun & verb* var. of CAROM.

carronade /karəˈneɪd/ *noun.* L18.
[ORIGIN from *Carron*, near Falkirk in Scotland, where orig. made + -ADE.]
hist. A (chiefly naval) short large-calibred gun.

carroon *noun* var. of CAROON.

carrot /ˈkarət/ *noun.* L15.
[ORIGIN Old French & mod. French *carotte* from Latin *carota* from Greek *karōton.*]
1 An umbelliferous plant, *Daucus carota*, having a large tapering root which in cultivated forms is orange-coloured and edible; a root of this, eaten as a vegetable. L15. ▸**b** *fig.* (with allus. to the traditional use of a carrot to induce a donkey to move, freq. opp. ***stick***). An enticement; a promised reward. L19.

b J. K. GALBRAITH Along with the carrot of pecuniary reward must go the stick of personal economic disaster.

2 Something carrot-shaped, esp. (*N. Amer.*) a plug of tobacco. M17.
3 In *pl.* Red hair; (a name for) a red-haired person. *slang.* L17.
■ **carroty** *adjective* like carrots; orange-red; red-haired: L17.

carrousel *noun* see CAROUSEL.

†**carrow** *noun. Irish.* L16–E19.
[ORIGIN Old Irish *cerrbach* (mod. *cearrbhach*).]
An itinerant gambler.

carrozzi *noun* see KARROZZIN.

carry /ˈkari/ *noun.* E17.
[ORIGIN from the verb.]
1 A vehicle, a cart, a barrow. *Scot.* & *N. English.* E17.
2 The drift of the clouds in the wind; the clouds collectively, the sky. *Scot.* L18.
3 The range of a gun; the distance traversed by a golf ball etc. before pitching; a trajectory. M19.
4 The action or an act of carrying, *spec.* of carrying a boat, supplies, etc., between rivers or around an obstacle to navigation. *N. Amer.* M19. ▸**b** *AMER. FOOTBALL.* The action or an act of running or rushing with the ball. M20.
5 A place or route between navigable points, over which boats, supplies, etc., have to be carried. *N. Amer.* M19.

carry /ˈkari/ *verb.* LME.
[ORIGIN Anglo-Norman, Old Northern French *carier* var. of *charier* (mod. *charrier* cart, drag) corresp. to Provençal *carrejar*, from *car* CAR.]
▸ **I** *verb trans.* **1** Bear from one place to another, convey, transport, (by vehicle, ship, aircraft, etc.; on horseback; on a river, the wind, etc., by its own motion; on the person, in the hand, or *fig.* in the mind). LME. ▸**b** Escort, lead, conduct, (a person, animal, etc.); take with one, esp. by force. Now *arch.* & *dial.* E16. ▸**c** Of a road, pipe, wire, etc.: conduct, convey, be traversed by (traffic, liquid, electric current, etc.). E17. ▸**d** *fig.* Continue to have with or beside one as one moves. L18.

SHAKES. *Temp.* I'll bear your logs . . I'll carry it to the pile. G. BERKELEY If we carry our thoughts from the corporeal to the moral world. LD MACAULAY The news . . had been carried to the Earl of Pembroke. E. HEMINGWAY He wore his overcoat and carried his wet hat. R. MACAULAY Carried out to sea by the tide. P. V. WHITE The master of the Osprey will carry you to Newcastle. R. DAVIES I went back . . as fast as my artificial leg would carry me. J. D. MACDONALD Offshore islands . . composed of the materials the rivers had carried down to the sea and deposited. **b** S. JOHNSON The lady carried her horse a thousand miles. J. GALSWORTHY After three days at Robin Hill she carried her father back with her to Town. **c** G. M. TREVELYAN The improved roads carried visitors . . far afield.

2 Cause to move or go, impel, drive; cause or enable to proceed; (of a journey etc.) lead, bring, *to* etc. LME. ▸**b** Urge, influence; deprive of self-control. (Now usu. ***carry away.***) *arch.* M16.

LD MACAULAY A scanty stock of silver, which . . was to carry the nation through the summer. E. A. FREEMAN The great march which carried Harold . . to Stamford Bridge. J. R. GREEN A mission carried him in early life to Italy. A. SCHLEE More and more people entered behind her and she was carried inevitably forward . . by their pressure.

3 Propel (a missile, ball, etc.) to a specified distance or on a specified course. LME. ▸**b** Propel a golf ball, cricket ball, etc., beyond (a point). L19.

b B. LOCKE It is important . . to be able to hit very high iron shots to carry formidable obstacles, such as big bunkers.

4 Hold up, while in motion; have on one's person, possess; bear with or within one; keep in mind. LME. ▸**b** Have as an attribute, property, meaning, consequence, etc.; display, exhibit; involve, imply. L16. ▸†**c** Wield (power, influence). L16–M17. ▸**d** Be pregnant with. L18. ▸**e** *MILITARY.* Hold (a weapon) in the position for saluting. L18. ▸**f** Keep on hand; stock. M19. ▸**g** Of a newspaper etc.: print (an article) in its pages, publish. Of a broadcasting station: put out (a programme). E20.

J. CONRAD A prisoner being partly carried, partly dragged along the hall. W. CATHER He can't carry a drink or two as he used. B. SPOCK This is a special memory problem (just the way some children can't carry a tune). M. PUZO He had a license to carry a gun. J. G. FARRELL Young men carrying Sinn Fein flags. **b** SHAKES. *Hen. VIII* Words cannot carry Authority so weighty. MILTON His habit carries peace, his brow defiance. E. R. CONDER A positive judgment carrying immense consequences. B. TRAPIDO He has about him the same confident ease but carries it with greater subtlety. **f** E. REVELEY Some sort of special medicine—I'm not even sure the chemists here carry it. **g** V. S. NAIPAUL Next morning the *Trinidad Sentinel* carried this story on page five.

5 Extend, prolong, or continue (a line, process, etc.) in a specified direction or way, or to a specified point. Chiefly *fig.* LME.

E. A. FREEMAN He did not tarry long in carrying his purpose into effect. C. P. SNOW The bedrooms . . carried comfort to such a point that it was difficult to sleep at all. C. HILL Laud's religious policy carried the re-catholicizing tendencies . . to their logical conclusion.

6 Bear the weight of; sustain, support, (*lit.* & *fig.*). LME. ▸†**b** Tolerate, endure. L16–L17. ▸**c** Support with financial or other assistance; help or compensate for (a team member etc. who does not pull his or her weight); be the major cause of the effectiveness of. L19.

J. RUSKIN Main arches . . carried by . . pillars. H. G. WELLS A red wooden curtain pole . . carried green and dust-coloured curtains. *Conservation News* The Zambesi region . . carries a very rich vegetation. **b** SHAKES. *Lear* Man's nature cannot carry Th' affliction nor the fear.

7 Bear (the body, head, etc., oneself) in a specified way. L16.
8 Conduct, manage (a matter, affair, etc.). (Now usu. ***carry on.***) *arch.* L16.
9 Obtain as the result of effort, win; take by assault, capture. L16. ▸**b** Gain victory or acceptance for; *esp.* get (a measure) passed or adopted in a vote. E17. ▸**c** Gain (a district etc.) in an election. Chiefly *US.* M19.

C. MERIVALE He strove to carry with his own hand the victory. D. L. SAYERS Better use shock tactics and carry the place by assault. **b** P. H. STANHOPE They carried their candidates in the centres of popular election. A. BRIGGS The bill . . was finally carried by 263 votes to 46. B. CASTLE We carried the vote in committee by nine votes to six.

10 Transfer (a figure etc.) to a new page or account (now usu. ***carry forward***); transfer (a figure) to the next column in an arithmetical operation. M18.

W. COBBETT You are to put down the 4 and carry 2.

▸ **II** *verb intrans.* †**11** Ride, move with speed or energy. LME–M16.
12 Bear loads; act as a carrier. L16.
13 *FALCONRY.* Fly away with the quarry. E17.
14 Propel a missile. M17.

JOHN PHILLIPS About as high as a crossbow can carry.

15 Of a missile, sound, etc.: travel or be propelled for a specified distance or in a specified manner (*absol.* far, well). M17.

W. MAXWELL A man cursing . . can be heard a long way. All sounds carry. G. M. FRASER Their rank stench carried a good half-mile.

†**16** Behave. M17–E18.

– PHRASES: **carry all before one** overcome all opposition, succeed. ***carry an M under one's girdle***: see M, M 7. ***carry a torch for***: see TORCH *noun*. ***carry coals to Newcastle***: see COAL *noun*. **carry conviction** be convincing. **carry it** (*a*) have the advantage, win the day; †(*b*) act, behave, in a specified way. ***carry one's bat***: see BAT *noun*[1] 2. **carry sail** have sails set. ***carry the bat***: see BAT *noun*[1] 2. ***carry the can*** (***back***): see CAN *noun* 1. **carry the day** win, succeed. ***carry the world before one***: see WORLD *noun*. **carry weight** (*a*) be influential or important; (*b*) *HORSE-RACING* carry weight as a handicap. **carry with one** persuade, convince (one's hearer etc.). ***cash and carry***: see CASH *noun*[1]. ***fetch and carry***: see FETCH *verb*.

– WITH ADVERBS IN SPECIALIZED SENSES: **carry away** (*a*) *verb phr. trans.* transport, remove, inspire, fire with (excessive) enthusiasm, deprive of self-control; (*b*) *verb phr. trans.* & *intrans.* (*NAUTICAL*) break off and remove (a ship's mast etc.) forcibly; be lost thus; †(*c*) ***carry it away***, have the advantage, win the day. **carry back** take (a person) back in thought to a past time. **carry forward** transfer (a figure etc.) to a new page or account. **carry off** (*a*) remove by force, abduct; be the cause of death of; (*b*) win, achieve; render (one's action, condition, etc.) acceptable or passable by one's manner; ***carry it off*** (***well***), do well under difficulties. **carry on** (*a*) *verb phr. trans.* continue, keep up, conduct (a conversation, a business, etc.), advance (a process etc.); (*b*) *verb phr. intrans.* go on with what one is doing, continue one's course, be continued; *colloq.* behave strangely or excitedly, speak angrily, flirt or have an affair (*with*). **carry out** perform, conduct to completion, put into practice. **carry over** transfer, esp. = ***carry forward*** above; postpone to a later time. **carry through** bring safely out of difficulties, perform to completion. **carry up** (*a*) continue (building etc.) to a given point; (*b*) trace back in time; †(*c*) bear, hold up.

– COMB.: **carryall** (*a*) a light carriage, a carriole; *N. Amer.* a car with sideways seats; (*b*) *N. Amer.* a large bag or case; **carrycot** a portable cot for a baby; **carry-forward** a balance of money carried forward; CARRY-ON; **carry-out** *noun & adjective* (a quantity of) prepared food, drink, etc.) bought for consumption off the premises; a takeaway meal, restaurant, etc.; **carry-over** (*a*) *STOCK EXCHANGE* postponement of payment to next settling day; (*b*) a sum held over or transferred; a transference; †**carry-tale** a telltale.

carrying /ˈkarɪɪŋ/ *verbal noun.* LME.
[ORIGIN from CARRY *verb* + -ING[1].]
1 The action of CARRY *verb.* LME.
2 ***carrying-on***, ***carryings-on***, excitement, commotion, questionable behaviour, flirtation. *colloq.* M17.
– COMB.: **carrying place** *N. Amer.* = CARRY *noun* 5; **carrying trade** the transportation of goods from one country to another by water or air as a business.

carry-on /ˈkarɪɒn; *in sense A.1 also* karɪˈɒn/ *noun & adjective.* L19.
[ORIGIN from CARRY *verb* + ON *adverb.*]
▸ **A** *noun.* **1** A fuss, a to-do; excitement, carryings-on. *colloq.* L19.
2 A bag or suitcase suitable for carrying on to an aircraft as hand luggage. M20.
▸ **B** *adjective.* That may be carried on; suitable for carrying on to an aircraft. M20.

carse /kɑːs/ *noun. Scot.* ME.
[ORIGIN Perh. pl. of CARR *noun*[2].]
(A stretch of) alluvial lowland beside a river.

Carshuni *noun* var. of GARSHUNI.

carstone /ˈkɑːstəʊn/ *noun.* E19.
[ORIGIN Prob. dial. var. of ***quernstone*** s.v. QUERN *noun.*]
GEOLOGY. Hard ferruginous sandstone of Lower Cretaceous age.

cart /kɑːt/ *noun & verb.* ME.
[ORIGIN Old Norse *kartr* (= Old English *cræt*), prob. infl. by Anglo-Norman, Old Northern French *carete* (mod. *charette*) dim. of *carre* CAR.]
▸ **A** *noun.* †**1** A chariot, a carriage. ME–E17.

SHAKES. *Haml.* Full thirty times hath Phoebus' cart gone round Neptune's salt wash and Tellus' orbed ground.

2 A strong two-wheeled or four-wheeled conveyance, usu. horse-drawn, used esp. in farming and for carrying heavy goods. ME.

ROBERT BURTON As good horses draw in carts as coaches. A. E. HOUSMAN Here the hangman stops his cart: Now the best of friends must part. DAY LEWIS The rest of the flat cart was filled with hens for the market.

bullock cart, ***handcart***, etc. ***dustcart***, ***hay cart***, etc.

3 A light two-wheeled one-horse vehicle for driving in. E19.
dogcart etc.

– PHRASES: **in the cart** *slang* in an awkward or losing position; in trouble. **put the cart before the horse** reverse the proper order of things; take an effect for a cause.

– COMB.: **cart body** the part of a cart in which the load is placed; **carthorse** (orig.) a horse used to draw a cart; (now) a strong thickset horse fit for heavy work; **cartload** a cartful; a large quantity of something (***a cartload of monkeys***: see MONKEY *noun*); **cartman** a man who drives a cart; **cart-road** a rough road suitable only for carts and other farm vehicles; **cart-rut** a deep rut cut in soft ground by the wheels of a cart; **cart's tail**, **cart tail** the rear of a cart, to which formerly offenders were tied to be dragged through the streets or flogged; **cart-track** (*a*) a rough track suitable only for carts and other farm vehicles; (*b*) a cart-rut; ***cart tail***: see ***cart's tail*** above; **cart-way** a rough way suitable only for carts and other farm vehicles; CARTWHEEL; **cart-whip** a long heavy horsewhip; **cartwright** a maker of carts.

▸ **B** *verb.* **1** *verb intrans.* Work with or use a cart. *rare.* LME.
2 *verb trans.* Convey or transport (as) in a cart; *colloq.* carry (esp. something cumbersome or heavy) over an unduly long distance, carry or take unceremoniously. LME. ▸**b** Convey publicly in a cart as a means of punishment. *obsolete* exc. *hist.* M16.

DE QUINCEY We were all carted to the little town. J. K. JEROME Harris and I . . carted out our luggage on to the doorstep. F. ASTAIRE She took on the challenging job of carting her two brats to New York in search of a career. **b** G. CRABBE Suspected, tried, condemned, and carted in a day.

cart off remove, esp. by force.
3 *verb trans.* Get (someone) into trouble; betray the hopes of, let down. Chiefly as ***carted*** *ppl adjective. slang.* L19.
4 *verb trans.* CRICKET. Hit hard. E20.
■ **cartage** *noun* (the cost of) conveyance by cart LME. **carter** *noun* †(*a*) a charioteer; (*b*) a person who drives a cart (formerly as a type of low birth or boorish manners): ME. **cartful** *noun* as much or as many as a cart will hold LME.

C

carte /kɑːt/ *noun*[1]. LME.
[ORIGIN French from Latin *c(h)arta*: see CARD *noun*[2], CHART *noun*.]
†1 A charter, a document; an exposition; a chart, a diagram. LME–M18.
2 A playing card; in *pl.*, a game of cards. *Scot.* L15.
3 A bill of fare. Cf. À LA CARTE. E19.
4 = CARTE DE VISITE. M19.

carte *noun*[2] see QUART *noun*[2].

carte blanche /kɑːt ˈblɑːnʃ, *foreign* kart(ə) ˈblɑ̃ːʃ/ *noun phr.* Pl. **cartes blanches** /kɑːts ˈblɑːnʃ, *foreign* kart(ə) blɑ̃ːʃ/. L17.
[ORIGIN French = blank paper.]
1 A blank sheet of paper to be filled in as a person wishes; *fig.* full discretionary power granted (now the usual sense). L17.
2 CARDS. In piquet and bezique, a hand containing no court cards as dealt, and attracting a compensatory score. E19.

carte de visite /ˌkɑːtdəvɪˈziːt/ *noun.* Now *arch.* or *hist.* Pl. **cartes de visite** (pronounced same). M19.
[ORIGIN French = visiting card.]
A small photographic portrait mounted on a card.

carte d'identité /kart didɑ̃tite/ *noun phr.* Pl. ***cartes d'identité*** (pronounced same). E20.
[ORIGIN French.]
An identity card.

carte du pays /kart dy pe(j)i/ *noun phr.* Pl. ***cartes du pays*** (pronounced same). M18.
[ORIGIN French, lit. 'map of the country'.]
(A statement of) the state of affairs.

cartel /*branch I* ˈkɑːt(ə)l, *branch II* kɑːˈtɛl/ *noun.* Branch I also †**ch-**. M16.
[ORIGIN French from Italian *cartello* placard, challenge, dim. of *carta* from Latin *c(h)arta* (see CARD *noun*[2], CHART *noun*). Branch II from German *Kartell* from French.]
► **I 1** In full ***cartel of defiance***. A written challenge. Now *arch.* or *hist.* M16.
2 *hist.* A written agreement relating to the exchange or ransom of prisoners; an exchange or ransom of prisoners; (in full ***cartel ship***) a ship commissioned for the exchange of prisoners. L17.
3 *gen.* A paper or card bearing writing or printing. L17.
► **II 4** A combination between political parties to promote a mutual interest. L19.
5 A manufacturers' agreement or association formed to control marketing arrangements, regulate prices, etc. E20.
■ **carteliˈzation**, **-ll-** *noun* formation of or into cartels E20. **cartelize**, **-ll-** *verb trans. & intrans.* form (into) a business etc. cartel E20.

cartes blanches *noun phr.* pl. of CARTE BLANCHE.

cartes d'identité, cartes du pays *noun phrs.* pls. of CARTE D'IDENTITÉ, CARTE DU PAYS.

Cartesian /kɑːˈtiːzjən, -ʒ(ə)n/ *adjective & noun.* M17.
[ORIGIN mod. Latin *Cartesianus*, from *Cartesius* Latinized form of the name of René *Descartes* (1596–1650), French philosopher and scientist: see -IAN.]
► **A** *adjective.* Pertaining to or characteristic of Descartes, his philosophy, or his mathematical methods. M17.

H. HALLAM *Cogito; Ergo sum*, this famous enthymem of the Cartesian philosophy.

Cartesian coordinate each of a set of coordinates describing the position of a point in relation to a set of intersecting straight axes (usu. in *pl.*). **Cartesian devil**, **Cartesian diver** a toy that rises and falls in a liquid when the vessel containing it is subjected to varying pressure.
► **B** *noun.* A follower of Descartes. M17.
■ **Cartesianism** *noun* the philosophy of Descartes M17.

Carthaginian /kɑːθəˈdʒɪnɪən/ *noun & adjective.* M16.
[ORIGIN from Latin *Carthago*, *-ginis* Carthage (see below) + -IAN.]
(A native or inhabitant) of Carthage, a powerful ancient city of N. Africa near Tunis, defeated and destroyed by Rome in 146 BC, but later recolonized.
Carthaginian peace a peace settlement which imposes very severe terms on the defeated side.

carthamus /ˈkɑːθəməs/ *noun.* M16.
[ORIGIN mod. Latin from Arabic *qirtim*, *qurtum* safflower.]
Any plant of the genus *Carthamus* of the composite family, *esp.* safflower, *C. tinctorius*.
■ **carthamin** *noun* (CHEMISTRY) a red quinonoid glycoside which is the colouring matter of safflower M19.

Carthusian /kɑːˈθjuːzɪən/ *noun & adjective.* M16.
[ORIGIN medieval Latin *Carthusianus*, from *Cart(h)usia* La Grande Chartreuse, a monastery near Grenoble, France: see -IAN. Cf. CHARTERHOUSE, CHARTREUSE, CHARTREUX.]
1 (A member) of the austere order of monks founded by St Bruno in 1084. M16.
2 (A past or present member) of Charterhouse School (see CHARTERHOUSE 2). M19.

cartilage /ˈkɑːt(ɪ)lɪdʒ/ *noun.* LME.
[ORIGIN French from Latin *cartilago*, *-agin-*.]
A firm, elastic, semi-opaque connective tissue of the vertebrate body; gristle. Also, a structure made of this.
hyaline cartilage, ***Meckel's cartilage***, ***nasal cartilage***, ***thyroid cartilage***, etc. **temporary cartilage** that cartilage in the young which later ossifies.
■ **cartilaginiﬁˈcation** *noun* formation of or conversion into cartilage M19. **cartiˈlaginoid** *adjective* of the form or nature of cartilage M19.

cartilaginous /kɑːtɪˈladʒɪnəs/ *adjective.* LME.
[ORIGIN Old French (also *-eus*), or Latin *cartilaginosus*, formed as CARTILAGE: see -OUS.]
1 Of, or of the nature of, cartilage. LME.
cartilaginous fish a fish with a skeleton of cartilage, i.e. a member of the class Selachii (or Chondrichthyes), which includes the sharks and rays.
2 BOTANY. Of the texture of cartilage. L17.

cartle *noun* see KATEL.

cartogram /ˈkɑːtəgram/ *noun.* L19.
[ORIGIN French *cartogramme*, from *carte* map: see CARD *noun*[2], -GRAM.]
A map with diagrammatic statistical information.

cartographer /kɑːˈtɒgrəfə/ *noun.* Also (now *rare*) **ch-**. M19.
[ORIGIN from CARTOGRAPHY or after French *cartographe*: see -GRAPHER, -ER[1]. Spelling with *ch-* after Latin *charta*.]
A person who draws maps; an expert in or practitioner of cartography.

cartography /kɑːˈtɒgrəfi/ *noun.* Also (now *rare*) **ch-**. M19.
[ORIGIN French *cartographie*, from *carte* map: see CARD *noun*[2], -OGRAPHY. Spelling with *ch-* after Latin *charta*.]
The drawing of maps or charts.
■ **cartoˈgraphic** *adjective* M19. **cartoˈgraphically** *adverb* M20.

cartomancy /ˈkɑːtəmansi/ *noun.* L19.
[ORIGIN French *cartomancie*, from *carte* CARD *noun*[2]: see -MANCY.]
Fortune-telling by playing cards.

carton /ˈkɑːt(ə)n/ *noun & verb.* E19.
[ORIGIN French formed as CARTOON.]
► **A** *noun* **1 a** A light cardboard or pasteboard box; a light container of waxed cardboard, plastic, etc., in which drinks and other foodstuffs are packaged. E19. ►**b** Cardboard, pasteboard; papier mâché. L19.

a J. THURBER Fifteen large cartons filled with old Christmas cards. R. LOWELL Milk cartons, . . Two plates sheathed with silver foil.

2 The disc within the bull's-eye of a target; a shot that hits this. M19.
► **B** *verb trans.* Pack in a carton. Chiefly as ***cartoned*** *ppl adjective.* E19.

cartonnage /ˈkɑːt(ə)nɪdʒ/ *noun.* Also **cartonage**. M19.
[ORIGIN French, formed as CARTON: see -AGE.]
EGYPTOLOGY. A mummy-case made of tightly fitting layers of linen or papyrus glued together.

carton-pierre /kartɔ̃pjɛr/ *noun.* M19.
[ORIGIN French, lit. 'cardboard (of) stone'.]
Papier mâché made to resemble stone or bronze.

cartoon /kɑːˈtuːn/ *noun & verb.* L16.
[ORIGIN Italian *cartone* augm. of *carta*: see CARTEL, -OON.]
► **A** *noun.* **1** A full-size drawing made on stout paper as a design for a painting, tapestry, mosaic, etc. L16.
2 An illustrative drawing (orig. full-page or large) in a newspaper or magazine, esp. as a vehicle for political satire or humour; an amusing drawing with or without a caption; a sequence of these in a strip. M19. ►**b** A film made by animating a series of drawings. E20.
strip cartoon: see STRIP *noun*[1] 3b.
► **B** *verb.* **1** *verb intrans.* Draw a cartoon or cartoons. Chiefly as ***cartooning*** *verbal noun.* M19.
2 *verb trans.* Represent in a cartoon; caricature in a cartoon. L19.
■ **cartoonery** *noun* cartoons collectively; the making of cartoons: M19. **cartoonish** *adjective* resembling (the style of) a cartoon (sense 2); showing simplification or exaggeration of some features: L20. **cartoonishly** *adverb* L20. **cartoonishness** *noun* L20. **cartoonist** *noun* a person who draws cartoons L19. **cartoony** *adjective* = CARTOONISH L20.

cartophily /kɑːˈtɒfɪli/ *noun.* M20.
[ORIGIN from French CARTE *noun*[1] or Italian *carta* (see CARTEL) + -O- + -PHILY.]
The collection of picture cards, as cigarette cards etc., as a pursuit or hobby.
■ **cartoˈphilic** *adjective & noun* (*rare*) L19. **cartophilist** *noun* a collector of cigarette cards etc. M20.

cartouche /kɑːˈtuːʃ/ *noun.* E17.
[ORIGIN French from Italian *cartoccio*, from *carta*: see CARTEL.]
► **I 1** = CARTRIDGE 1. *obsolete* exc. *hist.* E17. ►†**b** A case of wood, pasteboard, etc., for cannonballs. E17–M18.
► **II 2 a** ARCHITECTURE. A scroll-shaped ornament; a scroll-shaped corbel, mutule, or modillion; a tablet representing a scroll with rolled-up ends or edges, with or without an inscription. E17. ►**b** A painting or drawing of a scroll with rolled-up ends, with or without a text; an ornate frame in the shape of such a scroll. L18.
3 EGYPTOLOGY. An elongated oval with a straight bar at the end containing the hieroglyphic names and titles of kings. M19.
– COMB.: **cartouche-box** (*obsolete* exc. *hist.*) a cartridge box.

cartridge /ˈkɑːtrɪdʒ/ *noun.* L16.
[ORIGIN Alt. of CARTOUCHE.]
1 A paper, metal, etc. case containing a charge of propellent explosive for firearms or blasting, with a bullet or shot if intended for small arms. L16.
blank cartridge: see BLANK *adjective*.
2 A case and its contents prepared for more or less direct insertion into a particular mechanism, as a spool of photographic film or magnetic tape in a container, an ink container for a pen, etc. E20.
3 A removable pick-up head of a record player. M20.
turnover cartridge: see TURNOVER *adjective*.
– COMB.: **cartridge belt** a belt fitted with sockets for cartridges; **cartridge box** a box for storing or carrying cartridges; **cartridge case** (*a*) = ***cartridge box*** above; (*b*) the paper, metal, etc. shell of a cartridge; **cartridge paper** a thick, rough paper used for cartridges, drawing, and for making strong envelopes.

cartulary /ˈkɑːtjʊləri/ *noun.* Also **ch-**. LME.
[ORIGIN medieval Latin *c(h)artularium*, from *c(h)artula* dim. of *c(h)arta*: see CHARTA, CARD *noun*[2], -ULE, -ARY[1].]
†1 A collection of medical recipes. Only in LME.
2 A place where charters or records are kept; a collection of charters or records. M16.

cartwheel /ˈkɑːtwiːl/ *noun & verb.* Also **cart-wheel**. LME.
[ORIGIN from CART *noun* + WHEEL *noun*.]
► **A** *noun.* **1** A wheel of a cart. LME.
2 A lateral handspring with the arms and legs extended. M19.
turn a cartwheel, **turn cartwheels** execute one of, a succession of, these movements.
3 A large coin. M19.
4 In full ***cartwheel hat***. A hat with a wide circular brim. L19.
► **B** *verb intrans.* Move like a rotating wheel; turn a cartwheel or cartwheels; revolve. E20.

carucage /ˈkarjʊkɪdʒ/ *noun.* L16.
[ORIGIN medieval Latin *car(r)ucagium*, from *car(r)uca*: see CARUCATE, -AGE.]
hist. A feudal tax levied on each carucate of land.

carucate /ˈkarjʊkeɪt/ *noun.* LME.
[ORIGIN medieval Latin *car(r)ucata*, from *car(r)uca* (orig.) coach, chariot, in Gaul early applied to the wheel-plough, rel. to Latin *carrus* CAR *noun*: see -ATE[1].]
hist. A measure of land equivalent to the area that could be ploughed in a year by one plough and eight oxen; a ploughland.

caruncle /ˈkarəŋk(ə)l, kəˈrʌŋ-/ *noun.* L16.
[ORIGIN Obsolete French from Latin *caruncula* dim. of *caro* flesh: see -UNCLE.]
A fleshy excrescence or swelling, such as that at the inner corner of the eye (the ***lacrimal caruncle***), or the wattles of a turkey, etc., or (BOTANY) adjoining the micropyle of certain seeds.
■ **caˈruncular** *adjective* of the nature of or resembling a caruncle M19. **caˈrunculate** *adjective* having a caruncle or caruncles E19. **caˈrunculated** *adjective* (now *rare*) = CARUNCULATE E19.

carvacrol /ˈkɑːvəkrɒl/ *noun.* M19.
[ORIGIN from mod. Latin (*Carum*) *carvi* caraway + Latin *acris* ACRID *adjective* + -OL.]
CHEMISTRY. A fungicidal liquid phenol, $C_{10}H_{14}O$, present in many essential oils.

carval /ˈkɑːv(ə)l/ *noun.* L19.
[ORIGIN Manx.]
A Manx carol or ballad on a sacred subject.

carve /kɑːv/ *verb.* Pa. pple **carved**, (*arch. & poet.*) **carven** /ˈkɑːv(ə)n/.
[ORIGIN Old English *ċeorfan* = Old Frisian *kerva*, Middle Dutch & mod. Dutch *kerven*, Middle High German *kerben*, from West Germanic.]
1 *verb trans. & intrans.* Cut. Long *obsolete* in *gen.* sense. OE.
2 *verb trans.* Produce or shape by cutting, chiselling, or sculpturing, (a statue, portrait, representation in relief or intaglio, an inscription, a design, *out of*, *in*, or *on* a material). OE. ►**b** *verb trans.* Fashion (a material, *into* something) by cutting, chiselling, or sculpturing; cover or adorn with (or *with*) figures cut out, cut designs, etc. ME. ►**c** *verb intrans.* Cut figures, designs, etc.; practise sculpture, engraving, etc. M16.

TENNYSON An angel . . carved in stone. R. KIPLING I carved on the stone: '*After me cometh a Builder.*' **b** J. MARQUAND Sandal-wood, carved into a design of herons and lotus flowers. R. LEHMANN A crook-handled Alpenstock carved with edelweiss. K. CLARK He carved marble faster than any mason.

3 *verb intrans. & trans.* Cut up (meat etc.) into portions for serving; cut *into* (meat etc.) to produce servings. ME. ►†**b** *verb intrans.* Of a woman: be hospitable, be affable. *rare* (Shakes.). Only in L16. ►**c** *verb trans.* Slash or cut with a knife or razor. Also foll. by *up*. *slang.* E20.

J. WYNDHAM Over at a side-table three girls were . . carving chickens. J. GRIGSON As you carve into the chicken, sprinkle it lightly with salt.

†4 *verb trans.* Divide or part by cutting, cleave. LME–E17.
5 *verb trans. & intrans.* Cut (a way, passage, etc.). LME.

W. OWEN Swimmers carving thro' the sparkling cold.

†**6** *verb trans. & intrans.* Apportion; reserve, take, (*for*); minister *to*. **L16–M18.**
carve for oneself take at one's pleasure; indulge oneself.
7 *verb trans.* Divide into several pieces or portions; subdivide. **E18.**
– **WITH ADVERBS IN SPECIALIZED SENSES: carve out** (*a*) take from a larger whole (*LAW* esp. a smaller estate from a larger one); (*b*) cut out (a way, passage, etc.); create or bring about by much effort (a career, name, etc., *for* oneself or oneself and others). **carve up** (*a*) cut up into several pieces (see also sense 3c above); divide into several portions; (*b*) *slang* cheat, swindle.
– **COMB.: carve-up** *slang* (the result of) a sharing-out, esp. of dishonest gains.

carvel /ˈkɑːv(ə)l/ *noun*. **LME.**
[**ORIGIN** Old French *carvelle* (mod. *caravelle*) from Portuguese *caravela* dim. of *caravo* from late Latin *carabus* from Greek *karabos* horned beetle, crayfish, light ship.]
= **CARAVEL.**
– **COMB.: carvel-built, carvel-planked** *adjectives* (of a boat etc.) with planks that are set flush (opp. ***clinker-built***).

carver /ˈkɑːvə/ *noun*[1]. **LME.**
[**ORIGIN** from **CARVE** + **-ER**[1].]
1 A person who carves. **LME.**
2 A carving knife; (in *pl.*) a carving knife and fork. **M19.**
3 An armchair in a set of dining room chairs. **E20.**

Carver /ˈkɑːvə/ *noun*[2]. *US*. **E20.**
[**ORIGIN** John *Carver* (1576–1621), first governor of Plymouth Colony.]
In full ***Carver chair***. A chair with a rush seat, arms, and a back having horizontal and vertical spindles.

carvery /ˈkɑːvəri/ *noun*. **M19.**
[**ORIGIN** from **CARVE** + **-ERY**.]
1 Meat for carving. *rare*. **M19.**
2 Carved work. *rare*. **M19.**
3 A buffet or restaurant where meat is carved from a joint as required. **M20.**

carving /ˈkɑːvɪŋ/ *noun*. **ME.**
[**ORIGIN** from **CARVE** + **-ING**[1].]
1 The action of **CARVE**. **ME.**
2 Carved work; a carved figure, design, etc. **LME.**
– **COMB.: carving fork**: long-tined, used to steady a joint etc. and serve portions; **carving knife**: long-bladed, used for cutting portions of meat for serving.

carvone /ˈkɑːvəʊn/ *noun*. **L19.**
[**ORIGIN** formed as **CARVACROL** + **-ONE**.]
CHEMISTRY. A liquid cyclic ketone, $C_{10}H_{14}O$, with a characteristic odour, present in caraway and dill oils.

carwitchet *noun* var. of. **CARRIWITCHET**.

caryatid /karɪˈatɪd/ *noun*. Pl. **-ides** /-ɪdiːz/, **-ids** **M16.**
[**ORIGIN** (French *caryatide* from Italian *cariatide* from) Latin *caryatides* from Greek *karuatides* (pl.) priestesses of Artemis at *Karuai* (Caryae) in Laconia.]
ARCHITECTURE. A female figure used as a pillar to support an entablature. Cf. **TELAMON**.

caryophyllaceous /ˌkarɪəʊfɪˈleɪʃəs/ *adjective*. **M19.**
[**ORIGIN** from mod. Latin *Caryophyllaceae* (see below), from *caryophyllus* clove-pink from Greek *karuophullon*: see **-ACEOUS**.]
BOTANY. Of or pertaining to the family Caryophyllaceae, including the pinks, campions, and stitchworts.

caryopsis /karɪˈɒpsɪs/ *noun*. Pl. **-opses** /-ˈɒpsiːz/. **E19.**
[**ORIGIN** mod. Latin, from Greek *karuon* nut + *opsis* appearance.]
BOTANY. A one-seeded indehiscent fruit having the pericarp fused to the seed coat, as in wheat and maize.

CAS *abbreviation*.
Chief of the Air (Force) Staff.

ca. sa. /keɪ ˈseɪ, kɑː ˈsɑː/ *noun phr.* **L18.**
[**ORIGIN** Abbreviation.]
LAW. = **CAPIAS** ***ad satisfaciendum***.

casaba /kəˈsɑːbə/ *noun*. *N. Amer.* **L19.**
[**ORIGIN** from *Kasaba* (now Turgutlu) in Turkey, from where the melons were first exported.]
1 A winter melon of a variety with a wrinkled yellow rind and sweet flesh. **L19.**
2 In *pl.* A woman's breasts. *colloq.* **L20.**

A. MAUPIN The solitary blonde with the big casabas.

casale /kaˈsɑːle/ *noun*. Also ***-sal*** /-ˈsɑːl/. **E16.**
[**ORIGIN** Italian, from *casa* house.]
In Italy, Malta, etc.: a hamlet.

†**casamat** *noun* see **CASEMATE**.

Casanova /kasəˈnəʊvə, -z-/ *noun*. **E20.**
[**ORIGIN** Giovanni Jacopo *Casanova* de Seingalt (1725–98), Italian adventurer.]
A man who engages in promiscuous love affairs.

casbah *noun* var. of **KASBAH**.

cascabel /ˈkaskəb(ə)l/ *noun*. Also **-able**. **M17.**
[**ORIGIN** Spanish *cascabel*, from Catalan (Provençal) *cascavel* from medieval Latin *cascabellus* little bell.]
The knob at the rear end of a cannon; also, the whole section of a cannon behind the ring bolted to the emplacement.

cascade /kasˈkeɪd/ *noun & verb*. **M17.**
[**ORIGIN** French from Italian *cascata*, from *cascare* fall from Proto-Romance, from Latin *casus* fall: see **CASE** *noun*[1], **-ADE**.]
▸ **A** *noun*. **1** A waterfall, esp. a small one; a section of a large broken (esp. artificial) waterfall; a falling body of water. **M17.** ▸**b** *transf. & fig.* A quantity of material etc. falling; a falling stream *of*. **M19.**

F. TUOHY The rain . . fell in a solid cascade. **b** R. KIPLING A cascade of Survey-instruments, books, diaries, [etc.]. C. S. FORESTER The battle had begun in a muddle amid a cascade of vague orders.

2 A pyrotechnic device imitating a waterfall. **M18.**
3 A succession of electrical devices or stages in a process. **M19.**
4 A wavy arrangement of hanging lace etc. **L19.**
▸ **B** *verb*. **1** *verb intrans.* Fall in or like a cascade. **E18.**

R. CHANDLER From his outer breast pocket cascaded a show handkerchief. D. WELCH Short, sneering Chinese words cascaded out of his mouth. G. HUNTINGTON Down a little ravine a stream cascaded.

2 *verb intrans.* Vomit. *arch. colloq.* **L18.**
3 *verb trans.* Connect (electrical devices) in a cascade. **E20.**
4 *verb trans.* Pass (a thing) on to a succession of others. **L20.**

cascara /kaˈskɑːrə/ *noun*. **L19.**
[**ORIGIN** Spanish *cáscara* (*sagrada*) lit. '(sacred) bark'.]
In full ***cascara sagrada*** /səˈgrɑːdə/. The bark of a Californian buckthorn, *Rhamnus purshiana*; an extract of this, used as a purgative.

cascarilla /kaskəˈrɪlə/ *noun*. **L17.**
[**ORIGIN** Spanish, dim. of **CASCARA**.]
The aromatic bark of the W. Indian plant *Croton eluteria*. Also ***cascarilla bark***.

case /keɪs/ *noun*[1]. **ME.**
[**ORIGIN** Old French & mod. French *cas* from Latin *casus*, from base of *cadere* to fall. In branch II directly from Latin, translating Greek *ptōsis* lit. 'fall'.]
▸ **I** †**1** A thing that befalls or happens, an event, occurrence; chance, hazard. **ME–L16.**

CAXTON By caase of fortune. SPENSER I you recount a ruefull cace.

2 An instance of a thing's occurrence, a circumstance, a fact, etc. **ME.** ▸**b** A person (of a specified sort); an eccentric or comical person. *slang*. **M19.** ▸**c** An infatuation, an instance of falling in love. *slang*. **M19.**

R. DAVIES You get used to vanity, but Andro was a very special case. A. HAILEY A clear case of the women versus the men. **b** K. WATERHOUSE They laughed . . . shaking their heads. 'He's a case, i'n't he?' J. ARNOTT He was a bit of a sad case really.

3 Condition, state, plight; (good) physical condition. *arch.* exc. in certain phrs. (see below). **ME.**

AV *Exod.* 5:19 They were in euill case. SWIFT Their Horses large, but extreamly out of Case. R. BOLT I have . . been several times in such a case that I thought to die within the hour.

4 The state of matters relating to a given person or thing, one's circumstances or position; *the* actual state of affairs, *the* fact. **LME.**

JER. TAYLOR He hath no need to use them, as the case now stands. LD MACAULAY The case with me is the reverse. J. F. KENNEDY In Germany's case . . the old ideas and beliefs were completely destroyed. L. EDEL As has often been the case, changes in philosophical thought heralded technical innovations in the arts.

5 The condition of disease or injury of a person etc.; an instance of disease or injury; *colloq.* a patient, a person in need of (specified) treatment. **LME.**

W. H. DIXON At Deal they shipped a case of small-pox. W. C. WILLIAMS My first case was one of dandruff which I treated with some simple remedy. H. ROBBINS She's a mental case. T. S. ELIOT I will not discuss my case before another patient.

6 A legal action or suit, *esp.* one brought to trial; a statement of the facts in an adjudicated case, drawn up for a higher court's consideration; an action or suit that has been decided and may be cited. **E16.**

SHAKES. *Haml.* Why may that not be the skull of a lawyer? Where be his quiddities now, . . his cases, his tenures, and his tricks? F. RAPHAEL It was six months before the case came up.

7 The sum of arguments on one side of a legal cause or *transf.* of any matter of debate or controversy; a valid set of arguments. **L16.**

M. DRAYTON My doubtfull Case to plead. R. A. KNOX In arguing, never disguise from yourself the strength of the other man's case. T. BENN Let me try and make the case for fundamental changes to the way our economy is organised.

8 An incident or set of circumstances for investigation by police, a detective agency, a social worker, etc. **M19.**

L. LEE The police left . . with the case unsolved.

▸ **II 9** *GRAMMAR*. Any of the inflected forms of noun, adjective, or pronoun which express the varied relation in which the word may stand to other words in the sentence; this relation itself whether indicated by inflection or not. **LME.**
– **PHRASES: as the case may be** according to the situation. ***by the nature of the case, by the very nature of the case***: see **NATURE** *noun*. ***case in point***: see **POINT** *noun*[1]. ***case of conscience***. ***case stated***. ***from the nature of the case, from the very nature of the case***: see **NATURE** *noun*. ***hard case***: see **HARD** *adjective*. **have a case on** *slang* be infatuated or in love with. †**if case** = ***in case*** below. ***in any case***: see **ANY** *adjective* 1a. **in case** (*a*) if, in the event that, lest; (*b*) (as a precaution) against some possible occurrence. **in case of** in the event of. **in good case**, **in bad case**, etc., *arch.* in good, bad, etc., condition, well, badly, etc., off. **in no case** under no circumstances. **in that case** if that is true, should that happen. **in the case of** as regards. ***in the nature of the case, in the very nature of the case***: see **NATURE** *noun*. **just in case** = ***in case*** (b) above. **leading case** *LAW* a case serving as an especially significant precedent for deciding others. **make out a case (for)** put forward valid arguments (for). ***meet the case***: see **MEET** *verb*. **on the case** *hist.* (of a common-law action) based on a writ setting out fully details of a personal wrong not involving force. ***special case***: see **SPECIAL** *adjective*. ***state a case***: see **STATE** *verb*. ***STATED case***. ***subjective case***: see **SUBJECTIVE** *adjective* 5. ***test case***: see **TEST** *noun*[1]. ***the state of the case***: see **STATE** *noun*. ***trespass on the case***: see **TRESPASS** *noun* 3.
– **COMB.: casebook** a book containing records of legal, medical, or other cases; **case conference** a meeting of professionals (as doctors, teachers, social workers, etc.) to discuss a particular case; **case grammar** *LINGUISTICS* a form of transformational grammar in which the deep structure of sentences is analysed in terms of semantic case relationships; **case history** a record of a person's origins, personal history, and other information, for use in determining (esp. medical) treatment or other course of action; **case law** law as settled by decided cases; **caseload** the cases with which a doctor etc. is concerned at any one time; **case study** (a record of) an attempt to understand a person, matter, etc., from collected information about his, her, or its development; **casework** social work concerned with individual persons or small groups (also more fully ***social casework***); **caseworker** a social worker involved in casework (also more fully ***social caseworker***).

case /keɪs/ *noun*[2]. **LME.**
[**ORIGIN** Old French *casse* dial. var. of *chasse* (mod. *châsse* reliquary, frame) from Latin *capsa* box, bookcase, from base of *capere* to hold: in sense 5 perh. infl. by Italian *casa* house.]
1 A thing fitted to contain something else; a box, receptacle, bag, sheath, etc.; a glass box for displaying specimens, curiosities, etc. **LME.**
attaché case, bookcase, briefcase, card case, cigarette case, crankcase, dressing case, notecase, packing case, pillowcase, showcase, spectacle case, suitcase, etc. ***WARDIAN case***.
2 The outer protective or covering part of a natural or manufactured object, as a seed vessel, chrysalis, sausage, watch, book, etc. **LME.**

SHAKES. *Wint. T.* They seem'd almost, with staring on one another, to tear the cases of their eyes. OED Cloth cases . . for binding the volume will be issued with the December number.

3 The frame in which a door, stair, window, etc., is set. **E16.**
4 A box with its appropriate contents; hence, a brace (of pistols etc.), *gen.* a set. **M16.**

C. MARLOWE This case of rapiers. SIR W. SCOTT Cicely . . displayed a case of teeth which might have rivalled ivory. R. BRAUTIGAN A couple of cases of sweet wine.

5 The shell or carcass of a building; a house, esp. (*slang*) a brothel. **M16.**
6 *PRINTING* (now chiefly *hist.*). A receptacle divided into compartments for type. **L16.**
7 In full ***case-shot***. Bullets in an iron case fired from a cannon; shrapnel. **E17.**
8 In faro, the fourth card of a denomination, remaining in the box when the other three have been dealt. **M19.**
– **PHRASES: come down to cases, get down to cases** *US colloq.* come to the point. **keep cases** *US colloq.* note cards as they are dealt, keep a close watch. **lower case** (*a*) (chiefly *hist.*) a receptacle for type for small letters; (*b*) the small letters used in printing or (*loosely*) in writing, typing, etc. **upper case** (*a*) (chiefly *hist.*) a receptacle for type for capital letters; (*b*) the capital letters used in printing or (*loosely*) in writing, typing, etc.
– **COMB.: case-bottle** (*a*) a bottle that fits in a case with others; (*b*) a bottle with a protective case; **case-harden** *verb trans.* harden on the surface; *spec.* give a steel surface to (iron) by carburizing; *fig.* make callous; **case knife** a knife carried in a sheath; **case-oil** oil etc. transported in containers packed in wooden cases; **case-sensitive** *adjective* (*COMPUTING*) distinguishing between upper-case and lower-case letters for the purposes of searching files, sorting data, etc.; ***case-shot***: see sense 7 above; **case-weed** *dial.* shepherd's purse; **case worm** a caddis worm.

case /keɪs/ *verb trans.* **LME.**
[**ORIGIN** from **CASE** *noun*[2].]
1 Provide with a case; enclose in or as in a case; encase, surround *with*. **LME.**

POPE They case their limbs in brass; to arms they run. E. K. KANE Bones of seals, walrus, and whales—all now cased in ice. J. GWILT A brick wall . . cased with stone.

2 Strip of its case; skin. Now *dial. & N. Amer.* **L16.**
3 Examine beforehand, size up, spy out, esp. in preparation for robbery. *slang*. **E20.**

J. STEINBECK He was casing the field for a career.

■ **casing** *noun* (*a*) the action of the verb; (*b*) material or a structure that encases (***surface casing***: see **SURFACE** *noun & adjective*): **L16.**

caseation /keɪsɪˈeɪʃ(ə)n/ *noun*. **LME.**
[**ORIGIN** medieval Latin *caseatio(n-)*, from Latin *caseus* cheese: see **-ATION**.]
1 The coagulation of milk; conversion into cheese. Long *rare* or *obsolete*. **LME.**
2 *MEDICINE*. A form of necrosis characteristic of tuberculosis, in which diseased tissue forms a firm and dry mass like cheese in appearance. **M19.**

■ 'caseate *verb intrans.* [back-form.] undergo caseation (sense 2) L19.

casein /'keɪsiːn, -sɪɪn/ *noun.* M19.
[ORIGIN from Latin *caseus* cheese + -IN¹.]
The chief protein of milk; *esp.* this in coagulated form, as in cheese.
■ **caseinogen** /-'siːn-, -sɪ'ɪn-/ *noun* the soluble form in which casein occurs in milk L19.

C

casemate /'keɪsmeɪt/ *noun.* Also (earlier) †**casamat**. M16.
[ORIGIN (French from) Italian *casamatta*, earlier *camata*, perh. from Greek *khasma*, pl. *-mata*, CHASM.]
A chamber in the thickness of a wall of a fortress, provided with embrasures for defence. Also, an armoured enclosure protecting guns in a warship.
■ **casemated** *adjective* provided with casemates M18.

casement /'keɪsm(ə)nt/ *noun.* LME.
[ORIGIN Anglo-Latin *cassimentum*, from *cassa* (Latin *capsa* CASE *noun*²): see -MENT.]
1 ARCHITECTURE. A hollow moulding, *esp.* a cavetto. Also, a matrix made to receive a monumental brass. LME.
2 A vertically hinged frame with glass forming (part of) a window; *literary* a window. M16.

S. WEYMAN I had not seen the first moonbeams pierce the broken casement of the tower-room.

– COMB.: **casement cloth** plain fabric used chiefly for curtains; **casement window**: with a vertically hinged frame.

caseous /'keɪsɪəs/ *adjective.* M17.
[ORIGIN from Latin *caseus* cheese + -OUS.]
1 Of or like cheese, cheesy. M17.
2 MEDICINE. Like cheese in appearance; characterized by caseation. M18.

caser /'keɪsə/ *noun. slang.* E19.
[ORIGIN Prob. from Yiddish *keser* from Hebrew *keṯer* crown.]
A crown, five shillings or (now) 25 pence; *US* a dollar.

casern /kə'zəːn/ *noun.* Also **-z-**, **-ne**. L17.
[ORIGIN French *caserne* from Provençal *cazerna* from Proto-Romance from Latin *quaterna* (hut) for four.]
A barrack; *esp.* one erected temporarily in a garrison town.

casevac /'kasɪvak/ *noun. slang.* M20.
[ORIGIN from CASUALTY + EVACUATION. Cf. TACEVAL.]
The evacuation of casualties of battle by air.

cash /kaʃ/ *noun*¹. L16.
[ORIGIN French *casse* or its source Italian *cassa* from Latin *capsa* CASE *noun*².]
†**1 a** A box for money; a cash box. L16–M18. ▸**b** A sum of money. L17–M18.
2 Ready money, actual coins, notes, etc., (opp. ***credit***); (in banking and commerce) coins, or coins and banknotes, as opp. to cheques and orders; *gen.* (*colloq.*) money, wealth. L16.
cash and carry (designating) a system whereby the purchaser pays cash for (bulk orders of) goods and takes them away personally; (a store) trading thus. ***cash down***: see DOWN *adverb*. **cash on delivery** the forwarding of goods against cash to be paid to the postman or carrier; abbreviation ***COD***. **hard cash** (*a*) coins as opp. to paper money; (*b*) money as opp. to cheques etc. ***petty cash***: see PETTY *adjective*.
– COMB.: **cash account**: to which nothing is carried but cash received and cash paid; **cashback** (*a*) an incentive offered to buyers of cars or other products whereby they receive a cash refund after making their purchase; (*b*) a facility offered by retailers whereby customers may withdraw cash when making a debit card purchase, the amount withdrawn being added to their bill; **cash book** a book in which is entered a record of all cash paid and received; **cash box** a box where cash is kept; **cashcard** a coded card inserted into a cash dispenser to make a withdrawal; **cash cow** *colloq.* a business, project, etc., which provides a steady cash flow, *esp.* one considered as an attractive target for a takeover; **cash crop** (orig. *US*): cultivated primarily for its commercial value (as opp. to subsistence); **cash desk** a desk where cash is taken in a shop etc.; ***cash dispenser***: see DISPENSER 3; **cash flow** the movement of money as affecting liquidity, or as a measure of profitability; **cash nexus** *the* relationship constituted by monetary transactions; **cash payment**: in ready money; **cashpoint** (a location of) a cash dispenser; **cash price**: for payment in ready money (the lowest); **cash register** a till which visibly records the amount of each purchase, totals receipts, etc.; **cash sale**: for ready money; **cash-strapped** *adjective* (*colloq.*) short of money; **cash surrender value** the value of an insurance policy etc. cashed before it matures; **cash value** (*a*) the value in cash, *spec.* = ***cash surrender value*** above; (*b*) PHILOSOPHY the empirical content of a concept, word, or proposition.
■ **cashless** *adjective* M18.

cash /kaʃ/ *noun*². Pl. same. L16.
[ORIGIN Portuguese †*caxa*, *caixa* from Tamil *kācu*, infl. by CASH *noun*¹.]
hist. Any of various southern Indian, SE Asian, and Chinese coins of low value.

†**cash** *verb*¹ *trans.* M16–E19.
[ORIGIN Var. of CASS *verb*.]
= CASHIER *verb* 1, 2.

cash /kaʃ/ *verb*². E19.
[ORIGIN from CASH *noun*¹.]
1 *verb trans.* Give or obtain cash for (a note, cheque, etc.) E19. ▸**b** BRIDGE. Lead (a winning card); win (a trick) by leading a winning card. M20.
2 *cash up*: ▸**a** *verb intrans.* Pay the full amount of arrears, pay up. Now chiefly *US.* E19. ▸**b** *verb trans. & intrans.* Add up (takings etc.). M20.
3 *cash in*: ▸**a** *verb trans.* Exchange for cash. L19. ▸**b** *verb intrans.* Settle accounts (orig. at the end of a poker game); *fig.* die. E19. ▸**c** Foll. by *on*: realize profit on; *fig.* get advantage from. E20.
a cash in one's chips, **cash in one's checks**, etc., exchange counters for money on leaving the gaming table; settle accounts; *fig.* die.
■ **cashable** *adjective* able to be cashed L19.

†**casha** *noun* see KASHA *noun*¹.

cashel /'kaʃ(ə)l/ *noun.* M19.
[ORIGIN Irish *caiseal* from Latin *castellum* fortlet.]
In Ireland, an ancient circular wall enclosing a group of ecclesiastical buildings.

cashew /'kaʃuː, kə'ʃuː/ *noun.* L16.
[ORIGIN Portuguese from Tupi (*a*)*cajú*.]
(More fully ***cashew tree***) a large tree, *Anacardium occidentale*, native to tropical America and cultivated for its edible kidney-shaped nuts; (more fully ***cashew nut***) a nut of this tree; the fleshy receptacle bearing several such nuts.

cashier /ka'ʃɪə/ *noun.* L16.
[ORIGIN Dutch *cassier* or its source French *caissier*, from *caisse* CASH *noun*¹: see -IER.]
A person in charge of a bank's or business's cash; a person who handles customer payments in a shop etc.

cashier /kə'ʃɪə, ka-/ *verb trans.* L16.
[ORIGIN Early Flemish *kasseren* disband (soldiers), revoke (a will), from French *casser* break, dismiss, rescind = Italian *cassare* cancel, from Latin *quassare* QUASH *verb*.]
†**1** Discharge or disband (troops). L16–M18.
2 Dismiss from a position of command or authority, esp. with disgrace; depose. L16.

W. S. MAUGHAM He'd been kicked out of the Officers' Club at Warsaw and cashiered because he'd been caught cheating at cards.

3 *gen.* Dismiss. *obsolete* exc. as *fig.* use of sense 2. L16.

ADDISON The Ladies . . have already cashiered several of their Followers.

4 Discard; get rid of. *arch.* L16.
■ **cashierment** *noun* M17.

cashmere /kaʃ'mɪə, *esp. adjective* 'kaʃmɪə/ *noun & adjective.* L17.
[ORIGIN Early spelling of *Kashmir* in Asia (see KASHMIRI): cf. CASSIMERE.]
▸ **A** *noun.* **1** (Material made from) the fine soft wool of the Kashmir goat or the wild goat of Tibet; woollen fabric imitating this. L17.
2 A cashmere shawl etc. E19.
▸ **B** *adjective.* Made of cashmere. E19.
– NOTE: Rare before 19.

casino /kə'siːnəʊ/ *noun.* Pl. **-os**. See also CASSINO. M18.
[ORIGIN Italian, dim. of *casa* house from Latin *casa* cottage.]
1 Orig., a public room used for social meetings; *esp.* a public music or dancing saloon. Now, a building for gambling, often with other amenities. M18.
2 A summer house, esp. in Italy. M18.

casita /kə'sɪːtə/ *noun. N. Amer.* E19.
[ORIGIN Spanish, dim. of *casa* house, formed as CASINO.]
A small house or building, *esp.* a wooden cabin.

cask /kɑːsk/ *noun & verb.* E16.
[ORIGIN French *casque* or Spanish *casco* helmet, CASQUE. In sense 1 only in English.]
▸ **A** *noun.* **1** A wooden vessel of cylindrical form, usu. bulging in the middle, made of curved staves bound together by hoops, with flat ends, used esp. for alcoholic drinks; a similar vessel of metal, plastic, etc.; a barrel. E16. ▸**b** Such a vessel and its contents; the capacity of such a vessel as a measure for wine, spirits, etc. E18.
†**2 a** = CASKET *noun* 1. *rare* (Shakes.). Only in L16. ▸**b** A case; a shell. M17–E18.
†**3** = CASQUE 1. L16–L18.

fig.: SHAKES. *Coriol.* Not moving From th' cask to th' cushion, but commanding peace . . As he controll'd the war.

– COMB.: **cask-conditioned** *adjective* (of beer) matured naturally in a cask, without chemical processing.
▸ **B** *verb trans.* Put into a cask. M16.

casket /'kɑːskɪt/ *noun & verb.* LME.
[ORIGIN Perh. Anglo-Norman alt. of synon. Old French & mod. French CASSETTE.]
▸ **A** *noun.* **1** A small box or chest for jewels, letters, cremated ashes, or other things of value, itself often of value and richly ornamented. LME.

fig.: SHAKES. *John* They found him dead, . . An empty casket, where the jewel of life . . was . . ta'en away.

2 A (rectangular) coffin. Orig. *US.* M19.
▸ **B** *verb trans.* Enclose or store in a casket. E17.

†**Casleu** *noun* see KISLEV.

Caslon /'kazlən/ *noun.* M19.
[ORIGIN William *Caslon*, father (1692–1766) and son (1720–78), English type founders.]
More fully ***Caslon font***, ***Caslon type***, etc. A style of type cut by the Caslons or imitated from theirs.

Caspian /'kaspɪən/ *adjective & noun.* M16.
[ORIGIN from Latin *Caspius* (Greek *Kaspios*) + -AN.]
▸ **A** *adjective.* Designating, of, or pertaining to an inland sea of central Asia. M16.
▸ **B** *noun.* *The* Caspian Sea. L16.

casque /kɑːsk/ *noun.* L17.
[ORIGIN French from Spanish *casco*: cf. CASK.]
1 A piece of armour to cover the head; a helmet. Now *hist.* or *poet.* L17.
2 ZOOLOGY. A helmet-like structure, as in the cassowaries and hornbills. L18.

casquet /'kɑːskɪt; *foreign* kaːske (*pl. same*)/ *noun.* E17.
[ORIGIN French, dim. of CASQUE: see -ET¹.]
hist. A light and open helmet.

cass /kas/ *verb trans. obsolete* exc. *Scot.* LME.
[ORIGIN French *casser* from Latin *quassare* QUASH *verb*, the sense later infl. by *cassare* annul.]
1 Make void, annul, quash. LME.
2 Discharge; cashier. M16.

cassab /kə'sɑːb/ *noun.* L19.
[ORIGIN Urdu from Arabic *qaṣṣāb* player of a flute or pipe.]
An Asian merchant seaman.

cassada *noun* var. of. CASSAVA.

Cassandra /kə'sandrə/ *noun.* E17.
[ORIGIN Latin from Greek *Kas(s)andra*, daughter of Priam king of Troy, condemned by Apollo to prophesy correctly but never to be believed.]
A prophet of disaster, *esp.* one who is disbelieved.

cassareep /'kasəriːp/ *noun.* M19.
[ORIGIN Carib.]
A thick brown syrup prepared by boiling down the juice of the cassava with sugar, spices, etc.

cassata /kə'sɑːtə/ *noun.* E20.
[ORIGIN Italian.]
A Neapolitan ice cream containing fruit and nuts.

†**cassate** *verb trans.* L15–M18.
[ORIGIN Latin *cassat-* pa. ppl stem of *cassare*: see CASS *verb*, -ATE³.]
= CASS *verb*.

cassation /kə'seɪʃ(ə)n/ *noun*¹. LME.
[ORIGIN formed as CASSATE: see -ATION.]
Annulment, cancellation; an instance of this.
Court of Cassation a court of appeal in France etc.

cassation /kə'seɪʃ(ə)n/ *noun*². L19.
[ORIGIN German *Kassation* serenade from Italian *cassazione*.]
MUSIC. An eighteenth-century orchestral composition resembling a serenade.

cassava /kə'sɑːvə/ *noun.* Also **-da** /-də/. M16.
[ORIGIN Taino *casávi*, *cazábbi*, infl. by French *cassave*, Spanish *cassava*.]
1 A plant of the spurge family, *Manihot esculenta* (also called ***manioc***), much grown in the tropics for its edible tuberous roots and having two groups of cultivars, those containing high amounts of cyanide in their untreated roots (more fully ***bitter cassava***) and those with low amounts of cyanide (more fully ***sweet cassava***). M16.
2 Starch or flour obtained from the roots of this plant; bread made from this. L16.

casse /kas/ *noun*¹. L19.
[ORIGIN French, from *casser* to break.]
Souring of certain wines, accompanied by the loss of colour and the throwing of a sediment.

casse *noun*² var. of CASSIE *noun*¹.

Cassegrain /kasɪ'greɪn/ *noun.* L19.
[ORIGIN from Giovanni *Cassegrain* (1625–1712), French astronomer.]
ASTRONOMY. **1** Used *attrib.* with ref. to a kind of reflecting telescope having a convex secondary mirror which produces a focus at an aperture in the centre of the primary mirror, as ***Cassegrain focus***, ***Cassegrain telescope***, etc. L19.
2 A Cassegrain telescope. L19.
■ **Cassegrainian** *adjective* pertaining to or designating a telescope of this kind E19.

Casseiver /kə'siːvə/ *noun.* Also **c-**. L20.
[ORIGIN from CASSETTE + RECEIVER.]
(Proprietary name for) a combined cassette recorder and radio receiver.

casserole /'kasərəʊl/ *noun & verb.* E18.
[ORIGIN French, extension of *cassole* dim. of *casse* from Provençal *casa* from late Latin *cattia* ladle, pan from Greek *kuathion*, *-eion* dim. of *kuathos* cup: see -OLE¹.]
▸ **A** *noun.* **1** A covered heatproof vessel in which food is cooked and served (now also ***casserole dish***, ***casserole pan***, etc.); (a dish of) food cooked in this. E18.
2 The edging or outer portion of certain dressed dishes. Now *rare.* E18.

▸ **B** *verb trans.* Cook in a casserole. **M20.**

cassette /kəˈsɛt/ *noun.* **L18.**
[ORIGIN French, dim. of *casse*, *caisse* CASE *noun*[2]: see -ETTE.]
1 A casket. Now *rare.* **L18.**
2 A container for transporting photographic plates; a frame or holder for an X-ray plate or film. **L19.**
3 A container for a spool of magnetic tape, photographic film, etc., fashioned so as to be immediately usable on insertion into equipment designed for it; (now usu.) such a container together with its tape, film, etc.; a video or audio magnetic recording on such a tape. **M20.**
4 GENETICS. A block of genetic material which can be inserted or moved as a unit, *esp.* one which is expressed only at one location. **L20.**
– COMB.: **cassette deck**, **cassette player**, **cassette recorder**: designed to (record and) play back magnetic tapes.

cassia /ˈkasɪə/ *noun.* **OE.**
[ORIGIN Latin *cas(s)ia* from Greek *kasia* from Hebrew *qĕṣīʿāh*.]
1 An inferior kind of cinnamon; *esp.* the bark of the Far Eastern tree *Cinnamomum cassia*, of the bay family. Also ***cassia bark***. **OE.** ▸**b** The tree yielding this. Also ***cassia tree***. **LME.** ▸**c** A fragrant tree or shrub (cf. *Psalms* 45:8). *poet.* **L16.**
2 Any leguminous plant of the genus *Cassia*, *esp.* one yielding senna. Also called ***shower tree***. **LME.** ▸**b** Any medicinal product obtained from this. **M16.**

†**cassidony** *noun*[1]. **ME–M18.**
[ORIGIN Old French *cassidoine* popular var. of *calcidoine* formed as CHALCEDONY.]
= CHALCEDONY.

†**cassidony** *noun*[2]. **L16–M18.**
[ORIGIN Unknown.]
French lavender, *Lavandula stoechas.*

cassie /ˈkasi/ *noun*[1]. Also **casse** /kas/. **L17.**
[ORIGIN French (*papier*) *cassé* broken (paper).]
In full ***cassie paper***. The paper of the two outside quires of a ream.

cassie /ˈkasi/ *noun*[2]. *N. Amer.* **L19.**
[ORIGIN French from Provençal *cacio* acacia.]
The opopanax tree, *Acacia farnesiana.*

cassimere /ˈkasɪmɪə/ *noun.* **M18.**
[ORIGIN Var. of CASHMERE.]
A medium-weight twilled woollen cloth of soft texture. Cf. KERSEYMERE.

Cassinese /kasɪˈniːz/ *adjective & noun.* Pl. of noun same. **L19.**
[ORIGIN Italian, from Monte *Cassino* where the earliest Benedictine monastery was founded: see -ESE.]
(A monk) of the Benedictine order of Monte Cassino.

cassinette /kasɪˈnɛt/ *noun.* **E19.**
[ORIGIN Perh. alt. of CASSIMERE: see -ETTE.]
A thin fine twilled cloth with a cotton warp and a weft of wool or wool and silk.

Cassinian /kəˈsɪnɪən/ *adjective.* **E18.**
[ORIGIN from *Cassini* (see below) + -AN.]
MATH. Of or pertaining to the French astronomer G. D. Cassini (1625–1712) or other astronomers descended from him, or their work. Chiefly in ***Cassinian oval*** below.
Cassinian oval an oval with two foci such that the product of the focal distances of any point on the curve is a constant (instead of their sum being constant, as in an ellipse); any closed curve defined in this way.

cassino /kəˈsiːnəʊ/ *noun.* **L18.**
[ORIGIN Var. of CASINO.]
A two-handed card game in which players match or combine cards exposed on the table with cards from their hands. Also, either of two high-scoring cards in this game, (**a**) ***big cassino***, (now *rare*) ***great cassino***, the ten of diamonds, (**b**) ***little cassino***, the two of spades.

Cassiopeia /ˌkasɪəʊˈpiːə, kasɪˈəʊpɪə/ *noun.* **M16.**
[ORIGIN Mother of Andromeda in Greek mythol.]
(The name of) a conspicuous constellation of the northern hemisphere, between the Pole Star and Andromeda.

cassiri /kaˈsɪəri/ *noun.* **L18.**
[ORIGIN Carib: cf. CASSAREEP.]
An intoxicating liquor made in Guyana from sweet potatoes.

cassis /kaˈsiːs, ˈkasɪs/ *noun*[1]. **L19.**
[ORIGIN French = blackcurrant, app. from Latin CASSIA.]
A (freq. alcoholic) syrup made from blackcurrants and used to flavour drinks etc.

cassis /kaˈsi/ *noun*[2]. **L20.**
[ORIGIN See below.]
A wine produced in the region of Cassis, a small town near Marseilles.

cassiterite /kəˈsɪtərʌɪt/ *noun.* **M19.**
[ORIGIN from Greek *kassiteros* tin + -ITE[1].]
MINERALOGY. Native tin dioxide, SnO_2, which is the major ore of tin and is a tetragonal mineral usu. occurring as yellow, brown, or reddish prisms.

Cassius /ˈkasɪəs/ *noun.* **M19.**
[ORIGIN Andreas *Cassius* (c 1605–73), German physician and chemist.]
purple of Cassius, a purple pigment consisting of a colloidal mixture of metallic gold and tin(IV) dioxide.

cassock /ˈkasək/ *noun & verb.* **M16.**
[ORIGIN French *casaque* long coat from Italian *casacca* riding coat, prob. from Turkic *kazak*: see COSSACK.]
▸ **A** *noun.* **1** A long coat or cloak worn by soldiers. Long *obsolete* exc. *hist.* **M16.**
2 A kind of long loose coat or gown worn by men or women. Long *obsolete* exc. *hist.* **M16.**
3 A close-fitting garment with sleeves, fastened at the neck and reaching to the heels, worn under surplice, alb, or gown by clerics, choristers, etc., or as ordinary clerical costume. Also, a wearer of a cassock; *esp.* a member of the clergy. **E17.**
the cassock *fig.* the position or office of being a member of the clergy.
▸ **B** *verb trans.* Dress in or provide with a cassock. Chiefly as ***cassocked*** *ppl adjective.* **L18.**

cassolette /kasəˈlɛt/ *noun.* Also **-et**. **M17.**
[ORIGIN French from Provençal *casoleta* dim. of *casola*, from *casa*: see CASSEROLE, -ETTE.]
1 A vessel in which perfumes are burned. **M17.**
2 A box with a perforated cover for diffusing the odour of perfume in it. **E19.**
3 A small casserole dish; (a dish of) food cooked in this. **E19.**

†**cassonade** *noun.* **L16–E19.**
[ORIGIN French, from *casson* broken sugar, from *casser* break: see -ADE.]
Unrefined cane sugar (imported in casks).

cassone /kaˈsəʊni, *foreign* kasˈsoːne/ *noun.* Pl. **-nes** /-nɪz/, **-ni** /-ni/. **L19.**
[ORIGIN Italian, augm. of *cassa* chest.]
A large Italian coffer, esp. to hold a bride's trousseau.

cassoulet /ˈkasʊleɪ/ *noun.* **M20.**
[ORIGIN French, dim. of dial. *cassolo* stew-pan, tureen.]
A ragout of meat and beans.

cassowary /ˈkasəwəri, -wɛːri/ *noun.* **E17.**
[ORIGIN Malay *kesuari*.]
Any of the large flightless birds of the genus *Casuarius*, related to the emu and native to New Guinea, neighbouring islands, and Queensland.

Cassubian *noun & adjective* see KASHUBIAN.

cassumunar /kasəˈmjuːnə/ *noun.* Now *rare* or *obsolete*. Also †**-iar**. **L17.**
[ORIGIN App. of Eastern origin.]
The aromatic root of a plant of the ginger family used medicinally in the Indian subcontinent and eastern Asia, and probably a form of zedoary.

cast /kɑːst/ *noun*[1]. **ME.**
[ORIGIN from CAST *verb*.]
▸ **I** Senses connected with throwing or movement.
1 An act of casting, a throw of a missile, fishing line, net, etc.; the distance thrown; *spec.* a throw of dice, the number thrown. **ME.** ▸**b** ANGLING. That which is cast; (formerly) a length of gut with hook and fly, (now) a leader (usu. of nylon monofilament). Also (now *rare*), a place suited for casting. **E19.**

> AV *Luke* 22:41 He was withdrawen from them about a stones cast. W. ROBERTSON Their clothes, their arms, are staked . . upon a single cast. R. GRAVES As the hare doubled the leader killed it with a javelin cast.

measuring cast: see MEASURING *noun*.
2 A throw or stroke of fortune; chance, lot, fate. *obsolete* exc. *dial.* **ME.**
3 A turn of the eye in any direction; a look, a glance. **ME.**

> O. JOHNSON His big blue eyes had an upward cast toward the angels.

4 A throw in wrestling; a fall, an overthrow. Now *rare* or *obsolete*. **LME.**
5 That which is thrown, thrown out, or (chiefly *dial.*) produced; a quantity or amount thrown etc. at one time. **LME.** ▸**b** *spec.* A number of hawks flown off at a time (usu. a couple). **LME.** ▸**c** A warp (of herring). **L15.** ▸**d** A second swarm thrown off by a beehive in a season. **M17.** ▸**e** A mass of earth, mud, or sand thrown out from its hole by a worm etc. **E18.** ▸**f** A pellet regurgitated by a bird of prey. **M19.**

> MALORY Two cast of bread, with fat venison baked. DRYDEN A cast of scatter'd dust.

6 *fig.* A stroke, a touch; a sample. **M16.**

> W. WYCHERLEY If you hate Verses, I'll give you a cast of my Politics in Prose.

7 A lift in a vehicle. *obsolete* exc. *dial.* **M17.**

> S. RICHARDSON If . . you are for the Village, I'll give you a Cast.

8 A spreading out (as) of hunting hounds in search of a scent. **M19.** ▸**b** The sweep of a trained dog in sheep-mustering. *Austral. & NZ.* **E20.**

> R. SUTCLIFF To work their way north in a series of casts . . in the manner of a hound cutting across a scent.

▸ **II** Senses connected with arrangement, shaping, or appearance.
9 †**a** The plan or conformation of a building etc. **ME–L16.** ▸**b** The way in which something is laid out or drawn up; disposition, arrangement; *spec.* the assignment of parts in a play etc. to the various actors; the actors themselves; formerly also the part assigned to one actor. **L16.**

> **b** M. ARNOLD The happy cast and flow of the sentence. J. AGATE A . . musical comedy played by a sixteen-year-old cast.

†**10** Purpose, aim; a contrivance, a trick. **LME–E17.**
11 Calculation, reckoning; *esp.* the addition of columns of an account. **L15.**

> OED If the account does not balance now, there must be an error in the cast.

12 A model made by casting in a mould; a moulded mass of solidified material, esp. of plaster enclosing a fractured limb etc.; a negative impression of an object made in plaster, wax, etc. **E16.** ▸†**b** Casting, founding. *rare* (Shakes.). Only in **E17.** ▸**c** MEDICINE. A mass of dead cells and other matter formed in a diseased kidney and passed in the urine. **M19.** ▸**d** A fossil impression of the inside of a hollow structure. **L19.**

> W. SHENSTONE A most excellent figure, and I shall wish much to get a good cast of it. D. L. SAYERS When he makes a new key, he keeps a cast of it. E. BIRNEY The up-patients had gone about autographing all the casts with indelible pencils. **b** SHAKES. *Haml.* Why such daily cast of brazen cannon.

13 A permanent twist or inclination, *esp.* a squint (*in* an eye). **E16.**

> R. HOGGART Her left eye had a violent cast.

14 *fig.* Form, shape, appearance, (esp. of facial features); inclination; stamp, mould; nature, kind, style, quality. **M16.**

> I. WALTON This fish is of a fine cast and handsome shape. ADDISON The Mind that hath any Cast towards Devotion. S. JOHNSON A cast of talk, peculiar to their own fraternity. GIBBON Heroines of such a cast may claim our admiration. R. CHURCH A sallow skin that gave him a Spanish cast. S. KING His cast of mind makes it impossible for him to think otherwise.

15 A dash of some colour; a tinge, a shade. **E17.**

> SHAKES. *Haml.* Sicklied o'er with the pale cast of thought. J. GARDNER His blue eyes had a pink cast, as they always did when the light was strong.

– COMB.: **cast net** a fishing net which is cast and drawn immediately, rather than set and left.

†**cast** *noun*[2] var. of CASTE.

cast /kɑːst/ *ppl adjective.* **LME.**
[ORIGIN pa. pple of CAST *verb*.]
That has been cast.
– SPECIAL COLLOCATIONS & COMB.: **cast-for-age** *adjective* (*Austral. & NZ*) (of a sheep) disposed of because too old. **cast iron** a hard alloy of iron, carbon (in greater proportion than in steel), and silicon, cast in a mould (***malleable cast iron***: see MALLEABLE 1). **cast-iron** *adjective* made of cast iron; *fig.* hard, unchangeable, impregnable. **cast steel** steel made by melting and casting blister steel. See also CASTAWAY, CAST-OFF.

cast /kɑːst/ *verb.* Pa. t. & pple **cast**. See also KEST. **ME.**
[ORIGIN Old Norse *kasta*.]
▸ **I** Throw; throw down, defeat; put forcibly: generally replaced by THROW *verb*.
1 *verb trans.* Throw, move (as) by throwing, fling, hurl, toss. **ME.** ▸**b** *verb intrans.* Aim, throw; *esp.* †(**a**) shoot projectiles; (**b**) throw dice. **ME.**

> AV *John* 8:7 Hee that is without sinne among you, let him first cast a stone at her. T. HERBERT The wind blowing strongly, we were cast upon the shoales . . of Mozambique. EVELYN Never cast Water on things newly planted. C. S. FORESTER Tomorrow or the next day would see fate cast the dice—liberty or prison. **b** R. GRAVES He cast, and the javelin came darting surely down.

2 *verb refl.* Throw or project oneself. **ME.**
3 *verb trans.* Throw forth (a net, fishing line, sounding lead, etc.). **ME.** ▸**b** Throw a fishing line over (a piece of water). **L19.**

> *fig.*: K. TYNAN The lady might . . cast her net wider than her special talents would permit.

4 *verb trans.* Direct (one's eyes, a glance, etc.). **ME.**

> DRYDEN Th' unwary Lover cast his Eyes behind. E. F. BENSON Lucia cast him a quick glance.

5 *verb trans.* Cause (light, a shadow, etc.) to fall (*on*, *over*, etc.). **ME.**

> TENNYSON There is no bright form Doth not cast a shade. C. ODETS A traffic light . . casts its colours on the faces of the boy and girl.

†**6** *verb trans.* Emit, give out (heat, odour, etc.). **ME–M18.**
7 *verb trans.* Toss (the head). Long *obsolete* exc. *Scot.* **ME.**
8 *verb trans.* Place or apply hastily, forcefully, or decisively; place or cause to fall (doubt, blame, a spell, etc.) (*up*)*on*. **ME.** ▸†**b** Cover by applying mortar etc.; plaster, daub. Cf. ROUGHCAST. **L16–E19.**

C

W. RALEIGH Casting ungratefully on Moses all their misadventures. MILTON His ponderous shield behind him cast. S. WILBERFORCE My guide cast on my shoulders a beautiful mantle. A. MASON A spell to cast harm on a neighbour. M. EDWARDES The Committee also cast doubt on the value of the Ryder Report.

9 *verb trans.* Put, cause to be put, *into* prison etc., or (*arch.*) *into* a rage, sleep, etc. ME. ▸†**b** Set (a person) *upon doing*, *to do*. LME–M18.

W. DAMPIER Our continuing wet . . cast us all into Fevers. B. JOWETT They were being taken away to be cast into hell.

10 *verb trans.* Throw to the ground; overthrow, defeat. *arch.* & *dial.* ME. ▸**b** Throw (an animal) on its back or side. Usu. in *pass.* L16.

SHAKES. *Macb.* Though he took up my legs sometime, yet I made a shift to cast him. THACKERAY Low he lies . . who was cast lower than the poorest. **b** J. HERRIOT A horse which had got cast in its stall.

†**11** *verb trans.* Find guilty, convict; condemn. LME–M19.

T. STANLEY Socrates was cast by 281 voices. H. MACKENZIE I was tried for the crime, & was cast for transportation.

12 *verb trans.* Add, throw in *to*; bestow, confer, allot. Now *rare* or *obsolete*. LME.

13 *verb trans.* Give or deposit (one's vote) in a vote or election. L19.

H. WILSON Twelve members elected . . by 280-odd MPs each with twelve votes to cast.

▸ **II** Throw off, out, or up: except in sense 14b, now generally expressed with the use of adverbs (see below).

14 *verb trans.* Throw off, shed, slough, esp. in the process of growth; cease to wear (clothes). ME. ▸**b** Esp. of a tree, an animal, etc.: drop or shed out of due season; give birth to prematurely. LME.

J. SELDEN The Eagle had cast its feathers, and could towre no more. THACKERAY The horse had cast a shoe. **b** AV *Rev.* 6:13 As a figge tree casteth her vntimely figs when she is shaken of a mighty winde.

15 *verb trans.* & *intrans.* Throw up from within, vomit. Now chiefly *dial.* ME. ▸†**b** *verb trans.* Utter forcibly, ejaculate (words etc.). ME–E18. ▸**c** *verb trans.* & *intrans.* Of a bird of prey: regurgitate. L15.

b POPE Not louder shouts to pitying Heav'n are cast.

16 *verb trans.* Throw aside, reject, discard; dismiss, expel. ME.

SHAKES. *Oth.* The state . . Cannot with safety cast him.

17 *verb trans.* Throw up with a spade etc., dig up or out. Now chiefly *Scot.* LME. ▸†**b** Raise by digging, throw up (a mound etc.). L16–M17.

W. RALEIGH A newe ditch lately cast by Perseus. **b** MILTON Pioneers . . to trench a field Or cast a rampart.

▸ **III** Calculate, devise, design.

18 *verb trans.* & *intrans.* Reckon, calculate, sum up (accounts etc.); calculate and record the details of (a horoscope). ME. ▸†**b** Forecast, speculate. LME–M17.

D. BREWSTER Drawing an income from casting nativities. TENNYSON Who would cast and balance at a desk?

19 *verb trans.* & †*intrans.* (with inf.). Contrive, devise, scheme. ME.

I. WALTON Before you begin to angle, cast to have the wind on your back. E. B. BROWNING Do not cast Ambiguous paths . . for my feet.

†**20** *verb trans.* & *intrans.* Revolve in the mind, deliberate, ponder. LME–E18.

CAXTON They caste . . how they myght breng hym out of prison. ADDISON Casting in my thoughts the several unhappinesses of life.

†**21** *verb intrans.* Intend, determine *to do*. LME–E19.

SIR W. SCOTT The marshall and myself had cast To stop him.

▸ **IV** Arrange, shape; found.

22 *verb trans.* Put into shape, arrange, dispose, lay out; put *into* a particular form. Now only of abstract things, and passing into *fig.* use of sense 23. ME.

AV They did not cast the streets, nor proportion the houses in such comely fashion. ADDISON Casting into an Opera the Story of Whittington and his Cat. P. G. WODEHOUSE The thing was cast in narrative form.

23 *verb trans.* Form (a plastic or liquid substance, esp. molten metal) into a shape by pouring it into a mould; form (an object) of metal etc. in this way; found. L15.

R. EDEN They . . melte it & caste it fyrste into masses or wedges. W. HOGARTH A figure cast in soft wax. *fig.*: R. GRAVES These lieutenants . . were all cast in the same mould.

†**24** *verb trans.* Arrange or dispose (colours) in painting. M16–M17.

J. LYLY Cunning Painters who for the whitest worke, cast the blackest ground.

25 *verb trans.* Allocate (the roles in a play, film, etc.) to the actors; appoint (an actor) *in* or *for* a role, *as* a character. E18.

P. G. WODEHOUSE Cast for the part of Macbeth. L. HELLMAN I . . cast the play with a kind of abandoned belief that good actors can play anything.

▸ **V** Turn, twist; incline.

26 *verb intrans.* & *trans.* Turn, veer; bring (a ship) round. Now only *NAUTICAL*. LME.

F. MARRYAT Her foresail is loose, all ready to cast her. W. C. RUSSELL The wind has so got hold of her that she won't cast one way or the other.

27 *verb trans.* (in *pass.*) & *intrans.* Of timber: be warped, warp. M16.

28 *verb trans.* Turn (the scale or balance). Now only *fig.* Cf. ***casting vote*** s.v. CASTING *ppl adjective*. L16.

†**29** *verb intrans.* Incline, slant. L16–L18.

T. BEST Which way the ground casts.

30 *verb intrans.* Of hunters, hounds, etc.: go searching, spread out and search (in a given general direction). (Cf. ***cast about*** below.) L16.

G. J. WHYTE-MELVILLE Like a hound . . casting forward upon a vague speculation.

▸ **VI 31** *verb trans.* & *intrans.* Tie (a knot), make (a loop); entangle, catch. L16.

R. PRICE Struggling . . to hold off the snake from casting again. Two coils—you're lost.

– PHRASES, & WITH ADVERBS IN SPECIALIZED SENSES: **cast about** (*a*) go this way and that in search, seek to discover or devise means, (*for*, *to do*, *how*); (*b*) *arch.* change course or direction. ***cast accounts***: see ACCOUNT *noun*. ***cast a clout***: see CLOUT *noun*[1] 4. **cast adrift** leave to drift. ***cast anchor***: see ANCHOR *noun*[1]. **cast an eye** glance, have a quick look. **cast around** = ***cast about*** above. **cast ashore** (of waves etc.) deposit on the shore. **cast aside** discard, abandon. ***cast a slur on***: see SLUR *noun*[3] 1. **cast aspersions (on)** utter aspersions (regarding), slander. ***cast a stone (at)***: see STONE *noun*. **cast away** (*a*) throw away, squander, reject; (*b*) cast ashore, strand (cf. CASTAWAY); (in *pass.*, of a ship) be wrecked. †**cast by** discard. **cast down** (*a*) throw down, destroy, demolish, overthrow; (*b*) bend or turn downward; dispirit, depress, (usu. in *pass.*; cf. DOWNCAST *adjective*). **cast forth** throw out, expel, eject. ***cast in a heroic mould***: see MOULD *noun*[3]. ***cast in a person's dish***: see DISH *noun* 1. ***cast in a person's teeth***: see TOOTH *noun*. ***cast in one's lot with***: see LOT *noun*. ***cast light on***: see LIGHT *noun*. **cast loose** unfasten, set adrift, detach (oneself). ***cast lots***: see LOT *noun*. **cast off** (*a*) throw off, abandon, discard; (*b*) *KNITTING* take (a stitch) off a needle by looping it over the next; take off all stitches in this way to finish an edge; (*c*) *verb phr. trans.* & *intrans.* loosen and throw off (a mooring rope etc.); (*d*) *TYPOGRAPHY* calculate the space required in print by (copy). **cast on** *KNITTING* make (a stitch) on a needle; make the first row of stitches on a needle. ***cast one's bread upon the waters***: see WATER *noun*. ***cast one's mind back***: see MIND *noun*[1]. **cast out** (*a*) expel, eject; (*b*) *dial.* disagree, quarrel. ***cast pearls before swine***: see PEARL *noun*[1] 2. **cast round** = ***cast about*** above. ***cast stones (at)***: see STONE *noun*. ***cast the first stone***: see STONE *noun*. ***cast the glove***: see GLOVE *noun*. ***cast the gorge (at)***: see GORGE *noun*[1]. ***cast the lead***: see LEAD *noun*[1]. ***cast to the (four) winds***: see WIND *noun*[1]. **cast up** (*a*) throw up; (of the sea etc.) deposit on shore; raise up by digging etc.; (*dial.* or *obsolete*) vomit; ***cast up the gorge***: see GORGE *noun*[1]; (*b*) add (a column of figures etc.), count; (*c*) *dial.* utter as a reproach. †**cast water** diagnose disease by the inspection of urine. ***the die is cast***: see DIE *noun*[1].

Castalian /kaˈsteɪlɪən/ *adjective*. L16.
[ORIGIN from Latin *Castalia* (see below) from Greek *Kastalia*.]
Of or pertaining to Castalia, the fountain sacred to the Muses on Mount Parnassus; of or pertaining to the Muses.

Castalie /ˈkastəli/ *noun*. *arch.* or *poet.* Also **-ly**. E17.
[ORIGIN Alt. of *Castalia*: see CASTALIAN.]
A spring of pure water; a source of inspiration.

castaneous /kaˈsteɪnɪəs/ *adjective*. *rare*. L17.
[ORIGIN from Latin *castanea* chestnut (see CHESTEN) + -OUS: see -EOUS.]
Chestnut-coloured.

castanet /kastəˈnɛt/ *noun*. E17.
[ORIGIN Spanish *castañeta* (with later assim. to French *castagnette*) dim. of *castaña* from Latin *castanea* chestnut: see CHESTEN, -ET[1].]
A small concave piece of hardwood, ivory, etc., clicked or rattled in pairs as a rhythmic accompaniment to a Spanish dance etc. Usu. in *pl.*

castaway /ˈkɑːstəweɪ/ *noun* & *adjective*. E16.
[ORIGIN from CAST *ppl adjective* + AWAY *adverb*.]
▸ **A** *noun*. **1** A reprobate. *arch.* E16.
2 A shipwrecked person. L18.
3 An outcast; a drifter. M19.
▸ **B** *adjective*. Rejected, abandoned; shipwrecked, stranded; (*arch.*) reprobate. M16.

caste /kɑːst/ *noun*. Also †**cast**. M16.
[ORIGIN Spanish & Portuguese *casta* use as noun (sc. *raza*, *raça* race) of fem. of *casto* pure, unmixed from Latin *castus*: cf. CHASTE *adjective*.]
1 A race, a stock, a breed. *obsolete* in *gen.* sense. M16. ***half-caste***: see HALF-.
2 A Hindu hereditary class of socially equal persons, united in religion and usu. following similar occupations, distinguished from other castes in the hierarchy by its relative degree of purity or pollution. E17. ▸**b** Any more or less exclusive social class. E19.

b R. G. COLLINGWOOD The view that artists can or should form a special order or caste. B. R. O. ANDERSON Elimination of the samurai as a legal caste.

scheduled caste: see SCHEDULED.
3 The position conferred by membership of a caste. L18. **lose caste** be deprived of membership of one's caste; descend in the social scale.
4 The system of division of society into castes. M19.

MAX-MÜLLER In India caste . . has existed from the earliest times.

5 The form of a social insect having a particular function. M19.
– COMB.: **caste mark**: on the forehead, denoting membership of a particular Hindu caste; **caste system** a system of division of society into castes.
– NOTE: The four original Hindu castes, later greatly augmented, were priests, warriors, merchants, and artisans (see BRAHMIN, KSHATRIYA, VAISYA, SUDRA).
■ **casteless** *adjective* L19.

casteism /ˈkɑːstɪz(ə)m/ *noun*. Also **castism**. L19.
[ORIGIN from CASTE + -ISM.]
(Belief in or advocacy of) the system of division of society into castes.
■ **casteist** *noun* & *adjective* (*a*) *noun* a believer in or advocate of casteism; (*b*) *adjective* of or pertaining to casteism or casteists: M20.

castelet /ˈkastəlɪt/ *noun*. Also **-ll-**. ME.
[ORIGIN Old Northern French (mod. *châtelet*) dim. of *castel*: see CASTLE *noun*[1], -ET[1]. Cf. CASTLET, CHATELET.]
A small castle.

castellan /ˈkastələn/ *noun*. Also †**-ane**. See also CASTILIAN *noun*[2]. LME.
[ORIGIN Old Northern French *castelain* (mod. *châtelain*) from medieval Latin *castellanus* use as noun of Latin adjective, from *castellum* fortified place: see CASTLE *noun*[1], -AN, and cf. CHATELAIN. In sense 2 from medieval Latin.]
1 *hist.* The governor of a castle. LME.
†**2** = CASTILIAN *noun*[2]. *Scot.* E16–E17.
■ **castellany** *noun* the office or jurisdiction of a castellan; the territory subject to a castellan: LME.

castellar /kaˈstɛlə/ *adjective*. L18.
[ORIGIN from Latin *castellum* (see CASTLE *noun*[1]) + -AR[1].]
Pertaining to or of the nature of a castle.

castellate /ˈkastəleɪt/ *verb*. *rare*. M19.
[ORIGIN Back-form. from CASTELLATED.]
1 *verb intrans.* Take the form of a castle. M19.
2 *verb trans.* Build like a castle; build with battlements. M19.

castellated /ˈkastəleɪtɪd/ *adjective*. L17.
[ORIGIN from medieval Latin *castellatus*, from *castellum*: see CASTLE *noun*[1], -ATE[2], -ED[1].]
1 Built like a castle; battlemented; resembling a castle. L17.
2 Dotted with castles. E19.
■ Also **castellate** *adjective* (*rare*) M19.

castellation /kastəˈleɪʃ(ə)n/ *noun*. E19.
[ORIGIN from medieval Latin *castellat-* pa. ppl stem of *castellare* build castles, from *castellum*: see CASTLE *noun*[1], -ATION.]
The building of castles or battlements; a castellated structure, a battlement.

castellet *noun* var. of CASTELET.

castelry /ˈkast(ə)lri/ *noun*. *obsolete* exc. *hist.* L17.
[ORIGIN Old French *castelerie* from medieval Latin *castellaria*, from *castellum*: see CASTLE *noun*[1], -RY.]
(The territory subject to) the jurisdiction of a castle.

caster /ˈkɑːstə/ *noun*. In branch II also (& more usual in sense 4) **-or**. LME.
[ORIGIN from CAST *verb* + -ER[1].]
▸ **I 1** A person who casts something. LME.
2 A Monotype machine for casting type. E20.
▸ **II 3** A small bottle, jar, etc., with a perforated top, used for sprinkling pepper, sugar, etc., on food (in *pl.* sometimes including cruets for vinegar, oil, etc.). L17.
4 A small swivel wheel on the leg of a chair, table, etc. M18.
– COMB.: **castor action** the swivelling of vehicle wheels to ensure stability; **caster sugar** finely granulated white sugar.

castigate /ˈkastɪgeɪt/ *verb trans.* E17.
[ORIGIN Latin *castigat-* pa. ppl stem of *castigare*, from *castus* pure: see -ATE[3].]
1 Inflict suffering on to punish or subdue; chastise; rebuke severely. E17.

A. BRINK Castigating my body like some mediaeval nun. H. KISSINGER An editorial castigating the Nixon Administration for misleading the American people.

†**2** Reduce in intensity, moderate. M17–L18.

R. BURNS When your castigated pulse Gies now and then a wallop.

3 Correct, revise, and emend (a literary work etc.). *arch.* M17.

EVELYN Seneca's tragedies . . have . . been castigated abroad by several learned hands.

■ **castigator** *noun* E17. **castigatory** *adjective* & *noun* (*a*) *adjective* corrective, punitive; †(*b*) *noun* an instrument of chastisement: E17.

castigation /kastɪˈgeɪʃ(ə)n/ *noun*. LME.
[ORIGIN Latin *castigatio(n-)*, formed as CASTIGATE: see -ATION.]
The action or an act of castigating; chastisement; a rebuke; *arch.* (a) revision, (an) emendation.

Castile /kaˈstiːl/ *noun*. Also †**castle**. LME.
[ORIGIN *Castile* (see CASTILIAN *noun*¹ & *adjective*) in Spain, where orig. made.]
In full ***Castile soap***. A fine hard white or mottled soap made with olive oil and soda.

Castilian /kaˈstɪlɪən/ *noun*¹ & *adjective*. L15.
[ORIGIN Spanish *Castellano*, from *Castella* Castile (see below); later from *Castile*: see -AN, -IAN.]
▸ **A** *noun*. **1** A particular Spanish gold coin. Long *obsolete* exc. *hist.* L15.
2 The form of Spanish spoken in the province (earlier the kingdom) of Castile; standard literary Spanish. M16.
3 A native or inhabitant of Castile. L16.
▸ **B** *adjective*. Of or pertaining to Castile, Castilian, or Castilians. M16.

castilian /kaˈstɪlɪən/ *noun*². *obsolete* exc. *hist.* L16.
[ORIGIN Alt. of CASTELLAN.]
A member of the garrison of a castle; a person living in a castle.

casting /ˈkɑːstɪŋ/ *noun*. ME.
[ORIGIN from CAST *verb* + -ING¹.]
1 The action of CAST *verb*. ME.
2 **a** That which is cast up; a worm cast etc.; a pellet disgorged by a hawk etc. LME. ▸**b** An object cast in metal. L18.
– COMB.: **casting bottle** *hist.* a vinaigrette; **casting couch** *joc.*: on which actresses are said to be seduced in return for being awarded parts in films etc.; **casting director** one responsible for assigning roles in a film, play, etc.; **casting net** = *cast net* s.v. CAST *noun*¹.

casting /ˈkɑːstɪŋ/ *ppl adjective*. ME.
[ORIGIN formed as CASTING *noun* + -ING².]
1 That casts. ME.
2 Deciding, decisive. E17.
casting vote a vote that decides between two equal parties, esp. when (entitled to be) used by a chairman etc.

castle /ˈkɑːs(ə)l/ *noun*¹. LOE.
[ORIGIN Anglo-Norman, Old Northern French *castel* var. of *chastel* (mod. *château*) from Latin *castellum* dim. of *castrum* fortified place: see -LE². In branch II rendering late Latin (Vulgate) *castellum* village, Latin *castra* camp.]
▸ **I 1** A (usu. large) fortified building or set of buildings; a stronghold (*lit.* & *fig.*); (esp. in proper names) a mansion that was once such. Also (in proper names), a site of ancient earthworks. LOE. ▸**b** A model or representation of such a building or buildings. LME.

Proverb: An Englishman's house is his castle.

castle in the air, **castle in Spain** a visionary project, a daydream unlikely to be realized (see also ***build castles in the air*** s.v. AIR *noun*¹ 3). **the Castle** IRISH HISTORY the viceregal government and administration, of which Dublin Castle was the seat. **b bouncing castle**, **bouncy castle** a large inflatable in the form of a castle for people to throw themselves around in. ***sandcastle***: see SAND *noun*.
2 A tower mounted on an elephant's back; a movable tower formerly used in warfare. ME.
3 An elevated structure on the deck of a ship. *obsolete* exc. in FORECASTLE. ME.
4 A large ship, esp. of war. *literary*. L16.
5 CHESS. = ROOK *noun*². M17.
▸ †**II 6** In biblical translations and allusions: a village. LOE–M16.
†**7** *sing.* & (usu.) in *pl.* A camp. ME–L15.
– COMB.: **castle-builder** *fig.* a person who builds castles in the air, a daydreamer; **castle-building** *fig.* the building of castles in the air, daydreaming; **castle-guard** *hist.* a form of feudal service by which a tenant was bound to defend his lord's castle; the tenure of such service; a tax orig. paid in commutation of this service; **castle-nut** MECHANICS a nut with a notched extension for a locking pin; **castle pudding**: steamed or baked in a small mould; **castleward** *hist.* = ***castle-guard*** above.

†**castle** *noun*² var. of CASTILE.

castle /ˈkɑːs(ə)l/ *verb*. LME.
[ORIGIN from CASTLE *noun*¹.]
1 *verb trans.* Provide or equip with castles or battlements. Chiefly as ***castled*** *ppl adjective*. LME.
2 *verb trans.* Enclose (as) in a castle. L16.
3 *verb intrans.* CHESS. Move the king two squares towards a rook and the rook to the square which the king has crossed; (of the king) move thus in relation to a rook. M17. ▸**b** *verb trans.* Move (the king) thus in relation to a rook. M18.

castlet /ˈkɑːslɪt/ *noun*. M16.
[ORIGIN Var. of CASTELET assim. to CASTLE *noun*¹, or from CASTLE *noun*¹ + -LET.]
A small castle.

castling /ˈkɑːstlɪŋ/ *noun*. Long *obsolete* exc. *dial.* L16.
[ORIGIN from CAST *ppl adjective* or *noun*¹ + -LING¹.]
1 An aborted offspring. L16.
†**2** = CAST *noun*¹ 5d. E–M17.

castock /ˈkastɒk/ *noun*. *Scot.* & *N. English*. Also **cust-** /ˈkʌst-/. L15.
[ORIGIN Phonet. devel. of ***kale-stock*** s.v. KALE.]
A cabbage stalk or stem.

cast-off /ˈkɑːstɒf/ *ppl adjective* & *noun*. E18.
[ORIGIN from CAST *ppl adjective* + OFF *adverb*.]
▸ **A** *ppl adjective*. Thrown away, abandoned, rejected, discarded. E18.
▸ **B** *noun*. **1** A person who or thing which is cast off, *esp.* an unwanted garment. E18.
2 TYPOGRAPHY. A calculation of the space required for a given amount of copy in a particular typographic form. L19.

castor /ˈkɑːstə/ *noun*¹. LME.
[ORIGIN Old French & mod. French or Latin from Greek *kastōr*.]
1 The beaver; its pelt. Now *rare*. LME.
2 A pungent, bitter-tasting, reddish-brown substance obtained from two perineal sacs of the beaver, used in medicine and perfumery. E17.
3 A hat, orig. of (beaver's) fur. *arch. slang*. M17.

castor /ˈkɑːstə/ *noun*². M18.
[ORIGIN Uncertain: perh. = CASTOR *noun*¹ 2, as having succeeded it in medical use.]
castor oil, a pale yellow oil from the seeds of a tropical or subtropical shrub or tree, *Ricinus communis*, used as a purgative and lubricant.
– COMB.: **castor bean**, **castor oil bean** (a seed of) the castor oil plant; **castor oil plant** the plant that yields castor oil, esp. as grown as a pot plant.

castor *noun*³ see CASTER.

castoreum /kaˈstɔːrɪəm/ *noun*. Also †**-ry**. ME.
[ORIGIN Latin, formed as CASTOR *noun*¹.]
= CASTOR *noun*¹ 2.

castral /ˈkastr(ə)l/ *adjective*. *rare*. M16.
[ORIGIN from Latin *castra* camp + -AL¹.]
Of or pertaining to a camp.

castrametation /ˌkastrəmɪˈteɪʃ(ə)n/ *noun*. L17.
[ORIGIN French *castramétation*, from Latin *castra metari* measure or mark out a camp.]
The designing or laying out of military camps.

castrate /ˈkastreɪt/ *noun* & *adjective*. LME.
[ORIGIN Latin *castratus* pa. pple, formed as CASTRATE *verb*: see -ATE¹, -ATE².]
▸ **A** *noun*. A castrated man or animal. LME.
▸ **B** *adjective*. Castrated. Now *rare* or *obsolete*. E18.

castrate /kaˈstreɪt, ˈkastreɪt/ *verb trans*. M16.
[ORIGIN Latin *castrat-* pa. ppl stem of *castrare*: see -ATE³.]
1 Remove the testicles of; geld; *fig.* deprive of potency, vigour, or force. M16.
2 Expurgate (a text). *obsolete* exc. as passing into fig. use of sense 1. E17.
■ **caˈstrative** *adjective* of or pertaining to castration, tending to deprive of potency M20. **caˈstrator** *noun* E19.

castration /kaˈstreɪʃ(ə)n/ *noun*. LME.
[ORIGIN French, or Latin *castratio(n-)*, formed as CASTRATE *verb*: see -ATION.]
The action or an act of castrating someone or something; the fact of being castrated.
– COMB.: **castration complex** PSYCHOANALYSIS (*a*) a man's neurotic and unconscious fear of castration resulting from childhood fears of his father; (*b*) a woman's neurotic anxiety caused by her unconsciously feeling that she has been castrated.

castrato /kaˈstrɑːtəʊ/ *noun*. Pl. **-ti** /-ti/. M18.
[ORIGIN Italian, use as noun of pa. pple of *castrare* castrate.]
hist. An adult male singer castrated in boyhood so as to retain a soprano or alto voice.

castrensian /kaˈstrɛnsɪən/ *adjective*. M17.
[ORIGIN from Latin *castrensis* adjective, from *castra* camp, + -AN.]
Of or pertaining to a military camp.

Castroism /ˈkastrəʊɪz(ə)m/ *noun*. M20.
[ORIGIN from Fidel *Castro* Ruz (1927–), Cuban statesman + -ISM.]
The political principles or actions of Fidel Castro or his adherents or imitators. Cf. FIDELISM.

castrum /ˈkastrəm/ *noun*. Pl. **castra** /ˈkastrə/. M19.
[ORIGIN Latin.]
A Roman encampment or fortress.

casual /ˈkaʒjʊəl, -zj-/ *adjective* & *noun*. LME.
[ORIGIN Old French & mod. French *casuel* and Latin *casualis* (in its late and medieval uses), from *casus* CASE *noun*¹: see -AL¹.]
▸ **A** *adjective*. **1** Due to, characterized by, or subject to chance; accidental, fortuitous. LME. ▸†**b** Non-essential. LME–M17.

W. RALEIGH That which seemeth most casual and subject to fortune, is yet disposed by the ordinance of God. MILTON Where casual fire had wasted woods.

2 Occurring unpredictably; irregular; occasional. LME.

CLARENDON Both the known and casual Revenue. J. CARY The few shillings a week earned . . at casual and temporary jobs.

†**3** Frail, precarious, unreliable. E16–E18.

J. WORLIDGE In case . . the weather prove casual.

4 Occurring or brought about without design or premeditation; having no specific plan, method, motivation, or interest; performed or entered into casually; *spec.* designating or pertaining to sex between individuals who are not regular or established sexual partners. M17.

D. G. MITCHELL I made some casual remark about the weather. J. CONRAD A casual stroll or a casual spree on shore. CONAN DOYLE A problem without a solution may interest the student, but can hardly fail to annoy the casual reader.

5 Of a person, action, etc.: unmethodical, careless; unconcerned, uninterested; informal, unceremonious. L19. ▸**b** Of an item of clothing: suitable for informal wear. M20.

G. GREENE It needed only a casual inspection to realise how badly the office had been kept. A. LURIE We were both very strained, though we pretended to be casual. J. IRVING He puts up a casual hand to catch it.

– SPECIAL COLLOCATIONS: **casual acquaintance**: whom one met incidentally or whom one meets only occasionally. **casual labourer**: without permanent employment, working when the chance comes. **casual pauper**, **casual poor** *hist.*: receiving occasional relief, admitted temporarily to a workhouse, casual ward, etc. **casual ward** *hist.* a place for the temporary accommodation of vagrants. **casual water** GOLF a temporary accumulation of water not constituting one of the recognized hazards of the course.
▸ **B** *noun*. †**1** A chance. Usu. in *pl.* LME–M17.
2 A casual item of income. *rare*. E19.
3 A casual labourer. M19.
4 A casual pauper. Now *arch.* or *hist.* M19.
5 An introduced plant, animal, etc., which fails to establish itself. L19.
6 An item of casual clothing; *spec.* a low-heeled slip-on shoe. Usu. in *pl.* M20.
7 A hooligan who dresses conventionally in casual clothing. *slang*. L20.
■ **casualism** *noun* the doctrine that all things exist or happen by chance L19. **casually** *adverb* LME. **casualness** *noun* L19.

casuality /kaʒjʊˈalɪti, -zj-/ *noun*. Now *rare*. E16.
[ORIGIN French *casualité* from medieval Latin *casualitas*, from *casualis*: see CASUAL, -ITY.]
†**1** A casual item of income. E16–L17.
†**2** (A) chance; *esp.* an unfortunate accident. M16–L18.
3 The quality or state of being casual, casualness. L19.

casualty /ˈkaʒjʊəlti, -zj-/ *noun*. LME.
[ORIGIN Alt. of medieval Latin *casualitas* (see CASUALITY) after *penalty*, *royalty*, etc.: see -TY¹.]
1 Chance. Now *rare*. LME.

S. JOHNSON Combinations of skilful genius with happy casualty.

2 A chance occurrence; an accident, a mishap, a disaster. LME. ▸**b** A person killed or injured in war or an accident; a thing lost or destroyed. M19.

SHAKES. *Per.* Time hath rooted out my parentage, And to the world and awkward casualties Bound me in servitude. SWIFT Several casualties have happened this week, and the bill of mortality is very much increased. **b** S. SASSOON About 40 casualties; only 4 killed. J. T. STORY His own father's wool business was a casualty of the war years.

3 An incidental charge or payment; *spec.* (SCOTS LAW, now *hist.*) a payment due from a vassal in certain contingencies. LME.
†**4** Subjection to chance, uncertainty. E16–E19.
5 In full ***casualty department***, ***casualty ward***. The part of a hospital where casualties are attended to. M19.

casuarina /kasjʊəˈriːnə/ *noun*. L18.
[ORIGIN mod. Latin, from *casuarius* cassowary (from resemblance of the branches to the bird's feathers).]
A tree of the genus *Casuarina* (family Casuarinaceae), native to Australia and parts of SE Asia, with jointed branches resembling gigantic horsetail plants.

casuist /ˈkazjʊɪst, -ʒj-/ *noun*. E17.
[ORIGIN French *casuiste* from Spanish *casuista* from mod. Latin, from Latin *casus* CASE *noun*¹: see -IST.]
A person, esp. a theologian, who resolves cases of conscience, duty, etc.; a sophist, a quibbler.
■ **casuˈistic**, **casuˈistical** *adjectives* of or pertaining to casuists or casuistry M17. **casuˈistically** *adverb* L17. **casuistry** *noun* the reasoning of the casuist; the resolution of cases of conscience by the application of general rules to particular instances, freq. disclosing a conflict of duties; sophistry: E18.

†**casule** *noun*. OE–E19.
[ORIGIN (Old French from) late Latin *casula* hooded cloak: see CHASUBLE.]
= CHASUBLE.

casus belli /ˌkɑːsʊs ˈbɛliː, ˌkeɪsəs ˈbɛlʌɪ/ *noun phr.* Pl. same. M19.
[ORIGIN from Latin *casus* CASE *noun*¹ + *belli* genit. of *bellum* war.]
An act or situation justifying or precipitating war.

casus foederis /ˌkɑːsʊs ˈfɔɪdərɪs, ˌkeɪsəs ˈfiːdərɪs/ *noun phr.* Pl. same. L18.
[ORIGIN from Latin *casus* CASE *noun*¹ + *foederis* genit. of *foedus* treaty.]
An event which, under the terms of a treaty of alliance, entitles one of the allies to help from the other(s).

C

CAT /kat/ *abbreviation.*
1 Chiefly *hist.* College of Advanced Technology.
2 MEDICINE. Computed (or computerized) axial (or computer-assisted) tomography (cf. **CT**).

cat /kat/ *noun*[1].
[ORIGIN Old English *catt* masc. (= Old Norse *kọttr*), *catte* fem. (= Old Frisian, Middle Dutch *katte*, Dutch *kat*, Old High German *kazza*, German *katze*), reinforced in Middle English by Anglo-Norman, Old Northern French *cat* var. of Old French & mod. French *chat* from late Latin *cattus*.]
1 An agile, partly nocturnal, quadrupedal carnivorous mammal, *Felis catus*, with smooth fur and retractile claws, long domesticated as a pet. OE. ▸**b** Any of numerous related animals constituting the family Felidae, including the lion, tiger, leopard, lynx, etc. Also, any of various catlike animals of other taxa. M16. ▸**c** In full ***catfish***: (*a*) any of various mainly freshwater fishes of the order Siluriformes, having several sensory barbels and scaleless bodies; (*b*) = ***wolf fish*** s.v. WOLF *noun*; (*c*) a cuttlefish or other cephalopod. L16.
Maltese cat, Manx cat, Persian cat, Siamese cat, tortoiseshell cat, tabby cat, etc. **b *bearcat, big cat, bobcat, civet cat, native cat, polecat, sea cat, tiger cat, wild cat***, etc.
2 *fig.* A spiteful person, *esp.* (*derog.*) a spiteful or malicious woman; a prostitute (*obsolete* exc. in ***cathouse*** (a) below). ME. ▸**b** A person, a fellow (usu. of a specified kind); a jazz enthusiast. *slang.* E20.

b J. CAREW Was a time when that cat would run a mile if a woman smiled at him

b *hep-cat*: see HEP *adjective*. ***hip-cat***: see HIP *adjective*.
3 A small piece of wood tapering at each end, used in the game of tipcat; the game itself. LME.
4 *hist.* A movable penthouse used by besiegers for protection. L15.
5 NAUTICAL. (In full ***cathead***, †***cat's head***) a horizontal beam extending from each side of a ship's bow for raising and carrying an anchor; (in full ***cat-purchase***, ***cat-tackle***) a tackle used in hoisting an anchor to the cathead. L15.
6 *hist.* In full ***cat-o'-nine-tails***. A rope whip with nine knotted lashes for flogging sailors, soldiers, or criminals. L17.
7 A double tripod with six legs so placed that it always rests on three legs. E19.
– PHRASES: ***bell the cat***: see BELL *verb*[3]. **enough to make a cat laugh** extremely amusing. ***fat cat***: see FAT *adjective*. ***grin like a Cheshire cat***: see CHESHIRE 2. ***KILKENNY cat***. **let the cat out of the bag** reveal a secret, esp. involuntarily. **like a cat on hot bricks** & vars., (moving) quickly and uneasily. ***like a scalded cat***: see SCALDED *adjective*[1]. **like something the cat brought in** bedraggled, unkempt. ***no room to swing a cat in***: see ROOM *noun*[1]. **not a cat in hell's chance** no chance whatever. ***not room to swing a cat in***: see ROOM *noun*[1]. **play cat and mouse** toy with a weaker party; engage in prolonged wary manoeuvres. **put a cat among the pigeons**, **put the cat among the pigeons** create a violent intrusion, cause a severe upset. ***queen cat***: see QUEEN *noun* 6. **rain cats and dogs** rain very hard. **see which way the cat jumps** wait for an opinion or result to declare itself. ***shoot the cat***: see SHOOT *verb*. ***singed cat***: see SINGE *verb* 1. ***skin the cat***: see SKIN *verb*. ***suffering cats!***: see SUFFERING *ppl adjective* 3. ***tame cat***: see TAME *adjective* 1. ***tear a cat, tear the cat***: see TEAR *verb*[1]. **turn cat in pan, turn the cat in the pan** †(*a*) reverse the order or nature of things, make black seem white; (*b*) change sides, be a turncoat. ***whip the cat***: see WHIP *verb*.
– COMB.: **cat-and-dog** *adjective* quarrelsome, inharmonious; **cat-and-mouse** *adjective* involving playing cat and mouse (see above); **catbird** (*a*) any of various birds with mewing cries; *esp.* a N. American mockingbird, *Dumetella carolinensis*, with slaty-black plumage; (*Austral.*) any of a number of bowerbirds; (*b*) ***the catbird seat*** [the name of a short story (1942) by James Thurber], *US* a superior or advantageous position; **cat burglar**: who climbs a wall to enter an upper storey; **cat door** a small door which can be pushed open by a cat, enabling its entrances and exits; **catfight** *colloq.* a fight between women; ***catfish***: see sense 1c above (***walking catfish***: see WALKING *ppl adjective*); **cat flap** = ***cat door*** above; **cat foot** a dog's compact round foot, with the toes well knuckled up; **cat-foot** *verb trans.* with *it* (chiefly *N. Amer.*) walk stealthily or noiselessly; **cat-footed** *adjective* stealthy in movement; **cat-haul** *noun & verb* (*US*) (*a*) *noun* a punishment in which a cat is caused to maul the victim; (*b*) *verb trans.* subject to this punishment; *fig.* examine stringently; ***cathead***: see sense 5 above. **cat-hole** (*a*) a hole large enough to let a cat through; (*b*) NAUTICAL a hole at the stern of a ship, through which a cable or hawser can be passed; **cathouse** (*a*) a brothel; (*b*) a house for felines in a zoo; **cat ice** thin ice unsupported by water; **cat-lap** *slang* slops, weak tea, etc.; **catlick** *colloq.* a perfunctory wash; ***cat litter***: see LITTER *noun* 3. **catmint** [after medieval Latin *herba catti* or *cattaria*] an aromatic plant of the large genus *Nepeta*, of the mint family, esp. *N. cataria*, whose smell is irresistible to cats; **catnap** *noun & verb intrans.* (have) a brief sleep in a chair etc.; **catnip** [*nip*, var. of NEP *noun*[1]] catmint; ***cat-o'-nine-tails***: see sense 6 above; ***cat-purchase***: see sense 5 above; **cat's cradle** (a children's game with) string forming patterns held between the fingers and passed between players; **cat's ear** any of several composite plants constituting the genus *Hypochaeris*, with heads of yellow ligulate flowers and leaves in rosettes; esp. *H. radicata*, a common plant of grassland; **cat's foot** *fig.* †(*a*) = CAT'S PAW 2; (*b*) ground ivy, *Glechoma hederacea*; (*c*) a hill plant, *Antennaria dioica*, of the composite family, with heads of inconspicuous white flowers; **cat's head** *fig.* †(*a*) see sense 5 above; †(*b*) a variety of apple; (*c*) (now *rare*) = ***beakhead*** (c) s.v. BEAK *noun*[1]; †**cat-silver** mica; **cat's-meat** horseflesh or other meat prepared and sold as food for cats; **cat's meow**, **cat's pyjamas** *slang* (orig. & chiefly *US*) *the* acme of excellence, the cat's whiskers (see below); **catstick** a stick used in tipcat and trapball; **catsuit** an all-in-one, usu. close-fitting, garment with trouser legs; **cat's whisker** (*a*) (in *pl.*) *slang* (orig. *US*) *the* acme of excellence (cf. ***cat's meow***, ***cat's pyjamas*** above); (*b*) a fine adjustable wire in a crystal wireless receiver; ***cat-tackle***: see sense 5 above; ***cattail***: see CAT'S TAIL; **catwalk** a narrow footway or platform; **cat-witted** *adjective* (*arch.*) petty-minded and spiteful.
■ **catlike** *adjective* resembling (that of) a cat; stealthy; agile: L16.

cat /kat/ *noun*[2]. *obsolete* exc. (perh.) in CATBOAT. L17.
[ORIGIN Perh. same word as CAT *noun*[1]: cf. medieval Latin *catta* a kind of ship, Old French *chat* merchant ship.]
A strong merchant sailing vessel with a narrow stern, projecting quarters, and a deep waist, formerly used esp. in the coal and timber trade on the NE coast of England.

cat /kat/ *noun*[3]. *colloq.* L19.
[ORIGIN Abbreviation.]
= CATAMARAN *noun* 1.

cat /kat/ *adjective & noun*[4]. *colloq.* M20.
[ORIGIN Abbreviation of CATALYTIC *adjective*.]
▸ **A** *adjective*. ***cat cracker***, ***cat cracking***, (an installation for) the catalytic cracking of hydrocarbons. M20.
▸ **B** *noun*. = *CATALYTIC* ***converter***. L20.

cat /kat/ *verb trans.* Infl. **-tt-**. L16.
[ORIGIN from CAT *noun*[1].]
1 NAUTICAL. Raise (the anchor) from the surface of the water to the cathead. L16.
2 Flog with a cat-o'-nine-tails. M19.

cata- /ˈkatə/ *prefix*. Before a vowel or *h* usu. **cat-**. Also **k-**.
[ORIGIN Greek *kata*.]
Used in words adopted from Greek and in English words modelled on these, in senses (*a*) down, in position or in quantity or degree, as ***catadromous***, ***catalysis***, ***catastrophe***; (*b*) amiss, mis-, as ***catachresis***, ***catatonia***; (*c*) against, alongside, as ***catadioptric***, ***catechize***; (*d*) thoroughly, entirely, as ***catalepsy***, ***catalogue***.

catabaptist /katəˈbaptɪst/ *noun*. M16.
[ORIGIN medieval Greek *katabaptistēs* administrator of irregular or schismatic baptism, from *katabaptizein*, formed as CATA-, BAPTIZE.]
hist. (A 16th- and 17th-cent. nickname for) an opponent of the orthodox view of baptism.

catabatic *adjective* see KATABATIC.

catabolic /katəˈbɒlɪk/ *adjective*. Also **k-**. L19.
[ORIGIN formed as CATABOLISM + -IC.]
BIOLOGY. Pertaining to, involved in, or characterized by catabolism. Opp. ANABOLIC.

catabolism /kəˈtabəlɪz(ə)m/ *noun*. Also **k-**. L19.
[ORIGIN from Greek *katabolē* throwing down, ult. formed as CATA- + *ballein* throw: see -ISM.]
BIOLOGY. Destructive metabolism with the release of energy; the breakdown of complex substances within the body. Opp. ANABOLISM.
■ **catabolite** *noun* a product of catabolism M20. **catabolize** *verb trans.* break down by catabolism M20.

catabothron *noun* var. of KATAVOTHRON.

catacaustic /katəˈkɔːstɪk/ *adjective & noun*. E18.
[ORIGIN from CATA- + CAUSTIC.]
PHYSICS. ▸**A** *adjective*. Of a curve or surface: formed by the intersection of rays of light reflected from a curved surface. E18.
▸ **B** *noun*. A catacaustic curve or surface. Cf. DIACAUSTIC. E18.

catachresis /katəˈkriːsɪs/ *noun*. Pl. **-chreses** /-ˈkriːsiːz/. M16.
[ORIGIN Latin *catachresis* from Greek *katakhrēsis*, from *katakhrēsthai* to misuse, formed as CATA- + *khrēsthai* use.]
(An instance of) the incorrect use of words.
■ **catachrestic** /-ˈkrɛst-, -ˈkriː-/ *adjective* (of a word etc.) misused, misapplied; of the nature of catachresis: M17. **catachrestical** /-ˈkrɛst-, -ˈkriː-/ *adjective* E17. **catachrestically** /-ˈkrɛst-, -ˈkriː-/ *adverb* E17.

cataclasis /katəˈkleɪsɪs/ *noun*. Pl. **-clases** /-ˈkleɪsiːz/. M20.
[ORIGIN from CATA- + Greek *klasis* breaking.]
GEOLOGY. (A) crushing of rock.

cataclasm /ˈkatəklaz(ə)m/ *noun*. E19.
[ORIGIN Greek *kataklasma*, from *kataklan* break down, formed as CATA- + *klan* break.]
A violent break or disruption.

cataclastic /katəˈklastɪk/ *adjective*. L19.
[ORIGIN from CATA- + CLASTIC.]
GEOLOGY. Pertaining to, involving, or formed by crushing of rock.

cataclysm /ˈkatəklɪz(ə)m/ *noun*. E17.
[ORIGIN French *cataclysme* from Latin *cataclysmos* from Greek *kataklusmos* deluge, formed as CATA- + *kluzein* to wash.]
A violent geological or meteorological event; *the* Flood (in Genesis); *fig.* a political or social upheaval.
■ **cataˈclysmal** *adjective* M19. **cataˈclysmic** *adjective* M19. **cataˈclysmically** *adverb* L19.

catacomb /ˈkatəkuːm, -kəʊm/ *noun*. OE.
[ORIGIN Old French & mod. French *catacombes* from late Latin *catacumbas* = sense 1 below (so named in 5th cent. AD): ult. origin unknown.]
1 In *pl.* & †*sing.* An underground cemetery consisting of a subterranean gallery with recesses for tombs, orig. *spec.* the subterranean cemetery of St Sebastian near Rome. OE. ▸**b** *sing.* A single crypt or gallery in such works. *rare.* E18.
2 *transf.* A (wine) cellar. L18.

catacoustics /katəˈkuːstɪks/ *noun*. Now *rare* or *obsolete*. L17.
[ORIGIN from CATA- + ACOUSTICS.]
The science of reflected sound. Cf. DIACOUSTICS.

catadioptric /ˌkatədʌɪˈɒptrɪk/ *adjective*. E18.
[ORIGIN from CATA- + DIOPTRIC *adjective*.]
Pertaining to or involving both the reflection and the refraction of light.
■ **catadioptrical** *adjective* L17.

catadromous /katəˈdrəʊməs/ *adjective*. L19.
[ORIGIN from CATA- after ANADROMOUS *adjective*.]
Of fish: that descend rivers to lower reaches or to the sea to spawn.

†**catadupe** *noun*. L16–M18.
[ORIGIN French *catad(o)upe* from Latin *catadupa* (pl.) from Greek *katadoupoi* (pl.), formed as CATA- + *doupos* thud.]
A cataract, a waterfall, orig. of the Nile.

catafalque /ˈkatəfalk/ *noun*. Also (now *rare*) **catafalco** /katəˈfalkəʊ/, pl. **-o(e)s**. M17.
[ORIGIN French from Italian *catafalco* of unknown origin: cf. SCAFFOLD *noun*.]
1 A decorated structure fashioned so as to carry the coffin or effigy of a distinguished person during a funeral service or for a lying in state. M17.
2 A structure on which a coffin is drawn in procession. M19.

catagmatic /katəgˈmatɪk/ *noun & adjective*. Now *rare* or *obsolete*. M17.
[ORIGIN French †*catagmatique* from Greek *katagmatikos*, from *katagma* fracture: see -IC.]
MEDICINE. ▸**A** *noun*. A medicine used in healing fractures. M17.
▸ **B** *adjective*. Of or pertaining to fractures or their treatment. L17.

†**Cataian** *noun*. L16–M17.
[ORIGIN Var. of CATHAYAN *noun*.]
A swindler, a thief, a criminal.

Catalan /ˈkatəlan/ *noun & adjective*. LME.
[ORIGIN French from Provençal & Spanish, from Spanish *Cataluña*, Catalan *Catalunya* Catalonia (see below): see -AN.]
▸ **A** *noun*. **1** A native or inhabitant of Catalonia, a province of NE Spain, once an independent principality. LME.
2 The Romance language of Catalonia. L18.
▸ **B** *attrib.* or as *adjective*. Of or pertaining to Catalonia, its people, or their language. M19.
■ **Catalanist** *adjective & noun* (a person) favouring the independence of Catalonia E20.

catalase /ˈkatəleɪz/ *noun*. E20.
[ORIGIN from CATALYSIS *noun* + -ASE.]
BIOCHEMISTRY. An enzyme which catalyses the reduction of hydrogen peroxide.

catalectic /katəˈlɛktɪk/ *adjective & noun*. L16.
[ORIGIN Late Latin *catalecticus* from Greek *katalēktikos*, from *katalēgein* leave off, formed as CATA- + *lēgein* cease: see -IC.]
PROSODY. (A line or verse) lacking one syllable in the last foot.

catalepsy /ˈkat(ə)lɛpsi/ *noun*. LME.
[ORIGIN French *catalepsie* or late Latin *catalepsia*, from Greek *katalēpsis*, from *katalambanein* seize upon: see CATA-, -Y[3].]
1 MEDICINE. A condition of trance or seizure with loss of sensation or consciousness and abnormal maintenance of posture. LME.
†**2** PHILOSOPHY. Comprehension, apprehension. M17–M19.
■ **cataˈleptic** *adjective & noun* (*a*) *adjective* pertaining to, affected by, or of the nature of catalepsy; (*b*) *noun* a person suffering from catalepsy: L17.

catalexis /katəˈlɛksɪs/ *noun*. M19.
[ORIGIN Greek *katalēxis* termination, from *katalēgein*: see CATALECTIC.]
PROSODY. Absence of a syllable in the last foot of a line or verse.

catallactic /katəˈlaktɪk/ *adjective & noun*. M19.
[ORIGIN Greek *katallaktikos* (not in this sense), from *katallassein*, formed as CATA- + *allassein* change, exchange: see -IC.]
▸ **A** *adjective*. Pertaining to exchange of money etc. M19.
▸ **B** *noun*. In *pl.* (treated as *sing.*). Economics as the science of exchange. M19.

catalo *noun* var. of CATTALO.

catalogue /ˈkat(ə)lɒg/ *noun & verb*. Also ***-log**. LME.
[ORIGIN Old French & mod. French from late Latin *catalogus* from Greek *katalogos*, from *katalegein* pick out, enrol, formed as CATA- + *legein* choose.]
▸ **A** *noun*. **1** A list, register, or complete enumeration; now *spec.* one systematically or methodically arranged, often with brief particulars or descriptions aiding identification etc. LME.
Liberian catalogue: see LIBERIAN *adjective*[1]. ***thematic catalogue***: see THEMATIC *adjective* 2.
2 *fig.* An enumeration, series, etc. L16.

D. LODGE Mrs Zapp . . recited a catalogue of her husband's sins to me.

▸ **B** *verb trans.* **1** Make a catalogue or list of. L16.

J. STEINBECK His mind was cataloguing weak points and suspicious things about the car.

2 Inscribe or insert in a catalogue. M17.

HOR. WALPOLE If religion is thrown into the quarrel, the most innocent acts are catalogued with sins.

■ **cataloguer** *noun* M19. **cataloguist** *noun* L18. **cataloguize** *verb trans.* = CATALOGUE *verb* E17.

catalogue raisonné /ˌkat(ə)lɒg reɪzɒˈneɪ, *foreign* katalɔg rɛzɔne/ *noun phr.* Pl. **-s -s** (pronounced same). L18.
[ORIGIN French = reasoned catalogue.]
A descriptive catalogue with explanations or comments.

Catalonian /katəˈləʊnɪən/ *adjective & noun.* L16.
[ORIGIN from *Catalonia* (see CATALAN) + -AN.]
= CATALAN.

catalpa /kəˈtalpə/ *noun.* M18.
[ORIGIN Creek.]
An American or Asian tree of the genus *Catalpa*, of the bignonia family, with heart-shaped leaves, trumpet-shaped flowers, and long pods.

catalyse /ˈkat(ə)lʌɪz/ *verb trans.* Also ***-lyze**. L19.
[ORIGIN from CATALYSIS after *analyse*.]
CHEMISTRY. Accelerate or promote (a reaction or process) by catalysis.

fig.: *Nature* The technology bred of science has catalysed stupendous economic growth.

■ **catalysed** *adjective* (**a**) that has been catalysed; (**b**) (of a motor vehicle) having a catalytic converter: M20. **catalyser** *noun* a catalyst E20.

catalysis /kəˈtalɪsɪs/ *noun.* Pl. **-lyses** /-lɪsiːz/. M17.
[ORIGIN mod. Latin from Greek *katalusis*, from *kataluein* dissolve, formed as CATA- + *luein* set free.]
†**1** Dissolution, destruction. M–L17.
2 CHEMISTRY. The action or effect of a substance in increasing the rate of a reaction without itself being consumed; an instance of this. M19.
negative catalysis an analogous slowing of a reaction.

catalyst /ˈkat(ə)lɪst/ *noun.* E20.
[ORIGIN from CATALYSIS after *analyst*.]
CHEMISTRY. A substance which brings about catalysis. Also *fig.*, an agent that facilitates a change.

catalytic /katəˈlɪtɪk/ *adjective.* M19.
[ORIGIN from CATALYSIS after *analysis*, *analytic* etc.]
Of the nature of, involving, or pertaining to catalysis; acting as a catalyst.
catalytic converter a device fitted in the exhaust system of some motor vehicles which converts pollutant gases into less harmful ones by catalytic action. **catalytic cracker** a device for cracking petroleum oils by catalysis.
■ **catalytically** *adverb* M19.

catamaran /katəməˈran/ *noun.* E17.
[ORIGIN Tamil *kaṭṭu-maram* lit. 'tied wood'.]
1 A raft or float of logs tied side by side with the longest in the middle; a raft of two boats fastened side by side; a boat with two hulls side by side. E17.
2 *hist.* A naval weapon consisting of a floating chest packed with gunpowder. E19.
3 A quarrelsome woman. *colloq.* M19.

catamenia /katəˈmiːnɪə/ *noun pl.* Now *rare* or *obsolete*. M18.
[ORIGIN Greek, neut. pl. of *katamēnios* monthly, formed as CATA- + *mēn* month.]
The menstrual discharge.
■ **catamenial** *adjective* M19.

catamite /ˈkatəmʌɪt/ *noun.* L16.
[ORIGIN Latin *catamitus* (through Etruscan *catmite*) from Greek *Ganumēdēs* GANYMEDE.]
A boy kept for homosexual practices; the passive partner in anal intercourse.

catamount /ˈkatəmaʊnt/ *noun.* M17.
[ORIGIN Abbreviation of CATAMOUNTAIN.]
†**1** = CATAMOUNTAIN 1. M17–M18.
2 The puma. *N. Amer.* L18.

catamountain /katəˈmaʊntɪn/ *noun.* Also **cat o' mountain**. Orig. †**cat of the mountain**. LME.
[ORIGIN Rendering Latin *pardus*, Greek *pardos* PARD *noun*[1].]
1 A leopard, puma, or similar cat. LME.
2 *fig.* A wild aggressive person. E17.

catananche /katəˈnaŋki/ *noun.* E19.
[ORIGIN mod. Latin from Latin *catanance* plant used in love potions, from Greek *katanagkē*, formed as CATA- + *anagkē* compulsion.]
A plant of the genus *Catananche*, of the composite family, with blue or yellow flowers, native to the Mediterranean region.

catapan /ˈkatəpan/ *noun.* E18.
[ORIGIN medieval Latin *catapanus*, *cate-* from Greek *katepanō tōn axiōmatōn* (he who is) placed over the dignities.]
The governor of Calabria and Apulia under the Byzantine emperors.

cataphatic /katəˈfatɪk/ *adjective.* M19.
[ORIGIN Greek *kataphatikos* affirmative, from *kataphasis* affirmation, formed as CATA- + *phanai* speak: see -IC.]
THEOLOGY. Of knowledge of God: obtained through defining God with positive statements. Opp. APOPHATIC.

cataphora /kəˈtaf(ə)rə/ *noun.* M16.
[ORIGIN In sense 1 from Greek *kataphora*, formed as CATA- + *pherein* carry; in sense 2 from CATA- after ANAPHORA.]
1 MEDICINE. (An attack of) pathological sleepiness. Now *rare*. M16.
2 LINGUISTICS. The use of an expression which refers to or stands for a later word or group of words. L20.

cataphoresis /katəfəˈriːsɪs/ *noun.* L19.
[ORIGIN from CATA- + Greek *phorēsis* being carried.]
1 MEDICINE. The use of electricity to enable medicinal substances to pass through the skin. L19.
2 = ELECTROPHORESIS 1. M20.
■ **cataphoretic** /-ˈrɛt-/ *adjective* L19.

cataphoric /katəˈfɒrɪk/ *adjective.* L19.
[ORIGIN Greek *kataphorikos*, formed as CATAPHORESIS: see -IC.]
1 Of or pertaining to cataphoresis. L19.
2 LINGUISTICS. Referring to or standing for a later word or group of words. L20.

cataphract /ˈkatəfrakt/ *noun.* L16.
[ORIGIN Latin *cataphractes* (sense 1), *-tus* (sense 2) from Greek *kataphraktēs*, *-tos*, from *kataphrassein* clothe in mail.]
1 *hist.* An ancient coat of mail. L16.
2 A soldier in full armour. L17.

cataplasm /ˈkatəplaz(ə)m/ *noun.* LME.
[ORIGIN Old French & mod. French *cataplasme* or late Latin *cataplasma* from Greek *kataplasma*, from *kataplassein* plaster over, formed as CATA- + *plassein* to plaster.]
A plaster; a poultice.

cataplexy /ˈkatəplɛksi/ *noun.* L19.
[ORIGIN from Greek *kataplēxis* stupefaction, from *kataplēssein*, formed as CATA- + *plēssein* to strike.]
A sudden temporary paralysis due to fright or other strong emotion.
■ **cataˈplectic** *adjective* L19.

catapult /ˈkatəpʌlt/ *noun & verb.* L16.
[ORIGIN Old French & mod. French *catapulte* or Latin *catapulta* = Greek *katapeltēs*, formed as CATA- + var. of base of *pallein* hurl.]
▶ **A** *noun.* **1** *hist.* A military engine worked by levers and twisted rope for discharging darts, stones, etc. L16.
2 A contrivance of a forked stick and elastic for shooting small stones etc. M19.
3 A mechanical contrivance for launching a glider or other aircraft, esp. from the deck of a ship. E20.
▶ **B** *verb.* **1** *verb trans.* Launch with a catapult; hurl (as) from a catapult; fling forcibly (*lit.* & *fig.*). M19.
2 *verb intrans.* Move (as if) from a catapult. E20.

cataract /ˈkatərakt/ *noun & verb.* LME.
[ORIGIN Latin *cataracta* waterfall, floodgate, portcullis, from Greek *kataraktēs*, *-rrh-* down-rushing (water etc.), prob. from *katarassein*, formed as CATA- + *arassein* strike, smash. In sense 2 app. fig. use of sense 'portcullis'.]
▶ **A** *noun.* †**1** In *pl.* Floodgates, *spec.* of heaven (*Genesis* 7:11, 8:2). LME–L17. ▶†**b** *transf.* A waterspout. M16–M17.
2 MEDICINE. (A condition of) partial or complete opacity of the lens of the eye. LME.
3 A waterfall, *spec.* a large and sheer one; a torrent. L16.
†**4** A portcullis; the grating of a window. *rare*. M17–M19.
▶ **B** *verb.* **1** *verb trans.* Pour in a torrent. *rare*. L18.
2 *verb intrans.* Fall in or like a cataract. M19.
■ **cataractal** *adjective* of the nature of a cataract L19. †**cataractic** *adjective* (*rare*) cataractal L17–E19. **cataractous** /ˈkatəraktəs, katəˈraktəs/ *adjective* of or affected by cataract of the eye E19.

catarrh /kəˈtɑː/ *noun.* E16.
[ORIGIN French *catarrhe* from late Latin *catarrhus* from Greek *katarrhous*, from *katarrhein* run down, formed as CATA- + *rhein* flow.]
1 (An) excessive discharge of mucus from inflamed membranes, esp. in the nose and throat; (an) inflammation producing this. E16.
†**2** Cerebral effusion or haemorrhage; apoplexy. M16–E18.
■ **catarrhal** *adjective* of the nature of, involving, pertaining to, or affected with catarrh M17. **catarrhous** *adjective* = CATARRHAL L16.

catarrhine /ˈkatərʌɪn/ *noun & adjective.* M19.
[ORIGIN from CATA- + Greek *rhinos*, *rhis* nose.]
ZOOLOGY. ▶ **A** *noun.* A catarrhine primate. M19.
▶ **B** *adjective.* Pertaining to or designating a primate having nostrils close together and directed downwards (as in all the apes and Old World monkeys). M19.

catasetum /katəˈsiːtəm/ *noun.* E19.
[ORIGIN mod. Latin, formed as CATA- + Latin *seta* bristle (on account of the form of the rostellum).]
An epiphytic orchid of the genus *Catasetum*, native to tropical America.

catasta /kəˈtastə/ *noun.* Pl. **-stae** /-stiː/. M17.
[ORIGIN Latin = scaffold, stage.]
hist. A block on which slaves were exposed for sale.

catastasis /kəˈtastəsɪs/ *noun.* Pl. **-ases** /-əsiːz/. M16.
[ORIGIN Greek *katastasis* settling, appointment, formed as CATA- + STASIS.]
The third part of the ancient drama, in which the action is heightened for the catastrophe.

catastrophe /kəˈtastrəfi/ *noun.* M16.
[ORIGIN Latin *catastropha* from Greek *katastrophē* overturning, sudden turn, from *katastrephein*, formed as CATA- + *strephein* turn.]
1 The denouement of a play, esp. a tragedy; the final resolution of a novel etc. M16.
2 A disastrous conclusion; overthrow, ruin, calamitous fate. L16. ▶†**b** The buttocks. *joc. rare* (Shakes.). Only in L16.
3 A revolutionary event. L17. ▶**b** GEOLOGY. (An event causing) a sudden upheaval or discontinuity in the stratigraphic record. M19.
4 A sudden, widespread, or noteworthy disaster; an extreme misfortune. M18.

World Monitor Could a volcano trigger a global catastrophe?

– PHRASES: ***ultraviolet catastrophe***: see ULTRAVIOLET *adjective* 2.
– COMB.: **catastrophe theory** MATH. the topological description of systems which display abrupt discontinuous change.
■ **catastrophic** /-ˈstrɒfɪk/ *adjective* of or pertaining to a catastrophe; disastrous, dreadful: M19. **cataˈstrophical** *adjective* = CATASTROPHIC E19. **cataˈstrophically** *adverb* L19.

catastrophism /kəˈtastrəfɪz(ə)m/ *noun.* M19.
[ORIGIN from CATASTROPHE *noun* + -ISM.]
Belief in the occurrence of catastrophes; *esp.* the theory that geological or biological changes have occurred in sudden violent and unusual events (cf. UNIFORMITARIANISM).
■ **catastrophist** *noun & adjective* (**a**) *noun* a person who holds such a belief or theory; (**b**) *adjective* of or pertaining to catastrophism or catastrophists: M19.

catatonia /katəˈtəʊnɪə/ *noun.* Also †**k-**. L19.
[ORIGIN from CATA- + Greek *tonos* TONE *noun* + -IA[1].]
MEDICINE. Abnormal motor behaviour (esp. episodes of catalepsy or overactivity), associated esp. with a form of schizophrenia; catalepsy.
■ **catatoniac** *noun* a person affected with catatonia L19. **catatonic** /-ˈtɒnɪk/ *adjective & noun* pertaining to or characterized by catatonia; (a person) affected with catatonia: E20.

catavothron *noun* etc.: see KATAVOTHRON.

catawampus /katəˈwɒmpəs/ *adjective & noun. dial. & slang* (chiefly *N. Amer.*). As adjective also **-ous**. M19.
[ORIGIN Unknown.]
▶ **A** *adjective.* Fierce, destructive; askew, awry. M19.
▶ **B** *noun.* A fierce imaginary animal. M19.

catawba /kəˈtɔːbə/ *noun.* E19.
[ORIGIN from the *Catawba*, a river in the Carolinas, USA.]
(White wine from) a N. American variety of grape.

catboat /ˈkatbəʊt/ *noun.* L19.
[ORIGIN Perh. from CAT *noun*[2] + BOAT *noun*.]
A sailing boat with a single mast placed well forward and carrying only one sail.

catcall /ˈkatkɔːl/ *noun & verb.* M17.
[ORIGIN from CAT *noun*[1] + CALL *noun*.]
▶ **A** *noun.* **1** *hist.* A squeaking instrument or kind of whistle used esp. at a theatre to express impatience or disapproval. M17.
2 A shrill whistle (now usu. with the lips, formerly on the instrument) expressing impatience or disapproval at a theatre, public meeting, etc. M18.
▶ **B** *verb.* **1** *verb trans.* Subject to catcalls. L17.
2 *verb intrans.* Sound or make a catcall. M18.

catch /katʃ/ *noun*[1]. LME.
[ORIGIN from the verb.]
1 The amount of fish etc. caught at one time. LME.
2 That by which anything is caught and held, *esp.* a contrivance for checking the motion of a door. LME.
†**3** Real tennis. *Scot.* L15–L16.
4 The act or fact of catching. L16.
†**on the catch** in wait, on the lookout.
5 A thing or person caught or worth catching, esp. in matrimony by virtue of wealth, social position, etc. L16.
6 MUSIC. A round for three or more equal voices, occas. so devised as to produce punning or other humorous verbal combinations. L16.
†**7** A fragment or scrap of anything caught up; a snatch of song etc. Also, a short sight, a glimpse, a view. E17–M19.

J. GLANVILL We retain a catch of these pretty stories. S. JOHNSON Such houses as had any catch of the river.

8 A cunning question, esp. containing an element of deception or surprise; a concealed difficulty or drawback in a proposal or course of action; a snag. L17.

W. FREKE Most of their arguments . . are nothing but a few empty Catches in mere words. A. NIN I thought . . there must be a catch in it.

catch-22 [from a novel (1961) by J. Heller] a condition or consequence that precludes success, a dilemma where the victim cannot win.
9 In cricket, baseball, etc., a chance of or success in catching the ball, esp. (in cricket) so as to dismiss the batsman. Also with qualifying adjective: a player who is *good* etc. at catching the ball. L18.
10 A check or impediment in the voice, breath, throat, etc. L19.

A. HAILEY A catch in his voice, with tears not far away.

Scotch catch: see SCOTCH *adjective*.

catch /katʃ/ *noun*[2]. *obsolete* exc. *dial.* LME.
[ORIGIN Prob. from CATCH *verb* or *noun*[1]: cf. KETCH *noun*.]
A small boat; a ketch.

catch /katʃ/ *verb*. Pa. t. & pple **caught** /kɔːt/, (now *dial. & non-standard*) **catched**. Also (*dial.*) **ketch** /kɛtʃ/. ME.
[ORIGIN Anglo-Norman, Old French *cachier* var. of Old French *chacier* (mod. *chasser*): see CHASE *verb*[1]. Infl. in sense 'seize' and in forms by LATCH *verb*[1].]
▸ †**I 1** *verb trans. & intrans.* Chase. ME–M16.
▸ **II** Capture; reach.
2 *verb trans.* Capture (a person or animal that tries or would try to escape); ensnare, entrap; deceive, 'take in'. ME.

R. CAMPBELL We used to catch snakes for the Zoo. E. LONGFORD Lady Georgina Fane, unmarried daughter of Lord Westmorland, .. never gave up hope of catching him.

†**3** *verb trans.* Obtain by exertion; attain. ME–E17.

SHAKES. *3 Hen. VI* I .. Torment myself to catch the English crown. SHAKES. *Macb.* If th' assassination Could .. catch .. success.

4 *verb trans.* Hit (a person, usu. *on* a part of the body); land (a blow etc.) on. ME.

OED She caught him a sounding box on the ear. W. GASS His arm .. caught me on the side of the neck.

5 *verb trans.* Overtake, reach (an agent in motion; freq. foll. by *up*: see below); be in time to get to or reach (a thing, as a train etc., or person about to depart); in extended use, (be in time to) see or hear (a television or radio programme, etc.). E17.

ADDISON Caught in a shower. D. HAMMETT Not expecting to catch him in his office, but hoping to learn how to reach him at his home. R. MACAULAY She .. probably caught the night train. N. MAILER He .. kept racing back to his room to catch the news.

6 *verb trans.* Come upon (a person) unexpectedly; surprise, detect, (a person, *in* or *at* some activity, *doing*). In *pass.* also (*colloq.*) become pregnant. E17.

STEELE I catched her once .. at Chuck-Farthing among the Boys. E. O'NEILL He was caught red-handed and thrown off the force. D. HAMMETT When you catch her in a lie, she admits it. SLOAN WILSON Do you catch yourself wishing for her when you're making love to me?

▸ **III** Seize, take, grasp, snatch.
7 *verb trans.* Take hold of suddenly or forcibly; seize; (of fire) set alight; (of other natural agency) affect. ME.

SHAKES. *Oth.* Perdition catch my soul But I do love thee. J. CONRAD Catching me round the neck as any child almost will do. G. L. MALLORY The wind and sun .. have fairly caught us all. M. M. KAYE He watched the grass flare up and catch the sticks of wood.

8 *verb trans.* Take hold of suddenly or forcibly and remove. Now usu. foll. by *up*: see below. ME.

AV *Acts* 8:39 The Spirit of the Lord caught away Philip, that the eunuch saw him no more. TENNYSON He .. hastily caught His bundle .. and went his way.

9 *verb trans.* Entangle and hold; check suddenly; interrupt or intercept the motion of and hold; *spec.* in cricket, baseball, etc., prevent (the ball) from touching the ground after striking the bat. ME. ▸**b** In cricket, baseball, etc., dismiss (a batsman) by catching the ball after it has struck the bat and before it touches the ground. Also foll. by *out*. E18.

G. MACDONALD Find a basin or plate .. and put it to catch the drop here. R. KIPLING A grain-cart's axle caught them by the horns. I. MURDOCH Felix .. caught the falling Miranda in his arms. C. POTOK The ball was coming back to me, and I caught it neatly. **b** R. A. FITZGERALD Gilbert .. was also caught and bowled by Eastwood.

10 *verb trans.* Take, get, (rest, sleep, etc., now only for a brief period). ME.

R. WILBUR He'll catch a little nap.

†**11** *verb trans. gen.* Take. ME–M17.

CHAUCER Pryvely she kaughte forth a knyf. W. CAMDEN So they called parchment which wee have catcht from the Latine *Pergamentum*.

12 *verb trans.* Take advantage of (opportunity etc.) as it occurs. LME.
13 *verb trans.* Arrest the attention of; arrest (the attention etc., a faculty or organ of sense); captivate. LME.

DRYDEN The soothing arts that catch the fair. H. MARTINEAU A rustle .. caught her excited ear.

14 *verb intrans.* Of fire or something combustible: start to burn, take hold. Of an engine etc.: ignite, start up. M16.

V. WOOLF The flames had fairly caught. L. WOOLF Lizzy had put a large piece of newspaper 'to draw up the fire', the newspaper had 'caught'. J. GARDNER George .. ground on the starter a minute before the truck motor caught and roared.

15 *verb trans.* Grasp with the senses or mind; see, hear, etc., esp. by an effort; perceive; reveal to perception; apprehend and reproduce a likeness of. L16.

TOLKIEN They caught faintly the fragrance of woodland flowers. S. BECKETT I could not catch the words. J. T. STORY My headlights had caught what seemed to be spots of blood on the road. B. TRAPIDO Jonathan enacted the episode .., catching his grandmother's speech and gesture.

16 *verb intrans.* Snatch or grasp *at* (†*after*, †absol.). L16.

T. FULLER Mercy is a Grace which they hold the fastest, that most catch after it. W. COWPER Catching at his rein.

17 *verb intrans.* Become entangled or fixed (*in*, *on*, etc.); be impeded or checked. L18.

S. BELLOW His arm caught in the sleeve. T. WILLIAMS Her voice catches.

▸ **IV** Get or take passively.
18 *verb trans.* Receive, incur; be exposed to. Now esp. in phrases: see below. ME.

SHAKES. *3 Hen. VI* Fight closer or .. you'll catch a blow. GOLDSMITH Ye lakes, whose vessels catch the busy gale. I. COLEGATE The study caught the early morning sunshine.

19 *verb trans.* Become affected or inspired by (an emotion etc.). *obsolete* exc. as passing into fig. uses of sense 20. LME.

POPE Presumptuous Troy .. catch'd new fury at the voice divine.

20 *verb trans.* Take (as) by infection; contract (disease etc.); acquire by sympathy or imitation. LME.

G. GREENE He has caught mumps from the ambassador's son. E. O'NEILL They catch his excitement.

– PHRASES: ***a sprat to catch a herring***, ***a sprat to catch a mackerel***, ***a sprat to catch a whale***: see SPRAT *noun*[1]. ***be caught short***: see SHORT *adverb*. ***be caught with chaff***: see CHAFF *noun*[1]. **catch a cold**, **catch cold** contract a cold in the head; *fig.* encounter trouble or difficulties. ***catch a crab***: see CRAB *noun*[1]. **catch a glimpse of** see for a moment. **catch a likeness** reproduce a characteristic look in a picture etc. ***catch a packet***: see PACKET *noun* 3. ***catch a Tartar***: see TARTAR *noun*[2]. ***catch at a straw***, ***catch at straws***: see STRAW *noun*. ***catch bending***: see BEND *verb*. ***catch cold***: see ***catch a cold*** above. **catch fire** ignite, begin to burn, *fig.* be inflamed with passion, excitement, etc. **catch hold of** grasp, clutch at and seize. **catch it** *colloq.* incur a severe punishment. **catch me at —!**, **catch him doing —!**, etc., *colloq.* there is no possibility of my, his, etc. doing —. ***catch napping***: see NAP *verb*[1]. ***catch one's breath***, ***catch one's DEATH (of cold)***. ***catch on the hop***: see HOP *noun*[2] 1. ***catch sight of***: see SIGHT *noun*. **catch the eye of** meet the glance of (another person) with one's own, either by chance or design; *fig.* bring oneself to a person's notice, be noticed by. ***catch unawares***: see UNAWARES *adverb*.

– WITH ADVERBS IN SPECIALIZED SENSES: **catch on** (**a**) become popular or fashionable; (**b**) understand what is meant or what is happening (also foll. by *to*). **catch out** detect in a mistake etc., take unawares; (see also sense 9b above). **catch up** (**a**) *verb phr. trans.* raise suddenly aloft; pick up; raise and fasten up; (**b**) *verb phr. trans. & intrans.* (with *with*) overtake, reach (an agent in motion); (**c**) *verb phr. intrans.* make up arrears (*on*). **caught up** entangled or unwillingly involved *in*; completely absorbed *in*.

■ **catchable** *adjective* L17. **catcher** *noun* a person who or thing which catches; *spec.* the fielder in baseball who stands behind the batter; (***torpedo-boat catcher***: see TORPEDO *noun*): LME. **catching** *ppl adjective* that catches; *spec.* infectious (*lit.* & *fig.*): LME. **catchingness** *noun* (*rare*) M17. **catchy** *adjective* that catches; *esp.* attractive; (of a tune etc.) readily learned and remembered: E19.

catch- /katʃ/ *combining form*.
[ORIGIN from CATCH *verb* or *noun*[1].]
Mainly the verb in phraseological combs. as: (**a**) with nouns, in sense 'a person who or thing which catches (the object)', also in sense 'to catch, the catching of (the object)'; (**b**) in attrib. relation to nouns in sense 'that catches or for catching'.
■ **catch-all** *noun & adjective* (something) designed to catch or include various items, a general receptacle M19. **catch-as-catch-can** *noun & adjective* (designating or pertaining to) a wrestling style in which all holds are permissible L19. **catch crop** *noun* a crop grown between two staple crops (in position or time) L19. **catchfly** *noun* any of certain campions with sticky stems, chiefly of the genera *Silene* and *Lychnis* (***Nottingham catchfly***, ***sweet-william catchfly***: see SWEET *adjective & adverb*) L16. **catchline** *noun* a short eye-catching line of type, esp. one inserted by the compositor for identification M19. **catchpenny** *adjective & noun* (**a**) *adjective* intended merely to sell readily, superficially attractive but of little intrinsic worth; †(**b**) *noun* a publication etc. of this kind: M18. **catchphrase** *noun* a phrase in frequent current use M19. **catch points** *noun pl.* points to derail a train etc., e.g. when running away down a slope L19. **catch question** *noun* a question with a deliberate hidden difficulty, a trick question M19. **catch stitch** *noun* (**a**) BOOKBINDING kettle-stitch; (**b**) a cross stitch used for hems etc.: M19. **catch title** *noun* an abbreviated title at the foot of a page sufficient to identify the work to which it belongs L19. **catch-up** *noun* (*colloq.*) the action or process of catching up with someone; ***play catch-up***, try to make up arrears or a deficit: M20. **catch-water** *noun* (**a**) a drain or ditch for collecting surface or surplus water; also ***catch-water course***, ***catch-water drain***; (**b**) a vessel designed to catch water: L18. **catchweed** *noun* (now *rare* or *obsolete*) cleavers L18. **catchweight** *noun & adjective* (SPORT) (**a**) *noun* unrestricted weight; (**b**) *adjective* unrestricted as regards weight: E19. **catchword** *noun* (**a**) the first word of a page given at the foot of the previous one; (**b**) a word so placed as to draw attention, as the first or last headword repeated at the top of a dictionary etc. page, the rhyming word in a verse, the last word of an actor's speech which forms the cue, etc.; (**c**) a word or phrase caught up and repeated, esp. in connection with party politics, a slogan: E18.

catched *verb* see CATCH *verb*.

catchment /ˈkatʃm(ə)nt/ *noun*. M19.
[ORIGIN from CATCH *verb* + -MENT.]
In full ***catchment area***. The area from which rainfall flows into a river, reservoir, etc., *fig.* from which a hospital's patients, a school's pupils, etc. are drawn.

catchpole /ˈkatʃpəʊl/ *noun*. Also **-poll**. LOE.
[ORIGIN Anglo-Norman, Old French var. of Old French *chacepol*, or from Anglo-Latin *cacepollus*, from Proto-Romance var. of Latin *captare* (see CHASE *verb*[1]) + Latin *pullus* fowl.]
†**1** A tax gatherer; a Roman publican. LOE–M17.
2 *hist.* A sheriff's officer, esp. one who arrests for debt. LME.

catchup *noun* see KETCHUP.

cate /keɪt/ *noun*. *arch.* LME.
[ORIGIN Aphet. from ACATE.]
†**1** An act of selling something, a bargain. *rare*. Only in LME.
†**2** In *pl.* Provisions bought, victuals; = ACATE 2. L15–M19.
3 A choice article of food; a dainty, a delicacy. Usu. in *pl.* M16.

catechesis /katɪˈkiːsɪs/ *noun*. Pl. **-eses** /-iːsiːz/. M18.
[ORIGIN ecclesiastical Latin *catechesis* from Greek *katēkhēsis* instruction by word of mouth, from *katēkhein*: see CATECHIZE.]
1 Oral instruction given to catechumens; catechizing. M18.
2 A book for the instruction of catechumens. M18.

catechetic /katɪˈkɛtɪk/ *adjective & noun*. M17.
[ORIGIN ecclesiastical Greek *katēkhētikos*, from *katēkhētēs* catechist, from *katēkhein*: see CATECHIZE, -IC.]
▸ **A** *adjective*. Of or pertaining to catechesis; according to a catechism, esp. that of a Christian Church. M17.
▸ **B** *noun*. In *pl.* (treated as *sing.*). Christian theology as it deals with catechesis. M19.

catechetical /katɪˈkɛtɪk(ə)l/ *adjective*. E17.
[ORIGIN formed as CATECHETIC: see -ICAL.]
1 = CATECHETIC *adjective*. E17.
2 Consisting of questions and answers; proceeding by question and answer. L17.
■ **catechetically** *adverb* M18.

catechin /ˈkatɪtʃɪn/ *noun*. M19.
[ORIGIN from CATECHU + -IN[1].]
CHEMISTRY. The major constituent of catechu, a crystalline phenolic compound, $C_{15}H_{14}O_6$, of which there are several isomers.

catechise /ˈkatɪkiːz/ *noun*. *obsolete* exc. *dial.* M16.
[ORIGIN App. from French *catéchèse* CATECHESIS, conf. with CATECHIZE (French *catéchiser*).]
= CATECHESIS, CATECHISM.

catechise *verb* var. of CATECHIZE.

catechism /ˈkatɪkɪz(ə)m/ *noun*. E16.
[ORIGIN ecclesiastical Latin *catechismus* from ecclesiastical Greek, from *katēkhizein*: see CATECHIZE, -ISM.]
†**1** Catechetical instruction; catechesis. E16–E17.
2 A treatise for instruction in the principles of the Christian religion, in the form of question and answer. E16. **Church Catechism**: of the Anglican Church. **Longer Catechism**, **Shorter Catechism**: of Presbyterian Churches.
3 *transf.* & *fig.* **a** A course of question and answer; a series of questions put to anyone. L16. ▸**b** A book of instruction by question and answer. M17.
■ **cateˈchismal** *adjective* E19.

catechist /ˈkatɪkɪst/ *noun*. M16.
[ORIGIN ecclesiastical Latin *catechista* from ecclesiastical Greek *katēkhistēs*, from *katēkhizein*: see CATECHIZE.]
A teacher giving oral instruction in Christianity by means of a catechism. Also, a teacher of local origin in a mission church.
■ **cateˈchistic** *adjective* = CATECHISTICAL L17. **cateˈchistical** *adjective* of or pertaining to the office, teaching, or mode of instruction of a catechist; catechetical: L16. **cateˈchistically** *adverb* M17.

catechize /ˈkatɪkʌɪz/ *verb trans.* Also **-ise**. LME.
[ORIGIN ecclesiastical Latin *catechizare* from ecclesiastical Greek *katēkhizein*, from *katēkhein* sound through, instruct orally, formed as CATA- + *ēkhein* to sound, from *ēkhē*: see ECHO *noun*, -IZE.]
1 Instruct orally in the elements of the Christian religion by repetition (formerly) or by question and answer, esp. using a catechism; *transf.* instruct by question and answer. LME.
2 Question systematically or at length; interrogate; examine (as) with a catechism. E17.
■ **catechizer** *noun* LME.

catechol /ˈkatɪtʃɒl/ *noun*. L19.
[ORIGIN from CATECHU + -OL.]
CHEMISTRY. A crystalline dihydric phenol first obtained by distilling catechu; benzene-1,2-diol, $C_6H_4(OH)_2$.
■ **cateˈcholamine** /katɪˈkəʊləmiːn/ *noun* any of various catechol derivatives which have amine substituents and possess neurotransmitter and hormonal activity, e.g. dopamine, adrenalin M20. **catecholaminergic** /-ˌkəʊləmɪˈnəːdʒɪk/ *adjective* (PHYSIOLOGY) releasing or involving a catecholamine as a neurotransmitter L20.

catechu /ˈkatɪtʃuː/ *noun*. L17.
[ORIGIN mod. Latin, unexpl. deriv. of Malay *kacu*: cf. CACHOU.]
Any of various astringent tannin-rich vegetable extracts used esp. in tanning, e.g. gambier.

catechumen /katɪˈkjuːmɛn/ *noun*. LME.
[ORIGIN Old French & mod. French *catéchumène* or ecclesiastical Latin *catechumenus* from Greek *katēkhoumenos* being instructed, pres. pple pass. of *katēkhein*: see CATECHIZE.]
A Christian convert under instruction before baptism. Also, a young Christian preparing for confirmation.
■ **catechumenate** *noun* the position or condition of a catechumen L17. **catechuˈmenical** *adjective* L18.

categorem /ˈkatɪɡərɛm/ *noun*. Now *rare*. L16.
[ORIGIN Greek *katēgorēma*, *-mat-*, accusation, predicate, from *katēgorein* accuse.]
LOGIC. †**1** A predicate. L16–M17.
2 A categorematic word. M19.

categorematic /ˌkatɪɡ(ə)rɪˈmatɪk/ *adjective*. E19.
[ORIGIN formed as CATEGOREM + -IC.]
LOGIC & LINGUISTICS. Of a word: able to be used by itself as a term. Opp. ***syncategorematic***.
▪ **categorematical** *adjective* (*rare*) M17. **categorematically** *adverb* (*rare*) M17.

categorial /katɪˈɡɔːrɪəl/ *adjective*. E20.
[ORIGIN from CATEGORY + -AL[1], after German *kategorial*.]
Chiefly *LOGIC & LINGUISTICS*. Relating to or involving categories.

categoric /katɪˈɡɒrɪk/ *adjective & noun*. L17.
[ORIGIN French *catégorique* or late Latin *categoricus*, from Greek *katēgorikos* accusatory, affirmative, (later) categorical, from *katēgoria*: see CATEGORY, -IC.]
▸ **A** *adjective*. = CATEGORICAL. L17.
▸ †**B** *noun*. A categorical statement or proposition. L17–M19.

categorical /katɪˈɡɒrɪk(ə)l/ *adjective & noun*. L16.
[ORIGIN formed as CATEGORIC + -AL[1].]
▸ **A** *adjective*. Unconditional, absolute; explicit, direct, plain-speaking. L16.
categorical imperative *ETHICS* an unconditional moral obligation derived from pure reason. **categorical question** *GRAMMAR* a question answerable by a simple affirmation or negation, a yes-no question.
▸ **B** *noun*. A categorical proposition or statement. L17.
▪ **categorically** *adverb* E17.

category /ˈkatɪɡ(ə)ri/ *noun*. LME.
[ORIGIN French *catégorie* or its source late Latin *categoria* from Greek *katēgoria* statement, accusation, from *katēgorein* speak against, formed as CATA- + *agoreuein* speak in the assembly, formed as AGORA *noun*[1].]
▸ **I** *PHILOSOPHY*. **1** Any of a possibly exhaustive set of basic classes among which all things might be distributed (orig. each of ten classes postulated by Aristotle: cf. PREDICAMENT 1). LME.
2 Any of the a priori conceptions applied by the mind to sense impressions. (After Kant.) E19.
3 Any relatively fundamental philosophical concept. E20.
▸ **II** *gen.* **4** A class or division of people or things regarded as having particular shared characteristics. M17.

R. GODDEN I believe that, unconsciously, he relegated women to a different category. *New Scientist* Crustaceans of many kinds fall into this category.

5 *MATH*. An entity consisting of a class of abstract objects sharing a particular property together with a class of mappings which preserve that property. M20.
– COMB.: **category killer** a large store, esp. one of a chain, which becomes the dominant retailer in its category.
▪ **categoriˈzation** *noun* the action or an act of placing something in a category, classification L19. **categorize** *verb trans.* place in a category, classify E18.

catena /kəˈtiːnə/ *noun*. Pl. **-nae** /-niː/, **-nas**. M17.
[ORIGIN Latin = chain, as in ecclesiastical Latin *catena patrum* chain of the fathers (of the Church).]
A chain or connected series of things, esp. of the patristic comments on Scripture.

catenaccio /ˌkatəˈnatʃəʊ/ *noun*. M20.
[ORIGIN Italian, lit. 'bolt', from *catena* chain + the pejorative suffix *-accio*.]
SOCCER. A defensive system of play in which each attacking player is marked by one defender, with an additional defender, or sweeper, as cover.

catenane /ˈkatəneɪn/ *noun*. M20.
[ORIGIN from CATENA + -ANE 2.]
CHEMISTRY. A molecule which consists of two or more connected rings like links in a chain.

catenary /kəˈtiːnəri/ *noun & adjective*. M18.
[ORIGIN mod. Latin *catenaria* use as noun of fem. of Latin *catenarius* adjective, formed as CATENA: see -ARY[1].]
▸ **A** *noun*. A curve of the kind formed by a uniform chain hanging freely from two points not in the same vertical line. M18.
▸ **B** *adjective*. **1** Relating to a catena or series. M19.
2 Having the form of a catenary; pertaining to or characterized by a catenary. L19.
catenary bridge a suspension bridge hung by uniform chains from two points not in the same vertical line.
▪ **cateˈnarian** *adjective* (now *rare* or *obsolete*) = CATENARY *adjective* M18. ˈ**catenoid** *noun* a surface generated by rotation of a catenary about an axis L19.

catenate /ˈkatɪneɪt/ *verb trans.* E17.
[ORIGIN Latin *catenat-* pa. ppl stem of *catenare*, from *catena*: see CATENA, -ATE[3].]
Connect like the links of a chain.
▪ **cateˈnation** *noun* M17.

catenulate /kəˈtiːnjʊlət/ *adjective*. E19.
[ORIGIN from Latin *catena* CATENA + -ULE + -ATE[2].]
BOTANY & ZOOLOGY. Resembling a chain; having a chainlike series of projections.

†**cater** *noun*[1]. ME–M17.
[ORIGIN Aphet. from *acater* var. of ACATOUR.]
A buyer of provisions; a caterer.

cater /ˈkeɪtə/ *noun*[2]. LME.
[ORIGIN Old French & mod. French *quatre* four.]
1 The four on a die or (*arch.*) in a pack of cards; a throw of four at dice. LME.
2 *BELL-RINGING*. In *pl.* Changes on nine bells in which four couples of bells change places in the order of ringing. E19.

cater /ˈkeɪtə/ *verb*[1] *trans. & adverb*. *dial.* L16.
[ORIGIN from (the same root as) CATER *noun*[2].]
(Place, set) rhomboidally; (cut, move, etc.) diagonally.

cater /ˈkeɪtə/ *verb*[2]. L16.
[ORIGIN from CATER *noun*[1].]
1 *verb intrans.* Act as a caterer (*for*). L16.
2 *verb trans.* Provide or purvey as food. M17.
3 *verb intrans. gen.* Provide amusements, requisites, etc., *for*, *to*; make allowances *for*. M17. ▸**b** Pander *to* (evil inclinations etc.). M19.
▪ **catering** *noun* the action of the verb; the trade or work of a caterer: E19.

cateran /ˈkat(ə)r(ə)n/ *noun*. ME.
[ORIGIN medieval Latin *cateranus*, *kethernus* or its source Gaelic *ceathairne* peasantry (= Irish *ceithearn* KERN *noun*[1]).]
1 *hist.* An irregular fighting man of the Scottish Highlands. (Orig. in *pl.* & as *collect. sing.*) ME.
2 *transf.* A raider, a marauder. L19.

catercorner /ˈkeɪtəkɔːnə/ *adverb & adjective*. *N. Amer. & dial.* Also **catty-** /ˈkatɪ-/, **-cornered** /-kɔːnəd/, & other vars. M19.
[ORIGIN from CATER *adverb* + CORNER *noun* (+ -ED[2]).]
(Placed or situated) diagonally.

cater-cousin /ˈkeɪtəkʌz(ə)n/ *noun*. *arch.* E16.
[ORIGIN Origin of 1st elem. uncertain: perh. from CATER *noun*[1] with ref. to boarding together.]
An intimate friend.

caterer /ˈkeɪt(ə)rə/ *noun*. ME.
[ORIGIN from CATER *noun*[1] or *verb*[2] + -ER[1].]
1 A person who caters or provides provisions for a household, club, etc.; *esp.* a person whose trade is to supply, cook, serve, etc., food at a social function. ME.
2 *gen.* A person who provides amusements, requisites, etc. E18.

cateress /ˈkeɪt(ə)rɪs/ *noun*. M17.
[ORIGIN from CATER *noun*[1] or *verb*[2] + -ESS[1].]
A female caterer.

caterpillar /ˈkatəpɪlə/ *noun*. LME.
[ORIGIN Perh. from Anglo-Norman var. of Old French *chatepelose* lit. 'hairy cat', infl. by PILLAR.]
1 The larva of a butterfly or moth; *loosely* any of the similar larvae of various insects. LME.
lobster caterpillar: see LOBSTER *noun*[1] 3. ***nigger caterpillar***: see NIGGER *noun* 3. ***saddleback caterpillar***: see SADDLEBACK *noun* 2. **vegetable caterpillar** = AWHATO.
2 *fig.* A rapacious person; one who preys on society. Now *rare* or *obsolete*. M16.
3 *sing.* & (usu.) in *pl.* Any of several Mediterranean plants of the leguminous genus *Scorpiurus*, with spirally curved pods. Also ***caterpillar plant***. L16.
4 (Also **C-**.) (Proprietary name for) a vehicle with an endless articulated steel band (***Caterpillar track***, ***Caterpillar tread***, etc.) passing round and worked by two wheels, for travelling on rough ground. E20.

caterwaul /ˈkatəwɔːl/ *verb & noun*. LME.
[ORIGIN from CAT *noun*[1] + *-er-* connective + imit. final elem.]
▸ **A** *verb intrans.* **1** Of a cat: make the screaming noise characteristic of a cat on heat. LME. ▸**b** *transf.* Make a discordant screaming noise. L16.
2 Be in heat; behave lasciviously; pursue the opposite sex. *derog. arch.* M16.
▸ **B** *noun*. A screaming noise (as) of a cat during the mating season. E18.
▪ **caterwauler** *noun* (*rare*) E17.

catery /ˈkeɪt(ə)ri/ *noun*. Long *obsolete* exc. *hist.* LME.
[ORIGIN Aphet. from ACATERY.]
The office concerned with the provisioning of the royal household.

catgut /ˈkatɡʌt/ *noun*. L16.
[ORIGIN App. from CAT *noun*[1] (use unexpl.) + GUT *noun*.]
1 The dried and twisted intestines of the sheep, horse, or ass, used for the stringing of musical instruments, rackets, etc., and for surgical sutures. L16.
2 A violin; stringed instruments collectively. E18.
†**3** A coarse cloth of thick cord, used as a stiffening. M18–E19.

Cath. *abbreviation*.
1 Cathedral.
2 Catholic.

Cathar /ˈkaθɑː/ *noun*. Pl. **Cathars**, **Cathari** /ˈkaθɑːrʌɪ/. M17.
[ORIGIN medieval Latin *Cathari* (pl.) from Greek *katharoi* the pure.]
ECCLESIASTICAL HISTORY. A member of a sect seeking to achieve purity; *spec.* an Albigensian.
▪ **Catharist** *noun* E17. **Catharism** *noun* L16.

Catharine *noun* var. of CATHERINE.

catharsis /kəˈθɑːsɪs/ *noun*. In sense 2 also **k-**. Pl. **-tharses** /-ˈθɑːsiːz/. E19.
[ORIGIN mod. Latin from Greek *katharsis*, from *kathairein* cleanse, from *katharos* pure. In sense 2 from Aristotle's *Poetics*.]
1 *MEDICINE*. Purgation. E19.
2 (A) purification of the emotions by vicarious experience, esp. through drama, or, in psychotherapy, by abreaction. M19.

C

cathartic /kəˈθɑːtɪk/ *adjective & noun*. In sense 2 also **k-**. E17.
[ORIGIN Late Latin *catharticus* from Greek *kathartikos*, from *kathairein*: see CATHARSIS, -IC.]
▸ **A** *adjective*. **1** *MEDICINE*. Purgative. E17.
2 *gen.* Purifying; effecting catharsis. M17.
▸ **B** *noun*. A purgative. M17.
▪ **cathartical** *adjective* (now *rare*) M17. **cathartically** *adverb* E19.

Cathay /kaˈθeɪ/ *noun*. *arch. & poet.* M16.
[ORIGIN medieval Latin *Cat(h)aya* from Turkic *Khitāy*.]
The country of China.
▪ **Cathayan** *adjective & noun* L16.

cathectic /kaˈθɛktɪk/ *adjective*. E20.
[ORIGIN Greek *kathektikos* capable of holding.]
PSYCHOLOGY. Of or relating to cathexis.
▪ **cathect** *verb trans.* [back-form.] charge (an idea, impulse, etc.) with mental energy or emotion M20.

cathedra /kəˈθiːdrə/ *noun*. LME.
[ORIGIN Latin from Greek *kathedra* chair.]
A seat; *spec.* the chair of a bishop in his church; the episcopal see. See also EX CATHEDRA.

cathedral /kəˈθiːdr(ə)l/ *adjective & noun*. ME.
[ORIGIN Old French & mod. French *cathédral* from late Latin *cathedralis*, from Latin CATHEDRA: see -AL[1]. As noun short for ***cathedral church***.]
▸ **A** *adjective*. **1** Of or pertaining to a bishop's throne or see. (Not always distinguishable from the noun used attrib.) ME.
2 Of or pertaining to a chair of office or authority; *ex cathedra*. E17.

T. B. SHAW The style is too uniformly didactic, cathedral, and declamatory.

▸ **B** *noun*. **1** The principal church of a diocese, containing the bishop's throne. L16.
2 A principal Presbyterian church; any important, large, or imposing church. E19.
– SPECIAL COLLOCATIONS & COMB.: **cathedral church** a cathedral. **cathedral city**: in which there is a cathedral. **cathedral glass**: coloured and leaded like that of churches, for domestic etc. use.
▪ **catheˈdratic** *adjective* (now *rare*) = CATHEDRAL *adjective* M17.

catheretic /kaθəˈrɛtɪk/ *adjective & noun*. Now *rare* or *obsolete*. M17.
[ORIGIN Greek *kathairetikos* destructive, from *kathairein* destroy.]
MEDICINE. (An agent) having power to destroy, reduce, or consume.

Catherine /ˈkaθ(ə)rɪn/ *noun*. Also (less commonly) **-ar-**, **K-**. L16.
[ORIGIN Female forename, from mod. Latin *Catharina*, earlier *Katerina* repr. Greek *Aikaterina*, assim. to *katharos* pure. In sense 1 a legendary saint of Alexandria martyred on a spiked wheel.]
1 ***Catherine wheel***: ▸**a** Esp. *HERALDRY*. The figure of a wheel with curved spikes projecting from its circumference. L16. ▸**b** A firework which rotates in the manner of a wheel. M18. ▸**c** *ARCHITECTURE*. In full ***Catherine wheel window***. A circular window with radiating spokes. E19. ▸**d** A lateral handspring with the arms and legs extended. L19.
2 ***Catherine pear***, a small and early variety of pear. E17.

catheter /ˈkaθɪtə/ *noun*. Also **k-**. E17.
[ORIGIN Late Latin *catheter* from Greek *kathetēr*, from *kathienai* send or let down.]
MEDICINE. A tube which can be passed into the bladder or other body cavity or canal to allow the draining of fluid.
▪ **catheteriˈzation** *noun* the use of a catheter M19. **catheterize** *verb trans.* employ a catheter on (a patient); introduce a catheter into: L19. **catheterism** *noun* (now *rare* or *obsolete*) = CATHETERIZATION E18.

cathetometer /kaθɪˈtɒmɪtə/ *noun*. Also **k-**. M19.
[ORIGIN from CATHETUS + -OMETER.]
An instrument for measuring vertical distances, esp. small differences of level of liquid columns in tubes.

cathetus /ˈkaθətəs/ *noun*. Now *rare* or *obsolete*. Pl. **-ti** /-tʌɪ/. L16.
[ORIGIN Latin from Greek *kathetos* (*grammē*) perpendicular line, from *kathienai*: see CATHETER.]
A straight line falling perpendicularly on another straight line or surface.

cathexis /kəˈθɛksɪs/ *noun*. Pl. **-thexes** /-ˈθɛksiːz/. E20.
[ORIGIN Greek *kathexis* holding, retention, a rendering of German (*Libido*)*besetzung* (Freud).]
PSYCHOANALYSIS. The concentration or accumulation of libidinal energy on a particular object.

C

cathiodermie /kaθɪəʊˈdəːmiː/ *noun.* M20.
[ORIGIN French, perh. from CATHODE + *dermie* (formed as Greek *derma* + -Y³, with inserted *i*).]
(Proprietary name for) a beauty treatment in which an electric current is passed through a gel applied to a person's face, in order to cleanse the skin.

cathode /ˈkaθəʊd/ *noun.* Also †**k-**. M19.
[ORIGIN Greek *kathodos* way down, from *kata* CATA- + *hodos* way.]
A negative electrode or terminal. Opp. ANODE.
cold cathode: see COLD *adjective*. *hot cathode*: see HOT *adjective*. VIRTUAL *cathode*.
– COMB.: **cathode ray** a beam of electrons emitted from the cathode of a vacuum tube (*cathode-ray oscilloscope*: see OSCILLOSCOPE 2; *cathode-ray tube*, a vacuum tube in which cathode rays produce a luminous image on a fluorescent screen).
■ **cathodal** *adjective* of or pertaining to a cathode L19.

cathodic /kəˈθɒdɪk/ *adjective.* Also †**k-**. M19.
[ORIGIN from CATHODE + -IC.]
Of or pertaining to a cathode.
cathodic protection prevention of corrosion of a metal structure by making it act as the cathode of an electrolytic cell.
■ **cathodically** *adverb* M20.

cathodo- /ˈkaθədəʊ/ *combining form* of CATHODE: see -O-. Also †**k-**.
■ **cathodolumiˈnescence** *noun* luminescence excited by the impact of an electron beam E20.

Catholic /ˈkaθ(ə)lɪk/ *adjective & noun.* In branch II of the adjective **c-**. LME.
[ORIGIN Old French & mod. French *catholique* or its source Christian Latin *catholicus* from Greek *katholikos* general, universal, from *katholou* (*kath' holou*) in general, from *kata* in respect of, *holos* whole.]
▸ **A** *adjective.* **I** CHRISTIAN CHURCH.
1 Of, belonging to, or designating the ancient Church before the great schism between East and West, or any Church standing in historical continuity with it, as (*a*) the Western or Latin Church after the schism (distinguished from ***Eastern***, ***Orthodox***), (*b*) the Latin Church that remained under the Roman obedience after the Reformation (= ROMAN CATHOLIC *adjectival phr.*, opp. ***Protestant*** etc.), (*c*) the Anglican Church regarded as a continuation of both the Ancient and Latin Churches (= ANGLO-CATHOLIC *adjective*). LME.
2 Of, belonging to, or designating the Christian Church as a whole. M16.
3 Recognizing or having sympathies with all Christians. M17.

R. BAXTER The Lord Protector is noted as a man of a Catholic spirit, desirous of the unity and peace of all the servants of Christ.

▸ **II** *gen.* **4** Universal; of interest or use to everyone. M16. ▸†**b** Of a medicine, remedy, etc.: universally applicable. E17–M18. ▸†**c** Common, prevalent. Only in 17.

J. A. FROUDE What was of Catholic rather than national interest.

5 Having sympathies with all; all-embracing; broad-minded, tolerant. L16.

A. BURGESS I've got Catholic tastes. Catholic with a small 'c', of course.

▸ **B** *noun.* **1** A member of a Catholic Church; *esp.* = ROMAN CATHOLIC *noun phr.* LME.
†**2** = CATHOLICOS. E17–M18.
– PHRASES & COMB.: ANGLO-CATHOLIC. **Catholic and Apostolic Church**, **Catholic Apostolic Church** a religious body founded about 1835 according to the teachings of Edward Irving. ***Catholic Emancipation***: see EMANCIPATION. **Catholic Epistles**: those of James, Peter, and Jude, and the first of John, as not being addressed to particular Churches or persons. **Catholic King** *hist.* the King of Spain. **German Catholic** (*a*) *noun* a member of either of two religious parties who separated from the Roman Catholic communion in 19th-cent. Germany (usu. in *pl.*); (*b*) *adjective* of or pertaining to the German Catholics. **his Catholic Majesty** = ***Catholic King*** above. **Old Catholic** (*a*) *noun* a member of any of various religious parties who separated from the Roman Catholic communion, esp. the Church of Utrecht in the 18th cent. and the German Catholics (usu. in *pl.*); a member of a Roman Catholic family in England since the Reformation; (*b*) *adjective* of or pertaining to Old Catholics. ROMAN CATHOLIC. ***ROMISH Catholic***.
■ **Catholically** *adverb* E16. **Catholicism** /kəˈθɒlɪsɪz(ə)m/ *noun* (adherence to) the system, faith, and practice of a Catholic (esp. the Roman Catholic) Church L16. **Catholicization** /kəˌθɒlɪsʌɪˈzeɪʃ(ə)n/ *noun* the action of making Catholic E20. **Catholicize** /kəˈθɒlɪsʌɪz/ *verb trans. & intrans.* make Catholic or catholic; become (a) Catholic: E17. **Catholicly** *adverb* in accordance with the faith or teaching of the Catholic Church M16.

catholicate /kəˈθɒlɪkeɪt/ *noun.* M19.
[ORIGIN medieval Latin *catholicatus*, from *catholicus* CATHOLIC: cf. CATHOLICOS & see -ATE¹.]
The jurisdiction of a Catholicos.

catholicity /kaθəˈlɪsɪti/ *noun.* In sense 3 **C-**. E19.
[ORIGIN from CATHOLIC + -ITY: cf. French *catholicité*.]
1 The quality of having sympathies with all or being all-embracing; broad-mindedness, tolerance. E19.

H. REED It is important to cultivate a true catholicity of taste.

2 Universality; universal prevalence or recognition. E19.
3 The character of belonging to or being in accordance with a Catholic Church; *spec.* Roman Catholicism. E19.

E. B. PUSEY They wish to claim for the English Church the character of Catholicity.

catholicon /kəˈθɒlɪkɒn/ *noun.* LME.
[ORIGIN French *catholicon*, *-cum* from mod. Latin *catholicum* use as noun (sc. *remedium* remedy) of *catholicus*: see CATHOLIC. In sense 1 cf. medieval Latin *catholicon* dictionary.]
1 A comprehensive treatise. LME.
2 A universal remedy; a panacea. LME.

Catholicos /kəˈθɒlɪkɒs/ *noun.* Pl. **-coses**, **-coi** /-kɔɪ/. E17.
[ORIGIN medieval Greek *katholikos*: see CATHOLIC.]
CHRISTIAN CHURCH. The Patriarch of the Armenian or the Nestorian Church.
– COMB.: **Catholicos-Patriarch** the head of the Georgian Church.

Catiline /ˈkatɪlʌɪn/ *noun.* L16.
[ORIGIN Latin *Catilina*, cognomen of a Roman who conspired against the Roman republic in 63 BC: see -INE¹.]
A conspirator, esp. against government.
■ **Catilinarian** /ˌkatɪlɪˈnɛːrɪən/ *adjective & noun* (a person) resembling Catiline; conspiring, a conspirator, esp. against government: E19.

cation /ˈkatʌɪən/ *noun.* M19.
[ORIGIN from CAT(HODE or CATA- + ION.]
A positively charged ion, i.e. one which would be attracted to a cathode. Opp. ANION.
■ **catiˈonic** *adjective* of or pertaining to cations; of the nature of a cation: E20.

catkin /ˈkatkɪn/ *noun.* L16.
[ORIGIN Dutch †*katteken* lit. 'kitten': see CAT *noun*¹, -KIN.]
A cylindrical unisexual inflorescence, usu. pendent and downy or silky, borne by various trees.

catling /ˈkatlɪŋ/ *noun.* In sense 2 also **-in** /-ɪn/. E17.
[ORIGIN from CAT *noun*¹ + -LING¹.]
1 Catgut. E17.
2 SURGERY. A long, narrow, double-edged, straight knife for amputations. E17.
3 A kitten; a little cat. M17.

catlinite /ˈkatlɪnʌɪt/ *noun.* M19.
[ORIGIN from George *Catlin* (1796–1872), US artist + -ITE¹.]
The sacred pipestone of the American Indians, a red clay of the Upper Missouri region.

catocalid /katə(ʊ)ˈkeɪlɪd/ *adjective & noun.* L19.
[ORIGIN from mod. Latin *Catocala* (see below), from Greek *katō* below + *kalos* beautiful: see -ID³.]
(A moth) belonging to the noctuid genus *Catocala*, which includes the red underwing.

cat o' mountain *noun phr.* var. of CATAMOUNTAIN.

Catonian /keɪˈtəʊnɪən/ *noun & adjective.* M16.
[ORIGIN Latin *Catonianus*, from *Cato*, cognomen of Cato the Censor (234–149 BC and Cato of Utica (95–46 BC), both noted for the severity of their manners: see -IAN.]
▸ †**A** *noun.* A follower of either Cato. Only in M16.
▸ **B** *adjective.* Severe in manner, stern, austere. L17.

catoptric /kəˈtɒptrɪk/ *noun & adjective.* M16.
[ORIGIN Greek *katoptrikos* adjective, from *katoptron* mirror: see -IC.]
▸ **A** *noun sing.* & (now) usu. in *pl.* (treated as *sing.*). The branch of optics that deals with reflection. M16.
▸ **B** *adjective.* Of or relating to mirrors or reflection. E18.
■ **catoptrical** *adjective* (now *rare* or *obsolete*) L17.

catoptromancy /kəˈtɒptrəmansi/ *noun.* E17.
[ORIGIN from Greek *katoptron* (see CATOPTRIC) + -MANCY.]
Divination by means of a mirror or mirrors.

catostomid /kəˈtɒstəmɪd/ *noun & adjective.* L19.
[ORIGIN mod. Latin *Catostomidae* (see below), from *Catostomus* genus name, from Greek *katō* down + *stoma* mouth: see -ID³.]
(A freshwater fish) of the chiefly N. American family Catostomidae, which includes the suckers and buffaloes.

cat's eye /ˈkatsʌɪ/ *noun phr.* M16.
[ORIGIN from CAT *noun*¹ + -'S¹ + EYE *noun*.]
1 A gemstone, esp. a variety of chalcedony, which displays a lustre resembling the contracted pupil of a cat's eye. Also called ***sunstone***. M16.
2 A speedwell, forget-me-not, or similar bright flower. E19.
3 The operculum of a turban shell. L19.
4 Also **C-**. (Proprietary name for) a light-reflecting stud set into the surface of a road to demarcate traffic lanes etc. at night. M20.

†**catso** *noun & interjection.* *slang.* See also GADSO. E17.
[ORIGIN Italian *cazzo* lit. 'penis'.]
▸ **A** *noun.* Pl **-os**. A criminal or dishonest man. Only in 17.
▸ **B** *interjection.* = GADZOOKS. Only in E18.

cat's paw /ˈkatspɔː/ *noun.* *fig.* M18.
[ORIGIN from CAT *noun*¹ + -'S¹ + PAW *noun*¹.]
1 A light breeze that ripples the surface of water in places. M18.
2 A person used as a tool by another. Cf. ***cat's foot*** (a) s.v. CAT *noun*¹. L18.
3 NAUTICAL. A twisting hitch made in the bight of a rope to form two bights, to hook a tackle on. L18.

cat's tail /ˈkatsteɪl/ *noun.* *fig.* Also **cattail**. ME.
[ORIGIN from CAT *noun*¹ + -'S¹ + TAIL *noun*¹.]
1 Any of various plants with long thin parts suggestive of cats' tails, esp. (*a*) the reed mace; (*b*) a horsetail; (*c*) (more fully ***cat's tail grass***) a grass of the genus *Phleum*. ME.
2 A catkin. L16.

catsup *noun* var. of KETCHUP.

cattalo /ˈkatələʊ/ *noun.* *N. Amer.* Also **catalo**. Pl. **-o(e)s**. L19.
[ORIGIN from CATTLE + BUFFALO.]
A cross between a male buffalo and a domesticated cow.

†**cattan** *noun* see KATANA.

Cattern *noun & verb* var. of KATTERN.

cattery /ˈkatəri/ *noun.* L18.
[ORIGIN from CAT *noun*¹ + -ERY.]
A colony of cats; a place where cats are bred or looked after.

cattish /ˈkatɪʃ/ *adjective.* L16.
[ORIGIN from CAT *noun*¹ + -ISH¹.]
1 Of or like a cat. L16.
2 *spec.* Sly and spiteful; catty. L19.
■ **cattishly** *adverb* E20. **cattishness** *noun* L19.

cattle /ˈkat(ə)l/ *noun.* ME.
[ORIGIN from Anglo-Norman, Old Northern French *catel* var. of Old French *chatel* CHATTEL.]
▸ **I** Property.
†**1** (Personal) property; wealth, goods. ME–L15.
†**2** A chattel. L15–E18.
▸ **II** Treated as *pl.* Livestock.
3 Animals of the genus *Bos*, oxen; (now *arch. & dial.*) livestock, (in stables) horses. ME.
4 *derog.* People (likened to cattle). *arch.* L16.
†**5** Vermin; insects. Only in 17.
– COMB. & PHRASES: **black cattle** oxen of Scottish and Welsh highland breeds, orig. black. **cattle cake** concentrated food for cattle, in cake form; **cattle class** *joc.* economy class on an aircraft; **cattle dog** *Austral. & NZ* a dog bred or trained to work cattle; **cattle egret** a small white heron, *Bubulais ibis*, often associated with grazing cattle; **cattle grid**, (*US*) **cattle guard** a ditch covered by spaced bars to allow the passage of vehicles and pedestrians but not cattle etc.; **cattle lifter** a cattle thief; **cattleman** *N. Amer.* a person who tends or rears cattle; **cattle plague** rinderpest; **cattle rustler** a cattle thief; **cattle stop** *NZ* = ***cattle grid*** above; **cattle truck** a truck for the transport of cattle; *fig.* a crowded uncomfortable vehicle.

cattleya /ˈkatlɪə/ *noun.* E19.
[ORIGIN mod. Latin, from William *Cattley* (d. 1832), English patron of botany: see -A¹.]
An epiphytic neotropical orchid of the genus *Cattleya*, with handsome violet, pink, or yellow flowers.

catty /ˈkati/ *noun.* L16.
[ORIGIN Malay, Javanese *kati*. Cf. CADDY *noun*¹, KATI.]
Any of various weights of around 600 grams or 1⅓ lb, used in China and SE Asia.

catty /ˈkati/ *adjective.* L19.
[ORIGIN from CAT *noun*¹ + -Y¹.]
1 Sly and spiteful. L19.
2 Of or pertaining to cats. E20.
■ **cattily** *adverb* E20. **cattiness** *noun* E20.

cattycorner(ed) *adverbs & adjectives* see CATERCORNER.

Catullian /kəˈtʌlɪən/ *adjective.* M19.
[ORIGIN from *Catullus* (see below) + -IAN.]
Of, pertaining to, or characteristic of the Latin lyric poet Catullus (*c* 84–*c* 54 BC) or his writing.
■ Also **Catullan** *adjective* M20.

catydid *noun* var. of KATYDID.

caubeen /kɔːˈbiːn/ *noun.* *Irish & Canad. dial.* E19.
[ORIGIN Irish = old hat, old cap, from *cáibín* dim. of *cába* cape: see -EEN².]
A hat, a cap, *spec.* an Irish soldier's round flat cap resembling a beret.

Caucasian /kɔːˈkeɪzjən, -ʒ(ə)n/ *adjective & noun.* E17.
[ORIGIN from *Caucasus* (see below), *Caucasia*: see -IAN, -AN.]
▸ **A** *adjective.* **1** Of, pertaining to, or inhabiting the Caucasus, a mountainous region between the Black and Caspian Seas; of or pertaining to the non-Indo-European languages of this region, including Circassian and Georgian. E17.
2 Of, relating to, or designating the white or light-skinned division of humankind, formerly supposed to have originated in the Caucasus. E19.
▸ **B** *noun.* A white or light-skinned person. Also, a native or inhabitant of the Caucasus; the Caucasian languages collectively. M19.
Ibero-Caucasian, ***North Caucasian***, ***South Caucasian***, etc. (languages).
■ **Caucasic** /kɔːˈkasɪk/ *adjective* = CAUCASIAN *adjective* 2 L19. **ˈCaucasoid** *adjective & noun* (*a*) *adjective* of, pertaining to, or resembling the Caucasian division of humankind; (*b*) *noun* a Caucasoid person: E20.
– NOTE: In the racial classification developed by anthropologists in 19, ***Caucasian*** (or ***Caucasoid***) included peoples whose skin colour ranged from light (in northern Europe) to dark (in parts of North Africa and India). This classification is now outdated and not generally accepted as scientific, but ***Caucasian*** is now used, esp. in the US, as a synonym for 'white or of European origin'.

Cauchy /ˈkəʊʃi/ *noun*. L19.
[ORIGIN A.-L. *Cauchy* (1789–1857), French mathematician.]
MATH. **1** Used *attrib.* and in *possess.* to designate concepts introduced by Cauchy or arising out of his work. L19.
Cauchy integral (formula), **Cauchy's integral (formula)** a formula expressing the value of a function at a point in terms of an integral round a closed curve enclosing the point. **Cauchy sequence** any sequence of numbers a_n which satisfies the condition that, for any positive number ε, a value of *n* can be chosen so that any two members of the sequence after a_n differ by a quantity less than ε. **Cauchy's theorem** *spec.* the theorem that the integral of an analytic function of a complex variable round a closed curve which encloses no singularities is zero.
2 ***Cauchy–Riemann equation*** [RIEMANN], each of two partial differential equations which must be satisfied if a function of two variables is to be separable into a real part and an imaginary part. E20.
3 ***Cauchy–Schwarz inequality***, = ***SCHWARZ inequality***. M20.

caucus /ˈkɔːkəs/ *noun & verb*. Orig. *US*. M18.
[ORIGIN Perh. from Algonquian *cau'-cau'-as'u* adviser.]
▸ **A** *noun*. A committee of members of a political party, esp. elected representatives, meeting regularly to determine policy, select candidates, etc.; a group or bloc of such members; the systematic exercise of political control through such committees. Also (freq. *derog.*), a usu. secret meeting of a group active within a larger organization or party; a group of this kind. M18.

J. R. LOWELL In the Greek epic, the gods are partisans, they hold caucuses, they lobby and log-roll for their candidates. G. B. SHAW Mere politicians, the drudges of the caucus and the polling booth.

▸ **B** *verb intrans.* Hold or form a caucus. L18.

cauda /ˈkɔːdə/ *noun*. Pl. **-dae** /-diː/. L17.
[ORIGIN Latin = tail.]
ANATOMY & ZOOLOGY. A structure resembling a tail. Chiefly in ***cauda equina*** /ɪkˈwʌɪnə/, the bundle of nerves descending from the lower end of the spinal cord.

caudal /ˈkɔːd(ə)l/ *adjective & noun*. M17.
[ORIGIN mod. Latin *caudalis*, formed as CAUDA: see -AL¹.]
ANATOMY & ZOOLOGY. ▸ **A** *adjective*. Of, pertaining to, or of the nature of a tail; situated in or near the tail or posterior part of the body. M17.
▸ **B** *noun*. A caudal fin, vertebra, etc. M19.
■ **caudally** *adverb* L19.

caudate /ˈkɔːdeɪt/ *adjective*. E17.
[ORIGIN medieval Latin *caudatus*, formed as CAUDA: see -ATE².]
Having a tail or an appendage resembling a tail; tailed.
caudate nucleus *ANATOMY* the upper of the two grey nuclei of the corpus striatum.
■ Also **cauˈdated** *adjective* E19.

caudex /ˈkɔːdɛks/ *noun*. Pl. **-dices** /-dɪsiːz/. L18.
[ORIGIN Latin, earlier form of CODEX.]
BOTANY. The axis of a plant (esp. a palm or fern) consisting of stem and root.

caudicle /ˈkɔːdɪk(ə)l/ *noun*. M19.
[ORIGIN from Latin CAUDEX, *-dic-* after *caulicle* etc.: see -CULE.]
BOTANY. A small stalklike appendage to the pollinium of an orchid.

caudillo /kaʊˈdiːljəʊ/ *noun*. Pl. **-os**. M19.
[ORIGIN Spanish from late Latin *capitellum* dim. of *caput* head.]
In Spain and Spanish-speaking countries: a head of state, a military or political leader.
the Caudillo the title assumed by General Francisco Franco, ruler of Spain 1938–75.

caudle /ˈkɔːd(ə)l/ *noun & verb*. *arch.* ME.
[ORIGIN Old Northern French *caudel*, Old French *chaudel* (mod. *chaudeau*) from medieval Latin dim. of Latin *caldum* hot drink, from *cal(i)dus* warm.]
▸ **A** *noun*. A drink of warm gruel containing spice, sugar, and wine, for invalids. ME.
▸ **B** *verb trans.* **1** Administer a caudle to. Cf. CODDLE *verb*². E17.
2 Mix as in a caudle. L18.

caught *verb pa. t. & pple* of CATCH *verb*.

cauk /kɔːk/ *noun*. *obsolete* exc. *dial.* Also (esp. in sense 2) **cawk**. LME.
[ORIGIN Perh. north. var. of CHALK *noun*, or from Middle Dutch *calc* CHALK *noun*.]
1 Chalk. Also, lime, calcite, etc. LME.
2 Barytes. M17.

cauk *verb*¹ var. of COCK *verb*⁴.

†**cauk** *verb*² see CAULK *verb*¹.

caul /kɔːl/ *noun*¹. See also KELL. ME.
[ORIGIN Uncertain: perh. from Old French & mod. French *cale* head covering, but recorded earlier.]
1 A close-fitting netted headdress, esp. of a type worn by women indoors. Also, the plain back part of a woman's headdress. *obsolete* exc. *hist.* ME. ▸†**b** The netted substructure of a wig. L17–L18.
†**2** A spider's web. LME–M17.
3 a An enveloping membrane. Long *obsolete* in *gen.* sense. LME. ▸**b** The omentum. LME. ▸**c** The amnion or inner membrane enclosing the fetus before birth; a portion of this occas. found on a child's head at birth, thought to be lucky, and supposed to be a preservative against drowning. M16.
†**4** *gen.* A net. L15–L17.

caul /kɔːl/ *noun*². *Scot.* Also **cauld** /kɔːld/. M16.
[ORIGIN Unknown.]
A weir or dam for diverting river water.

†**caul** *noun*³ var. of COLE *noun*¹.

cauld *noun, adjective & adverb* see COLD *noun* etc.

cauldrife /ˈkɔːldrɪf/ *adjective*. *Scot.* M17.
[ORIGIN from CAUL *noun*² + RIFE. Cf. WASTRIFE.]
Causing cold, chilling; susceptible to cold.

cauldron /ˈkɔːldr(ə)n, ˈkɒl-/ *noun*. Also **cald-**. ME.
[ORIGIN Anglo-Norman, Old Northern French *caudron* (mod. *chaudron*) augm. of Proto-Romance var. of late Latin *cal(i)darium* cooking pot, from *cal(i)dus* hot. The spelling with *l* after Latin appeared in 15 and later infl. the pronunc., as in *fault*.]
A large cooking pot, usu. of a deep basin shape with a hoop handle and removable lid.

fig.: W. SHENSTONE Vesuvio's horrid cauldrons roar. N. MONSARRAT The harbour . . became a cauldron of smoke and flame and columns of erupting water.

– COMB.: **cauldron subsidence**: of a roughly cylindrical or conical mass of rock into a magma chamber.

caules *noun* pl. of CAULIS.

caulescent /kɔːˈlɛs(ə)nt/ *adjective*. M18.
[ORIGIN from Latin CAULIS + -ESCENT.]
BOTANY. Having an obvious stem.

caulicle /ˈkɔːlɪk(ə)l/ *noun*. M17.
[ORIGIN Latin *cauliculus*, formed as CAULIS: see -CULE.]
BOTANY. A little stalk, esp. a radicle.

caulicole /ˈkɔːlɪkəʊl/ *noun*. E19.
[ORIGIN French, or its source Italian *colicolo* from Latin *cauliculus*: see CAULICLE, -OLE¹.]
ARCHITECTURE. Any of the fluted stalks arising from the larger stalks of a Corinthian capital and bearing leaves or volutes.

cauliflory /ˈkɔːlɪflɔːri/ *noun*. E20.
[ORIGIN from Latin CAULIS + *flos*, *floris* flower + -Y³.]
BOTANY. The production of flowers directly from the main stem or branches.

cauliflower /ˈkɒlɪflaʊə/ *noun & verb*. L16.
[ORIGIN Alt. (by assim. to COLE *noun*¹, FLOWER *noun*) of French †*chou fleuri* (*flori*), prob. from Italian *cavolfiore*, pl. *cavoli fiori* or mod. Latin *cauliflora* 'flowered cabbage'.]
▸ **A** *noun*. **1** A cultivated variety of cabbage with a large, dense white flower head; the flower heads eaten as a vegetable. L16.
2 Something resembling a cauliflower in shape. M18.
– COMB.: **cauliflower cheese** a savoury dish made of cauliflower and cheese sauce; **cauliflower ear** an ear (esp. of a boxer) thickened and disfigured by repeated blows.
▸ **B** *verb trans.* **1** Powder (a wig). *rare*. L18.
2 Thicken or disfigure (an ear) by repeated blows, esp. in boxing. Chiefly as ***cauliflowered*** *ppl adjective*. M20.

cauline /ˈkɔːlʌɪn/ *adjective*. M18.
[ORIGIN from Latin CAULIS + -INE¹.]
BOTANY. Of or belonging to the stem; *esp.* (of a leaf) borne on the stem (opp. ***radical***).

caulis /ˈkɔːlɪs/ *noun*. Pl. **caules** /ˈkɔːliːz/. M16.
[ORIGIN Latin = stem, stalk.]
ARCHITECTURE. Each of the four principal stalks in a Corinthian capital.

caulk /kɔːk/ *noun*. *nautical slang*. M19.
[ORIGIN Perh. from the verb.]
1 A small drink of liquor, a dram. M19.
2 A short sleep, a nap. E20.

caulk /kɔːk/ *verb*¹. Also ***calk**. In branch I †**cauk**, †**cawk**. LME.
[ORIGIN Old Northern French *cauquer*, *caukier* var. of *cauchier* tread, press with force (mod. *côcher*) from Latin *calcare* tread, press, from *calx*, *calc-* heel.]
▸†**I 1** Of birds: copulate. LME–E18.
▸**II 2** *verb trans.* Stop up the seams of (a ship etc.) with oakum etc. and waterproofing material or by driving the plate-junctions together; stop up (seams) thus. L15.
caulking iron a tool for driving oakum etc. into the seams of a ship.
3 *verb trans.* Stop up or seal the crevices of (windows etc.); seal (crevices). E17.
4 *verb intrans.* Sleep, take a nap. *nautical slang*. E19.
■ **caulker** *noun* (**a**) a person who caulks ships; (**b**) an implement for caulking; (**c**) *nautical slang* = CAULK *noun* 1: L15.

caulk *verb*² var. of COCK *verb*⁴.

†**cauponate** *verb trans.* M17–E18.
[ORIGIN Latin *cauponat-* pa. ppl stem of *cauponari*, from *caupo*, *-on-* huckster, innkeeper: see -ATE³.]
Deal like a huckster with; traffic in (dishonestly) for gain.
■ †**cauponation** *noun* petty or unfair dealing; adulteration M16–E18.

†**cauponize** *verb trans.* Also **-ise**. M17–L18.
[ORIGIN from Latin *caupo*, *-on-*: see CAUPONATE, -IZE.]
= CAUPONATE Also, mix and adulterate for gain.

Caurus /ˈkɔːrəs/ *noun*. *arch.* LME.
[ORIGIN Latin.]
The stormy north-west wind, esp. personified.

causal /ˈkɔːz(ə)l/ *noun & adjective*. LME.
[ORIGIN Late Latin *causalis* adjective, from *causa*: see CAUSE *noun*, -AL¹.]
▸ **A** *noun*. A causal conjunction or particle. LME.
▸ **B** *adjective*. **1** *GRAMMAR & LOGIC.* Introducing or expressing a cause. M16.
2 Of or relating to a cause or causes; acting as a cause; of the nature of cause and effect. L16.

HENRY MORE As being a means to this end, and, therefore, Causal thereto. R. BLACKMORE The links of all the causal chain. P. DAVIES No signal could travel faster than light without producing causal chaos.

■ **causally** *adverb* in the manner of, or as being, the cause; by way of cause and effect: LME.

causalgia /kɔːˈzaldʒə/ *noun*. M19.
[ORIGIN from Greek *kausos* heat, fever + -ALGIA.]
MEDICINE. A severe burning pain in a limb caused by injury to a peripheral nerve.

causality /kɔːˈzalɪti/ *noun*. L15.
[ORIGIN French *causalité* or medieval Latin *causalitas*, formed as CAUSAL: see -ITY.]
1 Causal quality; the fact or state of acting as a cause. L15.
2 The operation or relation of cause and effect. M17.
3 *PHRENOLOGY.* A mental faculty of tracing effects to causes. L19.

causation /kɔːˈzeɪʃ(ə)n/ *noun*. L15.
[ORIGIN Old French & mod. French, or Latin *causatio(n-)* pretext etc., (in medieval Latin) action of causing, from *causat-* pa. ppl stem of *causari*, *-are*: see CAUSE *verb*, -ATION.]
The causing or producing of an effect; the relation of cause and effect.
social causation: see SOCIAL *adjective*.
■ **causational** *adjective* E20.

causative /ˈkɔːzətɪv/ *adjective & noun*. LME.
[ORIGIN Old French & mod. French *causatif*, *-ive* or late Latin *causativus*, from *causat-*: see CAUSATION, CAUSE *verb*, -ATIVE.]
▸ **A** *adjective*. **1** Effective as a cause, productive *of*. LME.
2 *GRAMMAR.* Expressing a cause or causation. E17.
▸ **B** *noun*. A causative agency; a causative word. L15.
■ **causatively** *adverb* M17. **causaˈtivity** *noun* = CAUSALITY 1 M19.

cause /kɔːz/ *noun*. ME.
[ORIGIN Old French & mod. French from Latin *causa* reason, motive, lawsuit.]
1 *gen.* That which produces an effect or consequence; an antecedent or antecedents followed by a certain phenomenon. ME. ▸**b** A person or other agent who occasions something, with or without intent. LME.

S. JOHNSON The greatest events may be often traced to slender causes. G. B. SHAW Bruno is buried, and his death from natural causes duly certified. H. INNES The sound of it falling must have been the cause of my waking. **b** G. BERKELEY God is the supreme and universal Cause of all things. TENNYSON Am I the cause . . that men Reproach you?

2 A fact, circumstance, or consideration which moves a person to action; ground for action, reason, motive; *esp.* adequate motive or justification. ME.

AV To amend it where he saw cause. J. R. GREEN The causes which drew students and teachers within the walls of Oxford. B. ENGLAND He was a hard man. But never without cause.

3 A matter about which a person goes to law, a subject of litigation; a legal case, (the case of one party in) a lawsuit. ME. ▸**b** *gen.* A matter of concern; the case as it concerns anyone, the situation. *obsolete* exc. *dial.* LME.

GOLDSMITH He that has most opinions is most likely to carry his cause. W. B. CARPENTER Further proceedings . . in a cause which he had heard some years previously. **b** SHAKES. *Lucr.* The cause craves haste.

4 That side of any question or controversy espoused by a person or party; a movement which inspires the efforts of its supporters. ME.

SHAKES. *John* Such temperate order in so fierce a cause. W. S. CHURCHILL The greatest of the European movements in these years was the cause of Italian unity. L. AUCHINCLOSS She had many causes, but currently she was absorbed in the fight against the Vietnamese war. H. CARPENTER A political rebel leaves his lover to fight for the cause.

†**5** Sickness, disease. LME–E17.

SHAKES. *Coriol.* Leave us to cure this cause.

– PHRASES: **cause and effect** (the operation or relation of) a cause and the effect it produces; the doctrine of causation. **efficient cause** *PHILOSOPHY* that which produces or occasions the thing caused. **final cause** *PHILOSOPHY* the purpose or end of the thing caused. **First Cause** the Creator of the universe. **formal cause** *PHILOSOPHY* that which defines the thing caused. †**for someone's cause** on someone's account, for the sake of someone. **good cause** (**a**) adequate justification; (**b**) a movement deserving support, esp. a charity. **in the cause of** to defend or support. **lost cause** a hopeless undertaking. **make common cause with** join forces with, ally oneself with. **material cause** *PHILOSOPHY* the matter that constitutes the thing caused. ***meritorious cause***: see MERITORIOUS *adjective*. ***occasional cause***: see OCCASIONAL *adjective* 4. ***primary cause***: see PRIMARY *adjective*.

probable cause: see PROBABLE *adjective*. ***secondary cause***: see SECONDARY *adjective*. **second cause** a cause which is itself caused.
– COMB.: **cause list** a list of cases awaiting trial.
■ **causeful** *adjective* (*rare*) (***a***) having (good) cause, well founded; (***b***) that is a cause *of*: LME. **causeless** *adjective* (***a***) having no antecedent cause; (***b***) *arch.* having no (legal) cause or reason; groundless, unjustifiable: LME. **causelessly** *adverb* M16.

cause /kɔːz/ *verb*. LME.
[ORIGIN Old French & mod. French *causer* or Latin *causari* give as a pretext etc., medieval Latin *-ari*, *-are* be the cause of, from *causa*: see CAUSE *noun*.]
1 *verb trans.* Be the cause of, effect, or bring about (a thing, esp. a bad thing); occasion, produce; induce or make (a person or thing *to do*, †*do*, a thing *to be done*, †*be done*); (arch.) bring it about *that*. LME.

SPENSER She caused them be led . . Into a bowre. AV *John* 11:37 Could not this man . . have caused that even this man should not have died? DRYDEN A Drench of Wine . . the Patient's Death did cause. C. BEATON The visitor pressed an electric button that caused a glass wall to roll back. L. DURRELL A cruel satirical short story, which . . caused me great pain.

cause havoc: see HAVOC *noun* 2.
†**2** *verb intrans.* Give reasons or excuses. *rare* (Spenser). Only in L16.
■ **causable** *adjective* (*rare*) that can be caused M17. **causer** *noun* a person who or thing which causes something LME.

'cause /kɒz, kəz/ *adverb & conjunction*. *colloq. & dial.* See also COS *adverb & conjunction*. LME.
[ORIGIN Abbreviation.]
= BECAUSE.

cause célèbre /ˌkɔːz sɛˈlɛbr(ə), *foreign* koːz selɛbr/ *noun phr.* Pl. **-s -s** (pronounced same). M18.
[ORIGIN French.]
A notorious legal case; a lawsuit that attracts much attention.

causerie /kozri/ *noun*. Pl. pronounced same. E19.
[ORIGIN French, from *causer* to talk.]
Informal (esp. literary) talk; a chatty article.

causes célèbres *noun phr.* pl. of CAUSE CÉLÈBRE.

causeuse /kozøːz/ *noun*. Pl. pronounced same. M19.
[ORIGIN French, from *causer*: see CAUSERIE.]
A small sofa for two people.

causeway /ˈkɔːzweɪ/ *noun & verb*. LME.
[ORIGIN from CAUSEY + WAY *noun*.]
▸ **A** *noun*. **1** A raised way, path, or road across a low or wet place or stretch of water; a raised footway beside a road. Formerly also, a mole or pier running into the sea or a river. LME.
2 A (paved) highway (*obsolete* exc. *hist.* & in proper names); a paved (part of a) path or road (now *dial.*). L16. ▸**b** *spec.* = CAUSEY *noun* 3b. *Scot.* E19.
▸ **B** *verb trans.* **1** Cross with a causeway; provide with a causeway. Freq. as ***causewayed*** *ppl adjective*. E18.
causewayed camp a type of Neolithic settlement in southern Britain, characterized by a series of concentric ditches crossed by one or more causeways.
2 = CAUSEY *verb*. M18.

causey /ˈkɔːzi, -si/ *noun & verb*. ME.
[ORIGIN Anglo-Norman var. of Old Northern French *caucíée* (mod. *chaussée*) from Proto-Romance fem. pa. pple (sc. *via* way, road) from Latin CALX, *calc-* lime.]
▸ **A** *noun*. †**1** A mound, embankment, or dam to retain the water of a river or pond. ME–L18.
2 = CAUSEWAY *noun* 1. ME.
3 = CAUSEWAY *noun* 2. Now *dial.* or *hist.* LME. ▸**b** *spec.* A cobbled (part of a) street or pavement; a paved area. Chiefly *Scot.* L15.
▸ **B** *verb trans.* Pave with small stones. Chiefly *Scot. & dial.* M16.

causidical /kɔːˈzɪdɪk(ə)l/ *adjective*. L18.
[ORIGIN from Latin *causidicus* pleader + -AL[1].]
Of or pertaining to a pleader of legal causes.

caustic /ˈkɔːstɪk, ˈkɒst-/ *adjective & noun*. LME.
[ORIGIN Latin *causticus* from Greek *kaustikos*, from *kaustos* combustible, from *kaiein* to burn: see -IC.]
▸ **A** *adjective*. **1** That burns or corrodes organic tissue. LME. ▸**b** *fig.* Sarcastic, sharp, biting. L18.
caustic bush *Austral.* a trailing succulent, *Sarcostemma australe*, containing milky juice toxic to livestock; also called ***milk-bush***. **caustic creeper** *Austral.* a spurge, *Euphorbia drummondii*, containing a milky juice poisonous to sheep. **caustic plant** = ***caustic bush*** above. ***caustic potash***: see POTASH 2. **caustic soda** sodium hydroxide, NaOH. **caustic vine** = ***caustic bush*** above. **caustic weed** = ***caustic creeper*** above.
2 PHYSICS. Of a curve or surface: formed by the intersection of rays of light reflected or refracted from a curved surface. E18.
▸ **B** *noun*. **1** A caustic substance. LME.
lunar caustic: see LUNAR *adjective*.
2 PHYSICS. A caustic curve or surface. E18.
■ **caustically** *adverb* M19. **causticity** /-ˈstɪsɪti/ *noun* L18.

cautel /ˈkɔːt(ə)l/ *noun*. LME.
[ORIGIN Old French & mod. French *cautèle* or Latin *cautela*, from *caut-* pa. ppl stem of *cavere* take heed.]
†**1** Cunning, trickery; a trick, a stratagem. LME–E17.
†**2** Caution, wariness. LME–M17.
3 A precautionary instruction or provision; *spec.* (CHRISTIAN CHURCH) a rubrical direction for the proper administration of the sacraments. LME.
■ **cautelous** *adjective* (*arch.*) crafty, deceitful, wily; cautious, wary, circumspect: LME.

cauter /ˈkɔːtə/ *noun*. M16.
[ORIGIN Old French & mod. French *cautère* from Latin *cauterium*: see CAUTERY.]
= CAUTERY 1.

cauterize /ˈkɔːtərʌɪz/ *verb trans.* Also **-ise**. LME.
[ORIGIN Old French & mod. French *cautériser* from late Latin *cauterizare* from Greek *kautēriazein*, from *kautērion*: see CAUTERY, -IZE.]
1 Burn or sear with heat or a caustic substance, esp. in surgical operations. LME.
2 *fig.* Deaden, make insensible or callous. L16.

SOUTHEY Custom soon cauterizes human sympathy.

■ **cauteri'zation** *noun* LME.

cautery /ˈkɔːt(ə)ri/ *noun*. LME.
[ORIGIN Latin *cauterium* from Greek *kautērion* branding iron, from *kaiein* to burn.]
1 A metal instrument or caustic substance for searing tissue. LME.
actual cautery *arch.* a hot iron for cauterizing. **potential cautery** *arch.* a caustic substance used for cauterizing.
2 The action of cauterizing. LME.

fig.: W. OWEN Their senses in some scorching cautery of battle Now long since ironed.

caution /ˈkɔːʃ(ə)n/ *noun & verb*. ME.
[ORIGIN Old French & mod. French from Latin *cautio(n-)*, from *caut-* pa. ppl stem of *cavere* take heed: see -ION.]
▸ **A** *noun*. **1** Security given, bail; a guarantee. Now chiefly *Scot. & US*. ME. ▸**b** A person who stands surety, a guarantor. L16.
†**2** A proviso. L16–L17.

MILTON What meant that caution joind, *if ye be found Obedient*?

3 A word of warning; a fact that acts as a warning; an official reprimand and warning regarding a person's future conduct. L16.

SHAKES. *Macb.* Whate'er thou art, for thy good caution, thanks. R. GRAVES The accused was at once dismissed with a caution.

†**4** A precaution, a taking of heed. E17–E19.
5 Prudence, taking care; attention to safety, avoidance of rashness. M17.

H. H. MILMAN Godfrey . . had learned caution by his eventful life; it had degenerated into craft. SLOAN WILSON He had almost gone charging . . to berate her, but an innate caution had stopped him. A. MACLEAN With infinite caution, a fraction of an inch at a time.

sound a note of caution: see NOTE *noun*[2].
6 A surprising or amusing person or thing. *colloq.* (orig. *US*). M19.

D. H. LAWRENCE Oh, he's a caution, that lad—but not bad, you know.

– COMB.: **caution money** money deposited as security for good conduct.
▸ **B** *verb trans.* & (*rare*) *intrans.* Warn (*against*; *to do*, *not to do*), advise; warn and reprove, esp. officially. E17.
■ **cautioner** *noun* (SCOTS LAW) a person who stands surety for another E16.

cautionary /ˈkɔːʃ(ə)n(ə)ri/ *adjective & noun*. L16.
[ORIGIN medieval Latin *cautionarius*, from Latin *cautio(n-)*: see CAUTION, -ARY[1].]
▸ **A** *adjective*. **1** Of, pertaining to, or of the nature of a pledge or security; held as a pledge or security. Now *hist.* exc. SCOTS LAW. L16.
†**2** Marked by caution; cautious. E17–M19.
3 Conveying a warning, admonitory. M17.

New Republic These outbreaks of violence against innocents ought to be cautionary tales.

†**4** Of the nature of a provision against danger; precautionary. L17–E19.
▸ **B** *noun*. A security, guarantee, bail; a surety. Now only in SCOTS LAW, an obligation undertaken to guarantee against or answer for the default of another. L16.

cautious /ˈkɔːʃəs/ *adjective*. M17.
[ORIGIN from CAUTION *noun* on the model of *ambition*, *ambitious*, etc.: see -TIOUS.]
Characterized by caution; wary, careful, circumspect.

T. FORREST I was very cautious of touching upon what had happened that morning. D. L. SAYERS Inclined to take a cautious view of rumours and suspicions. C. MILNE Let us buy not just our usual cautious one or two copies; let us take a dozen.

†**cautious to do** careful not to do.
■ **cautiously** *adverb* M17. **cautiousness** *noun* M17.

cava /ˈkeɪvə/ *noun*[1]. Pl. **cavae** /ˈkeɪviː/. E19.
[ORIGIN Abbreviation.]
MEDICINE. = ***VENA CAVA***.
■ **caval** *adjective* of or pertaining to one or both of the venae cavae L19.

cava /ˈkɑːvə/ *noun*[2]. L20.
[ORIGIN Spanish = cellar.]
A Spanish sparkling wine made in the same way as champagne.

cavalcade /kav(ə)lˈkeɪd, ˈkav(ə)lkeɪd/ *noun & verb*. L16.
[ORIGIN French from Italian *cavalcata*, from *cavalcare* to ride etc. from Proto-Romance, from Latin *caballus* horse.]
▸ **A** *noun*. †**1** A ride or raid on horseback. L16–L17.
2 A company or procession of riders, carriages, motor vehicles, etc., esp. on a festive or solemn occasion. M17.
▸ **B** *verb intrans.* Ride in a cavalcade. E18.

cavalier /kavəˈlɪə/ *noun & adjective*. M16.
[ORIGIN French, or its source Italian *cavaliere* deriv. of Latin *caballus* horse: see -IER. Cf. CHEVALIER.]
▸ **A** *noun*. **1** FORTIFICATION. A raised defence work on the level ground of a bastion, constructed to command the surrounding work and beyond. M16.
2 A horseman; *esp.* a cavalryman. *arch.* L16.
3 A lively military man; a courtly or fashionable gentleman, a gallant, esp. as an escort to a lady. L16.
4 *hist.* (Usu. **C-**.) A supporter of Charles I in the Civil War of 1642–9, a 17th-century Royalist. M17.
▸ **B** *adjective*. †**1** Gallant. *rare*. Only in M17.
2 Offhand; (esp. haughtily) careless in manner; curt; supercilious. M17.

CARLYLE This cavalier tone from an unknown person . . did not please me. H. ACTON Nancy's amiability with the French differed from her cavalier treatment of the American soldiers.

3 *hist.* (Usu. **C-**.) Supporting Charles I in the Civil War of 1642–9, Royalist; pertaining to or characteristic of the Cavaliers. E18.
cavalier cuff a cuff of gauntlet shape.
■ **cavalierish** *adjective* M17. **cavalierism** *noun* M17. **cavalierly** *adjective* characteristic of a cavalier, knightly M19. **cavalierly** *adverb* in a cavalier manner L17.

cavalier /kavəˈlɪə/ *verb intrans. & trans.* (with *it*). L16.
[ORIGIN from CAVALIER *noun & adjective*.]
Play the cavalier; pay court to women.

cavaliere servente /kavaˈljeːre serˈvɛnte/ *noun phr.* M18.
[ORIGIN Italian, lit. 'gentleman-in-waiting'.]
A (married) woman's lover or solicitous admirer.

cavallard *noun* var. of CAVAYARD.

cavally /kəˈvali/ *noun*. *arch.* Also **-llo** /-ləʊ/, pl. **-o(e)s**. E17.
[ORIGIN Spanish *caballo* lit. 'horse', perh. infl. by Italian *cavalli* pl. of *cavallo* mackerel.]
A horse mackerel or related marine fish.

cavalry /ˈkav(ə)lri/ *noun*. M16.
[ORIGIN French *cavallerie* from Italian *cavalleria*, from *cavallo* horse from Latin *caballus*: see -ERY, -RY.]
1 *collect.* (usu. treated as *pl.*). Soldiers on horseback; that part of a military force which consists of mounted troops. Now also, soldiers in motor vehicles. M16. ▸**b** A force or troop of cavalry. E17. ▸**c** *transf.* Horse-riders; horses for riding. L17.
†**2** Horsemanship. L16–L17.
– COMB.: **cavalryman** a soldier of a regiment of cavalry; **cavalry sword** a sword used by cavalry, *esp.* a sabre; **cavalry twill** a strong fabric woven in a double twill.

cavaquinho /ˌkavəˈkiːnjəʊ/ *noun*. M19.
[ORIGIN Portuguese, from *cavaco* wood chip.]
A type of small four-stringed guitar resembling a ukulele, popular in Brazil and Portugal.

cavass *noun* see KAVASS.

cavatina /kavəˈtiːnə/ *noun*. E19.
[ORIGIN Italian.]
MUSIC. A short simple song; a songlike piece of instrumental music, usu. slow and emotional.

cavayard /ˈkavɪjɑːd/ *noun*. *US*. Also **cavallard** /ˈkav(ə)ljɑːd/, **cavy-yard**, & other vars. E19.
[ORIGIN Alt. of Spanish CABALLADA.]
A drove of horses or mules; = CABALLADA.

cave /keɪv/ *noun*[1]. ME.
[ORIGIN Old French & mod. French from Latin *cava* use as noun of fem. sing. or neut. pl. of *cavus* hollow.]
1 A large natural underground hollow, usu. with a horizontal opening. ME.
idols of the cave: see IDOL *noun*.
2 POLITICS. A dissident group (cf. ADULLAMITE 2). M19.
– COMB.: **cave art**, **cave painting**: primitive or prehistoric, on the interiors of caves, esp. depicting animals; **cave bear**: of an extinct species known from remains found in caves; **cave-dweller**, **caveman**, **cavewoman**: prehistoric, living in a cave or caves; *fig.* of primitive or violent passions, instincts, and behaviour; **cavefish** = ***blind fish*** s.v. BLIND *adjective*.

cave /ˈkeɪvi/ *noun*[2] *& interjection*. LME.
[ORIGIN Latin, imper. sing. of *cavere* beware.]
▸ **A** *noun*. †**1** A warning; an injunction. LME–L15.
2 ***keep cave***, act as a lookout. *school slang*. E20.
▸ **B** *interjection*. As a warning cry: look out! *school slang*. M19.

cave /keɪv/ *verb*[1]. LME.
[ORIGIN from CAVE *noun*[1].]
1 *verb trans.* Hollow out, excavate. LME.
2 *verb intrans.* Lodge or lurk in a cave. E17.

3 *verb intrans.* Explore caves. Chiefly as ***caving verbal noun.*** M20.

cave /keɪv/ *verb*[2] *intrans. & trans. dial.* (chiefly *Scot. & N. English*). E16.
[ORIGIN Origin(s) unkn.]
1 Cause to fall clumsily or helplessly; tip over; topple. E16.
2 Toss (the head or other part of the body). L17.

cave /keɪv/ *verb*[3]. Also (*dial.*) **calve** /kɑːv/. E18.
[ORIGIN Perh. of Low German origin: cf. Western Flemish *inkalven* fall in, Dutch *afkalven* fall away, *uitkalven* fall out. Infl. by CAVE *verb*[1], *verb*[2].]
Usu. foll. by *in* (without *in* chiefly *US*).
1 *verb intrans.* Fall in over a hollow, subside; give way, yield to pressure, (*lit. & fig.*); submit, withdraw opposition. E18.

W. IRVING The earth caved in, so as to leave a vacant space. L. STEFFENS Men caved all around, but the women were firm. D. BAGLEY The front of the building caved in . . , seeming to collapse in slow motion.

2 *verb trans.* Cause to subside or yield to pressure; smash, bash, or beat in. E19.

B. HARTE Reckons she's caved in his head.

– COMB.: **cave-in** a fall of earth, an inward collapse under pressure.

†**cave** *verb*[4] var. of CHAVE.

cavea /ˈkeɪvɪə/ *noun*. Pl. **-eae** /-ɪiː/. E17.
[ORIGIN Latin = a hollow.]
ROMAN ANTIQUITIES. The (concave) auditorium of a theatre; a theatre.

caveat /ˈkavɪat, ˈkeɪ-/ *noun & verb*. M16.
[ORIGIN Latin, 3rd person sing. pres. subjunct. of *cavere* beware.]
▸ **A** *noun*. **1** A warning, a proviso; *spec.* in LAW (***a***) a process in an ecclesiastical court to suspend proceedings; (***b***) a notice to a court (esp. SCOTS LAW) or an entry in a register preventing a proceeding (as granting of a probate) until the objector's arguments have been heard. M16.
enter a caveat, put in a caveat.
†**2** A precaution. L16–L17.
▸ **B** *verb*. **1** *verb trans.* Enter a caveat against. *rare*. M17.
2 *verb intrans.* FENCING. Disengage. Now *rare* or *obsolete*. M17.
■ **cavea'tee** *noun* (LAW) a person against whose interests a caveat is entered E20. **caveator** *noun* (LAW) a person who enters a caveat L19.

†**caveer** *noun* var. of CAVIAR.

cavel /ˈkav(ə)l/ *noun & verb*. *Scot. & N. English*. ME.
[ORIGIN Corresp. to Dutch *kavel* lot, parcel (*kavelen* cast lots), Middle Dutch *cavele* lot: cf. Middle Low German *kavele* little stick (with runes) for casting lots.]
▸ **A** *noun*. **1** A lot (that is cast). ME.
2 A division made by lot. LME.
▸ **B** *verb intrans. & trans.* Infl. **-l(l)-**. Apportion (by lot). LME.

cavendish /ˈkav(ə)ndɪʃ/ *noun*. M19.
[ORIGIN Prob. from surname *Cavendish*.]
Tobacco softened, sweetened, and pressed into cakes.

caver /ˈkeɪvə/ *noun*. M17.
[ORIGIN from CAVE *noun*[1] or *verb*[1] + -ER[1].]
†**1** A person who frequents mines to take ore that has been left etc. M17–M19.
2 An explorer of caves. M20.

cavern /ˈkav(ə)n/ *noun & verb*. LME.
[ORIGIN Old French & mod. French *caverne* or Latin *caverna*, from *cavus* hollow: cf. CAVE *noun*[1].]
▸ **A** *noun*. An underground hollow, a (vast) cave; a dark cavity. LME.

COLERIDGE Where Alph, the sacred river, ran Through caverns measureless to man. L. P. HARTLEY Her eye sockets were caverns which revealed the skull.

▸ **B** *verb trans.* **1** Enclose (as) in a cavern. M17.
2 Hollow out into a cavern or caverns. M19.
■ **caverned** *adjective* (***a***) having caverns; hollowed out into caverns; (***b***) enclosed in a cavern: E18.

cavernicolous /kavəˈnɪkələs/ *adjective*. L19.
[ORIGIN from Latin *caverna* CAVERN *noun* + -I- + -COLOUS.]
BIOLOGY. Inhabiting caves.
■ **cavernicole** /kəˈvəːnɪkəʊl/ *noun* a cavernicolous animal M20.

cavernous /ˈkav(ə)nəs/ *adjective*. LME.
[ORIGIN Old French & mod. French *caverneux* or Latin *cavernosus*, from *caverna* CAVERN *noun*: see -OUS.]
1 Having many caverns. LME.
2 Full of cavities or interstices. LME.
3 Of or resembling a cavern; suggestive of a cavern. M19.

New Yorker Her voice echoed through the cavernous ballroom.

4 MEDICINE. Of respiration: marked by a prolonged hollow resonance. M19.
■ **cavernously** *adverb* M19.

cavernulous /kəˈvəːnjʊləs/ *adjective*. M18.
[ORIGIN from Latin *cavernula* dim. of *caverna*: see -ULOUS.]
Full of minute cavities; porous.

cavesson /ˈkavɪs(ə)n/ *noun*. L16.
[ORIGIN French *caveçon*, Italian *cavezzone* augm. of *cavezza* halter, from Proto-Romance, from medieval Latin *capitium* head covering, from Latin *caput, capit-* head.]
A noseband fitted with rings to which a lunge or reins may be attached, used in training young horses. In early use also, a similar noseband designed to bring a horse under control by inflicting pain on it.

cavetto /kəˈvɛtəʊ/ *noun*. Pl. **-tti** /-ti/. M17.
[ORIGIN Italian, dim. of *cavo* hollow from Latin *cavus* hollow: cf. CAVE *noun*[1].]
ARCHITECTURE. A hollow moulding with a quadrantal cross-section.

caviar /ˈkavɪɑː, kavɪˈɑː/ *noun*. Also **-iare**, †**-iary**, †**-eer**, & other vars. M16.
[ORIGIN Italian *caviale* (earlier & dial. *caviaro*, pl. *-ri*), French *caviar*, prob. from medieval Greek *khaviari* (whence also perh. Turkish *havyar*).]
The pickled roe of the sturgeon or other large fish, eaten as a delicacy.
caviar to the general [Shakes. *Haml.* II. ii] a good thing unappreciated by the ignorant. ***red caviar***: see RED *adjective*.

cavie /ˈkeɪvi/ *noun*. *Scot.* E16.
[ORIGIN App. from Middle Dutch *kēvie*, Dutch or Flemish *kevie*, ult. from Latin *cavea*: see CAGE *noun*.]
A hen coop.

cavil /ˈkav(ə)l/ *verb & noun*. M16.
[ORIGIN Old French & mod. French *caviller* from Latin *cavillari*, from *cavilla* scoffing, mockery.]
▸ **A** *verb*. Infl. **-ll-**, ***-l-**.
1 *verb intrans.* Raise a petty or unnecessary objection (*at*, *about*). M16.
2 *verb trans.* Object to (something) in a petty way. L16.
▸ **B** *noun*. A petty or unnecessary objection. L16.
■ **caviller** *noun* L16. †**cavillous** *adjective* full of cavils or cavilling; apt to cavil: L16–M19.

cavillation /kavɪˈleɪʃ(ə)n/ *noun*. LME.
[ORIGIN Old French & mod. French from Latin *cavillatio(n-)*, from *cavillat-* pa. ppl stem of *cavillari*: see CAVIL, -ATION.]
†**1** The use of legal quibbles; a legal quibble; chicanery, overreaching sophistry. LME–M17.
2 *gen.* The action of cavilling; a cavil. M16.

cavitary /ˈkavɪt(ə)ri/ *adjective*. M19.
[ORIGIN French *cavitaire*, from *cavité*: see CAVITY, -ARY[1].]
Of the nature of or pertaining to a cavity.

cavitation /kavɪˈteɪʃ(ə)n/ *noun*. L19.
[ORIGIN from CAVITY + -ATION.]
1 The formation of bubbles or cavities in a liquid caused by the rapid movement of a propeller etc. through it. L19.
2 MEDICINE. The formation of cavities in diseased tissue. E20.
■ **ˈcavitate** *verb intrans.* [back-form.] induce or undergo cavitation E20.

cavity /ˈkavɪti/ *noun*. M16.
[ORIGIN Old French & mod. French *cavité* or late Latin *cavitas*, from *cavus* hollow: see -ITY.]
A hollow place; a hollow; an empty space in a solid body, *spec.* in a decayed tooth.
COTYLOID ***cavity***. ***pit cavity***: see PIT *noun*[1]. ***resonant cavity***: see RESONANT *adjective*. *THORACIC* ***cavity***. ***tympanic cavity***: see TYMPANIC *adjective* 1. *VISCERAL* ***cavity***.
– COMB.: ***cavity resonator***: see RESONATOR 3b; **cavity wall** a double external wall with an internal cavity.

cavolo nero /ˌkavələʊ ˈnɛːrəʊ/ *noun*. L20.
[ORIGIN Italian, from *cavolo* cabbage + *nero* black.]
A dark-leaved variety of kale used esp. in Tuscan cookery.

cavort /kəˈvɔːt/ *verb intrans. colloq.* (orig. *US*). L18.
[ORIGIN Perh. alt. of CURVET *verb*.]
Prance, caper about.

†**cavous** *adjective*. LME–M18.
[ORIGIN Latin *cavosus*, from *cavus* hollow: see -OUS.]
Having a cavity; hollow; concave.

cavy /ˈkeɪvi/ *noun*. L18.
[ORIGIN mod. Latin *cavia* from Galibi *cabiai*.]
A rodent of the family Caviidae, native to S. America; *esp.* a guinea pig.
Patagonian cavy: see PATAGONIAN *adjective*.

cavy-yard *noun* var. of CAVAYARD.

caw /kɔː/ *verb, noun, & interjection*. L16.
[ORIGIN Imit.]
▸ **A** *verb intrans.* Of a rook, crow, raven, etc.: make its harsh natural cry. Of a person: make a sound contemptuously likened to this. L16.
▸ **B** *noun & interjection*. (Repr.) the cry of a rook, crow, raven, etc. M17.

cawk *noun*[1] var. of CAUK *noun*.

cawk /kɔːk/ *verb*[1] *intrans. & noun*[2]. M18.
[ORIGIN Imit.]
Caw; (utter) a harsh cry.

†**cawk** *verb*[2] see CAULK *verb*[1].

cawl /kɔːl/ *noun*. Long *obsolete* exc. *dial.*
[ORIGIN Old English *cawl*, *ceawl*.]
A basket; a Cornish creel.

†**caxon** *noun*. M18–M19.
[ORIGIN Perh. from the surname *Caxon*.]
A kind of wig.

cay /keɪ, kiː/ *noun*. L17.
[ORIGIN Spanish *cayo* from French *quai*, †*cay* QUAY *noun*. Cf. KEY *noun*[2].]
An insular bank or reef of coral, sand, etc.

cayenne /keɪˈɛn, attrib. ˈkeɪɛn/ *noun*. E18.
[ORIGIN Orig. from Tupi *kyynha*, *quiynha*, later assim. to *Cayenne*, chief town of French Guiana.]
In full ***cayenne pepper***. A pungent red powder prepared from ground dried chillies, used as a seasoning.
■ **cayenned** *adjective* seasoned with cayenne E19.

cayman *noun* var. of CAIMAN.

Cayuga /ˈkeɪjuːgə, ˈkʌɪ-/ *noun & adjective*. Pl. of noun **-s**, same. M18.
[ORIGIN Iroquoian place name.]
A member of, of or pertaining to, an Iroquois people, one of the five of the original Iroquois confederation, formerly inhabiting part of New York State; (of) the language of this people.

Cayuse /ˈkʌɪjuːs/ *noun & adjective*. In sense A.2 **c-**. E19.
[ORIGIN Penutian.]
▸ **A** *noun*. **1** Pl. same, **-s**. A member of a Penutian people of Washington State and Oregon; the language of this people. E19.
2 Pl. **-s**. An Indian pony; *colloq.* any horse. *N. Amer.* M19.
▸ **B** *attrib.* or as *adjective*. Of or pertaining to the Cayuse or their language. M19.

caza *noun* var. of KAZA.

cazern(e) *noun* vars. of CASERN.

CB *abbreviation*.
1 Citizens' Band (radio).
2 Companion (of the Order) of the Bath.
3 Confined, confinement, to barracks.

Cb *symbol*.
CHEMISTRY (now *hist.*). Columbium.

CBC *abbreviation*.
Canadian Broadcasting Corporation.

CBD *abbreviation*. *US*.
Cash before delivery.

CBE *abbreviation*.
Commander of (the Order of) the British Empire.

CBI *abbreviation*.
Confederation of British Industry.

CBS *abbreviation*.
Columbia Broadcasting System.

CBT *abbreviation*.
Cognitive behaviour therapy.

CBW *abbreviation*.
Chemical and biological warfare, weapons.

CC *abbreviation*[1].
1 City Council.
2 Companion of (the Order of) Canada.
3 County Council(lor).
4 Cricket Club.

cc *abbreviation*[2].
1 Carbon copy.
2 Cubic centimetre(s).

CCD *abbreviation*.
ELECTRONICS. Charge-coupled device.

CCJ *abbreviation*.
County court judgment.

CCTV *abbreviation*.
Closed-circuit television.

CCU *abbreviation*.
MEDICINE. **1** Cardiac care unit.
2 Coronary care unit.
3 Critical care unit.

CD *abbreviation*[1].
1 Civil Defence.
2 Compact disc, compact disc player.
3 French *corps diplomatique* diplomatic corps.
– COMB.: **CD video** a system of simultaneously reproducing sound and video pictures from a compact disc.

cd *abbreviation*[2].
Candela.

Cd *symbol*.
CHEMISTRY. Cadmium.

Cd. *abbreviation*.
Command Paper (third series, 1900–18).

CDC *abbreviation*. *US*.
Centers for Disease Control (and Prevention).

CD-I *abbreviation*.
Compact disc interactive.

CDMA *abbreviation*.
TELECOMMUNICATIONS. Code division multiple access.

cDNA *abbreviation*.
Complementary DNA.

C

Cdr *abbreviation.*
MILITARY. Commander.

CD-R *abbreviation.*
Compact disc recordable.

Cdre *abbreviation.*
Commodore.

CD-ROM /siːdiːˈrɒm/ *abbreviation.*
Compact disc (with) read-only memory.

CD-RW *abbreviation.*
Compact disc rewritable.

CDT *abbreviation. N. Amer.*
Central Daylight Time.

CDTV *abbreviation.*
Compact disc television.

CDV *abbreviation.*
CD video.

CE *abbreviation.*
1 Church of England.
2 Civil Engineer.
3 Common (or Christian) Era.

Ce *symbol.*
CHEMISTRY. Cerium.

ceanothus /siːəˈnəʊθəs/ *noun.* L18.
[ORIGIN mod. Latin from Greek *keanōthos* a kind of thistle.]
Any of various N. American shrubs, freq. grown for ornament, that constitute the genus *Ceanothus*, of the buckthorn family, and bear clusters of small starry blue or white flowers.

cease /siːs/ *noun.* Now *literary.* ME.
[ORIGIN Old French *ces*, formed as CEASE verb.]
Stopping, ending. Now only in ***without cease***.

cease /siːs/ *verb.* See also CESS *verb*[2]. ME.
[ORIGIN Old French & mod. French *cesser* from Latin *cessare* stop, from *cess-* pa. ppl stem of *cedere* CEDE.]
▸ **I** *verb intrans.* **1** Of people and other agents: stop, leave off, desist, discontinue. (Foll. by *from*, †*of*, *to do*.) ME. ▸†**b** (Take) rest, be or remain at rest. LME–M17.

SHELLEY Oh, cease! must hate and death return? Cease! Must men kill and die? TENNYSON Fold our wings, And cease from wanderings. G. VIDAL At five-thirty the world ceased to be official and became private.

2 Of actions, feelings, phenomena, etc.: come to or be at an end. ME.

QUILLER-COUCH Presently the turf ceased. Dismounting, I ran to the edge. J. STEINBECK When hostilities ceased everyone had his wounds.

3 No longer exist, become extinct; die. *literary.* LME.

V. WOOLF Did it matter that she must inevitably cease completely; all this must go on without her?

▸ **II** *verb trans.* †**4** Cause to leave off (*of* an action); appease, bring to rest. ME–L16.

TINDALE *Acts* 19:35 When the toune clarcke had ceased the people.

†**5** Put a stop to (the action of others, a state or condition of things). LME–L17.

MILTON He, her fears to cease, Sent down the meek-eyed Peace.

6 Leave off, discontinue (one's own action, feeling, etc.; *doing*). LME. ▸**b** BELL-RINGING. Bring (a peal) to an end; let (a bell) down. L17.

J. GALSWORTHY He did not believe her excuse, but ceased his opposition. J. UPDIKE Ezana would not cease his flirting with . . Mrs. Gibbs.

cease fire discontinue firing.
— COMB.: **ceasefire** a signal for the ceasing of active hostilities; an armistice, a period when hostilities are suspended.

ceaseless /ˈsiːslɪs/ *adjective.* L16.
[ORIGIN from CEASE *noun* + -LESS.]
Not ceasing, incessant, uninterrupted.
■ **ceaselessly** *adverb* L16. **ceaselessness** *noun* L19.

cebid /ˈsiːbɪd/ *noun & adjective.* L19.
[ORIGIN mod. Latin *Cebidae* (see below), from *Cebus* genus name: see -ID[3].]
ZOOLOGY. ▸**A** *noun.* A monkey of the family Cebidae, which includes most of the New World monkeys. L19.
▸ **B** *adjective.* Of, pertaining to, or designating this family. E20.
■ **ceboid** *adjective & noun* = CEBID E20.

cecidium /sɪˈsɪdɪəm/ *noun.* Pl. **-dia** /-dɪə/. E20.
[ORIGIN from Greek *kēkis* a gall + -IDIUM.]
= GALL *noun*[3]
■ **ceciˈdology** *noun* the scientific study of galls and their formation E20.

cecity /ˈsiːsɪti/ *noun. literary.* L15.
[ORIGIN Latin *caecitas*, from *caecus* blind: see -ITY. Cf. Old French & mod. French *cécité*.]
Blindness (chiefly *fig.*).

cecropia /sɪˈkrəʊpɪə/ *noun.* E19.
[ORIGIN mod. Latin (see sense 1), from *Cecrops* a king of Attica: see -IA[1].]
1 A tree of the tropical American genus *Cecropia*, which belongs to the mulberry family and includes some species yielding rubber. E19.
2 In full ***cecropia moth***. A N. American saturniid silk moth, *Platysamia cecropia*. M19.

cecum *noun* see CAECUM.

cedar /ˈsiːdə/ *noun.* OE.
[ORIGIN (Old French *cedre* from) Latin *cedrus* from Greek *kedros*.]
1 An evergreen conifer of the genus *Cedrus*; esp. *Cedrus libani* (more fully ***cedar of Lebanon***), native to Asia Minor. Also ***cedar tree***. OE. ▸**b** The fragrant durable wood of such a tree. ME.
Indian cedar = DEODAR.
2 Any of various trees more or less similar to this; the wood of these trees; *esp.* = ***red cedar*** (a) s.v. RED *adjective.* LME.
Bermuda cedar, ***Japanese cedar***, ***sharp cedar***, ***stinking cedar***, ***white cedar***, etc.
— COMB.: **cedar-bird** a N. American waxwing, *Bombycilla cedrorum*; ***cedar tree***: see sense 1 above; **cedar waxwing** = ***cedar-bird*** above.
■ **cedared** *adjective* (*poet.*) marked by the presence of cedars E19. **cedarn** *adjective* (*poet.*) of cedars or cedar wood M17. †**cedrine** *adjective* of or pertaining to cedar M–L18.

cede /siːd/ *verb.* E16.
[ORIGIN French *céder* or Latin *cedere* give way, yield, retreat.]
1 *verb trans.* Give up, surrender, yield (*to*); *esp.* grant (territory, *to*) by treaty etc. E16.
†**2** *verb intrans.* Give way, give place *to*. E17–M18.
■ **cedent** *noun* (SCOTS LAW) a person who assigns property to another L16.

cedi /ˈsiːdi/ *noun.* M20.
[ORIGIN Ghanaian, perh. from alt. of SHILLING.]
The basic monetary unit of Ghana, equal to 100 pesewas.

cedilla /sɪˈdɪlə/ *noun.* L16.
[ORIGIN Spanish (now *zedilla*), dim. of *zeda* letter Z. Cf. CERILLA.]
The diacritic mark ¸ written under *c* to show that it is sibilant /s/ or /ts/, as before *a*, *o*, *u* in French and Portuguese and (formerly) Spanish; a similar mark under *c* and *s* indicating a manner of articulation in various other contexts, as distinguishing the voiceless from the voiced consonants in modern Turkish.

cedrat /ˈsiːdrət/ *noun.* Also **-ate**. E18.
[ORIGIN French *cédrat* from Italian *cedrato*, from *cedro* citron, from Latin CITRUS.]
A variety of citron or lemon.

cedrela /sɪˈdriːlə/ *noun.* M19.
[ORIGIN mod. Latin from Spanish, dim. of *cedro*, *cedra* cedar.]
(The soft timber of) a tropical tree of the genus *Cedrela*, of the mahogany family.

cedula /ˈθɛdulə, s-/ *noun.* E18.
[ORIGIN Spanish *cédula* schedule.]
In Spain and some Spanish-speaking countries: an official permit or order; a government security.

Ceefax /ˈsiːfaks/ *noun.* L20.
[ORIGIN Repr. initial syllables of *seeing* + *facsimile*.]
(Proprietary name for) a teletext system developed and operated by the BBC.

Cefaut /siːfɑːˈʊt/ *noun. obsolete* exc. *hist.* Also **C fa ut**. LME.
[ORIGIN from *C* as a pitch letter + *fa* and *ut* designating tones in the solmization of Guido d'Arezzo (*c* 990–1050).]
MEDIEVAL MUSIC. The note C in Guido d'Arezzo's 1st and 2nd hexachords, where it was sung to the syllables *fa* and *ut* respectively. Cf. ALAMIRE, BEMI, CESOLFA, etc.

CEGB *abbreviation. hist.*
Central Electricity Generating Board.

ceiba /ˈsʌɪbə/ *noun.* E17.
[ORIGIN Spanish from Taino = giant tree.]
The kapok tree, *Ceiba pentandra*.

ceil /siːl/ *verb & noun.* Also **ciel**. LME.
[ORIGIN Uncertain: perh. rel. to Latin *celare*, French *céler*, hide, conceal.]
▸ **A** *verb trans.* †**1** Cover with a lining of woodwork, plaster, etc. LME–E17.
2 Line or plaster the roof of; construct an inner roof for. *arch.* E16.
▸ **B** *noun.* A ceiling. *poet. rare.* M19.

ceilidh /ˈkeɪli/ *noun.* L19.
[ORIGIN Irish *céilidhe* (now *céilí*), Gaelic *cēilidh*, from Old Irish *céilide* visit, act of visiting, from *céile* companion.]
An informal gathering for (esp. Scottish or Irish) folk music, dancing, song, etc.

ceiling /ˈsiːlɪŋ/ *noun.* Also **ciel-**. ME.
[ORIGIN from CEIL *verb* + -ING[1].]
1 The action of CEIL *verb. arch.* ME.
2 The wooden lining of a room; panelling; wainscoting. Long *obsolete* exc. *dial.* LME. ▸**b** NAUTICAL. The inside planking or lining of a ship's bottom and sides. LME.
†**3** A screen of tapestry; a curtain. LME–M17.
4 The upper interior surface of a room or other similar compartment. M16.

T. C. BOYLE It had a high ceiling and a big, walk-in closet.

hit the ceiling *colloq.* become very angry. ***suspended ceiling***: see SUSPENDED *ppl adjective.*
5 a AERONAUTICS. The maximum altitude which a given aircraft can attain under specified conditions. E20. ▸**b** METEOROLOGY. (The altitude of) the base of a cloud layer. M20. ▸**c** *gen.* An upper limit (to quantity, prices, etc.); a maximum. M20.
■ **ceilinged** *adjective* having a ceiling of a specified type E19.

ceinture /sɛ̃tyːr/ *noun.* Pl. pronounced same. LME.
[ORIGIN French formed as CINCTURE.]
= CINCTURE *noun.*
— NOTE: Fell into disuse after LME; reintroduced E19.

cel *noun* var. of CELL *noun*[2].

celadon /ˈsɛlədɒn/ *noun & adjective.* M18.
[ORIGIN French *céladon*, from the name of a character in D'Urfé's *L'Astrée*.]
▸ **A** *noun.* **1** A pale greyish shade of green. M18.
2 A glaze of this colour used on (esp. Chinese) pottery or porcelain; ceramic ware thus glazed. M19.
▸ **B** *attrib.* or as *adjective.* Of this colour; covered with this glaze. L19.

celandine /ˈsɛləndʌɪn/ *noun.* Orig. †**celidony** & other vars.; also (long *obsolete* exc. *dial.*) **saladine**. OE.
[ORIGIN Old French *celidoine*, from medieval Latin *celidonia* adjective, ult. from Greek *khelidōn* the swallow: for the inserted *-n-* (LME) cf. *passenger*.]
1 In full ***greater celandine***. A yellow-flowered plant of the poppy family, *Chelidonium majus*; a flowering stem of this plant. OE.
2 In full ***lesser celandine***. A common plant of the buttercup family, *Ranunculus ficaria*, bearing bright yellow flowers in early spring; a flowering stem of this plant. LME.

Celarent /sɪˈlɛːrənt/ *noun.* M16.
[ORIGIN Latin = they might hide, used as a mnemonic of scholastic philosophers, E indicating a universal negative proposition and A a universal affirmative proposition.]
LOGIC. The second mood of the first syllogistic figure, in which a universal negative major premiss and a universal affirmative minor premiss give a universal negative conclusion.

celature /ˈsiːlətjʊə/ *noun.* Now *rare* or *obsolete.* LME.
[ORIGIN Latin *caelatura*, from *caelare* emboss, engrave.]
Embossing; (an example of) embossed work.

†**cele** *noun.* L16–M18.
[ORIGIN formed as -CELE.]
MEDICINE. A swelling, *esp.* one in the groin.

-cele /siːl/ *suffix.* Also **-coele**.
[ORIGIN Greek *kēlē* tumour.]
Forming nouns denoting swellings, hernias, etc., as ***gastrocele***, ***mucocele***, ***urocele***, etc.

celeb /sɪˈlɛb/ *noun. colloq.* (orig. *US*). E20.
[ORIGIN Abbreviation.]
A celebrity.

celebrant /ˈsɛlɪbr(ə)nt/ *noun.* M19.
[ORIGIN French *célébrant*, or Latin *celebrant-* pres. ppl stem of *celebrare*: see CELEBRATE, -ANT[1].]
A person who celebrates; *esp.* the priest who officiates at the Eucharist.

celebrate /ˈsɛlɪbreɪt/ *verb.* LME.
[ORIGIN Latin *celebrat-* pa. ppl stem of *celebrare*, from *celeber*, *-bris* frequented, renowned: see -ATE[3].]
▸ **I** *verb trans.* **1** Perform (a religious ceremony) publicly and in due form; solemnize; officiate at (the Eucharist). LME.
2 Observe (a festival etc.) with due rites; honour or commemorate with ceremonies, festivities, etc. E16.

J. GALSWORTHY We must organize a little dinner to celebrate the event. A. C. BOULT Three concerts to celebrate Elgar's seventy-fifth birthday.

3 Make publicly known, proclaim; extol, praise widely. L16.

MILTON To celebrate his Throne With warbl'd Hymns. E. WILSON A succession of books . . that celebrate lyrically the marvels of nature.

▸ **II** *verb intrans.* **4** Officiate at the Eucharist. M16.
5 Engage in festivities; carouse. E20.
■ **celebrated** *adjective* (*a*) famous, renowned; †(*b*) performed with due rites: L16. **celebrative** *adjective* pertaining to or characterized by celebration M19. **celebrator**, †**-ter** *noun* a person who celebrates E17. **celebratory** *adjective* serving to celebrate, used in celebration E20.

celebration /sɛlɪˈbreɪʃ(ə)n/ *noun.* E16.
[ORIGIN Old French & mod. French *célébration* or Latin *celebratio(n-)*, from *celebrat-*: see CELEBRATE, -ATION.]
1 The observing of a feast etc.; the commemoration of an event with ceremonies or festivities; a social gathering held to celebrate something. E16.

M. DICKENS I say, don't you think this calls for a celebration? A. BARNETT Carter describes the celebration of 'Empire Day' at her south London primary school.

2 The performance of a solemn ceremony; *spec.* the action of celebrating the Eucharist. **M16.**
3 Making publicly known, proclamation; extolling. **M17.**
†**4** Renown, fame. Only in **18.**
■ **celebrational** *adjective* **E20.**

celebret /ˈsɛlɪbrɛt/ *noun.* **M19.**
[**ORIGIN** Latin = let him celebrate, 3rd person sing. pres. subjunct. of *celebrare* **CELEBRATE.**]
ROMAN CATHOLIC CHURCH. A document granting permission by a bishop to a priest to celebrate mass in a particular parish.

celebrious /sɪˈlɛbrɪəs/ *adjective.* **M16.**
[**ORIGIN** from Latin *celeber, -bris* (see **CELEBRATE**) + **-OUS.**]
†**1** Frequented, crowded, festive. **M16–L17.**
2 Renowned, famous. Now *arch. & dial.* **E17.**

celebrity /sɪˈlɛbrɪti/ *noun.* **LME.**
[**ORIGIN** Old French & mod. French *célébrité* or Latin *celebritas*, from *celeber, -bris*: see **CELEBRATE, -ITY.**]
†**1** A solemn ceremony; a celebration; due observance of ceremonies; pomp, solemnity. **LME–L18.**
2 The condition of being widely known or esteemed; fame, renown. **LME.**
3 A celebrated person; a (popular) public figure. **M19.**

celebutante /sɪˈlɛbjuːtɑːnt/ *noun.* **M20.**
[**ORIGIN** Blend of **CELEBRITY** and **DEBUTANTE.**]
A celebrity who is well known in fashionable society.

celeriac /sɪˈlɛrɪak/ *noun.* **M18.**
[**ORIGIN** from **CELERY**, with arbitrary use of **-AC.**]
A variety of celery with a root like a turnip.

celerity /sɪˈlɛrɪti/ *noun.* **L15.**
[**ORIGIN** Old French & mod. French *célérité* from Latin *celeritas*, from *celer* swift: see **-ITY.**]
1 Swiftness, speed. (Now chiefly of the actions of living beings.) **L15.**
†**2** A particular speed. **M–L18.**

celery /ˈsɛləri/ *noun.* **M17.**
[**ORIGIN** French *céleri* from Italian dial. *selleri* ult. from Greek *selinon* parsley.]
An umbelliferous plant, *Apium graveolens*, grown for its crisp blanched leaf stalks which are eaten raw in salads or cooked as a vegetable. Also (more fully ***wild celery***), the wild form of this, a Eurasian plant found chiefly in brackish ditches.
– **COMB.:** **celery salt** a mixture of salt and ground celery seed used for seasoning; **celery top**, **celery-top pine**, **celery-topped pine** an Australasian conifer of the genus *Phyllocladus*, with branchlets producing foliage like that of celery.

celesta /sɪˈlɛstə/ *noun.* **L19.**
[**ORIGIN** App. pseudo-Latinization of French *céleste*: see **CELESTE.**]
A small keyboard instrument in which hammers strike on steel plates, producing an ethereal bell-like sound.

celeste /sɪˈlɛst/ *noun.* **L19.**
[**ORIGIN** French *céleste* from Latin *caelestis*: see **CELESTIAL.**]
1 A stop on the organ and harmonium with a soft tremulous tone (French *voix céleste*). Also, a form of soft pedal on a piano. **L19.**
2 = **CELESTA. M20.**

celestial /sɪˈlɛstɪəl/ *adjective & noun.* **LME.**
[**ORIGIN** Old French *celestial*, *-el* from medieval Latin *caelestialis*, from Latin *caelestis*, from *caelum* heaven: see **-IAL.**]
▸ **A** *adjective.* **1** Of or pertaining to heaven, as the abode of God, angels, spirits, etc. **LME.**

> C. CULLEN She thinks that even up in Heaven Her class lies late and snores, While poor black cherubs rise at seven To do celestial chores.

2 Of or pertaining to the sky or material heavens. **LME.**
celestial body: see **BODY** *noun*. ***celestial equator***: see **EQUATOR** *noun* 1. ***celestial globe***: see **GLOBE** *noun* 3. ***celestial latitude***: see **LATITUDE** 5a. **celestial mechanics** the branch of theoretical astronomy that deals with the calculation of the motions of celestial objects. **celestial navigation**: using the observed positions of celestial objects. ***celestial pole***: see **POLE** *noun*[2] 1. ***celestial sphere***: see **SPHERE** *noun* 2.
3 Divine, heavenly; divinely beautiful, excellent. **LME.**

> W. STYRON A phrase of music, celestial and tender.

4 *hist.* Chinese. Chiefly in ***Celestial Empire***. **E19.**
▸ **B** *noun.* **1** An inhabitant of heaven. **L16.**
†**2** In *pl.* Heavenly objects, bodies, or attributes. **L16–M18.**
3 *hist.* A subject of the Celestial Empire; a Chinese person. **M19.**
■ **celestiˈality** *noun* **E19.** **celestially** *adverb* **LME.**

†**celestify** *verb trans. rare.* **M17–M18.**
[**ORIGIN** from Latin *caelestis* **CELESTIAL** + **-FY**: cf. Old French *celestifier*.]
Make heavenly.

Celestine /ˈsɛlɪstʌɪn, sɪˈlɛstʌɪn; -tɪn/ *noun*[1]. **L15.**
[**ORIGIN** medieval Latin *Caelestinus*, from name *Caelistinus* Celestine: see **-INE**[4].]
A member of a reformed branch of the Benedictine order, founded by Pope Celestine V in the 13th cent.

celestine /sɪˈlɛstiːn, ˈsɛlɪstiːn; -tʌɪn/ *noun*[2]. **E19.**
[**ORIGIN** from Latin *caelestis* **CELESTIAL** (on account of the colour) + **-INE**[5].]
MINERALOGY. Anhydrous strontium sulphate, occurring as colourless or sky-blue tabular orthorhombic crystals.
■ Also **celestite** *noun* **M19.**

celiac *adjective* see **COELIAC.**

celibacy /ˈsɛlɪbəsi/ *noun.* **M17.**
[**ORIGIN** from Latin *caelibatus*, from *caelebs, -ib-* unmarried, bachelor: see **-ACY.**]
The state of living unmarried, abstention from sexual intercourse, esp. by resolve or as an obligation.

celibatarian /ˌsɛlɪbəˈtɛːrɪən/ *adjective & noun.* **M19.**
[**ORIGIN** from French *célibataire*, from *célibat*: see **CELIBATE** *noun*[1], **-ARIAN.**]
▸ **A** *adjective.* Of or pertaining to celibacy; favouring celibacy. **M19.**
▸ **B** *noun.* A person who lives in or advocates celibacy. **M19.**

celibate /ˈsɛlɪbət/ *noun*[1]. *arch.* **E17.**
[**ORIGIN** French *célibat* or Latin *caelibatus* **CELIBACY**: see **-ATE**[1].]
The state of celibacy; an order of celibates.

celibate /ˈsɛlɪbət/ *adjective & noun*[2]. **E19.**
[**ORIGIN** from **CELIBACY**, after *magistracy, magistrate*, etc.: see **-ATE**[1], **-ATE**[2].]
▸ **A** *adjective.* Unmarried, single; abstaining from sexual intercourse; bound or resolved not to marry or have sexual intercourse. **E19.**
▸ **B** *noun.* A person who is celibate, esp. by resolve or as an obligation. **M19.**

†**celidony** *noun* see **CELANDINE.**

celio- *combining form* see **COELIO-.**

cell /sɛl/ *noun*[1]. **OE.**
[**ORIGIN** Old French *celle*, or its source Latin *cella* storeroom, chamber, small apartment, 'chapel' in a temple.]
▸ **I** A small room or dwelling.
1 A (small) monastery or nunnery, dependent on some larger house. **OE.**

> E. A. FREEMAN A priory of Lapley, which was a cell to Saint Remigius.

†**2** A cupboard. **ME–L16.**
3 A single-chambered dwelling inhabited by a hermit etc. **ME.**

> SHAKES. *Rom. & Jul.* There she shall at Friar Lawrence' cell Be shriv'd and married.

4 Any of a number of small chambers in a building; *spec.* a room for one person in a monastery etc.; a room for one or more prisoners. **ME.**

> R. KIPLING You 'ave been absent without leave an' you'll go into cells for that. E. WAUGH Left to herself in a concrete cell which she called her apartment.

condemned cell, ***death cell***, etc. ***padded cell***: see **PAD** *verb*[2] 1.
5 A humble dwelling; a lonely nook; an isolated retreat. Also, the grave. *poet.* **L16.**

> T. GRAY Each in his narrow cell for ever laid. SIR W. SCOTT Like hunted stag, in mountain cell.

▸ **II** *transf.* **6** A compartment in a cabinet, dovecote, bees' honeycomb, etc. **LME.**
7 An enclosed or circumscribed space, cavity, or volume, in an organism, mineral, fluid, etc., usu. distinguished by some property. **LME.** ▸**b** In *pl.* More fully ***cells of the brain***. The imaginary cavities of the brain, formerly or fancifully identified with particular faculties. **LME.**

> **b** W. COWPER The cells Where Mem'ry slept.

LANGMUIR cell.
8 *BIOLOGY.* The basic structural and functional unit of which living organisms and tissues are composed, usu. microscopic and consisting of cytoplasm bounded by a membrane, with genetic material (DNA) contained in a nucleus; a similar entity living independently, with or (in the case of bacteria) without a distinct nucleus. **L17.**

> R. DAWKINS As an adult, you consist of a thousand million million cells. D. LESSING To breed like cells under a microscope.

germ cell, ***nerve cell***, ***red cell***, ***sickle cell***, ***vegetative cell***, ***white cell***, etc. ***wandering cell***: see **WANDERING** *ppl adjective*.
9 A vessel containing electrodes for electricity generation or electrolysis. Also, a unit in a device for converting chemical or radiant energy into electrical energy. **E19.**
fuel cell, ***photocell***, ***photoelectric cell***, ***solar cell***, ***voltaic cell***, etc.
10 Any of the spaces into which a surface is divided by lines or a volume by surfaces; *spec.* a space between the ribs of a vaulted roof, or between the veins of an insect's wing. **M19.** ▸**b** A position or element in an arrangement in two or more dimensions. **M20.** ▸**c** The local area covered by one of the short-range radio stations in a cellular telephone system. **L20.**

> *Scientific American* Nine kings, eight bishops or eight rooks are needed to attack all vacant cells on a standard chessboard.

primitive cell, ***unit cell***, etc.
11 A container for a specimen or sample in microscopy, spectroscopy, etc. **L19.**
12 A small group of people (occas. one person) working, often clandestinely, as a nucleus of political (esp. revolutionary) activity; the headquarters of such a group. **E20.**
13 *COMPUTING.* A unit of data storage. **M20.**
14 A cellphone. *N. Amer.* **L20.**
– **COMB.:** ***cell membrane***: see **MEMBRANE** 1c; **cell-mediated** *adjective* relating to or denoting immunity resulting from the action of white blood cells, rather than that of circulating antibodies; **cellphone** a telephone giving access to a cellular radio system, a mobile phone.
■ **celled** *adjective* provided with cells, arranged or constructed in the form of cells (usu. of a specified kind or number) **L18.**

cell /sɛl/ *noun*[2]. Also **cel**. **M20.**
[**ORIGIN** Abbreviation of **CELLULOID.**]
A transparent sheet of celluloid or similar film material, which can be drawn on and used in combination with others in the production of cartoons etc.

cell /sɛl/ *verb.* **LME.**
[**ORIGIN** from **CELL** *noun*[1].]
1 *verb trans.* Shut up (as) in a cell. **LME.**
2 *verb intrans.* Live in a cell; *esp.* share a prison cell *with* another person. **L16.**
3 *verb trans.* Store in cells. **E19.**

cella /ˈkɛlə/ *noun.* Pl. **cellae** /ˈkɛliː/. **L17.**
[**ORIGIN** Latin: see **CELL** *noun*[1].]
The internal section of a Greek or Roman temple housing the hidden cult image; a similar part of other ancient temples.

cellar /ˈsɛlə/ *noun & verb.* **ME.**
[**ORIGIN** Anglo-Norman *celer* = Old French *celier* (mod. *cellier*) from late Latin *cellarium* set of cells, storehouse for food, from *cella* **CELL** *noun*[1]: see **-AR**[2].]
▸ **A** *noun.* **1** A storehouse or storeroom. *obsolete* in *gen.* sense. **ME.**
2 An underground room or vault, esp. for storage. **ME.**
beer cellar, ***coal cellar***, etc.
3 In full ***wine cellar***. A place in which wine is kept; *transf.* the contents of this, a person's stock of wines. **LME.**
†**4** A box, a case, esp. of bottles. (See also **SALT CELLAR.**) Only in **M17.**
– **COMB.:** **cellar beetle** any of several large slow-moving tenebrionid beetles of the genus *Blaps*; esp. *B. mucronata*, which frequents cellars etc.; **cellar-book**: for keeping a record of the stock of wines etc. in a cellar; **cellarman**: in charge of a cellar; **cellarway** a passage through cellars.
▸ **B** *verb trans.* Put into a cellar; store (as) in a cellar. **E16.**
■ **cellarage** *noun* (**a**) cellar accommodation, cellars; (**b**) *hist.* a feudal duty on wine in a cellar; (**c**) a charge for the use of a cellar: **E16.** **cellared** *adjective* (**a**) provided with a cellar or cellars; (**b**) stored or housed in a cellar: **M17.** **cellarer** *noun* (*hist.*) an officer in a monastery etc. in charge of food and drink **ME.** **cellaress** *noun* (*hist.*) a female cellarer **LME.** **cellaˈret** *noun* a case or sideboard for holding wine bottles in a dining room **E19.** **cellaring** *noun* (**a**) = **CELLARAGE** (a); (**b**) placing in a cellar or cellars: **LME.**

cellated /səˈleɪtɪd/ *adjective.* **M19.**
[**ORIGIN** from Latin *cellatus*, from *cella* **CELL** *noun*[1]: see **-ATE**[2], **-ED**[1].]
Divided into cells.

Cellnet /ˈsɛlnɛt/ *noun.* Also **c-**. **L20.**
[**ORIGIN** from **CELL** *noun*[1] or **CELLULAR** + **NET** *noun*[1].]
(Proprietary name for) a cellular telephone service. Occas. also, a cellular telephone.

cello /ˈtʃɛləʊ/ *noun.* Also **'cello**. Pl. **-llos**, (*rare*) **-lli** /-li/. **L19.**
[**ORIGIN** Abbreviation of **VIOLONCELLO.**]
A four-stringed bass instrument like a large violin, held resting on the floor by a seated player; a player on this in an orchestra etc.
■ **cellist** *noun* a player of the cello **L19.**

cellobiose /sɛləʊˈbʌɪəʊz, -s/ *noun.* **E20.**
[**ORIGIN** from **CELLULOSE** *noun* + **-O-** + **BI-** + **-OSE**[2].]
CHEMISTRY. A synthetic disaccharide which is a dimer of glucose and is obtained by partial hydrolysis of cellulose.

celloidin /sɛˈlɔɪdɪn/ *noun.* **L19.**
[**ORIGIN** from **CELLULOSE** *noun* + **-OID** + **-IN**[1].]
A pure form of pyroxylin used in microscopy to embed tissue specimens for sectioning.

Cellophane /ˈsɛləfeɪn/ *noun.* Also **c-**. **E20.**
[**ORIGIN** from **CELLULOSE** *noun* + **-O-** + *-phane* after **DIAPHANE.**]
(Proprietary name for) a glossy transparent material made from viscose, used chiefly for wrapping goods, food, etc.

cellotape *noun & verb* see **SELLOTAPE.**

cellular /ˈsɛljʊlə/ *adjective.* **M18.**
[**ORIGIN** French *cellulaire* from mod. Latin *cellularis*, from Latin *cellula*: see **CELLULE, -AR**[1].]
1 Of, pertaining to, characterized by, or consisting of biological cells; (of a plant) lacking a distinct stem, leaves, etc. (opp. ***vascular***). **M18.**
2 Of or pertaining to the cells of a monastery, prison, etc. **E19.**
3 Of or having small compartments, cavities, or divisions of area; porous; (of a fabric or garment) having an open texture. **E19.** ▸**b** Designating or pertaining to a mobile phone system that uses a number of short-range radio stations to cover the area it serves, the signal being automatically switched from one station to another as the user travels about. **L20.**
■ **celluˈlarity** *noun* **M19.**

cellulase /ˈsɛljʊleɪz/ *noun.* **E20.**
[**ORIGIN** from **CELLUL(OSE** + **-ASE.**]
BIOCHEMISTRY. An enzyme that converts cellulose into glucose or a disaccharide.

C

C

cellule /ˈsɛljuːl/ *noun*. LME.
[ORIGIN French, or Latin *cellula* dim. of *cella* CELL *noun*[1]: see -ULE.]
†**1** A small compartment, a pigeonhole; a 'cell of the brain'. LME–E19.
2 *BIOLOGY*. A minute cell, cavity, or pore. Now *rare*. M19.
■ **cellulate** *adjective* composed of or containing cells LME. **cellulated** *adjective* = CELLULATE L17.

cellulite /ˈsɛljʊlʌɪt/ *noun*. M20.
[ORIGIN French = CELLULITIS.]
Fatty tissue regarded as causing a dimpled or lumpy texture of (esp. a woman's) skin.

cellulitis /sɛljʊˈlʌɪtɪs/ *noun*. M19.
[ORIGIN formed as CELLULE + -ITIS.]
MEDICINE. Inflammation of loose subcutaneous connective tissue.
■ **cellulitic** /-ˈlɪtɪk/ *adjective* pertaining to or characterized by cellulitis E20.

celluloid /ˈsɛljʊlɔɪd/ *noun & adjective*. M19.
[ORIGIN from CELLULOSE *noun* + -OID. Cf. LOID.]
▸ **A** *noun*. A plastic made from camphor and nitrocellulose; a piece of this; *transf.* photographic film, the cinema. M19.
▸ **B** *adjective*. Made of celluloid; *fig.* of, pertaining to, or appearing in films; synthetic, unreal. M19.

cellulose /ˈsɛljʊləʊz, -s/ *noun & verb*. M19.
[ORIGIN French, formed as CELLULE + -OSE[2].]
▸ **A** *noun*. **1** A polymeric carbohydrate which forms the main constituent of the cell walls of plants. M19.
2 A compound of this; *esp.* the soluble thermoplastic acetate or nitrate used as the basis of paints, lacquers, etc. L19.
▸ **B** *verb trans*. Treat or coat with a cellulose-based material. M20.
■ **celluˈlosic** *adjective & noun* (**a**) *adjective* of the nature of or derived from (a compound of) cellulose; (**b**) *noun* a cellulosic compound or material: L19.

†**cellulose** *adjective*. M18–M19.
[ORIGIN mod. Latin *cellulosus*, formed as CELLULE + -OSE[1].]
= CELLULOUS.

cellulous /ˈsɛljʊləs/ *adjective*. E19.
[ORIGIN from CELLULE + -OUS.]
Consisting of cells; full of minute cavities.

celom *noun*, **celomate** *adjective & noun* see COELOM etc.

celosia /sɪˈləʊsɪə, -ʃə/ *noun*. E19.
[ORIGIN mod. Latin, from Greek *kēlos* burnt, dry (from the appearance of the flowers of some species): see -IA[1].]
A plant of the genus *Celosia*, of the amaranth family; *esp.* cockscomb, *C. cristata*.

celsian /ˈsɛlsɪən/ *noun*. L19.
[ORIGIN from CELSIUS + -AN.]
MINERALOGY. A barium aluminosilicate belonging to the feldspar group and occurring as colourless monoclinic crystals.

celsitude /ˈsɛlsɪtjuːd/ *noun*. Now *literary*. LME.
[ORIGIN Latin *celsitudo*, from *celsus* lofty: see -TUDE.]
Lofty position, eminence; loftiness; height.

Celsius /ˈsɛlsɪəs/ *adjective & noun*. M19.
[ORIGIN Anders *Celsius* (1701–44), Swedish astronomer.]
▸ **A** *adjective*. Designating or pertaining to the centigrade scale of temperature on which water freezes at 0° and boils at 100° under standard conditions; *postpositive* (with a specified temperature) on this scale. M19.
▸ **B** *noun*. The Celsius scale; a Celsius thermometer. E20.
– NOTE: The standard accepted term when giving temperatures, rather than *centigrade*.

Celt /kɛlt, s-/ *noun*[1]. Also **K-** /k-/. M16.
[ORIGIN Latin *Celtae* pl. from Greek *Keltoi* (later *Keltai*, perh. from Latin); later from French *Celte* Breton (as representative of the ancient Gauls).]
1 *hist.* A member of any of a group of ancient peoples of western Europe that included the Gauls and Britons. M16.
2 *gen.* A member of any of the peoples descended from the ancient Celts or speaking a Celtic language, as the Irish, Gaels, Manx, Welsh, Cornish, and Bretons. L18.

celt /sɛlt/ *noun*[2]. E18.
[ORIGIN medieval Latin *celtis* chisel.]
A stone or metal chisel-edged prehistoric implement; *loosely* any prehistoric stone axe.

Celtiberian /kɛltɪˈbɪərɪən/ *noun & adjective*. E17.
[ORIGIN from Latin *Celtiberia* (see below), formed as CELT *noun*[1], -I-, IBERIAN.]
(A native or inhabitant) of Celtiberia, an ancient province of Iberia lying between the Tagus and Ebro rivers.

Celtic /ˈkɛltɪk, ˈs-/ *adjective & noun*. Also **K-** /ˈk-/. L16.
[ORIGIN Latin *Celticus* (from *Celtae*) or French *Celtique* (from *Celte*): see CELT *noun*[1], -IC.]
▸ **A** *adjective*. Of or pertaining to the Celts and related peoples, or (with specification as for the noun, a stage or division of) their language group. L16.
Celtic cross a Latin cross with a circle around the centre. **Celtic fringe** (the land of) the Highland Scots, Irish, Welsh, and Cornish in relation to the rest of Britain. ***Celtic nard***: see NARD *noun* 2. **Celtic Sea** the area of sea south of Ireland and west of Cornwall. ***Celtic spikenard***: see SPIKENARD 2. **Celtic twilight** [the title of an anthology collected by W. B. Yeats] the romantic fairy tale atmosphere of Irish folklore; literature etc. conveying this. ***spike Celtic***: see SPIKE *noun*[2] 3.
▸ **B** *noun*. A branch of the Indo-European language family including Irish, Gaelic, Manx, Welsh, Cornish, and Breton, and the languages from which they have developed. E17.
Common Celtic, (*arch.*) **Old Celtic**: the undifferentiated Indo-European language branch. **P-Celtic** the group of Celtic languages (represented by Welsh, Cornish, and Breton) in which Common Celtic $*q^u$ developed to *p*; Brittonic. **Q-Celtic** the group of Celtic languages (represented by Irish, Gaelic, and Manx) in which Common Celtic $*q^u$ was retained; Goidelic.
– NOTE: In standard English the normal pronunc. is *kel-* rather than *sel-*, exc. in the name of the Glasgow football club.
■ **Celticism** /-sɪz(ə)m/ *noun* a Celtic custom or expression; devotion to Celtic customs; the branch of knowledge that deals with Celtic languages etc.: M19. **Celticist** /-sɪst/ *noun* a student of Celtic languages or other Celtic matters E20. **Celticize** /-sʌɪz/ *verb trans.* make Celtic in form, language, culture, etc. L19.

cembalo /ˈtʃɛmbələʊ/ *noun*. Pl. **-os**. M19.
[ORIGIN Italian, abbreviation of CLAVICEMBALO.]
A harpsichord.

cembra /ˈsɛmbrə/ *noun*. Also †**-bro**. M18.
[ORIGIN mod. Latin from German dial. *zember*, *zimber* TIMBER *noun*[1].]
In full ***cembra pine***. The Swiss stone pine, *Pinus cembra*.

cement /sɪˈmɛnt/ *noun*. ME.
[ORIGIN Old French & mod. French *ciment* from Latin *caementum* quarry stone, (in pl.) chips of stone, from *caedere* hew: see -MENT. Cf. SIMMON.]
1 A powdered substance mixed with water and applied as a paste which hardens into a stony consistency for binding together stones or bricks and for forming floors, walls, etc.; *esp.* a strong mortar of calcined lime and clay; *loosely* concrete. ME.
hydraulic cement, ***Keene's cement***, ***Parian cement***, ***Portland cement***, ***Roman cement***, etc.
2 Any substance applied in a soft form that later hardens, used for sticking things firmly together, filling cavities, etc.; *fig.* a principle, quality, etc., that unites. LME.
> E. IRVING Faith is the cement of all domestic and social union.

rubber cement: see RUBBER *noun*[1].
3 = CEMENTUM 2. M19.
4 *METALLURGY*. A powdered metal or other substance, esp. a precipitated metal. Usu. *attrib.*, as ***cement copper***, ***cement gold***, ***cement steel***, etc. L19.
– COMB.: **cement mixer** a machine (usu. with a revolving drum) for mixing cement (and freq. also sand, gravel, etc.) with water.

cement /sɪˈmɛnt/ *verb*. ME.
[ORIGIN Old French & mod. French *cimenter*, formed as CEMENT *noun*.]
1 *verb trans.* Unite (as) with cement (*lit.* & *fig.*). ME.
> SHAKES. *Ant. & Cl.* The fear of us May cement their divisions. N. GORDIMER The dented silver stopper . . was cemented to the glass neck by . . dried Silvo polish.

2 *verb intrans.* Cohere firmly (as) by the application of cement; stick. L17.
3 *verb trans.* Apply cement to; line or cover (as) with cement. L19.
■ **cementer** *noun* a person who or thing which cements M18. **cementing** *verbal noun* (**a**) the action of the verb; †(**b**) *ALCHEMY* the process of cementation: LME.

cementation /siːmɛnˈteɪʃ(ə)n/ *noun*. L16.
[ORIGIN from CEMENT *verb* + -ATION.]
1 The process by which one solid is made to combine with another by heating, without liquefaction; *spec.* the making of steel by heating iron with carbon. L16.
2 The action or process of cementing; the state thus produced. M17.

cementite /sɪˈmɛntʌɪt/ *noun*. L19.
[ORIGIN from CEMENT *noun* + -ITE[1].]
METALLURGY. A hard, brittle iron carbide, Fe_3C, present in cast iron and most steels.

cementitious /siːmɛnˈtɪʃəs/ *adjective*. E19.
[ORIGIN formed as CEMENTITE + -ITIOUS[1].]
Of the nature of cement.

cementum /sɪˈmɛntəm/ *noun*. E17.
[ORIGIN Latin form of CEMENT *noun*.]
†**1** *gen.* Cement. Only in E17.
2 *ANATOMY*. The hard bony tissue forming the outer layer of the root of a tooth. M19.

cemetery /ˈsɛmɪtri/ *noun*. LME.
[ORIGIN Late Latin *coemeterium* from Greek *koimētērion* dormitory, from *koiman* put to sleep.]
1 A place used for burials; *esp.* a usu. large area of public ground belonging to a town, city, etc., and laid out for the interment of the dead. LME.
> *fig.*: SWIFT It is with libraries as with other cœmeteries.

†**2** A churchyard. L15–E19.
■ **cemeˈterial** *adjective* relating to a cemetery; used for burial: E17.

cenacle /ˈsɛnək(ə)l/ *noun*. LME.
[ORIGIN Old French & mod. French *cénacle* from Latin *cenaculum*, from *cena* dinner: see -CULE.]
1 A dining room; *spec.* the room in which the Last Supper was held. LME.
2 A place where a discussion group, literary clique, etc., meets; the group itself. L19.

Cencibel /θɛnθɪˈbɛl, sɛnsɪˈbɛl/ *noun*. M20.
[ORIGIN Spanish, of unknown origin.]
In the Valdepeñas region of Spain: the Tempranillo grape.

ceneme /ˈkɛniːm/ *noun*. Also **k-**. M20.
[ORIGIN from Greek *kenos* empty + -EME.]
LINGUISTICS. A minimal unit of expression without content; a meaningless unit of sound. Opp. PLEREME.
■ **ceneˈmatic** *adjective* of or pertaining to cenemes M20. **ceneˈmatics** *noun* the branch of glossematics that deals with cenemes M20.

C.Eng. *abbreviation*.
Chartered engineer.

cenobite, **cenobium**, **cenoby** *nouns* see COENOBITE etc.

cenogenesis *noun* see CAENOGENESIS.

cenotaph /ˈsɛnətɑːf, -taf/ *noun & verb*. E17.
[ORIGIN French *cénotaphe* from late Latin *cenotaphium* from Greek *kenotaphion*, from *kenos* empty + *taphos* tomb.]
▸ **A** *noun*. An empty tomb; a sepulchral monument to honour someone whose body is elsewhere. E17.
the Cenotaph *spec.* that in Whitehall, London, commemorating the dead of the First and Second World Wars.
▸ **B** *verb trans.* Honour or commemorate with a cenotaph. M19.

cenote /seˈnote/ *noun*. M19.
[ORIGIN Yucatan Spanish from Maya *tzonot*.]
A natural underground reservoir of water, such as occurs in the limestone of Yucatan, Mexico.

Cenozoic /siːnəˈzəʊɪk/ *adjective & noun*. Also **Caen-**, **Cain-** /kʌɪn-/. M19.
[ORIGIN from Greek *kainos* new, recent + -ZOIC.]
GEOLOGY. ▸**A** *adjective*. Designating or pertaining to the latest era of geological time, following the Mesozoic and comprising the Tertiary and Quaternary periods (formerly, the Tertiary only). M19.
▸ **B** *noun*. The Cenozoic era; the rocks collectively dating from this time. L19.

cense /sɛns/ *noun*. ME.
[ORIGIN Old French from medieval Latin *censa* for Latin CENSUS (whence mod. French *cens*).]
†**1** = CENSUS *noun* 1. ME–M18.
2 = CENSUS *noun* 3. M16.
3 Income, taken as determining position or rank; rating. E17.

cense /sɛns/ *verb*[1]. LME.
[ORIGIN Aphet. from Old French & mod. French *encenser* INCENSE *verb*[1].]
1 *verb trans.* Perfume with the odour of burning incense; worship or honour with burning incense. LME.
2 *verb intrans.* Burn or offer incense. LME.

cense /sɛns/ *verb*[2] *trans.* Now *rare*. E17.
[ORIGIN Latin *censere* assess.]
Estimate, assess, judge.

censer /ˈsɛnsə/ *noun*. ME.
[ORIGIN Anglo-Norman (also *senser*), Old French *censier*, aphet. of *encensier*, from *encens* INCENSE *noun*.]
1 A vessel in which incense is burnt, esp. one that is swung during a religious ceremony. ME.
†**2** A cassolette; a perfume burner or diffuser. *rare* (Shakes.). Only in L16.

censor /ˈsɛnsə/ *noun & verb*. M16.
[ORIGIN Latin, from *censere* pronounce as an opinion, rate, assess: see -OR.]
▸ **A** *noun*. **1** Either of two magistrates in ancient Rome who compiled censuses of its citizens, etc., and supervised public morals. M16.
2 A person who exercises supervision or judgement over the conduct or morals of others. L16.
3 An adverse critic; a person who censures or finds fault. Now *rare*. L16.
4 An official with the power to suppress the whole or parts of books, plays, films, etc., on the grounds of obscenity, seditiousness, etc. M17. ▸**b** An official who, esp. in times of war, is empowered to censor private letters, news reports, etc. E20.
5 *PSYCHOLOGY*. [mistranslation of German *Zensur* censorship (Freud).] A mental power by which certain anxiety-provoking unconscious ideas and memories are prevented from emerging into consciousness. E20.
▸ **B** *verb trans.* Act as censor of; officially inspect and make deletions or changes in (a book, film, article, letter, etc.). L19.
> *Daily News* All news is being rigorously censored.

■ **censorable** *adjective* subject to censorship; in need of censorship: E20.

censorial /sɛnˈsɔːrɪəl/ *adjective*. L16.
[ORIGIN formed as CENSORIOUS + -AL[1].]
1 = CENSORIOUS 1. *rare*. L16.
2 Of, pertaining to, or characteristic of an official censor. L18.
■ Also **censorian** *adjective* L16.

censorious /sɛnˈsɔːrɪəs/ *adjective*. **M16.**
[ORIGIN from Latin *censorius* (formed as CENSOR) + -OUS.]
1 Fault-finding, severely critical; inclined to disapproval. **M16.**
C. ANSTEY Bath is a very censorious Place. E. WAUGH He felt these prejudices to be peculiar to himself; none of them made him at all censorious of anyone else.
2 Befitting a censor; grave, severe. Now *rare*. **M17.**
JONSON His [Bacon's] language . . was nobly censorious.
■ **censoriously** *adverb* **L17.** **censoriousness** *noun* **M17.**

censorship /ˈsɛnsəʃɪp/ *noun*. **L16.**
[ORIGIN from CENSOR *noun* + -SHIP.]
1 The action or function of a censor, esp. in controlling newspapers, films, letters, etc. **L16.** **2** *hist.* The office or function of a Roman censor. **E17.** **3** PSYCHOLOGY. The function of a subconscious mental censor. **E20.**

censual /ˈsɛnsjʊəl/ *adjective*. **E17.**
[ORIGIN Late Latin *censualis*, formed as CENSUS: see -AL[1]. Cf. Old French & mod. French *censuel*.]
Of or relating to a census.

censure /ˈsɛnʃə/ *noun*. **LME.**
[ORIGIN Old French & mod. French from Latin *censura* CENSUS: see -URE.]
†**1** A judicial (esp. ecclesiastical) sentence; a condemnatory judgement. **LME–M19.**
SWIFT The council thought the loss of your eyes too easy a censure.
2 The position or action of an official censor; censorship. Formerly also, a censor. **M16.**
3 Judgement, opinion; critical assessment. Now *rare*. **L16.**
W. RALEIGH To write my censure of this booke. W. H. AUDEN Greeks, in your censure, were rogues, / all teenagers delinquent.
4 Correction, esp. critical recension or revision. Now *rare*. **L16.**
H. HALLAM So arduous a task as the thorough censure of the Vulgate text.
5 (An) adverse judgement; (a) hostile criticism; an expression of disapproval or reprimand. **E17.**
SHAKES. *Meas. for M.* No might nor greatness in mortality Can censure scape. CONAN DOYLE Beyond a mild censure for the delay . . the lucky owner got away scatheless. SLOAN WILSON Misinterpreting his silence as censure.
vote of censure: see VOTE *noun*.
■ **censureship** *noun* (*rare*) = CENSORSHIP **E17.**

censure /ˈsɛnʃə/ *verb*. **L16.**
[ORIGIN French *censurer*, formed as CENSURE *noun*.]
1 *verb trans.* & *intrans.* Form or give an opinion (of); estimate, assess critically, judge. *obsolete* exc. *dial.* **L16.**
SHAKES. *Jul. Caes.* Censure me in your wisdom, and awake your senses, that you may the better judge. S. LATHAM Censure better of me. T. FULLER Eli . . censured Hannah . . to be drunk with wine.
2 *verb trans.* & *intrans.* Criticize unfavourably; find fault (with), reprove, blame. **L16.**
M. DRAYTON Duke Robert iustly censured stood, For Disobedience and unnaturall Pride. J. CHAMBERLAYNE They . . proceed accordingly to censure or commend, as they find cause. E. M. FORSTER Laura censured his immoral marriage.
†**3** *verb trans.* Pronounce judicial sentence on; sentence (*to*). Only in **17.**
CAPT. J. SMITH Some were censured to the whipping post.
■ **censurable** *adjective* **M17.** **censurableness** *noun* (*rare*) **M17.** **censurer** *noun* (*a*) a person who finds fault or blames; †(*b*) a censor, a judge: **L16.**

census /ˈsɛnsəs/ *noun* & *verb*. **E17.**
[ORIGIN Latin, from *censere* assess: cf. CENSE *noun*.]
▸ **A** *noun*. †**1** A tax, a tribute; *esp.* a poll tax. **E17–M19.**
2 *hist.* The registration of citizens and their property in ancient Rome, usu. for taxation purposes. **M17.**
3 An official enumeration of the population of a country etc., or of a class of things, usu. with statistics relating to them. **M18.**
▸ **B** *verb trans.* Conduct a census of; count, enumerate. **L19.**

cent /sɛnt/ *noun*[1]. **LME.**
[ORIGIN French, or Italian *cento*, Latin *centum*. Cf. SEN *noun*[2].]
1 A hundred. Now only in PER CENT. **LME.**
cent per cent: see PER CENT.
2 *gen.* A hundredth part. *rare*. **L17.**
3 A monetary unit equal to one-hundredth of a dollar in the US, Canada, Australia, New Zealand, and numerous other countries; one-hundredth of the basic monetary unit in certain other countries, as one-hundredth of a euro, of a shilling in Kenya, Somalia, Tanzania, and Uganda, of a rand in Namibia and South Africa, of a rupee in Mauritius and Sri Lanka, etc.; a coin of this value; *loosely* a small coin, the smallest sum possible. **L18.**
K. TENNANT If you marry that Alec, you don't get a cent.
like thirty cents: see THIRTY *adjective*. **not care a cent** not care at all. ***red cent***: see RED *adjective*.
■ **centage** *noun* (now *rare*) = PERCENTAGE **L18.**

cent /sɛnt/ *noun*[2]. *obsolete* exc. *hist.* **M16.**
[ORIGIN Uncertain: perh. same as CENT *noun*[1].]
1 A card game said to have resembled piquet, with a winning score of 100. **M16.**
2 A counter used in playing ombre. **M18.**

cental /ˈsɛnt(ə)l/ *noun*. **L19.**
[ORIGIN from Latin *centum* a hundred + -AL[1], perh. after *quintal*.]
A weight of one hundred pounds, used esp. for corn etc.

centas /ˈsɛntas/ *noun*. Pl. same. **M20.**
[ORIGIN Lithuanian.]
A monetary unit of Lithuania, equal to one-hundredth of a litas.

centaur /ˈsɛntɔː/ *noun*. **LME.**
[ORIGIN Latin *centaurus* from Greek *kentauros*, of unknown origin.]
1 GREEK MYTHOLOGY. A fabulous creature with the form of a horse, having a human body, arms, and head, in place of its neck and head. **LME.**
fig.: BYRON That moral centaur, man and wife.
2 (Usu. **C-**.) (The name of) *the* constellation Centaurus. **LME.**

centaurea /sɛnˈtɔːrɪə, sɛntəˈriːə/ *noun*. **E19.**
[ORIGIN mod. Latin, formed as CENTAURY.]
Any plant of the genus *Centaurea*, of the composite family, which includes the cornflower and knapweed.

Centaurus /sɛnˈtɔːrəs/ *noun*. **M17.**
[ORIGIN Latin: see CENTAUR.]
(The name of) a constellation of the southern hemisphere partly in the Milky Way and enclosing Crux; the Centaur.

centaury /ˈsɛntɔːri/ *noun*. **LME.**
[ORIGIN Late Latin *centauria*, *-ea*, ult. from Greek *kentauros* CENTAUR: the plant's medicinal properties were said to have been discovered by the centaur Chiron.]
1 A plant of the genus *Centaurium*, of the gentian family, usu. with pink flowers; esp. *Centaurium erythraea* (more fully ***common centaury***). Also (with specifying word), any of several plants of allied genera. **LME.**
yellow centaury: see YELLOW *adjective*.
2 = CENTAUREA. Now *rare* or *obsolete*. **LME.**

centavo /sɛnˈtɑːvəʊ/ *noun*. Pl. **-os**. **L19.**
[ORIGIN Spanish & Portuguese, from Latin *centum* a hundred.]
A monetary unit equal to one-hundredth of an escudo in Portugal (until the introduction of the euro in 2002) and the Cape Verde Islands, of a peso in Chile, Colombia, Cuba, Mexico, etc., of a sucre in Ecuador, of a colón in El Salvador, of a metical in Mozambique, and (formerly) of a cruzeiro in Brazil.

centenarian /sɛntɪˈnɛːrɪən/ *noun* & *adjective*. **M19.**
[ORIGIN formed as CENTENARY + -AN.]
(A person) a hundred or more years old.
■ **centenarianism** *noun* the state or fact of being a centenarian **L19.**

centenary /sɛnˈtiːnəri, -ˈtɛn-; ˈsɛntɪnəri/ *noun* & *adjective*. **E17.**
[ORIGIN Latin *centenarius* containing a hundred, from *centeni* a hundred each, from *centum* a hundred: see -ARY[1]. Cf. CENTENIER.]
▸ **A** *noun* **I 1** A space or duration of a hundred years; a century. **E17.**
2 A centennial anniversary; a celebration or festival in honour of this. (The usual sense.) **L18.**
▸ †**II 3** A hundredweight. **M17–L18.**
▸ **B** *adjective*. **1** Of or pertaining to the period of one hundred years; *esp.* of or pertaining to (the celebration of) a hundredth anniversary. **M17.**
2 *gen.* Of or belonging to a hundred. *rare*. **M18.**

centenier /ˈsɛntənɪə/ *noun*. Also (earlier) †**-ner**. **ME.**
[ORIGIN Anglo-Norman *centener*, Old French & mod. French *centenier*, from late Latin *centenarius* (formed as CENTENARY) for Latin CENTURION: see -IER. In branch II from Old French *centenaire* from Latin *centenarium*.]
▸ **I** †**1** A centurion. **ME–E17.**
2 A police officer on the island of Jersey. **M19.**
▸ †**II 3** A hundredweight. **LME–L16.**

centennial /sɛnˈtɛnɪəl/ *adjective* & *noun*. **L18.**
[ORIGIN from Latin *centum* a hundred, after *biennial*.]
▸ **A** *adjective*. Of or relating to (the completion of) a period of one hundred years; occurring every hundred years; relating to a centenary or its celebration. **L18.**
Centennial State *US* Colorado, admitted as a state in 1876, the centennial year of the United States.
▸ **B** *noun*. A hundredth anniversary or its celebration; a centenary. **L19.**

center *noun* & *adjective*, *verb* see CENTRE *noun* & *adjective*, *verb*.

centering *verbal noun* see CENTRING.

centesimal /sɛnˈtɛsɪm(ə)l/ *adjective* & *noun*. **L17.**
[ORIGIN from Latin *centesimus* hundredth, from *centum* a hundred: see -AL[1].]
▸ **A** *adjective*. †**1** Hundredfold. Only in **L17.**
2 Reckoning or reckoned by hundredths. **E19.**
▸ **B** *noun*. A hundredth part. Now *rare* or *obsolete*. **L17.**
■ **centesimally** *adverb* **E18.** **centesimate** *verb trans.* select every hundredth person in (a group) for punishment **M18.** **centesiˈmation** *noun* execution etc. of every hundredth person **M17.**

centesimo /tʃɛnˈteɪzɪməʊ/ *noun*. Pl. **-mi** /-mi/. **M19.**
[ORIGIN Italian.]
A former monetary unit of Italy, equal to one-hundredth of a lira.

centésimo /sɛnˈteɪzɪməʊ/ *noun*. Pl. **-os**. **E20.**
[ORIGIN Spanish.]
A monetary unit of Uruguay, equal to one-hundredth of a peso; a monetary unit of Panama, equal to one-hundredth of a balboa.

C

†**centesm** *noun*. **L15–E19.**
[ORIGIN Old French *cent(i)esme*, *-isme* (mod. *centième*), from Latin *centesimus*: see CENTESIMAL.]
A hundredth part.

centi- /ˈsɛnti/ *combining form*.
[ORIGIN Latin, from *centum* a hundred: see -I-.]
Used in names of units of measurement to denote a factor of one-hundredth, as ***centigram***, ***centilitre***, ***centipoise***. Abbreviation **c**.

centigrade /ˈsɛntɪɡreɪd/ *adjective* & *noun*. **E19.**
[ORIGIN French, formed as CENTI- + Latin *gradus* step, GRADE *noun*.]
▸ **A** *adjective*. Having a hundred divisions; *spec.* designating or pertaining to the Celsius scale of temperature, *postpositive* (with a specified temperature) on this scale. **E19.**
▸ **B** *noun*. A centigrade scale or thermometer. **M20.**
In giving temperatures *Celsius* is preferred.

centile /ˈsɛntʌɪl/ *noun* & *adjective*. **E20.**
[ORIGIN Abbreviation.]
= PERCENTILE.

centillion /sɛnˈtɪljən/ *noun*. *rare*. **L19.**
[ORIGIN from CENTI- after *million*, *billion*, etc.]
Orig. (esp. in the UK), the hundredth power of a million (10^{600}). Now usu. (orig. *US*), the 101st power of a thousand (10^{303}). Also *loosely*, an enormous number.
■ **centillionth** *noun* & *adjective* **M19.**

centime /ˈsɒntiːm; *foreign* sɑ̃tim (*pl. same*)/ *noun*. **E19.**
[ORIGIN French, formed as CENTESM.]
A monetary unit equal to one-hundredth of a franc in Switzerland and certain other countries (including France, Belgium, and Luxembourg until the introduction of the euro in 2002). Also, a monetary unit equal to one-hundredth of a gourde in Haiti or of a dirham in Morocco.

centimetre /ˈsɛntɪmiːtə/ *noun*. Also ***-meter**. **L18.**
[ORIGIN from CENTI- + METRE *noun*[2].]
One-hundredth of a metre, equal to 0.3937 inch.
– COMB.: **centimetre-gram-second** *adjective* designating or pertaining to a system of measurement in which these form the basic units of length, mass, and time respectively.
■ **centimetric** /sɛntɪˈmɛtrɪk/ *adjective* of the order of one centimetre in (wave-)length; pertaining to or involving electromagnetic radiation having a wavelength of 1 to 10 centimetres: **M20.**

céntimo /ˈsɛntɪməʊ, *foreign* ˈθentimo/ *noun*. Also **ce-**. Pl. **-os** /-əʊz, *foreign* -os/. **L19.**
[ORIGIN Spanish.]
A monetary unit of Spain until the introduction of the euro in 2002, equal to one-hundredth of a peseta. Also, a monetary unit equal to one-hundredth of the basic monetary unit in some Latin American countries, as one-hundredth of a colón in Costa Rica, of a guarani in Paraguay, or of a bolivar in Venezuela.

centimorgan /ˈsɛntɪˌmɔːɡ(ə)n/ *noun*. **M20.**
[ORIGIN from *centi-* (denoting a factor of one hundredth) + MORGAN *noun*[3].]
GENETICS. A unit used to express the distance between two gene loci on a chromosome, where a spacing of one centimorgan indicates a one per cent chance that two genes will be separated by crossing over.

†**centinel** *noun*, *verb* var. of SENTINEL *noun*, *verb*.

centipedal /sɛnˈtɪpɪd(ə)l/ *adjective*. **L19.**
[ORIGIN from Latin CENTI- + *ped-*, *pes* foot + -AL[1].]
PROSODY. Of one hundred metrical feet.

centipede /ˈsɛntɪpiːd/ *noun*. Also †**-pee**. **M17.**
[ORIGIN French *centipède* or Latin *centipeda*, formed as CENTI- + *ped-*, *pes* foot.]
Any of numerous predatory terrestrial arthropods belonging to the class Chilopoda, having an elongated body with many segments most of which bear a pair of legs.

centner /ˈsɛntnə/ *noun*. **M16.**
[ORIGIN German (now *Zentner*) from Latin *centenarius* CENTENARY.]
A German unit of weight usu. equal to 50 kg; a metric hundredweight.

cento /ˈsɛntəʊ/ *noun*. Pl. **-os**, †**-ones**. **E17.**
[ORIGIN Latin, lit. 'patchwork garment'.]
†**1** A piece of patchwork; a patchwork garment. **E–M17.**
2 A hotchpotch, a medley; *spec.* a composition made up of quotations from other authors. **E17.**

centra *noun pl.* see CENTRUM.

central /ˈsɛntr(ə)l/ *adjective & noun*. M17.
[ORIGIN French, or Latin *centralis*, from *centrum* CENTRE *noun*: see -AL[1].]
► **A** *adjective*. **1** Of or pertaining to the centre or middle; situated in, proceeding from, containing or constituting the centre of anything. M17.

J. HUGHES Around the central sun in circling eddies roll'd. R. SWINHOE The island.. from its central position would form a good depôt.

2 *fig.* Most important or significant; chief, leading, dominant; essential or fundamental *to*. M17. ▸**b** Of a body, office, association, etc.: controlling all branches of an organization etc. from a common centre. E19.

E. B. BROWNING The central truth. B. JOWETT Odysseus is the central figure of the one poem. N. FRYE Literature seems.. to be central to the arts. **b** GLADSTONE Commence not with local but central institutions. U. BENTLEY There's no central authority in this school.

3 *BIOLOGY & MEDICINE*. Involving or affecting the central nervous system (see below). M19.
4 *PHONETICS*. Of a vowel: formed with the centre of the tongue raised (towards the juncture of the soft and hard palates). M20.
– SPECIAL COLLOCATIONS: **Central America** the isthmus joining N. and S. America, extending from Mexico to Colombia. **Central American** (a native or inhabitant) of Central America. ***central bank***: see BANK *noun*[3] 3. **central casting** [from the *Central Casting* Corporation, a US organization established in 1926 to provide extras and bit-part players for films] (**a**) an agency or department which supplies actors for minor parts in films, television programmes, etc.; (**b**) a (notional) source for stereotypical or generic examples of particular types. **central force** a force attracting or repelling from a centre. **central heating** (the apparatus for) warming a building by hot water or hot air or steam conveyed by pipes from a central source, or by a general system of radiators etc. ***central lobby***: see LOBBY *noun* 3a. **central nervous system** the brain and spinal cord considered together. **Central Powers** Germany and Austria-Hungary before and during the First World War. **central processing unit** the part of a computer in which the control and execution of operations occur. ***central reservation***: see RESERVATION 8. ***central reserve***: see RESERVE *noun* 4c. **Central time** standard time used in central Canada and the US.
► **B** *noun*. Something central; *esp.* (*US*) a telephone exchange; *N. Amer. colloq.* a place characterized by a particular activity or type of person. L19.

New York Times A city that is quickly gaining the reputation as party central in Eastern Europe.

■ **centralism** *noun* a centralizing system; (support for) centralization: M19. **centralist** *noun & adjective* (**a**) *noun* an advocate of centralism; (**b**) *adjective* pertaining to or advocating centralism: E19. **centrally** *adverb* in a central manner or position; with regard to the centre; ***centrally heated***, equipped with central heating: LME. **centralness** *noun* L19.

centrale /sɛnˈtreɪli/ *noun*. Pl. **-lia** /-lɪə/. L19.
[ORIGIN Short for Latin *os centrale* central bone.]
ANATOMY. A central carpal bone which is possessed by many animals but is not usu. present in humans.

Centralia /sɛnˈtreɪlɪə/ *noun*[1]. L19.
[ORIGIN from CENTRAL *adjective* + *Australia*.]
Orig., a name proposed for the central strip of Australia comprising the present state of South Australia and the Northern Territory. Now, the central regions of Australia.

centralia *noun*[2] pl. of CENTRALE.

centralisation *noun*, **centralise** *verb* vars. of CENTRALIZATION, CENTRALIZE.

centrality /sɛnˈtralətі/ *noun*. M17.
[ORIGIN from CENTRAL *adjective* + -ITY.]
The quality or fact of being central (*lit. & fig.*); central nature or position.

F. W. FARRAR The centrality of its position.. made it a great commercial emporium. *Word* The centrality of languages to political life in Belgium.

centralization /sɛntrəlʌɪˈzeɪʃ(ə)n/ *noun*. Also **-isation**. E19.
[ORIGIN from CENTRALIZE + -ATION, or French *centralisation*.]
The fact or action of centralizing; *esp.* the concentration of administrative power in a central authority.

centralize /ˈsɛntrəlʌɪz/ *verb*. Also **-ise**. E19.
[ORIGIN from CENTRAL *adjective* + -IZE, or French *centraliser*.]
1 *verb intrans.* Come together at a centre; form a centre; be concentrated. E19.
2 *verb trans.* Bring to or locate in a centre; make central; concentrate (administrative powers etc.) in a single place. E19. ▸**b** *PHONETICS*. Make (a vowel) central, shift towards a central position. Chiefly as ***centralized*** *ppl adjective*. M20.

A. HELPS Business always tends to centralize itself. H. E. BATES One of those centralized courtyards.. enclosed on three sides by the house and on the fourth by a balustrade.

■ **centralizer** *noun* a person who centralizes or promotes centralization M19.

centre /ˈsɛntə/ *noun & adjective*. Also ***center**. LME.
[ORIGIN Old French & mod. French, or directly from Latin *centrum* from Greek *kentron* goad, peg, stationary point of a pair of compasses, from base of *kentein* to prick.]
► **A** *noun* **I 1** The middle point equidistant from all points on the circumference of an arc, circle, or sphere. LME. ▸**b** *ellipt.* The centre of the earth; the earth itself considered as the centre of the universe. *arch.* LME.

fig.: DONNE This bed thy center is, these wals thy spheare. **b** C. LAMB The feeling.. that all betwixt sky and centre was my own.

2 The point, pivot, or axis around which a body revolves. LME.

MILTON As a rock Of adamant, and as a centre, firm. *fig.*: CARLYLE Even an anarchy.. must have a centre to revolve around.

3 A point around which things group themselves; a focus of concentration or attraction; a point of dispersion, a nucleus, a source. E17. ▸**b** A building or group of buildings forming a central point, or constituting a main site for a particular activity; an installation etc. devoted to a particular activity. M19. ▸**c** *spec.* A location in the brain or nervous system responsible for a particular faculty etc. M19.

JOYCE Hell is the centre of evils. M. KLINE Great banking houses made Italy the financial center. R. L. FOX Pella.. was the centre of a tribal aristocracy. **c** P. PARISH The centres in the brain which control movement.

b ***attendance centre***, ***civic centre***, ***detention centre***, ***health centre***, ***jobcentre***, ***shopping centre***, ***youth centre***, etc.
4 In a lathe etc., a conical adjustable support for a workpiece. L18.
5 The area of a target located between the bull's eye and the outer; the hitting of this part. L19.
► **II 6** The middle point or point of equilibrium of a body or figure of any shape; the point equidistant or at a median distance from the extremities of a body or figure; the midpoint of a line; *gen.* the middle part or portion, the midst. LME. ▸**b** *spec.* The main body of troops occupying the space between the wings of an army; the middle division of a fleet. L16. ▸**c** (**C-**.) *The* remote central regions of Australia. Also ***Red Centre***. E20.

J. HOWELL They dwelt in the center of Spain not far from Toledo. D. WELCH The chocolate had a cream centre. J. JOHNSTON Steam.. hid the centre of the bridge. *fig.*: R. W. EMERSON If the man is off his centre, the eyes show it.

7 *ARCHITECTURE*. A temporary framework supporting a superstructure; *esp.* = CENTRING 2. E16.
8 *SPORT*. **a** A player whose position is in the middle of a line or field of players. M19. ▸**b** *SOCCER, HOCKEY*, etc. A kick or pass from either of the wings towards the middle of the pitch, esp. in the vicinity of the opponent's goal area. E20.
9 Orig., those deputies of moderate political opinions in the French Chamber who sit on central benches in front of the President. Now, (the views and aims of) any party or group holding moderate political views. M19.

Listener All three parties.. are now parties of the centre.

– PHRASES: **centre of attraction** (**a**) a point to which bodies tend by gravity; (**b**) a person or thing drawing general attention. **centre of buoyancy** the centroid of the volume of fluid displaced by a floating body. ***centre of curvature***: see CURVATURE 1b. **centre of flotation** (**a**) the centre of gravity of the waterplane of a floating body; (**b**) = ***centre of buoyancy*** above. **centre of gravity** (**a**) = ***centre of mass*** below; (**b**) *fig.* the point or object of greatest importance or interest. **centre of inertia**, **centre of mass** the point representing the mean position of the matter in an object or system. ***centre of ossification***: see OSSIFICATION 1. **centre of pressure** a point on a surface through which the resultant force due to pressure passes. ***dead centre***: see DEAD *adjective* etc. ***left centre***: see LEFT *adjective*. ***left, right, and centre***: see LEFT *adverb*. ***optical centre***: see OPTICAL *adjective*. ***right centre***: see RIGHT *adjective*. ***right, left, and centre***: see LEFT *adverb*. ***shifting centre***: see SHIFTING *adjective* 1. ***stage centre***: see STAGE *noun* 4.
► **B** *attrib.* or as *adjective*. Situated in or forming the centre; of or pertaining to the centre; central. L18.

J. BENTHAM The center one of the 5 uppermost Cells. R. K. DOUGLAS The centre figures of his philosophy.

– COMB. & SPECIAL COLLOCATIONS: **centre back** in *FOOTBALL & HOCKEY* etc., (the position of) a back who plays primarily in the centre of the pitch; **centre bit** a boring tool with a centre point and side cutters; **centreboard** a board for lowering through the keel of a sailing boat to prevent leeway; **centre field** *BASEBALL* (a fielder in) the central part of the outfield; **centre fielder** *BASEBALL* a fielder in the centre field; **centrefire** *adjective & noun* (a gun cartridge) having the primer in the centre of the base; (a gun) using such cartridges; **centrefold** a centre spread that folds out; a (usu. naked or scantily clad) model pictured on such a spread in a magazine; **centre forward** in *FOOTBALL & HOCKEY* etc., (the position of) the middle player in a forward line; **centre half** in *FOOTBALL & HOCKEY* etc., (the position of) the middle player in a halfback line; *loosely* = **centre back** above; **centre line** a real or imaginary line through the centre of something; **centrepiece** the principal item on display (*lit. & fig.*); *spec.* a glass or china ornament designed for the centre of a table; **centrepin** a relatively simple type of fishing reel with the line winding directly on to a revolving spool; **centre punch** a tool consisting of a metal rod with a conical point for making an indentation in an object, esp. to allow a drill to make a hole at the same spot without slipping; **centre-second** (a clock or watch with) a seconds hand mounted on the centre arbor; **centre spread** (the illustration, text, etc., occupying) the two facing middle pages of a newspaper etc.; **centre three-quarter** *RUGBY* either of two middle players in the line of three-quarters.
■ **centremost** *adjective* most central, midmost M19.

centre /ˈsɛntə/ *verb*. Also ***center**. Pres. pple **centring**, **-treing**, ***-tering**. L16.
[ORIGIN from the noun.]
1 *verb trans.* Place in the centre or a central position; make exactly central; concentrate or focus *in*, (*up*)*on*, (*a*)*round*; mark with a centre, constitute the centre of. Freq. in *pass.* L16. ▸**b** *verb trans. & intrans. SOCCER, HOCKEY*, etc. Kick or hit (the ball) from the wing to the centre of the pitch, esp. in the vicinity of the opponent's goal area. L19.

GOLDSMITH In reverie centred. C. HUTTON The necessity of well centring the object glass of a large telescope. K. LITTLE A plot of.. grass centred by a basin. R. CHURCH My universe was still centred in my mother's fragrant person.

2 *verb intrans.* Be situated (as) on a fixed centre; have its centre or be concentrated *in*, (*up*)*on*, (*a*)*round*; move (as) round a focal point. E17.

BUNYAN Here centreth Luke the Evangelist. W. SANSOM That strange figure around whom this account properly centres. B. BAINBRIDGE Tedious conversations centred on food.

centreing *verbal noun* var. of CENTRING.

centric /ˈsɛntrɪk/ *adjective*. L16.
[ORIGIN Greek *kentrikos*, from *kentron*: see CENTRE *noun & adjective*, -IC.]
1 That is in or at the centre, central. L16.

C. MARLOWE This centric earth.

2 Of, pertaining to, or characterized by a centre. E18.

R. BLACKMORE Orbs centric and excentrick.

3 *CYTOLOGY*. = CENTROMERIC. M20.
■ **centrical** *adjective* = CENTRIC M17. **centrically** *adverb* L18. **centricity** /sɛnˈtrɪsɪtі/ *noun* centric quality or position E19.

-centric /ˈsɛntrɪk/ *suffix*.
[ORIGIN After CONCENTRIC, ECCENTRIC, etc., from Greek *kentrikos*: see CENTRIC.]
Forming adjectives with the senses 'having a (specified) centre', 'having as its centre', as: ***anthropocentric***, ***heliocentric***, ***polycentric***, ***theocentric***, etc.

centrifugal /sɛnˈtrɪfjʊg(ə)l, ˈsɛntrɪfjuːg(ə)l, sɛntrɪˈfjuːg(ə)l/ *adjective & noun*. E18.
[ORIGIN from mod. Latin *centrifugus*, from *centrum* CENTRE *noun* + *-fugus* fleeing, from *fugere* flee: see -AL[1].]
► **A** *adjective*. **1** Moving or tending to move away from a centre (*lit. & fig.*; opp. ***centripetal***); ***centrifugal force***, (the inertial force causing) the tendency of a body rotating about a centre to move outwards from that centre. E18.
2 Of a machine, process, etc.: employing centrifugal force or motion. Of a product: obtained by the use of such a machine. M18.
3 Chiefly *BOTANY*. Developing or progressing from the centre outwards. M19.
► **B** *noun*. A centrifugal machine; a centrifuge. M19.
■ **centrifuˈgality** *noun* M20. **centrifugaliˈzation** *noun* the process of centrifugalizing E20. **centrifugalize** *verb trans.* subject to a centrifugal force or process L19. **centrifugally** *adverb* E19.

centrifugate /sɛnˈtrɪfjʊgeɪt/ *verb trans.* M19.
[ORIGIN formed as CENTRIFUGAL + -ATE[3].]
= CENTRIFUGE *verb*.
■ **centrifuˈgation** *noun* E19.

centrifuge /ˈsɛntrɪfjuːdʒ/ *adjective, noun, & verb*. E18.
[ORIGIN French, from mod. Latin *centrifugus* CENTRIFUGAL.]
► †**A** *adjective*. = CENTRIFUGAL *adjective* 1. E18–E19.
► **B** *noun*. A centrifugal machine; *esp.* a device for effecting separation, usu. of one liquid from another or of a solid from a liquid, by rapid rotation. L19.
► **C** *verb trans.* Subject to centrifugal motion; separate by means of a centrifuge. E20.
■ **cenˈtrifugate** *noun* material separated using a centrifuge E20.

†**centrinel** *noun* var. of SENTINEL *noun*.

centring /ˈsɛntrɪŋ/ *verbal noun*. Also **centering** (the usual form in sense 2), **centreing**, /-t(ə)rɪŋ/. M17.
[ORIGIN from CENTRE *verb* + -ING[1].]
1 The action of CENTRE *verb*; placing in the centre; making central; bringing centres into alignment. M17.
2 *ARCHITECTURE*. The temporary framework used to support an arch, dome, etc., while under construction. M18.

centriole /ˈsɛntrɪəʊl/ *noun*. L19.
[ORIGIN mod. Latin *centriolum* dim. of *centrum* centre: see -OLE[1].]
CYTOLOGY. A cylindrical organelle in the centrosome of a cell, involved esp. in the development of microtubular structures such as spindles and cilia.
■ **centriˈolar** *adjective* M20.

centripetal /sɛnˈtrɪpɪt(ə)l, ˈsɛntrɪpiːt(ə)l, sɛntrɪˈpiːt(ə)l/ *adjective*. E18.
[ORIGIN from mod. Latin *centripetus*, from *centrum* CENTRE *noun* + *-petus* seeking, from *petere* seek: see -AL[1].]
1 Moving or tending to move towards a centre (*lit. & fig.*; opp. ***centrifugal***); ***centripetal force***, the force directed towards the centre of rotation which acts upon a body in circular motion. E18.
2 Chiefly *BOTANY*. Developing or progressing from the periphery inwards. M19.
■ **centripetally** *adverb* M19.

centrist /ˈsɛntrɪst/ *noun & adjective*. **L19.**
[ORIGIN French *centriste*, formed as CENTRE *noun & adjective* + -IST.]
▶ **A** *noun*. Orig., a member of the French political centre (see CENTRE *noun* 9). Now, any holder of moderate (political) views. **L19.**
▶ **B** *adjective*. Of or pertaining to centrists; characterized by centrism. **E20.**
■ **centrism** *noun* (the policy of adopting) a middle position between extreme views **M20.**

centro- /ˈsɛntrəʊ/ *combining form* of Latin *centrum* CENTRE *noun*: see -O-.
■ **centroˈbaric** *adjective* (now *rare* or *obsolete*) relating to or possessing a centre of gravity **E18.** **centroˈlecithal** *adjective* (of an egg or egg cell) having a centrally placed yolk **L19.** **centromere** *noun* [Greek *meros* part] CYTOLOGY the part of a chromosome with which the spindle fibres become associated in cell division **E20.** **centroˈmeric** *adjective* pertaining to or associated with a centromere; having or involving a centromere: **M20.** **centrosome** *noun* (CYTOLOGY) a region of cytoplasm which is adjacent to the nucleus during interphase and forms the centre of an aster during division **L19.** **centrosphere** *noun* (CYTOLOGY) a centrosome; *spec.* the central part of an aster during division: **L19.**

centrode /ˈsɛntrəʊd/ *noun*. *rare*. **L19.**
[ORIGIN from CENTRO- + -ODE[2].]
MATH. The path traced by the instantaneous centre of rotation of a moving plane figure.

centroid /ˈsɛntrɔɪd/ *noun*. **L19.**
[ORIGIN formed as CENTRODE + -OID.]
MATH. A point defined in relation to a given figure in a manner analogous to the centre of mass of a corresponding body. Orig. also = CENTRODE.

†**centronel** *noun* var. of SENTINEL *noun*.

centrum /ˈsɛntrəm/ *noun*. Pl. **-trums**, **-tra** /-trə/. **M19.**
[ORIGIN Latin.]
A centre; *spec.* (ANATOMY) the solid central part of a vertebra, to which the arches and processes are attached.

†**centry** *noun*[1]. **E16.**
[ORIGIN Uncertain: cf. Anglo-Latin *centrie*, *-ii* (pl.).]
1 In *pl.* The centering of a bridge etc. **E16–M19.**
2 The centre, midst. Only in **L16.**

†**centry** *noun*[2] var. of SENTRY *noun*[1].

centum /ˈsɛntəm/ *noun*. **M17.**
[ORIGIN Latin.]
= CENT *noun*[1] 1. Chiefly in ***per centum***.

centum /ˈkɛntəm/ *adjective*. **E20.**
[ORIGIN Latin (see CENTUM *noun*): this word and SATEM exemplifying this distinction between the two groups.]
PHILOLOGY. Designating or pertaining to a chiefly western group of Indo-European languages having (voiceless) velar plosives where cognate words in the eastern group have sibilants.

centumvir /sɛnˈtʌmvə:, k-/ *noun*. Pl. **-viri** /-vəri/, **-virs**. **E17.**
[ORIGIN Latin, from *centum* a hundred + *viri* men.]
ROMAN HISTORY. Any of a body of (orig. 105) judges appointed to decide common causes among the Roman people.
■ **centumviral** *adjective* **L17.** **centumvirate** *noun* the position of being centumviri, the centumviri collectively; *transf.* any body of 100 men: **M18.**

centuple /ˈsɛntjʊp(ə)l/ *adjective*, *noun*, & *verb*. **E17.**
[ORIGIN French, or ecclesiastical Latin *centuplus* var. of *centuplex*, from *centum* hundred.]
▶ **A** *adjective & noun*. A hundredfold (amount). **E17.**
▶ **B** *verb trans*. Multiply by a hundred. **E17.**
■ **centuplicate** *verb*, *adjective*, & *noun* = CENTUPLE **M17.** **centupliˈcation** *noun* **L19.**

centurial /sɛnˈtjʊərɪəl/ *adjective*. **E17.**
[ORIGIN Latin *centurialis*, from *centuria* CENTURY: see -AL[1].]
Of or pertaining to a century.

centuriate /sɛnˈtjʊərɪət/ *adjective*. **E17.**
[ORIGIN Latin *centuriatus* pa. pple, formed as CENTURIATE *verb*: see -ATE[2].]
ROMAN HISTORY. Of, pertaining to, or divided into units of a hundred; *spec.* designating an assembly (Latin *comitia centuriata*) in which the people voted by units of a hundred.

centuriate /sɛnˈtjʊərɪeɪt/ *verb trans*. **E18.**
[ORIGIN Latin *centuriat-* pa. ppl stem of *centuriare* divide into centuries, from *centuria* CENTURY: see -ATE[3].]
ROMAN HISTORY. Divide into hundreds; *spec.* divide (land) into units of a hundred or so estates for assigning to colonists.
■ **centuriˈation** *noun* [Latin *centuriatio(n-)*] **M19.**

Centuriator /sɛnˈtjʊərɪeɪtə/ *noun*. **M17.**
[ORIGIN mod. Latin, formed as CENTURIATE *verb*: see -OR.]
Any of a number of 16th-cent. Protestant divines who compiled a thirteen-volume Church History of which each volume embraced a century. More fully ***Centuriator of Magdeburg***. Usu. in *pl.*

centurion /sɛnˈtjʊərɪən/ *noun*. **ME.**
[ORIGIN Latin *centurio(n-)*, from *centuria* CENTURY: see -ION.]
1 *hist*. A commander of a century in the ancient Roman army; an officer in command of 100 men. **ME.**
2 A person who has achieved a sporting century; *spec.* the scorer of a century in cricket. *colloq.* **L19.**

century /ˈsɛntʃʊri/ *noun*. **LME.**
[ORIGIN Latin *centuria*, from *centum* a hundred: see -Y[3].]
1 *hist*. A company in the ancient Roman army, consisting nominally of a hundred men. **LME.**
> *transf.*: DE QUINCEY Centuries of armed men . . firing from windows.

2 A group of a hundred things; a hundred. *arch.* exc. as below. **L16.** ▸**b** A sum of a hundred dollars, pounds, etc. *slang*. **M19.** ▸**c** A score of a hundred made in a sport or game; *esp.* a hundred or more runs made in one batsman's innings at cricket. **L19.**
> SHAKES. *Cymb.* A century of prayers.

double century: see DOUBLE *adjective & adverb*. ***triple century***: see TRIPLE *adjective & adverb*.
3 *hist*. Each of the 193 divisions by which the Roman people voted in the centuriate assembly. **E17.**
4 Orig. more fully ***century of years***. A period of 100 years. **E17.**
> A. ALISON Not years, but centuries must elapse.

5 Each of the hundred-year periods reckoned successively from an accepted epoch, esp. from the date assumed for the birth of Jesus. **M17.**
first century AD 1–100; **twentieth century** 1901–2000, *popularly*. 1900–1999; **second century** BC 200–101 BC; (etc.).
– COMB.: **century plant** = ***American aloe*** s.v. ALOE 4.
■ **centuried** *adjective* established for centuries; centuries old **E19.**

CEO *abbreviation*.
Chief executive officer.

ceorl *noun* see CHURL.

cep /sɛp/ *noun*. Also **cèpe** /sɛp (*pl. same*)/. **M19.**
[ORIGIN French *cèpe* from Gascon *cep* tree trunk, mushroom, from Latin *cippus* stake.]
An edible European mushroom, *Boletus edulis*.

'cep *preposition & conjunction* var. of 'CEPT.

cèpe *noun* var. of CEP.

cephal- *combining form* see CEPHALO-.

cephalalgy /ˈsɛfəlaldʒi/ *noun*. Now *rare*. Also in Latin form **-algia** /sɛfəˈlaldʒə/. **M16.**
[ORIGIN Latin *cephalalgia* from Greek *kephalalgia*, from *kephalē* head: see -ALGIA, -Y[3]. Cf. Old French & mod. French *céphalalgie*.]
(A) headache.

cephalic /sɪˈfalɪk, kɛˈfalɪk/ *adjective & noun*. **LME.**
[ORIGIN Old French & mod. French *céphalique* from Latin *cephalicus* from Greek *kephalikos*, from *kephalē* head: see -IC.]
▶ **A** *adjective*. **1** Of, relating, or pertaining to the head; situated in the head; of the nature of a head. **LME.**
cephalic index the ratio of the maximum breadth of a skull (multiplied by 100) to its maximum length. **cephalic presentation** the presentation of a fetus such that it is delivered head first. **cephalic vein** a major vein of the arm (so called because opening it was anciently supposed to relieve disorders of the head).
2 Curing or relieving disorders of the head. Now *rare* or *obsolete*. **M17.**
▶ †**B** *noun*. A medicine for ailments of the head. **LME–M18.**

-cephalic /sɪˈfalɪk, kɛ-/ *suffix*.
[ORIGIN from Greek *kephalē* head + -IC.]
= -CEPHALOUS.

cephalin /ˈsɛfəlɪn, ˈkɛ-/ *noun*. **L19.**
[ORIGIN from CEPHALO- + -IN[1].]
BIOCHEMISTRY. Any of a class of phospholipids present in cell membranes, esp. in the brain.

cephalization /sɛfəlʌɪˈzeɪʃ(ə)n, kɛ-/ *noun*. Also **-isa-**. **M19.**
[ORIGIN from CEPHALO- + -IZATION.]
A greater development of the head in relation to the rest of the body (as in an embryo); the extent of this.

cephalo- /ˈsɛfələʊ, ˈkɛ-/ *combining form*. Also (*rare*) **k-** /k-/. Before a vowel or *h* also **cephal-**.
[ORIGIN from Greek *kephalē* head: see -O-.]
1 Forming nouns and adjectives with the sense 'head, skull'.
2 PHARMACOLOGY. Forming names of drugs related to cephalosporin.
■ **cephalhaemaˈtoma** *noun*, pl. **-mas**, **-mata** /-mətə/, MEDICINE a swelling caused by a collection of blood between the skull and pericranium **E20.** **cephaˈlitis** *noun* (now *rare* or *obsolete*) = ENCEPHALITIS **E19.** **cephalocele** *noun* (MEDICINE, now *rare*) = ENCEPHALOCELE **L19.** **cephaloˈchordate** *adjective & noun* (ZOOLOGY) (of, pertaining to, or designating) a protochordate animal of the subphylum Cephalochordata, a lancelet **M20.** **cephaloˈmetric** *adjective* (MEDICINE) pertaining to or involving cephalometry **L19.** **cephaˈlometry** *noun* (MEDICINE) measurement of the head, esp. that of a fetus **L19.** **cephaloˈpelvic** *adjective* (MEDICINE) of the relation between the maternal pelvis and the fetal head **M20.** **cephalothin** *noun* [THIO-] PHARMACOLOGY an antibiotic related to cephalosporin, used to treat bacterial infections **M20.** **cephalothoˈracic** *adjective* of or pertaining to a cephalothorax **M19.** **cephaloˈthorax** *noun* (ZOOLOGY) the fused head and thorax possessed by chelicerate arthropods and some crustaceans **M19.**

cephalon /ˈsɛfəlɒn/ *noun*. **L19.**
[ORIGIN from Greek *kephalē* head.]
ZOOLOGY. The region of the head in some arthropods, esp. trilobites.

cephalopod /ˈsɛf(ə)ləpɒd, ˈkɛ-/ *noun & adjective*. **E19.**
[ORIGIN from mod. Latin *Cephalopoda* (see below), formed as CEPHALO- + -POD.]
(A mollusc) of the class Cephalopoda, members of which have a well-developed head surrounded by tentacles, and include the cuttlefish, octopus, nautilus, and extinct forms such as ammonites.
■ **cephaˈlopodal** *adjective* **L19.** **cephaˈlopodous** *adjective* (now *rare* or *obsolete*) **M19.**

cephalosporin /sɛfələ(ʊ)ˈspɔ:rɪn, kɛ-/ *noun*. **M20.**
[ORIGIN from mod. Latin *Cephalosporium* (see below) + -IN[1].]
Any of a class of natural and semi-synthetic antibiotics derived from a mould of the genus *Cephalosporium*.

-cephalous /ˈsɛf(ə)ləs, ˈkɛf-/ *suffix*.
[ORIGIN from Greek *kephalē* head + -OUS.]
Forming adjectives (chiefly ANTHROPOLOGY) in sense '-headed, having a head of a specified kind', as ***brachycephalous***, ***dolichocephalous***, etc.

cepheid /ˈsi:fɪɪd, ˈsɛ-/ *adjective & noun*. Also **C-**. **E20.**
[ORIGIN from CEPHEUS + -ID[3].]
ASTRONOMY. ▶**A** *adjective*. Belonging or pertaining to a class of variable stars, typified by δ Cephei, which have regular cycles of brightness which can be used to deduce their distances. **E20.**
▶ **B** *noun*. A star of this type. **E20.**

Cepheus /ˈsi:fɪəs, -fju:s/ *noun*. **M16.**
[ORIGIN Latin *Cepheus*, Greek *Kēpheus*, father of Andromeda in Greek mythol.]
(The name of) a constellation of the northern hemisphere on the edge of the Milky Way, near the Pole Star.

'cept /sɛpt/ *preposition & conjunction*. *colloq.* Also **'cep**. **M19.**
[ORIGIN Abbreviation.]
= EXCEPT *preposition*, *conjunction*.

ceraceous /sɪˈreɪʃəs/ *adjective*. Now *rare*. **M18.**
[ORIGIN from Latin *cera* wax + -ACEOUS.]
Of the nature of wax, waxy.

ceral /ˈsɪər(ə)l/ *adjective*. **L19.**
[ORIGIN Sense 1 from CERE *noun*; sense 2 from Latin *cera* wax: see -AL[1].]
1 Of or pertaining to the cere of a bird's bill. **L19.**
2 Of or relating to wax. **L19.**

cerambycid /sɛrəmˈbʌɪsɪd/ *noun & adjective*. **L19.**
[ORIGIN from mod. Latin *Cerambycidae* (see below), from *Cerambyx* genus name, from Greek *kerambux* a kind of beetle: see -ID[3].]
ENTOMOLOGY. ▶**A** *noun*. A beetle of the family Cerambycidae, which comprises the longhorn beetles. **L19.**
▶ **B** *adjective*. Of, pertaining to, or designating this family. **E20.**

ceramic /sɪˈramɪk/ *adjective & noun*. **E19.**
[ORIGIN Greek *keramikos*, from *keramos* potter's earth, pottery: see -IC.]
▶ **A** *adjective*. Of or relating to (the art of) pottery; designating or pertaining to hard brittle substances produced by the process of strong heating of clay etc. **E19.**
▶ **B** *noun*. An article made of pottery. In *pl.* also, pottery, the art of making pottery. **M19.**
■ **ceramicist** /-ɪsɪst/ *noun* (*a*) = CERAMIST; (*b*) an expert in or student of ceramics: **M20.** **ˈceramist** *noun* a person skilled in the art of pottery **M19.**

cerargyrite /sɪˈrɑ:dʒɪrʌɪt/ *noun*. **M19.**
[ORIGIN Irreg. from Greek *keras* horn + *arguros* silver + -ITE[1].]
MINERALOGY. A waxy mineral consisting of silver halides, esp. the chloride, and crystallizing in the cubic system; horn silver.

cerastes /sɪˈrasti:z/ *noun*. **LME.**
[ORIGIN Latin *cerastes* from Greek *kerastēs*, from *keras* horn.]
A viper of the genus *Cerastes*, of N. Africa; *esp.* the horned viper, *C. cornuta*.

cerastium /sɪˈrastɪəm/ *noun*. **L18.**
[ORIGIN mod. Latin, from Greek *kerastēs* horned (from the shape of the capsule in many species): see -IUM.]
A white-flowered plant of the genus *Cerastium*, which belongs to the pink family and includes mouse-ear chickweed.

cerate /ˈsɪərət/ *noun*. Now *rare* or *obsolete*. **LME.**
[ORIGIN Latin *ceratum* = Greek *kērōton* neut. of adjective *kērōtos*, covered with wax. Cf. French *cérat*.]
MEDICINE. A stiff ointment composed of wax, lard, or oil, and other ingredients.

ceration /sɪˈreɪʃ(ə)n/ *noun*. *obsolete* exc. *hist*. **E17.**
[ORIGIN medieval Latin *ceratio(n-)*, from *cerat-* pa. ppl stem of *cerare*, from *cera* wax: see -ION.]
ALCHEMY. The process of softening a hard substance.

ceratite /ˈsɛrətʌɪt, ˈsɪər-/ *noun*. **M19.**
[ORIGIN from mod. Latin *ceratites* (see below), from Greek *keras*, *kerat-* horn: see -ITE[1].]
PALAEONTOLOGY. An ammonoid fossil of the genus *Ceratites* or a related genus, common in Permo-Triassic rocks, and having usu. partly frilled, partly lobed suture lines. Cf. AMMONITE, GONIATITE.
■ **ceratitic** /-ˈtɪtɪk/ *adjective* pertaining to or characteristic of a ceratite **E20.**

cerato- /ˈsɛrətəʊ, k-/ *combining form* of Greek *keras*, *kerat-* horn, occas. as var. of KERATO-: see -O-.

C

■ **cerato'branchial** *adjective & noun* (of, pertaining to, or designating) any of the paired cartilaginous sections of the branchial arch (e.g. in fishes) M19. **cerato'hyal** *adjective & noun* (of, pertaining to, or designating) any of the paired sections of the hyoid arch of the vertebrate skeleton M19.

ceratopsian /sɛrəˈtɒpsɪən, kɛr-/ *adjective & noun.* E20.
[ORIGIN from mod. Latin *Ceratopsia* (see below), from Greek *keras, kerat-* horn + *ops* face: see -AN.]
PALAEONTOLOGY. ▶**A** *adjective.* Of, pertaining to, or designating the ornithischian infraorder Ceratopsia of chiefly quadrupedal dinosaurs, characterized by a parrot-like beak and frequently also horns and a bony frill at the back of the skull. E20.
▶ **B** *noun.* A dinosaur of this group. M20.

Cerberus /ˈsəːb(ə)rəs/ *noun. literary & joc.* Pl. **-ri** /-rʌɪ/. M17.
[ORIGIN Latin from Greek *Kerberos* the three-headed watchdog which guarded the entrance of Hades.]
A watchdog.
a sop to Cerberus something to propitiate a guard, official, etc.

cercaria /səːˈkɛːrɪə/ *noun.* Pl. **-iae** /-ɪiː/. M19.
[ORIGIN mod. Latin, irreg. from Greek *kerkos* tail: see -ARY[1].]
ZOOLOGY. A digenean trematode (fluke) in the free-swimming larval stage developed from the redia, in which form it passes from the intermediate to the definitive host. Cf. MIRACIDIUM.
■ **cercarial** *adjective* L19. **cercarian** *adjective* M19.

cerclage /səːˈklɑːʒ/ *noun.* Also **cir-**. M20.
[ORIGIN French, lit. 'encirclement'.]
MEDICINE. The use of a ring or loop to bind together the ends of an obliquely fractured bone or encircle the os of an incompetent cervix.

cercopithecoid /səːkəˈpɪθɪkɔɪd/ *adjective & noun.* L19.
[ORIGIN from Latin *cercopithecus* from Greek *kerkopithēkos* a long-tailed monkey, from *kerkos* tail + *pithēkos* ape: see -OID.]
ZOOLOGY. ▶**A** *adjective.* Of, pertaining to or characteristic of the superfamily Cercopithecoidea, which comprises the Old World monkeys. L19.
▶ **B** *noun.* A cercopithecoid monkey. M20.
■ **cercopithecine** /-siːn/ *adjective & noun* (*a*) *adjective* of, pertaining to, or designating the Cercopithecinae, a subfamily of the Cercopithoidea including the macaques, mangabeys, baboons, and guenons; (*b*) *noun* a cercopithecine monkey: M20.

cercus /ˈsəːkəs/ *noun.* Pl. **cerci** /ˈsəːkʌɪ/. E19.
[ORIGIN mod. Latin from Greek *kerkos* tail.]
ZOOLOGY. Either of a pair of small appendages at the end of the abdomen of certain insects and other arthropods.
■ **cercal** *adjective* L19.

cere /sɪə/ *noun.* Also †**s-**. L15.
[ORIGIN Latin *cera* wax.]
The soft waxlike covering of the base of the beak in certain birds (esp. birds of prey), in which the nostrils are pierced.

cere /sɪə/ *verb trans.* LME.
[ORIGIN Latin *cerare* to wax, from *cera* wax.]
1 Wrap in a cerecloth. LME. ▸†**b** Anoint with spices etc., embalm. L15–L16.
†**2** Smear, cover, or impregnate with wax. LME–M17.

cereal /ˈsɪərɪəl/ *adjective & noun.* E19.
[ORIGIN Latin *cerealis* pertaining to the cultivation of grain, from *Ceres* Roman goddess of agriculture: see -AL[1].]
▶ **A** *adjective.* Of, pertaining to, or of the nature of edible grain. E19.
cereal bar a prepackaged item of snack food made of cereal and usu. fruit.
▶ **B** *noun.* **1** Any of the plants of the grass family Gramineae which are cultivated for their edible seeds; a grain used for human food. Usu. in *pl.* M19.
2 Food made from wheat, maize, or another grain (usu. as a breakfast dish). L19.

cerebellum /sɛrɪˈbɛləm/ *noun.* M16.
[ORIGIN Latin, dim. of CEREBRUM: see -ELLUM.]
ANATOMY. The larger part of the hindbrain, responsible for the control of muscle tone and balance.
■ †**cerebel** *noun* = CEREBELLUM E17–M19. **cerebellar** *adjective* of or pertaining to the cerebellum E19.

cerebral /ˈsɛrɪbr(ə)l/ *adjective & noun.* E19.
[ORIGIN from Latin CEREBRUM + -AL[1]: cf. French *cérébral*.]
▶ **A** *adjective.* **1** Of or pertaining to the brain. E19. ▸**b** Appealing to the intellect rather than to the emotions; clever; intellectual. E20.
cerebral palsy a disorder chiefly characterized by spastic paralysis due to brain damage before or at birth.
2 *PHONETICS.* = CACUMINAL *adjective.* E19.
▶ **B** *noun. PHONETICS.* A cerebral consonant. E19.
■ **cerebralism** *noun* (*a*) intellectualism; (*b*) (now *rare*) the theory that mental processes arise from the action of the brain: L19. **cerebralist** *noun* (*a*) an intellectualist, an intellectual; (*b*) (now *rare*) a supporter of the theory of cerebralism: L19. **cerebrally** *adverb* L19.

cerebrate /ˈsɛrɪbreɪt/ *verb.* L19.
[ORIGIN formed as CEREBRATION + -ATE[3].]
1 *verb trans.* Subject to or produced by brain action. L19.
2 *verb intrans.* Cogitate. E20.

cerebration /sɛrɪˈbreɪʃ(ə)n/ *noun.* M19.
[ORIGIN from Latin CEREBRUM + -ATION.]
The working of the brain; *esp.* (in full ***unconscious cerebration***) the action of the brain in producing results without conscious thought.

cerebro- /ˈsɛrɪbrəʊ/ *combining form* of Latin CEREBRUM: see -O-.
■ **cerebro'centric** *adjective* centring on the brain M20. **cerebroside** *noun* [-OSE[2] + -IDE] *BIOCHEMISTRY* any of a group of glycolipids present in the sheaths of nerve fibres (cf. GANGLIOSIDE) L19. **cerebro'spinal** *adjective* of, pertaining to, or involving the brain and spinal cord (***cerebrospinal fluid***, the clear watery fluid occupying the space between the arachnoid membrane and the pia mater) E19. **cerebro'tonic** *adjective & noun* (*a*) *adjective* temperamentally resembling or characteristic of an ectomorph, with predominantly intellectual interests; (*b*) *noun* a cerebrotonic person: M20. **cerebro'vascular** *adjective* of or pertaining to the brain and the blood vessels which supply it M20.

cerebrum /ˈsɛrɪbrəm/ *noun.* E17.
[ORIGIN Latin = brain.]
ANATOMY. The larger, anterior part of the brain, responsible for voluntary activity and mental processes.

cerecloth /ˈsɪəklɒθ/ *noun & verb.* LME.
[ORIGIN from *cered cloth*: see CERE verb, CLOTH.]
▶ **A** *noun.* (A piece of) cloth made waterproof by smearing or impregnating with wax; *spec.* (*a*) one used for wrapping a corpse, a winding sheet; †(*b*) one used as a plaster. LME.
▶ †**B** *verb trans.* Wrap in or cover with a cerecloth. E–M17.

cerement /ˈsɪəm(ə)nt/ *noun. literary.* E17.
[ORIGIN App. from CERE *verb* + -MENT.]
1 In *pl.* (Waxed) wrappings for the dead; grave-clothes. E17.

SHAKES. *Haml.* Tell Why thy canoniz'd bones . . Have burst their cerements.

2 A cerecloth. *rare.* E19.
— NOTE: First recorded in Shakes.

ceremonial /sɛrɪˈməʊnɪəl/ *adjective & noun.* LME.
[ORIGIN Late Latin *caerimonialis*, from *caerimonia* CEREMONY: see -AL[1]. Cf. Old French & mod. French *cérémonial*.]
▶ **A** *adjective.* **1** Relating to or consisting of ceremonies or rites; ritual; formal. LME.

A. J. P. TAYLOR The upper-class uniform of top hat and tail coat was worn only on ceremonial occasions, such as weddings and race-meetings. E. H. PINTO Ceremonial tools of considerable elaboration were made for presentation to the notabilities invited to lay foundation stones.

2 Relating to or involving social formalities. M16.
ceremonial law: enforced by custom.
†**3** = CEREMONIOUS 2. L16–M17.
▶ **B** *noun.* †**1** A ceremonial commandment. LME–E17.
2 A system of rites; a rite or ceremony; the formalities proper to an occasion. LME.

HENRY FIELDING The two ladies . . after very short previous ceremonials, fell to business. I. D'ISRAELI The ceremonial prescribed in the Anglican service. J. BRONOWSKI A precise ceremonial which fixes the sequence of operations so that they are exact and memorable.

3 *ROMAN CATHOLIC CHURCH.* A book containing the order of ritual. E17.
4 The observance of ritual or convention; ceremonial display. M19.
■ **ceremonialism** *noun* addiction to or fondness for ceremonies; ritualism: M19. **ceremonialist** *noun* a ritualist, one given to ceremonies L17. **ceremonialize** *verb* (*a*) *verb trans.* render ceremonial or ritualistic; (*b*) *verb intrans.* carry out a ceremony: M19. **ceremonially** *adverb* M17.

ceremonious /sɛrɪˈməʊnɪəs/ *adjective.* M16.
[ORIGIN French *cérémonieux* or late Latin *caerimoniosus*, from *caerimonia*: see CEREMONY, -OUS.]
1 = CEREMONIAL *adjective* 1. M16.
2 Addicted or given to ceremony; punctilious. M16.
3 According to prescribed or customary formalities. L16.
4 Full of ceremony; accompanied by rites. E17.
■ **ceremoniously** *adverb* L16. **ceremoniousness** *noun* L16.

ceremony /ˈsɛrɪməni/ *noun.* LME.
[ORIGIN Latin *caerimonia* religious worship, (in pl.) ritual observances, perh. through Old French & mod. French *cérémonie*: see -MONY.]
1 An outward rite or observance; the performance of some solemn act according to a prescribed form. LME. ▸**b** (A rite regarded as) an empty form; a mere formality. M16.

R. W. EMERSON They repeated the ceremonies of the eleventh century in the coronation of the present Queen. A. N. WILSON It was not until she herself married that she became aware . . that this was a ceremony which her parents had never actually undergone. **b** ROBERT BURTON It is . . a meer flash, a ceremony, a toy, a thing of nought.

2 A formal act of politeness, courtesy, civility, etc. LME.

H. JAMES She went and knocked at his door—a ceremony without which she never crossed the threshold.

†**3** An object or symbolic attribute of worship, state, or pomp. L16–E18.
†**4** A portent, an omen. *rare* (Shakes.). Only in L16.
5 (Non-count.) Performance of (religious) rites; ceremonial display; pomp, state; precise observance of conventional forms; punctilious behaviour. L16.

SHAKES. *Hen. V* What have kings that privates have not too, Save ceremony. G. MACDONALD I was shown with much ceremony . . into the presence of two ladies.

— PHRASES: **master of ceremonies** a person in charge of ceremonies observed on state or public occasions; a person introducing speakers at a banquet, entertainers in a variety show, etc. ***sans cérémonie***: see SANS *preposition.* **stand on ceremony** insist on the observance of formalities. **without ceremony** informally, casually.

Cerenkov radiation /tʃəˈrɛŋkɒf reɪdɪˈeɪʃ(ə)n/ *noun phr.* Also **Cherenkov radiation.** M20.
[ORIGIN Pavel A. *Cherenkov* (1904–90), Soviet physicist.]
PHYSICS. Light emitted by a charged particle moving in a medium at a speed greater than that of light in the same medium.

cereologist /sɪərɪˈɒlədʒɪst/ *noun.* L20.
[ORIGIN from *Ceres* (see CEREAL) + -OLOGIST.]
A student or investigator of crop circles.
■ **cereology** *noun* L20.

cereopsis /sɛrɪˈɒpsɪs/ *noun.* M20.
[ORIGIN mod. Latin *Cereopsis* genus name, from Greek *kerinos* waxen (from *keros* wax) + *opsis* face, with ref. to the swollen waxy cere.]
In full ***cereopsis goose***. = ***Cape Barren goose*** s.v. CAPE *noun*[1].

cereous /ˈsɪərɪəs/ *adjective.* E17.
[ORIGIN from Latin *cereus* waxen, from *cera* wax: see -OUS.]
Of the nature of wax; waxen, waxy.

†**Ceres** *noun & adjective* see SERI.

ceresin /ˈsɛrɪsɪn/ *noun.* L19.
[ORIGIN from mod. Latin *ceres* from Latin *cera* wax + -IN[1].]
A hard whitish paraffin wax used with or instead of beeswax.

cereus /ˈsɪərɪəs/ *noun.* L17.
[ORIGIN Latin: see CEREOUS.]
Any of numerous neotropical cacti now or formerly included in the genus *Cereus*.
night-blooming cereus: see NIGHT *noun.*
— NOTE: Many species, esp. those designated 'night-blooming', are now placed in other genera.

ceric /ˈsɪərɪk/ *adjective.* M19.
[ORIGIN from CERIUM + -IC.]
CHEMISTRY. Of cerium in its higher valency (4). Cf. CEROUS.

†**cerilla** *noun.* L16–M19.
[ORIGIN Spanish, var. of CEDILLA.]
= CEDILLA.

cerin /ˈsɪərɪn/ *noun.* E19.
[ORIGIN from Latin *cera* wax + -IN[1].]
CHEMISTRY. **1** A terpenoid ketone extracted from cork. E19.
2 The alcohol-soluble part of beeswax. E19.

Cerinthian /sɪˈrɪnθɪən/ *noun & adjective.* LME.
[ORIGIN from *Cerinthus* (see below) + -IAN.]
ECCLESIASTICAL HISTORY. ▶**A** *noun.* An adherent of Cerinthus, a Gnostic of the 1st cent. AD who is usu. presented as antagonistic to the Apostle John. LME.
▶ **B** *adjective.* Of or pertaining to Cerinthus or his teaching. L16.

ceriph *noun* see SERIF.

†**Ceris** *noun & adjective* see SERI.

cerise /sɛˈriːz, -s/ *adjective & noun.* M19.
[ORIGIN French = cherry.]
(Of) a light clear red.

cerite /ˈsɪərʌɪt/ *noun.* E19.
[ORIGIN from CERIUM + -ITE[1].]
MINERALOGY. An orthorhombic hydrated silicate of cerium and other lanthanides, occurring as brown granular masses.

cerium /ˈsɪərɪəm/ *noun.* E19.
[ORIGIN from *Ceres*, an asteroid discovered shortly before this element + -IUM.]
A metallic chemical element, atomic no. 58, which is the most abundant of the lanthanide series (symbol Ce).

cermet /ˈsəːmɛt/ *noun.* M20.
[ORIGIN from CERAMIC + METAL *noun.*]
A heat-resistant material made by sintering a mixture of ceramic and metallic powders.

CERN /səːn/ *abbreviation.*
French *Conseil Européen pour la Recherche Nucléaire* European Organization for Nuclear Research (later European Laboratory for Particle Physics).

†**cern** *verb trans. rare* (Shakes.). Only in L16.
[ORIGIN Abbreviation.]
= CONCERN *verb.*

cernuous /ˈsəːnjʊəs/ *adjective.* M17.
[ORIGIN from Latin *cernuus* inclined forwards + -OUS.]
Chiefly *BOTANY.* Bowing downwards, drooping.

cero /ˈsɪərəʊ/ *noun.* Pl. **-os**, same. L19.
[ORIGIN Spanish *sierra* saw, sawfish.]
A mackerel, *Scomberomorus regalis*, found in warm parts of the western Atlantic. Also called ***sierra***.

cero- /ˈsɪərəʊ/ *combining form* of Latin *cera* or Greek *kēros* wax: see **-O-**.
■ **ceˈrography** *noun* writing, engraving, designing, or painting on or in wax **L16**. **ceroˈplastic** *adjective* of or relating to modelling in wax **E19**.

ceroc /sɪˈrɒk/ *noun*. **L20**.
[ORIGIN Invented word, appar. coined in English from French *ce* (as in *c'est*) + *roc* rock.]
A type of modern social dance having elements of rock and roll, jive, and salsa.

ceroon *noun* var. of **SERON**.

†**cerote** *noun*. **M16–M18**.
[ORIGIN Latin *cerotum* from Greek *kērōton*: see **CERATE**.]
= **CERATE**.

cerotic /sɪˈrɒtɪk/ *adjective*. **M19**.
[ORIGIN formed as **CEROTE** + **-IC**.]
CHEMISTRY. ***cerotic acid***, a fatty acid, $C_{26}H_{53}COOH$, present in insect waxes, usu. as the ceryl ester.
■ **ˈcerotate** *noun* a salt or ester of cerotic acid **L19**. **ˈcerotin** *noun* ceryl alcohol, $C_{27}H_{55}OH$, obtained from insect waxes **M19**.

cerous /ˈsɪərəs/ *adjective*. **M19**.
[ORIGIN from **CERIUM** + **-OUS**.]
CHEMISTRY. Of cerium in its lower valency (3). Cf. **CERIC**.

cert /sɜːt/ *noun*. *slang*. **L19**.
[ORIGIN Abbreviation of **CERTAIN** or **CERTAINTY**.]
A certainty, a sure thing; something bound to happen; a racehorse etc. regarded as certain to win. Freq. in ***dead cert***.
for cert = ***for certain*** (see **CERT.**).

cert. *abbreviation*.
1 Certificate.
2 Certified.

certain /ˈsɜːt(ə)n, -tɪn/ *adjective, noun, pronoun, & adverb*. **ME**.
[ORIGIN Old French & mod. French from Proto-Romance extension of Latin *certus* settled, sure.]
▸ **A** *adjective* **I 1** Determined, fixed; not variable. Occas. *postpositive*. **ME**. ▸**b** Definite, precise, exact. *arch*. **LME**.

H. J. STEPHEN Payment of money on a day certain. J. ARLOTT The fixed and certain oak. **b** MARVELL The answer is now much shorter and certainer.

2 Sure; inevitable; unfailing; wholly reliable. **ME**.

SPENSER Fearfull more of shame Then of the certeine perill he stood in. M. SOMERVILLE A certain indication of a coming tempest. H. CECIL An absolutely certain thing for the four o'clock had come in second.

3 Established as a truth or fact; not to be doubted. **LME**.

B. RUSSELL Is there any knowledge in the world which is so certain that no reasonable man could doubt it? J. STEINBECK Putting his certain ignorance against this man's possible knowledge.

make certain make sure.
4 Of a person: having no doubt, assured, convinced. **LME**. ▸**b** Destined, undoubtedly going *to do*. **M17**.

C. ISHERWOOD He can't be certain if Kenny answered his question or not. W. TREVOR One of the daily women was only a little sceptical, while the other was certain and adamant. I. MURDOCH He was quite certain that he was acting rightly. **b** OED We are certain to meet him in the course of our rambles.

morally certain so sure that one is justified in acting upon the conviction.
▸ **II 5** Known and particularized but not explicitly identified: (with sing. noun) a particular, (with pl. noun) some particular, some definite. **ME**. ▸**b** Of some extent at least; some though not much. **M16**. ▸**c** *euphem*. Which it is not polite or necessary to define further. **M18**. ▸**d** Of a person: unknown except by name; existing, but probably unknown to the reader or hearer. **L18**.

L. M. MONTGOMERY If it isn't carried in just a certain way the handle pulls out. M. FRAYN I shall want him to bring certain designated books and documents. **b** J. TYNDALL The ice is disintegrated to a certain depth. **d** SOUTHEY A certain Benjamin Franklin French writes to me from New Orleans.

up to a certain point: see **POINT** *noun*[1]. **c a certain age** an age when one is no longer young (usu. of a woman). **a certain disease** venereal disease. ***in a certain condition***: see **CONDITION** *noun* 8. **of a certain description** (of a woman) of the demimonde.
▸ **B** *ellipt*. as *noun* or *pl. pronoun*. **1** What is certain, certainty. *obsolete* exc. in ***for certain*** below. **ME**.

SHAKES. *Hen. V* I will live so long as I may, that's the certain of it.

for certain, (*dial*.) **for a certain**, (*arch*.) **of a certain**, **of certain** as a certainty, assuredly.
†**2** A particular quantity, amount, number, etc., *of*; *ellipt*. a particular sum of money. **ME–E17**.
3 Some but not all (*of*). **LME**.
▸ **C** *adverb*. Certainly; assuredly. Now *dial*. or *arch*. **ME**.
certain sure very certain.

certainly /ˈsɜːt(ə)nli, -tɪn-/ *adverb*. **ME**.
[ORIGIN from **CERTAIN** + **-LY**[2].]
1 In a manner that is certain; in a way that may be surely depended on. **ME**. ▸†**b** Exactly. **LME–E17**.
2 With certainty; unfailingly; indubitably, assuredly, admittedly; (in answers) without doubt, undeniably, yes (***certainly not***, (emphatically) no). **ME**. ▸**b** Fixedly. Now *rare*. **L16**.

certainty /ˈsɜːt(ə)nti, -tɪn-/ *noun*. **ME**.
[ORIGIN Anglo-Norman *certainté*, Old French *certaineté*: see **CERTAIN**, **-TY**[1].]
1 The quality or fact of being objectively certain. **ME**.

J. KEILL Geometry, which truly boasts the Beauty of Certainty.

2 The quality or state of being subjectively certain; assurance, confidence; certitude. **ME**.

BACON If a man will begin with certainties, hee shall end in doubts. R. P. WARREN He was filled with certainty, a . . conviction that engulfed him.

3 A definite number or quantity. *obsolete* exc. *THEATRICAL*, a flat rate. **LME**.
4 An undoubted fact; an indubitable prospect; a thing or person which may be relied on (*to do*). **E17**.

M. W. MONTAGU I would not advise you to neglect a certainty for an uncertainty. G. B. SHAW Though these are only risks to the individual, to the community they are certainties.

– PHRASES: **for a certainty** beyond possibility of doubt. ***moral certainty***: see **MORAL** *adjective*.

Cert.Ed. *abbreviation*.
Certificate in Education.

certes /ˈsɜːtɪz/ *adverb*. *arch*. **ME**.
[ORIGIN Old French & mod. French, prob. from Proto-Romance from Latin *certus*: see **CERTAIN**.]
Of a truth; assuredly, I assure you.

certie /ˈsɜːti/ *noun*. *Scot*. Also **-y**. **E19**.
[ORIGIN Perh. back-form. from **CERTES**, taken as pl.]
my certie (adverbial phr.), in good faith, on my word.

certifiable /ˈsɜːtɪfʌɪəb(ə)l/ *adjective*. **M19**.
[ORIGIN from **CERTIFY** + **-ABLE**.]
1 Able to be certified; *spec*. (of a person) so deranged as to be certifiably insane; (of mental illness) of such a type as to warrant certification. **M19**.
2 Of infectious disease: notifiable. *US*. **E20**.
■ **certifiably** *adverb* in a manner or degree warranting certification **L19**.

certificate /səˈtɪfɪkət/ *noun*. **LME**.
[ORIGIN French *certificat* or medieval Latin *certificatum* use as noun of neut. pa. pple of *certificare*: see **CERTIFY**, **-ATE**[1].]
†**1** The action or fact of certifying or giving assurance; certification, attestation. **LME–M17**.
2 A document in which a fact is formally certified or attested; *esp*. one formally attesting status, medical condition, abilities, fulfilment of requirements, ownership of shares, etc.; a licence. **M16**.
birth certificate, ***marriage certificate***, ***medical certificate***, ***X-certificate***, etc. ***certificate of origin***: see **ORIGIN** 1. **Certificate of Secondary Education** *hist*. (the certificate gained by passing) an examination for secondary-school pupils in England and Wales, usu. set and marked by individual schools; abbreviation ***CSE***. **General Certificate of Education** *hist*. (the certificate gained by passing) an examination esp. for secondary-school pupils in England and Wales, set and marked by an independent examination board; abbreviation ***GCE***. **General Certificate of Secondary Education** (the certificate gained by passing) an examination for secondary-school pupils in England and Wales, including coursework assessment by individual schools; abbreviation ***GCSE***. ***silver certificate***: see **SILVER** *noun & adjective*.
3 *LAW*. A writing made in one court, by which notice of its proceedings is given to another. Now *rare*. **E17**.

†**certificate** *pa. pple & ppl adjective*. **E–M16**.
[ORIGIN medieval Latin *certificatus* pa. pple of *certificare*: see **CERTIFY**, **-ATE**[2]. Cf. **CERTIFICATE** *verb*.]
Certified; assured.

certificate /səˈtɪfɪkeɪt/ *verb trans*. **M18**.
[ORIGIN from the noun: see **-ATE**[3]. Cf. **CERTIFICATE** *adjective*.]
1 Provide with a certificate; license or authorize by certificate. **M18**.
2 Attest by a certificate. **L19**.

certification /ˌsəːtɪfɪˈkeɪʃ(ə)n/ *noun*. **LME**.
[ORIGIN Old French & mod. French, or medieval Latin *certificatio(n-)*, from Latin *certificat-* pa. ppl stem of *certificare*: see **CERTIFY**, **-ATION**.]
▸ **I 1** Sure information; assurance. Now *rare*. **LME**.
2 *SCOTS LAW*. Notice or a warning to a party of the consequences of a failure to obey the summons or other writ. **L15**.
3 The action or an instance of certifying the truth of something. **M16**.
4 Provision of a formal or legal certificate, esp. of insanity; possession of a certificate. **L19**.
▸ **II 5** A certificate, now *esp*. one attesting to a qualification. **M16**.

certificatory /səˈtɪfɪkət(ə)ri/ *adjective*. **LME**.
[ORIGIN medieval Latin *certificatorius*, from Latin *certificat-*: see **CERTIFICATION**, **-ORY**[2].]
Serving to certify; of the nature of a certificate.
letter certificatory a written testimonial.

certified /ˈsɜːtɪfʌɪd/ *adjective*. **E17**.
[ORIGIN from **CERTIFY** + **-ED**[1].]
That has been certified; having a certificate, attested by certificate; *arch*. certain.
certified accountant, **certified public accountant** *US*: holding a certificate of professional competence. **certified cheque**: whose value is guaranteed by a bank. **certified mail** *US*: whose delivery is recorded. **certified milk**: guaranteed free from tuberculosis bacillus. ***certified public accountant***: see ***certified accountant*** above. **certified transfer** *STOCK EXCHANGE*: for which the shares are guaranteed to be available.

certify /ˈsɜːtɪfʌɪ/ *verb*. **ME**.
[ORIGIN Old French & mod. French *certifier* from late Latin *certificare*, from *certus*: see **CERTAIN**, **-FY**.]
1 *verb trans*. Make (a thing) certain; guarantee as certain; give certain information of. **ME**.
2 *verb trans*. Declare or attest by a formal or legal certificate. **ME**. ▸**b** *spec*. Declare (a person) officially insane. **L19**.
3 *verb trans*. Make (a person) certain (*of*); assure; give (a person) formal or legal attestation (*of*). *arch*. **ME**.
4 *verb intrans*. Testify *to*; vouch *for*. **ME**. ▸**b** *LAW*. Give a certificate for costs on a certain scale. Now *rare*. **L19**.
■ **certifier** *noun* **L16**.

C

certiorari /sɜːtɪəˈrɛːrʌɪ, -ˈrɑːri/ *noun*. **LME**.
[ORIGIN Law Latin, pass. of Latin *certiorare* inform, from *certior* compar. of *certus* **CERTAIN**. Cf. **SISERARY**.]
LAW. An order or (formerly) writ issuing from a superior court (in England the High Court) to an inferior court or tribunal and calling up the records and proceedings in some cause for review or a speedier judgement.

certiorate /ˈsɜːtɪəreɪt, ˈsɜːʃ-/ *verb trans*. Now *rare* or *obsolete*. **M16**.
[ORIGIN Late Latin *certiorat-* pa. ppl stem of *certiorare*: see **CERTIORARI**, **-ATE**[3].]
Inform authoritatively.

certitude /ˈsɜːtɪtjuːd/ *noun*. **LME**.
[ORIGIN Late Latin *certitudo*, from *certus*: see **CERTAIN**, **-TUDE**.]
1 Subjective certainty; assurance, confidence. **LME**. ▸**b** A feeling of certainty. Now *rare*. **E17**.
2 a Objective certainty. Now *rare* or *obsolete* in *gen*. sense. **M16**. ▸**b** Sureness of action, unfailing quality. **L16**.

certy *noun* var. of **CERTIE**.

cerulean /sɪˈruːlɪən/ *adjective & noun*. Chiefly *poet*. Also **cae-**. **M17**.
[ORIGIN from Latin *caeruleus* sky-blue, sea-blue (or -green), from *caelum* sky, heaven: see **-EAN**.]
(Of) the colour of the cloudless sky; deep blue, azure.
■ Also **cerule** *adjective & noun* (*poet*.) **L16**.

cerumen /sɪˈruːmən/ *noun*. **L17**.
[ORIGIN mod. Latin, from Latin *cera* wax.]
The yellow waxlike substance secreted in the outer ear.
■ **ceruminous** *adjective* **E19**.

ceruse /ˈsɪəruːs, sɪˈruːs/ *noun*. **LME**.
[ORIGIN Old French & mod. French *céruse* from Latin *cerussa*, perh. ult. from Greek *kēros* wax.]
White lead (basic lead carbonate), esp. as a cosmetic.

cerussite /ˈsɪərəsʌɪt/ *noun*. **M19**.
[ORIGIN from Latin *cerussa* (see **CERUSE**) + **-ITE**[1].]
MINERALOGY. Orthorhombic lead carbonate, most commonly occurring as white, grey, or yellowish crystals. Also called ***lead-spar***.

Cervantic /səːˈvantɪk/ *adjective*. **M18**.
[ORIGIN from *Cervantes* (see below) + **-IC**.]
Of, pertaining to, or characteristic of the Spanish novelist and dramatist Miguel de Cervantes Saavedra (1547–1616).

cervantite /səːˈvantʌɪt/ *noun*. **M19**.
[ORIGIN from *Cervantes*, a locality in Galicia, Spain + **-ITE**[1].]
MINERALOGY. Orthorhombic antimony tetroxide, usu. occurring as yellow or reddish needles.

cervelat /ˈsɜːvəlɑː/ *noun*. **E17**.
[ORIGIN French (now *cervelas*), from Italian *cervellata* Milanese sausage.]
A kind of smoked pork sausage.

cervical /ˈsɜːvɪk(ə)l, səːˈvʌɪk(ə)l/ *adjective & noun*. **L17**.
[ORIGIN French, or mod. Latin *cervicalis*, from Latin *cervicis*, **CERVIX**: see **-AL**[1].]
ANATOMY. ▸**A** *adjective*. **1** Of or pertaining to the neck. **L17**.
2 Of or pertaining to a cervix, *spec*. that of the womb. **M19**.
cervical smear: see **SMEAR** *noun* 2b.
▸ **B** *noun*. A cervical nerve, vertebra, etc. **M18**.

cervicitis /səːvɪˈsʌɪtɪs/ *noun*. **L19**.
[ORIGIN from Latin *cervic-*, **CERVIX** + **-ITIS**.]
MEDICINE. Inflammation of the neck of the womb.

cervico- /səːˈvʌɪkəʊ/ *combining form* of Latin *cervicis*, **CERVIX**: see **-O-**.
■ **cervicoˈfacial** *adjective* pertaining to the neck and face. **M19**.

cervid /ˈsɜːvɪd/ *noun & adjective*. **L19**.
[ORIGIN mod. Latin *Cervidae* (see below), from Latin *cervus* deer: see **-ID**[2].]
(A ruminant) of the family Cervidae, to which most deer belong.

cervine /ˈsɜːvʌɪn/ *adjective & noun*. **M19**.
[ORIGIN Latin *cervinus*, from *cervus* deer: see **-INE**[1].]
Of or like a deer; (an animal) of the deer family.

cervisial /səːˈvɪzɪəl/ *adjective*. *joc*. **L18**.
[ORIGIN from Latin *cervisia* beer + **-AL**[1].]
Of or pertaining to beer.

cervix /ˈsəːvɪks/ *noun*. Pl. **-vices** /-vɪsiːz/. **M18.**
[**ORIGIN** Latin.]
ANATOMY. The neck; a part of an organ resembling or forming a neck; *spec.* the narrow passage forming the lower end of the womb adjacent to the vagina.

ceryl /ˈsɪərʌɪl, -rɪl/ *noun*. **L19.**
[**ORIGIN** from Latin *cera* wax + **-YL**.]
CHEMISTRY. The straight-chain radical $C_{27}H_{55}$, present in cerotin. Usu. in *comb.*

Cesare /ˈsiːzəri/ *noun*. **M16.**
[**ORIGIN** A mnemonic of scholastic philosophers first used in medieval Latin, E indicating a universal negative proposition and A a universal affirmative proposition.]
LOGIC. The first mood of the second syllogistic figure, in which a universal negative major premiss and a universal affirmative minor premiss yield a universal negative conclusion.

Cesarean, **Cesarian** *nouns & adjectives* see **CAESAREAN**.

Cesarewitch /sɪˈzarəwɪtʃ/ *noun*. In sense 1 also **-vitch** /-vɪtʃ/, **c-**. **M19.**
[**ORIGIN** Russian *tsesarevich*, from *tsesar'* emperor (from Latin *Caesar*) + patronymic *-evich*. Cf. **TSAREVICH**.]
1 *hist.* = **TSAREVICH**. **M19.**
2 A long-distance handicap horse race run annually at Newmarket, England. **M19.**

cesium *noun* see **CAESIUM**.

Cesolfa /siːsɒlˈfɑː/ *noun*. *obsolete* exc. *hist.* Also **C sol fa**. **ME.**
[**ORIGIN** from *C* as a pitch letter + *sol* and *fa* designating tones in the solmization of Guido d'Arezzo (*c* 990–1050).]
MEDIEVAL MUSIC. The note C in Guido d'Arezzo's 3rd and 4th hexachords, where it was sung to the syllables *sol* and *fa* respectively. Cf. **ALAMIRE**, **BEFA**, **CEFAUT**, **CESOLFAUT**, etc.

Cesolfaut /siːsɒlfɑːˈʊt/ *noun*. *obsolete* exc. *hist.* Also **C sol fa ut**. **LME.**
[**ORIGIN** from *C* as a pitch letter + *sol*, *fa* and *ut* designating tones in the solmization of Guido d'Arezzo (*c* 990–1050).]
MEDIEVAL MUSIC. The note C in Guido d'Arezzo's 3rd, 4th, and 5th hexachords, where it was sung to the syllables *sol*, *fa*, and *ut* respectively. Cf. **ALAMIRE**, **BEFA**, **CESOLFA**, etc.

cespititious *adjective* see **CAESPITITIOUS**.

cespitose *adjective* see **CAESPITOSE**.

cess /sɛs/ *noun*[1]. Also †**s-**. **L15.**
[**ORIGIN** from **CESS** *verb*[1] or aphet. from **ASSESS** *noun*.]
1 *IRISH HISTORY*. The obligation to supply the Lord Deputy's household and soldiers with provisions at prices fixed by government. **L15.**
2 A local tax or rate; *Scot.* land tax. *obsolete* exc. *dial.* **M16.**
†**3** Assessment, estimation. Only in **L16.**

SHAKES. *1 Hen. IV* Poor jade is wrung in the withers out of all cess.

cess /sɛs/ *noun*[2]. *Irish*. **M19.**
[**ORIGIN** Perh. with ref. to **CESS** *noun*[1] 2.]
bad cess to, may evil befall.

cess /sɛs/ *verb*[1] *trans.* Also †**s-**. **LME.**
[**ORIGIN** Aphet. from **ASSESS** *verb*.]
†**1** = **ASSESS** *verb* 1. **LME–M18.**
2 = **ASSESS** *verb* 2. *obsolete* exc. *dial.* **L15.**
3 *verb trans.* *IRISH HISTORY*. Impose (soldiers etc.) on the community (see **CESS** *noun*[1] 2). **E17.**

†**cess** *verb*[2] *intrans.* **LME–M18.**
[**ORIGIN** Var. of **CEASE** *verb*.]
Cease to perform a legal duty. Cf. **CESSAVIT**.

cessation /sɛˈseɪʃ(ə)n/ *noun*. **LME.**
[**ORIGIN** Latin *cessatio(n-)*, from *cessat-* pa. ppl stem of *cessare*: see **CEASE** *verb*, **-ATION**.]
1 Ceasing; a pause, stoppage. **LME.** ▸†**b** *ellipt.* An armistice, a truce. **M17–M18.**
†**2** Inactivity. **E17–E19.**

cessavit /sɛˈseɪvɪt/ *noun*. **E16.**
[**ORIGIN** Latin, 3rd person sing. preterite of *cessare*: see **CEASE** *verb*.]
hist. A writ to recover lands, which lay when a tenant ceased to pay rent or perform legal duties for the space of two years.

cesser /ˈsɛsə/ *noun*. **M16.**
[**ORIGIN** Use as noun of Anglo-Norman, Old French & mod. French *cesser* **CEASE** *verb*: see **-ER**[4].]
LAW. **1** *hist.* Ceasing of a tenant to pay rent or perform legal duties for the space of two years (cf. **CESSAVIT**). **M16.**
2 Cessation, termination (of a term, liability, etc.). **E19.**

cessile /ˈsɛsʌɪl/ *adjective*. *rare*. **L16.**
[**ORIGIN** from Latin *cess-* (see **CESSION**) + **-ILE**.]
Of the air: yielding.

cession /ˈsɛʃ(ə)n/ *noun*. **LME.**
[**ORIGIN** Old French & mod. French, or its source Latin *cessio(n-)*, from *cess-* pa. ppl stem of *cedere* **CEDE**: see **-ION**.]
†**1** **a** The relinquishing of title or office. **LME–M18.** ▸**b** *ECCLESIASTICAL LAW*. The vacating of a benefice by taking another without dispensation. **L16.**
2 Ceding, giving up (*of* rights, property, etc., esp. *of* territory by a state). **LME.** ▸**b** *LAW*. The voluntary surrender by a debtor of all his or her effects to creditors. **L16.**
†**3** *gen.* Giving way, yielding. Only in **17.**

cessionary /ˈsɛʃ(ə)n(ə)ri/ *noun*. **L15.**
[**ORIGIN** medieval Latin *cessionarius* noun, from *cessio(n-)*: see **CESSION**, **-ARY**[1].]
1 An assignee. **L15.**
†**2** A bankrupt who makes cession. Only in **17.**

†**cessment** *noun* var. of **SESSMENT**.

†**cessor** *noun* var. of **SESSOR**.

cesspipe /ˈsɛspʌɪp/ *noun*. **L19.**
[**ORIGIN** from the imagined base of **CESSPOOL**, with implied sense 'sewage, liquid waste', + **PIPE** *noun*[1].]
A pipe leading to or from a cesspool.

cesspit /ˈsɛspɪt/ *noun*. **M19.**
[**ORIGIN** formed as **CESSPIPE** + **PIT** *noun*[1].]
A pit for the disposal of sewage.

cesspool /ˈsɛspuːl/ *noun*. **L17.**
[**ORIGIN** Prob. alt. of **SUSPIRAL**, with assim. to **POOL** *noun*[1].]
1 A trap made under a drain etc. to retain solid matter. Also, a rainwater head in guttering. **L17.**
2 An underground chamber for the temporary storage or disposal of foul water or sewage. **L18.**

fig. (*attrib.*): MALCOLM X I got my first schooling about the cesspool morals of the white man from the best source, from his own women.

cesspool of iniquity etc., a place of rampant vice.

cest /sɛst/ *noun*. *poet.* **L16.**
[**ORIGIN** French *ceste* or Latin **CESTUS** *noun*[1].]
= **CESTUS** *noun*[1].

c'est la vie /sɛ la vi, ˌseɪ lɑːˈviː/ *interjection*. **M20.**
[**ORIGIN** French.]
That's life (expr. acceptance of or resignation at a difficult or regrettable situation).

cestode /ˈsɛstəʊd/ *noun & adjective*. **M19.**
[**ORIGIN** from mod. Latin *Cestoda* (see below), from Latin **CESTUS** *noun*[1]: see **-ODE**[1].]
▸ **A** *noun*. A parasitic flatworm of the class Cestoda; a tapeworm. **M19.**
▸ **B** *adjective*. Of, pertaining to, or designating this class. **M19.**
■ Also **cestoid** *noun & adjective* (now *rare*) **M19.**

Cestrian /ˈsɛstrɪən/ *adjective*. **M17.**
[**ORIGIN** from *Cester*, Old English form of *Chester* + **-IAN**.]
Of or pertaining to the city of Chester or the county of Cheshire, in England.

cestui /ˈsɛti/ *noun*. **M16.**
[**ORIGIN** Anglo-Norman & Old French, from Proto-Romance, from Latin *ecce* lo! + *iste* that (one), with element *-ui* as in *cui* dat. of *quis* who.]
LAW. The person (who), he (who). Only in phrases.
cestui que trust /kɪ trʌst/, ***cestui que use*** /kɪ juːs/ the person for whose benefit anything is given in trust to another. ***cestui que vie*** /kɪ viː/ a person for whose life an estate or interest in property is held by another.

cestus /ˈsɛstəs/ *noun*[1]. Pl. **-ti** /-tʌɪ/. **M16.**
[**ORIGIN** Latin from Greek *kestos* use as noun of ppl adjective = stitched.]
A (bridal) belt or girdle for the waist, *esp.* that of Aphrodite or Venus.

cestus /ˈsɛstəs/ *noun*[2]. Pl. **-ti** /-tʌɪ/. **L17.**
[**ORIGIN** Latin *caestus*, from *caedere* to strike.]
hist. A covering for the hand made of thongs of bull-hide loaded with metallic strips, used by boxers in ancient Rome.

CET *abbreviation*.
Central European Time.

cetacean /sɪˈteɪʃ(ə)n/ *noun & adjective*. **M19.**
[**ORIGIN** from mod. Latin *Cetacea* (see below), from Latin *cetus* from Greek *kētos* whale: see **-ACEAN**.]
▸ **A** *noun*. A mammal of the order Cetacea, which includes the whales, dolphins, and porpoises. **M19.**
▸ **B** *adjective*. Of, pertaining to, or characteristic of cetacea. **M19.**

cetaceous /sɪˈteɪʃəs/ *adjective*. **M17.**
[**ORIGIN** from Latin *cetus* (see **CETACEAN**) + **-ACEOUS**.]
Of the nature of a whale; cetacean.

cetane /ˈsiːteɪn/ *noun*. **L19.**
[**ORIGIN** from **CETYL** + **-ANE**.]
CHEMISTRY. The liquid straight-chain isomer of hexadecane, used as a solvent and ignition standard.
– **COMB.**: **cetane number** a measure of the ignition properties of a diesel fuel.

cete /siːt/ *noun*[1]. *arch.* **ME.**
[**ORIGIN** Old French from Latin *cete* neut. pl. from Greek *kētē* (sing. *kēteos*) whales.]
A whale, a sea monster.

cete /siːt/ *noun*[2]. **LME.**
[**ORIGIN** Perh. from Latin *coetus* assembly, company.]
A group *of* badgers.

ceterach /ˈsɛtərak/ *noun*. **LME.**
[**ORIGIN** medieval Latin, of unknown origin.]
A fern of the genus *Ceterach*, of the spleenwort family, with scaly undersides to its fronds; *esp.* the rustyback fern, *C. officinarum*.

ceteris paribus /ˌkeɪtərɪs ˈparɪbəs, ˌsɛt-, ˌsiːt-/ *adverbial phr.* **E17.**
[**ORIGIN** mod. Latin.]
Other things being equal or unchanged.

cetology /siːˈtɒlədʒi/ *noun*. **M19.**
[**ORIGIN** from Latin *cetus* whale (see **CETACEAN**) + **-OLOGY**.]
The branch of zoology that deals with whales, dolphins, and porpoises.
■ **cetoˈlogical** *adjective* **M19.** **cetologist** *noun* **M20.**

cetrimide /ˈsɛtrɪmʌɪd/ *noun*. **M20.**
[**ORIGIN** from **CET(YL** + **TRI-** + **BRO)MIDE**.]
A detergent and antiseptic preparation based on the synthetic quaternary ammonium compound cetyltrimethylammonium bromide ($C_{19}H_{42}NBr$).

Cetti's warbler /ˈtʃɛtɪz ˈwɔːblə/ *noun phr.* **L19.**
[**ORIGIN** Francesco *Cetti*, 18th-cent. Italian ornithologist.]
A chestnut-brown warbler, *Cettia cetti*, resident in Britain since the 1970s, and noted for its strikingly loud and abrupt song.

Cetus /ˈsiːtəs/ *noun*. **M17.**
[**ORIGIN** Latin *cetus* whale: see **CETACEAN**.]
(The name of) a constellation on the celestial equator, between Taurus and Aquarius; the Whale.

cetyl /ˈsiːtʌɪl, -tɪl/ *noun*. **M19.**
[**ORIGIN** from Latin *cetus* whale + **-YL**: the first compounds were isolated from spermaceti.]
CHEMISTRY. The straight-chain radical $C_{16}H_{33}$·, *n*-hexadecyl. Usu. in *comb.*
– **COMB.**: **cetyl alcohol** a waxy alcohol, $CH_3(CH_2)_{15}OH$, occurring in faeces and (esterified) in spermaceti and wool-wax, and used in cosmetics and as an emulsifier.

ceviche /sɛˈviːtʃeɪ/ *noun*. Also **s-**. **M20.**
[**ORIGIN** S. Amer. Spanish *seviche*, *cebiche*.]
A S. American dish of marinaded raw fish or seafood, usu. garnished and served as a starter.

ceylanite *noun* var. of **CEYLONITE**.

Ceylon /sɪˈlɒn/ *noun*. **M19.**
[**ORIGIN** Former name of Sri Lanka: see **SRI LANKAN**.]
1 ***Ceylon moss***, a red seaweed of the Indian subcontinent, *Gracilaria lichenoides*, which is the major source of agar-agar. **M19.**
2 In full ***Ceylon tea***. A Pekoe tea produced in Sri Lanka. **L19.**

Ceylonese /sɪləˈniːz/ *adjective & noun*. Pl. of noun same. **L18.**
[**ORIGIN** from **CEYLON** + **-ESE**.]
= **SRI LANKAN**. Also *spec.*, = **SINHALESE**.

ceylonite /ˈsiːlənʌɪt/ *noun*. Also **ceylanite**. **E19.**
[**ORIGIN** French *ceylanite* from *Ceylan* **CEYLON**: see **-ITE**[1].]
MINERALOGY. A dark iron-rich variety of spinel.

CF *abbreviation*.
1 Chaplain to the Forces.
2 Cystic fibrosis.

Cf *symbol*.
CHEMISTRY. Californium.

cf. *abbreviation*.
Latin *confer* compare.

c.f. *abbreviation*.
Carried forward.

CFA *abbreviation*.
[**ORIGIN** French *Communauté Financière Africaine*.]
African Financial Community. Freq. as ***CFA franc***, the basic monetary unit of Cameroon, Congo, Gabon, and the Central African Republic.

CFC *abbreviation*.
Chlorofluorocarbon.

CFE *abbreviation*.
College of Further Education.

CFO *abbreviation*.
Chief financial officer.

CFS *abbreviation*[1].
Chronic fatigue syndrome.

cfs *abbreviation*[2].
Cubic feet per second.

cg *abbreviation*.
Centigram(s).

CGA *abbreviation*.
COMPUTING. Colour graphics adapter.

CGI *abbreviation*.
1 *COMPUTING*. Common Gateway Interface.
2 Compacted graphite iron.
3 *COMPUTING*. Computer-generated imagery.

CGM *abbreviation*.
Conspicuous Gallantry Medal.

CGS *abbreviation*[1].
1 Centimetre-gram-second (system).
2 Chief of the General Staff.

cgs *abbreviation*[2].
Centimetre-gram-second (system).

CGT *abbreviation*.
Capital gains tax.

ch.
A consonantal digraph introduced in early Middle English, at first used in adoptions of Old French words in *ch-*, and for Old English words in *c(e)-*, *c(i)-*. *ch* has the following principal values: /tʃ/ in all native Germanic words; /k/ in words taken from Greek (or Hebrew through Greek); /ʃ/ in words from mod.French; /x/ (for which /k/ is often substituted) in Scottish, Welsh, Irish, German, and some other foreign words.

CH *abbreviation*.
Companion of Honour.

Ch. *abbreviation*[1].
Church.

ch. *abbreviation*[2].
1 Chapter
2 Chestnut.

chabazite /ˈkabəzʌɪt/ *noun*. Also **-site**, †**-sie**, †**-zie**. E19.
[ORIGIN French *chabazie*, from Greek *khabazie* erron. reading for *khalazie*, voc. of *khalazios* hailstone, from *khalaza* hail: see -ITE[1].]
MINERALOGY. A colourless, pink, or yellow zeolite which usu. occurs as rhombohedral crystals.

Chablis /ˈʃabliː/ *noun*. M17.
[ORIGIN French (see below).]
A white burgundy wine, made at Chablis (Yonne), in central France.

chabootra *noun* var. of CHABUTRA.

†**chabuk** *noun* var. of CHAWBUCK *noun*.

chabutra /tʃəˈbuːtrə/ *noun*. Also **-boot-**. E19.
[ORIGIN Hindi *cabūtrā*, *-tarā*.]
In the Indian subcontinent: a platform or terrace, often adjoining a house or in a garden.

chace *noun*, *verb* see CHASE *noun*[1], *verb*[1].

chacha /ˈtʃʌtʃʌ/ *noun*. *Indian*. M20.
[ORIGIN Hindi *cācā*.]
Uncle.

cha-cha /ˈtʃɑːtʃɑː/ *noun* & *verb*. Also **cha-cha-cha** /tʃɑːtʃɑːˈtʃɑː/. M20.
[ORIGIN Amer. Spanish.]
▸ **A** *noun*. A type of ballroom dance to a Latin American rhythm; a piece of music for this dance. M20.
▸ **B** *verb intrans*. Perform this dance. M20.

chacham *noun* var. of HAHAM.

chack /tʃak/ *verb* & *noun*. Also **chak** (verb infl. **-kk-**). E16.
[ORIGIN Imit.]
▸ **A** *verb intrans*. **1** Snap or chatter with the teeth; suddenly shut the jaws or a door, window, drawer, etc. *Scot*. E16.
2 Of a bird: make a harsh call. E20.
▸ **B** *noun*. **1** A harsh note or call of a bird. L18. ▸**b** A wheatear. *dial*. E19.
2 A light meal, a snack. E19.

chacma /ˈtʃakmə/ *noun*. M19.
[ORIGIN Nama.]
A dark-furred baboon, *Papio ursinus*, of southern Africa. Also ***chacma baboon***. Also called ***ursine baboon***.

chaco *noun* see SHAKO.

chaconne /ʃəˈkɒn/ *noun*. L17.
[ORIGIN French from Spanish *chacona*.]
A moderately slow musical composition on a ground bass, usu. in triple time; a dance to this music.

chacun à son goût /ʃakœ̃ a sɔ̃ gu, ˌʃakəːn a sɒn ˈguː/ *interjection*. L18.
[ORIGIN French.]
Each to his (or her) own taste.

Chad /tʃad/ *noun*[1]. M20.
[ORIGIN Unknown.]
In full ***Mr Chad***. The figure of a human head looking over a wall, with a caption protesting against shortages etc. that usu. begins 'Wot, no —?'.

chad /tʃad/ *noun*[2]. M20.
[ORIGIN Unknown.]
COMPUTING. (A piece of) the waste material removed from punched cards or tape by punching.
■ **chadless** *adjective* not producing chads M20.

chad *noun*[3] var. of SHAD.

chadar *noun* var. of CHADOR.

Chadian /ˈtʃadɪən/ *adjective* & *noun*. M20.
[ORIGIN from *Chad* (see below) + -IAN.]
(A native or inhabitant) of the Republic of Chad, a state in north central Africa, formerly part of French Equatorial Africa.

Chadic /ˈtʃadɪk/ *adjective* & *noun*. L20.
[ORIGIN formed as CHADIAN + -IC.]
(Designating, of, or pertaining to) an Afro-Asiatic language group of western and central Africa.

chador /ˈtʃɑːdə/ *noun*. Also **chadar**, **chaddar**, **chuddar** /ˈtʃʌdə/, & other vars. E17.
[ORIGIN (Urdu *chādar*, *chaddar* from) Persian *čādar* sheet, veil.]
A large piece of material worn as a long shawl or cloak by Muslim women, and sometimes by Hindu or other women, esp. in the Indian subcontinent and Iran. Also, any of various similar garments worn by men in the Indian subcontinent.

chaebol /ˈtʃeɪbɒl/ *noun*. Pl. same, **-s**. L20.
[ORIGIN Korean, lit. 'money clan'.]
In the Republic of Korea: a large business conglomerate, esp. a family-owned one.

chaeta /ˈkiːtə/ *noun*. Pl. **-tae** /-tiː/. M19.
[ORIGIN mod. Latin from Greek *khaitē* long hair.]
A chitinous bristle; a seta.
■ **chaeˈtigerous** *adjective* = SETIGEROUS L19.

chaetodon /ˈkiːtədɒn/ *noun*. M18.
[ORIGIN mod. Latin, formed as CHAETA + -ODON.]
A brightly coloured marine fish of the family Chaetodontidae, with a deep, flattened body and bristle-like teeth. Also called ***butterfly fish***.
■ **chaetodont** *noun* & *adjective* (a fish) of the family Chaetodontidae M19.

chaetognath /ˈkiːtənaθ/ *noun*. L19.
[ORIGIN from mod. Latin *Chaetognatha* (see below), formed as CHAETA + Greek *gnathos* jaw.]
A small marine planktonic worm of the phylum Chaetognatha, with numerous spines on its head for seizing prey. Also called ***arrow worm***, ***sea-arrow***.

chafe /tʃeɪf/ *noun*. Also †**chaff**. M16.
[ORIGIN from the verb.]
1 A state of vexation or irritation; a rage, a temper. M16.
2 (An injury caused by) rubbing. M19.

chafe /tʃeɪf/ *verb*. Also †**chaff**. LME.
[ORIGIN Old French & mod. French *chauffer* from Proto-Romance var. of Latin *cal(e)facere* make warm, from *calere* be warm + *facere* make.]
▸ **I** *lit*. **1** *verb trans*. & *intrans*. Make or become warm. Long *obsolete* exc. in ***CHAFING dish***. LME.
2 *verb trans*. **a** Rub with the hand, esp. to restore warmth or sensation. LME. ▸**b** Abrade or injure by rubbing. E16.

> **a** T. WILSON Waxe chaufed with the handes is made softer. D. LODGE Chafing his chilled limbs . . to keep the circulation going. **b** B. MALAMUD The legholes were tight and chafed his flesh if he tried to turn.

3 *verb intrans*. Rub (*against*, *on*, etc.). E17.

> A. SCHLEE A rash on his neck where the stiff uniform had chafed.

▸ **II** *fig*. †**4** *verb trans*. Inflame (feelings); excite. LME–E18.
5 *verb trans*. & *intrans*. Make or become vexed or irritated; fret. LME.

> DICKENS Chafing like an angry sea, the crowd pressed after them. V. WOOLF Visitors do tend to chafe one, though impeccable as friends. K. M. E. MURRAY Furnivall appreciated the standard of James' work . . although he might chafe at his slowness. I. COLEGATE The . . horse and rider chafed to leave.

†**6** *verb trans*. Scold. LME–L17.
– COMB.: **chafe-wax** *hist*. an officer in Chancery who prepared the wax for sealing documents.

chafer /ˈtʃeɪfə/ *noun*[1]. Also †**-ff-**.
[ORIGIN Old English *ċeafor*, *ċefer* = Old Saxon, Middle Dutch & mod. Dutch *kever*, Old High German *chevar*, *-iro*, from Germanic: rel. to CHAFF *noun*[1], JOWL *noun*[1].]
A large beetle destructive to plants; *spec*. any of a group of scarabaeid beetles including the cockchafer and the rose chafer.

chafer /ˈtʃeɪfə/ *noun*[2]. See also CHAUFFER. LME.
[ORIGIN from CHAFE *verb* + -ER[1].]
1 A vessel for heating water etc.; a portable grate or chafing dish. LME.
2 *hist*. = ***chafe-wax*** s.v. CHAFE *verb*. L15.

chafery /ˈtʃeɪf(ə)ri/ *noun*. Now *rare* or *obsolete*. E17.
[ORIGIN Old French & mod. French *chaufferie*, formed as CHAFE *verb*: see -ERY.]
METALLURGY. A small hearth or furnace for reheating and reworking wrought iron.

†**chafeweed** *noun* see CHAFFWEED.

chaff /tʃɑːf, tʃaf/ *noun*[1] & *verb*[1].
[ORIGIN Old English *ċæf*, *ċeaf* = Middle Low German, Middle Dutch & mod. Dutch, Middle High German *kaf* (German dial. *kaff*), corresp. to Old High German *keva* husk, prob. from Germanic base with the sense 'gnaw, chew': rel. to CHAFER *noun*[1].]
▸ **A** *noun*. **1** The husks of corn etc. separated from the grain by threshing or winnowing. OE.
2 Cut hay (and straw) used for feeding cattle. OE.
3 *transf*. Refuse, worthless stuff or residue. LME.
4 BOTANY. Thin dry bracts or scales, esp. the bracts at the base of the florets in plants of the composite family. L18.
5 Strips of metal foil released in the air to obstruct radar detection. M20.
– PHRASES: **be caught with chaff** be easily deceived or trapped. **separate the wheat from the chaff** *fig*. distinguish good from bad.
– COMB.: **chaff-cutter** a machine for cutting hay and straw.
▸ **B** *verb trans*. Cut (hay etc.) for fodder. L19.

†**chaff** *noun*[2], *verb*[2] vars. of CHAFE *noun*, *verb*.

chaff /tʃɑːf, tʃaf/ *verb*[3] & *noun*[3]. E19.
[ORIGIN Perh. var. of CHAFE *verb*.]
▸ **A** *verb trans*. Banter or rail at, usu. in a light-hearted manner. E19.
▸ **B** *noun*. Banter, good-humoured raillery or repartee. M19.
■ **chaffingly** *adverb* L19.

chaffer /ˈtʃafə/ *noun*[1]. ME.
[ORIGIN formed as CHEAP *noun* + FARE *noun*[1], prob. after Old Norse *kaupfǫr* trading journey. In mod. use from the verb.]
1 Orig., trade, trading. Now *spec*. haggling, bargaining, barter. ME.
†2 Goods, wares. ME–L17.

†**chaffer** *noun*[2] var. of CHAFER *noun*[1].

chaffer /ˈtʃafə/ *verb*. ME.
[ORIGIN from CHAFFER *noun*[1].]
1 *verb intrans*. Orig., traffic, deal, trade. Now *spec*. bargain, haggle about terms or price. ME. ▸**b** *fig*. Bandy words, discuss terms, dispute. LME.
2 *verb trans*. Orig., traffic, deal, or trade in. Now *spec*. haggle over, barter. ME.
†**chaffer words** bandy words.
■ **chafferer** *noun* LME.

chaffinch /ˈtʃafɪn(t)ʃ/ *noun*. OE.
[ORIGIN from CHAFF *noun*[1] + FINCH.]
A common European finch, *Fringilla coelebs*.

chaffron *noun* var. of CHAMFRAIN.

chaffweed /ˈtʃafwiːd/ *noun*. In sense 1 also †**chafe-**. M16.
[ORIGIN Prob. from CHAFE *verb* + WEED *noun*[1].]
†1 Cudweed. M16–L19.
2 A pimpernel, *Anagallis minima*, with very small white or pink flowers. L18.

chaffy /ˈtʃɑːfi, ˈtʃafi/ *adjective*. M16.
[ORIGIN from CHAFF *noun*[1] + -Y[1].]
1 Of, pertaining to, resembling, or of the nature of chaff; *spec*. (BOTANY) paleaceous. M16.
2 *fig*. Light, empty, worthless. L16.

chafing /ˈtʃeɪfɪŋ/ *verbal noun*. LME.
[ORIGIN from CHAFE *verb* + -ING[1].]
The action of CHAFE *verb*.
– COMB.: **chafing dish** a vessel with an outer pan of hot water for keeping warm anything placed on top of it; a dish with a spirit lamp etc. for cooking at table.

chaft /tʃaft/ *noun*. Long *obsolete* exc. *Scot*. & *N. English*. ME.
[ORIGIN Old Norse (Swedish *käft*, Danish *kieft*, etc.), rel. to JOWL *noun*[1].]
Jaw. Usu. in *pl*.

Chaga *noun* & *adjective* var. of CHAGGA.

chagal /ˈtʃɑːg(ə)l/ *noun*. E20.
[ORIGIN Sanskrit *chāgala* coming from a goat.]
In the Indian subcontinent: a water bottle, usu. of canvas or leather.

chagan /kəˈgɑːn/ *noun*. L18.
[ORIGIN medieval Latin *c(h)aganus*, in Byzantine Greek *khaganos* from Old Turkish *qaġan* king, monarch: cf. CHAM *noun*, KHAN *noun*[1].]
hist. = KHAN *noun*[1]; *spec*. the monarch of the Avars in the 6th and 7th cents.

Chagas' disease /ˈtʃɑːgəs dɪˌziːz/ *noun phr*. Also **Chagas's disease** /ˈtʃɑːgəsɪz/. E20.
[ORIGIN from Carlos *Chagas* (1879–1934), Brazilian physician.]
MEDICINE. A progressive form of trypanosomiasis endemic in S. and Central America, transmitted by reduviid bugs.

Chagatai /dʒagəˈtʌɪ/ *noun* & *adjective*. Also (earlier) **J-**. M19.
[ORIGIN Name of a dynasty founded by Chaghatai a son of Genghis Khan, which reigned in Transoxiana 1227–1358.]
(Designating or pertaining to) the literary Turkic language of central Asia between the 15th and 19th cents.
■ **Chagataian** *adjective* M19. **Chagataic** *adjective* & *noun* M19.

Chagga /ˈtʃagə/ *noun* & *adjective*. Also **Chaga**. M19.
[ORIGIN Bantu.]
▸ **A** *noun*. Pl. same, **-s**, WACHAGGA.
1 A member of a people of northern Tanzania. M19.
2 The Bantu language of this people, Kichaga. L19.
3 Coffee grown by the Wachagga; *loosely*, Tanzanian coffee. M20.
▸ **B** *attrib*. or as *adjective*. Of or pertaining to the Wachagga or their language. L19.

chagigah *noun pl*. see HAGIGAH.

chagrin /ˈʃagrɪn/ *noun*. See also SHAGREEN. M17.
[ORIGIN French, lit. 'rough skin', of unknown origin.]
▸ **I** †**1** Worry, anxiety; melancholy. M17–M19.
2 Mortification arising from disappointment or failure; acute vexation or annoyance. E18.

> A. ROBERTS Much to his chagrin, no eulogies appeared about his long career in politics.

3 In *pl*. Troubles, vexations. M18.
▸ †**II** **4** = SHAGREEN. L17–M19.

C

†chagrin *adjective.* M17–E18.
[ORIGIN French, formed as CHAGRIN *noun*.]
Worried; melancholy; chagrined.

chagrin /ˈʃagrɪn, ʃəˈgriːn/ *verb trans.* M17.
[ORIGIN French *chagriner*, formed as CHAGRIN *noun*.]
Affect with chagrin. Usu. in *pass.*

chah *noun* var. of CHAR *noun*[2].

chai /tʃʌɪ/ *noun. Indian.* E20.
[ORIGIN A term in various Indian languages. Cf. CHAR *noun*[2].]
Tea.

chain /tʃeɪn/ *noun.* ME.
[ORIGIN Old French *chaine*, (earlier) *chaeine* (mod. *chaîne*) from Latin *catena*.]
1 A series of links (usu. metal) passing through each other, or otherwise jointed together, so as to form a strong but flexible means of connection. (Of various kinds for particular purposes etc., identified contextually or specified.) ME.
albert chain, bicycle-chain, daisy-chain, guard-chain, night chain, paper chain, safety-chain, tyre-chain, etc. ***drag the chain***: see DRAG *verb* 1.
2 (A chain as) a bond or fetter; in *pl.*, fetters, bonds, confinement, captivity. ME. ▸**b** *fig.* A thing which prevents freedom of action. LME.

MILTON To bottomless perdition, there to dwell In Adamantine Chains and penal Fire. P. HENRY Is life so dear . . as to be purchased at the price of chains and slavery? **b** HAZLITT The chain of habit.

ball and chain: see BALL *noun*[1] 3.
3 (A chain as) a barrier obstructing the entrance to a street, harbour, etc. ME.
4 A personal ornament in the form of a chain worn around the neck; such a chain worn as a badge of office. ME.
5 *fig.* A connected series, a sequence, a set, (of material or abstract things). LME. ▸**b** *spec.* A sequence of geographical features (as mountains, lakes, etc.) disposed in a linear series with actual or imagined connections. L17. ▸**c** A figure in a quadrille. M19. ▸**d** A group of associated shops, hotels, newspapers, etc. Orig. *US.* M19. ▸**e** *COMPUTING.* A set of files, data, program instructions, etc., related by chaining. M20.

C. M. YONGE I tried to get them to form a chain and drench the warehouses. E. MANNIN How far back could you go in the chain of causality?

food chain etc. ***Markov chain***.
6 A measuring line in land-surveying, consisting of one hundred jointed metal rods. E17. ▸**b** A length equal to this (66 feet, approx. 20.12 m.). M17.
7 *NAUTICAL.* = ***chainplate*** below. In *pl.* also, a small platform on either side of a ship from which the leadsman heaves the lead when sounding. E17.
8 The warp in weaving. E18.
9 *hist.* In full ***chain shot***. Two half or whole cannonballs joined by a chain, for cutting masts etc. E19.
10 A chain for fastening a door to its jamb as a security device. M19.
11 *CHEMISTRY.* A number of similar atoms, usu. carbon, joined in series in a molecule. L19.
long chain, open chain, etc.
– COMB.: **chain armour**: made of interlaced rings; **chain bridge** a suspension bridge on chains; **chain drive**: with transmission by endless chains; **chain gang**: of convicts, chained together, or forced to work in chains; **chain gear**: transmitting motion by an endless chain; **chain letter**: of which the recipient is asked to make copies to be sent to a (named) number of others (those being asked to do the like); **chain-link** *adjective* made of wire in a diamond-shaped mesh; **chainmail** = ***chain armour*** above; **chainplate** *NAUTICAL* a strong link or plate on a ship's side, to which the shrouds are secured; **chain printer** a line printer in which the printing types are carried on a moving endless chain; **chain pump**: to raise water, with a series of buckets etc. usu. passing through a tube on an endless chain; **chain reaction** a series of chemical or nuclear reactions each initiated by a product of the previous reaction; *fig.* a series of events each due to the previous one; **chainsaw**: with teeth on an endless chain; ***chain shot***: see sense 9 above; **chain-smoke** *verb trans. & intrans.* smoke (cigarettes etc.) continuously, esp. by lighting the next cigarette etc. from the one last smoked; **chain-smoker** a person who chain-smokes; **chain snake** a kingsnake with chainlike markings; **chain stitch** an ornamental crochet or embroidery stitch like a chain (***magic chain stitch***: see MAGIC *adjective* 3); **chain store** any of a series of shops owned by one firm and selling the same type of goods; **chain-wale** = CHANNEL *noun*[2]; **chain wheel**: transmitting power by a chain fitted to its edges; **chainwork** (*a*) chainlike ornamental work in sculpture etc.; (*b*) interlinked metal rings in a network; (*c*) a texture formed by knitting with a single thread.
■ **chainless** *adjective* E19. **chainlet** *noun* a little chain E19. **chainlike** *adjective* resembling a chain in appearance or structure L18.

chain /tʃeɪn/ *verb.* LME.
[ORIGIN from the noun.]
1 *verb trans.* Secure or confine with a chain (*lit.* & *fig.*). Also foll. by *up*. LME.

N. WHITTAKER The single luggage trolley was chained up. *Independent* Demonstrators chained themselves to trees.

2 *verb trans.* Obstruct or close with a chain. LME.
3 *verb trans.* Measure with a (surveyor's) chain. E17.
4 *verb trans. & intrans. COMPUTING.* Link or be linked by the inclusion in each file of an address by which a successor may be located. Chiefly as ***chaining*** *verbal noun.* M20.

chaîné /ʃɛne/ *noun.* Pl. pronounced same. M20.
[ORIGIN French = linked.]
BALLET. A quick step or turn from one foot to another, or a series of these, performed in a line.

chained /tʃeɪnd/ *adjective.* M16.
[ORIGIN from CHAIN *noun*, *verb*: see -ED[2], -ED[1].]
1 Provided or adorned with a chain or chains. M16.
2 That has been chained. E17.
3 Of lightning: having the form of a long zigzag line. M19.

chair /tʃɛː/ *noun*[1]. ME.
[ORIGIN Anglo-Norman *chaere*, Old French *chaiere* (mod. *chaire* bishop's throne etc.) from Latin CATHEDRA.]
1 A separate seat for one person, of various forms, usu. with a rest for the back and more or less comfortable. ME. ▸**b** *The* electric chair. *US.* E20.
armchair, Bath chair, deck chair, easy chair, garden chair, high chair, pushchair, rocking chair, wheelchair, etc. ***boatswain's chair***: see BOATSWAIN. ***chair of estate***: see ESTATE *noun* 4. ***electric chair***: see ELECTRIC *adjective*. ***musical chairs***: see MUSICAL *adjective*. **take a chair** sit down. ***wainscot chair***: see WAINSCOT *noun* 1.
2 A seat of authority, state, or dignity; *fig.* a place or situation of authority etc. ME. ▸**b** The seat from which a professor etc. delivers lectures. Now chiefly *fig.*, a professorship. LME. ▸**c** The seat of a bishop in his church; *fig.* episcopal dignity or authority. Now *arch.* or *hist.* L15. ▸**d** The seat of a person presiding at a meeting, public dinner, etc.; *fig.* the office of such a person; a chairman or chairwoman. M17. ▸**e** The seat of the chief elected official of a corporate town; *fig.* the office of such an official, a mayoralty. L17. ▸**f** A seat occupied by a Welsh bard at an Eisteddfod, *esp.* one awarded as a trophy; *fig.* a convention, now each of four, connected with the Eisteddfod. E19.
d be in the chair, **take the chair** be chairman. **e past the chair**, **above the chair** (of an alderman etc.) who has been mayor. **below the chair** (of an alderman etc.) who has not been mayor.
3 = SEDAN 1. *obsolete* exc. *hist.* LME.
†**4** A pulpit. M17–L19.
5 Chiefly *hist.* A kind of light chaise. M18.
6 An iron or steel socket fixed to a railway sleeper, securing a rail in place. E19.
– COMB.: **chair-bed** a chair that unfolds into a bed; **chair-borne** *adjective* (*colloq.*) administrative rather than active; **chair car** a railway carriage with chairs instead of long seats, a parlour car; **chairlady** a chairwoman; **chairlift** a series of chairs on an endless cable for carrying passengers up a mountain etc.; **chairoplane** a fairground roundabout with seats suspended on chains flung in a wide circle by the revolution of the machinery; **chair organ** = ***choir organ*** s.v. CHOIR *noun*; **chairperson** a chairman (of either sex) of a meeting etc.; **chairwoman** a female chairman of a meeting etc.

chair /tʃɛː/ *noun*[2]. *obsolete* exc. *hist.* Also (earlier) †**char**. ME.
[ORIGIN Old French & mod. French *char*, Old Northern French *charre*: see CHARIOT. Assim. to CHAIR *noun*[1].]
A chariot; a cart.

chair /tʃɛː/ *verb trans.* M16.
[ORIGIN from CHAIR *noun*[1].]
1 Install in a chair, esp. one of authority. M16.
2 Place (as if) in a chair and carry aloft (the winner of a contest etc.). M18.
3 Provide with a chair or chairs. M19.
4 Act as the chairman of, preside over (a meeting). E20.

chairman /ˈtʃɛːmən/ *noun.* Pl. **-men**. M17.
[ORIGIN from CHAIR *noun*[1] + MAN *noun*.]
1 A person chosen to preside over a meeting; a permanent president of a committee, board of directors, firm, country, etc.; the master of ceremonies at an entertainment. M17.
2 *hist.* **a** Either of the two sedan-bearers. L17. ▸**b** A person who wheels a Bath chair. M18.
■ **chairmanship** *noun* the office of chairman; the action of presiding as chairman: M19.

chaise /ʃeɪz/ *noun.* Pl. pronounced same. M17.
[ORIGIN French, var. of *chaire* CHAIR *noun*[1].]
1 Chiefly *hist.* A pleasure or travelling carriage, esp. a light open one for one or two people. See also POST-CHAISE. M17.
2 = CHAISE LONGUE. M20.

chaise longue /ʃeɪz ˈlɒŋ, *foreign* ʃɛːz lɔ̃ːg/ *noun phr.* Pl. **chaise longues** /ʃeɪz ˈlɒŋz/, **chaises longues** /ʃeɪz ˈlɒŋ(z), *foreign* ʃɛz lɔ̃ːg/. E19.
[ORIGIN French = long chair.]
A kind of sofa with a backrest at only one end.

chaise percée /ʃɛːz pɛrse/ *noun phr.* Pl. **-s -s** (pronounced same). M20.
[ORIGIN French = pierced chair.]
A chair incorporating a chamber pot.

chaises longues *noun phr. pl.* see CHAISE LONGUE.

chaises percées *noun phr.* pl. of CHAISE PERCÉE.

chaitya /ˈtʃʌɪtjə/ *noun.* L19.
[ORIGIN Sanskrit *caitya* (resembling) a funeral pile, mound, etc., from *citā* funeral mound.]
A Buddhist place or object of reverence.

chak *verb* & *noun* var. of CHACK.

chakra /ˈtʃʌkrə/ *noun.* L18.
[ORIGIN Sanskrit *cakra* (cogn. with WHEEL *noun*).]
1 A thin knife-edged disc of steel formerly used as a weapon by Sikhs. L18.
2 A discus or mystic circle depicted in the hands of Hindu deities. L19.
3 *YOGA.* Each of the centres of spiritual power in the human body. L19.
4 The circular emblem on the flag of the Indian Union. M20.

chal /tʃal/ *noun.* M19.
[ORIGIN Romany = person, fellow.]
A male Gypsy. Also ***Romany chal***.

chalan /tʃəˈlɑːn/ *noun.* M19.
[ORIGIN Urdu *chalān*, *chālan* from Persian *čalān*.]
In the Indian subcontinent: a waybill, a voucher; a draft of prisoners.

chalaza /kəˈleɪzə/ *noun.* Pl. **-zae** /-ziː/. E18.
[ORIGIN mod. Latin from Greek *khalaza* small knot.]
1 *ZOOLOGY.* Either of two twisted membranous strands which join the yolk to the ends of an egg. E18.
2 *BOTANY.* The region of the ovule where the nucellus joins the integuments. M19.
■ **chalazal** *adjective* (chiefly *BOTANY*) M19.

chalazion /kəˈleɪzɪən/ *noun.* Pl. **-zia** /-zɪə/. E18.
[ORIGIN Greek *khalazion* dim. of *khalaza*: see CHALAZA.]
MEDICINE. A swollen, inflamed sebaceous gland in the eyelid. Also called ***meibomian cyst***.

chalcanthite /kalˈkanθʌɪt/ *noun.* M19.
[ORIGIN from Latin *chalcanthum* from Greek *khalkanthon*, from *khalkos* copper + *anthos* flower: see -ITE[1].]
MINERALOGY. Native hydrated copper(II) sulphate, a blue triclinic mineral usu. occurring as tabular crystals.

Chalcedonian /kalsɪˈdəʊnɪən/ *noun* & *adjective.* M18.
[ORIGIN from *Chalcedon*, a city of ancient Bithynia, + -IAN.]
▸ **A** *noun.* A person upholding the canons etc. of the ecumenical council of Chalcedon (AD 451), which were eventually accepted by all except the Monophysite Churches. M18.
▸ **B** *adjective.* Of or pertaining to the council of Chalcedon, its canons, etc. L18.
Chalcedonian definition the declaration that there are two natures, divine and human, in the one person of Jesus Christ.

chalcedony /kalˈsɛdəni/ *noun.* Also †**cal-**. LME.
[ORIGIN Latin *c(h)alcedonius* from Greek *khalkēdōn*. Cf. CASSIDONY *noun*[1].]
MINERALOGY. A fine-grained fibrous variety of quartz having many precious or semi-precious forms such as agate, onyx, carnelian, and chrysoprase.
■ **chalceˈdonic** *adjective* E19.

chalcenterous /kalˈsɛnt(ə)rəs/ *adjective.* M20.
[ORIGIN from Greek *khalkenteros*, from *khalkos* copper, brass + *enteron* intestine: see -OUS.]
With bowels of bronze; tough.
■ Also **chalcenteric** *adjective* M20.

chalcid /ˈkalsɪd/ *adjective* & *noun.* L19.
[ORIGIN from mod. Latin *Chalcis* genus name from Greek *khalkos* copper, brass: see -ID[3].]
▸ **A** *adjective.* Of, pertaining to, or designating the superfamily Chalcidoidea of mostly parasitic hymenopterous insects, many of which have a metallic sheen. L19.
chalcid fly, **chalcid wasp** = sense B below.
▸ **B** *noun.* An insect of this superfamily. L19.
■ **chalcidid** *adjective* & *noun* = CHALCID; *spec.* (an insect) of the included family Chalcididae: L19.

Chalcidian /kalˈsɪdɪən/ *noun* & *adjective*[1]. M17.
[ORIGIN from Latin *Chalcis*, *Chalcid-* (see below) from Greek *Khalkis*, *Khalkid-*: see -IAN.]
(A native or inhabitant) of Chalcis, chief city of the Greek island of Euboea.

chalco- /ˈkalkəʊ/ *combining form* of Greek *khalkos* copper, brass: see -O-.
■ **chalcocite** *noun* (*MINERALOGY*) orthorhombic copper(I) sulphide, usu. occurring as black, fine-grained masses M19. **Chalcoˈlithic** *adjective* & *noun* (*ARCHAEOLOGY*) (designating or pertaining to) a brief period following the end of the Stone Age in some areas, during which copper implements were used as well as stone ones, before bronze technology was introduced E20. **chalˈcophanite** *noun* [Greek *phan-* showing] *MINERALOGY* a hydrated oxide of zinc and manganese, sometimes with a bronze lustre L19. **chalcophil(e)** *adjective* & *noun* (*GEOLOGY & CHEMISTRY*) (designating) an element which commonly occurs as a sulphide and is supposed to have become concentrated in the mantle E20.

chalcogen /ˈtʃalkədʒ(ə)n/ *noun.* M20.
[ORIGIN German *Chalkogen*, from Greek *khalkos* in supposed sense 'ore', after *halogen*.]
CHEMISTRY. Any of the elements of group VIA of the periodic table (oxygen, sulphur, selenium, tellurium, and polonium).
■ **chalˈcogenide** *noun* a binary compound of a chalcogen M20.

chalcography /kal'kɒgrəfi/ *noun*. **M17**.
[**ORIGIN** from Greek *khalkos* copper, brass + -**GRAPHY**: cf. French *chalcographie*.]
The art of engraving on copper.
■ **chalcographer** *noun* **M17**. **chalco'graphic** *adjective* of or pertaining to chalcography **L18**.

chalcopyrite /kalkə'pʌɪrʌɪt/ *noun*. **M19**.
[**ORIGIN** mod. Latin *chalcopyrites*, formed as **CHALCO-** + **PYRITE**.]
MINERALOGY. A tetragonal sulphide of copper and iron which is the principal ore of copper and usu. occurs as metallic brass-yellow masses. Also called ***copper pyrites***.

Chaldean /kal'diːən/ *noun & adjective*. **M16**.
[**ORIGIN** from Latin *Chaldaeus* from Greek *Khaldaios* masc., *Khaldaia* fem. (also as noun (sc. *gē* earth) Chaldea), from Assyrian *kaldū*: see -**AN**.]
▸ **A** *noun*. **1** A native or inhabitant of ancient Chaldea or Babylonia; *transf.* a person skilled in occult matters, an astrologer. **M16**.
2 The language of the Chaldeans. **L17**.
▸ **B** *adjective*. Of or pertaining to Chaldea, its inhabitants or their language; occult. **E17**.
■ Also **Chaldaic** /kal'deɪɪk/ *adjective* **M17**.

Chaldee /kal'diː, 'kaldiː/ *noun & adjective*. **LME**.
[**ORIGIN** Latin *Chaldaei* (pl.) Chaldeans, (sing.) Chaldea, formed as **CHALDEAN**.]
▸ **A** *noun*. **1** = **CHALDEAN** *noun* 1. **LME**.
2 = **CHALDEAN** *noun* 2. Also, Aramaic as used in books of the Bible. **LME**.
▸ **B** *adjective*. = **CHALDEAN** *adjective*. **L17**.

chalder /'tʃɔːldə/ *noun*. Chiefly *Scot. & N. English*. Now *arch.* or *hist.* **ME**.
[**ORIGIN** Old French & mod. French *chaudière*: see **CHALDRON** *noun*[1].]
A dry measure of capacity (of variable magnitude) for various materials, esp. coal, lime, grain, etc. Cf. **CHALDRON** *noun*[1] 2.

chaldron /'tʃɔːldrən/ *noun*[1]. **M16**.
[**ORIGIN** Old French *chauderon* (mod. *chaudron*) augm. of *chaud(i)ère* from late Latin *cal(i)darium* cooking pot: see -**OON**. Cf. **CAULDRON**.]
†**1** = **CAULDRON**. **M16–M18**.
2 A dry measure of capacity (cf. **CHALDER**). Now only *spec.* a measure for coals of approximately 36 bushels. **E17**.

†**chaldron** *noun*[2] var. of **CHAWDRON**.

chalet /'ʃaleɪ/ *noun*. **L18**.
[**ORIGIN** Swiss French, dim. of Old French *chasel* farmstead from Proto-Romance deriv. of Latin *casa* hut, cottage.]
A Swiss mountain cowherd's hut; a Swiss peasant's wooden cottage; a house with a widely overhanging roof; a small villa; a small house in a holiday camp etc.

chalice /'tʃalɪs/ *noun*. **OE**.
[**ORIGIN** Old French, or its source Latin **CALIX**, *-ic-*.]
1 A drinking cup, a goblet; the contents of this. Now *poet.* **OE**.
poisoned chalice: see **POISON** *verb* 2.
2 *spec.* The cup used in the administration of the Eucharist. **OE**.
3 The calyx of a flower. **M17**.
– **COMB.**: **chalice vine** a solandra, *Solandra maxima*, grown for ornament in the tropics.
■ **chaliced** *adjective* having cuplike blossom; contained in a chalice: **E17**.

chalicothere /'kalɪkəθɪə/ *noun*. **E20**.
[**ORIGIN** from mod. Latin *Chalicotherium* genus name, from Greek *khalik-*, *khalix* gravel + *thērion* wild animal.]
PALAEONTOLOGY. A perissodactyl of the extinct family Chalicotheriidae, similar to a horse but with clawed feet.

chalifa *noun* see **KHALIFA**.

chalk /tʃɔːk/ *noun*.
[**ORIGIN** Old English *ċealc* = Old Saxon *calc* (Dutch *kalk*), Old High German *kalk* (German *kalk*), from West Germanic from Latin **CALX**, *calc-*.]
†**1** Lime. (*rare* after Old English.) **OE–L16**.
2 A white soft earthy limestone consisting almost wholly of calcite. **OE**.
3 This or a substance of like texture or properties in prepared form, as for use in crayons for drawing, for writing on a blackboard, etc. **L15**. ▸**b** A piece or crayon of chalk. **E19**.
4 A mark, line, or score made with chalk; *spec.* (***a***) such a mark formerly used to record credit in a public house etc.; *arch.* a running account, credit; (***b***) (such a mark recording) a point scored in a game. **E16**.
5 Any of various earths resembling chalk (sense 2). Usu. with specifying word. **E17**.
6 *GEOLOGY*. A deposit or stratum composed mainly of chalk; *spec.* (**C-**) (the deposits of) the Upper Cretaceous system of western Europe. **E19**.
– **PHRASES**: **as different as chalk and cheese**, **as different as chalk from cheese** unlike in the essentials. **by a long chalk**, **by long chalks** by far, by a long way. **chalk and talk** teaching by traditional methods (employing blackboard, chalk, and dialogue). ***French chalk***: see **FRENCH** *adjective*. ***red chalk***: see **RED** *adjective*. ***Venetian chalk***: see **VENETIAN** *adjective*. ***walk the chalk***: see **WALK** *verb*[1].
– **ATTRIB. & COMB.**: In the sense 'made up or consisting (largely) of chalk', as ***chalk cliff***, ***chalk down***, etc. In the sense 'drawn with chalk, executed in chalk', as ***chalk drawing***, ***chalk head***, etc. Special combs., as **chalkboard** *N. Amer.* a blackboard; **chalkface** *colloq.* the day-to-day work of teaching in a school; **chalkhill blue** a lycaenid butterfly of chalk grassland, *Lysandra coridon*; **chalk-line** a line drawn in chalk; ***walk a chalk-line*** (*fig.*), behave with propriety, keep to a course of action or set of rules; **chalk pit** a quarry in which chalk is dug; **chalk-stone** a concretion of urates like chalk found in tissues and joints, esp. those of the hands and feet; **chalk-stripe** a pattern of thin white stripes on a dark background; **chalk-striped** *adjective* having a chalk-stripe; **chalk talk** *US* a talk, lecture, etc. in which the speaker uses blackboard and chalk.

chalk /tʃɔːk/ *verb trans*. **L15**.
[**ORIGIN** from the noun.]
1 Rub, mark, or inscribe (a surface) with chalk. **L15**.
2 Mix or treat with chalk. **L16**.
3 Write, draw, or record with chalk. (Foll. by *down*, *out*, *up*, etc.) **L16**.
– **WITH ADVERBS IN SPECIALIZED SENSES**: **chalk out** sketch, plan as a thing to be accomplished; (see also sense 3 above). **chalk up** charge, attribute, (*to* a person, account, experience, etc.); register (a success etc.); (see also sense 3 above).

chalky /'tʃɔːki/ *adjective*. **LME**.
[**ORIGIN** from **CHALK** *noun* + -**Y**[1].]
Having much chalk; resembling chalk, esp. in whiteness; like or containing chalk-stones.
■ **chalkiness** *noun* **E19**.

challah /'hɑːlə, xɑː'lɑː/ *noun*. Pl. **-s**, **chalot**, **-oth**, /xɑː'lɒt/. **E20**.
[**ORIGIN** Hebrew *hallah*.]
A loaf of white leavened bread, typically plaited in form, traditionally baked to celebrate the Jewish sabbath.

challenge /'tʃalɪn(d)ʒ/ *noun*. **ME**.
[**ORIGIN** Old French *c(h)alenge* from Latin *calumnia* **CALUMNY** *noun*.]
†**1** An accusation, a reproach, an objection. **ME–L17**.
†**2** A (false) claim; the act of demanding as a right. **ME–M18**.
3 An invitation or summons to take part in a trial or contest, *spec.* (***a***) to a duel, (***b***) to a sporting contest, esp. one issued to the reigning champion; a test of one's abilities, a demanding or difficult task. **ME**.

R. LYND My challenge to any of the great leaders of the Christian churches . . to come and debate the question of religion and free thought. D. ACHESON The tremendous challenge of his post, and the problems he faced. E. LONGFORD The Martyrs' Memorial . . an occasional challenge to the climbing skills of students.

4 A call to respond; *esp.* a sentry's demand for a password etc. **LME**.

E. BLUNDEN I heard the challenge 'Who goes there?'

5 *LAW*. An exception taken, to a person or thing; *spec.* an objection made to a juror. **LME**.
peremptory challenge: see **PEREMPTORY** *adjective* 1. ***principal challenge***: see **PRINCIPAL** *adjective*.
6 A calling in question; the state of being called in question. **E19**.

SIR W. SCOTT Schemes . . for bringing her title into challenge.

7 *IMMUNOLOGY*. A dose of antigen given to a previously exposed person or animal in order to detect immunity or hypersensitivity. **M20**.

challenge /'tʃalɪn(d)ʒ/ *verb*. **ME**.
[**ORIGIN** Old French *c(h)alengier* from Latin *calumniari*: see **CALUMNIATE** *verb*.]
▸ **I** *verb trans*. †**1** Accuse, bring a charge against; bring as a charge. **ME–L17**.

P. SIDNEY To be challenged of unkindness.

2 a Reprove; call to account. *obsolete* exc. *Scot.* **ME**. ▸**b** (Of a sentry etc.) ask (a person) for a password etc.; call to respond (*lit. & fig.*). **L18**.

a OED I have never been challenged for crossing these fields. **b** E. HEMINGWAY Orders to challenge all travellers and ask to see their papers.

3 a Lay claim to, demand as a right. (Foll. by †*that*, †*to do*.) *arch.* **ME**. ▸**b** Have a natural right or claim to, call for, (now *spec.* a responsive action or recognition, as attention, admiration, etc.). **LME**.

a T. HERBERT I challenge no thankes for what I publish. **b** T. BROWN Horace and Juvenal . . challenge a superiority above all the rest.

4 Invite or summon to take part in a trial, contest, duel, discussion, etc.; dare, defy; present a challenge to; stimulate. (Foll. by *to*, *to do*.) **LME**. ▸**b** Invite (emulous, hostile, or critical action of any kind). **E17**.

MILTON I . . challenge Dagon to the test. C. KINGSLEY He challenges all comers to wrestle with him. J. DICKEY A bad road always challenged him. J. ARCHER Inside the two-furlong marker—Highclere and Rosalie move up to challenge Buoy. **b** J. H. BLUNT Challenging controversy in every possible way.

5 Call into question; dispute, deny. **LME**.

T. H. HUXLEY I do not presume to challenge its wisdom.

6 *LAW*. Take exception or object to (a juror, evidence, etc.). **L16**.
7 *IMMUNOLOGY*. Give a dose that constitutes a challenge to (a person, an animal). **M20**.
▸ **II** *verb intrans*. **8** Issue a challenge to a duel etc. (*arch.*); present a challenge, offer interesting difficulties. **LME**.
†**9** Make or have a claim. *rare* (Shakes.). Only in **E17**.
10 *HUNTING*. Of a hound: give tongue on finding a scent. **L17**.
11 *LAW*. Take exception, object. **L19**.
■ **challengeable** *adjective* **LME**. **challenger** *noun* **LME**.

challenged /'tʃalɪndʒd/ *adjective*. *euphem.* (orig. *US*). **L20**.
[**ORIGIN** from **CHALLENGE** *verb* + -**ED**[1].]
(With prefixed adverb) having a disability of a specified kind. Hence (*joc.*), disadvantaged or lacking in some specified regard.
– **NOTE**: Introduced in the 1980s (in *physically challenged*) as a more positive alternative to *disabled* or *handicapped*, but soon began to be used with other adverbs in compounds such as *vertically challenged* (short) or *follicularly challenged* (bald) to make fun of euphemism and political correctness.

challenging /'tʃalɪn(d)ʒɪŋ/ *ppl adjective*. **M19**.
[**ORIGIN** from **CHALLENGE** *verb* + -**ING**[2].]
That challenges, *spec.* that presents a test of one's abilities; *euphem.* (of a person or their behaviour) difficult, demanding.

Times Applicants for this important, challenging and interesting post should have a degree. *Community Care* Women offenders who have complex issues in their lives and exhibit challenging behaviour.

■ **challengingly** *adverb* **E20**.

challis /'ʃalɪs, 'ʃali/ *noun*. **M19**.
[**ORIGIN** Perh. from the surname *Challis*.]
A lightweight soft clothing fabric of silk and worsted.

chalon /'ʃalən/ *noun*. Long *obsolete* exc. *hist.* **ME**.
[**ORIGIN** App. from *Châlons*-sur-Marne in NE France: cf. **SHALLOON**.]
A blanket or coverlet for a bed.
■ **chaloner** *noun* a maker of chalons **ME**.

chalone /'kaləʊn, 'keɪ-/ *noun*. **E20**.
[**ORIGIN** from Greek *khalōn* pres. pple of *khalaō* slacken, after **HORMONE**.]
PHYSIOLOGY. A substance secreted like a hormone but having the effect of inhibiting a bodily process; *spec.* an inhibitor of mitosis in particular tissues.
■ **cha'lonic** *adjective* **E20**.

chalot, **chaloth** *nouns* pls. of **CHALLAH**.

chaloupe *noun* var. of **SHALLOP**.

chalumeau /ʃalymo/ *noun*. Pl. ***-eaux*** /-o/. **E18**.
[**ORIGIN** French from late Latin *calamellus* dim. of *calamus* reed.]
A musical pipe of reed or straw; an instrument having a reed mouthpiece, *esp.* the forerunner of the clarinet. Also (in full ***chalumeau register***), the lowest register of the clarinet.

chalupa /tʃə'luːpə/ *noun*. **L19**.
[**ORIGIN** Spanish, rel. to **SHALLOP**.]
1 In Spain or Spanish America: a small light boat or canoe. **L19**.
2 A fried tortilla in the shape of a boat, with a spicy filling. **L20**.

Chalybean /kalɪ'biːən, *in Milton* kə'lɪbɪən/ *adjective*. *rare*. **L17**.
[**ORIGIN** from Latin *chalybeius* of steel, of the Chalybes (see below), from *chalybs*: see **CHALYBEATE** *adjective & noun*, -**AN**.]
Pertaining to the Chalybes, an ancient people of Asia Minor famous for their skill in working iron.
– **NOTE**: First recorded in Milton.

chalybeate /kə'lɪbɪət/ *adjective & noun*. **M17**.
[**ORIGIN** mod. Latin *chalybeatus*, from Latin *chalybs* from Greek *khalub-*, *khalups* steel: see -**ATE**[2].]
(A mineral water, a spring, etc.) impregnated with iron salts.

†**chalybeate** *verb trans*. **L16–E18**.
[**ORIGIN** formed as **CHALYBEATE** *adjective & noun* + -**ATE**[3].]
Impregnate with iron salts.

chalybite /'kalɪbʌɪt/ *noun*. **M19**.
[**ORIGIN** from Greek *khalub-*, *khalups* steel + -**ITE**[1].]
MINERALOGY. Siderite (native ferrous carbonate).

cham /kam/ *noun*. **LME**.
[**ORIGIN** French *cham*, *chan* from Turkic *ḳān* **KHAN** *noun*[1]. Cf. **CHAGAN**, **KHAN** *noun*[1].]
= **KHAN** *noun*[1]. Now only *transf. & fig.*, an autocrat, a dominant critic etc. (applied esp. to Samuel Johnson).

SMOLLETT That great Cham of literature, Samuel Johnson.

cham /tʃam/ *verb*. Long *obsolete* exc. *dial.* Infl. **-mm-**. **LME**.
[**ORIGIN** Prob. imit.: cf. **CHAMP** *verb*.]
1 *verb intrans. & trans.* = **CHAMP** *verb* 1, 2. **LME**.
2 *verb trans.* = **CHAMP** *verb* 3. Chiefly *Scot.* **E16**.

chama /'keɪmə/ *noun*. **M18**.
[**ORIGIN** Latin from Greek *khēmē* cockle.]
A sessile bivalve mollusc of the genus *Chama*, with rough, irregular valves, found in warm or tropical seas.

chamade /ʃə'mɑːd/ *noun*. **L17**.
[**ORIGIN** French from Portuguese *chamada*, from *chamar* from Latin *clamare*: see **CLAIM** *verb*, -**ADE** 1.]
MILITARY HISTORY. A signal by beat of drum or sound of trumpet inviting to a parley.

Chamaeleon *noun* see **CHAMELEON**.

chamaephyte /'kamɪfʌɪt/ *noun*. **E20**.
[**ORIGIN** from Greek *khamai* low, on the ground + -**PHYTE**.]
BOTANY. A plant which bears buds on or near the ground.

C

C

chamar /tʃə'mɑː/ *noun. Indian.* Also **chu-**. M19.
[ORIGIN Hindi *camār*.]
A member of a Hindu caste whose traditional occupation is leather-working; a tanner, a shoemaker.

chamber /'tʃeɪmbə/ *noun & verb.* ME.
[ORIGIN Old French & mod. French *chambre* from Latin CAMERA.]
▸ **A** *noun.* **1** An apartment in a house or other place of residence; a private room, *esp.* a bedroom. Now *arch.* or *poet.* exc. in *comb.* & as in sense b below. ME. ▸**b** In *pl.* A set of rooms in a larger building, esp. in the Inns of Court, let separately. Also, a judge's room for hearing cases, or for other official proceedings, out of court. M17.
audience chamber, ***bedchamber***, ***guest-chamber***, ***presence chamber***, etc. †**chamber of dais**, **chamber of deas** *Scot.* a parlour, a best bedroom. ***robe de chambre***: see ROBE *noun*[1].
2 (A hall used by) a deliberative or judicial body; *esp.* each of the houses of a parliament. LME.
council chamber, ***Star Chamber***, etc. **Chamber of Commerce** an association to promote and protect the interests of local commerce. **Chamber of Trade** a national organization representing local Chambers of Commerce. ***Lower Chamber***: see LOWER *adjective*. ***privy chamber***: see PRIVY *adjective*. ***Red Chamber***: see RED *adjective*. ***second chamber***: see SECOND *adjective*. SYNDICAL ***chamber***.
3 The hangings or furniture of a chamber. Now *rare* or *obsolete*. LME.
4 The treasury of a government, corporation, etc. Now *arch.* or *hist.* LME.
5 A cavity in the body of an animal or plant. LME.
P. PARISH The volume of blood in the heart chambers.
†**6 a** A detached charge piece put into the breech of a gun. LME–M19. ▸**b** A piece of ordnance standing on its breech, used to fire salutes etc. M16–M18.
†**7** A kingdom's chief city etc.; a royal residence; a royal port. M16–L17.
8 A relatively spacious underground hollow or section of such a hollow (dug out by an animal etc. or as a natural formation). L16. ▸**b** MINING. A large well-defined deposit of ore. L19.
F. HOYLE Although the cave is nearly 300 metres long, most of the paintings are in a chamber 18 by 9 metres.
9 A part of a firearm in which a charge is placed, as a space in the bore of old ordnance, each of the bores of an early revolver, (each section of) the cartridge compartment of a modern revolver, etc. L16.
10 *gen.* A space, cavity, or room constructed for various purposes (specified or identified contextually); an enclosed space or compartment in a structure, mechanism, etc. M18.
bubble chamber, ***cloud chamber***, ***decompression chamber***, ***gas chamber***, ***spark chamber***, etc. ***chamber of horrors***: see HORROR *noun*. ***lethal chamber***: see LETHAL *adjective*. ***torture chamber***: see TORTURE *noun*.
11 A chamber pot. L19.
– COMB.: **chamber concert** a concert of chamber music; †**chamber-council** a private concern; **chamber-deacon** *hist.* a poor clerk, esp. from Ireland, frequenting an English university in the 15th cent. and not belonging to any college or hall; **chamber-fellow** *arch.* one who shares a room or rooms with another; **chamber-lye** (*obsolete* exc. *dial.*) urine, esp. as formerly used for washing; **chambermaid** (*a*) a housemaid, esp. one in a hotel etc. who attends to the bedrooms; †(*b*) a lady's maid; **chamber music** music for a small group of instruments, particularly fitted for performance in a private room or a small hall; **chamber orchestra** a small orchestra; **chamber organ** a positive organ; an organ for domestic use, developed from the positive organ; **chamber pot** a receptacle for urine etc., for use in a bedroom or by a young child; **chamber-tomb** ARCHAEOLOGY a chambered tomb.
▸ **B** *verb.* **I** *verb trans.* **1** Place or shut (*up*) in or as in a chamber; *fig.* (*arch.*) restrain (one's words etc.). LME.
2 Provide with a chamber or chambers; form into a chamber or chambers. E17.
3 Hold in or as in a chamber. M19.
▸ **II** *verb intrans.* **4** Behave wantonly or lecherously. Long *arch.* E16.
■ **chambered** *adjective* having, formed into, or confined within a chamber or chambers; ARCHAEOLOGY (of a tomb) containing one or more burial chambers: LME. **chamberlet** *noun* a small chamber M19.

chamberer /'tʃeɪmb(ə)rə/ *noun. arch.* ME.
[ORIGIN Anglo-Norman *chamb(e)rer(e* = Old French *chamb(e)rier, -ière* (mod. *chambrier, -ière* chambermaid), formed as CHAMBER: see -ER[2].]
†**1** A chambermaid; a personal attendant, a valet. ME–E18.
2 A person who frequents ladies' chambers; a gallant. E17.

chamberlain /'tʃeɪmbəlɪn/ *noun.* ME.
[ORIGIN Old French *chamberlain, -lenc* (mod. *chambellan*) from Frankish (whence medieval Latin *camerlingus*), from Old Saxon *kamera* from Latin CAMERA: see -LING[1].]
1 A personal attendant of a king or nobleman in his bedroom (now *arch.* or *hist.*). Also, an officer managing the private chambers or household of a monarch, noble, etc. ME.
Lord Chamberlain (of the Household) the head of management of the royal household, formerly the licenser of plays for performance. **Lord Great Chamberlain (of England)** the hereditary holder of a ceremonial office, whose responsibilities include attendance on the monarch at a coronation.
2 A steward; an officer appointed to receive revenue etc.; *esp.* the treasurer of a corporation etc. LME.
†**3** An attendant at an inn, in charge of the bedrooms. M16–E19.
■ **chamberlainship** *noun* the position or office of chamberlain LME.

Chambertin /'ʃɒ̃bətã, *foreign* ʃɑ̃bɛrtɛ̃/ *noun.* L18.
[ORIGIN The vineyard of origin, in the Côte de Nuits, eastern France.]
A fine French red burgundy wine.

Chambéry /'ʃɒ̃bəriː, *foreign* ʃɑ̃beri/ *noun.* M20.
[ORIGIN The town of origin, in SE France.]
A dry French vermouth; a drink of this.

†**chamblet** *noun & verb* var. of CAMLET.

chambranle /ʃɑ̃brɑ̃ːl/ *noun.* Pl. pronounced same. E18.
[ORIGIN French.]
ARCHITECTURE. An ornamental bordering around a door, window, or fireplace.

chambray /'ʃambreɪ/ *noun & adjective.* Orig. *US.* E19.
[ORIGIN Irreg. from *Cambrai* (see CAMBRIC).]
(Made of) a type of gingham with white weft and coloured warp.

chambré /'ʃɒmbreɪ, *foreign* ʃɑ̃bre/ *adjective.* M20.
[ORIGIN French, pa. pple of *chambrer*, formed as CHAMBER.]
Of wine: at room temperature. Usu. *pred.*

†**chambrel** *noun* see CAMBREL.

chameleon /kə'miːlɪən/ *noun & adjective.* Also †**cam-**, (in sense 4) **-mael-**. ME.
[ORIGIN Latin *chamaeleon* from Greek *khamaileōn*, from *khamai* on the ground + *leōn* lion.]
▸ **A** *noun.* **1** Any of numerous small lizards of the Old World family Chamaeleontidae, with prehensile tails and the ability to change colour according to their surroundings. ME. ▸**b** An anole or other lizard able to change colour. *N. Amer.* L18.
†**2** BOTANY. Either of two plants of the composite family native to southern Europe, *Atractylis gummifera* (more fully ***white chameleon***) and *Cardopatium corymbosum* (more fully ***black chameleon***). E16–E18.
3 *fig.* Someone or something inconstant or variable. L16.
4 (Usu. **C-**.) (The name of) an inconspicuous circumpolar constellation of the southern hemisphere. Also ***the Chameleon***. L17.
†**5** CHEMISTRY. Potassium manganate, K_2MnO_4 (so called from the gradual change in colour of a solution from green to purple on exposure to air). Also ***mineral chameleon***. Only in 19.
▸ **B** *attrib.* or as *adjective.* = CHAMELEONIC. L16.
■ **chamele'onic** *adjective* chameleon-like; given to change, inconstant: E19. **chameleon-like** *adjective* resembling (that of) a chameleon; *fig.* inconstant: L16.

chametz *noun* var. of HAMETZ.

chamfer /'tʃamfə/ *verb & noun.* M16.
[ORIGIN Back-form. from CHAMFERING.]
▸ **A** *verb trans.* **1** Cut a channel or groove in; flute; furrow. *arch.* M16.
2 Bevel (a right-angled edge or corner) symmetrically. L17.
▸ **B** *noun.* †**1** A small groove, channel, etc. E17–E18.
2 A surface produced by bevelling a right-angled edge or corner symmetrically. M19.

chamfering /'tʃamf(ə)rɪŋ/ *noun.* M16.
[ORIGIN from French *chamfrain*, from *chant* edge (see CANT *noun*[1]) + *fraint* pa. pple of *fraindre* from Latin *frangere* break: assim. to -ING[1].]
†**1** Grooving, a groove, in wood, stone, etc. M16–E18.
2 The bevelling of a right-angled edge or corner symmetrically; a surface so produced. M18.

chamfrain /'tʃamfreɪn/ *noun. hist.* Also **chaffron** /'tʃafrən/, **chamfron** /'tʃamfrən/. LME.
[ORIGIN Old French & mod. French *chamfrein*, perh. from Old French *chafresner* (= Provençal *capfrenar*) put on a bridle, from *chef* head (see CHIEF *noun*) + *frein* from Latin *frenum* bridle, bit.]
The frontlet of a barded horse. Also, a piece of armour for a horse's face.

chamiso /tʃə'miːsəʊ/ *noun.* Pl. **-os**. Also **-mise** /-'miːz/. M19.
[ORIGIN Mexican Spanish.]
An evergreen shrub of the rose family, *Adenostoma fasciculatum*, native to California.

†**chamlet** *noun & verb* see CAMLET.

chamois /'ʃamwɑː; *in sense 2 of noun, adjective, usu.* 'ʃami/ *noun & adjective.* Pl. of noun same /'ʃamwɑːz, 'ʃamɪz/. Sense 2 of noun, adjective, also **shammy** /'ʃami/, (now *rare*) **shamoy** /'ʃamɔɪ, 'ʃami/. M16.
[ORIGIN Old French & mod. French, prob. ult. from Swiss Proto-Romance. Cf. Gallo-Latin *camox*.]
▸ **A** *noun.* **1** A goatlike antelope, *Rupicapra rupicapra*, found in the mountains of Europe and Asia Minor. M16.
2 More fully ***chamois leather***. Soft pliable leather from the chamois or (now more usu.) from sheep or lambs; a piece of this for polishing etc. L16.
▸ **B** *attrib.* or as *adjective.* **1** Made of chamois leather. E17.
2 Of the colour of chamois leather; yellowish brown. M17.

chamois /'ʃamwɑː, 'ʃami/ *verb.* Also (esp. sense 3) **shammy** /'ʃami/, (esp. sense 2) **shamoy** /'ʃamɔɪ, 'ʃami/. E17.
[ORIGIN French *chamoiser*, formed as CHAMOIS *noun & adjective*.]
†**1** *verb trans.* Make out of chamois leather. *rare.* Only in E17.
2 *verb intrans. & trans.* Prepare (leather, a skin) in imitation of true chamois leather. M18.
3 *verb trans.* Polish etc. with a chamois leather. M20.

†**chamoisite** *noun* see CHAMOSITE.

chamomile *noun* var. of CAMOMILE.

chamosite /'ʃaməzʌɪt/ *noun.* Orig. †**chamois-**. M19.
[ORIGIN from *Chamo(i)son*, a locality in Switzerland + -ITE[1].]
MINERALOGY. A greenish-grey or black clay mineral that is a monoclinic aluminosilicate of iron and occurs in oolitic and other bedded iron ores.
■ **chamo'sitic** *adjective* M20.

†**champ** *noun*[1]. ME.
[ORIGIN Old French & mod. French from Latin *campus*: see CAMP *noun*[2].]
1 A field, esp. of battle. ME–E19.
champ clos an enclosure for a judicial duel or tourney.
2 A ground in embroidery, painting, etc. ME–L16.

champ /tʃamp/ *noun*[2]. E17.
[ORIGIN from CHAMP *verb*.]
A champing action or noise.

champ /tʃamp/ *noun*[3]. M19.
[ORIGIN Hindi *cāp* CHAMPAC.]
The timber of the champac.

champ /tʃamp/ *noun*[4]. *colloq.* M19.
[ORIGIN Abbreviation.]
= CHAMPION *noun*[1] 3.

champ /tʃamp/ *verb.* LME.
[ORIGIN Prob. imit.: cf. CHAM *verb*, CHOMP.]
1 *verb intrans.* Make a noisy biting or chewing action (esp., of a horse etc., *at*, *on* the bit). LME.
champing at the bit *fig.* restlessly impatient to begin.
2 *verb trans.* **a** Munch (fodder etc.) noisily. M16. ▸**b** Bite noisily on (something hard); *esp.* (of a horse etc.) work (the bit) noisily in the teeth. L16.
3 *verb trans.* Mash, pound; crush under foot. *Scot.* L18.
■ **champer** *noun* L16.

champac /'tʃʌmpək, 'tʃam-/ *noun.* Also **chempaka** /'tʃɛmpəkə/ & other vars. L18.
[ORIGIN Sanskrit *campaka*, Malay *cempaka*.]
A southern Asian evergreen tree, *Michelia champaca*, of the magnolia family, which bears fragrant orange-coloured flowers and is sacred to Hindus and Buddhists. Also occas. applied to other trees with fragrant flowers.

champagne /ʃam'peɪn, attrib. 'ʃampeɪn/ *noun.* M17.
[ORIGIN *Champagne* (see below) formed as CHAMPAIGN.]
1 (A) wine from Champagne, a region (formerly a province) of NE France; *esp.* (a) naturally sparkling white wine from Champagne or elsewhere; *loosely* (a) sparkling white wine; a drink of any of these. M17.
oeil-de-perdrix champagne: see OEIL-DE-PERDRIX 2. ***pink champagne***: see PINK *adjective*[2].
2 *fig.* Something exhilarating or excellent. L19.
C. FRANCIS Its delicate flavour has earned it the description 'the champagne of teas'.
3 A pale straw colour. L19.
– COMB.: **champagne breakfast**, **champagne supper**, etc.: at which champagne is served; **Champagne Charlie** any noted (male) champagne-drinker; **champagne socialist** *derog.* a person who espouses socialist ideals while enjoying a wealthy and luxurious lifestyle.
■ **cham'pagney**, **-ny** *adjective* resembling champagne or its exhilarating qualities M19.

champaign /'tʃampeɪn/ *noun & adjective.* Now chiefly *literary.* Also **-ain**, †**-ian**, †**-ion**. LME.
[ORIGIN Old French & mod. French *champagne* from late Latin *campania* use as noun of fem. sing. & neut. pl. of *campanius* adjective, from Latin *campus*: see CAMP *noun*[2]. Cf. CAMPAGNA, CAMPAIGN.]
▸ **A** *noun.* **1** (An expanse of) level open country. LME.
†**2** The field of battle; a battlefield. LME–M19.
†**3** Unenclosed or common land. M16–M17.
4 *fig.* A field of enquiry, observation, etc.; a sphere of operation. L16.
▸ **B** *attrib.* or as *adjective.* †**1** Of, pertaining to, or designating unenclosed or common land. LME–E18.
2 Of, pertaining to, or designating level open country. E16.

†**champain** *noun*[1]. M16–E18.
[ORIGIN Cf. French *champagne* lower third of the shield.]
HERALDRY. An embattled line but with the top and bottom of each division pointed instead of square.

champain *noun*[2] var. of CHAMPAIGN.

champers /'ʃampəz/ *noun. slang.* M20.
[ORIGIN from CHAMPAGNE: see -ER[6].]
Champagne.

champerty /'tʃampəːti/ *noun.* LME.
[ORIGIN Anglo-Norman *champartie*, from Old French & mod. French *champart* the feudal lord's share of the produce, from Latin *campus* (see CAMP *noun*[2]) + *pars* PART *noun*.]
†**1** Partnership in power. LME–M16.

2 *LAW.* The action of assisting a party in a suit in which one is not naturally interested, with a view to receiving a share of the disputed property (an offence in the US and formerly in Britain). LME. ▸**b** An act or (now *US*) case of champerty. LME.
3 *fig.* A combination for an evil purpose. Now *rare.* E17.
■ **champertor** *noun* (now *rare*) a person engaged in champerty E16. **champertous** *adjective* (*rare*) of the nature of champerty M17.

†**champian** *noun & adjective* var. of CHAMPAIGN.

champignon /tʃam'pɪnjən, 'ʃampɪnjɔ̃; *foreign* ʃɑ̃piɲɔ̃ (*pl. same*)/ *noun.* Also †**-inion**. L16.
[ORIGIN French (earlier *champaignon*), dim. of *champagne*: see CHAMPAIGN.]
A mushroom; a toadstool. Now *spec.* (**a**) the edible field mushroom *Agaricus campestris*; (**b**) an agaric, *Marismius oreades*, which often forms fairy rings.

champion /'tʃampɪən/ *noun*[1], *adjective*[1], & *adverb.* ME.
[ORIGIN Old French & mod. French from medieval Latin *campio(n-)*, from Latin *campus* CAMP *noun*[2]. Cf. CAMP *noun*[1].]
▸ **A** *noun.* **1** A fighting man; a stout fighter. *arch.* ME.
2 A person who fights, argues, etc., on behalf of another or for a cause. ME.
J. R. ACKERLEY A formidable champion of the rights of her own sex.
3 An athlete, boxer, etc., who has defeated all competitors; an overall winner of a series of competitions; an animal, a plant, etc., adjudged to be superior to all others in a show. E18.
G. GREEN West Germany became the world champions against all the odds.
– PHRASES: **King's Champion**, **Queen's Champion**, **Champion of England** a hereditary official who offers to defend a new monarch's title to the crown at his or her coronation. ***seven champions***: see SEVEN *adjective.*
▸ **B** *adjective.* That is a champion (esp. sense 3); that has been adjudged to be superior in competition; *colloq.* first-rate, splendid. E19.
J. M. SYNGE They're cheering a young lad, the champion playboy of the Western World. K. A. PORTER An English bulldog of champion stock.
▸ **C** *adverb.* Splendidly. *colloq. & dial.* E20.
W. DEEPING We get on champion.
■ **championess** *noun* (now *rare*) a female champion L16. **championship** *noun* (**a**) the position or title of champion in a competition; a competition for this; (**b**) advocacy, defence: E19.

†**champion** *noun*[2] & *adjective*[2] var. of CHAMPAIGN.

champion /'tʃampɪən/ *verb trans.* E17.
[ORIGIN from CHAMPION *noun*[1].]
†**1** Challenge to a contest. *rare.* E17–E19.
2 Support the cause of; argue in favour of; defend. E19.

champlevé /'ʃampləveɪ, *foreign* ʃɑ̃ləve/ *adjective & noun.* M19.
[ORIGIN French, from *champ* field + *levé* raised.]
(Enamelwork) in which hollows made in the surface are filled with enamel colours.

chance /tʃɑːns/ *noun, adverb, & adjective.* ME.
[ORIGIN Anglo-Norman *ch(e)aunce*, Old French *chëance*, (mod. *chance*), from *chëoir* fall, befall, from Proto-Romance var. of Latin *cadere* fall.]
▸ **A** *noun.* **1** The way things happen of themselves; the absence of design or discoverable cause; the course of events regarded as a power; fortune, fate. ME. ▸†**b** *One's* fortune or lot. ME–E18.
W. C. BRYANT The chance of war Is equal, and the slayer oft is slain. W. PLOMER It was pure chance that was now to bring us together.
2 An event that is without apparent cause or unexpected; a casual circumstance; an accident. ME.
A. MCCOWEN By a happy chance [I] got a job almost immediately. D. ADAMS He hadn't done it deliberately, it was just a random chance.
3 An opportunity, as of escape, of dismissing a batsman in cricket, of scoring a goal in football, etc. ME.
BURKE A change of climate is his only chance. L. URIS I didn't even get a chance to tell you that your brother forgives you.
4 A possibility, a probability. Freq. in *pl.* L18.
E. HEMINGWAY The train was full and I knew there was no chance of a place. S. SASSOON The chances are about five to one against my ever using it.
– PHRASES: **by any chance** (in interrog. contexts) as is (just) possible. **by chance** as it happens or happened; without design or discoverable cause. ***chances are*** (***that***): see ***the chances are*** (***that***) below. **game of chance**: decided by luck not skill. ***leave nothing to chance***: see LEAVE *verb*[1]. ***long chance***: see LONG *adjective*[1]. ***main chance***: see MAIN *adjective*. ***not a cat in hell's chance***: see CAT *noun*[1]. ***not a chance in hell***: see HELL *noun*. ***not a dog's chance***: see DOG *noun*. ***not a snowball's chance*** (***in hell***): see SNOWBALL *noun* 1. ***off chance***: see OFF *preposition & adverb*. **on the chance** in view of the possibility (*of*, *that*). ***sporting chance***: see SPORTING *adjective*. ***stand a chance***: see STAND *verb*. **take a chance** (**a**) behave riskily; (**b**) let things go as they may, consent to take what comes (foll. by *on*, *with*). **take chances** behave riskily, esp. habitually. **take one's chance** let things go as they may, consent to take what comes (foll. by *on*, *with*). ***the chance of a lifetime***: see LIFETIME 1. **the chances are** (**that**), **chances are** (**that**) *colloq.* the likelihood is that. ***the main chance***: see MAIN *adjective*. ***treble chance***: see TREBLE *adjective*.
▸ **B** *adverb.* By chance. *arch.* M16.
▸ **C** *adjective.* That occurs or is by chance; casual, incidental. L17.
G. GREENE I had spoilt the occasion suddenly by a chance word. L. DURRELL I was something more than a chance traveller, . . I planned to stay in the island.
■ **chanceful** *adjective* (*arch.*) (**a**) casual, accidental; (**b**) unpredictable, eventful: L16. **chancefully** *adverb* (*arch. rare*) †(**a**) unfortunately; (**b**) in a chanceful manner: ME.

chance /tʃɑːns/ *verb.* LME.
[ORIGIN from the noun.]
1 *verb intrans.* Happen without design or discoverable cause. (With the event as subj. (†& the person or thing affected as indirect obj.); impers. subj. (esp. *it*) & *that* the event; the person or thing affected as subj. (†or indirect obj. with impers. subj.) & *to do* the event.) LME. ▸**b** Come *on*, *upon*, *across*, etc., by chance. M16.
SPENSER Him chaunst to meete . . A faithlesse Sarazin. M. TWAIN If it so chance that we be separated, let each make for London Bridge. H. JAMES An occasion chanced to present itself. TOLKIEN They fell silent, wondering what would chance. D. MURPHY My mother chanced to be passing. **b** SAKI The first crossing-sweeper . . she chanced across. J. G. COZZENS Mr. Hurst's librarian chanced on it in a completely forgotten portfolio.
†**how chance . . . ?** how is (or was) it that . . . ?
†**2** *verb intrans.* Fare, have luck (of a specified kind). LME–M16.
3 *verb trans.* Risk. *colloq.* M19.
R. RENDELL Occupants . . could come and go without . . chancing an encounter with porters.
chance one's arm take one's (possibly slight) chance of doing something successfully.
■ **chanceable** *adjective* (long *arch.*) happening by or subject to chance M16. **chancer** *noun* (*slang*) a person who takes chances or does risky things L19.

chancel /'tʃɑːns(ə)l/ *noun.* ME.
[ORIGIN Old French (mod. *cancel*) from Latin *cancelli* (pl.) dim. of *cancer* lattice, perh. dissimilated form of *carcer* barrier, prison.]
A part of a church near the altar, reserved for the clergy, choir, etc., and usu. enclosed.

chancellery /'tʃɑːns(ə)l(ə)ri, -sləri/ *noun.* Also **-ory**; **-elry** /-(ə)lri/. ME.
[ORIGIN Old French & mod. French *chancellerie*, from *chancelier*: see CHANCELLOR, -ERY.]
1 The position of a chancellor. ME.
2 The department, staff, or office of a chancellor. L17.
3 An office attached to an embassy or consulate. M19.

chancellor /'tʃɑːns(ə)lə/ *noun.* LOE.
[ORIGIN Anglo-Norman *c(h)anceler*, Old French *c(h)ancelier*, from late Latin *cancellarius* porter, secretary, from *cancelli* (see CHANCEL) + *-arius* -ER[2].]
1 *gen.* A secretary (of a king, foreign ruler, etc.). *obsolete* exc. *hist.* LOE.
2 A high-ranking state or law official of various kinds (specified by title or contextually identified). LOE.
Chancellor of England *hist.* = ***Lord Chancellor*** below, before the Union with Scotland. **Chancellor of the Duchy of Lancaster** the representative of the Crown as Duke of Lancaster, now a member of the British (earlier English) government, often a Cabinet minister employed on non-departmental work. **Chancellor of the Exchequer** the finance minister of the United Kingdom (earlier of England or Great Britain), orig. an official with custody of the seal of the exchequer. **Lord Chancellor**, **Lord High Chancellor** the highest officer of the Crown in the United Kingdom (earlier of England or Great Britain), formerly presiding over the House of Lords, the Chancery Division, and the Court of Appeal.
3 A titular head of a university, now usu. an honorary office, the actual duties being performed by a vice-chancellor. ME.
4 A foreman of a Scottish jury. Now *rare.* L15.
5 One of the four chief dignitaries in cathedrals of old foundation; a bishop's law officer. L16.
6 An officer of an order of knighthood who seals commissions etc. L16.
Chancellor of the Order of the Garter etc.
7 A chief minister of a European state, now only of the Federal Republic of Germany and of Austria. E17.
Iron Chancellor: see IRON *noun & adjective.*
8 The president of a chancery court. *US.* M18.
■ **chancellorship** *noun* the position of a chancellor L15.

chancelry *noun* var. of CHANCELLERY.

chance-medley /tʃɑːns'mɛdli/ *noun.* L15.
[ORIGIN Anglo-Norman *chance medlee*, formed as CHANCE *noun* + *medlee* fem. pa. pple of *medler* mix: see MEDDLE *verb.*]
1 *LAW* (now *hist.*). An action, esp. homicide, mainly but not entirely unintentional; a casual affray in which a person kills in self-defence after being assaulted and refusing to fight further (formerly regarded as excusable). L15.
2 *transf.* Inadvertency, haphazard or random action. L16.

chancery /'tʃɑːns(ə)ri/ *noun.* In sense 2 also **C-**. LME.
[ORIGIN Contr. of CHANCELLERY.]
†**1** = CHANCELLERY 1. LME–M17.
2 The court of the Lord Chancellor of the United Kingdom (earlier of England or Great Britain), now a division of the High Court of Justice. Also ***Court of Chancery***, ***High Court of Chancery***. LME. ▸**b** More fully ***chancery court***, ***court of chancery***. A similar court elsewhere; *US* a court of equity. M16.
3 An office for public records. E16.
4 = CHANCELLERY 2. M16.
5 = CHANCELLERY 3. (Now the official term in Brit. diplomatic use.) E20.
– PHRASES: **in chancery** (of the head of a boxer or wrestler) held under the opponent's arm and being pummelled. ***Inns of Chancery***: see INN *noun*. **ward in Chancery** a ward of court under the protection of the Court of Chancery.

chancre /'tʃaŋkə/ *noun.* L16.
[ORIGIN French, from Latin CANCER *noun*: cf. CANKER *noun*.]
MEDICINE. A painless ulcer, *esp.* one occurring on the genitals and resulting from syphilis.
soft chancre = CHANCROID *noun*.
■ **chancroid** *noun & adjective* (of) a venereal infection with the bacterium *Haemophilus ducreyi* causing enlarged, ulcerated lymph nodes of the groin (also called ***soft sore***) M19. **chancrous** *adjective* (now *rare* or *obsolete*) M18.

chancy /'tʃɑːnsi/ *adjective.* E16.
[ORIGIN from CHANCE *noun* + -Y[1].]
1 Lucky; safe to meddle with, 'canny'. *Scot.* E16.
2 Uncertain, risky. M19.
■ **chancily** *adverb* M20. **chanciness** *noun* L19.

chandelier /ʃandə'lɪə/ *noun.* M17.
[ORIGIN French, from *chandelle*: see CHANDELLE, -IER.]
1 *MILITARY.* A wooden frame filled with fascines to form a traverse in sapping. M17.
2 A branched hanging support for several lights, orig. candles. M18.

chandelle /ʃan'dɛl/ *noun.* E20.
[ORIGIN French, lit. 'candle'.]
A steep climbing turn executed in an aircraft to gain height while changing the direction of flight.

chandler /'tʃɑːndlə/ *noun.* ME.
[ORIGIN Anglo-Norman *chaundeler*, Old French *chandelier* candle-maker, -seller, from *c(h)andeile*, *c(h)andelle* (mod. *chandelle*) from Latin *candela*: see CANDLE *noun*, -ELLA, -ER[2].]
▸ **I** **1** A person who makes or sells candles. ME.
tallow-chandler, ***wax-chandler***.
2 An officer responsible for the supply of candles to a household. Long *obsolete* exc. *hist.* LME.
3 A retailer of provisions and items of equipment for a particular purpose, without specification (now *arch.* or *hist.*) usu. of candles, oil, soap, paint, groceries, etc., for households. L16.
corn chandler, ***ship's chandler***, etc.
▸ †**II** **4** A stand or support for a candle. LME–L18.
■ **chandlery** *noun* (**a**) (now chiefly *hist.*) a place where candles etc. are kept; (**b**) the goods produced or sold by a chandler: E17.

Chandler wobble /'tʃɑːndlə 'wɒb(ə)l/ *noun phr.* M20.
[ORIGIN Seth C. *Chandler* (1846–1913), US astronomer.]
A nutation of the earth's principal axis of inertia about its axis of rotation (with a period of approx. 14 months), manifested as a small oscillation in the latitude of points on the earth's surface.

chang /tʃaŋ/ *noun.* E19.
[ORIGIN Tibetan *chaṅ*.]
A Tibetan beer or wine made chiefly from barley or rice.

change /tʃeɪn(d)ʒ/ *noun.* ME.
[ORIGIN Anglo-Norman *chaunge*, Old French & mod. French *change*, formed as CHANGE *verb*.]
1 (An instance of) making or becoming different; the substitution of one thing or set of conditions for another; the following of one thing or set of conditions on another; (an) alteration in state or quality; variety; variation, mutation. ME. ▸**b** More fully ***change of the moon***. The arrival of the moon at a fresh phase, esp. at a new moon. LME. ▸**c** A round or sequence of steps within a dance. L16. ▸**d** *MUSIC.* Modulation. Now *rare* or *obsolete*. L16. ▸**e** One's death. *arch.* E17. ▸†**f** Changefulness; (a) caprice. Only in 17. ▸**g** *CRICKET.* The substitution of one bowler or type of bowling for another during the course of a match. E19. ▸**h** A gear change in a vehicle. M20.
R. B. SHERIDAN Do you really see any change in me? J. RHYS Her health was not good and she needed a change. A. TOFFLER He thrives on change, enjoys travel, new foods, [etc.]. **f** SHAKES. *Lear* You see how full of changes his age is.
change of address, ***change of key***, ***change of pace***, etc. ***social change***, ***sound change***, etc. ***change of air***: see AIR *noun*[1] 2. ***change of front***: see FRONT *noun* 5b. ***change of gear***, ***gear change***: see GEAR *noun*. ***change of heart***: see HEART *noun*. ***change of mind***: see MIND *noun*[1]. ***change of* SCENE**. ***change of the monsoon***: see MONSOON 1. ***chop and change***: see CHOP *noun*[5]. **for a change** *colloq.* for variety, as an exception to usual practice. ***grammatical change***: see GRAMMATICAL *adjective*. †**put the change upon** deceive (a person). ***SEA change***. **the change** (**of life**) the menopause.
2 A person who or thing which is or may be substituted for another of the same kind. ME. ▸**b** *CRICKET.* A change-bowler. M19.
R. GREENE Mistresse Lamilia, like a cunning Angler made readie her chaunge of baytes. A. HAILEY He would pause occasionally to pencil in a change.
change of clothes a second outfit in reserve.

C

3 Money given in exchange for notes, coins, etc., of a higher denomination or of a different currency; the balance returned when anything is paid for by an amount of money greater than its price. Hence, coins, esp. of low denominations. ME.

B. ALLWOOD The pub . . has change for a pound. E. BOWEN Shovelling into his pocket the change from a pound note. J. WAIN They jingle the hopeful change in their pockets.

get no change out of *slang* get no return, result, or satisfaction from; fail to get the better of (a person). **give change**, *N. Amer.* **make change** give money in exchange for notes, coins, etc., of a higher denomination, or in adjustment of a payment. ***loose change***: see LOOSE *adjective*. **small change** coins of low denominations; *fig.* trivial remarks.

†4 Exchange. ME–E17.

5 (Also **C-**.) A place where merchants meet for the transaction of business; an exchange. (From E19 also written ***'change*** as if for ***exchange***.) ME.

on change at the exchange.

6 *BELL-RINGING*. In *pl.* The different permutations in which a peal of bells may be rung. M17.

ring the changes (*a*) go through all the changes in ringing a peal of bells; (*b*) go through all the possible variations of any process (foll. by *on*); (*c*) *slang* substitute bad money for good.

– COMB.: **change-bowler** *CRICKET* a bowler who relieves the regular bowlers in a match; **change-house** *Scot.* (now *rare* or *obsolete*) a small inn or alehouse; **change-ringer**, **change-ringing** *BELL-RINGING* (a person who engages in) the ringing of a set of bells in a constantly varying order.

■ **changeful** *adjective* full of change; variable, inconstant: L16. **changefulness** *noun* L18. **changeless** *adjective* without change, unchanging, immutable L16. **changelessly** *adverb* E20. **changelessness** *noun* E19.

change /tʃeɪndʒ/ *verb*. ME.

[ORIGIN Old French & mod. French *changer* from late Latin *cambiare* from Latin *cambire* exchange, barter, prob. of Celtic origin.]

1 *verb trans.* Put, take, or use another or others instead of; give up, get rid of, *for*. ME. ▸**b** *spec.* Give or obtain money of smaller denomination or different currency in exchange for (money of a defined kind or amount). LME.

G. GREENE You changed your newspaper once and you soon got used to it. I. MURDOCH She had not changed her clothes. J. HERRIOT Stewie had changed his . . Austin Seven for a . . Ford V Eight. **b** E. NESBIT We would bring his share as soon as we could get the half-crown changed.

2 *verb trans.* Substitute one for another of (things of the same kind); go from one to another of (things of the same kind). ME. ▸**b** *verb intrans.* Change trains, boats, etc. L19.

T. STOPPARD The dancing farmhands changing partners. **b** OED Passengers for Cambridge change at Bletchley.

3 *verb trans.* Give and receive reciprocally (things of the same kind); exchange (*with*). Now *rare* exc. in ***change places*** (***with***). ME. ▸†**b** *verb intrans.* Make an exchange (*for, with*). M16–M17. ▸†**c** *verb trans.* Exchange (a thing) *with* (a person). L16–M17.

SIR W. SCOTT Her attendants changed expressive looks with each other. TENNYSON If you . . change a word with her he calls his wife.

4 *verb trans.* Make different, alter; turn or convert *into, to,* (*from*). ME.

V. WOOLF Experiences . . such as change a face . . from a pink innocent oval to a face lean, contracted, hostile. J. STEINBECK All night they walked and never changed their pace.

5 *verb intrans.* Become different; turn *into, to,* (*from*). ME. ▸**b** Of the moon: pass through phases; arrive at a fresh phase, esp. at a new moon. LME. ▸†**c** Change countenance; turn pale, blush, etc. L16–E17.

R. P. WARREN He watched the expression of her face change from pleasure to surprise. E. WAUGH Alastair . . had changed little since he joined the army. G. CHARLES He waited at the crossing for the traffic lights to change.

6 *verb intrans.* & (*rare*) *trans.* Shift, transfer, (usu. *from* one place *to* another); remove to another place or into other circumstances. LME.

D. H. LAWRENCE He changed his hat to his left hand. W. TREVOR Mrs Rush changed from second to third gear.

7 **a** *verb intrans.* & (now *Scot.*) *refl.* change one's clothes; *spec.* change into evening dress. L15. ▸**b** *verb trans.* Put fresh clothes on (another person); put fresh coverings on (a bed); *spec.* change the nappy of (a baby). E20.

– PHRASES, & WITH ADVERBS IN SPECIALIZED SENSES: ***change colour***: see COLOUR *noun*. **change down** engage a lower gear in a vehicle. ***change ends***: see END *noun*. ***change eyes***: see EYE *noun*. **change gear** engage a different gear in a vehicle. ***change hands***: see HAND *noun*. ***change horses in midstream***: see HORSE *noun*. ***change leg***: see LEG *noun*. ***change note***: see NOTE *noun*[2]. ***change one's condition***: see CONDITION *noun* 8. **change one's feet** *colloq.* put on other shoes etc. ***change one's mind***: see MIND *noun*[1]. ***change one's mood***: see MOOD *noun*[1]. ***change one's note***: see NOTE *noun*[2]. ***change one's skin***: see SKIN *noun*. ***change one's tune***: see TUNE *noun*. **change over** change from one system or situation to another (also foll. by *from, to*). ***change step***: see STEP *noun*[1]. ***change the subject***: see SUBJECT *noun*. **change up** engage a higher gear in a vehicle. **changing room** a room where one can change one's clothes, esp. at a sports ground. ***chop and change***: see CHOP *verb*[2] 2.

– COMB.: **changeover** a change from one system or situation to another; *spec.* the action of handing over the baton to the next runner in a relay race; **change-up** *BASEBALL* an unexpectedly slow pitch designed to deceive the batter's expectations.

changeable /ˈtʃeɪndʒəb(ə)l/ *adjective & noun*. ME.

[ORIGIN Old French & mod. French, formed as CHANGE *verb* + -ABLE.]

▸ **A** *adjective*. **1** That may change or be changed (by others); subject to change; mutable, variable, inconstant. ME.

2 Showing different colours under different aspects; shot. LME.

H. MCCLOY A ball dress of changeable silk, pale blue and rose.

▸ **B** *noun*. A changeable thing or person. Now *rare* or *obsolete*. E18.

■ **changea'bility**, **changeableness** *nouns* the quality of being changeable; mutability; inconstancy: LME.

changeling /ˈtʃeɪndʒlɪŋ/ *noun & adjective*. M16.

[ORIGIN from CHANGE *verb* + -LING[1].]

▸ **A** *noun*. **1** A person given to change; a waverer, a turncoat. *arch.* M16.

2 A person or thing (surreptitiously) put in exchange for another; *spec.* a child secretly substituted for another in infancy. M16.

3 A half-witted person. *arch.* E17.

▸ †**B** *adjective*. Changeable, variable, inconstant. M17–E18.

changement /ˈtʃeɪndʒm(ə)nt/ *noun*[1]. *rare*. LME.

[ORIGIN Old French & mod. French, formed as CHANGE *verb* + -MENT.]

(A) change, (an) alteration, (a) variation.

changement /ʃɑ̃ʒmɑ̃/ *noun*[2]. Pl. pronounced same. M19.

[ORIGIN French = CHANGEMENT *noun*[1].]

BALLET. In full ***changement de pieds*** /də pje/ [= of feet]. A jump during which the dancer changes the position of the feet.

changer /ˈtʃeɪndʒə/ *noun*. ME.

[ORIGIN Anglo-Norman *changëour*, Old French *changëor* (mod. *changeur*), in medieval Latin *cambiator*, formed as CHANGE *verb* + -ER[2]. Also immed. from CHANGE *verb* + -ER[1].]

1 A person who or thing which changes something (identified contextually or specified); *spec.* (the earliest use, now *rare*) one who exchanges money. ME.

2 A person who changes. *rare*. E17.

chank /tʃaŋk, tʃʌŋk/ *noun*. L17.

[ORIGIN Sanskrit *śaṅkha*, partly through Portuguese *chanco*, *chanquo*.]

The spiral shell of a gastropod, *Xancus pyrum*, used by Hindus for libation vessels and ornaments.

chank /tʃaŋk/ *verb trans.* Now *US & dial.* M16.

[ORIGIN Imit.: cf. CHAMP *verb*.]

= CHAMP *verb* 2.

channel /ˈtʃan(ə)l/ *noun*[1]. ME.

[ORIGIN Old French *chanel* partially Latinized var. of *chenel* from Latin *canalis* pipe, groove, channel, from *canna* CANE *noun*[1]: see -EL[2]. Cf. CANAL *noun*, CANNEL *noun*[1], KENNEL *noun*[2].]

▸ **I** Of water etc.

1 The hollow bed of running water (formerly also, of the sea). ME.

2 A gutter in a street etc. *obsolete* exc. *dial.* LME.

3 A natural or artificial tubular passage, esp. for liquids or fluids. LME.

†**4** A stream, a rivulet. L15–E18.

5 A navigable passage between shallows in an estuary or other waterway. E16.

6 A piece of water, wider than a strait, joining two larger pieces, usu. seas. M16.

the Channel, **the English Channel**: between England and France (***Chops of the Channel***: see CHOP *noun*[2] 3).

†**7** = CANAL *noun* 4. Only in 17.

▸ **II** *transf. & fig.* †**8** The neck, the throat. ME–L16.

9 That through which information, news, trade, etc., passes; a medium of communication; an agency. M16.

J. S. MILL No new . . channel for investment has been opened. T. STOPPARD The newspapers . . are the channel of the government's answerability to the governed.

the usual channels the approved or traditional modes of approach etc.

10 Gravel. *Scot. & N. English*. L16.

11 The course in which anything moves; a direction, a line. M17.

SWIFT The world went on in the old channel. M. MCCARTHY She managed to steer the conversation into safer channels.

green channel: see GREEN *adjective*. ***red channel***: see RED *adjective*.

12 A groove, a furrow; *spec.* in *ARCHITECTURE*, a fluting of a column. L17.

13 An electric circuit, band of radio frequencies, etc., used as a means of conveying or transmitting a signal in telecommunications, broadcasting, sound reproduction, etc.; a broadcasting service using a particular frequency band. M19.

second channel: see SECOND *adjective*.

– COMB.: †**channel-bone** the collarbone; **channel cat**, **channel catfish** *N. Amer.* a freshwater catfish, esp. *Ictalurus punctatus*; **Channel Fleet** *hist.* the portion of the British fleet detailed for service in the English Channel; **channel-hop** (*colloq.*) (*a*) change frequently from one television channel to another, using a remote control device; (*b*) travel across the English Channel and back to Britain frequently or for only a brief trip; **Channel Islander** a native or inhabitant of the Channel Islands; **Channel Islands** British Crown dependencies in the English Channel off the north-west coast of France, including Jersey, Guernsey, Alderney, and Sark; **channel-stone** a stone used in paving gutters; **channel-surf** *verb* (*colloq.*, chiefly *N. Amer.*) = ***channel-hop*** (*a*) above; **Channel Tunnel** a tunnel under the English Channel linking England and France (cf. CHUNNEL).

■ **channelly** *adjective* (*Scot. & N. English*) gravelly E17.

channel /ˈtʃan(ə)l/ *noun*[2]. M18.

[ORIGIN Alt. of ***chain-wale*** s.v. CHAIN *noun*: see WALE *noun*[1]. Cf. *gunnel*, *gunwale*.]

NAUTICAL. A broad thick plank projecting horizontally from a ship's side abreast of the mast, to widen the basis of support for the shrouds.

channel /ˈtʃan(ə)l/ *verb trans.* Infl. **-ll-**, ***-l-**. LME.

[ORIGIN from CHANNEL *noun*[1].]

1 Form channels in; groove. LME.

SHAKES. *1 Hen. IV* No more shall trenching war channel her fields.

2 Convey (as if) in a channel; guide, direct. M17. ▸**b** Serve as a medium for (a spirit or other paranormal influence). Freq. as ***channelling*** *verbal noun*. L20.

R. SCRUTON In so far as religious feeling exists, it is . . better that it be channelled towards its proper object. **b** T. ROBBINS I *have* been having psychic problems lately. I keep channeling Janis Joplin.

3 Excavate or cut out as a channel. E19.

4 Provide (a street) with gutters. L19.

■ **channeller** *noun* L19.

channelize /ˈtʃan(ə)lʌɪz/ *verb trans.* Chiefly *US*. Also **-ise**. E17.

[ORIGIN from CHANNEL *noun*[1] + -IZE.]

= CHANNEL *verb* 2.

– NOTE: In isolated use before M20.

■ **channeli'zation** *noun* E20.

channer /ˈtʃanə/ *verb intrans. Scot.* LME.

[ORIGIN Prob. imit.: cf. CHUNNER, CHUNTER.]

Mutter, grumble, murmur querulously.

chanson /ʃɑ̃sɔ̃/ *noun*. Pl. pronounced same. L15.

[ORIGIN Old French & mod. French from Latin *cantio(n-)*: see CANZONE.]

A French song.

chanson de geste /də ʒɛst/ [= of heroic deeds] any of a group of medieval French epic poems.

■ ***chansonette*** /ʃɑ̃sɔnɛt/ (*pl. same*)/ *noun* a short song E19. ***chansonnier*** /ʃɑ̃sɔnje/ (*pl. same*)/ *noun* (*a*) a writer or performer of esp. satirical songs (in France); (*b*) a collection of (French) songs: L19.

chant /tʃɑːnt/ *noun*. Also (now *Scot.*) **chaunt** /tʃɔːnt/. L17.

[ORIGIN from the verb: cf. Old French & mod. French *chant* from Latin CANTUS.]

1 A song; singing. L17.

MILTON Chant of tuneful birds.

2 *MUSIC*. A short musical passage in two or more phrases each with a reciting note to which any number of syllables may be sung, for singing unmetrical words; a psalm, canticle, etc., so sung. L18.

Ambrosian chant, ***Gregorian chant***, etc.

3 A measured monotonous song, a musical recitation of words; a singsong intonation in talk. E19.

GEO. ELIOT The clear-cut, emphatic chant which makes a truth doubly telling in Scottish utterance. R. HOGGART Rhyming chants survive, to accompany the games.

chant /tʃɑːnt/ *verb*. Also (now *Scot.*) **chaunt** /tʃɔːnt/. LME.

[ORIGIN Old French & mod. French *chanter* from Latin *cantare* frequentative of *canere* sing.]

1 *verb intrans. & trans. gen.* Sing. Chiefly *arch. & poet.* LME. ▸**b** *verb trans.* Sing of, celebrate in song. *poet.* L16.

R. BURNS How can ye chant, ye little birds. TENNYSON He . . chanted a melody.

chanting GOSHAWK.

2 *verb intrans. & trans.* Recite musically or rhythmically; intone; sing (to) a chant. LME.

SIR W. SCOTT With pious fools go chant and pray. B. CHATWIN He would . . chant the lines his mother taught him.

3 *verb intrans. & trans.* Talk or repeat (a statement) monotonously. L16.

MILTON Let them chaunt while they will of prerogatives.

4 *verb trans.* Praise (a horse) fraudulently to sell it. *arch. slang*. E19.

■ **chantable** *adjective* (*rare*) LME.

chantage /ʃɑ̃taːʒ, ˈtʃɑːntɪdʒ/ *noun*. L19.

[ORIGIN French.]

Extortion of money by blackmail.

chantarelle *noun* var. of CHANTERELLE *noun*[2].

chanter /ˈtʃɑːntə/ *noun*. Also (now *Scot.*) **chaunter** /ˈtʃɔːntə/. LME.

[ORIGIN Anglo-Norman *chauntour*, Old French *chantëor* (mod. *chanteur*), from Latin *cantator* singer, from *cantare*: see CHANT *verb*, -ER[2].]

1 A person who chants or sings; *spec.* (**a**) a chorister; (**b**) a precentor, a cantor; (**c**) a priest who sings masses in a chantry. LME.
2 The melody pipe, with finger holes, of a bagpipe. M17.
3 A person who fraudulently praises horses to sell them. *arch. slang.* M19.
■ **chantership** *noun* the office of a chanter or precentor E16.

chanterelle /ˈtʃɑːntərɛl, tʃɑːntəˈrɛl/ *noun*[1]. E17.
[ORIGIN French, formed as CHANT *verb*: see -EL[2].]
†**1** A decoy bird. Only in E17.
2 The highest-pitched string of a plucked or bowed musical instrument. L18.

chanterelle /ˈtʃɑːntərɛl/ *noun*[2]. Also **-tar-**. L18.
[ORIGIN French, from mod. Latin *cantharellus* dim. of *cantharus* from Greek *kantharos* drinking vessel: see -EL[2].]
A yellow funnel-shaped edible fungus, *Cantharellus cibarius*.
false chanterelle a fungus, *Hygrophoropsis aurantiaca*, resembling the chanterelle but inedible.

chanteuse /ʃɑːnˈtəːz, *foreign* ʃɑ̃tøːz/ *noun*. Pl. pronounced same. M19.
[ORIGIN French.]
A female singer of popular songs, esp. in France.

chantey *noun* var. of SHANTY *noun*[2].

chanticleer /ˈtʃɑːntɪklɪə/ *noun*. Also **C-**. ME.
[ORIGIN Old French *chantecler* (mod. *chanteclair*), the cock in *Reynard the Fox* and Chaucer's *Nun's Priest's Tale*. Cf. PARTLET *noun*[1].]
(A personal name for) a domestic cock.

Chantilly /ʃanˈtɪli; *foreign* ʃɑ̃tiji/ *noun & adjective*. L18.
[ORIGIN A town near Paris, France.]
1 (Designating) a soft-paste porcelain made at Chantilly in the 18th cent. L18.
2 (Designating) a delicate kind of bobbin lace, orig. made near Chantilly. M19.
3 (Designating a dish made with) sweetened whipped cream. M19.
crème Chantilly: see CRÈME 1. *meringue à la Chantilly*, *meringue Chantilly*: see MERINGUE *noun*[1].

chantress /ˈtʃɑːntrɪs/ *noun*. *arch.* LME.
[ORIGIN Old French *chanteresse*, formed as CHANTER: see -ESS[1].]
A female chanter or singer.

chantry /ˈtʃɑːntri/ *noun*. LME.
[ORIGIN Anglo-Norman *chaunterie*, Old French *chanterie*, from *chanter*: see CHANT *verb*, -ERY, -RY.]
†**1** Singing or chanting of the Mass etc. LME–L16.
2 An endowment for a priest or priests to sing Masses for the soul of the founder etc.; the priests, altar, chapel, etc., so endowed. LME.

chanty *noun* var. of SHANTY *noun*[2].

Chanuk(k)ah *nouns* vars. of HANUKKAH.

chaos /ˈkeɪɒs/ *noun*. L15.
[ORIGIN French or Latin from Greek *khaos* vast chasm, void.]
†**1** A gaping void, yawning gulf, chasm, abyss. L15–M17.
2 Formless primordial matter. Now *hist.* or *literary*. M16.
3 (A state of) utter confusion and disorder; *arch.* a confused mass or mixture. M16. ▸**b** SCIENCE. Behaviour of a system which is governed by deterministic laws but is so unpredictable as to appear random, owing to its extreme sensitivity to initial conditions. L20.

A. MILLER The very impulse to write . . springs from an inner chaos crying for order. K. CROSSLEY-HOLLAND The giants . . represent the forces of chaos. B. CASTLE Industrial action which can cause chaos in hospitals.

†**4** An amorphous lump. M–L16.
– COMB.: **chaos theory** the branch of mathematics that deals with complex systems whose behaviour is highly sensitive to slight changes in conditions.
■ **chaˈologist** *noun* an expert in or student of chaology L20. **chaˈology** *noun* the branch of science that deals with chaos L20.

chaotic /keɪˈɒtɪk/ *adjective*. E18.
[ORIGIN from CHAOS after *erotic*, *hypnotic*, etc.]
1 Of or pertaining to primordial chaos. Now *hist.* or *literary*. E18.
2 Utterly confused and disordered; SCIENCE exhibiting or characterized by chaos. M18.
chaotic attractor = *strange attractor* s.v. STRANGE *adjective*.
■ **chaotical** *adjective* (*rare*) L17. **chaotically** *adverb* E19.

chap /tʃap/ *noun*[1]. LME.
[ORIGIN Unknown: rel. to CHAP *verb*[2]. Cf. CHOP *noun*[1].]
1 A crack, an open seam, esp. in the skin or in dry ground. Usu. in *pl.* LME.
2 A stroke, a knock, a rap. *Scot. & N. English.* E16.
– COMB.: **ChapStick** *US* (proprietary name for) a stick of lipsalve.

chap /tʃap/ *noun*[2]. M16.
[ORIGIN Unknown: cf. CHOP *noun*[2].]
1 Either of the jaws of an animal or (*joc.* or *derog.*) a human, as forming part of the mouth. Usu. in *pl.* M16. ▸**b** Either half of the bill of a bird. M17. ▸†**c** In *pl.* The jaws of a vice etc. L17–M19.
2 Either side of the external jaw, a cheek. Usu. in *pl.* E18.
3 The lower jaw. M19.
4 The lower half of the cheek of a pig etc., as food. L19.
Bath chap: see BATH *noun*[1].
– COMB.: **chap-fallen** with the jaw hanging down; dispirited, dejected.
■ **chapless** *adjective* without the lower jaw L16.

chap /tʃap/ *noun*[3]. L16.
[ORIGIN Abbreviation of CHAPMAN.]
1 A buyer, a customer. Now *dial.* L16.
2 A man, a boy, a fellow; in *pl.* also, people. *colloq.* E18.

THACKERAY What sad wild fellows some of the chaps were. E. C. BENTLEY Geography is about Maps But Biography is about Chaps.

chap /tʃap/ *verb*[1] *trans. & intrans. obsolete* exc. *dial.* Infl. **-pp-**. ME.
[ORIGIN In early use, var. of CHEAP *verb*. Later, back-form. from CHAPMAN.]
Buy and sell, barter.

chap /tʃap/ *verb*[2]. Infl. **-pp-**. LME.
[ORIGIN Unknown: rel. to CHAP *noun*[1]. Cf. CHOP *verb*[1].]
▸ **I 1** *verb intrans. & trans.* (Cause to) crack or open in chaps; crack in fissures. LME.
2 *verb trans.* Chop. Long *obsolete* exc. *Scot.* LME.
▸ **II** Strike. *Scot. & N. English.*
3 *verb trans.* Strike. M16.
4 *verb intrans.* Of a clock, the hour: strike. L16.
5 *verb intrans.* Knock, rap, at a door etc. L18.
▸ **III 6** *verb intrans. & trans.* Choose. *Scot.* E18.

chaparejos /ʃapəˈreɪhəʊs, tʃ-/ *noun pl.* *US.* Also **-rreras** /-ˈrɛːrəs/. M19.
[ORIGIN Mexican Spanish *chaparreras*, from *chaparra*, *-o*: see CHAPARRAL. Later form *-ejos* prob. infl. by Spanish *aparejo* equipment.]
= CHAPS.

chaparral /ʃapəˈral, tʃ-/ *noun*. *US.* M19.
[ORIGIN Spanish, from *chaparra*, *-o* dwarf evergreen oak.]
Thicket of dwarf evergreen oaks; dense tangled brushwood.
– COMB.: **chaparral cock** the roadrunner, *Geococcyx californianus*.

chaparreras *noun pl.* see CHAPAREJOS.

chapatti /tʃəˈpɑːti, -ˈpati/ *noun*. Also **chapati**, **chupatti**, & other vars. E19.
[ORIGIN Hindi *capātī*, from *capānā* flatten, roll out, ult. from Dravidian.]
In Indian cookery, a small flat thin cake of coarse unleavened bread.

chapbook /ˈtʃapbʊk/ *noun*. E19.
[ORIGIN from CHAP(MAN + BOOK *noun*.]
Orig. (now *hist.*), a small pamphlet of tales, ballads, tracts, etc., hawked by chapmen. Now (chiefly *N. Amer.*), a small paper-covered booklet of poems, fiction, etc.

chape /tʃeɪp/ *noun & verb*. ME.
[ORIGIN Old French & mod. French = cape, hood (whence Spanish, Portuguese *chapa*) in techn. uses: see CAPE *noun*[1].]
▸ **A** *noun*. †**1** A plate of metal with which anything is overlaid or trimmed. Only in ME.
2 The metal plate of a scabbard, *esp.* that which covers the point. LME.
3 The tip of a fox's tail. L17.
4 The part of a buckle by which it is fastened to a strap. L17.
▸ **B** *verb trans.* Equip (a scabbard etc.) with a chape. LME.
■ **chapeless** *adjective* (*rare*) L16.

chapeau /ˈʃapəʊ/ *noun*. Pl. **-eaux** /-əʊ/. L15.
[ORIGIN French, in Old French *c(h)apel*, from Latin *cappellum* dim. of *cappa* CAP *noun*[1].]
Now chiefly HERALDRY. A cap, a hat; now *esp.* a cap of maintenance, usu. of red velvet turned up ermine.

chapeau-bras /ʃapobra/ *noun*. Pl. ***chapeaux-bras*** (pronounced same). M18.
[ORIGIN French, from CHAPEAU + *bras* arm.]
A three-cornered flat silk hat able to be carried under the arm.

chapeaux *noun* pl. of CHAPEAU.

chapeaux-bras *noun* pl. of CHAPEAU-BRAS.

chapel /ˈtʃap(ə)l/ *noun & adjective*. ME.
[ORIGIN Old French *chapele* from medieval Latin *cappella* dim. of *cappa* cape, cloak: see CAP *noun*[1], -EL[2] 1. Orig. the sanctuary in which the cloak of St Martin was kept.]
▸ **A** *noun*. **1** *gen.* A place of Christian worship other than a parish or cathedral church, *esp.* one attached to a private house or institution. ME.
2 A place for private worship in a larger building, with an altar; *esp.* such a part of a cathedral etc., separately dedicated. ME.
3 A place of public worship of the national episcopal Church subordinate to a parish church. LME.
4 *transf.* A lesser temple, fane, or sanctuary, with an altar to a god. Now *rare.* LME.
5 A choir attached to a chapel (usu. of a monarch or noble); hence, any group of singers or musicians attached to a church or institution. LME.
6 A non-Anglican, esp. Protestant Nonconformist, place of Christian worship. M17.
7 A chapel service; attendance at chapel. M17.

J. AUSTEN Without danger of reprobation because chapel was missed.

8 a A printing works. Now *rare.* L17. ▸**b** A meeting or association of the journeymen in a printing works; the smallest organized union group in a printing works, publishing house, etc. M18.
– PHRASES: **chapel of ease**: for the convenience of remote parishioners. **chapel of rest** an undertaker's mortuary. **chapel royal**: attached to a royal palace. **father of chapel**, **father of the chapel** the spokesman or shop steward of a printers' chapel. *Lady chapel*: see LADY *noun*. *Sistine Chapel*: see SISTINE *adjective*.
– COMB.: **chapel-master** the director of music at a royal etc. chapel; **chapelwarden** (now *rare*) a churchwarden at a chapel.
▸ **B** *adjective*. Belonging to or regularly attending a Nonconformist chapel. *colloq.* M20.

J. CARY Mrs. Wilmot was chapel. I'm sure she never went to a play.

chapelle ardente /ʃapɛl ardɑ̃t/ *noun phr.* Pl. **-s -s** (pronounced same). E19.
[ORIGIN French = burning chapel.]
A chamber prepared for the lying-in-state of a distinguished person, and lit up with candles, torches, etc.

chapelry /ˈtʃap(ə)lri/ *noun*. ME.
[ORIGIN Old French *chapelerie* (in medieval Latin *cappellaria*), formed as CHAPEL: see -ERY, -RY.]
1 A division of a parish, having its own chapel. ME.
2 A chapel with its precinct and accessory buildings. E19.

chaperon /ˈʃapərəʊn/ *noun & verb*. Also **-one**. LME.
[ORIGIN Old French & mod. French, formed as CHAPE.]
▸ **A** *noun*. **1** A hood, a cap. *obsolete* exc. *hist.* LME.
†**2** A small escutcheon placed esp. on the forehead of a horse drawing a hearse. L17–L18.
3 (Now usu. **-one**.) A person who accompanies and looks after a person or group of people; *esp.* a married or older woman accompanying a young unmarried woman to ensure propriety on social occasions. E18.
▸ **B** *verb trans.* Act as a chaperone to. L18.
■ **chaperonage** *noun* attendance as a chaperone. E19. **chaperonless** *adjective* M19.

chaperonin /ʃapəˈrəʊnɪn/ *noun*. L20.
[ORIGIN from CHAPERON + -IN[1].]
BIOCHEMISTRY. A protein that aids the assembly and folding of other protein molecules.

chapiter /ˈtʃapɪtə/ *noun*. See also CHAPTER *noun*. ME.
[ORIGIN Old French & mod. French *chapitre*: see CHAPTER *noun*.]
†**1** Early form of CHAPTER *noun*. ME–M17.
2 ARCHITECTURE. The capital of a column. LME.

†**chapiter** *verb* see CHAPTER *verb*.

chaplain /ˈtʃaplɪn/ *noun*. ME.
[ORIGIN Anglo-Norman, Old French *chapelain* from medieval Latin *cappellanus* (whence earlier CAPELLANE) orig. custodian of the cloak of St Martin, from *cappella*: see CHAPEL, -AN.]
1 The member of clergy attached to a chapel; *spec.* a member of the clergy officiating in the private chapel of a household or institution, on board ship, or for a regiment, school, etc. ME.
2 A nun who recites the inferior services in the chapel of a nunnery. LME.
■ **chaplaincy** *noun* the office or position of a chaplain M18. **chaplainry** *noun* (*obsolete* exc. SCOTTISH HISTORY) = CHAPLAINCY LME. **chaplainship** *noun* = CHAPLAINCY M16.

chaplet /ˈtʃaplɪt/ *noun*. LME
[ORIGIN Old French & mod. French *chapelet* dim. of *chapel* (mod. *chapeau* hat) from Proto-Romance dim. of *cappa* CAPE *noun*[2]: see -LET.]
1 A wreath of flowers, leaves, gold, gems, etc., for the head; a coronal. LME. ▸**b** HERALDRY. A charge representing a garland of leaves with four flowers at equal distances. L17.
2 ARCHITECTURE. A bead moulding. E17.
3 a A string of beads for counting prayers, of five decades. M17. ▸**b** A necklace. M19.
4 FOUNDING. A metal support of the core of a hollow moulding, as a cylindrical pipe. L19.

Chaplinesque /tʃaplɪnˈɛsk/ *adjective*. E20.
[ORIGIN from *Chaplin* (see below) + -ESQUE.]
Resembling or characteristic of the comedy and pathos of the English-born film actor Charles Spencer ('Charlie') Chaplin (1889–1977).

chapman /ˈtʃapmən/ *noun*. Now *arch.* or *hist.* Pl. **-men**.
[ORIGIN Old English *cēapman*, formed as CHEAP *noun* + MAN *noun*.]
1 A man who buys and sells; a merchant, a dealer. OE.
2 *spec.* A pedlar. ME.
†**3** A customer. ME–E19.
†**4** A broker. LME–M17.
■ **chapmanship** *noun* the occupation or activities of a chapman M16.

chappal /ˈtʃap(ə)l/ *noun*. Also **chappli** /ˈtʃapli/. L19.
[ORIGIN Hindi *cappal*, *caplī*.]
In the Indian subcontinent: a sandal, esp. of leather.

chappie /ˈtʃapi/ *noun*. *colloq.* (orig. *Scot.*). Also **-y**. E18.
[ORIGIN from CHAP *noun*[3] + -IE, -Y[6].]
A (little) chap or fellow.

chappli *noun* var. of CHAPPAL.

C

chappow /tʃa'paʊ/ *noun. Indian.* E19.
[ORIGIN Pashto.]
A plundering expedition; a raid.

chappy *noun* var. of CHAPPIE.

chappy /'tʃapi/ *adjective.* E17.
[ORIGIN from CHAP *noun*[1] + -Y[1].]
Full of chaps or clefts.

chaprassi /tʃə'prasi/ *noun.* Pl. **-i(e)s**. Also **chuprassy**. E19.
[ORIGIN Urdu *chaprāsī*, from *chaprās* official badge, from Persian *čaprāst*.]
In the Indian subcontinent: an attendant, a messenger, a household official.

chaps /ʃaps, tʃ-/ *noun pl. N. Amer.* L19.
[ORIGIN Abbreviation of CHAPAREJOS.]
Stout protective trousers for cowboys etc.

chaptalization /tʃaptəlʌɪ'zeɪʃ(ə)n/ *noun.* Also **-isation**. L19.
[ORIGIN from J. A. *Chaptal* (1756–1832), French chemist who invented the process, + -IZATION.]
In wine-making, the correction or improvement of must by the addition of calcium carbonate to neutralize acid or of sugar to increase alcoholic strength.
■ **chaptalize** *verb trans.* correct or improve by chaptalization E20.

chapter /'tʃaptə/ *noun.* Also (earlier) †**chapiter** & other vars. ME.
[ORIGIN Old French & mod. French *chapitre*, earlier *chapitle*, from Latin *capitulum* dim. of *caput* head.]
▸ **I 1** A main division of a book. ME. ▸**b** *ROMAN CATHOLIC CHURCH.* A short scriptural passage or lesson read at certain services. LME. ▸**c** An Act of Parliament numbered as part of a session's proceedings. M16.
2 *fig.* A category, a heading, a subject. *arch.* LME.

HOR. WALPOLE There are some chapters on which I still fear we shall not agree.

3 *transf. & fig.* A part, section, or period. E17.

R. W. EMERSON 'Tis a curious chapter in modern history, the growth of the machine-shop.

▸ **II 4** An assembly or the totality of the canons of a collegiate or cathedral church, or of the members of a monastic or knightly order. ME.
5 A local branch of a society. *N. Amer.* E19.
– PHRASES: **chapter and verse** *fig.* exact reference or authority. ***chapter of accidents***: see ACCIDENT 1b. **to the end of the chapter** *fig.* always, throughout.
– COMB.: **Chapter 11** [with allus. to chapter 11 of the US bankruptcy code] *US* protection from creditors given to a company in financial difficulties for a limited period to allow it to reorganize; **chapter house** a building where a chapter meets; **chapterman** a member of the chapter of a monastic order.

chapter /'tʃaptə/ *verb trans.* Earlier †**chapiter** etc. L15.
[ORIGIN Sense 1 from the noun; sense 2 from French *chapitrer*, formed as CHAPTER *noun*.]
1 Divide into chapters. L15.
2 Reprimand, take to task. *rare.* M16.

†**chapwoman** *noun.* Pl. **-women**. LME–E19.
[ORIGIN from CHAP(MAN + WOMAN *noun*.]
A female pedlar or dealer.

char /tʃɑː/ *noun*[1]. Also (now *rare*) **chare** /tʃɛː/. See also CHORE *noun*[2], JAR *noun*[3]
[ORIGIN Old English *ċerr*, (West Saxon) *ċierr*, late *ċyrr* rel. to CHAR *verb*[1].]
†**1** A return; a turn; an occasion, a time. Long only in ***a-char*** AJAR *adverb*[1] *& pred. adjective*[1]. OE–L18.
†**2** A turn of work; a deed; a piece of business. OE–L17.
3 An odd job, esp. of domestic work; in *pl.*, the housework of a domestic servant. Now only in *comb.* ME.
4 A charwoman. *colloq.* E20.
– COMB.: **charlady**, **charwoman** a woman hired by the hour or day or week to clean rooms in offices or houses.

char /tʃɑː/ *noun*[2]. Now *colloq.* Also **cha**, **chah**. L16.
[ORIGIN Chinese *chá*. Cf. CHAI.]
Tea.

J. COE The least you can do is stand me a cup of char.

– NOTE: Rare (and not naturalized) before E20.

char /tʃɑː/ *noun*[3]. Also **charr**. Pl. same. M17.
[ORIGIN Uncertain: perh. from Celtic.]
A small trout of the genus *Salvelinus*; esp. *S. alpinus* (also ***Arctic char***), of Arctic waters and northern lakes. Also (*N. Amer.*), the brook trout, *S. fontinalis*.

char /tʃɑː/ *noun*[4]. L19.
[ORIGIN from CHAR *verb*[2].]
A charred substance; *esp.* the residue resulting from the removal of volatile materials from coal.

†**char** *noun*[5] see CHAIR *noun*[2].

char /tʃɑː/ *verb*[1]. Infl. **-rr-**. Also (now *rare*) **chare** /tʃɛː/. See also CHORE *verb*.
[ORIGIN Old English *ċierran* rel. to CHAR *noun*[1].]
†**1** *verb trans. & intrans.* Turn; *esp.* turn away or aside. OE–L17.
†**2** *verb trans.* Do (a turn of work). L16–E19.
3 *verb intrans.* Do odd jobs, esp. of domestic work; work as a charwoman. E18.

char /tʃɑː/ *verb*[2]. Infl. **-rr-**. L17.
[ORIGIN App. back-form. from CHARCOAL: cf. CHARK *verb*[2].]
1 *verb trans.* Burn to charcoal; scorch, blacken with fire. L17.
2 *verb intrans.* Become reduced to charcoal. E18.

chara /'kɛːrə/ *noun*[1]. M18.
[ORIGIN Latin, name of an unkn. plant.]
A charophyte of the genus *Chara* (family Characeae), the members of which characteristically are encrusted with lime and have a fetid smell.
■ **cha'raceous** *adjective* resembling a chara; of or pertaining to the family Characeae (the stoneworts): M19.

chara /'ʃarə/ *noun*[2]. *colloq.* E20.
[ORIGIN Abbreviation of CHARABANC.]
A motor coach.

charabanc /'ʃarəbaŋ/ *noun. arch.* Also **char-à-banc**. E19.
[ORIGIN French *char-à-bancs* lit. 'carriage with seats'.]
A long and light vehicle with transverse seats looking forward; a motor coach.

characin /'karəsɪn/ *noun.* L19.
[ORIGIN mod. Latin *Characinus* genus name, from Greek *kharax* a kind of fish, lit. 'pointed stake'.]
A freshwater fish of the large family Characidae, most members of which (e.g. the piranhas, tetras) occur in S. and Central America.

charact /'karakt/ *noun. arch.* Also †**car-**. LME.
[ORIGIN Old French *c(h)aract* masc., *c(h)aracte* fem., perh. ult. from Greek *kharaktos* given or impressed as a mark, taken as noun.]
†**1** A mark, a sign; an engraved or impressed character. LME–M17.
2 A magical or kabbalistic sign or emblem. LME.

character /'karəktə/ *noun.* ME.
[ORIGIN Old French & mod. French *caractère* from Latin *character* from Greek *kharaktēr* instrument for marking, from *kharassein* engrave; assim. to Latin in 16.]
1 A distinctive mark impressed, engraved, or otherwise formed. *arch.* in *gen.* sense. ME.
2 = CHARACT 2. *arch.* LME. ▸†**b** *gen.* A symbol, an emblem; a representation. E17–E18.
3 A graphic symbol, *esp.* one denoting a sound or idea. Usu. in *pl.* L15. ▸**b** A writing system, a set of letters etc.; writing, printing; a style of writing or printing. *arch.* L16. ▸†**c** In *pl.* Shorthand. M17–E18. ▸†**d** A cipher for secret correspondence etc. M17–M18. ▸**e** *COMPUTING.* A letter, digit, or other symbol which can be read, stored, and output by a computer; a representation of such a symbol. M20.

F. KING Some in Western letters and some in Japanese characters. D. WALCOTT An old lady writes me in a spidery style, Each character trembling. **b** SPENSER The Saxons Character is the same with the Irish. SHAKES. *Meas. for M.* Here is the hand and seal of the Duke. You know the character, I doubt not.

4 *fig.* A token; a feature, trait, characteristic. *arch.* in *gen.* sense. E16. ▸**b** *BIOLOGY.* A distinguishing characteristic of a species etc. E18.

BURKE Tell me, what one character of liberty the Americans have.

5 A description; *spec.* a description or detailed report of a person's qualities, a testimonial. M16.

A. WILSON If you land back in the approved school don't come to me for a good character.

6 The estimate formed of a person's qualities; reputation; good repute. E17.

E. A. FREEMAN His character for sanctity.

†**7** Personal appearance. E17–M18.
8 Collective peculiarities; nature, sort, style; the distinctive mental or moral qualities of an individual, a people, etc.; distinction, individuality. E17.

A. CRUMP The amount and character of the deposits of English banks. M. INNES Inquiries on the character and habits of the missing girl. C. G. SELIGMAN In character the Tuareg are independent, brave, impulsive, and mendacious.

9 Recognized official rank; status, position; role. M17.

G. BURNET He had the appointments of an ambassador, but would not take the character.

10 a A person regarded as the possessor of specified qualities; a personage, a personality. M17. ▸**b** A person portrayed in a novel, a drama, etc; a part played by an actor or (*arch.*) a dissembler. M17. ▸**c** An eccentric or noticeable person. L18.

a L. P. HARTLEY Both were exceedingly strong characters. J. CANNAN The character who owns *Mab* . . leaves his gear out in her. **b** G. GREENE A story with a senior civil servant as the main character.

11 Moral strength, esp. if highly developed or evident. M18.

DAY LEWIS A delicate vivid face, giving an impression of character beyond her years.

– PHRASES: **in character** in accord with a person's nature and reputation. ***optical character reader***, ***optical character recognition***: see OPTICAL *adjective*. **out of character** at variance with a person's nature and reputation. ***social character***: see SOCIAL *adjective*. ***specific character***: see SPECIFIC *adjective*. ***titular character***: see TITULAR *adjective* 3. ***unit character***: see UNIT *noun*[1] & *adjective*.
– COMB.: **character actor**, **character actress**: specializing in character parts; **character assassination** deliberate destruction of a person's reputation; **character part** an acting part requiring strong delineation of individual, esp. eccentric or unusual, character; **character reference** a testimonial to a person's qualities; **character sketch** a brief (written) description of a person's qualities; **character string** a linear sequence of characters, esp. stored in or processed by a computer; **character witness** a person who attests to another person's good reputation.
■ **characterful** *adjective* full of character, individual E20. **characterless** *adjective* without character or individuality E17. **characterlessness** *noun* M19. **charactery**, **-try** *noun* (now *poet.*) expression of thought by symbols or characters; the symbols or characters collectively: L16.

character /'karəktə/ *verb trans. arch.* L16.
[ORIGIN from the noun.]
1 Engrave; inscribe. L16.
2 Represent, portray. L16.
3 Describe. (Foll. by †*as*, †*to be*.) Cf. CHARACTERIZE 2. E17.
4 = CHARACTERIZE 4. M17.
5 = CHARACTERIZE 5. M17.

†**characterical** *adjective.* E17.
[ORIGIN from Greek *kharaktērikos*, from *kharaktēr*: see CHARACTER *noun*, -ICAL.]
1 Characteristic, distinctive. E17–M18.
2 Of or pertaining to symbolic characters, magical symbols, or charms. M–L17.

characterisation *noun*, **characterise** *verb* vars. of CHARACTERIZATION, CHARACTERIZE.

†**characterism** *noun.* Also (earlier) in Latin form **-ismus**. M16.
[ORIGIN Late Latin *characterismus* from Greek *kharaktērismos*, from *kharaktēr*: see CHARACTER *noun*, -ISM.]
1 Characterization, description of character. M16–E19.
2 Characteristic quality; a characteristic. M17–L19.

characteristic /karəktə'rɪstɪk/ *adjective & noun.* M17.
[ORIGIN French *caractéristique* or medieval Latin *characteristicus* from late Greek *kharaktēristikos*, from Greek *kharaktēr*: see CHARACTER *noun*, -ISTIC.]
▸ **A** *adjective.* Indicative of character; typical; distinctive. (Foll. by *of*.) M17.
characteristic curve: showing the relation between two interdependent quantities (esp. properties of a device). ***STATIC characteristic curve***.
▸ **B** *noun.* **1** A distinctive mark; a distinguishing trait, peculiarity, or quality. M17.
2 *MATH.* The integral part of a logarithm. M17.
3 A characteristic curve. E20.
mutual characteristic: see MUTUAL *adjective*. ***STATIC characteristic***.
■ **characteristical** *adjective & noun* (**a**) *adjective* (*arch.*) = CHARACTERISTIC *adjective*; †(**b**) *noun* = CHARACTERISTIC *noun* 1: E17. **characteristically** *adverb* M17. **characteristicalness** *noun* (*arch.*) L18. **characteristicness** *noun* E19.

characterization /karəkt(ə)rʌɪ'zeɪʃ(ə)n/ *noun.* Also **-isation**. L16.
[ORIGIN from CHARACTERIZE + -ATION.]
The action or result of characterizing; *esp.* (**a**) portrayal in words etc., description; (**b**) the (effective) creation of a fictitious character or fictitious characters.

characterize /'karəktərʌɪz/ *verb.* Also **-ise**. L16.
[ORIGIN French *caractériser* or medieval Latin *characterizare*, from Greek *kharaktērizein*, from *kharaktēr*: see CHARACTER *noun*, -IZE.]
†**1** *verb trans.* Engrave, inscribe; = CHARACTER *verb* 1. L16–E19.
2 *verb trans.* Describe the character or peculiar qualities of; describe *as* (also †*to be*). E17.

J. BARNES Tasks which in human society might be characterized as 'female'.

†**3** Represent, portray; = CHARACTER *verb* 2. M17–E18.
4 *verb trans.* Mark or distinguish as a character does; be a characteristic of. M18.

Architectural Review The muscularly chunky buildings that characterize Dallas.

5 *verb intrans. & trans.* Impart character (to). E19.
■ **characterizer** *noun* M18.

characterology /karəktə'rɒlədʒi/ *noun.* E20.
[ORIGIN from CHARACTER *noun* + -OLOGY, translating German *Charakterologie*.]
The branch of psychology that deals with character, esp. its development and variation between individuals.
■ **charactero'logical** *adjective* E20. **characterologist** *noun* E20.

charade /ʃə'rɑːd/ *noun.* L18.
[ORIGIN French from mod. Provençal *charrado* conversation, from *charra* chatter, perh. of imit. origin.]
1 A written or (now usu.) acted clue from which a syllable of a word or a complete word is to be guessed. L18. ▸**b** (In *pl.* usu. treated as *sing.*) A game of guessing words from such clues. M19.
2 *fig.* An absurd pretence. L19.

charango /tʃəˈraŋɡəʊ/ *noun*. Pl. **-os**. **E20**.
[ORIGIN S. Amer. Spanish.]
A small South American musical instrument resembling a guitar, with a soundbox traditionally made from the shell of an armadillo.

charas /ˈtʃɑːrəs/ *noun*. Also **churrus** /ˈtʃʌrəs/. **M19**.
[ORIGIN Hindi *caras*.]
A narcotic resin from the flower heads of hemp; cannabis resin.

charbroil /ˈtʃɑːbrɔɪl/ *verb trans*. Orig. *US*. **M20**.
[ORIGIN from CHARCOAL *noun* + BROIL *verb*¹.]
Grill (meat etc.) on a rack over charcoal.

charchaf *noun* var. of CHARSHAF.

charcoal /ˈtʃɑːkəʊl/ *noun & verb*. **LME**.
[ORIGIN Uncertain: connected with COAL *noun* in sense 'charcoal'.]
▸ **A** *noun*. **1** *sing*. & †in *pl*. The black porous residue of partly burnt wood, bones, etc., a form of carbon. **LME**. ***activated charcoal***: see ACTIVATE *verb* 1. ***active charcoal***: see ACTIVE *adjective* 5. ***mineral charcoal***: see MINERAL *adjective*.
2 A charcoal pencil or crayon; a drawing in this medium. **L17**.
3 In full ***charcoal grey***. A dark grey. **E20**.
– COMB.: **charcoal biscuit**: containing wood charcoal as an aid to digestion; **charcoal burner** a maker of charcoal; **charcoal filter**: using charcoal to absorb impurities; ***charcoal grey***: see sense 3 above.
▸ **B** *verb trans*. **1** Mark, write, or blacken with charcoal. **M19**.
2 Suffocate with the fumes of charcoal. **M19**.

charcuterie /ʃɑːˈkuːt(ə)ri, *foreign* ʃarkytri/ *noun*. **M19**.
[ORIGIN French, from †*char* (mod. *chair*) *cuite* cooked flesh: see -ERY.]
Cold cooked meats; a shop selling these; a (French) pork butcher's shop.
■ ***charcutier*** /ʃarkytje (*pl. same*); ʃɑːˈkuːtɪeɪ/ *noun* a (French) pork butcher; a person who prepares or sells charcuterie: **L19**.

chard /tʃɑːd/ *noun*. Also **sh-** /ʃ-/. **M17**.
[ORIGIN French *carde*, perh. alt. by assoc. with *chardon* thistle: see CARDOON.]
The blanched shoots of globe artichoke or salsify. Also (more fully ***Swiss chard***), (the edible leaves and stalks of) seakale beet.

Chardonnay /ˈʃɑːdəneɪ/ *noun*. **E20**.
[ORIGIN French.]
(The vine bearing) a white grape used in wine-making; a dry white wine made from these grapes. Also ***Pinot Chardonnay***.

chare /tʃɛː/ *noun*¹. *N. English*. **ME**.
[ORIGIN Perh. same word as CHARE *noun*², CHAR *noun*¹.]
A narrow lane; an alley.

chare *noun*², *verb* see CHAR *noun*¹, *verb*¹.

charentais /ˈʃarənteɪ/ *noun*. **M20**.
[ORIGIN French, lit. 'from the Charentes region'.]
A melon of a small variety with a pale green rind and orange flesh.

charette /ʃaˈrɛt/ *noun*. Also †**-et**. **LME**.
[ORIGIN Old French & mod. French, formed as CHAIR *noun*²: see -ET¹, -ETTE.]
†**1** A cart; a chariot. **LME–E19**.
2 [With ref. to the use of a cart in the École des Beaux-Arts in Paris in the 19th cent. to collect students' work just prior to a deadline] *N. Amer*. ▸**a** A period designated for intense work, esp. in order to meet a deadline. **M20**. ▸**b** A meeting or conference devoted to a concerted effort to solve a problem or plan something. **M20**.

charge /tʃɑːdʒ/ *noun*. **ME**.
[ORIGIN Old French & mod. French from Proto-Romance, from late Latin *car(ri)care*: see CHARGE *verb*.]
▸ **I** †**1** A (material) load, burden, or weight. **ME–E18**.
2 *fig*. A load (of trouble, inconvenience, etc.); a source of trouble or inconvenience. **ME**.

A. FRASER The village was selfishly concerned that the baby should not be abandoned there, as a charge on the parish.

3 A task or duty laid upon one; commission, responsibility. **ME**.

W. S. CHURCHILL I have therefore laid down the charge which was placed upon me.

4 The duty or responsibility of taking care *of* (a person or thing); care, custody, control, superintendence. **LME**. ▸**b** A thing or person entrusted to the care of someone; *spec*. the people or district committed to the care of a member of the clergy. **M16**.

b J. FOWLES That sustained . . attention to her charges that a governess's duties require.

†**5** Importance, moment. **LME–L16**.

SHAKES. *Rom. & Jul.* The letter was not nice, but full of charge Of dear import.

6 a Pecuniary burden, cost. *arch*. **LME**. ▸**b** *sing*. & in *pl*. Expense. *arch*. **E16**. ▸**c** COMMERCE. In *pl*. Incidental expenses. **M16**. ▸**d** A price required or demanded for service rendered or goods supplied. **E19**.

b THACKERAY A . . cathedral built by the present bishop at his own charges. LD MACAULAY Well armed and mounted at their own charge. **d** A. C. BOULT The charge for admission . . was always one penny.

7 A liability to pay money laid on a person or estate. **LME**.
8 A precept, an order, *spec*. an official instruction or admonition given by a judge to a jury, by a bishop to his clergy, etc. **LME**.

H. JAMES The very words of the lady of Woollett . . ; her parting charge to her child.

9 An accusation; *spec*. that upon which a prisoner is brought up for trial. **L15**.

R. TRAVERS His warrant for the arrest of one Frank Harwood . . on the charge of wilful murder.

bring a charge (against), ***lay a charge (against)***, ***prefer a charge (against)***, etc.

10 HERALDRY. A device or bearing placed on a shield, crest, or supporter. **L16**.
11 FARRIERY. A thick adhesive plaster; a protective pad for the foot. **E17**.
12 The quantity of something which a receptacle, mechanism, etc., is designed to bear or receive at one time; *esp*. the appropriate quantity of explosive for a gun. **M17**. ▸**b** A quantity of explosive; an explosive device. **L19**.

POPE A charge of snuff the wily virgin threw. S. SASSOON The trigger . . had come loose . . and wouldn't fire the charge. **b** F. FITZGERALD The Viet Cong had set off plastic charges in the midst of the crowd.

13 a An accumulation of electricity on or in a body, or of chemical energy in a battery that is available for conversion to electricity; the amount of this, = ***electric charge*** s.v. ELECTRIC *adjective*. Also, the process of charging a battery. **M18**. ▸**b** *fig*. A concentration of emotion etc. **M19**. ▸**c** A quantity of electricity borne by an atom, molecule, or subatomic particle. **L19**.

b P. BROOK A verse play is half way between prose and the opera, . . yet with a higher charge than prose.

14 *slang*. **a** A dose or injection of a drug. **E20**. ▸**b** A thrill; a sharp stimulant effect; a feeling of excitement or satisfaction. **M20**. ▸**c** Marijuana. **M20**.

b J. RABAN It gives one a charge as strong as a snift of cocaine. **c** *Melody Maker* Smoking charge on the premises.

▸ **II 15** A rushing attack by soldiers, police, members of a team, an animal, etc.; an attack made by throwing oneself against an opponent in football etc. **M16**. ▸**b** MILITARY. A signal for attack sounded on a trumpet or other instrument. **M17**.

P. G. WODEHOUSE The Old Guard made their last desperate charge up the blood-soaked slopes of Waterloo. **b** C. S. FORESTER He yelled to his bugler to sound the charge.

†**16** The position of a weapon ready for action. **L16–M17**.
– PHRASES: **free of charge** without payment. **give in charge** hand over (a person) to the custody of the police. **in charge** in control, with overall responsibility. **in charge of** (*a*) under the supervision or control of; (*b*) having supervision or control of. **lay to someone's charge** impute to someone as a fault; charge someone with. **on a charge** accused of a particular offence under (esp. military) law. **on charge** (of a battery) being charged. ***prior charge***: see PRIOR *adjective*. **put in charge** cause (a person) to have supervision or control. **put on a charge** accuse of a particular offence under (esp. military) law. **return to the charge** *fig*. begin again, esp. in argument. ***reverse the charges***: see REVERSE *verb* 7. ***shaped charge***: see SHAPED 1. ***specific charge***: see SPECIFIC *adjective*. STRATIFIED ***charge***. **take charge** assume control or direction (*of*); *colloq*. (of things) get out of control, esp. with disastrous results.
– COMB.: **charge account** a credit account at a shop etc.; **charge-book**: in which are recorded cases and charges at a police court; **charge cap** an imposed upper limit on the amount that can be charged; **charge-cap** *verb trans*. subject to charge-capping; **charge-capping** imposition of an upper limit on the amount that can be charged, esp. by a local authority for public services; **charge card** a credit card, esp. for use at a particular store or chain of stores or for an account which must be cleared in full on receipt of a statement; **charge carrier** = CARRIER *noun* 9; **charge-coupled device** ELECTRONICS a sensitive semiconductor device used to record images (e.g. in large telescopes), in which the image is formed on a light-sensitive surface as small packets of electric charge, from which an array of pixels is created electronically; abbreviation *CCD*; **chargehand** a worker who is in charge of others; **charge house** †(*a*) a (boarding) school; (*b*) a workshop in which explosive is loaded into shells etc.; **charge nurse**: in charge of a ward etc.; **charge sheet**: on which are recorded cases and charges made at a police station.
■ †**chargeful** *adjective* burdensome; costly; full of responsibility: **LME–E17**. **chargeless** *adjective* (now *rare*) **L16**.

charge /tʃɑːdʒ/ *verb*. **ME**.
[ORIGIN Old French & mod. French *charger* from late Latin *car(ri)care* to load, from Latin *carrus* CAR.]
▸ **I 1** *verb trans*. Place a load on or in. *obsolete* exc. as passing into other senses. **ME**. ▸†**b** Overload. **LME–L18**.
2 *verb trans*. Load or fill (a thing) to the full or proper extent; *spec*. load (a gun) with explosive and shot. **ME**. ▸**b** Load, fill, saturate, *with* (*lit. & fig.*); imbue *with*. **L16**. ▸**c** Give an electric charge to (a body); store a charge in (a battery etc.). Also foll. by *up*. **M18**.

J. HERRIOT A bottle of Glenlivet Malt to charge Granville's glass. **b** E. A. PARKES Water highly charged with calcium carbonate. H. JAMES A table charged with purchases. T. COLLINS The air was still charged with dust. W. C. WILLIAMS Poetry is language charged with emotion. F. HERBERT Starlight displaced just enough of the night to charge each shadow with menace.

†**3** *verb trans*. Burden *with* sin, guilt, sickness, etc. **ME–M17**.
†**4** *verb trans*. Burden with or put to expense etc. **ME–M17**.
5 *verb trans*. Entrust or commission *with* as a duty, task, or responsibility. **ME**.

J. C. RANSOM The department of English is charged with . . the communication of literature.

6 *verb trans*. Command, order, *to do*, *that* (with subjunct.). **ME**. ▸**b** Deliver an official or formal instruction or exhortation to. **E17**.

SIR W. SCOTT He charged, That his array Should southward march. R. V. JONES Stafford Cripps was charged by Churchill to conduct an enquiry.

7 *verb trans*. Blame, censure; accuse, *spec*. of a particular offence under law. (Foll. by *with* an offence.) **ME**. ▸**b** Lay as a charge *against*, *on*, *upon*; state or assert in an indictment; make the charge *that*. **E17**.

F. RAPHAEL Cricklewood Police Station where his father had been charged. H. KISSINGER He had charged his predecessors with weakness. **b** DRYDEN Charge the crime, On native sloth. L. A. FIEDLER It has been charged against vulgar art that it is sadistic. S. KINGSLEY Mr. Reynolds charges you gave him money from the public treasuries.

†**8** *verb trans*. Attach weight or importance to; regard. **ME–M16**.
9 a *verb trans*. Subject or make liable (a person, estate, etc.) to a pecuniary obligation or liability. (Foll. by *with* the liability.) **ME**. ▸**b** *verb trans*. Require or demand (a price, *for* service rendered or goods supplied); impose as a liability or pecuniary charge (*on* a person, estate, etc.); put as a charge (*up*) *to*, *against*, *on*, an account; debit to an account. **L18**. ▸**c** *verb trans*. with double obj. Require or demand (a price) from (a person etc.). (Foll. by *for*.) **M19**. ▸**d** *verb intrans*. Make a pecuniary charge. **M19**.

a W. CRUISE: H. Lawson . . charged all his personal estate, with the payment of his debts. **b** A. LOOS They would charge up all the bills to Lady Francis Beekman. W. FAULKNER Have you been charging things at stores again? T. S. ELIOT The villages dirty and charging high prices. E. WAUGH This is the first time I've charged anything on expenses. G. M. FRASER Fifteen dollars a bottle they were charging for claret. **c** OED They were charged five shillings a head for dinner. **d** MRS H. WOOD I could not charge . . please say no more about payment.

10 HERALDRY. Place a bearing on (an escutcheon or another bearing). **L16**.
charged with bearing.
▸ **II 11** *verb trans*. & *intrans*. Make a rushing attack (on); rush or throw oneself (against or upon) with all one's force. **LME**.

M. MITCHELL Charging up the hill at his usual breakneck speed. M. ROBERTS I thought I was going to be killed when those police horses charged us.

12 *verb trans*. Place (a weapon) in position for action. **E16**.
■ **chargeable** *adjective* †(*a*) of the nature of a charge or burden; responsible; burdensome; costly; (*b*) able or liable to be charged: **LME**. **charged** *ppl adjective* that has been charged, now *spec*. with electricity or (*fig*.) emotion etc. **LME**.

chargé /ˈʃɑːʒeɪ, *foreign* ʃarʒe (*pl. same*)/ *noun*. **M19**.
[ORIGIN Abbreviation.]
= CHARGÉ D'AFFAIRES.

chargé d'affaires /ˌʃɑːʒeɪ daˈfɛː, *foreign* ʃarʒe dafɛːr/ *noun phr*. Pl. **chargés d'affaires** (pronounced same). Also †**chargé des affaires**. **M18**.
[ORIGIN French = (a person) in charge of affairs.]
1 A minister who transacts diplomatic business during the temporary absence of an ambassador; a state's representative at a minor foreign court or government. **M18**.
2 *gen*. A person temporarily in charge. **L18**.

chargee /tʃɑːˈdʒiː/ *noun*. **L19**.
[ORIGIN from CHARGE *verb* or *noun* + -EE¹.]
LAW. The person entitled to enforce a charge on land or other property to secure the repayment of a loan or other obligation

charger /ˈtʃɑːdʒə/ *noun*¹. **ME**.
[ORIGIN Anglo-Norman *chargeour* (cf. Old French *chargeoir* basket strapped on the back, *chargeoire* device for loading guns): see CHARGE *verb*, -OUR, -ER².]
A large plate or flat dish.

charger /ˈtʃɑːdʒə/ *noun*². **L15**.
[ORIGIN from CHARGE *verb* + -ER¹.]
1 An appliance for charging a gun, rifle, electric battery, etc. **L15**.
2 A person who makes a charge, an accuser. *rare*. **L16**.
3 A cavalry horse; *poet*. any horse. **M18**.
4 LAW. A person who must pay a charge on an estate etc. Now *rare*. **M19**.

chargrill /ˈtʃɑːɡrɪl/ *verb trans*. **L20**.
[ORIGIN from CHAR(COAL *noun* + GRILL *verb*.]
Grill (food, esp. meat or fish) quickly at a very high heat.

C

chariot /ˈtʃarɪət/ *noun & verb*. LME.
[ORIGIN Old French & mod. French, augm. of *char* ult. from Latin *carrum*, *-us*: see CAR. Cf. CHAIR *noun*², CHARETTE.]
▸ **A** *noun*. A wheeled conveyance, usu. horse-drawn, *spec.* †(**a**) a cart, a wagon; (**b**) *poet.* a stately or triumphal carriage; (**c**) a two-wheeled vehicle used in ancient warfare and racing; (**d**) (chiefly *hist.*) a light four-wheeled carriage with back seats only. LME.
▸ **B** *verb*. **1** *verb intrans.* Drive or ride in a chariot. M16.
2 *verb trans.* Carry or convey in or as a chariot. M17.
■ **charioˈtee** *noun* (US HISTORY) a light four-wheeled pleasure carriage with two seats E19. **chariotry** *noun* †(**a**) *rare* the art of driving a chariot; (**b**) the body of soldiers who fought from chariots: L17.

charioteer /tʃarɪəˈtɪə/ *noun & verb*. ME.
[ORIGIN Old French *charieter*, *charioteur*, formed as CHARIOT; later directly from CHARIOT.: see -EER.]
▸ **A** *noun*. **1** The driver of a chariot. ME.
2 (Usu. **C-**.) *The* constellation Auriga. E20.
▸ **B** *verb*. **1** *verb intrans. & trans.* Drive (a chariot). E19.
2 *verb trans.* Drive (a person) in a chariot. M19.
■ **charioteership** *noun* performance as a charioteer M19.

charism /ˈkarɪz(ə)m/ *noun*. L15.
[ORIGIN formed as CHARISMA.]
CHRISTIAN THEOLOGY. = CHARISMA 1.

charisma /kəˈrɪzmə/ *noun*. Pl. **-mata** /-mətə/. M17.
[ORIGIN ecclesiastical Latin from Greek *kharisma*, *-mat-*, from *kharis* favour, grace.]
1 CHRISTIAN THEOLOGY. A divinely conferred power or talent. M17.
2 A capacity to inspire devotion and enthusiasm; aura. M20.

charismatic /karɪzˈmatɪk/ *adjective & noun*. L19.
[ORIGIN from Greek *kharismat-* (see CHARISMA) + -IC.]
▸ **A** *adjective*. **1** CHRISTIAN THEOLOGY. Of or pertaining to a charisma; divinely conferred. L19. ▸**b** Designating, of, or pertaining to Christian worship marked by enthusiasm, spontaneity, ecstatic utterance, etc.; Pentecostal. M20.
2 Having charisma. M20.
▸ **B** *noun*. CHRISTIAN THEOLOGY. A person who claims divine inspiration; an adherent of charismatic worship. M20.
■ **charismatically** *adverb* M20.

charitable /ˈtʃarɪtəb(ə)l/ *adjective*. ME.
[ORIGIN Old French & mod. French, formed as CHARITY: see -ABLE.]
†**1** Showing Christian charity or the love of God and man. ME–M17.
†**2** Tender-hearted; loving; benevolent. LME–M17.
3 Full of active charity to others; *esp.* generous in giving to the poor. LME.
4 Connected with or devoted to a recognized object of charity; of the nature of a charity. L16.

I. MURDOCH A charitable organization supported mainly by American contributions.

5 Apt to judge favourably of persons, acts, motives, etc. E17.

BACON By a charitable construction it may be a sermon. A. F. DOUGLAS-HOME The most even-tempered and charitable of persons.

■ **charitableness** *noun* LME. **charitably** *adverb* LME.

charitarian /tʃarɪˈtɛːrɪən/ *noun*. *rare*. M19.
[ORIGIN from CHARITY + -ARIAN.]
A supporter of charities; a do-gooder.

charitative /ˈtʃarɪtətɪv/ *adjective*. Now *rare*. LME.
[ORIGIN Old French *charitatif* from medieval Latin *caritativus*, from Latin *caritat-*: see CHARITY, -IVE.]
1 Of the nature of or pertaining to charity. LME.
†**2** Of the nature of a charitable gift or donation. L16–E18.

charity /ˈtʃarɪti/ *noun*. LOE.
[ORIGIN Old French & mod. French *charité* from Latin *caritas*, from *carus* dear: see -ITY. Cf. CARITAS.]
1 Christian love; *esp.* Christian love of other people. LOE.
2 *gen.* Love, kindness, natural affection; spontaneous goodness. ME. ▸†**b** Fairness, equity. LME–M17. ▸**c** A disposition to think favourably of others, their actions, etc., and to make allowance for their shortcomings. L15. ▸**d** In *pl.* Feelings or acts of affection. M17.
3 Beneficence; liberality to or provision for those in need or distress; alms-giving. ME. ▸**b** Money, a gift, or other assistance to relieve need or distress. ME. ▸**c** A trust, foundation, organization, etc., for the benefit of those in need or distress; such trusts etc. viewed collectively. L16. ▸**d** In *pl.* Acts or works of liberality. E17.

R. H. TAWNEY Each town must organize charity for the support of the honest poor. *Proverb*: Charity begins at home. **c** P. AUSTER So much money pours in now, we give half of it to charity. *New Yorker* The Afghan Development Association is a charity funded by the government.

charity ball, ***charity concert***, etc. ***cold as charity*** (with allus. to the unsympathetic administration of charity). **Brother of Charity**, **Sister of Charity** a male, female, member of a religious order devoted to charity. ***legal charity***: see LEGAL *adjective*.
– COMB.: **Charity Commission**, **Charity Commissioners** (the members of) a board established to control charitable trusts; **charity school**: supported by charitable contributions; **charity shop** a shop where second-hand goods are sold to raise money for a charity; **charity walk** a sponsored walk to raise money for a charity; **charity walker** a participant in a charity walk.

charivari /ʃɑːrɪˈvɑːri/ *noun & verb*. See also SHIVAREE. M17.
[ORIGIN French, of unknown origin.]
▸ **A** *noun*. A cacophonous mock serenade in derision of an unpopular person, marriage, etc.; a discordant medley of sounds, a hubbub. M17.
▸ **B** *verb trans.* Greet or serenade with a charivari. E19.

chark /tʃɑːk/ *noun*. *obsolete* exc. *dial.* E18.
[ORIGIN App. from CHARK *verb*².]
Charred wood or coal; charcoal.

chark /tʃɑːk/ *verb*¹ *intrans.* *obsolete* exc. *dial.*
[ORIGIN Old English *ċearcian*: cf. CHIRK *verb*.]
1 Grind one's teeth; (of teeth) grind. OE.
†**2** Creak. Only in LME.
3 Complain querulously. *Scot.* E19.

chark /tʃɑːk/ *verb*² *trans.* M17.
[ORIGIN from CHARCOAL analysed as *chark coal*: cf. CHAR *verb*².]
Burn to charcoal or coke; char.

charkha /ˈtʃəːkə/ *noun*. Also **-ka**. L19.
[ORIGIN Urdu *charqa*, *-kā* spinning wheel from Persian *čarq(a)* rel. to Sanskrit *cakra* wheel.]
In the Indian subcontinent: a domestic spinning wheel, used chiefly for cotton.

charlatan /ˈʃɑːlət(ə)n/ *noun & adjective*. E17.
[ORIGIN French from Italian *ciarlatano*, from *ciarlare* to babble, patter, of imit. origin.]
▸ **A** *noun*. **1** A mountebank; *esp.* an itinerant vendor of medicines. *obsolete* exc. as passing into sense 2. E17.
2 A false pretender to knowledge or skill, orig. and esp. in medicine; a quack; a pretentious impostor. L17.
▸ **B** *adjective*. Of, pertaining to, or characteristic of a charlatan. L17.
■ **charlatanic** /ʃɑːləˈtanɪk/ *adjective* M19. **charlatanical** /ʃɑːləˈtanɪk(ə)l/ *adjective* M17. **charlatanism** *noun* the practice or method of a charlatan; the condition of being a charlatan: E19. **charlatanry** *noun* quackery, imposture M17.

Charles' law /ˈtʃɑːlz lɔː/ *noun phr.* Also **Charles's law** /ˈtʃɑːlzɪz lɔː/. L19.
[ORIGIN J. A. C. *Charles* (1746–1823), French physicist.]
CHEMISTRY. A law stating that the volume of an ideal gas at constant pressure is directly proportional to the absolute temperature.

Charles's Wain /tʃɑːlzɪz ˈweɪn/ *noun phr.*
[ORIGIN Old English *Carles wæġn* the wain of Carl or Charles (Charlemagne), perh. by assoc. of the star Arcturus with King Arthur, himself assoc. with Charlemagne.]
The Plough (PLOUGH *noun* 4).

Charleston /ˈtʃɑːlst(ə)n, -lz-/ *noun & verb*. Also **c-**. E20.
[ORIGIN A city and county in S. Carolina, USA.]
▸ **A** *noun*. A dance characterized by side-kicks from the knee. E20.
▸ **B** *verb intrans.* Dance the Charleston; kick sideways from the knee. E20.

Charley *noun* var. of CHARLIE.

charley horse /ˈtʃɑːli hɔːs/ *noun phr.* *N. Amer. slang*. L19.
[ORIGIN Unknown.]
Stiffness or cramp in an arm or a leg.

Charlie /ˈtʃɑːli/ *noun*. Also **-ley**, **c-**. E19.
[ORIGIN Dim. of male forename *Charles*: see -IE, -Y⁶.]
†**1** A night watchman. E–M19.
2 A small triangular beard, as worn by King Charles I. E19.
3 A name for the fox. M19.
4 In *pl.* A woman's breasts. *slang*. L19.
5 Cocaine. *slang*. M20.
6 A fool, an idiot. *slang*. M20.
7 A native or inhabitant, esp. a soldier, of (North) Vietnam. *US & Austral. slang*. M20.
– PHRASES: ***Champagne Charlie***: see CHAMPAGNE. TAIL-END ***Charlie***.

charlock /ˈtʃɑːlɒk/ *noun*.
[ORIGIN Old English *ċerlic*, *ċyrlic*, of unknown origin.]
Wild mustard, *Sinapis arvensis*, a yellow-flowered cruciferous weed of cultivated land. Formerly also, any of several other similar plants.

charlotte /ˈʃɑːlɒt/ *noun*. L18.
[ORIGIN French.]
A pudding made of stewed fruit with a casing or covering of bread, biscuits, sponge cake, or breadcrumbs.
charlotte russe /ruːs/ [French *russe* Russian.] a custard etc. enclosed in a sponge cake or sponge biscuits.

charm /tʃɑːm/ *noun*¹. ME.
[ORIGIN Old French & mod. French *charme* from Latin *carmen* song, verse, oracular response, incantation.]
1 The chanting of a verse supposedly having magic power; an incantation; any action, process, verse, etc., credited with such properties; a magic spell, a talisman. ME.
2 A quality or feature exciting love or admiration; attractiveness; the indefinable power of delighting; in *pl.*, sexual attractiveness. L16.

Argosy Extolling her charms so highly that Elizabeth experienced a pang of jealousy. A. CARTER His stock in trade is boyish charm.

3 A thing worn to avert evil etc.; an amulet; a trinket on a bracelet etc. L16.
4 PARTICLE PHYSICS. A quark flavour associated with a charge of +⅔. (Symbol *c*.) M20.
– PHRASES: **work like a charm** work perfectly.
– COMB.: **charm bracelet**: hung with charms; **charm school**: at which the social graces are taught.
■ **charmful** *adjective* full of charms or spells; charming: M17. **charmless** *adjective* lacking charm; unattractive or unpleasant: E18. **charmlessly** *adverb* L19. **charmlessness** *noun* E20.

charm *noun*² see CHIRM *noun*.

charm /tʃɑːm/ *verb*¹. ME.
[ORIGIN Old French & mod. French *charmer*, formed as CHARM *noun*¹. Sense 7 prob. infl. by CHARM *noun*¹.]
1 *verb intrans.* Work charms, use spells, practise magic. Now *rare*. ME.

SHAKES. *Haml.* No fairy takes, nor witch hath power to charm.

2 *verb trans.* Act upon (as) with a charm or magic; put a spell on; bewitch. LME. ▸**b** Bring *from* or *out* (*of*), send *away*, etc., by a charm or charms. M16.

E. K. KANE They wanted me to charm or cure him.

3 *verb trans.* Give (seemingly) magical powers or virtues to; give special good fortune or protection to. LME.
4 *verb trans.* Enthral, captivate, delight; give pleasure to. LME. ▸**b** *verb intrans.* Be enthralling; give pleasure. *poet.* E18.

ADDISON He every where charms and pleases us by the Force of his own Genius. P. G. WODEHOUSE 'Like you . . to meet my friends. Lady Underhill. Mr. Devereux.' 'Charmed,' said Ronnie affably.

5 *verb trans.* Subdue as if by magic power; soothe, allay. M16.

POPE Music the fiercest grief can charm.

†**6** *verb trans.* Invoke; entreat in the name of a power. L16–M18.
†**7** *verb trans.* Temper, tune, play, (an instrument or melody). L16–E17.
■ **charmer** *noun* a person who charms; *spec.* (**a**) an enchanter; (**b**) a particularly attractive or delightful person; (**c**) a person who subdues or controls as if by magic power (***snake-charmer***: see SNAKE *noun*): ME. **charming** *ppl adjective* that charms; *spec.* (**a**) (now *rare*) using charms, exercising magic power; (**b**) particularly attractive, delightful (freq. *iron.*) (***Prince Charming***: see PRINCE *noun*): LME. **charmingly** *adverb* E17. **charmingness** *noun* M18.

charm *verb*² see CHIRM *verb*.

Charmat /ˈʃɑːmɑː/ *noun*. M20.
[ORIGIN Eugène *Charmat*, French chemist who developed such a process.]
An inexpensive method of producing sparkling wine, by which the wine receives a second fermentation in large tanks rather than (as with champagne) in individual bottles.

charmed /tʃɑːmd/ *adjective*. LME.
[ORIGIN from CHARM *verb*¹, *noun*¹: see -ED¹, -ED².]
1 That has been charmed; enchanted; protected by a charm. LME.

E. P. THOMPSON Binns, who bore a charmed life, was acquitted of high treason.

2 PARTICLE PHYSICS. Designating a *c* quark; having the property charm. M20.

charmeuse /ʃɑːˈməːz, *foreign* ʃarmøːz/ *noun*. E20.
[ORIGIN French, fem. of *charmeur* charmer, formed as CHARM *verb*¹.]
A soft smooth silky dress fabric.

charmonium /tʃɑːˈməʊnɪəm/ *noun*. L20.
[ORIGIN from CHARM *noun*¹ + -ONIUM.]
PHYSICS. A combination of a charmed quark and antiquark.

†**charneco** *noun*. L16–M17.
[ORIGIN Said to be from the name of a village near Lisbon, Portugal]
A Portuguese wine.

charnel /ˈtʃɑːn(ə)l/ *noun*¹ *& adjective*. LME.
[ORIGIN Old French from medieval Latin *carnale* use as noun of neut. of *carnalis* CARNAL.]
▸ **A** *noun*. Orig., a cemetery. Now (more fully ***charnel house***) a house or vault in which dead bodies or bones are piled. LME.
▸ **B** *adjective*. Sepulchral, deathlike, ghastly. E19.

charnel /ˈtʃɑːn(ə)l/ *noun*². *obsolete* exc. *hist.* L15.
[ORIGIN Old French, prob. from Latin *cardinale* neut. of *cardinalis*, from *cardo*, *-in-* hinge: see -AL¹.]
A hinge, *esp.* that of a helmet.

charnockite /ˈtʃɑːnəkʌɪt/ *noun*. L19.
[ORIGIN from Job *Charnock* (d. 1693), the founder of Calcutta (now Kolkata), whose tombstone is made of this rock, + -ITE¹.]
GEOLOGY. A granite containing hypersthene.
■ **charnockitic** /tʃɑːnəˈkɪtɪk/ *adjective* M20.

Charolais /ˈʃarəʊleɪ, *foreign* ʃarɔlɛ/ *noun*. Also **-ll-**. Pl. same. L19.
[ORIGIN from Monts du *Charollais* in eastern France.]
(An animal of) a breed of large white beef cattle.

Charon /ˈkɛːrən/ *noun*. **L15**.
[**ORIGIN** Latin from Greek *Kharōn*.]
1 *GREEK MYTHOLOGY*. The ferryman conveying souls across the Styx to Hades. **L15**.
2 A ferryman. *joc.* **M19**.

charophyte /ˈkarəfʌɪt/ *noun*. **E20**.
[**ORIGIN** mod. Latin *Charophyta* former name of the Characeae, from **CHARA** *noun*[1]: see **-O-**, **-PHYTE**.]
A member of the Characeae, a group of macroscopic mainly freshwater algae marked by whorls of short branches arising from a main axis, often partly encrusted with calcium carbonate; a stonewort.
■ **charophytic** /-ˈfɪtɪk/ *adjective* **E20**.

charoset(h) *noun* var. of **HAROSETH**.

charpie /ˈʃɑːpi/ *noun*. **L18**.
[**ORIGIN** French: see **CARPET** *noun*.]
Old linen unravelled into short ends of thread for surgical dressings.

charpoy /ˈtʃɑːpɔɪ/ *noun*. **M17**.
[**ORIGIN** Urdu *chārpāī* from Persian.]
In the Indian subcontinent: a light bedstead.

charqui /ˈtʃɑːki/ *noun*. See also **JERKY** *noun*[1]. **E17**.
[**ORIGIN** (Amer. Spanish *charqui*, *charque* from) Quechua *cc'arki*: cf. **JERK** *verb*[2].]
Meat, esp. beef, cut into thin slices and dried in the wind and sun.

charr *noun* var. of **CHAR** *noun*[3].

charro /ˈtʃɑːrəʊ/ *noun*. Pl. **-os**. **E20**.
[**ORIGIN** Mexican Spanish from Spanish = rustic.]
A Mexican cowboy, *esp.* one elaborately dressed.

charry /ˈtʃɑːri/ *adjective*. **L18**.
[**ORIGIN** from **CHAR** *verb*[2] or **CHARCOAL**: see **-Y**[1].]
Of the nature of charcoal or a similar charred substance.

charshaf /ˈtʃarʃaf, ˈtʃɑːʃaf/ *noun*. Also ***-chaf*** /-tʃaf/. **E20**.
[**ORIGIN** Turkish *çarşaf* from Persian *čādor-šab* bedspread.]
A headscarf worn by Turkish and Balkan women (a remnant of the veil formerly worn).

chart /tʃɑːt/ *noun* & *verb*. **L16**.
[**ORIGIN** Old French & mod. French *charte* from Latin *charta*: see **CARD** *noun*[2].]
▸ **A** *noun* **I 1** A map. Now *spec.* (***a***) a navigator's sea map, showing coast outlines, rocks, shoals, depths of water, etc.; (***b***) an air navigator's map; (***c***) an outline map showing special features. **L16**.
plane chart: see **PLANE** *adjective*.
2 A sheet of tabulated or diagrammatic information; a set of curves on a graph etc. showing fluctuations in temperature, price, etc. **M19**. ▸**b** *spec.* A list of the currently most popular music recordings etc. Usu. in *pl.* **M20**.
test chart: see **TEST** *noun*[1].
▸ **II 3** A charter; a deed, document. *obsolete* exc. *Scot.* **E17**.
†**4** A card; *esp.* (***a***) a playing card; (***b***) a compass card. **L17–L18**.
▸ **B** *verb trans.* Make a chart of; record in a chart; map. **M19**.
– **COMB.**: **chartbuster** *colloq.* a very popular disc, tape, etc.; **chart-topping** *adjective* occupying the first place in a chart of discs, tapes, etc.

charta /ˈkɑːtə/ *noun*. Pl. **-tae** /-tiː/. *rare* exc. in var. of **MAGNA CARTA**. **M17**.
[**ORIGIN** medieval Latin = legal writing, charter, from Latin: see **CARD** *noun*[2].]
A charter.

chartaceous /kɑːˈteɪʃəs/ *adjective*. **M17**.
[**ORIGIN** from late Latin *chartaceus*, from Latin *charta*: see **CARD** *noun*[2], **-ACEOUS**.]
Of the nature of paper; papery.

chartae *noun* pl. of **CHARTA**.

†**chartel** *noun* see **CARTEL**.

charter /ˈtʃɑːtə/ *noun*. **ME**.
[**ORIGIN** Old French & mod. French *chartre* from Latin *chartula* dim. of *charta*: see **CARD** *noun*[2].]
1 A written document delivered by the monarch or legislature, esp. granting privileges or recognizing rights, or creating a borough, company, university, etc.; a written constitution. **ME**.
2 A written contract between individuals; *esp.* (***a***) *hist.* a deed conveying land; (***b***) = **CHARTER PARTY**. **ME**.
3 A publicly conceded right, a privilege; effective public permission; (a) licence. **M16**.

> **WORDSWORTH** And mighty forms seizing a youthful fancy Had given charter to irregular hopes. *Listener* 'It's the Scroungers' Charter,' said the man in the Liverpool jeweller's shop.

4 A chartered aircraft, boat, vehicle, etc. **M20**.
– **PHRASES**: ***Atlantic Charter***: see **ATLANTIC** *adjective* 2. ***blank charter***: see **BLANK** *adjective*. **Great Charter** = **MAGNA CARTA**. **People's Charter** the document embodying the principles and demands of the Chartists.
– **COMB.**: **charter flight**: by chartered aircraft; **charter-land** land held by charter, freehold land; **Charter Mark** (in the UK) an award granted to institutions for exceptional public service under the terms of the Citizen's Charter; **charter member** an original member of a society, corporation, etc.; **Charter school** *hist.* a school established by the Charter Society; **Charter Society** *hist.*: founded to provide Protestant education for the Catholic poor in Ireland.
■ **charterless** *adjective* **LME**.

charter /ˈtʃɑːtə/ *verb trans.* **LME**.
[**ORIGIN** from the noun.]
1 Grant a charter to; establish by charter. **LME**.
2 Privilege, license. **M16**.
3 Hire (a ship, vehicle, aircraft, etc.) as a conveyance. **L18**.

chartered /ˈtʃɑːtəd/ *ppl adjective*. **LME**.
[**ORIGIN** from **CHARTER** *verb* + **-ED**[1].]
1 That has been chartered. **LME**.
chartered libertine a person allowed to do as he pleases.
2 Having membership of a professional body with a royal charter. **M19**.
chartered accountant, ***chartered engineer***, ***chartered librarian***, ***chartered surveyor***, etc.

charterer /ˈtʃɑːt(ə)rə/ *noun*. **ME**.
[**ORIGIN** from **CHARTER** *noun*, *verb* + **-ER**[1].]
1 A freeholder; a freeman of a chartered borough. Now chiefly *hist.* **ME**.
2 A person who or organization which charters a ship, vehicle, aircraft, etc. **M19**.

Charterhouse /ˈtʃɑːtəhaʊs/ *noun* & *adjective*. **LME**.
[**ORIGIN** Anglo-Norman *Chartrous*, Old French & mod. French *Chartreuse* alt. of earlier Anglo-Norman *Chartous*, Old French *Charteuse*, from medieval Latin *Cart(h)usius*, from *Cart(h)usia*: see **CARTHUSIAN**. Assim. to **HOUSE** *noun*[1]. Cf. **CHARTREUX**.]
▸ **A** *noun*. **1** A Carthusian monastery. Now *arch.* or *hist.* **LME**.
2 In full ***Charterhouse School***, †***Charterhouse Hospital***. A charitable institution, later a public school, founded on the site of the Carthusian monastery in London (later moved to Godalming, Surrey). **M17**.
▸ **B** *adjective*. Carthusian. **LME**.

charter party /ˈtʃɑːtəpɑːti/ *noun*. **LME**.
[**ORIGIN** French *charte partie* from medieval Latin *charta partita* divided charter, indenture.]
A written contract made between a shipowner and a merchant for the hire of a ship and the delivery of the cargo.

Chartism /ˈtʃɑːtɪz(ə)m/ *noun*. **M19**.
[**ORIGIN** from medieval Latin **CHARTA** + **-ISM**, after the *People's Charter* (see **CHARTER** *noun*).]
The principles of a British democratic reform movement of 1837–48.

Chartist /ˈtʃɑːtɪst/ *noun* & *adjective*. *hist.* **M19**.
[**ORIGIN** formed as **CHARTISM** + **-IST**.]
▸ **A** *noun*. An adherent of Chartism. **M19**.
▸ **B** *adjective*. Of or pertaining to Chartism or Chartists. **M19**.

chartographer, **chartography** *nouns* etc., see **CARTOGRAPHER** etc.

chartreuse /ʃɑːˈtrəːz; *foreign* ʃartrøːz (*pl. same*)/ *noun*. **E19**.
[**ORIGIN** French, fem. of *Chartreux*: see **CHARTREUX**.]
1 *COOKERY*. A dish turned out from a mould, of meat, vegetables, or (now more usually) of fruit enclosed in jelly etc. **E19**.
2 A green or yellow liqueur of brandy and aromatic herbs etc., orig. made by the monks of La Grande Chartreuse, near Grenoble, France. **M19**.
3 An apple-green colour. **L19**.

Chartreux /ˈʃɑːtrəː, *foreign* ʃartrø/ *noun* & *adjective*. Now *rare* or *obsolete*. Pl. of noun **-eux** /-əːz, -ø/. **LME**.
[**ORIGIN** French, from Old French & mod. French *Chartreuse*: see **CHARTERHOUSE**.]
(A) Carthusian.

chartulary /ˈkɑːtjʊləri/ *noun*[1]. **L17**.
[**ORIGIN** medieval Latin *c(h)artularius*, from *c(h)artula*: see **CARTULARY**.]
An archivist.

chartulary *noun*[2] var. of **CARTULARY**.

chary /ˈtʃɛːri/ *adjective* & *adverb*.
[**ORIGIN** Old English *ċeariġ* = Old Saxon *carag*, Old High German *charag*, from West Germanic, from base of **CARE** *noun*: see **-Y**[1].]
▸ **A** *adjective*. †**1** Sorrowful, anxious; grievous. **OE–ME**.
†**2** Dear; cherished. **LME–E19**.
3 Cautious, wary; shy, fastidious; frugal, sparing, ungenerous. (Foll. by *about*, *in*, *of*, *(doing)*.) **M16**.

> **SHAKES.** *Haml.* The chariest maid is prodigal enough If she unmask her beauty to the moon. **SIR W. SCOTT** They were more chary of their royal presence. **V. GLENDINNING** One would be more chary about characterizing the Anglo-Irish were it not for the fact that they themselves have not been in the least chary about it.

▸ **B** *adverb*. Charily. Now *rare*. **L16**.
■ **charily** *adverb* **L16**. **chariness** *noun* **L16**.

Charybdis /kəˈrɪbdɪs/ *noun*. **LME**.
[**ORIGIN** Latin from Greek *kharubdis* a dangerous whirlpool in Greek mythol.]
A danger which threatens to engulf one; *esp.* (opp. **SCYLLA**) either of two dangers such that to avoid one increases the risk from the other.

Chas. *abbreviation*.
Charles.

chase /tʃeɪs/ *noun*[1]. Also (*arch.*) **chace**. **ME**.
[**ORIGIN** Old French *chace* (mod. *chasse*) from Proto-Romance, from verb whence **CHASE** *verb*[1].]
1 The action or an act of chasing; pursuit; hunting. **ME**. ▸**b** A steeplechase. **L19**.
paperchase, ***steeplechase***, etc. **give chase (to)** go in pursuit (of). ***lead a person a chase***: see **LEAD** *verb*[1]. ***the chase*** the sport of hunting. ***wild-goose chase***: see **WILD GOOSE**.
2 *The* or *one's* object of pursuit, as an animal, a ship, etc. **ME**.
3 A tract of unenclosed land reserved for hunting, *spec.* one owned by the Crown. Now chiefly *hist.* exc. in proper names. **ME**.
4 The right of hunting over or of keeping animals for hunting on a tract of land. **LME**.
5 *REAL TENNIS*. The second impact of an unreturned ball, for which the player scores unless the opponent betters it by a similar and subsequent unreturned impact which lands nearer the end wall where the chase was made. **LME**.
6 *hist.* The chase-guns of a ship; the part of a ship where the chase-ports are. **E17**.
– **COMB.**: **chase chorus** *JAZZ*: in which musicians improvise for a few bars in turn; **chase-gun**, **chase-port** *hist.* a gun, port, in the bow or stern of a vessel for use while chasing or being chased.

chase /tʃeɪs/ *noun*[2]. **L16**.
[**ORIGIN** French *châsse*: see **CASE** *noun*[2].]
PRINTING. A metal frame for holding composed type and blocks for printing a page or sheet.
rack chase: see **RACK** *noun*[2].

chase /tʃeɪs/ *noun*[3]. **E17**.
[**ORIGIN** French *chas* enclosed space from Provençal *ca(u)s* from medieval Latin *capsum* thorax, nave of a church.]
1 The cavity of a gun barrel; the part of a gun enclosing the bore. **E17**.
2 A groove or furrow cut in the face of a wall etc. to receive a pipe; a trench for drain tiles etc. **M19**.

chase /tʃeɪs/ *noun*[4]. *dial.* **M17**.
[**ORIGIN** Cf. French dial. (Norman) *chasse*.]
A green lane, *esp.* one leading up to a farmhouse or field.

chase /tʃeɪs/ *verb*[1]. Also (*arch.*) **chace**. **ME**.
[**ORIGIN** Old French *chacier* (mod. *chasser*) from Proto-Romance var. of Latin *captare* frequentative of *capere* take: cf. **CATCH** *verb*.]
1 *verb trans.* Follow with intent to kill, capture, overtake, attract, etc.; pursue, run after; appear to follow thus; try to attain or achieve. **ME**. ▸†**b** Persecute, harass. **ME–E17**. ▸**c** Follow (a drink etc.) with (or *with*) a chaser. *colloq.* **M20**.

> **SWIFT** We were chased by two pirates, who soon overtook us. **TENNYSON** Chasing each other merrily. **YEATS** I chased with hounds the flying deer. **P. G. WODEHOUSE** He drank like a fish and was always chasing girls. **J. SNOW** The Australians chased the 242 runs they needed to win.

chase one's tail: see **TAIL** *noun*[1]. ***chase the dragon***: see **DRAGON** *noun*. **chase up** *colloq.* pursue with a specific purpose. **go and chase oneself**, **chase oneself** *colloq.* (usu. in *imper.*) leave, go away.
2 *verb intrans.* †**a** Go hunting. **ME–E16**. ▸**b** Go in pursuit. Freq. foll. by *after*. **LME**. ▸**c** Hurry; move with speed. Usu. with adverb or preposition phr. **LME**.

> **b SIR W. SCOTT** 'Horse! horse!' the Douglas cried, 'and chase!' **E. O'NEILL** He doesn't give wild parties, doesn't chase after musical-comedy cuties. **c R. MACAULAY** Aunt Cynthia chased off after another exciting subject. **D. H. LAWRENCE** The wind chases by us and over the corn.

3 *verb trans.* Drive *away*, *out*, *from*, *out of*, etc. **ME**. ▸**b** Put to flight, rout; dispel. *arch.* **ME**. ▸**c** Drive (cattle etc.). Long *obsolete* exc. *dial.* **LME**.

> **J. CONRAD** The ship had been chased away. **G. B. SHAW** A flush of interest and delight suddenly chases the growing perplexity and boredom from her face.

■ **chaseable** *adjective* fit to be chased or hunted **LME**. **chasing** *verbal noun*[1] (***a***) the action of the verb (***contour-chasing***: see **CONTOUR** *noun*); (***b***) steeplechasing: **LME**.

chase /tʃeɪs/ *verb*[2] *trans.* **LME**.
[**ORIGIN** App. from **ENCHASE** *verb*[2].]
Ornament (metal) with embossed work, engrave in relief.
■ **chasing** *verbal noun*[2] (***a***) the action of the verb; (***b***) a chased design or figure: **M19**.

chase /tʃeɪs/ *verb*[3] *trans.* **E19**.
[**ORIGIN** from **CHASE** *noun*[3].]
Groove, indent.

chaser /ˈtʃeɪsə/ *noun*[1]. **ME**.
[**ORIGIN** Old French *chacë(o)ur* (mod. *chasseur*, formed as **CHASE** *verb*[1]: see **-ER**[2]. Later senses from **CHASE** *verb*[1] + **-ER**[1].]
1 A person who or thing which pursues, hunts, or drives away. (Foll. by *off*.) **ME**. ▸**b** *spec.* An amorous pursuer of women. *colloq.* (chiefly *US*). **L19**.
submarine chaser: see **SUBMARINE** *noun*.
†**2 a** A horse for hunting. **ME–M17**. ▸**b** A horse for steeplechasing. **L19**.
3 *hist.* A chase-gun. **E19**.
4 A drink following a drink of another kind, as water or beer after spirits, etc. *colloq.* **L19**.

C

B. ELTON He went straight to the bar and ordered beer with a bourbon chaser.

chaser /ˈtʃeɪsə/ *noun*². E18.
[ORIGIN from CHASE *verb*² + -ER¹.]
A person who chases metal.

chaser /ˈtʃeɪsə/ *noun*³. L19.
[ORIGIN from CHASE *verb*³ + -ER¹.]
A tool for cutting grooves.

C

Chasid *noun* var. of HASID.

chasm /ˈkaz(ə)m/ *noun*. Earlier †**chasma**, pl. **-mae**, **-mas**. L16.
[ORIGIN Latin *chasma* from Greek *khasma* gaping hollow.]
†**1 a** An opening up of the sea, or of the earth in an earthquake. L16–M17. ▸**b** A (supposed) rending of the firmament or vault of heaven. E17–M18.
2 A deep fissure, a wide crack. E17.
3 *fig.* A wide difference of feeling, interests, etc., a gulf; *arch.* a hiatus, a void. M17.
■ **chasmal** *adjective* belonging to or of the nature of a chasm M19. **chasmed** *adjective* having chasms, cleft into chasms L18. **chasmic** *adjective* = CHASMAL E20. **chasmy** *adjective* full of chasms; of the nature of a chasm: L18.

chasmogamy /kazˈmɒgəmi/ *noun*. E20.
[ORIGIN from CHASM + -O- + -GAMY.]
BOTANY. The opening of the perianth at the time of flowering. Opp. CLEISTOGAMY.
■ **chasmoˈgamic**, **chasmogamous** *adjectives* E20.

chasse /ʃas, ʃɑːs/ *noun*¹. LME.
[ORIGIN French *châsse*: see CASE *noun*².]
A case for the relics of a saint.

chasse /ʃas, ʃɑːs/ *noun*². Pl. ***chasses*** /ʃas, ˈʃɑːsɪz/. M18.
[ORIGIN French, abbreviation of CHASSE-CAFÉ.]
A liqueur taken after coffee, tobacco, etc.; a chaser.

chassé /ʃase (*pl. same*), ˈʃaseɪ/ *noun*. E19.
[ORIGIN French, lit. 'chasing, chase'.]
A sliding step in which one foot displaces the other in dancing.
chassé croisé /krwaze/ [lit. 'crossed'] a double *chassé* in which partners change position; *fig.* an elaborate reversal of position.

chassé /ˈʃaseɪ/ *verb*. Pa. t. & pple **-éd**, **-é'd**. M18.
[ORIGIN French *chasser* (imper. *chassez!*) lit. 'to chase, hunt'.]
1 *verb trans.* Dismiss. *arch. slang*. M18.
2 *verb intrans.* Execute a *chassé*. E19.

chasse-café /ʃaskafe/ *noun*. Now *rare*. Pl. pronounced same. E19.
[ORIGIN French, lit. 'chase-coffee'.]
A liqueur taken after coffee.

Chasselas /ʃaslɑ/ *noun*. M17.
[ORIGIN A village near Mâcon in France.]
A variety of white grape.

chasse-marée /ʃasmare/ *noun*. Pl. pronounced same. E19.
[ORIGIN French, lit. 'chase-tide'.]
A coasting lugger formerly used by the French for smuggling and privateering.

chassepot /ʃaspo/ *noun*. Pl. pronounced same. M19.
[ORIGIN Antoine A. *Chassepot* (1833–1905), its French designer.]
A type of bolt-action breech-loading rifle, used by the French army between 1866 and 1874.

chasseur /ʃaˈsəː; *foreign* ʃasœːr (*pl. same*)/ *noun*. M18.
[ORIGIN French, from *chasser* (see CHASE *verb*¹) + *-eur* -OR.]
1 *hist.* A soldier (esp. French) equipped and trained for rapid movement. M18.
2 a An attendant dressed in military style. Now *rare* or *obsolete*. M18. ▸**b** A hotel messenger, esp. in France. L19.
3 A huntsman. L18.
– COMB.: **chasseur sauce** a rich sauce with wine and mushrooms for poultry or game; **chicken chasseur** etc., chicken etc. cooked in chasseur sauce.

Chassid *noun* var. of HASID.

chassis /ˈʃasi, -iː/ *noun*. Pl. same /ˈʃasɪz, -iːz/. M17.
[ORIGIN French *châssis* from Proto-Romance, from Latin *capsa* CASE *noun*².]
†**1** A window frame, a sash. M17–E18.
2 The sliding base frame of a mounted gun. M19.
3 The base frame of a motor vehicle etc. E20.
4 A frame carrying radio etc. equipment. M20.
5 The human or animal frame, the body. *slang*. M20.
■ **chassisless** *adjective* M20.

chaste /tʃeɪst/ *adjective*. ME.
[ORIGIN Old French & mod. French from Latin *castus*.]
1 Abstaining from unlawful or immoral or all sexual intercourse; pure, virginal. ME. ▸†**b** Unmarried, single. ME–L16.
†**2** Free from guilt, innocent. ME–M16.
3 *fig.* Undefiled, stainless. E17.

SHAKES. *Oth.* Let me not name it to you, you chaste stars.

4 Decent, seemly, esp. in speech. E17.

L. STERNE The Hero's horse was a horse of chaste deportment.

5 Pure in taste or style, unadorned, simple; restrained, severe. M18.

J. WARTON So chaste and correct a writer. C. HAMPTON A large, chaste desk, its only ornament a large granite crucifix.

– COMB.: **chaste tree** [cf. AGNUS CASTUS] a violet-flowered aromatic shrub of the verbena family, *Vitex agnus-castus*, native to southern Europe, which is reputed to reduce sexual desire.
■ **chastely** *adverb* ME. **chasteness** *noun* LME.

†**chaste** *verb trans.* Also **chasty**. ME.
[ORIGIN Old French *chastier* (mod. *châtier*) from Latin *castigare* CASTIGATE.]
1 = CHASTEN. ME–E17.
2 Reprove, rebuke. Only in ME.

chastelain *noun* var. of CHATELAIN.

†**chastelet** *noun* see CHATELET.

chasten /ˈtʃeɪs(ə)n/ *verb trans.* E16.
[ORIGIN from CHASTE *verb* + -EN⁵.]
1 Esp. of God: discipline, punish by inflicting suffering, chastise. E16.

TENNYSON The love Wherewith we love the Heaven that chastens us.

2 Render pure in character or style. E18.
3 *fig.* Moderate; restrain, subdue. M19.

A. P. HERBERT Ernest hobbled on board, chastened by his fall, but cursing terribly.

■ **chastener** *noun* a person who or thing which chastens M16.

chastise /tʃaˈstʌɪz/ *verb trans.* ME.
[ORIGIN App. irreg. from CHASTE *verb*.]
†**1** Correct the faults of; reform. ME–L17.
2 Reprimand, rebuke. ME.

Guardian He chastises Renault for their failure to respond to BMW's challenge.

3 Punish, esp. by beating; inflict (esp. corporal) punishment on. ME. ▸**b** Inflict punishment for (an offence). *rare*. L16.
4 = CHASTEN 3. Now *rare* or *obsolete*. LME.
5 = CHASTEN 2. Now *rare* or *obsolete*. E17.
– NOTE: Orig., & usu. in Shakes., stressed on 1st syll.: cf. CHASTISEMENT.
■ **chastisable** *adjective* that may be, or deserves to be, chastised E17. **chastiser** *noun* LME.

chastisement /ˈtʃastɪzm(ə)nt, tʃaˈstʌɪz-/ *noun*. ME.
[ORIGIN from CHASTISE + -MENT.]
†**1** Correction of faults; (a) discipline. ME–E17.
2 Punishment, esp. corrective or disciplinary; thrashing. ME.

chastity /ˈtʃastɪti/ *noun*. ME.
[ORIGIN Old French & mod. French *chasteté* from Latin *castitas*, from *castus* CHASTE *adjective*: see -ITY.]
1 The quality or state of being chaste; virginity, celibacy. ME.
girdle of chastity: see GIRDLE *noun*¹.
2 Moderation, restraint; simplicity of style or taste. M18.
– COMB.: **chastity belt** a garment designed to prevent the woman wearing it from having sexual intercourse.

†**chasty** *verb* var. of CHASTE *verb*.

chasuble /ˈtʃazjʊb(ə)l/ *noun*. ME.
[ORIGIN Old French *chesible*, later Old French & mod. French *chasuble*, from late Latin *casubla* obscure alt. of Latin *casula* little cottage, hooded cloak, dim. of *casa* house.]
A sleeveless vestment worn by the celebrant at the Mass or Eucharist.

chat /tʃat/ *noun*¹. *obsolete* exc. *dial.* LME.
[ORIGIN French *chats* lit. 'cats'.]
1 A catkin. LME.
†**2** The winged fruit of the sycamore etc. M16–L17.
3 A small branch or twig, for kindling etc. M16.

chat /tʃat/ *noun*². M16.
[ORIGIN from CHAT *verb*.]
1 Idle or frivolous talk, small talk, gossip; (now usu.) easy familiar talk. M16.

SHAKES. *Tam. Shr.* O, how I long to have some chat with her! SWIFT Scarce list'ning to their idle chat. I. MURDOCH 'I am writing my memoirs.' 'Theatre chat?'

2 A light or (usu.) easy familiar conversation. M17.

E. M. FORSTER Dear, one moment—we may not have this chance for a chat again.

– COMB.: **chatline** a telephone service for conversation among a number of people on separate lines; **chat room** an area on the Internet or other computer network where users can communicate, typically one dedicated to a particular topic; **chat show** an entertainment of interviews, on television etc.

chat /tʃat/ *noun*³. L17.
[ORIGIN Prob. imit.]
1 Any of numerous small Old World thrushes with harsh calls and freq. boldly coloured plumage; *esp.* a stonechat, a whinchat. L17.
robin-chat: see ROBIN *noun*¹.
2 Any of various other small birds with harsh calls, esp. New World warblers of the genera *Granatellus* and *Icteria* (family Parulidae), and Australian birds of the family Ephthianuridae. L18.
woodchat: see WOOD *noun*¹. ***yellow-breasted chat***: see YELLOW *adjective*.

chat /tʃat/ *verb*. Infl. **-tt-**. LME.
[ORIGIN Abbreviation of CHATTER *verb*.]
1 *verb intrans.* Talk idly or frivolously or (now usu.) easily and familiarly. LME.

T. F. POWYS The remainder . . chatted with one another. M. LASKI They were chatted to in the streets. P. H. JOHNSON We sat . . chatting of nothing in particular.

†**2** *verb trans.* Talk idly or familiarly of; say idly or familiarly. L15–M18.
3 *verb trans.* Talk to (a person), esp. flirtatiously or with an ulterior motive. Freq. foll. by *up*. *slang*. L19.

V. S. PRITCHETT The girl in red, the one you were chatting up.

chateau /ˈʃatəʊ, *foreign* ʃɑːto/ *noun*. Also **château**. Pl. **-eaux** /-əʊz, *foreign* -o/. M18.
[ORIGIN French *château*: see CASTLE *noun*¹.]
A large country house in France (formerly also elsewhere); *esp.* one giving its name to wine made in its neighbourhood.
chateau in air, **chateau in Spain**, ***château en Espagne*** /ɒn ɛspaɲ/ = ***castle in the air***, ***castle in Spain*** s.v. CASTLE *noun*¹ 1.
– COMB.: **chateau-bottled** *adjective* (of wine) bottled at the vineyard.

Chateaubriand /ˌʃatəʊˈbriːɒ̃, *foreign* ʃatobrijɑ̃/ *noun*. Pl. pronounced same. L19.
[ORIGIN François René, Vicomte de *Chateaubriand* (1768–1848), French writer and statesman.]
A thick fillet beefsteak, grilled and garnished with herbs etc. Also ***Chateaubriand grill***, ***Chateaubriand steak***, etc.

chatelain /ˈʃatəleɪn/ *noun*. Also (earlier) **chast-** /ˈʃast-/. LME.
[ORIGIN Old French *chastelain* (mod. *châtelain*): see CASTELLAN.]
hist. = CASTELLAN 1.

chatelaine /ˈʃatəleɪn/ *noun*. M19.
[ORIGIN French *châtelaine* fem. of *châtelain*: see CHATELAIN.]
1 A female castellan (*hist.*); the mistress of a castle or country house. M19.
2 *hist.* A set of short chains attached to a woman's belt for carrying keys, a watch, a pencil, etc. M19.

chatelet /ˈʃatəlɪt/ *noun*. Also (earlier) †**chast-**. LME.
[ORIGIN Old French *chastelet* (mod. *châtelet*) dim. of *castel* CASTLE *noun*¹: see -ET¹. Cf. CASTELET.]
hist. A small castle; *spec.* a particular ancient prison in Paris.

chatellany /ˈʃatələni/ *noun*. M17.
[ORIGIN French *châtellenie*, assim. to CASTELLANY.]
hist. = CASTELLANY.

chaton /ʃatɔ̃/ *noun*. Pl. pronounced same. L16.
[ORIGIN French from German *Kasten* (Old High German, Middle High German *kasto*).]
The part of a ring in which a stone is set or on which a device is engraved.

chatoyant /ʃəˈtɔɪənt, *foreign* ʃatwajɑ̃/ *noun* & *adjective*. Now *rare*. L18.
[ORIGIN French, pres. pple of *chatoyer*: see -ANT¹.]
(Of) iridescent undulating lustre.

chatta /ˈtʃatə, ˈtʃɑːtə/ *noun*. L18.
[ORIGIN Hindi *chātā*.]
In the Indian subcontinent: an umbrella.

chattel /ˈtʃat(ə)l/ *noun*. ME.
[ORIGIN Old French *chatel* = Provençal *captal* from medieval Latin *capitale* use as noun of neut. of Latin *capitalis*: see CAPITAL *adjective* & *noun*². Cf. CATTLE.]
†**1 a** Property. Only in ME. ▸**b** Livestock. *rare*. Only in 17.
2 A movable possession (in LAW including abstract but transferable possessions, as leases etc.); (chiefly *rhet.*) a slave, a bondman. Usu. in *pl.* ME.
chattels personal LAW all movable goods. **chattels real** LAW: such as concern the realty, as leases etc. **goods and chattels** all kinds of personal property.
– COMB.: **chattel interest** (now *rare*) an interest in leasehold property; **chattel mortgage** *N. Amer.* the conveyance of chattels by mortgage as security for a debt; **chattel slave** a human being held as a chattel; **chattel slavery** = CHATTELISM.
■ **chattelism** *noun* the system of holding human beings as chattels M19.

chatter /ˈtʃatə/ *verb* & *noun*. ME.
[ORIGIN Imit., of frequentative formation: see -ER⁵. Cf. CHITTER.]
▸ **A** *verb*. **I** *verb intrans.* **1** Of a bird: utter quick series of short notes (now esp. notes approaching those of the human voice). ME.

WORDSWORTH The jay makes answer as the magpie chatters.

2 Of a person: talk quickly, incessantly, foolishly, or inopportunely. ME. ▸**b** Make sounds suggestive of human chattering. E17.

E. FERBER They chattered on and on about little inconsequential things. **b** SHAKES. *Temp.* Like apes, that mow and chatter at me. QUILLER-COUCH A hollow in the road, across which a tiny beck . . was chattering bravely.

chattering classes *colloq.* (*derog.*) the articulate professional people given to free expression of (esp. liberal) opinions on society and culture.
3 Of the teeth: rattle together. LME. ▸**b** Of a person: shiver, have chattering teeth. *rare*. E17. ▸**c** Rattle with vibration. L19.

J. Cary She dressed quickly, her teeth chattering, her fingers white and weak with cold. **b** I. Murdoch I was chattering with cold. **c** N. Gordimer A child bore over to me a cup of milky tea chattering against its saucer.

▸ **II** *verb trans.* **4** Utter or say chatteringly; chatter of. **ME.**

Tennyson They chatter'd trifles at the door.

5 Make (teeth) rattle. **E17.**

G. A. Sala Gibbering and chattering their teeth.

▸ **B** *noun.* **1** The chattering of birds etc.; a sound of chattering; rattling, noisy vibration. **ME.**

2 Incessant, trivial talk. **M19.**

– comb.: **chatterbox** a talkative person, esp. a child; **chattermag** *colloq. & dial.* a chatterbox; chatter.

■ **chatte'ration** *noun* prolonged chattering, noisy chatter **M19.** **chatterer** *noun* (*a*) a person who chatters; (*b*) orig. = waxwing (*waxen chatterer*: see waxen *adjective*); now more often, any of various other garrulous birds, *esp.* a babbler: **LME.** **chatteringly** *adverb* in a chattering manner **M19.** †**chattery** *noun* chat, chatter **L18–L19.** **chattery** *adjective* characterized by chattering, given to chattering **M19.**

chatterbot /ˈtʃatəbɒt/ *noun.* **L20.**
[origin from chatter *noun* + bot *noun*[4].]
computing. A program designed to interact with people by simulating human conversation.

Chattertonian /tʃatəˈtəʊnɪən/ *adjective & noun.* **M19.**
[origin from *Chatterton* (see below) + -ian.]
(An admirer or student) of the English poet Thomas Chatterton (1752–70) or his pseudo-archaic literary style.

chatty /ˈtʃati/ *noun.* **L18.**
[origin Hindi *cāṭī* from Tamil *caṭṭi*.]
In the Indian subcontinent: an earthenware pot for water.

chatty /ˈtʃati/ *adjective.* **M18.**
[origin from chat *noun*[2] + -y[1].]
Given to chat, fond of chatting; resembling chat.
■ **chattily** *adverb* **E19.** **chattiness** *noun* **L19.**

Chaucerian /tʃɔːˈsɪərɪən/ *adjective & noun.* **M17.**
[origin from *Chaucer* (see below) + -ian.]
(An admirer, imitator, or student) of the English poet Geoffrey Chaucer (*c* 1343–1400) or his writing.
Scottish Chaucerian: see Scottish *adjective.*
■ **Chaucerism** /ˈtʃɔːsərɪz(ə)m/ *noun* an expression used by or imitated from Chaucer **L16.**

chaud-froid /ʃəʊˈfrwɑː, *foreign* ʃofrwa (*pl. same*)/ *noun.* **L19.**
[origin French, lit. 'hot-cold.']
A dish of cold cooked meat or fish in a jelly or sauce.

chaud-mellé /ʃɔːdˈmɛli/ *noun.* **LME.**
[origin from Old French *chaud(e)* heated + *mellée* affray, mellay.]
scots law (now *hist.*). A sudden affray arising from heated emotions; a homicide committed in hot blood and without premeditation.

chauffer /ˈtʃɔːfə/ *noun.* **LME.**
[origin Var. of chafer *noun*[2]; later perh. infl. by French *chauffoir*, from *chauffer*: see chafe *verb*.]
†**1** = chafer *noun*[2] 1. **LME–E17.**
2 A small portable furnace, a brazier. **M19.**

chauffeur /ˈʃəʊfə, ʃəʊˈfəː/ *noun & verb.* **L19.**
[origin French = stoker, fireman, from *chauffer* (see chafe *verb*) + *-eur* -or.]
▸ **A** *noun.* †**1** A motorist. **L19–E20.**
2 A person employed to drive a private or hired car. **E20.**
▸ **B** *verb trans.* Drive (a car) as a chauffeur; convey (a person) by car. **E20.**
■ **chauffeuse** /ˈʃəʊfəːz, ʃəʊˈfəːz/ *noun* a female chauffeur **E20.**

chauki *noun* see choky *noun.*

chaukidar *noun* var. of chowkidar.

chaulmoogra /tʃɔːlˈmuːgrə/ *noun.* **E19.**
[origin Bengali *cāul-mugrā*.]
Any of several tropical Asian trees of the family Flacourtiaceae, esp. *Hydnocarpus kurzii*, whose seeds yield an oil (***chaulmoogra oil***) formerly used to treat skin diseases.
■ **chaulmoogric** *adjective* (chemistry): ***chaulmoogric acid***, a soft yellowish cyclopentene derivative, $C_{17}H_{31}COOH$, which is a major constituent of chaulmoogra oil **E20.**

chaung /tʃaʊŋ/ *noun.* **M20.**
[origin Burmese.]
In Myanmar (Burma): a watercourse.

chaunt *noun, verb* see chant *noun, verb.*

chaunter *noun* see chanter.

chaussée /ʃose/ *noun.* Pl. pronounced same. **E19.**
[origin French: see causey.]
In France, Belgium, etc.: a causeway; a high road.

chausses /ʃoːs/ *noun pl.* **L15.**
[origin French = clothing for the legs.]
hist. Pantaloons or tight coverings for the legs and feet, esp. of mail.
– note: Formerly naturalized.

chaussure /ʃosyːr/ *noun.* **LME.**
[origin Anglo-Norman *chaucer* = Old French *chaucier* (mod. *chaussure*), Provençal *causier* shoe. Cf. medieval Latin *calceatura*.]
Footwear.
– note: Formerly naturalized.

chautauqua /tʃɔːˈtɔːkwə, ʃ-/ *noun.* Orig. & chiefly *N. Amer.* (now *hist.*). **L19.**
[origin *Chautauqua*, a county and lake in New York State.]
A summer school or similar educational course.

chauvinism /ˈʃəʊv(ɪ)nɪz(ə)m/ *noun.* Also **C-.** **L19.**
[origin French *chauvinisme*, formed as chauvinist: see -ism.]
The state or quality of being a chauvinist; chauvinistic feeling or behaviour; an instance of this.

B. Cottle American hurricanes were always given women's names, a blatant piece of chauvinism.

male chauvinism: see male *adjective & noun.* ***social chauvinism***: see social *adjective.*

chauvinist /ˈʃəʊv(ɪ)nɪst/ *noun & adjective.* In sense A.1 also **C-.** **L19.**
[origin from Nicolas *Chauvin*, a Napoleonic veteran popularized as a character in *La cocarde tricolore* by the brothers Cogniard + -ist.]
▸ **A** *noun.* **1** A bellicose patriot; a fervent supporter of a cause. **L19.**
2 A person who is prejudiced against or inconsiderate of those of a different sex, class, nationality, culture, etc.; *esp.* = ***male chauvinist*** s.v. male *adjective & noun.* **M20.**
▸ **B** *adjective.* Of or pertaining to chauvinism or chauvinists; chauvinistic. **L19.**
■ **chauvi'nistic** *adjective* bellicosely patriotic; prejudiced against or inconsiderate of those of a different sex, nationality, etc. (***male-chauvinistic***: see male *adjective & noun*); showing such patriotism or prejudice: **L19.** **chauvi'nistically** *adverb* **L20.**

chav /tʃav/ *noun. slang.* **L20.**
[origin Uncertain: perh. from the name of *Chatham* in Kent, or from Polari *chavy* child, from Romany *chavi* or Polari *charver* a woman, esp. a prostitute, from Romany *charver* to copulate with.]
In the UK, a young lower-class person typified by brash and loutish behaviour and the wearing of (real or imitation) designer clothes.

†**chave** *verb trans. & intrans.* Also **cave.** **LME–L19.**
[origin from chaff *noun*[1].]
Separate chaff (from).

†**chavel** *noun* see jowl *noun*[1].

chavel /ˈtʃav(ə)l/ *verb.* Long *obsolete* exc. *dial.* Infl. **-ll-.** **ME.**
[origin from Middle English form of jowl *noun*[1].]
†**1** *verb intrans.* Talk idly, chatter. Only in **ME.**
2 *verb trans.* Mumble (food); chew. **E17.**

fig.: D. H. Lawrence The bracken . . , broken and chavelled by the restless wild winds of the long winter.

chavender /ˈtʃav(ə)ndə/ *noun.* Now *dial.* **L15.**
[origin Obscurely from (the same root as) chevin.]
The chub.

chaw /tʃɔː/ *noun*[1]. Long *obsolete* exc. *Scot.* **M16.**
[origin Var. of jaw *noun*[1].]
†**1** A jaw. Usu. in *pl.* **M16–L17.**
2 Loquacity; lecturing; cheek. *Scot.* **E20.**

chaw /tʃɔː/ *noun*[2]. *colloq. & dial.* **E18.**
[origin Var. of chew *noun*: cf. chow *noun*[1].]
An act of chewing, esp. something not for swallowing; something so chewed, *esp.* a quid of tobacco.

chaw /tʃɔː/ *verb.* Now *colloq. & dial.* **LME.**
[origin Var. of chew *verb*: cf. chow *verb*.]
1 *verb trans. & intrans.* Chew, now esp. without intending to swallow and in a vulgar manner. **LME.** ▸†**b** *verb trans.* Bite (a bullet) to make it jagged. Chiefly as ***chawed*** *ppl adjective.* **M17–M19.**
2 *verb trans. fig.* Brood over, ruminate on. **M16.**
– with adverbs in specialized senses: **chaw up** *US slang* destroy, put an end to.
– comb.: **chaw-bacon** *derog.* a bumpkin, a yokel; **chaw stick** a W. Indian climbing plant, *Gouania domingensis*, of the buckthorn family; the bark or a twig of this, chewed as a stimulant or stomachic.
■ **chawer** *noun* (*rare*) **E17.**

†**chawbuck** *verb trans. & noun.* As noun also **chabuk.** **E17–E19.**
[origin Urdu *chābuk* from Persian *čābuk* horsewhip.]
In India, Persia, etc.: (flog with) a whip.

chawdron /ˈʃɔːdrən/ *noun.* Long *obsolete* exc. *dial.* Also **chald-** /ˈʃɔːld-/. **LME.**
[origin Old French *chaudun* offal, pig's trotters, from medieval Latin *calduna*, app. from Latin *calidus* hot: assim. to chaldron *noun*[1].]
†**1** A kind of sauce made with chopped entrails, spices, etc. **LME–E17.**
2 *sing.* & in *pl.* Entrails, esp. as food. **L16.**

chawl /tʃɔːl/ *noun.* **L19.**
[origin Marathi *cāl* long narrow building.]
In the Indian subcontinent: a type of lodging house.

†**chawn** *noun.* **E17–L18.**
[origin Rel. to chine *noun*[1].]
= chine *noun*[1].

chay /tʃeɪ/ *noun*[1]. Also **chaya** /ˈtʃeɪə/. **L16.**
[origin Tamil *caya*.]
The root of an Indian plant, *Oldenlandia umbellata*, of the madder family, which yields a red dye.

chay *noun*[2] var. of shay *noun*[1].

chayote /ˈtʃeɪəʊti/ *noun.* **L19.**
[origin Spanish from Nahuatl *chayotli*.]
A vine, *Sechium edule*, native to tropical America and cultivated elsewhere for its fruit; the succulent squash-like fruit of this vine. Also called ***chocho***.

chazan *noun* var. of hazzan.

Chazar *noun & adjective* var. of Khazar.

chazzan *noun* var. of hazzan.

Ch.B. *abbreviation.*
Latin *Chirurgiae Baccalaureus* Bachelor of Surgery.

CHD *abbreviation.*
Coronary heart disease.

cheap /tʃiːp/ *noun.* Long *arch. rare.*
[origin Old English *ċēap* = Old Frisian *kāp*, Old Saxon *kōp* (Dutch *koop*), Old High German *kouf* (German *Kauf*), Old Norse *kaup*, from Germanic, from Latin *caupo* small tradesman, innkeeper. Cf. chapman.]
1 A (good) bargain; bargaining, trade; state of the market; abundance; price, value. After Middle English chiefly in ***good cheap***, good value, cheapness, advantageous terms, ease, plenty (passing into adjectival use). **OE.**
2 A place of buying and selling; a market. Long *obsolete* exc. as a component of proper names, as ***Cheapside***, ***Chepstow***, etc. **OE.**
†**3** Merchandise, chattels; *esp.* live cattle. Only in **OE.**

cheap /tʃiːp/ *adjective & adverb.* **L15.**
[origin Ellipt. for ***good cheap***: see cheap *noun*.]
▸ **A** *adjective.* **1** Low in price or charge made, absolutely or in relation to value; not costly, inexpensive. **L15.** ▸**b** Having or charging low prices. **L16.** ▸**c** Of a fare, rate, etc.: lower than the ordinary fare etc. **E18.** ▸**d** Of money: available on loan at a low rate of interest. **M19.**

Ld Macaulay The services of a Secretary of State . . well qualified for his post would have been cheap at five thousand. **b** OED He is not a cheap tailor.

2 Low in value, worthless, paltry. **L16.**

S. Johnson The cheap reward of empty praise. T. Stoppard A cynical pursuit of cheap sensationalism.

3 Lightly esteemed; *esp.* brought into contempt through overfamiliarity. **L16.**

S. Pepys Making the king cheap and ridiculous.

4 *fig.* Easily got or made; involving little labour, effort, etc. **E17.**

Shakes. *Meas. for M.* 'Twere the cheaper way: Better it were a brother died at once Than that a sister, by redeeming him, Should die for ever. J. Runciman My kisses ain't cheap.

5 In poor health, out of sorts. *slang.* **L19.**
▸ **B** *adverb.* At a low price, cheaply; easily. **M16.**
– phrases etc.: **cheap and cheerful** inexpensive but not unattractive. **cheap and nasty** of low cost and poor quality. **cheapjack** *noun & adjective* (*a*) *noun* a hawker at a fair; (*b*) *adjective* inferior, shoddy; ***cheapskate***: see skate *noun*[3]. ***dirt cheap***: see dirt *noun.* **feel cheap** *slang* feel ashamed or ill. **hold cheap** despise. **on the cheap** (too) cheaply.
■ **cheapie** *adjective & noun* (*dial. & slang*) = cheapo **L19.** **cheaply** *adverb* **M16.** **cheapness** *noun* **M16.** **cheapo** *adjective & noun* (*slang*), pl. **-os**, (something) inexpensive (cf. el cheapo) **M20.**

†**cheap** *verb.*
[origin Old English *ċēapian*, (from different base) *ċēapian* = Old Saxon *kopian*, *kopon*, Old High German *koufen*, *koufōn*, Old Norse *kaupa*, Goth *kaupōn*, from Germanic, from Latin *caupo*: see cheap *noun*.]
1 *verb intrans.* Barter; trade. **OE–ME.**
2 *verb trans.* **a** Buy. **OE–LME.** ▸**b** Bargain for; ask the price of. **ME–M19.**
3 *verb trans.* Offer for sale; offer *to sell*. **ME–L16.**
■ †**cheaping** *noun* (*a*) buying and selling, bargaining, trading; (*b*) a market, a marketplace, (surviving in place names as ***Chipping Campden***, ***Chipping Sodbury***, etc.): **OE–L16.**

cheapen /ˈtʃiːp(ə)n/ *verb.* **L16.**
[origin from cheap *adjective*, *verb* + -en[5].]
1 *verb trans.* Ask the price of, bid for. *arch.* **L16.**
2 *verb trans.* Lower the price of, make cheap; *fig.* depreciate, degrade. **M17.**
3 *verb intrans.* Become cheap (*lit. & fig.*). **E19.**
■ **cheapener** *noun* a person who cheapens something **M17.**

cheat /tʃiːt/ *noun*[1]. **LME.**
[origin Aphet. from escheat *noun*; sense 3 of unknown origin; later senses from the verb.]
†**1** An escheat. **LME–M17.**
†**2** An item of booty or spoil. **M16–E17.**
3 A thing, an article, (usu. of a specified description); *spec.* *the* gallows. *slang* (long *arch.*). **M16.**
†**4** **a** Cheating, fraudulence. **M–L17.** ▸**b** A fraud, a deception, a trick. **M17.**

5 A person who cheats (habitually); a swindler, a deceiver; an impostor; an unfair player. **M17.**

Independent on Sunday You are a liar, a cheat and a thief and I've come to expose you!

6 Darnel, chess, or other grass growing as a weed among cereal crops. *N. Amer. & dial.* **L18.**

7 A card game the point of which is to lie successfully and detect lying in others. **L19.**

†**cheat** *noun*². **LME–M17.**
[**ORIGIN** Unknown.]
Wheaten bread of the second quality, inferior to manchet.

cheat /tʃiːt/ *verb*. **LME.**
[**ORIGIN** Aphet. from **ESCHEAT** *verb*.]
†**1** *verb trans.* Escheat. Only in **LME.**
2 *verb intrans.* Act fraudulently, practise deception; play unfairly. **M16.** ▸**b** *spec.* Be sexually unfaithful. (Foll. by *on* the deceived person.) *N. Amer.* **M20.**

E. F. BENSON After dinner . . she permitted herself a game of patience, and since she never cheated, it was often ten o'clock before her game was over.

3 *verb trans.* Deprive *of* by deceit; defraud; deceive, trick (*into*, *out of*). **L16.**

SHAKES. *Rich. III* Cheated of feature by dissembling nature. W. CATHER I don't admire people who cheat Indians. TOLKIEN We are no phantoms, . . nor do your eyes cheat you.

4 *verb trans.* Beguile (time, weariness, etc.). **E18.**

STEELE No Lay unsung to cheat the tedious Way.

†**5** *verb trans.* Obtain by cheating. **E–M18.**
6 *verb trans. & intrans.* CINEMATOGRAPHY. Suppress or adapt (part of a film) during editing so as to create a desired illusion. **E20.**
■ **cheatable** *adjective* able to be cheated **M17.** **chea'tee** *noun* (*colloq.*) a person who is cheated **E17.** **cheater** *noun* †(**a**) an escheator; (**b**) a person who cheats; see also ***windcheater*** s.v. **WIND** *noun*¹; (**c**) in *pl.* (*US slang*), spectacles: **ME.** **cheatery** *noun* trickery, swindling **M16.**

†**chebec** *noun* var. of **XEBEC.**

chebule /kəˈbuːl/ *noun*. Now *rare* or *obsolete*. **LME.**
[**ORIGIN** French *chébule* from Italian *chebuli*, from Persian & Urdu *Kābulī* of Kabul.]
The astringent fruit of the Indian tree *Terminalia chebula*. Also ***chebule myrobalan***.
■ **chebulic** *adjective* **E18.**

Chechen /ˈtʃɛtʃ(ə)n/ *noun & adjective*. Pl. of noun **-s**, same. **E19.**
[**ORIGIN** Russian †*chechen* (mod. *chechenets*).]
A member of, of or pertaining to, a N. Caucasian people forming the main part of the population of the republic of Chechnya in SW Asia; (of) the language of this people.

chechia /ˈʃeɪʃɪə/ *noun*. **M19.**
[**ORIGIN** French *chéchia* from Maghribi pronunc. of Arabic *šāšiyya*, from Arabic *Šāš* Tashkent in Uzbekistan.]
A red felt cap worn in NW Africa.

check /tʃɛk/ *noun*¹. Also (long *arch.*) **cheque**. See also **CHEQUE** *noun*. **ME.**
[**ORIGIN** from **CHECK** *interjection*.]
▸ **I 1** In CHESS, the state or condition of a king (formerly also a queen or other powerful piece) exposed to direct attack; a move directly attacking a king etc. Formerly also *fig.*, an attack, a harmful act. **ME.**
2 FALCONRY. A false stoop when a hawk abandons its proper quarry and pursues crows, doves, or other prey; lesser game. **LME.**
†**3** A taunt; a rebuke. **E16–M18.**
4 A sudden stopping or slowing of motion; a rebuff, a repulse. **E16.** ▸**b** A stoppage, a pause. **M16.** ▸**c** HUNTING. The loss of a scent. **L18.** ▸**d** A crack or flaw in timber. **L19.**
†**5** A stoppage of wages or a fine imposed on servants in the royal household; the amount stopped. **E16–E18.**
6 Restraint on action; a restraining control. **M16.** ▸**b** A person who or thing which acts as a stop or restraint. **M17.**
7 Control by which accuracy is secured; the means or act of testing quality. **E17.**
8 A token, counterfoil, ticket, or other receipt for the identification of left luggage, the reserver of a seat, etc. Chiefly *N. Amer.* **E19.** ▸**b** A restaurant bill. Chiefly *US*. **M19.**
9 A counter used as a stake in a game of chance. *US*. **L19.**
10 A mark made against an item in an account or list indicating that it has been verified or noted; a tick. **L19.**
▸ **II** See **CHEQUE** *noun*.
– **PHRASES**: ***cash in one's checks***: see **CASH** *verb*² 3a. **checks and balances** (chiefly *US*) constitutional means of limiting or counteracting the wrongful use of governmental power; *gen.* guarantees and counterbalancing influences. **clerk of the cheque** (**a**) an officer of the royal household keeping the roll of royal staff and having control of the Yeomen of the Guard; †(**b**) an officer in control of a royal port, dockyard, etc. **hand in one's checks**, **pass in one's checks** *fig.* (*colloq.*) die. ***hatcheck boy***, ***hatcheck girl***: see **HAT** *noun*. **in check** (**a**) CHESS under direct attack; (**b**) under control. ***overdraw check***: see **OVERDRAW** *noun* 2. ***parity check***: see **PARITY** *noun*¹. ***pass in one's checks***: see ***hand in one's checks*** above. ***perpetual check***: see **PERPETUAL** *adjective*. ***rain check***: see **RAIN** *noun*¹.
■ **checkless** *adjective* (*rare*) unchecked **E17.**

check /tʃɛk/ *noun*² *& adjective*. **LME.**
[**ORIGIN** Prob. abbreviation of *checker* **CHEQUER** *noun*¹.]
▸ **A** *noun*. **1** A pattern of cross lines forming small squares. **LME.**
2 A fabric marked or woven with such a pattern. **E17.** ***tattersal check***: see **TATTERSALL** *noun*.
▸ **B** *adjective*. Marked or woven with such a pattern; made of such a fabric. **E16.**

check *noun*³ var. of **CHICK** *noun*².

check /tʃɛk/ *verb*¹. **LME.**
[**ORIGIN** Aphet. from Old French *eschequier* play chess, give check to, from *eschec* **CHECK** *noun*¹.]
1 *verb trans.* Directly threaten (an opponent's king, *transf.* one's opponent) at chess; put in check. **LME.**

fig.: SHAKES. *John* Thy bastard shall be king, That thou maynst be a queen and check the world.

2 *verb trans.* Suddenly stop or slow the motion of; physically obstruct (an opposing player) in ice hockey etc. **LME.**

S. BRETT As his finger moved towards the button, he checked it.

3 *verb intrans.* FALCONRY. Of a falcon etc.: recoil *at* or shy from the fist; abandon the quarry and fly at other prey. **E16.**
†**4** *verb trans.* Stop (a person) from receiving part of his or her wages. **E16–E19.**
5 *verb trans.* Rebuke, reprove, reprimand. Now *colloq.* **E16.**
†**6** *verb intrans. & trans.* Clash or collide *with* or with. **M16–M17.**
7 *verb trans.* Stay the onward course of, repress, restrain, (actions, growth, feelings, etc.); hold (an agent) in check or under restraint, curb; curb *oneself* in an action etc. **L16.**

J. CARY She began to laugh and then checked herself. C. MACKENZIE You will exercise your influence . . to check such criticism. E. BOWEN She checked or attempted to hide a shiver by wrapping her arms closely across her breast. ISAIAH BERLIN This does tend to check our arrogance, to induce humility.

8 *verb intrans.* Stop (short); restrain oneself. Formerly also *fig.*, take offence (*at*). **E17.** ▸**b** HUNTING. Of a dog: stop on losing a scent, or to make sure of one. **M18.**

R. KIPLING The lama turned to this and that, and finally checked . . before a large alto-relief. F. TUOHY The small movements of his body checked and became total stillness.

9 *verb trans.* Test (a statement, account, figures, work, a person working, etc.) by comparison or other investigation; examine the accuracy or condition of; inspect or investigate to ensure the satisfactoriness or suitability of. Now freq. foll. by *out*, *up*. **L17.** ▸**b** *verb intrans.* Make a comparison or investigation, conduct a check. Freq. foll. by *on*, *up* (*on*). **E20.**

BURKE I have checked this account . . and find it to be correct. A. LURIE My first reaction is to check my stockings for runs. **b** D. HAMMETT The District Attorney will have questioned him and checked up on him. J. DICKEY As we cleared each turn . . I kept looking for white water, and when I'd checked for that I looked along both banks.

b ***parity checking***: see **PARITY** *noun*¹.
10 *verb intrans.* Draw a cheque (*upon*, *for*). *US*. **E19.**
checking account *US* a current account at a bank etc.
11 *verb trans.* Deposit (luggage etc.) for storage or dispatch (in return for a check (see **CHECK** *noun*¹ 8)). Chiefly *N. Amer.* **M19.**
12 *verb trans.* Note with or indicate by a tick or other mark of verification. Also foll. by *off*. **M19.**
13 *verb intrans.* Agree when compared. Also foll. by *out*. **E20.**

M. M. ATWATER If there's finger-prints on it, and yours don't check, that'll let you out.

– **WITH ADVERBS & PREPOSITIONS IN SPECIALIZED SENSES**: **check in** arrive, and be recorded as arriving, at a hotel, factory, airport, etc.; record the arrival of (a person) at a hotel etc. **check into** arrive, and be recorded as arriving, at (a hotel etc.). **check out** depart, and be recorded as departing, from a hotel, factory, airport, etc.; *fig.* (*colloq.*) die; record the departure of (a person) at a hotel; prove to be true or correct (see also senses 9, 13 above). **check out of** depart, and be recorded as departing, from (a hotel etc.). **check over**, **check through** examine or verify successive items or parts of.
■ **checkable** *adjective* **L19.**

check /tʃɛk/ *verb*² *trans.* **LME.**
[**ORIGIN** from **CHECK** *noun*² or abbreviation of *checker* **CHEQUER** *verb*.]
Mark with a pattern of crossing lines or squares.

check /tʃɛk/ *interjection*. **ME.**
[**ORIGIN** Aphet. from Old French *eschec* (mod. *échec*) = Provençal *escac*, Italian *scacco* from Proto-Romance (medieval Latin) *scaccus* from Arabic from Persian *šāh* king, **SHAH**. Cf. **CHESS** *noun*¹, **EXCHEQUER.**]
1 In chess, notifying the exposure of an opponent's king to direct attack. **ME.**
2 Expr. assent or agreement. (Cf. **CHECK** *noun*¹ 10, its probable source.) *N. Amer. colloq.* **E20.**

N. MAILER 'No audience . . is going to trust a man whose wife takes a leap.' 'Check.'

check- /tʃɛk/ *combining form*. **LME.**
[**ORIGIN** from **CHECK** *noun*¹ or *verb*¹.]
In combs. in various relations with the senses 'that serves to check or control', 'an act of checking or being checked'.
check-action a mechanism restraining a piano hammer from striking a string twice. **check-in** the act of checking in. **checklist** a (complete) list for reference and verification. **check-nut** = *locknut* (a) s.v. **LOCK** *noun*². **checkout** (**a**) the act of checking out; a final check; (**b**) the pay desk in a supermarket etc. (also ***checkout counter***, ***checkout desk***, etc.). **checkpoint** a point at which documents, vehicles, etc., are checked or inspected; a time or stage at which progress etc. is assessed. **check rail** RAILWAYS an extra rail laid to resist sideways pressure on a sharp curve. **check rein** a rein attaching one horse's rein to another's bit, or preventing a horse from lowering its head. †**check roll** a list of the names and other details of people in the service of the royal or other large household; a muster roll. **checkroom**, **check stand** *N. Amer.* a room, a stand, in which 'checked' articles are placed. **check string** *hist.* a string used by a passenger in a carriage to signal the driver to stop. **checksum** COMPUTING a modular sum of the digits in a data item, transmitted with the item to provide a check of any errors that may arise in it. **check-taker** *US* a person who takes or collects the checks or tickets for admission to a theatre etc. **check-up** a careful examination, esp. of a person's general medical condition. **check valve** a valve preventing backward flow of liquid in a pipe etc. **checkweighman** a person who checks the weight of mined coal on behalf of miners.

checked /tʃɛkt/ *adjective*¹. Also †**chequed**. **LME.**
[**ORIGIN** from **CHECK** *noun*², *verb*²: see **-ED**², **-ED**¹.]
Marked with checks, having checks, chequered.

Time Young kids . . in checked shirts and baseball caps.

checked /tʃɛkt/ *adjective*². Also †**chequed**. **M18.**
[**ORIGIN** from **CHECK** *noun*¹, **CHEQUE** *noun*, or **CHECK** *verb*¹: see **-ED**², **-ED**¹.]
†**1** Of paper: having a counterfoil; for use as a cheque. Only in **M18.**
2 *gen.* That has been checked. Also ***checked-in***, ***checked-out***, ***checked-up***, etc. **L18.**
3 PHONETICS. Of a syllable: ending in a consonant, closed. Of a vowel: occurring in such a syllable. **L19.**

checker /ˈtʃɛkə/ *noun*¹. **M16.**
[**ORIGIN** from **CHECK** *verb*¹ + **-ER**¹.]
A person or device which checks; *spec.* (**a**) a person who works at the checkout of a supermarket etc.; (**b**) a player who checks an opponent in ice hockey etc.
SPELLING ***checker***.

checker *noun*², *verb* see **CHEQUER** *noun*¹, *verb*.

checkerberry /ˈtʃɛkəbɛri/ *noun*. **L18.**
[**ORIGIN** from *checker* var. of **CHEQUER** *noun*² + **BERRY** *noun*¹.]
A low creeping evergreen N. American shrub of the heath family, *Gaultheria procumbens*, with spicy-scented leaves and waxy white flowers (also called ***partidgeberry***, ***wintergreen***); the edible red fruit of this shrub.

checkered *adjective* see **CHEQUERED.**

†**checklaton** *noun*. *rare* (Spenser). Only in **L16.**
[**ORIGIN** Alt.]
= **CICLATOUN.**

checkmate /ˈtʃɛkmeɪt/ *interjection, noun, adjective, & verb*. **ME.**
[**ORIGIN** Aphet. from Old French *eschec mat* = Provençal *escac mat*, from Arabic *šāh māt(a)* repr. Persian *šāh māt* the king is defeated, the king is perplexed: see **CHECK** *interjection*, **MATE** *adjective*.]
▸ **A** *interjection*. In CHESS, notifying the putting of an opponent's king into inextricable check, by which the game is won; *transf.* notifying an adversary's defeat. **ME.**
▸ **B** *noun*. (The notifying to an opponent of) the inextricable check of a king in chess; *transf. & fig.* final defeat or deadlock. **LME.**
▸ **C** *pred. adjective*. In inextricable check; *fig.* defeated. **LME.**
▸ **D** *verb trans.* Give checkmate to; *fig.* defeat, frustrate. **LME.**

check-stone /ˈtʃɛkstəʊn/ *noun*. Now *dial. rare*. **L16.**
[**ORIGIN** Unknown.]
A smooth round pebble; *sing.* & in *pl.* a game played with such pebbles.

checky /ˈtʃɛki/ *adjective*. In HERALDRY also **che(c)quy**. **LME.**
[**ORIGIN** Aphet. from Old French *eschequié*, *eschequé*, later assim. to adjectives in **-Y**¹.]
Chiefly HERALDRY. Checked, chequered; (of a field or charge) divided into three or more rows of small squares of alternate tinctures.

chedarim *noun pl.* see **HEDER.**

Cheddar /ˈtʃɛdə/ *noun*. **M17.**
[**ORIGIN** A village in Somerset, England.]
1 In full ***Cheddar cheese***. A hard smooth-textured cheese made (orig. at Cheddar) by piling the curds and forming a smooth mass. **M17.**
2 ***Cheddar pink***, a pink, *Dianthus gratianopolitanus*, with dull greyish leaves, in Britain found only at Cheddar Gorge. **M19.**
■ **cheddaring** *noun* a process or stage in the manufacture of cheese, involving the piling of the curds to form a smooth mass **E20.**

cheder /ˈhɛdə, x-/ *noun*. Also **heder**. Pl. **-darim** /-ˈdɑːrɪm/, **-rs**. L19.
[ORIGIN Hebrew *ḥēder* room.]
A school for Jewish children in which Hebrew and religious knowledge are taught.

cheechako /tʃiːˈtʃɑːkəʊ/ *noun*. *N. Amer. colloq.* Pl. **-os**. L19.
[ORIGIN Chinook Jargon = newcomer.]
A newly arrived immigrant to the mining districts of N. America; a greenhorn, a tenderfoot.

chee-chee *adjective* var. of CHI-CHI.

cheek /tʃiːk/ *noun*.
[ORIGIN Old English *ċēoce* = Old Frisian *ziāke*, varying with Old English *ċēace*, *ċēce* = Middle & mod. Low German *kāke*, *kēke*, Middle Dutch *kāke* (Dutch *kaak*), from West Germanic.]
▸ **I** Of a person or animal.
†**1** The jaw, the jawbone; *sing.* & (usu.) in *pl.*, the chops, the fauces. OE–M16.
2 The side wall of the mouth; the side of the face below the eye; *fig.* something suggestive of the cheek in shape, colour, etc. OE.
BYRON Ocean's cheek Reflects the tints of many a peak.
3 A buttock. Usu. in *pl.* L16.
4 Impertinent speech; cool confidence, effrontery; insolence. M19.
GEORGE MOORE If he gives me any of his cheek I'll knock him down. J. FOWLES Some even had the cheek to push their cameras through the front gate.
▸ **II** *transf.* & *techn.* (All usu. in *pl.*)
5 The side post of a door, gate, etc. LME.
6 *gen.* A side. M16.
7 Either of the side pieces of a horse's bit; the strap of a bridle passing down each side of a horse's head, to connect the headpiece with the bit. E17.
8 NAUTICAL. On a square-rigged ship, each of the projections on either side of a mast on which the trestletrees rest; the outside wooden part of a block etc. E17.
9 Each of a pair of laterally arranged side pieces forming part of a machine; *esp.* each of the jaws of a vice. M17.
– PHRASES ETC.: **cheek by jowl**, †**cheek by cheek** side by side, close together, intimate(ly). **cheek to cheek** (in dancing) with the cheeks of partners (nearly) touching. ***of all the cheek*** etc.: see OF *preposition*. ***tongue-in-cheek***: see TONGUE *noun*. **to one's own cheek** without sharing or not shared with others. **turn the other cheek** [alluding to *Matthew* 5:39, *Luke* 6:29] permit or invite another blow, attack, etc.; refuse to retaliate. ***with one's tongue in one's cheek***, ***with tongue in cheek***: see TONGUE *noun*.
– COMB.: **cheekbone** (*a*) the bone above the cheek, forming the lower boundary of the orbits of the eyes; †(*b*) the jawbone; **cheek pouch** a pouchlike enlargement of the cheek, esp. in certain monkeys; **cheek tooth** a molar.
■ **cheeked** *adjective* having a cheek or cheeks (of a specified kind) M16.

cheek /tʃiːk/ *verb trans*. M16.
[ORIGIN from the noun.]
1 Form a cheek or side to. M16.
2 Address cheekily or saucily. *colloq.* M19.

cheeky /ˈtʃiːki/ *adjective*. E19.
[ORIGIN from CHEEK *noun* + -Y¹.]
Characterized by or showing cheek; insolent, impudent.
■ **cheekily** *adverb* E20. **cheekiness** *noun* M19.

cheep /tʃiːp/ *verb* & *noun*. Orig. *Scot.* E16.
[ORIGIN Imit.: cf. PEEP *verb*¹ & *noun*³.]
▸ **A** *verb*. **1** *verb intrans.* Utter shrill feeble sounds (like those) of a young bird. E16.
2 *verb trans.* Utter with a cheeping voice. M19.
▸ **B** *noun*. A shrill feeble sound (as) of a young bird. L18.
not a cheep *colloq.* not the slightest sound, not a word.
■ **cheeper** *noun* E17. **cheepy** *adjective* given to cheeping M19.

cheer /tʃɪə/ *noun*¹. See also CHEERS *interjection*. ME.
[ORIGIN Anglo-Norman *chere*, Old French *chiere* face, from late Latin *cara* from Greek *kara* head.]
†**1** The face; the expression of the face; countenance. ME–M19.
2 Disposition, frame of mind, mood. Now usu. with specifying word, esp. *good*. ME.
T. H. WHITE I rode away with heavy cheer.
of good cheer stout-hearted, hopeful. **what cheer?** how do you feel? (cf. WOTCHER *interjection*.).
3 Kindly welcome or reception, hospitable entertainment (passing into sense 5). *obsolete* exc. *dial.* ME.
SHAKES. *Lucr.* She securely gives good cheer And reverend welcome to her princely guest.
4 Cheerfulness, gladness, mirth, joy, gaiety. LME.
B. RUBENS He engaged a smile . . in preparation for the cheer he would put into his voice.
5 Provisions, viands, food (for entertainment). LME.
make good cheer feast, revel.
6 A thing which gives joy or gladness; comfort; encouragement. M16.
Times The market took cheer . . and marked the shares up 3p.
7 A shout of encouragement, welcome, approbation, or congratulation. L17.
J. HERRIOT The farm men didn't exactly break into a cheer but they were enormously pleased.
three cheers successive united hurrahs (*for* a person or thing honoured). **two cheers** *iron.* mild enthusiasm.
– COMB.: **cheerleader** (*a*) a member of a team of girls who perform organized cheering, chanting, and dancing at sporting events in the US; (*b*) an enthusiastic and vocal supporter of someone or something. **cheerleading** the action of behaving as a cheerleader.

cheer /tʃɪə/ *noun*². Also **chir**. E19.
[ORIGIN Nepali: imit.]
In full ***cheer pheasant***. A pheasant, *Catreus wallichii*, native to the Himalayan region.

cheer /tʃɪə/ *verb*. LME.
[ORIGIN from CHEER *noun*¹.]
†**1** *verb refl.* & *intrans.* With adverb: assume a particular disposition or state of mind. LME–E18.
SHAKES. *Merch. V.* How cheer'st thou, Jessica?
2 *verb trans.* Make of good cheer; comfort, console; make joyous, gladden, enliven. Freq. foll. by *up*. LME.
V. S. PRITCHETT It cheers me that I live on the frontier of Camden Town and Regent's Park. G. M. FRASER Grattan didn't cheer me up by remarking that the Cumanche are cannibals.
†**3 a** *verb trans.* Entertain with feasting. LME–L17. ▸**b** *verb trans.* & *intrans.* Solace or comfort as food does. M16.
a DRYDEN I myself the Guests with friendly Bowls will chear. **b** W. H. RUSSELL A cup . . which to my mind neither cheers nor inebriates.
4 *verb trans.* Encourage, inspirit, animate, incite, by word or deed (now esp. with cheers, passing into sense 7). Freq. foll. by *on*. LME.
C. THIRLWALL Cheering his troops by his presence and his words. K. GRAHAME His comrades cheered him on, Mole coaxed and encouraged him . . ; but nothing could overcome his stage-fright.
5 *verb intrans.* Be or grow cheerful, enjoy oneself. Now only foll. by *up*: become cheerful, take heart. L16.
W. FAULKNER When I gave him another sup . . , he cheered up some.
6 *verb trans.* Brighten up (one's face etc.). E17.
7 *verb trans.* & *intrans.* Salute with cheers, applause, or other indications of approbation or support. L18.
B. JOWETT Many of the audience cheered and applauded this. H. CARPENTER The boys were even forbidden to cheer at their own football matches.
■ **cheerer** *noun* a person who or thing which cheers L16. **cheeringly** *adverb* in a cheering manner, so as to cheer one E19.

cheerful /ˈtʃɪəfʊl, -f(ə)l/ *adjective*. LME.
[ORIGIN from CHEER *noun*¹ + -FUL.]
1 Contented, in good spirits, hopeful; willing, not reluctant. LME.
2 Inspiring contentment etc.; bright, pleasant. LME.
■ **cheerfully** *adverb* M16. **cheerfulness** *noun* LME.

cheerie-bye /tʃɪərɪˈbʌɪ/ *interjection*. *colloq.* M20.
[ORIGIN from CHEERIO + GOODBYE.]
Goodbye.

cheerio /tʃɪərɪˈəʊ/ *interjection*. *colloq.* Also **cheero** /tʃɪəˈrəʊ/. E20.
[ORIGIN from CHEERY + O *interjection*.]
Expr. good wishes on parting or before drinking; goodbye; good health.

cheerless /ˈtʃɪəlɪs/ *adjective*. L16.
[ORIGIN from CHEER *noun*¹ + -LESS.]
Devoid of comfort; dispiriting; gloomy.
■ **cheerlessly** *adverb* L19. **cheerlessness** *noun* M19.

cheerly /ˈtʃɪəli/ *adjective*. *arch.* L15.
[ORIGIN from CHEER *noun*¹ + -LY¹.]
Cheerful, lively.

cheerly /ˈtʃɪəli/ *adverb*. L15.
[ORIGIN from CHEER *noun*¹ + -LY².]
Cheerily; cheeringly; NAUTICAL heartily, with a will.

cheero *interjection* var. of CHEERIO.

cheers /tʃɪəz/ *interjection*. *colloq.* E20.
[ORIGIN pl. of CHEER *noun*¹.]
1 Expr. good wishes, esp. before drinking; cheerio, good health. Also, goodbye. E20.
2 Expr. thanks. L20.

cheery /ˈtʃɪəri/ *adjective*. LME.
[ORIGIN from CHEER *noun*¹ + -Y¹.]
Cheerful, in good spirits; genial, cheering.
■ **cheerily** *adverb* E17. **cheeriness** *noun* M19.

cheese /tʃiːz/ *noun*¹.
[ORIGIN Old English *ċēse*, *ċȳse* = Old Saxon *kāsi*, *k(i)ēsi* (Dutch *kaas*), Old High German *chāsi*, *kāsi* (German *Käse*), from West Germanic from Latin *caseus*.]
1 The curds of milk (coagulated by rennet) separated from the whey and pressed into a solid mass, eaten as food; a distinct kind of this. OE. ▸**b** A mass or cake of this within a rind. LME.
blue cheese, ***Cheddar cheese***, ***cottage cheese***, ***cream cheese***, ***Dutch cheese***, ***Lancashire cheese***, ***Limburger cheese***, ***Parmesan cheese***, ***processed cheese***, ***Swiss cheese***, etc. ***as different as chalk and cheese***, ***as different as chalk from cheese***: see CHALK *noun*. ***green cheese***: see GREEN *adjective*. ***hard cheese***: see HARD *adjective*. ***mousetrap cheese***: see MOUSETRAP 2.
2 The fruit of the common mallow, *Malva silvestris*, which has a round flattened shape like a cheese. E16.
3 A conserve of fruit etc. having the consistency or form of (cream) cheese. M16. ▸**b** A mass of crushed apples pressed together in the form of a cheese. E18.
damson cheese, ***lemon cheese***, etc.
4 Any object shaped like a cheese (usu. taken as being cylindrical or an oblate spheroid). M19.
5 The action of turning round rapidly and sinking down so that skirts and petticoats take the form of a cheese; a deep curtsy. (Cf. French *faire des fromages*.) *arch.* M19.
6 The word 'cheese' notionally or actually pronounced to form the lips into a smile, when one is being photographed. M20.
Z. MDA The photographer said 'Cheese!' but her face refused to break into a smile.
– COMB.: **cheeseboard** a board from which cheese is served; a selection of cheeses served with a meal; **cheeseburger** a hamburger with cheese in or on it; **cheesecake** (*a*) a tart(let) with a filling of sweetened curds on a pastry or biscuit-crumb base; (*b*) *slang* (orig. *US*) the display of shapely female form in advertisements, photographs, etc.; **cheesecloth** = ***butter muslin*** s.v. BUTTER *noun*¹; **cheese-cutter** (*a*) a knife with a curved blade used for cutting cheese; (*b*) a device for cutting cheese by pulling a wire through it; **cheese fly** a small black fly, *Piophila casei*, whose larvae feed on cheese; **cheese head** a squat cylindrical head of a screw etc.; **cheese knife** (*a*) = ***cheese-cutter*** (a) above; (*b*) a spatula used to break down curd in cheese-making; **cheese mite** a mite of the genus *Tyroglyphus*, feeding on old cheese; **cheesemonger** a dealer in cheese, butter, etc.; **cheese-pare** *verb intrans.* be stingy, make miserly economies; **cheese-paring** *adjective* & *noun* (*a*) *adjective* stingy; (*b*) *noun* stinginess; †**cheese-rennet**, †**cheese-running** lady's bedstraw, *Galium verum*, formerly used to curdle milk; **cheese skipper** the larva of the cheese fly; **cheesesteak** *US* a sandwich consisting of thinly sliced sautéed beef, melted cheese, and sautéed onions, served in a long bread roll; **cheese straw** a thin cheese-flavoured strip of pastry; **cheesewood** (the hard yellow wood of) an Australian tree of the genus *Pittosporum*.

cheese /tʃiːz/ *noun*². *slang.* E19.
[ORIGIN Prob. from Urdu from Persian *čīz* thing.]
1 *The* right or correct thing; something first-rate. E19.
2 An important or self-important person; *the* boss. Freq. as ***big cheese***. Orig. *US*. E20.

cheese /tʃiːz/ *verb trans.* *slang.* E19.
[ORIGIN Unknown.]
1 Stop *it*, leave off. Esp. in *imper.* E19.
2 Bore, exasperate. Chiefly as ***cheesed off***, browned off, fed up. M20.

cheeselip /ˈtʃiːzlɪp/ *noun*¹. *obsolete* exc. *dial.*
[ORIGIN Old English *ċēselyb(b)*, from CHEESE *noun*¹ + a word = Old Norse *lyf* herb, mod. German dial. *Lüpp* rennet.]
Rennet for cheese-making; the dried (calf's) stomach from which it is prepared.

cheeselip /ˈtʃiːzlɪp/ *noun*². *obsolete* exc. *dial.* M16.
[ORIGIN Unknown.]
A woodlouse or similar crustacean.

cheesy /ˈtʃiːzi/ *adjective*. In sense 3 also **cheesey**. LME.
[ORIGIN from CHEESE *noun*¹ + -Y¹.]
1 Of, belonging to, consisting of, or of the nature of cheese; containing cheese. LME.
2 Resembling cheese in appearance etc. M18.
3 Cheap and of low quality; hackneyed and sentimental; (of a smile) exaggerated and insincere. *colloq.* L19.
I. EDWARDS-JONES He's particularly fond of cheesy award ceremonies for cable companies. B. GRAHAM Johnny flashes his best cheeky, cheesy grin.
■ **cheesily** *adverb* L20. **cheesiness** *noun* M19.

cheetah /ˈtʃiːtə/ *noun*. L18.
[ORIGIN Hindi *cītā*, from Sanskrit *citraka* leopard.]
A swift-running spotted feline, *Acinonyx jubatus*, native to the plains of Africa and SW Asia.

cheetal *noun* var. of CHITAL.

cheewink *noun* var. of CHEWINK.

chef /ʃɛf/ *noun* & *verb*. E19.
[ORIGIN French = head.]
▸ **A** *noun*. A professional cook, *esp.* the chief cook in a restaurant or hotel. E19.
▸ **B** *verb intrans.* Infl. **-ff-**. Work as a chef. E20.

chef d'école /ʃɛf dekɔl/ *noun phr.* Pl. ***chefs d'école*** (pronounced same). M19.
[ORIGIN French = head of school.]
The initiator or leader of a school or style of music, painting, literature, etc.

chef-d'œuvre /ʃɛdœːvr/ *noun*. Pl. ***chefs-*** (pronounced same). E17.
[ORIGIN French = chief (piece) of work.]
The greatest work of an artist etc.; a masterpiece.

chef d'orchestre /ʃɛf dɔrkɛstr/ *noun phr.* Pl. ***chefs d'orchestre*** (pronounced same). M19.
[ORIGIN French = head of orchestra.]
The leader or conductor of an orchestra.

chefs d'école, ***chefs-d'œuvre***, ***chefs d'orchestre*** *nouns* pls. of CHEF D'ÉCOLE etc.

cheilo- /ˈkʌɪləʊ/ *combining form*. Also **chilo-**, (before a vowel) **ch(e)il-**.
Repr. Greek *kheilos* lip: see -O-.
■ **chei'litis** *noun* (MEDICINE) inflammation of the lips M19. **cheiloplastic** *adjective* of or pertaining to cheiloplasty M19. **cheiloplasty** *noun* (an instance of) surgical repair of injury or deformity of the lip M19.

cheir- *combining form* see CHIRO-.

cheiranthus /kʌɪˈranθəs/ *noun*. M19.
[ORIGIN mod. Latin (see below), from Greek *kheir* hand + *anthos* flower.]
A cruciferous plant of the genus *Cheiranthus* (now freq. included in the genus *Erysimum*), to which the wallflower belongs.

cheiro- *combining form* var. of CHIRO-.

cheirology *noun* var. of CHIROLOGY.

†**cheiropteran** *noun & adjective* var. of CHIROPTERAN.

Cheka /ˈtʃɛkə/ *noun*. Also **Tch-**. E20.
[ORIGIN Russian *Cheka*, from *Che*, *ka*, pronunc. of initials of *Chrezvychaĭnaya Komissiya* Extraordinary Commission (for combating Counter-revolution, Sabotage, and Speculation).]
An organization set up in 1917 in the USSR to investigate counter-revolutionary activities, superseded in 1922 by Ogpu.

Chekhovian /tʃɛˈkəʊvɪən/ *adjective*. Also **Tch-**. E20.
[ORIGIN from *Chekhov* (see below) + -IAN.]
Of, pertaining to, or characteristic of the work of the Russian author Anton Pavlovich Chekhov (1860–1904), esp. in attaching dramatic and symbolic significance to detail.

chela /ˈkiːlə/ *noun*[1]. Pl. **-lae** /-liː/. M17.
[ORIGIN mod. Latin from Latin *chele*, Greek *khēlē* claw.]
ZOOLOGY. A pincer-like claw of a crab, lobster, scorpion, etc.
■ **che'liferous** *adjective* bearing chelae or claws M18. **cheliform** *adjective* having the form of a chela L18.

chela /ˈtʃeɪlə/ *noun*[2]. M19.
[ORIGIN Hindi *celā*.]
A disciple, a pupil, *spec.* in Hinduism.

chelate /ˈkiːleɪt/ *adjective & noun*. E19.
[ORIGIN from CHELA *noun*[1] + -ATE[2].]
▸ **A** *adjective*. **1** ZOOLOGY. Having two opposing claws or pincer-like structures. E19.
2 CHEMISTRY. That is or involves a ligand which forms bonds to the same central atom at two or more points. E20.
▸ **B** *noun*. CHEMISTRY. A chelate compound. M20.

chelate /ˈkiːleɪt, kɪˈleɪt/ *verb trans*. E20.
[ORIGIN from the adjective.]
CHEMISTRY. Combine with in the manner of a chelate ligand.
■ **che'lation** *noun* the state or process of being chelated M20. **che'lator** *noun* a chelate ligand M20.

chelicera /kəˈlɪs(ə)rə/ *noun*. Pl. **-rae** /-riː/. Also anglicized as **chelicer** /ˈkɛlɪsə/. M19.
[ORIGIN mod. Latin, formed as CHELA *noun*[1] + Greek *keras* horn.]
ZOOLOGY. Each of the anterior pair of appendages of arachnids and some other arthropods, modified as pincer-like jaws.
■ **cheliceral** *adjective* L19. **chelicerate** *adjective & noun* (an arthropod) having chelicerae E20.

cheliped /ˈkiːlɪpɛd/ *noun*. M19.
[ORIGIN formed as CHELA *noun*[1] + -I- + Latin *ped-*, *pes* foot.]
ZOOLOGY. Either of a pair of limbs bearing claws or pincers, found in decapod crustaceans.

Chellean /ˈʃɛlɪən/ *adjective*. L19.
[ORIGIN French *Chelléen*, from *Chelles* near Paris: see -AN.]
= ABBEVILLIAN *adjective*.

†**cheloid** *noun & adjective* var. of KELOID.

chelonian /kɪˈləʊnɪən/ *adjective & noun*. E19.
[ORIGIN from mod. Latin *Chelonia*, from Greek *khelōnē* tortoise: see -IA[2], -AN.]
ZOOLOGY. ▸ **A** *adjective*. Of, pertaining to, or characteristic of the reptilian order Testudines (formerly Chelonia), which includes the tortoises, turtles, and terrapins. E19.
▸ **B** *noun*. A reptile of this order. E19.

chelp /tʃɛlp/ *verb & noun*. *dial*. E19.
[ORIGIN Uncertain: perh. imit.]
▸ **A** *verb trans. & intrans*. Chirp, squeak; chatter; cheep. E19.
▸ **B** *noun*. Chatter; backchat. L19.

Chelsea /ˈtʃɛlsi/ *noun*. E18.
[ORIGIN A district in London on the north bank of the Thames.]
1 ***Chelsea bun***, a kind of currant bun, originally made in Chelsea. E18.
2 More fully ***Chelsea ware***, ***Chelsea porcelain***, etc. A kind of porcelain made at Chelsea in the 18th cent. M18.
3 ***Chelsea pensioner***, an inmate of the Chelsea Royal Hospital for old or disabled soldiers. E19.
4 ***Chelsea boot***, a short elastic-sided boot. M20.
5 ***Chelsea tractor***, a large four-wheel-drive vehicle used in urban areas. *joc*. L20.

Cheltonian /tʃɛlˈtəʊnɪən/ *noun & adjective*. L19.
[ORIGIN from *Cheltenham* (see below) after ABERDONIAN etc.]
(A native or inhabitant) of the town of Cheltenham in Gloucestershire; (a member or former member) of Cheltenham College or Cheltenham Ladies' College.

chemi- /ˈkɛmi/ *combining form* of CHEMICAL *adjective*: see -I-. Cf. CHEMICO-, CHEMO-.
■ **chemilumi'nescence** *noun* the emission of (cold) light accompanying a chemical reaction L19. **chemilumi'nescent** *adjective* exhibiting chemiluminescence E20. **chemios'motic** *adjective* (BIOCHEMISTRY) pertaining to or involving the transfer of electrons, protons, or other species through membranes, as a mechanism of metabolic reactions M20. **chemisorb** *verb trans*. [back-form.] collect by chemisorption M20. **chemi'sorption** *noun* adsorption involving the formation of chemical bonds M20.

chemiatric /kɛmɪˈatrɪk/ *adjective & noun*. M19.
[ORIGIN from mod. Latin *chemiatria* iatrochemistry (Paracelsus), formed as CHEMI- + Greek *iatreia* medical treatment: see -IC.]
▸ **A** *adjective*. = IATROCHEMICAL. M19.
▸ **B** *noun*. = IATROCHEMIST. M19.

chemic /ˈkɛmɪk/ *adjective, noun, & verb*. Orig. †**chymic**. L16.
[ORIGIN French *chimique*, or mod. Latin *chimicus*, *chym-*, for medieval Latin *alchimicus*, from *alchimia* ALCHEMY: see -IC.]
▸ **A** *adjective*. **1** Alchemical. *arch*. L16.
†**2** = IATROCHEMICAL. E17–M18.
3 Of or belonging to chemistry. *poet*. M17.
▸ **B** *noun*. †**1** An alchemist. L16–L17.
†**2** = IATROCHEMIST. E–M17.
†**3** A chemist. M–L17.
4 Calcium or sodium hypochlorite used as bleach. *arch*. M19.
▸ **C** *verb trans*. Infl. **-ck-**.
†**1** Transmute (as) by alchemy. E17–E18.
2 Bleach with a solution of calcium or sodium hypochlorite. *arch*. M19.

chemical /ˈkɛmɪk(ə)l/ *adjective & noun*. Orig. †**chym-**. L16.
[ORIGIN formed as CHEMIC + -AL[1].]
▸ **A** *adjective*. †**1** Alchemical. L16–M18.
2 Of, made by, or relating to, chemistry; employing chemicals. L16. ▸**b** *spec*. Designating a lavatory or closet in which waste is decomposed by chemicals. M20.
†**3** = IATROCHEMICAL. L16–L18.
4 Of a person: engaged in the practice of chemistry; versed in chemistry. E17.
– SPECIAL COLLOCATIONS: ***chemical attraction***: see ATTRACTION 3. **chemical bond** = BOND *noun*[2] 11. **chemical engineer** an expert in chemical engineering. **chemical engineering** the science of the utilization of chemical processes in manufacturing. **chemical potential** a thermodynamic function pertaining to any one component present in a system, equal to the derivative of the free energy with respect to the quantity of that component. ***chemical shift***: see SHIFT *noun*. **chemical warfare**: employing chemical weapons. **chemical weapon** a weapon that depends for its effect on the release of a toxic or noxious substance.
▸ **B** *noun*. **1** A distinct substance obtained by or used in a chemical process. M18.
fine chemicals: used in small amounts and in a purified state. **heavy chemicals** bulk chemicals used in industry and agriculture.
2 A narcotic drug, *esp*. an addictive one. M20.
■ **chemicalize** *verb trans*. treat with chemicals; use chemicals in (an activity): E20. **chemically** *adverb* E17.

chemico- /ˈkɛmɪkəʊ/ *combining form* of CHEMICAL *adjective*: see -O-. Cf. CHEMI-, CHEMO-.
■ **chemico-'physical** *adjective* of or pertaining to chemistry and physics M19.

chemin de fer /ʃ(ə)mɛ̃ də fɛːr, ʃəˈmã də fɛː/ *noun*. L19.
[ORIGIN French = railway, lit. 'road of iron'.]
A form of baccarat.

chemise /ʃəˈmiːz/ *noun*. ME.
[ORIGIN Old French & mod. French from late Latin *camisia* shirt, nightgown.]
1 A garment for the upper body; *esp*. a woman's loose-fitting undergarment or dress hanging straight from the shoulders. ME.
2 *hist*. A wall with which a bastion etc. is lined as a fortification. E18.
3 *hist*. A loose covering for a book. L19.

chemisette /ʃɛmiːˈzɛt/ *noun*. E19.
[ORIGIN French, dim. of CHEMISE: see -ETTE.]
1 A bodice, resembling the upper part of a chemise. E19.
2 A piece of muslin, lace, etc., used to fill in the open front of a woman's dress. E19.

chemism /ˈkɛmɪz(ə)m/ *noun*. *rare*. E19.
[ORIGIN French *chimisme*, parallel to *chimiste* CHEMIST: see -ISM.]
Chemical action, activity, or force.

chemist /ˈkɛmɪst/ *noun*. Also (*arch*.) **chym-**. LME.
[ORIGIN French *chimiste*, †*chym-* from mod. Latin *chimysta*, *-ista* for *alchimista* ALCHEMIST.]
†**1** An alchemist. LME–M18.
†**2** = IATROCHEMIST. Only in E17.
3 A person skilled in chemistry; one who makes chemical investigations. E17.
4 A dealer in medicinal drugs, usu. also selling other medical goods and toiletries. M18.

chemistry /ˈkɛmɪstri/ *noun*. Also (*arch*.) **chym-**. L16.
[ORIGIN from CHEMIST + -RY.]
1 (The branch of science that deals with) the investigation of the substances of which matter is composed, and of the phenomena of combination and change which they display (cf. ALCHEMY); (a set of) chemical reactions or properties. Also *fig*., mysterious processes or change; (an) imponderable interaction. L16.

> R. W. EMERSON The world has a sure chemistry, by which it extracts what is excellent in its children. C. SAGAN Our chemistry is delicately attuned to the temperature of the planet on which we have evolved. R. JAFFE There just wasn't any chemistry between them anymore.

inorganic chemistry, ***organic chemistry***, ***physical chemistry***, ***surface chemistry***, etc.
†**2** = IATROCHEMISTRY. L17–E18.

chemmy /ˈʃɛmi/ *noun*. *colloq*. E20.
[ORIGIN Abbreviation.]
= CHEMIN DE FER.

chemo /ˈkiːməʊ/ *noun*. *colloq*. L20.
[ORIGIN Abbreviation.]
Chemotherapy.

chemo- /ˈkiːməʊ/ *combining form* of CHEMICAL *adjective*: see -O-. Cf. CHEMI-, CHEMICO-.
■ **chemoa'ttractant** *noun* (PHYSIOLOGY) a substance produced within the body which attracts motile cells of a particular type L20. **chemokine** *noun* (PHYSIOLOGY) any of a group of cytokines whose major function is the attraction of white blood cells to sites of inflammation L20. **chemoprophy'lactic** *adjective* of, pertaining to, or involving chemoprophylaxis M20. **chemoprophy'laxis** *noun* the prophylactic use of chemicals M20. **chemoreception** *noun* the response of an organism to a chemical change in its environment E20. **chemoreceptor** *noun* a sensory organ responsive to chemical stimuli E20. **chemostat** *noun* a system or device in which the chemical composition is kept at a controlled level; *esp*. one for the culture of micro-organisms, in which the nutrient medium is continually replenished: M20. **chemo'synthesis** *noun* the formation by living organisms of carbohydrates from inorganic compounds without the agency of light E20. **chemosyn'thetic** *adjective* of, pertaining to, or involving chemosynthesis M20.

chemoautotrophic /ˌkɛməʊɔːtəˈtrəʊfɪk, -ˈtrɒf-/ *adjective*. M20.
[ORIGIN from CHEMO- + AUTOTROPHIC.]
Of micro-organisms or their metabolism: deriving energy from the oxidation of inorganic compounds.
■ **chemo'autotroph** *noun* a chemoautotrophic organism M20. **chemoautotrophically** *adverb* M20. **chemoautotrophism** /-ˈtrəʊf-/ *noun* M20. **chemoautotrophy** /-ˈtrəʊf-/ *noun* M20.

chemokinesis /kɛmə(ʊ)kɪˈniːsɪs, -kʌɪ-/ *noun*. Pl. **-neses** /-ˈniːsiːz/. E20.
[ORIGIN from CHEMO- + KINESIS.]
BIOLOGY. (A) kinesis in response to a particular substance.
■ **chemokinetic** /-ˈnɛtɪk/ *adjective* of, pertaining to, or displaying chemokinesis E20.

chemosis /kɪˈməʊsɪs/ *noun*. E18.
[ORIGIN Greek *khēmōsis*, from *khēmē* cockleshell: see -OSIS.]
MEDICINE. Oedema of the conjunctiva.

chemotaxis /kɛmə(ʊ)ˈtaksɪs/ *noun*. L19.
[ORIGIN from CHEMO- + -TAXIS.]
BIOLOGY. Motion of a motile cell, organism, or part towards or away from an increasing concentration of a particular substance.
■ **chemotactic** *adjective* of, pertaining to, or displaying chemotaxis L19. **chemotactically** *adverb* E20.

chemotherapy /kiːmə(ʊ)ˈθɛrəpi, kɛm-/ *noun*. E20.
[ORIGIN from CHEMO- + THERAPY.]
The treatment of disease, esp. infections or cancer, by means of chemicals.
■ **chemothera'peutic**, **chemothera'peutical** *adjectives* of, pertaining to, or involving chemotherapy E20. **chemothera'peutically** *adverb* M20. **chemotherapist** *noun* M20.

chemotropism /kɛmə(ʊ)ˈtrəʊpɪz(ə)m/ *noun*. L19.
[ORIGIN from CHEMO- + Greek *tropos* turning + -ISM.]
BIOLOGY. A tropism, esp. of a plant, in response to a particular substance.
■ **chemotropic** /-ˈtrəʊpɪk, -ˈtrɒpɪk/ *adjective* of, pertaining to, or displaying chemotropism L19. **chemotropically** *adverb* L19.

chempaka *noun* see CHAMPAC.

chemurgy /ˈkɛməːdʒi/ *noun*. *US*. M20.
[ORIGIN from CHEMO- after *metallurgy*.]
The chemical and industrial use of agricultural products.
■ **che'murgic**, **che'murgical** *adjectives* M20.

chena /ˈtʃeɪnə/ *noun*. M19.
[ORIGIN Sinhalese *sēna*, *hēna*.]
In Sri Lanka: a clearing made for temporary cultivation; shrubby vegetation associated with shifting cultivation.

chenar *noun* var. of CHINAR.

chenille /ʃəˈniːl/ *noun*. M18.
[ORIGIN French, lit. 'hairy caterpillar', from Latin *canicula* dim. of *canis* dog.]
Velvety cord with pile all round, used in trimming and bordering dresses and furniture.

Chenin /ˈʃənã/ *noun*. L19.
[ORIGIN French, perh. from the name of the manor of Mont-*Chenin*, Touraine, where it was first imported from Anjou.]
1 In full ***Chenin noir*** /nwɑː/. A variety of black grape native to the Loire valley. L19.
2 In full ***Chenin blanc*** /blɑ̃/. A variety of white grape native to the Loire valley but widely cultivated elsewhere. Also, a white wine made from this grape. E20.

chenopodium /kɛnəˈpəʊdɪəm/ *noun*. L16.
[ORIGIN mod. Latin, from Greek *khēn* goose + *pod-*, *pous* foot, referring to the shape of the leaf.]
A plant of the large genus *Chenopodium* (family Chenopodiaceae); a goosefoot.
■ **ˌchenopodiˈaceous** *adjective* of or pertaining to the family Chenopodiaceae M19.

cheongsam /tʃɪɒŋˈsam, tʃɒŋ-/ *noun*. M20.
[ORIGIN Chinese (Cantonese) = Mandarin *chángshān*.]
A Chinese woman's garment with a high neck and a skirt slit at the side.

cheque /tʃɛk/ *noun*. Also ***check**. See also CHECK *noun*[1]. E18.
[ORIGIN Var. of CHECK *noun*[1].]
▸ **I** †**1** The counterfoil of a bank bill, draft, etc. Only in 18.
†**2** A draft form having a counterfoil. E18–M19.
3 A written order to a bank etc. to pay a named sum from the drawer's account to the bearer or to (the order of) a named person; a printed form on which such an order is to be written. L18.
blank cheque: see BLANK *adjective*. ***certified cheque***. ***marked cheque***. ***open cheque***: see OPEN *adjective*. ***rubber cheque***: see RUBBER *noun*[1]. ***traveller's cheque***: see TRAVELLER.
▸ **II** See CHECK *noun*[1] I.
– COMB.: **chequebook** a book of printed cheques, issued to the customers of banks etc.; *attrib.* (of journalism etc., *derog.*) spending money lavishly to procure stories; **cheque card** a card issued by a bank to guarantee the honouring of cheques up to a stated value.

†**chequed** *adjective*[1], *adjective*[2] vars. of CHECKED *adjective*[1], *adjective*[2].

chequeen *noun* see SEQUIN.

chequer /ˈtʃɛkə/ *noun*[1]. Also ***checker**. ME.
[ORIGIN Aphet. from EXCHEQUER *noun*.]
▸ **I** †**1** A chessboard; chess. ME–E19.
2 In *pl.* (usu. treated as *sing.*). The game of draughts. *dial.* & *N. Amer.* E18. ▸**b** In full ***checkerman***. A piece in the game of draughts. *N. Amer.* M19.
▸ **II** †**3** *The* Court of Exchequer. ME–L17.
†**4** *The* royal or national treasury. LME–L17.
5 A room, place, or table for accounts. *obsolete* exc. *hist.* LME.
▸ **III 6** A pattern made in squares, or with alternating colours. LME.
7 In *pl.* Squares or spots like or suggesting those which make up the design of a chessboard; *rare* the squares of an actual chessboard. E16.
– COMB.: ***checkerman***: see sense 2b above; **chequerboard** (the pattern of) a board for draughts or chess; **chequer-wise** *adverb* in the pattern of a chessboard; **chequer-work** work of a chequered pattern.

chequer /ˈtʃɛkə/ *noun*[2]. *dial.* M17.
[ORIGIN App. = CHEQUER *noun*[1], from their appearance.]
In *pl.* The berries of the wild service tree. Cf. CHECKERBERRY.

chequer /ˈtʃɛkə/ *verb trans.* Also ***checker**. LME.
[ORIGIN from CHEQUER *noun*[1].]
1 Diversify with a different colour or shade; variegate, mottle; break the uniformity of (*lit.* & *fig.*). LME.
> H. ALLEN Bright golden patches shimmered and chequered the road ahead. *fig.*: DICKENS His sleep was checkered with starts and moans.

2 Divide into or mark with squares, esp. of alternate colours. E17.
> C. LUCAS The other . . is checquered brown and black, in half-lozenges. J. MASEFIELD Chequered by tossing boughs the moon appeared.

†**3** Deposit (money) in an exchequer. E17–M18.
4 Arrange or distribute chequer-wise. L17.

chequered /ˈtʃɛkəd/ *adjective*. Also ***checkered**. LME.
[ORIGIN from CHEQUER *noun*[1], *verb*: see -ED[2], -ED[1].]
1 Marked like a chessboard; having a pattern of various crossing colours. LME.
chequered flag *MOTOR RACING* a flag with a black and white chequered pattern, displayed to drivers or riders at the moment of finishing a race.
2 Diversified in colour; marked with alternate light and shade; *fig.* undergoing varied fortunes, having discreditable episodes. L16.
> SOUTHEY Beneath the o'er-arching forests' chequer'd shade. J. BUCHAN Ancient families with chequered pasts. *Listener* My career with 20th Century Fox was somewhat chequered.

chequered skipper: see SKIPPER *noun*[1] 2.

†**chequin** *noun* see SEQUIN.

chequy *adjective* see CHECKY.

chère amie /ʃɛːr ami/ *noun phr.* Pl. ***chères amies*** /ʃɛːrz ami/. L18.
[ORIGIN French, lit. 'dear (woman) friend'.]
A female lover; a mistress.

cherem /ˈxerem, h-/ *noun*. Also **h-**. E19.
[ORIGIN Hebrew *ḥērem*, from *ḥāram* devote, put under a curse.]
Excommunication from the Synagogue and the Jewish community.

Cheremiss /ˈtʃɛrəmɪs/ *noun*. Also **-is**, **Tch-**. Pl. **-isses**, same. M17.
[ORIGIN Russian †*cheremis*.]
A member of a Finnic people living in Russia in the region of the middle Volga; the Finno-Ugric language of this people. Also called ***Mari***.

Cherenkov radiation *noun phr.* var. of CERENKOV RADIATION.

chères amies *noun phr.* pl. of CHÈRE AMIE.

cherimoya /tʃɛrɪˈmɔɪə/ *noun*. Also **chiri-** /tʃɪrɪ-/. M18.
[ORIGIN Spanish from Quechua, from *chiri* cold, refreshing + *muya* circle.]
(The pulpy edible fruit of) a small tree, *Annona cherimola*, native to the Andes of Peru and Ecuador.

cherish /ˈtʃɛrɪʃ/ *verb trans.* ME.
[ORIGIN Old French & mod. French *chériss-* lengthened stem of *chérir*, from *cher* dear from Latin *carus*: see -ISH[2].]
1 Treat or regard (a person) affectionately; make much of; fondle. *arch.* ME.
2 Protect or tend (a child, plant, etc.) lovingly; treat with fostering care. ME.
†**3** Entertain (a guest) kindly; cheer. LME–M18.
†**4** Keep warm; give ease or comfort to. LME–M18.
5 Value, hold dear, cling to, (esp. hopes, feelings, ideas, etc.). LME.
> HENRY MILLER The loss of something I had loved and cherished. P. SCOTT Both to cherish expectations and condition himself to sustain disappointments. M. LEITCH It was a good moment, one to be cherished, for he didn't know when the next one might present itself.

■ **cherishable** *adjective* M17. **cherisher** *noun* LME. **cherishingly** *adverb* in a cherishing manner, tenderly E17. **cherishment** *noun* (*a*) the process or fact of cherishing; †(*b*) an indulgence; nourishment: E16.

cher maître /ʃɛːr mɛːtr/ *noun phr.* Pl. **-s -s** (pronounced same). E20.
[ORIGIN French, lit. 'dear master'.]
(A flattering form of address to) a famous writer.

chernites /kəːˈnʌɪtiːz/ *noun*. E17.
[ORIGIN Greek *khernitēs*.]
hist. An ivory-like marble used by the ancients.

chernozem /ˈtʃəːnəzɛm/ *noun*. Also **-sem**, †**tch-**. M19.
[ORIGIN Russian, from *chërnyĭ* black + Slavonic base *zem-* (cf. Russian *zemlya*) earth.]
A dark, humus-rich, fertile soil characteristic of temperate or cool grassland.
■ **chernoˈzemic** *adjective* M20.

Cherokee /tʃɛrəˈkiː/ *adjective & noun*. L17.
[ORIGIN Cherokee †*tsaraki* (now *tsaliki*).]
▸ **A** *adjective*. Designating or pertaining to an Iroquoian people inhabiting Oklahoma and N. Carolina (and formerly a large part of the southern US), or their language. L17.
Cherokee rose a fragrant white-flowered climbing rose, *Rosa laevigata*, native to China and naturalized in the US.
▸ **B** *noun*. Pl. same, **-s**.
1 A Cherokee Indian. E18.
2 The language of the Cherokee. M18.

cheroot /ʃəˈruːt/ *noun*. L17.
[ORIGIN French *cheroute* from Tamil *curuṭṭu* roll of tobacco.]
A kind of cigar, orig. made in southern India, with both ends open.
Manila cheroot: see MANILA *adjective* 1.

cherry /ˈtʃɛri/ *noun & adjective*. ME.
[ORIGIN Old Northern French *cherise* (treated as pl.), mod. CERISE, from medieval Latin *ceresia*, perh. from orig. neut. pl. of adjective *ceraseus*, from Latin *cerasus* from Greek *kerasos*.]
▸ **A** *noun*. **1** The small edible stone fruit, dark red or yellow and red-flushed when ripe, borne by several trees of the genus *Prunus*, esp. the cultivated forms of *P. avium* (***sweet cherry***), *P. cerasus* (***sour cherry***, ***morello cherry***), or their hybrids. Also *fig.*, as a type of something red. ME.
> *fig.*: P. SIDNEY Opening the cherrie of her lips.

black cherry (*a*) a very dark ripe cherry; (*b*) *N. Amer.* (the dark fruit of) the rum-cherry, *Prunus serotina*. ***sour cherry***: see SOUR *adjective*. **two bites at the cherry**, **a second bite at the cherry** more than one attempt or opportunity to do something.
2 Any of the trees bearing this fruit, related to the plum but with flowers in umbels or racemes. Also (chiefly with specifying word), any of various related trees, some of which are grown for ornament; any of several other unrelated trees resembling the cherry in some respect. LME. ▸**b** More fully ***cherrywood***. The timber of any of these trees. L18.
bird cherry, ***choke cherry***, ***flowering cherry***, ***Hottentot cherry***, ***Japanese cherry***, ***Saint Lucie cherry***, ***Suriname cherry***, etc.
3 Virginity; a virgin. *slang*. E20.
– COMB.: **cherry-bob** two cherries with joined stems; **cherry-bounce** *arch.* cherry brandy; **cherry brandy** a dark-red liqueur of brandy in which cherries have been steeped; ***cherry laurel***: see LAUREL *noun* 3; **cherry-pick** *verb* selectively choose (the most beneficial or profitable items, opportunities, etc.) from what is available; **cherry picker** (*a*) a person who picks cherries; (*b*) in *pl.* (*hist. slang*), the 11th Hussars (so-called from their crimson trousers); (*c*) a crane for raising and lowering persons; **cherry pie** (*a*) a pie made with cherries; (*b*) a garden heliotrope; **cherry plum** (the fruit of) the small tree *Prunus cerasifera*; **cherry-red** (of) a bright deep red; **cherry tomato** (a plant bearing) a small deep-red variety of tomato; ***cherry tree***: see sense 2 above; ***cherrywood***: see sense 2b above.
▸ **B** *attrib.* or as *adjective*. **1** Bright deep red, of the typical colour of ripe cherries. LME.
2 Virgin. *slang*. M20.
■ **cherry-like** *adjective* resembling (that of) a cherry; bright deep red: M19.

†**cherry** *verb trans. rare* (Spenser). Only in L16.
[ORIGIN French *chérir* cherish.]
Cheer, delight.

chers maîtres *noun phr.* pl. of CHER MAÎTRE.

chersonese /ˈkəːsəniːs, -z/ *noun. poet.* or *rhet.* E17.
[ORIGIN Latin *chersonesus* from Greek *khersonēsos*, from *khersos* dry + *nēsos* island.]
A peninsula, *spec.* that of Thrace west of the Hellespont.

chert /tʃəːt/ *noun*. L17.
[ORIGIN Unknown: orig. dial.]
GEOLOGY. Hard dense rock formed of amorphous silica, occurring as several varieties.
radiolarian chert: see RADIOLARIAN *adjective*.
■ **cherty** *adjective* of the nature of or containing chert L18.

cherub /ˈtʃɛrəb/ *noun*. Also (now *rare*) **-bin** /-bɪn/, †**-bim**. Pl. **-rubs**, (in sense 2, also) **-rubim** /-rəbɪm/. OE.
[ORIGIN Ult. from Hebrew *kĕrūḇ*, pl. *kĕrūḇīm* (through Latin & Greek).]
1 In the Bible, a winged creature attending on God (and whose wings helped form the throne of God). In Christian theology, a member of the second order of the ninefold celestial hierarchy, ranking directly below the seraphim and above the thrones, and gifted with knowledge (usu. in *pl.*). Also, a conventional representation of such a being, esp. in the form of a winged (head of a) child. ME.
2 *transf.* A person, esp. a child, distinguished for cherubic qualities of beauty, innocence, etc. M16.
– NOTE: The representation of the cherub as a child is due to a rabbinic folk etymology explaining Hebrew *kĕrūḇ* as repr. Aramaic *kĕ-raḇyā* 'like a child'.
■ **cheˈrubic** *adjective* of, pertaining to, or resembling (a representation of) a cherub or cherubs; angelic; sweet and innocent: M17. †**cherubical** *adjective* = CHERUBIC: only in E17. **cheˈrubically** *adverb* M19. **cheruˈbimical** *adjective* = CHERUBIC L17. **cheruˈbinical** *adjective* (*rare*) = CHERUBIC E17.

chervil /ˈtʃəːvɪl/ *noun*. OE.
[ORIGIN Latin *chaerephylla*, *-phyllum* from Greek *khairephullon*.]
An umbelliferous herb, *Anthriscus cerefolium*, with aromatic leaves; the leaves of this plant as used to flavour soups, salads, etc. Also (with specifying word), any of various related umbelliferous plants; *esp.* (in full ***rough chervil***) *Chaerophyllum temulum*, a hedgerow plant with hairy red-spotted stems.
turnip-rooted chervil *Chaerophyllum bulbosum*, which has an edible root like a parsnip.

Ches. *abbreviation*.
Cheshire.

chesed /ˈhɛsɪd/ *noun*. L19.
[ORIGIN Hebrew *hesedh* grace, loving kindness.]
JUDAISM. The attribute of grace, benevolence, or compassion toward others; *spec.* in Kabbalah, this as one of the sephiroth.

Cheshire /ˈtʃɛʃə/ *noun & adjective*. L16.
[ORIGIN A county in England.]
1 In full ***Cheshire cheese***. A mild crumbly cheese of a type orig. made in Cheshire. L16.
2 ***grin like a Cheshire cat***, grin fixedly and broadly. L18.
3 ***Cheshire acre***, a unit of area formerly current in Cheshire, equal to 10,240 sq. yards (approx. 0.857 hectare). E19.

chesil /ˈtʃɛz(ə)l/ *noun*. Also (the usual form in sense 2) **chisel** /ˈtʃɪz(ə)l/.
[ORIGIN Old English *ċiosol*, *ċisel*, *ċysel* = Middle Dutch *kezel*, Low German *kesel*, Old High German *kisil* (German *Kiesel*), from West Germanic base, whence Middle High German *kis*, German *Kies* gravel.]
1 Gravel, shingle. Long *obsolete* exc. in the name (***Chesil Bank***, ***Chesil Beach***) of a long shingle ridge on the Dorset coast, SW England, enclosing a lagoon. OE.
2 Bran; coarse flour. *obsolete* exc. *dial.* L15.

†**chesnut** *noun* var. of CHESTNUT.

chess /tʃɛs/ *noun*[1]. ME.
[ORIGIN Aphet. from Old French *esches* (mod. *échecs*), pl. of *eschec* CHECK *noun*[1].]
1 A game for two players using a chequered board of sixty-four squares with eight pieces, viz. a king, queen, two rooks, knights, and bishops, and eight pawns each,

C

with the object of placing the opponent's king in checkmate. ME.
lightning chess: see LIGHTNING *noun & adjective*. ***living chess***: see LIVING *adjective*.
†**2** The pieces and pawns or the board used in playing. ME–E17.
3 *loosely*. Any of the various classical board games. LME.
– COMB.: **chessboard** *noun & adjective* (resembling) the board on which chess is played; **chess-clock**: displaying the accumulated time each player has expended on his or her moves; **chessman** any of the pieces or pawns with which chess is played (usu. in *pl.*).

chess /tʃɛs/ *noun*². *obsolete* exc. *dial.* LME.
[ORIGIN Unknown.]
1 A tier, layer, storey; a row. LME.
2 Each of the sections into which an apple etc. may be divided. *Scot.* L18.
3 In *pl.* The parallel planks of a pontoon bridge. E19.

chess /tʃɛs/ *noun*³. Chiefly *N. Amer.* M18.
[ORIGIN Unknown.]
A grass of the genus *Bromus*, commonly found as a weed among wheat.

chess-apple /ˈtʃɛsap(ə)l/ *noun*. M17.
[ORIGIN Uncertain: perh. from its spotty surface (cf. CHEQUER *noun*²).]
The fruit of the whitebeam, *Sorbus aria*.

chessel /ˈtʃɛs(ə)l/ *noun*. L17.
[ORIGIN App. from CHEESE *noun*¹ + WELL *noun*¹.]
A cheese-making mould.

chess-tree /ˈtʃɛstriː/ *noun*. ME.
[ORIGIN from unkn. 1st elem. + TREE *noun* (in sense 'wood').]
NAUTICAL. A piece of wood bolted perpendicularly on a ship's side, used to confine the clew of the mainsail.

chessylite /ˈtʃɛsɪlʌɪt/ *noun*. M19.
[ORIGIN from *Chessy*, near Lyons, France + -LITE.]
MINERALOGY. = AZURITE.

chest /tʃɛst/ *noun*.
[ORIGIN Old English *ċest*, *ċyst*, corresp. to Old Frisian, Middle Dutch *kiste* (Dutch *kist*), Old High German *kista* (German *Kiste*), Old Norse *kista*, from Germanic from Latin *cista* from Greek *kistē* box.]
1 A box, a coffer; a large box of strong construction for the custody of articles of value, *esp.* one for a sailor's belongings, for tools, for medicines, etc. OE.
2 A coffin. Now *dial.* OE.
3 That part of the human or of an animal's body that is enclosed by the ribs; the thorax; the front surface of a body from neck to waist. LME.
4 The treasury or coffer of an institution; *transf.* the money in one, the funds. LME.
5 A large case into which commodities (esp. tea) are packed for transport. E18.
– PHRASES: **chest of drawers** a piece of furniture with a set of drawers in a frame. **chest of viols** a set of viols kept in a chest. **get a thing off one's chest** *colloq.* relieve one's feelings by disclosing something. **hold one's cards close to one's chest**, **keep one's cards close to one's chest**, **play one's cards close to one's chest**, etc., be reluctant to reveal one's intentions or resources. ***military chest***: see MILITARY *adjective*.
– COMB.: **chest-expander** a piece of equipment for exercising and developing the muscles of the chest and arms; **chest freezer** a low freezer with an opening top; **chest protector** a covering or wrap of flannel etc. worn to protect the chest from cold; **chest voice**: of the lowest speaking or singing register.
■ **chested** *adjective* having a chest (of a specified kind) LME. **chestful** *noun* the quantity contained in a chest E18.

chest /tʃɛst/ *verb trans.* OE.
[ORIGIN from the noun.]
1 Put into a coffin. Now *dial.* OE.
2 Enclose in a chest; store away. OE.
3 Strike with the chest; guide or propel (a ball) with the chest. M19.

†**chesten** *noun*. OE–L17.
[ORIGIN Old French *chastaine* (mod. *châtaigne*) from Latin *castanea* from Greek *kastanea*, *-neion*, short for *kastaneion karuon* nut of Castanaea (Pontus) or Castana (Thessaly): cf. CHESTNUT.]
A chestnut; a chestnut tree.

chester /ˈtʃɛstə/ *noun*. *obsolete* exc. *hist.*
[ORIGIN Old English *ċeaster* ult. from Latin *castra*: a common elem. in place names (also in forms *-caster*, *-cester*).]
A walled town; *spec.* one that was formerly a Roman station.

chesterfield /ˈtʃɛstəfiːld/ *noun*. M19.
[ORIGIN from an Earl of *Chesterfield*.]
1 A plain overcoat usu. with a velvet collar. M19.
2 A sofa with a padded seat, back, and ends; *Canad.* any sofa. E20.

Chesterfieldian /tʃɛstəˈfiːldɪən/ *adjective*. L18.
[ORIGIN from *Chesterfield* (see below) + -IAN.]
Relating to or characteristic of Philip Stanhope, 4th Earl of Chesterfield (1694–1773), or his writings on manners and etiquette.

Chestertonian /tʃɛstəˈtəʊnɪən/ *adjective*. E20.
[ORIGIN from *Chesterton* (see below) + -IAN.]
Of, pertaining to, resembling, or characteristic of the English author Gilbert Keith Chesterton (1874–1936), or his writings.

chestnut /ˈtʃɛsnʌt/ *noun & adjective*. Also †**chesnut**. E16.
[ORIGIN from CHESTEN + NUT *noun*.]
► **A** *noun* **1 a** The edible nut of a tree of the genus *Castanea*, of the beech family; *esp.* that of *C. sativa* (also ***Spanish chestnut***, ***sweet chestnut***). Also (with specifying word), any of various fruits etc. resembling this nut. E16. ▸**b** (More fully ***chestnut tree***) the tree itself; (with specifying word) any of various similar trees. Also, the wood of these trees. L16. ▸**c** *ellipt.* A horse chestnut. L18.
2 A chestnut colour; a chestnut horse. (See sense B. below.) L16.
3 The small hard callosity in the skin of the horse at the inner side of the forelegs. M19.
4 A stale joke or anecdote; anything too often repeated. L19.
– PHRASES: ***Cape chestnut***: see CAPE *noun*¹. ***Chinese water chestnut***: see WATER *noun*. HORSE CHESTNUT. ***MORETON BAY chestnut***. **pull the chestnuts out of the fire** succeed in a hazardous undertaking on behalf of or through the agency of another (with ref. to the fable of a monkey using a cat's paw to get roasting chestnuts from a fire). ***TAHITI chestnut***. ***water chestnut***: see WATER *noun*. ***wild chestnut***: see WILD *adjective*.
– COMB.: **chestnut oak** any of various, chiefly N. American, oaks having leaves resembling those of the chestnut; ***chestnut tree***: see sense 1b above.
► **B** *adjective*. **1** Of the colour of a chestnut; deep reddish-brown. M16.
2 Of a horse: having reddish- or yellowish-brown coloration. L17.
■ **chestnutting** *noun* the gathering of chestnuts L18. **chestnutty** *adjective* (**a**) resembling the colour or flavour of a chestnut; (**b**) old and well known, frequently repeated: L19.

chesty /ˈtʃɛsti/ *adjective*. *colloq.* E20.
[ORIGIN from CHEST *noun* + -Y¹.]
1 Conceited, arrogant. *US.* E20.
2 Inclined to, marked by, or symptomatic of ailments of the chest. M20.
3 Having a large chest or prominent breasts. M20.
■ **chestily** *adverb* E20. **chestiness** *noun* E20.

Chesvan *noun* var. of HESVAN.

chétif /ʃetif/ *adjective*. E20.
[ORIGIN French.]
Puny, sickly, thin; miserable, wretched.

Chetnik /ˈtʃɛtnɪk/ *noun*. E20.
[ORIGIN Serbian *četnik*, from *četa* band, troop.]
A guerrilla fighter in the Balkans; *spec.* (*hist.*) one of a royalist force led by General Draža Mihajlović in occupied Yugoslavia, 1941–5.

chetrum /ˈtʃɛtruːm/ *noun*. Pl. same, **-s**. L20.
[ORIGIN Dzongkha.]
A monetary unit of Bhutan, equal to one-hundredth of a ngultrum.

chetty /ˈtʃɛti/ *noun*. L16.
[ORIGIN Tamil *ceṭṭi*.]
(A member of) any of a group of trading castes in southern India.

chevachee /tʃɛvəˈtʃiː/ *noun*. Long *obsolete* exc. *hist.* LME.
[ORIGIN Old French *chevauchiee*, pa. ppl formation on *chevauchier* (mod. *chevaucher*) from late Latin *caballicare* ride, from *caballus* horse.]
An expedition on horseback, a raid.

chevage /ˈtʃiːvɪdʒ/ *noun*. *obsolete* exc. *hist.* LME.
[ORIGIN Old French = capitation, from *chef* head: see CHIEF *noun*, -AGE.]
Capitation or poll money paid to a lord.

cheval /ʃəval, ʃəˈval/ *noun*. Pl. **-vaux** /-vo, -ˈvəʊ/. L15.
[ORIGIN French.]
The French for 'horse', also 'frame', occurring in various phrases used in English
■ ***cheval de bataille*** /də bataːj/ [lit. 'battle-horse'] an obsession, a pet subject E19. ***chevaux de frise*** /də friːz/ [lit. 'horses of Friesland': named iron. with ref. to their use by the Friesians, who had no cavalry] a number of metal spikes set in timber to repel cavalry, or set along the top of a fence, wall, etc., to repel intruders L17. See also À CHEVAL, ***pas de cheval*** s.v. PAS 2, ***petits chevaux*** s.v. PETIT *adjective*².

chevaleresque *adjective* see CHIVALRESQUE.

chevalet /ʃəvale/ *noun*. Pl. pronounced same. E19.
[ORIGIN French, dim. of CHEVAL.]
†**1** A trestle for a bridge. Only in E19.
2 The bridge of a bowed musical instrument. L19.

cheval glass /ʃəˈvalglɑːs/ *noun*. M19.
[ORIGIN from French CHEVAL + GLASS *noun*.]
A tall mirror swung on an upright frame.

chevalier /ʃɛvəˈlɪə, *foreign* ʃəvalje (*pl. same*)/ *noun*. LME.
[ORIGIN Anglo-Norman *chevaler*, Old French & mod. French *chevalier*, from medieval Latin *caballarius*, from Latin *caballus* horse: see -IER, -EER. Cf. CAVALIER *noun*.]
1 *hist.* A horseman, *esp.* a mounted knight. LME.
2 A chivalrous man, a gallant. M17.
3 A member of certain orders of knighthood, or of the French Legion of Honour, etc. E18.
– PHRASES: ***chevalier d'industrie*** /dɛ̃dystri/ [French, lit. 'knight of industry'] an adventurer, a swindler. ***PREUX chevalier***. **the Chevalier (de St George)** James Stuart, the Old Pretender. **the Young Chevalier** Charles Edward Stuart, the Young Pretender.

chevaline /ˈʃɛvəlɪn/ *adjective*. *rare*. M16.
[ORIGIN French, fem. of *chevalin*, from CHEVAL: see -INE¹.]
Of or pertaining to horses.

chevaux *noun pl.* see CHEVAL.

chevelure /ʃəvlyːr/ *noun*. Pl. pronounced same. LME.
[ORIGIN Old French *cheveleüre* (mod. *-elure*), from Latin *capillatura*, from *capillatus* haired, from *capillus* hair: see -URE.]
1 The hair of the head, a head of hair; (formerly) a wig. LME.
2 A halo around a star etc.; a comet's coma. L17.

cheverel /ˈʃɛv(ə)r(ə)l/ *noun & adjective*. LME.
[ORIGIN Old French *chevrele* dim. of *chèvre* goat.]
► †**A** *noun*. Kid leather, noted for its elasticity. LME–E17.
► **B** *adjective*. Of or pertaining to kid leather; *fig.* elastic, flexible, yielding. E16.

chevesaile /ˈtʃiːvəseɪl/ *noun*. *obsolete* exc. *hist.* LME.
[ORIGIN Old French *cheveçaille*, from *chevece* collar, from Latin *capitia* pl. of *capitium* opening for the head in a tunic etc.]
The collar of a coat, etc., often richly ornamented.

chevet /ʃəˈveɪ; *foreign* ʃəvɛ (*pl. same*)/ *noun*. E19.
[ORIGIN French = pillow.]
The apsidal termination of the east end of a church.

cheville /ʃəviːj/ *noun*. Pl. pronounced same. L19.
[ORIGIN French = peg, pin, plug.]
1 A meaningless or redundant word or phrase inserted to round off a sentence or complete a verse. L19.
2 A peg in a stringed musical instrument. L19.

chevin /ˈtʃɛvɪn/ *noun*. LME.
[ORIGIN Old French *chevenne*, *chevesne* (mod. *chevanne*), from Proto-Romance from Latin *capiton-*, *capito* (orig.) big-head, from *caput*, *-it-*, head.]
The chub.

Cheviot /ˈtʃɛvɪət/ *noun*. In sense 2 also **c-**. L18.
[ORIGIN from *Cheviot* Hills on the England–Scotland border.]
1 In full ***Cheviot sheep***. (An animal of) a breed of sheep from the Cheviot Hills. L18.
2 (Cloth made from) the wool of Cheviot sheep. M19.

chevisance /ˈʃɛvɪs(ə)ns/ *noun*. Long *arch.* ME.
[ORIGIN Old French, from *cheviss-* lengthened stem of *chevir* achieve, from *chef* head, chief: see CHIEF *noun*, -ANCE.]
†**1** A bringing to an end; furtherance; assistance. Only in ME.
†**2** Resource, remedy; an expedient. ME–M17.
†**3** Provision, supply; provisions; booty. ME–M17.
4 Raising money; borrowing; a loan; lending, usury; profiteering, gain. Freq. *derog.* LME.
5 (Confused by Spenser and others with ***chivalry*** and related words.) Enterprise, chivalry, prowess; an exploit. L16.

chevra *noun* var. of HEBRA.

chèvre /ʃɛːvr/ *noun*. M20.
[ORIGIN French = goat, esp. she-goat.]
French goat's-milk cheese.

chevrette /ʃəˈvrɛt/ *noun*. M18.
[ORIGIN French, dim. of CHÈVRE: see -ETTE.]
†**1** A machine for raising guns or mortars. M–L18.
2 A thin goatskin leather used for gloves. L19.

chevron /ˈʃɛvrən/ *noun*¹. LME.
[ORIGIN Old French & mod. French from Proto-Romance, from Latin *caper* goat: cf. Latin *capreoli* pair of rafters.]
1 HERALDRY. A charge consisting of a bent bar of an inverted V shape. LME. ▸**b** This shape used in decorative art etc. E17.
2 A beam or rafter; *esp.* in *pl.*, the rafters of a roof which meet at an angle at the ridge. L16.
3 A badge in a V shape (whether inverted or not) on the sleeve of a uniform, indicating rank or length of service; a V-shaped stripe. E19.
■ **chevronel** *noun* (HERALDRY) a bent bar on the escutcheon, half the breadth of the chevron L16.

†**chevron** *noun*². M16–E19.
[ORIGIN App. erron. for CHEVEREL.]
A glove.

chevron /ˈʃɛvrən/ *verb trans.* M16.
[ORIGIN from CHEVRON *noun*¹ or French *chevronner*.]
Provide with chevrons or things arranged in a chevron pattern; make with a chevron pattern.

chevronny /ˈʃɛvrəni/ *adjective*. In sense 2 also **-ony**. E18.
[ORIGIN French *chevronné* pa. pple of *chevronner*, formed as CHEVRON *noun*¹.]
1 HERALDRY. Charged with or formed by an even number of chevrons. E18.
2 *gen.* Zigzag. L19.

chevrotain /ˈʃɛvrəteɪn/ *noun*. Also **-tin** /-tɪn/. L18.
[ORIGIN French, dim. of Old French *chevrot* dim. of *chèvre* goat.]
A small deerlike ruminant of the mainly southern Asian family Tragulidae. Also called ***mouse deer***.

chevy *noun & verb* var. of CHIVVY *noun & verb*¹.

Chevy Chase /ˌtʃɛvi ˈtʃeɪs/ *noun phr.* *rhyming slang*. Now *rare*. M19.
[ORIGIN See CHIVVY *noun & verb*¹.]
The face.

chew /tʃuː/ *noun*. See also CHAW *noun*[2], CHOW *noun*[1]. ME.
[ORIGIN from the verb.]
1 An act of chewing. ME.
2 Something that is chewed; *spec.* a quid of tobacco. E18.
3 A chewy sweet. M20.

chew /tʃuː/ *verb*. See also CHAW *verb*, CHOW *verb*.
[ORIGIN Old English *ċēowan* = Middle Low German *keuwen* (Dutch *kauwen*), Old High German *kiuwan* (German *kauen*), from West Germanic.]
1 *verb trans.* Crush, bruise, and grind by the action of the molar teeth; grind to a pulp or indent by repeated biting; masticate (food). OE. ▸**b** Injure, break, or destroy with an action resembling that of the jaws. Freq. foll. by *off, up*. M19.

b C. RYAN The port wing . . was chewed off by the propeller of a Stirling bomber.

2 *verb trans. fig.* ▸**a** Examine or plan deliberately; meditate on; turn *over* in the mind; talk *over*. ME. ▸**b** Mumble; mutter inarticulately. E17. ▸**c** Foll. by *out*: reprimand. *N. Amer. colloq.* M20.

a M. PRIOR He chews Revenge.

3 *verb intrans.* Work food etc. with the teeth; champ, masticate. (Foll. by *(up)on* something.) LME.
4 *verb intrans.* Meditate, ruminate, exercise the mind, *(up)on, at*. L16.
– PHRASES: ***bite off more than one can chew***: see BITE *verb*. **chewing gum** a preparation of sweetened and flavoured gums and resins, used for prolonged chewing. ***chew the cud***: see CUD *noun*. **chew the fat**, **chew the rag** *slang* discuss a matter; persist in grumbling.
– COMB.: **chew stick** (*a*) = ***chaw stick*** s.v. CHAW *verb*; (*b*) the root or stem of various W. African plants, used to clean the teeth.
■ **chewable** *adjective* able to be chewed M19. **chewer** *noun* a person who or thing which chews E17. **chewy** *adjective* suitable for chewing; needing to be chewed: E20.

†**chewet** *noun*. M–L16.
[ORIGIN French *chouette*.]
A jackdaw, a chough; a chatterer.

Chewings fescue /ˈtʃuːɪŋz ˈfɛskjuː/ *noun phr.* E20.
[ORIGIN Charles *Chewings* (1859–1937), Austral. scientist who first marketed the grass (in NZ).]
A variety of red fescue (*Festuca rubra*) used as a pasture and lawn grass.

chewink /tʃiːˈwɪŋk/ *noun*. *N. Amer.* Also **chee-**. L18.
[ORIGIN Imit.]
The towhee *Pipilo erythrophthalmus*.

Cheyenne /ʃʌɪˈan/ *noun & adjective*. L18.
[ORIGIN Canad. French from Dakota *šahiyena*.]
▸ **A** *noun*. Pl. same, **-s**. A member of an Algonquian people living in Montana and Oklahoma (orig. living between the Missouri and Arkansas rivers); the language of this people. L18.
▸ **B** *attrib.* or as *adjective*. Of or pertaining to the Cheyenne or their language. E19.

Cheyne-Stokes /ˈtʃeɪnstəʊks/ *adjective*. L19.
[ORIGIN John *Cheyne* (1777–1836), Scot. physician, and William *Stokes* (1804–78), Irish physician.]
MEDICINE. Designating respiration characterized by a cyclical variation of rate involving gradual decrease, cessation, and gradual increase.

ARNOLD BENNETT Symptoms of 'Cheyne-Stokes breathing', the final and worst symptom of his disease.

†**cheyney** *noun*. L16–M18.
[ORIGIN Alt. of CHINA.]
A sort of worsted or woollen cloth.

chez /ʃeɪ, *foreign* ʃe, *before a vowel* ʃez/ *preposition*. M18.
[ORIGIN French from Old French *chiese* from Latin *casa* cottage.]
At the house or home of.

I. MURDOCH I thought it might not be very restful chez Dave.

chi /kʌɪ/ *noun*[1]. LME.
[ORIGIN Greek *khi*.]
The twenty-second letter (X, χ) of the Greek alphabet.
chi-rho [RHO] a monogram of chi and rho representing the first two letters of Greek *Khristos* Christ. See also CHI-SQUARE.

chi /tʃiː/ *noun*[2]. Also **qi**. M19.
[ORIGIN Chinese *qì* air, breath.]
The physical life force postulated by certain Chinese philosophers; the material principle.

chia /ˈtʃiːə/ *noun*. M19.
[ORIGIN Spanish *chía* from Nahuatl.]
A purple-flowered plant of the mint family, *Salvia hispanica*, native to Mexico and cultivated for its oily seed that is used in various foods and beverages.

chiack *noun & verb* var. of CHI-HIKE.

Chian /ˈkʌɪən, ˈkiːən/ *adjective & noun*. L16.
[ORIGIN from Latin *Chius* from Greek *Khios* adjective, from *Khios* Chios (see below): see -AN.]
▸ **A** *adjective*. Pertaining to or originating from the island of Chios in the Aegean. L16.
Chian turpentine: see TURPENTINE *noun* 1. **Chian wine** *hist.* wine from Chios, highly regarded in classical times.
▸ **B** *noun*. = ***Chian wine*** above. M17.

Chianina /kɪəˈniːnə/ *noun*. L20.
[ORIGIN Italian.]
(An animal of) a very large white breed of cattle, kept for its lean meat.

Chianti /kɪˈanti/ *noun*. M19.
[ORIGIN from the *Chianti* Mountains, Tuscany.]
A dry usu. red Italian wine, properly one made in the Chianti district of Tuscany.
– COMB.: **Chiantishire** a name for the Chianti region of Italy, or for Tuscany in general, with allusion to its popularity as a holiday destination for British tourists and as a domicile for British expatriates.

chiaroscuro /kɪˌɑːrəˈskʊərəʊ/ *noun & adjective*. M17.
[ORIGIN Italian, from *chiaro* clear, bright + *oscuro* dark, OBSCURE *adjective*.]
▸ **A** *noun*. Pl. **-os**.
1 A style of painting in which only light and shade are represented; black and white. M17.
2 The treatment or disposition of the light and shade, or brighter and darker masses, in a picture; an effect or contrast of light and shade in a picture or in nature. L17.

B. MOORE The sky was a shifting chiaroscuro of grays and blacks.

3 *fig.* The use of contrast in literature etc. E19.
▸ **B** *attrib.* or as *adjective*. In chiaroscuro, in black and white; *fig.* marked by stylistic etc. contrasts; half-revealed. M19.

J. GROSS Strip away the rant, and what remains is a daring chiaroscuro prose.

■ **chiaroscurist** *noun* an artist distinguished for or painting in chiaroscuro L18.

chiasma /kʌɪˈazmə/ *noun*. Pl. **-mas**, **-mata** /-mətə/. M19.
[ORIGIN mod. Latin from Greek *khiasma* crosspiece, decussation, from *khiazein*: see CHIASMUS.]
1 ANATOMY. An intercrossing or decussation; *esp.* (in full ***optic chiasma***) the commissure formed between the two optic nerves. M19.
2 CYTOLOGY. A structure formed by chromosomes during meiosis, at which crossing over occurs. E20.

chiasmus /kʌɪˈazməs, kɪ-/ *noun*. Pl. **-mi** /-mʌɪ/. M17.
[ORIGIN mod. Latin from Greek *khiasmos*, from *khiazein* mark with a chi, from *khi* CHI.]
1 *gen.* A diagonal or crosswise arrangement. *rare*. M17.
2 RHETORIC. The inversion in a second phrase or clause of the order of words in the first. L19.

chiastic /kʌɪˈastɪk, kɪ-/ *adjective*. M19.
[ORIGIN from Greek *khiastos* arranged crosswise, from *khiazein*: see CHIASMUS, -IC.]
Characterized by chiasmus; of the form of chiasmus, with reversal of order.

B. COTTLE 'Rhymney Beer—the Best Round Here' . . with the added trick of chiastic alliteration on R, B, B, R.

chiastolite /kʌɪˈastəlʌɪt, kɪ-/ *noun*. E19.
[ORIGIN formed as CHIASTIC + -LITE.]
MINERALOGY. A form of andalusite containing carbonaceous inclusions which cause some sections of the mineral to show the figure of a cross.

chiaus /tʃaʊs, -ʃ/ *noun*. Also **tchaush** /tʃaʊʃ/. L16.
[ORIGIN Turkish *çavuş*. See also CHOUSE *noun*.]
A Turkish messenger, herald, or sergeant.

chib /ˈtʃɪb/ *noun & verb*. *Scot. slang*. M20.
[ORIGIN Perh. a var. of CHIV.]
▸ **A** *noun*. A knife used as a weapon. M20.

I. WELSH The Yank . . jist wouldnae hand ower the wallet, even when Begbie pulled the chib.

▸ **B** *verb trans.* Stab (someone). L20.

I. RANKIN 'Nobody's going to leap from the shadows and chib you,' Rebus reassured him.

Chibcha /ˈtʃɪbtʃə/ *noun & adjective*. Pl. of noun same, **-s**. E19.
[ORIGIN Amer. Spanish from Chibcha *zipa* chief, hereditary leader.]
▸ **A** *noun*. A member of a S. American Indian people of Colombia, having an ancient civilization; the Chibchan language (now extinct) of this people. E19.
▸ **B** *attrib.* or as *adjective*. Of or pertaining to the Chibcha or their language. E19.

Chibchan /ˈtʃɪbtʃ(ə)n/ *noun & adjective*. E20.
[ORIGIN from CHIBCHA + -AN.]
(Of) a language family of Colombia and Central America.

chibol /ˈtʃɪb(ə)l/ *noun*. LME.
[ORIGIN North. var. of Old French *cibole* (mod. CIBOULE) from late Latin *caepulla* onion bed, from Latin *caepa*, *cepa* onion.]
†**1** = CIBOULE. LME–E18.
2 A spring onion. *dial.* M19.

chibouk /tʃɪˈbuːk/ *noun*. Also **-bouque**. E19.
[ORIGIN (French *chibouque* from) Turkish *çubuk*, (earlier) *çıbık* tube, pipe.]
A long Turkish tobacco pipe.

chic /ʃiːk/ *noun & adjective*. M19.
[ORIGIN French, prob. from German *Schick* skill.]
▸ **A** *noun*. Stylishness and elegance in dress, esp. of a specified kind. M19.

Independent My own daughter is burning with shame at my lack of chic. *Cherwell (online ed.)* Geek chic is back with a vengeance.

radical chic: see RADICAL *adjective* 2c.
▸ **B** *adjective*. Compar. **chic-er**; superl. **chic-est**. Stylish, elegant. M19.

Guardian A middle-class haven of chic bars and trendy boutiques.

■ **chicly** *adverb* E20. **chicness** *noun* L19.

C

chica /ˈtʃiːkə/ *noun*. M19.
[ORIGIN Amer. Spanish, prob. of Amer. Indian origin.]
A S. American climbing shrub, *Arrabidaea chica*, of the bignonia family; a red pigment obtained from this, and used as skin paint by peoples in the R. Orinoco region.

Chicagoan /ʃɪˈkɑːgəʊən/ *noun*. Also †**-ian**. M19.
[ORIGIN from *Chicago* (see below) + -AN, -IAN.]
A native or inhabitant of the city of Chicago in Illinois, USA.

Chicana *noun* see CHICANO.

chicane /ʃɪˈkeɪn/ *noun*. L17.
[ORIGIN French, formed as CHICANE *verb*.]
1 = CHICANERY 1. L17.
†**2** An instance of chicanery; a subterfuge, a quibble. L17–M18.
3 CARDS. A hand without trumps or without cards of one suit as dealt. L19.
4 An artificial barrier or obstacle, esp. a sharp double bend, on a motor-racing track. M20.

chicane /ʃɪˈkeɪn/ *verb*. L17.
[ORIGIN French *chicaner* pursue at law, quibble, of unknown origin.]
1 *verb intrans.* Employ chicanery; quibble, cavil. L17.
2 *verb trans.* Quibble over; argue *away* by chicanery. *rare*. L18.
3 *verb trans.* Deceive by chicanery, cheat, (*into, out of*, etc.). M19.
■ **chicaner** *noun* a person who practises chicanery; a quibbler, a shifty person: L17.

chicanery /ʃɪˈkeɪnəri/ *noun*. L16.
[ORIGIN French *chicanerie*, formed as CHICANE *verb*: see -ERY.]
1 Trickery in legal matters; the use of subterfuge and trickery in debate or action; deception; quibbling, sophistry. L16.
2 A dishonest artifice of law; a trick. L17.

Chicano /tʃɪˈkɑːnəʊ, ʃɪ-, -ˈkeɪn-/ *noun & adjective*. Also **c-**. M20.
[ORIGIN Alt. of Spanish *mejicano* Mexican, from *Méjico* Mexico.]
▸ **A** *noun*. Pl. **-os**. Fem. **-na** /-nə/. A N. American of Mexican origin. M20.
▸ **B** *adjective*. Of or pertaining to Chicanos; Mexican American. M20.

chich /tʃɪtʃ/ *noun*. *obsolete* exc. *dial.* Also †**cich**. LME.
[ORIGIN French *chiche* from Old French *cice* from Latin *cicer*.]
= CHICKPEA. Also †***chich-pease***.

chicha /ˈtʃɪtʃə/ *noun*. E17.
[ORIGIN Amer. Spanish from Kuna.]
A fermented liquor made from maize in S. and Central America.

chicharron /tʃiːtʃəˈrəʊn, *foreign* tʃitʃaˈrron/ *noun*. Pl. **-ones** /-əʊnɪz, *foreign* -ones/. M19.
[ORIGIN Amer. Spanish *chicharrón*.]
A piece of crackling, served as a delicacy in Mexico, parts of the southern US, etc.

chichi /ˈʃiːʃiː/ *noun & adjective*. E20.
[ORIGIN French.]
▸ **A** *noun*. Showiness, fussiness; affectation; a frilly or showy thing. E20.
▸ **B** *adjective*. Showy, frilly, fussy; affected. M20.

chi-chi /ˈtʃiːtʃiː/ *adjective*. *Indian* (somewhat *derog.*). Also **chee-chee**. L18.
[ORIGIN Perh. from Hindi *chī-chī* fie!, supposed to be used by Eurasians.]
(Esp. of a girl or woman) of mixed race; (of speech) characteristic of the English formerly spoken by some mixed-race people in India.

†**chichling** *noun* see CHICKLING.

chick /tʃɪk/ *noun*[1]. Pl. **-s**, (*dial.*) **-en** (see CHICKEN *noun*[1] II). ME.
[ORIGIN Abbreviation of CHICKEN *noun*[1].]
1 A child. *arch.* ME.

W. MORRIS No chick or child to bless his house.

2 A chicken; a young bird, esp. before or just after hatching. LME.

G. MAXWELL A moorhen chick of a few days old.

3 A young woman. *colloq.* E20.

M. AMIS This other girl of mine, this chick, this broad called Ursula.

– COMB.: **chick flick**, **chick lit** *colloq.* (chiefly *derog.*) a film, literature, which is perceived or marketed as appealing to young women.
■ **chicklet** *noun* (*a*) a young bird; a small chick; (*b*) *colloq.* a young woman: L19.

chick /tʃɪk/ *noun*[2]. Also **check** /tʃɛk/. L17.
[ORIGIN Urdu *chik* from Persian *čiğ*.]
In the Indian subcontinent: a screen for a doorway etc., made from split bamboo and twine.

chick /tʃɪk/ *noun*[3]. L18.
[ORIGIN Imit.]
1 A tick (of a clock etc.). *Scot.* L18.
2 The chirping call of a bird. M19.

chick /tʃɪk/ *verb intrans.* Long *obsolete* exc. *dial.* LME.
[ORIGIN Imit.: cf. CHIP *verb*[1].]
Sprout; crack as a seed does in sprouting.

chickabiddy /ˈtʃɪkəbɪdi/ *noun.* L18.
[ORIGIN from CHICK *noun*[1] + euphonic *-a-* + BIDDY *noun*[1].]
1 A child's word for a chicken or a chick. L18.
2 A little one, a dear child. E19.

chickadee /ˈtʃɪkədiː/ *noun. N. Amer.* M19.
[ORIGIN Imit.]
1 Any of various titmice native to N. America. M19.
2 Used as a term of endearment to a woman. M20.

chickaree /tʃɪkəˈriː/ *noun.* E19.
[ORIGIN Imit.]
A N. American red squirrel of the genus *Tamiasciurus*.

Chickasaw /ˈtʃɪkəsɔː/ *noun & adjective.* L17.
[ORIGIN Chickasaw *čikaša*.]
▸ **A** *noun.* Pl. **-s**, same.
1 A member of a Muskogean people formerly resident in Mississippi and Alabama, but subsequently in Oklahoma. L17.
2 The language of this people. L19.
▸ **B** *attrib.* or as *adjective*. Of or pertaining to the Chickasaws or their language. E18.
Chickasaw plum a wild plum, *Prunus angustifolia*, of the south-eastern US.

chicken /ˈtʃɪkɪn/ *noun*[1] *& adjective.*
[ORIGIN Old English *ċicen*, *ċȳcen*, prob. ult. rel. to COCK *noun*[1]. Cf. Middle Dutch & mod. Dutch *kieken*, Middle & mod. Low German *küken*, Middle High German *küchelīn* (German *Küchlein*), Old Norse *kjúklingr*.]
▸ **A** *noun.* **I** *sing.*, with pl. **-s**.
1 A young bird, esp. of the domestic fowl; (the flesh of) the domestic fowl as food. OE.
2 a A child. *arch.* LME. ▸**b** A young and inexperienced person. E18. ▸**c** A young woman. *slang.* M19.
3 A timorous or cowardly person. E17. ▸**b** (The name of) a game testing courage in the face of danger. M20.
▸ **II** *pl.* (*collect.*)
4 Poultry, fowl. *obsolete* exc. *dial.* E17.
– PHRASES: **chicken à la king** cooked breast of chicken in a cream sauce with mushrooms and peppers. ***chicken à la*** MARENGO. ***chicken à la Maryland***: see MARYLAND 2. ***chicken*** CHASSEUR. **chicken Kiev** chicken breast filled with garlic butter. ***chicken*** MARENGO. ***chicken Maryland***: see MARYLAND 2. **count one's chickens (before they are hatched)** be overoptimistic, be precipitate. DIGBY ***chicken***. ***like a hen with one chicken***: see HEN *noun* 1. ***Maryland chicken***: see MARYLAND 2. **Mother Carey's chicken** the storm petrel. **no chicken** = ***no spring chicken*** below. **spring chicken** (*a*) a young chicken for eating (orig. available only in spring); (*b*) *colloq.* a young person; chiefly in ***no spring chicken***, neither young nor inexperienced. ***Surrey chicken***: see SURREY *noun*[1] 2.
– COMB.: **chicken-and-egg** *adjective* designating a problem of which of two things, issues, etc., comes first, where each is viewed as the cause of the other; **chicken-breast** (*a*) a malformed projection of the breastbone; (*b*) the breast meat of a chicken; **chicken-breasted** *adjective* having a malformed projection of the breastbone; **chicken brick** an earthenware container in two halves, in which to cook a chicken etc.; **chickenburger** a cake of minced etc. chicken, usu. fried or grilled; ***chicken cholera***: see CHOLERA 3; **chicken feed** food for poultry; *colloq.* something trivial, esp. a small amount of money; **chicken hawk** (chiefly *N. Amer.*) any of various bird-eating raptors; **chicken-heart** *fig.* a timorous or cowardly person; **chicken-hearted** *adjective* timorous, cowardly; **Chicken Little**, **Chicken Licken** [name of a character in a nursery story who repeatedly warns that the sky is falling down] an alarmist; a person who panics at the first sign of a problem; **chicken-liver** *fig.* a coward; **chicken-livered** *adjective* cowardly; **chicken mite** = ***red mite*** (a) s.v. RED *adjective*; **chickenpox** [perh. from the mildness of the infection, as compared to smallpox] an infectious disease causing a mild fever and a rash of inflamed pimples, due to viral infection; also called ***varicella***; **chickenshit** *noun & adjective* (*slang*, chiefly *N. Amer.*) (*a*) *noun* a coward; nonsense, lies; (*b*) *adjective* cowardly; dishonest; **chicken weed** = CHICKWEED; **chicken wire** a light wire netting with a hexagonal mesh.
▸ **B** *adjective.* Cowardly; scared. *slang.* M20.

chicken *noun*[2] var. of CHIKAN.

chicken /tʃɪkɪn/ *verb intrans. slang.* M20.
[ORIGIN from CHICKEN *noun*[1] *& adjective.*]
Fail to act, back down, from motives of cowardice. Freq. foll. by *out*.

chickling /ˈtʃɪklɪŋ/ *noun.* Orig. **†c(h)ichling**. M16.
[ORIGIN from CHICH + -LING[1].]
= ***grass pea*** s.v. GRASS *noun.* Now usu. ***chickling pea***, ***chickling vetch***.

chickpea /ˈtʃɪkpiː/ *noun.* Also **†-pease**. E18.
[ORIGIN Alt. of *CHICH-pease*: see PEA *noun*[1], PEASE.]
(The seed of) a dwarf pea, *Cicer arietinum*, grown for food esp. in Asia.

chickweed /ˈtʃɪkwiːd/ *noun.* LME.
[ORIGIN from CHICK *noun*[1] + WEED *noun*[1].]
Any of numerous small white-flowered plants of the family Caryophyllaceae, and esp. of the genera *Cerastium* and *Stellaria*; spec. *S. media*, a common weed. Orig. more widely, any of various similar weedy plants.
jagged chickweed: see JAGGED *adjective*[1]. ***mouse-ear chickweed***: see MOUSE *noun*. ***water chickweed***: see WATER *noun*.
– COMB.: **chickweed wintergreen** a plant of the genus *Trientalis*, of the primrose family, bearing a starry white (occas. pink) flower above a whorl of obovate leaves, esp. *T. europaea* of Eurasian upland woods and moors (cf. ***starflower*** s.v. STAR *noun*[1]).

chicle /ˈtʃɪk(ə)l, -kli/ *noun.* L19.
[ORIGIN Amer. Spanish from Nahuatl *tzictli*.]
The coagulated latex of the sapodilla, *Manilkara zapota*, and several related trees, which forms the basis of chewing gum.

chicory /ˈtʃɪk(ə)ri/ *noun.* LME.
[ORIGIN from French †*cicorée* (mod. *chicorée*) endive, from medieval Latin *cic(h)orea*, ult. from Greek *kikhorion*: cf. SUCCORY.]
1 A Eurasian blue-flowered plant of the composite family, *Cichorium intybus*, found wild by roadsides and in pastures and cultivated for its roots and crowns of leaves which are eaten blanched in salads. Also (*N. Amer.*), (the leaves of) the endive, *C. endivia*. LME.
2 The root of *C. intybus* ground and roasted as a substitute for or an additive to coffee. E19.

chid, **chidden** *verb* see CHIDE *verb*.

chide /tʃʌɪd/ *noun.* Now *rare*. ME.
[ORIGIN from the verb.]
Wrangling; an angry rebuke.

chide /tʃʌɪd/ *verb.* Now *arch.* or *literary*. Pa. t. **chided**, **chid** /tʃɪd/; pa. pple **chided**, **chidden** /ˈtʃɪd(ə)n/, **chid**.
[ORIGIN Old English *ċīdan*, of unknown origin.]
1 *verb intrans.* †**a** Contend loudly, brawl, wrangle; quarrel or dispute angrily *with*. OE–M19. ▸**b** Give loud and angry expression to dissatisfaction; scold; rail (†*at*). ME.

> **b** SWIFT You came chiding into the world. *fig.*: KEATS The silver snarling trumpets 'gan to chide.

2 *verb trans.* Rail at, scold; rebuke; find fault with. ME.

> S. JOHNSON Having chidden her for undutifulness. GIBBON The emperor . . chided the tardiness of the senate.

3 *verb trans.* Drive, impel, or compel by chiding, *away*, *into* or *out of* a state, position, etc. L16.

> R. W. EMERSON Be neither chided nor flattered out of your position.

■ **chider** *noun* LME. **chiding** *noun* (*a*) the action of the verb; (*b*) a reproof, a rebuke: OE. **chidingly** *adverb* in a chiding manner L16.

chidlings *noun pl.* var. of CHITLINGS.

chief /tʃiːf/ *noun.* ME.
[ORIGIN Old French & mod. French *chef*, †*chief*, from Proto-Romance var. of Latin *caput* head.]
1 A leader, a ruler, a commander; a head of a tribe, clan, organization, etc.; the head of a department, the highest official. ME. ▸**b** NAUTICAL. *The* Chief Engineer of a (war)ship. *colloq.* L19.

> THACKERAY The chief of the kitchen. G. J. WHYTE-MELVILLE Our old chief . . has been appointed to a command in India. C. G. SELIGMAN The king was paramount lord over a confederation of provincial chiefs.

†2 The chief position; first place; pre-eminence. ME–E17.
†3 The head, the top, the upper end, (*of*). LME–L16.
4 HERALDRY. The top part of a shield, at most one third, often one fifth of the shield. LME.
†5 *The* best part *of*; *the* height *of*, *the* prime *of*. Cf. CHIEF *adjective* II. E16–E17.
6 In full ***chief rent***. Orig., a rent paid under a tenure in chief (see below). Later, a quit-rent. E16.
– PHRASES ETC.: **big chief**, **big white chief**, **great white chief** *joc.* [after Amer. Indian speech] a person in authority, an important person. **Chief of Staff** the senior staff officer of a service or of a commander. **in chief** (*a*) (holding tenure) directly from the lord paramount, the king (*hist.*); (holding tenure) by perpetual ground rent or feu duty; (*b*) *arch.* most of all, especially. **-in-chief** (*a*) supreme, principal, head (freq. in titles, as ***Colonel-in-Chief***, ***Commander-in-Chief***, ***Commodore-in-Chief***, ***Editor-in-Chief***); EXAMINATION-***in-chief***; (*b*) *hist.* holding directly from the king (as ***tenant-in-chief***). ***paramount chief***: see PARAMOUNT *adjective* 1.
■ **chiefdom** *noun* the estate, position, or dominion of a chief L16. **chiefry**, **-ery** *noun* IRISH HISTORY the office and territory of a chief; the dues belonging to the chief or to the lord superior: L16. **chiefess** *noun* a female chief L18. **chiefless** *adjective* M18. **chiefly** *adjective* of or pertaining to a chief L19. **chiefship** *noun* the office and function of a chief L17.

chief /tʃiːf/ *adjective & adverb.* ME.
[ORIGIN from the noun.]
▸ **A** *adjective.* **I** (Usu. *attrib.*)
1 Formally leading or most important. (Now only of people.) ME.

> R. GRAFTON Vienna, which is the chiefe Citie of the Countrie. M. LOWRY The chief cook regarded the . . second cook as a creature of completely inferior station.

Chief Justice, ***Chief Rabbi***, etc. ***Chief Constable***: see CONSTABLE 4. ***little chief hare***: see LITTLE *adjective*. ***Lord Chief Justice***: see JUSTICE *noun*.

2 Most important; principal, foremost, greatest. LME.

> N. HAWTHORNE A very dear friend . . who . . had been his chief intimate. J. BUCHAN His chief regret is that he is a miserable public speaker. W. S. CHURCHILL Madras . . was the chief trading centre.

chief good: see GOOD *noun*.
3 Prominent, leading; belonging to the highest group or the first rank. (With superl. & †compar.) LME.

> W. DAMPIER The Chinese are the chiefest merchants. LD MACAULAY A chief object of the expedition.

†4 Pre-eminent in excellence; best, finest, choice. E16–M17.
5 Intimate (as friends). *Scot.* M16.
▸ **II** *absol.* (with superl. & †compar.) Cf. CHIEF *noun* 5.
6 *pl.* The chief people. Long *arch.* M16.
7 The most or (*obsolete*) more important. E17.

> J. CHAMBERLAYNE There are six penny-post offices: the chiefest is in Threadneedle Street.

8 The main part, the bulk. L17.

> W. DAMPIER About which they spend the chiefest of their time. F. MARRYAT At night, when the chief of the inhabitants were in bed.

▸ **B** *adverb.* Chiefly, principally. *arch.* LME.
■ **chiefly** *adverb* pre-eminently; especially; above all; principally, mainly but not exclusively: LME.

chieftain /ˈtʃiːft(ə)n, -tɪn/ *noun.* ME.
[ORIGIN Old French *chevetaine* from late Latin *capitaneus* (see CAPTAIN), assim. to CHIEF *noun*.]
1 The head of a body of men, an organization, state, town, etc.; the ruler, the chief. *obsolete* in *gen.* sense. ME.
2 A military leader; a captain. Now *arch.* & *poet.* ME.
3 The chief of a clan or tribe. L16.
4 The captain of a band of robbers. M17.
■ **chieftaincy** *noun* the rank or position of a chieftain E17. **chieftainess** *noun* a female chieftain LME. **chieftainry** *noun* the rank, rule, or territory, of a chieftain; chieftains collectively: M18. **chieftainship** *noun* = CHIEFTAINCY L18.

chield /tʃiːld/ *noun. Scot.* Also **chiel** /tʃiːl/. LME.
[ORIGIN Var. of CHILD *noun*.]
A man, a lad, a fellow.

chiffchaff /ˈtʃɪftʃaf/ *noun.* L18.
[ORIGIN Imit.]
A common warbler, *Phylloscopus collybita*, with a highly characteristic repetitive song.

chiffon /ˈʃɪfɒn/ *noun & adjective.* M18.
[ORIGIN French, from *chiffe* rag.]
▸ **A** *noun.* **1** In *pl.* Trimmings or other adornments of women's dress. *arch.* M18.
2 A light diaphanous plain-woven fabric of silk, nylon, etc. L19.
▸ **B** *attrib.* or as *adjective*. Made of chiffon; light in weight. E20.
chiffon pie: with a light-textured filling flavoured with fruit etc.
■ **chiffony** *adjective* E20.

chiffonade /ʃɪfəˈnɑːd; *foreign* ʃifɔnad (*pl. same*)/ *noun.* Also **-nn-**. L19.
[ORIGIN French.]
A selection of shredded or finely cut vegetables, used esp. as a garnish for soup.

chiffonier /ʃɪfəˈnɪə/ *noun.* Also **†-n(n)ière**. M18.
[ORIGIN French *chiffonnier*, *-ière*, transf. use of CHIFFONNIER.]
A movable low cupboard with a sideboard top.

chiffonnier /ʃifɔnje/ *noun.* Pl. pronounced same. M19.
[ORIGIN French.]
A collector of scraps, a rag picker.

†chiffonnière *noun* var. of CHIFFONIER.

chifforobe /ˈʃɪfərəʊb/ *noun. US.* E20.
[ORIGIN from CHIFFO(NIER + WARD)ROBE.]
A piece of furniture with drawers in the lower part and hanging space in the upper part.

chigger *noun* var. of JIGGER *noun*[2].

chignon /ˈʃiːnjɒ̃/ *noun.* L18.
[ORIGIN French, orig. = nape of the neck, from Proto-Romance var. of Latin *catena* CHAIN *noun*: see -OON.]
A coil or mass of hair worn by women low on the back of the head.

chigoe /ˈtʃɪɡəʊ/ *noun.* Also (earlier) **†chique**. M17.
[ORIGIN (French *chique*) from a W. African lang.]
= JIGGER *noun*[2] 1.

chi-hike /ˈtʃʌɪ(h)ʌɪk/ *noun & verb.* Also **chi-ike**; (*Austral.* & *NZ*) **chiack** /ˈtʃʌɪak/. M19.
[ORIGIN Unknown.]
▸ **A** *noun.* A salutation; a noisy disturbance; jeering, banter. M19.
▸ **B** *verb.* **1** *verb trans.* Salute; jeer at, make fun of. M19.
2 *verb intrans.* Make a noisy demonstration; jeer, tease. L19.

chihuahua /tʃɪˈwɑːwə/ *noun.* Also **C-**. E19.
[ORIGIN *Chihuahua*, a city and state in Mexico.]
(An animal of) a breed of very small smooth-haired dog which originated in Mexico. Also ***chihuahua dog***.

chi-ike *noun & verb* var. of CHI-HIKE.

chikan /ˈtʃɪk(ə)n/ *noun*. Also **chicken**. **L19**.
[**ORIGIN** Urdu *chikan* from Persian *čikin*.]
A type of hand embroidery in the Indian subcontinent.

chikara *noun* var. of **CHINKARA**.

chikhor *noun* var. of **CHUKAR**.

chikungunya /tʃɪk(ə)nˈɡʌnjə/ *noun*. **M20**.
[**ORIGIN** Bantu (prob. Makonde).]
MEDICINE. A mosquito-borne viral disease resembling dengue, endemic in E. Africa and parts of Asia.

chil- *combining form* see **CHEILO-**.

chilblain /ˈtʃɪlbleɪn/ *noun*. **M16**.
[**ORIGIN** from **CHILL** *noun* + **BLAIN**.]
An itching swelling, esp. on the feet or hands, due to exposure to cold and poor blood circulation.
■ **chilblained** *adjective* **E17**.

Chilcat *noun & adjective* var. of **CHILKAT**.

child /tʃʌɪld/ *noun*. Also (*arch.*, esp. in sense 3) **childe**, **chylde**. Pl. **children** /ˈtʃɪldr(ə)n/. See also **CHIELD**.
[**ORIGIN** Old English *ċild* rel. to Gothic *kilþei* womb, *inkilþo* pregnant, as it were 'fruit of the womb'. The Middle English pl. *childre*, *childer* became *childeren*, *children*.]
▸ **I 1** A fetus; an infant; *spec.* (*dial.*) a female infant. **OE**.

SHAKES. *Wint. T.* A very pretty barne. A boy or a child, I wonder?

2 A boy or girl. **OE**. ▸**b** In biblical translations: a youth approaching or entering on manhood. **LME**.
3 *sing.* A youth of gentle birth. Chiefly as a title. *arch.* **OE**.

BYRON Childe Harold.

4 *transf.* A person who has (or is considered to have) the character, manners, or attainments of a child, esp. a person of immature experience or judgement; a childish person. **ME**.

J. CONRAD You are not fit for diplomatic work, you know, *ma chère*. You are a mere child at it.

5 A pupil at school. **ME**. ▸**b** *spec.* A chorister. **E16**.
†**6** A lad in service; a page, an attendant, etc. **LME–E17**.
7 A man, a lad, a fellow. Cf. **CHIELD**. Long *arch. rare*. **M16**.

L. G. GIBBON Chris waved to the old, kind childe as he bicycled down Blawearie brae.

▸ **II** As correlative to parent.
8 A son or daughter (at any age) *of* (or with *my* etc.); an offspring of human parents. (Used chiefly, & longer, of a daughter.) **OE**. ▸**b** A young animal. *rare*. **L16**.
9 In *pl.* Descendants; members of the tribe or clan. **ME**.
10 A disciple *of* a teacher; a follower or adherent *of*. Usu. in *pl.* **ME**.
11 *fig.* A product, derivative, extract, dependant, attachment, etc., *of*. **ME**.

SHAKES. *Rom. & Jul.* Dreams Which are the children of an idle brain. J. R. GREEN Elizabeth . . was a child of the Italian Renascence.

— **PHRASES**: **children of Israel** = **ISRAEL** 1. **from a child** since childhood. ***poor child***: see **POOR** *adjective*. ***quick with child***: see **QUICK** *adjective* 4a. ***red children***: see **RED** *adjective*. ***Sunday child***, ***Sunday's child***: see **SUNDAY**. **the child unborn**: a type of innocence, ignorance, etc. **this child** *slang* (orig. *US black English*) I, me. **with child** *arch.* (*a*) pregnant; †(*b*) *fig.* full *of*; eager, longing, *to do*.

— **COMB.**: **child abuse** severe maltreatment of a child, esp. by beating or neglect or sexual assault; **child allowance** a sum of money paid out or allowed against tax for a dependent child; **childbearing** giving birth to children; **child benefit** (in the UK) a state monetary allowance for each child in a family (replacing family allowance); **childbirth** giving birth to a child (***natural childbirth***: see **NATURAL** *adjective*); **child bride** a bride who is still a child, a very young bride; **childcare** the care or oversight of a child or children, esp. by a crèche or childminder in the temporary absence of a parent or guardian, or by a local authority when a normal home life is considered to be lacking; **child guidance** the supervision of the (esp. psychological) welfare of children and adolescents, the therapeutic treatment of maladjusted children and adolescents; **child labour** the (esp. inhumane or illegal) use of children in industry or business; **Childline** (a charitable organization running) a telephone helpline service offering help and advice to children experiencing problems, esp. physical or sexual abuse; **childminder** a person who takes care of a child or children, esp. in the temporary absence of a parent or guardian; *spec.* a person registered with the local authority to offer paid daytime care in his or her own home for children under the age of eight; **childminding** the oversight of a child or children in the temporary absence of a parent or guardian; *spec.* the work of a registered childminder; **child molestation** sexual abuse of a child by an adult; **child-molester** a person guilty of child-molestation; ***child* PORNOGRAPHY**; **childproof** *adjective* that cannot be operated, opened, damaged, etc., by a child; **child psychologist** a specialist in child psychology; **child psychology** the systematic study of the psychology of children; **children's hour** (chiefly *hist.*) an hour of recreation spent together by parents and their children in the evening; (***Children's Hour***), a BBC radio programme with this title, broadcast 1922–61; **child-resistant** *adjective* = ***childproof*** above; **child's play** (*a*) play befitting a child; (*b*) an easy task; **Child Support Agency** (in the UK and Australia) a government agency responsible for the assessment and collection of compulsory child maintenance payments from absent parents; **child-wife** a wife who is still a child, a very young wife; **child-woman** a person between childhood and womanhood; a woman who is still like a child.
■ **childed** *adjective* provided with a child or children **E17**. **childless** *adjective* **ME**. **childlessness** *noun* **M19**. **childlike** *adjective* (*a*) belonging to or becoming a child; filial; (*b*) resembling (that of) a child; possessing the qualities of a child (usu. in a good sense, as opp. ***childish***): **L16**. **childlikeness** *noun* childlike quality **E19**. **childly** *adjective* (*a*) childish; †(*b*) filial: **OE**. **childness** *noun* (*rare*) †(*a*) childish humour, childishness; (*b*) being a child: **E17**. **childship** *noun* (now *rare*) the relationship of child to parent; filiation, adoption: **M16**.

†**child** *verb*. **ME**.
[**ORIGIN** from the noun.]
1 *verb trans.* Give birth to (a child); bring forth. **ME–E17**.
2 *verb intrans.* Bear a child; be delivered of a child. **ME–E19**.

childbed /ˈtʃʌɪl(d)bɛd/ *noun*. **ME**.
[**ORIGIN** from **CHILD** *noun* + **BED** *noun*.]
1 The state of a woman in labour; giving birth to a child. **ME**.
2 The bed in which a child is born. **L16**.

childe *noun* see **CHILD** *noun*.

Childermas /ˈtʃɪldəmas/ *noun*. *arch.*
[**ORIGIN** Old English *ċildramæsse*, from *ċildra* genit. pl. of *ċild* **CHILD** *noun* + *mæsse* **MASS** *noun*[1].]
1 The festival of the Holy Innocents, 28 December, commemorating Herod's slaughter of the children (*Matthew* 2:16). **OE**.
2 The day of the week throughout the year corresponding to the day on which the festival last occurred. Now *dial.* **E17**.

childhood /ˈtʃʌɪldhʊd/ *noun*.
[**ORIGIN** Old English *ċildhād*: see **CHILD** *noun*, **-HOOD**.]
1 The state or stage of life of a child; the time during which one is a child; the time from birth to puberty. **OE**.

fig.: SHAKES. *Rom. & Jul.* Now I have stain'd the childhood of our joy.

second childhood the state of childishness incident to old age; dotage.
†**2** Childishness; a childish action. Only in **ME**.
†**3** The relationship of child to parent. Only in **E17**.

childish /ˈtʃʌɪldɪʃ/ *adjective*.
[**ORIGIN** Old English *ċildisċ*: see **CHILD** *noun*, **-ISH**[1].]
1 Of, belonging, or proper to a child or childhood; childlike. **OE**.
2 Not befitting mature age; puerile, silly. **LME**.
■ **childishly** *adverb* **LME**. **childishness** *noun* **E16**.

children *noun* pl. of **CHILD** *noun*.

Chile /ˈtʃɪli/ *noun*[1]. Also (*arch.*) **Chili**. **E19**.
[**ORIGIN** A S. American republic.]
Used *attrib.* to designate things found in or associated with Chile.
Chile hazel: see **HAZEL** *noun*[1]. **Chile nitre** natural sodium nitrate. **Chile pine** the monkey-puzzle tree, *Araucaria araucana*. **Chile saltpetre** = ***Chile nitre*** above.

chile *noun*[2] var. of **CHILLI**.

Chilean /ˈtʃɪlɪən/ *adjective & noun*. Also (*arch.*) **Chilian**. **E18**.
[**ORIGIN** from **CHILE** *noun*[1] + **-AN**.]
▸ **A** *adjective*. Of or pertaining to Chile or its inhabitants. **E18**.
***Chilean* JASMINE**.
▸ **B** *noun*. A native or inhabitant of Chile. **E19**.

chile ancho *noun phr.*: see **ANCHO**.

chili *noun*[1] var. of **CHILLI**.

Chili *noun*[2] see **CHILE** *noun*[1].

chiliad /ˈkɪlɪad/ *noun*. **LME**.
[**ORIGIN** Late Latin *chilias*, *-ad-* from Greek *khilias*, *-ad-*, from *khilioi* one thousand: see **-AD**[1].]
1 A period of one thousand years. **LME**. ▸**b** *spec.* The millennium. *rare*. **E18**.
2 A group of one thousand (things); a thousand. **L16**.

chiliagon /ˈkɪlɪag(ə)n/ *noun*. **L17**.
[**ORIGIN** from Greek *khiliagōnos*, from *khilioi* one thousand + *gōnia* angle.]
A plane figure with a thousand straight sides and a thousand angles.

chiliahedron /kɪlɪəˈhiːdr(ə)n, -ˈhɛd-/ *noun*. *rare*. Pl. **-dra** /-drə/, **-drons**. **L17**.
[**ORIGIN** from Greek *khilioi* one thousand + **-HEDRON**.]
A solid figure or object with a thousand plane faces.

Chilian *adjective & noun* see **CHILEAN**.

chiliarch /ˈkɪlɪɑːk/ *noun*. **L16**.
[**ORIGIN** Late Latin *chiliarches*, *-us* from Greek *khiliarkhēs*, *-os*, from *khilioi* one thousand: see **-ARCH**.]
A commander of a thousand men.
■ **chiliarchy** *noun* †(*a*) a body of a thousand men; (*b*) the post of chiliarch: **M17**.

chiliasm /ˈkɪlɪaz(ə)m/ *noun*. **E17**.
[**ORIGIN** Greek *khiliasmos*, from *khilias* **CHILIAD**.]
The doctrine of the millennium; the belief that Christ will reign in bodily presence on earth for a thousand years.

chiliast /ˈkɪlɪast/ *noun*. **L16**.
[**ORIGIN** Late Latin *chiliastes* from Greek *khiliastēs*, from *khilias* **CHILIAD**.]
An adherent of chiliasm; a millenarian.
■ **chiliˈastic** *adjective* of, pertaining to, or holding the doctrine of the millennium **L17**.

Chilkat /ˈtʃɪlkat/ *noun & adjective*. Also **Chilcat**. **M19**.
[**ORIGIN** Tlingit *jilḵáat*.]
▸ **A** *noun*. Pl. **-s**, same. A member of a subdivision of the Tlingit in Alaska. **M19**.
▸ **B** *adjective*. Of or pertaining to this people. **M19**.

chill /tʃɪl/ *noun*.
[**ORIGIN** Old English *ċele*, *ċiele*, of Germanic origin. Rel. to **COLD** *adjective*. In branch II also from the verb or adjective.]
▸ †**I 1** *gen.* Absence of heat, cold, coldness. **OE–LME**.
▸ **II 2** A lowered bodily temperature, marked by shivering; feverish shivering; a sudden sensation of physical cold, which is often a first stage or symptom of illness; a feverish cold. **ME**.

E. ROOSEVELT He began to complain that he felt a chill. P. F. BOLLER He contracted a chill that quickly became pneumonia.

3 A coldness of the air, water, etc., which may induce shivering; cold which has a depressing, benumbing, or penetrating effect on the body. **L18**.

G. MAXWELL She had recoiled at first from the biting chill of the water.

take the chill off warm slightly.
4 *fig.* **a** A depressing influence. **E19**. ▸**b** Absence of warmth of feeling or sympathy; coldness of manner. **M19**.

a J. MORLEY The . . prosaic results . . have thrown a chill over our political imaginations. **b** H. MARTINEAU To dissipate the chill by showing that we were ready to . . be sociable.

5 A metal mould, or piece of metal in a sand mould, used to cool quickly, and often to harden, the surface of molten metal brought into contact with it. **L19**.
6 A cloud or bloom on a surface, esp. caused by condensation. **L19**.

P. V. WHITE Basil returned with a green bottle. It was wearing a chill.

— **COMB.**: **chill factor** **METEOROLOGY** the apparent lowering of the air temperature by wind; **chill pill** *slang* an anti-depressant; anything intended to calm a person down (***take a chill pill***, calm down, relax).

chill /tʃɪl/ *adjective*. Now *literary*. **LME**.
[**ORIGIN** Prob. from the noun.]
1 Cold to touch or feel; now usu. unpleasantly or harmfully cold; that chills or causes shivering. **LME**.

ARNOLD BENNETT The atmosphere outside the stove was chill. W. BOYD He adored the chill green drink, clear and clinking with ice-cubes.

2 *fig.* That tends to repress warmth of feeling or enthusiasm; repressed in feeling, unemotional, austere. **LME**.

T. GRAY Chill Penury repress'd their noble rage. T. HARDY A chill self-reproach.

3 Depressingly affected by cold; having a pervading sensation of cold; sensitive or liable to cold. **L16**.

M. SHELLEY They had a fire to warm them when chill.

■ **chillness** *noun* **L16**.

chill /tʃɪl/ *verb*. **LME**.
[**ORIGIN** Prob. from the noun.]
▸ **I 1** *verb intrans.* Become cold. **LME**. ▸**b** Be seized with a sudden chill. **M19**.

DEFOE My very blood chills at the mention of the name of Newgate.

†**2** *verb intrans.* Shiver with cold. **LME–L16**.
3 *verb trans.* Make cold; affect harmfully with cold. **LME**. ▸**b** Deaden or destroy with cold. **E18**.

DRYDEN Ev'ry Lady's Blood with Fear was chill'd.

4 *verb trans. fig.* Affect as with cold; depress; deject, dispirit. **LME**.

H. KELLER Even now the thought of those dreadful days chills my heart.

5 *verb trans.* Cool and harden (molten metal) by contact with cold metal, or by casting in a metal mould. **M19**.
6 *verb trans.* Give a cloud or bloom to (a surface) by cold, condensation, etc. **M19**.
7 *verb trans.* Subject (food, esp. meat, etc.) to a low but not freezing temperature, esp. to preserve it. **L19**.

B. SPOCK You boil your milk . . cool it, then chill it in the refrigerator.

▸ **II 8** *verb trans. & intrans.* Warm slightly; raise or rise to temperate heat. *dial.* **E19**.

DICKENS A pint pot, the contents of which were 'chilling' on the hob.

▸ **III** *slang* (orig. *US*).
9 *verb intrans.* Freq. with *out*. Calm down, relax, take it easy. Freq. as *interjection*. **L20**. ▸**b** Pass time idly; hang around, esp. *with* other members of a group. **L20**.

Q. TARANTINO Tell her to chill. C. WILKINS Then Frank said, softly, 'Hey, Elliot, chill out, okay?' **b** B. CROSS Bored as hell . . , so I went to a place where the homeboys chill.

C

– COMB.: **chill-cast** *verb* rapidly solidify (cast iron or other metal) by contact with a cooled metal mould or other cold surface in order to produce a hard, dense surface; **chill-out** *adjective* (*colloq.*) intended to induce or enhance a relaxed mood, esp. denoting a room in a nightclub in which dancers may relax and where quiet or ambient music is played.

■ **chiller** *noun* a person who or thing which chills (***spine-chiller***: see SPINE *noun*) L18. **chillingly** *adverb* in a chilling manner L16.

C

chilli /ˈtʃɪli/ *noun*. Pl. **-i(e)s**. Also **chile**, pl. **chiles**, ***chili**. E17.
[ORIGIN Spanish *chile* from Nahuatl *chilli*.]
The (dried) red pod of the pepper *Capsicum annuum* var. *longum*, used in sauces, relishes, etc., and made into a hot cayenne; cayenne made from these dried pods. Also ***chilli pepper***.
chilli con carne /kɒn ˈkɑːni/ [Spanish = with meat] a Mexican dish of minced beef, beans, and chilli. **chilli relleno** /rɛˈljeɪnəʊ/ [Spanish = stuffed] a stuffed green pepper.
– COMB.: ***chilli pepper***: see above; **chilli powder** hot cayenne made from chillies.

chillsome /ˈtʃɪls(ə)m/ *adjective*. E20.
[ORIGIN from CHILL *noun* or *verb* + -SOME[1].]
Chilling, chilly.

chillum /ˈtʃɪləm/ *noun*. L18.
[ORIGIN Hindi *chilam*.]
The part of a hookah containing the tobacco etc.; *loosely* a hookah, or a pipe used for smoking cannabis.

chillumchee /ˈtʃɪləmtʃiː/ *noun*. E18.
[ORIGIN Urdu *chilamchī*.]
In the Indian subcontinent: a washbasin of brass or tinned copper.

chilly /ˈtʃɪli/ *adjective*. L16.
[ORIGIN from CHILL *noun* + -Y[1].]
1 That chills; disagreeably cold to touch or feel. L16.
chilly bin *NZ* a portable insulated container for keeping food or drink cool.
2 Affected by a chill; (feeling) rather cold; sensitive to cold. E17.
3 *fig.* Not genial; cold-mannered. M19.
■ **chillily** *adverb* M19. **chilliness** *noun* E18.

chilo- *combining form* var. of CHEILO-.

chilopod /ˈkʌɪləpɒd/ *noun & adjective*. M19.
[ORIGIN from mod. Latin *Chilopoda* pl. (see below): see CHEILO-, -POD.]
ZOOLOGY. ▸**A** *noun*. A myriapod of the class Chilopoda, a centipede. M19.
▸**B** *adjective*. Of, pertaining to, or characteristic of Chilopoda. L19.

Chiltern Hundreds /ˌtʃɪlt(ə)n ˈhʌndrədz/ *noun phr. pl.* ME.
[ORIGIN from *Chiltern* Hills in S. England + HUNDRED + -S[1].]
A crown manor, the administration of which is a nominal office under the Crown and so requires an MP to vacate his or her seat.
apply for the Chiltern Hundreds resign from the House of Commons.

chilver /ˈtʃɪlvə/ *noun*. Now *dial.*
[ORIGIN Old English *ċilfer-*, *ċilfor-lomb*, corresp. to Old High German *kilbur(ra)*, *-irra*: rel. to CALF *noun*[1].]
In full ***chilver-lamb***. A ewe lamb.

chimaera *noun* var. of CHIMERA.

chimaeroid /kʌɪˈmɪərɔɪd, kɪ-/ *noun & adjective*. M19.
[ORIGIN from CHILVER + -OID.]
(Relating to or characteristic of) a deep-sea fish of the subclass Holocephali (CHIMERA 4).

chimb *noun* var. of CHIME *noun*[2].

chime /tʃʌɪm/ *noun*[1]. ME.
[ORIGIN Prob. from Old English *ċimbal* CYMBAL, by analysis as *chime bell*.]
†**1** A cymbal. Only in ME.
2 An apparatus for striking a set of bells so as to make them chime; *spec.* (usu. in *pl.*) such an apparatus used as a doorbell. LME.
3 A set of bells, or of metal bars or tubes, so attuned as to chime when struck or slightly swung. LME.
musical chime: see MUSICAL *adjective*.
4 The series of musical sounds or tune played on such sets of bells; a chiming sound. M16.

> J. BETJEMAN The girl of my choice, with the tilt of her nose and the chime of her voice.

5 The rhythm or ring of verse; *derog.* jingle. M17.
6 *fig.* A system of which all the parts are in harmony. M17.

> MILTON Disproportion'd sin Jarr'd against natures chime, and with harsh din Broke the fair Musick.

7 *fig.* Harmony, accord, agreement. M19.

> H. MAUDSLEY Others have found no such happy chime of fact and theory.

– COMB.: **chime bars** a type of glockenspiel used esp. in schools.

chime /tʃʌɪm/ *noun*[2]. Also **chimb**. See also CHINE *noun*[3]. LME.
[ORIGIN Prob. identical with the noun occurring in Old English *ċimstān* base, pedestal, *ċimiren* clamp-iron, *ċimbing* joint, corresp. to Middle Dutch *kimme* (Dutch *kim*) edge of a cask, Middle Low German *kimme*, *kimm* (German *Kimme*).]
The rim at the ends of a cask, formed by the ends of the staves.

chime /tʃʌɪm/ *verb*[1]. ME.
[ORIGIN Uncertain: the relation to CHIME *noun*[1] is obscure.]
1 *verb intrans.* Resound when struck; ring out; tinkle; (of a set of bells) make a series of musical sounds. ME.

> E. WAUGH The bells of St. Bride's chimed unheard. L. DEIGHTON A clock chimed loudly. I. MCEWAN Ice chimed in glasses.

2 *verb intrans.* Produce a musical sound from a bell by striking it; make a series of musical sounds with a set of bells. LME.
3 *verb intrans. & trans.* Recite or repeat in cadence or mechanically. LME.

> BYRON Let simple Wordsworth chime his childish verse.

4 *verb trans.* **a** Of a set of bells etc.: indicate (the hour) by chiming. M16. ▸**b** Give out (a musical sound) when struck. *arch.* E17.

> **a** G. SWIFT The mantelpiece clock chimed one in the morning.

5 *verb trans.* Bring or put (into or out of a state or place) by chiming. L16.

> SOUTHEY His enemies had the indecency to chime him out of the church.

6 *verb trans.* Make a series of musical sounds on (a set of bells); strike (a bell etc.) so that a musical sound is given out. L16.
7 *verb intrans. & trans.* Jingle; rhyme (words). M17.
8 *verb intrans. fig.* Harmonize, agree, (*together*, *with*). L17.

> W. S. CHURCHILL Her endeavours chimed with the Imperial spirit of the age.

– WITH ADVERBS IN SPECIALIZED SENSES: **chime in** (***a***) *verb phr. intrans.* join in harmoniously or in unison; (***b***) *verb phr. intrans. & trans.* interject (as) a remark in agreement; (***c***) *verb phr. intrans.* be in complete (but usu. subordinate) accord *with*.

chime /tʃʌɪm/ *verb*[2] *trans.* M19.
[ORIGIN from CHIME *noun*[2].]
Groove or chamfer staves for the chime of (a cask).

chimenea /ˌtʃɪmɪˈneɪə, -ˈniːə/ *noun*. L19.
[ORIGIN Spanish, 'chimney']
Orig., in Spain or Spanish-speaking countries, a fireplace, esp. one with an open hearth and cone-shaped chimney. Now, a free-standing clay fireplace or oven consisting of a hollow bulbous body tapering to a short chimney-like smoke vent, often used as a source of heat outdoors.

chimer /ˈtʃʌɪmə/ *noun*[1]. E17.
[ORIGIN from CHIME *verb*[1] + -ER[1].]
A person who chimes bells etc.

chimer *noun*[2] var. of CHIMERE.

chimera /kʌɪˈmɪərə, kɪ-/ *noun*. Also **chimaera**. LME.
[ORIGIN Latin *chimaera* from Greek *khimaira* she-goat, monster, from *khimaros* he-goat.]
1 *GREEK MYTHOLOGY*. A fire-breathing monster, with a lion's head, a goat's body, and a serpent's tail. LME.
2 A grotesque monster represented in painting etc. LME.
3 **a** A bogey, a horrible phantasm. E16. ▸**b** A wild or fanciful conception. L16. ▸**c** A thing of hybrid character. M19.
4 (Usu. **chimaera**.) Any cartilaginous fish of the family Chimaeridae (order Holocephali), typically having erect pointed fins and a long tail. Also called ***rabbitfish***, ***ratfish***. E19.
5 *BIOLOGY*. An organism whose cells are not all derived from the same zygote. E20.
■ **chimeric** /-ˈmɛr-/, **chimerical** /-ˈmɛr-/ *adjectives* of the nature of a chimera; imaginary, fanciful, visionary; prone to entertain chimeras: M17. **chimerism** *noun* (*BIOLOGY*) the state of being a chimera (sense 5); the occurrence of chimeras: M20.

chimere /tʃɪˈmɪə/ *noun*. Also **chimer** /ˈtʃɪmə/. LME.
[ORIGIN Obscurely rel. to Spanish *zamarra* sheepskin cloak, Italian *zimarra*, *cimarra* long robe (whence French *simarre*, †*chimarre* loose gown): cf. SIMAR.]
A loose outer robe, *esp.* that worn by a bishop and having lawn sleeves attached.

chimichanga /tʃɪmɪˈtʃaŋɡə/ *noun*. M20.
[ORIGIN Mexican Spanish, lit. 'trinket'.]
A tortilla rolled round a savoury filling and deep-fried.

chiminage /ˈtʃɪmɪnɪdʒ/ *noun*. L16.
[ORIGIN Old French *cheminage* from *chemin* road: see -AGE. In Anglo-Latin *cheminagium*, *chim-*.]
FEUDAL LAW. A toll for liberty of passage through a forest.

chimney /ˈtʃɪmni/ *noun & verb*. ME.
[ORIGIN Old French & mod. French *cheminée* chimney, fireplace, from late Latin *caminata*, perh. orig. for *camera caminata* room with a fireplace, from Latin *caminus* forge, furnace, from Greek *kaminos* oven, furnace.]
▸**A** *noun*. **1** A fireplace, a hearth. *obsolete* exc. *dial.* ME.
†**2** A furnace. ME–E17.
†**3** A (portable) stove. LME–E17.
4 A channel or flue by which smoke from a fire, furnace, engine, etc. ascends; the part of this above a roof etc. LME.

> ARNOLD BENNETT To the east rose pitheads, chimneys, and kilns. P. V. WHITE The slow fire, upon which a dusty yellow light descended through the shaft that served them as a chimney.

smoke like a chimney smoke cigarettes etc. very heavily.
5 *transf.* A natural opening in the earth's surface, *esp.* that of a volcano. LME.
6 More fully ***lamp chimney***. A glass tube over the wick of a lamp protecting and providing a draught for the flame. M19.
7 *MINING*. An ore-shoot. M19.
8 *MOUNTAINEERING*. A steep and narrow cleft by which a cliff or mountain face may be climbed. L19.
– COMB.: **chimney-bar** an iron bar supporting the masonry above a fireplace; **chimney-board** a board used to close up a fireplace in summer; ***chimney breast***: see BREAST *noun* 8; **chimney corner** a warm seat within an old-fashioned fireplace; **chimney-money** *hist.* a tax on fire hearths, *spec.* that in England and Wales in the 17th cent.; **chimney nook** = *chimney corner* above; **chimney piece** †(***a***) a picture, piece of sculpture, etc., over a fireplace; (***b***) a mantelpiece; **chimney pot** (***a***) an earthenware or metal pipe, added to a chimney top; (***b***) *arch.* (more fully ***chimney pot hat***) a tall silk hat; **chimney stack** a number of chimneys standing together; a tall factory chimney; **chimney swallow** the common swallow, *Hirundo rustica*; (*N. Amer.*) = ***chimney swift*** below; **chimney sweep**, **chimney sweeper** a person whose business is to remove soot from chimneys; **chimney swift** *N. Amer.* a swift, *Chaetura pelagica*, often nesting in chimneys; **chimney top** the part of a chimney which rises above the roof, *esp.* the flat upper surface of this.
▸**B** *verb*. **1** *verb trans.* Provide with a chimney. E19.
2 *verb intrans. MOUNTAINEERING*. Climb *up* a chimney. M20.
■ **chimneyless** *adjective* M17.

chimonanthus /kʌɪməˈnanθəs/ *noun*. E19.
[ORIGIN mod. Latin, from Greek *kheimōn* winter + *anthos* flower.]
A shrub of the genus *Chimonanthus*, native to China; *esp.* wintersweet, *C. praecox*.

chimp /tʃɪmp/ *noun*. *colloq.* L19.
[ORIGIN Abbreviation.]
A chimpanzee.

chimpanzee /tʃɪmpanˈziː/ *noun*. M18.
[ORIGIN French *chimpanzé* from Kikongo.]
A Central and W. African anthropoid ape of the genus *Pan*, of which there are two species, *P. troglodytes*, which resembles humans more closely than does any other ape, and the pygmy chimpanzee or bonobo, *P. paniscus*.

chin /tʃɪn/ *noun*[1].
[ORIGIN Old English *ċin(n)* = Old Frisian *kin*, Old Saxon *kinni* (Dutch *kin*), Old Norse *kinn* chin, lower jaw, Gothic *kinnus* cheek, from Germanic: cogn. with Latin *gena* cheek, Greek *genus* jaw.]
1 The front of the lower jaw. OE.
double chin: see DOUBLE *adjective & adverb*. **keep one's chin up** remain cheerful. ***lead with one's chin***: see LEAD *verb*[1]. ***stick one's chin out***: see STICK *verb*[1]. **take it on the chin** *fig.* (***a***) suffer a severe blow; (***b***) meet misfortune courageously. **up to the chin** reaching to the chin; deeply immersed *in*.
2 A talk, a conversation. Also redupl. ***chin-chin***. *slang* (chiefly *US*). L19.
– COMB.: **chin music** (chiefly *US*) talk, chatter; **chinstrap** a strap for fastening a hat etc. under the chin; ***chins wag***: see WAG *verb*. **chinwag** *noun & verb* (*colloq.*) (***a***) *noun* chat, talk; a conversation; (***b***) *verb intrans.* talk, chat.
■ **chinless** *adjective* (***a***) without a chin; (***b***) *fig.* lacking firmness of character (esp. in ***chinless wonder***): E19. **chinned** *adjective* having a chin, esp. of a specified kind L16. **chinny** *adjective* marked by a conspicuous chin L19.

Chin /tʃɪn/ *noun*[2]. Pl. **-s**, same. L19.
[ORIGIN Burmese = hillman.]
A member of a people inhabiting the Chin hills and adjacent districts in Myanmar (Burma); the language of this people.

chin *noun*[3] var. of TCHIN.

Chin *noun*[4] *& adjective* var. of QIN.

chin /tʃɪn/ *verb*. Infl. **-nn-**. L16.
[ORIGIN from CHIN *noun*[1].]
▸**I** †**1** *verb intrans.* Press chin to chin. Only in L16.
2 *verb trans.* Bring (a fiddle etc.) up or *up* to the chin. M19.
3 *verb trans.* Draw one's body up so as to bring the chin up to or above (a horizontal bar etc.) with one's feet off the ground; *refl.* raise oneself thus. E20.

> H. ALLEN You take exercise by chinning yourself on the window bars. A. S. NEILL To ask a boy . . to chin a bar four times.

▸**II** **4** *verb intrans. & trans.* Talk, chat, (to). *US slang.* L19.

China /ˈtʃʌɪnə/ *noun*[1]. L16.
[ORIGIN A country in Asia: origin of the name unkn. (not native Chinese).]
▸**I** **1** Used *attrib.* to designate things found in, obtained from, or associated with China. L16.
China aster: see ASTER *noun* 2b. **China berry** *N. Amer.* (the fruit of) a China tree. ***China crêpe***: see CRÊPE *noun & adjective*. **China grass** ramie, *Boehmeria nivea*. **China ink** Indian ink. **China orange** the common orange, orig. from China. **China root** (the fleshy root of) a Far Eastern shrub, *Smilax china*; also, any of certain other plants or their roots. **China rose** (***a***) the monthly rose, *Rosa chinensis*, native to China; (***b***) an ornamental shrubby hibiscus, *H. rosa-sinensis*. **China silk** a light plain-woven silk fabric. **China syndrome** the imagined movement of a nuclear reactor deep into the earth after a meltdown. **China tea** a smoke-cured tea from a small-leaved tea plant grown in China. **Chinatown** a section of a town, esp. a seaport, where Chinese people live. **China tree** *N. Amer.* the azedarac; also, a wild soapberry, *Sapindus marginatus*, of the southern US.

▸ **II 2** *ellipt.* **a** = ***China root*** above. **L16.** ▸**b** = ***China rose*** (a) above **M19.** ▸**c** = ***China tea*** above. **E20.**
†**3** A Chinese person. **E–M17.**

china /ˈtʃʌɪnə/ *adjective & noun*[2]. Also **C-**. **L16.**
[**ORIGIN** Persian *čīnī* formed as **CHINA** *noun*[1] (from attrib. uses of which early uses of the adjective are indistinguishable).]
1 (Of) a fine semi-transparent or white ceramic material; porcelain. **L16.**
A. WILSON He knelt and carefully brushed up the minutest pieces of china. R. BRAUTIGAN We treat them all as if they were china.
Meissen china, ***Pinxton china***, ***Plymouth china***, ***Sèvres china***, etc.
2 Items made of this. **M17.**
R. RENDELL I just know she's going to be a vulgar lumpish creature who'll break the china.
3 In full ***china plate***. A mate, a friend. *rhyming slang*. **L19.**
B. BEHAN Two chinas from the same district or town.
– **COMB. & SPECIAL COLLOCATIONS:** **china blue** (of) a greyish blue; **china clay** kaolin; **china closet** a cabinet for keeping or displaying china; **china-mark (moth)** any of various delicately patterned pyralid moths whose larvae feed on water plants; †**china-metal** porcelain (so called when its composition was unknown); ***china plate***: see sense 3 above; **china shop**: selling china (***bull in a china shop***: see **BULL** *noun*[1]); **chinaware** = sense 2 above.
■ **chinagraph** *noun* a type of pencil for writing on glass, china, etc. (also ***chinagraph pencil***) **M20.**

Chinaman /ˈtʃʌɪnəmən/ *noun*. Pl. **-men**. **M18.**
[**ORIGIN** from **CHINA** *noun*[2] (branch I) or **CHINA** *noun*[1] (branch II) + **MAN** *noun*.]
▸ **I 1** A dealer in porcelain. Now *rare* or *obsolete*. **M18.**
▸ **II 2** A Chinese man. Now *arch.* or *derog.* **M19.**
3 *CRICKET*. A left-handed bowler's off break or googly to a right-handed batsman. **M20.**
– **PHRASES:** **Chinaman's chance** *US colloq.* a very slight chance (usu. in neg. contexts).
■ **Chinawoman** (now *arch.* or *derog.*) a Chinese woman.

chinar /tʃɪˈnɑː/ *noun*. Also **chenar**. **M17.**
[**ORIGIN** Persian *čenar*, *čīnār*.]
The oriental plane tree, *Platanus orientalis* (also ***chinar tree***); the wood of this tree.

chincapin *noun* var. of **CHINQUAPIN**.

chinch /tʃɪn(t)ʃ/ *noun*[1]. Also **chintz** /-ts/ & other vars. **E17.**
[**ORIGIN** Spanish *chinche* from Latin *cimex*, *cimic-*.]
More fully ***chinch bug***.
1 A bedbug. *obsolete* exc. *N. Amer.* **E17.**
2 A N. American bug, *Blissus leucopterus*, very destructive to cereals and other grasses. **M18.**

†**chinch** *adjective & noun*[2]. **ME.**
[**ORIGIN** Old French & mod. French *chi(n)che*.]
▸ **A** *adjective*. Mean, miserly. Only in **ME.**
▸ **B** *noun*. A miser; a wretch. **ME–L16.**
– **NOTE:** Survives in **CHINCHY**.

chinch *verb* see **CHINK** *verb*[2].

chincherinchee /tʃɪntʃərɪnˈtʃiː/ *noun*. Also **chink-** /tʃɪŋk-/; †**tintirinties** (earlier). **E20.**
[**ORIGIN** Imit. of the squeaky sound made by rubbing stalks together.]
A white-flowered bulbous plant, *Ornithogalum thyrsoides*, native to southern Africa.

chinchilla /tʃɪnˈtʃɪlə/ *noun*. **E17.**
[**ORIGIN** Spanish, prob. from Aymara or Quechua.]
▸ **I 1** A S. American rodent of the genus *Chinchilla*, with very soft grey fur. **E17.**
2 A cat of a silver-grey breed. **L19.**
3 A rabbit of a variety bred for its grey fur. Also ***chinchilla rabbit***. **E20.**
▸ **II 4** The fur of the S. American chinchilla or of the chinchilla rabbit. **E19.**

chin-chin *noun* see **CHIN** *noun*[1] 2.

chin-chin /tʃɪnˈtʃɪn/ *interjection & verb*. Now *colloq.* **L18.**
[**ORIGIN** Chinese *qing qing* (Wade–Giles *ch'ing ch'ing*).]
▸ **A** *interjection*. Used as a greeting, as a farewell, and as a toast. **L18.**
▸ **B** *verb*. Infl. **-nn-**.
1 *verb trans.* Greet. **L18.**
2 *verb intrans.* Say 'chin-chin'. **M19.**

chinchona *noun* var. of **CINCHONA**.

chinchy /ˈtʃɪntʃi/ *adjective*. Now chiefly *US colloq.* **LME.**
[**ORIGIN** from **CHINCH** *noun*[2] + **-Y**[1].]
Mean, miserly.
– **NOTE:** Not recorded between **M17** and **E20.**

chincough *noun* see **KINKCOUGH**.

Chindit /ˈtʃɪndɪt/ *noun*. **M20.**
[**ORIGIN** Burmese *chinthé*, a mythological creature.]
An Allied fighter behind the Japanese lines in Burma (Myanmar) (1943–5).

chine /tʃʌɪn/ *noun*[1].
[**ORIGIN** Old English *cinu* = Middle Dutch *kēne* (Dutch *keen*) from Germanic base of **CHINE** *verb*[1]. Cf. **CHAWN**, **CHINK** *noun*[2].]
†**1** *gen.* A fissure, a crack. **OE–L16.**
2 A fissure in the earth. Now only *spec.* a deep ravine in the Isle of Wight and in Dorset (chiefly in proper names). **OE.**

chine /tʃʌɪn/ *noun*[2]. **ME.**
[**ORIGIN** Aphet. from Old French *eschine* (mod. *échine*) from Proto-Romance blend of Germanic source of **SHIN** *noun* and Latin *spina* **SPINE** *noun*.]
1 The spine, the backbone. **ME.**
†**2** The back. **ME–L18.**
3 A joint of meat containing (part of) an animal's backbone. **ME.**
4 *transf.* A ridge, an arête. **M19.**
– **PHRASES:** ***mourning of the chine***: see **MOURNING** *noun*[2].

chine /tʃʌɪn/ *noun*[3]. **LME.**
[**ORIGIN** Alt. of **CHIME** *noun*[2].]
1 = **CHIME** *noun*[2]. **LME.**
2 *SHIPBUILDING*. **a** That part of the waterways projecting above the deck-plank. **M19.** ▸**b** The angle where the bottom lines of a ship's planking or plating meet the sides. **E20.**

chine /tʃʌɪn/ *verb*[1]. Long *obsolete* exc. *dial.*
[**ORIGIN** Old English *cīnan* = Old Saxon, Old High German *kīnan*, Gothic *keinan* sprout, from Germanic: cf. **CHINE** *noun*[1].]
1 *verb intrans.* Split open, crack; sprout. **OE.**
†**2** *verb trans.* Burst, split. **LME–E16.**

chine /tʃʌɪn/ *verb*[2] *trans.* **LME.**
[**ORIGIN** from **CHINE** *noun*[2]: cf. French *échiner* break the back of.]
1 Cut along or through the backbone of (a carcass). **LME.**
2 Break the back of. Now *rare* or *obsolete*. **L16.**

chiné /ʃiːˈneɪ/ *noun & adjective*. **M19.**
[**ORIGIN** French, pa. pple of *chiner*, from *Chine* China.]
(A fabric) given a mottled pattern of (supposedly) Chinese style by colouring the warp or weft threads, or both, before weaving.

Chinee /tʃʌɪˈniː/ *noun*. *arch. slang*. **L19.**
[**ORIGIN** from **CHINESE** *noun* taken as a pl.]
A Chinese person.

Chinese /tʃʌɪˈniːz/ *adjective & noun*. **L16.**
[**ORIGIN** from *China* (see **CHINA** *noun*[1]) + **-ESE**.]
▸ **A** *adjective*. Of or pertaining to China. **L16.**
Chinese anise: see **ANISE** 2. ***Chinese artichoke***: see **ARTICHOKE** 3. **Chinese block** an oblong slatted wooden block used esp. by jazz drummers. **Chinese box** each of a nest of boxes. **Chinese burn** *colloq.* an act of placing both hands on a person's arm and then twisting it with a wringing motion to produce a burning sensation. **Chinese cabbage** an oriental brassica; spec. *B. chinensis*, with smooth-edged tapering leaves, or *B. pekinensis*, which resembles lettuce. ***Chinese CHIPPENDALE***. **Chinese compliment** a pretended deference to the opinions of others, when one's mind is already made up. **Chinese copy** a slavish imitation. **Chinese gooseberry** = **KIWI** 4. ***Chinese jute***: see **JUTE** *noun*[2]. **Chinese lantern** (***a***) a collapsible lantern of thin coloured paper; (***b***) = **ALKEKENGI**. **Chinese laundry** a laundry operated by Chinese people. **Chinese layering** = ***air-layering*** s.v. **AIR** *noun*[1]. **Chinese leaf** = **PE TSAI**; in *pl.*, the leaves of this vegetable, used in salads. **Chinese mitten crab** an olive-green Asian crab, *Eriocheir sinensis*, with fur-covered pincers and hair on the legs, which has been introduced into European freshwater and estuaries where it can become a pest. ***Chinese olive***: see **OLIVE** *noun*[1] 1b. **Chinese puzzle** an intricate puzzle or problem. **Chinese restaurant**: operated by Chinese people, serving Chinese food. ***Chinese tallow tree***: see **TALLOW** *noun*. **Chinese wall** *fig.* an insurmountable barrier. ***Chinese water chestnut***: see **WATER** *noun*. **Chinese whispers** a game in which a message is distorted by being passed around in a whisper (also called ***Russian scandal***). **Chinese white** zinc oxide as a white pigment. ***Red Chinese*** see **RED** *adjective*. **TIBETO-CHINESE**.
▸ **B** *noun*. Pl. same, †**-eses**.
1 A native of China; a person of Chinese descent. **E17.**
overseas Chinese: see **OVERSEAS** *adjective*.
2 The Chinese language, a member of the Sino-Tibetan group, a tonal language with no inflections, declensions, or conjugations and having many dialects. **E18.**
■ **chinesery** *noun* = **CHINOISERIE** **L19.**

Ching *noun & adjective* var. of **QING**.

chink /tʃɪŋk/ *noun*[1]. **M16.**
[**ORIGIN** Obscurely rel. to **CHINE** *noun*[1]. Cf. **CHINK** *verb*[1].]
1 *gen.* A fissure, a crack. **M16.**
2 A long narrow opening, a slit, a peephole; a place not fully closed and admitting the light etc. **M16.**
■ **chinky** *adjective* characterized by or full of chinks **M17.**

chink /tʃɪŋk/ *noun*[2]. **L16.**
[**ORIGIN** Imit.: cf. **CHINK** *verb*[1].]
1 A short sharp ringing sound as of glasses or coins striking together. **L16.**
2 a Ready cash. *arch. colloq.* **L16.** ▸†**b** In *pl.* Coins. **L16–E17.**

Chink /tʃɪŋk/ *noun*[3]. *slang*. *offensive*. **L19.**
[**ORIGIN** Irreg. from *China* (see **CHINA** *noun*[1]): cf. **CHINKY**.]
A Chinese person.

chink *noun*[4] see **KINK** *noun*[1].

chink /tʃɪŋk/ *verb*[1]. **LME.**
[**ORIGIN** Imit.: cf. **CHINK** *noun*[2] and Dutch *kinken*.]
1 *verb intrans.* Emit a short, sharp ringing sound, as of coins, glasses, etc. striking together. **LME.**
A. CARTER Spoon chinked upon soup-plate.
2 *verb trans.* Cause to make this sound. **E17.**
POPE He chinks his purse.
■ **chinkle** *verb intrans. & trans.* chink continuously or lightly **M18.**

chink /tʃɪŋk/ *verb*[2] *intrans. & trans.* Also (*dial.*) **chinch** /tʃɪntʃ/; (esp. *NAUTICAL*) **chinse** /tʃɪns/. **E16.**
[**ORIGIN** Obscurely rel. to **CHINE** *verb*[1]: cf. **CHINK** *noun*[1].]
1 a *NAUTICAL*. (Chiefly ***chinse***.) Caulk (a ship, its seams), now *spec.* as a temporary measure. Also foll. by *up*. **E16.** ▸**b** Fill up (cracks, esp. between bricks, tiles, the logs of a log cabin, etc.); fill up the cracks of (a building). Also foll. by *up*. Chiefly *N. Amer.* **M18.**
†**2** (***chink*** only.) Open in cracks; crack, chap. **M16–L17.**

chink /tʃɪŋk/ *verb*[3] *trans. dial.* **E19.**
[**ORIGIN** Unknown: cf. **KINK** *noun*[2], *verb*[2].]
Give a twist to; sprain.

chink *verb*[4] see **KINK** *verb*[1].

chinkara /tʃɪˈkɑːrə/ *noun*. Also **chikara** /tʃɪŋˈkɑːrə/. **M19.**
[**ORIGIN** Hindi *cikārā* from Sanskrit *chikkāra*.]
In the Indian subcontinent: the mountain gazelle, *Gazella bennettii*.

chinkerinchee *noun* var. of **CHINCHERINCHEE**.

Chinky /ˈtʃɪŋki/ *noun*. *slang*. *offensive*. Also **-key**, **-kie**. **L19.**
[**ORIGIN** formed as **CHINK** *noun*[3] + **-Y**[6], **-IE**.]
A Chinese person (*derog.*); a Chinese restaurant.

chino /ˈtʃiːnəʊ/ *noun & adjective*. *US*. **M20.**
[**ORIGIN** Amer. Spanish = toasted.]
▸ **A** *noun*. Pl. **-os**. A cotton twill cloth, usu. khaki-coloured; in *pl.*, trousers made of this. **M20.**
▸ **B** *adjective*. Of this cloth. **M20.**

Chino- /ˈtʃʌɪnəʊ/ *combining form*.
[**ORIGIN** from *China* (see **CHINA** *noun*[1]) + **-O-**.]
Chinese and —, Sino-, as ***Chino-Japanese*** etc.

chinois /ʃɪnˈwɑː/ *noun*. **L20.**
[**ORIGIN** French, lit. 'Chinese'.]
A cone-shaped sieve with a closely woven mesh for straining sauces.

chinoiserie /ʃɪnˈwɑːzəri; *foreign* ʃinwazri (*pl. same*)/ *noun*. **L19.**
[**ORIGIN** French, from *chinois* Chinese + *-erie* **-ERY**.]
A decorative style in Western art, furniture, and architecture, esp. in the 18th cent., characterized by the use of Chinese motifs and techniques; a Chinese or imitation Chinese artistic object, piece of furniture, etc.

†**chinoline** *noun* var. of **QUINOLINE**.

Chinook /tʃɪˈnʊk/ *noun*. *N. Amer.* Also (exc. sense 1) **c-**. Pl. **-s**, same. **E19.**
[**ORIGIN** Salish *tsinúk*.]
1 A member of a N. American Indian people formerly living along the Columbia river; the language of this people. **E19.**
Lower Chinook, **Upper Chinook**: dialects of Chinook.
2 In full ***Chinook Jargon***. A pidgin composed of elements from Chinook, Nootka, English, French, and other languages, used in the Pacific north-west of N. America. **M19.**
3 In full ***Chinook salmon***. A salmon, *Oncorhynchus tshawytscha*, of the N. American Pacific coast. **M19.**
4 In full ***Chinook wind***. A warm dry wind which blows east of the Rocky Mountains. Also, a warm wet southerly wind west of them. **M19.**

chinovnik /tʃɪˈnɒvnɪk/ *noun*. Also **tch-**. Pl. **-s**, **-i** /-i/. **L19.**
[**ORIGIN** Russian.]
In Russia: a government official, *esp.* a minor functionary; a (mere) bureaucrat.

chinquapin /ˈtʃɪŋkəpɪn/ *noun*. Also **chincapin**. **E17.**
[**ORIGIN** from Virginia Algonquian.]
Any of various small N. American trees or their edible nuts; *esp.* the dwarf chestnut, *Castanea pumila*.
water chinquapin the American lotus, *Nelumbo lutea*.

chinse *verb* see **CHINK** *verb*[2].

chintz /tʃɪnts/ *noun*[1] *& adjective*. **E17.**
[**ORIGIN** Hindi *chīṭ* spattering, stain. Mod. form a fanciful spelling of original pl.]
▸ **A** *noun*. Pl. **chintzes**. Orig. †**chint**, pl. **chints**. Orig., a painted or stained calico from India. Now, a cotton cloth with a particoloured pattern, usu. fast-printed and glazed. **E17.**
▸ **B** *adjective*. Of chintz; covered with chintz. **E18.**
■ **chintzy** *adjective* (***a***) decorated or covered with chintz; *fig.* genteel, suburban; (***b***) *N. Amer. colloq.* cheap and of poor quality; (***c***) *N. Amer. colloq.* mean, miserly: **M19.**

chintz *noun*[2] var. of **CHINCH** *noun*[1].

chionodoxa /kʌɪənəˈdɒksə/ *noun*. **L19.**
[**ORIGIN** mod. Latin, from Greek *khiōn* snow + *doxa* glory.]
A blue-flowered early-blooming plant of the genus *Chionodoxa* of the lily family. Also called ***glory-of-the-snow***.

chip /tʃɪp/ *noun*.
[**ORIGIN** Old English *ċipp*, *ċyp* = Old Saxon *kip* post, *kipa* stave (Dutch *kip* beam of a plough), Old High German *kipfa* (German dial. *Kipf(e)*) axle, stave, Old Norse *keppr* stick, staff. Branch II perh. a different word, rel. to **CHIP** *verb*[1].]

C

C

▸ **I 1** The beam of a plough. *dial.* OE.

▸ **II 2** A thin piece cut from wood; a fragment broken from stone etc. ME.

3 A thin slice or piece of bread crust (*obsolete*), fruit, potato, etc.; *spec.* a (usu. oblong) piece of potato fried or for frying, (chiefly *N. Amer.*) a potato crisp; (orig. *US*) a cold thin crisp piece of food made from seasoned flour or meal (usu. with specifying word). LME. ***corn chip, potato chip, tortilla chip***, etc. CHOCOLATE ***chip***.

†**4** A key of a spinet or harpsichord. *rare* (Shakes.). Only in L16.

5 a Wood or woody fibre split into thin strips for making hats, bonnets, baskets, etc. L18. ▸**b** In full ***chip basket***. A basket made of strips of thin wood interwoven or joined. E20.

6 A piece of dried cow dung, used as fuel. Usu. in *pl.* *N. Amer.* M19.

7 A counter used for betting in a game of chance; a coin; in *pl.*, money. M19.

8 A blemish caused by chipping; a place on china etc. from which a chip has been knocked off. L19.

9 More fully ***chip shot***. In golf, a short lofted approach shot on to the putting green. In soccer etc., a short lofted kick. E20.

10 A tiny wafer of semiconducting material used to make an integrated circuit, *esp.* such a wafer of silicon (also ***silicon chip***). M20.

– PHRASES: **(as) dry as a chip** thoroughly dried up. ***bargaining chip***: see BARGAIN *verb* 1. ***blue chip***: see BLUE *adjective*. **burn to a chip** make inedible or useless by burning, burn up. ***cash in one's chips***: see CASH *verb*[2] 3a. **chip and PIN** a way of paying for goods by debit or credit card whereby one enters one's personal identification number in an electronic device. ***chip off the old block***, ***chip of the old block***: see BLOCK *noun* 1. ***fish and chips***: see FISH *noun*[1]. **hand in one's chips**, **pass in one's chips**, **throw in one's chips** *fig.* (*US colloq.*) die. **have a chip on one's shoulder** be touchy or embittered (from a former US practice of so placing a chip as a challenge to others to knock it off). **have had one's chips** *slang* be beaten, be finished; be unable to have what one wants. **in the chips** *slang* moneyed, affluent. **not care a chip** not care at all. ***pass in one's chips***: see ***hand in one's chips*** above. ***spit chips***: see SPIT *verb*[1]. ***throw in one's chips***: see ***hand in one's chips*** above. **when the chips are down** *colloq.* when it comes to the point.

– COMB.: **chip basket** (*a*) a wire basket used in deep-frying potato chips; (*b*) see sense 5b above; **chipboard** a thin pasteboard made of compressed wood chips and resin; **chipmaker** a company that makes microchips; **chip shop** a shop selling fish and chips; ***chip shot***: see sense 9 above.

chip /tʃɪp/ *verb*[1]. Infl. **-pp-**. LME.
[ORIGIN Rel. to Old English *forcippian* cut off, Middle & mod. Low German, Middle Dutch & mod. Dutch *kippen* hatch out by chipping the shell.]

†**1** *verb trans.* Remove the crust of (bread); remove (the crust of bread). LME–E18.

2 *verb trans.* Chap, crack. Long *obsolete* exc. *dial.* LME.

3 *verb intrans.* Of a seed or bud: break open, germinate. Long *obsolete* exc. *dial.* L15.

4 *verb trans.* Of a hatching chicken etc.: crack and break open (the eggshell). E17.

5 *verb trans.* Hew or cut with an axe, adze, or other implement. E17.

> G. SWIFT Dick . . chips ice from the lock-gates with fingers that do not seem to feel the cold.

6 a *verb intrans.* Break at the edge; lose a piece from the edge or surface; be apt to do so. M18. ▸**b** *verb trans.* Cut or break at the surface or edge; shape by so cutting; carve (an inscription etc.); cut or break (a piece) *off*, *from*, a surface or edge. M19. ▸**c** *verb intrans.* Make strokes *at* (as if) to cut or break pieces off; work *away at* so as to diminish or destroy. M19.

> **a** *Ladies Home Journal* (US) If nail color chips between manicures. **c** H. E. BATES Workmen were chipping at snow and ice with pickaxes. *Globe & Mail* (*Toronto*) Members will chip away at the coverage extended to the consumer, if there is no regulation.

7 *verb trans.* Harrow, hoe, (ground). *Austral. & NZ.* L18.

8 *verb trans.* Cut (esp. a potato) into chips; *US* slice (smoked dried beef) thinly. Chiefly as ***chipped*** *ppl adjective*. E19.

9 a *verb intrans.* Aim a blow *at* (*lit. & fig.*); poke fun *at*. E19. ▸**b** *verb trans.* Tease, chaff. *colloq.* L19.

> **b** J. HILTON Being chipped about that Chinese girl didn't appeal to my sense of humour.

10 *verb intrans. & trans.* Foll. by *in*: ▸**a** Put down (as) a stake, contribute (money etc.). M19. ▸**b** Contribute to a conversation, interpose. L19.

> **a** P. ACKROYD He insisted on paying the bill, he would not dream of having them chip in. R. CARVER All of us chipped in thirty-eight bucks for a funeral spray. **b** *Scottish Daily Express* Andrew quickly chipped in that there wasn't a 'bottomless pit of money'. *Stage & Television Today* Jack Lemmon and Walter Matthau—ready to chip in comments.

11 *verb intrans. & trans.* Kick or hit (a ball etc.) with a chip shot; bypass (an opposing player) with a chip shot. E20.

> G. GREEN Chipping home the free kick for goal number five. *Guardian* Bodak broke clear . . to chip Corrigan delightfully. *Los Angeles Times* A chance to chip and putt the ball.

– COMB.: **chip-axe** a small axe used in chipping timber etc. into shape; **chip-in** GOLF a chip shot by which the ball is holed.

■ **chipping** *noun* (*a*) a small piece of wood, stone, (*obsolete*) bread, etc., chipped or pared off, esp. in dressing or shaping (usu. in *pl.*); (*b*) the action of the verb: LME.

chip /tʃɪp/ *verb*[2] *intrans.* Chiefly *US*. Infl. **-pp-**. L18.
[ORIGIN Imit.]
Cheep, chirp.
chipping sparrow, †**chipping bird** a N. American sparrow, *Spizella passerina*. **chipping squirrel**, **chip squirrel** [by erron. identification of *chip* in CHIPMUNK] a chipmunk.

Chipewyan /tʃɪpəˈwʌɪən/ *adjective & noun*. Also **-pp-**. L18.
[ORIGIN Cree *ci:pwaya:n* lit. '(wearing) pointed-skin (garments)'.]
▸ **A** *adjective*. Designating or pertaining to an Athabaskan people of NW Canada or their language. L18.
▸ **B** *noun*. Pl. **-s**, same. A member of this people; the language of this people. E19.

chipmunk /ˈtʃɪpmʌŋk/ *noun*. Also †**-muck**. M19.
[ORIGIN from Ojibwa *ačitamo·n'?*.]
A N. American ground squirrel of the genus *Tamias*.
least chipmunk: see LEAST *adjective, noun, & adverb*.

chipolata /tʃɪpəˈlɑːtə/ *noun*. L19.
[ORIGIN French from Italian *cipollata* dish of onions, from *cipolla* onion.]
In full ***chipolata sausage***. A small, thin sausage.

Chippendale /ˈtʃɪp(ə)ndeɪl/ *adjective & noun*. L19.
[ORIGIN See below.]
▸ **A** *adjective*. Designating or pertaining to an elegant style of ornamental furniture popularized in the pattern books of the English cabinetmaker Thomas Chippendale (1718–79); designed by or in the style of Thomas Chippendale. L19.
▸ **B** *noun*. A piece of Chippendale furniture. L19.
Chinese Chippendale: combining square and angular outlines with Chinese motifs.

chipper /ˈtʃɪpə/ *noun*. E16.
[ORIGIN from CHIP *verb*[1] + -ER[1].]
A person who or thing which chips; *esp.* a machine for chipping timber.

chipper /ˈtʃɪpə/ *adjective*. *colloq.* (orig. *N. Amer.*). M19.
[ORIGIN Prob. var. of KIPPER *adjective*[2], infl. by CHIPPER *verb*.]
Cheerful, lively.

chipper /ˈtʃɪpə/ *verb*. *dial. & US*. E18.
[ORIGIN Imit.: partly a metathesis of CHIRRUP *verb*.]
1 *verb intrans.* Twitter; chatter. E18.
2 *verb trans.* Cheer *up*. L19.

Chippewa /ˈtʃɪpəwɔː, -wɑː/ *noun & adjective*. Also **-way** /-weɪ/. Pl. of noun same, **-s**. M18.
[ORIGIN Alt. of OJIBWA.]
= OJIBWA.
– NOTE: *Chippewa* refers esp. to the Ojibwa living to the east, south, and south-west of the Great Lakes.

Chippewyan *adjective & noun* var. of CHIPEWYAN.

chippie *noun*[1], *noun*[2] vars. of CHIPPY *noun*[1], *noun*[2].

chippy /ˈtʃɪpi/ *noun*[1]. Orig. *US*. Also **-ie**. M19.
[ORIGIN from CHIP *verb*[2] + -Y[6], -IE.]
1 A small bird; *spec.* = ***chipping sparrow*** s.v. CHIP *verb*[2]. M19.
2 A promiscuous or delinquent young woman; a prostitute; *derog.* a girl or young woman. *slang*. L19.

chippy /ˈtʃɪpi/ *noun*[2]. *colloq.* Also **-ie**. E20.
[ORIGIN from CHIP *noun* + -Y[6], -IE.]
1 A carpenter. Cf. CHIPS. E20.
2 A shop selling fish and chips. M20.

chippy /ˈtʃɪpi/ *adjective*. *dial. & slang*. E17.
[ORIGIN from CHIP *noun* or *verb*[1] + -Y[1].]
1 That chips or breaks into small pieces easily. E17.
2 As dry as a chip, thoroughly dried up. M19.
3 Unwell, esp. with a hangover. L19.
4 Irritable. L19. ▸**b** Of a game; characterized by rough and belligerent play. *N. Amer. colloq.* M20.
■ **chippiness** *noun* L19.

Chips /tʃɪps/ *noun*. *slang*. L18.
[ORIGIN Pl. of CHIP *noun*: see -S[1].]
(A nickname for) a carpenter, esp. on a ship.

†**chique** *noun* see CHIGOE.

chir /tʃɪə/ *noun*[1]. L19.
[ORIGIN Hindi *cīr*.]
A pine, *Pinus roxburghii*, native to the Himalayas. Also ***chir pine***.

chir *noun*[2] var. of CHEER *noun*[2].

chiragh /tʃɪˈrɑːɡ/ *noun*. L19.
[ORIGIN Urdu from Persian *čirāg* lamp, light.]
A simple oil lamp used in India and adjacent countries.

chiral /ˈkʌɪər(ə)l/ *adjective*. L19.
[ORIGIN from Greek *kheir* hand + -AL[1].]
Of a crystal, molecule, etc.: not superposable on its mirror image.
■ **chiˈrality** *noun* L19.

chirayta /tʃɪˈrʌɪtə/ *noun*. Also **-retta** /-ˈrɛtə/. M19.
[ORIGIN Hindi *cirāytā*, *ciraitā*.]
(A bitter infusion made from) an Indian plant of the gentian family, *Swertia chirata*.

†**chire** *noun* see CHIVE *noun*[1].

chiretta *noun* var. of CHIRAYTA.

Chiricahua /tʃɪrɪˈkɑːwə/ *noun & adjective*. E19.
[ORIGIN Apache, lit. 'great mountain'.]
▸ **A** *noun*. **1** A member of a N. American Indian people of SE Arizona. E19.
2 The Athabaskan language of this people. M19.
▸ **B** *adjective*. Of or pertaining to this people or their language. E20.

chirimoya *noun* var. of CHERIMOYA.

chirk /tʃəːk/ *adjective*. *US colloq.* L18.
[ORIGIN Prob. from CHIRK *verb*.]
Lively, in good spirits.

chirk /tʃəːk/ *verb*. LME.
[ORIGIN Imit.: cf. CHARK *verb*[1].]
1 *verb intrans.* Grate, grind; creak; croak. Long *obsolete* exc. *Scot. dial.* LME.
2 *verb intrans.* Chirp; squeak. LME.

> O. NASH The rural squirrel in his rage Chirks like a squirrel in a cage.

3 *verb intrans. & trans.* Cheer *up*. *US colloq.* M19.

chirl /tʃəːl/ *noun & verb*. Chiefly *Scot.* E17.
[ORIGIN Imit.]
▸ **A** *noun*. A warble. E17.
▸ **B** *verb trans. & intrans.* Warble. E19.

chirm /tʃəːm/ *noun*. Also (now the usual form in sense 2) **charm** /tʃɑːm/.
[ORIGIN Old English *ċearm*, *ċierm* = Old Saxon *karm*: cf. CHIRM *verb*.]
1 Noise, din; *esp.* (*a*) the blended singing of many birds; (*b*) the noise of many children etc. chattering. Now *dial.* OE.
2 A flock (*of* finches etc.). LME.

chirm /tʃəːm/ *verb intrans.* Now *dial.* Also **charm** /tʃɑːm/, **sharm** /ʃɑːm/.
[ORIGIN Old English *ċirman* = Middle Dutch *kermen*, *carmen* mourn, lament (Dutch *kermen*), Middle High German *karmen*.]
Cry out; *spec.* (of a bird, or a person likened to a bird) warble, chirp.

> W. OWEN The birds fifed on before, . . Right down to town; and there they ceased to charm.

chiro- /ˈkʌɪrəʊ/ *combining form*. Also **cheiro-**; (before a vowel) **chir-**, **cheir-**.
[ORIGIN Greek *kheiro-*, from *kheir* hand: see -O-.]
Of the hand.
■ **chiˈrognomist** *noun* one practising chirognomy L19. **chiˈrognomy** *noun* the supposed estimation of character by inspection of the hand M19. **chiroˈnomic** *adjective* of or pertaining to chironomy M18. **chiˈronomy** *noun* the art or science of gesticulation, or of moving the hands according to rule in oratory etc. L17.

chirograph /ˈkʌɪrəɡrɑːf/ *noun*. ME.
[ORIGIN French *chirographe* from Latin *chirographum* from Greek *kheirographon*, formed as CHIRO- + -GRAPH.]
Chiefly *hist.* A formal handwritten document, *esp.* an indenture of a fine.

chirographer /kʌɪˈrɒɡrəfə/ *noun*. LME.
[ORIGIN Anglo-Norman *cirographer*, medieval Latin *chirographarius*, from *chirographum*: see CHIROGRAPH, -ER[2]. In sense 2 from CHIRO- + -GRAPHER.]
1 *hist.* A legal officer appointed to engross fines in the Court of Common Pleas. LME.
2 A copying clerk; a person who employs handwriting. M18.

chirography /kʌɪˈrɒɡrəfi/ *noun*. M17.
[ORIGIN from CHIRO- + -GRAPHY.]
(The style or character of) handwriting.

chirology /kʌɪˈrɒlədʒi/ *noun*. Also **cheir-**. M17.
[ORIGIN (French *chirologie*,) formed as CHIRO- + -LOGY.]
†**1** The use of manual sign language. M–L17.
2 The branch of knowledge that deals with the hand. L19.
■ **chiroˈlogical** *adjective* of or pertaining to chirology (sense 2) M19. **chirologist** *noun* a person who makes the hand a subject of study M19.

chiromancy /ˈkʌɪrəmansi/ *noun*. LME.
[ORIGIN French *chiromancie* from Latin *chiromantia* from Greek *kheiromanteia*, formed as CHIRO- + -MANCY.]
Divination by (inspection of) the hand; palmistry.
■ **chiromancer** *noun* a practitioner of chiromancy M16. **chiroˈmantic** *adjective & noun* [from Greek *kheiromantis* chiromancer + -IC] (*a*) *adjective* of or pertaining to chiromancy; †(*b*) *noun* a chiromancer: E17. **chiroˈmantical** *adjective* (now *rare*) = CHIROMANTIC *adjective* M17. **chiromantist** *noun* (*rare*) a chiromancer M17.

chironomid /kʌɪˈrɒnəmɪd/ *adjective & noun*. L19.
[ORIGIN mod. Latin *Chironomidae* (see below), from *Chironomus* genus name from Greek *kheironomos* pantomime dancer: see -ID[3].]
▸ **A** *adjective*. Of, pertaining to, or designating the dipteran family Chironomidae, which includes many midges. L19.
▸ **B** *noun*. An insect of this family. L19.

chiropodist /kɪˈrɒpədɪst, ʃɪ-/ *noun*. L18.
[ORIGIN from CHIRO- + Greek *pod-*, *pous* foot + -IST.]
A person who treats ailments of the feet, esp. corns, bunions, etc., (and orig. those of the hands also).
■ **chiropody** *noun* the treatment of ailments of the feet L19.

chiropractic /kʌɪrəˈpraktɪk/ *adjective & noun*. L19.
[ORIGIN from CHIRO- + Greek *praktikos*: see PRACTIC *noun, adjective*.]
(Concerned with or pertaining to) the diagnosis and manipulative treatment of mechanical disorders of the joints, esp. of the spine.
■ **chiropractor** *noun* a person who practises chiropractic E20.

chiropteran /kʌɪˈrɒpt(ə) rən/ *noun & adjective*. Also †**cheir-**. M19.
[ORIGIN from mod. Latin *Chiroptera* bats, formed as CHIRO- + Greek *pteron* wing: see -AN.]
▸ **A** *noun*. A mammal of the order Chiroptera; a bat. M19.
▸ **B** *adjective*. Of this order; pertaining to bats. M19.
■ Also **chiropterous** *adjective* L19.

chirp /tʃəːp/ *verb & noun*. LME.
[ORIGIN Imit.]
▸ **A** *verb*. **1** *verb intrans*. Of a small bird, a grasshopper, etc.: make a characteristic short sharp thin sound. Of a person: make a sound imitative of or similar to this, esp. as a greeting or as encouragement; talk merrily; *colloq.* speak *up*. LME.

J. LAHIRI 'No need to worry,' he chirps, putting a stethoscope to Ashima's belly.

2 *verb trans*. Utter or express by chirping. E17.
3 *verb trans*. Greet or encourage by chirping. M19.
4 *verb trans. & intrans*. Cheer *up*. *US*. L19.
▸ **B** *noun*. A short sharp thin sound (as) of a small bird, a grasshopper, etc. E19.
■ **chirper** *noun* a person who or thing which chirps; a small bird: L16. **chirping** *ppl adjective* (**a**) that chirps; (**b**) merry, lively; (**c**) *arch.* producing merriment, cheering: M16.

chirpy /ˈtʃəːpi/ *adjective*. *colloq.* M19.
[ORIGIN from CHIRP + -Y[1].]
Given to chirping; lively; cheerful.
■ **chirpily** *adverb* E20. **chirpiness** *noun* M19.

chirr /tʃəː/ *noun & verb*. E17.
[ORIGIN Imit.: cf. CHURR.]
▸ **A** *noun*. A prolonged trilling sound (as) of a grasshopper etc. E17.
▸ **B** *verb intrans*. Make such a sound. E17.

chirrup /ˈtʃɪrəp/ *verb & noun*. L16.
[ORIGIN Alt. of CHIRP *verb* by trilling the *r*.]
▸ **A** *verb*. **1** *verb intrans*. Of a bird, grasshopper, etc.: make a series of chirps, twitter. Of a person: make a sound imitative of or similar to this, esp. as a greeting or as encouragement; sing or talk merrily. L16.
2 *verb trans*. Utter by chirruping. M17.
3 *verb trans*. Greet or encourage by chirruping. L18.
▸ **B** *noun*. A series of chirps; a twitter. M19.
■ **chirrupy** *adjective* (*colloq.*) given to chirruping; lively, cheerful; chirpy: E19.

chirt /tʃəːt/ *verb & noun*. *obsolete* exc. *Scot.* LME.
[ORIGIN Imit.]
▸ **A** *verb*. †**1** *verb intrans*. Chirp. Only in LME.
2 *verb intrans*. Spurt out. E16.
3 *verb trans*. Squeeze, press *out*. M17.
▸ **B** *noun*. †**1** A chirp. Only in E17.
2 A squeeze (ejecting liquid). M19.

chiru /ˈtʃɪruː/ *noun*. L19.
[ORIGIN Prob. from Tibetan.]
A gazelle, *Pantholops hodgsoni*, of high plateaux in Tibet, northern India, and parts of China, the male of which has very long straight horns.

chirurgeon /kʌɪˈrəːdʒ(ə)n, tʃɪ-/ *noun*. *arch.* ME.
[ORIGIN Old French *cirurgien* (mod. *chir-*): see SURGEON.]
A surgeon.

chirurgery /kʌɪˈrəːdʒ(ə)ri, tʃɪ-/ *noun*. *arch.* LME.
[ORIGIN Old French *cirurgerie*: see SURGERY.]
Surgery.
■ **chirurgic**, **chirurgical** *adjectives* surgical LME.

chisel /ˈtʃɪz(ə)l/ *noun*[1]. LME.
[ORIGIN Old Northern French (mod. *ciseau*, in pl. scissors) from Proto-Romance, from Latin *cis-* (as in late Latin *cisorium*) var. of *caes-* stem of *caedere* to cut: see -EL[2]. Cf. SCISSORS.]
1 A cutting tool having a square bevelled end for shaping wood, stone, or metal. LME.
cold chisel, **hot chisel**: suitable for cutting cold, hot, metal. **full chisel** *US colloq.* at full speed. ***skew chisel***: see SKEW *adjective*.
2 A similar surgical instrument for cutting bones. L17.
– COMB.: **chisel-toe** a squared toe of a shoe.
■ **chisel-like** /-l-l-/ *adjective* resembling (that of) a chisel M19.

chisel *noun*[2] var. of CHESIL *noun*.

chisel /ˈtʃɪz(ə)l/ *verb trans*. Infl. **-ll-**, *-**l-**. E16.
[ORIGIN from CHISEL *noun*[1].]
1 Cut, shape, etc., with a chisel; *transf.* shape, give form to. E16.

A. MILLER You can chisel the wood out around those bolts. *fig.*: R. MACAULAY Time chiselled delicate lines in her fine clear skin.

2 Cheat, defraud; treat unfairly. *slang*. E19.
■ **chiselled** *ppl adjective* cut or shaped with a chisel; *fig.* (of features etc.) finely or clearly cut: L16.

chiseller /ˈtʃɪz(ə)lə/ *noun*[1]. Also *-**eler**. E19.
[ORIGIN from CHISEL *verb* + -ER[1].]
A person who cuts or shapes with a chisel; *slang* a cheat, a swindler, a confidence trickster.

chiseller /ˈtʃɪz(ə)lə/ *noun*[2]. *Irish*. Also **-elur**, **chisler** /ˈtʃɪzlə/. E20.
[ORIGIN Unknown.]
A youngster, a child, a youth.

chi-square /kʌɪˈskwɛː/ *noun*. E20.
[ORIGIN from CHI + SQUARE *noun*: X is used conventionally to represent the square root of the sum of the squares of differences between observed and theoretical data.]
In full ***chi-square test***. A significance test used in the statistical comparison of observed and theoretical values.
■ **chi-squared** *adjective* designating such a test M20.

chit /tʃɪt/ *noun*[1]. LME.
[ORIGIN Uncertain: perh. same as CHIT *noun*[2].]
†**1** An animal's young; a whelp, a cub, a kitten. LME–E18.
2 A young child, a brat; a young, small, or slender woman. Usu. *derog.* E17.

G. SANTAYANA Some chit of a silly nurse-maid. SLOAN WILSON She was a proper woman. Not some little chit.

chit /tʃɪt/ *noun*[2]. *obsolete* exc. *dial.* E17.
[ORIGIN Perh. repr. obscurely Old English *ćīþ* shoot, sprout, seed, mote (in the eye), Old Saxon *kīþ* sprout, shoot, Middle Dutch *kijt*, Old High German *-kidi* sprout, from Germanic base also of CHINE *noun*[1].]
A shoot, a sprout.

chit /tʃɪt/ *noun*[3]. L18.
[ORIGIN Abbreviation of CHITTY *noun*.]
A written paper, a note; a note of an order, a sum owed, etc.

chit /tʃɪt/ *verb intrans*. Infl. **-tt-**. E17.
[ORIGIN from CHIT *noun*[2].]
Esp. of potatoes: sprout, germinate.

chital /ˈtʃiːt(ə)l/ *noun*. Also **chee-**. L19.
[ORIGIN Hindi *cītal*, *cittal* from Sanskrit *citrala* spotted.]
A white-spotted deer, *Axis axis*, of southern Asia. Also called ***axis* (*deer*)**, ***spotted deer***.

chitarrone /kɪtəˈrəʊni/ *noun*. Pl. **-ni** /-ni/. M18.
[ORIGIN Italian, augm. of *chitarra* guitar.]
A double-necked lute of great length, a theorbo.

chit-chat /ˈtʃɪttʃat/ *noun & verb*. L17.
[ORIGIN Redupl. of CHAT *noun*[2].]
▸ **A** *noun*. **1** Light familiar conversation. L17.
2 Subject matter of gossip or small talk. E18.
▸ **B** *verb intrans*. Infl. **-tt-**. Gossip, chat. E19.
■ **chit-chatty** *adjective* of the nature of chit-chat; gossipy: L19.

†**chithe** *noun* see CHIVE *noun*[1].

chitin /ˈkʌɪtɪn/ *noun*. Also †**-ine**. M19.
[ORIGIN French *chitine*, irreg. from Greek *khitōn*: see CHITON, -IN[1].]
An insoluble nitrogenous polysaccharide which is the main constituent of the exoskeleton of arthropods and also occurs in fungi.
■ **chitiniˈzation** *noun* conversion into chitin L19. **chitinize** *verb trans.* convert into chitin (usu. in *pass.*) L19. **chitinoid** *adjective* resembling chitin L19. **chitinous** *adjective* of the nature of or consisting of chitin M19.

chitlings /ˈtʃɪtlɪŋz/ *noun pl*. *dial.* & *US*. Also **chid-** /ˈtʃɪd-/. M19.
[ORIGIN Contr. of pl. of CHITTERLING.]
1 Chitterlings. M19.
2 Rags, tatters. *US*. M19.

chiton /ˈkʌɪtɒn, -t(ə)n/ *noun*. E19.
[ORIGIN Greek *khitōn*; in sense 1 through mod. Latin *Chiton* genus name.]
1 A mollusc of the class Polyplacophora, characterized by a broad oval foot and a symmetrical dorsal shell composed of a series of eight overlapping plates. E19.
2 A long woollen tunic worn in ancient Greece. M19.

chittack /ˈtʃɪtak/ *noun*. L19.
[ORIGIN Bengali *chaṭāk*.]
In the Indian subcontinent: a unit of weight equal to about 900 grains (approx. 58.3 grams).

chitter /ˈtʃɪtə/ *verb & noun*. ME.
[ORIGIN Imit., of frequentative formation: see -ER[5]. Cf. CHATTER.]
▸ **A** *verb*. **1** *verb intrans*. (Of a bird) utter quick series of short notes, twitter; (of a squirrel etc.) chatter; *gen.* make a twittering or chattering sound. ME.
2 *verb trans*. Utter by chittering. *rare*. LME.
3 *verb intrans*. Shiver with cold. E16.
4 *verb intrans*. Of the teeth: chatter. M16.
▸ **B** *noun*. Twittering. M19.

chitter-chatter /ˈtʃɪtətʃatə/ *noun*. E18.
[ORIGIN Redupl. of CHATTER *noun*: cf. CHIT-CHAT.]
Lively chattering, light gossip.

chitterling /ˈtʃɪtəlɪŋ/ *noun*. ME.
[ORIGIN Uncertain: perh. rel. to Middle High German *kutel* (German *Kutteln*) in same sense. In sense 3 treated as dim. of CHIT *noun*[1].]
1 *sing.* & (usu.) in *pl.* The smaller intestines of pigs etc., esp. when cooked as food. ME.
2 A frill, esp. down the front of a dress shirt. *obsolete* exc. *dial.* L16.
3 A little child, a brat. *derog.* L17.

chitty /ˈtʃɪti/ *noun*. E17.
[ORIGIN Hindi *ciṭṭhī* from Sanskrit *citra* spot, mark.]
= CHIT *noun*[3].

chitty /ˈtʃɪti/ *adjective*. Long *obsolete* exc. *dial.* E17.
[ORIGIN from CHITTY-FACE.]
Of a face: pinched; (later) baby-like.
– COMB.: **chitty-faced** *adjective* having a pinched face; baby-faced.

chitty-face /ˈtʃɪtɪfeɪs/ *noun*. Long *obsolete* exc. *dial.* E17.
[ORIGIN Perh. from French *chicheface* thin face: assoc. with CHIT *noun*[1].]
A person with a pinched face; (later) a baby-faced person.

chiule /tʃɪˈuːl/ *noun*. M19.
[ORIGIN Anglo-Latin *chiula*, *cyula* from Old English *ċīol*, *ċēol*: see KEEL *noun*[2].]
A warship of the early Germanic or Norse invaders of Britain.

chiv /tʃɪv/ *verb & noun*. *slang*. Also **sh-** /ʃ-/. E19.
[ORIGIN Var. of CHIVE *noun*[3] & *verb*.]
▸ **A** *verb trans*. Infl. **-vv-**. Knife, stab, slash. E19.
▸ **B** *noun*. A knife, a blade, a razor. M19.

chivalresque /ʃɪv(ə)lˈrɛsk/ *adjective*. Also **chevaleresque** /ʃɛvələˈrɛsk/. E19.
[ORIGIN (from CHIVALRY + -ESQUE after) French *chevaleresque*, from *chevalier*: see CHEVALIER.]
Characteristic or suggestive of the Age of Chivalry.

chivalric /ˈʃɪv(ə)lrɪk; *poet.* ʃɪˈvalrɪk/ *adjective*. L18.
[ORIGIN from CHIVALRY + -IC.]
Of or pertaining to chivalry; chivalrous.

chivalrous /ˈʃɪv(ə)lrəs/ *adjective*. LME.
[ORIGIN Old French *chevalerous*, from *chevalier*: see CHEVALIER, -OUS.]
†**1** Characteristic of a medieval knight or man-at-arms; valorous. LME–E17.
2 Of or pertaining to (a knight of) the Age of Chivalry. L18.
3 Pertaining to or characteristic of the ideal knight; gallant, honourable, courteous, disinterested; *derog.* quixotic. E19.
■ **chivalrously** *adverb* LME. **chivalrousness** *noun* M19.

chivalry /ˈʃɪv(ə)lri/ *noun*. ME.
[ORIGIN Old French & mod. French *chevalerie*, †*chiv-*, from medieval Latin *caballerius* for *caballarius*: see CHEVALIER, -ERY, -Y[3].]
1 *collect.* Knights or horsemen equipped for battle; medieval men-at-arms; gallant gentlemen. *arch.* ME. ▸†**b** The cavalry of ancient Greece and Rome. E16–L18.

GIBBON A valorous knight, who charged at the head of the Spanish chivalry . . against the Moors.

2 The qualities and abilities of a knight; knightly skill. *arch.* ME.

SIR W. SCOTT The last of all the Bards was he, who sung of Border Chivalry.

†**3** A feat of knightly valour; a gallant exploit. ME–E19.
4 Knighthood as a rank or order. *arch.* LME.
5 LAW. Tenure by knight service. *obsolete* exc. *hist.* L16.
6 The medieval knightly system with its religious, moral, and social code. M18.
7 The characteristics of an ideal knight; courage, honour, and courtesy; inclination to defend or help a weaker party. L18.

W. HOLTBY She had evoked some masculine sentiment of protective chivalry.

– PHRASES: **the Age of Chivalry** the period during which the knightly social and ethical system prevailed; the period during which men behaved with courage, honour, and courtesy.

†**chive** *noun*[1]. Earlier **chire**, **chithe**.
[ORIGIN Old English *ćīþ* from Germanic base also of CHINE *noun*[1], *verb*[1]. Intermediate *chire* unexpl.; *chive* perh. infl. by CHIVE *noun*[2].]
1 A tiny shoot, a sprout; a slender blade *of* grass etc. OE–M19.
2 A filamentous organ in a flower, a stamen or pistil; the filament of a stamen. OE–E19.

chive /tʃʌɪv/ *noun*[2]. Also (now *rare*) **cive** /sʌɪv/. LME.
[ORIGIN Old French dial. var. (whence Picard *chivot* green onion) of Old French & mod. French *cive* from Latin *cepa* onion. See also SITHE *noun*[2].]
1 *sing.* & (usu.) in *pl.* A small plant, *Allium schoenoprasum*, resembling the onion; the slender hollow leaves of this plant as used to flavour salads, soups, etc. LME.
†**2** A small bulb or bulbil, *esp.* a clove of garlic. M16–M18.

chive /tʃʌɪv, tʃɪv/ *noun*[3] *& verb*. *slang*. Also **sh-** /ʃ-/. See also CHIV. L17.
[ORIGIN Unknown.]
= CHIV.

chivvy /ˈtʃɪvi/ *noun & verb*[1]. Also **chivy**, **chevy** /ˈtʃɛvi/. L18.
[ORIGIN Prob. from *Chevy Chase*, scene of a skirmish celebrated in a Border ballad.]
▸ **A** *noun*. **1** A hunting cry. L18.
2 A chase, a pursuit, a hunt. E19.
3 [Abbreviation of CHEVY CHASE.] The face. *slang*. L19.
▸ **B** *verb*. **1** *verb trans*. Chase; harry; worry, trouble, harass. M19.
2 *verb intrans*. Race, scamper. M19.

chivvy /ˈtʃɪvi/ *verb*². *slang*. **M20.**
[**ORIGIN** from **CHIV** *verb*.]
= **CHIV** *verb*.

chivy *noun & verb* var. of **CHIVVY** *noun & verb*¹.

chiz /tʃɪz/ *verb & noun*. *school slang*. **M20.**
[**ORIGIN** Abbreviation of **CHISEL** *verb*.]
▸ **A** *verb intrans*. Infl. **-zz-**. Cheat or swindle. **M20.**
▸ **B** *noun*. Pl. **chizzes**. A swindle. **M20.**
■ **chizzer** *noun* **M20.**

chlamydia /kləˈmɪdɪə/ *noun*. Pl. **-ias**, **-iae** /-ɪiː/. **M20.**
[**ORIGIN** mod. Latin, formed as **CHLAMYDOSPORE**: see **-IA**¹.]
BACTERIOLOGY. A virus-like parasitic bacterium of the genus *Chlamydia*, some species of which cause diseases such as trachoma and psittacosis.
■ **chlamydial** *adjective* **M20.**

chlamydomonas /ˌklamɪdəˈməʊnəs/ *noun*. **L19.**
[**ORIGIN** mod. Latin, formed as **CHLAMYDOSPORE** + Greek *monas* **MONAD**.]
A unicellular green freshwater alga of the genus *Chlamydomonas*.

chlamydospore /ˈklamɪdəspɔː/ *noun*. **L19.**
[**ORIGIN** from Greek *khlamyd-* **CHLAMYS** + **-O-** + **SPORE** *noun*.]
BOTANY & ZOOLOGY. A spore with a thick protective coat.

chlamys /ˈklamɪs/ *noun*. **L17.**
[**ORIGIN** Greek *khlamus* mantle.]
A short cloak worn by men in ancient Greece.

chloanthite /kləʊˈanθʌɪt/ *noun*. **M19.**
[**ORIGIN** from Greek *khloanthēs* becoming green + **-ITE**¹.]
MINERALOGY. A nickel-rich variety of skutterudite. Also called ***white nickel*** (***ore***).

chloasma /kləʊˈazmə/ *noun*. Pl. **-mas**, **-mata** /-mətə/. **M19.**
[**ORIGIN** from Greek *khloazein* become green.]
MEDICINE. An area of skin, usu. on the face, which is temporarily abnormally pigmented, often owing to hormonal changes.

chlor- /klɔː/ *combining form*¹ of **CHLORINE** *noun*. Cf. **CHLORO-**².
■ **chloˈracne** *noun* (*MEDICINE*) a skin disease characterized by persistent lesions resembling acne, caused by regular exposure to chlorinated chemicals **E20.** **chloramine** *noun* an organic compound containing a chlorine atom bonded to nitrogen; *spec*. any of a group of sulphonamide derivatives used as antiseptics and disinfectants: **L19.** **chloˈrapatite** *noun* (*MINERALOGY*) a variety of apatite containing chlorine **M19.** **chlordiazeˈpoxide** *noun* a minor tranquillizer of the benzodiazepine group; (a proprietary name for the drug is **LIBRIUM**): **M20.** **chlortetraˈcycline** *noun* an antibiotic of the tetracycline group, obtained from the bacterium *Streptomyces aureofaciens* or prepared synthetically; (a proprietary name for the drug is **AUREOMYCIN**): **M20.**

chlor- *combining form*² see **CHLORO-**¹.

chloral /ˈklɔːral/ *noun*. **M19.**
[**ORIGIN** from **CHLOR-**¹ + **-AL**².]
CHEMISTRY. Trichloroacetaldehyde, CCl_3CHO, a pungent volatile liquid which is obtained by the action of chlorine on alcohol and is used esp. as a hypnotic (usu. in the form of its crystalline hydrate).

chloramphenicol /klɔːramˈfɛnɪkɒl/ *noun*. **M20.**
[**ORIGIN** formed as **CHLORAL** + **AMIDE** + **PHEN-** + **NITRO-** + **GLYCOL**.]
An antibiotic obtained from the bacterium *Streptomyces venezuelae* or prepared synthetically.
– **NOTE**: A proprietary name for this drug is **CHLOROMYCETIN**.

chlorate /ˈklɔːreɪt/ *noun*. **E19.**
[**ORIGIN** from **CHLORIC** + **-ATE**¹.]
CHEMISTRY. A salt of chloric acid.

chlordane /ˈklɔːdeɪn/ *noun*. **M20.**
[**ORIGIN** from **CHLOR-**¹ + **INDENE** + **-ANE**.]
A viscous chlorinated derivative of indene, $C_{10}H_6Cl_8$, used as an insecticide.

chlorella /kləˈrɛlə/ *noun*. **E20.**
[**ORIGIN** mod. Latin, dim. of Greek *khlōros* green.]
A unicellular green alga of the genus *Chlorella*.

chlorhexidine /klɔːˈhɛksɪdiːn/ *noun*. **M20.**
[**ORIGIN** from **CHLOR-**¹ + **HEX(ANE** + **-ID(E** + **AM)INE**.]
PHARMACOLOGY. A biguanide derivative, $C_{22}H_{30}Cl_2N_{10}$, used as a mild antiseptic, chiefly in skin creams and mouthwashes.

chloric /ˈklɔːrɪk/ *adjective*. **E19.**
[**ORIGIN** from **CHLORINE** *noun* + **-IC**: cf. **CHLOROUS**.]
CHEMISTRY. Of chlorine; ***chloric acid***, a strongly oxidizing acid, $HClO_3$, known only as an aqueous solution.

chloride /ˈklɔːrʌɪd/ *noun*. **E19.**
[**ORIGIN** from **CHLORINE** *noun* + **-IDE**.]
1 *CHEMISTRY*. A compound of chlorine with a less electrovalent element or radical; a salt or ester of hydrochloric acid. **E19.**
2 *loosely*. A bleach or disinfectant containing a hypochlorite. **E19.**
■ **chloridiˈzation** *noun* the process of chloridizing **L19.** **chloridize** *verb trans*. convert (esp. metal ores) into chloride **L19.**

chlorinate /ˈklɔːrɪneɪt, ˈklɒ-/ *verb trans*. **M19.**
[**ORIGIN** from **CHLORINE** *noun* + **-ATE**³.]
Treat or impregnate with chlorine (esp. as a means of disinfecting water); *CHEMISTRY* introduce one or more chlorine atoms into (a compound or molecule), usu. in place of hydrogen. Freq. as ***chlorinated*** *ppl adjective*.
■ **chloriˈnation** *noun* **M19.** **chlorinator** *noun* an apparatus for chlorinating water etc. **M20.**

chlorine /ˈklɔːriːn/ *noun*. **E19.**
[**ORIGIN** from Greek *khlōros* green + **-INE**⁵.]
A toxic yellowish-green gaseous chemical element, atomic no. 17, of the halogen group, with a strong pungent smell (symbol Cl).
■ **chloˈrinity** *noun* chloride concentration (of seawater etc.) **M20.**

chlorine /ˈklɔːrʌɪn/ *adjective*. *rare*. **M19.**
[**ORIGIN** formed as **CHLORINE** *noun* + **-INE**¹.]
Light-green.

chlorite /ˈklɔːrʌɪt/ *noun*¹. **L18.**
[**ORIGIN** from Latin *chloritis* from Greek *khlōritis* a green precious stone: see **CHLORO-**¹, **-ITE**¹.]
MINERALOGY. A monoclinic basic aluminosilicate of magnesium, iron, and often other elements, which is a constituent of many rocks and forms greenish platy crystals.
■ **chloˈritic** *adjective* consisting of or containing chlorite **E19.** **chloritiˈzation** *noun* conversion into (a form containing) chlorite **L19.** **chloritize** *verb trans*. bring about chloritization of (usu. in *pass*.) **E20.** **chloritous** *adjective* = **CHLORITIC** **M19.**

chlorite /ˈklɔːrʌɪt/ *noun*². **M19.**
[**ORIGIN** from **CHLORINE** *noun* + **-ITE**¹.]
CHEMISTRY. A salt of chlorous acid.

chloritoid /ˈklɔːrɪtɔɪd/ *noun*. **M19.**
[**ORIGIN** from **CHLORITE** *noun*¹ + **-OID**.]
MINERALOGY. A basic aluminosilicate of iron and usu. also magnesium, similar to mica and varying in colour from greenish black to grey.

chloro- /ˈklɔːrəʊ, ˈklɒrəʊ/ *combining form*¹ of Greek *khlōros* green: see **-O-**. Before a vowel also **chlor-**.
■ **chloroˈcruorin** *noun* a green respiratory pigment related to haemoglobin, present in the blood of some marine worms **L19.** **chloˈroma** *noun*, pl. **-mas**, **-mata** /-mətə/, *MEDICINE* (the occurrence of) a greenish tumour of bone associated with myeloid leukaemia **L19.** **chloroˈmelanite** *noun* [Greek *khlōromelan* dark green] *MINERALOGY* a greenish-black iron-containing variety of jadeite **L19.** **chloˈropal** *noun* (*MINERALOGY*) = **NONTRONITE** **E19.** **chlorophyte** *noun* *BOTANY* †(**a**) *rare* a green plant; (**b**) a green alga: **L19.**

chloro- /ˈklɔːrəʊ, ˈklɒrəʊ/ *combining form*² of **CHLORINE** *noun*: see **-O-**. Cf. **CHLOR-**¹.
Often denoting compounds formed by replacement of one or more hydrogen atoms by chlorine, as ***chlorobenzene***.
■ **chloroˈpicrin** *noun* [*picric acid*, from which orig. prepared] trichloronitromethane, CCl_3NO_2, a volatile, toxic, reactive liquid used as a disinfectant, pesticide, etc. **M19.** **chloroˈplatinate** *noun* a salt of chloroplatinic acid **M19.** **chloroplaˈtinic** *adjective*: ***chloroplatinic acid***, an acid, H_2PtCl_6, formed when platinum dissolves in aqua regia **L19.** **chloroprene** *noun* [**ISOPRENE**] 2-chloro-1,3-butadiene, C_4H_5Cl, a colourless liquid made from acetylene and hydrochloric acid, easily polymerized to neoprene **M20.** **chloroquine** /-kwiːn/ *noun* [**QUIN(OLINE)**] *PHARMACOLOGY* a quinoline derivative used esp. as an antimalarial **M20.** **chloroˈthiazide** *noun* (*PHARMACOLOGY*) a chlorinated thiazide used as a diuretic **M20.**

chlorodyne /ˈklɔːrədʌɪn, ˈklɒr-/ *noun*. **M19.**
[**ORIGIN** from **CHLOROFLUOROCARBON** + **ANODYNE**.]
A preparation containing chloroform and morphine, (esp. formerly) used as an anodyne.

chlorofluorocarbon /ˌklɔːrəʊflʊərəʊˈkɑːb(ə)n/ *noun*. **M20.**
[**ORIGIN** from **CHLORO-**² + **FLUORO-** + **CARBON** *noun*.]
Any of a group of exceptionally stable compounds containing carbon, fluorine, and chlorine (analogous to the hydrocarbons), which have been used esp. as refrigerants and aerosol propellants. Abbreviation ***CFC***.

chloroform /ˈklɔːrəfɔːm, ˈklɒr-/ *noun & verb*. **M19.**
[**ORIGIN** from **CHLORO-**² + **FORMIC**.]
▸ **A** *noun*. A thin colourless liquid, trichloromethane, $CHCl_3$, used as a solvent and as a general anaesthetic, its sweetish vapour producing narcosis when inhaled. **M19.**
▸ **B** *verb trans*. Treat with chloroform; render unconscious with chloroform. Freq. *fig*. **M19.**
■ **chloroˈformic** *adjective* of, pertaining to, or like chloroform **L19.**

Chloromycetin /klɔːrə(ʊ)ˈmʌɪsɪtɪn, klɒrə(ʊ)-, ˌklɔːrəʊmʌɪˈsiːtɪn/ *noun*. **M20.**
[**ORIGIN** from **CHLORO-**² + **MYCETO-** + **-IN**¹.]
(Proprietary name for) the drug chloramphenicol.

chlorophyll /ˈklɔːrəfɪl, ˈklɒr-/ *noun*. **E19.**
[**ORIGIN** French *chlorophylle* formed as **CHLORO-**¹ + Greek *phullon* leaf.]
Any of a group of magnesium-containing green pigments which occur in plants (giving the characteristic colour to foliage etc.) and act as absorbers of light for photosynthesis.
■ **chloroˈphyllous** *adjective* of the nature of, containing, or characteristic of chlorophyll **M19.**

chloroplast /ˈklɔːrəplast, -plɑːst, ˈklɒr-/ *noun*. **L19.**
[**ORIGIN** from **CHLORO-**¹ + **-PLAST**.]
BOTANY. A plastid containing chlorophyll.
■ †**chloroplastid** *noun* = **CHLOROPLAST** **L19–E20.**

chlorosis /klɒˈrəʊsɪs/ *noun*. Pl. **-roses** /-ˈrəʊsiːz/. **L17.**
[**ORIGIN** from **CHLORO-**¹ + **-OSIS**.]
1 *MEDICINE*. Severe anaemia due to iron deficiency, causing a characteristic greenish pallor. Also called ***greensickness***. **L17.**
2 *BOTANY*. The blanching of normally green parts of plants. Also, the abnormal turning green of other parts. **E19.**
■ **chlorotic** /-ˈrɒtɪk/ *adjective* pertaining to or affected with chlorosis (in either sense) **M18.**

chlorous /ˈklɔːrəs/ *adjective*. **M19.**
[**ORIGIN** from **CHLORINE** *noun* + **-OUS**: cf. **CHLORIC**.]
CHEMISTRY. Of chlorine; ***chlorous acid***, a weak acid, $HClO_2$, known only in aqueous solutions.

chlorpromazine /klɔːˈprəʊməzɪn, -ziːn/ *noun*. **M20.**
[**ORIGIN** from **CHLOR-**¹ + **PROMETHAZINE**.]
PHARMACOLOGY. A phenothiazine derivative used as a tranquillizer, sedative, and anti-emetic.
– **NOTE**: Proprietary names for this drug are **LARGACTIL**, **THORAZINE**.

Ch.M. *abbreviation*.
Latin *Chirurgiae Magister* Master of Surgery.

†**choak** *noun* var. of **CHOCK** *noun*¹.

†**choak** *verb* var. of **CHOKE** *verb*.

†**choaker** *noun* var. of **CHOKER**.

choak-full *adjective* var. of **CHOCK-FULL**.

†**choaky** *adjective* var. of **CHOKY** *adjective*.

choana /ˈkəʊənə/ *noun*. Pl. **-nae** /-niː/. **L19.**
[**ORIGIN** mod. Latin from Greek *khoanē* funnel.]
ANATOMY. A funnel-shaped opening, *esp*. either of those connecting the nasal cavities to the pharynx.

choano- /ˈkəʊənəʊ/ *combining form* of Greek *khoanē* funnel: see **-O-**.
■ **choanocyte** *noun* (*ZOOLOGY*) a flagellated cell with a collar of protoplasm at the base of the flagellum, e.g. in sponges **L19.**

choanoid /ˈkəʊənɔɪd/ *adjective*. **M19.**
[**ORIGIN** formed as **CHOANO-** + **-OID**.]
ANATOMY & BIOLOGY. Funnel-shaped.

choate /ˈkəʊeɪt/ *adjective*. **L19.**
[**ORIGIN** Back-form. from **INCHOATE** *adjective*, as if *in-* were **IN-**³.]
Finished, complete; fully developed.

chobdar /ˈtʃəʊbdɑː/ *noun*. **E18.**
[**ORIGIN** Urdu from Persian *čūbdār* mace-bearer.]
In the Indian subcontinent: an usher bearing a staff, attending on a dignitary.

choc /tʃɒk/ *noun*. *colloq*. **L19.**
[**ORIGIN** Abbreviation.]
= **CHOCOLATE** *noun*.
– **COMB.**: **choc bar**, **choc ice**, a small bar of ice cream enclosed in a thin layer of chocolate.

chocaholic *noun & adjective* var. of **CHOCOHOLIC**.

choccy /tʃɒki/ *noun*. *colloq*. Pl. **choccies**. **E20.**
[**ORIGIN** from **CHOC** + **-IE**.]
Chocolate; a chocolate sweet.

> *Face* Burdened by the pressure of fame . . unable to eat the choccy he loves so much.

chocho /ˈtʃəʊtʃəʊ/ *noun*. Also (chiefly *Austral. & NZ*) **choko** /ˈtʃəʊkəʊ/. Pl. **-os**. **M18.**
[**ORIGIN** Spanish, of Amer. Indian origin.]
= **CHAYOTE**.

chock /tʃɒk/ *noun*¹. Also †**choak**. See also **CHUCK** *noun*⁴. **ME.**
[**ORIGIN** Prob. from Old Northern French (mod. Picard *choke* big log, Norman *chouque*) var. of Old French *ço(u)che* (mod. *souche*) log, block of wood: ult. origin unknown.]
1 A block of wood, *esp*. a wedge for stopping the motion of a cask or wheel; a block (of wood or other material) placed in front of an aeroplane wheel as a brake. **ME.**
2 A log, esp. for burning. *dial*. **L17.**
3 = **CHUCK** *noun*⁴ 3 (now the usual form). **E18.**
– **COMB.**: **chockstone** *MOUNTAINEERING* a stone wedged in a vertical cleft, used as a belay point, stance, or hold.

chock /tʃɒk/ *noun*². **E20.**
[**ORIGIN** Imit.]
A hollow sound such as is made by an impact on wood.

chock /tʃɒk/ *verb*. **E17.**
[**ORIGIN** from **CHOCK** *noun*¹.]
†**1** *verb trans*. Drive in firmly. Only in **E17.**
†**2** *verb intrans*. Fit *in* tightly and exactly. **M17–L18.**
3 *verb trans*. Fit or make fast with a chock or chocks; wedge *up* tightly. **M19.**

chock /tʃɒk/ *adverb*. Also **choke** /tʃəʊk/. **L18.**
[**ORIGIN** Prob. from **CHOCK-FULL** *adjective*.]
Closely, tightly; close up.
chock-a-block (**a**) *NAUTICAL* (of two blocks) run close together in a tackle; (**b**) *transf. & fig*. jammed together, crammed *with*.

chocker /ˈtʃɒkə/ *adjective*. *slang*. Also **-cka**. **M20.**
[**ORIGIN** Abbreviation of *chock-a-block*: see **CHOCK** *adverb*.]
Fed up; very disgruntled.

chock-full /tʃɒkˈfʊl/ *adjective*. Also **choak-**, **choke-** /tʃəʊk-/; **chuck-** /tʃʌk-/. **LME.**
[**ORIGIN** Uncertain: later assoc. with **CHOCK** *noun*¹, *verb*.]
Crammed full (*of*); packed *with*; stuffed.

choco /ˈtʃɒkəʊ/ *noun*. *Austral. slang*. Also **-cko**. Pl. **-os**. M20.
[ORIGIN Abbreviation of CHOCOLATE *soldier*.]
A militiaman, a conscripted soldier.

chocoholic /tʃɒkəˈhɒlɪk/ *noun & adjective*. Also **choca-**. L20.
[ORIGIN from CHOCOLATE: see -AHOLIC.]
▸ **A** *noun*. A person addicted to or very fond of chocolate. L20.
▸ **B** *adjective*. Of or pertaining to chocoholics; addicted to or very fond of chocolate. L20.

chocolate /ˈtʃɒk(ə)lət/ *noun & adjective*. E17.
[ORIGIN French *chocolat* or Spanish *chocolate*, from Nahuatl *chocolatl* article of food made from cacao seeds; infl. by unrelated *cacaua-atl* drink made from cacao.]
▸ **A** *noun*. **1** A drink made of prepared chocolate (sense 2) dissolved in hot milk or water. E17.
2 An edible paste or solid made from cacao seeds by roasting, grinding, etc.; a small sweet or confection made of or covered with chocolate. M17.
milk chocolate: see MILK *noun*. *plain chocolate*: see PLAIN *adjective*[1] & *adverb*.
3 = CACAO *noun* 3 (cf. ***chocolate-tree*** below). Now *rare* or *obsolete*. M18.
4 A dark brown colour. L18.
▸ **B** *attrib*. or as *adjective*. Of or resembling the colour or flavour of chocolate; dark brown. L18.
– COMB. & SPECIAL COLLOCATIONS: **chocolate biscuit** a chocolate-coated biscuit; **chocolate-box** a decorated box filled with chocolates; *fig.* (usu. *attrib.*) a stereotyped romantic style of prettiness; **chocolate-boxy** *adjective* in chocolate-box style; **chocolate-brown** a dark rich brown; **chocolate chip** a small piece of chocolate used in making sweet biscuits and other confections; **chocolate drop** a small round sweet made of chocolate; **chocolate-house** *hist.* a house providing chocolate as a drink; ***chocolate mousse***: see MOUSSE *noun* 2, 2b; **chocolate soldier** a chocolate figurine of a soldier; *fig.* a soldier unwilling to fight; **chocolate-tree** = CACAO *noun* 3.

chocolatey /ˈtʃɒk(ə)ləti/ *adjective*. Also **-ty**. M20.
[ORIGIN from CHOCOLATE + -Y[1].]
Made of, containing, or resembling chocolate.

chocolatier /tʃɒkəˈlatɪə, *foreign* ʃɔkɔlatje (*pl. same*)/ *noun*. L19.
[ORIGIN French, formed as CHOCOLATE: see -IER.]
A maker or seller of chocolate.

chocolaty *adjective* var. of CHOCOLATEY.

Choctaw /ˈtʃɒktɔː/ *noun & adjective*. E18.
[ORIGIN Choctaw *čahta*.]
▸ **A** *noun*. Pl. **-s**, same.
1 A member of a Muskogean people originally inhabiting Mississippi and Alabama; the language of this people. E18. ▸**b** Used as a type of an unknown or difficult language. *colloq*. M19.
2 SKATING. A step from either edge of the skate to the other edge on the other foot in an opposite direction. Cf. MOHAWK *noun* 2. L19.
▸ **B** *attrib*. or as *adjective*. Of or pertaining to the Choctaws or their language. M18.

choenix /ˈkiːnɪks/ *noun*. E17.
[ORIGIN Late Latin from Greek *khoinix*.]
GREEK HISTORY. A dry measure equal to 1 quart or 1½ pints imperial measure.

choga /ˈtʃəʊɡə/ *noun*. M19.
[ORIGIN Urdu *chogha*, *-ā* from Persian *čūkā*.]
A loose Afghan garment with long sleeves.

choice /tʃɔɪs/ *noun*. ME.
[ORIGIN Old French *chois* (mod. *choix*) from *choisir* choose, from Proto-Gallo-Romance from Germanic base of CHOOSE.]
1 Choosing, deciding between possibilities; a necessity to choose, a selection. ME.

J. R. GREEN With this body too . . lay the choice of all future Protectors. R. L. STEVENSON At breakfast we had a choice between tea and coffee. J. BUCHAN I had before me a choice of routes, and I chose a ridge. A. LURIE You have already made your choices, taken the significant moral actions of your life.

2 The power, right, or faculty of choosing; option. ME.

E. W. LANE I have given thee thy choice of the Manner in which thou wilt die.

3 A person or thing (to be) specially chosen or selected; *the* elite; *the* best *of* a group etc.; *the* pick. LME.

MILTON The flower and choice of many Provinces. DRYDEN For me, the Wilds and Desarts are my Choice.

4 Variety and abundance to choose from; a scope or field of possibilities. L16. ▸**b** An abundant and well-chosen supply. L16.

E. HEATH Shops stocked with an immense choice of goods.

†**5** Care in choosing, judgement, discrimination. L16–M18.

BACON They were collected with Iudgement, and Choice.

†**6** Special value, estimation. *rare* (Shakes.). Only in E17.

SHAKES. *All's Well* This ring he holds In most rich choice.

7 An alternative. L18.

W. PALEY Death or conversion was the only choice offered to idolaters. J. D. SALINGER I didn't have any goddam choice except to leave.

– PHRASES: **by choice**, **for choice** preferably. **from choice** willingly, voluntarily. **have no choice** have no alternative. HOBSON'S CHOICE. **make one's choice** decide between possibilities. ***spoilt for choice***: see SPOIL *verb*. **take one's choice** = ***make one's choice*** above.

choice /tʃɔɪs/ *adjective*. ME.
[ORIGIN from the noun.]
1 Worthy of being chosen; of picked quality, select; exquisite; especially fine. ME.

POPE In a sea of folly toss'd, My choicest Hours of Life are lost.

2 Carefully chosen; (esp. of words) apt, appropriate. L16.

Times Literary Supplement These volumes contain some choice specimens.

3 Careful in choosing; discriminative; making much *of*. *obsolete* exc. *dial*. E17.

JER. TAYLOR He that is choice of his time, will also be choice of his company and choice of his actions.

■ **choicely** *adverb* LME. **choiceness** *noun* M17.

choil /tʃɔɪl/ *noun*. L19.
[ORIGIN Unknown.]
The indentation in a knife where the edge of the blade adjoins the tang; the point at which the cutting edge ends.

choir /ˈkwʌɪə/ *noun & verb*. Also (*arch.*, earlier) **quire**. ME.
[ORIGIN Old French *quer* (mod. *choeur*) from Latin *chorus*; spelling with *ch-* as in Latin & mod. French introduced in 17th cent.]
▸ **A** *noun*. **1** An organized body of singers performing or leading in the musical parts of a church service. ME.
2 That part of a church appropriated to singers; *esp.* the chancel of a cathedral, minster, or large church. ME.
3 Any company of singers, esp. an organized body performing at concerts etc., a choral society; a company of singing birds, angels, etc.; *gen.* a band or collection of similar persons or things. LME. ▸**b** A band of dancers or dancers and singers in non-Christian religious festivals etc. Cf. CHORUS *noun* 1b. M17.
4 (The players of) a group of musical instruments of the same class in an orchestra. E20.
– PHRASES: ***ritual choir***: see RITUAL *adjective*. ***ruler of the choir***: see RULER *noun*.
– COMB.: **choirboy** a boy who sings in a choir, esp. an ecclesiastical choir; **choirman** a man who sings in a choir; **choirmaster** the conductor of a choir; **choir nun** a nun professed to perform choir offices; **choir office** a divine service said or sung by a choir; **choir organ** [alt. of ***chair organ*** s.v. CHAIR *noun*[1]] the softest of three parts making up a large compound organ, with the lowest of three keyboards; **choir practice** the regular rehearsal of set pieces of music by a choir; **choir school** a school for choirboys (and other pupils) maintained by a cathedral etc.; **choir sister** = ***choir nun*** above; **choir stall** a fixed seat in the choir of a church etc.
▸ **B** *verb intrans. & trans*. Sing as a choir. *poet. rare*. L16.
■ **choired** *adjective* (*rare*) assembled in a choir; sung in chorus: L18.

choise /tʃɔɪs, -z/ *verb trans. & intrans*. Long *obsolete* exc. *Scot*. E16.
[ORIGIN Alt. of CHOOSE, prob. through assim. to French forms.]
= CHOOSE.

choisya /ˈʃwɑːzɪə/ *noun*. M19.
[ORIGIN mod. Latin, from M. J. D. *Choisy* (1799–1859), Swiss botanist: see -A[1].]
A white-flowered evergreen shrub of the genus *Choisya*, of the rue family, native to Mexico and Arizona; *esp.* Mexican orange, *C. ternata*.

choke /tʃəʊk/ *noun*[1]. *obsolete* exc. *dial*. Also (*Scot.*) **chowk** /tʃaʊk/. ME.
[ORIGIN Prob. var. of CHEEK *noun*; perh. also infl. by Old Norse *kjálki* jawbone.]
The fleshy part around and under the jaw; in *pl.*, the chops.

choke /tʃəʊk/ *noun*[2]. E16.
[ORIGIN from the verb.]
1 A thing which chokes. In *pl.* formerly also, quinsy. E16.
†**2** A block to progress, an obstruction. L17–E18.
3 [Perh. infl. by ending of ARTICHOKE.] The central part of an artichoke. L17.
4 A constriction; *esp.* a narrowed part of a gun bore etc. M18.
5 (The sound produced by) the action of choking. M19.
6 ELECTRICITY. A high-inductance coil which serves to smooth variations or change the phase of an alternating voltage applied to it. E20.
7 A valve in the air intake of a carburettor serving esp. to provide a richer mixture for engine starting. E20.

choke /tʃəʊk/ *verb*. Also †**choak**. ME.
[ORIGIN Aphet. from late Old English *ācēocian*, formed as A-[1] + CHEEK *noun*.]
▸ **I** *verb trans*. **1** Stop the breath of; suffocate, temporarily or finally, by squeezing the throat, blocking it up, or (of water, smoke, etc.) being unbreathable; (of emotion etc.) render speechless (often foll. by *up*). ME.

O. CLARK I got very choked up at the 5th prayer for the dead.

2 Smother, kill (a plant, fire, etc.) by deprivation of light, air, etc.; stop the vibration of (a cymbal); *fig.* suppress (feelings, aspirations, etc.). LME ▸†**b** Silence (an opponent) by an argument. M16–M17.
3 Block up (or *up*) wholly or partly; constrict (a tube) by narrowing part of it; obstruct (a channel) with sand, debris, etc. E17.

Audubon The basin was becoming choked with dirt.

4 Fill chock-full (*lit.* & *fig.*). E18.
5 Stop (a machine or its action) by clogging or jamming. E18.
6 Fit tightly *in*, ram *in*. M18.
7 Close the choke of (an internal-combustion engine, a vehicle). M20.
▸ **II** *verb intrans*. **8** Suffer a temporary or permanent stoppage of breath; become speechless through emotion etc. LME.
9 Undergo smothering, suppression, blockage, or obstruction. L16.

A. CROSS Kate choked on her wine.

– WITH ADVERBS IN SPECIALIZED SENSES: **choke back** conceal (emotion etc.) with difficulty. **choke down** swallow (food) with difficulty; restrain oneself with an effort from uttering (words etc.). **choke off** *colloq.* stop (a person, an attempt, etc.), esp. forcibly; dissuade, discourage, rebuke.
– COMB.: **chokeberry** (the red, black, or purple astringent fruit of) a N. American shrub of the genus *Aronia*, of the rose family; **choke cherry** (the astringent cherry of) a N. American tree, *Prunus virginiana*; **choke-coil** = CHOKE *noun*[2] 6; **choke-cymbal** a cymbal equipped or able to be rapidly damped; **choke-damp** asphyxiating gas, largely carbon dioxide, accumulated in a mine, well, etc.; **choke-pear** (now *rare* or *obsolete*) a hard or unpalatable pear; *fig.* something hard to accept, a difficulty; **choke-weed** a weed which chokes other plants, esp. (formerly) broomrape; **choking coil** = CHOKE *noun*[2] 6.
■ **chokingly** *adverb* in a choking manner, so as to choke E17.

choke *adverb* var. of CHOCK *adverb*.

choke-full *adjective* var. of CHOCK-FULL.

choker /ˈtʃəʊkə/ *noun*. Also †**choaker**. M16.
[ORIGIN from CHOKE *verb* + -ER[1].]
1 A person who or thing which chokes. M16.
2 A clerical or other high collar. *colloq.* M19.
3 A close-fitting necklace. E20.
4 A noose of wire rope etc. tied round a log for hauling it. E20.

chokey *noun, adjective* vars. of CHOKY *noun, adjective*.

chokidar *noun* var. of CHOWKIDAR.

choko *noun* var. of CHOCHO.

chokra /ˈtʃəʊkrə/ *noun*. L19.
[ORIGIN Hindi *chokrā*.]
In the Indian subcontinent: a boy, *esp.* one employed as a household or regimental servant.

choky /ˈtʃəʊki/ *noun*. Also **chokey**; (in sense 1) **chauki** /ˈtʃaʊki/. E17.
[ORIGIN Hindi *caukī*: in sense 2 infl. by CHOKE *verb* etc.]
1 In the Indian subcontinent: a custom or toll station; a station for horses etc.; a police station, a lock-up. E17.
2 Prison, imprisonment. *slang*. L19.

choky /ˈtʃəʊki/ *adjective*. Also †**choaky**; **chokey**. L16.
[ORIGIN from CHOKE *verb* + -Y[1].]
1 Apt to cause choking. L16.
2 Liable to or afflicted with choking. M19.
■ **chokiness** *noun* M19.

chol- *combining form* see CHOLE-.

chola *noun* see CHOLO.

cholate /ˈkəʊleɪt, ˈkɒl-/ *noun*. M19.
[ORIGIN from CHOLIC + -ATE[1].]
BIOCHEMISTRY. A salt or ester of cholic acid.

chole- /ˈkɒli/ *combining form* of Greek *kholē* bile, gall. Before a vowel **chol-**.
■ **chola·gogue** *noun* [Greek *kholagōgos* adjective, from *agōgos* leading, eliciting] a medicine supposed to promote the flow of bile from the gall bladder L17. **cholangi'ography** *noun* radiological examination of the bile ducts M20. **cholan'gitis** *noun* inflammation of the bile ducts L19. ˌ**cholecal'ciferol** *noun* (BIOCHEMISTRY) vitamin D_3, a compound related to calciferol, formed in the skin by ultraviolet light and present in egg yolk, liver, and fish-liver oils M20. †**choledoch** *adjective* [Greek *dokhos* containing, receiving] conveying or containing bile L17–M19. **choledo'chotomy** *noun* (an instance of) surgical opening of the bile duct draining into the duodenum L19. **choleli'thiasis** *noun*, pl. **-ases** /-əsiːz/, the formation of gallstones L19.

cholecyst- /ˈkɒlɪsɪst/ *combining form* of mod. Latin *cholecystis* gall bladder: see CHOLE-, CYST.
■ **cholecy'stectomy** *noun* (an instance of) surgical removal of the gall bladder L19. **cholecy'stitis** *noun* inflammation of the gall bladder M19. **cholecy'stography** *noun* radiological examination of the gall bladder E20. **cholecysto'kinin** *noun* (BIOCHEMISTRY) a hormone which is secreted by cells in the duodenum and stimulates the release of bile into the intestine and the secretion of enzymes by the pancreas M20. **cholecy'stotomy** *noun* (an instance of) surgical incision into the gall bladder L19.

cholent /ˈtʃɒl(ə)nt, ˈʃɒ-/ *noun*. M20.
[ORIGIN Yiddish *tsholnt*. Cf. SCHALET.]
A Jewish Sabbath dish of slowly baked meat and vegetables, prepared on a Friday and cooked overnight.

C

choler /ˈkɒlə/ *noun*. LME.
[ORIGIN Old French & mod. French *colère* from Latin CHOLERA.]
†**1** = CHOLERA 2a. LME–M18.
2 *hist.* Bile, orig. as that one of the four bodily humours believed to cause irascibility. LME. ▸†**b** Bilious disorder, biliousness. LME–L17.
choler adust a thick black fluid formerly supposed to be secreted by the suprarenal glands and to cause melancholy; black bile (cf. ATRABILIOUS).
3 Anger; irascibility, temper. M16.

cholera /ˈkɒlərə/ *noun*. LME.
[ORIGIN Latin from Greek *kholera*; in late Latin taking over the meanings of Greek *kholē* bile, anger.]
†**1** = CHOLER 2. LME–M16.
2 a *gen.* Any of various ailments involving severe vomiting and diarrhoea. Freq. with distinguishing word (see below). *obsolete* exc. *hist.* E17. ▸**b** *spec.* A dangerous infectious disease, endemic in Asia, which is caused by intestinal infection with the bacterium *Vibrio cholerae* and is characterized by severe vomiting and diarrhoea leading to dehydration. E19.
With distinguishing words (now largely *obsolete* exc. *hist.*): **Asiatic cholera** = sense 2b. **cholera infantum** /ɪnˈfantəm/ [Latin = of infants] gastroenteritis or a similar condition when occurring in a child; also called ***summer cholera***, ***summer diarrhoea***, etc. **cholera morbus** /ˈmɔːbəs/ [Latin = the disease cholera] = sense 2a, b. **epidemic cholera** = sense 2b. **summer cholera** = ***cholera infantum*** above.
3 ***chicken cholera***, ***fowl cholera***, infectious pasteurellosis of fowls (orig. thought to coincide with cholera epidemics). L19.
– COMB.: **cholera belt** *arch.* a flannel or silk waistband worn to prevent intestinal ailments.
■ **choleraic** /kɒləˈreɪɪk/ *adjective* pertaining to or of the nature of cholera M19.

choleric /ˈkɒlərɪk/ *adjective*. ME.
[ORIGIN Old French & mod. French *cholérique* from Latin *cholericus* bilious from Greek *kholerikos*, from *kholera* CHOLERA.]
1 *hist.* Having choler as the predominant humour; bilious. ME.
†**2** Subject to, involving or causing biliousness. M16–E18.
3 Irascible; hot-tempered. L16.
†**4** Angry, wrathful. L16–E18.
5 = CHOLERAIC. M19.

cholesterol /kəˈlɛstərɒl/ *noun*. L19.
[ORIGIN from CHOLE- + Greek *stereos* stiff + -OL.]
CHEMISTRY. A steroid alcohol, $C_{27}H_{45}OH$, which occurs widely in body cells and fluids, has several metabolic functions, and is a major component of atheromas and gallstones.
■ Also **cholesterin** *noun* (now *rare* or *obsolete*) E19.

choli /ˈtʃəʊli/ *noun*. E20.
[ORIGIN Hindi *colī*.]
A woman's short-sleeved bodice of a type worn in the Indian subcontinent.

choliamb /ˈkəʊlɪam(b)/ *noun*. M19.
[ORIGIN Late Latin *choliambus* from Greek *khōliambos*, from *khōlos* lame: see IAMBUS.]
PROSODY. = SCAZON.
■ **choliˈambic** *noun & adjective* (**a**) *noun* (in *pl.*) (poetry written in) this metre; (**b**) *adjective* of or pertaining to the choliamb; written in choliambs: L17.

cholic /ˈkəʊlɪk, ˈkɒl-/ *adjective*. M19.
[ORIGIN Greek *kholikos*: see CHOLE-, -IC.]
BIOCHEMISTRY. ***cholic acid***, a steroid acid, $C_{24}H_{40}O_5$, which is an oxidation product of cholesterol and is present (as salts) in bile.

choline /ˈkəʊliːn, -ɪn/ *noun*. Also **-in** /-ɪn/. M19.
[ORIGIN from CHOLE- + -INE[5].]
BIOCHEMISTRY. A strong base, $HO{\cdot}N(CH_3)_3{\cdot}CH_2CH_2OH$, which occurs widely in living organisms as a metabolic intermediate.
■ **choliˈnergic** *adjective* (PHYSIOLOGY) releasing or involving acetylcholine as a neurotransmitter (cf. ADRENERGIC) M20. **choliˈnesterase** *noun* an enzyme which hydrolyses esters of choline; *esp.* acetylcholinesterase: M20.

cholla /ˈtʃɔɪə/ *noun*. *US*. Also **choya**. M19.
[ORIGIN Mexican Spanish use of Spanish = skull, head, of unknown origin.]
Any of various opuntias of Mexico and the south-western US.

†**cholle** *noun*[1], *noun*[2] vars. of JOWL *noun*[2], *noun*[3].

cholo /ˈtʃəʊləʊ/ *noun*. Pl. **-os**. Fem. **chola** /ˈtʃəʊlə/. Also **C-**. M19.
[ORIGIN Amer. Spanish, from *Chololián*, now *Cholula*, a district of Mexico.]
An Indian of Latin America; a mestizo; *US* (freq. *derog.*) a lower-class Mexican.

chomer *noun* var. of HOMER *noun*[1].

chometz *noun* var. of HAMETZ.

chomp /tʃɒmp/ *verb intrans. & trans.* M17.
[ORIGIN Imit.]
= CHAMP *verb* 1, 2.

Chomskyan /ˈtʃɒmskɪən/ *adjective*. Also **-skian**. M20.
[ORIGIN from *Chomsky* (see below) + -AN.]
Of, pertaining to, or characteristic of Noam Avram Chomsky (1928–), US linguistic scholar, or his writings.

chon *noun* see JUN.

chondr- *combining form* see CHONDRO-.

chondrify /ˈkɒndrɪfʌɪ/ *verb trans.* L19.
[ORIGIN from Greek *khondros* cartilage + -FY.]
Convert into cartilage. Usu. in *pass.*
■ **chondrifiˈcation** *noun* L19.

chondrin /ˈkɒndrɪn/ *noun*. M19.
[ORIGIN formed as CHONDRIFY + -IN[1].]
A substance like gelatin, extracted from cartilage by boiling in water.

chondrite /ˈkɒndrʌɪt/ *noun*. M19.
[ORIGIN from Greek *khondros* granule + -ITE[1].]
A stony meteorite containing chondrules.
■ **chondritic** /kɒnˈdrɪtɪk/ *adjective* M19.

chondro- /ˈkɒndrəʊ/ *combining form* of Greek *khondros* cartilage, granule: see -O-. Before a vowel **chondr-**.
■ **chondroˈcranium** *noun* the cartilaginous skull of an embryo L19. **chondrocyte** *noun* a cartilage cell E20. **chondroˈgenesis** *noun* cartilage formation L19. **chonˈdroma** *noun*, pl. **-mas**, **-mata** /-mətə/, MEDICINE a benign tumour of cartilage M19. **chondrosarˈcoma** *noun*, pl. **-mas**, **-mata** /-mətə/, MEDICINE a malignant tumour arising from cartilage cells in bone L19.

chondrodite /ˈkɒndrədʌɪt/ *noun*. E19.
[ORIGIN from Greek *khondrōdēs* granular + -ITE[1].]
MINERALOGY. A monoclinic basic silicate and fluoride of magnesium and iron, usu. occurring as yellow to dark red prisms or granules.

chondroid /ˈkɒndrɔɪd/ *adjective*. M19.
[ORIGIN from Greek *khondros* cartilage + -OID.]
Resembling cartilage.

chondroitin /kɒnˈdrəʊɪtɪn/ *noun*. L19.
[ORIGIN from CHONDRO- + -ITE[1] + -IN[1].]
BIOCHEMISTRY. A polysaccharide which in the form of sulphate esters is a major component of cartilage and other connective tissue.

chondrophore /ˈkɒndrəfɔː/ *noun*. L19.
[ORIGIN from CHONDRO- + -PHORE, in sense 2 via mod. Latin *Chondrophora* (see below).]
ZOOLOGY. **1** A pit or projection that supports the internal hinge cartilage of a bivalve mollusc. L19.
2 Any of various pelagic hydroids of the suborder Chondrophora, consisting of polymorphic colonies or single large polyps with a chitinous float and a sail. L20.

chondrostean /kɒnˈdrɒstɪən/ *noun & adjective*. L19.
[ORIGIN from mod. Latin *Chondrostei* (see below), formed as CHONDRO- + Greek *osteon* bone: see -AN.]
▸ **A** *noun*. A bony fish of the superorder Chondrostei, which includes the sturgeons and many fossil forms. L19.
▸ **B** *adjective*. Of or pertaining to the Chondrostei. L19.

chondrule /ˈkɒndruːl/ *noun*. L19.
[ORIGIN from CHONDRITE + -ULE.]
A spheroidal mineral grain embedded in a meteorite.

choo-choo /ˈtʃuːtʃuː/ *noun*. E20.
[ORIGIN Imit.]
A child's word for a (steam) train or locomotive.

chook /tʃʊk/ *noun*. *Austral. & NZ colloq.* E20.
[ORIGIN cf. CHUCK *noun*[2], CHUCKY.]
A domestic fowl, a chicken.

chookie, **chooky** *nouns* see CHUCKY.

choola /ˈtʃuːlə/ *noun*. Also **chula**. E19.
[ORIGIN Hindi *cūlhā* from Sanskrit *culli*.]
In the Indian subcontinent: a fireplace, a cooking place.

choom /tʃʊm/ *noun*. *Austral. & NZ slang*. E20.
[ORIGIN Alt. of CHUM *noun*[1].]
An English soldier; an Englishman.

choose /tʃuːz/ *verb*. Also (*arch.*) **chuse**. Pa. t. **chose** /tʃəʊz/; pa. pple **chosen** /ˈtʃəʊz(ə)n/, (*arch. & non-standard*) **chose**.
[ORIGIN Old English *cēosan* = Old Frisian *kiāsa*, *ziāsa*, Old Saxon *kiosan* (Dutch *kiezen*), Old High German *kiosan*, Old Norse *kjósa*, Gothic *kiusan*, from Germanic, cogn. with Latin *gustare* to taste.]
▸ **I** *verb trans.* **1** Take by preference out of all that are available; select, pick (*out*); (with compl.) select as. OE.
S. FOOTE Have unanimously chosen you Mayor. A. L. ROWSE Sir Thomas Arundell, who chose out . . this spot. D. LODGE The Poles did not choose . . the political system under which they live.
2 Decide *to do* something (rather than something else); think fit *to do*; be determined *to do*. ME.
AV *Heb.* 11:25 Chusing rather to suffer affliction with the people of God, then to enioy the pleasures of sinne for a season. D. BOGARDE She . . didn't hear him. Or chose not to.
3 Wish to have, want. *obsolete* exc. *dial.* M18.
G. COLMAN Do you chuse any refreshment, Sir?
▸ **II** *verb intrans.* **4** Make a selection; exercise choice (*between*, *from*). ME.
E. F. BENSON She knew that she must act in one way or in another way, and she had to choose.
5 Do as one likes, take one's own way. *obsolete* or *dial.* LME.
– PHRASES: **cannot choose** *arch.* has or have no alternative (*but*). ***choose ends***: see END *noun*. **nothing to choose between** no difference between. ***pick and choose***: see PICK *verb*[1].
– NOTE: Formerly also with weak inflections.
■ **chooser** *noun* (**a**) *gen.* a person who chooses; †(**b**) *spec.* an elector: LME. **choosingly** *adverb* (*rare*) by choice M17.

choosy /ˈtʃuːzi/ *adjective*. *colloq.* Also **-sey**. M19.
[ORIGIN from CHOOSE + -Y[1].]
Particular in one's choice, fastidious.
■ **choosiness** *noun* M20.

chop /tʃɒp/ *noun*[1]. LME.
[ORIGIN from CHOP *verb*[1].]
1 An act of chopping; a cutting stroke made with an axe or similar implement. LME. ▸**b** A short sharp downward blow or stroke in boxing, cricket, tennis, etc. L19. ▸**c** *sing.* & (usu.) in *pl.* A wood-chopping contest. *Austral. & NZ*. E20.
the chop *slang* being killed or dismissed; sudden cancellation (of a project etc.). **b** ***KARATE-chop***.
2 A piece chopped off; *spec.* a thick slice of meat (esp. pork or lamb) usu. including a rib. LME.
chump chop, ***loin chop***, etc. ***Maintenon chop***: see MAINTENON 1.
†**3** A fissure, cleft, crack; a chap in the skin. L16–M19.
4 A broken motion of waves, usu. due to the action of the wind against the tide; choppiness. M19.
5 A person's share of something. *Austral. & NZ colloq.* E20.
– COMB.: **chophouse** a (cheap) restaurant.

chop /tʃɒp/ *noun*[2]. LME.
[ORIGIN Var. of CHAP *noun*[2].]
Usu. in *pl.* **1** Either of the jaws or cheeks of an animal or human; = CHAP *noun*[2] 1, 2. LME.
lick one's chops: see LICK *verb*.
†**2** (A name for) a fat-faced person. L16–E17.
SHAKES. *1 Hen. IV*: I'll hang you for going . . You will, chops?
3 The entrance or opening of a channel, valley, etc. M17.
Chops of the Channel the entrance from the Atlantic Ocean to the English Channel.
4 In *pl.* The technical skill of a musician, esp. one who plays jazz. *colloq.* M20.
S. RUSHDIE He's got the ear, he's got the chops.
– COMB.: **chop-fallen** *adjective* = ***chap-fallen*** s.v. CHAP *noun*[2].

chop /tʃɒp/ *noun*[3]. E17.
[ORIGIN Hindi *chāp* stamp, brand.]
1 In the Indian subcontinent, China, etc.: a seal, an official stamp. E17.
2 A licence, permit, etc., validated by an official stamp; an official permit. E17.
3 A trademark, a brand of goods (orig. in China). E19.
– PHRASES: **first chop**, **second chop** (*colloq.*) first class, second class. **no chop**, **not much chop** *Austral. & NZ colloq.* no good, not up to much.

chop /tʃɒp/ *noun*[4]. M17.
[ORIGIN from CHOP *verb*[1].]
A snap with the jaws or mouth.

chop /tʃɒp/ *noun*[5]. Now *rare* or *dial.* exc. in ***chop and change*** below. L17.
[ORIGIN from CHOP *verb*[2].]
An exchange, a barter.
chop and change a change, an alteration (usu. in *pl.*) (cf. CHOP *verb*[2] 2).

chop /tʃɒp/ *noun*[6]. *W. Afr. colloq.* E19.
[ORIGIN Unknown: cf. CHOP *verb*[4].]
(Prepared and cooked) food. Freq. in *comb.*

chop /tʃɒp/ *verb*[1]. Infl. **-pp-**. Pa. t. & pple **-pped**, (*arch.*) **-pt**. LME.
[ORIGIN Var. of CHAP *verb*[2].]
1 *verb trans.* Cut by one or more quick heavy blows, usu. with an axe or the like. Freq. with adverb or adverbial phr. LME. ▸**b** Strike (a ball, a person, etc.) with a short heavy (esp. edgewise) blow. L19.
AV *Micah* 3:3 They breake their bones, and chop them in pieces. E. CRISPIN I'll chop off your feet with these shears. **b** J. CLAVELL Mura had chopped his [another's] elbow with the side of his hand.
chopped liver (**a**) a dish of chopped (esp. chicken) liver, with onions, hard-boiled eggs, and seasonings; (**b**) *N. Amer. colloq.* a person or thing regarded as insignificant. **chopping block** a block for chopping wood etc. on; *fig.* something sustaining continual blows. **chopping board**: for preparing vegetables etc. on.
2 *verb trans.* Cut (*up*) into pieces, mince. LME.
E. M. FORSTER Euphemia . . will not . . chop the suet sufficiently small.
3 *verb intrans.* Strike a short heavy (esp. edgewise) blow *at* (occas. *on*), orig. in order to cut; cut *through* with such a blow. LME. ▸**b** In cricket, tennis, etc.: hit the ball with a short heavy (esp. edgewise) stroke. L19.
J. T. STORY Felix . . started chopping at the chain with an axe.

4 *verb trans. & intrans.* Thrust, go, or come, (*in, into*) with sudden impetus or violence; drop, fall, etc., suddenly. Long *obsolete* exc. *dial.* LME.

SHAKES. *Rich. III* Chop him in the malmsey-butt in the next room. SIR W. SCOTT Lest some passing stranger should chop in between me and the prize.

5 *verb trans. & intrans.* Strike, knock. Chiefly *Scot.* Now *rare* or *obsolete.* LME.
†**6** *verb intrans.* Break open in clefts or fissures; crack; chap. L16–M18.
7 *verb intrans.* Of the sea, waves, etc.: have a short jerky motion; break in short abrupt waves. Chiefly as ***chopping*** *ppl adjective.* M17.

R. H. DANA A stiff breeze . . directly against the course of the current, made an ugly, chopping sea.

chop /tʃɒp/ *verb*². Infl. **-pp-**. Pa. t. & pple **-pped**, (*arch.*) **-pt**. LME.
[ORIGIN Uncertain: perh. var. of CHAP *verb*¹. First evidenced in *chop-church* (see below).]
1 *verb intrans. & trans.* Barter, traffic (*with*); exchange by way of commerce. Long *obsolete* exc. *dial.* LME.
2 *chop and change*: ▸**a** *verb phr. intrans.* Barter, traffic, (*with*). Now chiefly *fig.*, change one's tactics, vacillate, be inconstant. L15. ▸**b** *verb phr. trans.* Barter, exchange; *fig.* make different, alter. Now *rare.* M16.
3 *verb trans.* ***chop logic***, engage in pedantically logical arguments. E16.
†**4** *verb intrans.* Exchange words; answer back. L16–E17.
5 *verb intrans.* Change, shift; esp. NAUTICAL (of the wind) veer *round, about*, suddenly. M17.
– COMB.: †**chop-church** a trafficker in ecclesiastical benefices; **chop-logic** (*a*) disputatious argument; (*b*) a person who argues pedantically or sophistically.

chop /tʃɒp/ *verb*³. Infl. **-pp-**. L16.
[ORIGIN App. from CHOP *noun*².]
†**1** *verb trans.* Take into the jaws and eat; snap *up*. L16–E18.
†**2** *verb intrans.* Snap, bite *at*. L16–L17.
3 *verb trans.* Of hounds etc.: seize (prey) before it is fairly away from cover. E17.

chop /tʃɒp/ *verb*⁴ *trans. & intrans. W. Afr. colloq.* Infl. **-pp-**. M19.
[ORIGIN Unknown: cf. CHOP *noun*⁶.]
Eat; kill to eat.

chop-chop /tʃɒpˈtʃɒp/ *adverb & interjection. colloq.* (orig. *Pidgin English*). M19.
[ORIGIN An obscure formation rendering Chinese dial. *kuai-kuai*.]
Quick, quickly; hurry up!

chopin /ˈtʃɒpɪn/ *noun*¹. Chiefly *Scot. obsolete* exc. *hist.* ME.
[ORIGIN Old French & mod. French *chopine* from Low German *schopen* an old measure = half a pint.]
A liquid measure of about one English quart.

chopin *noun*² var. of next.

chopine /tʃɒˈpiːn/ *noun. arch.* Also **chopin** /-pɪn/. L16.
[ORIGIN App. orig. from Spanish *chapín* = Portuguese *chapim*, Old French *chapin*.]
A kind of shoe raised above the ground by a cork sole or the like.

Chopinesque /ʃəʊpɪˈnɛsk/ *adjective.* E20.
[ORIGIN from *Chopin* (see below) + -ESQUE.]
MUSIC. Pertaining to or resembling the compositions or pianistic style of the Polish composer Frédéric Chopin (1809–49).

chopper /ˈtʃɒpə/ *noun*¹. L15.
[ORIGIN from CHOP *verb*² + -ER¹.]
A person who barters or exchanges, *esp.* (formerly) = ***chop-church*** s.v. CHOP *verb*²; a person who chops logic.

chopper /ˈtʃɒpə/ *noun*². M16.
[ORIGIN from CHOP *verb*¹ + -ER¹.]
1 A person who chops or cuts into pieces. M16. ▸**b** A person who fells trees; a lumberman. *US colloq.* E19.
2 An implement for chopping, *esp.* a large-bladed short axe; a butcher's cleaver. E19.
3 A device for regularly interrupting a light beam etc. E20.
4 A machine gun or gunner. *US slang.* E20.
5 A helicopter. *colloq.* M20.
6 A type of motorcycle with high handlebars and the front-wheel fork extended forwards. *slang* (orig. *US*). M20.

chopper /ˈtʃɒpə/ *noun*³. L18.
[ORIGIN Hindi *chappar*.]
In the Indian subcontinent: a thatched roof.
– COMB.: **chopper-cot** a camp bed with curtains.
■ **choppered** *adjective* thatched E19.

chopping /ˈtʃɒpɪŋ/ *adjective.* Now *rare* or *obsolete.* M16.
[ORIGIN from CHOP *verb*¹ + -ING².]
Big and vigorous; strapping; (of a baby) bouncing.

choppy /ˈtʃɒpi/ *adjective*¹. E17.
[ORIGIN from CHOP *noun*¹ + -Y¹.]
1 = CHAPPY *adjective. rare.* E17.
2 Of the sea etc.: breaking in short abrupt waves; giving a short jerky motion to things floating. M19.
■ **choppiness** *noun* L19.

choppy /ˈtʃɒpi/ *adjective*². M19.
[ORIGIN from CHOP *verb*¹ + -Y¹.]
Liable to change (like the wind); *fig.* unstable, vacillating.

chopsocky /ˈtʃɒpsɒki/ *noun. N. Amer. colloq.* L20.
[ORIGIN Perh. joc. from CHOP SUEY.]
Kung fu or a similar martial art, especially as depicted in violent action films. Freq. *attrib.*

chopstick /ˈtʃɒpstɪk/ *noun.* L17.
[ORIGIN from pidgin English *chop* quick (cf. CHOP-CHOP) + STICK *noun*¹, rendering Chinese dial. *kuaizi* lit. 'nimble ones'.]
1 Either of a pair of sticks of wood, ivory, etc., held in one hand, used by the Chinese etc. to lift food to the mouth. L17.
2 In *pl.* A simple tune for the piano, played with the forefinger of each hand. L19.

chop suey /tʃɒpˈsuːi/ *noun.* L19.
[ORIGIN Chinese (Cantonese) *tsaâp sui* mixed bits.]
A Chinese dish of pieces of meat or chicken fried with rice, onions, etc., often made with leftover food.

chopt *verb*¹, *verb*² *pa. t. & pple*: see CHOP *verb*¹, *verb*².

choragium /kɒˈreɪdʒɪəm/ *noun. rare.* Pl. **-ia** /-ɪə/. L17.
[ORIGIN Latin from Greek *khorēg(e)ion* place where a chorus was trained, formed as CHORAGUS.]
A dancing ground.

choragus /kɒˈreɪgəs/ *noun.* Also **-regus**. Pl. **-gi** /-gʌɪ, -giː/. E17.
[ORIGIN Latin from Greek *khoragos*, *-ēgos*, from *khoros* CHORUS *noun* + *agein* to lead.]
1 A functionary at Oxford University orig. appointed to supervise the practice of music. E17.
2 Chiefly GREEK HISTORY. The leader of a chorus, or of any group; *spec.* at Athens, a person who defrayed the cost of bringing out a chorus. E17.
■ **choragic** /-ˈradʒɪk, -ˈreɪdʒɪk/ *adjective* of or pertaining to a choragus M18.

choral *noun* var. of CHORALE.

choral /ˈkɔːr(ə)l/ *adjective.* L16.
[ORIGIN medieval Latin *choralis*, from Latin CHORUS *noun*: see -AL¹.]
1 Of or belonging to a choir; sung by a choir. L16.
2 Of, belonging to, or of the nature of a chorus; sung in chorus; containing a chorus or choruses. M17. ▸**b** Of poetry, drama, etc.: said or read by a group of voices. M20.
3 GREEK HISTORY. Pertaining to or forming a chorus as in ancient Greek religious festivals. M17.
– SPECIAL COLLOCATIONS: ***Choral Ode***: see ODE 1. **choral service** a religious service with canticles, anthems, etc., sung in chorus (also occas. with the versicles and responses being chanted). **choral society** a society of people interested in performing choral music. ***vicar choral***: see VICAR *noun* 4.
■ **choralism** *noun* choral composition; choral rendering and technique: E20. **choralist** *noun* a person who sings in a chorus M19. **chorally** *adverb* L18.

chorale /kɒˈrɑːl/ *noun.* Also **-ral**. M19.
[ORIGIN German *Choral(gesang)* translating medieval Latin *cantus choralis*.]
1 (A metrical hymn to) a simple tune usu. sung or played in unison, orig. in the Lutheran Church; the harmonized form of this. M19.
2 A group of singers. M20.
– COMB.: **chorale prelude** an organ piece based on a chorale.

Chorasmian /kɒˈrazmɪən/ *adjective. poet.* E19.
[ORIGIN from Greek *Khorasmioi* (pl.) name of a tribe of Sogdiana + -AN.]
Of, pertaining to, or designating a desert land south of the Aral Sea and about the lower course of the Oxus.

chord /kɔːd/ *noun*¹. Also †**cord**. ME.
[ORIGIN Aphet. from ACCORD *noun*, later infl. by CHORD *noun*².]
†**1** Agreement, reconciliation; an agreement, a peace treaty. Only in ME.
†**2** = ACCORD *noun* 4. LME–M17.
†**3** MUSIC. A concord; in *pl.*, the notes added to a bass to make up a chord (sense 4). L16–M18.
4 MUSIC. A group of notes sounded usu. together, combined according to some system. M18.
common chord any note with its major or minor third and perfect fifth. ***supplemental chord***: see SUPPLEMENTAL *adjective*.

chord /kɔːd/ *noun*². M16.
[ORIGIN Refashioning of CORD *noun*¹ after Latin *chorda*.]
1 ANATOMY. = CORD *noun*¹ 3, esp. in ***spinal chord***, ***vocal chord***. M16.
2 A straight line joining the extremities of an arc. Cf. earlier CORD *noun*¹ 5. L16. ▸**b** AERONAUTICS. The width of an aerofoil from leading to trailing edge. E20.
†**3** = CORD *noun*¹ 1. M17–E19.
4 The string of a harp or other instrument. Chiefly *poet.* or *fig.* M17.
strike a chord evoke some reaction in a person. **touch the right chord** appeal skilfully to emotion; evoke sympathy.
5 ENGINEERING. Either of the two principal members of the truss of a bridge. L19.

chord /kɔːd/ *verb intrans. rare.* M19.
[ORIGIN Prob. from CHORD *noun*¹, but perh. var. of CORD *verb*².]
Form a chord (*with*); harmonize.
■ **chording** *noun* the playing, singing, or arrangement of chords M19.

chorda /ˈkɔːdə/ *noun.* Pl. **-dae** /-diː/. E19.
[ORIGIN Latin.]
ANATOMY. = CORD *noun*¹ 3.
chorda tendinea /tɛnˈdɪnɪə/, pl. **-neae** /-nɪiː/, [mod. Latin = tendinous cord] any of the fine cords attaching the borders of the mitral and tricuspid valves of the heart to the papillary muscles.

chordal /ˈkɔːd(ə)l/ *adjective.* E17.
[ORIGIN from CHORD *noun*¹ or *noun*²: see -AL¹.]
Relating to, consisting of or of the nature of, a chord or chords.

C

chordate /ˈkɔːdeɪt/ *adjective & noun.* L19.
[ORIGIN from mod. Latin *Chordata*, from Latin CHORDA: see -ATE¹.]
ZOOLOGY. ▸**A** *adjective.* Of, pertaining to, or characteristic of the phylum Chordata of animals which possess a notochord (for at least some part of their lives). L19.
▸**B** *noun.* A member of this phylum, including all vertebrates, cephalochordates (lancelets), and (usu.) urochordates. E20.

chorded /ˈkɔːdɪd/ *adjective.* L17.
[ORIGIN from CHORD *noun*¹, *noun*², *verb* see -ED², -ED¹.]
Having chords; combined in chords, in harmony.

chordee /ˈkɔːdiː/ *noun.* E18.
[ORIGIN French (*chaudepisse*) *cordée* corded (urethral discharge).]
MEDICINE. (An) abnormal downward curvature of the erect penis.

chordophone /ˈkɔːdəfəʊn/ *noun.* M20.
[ORIGIN formed as CHORDOTONAL + -PHONE.]
Any musical instrument with strings.

chordotonal /kɔːdəʊˈtəʊn(ə)l/ *adjective.* L19.
[ORIGIN from CHORD *noun*² + -O- + TONAL *adjective*.]
ZOOLOGY. Of sense organs in insects: responsive to mechanical vibrations such as sound and bodily movements.

chore /kɔː/ *noun*¹. Long *obsolete* exc. *dial.* OE.
[ORIGIN Latin CHORUS *noun*. Cf. CORE *noun*².]
†**1** = CHOIR *noun* 2. OE–M17.
2 A band, a company; a group. OE.
†**3** A company of dancers or singers; a dance, a chorus. LME–L17.

chore /tʃɔː/ *noun*² & *verb.* Orig. *dial. & US.* M18.
[ORIGIN Unexpl. var. of CHAR *noun*¹.]
▸**A** *noun.* A small piece of domestic work (freq. in *pl.*); an odd job; a recurrent, routine, or tedious task. M18.

F. KIDMAN Sex on an empty stomach is always a bit of a chore.

▸**B** *verb intrans.* Do household work etc.; perform routine tasks. L18.
– COMB.: **chore-boy** *N. Amer.*: employed to do odd jobs.

-chore /kɔː/ *suffix.*
[ORIGIN from Greek *khōrein* to spread.]
BOTANY. Forming nouns denoting plants whose seeds are dispersed in a particular way, as *anemochore*, *hydrochore*.

chorea /kɒˈrɪə/ *noun.* L17.
[ORIGIN Latin from Greek *khoreia* dance.]
MEDICINE. Jerky involuntary movements; a disease with symptoms of this kind.
Huntington's chorea, SYDENHAM'S CHOREA.
■ **choreal** *adjective* = CHOREIC *adjective*¹ M19. **choreic** /kɒˈrɪɪk/ *adjective*¹ pertaining to or affected with chorea L19. **choreiform** /kɒˈrɪɪfɔːm/ *adjective* resembling the symptoms of chorea L19.

choree /kɒˈriː, ˈkɔːriː/ *noun. rare.* L16.
[ORIGIN French *chorée* from Latin *choreus* from Greek *khoreios* pertaining to a dance.]
= TROCHEE.
■ **choˈreic** *adjective*² characterized by trochees L19.

choregraph, **choregrapher** *nouns*, etc., see CHOREOGRAPH *noun* etc.

choregus *noun* var. of CHORAGUS.

choregy /kɒˈriːdʒi, ˈkɒrɪdʒi/ *noun.* M19.
[ORIGIN Greek *khorēgia*, from *khorēgos* CHORAGUS: see -Y³.]
GREEK HISTORY. The function or position of a choragus in ancient Athens.

choreograph /ˈkɒrɪəgrɑːf/ *noun. rare.* Also **choregraph** /ˈkɒrɪgrɑːf/. L19.
[ORIGIN formed as CHOREOGRAPHY + Greek *graphos* writer.]
= CHOREOGRAPHER.

choreograph /ˈkɒrɪəgrɑːf/ *verb.* M20.
[ORIGIN Back-form. from CHOREOGRAPHER.]
1 *verb trans.* Compose the choreography of (a ballet etc.); *fig.* arrange or combine harmoniously or for maximum effect. M20.
2 *verb intrans.* Compose choreography. M20.

choreographer /kɒrɪˈɒgrəfə/ *noun.* Also **choregrapher** /kɒˈrɛgrəfə/. L19.
[ORIGIN formed as CHOREOGRAPHY: see -GRAPHER.]
The creator or arranger of a ballet, stage dance, etc.; a person skilled in choreography.

choreographic /kɒrɪəˈgrafɪk/ *adjective.* Also **choregraphic** /kɒrɪˈgrafɪk/. E19.
[ORIGIN formed as CHOREOGRAPHY + -GRAPHIC.]
1 Of or pertaining to dancing. E19.
2 Of or pertaining to choreography or the devising of ballet or stage dances. E20.

▪ **choreographical** *adjective* L19. **choreographically** *adverb* E20.

choreography /kɒrɪˈɒɡrəfi/ *noun*. Also **choregraphy** /kɒˈrɛɡrəfi/. L18.
[ORIGIN from Greek *khoreia* choral dancing to music + -OGRAPHY.]
1 The written notation of dancing, choreology. L18.
2 The art of dancing. M19.
3 The creation or arrangement of a ballet or stage dance; the devising of steps and figures for a ballet or stage dance; the steps and figures of a particular ballet etc. E20.
▪ **choreographist** *noun* = CHOREOGRAPHER L19.

choreology /kɒrɪˈɒlədʒi/ *noun*. M20.
[ORIGIN formed as CHOREOGRAPHY + -OLOGY.]
The written notation of dancing; the study and description of the movements of dancing.

chorepiscopus /kɔːrɪˈpɪskəpəs/ *noun*. Pl. **-pi** /-pʌɪ, -piː/. L16.
[ORIGIN Late Latin from Greek *khōrepiskopos*, from *khōra*, *khōros* country + *episkopos* BISHOP *noun*.]
ECCLESIASTICAL HISTORY. A country or suffragan bishop of the early Church.
▪ **chorepiscopal** *adjective* of or pertaining to a chorepiscopus M19.

chori- /ˈkɔːri, ˈkɒri/ *combining form* of Greek *khōri*, *khōris* asunder, apart, used in *BOTANY*.
▪ **choriˈpetalous** *adjective* having separate petals L19.

choriamb /ˈkɒrɪam(b)/ *noun*. Also in Latin form **choriambus** /kɒrɪˈambəs/, pl. **-bi** /-bʌɪ/. L18.
[ORIGIN Late Latin *choriambus*, formed as CHOREE + IAMB.]
PROSODY. A metrical foot consisting of two short syllables between two long ones.
▪ **choriˈambic** *noun & adjective* [late Latin *choriambicus*] (*a*) *noun* a choriambic verse, a choriamb; (*b*) *adjective* consisting of a choriamb, containing choriambs: E17.

choric /ˈkɒrɪk, ˈkɔːrɪk/ *noun & adjective*. E19.
[ORIGIN Late Latin *choricus* from Greek *khorikos*, from *khoros* CHORUS *noun*: see -IC. As noun perh. after *heroics* etc.]
▸ **A** *noun*. In *pl*. The verses of a (Greek) chorus. *rare*. E19.
▸ **B** *adjective*. **1** Of, pertaining to, or resembling the chorus in a classical Greek play. M19.
2 Pertaining to a choir or chorus; choral. *rare*. L19.
▪ **chorically** *adverb* M20.

chorine /ˈkɔːriːn/ *noun*. Orig. & chiefly *US*. E20.
[ORIGIN from CHORUS *noun* + -INE³.]
A chorus girl.

chorio- /ˈkɔːrɪəʊ, ˈkɒrɪəʊ/ *combining form* of CHORION, and also occas. of CHOROID: see -O-.
▪ **chorioallanˈtoic** *adjective* of or pertaining to the chorioallantois E20. **chorioaˈllantois** *noun* the chorion and allantois fused together M20.phr: form changed **choriocarciˈnoma** *noun*, pl. **-mas**, **-mata** /-mətə/, = *chorionepithelioma* s.v. CHORION *noun* E20. **chorioretiˈnitis** *noun* = CHOROIDORETINITIS L19.

chorion /ˈkɔːrɪən/ *noun*. M16.
[ORIGIN Greek *khorion*.]
1 *ANATOMY*. The outermost membrane enveloping the fetus in mammals, birds, and reptiles. M16.
2 *ENTOMOLOGY*. The outer covering or shell of an insect's egg. M19.
– COMB.: **chorionepithelioma**, pl. **-mas**, **-mata** /-mətə/, *MEDICINE* a carcinoma of maternal tissue, originating in the chorion.
▪ **choriˈonic** *adjective* of or pertaining to the chorion; ***chorionic gonadotrophin***, a hormone secreted during pregnancy by the placenta which stimulates continued production of progesterone by the ovaries; ***chorionic villus sampling***, a procedure for obtaining information about a fetus in which a sample of tissue is taken from the villi of the chorion (abbreviation ***CVS***): L19.

chorist /ˈkɒrɪst, ˈkɔːrɪst/ *noun*. L15.
[ORIGIN Old French & mod. French *choriste* from medieval Latin *chorista*, formed as CHORUS *noun* + -IST.]
†**1** A member of a choir. L15–M18.
2 *GREEK HISTORY*. A member of the chorus in Greek drama. M18.
3 A person who sings in a chorus. M19.

chorister /ˈkɒrɪstə/ *noun*. LME.
[ORIGIN Anglo-Norman var. of Old French *cueriste*, from *quer* CHOIR; refashioned in 16 after CHORIST.]
A member of a choir, *esp*. a choirboy; *fig*. each of a group of angels, songbirds, etc. Also (*US*), the leader of a choir.
▪ **choristership** *noun* the office of chorister M16.

chorizo /tʃəˈriːzəʊ/ *noun*. Pl. **-os**. M19.
[ORIGIN Spanish.]
A Spanish sausage of which the chief ingredient is pork.

chorizont /kɔːrɪˈzɒnt/ *noun*. Also **C-**. Pl. **-tes** /-tiːz/. M19.
[ORIGIN Greek *khōrizontes* pl. of pres. pple of *khōrizein* to separate.]
hist. A grammarian who ascribed the *Iliad* and the *Odyssey* to different authors; *gen*. anyone ascribing a literary corpus to more than one author.

chorography /kɔːˈrɒɡrəfi/ *noun*¹. Now *rare* or *obsolete*. M16.
[ORIGIN French *chorographie* or Latin *chorographia* from Greek *khōrographia*, from *khōra*, *khōros* country, district: see -GRAPHY.]
The description and mapping of particular regions or districts; a description or delineation, or the natural configuration and features, of such a region.
– NOTE: Taken as intermediate in its scale between ***geography*** and ***topography***.

▪ **chorographer** *noun* E17. **choroˈgraphic** *adjective* L17. **choroˈgraphical** *adjective* L16. **choroˈgraphically** *adverb* L16.

chorography /kɔːˈrɒɡrəfi/ *noun*². Now *rare* or *obsolete*. E18.
[ORIGIN from Greek *khoros* dance + -GRAPHY.]
Dance notation; choreography.

choroid /ˈkɔːrɔɪd, ˈkɒr-/ *noun & adjective*. M17.
[ORIGIN Greek *khoroeidēs* adjective, for *khorioeidēs*, formed as CHORION + -OID.]
ANATOMY. ▸ **A** *noun*. The pigmented vascular layer of the eyeball, situated between the retina and the sclera. M17.
▸ **B** *adjective*. Resembling the chorion; choroidal. M18.
choroid coat, **choroid membrane** = CHOROID *noun*. **choroid plexus** a network of blood vessels in each ventricle of the brain.
▪ **choˈroidal** *adjective* of or pertaining to the choroid of the eye or the choroid plexus of the brain L17. **choroiˈditis** *noun* inflammation of the choroid M19.

choroido- /kəˈrɔɪdəʊ/ *combining form* of prec.: see -O-.
▪ **choroidoretiˈnitis** *noun* inflammation of the choroid and the retina M19.

chorology /kɔːˈrɒlədʒi/ *noun*. L19.
[ORIGIN from Greek *khōra* region + -OLOGY.]
(The knowledge of) the geographical distribution of an animal, plant, etc.
▪ **choroˈlogical** *adjective* M19.

choropleth /ˈkɒrəplɛθ/ *noun*. M20.
[ORIGIN formed as CHOROLOGY + Greek *plēthos* multitude, quantity.]
GEOGRAPHY. A symbol on a choropleth map (see below). Chiefly in ***choropleth map***.
– COMB.: **choropleth map** a map showing the geographical distribution of a property or quantity other than by isopleths, e.g. where an average value over an area is indicated by the way the area is shaded or coloured or by a symbol within the area.

chorten /ˈtʃɔːt(ə)n/ *noun*. L19.
[ORIGIN Tibetan.]
= CHAITYA.

chortle /ˈtʃɔːt(ə)l/ *verb & noun*. L19.
[ORIGIN Invented by Lewis Carroll: app. blend of CHUCKLE *verb* and SNORT *verb*².]
▸ **A** *verb intrans. & trans*. Utter (with) a loud gleeful chuckle; express pleasure or satisfaction in this way. L19.
▸ **B** *noun*. A chuckle of pleasure or satisfaction; an act of chortling. E20.

chorus /ˈkɔːrəs/ *noun*. M16.
[ORIGIN Latin from Greek *khoros*.]
1 a A character in a play whose function is to speak the prologue and epilogue and comment upon events. M16. ▸**b** *GREEK HISTORY*. A band of organized singers and dancers in religious festivals and dramatic performances; *esp*. in Attic tragedy, such a group providing a moral and religious commentary upon events; an utterance of such a group. L16.

> **a** SHAKES. *Hen. V* Admit me Chorus to this history.

b ***Greek chorus***: see GREEK *adjective*.
2 The refrain of a song in which the audience joins the performer in singing; the (repeated) main part of a popular song; a jazz improvisation on this. L16.

> G. DAWSON The chorus . . must be nonsense, or how could you expect the company to join in.

3 A band of singers, a choir; *spec*. in opera, oratorio, etc., the body of vocalists (as opp. to the soloists) who sing the choral parts. M17. ▸**b** A group of organized dancers and usu. singers who provide support for the main roles in musical comedy, variety shows, etc. M19.

> E. LINKLATER Her mother had been one of a chorus of villagers in Cavalleria Rusticana.

4 Anything sung by many at once; the simultaneous utterance of sounds by many persons, animals, etc. L17.

> ARNOLD BENNETT He disappeared amid a wailing chorus of 'Oh, dad!' G. ORWELL Utter silence except for the chorus of the frogs.

dawn chorus: see DAWN *noun*. **in chorus** in unison, all giving utterance together.
5 *MUSIC*. A composition in several (freq. four) parts each sung by several voices. L17.
Hallelujah Chorus: see HALLELUJAH *noun*.
6 (The sound produced by) a group of organ pipes or stops designed to be played together; a compound stop. L18.
– COMB.: **chorus girl** a young woman who sings and dances in the chorus of a musical comedy or the like; **chorus-master** the conductor of a chorus or choir.

chorus /ˈkɔːrəs/ *verb*. Infl. **-s-**, (now *rare*) **-ss-**. E18.
[ORIGIN from the noun.]
1 *verb trans*. Provide with a chorus. E18.
2 *verb trans. & intrans*. Sing, utter, or speak in chorus. M18.

chose /ʃəʊz/ *noun*. LME.
[ORIGIN Old French & mod. French from Latin *causa* matter, affair, thing.]
†**1** A thing (as a vague general term). LME–M17.
2 *LAW*. A thing, a chattel, a piece of property. L17.
chose in action a right enforceable by legal action. **chose in possession** a tangible good capable of being possessed and enjoyed, as a book, item of clothing, etc.

chose *verb pa. t. & pple*: see CHOOSE.

chose jugée /ʃoːz ʒyʒe/ *noun phr*. Pl. **-s -s** (pronounced same). L19.
[ORIGIN French.]
A settled or decided matter; something it is idle to discuss.

chosen /ˈtʃəʊz(ə)n/ *ppl adjective & noun*. ME.
[ORIGIN pa. pple of CHOOSE.]
Taken by preference, selected, picked out; *spec*. (*THEOLOGY*) elect of God. ***the chosen***, ***one's chosen***, a person or (usu.) people chosen, esp. by God.
chosen people, **chosen race** the Jews; *loosely* those specially favoured by God.

choses jugées *noun phr*. pl. of CHOSE JUGÉE.

chota /ˈtʃəʊtə/ *adjective*. *Indian*. E19.
[ORIGIN Hindi *choṭā*.]
Small, little; younger, junior.
chota hazri /ˈhɑːzri/ [Urdu *hāẓirī* breakfast] a light early breakfast. **chota peg** a small drink of whisky.

chott *noun* var. of SHOTT.

chou /ʃuː, *foreign* ʃu/ *noun*¹. Also **choux** (pronounced same). Pl. **choux**. E18.
[ORIGIN French = cabbage from Latin *caulis*.]
1 A small round cake of pastry filled with cream etc. E18.
2 A rosette or ornamental knot of ribbon, chiffon, etc., on a woman's hat or dress. L19.
– COMB.: **choux pastry** a very light pastry enriched with eggs.

Chou *noun*² *& adjective* var. of ZHOU.

Chouan /ʃwɑ̃/ *noun & adjective*. Pl. of noun pronounced same. L18.
[ORIGIN French, from 'Jean Chouan', an early Chouan leader, who used the cry of the *chouan* (dial.), a kind of owl.]
FRENCH HISTORY. A member of, of or pertaining to, the irregular forces who maintained a partisan resistance in the west of France against the Republican and Bonapartist governments; (a) Bourbon partisan.

choucroute /ˈʃuːkruːt, *foreign* ʃukrut/ *noun*. M19.
[ORIGIN French from German dial. *Surkrut* SAUERKRAUT, assim. to French CHOU.]
A kind of pickled cabbage.

chouette /ʃuːˈɛt/ *noun*. L19.
[ORIGIN French, lit. 'barn owl'.]
A player in a two-handed game (e.g. backgammon, piquet) who plays against a number of others successively or in combination, esp. as a means of enabling three players to compete with one another.

chough /tʃʌf/ *noun*. ME.
[ORIGIN Prob. imit.]
1 A jackdaw or related bird. Now *rare* exc. as below. ME.
2 A small crow of the genus *Pyrrhocorax*; *spec*. (*a*) the red-legged, red-billed *P. pyrrhocorax* (orig. called ***Cornish chough***), which in Britain frequents western cliffs; (*b*) ***alpine chough***, a yellow-billed chough, *P. graculus*, inhabiting mountains of Continental Europe and Asia. Also (in full ***white-winged chough***), an E. Australian magpie lark, *Corcorax melanorhamphos*. LME.

choultry /ˈtʃaʊltri/ *noun*. E17.
[ORIGIN from Malayalam *cāvaṭi*, Telugu *cāvaḍi*.]
In the Indian subcontinent: an open shed used as a travellers' rest house; the colonnade of a temple; a meeting house, a court house.

chou moellier /tʃaʊ ˈmɒlɪə/ *noun phr*. *Austral*. & *NZ*. E20.
[ORIGIN French = marrow-filled cabbage.]
= ***marrow-stem*** (***kale***) s.v. MARROW *noun*¹.

chouse /tʃaʊs/ *noun & verb*¹. *slang* (now *arch*. *rare*). Also †**chiaus**, **chowse**. E17.
[ORIGIN App. var. of CHIAUS *noun*, after a Turk who received hospitality in England after claiming to be a messenger or ambassador of the Sultan.]
▸ **A** *noun* **I** †**1** A cheat, a swindler. E–M17.
†**2** A person easily cheated, a dupe. M17–M18.
3 A trick, a swindle, a sham. E18.
▸ †**II 4** = CHIAUS. Only in M17.
▸ **B** *verb trans*. Dupe, trick, swindle; defraud *of*; cheat *out of*. M17.
▪ **chouser** *noun* a swindler, a cheat L19.

chouse /tʃaʊs/ *verb*² *trans*. *US colloq*. Also **chowse**. E20.
[ORIGIN Unknown.]
Disturb, harry (esp. cattle).

chout /tʃaʊt/ *noun*. L17.
[ORIGIN Marathi *cauth* a fourth part.]
hist. In India, the blackmail of a quarter of the revenue exacted from provinces by the Mahrattas.

choux *noun* see CHOU *noun*¹.

chow /tʃaʊ/ *noun*¹. *Scot*. E19.
[ORIGIN Var. of CHEW *noun*: cf. CHAW *noun*².]
An act of chewing; something for chewing, *esp*. a quid of tobacco.

chow /tʃaʊ/ *noun*². L19.
[ORIGIN Abbreviation of CHOW CHOW.]
1 A Chinese person. *slang* (chiefly *Austral.* & *NZ*). *derog.* L19.
2 Food. *slang* (orig. *Pidgin English*). L19.
3 A black-tongued dog of a Chinese breed, resembling a Pomeranian and usu. black or brown. L19.
– COMB.: **chowhound** *US slang* an excessively enthusiastic eater; a glutton.

chow /tʃaʊ/ *verb trans.* & *intrans. dial.* (chiefly *Scot.*). LME.
[ORIGIN Var. of CHEW *verb*: cf. CHAW *verb*.]
Chew.

chowchilla /tʃaʊˈtʃɪlə/ *noun. Austral.* M20.
[ORIGIN Imit. of the birds' calls.]
Either of two logrunners of the genus *Orthonyx*, which have stiffened tail feathers and are found in eastern Australia and New Guinea.

chow chow /ˈtʃaʊtʃaʊ/ *noun* & *adjective*. L18.
[ORIGIN Pidgin English: ult. origin unknown.]
▸ **A** *noun*. **1** A mixture or medley of food, as mixed pickles; *esp.* a Chinese preserve of orange peel, ginger, etc.; *gen.* (*colloq.*) food. L18.
2 = CHOW *noun*² 1. *Austral.* & *NZ slang. derog.* M19.
3 = CHOW *noun*² 3. L19.
▸ **B** *adjective*. Miscellaneous, mixed, assorted; (of water) broken, choppy. M19.

chowder /ˈtʃaʊdə/ *noun* & *verb*. Orig. & chiefly *N. Amer.* M18.
[ORIGIN Uncertain: perh. from French *faire la chaudière* supply a pot etc. for cooking a stew of fish etc. (*chaudière* pot, cauldron).]
▸ **A** *noun*. **1** A stew or thick soup of fish, clams, etc. M18.
2 More fully ***chowder party***. A (large) social gathering, freq. held in the open, at which chowder is cooked and served. E19.
▸ **B** *verb trans.* & *intrans.* Prepare a chowder (of). M18.

chowderhead /ˈtʃaʊdəhɛd/ *noun. colloq.* (chiefly *US*). M19.
[ORIGIN Prob. var. of JOLTER-HEAD.]
A blockhead, a muddle-headed person.
■ **chowderheaded** *adjective* stupid, blockheaded E19.

chowk /tʃaʊk/ *noun*¹. M19.
[ORIGIN Hindi *cauk*.]
In the Indian subcontinent: a city marketplace; a main street.

chowk *noun*² see CHOKE *noun*¹.

chowkidar /ˈtʃəʊkɪdɑː/ *noun*. Also **chauk-**, **chok-** /ˈtʃɒk-/. E17.
[ORIGIN Urdu *chaukīdār*, from Hindi *caukī* CHOKY *noun* + Urdu & Persian *-dār* holding, holder.]
In the Indian subcontinent: a watchman or gatekeeper.

chow mein /tʃaʊ ˈmeɪn/ *noun phr.* L19.
[ORIGIN Chinese *chǎo miàn* fried noodles.]
A Chinese dish of fried noodles usu. in a sauce with shredded meat and vegetables.

chowry /ˈtʃaʊri/ *noun*. Also **chowrie**. L18.
[ORIGIN Hindi *caũrī* from Sanskrit *camara* (tail of) yak.]
A fly whisk made of hair, feathers, or (orig.) the tail of the Tibetan yak.

chowse *noun* & *verb*¹, *verb*² vars. of CHOUSE *noun* & *verb*¹, *verb*².

choya *noun* var. of CHOLLA.

CHP *abbreviation*.
Combined heat and power.

Chr. *abbreviation*.
Chronicles (in the Bible).

chrematistic /kriːməˈtɪstɪk/ *adjective* & *noun*. M18.
[ORIGIN Greek *khrēmatistikos*, from *khrēmatizein* make money, from *khrēma*, *-mat-* money: see -IC.]
▸ **A** *adjective*. Of, pertaining to, or engaged in the accumulation of wealth. M18.
▸ **B** *noun*. In *pl.* (treated as *sing.*). The branch of knowledge that deals with wealth; economics. M19.

chrestomathy /krɛˈstɒməθi/ *noun*. M19.
[ORIGIN French *chrestomathie* or its source Greek *khrēstomatheia*, from *khrēstos* useful + *-matheia* learning.]
A collection of selected passages from an author or authors, *esp.* one compiled to assist in learning a language.
■ **chrestomathic** /krɛstə(ʊ)ˈmaθɪk/ *adjective* devoted to learning useful things E19.

Chrisake *noun* & *interjection* var. of CHRISSAKE.

chrism /ˈkrɪz(ə)m/ *noun*. OE.
[ORIGIN medieval Latin *crisma*, ecclesiastical Latin *chrisma*, from Greek *khrisma*, from *khriein* anoint.]
1 Oil mingled with balm, consecrated for use as an unguent in the administration of certain sacraments of the Christian Churches; an unguent. OE.
2 = CHRISOM 1, 2. OE.
3 A sacramental anointing; unction; *spec.* the ceremony of confirmation, esp. in the Orthodox Church. ME.
■ **chrismal** *adjective* & *noun* (**a**) *adjective* of or pertaining to chrism; (**b**) *noun* a chrisom or similar cloth; a vessel for holding the chrism: M17. **chrismation** /krɪzˈmeɪʃ(ə)n/ *noun* (*obsolete* exc. *hist.*) [medieval Latin *chrismatio(n-)*] application of the chrism, sacramental unction M16.

†**chrism** *verb trans.* LME–L18.
[ORIGIN medieval Latin *chrismare*, formed as CHRISM *noun*.]
Anoint with chrism.

chrismatory /ˈkrɪzmət(ə)ri/ *noun*. LME.
[ORIGIN medieval Latin *chrismatorium*, from *chrisma*, *-mat-* CHRISM *noun*: see -ORY¹.]
CHRISTIAN CHURCH. The vessel containing the chrism.

chrismon /ˈkrɪzmən/ *noun*. L19.
[ORIGIN medieval Latin, from *Christus* CHRIST + *monogramma* MONOGRAM.]
= *CHI-rho*.

chrisom /ˈkrɪz(ə)m/ *noun*. ME.
[ORIGIN Alt. of CHRISM *noun* through its popular pronunc. with two syll.]
1 In full ***chrisom-cloth***, ***chrisom-robe***, etc. A child's white robe at Christian baptism, used as a shroud if he or she died within a month. Now *hist.* ME.
2 In full ***chrisom-child***, ***chrisom-babe***, etc. A child that is less than one month old; a child that died at less than a month, or before baptism; *gen.* an infant, an innocent. ME.
†**3** = CHRISM *noun* 1, 3. LME–E18.

Chrissake /ˈkrʌɪseɪk/ *noun* & *interjection*. *colloq.* Also **Chrisake**. M20.
[ORIGIN Repr. a pronunc.]
Christ's sake; for Christ's sake! (See CHRIST.)

Christ /krʌɪst/ *noun* & *interjection*.
[ORIGIN Old English *Crīst* = Old Saxon, Old High German *Crist*, *Krist* from Latin *Christus* from Greek *Khristos*, use as noun of adjective meaning 'anointed', from *khriein* anoint, translating Hebrew *māšīaḥ* MESSIAH.]
▸ **A** *noun*. **1** The Messiah or Lord's Anointed of Jewish tradition. OE.
2 (The title, now usu. treated as a name, given to) Jesus of Nazareth, regarded by Christians as the fulfilment of Jewish prophecy. OE. ▸**b** An image or picture representing Jesus. M17.
†**3** In the Old Testament [rendering Latin *christus*]: a divinely appointed ruler or high priest. OE–E17.
– PHRASES & COMB.: *babe in Christ*: see BABE 2. ***body of Christ***: see BODY *noun*. **Christ's sake!** *colloq.* = ***for Christ's sake!*** below. **Christ's thorn** any of various thorny shrubs popularly supposed to have formed Jesus's crown of thorns; esp. *Ziziphus spina-christi* and *Paliurus spina-christi*, two shrubs of the buckthorn family. **for Christ's sake!** *colloq.* expr. exasperation, surprise, impatience, etc. ***soldier of Christ***: see SOLDIER *noun*. **the Christ child** Jesus as a child.
▸ **B** *interjection*. Expr. surprise, dismay, disbelief, etc. *colloq.* M18.
■ **Christed** *adjective* made one with Christ; made a partaker of Christ's nature: M17. **Christhood** *noun* the state or condition of being Christ LME. **Christless** *adjective* without Christ or his spirit M17. **Christlike** *adjective* resembling Christ; exhibiting the personal or spiritual qualities of Jesus: L17. **Christlikeness** *noun* L19. **Christly** *adjective* (**a**) Christlike; (**b**) *rare* of or pertaining to Christ: OE.

Christadelphian /krɪstəˈdɛlfɪən/ *adjective* & *noun*. M19.
[ORIGIN from late Greek *Khristadelphos* in brotherhood with Christ, from *Khristos* CHRIST + *adelphos* brother: see -IAN.]
Designating or pertaining to, a member of, a religious sect founded in the US, rejecting the Christian doctrine of the Trinity and expecting the Second Coming of Christ.

Christ-cross /ˈkrɪskrɒs, -krɔːs/ *noun*. See also CRISS-CROSS *noun*. LME.
[ORIGIN from *Christ's cross*.]
1 The figure of a cross (✠) in front of the alphabet in a hornbook. *obsolete* exc. *hist.* LME.
2 In full ***Christ-cross-row***. The alphabet. Now *arch.* & *dial.* M16.
3 The mark of a cross in general; *esp.* one used as a signature by an illiterate. Now *dial.* or *hist.* E17.

christen /ˈkrɪst(ə)n/ *adjective* & *noun*. Long *obsolete* exc. *dial.*
[ORIGIN Old English *crīsten* = Old Saxon, Old High German *kristin* from Latin *christianus* CHRISTIAN *adjective*.]
(A) Christian.

christen /ˈkrɪs(ə)n/ *verb trans.*
[ORIGIN Old English *crīstnian*, formed as CHRISTEN *adjective* & *noun*.]
1 Convert to Christianity; make Christian. Now *obsolete* or *arch.* OE.
2 Admit to the Christian Church by baptism; administer baptism to. ME.
3 Give a name to at baptism; name and dedicate (a bell, a ship, etc.) by a ceremony analogous to baptism; *gen.* give a name to. Freq. with compl.: give as a name at baptism; call by the name of. LME. ▸†**b** Stand as sponsor to at baptism. L15–M17.

P. NORMAN Both of Nanny Belmayne's sons were christened with very long names. Q. CRISP It has now been christened the New End Theatre. A. BLEASDALE He was christened here in this very Church as Patrick.

4 Use for the first time; soil etc. through use for the first time. *colloq.* E20.
■ **christener** *noun* a person who performs a christening or christenings OE. **christening** *verbal noun* (**a**) the action of the verb; (**b**) an instance of this; a ceremony of baptism: ME.

christendie /ˈkrɪs(ə)ndi/ *noun. Scot.* L18.
[ORIGIN App. from CHRISTIANITY, infl. by CHRISTENDOM.]
Christendom.

Christendom /ˈkrɪs(ə)ndəm/ *noun*. OE.
[ORIGIN from CHRISTEN *adjective* & *noun* + -DOM.]
†**1** The state or condition of being a Christian. OE–L17.
†**2** The Christian faith or religious system; Christianity. OE–M17.
3 Christians collectively; the Christian Church. OE. ▸**b** The nations professing Christianity collectively; the Christian domain. LME.
†**4** Baptism, christening; the giving of a name. ME–L17.

C

Christer /ˈkrʌɪstə/ *noun. N. Amer. slang.* E20.
[ORIGIN from CHRIST + -ER¹.]
An excessively zealous, pious, or sanctimonious person.

Christian /ˈkrɪstʃ(ə)n, -tɪən, *in sense 1b also* ˈkrʌɪstʃ(ə)n/ *noun*. E16.
[ORIGIN from the adjective.]
1 A member of the religion of Christ; an adherent of Christianity. E16. ▸**b** A member of a particular sect using this name. E19.
Bible Christian: see BIBLE. ***Liberal Christian***: see LIBERAL *adjective*. MUSCULAR ***Christian***.
2 A person who follows the precepts and example of Christ; a person of genuine piety. E16.
3 A (civilized) human being; a decent, respectable person. Now *colloq.* L16.
4 A variety of pear or plum. Now *rare* or *obsolete*. M17.
■ **Christianlike** *adjective* & *adverb* (in a manner) proper to or befitting a Christian L16.

Christian /ˈkrɪstʃ(ə)n, -tɪən/ *adjective*. LME.
[ORIGIN Latin *Christianus*, from *Christus* CHRIST: see -IAN.]
1 Of a person, community, etc.: believing in, professing, or belonging to the religion of Christ. LME.
2 Of a thing: pertaining to Christ or his religion; of or belonging to Christianity. M16.
3 Showing a character consistent with Christ's teaching; of genuine piety; Christlike. L16.
4 Of or belonging to a Christian or Christians. L16.
5 Civilized, decent. Now *colloq.* L16.
– SPECIAL COLLOCATIONS & COMB.: ***Christian antiquity***: see ANTIQUITY 1. ***Christian Brethren***: see BROTHER *noun*. **Christian burial** burial according to the ceremonies of the Christian Church. **Christian Democrat** a member of any of various moderate European political parties having a Roman Catholic base. **Christian Democratic** *adjective* designating, of or pertaining to, a party of Christian Democrats. **Christian era**: reckoned from the birth of Jesus. **Christian name** a name given (as) at baptism, a forename, a personal name. **Christian Science** the beliefs and practices of 'The Church of Christ, Scientist', a Christian body founded in the mid 19th cent. by Mary Baker Eddy in New Hampshire, USA, which holds that God and his perfect spiritual creation are the only ultimate reality, and that his law is always available to bring regeneration and healing to humanity. **Christian Scientist** an adherent of Christian Science. **Christian Socialism** a form of socialism, embracing Christianity, arising from an attempt to apply Christian precepts in everyday life. **Christian Socialist** an adherent of Christian Socialism. ***Christian year***: see YEAR *noun*¹ 3b. **Court Christian** (*obsolete* exc. *hist.*) an ecclesiastical court.
■ **Christianable** *adjective* (*colloq.*) [irreg.] fit to be or befitting a Christian L19. **Christianly** *adjective* & *adverb* (**a**) *adjective* characteristic of or befitting a Christian; (**b**) *adverb* in a Christianly manner: LME.

Christiania /krɪstɪˈɑːnɪə/ *noun*. Also **c-**. E20.
[ORIGIN Former name of Oslo, capital of Norway.]
A turn in skiing in which the skis are kept in parallel, used for stopping short.

Christianise *verb* var. of CHRISTIANIZE.

Christianism /ˈkrɪstʃ(ə)nɪz(ə)m, -tɪən-/ *noun*. L16.
[ORIGIN French *christianisme* or ecclesiastical Latin *christianismus* from Greek *khristianismos* Christianity: see -ISM.]
1 Christian belief, Christianity (chiefly when compared with other 'isms'). L16.
2 Christianity of a sort. L17.

Christianity /krɪstɪˈanɪti/ *noun*. ME.
[ORIGIN Old French *crestienté* (mod. *chrétienté*), from *crestien* CHRISTIAN *adjective*, assim. to late Latin *christianitas*: see -ITY.]
†**1** = CHRISTENDOM 3. ME–M17.
2 The Christian faith; the doctrines of Christ and his disciples. ME.
3 The state or fact of being Christian; Christian quality or character. ME.
MUSCULAR ***Christianity***.
4 *hist.* Ecclesiastical jurisdiction. L16.

Christianize /ˈkrɪstʃənʌɪz, -tɪən-/ *verb*. Also **-ise**. M16.
[ORIGIN from CHRISTIAN *adjective* + -IZE.]
1 *verb trans.* Make Christian; give a Christian character to. M16.
2 *verb intrans.* Become Christian; act according to Christianity. M16.
■ **Christiani'zation** *noun* L18.

Christiano- /krɪstɪˈɑːnəʊ/ *combining form* of Latin *Christianus* CHRISTIAN *adjective*: see -O-.

Christie /ˈkrɪsti/ *noun*. Also **-ty**. E20.
[ORIGIN Abbreviation.]
= CHRISTIANIA.

Christingle /ˈkrɪstɪŋɡ(ə)l/ *noun*. M20.
[ORIGIN Prob. alt. of German *Christkindl* Christmas present, (colloq.) Christ-child, after KRISS KRINGLE.]
CHRISTIAN CHURCH. A lighted candle set in an orange, symbolizing Christ as the light of the world, given to each child at a special children's Advent service (the ***Christingle service***) of a kind adopted from the Moravian Church.

C

Christmas /ˈkrɪsməs/ *noun & interjection*.
[ORIGIN Old English *Cristes mæsse* the mass of Christ.]
▸ **A** *noun*. The festival of Christ's birth celebrated by most Christian Churches on 25 December (one of the quarter days in England, Wales, and Ireland), devoted esp. to family reunion and jollification; the season around this date. OE.
Father Christmas Santa Claus; a jolly old man dressed in red, personifying Christmas festivities. ***merry Christmas***: see MERRY *adjective*. ***white Christmas***: see WHITE *adjective*.
– COMB.: **Christmas box** a small present or gratuity given at Christmas esp. to employees of firms providing regular services; **Christmas bush** (chiefly *Austral.*) any of various shrubs; esp. *Ceratopetalum gummiferum*, of the family Cunoniaceae, which bears decorative fruit at Christmas time; **Christmas cactus** a succulent S. American plant, *Schlumbergera bridgesii*, with red, pink, or white flowers, grown as a house plant and typically flowering in the northern midwinter; **Christmas card** a greetings card sent at or just before Christmas; ***Christmas carol***: see CAROL *noun* 3; **Christmas Day** 25 December; **Christmas Eve** (the evening of) 24 December; **Christmas flower** any of various plants flowering at Christmas time; *esp.* = ***Christmas rose*** below; **Christmas present** a gift given at Christmas; **Christmas pudding** a plum pudding eaten at Christmas; **Christmas rose** a hellebore, *Helleborus niger*, bearing white flowers in winter; **Christmas shopping**: for Christmas presents and seasonal fare; **Christmas stocking**: hung up by children on Christmas Eve for Father Christmas to fill with presents; **Christmastide**, **Christmas time** the period of some days around 25 December; **Christmas tree** (***a***) an evergreen tree (usu. a Norway spruce) or artificial tree set up indoors or in the open at Christmas time and hung with lights, presents, baubles, etc.; (***b***) *Austral. & NZ*, any of various trees or shrubs blooming at Christmas time; *esp.* = POHUTUKAWA; (***c***) a device or structure suggesting a Christmas tree in appearance; *spec.* a valve manifold situated on the casing of an oil or gas well (= TREE *noun* 7(d)).
▸ **B** *interjection*. [Alt. of *Christ*.] Expr. surprise, dismay, exasperation, etc. Freq. as ***Jiminy Christmas***. L19.
■ **Christmassy** *adjective* (*colloq.*) characteristic of or suitable for Christmas (festivities) L19.

Christmas /ˈkrɪsməs/ *verb*. *colloq.* Infl. **-s-**, **-ss-**. L16.
[ORIGIN from the noun.]
†**1** *verb trans.* Provide with Christmas cheer. *rare*. Only in L16.
2 *verb intrans.* Celebrate Christmas. E19.

Christmas disease /ˈkrɪsməs dɪˌziːz/ *noun phr*. M20.
[ORIGIN from Stephen *Christmas*, 20th-cent. English sufferer from the disease.]
MEDICINE. = ***HAEMOPHILIA B***.

Christo- /ˈkrɪstəʊ/ *combining form* of Latin *Christus* or Greek *Khristos* CHRIST: see **-O-**.
■ **Christoˈcentric** *adjective* having Christ as its centre L19. **Christocenˈtricity**, **Christoˈcentrism** *nouns* the state or condition of being Christocentric E20. **Christophany** /krɪˈstɒfəni/ *noun* a manifestation of Christ, esp. after the Resurrection M19.

Christology /krɪˈstɒlədʒi/ *noun*. L17.
[ORIGIN from CHRISTO- + -LOGY.]
That part of Christian theology dealing specifically with Christ; a doctrine or theory concerning Christ.
■ **Christoˈlogical** *adjective* M19. **Christologist** *noun* E19.

Christy *noun* var. of CHRISTIE.

chrom- /krəʊm/ *combining form* of CHROMIUM, used esp. in names of minerals (cf. CHROMO-).

chroma /ˈkrəʊmə/ *noun*. L19.
[ORIGIN Greek *khrōma* colour.]
Purity or intensity as a colour quality, esp. in colour television etc.

chromaffin /krə(ʊ)ˈmafɪn/ *adjective*. E20.
[ORIGIN from CHROMO- + Latin *affinis* akin.]
HISTOLOGY. Stained brown by chromates; *spec.* designating hormone-secreting granules in the adrenal medulla.

chromakey /ˈkrəʊməkiː/ *noun & verb*. M20.
[ORIGIN from CHROMA + KEY *noun*[1] or *verb*.]
▸ **A** *noun*. A technique by which a block of a particular colour in a video image can be replaced either by another colour or by a separate image, enabling, for example, a TV presenter to appear against a computer-generated background. M20.
▸ **B** *verb trans.* Manipulate (an image) using this technique. L20.

-chromasia /krəˈmeɪzɪə/ *suffix*.
[ORIGIN from CHROMO- + *-asia* mod. Latin ending on Greek model (cf. *-plasia*, *-stasia*, etc.) for nouns with a stem *-at-*: see -IA[1].]
MEDICINE & BIOLOGY. Forming nouns denoting a condition or property to do with colour, as ***hyperchromasia***.

-chromasy /ˈkrəʊməsi/ *suffix*.
[ORIGIN Anglicization.]
= -CHROMASIA.

chromat- *combining form* see CHROMATO-.

chromate /ˈkrəʊmeɪt/ *noun*. E19.
[ORIGIN from CHROMIC *adjective* + -ATE[1].]
CHEMISTRY. A salt of chromic acid.

chromatic /krə(ʊ)ˈmatɪk/ *noun & adjective*. LME.
[ORIGIN French *chromatique* or Latin *chromaticus* from Greek *khrōmatikos*, from *khrōma*, *-mat-* colour: see -IC.]
▸ **A** *noun*. †**1** A person who preserves his 'colour'; a person who is dyed-in-the-wool. Only in LME.
†**2** The art of colouring in painting. L17–M18.
3 MUSIC. In *pl.* Chromatic notes, harmonies, etc. E18.
4 In *pl.* (treated as *sing.*). The science of colour. L18.
▸ **B** *adjective*. **1** MUSIC. Orig. (*hist.*), designating one of three kinds of tetrachord in ancient Greek music, based on the intervals semitone, semitone, minor third. In modern music, designating, pertaining to, or including notes not belonging to the diatonic scale; (of an instrument) capable of producing (nearly) all the tones of the chromatic scale; (habitually) employing chromaticism. E17.
chromatic alteration: raising or lowering the pitch of a note. **chromatic scale**: proceeding by semitones. **chromatic semitone** the interval between a note and its sharp or flat.
2 Of or produced by colour. M19.
chromatic aberration: see ABERRATION *noun* 2.
3 Brightly coloured, colourful. M19.
■ **chromatically** *adverb* L18. **chromaticism** /-sɪz(ə)m/ *noun* (an instance of) the use of chromatic expressions, modulations, or harmonies in music L19. **chromaticity** /krəʊməˈtɪsɪti/ *noun* quality of colour determined independently of brightness E20.

chromatid /ˈkrəʊmətɪd/ *noun*. E20.
[ORIGIN from Greek *khrōma*, *-mat-* colour + -ID[2].]
BIOLOGY. Either of the two strands into which a chromosome divides longitudinally during cell division.

chromatin /ˈkrəʊmətɪn/ *noun*. L19.
[ORIGIN formed as CHROMATID + -IN[1].]
BIOLOGY. The readily stained material of the cell nucleus, consisting of DNA and protein (and RNA at certain times).

chromatism /ˈkrəʊmətɪz(ə)m/ *noun*. E18.
[ORIGIN Greek *khrōmatismos*, formed as CHROMATID + -ISM.]
1 Natural colouring. Now *rare* or *obsolete*. E18.
2 Chromatic aberration. M19.
3 Hallucinatory perception of colour. E20.

chromato- /ˈkrəʊmətəʊ/ *combining form* of Greek *khrōma*, *-mat-* colour: see **-O-**. Before a vowel **chromat-**. Cf. CHROMO-.
■ **chromatolysis** /-ˈtɒlɪsɪs/ *noun* (BIOLOGY) the solution and disintegration of the chromatin of cell nuclei L19. **chromatophore** *noun* (BIOLOGY) a cell or plastid containing pigment M19. **chromatoˈphoric** *adjective* (BIOLOGY) of or pertaining to a chromatophore L19. **chromaˈtopsia** *noun* (MEDICINE) abnormally coloured vision M19.

chromatogram /krəˈmatəɡram/ *noun*. M20.
[ORIGIN from CHROMATO- + -GRAM.]
A visible record of the result of a chromatographic separation.
paper chromatogram: see PAPER *noun & adjective*.

chromatograph /krəˈmatəɡrɑːf/ *verb & noun*. M19.
[ORIGIN from CHROMATO- + -GRAPH.]
▸ **A** *verb trans.* †**1** Represent in colours. *rare*. Only in M19.
2 Separate or analyse by chromatography. M20.
▸ **B** *noun*. An apparatus for chromatographic separation. M20.
■ **chromatographer** /krəʊməˈtɒɡrəfə/ *noun* a person who performs chromatography M20.

chromatography /krəʊməˈtɒɡrəfi/ *noun*. M18.
[ORIGIN from CHROMATO- + -GRAPHY: sense 2 from German *Chromatographie*.]
1 The description of colours. Now *rare* or *obsolete*. M18.
2 Any of various methods of chemical separation or analysis which depend on the different rates of passage of the components of a mixture through a sorbent medium (the sample being dissolved in a solvent or carried in a gas). M20.
paper chromatography: see PAPER *noun & adjective*.
– NOTE: So named because in the earliest chromatographic separations the result was displayed as a number of coloured bands or spots.
■ **chromatographic** /krəʊmətəˈɡrafɪk/ *adjective* of, pertaining to, or involving chromatography E20. **chromatoˈgraphical** *adjective* = CHROMATOGRAPHIC M20. **chromatoˈgraphically** *adverb* M20.

chromatoid /ˈkrəʊmətɔɪd/ *adjective*. E20.
[ORIGIN from CHROMATIN + -OID.]
BIOLOGY. Resembling chromatin in staining readily.

chromatology /krəʊməˈtɒlədʒi/ *noun*. *rare*. E19.
[ORIGIN from CHROMATO- + -LOGY.]
The science of colours.

chrome /krəʊm/ *noun & verb*. E19.
[ORIGIN French from Greek *khrōma* colour: so named from the brilliant colours of its compounds.]
▸ **A** *noun*. **1** Chromium; *esp.* chromium plate. E19.
2 A chromate or other chromium compound used in tanning or dyeing, or as a pigment. Also *ellipt.*, chrome leather. L19.
Oxford chrome: see OXFORD *adjective*.
– COMB.: ***chrome alum***: see ALUM *noun* 2; **chrome green** (***a***) chromium(III) oxide, Cr_2O_3, as a pigment; (***b***) a mixture of Prussian blue and chrome yellow (or sometimes cadmium yellow), used as a pigment (also called ***zinnober green***); **chrome leather** leather tanned with chromium compounds; **chrome moly** a strong steel alloy made principally of chrome and molybdenum; **chrome steel** a hard, fine-grained steel containing chromium; **chrome tanning** tanning of hides by immersion in acid solutions of chromates; **chrome yellow** lead chromate, $PbCrO_4$, used as a bright yellow pigment.
▸ **B** *verb trans.* (Chiefly as ***chromed ppl adjective*** or ***chroming verbal noun***.)
1 Treat (textiles, hides) with a chromium compound. L19.
2 Electroplate with chromium. M20.

chromic /ˈkrəʊmɪk/ *adjective*. E19.
[ORIGIN from CHROME + -IC.]
CHEMISTRY. Of or containing chromium, esp. in a higher valency (cf. CHROMOUS).
chromic acid a strongly oxidizing acid, H_2CrO_4, present in aqueous solutions of chromium(VI) oxide; this oxide itself. **chromic anhydride** chromium(VI) oxide, CrO_3, a dark red crystalline solid with powerful oxidizing properties. **chromic oxide** chromium(III) oxide, Cr_2O_3, a green amphoteric solid.

chrominance /ˈkrəʊmɪn(ə)ns/ *noun*. M20.
[ORIGIN from CHROMO- after *luminance*.]
In colour television, the colorimetric difference between a given colour and a standard colour of equal luminance.

chromite /ˈkrəʊmʌɪt/ *noun*. M19.
[ORIGIN from CHROME or CHROMIUM + -ITE[1].]
1 CHEMISTRY. A compound formed by reaction of chromium(III) oxide with a base. M19.
2 MINERALOGY. The major ore of chromium, a black oxide of chromium and ferrous iron that crystallizes in the cubic system but usu. occurs in massive form. M19.

chromium /ˈkrəʊmɪəm/ *noun*. E19.
[ORIGIN from CHROME + -IUM.]
A hard white lustrous metal which is a chemical element of the transition series, atomic no. 24, and is much used in alloys and corrosion-resistant coatings (symbol Cr).
– COMB.: **chromium-plate** *noun & verb* (***a***) *noun* an electrolytically deposited protective or decorative coating of chromium; (***b***) *verb trans.* electroplate with chromium; *fig.* embellish pretentiously or tastelessly.

chromo /ˈkrəʊməʊ/ *noun*[1]. *colloq.* (now chiefly *hist.*). Pl. **-os**. M19.
[ORIGIN Abbreviation.]
= CHROMOLITHOGRAPH *noun*.

chromo /ˈkrəʊməʊ/ *noun*[2]. *Austral. slang*. Pl. **-os**. L19.
[ORIGIN Prob. fig. use of CHROMO *noun*[1].]
A prostitute.

chromo- /ˈkrəʊməʊ/ *combining form* of Greek *khrōma* colour, or, less commonly, of CHROMIUM: see **-O-**.
■ **chromodyˈnamics** *noun* (PARTICLE PHYSICS) (more fully ***quantum chromodynamics***) a quantum field theory in which the strong interaction is described in terms of an interaction between quarks mediated by gluons, both quarks and gluons being assigned a quantum number called 'colour' L20. **chromogen** *noun* (CHEMISTRY) a substance which can be converted to a dyestuff by the introduction of a polar group M19. **chromoˈgenic** *adjective* colour-forming L19. **chromophil(e)** *adjective & noun* (HISTOLOGY) (a cell) that is readily stained L19. **chromoˈphilic** *adjective* (HISTOLOGY) readily stained L19. **chromophobe** *adjective & noun* (HISTOLOGY) (a cell) that is not readily stained E20. **chromoˈphobic** *adjective* (HISTOLOGY) not readily stained L19. **chromophore** *noun* (CHEMISTRY) that part of the molecule which is responsible for a compound's colour L19. **chromoˈphoric** *adjective* (CHEMISTRY) responsible for a compound's colour L19. **chromoˈprotein** *noun* (BIOCHEMISTRY) a compound consisting of a protein bound to a metal-containing pigment or a carotenoid E20.

chromolithograph /krəʊməʊˈlɪθəɡrɑːf/ *noun & verb*. M19.
[ORIGIN from CHROMO- + LITHOGRAPH *noun*, *verb*.]
Chiefly *hist.* ▸**A** *noun*. An image printed in colours by lithography and produced by hand separation of the colours. M19.
▸ **B** *verb trans.* Print in colours in this way. M19.
■ **chromoliˈthographer** *noun* M19. **chromolithoˈgraphic** *adjective* M19. **chromoliˈthography** *noun* M19.

chromone /ˈkrəʊməʊn/ *noun*. E20.
[ORIGIN from CHROMO- + -ONE.]
CHEMISTRY. A bicyclic ketone, $C_9H_6O_2$, e.g. coumarin; any derivative of this.

chromoplast /ˈkrəʊməplast, -plɑːst/ *noun*. E20.
[ORIGIN from CHROMO- + -PLAST.]
BOTANY. A coloured plastid other than a chloroplast, typically containing a yellow or orange pigment.
■ Also **chromoˈplastid** *noun* L19.

chromosome /ˈkrəʊməsəʊm/ *noun*. L19.
[ORIGIN German *Chromosom*: see CHROMO-, -SOME[3].]
BIOLOGY. A threadlike structure of nucleic acids and protein which carries a set of linked genes and occurs singly in prokaryotes and in characteristic numbers, usu. paired, in the cell nuclei of higher organisms.
PHILADELPHIA ***chromosome***.
– COMB.: **chromosome number** the characteristic number of chromosomes found in the cell nuclei of organisms of a particular species.
■ **chromoˈsomal** *adjective* of, pertaining to, or involving chromosomes E20. **chromoˈsomally** *adverb* as regards chromosomes, by means of chromosomes E20.

chromosphere /ˈkrəʊməsfɪə/ *noun*. M19.
[ORIGIN from CHROMO- + -SPHERE.]
ASTRONOMY. The reddish transparent gaseous envelope surrounding the photosphere of the sun or another star.
■ **chromoˈspheric** *adjective* M19.

chromous /ˈkrəʊməs/ *adjective*. M19.
[ORIGIN from CHROMIUM + -OUS.]
CHEMISTRY. Of divalent chromium. Cf. CHROMIC.

chromyl /ˈkrəʊmʌɪl, -mɪl/ *noun*. M19.
[ORIGIN from CHROM- + -YL.]
CHEMISTRY. The divalent radical :CrO_2. Usu. in *comb.*

Chron. *abbreviation*.
Chronicles (in the Bible).

chronal /ˈkrəʊn(ə)l/ *adjective*. L19.
[ORIGIN from Greek *khronos* time + -AL[1].]
Of or pertaining to time.

chronic /ˈkrɒnɪk/ *adjective & noun*. LME.
[ORIGIN French *chronique* from Latin *chronicus* from Greek *khronikos* of or pertaining to time, from *khronos* time: see -IC.]
▸ **A** *adjective*. **1** Of a disease etc.: lingering, lasting; of slow progression and often gradual onset. Cf. ***acute***. LME. ▸**b** Of an invalid: suffering from a chronic illness. M19.
chronic fatigue syndrome a medical condition of unknown cause, with fever, aching, and prolonged tiredness and depression, typically occurring after a viral infection (abbreviation ***CFS***; also called ***ME***).
2 *gen.* Continuous, constant, inveterate. M19.

J. S. MILL A state of chronic revolution and civil war. J. BUCHAN There was a chronic inaccuracy in him which vexed his father's soul.

3 Bad, intense, severe. *colloq.* E20.
something chronic *adverbial phr.* severely, badly.
▸ **B** *ellipt.* as *noun*. A chronic invalid, sufferer, etc. M19.
■ **chronicity** /krəˈnɪsɪti/ *noun* chronic quality or condition M19.

chronical /ˈkrɒnɪk(ə)l/ *adjective*. M16.
[ORIGIN formed as CHRONIC + -AL[1].]
†**1** Of or relating to verbal tense. Only in M16.
2 = CHRONIC *adjective* 1, 2. E17.
3 Of, pertaining to, or regulated by time. M17.
■ **chronically** *adverb* †(*a*) with regard to time; (*b*) in a chronic manner, inveterately, for a long period: M16.

chronicle /ˈkrɒnɪk(ə)l/ *noun & verb*. ME.
[ORIGIN Anglo-Norman *cronicle* var. of Old French *cronique* (mod. *chronique*) from Latin *chronica* from Greek *khronika* annals.]
▸ **A** *noun*. **1** A detailed and continuous record of events in order of time; a historical record in which facts are related usu. without interpretation etc. In *pl.* (treated as *sing.*) (**C-**), either of two historical books of the Old Testament and Hebrew Scriptures. ME.
2 A record, a register; a narrative, an account. Freq. in titles of newspapers. LME.

E. WAUGH Do realize that a letter need not be a bald chronicle of events.

– COMB.: **chronicle drama** drama, a play, based on historical accounts; **chronicle history** *arch.* a chronicle drama.
▸ **B** *verb trans.* Enter in a chronicle; put on record, register. LME.
■ **chronicler** *noun* a person who writes or compiles chronicles; a recorder of events: LME.

chronique /ˈkrɒniːk; *foreign* krɔnik (*pl. same*)/ *noun*. LME.
[ORIGIN Old French *cronique*: see CHRONICLE.]
A chronicle.

chronique scandaleuse /krɔnik skɑ̃daløːz/ *noun phr.* Pl. **-s -s** (pronounced same). M19.
[ORIGIN French.]
A compilation or body of gossip, scandal, etc.

chrono- /ˈkrɒnəʊ/ *combining form* of Greek *khronos* time: see -O-.
■ **chronobioˈlogic** *adjective* = CHRONOBIOLOGICAL M20. **chronobioˈlogical** *adjective* of or pertaining to chronobiology L20. **chronobiˈology** *noun* the biology of cyclical physiological phenomena M20. **chronostratiˈgraphic**, **chronostratiˈgraphical** *adjectives* of or pertaining to chronostratigraphy M20. **chronostraˈtigraphy** *noun* (*GEOLOGY*) the branch of stratigraphy that deals with the absolute ages of strata M20. **chronoˈtherapy** *noun* (*MEDICINE*) the treatment of an illness or disorder by administering a drug at a time of day believed to be in harmony with the body's natural rhythms L20. **chronotropic** /-ˈtrəʊpɪk, -ˈtrɒpɪk/ *adjective* (*PHYSIOLOGY*) affecting the rate at which the heart beats M20.

chronogram /ˈkrɒnəgram/ *noun*. E17.
[ORIGIN from CHRONO- + -GRAM.]
A phrase etc. of which the roman-numeral letters express a date when added together (e.g. LorD haVe MerCIe Vpon Vs = 50 + 500 + 5 + 1000 + 100 + 1 + 5 + 5 = 1666).
■ **chronograˈmmatic** *adjective* of or pertaining to chronograms; of the nature of a chronogram: M18. **chronograˈmmatical** *adjective* (now *rare* or *obsolete*) = CHRONOGRAMMATIC M17.

chronograph /ˈkrɒnəgrɑːf/ *noun*. M17.
[ORIGIN from CHRONO- + -GRAPH.]
1 = CHRONOGRAM Now *rare* or *obsolete*. M17.
2 An instrument for recording time with considerable accuracy; a stopwatch. M19.

chronographic /krɒnəˈgrafɪk/ *adjective*. M19.
[ORIGIN formed as CHRONOGRAPH + -IC.]
Of or pertaining to a chronograph or chronography.
■ **chronographical** *adjective* = CHRONOGRAPHIC L16. **chronographically** *adverb* M19.

chronography /krəˈnɒgrəfi/ *noun*. M16.
[ORIGIN Late Latin *chronographia* from Greek *khronographia*, formed as CHRONO- + -GRAPHY.]
A chronological description or arrangement of past events. Also, chronology.
■ **chronographer** *noun* a chronicler, a chronologist M16.

chronological /krɒnəˈlɒdʒɪk(ə)l/ *adjective*. E17.
[ORIGIN from CHRONOLOGY + -ICAL.]
Of, pertaining to, relating to, or dealing with chronology; in accordance with chronology; arranged in order of time.
■ **chronologic** *adjective* = CHRONOLOGICAL E17. **chronologically** *adverb* L17.

chronology /krəˈnɒlədʒi/ *noun*. L16.
[ORIGIN mod. Latin *chronologia*, formed as CHRONO- + -LOGY.]
1 The science of computing dates; the arrangement of events according to dates or times of occurrence. L16.

R. CUDWORTH If Chronology had not contradicted it, it would have been concluded, that he had been an Auditour of Pythagoras himself. C. S. LEWIS The chronology of this disaster is a little vague, but I know . . that it had not begun when I went there and that the process was complete very shortly after I left.

2 A chronological table, list, or treatise. E17.
■ **chronologer** *noun* = CHRONOLOGIST L16. **chronologist** *noun* a person versed in chronology, a person who investigates the dates of events E17. **chronologize** *verb trans.* †(*a*) chronicle, record; (*b*) apply chronology to, arrange chronologically: E17.

chronometer /krəˈnɒmɪtə/ *noun*. E18.
[ORIGIN from CHRONO- + -METER.]
†**1** *MUSIC*. = METRONOME. E18–M19.
2 An instrument for measuring time; *esp.* one designed to keep accurate time at all temperatures etc. and to be used at sea in determining longitude etc. by astronomical observation. E18.

chronometry /krəˈnɒmɪtri/ *noun*. M19.
[ORIGIN formed as CHRONOMETER + -METRY.]
(The science of) the accurate measurement of time.
■ **chronoˈmetric**, **chronoˈmetrical** *adjectives* of or pertaining to chronometry; relating to the measurement of time: M19. **chronoˈmetrically** *adverb* M19.

chronoscope /ˈkrɒnəskəʊp/ *noun*. E18.
[ORIGIN formed as CHRONOMETER + -SCOPE.]
A device for measuring (short) time intervals, esp. in determining (*a*) the velocity of projectiles, or (*b*) a person's reaction time.

†**chrony** *noun & verb* var. of CRONY.

chrys- *combining form* see CHRYSO-.

chrysalid /ˈkrɪs(ə)lɪd/ *noun & adjective*. L18.
[ORIGIN formed as CHRYSALIS.]
▸ **A** *noun*. A chrysalis. L18.
▸ **B** *adjective*. Of or pertaining to a chrysalis. E19.

chrysalides *noun pl.* see CHRYSALIS.

chrysalis /ˈkrɪs(ə)lɪs/ *noun*. Pl. **-ises** /-ɪsɪz/, (now *rare*) **-ides** /-ɪdiːz/. E17.
[ORIGIN Latin *chrysal(l)is*, *-id-* from Greek *khrūsallis*, from *khrūsos* gold.]
A pupa, esp. of a butterfly or moth; the hard sheath of this. Also *fig.*, a quiescent transitional form.
■ **chrysaline** *adjective* of, pertaining to, or of the nature of a chrysalis L18. **chrysalize** *verb intrans. & refl.* (*rare*) become a chrysalis; pupate: E19. **chrysaloid** *adjective* resembling a chrysalis E19.

chrysanth /krɪˈsanθ, -z-/ *noun*. *colloq.* E20.
[ORIGIN Abbreviation.]
= CHRYSANTHEMUM.

chrysanthemum /krɪˈsanθɪməm, -z-/ *noun*. M16.
[ORIGIN Latin *chrysanthemum* from Greek *khrūsanthemon*, formed as CHRYSO- + *anthemon* flower.]
Any plant of the large genus *Chrysanthemum*, of the composite family. Orig. *spec.* the corn marigold, *C. segetum*; now usu., any of numerous cultivated chiefly late-blooming species or varieties placed in the genus *Dendranthema*. Also, a flower or flowering stem of such a plant.
– PHRASES: **the Chrysanthemum Throne** the throne of Japan, the Japanese monarchy. ***KOREAN chrysanthemum***.

chryselephantine /ˌkrɪselɪˈfantʌɪn/ *adjective*. E19.
[ORIGIN Greek *khruselephantinos*, from *khrusos* gold + *elephant-*, *-as* elephant, ivory: see -INE[1].]
Overlaid with gold and ivory, as by ancient Greek sculptors.

chrysene /ˈkrʌɪsiːn/ *noun*. M19.
[ORIGIN French *chrysène*, formed as CHRYSO- + -ENE: the first, impure, specimens were yellow.]
CHEMISTRY. A polycyclic aromatic hydrocarbon, $C_{18}H_{12}$, present in coal tar and isolated as colourless crystals.

chrysid /ˈkrʌɪsɪd/ *noun & adjective*. L19.
[ORIGIN from mod. Latin *Chrysididae* (see below), from *Chrysis* genus name: see CHRYSO-, -ID[3].]
▸ **A** *noun*. A parasitic hymenopterous insect of the family Chrysididae, which includes the cuckoo wasps. L19.
▸ **B** *adjective*. Of, pertaining to, or designating this family. E20.

chryso- /ˈkrɪsəʊ/ *combining form* of Greek *khrūsos* gold: see -O-. Before a vowel **chrys-**.
■ **chrysarobin** /krɪsəˈrəʊbɪn/ *noun* [mod. Latin *araroba* from Portuguese from Tupi *arárowa*] a mixture of chrysophanic acid and related compounds obtained from a S. American leguminous tree, *Andira araroba*, used to treat skin ailments L19. **chrysophanic** /-ˈfanɪk/ *adjective* [Greek *phainein* to show] (*CHEMISTRY*): ***chrysophanic acid***, a yellow crystalline phenol, $C_{15}H_{12}O_4$, which is a derivative of anthraquinone and occurs in many plants and lichens M19. **chrysopoˈetic** *adjective & noun* (*rare*) (in *pl.*) [Greek *poiētikos* making] gold-making E18. **chrysotype** *noun* a photographic process employing gold chloride M19.

chrysoberyl /krɪsəˈbɛrɪl/ *noun*. M17.
[ORIGIN Latin *chrysoberyllus*, formed as CHRYSO- + BERYL.]
MINERALOGY. Orig., a yellow-tinged variety of beryl. Now, a yellowish-green orthorhombic oxide of beryllium and aluminium which occurs as tabular crystals often of gem quality.

chrysocolla /krɪsəˈkɒlə/ *noun*. In sense 1 also **chrysocoll** /ˈkrɪsəkɒl/. L16.
[ORIGIN Latin *chrysocolla* from Greek *khrūsokolla* 'gold-solder'.]
1 *hist.* A mineral used by the ancients for soldering gold, usu. identified with borax or malachite. L16.
2 *MINERALOGY*. A hydrated silicate of copper usu. occurring as green opaline crusts and masses. L18.

chrysoidine /krɪˈsəʊɪdiːn/ *noun*. L19.
[ORIGIN from Greek *khrūsoeidēs* like gold + -INE[5].]
A golden-yellow dye made by diazo coupling of aniline and *m*-phenylenediamine.

chrysolite /ˈkrɪsəlʌɪt/ *noun*. LME.
[ORIGIN Old French *crisolite* from medieval Latin *crisolitus*, ult. from Greek *khrūsolithos*, formed as CHRYSO- + -LITE.]
Orig., any of various green gemstones. Now (*MINERALOGY*), a yellow variety of olivine.

chrysomelid /krɪsə(ʊ)ˈmɛlɪd, -ˈmiːlɪd/ *adjective & noun*. L19.
[ORIGIN from mod. Latin *Chrysomelidae* (see below), from *Chrysomela* genus name, from Greek *khrusomēlon* quince (lit. 'golden apple') but infl. by Greek *khrusomēlolonthion* little golden chafer: see CHRYSO-, -ID[3].]
ZOOLOGY. ▸**A** *adjective*. Of, pertaining to, or designating the insect family Chrysomelidae, which comprises the leaf beetles. L19.
▸ **B** *noun*. A chrysomelid beetle, a leaf beetle. L19.

chrysoprase /ˈkrɪsəpreɪz/ *noun*. ME.
[ORIGIN Old French *crisopace* from Latin *chrysopassus*, *-prasus* from Greek *khrūsoprasos*, formed as CHRYSO- + *prason* leek.]
Orig., a golden-green precious stone, perh. a variety of beryl. Now (*MINERALOGY*), an apple-green variety of chalcedony.

chrysotile /ˈkrɪsətʌɪl/ *noun*. M19.
[ORIGIN from CHRYSO- + Greek *tilos* fibre.]
MINERALOGY. An asbestiform variety of serpentine.

†**chrystal** *noun & adjective*, *verb* vars. of CRYSTAL *noun & adjective*, *verb*.

†**chrystalline** *adjective & noun* var. of CRYSTALLINE.

chthonian /ˈkθəʊnɪən/ *adjective*. M19.
[ORIGIN from Greek *khthonios* (from *khthōn* earth) + -AN.]
= CHTHONIC.

chthonic /ˈkθɒnɪk/ *adjective*. L19.
[ORIGIN from Greek *khthōn* earth + -IC.]
Dwelling in or beneath the earth or in the underworld; of or pertaining to the underworld.

chub /tʃʌb/ *noun*. Pl. same. LME.
[ORIGIN Unknown.]
1 A thick-bodied coarse-fleshed river fish, *Leuciscus cephalus*, of the carp family. Also (*N. Amer.*), any of various freshwater fishes of the carp family; any of various similar marine fishes of the family Kyphosidae (also ***sea chub***). LME.
RED-TAIL chub.
†**2** A lazy person; a yokel, a dolt; a lad. M16–E19.
■ **chubbed** *adjective* (now *rare*) short and thick, chubby L17.

Chubb /tʃʌb/ *noun*. M19.
[ORIGIN Charles *Chubb* (1773–1845), London locksmith.]
In full ***Chubb lock***. (Proprietary name for) a patent lock with tumblers and a device for fixing the bolt immovably should an attempt be made to pick it.

chubby /ˈtʃʌbi/ *adjective*. E17.
[ORIGIN from CHUB + -Y[1].]
†**1** Short and thick like a chub. E17–L19.
2 Round-faced; plump. E18.
■ **chubbily** *adverb* E20. **chubbiness** *noun* M19.

chuck /tʃʌk/ *noun*[1]. LME.
[ORIGIN Imit.: cf. CHUCK *verb*[1].]
A soft clucking sound.

chuck /tʃʌk/ *noun*^{2}. L16.
[ORIGIN Alt. of CHICK *noun*^{1} after CHUCK *noun*^{1} Cf. CHOOK.]
1 A term of endearment, esp. as *voc.*: dear one, darling. Now *dial.* L16.
> E. BRONTË Will you come Chuck?

2 A chicken, a domestic fowl. *N. English.* L17.

chuck /tʃʌk/ *noun*^{3}. E17.
[ORIGIN from CHUCK *verb*^{2}.]
1 A playful touch under the chin. E17.
2 = ***chuck-farthing*** s.v. CHUCK *verb*^{2}. Now *dial.* E18.
3 = CHUCKIE *noun*^{1}. *Scot.* E19.
4 An abrupt movement, a jerk, a toss. M19.
5 A throw from the hand; *spec.* in CRICKET, a delivery considered to be a throw and so illegal. *colloq.* M19.
6 ***the chuck***, dismissal, rejection. *slang.* L19.

chuck /tʃʌk/ *noun*^{4}. L17.
[ORIGIN Var. of CHOCK *noun*^{1}: cf. CHUNK *noun*^{1}.]
1 A chock; a chunk. Chiefly *dial.* L17.
2 A cut of beef from the neck to the ribs. E18.
3 A contrivance in a lathe etc. for holding a workpiece. E19.

chuck /tʃʌk/ *noun*^{5}. Now *N. Amer. colloq.* M19.
[ORIGIN Perh. same word as CHUCK *noun*^{4}.]
1 Food, provisions. M19.
2 A meal; mealtime. M19.
– COMB.: **chuck wagon** a provision cart on a ranch etc.

chuck /tʃʌk/ *noun*^{6}. L19.
[ORIGIN Chinook Jargon = water.]
In Canada, a large body of water.
SKOOKUM *chuck*.

chuck /tʃʌk/ *verb*^{1} *intrans.* LME.
[ORIGIN Imit.: cf. CHUCK *noun*^{1}.]
1 Make a soft clucking noise. LME.
†**2** Chuckle. Only in L16.

chuck /tʃʌk/ *verb*^{2}. E16.
[ORIGIN Perh. from Old French *chuquer*, earlier form of *choquer* knock, bump, of unknown origin.]
1 *verb trans.* Give a playful touch under the chin to. E16.
2 *verb trans.* Throw, toss, fling, now esp. with contempt, carelessness, or ease; throw *away*, *out*, etc. (see also specialized senses below); throw or give up; throw out; reject, abandon. (Earliest in ***chuck-farthing*** below.) *colloq.* L17. ▸**b** CRICKET. Deliver (a ball) with an action considered to be a throw and so illegal. *colloq.* M19.
> TENNYSON England now Is but a ball chuck'd between France and Spain. W. GERHARDIE To chuck the army and enter a commercial life. P. H. GIBBS A girl who had chucked them for someone else. P. LIVELY He chucks me free concert tickets he can't use.

chuck in the towel: see TOWEL *noun* 1. **chuck it** *slang* stop, desist.
3 *verb intrans.* Play chuck-farthing. *rare.* M18.
4 *verb intrans.* Throw a ball etc.; *spec.* in CRICKET, deliver the ball with an action considered to be a throw and so illegal. *colloq.* E20.
– WITH ADVERBS IN SPECIALIZED SENSES: **chuck in** abandon (an activity), stop doing. **chuck off** *Austral. & NZ slang* sneer (*at*), chaff. **chuck out** eject, get rid of, (a troublesome or unwanted person) from a meeting, public house, etc. **chuck up** abandon, dismiss; throw over, jilt.
– COMB.: **chuck-farthing** (orig.) a game in which coins were pitched at a mark and then tossed at a hole; (later) any similar game; **chuckhole** *US* a hole or rut in a road or track.

chuck /tʃʌk/ *verb*^{3} *trans.* M19.
[ORIGIN from CHUCK *noun*^{4}.]
Fix on a lathe by means of a chuck.

chuck /tʃʌk/ *adverb.* M18.
[ORIGIN Imit.]
With direct impact.

chuck-a-luck /ˈtʃʌkəlʌk/ *noun. N. Amer.* M19.
[ORIGIN App. from CHUCK *verb*^{2} + connective *-a-* + LUCK *noun*.]
A gambling game played with dice.

chuckawalla *noun* see CHUCKWALLA.

chucker /ˈtʃʌkə/ *noun*^{1}. *colloq.* M18.
[ORIGIN from CHUCK *verb*^{2} + -ER^{1}.]
1 A small pebble. M18.
2 A person who throws; *spec.* in CRICKET, a bowler whose delivery of the ball is considered to be a throw and so illegal. L19.
3 ***chucker-out***, a person who ejects troublesome or unwanted persons, a bouncer. L19.

chucker *noun*^{2} var. of CHUKKA.

chuck-full *adjective* var. of CHOCK-FULL.

chuckie /ˈtʃʌki/ *noun*^{1}. *Scot.* M18.
[ORIGIN from CHUCK *verb*^{2} or *noun*^{3} + -IE.]
More fully ***chuckie-stane***, ***chuckie-stone***. A small pebble, a smooth stone, esp. as used in games, for skimming on water, etc.; in *pl.*, a game with pebbles or marbles.

chuckie *noun*^{2} var. of CHUCKY.

chuckle /ˈtʃʌk(ə)l/ *noun.* M18.
[ORIGIN from CHUCKLE *verb*.]
1 An act of chuckling; a suppressed (formerly, a loud or convulsive) laugh; a soft cackle or clucking sound. M18.
2 Private amusement, chuckling. M19.

chuckle /ˈtʃʌk(ə)l/ *adjective.* E18.
[ORIGIN Prob. rel. to CHUCK *noun*^{4}: see -LE^{1}.]
Esp. of the head: large, clumsy, blockish. Usu. in *comb.* as below.
– COMB.: **chucklehead** a stupid person, a blockhead; **chuckleheaded** *adjective* stupid, blockheaded; **chuckleheadedness** stupidity.

chuckle /ˈtʃʌk(ə)l/ *verb.* L16.
[ORIGIN from CHUCK *verb*^{1} + -LE^{3}.]
1 *verb trans.* †**a** Laugh vehemently or convulsively. L16–E19. ▸**b** Laugh to oneself; make suppressed sounds of glee etc. E19.
> **b** I. D'ISRAELI A tale which some antiquaries still chuckle over.

2 *verb trans.* Call (fowl etc.) together with a chucking sound. *rare.* L17.
3 *verb intrans.* Of a bird: cackle or cluck softly. E19.
> KEATS The chuckling linnet.

■ **chucklesome** *adjective* (orig. *US*) humorous, amusing: E20.

chuckler /ˈtʃʌklə/ *noun.* M18.
[ORIGIN Tamil *cakkili*.]
A person of a very low caste in southern India, whose members are tanners or cobblers; a southern Indian shoemaker.

chuckwalla /ˈtʃʌkwɒlə/ *noun.* Also **chuckawalla** /-kə-/. L19.
[ORIGIN Mexican Spanish *chacahuala* from Amer. Indian.]
An iguanid lizard, *Sauromalus obesus*, of Mexico and the south-western US.

chuck-will's-widow /tʃʌkwɪlzˈwɪdəʊ/ *noun.* L18.
[ORIGIN Imit.]
A large nightjar of eastern N. America, *Caprimulgus carolinensis*.

chucky /ˈtʃʌki/ *noun.* Also **chuckie**; *Austral. & NZ* (sense 2) **chookie**, **-y** /ˈtʃʊki/. E18.
[ORIGIN from CHUCK *noun*^{2} + -Y^{6}, -IE.]
1 A term of endearment: little one, dearie. Now *dial.* E18.
2 A chicken, a domestic fowl. *colloq.* L18.

chuddar *noun* var. of CHADOR.

chuddies /ˈtʃʌdiːz/ *noun pl.* Also **chuddis**. *Indian.* L20.
[ORIGIN Perh. alt. of CHURIDARS.]
Underpants.

chuddy /ˈtʃʌdi/ *noun. dial.* or *Austral. & NZ slang.* Also **chutty** /ˈtʃʌti/. M20.
[ORIGIN Uncertain: perh. alt. of *chewed*.]
Chewing gum.

chufa /ˈtʃuːfə/ *noun.* M19.
[ORIGIN Spanish.]
(The edible nutty tuber of) the nut-grass, *Cyperus esculentus*. Also called ***earth almond***.

chuff /tʃʌf/ *noun*^{1} *& adjective*^{1}. Now *dial.* LME.
[ORIGIN Unknown.]
▸ **A** *noun.* A rustic, a boor; a churlish person; a miser; *gen.* a person of the specified unpleasant kind. LME.
▸ **B** *adjective.* Surly, gruff, morose. L18.
■ **chuffy** *adjective*^{1} = CHUFF *adjective*^{1} E18.

chuff /ˈtʃʌf/ *noun*^{2} *& adjective*^{2}. Now *dial.* M16.
[ORIGIN Unknown.]
▸ †**A** *noun.* **1** A chubby cheek. Only in M16.
2 An animal's muzzle. Only in E17.
▸ **B** *adjective.* **1** Chubby, fat. M16.
2 Pleased, happy. M19.
■ **chuffy** *adjective*^{2} plump-cheeked, chubby E17.

chuff /tʃʌf/ *noun*^{3}, *interjection, & verb.* Also redupl. **chuff-chuff**. E20.
[ORIGIN Imit.]
▸ **A** *noun & interjection.* (Repr.) a sharp puffing sound, as of a steam engine. E20.
▸ **B** *verb intrans.* Of a steam engine etc.: work with or make a regular sharp puffing sound. E20.

chuff /tʃʌf/ *noun*^{4}. *slang.* M20.
[ORIGIN Unknown.]
A person's buttocks or anus.

chuffed /tʃʌft/ *adjective. slang.* M20.
[ORIGIN Cf. CHUFF *adjective*^{1}, *adjective*^{2}.]
1 Pleased. M20.
2 Displeased. M20.

chuffing /ˈtʃʌfɪŋ/ *adjective. N. English colloq.* L20.
[ORIGIN Uncertain: perh. infl. by CHUFF *noun*^{4}.]
Used for emphasis or as a mild expletive.
> N. BLINCOE Look around. You see what the place looks like? What it chuffing smells like?

chug /tʃʌg/ *noun, interjection, & verb.* Also redupl. **chug-chug**. M19.
[ORIGIN Imit.]
▸ **A** *noun & interjection.* (Repr.) a muffled explosive sound as of a slowly running internal-combustion engine or its exhaust. M19.
▸ **B** *verb intrans.* Infl. **-gg-**. Move with or make this sound. L19.

chukar /ˈtʃʊkɑː/ *noun.* Also **chikhor** /ˈtʃɪkɔː/ & other vars. E19.
[ORIGIN Sanskrit *cakor(a)*.]
A red-legged partridge, *Alectoris chukar*, native to Asia and SE Europe. Also ***chukar partridge***.

Chukchi /ˈtʃʊktʃi, -iː/ *noun & adjective.* Also **Chukchee**, **Tchuktchi**, & other vars. E18.
[ORIGIN Russian *Chukchi* pl. (sing. *-cha*).]
▸ **A** *noun.* Pl. **-s**, same. A member of a Palaeoasiatic people of extreme NE Siberia; the language of this people. E18.
▸ **B** *adjective.* Designating, of, or pertaining to this people or language. E19.

chukka /ˈtʃʌkə/ *noun.* Also **chucker**, **chukker**. L19.
[ORIGIN Hindi *cak(k)ar* from Sanskrit *cakra* circle, wheel.]
Each of the periods into which a game of polo is divided.
– COMB.: **chukka boot** an ankle-high leather boot, as worn by polo players.

chula *noun* var. of CHOOLA.

chulo /ˈtʃulo, ˈtʃuːləʊ/ *noun.* Pl. **-os** /-ɔs, -əʊz/. L18.
[ORIGIN Spanish.]
A bullfighter's assistant.

chum /tʃʌm/ *noun*^{1}. *colloq.* L17.
[ORIGIN Prob. short for *chamber-fellow*: orig. Oxford Univ. slang equiv. to Cambridge *crony*.]
A person who shares apartments with another or others; (now usu.) an intimate friend, esp. among schoolchildren.
new chum *Austral. & NZ* a recent immigrant, a greenhorn.
■ **chumship** *noun* the state or condition of being chums; (the period of) intimate friendship: M19.

chum /tʃʌm/ *noun*^{2}. *US.* M19.
[ORIGIN Unknown.]
1 Refuse from fish, *esp.* that remaining after expressing oil. M19.
2 Chopped fish thrown overboard as bait, as in trolling. L19.

chum /tʃʌm/ *noun*^{3}. L19.
[ORIGIN Perh. alt. of CHUMP *noun*.]
CERAMICS. A receptacle used for turning a form.

chum /tʃʌm/ *noun*^{4}. E20.
[ORIGIN Chinook Jargon *tzum* (*samun*) lit. 'spotted (salmon)'.]
A salmon, *Oncorhynchus keta*, of the N. American Pacific coast. Also ***chum salmon***.

chum /tʃʌm/ *verb*^{1}. *colloq.* Infl. **-mm-**. M18.
[ORIGIN from CHUM *noun*^{1}.]
1 *verb intrans.* Share rooms (*with*); be very friendly (*with*). M18. ▸**b** ***chum up***, form a close friendship (*with*). L19.
2 *verb trans.* Quarter (a person) *on* another to share rooms. M19.

chum /tʃʌm/ *verb*^{2} *trans. & intrans. US.* Infl. **-mm-**. L19.
[ORIGIN from CHUM *noun*^{2}.]
Bait (a fishing place) with chum; attract (fish) with chum.

chumar *noun* var. of CHAMAR.

Chumash /ˈtʃuːmaʃ/ *noun & adjective.* E20.
[ORIGIN Chumash, lit. 'islander'.]
▸ **A** *noun.* Pl. same, **-es**. A member of an American Indian people inhabiting coastal parts of southern California; the extinct Hokan language of this people. E20.
▸ **B** *adjective.* Of or relating to the Chumash people or their language. E20.

chumble /ˈtʃʌmb(ə)l/ *verb trans. & intrans. dial. & colloq.* E19.
[ORIGIN Prob. imit.]
Gnaw, nibble, peck, mumble, (*at*).

chummage /ˈtʃʌmɪdʒ/ *noun.* L18.
[ORIGIN from CHUM *noun*^{1} or *verb*^{1} + -AGE.]
1 *hist.* A fee demanded by prisoners from a new inmate; a fee paid by a person to another chummed on him, as an inducement to find alternative accommodation. L18.
2 The system of chumming one person on another. M19.

chummery /ˈtʃʌməri/ *noun.* L19.
[ORIGIN from CHUM *noun*^{1} + -ERY.]
1 Intimate friendship. L19.
2 In India: a house or apartment shared by individuals; shared quarters. L19.

chummy /ˈtʃʌmi/ *noun*^{1}. *arch. colloq.* M19.
[ORIGIN Alt. of CHIMNEY *noun*.]
A chimney sweeper's boy; a chimney sweeper.

chummy /ˈtʃʌmi/ *noun*^{2}. *colloq.* M19.
[ORIGIN from CHUM *noun*^{1} + -Y^{6}.]
1 = CHUM *noun*^{1}. M19.
2 A person accused or detained; a prisoner. *Police slang.* M20.

chummy /ˈtʃʌmi/ *adjective. colloq.* L19.
[ORIGIN from CHUM *noun*^{1} + -Y^{1}.]
Intimate, friendly, sociable.
■ **chummily** *adverb* M20.

chump /tʃʌmp/ *noun.* E18.
[ORIGIN Perh. blend of CHUNK *noun*^{1} and LUMP *noun*^{1} or STUMP *noun*^{1}.]
1 A short thick lump of wood; an end piece. E18.
2 The thick end, esp. of a loin of lamb or mutton. M19.
3 The head. *colloq.* M19.

off one's chump crazy, wild with excitement, etc.
4 A foolish person, a blockhead. *colloq.* **L19.**
– **COMB.**: **chump change** *colloq.* (chiefly *N. Amer.*) a small or insignificant amount of money; **chump chop** a chop from the chump end; **chump end** the thick end of a loin of lamb or mutton.

Chün /tʃuːn/ *adjective & noun.* **L19.**
[**ORIGIN** from *Chün Chou* (see below).]
(Designating) a type of thickly glazed coloured stoneware orig. made at Chün Chou in Honan province, China, during the Song dynasty.

chunam /tʃʊˈnam/ *noun & verb trans.* (infl. **-mm-**). **L17.**
[**ORIGIN** Tamil *cuṇṇāmbu* lime.]
(Cover with) a cement of shell lime and sea sand, used chiefly in the Indian subcontinent.

chunder /ˈtʃʌndə/ *verb intrans. & noun. slang,* chiefly *Austral. & NZ.* Also **-da**. **M20.**
[**ORIGIN** Prob. rhyming slang *Chunder Loo* for 'spew', after a cartoon figure *Chunder Loo of Akim Foo* appearing in advertisements for Cobra boot polish.]
Vomit.

chunk /tʃʌŋk/ *noun*[1] *& verb*[1]. **L17.**
[**ORIGIN** App. alt. of **CHUCK** *noun*[4].]
▸ **A** *noun.* **1** A thick lump (of wood, bread, cheese, etc.) cut or broken off. **L17.** ▸**b** A block of wood. Chiefly *US.* **L18.**
2 A sturdy person or horse; a sturdy specimen *of. US.* **E19.**
3 A substantial amount or portion (*of*). **L19.**
▸ **B** *verb trans.* **1** Hit with a missile; throw a missile at. *US colloq.* **M19.**
2 Replenish (a fire) with fuel; build (a fire) *up. US colloq.* **M19.**
■ **chunky** *adjective* comprising chunks; short and thick; small and sturdy; bulky: **M18.**

chunk /tʃʌŋk/ *verb*[2], *noun*[2], *& interjection.* Also redupl. **chunk-chunk**. **L19.**
[**ORIGIN** Imit.]
▸ **A** *verb intrans.* Move with or make a muffled metallic sound. **L19.**
▸ **B** *noun & interjection.* (Repr.) such a sound. **L19.**

Chunnel /ˈtʃʌn(ə)l/ *noun. colloq.* **E20.**
[**ORIGIN** Contr.]
= ***Channel Tunnel*** s.v. **CHANNEL** *noun*[1].

chunner /ˈtʃʌnə/ *verb trans. & intrans.* Chiefly *Scot. & US.* **L16.**
[**ORIGIN** Prob. imit.: cf. **CHANNER**, **CHUNTER**.]
Mutter, grumble, murmur querulously.

chuño /ˈtʃuɲo, ˈtʃuːnjəʊ/ *noun.* **E17.**
[**ORIGIN** Amer. Spanish from Quechua *ch'uñu*.]
(Flour prepared from) dried potatoes, as eaten by Andean Indians.

chunter /ˈtʃʌntə/ *verb intrans.* **L17.**
[**ORIGIN** Prob. imit.: cf. **CHANNER**, **CHUNNER**.]
Mutter, grumble, murmur querulously.

chupacabra /tʃuːpəˈkabrə/ *noun.* **L20.**
[**ORIGIN** Spanish, lit. 'goatsucker', from *chupar* to suck + *cabra* goat.]
A creature said to exist in parts of Central America and to attack animals, esp. goats.

chupatti *noun* var. of **CHAPATTI**.

chuppah /ˈxʊpə/ *noun.* Also **-a**. **L19.**
[**ORIGIN** Hebrew *huppāh* cover, canopy.]
A canopy beneath which Jewish marriage ceremonies are performed.

chuprassy *noun* var. of **CHAPRASSI**.

church /tʃəːtʃ/ *noun.*
[**ORIGIN** Old English *ċir(i)ċe, ċyr(i)ċe* = Old Frisian *szereke, szurka, tzierka*, Old Saxon *kirika, kerika* (Dutch *kerk*), Old High German *chirihha, kiricha* (German *Kirche*), from West Germanic from medieval Greek *kurikon* for *kuriakon* use as noun (sc. *dōma* house) of neut. of *kuriakos* pertaining to the Lord, from *kurios* master, lord. Cf. **KIRK** *noun*.]
▸ **I** (Usu. **c-**.) A building and extended uses.
1 A building for public Christian worship, esp. of the denomination recognized by the state (cf. ***chapel, oratory***); public Christian worship. **OE.**

> **STEELE** As soon as church was done, she immediately stepp'd out.

go to church *spec.* (*colloq.*) get married. ***CATHEDRAL church***. ***COLLEGIAL church***. ***collegiate church*** s.v. **COLLEGIATE** *adjective*. ***minster church***: see **MINSTER** 2. ***PARISH church***. ***Patriarchal church***: see **PATRIARCHAL** 1.
†**2** A temple; a mosque. **OE–M17.**
▸ **II** (Usu. **C-**.) A community or organization.
3 The body of all Christians. **OE.**
Doctors of the Church: see **DOCTOR** *noun*. ***Fathers of the Church***: see **FATHER** *noun*. **the Church Catholic**: emphasizing its universality. **the Church invisible** the whole body of Christians, past and present. **the Church militant** Christians on earth warring against evil. **the Church triumphant** Christians at peace in heaven. **the Church visible** the whole body of Christians on earth.
4 A particular organized Christian society, distinguished by special features of doctrine, worship, etc., or confined to territorial or historical limits. **OE.**
Ancient Church, ***Anglican Church***, ***Baptist Church***, ***Catholic Church***, ***Congregational Church***, ***Eastern Church***, ***Greek Church***, ***Latin Church***, ***Lutheran Church***, ***Methodist Church***, ***Nestorian Church***, ***Orthodox Church***, ***Presbyterian Church***, ***Roman Catholic Church***, ***Russian Church***, ***Western Church***, etc. ***Broad Church***: see **BROAD** *adjective*. **Church of England** the English branch of the Western or Latin Church which has rejected the Pope's supremacy since the Reformation but retained episcopacy. **Church-of-Englandism** adherence to the Church of England. **Church of Scotland** Scotland's national Presbyterian Church. ***High Church***: see **HIGH** *adjective*. ***Low Church***: see **LOW** *adjective*.
5 A congregation of Christians locally organized into a society for religious worship etc. **OE.**
6 The ecclesiastical and clerical organization of Christian society or a particular Christian society; the clergy and officers collectively or as a corporation; formerly esp. as an estate of the realm (opp. state). **OE.**
enter the Church, **go into the Church** take holy orders, become a minister or priest. **Holy Church** (*a*) the Church regarded as divinely instituted and guided; †(*b*) the clergy similarly regarded. **Mother Church** the Church, esp. the Roman Catholic Church, as having maternal authority or solicitude. ***Church and state***: see **STATE** *noun*. ***parochial church council***: see **PAROCHIAL** 1. ***Prince of the Church***, ***Prince of the Holy Roman Church***: see **PRINCE** *noun*.
7 (In biblical translations) the congregation of Israelites; the faithful Israelites of the Old Testament, regarded as analogous to the Christian Church. **OE.**
8 A non-Christian society or movement regarded as a religion or as having the social, ethical, or spiritual qualities of a religion. **LME.**
Church of Scientology etc.
– **ATTRIB. & COMB.**: In the senses 'of the Church, ecclesiastical, (in England often *spec.*) of the Church of England, of a church', as ***church assembly***, ***church bazaar***, ***church dignitary***, ***church door***, (US) ***church fair***, ***church fête***, ***church history***, ***church land***, ***church member***, ***church membership***, ***church officer***, ***church organ***, ***church organist***, ***church spire***, ***church steeple***, ***church tower***, ***church vestments***, ***church window***, etc. Special combs., as **church-ale** *hist.* a periodic festive gathering held in connection with a church; **Church Army** a Church of England organization for evangelism and welfare work; **church bell** a bell rung to call people to worship etc.; **church book** a book belonging to or used in connection with a church, as a service book, a parish register, etc.; ***Church Catechism***: see **CATECHISM** 2; **Church Commissioners** the body managing the finances of the Church of England; **Church Congress** *hist.* the annual meetings of the Church of England for discussion; ***Church Covenant***: see **COVENANT** *noun*; ***Church Establishment***: see **ESTABLISHMENT** 3; ***Church Fathers***: see **FATHER** *noun*; **churchgoer** a person who attends the services of a church, esp. regularly; **churchgoing** (esp. regular) attendance at the services of a church; **church-government** the government or organization of a Church, esp. with regard to the exercise of authority and discipline; ***church-grith***: see **GRITH** 2; **church-house** (*a*) a house belonging to a church or to the Church; (*b*) *US* a church, a meeting house; ***church-litten***: see **LITTEN** *noun*; **church key** *N. Amer.* a metal device with a bottle opener at one end and a triangular head at the other for punching a hole in cans; **church living** a benefice in the Established Church; **church mode** each of the eight modes used for plainsong and liturgical chant, each beginning on a different note and having a different pattern of tones and semitones; **church mouse**: inhabiting a church and proverbially poverty-stricken; **church owl** the barn owl; **church parade** attendance at church as a military etc. duty; attendance at church in a body by members of a society etc.; **church planting** the practice of sending parishioners from a thriving (esp. charismatic) Christian church to take over one with a dwindling congregation; **church-rate** a rate levied on parishioners for the maintenance of the church and its services (formerly compulsory, now voluntary but seldom requested); **church school** a school founded by or associated with a Church, esp. the Church of England; **church-scot**, **church-shot** *hist.* a contribution in kind or money made or demanded for the support of the clergy; **church service** a meeting for public worship, esp. following a stated form; the order of such worship, *spec.* the order of Common Prayer of the Church of England; ***Church Slavonic***: see **SLAVONIC** *noun*; **church-text** (now *rare*) black letter, Old English, or textura lettering and type; **churchwoman** a woman member of the Established Church; **church work** (*a*) work at building a church (proverbially slow); (*b*) work for or in connection with the Church; **churchyard** an enclosed ground in which a church stands, esp. as used for burials; ***churchyard cough*** a cough seeming to herald death; ***Church year***: see **YEAR** *noun*[1].
■ **churchdom** *noun* (*rare*) status as a Church; organization as a Church: **M17.** **churchiˈanity** *noun* (*derog.*) devotion to the Church rather than to Christianity itself **M19.** **churchless** *adjective* not having a church or an organized Church; not belonging to a Church: **M17.** **churchlet** *noun* (*rare*) a small church **M17.** **churchlike** *adjective* (*a*) befitting the Church; (*b*) like a church: **L16.** **churchly** *adjective* pertaining to or befitting a church or the Church, ecclesiastical: **OE.** **churchward** *adverb & adjective*, **churchwards** *adverb* [orig. *to churchward*] towards the church **LME.** **churchwise** *adjective & adverb* after the manner of a church **E17.**

church /tʃəːtʃ/ *verb trans.* **LME.**
[**ORIGIN** from the noun.]
1 Bring or take (esp. a woman after childbirth) to church to receive particular rites or ministrations (usu. in *pass.*); conduct a church service of thanksgiving for (esp. a woman after childbirth). **LME.**
2 Call to account in church. *US local.* **E19.**

Churchillian /tʃəːˈtʃɪlɪən/ *adjective.* **L19.**
[**ORIGIN** from family name Spencer-*Churchill* + **-IAN**.]
Of, pertaining to, or characteristic of any of the Churchills, esp. the British statesmen Lord Randolph Churchill (1849–95) and his son Sir Winston Churchill (1874–1965). Cf. **WINSTONIAN**.
■ **Churchilliˈana** *noun pl.* [-**ANA**] sayings by Sir Winston Churchill; publications or other items concerning or associated with Churchill: **M20.**

churchman /ˈtʃəːtʃmən/ *noun.* Pl. **-men**. **ME.**
[**ORIGIN** from **CHURCH** *noun* + **MAN** *noun*.]
1 A clergyman. **ME.**
†**2** A churchwarden. Only in **16.**
3 A supporter or member of a Church; *esp.* a member of the Established Church. **L17.**
■ **churchmanlike** *adjective* resembling or befitting a churchman **M19.** **churchmanly** *adjective* of or befitting a churchman **M19.** **churchmanship** *noun* the status or quality of a churchman; churchmanly behaviour: **L17.**

C

churchwarden /ˈtʃəːtʃwɔːd(ə)n/ *noun & adjective.* **LME.**
[**ORIGIN** from **CHURCH** *noun* + **WARDEN** *noun*[1].]
▸ **A** *noun.* **1** Either of two elected lay people in an Anglican parish who are the foremost representatives of the laity, with responsibility for maintaining order in the church and for looking after its movable property; *US* a church administrator. **LME.**
2 A long clay pipe. **M19.**
▸ **B** *attrib.* or as *adjective.* Designating a sham Gothic style affected in church building and restoration in the early 19th cent.; in this style. **M19.**
■ **churchwardenism** *noun* the practice of building or restoring churches in churchwarden style **M19.** **churchwardenize** *verb trans.* restore (a church) in churchwarden style **M19.** **churchwardenly** *adjective* of or befitting a churchwarden **L19.** **churchwardenship** *noun* the position or office of churchwarden **E17.**

churchy /ˈtʃəːtʃi/ *adjective. colloq.* **M19.**
[**ORIGIN** from **CHURCH** *noun* + **-Y**[1].]
1 Obtrusively or intolerantly devoted to the Church or opposed to religious dissent. **M19.**
2 Like a church. **L19.**
■ **churchiness** *noun* **L19.**

churel /tʃʊˈreɪl/ *noun.* **E20.**
[**ORIGIN** Hindi *curail*.]
In the Indian subcontinent: the malevolent ghost of a woman who has died in childbirth, believed to spread disease.

churidars /ˈtʃʊrɪdɑːz/ *noun pl.* Also **churidar**. **L20.**
[**ORIGIN** from Hindi *cūṛīdār* having a series of gathered rows (i.e. at the bottom of the trouser legs, traditionally worn too long and tucked up).]
Tight trousers worn by people from the Indian subcontinent, typically with a kameez or kurta.

churinga /tʃəˈrɪŋgə/ *noun.* Also **tjurunga** /tʃəˈrʊŋgə/. Pl. **-s**, same. **L19.**
[**ORIGIN** Arrernte *tywerrenge*, lit. 'object from the dreaming'.]
Among Australian Aborigines, a sacred object, *spec.* an amulet.

churl /tʃəːl/ *noun.* In sense 2 also **ceorl** /kjəːl, tʃ-/.
[**ORIGIN** Old English *ċeorl* = Old Frisian *tzerl, tzirl*, Middle Low German *kerle* (whence German *Kerl* fellow), Middle Dutch & mod. Dutch *kerel*, from West Germanic: rel. to **CARL** *noun*.]
†**1** A man, esp. as correlative to 'wife'. **OE–LME.**
2 In the Old English constitution: a man, a member of the lowest rank of freemen; an ordinary freeman ranking directly below a thane (**THANE** 3). After the Norman Conquest: a serf, a bondman. **OE.** ▸**b** *loosely.* A person of low birth. Passing into other senses. **LME.**
3 A peasant or rustic. *arch.* **ME.**
4 A bad-mannered and mean-spirited person. **ME.**
5 A miserly person. *arch.* **M16.**

churlish /ˈtʃəːlɪʃ/ *adjective.* **OE.**
[**ORIGIN** from **CHURL** + **-ISH**[1].]
1 Of or pertaining to a churl or churls; of the rank of a churl. Long *arch.* **OE.**
2 Boorish or rude in behaviour; surly. Also, miserly, grudging. **LME.**

> **K. ATKINSON** It seemed churlish not to comply with her heartfelt request.

3 Of an animal, natural agent, etc.: violent, rough. Also, of soil or other material: difficult to work, intractable. *obsolete* exc. as passing into fig. uses of sense 2. **L15.**
■ **churlishly** *adverb* **LME.** **churlishness** *noun* **E16.**

churn /tʃəːn/ *noun & verb.*
[**ORIGIN** Old English *ċyrin* = Middle Low German *kerne, kirne*, Middle Dutch *kerne*, Old Norse *kirna*, from Germanic. Sense A.2 from the verb.]
▸ **A** *noun.* **1** A butter-making machine in which milk or cream is agitated; a large milk can (orig. one shaped like a butter churn). **OE.**
2 A churning action or sensation. **L19.**
▸ **B** *verb.* **1** *verb trans. & intrans.* Agitate (milk or cream) in a churn; produce (butter) thus. **LME.**
2 *verb trans.* Stir (liquid etc.) about, cause to froth; agitate violently; turn or throw *up* violently. **L17.**

> **W. HOLTBY** The wagon wheels had churned the yard to treacly clay. **J. BETJEMAN** Bills to pay later churned up my insides.

3 *verb intrans.* Move churning up water, earth, etc.; turn like a churn; (of liquid etc.) wash to and fro, foam, seethe. **M18.**

> **S. O'FAOLÁIN** Rain-water churning down the rocky valleys. **R. CHANDLER** The ventilator churned dully. **C. S. FORESTER** Churning along over Salisbury Plain on a bicycle with worn sprocket wheels. **W. STYRON** I felt my stomach churn and heave.

4 *verb trans.* Foll. by *out*: produce in quantity rather than quality. **E20.**

– **COMB.**: **churn-milk** (now *dial.*) buttermilk; **churn-owl** (now *dial.*) the nightjar; **churn rate** the annual percentage rate at which customers discontinue using a service, esp. cable and satellite television; **churn-staff** a staff for agitating milk or cream in a standing churn.

■ **churnaˈbility** *noun* the readiness (of fats in milk or cream) to form butter in churning **L19.** **churnable** *adjective* (of fats in milk or cream) ready to form butter in churning **E20.** **churner** *noun* a person who or machine which churns **L19.** **churning** *verbal noun* (**a**) the action or process of the verb; (**b**) *colloq.* the buying and selling of a client's investments for the sole purpose of earning more commission: **LME.**

C

churr /tʃəː/ *verb & noun.* **M16.**
[**ORIGIN** Imit.: cf. **CHIRR.**]
▸ **A** *verb intrans.* Esp. of some birds, as the nightjar: make a deep prolonged trilling sound. **M16.**
▸ **B** *noun.* **1** Any of various birds that make such a sound, as the partridge, the nightjar. *dial.* **E17.**
2 Such a sound. **M19.**

churrasco /tʃʊˈraskəʊ/ *noun.* **M20.**
[**ORIGIN** S. Amer. Spanish, prob. from Spanish dial. *churrascar* to burn, rel. to Spanish *soccarar* to scorch.]
A South American dish consisting of steak barbecued over a wood or charcoal fire.
■ **churrascaria** /tʃʊˌraskəˈrɪə/ [Spanish *-aria* **-ERY**] a restaurant specializing in churrasco **L20.**

Churrigueresque /tʃʌrɪgəˈrɛsk/ *adjective.* **M19.**
[**ORIGIN** from *Churriguera* (see below) + **-ESQUE.**]
ARCHITECTURE. Lavishly ornamented in the late Spanish baroque style of José Churriguera (1665–1725).

churro /ˈtʃʊrəʊ/ *noun.* Pl. **-os.** **E20.**
[**ORIGIN** Spanish, of uncertain origin; perh. related to *churro* (adjective) coarse, rough.]
A Spanish sweet snack consisting of a strip of fried dough dusted with sugar or cinnamon.

churrus *noun* var. of **CHARAS.**

chuse *verb* arch. var. of **CHOOSE.**

chut /tʃʊt, ʃ-/ *interjection.* **E19.**
[**ORIGIN** Imit.: cf. French *chut.*]
Expr. impatience.

chute /ʃuːt/ *noun*[1] *& verb.* Orig. *N. Amer.* **E19.**
[**ORIGIN** French = fall (of water etc.) from Old French *cheoite* use as noun of fem. pa. pple of *cheoir* to fall from Latin *cadere*; extended to senses of **SHOOT** *noun*[1]. Cf. **SHUTE** *noun*[2].]
▸ **A** *noun.* **1** A cataract or cascade of water; a steep descent in a riverbed producing a swift current. *N. Amer.* **E19.**
2 A sloping channel or slide, with or without water, for conveying things to a lower level; a slope for shooting rubbish down. **E19.**
3 A narrow passage or enclosure for cattle or sheep. **L19.**
4 A steep slide or roller coaster, esp. with water at the foot, at a fairground etc. **E20.**
▸ **B** *verb trans.* **1** Send down through a chute; drive into or pen in a chute. **L19.**
2 ***chute the chute(s)***, ride on a chute at a fairground etc. **E20.**
– **PHRASES**: **chutes and ladders** *US* the game snakes and ladders; **chute-the-chutes** = sense A.4 above.

chute /ʃuːt/ *noun*[2]. *colloq.* Also **'chute.** **E20.**
[**ORIGIN** Abbreviation.]
A parachute.
■ **chutist** *noun* a parachutist **E20.**

chutney /ˈtʃʌtni/ *noun.* **E19.**
[**ORIGIN** Hindi *caṭnī.*]
A pungent, orig. Indian, condiment of fruits, vinegar, spices, etc.

chutter /ˈtʃʌtə/ *verb intrans.* **M20.**
[**ORIGIN** Imit.]
Make a muffled clattering or spluttering noise.

chutty *noun* var. of **CHUDDY.**

chutzpah /ˈxʊtspə, ˈhʊ-/ *noun. slang.* **L19.**
[**ORIGIN** Yiddish from Aramaic *ḥuṣpā.*]
Shameless audacity, gall.

chylde *noun* see **CHILD** *noun.*

chyle /kʌɪl/ *noun.* Also in Latin form †**chylus.** **LME.**
[**ORIGIN** Late Latin *chylus* from Greek *khūlos* animal or plant juice.]
A milky fluid containing fat droplets which drains from the lacteals of the small intestine into the lymphatic system during digestion.
receptacle of chyle: see **RECEPTACLE** 3a.
■ **chyliˈfactive**, **chyliˈfactory** *adjectives* (*rare*) producing chyle **M17.** **chyˈliferous** *adjective* bearing or containing chyle **M17.** **chyˈlific** *adjective* (now *rare* or *obsolete*) producing chyle **M19.** **chylifiˈcation** *noun* conversion into chyle **E17.** **chylify** *verb trans.* convert into chyle **M17.** **chylous** *adjective* pertaining to, full of, or of the nature of chyle **M17.** **chyˈluria** *noun* (*MEDICINE*) the presence of chyle in the urine **M19.**

chylo- /ˈkʌɪləʊ/ *combining form* of **CHYLE**: see **-O-.**
■ **chyloˈmicron** *noun* a droplet of fat present in the blood or lymph after absorption from the small intestine **E20.** †**chylopoietic** *adjective* producing chyle **M18–M19.**

chyme /kʌɪm/ *noun.* Also in Latin form †**chymus.** **LME.**
[**ORIGIN** Late Latin *chymus* from Greek *khūmos* animal or plant juice.]
†**1** A humour of the body; the humours collectively. Only in **LME.**
2 The pulpy acidic fluid which passes from the stomach to the small intestine, and consists of gastric juices and partly digested food. **E17.**
■ **chymous** *adjective* pertaining to or of the nature of chyme **L17.**

†**chymic** *adjective, noun, & verb* see **CHEMIC.**

†**chymical** *adjective & noun* see **CHEMICAL.**

chymist, **chymistry** *nouns* see **CHEMIST**, **CHEMISTRY.**

chymo- /ˈkʌɪməʊ/ *combining form* of **CHYME**: see **-O-.**
■ **chymoˈtrypsin** *noun* a proteolytic enzyme active in the small intestine **M20.** **chymotrypˈsinogen** *noun* an inactive precursor of chymotrypsin secreted by the pancreas and activated by trypsin **M20.**

†**chymus** *noun* var. of **CHYME.**

chypre /ʃiːpr(ə), *foreign* ʃipr/ *noun.* **L19.**
[**ORIGIN** French = Cyprus, where perh. orig. made.]
A heavy perfume made from sandalwood.

CI *abbreviation.*
1 Channel Islands.
2 *hist.* Order of the Crown of India.

CIA *abbreviation. US.*
Central Intelligence Agency.

ciabatta /tʃəˈbɑːtə, *foreign* tʃaˈbatta/ *noun.* Pl. **-ttas**, **-tte** /-tte/. **L20.**
[**ORIGIN** Italian dial., lit. 'slipper' (from the shape of the loaf).]
A type of moist aerated Italian bread made with olive oil; a loaf of this.

ciao /tʃaʊ/ *interjection. colloq.* **E20.**
[**ORIGIN** Italian dial. alt. of *schiavo* (I am your) slave from medieval Latin *sclavus* slave.]
Hello; goodbye.

cibarian /sɪˈbɛːrɪən/ *adjective.* **E17.**
[**ORIGIN** from Latin *cibarius*, from *cibus* food, + **-AN.**]
1 Of or pertaining to food. *rare.* **E17.**
2 *ENTOMOLOGY.* Of or pertaining to the mouthparts of an insect. **M19.**
■ **cibarial** *adjective* (*ENTOMOLOGY*) = **CIBARIAN** 2; *spec.* of or pertaining to the cibarium: **L19.** **cibarious** *adjective* (*rare*) (**a**) = **CIBARIAN** 1; (**b**) edible: **M17.** **cibarium** *noun* (*ENTOMOLOGY*) the preoral cavity of an insect, often specialized for the temporary storage of food or as a salivary pump **M20.**

†**cibation** *noun.* **L15.**
[**ORIGIN** Late Latin *cibatio(n-)*, from Latin *cibat-* pa. ppl stem of *cibare* to feed from *cibus* food see **-ATION.**]
1 *ALCHEMY.* The seventh process, 'feeding the matter'. **L15–M17.**
2 *gen.* Taking food, feeding. **M17–M19.**

cibol *noun* see **CIBOULE.**

ciborium /sɪˈbɔːrɪəm/ *noun.* Pl. **-ia** /-ɪə/. **M16.**
[**ORIGIN** medieval Latin from Greek *kibōrion* cup-shaped seed vessel of the Egyptian water lily, or a cup made from this. Sense 1 prob. infl. by Latin *cibus* food.]
1 *CHRISTIAN CHURCH.* A receptacle for the reservation of the Eucharist, shaped like a shrine, or a cup with an arched cover. **M16.**
2 *ARCHITECTURE.* A canopy; a canopied shrine. **M18.**

ciboule /ˈsɪb(ə)l/ *noun.* Also **cibol.** **M17.**
[**ORIGIN** French: see **CHIBOL.** Cf. earlier **SYBOW.**]
The Welsh onion, *Allium fistulosum*, which resembles a spring onion.

cicada /sɪˈkɑːdə/ *noun.* **LME.**
[**ORIGIN** Latin *cicada*, *cicala.*]
Any of the family Cicadidae of large-winged homopteran insects, the males of which make shrill chirping sounds.
periodical cicada: see **PERIODICAL** *adjective* 2. ***SEVENTEEN-year cicada.***
– **NOTE**: The usual name 17–18 was **CIGALA.**
■ **cicad** /ˈsɪkad/ *noun* a cicada **M19.** **cicala** *noun* a cicada **L18.**

cicatrice /ˈsɪkətrɪs/ *noun.* Also (esp. *MEDICINE & BOTANY*) **cicatrix** /ˈsɪkətrɪks/. Pl. **cicatrices** /ˈsɪkətrɪsɪz/; *esp. MEDICINE & BOTANY* sɪkəˈtrʌɪsiːz/. **LME.**
[**ORIGIN** Old French & mod. French, or Latin *cicatrix*, *-tric-.*]
1 The scar of a healed wound, burn, etc.; a scar on the bark of a tree. **LME.** ▸**b** *BOTANY.* = **SCAR** *noun*[2] 2. **E19.**
2 A mark or impression resembling a scar. **L16.**
■ **cicatricial** /sɪkəˈtrɪʃ(ə)l/ *adjective* pertaining to or of the nature of a scar; forming a scar: **L19.**

cicatricula /sɪkəˈtrɪkjʊlə/ *noun.* Pl. **-lae** /-liː/. Also anglicized as **cicatricle** /sɪˈkatrɪk(ə)l/. **M17.**
[**ORIGIN** Latin, dim. of *cicatrix*: see **CICATRICE**, **-CULE.**]
A small mark or scar; *esp.* the germinal region of an egg.

cicatrise *verb* var. of **CICATRIZE.**

cicatrix *noun* see **CICATRICE.**

cicatrize /ˈsɪkətrʌɪz/ *verb.* Also **-ise.** **LME.**
[**ORIGIN** Old French & mod. French *cicatriser*, †*-icer*, formed as **CICATRICE**; assim. to verbs in **-IZE.**]
1 *verb trans.* Heal (a wound etc.) by scarring; skin over. **LME.**
2 *verb intrans.* Of a wound etc.: become healed by forming a scar. **LME.**
3 *verb trans.* Mark with scars; scar. **E18.**
■ **cicaˈtrizant** *adjective & noun* (a medicine) that cicatrizes wounds etc. **M17.** **cicatriˈzation** *noun* the formation of a scar in the healing of a wound etc. **M16.** **cicatrizer** *noun* a person who or thing which cicatrizes wounds etc. **L16.**

cicely /ˈsɪsɪli/ *noun.* **L16.**
[**ORIGIN** App. from Latin *seselis* **SESELI** from Greek, with assim. to female forename *Cicely.*]
Any of various umbelliferous plants; *esp.* (**a**) (more fully ***sweet cicely***) a European plant, *Myrrhis odorata*, resembling cow parsley, with aromatic foliage and white flowers; (**b**) *N. Amer.* a member of the genus *Osmorhiza.*

cicer /ˈsɪsə/ *noun.* **LME.**
[**ORIGIN** Latin.]
A chickpea. Now only as mod. Latin genus name.

cicerone /tʃɪtʃəˈrəʊni, sɪsə-/ *noun.* Pl. **-ni** /-ni/, **-nes.** **E18.**
[**ORIGIN** Italian from Latin *Ciceron-*: see **CICERONIAN.**]
A guide who understands and explains antiquities etc.

cicerone /tʃɪtʃəˈrəʊn, sɪs-/ *verb trans.* **L18.**
[**ORIGIN** from the noun.]
Act as a cicerone to.

Ciceronian /sɪsəˈrəʊnɪən/ *adjective & noun.* **L16.**
[**ORIGIN** Latin *Ciceronianus*, from *Cicero*, *-on-* cognomen of Marcus Tullius *Cicero* (106–43 BC), Roman politician and orator: see **-IAN.**]
▸ **A** *adjective.* Pertaining to or in the style of Cicero; eloquent, classical, rhythmical. **L16.**
▸ **B** *noun.* An admirer, student, or imitator of Cicero or his works. **L16.**
■ **Ciceronianism** *noun* (an expression) imitating Cicero as a model of Latin style **L16.**

†**cich** *noun* var. of **CHICH.**

cichlid /ˈsɪklɪd/ *noun & adjective.* **L19.**
[**ORIGIN** mod. Latin *Cichlidae* (see below), from Greek *kikhlē* a kind of fish: see **-ID**[3].]
▸ **A** *noun.* A tropical freshwater fish of the family Cichlidae, of which many kinds are kept in aquaria. **L19.**
▸ **B** *adjective.* Of, pertaining to, or designating this family. **L19.**

†**cichling** *noun* see **CHICKLING.**

cicisbeo /tʃɪtʃɪzˈbeɪəʊ/ *noun.* Pl. **-bei** /-ˈbeiːi/, **-os.** **E18.**
[**ORIGIN** Italian, of unknown origin.]
A married (orig. Italian) woman's male companion or lover.
■ **cicisbeism** /-ˈbiːɪz(ə)m/ *noun* the practice of attending a married woman as a cicisbeo **M18.**

ciclatoun /ˈsɪklətən/ *noun.* Long *obsolete* exc. *hist.* **ME.**
[**ORIGIN** Old French *ciclaton*, perh. from Arabic *siqlāṭūn.*]
Cloth of gold or a similar rich material.

ciconiiform /sɪˈkəʊnɪɪfɔːm/ *adjective.* **L19.**
[**ORIGIN** mod. Latin *ciconiiformis*, from *ciconia* stork: see **-FORM.**]
ORNITHOLOGY. Belonging or pertaining to the order Ciconiiformes, which includes the herons, storks, ibises, flamingos, and related birds.

†**cicurate** *verb trans.* **E17–E18.**
[**ORIGIN** Latin *cicurat-* pa. ppl stem of *cicurare* to tame from *cicur* tame: see **-ATE**[3].]
Tame, domesticate.

cicuta /sɪˈkjuːtə/ *noun.* **LME.**
[**ORIGIN** Latin.]
Hemlock, esp. as a poison.
■ **cicuˈtoxin** *noun* a polyunsaturated alcohol that is the major toxin of water hemlock, *Cicuta virosa* **L19.**

CID *abbreviation.*
1 Criminal Investigation Department.
2 *hist.* Committee of Imperial Defence.

cidaris /ˈsɪdərɪs/ *noun.* **E17.**
[**ORIGIN** Latin from Greek *kidaris*, *kitaris*, = Hebrew *keṯer* (Persian) crown, diadem.]
The royal tiara or cap of state of the ancient Persians.

-cide /sʌɪd/ *suffix.*
[**ORIGIN** Sense 1 from French *-cide* from Latin *-cida*, sense 2 from French *-cide* from Latin *-cidium* cutting, killing, both from *caedere*, *-cidere* cut, kill.]
1 Forming (usu. with intermediate **-I-**) nouns with the sense 'a person or substance that kills', as ***fratricide***, ***insecticide***, etc.
2 Forming (usu. with intermediate **-I-**) nouns of action with the sense 'the killing of (the first element)', as ***suicide*** etc.

cider /ˈsʌɪdə/ *noun.* Also *arch.* **cyder.** **ME.**
[**ORIGIN** Old French *sidre*, earlier *cisdre* (mod. *cidre*), from ecclesiastical Latin *sicera* (medieval Latin *cisera*) from ecclesiastical Greek *sikera* from Hebrew *šēḵār* strong drink.]
A drink made from the juice of apples (and formerly other fruit) expressed and fermented; *N. Amer.* unfermented apple juice.
– **COMB.**: **cider apple**: from which cider is made. **cider press**: for squeezing juice from apples.
■ **ciderist** *noun* (now *rare*) a maker or connoisseur of cider **M17.** **ciderkin** *noun* a weak cider made from second pressings **L17.** **cidery** *adjective* of the nature of or resembling cider **L19.**

ci-devant /sidvɑ̃/ *adjective & adverb*. **E18**.
[**ORIGIN** French.]
Former(ly); that has been (with the person's earlier name or status).

CIE *abbreviation*.
Companion of (the Order of) the Indian Empire.

ciel *verb & noun* var. of **CEIL**.

cieling *noun* var. of **CEILING**.

cierge /sɪədʒ; *foreign* sjɛrʒ (*pl. same*)/ *noun*. **ME**.
[**ORIGIN** Old French *cerge*, (also mod.) *cierge*, from Latin *cereus* wax taper, from *cera* wax.]
A wax candle, *esp.* one used in religious ceremonies.

c.i.f. *abbreviation*.
Cost, insurance, freight (as being included in a price).

cig /sɪɡ/ *noun*. *colloq*. **L19**.
[**ORIGIN** Abbreviation.]
A cigarette; *occas.* a cigar, a cigarillo.

cigala /sɪˈɡɑːlə/ *noun*. Also **-ale** /-ɑːl/. **E17**.
[**ORIGIN** Old Provençal *cigala*, French *cigale*, formed as **CICADA**.]
= **CICADA**.

cigar /sɪˈɡɑː/ *noun*. Also **segar**, (now *US colloq. & dial.*) **seegar** /ˈsiːɡɑː/. **E18**.
[**ORIGIN** French *cigare* or its source Spanish *cigarro*, prob. from Maya *sik'ar* smoking.]
A compact roll of tobacco leaf for smoking.
close but no cigar *colloq.* (of an attempt) almost but not quite successful. ***Manila cigar***: see **MANILA** *adjective* 1. ***panatela cigar***: see **PANATELA** 1.
– **COMB.**: **cigar flower** a Mexican primulaceous plant, *Cuphea ignea*, with a scarlet tubular corolla tipped with black and white; **cigar-holder** a device for holding a cigar for smoking; **cigar-lighter** a device (esp. in a car) for lighting a cigar, cigarette, etc.; **cigar plant** = *cigar flower* above; **cigar-shaped** *adjective* cylindrical with a tapered end or tapered ends.
■ **ciga'resque** *adjective* (*joc.*) having a cigar or cigars as a prominent feature **M19**. **cigary** *adjective* of or pertaining to a heavy cigar-smoker **E20**.

cigarette /sɪɡəˈrɛt/ *noun*. Also ***-ret**. **M19**.
[**ORIGIN** French, from *cigare*: see **CIGAR**, **-ETTE**.]
A small cylinder of finely cut tobacco or of a narcotic or medicated substance rolled in paper for smoking.
RUSSIAN cigarette.
– **COMB.**: **cigarette card**, **cigarette coupon** a picture card or voucher inserted by the manufacturer into a packet or box of cigarettes; **cigarette case**: for holding cigarettes before use; **cigarette end** the unsmoked remainder of a cigarette; **cigarette holder** a device for holding a cigarette for smoking; **cigarette lighter** a device for lighting cigarettes; **cigarette machine**: that dispenses (boxes or packets of) cigarettes; **cigarette pants** women's trousers with straight, very narrow legs; **cigarette paper**: for rolling tobacco in to make a cigarette.

cigarillo /sɪɡəˈrɪləʊ, -ljəʊ/ *noun*. Pl. **-os**. **M19**.
[**ORIGIN** Spanish *cigarrillo*, dim. of *cigarro* **CIGAR**.]
A small cigar.

cigarito /sɪɡəˈriːtəʊ/ *noun*. Pl. **-os**. Also **-ta** /-tə/. **M19**.
[**ORIGIN** Amer. Spanish *cigarrito*, dim. of *cigarro* **CIGAR**.]
A cigarette.

ciggy /ˈsɪɡi/ *noun*. *colloq*. **M20**.
[**ORIGIN** Abbreviation: see **-Y**[6].]
A cigarette.

CIGS *abbreviation*.
hist. Chief of the Imperial General Staff.

ciguatera /sɪɡwəˈtɛːrə/ *noun*. **M19**.
[**ORIGIN** Amer. Spanish, from *cigua* sea snail.]
Poisoning due to ingestion of neurotoxins sometimes present in the flesh of tropical marine fish.

cilantro /sɪˈlantrəʊ/ *noun*. **E20**.
[**ORIGIN** Spanish, from Latin *coliandrum* coriander.]
Coriander, esp. the leaf used as a seasoning or garnish in Mexican cuisine.

cilery /ˈsɪləri/ *noun*. Now *rare* or *obsolete*. Also **-ll-**. **M16**.
[**ORIGIN** Uncertain: perh. rel. to **CEIL**.]
ARCHITECTURE. Drapery or foliage carved on the heads of pillars; such a carving.

cilia *noun* pl. of **CILIUM**.

ciliary /ˈsɪlɪəri/ *adjective*. **L17**.
[**ORIGIN** formed as **CILIUM** + **-ARY**[1].]
1 Of or pertaining to the eyelashes or eyelids. **L17**.
ciliary body the part of the eye connecting the choroid to the iris. **ciliary muscle** an annular muscle within the ciliary body controlling the shape of the lens of the eye.
2 Of, pertaining to, caused by, or involving cilia (sense 3). **M19**.
■ Also †**ciliar** *adjective* **E17–E19**.

ciliate /ˈsɪlɪeɪt/ *adjective & noun*. **M18**.
[**ORIGIN** formed as **CILIARY** + **-ATE**[2].]
▶ **A** *adjective*. Fringed or surrounded with cilia. **M18**.
▶ **B** *noun*. A protozoan of the phylum Ciliophora (formerly class Ciliophora), characterized by the presence of motile cilia. **L19**.
■ **ciliated** *adjective* = **CILIATE** *adjective* **M18**. **cili'ation** *noun* the presence or arrangement of cilia **M19**.

cilice /ˈsɪlɪs/ *noun*. **L16**.
[**ORIGIN** French from Latin *cilicium* from Greek *kilikion*, from *Kilikia* Cilicia (see **CILICIAN**).]
(A garment of) haircloth.

Cilician /sɪˈlɪʃ(ə)n/ *adjective & noun*. **L16**.
[**ORIGIN** from *Cilicia* (see below) + **-AN**.]
▶ **A** *adjective* of or pertaining to Cilicia, an ancient district of S. Anatolia, now in S. Turkey. **L16**.
▶ **B** *noun*. A native or inhabitant of Cilicia. **M18**.

Cilicism /ˈsɪlɪsɪz(ə)m/ *noun*. **M19**.
[**ORIGIN** formed as **CILICIAN** + **-ISM**.]
A word or expression characteristic of Cilicia.

ciliiform /ˈsɪlɪɪfɔːm/ *adjective*. **M19**.
[**ORIGIN** from **CILIUM** + **-I-** + **-FORM**.]
Having the form of cilia.

cilio- /ˈsɪlɪəʊ/ *combining form* of **CILIUM**: see **-O-**.
■ **cilio'retinal** *adjective* of or pertaining to the retina and ciliary body of the eye **L19**.

cilium /ˈsɪlɪəm/ *noun*. Pl. **-ia** /-ɪə/. **E18**.
[**ORIGIN** Latin.]
1 An eyelash; (the edge of) an eyelid. **E18**.
2 A delicate hair like an eyelash, e.g. on the margin of a leaf, or the wing of an insect. **L18**.
3 A hairlike appendage, usu. motile, which is found in numbers on the surfaces of some cells, and in many organisms is used in locomotion. **M19**.

cill *noun & verb* see **SILL** *noun*[1] *& verb*.

cillery *noun* var. of **CILERY**.

cimarron /ˈsɪmər(ə)n, sɪməˈrəʊn/ *noun*. *N. Amer.* Also **cimmaron**. **M19**.
[**ORIGIN** from Amer. Spanish *cimarrón* wild, untamed, (as noun) runaway slave, from *cima* peak.]
The Rocky Mountain sheep, *Ovis canadensis*.

cimbalom /ˈsɪmb(ə)l(ə)m/ *noun*. Also **z-** /z-/. **L19**.
[**ORIGIN** Hungarian from Italian *cembalo*, *cimbalo* **CYMBALO**.]
A dulcimer.

cimbia /ˈsɪmbɪə/ *noun*. **M17**.
[**ORIGIN** Italian.]
ARCHITECTURE. A fillet or ring round the shaft of a column; an apophyge.

Cimbrian /ˈsɪmbrɪən/ *noun & adjective*. **M16**.
[**ORIGIN** from Latin *Cimbri* + **-AN**.]
▶ **A** *noun*. A member of an ancient people of central Europe of unknown affinities. **M16**.
▶ **B** *adjective*. Of or pertaining to the Cimbrians. **L16**.

Cimbric /ˈsɪmbrɪk/ *noun & adjective*. **E17**.
[**ORIGIN** formed as **CIMBRIAN** + **-IC**.]
▶ **A** *noun*. †**1** A Cimbrian. *rare*. Only in **E17**.
2 The language of the Cimbrians. **M18**.
▶ **B** *adjective*. = **CIMBRIAN** *adjective*. **L18**.

†**cime** *noun* see **CYME**.

cimelia /sɪˈmiːlɪə/ *noun pl*. *rare*. **M17**.
[**ORIGIN** Late Latin, pl. of *cimelium* (church) treasure from Greek *keimēlion* anything stored up as valuable.]
Treasures laid up in store.
■ **cimeliarch** *noun* (*a*) a storehouse (for treasures); (*b*) a treasurer: **M17**.

cimetidine /sʌɪˈmɛtɪdiːn/ *noun*. **L20**.
[**ORIGIN** from *ci-* alt. of **CY(ANO-** + **MET(HYL** + **-IDINE**.]
PHARMACOLOGY. An antihistamine drug which is a sulphur-containing derivative of imidazole used to treat peptic ulcers.
– **NOTE**: A proprietary name for this drug is **TAGAMET**.

cimex /ˈsʌɪmɛks/ *noun*. Pl. †**cimices**. **L16**.
[**ORIGIN** Latin.]
A bedbug. Now only as mod. Latin genus name.

cimmaron *noun* var. of **CIMARRON**.

Cimmerian /sɪˈmɪərɪən/ *noun & adjective*. **L16**.
[**ORIGIN** from Latin *Cimmerius* (from Greek *Kimmerios*) + **-AN**.]
▶ **A** *noun*. **1** A member of a people fabled to live in perpetual darkness. **L16**.
2 A member of a nomadic people of antiquity, the earliest known inhabitants of the Crimea, who overran Asia Minor in the 7th cent. BC. **L18**.
▶ **B** *adjective*. **1** Of or pertaining to the legendary Cimmerians; (of darkness, night, etc.) thick, gloomy. **L16**.
2 Of or pertaining to the nomadic Cimmerians. **M19**.

C.-in-C. *abbreviation*.
Commander-in-chief.

cinch /sɪn(t)ʃ/ *noun & verb*. **M19**.
[**ORIGIN** Spanish *cincha* girth.]
▶ **A** *noun*. **1** A saddle-girth used in Mexico and the western US, usu. made of twisted horsehair or cord. **M19**.
2 *fig*. A firm hold; *slang* a sure, safe, or easy thing, a certainty. **L19**.

R. TREMAIN I had my piece of rope now. Getting out on to the roof was a cinch.

lead-pipe cinch: see **LEAD** *noun*[1] *& adjective*.
3 A variant of the card game all fours. **L19**.
▶ **B** *verb*. **1** *verb trans.* Fix (a saddle etc.) securely by means of a girth, fix (a girth); *transf.* girdle, pull *in*, (clothing). **M19**.
▸**b** *verb intrans.* Fix a saddle-girth. **L19**.
2 *verb trans. fig.* Get (a person) into a tight place; secure a hold upon. **L19**. ▸**b** Make certain of (something); render conclusive. *slang*. **E20**.
3 *verb trans.* In the card game cinch: protect (a trick) by playing a higher trump than the five. **L19**.

C

cinchocaine /ˈsɪŋkəʊkeɪn/ *noun*. **M20**.
[**ORIGIN** from **CINCHONA** + **-CAINE**.]
PHARMACOLOGY. A quinoline derivative used as a very powerful local anaesthetic for surface or spinal applications.
– **NOTE**: A proprietary name for this drug is **NUPERCAINE**.

cinchona /sɪŋˈkəʊnə/ *noun*. Also **chinchona** /tʃɪnˈtʃəʊnə/. **M18**.
[**ORIGIN** mod. Latin, from Countess of *Chinchón* (d. 1641), vicereine of Peru, who introduced the drug to Spain.]
1 An evergreen tree or shrub of the S. American genus *Cinchona*, of the madder family, with fragrant flowers. **M18**.
2 = ***cinchona bark*** below. Also, a drug made from cinchona bark. **L18**.
– **COMB.**: **cinchona bark** the dried bark of a cinchona (as a source of quinine and other medicinal alkaloids).
■ **cinchonicine**, **cinchonidine** *nouns* cinchona alkaloids isomeric with cinchonine **M19**. **cinchonine** *noun* an alkaloid, $C_{19}H_{22}ON_2$, with febrifuge properties, found with quinine in cinchona bark **E19**. **cinchonism** *noun* poisoning due to excessive ingestion of cinchona alkaloids **M19**.

cincinnus /sɪnˈsɪnəs/ *noun*. **M19**.
[**ORIGIN** Latin = curl, ringlet.]
BOTANY. A scorpioid cyme.

cinct /sɪŋkt/ *pred. adjective*. Chiefly *poet.* **LME**.
[**ORIGIN** Latin *cinctus* pa. pple of *cingere* gird.]
Girt, encircled, (*with*).

cincture /ˈsɪŋktʃə/ *noun & verb*. **L16**.
[**ORIGIN** Latin *cinctura*, formed as **CINCT** + *-ura* **-URE**.]
▶ **A** *noun*. **1** A girding, encompassing, or encircling; enclosure. **L16**.
2 A thing which girdles or encompasses; *spec.* a girdle or belt for the waist. **M17**. ▸**b** *ARCHITECTURE.* The ring at the top or bottom of a column which divides the shaft from the capital or base; a ring or band encircling a column or interrupting an architrave. **L17**.
▶ **B** *verb trans.* Gird; encompass, surround. **L18**.

cinder /ˈsɪndə/ *noun & verb*.
[**ORIGIN** Old English *sinder* = Middle Low German *sinder*, Old High German *sintar* (German *Sinter*), Old Norse *sindr*; with assim. since 16 to unrelated French *cendre* (Latin *cinis*, *ciner-* ashes).]
▶ **A** *noun*. **1** Slag, scoria. **OE**.
2 In *pl.* The residue of combustion; ashes. **LME**.
3 *spec.* A residual piece of coal, wood, etc., whether cold or not, that has ceased to flame but has still combustible matter in it. **M16**.
burn to a cinder make inedible or useless by burning.
– **COMB.**: **cinder cone** a cone formed round the mouth of a volcano by debris cast up during eruption; **cinder path**, **cinder track** a footpath or running track laid with fine cinders.
▶ **B** *verb trans.* Reduce to cinders. **LME**.
■ **cindery** *adjective* of the nature of a cinder; full of cinders: **M16**.

Cinderella /sɪndəˈrɛlə/ *noun*. **M19**.
[**ORIGIN** The heroine of a fairy tale, from **CINDER** *noun* + **-ELLA**, after French *Cendrillon*, from *cendre* cinders, ashes + dim. ending *-illon*.]
1 A drudge; a neglected or despised partner, member of a group, etc.; a person or thing of unrecognized or disregarded merit or beauty. **M19**.
2 In full ***Cinderella dance***. A dance stopping at midnight. **L19**.

cinderous /ˈsɪnd(ə)rəs/ *adjective*. Also **cindrous** /ˈsɪndrəs/. **E17**.
[**ORIGIN** from **CINDER** *noun* + **-OUS**.]
Cindery.

cine /ˈsɪni/ *adjective*. Also (now *rare*) **k-** /k-/. See also **CINE-**. **L19**.
[**ORIGIN** Abbreviation.]
Cinematographic.
cine camera, ***cine film***, ***cine projector***, etc.

cine- /ˈsɪni/ *combining form*.
[**ORIGIN** Abbreviation of **CINEMATOGRAPHIC**, **CINEMA**. Cf. **CINE**.]
1 Cinematographic.
2 With the sense 'cinema', as ***cine-goer***.
■ **cinefluoro'graphic** *adjective* of or pertaining to cinefluorography **M20**. **cinefluo'rography** *noun* the recording of a fluoroscopic image by cinephotography **M20**. **cinemicro'graphic** *adjective* of or pertaining to cinemicrography **M20**. **cinemi'crography** *noun* the making of a cine film of an object, process, etc., seen with the aid of a microscope **M20**. **cinephile** *noun* a person who is fond of the cinema **L20**. **cine'philia** *noun* interest in or liking for the cinema **L20**. **cinepho'tography** *noun* the making of a cine film **E20**. **cineplex** *noun* (chiefly *N. Amer.*) a cinema with several separate screens, a multiplex **L20**. **cine'radiograph** *noun* a series of cineradiographic photographs **M20**. **cineradio'graphic** *adjective* of or pertaining to cineradiography **M20**. **cineradi'ography** *noun* the taking of a

series of X-ray photographs which can be viewed in the manner of a cine film M20.

cinéaste /ˈsɪneɪast; *foreign* sineast (*pl. same*)/ *noun.* Also **cineast(e)** /ˈsɪnɪast/. E20.
[ORIGIN French, from *ciné* CINE + *-aste* as in *enthousiaste* enthusiast.]
An enthusiast for or devotee of the cinema.

C

cinema /ˈsɪnɪmə/ *noun.* Also (now *rare*) **k-** /k-/. E20.
[ORIGIN French *cinéma* abbreviation of *cinématographe* CINEMATOGRAPH *noun.* Initial *k-* after Greek.]
1 = CINEMATOGRAPH *noun.* E20.
2 A theatre in which cinematographic films are shown. E20.
3 Cinematography; the production of cinematographic films, esp. as an art or an industry. E20.
– COMB.: **cinema-goer** a person who frequents the cinema; **cinema organ**: with extra stops and effects.

CinemaScope /ˈsɪnɪməˌskəʊp/ *noun.* M20.
[ORIGIN from CINEMA + -SCOPE.]
(Proprietary name for) a cinematographic process in which special lenses are used to compress a wide image into a standard frame and then expand it again during projection, resulting in an image that is almost two and a half times as wide as it is high.

cinematheque /sɪnɪməˈtɛk/ *noun.* Also ***cinémathèque*** /sinematɛk (*pl. same*)/. M20.
[ORIGIN French *cinémathèque*, formed as CINEMA, after *bibliothèque* library.]
A library of cinema films; a (national) repository of old films. Also, a small cinema showing artistic films.

cinematic /sɪnɪˈmatɪk/ *adjective.* E20.
[ORIGIN from CINEMA after CINEMATOGRAPH: see -IC.]
Of or pertaining to the cinematograph; suitable for cinematography; suggestive of the technique, dialogue, etc., of the cinema.
■ **cinematically** *adverb* M20.

cinematize /ˈsɪnɪmətʌɪz/ *verb trans.* Also **-ise**. E20.
[ORIGIN formed as CINEMATIC + -IZE.]
Adapt (a play, story, etc.) to the cinema; make a film of.

cinematograph /sɪnɪˈmatəgrɑːf/ *noun & verb.* Also (now *rare*) **k-** /k-/. L19.
[ORIGIN French *cinématographe*, from Greek *kinēma*, *kinēmat-* movement: see -GRAPH. Initial *k-* after Greek.]
▸ **A** *noun.* An apparatus for producing an image in which persons and things appear to move, by rapidly projecting on to a screen a succession of photographs on a long film, often also with the reproduction of sound recorded on it; a film projector. L19.
▸ **B** *verb trans.* Make a cinematographic record of. L19.

cinematographic /ˌsɪnɪmatəˈgrafɪk/ *adjective.* Also (now *rare*) **k-** /k-/. L19.
[ORIGIN from CINEMATOGRAPH + -IC. Initial *k-* after Greek.]
Of or pertaining to cinematography or the cinematograph.
■ **cinematographical** *adjective* E20. **cinematographically** *adverb* L19.

cinematography /ˌsɪnɪməˈtɒgrəfi/ *noun.* Also (now *rare*) **k-** /k-/. L19.
[ORIGIN formed as CINEMATOGRAPHIC: see -GRAPHY. Initial *k-* after Greek.]
The art of taking and reproducing cinematographic films; the use of the cinematograph.
■ **cinematographer** *noun* a person who takes cinematographic films L19. **cinematographist** *noun* (now *rare*) = CINEMATOGRAPHER L19.

cinéma-vérité /sinemaverite, ˌsɪnɪməˈvɛrɪteɪ/ *noun.* M20.
[ORIGIN French.]
(The making of) films which avoid artificiality and have the appearance of real life.

cineole /ˈsɪnɪəʊl/ *noun.* Also **-ol** /-ɒl/. L19.
[ORIGIN from reversal of mod. Latin *oleum cinae* wormseed oil, from Latin *oleum* oil + *cynas* an Arabian tree: see -OLE[2].]
Either of two isomeric essential oils, 1,4- and 1,8-cineole; *esp.* the latter, = EUCALYPTOL.

cineraria /sɪnəˈrɛːrɪə/ *noun*[1]. L16.
[ORIGIN mod. Latin (former genus name), fem. of Latin *cinerarius* CINERARY.]
Orig., the silver ragwort, *Senecio cineraria*, grown for its hoary leaves. Now, any of various garden hybrids of the allied *Pericallis cruenta*, of the Canary Islands, with corymbs of daisy-like blue, purple, etc., flower heads, grown as pot plants.

cineraria *noun*[2] pl. of next.

cinerarium /sɪnəˈrɛːrɪəm/ *noun.* Pl. **-ria** /-rɪə/. L19.
[ORIGIN Late Latin *cinerarium* use as noun of neut. sing. of Latin *cinerarius*: see CINERARY, -ARIUM.]
A place for depositing the ashes of the dead after cremation.

cinerary /ˈsɪnərəri/ *adjective.* M18.
[ORIGIN Latin *cinerarius*, from *ciner-*, *cinis* ashes: see -ARY[1].]
Of or pertaining to ashes.
cinerary urn: holding the ashes of the dead after cremation.

cinereous /sɪˈnɪərɪəs/ *adjective.* LME.
[ORIGIN from Latin *cinereus*, from *cinis*, *ciner-* ashes, + -OUS.]
Of the nature of ashes; (esp. of a bird or plumage) ash-coloured.

cineritious /sɪnəˈrɪʃəs/ *adjective.* L17.
[ORIGIN from Latin *cinericius* from *cinis*, *ciner-* ashes, + -OUS: see -ITIOUS[1].]
1 Ash-grey; also formerly used of the grey matter of the brain and spinal cord. L17.
2 Of the nature of ashes or cinders. M18.

ciné-vérité /sineverite, sɪnɪˈvɛrɪteɪ/ *noun.* M20.
[ORIGIN French.]
= CINÉMA-VÉRITÉ.

Cingalese /sɪŋgəˈliːz/ *noun & adjective. arch.* Pl. of noun same. L16.
[ORIGIN formed as SINHALESE, partly through French *Cing(h)alais*.]
= SINHALESE.

cingle /ˈsɪŋg(ə)l/ *noun.* ME.
[ORIGIN Old French *cengle* (mod. *sangle*) from Latin *cingulum*, *-la* girdle, from *cingere* gird.]
A girdle; a girth; a belt.

cingulum /ˈsɪŋgjʊləm/ *noun.* Pl. **-la** /-lə/. M19.
[ORIGIN Latin: see CINGLE.]
Chiefly ANATOMY & ZOOLOGY. A girdle, belt, or analogous structure; *esp.* (***a***) a ridge surrounding the base of the crown of a tooth; (***b***) a gyrus of each cerebral hemisphere, partly encircling the corpus callosum.
■ **cingular** *adjective* of or pertaining to a cingulum E20. **cingulate** *adjective* having a cingulum; of the nature of a cingulum: E19.

cinnabar /ˈsɪnəbɑː/ *noun & adjective.* ME.
[ORIGIN Latin *cinnabaris* from Greek *kinnabari*, of oriental origin.]
▸ **A** *noun.* **1** Native mercury(II) sulphide, a bright red hexagonal mineral which usu. occurs in massive form and is the only important ore of mercury; this mineral used as a pigment, vermilion. ME.
2 A moth, *Tyria jacobaeae*, with bright red wing markings. Also ***cinnabar moth***. E19.
▸ **B** *adjective.* Of the colour of cinnabar; vermilion. E19.
■ **cinnabarine** *adjective* consisting of or containing cinnabar; of the colour of cinnabar: L17.

cinnamic /sɪˈnamɪk/ *adjective.* M19.
[ORIGIN from Latin *cinnamum* CINNAMON + -IC.]
CHEMISTRY. Of cinnamon; ***cinnamic acid***, the compound 3-phenylpropenoic acid, $C_6H_5·CHCHCOOH$, a crystalline unsaturated acid present in many resins and balsams.
■ **cinnaˈmaldehyde** *noun* the corresponding aldehyde, $C_6H_5CHCHCHO$, which is the major constituent of cinnamon and cassia oils L19. **ˈcinnamate** *noun* a salt or ester of cinnamic acid M19. **ˈcinnamyl** *noun* the radical $C_6H_5CHCHCH_2·$; usu. in *comb.*: M19.

cinnamon /ˈsɪnəmən/ *noun & adjective.* LME.
[ORIGIN Old French & mod. French *cinnamome* from Latin *cinnamomum* from Greek *kinnamōmon*, later refashioned after Latin *cinnamon*, *-mum* from Greek *kinnamon*, from Semitic, perh. ult. from Malay.]
▸ **A** *noun.* **1** The powdered aromatic inner bark of a southern Indian tree, *Cinnamomum zeylanicum*, used as a spice. Also, the bark of certain other trees, resembling this. LME.
2 A tree yielding cinnamon. LME.
3 The colour of cinnamon; a yellowish brown. L19.
– PHRASES: **wild cinnamon** an evergreen tree, *Canella winterana*, native to Florida and the W. Indies, whose bark is used as a spice; the bark of this tree. LME.
▸ **B** *adjective.* Of the colour of cinnamon; yellowish brown. L17.
– COMB.: **cinnamon bear** a cinnamon-coloured phase of the N. American black bear; **cinnamon fern** *N. Amer.* a large fern, *Osmunda cinnamomea*, often with cinnamon fronds; **cinnamon oil** an aromatic oil distilled from cinnamon bark; **cinnamon rose** a fragrant Eurasian rose, *Rosa majalis*; **cinnamon stone** a yellow-brown variety of garnet; **cinnamon toast** buttered toast spread with ground cinnamon and sugar.

cinq *noun* var. of CINQUE.

cinqfoil *noun & adjective* var. of CINQUEFOIL.

cinq trous /sɛ̃ːk tru/ *noun phr.* L19.
[ORIGIN French = five holes.]
A form of mesh in certain types of lace in which openings are set alternately in quincunx form.

cinquain /sɪŋˈkeɪn/ *noun.* E18.
[ORIGIN French, from *cinq* five + *-ain* -AN. Cf. QUATRAIN.]
†**1** A group of five battalions. *rare.* Only in E18.
2 A stanza of five lines. L19.

cinque /sɪŋk/ *noun.* Also **cinq**. LME.
[ORIGIN Old French *cinc*, *cink* (mod. *cinq*) from Latin *quinque* five. Cf. earlier CINQUE PORTS, also CINQ TROUS.]
1 The five on dice; a throw of five. LME.
2 BELL-RINGING. In *pl.* Changes on eleven bells in which five couples of bells change places in the order of ringing. L19.

cinquecento /tʃɪŋkwɪˈtʃɛntəʊ/ *noun.* M18.
[ORIGIN Italian = five hundred.]
The sixteenth century in Italy; the Italian style of art of this period, with reversion to classical forms.

■ **cinquecentist** *noun* a sixteenth-century Italian artist or writer L19.

cinquedea /tʃɪŋkwɪˈdeɪə/ *noun.* L19.
[ORIGIN Venetian Italian, from *cinque* five + *dea* = *dita* fingers, pl. of *dito* from Latin *digitus* DIGIT.]
An Italian broad-bladed dagger or short sword.

cinquefoil /ˈsɪŋkfɔɪl/ *noun & adjective.* Also **cinqfoil**. ME.
[ORIGIN from Latin *quinquefolium*: see CINQUE, FOIL *noun*[1].]
▸ **A** *noun.* **1** Any of various plants of the genus *Potentilla*, of the rose family, with compound leaves of five leaflets. ME.
2 An ornamental design resembling the leaf of a cinquefoil, esp. inscribed in an arch or circle. LME.
▸ **B** *adjective.* Shaped like the leaf of cinquefoil; decorated with cinquefoils. LME.
■ **cinquefoiled** *adjective* = CINQUEFOIL *adjective* E19.

†**cinquepace** *noun.* L16–M17.
[ORIGIN French *cinq pas* five paces.]
A lively dance, identified with the galliard.

Cinque Ports /sɪŋk ˈpɔːts/ *noun phr. pl.* ME.
[ORIGIN Old French *cink porz* repr. Latin *quinque portus* five ports.]
1 Certain ports on the SE coast of England (orig. five—Hastings, Sandwich, Dover, Romney, Hythe—later also Rye and Winchelsea) which formerly provided the chief part of the navy and in return had many important privileges and franchises. ME.
†**2** Barons of the Cinque Ports. Only in E17.

Cinzano /tʃɪnˈzɑːnəʊ/ *noun.* Pl. **-os**. E20.
[ORIGIN Name of the manufacturers.]
(Proprietary name for) an Italian vermouth; a drink of this.

CIO *abbreviation.*
Congress of Industrial Organizations.

cion *noun* see SCION.

cipher /ˈsʌɪfə/ *noun.* Also **cypher**. LME.
[ORIGIN Old French *cif(f)re* (mod. *chiffre*) from medieval Latin *cif(e)ra* partly through Italian *cifra*, †*cifera* from Arabic *ṣifr*: cf. ZERO *noun & adjective*. Branch II perh. a different word: cf. CIPHER *verb* I.]
▸ **I 1** An arithmetical symbol, 0, of no value by itself, but used to occupy a vacant place in decimal etc. numeration. LME. ▸**b** *fig.* A person who or thing which fills a place but is of no importance; a nonentity. L16.

b P. G. WODEHOUSE He was . . a cipher in the home.

2 A numeral; *esp.* an arabic numeral. LME. ▸†**b** A symbolic character; a hieroglyph; an astrological sign. M16–M19.
3 A secret or disguised system of writing, a code used in writing; a message etc. so written; a key to such a system. E16. ▸†**b** In *pl.* Shorthand. M16–M17.

L. STRACHEY She despatched a fulminating telegram to Mr. Gladstone, not in the usual cypher, but open.

PLAYFAIR *cipher*.
4 An interlacing of letters, esp. the initials of a name; a monogram. M16.
▸ **II 5** A continuous sounding of an organ pipe owing to a mechanical defect. L18.
■ **cipherdom** *noun* the state of being a nonentity E20.

cipher /ˈsʌɪfə/ *verb.* Also **cypher**. E16.
[ORIGIN Perh. two words. Branch II from the noun.]
▸ **I 1** *verb intrans.* Of an organ: sound a note continuously owing to a mechanical defect. E16.
▸ **II 2** *verb intrans.* Use arabic numerals; do arithmetic. *arch.* M16.
3 *verb trans. & intrans.* Write in cipher; express in a secret or disguised way; encipher. M16.
†**4** *verb trans. gen.* Express; delineate. (Foll. by *forth*, *out*.) L16–M17.
†**5** *verb trans.* Decipher. *rare* (Shakes.). Only in L16.
6 *verb trans.* Bevel *away*, *off*. Now *rare* or *obsolete*. L17.
7 *verb trans.* Calculate; work *out* arithmetically; think *out*. M19.
8 *verb trans.* CRICKET. Assign a zero to in the score; put out for no runs. L19.
■ **cipherable** *adjective* L19. **cipherer** *noun* M17.

cipolin /ˈsɪpəlɪn/ *noun.* Also **cipollino** /tʃɪpəˈliːnəʊ/, pl. **-os**. L18.
[ORIGIN (French *cipolin* from) Italian *cipollino*, from *cipolla* onion (Latin *cepa*); so called from the resemblance of its foliated structure to the coats of an onion.]
An Italian marble interfoliated with veins of talc, mica, quartz, etc., showing alternations of (esp. white and green) colourings.

cippus /ˈsɪpəs/ *noun.* Pl. **cippi** /ˈsɪpʌɪ/. E17.
[ORIGIN Latin = post, stake.]
1 The stocks. Now *rare* or *obsolete*. E17.
2 ARCHITECTURE. A low column, usu. bearing an inscription, used by the ancients as a landmark, funerary monument, etc. E18.

circa /ˈsəːkə/ *preposition.* M19.
[ORIGIN Latin.]
About, approximately in or at (with dates etc.).

circadian /səːˈkeɪdɪən/ *adjective*. **M20.**
[**ORIGIN** from Latin **CIRCA** + *dies* day + **-AN.**]
Of physiological activity etc.: occurring or recurring about once a day.

circar *noun* see **SIRKAR.**

Circassian /səːˈkasɪən/ *noun & adjective*. **M16.**
[**ORIGIN** from *Circassia* Latinized form of Russian *Cherkes*: see **-IA**[1], **-AN.**]
▸ **A** *noun*. **1** A native or inhabitant of Circassia, a region in the N. Caucasus; the Caucasian language of the people of this region. **M16.**
2 A thin worsted fabric. **E19.**
▸ **B** *adjective*. Of or pertaining to Circassia, the Circassians, or their language. **M17.**
the Circassian circle: a dance popular in the late 19th and early 20th cents.

Circe /ˈsəːsi/ *noun*. **LME.**
[**ORIGIN** Latin *Circe*, Greek *Kirkē*, an enchantress in Greek mythol.]
A dangerously attractive enchantress, a witch.
■ **Circean** /səːˈsiːən/ *adjective* bewitching, dangerously attractive **E17.**

circensian /səːˈsɛnsɪən/ *adjective*. **L16.**
[**ORIGIN** from Latin *circensis* + **-AN**: see **-IAN.**]
Of, pertaining to, or celebrated in the Circus in ancient Rome.

circinate /ˈsəːsɪnət, -eɪt/ *adjective*. **E19.**
[**ORIGIN** Latin *circinatus* pa. pple of *circinare* make round, formed as **CIRCINUS**: see **-ATE**[2].]
1 *BOTANY & ZOOLOGY*. Rolled up with its apex in the centre. **E19.**
2 *MEDICINE*. Circular in appearance; forming circular lesions. **L19.**
■ **circinately** *adverb* **M19.** **circiˈnation** *noun* (now *rare*) †(*a*) a circling or turning round; (*b*) *BOTANY* circinate vernation or foliation: **L16.**

Circinus /ˈsəːsɪnəs/ *noun*. **E19.**
[**ORIGIN** Latin *circinus* pair of compasses.]
(The name of) a small constellation of the southern hemisphere, in the Milky Way next to Centaurus; the Compasses.

circiter /ˈsəːsɪtə/ *preposition*. **L19.**
[**ORIGIN** Latin.]
With dates: about, circa.

circlage *noun* var. of **CERCLAGE.**

circle /ˈsəːk(ə)l/ *noun*. **OE.**
[**ORIGIN** Old French & mod. French *cercle* from Latin *circulus* dim. of **CIRCUS**: see **-ULE.** Respelt in 16 after Latin.]
▸ **I** A figure or appearance.
1 (The line enclosing) a perfectly round plane figure whose circumference is everywhere equidistant from its centre; *spec.* an imaginary circle on the celestial sphere or terrestrial globe, esp. connecting points of equal latitude, longitude, declination, etc. Also *loosely*, an imperfectly round plane figure, a ring, a closed loop. **OE.**
2 A luminous ring in the sky; a halo. **OE.** ▸**b** The round outline or surface of a celestial object. Chiefly *poet.* **M17.**
3 Formerly, the sphere in which a celestial object was supposed to revolve. Now, the orbit of a planet etc. **ME.**
4 A ringlike marking, e.g. a fairy ring. In various team games, a marked-off circular or semicircular area on the playing field, court, rink, etc., to which specific rules apply. **LME.** ▸**b** A dark circular mark around or below the eyes, esp. due to sickness or insufficient sleep. Usu. in *pl.* **M19.**
centre circle, *striking circle*, etc.
†**5** In urinalysis, the upper of the three layers of urine. **LME–E17.**
▸ **II** A material object.
6 A circular object, *esp.* a band; a ring; a crown, coronet, etc. **ME.**
transit circle: see **TRANSIT** *noun*.
7 The ring of a circus; *the* circus. *arch.* **E17.**
8 *ARCHAEOLOGY*. A field monument of circular shape, as a ring of standing stones, a circular ditch, a ring of pits, etc. **L18.**
9 A curved tier of seats in a theatre, concert hall, or cinema. **M19.**
dress circle, *family circle*, *upper circle*, etc.
▸ **III** *transf. & fig.* **10** The area, extent, or compass *of*. Now chiefly of non-material things: the area of influence or action *of*. **LME.**
11 A circular course, a complete revolution; a cyclic period. **LME.**

> A. H. SAYCE The circle of the year. J. B. PRIESTLEY It went round us once in a wide circle.

12 More fully ***vicious circle***. The fallacy of proving a proposition from another that rests on it for proof; an unbroken sequence of reciprocal cause and effect; an action and reaction that intensify each other. **LME.**
13 A completed series of parts forming a sequence. **M16.**
14 A set (*of* people), a coterie; a class or division of society. **M17.** ▸**b** A number of people grouped round a centre of interest. **E18.** ▸**c** A spiritualist seance. **M19.**

> P. G. WODEHOUSE The rest of his circle of acquaintance. M. GIROUARD More at home in donnish than country-house circles. **b** O. MANNING She started to rise, but the circle of women sat firm about her.

15 *hist.* A territorial division, esp. in Germany under the Holy Roman Empire. **L17.**
16 A railway, road, etc., forming a closed loop, allowing traffic to circulate continuously; *spec.* (**C-**) a London Underground line so constructed. **E19.**
– PHRASES: *Antarctic Circle*: see **ANTARCTIC** *adjective* 1. *Arctic Circle*: see **ARCTIC** *adjective* 1. **circle of confusion**, **circle of least confusion** the (smallest possible) circular area illuminated by the rays from a point object after refraction or reflection in a particular optical system (e.g. a camera). ***circle of position***: see **POSITION** *noun*. **circle of Willis** [Thomas *Willis* (1621–75), English physician] *ANATOMY* a circular structure on the underside of the brain formed by several linked arteries. **come full circle** return to starting point. **diurnal circle**: described by a celestial object in its apparent daily motion. **go round in circles** make no progress despite effort. **great circle** a circle on a sphere whose plane passes through the centre of the sphere. ***inner circle***: see **INNER** *adjective*. ***magic circle***: see **MAGIC** *adjective*. †**major circle** = ***great circle*** above. ***meridian circle***: see **MERIDIAN** *noun, adjective* 3. *PARHELIC* ***circle***. ***polar circle***: see **POLAR** *adjective*. ***Prague circle***, ***Prague linguistic circle***: see **PRAGUE**. ***primitive circle***: see **PRIMITIVE** *adjective & noun*. ***quality circle***: see **QUALITY** *noun & adjective*. *REPEATING* ***circle***. ***Rowland circle***, ***Rowland's circle***: see **ROWLAND**. **run round in circles**, **rush round in circles** *colloq.* be fussily busy with little result. ***sacred circle***: see **SACRED** *adjective*. ***segment of a circle***: see **SEGMENT** *noun* 1a. **small circle** any circle on a sphere other than a great circle. ***square the circle***: see **SQUARE** *verb*. ***swing around the circle***: see **SWING** *verb*. ***vertical circle***: see **VERTICAL** *adjective*. ***vicious circle***: see sense 12 above. ***Vienna Circle***: see **VIENNA** 1. ***virtuous circle***: see **VIRTUOUS** *adjective* 2.
– COMB.: **circle dance** = *ring dance* s.v. **RING** *noun*[1].
■ **circlewise** *adverb* in the manner or form of a circle **M16.**

circle /ˈsəːk(ə)l/ *verb*. **LME.**
[**ORIGIN** from the noun.]
▸ **I** *verb trans.* **1** Form a circle round; enclose in a circle. **LME.**

> B. PLAIN White lilacs circled the brim of her straw hat.

2 Move in a circle round. **L16.**

> P. F. BOLLER He circled the globe, visiting one country after another.

▸ **II** *verb intrans.* **3** Move in a circle (*round, about*, etc.). **LME.** ▸**b** *spec.* Of cavalry: sweep round on a moving flank as pivot (opp. ***wheel*** on a fixed flank). **E18.**

> POPE While the bowl circles, and the banquet warms. C. A. LINDBERGH I was circling preparatory to landing in a clover field.

circle back move in a wide loop towards the starting point.
4 *verb intrans.* Stand or extend in a circle. *rare.* **E17.**

> SIR W. SCOTT That proud ring Of peers who circled round the King.

■ **circled** *ppl adjective* (*a*) that has been circled; (*b*) rounded, circular; (*c*) marked with a circle or circles: **LME.** **circler** *noun* **E17.** **circling** *noun* (*a*) the action of the verb; (*b*) a circular formation: **LME.**

circlet /ˈsəːklɪt/ *noun*. **LME.**
[**ORIGIN** from **CIRCLE** *noun* + **-ET**[1]; perh. through French †*cerclet*.]
1 A ring, band, or hoop (*spec.* one of precious metal or jewels), worn as an ornament, esp. on the head. **LME.**
2 A small circle. **E16.**
†**3** A round piece of wood etc. put under a dish at table. **E17–M19.**

circlip /ˈsəːklɪp/ *noun*. **E20.**
[**ORIGIN** Blend of **CIRCULAR**, **CIRCLE** *noun*, etc. and **CLIP** *noun*[1].]
A metal ring sprung into a slot or groove in a bar etc. to hold something in place.

circs /səːks/ *noun pl.* *colloq.* **M19.**
[**ORIGIN** Abbreviation.]
Circumstances. Chiefly in ***under the circs***.

circuit /ˈsəːkɪt/ *noun & verb*. **LME.**
[**ORIGIN** Old French & mod. French from Latin *circuitus*, from *circuit-* pa. ppl stem of *circuire* var. of *circumire*, from *circum* around + *ire* go.]
▸ **A** *noun*. **1** A line that encloses an area; the distance round; the circumference. **LME.** ▸†**b** A circlet, a crown. *rare* (Shakes.). Only in **L16.**
2 A space enclosed by a line; an area; an extent. **LME.** ▸**b** *fig.* A sphere of action etc. **L16.**
3 The time during which a disease runs its course. *rare.* **LME.**
4 The action of going or moving around or about; a circular journey; a course through intermediate points back to the starting place; a roundabout journey or course. **LME.** ▸**b** *fig.* A revolution of time etc., a cyclic period. **E17.**

> R. L. STEVENSON The figure reappeared, and, making a wide circuit, began to head me off. C. P. SNOW Henry could perform a dignified circuit, Rome, Florence, Venice, . . being entertained by American acquaintances.

5 The journey of a judge etc. in a particular district to hold courts; the lawyers making the circuit. **L15.** ▸**b** A route followed by an itinerant entertainer or competitor in sporting events; a number of places of entertainment at which productions are presented successively; a sequence of sporting events; a chain of theatres, cinemas, etc., under a single management. **M19.**
b ***rubber-chicken circuit***: see **RUBBER** *noun*[1].
6 A roundabout process or mode (of reasoning, legal action, †expression, etc.). **M16.**
7 The district through which a judge etc. moves to hold courts. **L16.**
8 A group of local Methodist churches forming a minor administrative unit. **M18.**
9 The route followed by a confined electric current; an arrangement of interconnected devices such as transistors, resistors, etc., for achieving a particular electric effect. **M18.**
CLOSED-***circuit***. ***equivalent circuit***: see **EQUIVALENT** *adjective*. ***integrated circuit***: see **INTEGRATE** *verb*. ***metallic circuit***: see **METALLIC** *adjective*. ***open circuit***: see **OPEN** *adjective*. *PRINTED* ***circuit***. *SEQUENTIAL* ***circuit***. ***short circuit***: see **SHORT** *adjective*. ***solid circuit***: see **SOLID** *adjective & adverb*.
10 A road forming a closed loop built or used mainly for motor racing. **E20.**
11 A sequence of athletic exercises performed consecutively. **M20.**
– COMB.: **circuit board** a thin rigid board containing an electric circuit; *esp.* = *PRINTED* ***circuit***; **circuit-breaker** an apparatus for interrupting an electric circuit, usu. as a safety measure (***oil circuit-breaker***: see **OIL** *noun*); **circuit court** (*a*) a court held by a circuit judge of the High Court of Justiciary in Scotland outside Edinburgh; (*b*) *US* a Federal court of authority intermediate between a district court and the Supreme Court; **circuit judge** orig., a judge who makes a circuit to hold courts; now, a judge who primarily sits in the county courts and the Crown Court or who sits on a circuit court; **circuit-training** consecutive performances of a series of different athletic exercises.
▸ **B** *verb*. **1** *verb trans.* Go or travel round. **LME.**
2 *verb intrans.* Go or move in a circuit. **E17.**
■ **circuiˈteer** *noun & verb* (*a*) *noun* a judge etc. on circuit; †(*b*) *verb intrans.* go on a circuit: **M18.** **circuiter** *noun* = **CIRCUITEER** *noun* **M17.** **circuitor** *noun* a person who goes on rounds, a travelling inspector etc. **E19.** **circuitry** *noun* electric circuits collectively; equipment forming a circuit or circuits: **M20.**

circuition /səːkjʊˈɪʃ(ə)n/ *noun*. *arch.* **M16.**
[**ORIGIN** Latin *circuitio(n-)*, from *circuit-*: see **CIRCUIT**, **-ION.**]
A going round or about; *fig.* circumlocution.

circuitous /səːˈkjuːɪtəs/ *adjective*. **M17.**
[**ORIGIN** medieval Latin *circuitosus*, from *circuit-*: see **CIRCUIT**, **-OUS.**]
Going a long way round, indirect, roundabout.
■ **circuitously** *adverb* **L18.** **circuitousness** *noun* **E19.**

circuity /səːˈkjuːɪti/ *noun*. Now *rare*. **M16.**
[**ORIGIN** Old French *circuité*, from Latin *circuit-*: see **CIRCUIT**, **-Y**[5].]
†**1** Enclosure, compass, area. **M–L16.**
2 Circuitous quality; a circuitous process. **L16.**

circulable /ˈsəːkjʊləb(ə)l/ *adjective*. **L18.**
[**ORIGIN** from **CIRCULATE** *verb* + **-ABLE.**]
Able to be circulated.

circular /ˈsəːkjʊlə/ *adjective & noun*. **LME.**
[**ORIGIN** Anglo-Norman *circuler*, Old French *circulier* (mod. *-aire*), learned alt. of *cerclier* from late Latin *circularis*, from Latin *circulus* **CIRCLE** *noun*: see **-AR**[1].]
▸ **A** *adjective*. **1** Having the form of a circle. **LME.**
circular saw a toothed disc rotated by machinery for sawing.
2 Moving in or passing over a circle; taking place along a circle; describing a circle. **LME.**
circular tour: bringing the traveller back to the starting place.
3 (Of an argument) involving a vicious circle of reasoning; having the characteristics of a vicious circle. **LME.**
4 Of or pertaining to the circle as a mathematical figure. **L16.**
†**5** Perfect, full, complete. **E–M17.**
6 Circuitous, indirect. **E17.**
7 Moving or occurring in a cycle of repetition. **M17.**
8 Addressed to a circle of people, customers, etc. **M17.**
circular letter, *circular note*, etc.
▸ **B** *noun*. †**1** A circular figure or space. *rare.* **M16–E19.**
2 A letter, notice, advertisement, etc., of which many copies are made for distribution. **L18.**
■ **circularly** *adverb* in a circular manner; ***circularly polarized***, (of light) having a uniformly rotating plane of polarization: **LME.** **circularness** *noun* (*rare*) **L16.** †**circulary** *adjective* = **CIRCULAR** *adjective* **L16–M18.**

circularise *verb* var. of **CIRCULARIZE.**

circularity /səːkjʊˈlarɪti/ *noun*. **L16.**
[**ORIGIN** medieval Latin *circularitas*, from *circularis*: see **CIRCULAR** *adjective & noun*, **-ITY.**]
Circular quality, form, or movement.

> S. JOHNSON A hut is constructed with loose stones, ranged . . with some tendency to circularity. J. LYONS There is no circularity involved in the statement of the problem or its proposed solution.

circularize /ˈsəːkjʊlərʌɪz/ *verb trans.* Also **-ise.** **L18.**
[**ORIGIN** from **CIRCULAR** + **-IZE.**]
1 Make circular. **L18.**
2 = **CIRCULATE** 3. **L18.**
3 Send circulars to. **M19.**
■ **circulariˈzation** *noun* **L19.**

C

circulate /ˈsəːkjʊleɪt/ *verb*. L15.
[ORIGIN Latin *circulat-* pa. ppl stem of *circulare*, *-ari*, from *circulus* CIRCLE *noun*: see -ATE³.]
▸ **I** *verb trans.* †**1** ALCHEMY. Subject to continuous distillation in a closed vessel, fashioned so as to return the condensed vapour to the original liquid. L15–L17.
†**2** = CIRCLE *verb* 1. L16–L17.
3 Cause to go round, pass or hand round; put about, give currency to (a book, report, scandal, etc.); send out as a circular. L18.
E. BOWEN Portia had to circulate the cakes. M. L. KING An enthusiastic group had mimeographed leaflets . . and by evening these had been widely circulated.
4 = CIRCULARIZE 3. M20.
Daily Telegraph By using the . . mailing list it has circulated some 97,000 of the fund's members.
▸ **II** *verb intrans.* †**5** Gather in a circle. *rare*. Only in E16.
6 Move round in a circle or circuit; travel a course which ends at the starting point; *spec.* (of blood, sap, or other vital fluid) flow continuously round the body. M17.
J. F. W. HERSCHEL The moon circulates about the earth. G. ORWELL A large jug was circulating, and the mugs were being refilled with beer.
7 Pass from place to place freely and continuously; (of a newspaper etc.) pass into the hands of readers, be extensively read. M17.
EVELYN The Air . . circulates through . . to the Grate of the Stove.
8 MATH. Of a decimal fraction, esp. of more than one figure: recur. Now *rare* or *obsolete*. M18.
9 Of a person: go about in a social circle; move around at a social function, talking to different people. M19.
M. O. W. OLIPHANT He came . . by no means prepared to circulate among his flock. J. WAIN Shall we circulate a bit? . . Otherwise we shan't have spoken to a soul.
10 Travel or walk about. Chiefly *US*. M19.
– PHRASES: *circulating* LIBRARY. **circulating medium** the notes, gold, etc., used in exchange.
■ **circulative** *adjective* having the quality of circulating or producing circulation M17.

circulation /səːkjʊˈleɪʃ(ə)n/ *noun*. LME.
[ORIGIN Old French & mod. French, or Latin *circulatio(n-)*, formed as CIRCULATE: see -ATION.]
†**1** ALCHEMY. The continuous distillation of a liquid: see CIRCULATE 1. LME–M17.
2 Movement in a circle, circular motion or course. *obsolete* exc. *hist.* M16.
3 The continuous motion by which the blood travels through all parts of the body under the action of the heart; *transf.* the movement of sap in plants. M17.
E. HEMINGWAY I slapped my arms to keep the circulation going.
collateral circulation: see COLLATERAL *adjective*.
4 The movement of anything such that it returns to its previous position or state after a circuit of intermediate points. M17.
LANGMUIR *circulation*.
†**5** A continuous repetition of a series of actions, events, etc. L17–M18.
6 Movement to and fro or from hand to hand etc.; the movement or exchange of currency, coin, etc., transmission or distribution of news, books, etc.; the number of copies, esp. of a newspaper, that are sold. L17.
R. LARDNER A growing paper, with a big New York circulation. D. LODGE A wildly distorted . . version of an anecdote . . which I . . put into circulation.
bank of circulation: see BANK *noun*³ 3. **in circulation**, **out of circulation** *fig.* participating, not participating, in activities etc.
7 A circulating medium; a currency. L18.
medium of circulation: see MEDIUM *noun*.

circulator /ˈsəːkjʊleɪtə/ *noun*. E17.
[ORIGIN Latin *circulator* pedlar, quack (whence French †*circulateur*), formed as CIRCULATE: see -OR.]
†**1** A quack, a charlatan. E17–M19.
†**2** A person who travels round the world; a commercial traveller. M17–M18.
3 A person who circulates information etc.; a scandalmonger. L18.

†**circulatory** *noun*. M16–M18.
[ORIGIN medieval Latin *circulatorium*, formed as CIRCULATE: see -ORY¹.]
ALCHEMY. An alembic having its neck bent back so as to re-enter its lower part.

circulatory /ˈsəːkjʊlət(ə)ri, səːkjʊˈleɪt(ə)ri/ *adjective*. E17.
[ORIGIN from CIRCULATE + -ORY²: cf. French *circulatoire*. In branch II from Latin *circulatorius*, formed as CIRCULATOR.]
▸ **I 1** Of or pertaining to the circulation of the blood, sap, etc. E17.
†**2** ALCHEMY. For the purpose of continuous distillation. L17–E18.
▸ †**II 3** Of or pertaining to a quack or charlatan. M17–L18.

circulus vitiosus /ˌsəːkjʊləs vɪʃɪˈəʊsəs, vɪtɪ-/ *noun phr.* Pl. ***-li -osi*** /-lʌɪ -ˈəʊsʌɪ/. E20.
[ORIGIN Latin.]
A vicious circle.

circum- /ˈsəːkəm/ *prefix*.
[ORIGIN Latin, from *circum* preposition = around, about.]
Used in words adopted from Latin and in English words modelled on these with the sense 'around, about' adverbially, as ***circumfuse***, ***circumscribe***, and prepositionally, as ***circumlittoral*** etc.
■ **circumaˈdjacent** *adjective* lying immediately around E17. †**circumagitation** *noun* motion or impulsion round or about M17–L18. **circumˈambages** *noun pl.* (*rare*) roundabout methods or modes of speech M17. **circumˈgyrate** *verb trans.* & *intrans.* (now *rare*) (cause to) turn, wheel, or roll round M17. **circumgyˈration** *noun* the action or an act of turning, wheeling, or rolling round E17. **circumgyˈratory** *adjective* marked by circumgyration M19. **circumˈjovial** *adjective* & †*noun* (ASTRONOMY) (a satellite) revolving round Jupiter L17. **circumˈjovian** *adjective* = CIRCUMJOVIAL *adjective* M19. **circumˈlittoral** *adjective* bordering the shore L19. **circumˈlunar** *adjective* moving or situated round the moon E20. **circum-meˈridian** *adjective* (of a body when) at or near the meridian M19. **circumˈmure** *verb trans.* wall round E17. **circumnuˈtate** *verb intrans.* (BOTANY) perform circumnutation L19. **circumnuˈtation** *noun* (BOTANY) helical movement of the growing part of a plant L19. **circumˈoral** *adjective* (ANATOMY & ZOOLOGY) situated around the mouth M19. **circumpoˈsition** *noun* (HORTICULTURE) the propagation of plants in a particular surrounding environment or medium; *spec.* = ***air-layering*** s.v. AIR *noun*¹: M17. **circumroˈtation** *noun* †(*a*) a changing about in rotation; (*b*) a revolution as of a wheel or on an axis; a complete rotation: E17. **circumˈscissile** *adjective* (BOTANY) dehiscing or opening by a circular fissure M19. **circumˈsolar** *adjective* moving or situated round the sun M19. **circumˈtabular** *adjective* sitting round a table E20. **circumterˈrestrial** *adjective* moving or situated round the earth M19.

circumambient /səːkəmˈambɪənt/ *adjective* & *noun*. M17.
[ORIGIN from CIRCUM- + AMBIENT. Cf. late Latin *circumambire*.]
▸ **A** *adjective*. Esp. of the air or other fluid: surrounding, encompassing. M17.
▸ **B** *absol.* as *noun*. *The* surrounding air or atmosphere. L17.
■ **circumambience** *noun* the act or fact of surrounding E18. **circumambiency** *noun* surrounding quality or condition; an environment: M17.

circumambulate /səːkəmˈambjʊleɪt/ *verb trans.* & *intrans.* M17.
[ORIGIN from CIRCUM- + AMBULATE. Cf. late Latin *circumambulare*.]
Walk round or about.
■ **circumambuˈlation** *noun* E17. **circumambulator** *noun* a person who circumambulates L18. **circumambulatory** *adjective* M17.

circumbendibus /səːkəmˈbɛndɪbəs/ *noun*. L17.
[ORIGIN from CIRCUM- + BEND *noun*³ + Latin *-ibus* abl. pl. ending.]
A roundabout method; a twist, a turn; a circumlocution.

Circumcellion /səːkəmˈsɛlɪən/ *noun*. LME.
[ORIGIN ecclesiastical Latin *circumcelliones* pl., formed as CIRCUM- + *cella* CELL *noun*¹.]
1 ECCLESIASTICAL HISTORY. A Donatist fanatic in 4th-cent. Africa. Usu. in *pl.* LME.
†**2** A vagrant. LME–M17.

circumcircle /ˈsəːkəmsəːk(ə)l/ *noun*. L19.
[ORIGIN from CIRCUM- + CIRCLE *noun*.]
A circle passing through each vertex of a polygon.

circumcise /ˈsəːkəmsʌɪz/ *verb trans.* ME.
[ORIGIN Old French *circonciser* or *circoncis-* pa. ppl stem of *circoncire*, from Latin *circumcidere* (translating Greek *peritemnein*), formed as CIRCUM- + *caedere* to cut.]
1 Cut off the foreskin of (a male), as a religious rite (esp. Jewish or Muslim) or for medical reasons; cut off the clitoris or the labia minora of (a female). ME.
2 *fig.* In biblical translations and allusions: purify (the heart etc.). ME.
†**3** Cut round, trim. LME–L18.
†**4** *fig.* Cut short, curtail, limit. M16–L17.
■ **circumciser** *noun* M16.

circumcision /səːkəmˈsɪʒ(ə)n/ *noun*. ME.
[ORIGIN Old French & mod. French *circoncision*, from late Latin *circumcisio(n-)* (translating Greek *peritomē*), from *circumcis-* pa. ppl stem of *circumcidere*: see CIRCUMCISE, -ION.]
▸ **I 1** The act or rite of circumcising a person, for religious or medical reasons. ME.
female circumcision: see FEMALE *adjective*.
2 *fig.* In biblical translations and allusions: spiritual purification. LME.
3 In biblical translations and allusions: *the* Jews. LME.
4 ECCLESIASTICAL. The feast of the Circumcision of Jesus, 1 January. LME.
▸ †**II 5** Cutting round; a cut round. L16–M18.

circumduce /səːkəmˈdjuːs/ *verb trans.* M16.
[ORIGIN Latin *circumducere*, formed as CIRCUM- + *ducere* to lead.]
†**1** = CIRCUMDUCT. M16–M17.
2 SCOTS LAW (now *hist.*). Reject as legally invalid; *spec.* declare (the term) elapsed for producing proof or evidence in court proceedings. M16.

circumduct /səːkəmˈdʌkt/ *verb trans.* L16.
[ORIGIN Latin *circumduct-* pa. ppl stem of *circumducere*: see CIRCUMDUCE.]
Lead or move around or about. Now *spec.* in ANATOMY, cause (an eye, a limb, etc.) to make a circular movement.

circumduction /səːkəmˈdʌkʃ(ə)n/ *noun*. M16.
[ORIGIN Latin *circumductio(n-)*, formed as CIRCUMDUCT: see -ION.]
1 SCOTS LAW (now *hist.*). The action of circumducing. M16.
2 The action of circumducting. M16.

circumference /səˈkʌmf(ə)r(ə)ns/ *noun*. LME.
[ORIGIN Old French & mod. French *circonférence* from Latin *circumferentia*, from *circumferre*, formed as CIRCUM- + *ferre* to carry, bear: see -ENCE.]
1 An enclosing boundary, esp. of a circle or other figure enclosed by a curve; the distance round this. LME.
†**2** An arc; a circle; the surface of a sphere, cylinder, or other body of circular section. LME–L18.
3 Environment. *rare*. LME.
†**4** A circuit; a roundabout course. M16–E18.
5 Boundary, compass, enclosure. L16.
■ **circumfeˈrential** *adjective* of or pertaining to a circumference E17. **circumfeˈrentially** *adverb* M19.

circumferentor /səːˈkʌmfərɛntə/ *noun*. E17.
[ORIGIN from Latin *circumferent-* pres. ppl stem of *circumferre*: see CIRCUMFERENCE, -OR.]
A surveyor's instrument consisting of a flat bar with vertical sights at each end and a compass in the middle.

circumflex /ˈsəːkəmflɛks/ *adjective* & *noun*. L16.
[ORIGIN Latin *circumflexus* pa. pple of *circumflectere*, formed as CIRCUM- + *flectere* to bend, translating Greek *perispōmenos* drawn around.]
▸ **A** *adjective*. **1** GRAMMAR. Designating an angular or curved accent mark (ˆ, ˆ, or ˜) placed over a vowel in some languages (orig. Greek) to indicate rising and falling tone, contraction, length, or special quality (of the vowel or of an adjacent consonant). L16.
2 Bent, bending round. Now *rare* in *gen.* sense. E18.
3 ANATOMY. Curved; bent round another part; *spec.* designating a nerve and artery of the upper arm. M19.
▸ **B** *noun*. **1** A circumflex accent mark. E17.
†**2** Bending round, winding. E17–L18.
3 A curved line, (or {, bracketing two or more lines of writing etc. *rare*. E19.

circumflex /ˈsəːkəmflɛks/ *verb trans.* M16.
[ORIGIN Sense 1 from CIRCUMFLEX *adjective* & *noun*; sense 2 from Latin *circumflex-*, formed as CIRCUMFLEX *adjective* & *noun*.]
1 Write with a circumflex accent; pronounce as indicated by a circumflex accent. M16.
2 Bend or wind round. M17.

circumfluent /səːˈkʌmflʊənt/ *adjective*. L16.
[ORIGIN Latin *circumfluent-* pres. ppl stem of *circumfluere*, formed as CIRCUM- + *fluere* to flow: see -ENT.]
Flowing round; surrounding.
■ **circumfluence** *noun* L19.

circumfluous /səːˈkʌmflʊəs/ *adjective*. *literary*. E17.
[ORIGIN from Latin *circumfluus*, from *circumfluere*: see CIRCUMFLUENT, -OUS.]
1 Flowed round, surrounded by water. E17.
2 = CIRCUMFLUENT. M17.

circumforaneous /səːkəmfəˈreɪnɪəs/ *adjective*. Now *rare*. E17.
[ORIGIN from Latin *circumforaneus* (formed as CIRCUM- + FORUM) + -OUS.]
Strolling from market to market; vagrant.

circumfuse /səːkəmˈfjuːz/ *verb trans.* L16.
[ORIGIN Latin *circumfus-* pa. ppl stem of *circumfundere*, formed as CIRCUM- + *fundere* pour.]
Pour about, diffuse, (*around*, *about*); surround *with* or *in* a fluid medium etc.
■ **circumfusion** *noun* E17.

circumgestation /səːkəmdʒɛˈsteɪʃ(ə)n/ *noun*. Long *rare*. M16.
[ORIGIN from CIRCUM- + GESTATION.]
Carrying about (ceremonially or in procession).

circumincession /səːkəmɪnˈsɛʃ(ə)n/ *noun*. Also **-session**. M17.
[ORIGIN medieval Latin *circumincessio(n-)* (translating Greek *perikhōrēsis* going round), formed as CIRCUM- + *incessio(n-)*, from *incess-* pa. ppl stem of *incedere* move, proceed: see -ION. Spelling with *-s-* through misinterpretation as 'reciprocal indwelling'.]
CHRISTIAN THEOLOGY. The reciprocal existence of the persons of the Trinity in one another.

circumjacent /səːkəmˈdʒeɪs(ə)nt/ *adjective*. L15.
[ORIGIN Latin *circumjacent-* pres. ppl stem of *circumjacere*, formed as CIRCUM- + *jacere* lie down: see -ENT.]
Situated around, adjacent on all sides. (Foll. by *to*.)
■ **circumjacence** *noun* the fact or quality of being circumjacent L19. **circumjacency** *noun* (*a*) in *pl.*, circumjacent parts; (*b*) = CIRCUMJACENCE: M18.

circumlocution /səːkəmləˈkjuːʃ(ə)n/ *noun*. LME.
[ORIGIN French, or Latin *circumlocutio(n-)*, formed as CIRCUM- + *locutio(n-)* LOCUTION, translating Greek PERIPHRASIS.]
Expression of meaning indirectly or in more words than necessary; evasive talk; an instance of this, a roundabout expression.
■ **circumlocutional**, **circumlocutionary** *adjectives* pertaining to or given to circumlocution M19. **circumlocutionist** *noun* a person who uses circumlocution M19. **circumlocutory** /səːkəmˈlɒkjʊt(ə)ri, səːkəmləˈkjuːt(ə)ri/ *adjective* marked by circumlocution M17.

circumnavigate /səːkəmˈnavɪgeɪt/ *verb trans.* M17.
[ORIGIN from CIRCUM- + NAVIGATE. Cf. Latin *circumnavigare*.]
Sail round (esp. the world).
■ **circumnavigable** *adjective* able to be circumnavigated L17. **circumnaviˈgation** *noun* E18. **circumnavigator** *noun* L18.

circumpolar /səːkəm'pəʊlə/ *adjective*. L17.
[ORIGIN from CIRCUM- + POLAR.]
1 *ASTRONOMY*. Situated or occurring above the horizon at all times of the day in a given latitude. L17.
2 Around either pole of the earth; inhabiting such a region. L17.

circumscribe /'səːkəmskrʌɪb/ *verb trans*. LME.
[ORIGIN Latin *circumscribere*, formed as CIRCUM- + *scribere* draw lines, write.]
1 Lay down the limits of, confine; restrict; mark off, define logically. LME.
> SHAKES. *Haml.* Therefore must his choice be circumscrib'd. E. F. BENSON To play lawn-tennis . . in the exceedingly circumscribed court.

2 Draw a line round; form the boundary of; encircle, encompass. L16.
> W. HOGARTH The straight line and the circular line . . bound and circumscribe all visible objects. DEFOE I was alone, circumscribed by the . . ocean.

3 *GEOMETRY*. Draw (a figure) round another, meeting it at points but not cutting it. L16.
†**4** Inscribe around. Only in 17.
■ **circumscriber** *noun* (*arch.*) a person who or thing which circumscribes; *spec.* a person who signs a round robin: E17. **circumscript** *adjective* (now *rare*) circumscribed M16.

circumscription /səːkəm'skrɪpʃ(ə)n/ *noun*. LME.
[ORIGIN Latin *circumscriptio(n-)*, from *circumscript-* pa. ppl stem of *circumscribere*: see CIRCUMSCRIBE, -ION.]
1 An inscription around a coin etc. LME.
†**2** The fact or quality of being confined to definite limits of space, as a property of matter. L15–M19.
3 The action or an act of laying down limits; the fact of being limited; confinement; (a) restraint, (a) restriction; (a) definition, (a) description. M16.
> MILTON No injurious Alteration or Circumscription of Mens Lands. E. POUND Criticism is not a circumscription or a set of prohibitions.

4 A boundary, an outline, a periphery; a border, an edging. L16.
> M. BRADBURY The main horizon . . of their lives, the limit and circumscription of their world.

5 *GEOMETRY*. The action of circumscribing one figure around another. L16.
6 A circumscribed space; a district or region of definite limits. M19.
■ †**circumscriptive** *adjective* pertaining to or having the attribute of circumscription L15–M18. †**circumscriptively** *adverb* L15–M18.

circumspect /'səːkəmspɛkt/ *adjective*. LME.
[ORIGIN Latin *circumspectus* pa. pple of *circumspicere*, formed as CIRCUM- + *specere* to look.]
Showing caution; cautious, wary; taking everything into account.
> J. STEINBECK The brothels were quiet, orderly and circumspect. S. BELLOW He was a circumspect driver.

■ **circum'spection** *noun* cautious observation of circumstances; circumspect action or conduct: LME. **circum'spectious** *adjective* circumspect M17. **circum'spective** *adjective* looking around; given to circumspection: M17. **circum'spectively** *adverb* E17. **circumspectly** *adverb* LME. **circumspectness** *noun* M16.

circumsphere /'səːkəmsfɪə/ *noun*. M20.
[ORIGIN from CIRCUM- + SPHERE *noun*, after *circumcircle*.]
MATH. A sphere that touches all the vertices of a given polyhedron. Cf. IN-SPHERE.

circumstance /'səːkəmst(ə)ns/ *noun* & *verb*. ME.
[ORIGIN Old French & mod. French *circonstance* or Latin *circumstantia*, from *circumstant-* pres. ppl stem of *circumstare*, formed as CIRCUM- + *stare* to stand: see -ANCE.]
▸ **A** *noun*. **I** Something surrounding (*lit.* & *fig.*).
†**1** That which stands around or surrounds; surroundings. ME–L19.
2 In *pl.*, or *sing.* (as a non-count noun). The material, logical, or other environmental conditions of an act or event; the time, place, manner, cause, occasion, etc., of an act or event; the external conditions affecting or that might affect action, *spec.* as indicating criminality. ME. ▸**b** In *sing.* (as a count noun). Any of such conditions. M16. ▸**c** *spec.* In *pl.* State of financial or material welfare. E18.
> J. WEBSTER We have nought but circumstances To charge her with, about her husband's death. J. A. FROUDE Who found himself in circumstances to which he was unequal. L. P. HARTLEY A soldier has to change his mind when circumstances demand it. J. HELLER That men should die was a matter of necessity; *which* men should die, though, was a matter of circumstance. J. BARTH When I next saw her, it was under entirely different circumstances. J. FOWLES Ernestina . . was . . a victim of circumstances. **b** J. GALSWORTHY A solid and prolonged happiness such as perhaps no other circumstance in life had afforded him. **c** N. MITFORD Summer came and went without any change in Polly's circumstances.

3 Formality, ceremony, or fuss surrounding an act or event. Now chiefly in ***pomp and circumstance***. LME. ▸†**b** Importance. L16–L17.
4 Detail about the external conditions of an act or event; *arch.* circumlocution, indirectness. E16.
▸ **II** Something accessory.
5 An accessory matter; a particular, a detail. Usu. in *pl.* ME. ▸†**b** *spec.* A material adjunct; a physical feature. L16–L18.
> SWIFT The sentence of death with all the circumstances of hanging, beheading, quartering, embowelling and the like.

†**6** Subordinate matters or details. LME–E18.
7 The part(s) not of the essence or substance of something. *arch.* L16.
8 An incident, an occurrence; a fact. L16.
> T. CAPOTE A circumstance which explained the presence of perhaps a third of the immense congregation.

– PHRASES: **a mere circumstance**, **a poor circumstance**, **a remote circumstance** *US colloq.* a person or thing of little or no importance. ***creature of circumstance***: see CREATURE. **in no circumstances** not whatever happens; never. **in the circumstances** owing to or making allowance for circumstances. ***narrow circumstances***: see NARROW *adjective*. **not a circumstance to** *US colloq.* nothing in comparison with. **under no circumstances** = ***in no circumstances*** above. **under the circumstances** = ***in the circumstances*** above.
▸ **B** *verb trans*. †**1** Subject to conditions or circumstances. LME–M18.
2 Place with regard to circumstances or relations. Chiefly as ***circumstanced*** *ppl adjective*. E17.
†**3** = CIRCUMSTANTIATE 4. M17–L18.

circumstantial /səːkəm'stanʃ(ə)l/ *adjective* & *noun*. L16.
[ORIGIN from Latin *circumstantia* CIRCUMSTANCE *noun* + -AL[1].]
▸ **A** *adjective*. **1** Of, pertaining to, or dependent on circumstances; adventitious, incidental. L16.
> COLERIDGE Our political strength and circumstantial prosperity. J. R. LOWELL A principle of life is the first requirement of art; all else is circumstantial and secondary. O. SACKS The names of my patients, . . and certain other circumstantial details.

circumstantial evidence: tending to establish a conclusion by inference from known facts which are otherwise hard to explain.
2 Detailed; particular. E17.
> ADDISON We cannot be too minute and circumstantial in accounts of this nature. J. WAIN When telling a lie, make it circumstantial, load it with detail.

3 Full of ceremony or pomp. E18.
▸ **B** *noun*. In *pl.* Circumstantial matters; particulars, details; incidental or adventitious features. M17.
■ **circumstanti'ality** *noun* circumstantial quality, (a) particularity M18. **circumstantially** *adverb* M17. †**circumstantialness** *noun* M18–E19.

circumstantiate /səːkəm'stanʃɪeɪt/ *verb trans*. Now *rare*. LME.
[ORIGIN medieval Latin *circumstantiat-* pa. ppl stem of *circumstantiare* to condition, from Latin *circumstantia*: see CIRCUMSTANCE, -ATE[3].]
†**1** Accompany as a circumstance. Only in LME.
†**2** = CIRCUMSTANCE *verb* 2. Chiefly as ***circumstantiated*** *ppl adjective*. E17–L19.
†**3** = CIRCUMSTANCE *verb* 1. M17–E18.
4 Set forth or support with circumstances or details. M17.
■ **circumstantia'tion** *noun* M19.

circumvallate /səːkəm'valeɪt, -ət/ *adjective*. M17.
[ORIGIN Latin *circumvallatus* pa. pple, formed as CIRCUMVALLATE *verb*: see -ATE[2].]
Surrounded (as) with a rampart; *spec.* designating certain papillae near the back of the tongue, surrounded by taste receptors.

circumvallate /səːkəm'valeɪt/ *verb trans*. E19.
[ORIGIN Latin *circumvallat-* pa. ppl stem of *circumvallare*, formed as CIRCUM- + *vallare*, from *vallum* rampart: see -ATE[3].]
Surround (as) with a rampart or entrenchment.

circumvallation /səːkəmva'leɪʃ(ə)n/ *noun*. M17.
[ORIGIN Late Latin *circumvallatio(n-)*, formed as CIRCUMVALLATE *verb*: see -ATION.]
1 The making of a rampart or entrenchment. M17.
2 A rampart, an entrenchment; *fig.* a surrounding defence. M17.

circumvent /səːkəm'vɛnt/ *verb*. LME.
[ORIGIN Latin *circumvent-* pa. ppl stem of *circumvenire*, formed as CIRCUM- + *venire* come.]
1 *verb trans*. Deceive, outwit, overreach; find a way round, evade (a difficulty). LME. ▸**b** *verb intrans*. Employ deception or evasion. L16.
2 *verb trans*. Entrap by surrounding; beset (*with*). M16.
3 *verb trans*. Go round; enclose; make the circuit of. E19.
■ Also †**circumvene** *verb trans*. (chiefly *Scot.*) L15–L18.

circumvention /səːkəm'vɛnʃ(ə)n/ *noun*. LME.
[ORIGIN Late Latin *circumventio(n-)*, formed as CIRCUMVENT: see -ION.]
The action or an act of circumventing someone; *SCOTS LAW* deceitful or fraudulent conduct perpetrated against a facile person.

circumvolute /səː'kʌmvəluːt/ *verb trans*. Now *rare*. L16.
[ORIGIN Latin (*circumvolutare* frequentative of) *circumvolut-* pa. ppl stem of *circumvolvere* CIRCUMVOLVE.]
Roll or curl round; enwrap by twisting or winding something round.

circumvolution /səːkəmvə'luːʃ(ə)n/ *noun*. LME.
[ORIGIN from Latin *circumvolut-* (see CIRCUMVOLUTE) + -ION.]
1 Turning round an axis or centre; an instance of this; (a) revolution, (a) rotation. LME.
2 The winding or folding of one thing round another; a fold or turn of something so wound. L16.
3 A sinuous movement; a winding course; a twist, a coil. L16.

C

circumvolve /səːkəm'vɒlv/ *verb trans*. & *intrans*. Now *rare*. LME.
[ORIGIN Latin *circumvolvere*, formed as CIRCUM- + *volvere* to turn.]
1 Rotate, revolve. LME.
†**2** Wind, fold, or twist round; enwrap (*lit.* & *fig.*). L16–E19.

circus /'səːkəs/ *noun*. LME.
[ORIGIN Latin = circle, circus, corresp. to Greek *kirkos*, *krikos* ring, circle.]
▸ **I 1** *ROMAN ANTIQUITIES*. A rounded or oval arena lined with tiers of seats, for equestrian and other exhibitions. LME. **the Circus**: the largest at Rome.
†**2** A circle, a ring; a road forming a closed loop. E–M18.
3 An open, more or less circular, area in a town where streets converge; a circular range of houses. M18. ***Oxford Circus***, ***Piccadilly Circus***, (in London), etc.
4 A natural amphitheatre of hills etc. M19.
▸ **II 5** A travelling show of horses, riders, acrobats, clowns, performing animals, etc., usu. performing in a circular arena; the type of entertainment provided by such shows. L18. ***THREE-ring circus***.
6 A disturbance; a scene of lively action. *colloq.* M19.
7 An exhibition etc. at a Roman circus; *spec.* in ***bread and circuses*** [translating Latin PANEM ET CIRCENSES], public provision of food and entertainment, esp. to assuage the populace. E20.
8 More fully ***flying circus***. A squadron of aeroplanes; a group of aircraft or pilots engaged in spectacular flying. *slang*. E20.
9 A group of people performing in sports etc. together or in succession, usu. in a series of different places. *colloq.* (freq. *derog.*). M20.
10 (**C-**.) *The* British secret service. *slang*. M20.
■ **circussy** *adjective* resembling or characteristic of a circus L19.

ciré /'siːreɪ/ *adjective* & *noun*. E20.
[ORIGIN French = waxed.]
(Fabric) with a smooth polished surface, obtained esp. by heating and waxing.

cire perdue /siːr pɛrdy/ *noun phr*. L19.
[ORIGIN French = lost wax.]
A method of casting bronze by pouring metal over a core within a mould, into the space created by melting and running out the original wax surface of the model.

cirl bunting /səːl 'bʌntɪŋ/ *noun phr*. L18.
[ORIGIN from Italian *cirlo*, prob. from *zirlare* whistle as a thrush, + BUNTING *noun*[1].]
A bunting, *Emberiza cirlus*, which is resident in SW England and is distinguished by the yellow, black, and green head of the male.

†**ciron** *noun*. LME–L18.
[ORIGIN French.]
The itch mite, *Sarcoptes scabiei*. Also = JIGGER *noun*[2] 1.

cirque /səːk/ *noun*. E17.
[ORIGIN French from Latin CIRCUS.]
1 = CIRCUS 1. E17.
2 A circle, a ring, a circlet. *literary*. L17.
3 *PHYSICAL GEOGRAPHY*. A large bowl-shaped hollow of glacial origin at the head of a valley or on a mountainside. M19.

cirrhosis /sɪ'rəʊsɪs/ *noun*. Pl. **-rrhoses** /-'rəʊsiːz/. Formerly also in French form †**cirrhose**. E19.
[ORIGIN mod. Latin from Greek *kirrhos* orange-tawny (on account of the colour of the affected liver in many cases): see -OSIS.]
MEDICINE. A chronic disease in which much of the liver is replaced by fibrous tissue and the organ takes on a nodular appearance. Also occas., degeneration of another organ.
■ **cirrhotic** *adjective* & *noun* (**a**) *adjective* of the nature of or affected by cirrhosis; (**b**) *noun* a sufferer from cirrhosis: L19.

†**cirrhus** *noun* var. of CIRRUS.

cirri *noun* pl. of CIRRUS.

cirriferous /sɪ'rɪf(ə)rəs/ *adjective*. M18.
[ORIGIN from Latin *cirri-* CIRRUS + -FEROUS.]
Bearing cirri.

cirriform /'sɪrɪfɔːm/ *adjective*. E19.
[ORIGIN formed as CIRRIFEROUS + -FORM.]
1 *METEOROLOGY*. Having the form or appearance of cirrus. E19.
2 *ZOOLOGY*. Like cirri. M19.

cirrigerous /sɪ'rɪdʒərəs/ *adjective*. M18.
[ORIGIN formed as CIRRIFEROUS + -GEROUS.]
Bearing cirri.

cirripede /'sɪrɪpiːd/ *noun* & *adjective*. Also (earlier) **-ped** /-pɛd/. M19.
[ORIGIN mod. Latin *Cirripeda*, *-dia* pl., from Latin CIRRUS + *ped-*, *pes* foot: so called from the appearance of the legs when protruded from the valved shell.]

ZOOLOGY. (A marine crustacean) of the subclass Cirripedia, members of which (the barnacles) are generally sessile as adults and have limbs modified for filter-feeding.

cirro- /ˈsɪrəʊ/ *combining form* of CIRRUS: see -O-.
■ **cirro'cumulus** *noun*, pl. **-li**, /-lʌɪ, -liː/, *METEOROLOGY* a cloud or cloud type occurring at high altitude (usu. 5 to 13 km, 16,500 to 45,000 ft) and having the appearance of a rippled, granulated, or otherwise broken layer E19. **cirro'stratus** *noun* (*METEOROLOGY*) a cloud or cloud type occurring at high altitude (usu. 5 to 13 km, 3 to 8 miles) and forming a thin, more or less uniform layer E19.

cirrous /ˈsɪrəs/ *adjective*. M17.
[ORIGIN from CIRRUS + -OUS.]
1 *BOTANY & ZOOLOGY.* Bearing cirri; of the nature of a cirrus. M17.
2 *METEOROLOGY.* Of or pertaining to cirrus cloud. E19.
■ Also **cirrose** *adjective* E19.

cirrus /ˈsɪrəs/ *noun*. Also †**cirrhus**. Pl. **cirri** /ˈsɪrʌɪ, -riː/. E18.
[ORIGIN Latin = curl, fringe.]
1 A curl or tuft of hair. *rare*. E18.
2 *BOTANY.* A tendril. E18.
3 *ZOOLOGY.* A slender, filamentary appendage, e.g. the limb of a cirripede, a barbel of certain fishes. M18.
4 *METEOROLOGY.* A cloud type occurring at high altitude (usu. 5 to 13 km, 3 to 8 miles) and having the appearance of wispy filamentous tufts. E19.

†**cirsocele** *noun*. E18–L19.
[ORIGIN Greek *kirsokēlē*, from *kirsos* enlargement of a vein: see -CELE.]
= VARICOCELE.

cirsoid /ˈsəːsɔɪd/ *adjective*. M19.
[ORIGIN Greek *kirsoeidēs*, from *kirsos*: see CIRSOCELE, -OID.]
MEDICINE. Having the appearance of a varicose vein.

CIS *abbreviation*.
Commonwealth of Independent States.

cis- /sɪs/ *prefix*. In sense 2 also as attrib. adjective **cis**.
[ORIGIN Latin, from *cis* preposition.]
1 Used in words adopted from Latin and in English words modelled on these with the sense 'on this side of' (opp. TRANS-, ULTRA-), occas. retaining orientation from Rome (as ***cisalpine*** etc.), but usu. from the user's or the majority's position (as ***cisatlantic*** etc.); also occas. of time (as ***cis-Elizabethan***).
2 *CHEMISTRY.* (Usu. italicized.) Designating compounds in which two atoms or groups are situated on the same side of a given plane in the molecule (opp. TRANS-). L19.
■ **cisat'lantic** *adjective* on one's own side of the Atlantic L18. **cis'lunar** *adjective* on this side of the moon, between the earth and the moon L19. **cisoid** *adjective* (*CHEMISTRY*) designating a compound, group, or structure in which two like atoms or groups lie on the same side of a single bond or line of bonds M20. **cispadane** *adjective* on the south (Roman) side of the River Po L18. **cis'pontine** *adjective* on this side of the bridge or bridges; *spec.* on the north (orig. the better-known) side of the Thames bridges in London: M19. **cis-trans** *adjective* (*CHEMISTRY*) designating isomerism characterized by *cis* and *trans* isomers M20.

cisalpine /sɪsˈalpʌɪn/ *adjective & noun*. M16.
[ORIGIN Latin *cisalpinus*, formed as CIS-, ALPINE *adjective & noun*[2].]
▸ **A** *adjective*. **1** On this (the Roman) side of the Alps; south of the Alps. M16.
2 *CHRISTIAN CHURCH.* Of or pertaining to the Gallican Church movement. L18.
▸ **B** *noun*. A member of the Roman Catholic Church who accepts the principles of the Gallican Synod of 1682. L18.

cisco /ˈsɪskəʊ/ *noun*. Pl. **-oes**, same. M19.
[ORIGIN Unknown.]
Any of several freshwater salmonid fishes of the genus *Coregonus*.
Arctic cisco = OMUL.

Ciskeian /sɪˈskʌɪən/ *noun & adjective*. M20.
[ORIGIN from *Ciskei* (see below), from CIS- + *Kei*, a river in eastern South Africa, + -AN.]
(A native or inhabitant) of Ciskei, a former black African homeland within South Africa.

cismontane /sɪsˈmɒnteɪn/ *adjective*. E19.
[ORIGIN Latin *cismontanus*, formed as CIS-, MONTANE.]
On this side of the mountains; *esp.* = CISALPINE *adjective* 1.

cisplatin /sɪsˈplatɪn/ *noun*. L20.
[ORIGIN from CIS- 2 + PLATIN(UM *noun*.]
PHARMACOLOGY. A coordination compound of platinum, $Pt(NH_3)_2Cl_2$, which is cytotoxic and is used in cancer chemotherapy.

cissoid /ˈsɪsɔɪd/ *noun*. M17.
[ORIGIN Greek *kissoeidēs*, from *kissos* ivy: see -OID.]
MATH. A cubic curve of infinite length and having one cusp, that is the locus of certain points on the secants of a circle from a fixed point on its circumference (represented by the equation $r = a \sin^2 \theta/\cos \theta$).

cissy *noun & adjective* var. of SISSY.

cist /sɪst, kɪst/ *noun*[1]. E19.
[ORIGIN Welsh = chest.]
ARCHAEOLOGY. A prehistoric burial chamber made with stone slabs. Also, a hollowed tree-coffin.
long cist: see LONG *adjective*[1]. ***oak cist***: see OAK *noun & adjective*.

cist /sɪst/ *noun*[2]. M19.
[ORIGIN Latin *cista*: see CHEST *noun*.]
GREEK ANTIQUITIES. A box used for sacred utensils.

Cistercian /sɪˈstəːʃ(ə)n/ *adjective & noun*. LME.
[ORIGIN French *cistercien*, from Latin *Cistercium* Cîteaux, near Dijon, France (cf. medieval Latin *Cisterciensis*): see -IAN.]
▸ **A** *adjective*. Of or belonging to a monastic order founded at Cîteaux in 1098 by Robert, abbot of Molesme, as a stricter offshoot of the Benedictines. LME.
▸ **B** *noun*. A monk or nun of the Cistercian order. LME.

cistern /ˈsɪstən/ *noun*. ME.
[ORIGIN Old French *cisterne* (mod. *citerne*) from Latin *cisterna*, formed as CIST *noun*[2].]
1 An artificial reservoir for storing water, *esp.* one in the roof space of a building supplying the taps, or above a water closet. ME.
2 A large vessel for water or other liquid, *esp.* one used †(***a***) for personal washing, †(***b***) at the dinner table. L16.
3 A natural reservoir or depression containing water, e.g. a pond. E17.
4 A fluid-filled cavity in an organism or cell; *esp.* a reservoir of cerebrospinal fluid in the subarachnoid space. E17.

cisterna /sɪˈstəːnə/ *noun*. Pl. **-nae** /-niː/. L19.
[ORIGIN mod. Latin from Latin: see CISTERN.]
ANATOMY & BIOLOGY. = CISTERN 4.

cistophorus /sɪˈstɒfərəs/ *noun*. Pl. **-ri** /-rʌɪ/. M19.
[ORIGIN Latin from Greek *kistophoros*, from *kistē* CHEST *noun* + *-phoros* bearing.]
A Greek coin bearing an impression of a sacred chest.

cistron /ˈsɪstrɒn/ *noun*. M20.
[ORIGIN from CIS- + TRANS- (referring to the possibility of two genes being on the same or different chromosomes) + -ON.]
BIOLOGY. A section of a nucleic acid molecule that codes for a specific product of transcription.

cistus /ˈsɪstəs/ *noun*. M16.
[ORIGIN mod. Latin from Greek *kistos*, *-thos*.]
An evergreen shrub of the genus *Cistus*, of the Mediterranean region, with large white or red flowers. Also called ***rock rose***.

cistvaen *noun* var. of KISTVAEN.

cit /sɪt/ *noun*. *arch.* M17.
[ORIGIN Abbreviation of CITIZEN.]
1 A townsman; a shopkeeper, a trader. Occas. = CITESS 1. Usu. *derog.* M17.
2 In *pl.* Civilian clothes, 'civvies'. *US slang*. E19.

citadel /ˈsɪtəd(ə)l, -dɛl/ *noun*. M16.
[ORIGIN French *citadelle* or its source Italian *cittadella* dim. of †*cittade* (var. of *città*) from Latin *civitas* CITY.]
1 A fortress, *esp.* one guarding or dominating a city; *transf.* & *fig.* a stronghold. M16.

C. THIRLWALL To collect all the remaining strength . . in a mountain citadel. W. S. CHURCHILL The French had had to evacuate their troops from the citadel in Aleppo. L. TRILLING The university figured as the citadel of conservatism.

2 A meeting hall of the Salvation Army. L19.

citation /sʌɪˈteɪʃ(ə)n/ *noun*. ME.
[ORIGIN Old French & mod. French from Latin *citatio(n-)*, from *citat-pa.* ppl stem of *citare* CITE: see -ATION.]
1 *LAW.* A summons; a document containing a summons. ME.
2 The action of citing or quoting any words or a written passage. M16.
3 A passage cited, a quotation. M16.
4 A mention in an official dispatch; a descriptive announcement of an award. E20.

T. ROETHKE I was graduated . . with the highest possible degree citation.

citatory /ˈsʌɪtət(ə)ri/ *adjective*. *arch.* M16.
[ORIGIN medieval Latin *citatorius*, from Latin *citat-*: see CITATION, -ORY[2].]
Having the faculty of citing or summoning; concerned with citation. Esp. in ***letters citatory***.

cite /sʌɪt/ *verb trans*. LME.
[ORIGIN Old French & mod. French *citer* from Latin *citare* frequentative of *ciere*, *cire* set in motion, call.]
1 Summon officially before a court of (usu. ecclesiastical) law. LME.
2 *gen.* Summon; arouse, excite. Now *arch.* or *poet.* M16.
3 Quote (a book, passage, author, etc.), esp. as an authority in support of a position; adduce or mention as an example, precedent, or proof; call to mind; refer to (*as*). M16. ▸**b** *spec.* Mention in an official dispatch. E20.

POPE I cite the whole three verses. R. GRAVES He cited Ovid as having said this, and Meleager that, in praise of a fine head of hair. J. F. KENNEDY After announcing this new industrial plan the White Paper cited the need for skilled labour. I. HAMILTON The poem's last lines—sometimes cited as a memorable evocation of urban violence.

■ **citable** *adjective* able to be cited E18. †**cital** *noun* (*rare*) [-AL[1]] (***a***) an impeachment; (***b***) citation, summons: L16–M18. **citer** *noun* L16.

CITES *abbreviation*.
Convention on Trade in Endangered Species.

citess /ˈsɪtɛs, sɪˈtɛs/ *noun*. *arch.* L17.
[ORIGIN from (the same root as) CIT + -ESS[1].]
1 A townswoman; a female shopkeeper or trader. *derog. rare*. L17.
†**2** A female citizen. *US*. L18–E19.

cithara /ˈsɪθ(ə)rə, k-/ *noun*. Also **k-** /k-/. L18.
[ORIGIN Latin from Greek *kithara*.]
An ancient Greek and Roman stringed musical instrument akin to the lyre, having two arms rising vertically from the soundbox.

citharist /ˈsɪθ(ə)rɪst/ *noun*. LME.
[ORIGIN Latin *citharista* from Greek *kitharistēs*, from *kithara*: see CITHARA, -IST.]
A player on the cithara or (formerly) the cittern.

cither /ˈsɪθə/ *noun*. Now *rare*. E17.
[ORIGIN formed as CITHARA.]
A cithara; a cittern.

cithern, **citheren** *nouns* vars. of CITTERN.

citied /ˈsɪtɪd/ *adjective*. E17.
[ORIGIN from CITY + -ED[2].]
Made into or like a city; occupied by a city or cities.

citify /ˈsɪtɪfʌɪ/ *verb trans*. Also **cityfy**. E19.
[ORIGIN from CITY + -FY.]
Make urban in appearance or behaviour; impart features characteristic of a city to. Chiefly as ***citified*** *ppl adjective*.
■ **citifi'cation** *noun* E20.

citizen /ˈsɪtɪz(ə)n/ *noun & adjective*. ME.
[ORIGIN Anglo-Norman *citesein*, *-zein* alt. (prob. after *deinzein* DENIZEN *noun & adjective*) of Old French *citeain* (mod. *citoyen*) from Proto-Romance, from Latin *civitas* CITY.]
▸ **A** *noun*. **1** An inhabitant of a city or town; *esp.* one possessing civic rights, as a freeman etc.; a town-dweller. ME.
2 A member, native or naturalized, of a (usu. specified) state or commonwealth. LME. ▸**b** *spec.* As a title or form of address during the French Revolution: supporter of the republican order. *obsolete* exc. *hist.* L18.
3 An inhabitant, an occupant, (*of*). LME.
4 A civilian. *rare*. E17.
– PHRASES: **citizen of the world** a person who is at home anywhere, a cosmopolitan. **Citizens' Advice Bureau** a local office giving free advice to enquirers concerning their rights or about available aid. **citizen's arrest**: by a private citizen without a warrant, allowable in certain cases, as the witnessing of an arrestable offence. **Citizens' Band** (designating or pertaining to) a range of radio frequencies allocated for local communication by individuals. **Citizen's Charter** a document setting out the rights of citizens, *esp.* a British government document of 1991 guaranteeing citizens the right of redress where a public service fails to meet certain standards. ***John Citizen***. ***second class citizen***: see SECOND CLASS *adjective*. ***senior citizen***: see SENIOR *adjective*.
▸ †**B** *adjective*. Like a city- or town-dweller, city-bred. *rare* (Shakes.). Only in E17.
■ **citizeness** *noun* a female citizen L18. **citizenhood** *noun* (***a***) the state of being a citizen; (***b***) the body of citizens: L19. **citizenish** *adjective* of the nature of or relating to citizens E19. **citizenly** *adjective* pertaining to or characteristic of a citizen M19. **citizenry** *noun* a body of citizens, citizens collectively E19. **citizenship** *noun* the position or status of being a citizen E17.

citole /sɪˈtəʊl/ *noun*. LME.
[ORIGIN Old French (= Provençal *citola*), obscurely from Latin CITHARA: see -OLE[1].]
A medieval plucked musical instrument akin to the lute, a precursor of the cittern.

citral /ˈsɪtral/ *noun*. L19.
[ORIGIN from CITRUS + -AL[2].]
CHEMISTRY. A terpenoid aldehyde, $C_{10}H_{16}O$ (of which there are several isomers), which occurs widely in plants (esp. lemon grass and citrus fruit) and has an odour of lemons.

citrate /ˈsɪtreɪt/ *noun & verb*. L18.
[ORIGIN from CITRIC + -ATE[1].]
▸ **A** *noun*. *CHEMISTRY.* A salt or ester of citric acid. L18.
▸ **B** *verb trans*. Treat (blood) with a solution of a citrate, esp. to prevent coagulation. Chiefly as ***citrated*** *ppl adjective*. E20.

citric /ˈsɪtrɪk/ *adjective*. L18.
[ORIGIN from Latin CITRUS + -IC.]
CHEMISTRY. ***citric acid***, a sharp-tasting crystalline tribasic acid, $C_6H_8O_7$, present in the juice of citrus fruit and made commercially by the fermentation of sugar.

citriculture /ˈsɪtrɪˌkʌltʃə/ *noun*. E20.
[ORIGIN from Latin CITRUS + -I- + -CULTURE.]
The cultivation of citrus fruit trees.

citril /ˈsɪtrɪl/ *noun*. L17.
[ORIGIN App. from Italian *citrinella* dim. of *citrina* citrine-coloured (bird).]
More fully ***citril finch***. A yellow-green finch, *Serinus citrinella*, resident in southern Europe.

citrin /ˈsɪtrɪn/ *noun*. M20.
[ORIGIN from CITRUS + -IN[1].]
BIOCHEMISTRY. A substance consisting of one or more of a group of flavonoids which occur mainly in citrus fruit

and blackcurrants and were formerly thought to be essential in the diet. Also called ***vitamin P*** (chiefly *US*).

citrine /ˈsɪtrɪn/ *adjective & noun*. LME.

[ORIGIN Old French & mod. French *citrin(e)* lemon-coloured from medieval Latin *citrinus*, from Latin CITRUS: see -INE[1].]

▸ **A** *adjective*. Of a light greenish yellow; lemon-coloured. LME.

▸ **B** *noun*. **1** A glassy yellow variety of quartz; false topaz. L16.

2 Citrine colour. L19.

citron /ˈsɪtr(ə)n/ *noun & adjective*. E16.

[ORIGIN Old French & mod. French from Latin CITRUS, after *limon* lemon.]

▸ **A** *noun*. **1** A fruit resembling the lemon but larger, less acid, and with thicker rind. (Orig. also the lemon, and perh. the lime.) E16.

2 The tree, *Citrus medica*, which bears this fruit. Also ***citron tree***. M16.

3 A light greenish-yellow colour; citrine. E17.

†**4** The fragrant wood of an African tree, prob. a cypress, *Tetraclinis articulata*, prized in Roman times for making furniture. M17–M18.

†**5** Brandy flavoured with citron or lemon peel. E–M18.

▸ **B** *adjective*. Of a light greenish-yellow colour, citrine. E20.

citronella /sɪtrəˈnɛlə/ *noun*. M19.

[ORIGIN mod. Latin, dim. of CITRON.]

A fragrant southern Asian grass, *Cymbopogon nardus*; an oil distilled from this (also ***citronella oil***), often used to keep insects away.

■ **citronellal** *noun* [-AL[2]] a terpenoid aldehyde, $C_{10}H_{18}O$, found esp. in citronella, rose, and geranium oils L19. **citronellol** *noun* the corresponding alcohol, $C_{10}H_{20}O$, obtained from similar sources; also called ***rhodinol***: L19.

citrous /ˈsɪtrəs/ *adjective*. E20.

[ORIGIN from CITRUS + -OUS.]

Of the genus *Citrus*; from a tree of the genus *Citrus*.

†**citrul** *noun*. LME–M18.

[ORIGIN Old French *citrule* (mod. *citrouille*), ult. from Latin CITRUS with dim. suffix.]

The watermelon. Also, the pumpkin.

citrulline /ˈsɪtrʌliːn/ *noun*. Also **-in** /-ɪn/. M20.

[ORIGIN from medieval Latin *citrullus* watermelon, formed as CITRUL, + -INE[5].]

BIOCHEMISTRY. An amino acid, $NH_2CONH(CH_2)_3CHNH_2COOH$, which occurs in watermelons and is an intermediate in urea synthesis in animals.

citrus /ˈsɪtrəs/ *noun*. E19.

[ORIGIN Latin = citron tree, thuja.]

A tree of the genus *Citrus*, which includes the lemon, citron, lime, orange, grapefruit, etc.; (more fully ***citrus fruit***) a fruit of such a tree.

citrus root weevil = VAQUITA 1.

cittern /ˈsɪt(ə)n/ *noun*. Also **cithern** /ˈsɪθ(ə)n/, **cithren** /ˈsɪθr(ə)n/. M16.

[ORIGIN formed as CITHARA after GITTERN.]

A wire-stringed musical instrument akin to the lute and usu. played with a plectrum, much used in the 16th and 17th cents.

– COMB.: †**cittern-head** a term of abuse alluding to the grotesque carved head often found on a cittern.

city /ˈsɪti/ *noun*. ME.

[ORIGIN Old French & mod. French *cité* from Latin *civitas*, from *civis* citizen: see -TY[1].]

1 A town or other inhabited place. Long *obsolete* exc. *dial.* ME.

> AV *Luke* 7:11 He went into a city called Nain.

2 A large town; *spec.* a town created a 'city' by charter, esp. as containing a cathedral. Also (chiefly *US*), a municipal corporation occupying a definite area. ME.

> BROWNING Hamelin town's in Brunswick By famous Hanover city. E. A. FREEMAN Birmingham and Dundee, hitherto merely boroughs, were raised to the rank of cities.

Cities of the Plain: see PLAIN *noun*[1] 1. **city of refuge** *hist.* an Israelite town set apart for those who had committed manslaughter. ***free city***: see FREE *adjective*. ***Granite City***: see GRANITE *adjective*. ***Holy City***: see HOLY *adjective*. ***inner city***: see INNER *adjective*. ***Leonine City***: see LEONINE *adjective*[2] 1. ***Monumental City***: see MONUMENTAL. ***Mormon City***. ***mushroom city***: see MUSHROOM *noun & adjective*. ***open city***: see OPEN *adjective*. **the City of God** Paradise, an ideal community in Heaven. **the City of the Seven Hills**, **the Eternal City** Rome. **the Heavenly City** Paradise. ***the Windy City***: see WINDY *adjective*[1]. ***twin city***: see TWIN *adjective & noun*. ***Vatican City***.

3 The people or entire community of a city. ME.

> AV *Matt.* 21:10 All the city was moved, saying, Who is this?

4 ***the City***, that part of London situated within the ancient boundaries and governed by the Lord Mayor and Corporation, *esp.* its business part or community, in the neighbourhood of the Exchange and the Bank of England; *loosely* financial and commercial circles. M16.

5 *hist.* A self-governing city or city state. M16.

6 With preceding adjective or as 2nd elem. of comb.: used to emphasize the adjective or noun of quality. *N. Amer. slang*. M20.

> *Rolling Stone* I get talking and *whoa*! Trouble city!

– COMB.: **City Company** a corporation representing an ancient trade guild; **city desk** *N. Amer.* the newspaper department for local news; **city editor**: (*a*) *N. Amer.* dealing with local news for a newspaper; (*b*) (**C-**) dealing with financial news for a newspaper or journal; **city farm** (*a*) *US* a penal institution which also functions as a farm; (*b*) a farm established within an urban area for educational purposes, as a museum, etc.; **city fathers** the persons responsible for the administration of a city; **city gent** *colloq.* a typical businessman working in the City; **city hall** *N. Amer.* municipal offices or officers; **city marshal** (*a*) see MARSHAL *noun*[1] 5b; (*b*) *US* a law officer in some cities, whose duties include the serving of summonses; ***city mission***: see MISSION *noun* 4b; ***city missionary***: see MISSIONARY *noun* 1; **city page** the page in a newspaper or journal dealing with financial and business news; **cityscape** a view of a city, city scenery; **city slicker** *colloq.*, *derog.* a city-dweller seen as smart and sophisticated or smooth and persuasive; **city state** *hist.* a city that is also an independent sovereign state; **citywide** *adjective* extending throughout a city.

■ **cityful** *noun* as many as a city will contain E19. **cityless** *adjective* LME. **cityward** *adjective*, **cityward(s)** *adverb* [orig. *to the cityward*] in the direction of a city LME.

cityfy *verb* var. of CITIFY.

cive *noun* see CHIVE *noun*[2].

civet /ˈsɪvɪt/ *noun*[1]. M16.

[ORIGIN French *civette* from Italian *zibetto* from medieval Latin *zibethum* from Arabic *zabād* (= sense 2).]

1 Any of several carnivorous mammals of the Asian and African family Viverridae, which also includes the genets and mongooses; esp. *Viverra civetta*, of sub-Saharan Africa. Also ***civet cat***. M16.

2 A strong musky perfume obtained from the anal glands of these animals. M16.

†**civet** *noun*[2]. M16–E18.

[ORIGIN French *civette*, dim. of Old French & mod. French *cive*: see CHIVE *noun*[2], -ET[1].]

= CHIVE *noun*[2].

civet /sivɛ/ *noun*[3]. Pl. pronounced same. E18.

[ORIGIN French, earlier *civé*, from *cive* CHIVE *noun*[2].]

A highly seasoned stew of hare, venison, game, etc.

civet de lièvre /də ljɛːvr/ *civet* of hare.

civet /ˈsɪvɪt/ *verb trans*. E17.

[ORIGIN from CIVET *noun*[1].]

Perfume with civet.

civic /ˈsɪvɪk/ *adjective*. M16.

[ORIGIN French *civique* or Latin *civicus*, from *civis* citizen. In sense 1 translating Latin (*corona*) *civica*.]

1 *hist.* Designating a garland of oak leaves and acorns given in ancient Rome to one who saved a fellow citizen's life in war. M16.

> MARVELL Our civil warrs have lost the civick crowne.

2 Of or pertaining to a city; municipal; urban. M17.

> BYRON Butcher'd in a civic alley. R. H. TAWNEY The whole range of civic administration, from the regulations to be made for markets . . to the control of prices, . . and rents.

civic centre an area where municipal offices and other public buildings are situated, often in a united architectural scheme.

3 Of or pertaining to citizenship; civil (opp. military, ecclesiastical, etc.). L18.

> H. ARENDT A municipal law giving full civic, though not political, rights to the Jews.

4 Of or proper to a citizen or citizens. L18.

> J. S. BLACKIE He displayed a civic virtue on other occasions.

– COMB.: **civic-minded** *adjective* concerned with civic affairs, public-spirited.

■ †**civical** *adjective* E–M17. **civically** *adverb* M17.

civics /ˈsɪvɪks/ *noun pl*. (usu. treated as *sing.*) Orig. *US*. L19.

[ORIGIN from CIVIC + -S[1]: see -ICS.]

The rights and duties of citizenship, as a subject of study.

civil /ˈsɪv(ə)l, -ɪl/ *adjective, noun, & adverb*. LME.

[ORIGIN Old French & mod. French from Latin *civilis*, from *civis* citizen: see -IL, -ILE.]

▸ **A** *adjective*. ▸**I** *gen.* **1** Of or pertaining to citizens; relating to the internal organization of a society, state, etc. LME. ▸**b** Of disorder or conflict: occurring between citizens of the same country. LME.

> R. HOOKER To exercise civil dominion of their own. HOR. WALPOLE The instruction of heathen children in . . civil knowledge. **b** *Fortean Times* Civil conflicts have plagued Indonesia.

†**2** Civic, municipal; urban. *rare*. E16–E18.

3 Orderly; well-governed. Long *obsolete* exc. *N. Irish & Canad. dial.* M16.

> MILTON That Army, lately so renown'd for the civilest and best order'd in the world.

4 In a condition of advanced social development; civilized; educated, well-bred; refined. *arch.* M16.

> E. BREREWOOD Their own languages, which they held to be more civil than the Roman. SOUTHEY As in civil, so in barbarous states.

†**5** Seemly, decent, grave. L16–L17.

> T. DEKKER In lookes, graue; in attire, ciuill.

†**6** Humane, considerate, kind. Only in 17.

7 Polite, obliging; courteous; not rude. E17.

> G. SWIFT Quinn was actually civil to me, even amiable.

▸ **II** *spec.*

8 Not military or naval etc.; not ecclesiastical, secular. LME.

> MILTON Both in religious and civill Wisdome. B. RUSSELL The civil government had not discovered ways of preventing military insurrection.

9 Of law, a legal process, etc.: not criminal, political, or (formerly) ecclesiastical; relating to private relations between members of a community. LME. ▸**b** Of or pertaining to Roman law or the legal systems (as of France or Germany) historically influenced by it. L16.

10 Legal as distinguished from natural; legally recognized; *spec.* (of time measurement) fixed by custom or enactment, not natural or astronomical. E17.

†**11** THEOLOGY. Good or moral, but unregenerate. Only in 17.

– SPECIAL COLLOCATIONS: **civil aviation**: not military, *esp.* commercial. **civil commotion** ENGLISH LAW a riot or similar disturbance. **civil court** a court dealing with non-criminal cases. ***civil day***: see DAY *noun*. ***civil* DEATH**. **civil defence** the organization of civilians to preserve lives and property during and after enemy action, esp. air raids. **civil disobedience** the refusal to obey laws, pay taxes, etc., as part of a political campaign. ***civil engineer***: see ENGINEER *noun* 3. ***civil engineering***: see ENGINEERING *noun* 1. **civil law** *spec.* (also ***the civil law***) Roman law (opp. canon or common law) or the systems of private law (as of France or Germany) historically influenced by it (the sense meant when CIVIL LAW is used as a subject label in this dictionary); see also sense 9 above; **civil liberty** the state of being subject only to laws established for the good of the community; in *pl.*, one's rights to be only so subject. **civil list** (*a*) *hist.* a list of certain items of state expenditure on civil administration; the recipients of moneys voted on this list; (*b*) (with cap. initials) an annual allowance by Parliament for the British monarch's official expenses in his or her role as head of state. **civil marriage**: solemnized as a civil contract without a religious ceremony. ***civil parish***: see PARISH 2. **civil partnership**, **civil union** (in some countries) a legally recognized union of a same-sex couple, with rights similar to those of marriage. **civil rights** the rights of each citizen (*US* esp. of black people) to liberty, equality, etc. **civil servant** a member of the Civil Service. **Civil Service** (*a*) *hist.* that part of the service of the East India Company carried out by covenanted servants not belonging to the army or navy; (*b*) all the non-military branches of state administration. **civil state** marital status; being single, married, divorced, etc. **civil war**: between citizens of the same country, esp. (freq. with cap. initials) in England (1642–9), US (1861–5), or Spain (1936–9). **civil wrong** an infringement of a person's rights, as a tort of breach of contract. ***civil year***: see YEAR *noun*[1].

▸ **B** *noun*. †**1** = CIVILIAN *noun* 1. Only in LME.

†**2** In *pl.* Civil matters, concerns, or affairs. M17–E18.

3 ***do the civil***, act politely (*to* a person), behave in a properly polite manner. *arch. colloq.* M19.

▸ †**C** *adverb*. = CIVILLY. M17–L18.

■ †**civilist** *noun* (*a*) a civilian; (*b*) a politician: M16–M18. **civilly** *adverb* (*a*) in accordance with civil law; (*b*) with reference to civil matters; (*c*) in a civil manner: LME. **civilness** *noun* (*rare*) civility M16.

civilian /sɪˈvɪljən/ *noun & adjective*. LME.

[ORIGIN Old French *civilien* in *droit civilien* civil law, formed as CIVIL: see -IAN. Later directly from CIVIL.]

▸ **A** *noun*. **1** A student of, practitioner of, or expert in civil law. Now *rare*. LME.

†**2** THEOLOGY. A person who is good or moral, but unregenerate. E–M17.

3 A non-military employee of the East India Company; (later) a member of the Indian Civil Service. M18.

4 A person whose regular profession is non-military; one who is not in or of the army, navy, air force, or police. E19.

> M. KENNEDY Hopes of a brave new world . . filled the minds of servicemen and civilians alike.

▸ **B** *attrib.* or as *adjective*. Of or pertaining to civilians; not in or of the army, navy, air force, or police. M17.

> L. DE BERNIÈRES Rough-terrain vehicles . . for civilian and military purposes.

■ **civiliaˈnization** *noun* the action or result of civilianizing M20. **civilianize** *verb trans.* make civilian; *spec.* convert (an armed-service post) into a civilian post: L19.

civilisation *noun* var. of CIVILIZATION.

civilise *verb* var. of CIVILIZE.

civility /sɪˈvɪlɪti/ *noun*. LME.

[ORIGIN Old French & mod. French *civilité* from Latin *civilitas*, from *civilis*: see CIVIL, -ITY.]

▸ **I** Conn. with citizenship.

†**1** = CITIZENHOOD. LME–L16.

†**2** Civil power. LME–M16.

†**3** Polity, civil organization; *spec.* good polity, civil order. M16–L17.

4 Good citizenship; orderly behaviour. Long *obsolete* exc. *N. Irish*. M16.

†**5** THEOLOGY. Civil or moral righteousness. E–M17.

▸ **II** Conn. with civilization.

6 The state of being civilized, civilization; culture, refinement; polite or liberal education. *arch.* M16.

> W. RALEIGH From them the Greekes, then barbarous, received Civilitie. DE QUINCEY Our universities, all so many recurring centres of civility.

C

7 Politeness; consideration; an act or expression of politeness (usu. in *pl.*). M16.

LD MACAULAY He would not use the common forms of civility. J. I. M. STEWART A formally courteous person . . who felt obliged to stay put until adequate civilities had been exchanged.

†8 Decency, seemliness. Only in 17.
– COMB.: †**civility-money** a gratuity, a tip.

C

civilization /ˌsɪvɪlʌɪˈzeɪʃ(ə)n/ *noun*. Also **-isation**. E18.
[ORIGIN from CIVILIZE + -ATION. Cf. French *civilisation*.]
†1 LAW. The process of turning a criminal action or process into a civil one; the assimilation of common law to civil law. E18–E19.
2 The state or condition of being civilized; civilized society; a highly developed state of society; a particular form, stage, or type of social development. M18.

A. KOESTLER The breakdown of civilization during the Dark Ages. K. CLARK Of this ancient, rustic civilisation we have no record beyond the farmhouses themselves.

3 The action or process of civilizing or being civilized. L18.
■ **civilizational** *adjective* of or pertaining to civilization M19.

civilize /ˈsɪvɪlʌɪz/ *verb*. Also **-ise**. E17.
[ORIGIN French *civiliser* (earlier *-zer*), formed as CIVIL: see -IZE.]
1 *verb trans.* Bring out of barbarism; bring to conformity with the standards of behaviour and the tastes of a highly developed society; enlighten; refine and educate. E17.
†2 *verb trans.* Subject to civil authority. E17–E18.
3 *verb intrans.* †**a** Behave in a civilized fashion. Only in E17. ▸**b** Become civilized. M19.
■ **civilizable** *adjective* able to be civilized M19. **civilized** *ppl adjective* that has been civilized; pertaining to or characteristic of a highly developed society; refined, educated: E17. **civiliˈzee** *noun* (now *rare*) a civilized person M19. **civilizer** *noun* L17.

civism /ˈsɪvɪz(ə)m/ *noun*. L18.
[ORIGIN French *civisme*, from Latin *civis* citizen: see -ISM.]
The principles of good citizenship, esp. (& orig.) in relation to the republican order established by the French Revolution.

civvy /ˈsɪvi/ *noun & adjective*. *slang*. L19.
[ORIGIN Abbreviation of CIVILIAN.]
▸ **A** *noun*. 1 In *pl.* Civilian clothes. L19.
2 A civilian. E20.
▸ **B** *adjective*. Civilian. E20.
Civvy Street civilian (as opp. to Service) life.

CJ *abbreviation*.
Chief Justice.

CJD *abbreviation*.
Creutzfeldt–Jakob disease.

cl *abbreviation*.
Centilitre(s).

Cl *symbol*.
CHEMISTRY. Chlorine.

cl. *abbreviation*.
1 Class.
2 Clause.

clabber /ˈklabə/ *noun*¹. *Scot. & Irish*. Also **clauber** /ˈklɔːbə/. E19.
[ORIGIN Gaelic *clàbar*, Irish *clábar*.]
Mud, soft dirt, wet clay.
■ **clabbery** *adjective* L19.

clabber /ˈklabə/ *noun*² & *verb*. Chiefly *US*. E19.
[ORIGIN Abbreviation.]
▸ **A** *noun*. = BONNY-CLABBER. E19.
▸ **B** *verb intrans. & trans.* Curdle, turn sour. L19.

clachan /ˈklax(ə)n/ *noun*. *Scot. & N. Irish*. LME.
[ORIGIN Gaelic & Irish *clachán*.]
A small village, a hamlet.

clack /klak/ *noun & interjection*. LME.
[ORIGIN Imit.: cf. Old Norse *klak* chirping of birds, Dutch *klak*, Middle High German *klac*, CLAIK noun.]
▸ **I** *noun & interjection*. Also redupl. **clack-clack(-clack)**.
1 (Repr.) the noise of continual loud talking, loud chatter. LME.
2 (Repr.) a sharp sound as of boards struck together, a metal object striking stone or wood, etc. L16.
▸ **II** *noun*. 3 The clapper of a mill. *obsolete* exc. *dial.* LME.
4 The human tongue. Usu. *derog.* L16.
5 A flap valve in a pump etc. Also ***clack-valve***. M17.
6 An instrument that clacks to frighten birds away. L17.
7 A (loud) chat, a conversation. *colloq.* L18.

clack /klak/ *verb*. ME.
[ORIGIN Imit.: cf. Old Norse *klaka* twitter, (of birds) chatter, Dutch *klakken* crack, French *claquer*, CLAIK verb.]
1 *verb intrans.* Chatter loudly, talk continually. ME.

LD MACAULAY He will sit clacking with an old woman for hours.

2 *verb intrans. & trans.* (Cause to) make a clack; clatter. M16.

S. DELANEY The old clogs clacking along the cobbles. M. RICHLER Max clacked his tongue reproachfully.

3 *verb intrans.* Of a hen etc.: cluck, cackle. E18.
– COMB.: **clack dish** *hist.* = ***clap dish*** s.v. CLAP *verb*¹.
■ **clacker** *noun* M17.

clacket /ˈklakɪt/ *noun*. L16.
[ORIGIN French *claquet*, from *claquer* to clack: see -ET¹.]
†1 = CLACK *noun* 3, 6. L16–E17.
2 A light or repeated clacking sound; incessant chatter. E19.
■ **clackety** *adjective* making a light or repeated clacking sound M19.

clacket /ˈklakɪt/ *verb intrans.* M16.
[ORIGIN French *claqueter*, formed as CLACKET noun.]
Clack lightly or repeatedly.

Clactonian /klakˈtəʊnɪən/ *adjective & noun*. M20.
[ORIGIN from *Clacton* (see below) + -IAN.]
ARCHAEOLOGY. (The culture or industry) of an early Palaeolithic period represented by flint implements found at Clacton-on-Sea in SE England, dated to about 250,000–200,000 years ago.

clad /klad/ *verb*¹ *trans.* Infl. **-dd-**. M16.
[ORIGIN App. from CLADDAGH.]
1 Clothe. *arch.* M16.
2 Provide with cladding. M20.

clad *verb*² *pa. t. & pple*: see CLOTHE.

Claddagh /ˈkladə/ *noun*. E20.
[ORIGIN from *Claddagh*, a fishing village on the edge of Galway city, Ireland.]
A symbol formed from two hands holding a crowned heart, which represents friendship, love, and loyalty. Chiefly *attrib.*, designating jewellery bearing the symbol; ***Claddagh ring***, a ring given traditionally in Ireland as a token of love.

cladding /ˈkladɪŋ/ *noun*. L19.
[ORIGIN from CLAD *verb*¹ + -ING¹.]
1 In *pl.* Clothes. *rare*. L19.
2 A special coating or covering on a structure, material, etc.; the application of such a covering. M20.

clade /kleɪd/ *noun*. M20.
[ORIGIN Greek *klados* branch.]
BIOLOGY. A group of organisms believed to have evolved from a common ancestor.
■ **cladism** *noun* belief in cladistics M20. **cladist** *noun* [perh. back-form. from CLADISTIC] an exponent of cladistics M20.

cladistic /kləˈdɪstɪk/ *adjective*. M20.
[ORIGIN from CLADE + -ISTIC.]
BIOLOGY. Of or pertaining to clades or cladistics.
■ **cladistically** *adverb* in terms of cladistics; as regards cladistics or a cladistic relationship: M20.

cladistics /kləˈdɪstɪks/ *noun*. M20.
[ORIGIN from CLADISTIC: see -ICS.]
BIOLOGY. The systematic classification of groups of organisms on the basis of the order of their assumed divergence from ancestral species; systematics based on this.

clado- /ˈkleɪdəʊ, ˈkladəʊ/ *combining form* of Greek *klados* branch, shoot, or of CLADE: see -O-.
■ **cladoˈgenesis** *noun* (BIOLOGY) the formation of a new species by evolutionary divergence of an ancestral species and species derived from it (cf. ANAGENESIS) M20. **cladogeˈnetic** *adjective* (BIOLOGY) of, pertaining to, or arising through cladogenesis M20. **claˈdogenous** *adjective* (BOTANY) growing from or borne on branches L19. **cladogram** *noun* (BIOLOGY) a tree diagram of the cladistic relationship between a number of species M20.

cladoceran /kləˈdɒs(ə)r(ə)n/ *noun & adjective*. E20.
[ORIGIN from mod. Latin *Cladocera* (see below), formed as CLADO- + Greek *keras* horn (on account of the branched antennae): see -AN.]
(A branchiopod crustacean) of the group Cladocera, which includes the water fleas.

cladode /ˈkleɪdəʊd/ *noun*. L19.
[ORIGIN from late Greek *kladōdēs* with many shoots, from *klados* shoot.]
BOTANY. A flattened leaflike stem.

cladosporium /kladəʊˈspɔːrɪəm/ *noun*. Pl. **-ria** /-rɪə/. L19.
[ORIGIN mod. Latin (see below), formed as CLADO- + *spora* seed + -IUM.]
(Infestation with) a fungus of the genus *Cladosporium*, esp. causing leaf mould of tomatoes.

claes *noun pl.* see CLOTHES.

clafoutis /klaˈfuːti/ *noun*. Pl. same. M20.
[ORIGIN French dial., from *clafir* to fill.]
A type of flan made of fruit, esp. cherries, baked in a sweet batter.

clag /klag/ *verb & noun*. Chiefly *Scot. & N. English*. LME.
[ORIGIN Perh. of Scandinavian origin: cf. Danish *klag*, *klagge* sticky mud, clay, *klæg*, *klæget* viscous, rel. to CLAY noun.]
▸ **A** *verb*. Infl. **-gg-**.
1 *verb trans.* Bedaub or clot *with*; clog. LME.
2 *verb intrans.* Stick, adhere, (*to*). M16.
▸ **B** *noun*. 1 A flaw of character; a fault. *Scot.* L16.
2 A legal encumbrance on a property etc. *Scot.* Long *rare*. L16.
3 A mass of clotted dirt in a sheep's fleece etc. M17.
■ **claggum** *noun* treacle toffee M19. **claggy** *adjective* tending to form clots; sticky: L16.

claik /kleɪk/ *noun, interjection, & verb*. *Scot.* LME.
[ORIGIN Imit.: cf. CLACK *noun & interjection*, *verb*.]
▸ **A** *noun*. 1 More fully ***claik goose***. The barnacle goose. LME.
2 Also *interjection*. (Repr.) the harsh call of a goose, the cluck or cackle of a hen etc. L15.
3 Chatter, gossip; a gossipy person. L18.
▸ **B** *verb intrans.* 1 Of a goose: call harshly. Of a hen etc.: cluck, cackle. E16.
2 Chatter, talk tediously. M19.

claim /kleɪm/ *noun*. ME.
[ORIGIN Old French *claime*, from *clamer*: see CLAIM *verb*.]
▸ **I** 1 A demand for something as due; a statement of one's right *to* something; a contention, an assertion; *spec.* (***a***) a formal assertion of a right to a piece of land for mining etc.; (***b***) a demand for payment in accordance with law, an insurance policy, etc.; (***c***) (in full ***pay claim***) a demand for an increase in pay; (***d***) a formal statement of the novel features in a patent. ME.

C. DAY The telephone company sent us circulars in which they made large claims. C. HILL By arbitrary arrest and imprisonment he enforced his claim to tax without Parliamentary consent. A. BRINK The Department of Justice instituted a claim for libel against the newspaper.

Court of Claims: see COURT *noun*¹. **lay claim to** assert one's right to, claim. ***no-claim bonus***, ***no-claims bonus***: see NO *adjective*. ***quit claim to***: see QUIT *verb*. ***small claims court***: see SMALL *adjective*. ***statement of claim*** = ***claim form*** below.
2 A right or title (*to* something); a right to make a demand (*(up)on* a person etc.). ME.

J. B. PRIESTLEY Miss Trant had waived any claim to her part of the fee. R. S. THOMAS The claim Of wife and young ones. W. S. CHURCHILL His care for the Royal Navy is his chief claim upon the gratitude of his countrymen.

3 A piece of land allotted or taken for the purpose of mining etc. L18.
prospecting claim: see PROSPECT *verb* 4. **stake a claim**, **stake out a claim** make a claim to a piece of land for mining etc. by marking it with stakes; *fig.* make a statement of one's rights (*to*).
▸ †**II** 4 A call, a shout. *rare* (Spenser). Only in L16.
– COMB.: **claim form** ENGLISH LAW a pleading served by the plaintiff in a High Court action containing the allegations made against the defendant and the relief sought by the plaintiff. **claim-jumper** a person who appropriates a mining claim already taken by another.
■ **claimless** *adjective* E19.

claim /kleɪm/ *verb*. ME.
[ORIGIN Old French *claim-* tonic stem of *clamer* to cry, call, appeal, from Latin *clamare*. Cf. CLAMOUR *noun*.]
▸ **I** *verb trans.* 1 Demand as one's due or property, require as a right, (*arch.* foll. by *that*, *to be* + pa. ppl adjective); *fig.* have as a property, achievement, or consequence, *esp.* take by death. ME.

C. MERIVALE He claimed that his word should be law. J. R. GREEN Every townsman could claim to be tried by his fellow-townsman. B. PYM The television screen was beginning to claim their full attention. M. M. KAYE The cholera had claimed four more lives. *Which?* You should claim a refund of the repair cost from the shop.

2 Assert or demand recognition of (the fact *that*); represent oneself as having, oneself *to be*, *to have done*; represent oneself so as to seem *to do*; assert, contend, *that*. ME.

DEFOE Both sides claimed the victory. E. WAUGH Basil claimed to have eaten a girl once in Africa. G. GREENE She never claimed to like a thing that she disliked. M. HOLROYD He claimed to be a descendant of Owen Glendower. E. CRISPIN The Major could sense a journalist, or . . claimed he could.

†3 Name (as), proclaim (to be); represent (oneself) as. ME–L16.
4 Of a thing: have a right to, deserve, call for. E17.

J. TYNDALL One other point . . which claims our attention.

▸ **II** *verb intrans.* 5 Put forward a claim; assert a right; represent oneself to be. Now only *spec.* make a claim for indemnity on an insurance company. ME.

POPE Say from what scepter'd ancestry ye claim.

■ **claimable** *adjective* E17. **claimant** *noun* a person who makes a claim, esp. formally; a person who has a claim (*(up)on*): L17. **claimer** *noun* LME.

clairaudience /klɛːrˈɔːdɪəns/ *noun*. M19.
[ORIGIN from French *clair* clear + AUDIENCE, after CLAIRVOYANCE.]
The supposed faculty of perceiving, as if by hearing, what is inaudible.
■ **clairaudient** *adjective & noun* (***a***) *adjective* having the faculty of clairaudience; of the nature of or pertaining to clairaudience; (***b***) *noun* a clairaudient person: M19.

clair-de-lune /klɛːrdəlyn, klɛːdəˈluːn/ *noun*. L19.
[ORIGIN French, lit. 'moonlight'.]
A soft white or pale blue-grey colour; a Chinese porcelain glaze of this colour.

clair-obscure /klɛːrəbˈskjʊə/ *noun*. E18.
[ORIGIN French *clair-obscur* translating Italian CHIAROSCURO.]
Chiaroscuro.

clairschach /ˈklɑːʃəx/ *noun*. Also **clar-**. **L15.**
[**ORIGIN** Irish *cláirseach*, Gaelic *clàrsach*.]
The traditional Celtic harp strung with wire.
▪ **clairschacher** *noun* a person who plays the clairschach **E16.**

clairvoyance /klɛːˈvɔɪəns/ *noun*. **M19.**
[**ORIGIN** French, formed as **CLAIRVOYANT**: see **-ANCE**.]
1 The supposed faculty of perceiving, as if by seeing, what is happening or exists out of sight. **M19.**
2 Keenness of mental perception: exceptional insight. **M19.**

clairvoyant /klɛːˈvɔɪənt/ *adjective & noun*. Occas. fem. **-ante**. **L17.**
[**ORIGIN** French, from *clair* clear + *voyant* pres. ppl adjective of *voir* see: see **-ANT**[1].]
▸ **A** *adjective*. **1** Clear-sighted, perceptive. *rare*. **L17.**
2 Having or exercising the faculty of clairvoyance; pertaining to clairvoyance. **M19.**
▸ **B** *noun*. **1** A clear-sighted person. *rare*. **L18.**
2 A person having the faculty of clairvoyance. **M19.**
▪ **clairvoyantly** *adverb* **L19.**

clam /ˈklam/ *noun*[1].
[**ORIGIN** Old English *clam* = Old High German *klamma* (German dial. *Klamm*), Middle High German, German *klemme*, Dutch *klemme*, *klem*, from Germanic (rel. to **CLAMP** *noun*[1]).]
†**1** Anything that holds tight; in *pl.* bonds, bondage. Only in **OE.**
2 An instrument for clasping rigidly or holding fast; a clamp, vice, pair of pincers, etc.; also, a lining for the jaws of a vice. **LME.**
3 In *pl.* clutches, claws. Long *obsolete* exc. *dial.* **M16.**

clam /klam/ *noun*[2]. **E16.**
[**ORIGIN** App. from **CLAM** *noun*[1].]
1 A bivalve mollusc; *esp.* (***a***) *Scot.* a scallop; (***b***) an extremely large tropical bivalve, *Tridacna gigas* (usu. ***giant clam***); (***c***) either of two common bivalves valued as food on the east coast of N. America, the quahog *Venus mercenaria* (also ***hard clam***, ***round clam***) and *Mya arenaria*, which has a very long siphon (also ***long clam***, ***longneck clam***, ***soft clam***, ***steamer clam***). (Earliest in ***clamshell*** below.) **E16.**
(***as***) ***happy as a clam***: see **HAPPY** *adjective*. ***Venus clam***: see **VENUS** 9. ***Washington clam***: see **WASHINGTON** 1.
2 The mouth. *US slang*. **E19.**
3 A person who is close-minded, close-mouthed, etc.; a taciturn person. *US slang*. **M19.**
– **COMB.**: **clambake** *US* a social gathering for eating (esp. clams and fish) outdoors; a loud and lively gathering, a jam session; **clamdigger** (***a***) a person who digs for clams; (***b***) (***clamdiggers***) close-fitting calf-length trousers for women; **clamshell** (***a***) the shell of a clam; (***b***) *US slang* = sense 2 above.

clam /klam/ *noun*[3]. **M16.**
[**ORIGIN** Perh. back-form. from **CLAMMY**.]
†**1** A soft mass. Only in **M16.**
2 Clamminess. **L17.**

clam /klam/ *noun*[4]. **E18.**
[**ORIGIN** Prob. imit.: cf. **CLAM** *verb*[3].]
BELL-RINGING. The crash of two or more bells of a peal rung together.

clam /klam/ *adjective*. *obsolete* exc. *dial.* **ME.**
[**ORIGIN** Prob. rel. to **CLAM** *verb*[1], **CLOAM** *noun*.]
Sticky; cold and damp; clammy.

clam /klam/ *verb*[1]. *obsolete* exc. *dial.* Infl. **-mm-**. **LME.**
[**ORIGIN** Var. of **CLEAM**, perh. infl. by **CLAM** *adjective*.]
1 *verb trans.* Smear or spread (sticky or slimy matter) *on*; daub (*with*). **LME.**
2 *verb trans.* Clog or choke up. **E16.**
3 *verb intrans.* Be moist and sticky; stick, adhere. **M16.**
4 *verb trans.* Clog or entangle *with* or *in* anything sticky. **L16.**

clam /klam/ *verb*[2] *intrans.* Infl. **-mm-**. **M17.**
[**ORIGIN** from **CLAM** *noun*[2].]
1 Dig for clams, collect clams. *US*. **M17.**
2 Foll. by *up*: become silent, stop talking or otherwise communicating. *slang* (chiefly *N. Amer.*). **E20.**

clam /klam/ *verb*[3]. Infl. **-mm-**. **L17.**
[**ORIGIN** Prob. imit.: cf. **CLAM** *noun*[4], **CLAMOUR** *verb*[2].]
BELL-RINGING. **1** *verb intrans.* Of bells: sound or crash together. **L17.**
2 *verb trans.* Sound or crash (bells) together. **E18.**

clam *verb*[4] var. of **CLEM**.

clamant /ˈkleɪm(ə)nt, ˈklam-/ *adjective*. **M17.**
[**ORIGIN** from Latin *clamant-* pres. ppl stem of *clamare* cry out: see **-ANT**[1]. Cf. **CLAIM** *verb*.]
1 Clamorous, noisy. **M17.**
2 *fig.* Insistent, urgent. **E18.**

> *New Scientist* By 1920 the need for training and transfer of US technology was clamant.

▪ **clamantly** *adverb* **M19.**

†**clamb** *verb pa. t.*: see **CLIMB** *verb*.

clamber /ˈklambə/ *verb & noun*. **ME.**
[**ORIGIN** Of frequentative form, prob. from **CLAMANT**: see **-ER**[5].]
▸ **A** *verb*. **1** *verb intrans. & trans.* Climb using hands and feet; climb with difficulty and effort. **ME.**

> S. JOHNSON They can . . clamber the mountain. F. HERBERT The craft creaked as the others clambered aboard.

2 *verb intrans. transf. & fig.* ▸**a** Climb or struggle (*up*) into a position of eminence; attain with effort *to*. Now *rare*. **L16.** ▸**b** Rise upwards heavily, irregularly, or steeply. **E17.** ▸**c** Of a plant: climb by means of tendrils. **E17.**

> **b** N. HAWTHORNE A tall palace of gray, time-worn stone clambered skyward. TENNYSON The narrow street that clamber'd toward the mill. **c** C. RAINE Ivy clambers over the sides of a rusty cot.

▸ **B** *noun*. An act of clambering; a climb using hands and feet. **E19.**
▪ **clamberer** *noun* a person who or thing which clambers; formerly *esp.* a climbing plant: **L16.**

clame *verb* var. of **CLEAM**.

clamjamphrie /klamˈdʒamfri/ *noun*. *Scot. & N. English*. Also **clan-** /klan-/, **-fry**, & other vars. **E19.**
[**ORIGIN** Unknown.]
Worthless or vulgar people; a mob, a rabble.

clammer *verb* see **CLAMOUR** *verb*[2].

clammy /ˈklami/ *adjective*. **LME.**
[**ORIGIN** from **CLAM** *verb*[1] or *adjective* + **-Y**[1].]
Moist, usu. cold, and sticky or slimy; damp and cold.

> SOUTHEY The cold sweat stands Upon his clammy limbs. D. H. LAWRENCE The wind drifted a clammy fog across the hills. J. MASTERS The clammy sari was clinging to my body.

▪ **clammily** *adverb* **M19.** **clamminess** *noun* **E16.**

clamor *noun*, *verb*[1], *verb*[2] see **CLAMOUR** *noun*, *verb*[1], *verb*[2].

clamorous /ˈklam(ə)rəs/ *adjective*. **LME.**
[**ORIGIN** from late Latin *clamorosus*, from Latin *clamor*: see **CLAMOUR** *noun*, **-OUS**. Cf. Old French *clamoreus*.]
Of the nature of clamour; uttered with or accompanied by shouting; noisy; loudly and persistently complaining, appealing, or demanding; urgently claiming attention.

> SHAKES. *A.Y.L.* I will be . . more clamorous than a parrot against rain. D. H. LAWRENCE Her voice was loud and clamorous. W. STYRON The night was clamorous with frogs and katydids.

▪ **clamorously** *adverb* **M16.** **clamorousness** *noun* **E17.**

clamour /ˈklamə/ *noun*. Also ***-or**. **LME.**
[**ORIGIN** Anglo-Norman *clamur*, Old French *clamour* from Latin *clamor* rel. to *clamare*: see **-OUR**. Cf. **CLAIM** *verb*.]
1 Loud shouting (by one or, freq., many), esp. in complaint, appeal, or opposition; vehement expression of feeling, esp. of discontent or disapprobation; popular outcry. **LME.**

> R. WHATELY Attempts . . to silence a speaker by clamour. E. LONGFORD An important section of the Army . . fell a victim to the country's clamour for economy.

2 A loud shout, an outburst of noisy utterance; a popular outcry. **LME.**

> C. THIRLWALL Interrupted in a speech by clamours of disapprobation.

3 Any loud or confused noise. **L16.**

> W. IRVING The clamour of a troop of dogs. A. C. SWINBURNE The clamour of his storms. A. MACLEAN The sudden strident clamour of an alarm bell.

clamour /ˈklamə/ *verb*[1]. Also ***-or**. **LME.**
[**ORIGIN** from the noun.]
1 *verb intrans.* Make a clamour; raise an outcry; make a loud appeal, complaint, or demand, (*for*, *against*, *to do*). **LME.**

> SHAKES. *Macb.* The obscure bird Clamour'd the livelong night. A. BRIGGS The urban working classes came into the open to clamour for reform. R. SUTCLIFF If you tell me to do a thing, I will do it, without clamouring to know why.

2 *verb trans.* †**a** Disturb with clamour. Only in **17.** ▸**b** Move or drive *out of*, *into*, etc., by clamouring; put *down* by clamour. **M17.**
3 *verb trans.* Utter or assert clamorously. **M19.**
▪ **clamourer** *noun* **M17.**

clamour /ˈklamə/ *verb*[2] *trans.* Now *rare*. Also **-or**, **clammer**. **E17.**
[**ORIGIN** Uncertain: perh. rel. to **CLAM** *verb*[3] or a use of **CLAMOUR** *verb*[1].]
Silence, stop the noise of, (*spec.* bells).
– **NOTE**: First recorded in Shakes.

clamp /klamp/ *noun*[1] & *verb*[1]. **ME.**
[**ORIGIN** Prob. of Low German origin: cf. Dutch, Low German *klamp*, †*klampe* (whence German *Klampe*), from Germanic (rel. to **CLAM** *noun*[1]).]
▸ **A** *noun*. **1** A brace, clasp, or band, usu. of rigid material, used for strengthening or fastening things together. **ME.**
2 **NAUTICAL.** Each of the thick planks in a ship's side below the shelf-piece, which support the ends of the deck beams. **L15.**
3 An appliance or tool with parts which may be brought together by a screw etc. for holding or compressing. **L17.**
4 **ELECTRICITY.** A circuit which serves to maintain at prescribed levels the voltage limits of a signal. Also ***clamp circuit***. **M20.**
▸ **B** *verb*. **1** *verb trans.* Patch (*up*). *Scot.* **L15.**
2 *verb trans.* Make fast or strengthen (as) with a clamp or clamps; place or hold firmly. **L17.** ▸**b** Immobilize with a wheel clamp. **L20.**

> R. P. WARREN To . . clamp a cigar in his left jaw. W. GOLDING A heavy hand . . clamped me down. L. DEIGHTON The . . cables were roughly clamped across the charred ends as if with artery forceps.

3 *verb intrans.* **a** ***clamp down*** (***on***), press down hard (on), become stricter (regarding), call a halt (to). **E20.** ▸**b** ***clamp down***, (of cloud, fog, etc.) descend very low, so as to prevent flying etc. **M20.**

> **a** *Economist* The government clamped down firmly on all political agitation. L. LEE Suddenly the iron-frost of destitution would clamp down on the house.

4 *verb trans.* **ELECTRICITY.** Maintain the voltage limits of (a signal) at prescribed values. Freq. as ***clamping verbal noun***. **M20.**
– **COMB.**: **clampdown** an act of clamping down.

clamp /klamp/ *noun*[2] & *verb*[2]. **L16.**
[**ORIGIN** Prob. from (M)Du *klamp* heap, rel. to **CLUMP** *noun*.]
▸ **A** *noun*. **1** A stack or pile of bricks for burning. **L16.**
2 A heap or pile of straw and earth covering potatoes etc. during winter; a heap or pile of turf, peat, garden rubbish, etc. **E18.**
▸ **B** *verb trans.* Pile *up* in a clamp; store (potatoes etc.) in a clamp. **M19.**

clamp /klamp/ *noun*[3] & *verb*[3]. Chiefly *Scot. & N. English*. **L18.**
[**ORIGIN** Imit.: cf. **CLOMP**, **CLUMP** *noun*, *verb*.]
▸ **A** *noun*. A heavy step or tread; a stamp with the feet. **L18.**
▸ **B** *verb intrans.* Tread heavily, clump. **E19.**

clamper /ˈklampə/ *verb*[1] & *noun*. Now chiefly *Scot.* **M16.**
[**ORIGIN** from **CLAMP** *verb*[1] + **-ER**[5].]
▸ **A** *verb trans.* Put together hastily or clumsily, patch *up*, (*lit.* & *fig.*). **M16.**
▸ **B** *noun*. **1** A metal patch or plate. *Scot.* **E17.**
2 A botched-up argument or charge. **M17.**

clamper /ˈklampə/ *verb*[2] *intrans.* Chiefly *Scot. & dial.* **E19.**
[**ORIGIN** from **CLAMP** *verb*[3] + **-ER**[5].]
Walk or step heavily or noisily.

clan /klan/ *noun & verb*. **LME.**
[**ORIGIN** Gaelic *clann* offspring, family, stock, from Old Irish *cland* (mod. Irish *clann*) from Latin *planta* sprout, scion, **PLANT** *noun*.]
▸ **A** *noun*. **1** A group of (esp. Highland) Scots claiming descent from a common ancestor, acknowledging a patriarchal chief, and usu. all having the same surname. **LME.**
2 *gen.* Any similar tribal division or group; a (large) close-knit family. **E16.**
3 A group of people having shared attributes; a party, a coterie, a set. Usu. *derog.* **M16.**
4 A group of objects, animals, plants, etc., sharing common origins or attributes. **M17.** ▸**b** **ECOLOGY.** A small local group of a dominant plant species. **E20.** ▸**c** **GEOLOGY.** A group of igneous rocks of similar chemical composition. **E20.**
– **COMB.**: **clansfolk** (fellow) members of a clan. **clansman** a male (fellow) member of a clan. **clanswoman** a female (fellow) member of a clan.
▸ **B** *verb intrans.* Infl. **-nn-**. Combine (*together*) as members of a clan. **L17.**
▪ **clanism** *noun* clan system or feeling **M19.** **clanny** *adjective* = **CLANNISH** **L19.** **clanship** *noun* a clan system; clannish behaviour; clan membership or feeling: **M18.**

†**clancular** *adjective*. **E17–M18.**
[**ORIGIN** Latin *clancularius*, from *clanculum* adverb, dim. of *clam* in secret: see **-AR**[2].]
Secret; clandestine.
▪ †**clancularly** *adverb* **E17–M19.** †**clanculary** *adjective* = **CLANCULAR** **M16–M17.**

clandestine /klanˈdɛstɪn, ˈklandɛstɪn/ *adjective*. **M16.**
[**ORIGIN** French *clandestin* or Latin *clandestinus*, from *clam* in secret: see **-INE**[1].]
Surreptitious, secret.
▪ **clandestinely** *adverb* **M17.** **clandeˈstinity** *noun* (surreptitious) secrecy **L17.**

clang /klaŋ/ *noun & verb*. **L16.**
[**ORIGIN** Imit., but infl. by Latin *clangor*, *clangere* (see **CLANGOUR**); sense A.3 from German *Klang*. Cf. **CLANK**, **CLINK** *noun*[1], *verb*[1].]
▸ **A** *noun*. **1** A loud resonant metallic sound, as of a trumpet, armour, a large bell, etc. **L16.**
2 The loud harsh scream of certain birds, as geese. **M17.**
3 Chiefly **PSYCHOLOGY.** (The acoustic sensation of) a sound consisting of a fundamental tone and overtones. Now *rare*. **M19.**
– **COMB.**: **clang association** **PSYCHOLOGY** an association of words by sound rather than meaning.
▸ **B** *verb*. **1** *verb intrans.* Move with or make a loud resonant metallic sound. **L16.**

> J. STEINBECK Every day the red bus clangs back and forth. A. CARTER A voice that clanged like dustbin lids.

2 *verb trans.* Cause to make a clang; strike together with a clang. **E18.**
3 *verb intrans.* Of certain birds: utter their loud harsh cry. **M19.**

C

■ **clanger** *noun* (*slang*) a blunder (esp. in ***drop a clanger***, make a blunder) M20.

clangour /ˈklaŋɡə/ *noun & verb*. Also *-or. L16.
[ORIGIN Latin *clangor*, from *clangere* resound: see -OUR, -OR.]
▸ **A** *noun*. Clanging noise; a succession or prevalence of clanging noises. L16.

P. PULLMAN A loud jarring bell was filling the ship with its clangour.

▸ **B** *verb intrans*. Make a clangour. M19.
■ **clangorous** *adjective* full of clangour E18. **clangorously** *adverb* M19.

clanjamfry, **clanjamphrie** *nouns* vars. of CLAMJAMPHRIE.

clank /klaŋk/ *noun & verb*. LME.
[ORIGIN Imit., = Middle Low German, Middle Dutch & mod. Dutch *klank*, Old High German *klanc*, *klank-*. Cf. CLANG, CLINK *noun*[1], *verb*[1], CLONK, CLUNK *verb & noun*[2].]
▸ **A** *noun*. An abrupt heavy metallic sound, as of heavy pieces of metal meeting, a chain rattling, etc. LME.
▸ **B** *verb*. **1** *verb trans*. Deposit with a clank; put *down* heavily. E17.
2 *verb intrans*. Make an abrupt heavy metallic sound; move with a clank or clanks. M17.

E. DARWIN Dungeons dank Where . . fetters clank. J. GALSWORTHY The iron gates clanked open. C. P. SNOW Some undergraduates came clanking through in football boots.

3 *verb trans*. Cause to make a clank or clanks; proclaim by a clank or clanks. M18.

J. CLARE The beating snow-clad bell, with sounding dead, Hath clanked four. C. H. SISSON Gaolers . . Clanking their keys.

— NOTE: In isolated use before 17.
■ **clankety-clank** /ˌklaŋkɪtɪˈklaŋk/ *noun* a repeated clanking sound L19. **clankless** *adjective* (*rare*) E19.

clannish /ˈklanɪʃ/ *adjective*. M18.
[ORIGIN from CLAN *noun* + -ISH[1].]
Pertaining to or characteristic of a clan; (too much) attached to one's own clan, family, etc.
■ **clannishly** *adverb* L19. **clannishness** *noun* E19.

clap /klap/ *noun*[1]. ME.
[ORIGIN from CLAP *verb*[1].]
▸ **I** A noise or action.
1 Noisy talk, chatter. Long *obsolete* exc. *dial*. ME.
2 A sounding blow; a slap, a pat. ME.

S. JOHNSON All the forms of . . salutation, from the clap on the shoulder to the humble bow.

3 A sudden stroke (*lit. & fig.*). *obsolete* exc. *Scot.* & in ***afterclap*** s.v. AFTER-. ME.
4 An abrupt explosive noise, as of two hard surfaces striking one another; the report of a gun. LME. ▸**b** *spec.* A peal of thunder. LME. ▸**c** *spec.* The noise of the palms of the hands being struck together; (a round of) applause. L16.
▸ **II** A physical object.
5 = CLAPPER *noun*[1] 1; *esp.* the clapper of a mill. ME.
†**6** The human tongue. ME–L16.
7 The lower mandible of a hawk. L15.

clap /klap/ *noun*[2]. *coarse slang*. L16.
[ORIGIN from Old French *clapoir* venereal bubo.]
Venereal disease, *esp.* gonorrhoea, (also ***the clap***); an infection with this.

clap /klap/ *verb*[1]. Infl. **-pp-**. Pa. t. & pple **clapped**, (*arch.*) **clapt**.
[ORIGIN Old English *clappan* = Old Frisian *klappia*, Middle Low German *klappen*, Old High German *klapfōn*, Old Norse *klappa*, beside Old English *clæppan* = Old Frisian *kleppa*, Middle Low German *kleppen*, Old High German *klepfen*: of imit. origin.]
†**1** *verb intrans*. Throb, beat, pulsate. OE–LME.
2 *verb trans*. Strike with sounding blows. *arch.* OE.
3 *verb intrans*. Make an abrupt explosive noise; make a loud rattling noise; *spec.* (***a***) (of a door, window, etc.) close with a bang, slam; †(***b***) rap, knock at a door etc.; (see also sense 6b). Now *arch. & dial.* LME.
4 *verb intrans*. Chatter loudly, talk continually, (= CLACK *verb* 1). Now *rare*. LME.
5 *verb trans*. Cause to make an abrupt explosive noise, strike together; cause to make a loud rattling noise; *spec.* (***a***) close (a door, window, etc., *to*) with a bang, slam; †(***b***) strike (hands) reciprocally, in token of a bargain; (see also senses 6, 7). Now *arch. & dial.* LME.
6 *verb trans*. Strike (the hands) together loudly, esp. to show approval, for warmth, as a signal, etc.; show approval of (a person, an event, etc.) by doing this. LME. ▸**b** *verb intrans*. Clap the hands together; applaud by clapping hands. E16.

S. PEPYS It was very finely sung, so as to make the whole house clap her. D. PARKER The Swedish girl raised her hands . . and clapped them twice together to summon the waiter.

7 *verb trans*. Of a bird: flap (the wings) audibly. LME.
8 *verb trans*. Slap with the palm of the hand, as a sign of approval, in encouragement, etc.; *Scot. & N. English* pat fondly. LME. ▸**b** Smooth or flatten (*out*) with the palms or with a flat-surfaced object. Chiefly *N. English*. M16.
9 *verb trans*. Put or place quickly, energetically, or unceremoniously; impose (as) with authority (*up*)*on*. LME.

SHAKES. *Merry W.* Clap on more sails; pursue. BYRON I have . . clapt sentinels at the doors. R. W. EMERSON He has clapped copyright on the world. E. BOWEN The ices . . were clapped between wafers. J. CHEEVER I . . clapped my hat on my head, and marched out. A. FRASER The government speedily clapped the leaders in prison.

clap eyes on *colloq.* catch sight of, see (usu. in neg. contexts).
10 *verb intrans*. †**a** Come or go suddenly or decisively; enter *into* (an activity) with alacrity. M16–M18. ▸**b** Foll. by *on*: apply oneself energetically, set to. *colloq.* M19.
11 *verb intrans*. Press or lie close (*to*, *in*, etc.). Now chiefly *Scot.* L16.
12 *verb trans*. **a** Foll. by *up*: make or construct hastily or without much care; chiefly (& now only) *fig.*, arrange or settle (an agreement etc.) hastily or without much care. *arch.* L16. ▸†**b** Put or stick *together*. M17–E18.
— COMB.: (partly from CLAP *noun*[1]): **clap-bread** thin oatmeal cake; **clap dish** *hist.* a wooden alms dish with a lid, carried by beggars, lepers, etc., and rattled to attract notice; **clap-net** a fowler's or entomologist's net shut by pulling a string.
■ **clapped out** *adjectival phr.* (*slang*) worn out, exhausted, no longer functioning M20.

clap /klap/ *verb*[2] *trans. coarse slang*. Infl. **-pp-**. M17.
[ORIGIN from CLAP *noun*[2].]
Infect with venereal disease, esp. gonorrhoea.

clapboard /ˈklapbɔːd, ˈklabəd/ *noun & verb*. E16.
[ORIGIN Partial translation of CLAPHOLT.]
▸ **A** *noun* **1 a** A piece of split oak used for barrel staves and wainscoting. *obsolete* exc. *hist.* E16. ▸**b** A weatherboard. *N. Amer.* M17.
†**2** The material of such boards; such boards collectively. M16–L19.
▸ **B** *verb trans*. Cover or line with clapboards. *US*. M17.
■ **clapboarding** *verbal noun* (*US*) (***a***) the action of the verb; (***b***) a covering of clapboards on a building etc.: M17.

Clapham /ˈklap(ə)m/ *noun*. M19.
[ORIGIN A district of SW London.]
1 ***the Clapham Sect***, an early-19th-cent. group noted for evangelical opinions and philanthropic activity (some of whose chief members lived at Clapham). Somewhat *derog.* *obsolete* exc. *hist.* M19.
2 ***the man on the Clapham omnibus***, the average man. E20.

†**clapholt** *noun*. LME–E18.
[ORIGIN Low German *klappholt* = Dutch *klaphout*, from *klappen* crack + *holt* wood.]
= CLAPBOARD *noun* 2.

clapmatch /ˈklapmatʃ/ *noun*. Also **k-**. M18.
[ORIGIN Dutch *klapmuts(rob)* hooded seal, from *klapmuts* cap with flaps.]
Orig., a hooded or eared seal. Now, a female seal.

clapper /ˈklapə/ *noun*[1] & *verb*. ME.
[ORIGIN from CLAP *verb*[1] + -ER[1].]
▸ **A** *noun*. **1** A device that makes short repeated strokes or that makes a clapping or loud rattling noise; *spec.* (***a***) a contrivance in a mill for striking or shaking the hopper so as to make the grain move down to the millstones; (***b***) *hist.* the lid of a clap dish, or a rattle, used by beggars, lepers, etc., to attract attention; (***c***) the tongue or striker of a bell; (***d***) an instrument for frightening birds away; (***e***) CINEMATOGRAPHY (in full ***clapperboard***) a device making a sharp noise for the synchronization of picture and sound. ME. ▸**b** The human tongue. Usu. *derog.* M17.
like the clappers *slang* very fast, very hard.
2 A person who claps; a claqueur. E19.
— COMB.: ***clapperboard***: see sense 1 above; **clapperclaw** *verb trans.* (*arch.*) claw with the open hand and nails; *fig.* revile; **clapperdudgeon** *arch. slang.* [app. DUDGEON *noun*[1]] a person born a beggar, a low wretch; **clapper rail** a large greyish N. American rail, *Rallus longirostris*, of coastal marshes.
▸ **B** *verb*. **1** *verb trans*. **a** Fit a clapper to (a bell). *rare*. E16. ▸**b** Sound (a bell) by pulling the clapper. L19.
2 *verb intrans*. Make a noise like a clapper. M19.

clapper /ˈklapə/ *noun*[2]. ME.
[ORIGIN Anglo-Norman *claper* = Old French *clapier* from Provençal = heap of stones, rabbit warren, of Gaulish origin.]
1 More fully ***clapper bridge***. A rough bridge or raised path of stones. *dial.* ME.
†**2** A rabbit burrow; a place for keeping rabbits. LME–E18.

clapt *verb pa. t. & pple*: see CLAP *verb*[1].

claptrap /ˈklaptrap/ *noun*. M18.
[ORIGIN from CLAP *noun*[1] + TRAP *noun*[1].]
1 A device, expression, etc., to elicit applause. *arch.* M18.
2 Language used or sentiments expressed only to elicit applause; pretentious but empty assertions; nonsense. E19.
■ **claptrappy** *adjective* M19.

claque /klak, klɑːk; *foreign* klak (*pl. same*)/ *noun*. M19.
[ORIGIN French, from *claquer* to clap.]
A hired body of applauders; *transf.* a body of sycophantic followers.

claqueur /klɑːˈkəː; *foreign* klakœːr (*pl. same*)/ *noun*. M19.
[ORIGIN French, from *claquer* (see CLAQUE) + *-eur* -OR.]
A member of a claque.

clarabella /klarəˈbɛlə/ *noun*. M19.
[ORIGIN from Latin *clarus*, (fem.) *-ra* clear + *bellus*, (fem.) *-lla* beautiful.]
An organ stop having a flutelike quality.

clarain /ˈklareɪn/ *noun*. E20.
[ORIGIN from Latin *clarus* CLEAR *adjective*, after FUSAIN.]
GEOLOGY. One of the lithotypes of coal, a finely laminated material with a silky lustre.

Clare /klɛː/ *noun*. E17.
[ORIGIN from St *Clare* (see below).]
A nun of the Franciscan order founded by St Clare at Assisi *c* 1212. Freq. ***Poor Clare***.

clarence /ˈklar(ə)ns/ *noun*. M19.
[ORIGIN from the Duke of *Clarence*, later William IV.]
Chiefly *hist.* A four-wheeled closed carriage with seats for four inside and two on the box.

Clarenceux /ˈklar(ə)nsuː/ *noun*. Also †**-cieux**. LME.
[ORIGIN Anglo-Norman, from *Clarence*, an English dukedom named from Clare in Suffolk.]
The second English King of Arms, having jurisdiction south of the Trent.

Clarendon /ˈklar(ə)ndən/ *noun*. M19.
[ORIGIN Prob. from the *Clarendon* Press, Oxford.]
TYPOGRAPHY. A bold condensed type with bracketed serifs, used esp. for emphasis.

claret /ˈklarət/ *adjective & noun*. LME.
[ORIGIN Old French (*vin*) *claret* (mod. *clairet*) orig. of light-red wines, from *clarè*: see CLARY *noun*[1].]
▸ **A** *adjective*. †**1** ***claret wine*** = sense B.1 below. LME–E18.
2 Of the colour of claret. M16.
▸ **B** *noun*. **1** Orig., wine of a yellowish or light-red colour, as distinguished from white or red wine; later, red wine generally. Now, (a) red wine from Bordeaux in France; *transf.* (a) wine of the same character from some other country. Also, a drink of such wine. E16.
2 Blood. *slang*. E17.
3 The colour of claret, (now) a reddish violet. M17.
— PHRASES: ***riddle of claret***: see RIDDLE *noun*[2] 1. **tap a person's claret** *slang* make a person's nose bleed by a blow with the fist.
— COMB.: **claret colour** = sense 3 above; **claret-coloured** *adjective* of the colour claret.
■ **clare'teer** *noun* (now *rare* or *obsolete*) a drinker of claret L17. **clarety** *adjective* E18.

clarichord /ˈklarɪkɔːd/ *noun*. *obsolete* exc. *hist.* LME.
[ORIGIN Alt. of CLAVICHORD by assoc. with Latin *clarus* clear.]
= CLAVICHORD.

clarification /ˌklarɪfɪˈkeɪʃ(ə)n/ *noun*. E16.
[ORIGIN In branch I partly from CLARIFY, partly from French *clarification*, formed as CLARIFY: see -FICATION. In branch II from ecclesiastical Latin *clarificatio(n-)*, from *clarificat-* pa. ppl stem of *clarificare*: see CLARIFY, -ATION.]
▸ **I 1** The action of making clear or plain to the understanding; removal of complexity, ambiguity, or obscurity. E16.
2 The action of freeing from impurities or making transparent; the process of becoming free from impurities or transparent. E17.
▸ †**II 3** Glorification, transfiguration. M–L17.
■ **clarificatory** *adjective* tending to, having the purpose of, or relating to, clarification M20.

clarify /ˈklarɪfʌɪ/ *verb*. ME.
[ORIGIN Old French & mod. French *clarifier* from late Latin *clarificare*, from Latin *clarus* clear + *-ficare* -FY.]
†**1** *verb trans*. Declare, set forth clearly. Only in ME.
2 *verb trans*. Make pure and clean, physically or (*arch.*) morally; free from impurities; *spec.* make (a liquid, butter, etc.) transparent. ME.
†**3** *verb trans*. Free from darkness or gloom; brighten, illumine. LME–L17.
4 *verb trans*. Remove complexity, ambiguity, or obscurity from (a subject, statement, etc.); make clear or plain; remove ignorance, misconception, or error from (the mind etc.). LME.

Maclean's Magazine I would . . like to clarify a few points.

5 *verb trans*. Make unobstructed, clear, (the sight, eyes, mental vision; *arch.* the throat, the voice). LME.
†**6** *verb trans*. Make illustrious or glorious; exalt. LME–M17.
7 *verb intrans*. Become transparent; be made clear or pure (*lit. & fig.*). L16.
■ **clarifier** *noun* M16.

clarine /ˈklariːn/ *noun*. LME.
[ORIGIN Old French *clarin* (mod. *clarine* in sense 2 only) by-form of *claron* CLARION.]
†**1** = CLARION. LME–M18.
2 A cowbell. *rare*. E20.

clarinet /klarɪˈnɛt/ *noun*. M18.
[ORIGIN French *clarinette* dim. of *clarine*: see CLARINE, -ETTE.]
1 A woodwind instrument having a single-reed mouthpiece, holes, and keys; a player on this in an orchestra etc. M18.
2 An organ stop of similar sound quality. L19.
■ **clarinettist**, *-**etist** *noun* a player on the clarinet M19.

clarion /ˈklarɪən/ *noun & adjective*. ME.
[ORIGIN medieval Latin *clario(n-)*, from Latin *clarus* clear: cf. Old French *claron* (mod. *clairon*).]
▸ **A** *noun*. **1** *hist.* A shrill narrow-tubed war trumpet. ME.
2 The sound of a trumpet; any rousing sound. *poet.* M17.

MILTON The crested Cock whose clarion sounds The silent hours. K. TYNAN Her voice is a rallying-call. . a downright clarion.

3 An organ stop of sound quality similar to a clarion. L17.
▸ **B** *attrib.* or as *adjective*. Of a clarion; sounding like a clarion; loud and clear. LME.

clarionet /klarɪəˈnɛt/ *noun*. L18.
[ORIGIN from CLARION + -ET[1], partly from CLARINET.]
= CLARINET.

Clarisse /klaˈriːs/ *noun*. L17.
[ORIGIN French, formed as CLARE.]
= CLARE.

clarity /ˈklarɪti/ *noun*. ME.
[ORIGIN Latin *claritas*, from *clarus* clear: see -ITY.]
†**1** Glory, divine lustre. ME–L17.
†**2** Brightness, brilliance, splendour. LME–L17.
3 Clearness (of sight, judgement, colour, sky, atmosphere, etc.); lack of ambiguity (in literary style, ideas, etc.); an instance of this. E17.

Clark /klɑːk/ *noun*. E19.
[ORIGIN William *Clark* (1770–1838), US explorer.]
Clark's crow, ***Clark's nutcracker***, ***Clark nutcracker***, a black, grey, and white crow, *Nucifraga columbiana*, of western N. America.

clarkia /ˈklɑːkɪə/ *noun*. E19.
[ORIGIN mod. Latin (see below), from William *Clark* (1770–1838), US explorer: see -IA[1].]
A plant of the American genus *Clarkia*, which includes several annuals cultivated for their white, pink, or purple flowers.

claro /ˈklɑːrəʊ/ *noun*. Pl. **-os**. L19.
[ORIGIN Spanish = light, clear.]
A light-coloured cigar.

†**claro-obscuro** *noun*. Only in 18.
[ORIGIN Latinization of Italian CHIAROSCURO.]
Chiaroscuro.

clarschach *noun* var. of CLAIRSCHACH.

clart /klɑːt/ *verb & noun*. *Scot. & N. English*. L17.
[ORIGIN Unknown.]
▸ **A** *verb trans*. †**1** Smear or plaster (*up*)*on*. Only in L17.
2 Smear or daub with dirt. E19.
▸ **B** *noun*. **1** Sticky dirt, mud, filth; a daub of this. E19.
2 A dirty person; a nasty thing; hypocritical talk. E19.
– NOTE: Much older than the written record: *beclart* verb is evidenced in Middle English.
■ **clarty** *adjective* covered in or of the nature of sticky dirt; nasty: L16.

clary /ˈklɛːri/ *noun*[1]. ME.
[ORIGIN Old French *claré*, from medieval Latin *(vinum) claratum* clarified (wine), from *clarare*, from *clarus* clear: see -Y[5].]
Chiefly *hist.* A sweet drink made of wine, clarified honey, pepper, ginger, and other spices.

clary /ˈklɛːri/ *noun*[2]. LME.
[ORIGIN French †*clarie* from medieval Latin *sclarea*: loss of initial *s* is unexpl.]
An aromatic herb of the genus *Salvia*, of the mint family; esp. *S. sclarea*, native to southern Europe.

clash /klaʃ/ *noun*. E16.
[ORIGIN Imit.: cf. CLASH *verb*.]
1 A loud discordant resonant sound as of a collision, the striking of weapons, bells rung together, cymbals, etc.; *Scot.* a blow yielding such a sound. E16.

LD MACAULAY The clash of cymbals, and the rolling of drums.

2 A collision, a conflict, esp. of hostile opinions; a disagreement; being at variance or incompatible (*with*); a jarring or unpleasant contrast (of colour etc.). M17.

Independent Clashes between stone-throwing villagers and Israeli troops.

3 Chatter, idle talk; an item of (malicious) gossip. *Scot. & N. English*. M17.
4 A sudden and heavy fall of rain etc. *Scot. & N. English*. E19.

clash /klaʃ/ *verb*. E16.
[ORIGIN Imit.: cf. CLASH *noun*.]
▸ **I** *verb intrans*. **1** Make a loud discordant resonant sound, produce a clash; strike violently, esp. so as to produce a clash (*against*, *together*). E16.

MILTON Arms on Armour clashing. SIR W. SCOTT The swords clashed smartly together. O. MANNING Outside, a thunderstorm was roaring and clashing.

2 Come into conflict; disagree, be at variance, be incompatible; (of colours etc.) contrast jarringly. (Foll. by *with*.) E17.

D. CARNEGIE These two clashed on every debatable subject. W. S. CHURCHILL When pleasure clashed with royal duty it was usually pleasure that won. H. KISSINGER Soviet and Chinese troops clashed in the frozen Siberian tundra.

3 Talk recklessly or maliciously. *Scot.* L17.
▸ **II** *verb trans*. **4** Strike (together) so as to produce a clash; slam (a door etc.); *Scot.* throw violently so as to produce a clash. E16.

TENNYSON Sir Gareth's brand clashed his. TOLKIEN The armed men that stood near clashed their weapons. J. DICKEY I got in and clashed the car door.

5 Produce or express with a clash. M17.

R. ELLIS Let a gong clash glad emotion.

■ **clasher** *noun* E17.

†**clashee**, **clashy** *nouns* vars. of KHALASSI.

clasp /klɑːsp/ *noun & verb*. ME.
[ORIGIN Unknown: for the terminal sounds cf. *grasp*, *hasp*, Middle Dutch *gaspe*, *gespe* (Dutch *gesp* clasp, buckle).]
▸ **A** *noun*. **1** A contrivance of interlocking parts for fastening; a buckle, a brooch; a metal fastening of a book cover. ME.
†**2** = CLASPER 2. L16–E18.
3 An embrace; an encircling grip of the hand or arm; a handshake; grasp, reach. M17.
4 A bar of silver on a medal ribbon with the name of a battle etc. (fought during the campaign commemorated by the medal) at which the wearer was present. E19.
– COMB.: **clasp knife** a folding knife, usu. with a catch to fix the blade when open.
▸ **B** *verb*. **I** *verb trans*. **1** Fasten, secure, or close with or as a clasp; fasten (a clasp). LME.

W. SHENSTONE One modest em'rald clasp'd the robe she wore.

2 Provide or fit (a book etc.) with a clasp. LME.
3 *gen.* Encircle and hold closely; *loosely & poet.* surround, enfold. LME.

T. HOOD She stood. . Clasp'd by the golden light of morn. R. MACAULAY She clasped Helen's hand in both hers.

4 *spec.* Hold with close pressure of the curved hand; press (one's hands) closely together with fingers interlaced; hold closely in one's arms with hands joined; throw both arms round, embrace. LME.

GEO. ELIOT She should clasp her son again. A. G. GARDINER Two other children. . walk with the soldier, each clasping a hand. V. WOOLF She sank down. . , clasping her knees together. I. ASIMOV His hands, which had been clasped, drew apart.

clasp hands shake hands with fervour or affection.
5 Bend or fold tightly *around* or *over*. L18.
▸ **II** *verb intrans*. **6** Be fastened as a clasp; hold tight; embrace; (of hands) press tightly together, esp. with interlaced fingers. M16.

SHAKES. *Per.* Clasping to the mast. R. WARNER I saw his hands clasp and unclasp.

clasper /ˈklɑːspə/ *noun*. M16.
[ORIGIN from CLASP *verb* + -ER[1].]
1 A person who or thing which clasps; a means of holding fast. M16.
2 *BOTANY*. A tendril. L16.
3 *ZOOLOGY*. Either of a pair of appendages of the male used to hold the female in copulation, esp. in certain fishes and insects. Usu. in *pl.* M19.

class /klɑːs/ *noun & adjective*. M16.
[ORIGIN Latin *classis* assembly, division of the Roman people. Cf. Old French & mod. French *classe*.]
▸ **A** *noun*. **1** *ROMAN HISTORY*. Each of the divisions or orders of the Roman people in the constitution ascribed to Servius Tullius. M16.
2 A set of students or scholars taught together; a course of instruction for a group of students; a meeting of students for instruction. M16. ▸**b** All college or school students of the same standing. *N. Amer.* L17.

LYTTON I was in the head class when I left Eton. S. HEANEY My lesson note reads: Teacher will play Beethoven's Concerto Number Five And class will express themselves freely In writing. JO GRIMOND A class in first aid, which he attended.

in class (*a*) teaching or being taught in a class; (*b*) as a member of a class. ***senior class***: see SENIOR *adjective*. **b class of** (a specified year): all those graduating from a school or college in a particular year.
3 *gen.* A division according to grade or quality. E17.
high class, ***low class***, ***first class***, ***second class***, etc. **in a class of its own**, **in a class of one's own**, **in a class on its own**, **in a class on one's own** unequalled.
4 *gen.* A group of people or things having some attribute in common; a set, a category. M17.

COLERIDGE The class of readers, to which he means to address his communications. D. R. HOFSTADTER The class of numbers known to be producible.

class A, **class B**, **class C** designating an illegal narcotic drug classified as being of the most harmful and addictive (or a less harmful and addictive) kind. ***open class***: see OPEN *adjective*. ***SPECTRAL class***. ***SPECTRAL-luminosity class***.
5 **a** A presbytery in the Church of Scotland. Cf. CLASSIS 2. *obsolete* exc. *hist.* E18. ▸**b** A subdivision of a Methodist congregation, meeting together. M18.
6 A rank or order of a society; *sing.* & in *pl.*, the members of a specified social rank; in *pl.* also (*arch.*) *the* rich or educated. M18. ▸**b** The system or fact of the division of society into ranks or orders; social rank, *esp.* high rank. M19.
lower class(es), ***middle class(es)***, ***professional class(es)***, ***socio-economic class***, ***upper class(es)***, ***working class(es)***, etc.
7 *BIOLOGY*. The principal taxonomic grouping, ranking above order and below phylum or division. M18.
8 A division of candidates or competitors according to merit in an examination. E19.
take a class obtain an honours degree.
9 Distinction, high quality. *colloq.* L19.

T. DREISER This is a special coat . . . It has class.

no class *colloq.* quite inferior.
– COMB.: **class action** *US* a (single) legal action brought on behalf of all the members of a group with a common interest or grievance; **class-conscious** *adjective* conscious of class, *esp.* realizing and usu. participating in the conflict between one's own and other classes; **class consciousness** the state of being class-conscious; **class-fellow** = *classmate* below; ***class-leader***: see LEADER 7; **class list** *spec.* a list of the classes obtained by candidates in an examination; **classmate** a present or past member of the same school, college, etc., class as oneself; **class noun** *GRAMMAR* a count noun, a common noun referring to each member of a class; **classroom** a place where a class is taught (***open classroom***: see OPEN *adjective*); **class war**, **class warfare** conflict between social classes; **classwork** schoolwork done in class.
▸ **B** *adjective*. Having class, in the top class, classy. *colloq.* L19.

H. DE SÉLINCOURT If he'd had coaching, he'd be a class bowler. DAY LEWIS Real class your sister is.

– NOTE: See note s.v. CLASSIS.
■ **classless** *adjective* making or having no distinction of class L19. **classlessness** *noun* M20.

class /klɑːs/ *verb*. E18.
[ORIGIN from the noun.]
†**1** *verb trans*. Divide into classes. E18–E19.
2 *verb trans*. Place in a class; assign to its proper class or group. M18.
3 *verb intrans*. Rank; be classed. M18.
classed growth [translating French ***cru classé***] a Bordeaux wine belonging to one of the top official groupings.
■ **classable** *adjective* able to be classed M19. **classer** *noun* a person who classes E19.

classes *noun* pl. of CLASS *noun*, CLASSIS.

classic /ˈklasɪk/ *adjective & noun*. E17.
[ORIGIN French *classique* or Latin *classicus*, formed as CLASS *noun*: see -IC.]
▸ **A** *adjective* **I** **1** Of the first class, of acknowledged excellence; remarkably typical; outstandingly important. E17.

C. S. LEWIS The taste for what he called 'the good, solid, old books', the classic English novelists. C. HAMPTON They tell me I'm a classic case, because my uncle raped me when I was twelve.

classic races the five annual chief flat races for horses in England (the One Thousand Guineas, Two Thousand Guineas, Derby, Oaks, and St Leger).
2 Of or pertaining to the standard ancient Greek and Latin authors or their works, or the culture, art, architecture, etc. of Greek and Roman antiquity generally. Cf. CLASSICAL 2. E17.

C. KINGSLEY He had never felt the influence of classic civilization.

3 Known from ancient Greek or Latin authors; having literary or historic associations. E18.

R. BURNS A few pilgrimages over some of the classic ground of Caledonia.

4 Characteristic of the art, architecture, or literature of Greek and Roman antiquity; well-proportioned, with clarity of outline or formal design; (of style) restrained, harmonious and in accordance with established forms (cf. ***romantic***). M18. ▸**b** Of clothes: made in a simple style not much affected by changes in fashion. M20.

J. MORLEY That permanence, which is only secured by classic form. J. AGATE Wolfit has everything a great actor should have except classic features.

b ***classic tutu***: see TUTU *noun*[2].
5 (Usu. **C-**.) Of or pertaining to a high phase of ancient Meso-American civilization *c* 300–*c* 900. M20.
▸ †**II** **6** = CLASSICAL 8. Only in M17.
▸ **B** *noun*. **1** A writer, artist, composer, work, or example of the first rank, acknowledged excellence, or value; orig. & esp. an ancient Greek or Latin writer or work of literature. In *pl.* also, *the* body of Greek and Latin literature; *the* body of literature, art, music, etc. that is considered excellent, significant, or standard. E18. ▸**b** In *pl.* The branch of knowledge that deals with ancient Greek and Latin literature, or Greek and Roman antiquity generally. L19.

I. D'ISRAELI Dante was the classic of his country. G. B. SHAW The glees, madrigals, and motets . . are the five English classics. D. H. LAWRENCE We like to think of the old fashioned American classics as children's books. S. BRETT 'All they ever bloody want is the Barbershop Sketch.' 'Well, it is a classic'.

2 A scholar of Greek and Latin literature. *arch.* E19.

E. M. FORSTER He was not a good classic, but good enough to take the Lower Fifth.

senior classic: see SENIOR *adjective*.
3 A follower of classic models. L19.
4 A major sports tournament or competition, orig. *spec.* each of the five classic races (see sense A.1 above). E20.
5 A garment in a classic style. M20.

classical /ˈklasɪk(ə)l/ *adjective*. L16.
[ORIGIN from Latin *classicus* CLASSIC + -AL¹.]
▸ **I 1** = CLASSIC *adjective* 1. L16.

C. HILL He is a classical example of a man who ruined himself by unsuccessful investment in the court.

2 Designating, of, or pertaining to the standard ancient Greek and Latin authors or their works, or the culture, art, architecture, etc., of Greek and Roman antiquity generally; specializing in or based on the study of the Greek and Latin classics, or Greek and Roman antiquity generally. Cf. CLASSIC *adjective* 2. E17.

JOHN BRIGHT One of the faults of a high classical education. R. V. JONES Cambridge could not find . . a classical scholar who knew any engineering. G. EWART The multitudinous / classical allusions just fill them with boredom.

classical antiquity: see ANTIQUITY 1.
3 Designating the form or period of a language used by ancient standard authors. M19.
classical Arabic, *classical Greek*, *classical Hebrew*, *classical Latin*, etc.
4 = CLASSIC *adjective* 4. M19.

J. RUSKIN The classical landscape . . is . . the representative of perfectly trained and civilised human life. T. E. HULME I prophesy that a period of dry, hard classical verse is coming.

5 *spec.* Designating, of, or pertaining to music characterized by clarity, regularity, and use of established forms, *esp.* that of the late 18th and early 19th cents. marked esp. by sonata form (cf. ***romantic***); *loosely* designating so-called conventional or serious music as opp. to folk, jazz, pop, rock, etc. M19.
classical guitar: see GUITAR *noun*.
6 Designating, of, or pertaining to the form or period of an art etc. regarded as representing the height of achievement; in a long-established style of acknowledged excellence. E20.
classical ballet etc.
7 Designating, of, or pertaining to the first significant period of a department of study; *spec.* (PHYSICS etc.) relating to or based upon concepts and theories which predate (and hence are not subject to the postulates of) relativity and quantum mechanics, based on the theories and concepts of Newton, Maxwell, etc. E20.
classical mechanics: see MECHANICS 1b.
▸ **II 8** *hist.* Of or pertaining to a classis in a Presbyterian Church. L16.
■ **classicalism** *noun* adherence to classical ideals, styles, etc.; interest in the classics: M19. **classiˈcality** *noun* classical quality or character; classical scholarship; an instance of classical learning; a classical feature in art etc.: E19. **classically** *adverb* †(*a*) in classes, in order; (*b*) in (a) classical manner; in a classical style; (*c*) as regards the classics: M17.

classicise *verb* var. of CLASSICIZE.

classicism /ˈklasɪsɪz(ə)m/ *noun*. M19.
[ORIGIN from CLASSIC + -ISM.]
1 The principles of classic literature, art, etc.; adherence to classical ideals, styles, etc. M19.
2 A classical idiom or form. L19.
3 Classical scholarship; advocacy of classical education. L19.
■ **classicist** *noun* an upholder or imitator of classical style; a student or scholar of classics; an advocate of classical education: E19. **classiˈcistic** *adjective* characterized by classicism M19.

classicize /ˈklasɪsʌɪz/ *verb*. Also **-ise**. M19.
[ORIGIN formed as CLASSICISM + -IZE.]
1 *verb trans.* Make classic. M19.
2 *verb intrans.* Affect or imitate classical style etc. L19.

Classico /ˈklasɪkəʊ/ *adjective*. M20.
[ORIGIN Italian *classico* classic, traditional, genuine.]
In the classification of Italian wines (orig. of Chianti): designating a wine produced in the original district or near the town from which the type takes its name, and thus usu. made to higher standards than a regional wine without the designation.

classification /ˌklasɪfɪˈkeɪʃ(ə)n/ *noun*. L18.
[ORIGIN French, from *classe* CLASS *noun*: see -FICATION.]
1 The action of classifying. L18.
2 The result of classifying; a systematic distribution or arrangement in a class or classes. L18.
– PHRASES: ***decimal classification***: see DECIMAL *adjective*. ***periodic classification***: see PERIODIC *adjective*¹ 2.
■ **classificatory** *adjective* tending to, having the purpose of, or relating to classification M19.

classify /ˈklasɪfʌɪ/ *verb trans.* L18.
[ORIGIN Back-form. from CLASSIFICATION.]
1 Arrange in classes; assign to a class. L18.
2 Designate as officially secret or not for general disclosure. Chiefly as ***classified*** *ppl adjective*. M20.
■ **classifiable** *adjective* able to be classified M19. **classifier** *noun* (*a*) a person who or thing which classifies; (*b*) GRAMMAR an element attached to or associated with nouns in certain languages, esp. indicating the class of objects to which the referent belongs: E19.

classis /ˈklasɪs/ *noun*. Pl. **classes** /ˈklasiːz/. L16.
[ORIGIN Latin: see CLASS *noun*.]
†**1** A division according to rank; a class. L16–E18.
2 In certain Protestant Churches: an inferior judicial body consisting of the elders or pastors of the parishes or churches of a district; such a district. L16.
†**3** A bookcase at right angles to a wall in a library; a bay or alcove between two of these. E17–E18.
†**4** A school or college class. *US.* M17–M19.
– NOTE: Exc. in speech the pl. is usu. indistinguishable from that of CLASS *noun*. Ambiguous early exs. in all but sense 1 have been regarded as belonging here.

classism /ˈklɑːsɪz(ə)m/ *noun*. M19.
[ORIGIN from CLASS *noun* + -ISM.]
Distinction or discrimination on the grounds of social class; prejudice in favour of or against others on the basis of their social class.
■ **classist** *noun & adjective* (*a*) *noun* an adherent or practitioner of classism; (*b*) *adjective* of or pertaining to classism or classists: L20.

classy /ˈklɑːsi/ *adjective*. *colloq.* L19.
[ORIGIN from CLASS *noun* + -Y¹.]
Of a high or superior class; stylish, smart.
■ **classiness** *noun* E20.

clastic /ˈklastɪk/ *adjective & noun*. L19.
[ORIGIN French *clastique* from Greek *klastos* broken in pieces: see -IC.]
GEOLOGY. (Designating) a rock consisting of fragments of pre-existing rocks.
■ **clast** *noun* [back-form.] a constituent fragment of a clastic rock M20.

clat /klat/ *noun*. *dial.* E17.
[ORIGIN Uncertain: cf. CLART, CLOT *noun*.]
A clod, a piece of dirt or cow dung.
■ **clatty** *adjective* (chiefly *Scot.*) muddy, dirty; nasty, unappealing: E17.

clatch *noun* var. of CLETCH.

clathrate /ˈklaθreɪt/ *adjective & noun*. M19.
[ORIGIN Latin *clathratus* pa. pple of *clathrare*, from *clathri* (pl.) lattice from Greek *klēthra* bars: see -ATE².]
▸ **A** *adjective*. **1** Resembling latticework; cancellate. *rare*. M19.
2 CHEMISTRY. Of a compound: containing molecules of one substance physically enclosed within the structure of another. M20.
▸ **B** *noun*. CHEMISTRY. A clathrate compound. M20.
■ **claˈthration** *noun* formation of a clathrate compound M20.

clatter /ˈklatə/ *noun*. LME.
[ORIGIN Prob. from the verb: cf. Middle Dutch *klatere*, Dutch *klater* a rattle.]
1 Noisy rapid talk, loud chatter, gabble. LME. ▸**b** *sing.* & in *pl.* Gossip; tittle-tattle. Chiefly *Scot.* L16.

T. H. WHITE Shut yer trap, . . and leave this daft clatter about Sir Lancelot.

2 A rattling noise as of the rapidly repeated collision of sonorous bodies that do not ring. L16.

S. JOHNSON The clatter of empty pots.

■ **clattery** *adverb & adjective* (*a*) *adverb* (now *non-standard*, *rare*) in a clattery manner, clatteringly; (*b*) *adjective* tending to clatter, clattering: E19.

clatter /ˈklatə/ *verb*.
[ORIGIN Old English (as verbal noun). Cf. Middle Dutch & mod. Dutch *klateren* rattle, chatter.]
1 *verb intrans.* Make a clatter; move with a clatter (*along*, *down*, etc.). OE.

E. HEMINGWAY He fired two pans, the guns clattering. A. MASON The guards clattered to a halt.

2 *verb intrans.* Talk noisily and rapidly, chatter loudly; *Scot.* gossip. ME.
†**3** *verb trans.* Say noisily and rapidly; talk noisily or indiscreetly about. ME–M18.
4 *verb trans.* Cause to make a clatter. M16.
■ **clatterer** *noun* LME.

clauber *noun* var. of CLABBER *noun*¹.

claucht *verb* see CLEEK *verb*.

Claude Lorraine glass /klɔːd lɒˈreɪn glɑːs/ *noun phr.* Also **Claude glass**. L18.
[ORIGIN *Claude* Gelée (1600–82), known as *Lorraine*, French landscape painter.]
A convex dark or coloured glass that reflects an image of diminished size and subdued colour.

Claudian /ˈklɔːdɪən/ *adjective & noun*. E18.
[ORIGIN Latin *Claudianus*, from *Claudius*: see -AN.]
ROMAN HISTORY. ▸**A** *adjective*. Of or pertaining to any of several distinguished Romans of the name of Claudius or the gens to which they belonged (among whose members were the emperors Tiberius, Caligula, Claudius, and Nero). E18.
▸ **B** *noun*. A member of the Claudian gens. E20.

claudicant /ˈklɔːdɪk(ə)nt/ *adjective*. Now *rare* or *obsolete*. E17.
[ORIGIN Latin *claudicant-* pres. ppl stem of *claudicare*: see CLAUDICATION, -ANT¹.]
Lame, limping.

claudication /klɔːdɪˈkeɪʃ(ə)n/ *noun*. LME.
[ORIGIN Latin *claudicatio(n-)*, from *claudicat-* pa. ppl stem of *claudicare* to limp, from *claudus* lame: see -ATION.]
The action of limping; ***intermittent claudication***, a condition of the legs, due to arterial obstruction, in which pain is induced by walking and relieved by rest.

claught *verb* see CLEEK *verb*.

clause /klɔːz/ *noun & verb*. ME.
[ORIGIN Old French & mod. French = Provençal *clauza*, for Latin *clausula* close of a rhetorical period, (later) conclusion of a legal formula, section of law, fem. dim. of *claus-* pa. ppl stem of *claudere* CLOSE *verb*.]
▸ **A** *noun*. **1** A simple sentence; a distinct part of a sentence including a subject and predicate, or one resembling this; a single passage of discourse or writing. ME.
final clause: see FINAL *adjective*. ***subordinate clause***: see SUBORDINATE *adjective* 2.
2 A particular and separate article, stipulation, or proviso, in any formal or legal document. LME.
Clause Four the part of the constitution of the UK Labour Party which contained a commitment to the common ownership of industry and services (revised in 1995 to allow for the alternative of public accountability of privately owned services). ***PRAEMUNIENTES clause***. ***REOPENER clause***. ***resolutive clause***: see RESOLUTIVE 2. ***saving clause***: see SAVING *ppl adjective*. ***testimonium clause***: see TESTIMONIUM 2. ***VALENT clause***.
†**3** Conclusion, *esp.* the close of a sentence. L16–E18.
▸ **B** *verb intrans.* Construct clauses. L19.
■ **clausal** *adjective* E20.

†**clauster** *noun*. Also **-tre**. OE–E18.
[ORIGIN Latin *claustrum* CLOISTER *noun*.]
A cloister, cell, or monastery.

claustral /ˈklɔːstr(ə)l/ *adjective*. LME.
[ORIGIN Late Latin *claustralis*, formed as CLAUSTER: see -AL¹.]
1 Pertaining to a cloister or religious house; adjoining a cloister. LME.
2 Resembling (that of) a cloister; *fig.* narrow-minded. M19.

claustration /klɔːˈstreɪʃ(ə)n/ *noun*. M19.
[ORIGIN from Latin *claustrum*: see CLOISTER *noun*, -ATION.]
Enclosure or confinement (as) in a cloister.

†**claustre** *noun* var. of CLAUSTER.

claustrophilia /klɔːstrəˈfɪlɪə/ *noun*. E20.
[ORIGIN mod. Latin, from Latin *claustrum* (see CLOISTER *noun*) + -O- + -PHILIA.]
Irrational desire to be enclosed within a confined space.

claustrophobe /ˈklɔːstrəfəʊb/ *adjective & noun*. M20.
[ORIGIN Back-form. from CLAUSTROPHOBIA.]
▸ **A** *adjective*. = CLAUSTROPHOBIC *adjective* 2. *rare*. M20.
▸ **B** *noun*. = CLAUSTROPHOBIC *noun*. M20.

claustrophobia /klɔːstrəˈfəʊbɪə/ *noun*. L19.
[ORIGIN mod. Latin, from Latin *claustrum* (see CLOISTER *noun*) + -O- + -PHOBIA.]
Irrational fear of confined places.

claustrophobic /klɔːstrəˈfəʊbɪk/ *adjective & noun*. L19.
[ORIGIN from CLAUSTROPHOBIA + -IC.]
▸ **A** *adjective*. **1** Prone to or suffering from claustrophobia. L19.
2 Of a place etc.: confined, restricting; inducing claustrophobia. M20.
▸ **B** *noun*. A person who is prone to or suffers from claustrophobia. M20.
■ **claustrophobically** *adverb* in a claustrophobic manner; so as to induce claustrophobia: M20.

claustrum /ˈklɔːstrəm/ *noun*. Pl. **-stra** /-strə/. M19.
[ORIGIN Latin: see CLOISTER *noun*.]
ANATOMY. A thin layer of grey matter in each cerebral hemisphere between the lentiform nucleus and the insula.

clausula /ˈklɔːzjʊlə/ *noun*. Pl. **-lae** /-liː/. M17.
[ORIGIN Latin (in medieval Latin sense): see CLAUSE.]
1 MUSIC. The conclusion of a movement or phrase. M17.
2 GRAMMAR. The close or end of a period, esp. one in ancient or medieval Latin having a definable cadence. E20.
– NOTE: See also ***clausula*** REBUS SIC STANTIBUS.

†**clausure** *noun*. LME–E19.
[ORIGIN Late Latin *clausura*: see CLOSURE.]
The action of closing or enclosing; closed condition; that which encloses.

clavate /ˈkleɪveɪt/ *adjective*. M17.
[ORIGIN mod. Latin *clavatus*, from *clava* club: see -ATE².]
†**1** Knobbed. Only in M17.
2 Chiefly BOTANY. Club-shaped. E19.
■ Also **clavated** *adjective* E18.

clave /kleɪv, klɑːv/ *noun*. E20.
[ORIGIN Amer. Spanish from Spanish *clave* keystone from Latin *clavis* key.]
MUSIC. Either of a pair of hardwood sticks used to make a hollow sound. Usu. in *pl.*

clave *verb*¹, *verb*² see CLEAVE *verb*¹, *verb*².

clavecin /ˈklavɪsɪn/ *noun*. E19.
[ORIGIN French formed as CLAVICYMBAL.]
A harpsichord, esp. in or from France.
■ **clavecinist** *noun* a (French) harpsichordist M19.

clavel /ˈklav(ə)l/ *noun*. Now *dial*. L17.
[ORIGIN Old French (mod. *claveau*) from medieval Latin *clavellus* dim. of Latin *clavis* key: see -EL².]
The lintel over a fireplace.
– COMB.: **clavel-piece** a mantelpiece.

claver /ˈkleɪvə/ *noun*. *Scot*. & *N. English*. E18.
[ORIGIN from CLAVER *verb*².]
Idle garrulous talk; a piece of idle gossip.

claver /ˈklavə/ *verb*¹ *intrans*. Long *obsolete* exc. *dial*. ME.
[ORIGIN Uncertain: cf. Danish *klavre*, & mod. Dutch *klaveren* clamber.]
Climb, clamber.

claver /ˈkleɪvə/ *verb*² *intrans*. *Scot*. & *N. English*. L16.
[ORIGIN Unknown.]
Talk idly, gossip.

clavicembalo /klavɪˈtʃɛmbələʊ/ *noun*. Pl. **-os**. M18.
[ORIGIN Italian, formed as CLAVICYMBAL.]
A harpsichord, esp. in or from Italy.

clavichord /ˈklavɪkɔːd/ *noun*. LME.
[ORIGIN medieval Latin *clavichordium*, from Latin *clavis* key + *chorda* string (see CORD *noun*¹).]
A keyboard instrument with strings activated by brass blades fixed upright in the key levers.

clavicle /ˈklavɪk(ə)l/ *noun*. E17.
[ORIGIN Latin *clavicula* dim. of *clavis* key: see -CULE.]
ANATOMY. A collarbone.
■ **claˈvicular** *adjective* E19.

clavicymbal /klavɪˈsɪmb(ə)l/ *noun*. Now *arch*. or *hist*. L15.
[ORIGIN medieval Latin *clavicymbalum*, from *clavis* key + *cymbalum* CYMBAL.]
A harpsichord, esp. of early date.

clavicytherium /ˌklavɪsɪˈθɪərɪəm/ *noun*. Pl. **-ia** /-ɪə/. L18.
[ORIGIN mod. Latin, from Latin *clavis* key + CITHARA.]
hist. A keyboard instrument resembling an upright spinet.

clavier /ˈklavɪə; *in sense 2 also* kləˈvɪə/ *noun*. E18.
[ORIGIN (German *Klavier* from) French *clavier* from medieval Latin *claviarius* key-bearer, from *clavis* key: see -ER².]
MUSIC. **1** A keyboard. E18.
2 A keyboard instrument, esp. in or from Germany. M19.

claviform /ˈklavɪfɔːm/ *adjective*. E19.
[ORIGIN from Latin *clava* club + -I- + -FORM.]
Club-shaped.

claviger /ˈklavɪdʒə/ *noun*. *obsolete* exc. *hist*. M16.
[ORIGIN Latin *claviger* adjective, carrying a key or a club, from *clavis* key or *clava* club + *-ger*: see -GEROUS.]
A carrier or keeper of a key or keys

Clavioline /ˈklavɪəliːn/ *noun*. M20.
[ORIGIN After CLAVICHORD etc.]
(Proprietary name for) a small electronic keyboard instrument attachable to a piano.

clavis /ˈkleɪvɪs/ *noun*. *rare*. M17.
[ORIGIN Latin.]
A key.

clavus /ˈkleɪvəs/ *noun*. Pl. **-vi** /-vʌɪ/. E19.
[ORIGIN Latin = nail, wart.]
1 = ERGOT *noun* 1. Now *rare* or *obsolete*. E19.
2 MEDICINE. A corn, a callosity. E19.
3 = LATICLAVE. M19.
4 ZOOLOGY. A projection resembling a fingernail; *esp*. part of the hardened forewing of a heteropteran insect. M19.

claw /klɔː/ *noun*¹.
[ORIGIN Old English *clawu* (from the oblique cases, the orig. nom. being repr. by *clēa* CLEE) = Old Frisian *klē*, *klāwe*, Old Saxon *clāuua* (Dutch *klauw*), Old High German *klāwa* (German *Klaue*), from West Germanic.]
1 A sharp horny nail (often slender and curved) on the toes of birds and some animals; a similar structure in some arthropods; a foot with such a nail or nails. OE. ▸†**b** A hoof; one of the parts of a (cloven) hoof. OE–M17.
2 A contrivance resembling a claw, for grappling, holding, etc.; part of the mechanism of a lock. OE.
3 A hand (*derog*.); a bent disfigured hand. L16.

N. HAWTHORNE A yellow claw—the very same that had clawed together so much wealth—poked itself out of the coach-window.

4 BOTANY. In some flowers, the narrow tapering lower part of a petal, by which it is attached. L18.
– COMB.: **claw-and-ball** *adjective* (of furniture) having feet which represent a claw clasping a ball; **claw foot** (*a*) a foot on a piece of furniture, shaped to resemble a claw; (*b*) MEDICINE (a condition causing) an excessively arched foot with an unnaturally high instep; **claw hammer** a hammer with a curved split end for extracting nails.
■ **clawed** *adjective* (*a*) having a claw or claws; ***clawed toad***, a southern African toad, *Xenopus laevis*, freq. bred for scientific research; (*b*) (of a hand) bent and disfigured like a claw: ME. **clawless** *adjective* E19. **clawlike** *adjective* resembling (that of) a claw E19.

†**claw** *noun*² var. of CLOVE *noun*³.

claw /klɔː/ *verb*.
[ORIGIN Old English *clawian*, from CLAW *noun*¹.]
1 *verb trans*. Scratch or tear with or as with claws. OE.
2 *verb trans*. & *intrans*. Scratch gently, so as to relieve itching or soothe. Now *Scot*. ME.
claw the back of (now *dial*.) flatter, toady to.
3 *verb trans*. Flatter, cajole, wheedle, fawn upon. Now *dial*. LME.

T. ADAMS Claw me, and I will claw thee: Winke at mine, and I will not see thy faults.

4 *verb intrans*. Grasp, clutch, (*at* etc.); scratch *at*. LME.
5 *verb trans*. Seize, grip, clutch, or pull (as) with claws. M16.
6 *verb trans*. Strike as with claws; beat. Now *dial*. L16.
7 *verb intrans*. NAUTICAL. Beat to windward (*off*, *from*, a lee shore etc.). E17.
– WITH ADVERBS IN SPECIALIZED SENSES: **claw back** regain gradually or with great effort; take back (an allowance by additional taxation etc.) **claw off** (*a*) get rid of (as an itch); †(*b*) rate soundly, scold.
– COMB.: **clawback** (*a*) [BACK *noun*¹] a toady; (*b*) [BACK *adverb*] retrieval, recovery (of an allowance by additional taxation etc.).
■ **clawer** *noun* (*rare*) ME.

clay /kleɪ/ *noun*.
[ORIGIN Old English *clǣg* = Old Frisian *klāy*, Middle & mod. Low German, Middle Dutch & mod. Dutch *klei*, from West Germanic from Germanic base repr. also by CLEAM, CLEAVE *verb*², CLIMB *verb*.]
1 A stiff tenacious fine-grained earth consisting mainly of hydrated aluminosilicates, which becomes more plastic when water is added, and can be moulded and dried to make bricks, pottery, etc. OE. ▸†**b** Any substance of a tough sticky nature, as bitumen, pitch, etc. LME–L16.

YEATS Quiet as the clay-cold dead.

china clay, ***fireclay***, ***grafting clay***, ***pipeclay***, etc. ***London clay***, ***Oxford clay***, etc. ***feet of clay***: see FOOT *noun*. ***virgin clay***: see VIRGIN *adjective*. ***white clay***: see WHITE *adjective*.
2 (Moist) earth, mire, mud. ME.
3 (The material of) the human body. ME.
lump of clay: see LUMP *noun*¹. **moisten one's clay**, **wet one's clay** *arch*. *joc*. drink.
4 In full ***clay pipe***. A tobacco pipe made of clay. M19.
long clay: see LONG *adjective*¹.
5 In full ***clay pigeon***. A saucer-shaped piece of baked clay or other material, serving as a target in trapshooting. Orig. *US*. L19.
– COMB.: **clay court** a tennis court with a clay surface; **clay ironstone** clayey iron ore, esp. argillaceous siderite; **clay mineral** any of a number of aluminosilicate minerals which occur as colloidal crystals in clay; **claypan** *Austral*. a natural hollow formed of clayey soil and retaining water after rain; ***clay pigeon***: see sense 5 above; ***clay pipe***: see sense 4 above; **clay slate** an argillaceous sedimentary rock with a slaty cleavage; **claystone** any of various rocks consisting of or resembling clay, *esp*. fine-grained mudstone.
■ **clayen** *adjective* (*arch*.) of clay LME. **clayish** *adjective* more or less clayey LME. **claylike** *adjective* resembling clay E17.

clay /kleɪ/ *verb trans*. LME.
[ORIGIN from the noun.]
Treat, cover, or dress with clay.

clayey /ˈkleɪi/ *adjective*. OE.
[ORIGIN from CLAY *noun*: see -Y¹]
1 Full of clay; of the nature of clay; argillaceous. OE. ▸**b** Of mortal clay. L16.
2 Smeared or soiled with clay. LME.
3 Resembling clay. L17.
■ **clayeyness** *noun* L19.

claymation /kleɪˈmeɪʃ(ə)n/ *noun*. Also **C-**. L20.
[ORIGIN from CLAY *noun* + ANI)MATION.]
A method of animation in which clay figures are filmed using stop-motion photography.
– NOTE: Proprietary name in the US.

claymore /ˈkleɪmɔː/ *noun*. E18.
[ORIGIN from Gaelic *claidheamh* sword + *mór* great.]
1 *hist*. A broadsword used by Scottish Highlanders, either two-edged, or basket-hilted and single-edged (a form introduced in the 16th cent.). E18. ▸**b** A man armed with a claymore. M19.
2 In full ***claymore mine***. A type of anti-personnel mine. M20.

claytonia /kleɪˈtəʊnɪə/ *noun*. L18.
[ORIGIN mod. Latin, from John *Clayton* 18th-cent. Virginian botanist: see -IA¹.]
A small succulent plant of the chiefly N. American genus *Claytonia*, of the purslane family, with white or pink flowers. Also called ***spring beauty***.

-cle /k(ə)l, *after s* (ə)l/ *suffix* (not productive).
Repr. French *-cle* from Latin *-culus*, *-a*, *-um* -CULE, as in ***article***, ***corpuscle***, ***follicle***, ***ventricle***, etc.

cleach /kliːtʃ/ *verb*. Long *obsolete* exc. *dial*. ME.
[ORIGIN Prob. already in Old English: cf. corresp. north. CLEEK *verb*.]
1 *verb trans*. & †*intrans*. Clutch. ME.
2 *verb trans*. & *intrans*. Draw or get (water) in a shallow vessel. LME.

clead /kliːd/ *verb trans*. *Scot*. & *N. English*. Also **cleed**. Pa. t. & pple **cled** /klɛd/. ME.
[ORIGIN Old Norse *klæða*, pa. t. *klædda* rel. to CLOTH, CLOTHE.]
Clothe.
■ **cleading** *noun* (*a*) clothing; (*b*) a protective covering or casing, lagging: ME.

cleam /kliːm/ *verb trans*. Long *obsolete* exc. *dial*. Also **clame** /kleɪm/.
[ORIGIN Old English *clǣman* = Middle Dutch *klēmen*, Old High German *kleimen*, Old Norse *kleima* daub, plaster, from Germanic, ult. from base repr. also by CLAY *noun*, CLEAVE *verb*², CLIMB *verb*, CLOAM. See also CLAM *verb*¹.]
1 Smear, bedaub, plaster. OE.
2 Cause to stick. ME.

C

clean /kliːn/ *noun*. M19.
[ORIGIN from the verb.]
1 An act of cleaning. M19.
2 WEIGHTLIFTING. The action of raising a weight from the floor to shoulder level in a single movement. Freq. in ***clean and jerk***, ***clean and press***. E20.

clean /kliːn/ *adjective*.
[ORIGIN Old English *clǣne* = Old Frisian *klēne*, *kleine*, Old Saxon *klēni* (Dutch *kleen*, *klein* small), Old High German *kleini* clear, delicate, neat, small (German *klein* small), from West Germanic.]
1 Free from anything that dims lustre or transparency. *obsolete* exc. as passing into sense 2. OE.

SPENSER All of Diamond perfect pure and cleene.

2 Free from any polluting ingredient or foreign matter; unadulterated, pure, (*lit*. & *fig*.). OE. ▸**b** In good condition, unspoiled, essentially unchanged. *colloq*. M20.

Times Clean air, that is to say an atmosphere . . relatively free from pollution and contamination.

3 Free from or *of* dirt or contaminating matter; unsoiled. OE. ▸**b** Of a ship: having a bottom free of barnacles etc. Of a whaling or fishing vessel: with nothing in the hold, empty. M17. ▸**c** Of paper: blank. Of a printer's proof, a copy of writing, etc.: free from corrections or alterations. Of a document, report, etc.: bearing no adverse point or remark; listing no offence. L17. ▸**d** Of a deer, a deer's horns: having shed the velvet. M19. ▸**e** Of an animal, child, etc.: not fouling itself or its environment; habitually depositing or able to deposit excreta, esp. faeces, in the proper place. L19. ▸**f** Free from concealed weapons, illegal substances, etc. *slang*. E20. ▸**g** Of a nuclear weapon: causing relatively little fallout. M20.

R. W. EMERSON A Frenchman may possibly be clean; an Englishman is conscientiously clean. A. POWELL Why aren't you wearing a clean shirt? **e** G. GORER When should a young child start being trained to be clean? **f** M. PUZO They'll frisk me . . so I'll have to be clean.

4 Free from spiritual or moral pollution; chaste, innocent. (Foll. by †*of*, *from*.) OE. ▸**b** Guiltless of a charge or accusation. Now *slang*, free from involvement in criminal or otherwise undesirable activity, giving no cause for suspicion. (*obsolete* from E17; recorded again E20.) ME. ▸**c** Free from impropriety; not obscene. *colloq*. M19. ▸**d** Free from or cured of addiction to drugs. *slang*. M20.

TENNYSON I trust That I am whole, and clean, and meet for Heaven. **b** A. PRICE He's . . absolutely clean No contacts. No hint of anything.

c *good clean fun*.

5 Free from ceremonial defilement or from disease. OE. ▸**b** Of animals: not prohibited as food; suitable for use as food. OE. ▸**c** Of an animal: avoiding food regarded as unwholesome. *arch*. M16.
6 Free from obstructions, encumbrances, unevennesses, irregularities, or non-essentials; having a simple well-defined form or line. ME. ▸**b** Of timber: free from knots. E17. ▸**c** Of a ship, aircraft, etc.: with tapering lines, smooth, streamlined. E18. ▸**d** Of a pigeon: without feathers on the legs or feet. Of a draught horse: without long hair on the fetlocks. M19. ▸**e** Giving a distinct impression to the senses; sharp and fresh. E20.

E. K. KANE The clean abrupt edge of the fractures. J. STALLWORTHY Years overlap, have no clean start or end. D. BAGLEY Brooks's desk was clean, a vast expanse of solid teak unmarred by a single paper. **e** J. RHYS The strong taste of punch, the cleaner taste of champagne.

7 Complete, entire; decisive, thoroughgoing. ME.
8 a Of style or language: free from faults, correct, pure. *arch*. LME. ▸**b** Observing the rules or conventions of a sport or game; fair, sporting. M20.
9 Well-formed; slender and shapely; neatly made or done; skilful, adroit; smart, clever. In early use also as a vague term of approbation. LME.

E. WALLER Thy waist is straight and clean As Cupid's shaft. D. JUSTICE Ladies . . clean of limb. J. A. MICHENER To pick off the . . animals with a clean shot.

– SPECIAL COLLOCATIONS & PHRASES: (*as*) ***clean as a whistle***: see WHISTLE *noun*. ***clean bill of health***: see BILL *noun*³. **clean break** a quick and final break. **clean fingers** *fig*. absence of corruption or bribery. **clean hands** *fig*. absence of guilt. **clean sheet**, **clean slate** *fig*. a state free from commitments or imputations. ***clean sweep***: see SWEEP *noun*. ***clean ticket***: see TICKET *noun*. **come clean** *colloq*. (orig. *US*) confess, own up. ***keep one's nose clean***: see NOSE

noun. ***keep the party clean***: see PARTY *noun*. ***make a clean breast of***: see BREAST *noun*. **make a clean job of** *colloq*. do thoroughly. ***make a clean sweep (of)***: see SWEEP *noun*. **show a clean pair of heels** escape by speed. ***the clean potato***: see POTATO *noun*. **the clean thing** *US* the honest straightforward thing. ***wipe the slate clean***: see SLATE *noun*[1] 3b.
■ **cleanish** *adjective* fairly clean M18. **cleanness** /-n-n-/ *noun* OE.

clean /kliːn/ *verb*. LME.
[ORIGIN from the adjective.]
1 *verb trans*. Make clean (*of* dirt etc.); remove the internal organs of (fish or fowl) preparatory to serving as food; eat all the food on (one's plate). LME. ▸**b** Deprive (a person) of all his or her money. Cf. sense 4 below. *slang*. E20.
dry-clean: see DRY *adjective*.
2 *verb intrans*. Become clean; make oneself clean. E18.
3 *verb trans*. Foll. by *out*: Remove undesirable contents from; empty, strip; *slang* deprive of all available money or assets. M19. ▸**b** Deal effectively with; eject; eject the occupants from. *US*. M19.
4 *verb trans. & intrans*. Foll. by *up*: ▸**a** *verb trans. & intrans*. Make (a place, oneself, etc.) clean or tidy; clear away a mess (from). M19. ▸**b** *verb trans*. Acquire as gain or profit. *slang* (orig. *US*). M19. ▸**c** *verb trans*. Defeat; take all the money from. *slang*. L19. ▸**d** *verb intrans*. Make a large profit. *N. Amer. slang*. E20. ▸**e** *verb trans*. Remove disorder, crime, etc., from; remove remaining pockets of enemy resistance from (an area). E20.

a *New Scientist* The technique . . has been widely used to clean up contaminated land. **d** D. HAMMETT He had cleaned up heavily in a lumber deal.

5 WEIGHTLIFTING. Raise (a weight) from the floor to shoulder level in a single movement. Freq. in ***clean and jerk***, ***clean and press***. M20.
■ **cleanable** *adjective* able to be cleaned L19.

clean /kliːn/ *adverb*.
[ORIGIN Old English *clǣne*, *clēne*, from the adjective.]
1 In a clean manner (= CLEANLY *adverb* 1). OE.
2 Completely, outright, quite, simply. OE.

C. BRONTË Your proposal has almost driven me 'clean daft'. H. JAMES He had clean forgotten. R. MACAULAY The young man got clean away.

clean- /kliːn/ *combining form*. E16.
[ORIGIN Repr. CLEAN *adjective*, *adverb*.]
Clean(ly).
clean-bowl *verb trans*. (CRICKET) bowl out (a batsman) or bowl down (a wicket) with a ball that hits the wicket without having touched the bat or the body of the batsman. **clean-cut** *adjective* sharply outlined. **clean-living** *adjective* of upright character. **clean-limbed** *adjective* (of joints, a figure, etc.) well-formed, shapely. **clean-run** *adjective* (of a salmon) well-fed and bright-looking, newly returned to fresh water from the sea; *fig*. (of a person) with the bloom of youth, healthy and lively. **clean-shaven** *adjective* without a beard or moustache or whiskers. **cleanskin** *Austral. & NZ* an unbranded animal (cf. ***clearskin*** s.v. CLEAR *adjective*); *slang* a person without a police record.

cleaner /ˈkliːnə/ *noun*. LME.
[ORIGIN from CLEAN *verb* + -ER[1].]
1 A person who cleans, esp. rooms or clothes. LME. ▸**b** *sing*. & (freq.) in *pl*. A shop or firm that cleans clothes or household fabrics (= ***dry-cleaner*** s.v. DRY *adjective*). L19.
b send to the cleaners, **take to the cleaners** *colloq*. (*a*) rob or defraud of all available money or assets; (*b*) inflict a crushing defeat on.
2 An instrument or machine for cleaning. L19.
3 A small marine animal which cleans larger ones of parasites, bacteria, or dead tissue. Also ***cleaner fish***. M20.

cleanly /ˈklɛnli/ *adjective*. OE.
[ORIGIN from CLEAN *adjective* + -LY[1].]
†**1** Morally or spiritually clean. OE–L17.
†**2** Free of dirt, unsoiled. ME–L16.
3 Habitually clean. E16.
4 Of an action: adroit, deft. *obsolete* exc. *dial*. M16.
5 Conducing to or promoting cleanness. E17.
■ **cleanlily** *adverb* L17. **cleanliness** *noun* LME.

cleanly /ˈkliːnli/ *adverb*. OE.
[ORIGIN from CLEAN *adjective* + -LY[2].]
1 In a clean manner (= CLEAN *adverb* 1). OE.
†**2** = CLEAN *adverb* 2. OE–M17.

clean-out /ˈkliːnaʊt/ *noun*. L19.
[ORIGIN from CLEAN *verb* + OUT *adverb*: see CLEAN *verb* 4.]
An act of cleaning out; an emptying or removal of undesirable contents etc.

cleanse /klɛnz/ *verb*.
[ORIGIN Old English *clǣnsian*, from CLEAN *adjective*.]
1 *verb trans*. Make morally or spiritually clean (*of*, *from*, sin, guilt, etc.); expiate (sin or crime). OE.
2 *verb trans. & intrans*. Make (a thing, now esp. the skin) thoroughly clean. OE.
3 *verb trans*. Chiefly in biblical translations: make ceremonially clean; cure (a leper etc.). *arch*. OE.
4 *verb trans*. Purge, clear by evacuation. OE.
5 *verb trans*. Clear, rid (*of*, *from*). ME.
6 *verb intrans*. Of cattle: pass the afterbirth. *N. English*. E17.
– PHRASES: **cleansing cream**: for removing unwanted matter from the face, hands, etc. **cleansing department** a local service of refuse collection etc. **cleansing tissue**: for removing unwanted matter from the face, hands, etc.
■ **cleansable** *adjective* L15. **cleanser** *noun* a person who or thing which cleanses; *spec*. (*a*) *arch*. a purgative; (*b*) a cosmetic for cleaning the skin: OE.

clean-up /ˈkliːnʌp/ *noun*. M19.
[ORIGIN from CLEAN *verb* + UP *adverb*[1]: see CLEAN *verb* 5.]
1 MINING. An act of collecting the valuable material produced during a given period of operation; the value of such material. *US*. M19.
2 A profit; a financial success or gain. *slang* (orig. *US*). L19.
3 An act of making clean or tidy. L19.
4 An act of removing or putting an end to disorder, crime, etc., or remaining pockets of enemy resistance. E20.

clear /klɪə/ *noun*. ME.
[ORIGIN Branch I from the adjective, branch II from the verb.]
▸ **I** †**1** A beautiful woman. ME–M17.
†**2** Brightness, clearness; translucence. L15–E18.
3 ***in the clear***: ▸**a** In interior extent. L17. ▸**b** In profit. *N. Amer*. E20. ▸**c** Free of suspicion or difficulty. M20.
4 ***in clear***, not in cipher or code. M20.
▸ **II 5** A clearing of the sky, weather, fog, etc. L16.

clear /klɪə/ *adjective*. ME.
[ORIGIN Old French *cler* (mod. *clair*) from Latin *clarus* clear, bright, etc.]
1 Of light, a source of light: (orig.) brightly shining, brilliant; (now) pure, unclouded. Of fire: with little flame or smoke. Of a colour: pure, unmixed. ME.

AV *S. of S*. 6:10 Cleare as the sunne. J. B. PRIESTLEY The clearest azure.

2 Of the day, daylight, etc.: fully light (*arch*.). Of the weather, a period of time in respect of weather, etc.: (orig.) full of sunshine, bright; (now) free from cloud, mist, and haze. Of the sky: cloudless. ME. ▸**b** *fig*. Cheerful, serene. *arch*. LME.

D. H. LAWRENCE It was a clear morning. C. RYAN Unlike Holland, where the weather was clear, Britain was covered by fog.

3 Transparent; translucent; not turbid; free from sediment etc. ME.

SWIFT A dozen or two of good clear wine. COLERIDGE The harbour-bay was clear as glass. SCOTT FITZGERALD The air so clear you could see the leaves on Sunset Mountain.

4 Lustrous, having a shiny surface. ME. ▸**b** Of the complexion; fresh and unblemished. Formerly also of a person: having such a complexion. ME. ▸†**c** Of a woman: beautiful, fair. LME–L16. ▸†**d** Illustrious. LME–E17.
5 Easily seen (*lit. & fig*.); distinctly visible; intelligible, perspicuous, unambiguous; manifest, evident. ME. ▸**b** Not in cipher or code. E20.

G. ORWELL The great enemy of clear language is insincerity. J. B. PRIESTLEY Make it clear [that] I'm not trying to sell any pictures. I. MURDOCH All the elements of his case were clear to him. P. ROTH Either I'm not making myself clear or you don't even want to begin to understand me. A. THWAITE A clear vision of Christ in majesty.

6 Seeing distinctly (*lit. & fig*.); discerning, penetrating. ME. ▸**b** Confident, decided, certain. Foll. by *for*, *as to*, *on*, *about* (a fact, course of action, etc.), *that*, †*of* (a fact). E17.

J. MORLEY His sight was exquisitely keen and clear. **b** BOSWELL We were, by a great majority, clear for the experiment. E. A. FREEMAN I am not quite clear about the date. G. GREENE He would like to be clear in his own mind as to what had happened. J. BERRYMAN I'm fairly clear . . there's no such place.

7 Of a sound, a voice, etc.: ringing, pure and well-defined; distinctly audible. ME. ▸**b** PHONETICS. Not velarized or retracted; *spec*. designating the palatalized, as opp. to the 'dark' or velarized, lateral consonant (/l/). L19.

SHAKES. *Tr. & Cr*. Crack my clear voice with sobs. J. STEINBECK In Kino's head there was a song now, clear and soft.

8 Guileless, ingenuous; innocent, free from fault or guilt. ME.

SHAKES. *Macb*. Duncan Hath borne his faculties so meek, hath been so clear in his great office. MILTON Fame is the spur that the clear spirit doth raise.

9 Free from obstructions, obstacles, encumbrances, burden, contents, or occupants; open for passage or operations; free from the presence *of*. ME. ▸**b** Free from unevennesses or irregularities. M17.

POPE A clear stage is left for Jupiter to display his omnipotence. H. NELSON One of our Transports will be clear tonight. A. P. STANLEY The way was now clear to the Jordan. B. WEBB To leave the field clear for the younger men and remain a silent member. B. CHATWIN Providing the lanes were clear of ice. **b** W. COBBETT Several oaks . . with a clear stem of more than forty feet.

the coast is clear: see COAST *noun* 2.
10 Free from contact; disengaged; apart, out of reach. (Foll. by *of*, *from*.) LME.

DEFOE We were clear of the isles. BURKE My motives are clear from private interest. H. E. BATES Ice that had been swept clear.

11 Of income, gain, etc.: without deduction, net. LME.
12 Free from legal, pecuniary, or other complications. L15.
13 Free from limitation or qualification; absolute, complete, entire; sheer. E16.

R. L'ESTRANGE You will find in all Respects the clear contrary. H. CECIL Leading by a clear eighteen lengths.

14 Unadulterated, pure; of the highest quality. *techn. & slang*. M18.
– PHRASES: **(as) clear as a bell** heard very distinctly. **(as) clear as day** very clear, esp. to the understanding. **(as) clear as mud** not clear at all, completely unintelligible. ***(as) clear as a whistle***: see WHISTLE *noun*. ***clear conscience***. ***clear grit***: see GRIT *noun*[1]. **clear soup**: containing little solid matter. **out of a clear sky** *fig*. as a complete surprise. ***the clear grit***: see GRIT *noun*[1].
– COMB.: **clear-air** *adjective* designating atmospheric turbulence without visible signs; **clear-eyed** *adjective* (*fig*.) discerning, penetrating; **clear-headed** *adjective* having a clear head; able to think clearly; **clear-headedness** the quality or state of being clear-headed; **clear-obscure** = CHIAROSCURO; **clear-sighted** *adjective* having clear sight, discerning; **clear-sightedness** the quality or state of being clear-sighted; **clearskin** *Austral. & NZ* an unbranded animal (cf. ***cleanskin*** s.v. CLEAN-); **clear-starch** *verb intrans. & trans*. stiffen (linen) with colourless starch; **clearway** a road on which vehicles must not stop; **clearweed** *N. Amer*. a plant of the nettle family, *Pilea pumila*, with a semi-transparent stem; **clearwing** a day-flying moth of the family Sesiidae, members of which have largely transparent wings and mimic other insects, e.g. hornets.
■ **clearish** *adjective* somewhat clear E19. **clearness** *noun* ME.

clear /klɪə/ *verb*. ME.
[ORIGIN from the adjective.]
▸ **I 1** *verb trans*. Make morally or spiritually pure; expiate. *obsolete* exc. as *fig*. use of senses 9, 12. ME.

SHAKES. *Lucr*. The blackest sin is clear'd with absolution.

2 *verb trans*. Show or declare to be innocent; free from blame or suspicion. (Foll. by *of*, *from*.) LME.

ADDISON How! would'st thou clear rebellion! M. EDGEWORTH He must commit Mr. F. to gaol, unless he can clear himself.

3 *verb trans*. Approve or obtain approval of (a plan etc., a person to be entrusted with secret information etc.). (Foll. by *with* an authorizing person or body.) M20.

A. H. COMPTON If they cleared me it would be necessary for them to clear my wife as well. M. EDWARDES The appointment had been cleared with the Prime Minister.

▸ **II 4** *verb trans*. Explain, elucidate; enlighten, inform (the mind or understanding). *arch*. ME. ▸†**b** Prove, demonstrate. ME–L18.

GOLDSMITH Willing to clear the thing to his satisfaction.

5 *verb trans*. †**a** Fill with light; brighten (*lit. & fig*.). Also foll. by *up*. LME–L17. ▸**b** Make transparent or translucent; remove cloudiness or turbidity from; clarify (a liquid). LME.
6 *verb intrans*. Become clear or bright. Esp. of weather also foll. by *up*. LME.

THACKERAY The day did not clear up sufficiently. LD MACAULAY For a time the prospect seemed to clear. A. SILLITOE His head clearing with the sudden onset of fresh air.

7 *verb trans*. **a** Make (the voice) clear and distinct in sound. LME. ▸**b** Make (the eyes or eyesight) clear in vision. L16.
8 *verb trans*. Remove obstructions, obstacles, encumbrances, burden, contents, or occupants from; open for passage or operations; empty. (Foll. by *of*, †*from*.) Also foll. by *out*. See also ***clear up*** below. M16. ▸**b** *verb intrans*. Become empty or unobstructed. L19.

H. MAYHEW The strathes and glens of Sutherland have been cleared of their inhabitants. J. AGATE It entirely cleared my mind of any possible doubts. D. ABSE She cleared the tea-table. R. MACAULAY Sites would be cleared for rebuilding. D. JACOBSON The soldiers began to clear a way through the throng. F. ORMSBY Other chores—a path to clear, [etc.]. *fig*.: P. ACKROYD Clearing the ground . . before he began seriously to concentrate on the work to come.

clear one's throat rid the throat of phlegm, huskiness, etc., by slight coughing. **clear the air**: of sultriness; *fig*. of suspicion, tension, etc. ***clear the coast***: see COAST *noun* 2. **clear the decks (for action)** make ready to fight (*lit. & fig*.). ***clear the way***: see WAY *noun*.
9 *verb trans*. Settle, discharge, (a debt, a bill, etc.). Also foll. by *off*. L16. ▸†**b** *verb intrans*. Settle accounts *with*. L16–L18. ▸**c** *verb trans. & intrans*. Set (a person, an estate) free from debt. E17.
10 *verb trans*. Free from contact, disengage; get clear *of*, *from*. L16. ▸**b** *verb trans. & intrans*. FOOTBALL & HOCKEY etc. Of a defending player: kick or hit (the ball) away from a dangerous attacking position. L19.
11 *verb trans*. Remove (an obstruction, unwanted object, contents, etc.), disperse. Also foll. by *away*, *off*, *out*. See also ***clear up*** below. E17. ▸**b** *verb intrans*. Go away; disperse; disappear. Also foll. by *away*, *off*, *out*. E19.

SOUTHEY A gentle sea-breeze began to clear the mist. M. PUZO How did he get the cops to clear everybody out and where did they go? J. FRAME Clearing the weeds and preparing the garden. E. FIGES Breakfast had been cleared away. **b** A. RANSOME The smoke was clearing outside. J. T. STORY Felix suddenly cleared out and drove off. T. SHARPE The Dean sat in his car and waited for the traffic to clear.

12 *verb trans.* Pass clear of (an obstruction etc.); get clear through, away from, or over (a distance). E17. ▸**b** Pass over or by without touching, esp. by jumping. L18.

T. COLLINS Another mile, and I cleared the pine-ridge. **b** W. S. CHURCHILL Not only did he . . arrive at the fence, he cleared it in magnificent style.

13 *verb trans.* Make (a sum) as a net gain or to balance expenses. E18.
14 *verb trans. & intrans.* Pass through the formalities of (a customs office etc.). Also foll. by *out*. E18.
15 *verb trans.* Pass (a cheque, bill) through a clearing house. M19.
16 *verb intrans.* Remove the remains of a meal from a table etc. Also (earlier) foll. by *away*. M19.
– WITH ADVERBS IN SPECIALIZED SENSES: **clear up** (*a*) *verb phr. trans. & intrans.* put (an area) into order by removing obstructions, rubbish, etc.; remove (obstructions, rubbish, etc.) to leave an area tidy; (*b*) *verb phr. trans.* elucidate, solve (a mystery); cure (an infection etc.); (*c*) *verb phr. intrans.* (of an infection etc.) become cured, disappear; (see also senses 5, 6, 9 above).
– COMB.: **clear-out** an act or period of clearing out, a removal and disposal of unwanted items or material; **clear-up** an act or period of clearing up, a removal and tidying away of obstructions, rubbish, etc.
■ **clearage** *noun* (*a*) = CLEARANCE 2; (*b*) the action of clearing: M18. **clearer** *noun* L16.

clear /klɪə/ *adverb*. ME.
[ORIGIN Partly the adjective after verbs; partly after other flat adverbs, esp. CLEAN *adverb*.]
1 = CLEARLY 1. Now chiefly of sound, esp. in ***loud and clear*** s.v. LOUD *adverb* 1. ME.

MILTON Now clear I understand. G. STEIN To make Jeff Campbell see much clearer.

2 Completely; = CLEAN *adverb* 2. Now only modifying adverbs & adverbial phrs. ME.

R. L'ESTRANGE He is Now got into Clear Another story. A. LOOS The boat does not come clear up to London.

3 Brightly; with a clear light. LME.
4 So as to be clear (*of*). L16.

H. SECOMBE He leapt clear just before it plummeted down.

steer clear of: see STEER *verb*¹.
– COMB.: **clear-cut** *adjective* well-defined; **clear-cut** *verb trans.*, **clear-fell** *verb trans.* cut down and remove every tree from (an area).

clearance /ˈklɪər(ə)ns/ *noun*. M16.
[ORIGIN from CLEAR *verb* + -ANCE.]
1 An act of clearing or making clear; *esp.* (*a*) a removal of obstructions, encumbrances, contents, etc. (see CLEAR *verb* 8, 11); a removal of old buildings, persons, or objects, so as to clear land; (*b*) the clearing of a ship at customs; (*c*) the clearing of a cheque; (*d*) permission, authorization, esp. for an aircraft to land or take off or for a person to be entrusted with secret information etc. M16.
the Highland clearances, **the clearances** *hist.* the enforced depopulation of the Scottish Highlands.
2 A certificate that a ship has been cleared at customs. E18.
3 A clear space allowed for the passage of two objects or parts; the distance allowed. L18.
4 A cleared space, a clearing. Now *rare* or *obsolete*. E19.
5 FOOTBALL & HOCKEY etc. A defensive kick or hit away from a dangerous attacking position. E20.
– COMB.: **clearance order**: for the demolition of buildings; **clearance sale**: to effect clearance of superfluous stock.

clearcole /ˈklɪəkəʊl/ *noun & verb trans.* E19.
[ORIGIN French *claire colle* clear glue or size.]
(Paint with) size and whiting or white lead as a first coat in house painting.

clearing /ˈklɪərɪŋ/ *noun*. LME.
[ORIGIN from CLEAR *verb* + -ING¹.]
1 The action of CLEAR *verb*. LME. ▸**b** The washing of calico to remove excess dye. M19.
2 A piece of land in a forest cleared for cultivation; an open space in a forest. L17.
†**3** In *pl.* The balance of a military officer's pay after deductions. L17–E19.
4 In the UK, a system used by universities to fill the remaining available undergraduate places before the start of the academic year. L20.
– COMB.: **clearing bank** a bank that is a member of a clearing house, *spec.* of the London Clearing House; **clearing house** a bankers' institution where cheques and bills are exchanged, so that only the balances need be paid in cash; *transf.* an agency for collecting and distributing information etc.

clearly /ˈklɪəli/ *adverb*. ME.
[ORIGIN from CLEAR *adjective* + -LY².]
1 Distinctly; plainly; manifestly, obviously. ME.

J. TYNDALL The top of the mountain rose clearly above us. H. JAMES The moment of his mother's arrival was never clearly ascertained. G. VIDAL I remember that very clearly. I. MCEWAN It was clearly visiting time in the wards.

2 Brightly; with a clear light. Now *rare*. LME.

I. MURDOCH The moon shone clearly on to my bed.

†**3** Honestly, frankly. LME–L17.
†**4** Completely; = CLEAR *adverb* 2. LME–E19.
†**5** Without deduction, net. LME–M17.

clearstory *noun* see CLERESTORY.

cleat /kliːt/ *noun & verb*. ME.
[ORIGIN Corresp. to Dutch *kloot* ball, sphere, Old High German *klōz* clod, lump, wedge (German *Kloss* clod, dumpling), from West Germanic: prob. already in Old English. Rel. to CLOT *noun*, CLOUT *noun*¹.]
▸ **A** *noun*. **1** A wedge. ME.
2 a A projecting piece bolted on to a spar, gangway, boot, etc. to provide footing or to prevent a rope from slipping. LME. ▸**b** A piece of wood or iron bolted on for securing ropes to or for strengthening woodwork etc. M18.
3 A wedge-shaped or other piece fastened on, or left projecting, for any purpose: as a handle etc. E17.
▸ **B** *verb trans.* Fasten to, or with, a cleat; provide with cleats. E17.

cleavage /ˈkliːvɪdʒ/ *noun*. E19.
[ORIGIN from CLEAVE *verb*¹ + -AGE.]
1 The action of splitting a crystal or rock along a line of natural fissure; *gen.* the action of splitting or dividing. Also, the state of being split, a division; the manner or direction in which a mineral or rock or *gen.* a party, opinion, etc., tends to split. E19. ▸**b** BIOLOGY. Cell division; esp. of a fertilized egg cell. L19.

W. LIPPMANN There is some kind of radical cleavage between the Marxian theory and the historic Soviet state. W. S. CHURCHILL Anxious to avoid a total religious cleavage with the European Powers. J. BRONOWSKI Sometimes the stone had a natural grain, sometimes the tool-maker created the lines of cleavage.

b ***spiral cleavage***: see SPIRAL *adjective*¹.
2 The hollow between a woman's breasts, esp. as exposed by a low-cut garment. *colloq.* M20.

cleave /kliːv/ *noun*. Irish. M16.
[ORIGIN Irish *cliabh*.]
A basket.

cleave /kliːv/ *verb*¹. Now chiefly *literary*. Pa. t. **cleaved**, **cleft** /klɛft/, **clove** /kləʊv/, (*arch.*) **clave** /kleɪv/. Pa. pple **cleaved**, **cleft**, **clove**, **cloven** /ˈkləʊv(ə)n/. See also CLOVEN *ppl adjective*.
[ORIGIN Old English *clēofan* = Old Saxon *klioban* (Dutch *klieven*), Old High German *kliuban* (German *klieben*), Old Norse *kljúfa*, from Germanic.]
1 *verb trans.* Split, esp. along the grain or line of cleavage; intersect, fissure. OE. ▸**b** *verb trans.* Separate or sever *from* by dividing or splitting. ME.

AV *Gen.* 22:3 Abraham . . claue the wood. R. MACAULAY Cleaving the forests, deep valleys ran down to the sea.

2 *verb intrans.* Come apart, esp. along the grain or line of cleavage. ME.
3 *verb trans. & intrans.* Pierce and penetrate (air, water, etc.), make one's way through (air, water, etc.). M16. ▸**b** *verb trans.* Make (one's way, a channel, etc.) by piercing and penetrating. M19.

WORDSWORTH Through the inferior throng I clove Of the plain Burghers. E. MUIR Two towering birds cleaving the air. **b** E. BOWEN A steamer . . cleft a long bright furrow in the shadowy water.

■ **cleavable** *adjective* able to be cloven or split M19.

cleave /kliːv/ *verb*². Now *literary*. Pa. t. **clave** /kleɪv/, **cleaved**; pa. pple **cleaved**.
[ORIGIN Old English *cleofian*, *clifian* (weak), *clīfan* (strong) = (i) Old Saxon *klībon* (Dutch *kleven*), Old High German *klebēn* (German *kleben*), (ii) Old Saxon *biklīban* (Dutch *beklijven*), Old High German *klīban*, Old Norse *klífa*, from West Germanic base also of CLAY *noun*, CLIMB *verb*, CLOAM.]
1 *verb intrans.* Stick fast, adhere, or cling *to* (*lit. & fig.*). OE. ▸†**b** Remain steadfast, continue. ME–L16.

BACON Water in small quantity cleaveth to any thing that is solid. L. STRACHEY More closely than ever did she cleave to the side of her mistress. B. BETTELHEIM The English translations cleave to an early stage of Freud's thought.

2 *verb trans.* Attach *to* (esp. *fig.*). M20.

A. FRASER The real theme of the coronation—to cleave the Scottish people to their young King.

cleavelandite /ˈkliːvləndʌɪt/ *noun*. E19.
[ORIGIN from Parker *Cleaveland* (1780–1858), US mineralogist + -ITE¹.]
MINERALOGY. A variety of albite forming thin platy crystals.

cleaver /ˈkliːvə/ *noun*. LME.
[ORIGIN from CLEAVE *verb*¹ + -ER¹.]
1 A person who cleaves wood etc. LME.
2 An instrument for cleaving; *spec.* a butcher's chopping tool for carcasses. L16.

cleavers /ˈkliːvəz/ *noun* (treated as *sing.* or *pl.*). Also **clivers** /ˈklɪv-/.
[ORIGIN Old English *clīfe* = Old Saxon *klība*, Old High German *klība*, from base of CLEAVE *verb*².]
A climbing weed, *Galium aparine*, which adheres by minute hooked prickles to clothes, fur, etc. Also called ***goose-grass***.

cleck /klɛk/ *verb trans.* Chiefly *Scot.* LME.
[ORIGIN Old Norse *klekja*.]
Hatch (*lit. & fig.*).
■ **clecking** *noun* (*a*) hatching; (*b*) a brood: M16.

cled *verb pa. t. & pple* of CLEAD *verb*.

cledge /klɛdʒ/ *noun*. *dial.* E18.
[ORIGIN Prob. rel. to CLAG.]
Clay, clayey soil; a kind of fuller's earth.
■ **cledgy** *adjective* L16.

C

clee /kliː/ *noun*. *obsolete* exc. *dial.*
[ORIGIN Old English *clēa* (*clēo*): see CLAW *noun*¹.]
= CLAW *noun*¹ 1.

cleed *verb* var. of CLEAD.

cleek /kliːk/ *noun*. Chiefly *Scot.* LME.
[ORIGIN from the verb: cf. CLICK *noun*³.]
1 A large hook or crook (for catching hold of something). LME. ▸**b** A hold, a clutch. LME.
2 GOLF. An iron-headed club with a straight narrow face and a long shaft, as a number one iron. *arch.* E19.

cleek /kliːk/ *verb trans.* *Scot. & N. English.* Also **cleik**. Pa. t. & pple **claucht**, **-ght**, /klɔː(x)t/. LME.
[ORIGIN formed as CLEACH *verb*. Cf. CLICK *verb*².]
1 Clutch; grasp suddenly, firmly, or eagerly. LME.
2 Snatch (*out, up, off*). LME.
3 Lay hold of with a cleek. E19.

cleeve *noun* var. of CLEVE.

clef /klɛf/ *noun*. L16.
[ORIGIN French from Latin *clavis* key.]
MUSIC. Any of several symbols placed on a particular line of a stave to indicate the name and pitch of the notes standing on that line, and hence of the other notes.
alto clef: see ALTO *adjective*. ***bass clef***: see BASS *adjective*. ***C clef***: see C, C. ***F clef***: see F, F. ***G clef***: see G, G. ***soprano clef***: see SOPRANO *adjective*. ***tenor clef***: see TENOR *adjective*. ***treble clef***: see TREBLE *adjective*.

cleft /klɛft/ *noun*. Also (earlier) **clift** /klɪft/. ME.
[ORIGIN Corresp. to Old High German, Old Norse *kluft*, cogn. with CLEAVE *verb*¹: prob. already in Old English. Assim. to CLEFT *adjective*.]
1 A space or division made by cleaving; a split, a fissure, a crack, a crevice. ME.
natal cleft: see NATAL *adjective*². VISCERAL ***cleft***.
2 *spec.* ▸**a** The fork of the legs. *obsolete* exc. *dial.* ME. ▸**b** A split made in a tree, esp. to receive a graft. LME. ▸**c** A crack of the skin, a chap; a crack in a horse's foot. L16.
3 (A piece of) split wood, esp. for fuel. Now *dial.* L15.
■ **clefted** *adjective* having a cleft or clefts, split M16.

cleft /klɛft/ *ppl adjective*. LME.
[ORIGIN pa. pple of CLEAVE *verb*¹: cf. CLOVEN *ppl adjective*.]
Split apart; partly split; bifurcate.
cleft lip a congenital split in the upper lip on one or both sides of the centre, often associated with a cleft palate. **cleft palate** a congenital malformation in which there is a longitudinal fissure in the roof of the mouth. **cleft sentence** GRAMMAR a sentence in which an element is emphasized by being put in a separate clause and the use of an empty introductory word, usu. *it, that*, or *what*, e.g. *it's money we want, what we want is money; it was today that I saw him; that was the King you were talking to*. **in a cleft stick** in a position allowing neither retreat nor advance; in a fix.

cleft *verb pa. t. & pple* of CLEAVE *verb*¹.

cleg /klɛg/ *noun*. LME.
[ORIGIN Old Norse *kleggi* (Norwegian *klegg*, Danish *klæg*).]
A gadfly, a horsefly; *esp.* one of the common genus *Haematopota*.

cleidoic /klʌɪˈdəʊɪk/ *adjective*. M20.
[ORIGIN from Greek *kleidoō* lock up + -IC.]
BIOLOGY. Of the egg of an oviparous land animal: completely enclosed in a membrane or shell.

cleik *verb* var. of CLEEK *verb*.

cleistogamy /klʌɪˈstɒgəmi/ *noun*. L19.
[ORIGIN from Greek *kleistos* closed + -GAMY.]
BOTANY. The occurrence of permanently closed flowers in which self-fertilization occurs. Opp. CHASMOGAMY.
■ **cleistoˈgamic**, **cleistogamous** *adjectives* L19.

cleithral /ˈklʌɪθr(ə)l/ *adjective*. M19.
[ORIGIN from Greek *kleithron* bar for closing a door + -AL¹.]
GREEK ARCHITECTURE. Of a temple: covered in. Opp. HYPAETHRAL.

clem /klɛm/ *verb*. *dial.* Also **clam** /klam/. Infl. **-mm-**. M16.
[ORIGIN Repr. Old English *beclemman* confine, shut in, Old Saxon *klemmian* pinch, constrain, from West Germanic, from Germanic base also of CLAM *noun*¹.]
1 *verb trans.* Pinch or waste with hunger or thirst. M16.
2 *verb intrans.* Suffer the pangs of hunger or thirst; starve. L16.

clematis /ˈklɛmətɪs, kləˈmeɪtɪs/ *noun*. M16.
[ORIGIN Latin (also, periwinkle) from Greek *klēmatis*, from *klēma* vine-branch.]
A plant of the large genus *Clematis* of the buttercup family, with a showy calyx and no corolla, and seed vessels often with a feathery style, most species being woody climbing shrubs, as traveller's joy, *C. vitalba*; *esp.* any of the numerous cultivated varieties.

clemency /ˈklɛm(ə)nsi/ *noun*. LME.
[ORIGIN Latin *clementia*, formed as CLEMENT: see -ENCY.]
1 Mildness or gentleness of temper in the exercise of authority or power; mercy, leniency. LME.
2 Mildness of weather or climate. M17.
■ Also †**clemence** *noun* LME–L16.

clement /ˈklɛm(ə)nt/ *adjective*. LME.
[ORIGIN Latin *clement-*, *-ens*: see -ENT.]
1 Mild and humane in the exercise of power or authority; merciful, lenient, kindly. LME.
2 Of weather or climate: mild. M19.
■ **clemently** *adverb* M16.

Clementine /ˈklɛm(ə)ntʌɪn/ *noun*[1] & *adjective*. LME.
[ORIGIN medieval Latin *Clementinus*, from *Clemens* the adjective (see CLEMENT) used as a personal name: see -INE[1].]
▸ **A** *noun*. In *pl*. The constitutions collected by Pope Clement V (1264–1314), forming the seventh book of the decretals. Also, certain apocryphal writings once attributed to Clement of Rome, a bishop of the early Church (fl. *c* AD 96). LME.
▸ **B** *adjective*. Of or pertaining to one of the name of Clement, esp. (**a**) Clement of Rome, (**b**) Pope Clement V. E18.

clementine /ˈklɛm(ə)ntʌɪn, -tiːn/ *noun*[2]. E20.
[ORIGIN French *clémentine*.]
A variety of tangerine grown esp. in N. Africa and the Mediterranean.

clenbuterol /klɛnˈbjuːtərɒl/ *noun*. L20.
[ORIGIN Prob. from *cl-* (in CHLORO-) + PH)EN(YL + BUT(YL + *er* + -OL.]
PHARMACOLOGY. A synthetic compound having sympathomimetic and growth-promoting properties, $C_{12}H_{18}Cl_2N_2O$, used in the treatment of asthma and respiratory diseases and in veterinary obstetrics, and also as an illegal performance-enhancing drug.

clench /klɛn(t)ʃ/ *noun*. See also CLINCH *noun*. LME.
[ORIGIN from the verb.]
1 = CLINCH *noun* 1, 2, 3. LME.
2 A pun, a quibble; = CLINCH *noun* 4. *arch*. M17.
3 The action of clenching the fingers, fist, teeth, etc.; the state of being clenched together. M19.

clench /klɛn(t)ʃ/ *verb trans*. See also CLINCH *verb*, CLINK *verb*[2].
[ORIGIN Old English *-clenćan* = Old High German *klenken*, from Germanic, from base parallel to that of CLING *verb*.]
1 = CLINCH *verb* 1a. OE.

M. LEITCH Her hair was clenched in curlers.

2 Set firmly together, close (the fingers, fist, teeth, etc.) tightly. LME.

J. STEINBECK He struck her in the face with his clenched fist. F. KING She clenched her jaws until they ached.

clenched fist salute: see SALUTE *noun*[1].
■ **clencher** *noun* = CLINCHER LME.

cleome /klɪˈəʊmi/ *noun*. E19.
[ORIGIN mod. Latin from Greek (Theophrastus), name of a different plant.]
Any of various chiefly tropical American plants constituting the genus *Cleome*, of the caper family, notable for their very long stamens; *esp*. = ***spider flower*** s.v. SPIDER *noun*.

clepe /kliːp/ *verb*. *arch*. (long *rare* exc. as YCLEPT). Pa. t. & pple also †**clept**.
[ORIGIN Old English *cleopian*, *clipian* from Germanic, rel. to Old Frisian *klippa*, *kleppa* ring, Low German *klippen* sound, resound.]
†**1** *verb intrans*. Cry, call, (*on*, *to*, *for*, *after*). OE–M16.
†**2** *verb trans*. Call (a person); summon; speak to, address. OE–M16.
3 *verb trans*. Call by the name of, name. OE.

clepsydra /ˈklɛpsɪdrə/ *noun*. Pl. **-dras**, **-drae** /-driː/. LME.
[ORIGIN Latin from Greek *klepsudra*, from *kleps-* combining form of *kleptein* steal + *hudōr* water.]
An instrument used in antiquity to measure time by the flow of water; a water clock.

†**clept** *verb pa. t. & pple* of CLEPE *verb*.

cleptoparasite *noun* var. of KLEPTOPARASITE.

clerestory /ˈklɪəstɔːri/ *noun*. Also ***clearstory**. LME.
[ORIGIN from CLEAR *adjective* + STOREY: cf. Anglo-Latin *historia clara*.]
1 The upper part of the nave, choir, and transepts of any large church, containing a series of windows, clear of the roofs of the aisles, admitting light to the central parts of the building. LME. ▸**b** A similar feature in other buildings. E16.
2 A raised section of a railway carriage roof, containing small windows or ventilators. Chiefly *US*. L19.
– COMB.: **clerestory window**: with no crosspiece dividing the light.

clergess /ˈkləːdʒɛs/ *noun*. Long *arch*. *rare*. ME.
[ORIGIN Old French *clergesse* fem. of *clerc*: see CLERK *noun*, -ESS[1].]
†**1** A learned woman. Only in ME.
2 A female member of a religious order. LME.

clergy /ˈkləːdʒi/ *noun*. ME.
[ORIGIN Partly from Old French & mod. French *clergé* from ecclesiastical Latin *clericatus*, from *clericus* (see CLERK, -ATE[1]); partly from Old French & mod. French *clergie*, from *clerc* CLERK *noun* + *-ie* -Y[3], infl. by *clergé*.]
▸ **I 1** Learning, scholarship. Long *obsolete* exc. in proverb *an ounce of mother-wit is worth a pound of clergy*. ME.
†**2** The state of being ordained to the Christian ministry; membership of a clerical order. ME–M16.
▸ **II** Treated as *sing*. & (usu.) *collect. pl*.
3 The body of all persons ordained to the Christian ministry. Opp. ***laity***. ME. ▸†**b** Any priestly body. LME–E18.

R. DAVIES Members of the clergy . . are expected to be moral exemplars.

4 In biblical translations and allusions [translating Greek *klēros*, *klērōn* (1 *Peter* 5:3)]: the body of all Christians. *arch*. LME.
– PHRASES: **benefit of clergy** *hist*. exemption from ordinary courts of law because of membership of the clergy or (later) literacy or scholarship; also (later), exemption from the sentence for certain first offences because of literacy. ***regular clergy***: see REGULAR *adjective*. ***secular clergy***: see SECULAR *adjective* 1. **without benefit of clergy** *joc*. without formal marriage etc.
– COMB.: **clergy house** a dwelling house for the member or members of clergy having (sole or subordinate) charge of a particular living; **clergyman** a man ordained to the Christian ministry, a priest; *esp*. an ordained minister of the Church of England; ***clergyman's sore throat***, ***clergyman's throat***, a chronic sore throat afflicting those who speak much in public; **clergywoman** †(**a**) a nun; a priestess; (**b**) (chiefly *joc*.) the wife of a clergyman; (**c**) a female minister of religion.
■ **clergiable** *adjective* (*hist*.) (of an offence etc.) admitting benefit of clergy M18.

cleric /ˈklɛrɪk/ *adjective* & *noun*. E17.
[ORIGIN ecclesiastical Latin *clericus* from ecclesiastical Greek *klērikos* belonging to the Christian ministerial order, from *klēros* lot, heritage (as in *Acts* 1:17).]
▸ **A** *adjective*. Of or pertaining to the clergy, clerical. Now *rare*. E17.
▸ **B** *noun*. A person ordained to the Christian ministry. Now also, a priest or religious leader in any religion. E17.

clerical /ˈklɛrɪk(ə)l/ *adjective* & *noun*. L15.
[ORIGIN ecclesiastical Latin *clericalis*, formed as CLERIC: see -AL[1].]
▸ **A** *adjective*. **1** Orig., learned. Later *gen*., of, pertaining to, or characteristic of (a member of) the clergy. L15.
clerical collar an upright white collar, fastening at the back, worn by members of the clergy.
2 Of or pertaining to a clerk or clerks; involving copying out. L18.
clerical error an error made in copying or writing out.
▸ **B** *noun*. **1** A cleric. E17.
2 In *pl*. Clerical clothes. M19.
■ **clericalism** *noun* clerical principles, rule, or influence M19. **clericalist** *noun* an adherent of clericalism M19. **cleri'cality** *noun* (**a**) *rare* a clerical trait; (**b**) clerical quality or condition: M17. **clericali'zation** *noun* the action of clericalizing E20. **clericalize** *verb trans*. make clerical, subject to clerical rule or influence L19. **clerically** *adverb* L18.

clerico- /ˈklɛrɪkəʊ/ *combining form*. E19.
[ORIGIN formed as CLERIC: see -O-.]
Clerically, clerical and —, as ***clerico-liberal***, ***clerico-political*** adjectives.

clerid /ˈklɛrɪd/ *noun* & *adjective*. L19.
[ORIGIN mod. Latin *Cleridae* (see below), from *Clerus* genus name from Greek *klēros*: see -ID[3].]
(A beetle) of the family Cleridae.

clerihew /ˈklɛrɪhjuː/ *noun*. E20.
[ORIGIN Edmund *Clerihew* Bentley (1875–1956), English writer who devised the form.]
A short witty, comic, or nonsensical verse, usu. in two rhyming couplets with lines of unequal length.

clerisy /ˈklɛrɪsi/ *noun*. E19.
[ORIGIN App. after German *Klerisei*, formed as CLERIC.]
A distinct class of learned or literary persons.

clerk /klɑːk/ *noun* & *verb*. OE.
[ORIGIN formed as CLERIC, reinforced by Old French & mod. French *clerc* from same source.]
▸ **A** *noun*. **1** A man ordained to the Christian ministry, formerly esp. in minor orders, now (*arch*. or LAW) in holy orders. OE. ▸**b** A lay officer of a cathedral, parish church, university college chapel, etc. M16.
2 A literate person, a scholar. Now *arch*. or *hist*. OE.
3 An officer in charge of records etc.; the secretary or agent of a town council, corporation, court, etc.; *spec*. a senior official in Parliament. E16.
4 A person employed in a bank, office, shop, etc., to make entries, copy letters, keep accounts and files, etc. Also, a person being trained in law. E16.
5 An assistant in a shop or hotel. *N. Amer*. L18.
– PHRASES: ***articled clerk***: see ARTICLE *verb* 4. ***Clerk of the Closet***: see CLOSET *noun* 2. **clerk of the course** the judges' secretary etc. in horse-racing or motor racing. ***Clerk of the Irons***: see IRON *noun*. ***Clerk of the Pells***: see PELL *noun*[1]. **Clerk of the Scales** the official who weighs jockeys etc. **clerk of the works**, **clerk of works** an overseer of building works etc. ***criminous clerk***: see CRIMINOUS 3. ***Deputy Clerk Register***: see REGISTER *noun*[1]. ***lay clerk***: see LAY *adjective*. ***Lord Clerk Register***: see REGISTER *noun*[1]. ***Lord Justice Clerk***: see LORD *noun*. ***parish clerk***: see PARISH *noun*. ***reading clerk***: see READING *ppl adjective*[1]. ***St Nicholas' clerk***, ***St Nicholas's clerk***: see SAINT *noun* & *adjective*. ***tally clerk***: see TALLY *noun*[1]. ***town clerk***: see TOWN *noun*. ***treason of the clerks***: see TREASON *noun*.
▸ **B** *verb intrans*. Act or work as a clerk. M16.
■ **clerkage** *noun* (*rare*) the work of a clerk; clerks collectively: M16. **clerkdom** *noun* the status or function of a clerk; clerks as a class: M19. **clerkess** *noun* (*Scot*.) a female clerk E20. **clerkhood** *noun* the status or position of a clerk ME. **clerkish** *adjective* resembling or characteristic of a clerk M19. †**clerklike** *adverb* & *adjective* (*rare*) (**a**) *adverb* in the manner of a clerk; (**b**) *adjective* resembling (that of) a clerk: E17–E18.

clerkly /ˈklɑːkli/ *adjective*. LME.
[ORIGIN from CLERK *noun* + -LY[1], after CLERKLY *adverb*.]
1 Scholarly, learned. *arch*. LME.
2 Of or pertaining to the clergy, clerical. L15.
3 Of or pertaining to fine handwriting; skilled in copying. E19.
4 Of or pertaining to an office clerk. M19.
■ **clerkliness** *noun* M16.

clerkly /ˈklɑːkli/ *adverb*. LME.
[ORIGIN from CLERK *noun* + -LY[2], after late Latin *clericaliter*.]
1 In a scholarly way, learnedly. *arch*. LME. ▸†**b** Cleverly, artfully. L16–E17.
2 In fine handwriting, in the manner of a good copyist. E19.

clerkship /ˈklɑːkʃɪp/ *noun*. ME.
[ORIGIN from CLERK *noun* + -SHIP.]
†**1** The clergy. *rare*. Only in ME.
2 The status or position of a clerk. L15.
3 Writing by hand; style of handwriting, skilled copying. M16.
4 Scholarship, learning. *arch*. M17.

clerodendrum /klɪərəˈdɛndrəm/ *noun*. Also **-dron** /-dr(ə)n/. E19.
[ORIGIN mod. Latin, from Greek *klēros* chance, lot + *dendron* tree: prob. so called because of the variable medicinal properties of the genus.]
A shrub or small tree of the African and Asian genus *Clerodendrum*, of the verbena family, with fragrant showy flowers.

cleromancy /ˈklɪərəmansi/ *noun*. Now *rare*. E17.
[ORIGIN from Greek *klēros* chance, lot + -MANCY.]
Divination by lots.

cleruch /ˈklɪərʊk/ *noun*. Also **k-**. M19.
[ORIGIN Greek *klēroukhos* allottee, from *klēros* chance, lot + *ekhein* have, hold.]
GREEK HISTORY. An Athenian granted land in a foreign state but retaining rights as a citizen at home.
■ **cleruchy** *noun* the allotment of land among cleruchs, a body of cleruchs M19.

cletch /klɛtʃ/ *noun*. *dial*. Also **clatch** /klatʃ/. L17.
[ORIGIN from CLECK *verb*: cf. *bake*, *batch*, etc. Cf. CLUTCH *noun*[2].]
A clutch of eggs, chicks, etc.; *transf*. (usu. *derog*.) a family.

clethra /ˈkliːθrə, ˈklɛθrə/ *noun*. L18.
[ORIGIN mod. Latin from Greek *klēthra* alder, which it resembles in foliage.]
A tree or shrub of the genus *Clethra*, native to America and eastern Asia, with racemes of white or pink flowers. Cf. ***pepperbush*** s.v. PEPPER *noun*.

cleuch /kl(j)uːx/ *noun*. *Scot*. Also **-gh**. ME.
[ORIGIN Var. of CLOUGH *noun*[1].]
1 A steep-sided ravine (= CLOUGH *noun*[1]). Freq. in place names as ***Buccleuch*** etc. ME.
2 The precipitous side of a ravine; a steep descent. E16.

cleuk *noun* see CLUTCH *noun*[1].

cleve /kliːv/ *noun*. Long *obsolete* exc. *dial*. Also **cleeve**. ME.
[ORIGIN Var. of CLIFF *noun* after Old English pls. *cleofu*, *cleofum*.]
1 A cliff. ME.
2 A steep slope, a steep hillside. ME.

cleveite /ˈkliːvʌɪt/ *noun*. L19.
[ORIGIN from Per T. *Cleve* (1840–1905), Swedish chemist + -ITE[1].]
MINERALOGY. A variety of uraninite containing rare earth elements.

Cleveland bay /ˌkliːvlənd ˌbeɪ/ *noun phr*. L18.
[ORIGIN from *Cleveland*, a former county of England + BAY *noun*[6].]
A bay horse with black legs of a strong breed originating in the north of England.

clever /ˈklɛvə/ *adjective* & *adverb*. Also (*dial*.) **cliver** /ˈklɪvə/. ME.
[ORIGIN Perh. rel. to CLEAVE *verb*[2]. Cf. also Low German *klöver*, *klever*, Middle Dutch *klever* sprightly, brisk, smart.]
▸ **A** *adjective*. †**1** Quick or ready to catch hold. *rare*. Only in ME.
2 Manually dexterous; deft; possessing physical skill. L16.
3 Nimble, agile, active; in good health. Now *dial*. or *colloq*. L17.

C. NEWLAND But are you all right? You don't sound too clever, luv.

4 Lithe, clean-limbed; handsome. Now *dial*. L17.
5 Possessing mental skill or agility; talented; quick-witted. E18.
too clever by half: see HALF *noun*.
6 Of a thing or action: showing physical or mental skill or agility; ingenious. E18.
7 Handy; neat and convenient; well made. *obsolete* exc. *Canad. dial*. E18.

8 Pleasing, nice. Now *dial. & US colloq.* M18.
– COMB.: **clever-clever** *adjective* ostentatiously clever, eagerly seeking to appear clever; **clever clogs**, **clever Dick**, **clever sticks** *colloq.* a (would-be) smart and knowing person, a know-all.
▸ **B** *adverb.* Cleverly. Chiefly *colloq. & dial.* M17.
box clever: see BOX *verb*².
■ **clevе'rality** *noun* (*Scot. & N. English*) cleverness M18. **cleverish** *adjective* fairly clever E19. **cleverly** *adverb* (*a*) in a clever manner; (*b*) (now *dial. & US*) fully, completely: L17. **cleverness** *noun* the state or quality of being clever M18.

clevis /ˈklɛvɪs/ *noun.* L16.
[ORIGIN Perh. rel. to CLEAVE *verb*¹.]
A U-shaped piece of metal at the end of a beam for attaching tackle etc.; a connection in which a bolt holds one part that fits between the forked ends of another.

clew /kluː/ *noun.* See also CLUE *noun.*
[ORIGIN Old English *cliwen*, *cleowen* = Middle Low German, Dutch *kluwen*, from base also of Old High German *kliuwa*, *kliuwi* ball, sphere, prob. ult. rel. to CLAW *noun*¹.]
†**1** A globular body; a rounded mass. OE–L18. ▸**b** A round bunch or cluster. E17–E18.
2 A ball of thread or yarn. *arch.* OE.
3 *spec.* ▸**a** A ball of yarn etc. used to trace a path through a maze (as in the Greek myth of Theseus in the Labyrinth); a thing which guides through perplexity, a difficult investigation, an intricate structure, etc. LME. ▸**b** = CLUE *noun* 4a. E18.
4 The mythological thread of life spun by the Fates. E17.
5 NAUTICAL. The lower or after corner of a sail. (Earlier as CLUE *noun* 2.) E17.
6 NAUTICAL. The series of cords by which a hammock is suspended. M18.
– COMB.: **clew-garnet** NAUTICAL a tackle to clew up the courses or lower square sails in furling; **clew-line** NAUTICAL a tackle connecting the clew of a sail to the upper yard or mast; occas. = ***clew-garnet*** above.

clew /kluː/ *verb.* See also CLUE *verb.* LME.
[ORIGIN from the noun.]
1 *verb trans.* Coil *up* into a ball. LME.
2 *verb trans.* Point *out* or trace (as) by a clew or clue. *rare.* E17.
3 *verb trans. & intrans.* NAUTICAL. Draw the lower ends of (a sail) *up* to the upper yard or mast ready for furling; let *down* (a sail) by clews in unfurling. M18.

clianthus /klʌɪˈanθəs/ *noun.* M19.
[ORIGIN mod. Latin, app. from Greek *klei-*, *kleos* glory + *anthos* flower.]
An Australasian leguminous plant of the genus *Clianthus*, which includes the kaka-beak, *C. puniceus*, and Sturt's desert pea, *C. formosus*. Also called ***glory pea***.

cliché /ˈkliːʃeɪ/ *noun.* M19.
[ORIGIN French, use as noun of pa. pple of *clicher* to stereotype, perh. of imit. origin.]
1 *hist.* A metal stereotype or electrotype block. M19.
2 A stereotyped expression, a hackneyed phrase or opinion; a stereotyped character, style, etc. L19.

K. LETTE He was the complete two-legged Australian male cliché—bronzed, blonde, blue-eyed, biceps rippling. A. GARLAND Better the devil you know is a cliché I now despise.

■ **clichéd**, **cliché'd** *adjective* hackneyed, full of clichés E20.

click /klɪk/ *noun*¹. E17.
[ORIGIN Imit.: cf. Old French *clique* tick of clock, Dutch *klik* tick.]
1 A slight sharp sound of concussion as made by the latch of a door dropping, the impact of two billiard balls, etc. Also (*dial.*), a quick light blow, a tap. E17. ▸**b** *spec.* (Such a sound made by) a touching of a horse's fore and hind shoes, through overreaching. L19. ▸**c** RADIO. In *pl.* Atmospherics of short duration. E20.
2 A mechanism making this noise, e.g. the catch of a ratchet wheel etc. M18.
3 A sharp non-vocal suction, used as a speech sound in certain (chiefly African) languages. E19.
4 COMPUTING. An act of pressing one of the buttons on a mouse. L20.
– COMB.: **click beetle** a beetle of the large family Elateridae, members of which are able to spring up with a clicking sound when lying on their backs; **click-clack** *noun & verb intrans.* (make) a repeated sound like a click; **click language**: in which clicks are used; **clickstream** COMPUTING a series of mouse clicks made by a user while accessing the Internet, esp. as monitored to assess a person's interests for marketing purposes.
■ **clicky** *adjective* containing many clicks L19.

click /klɪk/ *noun*². E19.
[ORIGIN Anglicized from French CLIQUE.]
= CLIQUE.

click /klɪk/ *noun*³. E19.
[ORIGIN Var. of CLEEK *noun.*]
1 In full ***click-hook***. A large hook or crook. E19.
2 A jerk with a hook or crook. L19.
3 A manoeuvre in wrestling, whereby the opponent's foot is knocked sharply off the ground. Now *rare.* L19.

click /klɪk/ *verb*¹. L16.
[ORIGIN Imit.: cf. CLICK *noun*¹.]
1 *verb trans. & intrans.* (Cause to) make a slight sharp concussive sound; move with such a click; operate (a camera etc.) with a click. L16. ▸**b** *verb intrans.* Of a horse: overreach and make a click by the touching of fore and hind shoes. E18. ▸**c** *verb trans. & intrans.* COMPUTING. Press (one of the buttons on a mouse); select (an item on a screen, in a menu, etc.) by pressing a mouse button. L20.

D. H. LAWRENCE She heard a latch click. E. BOWEN She . . clicked open her bag. G. ORWELL The cage door had clicked shut. J. KOSINSKI The soldiers clicked their heels. B. HINES Clicking his tongue on the roof of his mouth.

2 *verb intrans. fig.* ▸**a** Be successful; secure one's object; be understood; become instantly friendly, strike up a rapport. (Foll. by *with.*) *slang.* E20. ▸**b** Be chosen *for*, come in *for. military slang.* E20. ▸**c** Become pregnant. *colloq.* M20. ▸**d** Fall into context; begin to revive a memory. *colloq.* M20.

a C. LAMBERT Attractive girls with whom he ultimately and triumphantly 'clicks'. D. CUSACK We don't seem to click. **d** A. BURGESS Then the name clicked, because somebody in the town had talked about Everett.

■ **clickable** *adjective* L20.

click /klɪk/ *verb*² *trans.* Chiefly *dial.* L17.
[ORIGIN Var. of CLEEK *verb.*]
Clutch; grasp suddenly, firmly, or eagerly; snatch (*up* etc.).

clicker /ˈklɪkə/ *noun.* L17.
[ORIGIN from CLICK *verb*¹ or *verb*² + -ER¹.]
1 A shopkeeper's (orig. a shoemaker's) tout. L17.
2 A foreman shoemaker who cuts out the leather. L17.
3 A compositor in charge of a companionship who distributes the copy etc. E19.

clicket /ˈklɪkɪt/ *noun. obsolete* exc. *dial.* LME.
[ORIGIN Old French & mod. French *cliquet*, from Old French *clique* door latch: see -ET¹.]
1 The latch of a door or gate. LME.
†**2** A latchkey. LME–L16.
†**3** A device for making a clicking sound, a clapper, a rattle. LME–M18.

clicket /ˈklɪkɪt/ *verb.* LME.
[ORIGIN from the noun: cf. French *cliqueter*. Branch II may be a different word.]
▸ **I 1** *verb trans.* Fasten with a latch, lock. *obsolete* exc. *dial.* LME.
2 *verb intrans.* Chatter. L16.
3 *verb intrans.* Make a light or repeated clicking sound. E20.
▸ **II 4** *verb intrans.* Of a fox: be in heat; copulate. L16.

clickety-clack /klɪkətɪˈklak/ *noun, interjection, & verb.* Also **-click** /-ˈklɪk/. L19.
[ORIGIN Imit.]
▸ **A** *noun & interjection.* (Repr.) a repeated clicking sound as of shoe heels on a hard surface. L19.
▸ **B** *verb intrans.* Move with a sound of this kind. M20.

cliency /ˈklʌɪənsi/ *noun. rare.* M17.
[ORIGIN Late Latin *clientia*, formed as CLIENT.]
= CLIENTSHIP.

client /ˈklʌɪənt/ *noun.* LME.
[ORIGIN Latin *client-*, *-ens*, earlier *cluens* use as noun of pres. pple of *cluere*, *cluere* hear, listen, obey: see -ENT.]
▸ **I 1** A person who is under the protection and patronage of another; a dependant, a hanger-on. *arch.* LME.
2 ROMAN HISTORY. A plebeian under the protection of a patrician. Cf. PATRON *noun* 4C. M16.
▸ **II 3** A person who employs the services of a legal adviser; a person whose cause an advocate pleads. LME.
4 *gen.* A person using the services of any professional; a customer. E17. ▸**b** A person assisted by a social worker etc. L19.

Guardian Licensed dealers often charge their clients a commission fee of 10 per cent or more.

▸ **III 5** COMPUTING. (In a network) a desktop computer or workstation that is capable of obtaining information and applications from a server. L20. ▸**b** More fully *client application*, *program*. A program that is capable of obtaining a service provided by another program. L20.
– COMB.: **client state**, **client nation**, etc.: dependent upon a larger one for trade, military aid, etc.
■ **clientage** *noun* (*a*) a body of clients; (*b*) the relation of client to patron: M17. **cliental** *adjective* (*rare*) of or pertaining to a client or clients M17. **clientry** *noun* = CLIENTAGE L16. **clientship** *noun* the state or relation of a client M17.

clientele /kliːɒnˈtɛl, *foreign* kliɑ̃tɛl/ *noun.* Also **-èle**. M16.
[ORIGIN Orig. from Latin *clientela*, formed as CLIENT Later from French *clientèle* from Latin.]
†**1** Clientship; patronage. M16–L19.
2 A body of clients, a following; the customers (of a shop); the patrons (of a theatre etc.); persons seeking the professional advice of a lawyer, architect, etc. L16.

clientelism /kliːɒnˈtɛlɪz(ə)m/ *noun.* Orig. in Italian form ***clientelismo*** /kliɛntiˈlizmo/. M20.
[ORIGIN Italian *clientelismo* patronage system.]
A social order which depends upon relations of patronage, esp. as a political approach which emphasizes or exploits such relations.
■ **cliente'listic** *adjective* M20.

Clifden nonpareil /klɪfd(ə)n ˈnɒnpərɛl/ *noun phr.* M18.
[ORIGIN from †*Clifden* (now *Cliveden*), a village in Buckinghamshire, central England + NONPAREIL.]
A large Eurasian noctuid moth, *Catocala fraxini*, with blue and black hindwings.

cliff /klɪf/ *noun.*
[ORIGIN Old English *clif* = Old Saxon (Dutch) *klif*, Old High German *klep*, Old Norse *klif*, from Germanic. Cf. CLEVE.]
1 A steep rock face, now *esp.* one facing the sea. OE.
†**2** A shore, a coast. OE–E17.
3 A steep slope, a steep hillside. Now *dial.* ME.
4 The strata of rock lying above or between coal seams. L17.
– COMB.: **cliffhanger** a serial film in which each episode ends in a desperate situation; a story etc. with the outcome excitingly uncertain; **cliffhanging** *adjective* full of suspense; **cliff swallow** a square-tailed swallow of N. and S. America, *Hirundo pyrrhonota*, which builds a jar-shaped nest of mud and straw; also called ***mud swallow***.
■ **clifflike** *adjective* resembling (that of) a cliff, steep and rocky M19. **cliffy** *adjective* having cliffs, craggy M16.

clift /klɪft/ *noun*¹. Now *dial.* LME.
[ORIGIN Var. of CLIFF, by assoc. with *clift* CLEFT *noun.*]
A cliff.
■ **clifty** *adjective* cliffy L16.

clift *noun*² var. of CLEFT *noun.*

climacteric /klʌɪˈmakt(ə)rɪk, klʌɪmakˈtɛrɪk/ *adjective & noun.* M16.
[ORIGIN French *climactérique* or Latin *climactericus*, from Greek *klimaktērikos*, from *klimaktēr* critical period, from *klimax*, *-mak-*: see CLIMAX, -IC.]
▸ **A** *adjective.* **1** Pertaining to or constituting a critical period in human life; critical, fatal. M16. ▸**b** MEDICINE. Occurring at or characteristic of a period of life when (male) fertility and sexual activity are in decline; (in women) menopausal. E19.
2 = CLIMACTIC. L18.
▸ **B** *noun.* A supposedly critical stage in human life, esp. occurring at ages that are multiples of seven years; a critical period, point, or epoch. M17.
– PHRASES: **grand climacteric** (designating) the 63rd year of life, supposed to be specially critical.
■ †**climacter** *noun* = CLIMACTERIC *noun* E–M17. **climac'terical** *adjective* & †*noun* = CLIMACTERIC L16.

climactic /klʌɪˈmaktɪk/ *adjective.* L19.
[ORIGIN Irreg. from CLIMAX, prob. infl. by CLIMACTERIC.]
Of or pertaining to a climax or ascending series; of the nature of a climax.
■ **climactically** *adverb* L19.

climate /ˈklʌɪmət/ *noun & verb.* LME.
[ORIGIN Old French & mod. French *climat* or late Latin *clima*, *-mat-* from Greek *klima*, *-mat-* slope of ground, zone, region, from *klinein* to lean, slope.]
▸ **A** *noun.* †**1** A belt of the earth's surface contained between two parallels of latitude. LME–L18. ▸**b** Any region of the earth. L15–L18.
2 A region considered with reference to its atmospheric conditions or its weather. E17.
3 The prevailing atmospheric phenomena and conditions of temperature, humidity, wind, etc., (of a country or region). E17. ▸**b** *fig.* The mental, moral, etc., environment prevailing in a body of people in respect of opinion, some aspect of life, etc. M17.
continental climate: see CONTINENTAL *adjective.* ***MEDITERRANEAN climate***.
▸ **B** *verb.* †**1** *verb intrans.* Sojourn in a particular climate. *rare* (Shakes.). Only in E17.
2 *verb trans.* = ACCLIMATIZE. *US.* M19.
■ **climatal** *adjective* = CLIMATIC M19. **climatize** *verb trans.* = ACCLIMATIZE E19. †**climature** *noun* (*a*) *rare* a region; (*b*) meteorological condition resulting from latitude: E17–E19.

climatic /klʌɪˈmatɪk/ *adjective.* E19.
[ORIGIN from CLIMATE + -IC.]
Of or pertaining to climate.
■ **climatical** *adjective* (*rare*) M17. **climatically** *adverb* in relation to climate L19.

climatology /klʌɪməˈtɒlədʒi/ *noun.* M19.
[ORIGIN from CLIMATE + -OLOGY.]
The branch of physical science that deals with climate.
■ **climato'logical** *adjective* M19. **climato'logically** *adverb* L19. **climatologist** *noun* L19.

climax /ˈklʌɪmaks/ *noun & verb.* M16.
[ORIGIN Late Latin *climax* from Greek *klimax* ladder, climax.]
▸ **A** *noun.* **1** RHETORIC. (A figure characterized by) the arrangement of propositions or ideas in order of increasing importance, force, or effectiveness of expression. M16.
†**2** An ascending series or scale. M–L18.
3 The highest point reached; a peak of intensity or interest; a culmination. L18. ▸**b** *spec.* The last or highest term of a rhetorical climax. M19. ▸**c** ECOLOGY. The final stage in a succession, at which a plant community reaches a state of equilibrium; a community that has attained this state. Freq. *attrib.* E20. ▸**d** A sexual orgasm. E20.
▸ **B** *verb intrans. & trans.* Come or bring to a climax. M19.

C

climb /klʌɪm/ *noun*. L16.
[ORIGIN from the verb.]
An act of climbing; a place (to be) climbed; an ascent by climbing.
at the climb *criminals' slang* engaged as a cat burglar.

climb /klʌɪm/ *verb*. Pa. t. & pple **climbed**, (*arch.*) **clomb** /kləʊm/. Pa. t. also †**clamb**.
[ORIGIN Old English *climban* = Middle & mod. Low German, Middle Dutch & mod. Dutch *klimmen*, Old High German *klimban* (German *klimmen*), from West Germanic nasalized var. of base of CLEAVE *verb*[2] (orig. = hold fast).]
▸ **I** *verb intrans.* **1** Raise oneself by grasping or clinging, or by the aid of hands and feet; ascend a steep place. Freq. foll. by *up* (adverb & preposition). OE. ▸**b** Rise with gradual or continuous motion; (of the sun, an aeroplane, etc.) go upwards, move towards the zenith; *fig.* increase steadily. OE. ▸**c** *fig.* Rise in dignity, rank, or state by continued effort; ascend in the intellectual, moral, or social scale. ME. ▸**d** Of a plant: creep up by the aid of tendrils or by twining. L18.

A. RANSOME John climbed to the topmost branches of the old ash tree. J. FOWLES I climbed up the goat-paths. **b** SHAKES. *Cymb.* Let our crooked smokes climb to their nostrils. TENNYSON The slow moon climbs. C. P. SNOW The cost of living was climbing. **c** H. L. MENCKEN The Japanese . . have climbed into the first rank of World Powers.

climbing frame a structure, usu. of pipes joined together, for children to climb on. **climbing iron** a set of spikes attachable to a boot for climbing trees or ice slopes. ***climbing perch***: see PERCH *noun*[1]. ***climb on the bandwagon***: see ***bandwagon*** s.v. BAND *noun*[1]. **c** ***social climb***: see SOCIAL *adjective*. **d** ***climbing bittersweet***: see BITTERSWEET *noun* 4.

2 Slope upwards. ME.

E. J. HOWARD The road . . climbed with a steepness only made possible by its tortuous method.

3 Foll. by *down*: (**a**) (adverb & preposition) lower oneself (along) by grasping or clinging, or by the aid of hands and feet; (**b**) *fig.* (adverb) withdraw, esp. with ignominy, from a position taken up, abandon a declared position. ME.

G. B. SHAW Climbing down the pipe. R. MACAULAY Makeshift opportunists, backing out and climbing down.

▸ **II** *verb trans.* **4** Ascend or mount by climbing. ME.

BYRON We . . clomb the high hill. R. MACAULAY The rich fruit orchards that climbed the wooded hills. K. VONNEGUT To climb a few rungs of the ladder of culture.

climb the ladder: see LADDER *noun* 1b.

5 Attain or achieve by climbing. L16.

A. WELBY I've climbed the summit of some breezy hill.

– COMB.: **climbdown** a withdrawal, esp. with ignominy, from a position taken up; abandonment of a declared position.
■ **climbable** *adjective* M16. **climber** *noun* a person who or thing which climbs; *spec.* (*a*) a climbing plant; (***b***) *criminals' slang* a cat burglar; (***c***) *fig.* a person who continually seeks (esp. social) advancement (***social climber***: see SOCIAL *adjective*): LME.

clime /klʌɪm/ *noun*. Now chiefly *literary*. LME.
[ORIGIN Late Latin *clima*: see CLIMATE.]
1 A region, esp. considered with reference to its climatic conditions. Cf. CLIMATE *noun* 1b, 2. LME.
†**2** = CLIMATE *noun* 1. L15–L17.
3 = CLIMATE *noun* 3; *fig.* atmosphere. L16.

clinamen /klʌɪˈneɪmɛn/ *noun*. *literary*. Pl. **-mina** /-mɪnə/. L17.
[ORIGIN Latin.]
An inclination, a bias.

clinch /klɪn(t)ʃ/ *noun*. L16.
[ORIGIN Var. of CLENCH *noun*: cf. CLINCH *verb*.]
1 A thing which clutches, grips, or fixes fast; a grip, a hold. L16.
2 NAUTICAL. A method of fastening large ropes by a half hitch with the end seized back on its own part; that part of a rope which is clinched. E17.
3 A fastening in which the end of a nail or bolt is beaten back or flattened after passing through something; the point of a clinched nail; a clinched nail or bolt, a nail for clinching something (also ***clinch-nail***). M17.
4 A pun, a quibble; (= CLENCH *noun* 2). M17.
5 An act of clinching or riveting together; the clinching of an argument etc.; the state of being clinched. M19.
6 A struggle or scuffle at close quarters; BOXING a position of being too close for a full-arm blow, an act of holding after an exchange of blows. M19.
7 An embrace, esp. a passionate one. Orig. *US*. E20.

Daily Star Anna . . was caught in a locker-room clinch with her best pal's boyfriend.

clinch /klɪn(t)ʃ/ *verb*. L16.
[ORIGIN Var. of CLENCH *verb*, prob. by assim. to CLINK *verb*[2].]
1 *verb trans.* **a** Fix securely (as) with a nail, bolt, rivet, etc.; secure (a nail, rivet, etc.) by driving the point sideways when through. L16. ▸**b** *fig.* Make firm and sure (an argument, bargain, etc.); drive home; make conclusive, establish. E18.

b ANTHONY SMITH His earlier, considered, authenticated and definite wish clinched the matter.

†**2** *verb trans.* = CLENCH *verb* 2. E17–E19.
3 *verb trans.* NAUTICAL. Fasten (a rope) with a clinch. M18.
4 *verb intrans.* Grapple at close quarters; (of boxers) come too close for a full-arm blow. E19. ▸**b** Embrace. *colloq.* (orig. *US*). L19.
■ **clincher** *noun* a person who or thing which clinches; *esp.* a conclusive statement, argument, etc.; ***clincher-built*** = ***clinker-built*** s.v. CLINKER *noun*[1]: ME.

cline /klʌɪn/ *noun*. M20.
[ORIGIN from Greek *klinein* to lean, slope.]
1 BIOLOGY. A gradation in one or more characters within a species or other taxon. M20.
2 *gen.* A continuum with an infinite number of gradations. M20.
■ **clinal** *adjective* M20.

cling /klɪŋ/ *noun*. M17.
[ORIGIN from the verb.]
1 The act of clinging; adhesion, adherence. M17.
2 A clasp; an embrace. *rare*. M17.
3 = ***clingstone*** s.v. CLING *verb*. Also ***cling peach***. M19.

cling /klɪŋ/ *verb*. Pa. t. & pple **clung** /klʌŋ/.
[ORIGIN Old English *clingan*, corresp. to Middle Dutch *klingen* stick, adhere. Middle High German *klingen* climb, from Germanic, from base parallel to that of CLENCH *verb*.]
1 *verb intrans.* Adhere together in a stiff mass. Long *obsolete* exc. as passing into senses 3 & 5 in ***cling together***. OE.
2 *verb intrans.* Of an animal or vegetable body: shrink up, shrivel, wither. Now *dial.* OE. ▸**b** *verb trans.* Cause (an animal or vegetable body) to shrink up, shrivel, or wither. Now *dial.* M16.

b SHAKES. *Macb.* Upon the next tree shalt thou hang alive, Till famine cling thee.

3 *verb intrans.* Adhere or be attached (*to*) by stickiness, suction, grasping, embracing, etc.; be or remain close *to*, as if attached. ME. ▸**b** *fig.* Adhere or cleave *to* in affection, fellowship, sympathy, practice, or idea; remain (stubbornly) faithful *to*. L16.

DICKENS The fog clings so. D. H. LAWRENCE He caught her hand and clung to it. D. WELCH The wet shorts clung to our thighs. *fig.*: JOHN BROOKE Some of the abuse heaped upon her still clings to her name. **b** H. L. MENCKEN The lawyers and judges cling to the idea of equality before the law.

†**4** *verb trans.* Cause to cling, make fast. L16–L18.
5 *verb trans.* Cause to adhere or stick *together*. Now *dial.* E17.
– COMB.: **cling film** thin plastic film that adheres to surfaces, used esp. for wrapping and covering foods; **clingfish** (orig. *N. Amer.*) a small marine fish of the family Gobiesocidae, having a ventral sucker enabling it to adhere to rocks etc.; also called ***sea-sucker***; **clingstone**, **clingstone nectarine**, **clingstone peach** a kind of nectarine or peach in which the flesh is firmly attached to the stone when ripe.
■ **clinger** *noun* E16. **clinginess** *noun* the state or quality of being clingy L18. **clinging** *adjective* that clings, clingy L16. **clingingly** *adverb* M19. **clingy** *adjective* tending to cling; sticky, adhesive, tenacious: E18.

clinic /ˈklɪnɪk/ *noun*[1] & *adjective*. Now *rare* or *obsolete*. E17.
[ORIGIN Latin *clinicus* from Greek *klinikos*, from *klinē* bed: see -IC.]
▸ **A** *noun*. **1** A person who is confined to bed by sickness etc. E17.
2 ECCLESIASTICAL HISTORY. A person who defers baptism until the deathbed. M17.
▸ **B** *adjective*. Of or pertaining to the sickbed; *spec.* designating deathbed baptism, conversion, etc. (cf. CLINICAL *adjective* 2). E17.

clinic /ˈklɪnɪk/ *noun*[2]. M19.
[ORIGIN French *clinique* from Greek *klinikē* the clinical art.]
1 The teaching of medicine or surgery at the bedside of a sick person, esp. in a hospital. M19.
2 A private or specialized hospital; a place or an occasion for giving medical treatment or advice, esp. in a hospital and devoted to one topic. L19.
family-planning clinic, ***fracture clinic***, ***immunization clinic***, ***postnatal clinic***, etc.
3 A conference, class, short course, etc., on a particular subject or activity. Chiefly *N. Amer.* E20.
■ **clinician** /klɪˈnɪʃ(ə)n/ *noun* orig., a clinical investigator; now, a doctor having direct contact with and responsibility for patients: L19.

clinical /ˈklɪnɪk(ə)l/ *adjective*. L18.
[ORIGIN formed as CLINIC *noun*[1] & *adjective* + -AL[1].]
1 MEDICINE. Designating or pertaining to teaching given at the bedside of a sick person, esp. in a hospital, and (branches of) medicine involving the study or care of actual patients. L18.
clinical death: judged by direct observation of the individual's condition. **clinical medicine**: based on the observed symptoms. ***clinical*** THERMOMETER.
2 ECCLESIASTICAL. Administered at the sickbed to one likely to die. Cf. CLINIC *adjective*. M19.
3 Coldly detached and impersonal; objective, dispassionate. E20. ▸**b** Bare and functional, like a hospital. M20.
■ **clinically** *adverb* in a clinical manner; as regards clinical medicine, from the point of view of clinical medicine: M19.

clink /klɪŋk/ *noun*[1]. LME.
[ORIGIN from CLINK *verb*[1].]
1 A sharp abrupt ringing sound, as of small metallic bodies or glasses struck together. LME.
2 Assonance, jingle. *derog.* E18.
3 A smart sharp blow. *dial.* E18.
4 Money; hard cash. *Scot. colloq.* E18.

clink /klɪŋk/ *noun*[2]. *slang*. E16.
[ORIGIN Unknown: orig. applied to a prison in Southwark, London.]
A prison. Esp. in ***in clink***, ***in the clink***.

clink /klɪŋk/ *noun*[3]. L19.
[ORIGIN Unknown: cf. CLINK *verb*[3].]
An internal crack in a block of metal caused by uneven heating or cooling.

clink /klɪŋk/ *verb*[1]. ME.
[ORIGIN Prob. from Middle Dutch & mod. Dutch *klinken* sound, ring, tinkle, rel. to Middle Low German, Middle Dutch & mod. Dutch *klank* sound. Cf. CLANG, CLANK.]
1 *verb trans.* Cause to make a sharp abrupt ringing sound; strike together with such a clink. ME.
2 *verb intrans.* Move with or make a clink or clinks. LME.
3 *verb intrans.* Of words: jingle together; rhyme. E18.
4 *verb trans. & intrans.* Put or sit *down*, go *off*, put *on*, abruptly or smartly. *Scot.* E18.
■ **clinking** *ppl adjective & adverb* (***a***) *ppl adjective* that clinks; *slang* (exceedingly) good; (***b***) *adverb* (*slang*) exceedingly: M17.

clink /klɪŋk/ *verb*[2] *trans. Scot. & N. English*. LME.
[ORIGIN Var. of CLENCH *verb*.]
Rivet; fix or fasten with nails; secure (a nail, rivet, etc.).

clink /klɪŋk/ *verb*[3] *trans.* E20.
[ORIGIN Unknown: cf. CLINK *noun*[3].]
Cause (metal) to fracture internally.

†**clinkard**, **clinkart** *nouns* vars. of CLINKER *noun*[2].

clink-clank /ˈklɪŋk-klaŋk/ *noun & verb*. L18.
[ORIGIN from CLINK *noun*[1], *verb*[1] + CLANK.]
▸ **A** *noun*. A repeated clinking sound. L18.
▸ **B** *verb intrans.* Move with or make such a sound. E20.

clinker /ˈklɪŋkə/ *noun*[1]. ME.
[ORIGIN from CLINK *verb*[2] + -ER[1].]
1 A person who or thing which rivets or puts in nails; *fig.* a clinching argument etc. ME.
2 A clinched nail, a nail for clinching something. L19.
– COMB.: **clinker-built** *adjective* (of a boat) made with external planks which overlap downwards and are fastened with clinched nails.

clinker /ˈklɪŋkə/ *noun*[2]. Also †**-ard**, †**-art**. M17.
[ORIGIN Early mod. Dutch *klinckaerd* (now *klinker*), from *klinken* to ring: see CLINK *verb*[1].]
1 A very hard kind of brick employed as paving in the Netherlands. M17.
2 A brick the surface of which has vitrified, or a mass of bricks that has fused, by exposure to intense heat. M17.
3 (A piece of) stony residue from burnt coal, a furnace, etc.; slag. M18.
4 (A piece of) rough scoriaceous lava resembling furnace slag. M19.
■ **clinkery** *adjective* L19.

clinker /ˈklɪŋkə/ *noun*[3]. L17.
[ORIGIN from CLINK *verb*[1] + -ER[1].]
1 A person who or thing which clinks. L17.
2 A thing, animal, or person of the first quality; an excellent specimen. Cf. CLINKING *ppl adjective*. *slang*. M19.
3 A wrong musical note, a discord; an error in performance, a blunder. *N. Amer. slang*. M20.

clinkstone /ˈklɪŋkstəʊn/ *noun*. E19.
[ORIGIN German *Klingstein*, formed as CLINK *verb*[1] + STONE *noun*.]
A compact greyish-blue feldspathic rock having a metallic resonance when struck.

clino- /ˈklʌɪnəʊ/ *combining form* of Greek *klinein* to lean, slope; in MINERALOGY & CRYSTALLOGRAPHY usu. with the sense 'monoclinic': see -O-. Cf. KLINO-.
■ **clinochlore** *noun* a hexagonal variety of chlorite rich in magnesium and aluminium and usu. poor in iron M19. **clinoˈgraphic** *adjective* (***a***) (of a projection) oblique, such that no surface (esp. of a crystal) is projected as a line; (***b***) of a curve) representing gradient as a function of altitude: L19. **clinoˈpinacoid** *noun* the plane perpendicular to the axis of symmetry in the monoclinic system L19. **clinopyˈroxene** *noun* any monoclinic pyroxene E20.

clinoid /ˈklʌɪnɔɪd/ *adjective*. M18.
[ORIGIN from Greek *klinē* bed + -OID.]
ANATOMY. Resembling a bed; *spec.* designating four processes of the sphenoid bone surrounding the base of the pituitary gland.

clinometer /klʌɪˈnɒmɪtə, klɪ-/ *noun*. E19.
[ORIGIN from CLINO- + -METER.]
Any of various instruments for measuring inclination or elevation, esp. of sloping ground, strata, etc.

clinquant /ˈklɪŋk(ə)nt/ *adjective & noun*. L16.
[ORIGIN French, pres. pple of †*clinquer* ring, glitter, from Low German *klinken* CLINK *verb*[1]: see -ANT[1].]
▸ **A** *adjective*. Glittering with gold and silver; tinselled. L16.
▸ **B** *noun*. Imitation gold leaf; *fig.* literary or artistic tinsel; false glitter. L17.

clint /klɪnt/ *noun*. ME.
[ORIGIN Danish & Swedish *klint*, from Old Swedish *klinter* rock.]
A hard or flinty rock; *spec.* (GEOLOGY) any of the masses of rock left standing between fissures (grikes) in a limestone pavement; also occas., a grike.

■ **clinty** *adjective* consisting of or characterized by clints E16.

Clintonite /ˈklɪntənaɪt/ *noun & adjective*. L20.
[ORIGIN from *Clinton* (see below) + -ITE¹.]
▸ **A** *noun*. A supporter or adherent of President William J. D. Clinton (b. 1946), US President 1993–2000, or his policies.
▸ **B** *adjective*. Of or pertaining to Clintonites or Clinton's policies.
■ **Clinˈtonian** *adjective & noun* L20. **Clintonism** *noun* L20.

cliometrics /klʌɪəˈmɛtrɪks/ *noun*. M20.
[ORIGIN from *Clio*, the Muse of history + METRIC *noun*¹: see -ICS.]
A method of historical research making much use of statistical information and methods.
■ **cliometric** *adjective* M20. **cliometrician** /klʌɪəmɛˈtrɪʃ(ə)n/ *noun* a practitioner of cliometrics M20.

clioquinol /klʌɪə(ʊ)ˈkwɪnɒl/ *noun*. M20.
[ORIGIN from *Cl*, chemical symbol for chlorine + IO(DINE + QUINOL(INE.]
PHARMACOLOGY. A quinoline derivative that has been used as an antiseptic to treat intestinal amoebiasis, diarrhoea, and ear and skin infections; 5-chloro-8-hydroxy-7-iodoquinoline, C_9H_5NOClI.

clip /klɪp/ *noun*¹. LME.
[ORIGIN from CLIP *verb*².]
1 In *pl.* Shears, esp. for wool. LME.
2 A thing which is clipped or cut; a clipping; the whole quantity of wool shorn in any place or season. E19. ▸**b** An extract from a motion picture, a television programme, etc. M20.

> **b** *Sunday Times* The illustrative clip shown on the night featured a large Chinese family.

3 An act of clipping or shearing; a haircut. E19.
4 A smart blow or stroke. M19.

> J. FOWLES I felt like giving her a good clip over the earhole.

5 A rate of (esp. rapid) motion. M19.

> H. ALLEN He splashed at a sharp clip through the ford.

clip /klɪp/ *noun*². L15.
[ORIGIN from CLIP *verb*¹.]
1 A thing which clips or clasps; an instrument or device (usu. worked by a spring) that holds an object or objects fast or together, or that attaches to an object as a marker. L15. ▸**b** A linked set of cartridges for a firearm. E20. ▸**c** A piece of jewellery fastened by a clip. M20.
bicycle-clip, ***crocodile-clip***, ***hair-clip***, ***paper clip***, etc.
†**2** Embracing; an embrace. M16–L17.
– COMB.: **clipboard** a small board with a sprung clip for holding papers etc.

clip /klɪp/ *verb*¹. Infl. **-pp-**. Pa. t. & pple **clipped**, (*arch.*) **clipt**.
[ORIGIN Old English *clyppan* = Old Frisian *kleppa*, from West Germanic.]
1 *verb trans. & intrans.* Clasp with the arms, embrace, hug. *arch. & dial.* OE.
2 *verb trans.* Surround closely, encircle, encompass. *arch.* OE.

> W. COWPER Yon fair sea, That clips thy shores.

3 *verb trans. & intrans.* Grip tightly; fasten with a clip; fasten (a clip). OE.

> E. HEMINGWAY Their carbines were clipped to the frame of the bicycles. A. MACLEAN They clipped their parachute snap catches on to the overhead wire. *Which Computer?* The ribbon . . has guides that clip onto the print head.

– COMB.: **clip-on** *adjective* that attaches by a clip.

clip /klɪp/ *verb*². Infl. **-pp-**. Pa. t. & pple **clipped**, (*arch.*) **clipt**. ME.
[ORIGIN Old Norse *klippa*, prob. imit.: cf. Low German, Frisian *klippen*.]
1 *verb trans.* Cut or trim with scissors or shears; take away (part of the hair, wool, etc.) with scissors or shears (foll. by *off*). ME. ▸**b** Form or mark by so cutting or trimming. L17.

> W. GASS She'd be clipping the hedge. W. BOYD A neatly clipped pencil moustache. *fig.*: P. G. WODEHOUSE How your grandfather clipped six seconds off Roger Bannister's mile. **b** P. PEARCE Each alcove and archway clipped in the yew-trees.

clip the wings of trim the feathers of (a bird) so as to disable from flight; *fig.* check the aspirations of, prevent (a person) from acting.
2 *spec.* ▸**a** *verb trans. & intrans.* Shear (sheep); cut off (a sheep's fleece etc.); cut off (a person's hair), poll. ME. ▸**b** *verb trans. & intrans.* Pare the edges of (coinage). LME. ▸**c** *verb trans.* Cut out (an article, coupon, etc.) from a newspaper etc. Chiefly *N. Amer.* L19. ▸**d** *verb trans.* Remove a small piece of (a train or bus ticket) to show that it has been used. L19. ▸**e** *verb trans.* COMPUTING. Process (an image) so as to remove the parts outside a certain area. M20.
3 *verb trans.* & (now *dial.*) *intrans.* Cut short, diminish; *spec.* pronounce hurriedly and imperfectly or in a staccato fashion, omit (letters or syllables) from words. E16.

> CARLYLE Pfalz must be reinstated, though with territories much clipped. D. CUSACK A habit of clipping her sentences till they resemble explosive bullets rather than conversation.
> I. MURDOCH He had given her clipped answers, minimizing everything.

4 *verb intrans.* **a** Move the wings rapidly, fly rapidly. *arch.* E17. ▸**b** Move or run quickly. *US colloq.* M19.
5 *verb trans.* Hit smartly; strike against in passing. *colloq.* M19.

> *New Statesman* He had 'clipped him round the earhole'. *Daily Express* Tony definitely had to snatch up the filly to avoid clipping the winner's heels.

6 *verb trans.* Swindle; rob, steal. *slang* (orig. *US*). E20.
7 *verb trans.* Kill, esp. by shooting. *N. Amer. slang.* E20.
– COMB.: **clip art** (*a*) pre-printed illustrations designed to be cut out and used in artwork; (*b*) COMPUTING pre-drawn pictures and symbols that computer users can add to their documents, often provided with word-processing software and drawing packages; **clip joint** *slang* a nightclub etc. charging exorbitant prices.

clip-clop /ˈklɪpklɒp/ *noun & verb*. L19.
[ORIGIN Imit.]
▸ **A** *noun*. An abrupt alternating sound as of the beating of a horse's hoofs on a hard surface. L19.
▸ **B** *verb intrans.* Infl. **-pp-**. Move with or make such a sound. E20.
■ Also **clippety-clop** *noun* E20.

clipe *verb & noun* var. of CLYPE.

clipper /ˈklɪpə/ *noun*. ME.
[ORIGIN from CLIP *verb*² + -ER¹.]
1 A person who clips fleeces, hair, coinage, etc. ME.
2 An instrument for clipping; in *pl.*, shears, scissors. L16.
3 a A fast sailing ship, *esp.* one with raking bows and masts. E19. ▸**b** A fast horse. M19. ▸**c** A first-rate person or thing, an excellent specimen. *slang.* M19.
– COMB.: **clipper-built** *adjective* (of a sailing ship) built for speed, with raking bows and masts; **clipper ship** = sense 3a above.

clippie /ˈklɪpi/ *noun*. *colloq.* Also **clippy**. M20.
[ORIGIN from CLIP *verb*² + -IE, -Y⁶.]
A bus conductress.

clipping /ˈklɪpɪŋ/ *noun*. ME.
[ORIGIN from CLIP *verb*² + -ING¹.]
1 The action of CLIP *verb*². ME.
2 A piece clipped off; a paring; a shred of cloth etc.; (chiefly *N. Amer.*) = CUTTING *noun* 2C. ME.

clipping /ˈklɪpɪŋ/ *adjective*. L16.
[ORIGIN from CLIP *verb*² + -ING².]
1 That clips. L16.
2 First-rate, excellent. *slang.* M19.
■ **clippingly** *adverb* M19.

clippy *noun* var. of CLIPPIE.

clipt *verb*¹, *verb*² *pa. t. & pple*: see CLIP *verb*¹, *verb*².

clique /kliːk/ *noun*. See also CLICK *noun*². E18.
[ORIGIN Old French & mod. French, from *cliquer* make a noise, from Middle Dutch *klikken* CLICK *verb*¹.]
A small exclusive group; a coterie.
■ **cliquish** *adjective* resembling or suggestive of a clique or cliques; pettily exclusive: M19. **cliquishness** *noun* M19. **cliquism** *noun* the practice of forming cliques; petty exclusiveness: M19.

cliquey /ˈkliːki/ *adjective*. Also **cliquy**. M19.
[ORIGIN from CLIQUE + -Y¹.]
Characterized by cliques; cliquish.

clish-clash /ˈklɪʃklaʃ/ *noun & interjection*. L16.
[ORIGIN Redupl. of CLASH *noun*.]
1 *noun & interjection* (Repr.) the reciprocal or alternate clash of weapons. L16.
2 *noun*. Idle gossip. *Scot.* L17.

clish-ma-claver /klɪʃməˈkleɪvə/ *noun*. *Scot.* E18.
[ORIGIN from *clish-* in CLISH-CLASH + euphonic *-ma-* + CLAVER *noun*.]
Idle gossip.

clit /klɪt/ *noun*. *slang.* M20.
[ORIGIN Abbreviation.]
= CLITORIS.

C.Lit. *abbreviation*.
Companion of Literature.

clitch /klɪtʃ/ *verb*. *obsolete* exc. *dial.* See also CLUTCH *verb*.
[ORIGIN Old English *clyččan* from Germanic.]
†**1 a** *verb trans.* Crook, bend; close (the hand); clench (the fist). OE–L16. ▸**b** *verb intrans.* Crook, bend at a joint, crouch. Only in ME.
2 *verb trans.* Grasp tightly, clutch. LME.
3 *verb trans.* Make fast; stick together. LME.

clitellum /klʌɪˈtɛləm/ *noun*. Pl. **-lla** /-lə/. M19.
[ORIGIN mod. Latin from Latin *clitellae* pl., packsaddle.]
ZOOLOGY. A raised band encircling the body of oligochaete worms and some leeches, made up of reproductive segments.
■ **clitellar** *adjective* L19.

clitic /ˈklɪtɪk/ *noun & adjective*. M20.
[ORIGIN from EN)CLITIC, PRO)CLITIC.]
GRAMMAR. = ENCLITIC, PROCLITIC.

clitoris /ˈklɪt(ə)rɪs/ *noun*. E17.
[ORIGIN mod. Latin from Greek *kleitoris*.]
A small erectile part of the female genitals in mammals and some other vertebrates.
■ **clitoral**, **cliˈtorial** *adjectives* M20. **clitoriˈdectomy** *noun* (an instance of) surgical removal of the clitoris M19.

clitter /ˈklɪtə/ *verb & noun*. E16.
[ORIGIN Imit.: cf. CLATTER *noun*, *verb*.]
▸ **A** *verb*. †**1** *verb intrans.* Chatter. *rare.* E16–M19.
2 *verb trans. & intrans.* (Cause to) make a thin vibratory rattling sound. M16.
▸ **B** *noun*. A thin vibratory rattling sound. L19.

clitter-clatter /ˈklɪtəklatə/ *noun*. M16.
[ORIGIN Redupl. of CLATTER *noun*.]
A light or repeated clatter; garrulous talk, idle gossip.

clivers *noun* var. of CLEAVERS.

clivia /ˈklʌɪvɪə/ *noun*. Also **-vea**. E19.
[ORIGIN mod. Latin, from *Clive*, maiden name of Charlotte, Duchess of Northumberland (1787–1866): see -IA¹.]
A southern African amaryllid of the genus *Clivia*, with orange, red, or yellow flowers. Also called ***Kaffir lily***. Cf. NATAL ***lily***.

Cllr *abbreviation*.
Councillor.

clo /kləʊ/ *noun*. Orig. *US*. Pl. same. M20.
[ORIGIN from CLO(THING. Cf. TOG *noun* 3.]
A unit expressing the heat-retaining power of clothing material.

clo' /kləʊ/ *noun pl. arch. colloq.* M19.
[ORIGIN Abbreviation.]
Clothes. Esp. in ***old clo'***.

cloaca /kləʊˈeɪkə/ *noun*. Pl. **-cae** /-siː, -kiː/, **-cas**. L16.
[ORIGIN Latin *cloaca*, *cluaca* rel. to *cluere* cleanse.]
1 An underground conduit for drainage, a sewer. Also, a water closet. L16.

> *fig.*: CARLYLE That tremendous Cloaca of Pauperism.

2 ZOOLOGY. A common cavity for the release of digestive and urogenital products in birds, reptiles, amphibians, most fish, and monotremes. M19.
■ **cloacal** *adjective* M17.

cloak /kləʊk/ *noun & verb*. Also (*arch.*) **cloke**. ME.
[ORIGIN Old French *cloke*, *cloque*, dial. var. of *cloche* (i) bell, (ii) cloak, from medieval Latin *clocca*: cf. CLOCK *noun*¹.]
▸ **A** *noun*. **1** A loose usu. sleeveless outdoor garment. ME. ▸**b** *fig.* A thing which covers over and conceals; a pretext; a pretence; a covering. E16.

> **b** R. W. EMERSON Tucking up . . the ground under a cloak of snow. E. WAUGH She pretends to be a painter, but you have only to look at her work to realise it is a cloak for other activities.

Inverness cloak: see INVERNESS 2. **b** ***Plymouth cloak***: see PLYMOUTH 1.
†**2** An academic or clerical gown, *esp.* a Geneva gown. M17–E18.
3 In *pl.* = ***cloakroom*** (b) below. M20.
– COMB.: **cloak-and-dagger** *adjective* [translating French *de cape et d'épée*] involving or characteristic of plot and intrigue, esp. espionage; **cloak-and-sword** *adjective* [translating Spanish (*comedia*) *de capa y espada*] involving or characteristic of fighting and romance; †**cloak-bag** a bag for a cloak or other clothes; a valise; **cloakroom** (*a*) a room in which to leave cloaks, coats, hats, etc., or luggage; (*b*) *euphem.* a lavatory; a room containing a number of lavatories.
▸ **B** *verb*. **1** *verb trans.* Cover with or wrap in a cloak; cover over, conceal, disguise. LME.
2 *verb intrans.* Put on a cloak; *fig.* dissemble. L16.
■ **cloaking** *noun* (*a*) the action or an act of wrapping someone or something in a cloak; (an act of) concealment; (*b*) (a) material for making cloaks: E16. **cloakless** *adjective* L16.

cloam /kləʊm/ *noun & adjective*. *obsolete* exc. *dial.*
[ORIGIN Old English *clām* = Middle Dutch *cleem* potter's clay, from West Germanic deriv. of Germanic base repr. also by CLAY *noun*, CLEAM, CLEAVE *verb*², CLIMB *verb*.]
▸ **A** *noun*. Orig. *gen.*, mud, clay. Later *spec.*, earthenware, potter's clay. OE.
▸ **B** *adjective*. Earthenware. OE.

†**cloath** *verb* var. of CLOTHE.

†**cloaths** *noun pl.* var. of CLOTHES.

clobber /ˈklɒbə/ *noun*¹ & *verb*¹. M19.
[ORIGIN Unknown.]
▸ **A** *noun*. A black paste used by cobblers to fill up and conceal cracks in leather. M19.
▸ **B** *verb trans.* **1** Patch *up*; cobble. M19.
2 Add enamelled decoration to (porcelain, esp. blue-and-white). L19.

clobber /ˈklɒbə/ *noun*² & *verb*². *slang.* L19.
[ORIGIN Unknown.]
▸ **A** *noun*. Clothing; gear, equipment. L19.
▸ **B** *verb trans.* Dress (oneself). Freq. foll. by *up*. Chiefly as ***clobbered*** *ppl adjective*. L19.

clobber /ˈklɒbə/ *verb*³ *trans.* *slang.* M20.
[ORIGIN Unknown.]
Hit, thrash; defeat; criticize severely.

clobiosh *noun* var. of KLABERJASS.

clochard /klɔʃaːr/ *noun*. Pl. pronounced same. M20.
[ORIGIN French, from *clocher* to limp.]
In France: a beggar, a vagrant.

C

cloche /klɒʃ, kləʊʃ/ *noun*. L19.
[ORIGIN French = bell: see CLOAK.]
1 A bell glass; a small translucent cover for forcing or protecting outdoor plants. L19.
2 In full ***cloche hat***. A woman's close-fitting bell-shaped hat. E20.

clocher /ˈkləʊʃə/ *noun*. LME.
[ORIGIN Anglo-Norman *clocher*, Old French *clochier*, (also mod.) *clocher*, from *cloche* bell (see CLOAK) + *-er* -ER².]
A bell tower; a belfry.

clock /klɒk/ *noun*¹. LME.
[ORIGIN Middle Low German, Middle Dutch *klocke* (Low German, Dutch *klok*), corresp. to Old English *clucge*, Old Frisian *klokke*, Old High German *glocka* (German *Glocke* bell), Old Norse *klokka*, *klucca*, from Germanic from medieval Latin *clocca*: cf. CLOAK.]
†**1** Orig., a bell. Later, the gong of a striking watch. LME–E18.
2 An instrument for indicating or measuring time, usu. utilizing the motion of wheels controlled by periodically wound-up springs or weights or by electricity etc., or (now) utilizing vibrating atoms, piezoelectric crystals, etc. to record and show hours, minutes, etc., by hands on a dial or by displayed figures. LME. ▸**b** (Usu. **C-**.) *The* constellation Horologium. M19.
3 A watch; *esp.* a stopwatch. Now *colloq.* M16.
†**4** The hour as struck by the clock. E17–M18.
5 The downy seed head of a dandelion etc. M19.
6 The human face. *slang*. E20. ▸**b** A punch (in the face). *slang*. M20.
7 A dial indicating pressure, consumption, etc.; *esp.* a taximeter, a speedometer, an odometer. *colloq.* M20.
8 COMPUTING. An electronic device, usu. a stable oscillator, used to initiate actions within, and to synchronize, sequential logic circuits. M20.
– PHRASES: ***Act of Parliament clock***: see PARLIAMENT *noun*. ***against the clock***: see AGAINST *preposition* 1. ***astronomical clock***: see ASTRONOMICAL 1. ***atomic clock***. **beat the clock** complete a task before a stated time. ***biological clock***. ***by Shrewsbury clock***: see SHREWSBURY 1. ***digital clock***: see DIGITAL *adjective* 1. ***French clock***: see FRENCH *adjective*. ***German clock***: see GERMAN *adjective*¹. **hold the clock on** ascertain the time taken by. ***Jack of the clock***: see JACK *noun*¹ 2. ***journeyman clock***: see JOURNEYMAN 3. ***master clock***: see MASTER *noun*¹ & *adjective*. ***musical clock***: see MUSICAL *adjective*. ***night clock***: see NIGHT *noun*. **O'CLOCK**. ***of the clock***: see OF *preposition*. ***punch the clock***: see PUNCH *verb*. **put the clock back** reset a clock to an earlier time; *fig.* go back to a past age or earlier state of affairs; take a retrograde step. ***regulator clock***: see REGULATOR 4. **round the clock** for 24 or 12 hours without intermission; all day and night; ceaselessly. **set the clock back** = ***put the clock back*** above. ***settler's clock***: see SETTLER 2. ***speaking clock***: see SPEAKING *ppl adjective*. ***talking clock***: see TALKING *ppl adjective*. **turn the clock back** = ***put the clock back*** above. **watch the clock** eagerly wait for a particular time, esp. the end of working hours. ***water clock***: see WATER *noun*.
– COMB.: **clock face** the dial-plate of a clock; **clock golf** a lawn game in which the players putt to a hole in the centre of a circle from successive points on its circumference; **clock radio** a combined clock and radio, which can be set so that the radio will come on at a desired time; **clock tower**: built for a large clock; **clock-watch** *verb intrans.* eagerly wait for a particular time, esp. the end of working hours; **clock-watcher** a person who clock-watches, a person who takes care not to exceed minimum working hours.
■ **clockwise** *adjective & adverb* in the direction of movement of the hands of a clock, moving in a curve from left to right as seen from a central position L19.

clock /klɒk/ *noun*². M16.
[ORIGIN Unknown.]
An ornamental pattern worked on (the side of) a sock or stocking.

clock /klɒk/ *noun*³. *dial.* M16.
[ORIGIN Unknown.]
A beetle; *esp.* a dor beetle or cockroach (also ***black clock***).

clock /klɒk/ *verb*¹. Now *Scot. & N. English*.
[ORIGIN Old English *cloccian*, cf. Middle Dutch *clocken* (Dutch *klokken*), Swedish dial. *klokka*: cf. CLUCK *verb*.]
1 *verb intrans.* Cluck. OE. ▸†**b** *verb trans.* Call (chickens etc.) by clucking. LME–E18.
2 *verb intrans.* Of the stomach, water, etc.: gurgle. OE.
3 *verb intrans. & trans.* Of a bird etc.: sit on eggs; incubate; hatch. *Scot. & N. English*. L17.

clock /klɒk/ *verb*² *trans.* M16.
[ORIGIN from CLOCK *noun*².]
Embroider with clocks (formerly also occas. with a similar pattern). Chiefly as ***clocked*** *ppl adjective*.

clock /klɒk/ *verb*³. L19.
[ORIGIN from CLOCK *noun*¹.]
▸ **I 1** *verb trans.* Time by a clock or stopwatch. L19.
2 *verb trans.* Attain or register (a stated time, distance, or speed in a race etc.). Also foll. by *up*. *colloq.* L19.
3 *verb intrans.* ***clock in*** or ***clock on***, ***clock out*** or ***clock off***, register arrival, departure, by means of an automatic recording clock; *transf.* start, stop, working; arrive, leave. E20.
4 *verb trans.* Look at, watch, observe, notice. *slang*. M20.

J. ARNOTT I clocked a few faces I vaguely remembered.

▸ **II 5** *verb trans.* = CLAPPER *verb* 1b. L19.
6 *verb trans.* Punch in the face; hit. *slang*. M20.

clocker /ˈklɒkə/ *noun*¹. *Scot. & N. English*. E19.
[ORIGIN from CLOCK *verb*¹ + -ER¹.]
A sitting hen.

clocker /ˈklɒkə/ *noun*². E20.
[ORIGIN from CLOCK *verb*².]
A person who embroiders clocks.

clocker /ˈklɒkə/ *noun*³. E20.
[ORIGIN from CLOCK *verb*³ + -ER¹.]
1 HORSE-RACING. A person (usu. employed by a racing magazine or paper) who times horses' training runs in order to give a guide to form. *US*.
2 A person who turns back the milometer of a motor vehicle so that it registers a falsely low mileage. *slang*. L20.
3 [Perh. because such dealers work around the clock.] A drug dealer, esp. one who works on the streets. *US slang*. L20.

clockwork /ˈklɒkwəːk/ *noun & adjective*. E17.
[ORIGIN from CLOCK *noun*¹ + WORK *noun*.]
▸ **A** *noun*. A mechanism utilizing the motion of wheels controlled by periodically wound up springs (as in a clock). E17.

fig.: G. BERKELEY The clockwork of nature. M. R. MITFORD This jewel of a valet, this matchless piece of clock-work.

(as) regular as clockwork, **like clockwork** smooth(ly), regular(ly), automatic(ally).
▸ **B** *attrib.* or as *adjective*. Operated by clockwork; of or like clockwork. M18.

S. E. FERRIER A very . . quiet, old-fashioned family, quite clockwork in our ways and hours. V. NABOKOV Mere springs and coils produced the movement of our clockwork man.

clod /klɒd/ *noun*. LME.
[ORIGIN Var. of CLOT *noun*.]
†**1** A coagulated mass; a clot of blood etc. LME–M18.
2 A mass *of* solid matter; a lump of earth, clay, loam, etc., *esp.* one formed by ploughing. LME. ▸**b** A sod, a turf. *obsolete* exc. *dial.* L16.

MILTON Two massie clods of Iron and Bras. W. SEWEL Clods and stones were thrown at him.

3 A coarse cut of meat from the lower neck of an ox. L15.
4 Earth, clay, lumpy soil. L16. ▸**b** MINING. Soft shale, esp. over a coal seam. M19.
the clod *spec.* the earth as a place for burial.
5 *fig.* A human body, a human being, as non-spiritual or mortal. L16.

SPENSER Us wretched earthly clods.

6 *fig.* A blockhead; a clumsy awkward person; a dull unresponsive person; a dolt. Cf. CLOT *noun* 3. Now *colloq.* L16.

R. D. BLACKMORE The Doones were of very high birth, as all we clods of Exmoor knew. J. RABAN His portrait of desert life is so loving . . that one would be a clod not to be moved by it.

7 A small loaf of (esp. coarse) bread. *Scot.* L18.
8 A copper coin. *slang*. E20.
– COMB.: **clodhopper** *colloq.* (*a*) a ploughman, an agricultural labourer; a country bumpkin; a clumsy awkward person; (*b*) a large clumsy shoe (usu. in *pl.*); **clodhopping** *adjective* (*colloq.*) large and clumsy, awkward, loutish; **clodpate** *arch.* a blockhead; **clodpated** *adjective* (*arch.*) blockheaded; **clodpole**, **clodpoll** a blockhead; a bumpkin, a lout.
■ **cloddish** *adjective* somewhat like a clod, boorishly stolid, clumsy and awkward M19. **cloddy** *adjective* †(*a*) characterized by clots, clotted, coagulated; (*b*) characterized by or full of clods; (*c*) like a clod, cloddish: LME.

clod /klɒd/ *verb*. Infl. **-dd-**. LME.
[ORIGIN from the noun: cf. CLOT *verb*.]
1 *verb trans.* Clear (land) of clods etc. *obsolete* exc. *Scot. dial.* LME.
†**2** *verb trans.* Cover with clods; enclose (as) in clods. LME–E17.
3 *verb intrans. & trans.* †**a** Clot, coagulate. LME–M18. ▸**b** Stick together in clods, form into clods. Chiefly as ***clodded*** *ppl adjective*. M16.
4 *verb trans.* Pelt with clods, throw clods, stones, etc., at; drive *away*, *out* with clods, stones, etc. Chiefly *Scot. & dial.* E16.
5 *verb trans.* Heave, throw heavily. *Scot. & N. English*. L18.

clodder /ˈklɒdə/ *noun*. Long *dial. rare*. LME.
[ORIGIN from CLOFF.]
A clotted or curdled mass; a clot.

clodder *verb* var. of CLOTTER.

cloff /klɒf/ *noun*. E16.
[ORIGIN Unknown.]
hist. A proportion of the weight of certain wholesale commodities given to cover inaccuracies in retailing in smaller quantities.

clog /klɒg/ *noun*. ME.
[ORIGIN Unknown.]
1 A block of wood etc. used to prevent or hinder movement, loss, or escape; *fig.* an impediment, an encumbrance. ME.

C. LAMB I never tied tin-kettle, clog, Or salt-box to the tail of dog. C. V. WEDGWOOD That clog on their action—the powerless, reduced but obstructive House of Lords.

2 A thick piece of wood, a log. *obsolete* exc. *Scot.* LME.
3 A heavy shoe or overshoe with a wooden sole; a heavy wooden shoe with an upturned pointed toe of a type traditionally worn in the Netherlands. LME.
†**4** A fir cone, a pine cone. L16–E18.
5 *hist.* A calendar cut on the sides of a square (usu. wooden) block. L17.
– PHRASES: **clogs to clogs in three generations** the return of a family to poverty after one generation of prosperity. ***pop one's clogs***: see POP *verb* 2.
– COMB.: **clog-almanac** *hist.* = sense 5 above; **clog dance** a dance performed in clogs with rhythmic beating of the feet; *transf.* a dance imitating this; **clog dancer** a person who performs a clog dance.
■ **clogger** *noun* (*a*) a maker of clogs; (*b*) *slang* a player in soccer who habitually fouls in tackling: M18. **clogginess** *noun* the state or quality of being cloggy L18. **cloggy** *adjective* lumpy, knotty; sticky; full of clogging matter: L16.

clog /klɒg/ *verb*. Infl. **-gg-**. LME.
[ORIGIN from the noun.]
1 *verb trans.* Fasten a clog to, impede (an animal etc.) with a clog; fasten by a clog; encumber, hamper, hinder. LME.

SHELLEY Superstition . . has . . clogged man to earth. A. W. KINGLAKE The whole flotilla would be clogged by the slowness of the sailing vessels. A. POWELL Extraneous detail that can clog a narrative.

2 *verb trans.* Obstruct or encumber by stickiness. E16.

A. T. ELLIS Her boots were clogged with mud.

3 a *verb trans.* Fill up or *up* so as to hinder free passage, action, or function. L16. ▸**b** *verb intrans.* Become filled (*up*) so as to hinder free passage, action, or function. M17.

a W. DUFTON When the Eustachian tube is clogged up with mucus. H. KISSINGER The White House switchboard was clogged with congratulatory phone calls. **b** F. L. WRIGHT Broken stone does not clog up.

4 *verb trans.* Satiate, surfeit, cloy. *obsolete* exc. *dial.* L16.
5 *verb trans.* Put wooden soles on (shoes etc.). M17.
6 *verb intrans.* Perform a clog dance. E20.

cloison /ˈklɔɪz(ə)n; *foreign* klwazɔ̃ (*pl. same*)/ *noun*. L17.
[ORIGIN French.]
A partition, a division.

cloisonné /klwazɔne/ *adjective & noun*. M19.
[ORIGIN French, pa. pple of *cloisonner* to partition, formed as CLOISON.]
More fully ***cloisonné enamel***. (Designating) enamelwork or ware in which the colours in the pattern are separated by thin strips of metal etc.

cloister /ˈklɔɪstə/ *noun & verb*. ME.
[ORIGIN Old French *clo(i)stre* (mod. *cloître*) from Latin *claustrum*, *clostrum* lock, bar, enclosed space, from *claus-* pa. ppl stem of *claudere* CLOSE *verb* + *-trum* instr. suffix.]
▸ **A** *noun*. **1** A place of religious seclusion; a convent, a monastic house. ME.
the cloister monastic life, seclusion.
2 *sing.* & (freq.) in *pl.* A covered place for walking, often round a quadrangle with a wall on the outer and a colonnade or windows on the inner side, esp. of convent, college, or cathedral buildings. ME.
3 An enclosed space, an enclosure. *obsolete* exc. as passing into fig. uses of senses 1, 2. LME.
– COMB.: **cloister-garth** the open court enclosed by a cloister.
▸ **B** *verb trans.* **1** Surround (as) with a cloister; convert into a cloister. LME.
2 Enclose or shut *up* in a cloister or religious house. L16.
3 Shut up in a secluded place. L16.
4 *fig.* Confine, restrain within narrow limits. E17.
■ **cloistered** *adjective* shut up (as) in a cloister; secluded, sheltered (*lit.* & *fig.*): L16. **cloisterer** *noun* (now *rare*) a person who lives in a cloister, a monk or nun ME. **cloisterless** *adjective* LME. **cloisterly** *adjective* of, pertaining to, or characteristic of a cloister L16. †**cloistress** *noun* (*rare*, Shakes.) a nun: only in E17.

cloistral /ˈklɔɪstr(ə)l/ *adjective*. E17.
[ORIGIN from CLOISTER *noun* + -AL¹; cf. medieval Latin *claustralis*, Old French & mod. French *claustral*.]
Of or pertaining to a cloister; monastic; belonging to a monastic order.

cloke *noun*¹ see CLUTCH *noun*¹.

cloke *noun*² & *verb* see CLOAK.

cloky *noun* see CLOQUÉ.

clomb *verb* see CLIMB *verb*.

clomp /klɒmp/ *verb & noun*. Also (*Scot.*) **clomph** /klɒmf/. E19.
[ORIGIN Imit.: cf. CLAMP *noun*³ & *verb*³, CLUMP *noun*, *verb*.]
▸ **A** *verb intrans.* = CLUMP *verb* 1. E19.
▸ **B** *noun*. = CLUMP *noun* 4. M19.

clone /kləʊn/ *noun & verb*. E20.
[ORIGIN Greek *klōn* twig, slip.]
▸ **A** *noun*. **1** A group of organisms (orig. plants) produced by asexual means from a single ancestor to which they are genetically identical. E20.
2 An individual organism so produced; an animal or person that develops from one somatic cell of its parent and is genetically identical to that parent. L20. ▸**b** Each of two or more identical people, an imitator, a double; a copy, *esp.* a microcomputer designed to simulate another (more expensive) model. L20.

3 Within gay culture: a homosexual man who adopts an exaggeratedly macho appearance and style of dress. **L20.**
▸ **B** *verb trans.* Propagate or produce as a clone; create genetically identical copies of. **M20.**
■ **clonal** *adjective* **E20.** **cloˈnality** *noun* **M20.** **clonally** *adverb* **M20.** **cloner** *noun* **L20.**

clonic /ˈklɒnɪk/ *adjective.* **M19.**
[ORIGIN from CLONUS + -IC.]
MEDICINE. Of, pertaining to, or of the nature of clonus. Opp. TONIC *adjective* 1.
tonic-clonic: see TONIC *adjective* 1.

clonk /klɒŋk/ *noun, interjection, & verb.* **M19.**
[ORIGIN Imit.: cf. CLANK, CLINK *noun*¹, *verb*¹, CLUNK *verb* & *noun*².]
▸ **A** *noun & interjection.* (Repr.) an abrupt heavy metallic sound of impact. **M19.**
▸ **B** *verb.* **1** *verb intrans.* Move with or make a clonk or clonks. **M19.**
2 *verb trans.* Hit forcibly. *colloq.* **M20.**

clonus /ˈkləʊnəs/ *noun.* **E19.**
[ORIGIN Latin from Greek *klonos* turmoil.]
MEDICINE. Muscular spasm involving repeated, often rhythmic, contractions.

†**clooch** *noun* see CLUTCH *noun*¹.

cloop /kluːp/ *noun & verb intrans.* **M19.**
[ORIGIN Imit.]
(Make) a muted popping sound, as of a cork being drawn from a bottle.

cloose *noun* see CLOW.

cloot /kluːt/ *noun. Scot. & N. English.* **E18.**
[ORIGIN Prob. from Old Norse *kló* CLAW *noun*¹.]
1 (A division of) a cloven hoof. **E18.**
2 In *pl.* **C-**. The Devil. **L18.**
■ **Clootie** *noun* the Devil **L18.**

clop /klɒp/ *noun & verb.* Freq. redupl. **clop-clop**. Also (now *rare*) **k-**. See also CLIP-CLOP. **M19.**
[ORIGIN Imit.]
▸ **A** *noun.* An abrupt sound as of heavy shoes or a horse's hoofs on a hard surface. **M19.**
▸ **B** *verb intrans.* Infl. **-pp-**. Move with or make such a sound. **M19.**

cloqué /ˈkləʊkeɪ/ *noun.* Also anglicized as **cloky** /ˈkləʊki/. **E20.**
[ORIGIN French, lit. 'blistered'.]
A fabric with an irregularly raised or embossed surface.

closable /ˈkləʊzəb(ə)l/ *adjective.* Also **close-**. **E20.**
[ORIGIN from CLOSE *verb* + -ABLE. Earlier in UNCLOSABLE.]
Able to be closed.

close /kləʊs/ *noun*¹. **ME.**
[ORIGIN Old French & mod. French *clos* from Latin *clausum* closed place, enclosure, use as noun of neut. pa. pple of *claudere* CLOSE *verb*.]
▸ **I** **1** *gen.* An enclosed place, an enclosure. **ME.**

TENNYSON I lay Pent in a roofless close of ragged stones.

break a close, **break a person's close** LAW trespass on another's land.
2 a An enclosure about or beside a building. Long *obsolete* in *gen.* sense. **ME.** ▸**b** *spec.* The precinct of a cathedral. Formerly also, the precinct of any sacred place, a cloister. **LME.** ▸**c** A farmyard. Now *dial.* **LME.**
3 a A field, an enclosed piece of land. Now *dial.* & LAW. **LME.** ▸**b** A playing field at certain English public schools. **L19.**

b H. NEWBOLT There's a breathless hush in the Close to-night, Ten to make and the match to win!

4 An entry, a passage, an alleyway. Chiefly *Scot.*, an entry from a street to a common stairway or a court at the back of a building; also, a common stairway or court with such an entry. **LME.**
5 A (usu. short) street closed at one end, a cul-de-sac. Freq. in proper names. **E18.**
▸ †**II** **6** An enclosing line, a circuit, a boundary. **ME–M17.**

close /kləʊz/ *noun*². **LME.**
[ORIGIN from CLOSE *verb*.]
1 An act of coming to an end; an end, a conclusion. **LME.**

L. GORDON The chill close of an October day.

†**2** The closing passage of a speech, argument, etc. **L16–M18.**
3 MUSIC. The conclusion of a phrase, a cadence. **L16.**
PLAGAL close.
4 A closing or uniting together; union, junction. Chiefly *poet.* **L16.**
5 A closing in fight, a grapple, a struggle. *arch.* **L16.**

close /kləʊs/ *adjective & adverb.* **LME.**
[ORIGIN Old French & mod. French *clos* from Latin *clausus* pa. pple of *claudere* CLOSE *verb*.]
▸ **A** *adjective.* **I** Of a closed condition or its results.
1 Closed, shut; having no part left open. **LME.** ▸**b** HERALDRY. Of wings: folded to the body. **E17.** ▸**c** PHONETICS. Of a vowel: articulated with the tongue in a relatively high position. **E17.**

A. TROLLOPE I've brought a close carriage for him.

2 Shut up in prison etc., under strict restraint. Of confinement: strict. **LME.**

WELLINGTON Captain—is in close arrest.

3 Concealed from observation; hidden, secret, secluded; *arch.* private, snug. **LME.**

S. JOHNSON A close room, an easy chair. I. MURDOCH She kept this interlude a close secret and never spoke of it to anyone.

4 Secretive, reticent, reserved. **LME.**

DICKENS He was too close to name his circumstances to me.

†**5** Rigorous, severe. **LME–L18.**

J. WESLEY She had close trials from her poor, apostate husband.

6 Enclosed, esp. with walls or barriers; shut *in* or away *from*; confined, contracted; narrow. **L15.**

W. OWEN Down the close, darkening lanes they sang their way.

7 Of air, atmosphere, etc.: stuffy, airless, stifling. **L16.**

A. PATON It was close and sultry, and soon there would be thunder. S. BELLOW The house was close and faintly sour with furniture polish.

8 Stingy, niggardly; grudging any expense. **M17.**

A. S. BYATT He would break a close northern habit of meanness to provide champagne.

9 Restricted or limited to a privileged few. **E19.**

BOSW. SMITH These . . filled up the vacancies . . from among themselves, like the members of a close college.

10 Under prohibition; during which something is prohibited. **E19.**
▸ **II** Of proximity of space or time.
11 Dense or compact in texture or arrangement; with no or only slight intervals. Cf. earlier B.4 below. **L15.** ▸**b** Detailed, concentrated, searching, thorough; leaving no gaps or weaknesses. **M17.**

DRYDEN In close plantations. T. HARDY Their vans . . were drawn up . . in close file. **b** COLERIDGE A close reasoner. E. A. BOND Under a close cross-questioning. F. R. LEAVIS *Close analytical* study of a few poems.

12 Of an item of clothing etc.: fitting exactly or tightly. **L15.**
13 Very near in relation or connection; intimate, confidential. Cf. earlier B.5 below. **L16.** ▸**b** Of a translation etc.: following or resembling the original to a large extent. **E18.**

W. PALEY In close conformity with the Scripture account. P. SCOTT No close friend by whom to be comforted. C. CONNOLLY With the sea . . his relations were always close and harmonious. P. V. WHITE We were a very close family.

14 Very near in position; in or nearly in contact; narrowly escaped. Cf. earlier B.5 below. **E17.**

J. HELLER The tables in the delicatessen were small and close.

15 Of a contest, its outcome, etc.: nearly equal, narrowly decided. **M19.**
▸ **B** *adverb.* (Some pred. uses of the adjective pass into this.)
1 In or into a closed position. **LME.**
2 In concealment, hiding, or strict confinement. **LME.**

A. S. BYATT We must keep our secrets close.

†**3** Secretly, covertly. **LME–M17.**
4 Tightly; fast; densely, compactly; so as to leave no interstices or openings; searchingly, thoroughly. **LME.**

C. THIRLWALL The closer they are examined, the more suspicious do they appear.

5 Very near in position, relation, or connection; in or into immediate proximity or intimacy. **LME.**

JOSEPH HALL Let us pile up all close together. J. C. POWYS The courage . . to move up close to him. I. MCEWAN They kissed and sat close.

6 *gen.* In a close manner; closely. **M17.**
— SPECIAL COLLOCATIONS, PHRASES, & COMB.: ***as close as it can stick***, ***as close as one can stick***: see STICK *verb*¹. ***at close range***: see RANGE *noun*¹. ***close as wax***: see WAX *noun*¹. ***close borough***: see BOROUGH *noun* 3. **close by** very near (to). **close call** *colloq.* = *close shave* below. **close-carpet** *verb trans.* cover the whole floor of (a room) with carpet. ***close communion***: see COMMUNION 5. **close-cropped** *adjective* (of hair) cut very short. **close encounter**: *spec.* a supposed encounter with a UFO or extraterrestrials; ***close encounter of the first, second, etc., kind***: involving increasing degrees of complexity and apparent exposure of the witness to aliens. †**close-fights** *pl.* = *close quarters* (a) below. **close-fisted** *adjective* that keeps the hand tightly shut; chiefly *fig.*, mean, grudging. **close-fitting** *adjective* (of a garment) fitting closely to the body. **close-grained** *adjective* without gaps between fibres etc. **close-handed** *adjective* (*arch.*) = ***close-fisted*** above. **close harmony** the singing of parts within an octave or twelfth. **close-hauled** *adjective* (of a ship) with sails hauled aft to sail close to the wind. **close-knit** *adjective* intimately united by common interests, marriage, etc. **close-lipped** *adjective* with tightly set lips; *fig.* reticent, discreet. **close mourning** *arch.* deep mourning. **close-mouthed** *adjective* = ***close-lipped*** above. **close on** very near to, nearly. ***close port***: see PORT *noun*¹. **close quarters** *pl.* (**a**) *hist.* barriers across a ship's decks providing a place of retreat for the crew and with holes for firing at a hostile boarding party; (**b**) direct contact, esp. with an enemy; uncomfortable nearness; (***at close quarters***, very near, from a very short distance). **close-reef** *verb trans.* (NAUTICAL) reef closely, take in all the reefs of (a sail or ship). **close season** a period when something is forbidden by law, as the killing of game, or does not take place, as the playing of cricket or another organized sport. **close shave** a narrow escape, a near thing. **close-stool** a chamber pot enclosed in a stool with a cover. **close thing** = ***close shave*** above. ***close to home***: see HOME *noun & adjective*. ***close to the bone***: see BONE *noun*. **close to the wind** NAUTICAL against the wind as nearly as is compatible with its filling the sails. **close upon** = ***close on*** above. ***hold one's cards close to one's chest***: see CHEST *noun*. ***MAISON close. pound close***: see POUND *noun*² 1a.
■ **closen** *verb trans. & intrans.* make or become close(r), close up **M19.** **closish** *adjective* fairly close **M19.**

close /kləʊz/ *verb.* **ME.**
[ORIGIN Old French & mod. French *clos-* pa. ppl stem of *clore* from Latin *claudere* shut, close.]
1 *verb trans.* Enclose, confine, encompass; *fig.* include, contain. (Foll. by *in*, *within*.) *arch.* **ME.**

W. PRYNNE They . . closed him in a monastery. TENNYSON I clung to all the present for the promise that it closed.

2 *verb trans.* Cover or block (an opening); move (a lid, door, etc.) so as to cover or block an opening; cover or block up the opening(s) of (a box, room, etc.); officially prohibit access to (a public building etc.), declare to be no longer open. **ME.**

T. GRAY Now my weary lips I close. LD MACAULAY An attempt . . to close the coffee houses. P. KAVANAGH The potato-stalks closed the alleys. T. KENEALLY They closed the . . pasture gates behind them. T. BERGER He sprinkled a bit of salt into the pot before closing it with the lid.

close a gap: see GAP *noun*. ***close one's eyes against***, ***close one's eyes to***: see EYE *noun*. ***close one's heart*** (***to***): see HEART *noun*. ***close one's mind*** (***to***): see MIND *noun*¹. ***close the books***: see BOOK *noun*. ***close the door on***, ***close the door to***: see DOOR *noun*. **closing order** ENGLISH LAW an order by a local authority prohibiting the use of premises for specified purposes.
3 *verb intrans.* Become enclosed, covered or blocked up, or (esp. officially) inaccessible; become or be declared to be no longer open; move so as to cover or block an opening (foll. by *over*, (*up*)*on* a person who or a thing which has entered). **LME.**

DICKENS On June 24th the eyes of the brilliant comedian closed upon the world. JAN MORRIS The Cowley works close for their annual holidays.

4 *verb trans.* Bring to an end; conclude, complete, settle (a bargain etc.). **LME.**

G. SAINTSBURY Dryden . . at once closed the period of his own contemporaries and opened a new one.

5 *verb intrans.* Come to an end; conclude, finish speaking or writing (*with* a particular remark etc.). **LME.** ▸**b** *verb intrans.* Of stocks or shares: be *at* a particular price at the close of a day's trading. **M19.**

D. J. ENRIGHT I want to close by reading three poems. C. IVES The day of leaders, as such, is gradually closing.

6 *verb trans.* Bring closer or into contact; draw together so as to eliminate gaps or openings. **LME.** ▸**b** Join together the uppers of (a boot or shoe). **E19.** ▸**c** Make (an electric circuit etc.) continuous. **L19.**

E. HEMINGWAY My hands were so sore I could hardly close them over the oars.

close ranks *fig.* maintain solidarity.
7 *verb intrans.* Come closer or into contact; coalesce, meet in a common centre; draw near, approach close. **LME.** ▸**b** Come within striking distance, come to close quarters, grapple (*with*). **L16.**

SHAKES. *Hen. V* As many lines close in the dial's centre. R. SUTCLIFF Closing round them as a wolf-pack closes round its prey. **b** C. ISHERWOOD They closed . . and staggered grappling about the room.

8 *verb intrans.* Come to terms, come to an agreement, (*with*); agree *with*, (*up*)*on* an offer, terms, etc. **E17.**

H. BELLOC Mr. Foley was glad that he came to a sensible business decision . . and closed with him. W. GOLDING I closed . . with this very advantageous offer.

9 *verb trans.* Chiefly NAUTICAL. Come close to or alongside of. **L17.**

F. MARRYAT We . . closed the admiral's ship, and the captain went on board.

— WITH ADVERBS IN SPECIALIZED SENSES: **close down** (**a**) *verb phr. trans.* close by forcing or fastening down; (**b**) *verb phr. trans. & intrans.* stop the functioning of, stop functioning, esp. permanently; (of a broadcasting station) end transmission until the next day. **close in** (**a**) *verb phr. trans.* confine by covering or blocking the means of egress, hem in, enclose; (**b**) *verb phr. trans.* shut with inward motion; †(**c**) *verb phr. intrans.* come to agreement *with*; (**d**) *verb phr. intrans.* come into contact or to close quarters *with*; (**e**) *verb phr. intrans.* come nearer so as to surround or envelop; (of days etc.) get successively shorter; (foll. by (*up*)*on*). **close off** *verb phr. trans.* prevent access to by covering or blocking the means of entrance. **close out** *verb phr. trans.* (*N. Amer.*) clear out (stock etc.), bring (a business etc.) to a close, dispose of, discontinue. **close up** (**a**) *verb phr. trans.* confine or prevent access to by covering or blocking the opening(s); cover or block up completely; shut, esp. temporarily; bring the parts of closer together or into contact; (**b**) *verb phr. trans.* (*arch.*) bring to an end; (**c**) *verb phr. intrans.* move closer (*to*); coalesce; become more dense or compact.

closeable *adjective* var. of CLOSABLE.

C

closed /kləʊzd/ *ppl adjective*. ME.
[ORIGIN from CLOSE *verb* + -ED¹.]
1 *gen.* That has been closed; not open. ME.
2 Limited in number or by certain conditions; self-contained, not communicating with others. M19. ▸**b** MATH. Limited in some specified way; *esp.* (of a set) having the property that the result of a specified operation on any element of the set is itself a member of the set; also, (of a set) containing all its limit points. M19.
– SPECIAL COLLOCATIONS & COMB.: *closed book*: see BOOK *noun*. **closed caption** (chiefly *N. Amer.*) *noun & verb* (**a**) *noun* one of a series of subtitles to a television programme, accessible through a decoder; (**b**) *verb* (**closed-caption**) provide (a programme) with such captions. **closed-circuit** *adjective* (of television) for a restricted number of receivers by use of wires not waves for transmission. **closed door** *fig.* an obstacle, an impasse, a restriction; ***behind closed doors***, in secret, in private. **closed-door** *adjective* restricted, obstructive, secret. **closed-end** *adjective* having a predetermined extent. ***closed loop***: see LOOP *noun*² 13. **closed season** *N. Amer.* = ***close season*** s.v. CLOSE *adjective & adverb*. **closed shop** (the system obtaining in) a workshop or other establishment where only members of a trade union may be employed. **closed society**: characterized by a rigid system of beliefs, resisting all contact with other systems, and hostile to any structural change. **closed syllable**: ending in a consonant.

closely /ˈkləʊsli/ *adverb*. LME.
[ORIGIN from CLOSE *adjective* + -LY².]
In a close manner; so as to be or make close.

SHAKES. *Haml.* We have closely sent for Hamlet hither. OED Henry was closely confined in the Tower. D. H. LAWRENCE He followed her closely. J. BUCHAN A sheet of yellowish parchment, covered closely with Greek characters. J. CARY He listened closely to the details of fashionable life. G. GREENE He leant closely to the canvas. J. MITCHELL The men were in closely tailored slacks or jeans.

closeness /ˈkləʊsnɪs/ *noun*. LME.
[ORIGIN from CLOSE *adjective* + -NESS.]
The state or quality of being close.

SWIFT Almost stifled by the closeness of the room. H. A. L. FISHER The old Norse literature . . stands out . . for . . its closeness to the facts of life. C. FREEMAN She felt a strange closeness to the actors on the stage.

closer /ˈkləʊzə/ *noun*. LME.
[ORIGIN from CLOSE *verb* + -ER¹.]
1 *gen.* A person who or thing which closes something; a person who or thing which forms a close. LME.
2 A worker who joins together the uppers of boots or shoes. E18.
3 A stone or brick smaller than the rest, used to end a course of brickwork etc. E18.

closet /ˈklɒzɪt/ *noun & adjective*. LME.
[ORIGIN Old French, dim. of *clos*: see CLOSE *noun*¹, -ET¹.]
▸**A** *noun*. **1** A private or small room, *esp.* one used for private interviews, devotions, or study. LME.
2 The private apartment of a monarch. Now *hist.* LME.
Clerk of the Closet the British monarch's principal chaplain.
3 A room etc. for urination and defecation; a lavatory. L15.
water closet: see WATER *noun*.
4 a A private repository of valuables, curiosities, etc.; a cabinet. Now chiefly in ***china closet*** (passing into sense b). E17. ▸**b** A cupboard, a recess for storage. Now *dial.* & *N. Amer.* E17.
b come out of the closet *fig.* stop hiding something about oneself, esp. one's homosexuality; come to public notice or view. ***skeleton in the closet***: see SKELETON *noun*.
– COMB.: **closet play** a play to be read rather than acted.
▸**B** *attrib.* or as *adjective*. Concealed, secret, private. E17.

Sunday Telegraph He was not a closet Papist intoxicated by bells and fancy vestments.

closet queen *slang* a man who conceals his homosexuality.

closet /ˈklɒzɪt/ *verb trans.* L16.
[ORIGIN from the noun.]
Shut up (or †*up*) in a closet; detain for a private consultation etc. Freq. in *pass.*, be in private consultation (*with*).

LD MACAULAY Some of the Churchmen whom he had closeted had offered to make large concessions. C. S. FORESTER He was closeted alone with Hudson for a long time.

close-up /ˈkləʊsʌp/ *noun*. E20.
[ORIGIN from CLOSE *adjective & adverb* + UP *adverb*¹.]
A photograph or film taken at short range and showing the subject on a large scale; *fig.* an intimate and detailed description.
medium close-up: see MEDIUM *adjective*.

closh /klɒʃ/ *noun*. E19.
[ORIGIN Unknown.]
A spiked upright block on the deck of a whaling vessel, on which blubber is cut up.

closing /ˈkləʊzɪŋ/ *noun*. LME.
[ORIGIN from CLOSE *verb* + -ING¹.]
The action of CLOSE *verb*, an act or instance of this; *esp.* the prohibition of access to a public building, the declaration that a shop etc. is no longer open.
early closing, ***Sunday closing***, etc.
– COMB.: **closing time** the set time at which a public building or place, *spec.* a public house, closes.

clostridium /klɒˈstrɪdɪəm/ *noun*. Pl. **-dia** /-dɪə/. L19.
[ORIGIN mod. Latin from Greek *klōstēr* spindle: see -IDIUM.]
A rod-shaped anaerobic bacterium of the large genus *Clostridium*, which includes many pathogenic species, e.g. those causing tetanus, gas gangrene, and botulism and other forms of food poisoning.
■ **clostridial** *adjective* of, pertaining to, or caused by such bacteria M20.

closure /ˈkləʊʒə/ *noun & verb*. LME.
[ORIGIN Old French from late Latin *clausura*, from *claus-* pa. ppl stem of *claudere* CLOSE *verb*: see -URE.]
▸**A** *noun* †**I 1** A thing which encloses, shuts in, or confines. LME–L19. ▸**b** Bound, limit, circuit. L16–M17.
2 An enclosed place; *spec.* a fortification, an entrenchment. LME–E17.
3 Enclosing. LME–E18.
▸**II 4** An act of closing or shutting. LME.
5 †**a** A fontanelle of the skull. LME–M16. ▸**b** A thing by which another thing is closed or fastened, a fastener. E17.
6 The state or condition of being closed. M19. ▸**b** MATH. The condition or property of being closed (sense 2b); a function, operation, etc., which produces this condition; the smallest closed set that contains a given set; the closed set obtained from a given set by adding all the limit points of the latter. E20.
▸**III 7** A bringing to an end; a conclusion; a close. LME.
8 In a legislative assembly, a decision, by vote or under rules, to put a question without further debate. L19.
kangaroo closure: see KANGAROO *noun* 3.
9 Orig. PSYCHOANALYSIS. (An act which brings about) a sense of resolution of a traumatic, emotional, or other experience. L20.

DAVID MITCHELL You need peace of mind, some closure.

▸†**IV 10** An agreement, a union, (*with*). Only in M17.
▸**B** *verb trans.* Apply closure to (a motion, speakers, etc.) in a legislative assembly. L19.

clot /klɒt/ *noun*. See also CLOD *noun*.
[ORIGIN Old English *clot(t)* = Middle High German *kloz* (German *Klotz*), from Germanic: cf. CLEAT, CLOUT *noun*¹.]
1 A mass of material stuck or matted together; a semi-solid lump of coagulated liquid, esp. one formed from blood exposed to air. OE.

R. ADAMS A flat, wet clot of dead leaves.

2 = CLOD *noun* 2. Long *dial.* ME.
3 = CLOD *noun* 4. Now *rare*. LME.
4 *fig.* A clumsy awkward person; (now more commonly) a stupid person, a dolt. Cf. CLOD *noun* 6. Now *colloq.* M17.

T. RATTIGAN Johnny, you clot! What about that beer?

– COMB.: †**clot-bird** the wheatear; **clotpole**, **clotpoll** *arch.* = ***clodpole*** s.v. CLOD *noun*.
■ **clottish** *adjective* (*colloq.*) stupid, somewhat blockheaded M20. **clotty** *adjective* (now *rare*) full of clots or lumps, inclined to clot LME.

clot /klɒt/ *verb*. Infl. **-tt-**. LME.
[ORIGIN from the noun: cf. CLOD *verb*.]
1 a *verb intrans.* Break up clods. Long *dial.* LME. ▸**b** *verb trans.* Clear (land) of clods. Long *dial.* M16.
2 a *verb intrans.* Form into clots; congeal, coagulate. LME. ▸**b** *verb trans.* Cause to form into clots; mat with sticky matter; cover with clots of dirt etc. L17.

a A. KOESTLER The people were clotting into groups, chattering excitedly. D. MORRIS Blood spilled . . will clot more quickly. **b** D. WELCH The autumn leaves were clotted into great coloured lumps. E. BOWEN Dead leaves clotted and marred the lake.

clotbur /ˈklɒtbəː/ *noun*. Now *dial.* M16.
[ORIGIN from CLOTE + BUR *noun*¹.]
Burdock.

clote /kləʊt/ *noun*. Now *dial.*
[ORIGIN Old English *clāte* from Germanic base meaning 'to stick': rel. to CLAY *noun*.]
Burdock, or another plant resembling it; the yellow water lily (also ***water clote***).

cloth /klɒθ/ *noun & adjective*.
[ORIGIN Old English *clāþ* = Old Frisian *klāth*, *klēth*, Middle Dutch *kleet* (Dutch *kleed*), Middle High German *kleit* (German *Kleid*), of unknown origin.]
▸**A** *noun*. Pl. **cloths**, CLOTHES.
▸**I** (A piece of) fabric.
1 A piece of woven or felted material used for wrapping, spreading, wiping, covering, etc. OE. ▸**b** A tablecloth. ME. ▸†**c** A canvas for painting on, a painted canvas. L17–E19. ▸**d** THEATRICAL. A large piece of painted scenery. See also BACKCLOTH 1. L19.
altar cloth, ***loincloth***, ***neckcloth***, ***tablecloth***, ***tea cloth***, etc. **cloth of estate**, **cloth of state** a cloth erected over a throne or chair as a sign of rank, a canopy. †**painted cloth** a painted or embroidered wall hanging, a tapestry.
2 NAUTICAL. †**a** A sail. Only in LME. ▸**b** The sails of a ship collectively. M17. ▸**c** Each of the breadths of canvas of which a sail is composed. L17.
3 A particular length or quantity of woven fabric; a 'piece'. *obsolete* exc. *dial.* LME.
4 Fabric woven or felted from animal, vegetable, mineral, or synthetic fibres; *esp.* woollen woven fabric used for clothes. LME.
broadcloth, ***Lancaster cloth***, ***long cloth***, ***oilcloth***, ***sackcloth***, etc. **cloth of gold**, **cloth of silver** tissue of gold, silver, threads interwoven with silk or wool. ***cloth of* TARS**. **cut one's coat according to one's cloth** adapt expenditure to resources, limit one's ambition to what is feasible.
▸**II** As clothing.
†**5 a** A garment. OE–LME. ▸**b** Clothing, dress. ME–E19.
†**6** The distinctive clothing worn by employees of the same person or members of the same profession; livery. LME–E19.
7 *transf.* One's profession as shown by clothes, esp. clerical. M17.
man of the cloth: see MAN *noun*. **the cloth** the clergy.
▸**B** *attrib.* or as *adjective*. Made of cloth. L16.
– COMB. & SPECIAL COLLOCATIONS: **cloth-binding** the cover of a book in cloth over boards; **cloth-bound** *adjective* having a cloth-binding; **cloth-cap** *adjective* pertaining to or characteristic of the working class; **cloth-eared** *adjective* (*colloq.*) having poor hearing, insensitive to sound; **cloth ears** *colloq.* (a person with) poor hearing; **cloth-head** *colloq.* a stupid person, a dolt; **cloth-headed** *adjective* (*colloq.*) stupid, foolish; **cloth-worker** a maker or manufacturer of cloth; **cloth-yard shaft** *hist.* an arrow a yard long.

clothe /kləʊð/ *verb*. Also †**cloath**. Pa. t. & pple **clothed**, (*arch., techn., & formal*) **clad** /klad/. See also YCLAD.
[ORIGIN Old English (*ge*)*claþod*, -*ed* ppl adjective, from CLOTH Infl. by Old Norse *klæða*, *klæddr* pa. t. & pple.]
▸**I** *lit.* **1** *verb trans.* Provide with clothes; put clothes upon; dress. (Foll. by *in*, *with*.) OE. ▸**b** *spec.* Invest in a religious habit. E17.

SPENSER In mighty armes he was yclad anon, And silver shield. MILTON He clad Thir nakedness with Skins of Beasts. TENNYSON The hand that . . often toil'd to clothe your little ones. B. TRAPIDO Jane would . . clothe herself . . in a dowdy two-piece.

†**2** *verb trans.* Put on as clothing, don. Only in ME.
3 *verb trans.* Cover with a cloth or cloths. LME. ▸**b** NAUTICAL. Rig (a ship, mast, etc.). E18.
4 *verb intrans.* Put clothes on, dress oneself; be clothed. Now *rare*. LME.
▸**II** *fig.* **5** *verb trans.* Cover as with clothes or a cloth. (Foll. by *in*, *with*.) ME.

SIR W. SCOTT Will spring return . . And blossoms clothe the hawthorn spray? CARLYLE Thus he [Man] is also said to be clothed with a body. H. BELLOC A wood . . clothing a rocky peak.

6 *verb trans.* Conceal the true nature or form of, disguise. (Foll. by *in*, *with*.) LME.

E. J. HOWARD Men had more practice at dressing up their lusts, or . . no need to clothe them.

7 *verb trans.* Invest or endue *with* a character, attributes, etc.; endow *with* power, a liability, etc. E17.

BUNYAN With such gravity cloath every page. T. JEFFERSON The clauses . . clothing consuls with privileges of the law of nations.

8 *verb trans.* Express (thoughts, ideas, etc.) *in*, *with*. L17.

clotheless /ˈkləʊðlɪs/ *adjective*. Also †**clothless**. LME.
[ORIGIN from CLOTH *noun* + -LESS.]
Without clothes, lacking clothing.

clothes /kləʊðz, kləʊz/ *noun pl.* Also †**cloaths**, (*Scot.* & *N. English*) **claes** /kleɪz/.
[ORIGIN Old English *clāþas* pl. of CLOTH *noun*.]
1 Things worn to cover the body and limbs. Freq. in comb. with word specifying purpose. OE. ▸**b** Clothing etc. for washing; laundry. LME.
bedclothes, ***swaddling clothes***, ***underclothes***, etc. ***change of clothes***: see CHANGE *noun* 2. ***old clothes man***: see OLD *adjective*. **b *drive a buck of clothes***: see DRIVE *verb*.
†**2** Swaddling clothes. ME–M18.
3 Bedclothes. ME.
– COMB.: **clothes bag**, **clothes basket**: for holding or conveying clothes to be washed; **clothes brush** a stiff brush for removing dust, dirt, etc., from clothes; **clothes-conscious** *adjective* aware of or concerned with clothes; **clothes drier** a device for drying washed or wet clothes; ***rotary clothes drier***: see ROTARY *adjective*; **clothes hanger** a shaped piece of wood, wire, etc., from which clothes can be hung in the normal shape, a coat hanger; **clothes horse** a frame for airing washed clothes; *fig.* an affectedly fashionable person; **clothes line** a rope, wire, etc., for hanging washed clothes etc. to dry (***rotary clothes line***: see ROTARY *adjective*); ***clothes moth***: see MOTH *noun*¹ 2a; **clothes peg**, (chiefly *N. Amer.*) **clothes pin** a clip or forked device of wood, plastic, etc., to hold washing on a clothes line; **clothes post**, **clothes prop** a support for a clothes line.
■ **clothesless** *adjective* = CLOTHELESS M19. **clotheslessness** *noun* L19.

clothier /ˈkləʊðɪə/ *noun*. ME.
[ORIGIN from CLOTH *noun*: see -ER¹, -IER.]
A person engaged in the cloth trade; *esp.* a seller of men's clothes.

clothing /ˈkləʊðɪŋ/ *noun*. ME.
[ORIGIN from CLOTHE *verb* + -ING¹.]
1 The action of CLOTHE *verb*. ME.
2 Clothes collectively, dress. ME. ▸†**b** Bedclothes. ME–L18. ▸†**c** Livery; a livery company. LME–E17.

Horse & Rider Some sort of protective clothing may be required. *Face* Girls in skimpy clothing.

wolf in sheep's clothing: see WOLF *noun*.

3 Cloth-making; the cloth trade. Now *rare*. M16. **4** A covering or casing of cloth etc.; *esp.* lagging, cladding. L18. **5** *NAUTICAL*. Sails, rigging. L18.

– COMB.: **clothing book** a ration book containing clothing coupons; **clothing club** a club for the purchase or exchange of clothing by small part-payments; **clothing coupon** a ration coupon entitling the holder to a specified quantity of clothes or clothing materials.

†**clothless** *adjective* var. of CLOTHELESS.

clotted /ˈklɒtɪd/ *ppl adjective*. E17.
[ORIGIN from CLOT *verb* + -ED[1]. In sense 1b prob. alt. of CLOUTED.]
1 Formed into clots or lumps; coagulated, congealed; matted in or with clots; covered with clots of blood etc. E17. ▸**b** Of cream: made by scalding milk. L19. **2** *fig.* Concentrated, dense, impenetrable. L17.

W. EMPSON I tried to defend my clotted kind of poetry.

clotter /ˈklɒtə/ *verb intrans. & trans.* Now *arch. & dial.* Also **clodder** /ˈklɒdə/. See also CLUTTER *verb*. LME.
[ORIGIN from CLOT *verb* + -ER[5].]
= CLOT *verb* 2.

cloture /ˈkləʊtjʊə/ *noun & verb*. Now chiefly *US*. L19.
[ORIGIN French *clôture* from Old French CLOSURE.]
▸ **A** *noun*. = CLOSURE *noun* 8. L19.
▸ **B** *verb trans*. = CLOSURE *verb*. L19.

clou /klu/ *noun*. L19.
[ORIGIN French, lit. 'nail, stud'.]
The chief attraction, the point of greatest interest, the central idea.

cloud /klaʊd/ *noun*.
[ORIGIN Old English *clūd*, prob. rel. to CLOT *noun*.]
1 A mass of rock, earth, etc.; a hill. Long *obsolete* exc. *local* in place names. OE. **2** (A mass of) visible condensed water vapour suspended in the atmosphere high over the general level of the ground; in *pl.* also, the sky, the heavens. ME.

SHAKES. *Rom. & Jul.* She is advanc'd Above the clouds, as high as heaven itself. L. DEIGHTON Big rain clouds raced across the moon. K. A. PORTER La Condesa rose lightly as a cloud. ANTHONY HUXLEY Cloud may reduce light intensity to as little as five per cent of that of the full sun.

a cloud on the horizon an indication of future trouble. **in the clouds** mystical, unreal, imaginary; (of a person) abstracted, inattentive. ***Land of the Long White Cloud***: see LAND *noun*[1]. *LENTICULAR* ***cloud***. **on cloud seven**, **on cloud nine** *colloq.* extremely happy. **with one's head in the clouds** unrealistic; living in a world of fantasy.

3 A thing that darkens or overshadows with gloom, trouble, suspicion, etc.; obscurity; a state of gloom, trouble, etc.; a frowning or depressed look. ME.

J. HEATH-STUBBS A dark cloud of suspicion broods over all.

under a cloud out of favour, discredited.

4 An airborne suspension of smoke, dust, etc.; a hazy aggregation of gas, particles, etc. LME. ▸**b** *ASTRONOMY*. A hazy area in the night sky produced by the light of distant stars; a nebula; a region of dust, gas, etc., in deep space appearing lighter or darker owing to the reflection, absorption, etc., of light. M16.

H. E. BATES The tractor seemed to draw behind it a brown and smoky cloud.

blow a cloud: see BLOW *verb*[1]. ***mushroom cloud***: see MUSHROOM *noun & adjective*. **b** *MAGELLANIC* ***Cloud***.

5 A great number *of* birds, insects, persons, etc., moving together. LME.

Oort cloud, ***Oort comet cloud***, ***Oort's cloud***, ***Oort's comet cloud***: see OORT 2.

6 A thing that obscures or conceals. E16. ▸**b** A region of dimness or obscurity in an otherwise clear or transparent body or liquid; a fuzzy patch or spot, *spec.* of another colour on the face of a horse. M16. ▸**c** A light loosely knitted woollen scarf or shawl. Now *arch. & Canad. dial.* L19.

C. V. WEDGWOOD The cloud of conjecture which obscures Cromwell's actions and motives.

– COMB.: **cloudburst** a sudden violent rainstorm; **cloud-castle** a daydream; **cloud chamber** *PHYSICS* a container of air or gas supersaturated with water vapour, used to detect charged particles by the condensation trails which they produce; **cloud cover** cloud that covers (much of) the sky; the extent to which the sky is covered by cloud; **cloud cuckoo land** [translating Greek *Nephelokokkugia* (*nephelē* cloud, *kokkux* cuckoo) in Aristophanes' *Birds*] a fanciful or ideal realm; **cloud hopping** (of aircraft) flying from cloud to cloud esp. for concealment; **cloudland** Utopia, fairyland; **cloudscape** a picture or picturesque grouping of clouds; **cloud seeder** a person or thing which seeds clouds with crystals to cause rain; **cloud seeding** the seeding of clouds with crystals; **cloud street** a line of cumulus clouds formed parallel to the wind direction.

■ **cloudless** *adjective* LME. **cloudlessness** *noun* M19. **cloudlet** *noun* a little cloud L18. **cloudlike** *adjective & adverb* (**a**) *adjective* resembling (that of) a cloud; (**b**) *adverb* in the manner of a cloud: M17.

cloud /klaʊd/ *verb*. LME.
[ORIGIN from the noun.]
1 *verb trans.* Overspread or darken with clouds, gloom, trouble, etc.; throw into the shade, surpass; make dim or obscure; mar, detract from; *arch.* defame. LME.

S. WEYMAN A shade of annoyance clouded her countenance. S. K. PENMAN His eyes were rheumy, clouded by cataracts.

2 *verb intrans.* Become overcast or gloomy. (Foll. by *over*, *up*.) M16. **3** *verb trans.* Hide, conceal. L17–E18.

clouded leopard a large, spotted, mainly arboreal feline, *Neofelis nebulosa*, of SE Asia. **clouded yellow** an orange or yellow and black pierid butterfly of the genus *Colias*, esp. *C. croceus*, known in Britain as a migrant from southern Europe.

4 *verb trans.* Variegate with vague patches of colour. L17.

cloudberry /ˈklaʊdbɛri, -b(ə)ri/ *noun*. L16.
[ORIGIN App. from CLOUD *noun* + BERRY *noun*[1].]
(The edible orange fruit of) a dwarf thornless bramble, *Rubus chamaemorus*, of mountain moorlands in north temperate regions.

cloudy /ˈklaʊdi/ *adjective*. OE.
[ORIGIN from CLOUD *noun* + -Y[1].]
†**1** Rocky, hilly. OE–LME. **2** Of or like cloud; of or pertaining to the clouds; characterized by clouds, having many clouds; obscured by cloud(s). ME. **3** Not transparent or clear. LME. ▸**b** Variegated with vague patches of colour. Now *rare*. L17. **4** Darkened by ignorance etc.; (of ideas etc.) unclear, indistinct, vague. LME. **5** Darkened by misfortune, grief, anger, etc.; gloomy, sullen, frowning. LME.
■ **cloudily** *adverb* L16. **cloudiness** *noun* L16.

clough /klʌf/ *noun*[1].
[ORIGIN Old English *clōh* (in place names) from Germanic, rel. to Old High German *klinga* (German dial. *Klinge*) ravine.]
1 A ravine, a steep valley usu. with a torrent bed. OE. **2** A cliff, a crag, a rock. Long *obsolete* exc. *Scot.* LME.

clough *noun*[2] var. of CLOW.

clour /ˈkluə/ *noun & verb*. *Scot. & N. English*. LME.
[ORIGIN Unknown.]
▸ **A** *noun*. †**1** A knoll, a mound. LME–M17. **2** A swelling or lump (on the head) caused by a heavy blow. E16. **3** A heavy blow. L18. **4** A dent caused by a heavy blow. E19.
▸ **B** *verb trans.* Dent; strike heavily; raise a swelling or lump on (the head) by a heavy blow. L16.

clout /klaʊt/ *noun*[1].
[ORIGIN Old English *clūt*, corresp. to Middle & mod. Low German, Middle Dutch *klūt(e)* (Dutch *kluit* lump, clod), Old Norse *klútr* kerchief: rel. to CLEAT, CLOT *noun*.]
▸ **I 1** A piece of cloth, leather, etc., for mending; a patch. OE. **2** A metal plate, *esp.* one fixed to an axle-tree to prevent wear. *obsolete* exc. *dial.* OE. †**3** A shred, esp. of cloth. ME–E17. **4** A piece of cloth (*gen.*); a cloth, *esp.* one put to squalid uses; a rag; an article of clothing. Now *arch. & dial.* ME. ▸**b** A handkerchief. Now *dial. & slang.* LME.

J. BANVILLE In her hospital clouts she sat up in bed . . and talked ecstatically of God.

†**babe of clouts** a doll. **cast a clout** remove a garment.

5 In *pl.* Swaddling clothes. Now *dial.* ME. **6** *ARCHERY*. Orig. (*hist.*), (a piece of canvas on a frame and laid on the ground as) the mark shot at in archery; a shot that hits the mark. Now *spec.* a target twelve times the usual size, used flat on the ground with a flag marking its centre. L16. **7** = CLOUT NAIL. E19.
▸ **II 8** A heavy blow. LME. **9** Personal or private influence; power of effective action, esp. in politics. *colloq.* M20.

clout /klaʊt/ *noun*[2]. Long *obsolete* exc. *dial.* ME.
[ORIGIN Perh. var. of CLOT *noun* or formed as CLOUT *noun*[1].]
1 A clot or clod of earth. ME. †**2** In *pl.* Cream curds, clotted cream. LME–M17. **3** A stupid person. E19.

clout /klaʊt/ *verb trans.* OE.
[ORIGIN from CLOUT *noun*[1].]
▸ **I 1** Mend with a patch, patch. OE. ▸†**b** Put *in*, *on*, *to*, as a patch. ME–L16. **2** Arm or protect with a metal plate; shoe with clout nails as protection against wear. LME.

clouted shoe: studded with clout nails as a protection against wear.

†**3** Put together clumsily; botch (*up*). LME–M17. **4** Cover with a cloth. *arch.* L16.
▸ **II 5** Hit hard. ME.

K. ATKINSON Frank clouted him for his language.

■ **clouter** *noun* a person who mends or patches; a botcher: ME. †**clouterly** *adjective* clumsy, awkward, clownish M17–E19.

clouted /ˈklaʊtɪd/ *adjective*. Now *dial.* M16.
[ORIGIN Perh. from CLOUT *noun*[2] + -ED[2].]
Of cream: clotted.

clout nail /ˈklaʊtneɪl/ *noun*. ME.
[ORIGIN from CLOUT *noun*[1] or *verb* + NAIL *noun*.]
A nail with a large flat head.

clove /kləʊv/ *noun*[1].
[ORIGIN Old English *clufu*, corresp. to the first elem. of Old Saxon *cluflōc* 'clove-leek', garlic, Old High German *klovolouh* (German *Knoblauch*), from Germanic base rel. to that of CLEAVE *verb*[1].]
1 Each of the small bulbs which make up the compound bulb of garlic, shallot, etc. OE. **2** A natural segment of a fruit. Now *rare*. M17.

clove /kləʊv/ *noun*[2]. ME.
[ORIGIN Old French *clou de girofle* lit. 'nail of gillyflower': cf. GILLYFLOWER.]
▸ **I** Orig. (long *rare* in sense 1) ***clove gillyflower*** & vars. **1** The dried flower bud of a tropical myrtle, *Syzygium aromaticum*, used as a pungent aromatic spice. Usu. in *pl.* ME.

oil of cloves a medicinal oil extracted from cloves.

2 A clove-scented pink, *Dianthus caryophyllus*, now known only as carnations and other cultivated forms. M16.
▸ **II 3** In full ***clove tree***. The tropical myrtle, *Syzygium aromaticum*, native to the Moluccas. L16.
4 In *pl.* A cordial flavoured with cloves. M19.

– COMB.: **clove-brown** (of) the colour of cloves; medium brown; **clove carnation** = sense 2 above; ***clove gillyflower***: see branch I above; **clove pink** = sense 2 above.

clove /kləʊv/ *noun*[3]. Also †**claw**. L15.
[ORIGIN Anglo-Latin *clavus*, Anglo-Norman *clou*, *clove*.]
hist. A weight of cheese or wool, equal to 7 or 8 lbs (approx. 3.2 to 3.6 kg).

clove /kləʊv/ *noun*[4]. *US*. L18.
[ORIGIN Dutch *klove*, also *kloof*, in Middle Dutch *clove*, Middle Low German *klove* split, cleft, rel. to CLEAVE *verb*[1].]
A rocky cleft or fissure; a gap, a ravine. Chiefly in place names.

clove *verb* see CLEAVE *verb*[1].

clove hitch /ˈkləʊv hɪtʃ/ *noun phr.* M18.
[ORIGIN from *clove* pa. pple of CLEAVE *verb*[1] (as showing parallel separate lines) + HITCH *noun*.]
A hitch by which a rope etc. is secured by passing it twice round a spar or rope etc. that it crosses at right angles.

cloven /ˈkləʊv(ə)n/ *ppl adjective*. ME.
[ORIGIN pa. pple of CLEAVE *verb*[1].]
Divided lengthwise; split (into pieces or to a certain depth); bifurcate.

cloven foot, **cloven hoof**: of ruminant quadrupeds, of the god Pan, of the Devil (***show the cloven foot***, ***show the cloven hoof***: see SHOW *verb*).

cloven *verb* see CLEAVE *verb*[1].

clover /ˈkləʊvə/ *noun & verb*.
[ORIGIN Old English *clāfre* = Middle & mod. Low German, Dutch *klāver*, from Germanic. First syll. corresp. to Old Saxon *klē*, Old High German *klēo* (German *Klee*).]
▸ **A** *noun*. Any of various leguminous plants constituting the genus *Trifolium*, with white, pink, etc., flowers in crowded heads and with trifoliate leaves; *esp.* any of several such plants grown as fodder, *T. repens* (more fully ***Dutch clover***, ***white clover***), *T. pratense* (more fully ***red clover***), and *T. hybridum* (more fully *ALSIKE* ***clover***). Cf. TREFOIL. OE.

Darling clover: see DARLING *noun*[2]. **four-leaf clover**, **four-leaved clover** (a representation of) a clover leaf with four leaflets, thought to bring good luck. **in clover** in ease and luxury. **Japan clover** = LESPEDEZA. ***rabbit-foot clover***: see RABBIT *noun*. ***subterranean clover***: see SUBTERRANEAN *adjective*. ***sweet clover***: see SWEET *adjective & adverb*.

– COMB.: **clover-grass** clover; **cloverleaf** (chiefly *N. Amer.*) a road intersection whose layout resembles a four-leaf clover; **clover weevil** any of various small weevils which feed on leguminous crops.
▸ **B** *verb trans.* Sow or cover with clover. Chiefly as ***clovered*** *ppl adjective*. M17.
■ **clovery** *adjective* having much clover; of the nature of clover: M17.

Clovis /ˈkləʊvɪs/ *adjective*. M20.
[ORIGIN See below.]
Designating a prehistoric culture first found near Clovis in eastern New Mexico, USA, or its remains, esp. the typical stone projectile points with fluting at the base, which are earlier than the Folsom points (see FOLSOM).

clow /klaʊ/ *noun*. Now *dial.* Also **clough**, (*Scot. & N. English*) **close** /kluːs/.
[ORIGIN Old English *clūse* from late Latin *clusa* var. of *clausa* closed place or way, later taken as pl.]
†**1** A narrow pass. Only in OE. **2** A dam for water, a sluice. ME.

clown /klaʊn/ *noun & verb*. M16.
[ORIGIN Perh. of Low German origin: cf. Northern Frisian *klönne*, *klünne*, clumsy fellow, *klünj* clod, lump, etc.]
▸ **A** *noun*. **1** A countryman, a rustic, a peasant, esp. when regarded as ignorant, crass, or rude. M16. **2** A person without refinement or culture; an ignoramus, a boor, an uncouth or ill-bred person. L16. **3** A fool or jester, esp. in a pantomime or circus. E17.

– COMB.: **clown fish** an anemone fish, *Amphiprion percula*, which is orange-brown with black-bordered white stripes and occurs in the Indian and Pacific Oceans.
▸ **B** *verb*. **1** *verb* †*trans.* with *it* & *intrans.* Play the clown; perform as a clown. L16. **2** *verb trans.* Play the clown in; portray like a clown. L19.

C

■ **clownery** *noun* the behaviour or acts of a clown, clownish behaviour L16. **clownish** *adjective* pertaining to or characteristic of a clown; ignorant, crass, rude; jesting, boisterously comic: L16. **clownishly** *adverb* L16. **clownishness** *noun* L16. **clownship** *noun* (*a*) the estate or condition of a clown or clowns; (*b*) (with possess. adjective, as ***your clownship*** etc.) a mock title of respect given to a clown: E17.

cloy /klɔɪ/ *verb*. LME.
[ORIGIN Aphet. from ACCLOY.]
†**1** *verb trans.* Pierce (as) with a nail; *esp.* = ACCLOY 1. LME–E18.
2 *verb trans.* †**a** Stop *up*, block (a passage etc.); choke, fill *up*; clog, encumber. LME–M17. ▸**b** Spike (a gun). Now *rare*. E17.
3 *verb trans. & intrans.* Satiate, weary, or nauseate by richness, sweetness, sameness, or excess, of food, pleasure, attention, etc. (Foll. by *with*.) M16.
■ **cloyingly** *adverb* in a cloying manner or degree E20. **cloyless** *adjective* that does not cloy E17. †**cloyment** *noun* (*rare*, Shakes.) satiety: only in E17. **cloysome** *adjective* (*rare*) tending to cloy E17.

clozapine /ˈkləʊzəpiːn/ *noun*. M20.
[ORIGIN from C(H)LO(RO-² + elems. of *benzodiazepine*.]
PHARMACOLOGY. A sedative of the benzodiazepine group used to treat schizophrenia.

cloze /kləʊz/ *adjective*. M20.
[ORIGIN Repr. abbreviation of CLOSURE *noun*.]
Designating a comprehension test or testing procedure in which the subject is asked to supply words deleted from a text.

club /klʌb/ *noun*. ME.
[ORIGIN Old Norse *clubba* assim. form of *klumba* (cf. *klumbu-*, *klubbufótr* club-footed), rel. to CLUMP *noun*.]
▸ **I 1** A heavy stick which increases in thickness and weight towards one end, used as a weapon etc. ME.
2 A stick or bat used in various ball games, esp. golf. LME.
3 Any organ, structure, etc., shaped like a club or with a knob at the end. LME. ▸**b** The butt end of a gun. E18. ▸**c** Chiefly *hist.* (A wig with) a club-shaped pigtail. L18.
4 CARDS. [translating Spanish *basto*, Italian *bastone* (cf. BASTO, BATON *noun*) the club or cudgel figured on Spanish or Italian cards.] In *pl.* (occas. treated as *sing.*), one of the four suits into which a pack of playing cards is divided, distinguished in British cards by a trefoil leaf in black; *sing.* a card of this suit. Also occas. a card or (in *pl.*) the suit distinguished in Spanish and Italian cards by cudgels or batons. M16.
▸ **II** †**5** Combination into one mass; *esp.* combination of contributions to make up a total sum; one share of such joint expense. M17–L18.
†**6** A social meeting the expenses of which are jointly defrayed. M17–E19.
†**7** A secret society, esp. with a political object. L17–M18.
8 An association of people united by some common interest; *esp.* (*a*) an association meeting periodically for a shared activity or for social purposes; (*b*) an association in which members make regular payments to a central fund or regular purchases from a central source to acquire some benefit. (Freq. with specification of purpose, nature, or membership.) L17. ▸**b** *spec.* An association of people formed mainly for social purposes and having premises providing meals, temporary residence, etc., for the use of members. L18. ▸**c** A group of people, nations, etc., having something in common. M20.

b A. TROLLOPE The club went on its way like other clubs, and men dined and smoked and played billiards and pretended to read.

athletic club, ***benefit club***, ***book club***, ***Christmas club***, ***fan club***, ***football club***, ***social club***, ***working men's club***, etc.
9 A building, rooms, or other premises occupied or owned by a club; an establishment providing entertainment etc. to members and guests. Also, a nightclub, *esp.* one playing fashionable dance music. (Freq. with specification as in sense 8 above.) M19.

R. HOGGART Going with her husband to his pub or club. S. STEWART I decided that the only solution was to leave and exited the smoky club.

– PHRASES: ***Indian clubs***: see INDIAN *adjective*. **in the club**, **in the pudding club** *slang* pregnant. ***nuclear club***: see NUCLEAR *adjective*. **on the club** *colloq.* through a benefit club etc. **the best club in London** *joc.* the House of Commons.
– COMB.: **club armchair**, **club chair** a thickly upholstered armchair of the type often found in clubs; **club class** an intermediate class of fare and accommodation on a passenger aircraft; **club foot** a congenitally distorted foot, = TALIPES; also, a foot of stunted lumpy appearance; **club-footed** *adjective* having a club foot; **club-haul** *verb trans. & intrans.* (NAUTICAL) tack (a ship) by letting the lee-anchor down as soon as the wind is out of the sails, so bringing the head to wind, then cutting the cable and trimming the sails to the other tack when the ship pays off (a last resort); **clubhouse** the premises occupied by a club; *esp.* those attached to a golf course; **clubland** *colloq.* the vicinity of St James's in London; any area where there are many clubs; **club-law** the use of physical force as contrasted with argument; the law of the physically stronger; **clubman** (*a*) a man armed with a club; (*b*) a member of one or more clubs; **clubmoss** any of various pteridophytes constituting the genus *Lycopodium* (family Lycopodiaceae) or formerly included in it, which are small creeping plants (unrelated to mosses) with needle-like or scalelike leaves; ***lesser clubmoss***, an allied smaller mosslike plant, *Selaginella selaginoides*; **clubroot** a fungal disease of turnips and other root crops, in which root galls are produced; **clubrush** a marsh or aquatic plant of the genus *Scirpus* or certain related genera of the sedge family; **club sandwich** (orig. *US*) a sandwich with two layers of filling between three slices of toast or bread, *esp.* one containing bacon, chicken, and tomato; **Club Soda** (proprietary name for) a variety of soda water.
■ **clubbish** *adjective* (*a*) resembling a club; clumsy; (now *dial.*) clownish, boorish; (*b*) fond of clubs, given to frequenting clubs: E16. **clubbism** *noun* the club system, the practice of forming clubs (orig. political clubs of the French Revolution) M19. **clubbist** *noun* (*a*) a member or supporter of the political clubs of the French Revolution, or of their principles; (*b*) a member of a club: L18. **clubby** *adjective* (*US*) (*a*) identified with a club, characteristic of a club; (*b*) friendly, sociable: M19. **clublike** *adjective* resembling a club; having a swelling at one end: M19. **clubster** *noun* (*a*) = *clubman* above; (*b*) *dial.* a stoat: E18.

club /klʌb/ *verb*. Infl. **-bb-**. L16.
[ORIGIN from the noun.]
1 *verb trans.* Beat with or as with a club. L16. ▸**b** Use (esp. a musket) as a club. E18.

C. G. SELIGMAN Kinnyole was clubbed to death by his own people.

2 *verb trans.* Gather into a clublike mass, gather together, (foll. by *together*); (chiefly *hist.*) dress (hair) in a club-shaped pigtail. E17.

J. PAYN London which is equal to half a dozen great towns clubbed together.

3 *verb trans.* Combine into a common stock or to a common end (foll. by *together*); contribute (money etc.) as one's share of a common stock; make *up* or put *together* (a sum of money etc.) by joint contributions. M17.

P. A. MOTTEUX Let every Man club his Penny towards it. G. GREENE We clubbed our butter rations.

4 *verb intrans.* Combine, form into a club or mass; *esp.* combine for joint action, to make up a sum of money for a particular purpose, or (formerly) as members of a secret society. (Foll. by *together*, *with*.) M17.

S. PEPYS How he did endeavour to find out a ninepence to club with me for the coach. E. HUXLEY A group of Pakistanis . . have clubbed together to buy a joint house.

5 *verb trans.* MILITARY. Throw into a confused mass. E19.
6 *verb intrans.* Visit a nightclub or nightclubs, esp. to dance. Freq. in ***go (out) clubbing***. M20.

S. STEWART I hadn't been clubbing . . since the last New Year's Eve disaster.

clubbable /ˈklʌbəb(ə)l/ *adjective*. Also **clubable**. L18.
[ORIGIN from CLUB *noun* + -ABLE.]
Fit to be a member of a club, sociable.
■ **clubbaˈbility** *noun* L19. **clubbableness** *noun* M20.

clubbed /klʌbd/ *adjective*. LME.
[ORIGIN from CLUB *noun*, *verb*: see -ED², -ED¹.]
1 Shaped like a club; thickset. LME.
2 That has been clubbed; formed into a club; used as a club. E17.

clubber /ˈklʌbə/ *noun*. M17.
[ORIGIN from CLUB *verb* or *noun* + -ER¹.]
1 a A person who clubs or combines with others for any object; a person who belongs to a club. M17. ▸**b** A person who goes clubbing. M20.
2 A person who wields a club. L19.

cluck /klʌk/ *noun & interjection*. E18.
[ORIGIN from the verb, or imit.]
▸ **A** *noun*. **1** The abrupt hollow guttural sound made by a hen desiring to sit or calling its chicks. Also, any similar sound, *esp.* the click of African etc. languages (see CLICK *noun*¹ 3). E18.
2 A stupid person. Esp. in ***dumb cluck***. *slang*. M20.
▸ **B** *interjection*. Repr. the cluck of a hen (see above). E19.

cluck /klʌk/ *verb*. L15.
[ORIGIN Imit., corresp. to Middle High German *klukken*, Danish *klukke*, Swedish *klucka*: cf. CLOCK *verb*¹.]
1 *verb trans.* (Of a hen) summon (chicks) with clucks; summon or encourage as a hen its chicks. L15.
2 *verb intrans.* Utter a cluck; *fig.* express fussy concern, disapproval, etc. L16.

J. DOS PASSOS Fainy clacked the reins . . and clucked with his tongue. S. MILES The . . nurse . . is clucking distressedly.

■ **clucky** *adjective* (of a hen) sitting or ready to sit on eggs E20.

clue /kluː/ *noun*. LME.
[ORIGIN Var. of CLEW *noun*.]
1 = CLEW *noun* 3a. LME.
2 = CLEW *noun* 5. L16.
3 = CLEW *noun* 2. *arch.* E17.
4 A fact or principle that serves as a guide, or suggests a line of inquiry, in a problem or investigation, an intricate structure, etc. E17. ▸**b** A word, phrase, etc., indicating a word or words to be inserted in a crossword puzzle. E20.

Independent He does not readily give clues about his character or inner thoughts. A. GHOSH An examination of the boy might yield a clue to what had happened.

not have a clue *colloq.* be ignorant or incompetent, be at a complete loss.
5 The thread of a story; a train of thought. M17.
†**6** = CLEW *noun* 1b. L17–E18.
7 = CLEW *noun* 5. L17.
8 = CLEW *noun* 6. M18.
■ **clueful** *adjective* (*a*) *rare* full of clues, informative; (*b*) *colloq.* well informed, knowledgeable: E20. **clueless** without a clue; *colloq.* ignorant, stupid: M19. **cluelessness** *noun* M20.

clue /kluː/ *verb*. M17. Pres. pple & verbal noun **clueing**.
[ORIGIN Var. of CLEW *verb*.]
†**1** *verb trans.* Follow, track. Only in M17.
2 *verb trans. & intrans.* = CLEW *verb* 3. M18.
3 *verb trans.* = CLEW *verb* 1. M19.
4 *verb trans.* Provide a clue to (a line in a crossword puzzle etc.). M20.
5 *verb trans.* Inform, tell (a person). Freq. foll. by *in*, *up*. *slang*. M20.

Clumber /ˈklʌmbə/ *noun*. M19.
[ORIGIN from *Clumber* Park in Nottinghamshire.]
More fully ***Clumber spaniel***. A spaniel of a slow heavily built breed.

clump /klʌmp/ *noun*. ME.
[ORIGIN Partly from Middle Low German *klumpe* (Low German *klump*) rel. to Middle Dutch *klompe* (Dutch *klomp*) lump, mass, & CLUMPER, CLAMP *noun*², CLUB *noun*; partly imit.]
1 A compact shapeless mass, a heap, a lump. ME. ▸**b** *spec.* An agglutinated mass of blood cells, bacteria, etc. L19.

E. GARRETT A baker gave me a clump o' bread.

2 A cluster or compact group of or *of* trees, shrubs, or other growing things, or (*transf.*) buildings, people, etc. L16.

V. WOOLF The fine clump of St John's wort that grew beside it. A. CARTER Discontented tradespeople stood in fretful clumps in the street.

3 More fully ***clump-sole***. A thick extra sole on a shoe. M19.
4 A heavy blow. *colloq.* L19.
5 A noise of a heavy step or tread, a non-resonant sound as of a heavy blow. Cf. CLAMP *noun*³, CLOMP *noun*. L19.

W. BOYD Acutely aware of the clump of his boots on the wood.

6 In *pl.* A game in which two teams try to guess an agreed word. L19.
■ **clumpish** *adjective* heavy and clumsy L17. **clumpy** *adjective* forming clumps; having many clumps; clumpish: E19.

clump /klʌmp/ *verb*. M17.
[ORIGIN Partly from the noun, partly imit.]
1 *verb intrans.* Move with or make a heavy non-resonant sound; tread heavily. Cf. CLAMP *verb*³, CLOMP *verb*. M17.

BUNYAN Every clown with his clumping dirty shoes. F. TUOHY They clumped around in tweeds and brogues.

2 a *verb trans.* Arrange or plant in a clump or mass. L18. ▸**b** *verb trans.* Provide with clumps of trees or other growing things. Chiefly as ***clumped*** *ppl adjective*. E19. ▸**c** *verb intrans.* Form a clump or clumps. L19.

a C. BEATON Three carnations clumped together. **b** E. BOWEN A sort of outdoor drawing-room clumped with mauve rhododendrons. **c** ANTHONY SMITH Further aggregation, or clumping, of the blood platelets.

3 *verb trans.* Hit, strike. *colloq.* M19.

clumper /ˈklʌmpə/ *noun & verb*. Long *obsolete* exc. *dial.*
[ORIGIN Old English *clympre* rel. to CLUMP *noun*.]
▸ **A** *noun*. = CLUMP *noun* 1. OE.
▸ †**B** *verb trans.* Form into lumps or masses, clot. M16–M17.

clumps /klʌmps/ *adjective*. Long *obsolete* exc. *dial.* Also †**clumse**. E17.
[ORIGIN Rel. to CLUMSE: cf. Icelandic *klumsa* lockjawed, Swedish dial. *klumsen* benumbed, dazed.]
Numb with cold; awkward, stupid, lazy; gruff, surly.

clumse /klʌmz/ *verb*. Long *obsolete* exc. *dial.* Also **clumps** /klʌmps/. ME.
[ORIGIN Prob. of Scandinavian origin: cf. Norwegian dial. *klumsen* strike dumb, clog, hamper, *klumst* clumsy.]
1 *verb trans.* Numb (*lit.* & *fig.*); daze, stupefy, dumbfound. Orig. & chiefly as ***clumsed***, ***clumst*** *ppl adjective*. ME.
†**2** *verb intrans.* Be or become numb with cold. Only in LME.

clumsy /ˈklʌmzi/ *adjective*. L16.
[ORIGIN from CLUMSE + -Y¹: cf. Swedish *klumsig* numb, clumsy.]
1 Heavy and awkward in motion or action; awkward in shape; ungainly; lacking in grace or skill; rudely constructed; without tact. L16.

I. D'ISRAELI A clumsy forgery. G. ORWELL He wrote in large clumsy capitals. A. WILSON Tom was . . clumsy; he . . knocked over full ashtrays.

†**2** Numb or stiffened with cold. Only in E17.
■ **clumsily** *adverb* L17. **clumsiness** *noun* M17.

clunch /klʌn(t)ʃ/ *noun*. LME.
[ORIGIN Perh. from CLUNCH *adjective*, or rel. to CLUMP *noun* as *bump*:*bunch*, *hump*:*hunch*.]
1 A lump. Long *obsolete* exc. *dial.* LME.
2 A lumpish fellow, a lout. *obsolete* exc. *dial.* E17.
3 a Any of various stiff clays. Also ***clunch clay***. *local*. L17. ▸**b** A soft limestone used esp. for internal carved building work. E19.

clunch /klʌn(t)ʃ/ *adjective*. *obsolete* exc. *dial.* L18.
[ORIGIN Prob. from Low German *Klunt*, Dutch *klont* lump, clod.]
Lumpy; heavy and stiff in consistency; thickset.

clung /klʌŋ/ *ppl adjective. arch. & dial.* ME.
[ORIGIN pa. pple of CLING *verb*.]
Drawn together, shrunken; pinched with hunger. Of soil: stiff, tenacious.

clung *verb pa. t. & pple* of CLING *verb*.

Cluniac /ˈkluːnɪak/ *noun & adjective.* L16.
[ORIGIN medieval Latin *Cluniacus*, from *Clun(i)aeum* Cluny (or Clugny), France: see -AC.]
▸ **A** *noun.* A monk of the monastery of Cluny, near Mâcon in France, or of the reformed Benedictine order which developed from it. L16.
▸ **B** *adjective.* Of or pertaining to this monastery or order. L19.

clunk *noun*[1] var. of KLUNK *noun*.

clunk /klʌŋk/ *verb & noun*[2]. Orig. *Scot.* L18.
[ORIGIN Imit.: cf. CLANK, CLINK *noun*[1], *verb*[1], CLONK.]
▸ **A** *verb intrans.* Make a hollow gurgling sound, as liquid poured from a bottle; make a dull clanking sound. L18.
▸ **B** *noun.* Such a sound. E19.

clunker /ˈklʌŋkə/ *noun. N. Amer. colloq.* M20.
[ORIGIN from CLUNK *verb* + -ER[1].]
1 A dilapidated vehicle or machine. M20.
2 A thing that is totally unsuccessful. L20.

clunky /ˈklʌŋki/ *adjective. colloq.* (orig. *N. Amer.*). M20.
[ORIGIN from CLUNK *noun*[1] or *noun*[2] + -Y[1].]
Poorly constructed, clumsy; inferior. Also, solid, heavy, and somewhat inelegant (freq. of shoes).

L. O'KEEFFE In the '50s.. teenage girls rocked and rolled in clunky saddle shoes. Y. MARTEL Stupid script, clunky dialogue, cardboard characters.

■ ˈ**clunkily** *adverb* L20.

Cluny /ˈkluːni/ *noun.* L19.
[ORIGIN See CLUNIAC.]
In full ***Cluny lace***. A kind of bobbin lace for clothing etc.

clupeoid /ˈkluːpɪɔɪd/ *noun & adjective.* M19.
[ORIGIN from mod. Latin *Clupea* genus name from Latin *clupea*, name of a river fish + -OID.]
(A fish) of the family Clupeidae, which includes the herring, sprat, anchovy, etc.
■ Also **clupeid** *noun & adjective* L19.

cluster /ˈklʌstə/ *noun.*
[ORIGIN Old English *clyster*, rarely *cluster*, also *ġeclystre*, prob. from Germanic base also of CLOT *noun*.]
1 A collection of fruit (orig. grapes), flowers, etc., growing closely together; a bunch. OE.
2 A compact group of other similar things, as persons, animals, gems, etc. LME. ▸**b** ASTRONOMY. A group of stars or galaxies forming a relatively close association. E18. ▸**c** LINGUISTICS. A group of successive consonants. E20.

A. P. HERBERT There was a lock every quarter of a mile, and sometimes a cluster of two or three. B. MOORE The other monks bunched in a cluster.

LAYGEAR *cluster*. **b** GLOBULAR *cluster*. ***local cluster***: see LOCAL *adjective*. ***open cluster***: see OPEN *adjective*.
– COMB.: **cluster bomb** an anti-personnel bomb spraying metal pellets on impact; **cluster compound** CHEMISTRY a compound whose structure involves a polycyclic aggregate of atoms of one (sometimes, more than one) element bonded together; **cluster pine** the maritime pine, *Pinus pinaster*.

cluster /ˈklʌstə/ *verb.* LME.
[ORIGIN from the noun.]
▸ **I** *verb trans.* Orig. & chiefly as ***clustered*** *pa. pple & ppl adjective.*
1 Arrange in a cluster, group closely. LME.
clustered columns, **clustered pillars**, **clustered shafts**: several close together, or disposed round and half detached from the pier.
2 Provide or cover with clusters. (Foll. by *with*.) LME.

SOUTHEY Mountains clustered with the fruitful pines.

†**3** Coagulate, clot. Only in M16.
▸ **II** *verb intrans.* **4** Congregate in a cluster or clusters; grow or be situated in a cluster or clusters; gather *(a)round*. LME.

M. F. MAURY The.. icebergs which cluster off the Falkland Islands. K. MANSFIELD Round the ice-cream cart.. the children cluster. R. ELLISON We were a small tight group, clustered together.

†**5** Coagulate, clot. L15–M16.

clutch /klʌtʃ/ *noun*[1]. Branch I also (all earlier) (*Scot. & N. English*) **cleuk** /kluːk, klyk/, (now *dial.*) **cloke** /kləʊk/, †**clooch**, & other vars. ME.
[ORIGIN Unknown: mod. form from CLUTCH *verb*. The relationship of the various early forms is obscure.]
▸ **I** **1** A claw; *derog.* a hand. Usu. in *pl.* Now chiefly *Scot.* in *gen.* sense. ME.
2 *spec.* A hand as an instrument of rapacity or cruelty, a grasping hand. Usu. in *pl.*, & in ***in a person's clutches***, ***into a person's clutches***, ***out of a person's clutches***, etc. (passing into sense 3). E16.

SHAKES. *Haml.* But age.. hath caught me in his clutch. STEELE [He] escapes the Clutches of the Hangman.

3 a Tight hold or grip; relentless control. L18. ▸**b** An act of grasping *at*. M19.

a F. MARRYAT I can't hold on ten seconds more... my clutch is going now.

▸ **II** ***clutch*** only.
4 MECHANICS. An arrangement for connecting or disconnecting working parts. E19. ▸**b** In a motor vehicle: a device for connecting the engine to the transmission; the pedal operating this. L19.
b ***ride the clutch***: see RIDE *verb*. ***slip in the clutch***, ***slip the clutch***: see SLIP *verb*[1].

clutch /klʌtʃ/ *noun*[2]. E18.
[ORIGIN Prob. southern var. of CLETCH.]
A set of eggs for hatching, or of birds hatched, at a single time; *transf.* (usu. *derog.*) a closely associated group *of*.

A. L. ROWSE A clutch of leering women. D. ATTENBOROUGH The female can only lay a relatively small number of eggs in a clutch.

clutch /klʌtʃ/ *verb.* ME.
[ORIGIN Var. of CLITCH *verb*.]
†**1 a** *verb intrans.* Bend or crook at the joint. Only in ME. ▸**b** *verb trans.* Incurve (the fingers), clench (the hand). L16–E18.
2 *verb trans.* Seize eagerly or convulsively with the claws or fingers. LME.

SIR W. SCOTT With all the fingers spread out as if to clutch it.

3 *verb trans.* Hold firmly in one's grasp, grip. E17.

D. H. LAWRENCE Alvina counted it [money] and kept it clutched in her hand. J. BERGER She dances like a bear, clutching her partner close to her.

4 *verb intrans.* Grasp or snatch *at*. M19.

H. JAMES She.. could only clutch at the hope of some inspiration. L. DURRELL The sleeper awoke and clutched at my hand.

– PHRASES: ***clutch at a straw***, ***clutch a straw***, ***clutch at straws***, ***clutch straws***: see STRAW *noun*.
– COMB.: **clutch bag** a handbag with no handle or strap.

clutter /ˈklʌtə/ *noun.* L16.
[ORIGIN Var. of CLODDER *noun* or from the verb: assoc. with *cluster*, *clatter*.]
†**1** A clotted mass. L16–E17.
2 A confused collection; crowded disorder, untidy state, litter. M17.

G. HEYER An open book lay on the ground beside it, with a clutter of newspapers and magazines. H. ACTON She was surrounded by neatness and order: there was a complete absence of clutter. F. KIDMAN A clutter of ramshackle cottages with wet washing flapping on the clotheslines.

3 Bustle, commotion; hubbub, disturbance; mingled rattle. Now *arch. & dial.* M17.

MILTON The clutter of their Horse, and of their Wheels. SWIFT Those ladies, who are apt to make the greatest clutter on such occasions.

clutter /ˈklʌtə/ *verb.* LME.
[ORIGIN Var. of CLOTTER *verb*, assoc. with *cluster*, *clatter*.]
1 *verb trans. & intrans.* Clot, coagulate. *obsolete* exc. *dial.* LME.
2 a *verb intrans.* Run (*together*) in confused groups, crowd (*together*). Now *rare* or *obsolete*. M16. ▸**b** *verb trans.* Heap together in confusion. *obsolete* exc. *dial.* M17.
3 *verb intrans.* Run in bustling disorder or with a confused noise. Now chiefly *dial.* E17.

DEFOE The coaches, horsemen and crowd, cluttered away, to be out of harm's way.

4 *verb trans. & intrans.* Utter or speak confusedly, esp. habitually. M17.
5 *verb trans.* Crowd untidily (*with*), litter *with*. Freq. foll. by *up*. L17.

C. MCCULLERS The four walls were cluttered with calendars and crudely painted advertisements. J. FRAME Who wanted an ugly old broken-down alcoholic cluttering up precious hospital cubic feet?

†**cly** *verb & noun. slang.* M16.
[ORIGIN Perh. of Low German origin: cf. Low German *kleien* to scratch, claw.]
▸ **A** *verb trans.* Take; *esp.* steal, pocket. M16–M19.
▸ **B** *noun.* A pocket; money. L17–L19.
– COMB.: **cly-faker** a pickpocket; **cly-faking** picking pockets.

Clydesdale /ˈklʌɪdzdeɪl/ *noun.* L18.
[ORIGIN The area of the River Clyde in Scotland.]
1 More fully ***Clydesdale horse***. A horse of a heavy draught breed originating around Clydesdale. L18.
2 More fully ***Clydesdale terrier***. A terrier of a small smooth-haired breed originating around Clydesdale. L19.

clype /klʌɪp/ *verb & noun. Scot.* Also **clipe**. E18.
[ORIGIN Obscurely from CLEPE.]
▸ **A** *verb intrans.* Tell tales, tattle (*on*). E18.
▸ **B** *noun.* A telltale. E19.

clypeate /ˈklɪpɪeɪt/ *adjective.* M19.
[ORIGIN formed as CLYPEUS + -ATE[2].]
BOTANY & ZOOLOGY. Resembling a round shield.
■ Also **clypeated** *adjective* (*rare*) E18.

clypeus /ˈklɪpɪəs/ *noun.* Pl. **-ei** /-ɪʌɪ/. M19.
[ORIGIN Latin *clipeus*, *clupeus* round shield.]
The broad shield-shaped frontal part of an insect's head, above the labrum.
■ **clypeal** *adjective* L19.

clyster /ˈklɪstə/ *noun & verb. arch.* LME.
[ORIGIN Old French & mod. French *clystère* or Latin *clyster* from Greek *klustēr* syringe, from *kluzein* rinse out.]
▸ **A** *noun.* A medicine injected into the rectum, an enema; occas., a suppository. LME.
▸ **B** *verb trans.* Treat with a clyster. L15.

CM *abbreviation*[1].
Member of the Order of Canada.

cm *abbreviation*[2].
Centimetre(s).

Cm *symbol.*
CHEMISTRY. Curium.

Cm. *abbreviation.*
Command Paper (sixth series, 1986–).

Cmd. *abbreviation.*
Command Paper (fourth series, 1918–56).

Cmdr *abbreviation.*
Commander.

Cmdre *abbreviation.*
Commodore.

CMEA *abbreviation.*
Council for Mutual Economic Assistance.

CMG *abbreviation.*
Companion of (the Order of) St Michael and St George.

Cmnd. *abbreviation.*
Command Paper (fifth series 1956–86).

CMOS *abbreviation.*
ELECTRONICS. Complementary metal oxide semiconductor, denoting a technology for making low-power integrated circuits.

CMV *abbreviation.*
MEDICINE. Cytomegalovirus.

CNAA *abbreviation.*
Council for National Academic Awards.

CND *abbreviation.*
Campaign for Nuclear Disarmament.
■ **CNDer** *noun* a member or supporter of CND L20.

cnemial /ˈkniːmɪəl/ *adjective.* L19.
[ORIGIN from Greek *knēmē* tibia + -AL[1].]
ORNITHOLOGY. Of or pertaining to the tibia.

CNG *abbreviation.*
Compressed natural gas.

cnidarian /nʌɪˈdɛːrɪən, nɪ-/ *noun & adjective.* M20.
[ORIGIN from mod. Latin *Cnidaria* (see below), formed as CNIDO- + *-aria* pl. of Latin *-arium* -ARY[1] (cf. -ARIAN): see -AN.]
ZOOLOGY. ▸**A** *noun.* An animal of the invertebrate phylum Cnidaria (cf. COELENTERATE *noun*). M20.
▸ **B** *adjective.* Of or pertaining to this phylum. M20.

cnido- /ˈknʌɪdəʊ/ *combining form.*
[ORIGIN from Greek *knidē* nettle: see -O-.]
ZOOLOGY. Used in terms relating to stinging cells of coelenterates etc.
■ **cnidoblast** *noun* a cell in which a nematocyst develops L19. **cnidocil** *noun* [Latin CILIUM] the external irritable process of a nematocyst L19.

CNN *abbreviation.*
Cable News Network.

cnr *abbreviation.*
Corner.

CNS *abbreviation.*
1 Central nervous system.
2 Chief of the Naval Staff.

CO *abbreviation.*
1 Colorado.
2 Commanding Officer.
3 Conscientious objector.

Co *symbol.*
CHEMISTRY. Cobalt.

co- /kəʊ/ *prefix.*
[ORIGIN Latin, var. of COM- esp. before vowels, *h*, and *gn*: cf. COL-, CON-, COR-.]
1 Used in words adopted from Latin and in English words modelled on these, and as a productive prefix, forming: (*a*) verbs from verbs with the sense 'with others', as ***co-edit***, ***cooperate***; (*b*) adjectives from adjectives and adverbs from adverbs with the senses 'jointly', 'mutually', as ***co-belligerent***, ***coequal***, ***coequally***; (*c*) nouns from nouns with the senses 'joint', as ***co-author***, ***co-precipitation***, and 'mutual', as ***coequality***. ▸**b** BIOLOGY. Forming names of substances which combine with others to produce an effect, or enhance the action of others, but are individually inactive, as ***co-carcinogen***, ***coenzyme***.

2 *MATH.* Short for *complement*, in the sense 'of the complement' (as *cosine*) or 'complement of' (as *co-latitude*).
■ **coadap'tation** *noun* mutual adaptation **E19.** **coa'dapted** *adjective* mutually adapted **M19.** **coa'djust** *verb trans.* adjust to each other **M19.** **co'adjutant** *adjective & noun* (a person) helping another or others or with another or others **E18.** **co-a'dore** *verb trans.* adore conjointly (*with*) **E17.** **co-ad'venturer** *noun* a fellow adventurer **M17.** **co'agency** *noun* joint or combined agency **E17.** **co'agent** *noun* a joint agent **L16.** **co-a'ration** *noun* cooperative ploughing or tillage, esp. as practised in Wales in ancient times **L19.** **co'arbiter** *noun* a joint arbiter **L16.** **co-a'ssessor** *noun* a joint assessor **M17.** **co-a'ssume** *verb trans.* assume together or conjointly (*with*) **E17.** **co-a'ttest** *verb trans.* attest together or conjointly (*with*) **M17.** **co'branded** *adjective* marketed under or carrying two or more brand names **L20.** **co-de'fendant** *noun* a joint defendant **M17.** **co-de'pendency** *noun* emotional dependency on supporting or caring for another person or other people **L20.** **co-de'terminant** *noun* each of a set of determining factors **L19.** **co-determi'nation** *noun* joint determination; *spec.* of company policies by unions and workers as well as management **E20.** **co-de'termine** *verb trans.* jointly determine **E20.** **codi'rector** *noun* a joint director **M19.** **co-'driver** *noun* a person who takes turns in driving a vehicle, esp. in a race, rally, etc. **M20.** **co-'editor** *noun* a joint editor **L19.** **co-e'ffect** *noun* a joint or concomitant effect **M18.** **co'enzyme** *noun* (*BIOCHEMISTRY*) an organic compound which combines with an enzyme to activate it **E20.** **co-e'state** *noun* an estate or state possessing equal authority or rank with another **M18.** **co-'favourite** *noun* an equal or joint favourite, esp. in a sporting contest **E20.** **co-feo'ffee** *noun* (*hist.*) a joint feoffee **LME.** **co-'founder** *noun* a joint founder **E17.** **co-'foundress** *noun* a joint foundress, a female joint founder **M17.** **co-'guardian** *noun* a joint guardian **M17.** **co-'guardianship** *noun* joint guardianship **L19.** **co-'head** *noun* a joint leader or principal **L19.** **co'heir** *noun* a joint heir **LME.** **co'heiress** *noun* a joint heiress, a female coheir **M17.** **co'heirship** *noun* joint heirship **E17.** **co'helper** *noun* a joint helper **M16.** **co-'heritor** *noun* a joint inheritor **M16.** **co-host** (*a*) *noun* a person who hosts an event or broadcast with another or others; (*b*) *verb trans.* be the co-host of: **E20.** **coindi'cation** *noun* (a) conjoint or concurrent indication **E17.** **co-'infinite** *adjective* equally or conjointly infinite **M17.** **co-in'habitant** *noun* a joint inhabitant **M16.** **co-in'here** *verb intrans.* inhere together **M19.** **co-in'herence** *noun* joint inherence **E19.** **co-in'herent** *adjective* jointly inherent **E19.** **co-in'heritance** *noun* (a) joint inheritance **L16.** **co-in'heritor** *noun* a joint inheritor **E16.** **co-instan'taneous** *adjective* occurring or existing at the same moment **M18.** **co-instan'taneously** *adverb* simultaneously **E19.** **co'juror** *noun* (chiefly *hist.*) a fellow oath taker, one who confirms under oath the oath of another **M18.** **co-'labourer** *noun* a fellow labourer **M19.** **co-'morbid** *adjective* (*MEDICINE*) pertaining to or designating a medical condition that co-occurs with another **L20.** **co-mor'bidity** *noun* (*MEDICINE*) the quality of being co-morbid **L20.** **co-'obligant** *noun* a person under joint obligation **E19.** **co-'obligor** *noun* (*LAW*) a person who accepts an obligation or makes a commitment along with others **L18.** **co-o'ccur** *verb intrans.* occur together or simultaneously (*with*) **M20.** **co-o'ccurrence** *noun* simultaneous or joint occurrence **M20.** **co-o'ccurrent** *adjective & noun* (each of two or more things) occurring together or simultaneously **M20.** **co-om'nipotent** *adjective* conjointly omnipotent **M16.** **co-'ossify** *verb intrans. & trans.* ossify together **L19.** **co-'owner** *noun* a joint owner **M19.** **co-'ownership** *noun* joint ownership **L19.** **co'pastor** *noun* a joint pastor **E19.** **co-'payment** *noun* (in medical insurance) a contribution made by an insured person towards medical treatment; the payment of such contributions: **M20.** **co-pro'duction** *noun* (a) joint production; *esp.* a cinematographic film produced by teams from more than one country: **M20.** **co-pro'moter** *noun* a joint promoter **E19.** **co-pro'prietor** *noun* a joint proprietor **L18.** **co-'regency** *noun* a joint regency **M17.** **co-'regent** *adjective & noun* (a person) ruling jointly with another **L18.** **co-'regnant** *noun & adjective* (a person) reigning jointly with another **M17.** **co-'residence** *noun* residence together, joint residence **M17.** **co-'ruler** *noun* a joint ruler **L17.** **co'seismal** *adjective & noun* (*a*) *adjective* relating to points affected simultaneously by an earthquake; (*b*) *noun* a line or curve connecting such points: **M19.** **co-'sleep** *verb intrans.* sleep in the same bed or room as one's parent or child **M20.** **co-'sovereign** *noun* a joint sovereign, a fellow sovereign **L18.** **co-'sovereignty** *noun* joint sovereignty **E18.** **co-spe'cific** *adjective* = CONSPECIFIC *adjective* **L19.** **co'tectic** *adjective* [after EUTECTIC] *PETROGRAPHY* representing conditions under which two or more minerals etc. crystallize simultaneously from a liquid **E20.** **co-'tenancy** *noun* joint tenancy **L19.** **co-'tenant** *noun* a joint tenant **M19.** **co-text** *noun* the text surrounding a particular word etc. **M20.** **co-u'nite** *verb trans. & intrans.* (*arch.*) unite together, conjoin **M16.** **co-'work** *verb intrans.* work together, cooperate **E17.** **co-'worker** *noun* a person who works in collaboration with another; a fellow worker: **M17.**

Co. *abbreviation.*
1 Company.
2 County.
– **PHRASES:** **and Co.** /kəʊ/ *colloq.* and the rest of them, and similar things, etcetera.

c/o *abbreviation.*
Care of.

coacervate /kəʊˈasəveɪt/ *noun.* **E20.**
[ORIGIN Back-form. from COACERVATION: see -ATE[1].]
CHEMISTRY. A colloid-rich viscous liquid phase which may separate from a colloidal solution on addition of a third component.

coacervate /kəʊˈasəveɪt/ *verb trans.* **E17.**
[ORIGIN Latin *coacervat-* pa. ppl stem of *coacervare*, formed as CO- + *acervare*, from *acervus* heap: see -ATE[3].]
1 Heap together, gather into a heap. Now *rare.* **E17.**
2 *CHEMISTRY.* Cause coacervation of. **M20.**

coacervation /kəʊˌasəˈveɪʃ(ə)n/ *noun.* **LME.**
[ORIGIN Latin *coacervatio(n-)*, formed as COACERVATE *verb*: see -ATION.]
1 The action of heaping together; accumulation; an accumulated mass. Now *rare.* **LME.**
2 *CHEMISTRY.* The separation of a coacervate from a colloidal solution. **E20.**

coach /kəʊtʃ/ *noun.* **M16.**
[ORIGIN French *coche* from Hungarian *kocsi* (*szekér*) (cart) from *Kocs*, a town in Hungary.]
1 A large horse-drawn carriage; *esp.* (*a*) a state carriage; (*b*) (chiefly *hist.*) a privately owned carriage for personal use; (*c*) *hist.* a large closed carriage for public conveyance of passengers. **M16.** ▸**b** A railway passenger or mail carriage; *esp.* (*US*) one not provided with beds or berths. **M19.** ▸**c** A chartered or long-distance usu. single-decker bus. Also called *motor coach*. **E20.** ▸**d** Economy-class seating in an aircraft. *N. Amer.* **M20.**
hackney coach, *stagecoach*, etc. **drive a coach and horses through**, **drive a coach and six through**, etc., *fig.* render (legislation etc.) useless. *sociable coach*: see SOCIABLE *adjective*.
2 A cabin at the stern of a man-of-war, usu. occupied by the captain. **M17.**
3 A private tutor. **M19.** ▸**b** An instructor of an athletics team, rowing crew, etc. **L19.** ▸**c** A tame bullock, horse, etc., used as a decoy in catching wild livestock. *Austral.* **L19.**
– **COMB.:** **coach-box** a coachman's seat; **coach-building** the building of motor-vehicle bodies; **coach-built** *adjective* (of a motor-vehicle body) built by craftsmen, orig. using wood; **coach-dog** a Dalmatian; **coach horse**: used for drawing a coach; *devil's coach horse*: see DEVIL *noun*; **coach house** an outhouse for carriages; **coachload** a large number of people travelling by coach, a coachful; **coachman** a driver of a horse-drawn carriage; **coachmanship** skill in driving a coach; *coach station*: see STATION *noun*; **coach whip** [from its whiplike stems] the ocotillo, *Fouquieria splendens*; **coachwood** *Austral.* (a tree, esp. *Ceratopetalum apetalum*, yielding) close-grained timber suitable for cabinetmaking; **coachwork** the bodywork of a road or rail vehicle.
■ **coachee** *noun*[1] (*a*) *arch. colloq.* a coachman; (*b*) *US* (chiefly *hist.*) a long lightweight horse-drawn carriage: **L18.** **coachful** *noun* a coach's full complement of passengers **M17.** **coachy** *noun* (*arch. colloq.*) a coachman **E19.**

coach /kəʊtʃ/ *verb.* **E17.**
[ORIGIN from the noun.]
1 *verb trans.* Convey in, seat in, or provide with a coach. Now *rare.* **E17.**
2 *verb intrans.* Ride or drive in a coach. **M17.**

J. HATTON The . . inn of the old coaching days.

3 *verb trans.* Tutor, train, esp. individually or intensively (*for* an examination, competition, etc.); give hints to; prime with facts. **E18.** ▸**b** Decoy (wild cattle, horses, etc.) with tame animals. *Austral.* **L19.**

C. CHAPLIN Sydney had so zealously coached me that I was almost word-perfect. H. MACMILLAN Expert scientists who . . tried to coach me in the profound mysteries of atomic theory.

■ **coachee** *noun*[2] a person who is coached **M19.**

coacher /ˈkəʊtʃə/ *noun.* **L16.**
[ORIGIN from COACH *noun* or *verb* + -ER[1].]
†1 A coachman. **L16–E17.**
2 A coach horse. **E18.**
3 A person who coaches a pupil, a team, etc. **L19.** ▸**b** = COACH *noun* 3c. *Austral. & NZ.* **L19.**

coachwhip /ˈkəʊtʃwɪp/ *noun.* **M18.**
[ORIGIN from COACH *noun* + WHIP *noun*.]
1 A whip used by a coachman. **M18.**
2 More fully *coachwhip snake*. A fast-moving black or brown N. American snake, *Masticophis flagellum*. **M18.**
3 More fully *coachwhip bird*. The Australian whipbird. **L18.**

coact /kəʊˈakt/ *verb.* **LME.**
[ORIGIN Branch I from Latin *coact-* pa. ppl stem of *cogere* compel (see COGENT); branch II from CO- + ACT *verb*.]
▸ **I** †1 *verb trans.* Compel, constrain. **LME–M17.**
2 *verb trans.* Control. *rare.* **M19.**
▸ **II** †3 *verb trans.* Enact together. *rare.* Only in **L16.**
4 *verb intrans.* Act together, cooperate. **E17.**
■ **coaction** *noun* (*a*) (now *rare*) compulsion, restraint, coercion; (*b*) concerted action, acting together: **LME.**

coactive /kəʊˈaktɪv/ *noun & adjective.* **E16.**
[ORIGIN Late Latin *coactivus* compulsory, from *coact-* (see COACT, -IVE), or Old French & mod. French *coactif*, *-ive*. Sense B.2 from CO- + ACTIVE *adjective*, infl. by Anglo-Latin *coactivus* acting jointly.]
▸ †**A** *noun.* A compelling cause. *rare.* Only in **E16.**
▸ **B** *adjective* †1 **a** Enforced, compulsory. **L16–M17.** ▸**b** Compelling, coercive. Now *rare.* **E17.**
2 Acting in concert, taking place together. *rare.* **E17.**

Coade stone /ˈkəʊd stəʊn/ *noun phr.* **E20.**
[ORIGIN *Coade*, the name of a family whose company manufactured the stone.]
An artificial stone claimed to have greater frost and heat resistance than natural stone and formerly much used for statues, decorative work, etc.

coadjutor /kəʊˈadʒʊtə/ *noun.* **LME.**
[ORIGIN Old French & mod. French *coadjuteur*, †*-tor*, from late Latin *coadjutor*, formed as CO- + ADJUTOR.]
An assistant, *esp.* one appointed to assist a bishop.
■ **coadjutorship** *noun* (*a*) the office of coadjutor; (*b*) helping cooperation: **M17.** **coadjutress** *noun* a female coadjutor **E17.** †**coadjutrice** *noun* = COADJUTRESS **M16–M18.** **coadjutrix** *noun* = COADJUTRESS **M17.**

coadunate /kəʊˈadjʊneɪt/ *verb trans.* **E17.**
[ORIGIN Latin *coadunat-* pa. ppl stem of *coadunare*, formed as CO- + *adunare*, formed as AD- + *unare*, from *unus* one: see -ATE[3].]
Unite, combine. Chiefly as *coadunated ppl adjective.*

coadunation /kəʊˌadjʊˈneɪʃ(ə)n/ *noun.* **M16.**
[ORIGIN Late Latin *coadunatio(n-)*, formed as COADUNATE: see -ATION.]
Union, combination.

coagment /kəʊagˈmɛnt/ *verb trans.* Now *rare* or *obsolete.* **E17.**
[ORIGIN Latin *coagmentare*, from *coagmentum* joining: see -MENT.]
Stick together; cement. Only as *coagmented ppl adjective.*

coagulable /kəʊˈagjʊləb(ə)l/ *adjective.* **M17.**
[ORIGIN French, or medieval Latin *coagulabilis*, from *coagulare* COAGULATE *verb*: see -ABLE.]
Able to be coagulated.
■ **coagula'bility** *noun* **L18.**

coagulant /kəʊˈagjʊl(ə)nt/ *noun & adjective.* **L18.**
[ORIGIN Latin *coagulant-* pres. ppl stem of *coagulare* COAGULATE *verb*: see -ANT[1].]
(An agent, as rennet) that brings about coagulation.

coagulase /kəʊˈagjʊleɪz, -s/ *noun.* **E20.**
[ORIGIN from COAGULATE *adjective* + -ASE.]
BIOCHEMISTRY. A bacterial enzyme which brings about coagulation of the blood.

†**coagulate** *adjective.* **LME–M19.**
[ORIGIN Latin *coagulatus*, formed as COAGULATE *verb*: see -ATE[2].]
Coagulated.

coagulate /kəʊˈagjʊleɪt/ *verb.* **LME.**
[ORIGIN Latin *coagulat-* pa. ppl stem of *coagulare*, formed as COAGULUM: see -ATE[3].]
1 *verb trans. & intrans.* Change from a fluid to a more or less solid state, esp. by a chemical reaction; set, solidify. **LME.** ▸†**b** *verb intrans.* Solidify by evaporation; crystallize. **M17–E18.**

ROBERT KNOX Albumen . . is coagulated by heat, alcohol and the stronger acids. E. HEMINGWAY I stopped the bleeding by lying still and letting it coagulate.

2 *verb trans. & intrans.* Form as a mass; unite into a mass. **E17.**

J. HOWELL Venus . . was . . coagulated of that foam. *fig.*: J. STEINBECK Gradually their wills coagulated.

■ **coagulative** *adjective* having the property of coagulating; involving or producing coagulation: **E17.** **coagulator** *noun* = COAGULANT *noun* **E17.**

coagulation /kəʊagjʊˈleɪʃ(ə)n/ *noun.* **LME.**
[ORIGIN Old French & mod. French, or Latin *coagulatio(n-)*, formed as COAGULATE *verb*: see -ATION.]
1 The action or process of coagulating. **LME.** ▸†**b** Solidification by evaporation; precipitation from a solution; crystallization. **L15–E18.**
2 A coagulated mass. **M17.**

coagulin /kəʊˈagjʊlɪn/ *noun.* **E20.**
[ORIGIN from COAGULATE *verb* + -IN[1].]
BIOLOGY. Any substance produced in the body which accelerates the coagulation of foreign proteins or of blood.

coagulometer /kəʊˌagjʊˈlɒmɪtə/ *noun.* **E20.**
[ORIGIN from COAGULATE *verb* + -OMETER.]
An instrument for measuring the ease or rate of coagulation of blood.

coagulum /kəʊˈagjʊləm/ *noun.* Pl. **-la** /-lə/. **M16.**
[ORIGIN Latin.]
1 A coagulant; rennet; that part of the blood that coagulates, the clotting element. Now *rare* or *obsolete.* **M16.**
2 A coagulated mass. **M17.**

coaita /kəʊˈʌɪtə/ *noun.* **L18.**
[ORIGIN Spanish from Tupi-Guarani *coatá* monkey.]
A spider monkey.

coak /kəʊk/ *noun & verb.* **L15.**
[ORIGIN Perh. repr. Old Northern French var. of Old French *coche*, Italian *cocca* notch: cf. COCK *verb*[4].]
▸ **A** *noun.* A tabular projection on the face of a piece of scarfed timber, to fit into a recess in the face of another which is to be joined to it, to make a firmer joint; a metal lining to such a recess. **L15.**
▸ **B** *verb trans.* Join by means of coaks. **L18.**

coal /kəʊl/ *noun & verb.*
[ORIGIN Old English *col* = Old Frisian, Middle Low German *kole* (Low German *kale*), Middle Dutch *cole* (Dutch *kool*), Old High German *kol(o)* (German *Kohle*), Old Norse *kol*, from Germanic.]
▸ **A** *noun.* 1 A red-hot piece of carbon, charred wood, etc.; a glowing ember. Also more fully *coal of fire* (arch.), *live coal*, etc. **OE.**
†2 A charred remnant, a cinder; cinders, ashes. Also more fully *dead coal* etc. **OE–M17.**
†3 *sing.* & in *pl.* Charcoal. **ME–M19.**
4 *sing.* & (now *rare*) in *pl.* A hard opaque black or blackish mineral, mainly carbonized plant matter, found in seams or strata at or below the earth's surface and used as fuel and in the manufacture of gas, tar, etc. (With *pl.*) a piece of this ready for burning in a fire. **ME.**

P. H. JOHNSON She . . went over to the fire, throwing more coals upon it. N. CALDER Fossil fuels like coal and oil. W. BRONK The coal, . . I put it on the fire.

bituminous coal, black coal, brown coal, cannel coal, coking coal, mineral coal, sea coal, etc.

– PHRASES: **call over the coals** = *haul over the coals* below. ***coal of fire***: see sense 1 above. **(carry) coals to Newcastle** (bring) a thing of which there is already a plentiful supply; (do) something absurdly superfluous. **haul over the coals** [from the treatment of heretics] call to account and convict, reprimand. **heap coals on a person's head, heap coals of fire on a person's head** cause remorse by returning good for evil. ***live coal***: see sense 1 above. ***small coal***: see SMALL *adjective*. ***white coal***: see WHITE *adjective*.

– COMB.: **coal-bed** a stratum of coal; **coal-black** *adjective* completely black; **coal box** a receptacle for coal to supply the fire of a room; **coal bunker** a place for storing coal in a ship etc.; **coal cellar** a basement storage place for coal; **coal dust** powdered coal; **coalface** an exposed surface of coal in a mine; **coalfield** a district with a series of coal strata; **coal fire** a fire made (primarily) of coal; **coal-fired** *adjective* heated or driven by coal; **coalfish** = SAITHE; **coal gas** a mixture of gases (chiefly hydrogen and methane) obtained by destructive distillation of coal and used for fuel; **coal-heaver** a person employed in moving coal; **coal-heugh** *Scot.* a coalmine; **coal-hole** a small coal cellar; **coalhouse** a building etc. for the storage of coal; **coalman** a man who carries, sells, or delivers coal; **coal-master** *hist.* the owner or lessee of a coalmine; **coal measures** the series of rocks comprising coal seams and the intervening strata; **coal merchant** a retail seller of coal; **coal-meter** (now *arch.* or *hist.*) a person who measures or weighs coal (formerly *spec.*, an official of the corporation of London); **coalmine** a mine in which coal is dug; **coalminer** a person who digs for coal; **coalmining** digging for coal; **coal oil** *N. Amer.* (*a*) petroleum; (*b*) paraffin; **coal-owner** *hist.* = *coal-master* above; **coal pit** (*a*) (now *US*) a place where charcoal is made; (*b*) a coalmine; **coal sack** (*a*) a sack for carrying coal; (*b*) a dark patch in the Milky Way, *spec.* (also **C-**) one near the Southern Cross; **coal scuttle** a coal box; a bucket, usu. with a sloping lip for pouring, for carrying and holding coal for the fire of a room; **coal seam** a stratum of coal; **coal tar** a thick black viscid liquid produced by the destructive distillation of bituminous coal, containing benzene, naphthalene, phenols, aniline, and many other organic chemicals; **coal-whipper** *hist.* a person or apparatus raising coal from a ship's hold by means of a pulley; **coal-worker** a coalminer; a worker at a colliery; **coal-works** a colliery.

▸ **B** *verb* **1 a** *verb intrans.* Get coal; take in a supply of coal. LME. ▸**b** *verb trans.* Supply with coal; put coal into (a ship etc.). M19.

> **a** E. WAUGH A . . sloop which was coaling for a cruise in the Persian Gulf.

2 *verb trans.* Convert into charcoal. *arch.* L16.

– NOTE: The vowel was short in Old English and remained so in many derivatives.

■ **coaler** *noun* a ship or railway transporting coal; a tender supplying coal to a steamship: L19. **coalifiˈcation** *noun* the process by which plant remains become coal E20.

coalesce /kəʊəˈlɛs/ *verb*. M16.

[ORIGIN Latin *coalescere*, formed as CO- + *alescere* grow up, from *alere* nourish: see -ESCE.]

†**1** *verb trans.* Cause to grow together, unite. M16–L18.

2 *verb intrans.* Grow or come together to form one whole; unite; combine in a coalition. M17.

> LD MACAULAY Who had bound himself . . never to coalesce with Pitt. C. DARWIN The granules coalesce into larger masses. M. GIROUARD The elements that were to coalesce as 'Queen Anne'.

■ **coalescence** *noun* the action or process of coalescing; union; combination in a coalition: M16. **coalescent** *adjective* that coalesces M17.

coalise *verb* var. of COALIZE.

Coalite /ˈkəʊlʌɪt/ *noun*. E20.

[ORIGIN from COAL *noun* + -ITE[1].]

(Proprietary name for) a kind of smokeless fuel made by refining coal.

coalition /kəʊəˈlɪʃ(ə)n/ *noun*. E17.

[ORIGIN medieval Latin *coalitio(n-)*, from *coalit-* pa. ppl stem of *coalescere* COALESCE: see -ION.]

1 Coalescence; union, fusion, combination. E17.

> J. TRAPP Water and oil violently shaken together may seem to mingle, but . . there is no coalition. B. COTTLE The coalition of an emphatic name and a clear symbol has often made for fine visual advertising.

2 POLITICS. A temporary combination of parties etc. that retain distinctive principles. E18.

> T. BENN All major political parties are coming to be seen for what they are—broad coalitions.

■ **coalitioner** *noun* a person who forms or joins a coalition E19. **coalitionism** *noun* the principles or advocacy of government by coalition of parties E20. **coalitionist** *noun* an adherent of a coalition or of coalitionism L18.

coalize /ˈkəʊəlʌɪz/ *verb intrans.* Now *rare*. Also **-ise**. L18.

[ORIGIN French *coaliser*, from *coalition* formed as COALITION: see -IZE.]

Form a coalition.

■ **coalizer** *noun* L18.

coalmouse /ˈkəʊlmaʊs/ *noun*. Also **cole-**. Pl. **-mice** /-mʌɪs/.

[ORIGIN Old English *colmāse*: see COAL, TITMOUSE.]

= COAL TIT.

Coalport /ˈkəʊlpɔːt/ *noun*. L19.

[ORIGIN See below.]

A kind of porcelain, freq. decorated with floral designs, produced at Coalport in Shropshire.

coal tit /ˈkəʊltɪt/ *noun*. Also **cole-**. M19.

[ORIGIN from COAL *noun* (on account of its dark colouring) + TIT *noun*[4].]

A small greyish tit, *Parus ater*. Also called ***coalmouse***.

■ Also **coal-titmouse** *noun*, pl. **-mice**, *arch.* L18.

coaly /ˈkəʊli/ *adjective*. See also COLLY *adjective & noun*[2]. L16.

[ORIGIN from COAL *noun* + -Y[1].]

Having much coal; covered with coal; of the nature or colour of coal.

– NOTE: Place name evidence and the short-vowel var. *colly* suggest that the word was already in Old English.

coaming /ˈkəʊmɪŋ/ *noun*. E17.

[ORIGIN Unknown.]

A raised border round the hatches etc. of a ship to keep out water. Usu. in *pl.*

coapt /kəʊˈapt/ *verb trans.* Now *rare*. L16.

[ORIGIN Late Latin *coaptare*, formed as CO- + *aptare*, from *aptus* APT.]

Fit or join together.

coaptation /kəʊapˈteɪʃ(ə)n/ *noun*. M16.

[ORIGIN Late Latin *coaptatio(n-)*, formed as COAPT: see -ATION.]

The adaptation or adjustment of things, parts, etc., to each other; *spec.* in MEDICINE, the drawing together of separated tissue, e.g. in a wound or fracture.

coarb /ˈkəʊɑːb/ *noun*. M17.

[ORIGIN Irish *comharba*.]

hist. A successor in an ecclesiastical office of the Celtic Church.

†**coarct** *verb trans.* LME.

[ORIGIN Latin *coar(c)tare*, formed as CO- + *artare*, from *artus* confined.]

1 Press or draw together. LME–E17.

2 Restrict the action of (a person). LME–E19.

3 Confine within narrow limits. LME–M17.

coarctate /kəʊˈɑːkteɪt/ *adjective*. LME.

[ORIGIN Latin *coar(c)tatus* pa. pple of *coar(c)tare*: see COARCT, -ATE[2].]

1 Pressed close together, contracted, confined. LME.

2 ENTOMOLOGY. (Of a pupa) formed within and remaining concealed by the larval cuticle; (of metamorphosis) resulting in such a pupa. E19.

coarctation /kəʊɑːkˈteɪʃ(ə)n/ *noun*. LME.

[ORIGIN Latin *coar(c)tatio(n-)*, from *coar(c)tat-* pa. ppl stem of *coar(c)tare*: see COARCT, -ATION.]

1 The action of compressing tightly; the state of being tightly compressed; *spec.* (MEDICINE) congenital narrowing of a short section of the aorta. LME.

2 Confinement or restriction as to limits. Now *rare*. E17.

coarse /kɔːs/ *adjective*. LME.

[ORIGIN Unknown.]

▸ **I 1** Ordinary, common, inferior. Largely *obsolete* exc. as passing into other senses. LME.

> SHAKES. *Hen. VIII* Now I feel Of what coarse metal ye are moulded—envy.

▸ **II** (Often inherent in earlier uses of sense 1.)

2 Rough, loose, or large in texture, grain, or features; in a natural or raw state; rough or harsh to the senses. L16. ▸**b** Of weather: rough, stormy. Now *dial.* L18.

> R. W. EMERSON They are full of coarse strength, rude exercise . . and sound sleep. TENNYSON Thou, My Lord, eat also, tho' the fare is coarse. J. STEINBECK His mustache was thin and coarse. A. LURIE The fine sheet . . weighed on me like a coarse blanket. C. CONRAN Spread a layer of coarse salt over the bottom of a heavy frying-pan.

3 Not delicate in perception, manner, or taste; unrefined; rude, uncivil, vulgar; (esp. of language) obscene. L17.

> L. STEPHEN That style of coarse personal satire of which Swift was a master. L. G. GIBBON That coarse young Guthrie brute would never thrive.

– SPECIAL COLLOCATIONS & COMB.: **coarse-fibred** *adjective* = *coarse-grained* below. **coarse fish** any freshwater fish other than salmon or trout. **coarse fishing**: for coarse fish. **coarse-grained** *adjective* (*fig.*, of a person) having a coarse nature, unrefined.

■ **coarsely** *adverb* M16. **coarsen** *verb trans. & intrans.* make or become (more) coarse E19. **coarseness** *noun* M16. **coarsish** *adjective* somewhat coarse M18.

coarticulate /kəʊɑːˈtɪkjʊleɪt/ *verb*. L16.

[ORIGIN from CO- + ARTICULATE *verb*.]

1 *verb intrans.* ANATOMY. Unite to form a joint. *rare*. L16.

2 *verb trans.* PHONETICS. Articulate together. M20.

coarticulation /ˌkəʊɑːtɪkjʊˈleɪʃ(ə)n/ *noun*. L16.

[ORIGIN from CO- + ARTICULATION. Sense 1 translating Greek *sunarthrōsis*.]

†**1** Jointing together of two bones. L16–M17.

2 PHONETICS. (An) articulation of two sounds together. M20.

coast /kəʊst/ *noun*. OE.

[ORIGIN Old French *coste* (mod. *côte*) or (in earliest use) its source Latin *costa* rib, flank, side. In branch II repr. mod. French *côte* with the sense 'slope, hillside', infl. by the verb.]

▸ **I** †**1** A rib; the side of any body (human or animal); the side of anything. OE–E19.

2 Orig. more fully ***coast of the sea***, ***sea coast***. The border of land near the sea; the seashore. ME.

> A. L. ROWSE We drove out to the coast. *Times* The seas off the Ayrshire coast.

clear the coast remove an enemy or other obstacle to (dis)embarkation etc. **coast to coast**, **from coast to coast** across a whole island or continent. ***Slave Coast***: see SLAVE *noun & adjective*. **the Coast** *esp.* (*US*) the Pacific coast of N. America. **the coast is clear** the enemy is not about to obstruct (dis)embarkation etc.; there is no chance of being hindered or observed.

†**3** A region of the earth or the heavens; a tract, a district; a part of the world. ME–M17.

†**4** An area or direction in relation to a person or thing; a point of the compass; a quarter. ME–E18.

†**5** The border of a country etc., frontier territory. Usu. in *pl.* LME–E17.

▸ **II 6** A slide for tobogganing; a slide downhill on a toboggan. *N. Amer.* L18.

7 A (usu. downhill) run on a bicycle etc. without pedalling or in a motor vehicle without using the engine. L19.

– COMB.: **coast disease** *Austral.* a mineral deficiency disease of sheep and cattle; **coastguard** (one of) a body of people employed to keep watch on the coasts and thus save life, prevent smuggling, etc.; **coast sickness** *Austral.* = ***coast disease*** above.

■ **coastal** *adjective* of or pertaining to a coast M19. **coastward** *adjective*, **coastward(s)** *adverb* toward or in the direction of a coast M19. **coastways** *adverb* (*arch.*) = COASTWISE *adverb* E18. **coastwise** *adverb & adjective* (*a*) *adverb* by way of or along a coast; (*b*) *adjective* following or carried along a coast: L17.

coast /kəʊst/ *verb*. LME.

[ORIGIN Old French *costeier* (mod. *côtoyer*), formed as COAST *noun*.]

▸ **I** †**1** *verb trans. & intrans.* Keep by the side of (a person etc. moving). LME–L17.

†**2 a** *verb trans.* Go or move by the side of (a place etc.); skirt. LME–M18. ▸**b** *verb intrans.* Lie or lead alongside; go, pass, *along, by, round*, etc. LME–M19. ▸**c** *verb intrans.* Move in a roundabout course. *rare* (Shakes.). Only in E17.

3 *verb trans. & intrans.* Proceed or travel by the edge of (the sea, a lake, a river, etc.). Now *arch. & dial.* LME.

4 a *verb trans.* Sail by the coast of, skirt the shore of. LME. ▸**b** *verb intrans.* Sail *along, by*, etc., a coast; sail along a coast from port to port. M16.

b coasting vessel = COASTER 3.

†**5** *verb trans. & intrans.* Travel around, move about, explore, scour. LME–L17.

†**6 a** *verb trans.* Border, adjoin; approach, esp. with hostility. LME–M17. ▸**b** *verb intrans.* Border (*up*)*on*; come or be near *to*; make one's way *to, towards*; approach. *lit. & fig.* LME–E18.

7 *verb intrans.* Of a hawk, hound, etc.: not fly or run straight at the prey. M16.

▸ **II 8** *verb intrans.* Slide downhill on a toboggan. *N. Amer.* L18.

9 *verb intrans.* Of a person or vehicle: move easily without the use of power. L19.

> J. COE Successive buses coasted by.

10 *verb intrans. fig.* Make progress without any exertion. M20.

> *www.fictionpress.com* I thought I could coast through life on my parent's money and never support myself. *Cherwell (online ed.)* The Oxford team deservedly and easily coasted to another victory.

coasteering /kəʊˈstɪːrɪŋ/ *noun*. L20.

[ORIGIN Blend of COAST *noun* and *-eering* as in *mountaineering* and *orienteering*.]

The sport of travelling along a rocky coast by climbing, scrambling, and swimming in the sea.

coastel /kəʊsˈtɛl/ *noun*. L20.

[ORIGIN Blend of COAST *noun* and HOTEL.]

An accommodation barge for off-shore workers, troops, etc.; a floating barracks or hotel.

coaster /ˈkəʊstə/ *noun*. L16.

[ORIGIN from COAST *verb* + -ER[1].]

1 A person who sails along a coast. L16.

2 A person who lives by a coast. E17.

3 A vessel employed in sailing along a coast, trading from port to port, esp. of the same country. L17.

4 a A toboggan for coasting. *N. Amer.* M19. ▸**b** A roller coaster. *N. Amer.* E20.

5 A silver tray for a decanter; a small mat for a drinking glass. L19.

coat /kəʊt/ *noun & verb*. ME.

[ORIGIN Old French *cote* (mod. *cotte* petticoat), from Proto-Romance from Frankish, of unknown origin.]

▸ **A** *noun*. **1** An outer garment, usu. made of cloth and having long sleeves, and orig. worn by men and boys. Without specification now *esp.* a sleeved outdoor garment worn over indoor clothes for warmth; also (esp. in ***coat and skirt***) a woman's tailored jacket worn with a skirt; formerly also, a close-fitting tunic coming no lower than the waist. ME. ▸**b** *transf.* With qualifying colour adjective: a person wearing a coat of the specified colour, esp. as a uniform. E16. ▸†**c** = ***coat card*** below. L16–M17. ▸†**d** = ***coat-money*** below. E17–E18.

car coat, dress coat, frock coat, greatcoat, housecoat, Mackintosh coat, mandarin coat, Melton coat, overcoat, raincoat, russet coat, surcoat, tailcoat, trench coat, tuxedo coat, waistcoat, etc. **coat of arms** a coat or vest embroidered with heraldic arms, a herald's tabard; (see also sense 4 above). **coat of mail** a linen or leather jacket quilted with interlaced rings or overlapping plates of steel, as defensive armour. ***cut one's coat according to one's cloth***: see CLOTH *noun* 4. ***pull a***

C

person's coat: see PULL *verb*. **trail one's coat** = *trail one's coat-tails* below. **turn one's coat** desert, change sides. **b** *blue-coat*, *redcoat*, etc.
2 A petticoat. Usu. in *pl. obsolete* exc. *dial.* LME.
3 In translations of ancient languages: any of various styles of tunic or other outer garment for the body. LME.
4 More fully ***coat of arms***. A person's or corporation's distinctive heraldic bearings or shield. LME.
5 A natural covering or integument: ▸**a** An animal's covering of hair, fur, feathers, etc. Also (*rare*), an animal's hide. LME. ▸**b** ANATOMY. A membrane etc. enclosing or lining an organ. LME. ▸**c** A skin, a rind, a husk; a layer of a bulb etc. M16.
†**6** Clothing as indicating a profession, class, etc. L16–L18.
7 NAUTICAL. A piece of tarred canvas or (now usu.) of rubber fixed around a mast, bowsprits, etc., where they enter the deck, to keep water out. E17.
8 A layer of any substance, esp. paint, covering a surface; a covering laid on at one time. E17.
FIRST *coat*. *rough coat*: see ROUGH *adjective*.
9 *fig.* Anything that covers or conceals. E17.
– COMB.: **coat armour** †(*a*) a coat of arms (both senses); (*b*) blazonry, heraldic arms; †**coat card** a court card; **coat dress** a woman's tailored dress resembling a coat; **coat hanger** a clothes hanger; **coat-money** *hist.* money for providing a coat for each man in military service, *esp.* a non-parliamentary tax exacted by Charles I; **coat-tail** a tail of a coat; ***on a person's coat-tails***, undeservedly benefiting from someone's progress; ***trail one's coat-tails*** (for someone to tread on), seek to pick a quarrel.
▸ **B** *verb trans.* **1** Provide with or clothe in a coat; dress. LME.
2 Cover with a surface layer or successive layers of a substance as paint, tin, etc.; (of a substance) cover (a surface) in a coat. M18.
■ **coated** *adjective* wearing a coat; having a coat (of a specified kind) (*wavy-coated*: see WAVY *adjective* 1d); covered *with*, *in*, a coat or coating of some substance: L16. **coa'tee** *noun* (*a*) *arch.* a close-fitting short-tailed chiefly military coat; (*b*) a woman's or infant's short coat: L18. **coatless** *adjective* L16.

coath *noun* var. of COTHE *noun*.

coati /kəʊˈɑːti/ *noun*. Pl. **-s**, same. E17.
[ORIGIN Spanish & Portuguese from Tupi *kua'ti*.]
A Central and S. American carnivore of the genera *Nasua* or *Nasuella*, resembling a raccoon and with a long flexible snout.
■ Also **coatimundi** /kəʊˌɑːtɪˈmʌndi/ *noun* [Portuguese *cuatimundi* from Tupi *kuatimu'ne*, from *kua'ti* + *mu'ne* snare, trick] L17.

coating /ˈkəʊtɪŋ/ *noun*. L16.
[ORIGIN from COAT + -ING¹.]
1 Material for coats. L16.
2 (An article of) clothing of the nature of a coat. L18.
3 A layer of any substance, as paint, tin, etc., spread over or covering a surface. L18.

co-author /kəʊˈɔːθə/ *noun & verb*. L19.
[ORIGIN from CO- + AUTHOR.]
▸ **A** *noun*. A joint author. L19.
▸ **B** *verb trans.* Be a co-author of. M20.
■ **co-authorship** *noun* L19.

coax /ˈkəʊaks/ *noun*. *colloq.* M20.
[ORIGIN Abbreviation.]
Coaxial cable.

coax /kəʊks/ *verb*. Orig. †**cokes**. L16.
[ORIGIN from COKES *noun*.]
1 *verb trans.* Pet, fondle, caress; treat endearingly. *obsolete* exc. *dial.* L16.
2 *verb trans.* Persuade gradually by flattery, caresses, etc., or by continued patient trial (*to do*, *into doing*, (*in*)*to* or *out of* an action or state); get (a thing) *out of*, *from* a person by such gradual persuasion. M17. ▸**b** *verb intrans.* Employ persuasive flattery, caresses, etc., or continued patient trial. M17.

> L. M. MONTGOMERY I had ever such a time coaxing her to let me come down and say good-bye. P. KAVANAGH How to coax a cheer or a laugh from a lazy crowd. DAY LEWIS A recalcitrance I could always be coaxed out of by my father's pretending I was a bear. I. COLEGATE To rake out the embers of his stove and coax it back into flame.

†**3** *verb trans.* Make a fool of. L17–E19.
– NOTE: Described by Samuel Johnson as 'a low word' and prob. in use long before it is recorded in literature. Sense 3 is prob. the original.
■ **coaxer** *noun* E18. **coaxingly** *adverb* in a coaxing manner E18.

coaxial /kəʊˈaksɪəl/ *adjective*. L19.
[ORIGIN from CO- + AXIAL.]
Sharing a common axis; situated on or rotating about the same axis. Also, using or involving coaxial cable.
coaxial cable a coaxial line; a cable consisting of several coaxial lines. **coaxial line** an electrical transmission line with two concentric conductors separated by an insulator.
■ **coaxially** *adverb* L19.

cob /kɒb/ *noun*¹. LME.
[ORIGIN Unknown.]
▸ **I** With the notion 'big', 'stout'.
1 A great man, a leading man. Now *dial.* LME. ▸†**b** A wealthy man, a miser. M16–L17.
2 A male swan. Also ***cob-swan***. LME.
3 A sturdy short-legged riding horse. E19.
▸ **II** With the notion 'rounded'.
4 a In full ***cobnut***. A large kind of hazelnut; (as ***cobnut(s)***), any of various children's games using nuts. M16. ▸**b** In full ***cob-loaf***. A round loaf of bread. E17. ▸**c** In full (now *dial.*) ***cob-coal***. A large roundish piece of coal. E19. ▸**d** A testicle. Usu. in *pl. dial.* E19. ▸**e** A (baked apple) dumpling. *dial.* L19.
5 a A small stack of hay or corn. *dial.* E17. ▸**b** A bunch or knot of hair; a chignon. M19.
6 *gen.* A lump or heap *of*. *dial.* L19.
▸ **III** With the notion 'head', 'top'.
†**7 a** The head of a (red) herring. L16–M17. ▸**b** In *pl.* Young herring. *Scot.* L19.
8 = CORNCOB 1. L17.
corn on the cob maize cooked and eaten attached to the cob.
9 The seeding head of wheat, clover, etc. *dial.* M19.
– COMB.: *cob coal*: see sense 4c above; **cob-iron** (*a*) in *pl.* (*hist.*), the irons supporting a spit; (*b*) an andiron; *cob-loaf*: see sense 4b above; **cob-meal** *US* corncobs ground down; *cobnut(s)*: see sense 4a above; **cob pipe** = CORNCOB 2.

cob /kɒb/ *noun*². Also **cobb**. M16.
[ORIGIN Perh. of Low German origin: cf. Dutch *kobbe*, *kobmeeuw*, East Frisian *sê-kobbe*.]
More fully ***sea-cob***. A gull, *esp.* a greater black-backed gull.

cob /kɒb/ *noun*³. E17.
[ORIGIN Unknown.]
A composition of clay, gravel, and straw, used for building walls etc.

cob /kɒb/ *noun*⁴. Also **cobb**. E17.
[ORIGIN Perh. abbreviation of COBBLE *noun*.]
A mole or pier (as constructed of cobblestones).

cob /kɒb/ *noun*⁵. Chiefly *Irish. obsolete* exc. *hist.* L17.
[ORIGIN Perh. from COB *noun*¹ I (as the largest silver coin).]
A Spanish dollar or piece of eight.

cob /kɒb/ *noun*⁶. *dial.* Also **cobb**. L17.
[ORIGIN Unknown.]
A wicker basket carried on the arm.

cob /kɒb/ *noun*⁷. *US & dial.* Also **cobb**. E19.
[ORIGIN from COB *verb*¹.]
A blow, a knock.

cob /kɒb/ *noun*⁸. *slang*. M20.
[ORIGIN Unknown.]
A fit of annoyance or anger. Only in ***have a cob on***, ***get a cob on***, be annoyed, become angry.

cob *noun*⁹ var. of KOB *noun*¹.

cob /kɒb/ *verb*¹. Infl. **-bb-**. LME.
[ORIGIN Uncertain: perh. imit.]
†**1** *verb intrans.* Fight; give blows. Only in LME.
2 a *verb trans.* NAUTICAL. Strike on the buttocks with a flat instrument, as a punishment. Now *hist.* M18. ▸**b** *gen.* Strike. *dial.* E19.
3 *verb trans.* Crush or bruise (ore). L18.
4 a *verb intrans.* Of seed: undergo threshing (*well* etc.). L18. ▸**b** *verb trans.* Thresh or beat out (seed). E19.

cob /kɒb/ *verb*² *intrans. & trans. dial.* Infl. **-bb-**. L19.
[ORIGIN Unknown.]
Take a liking to (each other), get on well *together*.

cobalamin /kəˈbɒləmɪn/ *noun*. M20.
[ORIGIN from COBALT + VIT)AMIN.]
BIOCHEMISTRY. Any of a group of cobalt-containing substances including vitamin B_{12}.

cobalt /ˈkəʊbɒlt, -ɔːlt/ *noun & adjective*. L17.
[ORIGIN German *Kobalt*, KOBOLD, lit. 'fairy, demon': so called from the belief that cobalt ore was deleterious to the silver ores with which it occurred: cf. NICKEL *noun & adjective*, WOLFRAM.]
▸ **A** *noun*. **1** A hard, weakly magnetic metal which is a chemical element of the transition series, atomic no. 27, used widely in alloys (symbol Co).L17.
red cobalt (*ore*): see RED *adjective*. *speiss-cobalt*: see SPEISS 2.
2 In full ***cobalt blue***. A deep blue pigment containing cobalt(II) oxide and alumina; the colour of such a pigment. M19.
– COMB.: **cobalt bloom** = ERYTHRITE; *cobalt blue*: see sense 2 above; **cobalt bomb** (*a*) a container of a cobalt radioisotope for therapeutic use; (*b*) a hydrogen bomb designed to disperse radioactive cobalt; **cobalt glance** = COBALTITE.
▸ **B** *adjective*. Of cobalt blue. M19.
■ **co'baltic** *adjective* of or pertaining to cobalt; *spec.* of trivalent cobalt: L18. **cobal'tiferous** *adjective* containing or yielding cobalt M19. **co'baltous** *adjective* of divalent cobalt M19.

cobalti- /kəˈbɒlti, -ˈbɔːlti/ *combining form* of COBALT: see -I-. Esp. of trivalent cobalt (cf. COBALTO-).
■ **cobalti'cyanide** *noun* a salt of the complex anion $Co(CN)_6^{3-}$ L19.

cobaltite /ˈkəʊb(ə)ltʌɪt/ *noun*. M19.
[ORIGIN from COBALT *noun* + -ITE¹.]
MINERALOGY. A cubic sulpharsenide of cobalt which usu. occurs as silvery-white metallic cubic or polyhedral crystals.
■ Earlier †**cobaltine** *noun* L18–L19.

cobalto- /kəˈbɒltəʊ, -ˈbɔːlt-/ *combining form* of COBALT: see -O-. Esp. of divalent cobalt (cf. COBALTI-). Freq. forming names of minerals.

cobb *noun* var. of COB *noun*², *noun*⁴, *noun*⁶, *noun*⁷.

cobber /ˈkɒbə/ *noun*¹. L18.
[ORIGIN from COB *verb*¹ or *noun*¹ + -ER¹.]
A person who breaks ore into small pieces.

cobber /ˈkɒbə/ *noun*² *& verb*. *Austral. & NZ colloq.* L19.
[ORIGIN Perh. from COB *verb*² + -ER¹.]
▸ **A** *noun*. A companion; a mate; a friend. L19.
▸ **B** *verb intrans.* Foll. by *up*: make friends (*with*). E20.

cobble /ˈkɒb(ə)l/ *noun*. LME.
[ORIGIN from COB *noun*¹ II + -LE¹.]
1 In full ***cobblestone***. A water-worn rounded stone, esp. of the size used for paving. LME.
2 In *pl.* Coal in lumps of this size. E19.
■ **cobbly** *adjective* paved with cobbles L19.

cobble /ˈkɒb(ə)l/ *verb*¹. L15.
[ORIGIN Back-form. from COBBLER.]
1 *verb trans. & intrans.* Mend (esp. shoes); mend roughly or clumsily; patch (*up*). L15.
2 *verb trans.* Put *together* roughly or clumsily. L16.
3 *verb trans.* Make by putting things together roughly or clumsily. Also foll. by *together*. M18.

cobble /ˈkɒb(ə)l/ *verb*² *trans.* L17.
[ORIGIN from COBBLE *noun*.]
1 Pelt with stones etc. *dial.* L17.
2 Pave with cobbles. M19.

cobbler /ˈkɒblə/ *noun*. ME.
[ORIGIN Unknown.]
1 A person who mends shoes. ME. ▸**b** The last sheep to be sheared, an awkward sheep to shear, (in punning allusion to a cobbler's last). *Austral. & NZ colloq.* L19. ▸**c** In *pl.* [abbreviation of ***cobbler's awls*** below]. Testicles; nonsense, rubbish. *slang*. M20.
2 A clumsy worker, a botcher. L16.
3 An iced drink of wine, sugar, and lemon, in a tall glass. E19.
4 A dish of fruit, or occas. other ingredients, baked with a cake topping. Orig. *US*. M19.
5 A horse chestnut used in the children's game of conkers. *dial.* L19.
– COMB.: **cobbler's awls** *rhyming slang* balls, testicles; **cobbler's peg(s)** *Austral.* a weed of the composite family with sharp-pointed seeds, spec. *Bidens pilosa*; **cobbler's wax** a resinous substance used for waxing thread.

cobbra /ˈkɒbrə/ *noun*. *Austral.* Now *rare*. Also **cobra**. M19.
[ORIGIN Dharuk *gabarra*.]
The head; the skull.

cobby /ˈkɒbi/ *adjective*. L17.
[ORIGIN from COB *noun*¹ I + -Y¹.]
1 Stout, hearty. *dial.* L17.
2 Headstrong; arrogant. *dial.* L18.
3 Of the nature of or like a cob (horse); shortish and thickset; stocky. L19.

Cobdenism /ˈkɒbd(ə)nɪz(ə)m/ *noun*. M19.
[ORIGIN from Richard *Cobden* (1804–65), English statesman and economist, its leading advocate + -ISM.]
hist. A policy advocating free trade, peace, and international collaboration.
■ **Cobdenite** *noun* a supporter of Cobdenism L19.

co-belligerent /kəʊbɪˈlɪdʒ(ə)r(ə)nt/ *adjective & noun*. E19.
[ORIGIN from CO- + BELLIGERENT.]
(A nation etc.) jointly waging war.
■ **co-belligerence**, **co-belligerency** *nouns* the quality or state of being (a) co-belligerent M20.

cobia /ˈkəʊbɪə/ *noun*. M19.
[ORIGIN Unknown.]
A large slender predatory game fish, *Rachycentron canadum*, of the tropical Atlantic, Indian, and western Pacific Oceans. Also called ***runner***, ***sergeant fish***.

coble /ˈkəʊb(ə)l/ *noun*. OE.
[ORIGIN Perh. from Celtic: cf. Welsh *ceubal* ferryboat, skiff, wherry, Old Breton *caubal*.]
A flat-bottomed boat used esp. for fishing in Scotland and NE England: in Scotland usu. a rowing boat used on rivers and lakes, in NE England a seagoing boat with oars and a lug sail.

Cobol /ˈkəʊbɒl/ *noun*. M20.
[ORIGIN Acronym, from common business-oriented language.]
(The name of) a programming language designed for use in business operations.

cobra /ˈkəʊbrə, ˈkɒbrə/ *noun*¹. M17.
[ORIGIN Portuguese *cobra de capello* lit. 'snake with hood', ult. from Latin *colubra* snake.]
Orig. more fully ***cobra de capello*** /də kaˈpɛləʊ/. Any of a number of venomous Asian and African snakes esp. of the genus *Naja*, which can dilate their necks to form a hood when excited.
king cobra, ***spectacled cobra***, etc.

cobra *noun*² var. of COBBRA.

co-brother /kəʊˈbrʌðə/ *noun*. Pl. **-brothers**, **-brethren** /-ˈbrɛðr(ə)n/. **L16**.
[**ORIGIN** from **CO-** + **BROTHER** *noun*.]
Brother in the same craft or occupation; confrère.

Coburg /ˈkəʊbəːg/ *noun*. **E19**.
[**ORIGIN** from Prince Albert of Saxe-*Coburg* (1819–61), consort of Queen Victoria.]
Chiefly *hist.* **1** A two-wheeled covered carriage or cart, used esp. in the country. **E19**.
2 In full ***Coburg loaf***. A kind of loaf. **M19**.
3 A thin fabric used for dresses and coat linings. **M19**.

cobweb /ˈkɒbwɛb/ *noun*. Orig. †**cop(pe)-**. **ME**.
[**ORIGIN** from **COP** *noun*[2] + **WEB** *noun*.]
1 The fine network spun by a spider to catch its prey; the material of this; *spec.* (*a*) an old web covered with dirt and dust (usu. in *pl.*); (*b*) *ZOOLOGY* the type of web built by a cobweb spider. **ME**. ▸**b** A single thread spun by a spider. **M19**.
†**2** Threads similar to the spider's, produced by insects etc. **LME–E17**.
3 *fig.* Anything of flimsy, frail, or unsubstantial texture. **L16**. ▸**b** *sing.* & (usu.) in *pl.* Musty rubbish. **L16**. ▸**c** A subtly woven snare; an entangling mesh. **M17**.
b blow away the cobwebs, **clear away the cobwebs** remove fustiness or lethargy.
4 In full ***cobweb bird***. The spotted flycatcher, which uses spiders' webs in constructing its nest. **E18**.
– **COMB.**: ***cobweb bird***: see sense 4 above; **cobweb law** *arch.* a law which can be broken by the rich or powerful; **cobweb micrometer**: with spider's threads instead of wires; **cobweb spider** any of various spiders of the family Theridiidae, which build tangled three-dimensional webs.
■ **cobwebbed** *adjective* covered or hung (as) with cobwebs **E17**. **cobwebbery** *noun* a structure of cobweb, *fig.* (a) subtle entangling argument: **M19**. **cobwebby** *adjective* cobwebbed; resembling cobwebs: **M18**. **cobweblike** *adjective* resembling (that of) a cobweb or cobwebs, cobwebby **M17**.

coca /ˈkəʊkə/ *noun*. **L16**.
[**ORIGIN** Spanish from Aymara *kuka* or Quechua *koka*.]
A S. American shrub, *Erythroxylum coca*; the dried leaves of this, chewed as a stimulant.

Coca-Cola /kəʊkəˈkəʊlə/ *noun*. **L19**.
[**ORIGIN** from **COCA** + **COLA** *noun*[1].]
(Proprietary name for) an American aerated soft drink.
■ **coca-colonization** /ˌkəʊkəkɒlənʌɪˈzeɪʃ(ə)n/ *noun* the spread of American culture as represented by Coca-Cola **M20**.

cocaine /kəˈkeɪn/ *noun*. **M19**.
[**ORIGIN** from **COCA** + **-INE**[5].]
An alkaloid, $C_{17}H_{21}NO_4$, which is present in the leaves and other parts of the coca shrub and is used as a local anaesthetic and as a stimulant.
■ **cocainism** *noun* (the condition due to) excessive use of or addiction to cocaine **L19**. **cocaini'zation** *noun* treatment with cocaine **L19**. **cocainize** *verb trans.* treat with cocaine **L19**.

cocarcinogen /kəʊkɑːˈsɪnədʒ(ə)n/ *noun*. **M20**.
[**ORIGIN** from **CO-** + **CARCINOGEN**.]
A substance that increases the carcinogenic effect of another.
■ **cocarcino'genic** *adjective* **M20**.

cocasse /kɔkas/ *adjective*. **M19**.
[**ORIGIN** French.]
Droll; ridiculous.

coccagee /kɒkəˈdʒiː/ *noun*. **E18**.
[**ORIGIN** Irish *cac an ghéidh* goose-dung (from its greenish-yellow colour).]
A cider apple formerly in repute; cider made from it.

Cocceian /kɒkˈsiːən/ *noun & adjective*. **L17**.
[**ORIGIN** from *Cocceius* (see below) Latinized form of the German surname *Koch* + **-AN**.]
ECCLESIASTICAL HISTORY. An adherent of, of or pertaining to, the beliefs of the German-born dogmatic theologian Johannes Cocceius (1603–69), who held that Old Testament history was a foreshadowing of the history of Christ and his Church.

coccid /ˈkɒksɪd/ *noun & adjective*. **L19**.
[**ORIGIN** from **COCCUS** + **-ID**[3].]
▸ **A** *noun*. A homopteran insect of the family Coccidae; a scale insect. **L19**.
▸ **B** *adjective*. Of, pertaining to, or designating this family. **E20**.

coccidia *noun* pl. of **COCCIDIUM**.

coccidioidomycosis /kɒksɪdɪˌɔɪdəʊmʌɪˈkəʊsɪs/ *noun*. Pl. **-coses** /-ˈkəʊsiːz/. **M20**.
[**ORIGIN** from mod. Latin *Coccidioides* (see below) + **-O-** + **MYCOSIS**.]
MEDICINE. Infection with the fungus *Coccidioides immitis*, which usu. affects the lungs and is endemic in the warmer, arid regions of America. Also called ***San Joaquin Valley fever***, ***valley fever***.

coccidiosis /kɒkˌsɪdɪˈəʊsɪs/ *noun*. Pl. **-oses** /-ˈəʊsiːz/. **L19**.
[**ORIGIN** from **COCCIDIUM** + **-OSIS**.]
A disease of birds or mammals caused by the presence of coccidia.

coccidiostat /kɒkˈsɪdɪə(ʊ)stat/ *noun*. **M20**.
[**ORIGIN** formed as **COCCIDIUM** + **-O-** + **-STAT**.]
A substance administered usu. to poultry to retard the growth and reproduction of pathogenic coccidia.

coccidium /kɒkˈsɪdɪəm/ *noun*. Pl. **-ia** /-ɪə/. **M19**.
[**ORIGIN** mod. Latin, from Greek *kokkid-*, *-is* dim. of *kokkos*: see **COCCUS**, **-IUM**.]
†**1** *BOTANY*. A spherical or hemispherical conceptacle in some algae. **M–L19**.
2 A sporozoan of the subclass Coccidia (or suborder Eimeriorina), which includes toxoplasmas and other intracellular parasites including those of malaria (plasmodia). **L19**.
■ **coccidian** *noun & adjective* (*a*) *noun* = **COCCIDIUM** 2; (*b*) *adjective* designating or pertaining to (parasitic) coccidia: **E20**.

coccinellid /kɒksɪˈnɛlɪd/ *noun & adjective*. **L19**.
[**ORIGIN** mod. Latin *Coccinellidae* (see below), from *Coccinella* genus name, from Latin *coccineus* scarlet: see **-ID**[3].]
▸ **A** *noun*. A beetle of the family Coccinellidae; a ladybird. **L19**.
▸ **B** *adjective*. Of, pertaining to, or designating this family. **E20**.

coccolith /ˈkɒkəlɪθ/ *noun*. **M19**.
[**ORIGIN** from Greek *kokkos* (see **COCCUS**) + **-LITH**.]
A minute rounded calcareous platelet, numbers of which form the spherical shells of unicellular marine flagellates of the order Coccolithophorida.
■ **cocco'lithophore** *noun* an organism of this order **M20**. **coccolitho'phorid** *noun & adjective* **M20**.

coccosphere /ˈkɒkəsfɪə/ *noun*. **M19**.
[**ORIGIN** formed as **COCCOLITH** + **SPHERE** *noun*.]
The shell of a coccolithophore.

cocculus indicus /ˌkɒkjʊləs ˈɪndɪkəs/ *noun phr.* Also †**cocculus india**. **L16**.
[**ORIGIN** mod. Latin *cocculus* irreg. dim. of Latin *coccum* kermes, berry + *indicus* Indian.]
The toxic dried berries of a SE Asian climbing shrub, *Anamirta cocculus* (family Menispermaceae).

coccus /ˈkɒkəs/ *noun*. In sense 2 orig. †**-um**. Pl. **cocci** /ˈkɒk(s)ʌɪ, ˈkɒk(s)iː/. **M18**.
[**ORIGIN** mod. Latin from Greek *kokkos* grain, berry, seed.]
1 A scale insect, *esp.* any of those yielding cochineal, kermes, or lac. Now *rare* or *obsolete*. **M18**.
2 *BOTANY*. One of the separable carpels of a dry fruit. **E19**.
3 Any more or less spherical bacterium. **L19**.
■ **coccal** *adjective* of or pertaining to a (bacterial) coccus; of the nature of or resembling a coccus: **E20**. **coccoid** *adjective* of the nature of or resembling a coccus (usu. a bacterial coccus) **E20**.

coccy- /ˈkɒksi/ *combining form* of **COCCYX**. Before a vowel also **coccyg-** /ˈkɒksɪdʒ, -ɪg/, **coccygo-** /ˈkɒksɪgəʊ/ (see **-O-**).
■ **coccy'dynia** *noun* pain in the coccygeal region **L19**.

coccygeal /kɒkˈsɪdʒɪəl/ *adjective*. **L18**.
[**ORIGIN** formed as **COCCYX** + **-AL**[1].]
ANATOMY. Of or pertaining to the coccyx.

coccyx /ˈkɒksɪks/ *noun*. Pl. **-yxes**, **-yges** /-ɪdʒiːz/. **L16**.
[**ORIGIN** Latin from Greek *kokkux*, *-ug-* (orig.) cuckoo: from its resemblance (in humans) to a cuckoo's beak.]
ANATOMY. The small triangular bone forming the lower end of the spinal column in humans and some apes; the analogous part in birds or other vertebrates.

Cochin /ˈkɒtʃɪn/ *noun*. **M19**.
[**ORIGIN** *Cochin*-China, formerly a part of French Indo-China, now of Vietnam.]
More fully ***Cochin-China*** (***fowl***). A breed of poultry from Cochin-China, with feathery legs.

cochineal /ˈkɒtʃɪniːl/ *noun*. **L16**.
[**ORIGIN** French *cochenille*, perh. from Latin *coccinus* scarlet from Greek *kokkos* **COCCUS**or from Spanish *cochinilla* woodlouse.]
1 (A scarlet dye made from) the dried bodies of females of a scale insect, *Dactylopius coccus*, which lives on certain cacti in Mexico and (when cultivated) elsewhere. **L16**.
2 The insect itself. **L16**.
– **COMB.**: **cochineal insect** = sense 2 above; **cochineal plant** a shrubby cactus, *Nopalea cochenillifera*, which is the principal species on which the insect feeds.

cochlea /ˈkɒklɪə/ *noun*. Pl. **-eae** /-ɪiː/. **M16**.
[**ORIGIN** Latin *coc(h)lea* snail shell, screw from Greek *kokhlias*, prob. rel. to *kogkhē* **CONCH**.]
†**1** A spiral staircase; an Archimedean screw. **M16–L17**.
2 *ANATOMY*. The spiral cavity of the inner ear, in which the sensory reception of sound occurs. **L17**.
3 A snail shell. *rare*. **L17**.
■ **cochlear** *adjective* of or pertaining to the cochlea of the ear; *spec.* designating or pertaining to a branch of the vestibulocochlear nerve concerned with hearing (***TECTORIAL membrane of the cochlear duct***): **M19**. **cochleate** *adjective* (chiefly *BOTANY*) twisted, spiral **M19**. **cochleated** *adjective* **E18**.

cochleariform /kɒklɪˈɛːrɪfɔːm/ *adjective*. **M19**.
[**ORIGIN** from Latin *coc(h)leare* spoon + **-I-** + **-FORM**.]
Spoon-shaped.

cochlite /ˈkɒklʌɪt/ *noun*. **L17**.
[**ORIGIN** from Greek *kokhlos* spiral seashell + **-ITE**[1].]
PALAEONTOLOGY. A fossil spiral shell.

cock /kɒk/ *noun*[1].
[**ORIGIN** Old English *cocc*, *kok* = Old Norse *kokkr*, prob. from medieval Latin *coccus* (Salic Laws), of imit. origin; reinforced in Middle English by Old French & mod. French *coq*.]
▸ **I 1** A male bird, *esp.* a male domestic fowl. As 2nd elem. of comb. also in specific names of birds (usu. distinctively of the male). **OE**. ▸**b** A weathercock. **LME**. ▸**c** A woodcock. **M16**.
blackcock, ***gorcock***, ***heath-cock***, ***moorcock***, ***peacock***, ***woodcock***, etc. **a story of a cock and a bull** a rambling inconsequential tale, an incredible tale (hence ***cock and bull story*** below). **fighting cock** a gamecock (***live like fighting cocks***, get the best of fare). ***gamecock***: see **GAME** *noun*. **talk of a cock and a bull** tell a cock and bull story. See also **WEATHERCOCK**.
2 The crowing of a domestic cock. **LME**.

SHAKES. *Lear* This is the foul fiend Flibbertigibbet; he begins at curfew, and walks till the first cock.

3 The leader, the chief, the best. Usu. foll. by *of*. **M16**.
4 Orig., a person who fights pluckily. Now, a familiar form of address to a man, esp. in ***old cock***. **M17**.

DICKENS Do you always smoke arter you goes to bed, old cock?

5 A male lobster, crab, or salmon. **L17**.
▸ **II 6** A tapped spout; a tap, a valve for controlling flow. **L15**.
full cock with the cock fully open. **STOPCOCK**. ***THREE-way cock***. **turn the cock**: open it.
7 A lever in a gun raised ready to be released by the trigger. **M16**.
8 a The pointer of a balance. **E17**. ▸**b** The gnomon of a sundial. **E17**. ▸**c** An overhanging bracket in a clock or watch supporting the outer end of the pivot of a wheel or pendulum. **L17**.
9 The penis. Cf. earlier **PILLICOCK**. *coarse slang*. **E17**.
10 *CURLING*. The circle at the end of the rink at which stones are aimed. **L18**.
11 A cock and bull story; nonsense. Cf. **POPPYCOCK**. *slang*. **M19**.
▸ **III** [Partly from **COCK** *verb*[1].]
12 The state of being cocked; a pronounced upward turn or bend; *spec.* an upward turn to the brim of a hat; a turned-up part of the brim of a hat. **E17**.
at full cock (of a firearm) with the cock lifted to the position at which the trigger will act. **at half cock** (of a firearm) with the cock lifted but not to the position at which the trigger will act; *fig.* when only half ready. ***KEVENHULLER cock***.
– **COMB. & PHRASES**: **cock and bull story** [from ***a story of a cock and a bull*** above] an incredible tale, a false story; **cock-and-hen** *adjective* including both men and women, for both sexes; **cock-bead** *CABINETMAKING* a quirked or projecting bead; **cock-beaded** *adjective* decorated with cock-beads; **cock-brained** *adjective* foolish and light-headed, silly; **cockcrow** dawn; **cockfight**: *esp.* between cocks set to fight, as a sport; **cockfighting** setting cocks to fight, as a sport; **cock-laird** *Scot.* a small landowner; **cock-light** *dial.* (*a*) dawn; (*b*) evening twilight; **cockmaster** *hist.* a person who rears gamecocks; †**cock-match** a cockfighting match; **cock-of-the-north** the brambling; **cock-of-the-plains** *N. Amer.* the sage grouse, *Centrocercus urophasianus*; **cock-of-the-rock** a S. American cotinga of the genus *Rupicola*, the male of which is bright red or orange with a prominent crest; **cock of the walk** a dominant person, a person whose supremacy in a particular circle or sphere is undisputed; **cock-of-the-wood** (*a*) the capercaillie; (*b*) *N. Amer.* the red-crested woodpecker; **cock-paddle** *Scot.* & *N. English* the lumpfish; **cock-penny** *hist.* a customary payment at Shrovetide, formerly made to the schoolmaster in certain schools in the north of England, orig. to defray cock-fighting or cock-throwing expenses; **cock robin** (a familiar name for) a male robin; **cock's egg** *dial.* a small misshapen egg; **cocksfoot** (**grass**) a pasture grass, *Dactylis glomerata*, with a large branched panicle; **cockshead** *dial.* any of various meadow plants with reddish flowers, *esp.* sainfoin and red clover; **cockshoot** (now *dial.*) a broad woodland glade with nets stretched across the opening to catch woodcock; **cock-shut** (**time**) (now *dial.*) twilight; **cockshy** (a throw at) an object (orig. a cock) set up to be thrown at with sticks, stones, etc.; *fig.* an object of ridicule or criticism; **cock sparrow** a male sparrow; a small lively pugnacious person; **cock-stand** *coarse slang* an erection of the penis; **cocksucker** *coarse slang* a fellator; freq. as a generalized term of abuse; **cock-teaser** = ***prick-teaser*** s.v. **PRICK** *noun*; **cock-thropped**, **cock-throttled** *adjectives* (of a horse) having a long excessively curved neck; **cock-throwing** *hist.* throwing sticks etc. at a cock tied to a post to knock it down or kill it, as a sport esp. at Shrovetide. **set cock on hoop**, †**set cock a hoop**, †**set the cock on the hoop** [perh. repr. sense 6 but difficult to explain] (app.) turn on the tap and let the liquor run; drink without stint; abandon oneself to reckless enjoyment.
■ **cock-a-doodle-doo** /ˌkɒkəduːd(ə)lˈduː/ *noun & interjection* (repr.) a cock's crow; (*nursery* & *joc.*) a cock: **L16**. **cockish** *adjective* (*a*) strutting, self-assertive, cocky; (*b*) (now *dial.*) lecherous; (*c*) *joc.* resembling a cock: **M16**.

cock /kɒk/ *noun*[2]. *obsolete* exc. in **COCKBOAT**, **COXSWAIN**. **ME**.
[**ORIGIN** Old French *coque* dial. var. of *coche* = Provençal *coca*, Old Italian *cocca*, from medieval Latin *caudica*, from Latin *caudex*, *codex* block of wood: cf. **COG** *noun*[1].]
= **COCKBOAT**.

cock /kɒk/ *noun*[3]. **LME**.
[**ORIGIN** Perh. from Scandinavian (cf. Norwegian *kok* heap, lump, Danish dial. *kok* haycock, Swedish *koka* clod), but an Old English word = 'hill' has been assumed for the place names *Cockhampstead*, *Cookham*, etc.]
A small conical heap of hay etc. in a field.

cock /kɒk/ *noun*[4]. Now *arch.* & *dial.* **LME**.
[**ORIGIN** Alt.]
God: used esp. in oaths and exclamations.

C

JONSON Cock's bodikins! we must not lose John Clay. SIR W. SCOTT Is he?.. ay, by cock and pie is he.

cock /kɒk/ *verb*¹. ME.
[ORIGIN from COCK *noun*¹.]
▸ †I **1** *verb intrans. & trans.* (with *it*). Fight, quarrel. ME–E17.
▸ II **2** *verb intrans.* Train or use gamecocks. Chiefly as ***cocking*** *verbal noun*. M16.

C

3 *verb intrans.* Strut, swagger; brag, crow *over*. *obsolete* exc. *dial.* L16.
4 *verb intrans.* Shoot woodcocks. Chiefly as ***cocking*** *verbal noun*. L17.
▸ III **5** †**a** *verb trans.* Place (a match) in the cock of a matchlock gun. L16–M17. ▸**b** *verb trans.* Put (a firearm) in readiness for firing by raising the cock etc.; raise (the cock), draw back (the hammer), set (the trigger), in readiness for firing. M17.
6 *verb trans.* Erect, stick or stand up (or *up*), jauntily or defiantly; turn or tip to one side alertly, jauntily, or defiantly; bend (a limb, a joint, etc.) at an angle. E17. ▸**b** Turn up the brim of (a hat). M17.

SIR W. SCOTT The wisest Captain that ever cocked the sweet gale in his bonnet. E. FIGES A small bird.. stopped to listen, its head cocked to one side.

cock an eyebrow look quizzically (*at*). ***cock a snook***: see SNOOK *noun*². **cock one's ears** raise or turn the ears in attention, begin to listen. **cock one's eye** glance knowingly, wink, (*at*). **cock one's eyebrows** = ***cock an eyebrow*** above. **cock one's hat** set one's hat jauntily on one side of the head; tip or raise one's hat jauntily, as a salutation; (see also sense 6b above). **cock one's nose** turn up one's nose in contempt or indifference. **cock the ears** = ***cock one's ears*** above. **cock the nose** = ***cock one's nose*** above. **b cocked hat** (**a**) formerly, a (three-cornered) hat with the brim permanently turned up; now, a brimless triangular hat pointed at front and back and rising to a point at the crown; ***knock into a cocked hat***, defeat utterly, damage irreparably; (**b**) a note, napkin, etc., folded into the shape of a cocked hat.
7 *verb intrans.* Stick or stand up (or *up*) conspicuously. E17.
8 *verb trans.* Foll. by *up*: bungle, make a mess of. *slang.* M20.
■ **cocking** *noun* (**a**) the action of the verb; (**b**) *arch.* a cockfight: ME.

cock /kɒk/ *verb*² *trans. & intrans.* LME.
[ORIGIN from COCK *noun*³.]
Pile (hay etc.) into cocks.

cock /kɒk/ *verb*³ *trans. colloq. & dial.* L16.
[ORIGIN Perh. abbreviation of COCKER *verb*¹.]
Pamper, indulge; reward disproportionately. Freq. foll. by *up*.

cock /kɒk/ *verb*⁴ *trans.* Also **cau(l)k** /kɔːk/. M17.
[ORIGIN Perh. from COAK *noun*: cf. COG *verb*³.]
Secure by a dovetail, mortise and tenon, etc.

cockabully /ˈkɒkəbʊli/ *noun. NZ.* L19.
[ORIGIN Maori *kokopu*, *kokopara*: cf. BULLY *noun*⁴.]
Any of various small blunt-nosed freshwater fishes, esp. of the genus *Gobiomorphus*.

cockade /kɒˈkeɪd/ *noun.* Also †**-ard**. M17.
[ORIGIN French *cocarde* orig. in *bonnet à la coquarde* from fem. of †*coquard* proud, saucy, from *coq* COCK *noun*¹: see -ARD. Assim. to -ADE.]
A rosette, knot of ribbons, etc., worn in the hat as a badge of office or party, or as part of a livery.
■ **cockaded** *adjective* having or wearing a cockade M18.

cock-a-hoop /kɒkəˈhuːp/ *adjective & adverb.* M17.
[ORIGIN from ***set cock a hoop*** s.v. COCK *noun*¹, infl. by sense 1 of COCK *noun*¹.]
▸ **A** *adjective.* Elated, boastfully triumphant. M17.
▸ **B** *adverb.* †**1** ***set cock-a-hoop***, elate, make boastfully triumphant. L17–E18.
2 Elatedly, with boastful triumph. E19.

Cockaigne /kɒˈkeɪn/ *noun.* Also **-ayne**. ME.
[ORIGIN Old French *cocaigne*, as in *pais de cocaigne* fool's paradise (mod. *cocagne*), corresp. to Spanish *cucaña*, Portuguese *cucanha*, Italian *cuccagna*, from Middle Low German *kokenje* small very sweet cake, dim. of *koke* CAKE *noun*.]
1 An imaginary land of idleness and luxury. ME.
2 London (punningly with reference to COCKNEY). *joc.* E19.

cockal *noun* var. of COCKALL.

cock-a-leekie /kɒkəˈliːki/ *noun.* Also **cocky-** /kɒki-/, **-leeky**. M18.
[ORIGIN from COCK *noun*¹ + LEEK: see -IE, -Y⁶.]
A Scottish soup made with chicken and leeks.

cockall /ˈkɒkɔːl/ *noun. obsolete* exc. *dial.* Also **-al** /-(ə)l/. M16.
[ORIGIN Unknown.]
†**1** A knuckle bone, esp. (in *pl.*) as used in various games. M16–L17.
2 *sing. & in pl.* Any of various games using knuckle bones. L16.

cockalorum /kɒkəˈlɔːrəm/ *noun. colloq.* E18.
[ORIGIN Arbitrary, from COCK *noun*¹.]
A self-important little man.
hey cockalorum, **hi cockalorum**, **high cockalorum**: (the cry in) a game like leapfrog.

cockamamie /ˈkɒkəmeɪmi/ *noun & adjective. slang* (orig. *US*). Also **-my**. M20.
[ORIGIN Prob. alt. of DECALCOMANIA.]
▸ **A** *noun.* A picture or design left on the skin as a transfer. M20.
▸ **B** *adjective.* Muddled; implausible, incredible. M20.

cockamaroo /kɒkəməˈruː/ *noun.* M19.
[ORIGIN Unknown.]
A variety of bagatelle played on a board or table with pins, holes, arches, and bells. Also called ***Russian bagatelle***.

cockapoo /kɒkəˈpuː/ *noun.* M20.
[ORIGIN from COCKER *noun*² + POO(DLE *noun*.]
A dog that is a cross-breed of an American cocker spaniel and a miniature poodle.

†**cockard** *noun* var. of COCKADE.

cockatiel /kɒkəˈtiːl/ *noun.* Also **-teel**. L19.
[ORIGIN Dutch *kakatielje*, prob. dim. formed as COCKATOO.]
A small, delicately crested Australian parrot, *Nymphicus hollandicus*. Cf. QUARRION.

cockatoo /kɒkəˈtuː/ *noun.* M17.
[ORIGIN Dutch *kaketoe* from Malay *kakatua*: infl. by COCK *noun*¹.]
1 Any of various Australasian parrots of the family Cacatuidae, with an erectile crest. M17.
Leadbeater's cockatoo, ***rose-breasted cockatoo***, ***sulphur-crested cockatoo***, etc.
2 A lookout usu. acting on behalf of those engaged in some illegal activity. *Austral. slang.* E19.
3 A small farmer. Also ***cockatoo farmer***. Cf. COCKY *noun*². *Austral. & NZ colloq.* M19.
– COMB.: ***cockatoo farmer***: see sense 3 above; **cockatoo fence** *Austral.* a rough fence of logs and saplings.

cockatrice /ˈkɒkətrʌɪs, -trɪs/ *noun.* LME.
[ORIGIN Old French *cocatris* from medieval Latin *calcatrix*, *cauc-* fem. agent noun from Latin *calcare* to tread, track, from *calx* heel, rendering Greek *ikhneumōn* tracker (see ICHNEUMON).]
1 A fabulous reptile, whose gaze or breath is fatal, hatched by a serpent from a cock's egg; a basilisk. LME. ▸**b** Chiefly HERALDRY. A monster represented as a two-legged dragon (or wyvern) with a cock's head and a barbed tongue. E16.
2 *fig.* **a** A malicious or destructive person. Cf. BASILISK 2. E16. ▸†**b** A prostitute. L16–M18.

cock-bill /ˈkɒkbɪl/ *noun & verb.* Also †**-bell**. L16.
[ORIGIN Unknown.]
NAUTICAL. ▸**A** *noun.* The position of an anchor hanging from the cathead ready for dropping, or of the yards of a vessel when placed at an angle with the deck, as a sign of mourning. Only in ***a-cock-bill*** *adverb* [A *preposition*¹], in this position. L16.
▸ **B** *verb trans.* Place a-cock-bill. M19.

cockboat /ˈkɒkbəʊt/ *noun.* LME.
[ORIGIN from COCK *noun*² + BOAT *noun*.]
A ship's small boat, *esp.* one towed behind a vessel going up or down river.

cockchafer /ˈkɒktʃeɪfə/ *noun.* E18.
[ORIGIN from COCK *noun*¹ + CHAFER *noun*¹.]
A large pale brown chafer, *Melolontha melolontha*, which often flies at night with a whirring sound. Also called ***may-bug***.

cocker /ˈkɒkə/ *noun*¹. Now *dial.*
[ORIGIN Old English *cocor* = Old Frisian *koker*, Old Saxon *cocăr(i* (Dutch *koker*), Old High German *kohhar(i* (German *Köcher*).]
†**1** A quiver for arrows. OE–ME.
2 A high laced boot; a kind of legging. LME.

cocker /ˈkɒkə/ *noun*². ME.
[ORIGIN from COCK *verb*¹ + -ER¹.]
†**1** A fighter; a quarrelsome person. Only in ME.
2 A patron of cockfighting; a breeder or trainer of gamecocks. L17.
3 More fully ***cocker spaniel***. A small spaniel of a type bred to rouse woodcock etc. E19.

cocker /ˈkɒkə/ *noun*³. Now *dial.* Also **coker**. ME.
[ORIGIN from COCK *verb*² + -ER¹.]
A person who piles hay into cocks; *gen.* a harvest labourer.

Cocker /ˈkɒkə/ *noun*⁴. E19.
[ORIGIN Edward *Cocker* (1631–75), English arithmetician, reputed author of a widely used text.]
according to Cocker, exact(ly), correct(ly).

cocker /ˈkɒkə/ *noun*⁵. *slang & dial.* L19.
[ORIGIN Cf. COCK *noun*¹ 4.]
Used as a form of address.

cocker /ˈkɒkə/ *verb*¹ *trans.* LME.
[ORIGIN Unknown: cf. COCK *verb*³.]
Pamper, indulge, coddle. Also foll. by *up*.

AV *Ecclus* 30:9 Cocker thy childe, and hee shall make thee afraid. S. RICHARDSON [He] cockers up that dangerous Propensity, which he ought.. to subdue. SIR W. SCOTT I have not been cockered in wantonness or indulgence.

cocker /ˈkɒkə/ *verb*² *intrans. obsolete* exc. *Scot.* M16.
[ORIGIN Rel. to COCKLE *verb*²: see -ER⁵.]
Rock unsteadily, totter.

cockerel /ˈkɒk(ə)r(ə)l/ *noun.* ME.
[ORIGIN Dim. of COCK *noun*¹: see -REL.]
1 A young cock. ME.
2 A young man. *arch.* L16.

cockernony /kɒkəˈnəʊni/ *noun. Scot. arch.* E18.
[ORIGIN Unknown.]
The gathering up of a young woman's hair in a snood.

cocket /ˈkɒkɪt/ *noun.* ME.
[ORIGIN Perh. from Latin *quo quietus est* by which he is quit, the last words of the custom-house officer's receipt. Cf. Anglo-Norman *cokete*, Anglo-Latin *coketa*, *-tum*.]
1 *hist.* A seal of the King's Custom House. ME.
2 Customs duty. *arch.* ME.
3 *hist.* A sealed document certifying the payment of duty. LME.

cocket /ˈkɒkɪt/ *adjective.* Now *dial.* M16.
[ORIGIN Perh. from French *coquet*, *-ette* gallant; in English infl. by COCK *noun*¹, but cf. French *coqueter* strut.]
Orig., proud, arrogant. Now, merry, perky.

cockeye /ˈkɒkʌɪ/ *noun & adjective. colloq.* E19.
[ORIGIN App. from COCK *verb*¹ + EYE *noun*.]
▸ **A** *noun.* A squinting eye. E19.
▸ **B** *adjective.* = COCKEYED *adjective*. L19.
cockeye pilot = BEAU GREGORY.

cockeyed /ˈkɒkʌɪd/ *adjective. colloq.* E19.
[ORIGIN from COCKEYE + -ED².]
1 Having a squint. E19.
2 Crooked, set aslant, not level; absurd. L19.
3 Drunk. Orig. *US.* E20.

cock-horse /ˈkɒkhɔːs, kɒkˈhɔːs/ *noun & adverb.* M16.
[ORIGIN from COCK *noun*¹ or *verb*¹ + HORSE *noun*.]
▸ **A** *noun.* **1** A child's hobby horse; anything a child rides astride, as a person's knee. Now chiefly in A-COCK-HORSE. M16.
†**2** An exalted position, a place of triumph. Chiefly in A-COCK-HORSE. L16–E19.
3 A high-spirited horse, a stallion. L16.
4 Chiefly *hist.* An additional horse for helping a coach uphill. L19.
▸ **B** *adverb.* = A-COCK-HORSE 1. M16.

cockle /ˈkɒk(ə)l/ *noun*¹.
[ORIGIN Old English *coccul*, *-el* perh. from medieval Latin dim. of Latin *coccum* berry: see -LE².]
1 Now usu. more fully ***corncockle***. A purple-flowered plant, *Agrostemma githago*, of the pink family, formerly a common weed of cornfields. OE.
2 [Orig. as mistranslation of Greek *zizania*, Latin *lolium* darnel (*Matthew* 13:25).] A harmful weed of corn; a disease of corn which turns the grains black. OE.

fig.: SHAKES. *Coriol.* The cockle of rebellion, insolence, sedition.

– COMB.: **cocklebur(r)** a weed of the genus *Xanthium*, of the composite family, producing fruit covered with hooked bristles.

cockle /ˈkɒk(ə)l/ *noun*². ME.
[ORIGIN Old French & mod. French *coquille* shell from medieval Latin from medieval Greek *kokhulia* pl. of *kokhulion*, for Greek *kogkhulion*, from *kogkhē* CONCH.]
1 An edible bivalve mollusc of the genus *Cardium*, common on sandy coasts. Formerly also, any of various other bivalves. ME.
2 The shell, or a valve of the shell, of a cockle. LME.
3 A small shallow boat. M19.
– PHRASES: **the cockles of one's heart** one's deepest feelings (esp. in ***rejoice the cockles of one's heart***, ***warm the cockles of one's heart***).
– COMB.: **cockle-hat** *hist.* a hat with a cockle or scallop shell in it, worn by pilgrims; **cockleshell** = senses 2, 3 above.
■ **cockler** *noun* a person who gathers cockles M18. **cockling** *noun* the activity or occupation of gathering cockles L18.

cockle /ˈkɒk(ə)l/ *noun*³. LME.
[ORIGIN Rel. to COCKLE *verb*¹.]
A bulge or wrinkle in paper, glass, etc.; a pucker.
■ **cockly** *adjective* wrinkled, puckered E16.

cockle /ˈkɒk(ə)l/ *noun*⁴. L17.
[ORIGIN Perh. from Dutch *kākel*, *kaekel*, *kāchel*, esp. in *kacheloven*, from German *Kachel* stove-tile, *Kachelofen* stove made of these.]
1 The fire chamber of a hop or malt kiln. Also ***cockle-oast***. L17.
2 A kind of large heating stove, *spec.* one with radiating plates or chambers around which air is passed before entering for heating. Also ***cockle-stove***. L18.

†**cockle** *adjective.* E18–E19.
[ORIGIN Perh. from COCKLE *noun*².]
Whimsical.

cockle /ˈkɒk(ə)l/ *verb*¹ *intrans. & trans.* M16.
[ORIGIN French *coquiller* blister (bread) in cooking (cf. *recoquiller* turn or curl up), from *coquille* shell etc.: see COCKLE *noun*².]
(Cause to) bulge, curl up, pucker.

cockle /ˈkɒk(ə)l/ *verb*² *intrans. dial.* L18.
[ORIGIN Rel. to COCKER *verb*²: see -LE³. Cf. also COGGLE *verb*.]
Rock unsteadily; totter.

†**cockloche** *noun.* Also **cockoloach**. E17–M19.
[ORIGIN Unknown.]
A silly coxcomb.

cockloft /ˈkɒklɒft/ *noun.* L16.
[ORIGIN Perh. from COCK *noun*¹ + LOFT *noun*.]
A small upper loft.

cockney /ˈkɒkni/ *noun & adjective*. In senses A.4, B.2 also **C-**. LME.
[ORIGIN Prob. from COCK *noun*[1] + *-n-* of genit. pl. + EY *noun*, = cock's egg: cf. German *Hahnenei*. Sense 2 assoc. with COCKER *verb*[1].]
▸ **A** *noun*. †**1** An egg; a small misshapen egg (= ***cock's egg*** s.v. COCK *noun*[1]). LME.
2 A pampered child; a milksop. Long *obsolete* exc. *dial.* LME. ▸†**b** A wanton or squeamish woman. Only in E17.
†**3** A person who lives in a town, regarded as effeminate, affected, or weakly. L16–E19.
4 A native of London, esp. of the East End or speaking its dialect; the dialect of the East End of London. Formerly somewhat *derog.* E17.
5 A young snapper fish. *Austral.* E20.
▸ **B** *adjective*. **1** Pampered, effeminate, squeamish; *derog.* characteristic of a town-dweller. Now *arch. & dial.* L16.
2 Pertaining to or characteristic of the London cockney. M17.
Cockney School (somewhat *derog.*) a group of 19th-cent. writers belonging to London, of whom Leigh Hunt was taken as the representative.
■ **cockneydom** *noun* the domain of cockneys; cockneys collectively: M19. **cockney'ess** *noun* (now *rare*) a female cockney M19. **cockneyfi'cation** *noun* making or becoming cockney in character L19. **cockneyfy** *verb trans. & intrans.* make or become cockney in character E19. **cockneyish** *adjective* somewhat cockney in character E19. **cockneyism** *noun* (*a*) cockney quality; (*b*) a cockney characteristic (in idiom, pronunciation, etc.): E19. **cockneyize** *verb* (*a*) *verb trans.* make cockney; (*b*) *verb intrans.* use cockneyisms: E19.

†**cockoloach** *noun* var. of COCKLOCHE.

cockpit /ˈkɒkpɪt/ *noun*. L16.
[ORIGIN from COCK *noun*[1] + PIT *noun*[1].]
1 A pit or other place made for cockfights. L16.
2 An arena for any struggle. L16.
†**3** A theatre; the pit of a theatre. L16–M17.
4 NAUTICAL. The after part of the orlop deck of a man-of-war, to which the wounded were carried for treatment; the well of a sailing yacht where the steering wheel or tiller is located. E18.
5 The space for a pilot etc. in the fuselage of an aircraft or in a spacecraft. E20.
6 The driver's seat in a racing car. M20.

cockroach /ˈkɒkrəʊtʃ/ *noun*. Orig. †**cacaroch** & other vars. E17.
[ORIGIN Spanish *cucaracha*, assim. (by 19) to COCK *noun*[1], ROACH *noun*[4].]
An insect of the suborder Blattaria (order Dictyoptera), typically a stout-bodied scavenger resembling a beetle, with hardened forewings; *esp.* the large dark brown *Blatta orientalis* and *Periplaneta americana*, which infest kitchens, warehouses, etc.
German cockroach: see GERMAN *adjective*[1].

cockscomb /ˈkɒkskəʊm/ *noun*. Also **cock's comb**, †**coxcomb**. See also COXCOMB. LME.
[ORIGIN from COCK *noun*[1] + -'S[1] + COMB *noun*[1].]
▸ **I 1** The comb of a cock. LME.
▸ **II 2** Any of various plants having some resemblance to a cock's comb, *esp.* (*a*) the yellow rattle; (*b*) *Celosia cristata*, of the amaranth family, cultivated for its feathery flowers. LME.
3 A jester's cap, resembling a cock's comb. E16.
†**4** The head. *joc.* L16–M19.
▸ **III** See COXCOMB 1.

cocksman /ˈkɒksmən/ *noun*. Orig. & chiefly *US*. L19.
[ORIGIN from COCK *noun*[1] + MAN *noun*.]
A man considered in terms of sexual prowess; a man (reputedly) of exceptional virility or sexual accomplishment, a stud.
■ **cocksmanship** *noun* L20.

cockspur /ˈkɒkspəː/ *noun*. In sense 1 also **cock's spur**. L16.
[ORIGIN from COCK *noun*[1] + -'S[1] + SPUR *noun*[1].]
1 The spur of a cock. L16.
2 ANGLING. A kind of worm. M17.
3 = FINGRIGO. M18.
– COMB.: **cockspur grass** a millet, *Echinochloa crusgalli*, which is a common weed in warmer parts of the world; also called ***barnyard grass***; **cockspur thorn** a N. American hawthorn, *Crataegus crus-galli*.

cocksure /kɒkˈʃʊə/ *adjective & adverb*. E16.
[ORIGIN from COCK *noun*[4] + SURE *adjective*: assoc. with COCK *noun*[1] is later.]
▸ **A** *adjective*. **I** Of objective sureness.
†**1** Absolutely safe (from danger, interference, etc.). E16–L17.
†**2** Absolutely to be depended on; absolutely certain *of*, *to do*. (Of a person passing into sense 3.) E16–M19.
▸ **II** Of subjective sureness.
3 Quite convinced (*of*, *about*) in one's own mind. L17.
F. MARRYAT 'I do believe that—I'm drunk.' 'And I'm cock sure of it.'
4 Self-confident, dogmatic, presumptuous. M18.
Spectator It was Lord Melbourne . . who said, 'I wish I was as cock-sure of anything as Tom Macaulay is cock-sure of everything.' G. GREENE He was happy, he was conceited, he was cocksure. M. RENAULT I didn't say so. I've had training enough not to make that sort of cocksure prognosis.
▸ **B** *adverb*. With perfect security or certainty. *arch.* L16.
■ **cocksureness** *noun* L19.

cockswain *noun* var. of COXSWAIN.

cocksy *adjective* var. of COXY.

cocktail /ˈkɒkteɪl/ *adjective, noun, & verb*. E17.
[ORIGIN from COCK *noun*[1], *verb*[1] + TAIL *noun*[1].]
▸ **A** *adjective*. **1** That cocks the tail or hinder part. E17.
cocktail beetle = sense B.3 below.
2 (Of a horse) not thoroughbred; *fig.* (*arch.*) characteristic of an upstart, lacking in true gentility. M19.
▸ **B** *noun*. **1** A cock-tailed horse; a racehorse that is not thoroughbred; *fig.* (*arch.*) a person pretending to gentility but lacking in breeding, an upstart. E19.
2 An alcoholic drink consisting of a spirit or spirits mixed with fruit juice, bitters, sugar, etc. Orig. *US*. E19.
Manhattan cocktail, ***old-fashioned cocktail***, ***rattlesnake cocktail***, ***Sazarac cocktail***, etc.
3 = ***devil's coach horse*** s.v. DEVIL *noun*. L19.
4 A dish such as chopped fruit salad, shellfish in a sauce, etc., served as an appetizer at the beginning of a meal or as a light refreshment. E20.
fruit cocktail, ***prawn cocktail***, ***shrimp cocktail***, etc.
5 *fig.* Any (esp. unpleasant or dangerous) mixture of substances or factors. M20.
Daily Telegraph A 'cocktail' of drugs which included cannabis.
Molotov cocktail: see MOLOTOV 1.
– COMB.: **cocktail cabinet**: for storing alcoholic drinks; **cocktail dress**: semiformal, suitable for wearing at a cocktail party; **cocktail-mixer** a container in which a cocktail is mixed by vigorous shaking; **cocktail onion** a small pickled onion; **cocktail party**: at which cocktails or other alcoholic drinks are the principal refreshments provided; **cocktail sausage** a small sausage suitable for serving on a cocktail stick; **cocktail-shaker** = *cocktail-mixer* above; **cocktail stick** a small pointed stick on which articles of food, as onions, small sausages, etc., are served.
▸ **C** *verb*. **1** *verb trans.* Affect with cocktails; provide with cocktails. M19.
2 *verb intrans.* Drink cocktails; attend cocktail parties. M20.

cock-tailed /ˈkɒkteɪld/ *adjective*. M18.
[ORIGIN formed as COCKTAIL + -ED[2].]
1 Of a horse: having a docked tail. M18.
2 Having the tail or hinder part cocked up. L18.

cock-up /ˈkɒkʌp/ *noun*. L17.
[ORIGIN from *cock up*: see COCK *verb*[1].]
1 A hat or cap cocked up in front. Now *rare*. L17.
2 A bungle, a mistake, a muddle. *slang*. M20.

cocky /ˈkɒki/ *noun*[1]. *arch.* L17.
[ORIGIN from COCK *noun*[1] + -Y[6].]
A little cock: used as a term of endearment.

cocky /ˈkɒki/ *noun*[2]. *colloq.* M19.
[ORIGIN from COCK(ATOO + -Y[6].]
1 = COCKATOO 1. *Austral.* M19.
2 = COCKATOO 3. Also ***cocky farmer***. *Austral. & NZ* L19.
cocky's joy *slang* (*a*) golden syrup; (*b*) treacle, molasses.

cocky /ˈkɒki/ *adjective*. M16.
[ORIGIN from COCK *noun*[1] + -Y[1].]
†**1** Lecherous. Only in M16.
2 Arrogant, conceited; cheeky, impertinent. M18.

cocky-leekie, **cocky-leeky** *nouns* vars. of COCK-A-LEEKIE.

cockyolly /kɒkɪˈɒli/ *noun*. M19.
[ORIGIN Fanciful from COCK *noun*[1].]
More fully ***cockyolly bird***. A child's word for a small bird.

coco /ˈkəʊkəʊ/ *noun*. Pl. **-os**. Also **cocoa**. M16.
[ORIGIN Portuguese & Spanish *coco* (orig.) grinning face, alluding to the appearance of the base of the shell. The form *cocoa* arises (app. by accident) from Johnson's Dictionary.]
▸ **I** †**1** = COCONUT 1. M16–M18.
2 = COCONUT 2. M16.
3 = COCONUT 3. *slang*. E19.
▸ **II 4** The root of the taro. *W. Indian*. M18.
– COMB.: **coco fibre** the fibre of the coconut husk; **coco-grass** *N. Amer.* a nut-grass, *Cyperus rotundus*; **coco matting** = *COCONUT matting*; **coco palm**, **coco tree** = sense 2 above.

coco *verb* var. of COCOA *verb*.

cocoa /ˈkəʊkəʊ/ *noun*[1]. E18.
[ORIGIN Alt. of CACAO.]
1 = CACAO 1. Now only more fully ***cocoa bean***. E18.
2 The powder produced by crushing and grinding cacao beans (often with other ingredients); a drink made from this. L18. ▸**b** A shade of brown resembling the colour of this powder. E20.
3 = CACAO 3. *rare*. L19.
– COMB.: ***cocoa bean***: see sense 1 above; **cocoa butter** = *CACAO butter*; **cocoa moth** = *TOBACCO moth*; **cocoa nibs**: see NIB *noun*[1] 6; **cocoa tree** = *CACAO tree*.

cocoa *noun*[2] var. of COCO *noun*.

cocoa /ˈkəʊkəʊ/ *verb intrans. slang*. Also **coco**. M20.
[ORIGIN Rhyming slang.]
Say so. Only in ***I should cocoa***.
Times (online ed.) Do the American customers feel cheated by this? I should cocoa.

cocoanut *noun* var. of COCONUT.

cocobay /ˈkəʊkəʊbeɪ/ *noun*. *W. Indian*. L18.
[ORIGIN Twi *kokobé*.]
Leprosy or other skin disease.

cocobolo /kəʊkəʊˈbəʊləʊ/ *noun*. Pl. **-os**. Also **-la** /-lə/. M19.
[ORIGIN Spanish from Arawak *kakabali*.]
(The hard red wood of) a tropical American tree of the genus *Dalbergia*.

coco de mer /ˌkəʊkəʊdəˈmɛː/ *noun*. E19.
[ORIGIN French = coco from the sea (as having been first known from the nuts found floating in the sea).]
A tall palm tree *Lodoicea maldivica*, native to the Seychelles; its immense woody nut.

co-conscious /kəʊˈkɒnʃəs/ *adjective & noun*. E20.
[ORIGIN from CO- + CONSCIOUS.]
PSYCHOLOGY. ▸**A** *adjective*. Pertaining to the conjunction of experiences within a single consciousness (applied to the supposed knowledge an omniscient god would have of the conscious acts and states of all beings). Also, of or pertaining to the experiences that are split from one another in a multiple personality. E20.
▸ **B** *noun*. A hypothetical part of the subconscious. E20.
■ **co-consciously** *adverb* E20. **co-consciousness** *noun* E20.

coconut /ˈkəʊkənʌt/ *noun*. Also **cocoanut**. E17.
[ORIGIN from COCO *noun* + NUT *noun*.]
▸ **I 1** The large ovate brown hard-shelled seed of the tropical palm tree *Cocos nucifera*, which has an edible white lining enclosing a white liquid; the flesh of this. E17.
SEA ***coconut***. ***the milk in the coconut***: see MILK *noun*.
2 The tree itself. M19.
3 The human head. *slang*. M19.
▸ **II 4** ***double coconut***, = COCO DE MER. E19.
– COMB.: **coconut butter** the solid oil obtained from the flesh of the coconut, used in soap, candles, ointment, etc.; **coconut crab** a large terrestrial pagurid crab, *Birgus latro*, which climbs palm trees to get coconuts; also called ***palm-crab***, ***robber crab***; **coconut ice** a sweet of sugar and desiccated coconut; **coconut matting**: made from the fibre of the nut's outer husk; **coconut milk** the liquid found inside the coconut; **coconut palm** = sense 2 above; **coconut shy** a sideshow in a fairground where balls are thrown to try to dislodge coconuts; **coconut tree** = sense 2 above.

cocoon /kəˈkuːn/ *noun & verb*. L17.
[ORIGIN French *cocon*, †*coucon* from medieval Provençal *coucoun* eggshell, cocoon, dim. of *coca* shell.]
▸ **A** *noun*. **1** A silky case spun by an insect larva to protect it as a pupa, *esp.* and orig. that of the silkworm. L17.
2 *transf. & fig.* A similar structure made by other animals; something which encloses like a cocoon; a protective covering, esp. to prevent the corrosion of metal equipment. M19.
K. TYNAN Each lives in a cocoon of fantasy which the outside world can hardly penetrate. C. FRANCIS As the darkness envelops you, it is easy to believe your boat is a cocoon of safety.
▸ **B** *verb*. **1** *verb trans.* Wrap (as) in a cocoon; spray with a protective covering. M19.
Listener Cocooned in their bungalows, isolated in their club.
2 *verb intrans.* Form a cocoon. L19.
■ **cocoonery** *noun* (*US*) a building or room for rearing silkworms M19.

cocopan /ˈkəʊkəʊpan/ *noun*. *S. Afr.* E20.
[ORIGIN Zulu *i-ngqukumbana*, *-bane* stumpy wagon.]
A small steel truck which runs on rails, used esp. in gold mines.

coco-plum /ˈkəʊkəʊplʌm/ *noun*. L17.
[ORIGIN from ICACO + PLUM *noun*.]
= ICACO.

cocorite /ˈkəʊkərʌɪt/ *noun*. L18.
[ORIGIN from a Brazilian or Guyanese lang.]
A small S. American palm, *Maximiliana maripa*. Also ***cocorite palm***.

cocotte /kɒˈkɒt/ *noun*. M19.
[ORIGIN French: sense 1 from a child's name for a hen; sense 2 from French *cocasse* from Latin *cucuma* cooking vessel.]
1 A fashionable prostitute. *arch.* M19.
2 A small fireproof dish for cooking and serving one portion of food. E20.

cocoyam /ˈkəʊkəʊjam/ *noun*. E20.
[ORIGIN Prob. from COCO *noun* 4 + YAM *noun*[1].]
The edible root of taro, *Colocasia esculenta*, or of a related plant, *Xanthosoma sagittifolium*.

coctile /ˈkɒktʌɪl/ *adjective*. L17.
[ORIGIN Latin *coctilis* baked, burnt, from *coct-* pa. ppl stem of *coquere* to cook: see -ILE.]
Of baked brick; baked.

coction /ˈkɒkʃ(ə)n/ *noun*. Now *rare* or *obsolete*. LME.
[ORIGIN Latin *coctio(n-)* digestion, (in late Latin) cooking, from *coct-*: see COCTILE, -ION.]
1 Cooking; boiling. LME.
†**2** Suppuration as a process regarded as necessary for the healing of wounds or diseases. L16–M19.
†**3** Digestion of food. E17–L19.
†**4** The action of heat in preparing any substance. L17–M18.

C

†**5** Preparation by a natural process leading to perfection. **L17–E18.**

cocus /ˈkəʊkəs/ *noun*. **M17.**
[**ORIGIN** Unknown.]
The hard, dark, heavy wood of a W. Indian leguminous tree, *Brya ebenus*, used in turnery. Also ***cocus wood***.

COD *abbreviation*.
1 Cash (or (*US*) collect) on delivery.
2 Concise Oxford Dictionary.

cod /kɒd/ *noun*[1].
[**ORIGIN** Old English *cod(d)* = Old Norse *koddi*, Old Danish *kodde* (cf. **COD** *noun*[3]), Swedish *kudde* cushion, pillow, pad, Norwegian *kodd* testicle, scrotum, from Germanic.]
1 A bag, a wallet. Long *obsolete* exc. *dial.* **OE.**
2 A husk, a pod. Cf. **PEASECOD.** *obsolete* exc. *dial.* **OE.**
3 The scrotum; in *pl.*, the testicles. *arch.* **LME.**
4 The narrow-necked bag at the end of a trawl net etc. Now usu. more fully ***cod end***. **M16.** ▸†**b** The innermost recess of a bay or inlet. **L17–M18.**
†**5** A cocoon. **E17–E19.**
■ **codded** *adjective* (now *dial.*) (***a***) bearing pods; (***b***) in the pod or (of corn) the ear: **LME.**

cod /kɒd/ *noun*[2]. Pl. same. **ME.**
[**ORIGIN** Unknown.]
More fully ***codfish***. A large marine fish, *Gadus morhua*, which inhabits the N. Atlantic and adjacent seas, and has considerable economic importance as a food fish. Also (usu. with specifying word), any of various other fishes related to this (in the family Gadidae) or of corresponding value in other regions.
Murray cod: see **MURRAY** *noun*[2]. ***red rock-cod***: see **RED** *adjective*.
– **COMB.**: **cod-bank** a submarine bank frequented by cod; ***codfish***: see above; **cod-line** a line used in fishing for cod; **cod liver oil** oil expressed from the liver of the cod or a related fish, used as a rich source of vitamins A and D; **cod's-head** *fig.* a stupid person; **cod war** *colloq.* any of a number of disputes between Britain and Iceland in the period 1958–76, concerning fishing rights in Icelandic waters.

cod /kɒd/ *noun*[3]. *Scot. & N. English*. **LME.**
[**ORIGIN** Old Danish *kodde*, Old Norse *koddi* cushion, pillow (cf. **COD** *noun*[1]).]
1 A pillow. **LME.**
2 The bearing of an axle. **LME.**

cod /kɒd/ *noun*[4] *& adjective*. *slang*. **L17.**
[**ORIGIN** Unknown: **CODGER** appears much later.]
▸ **A** *noun*. **1** A person; *esp.* an old fool, an idiot. **L17.**
2 A joke, a hoax; a parody. **E20.**
▸ **B** *adjective*. Parodying, mock. **M20.**

cod /kɒd/ *noun*[5]. *slang*. Also **cod(')s** /kɒdz/. **M20.**
[**ORIGIN** Abbreviation.]
= **CODSWALLOP.**

cod /kɒd/ *verb*[1]. *obsolete* exc. *dial.* Infl. **-dd-**. **M16.**
[**ORIGIN** from **COD** *noun*[1].]
1 *verb intrans.* Produce pods. **M16.**
2 *verb trans.* Gather the pods of. **L16.**

cod /kɒd/ *verb*[2] *trans. & intrans. dial. & slang*. Infl. **-dd-**. **L19.**
[**ORIGIN** Perh. from **COD** *noun*[4].]
Hoax; parody; play a joke (on).

coda /ˈkəʊdə/ *noun*. **M18.**
[**ORIGIN** Italian from Latin *cauda* tail.]
1 *MUSIC*. An independent and often elaborate passage introduced after the end of the main part of a movement. **M18.** ▸**b** *transf. & fig.* A concluding event, remark, literary passage, etc. **L19.**
2 *BALLET*. The final section of a classical *pas de deux*; the concluding dance of a whole ballet. **E20.**

cod-bait *noun* see **CAD-BAIT.**

codder /ˈkɒdə/ *noun*[1]. Now *dial.* **E16.**
[**ORIGIN** from **COD** *noun*[3] + **-ER**[1].]
A worker in leather; a saddler.

codder /ˈkɒdə/ *noun*[2]. *dial.* **L17.**
[**ORIGIN** from **COD** *noun*[1] or *verb*[1] + **-ER**[1].]
A person who gathers pea pods.

codder /ˈkɒdə/ *noun*[3]. *US*. **M19.**
[**ORIGIN** from **COD** *noun*[2] + **-ER**[1].]
A person or vessel engaged in fishing for cod.

†**codding** *adjective*. *rare* (Shakes.). Only in **L16.**
[**ORIGIN** Perh. from **COD** *noun*[1] 3.]
Lustful.

coddle /ˈkɒd(ə)l/ *verb*[1] *trans. & intrans.* **L16.**
[**ORIGIN** Unknown: cf. **CODDLE** *verb*[2] *& noun*.]
Boil gently, parboil, stew.

coddle /ˈkɒd(ə)l/ *verb*[2] *& noun*. **E19.**
[**ORIGIN** Prob. dial. var. of **CAUDLE** *verb*, but perh. fig. use of **CODDLE** *verb*[1] Cf. **MOLLYCODDLE.**]
▸ **A** *verb trans.* Treat as an invalid, keep from cold and exertion, feed *up*. **E19.**
▸ **B** *noun*. A person who coddles himself or herself or is coddled by others. *colloq.* **M19.**
■ **coddler** *noun* (***a***) *rare* = **CODDLE** *noun*; (***b***) ***egg-coddler***: see **EGG** *noun*: **M19.**

code /kəʊd/ *noun*. **ME.**
[**ORIGIN** Old French & mod. French from Latin *codex*: see **CODEX.**]
1 **a** *ROMAN LAW*. Any of the systematic collections of statutes made by or for the later emperors, *esp.* that of Justinian. **ME.** ▸**b** A systematic collection or digest of laws; a body of laws so arranged as to avoid inconsistency and overlapping. **M18.**
b criminal code: see **CRIMINAL** *adjective* 2. ***Salic code***: see **SALIC** *adjective*[1] 2.
†**2** A collection of (chiefly religious) writings forming a book. Only in **18.**
3 A set of rules on any subject; *esp.* the prevalent morality of a society or class; an individual's standard of moral behaviour. **E19.**

> G. ORWELL In all questions of morals they were allowed to follow their ancestral code. G. STEINER Fascism is the ultimate code of the hoodlum.

code of honour: see **HONOUR** *noun*.
4 A system of military etc. signals esp. used to ensure secrecy; a cipher; a systematic modification of a language, information, etc., into letter, figure, or word groups or symbols for the purposes of brevity, secrecy, or the machine-processing of information; *transf.* a system by which genetic etc. information is stored. **E19.**

> U. LE GUIN He took pleasure only in writing to his friends . . in a code they had worked out at the Institute. N. CHOMSKY The phrase 'contain the expansion of China' must be understood as code for . . 'repress movements for national independence and social reconstruction in SE Asia'.

dialling code, ***genetic code***, ***machine code***, ***Morse code***, ***Playfair code***, ***postcode***, ***shift code***, ***zip code***, etc.
– **COMB.**: **code-book** a list of symbols etc. used in a code; **code-breaker** a person who solves or breaks a code or codes; a device for breaking codes; **code name**, **code number** a word, symbol, or number used for secrecy or convenience instead of an ordinary name; **code-sharing** agreement between two or more airlines to list certain flights in a reservation system under each other's names.

code /kəʊd/ *verb*. **E19.**
[**ORIGIN** from the noun.]
1 *verb trans.* Put (a message etc.) into code; represent by means of a code. **E19.**
2 *verb intrans. BIOLOGY*. Foll. by *for*: be the genetic code for (an amino acid etc.), be the genetic determiner of (a character etc.). **M20.**
3 *verb trans.* Write code for (a computer program). **L20.**
■ **coda'bility** *noun* ability to be coded **M20.** **coder** *noun* **E20.**

codec /ˈkəʊdɛk/ *noun*. **M20.**
[**ORIGIN** Blend of *coder* and *decoder*.]
A device which can encode and decode or compress and decompress a signal or block of data to make it more suitable for efficient transmission, processing, storage, etc.; *esp.* a device which converts analog video into compressed video, or analog sound into digital sound.

codeine /ˈkəʊdiːn, -dɪiːn/ *noun*. **M19.**
[**ORIGIN** from Greek *kōdeia* head, poppy head + **-INE**[5].]
CHEMISTRY. A crystalline alkaloid, $C_{18}H_{21}NO_3$, obtained from opium and used as a hypnotic and analgesic.

codependent /kəʊdɪˈpɛnd(ə)nt/ *adjective & noun*. **M20.**
[**ORIGIN** from **CO-** + **DEPENDENT** *adjective*.]
▸ **A** *adjective*. **1** Of two or more entities, mathematical or logical objects, or their values: dependent on each other; dependent in the same way on some common factor or principle. **M20.**
2 *PSYCHOANALYSIS*. Of or relating to codependency; displaying codependency. Orig. *US*. **L20.**
▸ **B** *noun*. *PSYCHOANALYSIS*. A person with an excessive emotional or psychological reliance on someone (typically a partner or close relative) who requires their care or support. **L20.**
■ **codependence** *noun* (***a***) joint dependence of two factors, mathematical quantities, etc. on each other or on a common factor; dependence on two or more factors simultaneously; (***b***) *PSYCHOANALYSIS* = **CODEPENDENCY**: **L20.** **codependency** *noun* (*PSYCHOANALYSIS*) excessive emotional or psychological reliance on another person who requires care or support **L20.**

codetta /kəʊˈdɛtə/ *noun*. **M19.**
[**ORIGIN** Italian, dim. of **CODA.**]
MUSIC. A short coda; a short passage connecting sections of a movement or fugue.

codex /ˈkəʊdɛks/ *noun*. Pl. **codices** /ˈkəʊdɪsiːz, ˈkɒd-/. **L16.**
[**ORIGIN** Latin *codex*, *codic-* block of wood, block split into leaves or tablets, book.]
†**1** = **CODE** *noun* 1, 3. **L16–M18.**
2 A manuscript volume, esp. of ancient texts. **L18.**
3 A collection of pharmaceutical descriptions of drugs, preparations, etc. **M19.**

codger /ˈkɒdʒə/ *noun*. **M18.**
[**ORIGIN** Perh. var. of **CADGER** *noun*[1].]
1 A fellow, a person, esp. a strange one; an elderly man (freq. in ***old codger***). *colloq.* **M18.**
2 A mean, stingy, or miserly (old) person; a tramp; a beggar. *dial.* **L18.**

codiaeum /kəʊdɪˈiːəm/ *noun*. **M19.**
[**ORIGIN** mod. Latin from an Indonesian lang.]
BOTANY. = **CROTON** *noun*[1] 2.

codices *noun* pl. of **CODEX.**

codicil /ˈkɒdɪsɪl, ˈkəʊ-/ *noun*. **LME.**
[**ORIGIN** Latin *codicillus* (chiefly in pl.) dim. of *codex*: see **CODEX.**]
1 A supplement to a will, added by the testator for the purpose of explanation, alteration, etc., of the original contents. **LME.** ▸**b** *transf. & fig.* A supplementary addition, an appendix. **L18.**
†**2** (A letter on) a writing tablet; a letter granting a patent. **M17–L18.**
■ **codi'cillary** *adjective* of the nature of or belonging to a codicil **E18.**

codicology /kəʊdɪˈkɒlədʒi/ *noun*. **M20.**
[**ORIGIN** French *codicologie*, from Latin *codic-*, **CODEX**: see **-OLOGY.**]
The branch of knowledge that deals with manuscripts and their interrelationships.
■ **codico'logical** *adjective* **M20.** **codico'logically** *adverb* **M20.**

codify /ˈkəʊdɪfʌɪ/ *verb trans.* **M19.**
[**ORIGIN** from **CODE** *noun*: see **-FY.** Cf. French *codifier*.]
1 Reduce (laws) to a code. **M19.**
2 Reduce to a general system; systematize. **M19.**
■ **codifi'cation** *noun* **E19.** **codifier** *noun* **M19.**

codilla /kəʊˈdɪlə/ *noun*. **L18.**
[**ORIGIN** App. dim. of Italian **CODA.**]
The coarse tow of flax or hemp.

codille /ˈkəʊdɪl/ *noun*. **L17.**
[**ORIGIN** French from Spanish *codillo* lit. 'elbow joint', dim. of *codo* elbow.]
In ombre, the losing of the game by the person who undertakes to win it.

codlin *noun* var. of **CODLING** *noun*[2].

codling /ˈkɒdlɪŋ/ *noun*[1]. Pl. same. **ME.**
[**ORIGIN** from **COD** *noun*[2] + **-LING**[1].]
A young or small cod.

codling /ˈkɒdlɪŋ/ *noun*[2]. Also **-lin** /-lɪn/. **LME.**
[**ORIGIN** Anglo-Norman *Quer de lion* (French *Cœur de lion*) lionheart.]
1 A cooking apple of a long tapering shape; the tree bearing this type of apple. Formerly also, any hard or unripe apple. **LME.**
KESWICK codling.
†**2** A raw youth. **E–M17.**
– **COMB.**: **codling moth** a small moth, *Cydia pomonella*, whose larvae feed on apples; **codlings-and-cream** great hairy willowherb, *Epilobium hirsutum*.

codology /kɒˈdɒlədʒi/ *noun*. *Irish colloq.* **E20.**
[**ORIGIN** from **COD** *noun*[4] + **-OLOGY.**]
Hoaxing, leg-pulling.

codominant /kəʊˈdɒmɪn(ə)nt/ *adjective & noun*. **E20.**
[**ORIGIN** from **CO-** + **DOMINANT.**]
▸ **A** *adjective*. **1** Chiefly *ECOLOGY*. Sharing dominance; of equal dominance. **E20.**
2 *GENETICS*. Of characters, alleles: expressed independently in heterozygous offspring, without displaying dominance or recessiveness. **M20.**
▸ **B** *noun*. A species etc. that is codominant. **M20.**

co-domini /kəʊˈdɒmɪnʌɪ/ *noun pl.* **M20.**
[**ORIGIN** from **CO-** + Latin *domini* pl. of *dominus* lord, ruler.]
Condominium powers, *spec.* the UK and Egypt in relation to Sudan between 1899 and 1966.

codon /ˈkəʊdɒn/ *noun*. **M20.**
[**ORIGIN** from **CODE** *noun* + **-ON.**]
GENETICS. A group of three consecutive nucleotides which together form a unit of the genetic code and determine which amino acid is added at a particular point in protein synthesis.

codpiece /ˈkɒdpiːs/ *noun*. *obsolete* exc. *hist.* **LME.**
[**ORIGIN** from **COD** *noun*[1] 3 + **PIECE** *noun*.]
A bagged appendage to the front of a man's breeches or close-fitting hose.

codswallop /ˈkɒdzwɒləp/ *noun*. *slang*. **M20.**
[**ORIGIN** Unknown: often said to be from the name of Hiram *Codd* (1838–87), Brit. soft drinks manufacturer + **WALLOP** *noun* in the slang sense 'beer'.]
Nonsense, drivel.

†**cod-worm** *noun* see **CAD-WORM.**

coecilian *noun* var. of **CAECILIAN.**

coed /ˈkəʊɛd, kəʊˈɛd/ *noun & adjective*. *colloq.* (orig. *US*). **L19.**
[**ORIGIN** from **CO-EDUCATION(AL).**]
▸ **A** *noun*. **1** A co-educational institution or system; co-education. **L19.**
2 A female student at a co-educational institution. **L19.**
▸ **B** *adjective*. Co-educational; of or pertaining to a coed (sense 2). **L19.**

co-educate /kəʊˈɛdjʊkeɪt/ *verb trans.* Orig. *US*. **M19.**
[**ORIGIN** Back-form. from **CO-EDUCATION.**]
Educate (persons of both sexes) together; educate in a co-educational institution.
■ **co-educator** *noun* a proponent or practitioner of co-education **E20.**

co-education /ˌkəʊɛdjʊˈkeɪʃ(ə)n/ *noun*. **M19.**
[**ORIGIN** from **CO-** + **EDUCATION.**]
The education of both sexes together.
■ **co-educational** *adjective* of or pertaining to co-education, practising co-education **L19.**

coefficient /kəʊɪˈfɪʃ(ə)nt/ *adjective & noun*. M17.
[ORIGIN mod. Latin *coefficient-*: see CO-, EFFICIENT.]
▸ **A** *adjective*. Cooperating to produce a result. Now *rare* or *obsolete*. M17.
▸ **B** *noun*. **1** A joint or cooperating agent or factor in producing a cause. E18.
2 a MATH. A known or constant quantity placed before and multiplying another. E18. ▸**b** Chiefly PHYSICS. A multiplier or factor which expresses the magnitude of some property of a particular substance etc. E19.
a differential coefficient = DERIVATIVE *noun* 3. **b** ***absorption coefficient***, ***coefficient of expansion***, ***coefficient of friction***, ***coefficient of permeability***, ***pluviometric coefficient***, ***Racah coefficient***, ***virial coefficient***, etc.

coehorn /ˈkəʊhɔːn/ *noun*. Also **cohorn**. E18.
[ORIGIN from Menno, Baron van *Coehoorn* (1641–1704), Dutch soldier and military engineer.]
MILITARY HISTORY. A small bronze mortar for throwing grenades, introduced by van Coehoorn.

coelacanth /ˈsiːləkanθ/ *noun*. M19.
[ORIGIN mod. Latin *Coelacanthus* genus name, from Greek *koilos* hollow + *akantha* spine, on account of its hollow-spined fins.]
A crossopterygian fish of the order Actinistia, which was believed to include only fossil forms until the discovery of *Latimeria chalumnae* in the Indian Ocean in 1938.
■ **coela'canthid** *noun & adjective* L19. **coela'canthine** *adjective* L19.

-coele *suffix* var. of -CELE.

coelenterate /siːˈlɛnt(ə)rət/ *noun & adjective*. L19.
[ORIGIN from mod. Latin *Coelenterata* (see below), from Greek *koilos* hollow + *enteron* intestine: see -ATE².]
ZOOLOGY. ▸**A** *noun*. Orig., an animal of the invertebrate phylum Coelenterata, which comprised the present-day phyla Cnidaria, Ctenophora, and sometimes Porifera (sponges). Now usu., an animal of the phylum Cnidaria (also called Coelenterata), which includes jellyfishes, hydras, sea anemones, and corals. Cf. CNIDARIAN. L19.
▸ **B** *adjective*. Of or pertaining to this group of animals. L19.
■ **coelenteron** *noun* the central gastric cavity of a coelenterate L19.

coeliac /ˈsiːlɪak/ *adjective*. Also ***celiac**. M17.
[ORIGIN Latin *coeliacus* from Greek *koiliakos* from *koilia* belly: see -AC.]
MEDICINE. Of or pertaining to the abdominal cavity; pertaining to or suffering from coeliac disease (see below).
coeliac disease sensitivity of the lining of the small intestine to gluten, causing chronic failure to digest food properly unless gluten is strictly excluded from the diet.
■ †**coeliacal** *adjective* E17–E18.

coelio- /ˈsiːlɪəʊ/ *combining form* of Greek *koilia* belly: see -O-. Also ***celio-**.
■ **coeli'otomy** *noun* (MEDICINE) = LAPAROTOMY L19.

coelom /ˈsiːləm/ *noun*. Also **-ome** /-əʊm/, ***cel-**, & in mod. Latin form **coeloma** /siːˈləʊmə/, pl. **-mata** /-mətə/. L19.
[ORIGIN Greek *koilōma*, *-mat-* hollow, cavity.]
ZOOLOGY. The secondary body cavity of an animal, between the body wall and the gut, *spec.* one surrounded by mesoderm.
■ **coe'lomic** *adjective* pertaining to or of the nature of a coelom L19.

coelomate /ˈsiːləmeɪt/ *adjective & noun*. Also ***celomate**. L19.
[ORIGIN from COELOM + -ATE².]
ZOOLOGY. ▸**A** *adjective*. Having a coelom. L19.
▸ **B** *noun*. An animal having a coelom, of the group Coelomata, which includes the annelids, molluscs, arthropods, echinoderms, and chordates. L19.

coelostat /ˈsiːlə(ʊ)stat/ *noun*. L19.
[ORIGIN Irreg. from Latin *caelum* sky + -O- + -STAT.]
ASTRONOMY. An instrument which by means of a rotating mirror enables celestial objects to be photographed without their diurnal motion.

coelurosaur /sɪˈljʊərəsɔː/ *noun*. M20.
[ORIGIN from Greek *koilos* hollow + URO-² + -SAUR.]
Any of a group of small slender theropod dinosaurs with long forelimbs.

coemption /kəʊˈɛm(p)ʃ(ə)n/ *noun*. LME.
[ORIGIN Latin *coemptio(n-)*, from *coempt-* pa. ppl stem of *coemere* buy up: see -ION.]
1 The buying up of the whole supply of any commodity in the market. LME.
2 ROMAN LAW. The fictitious sale of a woman by herself or her father, usu. to her husband. L17.

coen- *combining form* see COENO-.

coenaesthesis /siːnɛsˈθiːsɪs/ *noun*. Also ***-nesth-**. Pl. **-theses** /-ˈθiːsiːz/. M19.
[ORIGIN from Greek *kainos* common + *aisthēsis* sensation, perception.]
PSYCHOLOGY. The perception of one's whole bodily state arising from the sum of somatic sensations.
■ Also **coenaesthesia** *noun* L19.

coeno- /ˈsiːnəʊ/ *combining form* of Greek *koinos* common: see -O-. Before a vowel **coen-**.
■ **coen'enchyme** *noun* [Greek *egkhuma* infusion] ZOOLOGY (**a**) a usu. calcified substance secreted by the coenosarc of some anthozoans; (**b**) = COENOSARC: L19. **coenocyte** *noun* a body of algal or fungal cytoplasm containing several nuclei, enclosed in a single membrane E20. **coeno'cytic** *adjective* of, pertaining to, or having the structure of a coenocyte E20. **coenosarc** *noun* [Greek *sarx*, *sark-* flesh] ZOOLOGY the soft tissue connecting the polyps of colonial coelenterates M19.

coenobite /ˈsiːnəbʌɪt/ *noun*. Also ***cen-** /ˈsiːn-, ˈsɛn-/. LME.
[ORIGIN Old French & mod. French *cénobite* or ecclesiastical Latin *coenobita*, from *coenobium* from Greek *koinobion* community life, convent, from *koinos* common + *bios* life: see -ITE¹.]
A member of a monastic community.
■ **coenobitic** /siːnəˈbɪtɪk/, **coenobitical** /siːnəˈbɪtɪk(ə)l/ *adjectives* of or pertaining to a coenobite or coenobites, or a monastic community M17.

coenobium /sɪˈnəʊbɪəm/ *noun*. Also ***cen-**. Pl. **-bia** /-bɪə/. E19.
[ORIGIN ecclesiastical Latin: see COENOBITE.]
1 = COENOBY. E19.
2 BIOLOGY. A cluster of unicellular organisms, e.g. green algae, that behaves as a colony. L19.

coenoby /ˈsiːnəbi/ *noun*. Also ***cen-** /ˈsiːn-, ˈsɛn-/. L15.
[ORIGIN formed as COENOBIUM.]
A monastic house.

coenurus /sɪˈnjʊərəs/ *noun*. Pl. **-ri** /-rʌɪ/. Orig. anglicized as †**coenure**. M19.
[ORIGIN mod. Latin from Greek *koinos* common + *oura* tail.]
The hydatid of a canine tapeworm, *Multiceps multiceps*, which occurs in various intermediate hosts, esp. sheep, in which it causes staggers.

coequal /kəʊˈiːkw(ə)l/ *adjective & noun*. Now *arch.* or *literary*. LME.
[ORIGIN Latin *coaequalis* of the same age: see CO-, EQUAL *adjective, adverb, & noun*.]
▸ **A** *adjective*. †**1** Of the same age, coeval. LME–E17.
2 Equal in rank, power, importance, etc. (*with*). LME.
3 Equivalent, coextensive (*with*). M19.
▸ **B** *noun*. A person who is the equal of another. L16.
■ **coe'quality** *noun* L16. **coequally** *adverb* M17.

†**coequate** *adjective*. E17–M18.
[ORIGIN Latin *coaequatus* pa. pple of *coaequare*, formed as CO- + *aequare*: see EQUATE.]
Made equal with something else.
coequate anomaly the true anomaly of a planet.
■ Also †**coequated** *adjective* L16–E18.

coerce /kəʊˈəːs/ *verb*. LME.
[ORIGIN Latin *coercere*, formed as CO- + *arcere* restrain.]
1 *verb trans.* Forcibly constrain or impel (*into* obedience, compliance, etc.); force or compel *to do*. LME. ▸**b** Enforce. Chiefly *US*. M19.
2 *verb intrans.* Enforce obedience; use coercive measures. L17.
■ **coercer** *noun* E19. **coercible** *adjective* M17.

coercion /kəʊˈəːʃ(ə)n/ *noun*. LME.
[ORIGIN Old French *cohercion*, *-tion* from Latin *coer(c)tio(n-)* (medieval Latin *coercio(n-)*) var. of *coercitio(n-)*, from *coercit-* pa. ppl stem of *coercere*: see COERCE, -ION.]
1 Constraint, restraint, compulsion; the controlling of a voluntary agent or action by force. LME.
J. R. GREEN Justice is degraded by . . the coercion of juries.
†**2** The faculty or power of coercing or punishing; the power to compel assent. E16–E18.
3 Government by force; the employment of force to suppress political disaffection and disorder. L18.
4 Physical pressure; compression. Now *rare*. M19.
■ **coercionist** *noun* a person who advocates or supports government by coercion M19.

coercive /kəʊˈəːsɪv/ *adjective & noun*. L16.
[ORIGIN from COERCE + -IVE.]
▸ **A** *adjective*. **1** Of the nature of coercion; having the attribute of coercing. L16.
2 Compelling assent or belief, convincing. M17.
3 Having the power of physical pressure or compression. M17.
coercive force PHYSICS = COERCIVITY.
▸ **B** *noun*. A coercive means or measure. M17.
■ **coercitive** *adjective* (now *rare*) = COERCIVE *adjective* M17. **coercively** *adverb* M17. **coerciveness** *noun* M18. **coer'civity** *noun* (PHYSICS) the resistance of a magnetic material to changes in magnetization; *spec.* the magnetic field intensity necessary to demagnetize a given fully magnetized substance: L19.

coessential /kəʊɪˈsɛnʃ(ə)l/ *adjective*. L15.
[ORIGIN ecclesiastical Latin *coessentialis* (translating Greek *homoousios* of the same substance), predicated attribute of the persons of the Trinity: see CO-, ESSENTIAL.]
1 United or inseparable in essence or being. L15.
2 Having the same substance or essence; consubstantial. L16.
■ **coessenti'ality** *noun* L17. **coessentially** *adverb* E19.

coetaneous /kəʊɪˈteɪnɪəs/ *adjective*. E17.
[ORIGIN from Latin *coaetaneus* contemporaneous, formed as CO- + *aetaneus*, from *aetas* age: see -OUS.]
= COEVAL *adjective*.
■ **coetaneously** *adverb* E19. **coetaneousness** *noun* M18.

coeternal /kəʊɪˈtəːn(ə)l/ *adjective*. LME.
[ORIGIN from ecclesiastical Latin *coaeternus* (also *coaeternalis*) + -AL¹: see CO-, ETERNAL.]
Equally eternal; existing *with* another eternally.
■ **coeternally** *adverb* L16.

coeternity /kəʊɪˈtəːnɪti/ *noun*. L16.
[ORIGIN Late Latin *coaeternitas*: see CO-, ETERNITY.]
Coeternal existence or quality; eternal existence with another.

coeval /kəʊˈiːv(ə)l/ *noun & adjective*. E17.
[ORIGIN from late Latin *coaevus*, formed as CO- + *aevum* age: see -AL¹.]
▸ **A** *noun*. **1** A person (or thing) belonging to the same period. E17.
2 A person who is of the same age as another. M17.
▸ **B** *adjective*. Foll. by *with*, †*to*.
1 Of equal antiquity, of contemporaneous origin. M17.
2 Of the same age, equally old. L17.
3 Existing at the same epoch; contemporary. E18.
4 Of the same duration. M18.
■ **coe'vality** *noun* coeval quality; equality of age: M17. **coevally** *adverb* E18.

coevolution /kəʊɛvəˈljuːʃən, kəʊiːvəˈljuːʃən/ *noun*. E20.
[ORIGIN from CO- + EVOLUTION.]
The evolution of two or more things jointly and reciprocally; *esp.* (BIOLOGY) the influence of closely associated species on each other in their evolution.
■ **coe'volve** *verb* M20. **coevolutionary** *adjective* M20.

co-executor /kəʊɪgˈzɛkjʊtə/ *noun*. LME.
[ORIGIN medieval Latin *coexecutor*: see CO-, EXECUTOR.]
A joint executor.
■ **co-executrix** *noun* a joint executrix LME.

coexist /kəʊɪgˈzɪst/ *verb intrans.* M17.
[ORIGIN Late Latin *coexistere*: see CO-, EXIST. Cf. Old French & mod. French *coexister*.]
Exist at the same time, in the same place, etc. (*with* another or others). Esp. of states with different ideologies: exist peacefully side by side.

coexistence /kəʊɪgˈzɪst(ə)ns/ *noun*. LME.
[ORIGIN medieval Latin *coexistentia*: see CO-, EXISTENCE. Cf. French *coexistence*.]
1 Existence together or in conjunction. LME.
2 *spec.* Existence side by side in mutual toleration of states, groups, etc., professing different ideologies. Also more fully ***peaceful coexistence***. M20.

coexistent /kəʊɪgˈzɪst(ə)nt/ *adjective & noun*. M17.
[ORIGIN formed as COEXIST: see -ENT. Cf. French *coexistant*.]
▸ **A** *adjective*. Existing together or in conjunction. M17.
▸ **B** *noun*. A thing which coexists with something else; a concomitant. M19.

coextend /kəʊɪkˈstɛnd/ *verb trans. & intrans.* E17.
[ORIGIN from CO- + EXTEND: cf. medieval Latin *coextendere*.]
Make or be coextensive.
■ **coextension** *noun* coincidence in extension L17.

coextensive /kəʊɪkˈstɛnsɪv/ *adjective*. L18.
[ORIGIN from CO- + EXTENSIVE.]
Extending over the same space or time; coinciding in limits; of equal extension.
■ **coextensively** *adverb* M19. **coextensiveness** *noun* L17.

cofactor /ˈkəʊfaktə/ *noun*. L19.
[ORIGIN from CO- + FACTOR *noun*.]
1 MATH. A coefficient; *spec.* the quantity obtained from a determinant or square matrix by removal of the row and column containing a given element. L19.
2 BIOCHEMISTRY. A non-protein substance whose presence is essential for the activity of an enzyme. M20.

C of E *abbreviation*.
Church of England.

coff /kɒf/ *verb trans. Scot. arch.* Pa. t. & pple **coft** /kɒft/. LME.
[ORIGIN Orig. only as pa. t. & pple, prob. from Middle Dutch *coft(e)* pa. pple of *cōpen* COPE *verb*³.]
Buy, purchase.

coffee /ˈkɒfi/ *noun & adjective*. L16.
[ORIGIN Turkish *kahve* ult. from Arabic *qahwa*, prob. through Dutch *koffie*.]
▸ **A** *noun*. **1** A drink made by infusion from the seeds of a shrub (see sense 3) roasted and ground or (in the East) pounded. L16. ▸**b** A cup of, or light refreshments including, this drink. L18.
2 Seeds of this shrub, either raw or roasted (and ground). E17.
3 The shrub or tree from which the seeds are obtained: any of certain members of the palaeotropical genus *Coffea* (esp. *C. arabica*), of the madder family, which bear white flowers succeeded by red berries each containing two seeds. E17.
4 The light brown colour of white coffee. E19.
– PHRASES: **black coffee**: served without milk or cream. **Gaelic coffee**: served with cream and (now usu. Scotch) whisky. **Irish coffee**: served with cream and Irish whiskey. ***KENYA coffee***. ***ROBUSTA coffee***. ***Scotch coffee***: see SCOTCH *adjective*. ***sergeant major's coffee***: see SERGEANT MAJOR *noun* 4. ***Turkish coffee***: see TURKISH *adjective*. ***Viennese coffee***: see VIENNESE *adjective*. **white coffee**: served with milk or cream.
– COMB.: **coffee-and** *US slang* coffee and doughnuts; **coffee bar** a cafe serving coffee and light refreshments; **coffee bean** the seed of the coffee tree; **coffee-berry** (**a**) the fruit or (loosely) the seed of the coffee tree; (**b**) *US* the Kentucky coffee tree; **coffee-break** an interval, usu. between periods of work, esp. mid-morning,

C

when coffee is drunk; **coffee cake** (*a*) *N. Amer.* a cake or sweet bread flavoured with cinnamon or topped or filled with cinnamon sugar, usu. eaten with coffee; (*b*) a coffee-flavoured cake; **coffee-coloured** *adjective* (*a*) of the colour of white coffee; (*b*) (of a person) having a light brown skin colour; **coffee cup** a cup of a special shape or size for holding coffee; **coffee essence** concentrated extract of coffee; **coffee grounds** the granular sediment remaining in coffee after infusion; **coffee house** *noun & verb* (*a*) *noun* a place where coffee and other refreshments are provided, *esp.* one used in the 17th and 18th cents. as a centre for political and literary conversation, circulation of news, etc.; (*b*) *verb intrans.* (*slang*) stand about gossiping, orig. while waiting for the hounds at a meet; **coffee-maker** *spec.* a device for brewing coffee; **coffee mill** a hand mill for grinding roasted coffee beans; **coffee morning** a morning gathering, often in aid of charity, at which coffee is served; ***coffee nibs***: see NIB *noun*[1] 6; **coffee pot** a tall covered pot with a spout, in which coffee is made or served; **coffee room** a public room where coffee etc. is served; formerly, the dining room in a hotel; **coffee shop** (*a*) a shop selling coffee beans or ground coffee; (*b*) a small restaurant, usu. attached to a hotel; **coffee spoon** a small spoon for stirring coffee in a cup; **coffee stall** a movable structure at which coffee and other refreshments are sold; **coffee table** a small low table for serving coffee (***coffee-table book*** (usu. *derog.*), a large expensive lavishly illustrated book); **coffee tree** (*a*) a tree or shrub from which coffee is obtained (= sense 3 above); (*b*) *N. Amer.* a leguminous tree, *Gymnocladus dioica*, whose seeds can be used as a substitute for coffee (also more fully ***Kentucky coffee tree***).

▸ **B** *adjective.* Of the light brown colour of white coffee. **E20.**

coffer /ˈkɒfə/ *noun.* **ME.**

[ORIGIN Old French & mod. French *coffre* from Latin *cophinus*: see COFFIN *noun*.]

1 A box, a chest; *esp.* a strongbox in which money or valuables are kept. In *pl.* also, treasury, funds. **ME.**

S. SMILES Efforts to fill the coffers of Rome by the sale of indulgences.

†**2** A coffin. **ME–M16.**

†**3** An ark. **ME–E18.**

4 *ARCHITECTURE.* An ornamental sunk panel in a ceiling or soffit. **M17.**

– COMB.: **cofferdam** a watertight enclosure used in the construction of bridges, in harbour works, etc.; also, a double bulkhead in a large merchant vessel, esp. a tanker, built as a safety measure between holds or oil tanks.

coffer /ˈkɒfə/ *verb trans.* **LME.**

[ORIGIN from the noun.]

1 Enclose (as) in a coffer; treasure *up*. *arch.* **LME.**

2 *ARCHITECTURE.* Adorn with coffers (see COFFER *noun* 4). **M19.**

■ **coffering** *noun* (*a*) the action of the verb; (*b*) (chiefly *ARCHITECTURE*) an arrangement or structure of coffers: **L18.**

cofferer /ˈkɒfərə/ *noun.* **ME.**

[ORIGIN Anglo-Norman *cofrere* treasurer (= Anglo-Latin *cofferarius*) corresp. to Old French *cofrier* box-maker (medieval Latin *cofferarius*), formed as COFFER *noun*, -ER[2].]

1 *hist.* A treasurer; *spec.* one of the treasurers of the royal household. **ME.**

†**2** A person who makes coffers. **ME–E16.**

cofferet *noun* var. of COFFRET.

coffin /ˈkɒfɪn/ *noun.* **ME.**

[ORIGIN Old French *cof(f)in* little basket, case from Latin *cophinus* from Greek *kophinos* basket: cf. COFFER *noun*.]

1 Orig., a chest, a casket, a box. Now *spec.* a long box in which a corpse is buried or cremated. **ME.** ▸**b** *fig.* An old and unseaworthy vessel; an aircraft etc. thought likely to crash. Usu. more fully ***floating coffin***, ***flying coffin***, etc. *colloq.* **E19.**

a nail in the coffin of *fig.* something which tends to hasten or ensure the death or end of. ***oak coffin***: see OAK *noun & adjective*.

†**2** A basket. **LME–M16.**

†**3** A pastry mould for a pie, a piecrust; a pie dish. **LME–M18.**

4 A paper case or receptacle, esp. of conical shape. Now *rare* or *obsolete*. **L16.**

5 The whole of a horse's hoof below the coronet. **E17.**

6 The wooden frame enclosing the stone on which type was placed in a wooden printing press. Also, the bed of a printing machine. **M17.**

†**7** A case in which articles are fired in a furnace. **L17–L18.**

– COMB.: **coffin bone** the distal phalangeal bone of a horse, enclosed within the hoof; **coffin corner** *AMER. FOOTBALL* the angle between goal line and sideline; **coffin joint** the joint at the top of a horse's hoof; **coffin nail** *fig.* (*slang*) a cigarette; **coffin plate** a metal plate set in a coffin lid, bearing the name etc. of the deceased; **coffin ship** *colloq.* an old and unseaworthy ship (cf. sense 1c above); **coffin stool** a stand or support for a coffin.

■ **coffinless** *adjective* **E19.**

coffin /ˈkɒfɪn/ *verb trans.* **M16.**

[ORIGIN from the noun.]

Enclose (as) in a coffin.

JONSON Coffin them alive In some kind clasping prison. A. P. STANLEY The coffined body lay in state at Westminster.

coffle /ˈkɒf(ə)l/ *noun.* **M18.**

[ORIGIN Arabic *qāfila* CAFILA.]

A line of or *of* slaves or animals driven along together.

coffret /ˈkɒfrɪt/ *noun.* Also **cofferet** /ˈkɒfərɪt/. **L15.**

[ORIGIN Old French, dim. of *coffre*: see COFFER *noun*, -ET[1].]

A small coffer.

coft *verb pa. t. & pple* of COFF.

cog /kɒg/ *noun*[1]. **ME.**

[ORIGIN Middle Low German, Middle Dutch *kogge* (Dutch *kog*), whence also Old French *cogue*, *koge*.]

1 *hist.* A medieval broadly built ship with rounded prow and stern. **ME.** ▸**b** A kind of craft formerly used for local commerce on the Rivers Humber and Ouse in NE England. *obsolete* exc. *dial.* **M16.**

2 More fully ***cogboat***. = COCKBOAT. **LME.**

cog /kɒg/ *noun*[2]. **ME.**

[ORIGIN Prob. of Scandinavian origin: cf. synon. Swedish *kugge*, *kughjul* cogwheel, Norwegian *kug*.]

1 Each of a series of projections on the edge of a wheel or the side of a bar transferring motion by engaging with another such series; *fig.* an unimportant member of a large organization etc. Also, a wheel with such projections. **ME.**

J. ARGENTI The larger the company the greater is the feeling amongst the junior employees that they are merely small cogs in a giant wheel.

2 Each of the short handles of the pole of a scythe. Long *dial.* **L17.**

3 A wedge or support fixed under anything. Chiefly *N. English.* **L19.**

– COMB.: **cog rail**, **cog railway**: with cogs or teeth, for very steep gradients; **cogwheel**: with cogs or teeth.

cog /kɒg/ *noun*[3]. **M16.**

[ORIGIN Rel. to COG *verb*[2].]

†**1** An act or way of cogging at dice. **M16–M17.**

2 A small coin. Formerly also *gen.* (*slang*) anything used by a trickster to entice a victim. Long *obsolete* exc. (*rare*) *Jamaican dial.* **M16.**

†**3** A deception, a trick, a fraud, an imposture. **E–M17.**

cog /kɒg/ *noun*[4]. **M19.**

[ORIGIN from COG *verb*[3].]

A tenon on the end of a beam.

cog *noun*[5] var. of COGUE.

cog /kɒg/ *verb*[1]. Infl. **-gg-**. **L15.**

[ORIGIN from COG *noun*[2].]

1 *verb trans.* Equip (a wheel etc.) with cogs. **L15.**

2 *verb trans.* Chock (a wheel etc.); steady with a wedge or wedges. Chiefly *N. English.* **M17.**

3 *verb trans.* Roll or bloom (ingots). Also foll. by *down*. **L19.**

4 *verb intrans.* Engage with corresponding cogs or projections; *fig.* fit in, agree, work (*together*) in harmony. **L19.**

cog /kɒg/ *verb*[2]. Infl. **-gg-**. **M16.**

[ORIGIN Unknown.]

1 *arch.* ▸**a** *verb intrans.* Cheat in throwing dice. **M16.** ▸**b** *verb trans.* Throw (a die, dice) fraudulently to direct or control their fall. **M16.**

†**2** *verb intrans.* Employ fraud or deceit, cheat; employ flattery, wheedle; jest or quibble (*with*). **M16–L19.**

†**3** *verb trans.* Cheat, flatter, (*into*, *out of*); get *from* a person by fraud or flattery; produce cunningly or fraudulently; foist *in* (adverb); palm off (*up*)*on*. **L16–L19.**

4 *verb trans.* Copy (the work of another person) illicitly or without acknowledgement. *Irish.* **M20.**

■ **cogger** *noun* **M16.**

cog /kɒg/ *verb*[3] *trans. & intrans.* Infl. **-gg-**. **E19.**

[ORIGIN App. var. of COCK *verb*[3].]

Join (a beam), connect timbers etc., by means of a cog or tenon. Chiefly as ***cogging*** *verbal noun*.

cogency /ˈkəʊdʒ(ə)nsi/ *noun.* **M17.**

[ORIGIN from COGENT: see -ENCY.]

1 The quality of being cogent; the power of compelling conviction or assent. **M17.**

2 A convincing argument. *rare.* **M19.**

■ **cogence** *noun* (*rare*) cogency **L18.**

cogeneration /ˌkəʊdʒɛnəˈreɪʃ(ə)n/ *noun.* **L20.**

[ORIGIN from CO- + GENERATION.]

The generation of electricity and useful heat jointly; the utilization of the steam left over from electricity generation for heating.

■ **coˈgenerated** *adjective* produced by cogeneration **L20.** **coˈgenerator** *noun* a system or plant for cogeneration **L20.**

cogent /ˈkəʊdʒ(ə)nt/ *adjective.* **M17.**

[ORIGIN Latin *cogent-* pres. ppl stem of *cogere* drive together, compel, formed as CO- + *agere* drive: see -ENT.]

1 Able to compel assent or belief; *esp.* (of an argument, explanation, etc.) persuasive, expounded clearly and logically, convincing. **M17.**

2 *gen.* Constraining, impelling; forcible. **L17.**

■ **cogently** *adverb* **M17.**

coggie *noun* var. of COGIE.

coggle /ˈkɒg(ə)l/ *noun. obsolete* exc. *dial.* **LME.**

[ORIGIN Perh. var. of COBBLE *noun*.]

A rounded water-worn stone; a cobble.

coggle /ˈkɒg(ə)l/ *verb intrans. & trans. Scot. & N. English.* **M18.**

[ORIGIN Perh. from COGGLE *noun*, but cf. COCKLE *verb*[2].]

Shake from side to side; totter; wobble.

coggly /ˈkɒgli/ *adjective. Scot. & N. English.* **E19.**

[ORIGIN from COGGLE *noun* or *verb* + -Y[1].]

Shaky, unstable; liable to overturn.

cogida /koˈxiða, kəˈhiːdə/ *noun.* **E20.**

[ORIGIN Spanish, lit. 'a gathering of the harvest', use as noun of fem. pa. pple of *coger* seize from Latin *colligare*: see COLLIGATE *verb*.]

A tossing of a bullfighter by a bull.

cogie /ˈkəʊgi/ *noun. Scot.* Also **coggie** /ˈkɒgi/. **M18.**

[ORIGIN from COGUE + -IE.]

(The contents of) a small wooden bowl.

cogitable /ˈkɒdʒɪtəb(ə)l/ *adjective & noun.* **LME.**

[ORIGIN Latin *cogitabilis*, from *cogitare*: see COGITATE *verb*, -ABLE.]

▸ **A** *adjective.* Able to be grasped by the mind; conceivable. **LME.**

▸ **B** *noun.* A conceivable thing. Now *rare.* **E17.**

cogitabund /ˈkɒdʒɪtəbʌnd/ *adjective.* Now *rare.* **M17.**

[ORIGIN Latin *cogitabundus*, from *cogitare* COGITATE *verb*.]

Meditative, deep in thought.

cogitate /ˈkɒdʒɪteɪt/ *verb.* **L16.**

[ORIGIN Latin *cogitat-* pa. ppl stem of *cogitare* think, formed as CO- + *agitare*: see AGITATE *verb*, -ATE[3].]

1 *verb intrans. & trans.* Think, ponder, meditate; devise, plan. **L16.**

DICKENS Still cogitating and looking for an explanation in the fire. OED The man is cogitating mischief against us.

2 *verb trans. PHILOSOPHY.* Form a conception of (an object). Now *rare.* **M19.**

■ **cogitator** *noun* **M19.**

cogitation /kɒdʒɪˈteɪʃ(ə)n/ *noun.* **ME.**

[ORIGIN Old French *cogitacion* from Latin *cogitatio(n-)*, formed as COGITATE: see -ATION.]

1 The action of thinking; attentive consideration, reflection, meditation. **ME.** ▸**b** The faculty of thinking; thought. **M16.**

2 A thought, a reflection. **ME.** ▸**b** A plan, a design. **M16.**

cogitative /ˈkɒdʒɪtətɪv/ *adjective.* **LME.**

[ORIGIN French †*cogitatif*, *-ive*, or late Latin *cogitativus*, formed as COGITATE: see -IVE.]

1 Having the power or faculty of thought; thinking (as a characteristic attribute). **LME.**

2 Given to cogitation; thoughtful; meditative. **E17.**

■ **cogitatively** *adverb* **M18.** **cogitativeness** *noun* **E19.**

cogito /ˈkɒdʒɪtəʊ/ *noun.* **M19.**

[ORIGIN Latin = I think, lst pers. pres. of *cogitare* COGITATE, from the formula *cogito, ergo sum* 'I think (or I am thinking), therefore I am' of the French philosopher René Descartes (1596–1650).]

PHILOSOPHY. The principle establishing the existence of the thinker from the fact of his or her thinking or awareness.

cognac /ˈkɒnjak; *foreign* kɔɲak (*pl. same*)/ *noun.* Also **C-**. **L16.**

[ORIGIN *Cognac* in western France.]

1 In full ***Cognac wine***. A white wine produced at Cognac. **L16.**

2 Orig. ***cognac brandy***. French brandy, properly that distilled from the wine of Cognac; a drink of this. **L17.**

cognate /ˈkɒgneɪt/ *adjective & noun.* **E17.**

[ORIGIN Latin *cognatus*, formed as CO- + *gnatus* born.]

▸ **A** *adjective.* **1** Of or pertaining to kinship; descended from a common ancestor. **E17.** ▸**b** *spec. LINGUISTICS.* Of the same linguistic family; representing the same original word or root; of parallel development in different allied languages (as English *father*, German *Vater*, Latin *pater*). **E19.**

b B. COTTLE Broom is cognate with Bramble, so the word must have something to do with spikiness.

2 Akin in origin, nature, or quality. **M17.**

J. GOAD Comets and Fiery Meteors are cognate. B. JOWETT Geometry and the cognate sciences.

– SPECIAL COLLOCATIONS: **cognate accusative**, **cognate object** *GRAMMAR* a direct object whose meaning is not distinct from that of its verb (*live a good life* = live virtuously).

▸ **B** *noun.* **1** Chiefly *LAW.* A person related by blood to another; *esp.* a relative on the mother's side; in *pl.*, descendants of a common ancestor. Cf. AGNATE. **M18.**

2 A cognate word. **M19.**

■ **cognately** *adverb* **M20.** **cognateness** *noun* **E19.** **cognatic** /kɒgˈnatɪk/ *adjective* of, pertaining to, or reckoned through cognates (COGNATE *noun* 1) **M18.**

cognation /kɒgˈneɪʃ(ə)n/ *noun.* Now *rare.* **LME.**

[ORIGIN Latin *cognatio(n-)*, formed as COGNATE: see -ATION.]

1 The relationship of cognate persons. **LME.**

†**2** *collect.* Kindred, relations. **LME–M16.**

3 Affinity, connection, relation, likeness. **M16.**

4 The relationship of cognate words etc. **M19.**

cognisable *adjective*, **cognisance** *noun*, etc., vars. of COGNIZABLE etc.

cognita *noun* pl. of COGNITUM.

cognition /kɒgˈnɪʃ(ə)n/ *noun.* **LME.**

[ORIGIN Latin *cognitio(n-)*, from *cognit-* pa. ppl stem of *cognoscere* get to know, investigate, formed as CO- + (*g*)*noscere* know: see -ION.]

1 The action or faculty of knowing, now *spec.* including perceiving, conceiving, etc., as opp. to emotion and volition; the acquisition and possession of empirical factual knowledge. **LME.** ▸**b** A perception, a sensation, a notion, an intuition. **L18.**

2 = COGNIZANCE 4. Chiefly *Scot.* L15.
■ **cognitional** *adjective* E19.

cognitive /ˈkɒɡnɪtɪv/ *adjective.* L16.
[ORIGIN medieval Latin *cognitivus*, from *cognit-*: see COGNITION, -IVE.]
Of or pertaining to cognition; based on or pertaining to empirical factual knowledge.
cognitive behaviour therapy, **cognitive therapy** a type of psychotherapy in which negative patterns of thought about the self and the world are challenged in order to alter behaviour or mood. **cognitive dissonance** the state of having inconsistent thoughts, beliefs, or attitudes, especially as relating to behavioural decisions and attitude change. **cognitive science** the science or study of cognition or intelligence. **cognitive scientist** an expert in or student of cognitive science.
■ **cognitively** *adverb* in a cognitive manner; with regard to or from the point of view of cognition: L19.

cognitum /ˈkɒɡnɪtəm/ *noun. rare.* Pl. ***-ta*** /-tə/. L19.
[ORIGIN Latin, neut. pa. pple of *cognoscere*: see COGNITION.]
PHILOSOPHY. An object of cognition.

cognizable /ˈkɒ(ɡ)nɪzəb(ə)l/ *adjective.* Also **-isable**, †**conusable**. L17.
[ORIGIN from (the same root as) COGNIZE *verb* + -ABLE.]
1 Able to be known; perceptible; recognizable. L17.
2 Able or liable to be judicially examined or tried; within the jurisdiction of a court etc. L17.
■ **cogniza'bility** *noun* M19. **cognizableness** *noun* L19. **cognizably** *adverb* E19.

cognizance /ˈkɒ(ɡ)nɪz(ə)ns/ *noun.* Also **-isance**, †**conusance**. ME.
[ORIGIN Old French *conis(s)aunce*, *conus-* vars. of *conoi(s)sance* (mod. *connaissance*), from Proto-Romance, from Latin *cognoscent-* pres. ppl stem of *cognoscere*: see COGNITION, -ANCE.]
1 A distinctive device or mark, as a crest, heraldic bearing, etc.; *spec.* (HERALDRY) an emblem borne by all the retainers of a noble house, a badge. ME.

T. H. WHITE The cognizance was of a silver woman on a sable field.

†**2** Recognition. *rare.* ME–L16.
3 Knowledge, understanding, acquaintance, awareness, now *spec.* as attained by observation or information; notice; a sphere of observation or concern. LME.

HOBBES The tree of cognizance of Good and Evill. R. SCRUTON A promise is made, another given, knowingly and in full cognizance of consequences.

have cognizance of know, esp. in a legitimate or official way. **take cognizance of** attend to, not allow to go unobserved.
4 (The right of) dealing with a matter legally or judicially; taking judicial or authoritative notice. LME.

BURKE To introduce courts of justice for the cognizance of crimes.

5 LAW. Acknowledgement, esp. of a fine; admission of an alleged fact. Also, a plea in replevin that a defendant holds goods in the right of another as his bailee. L16.

cognizant /ˈkɒ(ɡ)nɪz(ə)nt/ *adjective.* Also **-isant**. E19.
[ORIGIN from COGNIZANCE: see -ANT[1]. Cf. earlier CONUSANT.]
1 Having knowledge, being aware (*of*). E19. ▸**b** Having cognition. M19.
2 LAW. Having cognizance or jurisdiction. M19.

cognize /kɒɡˈnʌɪz/ *verb.* Also **-ise**. M17.
[ORIGIN from COGNIZANCE after *recognize* etc.]
†**1** *verb intrans.* Take judicial notice. Only in M17.
2 *verb trans.* Take or have cognizance of; notice, observe; know, perceive. E19.

cognizee /kɒ(ɡ)nɪˈziː/ *noun.* Also **-isee**, †**conusee**. M16.
[ORIGIN After COGNIZOR or its source: see -EE[1].]
LAW (now *hist.*). The party in whose favour a fine of land was levied.

cognizor /ˈkɒ(ɡ)nɪzɔː/ *noun.* Also **-isor**, †**conusor**. M16.
[ORIGIN Anglo-Norman *coniso(u)r* = Old French *conoisseur* (later CONNOISSEUR).]
LAW (now *hist.*). The party who levied a fine of land.

cognomen /kɒɡˈnəʊmən/ *noun.* Pl. **-mens**, (earlier) †**-mina**. E17.
[ORIGIN Latin *cognomen*, *-min-*, formed as CO- + (*g*)*nomen* name.]
1 A surname; a nickname; *loosely* an appellation, a name. E17.
2 ROMAN HISTORY. The third personal name of a Roman citizen (as Marcus Tullius *Cicero*); a fourth name or personal epithet (as Publius Cornelius Scipio *Africanus*). L19.

cognominal /kɒɡˈnɒmɪn(ə)l/ *adjective.* M17.
[ORIGIN from Latin *cognominis* having the same name or from *cognomin-*, *-men* COGNOMEN: see -AL[1].]
1 Having the same name or cognomen. M17.
2 Of or pertaining to a cognomen or surname. M17.

cognominate /kɒɡˈnɒmɪneɪt/ *verb trans.* E17.
[ORIGIN Latin *cognominat-* pa. ppl stem of *cognominare*, formed as COGNOMEN: see -ATE[3].]
Give a cognomen to; nickname; *loosely* call, style.
■ **cognomi'nation** *noun* (**a**) cognominating; (**b**) a cognomen: E17.

cognosce /kɒɡˈnɒs/ *verb.* Chiefly SCOTS LAW. M16.
[ORIGIN Latin *cognoscere*: see COGNITION.]
1 *verb intrans.* Make an inquiry; take judicial cognizance of a cause etc. Now *rare* or *obsolete.* M16.
2 *verb trans.* Judicially examine and pronounce (a person) to be of a specified status. Without compl.: declare insane. M16.
3 *verb trans.* Take judicial cognizance of (a matter); investigate, examine. E17.

cognoscence /kɒɡˈnɒs(ə)ns/ *noun.* Now *rare.* LME.
[ORIGIN (Old French *cognoissance* from) late Latin *cognoscentia*, from *cognoscere*: see COGNITION, -ENCE.]
1 A heraldic cognizance or badge. LME.
2 Cognition; cognizance. L15.
■ **cognoscent** *adjective* (*rare*) cognitive; cognizant: M17.

cognoscente /kɒnjəˈʃɛnti, *foreign* koɲoˈʃɛnte/ *noun.* Pl. **-ti** /-ti/. M18.
[ORIGIN Italian (now CONOSCENTE), lit. 'person who knows', Latinized form of *conoscente* from Latin *cognoscent-* pres. ppl stem of *cognoscere*: see COGNITION, -ENT.]
A connoisseur; a discerning expert.

Campaign It is written for the cognoscenti and has a tendency towards in-jokes.

cognoscible /kɒɡˈnɒsɪb(ə)l/ *adjective.* M17.
[ORIGIN Late Latin *cognoscibilis*, from *cognoscere*: see COGNITION, -IBLE.]
1 Knowable; recognizable. M17.
†**2** = COGNIZABLE 2. M17–M18.
■ **cognosci'bility** *noun* M17.

cognoscitive /kɒɡˈnɒsɪtɪv/ *adjective.* Now *rare.* M17.
[ORIGIN from COGNITIVE after Latin *cognoscere* (see COGNITION).]
= COGNITIVE.

cognovit /kɒɡˈnəʊvɪt/ *noun.* E18.
[ORIGIN Latin *cognovit* (*actionem*) he has acknowledged (the action).]
LAW (now *hist.*). In full ***cognovit actionem*** /aktɪˈəʊnɛm/. A defendant's acknowledgement that the plaintiff's cause is just; an acknowledgement of a debt.

cogon /ˈkəʊɡɒn/ *noun. N. Amer.* E20.
[ORIGIN Tagalog *kugon*.]
In full ***cogon grass***. A coarse grass, *Imperata cylindrica*, native to SW Asia and found worldwide as an invasive weed.

cogue /kəʊɡ, kɒɡ/ *noun & verb.* Chiefly *Scot.* Also **cog** (verb infl. **-gg-**). E16.
[ORIGIN Unknown.]
▸ **A** *noun.* **1** A wooden pail used for milking etc. E16.
2 A small wooden cup; a small measure of spirits etc. L17.
3 A dry measure equivalent to a quarter of a peck. M18.
▸ **B** *verb.* †**1** *verb intrans.* Drink spirits. M–L18.
2 *verb trans.* Put into a cogue. M18.
■ **cogueful** *noun* as much as a cogue will hold L17.

cog-wood /ˈkɒɡwʊd/ *noun.* E18.
[ORIGIN from COG *noun*[2] + WOOD *noun*[1].]
(The hard timber of) a W. Indian tree, *Ziziphus chloroxylon*, of the buckthorn family.

cohabit /kəʊˈhabɪt/ *verb intrans.* M16.
[ORIGIN Late Latin *cohabitare*, formed as CO- + *habitare* HABIT *verb*.]
1 *gen.* Live together (*with*). *arch.* M16.
2 *spec.* Live together as husband and wife, esp. when not legally married. M16.
■ **cohabitant** *noun* a person who lives together with another or others L16. **cohabi'tee** *noun* a person who lives with another as husband or wife without legal marriage L20. **cohabiter** *noun* a cohabitant or cohabitee E17. **cohabitor** *noun* a cohabitee L20.

cohabitation /kəʊhabɪˈteɪʃ(ə)n/ *noun.* LME.
[ORIGIN Late Latin *cohabitatio(n-)*, formed as CO- + *habitatio(n-)* HABITATION. Cf. Old French & mod. French *cohabitation*.]
1 *gen.* Living together; community of life. *arch.* LME.
2 *spec.* Living together as husband and wife, esp. without legal marriage. M16.
3 Coexistence of or cooperation between office-holders of different political persuasions, orig. in France. L20.
■ **cohabitational** *adjective* M20.

cohen *noun* var. of KOHEN.

cohere /kə(ʊ)ˈhɪə/ *verb.* M16.
[ORIGIN Latin *cohaerere*, formed as CO- + *haerere* to stick.]
1 *verb intrans.* Of parts or individuals, or of a whole: stick together (*lit. & fig.*); become or remain united. M16.

C. COTTON By cohering with other persons of condition. A. W. KINGLAKE The hard mass became fluid. It still cohered. W. E. H. LECKY A . . dissolution of the moral principles by which society coheres.

2 *verb intrans.* Be consistent; be congruous in substance, tenor, or general effect. L16. ▸†**b** Coincide, come together in agreement. E–M17.

T. SHADWELL That trimming . . does not cohere with your complexion at all.

3 *verb trans.* Unite, cause to form a whole. *rare.* E17.
■ **coherer** *noun* an early form of radio detector, usu. consisting of a glass tube loosely filled with metal filings whose bulk electrical resistance decreased in the presence of radio waves L19. **cohering** *adjective* that cohere(s); BOTANY united externally: M17.

coherence /kə(ʊ)ˈhɪər(ə)ns/ *noun.* M16.
[ORIGIN Latin *cohaerentia*, formed as COHERENT: see -ENCE.]
1 The action or fact of sticking together (*lit. & fig.*); cohesion, union. M16.
2 Logical or clear interconnection or relation; consistency; congruity of substance, tenor, or general effect. L16. ▸†**b** Coincidence, agreement. L16–L17.
†**3** Context; immediately surrounding discourse. L16–M18.
4 PHYSICS. The property (of waveforms) of being coherent. E20.
– COMB.: **coherence theory** PHILOSOPHY either of two theories of truth positing (**a**) that coherence is the definition or criterion of truth, or (**b**) that the truth of a proposition consists in the coherence of that proposition with the set of all other true propositions.
■ **coherency** *noun* the quality of being coherent E17.

coherent /kə(ʊ)ˈhɪər(ə)nt/ *adjective.* M16.
[ORIGIN from Latin *cohaerent-* pres. ppl stem of *cohaerere*: see COHERE, -ENT.]
†**1** Logically related *to*; accordant *with*. M16–E17.
2 Of an argument, discourse, reasoning, etc.: consistent, non-contradictory, logical, in the relation of its parts; easily followed, complete and intelligible. L16. ▸**b** Of a person: logical or clear in argument or expression, intelligible. E18.

H. READ Too inarticulate to give a coherent account of his ambitions. P. G. WODEHOUSE A great coherent, purposeful plan. C. P. SNOW 'Are you part of a dream?' . . They were his first coherent words. **b** DICKENS Be plain and coherent, if you please.

3 Sticking together (*lit. & fig.*); united, exhibiting cohesion. L16.

T. H. HUXLEY These rocks are sufficiently coherent to form durable building stones. R. P. JHABVALA Their differences melted away and they became a coherent smiling group.

4 PHYSICS. (Of waves and radiation) having a constant phase relationship between different parts and so able to interfere with other waves having this property; producing such radiation. E19.
■ **coherently** *adverb* E17.

cohesion /kə(ʊ)ˈhiːʒ(ə)n/ *noun.* M17.
[ORIGIN from Latin *cohaes-* pa. ppl stem of *cohaerere*: see COHERE, -ION.]
The action or condition of sticking together or cohering; a tendency to remain united; *spec.* (PHYSICS) the sticking together of particles or molecules of the same substance (cf. ADHESION).

A. GEIKIE Water . . loosens the cohesion of a steep bank. A. S. EDDINGTON The forces of cohesion between its particles. J. GROSS Social cohesion can never be as absolute as artistic unity. M. BRADBURY They had acquired a cohesion, a closeness.

cohesive /kə(ʊ)ˈhiːsɪv/ *adjective.* E18.
[ORIGIN formed as COHESION + -IVE.]
Having the property of cohering; characterized by cohesion.
■ **cohesively** *adverb* E19. **cohesiveness** *noun* M18.

cohibit /kəʊˈhɪbɪt/ *verb trans.* Now *rare.* M16.
[ORIGIN Latin *cohibit-* pa. ppl stem of *cohibere* restrain, formed as CO- + *habere* have.]
Restrain; restrict.
■ **cohi'bition** *noun* M16.

†**Cohi Noor** *noun* see KOH-I-NOOR.

coho /ˈkəʊhəʊ/ *noun.* Pl. same, **-os**. Also **-oe**. M19.
[ORIGIN Unknown.]
A salmon, *Oncorhynchus kisutch*, of N. American coasts and rivers; also ***coho salmon***. Also called ***silver salmon***.

cohobate /ˈkəʊhəʊbeɪt/ *verb trans.* Long *arch.* L16.
[ORIGIN from mod. Latin *cohobare* = French *cohober*: see -ATE[3].]
CHEMISTRY. Subject to repeated distillation by returning the distillate to the liquid being distilled; reflux.
■ †**cohobation** *noun* E17–L18.

cohog *noun & verb* see QUAHOG.

cohorn *noun* var. of COEHORN.

cohort /ˈkəʊhɔːt/ *noun.* LME.
[ORIGIN Old French *cohorte* or Latin *cohors*, *-hort-* enclosure, company, crowd, formed as CO- + *hort-* as in *hortus* garden.]
1 ROMAN HISTORY. A body of infantry of the Roman army, ten of which made up a legion; a body of auxiliary troops or (later) of cavalry of similar strength. LME.
2 A similar division of any other army; a band of warriors. E16.
3 A company or band, esp. of people united in some common purpose. E18. ▸**b** A group of people having a common statistical characteristic, esp. that of being born in the same year. M20.

W. HUTTON The public schools turn out cohorts of Conservative supporters. **b** *Independent* They are from the first cohort not to have been scarred by China's recent political catastrophes.

4 A taxonomic grouping ranking above superorder and below subclass. Formerly, a grouping above order but of no fixed rank. M19.
5 An assistant, a colleague, an accomplice. Chiefly *N. Amer.* M20.

M. SYAL Her constant cohorts were Fat Sally . . and Sherrie.

cohortation /kəʊhɔːˈteɪʃ(ə)n/ *noun.* Now *rare* or *obsolete.* LME.
[ORIGIN Latin *cohortatio(n-)*, formed as CO-, HORTATION.]
(An) exhortation.

cohosh /kəˈhɒʃ/ *noun. N. Amer.* L18.
[ORIGIN Eastern Abnaki *kkʷàhas*.]
Any of various plants having medicinal uses.
black cohosh a bugbane, *Cimicifuga racemosa*. **blue cohosh** *Caulophyllum thalictroides*, of the barberry family. **white cohosh** white baneberry, *Actaea pachypoda*.

COHSE /ˈkəʊzi/ *abbreviation.*
Confederation of Health Service Employees.

cohue /kɔy/ *noun.* Pl. pronounced same. M19.
[ORIGIN French.]
A mob, an unruly crowd.

cohune /kəˈhuːn/ *noun.* Also **cahoun**. M18.
[ORIGIN Miskito.]
A Central American palm, *Orbignya cohune*. Also ***cohune palm***.

COI *abbreviation.*
Central Office of Information.

coif /kɔɪf/ *noun.* ME.
[ORIGIN Old French *coife* (mod. *coiffe*) headdress from late Latin *cofia* helmet.]
1 A close-fitting cap covering the top, back, and sides of the head. Now *hist.* except as worn by nuns. ME.
2 A close-fitting skullcap worn under a helmet. *obsolete* exc. *hist.* ME.
3 A white cap worn by lawyers as a distinctive mark of their profession, *esp.* & later only that worn by a serjeant-at-law. *obsolete* exc. *hist.* LME.
the coif *hist.* the position of serjeant-at-law (SERGEANT ***of the coif***).

coif /kɔɪf/ *verb trans.* LME.
[ORIGIN Partly from Old French *coifer* (mod. *coiffer*), formed as COIF *noun*; partly from the noun.]
Provide or cover with a coif; (*obsolete* exc. *hist.*) invest with a serjeant-at-law's coif.

coiff /kwɑːf, kwɒf/ *verb trans.* M19.
[ORIGIN French *coiffer*: see COIF *verb*.]
Dress or arrange (the hair). Chiefly as ***coiffed*** *ppl adjective*.
■ Also **coiffé** /-feɪ/ *verb trans.* M19.

coiffeur /kwɑːˈfəː, kwɒ-; *foreign* kwafœːr (*pl. same*)/ *noun.* M19.
[ORIGIN French, formed as COIFF + *-eur* -OR.]
A hairdresser.
■ **coiffeuse** /-əːz; *foreign* -øːz (*pl. same*)/ *noun* a female hairdresser L18.

coiffure /kwɑːˈfjʊə, kwɒ-; noun *also foreign* kwafyːr (*pl. same*)/ *noun & verb.* M17.
[ORIGIN French, formed as COIFF: see -URE.]
▸ **A** *noun.* The way the hair is arranged or (formerly) the head decorated or covered; a hairstyle, a headdress. M17.
▸ **B** *verb trans.* = COIFF. Chiefly as ***coiffured*** *ppl adjective*. E20.

coign /kɔɪn/ *noun.* Also **coigne**. LME.
[ORIGIN Var. of COIN *noun*: cf. QUOIN *noun*.]
▸ **I** = QUOIN *noun*.
1 A projecting corner; a cornerstone; an angle. LME.

R. LEHMANN They sat in a coign of the cliff.

coign of vantage [from Shakes. *Macb.*] a place affording a good view of something.
2 A wedge. M18.
▸ †**II 3** = COIN *noun* II. LME–E16.

coign *verb* see QUOIN *verb*.

coigning *noun* see QUOINING.

coignye *noun* var. of COYNYE.

coil /kɔɪl/ *noun*[1]. Now *arch. & dial.* M16.
[ORIGIN Unknown.]
A noisy disturbance, a turmoil, a confused noise, a fuss.
keep a coil make a fuss, disturbance, etc. **this mortal coil** [from Shakes. *Haml.*] the turmoil of life.

coil /kɔɪl/ *noun*[2]. L16.
[ORIGIN from COIL *verb*.]
1 A length of rope, cable, etc., gathered up into a number of concentric rings; the quantity of cable etc. usually wound up. L16.
Flemish coil: see FLEMISH *adjective & noun*.
2 An arrangement of a thing in a spiral or a series of concentric circles or rings; a thing so arranged. M17.
3 A single turn of a coiled thing, esp. of a snake. E19.
4 *spec.* ▸**a** A piece of wire, piping, etc., wound spirally or helically. E19. ▸**b** A helix of wire for the passage of electric current, esp. for the ignition in an internal-combustion engine, or around a magnetic metal core as in an electromagnet or transformer. M19. ▸**c** A lock of hair twisted and made into a spiral. L19. ▸**d** A roll of postage stamps. E20. ▸**e** A flexible loop of material used as an intrauterine contraceptive device. M20. ▸**f** In full ***mosquito coil***. A slowly burning spiral made with a dried paste of pyrethrum powder, which produces a smoke that inhibits mosquitoes from biting. M20.
b *exploring coil*, *induction coil*, *repeating coil*, *Tesla coil*, *tickler coil*, etc.

coil /kɔɪl/ *verb.* E16.
[ORIGIN Old French *coillir* (mod. *cueillir* gather) = Provençal *colhir*, Spanish *coger*, Portuguese *colher* (also) furl, coil rope, from Latin *colligere*: see COLLECT *verb*.]
1 *verb trans.* Arrange (a rope etc.) in concentric rings, either on top of each other or as a flat spiral. Also foll. by *up*. E16.
2 *verb trans.* Wrap or encircle in a coil or coils. *obsolete* exc. *dial.* E17.
3 *verb trans. & intrans.* Twist in or into a circular, spiral, or winding shape. Also foll. by *up*. M17.

TENNYSON The long convolvuluses That coil'd around the stately stems. I. MURDOCH She coiled the . . hair into an artful bun. R. L. FOX Long tame snakes . . would . . coil themselves around the wands and garlands.

4 *verb intrans.* Move in a spiral course or in a sinuous fashion. E19.

S. NAIPAUL The smoke coiling up from the incinerator pit.

■ **coiled** *ppl adjective* that has been coiled, disposed in a coil; (of basketry, a basket) made by coiling the fibre; (of pottery, a pot) made by building up coils of clay: E17.

coin /kɔɪn/ *noun.* See also COIGN *noun*, QUOIN *noun*. ME.
[ORIGIN Old French & mod. French *coin*, †*coing* wedge, corner, †stamping die, from Latin *cuneus* wedge.]
▸ **I 1** See QUOIN *noun*. ME.
▸ †**II 2** A die for stamping money; a stamped device, an impress. LME–L17.
3 A piece of metal, usu. a disc, made into money by an official stamp. LME.

fig.: F. W. ROBERTSON Words are . . the coins of intellectual exchange.

obsidional coin: see OBSIDIONAL. **the other side of the coin** *fig.* the opposite view of a matter (cf. ***the reverse of the medal*** s.v. REVERSE *noun*).
4 Metal money; *slang* money, cash. LME.

A. MARS-JONES In coin, two hundred pounds.

bad coin debased currency. **false coin** imitation coin in base metal; *fig.* something spurious. **pay a person in his or her own coin** retaliate by similar behaviour.
– COMB.: **coin box** (a receptacle for coins in) a coin-operated telephone; **coin-op** *adjective & noun* (*a*) *adjective* coin-operated; (*b*) *noun* a launderette etc. with automatic coin-operated machines; **coin-operated** *adjective* (of a machine, lock, etc.) operated by a coin or coins.

coin /kɔɪn/ *verb*[1] *trans.* ME.
[ORIGIN Old French *coignier* mint, formed as COIN *noun*.]
▸ **I 1** Make (money) by stamping metal. ME.
coin money *fig.* get money fast.
2 Make (metal) into money by stamping pieces of definite weight and value with authorized marks or characters. LME.
3 *fig.* **a** Devise, produce; fabricate, invent (esp. a new word etc.). M16. ▸**b** *fig.* Make money out of or by means of. L16. ▸**c** Fashion or convert (*in*)*to*. E17.

a DISRAELI He would coin a smile for the instant. R. D. LAING The word 'psychiatry' was coined to refer to the institution of a discipline within medicine. **b** W. IRVING He coined the brains of his authors. **c** BYRON I have not . . coin'd my cheek to smiles.

a to coin a phrase *iron.*: accompanying a banal remark.
†**4** Stamp on a coin; figure in or on a coin. E–M17.
▸ **II** See QUOIN *verb*.
■ **coinable** *adjective* M19. **coiner** *noun* (*a*) a person who coins money etc.; *esp.* a maker of counterfeit coins; (*b*) an inventor, a fabricator: ME.

coin *verb*[2] see QUOIN *verb*.

coinage /ˈkɔɪnɪdʒ/ *noun.* LME.
[ORIGIN Old French *coigniage*, formed as COIN *noun*: see -AGE.]
1 The action or process of coining money; the right to coin money. LME.
2 Coins collectively; a system of coins in use. LME.
decimal coinage: see DECIMAL *adjective*.
3 *hist.* The official stamping of blocks of tin; the right of doing this. LME.
4 *fig.* An invention; a coined word; the action or process of inventing or of coining words etc. E17.

coincide /kəʊɪnˈsʌɪd/ *verb intrans.* E18.
[ORIGIN medieval Latin *coincidere* (in Astrol.), formed as CO- + *incidere* fall upon or into. Cf. Old French & mod. French *coïncider*.]
1 Occupy the same portion of space. E18.
2 Correspond in substance, nature, or character; agree exactly together or *with*. E18. ▸**b** Concur *in* opinion etc. M18.

GIBBON The true interest of an absolute monarch generally coincides with that of his people. R. D. LAING The person you take me to be, and the identity that I reckon myself to have, will coincide, by and large.

3 Occur at or during the same time. (Foll. by *with*.) E19.

W. TREVOR The marriage had been arranged to coincide with the end of the Easter term.

coincidence /kəʊˈɪnsɪd(ə)ns/ *noun.* E17.
[ORIGIN medieval Latin *coincidentia*, formed as COINCIDE: see -ENCE.]
1 Occupation of the same portion of space. E17.
2 Correspondence in substance, nature, character, value, etc.; (an instance of) exact agreement. E17. ▸**b** Concurrence in opinion etc. L18.
3 Simultaneous occurrence or existence; an instance of this. M17. ▸**b** PHYSICS. The presence of ionizing particles etc. in two or more detectors simultaneously, or of two or more signals simultaneously in a circuit. M20.

Fortean Times The coincidence of winged or tailed figures in the art of far-separated regions.

4 A notable concurrence of events or circumstances without apparent causal connection. L17.

Field By a strange sartorial coincidence, my host and I were both in matching brown shooting suits. T. CLANCY We can't tell if it's just coincidence or part of a plan.

■ †**coincidency** *noun* (an instance of) correspondence or exact agreement E17–L18.

coincident /kəʊˈɪnsɪd(ə)nt/ *adjective & noun.* M16.
[ORIGIN medieval Latin *coincident-* pres. ppl stem of *coincidere*: see COINCIDE, -ENT.]
▸ **A** *adjective.* **1** Having the same substance, nature, character, value, etc.; in exact agreement *with*. M16.
2 Simultaneous, exactly contemporaneous. L16.
3 Occupying the same portion of space. M17.
▸ †**B** *noun.* A coinciding thing. Usu. in *pl.* E17–M18.
■ **coincidently** *adverb* in a coincident manner, correspondingly, concurrently E17.

coincidental /kəʊɪnsɪˈdɛnt(ə)l/ *adjective.* E19.
[ORIGIN from COINCIDENT + -AL[1].]
Of the nature of (a) coincidence; coinciding, esp. without apparent causal connection.
■ **coincidentally** *adverb* (*a*) = COINCIDENTLY; (*b*) by coincidence, without apparent causal connection: M19.

coining *noun* see QUOINING.

Cointreau /ˈkwɑːntrəʊ, *foreign* kwɛ̃tro/ *noun.* E20.
[ORIGIN French.]
(Proprietary name for) a colourless orange-flavoured liqueur; a drink of this.

coir /ˈkɔɪə/ *noun.* L16.
[ORIGIN Malayalam *kāyaṟu* cord, coir.]
The fibre from the outer husk of the coconut, used for ropes, matting, etc., and as a substitute for peat in horticulture; light rope made from this.

coistrel *noun* var. of CUSTREL.

†**coit** *noun.* LME–M18.
[ORIGIN formed as COITUS.]
= COITUS.

coition /kəʊˈɪʃ(ə)n/ *noun.* M16.
[ORIGIN Latin *coitio(n-)*, from *coit-* pa. ppl stem of *coire*, formed as CO- + *ire* go: see -ION.]
†**1** Going or coming together; mutual attraction; conjunction of planets. M16–M18.
2 = COPULATION 2. E17.

coitus /ˈkəʊɪtəs/ *noun.* M19.
[ORIGIN Latin, from *coit-*: see COITION.]
= COPULATION 2.
coitus interruptus /ɪntəˈrʌptəs/ withdrawal of the penis from the vagina before ejaculation. **coitus reservatus** /rɛzəˈvɑːtəs/ postponement or avoidance of orgasm, to prolong sexual intercourse.
■ **coital** *adjective* L19.

cojones /koˈxones, kəˈhəʊneɪs/ *noun pl. colloq.* M20.
[ORIGIN Spanish, pl. of *cojón* testicle.]
Testicles; *fig.* courage, guts.

coke /kəʊk/ *noun*[1] & *verb*[1]. LME.
[ORIGIN Perh. same word as COLK.]
▸ **A** *noun.* †**1** Charcoal. Only in LME.
2 *sing.* & †in *pl.* Coal deprived by dry distillation of its volatile constituents; the solid substance left after heating petrol etc. LME.
go and eat coke *slang* go away!
– COMB.: **cokeman** a workman who handles coke; **coke oven**: producing coke from coal.
▸ **B** *verb trans. & intrans.* Convert into coke. L18.
coking coal coal suitable for making into coke.

coke /kəʊk/ *noun*[2] & *verb*[2]. *colloq.* E20.
[ORIGIN Abbreviation.]
▸ **A** *noun.* Cocaine, as a drug. E20.
▸ **B** *verb trans.* Drug (oneself) with cocaine. Also foll. by *up*. E20.
■ **cokey** *noun* a cocaine addict E20.

Coke /kəʊk/ *noun*[3]. Also **c-**. E20.
[ORIGIN Abbreviation.]
Proprietary name, = COCA-COLA.

coker /ˈkəʊkə/ *noun*[1]. L18.
[ORIGIN from COKE *noun*[1] & *verb*[1] + -ER[1].]
A person who supervises the coking of coal; a cokeman.

coker *noun*[2] var. of COCKER *noun*[2].

†**cokes** *noun.* M16–L17.
[ORIGIN Unknown.]
A gullible or foolish man, a simpleton.

†**cokes** *verb* see COAX *verb*.

col /kɒl/ *noun.* M19.
[ORIGIN French from Latin *collum* neck.]
1 A depression in the summit-line of a mountain chain; a saddle between two peaks. M19.
2 METEOROLOGY. An area of lower pressure between two anticyclones. L19.

col- /kɒl, *unstressed* kəl/ *prefix*.
Var. of Latin **COM-** before *l*. Cf. **CO-**, **CON-**, **COR-**.

Col. *abbreviation*.
1 Colonel.
2 Colorado.
3 Colossians (New Testament).

col. /kɒl/ *noun*. Pl. **cols.** (point). **E20**.
[**ORIGIN** Abbreviation.]
= **COLUMN** 2.

cola /ˈkəʊlə/ *noun*[1]. Also **k-**. **E17**.
[**ORIGIN** Temne *k'ola* cola nut.]
1 A tree of the genus *Cola*, native to W. Africa, esp. *C. acuminata*; the bitter seed of such a tree (also ***cola nut***, ***cola seed***). **E17**.
2 A carbonated drink flavoured with cola seeds. Earliest in **COCA-COLA**, **PEPSI-COLA**. **L19**.

cola *noun*[2] *pl.* see **COLON** *noun*[2].

colander /ˈkʌləndə/ *noun & verb*. Also **cullender**. **ME**.
[**ORIGIN** Perh. from Old Provençal *colador* (mod. Provençal *couladou*) = Spanish *colador*, from Proto-Romance, from Latin *colat-* pa. ppl stem of *colare* strain: see **-OR**. Cf. medieval Latin *colatorium*, French *couloir*. For the intrusive *n* cf. *messenger*, *passenger*, etc.]
▸ **A** *noun*. A perforated vessel used as a strainer in cookery; *transf.* a similar vessel used in other processes. **ME**.
▸ **B** *verb trans.* **1** Perforate with holes. **E18**.
2 Pass through a colander, strain. **L19**.

colation /kəˈleɪʃ(ə)n/ *noun*. Long *rare*. **E17**.
[**ORIGIN** medieval Latin *colatio(n-)*, from Latin *colat-*: see **COLANDER**, **-ATION**.]
The action of straining or passing through a strainer.

co-latitude /kəʊˈlatɪtjuːd/ *noun*. **L18**.
[**ORIGIN** from **CO-** + **LATITUDE**.]
ASTRONOMY. The complement of latitude, i.e. the difference between latitude and 90 degrees.

†**colature** *noun*. **LME**.
[**ORIGIN** Old French & mod. French, or late Latin *colatura*, from *colat-*: see **COLANDER**, **-URE**.]
1 The product of straining. **LME–E17**.
2 A strainer; *ANATOMY* a sphenoidal sinus. **L16–L17**.
3 = **COLATION**. **M17–L18**.
■ †**colatory** *noun* = **COLATURE** 2 **LME–E18**.

†**colbertine** *noun*. Also **-een**. **L17–M19**.
[**ORIGIN** from *Colbert* French surname + **-INE**[4].]
Open lace with a square ground.

colcannon /kɒlˈkanən/ *noun*. **L18**.
[**ORIGIN** Perh. from **COLE** *noun*[1].]
An Irish and Scottish dish of cabbage and potatoes boiled and pounded.

Colchian /ˈkɒlkɪən/ *adjective*. **E17**.
[**ORIGIN** from Latin *Colchis* (see below) from Greek *Kolkhis* + **-AN**.]
Of Colchis, the ancient name of a region east of the Black Sea, associated in Greek mythology with the quest of the Golden Fleece.
■ Also **Colchic** *adjective* **L16**.

colchicine /ˈkɒltʃɪsiːn/ *noun*. **M19**.
[**ORIGIN** from **COLCHICUM** + **-INE**[5].]
CHEMISTRY. A toxic yellow alkaloid, $C_{22}H_{25}NO_6$, present esp. in colchicum corms, which is used to treat gout and in plant-breeding to induce mutations.
■ Also †**colchicia** *noun* **M–L19**.

colchicum /ˈkɒltʃɪkəm, ˈkɒlk-/ *noun*. **L16**.
[**ORIGIN** Latin from Greek *kolkhikon* use as noun of neut. of *Kolkhikos*, from *Kolkhis* (with ref. to the poisonous arts of Medea): see **COLCHIAN**.]
1 A plant of the genus *Colchicum* of the lily family, *esp.* meadow saffron, *C. autumnale*. **L16**.
2 The dried corm or seed of such a plant used medicinally. **L18**.

†**colcothar** *noun*. **E17–M19**.
[**ORIGIN** Arabic *qulquṭār*.]
Ferric oxide, rouge, formed as a residue in the distillation of sulphuric acid from ferrous sulphate.

cold /kəʊld/ *noun*. Also (*Scot. & N. English*) **cauld** /kɔːld/.
[**ORIGIN** Old English *cald*, *ċeald* neut., from the adjective.]
1 The opposite or the absence of heat; the prevalence of low temperature, esp. in the atmosphere; cold weather; a condition of low temperature, a cold spell. **OE**.
2 The sensation produced by loss of heat from the body or by exposure to a lower temperature; a cold condition of the body. **OE**. ▸**b** *fig.* Lack of zeal, enthusiasm, or heartiness. **ME**.
3 An indisposition supposed to be caused by exposure to cold; *spec.* (also ***common cold***, ***cold in the head***) a viral infection causing inflammation of the mucous membranes of the nose and throat, usu. with hoarseness, running at the nose, coughing, etc. **ME**.
4 Cold water. Chiefly in ***hot and cold***. **E20**.
– **PHRASES**: ***catch a cold***, ***catch cold***: see **CATCH** *verb*. ***catch one's DEATH of cold***. ***cold in the head***, ***common cold***: see sense 3 above. **degrees of cold** degrees below freezing point. **left out in the cold** *fig.* ignored, not looked after. ***streaming cold***: see **STREAMING** *ppl adjective*.
– **COMB.**: **cold sore** an inflamed blister, esp. in or near the mouth, due to herpes simplex infection; **cold wave** *noun*[1] a spell of cold weather; a fall of temperature travelling over a large area.

cold /kəʊld/ *adjective & adverb*. Also (*Scot. & N. English*) **cauld** /kɔːld/.
[**ORIGIN** Old English *cald*, (West Saxon) *ċeald* = Old Frisian, Old Saxon *cald* (Dutch *koud*), Old High German *kalt* (German *kalt*), Old Norse *kaldr*, Gothic *kalds*, from Germanic, rel. to Latin *gelu* frost.]
▸ **A** *adjective*. **1** Of or at a temperature perceptibly lower than that of the living human body; of or at a relatively low temperature; characteristically or naturally so. **OE**. ▸**b** Dead; *slang* unconscious. **ME**.

> **GOLDSMITH** In the cold regions of the north. **E. O'BRIEN** The linoleum was cold on the soles of my feet. **N. MOSLEY** A spell of cold weather in which the pavements froze.

2 Not heated; having been allowed to cool after heating; (of a hearth etc.) with no fire burning; (of a tobacco pipe etc.) not lit. **OE**.

> **SCOTT FITZGERALD** A plate of cold fried chicken between them.

3 *fig.* Void of warmth or intensity of feeling; indifferent, apathetic; cool; not cordial or friendly; (more positively) feelingless, callous. **OE**. ▸**b** Sexually frigid, without sensual passion. **L16**.

> **STEELE** Cold to what his friends think of him. **T. HARDY** An unprotected childhood in a cold world has beaten gentleness out of me. **R. LEHMANN** Cold natures are always secretive. **A. C. BOULT** A wonderful collection of stories which he told with such relish . . that one hesitates to retell them in cold print.

4 *hist.* Designating a quality associated with coldness and regarded in medieval and later times as one of four qualities inherent in all things; having a preponderance of this quality. Cf. ***hot***, ***dry***, ***moist***. **OE**.
5 Gloomy, dispiriting, depressing; chilling. **ME**.

> **W. COWPER** She feels . . A cold misgiving. **LD MACAULAY** Preston brought cold news.

6 Of a person or animal, or a part of the body: feeling cold. Chiefly *pred.* **LME**.

> **D. H. LAWRENCE** I was very cold, so I went downstairs. **G. SWIFT** His hands . . were still cold from walking home in the rain.

7 Of soil: slow to absorb heat. **LME**.
8 Without power to influence; having lost the power of exciting the emotions; stale. **L16**.

> **D. L. SAYERS** The news was already 'cold'.

9 **a** *HUNTING*. Of a scent: weakened by the passage of time, faint. **L16**. ▸**b** Of a participant in a children's seeking or guessing game: far from finding or guessing what is sought. **M19**.
10 Of a colour or colouring: suggestive of cold or a sunless day; not suggestive of light and warmth; *esp.* of a pale blue or grey tint. **E18**.
11 Without preparation, preliminary performance, etc.; unrehearsed. Orig. & chiefly *N. Amer.* **L19**.
12 At one's mercy. *colloq.* **E20**.
– **PHRASES**: **as cold as ice** very cold (*lit. & fig.*). ***blow hot and cold***: see **BLOW** *verb*[1]. ***cauld kale het again***: see **KALE** *noun*. ***cold as CHARITY***. ***go hot and cold***: see **HOT** *adjective*. **knock cold**, **lay cold**, **lay out cold** *slang* knock unconscious, stun, shock severely. **leave a person cold** fail to interest or excite a person. ***stone-cold sober***: see **STONE** *adverb*.
– **SPECIAL COLLOCATIONS & COMB.**: **cold bath**: in cold water. ***cold blood***: see **BLOOD** *noun*. **cold-blooded** *adjective* (**a**) = **ECTOTHERMIC**; (**b**) *fig.* without excitement or sensibility; callous, deliberately cruel. **cold call** *verb intrans. & trans.* make an unsolicited call to or on (a person) to sell goods or services. **cold cathode**: that emits electrons without being heated. ***cold chisel***: see **CHISEL** *noun*[1] 1. **cold-cock** *verb trans.* (*N. Amer. colloq.*) knock (a person) out with a blow to the head. **cold comfort** poor consolation. ***cold compress***: see **COMPRESS** *noun* 1. **cold cream** a cooling cosmetic cream, used also for softening and cleansing the skin. **cold-cream** *verb trans.* apply cold cream to; take *off* by means of cold cream. **cold cuts** an assortment of cooked meats, sliced and served cold. ***cold dark matter***: see ***dark matter*** s.v. **DARK** *adjective*. **cold deck** *US slang* a pack of cards in which the cards have been arranged beforehand. **cold-deck** *verb trans.* (*US slang*) cheat (a person) by using a cold deck. **cold-drawn** *adjective* (of metal) drawn out into a wire or bar while cold. **cold feet** *colloq.*: a sign of fear or cowardice; esp. in ***get cold feet***, ***have cold feet***, refuse to proceed through fear or cowardice. **cold-finch** (*obsolete* exc. *dial.*) the pied flycatcher, *Ficedula hypoleuca*. **cold frame** *HORTICULTURE*: in which small plants are grown without artificial heat. ***cold front***: see **FRONT** *noun* 11b. **cold fusion** nuclear fusion supposedly brought about at a much lower temperature than is usually required, esp. a temperature near room temperature. ***cold harbour***: see **HARBOUR** *noun*[1]. **cold-hearted** *adjective* lacking in sensibility or natural affection; unkind. ***cold lead***: see **LEAD** *noun*[1]. **cold light** light accompanied by little or no heat, e.g. luminescence. **cold meat** (**a**) meat cooled after cooking; (**b**) *slang* a corpse, corpses. **cold-moulded** *adjective* (of an object) moulded from a resin that hardens without being heated. ***cold OBSTRUCTION***. **cold-rolled** *adjective* (of metal) having been rolled into sheets while cold, resulting in a smooth hard finish. **cold shoulder** *fig.* intentionally unfriendly treatment; esp. in ***give a person the cold shoulder***. **cold-shoulder** *verb trans.* treat with intentional coldness or contemptuous neglect. **cold shower**: in cold water. ***cold-slaw***: see **COLESLAW**. ***cold snap***: see **SNAP** *noun* 10. **cold start**, **cold starting**: of an internal-combustion engine at ambient temperature. ***cold steel***: see **STEEL** *noun*[1]. **cold storage** storage in a refrigerator; *fig.* a state of abeyance. ***cold sweat***: see **SWEAT** *noun*. **cold table** (a table bearing) dishes of cold food. **cold tap**: dispensing cold water. **cold turkey** *slang* (**a**) *US* blunt statements; (**b**) abrupt withdrawal of drugs from an addict; the symptoms of this. **cold war** hostilities short of armed conflict, consisting in threats, violent propaganda, subversive political activities, etc.; *spec.* those formerly between the USSR and the western powers after the Second World War. **cold warrior** a participant in a cold war. **cold water** *fig.* discouragement, disparagement; esp. in ***pour cold water on***, ***throw cold water on***, discourage, disparage, (a scheme etc.). **cold-water** *adjective* (**a**) using or containing unheated water; (**b**) living in or characteristic of the seas of cool or polar regions; (**c**) *US* (of a house etc.) without central heating. **cold wave** *noun*[2] a kind of permanent hair wave produced by a cold process. **cold-weld** *verb trans.* join (a piece of metal) to another without the use of heat, by forcing them together so hard that the surface oxide films are disrupted and adhesion occurs. **cold work** the working of metal while it is cold. **cold-work** *verb trans.* shape (metal) while it is cold. ***ice-cold***: see **ICE** *noun*. ***stone-cold***: see **STONE** *noun*.
▸ **B** *adverb*. Without any mitigation; absolutely, entirely. *US slang*. **L19**.
■ **coldly** *adverb* **ME**. **coldness** *noun* **LME**.

C

cold /kəʊld/ *verb*.
[**ORIGIN** Old English (*a*)*caldian*, *ċealdian*, from the adjective.]
1 *verb intrans.* Become or be cold. Long *rare*. **OE**.
†**2** *verb trans.* Make cold; chill. **LME–L16**.
3 *verb trans.* Afflict with a cold or chill. Chiefly as ***colded*** *ppl adjective*. *dial.* **E19**.

cold-short /ˈkəʊldʃɔːt/ *adjective*. **E17**.
[**ORIGIN** Swedish *kallskör* (= Norwegian, Danish *koldskjør*), neut. *kallskört* (sc. *jern* iron), from *kallr* cold + *skör* brittle, later assoc. with **SHORT** *adjective* 'brittle'.]
Of metal: brittle in its cold state.

coldslaw *noun* var. of **COLESLAW**.

cole /kəʊl/ *noun*[1]. Now *rare* exc. in comb. Also †**caul**.
[**ORIGIN** Old English *cāwel*, *caul* = Middle Dutch *cōle* (Dutch *kool*), Old High German *chōl(i)*, *chōlo*, *-a* (German *Kohl*), from Latin *caulis* (later *caulus*, *-a*) stem, stalk, cabbage; reinforced by forms from cogn. Old Norse *kál* (cf. **KALE**).]
1 Cabbage, brassica. **OE**.
2 Soup; broth; stew. Long *obsolete* exc. *dial.* **LME**.
– **COMB.**: **colewort** cabbage, brassica, *esp.* a kind that does not heart. Cf. also **COLESEED**, **COLESLAW**.

cole /kəʊl/ *noun*[2]. *slang*. **L17**.
[**ORIGIN** Perh. from **COAL** *noun*.]
Money.

-cole /kəʊl/ *suffix*.
[**ORIGIN** formed as **-COLOUS**.]
Forming (**a**) nouns with the sense 'an organism that lives or grows in or on a specified kind of habitat or material', as ***limnicole***, and (**b**) adjectives with the sense of **-COLOUS**, as ***muscicole***.

colectomy /kəʊˈlɛktəmi/ *noun*. **L19**.
[**ORIGIN** from **COLON** *noun*[1] + **-ECTOMY**.]
Surgical removal of all or part of the colon; an instance of this.

colemanite /ˈkəʊlmənʌɪt/ *noun*. **L19**.
[**ORIGIN** from William T. *Coleman* (1824–93), US mine-owner + **-ITE**[1].]
MINERALOGY. A monoclinic hydrated borate of calcium usu. occurring as white glassy prisms.

colemouse *noun* var. of **COALMOUSE**.

Coleoptera /kɒlɪˈɒpt(ə)rə/ *noun pl.* Rarely in sing. **-ron** /-rən/. **M18**.
[**ORIGIN** mod. Latin, from Greek *koleopteros* sheath-winged, from *koleos* sheath + *pteron* wing: see **-A**[3].]
(Members of) a large order of insects having the front wings modified as hard wing cases, and comprising the beetles (including weevils).
■ **coleopteran** *noun & adjective* (a member) of the order Coleoptera **M19**. **coleopterist** *noun* a person who studies beetles **M19**. **coleopteroid** *adjective* resembling or akin to a member of the order Coleoptera **L19**. **coleopterous** *adjective* belonging or pertaining to the order Coleoptera **L18**.

coleoptile /kɒlɪˈɒptʌɪl/ *noun*. **M19**.
[**ORIGIN** from Greek *koleos* sheath + *ptilon* feather.]
BOTANY. A hollow organ enclosing the first leaf of a germinating cereal grain.

coleorhiza /ˌkɒlɪə(ʊ)ˈrʌɪzə/ *noun*. **M19**.
[**ORIGIN** formed as **COLEOPTILE** + Greek *rhiza* root.]
BOTANY. The root sheath of a germinating cereal grain.

colerake /ˈkəʊlreɪk/ *noun*. Now *rare* or *obsolete*. Also **colrake**. **LME**.
[**ORIGIN** Perh. from **COAL** *noun* (in sense 'cinder') + **RAKE** *noun*[1].]
An instrument for raking ashes out of an oven or furnace; a similar instrument for other purposes.

Coleridgian /kəʊlˈrɪdʒɪən/ *adjective & noun*. Also **-ean**. **E19**.
[**ORIGIN** from *Coleridge* (see below) + **-IAN**.]
▸ **A** *adjective*. Of, pertaining to, or characteristic of the English poet and philosopher Samuel Taylor Coleridge (1772–1834) or his writings, opinions, etc. **E19**.
▸ **B** *noun*. An admirer or student of Coleridge or his writing. **E19**.

coleseed /ˈkəʊlsiːd/ *noun*. **OE**.
[**ORIGIN** from **COLE** *noun*[1] + **SEED** *noun*. In sense 2 prob. partly from Dutch *koolzaad*: see **COLZA**.]
†**1** Cabbage seed. Only in **OE**.
2 Rapeseed; rape; = **COLZA**. **LME**.

coleslaw /ˈkəʊlslɔː/ *noun*. Orig. *US*. Also **cold-** /kəʊld-/. L18.
[ORIGIN Dutch *koolsla*, from *kool* COLE *noun*[1] + *sla* SLAW.]
A salad of sliced raw cabbage, now usu. with mayonnaise etc.

†**colet** *noun*. LME–M18.
[ORIGIN Abbreviation.]
= ACOLYTE.

coleta /kəˈleɪtə/ *noun*. E20.
[ORIGIN Spanish, dim. of *cola* tail, from Latin *coda*, *cauda* tail.]
A pigtail, worn by a bullfighter as a mark of his profession.

cole tit *noun* var. of COAL TIT.

coleus /ˈkəʊlɪəs/ *noun*. M19.
[ORIGIN mod. Latin from Greek *koleos* sheath: from the form of its united filaments.]
A plant of the genus *Solenostemon*, of the mint family, usu. with variegated coloured leaves.

coley /ˈkəʊli/ *noun*. M20.
[ORIGIN Prob. from *coalfish* s.v. COAL *noun* + -Y[1].]
= SAITHE.

coli /ˈkəʊlʌɪ/ *noun*. Pl. same. L19.
[ORIGIN mod. Latin (*Bacillus* or *Escherichia*) *coli* (species name), from Latin genit. of COLON *noun*[1].]
A bacterium, *Escherichia coli*, which inhabits the large intestine of humans and animals. Freq. in *comb.*
■ **coliform** *adjective* belonging to a group of rod-shaped bacteria typified by *Escherichia coli* E20. **coliphage** *noun* a bacteriophage that attacks *E. coli* M20.

colibri /ˈkɒlɪbri/ *noun*. L17.
[ORIGIN French, Spanish from Carib.]
A large violet-eared hummingbird of the genus *Colibri*.

colic /ˈkɒlɪk/ *noun & adjective*. LME.
[ORIGIN Old French & mod. French *colique* from late Latin *colicus* adjective from COLON *noun*[1]: see -IC.]
▶ **A** *noun*. An acute episodic abdominal pain, now *esp.* one arising from the twisting, obstruction, or spasm of a hollow organ. LME.
painter's colic: see PAINTER *noun*[1]. ***RENAL colic***.
– COMB.: **colic root** *N. Amer.* any of certain medicinal plants, *esp.* star-grass, *Aletris farinosa*.
▶ **B** *adjective*. **1** (Now taken to be the noun used *attrib.*) Affecting the colon; of the nature of colic. LME.
2 Pertaining to the colon. E17.
■ †**colical** *adjective* = COLIC *adjective* E17–M18. **colicky** *adjective* pertaining to or of the nature of colic; subject to or producing colic: M18.

colicin /ˈkɒlɪsɪn/ *noun*. Also **-ine** /-iːn/. M20.
[ORIGIN French *colicine*, from COLI + -*c*-: see -IN[1], -INE[5].]
BACTERIOLOGY. A bacteriocin produced by a coliform bacterium.

colin /ˈkɒlɪn/ *noun*. L17.
[ORIGIN Erron. form of Nahuatl *çolin*.]
= BOBWHITE.

coliseum /kɒlɪˈsiːəm/ *noun*. Also (now usual in sense 1) **colosseum**; (earlier) †**-ee**, †**-eo**. E16.
[ORIGIN medieval Latin *coliseum* use as noun of Latin *colosseus* colossal, formed as COLOSSUS. Earliest forms from French *colisée*, Italian *coliseo*, from medieval Latin.]
1 ***the Colosseum***, the amphitheatre of Vespasian at Rome. E16.
†**2** Any ancient Roman amphitheatre. *rare*. L16–L18.
3 (A name given to) a large theatre or *esp.* (*N. Amer.*) a large stadium etc. L19.

colitis /kəˈlʌɪtɪs/ *noun*. M19.
[ORIGIN from COLON *noun*[1] + -ITIS.]
MEDICINE. Inflammation of the colon.

colk /kɒlk/ *noun*. *obsolete* exc. *dial.* LME.
[ORIGIN Unknown: cf. COKE *noun*[1].]
The core of an apple, of a horn, a heart of wood, etc.

coll /kɒl/ *verb*[1] *trans*. Long *obsolete* exc. *dial.* Also **cull** /kʌl/. ME.
[ORIGIN French *coler* = *accoler* ACCOLL or aphet. from ACCOLL.]
Embrace, hug.

coll /kɒl/ *verb*[2] *trans*. *obsolete* exc. *Scot.* L15.
[ORIGIN Perh. of Scandinavian origin: cf. Old Norse *kollr* head, poll, shaven crown, *kolla* beast without horns, Norwegian *kylla* poll, prune, cut. Cf. COW *verb*[1].]
Cut off the hair of, clip, cut close.

collaborate /kəˈlabəreɪt/ *verb intrans*. L19.
[ORIGIN Late Latin *collaborat-* pa. ppl stem of *collaborare*, formed as COL- + *laborare* LABOUR *verb*: see -ATE[3].]
1 Work jointly (*with*), esp. on a literary or scientific project. L19.
2 *spec.* Cooperate traitorously with (or *with*) an enemy. M20.
■ ***collaborateur*** /kɔlabɔratœːr (*pl. same*)/ *noun* = COLLABORATOR E19. **collaboˈration** *noun* M19. **collaboˈrationist** *noun & adjective* (a person) advocating or practising collaboration E20. **collaborative** *adjective* E20. **collaboratively** *adverb* L20. **collaborator** *noun* a person who collaborates E19.

collage /kɒˈlɑːʒ/ *noun*. E20.
[ORIGIN French = gluing.]
An abstract form of art in which photographs, pieces of paper, string, matchsticks, etc., are placed in juxtaposition and glued to a surface; a work in this form; *fig.* a jumbled collection of impressions, events, styles, etc.
■ **collagist** *noun* a person who makes collages M20.

collagen /ˈkɒlədʒ(ə)n/ *noun*. M19.
[ORIGIN French *collagène* from Greek *kolla* glue: see -GEN.]
Any of a group of insoluble fibrous proteins that are the chief constituent of connective tissue and yield gelatin on boiling.
■ **coˈllagenous** *adjective* of the nature of or containing collagen M19.

collapsar /kəˈlapsɑː/ *noun*. L20.
[ORIGIN from COLLAPSE *verb* after *pulsar*, *quasar*.]
ASTRONOMY. A black hole formed by gravitational collapse of a star.

collapse /kəˈlaps/ *noun*. E19.
[ORIGIN Medical Latin *collapsus* use as noun of pa. pple: see COLLAPSED.]
(An action or instance of) collapsing; a collapsed condition.

> A. J. CRONIN The operation might induce an immediate collapse. A. MARS-JONES The marshal . . waits in collapse on a chair. P. ACKROYD The entire collapse of his career.

collapse of a stout party: see STOUT *adjective*.

collapse /kəˈlaps/ *verb*. M18.
[ORIGIN Back-form. from COLLAPSED.]
1 *verb intrans.* Undergo or experience a falling in (as with the puncture of an inflated hollow body); shrink suddenly together; break down, give way, cave in. M18.

> E. WAUGH The camp bed . . collapsed repeatedly. I. F. ELIS The side collapsed and half filled the pit with earth.

2 *verb intrans. transf. & fig.* Come to nothing, fail; experience prostration through loss of muscular or nervous power; experience a breakdown of mental energy. E19.

> B. CHATWIN When she could work no more, she would collapse into the rocking chair. A. MOOREHEAD The little township . . has collapsed through want of trade. A. MASON The landowner collapsed where he stood, and . . was found to be dead.

3 *verb trans.* Cause to collapse. L19.
■ **collapsiˈbility** *noun* the quality of being collapsible L19. **collapsible** *adjective* able to be collapsed M19. †**collapsion** *noun* = COLLAPSE *noun* E17–E19.

collapsed /kəˈlapst/ *adjective*. E17.
[ORIGIN from Latin *collapsus* pa. pple of *collabi*, formed as COL- + *labi* fall (see LAPSE *noun*) + -ED[1].]
1 Fallen in, shrunk together, broken down. E17.
2 Ruined, fallen into decay; failed. E17.
†**3** Lapsed in religion etc.; in a state of sin, fallen. E–M17.
4 Prostrated; completely broken down in mental energy. M17.

collar /ˈkɒlə/ *noun*. ME.
[ORIGIN Anglo-Norman *coler*, Old French *colier* (mod. *collier*) from Latin *collare*, from *collum* neck: see -AR[1].]
1 The upright or turned-over neckband of a coat, dress, shirt, etc.; a band of linen, lace, etc., completing the upper part of a costume. Also, an ornamental chain or band worn around the neck as a badge of office etc., now *spec.* one forming part of the insignia of an order of knighthood. ME.
Eton collar, ***mandarin collar***, ***Medici collar***, ***Prussian collar***, ***Shakespeare collar***, ***toby collar***, etc.
†**2** A piece of armour for protecting the neck. ME–L16.
3 A roll around a draught animal's neck forming part of the harness through which the power of drawing is directly exerted. See also ***breast collar*** s.v. BREAST *noun*. ME.
horse collar: see HORSE *noun*.
4 A band put around the neck of an animal (esp. a dog) to control, identify, or ornament it. LME.
dog collar: see DOG *noun*.
5 A metal band fixed round the neck of prisoners, slaves, servants, etc. *obsolete* exc. *hist.* LME.
6 NAUTICAL. (Orig.) the lower end of the principal stays of a mast; (later) the rope, with a deadeye in its end, to which the stay is secured. Also, the eye in the upper end of a stay or the bight of the shrouds, which is threaded over the masthead before being set taut to hold the mast secure. LME.
7 **a** Orig., a boar's or pig's neck cut as a piece of meat. Now, the part of a flitch of bacon nearest the neck. L15. ▸**b** A piece of meat (esp. from a pig's neck) or a fish rolled up and usu. tied. M17.
8 An encompassing or restraining strap or band; a ring, circle, flange, etc. in a machine. E16.
9 A wrestling move in which the opponent is tackled by the neck. L16.
10 A marking or structure resembling a collar; *esp.* a coloured stripe around an animal's or bird's neck. M17.
11 An arrest, legal apprehension. *slang*. M19.
– PHRASES: ***clerical collar***: see CLERICAL *adjective* 1. **collar of esses**, **collar of SS** a chain consisting of a series of S's: the former badge of the House of Lancaster, still used in the costumes of some officials. **feel a person's collar** *slang* arrest or legally apprehend a person; freq. in pass. ***have one's collar felt***. ***hot under the collar***: see HOT *adjective*. **put the collar on** *slang* arrest, legally apprehend.
– COMB.: **collar beam** a horizontal beam connecting two rafters and forming with them an A-shaped roof truss; **collarbone** the curved bone joining the shoulder blade to the breastbone; the clavicle; **collar day** *hist.*: on which knights wore the collar of their order, when taking part in any court ceremony; **collar stud**: to fasten a detachable collar to a shirt; **collar-work** work in which a draught animal has to strain hard against the collar; *fig.* severe and close work.
■ **collarless** *adjective* E17.

collar /ˈkɒlə/ *verb*. M16.
[ORIGIN from the noun.]
1 *verb trans.* Put a collar on; fasten or surround as with a collar. M16. ▸**b** *spec.* Put a collar on (a horse), esp. for the first time; break (a horse) in. L17.
2 *verb intrans.* Lay hold of the opponent's neck or collar in wrestling. Now *rare* or *obsolete*. M16.
3 *verb trans.* Seize or take hold of by the collar; capture, arrest; stop and detain; RUGBY lay hold of and stop (an opponent holding the ball); *slang* grab, take, appropriate, esp. illicitly. E17.

> F. MARRYAT He was collared by two French soldiers, and dragged back into the battery. V. WOOLF He would collar Miss Whatshername and ask for a synopsis. JO GRIMOND The Stewart Earls and their grasping followers . . collared much of the land.

4 *verb trans.* Roll up (a cut of meat, a fish, etc.) and tie with string. L17.

collard /ˈkɒləd/ *noun*. *N. Amer. & dial.* M18.
[ORIGIN Reduced form of *colewort* s.v. COLE *noun*[1].]
A variety of cabbage which does not develop a heart, used for greens (also ***collard greens***).

collared /ˈkɒləd/ *adjective*. LME.
[ORIGIN from COLLAR *noun*, *verb*: see -ED[2], -ED[1].]
1 Wearing a collar. LME.
2 That has been collared. M17.
3 Of an animal or bird: having a bandlike marking, esp. round the neck. E19.
collared dove a grey-brown dove, *Streptopelia decaocto*, that began to colonize Britain from Europe in the 1950s and is now common. ***collared lemming***: see LEMMING 1. ***collared PECCARY***.

collarette /kɒləˈrɛt/ *noun*. L17.
[ORIGIN French *collerette* dim. of *collier* COLLAR *noun*: see -ETTE.]
1 A woman's ornamental collar of lace, fur, etc. L17.
2 A dahlia with shortened petals immediately surrounding the centre, and flat outer petals. E20.

collate /kɒˈleɪt/ *verb*. M16.
[ORIGIN Latin *collat-* pa. ppl stem of *conferre*: see CONFER *verb*, -ATE[3].]
1 ECCLESIASTICAL. †**a** *verb trans.* Confer (a benefice) *on* a person. M16–L17. ▸**b** *verb trans.* Esp. of an Ordinary: appoint (a cleric) *to* a benefice. E17. ▸**c** *verb intrans.* Make an appointment to a benefice; make appointments to benefices. E17.
†**2** *verb trans. gen.* Confer or bestow (*up*)*on*; grant *to*. L16–E18.
3 *verb trans.* Bring together for comparison; compare carefully and exactly (esp. copies of a text or document, one such copy *with* another); put together (esp. information, or sheets to form two or more copies of a document). E17.
4 *verb trans.* Examine and check the order etc. of (the sheets of a printed book, a book) by signatures; check the printed appearance and order of. L18.
■ **collatable** *adjective* M19.

collateral /kɒˈlat(ə)r(ə)l/ *adjective & noun*. LME.
[ORIGIN medieval Latin *collateralis*: see COL-, LATERAL.]
▶ **A** *adjective*. **1** Situated or placed side by side; parallel. LME.
2 *fig.* Accompanying, attendant, concomitant. LME. ▸†**b** Of equal rank. LME–M17. ▸**c** Parallel in time, order, development, etc.; corresponding. E16.
3 Lying aside from the main subject, issue, purpose, etc.; subordinate. LME.
4 Descended from the same ancestors but by a different line (opp. ***lineal***). LME.
– SPECIAL COLLOCATIONS: **collateral bundle** BOTANY a vascular bundle in which the xylem and phloem lie side by side. **collateral circulation** ANATOMY an alternative route for blood when primary vessels are blocked; the channel. **collateral contract** a subsidiary contract which induces a person to enter into a main contract. **collateral damage** destruction or injury beyond that intended or expected, esp. in the vicinity of a military target. **collateral issue** LAW a question not directly at issue. **collateral security** property pledged as a guarantee for the repayment of money.
▶ **B** *noun*. †**1** An associate in some office, function, etc. L16–E18.
†**2** An equal (in rank). E–M17.
3 A collateral kinsman or kinswoman. L17.
4 Property pledged as a guarantee for the repayment of money; collateral security. M19.

> *Boston Globe* Loans in which the equity in a person's house is used as collateral.

5 ANATOMY. A branch of a nerve fibre at right angles to the main part. L19.
■ **collateˈrality** *noun* E17. **collaterally** *adverb* LME.

collation /kɒˈleɪʃ(ə)n/ *noun*. ME.
[ORIGIN Old French *collacion*, -*tion* from Latin *collatio(n-)* collection, comparison, (in medieval Latin) conference, repast, formed as COLLATE *verb*: see -ATION.]
▶ **I** Conference.
1 **a** In *pl.*, John Cassian's *Collationes Patrum in Scetica Eremo Commorantium*, Conferences of (and with) the Egyptian Hermits (AD 415–20); *sing.* a section of this work. ME. ▸**b** A

reading in a Benedictine monastery from this work, later also from any other edifying text, before the light meal taken at the end of the day; this meal; *transf.* (in mod. Roman Catholic usage) a light meal in the evening of a fast day. ME.

†**2** A (private or informal) conference; a discourse, a homily, a treatise. LME–M17.

3 A light meal, esp. at an unusual time. Now chiefly in ***cold collation***. E16.

▸ **II** Bringing together.

4 a A collection, esp. of money; a contribution. *obsolete* exc. *Scot.* ME. ▸**b** *ROMAN & SCOTS LAW.* A bringing together of the whole estate and funds on which the children of a deceased parent have a claim in succession, including any funds etc. advanced previously to any of the children, for its subsequent equal division among them. E19.

5 The act of collating; comparison; *esp.* the textual or critical comparison of various documents, editions, etc. LME. ▸**b** The recorded result of such textual etc. comparison; a set of corrections compiled after such comparison. L17.

6 The action of collating the sheets etc. of a document or printed book. M18.

▸ **III 7** Conferring or bestowal (esp. of a dignity, honour, etc.). Now only *ECCLESIASTICAL*, the bestowal *of* a benefice on a member of the clergy; the appointment (by the Ordinary) of a member of the clergy *to* a benefice. LME. ▸**b** The right of institution to a benefice. Now *rare*. L15.

■ **coˈllational** *adjective* of or pertaining to collation M20.

†**collation** *verb*. M16.

[ORIGIN from the noun.]

1 *verb trans.* = COLLATE 3, 4. M16–E18.

2 *verb trans. & intrans.* Entertain with or have lunch. E17–M18.

■ †**collationer** *noun* a collator; a person who lunches or has a collation: L17–L18.

collative /kɒˈleɪtɪv/ *adjective*. E17.

[ORIGIN In sense 1 from Latin *collativus*, formed as COLLATE + -IVE; in senses 2, 3 from COLLATE + -IVE, perh. through French *collatif*.]

†**1** Of a conferred or bestowed kind. Only in E17.

†**2** Of the nature of or formed by contribution. M17–E19.

3 That confers or can confer. (Foll. by *of*.) M17.

4 *ECCLESIASTICAL.* Where the Ordinary collates. E18.

collator /kɒˈleɪtə/ *noun*. LME.

[ORIGIN Latin *collator*, formed as COLLATE: see -OR. In senses 2, 3 = medieval Latin *collator*, French *collateur*.]

†**1** A collector. *rare*. Only in LME.

2 A person who collates a text, edition, etc.; a person who collates the sheets of a printed book etc. E17.

3 *ECCLESIASTICAL.* A person who collates to a benefice. E17.

4 A person who bestows. M17.

5 A machine for combining sets of punched cards, or sheets to form copies of a document. M20.

collaudation /kɒlɔːˈdeɪʃ(ə)n/ *noun*. *arch.* E17.

[ORIGIN Latin *collaudatio(n-)*, from *collaudare*, formed as COL- + *laudare* to praise: see -ATION.]

Warm praise, high commendation; an instance of this.

colleague /ˈkɒliːɡ/ *noun*. E16.

[ORIGIN French *collègue* from Latin *collega* partner in office, formed as COL- + *leg-* stem of *lex* law, *legare* depute.]

A fellow official or worker, esp. in a profession or business.

■ **colleagueship** *noun* the position or relation of a colleague M17.

colleague /kəˈliːɡ/ *verb*. *obsolete* exc. *Scot.* M16.

[ORIGIN Old French *colliguer*, later *collèguer* from Latin *colligare* bind together, formed as COL- + *ligare* bind.]

†**1** *verb trans.* Join in alliance, associate. M16–M18.

2 *verb intrans.* Unite, cooperate; conspire. (Foll. by *with*, *together*.) M16.

collect /ˈkɒlɛkt, -lɪkt/ *noun*. ME.

[ORIGIN Old French & mod. French *collecte* from Latin *collecta* gathering, collection, (in late Latin) assembly, meeting, use as noun of fem. pa. pple of *colligere*: see COLLECT *verb*.]

1 A short prayer said by the minister in Anglican and Roman Catholic liturgies, *esp.* one before the first reading in the Eucharist and varying according to the day or season. ME.

†**2** The action or an act of collecting (esp. money). LME–M16.

†**3** A meeting, esp. for worship. LME–E18.

†**4** A group of things collected or occurring together. LME–L19.

collect /kəˈlɛkt/ *pa. pple & ppl adjective*. Long *arch.* LME.

[ORIGIN Latin *collectus* pa. pple of *colligere*: see COLLECT *verb*.]

Collected.

collect /kəˈlɛkt/ *verb*. LME.

[ORIGIN Old French & mod. French *collecter* or medieval Latin *collectare*, from Latin *collect-* pa. ppl stem of *colligere*, formed as COL- + *legere* collect, assemble, choose, read.]

▸ **I 1** *verb trans.* Assemble into one place or group. LME. ▸**b** *verb trans.* Obtain or seek out (specimens, stamps, books, etc.) to add to others, esp. as a hobby. M18. ▸**c** *verb intrans.* Maintain and add to a collection of similar things, esp. as a hobby. L19.

J. RUSKIN Collecting materials for my work on Venetian architecture.

collect eyes intentionally attract several people's attention.

2 a *verb trans.* Get or receive (money, contributions, etc.) from a number of people. M17. ▸**b** *verb intrans.* Receive donations or (*colloq.*) a payment. M19.

b J. JOHNSTON Those collecting for some charity.

3 *verb trans.* Get from a place of deposit; call for. *colloq.* L19.

4 *verb trans.* Attract (a group of people) to oneself, serve as a focus for. M20.

▸ **II 5** *verb trans.* Deduce, infer, gather. Foll. by simple obj. subord. clause, obj. and inf. LME.

G. HEYER I collect, from something Stavely said to me, that already she doesn't like it.

6 *verb trans.* Regain control over (one's thoughts or feelings, oneself); summon up (courage). E17.

7 *verb intrans.* Come together, gather, assemble; accumulate. L18.

LD MACAULAY A force was collecting at Bridport.

8 *verb trans.* Cause (a horse) to bring its legs compactly under itself and be better able to respond to the rider. M19.

collect /kəˈlɛkt/ *adverb & adjective*. Orig. *US*. E20.

[ORIGIN Imper. of COLLECT *verb*.]

▸ **A** *adverb*. On the condition that the recipient (of a parcel, telephone call, etc.) pays, in some cases at the time of delivery. E20.

M. DE LA ROCHE She arranged for coal to be sent collect.

▸ **B** *adjective*. Sent in this way. E20.

collectable /kəˈlɛktəb(ə)l/ *adjective & noun*. Also **-ible**. M17.

[ORIGIN from COLLECT *verb* + -ABLE, -IBLE.]

▸ **A** *adjective*. **1** Able to be collected. M17.

2 Worth collecting; of interest to a collector. L19.

▸ **B** *noun*. A book etc. worth collecting. Usu. in *pl.* M20.

collectanea /kɒlɛkˈtɑːnɪə, -ˈteɪn-/ *noun*. M17.

[ORIGIN Latin *collectanea* neut. pl., from *collect-* (see COLLECT *verb*), as used as adjective in *Dicta collectanea* of Caesar, and as noun in *Collectanea* of Solinus.]

As *pl.*, passages, remarks, etc., collected from various sources. As *sing.*, a miscellany.

collectar /ˈkɒlɛktɑː/ *noun*. Also **-are**. ME.

[ORIGIN medieval Latin *collectarium*, from *collecta* COLLECT *noun*: see -ARIUM.]

CHRISTIAN CHURCH. A book of collects.

■ Also **collectarium** /kɒlɛkˈtɑːrɪəm, -ˈtɛːr-/ *noun*, pl. **-ia** /-ɪə/, **-iums** M19.

collected /kəˈlɛktɪd/ *ppl adjective*. E17.

[ORIGIN from COLLECT *verb* + -ED[1].]

1 In command of one's thoughts or feelings; self-possessed. E17.

2 Gathered together; *spec.* (of a horse) with its legs brought compactly under itself. L17.

■ **collectedly** *adverb* L17. **collectedness** *noun* M17.

collectible *adjective & noun* see COLLECTABLE.

collection /kəˈlɛkʃ(ə)n/ *noun*. LME.

[ORIGIN Old French & mod. French from Latin *collectio(n-)*, from *collect-*: see COLLECT *verb*, -ION.]

1 The action or an act of collecting or gathering together. LME. ▸**b** The action or an act of collecting taxes, or money for a definite purpose (e.g. in church or at a meeting); money so collected. L15.

L. MACNEICE A red letter-box fastened to a telegraph pole—four collections a week. A. THWAITE Parcelling up the garbage for Collection. **b** D. H. LAWRENCE The collection arrived with the last hymn.

†**2** A summary, an abstract. LME–E18.

3 A group of things collected or gathered together, e.g. literary items, specimens, works of art, or fashionable clothes. LME. ▸**b** An accumulation of material. L17.

R. G. COLLINGWOOD A new collection of all the Roman inscriptions . . in Britain. P. ROTH We have an excellent classical record collection.

4 The district under the jurisdiction of a collector of taxes or customs. L15.

†**5** The action of inferring; an inference. E16–E18.

6 In *pl.* A college examination held at the beginning or end of each term at Oxford (hence occas. elsewhere). L18.

collective /kəˈlɛktɪv/ *adjective & noun*. LME.

[ORIGIN Old French & mod. French *collectif*, -*ive* or Latin *collectivus*, from *collect-*: see COLLECT *verb*, -IVE.]

▸ **A** *adjective*. **1** Denoting or representing a number of individuals or items. LME.

J. LOCKE The great collective idea of all bodies whatsoever, signified by the name *world*.

collective noun: denoting, in the singular, more than one individual, e.g. *committee*, *flock*.

2 Formed by collection; constituting a collection; taken as a whole, aggregate. L16.

W. TAYLOR A collective edition of his works.

collective fruit *BOTANY* a fruit formed by the aggregation of carpels from several flowers, as in the mulberry.

†**3** That deduces or infers. *rare*. Only in M17.

4 Pertaining to or derived from a number of individuals taken or acting together. M17.

W. LIPPMANN The socialist contention that the collective ownership of the means of production will produce . . men who are purged of acquisitiveness and aggression.

collective bargaining negotiation of wages etc. by an organized body of employees. **collective farm**: consisting of the holdings of several farmers run as a joint enterprise, esp. in the former USSR. **collective ownership** State ownership (of land, the means of production) for the benefit of all. **collective security** *POLITICS* the policy or principle of the alliance of several countries to strengthen the security of each. **collective unconscious** *JUNGIAN PSYCHOLOGY* the part of the unconscious that derives from ancient ancestral experience and is common to all.

▸ **B** *noun*. **1** A collective noun. E17.

2 A collective body, whole, or organization; *esp.* a collective farm. M17.

■ **collectively** *adverb* in a collective manner; in a body, jointly: L16. **collectiveness** *noun* M17.

collectivise *verb* var. of COLLECTIVIZE.

collectivism /kəˈlɛktɪvɪz(ə)m/ *noun*. M19.

[ORIGIN from COLLECTIVE + -ISM, after French *collectivisme*.]

Collective ownership of land and the means of production, as a political principle; the practice or principle of giving the group priority over the individual.

■ **collectivist** *noun & adjective* (**a**) *noun* an advocate of collectivism; (**b**) *adjective* of or pertaining to collectivism or collectivists: L19. **collectiˈvistic** *adjective* L19.

collectivity /kɒlɛkˈtɪvɪti/ *noun*. M19.

[ORIGIN from COLLECTIVE + -ITY: in senses 2 and 3 after French *collectivité*.]

1 Collective quality. M19.

2 Collectivism. L19.

3 A group or community of people bound together by common beliefs or interests. L19.

S. NEILL He uses the term . . in the plural . . for the churches as a collectivity in which a common faith and a common order prevail.

4 An aggregate, a whole. L19.

J. Z. YOUNG The relation of the individual to the collectivity of men.

collectivize /kəˈlɛktɪvʌɪz/ *verb trans.* Also **-ise**. L19.

[ORIGIN from COLLECTIVE + -IZE.]

Establish or organize in accordance with principles of collectivism.

■ **coˌllectiviˈzation** *noun* the process or policy of collectivizing L19.

collector /kəˈlɛktə/ *noun*. LME.

[ORIGIN Anglo-Norman *collectour* from medieval Latin *collector*, from *collect-*: see COLLECT *verb*, -OR.]

1 A person who collects money; an official who receives money due, as taxes or rent. LME. ▸**b** *hist.* In India, the chief administrative official of a district, whose special duty was the collection of revenue. L18.

2 A person or thing which collects or gathers together; *spec.* a person who collects and keeps specimens, works of art, etc.; formerly also, a compiler. M16. ▸**b** A part of various electrical machines that receives or attracts current. L18. ▸**c** The part of a transistor into which charge carriers flow from the base. M20.

collector's item, **collector's piece** a thing of sufficient beauty, rarity, or interest to be placed in a collection. ***ticket-collector***: see TICKET *noun*.

■ **collectorate** *noun* the district in which a collector (sense 1) has jurisdiction L18. **collectorship** *noun* (**a**) the position or office of a collector; (**b**) an Indian collectorate: E16.

colleen /kɒˈliːn, ˈkɒliːn/ *noun*. *Irish.* E19.

[ORIGIN Irish *cailín* dim. of *caile* countrywoman, girl: see -EEN[2].]

A girl.

college /ˈkɒlɪdʒ/ *noun*. LME.

[ORIGIN Old French & mod. French *collège* or its source Latin *collegium* association, partnership, guild, corporation, from *collega* COLLEAGUE *noun*.]

1 An organized body of people performing certain common functions and sharing special privileges. LME.

College of Arms, (*colloq.*) **College of Heralds** a corporation recording armorial bearings and lineages. **College of Justice** all those who participate in the administration of justice in the Court of Session in Scotland (***Senator of the College of Justice***: see SENATOR 3). *ELECTORAL* ***college***. **Heralds' College** = ***College of Arms*** above. **Sacred College** the Pope's council of cardinals, which elects a new pope, usu. from amongst their number (***Dean of the Sacred College***: see DEAN *noun*[1] 6). ***College of Preceptors***, ***College of Surgeons***, etc.

†**2** An assemblage or company *of* individuals. LME–M18. ▸**b** [Repr. German *Collegium*.] A reunion, a meeting of companions. E18.

DRYDEN Thick as the college of the bees in May.

3 A community of clergy living together on a foundation for religious service etc. Now chiefly *hist.* LME.

College of the Propaganda: see PROPAGANDA *noun* 1.

4 a An independent self-governing corporation of teachers and scholars, *esp.* one within or associated with a university; an American or (formerly) Scottish university, *esp.* a small US university that offers a limited curriculum or teaches only to the first degree. LME. ▸**b** An institution for professional or vocational training or

C

study, e.g. in music, agriculture, or theology; a higher educational institution for those who have left school, other than a university (sometimes also other than a polytechnic), usu. having a bias towards technical or vocational subjects; a school for pupils over the school-leaving age. Also, the name of some modern public schools and smaller private ones. M19.

a *Eton College*, *Harvard College*, *New College*, etc. **college of education** an institution for training schoolteachers. *junior college*: see JUNIOR adjective. *senior college*: see SENIOR adjective. **b** *Cheltenham Ladies' College*, *Lancing College*, *sixth-form college*, *tertiary college*, etc. *military college*, *technical college*, etc.

C

5 a The building or set of buildings occupied by a college (sense 4). LME. **›b** Without article: some college, known or unknown; attendance at a college or university. M18.

b DISRAELI College had ruined me. *New Society* A young social worker, fresh out of college and with all the right letters after his name.

6 *hist.* A hospital, almshouse, or similar charitable foundation. L17.
7 A prison, a reformatory. *slang.* L17.
8 A course of lectures at a foreign university. E18.
– COMB.: **college living** a benefice in the gift of a college; **college pudding** a small plum pudding for one person.
■ **colleger** *noun* (*a*) a member of a college or (formerly) of the same college; *spec.* each of the 70 foundation scholars at Eton College; (*b*) *slang* a mortarboard: M16.

collegial /kəˈliːdʒɪəl, -dʒ(ə)l/ *adjective.* LME.
[ORIGIN Old French & mod. French *collégial* or late Latin *collegialis*, from *collegium*: see COLLEGE, -IAL.]
1 = COLLEGIATE *adjective* 1. LME.
collegial church a collegiate church.
2 Of or pertaining to a (university etc.) college. E17.
3 Pertaining to or involving a body of people associated as colleagues. E17.
■ **collegiˈality** *noun* the relationship of, or appropriate to, colleagues; *spec.* joint responsibility, esp. of Roman Catholic bishops in church government: L19. **collegially** *adverb* M17.

collegian /kəˈliːdʒɪən, -dʒ(ə)n/ *noun & adjective.* LME.
[ORIGIN medieval Latin *collegianus*, from *collegium*: see COLLEGE, -IAN.]
► **A** *noun.* **1** A past or present member of a college; a foundation scholar, a colleger. LME.
2 A prisoner. *slang.* E19.
► **B** *adjective.* = COLLEGIAL. *rare.* M17.
■ **collegianer** *noun* (*a*) (*obsolete* exc. *Scot.*) = COLLEGIAN *noun* 1; †(*b*) a colleague: M16.

collegiate /kəˈliːdʒ(ɪ)ət/ *adjective & noun.* LME.
[ORIGIN Late Latin *collegiatus* member of a college (in medieval Latin as adjective), from *collegium* COLLEGE: see -ATE[1], -ATE[2].]
► **A** *adjective.* **1** Of the nature of, constituted as, a college. LME.
2 Of or pertaining to colleagues; corporate, combined. LME.
3 Of, pertaining to, or characteristic of a college or college students. M16. **›b** *spec.* Designed for use by college students or others of similar educational standard. *US.* L19.

DEFOE A collegiate life did not suit me. J. KEROUAC He liked to dress sharp, slightly on the collegiate side.

4 Composed of colleges. M19.
– SPECIAL COLLOCATIONS: **collegiate church** (*a*) a church that is endowed for a chapter of canons or prebends but is not a cathedral; (*b*) *Scot. & US* a church in the joint charge of two ministers. **collegiate Gothic** *US* (in) a style of Gothic architecture associated with old colleges.
► **B** *noun.* **1** A member of a college. *obsolete* exc. *US.* E17. **›†b** An inmate of a prison or asylum. *slang.* L17–M18.
†**2** A colleague. Only in 17.
3 A collegiate dictionary. *US.* L19.
■ **collegiately** *adverb* E17.

collegiate /kəˈliːdʒɪeɪt/ *verb trans.* M16.
[ORIGIN from COLLEGIATE *adjective & noun*: see -ATE[3].]
Constitute as a college or a collegiate church.

collegium /kəˈliːdʒɪəm/ *noun.* Pl. **-ia** /-ɪə/. L19.
[ORIGIN Latin: see COLLEGE.]
1 In full ***collegium musicum*** /ˈmjuːzɪkəm/, pl. ***collegia musica*** /ˈmjuːzɪkə/. A society of amateurs for performing music, now *esp.* one attached to a German or US university. L19.
2 *hist.* [Repr. Russian *kollegiya*.] An advisory or administrative board in Russia. E20.

collembolan /kəˈlɛmbələn/ *noun & adjective.* L19.
[ORIGIN from mod. Latin *Collembola* (see below), from Greek *kolla* glue + *embolon* peg, stopper (with ref. to the insect's ventral tube, which can secrete an adhesive substance): see -AN.]
► **A** *noun.* A minute wingless insect of the order Collembola; a springtail. L19.
► **B** *adjective.* Of or pertaining to the order Collembola or collembolans. L19.

collenchyma /kəˈlɛŋkɪmə/ *noun.* M19.
[ORIGIN from Greek *kolla* glue + *egkhuma* infusion.]
BOTANY. Tissue strengthened by the thickening of cell walls, as in young shoots.
■ **collenˈchymatous** *adjective* L19.

Colleries /ˈkɒlərɪz/ *noun pl.* M18.
[ORIGIN Tamil *kallar* thieves.]
A Dravidian people of SE India.

Colles fracture /ˈkɒlɪs ˈfraktʃə/ *noun phr.* Also **Colles's fracture** /ˈkɒlɪsɪz/. L19.
[ORIGIN Abraham *Colles* (1773–1843), Irish surgeon.]
MEDICINE. Fracture of the lower end of the radius accompanied by backward displacement of the hand.

collet /ˈkɒlɪt/ *noun*[1] *& verb.* LME.
[ORIGIN Old French & mod. French, dim. of *col* from Latin *collum* neck: see -ET[1].]
► **A** *noun* †**1 a** A piece of armour for the neck. *Scot.* LME–E17. **›b** The neckband of a garment; a necklet. M16–M17.
2 A circular metal ring on a spindle or lining in a hole; ENGINEERING a slit sleeve with an external taper which tightens when pushed into an internally tapered socket in a lathe mandrel etc. E16.
3 A metal flange or setting for a precious stone. E16.
†**4** GLASS-MAKING. The portion of glass left on the end of a blowing iron after the removal of the finished article. See also CULLET. M17–L18.
► **B** *verb trans.* Set in or provide with a collet. E17.

collet *noun*[2] see CULET *noun*[2].

colleterial /kɒlɪˈtɪərɪəl/ *adjective.* L19.
[ORIGIN from Greek *kollan* to glue + *-ētēr* agent-suff. + -IAL.]
ENTOMOLOGY. Of a gland: secreting the materials which form the ootheca.

†**colley** *noun* var. of COLLIE.

colliculus /kəˈlɪkjʊləs/ *noun.* Pl. **-li** /-lʌɪ, -liː/. M19.
[ORIGIN Latin, dim. of *collis* hill: see -CULE.]
ANATOMY. A small protuberance; *spec.* any of those of the roof of the midbrain, of which there are two pairs involved respectively in vision and hearing.
■ **collicular** *adjective* L19.

collide /kəˈlʌɪd/ *verb.* E17.
[ORIGIN Latin *collidere* clash together, formed as COL- + *laedere* hurt by striking.]
1 *verb trans.* Bring into violent contact, strike together. Now *rare* or *obsolete* exc. *techn.* E17.
2 *verb intrans.* Come into collision (*with*); strike or dash together. E18. **›b** *fig.* Be in conflict, clash, conflict. M19.
■ **collider** *noun* (PHYSICS) a particle accelerator in which two beams are made to collide L20.

collidine /ˈkɒlɪdiːn/ *noun.* M19.
[ORIGIN from Greek *kolla* glue + -IDINE.]
CHEMISTRY. Any of a number of isomeric trimethyl and methylethyl derivatives of pyridine, found in coal tar.

collie /ˈkɒli/ *noun.* Also **-y**, †**-ey**. M17.
[ORIGIN Perh. from COAL (from its colour) + -IE, -Y[6]: cf. COLLY *adjective & noun*[2].]
A sheepdog of an orig. Scottish breed with a long pointed nose and usu. long hair. Also ***collie-dog***.
bearded collie: see BEARDED 1. ***border collie***: see BORDER *noun*. ***rough collie***: see ROUGH *adjective*.

collier /ˈkɒlɪə/ *noun.* ME.
[ORIGIN from COAL + -IER.]
1 A maker of wood charcoal. *obsolete* exc. *US.* ME.
†**2** A person who carries coal or charcoal for sale. L15–E19.
3 A person who works in a coalmine; a coalminer. M16.
4 A ship carrying coal; a member of the crew of such a ship. E17.
5 In full ***collier aphid***, ***collier fly***, etc. A black aphid, *Aphis fabae*. *obsolete* exc. *US.* M18.
6 The swift. *dial.* L18.

colliery /ˈkɒlɪəri/ *noun.* M17.
[ORIGIN from COLLIER + -Y[3].]
1 A place where coal is worked; a coalmine and its buildings. M17.
†**2** Ships employed in the coal trade; one such vessel. E–M18.

collieshangie /kɒlɪˈʃaŋi/ *noun. Scot.* M18.
[ORIGIN Unknown.]
A noisy quarrel; a confused fight.

colligable /ˈkɒlɪgəb(ə)l/ *adjective.* M20.
[ORIGIN from COLLIGATE *verb* + -ABLE.]
LINGUISTICS. Capable of forming part of a colligation.
■ **colligaˈbility** *noun* M20.

†**colligance** *noun.* LME–E18.
[ORIGIN Old French, or medieval Latin *colligantia* from Latin *colligare*: see COLLEAGUE *verb*, -ANCE.]
Attachment together; connection.

colligate /ˈkɒlɪgət/ *adjective.* Long *rare.* L15.
[ORIGIN Latin *colligatus* pa. pple, formed as COLLIGATE *verb*: see -ATE[2].]
Bound together, attached.

colligate /ˈkɒlɪgeɪt/ *verb.* M16.
[ORIGIN Latin *colligat-* pa. ppl stem of *colligare*, formed as COL- + *ligare* bind: see -ATE[3].]
†**1** *verb trans.* Bind or fasten together. M16–L18.
2 *verb trans.* Join or unite *with.* E17.
3 *verb trans.* Unite in a class or order; *spec.* in LOGIC, connect together (isolated facts) by a general notion or hypothesis. L17.
4 *verb intrans.* LINGUISTICS. Of a word class or other functional category: be in colligation *with.* M20.
■ **coˈlligative** *adjective* of or pertaining to the binding together of molecules E20.

colligation /kɒlɪˈgeɪʃ(ə)n/ *noun.* LME.
[ORIGIN Old French, or Latin *colligatio(n-)*, formed as COLLIGATE *verb*: see -ATION.]
†**1** Physical binding together; connection. LME–M17.
2 Conjunction, alliance; union. M17.
3 LOGIC. The connection of a number of isolated facts by a general notion or hypothesis; a group of facts so connected. M19.
4 LINGUISTICS. Juxtaposition or grouping in syntactic relation of particular word classes or other functional categories; a sequence of word classes etc. in syntactic relation. M20.

colligible /ˈkɒlɪdʒɪb(ə)l/ *adjective.* Now *rare.* M17.
[ORIGIN from stem of Latin *colligere* COLLECT *verb* + -IBLE.]
That may be collected.

collimate /ˈkɒlɪmeɪt/ *verb.* E17.
[ORIGIN from Latin *collimare* erron. reading in some eds. of Cicero for *collineare* aim: see -ATE[3].]
†**1** *verb intrans.* Level or aim at a mark. Only in Dicts. E17–L18.
2 *verb trans.* Orig. ASTRONOMY. Correct the direction of (telescopes or other devices, rays of light, etc.); make accurately parallel. M19.
■ **collimator** *noun* a device for collimating; *esp.* (*a*) a small telescope for collimating another; (*b*) a device for producing a beam of parallel rays: M19.

collimation /kɒlɪˈmeɪʃ(ə)n/ *noun.* L17.
[ORIGIN formed as COLLIMATE: see -ATION.]
The action of collimating (sense 2) a telescope, light beam, etc. Also, correct or parallel alignment, absence of divergence.

collinear /kɒˈlɪnɪə/ *adjective.* M18.
[ORIGIN from COL- + LINEAR.]
†**1** Lying in the same plane. *rare.* Only in M18.
2 In the same straight line. M19.
■ **collineˈarity** *noun* M19. **collinearly** *adverb* M19.

Collins /ˈkɒlɪnz/ *noun*[1]. M19.
[ORIGIN A surname.]
(In full ***John Collins***, ***Tom Collins***) a cocktail consisting of gin mixed with soda, lemon or lime juice, and sugar; (usu. with specifying word, as ***brandy Collins***) this cocktail made with a different spirit.

Collins /ˈkɒlɪnz/ *noun*[2]. *colloq.* E20.
[ORIGIN William *Collins*, a character in Jane Austen's *Pride & Prejudice*.]
A letter of thanks for hospitality or entertainment, sent by a departed guest.

†**colliquation** *noun.* E17.
[ORIGIN medieval Latin *colliquatio(n-)*, formed as COLLIQUATIVE: see -ATION. Cf. French †*colliquation*.]
1 Melting, fusion, liquefaction. E17–M18.
2 MEDICINE. Wasting away of the body; disintegration of tissue into pus etc.; excessive fluidification of the bodily humours, esp. the blood; an instance of this. E17–M18.

colliquative /kɒˈlɪkwətɪv/ *noun & adjective.* Now *rare.* LME.
[ORIGIN from medieval Latin *colliquat-* pa. ppl stem of *colliquare*, formed as COL- + *liquare* liquefy, melt, + -IVE. Cf. French †*colliquatif*.]
► †**A** *noun.* A medicine to dissolve or reduce bodily solids. *rare.* Only in LME.
► **B** *adjective.* Having the power or effect of liquefying; MEDICINE causing the body to waste away, characterized by wasting away of the body. M17.

collision /kəˈlɪʒ(ə)n/ *noun.* LME.
[ORIGIN Late Latin *collisio(n-)*, from *collis-* pa. ppl stem of *collidere* COLLIDE *verb*: see -ION.]
1 The action of striking against something with force; the action or an act of colliding; (a) violent encounter of a moving body, esp. a ship or vehicle, with another or with a fixed object. LME. **›b** COMPUTING. An instance of two or more records being assigned the same location in memory. Also, an instance of different sources or nodes attempting to send a signal simultaneously along a shared line. M20.

E. RUTHERFORD The number of collisions of the particle with the atom. J. WAIN His head came into painful collision with a wooden crate. M. SHADBOLT His brakes squealed, to avoid a collision with a truck.

†**2 a** Syneresis of two vowels. M16–L17. **›b** Dissonant conjunction of speech sounds. M17.
3 *fig.* The encounter of opposed ideas, interests, factions, etc.; a clash, a conflict. M17. **›b** The action of coming into contact (with no notion of violence or hostility); coincidence, conjunction. Now *rare* or *obsolete.* M17.

b S. JOHNSON By the fortuitous collision of happy incidents.

– COMB.: **collision bulkhead** a strong watertight bulkhead built in the bows of a ship to prevent flooding after a collision; **collision course** a course or action bound to end in a collision (*lit.* & *fig.*); **collision-mat** NAUTICAL a mat with oakum on one face for putting over a hole made by a collision; **collision quarters**, **collision stations** pre-assigned positions to be taken up by the crew and passengers of a ship etc. in the event of a collision.

■ **collisional** *adjective* pertaining to or resulting from collision, esp. of microscopic particles L19. **collisionally** *adverb* M20. **collisionless** *adjective* M20.

colloblast /ˈkɒləʊblast/ *noun*. E20.
[ORIGIN from Greek *kolla* glue + -O- + -BLAST.]
ZOOLOGY. = ***lasso-cell*** s.v. LASSO *noun*.

collocable /ˈkɒləkəb(ə)l/ *adjective*. M20.
[ORIGIN from COLLOCATE + -ABLE.]
LINGUISTICS. Capable of forming part of a collocation.
■ **colloca'bility** *noun* M20.

collocate /ˈkɒləkeɪt/ *verb*. E16.
[ORIGIN Latin *collocat-* pa. ppl stem of *collocare*, formed as COL- + *locare* to place, LOCATE: see -ATE³.]
1 *verb trans.* Place side by side or in some relation; set in a place or position; *spec.* in *LINGUISTICS*, juxtapose (a word) with another so as to form a collocation. E16.
2 *verb intrans. LINGUISTICS*. Be habitually juxtaposed *with*, form a collocation. M20.
■ **collocative** *adjective* of the nature of or pertaining to collocation E19.

collocation /kɒləˈkeɪʃ(ə)n/ *noun*. LME.
[ORIGIN Latin *collocatio(n-)*, formed as COLLOCATE: see -ATION.]
The action of collocating; the state of being collocated; a disposition, an arrangement; *spec.* in *LINGUISTICS*, (esp. habitual) juxtaposition or association of a particular word with other particular words, a group of words so associated.
■ **collo'cational** *adjective* of or pertaining to collocation L19.

collocutor /ˈkɒləkjuːtə, kəˈlɒkjʊtə/ *noun*. M16.
[ORIGIN Late Latin *collocutor*, from *collocut-* pa. ppl stem of *colloqui*, formed as COL- + *loqui* talk: see -OR.]
A participant in a conversation or dialogue.
one's collocutor the person with whom one is talking.
■ **col'locutory** *adjective* of the nature of conversation or dialogue L18.

collodion /kəˈləʊdɪən/ *noun*. Also (*rare*) **-ium** /-ɪəm/. M19.
[ORIGIN from Greek *kollōdēs* gluelike, from *kolla* glue: cf. -ODE¹.]
A solution of pyroxylin in ether, used to apply a thin gummy film in photography and surgery.
■ **collodionize** *verb trans.* treat with collodion M19.

collogue /kɒˈləʊg/ *verb*. E17.
[ORIGIN Prob. alt., by assoc. with Latin *colloqui*, of COLLEAGUE *verb*.]
†**1** *verb intrans.* **a** Speak flatteringly; deal flatteringly *with*. E17–E18. ▸**b** Feign agreement or belief. E–M17.
2 *verb intrans.* **a** Intrigue, collude, conspire, (*with*). Now *dial.* M17. ▸**b** Talk confidentially (*with*). E19.
3 *verb trans.* Influence by flattery, coax. *obsolete* exc. *dial.* L17.

colloid /ˈkɒlɔɪd/ *adjective & noun*. M19.
[ORIGIN from Greek *kolla* glue + -OID.]
▸ **A** *adjective*. Of the nature or appearance of glue; *MEDICINE* characterized by the formation of colloid; *CHEMISTRY* = COLLOIDAL. *rare* in *gen.* sense. M19.
▸ **B** *noun*. **1** *ANATOMY & MEDICINE*. A jelly-like substance; *esp.* (*a*) one characteristic of certain cancers; (*b*) one normally present in the follicles of the thyroid gland. M19.
2 *CHEMISTRY*. A non-crystalline substance consisting of ultramicroscopic particles (often large single molecules); such a substance dispersed in another phase, esp. to form a viscous solution having special properties. M19.
protective colloid: see PROTECTIVE *adjective* 3a.

colloidal /kəˈlɔɪd(ə)l/ *adjective*. M19.
[ORIGIN from COLLOID + -AL¹.]
CHEMISTRY. Of, pertaining to, or of the nature of a colloid.
■ **colloi'dality** *noun* M19. **colloidally** *adverb* as a colloid; in the manner of a colloid: E20.

collop /ˈkɒləp/ *noun*¹. LME.
[ORIGIN from Scandinavian word repr. by Old Swedish *kolhuppadher* roasted on coals (from *kol* COAL *noun* + *huppa* leap, cf. SAUTÉ), Swedish *kalops*, dial. *kollops* dish of stewed meat.]
1 In *pl.* Orig., fried bacon and eggs. Later (in ***collops and eggs***), fried bacon. Now *dial.* LME.
2 A slice of meat (orig. fried or grilled); an escalope. LME. ▸**b** In *pl.* (A dish of) minced or chopped meat. *dial.* M17.
b *Scotch collops*: see SCOTCH *adjective*.
†**3** A piece of flesh; *fig.* an offspring. E16–M17.
4 A thick fold of flesh on the body. Now *Scot. & dial.* M16.
5 *fig.* A slice; a piece cut off. L16.
– COMB.: **Collop Monday** (now *dial.*) the Monday before Shrove Tuesday, on which bacon and eggs would be served.

collop /ˈkɒləp/ *noun*². *Irish*. L17.
[ORIGIN Irish *colp(th)ach* heifer, bullock.]
A full-grown cow or horse; *transf.* the quantity of grass or area of pasture needed for a cow for one year.

collophane /ˈkɒləfeɪn/ *noun*. E20.
[ORIGIN German *Kollophan*, formed as COLLOID + Greek *-phanēs* showing, from *phainein* to show.]
MINERALOGY. A cryptocrystalline calciferous form of apatite which occurs in fossilized bone and other organic deposits.
■ Also **co'llophanite** *noun* M19.

colloque /kəˈləʊk/ *noun*. Now *rare*. L15.
[ORIGIN French from Latin COLLOQUIUM.]
†**1** A place for conversation. *rare*. Only in L15.
†**2** A conversation, a conference. L16–L17.
3 = COLLOQUY 2. M19.

colloquial /kəˈləʊkwɪəl/ *adjective & noun*. M18.
[ORIGIN from Latin COLLOQUIUM + -AL¹.]
▸ **A** *adjective*. **1** Conversational; in or of talk, oral. M18.
2 Belonging to familiar speech and writing; not used in formal or elevated language. M18.
▸ **B** *noun*. Colloquial speech or language. E20.
■ **colloquialism** *noun* colloquial style, esp. of language; a colloquial expression: L18. **colloquialist** *noun* (*a*) a person who uses colloquialisms; (*b*) a good talker: E19. **colloqui'ality** *noun* (now *rare*) = COLLOQUIALISM E19. **colloquially** *adverb* L18.

colloquise *verb* var. of COLLOQUIZE.

colloquist /ˈkɒləkwɪst/ *noun*. L18.
[ORIGIN formed as COLLOQUIAL + -IST.]
An interlocutor.

colloquium /kəˈləʊkwɪəm/ *noun*. Pl. **-ia** /-ɪə/, **-iums**. L16.
[ORIGIN Latin, formed as COL- + *loqui* speak.]
†**1** A conversation, a dialogue. L16–M18.
2 A conference; *spec.* an academic conference or seminar. M19.

colloquize /ˈkɒləkwʌɪz/ *verb intrans.* Also **-ise**. E19.
[ORIGIN formed as COLLOQUIUM + -IZE.]
Engage in colloquy.

colloquy /ˈkɒləkwi/ *noun*. LME.
[ORIGIN Latin COLLOQUIUM: see -Y⁴.]
1 A discourse, a dialogue, (spoken or written); an act of conversing; a conversation. LME. ▸**b** Conversation, dialogue. E19.
2 *ECCLESIASTICAL*. A judicial and legislative court in a Reformed or Presbyterian Church. L17.

collotype /ˈkɒlətʌɪp/ *noun*. L19.
[ORIGIN from Greek *kolla* glue + -O- + -TYPE.]
A thin sheet of gelatin which may be exposed to light, treated with reagents, and used to make a print by lithography; a print so made.

collow /ˈkɒləʊ/ *verb & noun*. *obsolete* exc. *dial.* ME.
[ORIGIN Uncertain: perh. repr. Old English verb from COALY (see note s.v.). Cf. COLLY *adjective & noun*², *verb*².]
▸ **A** *verb trans.* Make black with coal dust; blacken, begrime. ME.
▸ **B** *noun*. Soot; smut; grime. L17.

colluctation /kɒlʌkˈteɪʃ(ə)n/ *noun*. *arch.* E17.
[ORIGIN Latin *colluctatio(n-)*, from *colluctat-* pa. ppl stem of *colluctari*, formed as COL- + *luctari* wrestle, strive.]
A wrestling or struggling together; a conflict, opposition.

collude /kəˈl(j)uːd/ *verb*. E16.
[ORIGIN from Latin *colludere* have a secret agreement, formed as COL- + *ludere* play.]
1 *verb intrans.* Conspire, plot, connive; act in secret concert. (Foll. by *with* a person, *in* an act etc.) E16.
†**2** *verb trans.* Stir up or bring about by collusion. L18–M19.
■ **colluder** *noun* M17.

collusion /kəˈl(j)uːʒ(ə)n/ *noun*. LME.
[ORIGIN Old French & mod. French, or Latin *collusio(n-)*, from *collus-* pa. ppl stem of *colludere*: see COLLUDE, -ION.]
1 Secret agreement or understanding for nefarious purposes; conspiracy; fraud, trickery. LME. ▸**b** An instance of this. Now *rare*. L16.
2 *LAW*. An agreement between two or more people, esp. ostensible opponents in a suit, to act to the prejudice of a third party or for an improper purpose. LME.

collusive /kəˈl(j)uːsɪv/ *adjective*. L17.
[ORIGIN from Latin *collus-* (see COLLUSION) + -IVE.]
Characterized by or given to collusion.
■ **collusively** *adverb* M18.

collusory /kɒˈluːz(ə)ri/ *adjective*. Now *rare*. E18.
[ORIGIN Late Latin *collusorius*, formed as COLLUSIVE: see -ORY².]
= COLLUSIVE.

colluvial /kəˈl(j)uːvɪəl/ *adjective*. E19.
[ORIGIN from COLLUVIES + -AL¹.]
1 Of or pertaining to a colluvies. *rare*. E19.
2 *PHYSICAL GEOGRAPHY*. Of, pertaining to, or of the nature of colluvium. L19.

colluvies /kəˈl(j)uːvɪiːz/ *noun*. Now *rare* or *obsolete*. Pl. same. M17.
[ORIGIN Latin *colluvies*, from *colluere* rinse, formed as COL- + *luere* wash.]
1 A collection of foul matter, *esp.* a discharge from an ulcer. M17.
2 A confluence (of waters etc.). M17.
3 *fig.* A rabble, a hotchpotch. M17.

colluvium /kəˈl(j)uːvɪəm/ *noun*. M20.
[ORIGIN Latin, formed as COLLUVIES: see -IUM.]
PHYSICAL GEOGRAPHY. Material which accumulates at the foot of a steep slope.

colly *noun*¹ var. of COLLIE.

colly /ˈkɒli/ *adjective & noun*². Long *dial.* E17.
[ORIGIN Var. of COALY.]
▸ **A** *adjective*. Sooty, grimy; coal-black. E17.
▸ **B** *noun*. **1** Soot, smut. E18.
2 The blackbird. E19.

†**colly** *verb*¹ *intrans.* LME–L18.
[ORIGIN Old French *coleier*, *coloier* turn the neck, from *col* neck.]
Move the neck; (of a bird) turn the head from side to side.

colly /ˈkɒli/ *verb*² *trans.* Now *arch. & dial.* L16.
[ORIGIN Var. of COLLOW *verb*.]
Blacken with coal dust or soot; begrime.

Collyridian /kɒlɪˈrɪdɪən/ *noun & adjective*. M16.
[ORIGIN Late Latin *collyridianus*, from *collyrida* from Greek *kollūris*, *-id-* cake, dim. of *kollura* roll of coarse bread: see -AN.]
ECCLESIASTICAL HISTORY. ▸**A** *noun*. A member of a sect idolatrously offering cakes to the Blessed Virgin, which consisted mainly of women and originated in Thrace in the 4th cent. AD. M16.
▸ **B** *adjective*. Of or pertaining to this sect. E19.

C

collyrium /kəˈlɪrɪəm/ *noun*. Pl. **-ia** /-ɪə/. LME.
[ORIGIN Latin *collyrium* from Greek *kollurion* poultice, eye ointment, from *kollura* (see COLLYRIDIAN).]
1 A medicinal application for the eyes, an eye lotion. LME.
2 A cosmetic application for the eyes, as kohl. *rare*. E17.
3 A suppository. M18.

Colly-west /ˈkɒlɪwɛst/ *adverb, noun, & adjective*. *dial.* Also **Collywest**. E19.
[ORIGIN from *Collyweston*, a village in Northamptonshire.]
▸ **A** *adverb*. Awry, askew. E19.
▸ **B** *noun*. Nonsense. M19.
▸ **C** *adjective*. Contrary, contradictory. L19.

collywobbles /ˈkɒlɪwɒb(ə)lz/ *noun pl. colloq.* E19.
[ORIGIN Fanciful formation from COLIC + WOBBLE *noun*.]
Rumbling in the intestines; stomach ache; a feeling of apprehension (with intestinal symptoms).

Colmar /ˈkɒlmɑː/ *noun*. E18.
[ORIGIN Perh. from the town in Alsace.]
1 A fan fashionable in Queen Anne's reign. †**2** A variety of pear. Only in M18.

colobine /ˈkɒləbʌɪn/ *adjective & noun*. M20.
[ORIGIN from mod. Latin *Colobinae* (see below), formed as COLOBUS: see -INE¹.]
ZOOLOGY. ▸**A** *adjective*. Of, pertaining to, or characteristic of the subfamily Colobinae (family Cercopithecidae) of mainly leaf-eating Old World monkeys, which have sacculated stomachs and lack cheek pouches. M20.
▸ **B** *noun*. A monkey of this subfamily, a leaf monkey. M20.

colobium /kəˈləʊbɪəm/ *noun*. Pl. **-ia** /-ɪə/. E17.
[ORIGIN Late Latin from Greek *kolobion*, from *kolobos* curtailed.]
A half-sleeved or sleeveless tunic worn by the early clergy, by monks, and by monarchs at their coronation.

coloboma /kɒləʊˈbəʊmə/ *noun*. Pl. **-mas**, **-mata** /-mətə/. M19.
[ORIGIN mod. Latin from Greek *kolobōma* the part removed in mutilation, from *kolobos* curtailed: see -OMA.]
MEDICINE. A congenital malformation of the eye causing e.g. a notch in the iris or in an eyelid.

colobus /ˈkɒləbəs/ *noun*. M19.
[ORIGIN mod. Latin from Greek *kolobos* curtailed (on account of the shortened thumbs).]
An African leaf-eating monkey of the genus *Colobus*. Also ***colobus monkey***.

colocasia /kɒləʊˈkeɪzɪə/ *noun*. LME.
[ORIGIN Latin, from Greek *kolokasia* (rhizome of) the Egyptian water lily.]
A plant of the genus *Colocasia*, spec. = TARO.

colocynth /ˈkɒləsɪnθ/ *noun*. Orig. also in Latin form †**colocynthis**. M16.
[ORIGIN Latin *colocynthis* from Greek *kolokunthis*, *-id-*: cf. COLOQUINTIDA.]
The bitter-apple, *Citrullus colocynthis*, a plant of the gourd family, whose pulpy fruit provides a bitter purgative drug. Also, the fruit or the drug.

Cologne /kəˈləʊn/ *noun*. In sense 2 now usu. **c-**. M17.
[ORIGIN French = German *Köln*, from Latin *Colonia* (*Agrippina*), a German city on the Rhine.]
1 ***Cologne earth***, †***Cologne's earth***, a brown pigment prepared from lignite, orig. from near Cologne. M17.
2 Eau de Cologne or other lightly scented toilet water. Also ***Cologne water***. E19.

colombophile /kəˈlʌmbəfʌɪl/ *noun & adjective*. L19.
[ORIGIN French, from *colombe* pigeon formed as COLUMBA: see -PHIL.]
▸ **A** *noun*. A pigeon-fancier. L19.
▸ **B** *adjective*. Pigeon-fancying. L19.

colometry /kəʊˈlɒmɪtri/ *noun*. L19.
[ORIGIN Greek *kōlometria*, from *kōlon* limb, clause: see -METRY.]
PALAEOGRAPHY. The division of texts by cola.
■ **colo'metric** *adjective* L19. **colo'metrical** *adjective* E20. **colo'metrically** *adverb* E20.

colon /ˈkəʊlən, -lɒn/ *noun*¹. LME.
[ORIGIN Latin from Greek *kolon*, (also) food, meat.]
ANATOMY. The greater part of the large intestine extending from the caecum to the rectum. Formerly (*popularly*), the belly, the guts.
sigmoid colon: see SIGMOID *adjective* 2. ***transverse colon***: see TRANSVERSE *adjective*.

colon /ˈkəʊlən/ *noun*². Pl. in sense 1 **cola** /ˈkəʊlə/, in sense 2 **-s**. **M16**.
[ORIGIN Latin from Greek *kōlon* limb, clause.]
1 In *CLASSICAL PROSODY & RHETORIC*, (a pause of intermediate length before) a distinct section of a complex sentence or rhythmical period. In *PALAEOGRAPHY*, a clause or group of clauses written as a line or taken as a standard of measure in ancient manuscripts or texts. **M16**.
2 A punctuation mark consisting of two dots placed one above the other (:), indicating a discontinuity of grammatical construction, though one less than that indicated by a period or full stop, and now esp. marking antithesis, illustration, quotation, or listing (sometimes with a dash :—), or between numbers in a proportion, reference, etc. See also SEMICOLON. **E17**.

colon /kɒˈlən/ *noun*³. **E17**.
[ORIGIN French from Latin *colonus*: see COLONY.]
1 A husbandman. *rare*. **E17**.
2 *hist*. A colonial settler or farmer, esp. in a French colony. **M20**.

colón /kəʊˈləʊn/ *noun*. Pl. **colones** /kəʊˈləʊnɪz/, **colons**. **L19**.
[ORIGIN from Spanish Cristóbal *Colón* Christopher Columbus (see COLUMBUS).]
The basic monetary unit of Costa Rica and of El Salvador, equal to 100 céntimos in Costa Rica and 100 centavos in El Salvador.

colonel /ˈkəːn(ə)l/ *noun*. Also †**coro-**, (esp. in titles) **C-**. **M16**.
[ORIGIN French †*coronel*, later *colonnel* (now *colonel*), from Italian *colonnello*, from *colonna* COLUMN.]
1 The highest-ranking officer of a regiment; an officer ranking next above a lieutenant colonel and next below a brigadier in military rank. Also (esp. in the southern US) used as a courtesy title to minor government officials and to former military men. **M16**.
Colonel Blimp: see BLIMP 3. **colonel-general** an officer in charge of all the regiments of an (esp. foreign) army: freq. an honorary rank. **Colonel-in-Chief**: an honorary rank. *LIEUTENANT colonel*.
2 A holder of any of various military ranks in ancient armies. **M16**.
– NOTE: The form *coronel* prevailed in writing until **M17** and is also the source of the mod. pronunc. The 1773 edition of Johnson's *Dictionary* records only /ˈkɒl-/.
■ **colonelcy** *noun* the post, rank, or commission of a colonel **L18**. **colonelling** *noun* playing the colonel; trying to raise a regiment: **M17**. **colonelship** *noun* = COLONELCY **L16**.

colonial /kəˈləʊnɪəl/ *adjective & noun*. **L18**.
[ORIGIN from COLONY + -AL¹, perh. after French *colonial*.]
▶ **A** *adjective*. **1** Of or pertaining to a colony or colonies, esp. a British Crown Colony. Now freq. *derog*. **L18**. ▸**b** Pertaining to or characteristic of the period of the British colonies in America before they became the US; built or designed in a style of this period. *N. Amer*. **L18**. ▸**c** Dealing in produce from a colony or colonies. **L19**.
R. CONQUEST A state ruled by a foreign marshal condemns colonial oppression.
colonial goose *Austral. & NZ* stuffed boned roast leg of mutton. **Colonial Office** *hist*. the Government department in charge of colonies.
2 Of animals or plants: living in colonies. **L19**.
N. TINBERGEN Like many colonial birds, gulls are very vociferous.
▶ **B** *noun*. **1** A native or inhabitant of a colony. **M19**.
2 A house etc. built in colonial style. *N. Amer*. **M20**.
■ **colonially** *adverb* **M19**.

colonialism /kəˈləʊnɪəlɪz(ə)m/ *noun*. **L18**.
[ORIGIN from COLONIAL + -ISM.]
1 The practice or policy of maintaining colonies; now freq. *derog*., the alleged policy of exploitation of backward or weak peoples. **L18**.
2 Colonial manners or practices. Now *rare*. **M19**.
3 A colonial expression or idiom. **L19**.
■ **colonialist** *noun & adjective* (**a**) *noun* an adherent of colonialism; (**b**) *adjective* of or pertaining to colonialists or colonialism: **E19**.

colonic /kəʊˈlɒnɪk/ *adjective*. **E20**.
[ORIGIN from COLON *noun*¹ + -IC.]
Of or pertaining to the colon; affecting the colon.
colonic irrigation the application of water via the anus to flush out the colon.

colonisation *noun*, **colonise** *verb* vars. of COLONIZATION, COLONIZE.

colonist /ˈkɒlənɪst/ *noun*. **E18**.
[ORIGIN from COLONIZE: see -IST.]
1 A settler in a new country; an inhabitant of a colony. **E18**. ▸**b** An established but non-indigenous plant or animal. **L19**.
2 *US POLITICS*. A party supporter planted in a district to increase the party's vote in an election. **M19**.

colonization /kɒlənʌɪˈzeɪʃ(ə)n/ *noun*. Also **-isation**. **L18**.
[ORIGIN from COLONIST + -ATION.]
1 The establishment of a colony or colonies. (Foll. by *of* a place.) **L18**. ▸**b** The occupation by a plant or animal species of an area from which it was formerly absent. **E20**.
2 *US POLITICS*. The planting of party supporters in a district to increase the party's vote at an election. **M19**.
■ **colonizationism** *noun* (*US HISTORY*) the principles of colonizationists **M19**. **colonizationist** *noun* (*US HISTORY*) an advocate of the colonization of Africa by black Americans. **M19**.

colonize /ˈkɒlənʌɪz/ *verb*. Also **-ise**. **E17**.
[ORIGIN from COLONY: see -IZE.]
1 *verb trans*. Establish a colony in. **E17**. ▸**b** Of plants or animals: establish themselves in (an area). Cf. COLONIZATION 1b. **M19**.
G. STEINER The uprooted peoples began colonizing Asia Minor.
2 *verb trans*. Establish in a colony. **M17**.
Encycl. Brit. Permission . . to colonize 300 families.
3 *verb intrans*. Establish a colony or colonies; join a colony. **E19**.
4 *verb intrans. & trans. US POLITICS*. Plant (party supporters) in a district, plant party supporters in (a district), to increase the party's vote at an election. **M19**.
■ **colonizable** *adjective* **M19**. **colonizer** *noun* **L18**.

colonnade /kɒləˈneɪd/ *noun*. **E18**.
[ORIGIN French (earlier †*-ate*), from *colonne* COLUMN, after Italian *colonnato*, †*-ata*: see -ADE.]
1 *ARCHITECTURE*. A series of columns placed at regular intervals and supporting an entablature. **E18**.
2 *transf*. A row of trees etc. **M18**.
■ **colonnaded** *adjective* having a colonnade **E19**.

colonnette /kɒləˈnɛt/ *noun*. **L19**.
[ORIGIN French, dim. of *colonne* COLUMN: see -ETTE.]
ARCHITECTURE. A small column.

colonoscope /kəˈlɒnəskəʊp/ *noun*. **M20**.
[ORIGIN from COLON *noun*¹ + -O- + -SCOPE.]
A flexible fibre-optic instrument inserted through the anus in order to allow visual examination of the colon.
■ **colonoˈscopic** *adjective* **L20**. **coloˈnoscopy** *noun* (an instance of) visual examination of the colon with a colonoscope **M20**.

colony /ˈkɒləni/ *noun*. **LME**.
[ORIGIN Latin *colonia* farm, settlement, from *colonus* tiller, settler, from *colere* cultivate: see -Y³.]
▶ **I 1** *ROMAN HISTORY*. A garrison settlement, usu. of veteran soldiers, in a conquered territory. **LME**.
†**2** A farm; a rural settlement. **M16–M17**.
3 *GREEK HISTORY*. An independent city founded by emigrants **L16**.
▶ **II 4** A settlement in a new country; a body of settlers forming a community fully or partly subject to the mother state; the territory of such settlers. **M16**.
HOBBES Colonies sent from England, to plant Virginia. S. JOHNSON A ship stored for a voyage to the colonies.
5 A community of animals or plants of one kind forming a physically connected structure or otherwise living in close proximity; the place of habitation of such a group. **L17**.
R. DAWKINS Blackheaded gulls nest in large colonies. D. ATTENBOROUGH Coral polyps . . working together in colonies.
6 A body of people of a particular nationality or occupation in a city or country, esp. if living more or less in isolation or in a special quarter; a segregated group; the district, quarter, etc., inhabited by such a group. **E18**.
Time The Nudist colony on an island in the Seine.

colopexy /ˈkəʊləpɛksi, kəʊləˈpɛksi/ *noun*. **L19**.
[ORIGIN mod. Latin *colopexia*, formed as COLON *noun*¹ + -O- + Greek *pēxis* fixing: see -Y³.]
The surgical attachment of part of the colon to the abdominal wall; an instance of this.

colophon /ˈkɒləf(ə)n/ *noun*. **E17**.
[ORIGIN Late Latin *colophon* from Greek *kolophōn* summit, finishing touch.]
1 A crowning or finishing touch. *rare*. **E17**.
C. CONNOLLY One of the colophons of literature, one of those great writers who put full stop to a form of art, was Marcel Proust.
2 A statement, sometimes with a device, at the end of a manuscript or printed book, giving information about its authorship, production, etc. (as the printer's name and date and place of printing). **L18**. ▸**b** A publisher's or printer's imprint; *loosely* a publisher's device, esp. on a title page. **M20**.

colophony /kəˈlɒfəni, ˈkɒləfəʊni/ *noun*. **ME**.
[ORIGIN Latin *colophonia* for *Colophonia resina* resin of Colophon (a town in Lydia).]
Rosin.

coloquintida /kɒləˈkwɪntɪdə/ *noun*. Now *rare* or *obsolete*. **LME**.
[ORIGIN medieval Latin, formed as COLOCYNTH.]
= COLOCYNTH. Also *fig*., a bitter medicine.

color *noun*, *verb*, **colorable** *adjective* see COLOUR *noun*, *verb*, COLOURABLE.

Coloradan /kɒləˈrɑːd(ə)n/ *noun & adjective*. **L19**.
[ORIGIN from *Colorado* (see below) + -AN.]
A native or inhabitant of, of or pertaining to, the state of Colorado, USA.
■ Also **Coloradian**, **Coloradoan** *noun & adjective* **M19**.

Colorado beetle /kɒləˌrɑːdəʊ ˈbiːt(ə)l/ *noun phr*. **M19**.
[ORIGIN *Colorado*, a state of the US.]
A yellow black-striped beetle, *Leptinotarsa decemlineata*, which is native to N. America and is a serious pest of potato crops. Also *Colorado potato beetle*.

colorant *noun* see COLOURANT.

coloration /kʌləˈreɪʃ(ə)n/ *noun*. Also **colour-**. **E17**.
[ORIGIN French, or late Latin *coloratio(n-)*, from *colorat-* pa. ppl stem of *colorare* COLOUR *verb*: see -ATION.]
Colouring, the method of putting on or arranging colour; the natural, esp. variegated, colouring of plants and animals.
protective coloration: see PROTECTIVE *adjective*. *warning coloration*: see WARNING *ppl adjective*.

coloratura /kɒlərəˈtjʊərə, -ˈtʊ-/ *noun*. **M18**.
[ORIGIN Italian from late Latin *coloratura*, from *colorat-*: see COLORATION, -URE.]
1 Florid passages in vocal music, with runs, trills, etc.; the singing of these. **M18**.
2 A singer of coloratura, esp. a soprano. **M20**.
■ Also **colorature** *noun* (*rare*) [German *Coloratur*] **E19**.

colorectal /kəʊləʊˈrɛkt(ə)l/ *adjective*. **M20**.
[ORIGIN from COLON *noun*¹ + RECTAL: see -O-.]
MEDICINE. Pertaining to or affecting the colon and the rectum.

colored *adjective & noun* see COLOURED.

colorific /kʌləˈrɪfɪk, kɒl-/ *adjective*. **L17**.
[ORIGIN French *colorifique* or mod. Latin *colorificus*, from Latin *color* COLOUR *noun*: see -FIC.]
Producing colour(s); highly coloured (*lit. & fig.*).

colorimeter /kʌləˈrɪmɪtə, kɒl-/ *noun*. **M19**.
[ORIGIN from Latin *color* COLOUR *noun* + -IMETER. Cf. French *colorimètre*.]
An instrument for measuring intensity of colour.
■ **coloriˈmetric**, **coloriˈmetrical** *adjectives* of or pertaining to a colorimeter or colorimetry **L19**. **coloriˈmetrically** *adverb* by means of a colorimeter **E20**. **colorimetry** *noun* the measurement of intensity of colour **L19**.

coloring, **colorist** *nouns* see COLOURING, COLOURIST.

colorize /ˈkʌlərʌɪz/ *verb trans*. Also **colour-**; **-ise**. **E17**.
[ORIGIN from COLOUR *noun* + -IZE.]
Colour (a thing), add colour to; *spec*. colour (a black and white film) by means of a computer.
■ **coloriˈzation** *noun* coloration, colouring; (as *Colorization*, US proprietary name for) the process or technique of colorizing: **M18**. **colorizer** *noun* a colouring agent or process; (as *Colorizer*, US proprietary name for) a colorizing process: **L19**.

coloss /kəˈlɒs/ *noun*. *arch*. Also **-osse**. **M16**.
[ORIGIN French *colosse* from Latin COLOSSUS.]
= COLOSSUS.

colossal /kəˈlɒs(ə)l/ *adjective*. **E18**.
[ORIGIN French, formed as COLOSS: see -AL¹.]
1 Of or like a colossus; gigantic, huge, (in scope, extent, or amount). **E18**.
2 Tremendous; remarkable, splendid, delightful. *colloq*. **L19**.
3 *ARCHITECTURE*. Of an order: more than one storey high. **M20**.
■ **colossally** *adverb* **M19**.

colosse *noun* var. of COLOSS.

colossean /kəˈlɒsɪən/ *adjective*. *arch*. Also †**-ian**. **E17**.
[ORIGIN from Latin *colosseus*, formed as COLOSSUS: see -EAN, -IAN.]
= COLOSSAL 1.

colosseum *noun* see COLISEUM.

Colossian /kəˈlɒsɪən/ *noun & adjective*¹. **E16**.
[ORIGIN from *Colossae* (see below) + -IAN.]
▶ **A** *noun*. A native or inhabitant of Colossae, an ancient city in Phrygia, Asia Minor. In *pl*. (treated as *sing*.), St Paul's Epistle to the Colossians, a book of the New Testament. **E16**.
▶ **B** *adjective*. Of or pertaining to Colossae or the Colossians. **L19**.

†**colossian** *adjective*² see COLOSSEAN.

colossus /kəˈlɒsəs/ *noun*. Pl. **-ssi** /-sʌɪ/, **-ssuses**. **LME**.
[ORIGIN Latin from Greek *kolossos* applied by Herodotus to the statues of Egyptian temples.]
1 A statue of much more than life-size, as that said to have stood astride the entrance to the harbour of Rhodes in ancient Greece. **LME**.
2 A gigantic or overawing person or thing; an empire etc. personified as standing astride over dominions. **E17**.

colostomy /kəˈlɒstəmi/ *noun*. **L19**.
[ORIGIN from COLON *noun*¹ + Greek *stoma* mouth + -Y³.]
(The making of) a surgical incision in the colon to provide an artificial anus through the abdominal wall in cases of stricture etc.

colostrum /kəˈlɒstrəm/ *noun*. Also (earlier) †**-tra**. **L16**.
[ORIGIN Latin.]
The first milk of a mammal after parturition.

colotomy /kəˈlɒtəmi/ *noun*. **M19**.
[ORIGIN from COLON *noun*¹ + -TOMY.]
Surgical incision into the colon; an instance of this.

colour /ˈkʌlə/ *noun*. Also ***color**. ME.
[ORIGIN Old French *colur, colour* (mod. *couleur*) from Latin *color*: see -OUR.]
▸ **I 1** A particular tint; one, or any mixture, of the constituents into which light can be separated as in the spectrum, including (loosely) black and white. ME. ▸**b** A conventional colour used in heraldry, as gules, vert, etc.; a tincture, *esp.* one other than a metal or a fur. LME. ▸**c** *BOTANY*. A colour other than green. M19.

DAY LEWIS Her hair . . was a rich auburn colour. E. LONGFORD The colours the Duke preferred were gay and warm; no greens, blues, black or white.

liver colour, ***mouse-colour***, ***stone-colour***, ***strawberry colour***, etc.

2 Facial complexion; hue of the skin as reflecting a physical or mental state. ME. ▸**b** *spec.* Ruddiness of face. Also, a flush, a blush. ME. ▸**c** Hue of skin pigmentation; (dark) skin pigmentation, esp. as giving rise to prejudice, discrimination, etc. LME.

b S. O'FAOLÁIN A sturdy woman with fresh colour in her cheeks. ALAN JACKSON A word of praise would bring A colour to her cheek. **c** L. VAN DER POST A spirit . . at work among us all no matter what our race or colour.

3 The sensation produced on the eye by spectral resolution or (selective) surface reflection etc. of rays of light; the property of so producing different sensations on the eye. Cf. ***black***, ***white***. LME.

E. BOWEN The façade, dun stucco, . . never altered in colour except at sunset.

4 a *ART*. The general effect produced by all the colours of a picture. M17. ▸**b** The representation of colour by contrasts of light and dark in an engraving or monochrome. Also, the (relative) blackness of printed type. L18. ▸**c** (The use of) two or more colours, not just black and white, in photography or cinematography; (the use of) nearly natural colours in a reproductive medium. L19.

▸ **II 5** A colouring matter; pigment; paint. ME.

Ladies Home Journal (US) If nail color chips between manicures, simply brush on a fresh coat of color.

6 *sing.* & (usu.) in *pl.* A coloured device, badge, article or set of clothing, etc., worn as a symbol of a party, membership of a club, a jockey's employer, etc. LME. ▸**b** In *pl.* The distinctive colours of a school, college, club, etc., team, crew, or the like, as conferred to denote selection as a representative member; selection to represent a school etc. L19. ▸**c** A person who has gained colours. M20.

SIR W. SCOTT The servants . . wore the colours of the Prince's household. *National Review (US)* Its green, yellow, and white colors are splashed over public buildings.

7 A naval or nautical flag; either of the pair of silk flags (***the King's colour*** or ***the Queen's colour*** and ***the regimental colour***) carried by a regiment. In *pl.* also, a regiment, the armed forces, (now chiefly in ***with the colours***). L16. ▸**b** In *pl.* More fully ***pair of colours***. An ensign's commission. *arch.* E18. ▸**c** In *pl.* A national flag. Also, two or more symbolic flags usually displayed or carried together. L19. ▸**d** In *pl.* A nautical ceremony at which a flag is saluted as it is raised or lowered. E20.

SHAKES. *3 Hen. VI* Sound trumpets; let our bloody colours wave. **c** J. DOS PASSOS The Commanding General never permits a flag to be carried past him without uncovering and remaining so until the colors have passed.

8 *MINING*. (A particle of) gold. M19.
9 *SNOOKER*. Any of the balls other than the white cue ball and the reds. E20.
▸ **III 10** (An) outward appearance, (a) show, (a) semblance *of*. ME.
11 General complexion or tone; character, kind, mood; import, shade of meaning. ME.

O. CROMWELL Nor can it be urged that my words have the least colour that way. THACKERAY Pendennis . . took his colour very readily from his neighbour. T. KENEALLY The colour of his opinion . . was generally anti-monarchist and Papist.

12 A specious or plausible reason; a pretext; an excuse. LME. ▸**b** *LAW*. An apparent or *prima facie* right, as ***colour of title***; a plausible but really false plea intended to make the point to be decided appear to be one of law and not of fact. M16.

JAS. MILL An enterprise . . which . . afforded a colour for detaining the troops.

13 In *pl.* Rhetorical modes or figures; ornaments of style or diction. LME.
14 Timbre, sound quality; variety of musical expression, modulation (of the voice etc.). L16.

S. HAZZARD His voice . . had a mature colour, resonant, almost beautiful. *Los Angeles Times* The reading had vitality and color, balances that brought the all-important flute part . . to the fore.

15 Evocative description, detailed characterization; picturesqueness in literature. Earliest in ***local colour***: see LOCAL *adjective*. L19.
16 *PARTICLE PHYSICS*. A quantized property of quarks which differentiates them into three varieties (called blue, green, and red) and is thought to be the source of the strong interaction. L20.

– PHRASES ETC.: **change colour** *spec.* of a person: (**a**) turn pale; (**b**) blush, flush. **come off with flying colours**, **come through with flying colours** come successfully through a test etc., win credit. **complementary colour** a colour that combined with a given colour makes white or black. ***dead colour***: see DEAD *adjective & adverb*. ***false colours***: see FALSE *adjective*. ***FOUR-colour problem***. ***full-colour***: see FULL *adjective*. **gain one's colours**, **get one's colours** be included in a sports team, esp. as a regular member. **give a person his or her colours** include a person in a sports team, esp. as a regular member. **give colour to** = ***lend colour to*** below. **haul down one's colours** admit defeat. ***high colour***: see HIGH *adjective*. ***horse of another colour***: see HORSE *noun*. **lend colour to** (**a**) afford a pretext to; (**b**) give plausibility to. ***liturgical colours***: see LITURGICAL *adjective*. ***local colour***: see LOCAL *adjective*. **nail one's colours to the mast** (**a**) persist, refuse to give in; (**b**) commit oneself to some party or plan of action. ***off colour***: see OFF *preposition & adjective*. **paint in bright colours** *fig.* describe optimistically. **person of colour** (now chiefly *US*) a non-white person. ***primary colour***: see PRIMARY *adjective*. ***primitive colour***: see PRIMITIVE *adjective & noun*. ***RACING colours***. ***r-colour***: see R, R 1. ***scheme of colour***: see SCHEME *noun*[1] 7b. ***secondary colour***: see SECONDARY *adjective*. **see the colour of a person's money** receive some evidence of forthcoming payment from a person. **show one's colours**, **show one's true colours** reveal one's (true) party or character. ***solid colour***: see SOLID *adjective & adverb*. ***stand of colours***: see STAND *noun*[1] 15b. ***strike one's colours***: see STRIKE *verb*. ***the King's colour***, ***the Queen's colour***, ***the regimental colour***: see sense 7 above. ***turn colour***: see TURN *verb*. **under colour of** under pretext or pretence of; under the alleged authority of. ***vowel colour***: see VOWEL *noun*. **with the colours** serving in the armed forces.

– ATTRIB. & COMB.: Esp. with ref. to photographic etc. reproduction in colour, as ***colour camera***, ***colour photograph***, ***colour photography***, ***colour print***, ***colour slide***, ***colour transparency***, etc. Special combs., as **colour atlas** a chart giving examples of a series of shades of colour; **colour bar** legal or social discrimination between white and non-white persons; **colour-blind** *adjective* unable to distinguish certain colours; (esp. of animals) unable to distinguish colours at all; **colour blindness** the condition of being colour-blind; **colour-box** a paintbox; **colour-change** *spec.* a change in the colour of an animal's coat, skin, etc., for camouflage or protection; **colour code** a guide or code using certain colours as a standard method of identification; **colour-code** *verb trans.* identify by means of a standard colour; **colour constancy** the effect whereby the intrinsic colour of an object is perceived as almost constant despite changes in the colour of the illumination; **colour-fast** *adjective* dyed in colours that will not easily fade or wash out; **colour fastness** the quality of being colour-fast; **colour-field painting** a style of American abstract painting prominent from the late 1940s to the 1960s featuring large expanses of unmodulated colour covering the greater part of the canvas; **colour film** (**a**) a cinema film produced in nearly natural colours; (**b**) a film suitable for producing colour photographs; **colour filter** a photographic filter that absorbs light of certain colours; **colour guard** an honour guard carrying colours; **colour hearing** = ***coloured hearing*** s.v. COLOURED *adjective* 1; **colour-index** a measure of colour; *spec.* (**a**) *ASTRONOMY* the difference between the photographic and visual magnitudes of a star, or between the apparent magnitudes at two standard wavelengths; (**b**) *GEOLOGY* a number representing the relative proportions of dark-coloured (ferromagnesian) and pale-coloured minerals in an igneous rock; **colour-light** *adjective* designating (esp. railway) signals using coloured electric lights; **colour line** a social or occupational demarcation between white and non-white persons; **colour-man** (**a**) a dealer in paints; (**b**) a dye-worker; **colour phase** a genetic or seasonal variation in the colour of the skin, pelt, or feathers of an animal or bird; **colour-plate** each of a set of plates used in printing in colour; a print made from such plates; **colourpoint** a cat of a long-haired breed having a pale coat with dark points, and blue eyes, developed by crossing Persian and Siamese cats; **colour prejudice**: against persons of particular skin colour; **colour scheme** a (deliberate) conjunction of colours, esp. in interior decoration or garden-planting; **colour separation** any of three negative images of the same subject made using green, red, and blue filters and combined to reproduce the full colour of the original; the production of such images; **colour sergeant** the senior sergeant of an infantry company; a sergeant in an honour guard who carries one of the colours; **colour supplement** a supplement containing coloured illustrations, published with a newspaper etc. otherwise printed without colour; **colour television**: reproducing nearly natural colours, not just black and white; **colour temperature** *ASTRONOMY & PHOTOGRAPHY* the temperature at which a black body would emit radiation of the same colour as the body in question; **colour therapy** a system of alternative medicine based on the use of colour, esp. in the form of coloured light, to promote physical or mental well-being; **colourtype (process)** = ***THREE-colour process***; **colour-wash** *noun & verb trans.* (paint with) coloured distemper; **colourway** a coordinated combination of colours.
▪ **colourful** *adjective* full of colour; *fig.* full of interest, excitement, force, etc., flamboyant: L19. **colourfully** *adverb* E20. **colourfulness** *noun* E20. **colourless** *adjective* (**a**) *gen.* without colour; (**b**) without distinctive character, vividness, or picturesqueness; neutral: LME. **colourlessly** *adverb* L19. **colourlessness** *noun* L17. **coloury** *adjective* (**a**) *colloq.* characterized by or rich in colour; (**b**) (of hops, coffee beans, etc.) having a colour indicative of good quality: M19.

colour /ˈkʌlə/ *verb*. Also ***color**. ME.
[ORIGIN Old French *colourer* (mod. *colorer*) from Latin *colorare*, from *color* COLOUR *noun*.]
1 *verb trans.* Give colour to; paint, stain, dye. Also *fig.*, embellish, adorn, make vivid or picturesque. ME.

Church Times Finish the picture by joining the dots . . . Colour it with crayons or felt-tips. *Globe & Mail (Toronto)* Her dances are romantically coloring the world after nature.

2 *verb trans.* Disguise; render specious or plausible; misrepresent. LME.

DICKENS The evidence has been suppressed and coloured.

†**3** *verb trans.* Lend one's name to; represent or deal with as one's own. LME–E18.
4 *verb intrans.* Turn red in the face, blush. Also foll. by *up*. E17.

D. LESSING Anna, conscious that she was colouring, met his eyes with an effort.

5 *verb intrans. gen.* Take on colour; change colour; become coloured. M17.
6 *verb trans.* Imbue with its own tone or character; condition, influence. M19.

G. M. TREVELYAN The aristocratic influence which coloured many aspects of life.

– WITH ADVERBS IN SPECIALIZED SENSES: **colour in** fill in by colouring. **colour over** cover by colouring.
▪ **colourer** *noun* E17.

colourable /ˈkʌlərəb(ə)l/ *adjective*. Also ***color-**. LME.
[ORIGIN Old French *colorable* having bright colours; in sense 2 from COLOUR *noun*: see COLOUR *noun*, -ABLE.]
1 Having an appearance of truth or right; specious, plausible. LME. ▸**b** Pretended; feigned; counterfeit. LME.
†**2** Possessed of colour; having much colour. E17–E18.
▪ **colourаˈbility** *noun* L19. **colourably** *adverb* LME.

colourant /ˈkʌlər(ə)nt/ *noun*. Also ***color-**. L19.
[ORIGIN from COLOUR *verb* + -ANT[1].]
A colouring agent.

colouration *noun* var. of COLORATION.

coloured /ˈkʌləd/ *adjective & noun*. Also ***color-**. LME.
[ORIGIN from COLOUR *verb, noun*: see -ED[1], -ED[2].]
▸ **A** *adjective*. **1** Having colour (strictly, exclusive of black or white); having been coloured. Also *fig.*, (of literary style etc.) embellished, adorned, made picturesque; imbued with a particular tone or character, conditioned, influenced. LME.

W. GASS They have some colored sheets—one lavender, one rose, one wine. C. HAYES Coloured pencils have the same graphic qualities as pastels.

coloured hearing accompaniment of the hearing of sounds with the perception of certain colours.

†**2** Made to look well; specious; feigned. LME–E17.
3 Having a specified colour or type of complexion. LME. ***cream-coloured***, ***flesh-coloured***, ***fresh-coloured***, ***mulberry-coloured***, ***pink-coloured***, ***sky-coloured***, ***tabby-coloured***, etc.
4 Having a skin of a colour other than white; wholly or partly of non-white descent; of or belonging to a black people; for the separate use of black people. (Cf. BLACK *adjective* 2b.) Now considered *offensive*. E17. ▸**b** *spec.* (usu. **C-**.) Formerly used as an official ethnic label in South Africa for people of mixed ethnic origin, including Khoisan, African, Malay, Chinese, and white. E19.

S. LONGSTREET Poor white and colored high yaller. *New Yorker* The 'colored balcony', with its separate entrance, once a regular feature of Southern theatres.

b ***Cape Coloured***: see CAPE *noun*[1].

▸ **B** *noun*. A person wholly or partly of non-white descent. Now considered *offensive*. M20.

colouring /ˈkʌlərɪŋ/ *noun*. Also ***color-**. LME.
[ORIGIN from COLOUR *verb* + -ING[1].]
1 The action of COLOUR *verb*. LME.
2 Matter which imparts colour. LME.
3 The effect of the application of colour; the style in which anything is coloured, or in which an artist employs colour. Also, a coloured drawing, a painting. E18. ▸**b** Pervading character, tone, or aspect. M18. ▸**c** Facial complexion; usual hue of the skin. M20.
c ***protective colouring***: see PROTECTIVE *adjective*.
– COMB.: **colouring book** a book of outline drawings designed to be coloured in (usu. by children).

colourist /ˈkʌlərɪst/ *noun*. Also ***color-**. L17.
[ORIGIN from COLOUR *noun* + -IST, after Italian *colorista* (whence French *coloriste*).]
A painter skilful in colouring; an adept user of colour (*lit.* & *fig.*).
▪ **colouˈristic** *adjective* of or pertaining to a colourist or artistic colouring L19.

colourize *verb* var. of COLORIZE.

-colous /ˈkʌləs/ *suffix*.
[ORIGIN from Latin *-colus* inhabiting, from *colere* inhabit: see -OUS.]
Forming adjectives with the senses 'living or growing in or on', 'frequenting', as ***calcicolous***, ***nidicolous***.

colpo- /ˈkɒlpəʊ/ *combining form*. Before a vowel **colp-**.
[ORIGIN from Greek *kolpos* womb: see -O-.]
Forming nouns (and their derivs.) with the sense 'of the vagina'.
▪ **colposcope** *noun* an instrument which can be inserted into the vagina for examination of the cervix of the womb M20. **colˈposcopy** *noun* internal examination by means of a colposcope M20. **colˈpotomy** *noun* (an instance of) surgical incision into the wall of the vagina E20.

colportage /ˈkɒlpɔːtɪdʒ/ *noun*. M19.
[ORIGIN French, from *colporter*: see COLPORTEUR, -AGE.]
The work of a colporteur; the peddling of books, newspapers, bibles, etc.

C

colporteur /ˈkɒlpɔːtə, kɒlpɔːˈtəː/ *noun*. L18.
[ORIGIN French, from *colporter* prob. alt. of *comporter* from Latin *comportare* transport, formed as COM- + *portare* carry (cf. PORTER *noun*[2]).]
A pedlar of books, newspapers, etc., *esp*. one employed by a religious society to distribute bibles and other religious tracts.

colrake *noun* var. of COLERAKE.

colsa *noun* var. of COLZA.

colt /kəʊlt/ *noun*[1]. OE.
[ORIGIN Uncertain: cf. Swedish *kult, kulter, kulting*, applied to half-grown animals and boys.]
1 Orig., a young horse or animal of the horse kind; in early biblical translations, a young camel. Now, a young male horse that has been taken from the dam but is not fully grown, *spec*. (esp. of a racehorse) that is under the age of 4 or 5. Cf. FILLY, FOAL *noun*. OE.
2 A person likened to a colt; *spec*. †(*a*) a lascivious person; (*b*) a young or inexperienced person, esp. in sports; a member of a junior team; *esp*. a cricketer during his first season; (*c*) a frisky or frolicsome person. ME.
3 The barrister who attended on a serjeant-at-law at his induction. *slang*. *obsolete* exc. *hist*. M18.
4 A short piece of weighted rope used as a weapon, *spec*. (NAUTICAL) a similar instrument used for corporal punishment. *slang*. M18.
– COMB.: **colt foal** a male foal; **colt-pixie** a mischievous sprite in the form of a ragged colt; **coltsfoot** [translating medieval Latin *pes pulli*] a plant of the composite family, *Tussilago farfara*, with yellow flowers and heart-shaped leaves; also occas., any of certain other plants resembling this (***sweet coltsfoot***: see SWEET *adjective & adverb*); **colt's tail** a cloud with a ragged edge, regarded as portending rain; **colt's tooth** (*a*) one of the first set of teeth of a horse; (*b*) youthful desires; inclination to friskiness, frolicking, or lasciviousness.
■ **colthood** *noun* M19. **coltish** *adjective* (*a*) of, pertaining to, or like a colt or colts; wild, frisky, untamed; †(*b*) lascivious, salacious: LME. **coltishly** *adverb* M16. **coltishness** *noun* M17.

Colt /kəʊlt/ *noun*[2]. M19.
[ORIGIN Samuel *Colt* (1814–62), US inventor.]
(Proprietary name for) a type of firearm, *esp*. a type of repeating pistol.

colt /kəʊlt/ *verb*. L16.
[ORIGIN from COLT *noun*[1].]
1 *verb intrans*. Frisk or run wild as a colt (usu. implying wantonness). *obsolete* exc. *dial*. L16.
†**2** *verb trans*. Make a fool of; cheat. L16–E17.
†**3** *verb trans*. Copulate with. *rare* (Shakes.). Only in E17.
4 *verb intrans*. Fall in, cave in; collapse. *dial*. L17.
5 *verb trans*. Beat with a colt (see COLT *noun*[1] 4). *slang*. M18.
■ **colting** *noun* (*a*) the action of the verb; (*b*) *slang* a beating with a colt: M19.

coltan /ˈkɒltan/ *noun*. L20.
[ORIGIN from COL(UMBITE + TAN(TALITE.]
A mineral which is a combination of columbite and tantalite and which is refined to produce tantalum.

colter *noun* see COULTER.

coluber /ˈkɒljʊbə/ *noun*. LME.
[ORIGIN Latin *coluber, -bris*.]
A snake; *spec*. a colubrid. Now only as mod. Latin genus name.

colubrid /ˈkɒljʊbrɪd/ *noun & adjective*. L19.
[ORIGIN mod. Latin *Colubridae* (see below), formed as COLUBER: see -ID[3].]
ZOOLOGY. ▸**A** *noun*. A snake of the large family Colubridae, to which most typical non-venomous snakes belong. L19.
▸ **B** *adjective*. Of, pertaining to, or designating this family. L19.

colubrine /ˈkɒljʊbrʌɪn/ *adjective*. E16.
[ORIGIN Latin *colubrinus*, formed as COLUBER: see -INE[1].]
1 Of or belonging to a snake; snakelike. E16.
2 ZOOLOGY. Colubrid; *spec*. of or pertaining to the subfamily Colubrinae of colubrid snakes with solid teeth. M19.

colugo /kəˈluːɡəʊ/ *noun*. Pl. **-os**. L18.
[ORIGIN Unknown.]
A flying lemur.

colulus /ˈkɒljʊləs/ *noun*. Pl. **-li** /-lʌɪ, -liː/. E20.
[ORIGIN mod. Latin, dim. of *colus* distaff.]
ZOOLOGY. A sclerite at the base of and between the front spinnerets in many spiders.

Columba /kəˈlʌmbə/ *noun*. L18.
[ORIGIN Latin *columba* dove, pigeon.]
(The name of) a constellation of the southern hemisphere near Canis Major; the Dove.

columbaceous /kɒl(ə)mˈbeɪʃəs/ *adjective*. L17.
[ORIGIN formed as COLUMBA + -ACEOUS.]
Of the nature of a dove or pigeon; dovelike.

Columban /kəˈlʌmb(ə)n/ *adjective & noun*. L19.
[ORIGIN from *Columba* (see below) + -AN.]
▸ **A** *adjective*. Of, pertaining to, or characteristic of the Irish missionary St Columba of Iona (*c* 521–97), or his followers. L19.
▸ **B** *noun*. A disciple of St Columba. L19.

columbarium /kɒl(ə)mˈbɛːrɪəm/ *noun*. Pl. **-ia** /-ɪə/, **-iums**. M18.
[ORIGIN Latin *columbarium*, formed as COLUMBA: see -ARIUM.]
1 A vault or building with niches for the reception of cinerary urns; a niche in such a vault etc. M18.
2 A pigeonhole; a columbary. E19.

columbary /ˈkɒl(ə)mb(ə)ri/ *noun*. M16.
[ORIGIN formed as COLUMBARIUM: see -ARY[1].]
A pigeon house, a dovecote.

columbiad /kəˈlʌmbɪad/ *noun*. L18.
[ORIGIN formed as COLUMBIAN + -AD[1].]
1 An epic of America. Chiefly as a poem title. L18.
2 A kind of heavy cast-iron cannon formerly used in the US army. E19.

Columbian /kəˈlʌmbɪən/ *adjective & noun*. M18.
[ORIGIN from mod. Latin *Columbia* poet. name for America, formed as COLUMBUS: see -AN.]
▸ **A** *adjective*. Of or pertaining to America, esp. at the time of its discovery by Christopher Columbus; *spec*. of or pertaining to the United States. M18.
▸ **B** *noun*. An American; a native or inhabitant of the United States. *obsolete* exc. *hist*. L18.

columbic /kəˈlʌmbɪk/ *adjective*. Now *rare* or *obsolete*. E19.
[ORIGIN from COLUMBIUM + -IC.]
CHEMISTRY. Of or pertaining to columbium (niobium).
columbic acid = NIOBIC *acid*.
■ **columbate** *noun* = NIOBATE E19.

columbine /ˈkɒl(ə)mbʌɪn/ *noun*[1]. ME.
[ORIGIN Old French *colombine* from medieval Latin *columbina* (*herba*) dovelike (plant), from *columba* pigeon, the flower being likened to five clustered pigeons: see -INE[1].]
Aquilegia, esp. *Aquilegia vulgaris*.

Columbine /ˈkɒl(ə)mbʌɪn/ *noun*[2]. E18.
[ORIGIN French from Italian *Colombina* use as noun of fem. of *colombino* dovelike in gentleness.]
Orig., a servant girl in *commedia dell'arte*. Now, the sweetheart of Harlequin in pantomime.

columbine /ˈkɒl(ə)mbʌɪn/ *adjective & noun*[3]. Now *rare*. LME.
[ORIGIN Old French & mod. French *columbin(e)* from Latin *columbinus* from *columba* dove: see -INE[1].]
▸ **A** *adjective*. **1** Of, pertaining to, or of the nature of a dove; dovelike. LME.
2 Dove-coloured. LME.
▸ **B** *noun*. Dove-colour. E17.

columbite /kəˈlʌmbʌɪt/ *noun*. E19.
[ORIGIN from COLUMBIUM + -ITE[1].]
MINERALOGY. The chief ore of niobium, an orthorhombic oxide of iron, manganese, and niobium (usu. with some tantalum), occurring usu. as red prismatic crystals.

columbium /kəˈlʌmbɪəm/ *noun*. Chiefly *US*. Now *rare* or *obsolete*. E19.
[ORIGIN from mod. Latin *Columbia* poet. name for America, from *Columbus* (see COLUMBUS), + -IUM.]
CHEMISTRY. = NIOBIUM (symbol Cb).

Columbus /kəˈlʌmbəs/ *noun*. L16.
[ORIGIN Christopher *Columbus* (1451–1506), Genoese explorer, discoverer of America.]
An explorer, a discoverer.

columel /ˈkɒljʊmɛl/ *noun*. *rare*. E17.
[ORIGIN Latin *columella*, dim. of *columna*: see COLUMN, -EL[2].]
A small column.

columella /kɒljʊˈmɛlə/ *noun*. Pl. **-llae** /-liː/. L16.
[ORIGIN Latin: see COLUMEL.]
A structure or organ resembling a small column; *esp*. †(*a*) the uvula; (*b*) the axis of the cochlea; (*c*) the axis of a spiral shell; (*d*) BOTANY the axis of a fruit composed of several carpels; the axis of the spore-producing body of certain plants; (*e*) ZOOLOGY one of the ossicles of the middle ear of birds, reptiles, and amphibians.
■ **columellar** *adjective* E19.

column /ˈkɒləm/ *noun*. LME.
[ORIGIN Partly from Old French *columpne* (mod. *colonne*, after Italian *colonna*), partly from its source Latin *columna* pillar.]
1 ARCHITECTURE. A long vertical, often slightly tapering, cylinder usu. surmounted by an entablature and forming part of an arcade or colonnade, or standing alone as a monument. LME. ▸**b** *fig*. A support, a prop. E17.

W. S. MAUGHAM Long halls, the roof supported by sculptured columns. A. WILSON The towering column of the Duke of York.

coupled columns. *Osiride column*.

2 A vertical division of text on a page; a vertical array of figures or other information in a table. LME. ▸**b** A part of a newspaper, sometimes more or less than a column of print, devoted (esp. regularly) to a special subject or writer. M19.

G. K. CHESTERTON Adding up a column in a ledger. **b** R. CAMPBELL Then through my weekly columns I may pour The sentiments that dowagers adore.

b ***advertisement column***, ***agony column***, ***gossip column***, etc. ***funny column***: see FUNNY *adjective*. ***personal column***: see PERSONAL *adjective*. ***social column***: see SOCIAL *adjective*. **the columns of** the contents of (a newspaper); (***our columns***, used by a newspaper itself).

3 A structure or object likened to a column (sense 1), as part of an animal body, part of a machine, etc. LME. ▸**b** BOTANY. The structure formed by the union of the style and stamens, or of staminal filaments, esp. in the orchids. E19.

TENNYSON The knotted column of his throat.

pulsed column: see PULSED *ppl adjective*. ***rectifying column***: see RECTIFY *verb* 2. ***spinal column***: see SPINAL *adjective*. ***vertebral column***: see VERTEBRAL *adjective* 2.

4 MILITARY. A narrow-fronted deep formation of troops or armoured vehicles etc. in successive lines. LME. ▸**b** NAUTICAL. A body or division of ships. E19.

transf.: R. LOWELL A mother skunk with her column of kittens.

column of ROUTE. **dodge the column** *colloq*. shirk a duty; avoid work. ***fifth column***: see FIFTH *adjective*.

5 A vertical cylindrical mass of liquid or vapour. L17.

L. VAN DER POST I spotted two more columns of smoke.

6 A party, a faction. Chiefly *US*. E20.
– COMB.: **column inch** the quantity of print occupying one inch length of column.
■ **columniform** /kəˈlʌmnɪfɔːm/ *adjective* shaped like a column E19.

columna /kəˈlʌmnə/ *noun*. *rare*. Pl. **-nae** /-niː/. L17.
[ORIGIN Latin: see COLUMN *noun*.]
1 BOTANY. = COLUMN 3b. L17.
2 ANATOMY. A column-shaped part of the body. M18.

columnal /kəˈlʌmn(ə)l/ *adjective & noun*. M18.
[ORIGIN from COLUMN + -AL[1].]
▸ **A** *adjective*. Columnar. Now *rare*. M18.
▸ **B** *noun*. ZOOLOGY. A segment or joint of the stem of a crinoid. L19.

columnar /kəˈlʌmnə/ *adjective*. E18.
[ORIGIN Late Latin *columnaris*, from *columna* COLUMN: see -AR[1].]
1 Of the nature or form of a column or columns. E18.
2 Written or printed in columns. M19.
3 Characterized by or raised on columns. M19.
■ Also †**columnary** *adjective* L16–E18.

columnated /ˈkɒl(ə)mneɪtɪd/ *adjective*. Also **-iated** /-ɪeɪtɪd/. E18.
[ORIGIN from Latin *columnatus*, from *columna* COLUMN, + -ED[1]. Form with *-i-* after COLUMNIATION.]
= COLUMNED 1.

columned /ˈkɒl(ə)md/ *adjective*. L18.
[ORIGIN from COLUMN *noun* + -ED[2].]
1 Having columns; supported on columns. L18.
2 Divided into columns. E19.
3 Like a column, columnar. M19.

columniated *adjective* see COLUMNATED.

columniation /kəlʌmnɪˈeɪʃ(ə)n/ *noun*. M17.
[ORIGIN from Latin *columnatio(n-)*, from *columna* COLUMN, after INTERCOLUMNIATION.]
ARCHITECTURE. The employment of columns; the arrangement of columns.

columnist /ˈkɒl(ə)m(n)ɪst/ *noun*. E20.
[ORIGIN from COLUMN + -IST.]
A journalist who regularly contributes to a newspaper a column, esp. of miscellaneous comment on people and events.

colure /kəˈljʊə/ *noun*. LME.
[ORIGIN Late Latin *coluri* pl. from Greek *kolourai* (sc. *grammai* lines) pl. of *kolouros* truncated, from *kolos* docked + *oura* tail (so called because their lower part is permanently cut off from view).]
ASTRONOMY. Either of the two great circles passing through the celestial poles and intersecting the ecliptic at either the equinoxes or the solstices.

coly /ˈkəʊli/ *noun*. M19.
[ORIGIN from mod. Latin *Colius* from Greek *kolios* a kind of woodpecker.]
= ***mousebird*** s.v. MOUSE *noun*.

colza /ˈkɒlzə/ *noun*. Also **colsa**. E18.
[ORIGIN French (Walloon) *kolza*, earlier *colzat* from Low German *kōlsāt*, Dutch *koolzaad*, from *kool* COLE *noun*[1] + *zaad* SEED *noun*.]
Rape, rapeseed; = COLESEED 2.

COM *abbreviation*.
Computer output on microfilm or microfiche.

com- /kɒm, *unstressed* kəm/ *prefix*.
Repr. Latin *com-* (= *cum* preposition 'with') in senses 'with', 'together', 'jointly'; also 'completely', and hence *intensive*. Used before *b*, *p*, *m*, and a few words beginning with vowels or *f*; assim. to COL- before *l*, COR- before *r*; reduced to CO- before vowels generally, *h*, and *gn*; as CON- before other consonants. As a living prefix chiefly in form CO-.

coma /ˈkəʊmə/ *noun*[1]. Pl. **-mae** /-miː/. E17.
[ORIGIN Latin from Greek *komē* hair of the head.]
1 BOTANY. The top of a plant; *esp*. a terminal tuft of bracts or leaves; a leafy crown of branches; a tuft of silky hairs at the end of some seeds. E17.
2 ASTRONOMY. The diffuse hazy region surrounding the nucleus of a comet. M18.

3 An optical aberration causing the image of an off-axis point to be flared, like a comet with a diverging tail; the flared image itself. **M19.**
■ **co'matic** *adjective* **E20.**

coma /ˈkəʊmə/ *noun*². **M17.**
[ORIGIN mod. Latin from Greek *kōma*, *-mat-*, rel. to *koitē* bed, *keisthai* lie down.]
MEDICINE. A prolonged state of unconsciousness from which the patient cannot be roused. Formerly also, an unnatural heavy sleep.
– COMB.: **coma vigil** †(*a*) a prolonged state of drowsiness in which the patient nevertheless cannot sleep; (*b*) a state in typhus fever etc. in which the patient lies unconscious but with eyes wide open.

Coma Berenices /ˌkəʊmə bɛrɪˈnʌɪsiːz/ *noun phr.* **M17.**
[ORIGIN Latin, formed as COMA *noun*¹ + *Berenice* (*c* 273–221 BC), wife of Ptolemy III of Egypt; her hair was said to have been stolen from the temple of Venus and afterwards placed in the heavens.]
(The name of) an inconspicuous constellation of the northern hemisphere, between Boötes and Virgo; = BERENICE'S HAIR.

comae *noun* pl. of COMA *noun*².

Comanche /kəˈmantʃi/ *noun & adjective.* **E19.**
[ORIGIN Spanish from Shoshonean.]
▸ **A** *noun.* Pl. **-s**, same.
1 A member of a Shoshonean people of Texas and Oklahoma. **E19.**
2 The language of this people. **M19.**
▸ **B** *attrib.* or as *adjective.* Of or pertaining to the Comanches or their language. **E19.**

co-mate /ˈkəʊmeɪt, kəʊˈmeɪt/ *noun.* **L16.**
[ORIGIN from CO- + MATE *noun*².]
A companion, a mate.

comatose /ˈkəʊmətəʊs/ *adjective.* **L17.**
[ORIGIN from Greek *kōmat-* (see COMA *noun*¹) + -OSE¹.]
1 In a coma; of the nature of coma. **L17.**
2 *transf.* Drowsy, lethargic. **E19.**
■ Also †**comatous** *adjective* **M17–L18.**

comb /kəʊm/ *noun*¹. See also KAME.
[ORIGIN Old English *camb*, *comb* = Old Saxon *camb* (Dutch *kam*), Old High German *kamb* (German *Kamm*), Old Norse *kambr*, from Germanic.]
▸ **I 1** A toothed strip of bone, horn, metal, plastic, etc., for untangling, arranging, or keeping in place the hair. See also CURRY COMB *noun*, ***horse-comb*** s.v. HORSE *noun*. **OE.**
fine-tooth comb: see FINE *adjective*. ***redding comb***: see REDD *verb*². ***Spanish comb***: see SPANISH *adjective*. ***toothcomb***: see TOOTH *noun*.
2 Something resembling this in function, structure, etc., as (*a*) a toothed instrument for separating and dressing textile fibres; (*b*) a toothed structure for graining painted work; (*c*) the pair of abdominal appendages in a scorpion; an analogous structure in other animals; (*d*) a row of brass points for collecting the electricity in an electrostatic generator; (*e*) *Austral. & NZ* the lower, fixed cutting piece of a sheep-shearing machine. **ME.**
3 The action or an act of combing. **E20.**
▸ **II 4** The red fleshy crest on the head of the domestic fowl, esp. the male; so called from its serrated form (cf. COCKSCOMB 1); an analogous growth in other birds. **OE.**
cut the comb of humiliate, make less conceited. ***white comb***: see WHITE *adjective*.
5 Something resembling a cock's comb in position or appearance, as (*a*) the crest of a helmet; the upright blade on a morion; (*b*) (now *dial.*) the crest or top of a bank, hill, etc.; the ridge formed between ruts; (*c*) the upper corner of a gun stock, against which the cheek is placed in firing; (*d*) the crest of a wave. **OE.**
▸ **III** (Not found in the cognates.)
6 = HONEYCOMB *noun* 1 (earlier). **ME.**
virgin comb: see VIRGIN *adjective*.
– COMB.: **comb-back** a high-backed Windsor chair with a straight top rail; **comb-brush** (*a*) a brush to clean combs; †(*b*) a lady's maid; **comb jelly** *ZOOLOGY* a ctenophore; **comb-over** a strip of hair combed over a bald patch on a man's head in an attempt to conceal it; ***comb-tailed paradise fish***: see PARADISE *noun*.
■ **combed** *adjective* (esp. of a cock) having a comb **M16.** **combless** *adjective* without a comb or crest **L16.** **comblike** *adjective* resembling (that of) a comb **E17.** **comby** *adjective* (*a*) full of holes like a honeycomb; (*b*) *GEOLOGY* having layers with parallel crystals like the teeth of a comb: **L18.**

comb /kəʊm/ *noun*². Now chiefly *dial.* Also **come** /kəʊm, kuːm/, **coomb** /kuːm/. **LME.**
[ORIGIN Prob. from Germanic base repr. also by German *Keim*.]
The radicle of the grain, which develops during malting and is then dried up by roasting and separated.

comb *noun*³, *noun*⁴ vars. of COOMB *noun*¹, COMBE.

comb /kəʊm/ *verb.* **LME.**
[ORIGIN from COMB *noun*¹, repl. KEMB *verb*.]
1 *verb trans.* **a** Draw a comb through (the hair); curry (a horse). **LME.** ▸**b** Dress (wool, flax, etc.) with a comb, so as to separate and arrange the fibres. **L16.** ▸**c** Scrape or rake with an action like that of a comb. **M17.**

> **c** R. HUGHES The wind had combed up some quite hearty waves.

comb a person's head with a three-legged stool & vars. (now *dial.*), give a person a thrashing. **comb out** comb through (the hair) after setting and drying it, or to remove knots; *fig.* search or bombard systematically; single out for removal (orig. persons fit for military service).
2 *verb intrans.* Of a wave: roll over and break with a foamy crest. Orig. *US.* **E19.**

> K. KESEY The swells at the mouth of the jetty were combing higher than the boat.

3 *verb trans.* Search minutely and systematically. (Earlier in BEACHCOMBING.) *colloq.* **E20.**

> H. INNES I combed the 'Situations Vacant' columns of the papers. B. MALAMUD He combed the crowded streets, searching for Susskind.

4 *verb trans.* Of a ship: turn into line with (the track of a torpedo) to avoid being hit. **M20.**
– COMB.: **comb-out** an act of combing something out (*lit. & fig.*).

combat /ˈkɒmbat, ˈkʌm-, -ət/ *noun.* **M16.**
[ORIGIN French, from *combattre* from late Latin *combattere*, formed as COM- + var. of *batuere* fight.]
1 A fight or armed encounter between two persons, parties, animals, etc.; a duel. More explicitly ***single combat***. **M16.**
judicial combat: see JUDICIAL *adjective*. ***judiciary combat***: see JUDICIARY *adjective* 3. **trial by combat** *hist.* legal decision of a dispute by single combat.
2 *gen.* A fight, fighting, between opposing forces (usu. on a smaller scale than (a) battle); a conflict, strife. **L16.**

> B. JOWETT Is courage only a combat against fear and pain? H. WOUK Her life passed in combat with an incompetent world. *attrib.*: F. FITZGERALD These officers were professional soldiers. Most of them had combat experience.

UNARMED ***combat***.
– COMB.: **combat boots**, **combat jacket**: (of a type) worn by soldiers in actual combat; **combat fatigue** mental illness due to stress in wartime combat (= ***battle fatigue***); ***combat jacket***: see ***combat boots*** above; **combat trousers** loose trousers with large patch pockets halfway down each leg, typically made of hard-wearing cotton.

combat /ˈkɒmbat, ˈkʌ-, -ət/ *verb.* **M16.**
[ORIGIN French *combattre*: see COMBAT *noun*.]
1 *verb intrans.* Fight or do battle (*with*, *against*), esp. in single combat. **M16.**
2 *verb trans.* Fight with, oppose in armed conflict. Now chiefly *fig.* **L16.**

> A. HAILEY Details of the types of offences involved and methods being used to combat them.

■ **combater** *noun* (*rare*) **L16.**

combatant /ˈkɒmbət(ə)nt, ˈkʌm-/ *adjective & noun.* In sense A.1 freq. **-tt-**. **LME.**
[ORIGIN Old French, pres. pple of *combattre*: see COMBAT *noun*, -ANT¹.]
▸ **A** *adjective.* **1** *HERALDRY.* Poised for combat; *esp.* rampant with the forepaws raised as if in fight (usu. said of two lions facing each other). **LME.**
2 *gen.* Fighting, ready to fight; *esp.* taking part in active fighting during a war (opp. ***non-combatant***). **M17.**
▸ **B** *noun.* A participant in an armed contest, in early use esp. in single combat; a participant in active fighting during a war (opp. ***non-combatant***); *gen.* a contender, an opponent. **L15.**

combative /ˈkɒmbətɪv, ˈkʌm-/ *adjective.* **M19.**
[ORIGIN from COMBAT *verb* + -IVE.]
Having a propensity for combat, pugnacious.
■ **combatively** *adverb* **M19.** **combativeness** *noun* (orig. *PHRENOLOGY*) **E19.** **combativity** /-ˈtɪvɪti/ *noun* **E20.**

combattant *adjective* see COMBATANT.

combe /kuːm/ *noun.* Also **comb**, **coomb**.
[ORIGIN Old English *cum(b)* from British: cf. CWM.]
A deep hollow or valley, esp. on the side of a hill; a valley running up from the sea.
– NOTE: Not found in Old English or Middle English literature, but occurring from early times in charters in place names belonging to the south of England, many of which survive, e.g. *Batscombe*, *Southcombe*. Its present general use goes back to **L16.**

comber /ˈkəʊmə/ *noun*¹. **ME.**
[ORIGIN from COMB *verb* + -ER¹.]
1 A person who or machine which combs wool, cotton, etc. **ME.**
2 A long curling wave, a breaker. Cf. BEACHCOMBER 2. **M19.**
3 A person who searches minutely and systematically. Earliest & chiefly in BEACHCOMBER 1. **M19.**

comber /ˈkɒmbə/ *noun*². **M18.**
[ORIGIN Unknown.]
A fish of the sea perch family, *Serranus cabrilla*. Cf. GAPER 3.

combi /ˈkɒmbi/ *noun. colloq.* Pl. **-ies**, (sense 2) **-is**. **L19.**
[ORIGIN Abbreviation: cf. COMBS.]
1 *sing.* & (usu.) in *pl.* A combination garment, combinations. **L19.**
2 A vehicle, machine, etc. with two or more functions. **L20.**

combinable /kəmˈbʌɪnəb(ə)l/ *adjective.* **M18.**
[ORIGIN from COMBINE *verb*¹ + -ABLE.]
Able to be combined.
■ **combina'bility** *noun* **E20.**

combinate /ˈkɒmbɪnət/ *adjective. rare.* **L16.**
[ORIGIN Late Latin *combinatus* pa. pple of *combinare* COMBINE *verb*¹: see -ATE².]
1 Combined. **L16.**
†**2** Betrothed, bound by oath. Cf. COMBINE *verb*¹ 2. *rare* (Shakes.). Only in **E17.**

combination /kɒmbɪˈneɪʃ(ə)n/ *noun.* **LME.**
[ORIGIN Old French (mod. *combinaison*) or Latin *combinatio(n-)*, from *combinat-* pa. ppl stem of *combinare*: see COMBINE *verb*¹, -ATION.]
1 The action of combining two or more things; combined state. **LME.** ▸**b** A combined set or series of things; a compound thing, *esp.* a compound word or taxonomic name. **M16.**

> E. O'NEILL Consider these two inventions of mine in combination. C. FRANCIS Bad visibility and a sudden squall are a dangerous combination.

2 The association of people for a common (formerly usu. illegal) purpose; an association of people so formed. **LME.** ▸†**b** Agreement, compact. *rare* (Shakes.). Only in **E17.** ▸**c** A small instrumental band. Cf. COMBO. **E20.**
3 **a** *MATH.* A selection of a given number of elements from a larger number of elements, without regard to the order of the elements chosen. Cf. PERMUTATION. **L17.** ▸**b** A particular sequence of letters or numbers chosen in setting a combination lock (see below); the lock itself. **M19.** ▸**c** *CHESS.* A sequence of forcing moves with a specific goal. **L19.**
4 *CHEMISTRY.* The union of substances to form a compound (whose properties differ from those of the original substances); the state of being united in a compound; a compound so formed. **M18.**
5 In *pl.* A single undergarment for the body and legs (= ***combination garment*** below). **L19.**
6 A motorcycle with sidecar attached. **E20.**
– COMB.: **combination garment** = sense 5 above; **combination laws** laws (repealed in 1824) directed against workpeople combining to obtain an increase in wages etc.; **combination lock** a lock (as of a safe or strongroom) controlled by a dial or dials, in which letters or numbers have to be arranged in a particular sequence to release the lock; **combination room** at Cambridge University, a common room, *esp.* a senior common room (***senior combination room***: see SENIOR *adjective*); **combination therapy** the treatment of a disease, esp. cancer or AIDS, by giving the patient two or more drugs (or other therapeutic agents) simultaneously; **combination tone** a note produced by the combined sounding of two other notes, a resultant tone.
■ **combinational** *adjective* **L17.**

combinative /ˈkɒmbɪnətɪv/ *adjective.* **M19.**
[ORIGIN from COMBINATION + -IVE: see -ATIVE.]
1 Able or tending to combine; relating to combination. **M19.**
2 *PHILOLOGY.* Of a sound change: occurring under the influence of adjoining sounds. Opp. ISOLATIVE 2. **L19.**
3 *CHESS.* Using combinations. **E20.**

combinatorial /ˌkɒmbɪnəˈtɔːrɪəl/ *adjective.* **E19.**
[ORIGIN formed as COMBINATORY + -AL¹.]
Of or pertaining to mathematical combinations. Esp. in ***combinatorial analysis***.
■ ˌ**combinatori'ality** *noun* **M20.** **combinatorially** *adverb* **M20.**

combinatory /ˈkɒmbɪnət(ə)ri, kɒmbɪˈneɪt(ə)ri/ *adjective.* **M17.**
[ORIGIN from COMBINATION + -ORY¹.]
1 = COMBINATIVE 1. **M17.**
2 *LOGIC.* Designating or pertaining to a branch of symbolic logic concerned esp. with substitution and elimination of variables. **E20.**
■ **combinatorics** /-ˈtɒrɪks/ *noun* the study of possible combinations or configurations **M20.**

combine /ˈkɒmbʌɪn/ *noun.* **E17.**
[ORIGIN from COMBINE *verb*¹.]
†**1** A conspiracy, a plot. Only in **E17.**
2 An alliance of people or organizations to further their commercial, political, etc., ends, freq. by underhand means. **L19.**
3 In full ***combine harvester***. A combined reaping and threshing machine. **E20.**

combine /kəmˈbʌɪn/ *verb*¹. **LME.**
[ORIGIN Old French *combiner* or late Latin *combinare* join two by two, formed as COM- + *bini* two at a time.]
1 *verb trans.* Unite, join together; associate (persons etc.) in a joint action, feeling, etc. **LME.** ▸**b** Cause to coalesce or form one body; *CHEMISTRY* cause to enter into combination. **L18.** ▸**c** Possess or show (esp. disparate qualities or features) at the same time. **E19.**

> JAS. MILL A sense of common danger might . . combine them in operations of defence. **c** W. S. MAUGHAM She combined great good nature with a proper degree of toughness.

†**2** *verb trans.* Bind by oath. Cf. COMBINATE 2. *rare* (Shakes.). Only in **E17.**

> SHAKES. *Meas. for M.* For my poor self, I am combined by a sacred vow, and shall be absent.

3 *verb intrans.* Unite together for a common purpose; form an association, esp. for some economic, social, or political objective. **E17.**

> G. B. SHAW When wolves combine to kill a horse.

C

4 *verb intrans.* Come together in one body, coalesce; CHEMISTRY unite to form a compound, enter into combination. E18.

combining weight CHEMISTRY the equivalent of an element.

■ †**combinement** *noun* = COMBINATION *noun* E17–E19. **combiner** *noun* †(*a*) a conspirator; (*b*) a person who or thing which combines: E16.

combine /ˈkɒmbʌɪn/ *verb*² *trans.* E20.
[ORIGIN from COMBINE *noun* 3.]
Harvest with a combine harvester.

combined /kəmˈbʌɪnd/ *adjective.* LME.
[ORIGIN from COMBINE *verb*¹ + -ED¹.]
1 United or coupled; resulting from a combination. LME.

A. KNOX When a collective and combined effect is to be produced. B. SPOCK Inoculations against these three diseases can be given together in a combined form. R. K. NARAYAN The hall was a passage, . . drawing-room, study, everything combined.

combined pill an oral contraceptive containing both an oestrogen and a progestogen.

2 Performed by agents acting in concert. E17.

LD MACAULAY One vigorous and combined struggle for emancipation.

combined operation: in which several branches of the armed forces (or some other organization) cooperate.

■ **combinedly** /-nɪd-/ *adverb* M17. **combinedness** /-nɪd-/ *noun* M19.

combing /ˈkəʊmɪŋ/ *noun.* M16.
[ORIGIN from COMB *verb* + -ING¹.]
1 The action of COMB *verb.* M16.
BEACHCOMBING.
2 In *pl.* Hairs combed off. M17.
– COMB.: **combing wool** long-stapled wool suitable for combing and spinning into worsted.

combining /kəmˈbʌɪnɪŋ/ *noun.* M16.
[ORIGIN from COMBINE *verb*¹ + -ING¹.]
The action of COMBINE *verb*¹. Also (*rare*), an instance of combining.
– COMB.: **combining form** a form of a word used (only) in compounds, as *Indo-* repr. *Indian* in *Indo-European.*

comble /kɔ̃ːbl/ *noun.* Pl. pronounced same. M19.
[ORIGIN French from Latin *cumulus* heap.]
A culminating point, a crowning touch.

combo /ˈkɒmbəʊ/ *noun. slang.* Pl. **-os.** L19.
[ORIGIN from COMB(INATION + -O.]
1 A white man who lives with an Aboriginal woman. *Austral.* L19.
2 Combination, partnership (in various senses). Chiefly *N. Amer.* E20.
3 A small instrumental band, esp. of jazz musicians. Cf. COMBINATION 2C. E20.

comboloio /kɒmbəˈləʊjəʊ, kɒmvəˈlɔɪjəʊ/ *noun.* Pl. **-os.** E19.
[ORIGIN mod. Greek *kompoloi.*]
A Muslim rosary of ninety-nine beads.

combretaceous /kɒmbrɪˈteɪʃəs/ *adjective.* M19.
[ORIGIN from mod. Latin *Combretaceae*, from genus name *Combretum*: see COMBRETUM, -ACEOUS.]
Of or pertaining to the Combretaceae, a family of tropical trees and shrubs allied to the myrtles.

combretum /kɒmˈbriːtəm/ *noun.* E19.
[ORIGIN mod. Latin from Latin *combretum* (Pliny), an unidentified plant.]
A tree or (often climbing or trailing) shrub of the genus *Combretum*, of the family Combretaceae (see COMBRETACEOUS).

combs /kɒmz/ *noun pl. colloq.* Also **coms.** M20.
[ORIGIN Abbreviation: cf. COMBI.]
A combination garment, combinations.

comburent /kəmˈbjʊər(ə)nt/ *adjective & noun. rare.* Also **-ant.** L16.
[ORIGIN Latin *comburent-* pres. ppl stem of *comburere* burn up: see -ENT.]
► **A** *adjective.* Burning; causing combustion. L16.
► **B** *noun.* A substance that causes combustion. M19.

comburgess /kɒmˈbəːdʒɪs/ *noun.* LME.
[ORIGIN from COM- + BURGESS *noun*, after medieval Latin *comburgensis.*]
hist. **1** A fellow citizen or freeman of a borough; a fellow burgess. LME.
2 In certain English boroughs, up to 1835: any of the municipal magistrates chosen by and from among their fellow burgesses, and associated with the alderman. M17.

combust /kəmˈbʌst/ *adjective.* LME.
[ORIGIN Latin *combustus* pa. pple of *comburere* burn up: cf. Old French *combust.*]
†**1** Burnt; *spec.* acted on by fire, calcined. LME–E19.
2 ASTROLOGY. Of planets in or near conjunction: so near the sun (*spec.* within 8° 30′) as to have their influence destroyed by it. LME.

combust /kəmˈbʌst/ *verb.* L15.
[ORIGIN from (the same root as) COMBUST *adjective.*]
1 *verb trans.* Now chiefly SCIENCE. Subject to combustion; *spec.* (*arch.*) calcine. L15.
2 *verb intrans.* Chiefly SCIENCE. Undergo combustion. M20.
■ **combustor** *noun* M20.

combustible /kəmˈbʌstɪb(ə)l/ *adjective & noun.* E16.
[ORIGIN Old French & mod. French, or medieval Latin *combustibilis*, from *combust-*: see COMBUSTION, -IBLE. Cf. earlier INCOMBUSTIBLE.]
► **A** *adjective.* **1** Able to be consumed by fire, suitable for burning. E16.
2 *fig.* Easily kindled to violence or passion. M17.
► **B** *noun.* A combustible substance. L17.
■ **combustiˈbility** *noun* L15. **combustibleness** *noun* (*rare*) M17. **combustibly** *adverb* (*rare*) L16.

combustion /kəmˈbʌstʃ(ə)n/ *noun.* LME.
[ORIGIN Old French & mod. French, or late Latin *combustio(n-)*, from *combust-*, pa. ppl stem of *comburere* burn up.]
1 Consumption or destruction by fire. LME.
2 CHEMISTRY. Chemical change, *spec.* oxidation, marked by the production of heat and light. Also, a process of slow oxidation not accompanied by light, as in the animal body, in the decomposition of organic matter, etc. LME.
internal-combustion engine: see INTERNAL *adjective.* ***spontaneous combustion***: see SPONTANEOUS *adjective* 3.
†**3** MEDICINE. A burn; inflammation. LME–M17.
†**4** ASTROLOGY. Obscuration by proximity to the sun (see COMBUST *adjective* 2). LME–M18.
5 *fig.* Violent excitement or commotion. Now *rare.* L16.

MALCOLM X This is the situation which permitted Negro combustion to slowly build up to the revolution-point.

– COMB.: **combustion chamber** a space in which combustion takes place, as of gases in a boiler furnace or fuel in an internal-combustion engine; **combustion tube** a heat-resistant tube in which organic compounds are burnt (used in quantitative analysis).
■ †**combustious** *adjective* combustible; marked by combustion; *fig.* raging, turbulent: L16–E19.

combustive /kəmˈbʌstɪv/ *adjective.* L16.
[ORIGIN from Latin *combust-* (see COMBUSTION) + -IVE.]
†**1** MEDICINE. Pertaining to a boil (cf. COMBUSTION *noun* 3). Only in L16.
2 †**a** Having the quality of causing combustion. M17–E19.
▸**b** Pertaining to or marked by combustion. M19.

come /kʌm/ *noun*¹.
[ORIGIN Old English *cyme* from Germanic, from base of COME *verb*; assim. to the verb in Middle English. Later from the verb.]
†**1** Approach, arrival, coming. OE–LME.
2 ***come-and-go***, passage to and fro. L18.
3 A flow or flood *of* water. M19.
4 Semen; sexual fluid. *slang.* M20.

come *noun*² var. of COMB *noun*².

come /kʌm/ *verb.* Pa. t. **came** /keɪm/; pa. pple **come.**
[ORIGIN Old English *cuman* = Old Frisian *kuma*, Old Saxon *cuman* (Dutch *komen*), Old High German *queman*, *coman* (German *kommen*), Old Norse *koma*, Gothic *qiman*, from Germanic.]
gen. An elementary intrans. verb of motion expressing movement towards the speaker or a point where he or she mentally places himself or herself, towards the person spoken to, or towards the person spoken of. Opp. ***go.***
► **I** *verb intrans.* Of (actual or attributed) spatial motion.
1 Move towards one; *esp.* reach one thus; arrive. (Foll. by *to do*, *and do*, verbal noun in A *preposition*¹ 8, pple in -ING².) OE.

MILTON He at their invoking came. DICKENS When will you come to see me? TENNYSON I never came a-begging for myself. OED Come and see us. J. FOWLES If someone came looking for them.

2 Of an inanimate thing or involuntary agent: move or be brought hither, or *to* a specified place. (Following constructions as sense 1.) ME.

J. CONRAD The scented air of the garden came to us.

3 Be reached, pass *into* view, as a result of a person's actual or notional advance; take a specified position in relation to something else. ME.

W. STUBBS Beneath these comes the free class of labourers.

4 Reach or extend without actual motion (as far as or *to* a specified point or level). LME.

R. H. MOTTRAM The bed came so far down the little room.

► **II** *verb intrans.* With the idea of movement subordinated.
5 Of an event, a fate, etc.: happen *to* a person or thing. OE.
6 Pass into the possession of a person etc. (Foll. by *to.*) ME.
▸**b** Of a thing: be normally available or on sale (*in* a size, colour, etc., or *with* certain features etc.). M20.
easy come, easy go.
7 Be perceived or thought. (Foll. by *into, to.*) ME. ▸**b** Take shape in one's imagination or mind; issue as speech. M18.

TENNYSON There came a sound. **b** G. GREENE Trying to write a book that simply would not come.

8 Be derived, emanate, (*from*); be the result or descendant *of.* ME.

V. WOOLF That's what comes of putting things off.

9 Pass or be brought *into* or *to* a situation or state. E16.

C. HILL Laud had come into favour at court.

come into contact, come into fashion, come into play, come into prominence, etc.
10 Of butter: form. Of a liquid: solidify, coagulate. M17.

► **III** *verb intrans.* With an idea of time or succession involved.
11 **a** Foll. by *to, to do*: reach in the course of orderly treatment. ME. ▸**b** Foll. by *to*: reach, as an end or result. L15.

a DEFOE When I come to consider that part. **b** V. WOOLF How difficult to come to any conclusion!

12 Arrive or occur in due course. ME. ▸**b** With following future date (*colloq.*) or period of time (*dial.*): when that date comes, when that period has elapsed. ME.

SWIFT The day came for my departure. G. GREENE After the steak-and-kidney pie came a treacle tart. **b** T. COLLINS He was married, three years ago come Boxing Day.

13 Happen, come about. ME.

COVERDALE 1 *Sam.* 1:4 Whan it came vpon a daye that Elcana offred.

14 Foll. by *to, to do*: attain or be brought to (a specified state) by events or development. ME.

E. HEMINGWAY Later he had come to like it. I. MURDOCH It came to rest.

15 With compl.: become, get to be (in a specified condition); turn out by experience to be. ME.

DICKENS The brown-paper parcel had 'come untied'.

16 Reach orgasm. Also foll. by *off. slang.* E17.
► **IV** *verb trans.* **17** Traverse (a route, a distance). E17.
18 Approach (a specified age) as the next birthday. Chiefly as ***coming*** pres. pple. L17.
19 Play (a dodge, a trick); behave as. (Foll. by *over* the person taken in.) L18.

J. CARY She apologised for coming the don.

20 Achieve; succeed in doing. Chiefly as ***come it.*** *US & dial.* E19.
► **V** *spec.* uses of parts of the verb.
21 In *imper.* ▸**a** An invitation or encouragement to do something, usu. with the speaker. OE. ▸**b** An exclam. expressing mild protest, remonstrance, or impatience at someone. ME.
22 ***coming*** pres. pple: a response to a call, 'I am coming.' E18.
– PHRASES: (A selection of cross-refs. only is included.) **as — as they come** *colloq.*: supremely —. ***come a cropper***: see CROPPER *noun*². ***come a gutser***: see GUTSER *noun.* ***come a long way***: see WAY *noun.* **come and go** (*a*) come to a place and depart again; (*b*) be first present and then absent; (of time) arrive and pass. ***come a purler***: see PURLER 1. ***come a stumer***: see STUMER 1b. ***come clean***: see CLEAN *adjective.* ***come easy to***: see EASY *adverb* 1. ***come home (to)***: see HOME *adverb.* ***come home to roost***: see ROOST *noun*¹. ***come home with the milk***: see MILK *noun.* ***come in one's way***: see WAY *noun.* **come into one's head** occur to one. ***come into question***: see QUESTION *noun.* ***come into the world***: see WORLD *noun.* **come it over** *colloq.* seek to impose on or to impress deceptively. **come it strong** *slang* go to excessive lengths, use exaggeration. ***come naturally to***: see NATURALLY 1. ***come of age***: see AGE *noun* 2. **come off it** *colloq.* stop talking or acting like that; stop trying to fool the hearer; (usu. in *imper.*). **come one's way** become available or accessible to one; happen to one. ***come one's ways***: see WAY *noun.* ***come on strong, come out strong***: see STRONG *adverb.* ***come out in the wash***: see WASH *noun.* ***come rain or shine***: see RAIN *noun*¹. ***come short***: see SHORT *adverb.* ***come short home***: see HOME *adverb.* ***come tardy off***: see TARDY *adverb.* **come the old soldier over** *slang* seek to impose on (someone), esp. on grounds of greater experience or age. ***come the raw prawn***: see PRAWN *noun.* ***come the* Rothschild.** **come to a bad end** meet with ruin or disgrace. **come to an end** terminate, end. **come to a point** taper. **come to think of it** *colloq.* when one considers; on reflection. ***come true***: see TRUE *adjective, noun, & adverb.* ***come unstuck***: see UNSTICK *verb.* **come what may** whatever may happen. ***everything coming one's way***: see WAY *noun.* ***have another think coming***: see THINK *noun.* **have it coming to one** *colloq.* have one's just deserts coming. ***how come?***: see HOW *adverb.* ***kingdom come***: see KINGDOM *noun* 4. ***let 'em all come***: see LET *verb*¹. ***not come to much***: see MUCH. ***see a person coming***: see SEE *verb.* ***see it coming***: see SEE *verb.* ***shape of things to come***: see SHAPE *noun*¹. ***take things as they come***: see TAKE *verb.* ***the world to come***: see WORLD *noun.* **to come** (*a*) *pred.* in the future; (*b*) *postpositive* future; (*c*) *absol.* the future. ***when a person's ship comes home, when a person's ship comes in***: see SHIP *noun* 1.
– WITH ADVERBS IN SPECIALIZED SENSES: (See also Phrases above.) **come about** (*a*) happen, come to pass; (*b*) = ***come round*** (a) below; (*c*) (now *rare* or *obsolete*) (of the wind) = ***come round*** (d) below; (of a boat) change direction. **come abroad** *arch.* come out from seclusion, appear. ***come across***: see ACROSS *adverb* 2. **come again** (*a*) return; (*b*) recover from faintness etc.; (*c*) (as *interrog. imper.*) what did you say?; (*d*) (of a racehorse) regain speed. **come along** (*a*) move onward (toward or with the speaker); freq. in *imper.* (*colloq.*), make haste or an effort; (*b*) make progress; (*c*) arrive, turn up. **come amiss** happen out of order; be unacceptable; (usu. in neg.). **come apart** fall into pieces (***come apart at the seams***: see SEAM *noun*¹). **come away** (*a*) (of a plant) grow rapidly; (*b*) become detached; (*c*) be left *with* an impression, feeling, etc. **come back** (*a*) return, esp. to memory, or to a former state of popularity; (*b*) regain consciousness; (*c*) *N. Amer.* retort, retaliate; (*d*) (of an athlete) regain form, or the initiative in an event. **come by** pass by. **come down** (*a*) come to a place regarded as lower; *spec.* fall, (of an aircraft) land; ***come down to earth*** (colloq.), return to reality; (*b*) lose social status; (*c*) become lower in cost or value; (*d*) ***come down on, come down upon***: attack suddenly or severely; make a heavy call on; punish, reprimand; (*e*) survive from an earlier time, be handed down; (*f*) *colloq.* pay out, give money, (foll. by *with* money etc.); (*g*) *Austral., NZ, & S. Afr.* (of a river) flow in flood; (*h*) ***come down to***: be basically a matter of; amount to, mean in essence; ***come down to it***, get to

basic principles; (*i*) become ill (*with*); (*j*) decide (*in favour of* etc.); (*k*) end a period of residence in a university. **come forward** approach the front; offer oneself for a task, post, etc.; make advances (*lit. & fig.*). **come in** (*a*) enter a house or a room; (*b*) come into use; become fashionable or seasonable; (*c*) invade, occupy; become a partner in a company; ***come in on***, join (an enterprise); †(*d*) ***come in unto***, have sexual intercourse with; †(*e*) submit (*to* an adversary); (*f*) (of a time or a season) begin; †(*g*) ***come in with***, meet, fall in with; (*h*) be brought or given in; be received as income; (*i*) enter into a narrative, list, etc.; find a place, esp. with reference to manner or position; ***where a person comes in***, what his or her role is, how his or her interests are advanced, (usu. in *interrog.*); ***where a person came in*** (colloq.), back where he or she started or at a stage reached previously; ***come in nowhere***: see NOWHERE *adverb* 3; †(*j*) FENCING get within the opponent's guard; (*k*) arrive, reach a destination; take a specified place in a race; (*l*) ***come in for***: receive, esp. incidentally; attract (criticism etc.); ***come in for it*** (colloq.), incur punishment or a rebuke; (*m*) come to power, be elected; (*n*) *dial. & US* (of a cow) calve; (*o*) CRICKET begin an innings; (*p*) (of the tide) advance; (*q*) be (useful etc.) as something to have available; (*r*) ***come in on***, ***come in upon***, enter one's thoughts; (*s*) begin radio transmission; start speaking, in a discussion. ***come near***: see NEAR *adverb*². **come off** (*a*) come away from, leave (esp. a port or mooring); (*b*) emerge from a contest etc. in a specified manner or state; (***come off second best***: see SECOND BEST *adjective & adverb*, ***come off with flying colours***: see COLOUR *noun*); †(*c*) (of a thing) turn out, come to a result; (*d*) take place; †(*e*) pay; †(*f*) get off, escape; (*g*) become detached; be detachable; (*h*) *colloq.* be successful or effective; (*i*) *US slang* = ***come off it*** in Phrases above; (*j*) fall from a horse, a bicycle, etc.; (*k*) CRICKET cease bowling; (*l*) (of a show) reach the end of its run; (*m*) cease to be assigned to (a task etc.); cease to use (***come off the pill***: see PILL *noun*³ 1c); (see also sense 15 above). **come on** (*a*) continue coming; advance, esp. to attack; arrive having come *from* a previous place of arrival; (*b*) supervene; begin *to* rain or blow; (*c*) make progress, improve; thrive; (*d*) arise to be discussed or dealt with; (*e*) appear on stage or a scene of action; begin to be heard on the radio or telephone, or be seen on a cinema or television screen; (*f*) CRICKET begin to bowl; (*g*) in *imper.*: hurry up; follow me; please do what I ask; I defy you. **come out** (*a*) come out of a place, *spec.* to fight; begin a strike; leave a place where it was fixed or held; (*b*) become public, become known; (of a card) be played; (of a game of patience) go to the finish, with all cards played and their desired arrangement achieved; (*c*) be published; (*d*) (of a plant, disease, etc.) come into visible development; PHOTOGRAPHY give rise to a satisfactory image; become covered *in* a rash etc.; (*e*) show or declare oneself publicly (*for* or *against* something); *spec.* cease to conceal one's homosexuality; (*f*) (of a girl) make her formal entry into upper-class society; make a debut on stage; (*g*) (of the sun etc.) emerge from cloud; become visible; (*h*) show itself prominently; become explicit; (*i*) finish up (in a certain way or at a certain value), esp. after a contest or a calculation; (*j*) extend, project; (*k*) (of a stain or mark) be removed; (*l*) ***come right out (with it)*** (N. Amer. colloq.), speak frankly or tactlessly; (*m*) ***come out of***: emerge from (a place); be brought from; pass out of (a state); proceed or result from; (*n*) ***come out with***, utter; blurt. **come over** (*a*) come, in the process crossing an obstacle or travelling a distance; (*b*) change sides, to one's own; (*c*) pass over during distillation; (*d*) *colloq.* (with following adjective) have a specified feeling come over one; adopt a specified manner; (***come over all unnecessary***: see UNNECESSARY *adjective* 1); (*e*) convey one's meaning or an impression; (***come over big***: see BIG *adverb*). **come round** (*a*) come with the passage of time, recur; (*b*) come in the course of a circuit or a circuitous route; (*c*) make an informal or casual visit; (*d*) (of the wind) change to a more favourable quarter; hence, change for the better, esp. after faintness, bad temper, etc.; be converted to another person's opinion. ***come short***: see SHORT *adverb*. **come through** (*a*) survive an experience; attain an end; (***come through with flying colours***: see COLOUR *noun*); (*b*) arrive after passing through a system, process, etc.; (*c*) act as desired or expected; provide what is required; (*d*) succeed in giving a favourable impression. **come to** (*a*) NAUTICAL cease moving, heave to; (*b*) (*obsolete* exc. *dial.*) recover one's calmness or good humour; (*c*) regain consciousness; revive. **come up** (*a*) come to a place regarded as higher, *spec.* to London; come into residence at a university; (of food) be vomited; (*b*) approach close *to*; ***be coming up***, be approached in the course of travel; ***come up smiling***, emerge cheerfully and undaunted from an unpleasant experience; (*c*) originate; come into use or fashion; (*d*) appear above the soil; rise through water or above its surface; (*e*) attain or be equal *to* a certain standard; (*f*) NAUTICAL come to a specified direction; change course towards the wind; (*g*) come forward from the rear; get abreast (*with*); ***be come up with*** (US), be outwitted; (*h*) be presented in court, or *for* a decision, sale, etc.; (*i*) arise, occur; be mentioned in talk; (*j*) (of theatre lights) become brighter; (of something cleaned or renovated) look cleaner or brighter; (*k*) ***coming up*** (colloq.): said when food is about to be served; (*l*) ***marry come up!***: see MARRY *interjection*; (*m*) ***come up with*** (colloq.), produce in response to a challenge.

– WITH PREPOSITIONS IN SPECIALIZED SENSES: (See also Phrases above.) **come across** meet or find by chance. **come at** (*a*) (now *dial.*) approach, come to; (*b*) reach, get access to, esp. with effort; (*c*) come suddenly and aggressively towards; (*d*) *Austral. & NZ colloq.* agree to do or accept. **come before** (*a*) be presented for consideration by (a judge, court, etc.); (*b*) be given priority over. ***come between***: see BETWEEN *preposition* 5. **come by** get hold of, obtain; receive. **come for** = *come at* (c) above. **come into** †(*a*) accede to, fall in with; (*b*) come into possession of, esp. as an heir; (see also sense 9 above). **come of** become of, happen to; (see also sense 8 above). **come on** = *come upon* below. **come over** †(*a*) surpass; (*b*) take possession of (*fig.*), affect persuasively; (*c*) happen to, befall (a person); influence for the worse; (*d*) *colloq.* get the better of by craft. **come to** (*a*) ***come to oneself***, ***come to one's senses***: regain consciousness; recover from excitement, passion, etc.; (*b*) add up to, cost, amount to (*lit. & fig.*), be equivalent to; ***if it comes to that***, ***come to that*** (colloq.), in fact; (*c*) result in; tend towards (a condition disapproved of). **come under** (*a*) be classed as, be included under; (*b*) become subject to (an influence etc.). **come upon** (*a*) attack, esp. suddenly; (*b*) affect in an overwhelming or supernatural way; (*c*) make a demand or claim upon; (*d*) = ***come across*** above; (*e*) become a burden or charge on.

– COMB.: **come-at-able** *adjective* (colloq.) accessible; obtainable; **come-between** a person or thing which intervenes; **come-by-chance** *colloq.* an illegitimate child; **comedown** a downfall; a drop in status or official position; **come-hither** *noun & adjective* (colloq.) (*a*) *noun* enticement, allure; (*b*) *adjective* enticing, flirtatious; **come-off** (*a*) a conclusion, finish; (*b*) an excuse for non-performance; **come-outer** *US* a person who dissociates himself or herself from an organization; **come-o'-will** *Scot.* a thing that comes of its own accord; an illegitimate child.

comeback /ˈkʌmbak/ *noun*. L19.
[ORIGIN from *come back* s.v. COME *verb*.]
1 An act of retaliation; a retort, a critical reaction; an opportunity to seek redress. *colloq.* L19.

> *Horse & Rider* You don't get a warranty, so if something goes wrong with them, you have no comeback.

2 A sheep three-quarters merino and one quarter crossbred; the skin or fleece of such a sheep. *Austral. & NZ*. L19.
3 A return to a former favourable position; a reinstatement. E20.

> *Independent* Such gastronomic clichés are making a comeback.
> S. RUSHDIE Her attempted comeback had hardly been a triumph.

4 A person who has come back; *spec.* a ghost. E20.

Comecon /ˈkɒmɪkɒn/ *noun*. M20.
[ORIGIN Abbreviation of *Council for Mutual Economic Assistance* (or *Aid*), translating Russian *Sovet Ėkonomicheskoĭ Vzaimopomoshchi*.]
An economic association of Communist countries, chiefly in eastern Europe.

†**co-meddle** *verb trans. rare*. Also **commeddle**. Only in E17.
[ORIGIN from CO-, COM- + MEDDLE *verb*.]
Mix or mingle together.

comedian /kəˈmiːdɪən/ *noun*. L16.
[ORIGIN French *comédien*, from *comédie* COMEDY: see -IAN.]
1 A writer of comedies. L16.
2 A comic actor; occas., any actor. E17.
low comedian: see LOW *adjective & noun*⁴.
3 An entertainer whose act is designed to make the audience laugh; an amusing person (freq. *iron.*). L19.
alternative comedian: see ALTERNATIVE *adjective* 3b.

comedic /kəˈmiːdɪk, -ˈmɛ-/ *adjective*. M17.
[ORIGIN Latin *comoedicus* from Greek *kōmōdikos*, from *kōmōdia* COMEDY: see -IC.]
Of or pertaining to comedy; comic.

comédie /kɔmedi/ *noun*. Pl. pronounced same. E19.
[ORIGIN French: see COMEDY.]
1 ***comédie larmoyante*** /larmwajɑ̃t/, pl. *-antes* /-ɑ̃t/ [French *larmoyant* weeping], a sentimental, moralizing comedy. E19.
2 ***comédie humaine*** /ymɛn/, pl. *-aines* /-ɛn/ [French *humain* HUMAN *adjective*, humane], the sum of human activities; a literary portrait of this. L19.
3 ***comédie noire*** /nwaːr/, pl. *-res* /-r/ [French *noir* black], a macabre or farcical rendering of a violent or tragic theme. Cf. BLACK *adjective* 8b. M20.

comedienne /kəmiːdɪˈɛn, -mɛ-/ *noun*. Also **-éd-** /-eɪd-/. M19.
[ORIGIN French, fem. of *comédien* COMEDIAN.]
A female comedian.
alternative comedienne: see ALTERNATIVE *adjective* 3b.

comedietta /kəmiːdɪˈɛtə/ *noun*. M19.
[ORIGIN Italian, from *comedia* (now *-mm-*) from Latin *comoedia* COMEDY + *-etta* -ET¹.]
A short or slight comedy.

comedist /ˈkɒmədɪst/ *noun*. E19.
[ORIGIN from COMEDY + -IST.]
A writer of comedies.

comedo /ˈkɒmɪdəʊ, kəˈmiːdəʊ/ *noun*. Pl. **comedos**, **comedones** /kɒmɪˈdəʊniːz/. M19.
[ORIGIN Latin = glutton, from *comedere* eat up (see COMESTIBLE).]
MEDICINE. A blackhead.

comedy /ˈkɒmɪdi/ *noun*. LME.
[ORIGIN Old French & mod. French *comédie* from Latin *comoedia* from Greek *kōmōidia*, from *kōmōidos* comic actor, comic poet, from *kōmos* revel + *aoidos* singer (from *aeidein* sing).]
1 a A narrative poem with a happy ending. *obsolete* exc. in ***The Divine Comedy*** [translating *La Divina Commedia*] of Dante. LME. ▸**b** A drama (on stage, film, or radio) with a happy ending, chiefly representing everyday life and of a light, amusing, and often satirical character; any literary composition with similar characteristics. E16.

> **b** SHAKES. *L.L.L.* A consent, Knowing aforehand, of our merriment, To dash it like a Christmas comedy. T. RANDOLPH A pleasant Comedie entituled Hey for Honesty. BYRON All comedies are ended by a marriage.

2 a A genre of drama etc. characterized by its depiction of amusing characters or incidents and an informal style. LME. ▸**b** Humour; humorous behaviour. L19.

> **b** F. HURST Come on. . . cut the comedy.

3 A humorous or farcical incident in life; such incidents collectively. L16.
– PHRASES: ***alternative comedy***: see ALTERNATIVE *adjective* 3b. **comedy of manners**: in which modes and manners of society are satirically or amusingly portrayed. ***low comedy***: see LOW *adjective & noun*⁴. ***musical comedy***: see MUSICAL *adjective*. ***situation comedy***.

comeling /ˈkʌmlɪŋ/ *noun*. Now *arch. & dial.* ME.
[ORIGIN from COME *verb* + -LING¹.]
A newcomer, an immigrant; a stranger.

comely /ˈkʌmli/ *adjective*. ME.
[ORIGIN Prob. aphet. from BECOMELY. Cf. Middle High German *komlich* suitable (beside *bekōme* suitably; German dial. *komm-*, *kömmlich*), Dutch †*komlick* fitting.]
1 Pleasing to the eye; *esp.* (of a person) attractive without being beautiful. ME.
2 Pleasing to the moral sense or aesthetic taste; becoming, proper, decorous. ME.

> R. HOGGART A good and comely life.

3 *gen.* Pleasing, agreeable. *arch.* ME.
■ **comelily** *adverb* (now *rare* or *obsolete*) ME. **comeliness** *noun* LME.

come-on /ˈkʌmɒn/ *noun & adjective*. *slang*. L19.
[ORIGIN from *come on* s.v. COME *verb*.]
▸ **A** *noun*. **1** A dupe. L19.
2 A swindler. E20.
3 An enticement, an invitation to approach. E20.
▸ **B** *adjective*. Enticing. E20.

comer /ˈkʌmə/ *noun*. LME.
[ORIGIN from COME *verb* + -ER¹.]
1 A person who comes; a visitor. Usu. qualified by prec. adjective or prefix. LME.
first comer, ***home-comer***, ***incomer***, ***newcomer***, etc. **all comers** anyone who chooses to come or take part; a sporting event open to anyone. ***late comer***: see LATE *adjective*.
2 A person who shows promise. *colloq.* L19.

comes /ˈkəʊmiːz/ *noun*. Pl. **comites** /-ɪtiːz/. M18.
[ORIGIN Latin = companion, formed as COM- + *ire*, *it-* go.]
MUSIC. An answering or imitating voice in a canon or fugue; the answer itself. Opp. DUX 1.

comestible /kəˈmɛstɪb(ə)l/ *adjective & noun*. L15.
[ORIGIN Old French & mod. French from medieval Latin *comestibilis*, from Latin *comest-* pa. ppl stem of *comedere* eat up, formed as COM- + *edere* eat: see -IBLE.]
▸ †**A** *adjective*. Edible. L15–L17.
▸ **B** *noun*. An article of food. Usu. in *pl.* Usu. *formal* or *joc.* M19.

comet /ˈkɒmɪt/ *noun & adjective*. Also †**-eta**. LOE.
[ORIGIN (Old French & mod. French *comète* from) Latin *cometa* from Greek *komētēs* long-haired (star), from *komaein* wear the hair long, from *komē* hair.]
▸ **A** *noun*. **1** ASTRONOMY. A celestial object that orbits the sun in a highly elliptical path and, when in the vicinity of the sun, usu. has a bright hazy head and a long, more diffuse tail. LOE. ▸**b** *fig.* A portent; a herald. L16.
Oort comet cloud, ***Oort's comet cloud***: see OORT 2.
2 A card game ancestral to Newmarket. L17.
– COMB.: **comet-finder**, **comet-seeker** a telescope of low power and large field of view, used in searching for comets; **comet-year**: in which a notable comet has appeared.
▸ **B** *adjective*. Designating wine made in a comet-year, supposed to have superior qualities. M19.
■ **cometary** *adjective* of or pertaining to a comet or comets; like a comet: M17. **coˈmetic**, **coˈmetical** *adjectives* cometary; *fig.* blazing; portentous; erratic: M17.

comeuppance /kʌmˈʌp(ə)ns/ *noun*. *colloq.* M19.
[ORIGIN from COME *verb* + UP *adverb*¹ + -ANCE.]
One's deserts (for misbehaviour etc.).

comfit /ˈkʌmfɪt/ *noun & verb*. ME.
[ORIGIN Old French *confit(e)* from Latin *confectum*, *-ta* use as noun of neut. and fem. of *confectus* pa. pple of *conficere* prepare: see CONFECT *verb*.]
▸ **A** *noun*. A sweet containing a nut, seed, etc., preserved with sugar. ME.
▸ †**B** *verb trans.* Preserve, pickle; make (a nut, fruit, etc.) into a comfit. LME–M18.

†**comfiture** *noun* var. of CONFITURE.

comfort /ˈkʌmfət/ *noun*. ME.
[ORIGIN Old French *confort* from Proto-Romance, from late Latin *confortare*: see COMFORT *verb*.]
1 Strengthening, encouragement; aid, support; a support, a source of strength; refreshment. Now only in ***aid and comfort*** (*arch.*, in LAW). ME.
†**2** Pleasure, enjoyment; gladness. ME–M16.
3 Relief or support in distress or affliction; consolation, solace; the state of being consoled. ME.

> HENRY FIELDING Others applying for comfort to strong liquors.
> GEO. ELIOT She had . . a sense of solemn comfort.

4 A person who or thing which affords consolation; a cause of satisfaction or relief. LME.

> D. M. MULOCK Growing up to be a help and comfort to my father. E. M. FORSTER His comfort was that the pater's eyes were opened at last.

5 A thing that produces or ministers to a state of physical and mental ease; a thing that makes life easy. Usu. in *pl.* M17.

> S. JOHNSON Before they quit the comforts of a warm home.
> J. HELLER Some new comfort Orr had installed . . running water, wood-burning fireplace, cement floor.

C

6 A state of physical and material well-being; the condition of being comfortable. E19.

> JAN MORRIS The heads of colleges live in almost unrivalled comfort, in lovely old houses with attentive servants. R. COBB Edward driving, which he did much too fast for my comfort.

7 A warm quilt. *US*. M19.

– PHRASES: ***cold comfort***: see COLD *adjective*. **creature comforts** good food, clothes, etc. ***curate's comfort***: see CURATE *noun*. ***letter of comfort***: see LETTER *noun*[1]. ***Southern Comfort***: see SOUTHERN *adjective*.

– COMB.: **comfort eating** eating to make oneself feel happier rather than to satisfy hunger; **comfort food** (a) food that provides consolation or a feeling of well-being, esp. one with a high sugar or carbohydrate content and associated with childhood or home cooking; **comfort station** *US* a public lavatory; **comfort zone** (*a*) a place or situation where one feels at ease; (*b*) a method of working that requires little effort and yields only barely acceptable results.

■ **comfortful** *adjective* full of comfort, comforting M16. **comfortless** *adjective* without comfort; dreary, cheerless: LME. **comfortlessly** *adverb* M16.

comfort /ˈkʌmfət/ *verb*. ME.
[ORIGIN Old French *conforter* from late Latin *confortare* strengthen, formed as COM- + *fortis* strong.]

†1 *verb trans.* Strengthen (morally or physically); encourage, hearten; invigorate, refresh. ME–E18.

> COVERDALE *2 Sam.* 2:7 Let youre hande now therfore be comforted, and be ye stronge. R. COPLAND The water . . that conforteth and clereth the syght.

†2 *verb trans.* Give delight or pleasure to; gladden; entertain. ME–E17.

> SHAKES. *Jul. Caes.* To keep with you at meals, comfort your bed, and talk to you sometimes.

†3 *verb trans.* Lend support to; give relief to; assist, aid. ME–L18.

> J. AYLIFFE Guilty of comforting and assisting the Rebels. WORDSWORTH She quite forgot to send the Doctor To comfort poor old Susan Gale.

4 *verb trans.* Soothe in grief and trouble; console; solace. ME. ▸†**b** *verb intrans.* Take comfort. *rare* (Shakes.). Only in E17.

> S. RICHARDSON She comforted herself, that Sir Charles would be able to soften their resentments. E. HEMINGWAY I comforted her and she stopped crying.

5 *verb trans.* Allay physical discomfort; make comfortable. L19.

> M. E. BRADDON Refreshed by the coffee and comforted by the warmth of the stove.

comfortable /ˈkʌmf(ə)təb(ə)l/ *adjective & noun*. ME.
[ORIGIN Anglo-Norman *confortable*, formed as COMFORT *verb*: see -ABLE.]

▸ **A** *adjective*. **I** Active.

†1 Giving mental or spiritual delight; pleasant; pleasing to the senses. ME–M18. ▸†**b** Satisfactory; *colloq.* tolerable, fairly good. M17–E18.

2 Strengthening (morally, spiritually, or †physically); sustaining; encouraging, reassuring. *arch.* LME. ▸†**b** Helpful, serviceable. L16–E18.

> G. BERKELEY The comfortable expectation of Immortality. **b** DEFOE Their . . canoes which had been so comfortable to them.

the Comfortable Words four scriptural passages following and confirming the absolution in some Eucharistic rites.

3 Affording or conveying consolation; comforting; consolatory. *arch.* LME.

> SHAKES. *All's Well* Be comfortable to my mother . . , and make much of her.

4 Such as to obviate hardship, save trouble, and promote content; ministering to comfort; freeing from anxiety or concern. M18. ▸**b** (Of a margin) large enough to avoid any challenge or doubt; (of a victory) achieved with ease. M20.

> N. SHUTE On the table at a comfortable height for Elspeth. P. REDGROVE A very comfortable income.

▸ **II** Passive & neutral.

†5 Consoled; cheerful. L16–M18.

6 At ease, free from hardship, pain, and trouble; enjoying comfort; having ample money for one's needs; having an easy conscience. L18. ▸**b** Undisturbed; complacent; placidly self-satisfied. *colloq.* M19.

> OED I am not . . quite comfortable about the matter. E. M. FORSTER Would she not be more comfortable . . at the hotel? W. FAULKNER She was of comfortable people—not the best in Jefferson, but good people enough. **b** B. PYM The comfortable assumption of so much that could be left to the women.

▸ **B** *noun*. †1 A source of comfort; a creature comfort. M17–L18.

2 A warm article of clothing, a comforter; *US* a warm quilt. M19.

■ **comfortableness** *noun* L16. **comfortably** *adverb* in a comfortable manner; so as to be comfortable; (***comfortably off***, having ample money for one's needs): LME.

†**comfortative** *adjective & noun*. LME.
[ORIGIN Old French *confortatif, -ive* from late Latin *confortativus*, from *confortare*: see COMFORT *verb*, -ATIVE.]

▸ **A** *adjective*. Strengthening, reviving; cheering. LME–L17.

▸ **B** *noun*. A thing which strengthens or revives, *esp.* a restorative medicine or cordial. LME–L19.

comforter /ˈkʌmfətə/ *noun*. LME.
[ORIGIN Partly from Anglo-Norman *confortour* = Old French *conforteor*, formed as COMFORT *verb*, -OUR, -ER[2]; partly (as a title of the Holy Spirit) translating ecclesiastical Latin *consolator* rendering Greek *paraklētos* PARACLETE.]

1 A person who or thing which gives comfort. LME.
Job's comforter: see JOB *noun*[3]. **the Comforter** CHRISTIAN THEOLOGY the Holy Spirit.

†2 A small kind of spaniel. L16–E19.

3 **a** A warm garment; *spec.* a long woollen scarf. E19. ▸**b** A warm quilt. *N. Amer.* M19.

4 A baby's dummy teat of rubber etc. L19.

†**comfortive** *adjective & noun*. LME–E19.
[ORIGIN from COMFORT *verb* + -IVE.]
= COMFORTATIVE.

comfortress /ˈkʌmfətrɪs/ *noun*. Now *rare*. LME.
[ORIGIN Old French *conforteresse* fem. of *confortère* comforter: see -ESS[1].]
A female comforter.

comfrey /ˈkʌmfri/ *noun*. ME.
[ORIGIN Anglo-Norman *cumfirie*, Old French *confi(e)re* (mod. dial. *confier* etc.), also *confierge*, from medieval Latin *cumfiria* for Latin *conferva*, from *confervere* heal, (lit.) boil together, formed as CON- + *fervere* boil.]
A plant of the genus *Symphytum*, of the borage family; esp. *S. officinale*, which has rough leaves and bears drooping clusters of white or purple flowers, and was formerly much used to treat wounds.

comfy /ˈkʌmfi/ *adjective*. *colloq.* E19.
[ORIGIN Abbreviation: see -Y[1].]
Comfortable.
■ **comfily** *adverb* E20.

comic /ˈkɒmɪk/ *adjective & noun*. L16.
[ORIGIN Latin *comicus* from Greek *kōmikos* from *kōmos* revel: see -IC.]

▸ **A** *adjective*. 1 Pertaining to or in the style of comedy. L16.

2 Causing or meant to cause laughter; facetious; burlesque; funny. M18.

> W. S. MAUGHAM Our use of the same word . . had a comic effect, so that we were obliged to laugh. J. IRVING I promise . . to perform comic stunts and make you laugh all night.

– SPECIAL COLLOCATIONS: **comic book** a book of strip cartoons. **comic opera**: with much spoken dialogue, and usu. humorous treatment. **comic paper** = sense B.3 below. **comic relief** comic episodes in a play etc. intended to offset more serious portions; the relaxation of tension etc. provided by such episodes. **comic strip** a strip cartoon telling a comic story.

▸ **B** *noun*. †1 A comic writer; = COMEDIAN 1. E17–M18.

†2 **a** A comic actor; = COMEDIAN 2. E17–E18. ▸**b** An entertainer whose act is designed to make the audience laugh; an amusing person. Cf. COMEDIAN 3. E20.

3 A light or amusing paper; a periodical with narrative mainly in pictures (orig. and chiefly for children); in *pl.* also, comic strips in a newspaper etc. L19. ▸**b** A comic film, television programme, etc. E20.
HORROR comic.

comical /ˈkɒmɪk(ə)l/ *adjective*. LME.
[ORIGIN formed as COMIC + -AL[1].]

†1 = COMIC *adjective* 1. LME–E18.

†2 Of style, subject, etc.: befitting comedy, trivial, low. L16–L17.

†3 Like the ending of a comedy, happy, fortunate. L16–L17.

4 Causing laughter; humorous, funny; ludicrous, risible. L17.

> S. K. PENMAN Bennet did a comical double-take upon being introduced to Rob.

5 Strange, odd; difficult to deal with; out of sorts, unwell. *colloq. & dial.* L18.

■ **comiˈcality** *noun* comic quality; a comical thing: L18. **comically** *adverb* E17. **comicalness** *noun* L17.

Comice /ˈkɒmɪs/ *noun*. L20.
[ORIGIN French = association, cooperative, spec. the *Comice Horticole* of Angers, France, where the variety was developed.]
A kind of pear, = ***Doyenne du Comice*** s.v. DOYENNE *noun*[1].

comico- /ˈkɒmɪkəʊ/ *combining form*.
[ORIGIN from Latin *comicus*, Greek *kōmikos*: see COMIC, -O-.]
Forming chiefly adjectives with the sense 'comic and —', as ***comico-tragic(al)*** etc.

†**comilitant** *noun & adjective* var. of COMMILITANT.

Cominform /ˈkɒmɪnfɔːm/ *noun*. M20.
[ORIGIN from *Com(munist) Inform(ation (Bureau)*.]
hist. A former Soviet-led agency of international Communism in Europe.
■ **Cominformist** *adjective & noun* supporting, a supporter of, the Cominform or Soviet rather than national (esp. Yugoslavian) Communist policy M20.

coming /ˈkʌmɪŋ/ *noun*. ME.
[ORIGIN from COME *verb* + -ING[1].]

1 The action of COME *verb*; a movement towards or arrival at a specified or understood point, time, or result. Also foll. by adverb or preposition. ME.

> MILTON At his coming to the Crown. T. S. ELIOT A cold coming we had of it. R. GITTINGS His financial position at coming-of-age. A. POWELL A . . dance on the 'coming out' of a daughter.

Second Coming: see SECOND *adjective*.

†2 A means of access, an approach; ***coming in***, a means of entrance, an entry. LME–E18.

3 ***comings in***, revenues, receipts. L16.

coming /ˈkʌmɪŋ/ *adjective*. LME.
[ORIGIN from COME *verb* + -ING[2].]

1 That comes. Also foll. by adverb. LME.
have another guess coming, ***have got another guess coming***: see GUESS *noun*.

2 Inclined to make or meet advances; ready, eager, complaisant, forward. *arch.* L16.

3 Likely to be important in the future, rising into prominence. M19.

> H. ROBBINS People will pay to see the pictures . . . It's the coming thing.

comingle *verb* var. of COMMINGLE.

Comintern /ˈkɒmɪntəːn/ *noun*. E20.
[ORIGIN Russian *Komintern*, from *kom(munisticheskiĭ* communist + *intern(atsional'nyĭ* international.]
The Third International (see INTERNATIONAL *noun* 2).

comitadji /kɒmɪˈtadʒi/ *noun*. Also **komita(d)ji**. E20.
[ORIGIN Turkish *komitacı* lit. 'member of a (revolutionary) committee'.]
A member of a band of irregular soldiers in the Balkans; *spec.* (*hist.*) a Balkan rebel against the Ottoman Empire before the First World War.

comital /ˈkɒmɪt(ə)l/ *adjective*. M19.
[ORIGIN medieval Latin *comitalis*, from *comit-*, *comes* in sense 'a count': see -AL[1].]
Of or pertaining to a count or earl; of the rank of a count or earl.

comitant /ˈkɒmɪt(ə)nt/ *adjective & noun*. *rare*. E17.
[ORIGIN Latin *comitant-* pres. ppl stem of *comitari* accompany, from *comit-* *comes* companion: see -ANT[1].]
(Something) accompanying; (a) concomitant.

comitative /ˈkɒmɪtətɪv/ *adjective*. M19.
[ORIGIN from Latin *comitat-* pa. ppl stem of *comitari* (see COMITANT), + -IVE.]
GRAMMAR. Expressing accompaniment or association.

comitatus /kɒmɪˈteɪtəs/ *noun*. Pl. same. L19.
[ORIGIN Latin *comitatus*, from *comit-*, *comes* companion: see -ATE[1].]
hist. A body of warriors, nobles, etc., attached to the person of a king or chieftain; the status of such a body. See also POSSE COMITATUS.

comites *noun* pl. of COMES.

comitia /kəˈmɪʃə, -ʃɪə/ *noun pl.* (also treated as *sing.*). E17.
[ORIGIN Latin, pl. of *comitium* assembly, formed as COM- + *-itium*, from *it-*, *ire* go.]

1 *gen.* An assembly. *rare*. E17.

2 An assembly of the Fellows of the Royal College of Physicians, London. L17.

3 ROMAN HISTORY. An assembly of the Roman people to elect magistrates and pass legislation. M18.

comitial /kəˈmɪʃ(ə)l, -ʃɪəl/ *adjective*. M16.
[ORIGIN Latin *comitialis*, formed as COMITIA: see -AL[1].]

1 ROMAN HISTORY. Of or pertaining to the comitia. M16.

†2 Designating or pertaining to any of various Presbyterian or political assemblies. L16–L18.

comitology /kɒmɪˈtɒlədʒi/ *noun*. M20.
[ORIGIN from COMMIT(TEE + -OLOGY.]
Orig., the study of committees. Now, any of various committees which oversee the implementation of European Union legislation and policy; the work of these committees.

comity /ˈkɒmɪti/ *noun*. M16.
[ORIGIN Latin *comitas*, from *comis* courteous: see -ITY.]

1 Courtesy, civility; kindly and considerate behaviour towards others. M16.

2 **a** ***comity of nations***, ***international comity***, the friendly recognition as far as is practicable by nations of each other's laws and usages. M19. ▸**b** An association of or *of* nations etc. for mutual benefit; the community of civilized nations. M19.

> **b** C. R. ATTLEE Germany was back in the comity of nations. P. USTINOV Voices which spoke for Russia in the comity of civilised people.

comma /ˈkɒmə/ *noun*. L16.
[ORIGIN Latin from Greek *komma* piece cut off, short clause.]

1 In CLASSICAL PROSODY & RHETORIC, a phrase or group of words shorter than a colon (COLON *noun*[2] 1); *loosely* (now *rare* or *obsolete*) a short clause or phrase within a sentence. L16. ▸†**b** A clause or short passage of a treatise or argument. L16–L17.

2 A punctuation mark (now ,) indicating a pause between parts of a sentence or separating items in a list, also used to separate (groups of) figures etc. L16. ▸b A short pause such as may be indicated by a comma. L16. ▸c *fig.* A break of continuity, an interval, a pause. E17.
3 MUSIC. A definite minute interval or difference of pitch. L16.
4 In full ***inverted comma***. A comma (sense 2) placed upside down (single or paired) above the line before a quotation; in *pl.* also, quotation marks (including the erect comma(s) or apostrophe(s) above the line closing a quotation). E18.
5 In full ***comma butterfly***. A nymphalid butterfly, *Polygonia c-album*, having a white comma-shaped mark on the underside of the wing. M18.
6 In full ***comma bacillus***. A cholera bacillus (of curved shape). L19.

command /kəˈmɑːnd/ *noun*. LME.
[ORIGIN from the verb.]
1 The act of commanding; an authoritative statement that a person must do something; an order, bidding; a commandment. LME. ▸b A symbolic expression which defines an operation in a computer; a signal initiating the performance of such an operation. M20.
at a person's command, **by a person's command** in pursuance of a person's bidding. **word of command** the customary order for movement in drill; spoken signal to begin.
2 The faculty of commanding; rule, control; the exercise or tenure of authority, esp. naval or military. Also, a commander's position. LME. ▸b Those in command. Esp. in ***the high command***, ***the higher command***, the army commander-in-chief and his staff. E20.

DRYDEN He assumed an absolute command over his readers. LD MACAULAY The places and commands which he held under the Crown. C. S. FORESTER The command of a regular brigade of cavalry.

in command (of) commanding, in control (of). ***second in command***: see SECOND *adjective*. **under command of**, **under the command of** commanded by.
3 Power of control, sway, mastery, possession. M16. ▸b Domination from an elevated or superior strategic position; range of vision, outlook, prospect. E17. ▸c Despotism, coercion. *rare*. L17.

B. JOWETT Having gifts of courage . . and command of money and friends. I. COMPTON-BURNETT Duncan . . had lost his command of himself. b K. DIGBY I . . gott my fleete out of command of the fortes. DRYDEN The steepy stand, which overlooks the vale with wide command.

at command ready to be used at will. **command of language** skill in speech, articulacy.
4 A body of troops, a district, etc., under a commander (esp. naval or military) or one particular authority; a unit of an army, air force, etc., organized for a particular duty or operating in a particular area. L16.

G. CATLIN Colonel Dodge ordered the command to halt. B. HORROCKS Before the war Western Command had always been regarded as a backwater.

Bomber Command, ***Coastal Command***, ***Fighter Command***, ***Strike Command***, ***Support Command***, ***Transport Command***, etc.
– COMB.: **command economy** ECONOMICS = ***planned economy*** s.v. PLANNED *ppl adjective*; **command language** COMPUTING a source language composed chiefly of a set of commands or operators, used esp. for communicating with the operating system of a computer; *spec.* a job control language; **command line** an interface for typing commands directly to a computer's operating system; **command module** the control compartment of a spacecraft; **Command Paper** a paper laid by command of the Crown before Parliament etc.; **command performance** a theatrical or musical performance given by royal command; **command post** the headquarters of a military unit.

command /kəˈmɑːnd/ *verb*. ME.
[ORIGIN Anglo-Norman *comaunder*, Old French *comander* (mod. *commander*) from late Latin *commandare*, formed as COM- + *mandare* commit, enjoin: cf. COMMEND *verb*.]
▸ I 1 *verb trans.* Lay down as a command; give a command or commands to; order, bid, enjoin, with authority and influence. (With a command, a person etc. given a command (historically an indirect obj.), or both as object(s); a person etc. *to do*, (arch.) *do*, †*to* a thing; *that* something (*should*) *be* done; a person or thing *to be* + pa. pple.) ME. ▸b *verb intrans.* Issue commands. LME.

AV *Acts* 25:6 He . . commanded Paul to be brought. W. BLACKSTONE The rule of life which religion commands. J. B. PRIESTLEY 'Go to Liverpool at once,' he commanded. E. O'NEILL His Imperial Majesty commands that you stop talking. T. CAPOTE When the next boy commanded him to halt, he at once obeyed.

2 *verb trans. ellipt.* a Order to come or go *to*, *from*, *away*, etc. *arch.* LME. ▸†b Order to be sent or given; demand. L16–L18.

a MILTON Commanded home for doing too much. b SHAKES. *Cymb.* You have commanded of me these most poisonous compounds.

3 *verb trans.* Have authority over; be in command of (forces, a ship, etc.); be in control of; master, restrain, (oneself, one's passions, etc.). LME. ▸b *verb intrans.* Have authority or control; be in command, be supreme. L16.

C. MARLOWE The haughty Dane commands the narrow seas. M. EDGEWORTH: F. commanded his temper. b DEFOE Colonel Forbes . . commanded at the siege.

4 *verb trans.* Have (a person etc.) at one's call; have (money, skill, etc.) at one's disposal or within easy reach. M16.

A. C. BOULT Eugène Ysaÿe commanded a breadth of tone as a violinist which remains unmatched. H. WILSON Whether A or B can in fact command a majority in the House of Commons.

yours to command *arch.*: a formula used for closing a letter.
5 *verb trans.* Deserve and get; exact, compel. L16.

K. TYNAN He could not command my sympathy nor even . . my interest. F. HERBERT He . . commanded their attention with a knuckle rap against the table.

6 *verb trans.* Dominate from an elevated or superior strategic position; look down on or over. E17. ▸b *verb intrans.* Dominate by looking down *over*; have a commanding position. E17.

J. RUSKIN My bedroom window commanded . . a very lovely view. E. BOWEN Combe Farm commanded the valley.

▸†II 7 *verb trans.* Commend, recommend, confide. LME–M16.
■ **commandable** *adjective* LME.

commandant /kɒmənˈdant, ˈkɒməndant; -ɑːnt/ *noun*. L17.
[ORIGIN French *commandant*, Italian, Spanish *commandante*; in sense 2 Afrikaans *kommandant*: see COMMAND *verb*, -ANT[1].]
1 A commanding officer, esp. of a particular force, a military academy, etc. L17.
2 In *S. AFR. HISTORY*, the leader of a Boer commando. Now, an officer in the South African armed forces ranking between a major and a colonel. L18.
commandant-general a commander-in-chief.
■ **commandantship** *noun* the office or position of commandant M19.

Commandaria /kɒmənˈdɛːrɪə/ *noun*. Also **-eria** /-ɪərɪə/. E20.
[ORIGIN medieval Latin *commandaria* (from being made on the former commanderies): see COMMANDERY 1.]
A sweet red or dark brown wine from Cyprus.

commandeer /kɒmənˈdɪə/ *verb trans.* E19.
[ORIGIN Afrikaans *kommandeer* from Dutch *commanderen* from French *commander* COMMAND *verb*.]
Seize (men or goods) for military service; take arbitrary possession of.

commander /kəˈmɑːndə/ *noun*. ME.
[ORIGIN Old French *comandere*, *-eor*, Anglo-Norman *comandour*, (mod. *commandeur*), from Proto-Romance, from late Latin *commandare*: see COMMAND *verb*, -ER[2].]
1 A person who commands; a person who has the control or disposal *of*; a ruler, a leader. ME.
Commander of the Faithful: a title of the Caliphs.
2 *spec.* ▸a An officer in command of a ship, a military force, etc.; a naval officer ranking next below a captain; an officer in charge of a London police district. LME. ▸b *hist.* The administrator of a commandery of a knightly order. E17. ▸c More fully ***knight commander***. A member of a higher class in some orders of knighthood. E19.
a master and commander: see MASTER *noun*[1]. ***wing commander***: see WING *noun*.
3 A large wooden mallet. L16.
†4 a A surgical instrument for reducing dislocations. L17–L18. ▸b A mechanical device for straightening, reshaping, etc. L19.
– COMB.: **commander-in-chief** a supreme commander.
■ **commandership** *noun* the office or position of commander E17.

Commanderia *noun* var. of COMMANDARIA.

commandery /kəˈmɑːndəri/ *noun*. Also **-dry** /-dri/. LME.
[ORIGIN French *commanderie*, formed as COMMANDER: see -ERY. Partly from medieval Latin *commendaria*, from *commenda* benefice.]
1 *hist.* An estate, manor, etc., belonging to a religious and military order of knights, as the Knights Hospitaller. LME. ▸b A conventual priory of a non-military religious order. M16.
†2 An ecclesiastical or other benefice held *in commendam*. M16–E19.
†3 The tenure of command. L16–M17.
4 The rank of commander in an order of knighthood; a benefice or pension attached to such a commandership. E17.
†5 A district under a commander. M17–E19.

commanding /kəˈmɑːndɪŋ/ *adjective*. L15.
[ORIGIN from COMMAND *verb* + -ING[2].]
1 Possessing or exercising command; ruling; controlling. L15.
2 Indicating or expressing command; (of a person, looks, ability, etc.) dignified, exalted, impressive. L16.
3 Dominating by an elevated or superior strategic position; (of a hill, position, etc.) affording command, giving a wide view. M17.
■ **commandingly** *adverb* LME. **commandingness** *noun* (*rare*) commanding quality L19.

commandite /kɒmənˈdiːt; *foreign* kɔmɑ̃dit/ *noun*. M19.
[ORIGIN French, from *commander* in sense 'entrust'.]
A form of partnership in which a person may advance capital with no functions and strictly limited liability.

commandment /kəˈmɑːn(d)m(ə)nt/ *noun*. ME.
[ORIGIN Old French *comandement* (mod. *comm-*), from *comander* COMMAND *verb*: see -MENT.]
1 *gen.* An authoritative order or injunction. *arch.* ME.
2 *spec.* A divine command. ME.
eleventh commandment: see ELEVENTH *adjective*. **the Ten Commandments** those given by God to Moses on Mount Sinai (*Exodus* 20:1–7); *arch. colloq.* the ten fingernails (esp. of a woman).
†3 The action or fact of commanding; bidding. LME–L17.
†4 Authority, sway, rule; military command. LME–M17.
5 LAW. The offence of inducing another to break the law. *obsolete* exc. *hist.* E17.

commando /kəˈmɑːndəʊ/ *noun*. Pl. **-os**. L18.
[ORIGIN Portuguese (now *comando*), from *commandar* COMMAND *verb*.]
1 A party, orig. of Boers or burghers in South Africa, called out for military purposes, a militia; *S. AFR. HISTORY* a unit of the Boer army made up of the militia of an electoral district; a raiding party, a raid, orig. against black tribesmen; participation in such a raid. L18.
2 (A member of) a unit of British amphibious shock troops; (a member of) a similar unit elsewhere. M20.
– PHRASES: **go commando** *colloq.* wear no underpants. **on commando**, **upon commando** *hist.* on militia service in the Boer army.

†**commandore** *noun* see COMMODORE.

commandress /kəˈmɑːndrɪs/ *noun*. Now *rare*. L16.
[ORIGIN from COMMANDER + -ESS[1].]
A female commander.

commandry *noun* var. of COMMANDERY.

commeasurable /kɒˈmɛʒ(ə)rəb(ə)l/ *adjective*. L17.
[ORIGIN from COM- + MEASURABLE.]
= COMMENSURABLE.

commeasure /kəˈmɛʒə/ *verb trans.* E17.
[ORIGIN from COM- + MEASURE *verb*.]
Measure as an exact equivalent; be equal to in measure, be coextensive with.

comme ci, comme ça /kɔm si kɔm sa/ *adverbial & adjectival phr.* M20.
[ORIGIN French, lit. 'like this like that'.]
So-so, middling(ly).

†**commeddle** *verb* var. of CO-MEDDLE.

commedia dell'arte /kɒmˈmeːdia dɛlˈarte, kɒˈmɛdɪə dɛlˈɑːteɪ/ *noun phr.* L19.
[ORIGIN Italian = comedy of art.]
The improvised popular comedy in Italian theatres between the 16th and 18th cents. with stock characters.

comme il faut /kɔm il fo, kɒm iːl fəʊ/ *adverbial & pred. adjectival phr.* M18.
[ORIGIN French, lit. 'as it is necessary'.]
Proper(ly), correct(ly), as it should be (esp. of behaviour).

commemorate /kəˈmɛməreɪt/ *verb trans.* L16.
[ORIGIN Latin *commemorat-* pa. ppl stem of *commemorare*, formed as COM- + *memorare* relate, from *memor* (see MEMORY): see -ATE[3].]
1 Mention. Now *spec.* mention as worthy of remembrance; celebrate in speech or writing. L16.
2 Preserve in memory by some solemnity or celebration. M17.
3 Of a thing: be a memorial of. M18.
■ **commemorative** *adjective* that commemorates a person, event, etc. L16. **commemoratively** *adverb* M17. **commemorator** *noun* a person who commemorates a person, event, etc. M19.

commemoration /kəmɛməˈreɪʃ(ə)n/ *noun*. LME.
[ORIGIN Old French & mod. French, or Latin *commemoratio(n-)*, formed as COMMEMORATE: see -ATION.]
1 An act of commemorating by some solemnity or celebration. LME. ▸b CHRISTIAN CHURCH. A service or part of a service in memory of a saint or some sacred event. LME. ▸c A public memorial. M17. ▸d An annual celebration at Oxford University in memory of the founders and benefactors of a college or the university. Cf. ENCAENIA. M18.
2 Recital, mention. Now *spec.* eulogistic or honourable mention. L16.
– COMB.: **commemoration ball** an Oxford college dance held at a time close to commemoration.

commence /kəˈmɛns/ *verb*. ME.
[ORIGIN Old French *com(m)encier* (mod. *commencer*) from Proto-Romance, from Latin COM- + *initiare* INITIATE *verb*. In sense 3 translating medieval Latin *incipere*.]
1 *verb trans.* Begin (an action, *doing*, *to do*), enter upon. ME.
2 *verb intrans.* Make a start or a beginning; come into operation. LME.
3 *verb intrans. & trans.* Take an academic degree, esp. a higher degree, (*in* a particular faculty etc.); take the academic degree of (MA etc.); graduate from university etc. LME.
4 As *copular verb*. Begin to be or with being; begin to act or work as. *arch.* M17.

J. WESLEY The wandering thoughts . . then commence sinful. A. DOBSON Who had already commenced poet as an Eton boy.

■ **commenceable** *adjective* M17. **commencer** *noun* (*a*) *gen.* a person who commences; †(*b*) *spec.* a person taking an academic degree, esp. a higher degree; *US* a college student about to graduate: LME.

C

commencement /kəˈmɛnsm(ə)nt/ *noun*. ME.
[ORIGIN Old French & mod. French, formed as COMMENCE: see -MENT.]
1 The action, process, or time of beginning. ME.
2 The taking of an academic degree, esp. a higher degree; (at certain universities, esp. in the US) the ceremony of degree conferment. LME.

†**commend** *noun*. L15.
[ORIGIN Partly from French *commende*, partly from the verb.]
1 (A) commendation. L15–M17.
SHAKES. *Per.* He had need mean better than his outward show Can any way speak in his just commend.
2 A greeting, a compliment. L15–M17.
3 = COMMENDAM. *Scot.* L15–E16.

commend /kəˈmɛnd/ *verb*. ME.
[ORIGIN Latin *commendare*, formed as COM- + *mandare* commit, entrust: cf. COMMAND *verb*.]
1 *verb trans.* Mention or present as worthy of acceptance or approval; praise, extol; recommend. ME. ▸**b** *verb trans.* Esp. in greetings: recommend (oneself, another) to kindly remembrance, convey kind greetings from (a person) *to* another. *arch.* LME. ▸**c** *verb intrans.* Give praise. M18.
J. LONDON He had been commended for his brilliant description of the Socialist meeting. F. M. NICHOLS It commends itself to all the theologians who are either learned, or honest and candid. E. BOWEN Mr. Lee-Mittison . . commended him to their good graces with a general wave of the hand.
highly commended (of a competitor) just missing the prize list. **b commend me to** give my kind greetings to; *colloq.* give me by choice, (*iron.*) I prefer.
2 *verb trans.* Entrust, commit, (*to*, now only *to* a person's care or keeping). LME.
T. BECON Commend to memory the fifteenth chapter of Corinthians. J. BUCHAN I commended my soul to my Maker.
†**3** *verb trans.* Adorn, grace. M16–M17.
4 *verb trans.* ECCLESIASTICAL HISTORY. Bestow *in commendam*. E17.
5 *verb trans. hist.* Place under the personal protection of a feudal lord. M19.
■ **commender** *noun* (now *rare*) L16.

commenda *noun* see COMMENDAM.

commendable /kəˈmɛndəb(ə)l/ *adjective*. LME.
[ORIGIN Old French & mod. French from Latin *commendabilis*, formed as COMMEND *verb*: see -ABLE.]
Deserving of commendation or approval; laudable.
■ **commendableness** *noun* M17. **commendably** *adverb* LME.

commendador /kɒmɛndəˈdɔː/ *noun*. L16.
[ORIGIN Spanish *comendador* COMMANDER.]
Chiefly *hist.* A Spanish or Venetian commander.

commendam /kəˈmɛndam/ *noun*. Also (now *rare*) **-da** /-də/, †**-dum**. M16.
[ORIGIN ecclesiastical Latin, accus. sing. of *commenda* in *dare* etc. IN COMMENDAM.]
ECCLESIASTICAL HISTORY. The custody of a benefice in the absence of a regular incumbent; the benefice or office so held.

commendatary /kəˈmɛndət(ə)ri/ *noun & adjective*. Now *rare*. M16.
[ORIGIN medieval Latin *commendatarius*, from *commendat-*: see COMMENDATION, -ARY[1].]
▸ **A** *noun*. In ECCLESIASTICAL HISTORY, = COMMENDATOR 1; *gen.* a commissioner. M16.
▸ **B** *adjective*. = COMMENDATORY *adjective* 2. E17.

commendation /kɒmɛnˈdeɪʃ(ə)n/ *noun*. ME.
[ORIGIN Old French & mod. French from Latin *commendatio(n-)*, from *commendat-* pa. ppl stem of *commendare* COMMEND *verb*: see -ATION.]
1 CHRISTIAN CHURCH. Usu. in *pl.* A liturgical office, orig. ending with the prayer *Tibi, Domine, commendamus* (to You, Lord, we commend), commending the souls of the dead to God, said before burial or cremation and at any subsequent memorial service. ME.
2 The action of commending; approval, praise; recommendation. LME.
3 An expression of approval; a recommendation; in *pl.* also (*arch.*), respects, compliments, greetings. L15.
4 *hist.* The delivery by a freeman of himself and his possessions to the protection of a feudal lord. E19.

commendator /ˈkɒməndeɪtə/ *noun*. E16.
[ORIGIN Latin *commendator* formed as COMMENDATION: see -OR.]
1 ECCLESIASTICAL HISTORY. A person holding a benefice *in commendam*. E16.
2 A Spanish commander. Now *rare* or *obsolete*. L16.

Commendatore /kɒmɛndəˈtɔːri/ *noun*. L19.
[ORIGIN Italian, formed as COMMENDATOR.]
A knight of an Italian order of chivalry.

commendatory /kɒˈmɛndət(ə)ri/ *adjective & noun*. M16.
[ORIGIN Late Latin *commendatorius*, formed as COMMENDATOR: see -ORY[2].]
▸ **A** *adjective*. **1** Commending, recommending. M16.
2 ECCLESIASTICAL HISTORY. Holding a benefice *in commendam*. L17.
▸ †**B** *noun*. **1** = COMMANDER 2b. M16–M18.
2 = COMMANDERY 1. L16–M18.
3 = COMMENDATOR 1. L16–E18.
4 A commendatory fact or word. M17–E18.
5 = COMMENDAM. M18–M19.

commensal /kəˈmɛns(ə)l/ *adjective & noun*. LME.
[ORIGIN French, or its source medieval Latin *commensalis*, formed as COM- + *mensa* table: see -AL[1].]
▸ **A** *adjective*. **1** Eating at or pertaining to the same table. LME.
2 BIOLOGY. Of, pertaining to, or exhibiting commensalism. L19.
▸ **B** *noun*. **1** Any of a company eating at the same table. Formerly also *spec.*, an oppidan at Eton College. LME.
2 BIOLOGY. A commensal organism. L19.
■ **commensalism** *noun* (BIOLOGY) an association between two species in which one benefits and the other is neither harmed nor benefited (cf. SYMBIOSIS) L19. **commenˈsality** *noun* the habit of eating at the same table E17.

commensurable /kəˈmɛnʃ(ə)rəb(ə)l, -sjə-/ *adjective*. M16.
[ORIGIN Late Latin *commensurabilis*, formed as COM- + *mensurabilis* MENSURABLE: see -ABLE.]
1 Measurable by the same standard (*to*, *with*); (of numbers, magnitudes, etc.) having a ratio that may be expressed as a ratio of two integers. M16.
2 Proportionate (*to*). Now *rare*. M17.
■ **commensuraˈbility** *noun* L16. **commensurableness** *noun* M16. **commensurably** *adverb* M17.

commensurate /kəˈmɛnʃ(ə)rət, -sjə-/ *adjective*. M17.
[ORIGIN Late Latin *commensuratus*, formed as COM- + *mensuratus* pa. pple of *mensurare*: see MEASURE *verb*, -ATE[2].]
1 Of equal extent, coextensive, (*with*, *to*). M17.
2 Proportionate (*to*, *with*). M17.
3 Corresponding in nature (*with*, *to*); belonging to the same category. Now *rare*. M17.
■ **commensurately** *adverb* L17. **commensurateness** *noun* M17.

†**commensurate** *verb trans*. M17.
[ORIGIN from (the same root as) COMMENSURATE *adjective*: see -ATE[3].]
1 Make commensurate *to*. M17–E18.
2 Reduce to a measure or standard, measure. Only in M17.

commensuration /kəmɛnʃəˈreɪʃ(ə)n, -sjə-/ *noun*. Now *rare*. E16.
[ORIGIN Senses 1, 2 from COM- + MENSURATION; sense 3 from late Latin *commensuratio(n-)*, formed as COMMENSURATE *verb*: see -ATION.]
1 The measuring of things against or in comparison with each other. E16.
†**2** An act of measuring; a measurement. M16–L17.
3 Relationship of measurements etc., proportion. E17.

comment /ˈkɒmɛnt/ *noun*. LME.
[ORIGIN Latin *commentum* invention, contrivance, interpretation, comment, from *comment-* pa. ppl stem of *comminisci* devise, contrive.]
†**1** An expository treatise; a commentary. LME–L19.
2 An explanatory note; a remark; a criticism; an opinion, now esp. as conveyed by the media; *fig.* (of an event etc.) an illustration, an elucidating example. LME.
G. CRABBE Bibles with cuts and comments. V. GLENDINNING No one can go and post a letter without a comment being made.
3 Critical matter added to illustrate the text of a book etc. L16.
4 Animadversion, criticism, remark. M19.
E. ROOSEVELT It would cause great comment if I cancelled them [engagements] at the last moment.
5 LINGUISTICS. The part of a sentence giving new information about the topic or theme of an utterance or discourse. Cf. RHEME 2. M20.
– PHRASES: **no comment** *colloq.* (*a*) I decline to answer the question; (*b*) there is no need for me to express an opinion. ***social comment***: see SOCIAL *adjective*.

comment /ˈkɒmɛnt/ *verb*. LME.
[ORIGIN from COMMENT *noun* or French *commenter*; in sense 1, from medieval Latin *commentare*, Latin *-ari* frequentative of Latin *comminisci* (see COMMENT *noun*).]
†**1** *verb trans.* Devise, contrive, invent. LME–L16.
2 *verb intrans.* Write explanatory notes (*up*)*on*; make (esp. unfavourable) remarks (*on*, *upon*, *that*). LME.
DAY LEWIS He would act the biblical stories on which he was commenting. C. RYAN Eisenhower never commented on him except in private.
3 *verb trans.* Provide with comments, make comments on; annotate. *arch.* L16.
†**4** *verb intrans.* Remark mentally; meditate. L16–E17.
■ **commenter**, **-or** *noun* a person who comments; a commentator: LME.

commentariat /ˌkɒmənˈtɛːrɪət/ *noun*. L20.
[ORIGIN Blend of COMMENTARY and PROLETARIAT.]
Chiefly *US* POLITICS. Members of the news media as a class.

commentary /ˈkɒmənt(ə)ri/ *noun & verb*. LME.
[ORIGIN Latin *commentarius*, *-ium* use as noun (sc. *liber* book, *volumen* volume) of adjective from *commentari*: see COMMENT *verb*, -ARY[1].]
▸ **A** *noun*. **1** An expository treatise; a series of comments or annotations on a text. LME. ▸**b** Chiefly *hist.* A memoir, an informal historical record. Usu. in *pl.* L15. ▸**c** A spoken description of an event, performance, etc., accompanying a radio or television broadcast, a cinema film, etc. L19.
c running commentary: see RUNNING *ppl adjective*.
2 *transf.* & *fig.* A comment, a remark, an illustration. M16.
T. GUNN There will be no speech from / the scaffold, the scene must / be its own commentary.
3 Exposition, annotation, systematic commenting, acting as commentator. M17.
▸ **B** *verb*. †**1** *verb intrans.* Comment (*up*)*on*. Only in E17.
2 *verb trans.* Annotate. *rare*. M17.

commentate /ˈkɒmənteɪt/ *verb*. LME.
[ORIGIN In isolated early use from Latin *commentat-*: see COMMENTATION, -ATE[3]. In mod. use back-form. from COMMENTATOR.]
1 *verb trans.* = COMMENT *verb* 3. *rare*. LME.
2 *verb intrans.* Act as a commentator. M19.

commentation /kɒmənˈteɪʃ(ə)n/ *noun*. LME.
[ORIGIN Latin *commentatio(n-)*, from *commentat-* pa. ppl stem of *commentari*: see COMMENT *verb*, -ATION.]
†**1** A comment; a commentary. LME–E18.
†**2** (Comment which is) mere invention or concoction. M17–M18.
3 Commenting. M19.

commentator /ˈkɒmənteɪtə/ *noun*. LME.
[ORIGIN Latin *commentator*, from *commentat-*: see COMMENTATION, -OR.]
A writer or speaker of a commentary; a person who comments on current events, esp. on radio or television.
■ **commentaˈtorial** *adjective* of, pertaining to, or characteristic of a commentator or commentators E19. **commentatorship** *noun* M18.

commentitious /kɒmɛnˈtɪʃəs/ *adjective*. Now *rare* or *obsolete*. E17.
[ORIGIN from Latin *commenticius*, *-tius*, from *comment-*: see COMMENT *noun*, -ITIOUS[1].]
Fictitious, lying.

commerce /ˈkɒməːs/ *noun*. M16.
[ORIGIN French *commerce* or Latin *commercium* trade, trafficking, formed as COM- + *merx*, *merc-* merchandise.]
1 Dealings, social intercourse; converse with God, with spirits, thoughts, etc. M16.
2 Buying and selling; the exchange of merchandise or services, esp. on a large scale. L16. ▸**b** A gambling card game in which players exchange cards with a spare hand. Also, a derivative of this in which cards are obtained by purchase from the dealer or by exchange with one's neighbour. E18.
A. HOURANI The main centres of finance and commerce.
Chamber of Commerce: see CHAMBER *noun* 2. ***standard of commerce***: see STANDARD *noun* 7b.
†**3** A mercantile transaction; an affair, a concern. L16–E18.
4 Sexual intercourse. *arch.* E17.
A. THEROUX The woman has no commerce with a man.
†**5** Interchange (of ideas, letters, etc.). E17–M18.
†**6** Means of communication. M17–M18.

commerce /kəˈməːs/ *verb intrans. arch.* L16.
[ORIGIN Partly from the noun, partly from French *commercer*.]
†**1** Carry on trade. L16–M17.
2 Communicate or associate *with*. L16.

commercial /kəˈməːʃ(ə)l/ *adjective & noun*. L16.
[ORIGIN from COMMERCE *noun* + -IAL.]
▸ **A** *adjective*. **1** Of, pertaining to, or engaged in commerce. L16.
2 Of a chemical etc.: unpurified. M18.
3 Interested in financial return rather than artistry; likely to make a profit; regarded as a mere matter of business. L19.
C. PEBODY The first English newspaper that proved a commercial success.
4 Of radio or television broadcasting: funded by the revenue from broadcast advertising. M20.
– SPECIAL COLLOCATIONS: **commercial art**: used in advertising etc. **commercial college**, **commercial school**, etc.: giving instruction in commercial subjects. ***commercial docks***: see DOCK *noun*[3]. ***commercial school***: see ***commercial college*** above. ***commercial traveller***: see TRAVELLER 2c. **commercial vehicle**: used or suitable for transporting fare-paying passengers or merchandise.
▸ **B** *noun*. **1** A commercial traveller; a person engaged in commerce. *arch.* M19.
2 A broadcast advertisement; a broadcast programme containing an advertisement. M20.
spot commercial: see SPOT *noun & adjective*.
■ **commerciaˈlese** *noun* (an instance of) the language or diction of the commercial world E20. **commercialism** *noun* (*a*) the principles and practice of commerce; excessive adherence to financial return as a measure of worth; (*b*) a commercial custom or expression: M19. **commercialist** *noun* a person engaged in commerce; an adherent of commercialism: E19. **commerciˈality** *noun* M19. **commercialize** *verb trans.* render (merely) commercial, derive commercial profit from M19. **commercially** *adverb* L18.

commère /kɒmɛːr, ˈkɒmɛː/ *noun*. Pl. pronounced /-ɛːr, -ɛːz/. E20.
[ORIGIN French (see CUMMER), fem. of COMPÈRE.]
A female compère.

Commie /ˈkɒmi/ *noun & adjective*. *colloq*. **M20**.
[**ORIGIN** Abbreviation: see **-IE**.]
(A) Communist.

†**commigration** *noun*. **E17–M18**.
[**ORIGIN** Latin *commigratio(n-)*, from *commigrat-* pa. ppl stem of *commigrare*: see **COM-**, **MIGRATE**, **-ATION**.]
(A) migration, esp. on a large scale.

†**commilitant** *noun & adjective*. Also **comil-**. **L16**.
[**ORIGIN** Latin *commilitant-* pres. ppl stem of *commilitare* soldier with: see **COM-**, **MILITATE**, **-ANT**[1].]
▸ **A** *noun*. A fellow soldier. **L16–E18**.
▸ **B** *adjective*. Fighting in alliance. *rare*. Only in **M19**.

commilito /kəˈmɪlɪtəʊ/ *noun*. Pl. ***commilitones*** /kəmɪlɪˈtəʊniːz/. Also anglicized as †**-ton**. **LME**.
[**ORIGIN** Latin, formed as **COM-** + *milit-*, *miles* soldier.]
A fellow soldier, a comrade in arms.

comminate /ˈkɒmɪneɪt/ *verb trans. & intrans*. **E17**.
[**ORIGIN** from Latin *comminat-*: see **COMMINATION**, **-ATE**[3].]
Anathematize.
■ **comminator** *noun* **L17**.

commination /kɒmɪˈneɪʃ(ə)n/ *noun*. **LME**.
[**ORIGIN** Latin *comminatio(n-)*, from *comminat-* pa. ppl stem of *comminari*, formed as **COM-** + *minari* threaten: see **-ATION**.]
1 Threatening of divine vengeance; denunciation. **LME**.
2 A recital of divine threats against sinners in the Anglican liturgy for Ash Wednesday; the service that includes this. **M16**.

comminatory /ˈkɒmɪnət(ə)ri/ *adjective*. **E16**.
[**ORIGIN** medieval Latin *comminatorius*, from *comminat-*: see **COMMINATION**, **-ORY**[2].]
Threatening; denunciatory.

commingle /kɒˈmɪŋg(ə)l/ *verb intrans. & trans. literary*. Also **comingle** /kəʊˈmɪŋg(ə)l/. **E17**.
[**ORIGIN** from **COM-**, **CO-** + **MINGLE** *verb*.]
Mingle together.

comminute /ˈkɒmɪnjuːt/ *verb trans*. **E17**.
[**ORIGIN** Latin *comminut-* pa. ppl stem of *comminuere*, formed as **COM-** + *minuere* lessen.]
1 Reduce to small fragments; break down or grind into small particles. **E17**.
comminuted fracture: producing multiple fragments of bone.
2 Divide (property etc.) into small portions. **M19**.
■ **commiˈnution** *noun* **L16**. **comminutor** *noun* a machine that breaks up solids, esp. of sewage **M19**.

commis /ˈkɒmi/ *noun*. Pl. same (pronounced same, /-iːz/). **L16**.
[**ORIGIN** French, use as noun of pa. pple of *commettre* entrust, formed as **COMMIT**.]
†**1** A deputy, a clerk. **L16–E19**.
2 A junior waiter or chef. **M20**.

commiserable /kəˈmɪz(ə)rəb(ə)l/ *adjective*. **E17**.
[**ORIGIN** from **COMMISERATE** + **-ABLE**.]
Deserving commiseration.

commiserate /kəˈmɪzəreɪt/ *verb*. **L16**.
[**ORIGIN** Latin *commiserat-* pa. ppl stem of *commiserari*, *-are*, formed as **COM-** + *miserari* lament, pity, from *miser* wretched: see **-ATE**[3].]
1 *verb intrans*. Feel compassion (*arch*.); condole (*with*). **L16**.
V. SACKVILLE-WEST They would commiserate now with her in being left alone. W. GOLDING Philip commiserated; . . pointed out the agony of my choice.
2 *verb trans*. Feel or express compassion for; condole with. *arch*. **E17**.
■ **commiseratingly** *adverb* with commiseration **M19**. **commiserative** *adjective* given to or showing commiseration, compassionate **E17**. **commiseratively** *adverb* **E17**.

commiseration /kəmɪzəˈreɪʃ(ə)n/ *noun*. **M16**.
[**ORIGIN** Latin *commiseratio(n-)*, formed as **COMMISERATE**: see **-ATION**.]
1 The action of commiserating; (the expression of) compassion; pity. **M16**.
A. TOFFLER Moving one's household . . is a cause for commiseration rather than congratulation.
2 A feeling or expression of compassion; a condolence. Usu. in *pl*. **E17**.
W. GOLDING I asked that my commiserations for his sickness . . should be conveyed.

commish /kəˈmɪʃ/ *noun*. *colloq*. **E20**.
[**ORIGIN** Abbreviation.]
(A) commission.

commissaire /kɒmɪˈsɛː/ *noun*. **M18**.
[**ORIGIN** French: see **COMMISSAR**.]
= **COMMISSARY**.

commissar /kɒmɪˈsɑː/ *noun*. **LME**.
[**ORIGIN** French *commissaire* from medieval Latin *commissarius* **COMMISSARY**. In sense 2 from Russian *komissar* from French.]
†**1** A deputy, a delegate, a commissary. Chiefly *Scot*. **LME–M18**.
2 *hist*. The head of a government department in the USSR. **E20**.

commissarial /kɒmɪˈsɛːrɪəl/ *adjective*. **E18**.
[**ORIGIN** from medieval Latin *commissarius* **COMMISSARY** + **-AL**[1].]
Of or pertaining to a commissary.

commissariat /kɒmɪˈsɛːrɪət/ *noun*. In sense 1 usu. **-ot**. **L16**.
[**ORIGIN** Partly from medieval Latin *commissariatus*, formed as **COMMISSARY**; partly from French *commissariat*: see **-ATE**[1].]
1 *SCOTS LAW* (now *hist*.). The office, jurisdiction, or district of a commissary. **L16**.
2 A department, esp. military, for the supply of food etc.; food supplied. **L18**.
3 *hist*. A government department in the USSR. **E20**.

commissary /ˈkɒmɪs(ə)ri/ *noun*. **LME**.
[**ORIGIN** medieval Latin *commissarius* officer in charge, from *commiss-*: see **COMMISSION** *noun*, **-ARY**[1].]
1 A deputy, a delegate, a commissioned representative. **LME**.
2 *ECCLESIASTICAL*. The representative of the bishop in part of his diocese, or of an absent bishop. **LME**.
3 **a** The Vice-Chancellor of Oxford University. *obsolete* exc. *hist*. **LME**. ▸**b** An assessor in the Vice-Chancellor's court at Cambridge University. **L18**.
4 **a** *MILITARY*. An officer charged with the supply of food etc. to soldiers. **L15**. ▸**b** A store for provisions etc.; *spec*. a restaurant in a film studio etc. *US*. **L19**.
5 A senior police officer in France. **L18**.
6 *SCOTS LAW* (now *hist*.). A judge in a commissary court. **E19**.
7 = **COMMISSAR** 2. **E20**.
– **COMB. & PHRASES**: **commissary court** *SCOTS LAW* (now *hist*.) a court which exercised jurisdiction in marriage, testamentary affairs, etc.; **commissary general** a chief or head commissary.
■ **commissaryship** *noun* **L16**.

commission /kəˈmɪʃ(ə)n/ *noun*. **ME**.
[**ORIGIN** Old French & mod. French from Latin *commissio(n-)*, from *commiss-* pa. ppl stem of *committere* **COMMIT**: see **-ION**.]
▸ **I** **1** Authority; *esp*. delegated authority to act in a specific capacity or manner. **ME**. ▸**b** *spec*. Authority to act as agent for another in trade; (a) payment to an agent proportional to the amount involved in a transaction, a percentage on the amount involved. **E17**.
LD MACAULAY Dundee . . had summoned all the clans which acknowledged his commission. **b** V. S. NAIPAUL Some of them wanted a fifteen-cent commission on every copy. W. C. KETCHUM Galleries . . have been known to take merchandise at no commission.
2 A command, an instruction. **LME**.
E. A. FREEMAN They gave him no direct commission to bind them to any consent.
3 A warrant conferring authority, *esp*. that of officers in the army, navy, and air force, above a certain rank; an office or rank conferred by such a warrant. **LME**.
H. COX Commissions of inquiry are issued by the Crown. B. CHATWIN The colonel had recently resigned his commission.
4 A body of people with delegated authority to act in a specific capacity or manner; the office or department of such a body or of a commissioner. **L15**.
5 A charge or matter entrusted to a person to perform; an order for the execution of a particular work. **L16**.
M. HOLROYD His first commission in portraiture was to paint an old lady living in Eaton Square. J. RATHBONE I have a commission to find you.
6 The entrusting of or *of* authority, a charge, etc. (*to*); the admitting of a warship etc. to active service. **L19**.
▸ **II** **7** The committing of or *of* a crime, sin, etc. **LME**.
8 An offence, crime, etc., committed. *rare*. **M17**.
– **PHRASES**: ***Commission of Array***: see **ARRAY** *noun* 3. ***commission of lunacy***: see **LUNACY** 1. ***commission of oy and terminer***: see **OY** *interjection*[2]. ***commission of sewers***: see **SEWER** *noun*[1]. **commission of the peace** (the authority given to) Justices of the Peace. ***High Commission***: see **HIGH** *adjective*. **in commission** (**a**) in the exercise of (delegated authority); (**b**) (of an office) placed by warrant in the charge of a body of people, instead of the ordinary constitutional administrator; (**c**) (of a warship, aircraft, etc.) manned, armed, and ready for active service. **on commission** with payment proportional to the amount involved in a transaction, (paid) on a pro rata basis. **out of commission** not in service; not in working order, unable to function. ***override one's commission***: see **OVERRIDE** *verb*. ***overriding commission***: see **OVERRIDE** *verb*. **Royal Commission** a commission of inquiry or a committee appointed by the Crown at the instance of the Government. **sin of commission** the doing of a thing which ought not to have been done (opp. ***sin of omission***).
– **COMB.**: **commission agent** a person who transacts business for another on commission; *spec*. a bookmaker; †**commission officer** a commissioned officer.

commission /kəˈmɪʃ(ə)n/ *verb*. **M17**.
[**ORIGIN** from the noun.]
1 *verb trans*. Empower by a commission, give authority; entrust with an office or duty. Foll. by *to do*. **M17**. ▸**b** Send on a mission *to*, *to do*. **L17**. ▸**c** Give (an artist etc.) a commission *to do*. **E19**.
G. VIDAL Giles was commissioned to find a boat. **c** G. GREENE I've been commissioned to do a Life of General Gordon.
2 *verb trans*. Give (a person) a commission for a rank in the army, navy, or air force. Cf. earlier **COMMISSIONED** 1. **E18**.
F. CHICHESTER I was commissioned as a Flying Officer.
3 *verb trans*. Give (an officer) command of a ship. **L18**.
4 *verb trans*. Admit (a warship, aircraft, etc.) to active service; prepare (a warship, aircraft, etc.) for active service; bring (a machine, equipment, etc.) into operation. **L18**. ▸**b** *verb intrans*. Of a warship, aircraft, etc.: commence active service. **E20**.
5 *verb trans*. Give a commission for, order, (a particular piece of work, the execution of a work, †an article of merchandise). **L18**.
R. BURNS The books I commissioned in my last. K. CLARK The princely patrons . . commissioned quantities of manuscripts.
■ **commissional** *adjective* of or pertaining to a commission **M16**. †**commissionate** *verb trans. & intrans*. = **COMMISSION** *verb* **L16–E19**.

C

commissionaire /kəmɪʃəˈnɛː/ *noun*. **M17**.
[**ORIGIN** French *commissionnaire* formed as **COMMISSIONER**.]
1 A person entrusted with small commissions; a messenger. Now *rare*. **M17**.
2 A member of an association of pensioned soldiers organized for employment as messengers, porters, etc. (now *hist*.). Hence, a uniformed door attendant at a theatre, cinema, large shop, office, etc. **M19**.

commissioned /kəˈmɪʃ(ə)nd/ *adjective*. **L17**.
[**ORIGIN** from **COMMISSION** *noun*, *verb*: see **-ED**[2], **-ED**[1].]
1 Of an officer in the army, navy, or air force: holding a rank conferred by a commission. Opp. ***non-commissioned***. **L17**.
2 *gen*. That has been commissioned. **M18**.

commissioner /kəˈmɪʃ(ə)nə/ *noun*. **LME**.
[**ORIGIN** medieval Latin *commissionarius* noun, from *commissio(n-)*: see **COMMISSION** *noun*, **-ER**[2].]
1 A person appointed by commission, as the head of the Metropolitan Police in London, a delegate to the General Assembly of the Church of Scotland, etc.; a member of a commission or of any of certain government boards. **LME**. ▸**b** A representative of supreme authority in a district, department, etc. **L15**.
Charity Commissioner, ***Civil Service Commissioner***, ***commissioner of sewers***, ***Parliamentary Commissioner for Administration***, etc. **Commissioner for Oaths** a solicitor authorized to administer an oath to a person making an affidavit. ***High Commissioner***: see **HIGH** *adjective*. **Lord Commissioner**, **Lord High Commissioner** the representative of the Crown at the General Assembly of the Church of Scotland.
2 A bookmaker. *slang*. Now *rare*. **M19**.
■ **commissionership** *noun* **E19**.

commissive /kəˈmɪsɪv/ *adjective*. **E19**.
[**ORIGIN** from **COMMISSION** *noun* + **-IVE**, after *omissive*.]
Of an act etc.: actually done or committed, involving active agency.

commissure /ˈkɒmɪsjʊə/ *noun*. **LME**.
[**ORIGIN** Latin *commissura*, from *commiss-*: see **COMMISSION** *noun*, **-URE**.]
1 *gen*. A juncture, a seam. **LME**.
2 A joint between two bones; *esp*. a suture. Now *rare* or *obsolete*. **M16**.
3 The line or point where lips or eyelids meet. **M18**.
4 Any of several bundles of nerve tissue which connect the two sides of the central nervous system in the brain or spinal cord. **E19**.
5 *BOTANY*. The line of junction of the cohering faces of two carpels (in umbellifers). **M19**.

commis-voyageur /kɒmi vwajaʒœːr/ *noun*. Pl. pronounced same. **M19**.
[**ORIGIN** French.]
A commercial traveller.

commit /kəˈmɪt/ *verb*. Infl. **-tt-**. **LME**.
[**ORIGIN** Latin *committere* join, practise, entrust, (in medieval Latin) consign to custody, formed as **COM-** + *mittere* put, send (see **MISSION** *noun*, *verb*).]
▸ **I** *verb trans*. **1** Entrust or consign for treatment or safe keeping (*to* a person, a person's care, etc., *to* the earth, the flames, etc.). **LME**.
commit to memory learn so as to be able to recall. ***commit to paper***: see **PAPER** *noun & adjective*. **commit to writing** record in writing.
2 Consign officially to custody as a (suspected) criminal or as insane; send to prison etc., esp. until trial. (Foll. by *to*.) **LME**.
H. MARTINEAU The magistrates committed the prisoners to the House of Correction for one month each. E. ALBEE I'm rather worried about you. About your mind . . . I think I'll have you committed. R. TRAVERS He was charged with wilful murder and formally committed for trial.
†**3** Charge with a duty or office. **LME–M16**.
4 Be the doer of (a crime, a sin, a blunder, etc.). **LME**.
commit adultery, ***commit mayhem***, ***commit murder***, ***commit suicide***, etc.
†**5** Connect, fasten. **M16–L17**.
6 Refer (a parliamentary bill etc.) to a committee. **L16**.
7 Engage (parties) as opponents; embroil. *arch*. **E17**.
8 Expose to risk; involve (character, honour, etc.). **L18**. ▸**b** Pledge (oneself) by implication; bind (a person, oneself, *to* a course of action); dedicate (oneself) morally (*to* a doctrine or cause). **L18**.
T. JEFFERSON The importance of restraining individuals from committing the peace and honor of the two nations. **b** H. JAMES Your offer has been before me only these few minutes, and it's too soon for me to commit myself to anything. SLOAN WILSON He had written, 'Maybe—don't commit us.'

▸ **II** *verb intrans.* †**9** Commit an offence; commit adultery. M16–M17.

10 Commit a (suspected) criminal to prison etc. E19.

■ **committable** *adjective* M17. **committed** *ppl adjective* that has been committed; *spec.* obliged to adhere (*to* a course of action), morally dedicated (*to* a doctrine or cause), having a political, artistic, etc., commitment: LME. **committer** *noun* E16. **committible** *adjective* M17.

C

commitment /kəˈmɪtm(ə)nt/ *noun*. L16.
[ORIGIN from COMMIT + -MENT.]
1 The action of officially consigning a person to custody; imprisonment, esp. until trial. L16. ▸**b** A warrant or order consigning a person to prison etc. M18.
†**2** The action of committing an offence etc. E17–M18.
3 The action of referring a parliamentary bill etc. to a committee. E17.
4 *gen.* The action of entrusting or consigning for treatment or safe keeping. L17.
5 The state or quality of being dedicated to a particular cause or activity; an instance of this. L18. ▸**b** [translating French *engagement*.] (Moral, political, artistic, etc.) involvement restricting freedom of action. M20.

New York Times A guy who sleeps around and avoids commitment. *Outlook* I have a commitment to bring art to the people.

6 An engagement, an obligation. M19.

Applied Linguistics People who were young, free of family commitments, and able to move.

committal /kəˈmɪt(ə)l/ *noun*. E17.
[ORIGIN formed as COMMITMENT + -AL[1].]
The action of committing; commitment, esp. (*a*) of an offence, (*b*) of a person to custody or confinement, (*c*) of a body or ashes to the grave or the sea at burial or to the fire at cremation.
– COMB.: **committal proceedings**: in a magistrates' court to determine whether a case should go for trial to a Crown Court.

committee /*in branch* I kɒmɪˈtiː; *in branch* II kəˈmɪti/ *noun*. L15.
[ORIGIN from COMMIT + -EE[1].]
▸ **I** An individual.
1 A person to whom some charge, trust, or function is committed. *obsolete* in *gen.* sense. L15. ▸**b** *hist.* A director of the East India Company. L17. ▸**c** *hist.* A member of the highest management board of Guy's Hospital, London. E18.
2 LAW. A person entrusted with the charge of another or of his or her property; *US* a person who has been judicially committed to the charge of another because of insanity or mental disability. M18.
▸ **II** An aggregate of people.
3 A body of two or more people appointed for some special function by, and usu. out of, a (usu. larger) body; *esp.* such a body appointed by Parliament etc. to consider details of proposed legislation. L16.

Speedway Star The youth committee are trying to organise a team event. P. GREGORY The committee is chaired by a graduate of this university.

Committee of the whole House the whole House of Commons when sitting as a committee. ***joint committee***: see JOINT *adjective*. ***National Hunt Committee***: see NATIONAL *adjective*. ***Rules Committee***: see RULE *noun*. ***select committee***: see SELECT *adjective*. ***standing committee***: see STANDING *adjective*. ***steering committee***: see STEER *verb*[1].

†**4** A meeting or session of such a body. M17–M18.
– COMB.: **committee man**, **committee woman**: a member of a committee or committees.

commix /kɒˈmɪks/ *verb trans. & intrans.* Now *arch.* or *poet.* Pa. pple **-mixed**, **-mixt**. LME.
[ORIGIN Orig. pa. pple, from Latin *commixtus*, formed as COM- + *mixtus* (see MIX *verb*).]
Mix, blend.

commixtion /kɒˈmɪkstʃ(ə)n/ *noun*. Also †**-mixion**. LME.
[ORIGIN Late Latin *commixtio(n-)*, from Latin *commixt-* pa. ppl stem of *commiscere*, formed as COM- + *miscere* (see MIX *verb*).]
1 = COMMIXTURE 1. *obsolete* exc. SCOTS LAW, the mixing together of materials belonging to different owners. LME.
†**2** Sexual intercourse. LME–L17.
†**3** = COMMIXTURE 2. LME–M17.

commixture /kɒˈmɪkstʃə/ *noun*. L16.
[ORIGIN Late Latin *commixtura*, from *commixt-*: see COMMIXTION, -URE.]
1 The action or an act of mixing together. L16.
2 The state of being mixed together; a mixture, a compound. L16.
†**3** = COMPLEXION *noun* 1. *rare* (Shakes.). Only in L16.

Commo /ˈkɒməʊ/ *noun*. *Austral. & NZ colloq.* Also **c-**. Pl. **-os**. M20.
[ORIGIN Abbreviation: see -O-.]
A Communist.

commodatum /kɒməˈdeɪtəm/ *noun*. Pl. **-ta** /-tə/. L17.
[ORIGIN Latin, use as noun of neut. of *commodatus* pa. pple of *commodare* accommodate, lend.]
ROMAN & SCOTS LAW. A free loan, for use, of anything not perishable or consumable.

■ Also **commodate** /ˈkɒmədət/ *noun* (now *rare* or *obsolete*) E18.

commode /kəˈməʊd/ *noun*. L17.
[ORIGIN French, use as noun of *commode* adjective: see COMMODE *adjective*.]
1 A tall headdress formerly worn by women, consisting of a wire framework covered with silk or lace. L17.
2 A chest of drawers or chiffonier of the decorative kind found esp. in 18th-cent. drawing rooms. M18.
3 A lavatory, a privy. *arch. rare*. E19.
4 A chamber pot enclosed in a chair or box with a cover. M19.

†**commode** *adjective*. M17.
[ORIGIN French from Latin *commodus*: see COMMODIOUS.]
1 Convenient, suitable. M17–M18.
2 Accommodating; usu. in a bad sense. E–M18.

commodification /kəˌmɒdɪfɪˈkeɪʃ(ə)n/ *noun*. L20.
[ORIGIN from COMMODITY: see -FICATION.]
The action of turning something into or treating something as a (mere) commodity.
■ **coˈmmodified** *adjective* L20. **coˈmmodify** *verb* L20.

commodious /kəˈməʊdɪəs/ *adjective*. LME.
[ORIGIN French *commodieux* or medieval Latin *commodiosus*, from Latin *commodus* convenient, formed as COM- + *modus* measure: see -OUS.]
†**1** Beneficial, profitable, useful. LME–M18.
2 a Convenient, serviceable; *spec.* convenient as accommodation or shelter. Foll. by *for*, *to*. *arch.* M16. ▸**b** Conveniently roomy, spacious. M16.

a DEFOE The Isle of Caldey . . safe and commodious for Men of War. **b** H. JAMES The smoking-room . . was . . high, light, commodious.

†**3** Of life, living: endowed with conveniences. M16–M17.
†**4** Opportune. E17–M18.
†**5** Of a person: accommodating. *rare* (Shakes.). Only in E17.
■ **commodiously** *adverb* LME. **commodiousness** *noun* M16.

commoditization /kəˌmɒdɪtʌɪˈzeɪʃ(ə)n/ *noun*. L20.
[ORIGIN from COMMODITY + -IZATION.]
= COMMODIFICATION *noun*.
■ **coˈmmoditize** *verb* L20. **coˈmmoditized** *adjective* L20.

commodity /kəˈmɒdɪti/ *noun*. LME.
[ORIGIN Old French & mod. French *commodité* or Latin *commoditas*, from *commodus*: see COMMODIOUS, -ITY.]
▸ †**I** **1** Suitability; fitting utility; convenience, as a property of something. LME–L17.
2 a A person's convenience. LME–M19. ▸**b** (An) advantage, (a) benefit; (selfish) interest. E16–M19. ▸**c** Expediency. L16–L18. ▸**d** Profit, gain. L16–M17.
3 Opportunity, occasion. M16–M17.
▸ **II** **4** A thing of use or value; *spec.* a thing that is an object of trade, *esp.* a raw material or agricultural crop. LME. ▸**b** *fig.* A thing one deals in or makes use of. L16.

R. K. NARAYAN Bullock carts . . loaded with coconut, rice and other commodities for the market. **b** A. G. GARDINER Prettiness is the women's commodity.

†**5** A quantity *of* wares; *spec.* one lent on credit by a usurer for resale, usu. to the usurer himself. L16–M17.

SHAKES. *Meas. for M.* Here's young Master Rash; he's in for a commodity of brown paper and old ginger, . . of which he made five marks ready money.

commodore /ˈkɒmədɔː/ *noun*. Orig. also †**commandore**. L17.
[ORIGIN Prob. from Dutch *komandeur* from French *commandeur* COMMANDER.]
1 A naval officer ranking above a captain and below a rear admiral. L17. ▸**b** A commodore's ship; the principal or the second ship of a group. Now *rare* or *obsolete*. L17.
2 The senior captain of a company of ships or of a shipping line. M19.
3 The senior officer of a yacht club. M19.
4 ***air commodore***, a commissioned rank in the Royal Air Force, above a group captain and below an air vice-marshal. E20.

common /ˈkɒmən/ *noun*. See also COMMONS. ME.
[ORIGIN Partly repr. French *commune* (see COMMUNE *noun*[1]); partly Latin *commune* use as noun of neut. of *communis*; partly from the adjective.]
†**1** The community, the general body of people; occas., the state. ME–M17.
†**2** The common people, often as an estate of the realm. ME–M18.
3 An area of land held jointly by all the members of a community; in mod. use, a piece of open waste land or of common land. ME.
4 CHRISTIAN CHURCH. The parts of a service used for each of a certain class of occasions, e.g. saint's days, where no individual psalm, lesson, etc., is appointed. Cf. PROPER *noun* 2. ME.
5 ENGLISH LAW. A right to make a particular kind of use of land or water owned by another. Also ***right of common***. LME.
common of pasture, ***common of piscary***, ***common of turbary***, etc.
6 *ellipt.* Common sense. *slang*. E20.
– PHRASES: **in common** †(*a*) generally; ordinarily; (*b*) in joint use or possession; (*c*) LAW (held or owned) by two or more people each having undivided possession but with distinct, separately transferable interests (***TENANCY in common***); (cf. ***in severalty*** (a) s.v. SEVERALTY, ***joint tenancy*** s.v. JOINT *adjective*); (*d*) that is common to both or all; jointly *with*. **the common** what is usual or ordinary; now chiefly in ***out of the common***, unusual.

common /ˈkɒmən/ *adjective & adverb*. ME.
[ORIGIN Old French *comun* from Latin *communis*.]
▸ **A** *adjective*. **I** Of a public or non-private nature.
1 Shared alike by all the persons or things in question, or by all humankind (foll. by *to*, (rare) *between*); having the same relationship to all the persons or things in question. ME.

ADDISON Faults common to both Parties. H. E. BATES Weeping to each other in common grief.

Common Celtic, ***Common Germanic***, etc.

2 Belonging to more than one as a result of joint action or agreement. ME.

CHAUCER This was the commune voys of every man. W. TREVOR They walked towards a common goal.

3 Of or belonging to the community or a civic authority. ME.

TENNYSON He sow'd a slander in the common ear.

common council, ***common hall***, ***common hangman***, ***common seal***, etc.

4 Free to be used by everyone; public. ME.
common alehouse, ***common lodging house***, etc.
5 Generally known; *spec.* (of an offender or offence) public, notorious, habitual. ME.

J. WESLEY Baptized liars and common swearers.

common nuisance etc.

6 Of general application. LME.
†**7** [Latin *communis*.] Generally accessible, affable. LME–E17.
▸ **II** Of ordinary occurrence or quality.
8 Of frequent or ordinary occurrence; prevalent, not rare; usual. ME.

J. WESLEY The horrid crime of self-murder is so common . . in England. T. HARDY The Coggans . . were as common among the families of this district as the Avons and Derwents among our rivers. D. DU MAURIER That endless yattering, so common in women.

9 a Of a person: undistinguished by rank or position; belonging to the general body of people. ME. ▸**b** Unrefined, vulgar. M19.

a ADDISON Songs and Fables . . in Vogue among the common People. R. WEST Even common soldiers had considerable opportunity for advancement. **b** JILLY COOPER Nanny Ellis said it was . . common to play with children whose friends were in trade.

10 Undistinguished by any special or superior quality; ordinary. LME.

JOSEPH HALL Dayes, whether common or sacred. G. MACDONALD Here . . was no common mind.

11 Of the most familiar type. LME.

B. FRANKLIN Common fire . . as well as electrical fire. G. WHITE Flocks of the common linnet.

▸ **III** **12** In New Testament and derived use [= Hellenistic Greek *koinos*]: not ceremonially clean. ME.
▸ **IV** Technical uses.
13 MATH. Of a quantity: belonging equally to two or more quantities. LME.
common factor, ***common multiple***, etc.
14 GRAMMAR. **a** Of a noun: applicable to any of an indefinite class of entities, not just one, or denoting a general property or quality. Opp. ***proper***. LME. ▸**b** Designating a gender to which both masculine and feminine words belong; (of a word) belonging to this gender. M16.
15 PROSODY. Of a syllable: optionally either short or long. L17.
– PHRASES & SPECIAL COLLOCATIONS: ***by common consent***: see CONSENT *noun* 2. ***common astrologer***: see ASTROLOGER 2. **common carrier** a person who undertakes as a business to transport any goods or any person in a specified category. ***common centaury***: see CENTAURY 2. ***common chord***: see CHORD *noun*[1] 4. ***common cold***: see COLD *noun* 3. **Common Council** a town or city council, now only in London or US. **Common Councilman** a member of a Common Council. **common crier** a town crier. ***common denominator***: see DENOMINATOR 1. **Common Era** the Christian era. **common field** *hist.* a field belonging to the members of a local community as a whole. **common form** what is usually done and of no special significance, accepted procedure. **common ground** something on which two parties agree or in which both are interested in negotiation, conversation, etc. **common ground dove** = ***TOBACCO dove***. **common gull** a migratory gull, *Larus canus*, widespread on coasts and lowlands in northern and eastern Eurasia and north-west N. America. ***common hunt***: see HUNT *noun*[1]. **common informer** *hist.* a person who sued for the penalty payable by an offender in cases where part or all of the penalty was given to anyone who would sue for it, not only the aggrieved party. ***common jackal***: see JACKAL *noun* 1. **common jury** *hist.*: for which no qualification of rank or property was required. **common knowledge** something known to most people. **common land** (*a*) land subject to rights of common; (*b*) open waste land. ***common laurel***: see LAUREL *noun* 3. **common lizard** = ***viviparous lizard*** s.v. VIVIPAROUS 1. ***common LOGARITHM***. ***common MALLOW***. ***common maple***: see MAPLE *noun* 1. **Common Market** a former name for the European Economic

Community, or European Union. ***common* MERGANSER**. ***common* metre** an iambic metre for hymns in which the verse has four lines with 8, 6, 8, and 6 syllables. ***common* MICA**. ***common opal***: see OPAL *noun* 1. **common or garden** *colloq.* ordinary. ***common* PEAFOWL**. ***common pleas***: see PLEA *noun*. ***common* POMPANO**. **common prayer** prayer in which worshippers publicly unite; *esp.* (*C- P-*) the public worship of the Church of England as prescribed in the *Book of Common Prayer*, orig. in 1549. ***common privet***: see PRIVET 1. **common property** *fig.* = *common knowledge* above. ***common* REDSTART**. ***common recovery***: see RECOVERY 4. ***common roller***: see ROLLER *noun*[2]. ***common* ROOIBEKKIE**. **common room** a room in a college, school, etc., to which all members in a certain category have common access for social or business purposes; the members using it; (***junior common room***: see JUNIOR *adjective*, ***middle common room***: see MIDDLE *adjective*, ***senior common room***: see SENIOR *adjective*). ***common* RORQUAL**. ***common ryegrass***: see RYEGRASS 2. ***common salt***: see SALT *noun*[1] 1. **common sandpiper** a migratory Old World sandpiper, *Actitis hypoleucos*, with olive-brown and white plumage. ***common scold***: see SCOLD *noun* 1. ***common scrubfowl***: see SCRUB *noun*[1]. ***common scurvy grass***: see SCURVY *noun*. **common seal** a seal with a mottled grey coat, *Phoca vitulina*, of N. Atlantic and N. Pacific coasts. ***common* SENSORIUM**. ***common sensory***: see SENSORY *noun* 2. **Common Serjeant** a circuit judge who has duties in the City of London and sits in the Central Criminal Court. ***common shore***: see SHORE *noun*[3]. ***common shoveler***: see SHOVELER *noun*[1] 2. ***common shrimp***: see SHRIMP *noun* 1. ***common silverbill***: see SILVER *noun & adjective*. ***common situs***: see SITUS 2b. ***common snapping turtle***: see SNAPPING *ppl adjective* 3. ***common snipe***: see SNIPE *noun* 1. ***common soldier***: see SOLDIER *noun* 1. ***common sole***: see SOLE *noun*[3]. ***common St John's wort***: see SAINT *noun & adjective*. **common stock** *N. Amer.* the ordinary shares of a company. ***common storksbill***: see STORK *noun*. ***common suit***: see SUIT *noun* 1b. ***common* TEGU**. **common tern** the widespread migratory tern *Sterna hirundo*. **common time** MUSIC: in which there are two or four beats, esp. four crotchets, in a bar. ***common toadfish***: see TOADFISH 1. **common touch** *the* ability to get on with or appeal to ordinary people. ***common twayblade***: see TWAYBLADE 1. ***common valerian***: see VALERIAN 1. ***common violet***: see VIOLET *noun* 1. ***common vole***: see VOLE *noun*[2]. ***common* WALLAROO**. ***common* WOMBAT**. **common year** a year of 365 days beginning on 1 January. ***least common multiple***, ***lowest common multiple***: see MULTIPLE *noun*. ***make common cause with***: see CAUSE *noun*. ***the common rustic***: see RUSTIC *noun* 3.

▸ **B** *adverb*. Commonly. *obsolete* exc. *US colloq.* ME.

■ **commonish** *adjective* rather common L18.

†common *verb*. ME.

[ORIGIN Orig. a form of COMMUNE *verb*, with stress shifted to 1st syll. In branch III from COMMON *noun*, *adjective*, COMMONS.]

▸ **I 1** *verb intrans.* Associate *with*, have (esp. sexual) intercourse *with*. ME–M16.
2 *verb trans.* Share (*with*), communicate (*to*). LME–M16.
3 *verb trans.* Tell, declare, publish. LME–M16.
4 *verb intrans.* Participate, share *in*, *with*. LME–E17.
▸ **II** = COMMUNE *verb* II.
5 *verb trans. & intrans.* = COMMUNE *verb* 6. LME–E16.
6 a *verb intrans.* = COMMUNE *verb* 5a. LME–M18. ▸**b** *verb trans.* = COMMUNE *verb* 5c. LME–E17.
▸ **III 7** *verb intrans.* Exercise a right of common. E16–E19.
8 *verb intrans.* Eat at a common table. L16–M18.

commonable /ˈkɒmənəb(ə)l/ *adjective*. E17.

[ORIGIN from COMMON *verb* + -ABLE.]

1 Of an animal: able to be pastured on common land. E17.
2 Of land: able to be held in common; suitable for the exercise of rights of common. M17.

commonage /ˈkɒmənɪdʒ/ *noun*. E17.

[ORIGIN from COMMON *noun*, *verb* + -AGE.]

1 a = COMMON *noun* 5, *esp.* common of pasture. E17. ▸**b** Common land; a common. L18. ▸**c** The condition of being subject to rights of common. E19.
2 The common people. M17.

commonality /kɒməˈnalɪti/ *noun*. LME.

[ORIGIN By-form of COMMONALTY.]

†1 a = COMMONALTY 1a. LME–L17. ▸**b** = COMMONALTY 1b. Only in L17. ▸**c** = COMMONALTY 3. Only in L17.
2 a Possession in common; the sharing of features or attributes; the state of having something in common (*with*). (*rare* before M20.) M16. ▸**b** A shared feature or attribute. L20.
3 = COMMONALTY 2. L16.

commonalty /ˈkɒmən(ə)lti/ *noun*. ME.

[ORIGIN Old French *comunalté* from medieval Latin *communalitas*, from Latin *communis*: see COMMON *adjective*, -ALITY.]

†1 a The people of a nation, city, etc.; a community, a body politic. ME–M17. ▸**b** A republic, a democracy. E–M17.
2 The common people. ME.
3 A corporate body. LME.
4 The general body *of* humankind etc. M16.

commoner /ˈkɒmənə/ *noun*. ME.

[ORIGIN medieval Latin *communarius*, from *communa* COMMUNE *noun*[1]: see -ER[2].]

†1 A citizen, a burgess. ME–M17.
2 Any of the common people; now, anyone below the rank of peer. LME.
†3 A person who shares in anything. LME–M17.
4 A member of the House of Commons. Now *rare*. LME.
5 A person who has a right of common. LME.
†6 A prostitute. Only in 17.
7 At some English educational institutions: a student without financial support from his college, paying for his own commons; a student without a college scholarship etc. Cf. PENSIONER 5. E17.

■ **commonership** *noun* the situation of being a commoner E20.

commonhold /ˈkɒmənhəʊld/ *noun*. L20.

[ORIGIN from COMMON *adjective* + HOLD *noun*[1].]

LAW. In England and Wales: a scheme of ownership under which tenants own their flat on a freehold basis but share certain responsibilities and pay for certain services in common.

■ **commonholder** *noun* L20.

commonise *verb* var. of COMMONIZE.

†commonitory *adjective & noun*. M16.

[ORIGIN Late Latin *commonitorius*, from Latin *commonit-* pa. ppl stem of *commonere* remind forcibly, formed as COM- + *monere* advise: see -ORY[2].]

▸ **A** *adjective*. Serving to advise or admonish. M16–M18.
▸ **B** *noun*. A warning. E18–M19.

■ **†commonition** *noun* (*rare*) (giving of) a formal admonition M18–M19.

commonize /ˈkɒmənʌɪz/ *verb*. Also **-ise**. M19.

[ORIGIN from COMMON *adjective* + -IZE.]

1 *verb intrans.* Pool food and share a meal (*with*). *colloq.* M19.
2 *verb trans.* Make common; *spec.* give (a proper noun) a meaning other than as a proper noun. M19.

■ **communiˈzation** *noun* M20.

common law /ˈkɒmən lɔː/ *noun phr*. ME.

[ORIGIN translating medieval Latin *jus commune*.]

1 The part of English law that is applied by national courts but is not fully prescribed by statute, purporting instead to be derived from ancient usage and judicial decisions. Opp. ***equity***, ***civil law***, ***statute law***. ME. ▸**b** The body of English law as adopted and adapted by the different states of the US. E19.
†2 The general law of a community or of the Church, as opp. to local or personal rules and customs. LME–M16.

– COMB.: **common-law husband**: in a common-law marriage; **common-law lawyer** = COMMON LAWYER; **common-law marriage** a marriage recognized in some jurisdictions as valid under common law though not brought about by a civil or ecclesiastical ceremony; *popularly* a relationship in which a man and woman cohabit for a period long enough to suggest stability; **common-law wife**: in a common-law marriage.

■ **common lawyer** *noun phr.* a lawyer versed in, or practising, common law L16.

commonly /ˈkɒmənli/ *adverb*. ME.

[ORIGIN from COMMON *adjective* + -LY[2].]

†1 Generally, universally. ME–M17.
†2 Together. ME–M16.
3 As a general thing; usually, ordinarily. ME.

> GIBBON More than commonly deficient in those qualities. B. JOWETT Writings commonly attributed to Plato.

†4 Closely, familiarly. ME–L16.
†5 Publicly. LME–L16.

> AV *Matt.* 28:15 This saying is commonly reported among the Iewes vntill this day.

commonness /ˈkɒmənnɪs/ *noun*. M16.

[ORIGIN from COMMON *adjective* + -NESS.]

1 The state or quality of being common. M16.
2 *spec.* Lack of excellence or distinction. E19.

commonplace /ˈkɒmənpleɪs/ *noun*, *adjective*, & *verb*. M16.

[ORIGIN Orig. two words, translating Latin *locus communis* translating Greek *koinos topos* general theme.]

▸ **A** *noun*. **†1** RHETORIC. A passage of general application; a leading text. M–L16.
2 a A notable passage or quotation entered in a book for future use. M16. ▸**†b** A commonplace book. M16–M18.
3 An ordinary topic; an opinion or statement generally accepted; a platitude. M16.

> D. H. LAWRENCE He was nervous . . , chattering the conventional commonplaces. JOHN BROOKE A commonplace of school history books.

†4 A thesis or discourse on a set theme. M17–E18.
5 Anything usual or trite; ordinary or trite matter. M18.

> S. RICHARDSON Common subjects afford only commonplace.

6 Ordinariness; lack of distinction. M19.

> G. M. TREVELYAN Local traditions were yielding to nationwide commonplace.

7 ***the commonplace***, that which is ordinary and without novelty. M19.

– COMB.: **commonplace book** a book of commonplaces (sense 2a).

▸ **B** *adjective*. Of the nature of a commonplace; lacking originality, trite. E17.
▸ **C** *verb*. **1** *verb intrans.* Utter commonplaces. E17.
†2 *verb intrans.* Speak in support of a thesis. M17–M18.
3 *verb trans.* Extract noteworthy items from (a text); arrange under general headings; enter in a commonplace book. M17.

■ **commonplaceness** *noun* E19. **commonplacer** *noun* †(*a*) a commonplace book; (*b*) a person who keeps a commonplace book: M17.

commons /ˈkɒmənz/ *noun pl*. ME.

[ORIGIN Pl. of COMMON *noun*.]

▸ **I** Common people.
1 *hist.* The common people, as distinguished from those of noble, knightly, or gentle rank. ME.
†2 The burgesses of a town. ME–E18.
3 a The third estate in the English or other similar constitution (in early use excluding the clergy), as represented by the Lower House of Parliament. ME. ▸**b** (**C-**.) The representatives in Parliament of this estate; the Lower House. ME.

b House of Commons the Lower House of Parliament in the UK.

▸ **II** Provisions in common.
4 a Provisions shared in common, esp. in a college or a religious community; the share due to each person; formerly also, the cost of this. ME. ▸**b** Treated as *sing.* A common table; a dining hall; formerly, at Oxford University, a definite portion of food supplied by one's college at a set price. M17.

> **b** T. C. WOLFE Food was . . very cheap: at the college commons, twelve dollars a month.

5 Rations; daily fare. M16.

short commons insufficient food.

common sense /kɒmən ˈsɛns/ *noun phr. & adjective*. Also **common-sense**, **commonsense**. M16.

[ORIGIN Repr. Greek *koinē aisthēsis*, Latin *sensus communis*.]

▸ **A** *noun phr.* **1** An internal sense formerly regarded as uniting the impressions of the five senses in a common consciousness. *obsolete* exc. *hist.* M16.
2 a Ordinary or normal understanding. M16. ▸**b** Good sound practical sense in everyday matters; general sagacity. E18. ▸**c** A thing in accordance with common sense. E19.
3 The collective sense or judgement of humankind or of a community. L16.
4 PHILOSOPHY. The faculty by which certain beliefs are generally accepted without philosophical enquiry or influence from religious teaching etc. M18.

▸ **B** *adjective*. (With hyphen or as one word.) Based on common sense; that is in accord with common sense. M19.

> R. G. COLLINGWOOD The world they represent is not the common-sense world, it is the world of delirium.

■ **commonˈsensible** *adjective* = COMMONSENSICAL M19. **commonˈsensibly** *adverb* L19. **commonˈsensical** *adjective* possessing or marked by common sense M19. **ˌcommonsensiˈcality** *noun* E20. **commonˈsensically** *adverb* L19.

commonty /ˈkɒmənti/ *noun*. Now only *Scot.* LME.

[ORIGIN Old French *comuneté*: see COMMUNITY.]

†1 = COMMONALTY 2. LME–M17.
†2 A community, a body politic. LME–E16.
3 Common possession. LME.
4 = COMMON *noun* 5. *Scot.* LME.
5 = COMMON *noun* 3. *Scot.* LME.

commonweal /ˈkɒmənwiːl/ *noun*. *arch.* ME.

[ORIGIN Orig. two words, from COMMON *adjective* + WEAL *noun*[1].]

1 = COMMONWEALTH 2. ME.
2 (Usu. two words.) Common well-being; the general good. LME.

commonwealth /ˈkɒmənwɛlθ/ *noun*. LME.

[ORIGIN Orig. two words, from COMMON *adjective* + WEALTH.]

1 = COMMONWEAL 2. *arch.* LME.
2 The body politic; a nation, viewed as a community in which everyone has an interest. E16.
3 *fig.* Any aggregate of persons or things united by some common factor. M16. ▸**b** A company of actors who share the takings instead of receiving a salary. E19.

> BURKE Writers on publick law have often called this aggregate of nations a commonwealth.

commonwealth of learning learned people collectively. ***commonwealth of letters***: see LETTER *noun*[1]. **commonwealth of nations** the nations viewed as a community of states.

4 A republic; a democracy. E17. ▸**b** A state of the US, esp. as a formal title of some of them. L18.
5 ***the Commonwealth***: ▸**a** *hist.* The republican government in England between 1649 and 1660. M17. ▸**b** The federated states of Australia. L19. ▸**c** [from sense 3.] A free association of the UK with certain independent states (orig. subject to Britain) and dependencies which all acknowledge the British monarch as its Head. Also ***British Commonwealth*** (***of Nations***). E20.

a Lord Protector of the Commonwealth: see PROTECTOR 2b. **c the New Commonwealth** countries of the British Commonwealth that have become independent since 1945. **the Old Commonwealth** Canada, Australia, and New Zealand.

– COMB.: **Commonwealth Day** a day each year commemorating the British Commonwealth (formerly called Empire Day); **Commonwealth preference** the practice of charging lower tariffs on imports from Commonwealth countries; **commonwealth's-man** †(*a*) a person devoted to the public good; (*b*) *hist.* an adherent of the Commonwealth in the 17th cent.; †(*c*) a republican.

commorant /ˈkɒmər(ə)nt/ *adjective*. Now *rare* or *obsolete*. M16.
[ORIGIN Latin *commorant-* pres. ppl stem of *commorari* tarry, abide, formed as COM- + *morari* delay: see -ANT¹.]
Resident.
■ **commorancy** *noun* (a) residence, (an) abode L16. †**commoration** *noun* residing, abiding E17–M19.

commorient /kəˈmɔːrɪənt/ *adjective & noun*. M17.
[ORIGIN Latin *commorient-* pres. ppl stem of *commori*, formed as COM- + *mori* die: see -ENT.]
▶ †**A** *adjective*. Of or pertaining to simultaneous death. Only in M17.
▶ **B** *noun*. Pl. **commorientes** /kəmɔːrɪˈɛntiːz/, **commorients**. A person who dies at the same time as another; LAW each of two or more people dying on the same occasion (as in the same accident or other disaster) and connected by way of disposing of assets one to the other on death (usu. in *pl.*). M18.

commot /ˈkɒmət/ *noun*. Also **-ote** /-əʊt/. L15.
[ORIGIN Welsh *cymwd*, *kymwt* (now *cwmwd*) neighbourhood, locality.]
hist. In Wales, a territorial division subordinate to a cantred.

commotion /kəˈməʊʃ(ə)n/ *noun*. LME.
[ORIGIN Old French & mod. French, or Latin *commotio(n-)*, formed as COM- + *motio(n-)* MOTION *noun*.]
†**1** Mental or emotional disturbance. LME–M18.
2 Public disorder; (an) insurrection. LME.
3 a (A) physical disturbance, more or less violent. LME. ▸**b** (A) bustle; (a) noisy confusion. E17.

> **a** SOUTHEY The billows' commotion. **b** P. PEARCE There was a commotion of voices and footsteps.

†**4** Continuous or recurring motion. E16–M17.

commove /kəˈmuːv/ *verb trans.* *arch.* LME.
[ORIGIN Orig. from Old French *commovoir* (see COM-, MOVE *verb*); later from MOVE *verb* after Latin *commovere*.]
Move violently; agitate, arouse, (*lit.* & *fig.*); excite. Chiefly as ***commoved*** *ppl adjective*.

> R. L. STEVENSON He who has seen the sea commoved with a great hurricane.

communal /ˈkɒmjʊn(ə)l, kəˈmjuː-/ *adjective*. L15.
[ORIGIN Old French *communel* (mod. *-al*) from late Latin *communalis*, from *communis* COMMON *adjective*: see -AL¹.]
†**1** Unanimous. *rare*. Only in L15.
2 Of, pertaining to, or belonging to a commune, esp. (**C-**) the Paris Commune. E19.
3 Of or for the community or a community, for common use; shared by all, general. M19.

> R. FRY The greatest art has always been communal. C. MCCULLOUGH The bathroom and kitchen were communal, shared by all the tenants. F. WELDON The communal guilt which the male sex appears to bear in relation to women.

communal MARRIAGE.
■ **commuˈnality** *noun* community of feeling, solidarity E20. **communaliˈzation** *noun* the action of communalizing L19. **communalize** *verb trans.* make (esp. land) communal L19. **communally** *adverb* L19.

communalism /ˈkɒmjʊn(ə)lɪz(ə)m/ *noun*. L19.
[ORIGIN from COMMUNAL + -ISM.]
The principle of the communal organization of society.
■ **communalist** *noun* an adherent of communalism L19. **communaˈlistic** *adjective* L19.

communard /ˈkɒmjʊnɑːd/ *noun*. L19.
[ORIGIN French, formed as COMMUNE *noun*¹ + -ARD.]
A member of a commune; *esp.* (**C-**) an adherent of the Paris Commune; a communalist.

commune /ˈkɒmjuːn/ *noun*¹. L17.
[ORIGIN French from medieval Latin *communia* neut. pl. of Latin *communis* COMMON *adjective* taken as fem. sing. in sense 'group of people having a common life'.]
▶ **I 1** A French territorial division, the smallest for administrative purposes; a similar division elsewhere. L17.
2 ***the Commune*** (***of Paris***), ***the Paris Commune***: (**a**) a body which usurped the municipal government of Paris during the French Revolution; (**b**) the communalistic government temporarily established in Paris in 1871. L18.
3 A communal settlement, orig. in a Communist country; a group of people not all of one family sharing living accommodation and goods. E20.
▶ **II 4** *hist.* The commonalty; a corporate body. E19.

commune /ˈkɒmjuːn/ *noun*². E19.
[ORIGIN from COMMUNE *verb*.]
The action of communing; converse, communion.

commune /kəˈmjuːn, ˈkɒmjuːn/ *verb*. ME.
[ORIGIN Old French *comuner* share, from *comun* COMMON *adjective*: cf. COMMON *verb*.]
▶ **I** = COMMON *verb* I.
†**1** *verb intrans.* = COMMON *verb* 1. ME–E19.
†**2** *verb trans.* = COMMON *verb* 2. ME–M16.
†**3** *verb trans.* = COMMON *verb* 3. LME–M16.
†**4** = COMMON *verb* 4. Only in LME.
▶ **II** †**5 a** *verb intrans.* Confer, consult, converse, (*with* a person, *of*, (*up*)*on* a matter). ME–M18. ▸**b** *verb trans.* Confer about, discuss, debate. L16–M17.
6 *verb intrans.* Have an intimate (esp. mental or spiritual) exchange or discussion (*with* a friend, one's heart, etc., *together*); feel in close touch *with* (nature etc.). LME.

> *Vanity Fair* The guests would sit around a bonfire, communing with nature.

7 †**a** *verb trans.* Administer Holy Communion to; = COMMUNICATE *verb* 3b. ME–E16. ▸**b** *verb intrans.* Receive Holy Communion; = COMMUNICATE *verb* 3a. Now chiefly *US*. M16.
■ **communer** *noun* (long *rare*) LME.

communicable /kəˈmjuːnɪkəb(ə)l/ *adjective*. LME.
[ORIGIN Old French & mod. French, or late Latin *communicabilis*, from *communicare*: see COMMUNICATE *verb*, -ABLE.]
†**1** Communicating, having intercommunication. LME–L17.
2 Able to be communicated to others. M16.

> E. A. PARKES An animal poison . . communicable from person to person. H. READ A vision . . too mystical to be wholly communicable.

3 Communicative, affable. *arch.* M16.
■ **communicaˈbility** *noun* M17. **communicableness** *noun* E17. **communicably** *adverb* E17.

communicant /kəˈmjuːnɪk(ə)nt/ *adjective & noun*. L15.
[ORIGIN Latin *communicant-* pres. ppl stem of *communicare*: see COMMUNICATE *verb*, -ANT¹.]
▶ **A** *adjective*. †**1** Of existence: shared *with*. *rare*. Only in L15.
2 Sharing, participating; having a part in common. *rare*. M16.
3 Providing communication, communicating. *rare*. L17.
4 Receiving Holy Communion, esp. regularly. *rare*. M19.
▶ **B** *noun*. **1** A person who receives Holy Communion, esp. regularly. M16.
2 A person who or thing which makes a communication; a person who imparts information. L16.

†**communicate** *adjective*. LME–E18.
[ORIGIN Latin *communicatus* pa. pple, formed as COMMUNICATE *verb*: see -ATE².]
Extrinsic; communicated.

communicate /kəˈmjuːnɪkeɪt/ *verb*. E16.
[ORIGIN Latin *communicat-* pa. ppl stem of *communicare* impart, share, etc., from *communis* COMMON *adjective* + *-ic-* formative of factitive verbs: see -ATE³.]
1 *verb trans.* Impart, transmit, (something intangible or abstract, as heat, motion, feeling, disease, etc., *to*, *spec.* information, news, etc., *to*, †*with*). E16. ▸†**b** Give, bestow, (something material). L16–M18.

> E. F. BENSON She read her other letter . . and communicated the contents. V. BRITTAIN I tried to communicate my enthusiasm for Oxford to the family circle. A. POWELL The stagnant character of those streets seemed to communicate itself to one's limbs.

2 *verb trans.* Share in, partake of; use or enjoy in common (*with*); share *with*. *arch.* E16. ▸†**b** *verb intrans.* Have a share, participate. (Foll. by *in*, *with*.) L16–E18.

> JONSON Thousands, that communicate our loss. WILLIAM WALLACE Nor was he the only acquaintance with whom Schopenhauer communicated some of his . . means.

3 a *verb intrans.* Receive Holy Communion. M16. ▸**b** *verb trans.* Administer Holy Communion to. M16. ▸†**c** *verb trans.* Celebrate, give, or receive (the Eucharist). M17–E18.
†**4** *verb refl.* Make oneself familiar; have intercourse or converse. (Foll. by *to*, *with*.) M16–L18.
5 *verb intrans.* Make or maintain social contact; convey or exchange information etc.; succeed in evoking understanding. (Foll. by *with*.) L16.

> E. B. TYLOR No means of communicating with others but by signs. *Listener* They buy only pictures that will communicate readily. B. EMECHETA She and Francis communicated only in monosyllables. *Acorn User* There are many variable parameters to be agreed before two computers can communicate.

6 *verb intrans.* Of rooms, vessels, etc.: have a common connecting door, aperture, channel, etc., (*with*); open into one another. M18.

> H. JAMES The library, which communicated with the office. OED Their apartments are separate, but they communicate by a door.

communication /kəmjuːnɪˈkeɪʃ(ə)n/ *noun*. LME.
[ORIGIN formed as COMMUNICATE *verb*: see -ATION.]
1 The action of communicating heat, feeling, motion, etc.; *spec.* the transmission or exchange of information, news, etc. LME. ▸**b** In *pl.* The science and practice of transmitting information. M20.

> J. B. PRIESTLEY The telegram was . . the common method of communication.

†**2** Conference; a conversation. LME–E17.
3 Social contact, personal intercourse. LME. ▸**b** Sexual intercourse. Long *arch.* L18.

> DEFOE They had little knowledge or communication one with another.

†**4** Shared possession, common participation; a similarity; a sharing. LME–L18.
5 Something communicated; (a piece of) information; a letter or message containing information or news. L15.

> M. PEAKE Very little communication passed between . . these outer quarters and those who lived *within* the walls. D. BROWN I am familiar enough with electronic communications to know they can be intercepted.

6 Access or means of access between persons or places; a means of communicating; a connecting door, passage, road, telephone line, etc.; in *pl.* spec. MILITARY, the means of transport between a base and a front. L17.

> J. LUBBOCK To protect our communications with India and Australia.

7 A meeting of a Masonic lodge. L19.
– PHRASES: **in communication (with)** †(**a**) in conference with; (**b**) actively communicating (with), able to communicate actively (with). PRIVILEGED ***communication***.
– COMB.: **communication cord** a cord or chain for pulling by a passenger to stop a train in an emergency; **communication satellite**, **communications satellite** an artificial satellite for broadcast communications; **communications theory**, **communication theory** the branch of knowledge that deals with language and other means of conveying or exchanging information.
■ **communicational** *adjective* M20. **communicationally** *adverb* L20.

communicative /kəˈmjuːnɪkətɪv/ *adjective*. LME.
[ORIGIN Late Latin *communicativus*, formed as COMMUNICATE *verb*: see -IVE. Cf. Old French & mod. French *communicatif*, *-ive*.]
1 Having the quality or habit of communicating. Now *spec.* ready to impart information etc.; open, talkative. LME.

> JER. TAYLOR An evil so communicative that it doth . . work like poison. W. COWPER Communicative of the good he owns. A. LURIE When drinks are served people become more lively and communicative.

†**2** Able to be communicated. E17–M18.
3 Of or pertaining to communication. L17.
■ **communicatively** *adverb* M17. **communicativeness** *noun* M17.

communicator /kəˈmjuːnɪkeɪtə/ *noun*. M17.
[ORIGIN from COMMUNICATE *verb* + -OR.]
A person who or thing which communicates.

> *attrib.*: D. ADAMS The . . Captain pressed a communicator button.

■ **communicatory** *adjective* (now *rare*) tending or pertaining to communication M17.

communion /kəˈmjuːnjən/ *noun*. LME.
[ORIGIN Old French & mod. French, or Latin *communio(n-)*, from *communis* COMMON *adjective*: see -ION. The religious uses depend on ecclesiastical Latin.]
▶ **I 1** Sharing, holding or being held in common, community; fellowship; (an) association in action, relation, or function. LME.

> AV *2 Cor.* 6:14 What fellowship hath righteousness with unrighteousness? and what communion hath light with darkness? A. WILSON Three elderly English scholars with no real communion of feeling except their nationality.

2 Communication, social contact. E17.

> W. RALEIGH The Israelites never had any communion or affairs with the Ethiopians.

3 Intimate mental or spiritual communing. *literary*. E19.

> R. FORD That health of body and soul which ever rewards a close communion with Nature.

▶ **II 4** The fellowship or mutual recognition between members of one Church, esp. between branches of the Catholic Church. Also, an organized body of people united by common religious faith and rites; *esp.* a body professing one branch of the Christian faith. LME.
communion of saints: see SAINT *noun & adjective*. ***lay communion***: see LAY *adjective*.
5 Also **C-**. (Participation in) the Eucharist. Also more fully ***Holy Communion***. LME.
close Communion: restricted to selected Church members; esp. among Baptists, to those baptized by immersion. **Communion in both kinds**: in which both the consecrated elements of bread and wine are administered. **Communion in one kind**: in which only one consecrated element is administered. **free Communion** = ***open Communion*** below. ***lay communion***: see LAY *adjective*. **open Communion**: administered to any Christian believer. **strict Communion** = ***close Communion*** above.
– COMB.: **Communion cloth** = ***altar cloth*** s.v. ALTAR *noun*; **Communion cup**, **Communion plate**, etc.: used for the consecrated elements at Holy Communion; **Communion rail** a rail in front of an altar or Communion table behind which people can receive Communion; **Communion table** the table or altar at which Holy Communion is celebrated.
■ **communionist** *noun* (**a**) *rare* = COMMUNICANT *noun* 1; (**b**) an adherent of a specified (*strict* etc.) type of Communion: M17.

communiqué /kəˈmjuːnɪkeɪ/ *noun*. M19.
[ORIGIN French, use as noun of pa. pple of *communiquer* communicate.]
An official communication; *esp.* an official statement reporting on a meeting, conference; etc.

communise *verb* var. of COMMUNIZE.

communism /ˈkɒmjʊnɪz(ə)m/ *noun*. M19.
[ORIGIN French *communisme*, from *commun* COMMON *adjective*: see -ISM.]
(A theory advocating) a system of society with property vested in the community and each member working for the common benefit according to his or her capacity and

receiving according to his or her needs; *spec.* (usu. **C-**) the movement or political party advocating such a system, esp. as derived from Marxism and seeking the overthrow of capitalism by a proletarian revolution; the communistic form of society established in the 20th cent. in the former USSR and elsewhere.

communist /ˈkɒmjʊnɪst/ *noun & adjective*. Also **C-**. **M19**.
[**ORIGIN** French *communiste*, formed as **COMMUNISM**: see **-IST**.]
▸ **A** *noun*. An adherent of communism. **M19**.
▸ **B** *adjective*. Of or pertaining to communists or communism; adhering to communism. **M19**.
■ **commuˈnistic** *adjective* of, pertaining to, or characteristic of communism **M19**. **commuˈnistically** *adverb* **L19**.

communitarian /kəmjuːnɪˈtɛːrɪən/ *noun & adjective*. **M19**.
[**ORIGIN** from **COMMUNITY** + **-ARIAN**, after *unitarian* etc.]
▸ **A** *noun*. **1** A member of a community practising cooperation and some communism. **M19**.
2 A supporter of an ideology which emphasizes the responsibility of the individual to the community and the social importance of the family unit. **L20**.
▸ **B** *adjective*. Of, pertaining to, or characteristic of communitarians or their type of community. **E20**.
■ **communitarianism** *noun* **M19**. **communitorium** *noun* a communitarian residence or settlement **M19**.

community /kəˈmjuːnɪti/ *noun*. **LME**.
[**ORIGIN** Old French *comuneté* (mod. *communité*), assim. to its source Latin *communitas*, from *communis* **COMMON** *adjective*: see **-ITY**. Cf. **COMMONTY**.]
▸ **I** A body of individuals.
†**1** The commons as opp. to peers etc.; the common people. **LME–E18**.
2 An organized political, municipal, or social body; a body of people living in the same locality; a body of people having religion, profession, etc., in common; a body of nations unified by common interests (freq., with cap. initial, in the title of an international organization). **LME**. ▸**b** *The* members of such a body collectively. **L18**.

> C. G. SELIGMAN They live in small communities or hunting bands. J. BRAINE The Thespians gave me . . the sense of belonging, of being part of a community. DAY LEWIS We were an ordered little unit . . , a Protestant enclave in a Catholic community. **b** B. HEAD Everybody made sacrifices for the community.

European Defence Community, ***European Economic Community***, etc. ***satellite community***: see **SATELLITE** *noun* 3b.
3 A monastic, socialistic, etc., body of people living together and holding goods in common. **E18**.
4 A group of animals etc. living or acting together; *ECOLOGY* a group of interdependent plants or animals growing or living together in natural conditions or inhabiting a specified locality. **M18**.
open community: see **OPEN** *adjective*.
▸ **II** A quality or state.
5 The state of being shared or held in common; joint ownership or liability. **M16**.

> H. G. WELLS Our community of blood with all mankind. H. J. LASKI Wallace traces these evils to private property and . . sees no remedy save community of possessions.

6 (A) common character; (an) agreement; (an) identity. **L16**.

> WORDSWORTH The points of community in their nature. A. STORR Men who form a close association based upon a community of ideas cannot avoid passionate controversy.

7 Social intercourse; communion; fellowship, sense of common identity. **L16**.

> M. SHELLEY There can be no community between you and me; we are enemies. P. GOODMAN During depression . . there is more community.

†**8** Commonness, ordinary occurrence. **L16–M17**.
9 Life in association with others; society; the social state. **M17**.

> STEELE [Marriage] is the foundation of community, and the chief band of society. S. NAIPAUL The decaying cities where the sense of community, of human belongingness, had been destroyed.

– COMB.: **community architect**: working in consultation with the local community in designing housing and other amenities; **community architecture**: as practised by community architects; **community care** long-term care for the mentally ill, the elderly, and people with disabilities which is provided within the community rather than in hospitals or institutions; **community centre** (a part of) a building providing social, recreational, and educational facilities for a neighbourhood; **community charge** a community tax; *spec.* (*hist.*) in Britain, a tax levied 1990–93 (1989–93 in Scotland) by local authorities on every adult (cf. ***poll tax*** s.v. **POLL** *noun*[1]); **community chest** *US* a fund for charity and welfare work in a community; **community college** (***a***) *N. Amer.* a college providing further and higher education esp. for members of the local community; (***b***) a secondary school whose educational and recreational facilities are available to adults in the local community; **community home** an institution for young offenders and other juveniles in need of custodial care; **community hospital** *US* a local general hospital esp. for short-term patients; **community leader** a prominent and active member or office-holder within a particular community; **community medicine** the branch of medicine that deals with matters of health and disease as they affect communities as a whole; **community order** *ENGLISH LAW* a sentence whereby a convicted person is required to perform community service, undergo treatment, observe a curfew, etc. rather than be imprisoned; **community policeman**, **community police officer**, etc.: involved in community policing; **community policing**: by officers intended to have personal knowledge of and involvement in the community which they police; **community property** *LAW* assets originally belonging to either or both of the partners in a marriage, but considered to be the joint property of both partners by virtue of their marriage; **community sentence** *ENGLISH LAW* a sentence whereby a convicted person is required to perform community service; **community service** socially useful voluntary work; *spec.* (*ENGLISH LAW*) work that an offender is required to do instead of going to prison; **community singing**: in chorus by a large gathering of people; **community spirit** a feeling of membership of a community; **community tax** (a) local tax on members of a community; **community worker** a person who works in a community to promote its welfare.

communize /ˈkɒmjʊnʌɪz/ *verb trans*. Also **-ise**. **L19**.
[**ORIGIN** from Latin *communis* **COMMON** *adjective* + **-IZE**.]
Make (land etc.) common property; make communistic.
■ **communiˈzation** *noun* **M19**.

commutable /kəˈmjuːtəb(ə)l/ *adjective*. **M17**.
[**ORIGIN** Latin *commutabilis*, formed as **COMMUTE** *verb*; in sense 2 from **COMMUTE** *verb*: see **-ABLE**. Cf. earlier **INCOMMUTABLE**.]
1 Exchangeable; convertible into money; that can be compounded for. **M17**.
2 Of a place: able to be commuted from or to; within commuting distance. (Foll. by *from* (a place), *to*.) **L20**.
■ **commutaˈbility** *noun* **L18**.

commutate /ˈkɒmjuːteɪt/ *verb*. **M17**.
[**ORIGIN** Latin *commutat-* pa. ppl stem of *commutare*: see **COMMUTE** *verb*, **-ATE**[3].]
†**1** *verb intrans*. Change. *rare*. Only in **M17**.
2 *verb trans*. Regulate the direction of (an electric current), esp. to make it a direct current. **L19**.

commutation /kɒmjʊˈteɪʃ(ə)n/ *noun*. **LME**.
[**ORIGIN** Old French & mod. French, or Latin *commutatio(n-)*, formed as **COMMUTATE**: see **-ATION**.]
†**1** Exchange, barter. **LME–M18**.
†**2** Change, alteration. **E16–M19**.
3 *RHETORIC*. A figure of speech involving a reversal of word order. *rare*. **M16**.
4 Interchange, replacement, substitution; *spec.* (***a***) substitution of one kind of payment or penalty for another; *LAW* a reduction in severity in the penalty imposed; (***b***) *MATH.* interchange of the order of two quantities added, operated on, multiplied, etc.; (***c***) *LINGUISTICS* substitution of one sound for another to produce a different word, as a test of separate phonemes. **L16**.
5 Regulation of the direction of an electric current; the action of a commutator. **L19**.
– COMB.: **commutation ticket** *US* a season ticket.

commutative /kəˈmjuːtətɪv, ˈkɒmjʊtətɪv/ *adjective*. **M16**.
[**ORIGIN** Old French & mod. French *commutatif*, *-ive* or Latin *commutativus*, formed as **COMMUTATE**: see **-IVE**.]
1 Of or pertaining to exchange or transactions between people. Chiefly & now only in ***commutative justice***. **M16**.
2 Pertaining to or involving substitution; *MATH.* governed by or stating the condition that the result of a binary operation is unchanged by interchange of the order of quantities, e.g. that $a \times b = b \times a$. **M19**.

> B. RUSSELL The associative, commutative and distributive laws.

3 Pertaining to or involving commutation of a penalty etc. **M19**.
■ **commutatively** *adverb* **L17**. **commutativeness** *noun* = **COMMUTATIVITY** **L19**. **commutaˈtivity** *noun* the ability of two or more quantities to commute **E20**.

commutator /ˈkɒmjʊteɪtə/ *noun*. **M19**.
[**ORIGIN** from (the same root as) **COMMUTATE** + **-OR**.]
A thing which commutes; *spec.* a device for commutating an electric current.

commute /kəˈmjuːt/ *verb & noun*. **LME**.
[**ORIGIN** Latin *commutare* change wholly, exchange, formed as **COM-** + *mutare* change.]
▸ **A** *verb*. **1** *verb trans*. Change (*into*); exchange, substitute, (*for*); interchange (two things). **LME**.

> T. KEN He and the Beasts seem Natures to commute, They act like Reason, and he like the Brute.

2 *verb trans*. *spec.* Change (an obligation etc.) *for*, *into* another by making a payment etc.; change (one kind of payment or penalty) *for*, *into* another; change (a punishment) *to* another less severe; convert into money. **M17**.

> J. S. MILL The legislature . . might commute the average receipts of Irish landowners into a fixed rent charge. E. BOWEN I commuted my pension. A. KOESTLER He waited a year for his execution, then the sentence was commuted to lifelong imprisonment.

3 *verb intrans*. Compensate *for*; serve as a substitute *for*. Now *rare*. **M17**.
4 *verb trans*. Commutate (an electric current). **L19**.
5 *verb intrans*. Buy and use a commutation ticket (*US*); travel by public or private conveyance between one's home and one's place of work; travel *between* regularly or frequently. (Earlier in **COMMUTER**.) **L19**.

> J. ARCHER The 8.17 train so favoured by those who commute from Oxford to London every day.

6 *verb intrans*. *MATH*. Have a commutative relation (*with*). **E20**.
▸ **B** *noun*. A journey on a commutation ticket (*US*); a journey by public or private conveyance between one's home and one's place of work. **M20**.

commuter /kəˈmjuːtə/ *noun*. Orig. *US*. **M19**.
[**ORIGIN** from **COMMUTE** *verb* + **-ER**[1].]
A person who commutes to work.

commutual /kəˈmjuːtʃʊəl, -tjʊəl/ *adjective*. Chiefly *poet*. Also †**comutual**. **E17**.
[**ORIGIN** from **COM-**, **CO-** + **MUTUAL** *adjective*.]
Mutual, reciprocal.

C

comose /ˈkəʊməʊs/ *adjective*. **L18**.
[**ORIGIN** Latin *comosus*, formed as **COMA** *noun*[2]: see **-OSE**[1].]
Of seeds etc.: hairy, downy.
■ Also **comous** *adjective* **M17**.

comozant *noun* see **CORPOSANT**.

comp /kɒmp/ *noun*. *colloq*. **L17**.
[**ORIGIN** Abbreviation.]
1 = **COMPANY** *noun* 3d. **L17**.
2 = **COMPOSITOR** 3. **L19**.
3 = **COMPETITION** 2. **E20**.
4 = **ACCOMPANIMENT** 1. **M20**.

comp /kɒmp/ *verb intrans. & trans*. *colloq*. **L19**.
[**ORIGIN** Abbreviation.]
1 Work as a compositor (on), compose. **L19**.
2 Play an accompaniment (to); accompany. **M20**.

Compa *abbreviation*. Also **Comp^a^**.
Company (esp. on banknotes).

compact /ˈkɒmpakt/ *noun*[1]. **L16**.
[**ORIGIN** Latin *compactum* use as noun of neut. pa. pple of *compacisci* make an agreement: see **COM-**, **PACT** *noun*. Cf. Old French *compact*.]
1 An agreement or contract made between two or more parties. **L16**.
social compact: see **SOCIAL** *adjective*.
†**2** Confederacy, plot, conspiracy. **L16–M17**.

compact /ˈkɒmpakt/ *noun*[2]. **L16**.
[**ORIGIN** from **COMPACT** *adjective*.]
1 An object or body of compacted material; a combination; a compact state. Now *rare*. **L16**.
2 A small flat case for face powder etc., usu. with a mirror in the lid. Also ***powder compact***. **E20**.
3 A medium-sized car. *N. Amer.* **M20**.

compact /kəmˈpakt, *in sense 1 also* ˈkɒmpakt/ *adjective*. **LME**.
[**ORIGIN** Latin *compactus* pa. pple, formed as **COMPACT** *verb*[1]. Cf. Old French & mod. French *compact* adjective.]
1 Closely or neatly packed together; dense; economical of space; not straggling or gangling; not diffuse; (of style etc.) condensed, terse. **LME**.

> K. AMIS A compact city with no suburbs to speak of. P. DAVIES A star that has imploded . . and become so compact that even its atoms are crushed.

compact car *N. Amer.* a medium-sized car. **compact disc**: on which sound, information, etc., is recorded digitally as a spiral pattern of pits and bumps for reproduction or retrieval using a laser beam.
2 Made up *of*, composed *of*. **M16**.

> V. SACKVILLE-WEST Of such small . . and mutual courtesies was their relationship compact.

■ **compactly** *adverb* **E17**. **compactness** *noun* **M17**.

compact /kəmˈpakt/ *verb*[1] *trans*. Pa. pple (earlier) **compact** (*arch.*), **-ed**. **LME**.
[**ORIGIN** Latin *compact-* pa. ppl stem of *compingere*, formed as **COM-** + *pangere* fasten. Cf. **COMPACT** *adjective*.]
1 Join or press firmly together; combine closely; compress, condense. **LME**.
2 Devise; make up (or †*up*), compose (*of*). **M16**.
†**3** Confirm, give consistency to. *rare* (Shakes.) Only in **E17**.
■ **compactedly** *adverb* (*rare*) compactly **M17**. **compactedness** *noun* compactness **M17**. **compactor** *noun* a person who or thing which compacts. **L16**.

†**compact** *verb*[2]. Pa. pple **compact**, **-ed**. **M16**.
[**ORIGIN** Latin *compact-* pa. ppl stem of *compacisci*: see **COMPACT** *noun*[1].]
1 *verb intrans*. Make a compact or agreement (*with*). **M16–L17**.
2 *verb trans*. Join in a compact; plan by a compact. **L16–M17**.

compaction /kəmˈpakʃ(ə)n/ *noun*. **LME**.
[**ORIGIN** Latin *compactio(n-)*, formed as **COMPACT** *verb*[1]: see **-ION**. Cf. Old French *compaction*.]
The action, process, or result of making or becoming compact; *spec.* the action or process of inducing the particles of a substance (as soil, concrete, etc.) to combine more tightly.

compactum /kəmˈpaktəm/ *noun*. **E20**.
[**ORIGIN** Latin, use as noun of neut. of *compactus*: see **COMPACT** *adjective*.]
A structure or device intended to hold a number of articles; a container; *spec.* a wardrobe.

†**compacture** *noun*. **L15–M17**.
[**ORIGIN** Latin *compactura*, formed as **COMPACT** *verb*[1]: see **-URE**.]
Manner of putting closely together; compact structure.

C

compadre /kɒm'pɑːdri/ *noun*. Chiefly *US*. M19.
[ORIGIN Spanish = godfather, hence benefactor, friend. Cf. GOSSIP *noun*.]
Companion, friend, (freq. as a form of address).

compages /kəm'peɪdʒiːz/ *noun*. Pl. same. Also (earlier) †**-age**. M16.
[ORIGIN Latin *compages*, formed as COM- + *pag-* base of *pangere* fasten, fix. Earliest form assoc. with nouns in -AGE.]
1 The joining of parts into a whole; solid structure; consistency. Now *rare*. M16.
2 A whole formed by the joining of parts; a framework, a complex structure, (*lit.* & *fig.*). M17.

compaginate /kəm'padʒɪneɪt/ *verb trans*. Now *rare*. E17.
[ORIGIN Late Latin *compaginat-* pa. ppl stem of *compaginare*, from *compago*, *-agin-* compages: see -ATE³.]
Join or fit firmly together; connect, unite, (*lit.* & *fig.*).
■ **compagi'nation** *noun* M17.

compagnon de voyage /kɔ̃paɲɔ̃ də vwajaːʒ/ *noun phr*. Pl. ***compagnons de voyage*** (pronounced same). Also ***compagnon du voyage*** /dy/. M18.
[ORIGIN French.]
A travelling companion, a fellow traveller.

compand /kəm'pand/ *verb trans*. M20.
[ORIGIN Back-form. from COMPANDER.]
TELECOMMUNICATIONS. Subject to the action of a compander.

compander /kəm'pandə/ *noun*. Also **-or**. M20.
[ORIGIN Blend of COMPRESSOR and EXPANDER.]
TELECOMMUNICATIONS. A device that improves the signal-to-noise ratio of reproduced or transmitted sound by compressing the range of amplitudes of the signal before transmission, and then expanding it on reproduction or reception.

†**companiable** *adjective*. Also **-anable**. ME–E19.
[ORIGIN Old French *compaignable*, formed as COMPANY *verb*: see -ABLE.]
Sociable, companionable.
■ †**companiableness** *noun* L16–L18.

companion /kəm'panjən/ *noun*¹ & *verb*. ME.
[ORIGIN Old French *compaignon* from Proto-Romance, from Latin COM- + *panis* bread.]
▶ **A** *noun* **I 1** A person or animal who associates with or accompanies another; an associate *in*, a sharer *of*. ME. ▸†**b** A (worthless) person, a fellow. L16–M18.

W. S. CHURCHILL My sole companion was a gigantic vulture. P. AUSTER He was more than just a potential drinking companion . . more than just another acquaintance.

†**2** Each of two or more people associated in a specific or legal relation. M16–M18.
3 (Also **C-**.) A member of an order of knighthood. Now *spec*. a member of the lowest grade of some orders of distinction. M16.
Companion of the Bath etc.
4 A person, usu. a woman, who is paid to live with and accompany another. M18.
▶ **II 5** A necessary guide or aid to a particular pursuit; *esp*. (**a**) a handbook or reference book to a specific subject, locality, etc. (freq. as part of the title); (**b**) (a piece of) equipment combining several requisites. E18.
6 A thing that matches or closely resembles another. L18.
7 A star etc. that accompanies another; *esp*. the fainter component of a double star system. E19.
– PHRASES: ***boon companion***: see BOON *adjective*. **companion in arms** a fellow soldier. **Companion of Honour** a member of a British order for those who have rendered conspicuous service to the nation. **Companion of Literature** (a recipient of) an honour conferred by the Royal Society of Literature. ***free companion***: see FREE *adjective*. ***lady's companion***: see LADY *noun* & *adjective*. ***native companion***: see NATIVE *adjective*.
– ATTRIB. & COMB.: In the sense 'that is a companion, that matches', as ***companion piece***, ***companion volume***, etc. Special combs., as **companion animal** a pet; **companion cell** BOTANY a specialized elongated parenchymatous cell connected to a sieve tube in the phloem of some flowering plants; **companion set** a set of fireside implements on a stand; **companion star** = sense 7 above.
▶ **B** *verb*. **1** *verb* †*refl*. & *intrans*. Keep company, consort, *with*. *literary*. E17.
2 *verb trans*. Go or be with as a companion; accompany (*lit*. & *fig*.). E17.
■ **companionage** *noun* (a list of) the body of companions of various orders L19. **companionhood** *noun* companionship M19. **companionless** *adjective* E19. †**companionry** *noun* (chiefly *Scot*.) companionship L16–E18.

companion /kəm'panjən/ *noun*². M18.
[ORIGIN Alt., by assoc. with COMPANION *noun*¹ & *verb*, of Dutch †*kompanje* (now *kampanje*) quarterdeck from Old French *compagne* from Italian (*camera della*) *compagna* storeroom for provisions.]
NAUTICAL. **1** A raised window frame on a quarterdeck for lighting cabins etc. below. Also, a wooden covering over the entrance to the master's cabin in some small ships. M18.
2 In full ***companion ladder***. A ladder giving access from deck to deck; the ladder to the quarterdeck used by officers. M19.
3 In full ***companionway***. The staircase to a cabin. M19.
– COMB.: **companion hatch** a wooden covering over the companionway; **companion hatchway** an opening in a deck leading to a cabin; ***companion ladder***: see sense 2 above; ***companionway***: see sense 3 above.

companionable /kəm'panjənəb(ə)l/ *adjective*. E17.
[ORIGIN Alt. of COMPAN(I)ABLE after COMPANION *noun*¹.]
1 Fitted for companionship; sociable, friendly; agreeable as company. E17.
2 Fitted to go *with* or match. *rare*. E19.
■ **companiona'bility** *noun* E19. **companionableness** *noun* L17. **companionably** *adverb* L17.

companionate /kəm'panjənət/ *adjective*. M17.
[ORIGIN from COMPANION *noun*¹ + -ATE².]
†**1** Companioned. Only in M17.
2 Designating a proposed form of marriage providing for divorce by mutual consent without any further legal obligations. E20.

companioned /kəm'panjənd/ *adjective*. E19.
[ORIGIN from COMPANION *noun*¹, *verb*: see -ED², -ED¹. Earlier in UNCOMPANIONED (in different sense).]
Having, or accompanied by, a companion or companions.

companionship /kəm'panjənʃɪp/ *noun*. M16.
[ORIGIN from COMPANION *noun*¹ + -SHIP.]
1 The state of being or having a companion or companions; association or presence as a companion or companions; fellowship. M16. ▸**b** An association, a fellowship. M19.
2 *hist*. The state of being a journeyman. L18.
3 An organized group of people; *spec*. (PRINTING HISTORY) a company of compositors working together under a clicker. E19.
4 Usu. **C-**. The dignity of a Companion in an order of knighthood etc. L19.

company /'kʌmp(ə)ni/ *noun*. ME.
[ORIGIN Anglo-Norman *compainie*, Old French *compa(i)gnie*, from Proto-Romance source of COMPANION *noun*¹: see -Y³. Infl. in commercial sense by Italian *compagnia*, in military sense by French *compagnie*.]
1 Companionship, fellowship, society. ME. ▸†**b** Sexual intercourse. ME–E17.

H. JAMES He found his own company quite absorbing. N. MOSLEY My child was quiet in the company of the others.

2 A number of individuals assembled or associated together; a body of people combined for some common object. ME.

V. WOOLF Gulls rode gently swaying in little companies of two or three.

3 *esp*. ▸**a** A body of soldiers; *spec*. a subdivision of an infantry battalion usu. commanded by a major or a captain. ME. ▸**b** (A corporation historically representing) a medieval trade guild. LME. ▸**c** A party of actors, entertainers, (formerly) musicians, etc. E16. ▸**d** A legal association formed to carry on some commercial or industrial undertaking. M16. ▸**e** In full ***ship's company***. The entire crew of a ship. E17. ▸**f** A social party or assembly. M17. ▸**g** A unit of Guides. E20.
4 Persons assembled or associated together; the social world (*arch*.); persons or a person whose presence prevents solitude or privacy; *esp*. guests. LME. ▸**b** The partner(s) whose names do not appear in the style or title of a firm. Chiefly in ***and Company***. M16. ▸**c** The person or persons with whom one voluntarily or habitually associates. E17.

OED I hoped we should be private here, but I find we have company. R. LARDNER I do love to have company once in a while, just a few congenial friends. E. BURKE Unfortunate in the choice of his political company.

– PHRASES: **bad company**, **good company**, etc., (**a**) a dull, lively, etc., companion; (**b**) unsuitable, suitable, etc., companions. ***bear company***: see BEAR *verb*¹. **err in good company** do no more than better people have done. ***free company***: see FREE *adjective*. ***good company***: see ***bad company*** above. **in company with** together with. ***John Company***. ***join company***: see JOIN *verb* 2. ***joint-stock company***: see JOINT *adjective*. **keep company (with)** associate habitually (with); *arch. colloq.* court. **keep a person company** accompany or stay with a person. **know a person by his or her company**, **know a person by the company he or she keeps** deduce a person's character from his or her habitual companions, resorts, etc. ***LIMITED company***. ***LIMITED-liability company***. ***MIXED company***. ***parent company***: see PARENT *noun* 3b. ***part company***: see PART *verb*. ***present company excepted***: see PRESENT *adjective*. ***private company***: see PRIVATE *adjective*. ***proprietary company***: see PROPRIETARY *adjective* 2. ***public company***: see PUBLIC *adjective* & *noun*. ***repertory company***: see REPERTORY 3c. ***ship's company***: see sense 3e above. ***STATUTORY company***. ***subsidiary company***: see SUBSIDIARY *adjective* 1. **the Company** *US slang* the Central Intelligence Agency. ***transfer company***: see TRANSFER *noun*.
– COMB.: **company car**: owned (or leased) and maintained by a commercial company for the use of an employee; **company law**: concerned with legally established companies; **company officer** a captain or lower commissioned officer; ***company promoter***: see PROMOTER 1b; ***company sergeant major***: see SERGEANT MAJOR *noun* 2.

company /'kʌmp(ə)ni/ *verb*. Now *arch*. & *dial*. ME.
[ORIGIN Old French *compaignier*, from *compaing* nom. of (the accus. form) *compaignon* COMPANION *noun*¹.]
1 *verb trans*. Accompany. ME.
†**2** *verb trans*. Associate in companionship (*with*). LME–L16.
3 *verb intrans*. Keep company (*with*, *together*). LME. ▸†**b** Cohabit *with*. LME–L17.

comparable /'kɒmp(ə)rəb(ə)l/ *adjective*. LME.
[ORIGIN Old French & mod. French from Latin *comparabilis*, from *comparare*: see COMPARE *verb*¹, -ABLE.]
1 Able to be compared (*with*). LME.
2 Worthy of comparison; fit to be compared (*to*). LME.
■ **compara'bility** *noun* M19. **comparableness** *noun* M18. **comparably** *adverb* LME.

comparatist /kəm'parətɪst/ *noun*. M20.
[ORIGIN from COMPARATIVE + -IST. Cf. French *comparatiste*.]
A user of comparative methods, esp. in the study of language and literature.

comparative /kəm'parətɪv/ *adjective* & *noun*. LME.
[ORIGIN Latin *comparativus*, from *comparat-* pa. ppl stem of *comparare*: see COMPARE *verb*¹, -ATIVE.]
▶ **A** *adjective*. **1** GRAMMAR. Designating the degree of comparison expressing more (or less) of a quality or attribute; designating a form etc. of an adjective or adverb expressing this degree of comparison (e.g. with inflection, as English -ER³; with modifier, as English ***more***; with a word from a different root, as English ***better*** corresponding to ***good***). Cf. ***superlative***. LME.
2 Considered, estimated, or perceptible by comparison; relative. L16.

B. JOWETT The comparative claims of pleasure and wisdom. C. S. FORESTER From the peril of the top to the comparative safety of the mainyard.

†**3** Fertile in (insulting) comparisons. *rare* (Shakes.). Only in L16.
4 Of or involving comparison; *esp*. involving comparison across different branches of a science or subject of study. E17.
comparative anatomy, ***comparative grammar***, ***comparative law***, ***comparative linguistics***, ***comparative philology***, ***comparative religion***, etc.
†**5** Serving as a basis for comparison. *rare* (Shakes.). Only in E17.
†**6** Comparable, worthy to be compared, (*to*). M17–E19.
▶ **B** *noun*. †**1** A thing or person to be compared, a rival, an equal. L15–E17.
2 GRAMMAR. A comparative form etc. of an adjective or adverb; the comparative degree. M16.
■ **comparatively** *adverb* by way of comparison; somewhat, rather: L16. **comparativist** *noun* a comparatist; a student of comparative linguistics or literature: L19.

comparator /kəm'parətə/ *noun*. L19.
[ORIGIN from Latin *comparat-* (see COMPARATIVE) + -OR.]
A device for making comparative measurements, esp. against a standard.
optical comparator: see OPTICAL *adjective*.

compare /kəm'pɛː/ *noun*¹. Now *literary*. E16.
[ORIGIN Var. of COMPEER *noun*, assim. to COMPARE *verb*¹. Cf. COMPARE *noun*².]
An equal, a rival. Chiefly in ***have no compare***, ***without compare*** (in which merges into next).

compare /kəm'pɛː/ *noun*². Chiefly *literary*. E16.
[ORIGIN from COMPARE *verb*¹, perh. also infl. by *without compare* (see COMPARE *noun*¹).]
Comparison. Chiefly in ***beyond compare***, ***past compare***, etc.

compare /kəm'pɛː/ *verb*¹. LME.
[ORIGIN Old French & mod. French *comparer* from Latin *comparare* pair, match, from *compar* like, equal, formed as COM- + *par* equal.]
1 *verb trans*. Liken, pronounce similar, (*to*). LME.

R. GRAVES It is hardly complimentary to Parrot, an undeniably handsome bird, to compare my grandson to him.

not to be compared to greatly inferior or superior to.
2 *verb intrans*. Be compared; bear comparison; be on terms of equality *with*. LME.

SPENSER Art, stryving to compare with Nature. OED This compares favourably with the inertness of England.

3 *verb trans*. Consider or estimate the similarity or dissimilarity of (one thing or person *to* another esp. in quality, *with* another esp. in quantity or detailed nature, two things or persons); observe the similarity or relation between (passages in a book etc.). L15.

R. G. COLLINGWOOD To compare the two accounts . . given by Thucydides and Aristotle. G. VIDAL How dull he is, thought Caroline, comparing him unfavourably with Jim.

compare notes compare each other's observations etc., exchange ideas and opinions.
4 *verb intrans*. Draw a comparison; make comparisons. L16.

C. S. LEWIS The pernicious tendency to compare and to prefer.

5 *verb trans*. GRAMMAR. Form the comparative and superlative degrees of (an adjective or adverb). E17.

W. WARD Words of one syllable are usually compared by *er*, and *est*.

■ **comparer** *noun* M17.

†**compare** *verb*² *trans*. *rare*. M–L16.
[ORIGIN Latin *comparare*, formed as COM- + *parare* get ready, provide, etc. Cf. Old French *comparer*.]
Get, obtain, acquire.

SPENSER To fill his bags, and richesse to compare.

comparison /kəmˈparɪs(ə)n/ *noun*. ME.
[ORIGIN Old French *comparesoun* (mod. *-aison*) from Latin *comparatio(n-)*, from *comparat-* pa. ppl stem of *comparare*: see COMPARE *verb*[1], -ISON.]
1 The action or an act of likening, or representing as similar. ME.

B. JOWETT The comparison of philosophy to a yelping she-dog.

2 Capacity of being likened or compared; comparable condition or character. (Always with negative expressed or implied.) ME.

SHAKES. *Tr. & Cr.* Troilus is the better man of the two . . O Jupiter! There's no comparison.

3 The action or an instance of observing and estimating similarities, differences, etc. LME.
bear comparison (with), **stand comparison (with)** admit of being compared favourably (with). **beyond comparison**, **beyond all comparison** totally different in quality. **in comparison with** compared to. PAIRED *comparison*.
4 GRAMMAR. The action of comparing an adjective or adverb; the relationship expressed in the (potential) comparing of qualities or attributes. Now chiefly in ***degree of comparison***, ***grade of comparison*** below. LME.
degree of comparison, **grade of comparison** each of the degrees of relationship expressed in the (potential) comparing of qualities or attributes: the positive or absolute, when no comparison is made; the comparative, when two are compared; the superlative, when more than two are compared.
5 A simile; an illustrative instance, a parallel, an analogy. LME.

A. P. HERBERT It was like an unconvincing third act of a promising play—though this comparison did not occur to Jane.

– COMB.: **comparison-shop** *verb intrans.* (*N. Amer.*) compare the price of goods or services provided by different shops or companies.

compart /kəmˈpɑːt/ *verb trans*. L16.
[ORIGIN Old French *compartir* or late Latin *compartiri* share with another, formed as COM- + *partiri* divide, share.]
†**1** Divide and share. L16–E17.
2 Lay out in accordance with a plan. E17.
3 Subdivide; partition; divide into compartments. L18.

compartition /kɒmpɑːˈtɪʃ(ə)n/ *noun*. E17.
[ORIGIN medieval Latin *compartitio(n-)*, from *compartit-* pa. ppl stem of *compartiri*: see COMPART, -ION.]
1 The distribution and disposition of the parts of a plan. E17.
†**2** Division and sharing with another. Only in M17.

compartment /kəmˈpɑːtm(ə)nt/ *noun & verb*. As noun also †**copart(i)ment**. M16.
[ORIGIN French *compartiment* from Italian *compartimento*, from *compartire* from late Latin *compartiri*: see COMPART *verb*, -MENT.]
▸ **A** *noun*. **1** A division or separate part, orig. of a design; a division separated by partitions; *spec.* (***a***) HERALDRY a panel, grassy mount, etc., below a shield; †(***b***) a discrete section or feature of a formal garden; (***c***) a partitioned-off division of a railway carriage; (***d***) a watertight division of a ship; (***e***) a section of a parliamentary bill with an allotted time for consideration. M16.

J. F. W. HERSCHEL They divide the spectrum into compartments. S. T. WARNER The most peculiar stockings, like gloves, with a compartment for each toe. R. P. GRAVES Housman began to keep his friendships in separate compartments.

watertight compartment: see WATERTIGHT *adjective*.
†**2** = COMPARTITION 1. E–M18.
– COMB.: **compartment syndrome** MEDICINE any of various conditions resulting from increased pressure within a confined body space, esp. of the leg or forearm.
▸ **B** *verb trans*. Divide or put into compartments (*lit. & fig.*). M19.
■ **compartmenˈtation** *noun* division into compartments M20.

compartmental /kɒmpɑːtˈmɛnt(ə)l/ *adjective*. M19.
[ORIGIN from COMPARTMENT + -AL[1].]
Consisting of or pertaining to a compartment or compartments; characterized by division into compartments.
■ ˌ**compartmentaliˈzation** *noun* division or separation into compartments (*lit. & fig.*) E20. **compartmentalize** *verb trans.* divide into compartments, place in separate compartments, (*lit. & fig.*) E20. **compartmentally** *adverb* M20.

†**compartner** *noun*. L16–E18.
[ORIGIN from COM- + PARTNER *noun*.]
A co-partner.

compass /ˈkʌmpəs/ *noun, adverb, & adjective*. ME.
[ORIGIN Old French & mod. French *compas*, from *compasser*: see COMPASS *verb*.]
▸ **A** *noun*. †**1** (Skilful or crafty) contriving; ingenuity, cunning; a crafty contrivance. ME–L16.
2 *sing.* & (usu.) in *pl.* An instrument for drawing circles and arcs or measuring distances between points, most commonly consisting of two legs connected at one end by a movable joint. Also ***pair of compasses***. ME. ▸**b** In *pl.* (Usu. **C-**.) *The* constellation Circinus. E19.
beam compass(es), ***bow compass(es)***, ***caliper compasses***, etc. ***universal compass***: see UNIVERSAL *adjective*.
†**3** **a** A circle; a circular thing. ME–L17. ▸**b** An arc (*obsolete* in *gen.* use); *spec.* the curved path of an arrow, or the angle of elevation determining this. LME. ▸**c** A circular course, a round; a roundabout journey, a detour. *arch.* LME.
c fetch a compass *arch.* make a circuit or detour, *fig.* act or speak in a roundabout way.
4 The line or boundary enclosing an area, the perimeter; measurement round, circumference. ME.

T. HERBERT The Caspian Sea is in compasse neere three thousand miles.

5 A circumscribed area or space; area, extent. ME.

C. THIRLWALL The . . towering hopes of Athens demanded that the new wall should inclose a larger compass.

6 An instrument for navigation or orientation showing the magnetic or true north, and bearings from it (in its simplest form a magnetized needle turning on a pivot). LME.
box the compass: see BOX *verb*[3]. GYROCOMPASS. ***liquid compass***: see LIQUID *adjective & noun*. ***magnetic compass***: see MAGNETIC *adjective*. MARINER'S ***compass***. ***point of the compass***: see POINT *noun*[1] 16. PRISMATIC ***compass***. ***variation of the compass***: see VARIATION 8.
7 *fig.* Limits, range, scope. M16. ▸**b** MUSIC. The range of tones of a voice or musical instrument. L16. ▸**c** Moderation, due limits. *obsolete* exc. *dial.* L16.

H. JAMES A peculiar girl, but the full compass of whose peculiarities had not been exhibited before. A. G. GARDINER Things to which we can give no name . . because they are outside the compass of our speech.

▸ †**B** *adverb*. **1** In circumference. ME–L16.
2 In an arc, curvedly. LME–M17.
▸ **C** *adjective*. Round, circular, curved. Now only in technical collocations (see below). E16.
– COMB. & SPECIAL COLLOCATIONS: ***compass card***: see CARD *noun*[2] 2b; **compass course**: indicated by a compass, but not actually followed because of deviation caused by wind, currents, etc.; **compass plane** a convex plane for smoothing curved surfaces; **compass-plant** *N. Amer.* any of various plants in which the leaves or branches are aligned north and south so as to avoid the midday sun, *esp.* the plant *Silphium laciniatum*, of the composite family; **compass rose** a graduated circle on a chart, from which bearings can be taken; **compass saw** a handsaw with a narrow blade for cutting curves; **compass timber** SHIPBUILDING timber steamed and curved to take the desired shape; **compass window** a bay window with a semicircular curve.
■ **compassless** *adjective* without a (mariner's) compass. M19.

compass /ˈkʌmpəs/ *verb*. Now chiefly *literary*. ME.
[ORIGIN Old French & mod. French *compasser* (now only) measure as with compasses, repr. Proto-Romance verb from Latin COM- + *passus* step, PACE *noun*[1]. Branch II from COMPASS *noun, adverb, & adjective*.]
▸ **I 1** *verb trans.* Contrive or devise, esp. by underhand means. ME.

J. L. MOTLEY England, whose desolation is thus sought and compassed.

2 *verb trans.* **a** Surround or hem in on all sides, enclose. Freq. extended by *round, about.* ME. ▸**b** Encircle or surround *with* something, †*in* the arms. LME.

a AV *Ps.* 118:12 They compassed mee about like Bees. POPE Like the sea they compass all the land.

3 *verb trans.* & †*intrans.* Go round, make a circuit of; traverse from end to end. LME.

C. KINGSLEY A generation which will compass land and sea to make one proselyte.

†**4** *verb trans. & intrans.* Consider, ponder. LME–M16.
5 *verb trans.* Seize, grasp. Now only *fig.*, grasp with the mind, comprehend. E16.

SHELLEY Why this should be, my mind can compass not.

6 *verb trans.* Accomplish, achieve (an objective); succeed in obtaining (something desired). M16.

T. KYD We, for all our wrongs, can compasse no redresse. LD MACAULAY Men who would unscrupulously employ corruption . . to compass their ends. G. MAXWELL They painted . . as much of the walls as their diminutive statures and a broken ladder could compass.

▸ **II 7** *verb trans. & intrans.* Bend round or into a circle, curve. Now chiefly of timber. M16.
■ **compassable** *adjective* attainable L16. **compasser** *noun* (now *rare*) L15.

compassion /kəmˈpaʃ(ə)n/ *noun*. ME.
[ORIGIN Old French & mod. French from ecclesiastical Latin *compassio(n-)*, from *compass-* pa. ppl stem of *compati* suffer with: see COM-, PASSION *noun*.]
†**1** Participation in another's suffering; fellow feeling, sympathy. ME–E17.
2 Pity inclining one to show mercy or give aid. Freq. in ***have compassion on***. ME.
†**3** Sorrowful emotion, grief. ME–L16.
– COMB.: **compassion fatigue** indifference to charitable appeals resulting from the frequency of such appeals.

compassion /kəmˈpaʃ(ə)n/ *verb trans. rare.* L16.
[ORIGIN from COMPASSION *noun*, or French †*compassionner*, formed as COMPASSION *noun*.]
Have compassion on, pity.
■ **compassionable** *adjective* †(***a***) compassionate; (***b***) deserving compassion, pitiable: M16.

compassionate /kəmˈpaʃ(ə)nət/ *adjective*. L16.
[ORIGIN from French *compassionné* pa. pple of †*compassionner* (see COMPASSION *verb*) + -ATE[2].]
1 Feeling or showing compassion or sympathy for others. L16. ▸**b** Granted out of compassion rather than from legal obligation. M19.
b compassionate allowance: granted when an ordinary pension or allowance is not permissible under official rules. **compassionate leave**: granted on grounds of bereavement, family illness, etc.
†**2** Displaying sorrowful emotion. *rare* (Shakes.). Only in L16.
†**3** Exciting compassion, pitiable. M17–M18.
■ **compassionately** *adverb* E17. **compassionateness** *noun* E17.

compassionate /kəmˈpaʃəneɪt/ *verb trans. arch.* L16.
[ORIGIN from COMPASSIONATE *adjective*, or French †*compassionner*: see COMPASSION *verb*, -ATE[3].]
Regard or treat with compassion, feel pity for.

compassive /kəmˈpasɪv/ *adjective. arch.* LME.
[ORIGIN Anglo-Norman, Old French *compassif, -ive* or late Latin *compassivus*, from *compass-*: see COMPASSION *noun*, -IVE.]
Compassionate, sympathetic.

compaternity /kɒmpəˈtəːnɪti/ *noun*. LME.
[ORIGIN medieval Latin *compaternitas*, from *compater* godfather, formed as COM- + *pater* father: see -ITY.]
The (spiritual) relationship between a child's godfathers (or godparents), or between them and the actual parents.

compatible /kəmˈpatɪb(ə)l/ *adjective*. LME.
[ORIGIN French from medieval Latin *compatibilis*, from late Latin *compati* suffer with: see COMPASSION *noun*, -IBLE.]
▸ **I 1** Able to be admitted or employed together or to coexist in the same subject; consistent, congruous. Of people: able to live or work in harmony together, mutually congenial, well-suited. (Foll. by *with*, †*to*.) LME.

W. BROOME Our poets have joined together such qualities as are by nature the most compatible. V. SACKVILLE-WEST To keep your estimate as low as is compatible with your own reasonable profit. S. HILL How many tastes we share, how compatible we are, Mrs Clemency!

2 *spec.* ▸**a** Of substances, esp. drugs: able to be used together without altering or adversely affecting the individual properties of each. L19. ▸**b** Of blood, organs, etc.: able to be introduced into the body by transfusion, transplantation, etc., without immune response. E20. ▸**c** Of two flowers (on the same or different plants): able to fertilize each other. See also SELF-COMPATIBLE *adjective*. E20. ▸**d** Of television pictures transmitted in colour: able to be received in black and white by a monochrome set. M20. ▸**e** Of computer hardware or software: able to be used on more than one system without special modification. L20.
e ***upward-compatible***: see UPWARD *adverb*.
▸ †**II 3** Participating in another's sufferings; sympathetic. L15–E17.
■ **compatiˈbility** *noun* the quality or state of being compatible (UPWARD ***compatibility***) E17. **compatibleness** *noun* (now *rare*) E17. **compatibly** *adverb* M18.

compatriot /kəmˈpatrɪət, -ˈpeɪt-/ *noun & adjective*. L16.
[ORIGIN Old French & mod. French *compatriote* from late Latin *compatriota* (translating Greek *sumpatriōtēs*): see COM-, PATRIOT *noun*.]
▸ **A** *noun*. A fellow countryman or countrywoman. L16.
▸ **B** *adjective*. Belonging to the same country. M18.
■ **compatriˈotic** *adjective* of or pertaining to compatriots; belonging to the same country: E19. **compatriotism** *noun* the position of being compatriots; compatriotic feeling: L18.

compear /kəmˈpɪə/ *verb intrans. Scot. obsolete* exc. LAW. LME.
[ORIGIN Old French *comper-* tonic stem of *compareir* from Latin *comparere*, formed as COM- + *parere* come into view: cf. APPEAR *verb*.]
Appear, present oneself; *esp.* (LAW) appear in court, either in person or by counsel.
■ **compearance** *noun* appearance, esp. in court LME.

compeer /kəmˈpɪə/ *noun & verb*. LME.
[ORIGIN Old French *comper*: see COM-, PEER *noun*[1].]
▸ **A** *noun*. **1** A person of equal rank or standing. See also COMPARE *noun*[1]. LME.
2 A companion, an associate. LME.
▸ †**B** *verb trans.* Be the equal of, rival. E17–M19.

compel /kəmˈpɛl/ *verb trans.* Infl. **-ll-**. LME.
[ORIGIN Latin *compellere*, formed as COM- + *pellere* drive.]
1 Constrain, force, oblige, (a person). (Foll. by *to do*, (*in*)*to* an action etc.). LME.

J. S. C. ABBOTT Russia should unite her arms with ours, and compel that power to peace. R. SCRUTON A law-making body is powerless unless it can compel the judges to apply its laws.

2 Force to come or go (in some direction); drive or force together. Now *literary*. LME.

DRYDEN Attended by the chiefs who sought the field, (Now friendly mix'd, and in one troop compell'd). SCOTT FITZGERALD Wedging his . . arm imperatively under mine, Tom Buchanan compelled me from the room.

†**3** Take by force, extort, requisition. LME–E19.
4 Bring about or evoke by force. L17.

P. LARKIN His passionate sincerity compelled complete attention.

■ **compellaˈbility** *noun* the quality or state of being (esp. legally) compellable L19. **compellable** *adjective* that may be compelled or constrained (*to do, to*); *spec.* (LAW) that may be made to attend court to give evidence: LME. **compeller** *noun* L16. **compelling** *ppl adjective* that compels; *spec.* that compels strong interest or feeling or admiration: E17. **compellingly** *adverb* M17.

compellation /kɒmpəˈleɪʃ(ə)n/ *noun. arch.* E17.
[ORIGIN Latin *compellatio(n-)*, from *compellat-* pa. ppl stem of *compellare* accost, address, from stem of *compellere*: see COMPEL, -ATION, and cf. APPELLATION.]
1 Addressing or calling upon anyone; a salutation, an address. E17.
2 Addressing by a particular name or title; style of address; a name or title used in speaking of a person or thing, an appellation. M17.

compend /ˈkɒmpɛnd/ *noun.* Now *rare* or *obsolete.* L16.
[ORIGIN Latin COMPENDIUM: cf. STIPEND.]
A compendium, an epitome.

compendia *noun pl.* see COMPENDIUM.

†**compendiary** *noun & adjective.* L16.
[ORIGIN Latin *compendiarius* short, and *-arium* neut. sing. used as noun; formed as COMPENDIUM, -ARY[1].]
► **A** *noun.* A compendium, an epitome. L16–E17.
► **B** *adjective.* Compendious, brief; expeditious. E17–E19.

compendiate /kɒmˈpɛndɪeɪt/ *verb trans.* Long *rare.* E17.
[ORIGIN Latin *compendiat-* pa. ppl stem of *compendiare* shorten, abridge, formed as COMPENDIUM: see -ATE[3].]
Sum up concisely.

V. NABOKOV Seldom does a casual snapshot compendiate a life so precisely.

compendious /kəmˈpɛndɪəs/ *adjective.* LME.
[ORIGIN Old French & mod. French *compendieux* from Latin *compendiosus*, formed as COMPENDIUM: see -OUS.]
†**1** Of a route, method, etc.: saving time or space, expeditious. LME–L18.
2 Containing the essential facts in a small compass; comprehensive but fairly brief. LME.
■ **compendiously** *adverb* LME. **compendiousness** *noun* LME.

compendium /kəmˈpɛndɪəm/ *noun.* Pl. **-iums**, **-ia** /-ɪə/. L16.
[ORIGIN Latin, orig. 'profit, saving', formed as COM- + *pendere* weigh.]
► **I 1** A work presenting in brief the essential points of a subject; a digest, an epitome. L16.
2 *fig.* An embodiment in miniature. E17.
†**3** Saving of labour, space, etc. M17–E19.
► **II 4** An assortment, a varied collection. L19.
5 a In full ***compendium of games***. A box containing assorted table games. L19. ▸**b** A package of stationery for letter-writing. E20.

compenetrate /kəmˈpɛnɪtreɪt/ *verb trans.* L17.
[ORIGIN from COM- + PENETRATE.]
Penetrate in every part, pervade; penetrate mutually.
■ **compeneˈtration** *noun* E19.

compensable /kəmˈpɛnsəb(ə)l/ *adjective.* M17.
[ORIGIN French, from *compenser* from Latin *compensare*: see COMPENSATE, -ABLE.]
Chiefly LAW. Able to be compensated for, justifying compensation.

compensate /ˈkɒmpɛnseɪt/ *verb.* M17.
[ORIGIN Latin *compensat-* pa. ppl stem of *compensare* weigh (one) against another, formed as COM- + *pensare*, frequentative of *pendere* weigh: see -ATE[3].]
1 *verb trans.* Counterbalance, make amends for. (Foll. by *with, by.*) M17. ▸**b** Provide (a pendulum etc.) with an arrangement to neutralize the effects of variations in temperature. E19. ▸**c** ELECTRICITY. Neutralize (a magnetomotive or electromotive force); correct (an undesired characteristic or effect) in a device or circuit. M19.

W. DAMPIER The benefit of it would not compensate the danger.

2 *verb intrans.* Serve as a recompense or adequate substitute (*for*); make up *for.* M17. ▸**b** PSYCHOLOGY. Offset a supposed deficiency or a frustration by developing another characteristic. E20.

I. COMPTON-BURNETT The hard moments were more than compensated for by the good ones.

3 *verb trans.* Make amends to, recompense. (Foll. by *for.*) E19.

R. WARNER Nothing could compensate him for what he was about to lose.

4 *verb trans.* Pay the salary or wages of; pay (a person) for work. Chiefly *N. Amer.* E20.
– NOTE: Formerly pronounced with stress on 2nd syll.
■ **compensatingly** *adverb* so as to compensate E19. **compensative** /kəmˈpɛnsətɪv, kɒmpɛnˈseɪtɪv/ *adjective* = COMPENSATORY M17. **compensator** *noun* a person who or thing which compensates M19. **compensatory** /kəmˈpɛnsət(ə)ri, kɒmpɛnˈseɪt(ə)ri/ *adjective* providing, effecting, or aiming at compensation E17.

compensation /kɒmpɛnˈseɪʃ(ə)n/ *noun.* LME.
[ORIGIN Old French & mod. French from Latin *compensatio(n-)*, formed as COMPENSATE: see -ATION.]
1 The action of compensating; the condition of being compensated. LME. ▸**b** PHYSIOLOGY. The counterbalancing of a deficiency by an increase in functional power elsewhere. M19. ▸**c** ELECTRICITY. Neutralization of a magnetomotive or electromotive force; correction of an undesired characteristic or effect in a device or circuit. M19. ▸**d** PSYCHOLOGY. (The result of) offsetting a supposed deficiency or a frustration by development of another characteristic. E20.

W. J. BATE When we cannot attain wealth, and therefore, by compensation, dismiss it as unimportant.

2 A thing that compensates or is given to compensate (*for*); a counterbalancing feature or factor; amends, recompense; *spec.* money given to compensate loss or injury, or for requisitioned property. L16.

D. CUSACK This place [a girls' school] has all the disadvantages of a nunnery with none of the compensations. G. BROWN The Germans made available a million pounds for compensation to British subjects for their sufferings under Nazi persecution.

3 Salary, wages, remuneration. Chiefly *N. Amer.* L18.
– COMB.: **compensation balance**, **compensation pendulum**: designed so as to neutralize the effects of temperature variation; **compensation water**: supplied from a reservoir to a stream in time of drought.
■ **compensational** *adjective* E19.

comper /ˈkɒmpə/ *noun.* L20.
[ORIGIN from COMP *noun* + -ER[1].]
A person who habitually enters competitions (esp. those promoting consumer goods) in order to win as many prizes as possible.

compère /ˈkɒmpɛː/ *noun & verb.* Also **compere**. M18.
[ORIGIN French, orig. 'godfather in relation to the actual parents', from medieval Latin *compater*: see COMPATERNITY.]
► **A** *noun.* †**1** An elderly man who lavishes gifts on a younger woman. Only in M18.
2 A person in a cabaret act, radio or television show, etc., who introduces the performers, comments on the turns, etc. E20.
► **B** *verb trans. & intrans.* Act as compère (to). M20.

compesce /kəmˈpɛs/ *verb trans. arch.* Long only *Scot.* LME.
[ORIGIN Latin *compescere.*]
Restrain, repress.

compete /kəmˈpiːt/ *verb intrans.* E17.
[ORIGIN Latin *competere* in its late sense of 'strive for (something) together with another', formed as COM- + *petere* aim at.]
Be a rival, bear comparison (*with* another, *in* a quality); strive, contend, take part in a competition, (*with* or *against* another, *for* a thing, *in doing*); strive for superiority *in*; be commercially competitive.

R. HEBER There was none who could compete with him in renown of learning. W. S. JEVONS The stores . . compete with shopkeepers, and induce them to lower their prices. A. STORR If an animal is competing with another for food, it needs to be aggressive. A. C. BOULT To compete at Henley is a wholly delightful experience. *Washington Post* If the Mexican industry is able to compete in its own market, that will guarantee that it will be able to compete in foreign markets.

competence /ˈkɒmpɪt(ə)ns/ *noun.* L16.
[ORIGIN from COMPETENT *adjective*: see -ENCE.]
†**1** = COMPETENCY 1. L16–M18.
2 An income adequate to support life; the condition of having this, easy circumstances. M17.

S. JOHNSON They . . growled away their latter years in discontented competence. R. H. TAWNEY To be content with a modest competence and to shun the allurements of riches.

3 Power, ability, capacity, (*to do*, *for* a task etc.); *spec.* legal authority, qualification, or admissibility, right to take cognizance. E18. ▸**b** The ability of a stream or current to carry fragments of a certain size. L19.

H. HALLAM The court of session . . . possessed no competence in criminal proceedings. N. CHOMSKY What the speaker of a language knows implicitly (what we may call his *competence*). R. V. JONES The construction of radio receivers was just within the competence of the average man.

competency /ˈkɒmpɪt(ə)nsi/ *noun.* L15.
[ORIGIN formed as COMPETENCE: see -ENCY. Sense 4 from Latin *competent-* in the earlier sense of *competere* (see COMPETENT *adjective*).]
†**1** An adequate supply (*of*). L15–M18.
2 = COMPETENCE 2. L16.
3 = COMPETENCE 3. L16.
†**4** Rivalry, competition. L16–M17.

competent /ˈkɒmpɪt(ə)nt/ *noun.* M17.
[ORIGIN ecclesiastical Latin *competent-, -ens* use as noun of pres. pple of *competere* in its later sense: see COMPETE, -ENT.]
ECCLESIASTICAL HISTORY. A candidate for baptism.

competent /ˈkɒmpɪt(ə)nt/ *adjective.* LME.
[ORIGIN Old French & mod. French *compétent* or its source Latin *competent-* pres. ppl stem of *competere* in its earlier sense 'coincide, be fitting' (cf. COMPETE): see -ENT.]
†**1 a** *gen.* Suitable, appropriate. LME–L18. ▸**b** *spec.* Appropriate to a person's rank or status. *arch.* LME.

b K. E. DIGBY If she [a widow] depart from the castle, then a competent house shall be provided for her.

2 Sufficient or adequate in amount, extent, or degree. LME. ▸†**b** Moderate, no more than adequate. E16–L18.

JAS. MILL Mr. Pitt's bill . . being now supported by a competent majority.

3 LAW. Legally authorized or qualified, able to take cognizance, (of a witness, evidence) eligible, admissible. LME.
4 *gen.* Belonging *to* as a rightful possession; permissible, legitimate. E17.

W. BLACKSTONE It is not competent to the defendant to allege fraud in the plaintiff.

5 *gen.* Having adequate skill, properly qualified, effective. (Foll. by *to do, at, for, in.*) M17. ▸**b** Of a stream, current: able to carry fragments of a certain size. L19. ▸**c** MEDICINE. Esp. of a valve or sphincter: functioning normally. L19.

G. B. SHAW I should not be competent to deal with it, as I am not a technical expert in medicine. D. H. LAWRENCE Extremely competent at motor-cars and farming. R. WARNER He was never brilliant but he used to be competent enough.

■ **competently** *adverb* LME.

competition /kɒmpɪˈtɪʃ(ə)n/ *noun.* E17.
[ORIGIN Late Latin *competitio(n-)*, from *competit-* pa. ppl stem of *competere*: see COMPETE *verb*, -ITION.]
1 The action of competing or contending with others (*for* supremacy, a position, a prize, etc.). E17. ▸**b** *spec.* Striving for custom between rival traders in the same commodity. L18. ▸**c** BIOLOGY. The interaction between two or more organisms, populations, or species that share a limited environmental resource. M19.

J. S. MILL Opening all objects of ambition . . to general competition. J. RABAN Ice-cream vans . . playing different tunes in furious competition.

b *imperfect competition*: see IMPERFECT *adjective.*
2 An event in which persons or teams compete; a match, a contest, a trial of ability. E17.

JO GRIMOND They played together . . in the foursomes competition known as the Calcutta Cup.

3 The person or persons competing with one; the opposition in a contest. E20.
– COMB.: **competition-wallah** *Indian colloq.* an Indian Civil Servant appointed by competitive examination.
■ **competitioner** *noun* a competitor; a person who enters a service etc. by competition: M17.

competitive /kəmˈpɛtɪtɪv/ *adjective.* E19.
[ORIGIN from Latin *competit-* (see COMPETITION) + -IVE.]
1 Of, pertaining to, involving, characterized by, or decided by competition. Of a person: with a strong urge to compete. E19.
competitive examination: for a position, office, bursary, etc.
2 Of a price etc.: comparing favourably with that of other traders. E20.
■ **competitively** *adverb* M19. **competitiveness** *noun* L19. **competiˈtivity** *noun* M20.

competitor /kəmˈpɛtɪtə/ *noun.* E16.
[ORIGIN French *compétiteur* or Latin *competitor*, formed as COMPETE: see -OR.]
1 A person who competes, a contestant; a rival, esp. in trade. E16.
†**2** An associate, a partner. L16–L17.
■ **competitorship** *noun* E17. **competitory** *adjective* marked by or subject to competition; competitive: E18. **competitress** *noun* (now *rare*) a female competitor M17.

compilation /kɒmpɪˈleɪʃ(ə)n/ *noun.* LME.
[ORIGIN Old French & mod. French from Latin *compilatio(n-)*, from *compilat-* pa. ppl stem of *compilare*: see COMPILE, -ATION.]
1 The act of compiling; the state of being compiled. LME.
2 A thing compiled; a collection from various sources. LME.
– COMB.: **compilation film** a film, esp. a documentary, compiled from various pieces (chiefly) shot for a different purpose.
■ **ˈcompilator** *noun* a compiler LME. **compilatory** /kəmˈpʌɪlət(ə)ri/ *adjective* of a compiler or a compilation E19.

compile /kəmˈpʌɪl/ *verb trans.* ME.
[ORIGIN Old French & mod. French *compiler* put together, collect, or its presumed source Latin *compilare* plunder, plagiarize.]
1 Collect (materials) into a list, volume, etc. ME.

L. STEPHEN Compiling notes to the Iliad from Eustathius.

2 Make up (a volume etc.) of materials from various sources. LME.

V. CRONIN The Princess began compiling a Russian dictionary.

†**3** Compose (a poem, story, etc.). LME–L16.
†**4** Make up, build. L15–L17.
†**5** Heap or gather together. L16–E19.
6 In CRICKET etc., accumulate (a specified high score). L19.
7 COMPUTING. Cause (a program etc.) to be changed from a high-level language into machine language or a low-level language designed for execution. M20.
■ †**compilement** *noun* (*a*) a structure; an accumulation; (*b*) = COMPILATION: E17–M19. **compiler** *noun* (*a*) a person who compiles materials, a volume, etc.; †(*b*) an author, a composer; (*c*) COMPUTING a program for putting other programs into a form suitable for a particular computer: ME.

comping /ˈkɒmpɪŋ/ *noun*. **L20.**
[**ORIGIN** from **COMP** *noun* + **-ING**[1].]
The practice of entering numerous competitions (esp. those promoting consumer goods) in order to win as many prizes as possible.

compital /ˈkɒmpɪt(ə)l/ *adjective*. **M17.**
[**ORIGIN** Latin *compitalis*, from *compitum* place where roads cross: see **-AL**[1].]
ROMAN ANTIQUITIES. Of or pertaining to crossroads; *spec.* designating shrines of domestic gods placed at street corners.

complacence /kəmˈpleɪs(ə)ns/ *noun*. **LME.**
[**ORIGIN** medieval Latin *complacentia*, formed as **COMPLACENT**: see **-ENCE**.]
†**1** Pleasure; (a) satisfaction. **LME–M18.** ▸**b** An object or source of pleasure and satisfaction. *rare* (Milton). Only in **M17.**
2 = **COMPLACENCY 1. L15.**
†**3** Complaisance. **E17–M18.**

complacency /kəmˈpleɪs(ə)nsi/ *noun*. **M17.**
[**ORIGIN** formed as **COMPLACENCE**: see **-ENCY**.]
1 Tranquil pleasure, self-satisfaction, esp. when uncritical or unwarranted. **M17.**
†**2** = **COMPLACENCE** 1. **M17–L19.**
†**3** (A) contented acquiescence or consent. **M17–E18.**
4 Complaisance. *arch.* **M17.**

complacent /kəmˈpleɪs(ə)nt/ *adjective*. **M17.**
[**ORIGIN** Latin *complacent-* pres. ppl stem of *complacere*, formed as **COM-** + *placere* please: see **-ENT**.]
†**1** Pleasant. **M17–L18.**
2 Tranquilly pleased, self-satisfied, esp. uncritically or unwarrantedly. **M18.**
3 Complaisant. *arch.* **L18.**
■ †**complacential** *adjective* characterized by complacency; complaisant: **M17–M19. complacently** *adverb* **E19.**

complain /kəmˈpleɪn/ *verb* & *noun*. **LME.**
[**ORIGIN** Old French & mod. French *complaign-* pres. stem of *complaindre*, from Proto-Romance (medieval Latin) *complangere*, from Latin **COM-** + *plangere* lament: cf. **PLAIN** *verb*.]
▸ **A** *verb*. †**1** *verb trans.* Bewail, lament. **LME–E18.**
†**2** *verb intrans.* & *refl.* Give expression to sorrow. **LME–M17.**
3 *verb intrans.* & †*refl.* Express dissatisfaction. (Foll. by *about*, (arch.) *against*, *at*, *of*, *that*, †*(up)on*.) **LME.** ▸**b** Make a formal statement of a grievance; lodge a complaint, bring a charge. **LME.**

E. WAUGH Everyone I met complained bitterly about the injustice of having to earn a living.

†**4** *verb trans.* Express dissatisfaction with. Only in **16.**
5 *verb intrans.* & †*refl.* Suffer physically, be unwell. *obsolete* exc. *dial.* **E17.**
6 *verb intrans. transf.* & *fig.* Emit a mournful sound; (of a mast, rudder, etc.) groan, creak. **L17.**
– **WITH PREPOSITIONS IN SPECIALIZED SENSES: complain of** announce that one is suffering from (a headache, an illness, etc.); (see also sense 3 above).
▸ **B** *noun*. (A) complaint. Now *poet.* **L15.**
■ **complainable** *adjective* (*rare*) lamentable, to be complained of **LME. complainer** *noun* (*a*) *LAW* (esp. *Scot.*) = **COMPLAINANT** *noun* 1; (*b*) a person who complains: **LME. complainingly** *adverb* in a complaining manner, querulously **LME.**

complainant /kəmˈpleɪnənt/ *adjective* & *noun*. **LME.**
[**ORIGIN** French *complaignant* pres. pple of *complaindre*: see **COMPLAIN**, **-ANT**[1].]
▸ **A** *adjective*. (Formally) complaining. Now *rare*. **LME.**
▸ **B** *noun*. **1** *LAW*. The person applying to the court in certain proceedings, esp. in a magistrates' court. **LME.**
2 *gen.* A person who complains. **E16.**

complaint /kəmˈpleɪnt/ *noun*. **LME.**
[**ORIGIN** Old French & mod. French *complainte* use as noun of fem. pa. pple of *complaindre*: see **COMPLAIN**.]
1 The expressing or an expression of grief; (a) lamentation; *spec.* a plaintive poem, a plaint. *arch.* **LME.**
2 The expressing or an expression of grievance or injustice suffered; *spec.* a formal accusation or charge, an allegation of a crime; the plaintiff's initial pleading in a civil action. **LME.**

O. MANNING Veering between complaint and a tolerant acceptance of suffering. A. POWELL One of Uncle Giles's chief complaints was that he had been 'put' into the army.

3 A bodily ailment. **E18.**
4 A subject or ground of dissatisfaction or grievance; a grievance that one wishes to express. **M18.**

D. JACOBSON Everything is fine. He has no complaints.

■ **complaintive** *adjective* (*rare*) given to complaint **M17.**

complaisance /kəmˈpleɪz(ə)ns/ *noun*. **M17.**
[**ORIGIN** Old French & mod. French, formed as **COMPLAISANT**: see **-ANCE**.]
1 Politeness; deference; willingness to please others; acquiescence. **M17.**
2 An act showing complaisance. **M18.**

complaisant /kəmˈpleɪz(ə)nt/ *adjective*. **M17.**
[**ORIGIN** French = obliging, pres. pple of *complaire* acquiesce in order to please, repr. Latin *complacere*: see **COMPLACENT**, **-ANT**[1].]
Disposed to please; obliging, courteous; accommodating.

E. M. FORSTER So she did want to talk about her broken engagement. Always complaisant, he put the letter away.

complaisant husband = **MARI COMPLAISANT**.

complanate /ˈkɒmplənеɪt/ *verb* & *adjective*. **M17.**
[**ORIGIN** Latin *complanat-* pa. ppl stem of *complanare* make level, formed as **COM-** + *planare*, from *planus* flat, level: see **-ATE**[3], **-ATE**[2].]
▸ †**A** *verb trans.* Make plane, flatten. **M17–E18.**
▸ **B** *adjective*. Made plane, flattened. **M19.**
■ **complaˈnation** *noun* **L17.**

compleat *adjective* & *adverb* see **COMPLETE** *adjective* & *adverb*.

complect /kəmˈplɛkt/ *verb trans.* **E16.**
[**ORIGIN** Latin *complecti*, *-ere* embrace, encircle, formed as **COM-** + *plectere* plait, twine.]
†**1** Embrace (*lit.* & *fig.*). **E16–M17.**
2 Connect together; interweave (*lit.* & *fig.*). **L16.**

complected /kəmˈplɛktɪd/ *adjective*. *US dial.* & *colloq.* **E19.**
[**ORIGIN** App. from **COMPLEXION**.]
Having a (specified) complexion.

complement /ˈkɒmplɪm(ə)nt/ *noun*. **LME.**
[**ORIGIN** Latin *complementum*, from *complere*: see **COMPLETE** *adjective* & *adverb*, **-MENT**. Cf. **COMPLIMENT** *noun*.]
†**1** **a** Completing, fulfilling. **LME–E18.** ▸**b** Completeness, fullness. Chiefly & now only *HERALDRY* of the moon. **E17.**
2 A thing which puts the finishing touches to a thing; the perfection, the consummation, the culmination. (Foll. by *of*.) **LME.**

STEELE Men rather seek for Money as the Complement of all their Desires.

3 The quantity or amount that completes or fills, the totality. (Foll. by *of*.) **L16.** ▸**b** The full number required (to man a ship, fill a conveyance, etc.). **E17.**

ADAM SMITH That full complement of riches which is consistent with the nature of its laws. **b** G. GREENE A full complement of passengers would have numbered only fourteen.

4 A thing which, when added, completes or makes up a whole; either of two mutually completing parts. **L16.** ▸**b** *MATH.* & *ASTRONOMY.* The angle which when added to a given angle makes 90 degrees. Cf. **SUPPLEMENT** *noun* 1c. **L16.** ▸**c** That colour which, mixed with another, produces white. **M19.** ▸**d** *GRAMMAR.* A word, phrase, or clause added to the verb of a sentence to complete the predicate, esp. to a verb of incomplete predication. Also, a restrictive relative clause identifying or defining the noun (in English often introduced by *that*, as in *the fact that*). **L19.** ▸**e** *PHYSIOLOGY.* A group of proteins present in blood plasma and tissue fluid, which by combining with an antigen–antibody complex can bring about the lysis of foreign cells. **E20.** ▸**f** *COMPUTING.* The number related to a given number in such a way that their sum is a number consisting entirely of 9s (in the decimal system), 1s (in the binary system), etc. Also, such a number increased by one. **M20.**

T. ROETHKE Such a course could provide a real complement to existing courses.

d *objective complement*: see **OBJECTIVE** *adjective* & *noun*.
†**5** A completing accessory. **L16–L17.**
†**6** A personal accomplishment or quality. **L16–M17.**
†**7** **a** A ceremony, a formal observance. **L16–M17.** ▸**b** Civility, politeness. Cf. **COMPLIMENT** *noun* 3. **L16–L17.** ▸**c** = **COMPLIMENT** *noun* 1, 2. **L16–E18.**
– **COMB.: complement-fixation**, **complement-fixing** *MEDICINE* the reaction of complement (sense 4e) with an antigen–antibody complex, freq. as the basis of a diagnostic test.
■ **complementizer** *noun* (*GRAMMAR*) a word, suffix, etc., that introduces a complement clause **M20.**

complement /ˈkɒmplɪmɛnt/ *verb*. **E17.**
[**ORIGIN** from the noun.]
†**1** *verb intrans.* & *trans.* (with *it*). Employ ceremony or formal courtesy. Cf. **COMPLIMENT** *verb* 1. Only in **17.**
†**2** *verb trans.* = **COMPLIMENT** *verb* 2. **M17–M18.**
3 *verb trans.* Complete, form the complement to. **M17.**
■ **complementer** *noun* **E17.**

complemental /kɒmplɪˈmɛnt(ə)l/ *adjective*. **L16.**
[**ORIGIN** from **COMPLEMENT** *noun* + **-AL**[1]. Cf. **COMPLIMENTAL**.]
▸ **I** †**1** Formal, ceremonious. **L16–L17.**
2 Of the nature of a complement; complementary (*to*). **E17.**
complemental male *ZOOLOGY* a small, often degenerate, male which may accompany hermaphrodite or female specimens of some cirripedes.
†**3** Accessory. Only in **M17.**
†**4** Personally accomplished. Only in **M17.**
▸ †**II** **5** Complimentary. **E17–E18.**
■ **complementally** *adverb* **L16.**

complementary /kɒmplɪˈmɛnt(ə)ri/ *adjective*. **E17.**
[**ORIGIN** formed as **COMPLEMENTAL** + **-ARY**[1].]
†**1** Formal, ceremonious. **E–M17.**
2 Forming a complement (*to*), completing; (of two or more things) complementing each other. **E19.**
complementary angles: whose sum is 90 degrees. *complementary colour*: see **COLOUR** *noun*. **complementary distribution** *LINGUISTICS*: of sounds, forms, etc., in mutually exclusive contexts. **complementary DNA** synthetic DNA in which the sequence of bases is complementary to that of a given sequence of messenger RNA. **complementary function** *MATH.* that part of the general solution of a linear differential equation which is the general solution of the associated homogeneous equation obtained by substituting zero for the terms not containing the dependent variable.
3 Designating or pertaining to medicine that involves methods or means not recognized by the majority of medical practitioners, not given full official recognition, or not based on modern scientific knowledge. **L20.**
■ **complementarily** *adverb* **E20. complemenˈtarity** *noun* complementary relationship; *spec.* (*PHYSICS*) the capacity of two contrasted theories (e.g. the wave and particle theories of light) together to explain a body of phenomena, although each separately accounts for only some aspects: **E20.**

complementation /ˌkɒmplɪmɛnˈteɪʃ(ə)n/ *noun*. **M20.**
[**ORIGIN** from **COMPLEMENT** *verb*, *noun* + **-ATION**.]
1 *GRAMMAR.* Complementary distribution. Also, addition of a word, phrase, or clause as a complement. **M20.**
2 *GENETICS.* The phenomenon by which the effects of two different non-allelic mutations in a gene are partly or entirely cancelled out when they occur together. **M20.**
3 *MATH.* & *COMPUTING.* The action of finding the complement of a numerical quantity. **M20.**
4 The action of doing something that is complementary to something else. **L20.**

completable /kəmˈpliːtəb(ə)l/ *adjective*. **M19.**
[**ORIGIN** from **COMPLETE** *verb* + **-ABLE**.]
Able to be completed.

complete /kəmˈpliːt/ *adjective* & *adverb*. Also (now only in sense A.4, *arch.*) **compleat**. **LME.**
[**ORIGIN** Old French & mod. French *complet* or Latin *completus* pa. pple of *complere* fill up, finish, fulfil, formed as **COM-** + base of *plenus* full.]
▸ **A** *adjective*. **1** Having all its parts or elements; entire, full, total. **LME.** ▸**b** Of a formal logical or mathematical system: such that no new axiom can be added that is independent of the existing axioms and consistent with them. **M20.**

G. CHAPMAN A coach . . Stately and complete. A. SILLITOE The drawn curtains . . made the blackout complete.

2 Finished, concluded, having run its full course. **LME.**

POPE Behold Villario's ten years toil compleat.

3 Without defect, perfect. **LME.**

S. JOHNSON The praise had been compleat had his friend's virtue been equal to his wit.

4 Fully accomplished, consummate. **E16.**

I. WALTON The Compleat Angler.

5 Having the maximum extent or degree, thorough. **M17.**

DEFOE The greatest and best principles are often illustrated . . by their completest contraries. A. N. WILSON The Bodger's action made Monty look a complete fool.

– **PHRASES: complete with** having as an important accompaniment.
▸ **B** *adverb*. Completely. Now *dial.* **LME.**
– **NOTE:** In **L16**, **E17** freq. stressed on 1st syll.
■ **completely** *adverb* **LME. completeness** *noun* **E17.**

complete /kəmˈpliːt/ *verb*. **LME.**
[**ORIGIN** from the adjective. Cf. French *compléter*.]
1 *verb trans.* Bring to an end, finish, conclude. **LME.** ▸**b** *verb intrans.* Conclude the legal transfer or sale of real estate. **E19.**

M. MEYER He never completed the work. P. ACKROYD He decided to complete his course for a bachelor's degree in three years.

2 *verb trans.* Make whole or perfect; fill up the amount or number of; add what is required to (a questionnaire etc.). **LME.** ▸†**b** Give a full title or degree to; invest fully with a rank or office. **M17–E18.**

WORDSWORTH All that love can do . . to complete the man, Perfect him, made imperfect in himself.

3 *verb trans.* Accomplish, fulfil (a vow, hope, etc.). *rare*. **LME.**

POPE To town he comes, compleats the nation's hope.

■ †**completement** *noun* completion **M17–L19. completer** *noun* **E18. completive** *adjective* having the attribute of completing, serving for completion (*of*) **M17.**

completion /kəmˈpliːʃ(ə)n/ *noun*. **L15.**
[**ORIGIN** Latin *completio(n-)*, from *complet-* pa. ppl stem of *complere*: see **COMPLETE** *adjective* & *adverb*, **-ION**.]
1 Accomplishment, fulfilment. **L15.**
2 *gen.* The action or an act of completing; the condition of being completed. **L15.** ▸**b** *ellipt.* Completion of the purchase of property. **E20.**

completist /kəmˈpliːtɪst/ *noun* & *adjective*. **M20.**
[**ORIGIN** from **COMPLET(E** *adjective* + **-IST**.]
▸ **A** *noun*. An obsessive (and often indiscriminate) collector.
▸ **B** *adjective*. Intent on completeness or comprehensiveness.

completory /kəmˈpliːt(ə)ri/ *noun* & *adjective*. **L15.**
[**ORIGIN** Late and medieval (eccl.) Latin *completorius*, (noun) *-ium*, formed as **COMPLETION**: see **-ORY**[1], **-ORY**[2].]
▸ **A** *noun*. **1** = **COMPLINE**. **L15.**
2 A thing which affords completion. **M17.**
▸ **B** *adjective*. Affording completion (*of*). **M17.**

C

complex /ˈkɒmplɛks/ *noun*. **M17.**
[**ORIGIN** Latin *complexus* noun, from pa. ppl stem of *complectere* (see **COMPLEX** *adjective*); later interpreted as use as noun of **COMPLEX** *adjective*.]
1 A complex whole; a group of related elements; an assemblage of related buildings, units, etc. **M17.**

A. TUCKER Names being . . necessary for gathering our ideas, and holding them together in a complex. *Downside Review* Russia is a culture-complex in itself. K. CLARK That complex of memories and instincts which are awakened . . by the word 'beauty'. D. LODGE The Inner Ring, an exhilarating complex of tunnels and flyovers.

leisure complex: see **LEISURE** *noun & adjective*.
2 *CHEMISTRY*. A substance or species formed by the combination of simpler ones; *spec.* a species (charged or neutral) in which a central usu. metal atom is bonded to a set of outer or ligand atoms, ions, or molecules (cf. ***COORDINATION* compound**). **L19.**
***SYNAPTONEMAL* complex.**
3 In *PSYCHOANALYSIS*, a related group of usu. repressed ideas, attitudes, and desires causing mental or behavioural abnormality; *colloq.* an obsession. **E20.**
inferiority complex, ***Oedipus complex***, etc.
■ **comˈplexant** *noun* (*CHEMISTRY*) a constituent of a complex; a species which forms a complex: **M20.**

complex /ˈkɒmplɛks/ *adjective*. **M17.**
[**ORIGIN** French *complexe* or its source Latin *complexus* pa. pple of *complectere*, *complecti* encompass, embrace, comprehend, comprise, assoc. with *complexus* plaited.]
1 Consisting of parts, formed by combination, composite. **M17.** ▸**b** *CHEMISTRY*. Of a substance or species: formed by combination of compounds, of the nature of a complex (**COMPLEX** *noun* 2). **L20.**
complex sentence *GRAMMAR*: with a subordinate clause or subordinate clauses.
2 Intricate, not easily analysed or disentangled, complicated. **E18.**

SOUTHEY As they weave The complex crossings of the mazy dance. C. FRANCIS He was a complex personality, with glaring faults as well as superhuman virtues.

3 *MATH*. Containing real and imaginary parts. **M19.**
complex conjugate each of two complex numbers having their real parts identical and their imaginary parts of equal magnitude but opposite sign. **complex number**: of the form $a + ib$ where a and b are real numbers and i is the square root of -1.
■ **com͵plexifiˈcation** *noun* the action of complexifying **E20.** **comˈplexify** *verb trans. & intrans.* make or become (more) complex **M19.** **complexly** *adverb* †(*a*) collectively; (*b*) in a complex manner: **M17.** **complexness** *noun* **E18.**

complex /kəmˈplɛks, ˈkɒmplɛks/ *verb*. **L15.**
[**ORIGIN** Latin *complex-* stem of *complexus*: see **COMPLEX** *adjective* Later senses prob. from the adjective or noun.]
†**1** *verb trans.* Join, attach. Only in **L15.**
2 *verb trans.* Combine into a complex whole; complicate. *rare*. **M17.**
3 *CHEMISTRY*. **a** *verb trans.* (Cause to) form a complex with. **M20.** ▸**b** *verb intrans.* Form a complex (*with*). **M20.**

complexion /kəmˈplɛkʃ(ə)n/ *noun & verb*. **ME.**
[**ORIGIN** Old French & mod. French from Latin *complexio(n-)* combination, association, (in late Latin) physical constitution, formed as **COMPLEX** *verb*: see **-ION**.]
▸ **A** *noun*. †**1** Physical constitution or nature (orig. as constituted by the bodily humours). **ME–M18.**
2 *hist.* The combination of supposed qualities (*cold* or *hot*, *moist* or *dry*), or of the four bodily humours, in a certain proportion, regarded in medieval and later times as determining the nature of a body, plant, etc.; the type of constitution attributed to this combination. **LME.** ▸†**b** A bodily humour; a collection of humours. **LME–L17.**
3 A habit of mind, a disposition. *obsolete* exc. as *fig.* use of sense 4. **LME.**
4 The natural colour, texture, and appearance, of the skin, esp. of the face. **L16.** ▸**b** *transf.* Colour, visible aspect, appearance. **L16.**
5 *fig.* Character, aspect. **L16.**

G. B. SHAW What you say puts a very different complexion on the matter. L. WOOLF People of varying political complexion.

†**6** Complication; (a) combination. **E17–M19.**
▸ **B** *verb trans.* †**1** Constitute by combination of various elements. **LME–M17.**
2 Give a colour or tinge to. **E17.**
■ **complexional** *adjective* †(*a*) of or pertaining to physical or mental constitution; (*b*) of or pertaining to skin colour and texture: **LME.** **complexionally** *adverb* **M17.** †**complexionary** *adjective* **M17–E18.** **complexioned** *adjective* †(*a*) having a (specified) physical or mental constitution; (*b*) having a (specified) colour and texture of skin; having a (specified) character or aspect: **LME.** **complexionless** *adjective* (of a person) pale, colourless **M19.**

complexity /kəmˈplɛksɪti/ *noun*. **L17.**
[**ORIGIN** from **COMPLEX** *adjective* + **-ITY**. Cf. French *complexité*.]
1 Complex nature or structure. **L17.**
2 A complex condition; a complication. **L18.**

†**complexive** *adjective*. **M17–M19.**
[**ORIGIN** Latin *complexivus*, from *complex-* stem of *complexus*: see **COMPLEX** *adjective*, **-IVE**.]
Comprehensive.

complexus /kəmˈplɛksəs/ *noun*. **L19.**
[**ORIGIN** formed as **COM-** + **PLEXUS**.]
A complicated system; a complex.

compliable /kəmˈplʌɪəb(ə)l/ *adjective*. *arch.* **M17.**
[**ORIGIN** from **COMPLY** + **-ABLE**.]
1 Compliant. **M17.**
†**2** Reconcilable, accordant. **M17–M18.**

compliance /kəmˈplʌɪəns/ *noun*. **M17.**
[**ORIGIN** from **COMPLY** + **-ANCE**.]
†**1** Complaisance. **M17–M18.**
†**2** Agreement; accord. **M17–M19.**
3 The action of complying with a request, command, etc.; an instance of so complying. (Foll. by *with*, (arch.) *to*.) **M17.** ▸†**b** *spec.* (Expedient) conformism in religion or politics. **L17–M19.** ▸**c** (An instance of) unworthy submission to a request, command, etc. **E18.**

Guardian Further measures to achieve proper compliance with agreed safety standards.

4 *PHYSICS*. The property of a body or material of undergoing elastic deformation, or (of gases) change in volume, when a force is applied; the extent of this under specified conditions. **M20.**
– **COMB.**: **compliance officer** a person who is employed to ensure that a company does not contravene any statutes or regulations which apply to its activities.
■ Also **compliancy** *noun* **M17.**

compliant /kəmˈplʌɪənt/ *adjective & noun*. **M17.**
[**ORIGIN** from **COMPLY** + **-ANT**[1].]
▸ **A** *adjective*. **1** Disposed to comply, yielding. **M17.**
†**2** Pliant, yielding to physical pressure. **M17–L18.**
▸ †**B** *noun*. A person who complies. Only in **M17.**
■ **compliantly** *adverb* **E19.**

complicacy /ˈkɒmplɪkəsi/ *noun*. **E19.**
[**ORIGIN** from **COMPLICATE** *verb*: see **-ACY**.]
1 Complexity. **E19.**
2 A complicated structure or condition. **M19.**

complicate /ˈkɒmplɪkət/ *adjective*. *arch.* **LME.**
[**ORIGIN** Latin *complicatus* pa. pple, formed as **COMPLICATE** *verb*: see **-ATE**[2].]
Compound, complex; intricate; involved. Also, interwoven.
■ †**complicateness** *noun* **M17–E19.**

complicate /ˈkɒmplɪkeɪt/ *verb trans.* **E17.**
[**ORIGIN** Latin *complicat-* pa. ppl stem of *complicare*, formed as **COM-** + *plicare* fold: see **-ATE**[3].]
†**1** Combine intimately, intertwine; fold together; entangle. **E17–E18.**
†**2** Compose or compound *of*. **E17–E18.**
3 Make (more) complex or intricate. **M17.**

Sunday Times The exercise was complicated by the fact that the letters . . were often warped and highly fragile.

4 Combine or mix up *with* in a complex or involved way. Also, introduce medical complications in. **L17.**

LD MACAULAY The history of the great English revolution begins to be complicated with the history of foreign politics.

■ **complicative** *noun & adjective* †(*a*) *noun* (*rare*) a complicating force, principle, etc.; (*b*) *adjective* complicating, causing complication: **M17.**

complicated /ˈkɒmplɪkeɪtɪd/ *adjective*. **M17.**
[**ORIGIN** from **COMPLICATE** + **-ED** *suffix*[1].]
†**1** Folded together; tangled. **M17–E18.**
2 Consisting of many interconnecting parts or elements, intricate. **M17.**

K. LETTE High-tech, all-in-one tracksuits and complicated air-cushioned training shoes. I. SINCLAIR Autumnal foliage draped itself over complicated ironwork at the edge of the terrace.

3 Involving many different and confusing aspects, complex. **M17.**

M. HADDON Numbers are sometimes very complicated and not very straightforward at all. A. M. SMITH Life has been getting rather complicated.

4 *MEDICINE*. Involving complications. **M18.**
■ **complicatedly** *adverb* **L19.** **complicatedness** *noun* **M18.**

complication /kɒmplɪˈkeɪʃ(ə)n/ *noun*. **LME.**
[**ORIGIN** Old French & mod. French, or late Latin *complicatio(n-)*, formed as **COMPLICATE** *verb*: see **-ATION**.]
1 An involved condition or structure; an entangled state of affairs; a complicating circumstance; *MEDICINE* a secondary disease or condition aggravating a previous one. **LME.**

W. PALEY That complication of probabilities by which the Christian history is attested. T. ROETHKE I've had pharyngitis with complications.

†**2** **a** The action of combining intimately, folding together, or compounding; the condition of being so combined etc. Only in **17.** ▸**b** The action of making (more) complicated; the condition of being complicated, complexity. **L18.**

b R. L. STEVENSON A woodyard of unusual extent and complication.

complice /ˈkʌmplɪs/ *noun*. *arch.* **LME.**
[**ORIGIN** Old French & mod. French from late Latin *complex*, *complic-* (adjective) confederate, formed as **COM-** + *plic-* as in *plicare* to fold.]
†**1** *gen.* An associate. **LME–L19.**
2 *spec.* An accomplice. **LME.**

complicit /kəmˈplɪsɪt/ *adjective*. **L20.**
[**ORIGIN** Back-form. from **COMPLICITY**.]
Having or showing complicity, that is a party to or involved *in* wrongdoing.

Independent The absurd notion . . that all these people are complicit in some criminal conspiracy.

complicity /kəmˈplɪsɪti/ *noun*. **M17.**
[**ORIGIN** Sense 1 from **COMPLICIT**, sense 2 from **COMPLICATE** *verb*: see **-ITY**.]
1 Partnership or involvement in wrongdoing. **M17.**
2 Complexity. Now *rare*. **M19.**

complier /kəmˈplʌɪə/ *noun*. **E17.**
[**ORIGIN** from **COMPLY** + **-ER**[1].]
†**1** An accomplice. **E–M17.**
2 A person who complies *with* a request, command, etc., (formerly) a fashion etc. **M17.** ▸†**b** *spec.* A conformist in religion or politics, esp. for expediency. **M17–M18.**

compliment /ˈkɒmplɪm(ə)nt/ *noun*. **M17.**
[**ORIGIN** French from Italian *complimento* repr. Proto-Romance var. of Latin *complementum* **COMPLEMENT** *noun*.]
1 A polite expression of praise or approval; a neatly phrased remark or an act implying praise or approval. **M17.**

B. OKRI Women clustered round, showering her with compliments.

pay a compliment, (*arch.*) ***make a compliment***, (*arch.*) ***pass a compliment***.
2 Polite praise, complimentary language. **M17.**
3 A formal greeting, esp. as the accompaniment to a message, note, present, etc. Usu. in *pl.* (Formerly foll. by *of*.) **M17.**
make one's compliments, ***pay one's compliments***, ***present one's compliments***, ***send one's compliments***, etc.
4 A gift, a present. Now *arch. & dial.* **E18.**
– **PHRASES**: ***Chinese compliment***: see **CHINESE** *adjective*. **compliments of the season** greetings appropriate to the (Christmas) season. **return the compliment** give one compliment in return for another; *fig.* retaliate or give a benefit in a similar way.
– **COMB.**: **compliment slip** a small piece of paper conveying formal greetings.

compliment /ˈkɒmplɪmɛnt/ *verb*. **L17.**
[**ORIGIN** French *complimenter*, formed as **COMPLIMENT** *noun* Cf. earlier **COMPLEMENT** *verb*.]
1 *verb intrans.* Employ ceremony or formal courtesy; pay compliments. **L17.**
2 *verb trans.* Address with formal courtesy; pay a compliment to (a person, *on* a thing), congratulate (*up*)*on*; present (a person *with* a thing) as a mark of courtesy. **E18.**
■ **complimenter** *noun* **M18.**

complimental /kɒmplɪˈmɛnt(ə)l/ *adjective*. Now *arch. & dial.* **L17.**
[**ORIGIN** from **COMPLIMENT** *noun* + **-AL**[1]. Cf. **COMPLEMENTAL**.]
†**1** Formal, ceremonious. **L17–E18.**
2 Complimentary. **E18.**
■ **complimentally** *adverb* **L17.**

complimentary /kɒmplɪˈmɛnt(ə)ri/ *adjective*. **E18.**
[**ORIGIN** formed as **COMPLIMENTAL** + **-ARY**[1].]
Expressive of or implying praise or approval; (of a person) given to paying compliments, paying a compliment; of the nature of a compliment, given free of charge by way of a compliment.
■ **complimentarily** *adverb* **E19.**

compline /ˈkɒmplɪn, -ʌɪn/ *noun*. Also **-in** /-ɪn/. **ME.**
[**ORIGIN** Alt., prob. after *matines*, *matins*, of Old French & mod. French *complie* (now *complies*), use as noun of fem. pa. pple of †*complir* complete, from Proto-Romance var. of Latin *complere* (see **COMPLETE** *adjective & adverb*).]
ECCLESIASTICAL. The seventh and last of the daytime canonical hours of prayer; the office, orig. directed to be said immediately before retiring for the night, appointed for this hour.

complish /ˈkʌmplɪʃ/ *verb trans.* Long *arch. rare*. **LME.**
[**ORIGIN** Old French *compliss-* lengthened stem of *complir* complete: see **COMPLINE**, **-ISH**[2]. Later perh. aphet. from **ACCOMPLISH**.]
Fulfil, accomplish.

complot /ˈkɒmplɒt/ *noun*. Now *rare*. **M16.**
[**ORIGIN** Old French & mod. French = †dense crowd, secret project, of unknown origin: assoc. with **PLOT** *noun*.]
A conspiracy, a plot; an intrigue.

complot /kəmˈplɒt/ *verb trans. & intrans.* Now *rare*. Infl. **-tt-**. **L16.**
[**ORIGIN** French *comploter*, formed as **COMPLOT** *noun*.]
Combine in plotting (some act, usu. criminal).
■ †**complotment** *noun* a conspiracy, a plot **L16–E18.** **complotter** *noun* **L16.**

Complutensian /kɒmpluːˈtɛnsɪən/ *adjective*. **M17.**
[**ORIGIN** from Latin *Complutensis*, from *Complutum* (see below), + -IAN.]
Of or pertaining to the Spanish town of Complutum (later Alcalá de Henares); *spec.* designating the earliest polyglot bible, published there in the early 16th cent.

compluvium /kəmˈpluːvɪəm/ *noun*. Pl. **-ia** /-ɪə/. **M19.**
[**ORIGIN** Latin, from *compluere* flow together.]
ROMAN ANTIQUITIES. A square opening in the roof of the atrium, through which fell the rainwater collected from the roof.

comply /kəmˈplʌɪ/ *verb*. **L16.**
[**ORIGIN** from Italian *complire* from Catalan *complir*, Spanish *cumplir*, from Latin *complere*: see COMPLETE *adjective & adverb*.]
†**1** *verb trans.* Fulfil, accomplish. *rare.* **L16–M17.**
†**2** *verb intrans.* Observe the formalities of courtesy and politeness. (Foll. by *with* a person.) **E–M17.**
†**3** *verb intrans.* Agree *with*, *together*; (foll. by *with*) suit. Only in **17.**
4 *verb intrans.* Foll. by *with*: accommodate oneself to (a person, circumstances, customs, etc.). *obsolete* exc. as passing into sense 5. **M17.** ▸†**b** Conform in religion or politics. Only in **M17.**
5 *verb intrans.* Act in accordance with or *with* a request, command, etc. **M17.** ▸†**b** Consent or agree *to*, *to do*. **L17–E18.**

> H. JAMES She . . prepared to comply with their aunt's demands. H. WILSON The Ministry did not agree with it and did not propose to comply. ANTHONY SMITH Friends do not always comply with expectation.

†**6** *verb intrans.* Ally oneself *with*. Only in **M17.**
†**7** *verb trans.* Make conform *to*. **M–L17.**
8 *verb intrans.* Of a thing: fit *with*, adapt itself *to*. Long *obsolete* exc. *dial.* **L17.**

compo /ˈkɒmpəʊ/ *noun*¹. Pl. **-os**. **E19.**
[**ORIGIN** Abbreviation of COMPOSITION.]
Stucco, plaster.

compo /ˈkɒmpəʊ/ *noun*². *Austral. & NZ slang*. **M20.**
[**ORIGIN** Abbreviation of COMPENSATION.]
Compensation, *esp.* that paid for an accident or industrial injury.

compo /ˈkɒmpəʊ/ *adjective*. **L19.**
[**ORIGIN** Abbreviation.]
= COMPOSITE *adjective*
compo rations: made up of various tinned foods, designed to last several days, and carried in a large pack.

†**compone** *verb* see COMPOUND *verb*.

componé *adjective* var. of COMPONY.

component /kəmˈpəʊnənt/ *noun & adjective*. **M16.**
[**ORIGIN** Latin *component-* pres. ppl stem of *componere*: see COMPOUND *verb*, -ENT.]
▸ **A** *noun*. †**1** A compounder. Only in **M16.**
2 A constituent part; *spec.*: (*a*) any of the separate parts of a motor vehicle, machine, etc.; (*b*) MATH. & PHYSICS each of a set of vectors (e.g. forces) which when combined are equivalent to a given vector; (*c*) CHEMISTRY each of the constituents of a phase system which together constitute the minimum number necessary in specifying the composition of the system. **M17.**
▸ **B** *adjective*. Composing, constituting, making up, constituent. **M17.**
■ **componential** /kɒmpəˈnɛnʃ(ə)l/ *adjective* of or pertaining to components; *spec.* (LINGUISTICS) designating the analysis of distinctive sound units or grammatical elements into phonetic or semantic components: **M20.** **componentry** *noun* components collectively **M20.**

compony /kɒmˈpɒni/ *adjective*. Also **-né**. **L16.**
[**ORIGIN** Old French & mod. French *componé*: see -Y⁵.]
HERALDRY. Composed of a single row of squares of two alternate tinctures, gobony.

comport /ˈkɒmpɔːt/ *noun*. **L19.**
[**ORIGIN** App. abbreviation of French *comportier* var. of COMPOTIER.]
= COMPOTE 3, COMPOTIER.

comport /kəmˈpɔːt/ *verb*. Now *literary*. **LME.**
[**ORIGIN** Latin *comportare*, formed as COM- + *portare* carry, bear. Cf. Old French & mod. French *comporter*.]
†**1** *verb trans. & intrans.* foll. by *with*. Endure, tolerate. **LME–M19.**
2 *verb intrans.* Foll. by *with*: agree with, suit, befit. **L16.**
3 *verb refl.* & †*intrans.* Behave. **E17.**
■ †**comportance** *noun* carriage, bearing, behaviour; agreement, compliance: **L16–M17.**

comportment /kəmˈpɔːtm(ə)nt/ *noun*. **L16.**
[**ORIGIN** French, from *comporter* formed as COMPORT *verb*: see -MENT.]
Personal bearing, demeanour; behaviour.

compos /ˈkɒmpɒs/ *adjective*. **E19.**
[**ORIGIN** Abbreviation.]
= COMPOS MENTIS.

composant *noun* see CORPOSANT.

compose /kəmˈpəʊz/ *verb*. **LME.**
[**ORIGIN** Old French & mod. French *composer*, based on Latin *componere* (see COMPOUND *verb*) but re-formed after Latin pa. pple *compositus* and Old French & mod. French *poser*: see POSE *verb*¹.]
▸ **I** Put together.
1 *verb trans.* Make by assembling parts; make up, construct. *obsolete* exc. as below. **LME.** ▸†**b** Fashion, frame. **L15–L17.**
2 *spec.* ▸**a** *verb trans.* Construct in words, write as author, produce in literary form. **LME.** ▸**b** *verb trans.* Construct in notes of music, produce in musical form; set (words) to music. **L16.** ▸**c** *verb intrans.* Construct a work or works in words or music; engage in literary or musical creation. **E17.**

> **a** DAY LEWIS A few poems in her own handwriting, composed after her marriage. P. ROTH To compose in my head . . the first lines of an introductory lecture. **b** J. GLASSCO She busied herself composing a sonata for violin.

3 *verb trans.* In *pass.* (orig. of sense 1, but now assoc. with sense 6). Be made up, be formed; be constituted *of*, consist *of*. **M16.**

> SHAKES. *Much Ado* He is compos'd and fram'd of treachery. JO GRIMOND The British Army was composed of Generals and 3-ton lorries.

4 *verb trans.* PRINTING & TYPOGRAPHY. Arrange (characters) by hand or machine, or electronically, in the order to be reproduced in print; set (an article, book, etc.) in type or otherwise prepare for printing. **M17.**
composing stick an instrument, usu. of adjustable width, in which metal type is assembled with spaces to form lines before being put on a galley.
5 *verb trans.* Put together to form a whole; *spec.* arrange artistically. **M17.**
6 *verb trans.* Constitute, make up, be the constituents or material of. (See also sense 3 above.) **M17.**

> B. RUSSELL A good society is a means to a good life for those who compose it.

▸ **II** Arrange, adjust.
7 *verb trans.* Settle (a dispute), pacify (contending persons, a region); arrange (any matter) properly or successfully. **LME.** ▸**b** *verb intrans.* Come to a settlement. *rare* (Shakes.). **E17.**

> TENNYSON It then remains . . to compose the event. L. VAN DER POST You must compose your differences with one another.

8 *verb trans.* Arrange in a particular manner or for a particular purpose (specified or understood, esp. in proper order or in a position of rest); arrange (one's face, features, etc.) so as to conceal one's feelings. **M16.** ▸**b** Lay out (a corpse). **L17.**

> L. A. G. STRONG She had been able to compose herself in a suitable attitude of meditation. N. ALGREN She composed her features and her hair.

9 *verb trans.* Dispose (esp. the mind, oneself) calmly and collectedly (*to* or *for* an action or state, *to do* something); calm, pacify, tranquillize. **E17.**

> SOUTHEY I would fain compose my thoughts for action. W. MARCH She sat down to compose herself. J. BARZUN Intellect . . should calm and compose the soul.

10 *verb trans.* Quiet (a noise etc.). *arch.* **E17.**
■ **composable** *adjective* †(*a*) *rare* adapted for composition; (*b*) able to be composed; suitable for setting to music: **E17.** **composal** *noun* (now *rare*) the act or action of composing **M17.** **composed** *adjective* that has been composed; *spec.* †(*a*) compound, composite; (*b*) calm and self-possessed; expressive of calm and self-possession: **L15.** **composedly** *adverb* **M17.** **composedness** *noun* **E17.**

composer /kəmˈpəʊzə/ *noun*. **M16.**
[**ORIGIN** from COMPOSE + -ER¹.]
1 *gen.* A person who or thing which composes. (Foll. by *of*.) **M16.**
2 *esp.* ▸†**a** A compositor. **L16–E18.** ▸**b** A person who composes music. **L16.** ▸**c** An author, a writer, (*of*). **E17.**

composite /ˈkɒmpəzɪt; *in sense B.5* -zʌɪt/ *adjective & noun*. In ARCHITECTURE orig. †**-ita**. **LME.**
[**ORIGIN** French, or Latin *compositus* pa. pple of *componere*: see COMPOUND *verb*, -ITE².]
▸ **A** *adjective*. **1** MATH. ▸†**a** Of a number: composed of more than one digit. Only in **LME.** ▸**b** Of a number: being the product of two or more factors greater than unity; not prime. **M18.**
2 ARCHITECTURE. Designating the fifth classical order, a compound of Ionic and Corinthian. **M16.**
3 *gen.* Made up of various parts or elements, compound; made of constituents that remain recognizable. **L17.**
4 BIOLOGY. Made up of a number of separate simple parts or individual organisms; *spec.* (BOTANY) belonging to or designating the large plant family Compositae, in which the so-called flower is a head of many florets sessile on a common receptacle and surrounded by a common involucre of bracts, as in the daisy, dandelion, etc. **M18.**
5 Of a railway carriage: having compartments of different classes. **M19.**
▸ **B** *noun*. †**1** MATH. A number composed of more than one digit. Only in **LME.**
2 ARCHITECTURE. The composite order. **M16.**
3 *gen.* A composite thing, a composite material, a compound. **M17.**
4 A composite plant. **M19.**
5 A resolution compiled from several independent resolutions, put before a Party Conference, Trades Union Congress, etc. Cf. earlier COMPOSITE *verb*. **L20.**
■ **compositely** *adverb* **M19.** **compositeness** *noun* **L19.**

composite /ˈkɒmpəzʌɪt/ *verb trans. & intrans*. **M20.**
[**ORIGIN** from the noun.]
Combine (independent resolutions) into one resolution for putting before a Party Conference, Trades Union Congress, etc.

composition /kɒmpəˈzɪʃ(ə)n/ *noun*. **LME.**
[**ORIGIN** Old French & mod. French from Latin *compositio(n-)*, from *composit-* pa. ppl stem of *componere*: see COMPOUND *verb*, -ION.]
▸ **I** The action.
1 The action of combining; the fact of being combined; combination. **LME.**
2 The forming of or *of* a thing by the combination of parts etc.; formation, construction. **LME.**
3 The combination of mathematical quantities, forces, etc. **L15.**
4 The settling of a debt etc. by some arrangement. **L15.**
5 a The combination (according to various rules and principles) of lexical items into a compound word. **M16.** ▸**b** The arrangement of words into sentences, and sentences into poetry or prose. **M16.**
†**6** The putting (of things) into proper order. **L16–M19.**
7 PHILOSOPHY. †**a** Synthetic reasoning; reasoning from the universal to the particular. **L16–M18.** ▸**b** The combination of two terms or propositions to form a compound term or proposition; (chiefly as ***fallacy of composition***) the invalid move from a proposition about individual members or subsets of a set or class taken separately to a proposition about the set or class itself. **E18.**
8 The composing of anything to be recited or read; the practice or art of literary production. **L16.**

> ARNOLD BENNETT He sat down to the composition of his letter.

9 The action or art of composing music. **L16.**

> M. TIPPETT What Mozart wrote in a letter about composition.

10 The arranging of the elements of a drawing, painting, sculpture, photograph, etc., so as to form an aesthetically pleasing whole. **L16.**

> E. H. GOMBRICH This . . gave the artist of the Middle Ages a new freedom to experiment with more complex forms of composition.

11 PRINTING & TYPOGRAPHY. The setting of type by hand or machine. See also PHOTOCOMPOSITION. **M19.**
▸ **II** The mode, with the resulting condition or state.
12 The manner in which a thing is composed or made up; the state or condition resulting from or constituted by combination; the combination of physical and mental qualities that make up a person. **LME.**

> H. JAMES Her stature, like most other points in her composition, was not unusual. J. REED Trotsky announced its composition: 100 members, of which 70 Bolsheviki. B. SPOCK The water and sugar are put in to make the mixture more like mother's milk in composition.

organic composition (of capital): see ORGANIC *adjective*.
13 The state or quality of being composite. **M16.**
14 The artistic manner or style in which words, visual elements, or musical notes, are put together. **M16.**
†**15** Consistency. *rare* (Shakes.). Only in **E17.**
▸ **III** The product.
16 A substance or preparation formed by the combination or mixture of various ingredients; *esp.* a compound artificial substance serving the purpose of a natural one. **LME.**

> *attrib.*: R. CHANDLER The gates folded back on a black composition driveway.

17 a An agreement, a contract; a treaty, a truce. *arch.* **LME.** ▸**b** A compromise. **L16.**
18 A condition consisting in the combination (material, practical, or ideal) *of* several things; a combination, an aggregate, a mixture. **M16.**

> R. W. EMERSON He seemed . . to be a composition of several persons.

19 a A piece of writing, a literary production; in schools etc., a piece of writing as an exercise in expressing oneself in prose. **L16.** ▸**b** A piece of music. **M17.** ▸**c** A painting, drawing, sculpture, photograph, etc., consisting of several elements aesthetically combined; *transf.* a harmonious natural scene. **M18.**

> **a** J. D. SALINGER I didn't have to do any work in English at all hardly, except write compositions once in a while. **b** Y. MENUHIN The Solo Sonata is . . the most important composition for violin alone since Bach. **c** K. CLARK The carefully constructed compositions of the later Giotto.

20 An agreement for the payment of a sum of money in lieu of a larger sum or some other obligation; payment of this by agreement; the sum of money so paid. **L16.**
■ **compositional** *adjective* **E19.** **compositionally** *adverb* **M20.** †**compositure** *noun* = COMPOSITION 12 **E17–E18.**

C

compositive /kəmˈpɒzɪtɪv/ *adjective*. **L16.**
[ORIGIN from COMPOSITE *adjective & noun* or COMPOSITION: see -IVE.]
Involving or using composition; synthetic.

compositor /kəmˈpɒzɪtə/ *noun*. **LME.**
[ORIGIN Anglo-Norman *compositour* = Old French & mod. French *-eur*, from Latin *compositor*, from *composit-*: see COMPOSITION, -OR.]
†**1** An umpire, an arbiter, a peacemaker. *Scot.* **LME–E18.**
2 The composer or compiler of a literary work. *rare.* **M16.**
3 *PRINTING.* A person who sets type by hand, corrects composed matter, makes up pages, and assembles them for printing; *loosely* a person who sets type by machine. **M16.**
■ **composiˈtorial** *adjective* of or pertaining to composers or compositors **E19.**

compositum /kəmˈpɒzɪtəm/ *noun*. Pl. **-ta** /-tə/, **-tums**. **M17.**
[ORIGIN Latin, neut. pa. pple of *componere*: see COMPOUND *verb*.]
= COMPOSITION 16, 18.

compos mentis /ˌkɒmpɒs ˈmɛntɪs/ *pred. adjectival phr.* **E17.**
[ORIGIN Latin.]
In one's right mind, having control of one's mind, not mad.

compossible /kəmˈpɒsɪb(ə)l/ *adjective*. **M17.**
[ORIGIN Old French from medieval Latin *compossibilis*: see COM-, POSSIBLE. Cf. earlier INCOMPOSSIBLE.]
Possible in conjunction, compatible, (*with*).
■ **compossiˈbility** *noun* **M17.**

compost /ˈkɒmpɒst/ *noun*. **LME.**
[ORIGIN Old French *composte* (mod. COMPOTE) from Latin *compos(i)ta*, *-tum* use as noun of fem. and neut. pa. pple of *componere* COMPOUND *verb*.]
1 A composition, a combination, a compound. **LME.**
†**2** A preparation of preserved fruit etc.; = COMPOTE 1. **LME–E18.**
3 A mixed manure of organic origin; loam soil or some other medium with added organic matter to grow plants in; *fig.* a mixture of ingredients. **LME.**
– COMB.: **compost heap**, **compost pile**: of garden refuse, soil, etc., used for the quick production of compost.

compost /ˈkɒmpɒst/ *verb trans.* **L15.**
[ORIGIN Old French *composter*, formed as COMPOST *noun*.]
Treat with or make into compost.
■ **compostable** *adjective* **L20.** **composter** *noun* **M19.**

composture /kəmˈpɒstʃə/ *noun*. Long *obsolete* exc. *dial.* **E17.**
[ORIGIN Old French, formed as COMPOST *verb*: see -URE.]
1 Composition. **E17.**
†**2** Compost, manure. *rare* (Shakes.). Only in **E17.**

composure /kəmˈpəʊʒə/ *noun*. **L16.**
[ORIGIN from COMPOSE *verb* + -URE.]
†**1** The action of composing or compounding; = COMPOSITION I. **L16–M18.**
†**2** **a** *gen.* The mode or form of composition, the state of being composed; = COMPOSITION II. **E17–M19.** ▸**b** *spec.* Calmness and self-possession, tranquil demeanour. **M17.**
†**3** A product of composing; = COMPOSITION III. **E17–L18.**

compotation /kɒmpə(ʊ)ˈteɪʃ(ə)n/ *noun*. **L16.**
[ORIGIN Latin *compotatio(n-)* (in Cicero translating Greek *sumposion* SYMPOSIUM): see COM-, POTATION.]
A drinking session, a carouse.
■ **ˈcompotator** *noun* a fellow drinker **M18.** **comˈpotatory** *adjective* **E19.**

compote /ˈkɒmpəʊt, -ɒt/ *noun*. Also **-ôte**. **L17.**
[ORIGIN French: see COMPOST *noun*.]
1 (A dish of) fruit preserved or cooked in a syrup; a fruit salad, stewed fruit, esp. with or in a syrup. **L17.**
2 A dish of stewed pigeon. **M18.**
3 A bowl-shaped dessert dish with a stem; a dish for stewed fruit etc. Cf. COMPORT *noun*, next. **L19.**

compotier /kɔ̃pɔtje/ *noun*. Pl. pronounced same. **M18.**
[ORIGIN French, formed as COMPOTE: see -IER.]
= COMPOTE 3.

compotus *noun* var. of COMPUTUS.

compound /ˈkɒmpaʊnd/ *noun*¹. **M16.**
[ORIGIN from COMPOUND *adjective*.]
1 A compound thing, a compound substance; *spec.* (**a**) a compound word; (**b**) *CHEMISTRY* a substance consisting of two or more elements chemically combined in fixed proportions by weight; (**c**) a compound (steam) locomotive. **M16.**

R. FRY This attempt to isolate the elusive element of the pure aesthetic reaction from the compounds in which it occurs. N. G. CLARK A group of compounds known as paraffin hydrocarbons.

BINARY **compound**. **open compound**: see OPEN *adjective*.
2 A union, combination, or mixture *of* ingredients, parts, etc. **E17.**

S. BRETT The smell of the house—a compound of used cooking oil, beer and wet cardboard.

3 Compounding, composition. **L17.**

compound /ˈkɒmpaʊnd/ *noun*². **L17.**
[ORIGIN Portuguese *campon* or Dutch *kampoeng*, from Malay *kampung*, *-ong* enclosure, small village.]
1 In SE Asia, the Indian subcontinent, etc.: an enclosure in which a house or factory stands. **L17.**
2 In S. Africa: an enclosure in which miners live. **L19.**
3 A large fenced-in space in a prison, concentration camp, etc.; a pound. **E20.**

compound /ˈkɒmpaʊnd/ *adjective*. **LME.**
[ORIGIN Orig. pa. pple of †*compo(u)ne*: see COMPOUND *verb*, -ED¹.]
1 Made up of several ingredients; consisting of several parts or elements; *spec.* (**a**) *BIOLOGY* consisting of a number of distinct units, organisms, etc.; (**b**) *GRAMMAR* (of a word) made up of more than one word or root; (of a tense) formed using an auxiliary verb; (**c**) *OPTICS* (of a lens) consisting of two or more different lenses mounted as a single unit. **LME.**
2 Combined, collective. **E18.**
– SPECIAL COLLOCATIONS: **compound engine** (**a**) a steam engine in which the same steam is made to expand successively in different sets of cylinders; (**b**) an aeroengine utilizing the kinetic energy of the exhaust (as a turbofan or turboprop). **compound eye** *ZOOLOGY* an eye (e.g. of an insect) composed of many simple units (ommatidia) each forming a facet of the whole organ. **compound fracture**: with the skin pierced by a bone end and involving a risk of infection. ***compound interest***: see INTEREST *noun*. **compound interval** *MUSIC*: exceeding one octave. **compound leaf**: divided into a number of leaflets (which may themselves be further divided). **compound locomotive**: working on the principle of the compound (steam) engine. ***compound machine***: see MACHINE *noun* 4b. **compound order** *ARCHITECTURE* the composite order. ***compound pendulum***: see PENDULUM *noun*. ***compound*** *PISTIL*. ***compound*** *RACEME*. **compound sentence** *GRAMMAR*: formed by coordination of two or more simple sentences. **compound time** *MUSIC*: having beats with the value of a dotted note. ***compound umbel***: see UMBEL 1.
■ **compoundness** *noun* **M18.**

compound /kəmˈpaʊnd/ *verb*. Also (earlier) †**-o(u)ne**. **LME.**
[ORIGIN Old French & mod. French *compo(u)n-* pres. stem of *compondre* from Latin *componere*, formed as COM- + *ponere* to place. Mod. form (**E16**) after EXPOUND.]
▸ **I** †**1** *verb trans.* Put together, join. **LME–M17.**
2 *verb trans.* Combine, mix, (material or abstract elements). (Foll. by *with*.) **LME.** ▸**b** *GRAMMAR.* Combine (words or roots) to form a larger word. **M16.** ▸**c** Combine (mathematical quantities etc.) so as to obtain a resultant or composite quantity. Also, reckon as compound interest, increase (as) by compound interest. **L16.** ▸**d** Add to, increase, complicate, (esp. difficulties etc.). **M20.**

SHAKES. *2 Hen. IV* Only compound me with forgotten dust. I. MURDOCH A vague . . pain in which portions of jealousy and wounded pride were compounded with a profound sense of homelessness. **d** A. HAILEY If the first was a mistake, then at least we need not compound it.

3 *verb trans.* Make up by the combination of various ingredients or elements. (Foll. by *of*, *from*.) **LME.**

A. J. CRONIN Andrew . . began . . to compound an anti-pyretic mixture. JO GRIMOND The feeling was compounded of several fears.

4 *verb trans.* Construct, form, compose. *obsolete* exc. as passing into sense 3. **LME.**

B. JOWETT Meletus . . has been compounding a riddle.

†**5** *verb trans.* Go to make up, constitute. **E17–E18.**
▸ **II 6** *verb intrans.* Agree, come to terms, settle a matter, now *spec.* by mutual concession or compromise or as in sense 7. (Foll. by *with* a person, *for* a thing.) **LME.**
7 *verb intrans. spec.* ▸**a** Come to a settlement by paying money, agree on a payment, (*with* a person, *for* a thing); substitute a money payment or some other lighter performance for or *for* a liability or obligation; settle a debt by partial repayment; discharge a recurrent payment in a lump sum. **L15.** ▸**b** Accept terms of settlement in lieu of prosecution; accept payment in lieu of one's full claims. (Foll. by *for*.) **L16.**
8 *verb trans.* Settle, compose, (a matter, esp. a dispute etc.), now *spec.* by mutual concession or compromise or as in sense 9. **E16.**
9 *verb trans. spec.* ▸**a** Settle (a debt) by partial repayment; settle (any matter) by payment of money. **M17.** ▸**b** Accept money for; condone (an offence etc.) for money; settle privately; forbear prosecution of (a felony) from private motives. **L17.**
■ **compoundable** *adjective* **E17.** **compounded** *adjective* (**a**) that has been compounded; formed by combination of various ingredients or elements; †(**b**) compound, composite, complex: **L16.**

compounder /kəmˈpaʊndə/ *noun*. **M16.**
[ORIGIN from COMPOUND *verb* + -ER¹.]
1 A person who settles quarrels; *derog.*, a compromiser. *obsolete* exc. *hist.*, a supporter of the conditional restoration of James II. **M16.**
2 A person who compounds for a liability, debt, or charge; one who compounds a felony or offence. **M16.**
3 A person who makes a compound of ingredients. **E17.**

†**compoune** *verb* see COMPOUND *verb*.

comprador /kɒmprəˈdɔː/ *noun*. Also **-ore**. **E17.**
[ORIGIN Portuguese = buyer, from late Latin *comparator*, from *comparare* purchase, formed as COM- + *parare* provide.]
†**1** A house steward in the European households of SE Asia, the Indian subcontinent, etc. **E17–E19.**
2 The Chinese chief agent of a foreign business house in China; *fig.* an agent of a foreign power. **M19.**

comprecation /kɒmprɪˈkeɪʃ(ə)n/ *noun*. **E17.**
[ORIGIN Latin *comprecatio(n-)*, from *comprecat-* pa. ppl stem of *comprecari*, formed as COM- + *precari* pray: see -ATION.]
(An act of) communal prayer; (a) joint supplication.

comprehend /kɒmprɪˈhɛnd/ *verb trans.* **ME.**
[ORIGIN Old French *comprehender* or Latin *comprehendere*, formed as COM- + *prehendere* seize.]
▸ **I 1** Grasp mentally, understand. **ME.**

J. S. MILL The majority . . cannot comprehend why those ways should not be good enough for everybody. S. KAUFFMANN To know him better than anyone, to comprehend him. B. MALAMUD Speak more slowly so that we can comprehend everything you say.

2 Apprehend with the senses, esp. the sight. *arch.* **LME.**
†**3** Accomplish, overtake, attain (*lit.* & *fig.*). **LME–E17.**
†**4** *lit.* Lay hold of, seize. *rare.* **L16–M17.**
▸ **II** †**5** Summarize; sum up. **LME–E17.**
6 Include, contain, comprise, take in; encompass. **LME.**

COVERDALE *2 Chron.* 2:6 The heauens of all heauens maye not comprehende him. M. DRAYTON Some swelling source (Whose plentie none can comprehend in bounds). R. HAKLUYT The second Volume comprehendeth the principall Navigations . . to the South. J. AUSTEN Far from comprehending him or his sister in their father's misconduct. M. H. ABRAMS In many later mimetic theories everything is comprehended in two categories.

■ **comprehendingly** *adverb* in a comprehending manner, intelligently **M19.**

comprehensible /kɒmprɪˈhɛnsɪb(ə)l/ *adjective*. **L15.**
[ORIGIN French *compréhensible* or Latin *comprehensibilis*, from *comprehens-* pa. ppl stem of *comprehendere*: see COMPREHEND, -IBLE. Cf. earlier INCOMPREHENSIBLE.]
1 That may be understood; conceivable, intelligible. (Foll. by *to*.) **L15.**
2 That may be included, contained, or comprised. **E16.**
■ **comprehensiˈbility** *noun* **M18.** **comprehensibly** *adverb* **M18.**

comprehension /kɒmprɪˈhɛnʃ(ə)n/ *noun*. **LME.**
[ORIGIN French *compréhension* or Latin *comprehensio(n-)*, from *comprehens-*: see COMPREHENSIBLE, -ION.]
▸ **I 1** The act, fact, or faculty of understanding, esp. of writing or speech; mental grasp. **LME.** ▸**b** *spec.* The setting or answering of questions on a set passage to test or improve linguistic understanding, esp. as a school exercise. **M20.**

Wall Street Journal There are just so many things people do that are just beyond comprehension.

2 An understanding, an adequate notion, (*of*). **L16.**
†**3** An act of grasping physically. *rare.* **M17–M18.**
▸ **II 4** The action of including, containing, or comprising; the fact or condition of being so included etc. **LME.** ▸**b** *ECCLESIASTICAL HISTORY.* The inclusion of Nonconformists in the Church of England. **M17.**
5 The faculty or quality of including; inclusiveness. **E17.**
6 *LOGIC.* The sum of the attributes included in a concept; intension. **E18.**

comprehensive /kɒmprɪˈhɛnsɪv/ *adjective & noun*. **E17.**
[ORIGIN French *compréhensif*, *-ive* or late Latin *comprehensivus*, from *comprehens-*: see COMPREHENSIBLE, -IVE.]
▸ **A** *adjective*. **1** Comprising or including much or all; of large content or scope; *spec.* (of motor vehicle insurance) providing cover for most risks, including damage to the policyholder's own vehicle. **E17.** ▸**b** Inclusive *of*. **M17.** ▸**c** *spec.* Designating a secondary school or a system of education which provides for children of all intellectual or other abilities. **M20.**

M. FRAYN A comprehensive lexicon of all the multi-purpose monosyllables used by headline-writers. D. HALBERSTAM He wanted more coverage than any other paper; he was determined . . to be comprehensive.

2 Characterized by mental comprehension; embracing many mental sympathies etc. **E17.**
3 *LOGIC.* Understood in intension as opp. to extension. Now *rare* or *obsolete.* **E18.**
▸ **B** *noun*. A comprehensive school. **M20.**
■ **comprehensively** *adverb* **LME.** **comprehensiveness** *noun* **M17.** **comprehensiviˈzation** *noun* the action of comprehensivizing **M20.** **comprehensivize** *verb trans.* make (a school, an education system) comprehensive **M20.**

†**comprehensor** *noun*. **M17–E18.**
[ORIGIN from Latin *comprehens-* (see COMPREHENSIBLE) + -OR.]
A person who has attained to full (religious) comprehension.

†**compresbyter** *noun*. **L16–E18.**
[ORIGIN ecclesiastical Latin, formed as COM-, PRESBYTER.]
A fellow presbyter.

compresence /kɒmˈprɛz(ə)ns/ *noun*. **M17.**
[ORIGIN from COM- + PRESENCE.]
Presence together; co-presence.
■ **compresent** *adjective* present together; co-present: **E20.**

compress /ˈkɒmprɛs/ *noun*. **L16.**
[ORIGIN French *compresse*, formed as COMPRESS *verb*.]
1 A soft linen pad for compressing an artery, applying a medicine, etc.; a piece of cloth, usu. wet and covered with a waterproof bandage, applied to reduce inflammation etc. (also ***cold compress***, ***water compress***). **L16.**

2 A machine for pressing cotton bales etc. in a compact form for transport etc. **M19**.

compress /kəmˈprɛs/ *verb trans.* **LME**.
[**ORIGIN** Old French *compresser* or late Latin *compressare* frequentative of Latin *comprimere*, or from *compress-* pa. ppl stem of *comprimere*: see **COM-**, **PRESS** *verb*[1].]
1 Press together, squeeze, (separate things, a hollow thing reducing its capacity, a substance making it more dense); flatten (as) by pressure; reduce to smaller volume; *fig.* condense, concentrate. **LME**. ▸**b** Increase the density of (a fluid) mechanically by increasing the mass contained in a fixed volume or reducing the volume of a fixed mass. **L17**.

R. C. HUTCHINSON Bickerings at Westminster could be compressed . . into a few columns of the big daily newspapers. M. FRAYN As if he had compressed a whole week's emotional energy into that one burst of anger.

†**2** Repress, keep under restraint. **E16–M19**.
†**3** Embrace sexually. **E17–E18**.
4 *COMPUTING*. Alter the form of (data) to reduce the amount of storage necessary. **M20**.
■ **compressed** *adjective* (**a**) that has been compressed; ***compressed air***, air that is at greater than atmospheric pressure; (**b**) *ZOOLOGY & BOTANY* flattened laterally: **L16**.

compressible /kəmˈprɛsɪb(ə)l/ *adjective*. **L17**.
[**ORIGIN** from **COMPRESS** *verb* + **-IBLE**.]
1 Able to be compressed. **L17**.
2 *MEDICINE*. Of the pulse: so faint that it appears to vanish under the pressure of the finger; thready. Now *rare*. **M19**.
■ **compressiˈbility** *noun* the quality of being compressible; *PHYSICS* (a measure of) the ability of a fluid to be compressed: **L17**.

compression /kəmˈprɛʃ(ə)n/ *noun*. **LME**.
[**ORIGIN** Old French & mod. French from Latin *compressio(n-)*, from *compress-*: see **COMPRESS** *verb*, **-ION**.]
1 The action or act of compressing; the state or condition of being compressed. **LME**.
2 a In a steam engine, the reduction in volume of the steam left in the cylinder after the exhaust is closed at the end of the exhaust stroke. **M19**. ▸**b** The (amount of) reduction in volume of the air–fuel mixture in an internal-combustion engine before ignition. **L19**.
3 *COMPUTING*. The process of reducing the amount of space occupied by data that is being stored or transmitted, by minimizing redundant information. **M20**.
– **COMB.**: **compression ratio** the ratio of the maximum to minimum volume in the cylinder of an internal-combustion engine measured before and after compression; **compression stroke** the stroke of the piston compressing the air–fuel mixture in the cylinder of an internal-combustion engine.
■ **compressional** *adjective* **L19**.

compressive /kəmˈprɛsɪv/ *adjective*. **LME**.
[**ORIGIN** Old French & mod. French *compressif*, *-ive*, or medieval Latin *compressivus*, from *compress-*: see **COMPRESS** *verb*, **-IVE**.]
1 Having the attribute or function of compressing; tending to compress. **LME**.
†**2** Consisting in or caused by compression. **LME–M17**.

compressor /kəmˈprɛsə/ *noun*. **M19**.
[**ORIGIN** from **COMPRESS** *verb* + **-OR**.]
An instrument or device for compressing; *spec.* a machine, or part of a machine, for compressing air or other gases, esp. for motive power.

compressure /kəmˈprɛʃə/ *noun*. **M17**.
[**ORIGIN** medieval Latin *compressura*, from *compress-*: see **COMPRESS** *verb*, **-URE**.]
Compression; (a) pressing together.

comprise /kəmˈprʌɪz/ *verb*. Also **-ize**. **LME**.
[**ORIGIN** French *compris(e)* pa. pple of *comprendre* **COMPREHEND**. Cf. **APPRISE** *verb*[1].]
†**1** *verb trans.* **a** Lay hold of, seize; *Scot.* seize legally. **LME–L17**. ▸†**b** Grasp mentally, perceive, comprehend. **LME–L17**.
2 *verb trans.* Include, contain, esp. as making up the whole; extend to, encompass; consist of, be made up of. **LME**. ▸†**b** Enclose, hold. **L15–M17**. ▸**c** Summarize, sum up. **E16**.

C. BRONTË In her own single person she could have comprised the duties of a first minister and a superintendent of police. MAX-MÜLLER The registers . . comprised a period of 200,000 years. M. MEYER The ground floor comprised the shop, a tiny waiting room and the kitchen. **c** W. PALEY Comprising what he delivered within a small compass.

†**3** *verb trans.* Write as author, compile, compose. **L15–E17**.
4 *verb trans.* Make up, constitute, compose. **L18**.

L. DURRELL A few such sketches comprise the whole portrait of the author.

5 *be comprised of*, be composed or made up of. **L19**.
6 *verb intrans.* Be made up *of*. **M20**.
– **NOTE**: Senses 5 and (now esp.) 6 are often regarded as erroneous uses.
■ **comprisable** *adjective* **E17**.

compromise /ˈkɒmprəmʌɪz/ *noun & adjective*. **LME**.
[**ORIGIN** Old French & mod. French *compromis* from Latin *compromissum* use as noun of neut. pa. pple of *compromittere* consent to arbitration, formed as **COM-** + *promittere* **PROMISE** *verb*.]
▸ **A** *noun* **I** †**1** A joint agreement made by contending parties to abide by the decision of an arbitrator. **LME–L16**. ▸**b** = **COMPROMISSION** 2. **E18–L19**.
2 Settlement by an arbitrator; arbitration. Now *rare* or *obsolete*. **LME**.
3 Settlement of a dispute by mutual concession; a concession offered to settle a dispute. **E16**.

SHAKES. *Rich. II* Warr'd he hath not, But basely yielded upon compromise That which his noble ancestors achiev'd with blows.

4 The finding of an intermediate way between (or *between*) conflicting requirements, courses of action, etc., by modification of each; a thing that results from or embodies such an arrangement. **E18**.

LD MACAULAY Logic admits of no compromise. The essence of politics is compromise. SCOTT FITZGERALD A compromise between the serious and the trivial.

▸ **II 5** A putting in peril; an exposure to risk. **E17**.
▸ **B** *adjective*. That is, or serves as, a compromise (sense A.4 above). **M19**.

compromise /ˈkɒmprəmʌɪz/ *verb*. **LME**.
[**ORIGIN** from the noun.]
▸ **I** †**1** *verb trans.* Refer (something) *to* another for decision. **LME–M17**.
†**2** *verb trans.* In *pass.* Be agreed by mutual concession. **LME–L18**.
3 *verb intrans.* Come to terms by mutual concession; make a compromise. **LME**.

S. RICHARDSON To induce him to compromise on those terms. M. MEYER Politicians . . invariably compromised with their ideals.

4 *verb trans.* †**a** Settle (a matter in dispute between others). **L16–L18**. ▸**b** Of a contending party: settle (a difference with or *with* another) by mutual concession; come to terms about. **L17**.
▸ **II 5** *verb trans.* Bring under suspicion or into danger, esp. by indiscreet action; imperil (a reputation etc.). **L17**.

R. CHURCH The spot of ink on his trousers . . did not compromise his dignity. T. SHARPE The shopgirls they had compromised.

■ **compromiser** *noun* †(**a**) an arbitrator in a dispute; (**b**) a person who compromises or advocates compromise: **L15**.

compromission /kɒmprəˈmɪʃ(ə)n/ *noun*. **LME**.
[**ORIGIN** Old French & mod. French, or medieval Latin *compromissio(n-)*, from Latin *compromiss-* pa. ppl stem of *compromittere*: see **COMPROMISE** *noun & adjective*, **-ION**.]
1 (An instance of) submission of a dispute to arbitration. **LME**.
2 (An instance of) delegation of the responsibility of electing to chosen representatives. **LME**.

†**compromit** *verb*. Infl. **-tt-**. **LME**.
[**ORIGIN** Latin *compromittere*: see **COMPROMISE** *noun & adjective*.]
1 *verb trans.* (*refl.* & in *pass.*). Bind themselves etc., be bound, jointly to accept an arbitrator's decision. **LME–M16**.
2 *verb trans.* Refer to arbitration; settle by arbitration or compromise. **LME–L17**.
3 *verb intrans. & trans.* Delegate (an election or one's right to vote). Only in **16**.
4 *verb trans.* = **COMPROMISE** *verb* 5. *US*. **L18–L19**.

†**comprotector** *noun*. **M17–M18**.
[**ORIGIN** from **COM-** + **PROTECTOR**.]
A joint protector.

comprovincial /kɒmprəˈvɪnʃ(ə)l/ *noun & adjective*. **LME**.
[**ORIGIN** Late Latin *comprovincialis* from Latin **COM-** + *provincialis* **PROVINCIAL**.]
▸ **A** *noun*. A bishop of the same province. **LME**.
▸ **B** *adjective*. Belonging to the same province. **M16**.

†**compt** *noun* var. of **COUNT** *noun*[1].

†**compt** *adjective*. **LME–L18**.
[**ORIGIN** Latin *comptus* pa. pple of *comere* dress (hair), adorn.]
Having the hair dressed. Of a person, a style of discourse: elegant, polished.

†**compt** *verb* var. of **COUNT** *verb*.

†**comptable** *adjective & noun* var. of **COUNTABLE** *adjective & noun*.

compter *noun* see **COUNTER** *noun*[1].

compte rendu /kɔ̃t rɑ̃dy/ *noun phr.* Pl. **-s -s** (pronounced same). **E19**.
[**ORIGIN** French = account rendered.]
A report, a review, a statement.

comptes rendus *noun phr.* pl. of **COMPTE RENDU**.

†**compting** *verbal noun* var. of **COUNTING**.

comptoir /kɔ̃twaːr/ *noun*. Pl. pronounced same. **E18**.
[**ORIGIN** French: see **COUNTER** *noun*[1].]
A commercial agency or factory in a foreign country.

Comptometer /kɒm(p)ˈtɒmɪtə/ *noun*. **L19**.
[**ORIGIN** App. from French *compte* **COUNT** *noun*[1] + **-OMETER**.]
(Proprietary name for) a type of calculating machine.

Compton effect /ˈkɒm(p)tən ɪˌfɛkt/ *noun phr.* **E20**.
[**ORIGIN** from A. H. *Compton* (1892–1962), US physicist.]
PHYSICS. The increase in wavelength that occurs when X-rays and gamma rays are scattered.

†**comptrol** *verb* var. of **CONTROL** *verb*.

comptroller /kənˈtrəʊlə/ *noun*. **L15**.
[**ORIGIN** Var. of **CONTROLLER** by erron. assoc. with **COUNT** *noun*[1] (late Latin **COMPUTUS**).]
A controller: now only in the titles of some financial and legal officers in government and the royal household. ***Comptroller and Auditor General***.

†**comptrolment** *noun* var. of **CONTROLMENT**.

compulsative /kəmˈpʌlsətɪv/ *adjective*. *rare* (Shakes.). **E17**.
[**ORIGIN** from Latin *compulsat-* pa. ppl stem of *compulsare* frequentative of *compellere* **COMPEL** + **-IVE**.]
Of the nature of compulsion.
■ **compulsatively** *adverb* **M19**.

†**compulsator** *noun* see **COMPULSITOR**.

†**compulsatory** *adjective*. **E16–E19**.
[**ORIGIN** formed as **COMPULSATIVE**: see **-ORY**[2].]
Of the nature of compulsion; compulsory.
■ †**compulsatorily** *adverb* **M–L18**.

compulse /kəmˈpʌls/ *verb trans.* *rare*. **LME**.
[**ORIGIN** Old French *compulser* from Latin *compulsare*: see **COMPULSATIVE**.]
Compel, oblige.

compulsion /kəmˈpʌlʃ(ə)n/ *noun*. **LME**.
[**ORIGIN** Old French & mod. French from late Latin *compulsio(n-)*, from Latin *compuls-* pa. ppl stem of *compellere* **COMPEL**: see **-ION**.]
1 The action, or an act, of compelling; the condition of being compelled; coercion, obligation. **LME**.

T. LEWIN The tribute . . would not be forthcoming except on compulsion.

under compulsion because one is compelled.
2 *PSYCHOLOGY*. An irresistible impulse to behave in a certain way, esp. despite one's conscious intent or wish. **E20**.

A. J. CRONIN An inner compulsion so powerful as to be irresistible.

compulsitor /kəmˈpʌlsɪtə/ *noun*. Orig. †**-ator**. **E16**.
[**ORIGIN** medieval Latin *compulsatorius* adjective, from Latin *compulsat-*: see **COMPULSATIVE**, **-OR**.]
SCOTS LAW. An act, instrument, or proceeding that orders or compels.

compulsive /kəmˈpʌlsɪv/ *adjective & noun*. **L16**.
[**ORIGIN** medieval Latin *compulsivus*, from Latin *compuls-*: see **COMPULSION**, **-IVE**.]
▸ **A** *adjective*. **1** = **COMPULSORY** *adjective* 2. **L16**.
†**2** = **COMPULSORY** *adjective* 1. **E17–M19**.
3 *PSYCHOLOGY*. Of the nature of or resulting from a compulsion; characterized by a compulsion. **E20**.

R. D. LAING His compulsive tendency to act in a feminine way. R. HAYMAN He was compulsive about personal cleanliness.

4 Of an entertainment etc.: that compels one's continued attention. **M20**.

Listener John Cole, Gerald Kaufman and Took's Endpiece are all compulsive reading.

▸ **B** *noun*. **1** A compelling force. *rare*. **M17**.
2 A person subject to a psychological compulsion. **M20**.
■ **compulsively** *adverb* **E17**. **compulsiveness** *noun* **E18**.

compulsory /kəmˈpʌls(ə)ri/ *noun & adjective*. **E16**.
[**ORIGIN** medieval Latin *compulsorius*, from Latin *compuls-*: see **COMPULSION**, **-ORY**[2].]
▸ **A** *noun*. Something that compels or is obligatory; *esp.* a legal mandate compelling obedience. **E16**.
▸ **B** *adjective*. **1** Produced by compulsion; enforced; compelled. **L16**.
compulsory purchase: see **PURCHASE** *noun* 6a.
2 Compelling, coercive. **M17**.
■ **compulsorily** *adverb* **M17**. **compulsoriness** *noun* **M19**.

compunction /kəmˈpʌŋkʃ(ə)n/ *noun*. **ME**.
[**ORIGIN** Old French & mod. French *componction* from ecclesiastical Latin *compunctio(n-)*, from Latin *compunct-* pa. ppl stem of *compungere* prick sharply, sting, formed as **COM-** + *pungere* prick: see **-ION**.]
1 Pricking or stinging of the conscience or the heart; uneasiness of mind after wrongdoing; remorse. **ME**. ▸**b** In weakened sense: a slight or passing regret for a minor misdeed, a scruple (sometimes including pity for the person wronged). **E18**.
†**2** Pity. **LME–L18**.
†**3** The action of pricking or puncturing. **LME–M17**.

compunctious /kəmˈpʌŋkʃəs/ *adjective*. **E17**.
[**ORIGIN** from **COMPUNCTION** + **-OUS**.]
1 Of the nature of, expressive of, compunction. **E17**.
2 Having compunction. **E19**.
■ **compunctiously** *adverb* **M19**.

compurgation /kɒmpəːˈgeɪʃ(ə)n/ *noun*. **M17**.
[**ORIGIN** medieval Latin *compurgatio(n-)*, from Latin *compurgat-* pa. ppl stem of *compurgare* purge completely: see **COM-**, **PURGATION**.]
1 The action of clearing a person from a charge by the oaths of a number of others; *gen.* vindication; vindicating evidence. **M17**.

SIR W. SCOTT My evidence is necessary to the compurgation of ane honest gentleman.

2 *hist.* The ancient mode of trial and purgation by means of a number of compurgators. **M19**.

C

C

compurgator /ˈkɒmpəːɡeɪtə/ *noun.* **M16.**
[ORIGIN medieval Latin, from Latin COM- + *purgator*, from *purgat-*: see PURGATION, -OR. Cf. Old French *compurgateur*.]
1 *hist.* A person who swore in favour of the character or credibility of an accused person when the latter swore an oath declaring his innocence. **M16.**
2 *gen.* A person who vouches for another; a character witness. **E17.**
■ **comˈpurgatory** *adjective* **E17.**

computable /kəmˈpjuːtəb(ə)l/ *adjective.* **E17.**
[ORIGIN Latin *computabilis*, from *computare*: see COMPUTE *verb*, -ABLE.]
Able to be computed.
■ **computaˈbility** *noun* **L19.**

computation /kɒmpjʊˈteɪʃ(ə)n/ *noun.* **LME.**
[ORIGIN Latin *computatio(n-)*, from *computat-* pa. ppl stem of *computare*: see COMPUTE *verb*, -ATION.]
1 The action or process of reckoning; calculation; the use of a computer. **LME.**
2 A result got by calculation. **E18.**
■ **computational** *adjective* **L19.** **computationally** *adverb* **M20.**

†**computator** *noun.* **L16–M18.**
[ORIGIN Latin, from *computat-*: see COMPUTATION, -OR.]
A person who calculates.

compute /kəmˈpjuːt/ *noun.* Now *rare.* **LME.**
[ORIGIN In sense 1 from French *comput*; in sense 2, from COMPUTE *verb*.]
†**1** = COMPUTUS 1. **LME–M16.**
2 Calculation. Now chiefly in ***beyond compute***. **L16.**

compute /kəmˈpjuːt/ *verb.* **E17.**
[ORIGIN French *computer* or Latin *computare*, formed as COM- + *putare* settle (an account), reckon.]
1 *verb trans.* Determine by calculation or computation; estimate, reckon. **E17.**
S. PEPYS He hath computed that the rents . . comes to 600,000l. per annum. SWIFT The souls in this kingdom are computed to be 1,500,000. F. CHICHESTER I uncased the slide rule, and computed the sun's true bearing.
computed axial tomography, **computed tomography** = ***computerized axial tomography*** s.v. COMPUTERIZE; abbrevs. *CAT*, *CT*.
2 *verb intrans.* Make reckoning; use a computer. **M17.**
†**3** *verb intrans.* Of numbers: make up, count. *rare* (Milton). Only in **M17.**

computer /kəmˈpjuːtə/ *noun.* Also **-or.** **M17.**
[ORIGIN from COMPUTE *verb* + -ER¹.]
1 A person who makes calculations; *spec.* a person employed for this in an observatory etc. **M17.**
2 An apparatus for making calculations; *spec.* an automatic electronic machine for making rapid calculations or controlling operations that are expressible in numerical or logical terms. **L19.**
computer program, ***computer programmer***, ***computer terminal***, etc. ***personal computer***: see PERSONAL *adjective*.
– COMB.: **computer-aided**, **computer-assisted** *adjectives* performed with the aid of a computer, esp. when previously performed without; **computer dating** the use of facilities provided by a computer to find potential partners for people; **computer-friendly** *adjective* suitable for use with computers, compatible with computers; (of a person) well-disposed towards computers, computerate; **computer game** (a software package for) a game played on a computer; ***computer graphics***: see GRAPHIC *noun* 1b, 4; **computer language** any of numerous systems of rules, words, and symbols for writing computer programs or representing instructions etc.; **computer literacy** = COMPUTERACY; **computer-literate** *adjective* = COMPUTERATE; **computer-readable** *adjective* = ***machine-readable*** *adjective* s.v. MACHINE *noun*; **computer science** the branch of knowledge that deals with the construction, operation, programming, and applications of computers; **computer scientist** a specialist in computer science; **computer virus** = VIRUS 4.
■ **computeracy** *noun* [after LITERACY] the quality of being computerate **L20.** **computerate** *adjective* [after LITERATE *adjective*] able to use computers, familiar with the operation of computers **L20.** **computeˈrese** *noun* (*a*) the symbols and rules of a programming language; (*b*) the jargon associated with computers: **M20.** **computerist** *noun* a (frequent) user of computers **L20.** **computeriˈzation** *noun* the action or result of computerizing something **M20.** **computerize** *verb trans.* equip with a computer; perform or produce by computer; ***computerized axial tomography***, ***computerized tomography***, tomography in which the X-ray scanner makes many sweeps of the body and the results are processed by computer to give a cross-sectional image (abbrevs. *CAT*, *CT*): **M20.**

computist /ˈkɒmpjʊtɪst/ *noun.* **LME.**
[ORIGIN medieval Latin *computista*, from late Latin COMPUTUS: see -IST.]
1 A person skilled in calendrical or astronomical reckoning. **LME.**
†**2** A keeper of accounts. **L16–L17.**
■ **compuˈtistic**, **compuˈtistical** *adjectives* **M20.**

computor *noun* var. of COMPUTER.

computus /ˈkɒmpjʊtəs/ *noun.* Also **-pot-** /-pɒt-/. **M19.**
[ORIGIN Late Latin = computation, from Latin *computare* COMPUTE *verb*.]
hist. **1** A medieval set of tables for astronomical and calendrical calculations. **M19.**
2 A reckoning; an account. **M19.**

comrade /ˈkɒmreɪd/ *noun.* Orig. also †**camerade.** **M16.**
[ORIGIN French *camerade*, *camarade* from Spanish *camarada* barrack-room, chamber-fellow, from *camara* chamber from Latin CAMERA: see -ADE.]
1 Orig., a person who shared the same room or tent, *esp.* (also ***comrade-in-arms***) a fellow soldier; hence, an associate (usu. male) in friendship, occupation, or fortune; an equal with whom one is on familiar terms. **M16.**
2 *spec.* A fellow socialist or communist. Freq. used before a name and as a form of address or reference. **L19.**
3 A (young) black radical political activist in South Africa. **L20.**
■ **comradeliness** *noun* comradely nature or behaviour **M20.** **comradely** *adjective* characteristic of or befitting a comrade **L19.** **comradery** *noun* = COMRADESHIP **L19.** **comradeship** *noun* the relationship of comrades; camaraderie: **E19.**

comrogue /ˈkɒmrəʊɡ/ *noun. arch.* **E17.**
[ORIGIN from COM- + ROGUE *noun*.]
A fellow rogue.

coms *noun pl.* var. of COMBS.

Comsat /ˈkɒmsat/ *noun.* **M20.**
[ORIGIN Abbreviation of *communication satellite*.]
(Proprietary name for) a satellite used for telecommunication.

Comstockery /ˈkɒmstɒk(ə)ri/ *noun.* Also **c-.** **E20.**
[ORIGIN from Anthony *Comstock* (1844–1915), member of the New York Society for the Suppression of Vice + -ERY.]
Excessive opposition to supposed immorality in the arts; prudery.
■ **Comstocker** *noun* a person who advocates or practises Comstockery **E20.**

comte /kɔ̃ːt/ (*pl. same*); kɔːnt, kɒmt/ *noun.* **E17.**
[ORIGIN French: see COUNT *noun*².]
A French nobleman corresponding in rank to an English earl.
– NOTE: Rare before **L19.**

Comtean *adjective* var. of COMTIAN.

comtesse /kɔ̃tes/ (*pl. same*); kɔːnˈtɛs, kɒm-/ *noun.* **E20.**
[ORIGIN French, formed as COMTE + -ESS¹.]
A French noblewoman corresponding in rank to an English countess.

Comtian /ˈkɔ̃ːntɪən, ˈkɒmt-/ *adjective.* Also **-ean**, **c-.** **M19.**
[ORIGIN from *Comte* (see below) + -IAN, -EAN.]
Of or deriving from Auguste Comte (1798–1857), French philosopher and founder of positivism.
■ **Comtism** *noun* Comtian philosophy, positivism **M19.** **Comtist** *noun* & *adjective* (*a*) *noun* an advocate or follower of Comtism; (*b*) *adjective* = COMTIAN: **M19.**

Comus /ˈkəʊməs/ *noun.* **L16.**
[ORIGIN Latin from Greek *kōmos* revel.]
Revelry personified; a revel.

†**comutual** *adjective* var. of COMMUTUAL.

con /kɒn/ *noun*¹. **L16.**
[ORIGIN from CON *adverb*.]
A reason, argument, or arguer against. Chiefly in ***pros and cons*** s.v. PRO *preposition* etc.

con /kɒn/ *noun*². *obsolete* exc. *dial.* **E17.**
[ORIGIN Perh. from French *cogner* strike, thump.]
A rap with the knuckles, a knock.

con /kɒn/ *noun*³. Also **conn.** **E19.**
[ORIGIN from CON *verb*².]
The action or post of conning a ship.

con /kɒn/ *noun*⁴. *colloq.* (orig. *US*). **L19.**
[ORIGIN Abbreviation.]
In *comb.* = CONFIDENCE, as ***con artist***, ***con man***, ***con trick***, etc.; *ellipt.* a confidence trick, a confidence trickster.
short con: see SHORT *adjective*.

con /kɒn/ *noun*⁵. *slang.* **L19.**
[ORIGIN Abbreviation.]
A convict; a criminal conviction.

con /kɒn/ *noun*⁶. *slang.* **E20.**
[ORIGIN Abbreviation.]
= CONSTRUE *noun*.

con /kɒn/ *noun*⁷. *colloq.* **M20.**
[ORIGIN Abbreviation.]
A convenience: only in MOD CON.

con /kɒn/ *noun*⁸. *colloq.* **L20.**
[ORIGIN Abbreviation.]
= CONVENTION *noun* 1; *esp.* an organized meeting of enthusiasts for science fiction or other genre, hobby, etc.

con /kɒn/ *verb*¹. Also (long *obsolete* exc. *dial.*) **cun** /kʌn/. **OE.**
[ORIGIN Partly form of CAN *verb*¹, with vowel extended from Old English 1st & 3rd person sing. pres.; partly Old English *cunnian*, *-ode* (weak) from West Germanic deriv. of base of CAN *verb*¹.]
▸ †**I** Senses repl. by CAN *verb*¹. Infl. as CAN *verb*¹.
1 *verb trans.* & *intrans.* Know. **OE–L17.**
N. FAIRFAX That [this] should be . . I no more conne, than that.
2 *verb intrans.* (usu. with inf.). Know how to; have the capacity or be able to. **ME–L15.**
CAXTON I sholde not conne telle the harme . . that he hath doon.
▸ **II** Senses not repl. by CAN *verb*¹. Infl. **-nn-.**
3 *verb trans.* Express, make known (gratitude, displeasure, etc.). *obsolete* exc. in ***con thanks*** below. **OE.**
ELIZABETH I We con you many laudes for having so neerely approched the villainous Rebel.
con thanks (now *arch.* & *dial.*) acknowledge one's gratitude; thank.
4 *verb trans.* Study, learn by heart; peruse; scan. Freq. foll. by *over*. **LME.**
S. BUTLER To con the Authors Names by rote. R. S. SURTEES The Baronet conned the . . matter over in his mind. J. GALSWORTHY He opened *The Times* . . and . . set himself steadily to con the news.

con /kɒn/ *verb*² *trans.* & *intrans.* Also †**cann**, ***conn**, †**cun.** Infl. **-nn-.** **E17.**
[ORIGIN App. weakened form of COND.]
Direct the steering of (a ship).

con /kɒn/ *verb*³ *trans. slang.* Infl. **-nn-.** **L19.**
[ORIGIN from CON *noun*⁴.]
Persuade; dupe, swindle.

con /kɒn/ *adverb.* **L16.**
[ORIGIN Abbreviation of CONTRA.]
Against a proposition etc. Chiefly in ***pro and con*** (occas. ***con and pro***) s.v. PRO *preposition, adverb*, etc.

con- /kɒn, *unstressed* kən/ *prefix.*
Var. of Latin COM- before *c, d, f, g, j, n, q, s, t, v*, and occas. before vowels (***conurbation***). Cf. CO-, COL-, COR-.

conacre /ˈkɒneɪkə/ *noun* & *verb.* **E19.**
[ORIGIN from CORN *noun*¹ + ACRE *noun*.]
IRISH HISTORY. ▸**A** *noun.* The letting by a tenant of small portions of land prepared for crop or grazing. **E19.**
▸ **B** *verb trans.* Sublet (land) in this manner. **M19.**

conalbumin /kənˈalbjʊmɪn/ *noun.* **E20.**
[ORIGIN from CON- + ALBUMIN.]
BIOCHEMISTRY. An iron-binding albumin present in egg white, resembling transferrin.

con amore /kɒn əˈmɔːreɪ, *foreign* kɔn aˈmoːrɛ/ *adverbial phr.* **M18.**
[ORIGIN Italian = with love.]
With devotion or zeal; *MUSIC* (as a direction) with tenderness.

conarium /kəˈnɛːrɪəm/ *noun. obsolete* exc. *hist.* Also †**-ion.** **M17.**
[ORIGIN mod. Latin from Greek *kōnarion* dim. of *kōnos* pine cone.]
ANATOMY. The pineal gland.

conation /kəˈneɪʃ(ə)n/ *noun.* **E17.**
[ORIGIN Latin *conatio(n-)*, from *conat-* pa. ppl stem of *conari* endeavour: see -ATION.]
†**1** An attempt, an endeavour. Only in **E17.**
2 *PHILOSOPHY.* The desire to perform an action; volition; (a) voluntary or purposive action. **M19.**
■ **conative** /ˈkɒnətɪv, ˈkəʊ-/ *noun* & *adjective* †(*a*) *noun* (*rare*) an endeavour, striving; (*b*) *adjective* of, pertaining to, or characteristic of conation: **L17.** ˈ**conatively** *adverb* **M20.**

conatus /kəˈneɪtəs/ *noun.* Pl. same /-tuːs/, **-tuses.** **M17.**
[ORIGIN Latin, from *conari*: see CONATION.]
A purposive or seemingly purposive force or impulse; an effort, striving.

con brio /kɒn ˈbriːəʊ, *foreign* kɔn ˈbrio/ *adverbial phr.* **E19.**
[ORIGIN Italian.]
MUSIC. A direction: with vigour.

concamerate /kɒnˈkaməreɪt/ *verb trans.* **E17.**
[ORIGIN Latin *concamerat-* pa. ppl stem of *concamerare* vault: see CON-, CAMERA, -ATE³.]
1 Vault, arch over. Now *rare* or *obsolete*. **E17.**
2 Divide into chambers or cells. Chiefly as ***concamerated*** *ppl adjective.* **M18.**
■ **concameˈration** *noun* (*a*) vaulting, a vaulted roof etc. (*lit.* & *fig.*); (*b*) (each of the chambers or the chambered formation resulting from) division into a number of separate cells: **M17.**

concatenate /kənˈkatɪneɪt/ *adjective.* **L15.**
[ORIGIN Late Latin *concatenatus* pa. pple, formed as CONCATENATE *verb*: see -ATE².]
Linked together, concatenated.

concatenate /kənˈkatɪneɪt/ *verb trans.* **L16.**
[ORIGIN Late Latin *concatenat-* pa. ppl stem of *concatenare*, formed as CON- + *catena* CHAIN *noun*: see -ATE³.]
Link together (chiefly *fig.*); connect as by a chain.

concatenation /kənkatɪˈneɪʃ(ə)n/ *noun.* **E17.**
[ORIGIN French *concaténation* or late Latin *concatenatio(n-)*, formed as CONCATENATE *verb*: see -ATION.]
1 Union by linking together, esp. in a series or chain; concatenated condition. **E17.**
G. H. LEWES The necessary concatenation of ideas which should reproduce the concatenation of objects.
2 A concatenated series or system; an interdependent or unbroken sequence. **M17.**

J. RUSKIN This vile concatenation of straight lines. U. LE GUIN Obscure concatenations of effect/cause/effect.

concaulescence /kɒnkɔːˈlɛs(ə)ns/ *noun.* L19.
[ORIGIN from CON- + CAULESCENT + -ENCE.]
BOTANY. Coalescence of two axes, e.g. of a leaf stalk and main stem.

concause /ˈkɒnkɔːz/ *noun.* E17.
[ORIGIN medieval Latin *concausa*, formed as CON- + CAUSE *noun.*]
A cooperating cause.
■ **conˈcausal** *adjective* M17.

concave /ˈkɒnkeɪv, kɒnˈkeɪv/ *noun.* M16.
[ORIGIN Old French from the adjective (see CONCAVE *adjective*: cf. Latin *concava* hollows), or ellipt. use of CONCAVE *adjective.*]
†**1** A hollow; a (cylindrical or spherical) cavity, the bore of a gun etc. M16–E19.
2 The concave inner surface of a vault, arch, hemisphere, etc.; freq. the vault of the sky, the vault of heaven. Chiefly *poet.* M16.
3 A concave lens, mirror, etc. E17.
4 A concave piece of a machine, as the part of a thresher in which the cylinder works etc. Chiefly *US.* L19.

concave /ˈkɒnkeɪv, pred. *also* kɒnˈkeɪv/ *adjective.* LME.
[ORIGIN Latin *concavus*, formed as CON- + *cavus* hollow (perh. through Old French & mod. French *concave*).]
†**1** Having an internal cavity; hollow. LME–M17.
2 Having an outline or surface curved like the interior of a circle or sphere; the reverse of convex. LME.
concave lens, ***concave mirror***, etc.
■ **concavely** *adverb* L19. **concaveness** *noun* M18.

concave /ˈkɒnkeɪv/ *verb trans.* LME.
[ORIGIN Old French *concaver* or Latin *concavare*, formed as CONCAVE *adjective.*]
Make concave; hollow out; *rare* vault, arch over. Orig. & chiefly as ***concaved*** *ppl adjective.*

concavity /kɒnˈkavɪti/ *noun.* LME.
[ORIGIN Old French & mod. French *concavité* or late Latin *concavitas*, formed as CONCAVE *adjective*: see -ITY.]
1 A hollow, a cavity. LME.
2 The concave surface or side of an arch, a sphere, etc.; a hollow vault. L15.
3 The quality or condition of being concave. L16.

concavo- /kɒnˈkeɪvəʊ/ *combining form.*
[ORIGIN from CONCAVE *adjective* + -O-.]
Concavely, concave and —.
■ **concavo-ˈconcave** *adjective* concave on both sides L19. **concavo-ˈconvex** *adjective* concave on one side and convex on the other (and thinnest in the centre: cf. CONVEXO-CONCAVE) L17.

conceal /kənˈsiːl/ *verb trans.* ME.
[ORIGIN Old French *conceler* from Latin *concelare*, formed as CON- + *celare* hide.]
1 Keep secret (*from*); refrain from disclosing or divulging. ME.

SIR W. SCOTT Concealing from him all knowledge of who or what he was. R. GRAVES Augustus had always great difficulty in concealing his dislike for Tiberius as a son-in-law.

concealed land (*obsolete* exc. *hist.*) land withheld from the monarch without a proper title (used esp. of land that had been in monastic possession before the Reformation).
2 Put, remove, or keep out of sight or notice; hide. LME.

SMOLLETT There was a blind that concealed us from the view. I. FLEMING He had a vast belly that he concealed behind roomy trousers and well-cut.. suits. M. GIROUARD Their apparent artlessness concealed a great deal of sophistication. *transf.*: W. TREVOR He pressed his face into the pillow to conceal the sound of.. sobbing.

concealed lighting artificial lighting in which the fitments are hidden from view.
■ **concealable** *adjective* (*rare*) able to be concealed M17.

concealer /kənˈsiːlə/ *noun.* L15.
[ORIGIN Anglo-Norman *concelour*, formed as CONCEAL: see -OUR, -ER[2].]
1 A person who conceals. L15.
2 *LAW* (now *hist.*). A person who sought to disturb possessors of concealed lands (see CONCEAL) by surreptitiously procuring spurious grants of Crown rights. L16.
3 A flesh-toned cosmetic stick used to cover spots, blemishes, and dark under-eye circles. L20.

concealment /kənˈsiːlm(ə)nt/ *noun.* ME.
[ORIGIN Old French *concelement*, formed as CONCEAL: see -MENT.]
1 The concealing or keeping secret (of information); *LAW* the non-disclosure of a known fact by a party to a contract. ME. ▸**b** The holding of land against the monarch's rights, without a proper title. *obsolete* exc. *hist.* E17.

A. S. TAYLOR The concealment of pregnancy is no offence in the English Law, but the concealment of.. the *birth* of a child is a misdemeanour.

2 *gen.* The action of concealing or keeping secret; the action of hiding or obscuring anything from view. L16.

J. GALSWORTHY The concealment of his satisfaction had been merely instinctive.

†**3** Secret knowledge; a secret, a mystery. L16–E17.

SHAKES. *1 Hen. IV* A worthy gentleman, Exceedingly well read, and profited In strange concealments.

4 The condition of being concealed; the capacity for concealing; in *pl.*, conditions or surroundings that conceal. E17.

OED He has absconded, and is still in concealment. C. MORGAN He is like a man secretly in love; .. speak her name, and his agony shines through all his concealments. R. WARNER I stepped forward a little from my place of concealment.

concede /kənˈsiːd/ *verb.* L15.
[ORIGIN French *concéder* or Latin *concedere* withdraw, yield, formed as CON- + *cedere* CEDE.]
1 *verb trans.* Admit to be true, allow, grant (a proposition); acknowledge the justice, propriety, etc., of (a statement, claim, etc.); (occas.) allow formally for the sake of argument. L15. ▸**b** *verb trans.* & *intrans.* Acknowledge (defeat) esp. in an election; admit defeat in (an election, a constituency, etc.). Orig. *US.* E19.

J. GILBERT The law itself was not conceded to have been unjust. DICKENS Conceding, for a moment, that there is any analogy between a bee and a man. H. JAMES Her claim to figure was questioned, but she was conceded presence. HARPER LEE If you'll concede the necessity of going to school. T. BENN Government and industry will have to concede that workers have a part to play in the management of the economy.

2 *verb trans.* Grant, yield, or surrender (anything asked for or claimed, as a right, privilege, etc.); fail to prevent an opponent in a contest from scoring (a goal, points, runs, etc.), lose (a game, match, etc.). M17.

H. T. BUCKLE Free trade was conceded to the West Indian Islands. H. READ Perhaps he conceded too much to the romantic idealism of his public.

3 *verb intrans.* Make a concession. *rare.* L18.

BURKE When.. I wished you to concede to America, at a time when she prayed concession at our feet.

■ **conceder** *noun* M19.

conceit /kənˈsiːt/ *noun.* LME.
[ORIGIN from CONCEIVE *verb* after *deceit* etc.]
▸**I** **1** That which is conceived in the mind, a conception, a notion, an idea. *obsolete* exc. *Scot.* LME.

T. FULLER Fluent in language to express their conceits. C. LAMB A glimmering conceit of some such thing.

†**2** The faculty of mental conception; apprehension, understanding. LME–E19.

WORDSWORTH His own conceit the figure planned.

3 Personal opinion, judgement, estimation. Usu. with qualifying adjective, as ***good conceit*** (***of oneself***), ***bad conceit*** (***of oneself***), etc. *arch.* & *dial.* LME.

B. FRANKLIN A remonstrance.. containing a submissive conceit, that one hundred thousand pounds.. would answer. F. KING She always had a good conceit of herself, that one.

in one's own conceit in one's own judgement.
4 Favourable opinion, esteem. Now *dial.* exc. in ***out of conceit*** below. LME.

ADAM SMITH The landlord's conceit of his own superior knowledge.

out of conceit no longer pleased *with.*
5 Overestimation of oneself or one's personal qualities; personal vanity. E17.

K. GRAHAME He got so puffed up with conceit that he made up a song.. in praise of himself.

▸**II** **6** A fancy article; anything quaintly decorative; a pretty trifle. *obsolete* exc. *Scot.* LME.
7 A fanciful, ingenious, or witty expression; *esp.* a far-fetched comparison or elaborate and intricate figure of speech, image, etc. Also, the use of such expressions etc. E16.

POPE Some to conceit alone their taste confine. J. R. GREEN Religious enthusiasm had degenerated into the pretty conceits of Mariolatry.

8 A fanciful notion; a fancy; a whim; the faculty of imagination. M16.

R. GREENE In conceit build castles in the sky. D. WELCH It was an old conceit of my aunt's to carry the predominant colour of her party decorations into the food itself.

▸†**III** **9** Conception of offspring. LME–L16.
10 An illness or affliction of the mind or the body. M16–E17.

H. PEACHAM Hee tooke a conceipt and dyed.

■ **conceitless** *adjective* (*rare*) without conceit LME. **conceity** *adjective* (chiefly *Scot.*) full of conceits, conceited L16.

conceit /kənˈsiːt/ *verb. arch.* & *dial.* M16.
[ORIGIN from the noun.]
▸**I** *verb trans.* †**1** Form a conception of; apprehend. M16–E17.

SHAKES. *Jul. Caes.* Him and his worth and our great need of him You have right well conceited.

2 Fill or inspire with a conceit or fancy. L16.

F. HALL To conceit ourselves that our progeny will be satisfied with our English.

3 Take a fancy to, like. L16.

M. R. MITFORD I shall never conceit the sight of a perch again.

4 Imagine, fancy, think. E17.

J. PRIESTLEY Arts of sorcery which they conceit that he learned in Egypt. J. R. SEELEY Conceiting himself to be made of better clay than other men.

†**5** Conceive as a purpose or design, plan. E–M17.
▸†**II** **6** *verb intrans.* Form a conception; think, imagine, consider. L16–E19.

C

conceited /kənˈsiːtɪd/ *adjective.* M16.
[ORIGIN from CONCEIT *noun, verb*: see -ED[2], -ED[1].]
▸**I** Chiefly from the noun.
†**1** **a** Having intelligence, wit, a mind, of a particular kind; clever, witty, amusing. M16–L17. ▸**b** Of a person, a person's work: ingenious, clever; *spec.* (of a writer, literary style, etc.) characterized by a use of literary conceits (see CONCEIT *noun* 7). Only in L16.

a ROBERT BURTON The Egyptians.. are commended to be.. a conceited merry Nation. W. LILLY Humane, rationall, and pleasantly conceited. **b** SHAKES. *Lucr.* A piece Of skilful painting .. Which the conceited painter drew so proud.

2 Fanciful or fantastical in manner, habit, etc.; whimsical; fastidious. L16.
3 Having an opinion (of a particular kind; †*absol.* good); -minded, -disposed. Long *dial.* L16.

J. SELDEN The people well-conceited of the King's aims.

4 Having too high an opinion of or (*rare*) *of* one's own beauty, ability, etc.; vain, self-satisfied. (See also SELF-CONCEITED.) E17.

J. H. NEWMAN The less a man knows, the more conceited he is of his proficiency. G. GREENE 'You ought to be grateful,' he told her in his light cocksure conceited manner.

▸**II** from the verb.
5 Conceived, devised; fancied; imaginary. Now *rare* or *obsolete.* L16.
†**6** Ingenious; fancy. L16–L17.
■ **conceitedly** *adverb* L16. **conceitedness** *noun* †(*a*) cleverness, imagination; (*b*) self-conceit, vanity: E17.

conceivable /kənˈsiːvəb(ə)l/ *adjective* & *noun.* LME.
[ORIGIN from CONCEIVE + -ABLE. Cf. French *concevable.*]
▸**A** *adjective.* Able to be (mentally) conceived; imaginable; supposable; (just) possible. LME.

E. A. FREEMAN It is just conceivable that Duncan refused homage to Cnut. L. DURRELL They are coming in from everywhere now, at every conceivable angle and speed.

▸**B** *noun.* A conceivable thing. M17.
■ **conceivaˈbility** *noun* E19. **conceivableness** *noun* LME. **conceivably** *adverb* E17.

conceive /kənˈsiːv/ *verb.* ME.
[ORIGIN Old French & mod. French *conceiv-* tonic stem of *concevoir* repr. Latin *concipere*, formed as CON- + *capere* take.]
▸**I** In a physical sense.
1 *verb trans.* & *intrans.* Become pregnant (with); in *pass.*, be created in the womb, be engendered. ME.

AV *Gen.* 30:19 And Leah conceived againe, and bare Iacob the sixth sonne. W. F. HOOK He preached the Lord Jesus Christ, who .. was conceived by the Holy Ghost. F. RAPHAEL In those two years Rachel conceived two children.

†**2** *verb trans.* In *pass.* Be made or become pregnant. LME–M17.

C. MARLOWE A princess-priest, Conceiv'd by Mars, Shall yield to dignity a double birth.

†**3** *verb trans. transf.* Take on (any state or condition); catch (fire etc.). LME–M18.

C. LUCAS The lightest waters most readily conceive igneous motion.

▸**II** Of mental processes.
4 *verb trans.* Take or admit into the mind; become affected or possessed with. ME.

M. EDGEWORTH He had conceived a dislike.. for this lady.

5 *verb trans.* & *intrans.* Form a mental representation (of or *of*); devise (a purpose, idea, plan, etc.); think, imagine. ME.

BUNYAN I can better conceive of them with my Mind, then speak of them with my Tongue. W. COWPER He first conceives, then perfects his design. R. J. SULLIVAN His system.. ill conceived and worse arranged. G. GREENE He was incapable of conceiving the pain he might cause others. I. MURDOCH He could not conceive of anybody enjoying Danby's company.

6 *verb trans.* Grasp mentally; take in, comprehend; understand. *arch.* LME.

SHAKES. *Merry W.* Nay, conceive me, conceive me, sweet coz. B. MARTIN All this I conceive perfectly well.

7 *verb trans.* & †*intrans.* Take into one's head; be of the opinion; fancy. LME.

J. SELDEN I am the rather induced to conceive charitably of those times. J. S. MILL He ought, I conceive, to be warned of the danger. R. H. MOTTRAM Words.. in what he conceived to be French.

▸**III** Other senses after Latin.
†**8** *verb trans.* Encompass, comprise, comprehend. LME–L16.

†**9** *verb trans.* Institute (an action at law). LME–L16.
10 *verb trans.* Formulate, express in words etc.; couch. Usu. in *pass.* LME.

GIBBON His answer was conceived in the tone of insult and defiance.

■ **conceivement** *noun* (*rare*) (a) conception E17. **conceiver** *noun* L16.

C

concelebrate /kɒnˈsɛlɪbreɪt/ *verb.* L16.
[ORIGIN Latin *concelebrat-* pa. ppl stem of *concelebrare*, formed as CON-, CELEBRATE: see -ATE[3].]
†**1** *verb trans.* Celebrate together or in great numbers; extol loudly. L16–E17.
2 *verb intrans.* (Of priests) celebrate mass, the Eucharist, etc., together; *esp.* (of a newly ordained priest) celebrate mass etc. *with* the ordaining bishop. L19.
■ **conceleˈbration** *noun* M19.

concent /kənˈsɛnt/ *noun & verb.* Now *rare* or *obsolete.* L16.
[ORIGIN Latin *concentus*, from *concinere* sing together, harmonize, formed as CON- + *canere* sing. Cf. CONCINNATE *verb.*]
▸ **A** *noun.* Harmony (of sounds, or *fig.*), concord, accord; a harmonious combination of voices etc. L16.
▸ †**B** *verb trans. & intrans.* Harmonize. L16–M17.

concenter *verb* see CONCENTRE.

concentrate /ˈkɒns(ə)ntreɪt/ *adjective & noun.* M17.
[ORIGIN formed as CONCENTRATE *verb* + -ATE[2], or directly from the verb.]
▸ **A** *adjective.* Concentrated. *arch.* M17.
▸ **B** *noun.* A concentrated substance; a concentrated form of something, esp. animal foodstuff. L19.

concentrate /ˈkɒns(ə)ntreɪt/ *verb.* M17.
[ORIGIN Latinized form of CONCENTRE, or analogical formation on French *concentrer*: see -ATE[3].]
▸ **I** *verb trans.* **1** Bring towards or collect at a centre; cause to converge or be focused (*on* a point, objective, etc.). M17.

D. BREWSTER The different rays concentrated by the lens. BOSW. SMITH Here Hannibal.. concentrated the forces which had been gathered from such distant countries. G. CLARE To concentrate over-powering affection exclusively on one other human being. R. DAHL Fury and hate can concentrate a man's mind to an astonishing degree.

2 *CHEMISTRY.* Increase the strength of (a solution, mixture, etc.), e.g. by evaporation of solvent. L17. ▸**b** Bring (ore etc.) to a state of greater purity by mechanical means. L19.

C. DARWIN The sap is concentrated by boiling, and is then called treacle.

3 Bring into closer union the parts of; reduce in compass (with concomitant increase in intensity etc.). M18.

C. BRONTË The obstinacy of my whole sex.. was concentrated in me.

▸ **II** *verb intrans.* **4** Collect or come together at a centre; become intensified. M17.

ISAAC TAYLOR Church Power.. concentrating around the See of Rome.

5 Employ all one's power or attention *on*; focus one's mental efforts (*on*). E20.

I. COMPTON-BURNETT He.. put the matter aside to concentrate on other things. J. H. BURN Morphine may produce drowsiness and inability to concentrate.

■ **concentrated** *adjective* (**a**) brought together, wholly directed towards one point or thing, intensified; (**b**) *CHEMISTRY* (of solutions etc.) relatively strong (opp. ***dilute***), *fig.* intense: L17. **concentratedly** *adverb* L19. **concentratedness** *noun* (*rare*) L19. **concentrator** *noun* a person who or thing which concentrates; *esp.* an apparatus which concentrates liquids etc.: M19.

concentration /kɒns(ə)nˈtreɪʃ(ə)n/ *noun.* M17.
[ORIGIN from CONCENTRATE *verb* + -ATION.]
1 The action of concentrating; the state of being concentrated; a concentrated collection or mass. M17.

WELLINGTON The concentration of your force in one position. J. R. GREEN This concentration of all power in the hands of a single man. E. MOONMAN The main concentration of West Indians is to be found in Brixton, London.

†**2** **a** The chemical separation of gold etc. from an alloy. L17–L18. ▸**b** *CHEMISTRY.* The strengthening of a solution by removal (e.g. by evaporation) of solvent; the condition so produced; the amount of solute per unit volume of a solution. L18. ▸**c** The mechanical removal of unwanted portions from an ore etc. L19.

b P. PARISH Injections ensure that the drug reaches a high concentration in the blood.

3 The bringing of parts or elements closer together; the act of condensing. M19.

M. ARNOLD Epochs of concentration cannot well endure for ever; epochs of expansion.. follow them. J. RUSKIN My affected concentration of language.

4 The continued focusing of mental powers and faculties on a particular object. M19.

DAY LEWIS Aged voters who.. through failing sight or powers of concentration confused C. S. with C. D. Lewis.

– COMB.: **concentration camp**: for the detention of non-combatants, political prisoners, internees, etc., esp. in Nazi Germany (with connotations of inhuman privations endured by the inhabitants).

concentrative /ˈkɒns(ə)ntreɪtɪv/ *adjective.* E19.
[ORIGIN from CONCENTRATE *adjective & noun* + -IVE.]
That concentrates; characterized by concentration.
■ **concentrativeness** *noun* E19.

concentre /kɒnˈsɛntə/ *verb.* Also *-ter. L16.
[ORIGIN French *concentrer*, formed as CON- + CENTRE *verb*: cf. CONCENTRATE *verb.*]
▸ **I** *verb trans.* **1** Bring into closer union, draw into a smaller space or area; intensify or strengthen in this way. L16.
2 Bring to or draw towards a common centre; collect (thoughts, faculties, etc.) and give them a common direction or purpose; form a centre or meeting point for. M17.
†**3** *CHEMISTRY.* = CONCENTRATE *verb* 2. M17–E19.
▸ **II** *verb intrans.* †**4** Agree, coincide. L16–M18.
5 Converge; collect at, move towards a common centre. M17.

concentric /kənˈsɛntrɪk/ *adjective.* LME.
[ORIGIN Old French & mod. French *concentrique* or medieval Latin *concentricus*, formed as CON- + CENTRE *noun*: see -IC.]
Having a common centre (*with*, *to*); situated or occurring around the same centre; consisting of more or less circular parts surrounding a common centre.

R. BENTLEY The concentric Revolutions of the Planets about the Sun. P. WARNER A concentric castle broke away from the old pattern of linear defence.. and instead had a system of enclosed squares.

concentric bundle *BOTANY* a vascular bundle in which one kind of vascular tissue completely surrounds the other. **concentric cable** = *COAXIAL* ***cable.***
■ **concentrical** *adjective* = CONCENTRIC M16. **concentrically** *adverb* E18. †**concentricate** *verb trans.* = CONCENTRATE *verb* 1, 3 M17–L18. **concentricity** /-ˈtrɪsɪti/ *noun* the state or quality of being concentric E19.

concentus /kɒnˈsɛntəs/ *noun. rare.* E17.
[ORIGIN Latin: see CONCENT.]
Singing together in harmony; a harmonious combination of voices etc.

concept /ˈkɒnsɛpt/ *noun.* M16.
[ORIGIN Late Latin *conceptus*, from pa. ppl stem of *concipere*: see CONCEIVE.]
†**1** = CONCEIT *noun.* M–L16.
2 A product of the faculty of conception; an idea of a class of objects, a general notion; a theme, a design. M17.

B. RUSSELL Awareness of universals is called *conceiving*, and a universal of which we are aware is called a *concept*. R. M. PIRSIG The motorcycle.. a system of concepts worked out in steel. D. LESSING The concept of ownership of land was unknown to them: land belonged to itself. *attrib.*: S. BRETT Great Expectations.. was a concept restaurant, themed wittily around the works of Dickens.

conceptacle /kənˈsɛptək(ə)l/ *noun.* E17.
[ORIGIN French, or Latin *conceptaculum*: see CON-, RECEPTACLE.]
†**1** A receptacle. E17–M19.
2 †**a** *ANATOMY.* A vessel or cavity of the body. E–M17. ▸**b** *BIOLOGY.* A structure resembling a cavity that contains the reproductive cells in some plants and animals of simple organization. M18.

conception /kənˈsɛpʃ(ə)n/ *noun.* ME.
[ORIGIN Old French & mod. French from Latin *conceptio(n-)*, from *concept-* pa. ppl stem of *concipere*: see CONCEIVE, -ION.]
1 The action of conceiving, or the fact of being conceived, in the womb. ME.

R. DAWKINS Our genes are doled out to us at conception.

Immaculate Conception: see IMMACULATE.
2 That which is conceived: (**a**) an embryo, a fetus; †(**b**) a child. LME.
false conception: see FALSE *adjective.*
3 The action or faculty of conceiving in the mind; apprehension, imagination; the formation of a concept. LME.

A. EINSTEIN We are drifting toward a catastrophe beyond conception.

in my conception to my mind, in my view.
4 That which is conceived in the mind; an idea, a notion; a concept. E17. ▸†**b** A mere fancy. *rare* (Shakes.). Only in E17.

J. BUTLER As impossible.. as for a blind man to have a conception of colours. *Washington Post* Ronald Reagan has.. altered the conception of the President's role.

have no conception of be unable to imagine.
5 Something originated in the mind; a design, plan; an original idea; a mental product of invention. E17. ▸**b** Origination in the mind; planning. E19.

W. H. PRESCOTT It was a bold conception, that of constructing a fleet to be transported across forest and mountain before it was launched.

†**6** The generation or production of plants and minerals. Only in M17.
■ **conceptional** *adjective* pertaining to, or of the nature of, a conception or idea M19. **conceptionist** *noun* (**a**) a person who deals with conceptions; (**b**) (**C-**) a member of a Catholic order named in honour of the Immaculate Conception: L18. †**conceptious** *adjective* (*rare*, Shakes.) apt to conceive, prolific: only in E17.

conceptive /kənˈsɛptɪv/ *adjective.* M17.
[ORIGIN Latin *conceptivus*, from *concept-*: see CONCEPTION, -IVE.]
That conceives; apt to conceive; of or pertaining to conception. (Rarely in a physical sense.)
■ **conceptively** *adverb* in a (mentally) conceptive manner M19. **conceptiveness** *noun* E19.

conceptual /kənˈsɛptjʊəl/ *adjective.* M17.
[ORIGIN medieval Latin *conceptualis*, formed as CONCEPT *noun*: see -AL[1].]
Of or pertaining to mental conception or concepts.
conceptual art art in which the idea or concept presented by the artist is considered more important than the finished product, if any such exists.
– NOTE: Rare before M19.
■ **conceptualism** *noun* (**a**) the scholastic doctrine that universals exist as mental concepts (only); (**b**) the doctrine that the mind is capable of forming a mental image corresponding to a general term: M19. **conceptualist** *noun & adjective* an adherent of, pertaining to or marked by, conceptualism M19. **conceptuaˈlistic** *adjective* L19. **conceptuaˈlistically** *adverb* M20. **conceptually** *adverb* as a concept L19.

conceptualize /kənˈsɛptjʊəlʌɪz/ *verb trans. & intrans.* Also **-ise.** L19.
[ORIGIN from CONCEPTUAL + -IZE.]
Form a concept or idea (of).
■ **conceptuaˈlizable** *adjective* M20. **conceptualiˈzation** *noun* E20. **conceptualizer** *noun* L20.

conceptus /kənˈsɛptəs/ *noun.* M18.
[ORIGIN Latin = conception, embryo, from *concept-* pa. ppl stem of *concipere*: see CONCEIVE.]
The product of conception in the womb, esp. in the early stages of pregnancy.

concern /kənˈsəːn/ *noun.* L16.
[ORIGIN from the verb. Cf. *regard*, *respect*.]
▸ **I** **1** Reference, respect, relation. Now *spec.* important relation, importance, interest, (chiefly in ***of concern*** (***to***)). L16.

A. W. HADDAN A truth of deep concern to men's souls.

2 A practical or business relation. Usu. in *pl.* L17.

HENRY FIELDING I know Mr. Nightingale.. and have formerly had concerns with him. DAY LEWIS His proper concern is with the object to be created.

have no concern with have nothing to do with.
3 Solicitous regard, anxiety. L17. ▸**b** In the Society of Friends, a conviction of the divine will. E18.

DRYDEN Without concern he hears.. Of.. distant war. M. AMIS She looks at me with such gentle concern, such protective concern.

4 Active interest, a share *in*. E18.
have a concern in have an interest or share in.
▸ **II** **5** A matter that relates to some person or thing; in *pl.* affairs. L17.

R. L. CHALONER The Battery subalterns.. Chat about minor military concerns.

6 A matter that affects or touches one; a subject that excites one's interest, attention, or care. L17.

A. MACLEAN The Treasury's basic concern is money. A. MCCOWEN It was no concern of mine if his mother had married his uncle.

7 A business organization; a firm. L17.

J. CHEEVER Mr. Nudd had inherited.. a wool concern.

going concern: see GOING *ppl adjective.*
8 An affair, an intrigue; an incident. Now *dial.* L17.
9 A material contrivance; a (complicated or cumbrous) thing. *colloq.* E19.

J. CARLYLE A steel-pen, which is a very unpliable concern.

concern /kənˈsəːn/ *verb.* Also (*dial.*, esp. in sense 5) **consarn** /kənˈsɑːn/. LME.
[ORIGIN Old French & mod. French *concerner* or late Latin *concernere* sift, distinguish, (in medieval Latin) have respect or reference to, formed as CON- + *cernere* sift.]
▸ **I** **1** *verb trans.* Have relation or reference to. LME.

TINDALE *Acts* 28:31 Teachynge those thinges which concerned the lorde Jesus.

as concerns with regard to.
2 *verb trans.* Affect; have a bearing on; involve. LME.

B. JOWETT Music is concerned with harmony and rhythm. R. G. COLLINGWOOD What the different people concerned were trying to do. W. CATHER It's a confidential matter, and concerns another person.

3 *verb trans.* & †*intrans.* Be of importance (to); be the concern of. L15.

SHAKES. *Oth.* The importancy of Cyprus to the Turk.. it more concerns the Turk than Rhodes.

4 *verb trans.* Engage the attention of; implicate; cause anxiety to. Usu. in *pass.* L16. ▸**b** *refl.* Interest oneself *with*, *in*, *about*, *to do*. M17.

M. EDGEWORTH Accused of being concerned in a riot. E. BOWEN At the minute, breakfast was what concerned her. LYNDON B. JOHNSON Eisenhower was deeply concerned about the disintegration in Laos. **b** R. GRAVES I never concern myself with high politics.

to whom it may concern: used to introduce a statement or testimonial.

5 *verb trans.* in *imper.* (expr. impatience). Confound, bother. *US & dial.* E19.

▸ †**II 6** *verb trans.* Distinguish, discern. LME–L16.

†**concernancy** *noun. rare* (Shakes.). Only in E17.
[ORIGIN from CONCERN *verb* + -ANCY.]
= CONCERNMENT.

concerned /kən'sə:nd/ *ppl adjective.* Also (*dial.*, esp. in sense 2) **consarned** /kən'sɑ:nd/. M17.
[ORIGIN from CONCERN *verb* + -ED[1].]
1 Interested, involved; troubled, anxious; showing concern. (Foll. by *about, for, in, with*, etc., (now usu. in neg. & interrog. contexts) *to do*.) M17. ▸**b** *spec.* Having a social conscience, involved in social or moral issues. M20.

E. M. FORSTER I am really concerned at the way those girls go on. E. BOWEN Braithwaite was clearing tea away with a concerned face.

as far as one is concerned, **so far as one is concerned** as regards one's interests.

2 Confounded, deuced. *US & dial.* M19.
■ **concernedly** /-nɪdli/ *adverb* M17. **concernedness** /-nɪdnɪs/ *noun* L17.

†**concerning** *noun.* L16–M17.
[ORIGIN from CONCERN *verb* + -ING[1].]
The taking of concern; concernment; a concern.

concerning /kən'sə:nɪŋ/ *ppl adjective. arch.* M17.
[ORIGIN from CONCERN *verb* + -ING[2]. Cf. earlier UNCONCERNING.]
That is of concern; distressing; important.

concerning /kən'sə:nɪŋ/ *preposition.* LME.
[ORIGIN from CONCERNING *adjective*, prob. modelled on a similar use of French *concernant*.]
Regarding, touching, in reference or relation to; about.

concernment /kən'sə:nm(ə)nt/ *noun.* E17.
[ORIGIN from CONCERN *verb* + -MENT.]
1 A matter concerning a person or thing; an interest. *arch.* E17.
2 An affair; a business; a concern. E17.

DRYDEN I do not think it my Concernment to defend it.

3 The fact of concerning or having reference; relation. M17.

R. BURTHOGGE Mind . . free from all . . concernment with matter.

4 Importance, weight, moment. M17.

R. W. EMERSON Secrets of highest concernment.

5 Participation *in*, involvement *with*; interference. M17.
6 A feeling of interest, solicitude, anxiety, etc. M17.

R. LOWELL He showed concernment for his soul.

concert /'kɒnsət/ *noun.* E17.
[ORIGIN French from Italian *concerto*, from *concertare*: see CONCERT *verb*. See also earlier CONSORT *noun*[2].]
1 Accordance of sounds; a (harmonious) combination of voices, instruments, etc. (Now only as a *transf.* or *fig.* use of another sense.) E17.

W. S. CHURCHILL The foundations were laid for a closer concert between the two peoples in facing the problems of the world.

2 Agreement in a plan or design; union formed by such agreement; accordance, harmony. M17.

W. C. BRYANT The linden . . Hums with a louder concert.

3 A musical performance in which several performers take part; *loosely* a solo recital. L17. ▸**b** A dancing performance consisting of single items, folk dances, etc. (in contrast to a full-scale ballet). E20.
†**4** A company or set of musicians; a choir. E–M18.
– PHRASES: **Concert of Europe** *hist.* the chief European powers acting together. **in concert** (*a*) acting jointly and in harmony (*with*); (*b*) performing music before a live audience, not in a recording studio etc. ***sacred concert***: see SACRED *adjective*.
– COMB.: **concert-goer** a person who regularly attends concerts; **concert grand** a grand piano of the largest size, suitable for concerts; **concert hall** a hall for the public performance of concerts; **concertmaster** the leader of an (esp. American or Continental) orchestra; **concert overture** MUSIC a piece like an operatic overture but intended for independent performance; **concert party** (*a*) a group of performers who give variety concerts; (*b*) STOCK EXCHANGE a number of parties who separately invest in a company with the concealed intention of using their holdings as a single block; **concert performance** (of an opera etc.): without scenery, costume, or action; **concert pitch** the (international standard) pitch to which musical instruments are tuned for concerts; *fig.* a state of unusual efficiency or readiness.
■ **concertize** *verb* (*a*) *verb intrans.* give a concert or concerts; (*b*) *verb trans.* arrange for performance in concert: L19.

concert /kən'sə:t/ *verb.* L16.
[ORIGIN French *concerter* from Italian *concertare* bring into agreement or harmony, of unknown origin.]
†**1** *verb trans.* Bring to agreement or unity. L16–L17.
2 *verb trans.* Arrange to carry out, agree (plans, action, etc.) with or *with* another person etc. or others; contrive by mutual agreement; plan or effect (coordinated action). L17.

C. THIRLWALL The insurrection seems not to have been judiciously concerted. D. ACHESON I hoped that the North Atlantic Treaty countries would concert their policies. J. G. FARRELL The inability of the sepoys to concert an attack with all their disparate forces.

3 *verb intrans.* Arrange a matter by agreement *with* someone; act in harmony *with*. E18.

A. F. DOUGLAS-HOME The Homes were the peacemakers, . . charged to concert with their English opposite number to keep order.

4 *verb intrans.* Sing or play in concert. *rare.* E19.
■ **concerted** *ppl adjective* (*a*) arranged by mutual agreement, done in concert, coordinated; (*b*) MUSIC arranged in parts for several voices or instruments; (*c*) united in action or intention; earlier in UNCONCERTED: E18.

concertante /kɒntʃə'tanti/ *adjective & noun.* Pl. of noun **-ti** /-ti/. E18.
[ORIGIN Italian, ppl adjective of *concertare*: see CONCERT *verb*.]
MUSIC. Formerly, (designating) those instrumental parts present throughout a piece of music. Now, (a piece of music) containing one or more solo parts (usu. of less prominence or weight than in a concerto) playing with an orchestra; also, designating such a part.
sinfonia concertante: see SINFONIA 1.

concerti *noun pl.* see CONCERTO.

concerti grossi *noun phr. pl.* see CONCERTO GROSSO.

concertina /kɒnsə'ti:nə/ *noun, adjective, & verb.* M19.
[ORIGIN from CONCERT *noun* + -INA[1].]
▸ **A** *noun.* **1** A portable free-reed musical instrument consisting of a pair of bellows usu. polygonal in form, with a set of finger studs at each end controlling valves which admit wind to the reeds. M19.
2 In full ***concertina wire***. Wire used for entanglements. E20.
▸ **B** *attrib.* or as *adjective.* (Able to be) compressed or closed like a concertina; involving such action. E20.
▸ **C** *verb trans. & intrans.* Shut up like a concertina; compress; collapse; wrinkle. E20.
■ **concertinist** *noun* a person who plays the concertina L19.

concertino /kɒntʃə'ti:nəʊ/ *noun.* Pl. **-os.** L18.
[ORIGIN Italian, dim. of CONCERTO.]
MUSIC. **1** A small or short concert. *rare.* L18.
2 The solo instrument(s) in a concerto. E19.
3 A simple or short concerto. L19.

concerto /kən'tʃə:təʊ, -tʃɛ:təʊ/ *noun.* Pl. **-tos**, **-ti** /-ti/. E18.
[ORIGIN Italian, from *concertare*: see CONCERT *verb*.]
MUSIC. Orig., a composition for various combinations of instruments. Now, a composition (in the classical form usu. in three movements) for one, or sometimes more, solo instruments accompanied by orchestra.

fig.: J. T. STORY A mad concerto of wildly excited bees and birds.

double concerto, **triple concerto**: for two, three, solo instruments.

concerto grosso /kən,tʃə:təʊ 'grɒsəʊ/ *noun phr.* Pl. **-ti -ssi** /-ti: -si:/. E18.
[ORIGIN Italian = big concerto.]
MUSIC. A baroque concerto characterized by the use of a small group of solo instruments alternately with the full orchestra; a modern imitation of this.

concessible /kən'sɛsɪb(ə)l/ *adjective.* M18.
[ORIGIN from Latin *concess-* (see CONCESSION) + -IBLE.]
That can be conceded.

concession /kən'sɛʃ(ə)n/ *noun.* LME.
[ORIGIN Old French & mod. French, or Latin *concessio(n-)*, from *concess-* pa. ppl stem of *concedere*: see CONCEDE, -ION.]
1 The action or an act of conceding something asked or required. LME.

HOBBES The Right whereby the Kings did rule, was founded in the very concession of the People. E. LANGLEY Jim's concession to the evening was to wash his sweater.

2 A grant of land or other property made by a government or ruling power. LME. ▸**b** A piece of land or territory so allotted. M18. ▸**c** A grant or lease of a small area or of a portion of premises for some specified purpose; the business premises etc. established there. *N. Amer.* E20.
3 A right or privilege granted by a government or ruling power. M16. ▸**b** A right or privilege granted by a commercial organization to an individual or company; a reduction in price for a certain category of person. M20.
4 Admission of a point claimed in argument. E17.

SIR T. BROWNE He [Satan] endeavours to propagate the unbelief of witches, whose concession infers his coexistency.

■ **concessional** *adjective* M20. **concessionary** *adjective & noun* (*a*) *adjective* pertaining to or of the nature of concession; (*b*) *noun* = CONCESSIONAIRE: M18. **concessioner** *noun* (*US*) = CONCESSIONAIRE L19. **concessionist** *noun* a person who advocates concession E19.

concessionaire /kənsɛʃə'nɛ:/ *noun.* Also **-nn-**. M19.
[ORIGIN French *concessionnaire*, formed as CONCESSION + *-aire* -ARY[1].]
The holder of a concession or grant, esp. of the use of land or trading rights.

concessive /kən'sɛsɪv/ *adjective & noun.* E18.
[ORIGIN Late Latin *concessivus*, from *concess-*: see CONCESSION, -IVE.]
▸ **A** *adjective.* **1** GRAMMAR. (Of a preposition or conjunction) introducing a phrase or clause which might be expected to preclude the action of the main clause but does not; designating such a phrase or clause. E18.
2 *gen.* Of the nature of or tending to concession. L19.
▸ **B** *noun.* GRAMMAR. A concessive particle, clause, etc. M18.
■ **concessively** *adverb* M17. **concessiveness** *noun* L19.

concessor /kən'sɛsə/ *noun. rare.* M17.
[ORIGIN Late Latin, from *concess-*: see CONCESSION, -OR.]
A person who concedes.

concetto /kən'tʃɛtəʊ/ *noun.* Pl. **-tti** /-ti/. M18.
[ORIGIN Italian, formed as CONCEPT.]
= CONCEIT *noun* 7.
■ **concettism** *noun* use of or fondness for conceits in literature M19. **concettist** *noun* a writer who makes use of conceits L19.

conch /kɒŋk, kɒn(t)ʃ/ *noun.* Pl. **conchs** /kɒŋks/, **conches** /'kɒn(t)ʃɪz/. Also ***conk** /kɒŋk/, pl. **-s**. LME.
[ORIGIN Latin CONCHA from Greek *kogkhē* mussel, cockle, shell-like cavity.]
1 Orig., a bivalve mollusc such as the oyster or mussel. Now, any of various prosobranchiate marine snails chiefly of the family Strombidae and Melongenidae, esp. of the genus *Strombus*, in which the outer whorl of the shell has a triangular outline and a wide lip, and often juts towards the apex; the shell of this or any other large gastropod. LME. ▸**b** Such a shell used as a wind instrument, e.g. in Hindu temples; *esp.* (ROMAN MYTHOLOGY) the shell blown by the Tritons in place of a trumpet. M18.
crown conch either of two Caribbean gastropods of the genus *Melongena* (family Melongenidae), which have heavy spiny shells. **fighting conch** either of two heavy Caribbean conches of the genus *Strombus*. ***queen conch***: see QUEEN *noun*. **spider conch** = SCORPION ***shell***.
2 An ancient Roman shallow bowl or vessel. LME.
3 ARCHITECTURE. (The domed roof of) a semicircular apse. M19.
4 ANATOMY. The concha of the ear. Now *rare* or *obsolete*. M19.
5 A white person of low social status inhabiting the Florida Keys or N. Carolina, *esp.* one of Bahamian origin. *US colloq.* M19.
■ **conched** *adjective* having a conch or conchs M19.

concha /'kɒŋkə/ *noun.* Pl. **-chae** /-ki:/, (esp. in sense 3) **-s**. L16.
[ORIGIN Latin: see CONCH.]
1 ANATOMY & ZOOLOGY. A part or structure resembling a shell, *esp.* (*a*) the central concavity of the auricle leading to the auditory meatus; (*b*) (more fully ***nasal concha***) the turbinate bone. L16.
2 ARCHITECTURE. = CONCH 3. E17.
3 = CONCHO. L19.
■ **con'chiferous** *adjective* producing or bearing shells, characterized by the presence of shells E19.

conche /kɒntʃ/ *noun & verb.* E20.
[ORIGIN French = CONCH.]
▸ **A** *noun.* A shell-shaped part of a machine used to work chocolate during its manufacture. E20.
▸ **B** *verb trans.* Mix or knead (chocolate) in such a machine. E20.

conchie /'kɒnʃi/ *noun. slang.* Also **conchy**. E20.
[ORIGIN Abbreviation.]
A conscientious objector.

conchiglie /kɒn'ki:ljeɪ/ *noun pl.* M20.
[ORIGIN Italian, pl. of *conchiglia* conch shell.]
Pasta in the form of small conch shells.

conchiolin /'kɒntʃɪəʊlɪn/ *noun.* L19.
[ORIGIN from Latin CONCHA + *-iola* dim. suffix + -IN[1].]
BIOCHEMISTRY. A scleroprotein forming the basis of the shells of molluscs.

†**conchite** *noun.* L17–M18.
[ORIGIN Greek *kogkhitēs* (*lithos*) shelly (stone): see -ITE[1].]
PALAEONTOLOGY. A fossil shell; a petrified shell.

conchitic /kɒŋ'kɪtɪk/ *adjective.* E19.
[ORIGIN formed as CONCHITE + -IC.]
GEOLOGY. Having many (fossil) shells.

concho /'kɒn(t)ʃəʊ/ *noun.* Chiefly *US*. L20.
[ORIGIN Spanish *concha* shell. Cf. CONCHA.]
A decorative piece of silver used to adorn clothing, as jewellery, or strung together with similar pieces to form a belt.

conchoid /'kɒŋkɔɪd/ *noun.* E18.
[ORIGIN from CONCH + -OID.]
MATH. Any of a family of quartic curves resembling a conch shell in outline, represented by the equation $(x - a)^2(x^2 + y^2) = b^2x^2$.

conchoidal /kɒŋ'kɔɪd(ə)l/ *adjective.* M17.
[ORIGIN formed as CONCHOID + -AL[1].]
1 MATH. Pertaining to or resembling a conchoid. M17.
2 GEOLOGY. Designating or displaying a fracture (of a rock or mineral) characterized by smooth shell-like convexities and concavities. E19.

■ **conchoidally** *adverb* in a conchoidal form L19.

conchology /kɒŋˈkɒlədʒi/ *noun.* L18.
[ORIGIN from Greek *kogkho-*, *kogkhē* shell + -LOGY.]
The branch of zoology that deals with shells and shellfish.
■ **concho'logical** *adjective* E19. **concho'logically** *adverb* M19. **conchologist** *noun* L18.

C

conchy *noun* var. of CONCHIE.

†**conchyliology** *noun.* L18–L19.
[ORIGIN from Latin *conchylium* shellfish from Greek *kogkhulion* dim. of *kogkhulē* = *kogkhē* CONCH: see -OLOGY.]
= CONCHOLOGY.

concierge /ˈkɒnsɪɛːʒ; *foreign* kɔ̃sjɛrʒ (*pl. same*)/ *noun.* M16.
[ORIGIN French from Old French *cumcerges* etc. = medieval Latin *consergius*, prob. ult. from Latin *conservus* fellow slave.]
1 The warden of a house, castle, or prison; (the title of) a high official in France and other European states, having custody of a royal palace etc. *obsolete* exc. *hist.* M16.
2 In France etc.: a doorkeeper, porter, etc., for a building, esp. a block of flats. L17.

†**concile** *verb trans.* LME–M18.
[ORIGIN Latin *conciliare*: see CONCILIATE.]
Reconcile; conciliate.

†**conciliable** *noun* see CONCILIABULE.

conciliable /kənˈsɪlɪəb(ə)l/ *adjective. rare.* M17.
[ORIGIN formed as CONCILE + -ABLE.]
Able to be conciliated; reconcilable.

conciliabule /kənˈsɪlɪəbjuːl/ *noun.* Also (earlier) †**-able.** E16.
[ORIGIN Latin *conciliabulum* place of assembly, from *concilium* assembly.]
A small or secret assembly; a conventicle.

conciliar /kənˈsɪlɪə/ *adjective.* L17.
[ORIGIN medieval Latin *conciliarius* counsellor: see -AR².]
Of or pertaining to (esp. ecclesiastical) councils.
■ **conciliarism** *noun* a theory of ecclesiastical government embodying the principle that Church councils constitute the highest authority M20. **conciliarist** *noun* a supporter of conciliarism M20. **conciliarly** *adverb* by a council M17.

conciliate /kənˈsɪlɪeɪt/ *verb.* M16.
[ORIGIN Latin *conciliat-* pa. ppl stem of *conciliare* combine, unite physically, procure, win, from *concilium* COUNCIL: see -ATE³.]
†**1** *verb trans.* Procure, get as an addition. M16–L18.
2 *verb trans.* Gain (goodwill, esteem, etc.) by soothing or pacifying acts. M16.

LD MACAULAY The arts which conciliate popularity.

3 *verb trans.* Reconcile, make accordant or compatible. L16. ▸**b** *verb intrans.* Effect a reconciliation, arbitrate, mediate, (*between*). L20.

GIBBON Conciliating the qualities of a soldier with those of a philosopher.

4 *verb intrans.* Make friends (*with*). *rare.* M18.
5 *verb trans.* Overcome the distrust or hostility of; placate, pacify. L18.

A. FRASER The acute financial demands of his foreign policy left him no choice but to conciliate Parliament.

■ **conciliative** *adjective* = CONCILIATORY E19. **conciliator** *noun* a person who or thing which conciliates L16.

conciliation /kənsɪlɪˈeɪʃ(ə)n/ *noun.* M16.
[ORIGIN Latin *conciliatio(n-)*, formed as CONCILIATE; see -ION.]
1 The action of conciliating; reconcilement; the use of conciliating measures. M16.
2 *spec.* The process of seeking agreement between the parties in an industrial dispute, without recourse to arbitration. L19.

conciliatory /kənˈsɪlɪət(ə)ri/ *adjective.* L16.
[ORIGIN formed as CONCILIATE + -ORY².]
Tending or calculated to conciliate; showing a spirit of conciliation.
■ **conciliatorily** *adverb* E20. **conciliatoriness** *noun* M19.

concinnate /kənˈsɪnət/ *adjective. rare.* M16.
[ORIGIN Latin *concinnatus* pa. pple, formed as CONCINNITY: see -ATE².]
Concinnated.

concinnate /kənˈsɪneɪt/ *verb trans.* Now *rare.* E17.
[ORIGIN Latin *concinnat-* pa. ppl stem of *concinnare* formed as CONCINNITY: see -ATE³.]
Put together fitly; arrange skilfully or neatly; set right.

concinnity /kənˈsɪnɪti/ *noun.* M16.
[ORIGIN Latin *concinnitas*, from *concinnus* skilfully put together: see -ITY.]
1 Skilful fitting together; (a) harmonious arrangement. M16.
2 (An instance of) studied elegance of style. L16.
■ **concinnous** *adjective* †(**a**) MUSIC harmonious; (**b**) of elegant style: M17.

†**concional** *adjective.* M17–E18.
[ORIGIN Latin *contionalis*, *conc-*, from *contio(n-)* (later *conc-*) contr. of *conventio(n-)* CONVENTION: see -AL¹.]
Of or pertaining to a public assembly or public speaking.

■ †**concionary** *adjective* = CONCIONAL M17–E18. †**concionator** *noun* [Latin *contionator*] a person who makes speeches, a preacher E17–M19.

concipient /kənˈsɪpɪənt/ *adjective. rare.* E19.
[ORIGIN Latin *concipient-* pres. ppl stem of *concipere* CONCEIVE.]
That conceives, conceiving.

concise /kənˈsʌɪs/ *adjective.* L16.
[ORIGIN French *concis(e)* or Latin *concisus* divided, broken up, brief, pa. pple of *concidere*, formed as CON- + *caedere* to cut.]
Of speech, writing, a person, style, etc.: brief but comprehensive in expression.
■ **concisely** *adverb* L17. **conciseness** *noun* M17.

concision /kənˈsɪʒ(ə)n/ *noun.* LME.
[ORIGIN Latin *concisio(n-)*, from *concisus*: see CONCISE, -ION.]
1 A cutting to pieces, a cutting up; *spec.* (in biblical translations and allusions) circumcision. LME. ▸†**b** A schism. M16–E18.
2 The quality or state of being concise; conciseness. L18.

concitation /kɒnsɪˈteɪʃ(ə)n/ *noun.* Long *rare.* M16.
[ORIGIN Latin *concitatio(n-)*, from *concitat-* pa. ppl stem of *concitare* stir up, excite, formed as CON- + CITE: see -ATION.]
Stirring up, agitation.

conclamation /kɒŋkləˈmeɪʃ(ə)n/ *noun.* E17.
[ORIGIN Latin *conclamatio(n-)*, from *conclamat-* pa. ppl stem of *conclamare*, formed as CON- + *clamare* shout: see -ATION.]
A loud calling out of many together, esp. in lamentation for the dead.

conclave /ˈkɒŋkleɪv/ *noun.* LME.
[ORIGIN French from Latin *conclave*, formed as CON- + *clavis* key.]
†**1 a** *gen.* A private room, an inner chamber. LME–M18. ▸**b** *spec.* The meeting place of the cardinals of the Roman Catholic Church for the election of a pope. LME.
2 A private meeting or close assembly. M16. ▸**b** *spec.* An assembly of cardinals for the election of a pope; *loosely* the body of cardinals. E17.
in conclave (of cardinals or *gen.*) meeting privately or behind closed doors.
■ **conclavist** *noun* †(**a**) any of the cardinals in conclave; (**b**) a person attendant upon a cardinal in conclave: E17.

conclude /kənˈkluːd/ *verb.* ME.
[ORIGIN Latin *concludere*, formed as CON- + *claudere* close, shut.]
▸ **I** †**1** *verb trans.* Overcome in argument, convince. ME–E18.
2 *verb trans.* Shut up, enclose; include, comprise. *arch.* LME. ▸†**b** Restrict, confine. M16–L17.

TENNYSON I dreamt Of some vast charm concluded in that star.

3 *verb trans.* †**a** Debar, restrain (*from*). LME–E18. ▸**b** Bind, oblige. *obsolete* exc. *LAW.* LME.

b J. LOCKE The consent of the majority shall . . conclude every individual.

▸ **II 4** *verb trans.* Bring to a close or end; wind up; finish; say or write in conclusion. LME.

SHAKES. *Rom. & Jul.* His fault concludes . . The life of Tybalt. DAY LEWIS Invariably concluding my discourse with 'In the name of the Father [etc.]'. J. CONRAD 'Aren't you astonished?' concluded the gaunt student.

5 *verb intrans.* Of a thing: come to a close or end; terminate. LME.

SHAKES. *Ven. & Ad.* Her heavy anthem still concludes in woe.

6 *verb intrans.* Make an end of an action; finish, close. Freq. foll. by *by*, *with*. E16.

T. HOOD My paper being filled . . I must conclude with kind regards to Emily.

▸ **III 7** *verb trans.* Arrive at as a judgement or opinion by reasoning; infer, deduce. Foll. by simple obj., the obj. *to be* something, *that*. LME.

H. POWER We cannot but conclude such Prognostics to be within the circle of possibilities. BURKE The greatest part of the governments . . must be concluded tyrannies. E. M. FORSTER Am I to conclude . . that he is a Socialist?

†**8** *verb trans.* Of a person, argument, etc.: demonstrate, prove. With constructions as sense 7. LME–L18.
†**9** *verb intrans.* Be conclusive. E16–E18.
10 *verb intrans.* Form a conclusion (*from*, *to*, *(up)on*). E16.

M. NOVAK So one must conclude from the eagerness with which Americans purchase 'how to' books.

▸ **IV 11** *verb trans.* Bring (a matter) to a decision; settle, arrange finally. LME.

H. MACMILLAN He wished to conclude a German peace treaty.

12 *verb trans.* & †*intrans.* Come to a decision, determine, resolve. Foll. by *that*, *to do*, †*of*, †*(up)on*. LME. ▸†**b** *verb intrans.* Agree, make terms (*with*). LME–L17.

SHAKES. *Lucr.* They did conclude to bear dead Lucrece thence. S. PEPYS We judged a third man is necessary, and concluded on . . Warren. C. M. YONGE She . . concluded that she would wait.

■ **concludent** *adjective* (now *rare* or *obsolete*) [Latin *concludent-*: see -ENT] conclusive, decisive L16. **concluder** *noun* E17.

conclusible /kənˈkluːzɪb(ə)l/ *adjective. rare.* M17.
[ORIGIN from Latin *conclus-* (see CONCLUSION) + -IBLE.]
Able to be concluded.

conclusion /kənˈkluːʒ(ə)n/ *noun.* LME.
[ORIGIN Old French & mod. French, or Latin *conclusio(n-)*, from *conclus-* pa. ppl stem of *concludere*: see CONCLUDE, -ION.]
1 The end, finish, or termination of a speech, writing, etc.; *esp.* a final section summarizing the main points. LME.
2 The issue, the final result, the outcome. LME.

I. MURDOCH One who has brought a difficult piece of navigation to a successful conclusion.

3 The result of a discussion or examination of an issue; final resolution, decision, agreement. LME.

W. RALEIGH Their standing out, hindred not the rest from proceeding to conclusion.

4 A judgement or statement arrived at by reasoning; an inference, a deduction. LME. ▸**b** *LOGIC.* A proposition derived from two previous propositions (the premisses) in a syllogism; a deduction from premisses. L15. ▸†**c** The action of concluding or inferring. *rare.* M16–M17.

J. TYNDALL The sober conclusions of science. G. BROWN People soon came to the conclusion that the letter must have been written by me.

†**5** A proposition, a dictum, a dogma; a problem, a riddle; an experiment. LME–L17.
6 The settling or final arranging (of a treaty etc.). M16.

E. HEATH The conclusion of the Test Ban Treaty was a diplomatic triumph.

7 *LAW.* **a** An act by which a person debars himself or herself; an estoppel. M16. ▸**b** *SCOTS LAW.* The clause of a summons which states the remedy sought. E19.
– PHRASES: ***foregone conclusion***: see FOREGONE *ppl adjective*¹. **in conclusion** in the end, finally, to conclude. ***jump to conclusions***: see JUMP *verb*. **try conclusions with** engage in a trial of skill etc. with.

conclusive /kənˈkluːsɪv/ *adjective.* L16.
[ORIGIN Late Latin *conclusivus*, formed as CONCLUSION: see -IVE.]
†**1** Summing up. Only in L16.
2 Concluding; occurring at or forming the end; final. Now *rare.* E17.
3 Ending all argument; decisive, convincing. M17.

R. GRAVES They should have provided more conclusive evidence of poisoning. P. H. JOHNSON The brisk and conclusive tone of a dentist who has completed a patient's fillings.

■ **conclusively** *adverb* M16. **conclusiveness** *noun* L17. **conclusory** *adjective* relating or tending to a conclusion M19.

concoct /kənˈkɒkt/ *verb.* Pa. pple **concocted**, †**concoct.** M16.
[ORIGIN Latin *concoct-* pa. ppl stem of *concoquere* lit. 'cook together', formed as CON- + *coquere* cook.]
†**1** *verb trans.* Digest (food): see CONCOCTION *noun*. M16–E19.
†**2 a** *verb trans.* Refine, purify (metals, minerals, etc.) by the action of heat. M16–M19. ▸**b** *verb trans. & intrans.* Cook, bake, boil; undergo cooking. L16–M19.
†**3** *verb trans. & intrans.* Ripen, bring or come to maturity. L16–E19. ▸**b** *verb trans.* Produce naturally, secrete. E17–M18.
4 *verb trans.* Prepare (esp. a soup, a drink) from a variety of ingredients. L17.

M. MITCHELL Eating . . the dessert concocted by Mammy from corn meal and dried huckleberries. J. B. MORTON An Indian . . concocted the foulest smell on earth to drive the snake out.

5 *verb trans.* Devise or make up (a story, scheme, etc.) by elaborate or concerted planning; fabricate. L18.

C. THIRLWALL The whole project, concocted with such elaborate preparations. T. DREISER He would have to concoct some excuse.

■ **concocter**, **-or** *noun* M17. **concoctive** *adjective* †(**a**) digestive; (**b**) pertaining to the concoction of a mixture, a story, etc.: L16.

concoction /kənˈkɒkʃ(ə)n/ *noun.* M16.
[ORIGIN Latin *concoctio(n-)*, formed as CONCOCT: see -ION.]
†**1** Digestion (of food). M16–E19.
first concoction, **second concoction**, **third concoction**: the three stages of digestion formerly recognized (***a fault in the first concoction***, ***an error in the first concoction*** (*fig.*), a fault etc. in the initial stage).
†**2** Ripening, maturation. M16–M19.
3 The elaborate composition of a story, scheme, etc. to suit a purpose; a fabricated story etc. E19.
4 The preparation of a dish, potion, etc., from a variety of ingredients; a thing so concocted. M19.

Guardian Solomongundy . . is an amazing concoction of ingredients picked up at the market.

concolorous /kənˈkʌlərəs/ *adjective.* M19.
[ORIGIN from Latin *concolor*, formed as CON- + *color* COLOUR *noun*: see -OUS.]
BOTANY & ZOOLOGY. Of a uniform colour; of an identical colour with.

concomitance /kənˈkɒmɪt(ə)ns/ *noun.* M16.
[ORIGIN medieval Latin *concomitantia*: see CONCOMITANT, -ANCE.]
1 The fact of being concomitant; subsistence together; an instance of this. M16.
2 *THEOLOGY.* (The doctrine of) the coexistence of the body and blood of Christ in each Eucharistic element singly (esp. the bread). M16.
■ Also **concomitancy** *noun* M17.

concomitant /kənˈkɒmɪt(ə)nt/ *adjective & noun*. E17.
[ORIGIN Late Latin *concomitant-* pres. ppl stem of *concomitari* accompany: see -ANT¹.]
▸ **A** *adjective*. Of a quality, circumstance, etc.: occurring along with something else, accompanying. (Foll. by *with*, (now *rare*) *of*, †*to*.) E17.
M. L. KING A numerical growth in church membership does not necessarily reflect a concomitant increase in ethical commitment.
▸ **B** *noun*. **1** An attendant quality, state, circumstance, etc.; an accompaniment. (Foll. by *of*.) E17.
E. FROMM Joy is the concomitant of productive activity.
†**2** A person who accompanies another; a companion. M17–L18.
■ **concomitantly** *adverb* M17.

concord /ˈkɒŋkɔːd/ *noun*¹. ME.
[ORIGIN Old French & mod. French *concorde* from Latin *concordia*, from *concors*, *concord-* of one mind, formed as CON- + *cor*, *cord-* heart.]
1 Agreement or harmonious relations between persons, nations, etc. ME. ▸**b** A treaty establishing harmony between nations. LME.
MILTON Love-quarrels oft in pleasing concord end. **b** W. H. PRESCOTT Abiding by the concord of Salamanca.
2 Agreement or harmony between things, esp. musical notes sounded together. ME. ▸**b** MUSIC. A chord which is in itself satisfying to the ear and does not require resolution. Cf. DISCORD *noun* 3. L16.
SHAKES. *Merch. V.* The man that . . is not mov'd with concord of sweet sounds.
3 LAW. A collusive court procedure for ensuring that a transfer of land was effective. *obsolete* exc. *hist.* L15.
4 GRAMMAR. Agreement between words in gender, number, case, person, etc. M16.
false concord: see FALSE *adjective*.

Concord /ˈkɒŋkɔːd/ *noun*². M19.
[ORIGIN US place name.]
1 In full ***Concord coach***, ***Concord wagon***. A type of stagecoach orig. made at Concord, New Hampshire. M19.
2 In full ***Concord grape***. A variety of dessert grape developed at Concord, Massachusetts. M19.

concord /kənˈkɔːd/ *verb*. LME.
[ORIGIN Old French & mod. French *concorder* from Latin *concordare*, from *concord-*: see CONCORD *noun*¹. Sense 3 is back-form. from CONCORDANCE.]
1 *verb intrans.* Be in or come into agreement or harmony. LME.
2 *verb trans.* Bring into harmony, reconcile. Now *rare*. LME. ▸†**b** Agree upon, decide by agreement. LME–M17.
3 *verb trans.* Make a concordance to (a text); arrange in a concordance. M20.
■ **concordable** *adjective* (now *rare* or *obsolete*) in full accord LME.

concordance /kənˈkɔːd(ə)ns/ *noun & verb*. LME.
[ORIGIN Old French & mod. French from medieval Latin *concordantia*, from *concordant-*: see CONCORDANT, -ANCE.]
▸ **A** *noun*. **1** Agreement, concord; an instance of this. LME. ▸†**b** Harmony of sounds. L15–L17.
†**2 a** A parallel passage in a book, esp. the Bible; a citation of such passages. LME–E18. ▸**b** An alphabetical arrangement of the principal words in a book (orig. the Bible) or author, with a list (and usu. citations) of the passages in which each occurs. Orig. in *pl.* LME.
▸ **B** *verb trans.* Make a concordance to (a book etc.). L19.
■ **concordancer** *noun* a compiler of a concordance L19.

concordancy /kənˈkɔːd(ə)nsi/ *noun*. Now *rare*. L16.
[ORIGIN formed as CONCORDANCE: see -ANCY.]
Agreement, concord.

concordant /kənˈkɔːd(ə)nt/ *adjective*. L15.
[ORIGIN Old French & mod. French from Latin *concordant-* pres. ppl stem of *concordare*, from *concord-*: see CONCORD *noun*¹, -ANT¹.]
1 Agreeing; harmonious; unanimous; consistent. L15.
SHELLEY Then dulcet music swelled Concordant with the life-strings of the soul. J. TYNDALL These different methods have given concordant results. W. STUBBS The common concordant and unanimous consent of all and singular.
2 GEOLOGY. Corresponding in direction with the planes of adjacent or underlying strata. E20.
■ **concordantly** *adverb* LME.

concordantial /kɒŋkɔːˈdanʃ(ə)l/ *adjective*. M17.
[ORIGIN from medieval Latin *concordantia*: see CONCORDANCE, -AL¹.]
Pertaining to a literary concordance.

concordat /kənˈkɔːdat/ *noun*. E17.
[ORIGIN French, or Latin *concordatum* use as noun of neut. pa. pple of *concordare* agree on: see CONCORDATUM, -AT¹.]
An agreement, a compact; now *esp.* one between the Vatican and a secular government relating to matters of mutual interest.
■ **concordatory** /-dət-/ *adjective* L19.

concordatum /kɒŋkɔːˈdɑːtəm/ *noun*. E17.
[ORIGIN Latin = 'a thing agreed upon': see CONCORDAT.]
hist. An Order in Council relating to the disposal of a special fund (the ***concordatum-fund***) for extraordinary expenses in Ireland voted annually by the British Parliament; a payment made under such an order.

concorporate /kənˈkɔːp(ə)rət/ *adjective*. LME.
[ORIGIN Latin *concorporatus* pa. pple of *concorporare* incorporate, formed as CON- + *corpus*, *corpor-* body: see -ATE².]
United in one body.

concorporate /kənˈkɔːpəreɪt/ *verb*. *arch.* M16.
[ORIGIN Latin *concorporat-* pa. ppl stem of *concorporare*: see CONCORPORATE *adjective*, -ATE³.]
1 *verb trans.* Form into one body. M16.
†**2** *verb intrans.* Coalesce into one body. E17–E18.
■ **concorpoˈration** *noun* E17.

concours d'élégance /kɔ̃kur delegɑ̃ːs/ *noun phr.* Pl. same. M20.
[ORIGIN French = contest of elegance.]
A parade of motor vehicles in which prizes are awarded for the most elegant-looking.

concourse /ˈkɒŋkɔːs/ *noun*. LME.
[ORIGIN Old French & mod. French *concours* from Latin *concursus*, from *concurs-* pa. ppl stem of *concurrere* CONCUR.]
1 A flocking or meeting together; a running or flowing together; confluence. LME. ▸†**b** A concurrence of times or circumstances; process (of time, events). Also, a conjunction of planets etc. LME–L18.
M. HALE The product of chance, or fortuitous concourse of particles of matter. DRYDEN Hears . . The noise and busy concourse of the mart.
2 An assemblage of persons or things; a crowd, throng. LME.
MILTON Under some concourse of shades. M. HOLROYD A great concourse of people gathered at the grave.
†**3** The (place of) meeting of lines, surfaces, etc. LME–E19.
†**4** Concurrence in action or causation, cooperation. LME–M19.
5 An open central area in a large public building, railway station, etc. Orig. *US*. M19.
M. BRADBURY He crosses the main concourse of the university . . where paths cross, crowds gather.

concreate /kɒŋkriːˈeɪt/ *verb trans.* Now *rare* or *obsolete*. E17.
[ORIGIN ecclesiastical Latin *concreat-* pa. ppl stem of *concreare*: see CON-, CREATE *verb*.]
Create together. Chiefly as ***concreated*** *ppl adjective*.
■ **concreative** *adjective* created or creating together M17.

†**concredit** *verb trans.* L16–E19.
[ORIGIN Latin *concredit-* pa. ppl stem of *concredere*: see CON-, CREDIT *noun*.]
Commit, entrust.

concremation /kɒŋkrɪˈmeɪʃ(ə)n/ *noun*. *rare*. M18.
[ORIGIN from CON- + CREMATION.]
1 Cremation together. M18.
2 Burning to ashes. M19.

concrement /ˈkɒŋkrɪm(ə)nt/ *noun*. *rare*. M17.
[ORIGIN from CON- + *-crement*, after *increment* etc.]
A growing together; a concretion.

concrescence /kənˈkrɛs(ə)ns/ *noun*. E17.
[ORIGIN from CON- + *-crescence*, after *excrescence* etc.]
†**1** Growth by assimilation. Only in E17.
2 A concretion. Now *rare* or *obsolete*. E17.
3 BIOLOGY. The coalescence or growing together of parts originally separate; *spec.* that of the lips of the blastopore to form the body of an embryo. L19.
■ **concrescent** *adjective* growing together E20.

concrete /ˈkɒŋkriːt/ *adjective & noun*. LME.
[ORIGIN French *concret* or Latin *concretus* pa. pple of *concrescere* grow together, formed as CON- + *crescere* grow.]
▸ **A** *adjective*. **1** Formed by cohesion of parts into a mass, solidified, solid; grown together. Also, compounded of various ingredients, composite. Now *rare* or *obsolete*. LME.
2 GRAMMAR & LOGIC. Of a term or noun: denoting a substance or thing as distinct from a quality, state, or action (opp. ***abstract***). Formerly also, designating a quality regarded as adherent to a substance, or a term expressing such a quality, i.e. the adjective, e.g. *white* (paper etc.), as distinct from the quality abstracted from the substance and expressed by an abstract noun, e.g. *whiteness*. LME.
3 Embodied in material form or existing as an actual example; real, tangible: opp. ***abstract***. Of an idea, proposal, etc.: relating to realities or actual instances; specific, definite. M17.
R. FRY Metaphysical ideas so vague as to be inapplicable to concrete cases. Y. WINTERS The concept is rendered concrete by the image of Cupid. H. MACMILLAN I was to announce the Bond as a concrete proposal. R. MACDONALD My witnesses aren't entirely dependable. We need concrete evidence.
concrete music = MUSIQUE CONCRÈTE. ***concrete operations***: see OPERATION 6b. **concrete poetry**, **concrete verse**: in which the meaning is conveyed visually, by means of patterns of words or letters and other typographical devices. **concrete universal** (PHILOSOPHY etc.) (something expressing) a universal in which the general and the particular or individual are combined; an organized unity. ***concrete verse***: see ***concrete poetry*** above.
4 [the noun used attrib.] Made or consisting of concrete. L19.
D. MORRIS The city is not a concrete jungle, it is a human zoo.
▸ **B** *noun* **I 1** A concrete noun or term. *rare*. LME.
2 A concreted mass; a concretion. Now *rare* or *obsolete* exc. as below. M17.
3 A heavy-duty building material made from a mixture of broken stone or gravel, sand, cement, and water, which forms a stonelike mass on hardening; paving etc. made of this. M19.
E. FERBER Tramping of restless feet on the concrete.
reinforced concrete: see REINFORCE *verb*.
▸ **II 4** *absol.* That which is concrete. Esp. in ***in the concrete***, in the sphere of concrete reality, concretely. M16.
– COMB.: **concrete mixer** = ***cement mixer*** s.v. CEMENT *noun*.
■ **concretely** *adverb* in a concrete form, manner, or sense M17. **concreteness** *noun* M18. **concretize** *verb trans.* render concrete, esp. opp. abstract L19. **concretiˈzation** *noun* the action of concretizing; the state of being concretized: M20.

concrete /kənˈkriːt; *in sense 3* ˈkɒŋkriːt/ *verb*. L16.
[ORIGIN from CONCRETE *adjective & noun*.]
1 *verb trans.* (freq. in *pass.*) & *intrans.* Unite into a mass by cohesion or coalescence of particles; make or become solid. L16. ▸†**b** *verb trans.* Unite, combine (sensations, ideas, etc.). E18–E19.
C. LYELL Ochreous sand, concreted . . into a kind of stone.
2 *verb trans.* Give concrete expression to (an abstract thing). M17.
J. CONRAD Precious dreams that concrete the most cherished . . of his illusions.
3 *verb trans.* Cover or pave with concrete; embed or set in concrete. L19.
■ ˈ**concreter** *noun* a builder or worker with concrete L19.

concretion /kənˈkriːʃ(ə)n/ *noun*. M16.
[ORIGIN French *concrétion* or Latin *concretio(n-)*, from *concret-* pa. ppl stem of *concrescere*: see CONCRETE *adjective & noun*.]
1 The action or process of growing together or uniting in one mass; coalescence. M16. ▸**b** Congelation or coagulation of a liquid. E17.
†**2** Union with a material thing. E17–M18.
3 A concreted mass (*of*); a lump, a nodule. E17. ▸**b** *spec.* MEDICINE. A calculus or hardened deposit in the body. M17. ▸**c** GEOLOGY. A nodule of distinct mineral composition occurring (usu. around a nucleus) in sedimentary rock. M19.
4 The action of expressing (an idea etc.) in concrete form; an embodiment in concrete form. M17.
■ **concretionary** *adjective* (esp. GEOLOGY) formed by concretion; marked by or consisting of concretions: M19.

†**concrew** *verb intrans.* *rare* (Spenser). Only in L16.
[ORIGIN from ACCRUE by substitution of CON-, perh. after Old French *concreü*.]
Grow into a mass.

concubinage /kɒnˈkjuːbɪnɪdʒ/ *noun*. LME.
[ORIGIN French, formed as CONCUBINE: see -AGE.]
The cohabiting of a man and a woman who are not legally married; the practice of keeping, or the state of being, a concubine.

concubinary /kɒnˈkjuːbɪnəri/ *adjective & noun*. E16.
[ORIGIN medieval Latin *concubinarius*, from Latin *concubina*: see CONCUBINE, -ARY¹.]
▸ **A** *adjective*. Relating to concubinage. Of a person: living or born in concubinage. E16.
▸ **B** *noun*. A person who lives in concubinage. L16.

concubine /ˈkɒŋkjʊbʌɪn/ *noun & verb*. ME.
[ORIGIN Old French & mod. French from Latin *concubina*, *concubinus*, formed as CON- + *cubare* to lie.]
▸ **A** *noun*. **1** A woman who cohabits with a man without being his wife, a kept mistress; (in polygamous societies) a secondary wife. ME.
†**2** A woman's lover. LME–M16.
▸ **B** *verb trans.* †**1** Take as a concubine. Only in L16.
2 Provide with a concubine or concubines. *rare*. E19.
■ **conˈcubinal** *adjective* (*rare*) M17.

†**conculcate** *verb trans.* M16–E18.
[ORIGIN Latin *conculcat-* pa. ppl stem of *conculcare*, formed as CON- + *calcare* tread: see INCULCATE.]
Trample under foot.
■ †**conculcation** *noun* LME–E19.

concupiscence /kənˈkjuːpɪs(ə)ns/ *noun*. ME.
[ORIGIN Old French & mod. French from late Latin *concupiscentia*, from *concupiscent-* pres. ppl stem of *concupiscere* inceptive of *concupere*, formed as CON- + *cupere* desire.]
Eager or inordinate desire; immoderate sexual desire, lust; THEOLOGY desire for worldly things.
C. CHAPLIN There's a dame that arouses my concupiscence. But she looks very expensive.
■ **concupiscent** *adjective* eagerly desirous, lustful M18. **concupiscently** *adverb* LME.

concupiscible /kənˈkjuːpɪsɪb(ə)l/ *adjective*. LME.
[ORIGIN Late Latin *concupiscibilis*, from *concupiscere*: see CONCUPISCENCE, -IBLE.]
1 Of the nature of concupiscence; vehemently desirous, lustful. LME.

concupiscible principle etc.: (in Platonic philosophy) one of the two parts of irrational human nature (the other being the *irascible*).
†2 Greatly to be desired or lusted after. L15–M18.

L. STERNE Never did thy eyes behold . . anything . . more concupiscible.

†concupy *noun. rare* (Shakes.). Only in E17.
[ORIGIN Perh. abbreviation of CONCUPISCENCE; sometimes interpreted as an alt. of CONCUBINE *noun*.]
Lust, concupiscence.

concur /kən'kəː/ *verb intrans.* Infl. **-rr-**. LME.
[ORIGIN Latin *concurrere*, formed as CON- + *currere* run.]
†1 **a** Run together violently, collide; rush together in battle. LME–L17. ▸†**b** Run or flow together to a meeting point. Of lines etc.: converge. M16–E19.
2 Act in concert, cooperate. Of causes etc.: combine (to produce a result). LME.

R. JAMESON One of the plane angles which concur to the formation of the solid angle. GEO. ELIOT I concurred with our incumbent in getting up a petition against the Reform Bill.

3 Agree or express agreement. (Usu. foll. by *with*.) LME. ▸†**b** Of things: agree in character etc., accord (*with*). M16–L18.

HENRY FIELDING Mr. Alworthy by no means concurred with the opinion of those parents. G. VIDAL Let me know . . if you concur in my plan. G. SWIFT We concur It's Sunday, without a doubt. **b** HOR. WALPOLE It was now twilight, concurring with the disorder of his mind.

4 Happen or occur together, coincide. Of characteristics: be combined in the same person or thing. L16.

A. BAIN When two pleasures concur, the result is a greater pleasure.

concurrence /kən'kʌr(ə)ns/ *noun*. LME.
[ORIGIN from CONCURRENT or medieval Latin *concurrentia*: see -ENCE.]
†1 Concentration (of mind). Only in LME.
2 **a** Joint action, cooperation. E16. ▸**b** Agreement, assent. M17.

b BURKE I had the fortune to find myself in perfect concurrence with a large majority in the house. T. HARDY With a mutual glance of concurrence the two men went into the night together.

3 A running together in time or space: ▸**a** Coincidence of events or circumstances. E17. ▸**b** The (point of) meeting of lines. M17.

a JOHN FOSTER The most opportune concurrence of circumstances.

4 Rivalry, competition. (In later use a Gallicism.) *arch.* E17.
■ Also **concurrency** *noun* L16.

concurrent /kən'kʌr(ə)nt/ *adjective & noun*. LME.
[ORIGIN Latin *concurrent-* pres. ppl stem of *concurrere*: see CONCUR, -ENT.]
▸ **A** *adjective*. **1** Occurring or operating simultaneously or side by side. LME. ▸**b** Of lines etc.: meeting in or tending towards the same point. E18.

J. WILLIAMS The concurrent existence of two distinct systems of jurisprudence.

2 Acting in conjunction; cooperating. M16.

H. E. MANNING He . . gives them the concurrent assistance of his own power.

3 Expressing agreement. Of things: accordant, consistent. M16.

J. BROWN By Shouts of Sympathy or concurrent Approbation.

▸ **B** *noun*. **1** A rival claimant, a competitor. (In later use a Gallicism.) *arch.* L16.
2 A concurrent circumstance, a contributory cause. M17.
■ **concurrently** *adverb* LME.

concursion /kən'kəːʃ(ə)n/ *noun*. Now *rare* or *obsolete*. M16.
[ORIGIN Latin *concursio(n-)*, from *concurs-* pa. ppl stem of *concurrere*: see CONCUR, -ION.]
A running or rushing together.

concuss /kən'kʌs/ *verb trans.* L16.
[ORIGIN Latin *concuss-* pa. ppl stem of *concutere*, formed as CON- + *quatere* shake.]
1 Shake violently, disturb. Chiefly *fig.* L16. ▸**b** MEDICINE. Affect with concussion. L17.
2 Force by threats (*into*, *to do*); intimidate. *arch.* (chiefly *Scot.*). E19.
■ **concussive** *adjective* of the nature of, producing, or pertaining to concussion L16.

concussion /kən'kʌʃ(ə)n/ *noun*. LME.
[ORIGIN Latin *concussio(n-)*, formed as CONCUSS; see -ION.]
1 MEDICINE. Temporary unconsciousness or incapacity due to a blow on the head. LME.
2 *gen.* The action of shaking violently; the shock of impact. L15.

R. BRADBURY The ocean rose and fell with prolonged concussions. C. RYAN The ground shook constantly from the concussion of heavy explosives.

3 Extortion by threats or violence, esp. by a ruling power. Now *rare* or *obsolete*. L16.

†cond *verb trans.* Also **cund**. Orig. **condie**, **-due**. ME.
[ORIGIN Old French & mod. French *conduire* from Latin *conducere* CONDUCT *verb*.]
1 Conduct, guide. Only in ME.
2 = CON *verb*². E17–E19.
3 Direct (fishing boats etc.) towards a shoal of herring etc. E17–M19.

conde /'kɒnde/ *noun*. Also **C-**. M17.
[ORIGIN Spanish from Latin *comes*, *comitis*: see COUNT *noun*².]
A Spanish count.

condemn /kən'dɛm/ *verb trans.* ME.
[ORIGIN Old French *condem(p)ner* (mod. *condamner*) from Latin *condem(p)nare*, formed as CON- + DAMN *verb*.]
1 Give judgement against, convict; sentence *to* punishment, *to be* punished; *esp.* sentence to death. ME.

POPE The thief condemn'd, in law already dead.

2 Pronounce an adverse judgement on; express strong disapproval of; censure, blame; reject. Of words, looks, actions, etc.: incur or bring about condemnation of. LME.

OED Their looks condemn them. W. S. CHURCHILL Opinion . . has on the whole condemned Rupert's resolve to fight. C. HAUGHEY I condemn the Provisional I.R.A. and all its activities.

3 **a** Consign to perdition; damn. LME. ▸**b** Force into or limit to an unwelcome or unpleasant action or state; *esp.* in *pass.*, be doomed *to* some condition or *to do* something. M17.

b J. MORSE A tract of sea . . condemned to perpetual calms. A. S. NEILL A society that condemns poor women to slave for sixteen hours a day.

4 Pronounce guilty *of* (a crime, fault, etc.). *arch.* M16.

T. HEYWOOD She was condemned of incest and buried alive.

5 Close permanently, block up (a door, window). M16.
6 Pronounce (smuggled goods, prizes of war, etc.) legally forfeited. E18.
7 Pronounce officially to be unfit for use, consumption, or habitation. E18. ▸**b** Pronounce judicially (land etc.) as converted or convertible to public use. *US*. M19.

E. COXHEAD Though it had been condemned twenty years before, a house is a house. I. MURDOCH These trees had . . been condemned as unsafe.

8 Pronounce incurable. M19.
■ **condemnable** /-mn-/ *adjective* M16. **condemnee** /-mn-/ *noun* (*US Law*) a person whose property is expropriated for public purposes and who is therefore eligible for compensation E20. **condemningly** *adverb* with condemnation M19. **condemnor** /-mn-/ *noun* (*US Law*) a person who expropriates private property for public purposes and evaluates it for compensation paid to the owner E20.

condemnation /kɒndɛm'neɪʃ(ə)n/ *noun*. LME.
[ORIGIN Late Latin *condemnatio(n-)*, from *condemnat-* pa. ppl stem of *condemnare*: see CONDEMN, -ATION.]
1 The action of condemning; judicial conviction; censure; the fact of being condemned. LME.

J. R. ACKERLEY Irregular relationships were regarded with far greater condemnation in Victorian times. R. A. KNOX The condemnation to hell of all infants that had died without baptism.

2 The state or condition of being condemned. M16.

MILTON To whom belongs But condemnation, ignominy and shame.

3 A ground or reason for condemning. M16.

SHAKES. *Cymb.* Speak, or thy silence on the instant is Thy condemnation and thy death.

4 A sentence of forfeiture; *spec.* (*US*) the judicial assignment of property to public purposes, or in payment of a debt. M19.

condemnator /kən'dɛmnətə/ *adjective & noun*. Chiefly *Scot.* E16.
[ORIGIN French †*condemnatoire* formed as CONDEMNATORY.]
LAW. ▸**A** *adjective*. Condemnatory; *esp.* (of a decree) in favour of the plaintiff. E16.
▸ †**B** *noun*. A condemnatory sentence or decree. M16–M17.

condemnatory /kən'dɛmnət(ə)ri/ *adjective*. L16.
[ORIGIN medieval Latin *condemnatorius*, from *condemnat-*: see CONDEMNATION, -ORY². Cf. CONDEMNATOR.]
Having the character of condemning; expressing condemnation.

condemned /kən'dɛmd/ *adjective*. LME.
[ORIGIN from CONDEMN + -ED¹.]
1 Pronounced to be at fault or guilty; under sentence of condemnation. LME. ▸**b** Confounded, damned. *arch. colloq.* (chiefly *US*). M19.
2 Set aside for or pertaining to persons sentenced to death. Chiefly in ***condemned cell***. L17.
3 Officially pronounced unfit for use, consumption, or habitation. L18.

condensate /'kɒnd(ə)nseɪt/ *noun*. L19.
[ORIGIN from CONDENSE *verb* + -ATE².]
A product of chemical or physical condensation.

condensate /kən'dɛnsət, -seɪt/ *adjective*. Now *rare* or *obsolete*. L15.
[ORIGIN Latin *condensat-* pa. ppl stem of *condensare*: see CONDENSE *verb*, -ATE².]
Condensed, thickened, increased in density.

condensate /kən'dɛnseɪt/ *verb trans. & intrans.* Now *rare* or *obsolete*. M16.
[ORIGIN formed as CONDENSATE *adjective*: see -ATE³.]
Condense.
■ **condensator** *noun* (*rare*) a condenser E19.

condensation /kɒndɛn'seɪʃ(ə)n/ *noun*. E17.
[ORIGIN Late Latin *condensatio(n-)*, formed as CONDENSATE *adjective*: see -ATION. Cf. Old French & mod. French *condensation*.]
1 The act or process of condensing; *spec.* the conversion of a substance from a state of gas or vapour to a liquid (occas., a solid) condition. E17.
2 Condensed condition; a condensed mass; condensed material, esp. of water on the inside of cold windows etc. E17.
3 The compression of thought or meaning into a few words; *esp.* the abridgement of a book etc.; the result of this. L18.
4 CHEMISTRY. In full ***condensation reaction***. A reaction in which two molecules combine to form a larger molecule, strictly with the elimination of a small molecule such as H_2O. L19.
5 PSYCHOANALYSIS. The fusion of two or more images or ideas into a single composite or new image, esp. in a dream; the carrying of more than one symbolic meaning by an image. E20.
– PHRASES: ***Knoevenagel condensation***. ***surface condensation***: see SURFACE *adjective*.
– COMB.: ***condensation reaction***: see sense 4 above; **condensation trail** = ***vapour trail*** s.v. VAPOUR *noun*.

†condense *adjective*. LME–L18.
[ORIGIN Latin *condensus*: see CONDENSE *verb*.]
Dense, condensed.

condense /kən'dɛns/ *verb trans. & intrans.* LME.
[ORIGIN Old French & mod. French *condenser* or Latin *condensare*, from *condensus* very dense: see CON-, DENSE *adjective*.]
1 Make or become (more) dense; increase in density; thicken; concentrate. LME.

B. LOVELL The contemporary view that the stars condensed from the interstellar gas clouds.

condensed milk: thickened by evaporation and sweetened.
2 Reduce or be reduced from gas or vapour to a liquid (occas. a solid) condition. M17.

E. STILLINGFLEET The air was condensed into clouds. D. LODGE Their breath condenses on the chill, damp air.

3 Bring or come together closely; *esp.* express (writing, speech, etc.) in few(er) words, make concise. E19.

CONAN DOYLE Is this too condensed, or can you follow it clearly? J. HELLER Gold condensed the piece further by four hundred words.

■ **condensa'bility** *noun* the quality of being condensable E19. **condensable** *adjective* that may be condensed M17. **condensedly** *adverb* with condensation (esp. of expression) L19. **condensery** *noun* a factory for making condensed milk E20. **condensible** *adjective* = CONDENSABLE L18.

condenser /kən'dɛnsə/ *noun*. L17.
[ORIGIN from CONDENSE *verb* + -ER¹. Cf. French *condenseur*.]
1 *gen.* A person who or thing which condenses. L17.
2 A vessel, apparatus, etc., in which vapour is reduced to liquid (occas. solid) form; *esp.* a chamber in a steam engine in which steam is condensed on leaving the cylinder; CHEMISTRY a device for condensing vapour during distillation etc. M18.
Liebig condenser, ***Liebig's condenser***: see LIEBIG 2.
3 ELECTRICITY. = CAPACITOR. L18.
padder condenser: see PADDER *noun*² 3.
4 A lens or system of lenses for concentrating light. L18.

condensity /kən'dɛnsɪti/ *noun*. E17.
[ORIGIN French †*condensité* or late Latin *condensitas*, from *condensus*: see CONDENSE *verb*, -ITY.]
†1 Density. E17–E19.
2 Condensed quality, pithiness. L19.

†conder *noun*. E17.
[ORIGIN from COND *verb* + -ER¹.]
1 A person who, stationed on high ground, signals the direction taken by shoals of herring etc. to fishing boats. E17–M19.
2 A person who cons a ship. L17–E19.

condescend /kɒndɪ'sɛnd/ *verb*. ME.
[ORIGIN Old French & mod. French *condescendre* from ecclesiastical Latin *condescendere* stoop (fig.), (in medieval Latin) accede, agree to, formed as CON- + DESCEND.]
▸ **I** Make concession (to).
†1 *verb intrans.* & (*rare*) *refl.* Yield, defer, accommodate oneself (*to*); accede, consent (*to*); come to agreement, concur. ME–L18.

G. DOUGLAS Thay [singers] condiscend sa weill in ane accord. W. DRUMMOND The three estates . . together condescended to the raising of an army. W. GODWIN He was resolved to condescend no further to the whims of a person.

†**2** *verb trans.* Concede, vouchsafe; agree upon, consent to. LME–L18.

J. SPALDING It was condescended among his friends, that twenty-four gentlemen . . should weekly attend. T. JEFFERSON No answers having yet been condescended.

▸ **II** Come down voluntarily.
†**3** *verb intrans.* Come or go down, descend. LME–L17.
4 *verb intrans.* Be gracious enough *to do* something, stoop voluntarily *to* an action, though showing one's feelings of dignity or superiority. Now freq. *iron.* LME.

S. SMILES [They] condescended to the meanest employments, for the purpose of disarming suspicion. E. F. BENSON Dismiss Johnson . . and get somebody who will condescend to garden.

5 *verb intrans.* Disregard one's superiority *to* a person; show kindness to an inferior; behave patronizingly (*to*). E17.

P. S. WORSLEY The god, condescending to his child. P. SCOTT The . . subalterns . . gave themselves airs . . . They even condescended to the Area Commander.

▸ **III** Come to a point.
†**6** *verb intrans.* Come *to* a particular point (in narration etc.). LME–E16.
7 *verb intrans.* Come to particulars; particularize, elaborate (*up*)*on*. *obsolete* exc. *Scot.* LME.
■ **condescendence** *noun* (**a**) condescension; compliance; (**b**) *Scot.* a specification of particulars: E17. **condescendency** *noun* (now *rare* or *obsolete*) condescension M17. **condescender** *noun* (*rare*) M17.

condescending /kɒndɪˈsɛndɪŋ/ *adjective*. M17.
[ORIGIN from CONDESCEND + -ING[2].]
†**1** Consenting. Only in M17.
2 That condescends, characterized by condescension; patronizing. E18.
3 Going into details, particularizing. *Scot.* L18.
■ **condescendingly** *adverb* M17.

condescension /kɒndɪˈsɛnʃ(ə)n/ *noun*. M17.
[ORIGIN Obsolete French (now *condescendance*), from (orig.) ecclesiastical Latin *condescensio(n-)*, from Latin *condescens-* pa. ppl stem of *condescendere*: see CONDESCEND, -ION.]
†**1** The fact or action of acceding or consenting; concession. M17–E18.
†**2** The action of stooping to something unworthy. M17–L18.
3 Voluntary disregarding of a superior position; affability to inferiors; a consciously gracious or patronizing act or manner. M17.

R. L. STEVENSON I had come . . to prove in a thousand condescensions that I was no sharer in the prejudice of race. I. MURDOCH I had never been spontaneously approached by a publisher before and such condescension rather turned my head.

4 Gracious, considerate, or submissive deference shown to another; complaisance. Now *rare* or *obsolete*. M17.

HENRY FIELDING Their extreme servility and condescension to their superiors.

■ †**condescensive** *adjective* characterized by or given to condescension M17–E19.

condictio /kənˈdɪkʃɪəʊ/ *noun*. Pl. **-dictiones** /-dɪkʃɪˈəʊniːz/. Also anglicized as †**-diction**. L18.
[ORIGIN Latin *condictio(n-)*, from *condict-* pa. ppl stem of *condicere*, formed as CON- + *dicere* say: see -ION.]
ROMAN LAW. A formal claim of debt or restitution.

†**condie** *verb* see COND.

condign /kənˈdʌɪn/ *adjective*. LME.
[ORIGIN Old French & mod. French *condigne* from Latin *condignus* wholly worthy, formed as CON- + *dignus* worthy.]
†**1** Equal in worth or dignity (*to*). LME–M19.

S. DOBELL Rank after mingling rank . . but each condign.

2 Of a person or thing: worthy, deserving. Now *rare* or *obsolete*. LME.

H. BRADSHAW As most condigne to beare the principalitie.

3 Worthily deserved, merited, appropriate; adequate. *obsolete* in *gen.* sense. LME. ▸**b** *spec.* Of punishment, retribution, etc.: appropriate to the crime, well-deserved and severe. E16.

SHAKES. *L.L.L.* Speak you this in my praise? . . In thy condign praise. **b** BOSW. SMITH To wreak condign vengeance on the common oppressor. *Times* Punishment for perjury had to be condign and commensurate with the gravity of the offence.

■ **condignly** *adverb* LME. **condignness** /-n-n-/ *noun* L16.

condignity /kənˈdɪgnɪti/ *noun*. M16.
[ORIGIN medieval Latin *condignitas*, from *condignus*: see CONDIGN, -ITY.]
1 SCHOLASTIC THEOLOGY. Merit acquired by humans through actions performed in reliance on the Holy Spirit; grace earned by works, as opp. to that freely given. M16.
†**2** *gen.* Worthiness, merit; what one deserves. L16–M17.

condiment /ˈkɒndɪm(ə)nt/ *noun & verb*. LME.
[ORIGIN Latin *condimentum*, from *condire* preserve, pickle, embalm, by-form of *condere* preserve: see -MENT.]
▸ **A** *noun*. A substance such as salt, mustard, or pickle that is used to add flavour to food. LME.
▸ **B** *verb trans.* Season or flavour with a condiment; spice. *rare*. LME.
■ **condimental** /kɒndɪˈmɛnt(ə)l/ *adjective* of or belonging to a condiment; spicy: E17.

condisciple /kɒndɪˈsʌɪp(ə)l/ *noun*. *arch.* LME.
[ORIGIN Latin *condiscipulus* fellow-scholar: see CON-, DISCIPLE *noun*.]
A fellow disciple; a fellow scholar or student.

†**condite** *verb trans.* LME.
[ORIGIN Latin *condit-* pa. ppl stem of *condire*: see CONDIMENT.]
1 Preserve with salt, spices, etc.; pickle. LME–E18.
2 Embalm. Only in M17.
3 Season, flavour. M–L17.

condition /kənˈdɪʃ(ə)n/ *noun*. ME.
[ORIGIN Old French *condicion* (mod. *condition*) from Latin *condicio(n-)* agreement, situation, etc., rel. to *condicere* agree upon, promise, formed as CON- + *dicere* declare, say: see -ION.]
▸ **I** A convention, proviso, etc.
1 A thing demanded or required as a prerequisite to the granting or performance of something else; a stipulation. ME. ▸†**b** *ellipt.* As conjunction = ***on condition that*** below. Only in E17.

MILTON Wilt thou enjoy the good, Then cavil the conditions? G. F. KENNAN A list of twenty-one conditions on which . . Communist groups . . would be admitted to the Third International. **b** SHAKES. *Tr. & Cr.* Condition I had gone barefoot to India.

on condition that with the condition that, provided that. POTESTATIVE ***condition***. ***resolutive condition***: see RESOLUTIVE 2.

2 A thing on whose existence or fulfilment that of another depends; a prerequisite. In *pl.*, circumstances, *esp.* those necessary for a thing's existence. ME.

G. J. ROMANES Environment . . or the sum total of the external conditions of life. G. MURRAY It is . . a necessary condition of social living, that we are individuals as well as members of a social whole.

†**3** A restriction, a qualification, a limitation. LME–M19.

J. BRAMHALL We are absolutely without condition glad of our own liberty.

†**4** An agreement; a covenant, a treaty. L15–E18.

SHAKES. *Merch. V.* If you repay me not . . such sum or sums as are Express'd in the condition.

5 A provision in a will, contract, etc., on which the legal force or effect of the document depends. L16.
conditions of sale the provisions under which a sale by auction takes place.
6 GRAMMAR. A conditional clause. M19.
7 A subject, course, etc., in which a student must pass an examination within a stated time to maintain provisionally granted status. *US.* M19.
▸ **II** State, mode of being.
8 A particular mode of being of a person or thing; a state; circumstances of wealth; social position. ME. ▸**b** *spec.* A state resulting from a physical or mental illness; sickness, a malady. E20.

W. H. PRESCOTT In the middle classes; and even in those of humbler condition. M. ESSLIN The act of waiting as an essential and characteristic aspect of the human condition. **b** T. S. ELIOT The condition is curable.

change one's condition (now *arch.* & *dial.*) get married. **in a certain condition**, **in a delicate condition**, **in an interesting condition** *euphem.* pregnant. **in condition** in good condition; physically fit. **in no condition** certainly not fit enough *to do*. ***mint condition***: see MINT *noun*[1]. **out of condition** in bad condition; physically unfit. ***race condition***: see RACE *noun*[1] 3C. ***spheroidal condition***: see SPHEROIDAL 2.

†**9** Mental disposition; moral nature; temper. In *pl.*, personal qualities; ways, morals; behaviour. LME–M19.

AV *2 Macc.* 15:12 A good man, . . gentle in condition, well spoken also. SIR W. SCOTT Miss Bell Fergusson, a woman of the most excellent conditions.

†**10** Nature, character, quality; a characteristic, an attribute. LME–E18.

A. DAY A man shaped as you see, and as bold in condition as he appeareth in shew.

condition /kənˈdɪʃ(ə)n/ *verb*. L15.
[ORIGIN Old French *condicionner* (mod. *-tionner*) or medieval Latin *condicionare* (*-tion-*), from *condicio(n-)*: see CONDITION *noun*.]
▸ **I** *verb intrans.* **1** Negotiate about conditions; make conditions; bargain *with*, *for*. *arch.* L15.
▸ **II** *verb trans.* **2** Stipulate for; make (something) a condition; agree by stipulation *to do* something. *arch.* M16.
3 Make conditional. Usu. foll. by *on*, *upon*. M16.
4 Govern, determine; impose conditions on; be essential to. E17.

M. GIROUARD Their ideas of beauty were conditioned by what they disliked about their parents.

5 Charge (a bond) with clauses or conditions. L17.
6 PHILOSOPHY. Subject to the qualifying conditions of finite existence or cognition. Now *rare*. E19.
7 Admit (a student) to a class on the condition of passing an examination within a stated time. (Cf. CONDITION *noun* 7.) *US.* M19.
8 Test the condition, state, or quality of (a textile etc.). M19.
9 Bring into a desired state or condition (*for*); make fit (esp. dogs, horses, etc.). M19. ▸**b** Teach, accustom (a person, animal, etc.) to adopt certain habits, attitudes, etc.; establish a conditioned reflex or response in. (Foll. by *to do*, *to* a thing etc.) E20.

b ALDOUS HUXLEY His conditioning has laid down rails along which he's got to run. He can't help himself. A. STORR Repeated positive reinforcement has conditioned him to favourable self-appraisal.

air conditioning: see AIR *noun*[1]. **b** ***verbal conditioning***: see VERBAL *adjective* 2.

conditional /kənˈdɪʃ(ə)n(ə)l/ *adjective & noun*. LME.
[ORIGIN Old French *condicionel* (mod. *-tionnel*) or late Latin *condicionalis*, from *condicio(n-)*: see CONDITION *noun*, -AL[1].]
▸ **A** *adjective*. **1** Subject to one or more conditions; depending (*on*, *upon*); not absolute; made or granted on certain conditions or terms. LME.

W. LIPPMANN The fulfillment of this promise is . . conditional upon the ability . . to define equality. P. BLANCHARD Such conditional endearments as, 'My love to the little Sarah Margaret. I love her if she is a good girl and learns to read.' A. LURIE His parents' affection . . was always conditional on good behaviour.

conditional agreement LAW an agreement dependent on the happening of an uncertain event. **conditional discharge** LAW an order made by a criminal court whereby an offender may be sentenced for the original offence if a further offence is committed within a fixed period. **conditional offer** *spec.* of a place at a university, college, etc., subject to the attainment of specified grades in forthcoming examinations. **conditional sale agreement** LAW a contract for the sale of goods under which ownership does not pass to the buyer until the instalments have been paid, although the buyer has possession.

2 GRAMMAR & LOGIC. Expressing or including a condition or supposition. M16.

A. BAIN The conditional clause is introduced by 'if'.

conditional mood GRAMMAR: used in the consequent clause of a conditional sentence.

▸ **B** *noun*. Chiefly GRAMMAR & LOGIC. A word, clause, proposition, etc., expressing or including a condition; the conditional mood. M16.
■ **conditionalism** *noun* (THEOLOGY) the doctrine of conditional survival after death L19. **conditionalist** *adjective & noun* of or pertaining to, a believer in, conditionalism L19. **conditioˈnality** *noun* the state or quality of being conditional M17. **conditionally** *adverb* (**a**) in a conditional manner, subject to conditions; †(**b**) on condition (*that*): LME.

conditionate /kənˈdɪʃ(ə)nət/ *adjective & noun*. LME.
[ORIGIN medieval Latin *condicionatus* (*-tion-*) pa. pple, formed as CONDITIONATE *verb*: see -ATE[2].]
▸ **A** *adjective*. Conditioned; subject to or limited by conditions. Now *rare* or *obsolete*. LME.
▸ **B** *noun*. A conditional thing, a contingency. L17.

conditionate /kənˈdɪʃ(ə)neɪt/ *verb*. M16.
[ORIGIN medieval Latin *condicionat-* pa. ppl stem of *condicionare*: see CONDITION *verb*, -ATE[3].]
†**1** *verb trans. & intrans.* Agree on (conditions); stipulate. M16–M17.
2 *verb trans.* Limit as a condition; be, or act as, a condition of. L16.

conditioned /kənˈdɪʃ(ə)nd/ *adjective*. LME.
[ORIGIN from CONDITION *noun*, *verb*: see -ED[2], -ED[1].]
▸ **I** From the noun.
1 Having a (specified) disposition or temperament; in a particular condition or state. LME.

SHAKES. *Merch. V.* The kindest man, the best condition'd and unwearied spirit In doing courtesies.

ill-conditioned, ***well-conditioned***, etc.

2 Placed in certain conditions; circumstanced, situated. M19.

COLERIDGE In countries well governed and happily conditioned.

▸ **II** From the verb.
3 Subject to conditions or limitations; dependent on a condition; not absolute or infinite. M17.

absol.: W. HAMILTON The Conditioned is that which is alone conceivable or cogitable.

4 Brought into a desired state; with the balance of certain qualities adjusted. E20.

H. G. WELLS They had no properly mixed and conditioned air.

conditioned reflex a reflex response to a non-natural stimulus established by training in a person, animal, etc. ***air-conditioned***: see AIR *noun*[1].

5 Taught to accept certain habits, attitudes, standards, etc.; accustomed *to*. M20.

R. CHURCH My father, long conditioned to bullying, refused to be intimidated.

conditioner /kənˈdɪʃ(ə)nə/ *noun*. L16.
[ORIGIN from CONDITION *verb* + -ER[1].]
†**1** A person who makes conditions. Only in L16.
2 A substance, appliance, etc., the use of which improves the condition of something. L19.
air conditioner, ***hair conditioner***, etc.

C

condo /ˈkɒndəʊ/ *noun. colloq.* (orig. *US*). Pl. **-os**. M20.
[ORIGIN Abbreviation.]
= CONDOMINIUM 2.

condolatory /kənˈdəʊlət(ə)ri/ *adjective*. M18.
[ORIGIN from CONDOLE after *consolatory*.]
Expressive of or intending condolence.

condole /kənˈdəʊl/ *verb*. L16.
[ORIGIN Christian Latin *condolere*, formed as CON- + *dolere* suffer pain, grieve.]
▸ **I** *verb intrans.* †**1** Sorrow greatly, grieve, lament. L16–M17.
R. TOFTE For my Sinnes fore Heauen I do condole.
2 Grieve *with*; express sympathy *with* a person *on* a loss etc.; express condolence. L16.
H. MARTINEAU Three quarters of her acquaintance came to condole. S. T. WARNER Condole with her, and listen to her sorrows.
▸ **II** *verb trans.* †**3** Grieve over, bewail, lament (a loss, misfortune, etc.); *refl.* grieve, lament. L16–L18.
S. RICHARDSON A person . . whose sufferings I condole.
†**4** Grieve with (a person); express commiseration of or sympathy with. L16–L18.
ADDISON They are comforted and condoled . . by their fellow-citizens.
5 Express formal regret at (a bereavement etc.). Now *rare*. L16.
H. ELLIS Elizabeth had sent to condole the death of Frederick the Second.
■ **condolement** *noun* †(**a**) lamentation; (**b**) (an expression of) condolence: L16. **condoler** *noun* E18. **condolingly** *adverb* in a condoling manner, with condolence E18.

condolence /kənˈdəʊl(ə)ns/ *noun*. E17.
[ORIGIN from CONDOLE + -ENCE. In sense 2 also infl. by French *condoléance*.]
†**1** Sympathetic grief; sorrowing with and for others. E17–E18.
2 Outward expression of sympathy for another's grief; *esp.* a formal declaration of regret for a person's bereavement, misfortune, etc. Freq. in *pl.* E17.
J. GALSWORTHY Kindness . . would frequently result in visits of condolence being made. H. CECIL The usual congratulations between the plaintiff and his legal advisers and . . condolences between Martin and his legal advisers.
■ †**condolency** *noun* (**a**) = CONDOLENCE; (**b**) compassion, commiseration: E17–E19.

condolent /kənˈdəʊl(ə)nt/ *adjective*. LME.
[ORIGIN Latin *condolent-* pres. ppl stem of *condolere*: see CONDOLE, -ENT.]
†**1** Sorrowing greatly. LME–L15.
2 Compassionate; expressing sympathetic grief. L15.

condom /ˈkɒndəm/ *noun*. E18.
[ORIGIN Unknown.]
A contraceptive or prophylactic sheath that can be worn on the penis during sexual intercourse or (***female condom***) that can be inserted into the vagina before sexual intercourse.

condominium /kɒndəˈmɪnɪəm/ *noun*. E18.
[ORIGIN mod. Latin, formed as CON- + DOMINIUM.]
1 Joint control of a state's affairs vested in two or more other states. E18.
2 A set of flats, group of cottages, etc., rented or bought by a group of people; a unit of property so held. *N. Amer.* M20.

condonation /kɒndəʊˈneɪʃ(ə)n/ *noun*. E17.
[ORIGIN Latin *condonatio(n-)*, formed as CONDONE: see CON-, DONATION.]
The forgiveness or overlooking, esp. by implication, of an offence.

condone /kənˈdəʊn/ *verb trans.* M19.
[ORIGIN Latin *condonare* deliver up, surrender, favour by not punishing, formed as CON- + *donare* give.]
1 Forgive or overlook (an offence; freq. a spouse's adultery); *esp.* forgive tacitly by not allowing the offence to affect one's relations with the offender. M19.
G. B. SHAW Is it your intention not only to condone my son's frauds, but to take advantage of them?
2 Of an action, fact, etc.: atone for (an offence); make (a wrong) appear forgivable. L19.
I. MURDOCH The vague illumination of lofty notions which may seem to condone all kinds of extravagance.
3 Approve, sanction, esp. reluctantly; acquiesce in. M20.
K. KESEY Like the whole thing had been planned by him, or at least condoned and authorized.
■ **condonable** *adjective* L19. **condoner** *noun* M19.

condor /ˈkɒndɔː/ *noun*. E17.
[ORIGIN Spanish *cóndor* from Quechua *kuntur*.]
Either of two very large vultures, *Vultur gryphus*, native to the Andes of S. America (more fully ***Andean condor***), and *Gymnogyps californianus*, of the mountains of California (more fully ***Californian condor***).

condottiere /kɒndɒtˈtjere/ *noun*. Pl. **-ri** /-ri/. Also †**-iero**. L18.
[ORIGIN Italian, from *condotta* a contract, from fem. pa. pple of *condurre* conduct, formed as CONDUCE.]
hist. A leader or member of a troop of mercenaries (orig. and esp. in Italy).

conduce /kənˈdjuːs/ *verb*. LME.
[ORIGIN Latin *conducere* bring together, hire, contribute, formed as CON- + *ducere* to lead.]
▸ **I** *verb trans.* †**1** Lead, conduct, bring (*lit.* & *fig.*). Foll. by *to*. LME–M17.
†**2** Engage for money, hire. *Scot.* L15–L17.
†**3** Bring about, bring to effect. Only in E16.
▸ **II** *verb intrans.* **4** Foll. by *to*: lead or tend towards, contribute to; promote, encourage. L15.
W. S. CHURCHILL This has not conduced to the national interest. R. WILBUR All bitter things conduce to sweet. Y. MENUHIN These circumstances not conducing to slumber, I spent the rest hour holding forth.
†**5** Gather together, start. *rare* (Shakes.). Only in E16.
SHAKES. *Tr. & Cr.* Within my soul there doth conduce a fight Of this strange nature.
■ **conducement** *noun* (long *rare*) (**a**) the action or quality of conducing (*to*); (**b**) a thing that conduces, tendency: M16. **conducible** *adjective* (*obsolete* exc. *Scot.*) that conduces; expedient, serviceable M16.

conducive /kənˈdjuːsɪv/ *adjective* & *noun*. M17.
[ORIGIN from CONDUCE after *conductive* etc.: see -IVE.]
▸ **A** *adjective*. Foll. by *to*: conducing or tending to (a specified end); tending to promote or encourage. M17.
▸ **B** *noun*. A thing which conduces (*to*). *rare*. L18.
■ **conduciveness** *noun* L17.

conduct /ˈkɒndʌkt/ *noun*[1]. Orig. †**conduit**. See also CONDUIT *noun*. ME.
[ORIGIN (Old French *conduit* from) Latin *conductus*, from *conduct-* pa. ppl stem of *conducere*: see CONDUCE.]
▸ **I** **1** Provision for guidance or conveyance; an escort, a convoy; a pass. *obsolete* exc. in SAFE CONDUCT. ME.
SHAKES. *Cymb.* I desire of you a conduct overland to Milford Haven.
2 The action of conducting; guidance, leading (*lit.* & *fig.*). LME.
S. JOHNSON Travelling together under the conduct of chance. W. GILPIN Under his conduct we climbed the steep.
†**3** A guide, a leader (*lit.* & *fig.*). LME–L18.
4 More fully ***conduct money***. Money paid for travelling expenses, esp. (*hist.*) for men on military service; a payment levied for this purpose by Charles I. E16.
5 Conveyance, esp. of liquid by a channel. *rare*. M16.
▸ **II** **6** Leadership, command, management. LME.
W. ROBERTSON The conduct of these troops was committed to Andrew de Foix.
7 The action or manner of carrying on a proceeding, business, etc.; management, handling; the execution of a work of art or literature, etc. LME.
J. REYNOLDS He perfectly understood . . the conduct of the background. T. ARNOLD Those engaged in the conduct of the school. R. V. JONES Those responsible for the conduct of the war.
8 Aptitude for leadership; skill in managing affairs; practical address, discretion. *arch.* M16.
DRYDEN Thus conduct won the prize when courage fail'd.
9 Manner of conducting oneself; behaviour, esp. in its moral aspect. M16. ▸**b** A proceeding, a course of conduct. Now *rare* or *obsolete*. E18.
A. POWELL Conduct obnoxious . . in one person may be . . tolerated in another. **b** JAS. MILL A conduct which demanded the most serious consideration.
disorderly conduct: see DISORDERLY *adjective* 1.
▸ †**III** See CONDUIT *noun*.
– COMB.: **conduct book** etc.: for recording a person's offences and punishments; ***conduct money***: see sense 4 above.

conduct /ˈkɒndʌkt/ *noun*[2]. LME.
[ORIGIN Latin *conductus* pa. pple of *conducere* hire.]
1 In full ***conduct priest***. A hired or salaried chaplain. *obsolete* exc. *hist.* LME. ▸**b** An Eton College chaplain. E18.
†**2** A hired workman. L15–M17.

conduct /kənˈdʌkt/ *verb*. Pa. t. & pple **conducted**, †**conduct**. Orig. †**conduit**. See also CONDUIT *verb*. LME.
[ORIGIN Old French & mod. French *conduite* pa. pple of *conduire* from Latin *conducere* CONDUCE, assim. to Latin *conductus*: see CONDUCT *noun*[1].]
▸ **I** **1** *verb trans.* Lead, guide (*lit.* & *fig.*); escort. LME. ▸**b** *verb intrans.* Lead *to*, conduce *to*. M19.
P. MORTIMER He conducted me round the factory. **b** R. FIRBANK An elm-lined lane that conducted to the farmyard gates.
conducted tour: led by a guide on a fixed itinerary.
2 **a** *verb trans.* Direct, be the commander of (an army, siege, etc.). *arch.* LME. ▸**b** *verb trans.* Manage, carry on (a business, transaction, process, etc.); preside over (a meeting etc.). M17. ▸**c** *verb trans.* & *intrans.* Act as conductor of (an orchestra, choir, musical performance, etc.). L18.
b E. BOWEN She saw him conducting a funeral . . leaning . . over the yawn of the grave to scatter his handful of earth. P. G. WODEHOUSE You can't conduct a delicate negotiation like this over the telephone. D. ADAMS The greatest experiment ever conducted—to find . . the Ultimate Answer of Life, the Universe, and Everything.
3 **a** *verb trans.* Convey, serve as a channel for (fluids etc.). LME. ▸**b** *verb trans.* & *intrans.* Transmit (heat, electricity, etc.) by conduction; be a conductor of heat or electricity. M18.
a H. MARTINEAU Air would be conducted into the recesses of the groves.
†**4** *verb trans.* = CONDUCE *verb* 2. L15–M16.
5 *verb refl.* Behave oneself in a specified way. E18.
▸ †**II** See CONDUIT *verb*.
■ **conducting** *verbal noun* the action of the verb; *esp.* the directing of an orchestra by a conductor: L15. **conducting** *ppl adjective* that conducts; *esp.* = CONDUCTIVE *adjective* 2: M17.

conductance /kənˈdʌkt(ə)ns/ *noun*. L19.
[ORIGIN from CONDUCT *verb* + -ANCE.]
The conducting power of an electrical conductor or component, equal (for direct currents) to the reciprocal of resistance.
mutual conductance: see MUTUAL *adjective*. ***specific conductance***: see SPECIFIC *adjective*.

conductible /kənˈdʌktɪb(ə)l/ *adjective*. *rare*. M19.
[ORIGIN from CONDUCT *verb* + -IBLE.]
Capable of conducting heat etc.; able to be conducted.
■ **conductiˈbility** *noun* M19.

conductimetric /kɒndʌktɪˈmɛtrɪk/ *adjective*. M20.
[ORIGIN from CONDUCTIVITY + -METRIC.]
CHEMISTRY. = CONDUCTOMETRIC.

conduction /kənˈdʌkʃ(ə)n/ *noun*. M16.
[ORIGIN Old French & mod. French, or Latin *conductio(n-)*, from *conduct-*: see CONDUCT *noun*[1], -ION.]
†**1** = CONDUCT *noun*[1] 1. M16–M17.
†**2** = CONDUCT *noun*[1] 6, 7, 8. M16–M19.
3 Hiring. *obsolete* exc. *ROMAN LAW*. M16.
4 The conveyance *of* fluid through a pipe etc. (usu. with ref. to natural processes). E17.
5 Transmission (of heat, electricity, etc.) by contact between the particles of matter; the transmission of impulses along nerves. E19.
– COMB.: **conduction band** *PHYSICS* an energy band partly filled by electrons, which can move freely and so conduct electricity.

conductitious /kɒndʌkˈtɪʃəs/ *adjective*. Now *rare* or *obsolete*. E17.
[ORIGIN Latin *conducticius*, *-tius*, from *conduct-* pa. ppl stem of *conducere* hire: see -ITIOUS[1]. Cf. CONDUCT *noun*[2].]
Hired, for hire.

conductive /kənˈdʌktɪv/ *adjective*. E16.
[ORIGIN from CONDUCT *verb* + -IVE.]
†**1** **a** *gen.* Having the property of conducting or leading (*lit.* & *fig.*). E16–M17. ▸**b** *spec.* Having the power of conducting heat, electricity, etc.; of, pertaining to, or involving the conduction of heat, electricity, etc. M19.
†**2** Conducive (*to*). E17–E18.
■ **conductively** *adverb* by means of conduction L19.

conductivity /kɒndʌkˈtɪvɪti/ *noun*. M19.
[ORIGIN from CONDUCTIVE + -ITY.]
PHYSICS etc. (A measure of) the property or power of a substance of conducting heat or electricity; conductance per unit volume; the property of tissue of conveying nerve impulses.
ELECTRICAL ***conductivity***. ***specific conductivity***: see SPECIFIC *adjective*. ***thermal conductivity***: see THERMAL *adjective*.
– COMB.: **conductivity water** water of high purity (and hence extremely low electrical conductivity) used in laboratory measurements of conductivity of solutions.

conductometer /kɒndʌkˈtɒmɪtə/ *noun*. L19.
[ORIGIN from CONDUCTIVITY + -OMETER.]
An instrument for measuring electrical conductivity.
■ **conductoˈmetric** *adjective* (*CHEMISTRY*) of, pertaining to, or involving the measurement of electrical conductivity, esp. as the means of determining the end point in titration E20. **conductometry** *noun* E20.

conductor /kənˈdʌktə/ *noun*. LME.
[ORIGIN Old French *conduitor*, (also mod.) *conducteur*, from Latin *conductor*, from *conduct-*: see CONDUCT *noun*[1], -OR.]
1 A (military) commander. Long *obsolete* exc. *hist.* LME.
2 A leader, a guide. L15.
3 A person who directs or manages. L16. ▸**b** The director of an orchestra, choir, etc., who indicates rhythm etc. by gestures made with the hands or a baton. L18.
4 A person who hires; a tenant. *obsolete* exc. *ROMAN LAW*. M17.
5 A thing which conducts or forms a channel for the passage of something; *esp.* a substance or device which conducts heat or electricity (freq. with specifying word). M18.
bus conductor, ***tram conductor***.
6 An official responsible for collecting fares and general supervision on a bus, tram, etc.; *US* a guard on a train. E19.
bad conductor, ***good conductor***, ***non-conductor***, etc. ***lightning conductor***: see LIGHTNING *noun* & *adjective*. SEMICONDUCTOR.
– COMB.: **conductor rail**: transmitting the current to an electric train.

■ **conduc'torial** *adjective* of, pertaining to, or characteristic of a conductor (esp. of music) M19. **conductorship** *noun* the office or function of (musical) conductor E19.

conductress /kən'dʌktrɪs/ *noun*. E17.
[ORIGIN from CONDUCTOR: see -ESS[1].]
A female conductor (esp. in a bus etc.).

conductus /kən'dʌktəs/ *noun*. Pl. **-ti** /-tʌɪ/. E19.
[ORIGIN medieval Latin: see CONDUCT *noun*[1].]
MEDIEVAL MUSIC. A type of composition of the 12th and 13th cents. with metrical Latin text.

conduit /'kɒndɪt, -djʊɪt/ *noun*. Also †**conduct**. See also CONDUCT *noun*[1]. ME.
[ORIGIN Orig. form of CONDUCT *noun*[1].]
▸ **I 1** A (natural or artificial) channel or pipe for conveying liquids etc. ME. ▸**b** A tube or trough for protecting insulated wires; a length of this. L19.

W. D. THORNBURY The volcanic plug formed when lava in the conduit of a volcano solidifies. P. MATTHIESSEN Water . . dripping sonorously onto slate conduits that conduct it to a . . caldron. *fig.*: L. TRILLING The family is the conduit of cultural influences.

2 A fountain. *arch.* ME.

D. G. ROSSETTI The conduits round the garden sing.

3 ARCHITECTURE. A passage, esp. underground. *rare*. E17.
▸ †**II** See CONDUCT *noun*[1].
– COMB.: **conduit-pipe** a tubular conduit.

†**conduit** *verb*. LME.
[ORIGIN Orig. form of CONDUCT *verb*. Sense 2 from CONDUIT *noun*.]
1 See CONDUCT *verb*. LME.
2 *verb trans.* Convey (as) through a conduit. LME–E17.

conduplicate /kən'djuːplɪkət/ *adjective*. L18.
[ORIGIN Latin *conduplicatus* pa. pple of *conduplicare*, formed as CON- + DUPLICATE *verb*: see -ATE[2].]
BOTANY. Of a leaf: folded lengthwise along the middle.

conduplication /kəndjuːplɪ'keɪʃ(ə)n/ *noun*. Now *rare*. E17.
[ORIGIN Latin *conduplicatio(n-)*, formed as CONDUPLICATE: see -ATION.]
A doubling, a repetition.

condurango *noun* var. of CUNDURANGO.

condylarth /'kɒndɪlɑːθ/ *noun*. L19.
[ORIGIN from *Condylarthra* (see below), from Greek *kondulus* knuckle, CONDYLE + *arthron* joint.]
A member of the order Condylarthra of extinct mammals of the Palaeocene and Eocene periods, the ancestors of some recent ungulates.

condylarthrosis /ˌkɒndɪlɑː'θrəʊsɪs/ *noun*. Pl. **-throses** /-'θrəʊsiːz/. M19.
[ORIGIN from CONDYLE + ARTHROSIS.]
ANATOMY. (A) condyloid articulation.

condyle /'kɒndɪl, -dʌɪl/ *noun*. M17.
[ORIGIN French from Latin *condylus* from Greek *kondulos* knuckle.]
ANATOMY. A rounded usu. cartilage-covered process at the end of a bone, articulating with another bone.
OCCIPITAL *condyle*.
■ **condylar** *adjective* of or pertaining to a condyle L19. **condyloid** *adjective* resembling, pertaining to, or (of articulation) involving a condyle M18.

condyloma /kɒndɪ'ləʊmə/ *noun*. Pl. **-mas**, **-mata** /-mətə/. LME.
[ORIGIN Latin from Greek *kondulōma* callous knob or lump, from *kondulos*: see CONDYLE, -OMA.]
MEDICINE. A large papilloma or warty growth of the skin, usu. in the genital region, of viral or syphilitic origin.
■ **condylomatous** *adjective* of the nature of a condyloma M19.

Condy's fluid /'kɒndɪz 'fluːɪd/ *noun phr.* M19.
[ORIGIN Henry Bollmann *Condy*, 19th-cent. English chemical manufacturer.]
A strong solution of sodium manganate or permanganate, used as a disinfectant.

cone /kəʊn/ *noun*. LME.
[ORIGIN French *cône* from Latin *conus* from Greek *kōnos* pine cone, geometrical cone, apex, etc.]
▸ **I 1** †**a** An apex, a vertex, an angle. LME–E18. ▸**b** The pointed tip of a helmet etc. E17.
2 A more or less conical reproductive structure found in the conifers and related plants, consisting of overlapping scales; a strobilus. M16.
3 MATH. A surface or solid figure generated by the straight lines drawn from a fixed point (the vertex) to a circle or other closed curve in a plane not containing the vertex. M16.
oblique circular cone, **oblique cone**: in which the vertex does not lie perpendicularly above the centre of the circle. **right circular cone**, **right cone**: in which the vertex lies perpendicularly above the centre of the circle. ***scalene cone***: see SCALENE *adjective* 1.
4 A cocoon. Now *rare* or *obsolete*. L18.
▸ **II** *transf.* from sense 3.
5 Any object or structure having a shape resembling that of a geometrical cone; a conical mass *of* any substance. L16.
null cone: see NULL *adjective*. PYROMETRIC **cone**. SEGER CONE. ***Southern Cone***: see SOUTHERN *adjective*. ***Staffordshire cone***: see STAFFORDSHIRE 1.
6 In full ***cone shell***. (The conical shell of) a marine gastropod of the family Conidae and esp. of the genus *Conus*. L18.
textile cone: see TEXTILE *adjective* 1.
7 A cone-shaped mountain or peak; *esp.* one of volcanic origin. M19.
8 ANATOMY. Any of the cone-shaped red-, green-, or blue-sensitive cells in the retina of the eye which function best in bright light and are essential for acute vision. Cf. ROD *noun* 9b. M19.
9 A black conical object hoisted by coastguards as a gale warning, the position of the cone conveying information about wind direction etc. M19.
10 = CORNET *noun*[1] 3b. E20.
11 A conical marker used to direct traffic. M20.
– COMB.: **coneflower** any of several N. American plants belonging to the genus *Rudbeckia* and related genera of the composite family, having flowers with conelike centres; **cone-in-cone** GEOLOGY a structure of concentric cones displayed by some concretions in sedimentary rocks, due to crystallization around an axis; **cone sheet** GEOLOGY a discordant igneous intrusion or dyke (usu. one of a concentric series), having the form of an inverted hollow cone; ***cone shell***: see sense 6 above; **cone wheat** = RIVET *noun*[2].
■ **conelike** *adjective* resembling (that of) a cone, cone-shaped, conical M17.

cone /kəʊn/ *verb*. L15.
[ORIGIN from the noun.]
1 *verb trans.* Shape like a cone; provide with a cone. Chiefly as ***coned*** *ppl adjective*. L15.
2 *verb intrans.* Of a tree: bear or produce cones. L19.
3 *verb trans.* Concentrate a number of searchlight beams (or streams of tracer shells) upon (an aircraft). M20.
4 *verb trans.* Mark or close *off* (an area, esp. of road) with conical markers. L20.
■ **coning** *verbal noun* (**a**) the action of the verb; the condition of being coned, esp. (of a wheel) in having a tapering tread; (**b**) the slanting upwards of helicopter rotor blades when in motion: M19.

conessine /kə'nɛsiːn/ *noun*. M19.
[ORIGIN from *Conessi* (see below) + -INE[5].]
A bitter alkaloid, $C_{24}H_{40}N_2$, obtained chiefly from the seeds and bark of an Asian tree, *Holarrhena* (formerly *Conessi*) *antidysenterica*, and used to treat amoebic dysentery.

Conestoga /kɒnɪ'stəʊgə/ *noun & adjective*. Pl. **-s**, (in sense 1, also) same. L17.
[ORIGIN Prob. from Iroquoian; in senses 2 & 3 from *Conestoga*, a town in Pennsylvania.]
1 A member of, of or pertaining to, an Iroquoian people formerly inhabiting parts of Pennsylvania and Maryland. Also called ***Susquehannock***. L17.
2 In full ***Conestoga wagon***. A large travelling wagon. *obsolete* exc. N. AMER. HISTORY. E18.
3 A heavy American breed of horse. Also ***Conestoga horse*** etc. E19.

coney *noun* see CONY.

confab /'kɒnfab/ *noun & verb*. *colloq.* E18.
[ORIGIN Abbreviation.]
▸ **A** *noun*. = CONFABULATION 1. E18.
▸ **B** *verb intrans.* Infl. **-bb-**. = CONFABULATE 1. M18.

confabulate /kən'fabjʊleɪt/ *verb intrans.* E17.
[ORIGIN Latin *confabulat-* pa. ppl stem of *confabulari* to converse, formed as CON-, FABLE *verb*: see -ATE[3].]
1 Converse together, chat (*with*). E17.
2 PSYCHIATRY. Fabricate imaginary experiences as a compensation for loss of memory. E20.
■ **confabulator** *noun* a person who confabulates M17. **confabulatory** *adjective* of confabulation; chatty, colloquial: M17.

confabulation /kənfabjʊ'leɪʃ(ə)n/ *noun*. LME.
[ORIGIN Latin *confabulatio(n-)*, formed as CONFABULATE: see -ATION.]
1 Talking together, conversation, chat; a familiar conversation. LME.

M. KEANE Delicious confabulations with her sisters on the endless subject of clothes. P. L. FERMOR After some whispered confabulation, they decided to have pity on me.

2 PSYCHIATRY. The invention of imaginary experiences to fill gaps in memory; an account so fabricated. E20.

confarreation /kənfarɪ'eɪʃ(ə)n/ *noun*. L16.
[ORIGIN Latin *confarreatio(n-)*, from *confarreat-* pa. ppl stem of *confarreare* unite in marriage by offering bread, formed as CON- + *farreum* spelt-cake: see -ATION.]
ROMAN HISTORY. The highest and most solemn form of marriage among the patricians of ancient Rome, made by offering a cake made of spelt in the presence of the Pontifex Maximus or Flamen Dialis and ten witnesses. Cf. DIFFARREATION.

confect /'kɒnfɛkt/ *noun*. E16.
[ORIGIN medieval Latin *confectum*, *-ta* use as noun of pa. pple of *conficere*: see CONFECT *verb*. Cf. COMFIT.]
A confection, a comfit.

confect /kən'fɛkt/ *verb trans.* Now chiefly *literary*. LME.
[ORIGIN Latin *confect-* pa. ppl stem of *conficere* put together, formed as CON- + *facere* make.]
1 Put together from various ingredients, make up. LME.

BACON The Confecting of the Ointment. D. ATTENBOROUGH Faked monsters . . confected in the Far East from bits and pieces of dissimilar creatures and . . sold to gullible travellers.

2 Make into a confection; prepare (food). Now *rare* or *obsolete*. LME.

confection /kən'fɛkʃ(ə)n/ *noun*. ME.
[ORIGIN Old French & mod. French from Latin *confectio(n-)* preparation, formed as CONFECT *verb*: see -ION.]
1 A preparation made by mixing; *esp.* a medicinal preparation of various drugs (often with a sweetening and preserving agent). Now *rare* or *obsolete* exc. as below. ME. ▸**b** A prepared dish or delicacy; *esp.* a sweet preparation of fruit, spices, sugar, chocolate, etc. Also *fig.*, a light and pleasing piece of music, literature, etc. LME. ▸†**c** A deadly potion. L15–M17.

b *fig.*: J. CAREY He knew he could manufacture the high-souled confection that his readers wanted.

2 Making or preparation by mixture of ingredients; mixing, compounding; the making of preserves or confectionery. LME.

THACKERAY Pots of jam of her confection.

†**3** State of preparation; composition, constitution. LME–L17.
4 A fashionable article of women's dress. (Orig. a Gallicism.) L19.

G. HEYER A dazzling confection with a high crown, a huge, upstanding poke-front, pomona green ribbons, and . . ostrich plumes.

confection /kən'fɛkʃ(ə)n/ *verb trans.* M16.
[ORIGIN from the noun: cf. French *confectionner*.]
1 Make into a confection; make up as a seasoned delicacy etc. M16.
2 Put together (a fashionable article of clothing). (Orig. a Gallicism.) M19.

confectionary /kən'fɛkʃ(ə)n(ə)ri/ *noun & adjective*. L16.
[ORIGIN from CONFECTION *noun* + -ARY[1]. Cf. medieval Latin *confectionarius* a maker of confections, apothecary.]
▸ **A** *noun*. **1** A confection, a sweet delicacy. Now *rare*. L16.
†**2** A maker of confections. E–M17.
3 A place where confections are kept or prepared. Now *rare*. E17.
4 The art or business of a confectioner, confectionery. *non-standard*. M18.
▸ **B** *adjective*. Of the nature of a confection; of or pertaining to confections or confectionery. M17.

confectioner /kən'fɛkʃ(ə)nə/ *noun*. L16.
[ORIGIN from CONFECTION *verb* + -ER[1].]
A maker of confections, cakes, chocolates, pastries, etc., now esp. for public sale.

confectionery /kən'fɛkʃ(ə)n(ə)ri/ *noun*. M18.
[ORIGIN from CONFECTIONER + -Y[3]: see -ERY.]
1 A thing, *collect.* things, made or sold by a confectioner. M18.
2 The art or business of a confectioner (cf. CONFECTIONARY *noun* 4); a confectioner's shop. E19.

†**confeder** *verb trans. & intrans.* LME–E17.
[ORIGIN Old French & mod. French *confédérer* from Latin *confoederare*: see CONFEDERATION.]
= CONFEDERATE *verb*.

confederacy /kən'fɛd(ə)rəsi/ *noun*. LME.
[ORIGIN Anglo-Norman, Old French *confederacie*, from stem of *confederer*, *confederacion*: see CONFEDERATION, -ACY.]
1 A union between persons, groups, states, etc., for mutual support or joint action; a league, an alliance. LME. ▸**b** A league etc. for an unlawful purpose; a conspiracy. LME.

W. ROBERTSON A general confederacy against the Ottoman power.

2 The condition or fact of being confederate; union for joint action; conspiracy. LME.

V. SACKVILLE-WEST They looked at each other with a glance of confederacy.

3 A collective body of people, groups, etc., united by league; *esp.* a union of states, a confederation. L17.

W. IRVING The literary world is made up of little confederacies.

confederal /kən'fɛd(ə)r(ə)l/ *adjective*. L18.
[ORIGIN from CONFEDERATION after *federal*.]
Pertaining to a confederation, *spec.* (US HISTORY) to the early organization of the US under the Articles of Confederation of 1781.

confederate /kən'fɛd(ə)rət/ *adjective & noun*. LME.
[ORIGIN Late (eccl.) Latin *confoederatus*, formed as CON- + FEDERATE *adjective*.]
▸ **A** *adjective*. **1** Allied; united in a confederacy. LME.
2 *hist.* (**C-**.) Designating, of, or pertaining to the eleven southern states of the US that seceded from the Union 1861–65. M19.
▸ **B** *noun*. **1** A person confederated with another or others; an ally; a conspirator, an accomplice. L15.
2 *hist.* (**C-**.) A person belonging to or supporting the Confederate States of America. M19.

confederate /kən'fɛdərеɪt/ *verb trans. & intrans.* **M16.**
[**ORIGIN** Prob. from **CONFEDERATE** *adjective & noun*: see **-ATE**[3].]
Bring, form, or come into a league, alliance, confederacy, or conspiracy (*with*).
■ **confederator** *noun* (now *rare* or *obsolete*) [Anglo-Norman *confederatour*] a confederate, a conspirator **LME.**

confederation /kənfɛdə'reɪʃ(ə)n/ *noun.* **LME.**
[**ORIGIN** Old French *confederacion* (mod. *-tion*) or late Latin *confederatio(n-)*, from Latin *confederat-* pa. ppl stem of *confoederare*, formed as **CON-** + *foederare* league together, from *foedus*, *foeder-* league, treaty.]
1 The action of confederating; the condition of being confederated: union (esp. of states) for mutual support or joint action; a league, an alliance. **LME.**
2 A number of parties united in an alliance or league; *esp.* a body of states joined in more or less permanent union. **E17.**
– **PHRASES**: **articles of confederation** provisions by which parties confederate; *spec.* (*US HISTORY*) those adopted by the thirteen original colonies at the Continental Congress of 1777.

confederative /kən'fɛd(ə)rətɪv/ *adjective.* **E19.**
[**ORIGIN** French *confédératif*, *-ive*, from *confédération*: see **CONFEDERATION**, **-IVE**.]
Of or relating to confederates or confederating.

confer /kən'fəː/ *verb.* Infl. **-rr-**. **LME.**
[**ORIGIN** Latin *conferre*, formed as **CON-** + *ferre* bring.]
†**1** *verb trans.* Bring together, gather, collect. **LME–E17.**
2 *verb intrans.* Converse, hold conference, take counsel, (*with*). **LME.** ▸†**b** *verb trans.* Discuss. **M16–L17.**
†**3** *verb intrans.* Contribute (*unto*, *to*). **E16–E18.**
†**4** *verb trans.* Bring into comparison (*with*). **E16–M18.**
5 *verb trans.* Give, grant, or bestow (a title, degree, favour, etc.). (Foll. by *on*, *upon*, †*to*, †*unto*.) **M16.**

> **SHAKES.** *Temp.* Confer fair Milan With all the honours on my brother. **H. JAMES** The character conferred on the scene by a cold spring rain. **R. SCRUTON** The Rent Acts confer powers to interfere in contractual bargaining.

■ **confe'ree** *noun* a participant in a conference; the recipient of a grant, honour, etc.: **L18.** **conferment** *noun* the action of granting or bestowing **M17.** **conferrable** *adjective* that may be conferred **M17.** **conferrer** *noun* **M16.**

conference /'kɒnf(ə)r(ə)ns/ *noun & verb.* **E16.**
[**ORIGIN** French *conférence*, or medieval Latin *conferentia*, formed as **CONFER** + **-ENCE**.]
▸ **A** *noun.* **1** Orig., conversation, talk. Now, the action of conversing or taking counsel on serious or important matters. **E16.** ▸**b** (The facility for) telephonic conversation among more than two people on separate lines. Usu. *attrib.* **M20.**

> **SHAKES.** *Jul. Caes.* Nor with such free and friendly conference As . . of old. **S. LEWIS** There was a conference of four union officials as to whether the . . coal-miners . . should strike.

news conference, ***press conference***, etc. **in conference** engaged in consultation, at a meeting.
†**2** Bringing together, collection; collation, comparison. **M16–M17.**
3 A formal (esp. annual) meeting held by any organization, association, etc., for consultation and discussion. **L16.**
Lambeth Conference: see **LAMBETH** 1.
4 (**C-**.) (The annual assembly of) the central governing body of the Methodist Church or of some other religious groups. **M18.**
5 = **CONFERRENCE**. **M19.**
6 An association in commerce (esp. of shipping companies) etc.; an association of sports teams or athletic clubs which usually play each other. **L19.**
7 (Usu. **C-**.) A late variety of pear with a flecked dark green skin. **L19.**
– **COMB.**: **conference centre** a building or complex for the holding of conferences; a place where a conference is held.
▸ **B** *verb intrans.* Confer; hold or attend a conference. Freq. as ***conferencing*** *verbal noun.* **M19.**

conférencier /kɔ̃ferɑ̃sje/ *noun.* Pl. pronounced same. **L19.**
[**ORIGIN** French.]
A lecturer, a public speaker; a (leading) member of a conference; a compère.

conferential /kɒnfə'rɛnʃ(ə)l/ *adjective.* **M19.**
[**ORIGIN** from medieval Latin *conferentia*: see **CONFERENCE**, **-AL**[1].]
Of or relating to (a) conference.

conferral /kən'fəːr(ə)l/ *noun.* Chiefly *US.* **L19.**
[**ORIGIN** formed as **CONFERRENCE** + **-AL**[1].]
Conferment, conferrence; an instance of this.

conferrence /kən'fəːr(ə)ns/ *noun.* **L19.**
[**ORIGIN** from **CONFER** + **-ENCE**.]
Conferment, bestowal, (esp. of degrees). Cf. **CONFERENCE** 5.

conferva /kən'fəːvə/ *noun. obsolete* exc. *hist.* Pl. **-vae** /-viː/. **M18.**
[**ORIGIN** Latin, perh. = comfrey.]
BOTANY. Any of a large group of filamentous cryptogams, esp. simple freshwater green algae, formerly constituting a heterogeneous and variously defined genus *Conferva*.

confess /kən'fɛs/ *verb.* **LME.**
[**ORIGIN** Old French *confesser* from Proto-Romance, from Latin *confessus* pa. pple of *confiteri* acknowledge, formed as **CON-** + *fateri* declare, avow.]
1 *verb trans.* Acknowledge; declare, disclose, (a secret, one's sins, esp. to a priest); admit (a crime, fault, weakness, etc.); concede, grant. Foll. by simple obj., *that*, a person or thing *to be*, †*to have done*, oneself to be. **LME.**

> **SHAKES.** *Per.* I here confess myself the King of Tyre. **E. PEACOCK** A distorted knowledge, it must be confessed, of religious duty. **J. STEINBECK** It would be interesting to know what sins she confessed. **G. F. KENNAN** Instead . . of confessing their real plight, they made efforts to conceal it. **N. MAILER** I must confess that this conversation bores me. **M. BRADBURY** They confessed things to each other.

2 *verb trans.* Acknowledge one's belief in, *that*; acknowledge the character or claims of; admit as legally valid. **LME.**

> **WYCLIF** My soule magnefieþ þe Lord, for I confesse þat he is greet. *Alternative Service Book* Grant that we . . who confess thy name may be united in thy truth.

3 *verb refl. & intrans.* Make a formal confession of one's sins, esp. to a priest. **LME.**

> *Book of Common Prayer* Bewail your own sinful lives, confess yourselves to Almighty God with full purpose of amendment of life. **SHAKES.** *Rom. & Jul.* Come you to make confession to this Father? . . To answer that, I should confess to you.

4 *verb trans.* Of a priest etc.: hear the confession of, act as confessor to. **LME.**
5 *verb trans.* Make known by circumstances; be evidence of; attest. Now *poet.* **L16.**

> **SIR W. SCOTT** Even . . Magnus himself had confessed the influence of the sleepy god.

6 *verb intrans.* Admit the truth of a (criminal) charge. **L16.**
7 *verb intrans.* Foll. by *to*: admit, acknowledge, (a charge, fault, weakness, etc.). **L18.**

> **SOUTHEY** I confess to having made free with his tail and his hoofs and his horns. **G. B. SHAW** A young fellow who is manly enough to confess to an obvious disadvantage.

■ **confessant** *noun* a person who confesses or makes a confession, esp. as a religious duty **E17.** **confessedly** /-sɪdli/ *adverb* admittedly; avowedly: **M17.** **confe'ssee** *noun* a person who is confessed by a priest; the priest to whom a person confesses: **E17.**

confessio /kən'fɛsɪəʊ/ *noun.* Pl. **-os**. **M19.**
[**ORIGIN** medieval Latin *confessio(n-)* **CONFESSION**.]
= **CONFESSION** 8.

confession /kən'fɛʃ(ə)n/ *noun.* **LME.**
[**ORIGIN** Old French & mod. French from Latin *confessio(n-)*, from *confess-* pa. ppl stem of *confiteri* **CONFESS** *verb*: see **-ION**.]
1 The making known or acknowledging of one's own fault, offence, etc.; acknowledgement before proper authority of the truth of a criminal charge. **LME.**

> **L. KENNEDY** It was vital to get confessions; and no attention was paid to recantations afterwards.

2 The acknowledging of sin or sinfulness with repentance and desire of absolution, either as a formal public religious act or privately to a priest as a religious duty. **LME.**

> **F. MCCOURT** Surely I'm in a state of grace just for going to confession.

3 Concession of the truth of a statement, agreement. Now *rare* or *obsolete.* **LME.**
4 The declaration of a belief; avowal, profession (of faith etc.). **LME.**
5 That which is confessed; the matter confessed; *esp.* a statement of one's guilt in a crime etc. **LME.**
6 That part of the public litany of most Christian Churches in which a general acknowledgement of sinfulness is made. **LME.**
7 In full ***confession of faith***. A statement setting out essential religious doctrine, a creed; a statement of one's principles in any matter. **M16.** ▸**b** The body of people sharing a confession of faith. **M17.**
8 A tomb in which a martyr etc. is buried, the whole structure erected over such a tomb; a part of, or the crypt or shrine under, the altar in which relics are placed. **L17.**
■ **confessionary** *noun* †(**a**) = **CONFESSIONAL** *noun* 2; (**b**) = **CONFESSION** 8: **M17.** **confessionary** *adjective* of or pertaining to confession **E17.** **confessionist** *noun* an adherent of a particular religious confession or sect **M16.** **confessionless** *adjective* without a confession; faithless: **L19.**

confessional /kən'fɛʃ(ə)n(ə)l/ *noun.* **L16.**
[**ORIGIN** French from Italian *confessionale* from medieval Latin *confessionale* neut. sing. of adjective *confessionalis*, from *confessio(n-)*: see **CONFESSION**, **-AL**[1].]
†**1** A payment for hearing or giving permission to hear confession. Only in **L16.**
2 A stall, desk, etc., where a priest (usu. of the Roman Catholic Church) hears confessions. **E18.** ▸**b** The act or practice of confessing to a priest. **E19.**

confessional /kən'fɛʃ(ə)n(ə)l/ *adjective.* **LME.**
[**ORIGIN** from **CONFESSION** + **-AL**[1].]
1 Of the nature of or pertaining to confession. **LME.**
2 Of or pertaining to confessions of faith or doctrinal systems; denominational; holding or according with certain doctrines or beliefs. **L19.**

confessor /kən'fɛsə, *in sense 3 also* 'kɒnfɛsə/ *noun.* **OE.**
[**ORIGIN** Anglo-Norman *confessur*, Old French *confessour* (mod. *-eur*) from ecclesiastical Latin *confessor*, from *confess-*: see **CONFESSION**, **-OR**.]
1 A person avowing his religion in the face of danger, and adhering to it despite persecution, but not suffering martyrdom. **OE.**
Edward the Confessor, **the Confessor** Edward, King of England 1042–66, canonized in 1161.
2 A person who makes confession or public acknowledgement of religious belief etc., or (later) of a crime, sin, etc. **ME.**
3 A priest who hears confessions. **ME.**
■ **confe'ssorial** *adjective* of or pertaining to a confessor **M19.** **confessorship** *noun* the function or office of confessor **M17.**

confetti /kən'fɛti/ *noun* (orig. *pl.* but now usu. treated as *sing.*). **E19.**
[**ORIGIN** Italian, pl. of *confetto* **COMFIT**.]
Coloured paper shapes showered on the bride and bridegroom by the guests at a wedding. In Italy (the earlier sense), real or imitation bonbons thrown during carnival etc.

confidant /kɒnfɪ'dant, 'kɒnfɪdant/ *noun.* Fem. & in sense 2 **-ante**. **M17.**
[**ORIGIN** Alt. of **CONFIDENT** *noun*, prob. to repr. pronunc. of French *confidente*: see **CONFIDENT**, **-ANT**[1].]
1 A person entrusted with knowledge of one's private affairs (orig. esp. one's love affairs) or thoughts. **M17.**
2 A type of settee usu. with seats at each end separated from the main seat by upholstered divisions. Also, a sociable. **L18.**

confide /kən'fʌɪd/ *verb.* **LME.**
[**ORIGIN** Latin *confidere*, formed as **CON-** + *fidere* trust.]
1 *verb intrans.* Trust or have faith; place trust or confidence *in*. **LME.**

> **HOBBES** Some other whom they confide in for protection.

2 *verb intrans. & trans.* Trust, believe, have confidence, (*that*). *arch.* **L15.**

> **T. JEFFERSON** They confide that the next election gives a decided majority in the two Houses.

3 *verb trans.* Impart as a secret or in confidence *to* (now also *in*) a person; entrust (an object of care, a task, etc.) *to*. **M18.**

> **E. M. FORSTER** He was confiding secrets to people whom he had scarcely seen. **J. REED** One confided to me . . that the counter-revolution would begin at midnight. **J. W. KRUTCH** He must . . confide his destiny to the whims of developing technology. **A. HALEY** To confide in his mother something he had kept carefully guarded from anyone.

4 *verb intrans.* Foll. by *in*: take (a person) into one's confidence, talk confidentially to. **L19.**

> **S. BELLOW** We no longer confide in each other; in fact, there are many things I could not mention to her.

■ **confider** *noun* **M17.** **confiding** *adjective* †(**a**) trusty, trustworthy; (**b**) trustful; imparting or inclined to impart confidences: **M17.** **confidingly** *adverb* **L19.** **confidingness** *noun* **L17.**

confidence /'kɒnfɪd(ə)ns/ *noun & verb.* **LME.**
[**ORIGIN** Latin *confidentia*, from *confident-* pres. ppl stem of *confidere* **CONFIDE**: see **-ENCE**. Cf. Old French & mod. French *confidence*.]
▸ **A** *noun.* **1** Firm trust, reliance, faith (*in*). **LME.**

> **SHAKES.** *Rich. II* The King reposeth all his confidence in thee. **H. JAMES** She had but a limited confidence in her brother's judgement.

level of confidence: see **LEVEL** *noun* 4d. ***vote of confidence***, ***vote of no confidence***: see **VOTE** *noun*.
2 Assurance arising from reliance on oneself, circumstances, etc.; self-reliance, boldness. **LME.** ▸**b** Excessive assurance; presumption, impudence. *arch.* **L16.**

> **S. JOHNSON** He . . was able to address those whom he never saw before with ease and confidence. **M. DRABBLE** The dress gave me a certain superficial confidence. **D. ADAMS** Feeling that he was the most important person in the Universe gave him the confidence to believe that something would turn up. **b** **S. PEPYS** Willetts confidence in sitting cheek by jowl by us.

3 A source of trust. *arch.* **LME.**

> **AV** *Prov.* 3:26 For the Lord shalbe thy confidence.

4 Assured expectation; the state of feeling certain (*of*). **M16.**

> **W. TEMPLE** The very Confidence of Victory . . makes Armies victorious.

5 The confiding of private matters with mutual trust; confidential intimacy. **L16.**
in confidence confidentially, as a secret. **in the confidence of** allowed to know the private thoughts or affairs of. **take into one's confidence** confide in.
†**6** Trustworthiness. **M17–E19.**
person of confidence a confidential agent.

7 A confidential communication. **M18.**

B. CASTLE Elizabeth tends to make a lot of confidences at these times.

– **COMB.**: **confidence coefficient** *STATISTICS* the particular probability used in defining a confidence interval, representing the likelihood that the interval will contain the parameter; **confidence game** *US* = *confidence trick* below; **confidence interval** *STATISTICS* a range of values so defined that there is a specified probability that the value of a parameter of a population lies within it; **confidence level** = *confidence coefficient* above; **confidence limit** *STATISTICS* either of the extreme values of a confidence interval; **confidence man**: who practises a confidence trick; **confidence trick** a swindle in which the victim is persuaded to entrust money or valuables to the swindler; **confidence trickster** a person who practises a confidence trick.

▸ **B** *verb trans.* Swindle by means of a confidence trick. *US slang*. **L19.**

■ Also **confidency** *noun* (*rare*) **E17.**

confident /ˈkɒnfɪd(ə)nt/ *adjective & noun*. **L16.**

[**ORIGIN** In sense 1 from Latin *confident-* (see **CONFIDENCE**); in later senses and as noun from French *confident(e)* from Italian *confidente* from Latin.]

▸ **A** *adjective*. †**1** Trustful, confiding. **L16–M17.**

2 Having firm trust or expectation; fully assured, certain. (Foll. by *of*, *in*, *that*.) **L16.**

SHAKES. *Cymb.* Confident I am Last night 'twas on mine arm. G. VIDAL My father died, confident that death did not exist.

3 Self-reliant, bold; sure of oneself, one's course, etc.; having no fear of failure. **L16.** ▸**b** Overbold; presumptuous, impudent. *arch.* **L16.** ▸**c** Assertive; dogmatic. **E17.**

S. JOHNSON His accusers were confident and loud. N. ALGREN He left with a confident, executive stride, a man who'd be rich in six weeks if not in five. **b** HENRY FIELDING A confident slut. **c** G. BERKELEY Your confident and positive way of talking.

†**4** Trustworthy, dependable. **E17–E18.**

5 Confidential, entrusted with secrets. Now *rare* or *obsolete*. **E17.**

▸ **B** *noun*. A person in whom another confides; a confidant. **E17.**

■ **confidently** *adverb* **L16.**

confidential /kɒnfɪˈdɛnʃ(ə)l/ *adjective*. **M17.**

[**ORIGIN** from **CONFIDENT** + **-IAL**, infl. by **CONFIDENCE**.]

†**1** Confident, bold. *rare*. **M–L17.**

2 Indicating private intimacy; inclined to impart confidences, confiding. **M18.**

3 Spoken or written in confidence; not intended for public knowledge. **L18.**

J. SYMONS Although it was supposed to be confidential information he saw no harm in repeating it.

4 Enjoying another's confidence; entrusted with secrets; charged with a secret task. **E19.**

■ **confidentiˈality** *noun* **M19.** **confidentially** *adverb* in a confidential manner; as a confidence: **L17.** **confidentialness** *noun* **L19.**

configurate /kənˈfɪɡjʊreɪt/ *verb trans.* Now *rare*. **M16.**

[**ORIGIN** Latin *configurat-* pa. ppl stem of *configurare*: see **CONFIGURE**, **-ATE**[3].]

Frame; give a configuration to.

■ **configurative** /-rətɪv/ *adjective* of or pertaining to configuration **L18.**

configuration /kənfɪɡəˈreɪʃ(ə)n, -ɡjʊ-/ *noun*. **M16.**

[**ORIGIN** Latin *configuratio(n-)*, formed as **CONFIGURATE**: see **-ATION**. Cf. Old French & mod. French *configuration*.]

1 *ASTRONOMY & ASTROLOGY.* Relative position, apparent or actual, of celestial objects; *esp.* = **ASPECT** *noun* 4. **M16.**

2 *gen.* The (result of) arrangement of the parts or elements of something; internal structure, conformation, outline. **M17.**

3 *CHEMISTRY.* The fixed three-dimensional relationship of the atoms in a molecule. **L19.**

4 *PHYSICS.* The distribution of electrons among the energy levels of an atom, or of nucleons among the energy levels of a nucleus, as specified by quantum numbers. **E20.**

5 *PSYCHOLOGY.* = **GESTALT**. **E20.**

6 *COMPUTING.* The configuring of (the constituent parts of) a computer system; the way the constituent parts of a computer system are configured, the units or devices required for this. **M20.**

■ **configurational** *adjective* **E20.** **configurationally** *adverb* **E20.** **configurationism** *noun* a theory that stresses configurations, *esp.* gestalt psychology **E20.**

configure /kənˈfɪɡə/ *verb trans.* **LME.**

[**ORIGIN** Latin *configurare* fashion after a pattern, formed as **CON-** + *figurare* **FIGURE** *verb*.]

1 Fashion according *to* a model (esp. with allus. to *Philippians* 3:10). Now *rare*. **LME.**

2 Put together in a certain configuration; shape, fashion. **M17.**

3 *spec.* *COMPUTING.* Interconnect or interrelate (a computer system or elements of it) so as to fit it for a designated task. **M20.**

confine /ˈkɒnfʌɪn, *poet. also* kɒnˈfʌɪn/ *noun*. **LME.**

[**ORIGIN** French *confins*, †*confines*, from Latin *confinia* pl. of *confine* and *confinium*, from *confinis* bordering, formed as **CON-** + *finis* end, limit (pl. *fines* territory). Branch II from Latin *confinis* noun from adjective.]

▸ **I 1** A boundary, a frontier, a limit, a borderland, (*lit.* & *fig.*). Usu. in *pl.* **LME.**

R. L. STEVENSON That . . sort of tragedy which lies on the confines of farce. P. S. BUCK His heart swelled and stopped as though it met sudden confines. B. LOVELL Star systems . . outside the confines of the Milky Way.

†**2** A region, a territory. Usu. in *pl.* **LME–L17.**

3 Confinement, limitation. *poet.* **L16.** ▸**b** A place of confinement. Now *rare*. **E17.**

R. BURNS Think on the dungeon's grim confine.

▸ †**II 4** In *pl.* Neighbours. **M–L16.**

■ **confineless** *adjective* (*rare*) unlimited **E17.**

confine /kənˈfʌɪn/ *verb*. **E16.**

[**ORIGIN** French *confiner*, formed as **CONFINE** *noun*, prob. after Italian *confinare*.]

1 a *verb intrans.* Have a common boundary *with*; border *on*, be adjacent *to*. Now *rare*. **E16.** ▸†**b** *verb trans.* Border on. Only in 17.

†**2** *verb trans.* Banish. **L16–M17.**

3 *verb trans.* Keep in a place, *within* or *to* limits or a defined area; restrict, secure. (*lit.* & *fig.*) **L16.** ▸**b** Shut up, imprison (*in*, †*into*). **E17.**

B. T. WASHINGTON He . . had to confine himself to the deck of the ship. W. S. CHURCHILL In the Middle Ages education had largely been confined to training the clergy. J. UPDIKE Border patrols have been instituted to confine the nomads. **b** SHAKES. *Temp.* She did confine thee . . Into a cloven pine. C. S. FORESTER It is here that the slaves were confined during the middle passage.

4 *verb trans.* Oblige (a person) to remain indoors, in bed, etc., through illness, bad weather, etc. (Foll. by *to*.) Usu. in *pass.* **M17.** ▸**b** In *pass.* Be in childbirth. **L18.**

G. BERKELEY I have been confined three weeks by gout. P. BARKER Gradually . . her health got worse, until she was confined to the house and almost bedridden.

■ **confinable** *adjective* able to be confined (earlier in **UNCONFINABLE**) **E17.** **confined** *adjective* that has been confined; (of a space) cramped, restricted: **L16.** **confinedly** /-nɪdli/ *adverb* (earlier in **UNCONFINEDLY**) **L17.** **confinedness** /-nɪdnɪs/ *noun* **M17.**

confinement /kənˈfʌɪnm(ə)nt/ *noun*. **M17.**

[**ORIGIN** from **CONFINE** *verb* + **-MENT**.]

1 The action of confining; the state or condition of being confined; imprisonment; restriction, limitation. **M17.**

solitary confinement: see **SOLITARY** *adjective*.

2 The condition of being in childbirth; delivery, *accouchement*. **L18.**

confiner /kənˈfʌɪnə/ *noun*. **L16.**

[**ORIGIN** from **CONFINE** *noun* or *verb* + **-ER**[1].]

†**1** A borderer, a neighbour. **L16–L17.**

†**2** An inhabitant. **L16–E17.**

3 A person who or thing which confines. *rare*. **M17.**

confinity /kənˈfɪnɪti/ *noun*. Now *rare*. **M16.**

[**ORIGIN** Old French & mod. French *confinité* or medieval Latin *confinitas*, from *confinis*: see **CONFINE** *noun*, **-ITY**.]

The position of bordering, contiguity.

confirm /kənˈfəːm/ *verb trans.* **ME.**

[**ORIGIN** Old French *confermer* (later *confirmer*) from Latin *confirmare*, formed as **CON-** + *firmare* strengthen, from *firmus* **FIRM** *adjective*.]

1 Make firm or firmer; establish (power, possession, etc.) more firmly, settle. **ME.**

SHAKES. *1 Hen. VI* His alliance will confirm our peace.

2 Make valid by formal assent; ratify, sanction; ratify the appointment etc. of (a person) *to* or *in* a position etc.; ratify the bestowal etc. of (a dignity, estate, etc.) *to* a person. **ME.**

R. HOLINSHED He was confirmed bishop of Couentrie. SHAKES. *3 Hen. VI* Confirm the crown to me and to mine heirs. GIBBON This modest sentence was confirmed by the emperor.

3 Administer the religious rite of confirmation to. **ME.**

4 Strengthen, establish, encourage (a person) *in* a habit, opinion, disposition, etc. Also *absol.* (now *rare*), strengthen morally or (formerly) physically. **ME.**

BYRON To laugh him out of his supposed dismay . . Perhaps . . to confirm him in it. J. RUSKIN Men . . whose hearts [were] confirmed, in the calm of these holy places.

5 Corroborate, verify, put beyond doubt. **LME.**

E. M. FORSTER Inside, the clock struck ten . . . Other clocks confirmed it. A. KOESTLER This suspicion is confirmed by the inquiry. B. BAINBRIDGE Before Adolf could confirm or deny that he had any such problem.

†**6** Affirm, maintain *that*. **LME–M17.**

†**7** Assure, convince. **E17–L18.**

J. FLETCHER We are all confirm'd 'twas a sought quarrel.

■ **confirmaˈbility** *noun* (*PHILOSOPHY*) the quality or condition of being confirmable **M20.** **confirmable** *adjective* able to be confirmed **M17.** **confirˈmand** *noun* a candidate for (religious) confirmation **M18.** **confirmatory** *adjective* tending to confirm; confirmative: **M17.** **confirmed** *adjective* that has been confirmed; firmly established, permanent, unlikely to change, inveterate: **LME.** **confirˈmee** *noun* (**a**) *LAW* a person to whom a confirmation is made; (**b**) *ECCLESIASTICAL* a person who is confirmed: **E17.** **confirmer** *noun* a person who or thing which confirms **L16.** **confirmor** *noun* (*LAW*) a party who confirms a voidable estate etc. **E17.**

confirmation /kɒnfəˈmeɪʃ(ə)n/ *noun*. **ME.**

[**ORIGIN** Old French & mod. French from Latin *confirmatio(n-)*, from *confirmat-* pa. ppl stem of *confirmare*: see **CONFIRM**, **-ATION**.]

1 A rite administered to baptized persons, esp. at the age of discretion to admit to full membership in various Christian Churches. In Judaism, the ceremony of bar mitzvah or bat mitzvah. **ME.**

2 The formal act of ratifying an appointment, election, decision, etc. **ME.**

3 The action of making (more) firm; establishing, settling. **LME.**

4 The action of corroborating or verifying; proof; a confirmatory statement or circumstance. **LME.**

Independent Further confirmation that the economy is in recession.

5 *LAW.* An act by a person ratifying a voidable disposition. **L15.** ▸**b** *SCOTS LAW.* A ratification of the testamentary appointment of an executor, or the first appointment for a case of intestacy, by court order. **L15.**

– **COMB.**: **confirmation theory** inductive logic.

confirmative /kənˈfəːmətɪv/ *noun & adjective*. **L16.**

[**ORIGIN** Latin *confirmativus* adjective, from *confirmat-*: see **CONFIRMATION**, **-IVE**.]

▸ †**A** *noun*. A thing that expresses confirmation. Only in **L16.**

▸ **B** *adjective*. Having the property of confirming. **M17.**

■ **confirmatively** *adverb* **M19.**

confiscate /ˈkɒnfɪskeɪt/ *verb trans.* Pa. pple & ppl adjective **-ated**, (*arch.*) **-ate** /-ət/. **M16.**

[**ORIGIN** Latin *confiscat-* pa. ppl stem of *confiscare*, formed as **CON-** + *fiscus* chest, treasury: see **-ATE**[3].]

1 Appropriate to the public treasury (as a penalty); adjudge to be forfeited to the state. **M16.**

2 Deprive of property as forfeited to the state. *arch.* **E17.**

3 Seize as by authority or summarily. **E19.**

A. MCCOWEN When he discovered me reading Dostoievsky . . he turned white and confiscated the book.

■ **conˈfiscable** *adjective* liable to confiscation **M18.** **confiˈscatable** *adjective* **M19.** **confiscator** *noun* a person who confiscates **M18.** **confiscatory** /kɒnˈfɪskət(ə)ri/ *adjective* of the nature of or tending to confiscation **L18.**

confiscation /kɒnfɪˈskeɪʃ(ə)n/ *noun*. **L15.**

[**ORIGIN** Latin *confiscatio(n-)*, formed as **CONFISCATE**: see **-ATION**.]

1 The action of **CONFISCATE** *verb*; seizure (of property) as legally forfeited, summary appropriation. **L15.** ▸**b** Unjust seizure; robbery under legal sanction. **M19.**

2 Confiscated property. *rare*. **L18.**

†**confisk** *verb trans.* **LME–E17.**

[**ORIGIN** Old French *confisquer* from Latin *confiscare*: see **CONFISCATE**.]

= **CONFISCATE**.

confitent /ˈkɒnfɪt(ə)nt/ *noun*. **E17.**

[**ORIGIN** Latin *confitent-* pres. ppl stem of *confiteri*: see **CONFESS**, **-ENT**.]

A person who confesses; a penitent.

Confiteor /kɒnˈfɪtɪɔː/ *noun*. **ME.**

[**ORIGIN** Latin = I confess, first word of the formula *Confiteor Deo Omnipotenti* I confess to Almighty God, etc.]

ROMAN CATHOLIC CHURCH. A form of prayer confessing sins, used in the Mass and some other sacraments.

confiture /ˈkɒnfɪtjʊə; *foreign* kɔ̃fityːr (*pl. same*)/ *noun*. Also †**comf-**. **LME.**

[**ORIGIN** Old French & mod. French, from *confit*: see **COMFIT**, **-URE**. Readopted in 19 from mod. French.]

†**1** A preparation of drugs. *rare*. Only in **LME.**

2 A preparation of preserved fruit etc.; a confection. **M16.**

confix /kənˈfɪks/ *verb trans.* **E17.**

[**ORIGIN** from **CON-** + **FIX** *verb*.]

Fix firmly, fasten.

conflab /ˈkɒnflab/ *noun*. *colloq.* (chiefly *US*). **L19.**

[**ORIGIN** Alt.]

= **CONFAB** *noun*.

conflagrate /ˈkɒnfləɡreɪt/ *verb*. **M17.**

[**ORIGIN** Latin *conflagrat-* pa. ppl stem of *conflagrare* burn up, formed as **CON-** + *flagrare* blaze: see **-ATE**[3].]

1 *verb intrans.* Catch fire. **M17.**

2 *verb trans.* Set ablaze; burn up. **L18.**

■ **conflagrant** /kənˈfleɪɡrənt/ *adjective* on fire, blazing **M17.** **conflagrator** *noun* an incendiary (person) **M17.**

conflagration /kɒnfləˈɡreɪʃ(ə)n/ *noun*. **L15.**

[**ORIGIN** Latin *conflagratio(n-)*, formed as **CONFLAGRATE**: see **-ATION**.]

1 The burning up *of* anything; consumption by fire. **L15.**

HOBBES The day of Judgment, and Conflagration of the present world.

2 A great and destructive fire. **M17.**

P. ACKROYD Warehouse after warehouse going up in the general conflagration.

†**3** *transf.* Severe inflammation; (a) high fever. **L17–E19.**

■ ˈ**conflagrative** *adjective* productive of conflagration **E19.**

conflate /ˈkɒnfleɪt/ *adjective*. **L16.**

[**ORIGIN** Latin *conflatus* pa. pple, formed as **CONFLATE** *verb*: see **-ATE**[2].]

Put together from various elements. Now *spec.* formed by fusion of two textual readings.

conflate /kən'fleɪt/ *verb trans.* LME.
[ORIGIN Latin *conflat-* pa. ppl stem of *conflare* kindle, achieve, fuse, formed as CON- + *flare* blow.]
†**1** Fuse, melt down (metal). LME–M17.
2 Put together; compose; bring about. E17.

D. PIPER Attempts . . to conflate an ideal poet, with Pope's image dominant.

3 Combine, blend (two things, esp. two variant texts etc.) into one. L19.

A. H. MCNEILE The custom of the former [Matthew] was to conflate the language of his sources when they overlapped.

conflation /kən'fleɪʃ(ə)n/ *noun.* LME.
[ORIGIN Late Latin *conflatio(n-)* fanning (of fire), fusion, formed as CONFLATE *verb*: see -ATION.]
The action or process of CONFLATE *verb*; the result of conflating, *esp.* a composite textual reading.

conflict /'kɒnflɪkt/ *noun.* LME.
[ORIGIN Latin *conflictus*, from *conflict-* pa. ppl stem of *confligere* strike together, clash, contend, fight, formed as CON- + *fligere* strike.]
1 A fight, a battle, a (prolonged) struggle between opposing forces (*lit. & fig.*); fighting, strife; the clashing or variance of opposed principles, beliefs, etc.; *PSYCHOLOGY* (the emotional distress due to) the opposition of incompatible wishes etc. in a person. LME.

W. S. CHURCHILL At every point . . the opposing causes came into conflict. JOHN BROOKE The conflict between successive generations is part of the law of life. F. FITZGERALD Many Americans persisted in thinking of the Vietnamese conflict as a civil war. D. HALBERSTAM He felt a powerful conflict of loyalties and interests.

2 Collision (of physical bodies), dashing together. Now *rare*. M16.
■ **conflictful** *adjective* M20. **conflictual** /kən'flɪktʃʊəl/ *adjective* pertaining to, characterized by, or involving conflict M20.

conflict /kən'flɪkt/ *verb.* LME.
[ORIGIN Latin *conflict-*: see CONFLICT *noun*.]
1 *verb intrans.* Fight, struggle (*with*). *lit. & fig.* LME.

W. COWPER These Two with Hector and his host Conflicted.

†**2** *verb trans.* Engage in battle, assault; *fig.* buffet with adversity. L16–M17.
3 *verb intrans.* Of principles, interests, etc.: clash; be incompatible. M17.

T. H. GREEN The perplexities of conscience . . in which duties appear to conflict with each other. H. MOORE Many other artists have had the same two conflicting sides in their natures.

■ **confliction** *noun* the action or condition of conflicting L17. **conflictive** *adjective* (*rare*) of a conflicting nature or tendency M19.

conflow /kɒn'fləʊ/ *verb intrans.* E17.
[ORIGIN from CON- + FLOW *verb*.]
Flow together (*with*).

confluence /'kɒnflʊəns/ *noun.* LME.
[ORIGIN Late Latin *confluentia*, formed as CONFLUENT: see -ENCE.]
1 a A flowing together or union of rivers etc. LME. ▸**b** The place where two or more rivers etc. unite. M16. ▸**c** A combined flow or flood. E17.
2 a A gathering together or flocking of people etc. LME. ▸**b** A numerous concourse or assemblage of people etc.; a multitude. LME.

confluent /'kɒnflʊənt/ *adjective & noun.* L15.
[ORIGIN Latin *confluent-* pres. ppl stem of *confluere*, formed as CON- + *fluere* flow: see -ENT.]
▸ **A** *adjective.* **1** Coalescing with one another so as to form one continuous mass or surface. L15.

C. DARWIN The surrounding dark zones become confluent.

2 Of streams, roads, etc.: flowing or running together so as to form one, uniting. E17.

A. GEIKIE Numerous confluent valleys, whose united waters . . enter the sea.

3 Flowing together in a body. E18.

M. PRIOR The whole ocean's confluent waters swell.

▸ **B** *noun.* †**1** The place where rivers etc. unite. Only in E17.
2 A stream etc. joining another, *spec.* one of nearly equal size. M17.
■ **confluently** *adverb* L19.

conflux /'kɒnflʌks/ *noun.* E17.
[ORIGIN Late Latin *confluxus*, formed as CON- + *fluxus* FLUX *noun*.]
= CONFLUENCE.

confocal /kɒn'fəʊk(ə)l/ *adjective & noun.* M19.
[ORIGIN from CON- + FOCAL.]
▸ **A** *adjective.* Having a common focus or common foci. M19.
▸ **B** *noun.* A figure having the same focus as another. E20.

conform /kən'fɔːm/ *adjective & adverb.* LME.
[ORIGIN French *conforme* from late Latin *conformis*, from Latin CON- + *forma* shape, FORM *noun*.]
▸ **A** *adjective.* **1** = CONFORMABLE *adjective* 1, 2. Now *rare* or *obsolete*. LME.
†**2** Conforming religiously, conformist. M17–E18.
▸ **B** *adverb.* In conformity *with*, *to*. *Scot.* E16.
■ †**conformly** *adverb* LME–M18.

conform /kən'fɔːm/ *verb.* ME.
[ORIGIN Old French & mod. French *conformer* from Latin *conformare*, formed as CON- + *formare* FORM *verb*[1].]
1 *verb trans.* Foll. by *to*: form (something) according to (some model); make like. ME.

R. HOOKER It truly conformeth us unto the image of Jesus Christ.

2 *verb trans.* (freq. *refl.*). Bring into harmony or conformity; adapt. ME.

J. R. LOWELL The life of a nation . . should be conformed to certain principles.

3 *verb intrans.* Act conformably or in conformity *to*; comply with rules or general custom; yield or show compliance. LME. ▸**b** *spec.* Chiefly *hist.* Comply with the usages of the Church of England. E17.

M. MCCARTHY He had tried to conform to an ideal of the English butler. E. FROMM Most people are not even aware of their need to conform.

4 *verb intrans.* Foll. by *to*, *with* (of things): follow in form or nature. L15.

R. DODSLEY The path . . conforms to the water . . accompanying this semicircular lake into another winding valley. H. NEMEROV Bent To conform with the curve of the rim.

†**5** *verb trans.* Bring into accord or mutual agreement. M17–E18.
■ **conformance** *noun* the action of conforming, conformity E17.

conformability /kənfɔːmə'bɪlɪti/ *noun.* M19.
[ORIGIN from CONFORMABLE + -ITY.]
The quality or condition of being conformable; *spec.* (*GEOLOGY*) the relation of strata, one of which rests on, and lies parallel to, the other.

conformable /kən'fɔːməb(ə)l/ *adjective & adverb.* L15.
[ORIGIN medieval Latin *conformabilis*, from *conformare*: see CONFORM *verb*, -ABLE.]
▸ **A** *adjective.* **1** Disposed or accustomed to conform; tractable; compliant *to*. L15. ▸**b** *spec.* Chiefly *hist.* Conforming to the usages of the Church of England. L16.

SHAKES. *Tam. Shr.* And bring you from a wild Kate to a Kate Conformable as other household Kates.

2 According in form or character *to*; similar *to*. E16.

G. BERKELEY The supposed circulation of the sap . . is in no sort conformable or analagous to the circulation of the blood.

3 Corresponding so as to fit; consistent; harmonious; fitting. (Foll. by *to*, *with*.) M16.

J. BUCHAN He felt it necessary to erect his own sanctuary, conformable to his modest but peculiar tastes.

4 *GEOLOGY.* Of strata in contact: lying in the same direction. Of a formation etc.: displaying conformability. E19.
▸ **B** *adverb.* In conformity with; conformably *to*. L16.
■ **conformableness** *noun* M16. **conformably** *adverb* in a conformable manner, in conformity *with*, according *to*, compliantly; *GEOLOGY* with conformability: E16.

conformal /kən'fɔːm(ə)l/ *adjective.* M17.
[ORIGIN In sense 1 from Latin *conformalis*, formed as CON- + *formalis* formal. In sense 2 from German *conform* + -AL[1].]
1 = CONFORMABLE. *rare*. M17.
2 *MATH.* Conserving the size of all angles in the representation of one surface on another; *spec.* (in mapmaking) orthomorphic. L19.
■ **conformally** *adverb* L19.

conformation /kɒnfɔː'meɪʃ(ə)n/ *noun.* E16.
[ORIGIN Latin *conformatio(n-)*, from *conformat-* pa. ppl stem of *conformare* CONFORM *verb*: see -ATION.]
1 The action of coming or bringing into conformity (*to*); adjustment, adaptation (*to*). E16.
2 The forming or fashioning of a thing in all its parts. E17.
3 The manner in which a thing is formed; structure, organization. M17. ▸**b** *CHEMISTRY.* Each of the three-dimensional structures that may be adopted by a particular molecule and can interconvert freely esp. by rotations around single bonds. M20.
– PHRASES: ***vice of conformation***: see VICE *noun*[1] 2b.
■ **conformational** *adjective* M20. **conformationally** *adverb* M20.

conformer /kən'fɔːmə/ *noun*[1]. E17.
[ORIGIN from CONFORM *verb* + -ER[1].]
A person who conforms, a conformist.

conformer /'kɒnfɔːmə/ *noun*[2]. M20.
[ORIGIN from CONFOR(MATIONAL + ISO)MER.]
CHEMISTRY. A form of a compound having a particular molecular conformation.

conformism /kən'fɔːmɪz(ə)m/ *noun.* E20.
[ORIGIN French *conformisme* or from (the same root as) CONFORMIST + -ISM. Cf. earlier NONCONFORMISM.]
The action, practice, or principle of conforming; belief in conforming.

conformist /kən'fɔːmɪst/ *noun & adjective.* M17.
[ORIGIN from CONFORM *verb* + -IST.]
▸ **A** *noun.* A person who conforms *to* any usage or practice; *spec.* (chiefly *hist.*) a person who conforms to the usages of the Church of England. (Cf. NONCONFORMIST.) M17.
occasional conformist: see OCCASIONAL *adjective* 1.
▸ **B** *adjective.* That conforms; of or pertaining to conformists. M17.

conformity /kən'fɔːmɪti/ *noun.* LME.
[ORIGIN Old French & mod. French *conformité* or late Latin *conformitas*, from *conformare*: see CONFORM *verb*, -ITY.]
1 Correspondence in form or manner (*to*, *with*); agreement in character; likeness; congruity. LME.
2 Action in accordance with some standard; compliance (*with*, *to*); acquiescence; an instance of this. L15. ▸**b** *spec.* Chiefly *hist.* Compliance with the usages of the Church of England. E17.
b ***occasional conformity***: see OCCASIONAL *adjective* 1.

confound /kən'faʊnd/ *verb trans.* ME.
[ORIGIN Anglo-Norman *confundre*, *-foundre*, Old French & mod. French *confondre* from Latin *confundere* pour together, mix up, formed as CON- + *fundere* pour.]
1 Overthrow, defeat, ruin, (now usu. a scheme, hope, etc.). ME. ▸†**b** Waste; spend. L16–E18.

F. WELDON A further confounding of Hilda's ill-wishes. A. S. BYATT The local prodigy returning . . to astonish and confound prophecy. **b** SHAKES. *1 Hen. IV* He did confound the best part of an hour In changing hardiment with great Glendower.

2 As a (mild) imprecation: curse, damn. ME.

O. CROMWELL One of them was heard to say . . 'God damn me, God confound me; I burn, I burn.' J. BUCHAN Confound the day I ever left the herdin'!

3 Discomfit; abash; put to shame. Usu. in *pass.* (Chiefly with allus. to biblical use.) ME.

MILTON Silent, and in face Confounded long they sate.

4 Throw into confusion or disorder; perplex. LME.

C. DARWIN This difficulty for a long time quite confounded me.

5 Mix up so that the elements become difficult to distinguish; confuse. LME.

S. JOHNSON I came by it [the money] in a very uncommon manner, and would not confound it with the rest.

6 Mix up in idea; fail to distinguish. L16.

K. DOUGLAS I see men as trees suffering/ or confound the detail and the horizon.

■ **confoundable** *adjective* (*rare*) E19. **confounded** *adjective & adverb* (*a*) *adjective* that has been confounded; accursed, damnable; (*b*) *adverb* confoundedly: LME. **confoundedly** *adverb* †(*a*) in a perplexed or confused manner; (*b*) cursedly, damnably: L17. **confoundedness** *noun* M17. **confounder** *noun* a person who confounds LME.

†**confrairy** *noun.* LME–M18.
[ORIGIN Old French *confra(i)rie*, formed as CONFRÈRE: see -Y[3].]
= CONFRATERNITY 1.

confrater /kən'freɪtə/ *noun.* L16.
[ORIGIN medieval Latin *confrater*: see CONFRÈRE.]
A member of a brotherhood, esp. of monks.

confraternity /kɒnfrə'təːnɪti/ *noun.* LME.
[ORIGIN Old French & mod. French *confraternité* from medieval Latin *confraternitas*, from *confrater*: see CONFRÈRE, FRATERNITY.]
1 A brotherhood; an association of men united for some (esp. religious) purpose, or in some profession. LME.
2 Brotherly union or communion. L17.

confrère /'kɒnfrɛː/ *noun.* LME.
[ORIGIN Old French & mod. French from medieval Latin *confrater*: see CON-, FRIAR.]
†**1** A fellow member of a fraternity. LME–L17.
2 A fellow member of a profession, scientific body, etc. M18.

confrérie /kɔ̃freri/ *noun.* Pl. pronounced same. E19.
[ORIGIN French, formed as CONFRÈRE.]
A religious brotherhood; an association or group of people having similar interests, jobs, etc.

†**confrication** *noun.* LME–L18.
[ORIGIN Late Latin *confricatio(n-)*, from *confricat-* pa. ppl stem of *confricare*, formed as CON- + *fricare* rub: see -ATION.]
Rubbing together, friction; an instance of this.

confront /kən'frʌnt/ *verb trans.* M16.
[ORIGIN French *confronter* from medieval Latin *confrontare*, from Latin CON- + *frons*, *front-* forehead, face, FRONT *noun*.]
1 Stand or meet facing, esp. in hostility or defiance; stand against, oppose. M16.

LD MACAULAY John Hampden . . had the courage . . to confront the whole power of the government. QUILLER-COUCH I am only coarse when confronted by respectability.

2 Bring together face to face; bring face to face *with*. M16. ▸**b** Set (a thing) face to face or side by side *with* another for purposes of comparison; compare. E17.

BURKE When and where the parties might be examined and confronted. G. GREENE A criminal should be confronted with his crime, for he may . . betray himself. **b** B. JOWETT The old order of things makes so poor a figure when confronted with the new.

3 Place (a thing) facing *to*; set in contrast *to*. *rare*. M17.
■ **confronter** *noun* a person or thing which confronts L16. **confrontment** *noun* (now *rare*) E17.

confrontation /kɒnfrən'teɪʃ(ə)n/ *noun.* E17.
[ORIGIN from CONFRONT + -ATION. Cf. medieval Latin *confrontatio(n-)* boundary, French *confrontation*.]
1 The bringing of people face to face, esp. of an accused and the accuser(s), etc., for the purpose of establishing the truth. E17.

2 The action of bringing things together for comparison. M17.
3 Hostile opposition of countries, parties, etc., with or without actual conflict. M20.
■ **confrontational** *adjective* characterized by or leading to (hostile) confrontation; aggressive, uncompromising: L20.

Confucian /kənˈfjuːʃ(ə)n/ *noun & adjective*. M19.
[ORIGIN from *Confucius* (see below, Latinization of *Kongfuze* Kong the master) + -AN.]
▸ **A** *noun*. A follower of the Chinese philosopher Confucius (551–479 BC). M19.
▸ **B** *adjective*. Of or pertaining to Confucius, his teaching, or his followers. M19.
■ **Confucianism** *noun* the doctrines or system of Confucius and his followers M19. **Confucianist** *noun & adjective* an adherent of, of or pertaining to, Confucianism M19.

confusable /kənˈfjuːzəb(ə)l/ *adjective & noun*. M19.
[ORIGIN from CONFUSE *verb* + -ABLE. Cf. CONFUSIBLE.]
▸ **A** *adjective*. Able to be, or liable to be, confused. M19.
▸ **B** *noun*. A thing, esp. a word, that is liable to be confused with another. Usu. in *pl.* L20.
■ **confusaˈbility** *noun* M19.

†**confuse** *adjective*. ME–M18.
[ORIGIN Old French & mod. French *confus(e)* from Latin *confusus* pa. pple of *confundere* CONFOUND.]
Confused.
■ †**confusely** *adverb* LME–M18.

confuse /kənˈfjuːz/ *verb trans*. ME.
[ORIGIN Orig. *confused* pa. pple, formed as CONFUSE *adjective* + -ED[1]; active voice is back-form., only in isolated use before 19.]
†**1** Rout, bring to ruin. Only in ME.
2 Discomfit in mind or feelings; abash, bewilder, perplex. LME.

R. HUGHES Question her . . , perhaps frighten her, at any rate confuse her and make her contradict herself. F. WELDON The signposts were turned the wrong way round to confuse German spies.

3 Throw into disorder or confusion. LME.

DICKENS I fear I might confuse your arrangements by interfering. ALDOUS HUXLEY His thoughts were confused, but the muddle was bright and violent . . not foggily languid.

4 Mix up or mingle physically. Only in *pass.* M16.

T. MEDWIN Their arms, legs, and bodies were confused together.

5 Mix up in the mind; fail to distinguish. E17.

J. RUSKIN We in reality confuse wealth with money. DAY LEWIS I have been confused with the . . aviator, Cecil Lewis.

■ **confused** *adjective* that has been confused; bewildered, perplexed; disorderly, chaotic, lacking clear distinction of elements: LME. **confusedly** /-zɪdli/ *adverb* E16. **confusedness** /-zɪdnɪs/ *noun* L16. **confusible** *adjective* (*a*) = CONFUSABLE; †(*b*) confusing, involving confusion: LME. **confusing** *ppl adjective* perplexing, bewildering M19. **confusingly** *adverb* M19. †**confusive** *adjective* that tends to confuse E17–L18.

confusible /kənˈfjuːzɪb(ə)l/ *adjective & noun*. LME.
[ORIGIN from CONFUSE *verb* + -IBLE.]
▸ **A** *adjective*. †**1** Confusing; involving confusion. *rare*. LME–E16.
2 = CONFUSABLE *adjective*. M19.
▸ **B** *noun*. = CONFUSABLE *noun*. Usu. in *pl.* L20.

confusion /kənˈfjuːʒ(ə)n/ *noun*. ME.
[ORIGIN Old French & mod. French, or Latin *confusio(n-)*: see CON-, FUSION.]
1 Discomfiture, ruin. *arch.* ME.

MILTON With ruin upon ruin, rout on rout, Confusion worse confounded. P. O'BRIAN 'Confusion to Boney,' they said, and drank their glasses dry.

2 Mental discomfiture, putting to shame; embarrassment, perplexity. ME.

COVERDALE *Ps.* 30:1 In the, O Lorde, is my trust: let me neuer be put to confucion. G. GREENE The woman . . rose in confusion at the sight of the strangers coming in.

3 Mixture in which the distinction of the elements is lost. Now *rare* or *obsolete*. ME.

Book of Common Prayer One altogether, not by confusion of substaunce: but by vnitie of person.

4 The action of throwing into disorder. LME.

BACON The first great judgement of God upon the ambition of man was the confusion of tongues.

5 A disordered condition; disorder. LME. ▸**b** Tumult; civil commotion. M16.

S. BECKETT In this immense confusion one thing alone is clear.

6 Failure to distinguish. LME.

E. CLODD That confusion between names and things which marks all primitive thinking.

7 The quality of being confused, indistinct or obscure. E18.

ALBAN BUTLER Confusion . . in writing is indeed without excuse.

circle of confusion, ***circle of least confusion***: see CIRCLE *noun* 1.
■ **confusional** *adjective* characterized by (mental) confusion L19.

confusticate /kənˈfʌstɪkeɪt/ *verb trans. colloq.* L19.
[ORIGIN Fanciful alt. of CONFOUND or CONFUSE *verb*.]
Confuse, confound, perplex.

confutation /kɒnfjʊˈteɪʃ(ə)n/ *noun*. LME.
[ORIGIN French, or Latin *confutatio(n-)*, from *confutat-* pa. ppl stem of *confutare*: see CONFUTE, -ATION.]
The action or an instance of confuting; disproof; the complete argument in which a thing is confuted.

confute /kənˈfjuːt/ *verb trans*. E16.
[ORIGIN Latin *confutare* check, restrain, answer conclusively, formed as CON- + base of *refutare* refute.]
1 Prove (an argument or opinion) to be false, invalid, or defective; refute. E16.

H. ALLEN There are certain expressions at times upon the faces of some women that utterly confute the doctrine of original sin but confirm predestination.

2 Prove (a person) to be wrong; convict of error by argument or proof. M16.

MILTON Satan stood A while as mute confounded what to say . . confuted and convinced.

3 Render futile, bring to naught. L16.
■ **confutable** *adjective* able to be confuted M17. **confutative** *adjective* tending to confutation M17. **confuter** *noun* a person who confutes L16.

conga /ˈkɒŋgə/ *noun & verb*. M20.
[ORIGIN Amer. Spanish from Spanish fem. of *congo* of or pertaining to Congo.]
▸ **A** *noun*. **1** A Latin American dance usu. performed by people in single file who take three steps forward and then kick. M20.
2 In full ***conga drum***. A tall, narrow, low-toned drum that is beaten with the hands. M20.
▸ **B** *verb intrans*. Pa. t. & pple **conga'd**, **congaed**. Perform the conga. L20.

congé /kɔ̃ʒe (*pl. same*); ˈkɔːʒeɪ, ˈkɒnʒeɪ/ *noun*. Also (now *rare*) **congee** /ˈkɒndʒiː/. LME.
[ORIGIN Old French *congié* (mod. *congé*) from Latin *commeatus* passage, leave to pass, furlough, from *commeare* go and come, formed as CON- + *meare* go, pass.]
1 Permission (for any act). Now *rare* or *obsolete*. LME.
2 Ceremonious leave-taking. LME.

QUILLER-COUCH You don't stop to touch your hat when you makes your congees.

†**3** Formal permission to depart. L15–L18.
4 A bow. *arch.* L16.
5 [from mod. French.] Unceremonious dismissal. Chiefly *joc.* M19.
– PHRASES: ***congé d'élire*** /ˌkɒnʒeɪ deˈlɪə/ [French = to elect] royal permission to a cathedral chapter or a monastic body to fill a vacant see or abbacy by election.
– NOTE: Formerly naturalized, but now usu. treated as mod. French in the current senses.

congé *verb* var. of CONGEE *verb*[2].

congeal /kənˈdʒiːl/ *verb*. LME.
[ORIGIN Old French & mod. French *congeler* from Latin *congelare*, formed as CON- + *gelare* freeze, from *gelu* frost.]
▸ **I** *verb trans*. **1** Convert by cooling from a soft or fluid state to a solid one; freeze. LME.

fig.: S. JOHNSON Curiosity . . may be dissipated in trifles or congealed by indolence.

†**2** Make crystalline or solid by any means. LME–E18.
3 Make (a liquid, esp. the blood) viscid or jelly-like. LME.

fig.: SHAKES. *Tam. Shr.* Too much sadness hath congeal'd your blood.

▸ **II** *verb intrans*. **4** Become solid by cooling; freeze. LME.
5 Become solid by any process. LME.
6 Of a liquid: stiffen into a viscid or jelly-like consistency; coagulate. LME.
■ **congealable** *adjective* E17. **congealment** *noun* (*a*) the act or process of congealing; (*b*) a congealed mass: LME.

congee /ˈkɒndʒiː/ *noun*[1] & *verb*[1]. Also **conjee**. L17.
[ORIGIN Tamil *kañci*.]
▸ **A** *noun*. Water in which rice has been boiled. L17.
– COMB.: **congee-house** *arch. slang* a military detention room or cell (where inmates are fed on congee).
▸ **B** *verb trans*. Pa. t. & pple **congeed**. Starch with rice water. L17.

congee *noun*[2] see CONGÉ *noun*.

congee /ˈkɒndʒiː/ *verb*[2]. Also **congé**. Pa. t. & pple **congeed**. ME.
[ORIGIN Old French *congeer*, *congier*, formed as CONGÉ *noun*.]
†**1** *verb trans*. Dismiss. ME–M16.
†**2** *verb trans*. Give official permission to. LME–M16.
3 *verb intrans*. Pay one's respects on leaving; say goodbye. *obsolete* exc. *dial.* E17.
4 *verb intrans*. Bow in courtesy or deferential respect. *arch.* E17.

congelation /kɒndʒɪˈleɪʃ(ə)n/ *noun*. LME.
[ORIGIN Old French & mod. French, or Latin *congelatio(n-)*, from *congelat-* pa. ppl stem of *congelare* CONGEAL: see -ATION.]
1 a The action or process of freezing. LME. ▸**b** A frozen condition; a frozen mass. L17.
2 a Solidification; *spec.* crystallization. LME. ▸**b** A concretion. E17.
3 Coagulation, clotting. LME.
■ †**congelative** *adjective* producing cold; tending to congeal or to crystallize: LME–E18.

congener /ˈkɒndʒɪnə, kɒnˈdʒiːnə/ *noun & adjective*. M18.
[ORIGIN Latin, formed as CON- + *gener-*, *genus* race, stock.]
▸ **A** *noun*. **1** A thing or person of the same kind or class as another. M18.
2 A by-product in the making of spirits or wines which gives the drink a distinctive character. *US*. M20.
▸ **B** *adjective*. Congeneric; akin. M19.
■ **conˈgenerate** *adjective* (*rare*) congeneric M17.

congeneric /kɒndʒɪˈnɛrɪk/ *adjective*. M19.
[ORIGIN formed as CONGENER + -IC.]
Of the same genus, kind, or race; allied in nature or origin.
■ Also **conˈgenerous** *adjective* M17.

congenial /kənˈdʒiːnɪəl/ *adjective*. E17.
[ORIGIN from CON- + GENIAL *adjective*[1].]
1 Of a person: sharing the same disposition or temperament. Of a thing or attribute: kindred; of similar character. (Foll. by *with*, *to*.) E17. ▸**b** Suited to the nature of anything. (Foll. by *to*.) M18. ▸**c** Agreeable; matching one's taste or inclination. (Foll. by *to*.) L18.
†**2 a** Innate; congenital. M17–L18. ▸**b** Connected with one's birth. L17–L18.
†**3** = CONGENERIC. M17–E19.
■ **congeniˈality** *noun* E17. **congenially** *adverb* M18.

congenital /kənˈdʒɛnɪt(ə)l/ *adjective*. L18.
[ORIGIN from Latin *congenitus*, formed as CON- + *genitus* pa. pple of *gignere* beget: see -AL[1].]
Existing from birth; that is such from birth.

M. LOWRY I was not a congenital idiot. G. BOURNE The delivery of a child suffering from congenital syphilis.

■ **congenitally** *adverb* M19. †**congenite** *adjective* connate; congenital; innate: E17–E19.

conger /ˈkɒŋgə/ *noun*[1]. ME.
[ORIGIN Old French & mod. French *congre* from Latin *congrus*, *conger* from Greek *goggros*.]
More fully ***conger eel***. Any eel of the family Congridae, comprising scaleless sea eels usu. found in coastal waters; spec. *Conger conger*, a European conger reaching up to 3 metres in length and caught for food.

conger /ˈkɒŋgə/ *noun*[2]. L17.
[ORIGIN Unknown.]
hist. An association of booksellers who sold or printed books for their common advantage.

congeries /kɒnˈdʒɪəriːz, -ɪz, -ɪiːz/ *noun*. Pl. same. M16.
[ORIGIN Latin *congeries* heap, pile, from *congerere*: see CONGEST *verb*.]
A collection of disparate or unsorted items; a ragbag.

C. JAMES It was a congeries of remembered sense impressions, a symposium of subtleties.

■ Also ˈ**congery** *noun* M19.

congest /kənˈdʒɛst/ *verb*. LME.
[ORIGIN Latin *congest-* pa. ppl stem of *congerere* collect, heap up, formed as CON- + *gerere* bear, carry.]
†**1** *verb trans*. Bring or gather together; heap up, accumulate. LME–M19.
2 *verb trans*. Affect with congestion. Chiefly as ***congested*** *ppl adjective*. M19.

Daily Telegraph Congested town centres.

3 *verb intrans*. Gather together; congregate. L19.
■ **congestive** *adjective* involving or produced by congestion M19.

congestion /kənˈdʒɛstʃ(ə)n/ *noun*. LME.
[ORIGIN Old French & mod. French from Latin *congestio(n-)*, formed as CONGEST: see -ION.]
1 Excessive accumulation of fluid in a part of the body: now only of blood in blood vessels or of mucus in the respiratory tract. LME.
2 a The action of heaping together in a mass; accumulation. L16. ▸**b** A heap, a pile. M17.

a C. IVES Congestion of personal property tends to limit the progress of the soul.

3 Obstructive or disruptive overcrowding with traffic or people. M19.

J. CHEEVER The noise and congestion of the city.

– COMB.: **congestion charge** a charge made for driving into an area that suffers heavy traffic.

congiary /ˈkɒndʒɪəri/ *noun*. E17.
[ORIGIN Latin *congiarium*, formed as CONGIUS: see -ARY[1].]
ROMAN HISTORY. A quantity of oil, wine, etc., or money given for distribution as a gift among the people or the soldiers.

congius /ˈkɒndʒɪəs/ *noun*. Pl. **-ii** /-ɪʌɪ/. LME.
[ORIGIN Latin.]
ROMAN HISTORY. A liquid measure of one eighth of an amphora, equal to about 6 imperial pints.

†**conglaciate** *verb*. M17.
[ORIGIN Latin *conglaciat-* pa. ppl stem of *conglaciare* freeze up, formed as CON- + *glaciare* turn to ice, from *glacies* ice: see -ATE[3].]
1 *verb trans*. Make into or like ice. M17–E19.

C

2 *verb intrans.* Become ice, freeze. **M17–E19.**
■ **†conglaciation** *noun* **M17–M18.**

conglobate /ˈkɒŋgləbeɪt, -ət/ *adjective.* **M17.**
[ORIGIN Latin *conglobatus* pa. pple, formed as CONGLOBATE *verb*: see -ATE[2].]
Formed or gathered into a ball; rounded, globular.

conglobate /ˈkɒŋgləbeɪt/ *verb trans. & intrans.* **M17.**
[ORIGIN Latin *conglobat-* pa. ppl stem of *conglobare*, formed as CON- + *globare* make into a ball, from *globus* ball, GLOBE: see -ATE[3].]
= CONGLOBE.
■ **congloˈbation** *noun* the action of conglobating; a rounded formation: **L16.**

conglobe /kɒnˈgləʊb/ *verb trans. & intrans.* **M16.**
[ORIGIN French *conglober* or Latin *conglobare*: see CONGLOBATE *verb*.]
Gather or form into a rounded compact mass.

conglobulate /kɒnˈglɒbjʊleɪt/ *verb intrans. rare.* **M18.**
[ORIGIN from Latin *globulus* GLOBULE after CONGLOBATE *verb*.]
Collect into a rounded or compact mass.
■ **conglobuˈlation** *noun* **E20.**

conglomerate /kənˈglɒm(ə)rət/ *adjective & noun.* **LME.**
[ORIGIN Latin *conglomeratus* pa. pple of *conglomerare*, formed as CON- + *glomer-*, *glomus* ball: see -ATE[2].]
▸ **A** *adjective.* **1** Consisting of distinct parts gathered together into a more or less rounded mass; clustered. **LME.**
2 *GEOLOGY.* Of the nature of or forming a conglomerate. **E19.**
▸ **B** *noun.* **1** *GEOLOGY.* A coarse-grained sedimentary rock composed of rounded fragments embedded in a matrix of a cementing material such as silica. **E19.**
2 A mixture of heterogeneous elements. **M19.**
3 A commercial or industrial corporation formed by the merger or takeover of a number of diverse enterprises; a company with subsidiaries operating in different, unrelated markets. **M20.**
■ **conglomeˈratic** *adjective* (*GEOLOGY*) of the nature or character of conglomerate **M19.** **conglomerator** *noun* an industrialist who manages a conglomerate or forms conglomerates **L20.** **conglomeˈritic** *adjective* = CONGLOMERATIC **M19.**

conglomerate /kənˈglɒməreɪt/ *verb.* **L16.**
[ORIGIN Latin *conglomerat-* pa. ppl stem of *conglomerare*: see CONGLOMERATE *adjective & noun*, -ATE[3].]
1 *verb trans.* Form into a more or less rounded mass; heap together. Now *rare* or *obsolete.* **L16.**
2 *verb trans. & intrans.* Collect into a coherent or compact body (*lit. & fig.*). **L16.**

> V. WOOLF Infinite numbers of dull people conglomerated round her.

conglomeration /kənglɒməˈreɪʃ(ə)n/ *noun.* **E17.**
[ORIGIN Late Latin *conglomeratio(n-)*, formed as CONGLOMERATE *verb*: see -ATION.]
1 The action of conglomerating. **E17.**
2 A cluster; a heterogeneous mixture. **M19.**

conglutinate /kɒnˈgluːtɪneɪt/ *verb.* Now *rare.* **LME.**
[ORIGIN Latin *conglutinat-* pa. ppl stem of *conglutinare*, formed as CON- + *glutinare* to glue, from *glutin-*, *gluten* glue: see -ATE[3].]
1 *verb intrans.* Stick together, cohere (*lit. & fig.*). Orig. (now *obsolete*) of a fracture or wound: knit together, close and heal. **LME.**
2 *verb trans.* Unite (a wounded part, broken bone, etc.); heal. **LME.**
3 *verb trans.* Cause to cohere; fasten firmly together. **LME.**
■ **conglutiˈnation** *noun* **LME.**

Congo /ˈkɒŋgəʊ/ *noun*[1]. Pl. **-oes.** **E19.**
[ORIGIN Place name: see branch I.]
▸ **I 1** Used *attrib.* to designate things associated with the Congo, a region in west central Africa on either side of the Congo (Zaire) River, or with any of the countries in it called Congo (the Democratic Republic of Congo, formerly Zaire, and the Republic of Congo). **E19.**
Congo pea (an edible seed of) a cajan, *Cajanus cajan*. **Congo** PEAFOWL.
2 In full ***Congo dance***. A kind of dance formerly performed by black Americans and subsequently white people of the southern US. **E19.**
3 In full ***Congo eel***, ***Congo snake***. Any of various large salamanders found in shallow water in the south-eastern and central US and having tiny, inconspicuous legs: *Amphius means*, with four legs, or *Siren lacertina* or *S. intermedia*, each with two forelegs only. **M19.**
4 *hist.* A person from the Congo. **M19.**
▸ **II 5** Used *attrib.* to designate various azo dyes mostly derived from benzidine or tolidine. **L19.**
■ **Congoˈese** *adjective & noun* (now *rare*) = CONGOLESE **L18.**

†congo *noun*[2] *& verb* see CANGUE.

congo *noun*[3] var. of CONGOU.

Congolese /kɒŋgəˈliːz/ *adjective & noun.* **E20.**
[ORIGIN French *Congolais*, formed as CONGO *noun*[1]: see -ESE.]
▸ **A** *adjective.* Of or pertaining to (the) Congo (see CONGO *noun*[1] I) or its people. **E20.**
▸ **B** *noun.* Pl. same. A native or inhabitant of (the) Congo; the Bantu language of (the) Congo. **E20.**

congou /ˈkɒŋguː, -gəʊ/ *noun.* Also **C-**, **congo**, **k-**. **E18.**
[ORIGIN Abbreviation from Chinese (Cantonese) *kungfuch'a*, (Mandarin) *gōngfu chá* tea made for refined tastes, from *gōngfu* effort + *chá* TEA *noun*.]
A kind of black China tea. Also ***congou tea***.

congrats /kənˈgrats/ *noun pl. colloq.* **L19.**
[ORIGIN Abbreviation.]
Congratulations. Usu. as *interjection*.
■ Also **congratters** *noun pl.* [-ER[6]] **E20.**

congratulate /kənˈgratjʊleɪt/ *verb.* **M16.**
[ORIGIN Latin *congratulat-* pa. ppl stem of *congratulari*, formed as CON- + *gratulari* manifest one's joy, from *gratus* pleasing: see -ATE[3].]
†1 *verb trans.* Express joy or satisfaction at (an event or circumstance, *to* or *with* a person); celebrate *with* some act. **M16–E19.**
2 a *verb trans.* Express sympathetic joy to (a person, *on*, *upon*, *for* an event or circumstance). **M16.** ▸**b** *verb intrans.* Offer congratulations. **M17.** ▸**c** *verb refl.* Think oneself fortunate; feel satisfaction at an achievement. (Foll. by *on*, *upon*, *for*.) **M17.**

> **a** *Vanity Fair* The president . . congratulated him on his retirement after 38 years' service. **c** A. ROY Mathew congratulated himself for the way it had all turned out.

†3 *verb intrans.* Rejoice along *with* another. (Foll. by *on*, *upon*, *for*.) **L16–E19.**
†4 *verb trans.* Give a salutation to. **L16–E17.**
†5 *verb trans.* Rejoice at, welcome (an event). **E17–M18.**
■ **congratulant** *adjective & noun* (**a**) *adjective* that congratulates; (**b**) *noun* a congratulator: **M17.** **congratulative** *adjective* (*rare*) congratulatory **M19.** **congratulator** *noun* a person who congratulates **M17.** **congratulatory** *adjective* conveying congratulations **E16.**

congratulation /kəngratjʊˈleɪʃ(ə)n/ *noun.* **LME.**
[ORIGIN Latin *congratulatio(n-)*, formed as CONGRATULATE: see -ATION.]
1 The action of congratulating. **LME.**
2 In *pl.* Congratulatory expressions. Freq. as *interjection*, well done! **M17.**

†congree *verb intrans. rare.* **L16–M19.**
[ORIGIN from CON- + GREE *verb*.]
Accord.

†congreet *verb intrans. rare* (Shakes.). Only in **L16.**
[ORIGIN from CON- + GREET *verb*[1].]
Greet mutually.

congregant /ˈkɒŋgrɪg(ə)nt/ *noun.* **L19.**
[ORIGIN Latin *congregant-* pres. ppl stem of *congregare*: see CONGREGATE *verb*, -ANT[1].]
A member of a (Jewish) congregation.

congregate /ˈkɒŋgrɪgət/ *adjective.* Now *rare.* **LME.**
[ORIGIN Latin *congregatus* pa. pple, formed as CONGREGATE *verb*: see -ATE[2].]
Congregated. Also, collective.

congregate /ˈkɒŋgrɪgeɪt/ *verb trans. & intrans.* **LME.**
[ORIGIN Latin *congregat-* pa. ppl stem of *congregare* collect together, formed as CON- + *greg-*, *grex*, flock: see -ATE[3].]
Collect or gather together into a crowd or mass; meet or assemble in a body, flock.

> SHELLEY The north wind congregates in crowds The floating mountains of the silver clouds. R. L. STEVENSON That city of gold to which adventurers congregated. R. P. WARREN People, almost a crowd, were beginning to congregate.

■ **congregated** *ppl adjective* (**a**) assembled or collected together; †(**b**) organized congregationally: **E17.** **congregative** *adjective* tending to congregate **L16.** **congregator** *noun* a person who congregates **M17.**

congregation /kɒŋgrɪˈgeɪʃ(ə)n/ *noun.* **LME.**
[ORIGIN Old French & mod. French *congrégation* or Latin *congregatio(n-)*, formed as CONGREGATE *verb*: see -ATION.]
1 The action of congregating or collecting into a crowd or mass. **LME.**
2 *gen.* A gathering, an assemblage, a company. **LME.**

> SHAKES. *Haml.* A foul and pestilent congregation of vapours. O. HENRY The . . outlaws seemed to be nothing more than a congregation of country bumpkins. J. S. HUXLEY A congregation of black snakes . . convoluted in their mating ceremonies.

3 (Freq. **C-**.) A general assembly of (certain, esp. senior resident) members of a university. **LME.**
4 In the Bible, the collective body, or an actual assembly, of the Israelites in the wilderness. **LME.**
5 *ROMAN CATHOLIC CHURCH.* A body of people obeying a common religious rule. **LME.** ▸**b** An administrative subdivision of the papal Curia, *spec.* a permanent committee of cardinals. **L17.**
Congregation of the Propaganda: see PROPAGANDA *noun* 1.
6 A body of people assembled for religious worship or to hear a preacher; the body of people regularly attending a particular church etc. **E16.**

> I. COMPTON-BURNETT We shall see you all in church this evening, I hope? We want very much to have a full congregation.

lead the prayers of a congregation: see LEAD *verb*[1].
7 *SCOTTISH HISTORY.* The party of Protestant Reformers during the reign of Mary Stuart. **M16.**
■ **congregationer** *noun* †(**a**) = CONGREGATIONALIST; (**b**) *SCOTTISH HISTORY* a member of the party of Protestant Reformers (see CONGREGATION *noun* 7): **M17.** **congregationist** *noun* †(**a**) = CONGREGATIONALIST; (**b**) a member of a Roman Catholic congregation (see CONGREGATION 5): **M17.**

congregational /kɒŋgrɪˈgeɪʃ(ə)n(ə)l/ *adjective & noun.* **M17.**
[ORIGIN from CONGREGATION + -AL[1].]
▸ **A** *adjective.* **1** Of or pertaining to a congregation; performed by a congregation. **M17.**
2 (**C-**.) Of, pertaining or adhering to, Congregationalism. **M17.**
▸ **B** *noun.* (**C-**.) A Congregationalist. *rare.* **M17.**
■ **Congregationalist** *noun* a member or adherent of a Congregational church **L17.** **congregationalize** *verb trans.* make congregational **M19.** **congregationally** *adverb* **L19.**

Congregationalism /kɒŋgrɪˈgeɪʃ(ə)n(ə)lɪz(ə)m/ *noun.* **E18.**
[ORIGIN from CONGREGATIONAL + -ISM.]
A system of ecclesiastical organization that leaves the legislative, disciplinary, and judicial functions to the individual churches and congregations; adherence to a Congregational church (in England and Wales such churches were largely merged in the United Reformed Church from 1972).

congress /ˈkɒŋgrɛs/ *noun & verb.* **LME.**
[ORIGIN Latin *congressus*, from *congress-* pa. ppl stem of *congredi* go together, meet, formed as CON- + *gradi* proceed, step.]
▸ **A** *noun.* **†1** An encounter in combat. **LME–E18.**
2 A coming together (of persons, †of things); a meeting. **E16.**

> J. WOODWARD A fortuitous Congress of Atoms. DISRAELI Never was a congress of friendship wherein more was said and felt.

3 = COPULATION 2. Now *arch.* or *literary.* **L16.**

> J. R. ACKERLEY It did not enter my head . . that my father might still be having congress with my mother.

4 Social intercourse. *arch.* **E17.**
5 A formal meeting or assembly of delegates etc. for discussion, esp. of people belonging to a particular body or engaged in special studies. **L17.**
Church Congress: see CHURCH *noun*.
6 (**C-**.) The national legislative body of the US during any two-year term, comprising the House of Representatives and the Senate. Also, the corresponding body in some other countries. **L18.**
Continental Congress: see CONTINENTAL *adjective*. ***Member of Congress***: see MEMBER *noun* 2.
– COMB.: **congress boot** a high boot with elastic sides; **Congressman**: belonging to the US Congress; **Congress Party** a broadly based political party in India, arising directly from the Indian independence movement (which met as the *Indian National Congress* from 1885); **Congresswoman**: belonging to the US Congress.
▸ **B** *verb intrans.* Meet in congress, come together, assemble. *rare.* **M19.**
■ **conˈgression** *noun* (*rare*) [Latin *congressio(n-)*] †(**a**) hostile encounter; †(**b**) = CONGRESS *noun* 3; (**c**) = CONGRESS *noun* 2: **LME.** **congressist** *noun* (*rare*) a member or supporter of a congress **L19.**

congressional /kənˈgrɛʃ(ə)n(ə)l/ *adjective.* **L17.**
[ORIGIN from CONGRESS after Latin *congressio(n-)*; see -ION, -AL[1].]
Of or pertaining to a congress, esp. (**C-**) the legislative Congress of the US.
■ **congressionalist** *noun* a supporter of a congress **L19.** **congressionally** *adverb* **M19.**

Congreve /ˈkɒŋgriːv/ *noun.* **E19.**
[ORIGIN Sir William *Congreve* (1772–1828), English inventor.]
hist. **1** In full ***Congreve rocket***. A military rocket of a kind invented by Congreve. **E19.**
2 In full ***Congreve match***. A friction match of a kind invented by Congreve. **M19.**

†congrue *verb intrans. rare* (Shakes.). Only in **E17.**
[ORIGIN Old French *congruer* or Latin *congruere*: see CONGRUENT.]
Agree, accord.

congruence /ˈkɒŋgrʊəns/ *noun.* **LME.**
[ORIGIN Latin *congruentia*, from *congruent-*: see CONGRUENT, -ENCE.]
1 = CONGRUITY 2. **LME.**
†2 *THEOLOGY.* = CONGRUITY 4. **LME–M17.**
3 Accordance, correspondence, consistency. **M16.**
4 Grammatical agreement or correctness. **E18.**
5 *MATH.* The relationship between two congruent numbers; an equation expressing this. **L19.**
■ **congruency** *noun* (**a**) congruence; (**b**) *MATH.* a system of lines depending on two parameters: **L15.**

congruent /ˈkɒŋgrʊənt/ *adjective.* **LME.**
[ORIGIN Latin *congruent-* pres. ppl stem of *congruere* meet together, agree, correspond, formed as CON- + *ruere* fall, rush: see -ENT.]
1 Agreeing or corresponding (*with*) in character, accordant. **LME.** ▸**†b** Fitting, proper. **LME–E18.**
2 *MATH.* **a** Of geometrical figures: coinciding exactly when superimposed. **E18.** ▸**b** Of numbers: giving the same remainder when divided by a given number, called the modulus. Cf. RESIDUE *noun* 4. **L19.**
■ **congruently** *adverb* **LME.**

Congruism /ˈkɒŋgrʊɪz(ə)m/ *noun.* **L19.**
[ORIGIN French *congruisme*, from *congru* from Latin *congruus*: see CONGRUOUS, -ISM.]
THEOLOGY. The doctrine which derives the efficacy of grace from its adaptation to the character and circumstances of the person called.

■ **Congruist** *noun* a person who holds the doctrine of Congruism E18.

congruity /kən'gruːɪti/ *noun*. LME.
[ORIGIN French *congruité* or late Latin *congruitas*, formed as CONGRUOUS: see -ITY.]
1 The quality of being congruous; agreement in character or qualities; accordance, harmony. LME. ▸**b** An instance or point of correspondence, agreement, etc. Usu. in *pl.* E17.
2 Accordance with what is right or appropriate; fitness, propriety. LME.
†**3** Grammatical agreement or correctness; propriety of speech. LME–E18.
4 a SCHOLASTIC THEOLOGY. The appropriateness of God's conferment of grace as a reward for the performance of good works. (Cf. ***condignity***.) M16. ▸**b** = CONGRUISM. M17.
†**5** MATH. Coincidence, congruence. M17–M18.
6 Harmony of the parts of a whole, coherence. E19.

congruous /'kɒŋgrʊəs/ *adjective*. L16.
[ORIGIN from Latin *congruus* agreeing, suitable + -OUS.]
1 Accordant, conformable, *with*. L16.
2 Fitting, appropriate. L16.
†**3** Grammatically correct. Only in M17.
4 MATH. Coincident, congruent. Now *rare* or *obsolete*. M17.
5 Coherent. M18.
■ **congruously** *adverb* L16. **congruousness** *noun* M18.

conhydrine /kən'hʌɪdriːn/ *noun*. M19.
[ORIGIN from CONIINE + HYDRATE *noun* + -INE[5].]
CHEMISTRY. A piperidine derivative, $C_8H_{17}NO$, found together with coniine in hemlock.

coni *noun* pl. of CONUS.

conic /'kɒnɪk/ *adjective & noun*. L16.
[ORIGIN mod. Latin *conicus* from Greek *kōnikos*, from *kōnos*: see CONE *noun*, -IC.]
▸ **A** *adjective*. **1** Of or pertaining to a cone. L16.
conic section any of a group of curves (circle, ellipse, parabola, hyperbola) formed by the intersection of a right circular cone and a plane.
2 = CONICAL *adjective* 1. E17.
▸ **B** *noun*. **1** In *pl.* (treated as *sing.*). The branch of mathematics that deals with the cone and the figures that may be generated from it. Now *rare*. L16.
2 A conic section. L19.
■ **conicity** /kə'nɪsɪti/ *noun* conicalness L19. **conicoid** *noun* any of the bodies or surfaces that can be generated by the rotation of conic sections M19.

conic- *combining form* see CONICO-.

conical /'kɒnɪk(ə)l/ *adjective*. L16.
[ORIGIN formed as CONIC + -AL[1].]
1 Shaped like a cone; tapering regularly to a point from a more or less circular base. L16.
conical pendulum: see PENDULUM *noun*.
2 = CONIC *adjective* 1. L16.
conical projection a map projection in which a spherical surface is projected on to a cone (usu. with its vertex above one of the poles).
■ **conically** *adverb* M17. **conicalness** *noun* M18.

conico- /'kɒnɪkəʊ/ *combining form*. Before a vowel also **conic-**. E19.
[ORIGIN Repr. Greek *kōniko-*, -*kos* CONIC: see -O-.]
Used adverbially to form adjectives with the sense 'nearly —, but with a tendency to be conical', as ***conico-cylindrical***, ***conico-hemispherical***, etc.

conicopoly /kɒnɪ'kɒpəli/ *noun*. *obsolete* exc. *hist*. L17.
[ORIGIN Tamil *kanakka-pillai* account-man.]
A non-European clerk or accountant in the Indian subcontinent.

conidium /kəʊ'nɪdɪəm/ *noun*. Pl. **-ia** /-ɪə/. L19.
[ORIGIN mod. Latin, from Greek *konis* dust: see -IDIUM.]
An asexual spore in certain fungi (where it forms at the tip of a specialized hypha) and in some bacteria resembling fungi.
■ **conidial** *adjective* of, pertaining to, or of the nature of a conidium or conidia L19. **conidiophore** *noun* a hypha bearing a conidium L19. **conidi'ophorous** *adjective* bearing conidia L19.

conifer /'kɒnɪfə, 'kəʊn-/ *noun*. M19.
[ORIGIN Latin *conifer* adjective, cone-bearing, from *conus* CONE *noun*: see -FER.]
A gymnospermous tree or shrub of the order Coniferales, members of which typically bear cones and evergreen needle-like leaves and include the pines, firs, cedars, larches, spruces, yews, etc.
■ **coniferi'zation** *noun* conversion of woodland to coniferous forest; planting with coniferous trees: M20.

coniferous /kə'nɪf(ə)rəs/ *adjective*. M17.
[ORIGIN formed as CONIFER: see -FEROUS.]
Cone-bearing, that is a conifer; pertaining to or consisting (predominantly) of conifers.

coniform /'kəʊnɪfɔːm/ *adjective*. L18.
[ORIGIN from Latin *conus*, *coni-* CONE *noun* + -FORM.]
Cone-shaped, conical.

coniine /'kəʊnɪiːn/ *noun*. M19.
[ORIGIN from Latin CONIUM + -INE[5].]
CHEMISTRY. A volatile oily liquid alkaloid, 2-propylpiperidine, $C_8H_{17}N$, which is the active principle of hemlock, *Conium maculatum*.

conium /'kəʊnɪəm/ *noun*. M19.
[ORIGIN Latin from Greek *kōneion* hemlock.]
An umbelliferous plant of the genus *Conium*; *esp.* hemlock, *C. maculatum*; an extract of any plant of this genus used medicinally.

†**conject** *verb trans. & intrans*. LME.
[ORIGIN Latin *conjectare* frequentative of *conjicere* throw together, put together in speech or thought, conclude, formed as CON- + *jacere* throw.]
1 = CONJECTURE *verb* 3, 4. LME–M18.
2 Plot, plan. LME–M16.
3 = CONJECTURE *verb* 1. LME–E17.
■ †**conjector** *noun* [Anglo-Norman *conjectour*, Old French -*eur*] a person who conjectures; a soothsayer, a guesser: LME–M18.

conjectural /kən'dʒɛktʃ(ə)r(ə)l/ *adjective*. M16.
[ORIGIN French from Latin *conjecturalis*, from *conjectura*: see CONJECTURE *noun*, -AL[1].]
1 Of the nature of, involving, or depending on conjecture. M16.
2 Given to making conjectures. M17.
■ **conjectu'rality** *noun* (*rare*) M17. **conjecturally** *adverb* LME.

conjecture /kən'dʒɛktʃə/ *noun*. LME.
[ORIGIN Old French & mod. French, or Latin *conjectura* conclusion, inference, from *conject-* pa. ppl stem of *conjicere*: see CONJECT, -URE.]
†**1** The interpretation of signs or omens; divination; (a) prognostication. LME–L17.
> MILTON To cast Ominous conjecture on the whole success.

†**2** Supposition. *rare*. LME–L16.
> SHAKES. *Hen. V* Now entertain conjecture of a time When creeping murmur.. Fills.. the universe.

3 (The formation or offering of) an opinion or conclusion based on insufficient evidence or on what is thought probable; guesswork, a guess, (a) surmise; *spec.* in textual criticism, (the proposal of) a reading not actually found in the text. E16.
> G. MURRAY You cannot study the future. You can only make conjectures about it. C. V. WEDGWOOD Contemporary hearsay and conjecture (of which there was much).

†**4** A ground or reason for conclusion (short of proof). E16–M17.

conjecture /kən'dʒɛktʃə/ *verb*. LME.
[ORIGIN Old French & mod. French *conjecturer* from late Latin *conjecturare*, from Latin *conjectura* (see CONJECTURE *noun*). Cf. CONJECT.]
†**1** *verb trans. & intrans.* Infer from signs or omens; divine, prognosticate. LME–M17.
†**2** *verb trans.* Conclude, infer, or judge from appearances or probabilities. LME–E17.
3 *verb trans.* Form or offer as an opinion or conclusion on admittedly insufficient grounds; guess, surmise; propose as a conjectural reading. M16.
> M. W. MONTAGU I conjecture them to be the remains of that city. T. HARDY I.. conjectured that these hours of absence were spent in furtherance of his plan. V. CRONIN Catherine's feelings .. can only be conjectured.

4 *verb intrans.* Form a conjecture; indulge in guesswork. (Foll. by *about*, (arch.) *of*, †*at*.) L16.
> BARONESS ORCZY Perhaps he was going to Greenwich, or . . . but Marguerite ceased to conjecture.

■ **conjecturable** *adjective* that may be conjectured L16. **conjecturer** *noun* †(*a*) a fortune-teller, an augur; (*b*) a maker of conjectures: E17.

conjee *noun & verb* var. of CONGEE *noun*[1] *& verb*[1].

conjobble /kən'dʒɒb(ə)l/ *verb trans. & intrans. colloq.* Now *rare* or *obsolete*. L17.
[ORIGIN from CON- and perh. JOB *noun*[1], *verb*[2] or JABBER, + -LE[3].]
Arrange (matters); discuss.

conjoin /kən'dʒɔɪn/ *verb*. LME.
[ORIGIN Old French & mod. French *conjoign-* pres. stem of *conjoindre* from Latin *conjungere*, formed as CON- + *jungere* JOIN *verb*.]
▸ **I** *gen.* **1** *verb trans. & intrans.* Join or become joined together; unite, combine. LME.
> J. SPEED Many fresh springs.. meet and conjoine in the vallies. A. J. AYER It is common to find belief in a transcendent god conjoined with belief in an after-life.

▸ **II** *spec.* **2** *verb trans. & intrans.* Of planets: be or come into conjunction (with). LME.
3 *verb trans.* & †*intrans.* Join or combine in action or purpose; ally. LME.
†**4** *verb trans.* Join in marriage. LME–M17.
†**5** *verb intrans.* = COPULATE 2. L16–E17.
■ **conjoined** *ppl adjective* joined together, combined, allied; HERALDRY (of charges) connected together, placed so as to touch; ***conjoined twin*** (MEDICINE) = SIAMESE ***twin***: L16. **conjoiner** *noun* M17.

conjoint /kən'dʒɔɪnt/ *adjective* (orig. *pa. pple*). LME.
[ORIGIN Old French & mod. French, pa. pple of *conjoindre*: see CONJOIN.]
Conjoined; united, combined; conjunct.
■ **conjointly** *adverb* ME.

conjubilant /kən'dʒuːbɪlənt/ *adjective*. *rare*. M19.
[ORIGIN medieval Latin *conjubilant-*, formed as CON- + JUBILANT.]
Jubilant or rejoicing together.

conjugacy /'kɒndʒəgəsi/ *noun*. M17.
[ORIGIN from CONJUGATE *adjective* + -ACY.]
†**1** Married state. *rare*. Only in M17.
2 Chiefly MATH. Conjugate condition. L19.

conjugal /'kɒndʒʊg(ə)l/ *adjective*. E16.
[ORIGIN Latin *conjugalis*, from *conjug-*, -*ju(n)x* consort, spouse, formed as CON- + stem of *jugum* yoke: see -AL[1]. Cf. Old French & mod. French *conjugal*.]
Of or relating to marriage, matrimonial; of or pertaining to a husband or wife in their relationship to each other.
> I. WALTON The hearing of such conjugal faithfulness will be Musick to all chaste ears.

conjugal rights those rights (esp. to sexual relations) supposedly exercisable in law by each partner in a marriage on the other. **conjugal rites** the wedding ceremony; *arch.* sexual intercourse.
■ **conju'gality** *noun* M17. **conjugally** *adverb* E17.

conjugate /'kɒndʒʊgət/ *adjective & noun*. L15.
[ORIGIN Latin *conjugatus* pa. pple of *conjugare*: see CONJUGATE *verb*, -ATE[2].]
▸ **A** *adjective*. **1** *gen.* Joined together, *esp.* coupled; connected, related. L15.
2 MATH. & PHYSICS. Joined or paired in some reciprocal relation (*to*); *spec.* (of two complex numbers) such that each is the complex conjugate of the other. L17.
3 BOTANY. Of leaves etc.: growing in or as a pair. L18.
4 GRAMMAR. Of words: derived from the same root (as one another). M19.
5 BIOLOGY. Of gametes: fused. M19.
6 BIBLIOGRAPHY. Of a pair of leaves: united with each other in being part of a single sheet of paper. L19.
– SPECIAL COLLOCATIONS: **conjugate acid**, **conjugate base** (CHEMISTRY): related to each other by the gain or loss of a proton (e.g. acetate ion is the conjugate base of acetic acid, the latter the conjugate acid of the former). **conjugate angle**, **conjugate arc** MATH.: either of a pair whose sum is 360°. **conjugate axis** MATH. the axis of a conic that bisects the principal or transverse axis. ***conjugate base***: see ***conjugate acid*** above. **conjugate deviation** OPHTHALMOLOGY a forced, persistent turning of the eyes to one side, their direction in relation to each other remaining unaltered. **conjugate diameter** (*a*) ANATOMY the distance between the front and rear of the pelvis, *spec.* determined from the sacral promontory to the back of the pubic symphysis; (*b*) MATH. = ***conjugate axis*** above. **conjugate focus** either of two points so situated in relation to a lens that light from an object placed at one of them forms an image at the other. **conjugate solution** CHEMISTRY either of a pair of solutions which may be formed by two partially miscible liquids and exist together in equilibrium at a given temperature, the solute in one solution being the solvent in the other.
▸ **B** *noun*. **1** GRAMMAR. Either of a group of words sharing the same root. L16.
2 Any conjugated thing. E17.
complex conjugate: see COMPLEX *adjective* 3.

conjugate /'kɒndʒʊgeɪt/ *verb*. M16.
[ORIGIN Latin *conjugat-* pa. ppl stem of *conjugare*, formed as CON- + *jugare* join, yoke, marry, from *jugum* yoke: see -ATE[3].]
1 *verb trans.* GRAMMAR. Inflect (a verb) in its various forms of voice, mood, tense, number, and person. M16.
2 *verb trans.* Yoke together, join, unite. *rare*. L16.
3 *verb intrans.* Unite sexually. Now chiefly BIOLOGY, unite in conjugation (sense 4). L18.
4 *verb trans.* BIOCHEMISTRY. Bring into conjugation (sense 5) *with*. Usu. in *pass.* M20.

conjugated /'kɒndʒʊgeɪtɪd/ *adjective*. L16.
[ORIGIN from CONJUGATE *verb* + -ED[1].]
1 That has been conjugated; conjugate. L16.
2 CHEMISTRY. Of, pertaining to, designating, or containing a (chain or ring) system of two or more double bonds linked by alternate single bonds. L19.

conjugation /kɒndʒʊ'geɪʃ(ə)n/ *noun*. LME.
[ORIGIN Latin *conjugatio(n-)*, from *conjugat-*: see CONJUGATE *verb*, -ATION.]
1 GRAMMAR. The scheme of all the inflectional forms belonging to a verb; a division of verbs according to general inflectional differences. LME. ▸**b** The setting forth (in speech or writing) of a verb's conjugation. M16. ▸**c** In Semitic languages, any of several sets of inflectional forms that give a passive, reflexive, causative, etc., meaning to the simple verb. L16.
> RICHARD MORRIS The verbs of the strong conjugation.. form the past tense by a change of the root-vowel. V. S. NAIPAUL Her grammar.. included a highly personal conjugation of the verb to be.

†**2** ANATOMY. A group of conjoined parts; *esp.* each of the several pairs of cerebral nerves. L16–E18.
3 The action of joining together or uniting; the condition of being conjugated or joined together; conjunction, union. E17. ▸†**b** An assemblage, a combination. E17–E18.

C

4 *BIOLOGY*. The fusion of gametes in sexual reproduction; the union of simple organisms for the exchange of genetic material. M19.
5 *BIOCHEMISTRY*. The (reversible) combination of a substance such as a protein with one of a different kind. M20.
■ **conjugational** *adjective* M19. **conjugationally** *adverb* L19.

conjunct /ˈkɒndʒʌŋkt/ *noun*. L16.
[ORIGIN from CONJUNCT *adjective*.]
†**1** A conjoined whole. *rare*. Only in L16.
2 A person or thing conjoined or associated with another. M17.
3 = CONJUNCTURE. M19.

conjunct /kənˈdʒʌŋkt/ *adjective* (orig. *pa. pple*). LME.
[ORIGIN Latin *conjunctus* pa. pple of *conjungere*, formed as CON- + *jungere* join. Cf. CONJOINT.]
1 Joined together; conjoined, combined; associated, esp. in a subordinate capacity. Also (*SCOTS LAW*), immediately associated. LME.
conjunct person *SCOTS LAW* an associate in an offence; *esp.* a person so closely involved with another as to be liable to the presumption of collusion or connivance. **conjunct probation**, **conjunct proof** *SCOTS LAW* (leading of) evidence restricted to the rebuttal of the averments of the opposing party in an action, but not introducing new points.
2 *LAW* (chiefly *Scot.*). Pertaining to or involving several persons jointly. L15.
3 Constituted by the conjunction of several elements; united, joint. E16.
4 *MUSIC*. Designating motion by steps from one degree of a scale to the next (i.e. by intervals of a second); proceeding by or involving such steps. Opp. DISJUNCT *adjective* 3. L17.
■ **conjunctly** *adverb* jointly LME.

conjunction /kənˈdʒʌŋkʃ(ə)n/ *noun*. LME.
[ORIGIN Old French & mod. French *conjonction* from Latin *conjunctio(n-)*, from *conjunct-* pa. ppl stem of *conjungere*: see CONJUNCT *adjective*, -ION.]
1 The action or an act of conjoining; the fact or condition of being conjoined; (a) union, (a) connection. LME. ▸**b** *ALCHEMY*. A mixing or union of substances. LME. ▸†**c** Union in marriage; sexual union. M16–E19.

A. BRIGGS A conjunction of some of his own supporters with his enemies.

in conjunction together, jointly, (*with*).
2 *ASTRONOMY & ASTROLOGY*. An alignment of three celestial objects; *spec.* the apparent coincidence or proximity of two celestial objects as viewed from the earth. LME.
inferior conjunction, **superior conjunction**: of an inferior planet with the sun, when the planet and the earth are on the same side, opposite sides, of the sun.
3 *GRAMMAR*. An uninflected word, other than a relative pronoun, used to connect clauses or sentences, or to coordinate words in the same clause. (One of the parts of speech.) LME.
subordinating conjunction: see SUBORDINATE *verb*.
†**4** A junction; a joint. LME–L17.
5 A number of things, persons, etc., conjoined or associated together; a combination, an association. M16.

A. W. KINGLAKE A strong man and a good cause make a formidable conjunction.

6 An occurrence of events or circumstances in combination. L17.

H. T. BUCKLE [This] required a peculiar conjunction of events.

7 *LOGIC*. A proposition of the form (p and q), which is true only when both p and q (and any further conjoined statements) are true. E20.
■ **conjunctional** *adjective* of the nature of or pertaining to a conjunction M17. **conjunctionally** *adverb* M19.

conjunctiva /kɒndʒʌŋkˈtʌɪvə, kənˈdʒʌŋktɪvə/ *noun*. LME.
[ORIGIN medieval Latin (*tunica*) *conjunctiva* conjunctive (membrane): see CONJUNCTIVE.]
The delicate mucous membrane that covers the front of the eye (except over the cornea) and lines the inside of the eyelids.
■ **conjunctival** *adjective* of or pertaining to the conjunctiva M19.

conjunctive /kənˈdʒʌŋktɪv/ *adjective & noun*. LME.
[ORIGIN Late Latin *conjunctivus*, from *conjunct-*: see CONJUNCTION, -IVE.]
▸ **A** *adjective*. **1** *GRAMMAR*. Of the nature of a conjunction; having the function of connecting, *spec.* uniting the sense as well as the construction. LME. ▸**b** Of the mood of a verb: used only in conjunction with another verb, subjunctive. M18.
2 *gen.* Having the property or effect of uniting or joining; connective. L15.
3 Conjunct, conjoined, united. E17.
4 *LOGIC*. Of, pertaining to, or characterized by the conjunction of statements etc. L17.
▸ **B** *noun*. **1** *GRAMMAR*. A conjunction; *spec.* one uniting the sense as well as the construction. L16. ▸**b** (A verb in) the conjunctive mood. E19.
†**2** = CONJUNCTIVA. M17–M18.
3 *LOGIC*. A conjunctive proposition or syllogism. M19.
■ **conjunctively** *adverb* E17. **conjunctiveness** *noun* M18.

conjunctivitis /kəndʒʌŋktɪˈvʌɪtɪs/ *noun*. M19.
[ORIGIN from CONJUNCTIVA + -ITIS.]
Inflammation of the conjunctiva.

conjuncture /kənˈdʒʌŋktʃə/ *noun*. E17.
[ORIGIN from CONJUNCTION by suffix-substitution, partly after French (mod. *conjoncture*) from Italian *congiuntura*, formed as CONJUNCT *noun* + -URE.]
1 A meeting *of* circumstances or events; a state of affairs, a juncture. E17.
†**2** = CONJUNCTION 2. E17–E19.
†**3** The action of joining together; the fact or state of being joined; a joining, a combination. M17–L18.

conjunto /kɒnˈhʌntəʊ/ *noun*. Pl. **-os**. M20.
[ORIGIN Spanish, lit. 'ensemble, group'.]
In Latin America or among Hispanic communities: a small musical group or band.

conjuration /kʌndʒəˈreɪʃ(ə)n, (*esp. in sense* 1) kɒndʒʊ(ə)-/ *noun*. LME.
[ORIGIN Old French *conjuracion*, (also mod.) *-ation*, from Latin *conjuratio(n-)*, from *conjurat-* pa. ppl stem of *conjurare* CONJURE *verb*: see -ATION.]
1 An act of swearing together; a making of a common oath; a banding together, a conspiracy. *arch.* LME.
2 A solemn appeal to something sacred or binding; a solemn entreaty. *arch.* LME.
3 The effecting of something supernatural by the invocation of a name of power or by an incantation. LME.
4 An incantation, a spell, a charm; a form of words used in conjuring. LME.
5 The performance of magic tricks, conjuring; a conjuring trick. M18.

conjurator /ˈkɒndʒʊ(ə)reɪtə/ *noun*. LME.
[ORIGIN Anglo-Norman *conjuratour* or medieval Latin *conjurator*, from *conjurat-*: see CONJURATION, -ATOR.]
A person joined with others by an oath; a fellow conspirator.

conjure /ˈkʌndʒə/ *noun*. LME.
[ORIGIN In isolated early use from Old French; later (L19) from the verb.]
†**1** = CONJURATION 3. Only in LME.
†**2** = CONJURATION 1. Only in M16.
3 Magic. *W. Indian & US black English*. L19.
– COMB.: **conjure doctor**, **conjure man** a witch doctor; **conjure woman** a witch.

conjure /ˈkʌndʒə; *in senses* 1, 2 kɒnˈdʒʊə/ *verb*. ME.
[ORIGIN Old French & mod. French *conjurer* plot, exorcise, adjure from Latin *conjurare* band together by an oath, conspire, (in medieval Latin) invoke, formed as CON- + *jurare* swear.]
▸ **I** **1** *verb trans.* Constrain (a person to some action) by appeal to an oath or something sacred; call upon in the name of some supernatural being. ME.
2 *verb trans.* Appeal solemnly to (a person) *to do* something; beseech, implore. ME.

CARLYLE A Letter from the Queen, conjuring him to return without delay.

3 *verb trans.* Call upon (a demon, spirit, etc.) to appear or act, by invocation or incantation. ME.
4 *verb intrans.* Orig., invoke a demon etc., use incantation or spells. Now, produce magical effects by trickery. ME.
a name to conjure with: of great importance. **conjuring trick** a magical effect achieved by sleight of hand or other natural means.
†**5** *verb trans.* Affect by incantation; charm, bewitch. LME–M19.
6 *verb trans.* Effect, produce, bring (*out*), convey (*away*), by magic or a conjuror's trick; evoke. Freq. *fig.* M16.

R. B. SHERIDAN What has conjured you to Bath? W. COWPER To conjure clean away the gold they touch. A. RANSOME As if she had somehow herself conjured the whole of High Topps into existence. S. HAZZARD Having perpetually conjured the sight of him in fancy.

conjure up bring into existence as if by magic, cause to appear to the mind or eye, evoke.
▸ †**II** **7** *verb intrans.* Swear together; band together by oath; conspire. LME–M17.
8 *verb trans.* Link by oath in an association or conspiracy. Usu. in *pass.* M16–E18.

MILTON The third part of Heav'ns Sons Conjur'd against the highest.

conjuror /ˈkʌndʒərə; *in sense* 3 kɒnˈdʒʊərə/ *noun*. Also **-er**. ME.
[ORIGIN Partly from CONJURE *verb*, partly from Anglo-Norman *conjurour*, Old French *conjurere*, *-eor* from medieval Latin *conjurator* CONJURATOR: see -OR, -ER[1], -ER[2].]
1 A person who practises conjuration; a magician, a wizard, a sorcerer. ME.
no conjuror a person of limited intelligence or ability.
2 A person who performs conjuring tricks. E18.
3 A person who is bound with others by an oath. Only in Dicts. M19.
■ **conjuress** *noun* a female conjuror; a sorceress: L16. **conjurorship** *noun* L17.

conjury /ˈkʌndʒəri/ *noun*. M19.
[ORIGIN from CONJURE *verb* after *augury*, *injury*, etc.]
Conjurors' tricks, magic.

conk /kɒŋk/ *noun*[1]. *slang*. E19.
[ORIGIN Perh. alt. of CONCH.]
1 The nose; the head. E19.
2 A punch on the nose or head; a blow. L19.

conk /kɒŋk/ *noun*[2]. Orig. *US*. M19.
[ORIGIN App. var. of CONCH.]
The fruiting body of a bracket fungus, esp. the fungus *Trametes pini*; infestation of timber by such a fungus.
■ **conky** *adjective* affected with conk E20.

conk *noun*[3] var. of CONCH.

conk /kɒŋk/ *verb*[1] *trans. slang*. E19.
[ORIGIN from CONK *noun*[1].]
Punch, esp. on the nose or head; hit, strike; kill.

conk /kɒŋk/ *verb*[2] *intrans. slang*. E20.
[ORIGIN Unknown.]
Of a machine etc.: break down, fail or show signs of failing. Of a person: collapse, die. Usu. foll. by *out*.

conker /ˈkɒŋkə/ *noun*. Also occas. **conquer**. M19.
[ORIGIN Perh. from CONCH, assoc. with CONQUER *verb*.]
Orig., a snail shell; now, a horse chestnut. In *pl.*, a game played orig. with snail shells, now with horse chestnuts on strings, in which each player tries to break with his or her own that held by the opponent. Cf. earlier CONQUEROR 2.

conkering *verbal noun* see CONQUERING.

con moto /kɒn ˈməʊtəʊ, *foreign* kɔn ˈmoto/ *adverbial phr.* E19.
[ORIGIN Italian = with movement.]
MUSIC. A direction: with spirited movement.

conn *noun* var. of CON *noun*[3].

conn *verb* see CON *verb*[2].

Conn. *abbreviation*.
Connecticut.

connate /ˈkɒneɪt/ *adjective*. M17.
[ORIGIN Late Latin *connatus* pa. pple of *connasci*, formed as CON- + *nasci* be born: see -ATE[2].]
1 Existing in a person from birth; innate, congenital. M17.
2 Of the same or similar nature; allied; congenial. M17.
3 *BOTANY & ZOOLOGY*. Of parts or organs: congenitally united, so as to form one part or organ. L18.
4 Formed at the same time, coeval. E19.
5 *GEOLOGY*. Of water: trapped in a sedimentary rock during its deposition. E20.
■ **connately** *adverb* L19. **connateness** *noun* M17.

connation /kəˈneɪʃ(ə)n/ *noun*. M19.
[ORIGIN formed as CONNATE: see -ATION.]
BIOLOGY. Connate condition (see CONNATE 3).

connatural /kəˈnatʃ(ə)r(ə)l/ *adjective*. L16.
[ORIGIN Late Latin *connaturalis*, formed as CON- + NATURAL *adjective*.]
1 Innate; belonging inherently or naturally (*to*). L16.
2 Of the same or similar nature, cognate. E17.
■ **connatuˈrality** *noun* E17. **connaturalize** *verb trans.* make connatural M17. **connaturally** *adverb* M17. **connaturalness** *noun* E17.

connect /kəˈnɛkt/ *verb*. LME.
[ORIGIN Latin *connectere*, formed as CON- + *nectere* bind, fasten.]
▸ **I** *verb intrans.* Usu. foll. by *with*.
1 Be united physically, make contact, join on; be related or associated; form a logical sequence. (*rare* before 18.) LME. ▸**b** Of a train, aeroplane, etc.: have its arrival timed to allow passengers in it to transfer to another (specified) train etc. M19. ▸**c** Hit the target (*with* a blow, kick, etc.). *colloq.* E20. ▸**d** Make a mental or practical connection; realize interconnections. E20. ▸**e** Make contact with a person, esp. for the purpose of buying drugs: cf. CONNECTION 9. *slang* (orig. *US*). E20. ▸**f** Succeed in communicating with the audience or reader; be meaningful. M20.

A. TUCKER One all-comprehensive plan; wherein . . all the parts connect with one another. F. TUOHY For her the word connected still with guilt. **b** F. L. OLMSTED The train was advertised to connect here with a steamboat for Norfolk. **d** E. M. FORSTER Live in fragments no longer. Only connect, and the beast and the monk, robbed of the isolation that is life to either, will die. **f** *Listener* A magazine programme . . has probably done its job if one of its items connects.

▸ **II** *verb trans.* **2** Join, link, fasten together, (two things, one thing *to* or *with* another); link in sequence or coherence. M16.

S. JOHNSON The authour connects his reasons well. JAS. MILL The Conjunctions are distinguished from the Prepositions by connecting Predications. DAY LEWIS The ponds . . were connected one to another by a tiny . . stream. L. DEIGHTON The super highway that connects Reggio to Naples.

3 Associate in occurrence or action. Usu. in *pass.*, be to do *with*. E18. ▸**b** Associate mentally. M18.

J. BENTHAM A very busy amateur in everything that is in any way connected with mechanics. W. F. HARVEY For some time there was nothing to connect me with the crime. **b** D. H. LAWRENCE It did not occur to her to connect the train's moving on with the sound of the trumpet.

4 Unite (a person) with another or others by relationship or marriage, by common interests, etc. Usu. in *pass.* or *refl.* M18.

5 Establish telephone communication for (a person) (*with*). **E20.**
■ **connectable** *adjective* = CONNECTIBLE **L19.** **connectiˈbility** *noun* the quality of being connectible **E20.** **connectible** *adjective* able to be connected **M18.** **connecting** *ppl adjective* serving to connect or join (***connecting rod***: transmitting motion from the piston to the crankpin etc. in an engine) **L17.**

connected /kəˈnɛktɪd/ *adjective.* **E18.**
[ORIGIN from CONNECT + -ED[1].]
1 Joined together, conjoined; *esp.* joined in sequence, coherent. **E18.**
SIMPLY connected. T-connected: see T, T 2.
2 Related; having relationships or associations (of a specified nature). **L18.**
well connected related to or associated with persons of good social position or influence.
■ **connectedly** *adverb* **L18.** **connectedness** *noun* **L17.**

connecter *noun* see CONNECTOR.

Connecticutter /kəˈnɛtɪkʌtə/ *noun.* **L19.**
[ORIGIN from *Connecticut* (see below) + -ER[1].]
A native or inhabitant of the state of Connecticut, USA.

connection /kəˈnɛkʃ(ə)n/ *noun.* Also (earlier, now usual only in sense 6b) **-nex-**. **LME.**
[ORIGIN Latin *connexio(n-)*, from *connex-* pa. ppl stem of *connectere*: see CONNECT, -ION. Mod. spelling after *connect*.]
1 *gen.* The action or an act of connecting or joining; the state of being connected. **LME.** ▸**b** The connecting of parts of an electric circuit; the making of electrical contact. **M19.** ▸**c** A linking by telephone communication. **L19.**

C. DARWIN This connection of the former and present buds by ramifying branches. J. BRYCE The connection of Church and State.

b SCOTT CONNECTION.
2 A connecting part; *spec.* a link between electrical components, a means of making electrical contact. **LME.**
3 (A) causal or logical relationship or association; (an) interdependence. **E17.**

E. W. ROBERTSON There was a close connexion during the early feudal period between rank and wealth. J. CONRAD The voice returned, stammering words without connection.

4 (A) contextual relation. Esp. in ***in this connection***, ***in the same connection***, ***in another connection***. **E18.**

R. PORSON Martin took the sentence out of its connection.

5 Personal dealing; a personal relationship or association. (Foll. by *with*.) **M18.** ▸**b** A sexual relationship, sexual intercourse. *arch.* **L18.**

F. RAPHAEL She cared little for her parents' world and had no connexion with it.

6 A body of people united by political, commercial, or other ties; a body of customers or clients. **M18.** ▸**b** *spec.* (**-nex-**.) In the Methodist Church or its offshoots: a denomination, an interrelated system of congregations. **M18.**

LD MACAULAY At the head of a strong parliamentary connection.

7 (A) family relationship, as by marriage or distant consanguinity. Freq. in *pl.* **L18.** ▸**b** A person connected with another or others by marriage or distant consanguinity; an acquaintance, *esp.* one who has prestige or influence. **L18.**

LD MACAULAY He was, by hereditary connection, a Cavalier. J. FENTON He was always Boasting of his connections. **b** S. H. ADAMS [John Quincy Adams] may well have been a connection of our line.

8 The scheduled meeting of one train, aeroplane, etc., with another on another route, for the transfer of passengers; the facilities or arrangements for this. **M19.**

L. MACNEICE I missed my connection in Glasgow and had to spend the day there.

9 A purchase of illegal drugs; a person who peddles or supplies these; an organization dealing in illegal drugs. *slang* (orig. *US*). **M20.**

connectional /kəˈnɛkʃ(ə)n(ə)l/ *adjective.* Also (in sense 2 always) **-nex-**. **M19.**
[ORIGIN from CONNECTION + -AL[1].]
1 Of, pertaining to, or of the nature of a connection. **M19.**
2 *spec.* Of or pertaining to a Methodist connection. **M19.**
■ **connectionalism** *noun* the organization of a Church by a system of connections **L19.**

connectionism /kəˈnɛkʃ(ə)nɪz(ə)m/ *noun.* Also **-nex-**. **M20.**
[ORIGIN from CONNECTION + -ISM.]
The doctrine that mental processes involve a bond or connection between stimulus and response; the theory that learning occurs by the formation of such connections.

connective /kəˈnɛktɪv/ *adjective & noun.* **M17.**
[ORIGIN from CONNECT *verb* + -IVE, repl. earlier CONNEXIVE.]
▸ **A** *adjective.* Serving or tending to connect. **M17.**
connective tissue *ANATOMY* tissue connecting and binding other tissues and organs of the body and containing relatively few cells in a non-living matrix, e.g. fibrous tissue and elastic tissue.
▸ **B** *noun.* **1** *GRAMMAR & LOGIC.* A connecting word or particle. **M18.**
2 *BOTANY.* The part of the filament which connects the lobes of the anther. **M19.**
■ **connectival** /kɒnɛkˈtʌɪv(ə)l/ *adjective* (*BOTANY*) of the connective **M19.** **connectively** *adverb* **L16.** **connecˈtivity** *noun* (chiefly *MATH. & LOGIC*) the state, property, or degree of being (inter)connected **L19.**

connector /kəˈnɛktə/ *noun.* Also (esp. of a person) **-er**. **L18.**
[ORIGIN formed as CONNECTIVE + -OR, -ER[1].]
A person or thing which connects; *esp.* a device for keeping two parts of an electrical conductor in contact.

Connemara /kɒnɪˈmɑːrə/ *noun.* **M19.**
[ORIGIN A region in the west of Co. Galway, Republic of Ireland.]
Used *attrib.* to designate things found in or associated with Connemara.
Connemara marble a banded serpentinous marble. **Connemara pony** a small hardy breed of horse.

conner /ˈkɒnə, *in sense 1 also* ˈkʌn-/ *noun*[1]. **OE.**
[ORIGIN from CON *verb*[1] + -ER[1].]
1 A person who tests or examines; an inspector. Cf. ***aleconner*** s.v. ALE *noun*. *arch.* **OE.**
2 A person who cons or studies diligently. **E19.**

conner *noun*[2] var. of CUNNER.

connex /ˈkɒnɛks/ *noun.* **LME.**
[ORIGIN Old French *connexe* annexe, dependence, from medieval Latin, from pa. pple of Latin *connectere*: see CONNECT *verb*.]
†**1** A connected circumstance or property. **LME–L17.**
2 *SCOTS LAW* (now *hist.*). An item of property connected with another. Always in conjunction with ***annex***. **M16.**

†**connex** *verb trans.* **M16.**
[ORIGIN Old French *connexer*, app. from *connexe* adjective, from Latin *connexus* pa. pple of *connectere*: see CONNECT.]
1 Join or fasten together. **M16–E18.**
2 Connect logically or practically; associate. **M16–M19.**

connexion *noun* see CONNECTION.

connexional *adjective* see CONNECTIONAL.

connexionism *noun* var. of CONNECTIONISM.

connexity /kəˈnɛksɪti/ *noun.* **E17.**
[ORIGIN Old French & mod. French *connexité*, from *connexe*: see CONNEX *verb*, -ITY.]
Connected quality, connectedness.

†**connexive** *adjective.* **L16.**
[ORIGIN Latin *connexivus*, from *connex-* pa. ppl stem of *connectere*: see CONNECT, -IVE.]
1 *LOGIC.* Conditional; (of a proposition) whose clauses are connected together as antecedent and consequent. **L16–E18.**
2 *GRAMMAR.* Conjunctive. **M17–L18.**
3 Connective. **L18–M19.**

conning tower /ˈkɒnɪŋtaʊə/ *noun.* **L19.**
[ORIGIN from CON *verb*[2] + -ING[1] + TOWER *noun*[1].]
The (armoured) pilot house of a warship; the superstructure of a submarine from which the vessel may be directed when on or near the surface.

conniption /kəˈnɪpʃ(ə)n/ *noun. N. Amer. colloq.* **M19.**
[ORIGIN Prob. invented.]
A fit of rage or hysteria; in *pl.*, hysterics. Also ***conniption-fit***.

connivance /kəˈnʌɪv(ə)ns/ *noun.* Also (earlier, now only in sense 3) **-vence**. **L16.**
[ORIGIN French *connivence* or Latin *conniventia*, from *connivere*: see CONNIVE, -ENCE.]
†**1** *lit.* Winking. **L16–E17.**
2 The action of conniving (*at* or *in* a person's misconduct); assistance in wrongdoing by conscious failure to prevent or condemn; tacit permission. **L16.**
3 *BOTANY & ZOOLOGY.* (Usu. **-vence**.) Tendency to converge. **M19.**
■ **connivancy** *noun* (*arch.*) connivance **E17.**

connive /kəˈnʌɪv/ *verb.* **E17.**
[ORIGIN French *conniver* from Latin *connivere*, formed as CON- + a stem rel. to *nictare* (see NICTITATE).]
▸ **I** *verb intrans.* **1** Foll. by *at*: shut one's eyes to (a thing one dislikes but is resigned to), pretend ignorance of, overlook. *arch.* **E17.**

LD MACAULAY The government thought it expedient occasionally to connive at the violation of this rule.

†**2** Foll. by *at*: regard (an offender) sympathetically. **E17–M18.**

CHESTERFIELD You must renounce courts, if you will not connive at knaves and tolerate fools.

3 Foll. by *at*: turn a blind eye to (an action one ought to oppose, but which one secretly sympathizes with); be secretly accessory to. **M17.**

S. SMILES The maritime population . . actively connived at their escape.

†**4** Remain inactive or dormant. *rare* (Milton). **M–L17.**
5 Be in secret complicity, conspire, (*with*). **L18.**

SIR W. SCOTT Dost thou connive with the wolves in robbing thine own fold?

6 *BOTANY & ZOOLOGY.* Converge (gradually). *rare.* **M19.**
▸ **II** *verb trans.* †**7** Connive at (a fault, offence, etc.). **E17–M19.**
■ **conniver** *noun* **M17.**

connivence *noun* see CONNIVANCE.

connivent /kəˈnʌɪv(ə)nt/ *adjective.* **E17.**
[ORIGIN Latin *connivent-* pres. ppl stem of *connivere* CONNIVE: see -ENT.]
†**1** Disposed to connive at or overlook offences. **E–M17.**
2 *ANATOMY.* Designating the circular folds (now usu. called ***plicae circulares***) in the mucous membrane of the small intestine. Long *rare* or *obsolete*. **L17.**
3 *BOTANY & ZOOLOGY.* Of parts: gradually convergent, approaching at the extremity. **M18.**

connoisseur /kɒnəˈsəː/ *noun & verb.* **E18.**
[ORIGIN Old French & mod. French (now *connaisseur*), from Old French *conoiss-* pres. ppl stem of *conoistre* (mod. *connaître*) know + *-eur* -OR.]
▸ **A** *noun.* A person with a thorough knowledge and critical judgement of a subject, esp. one of the fine arts; an expert in any matter of taste, e.g. wines, foods. (Foll. by *of*, *in*.) **E18.**

R. CHURCH I loved pencils . . . I collected them as a connoisseur. K. CLARK Lord Burlington was a connoisseur, collector and arbiter of taste.

▸ **B** *verb intrans. & trans.* Be a connoisseur (of). *rare.* **E19.**
■ **connoisseurship** *noun* the role or activity of a connoisseur; proficiency as a connoisseur: **M18.**

connotation /kɒnəˈteɪʃ(ə)n/ *noun.* **LME.**
[ORIGIN medieval Latin *connotatio(n-)*, from *connotat-* pa. ppl stem of *connotare*: see CONNOTE, -ATION.]
†**1** Something implied as a condition or accompaniment; a concomitant symptom. Only in **LME.**
2 An association or idea suggested by a word in addition to its primary meaning; implication. **M16.**

V. PACKARD The words instant coffee seemed loaded with unfortunate connotations.

3 *LOGIC.* Orig., the subject of which an attribute is predicated. Later, the attribute connoted by a term. **M17.**
4 The sum of what a word implies; meaning, signification. **M19.**
■ **connotational** *adjective* pertaining to or involving connotation **M20.**

connotative /ˈkɒnəteɪtɪv, kəˈnəʊtətɪv/ *adjective.* **E17.**
[ORIGIN medieval Latin *connotativus*, from *connotat-*: see CONNOTATION, -IVE.]
Having the quality of connoting; *esp.* implying or implied in addition to the primary meaning.
connotative term *LOGIC* a term which, while denoting a subject, also connotes its attributes.
■ **connotatively** *adverb* **M19.**

connote /kəˈnəʊt/ *verb trans.* **M17.**
[ORIGIN medieval Latin *connotare*, formed as CON- + *notare* NOTE *verb*[1].]
1 Of a word etc.: signify or imply in addition to the primary meaning. **M17.**

M. PATTISON Deism . . connotes along with natural religion a negation of the . . Christian revelation.

2 Of a fact etc.: imply as a consequence or condition; suggest. **M17.**

IDWAL JONES A gate that connoted landed respectability.

3 *LOGIC.* Orig., imply (the subject) in which an attribute inheres, while primarily signifying the attribute itself. Now, with inverted use: imply (the attributes involved), while denoting the subject. **E19.**
4 Include in its signification; mean, signify. **M19.**

connubial /kəˈnjuːbɪəl/ *adjective.* **M17.**
[ORIGIN Latin *connubialis*, from *connubium* wedlock, formed as CON- + *nubere* marry: see -AL[1].]
1 Of or pertaining to marriage or the married state; matrimonial. **M17.**
2 Married, wedded; of or pertaining to a spouse. **E19.**
■ **connubiˈality** *noun* the married state, wedlock; in *pl.*, customs characteristic of wedlock: **M19.** **connubially** *adverb* **M19.**

connumerate /kəˈnjuːməreɪt/ *verb trans. rare.* Pa. pple & ppl adjective **-ated**, †**-ate**. **LME.**
[ORIGIN Late Latin *connumerat-* pa. ppl stem of *connumerare*, formed as CON- + NUMERATE *verb*.]
Reckon or count together.
■ **connumeˈration** *noun* **M17.**

conodont /ˈkəʊnədɒnt/ *noun.* **M19.**
[ORIGIN from Greek *kōnos* cone + -ODONT.]
A fossil marine animal of the Cambrian to Triassic periods, with a long wormlike body and numerous small teeth, now believed to be the earliest vertebrate.

conoid /ˈkəʊnɔɪd/ *adjective & noun.* **L16.**
[ORIGIN Greek *kōnoeidēs* cone-shaped; from *kōnos* CONE *noun*: see -OID.]
▸ **A** *adjective.* Resembling a cone in shape; more or less conical. **L16.**
▸ **B** *noun.* **1** A solid generated by the revolution of a conic section about its axis; *esp.* a paraboloid or hyperboloid. **L16.**
2 A body of similar shape to a cone. **L18.**

■ co'**noidal** *adjective* pertaining to, of the shape of, or resembling a conoid L16. co'**noidic** *adjective* (*rare*) = CONOIDAL E19. co'**noidical** *adjective* (*rare*) = CONOIDAL L17.

conoscente /kɒnoʃ'ʃɛnte/ *noun.* Pl. ***-ti*** /-ti/. M18.
[ORIGIN Italian.]
= COGNOSCENTE.

†**conquassate** *verb trans.* M17–M18.
[ORIGIN Latin *conquassat-*: see CONQUASSATION, -ATE³.]
Shake hard, agitate.

†**conquassation** *noun.* LME–L18.
[ORIGIN Latin *conquassatio(n-)*, from *conquassat-* pa. ppl stem of *conquassare*, formed as CON- + *quassare* frequentative of *quatere* shake: see -ATION.]
Severe shaking; agitation; an instance of this.

conquer *noun* var. of CONKER *noun*.

conquer /'kɒŋkə/ *verb.* ME.
[ORIGIN Old French *conquerre* from Proto-Romance from Latin *conquirere* seek for, procure, gain, win, formed as CON- + *quaerere* seek.]
▶ **I** *verb trans.* †**1** Acquire, get possession of; attain to. ME–M16.

CAXTON Brenne had . . conquerd a grete lordship thurgh maryage.

2 Acquire by force of arms, win in war; subjugate (a country etc.) by force. ME.

A. ALISON At all hazards we must conquer a maritime peace. H. A. L. FISHER They had conquered Syria and Egypt.

3 Overcome (an opponent) by force; vanquish. ME.

R. W. EMERSON The Germans, whom the Romans found hard to conquer in two hundred . . years.

4 *transf. & fig.* Overcome or subdue (habit, passion, etc.) by an effort of will; get the better of; master; gain by a struggle; win the affections or sexual favours of. LME. ▸**b** Climb successfully and reach the top of (a mountain). L19.

C. HILL The idea of conquering poverty through conquering idleness. A. LURIE I conquered the impulse to hide in my room.

▶ **II** *verb intrans.* **5** Be the conqueror; make conquests; be victorious. ME.

SHAKES. *Rich. III* Arm, fight, and conquer, for fair England's sake! W. H. PRESCOTT Cortez . . did not conquer from the mere ambition of conquest.

■ **conquerable** *adjective* able to be conquered L15. **conqueress** *noun* (now *rare*) a female conqueror LME. **conqueringly** *adverb* (*rare*) in a conquering manner, victoriously E17. **conquerless** *adjective* (*poet. rare*) invincible L16.

conquering /'kɒnk(ə)rɪŋ/ *verbal noun.* In sense 2 usu. **conk-**. ME.
[ORIGIN from CONQUER *verb* + -ING¹. See also CONQUEROR 2, CONKER.]
1 The action of CONQUER *verb*. ME.
2 Playing at conkers. *colloq.* E19.

conqueror /'kɒŋk(ə)rə/ *noun.* ME.
[ORIGIN Anglo-Norman *conquerour*, Old French *-eor* (oblique), formed as CONQUER *verb*: see -OR.]
1 A person who conquers; a person who subjugates a nation; a victor. ME.
William the Conqueror, **the Conqueror** King William I of England, who effected the Norman Conquest in 1066.
2 = CONKER. E19.

conquest /'kɒŋkwɛst/ *noun.* ME.
[ORIGIN Old French *conquest(e)* (mod. *conquête*), repr. use as noun of neut. and fem. of Proto-Romance pa. pple of CONQUER *verb*.]
1 The action or an act of gaining by force of arms; military subjugation (of a country etc.). ME.

HOBBES Conquest . . is the Acquiring of the Right of Soveraignty by Victory.

the Norman Conquest, **the Conquest** the acquisition of the English crown by William of Normandy in 1066.
2 The action or an act of overcoming by force or by an effort of will; mastery; (a) winning of a person's affections or sexual favours; (a) successful climbing to the top of a mountain. ME.

SHAKES. *3 Hen. VI* I must yield . . by my fall, the conquest to my foe. W. S. MAUGHAM When he made the customary advances he discovered to his relief, for he was not a man who considered that resistance added a flavour to conquest, that she was no prude. ALDOUS HUXLEY The so-called 'conquest of space'.

3 Something acquired by force of arms; *esp.* conquered territory; *fig.* a person whose affections or sexual favours have been won. ME.

SHAKES. *Jul. Caes.* What conquest brings he home? What tributaries follow him to Rome. G. SANTAYANA Young boys . . look for some easy conquest among . . country wenches.

4 SCOTS LAW. (The acquisition of) property gained otherwise than by inheritance. *obsolete* exc. *hist.* LME.

conquest /'kɒŋkwɛst/ *verb trans.* Chiefly *Scot. & N. English.* Pa. t. & pple **-quested**, †**-quest**. ME.
[ORIGIN from the noun.]
1 Acquire, get possession of. Long only SCOTS LAW (now *hist.*), acquire (property) otherwise than by inheritance. ME.
†**2** Conquer; vanquish. LME–M17.

conquistador /kɒŋ'kwɪstədɔː/ *noun.* Pl. **-dors**, **-dores** /-dɔːrɪz/. M19.
[ORIGIN Spanish.]
A conqueror; *spec.* any of the Spanish conquerors of Mexico and Peru in the 16th cent.

Conradian /kɒn'radɪən/ *adjective.* E20.
[ORIGIN from Joseph *Conrad* (original name Teodor Józef Konrad Korzeniowski: see below) + -IAN.]
Of, pertaining to, or characteristic of Joseph Conrad (1857–1924), Polish-born writer of novels in English, or his work.

con rod /'kɒnrɒd/ *noun. colloq.* M20.
[ORIGIN Abbreviation.]
A connecting rod.

Cons. *abbreviation.*
Conservative.

consanguine /kɒn'saŋgwɪn/ *adjective.* E17.
[ORIGIN French *consanguin(e)* from Latin *consanguineus*: see CONSANGUINEOUS.]
Consanguineous.

consanguineous /kɒnsaŋ'gwɪnɪəs/ *adjective.* E17.
[ORIGIN from Latin *consanguineus* of the same blood, formed as CON- + *sanguis*, *-inis* blood: see -OUS.]
Related by descent from a common ancestor; of or pertaining to blood relationship; *spec.* (LAW) related as children of the same father (opp. ***uterine***). E17.
brother consanguineous, ***consanguineous brother***: see BROTHER *noun*.
■ **consanguineal** *adjective* = CONSANGUINEOUS 1 L18. **consanguinean** *adjective* = CONSANGUINEOUS E18. **consanguineously** *adverb* L19.

consanguinity /kɒnsaŋ'gwɪnɪti/ *noun.* LME.
[ORIGIN Latin *consanguinitas*, from *consanguineus*: see CONSANGUINEOUS, -ITY.]
1 Relationship by descent from a common ancestor; blood relationship. LME.

fig.: S. JOHNSON Such is the consanguinity of our intellects.

†**2** *collect.* Blood relations, kin. *rare.* LME–E18.

consarcination /kɒn,sɑːsɪ'neɪʃ(ə)n/ *noun.* Now *rare* or *obsolete.* M17.
[ORIGIN from Latin *consarcinat-* pa. ppl stem of *consarcinare* patch together, formed as CON- + *sarcinare* to patch: see -ATION.]
Patching together; a heterogeneous combination.

consarn *verb*, **consarned** *ppl adjective* see CONCERN *verb*, CONCERNED.

conscience /'kɒnʃ(ə)ns/ *noun.* ME.
[ORIGIN Old French & mod. French from Latin *conscientia* privity of knowledge, consciousness, from *conscire* be privy to, formed as CON- + *scire* know: see -ENCE.]
▶ †**I** **1** One's inmost thought, one's mind or heart. ME–E17.

SHAKES. *Hen. V* I will speak my conscience of the King: I think he would not wish himself anywhere but where he is.

2 (An) inward knowledge or consciousness; (an) internal conviction; mental recognition or acknowledgement (*of*). LME–M19.

HOBBES Mankind, from conscience of its own weaknesse.

3 Reasonableness, understanding. *rare* (Shakes.). Only in E17.
▶ **II** **4** A moral sense of right or wrong; a sense of responsibility felt for private or public actions, motives, etc.; the faculty or principle that leads to the approval of right thought or action and condemnation of wrong. ME.

E. PEACOCK With several twinges of conscience. R. MACAULAY David can do as he likes . . , it is between him and his conscience. E. ROOSEVELT Working conditions which no one with any social conscience would tolerate today.

†**5** Conscientious observance *of*, regard *to*. LME–L17.
6 Practice of or conformity to what is considered right; conscientiousness. *arch.* LME.

A. C. SWINBURNE The care and conscience with which their scenes were wrought out.

†**7** Sense of guilt with regard to a thought or action; scruple, compunction, remorse. LME–E17.
– PHRASES: **bad conscience**, **guilty conscience** a conscience troubled by feelings of remorse, guilt, or sin; a consciousness that one's thoughts or actions are or have been wrong. **case of conscience** [translating Latin *casus conscientiae*] a matter in which a conflict of principles has to be resolved by one's conscience. **clear conscience**, **good conscience** a conscience untroubled by feelings of remorse, guilt, or sin; a consciousness that one's thoughts or actions are or have been right. **for conscience sake**, **for conscience' sake** in order to satisfy one's conscience. **freedom of conscience**, **liberty of conscience** freedom of all citizens of a state to practise the religion of their choice. ***good conscience***: see ***clear conscience*** above. ***guilty conscience***: see ***bad conscience*** above. **have on one's conscience** feel guilty about. **in all conscience** *colloq.* by any reasonable standard. **keep a person's conscience** ensure that he or she forms sound moral judgements. ***liberty of conscience***: see ***freedom of conscience*** above. †**make a conscience of**, †**make conscience of** have scruples about. ***prick of conscience***: see PRICK *noun*. **prisoner of conscience** a person detained or imprisoned because of his or her religious or political beliefs. ***social conscience***: see SOCIAL *adjective*. ***soul and conscience***: see SOUL *noun*.
– COMB.: **conscience clause**: (in a law etc.) ensuring respect for the consciences of those affected; **conscience money**: sent to relieve the conscience, esp. in payment of evaded income tax; **conscience-smitten**, **conscience-stricken**, **conscience-struck** *adjectives* made uneasy by a bad conscience.
■ **conscienced** *adjective* having a conscience (of a specified nature) M16. **conscienceless** *adjective* LME.

conscient /'kɒnʃɪənt/ *adjective.* Now *literary.* E17.
[ORIGIN Latin *conscient-* pres. ppl stem of *conscire*: see CONSCIENCE, -ENT.]
Conscious.

conscientious /kɒnʃɪ'ɛnʃəs/ *adjective.* E17.
[ORIGIN French *conscienciеux* from medieval Latin *conscientiosus*, from Latin *conscientia*: see CONSCIENCE, -OUS.]
Obedient to conscience, (habitually) governed by a sense of duty; done according to conscience; scrupulous, painstaking; of or pertaining to conscience.

C. KINGSLEY She became a Baptist from conscientious scruples. T. COLLINS Ida was an untiring and conscientious worker.

conscientious objector a person who makes use of a conscience clause to refuse to conform to a regulation etc.; *esp.* a person who for reasons of conscience objects to military service.
■ **conscientiously** *adverb* M17. **conscientiousness** *noun* M17.

conscionable /'kɒnʃ(ə)nəb(ə)l/ *adjective.* Now *rare* or *obsolete.* M16.
[ORIGIN from CONSCIENCE (with /-s/ erron. taken as pl. suffix -S¹) + -ABLE.]
Having a conscience; showing a regard for conscience; conscientious, scrupulous.
■ **conscionableness** *noun* E17. **conscionably** *adverb* M16.

conscious /'kɒnʃəs/ *adjective & noun.* L16.
[ORIGIN from Latin *conscius* knowing something with others, knowing in oneself, from *conscire*: see CONSCIENCE, -OUS.]
▶ **A** *adjective.* †**1** Having guilty knowledge (*of*). L16–E19.

HENRY MORE She being conscious, did . . make confession of her wickedness.

2 Orig. more fully †***conscious to oneself***. Knowing or perceiving within oneself, aware. Foll. by *of* a fact, one's sensations, thoughts, etc., external circumstances, an external object, *that*. Also *absol.* (*poet.*), well aware. E17. ▸**b** As 2nd elem. of comb.: aware of, concerned about. E20.

LD MACAULAY He must have been conscious that, though he thought adultery sinful, he was an adulterer. T. HARDY Conscious that . . his accents and manner wore a roughness not observable in the street. I. MCEWAN He walked towards them slowly, . . conscious of their attention. S. HAZZARD She found them insufficiently conscious of their disadvantage.

SELF-CONSCIOUS. **b** ***class-conscious***, ***clothes-conscious***, ***health-conscious***, etc.
3 Of an inanimate thing: privy to, sharing in, or witnessing human thoughts and actions, external events, etc. Chiefly *poet.* E17.

SOUTHEY If the conscious air had caught the sound.

†**4** Foll. by *to*: sharing in the knowledge of, aware of, privy to. M17–E19.
5 Of an emotion, quality, etc.: of which one is aware; felt, sensible. M17.

GOLDSMITH His face became pale with conscious guilt. B. RUSSELL Fear—deep, scarcely conscious fear.

6 Having or manifesting the faculty of consciousness (CONSCIOUSNESS 3). L17.

J. B. MOZLEY Man . . as a conscious being.

conscious subject: see SUBJECT *noun* 5c.
7 Self-conscious, affected. E18.

POPE The conscious simper, and the jealous leer. L. P. HARTLEY This florid woman, with her air of conscious Edwardian gentility.

8 Aware of what one is doing or intends to do. Of an action etc.: realized by the doer, planned, deliberate. M19.

B. F. WESTCOTT A . . sequence . . which few will attribute to . . a conscious design. L. STEPHEN Pope was . . a conscious and deliberate artist.

9 Having the mental faculties in an active and waking state. M19.

T. HOLMES The sister reported that he had become conscious, having recognized her.

▶ **B** *noun. The* conscious mind. E20.
■ **consciously** *adverb* L17.

consciousness /'kɒnʃəsnɪs/ *noun.* M17.
[ORIGIN from CONSCIOUS + -NESS.]
1 Internal knowledge or conviction, esp. of one's own guilt, innocence, deficiencies, etc. M17.

B. JOWETT Happy in the consciousness of a well-spent life.

2 The state or fact of being mentally aware *of* anything; the perception *that*. L17.

ADAM SMITH A consciousness that . . this species of cultivation . . is more profitable. H. JAMES He enjoyed the consciousness of their having a secret together.

3 The state or faculty, or a particular state, of being aware of one's thoughts, feelings, actions, etc. L17.

J. LOCKE Consciousness is the perception of what passes in a Man's own mind. WORDSWORTH Consciousnesses not to be subdued.

4 The totality of the thoughts, feelings, impressions, etc., of a person or group; such a body of thoughts etc. relating to a particular sphere; a collective awareness or sense. **L17.**

M. HOWITT The commencement of a moral consciousness.

stream of consciousness: see STREAM *noun*.

5 The state of having the mental faculties awake and active; the waking state. **E19.**

D. L. SAYERS He became gradually weaker and lost consciousness.

– COMB.: **consciousness-raising** increasing (esp. social, political, or moral) sensitivity or awareness.

conscribe /kənˈskrʌɪb/ *verb trans.* **L15.**
[ORIGIN Latin *conscribere*: see CONSCRIPT *adjective*.]
†**1** Write, compose. *rare*. Only in **L15.**
†**2 a** *gen.* Enrol, levy (an army); enlist (a soldier). **M16–M17.** ▸**b** *spec.* = CONSCRIPT *verb*. **E19.**
†**3** Circumscribe, limit. **L16–E18.**

conscript /ˈkɒnskrɪpt/ *noun*. **L18.**
[ORIGIN French *conscrit* from Latin *conscriptus*: see CONSCRIPT *adjective*.]
A person enlisted by conscription for military etc. service.

conscript /ˈkɒnskrɪpt/ *adjective*. **LME.**
[ORIGIN Latin *conscriptus* pa. pple of *conscribere* write down, list, enrol, formed as CON- + *scribere* write.]
1 Enrolled or elected as a Roman senator or *transf.* as a member of any legislative or administrative body. Chiefly in ***conscript fathers*** [Latin *patres conscripti*, orig. *patres et conscripti*], Roman senators, legislators, etc., collectively. **LME.**
2 Of a soldier, an army, etc.: enlisted or raised by conscription. **E19.**

conscript /kənˈskrɪpt/ *verb trans.* Orig. *US*. **E19.**
[ORIGIN Back-form. from CONSCRIPTION.]
Enlist by conscription; recruit compulsorily.

C. RYAN Conscripted into the *Wehrmacht*. *fig.*: L. LEE Winter and summer.. conscripted our thoughts.

conscription /kənˈskrɪpʃ(ə)n/ *noun*. **LME.**
[ORIGIN Late Latin *conscriptio(n-)* levying of troops, formed as CONSCRIPT *adjective*: see -ION. In sense 3 after French.]
†**1** Writing down together, putting in writing. Also (*rare*), conjoint signature. **LME–E17.**
†**2** *gen.* Enrolment or enlistment of soldiers. **E16–M17.**
3 Compulsory enlistment for state service, esp. military service. **E19.**
■ **conscriptionist** *noun* an advocate of (military) conscription **E20.** **conscriptive** *adjective* involving or having (military) conscription **E20.**

consecrate /ˈkɒnsɪkrət/ *adjective*. *arch. rare*. **LME.**
[ORIGIN Latin *consecratus* pa. pple, formed as CONSECRATE *verb*: see -ATE[2].]
Consecrated, hallowed.

consecrate /ˈkɒnsɪkreɪt/ *verb trans.* **LME.**
[ORIGIN Latin *consecrat-* pa. ppl stem of *consecrare*, formed as CON- + *sacrare* dedicate, from *sacer* SACRED *adjective*: see -ATE[3].]
1 Set apart as sacred (*to*); dedicate solemnly to a sacred or religious purpose; make fit for religious use. **LME.** ▸**b** *spec.* Give sacramental character to (the Eucharistic elements of bread and wine) by performing the appropriate rite. **E16.**

R. HOOKER The custom of the primitive church in consecrating holy virgins.. unto the service of God. *Book of Common Prayer* If the consecrated bread or wine be all spent.. the Priest is to consecrate more.

2 Ordain (a bishop, monarch, etc.) to office. **LME.**
3 Dedicate or devote *to* a particular purpose or pursuit. **M16.**

W. H. PRESCOTT His whole life was consecrated to letters.

†**4** Devote or doom *to* destruction etc. **L16–M17.**
†**5** Apotheosize, deify. **E17–M18.**
6 Make an object of veneration or regard; sanctify; sanction by usage. **L17.**

J. LINGARD Writers, whose reputation consecrates their opinions.

■ **consecrated** *ppl adjective* that has been consecrated; *esp.* (of a church, churchyard, ground, etc.) set apart by episcopal dedication for public worship or the burial of the dead, and having the ecclesiastical and legal status thus conferred: **M16.** **consecrator** *noun* **M16.** **consecratory** *adjective* that consecrates **E17.**

consecration /kɒnsɪˈkreɪʃ(ə)n/ *noun*. **LME.**
[ORIGIN Old French & mod. French *consécration* or Latin *consecratio(n-)*, formed as CONSECRATE *verb*: see -ATION.]
1 The action of consecrating to a sacred or religious purpose; setting apart as sacred, devoting to religious use; *esp.* (***a***) the formal dedication of a church, churchyard, ground, etc., by a bishop for public worship or the burial of the dead; (***b***) the giving of the sacramental character to the Eucharistic elements of bread and wine. **LME.** ▸**b** An act of so consecrating; in *pl.* also, consecrated things. Long *arch.* **M16.**
2 (The ceremony of) ordination to a holy office. **LME.**
3 ROMAN HISTORY. Apotheosis, deification. **L15.**
4 Dedication or devotion to a particular purpose or pursuit. **L18.**
5 Sanction by law, custom, or usage. **M19.**

consectary /kənˈsɛktəri/ *noun*. **L16.**
[ORIGIN from Latin *consectarius* adjective, logically following (also *consectaria* noun pl.), from *consectari* frequentative of *consequi*: see CONSECUTION, -ARY[1].]
A consequence; a deduction, a conclusion, a corollary.

consecution /kɒnsɪˈkjuːʃ(ə)n/ *noun*. **LME.**
[ORIGIN Latin *consecutio(n-)*, from *consecut-* pa. ppl stem of *consequi* follow closely, overtake, formed as CON- + *sequi* pursue: see -ION.]
†**1** Attainment. *rare*. **LME–E17.**
2 (A) logical sequence; (an) inference; a train of reasoning. **M16.**
3 (A) succession, (a) sequence of events, phenomena, etc. **M16.** ▸**b** MUSIC. (A) succession of similar intervals. **M17.**

consecutive /kənˈsɛkjʊtɪv/ *adjective*. **E17.**
[ORIGIN French *consécutif*, *-ive*, from medieval Latin *consecutivus*, from *consecut-*: see CONSECUTION, -IVE.]
1 Following continuously; following one's or its predecessor in uninterrupted sequence. **E17.**

T. COLLINS Mrs. B. has.. three consecutive husbands in heaven.

†**2** Consequent (*to*). **M17–M19.**
3 Proceeding in logical sequence. **M18.**

CONAN DOYLE The first consecutive account of the affair.

4 MUSIC. Of intervals of the same kind, esp. fifths or octaves: occurring adjacently between the same two parts. **E19.**
5 GRAMMAR. Expressing consequence or result. **L19.**

C. T. ONIONS Relative Clauses with Final or Consecutive meaning sometimes take *shall* (*should*).

– SPECIAL COLLOCATIONS & PHRASES: **consecutive points**, **consecutive poles** = ***consequent points*** s.v. CONSEQUENT *adjective*. ***waw consecutive***: see WAW *noun*[3].
■ **consecutively** *adverb* **M17.** **consecutiveness** *noun* **E19.**

consenescence /kɒnsɪˈnɛs(ə)ns/ *noun*. *rare*. **L17.**
[ORIGIN from CON- (intensifier) + SENESCENCE.]
Simultaneous or parallel senescence; general decay.

consension /kənˈsɛnʃ(ə)n/ *noun*. *rare*. **L16.**
[ORIGIN Latin *consensio(n-)*, formed as CONSENSUS: see -ION.]
An agreement.

consensual /kənˈsɛnsjʊəl, -ʃʊəl/ *adjective*. **M18.**
[ORIGIN formed as CONSENSUS + -AL[1].]
1 Relating to or involving consent or consensus. **M18.**
consensual contract ROMAN LAW: requiring only the consent of the parties.
2 PHYSIOLOGY. Involving reflex response of the nervous system to stimulation of a sense organ; *spec.* designating the reaction of both eyes to a stimulus applied only to one. **E19.**
■ **consensually** *adverb* **L19.**

consensus /kənˈsɛnsəs/ *noun*. **M17.**
[ORIGIN Latin = agreement, from *consens-* pa. ppl stem of *consentire*: see CONSENT *verb*.]
1 Agreement or unity of or *of* opinion, testimony, etc.; the majority view, a collective opinion; (an agreement by different parties to) a shared body of views. **M17.**

M. HUNTER No single group has the right to ignore a consensus of thoughtful opinion. C. P. SNOW The general consensus appears to be that the murder story is unproven. *attrib.*: T. BENN Consensus politics draws its inspiration from many sources in all political parties.

2 Sympathetic or concordant action (of bodily organs etc.). Now *rare* or *obsolete*. **M19.**
– NOTE: Rare before **M19.**

consent /kənˈsɛnt/ *noun*. **ME.**
[ORIGIN Old French *consente*, formed as CONSENT *verb*.]
1 Voluntary agreement to or acquiescence in a proposition etc.; compliance, permission. **ME.**

HOBBES The Consent of a Subject to Soveraign Power. N. MITFORD I must have your consent as I'm not of age until May. *Proverb*: Silence gives consent.

age of consent the age at or above which consent, esp. of a girl to sexual intercourse, is valid in law.
2 Agreement by a number of people as to a course of action etc. Now only in ***by common consent***, (arch.) ***with one consent***, unanimously. **LME.**

W. COWPER But sing and shine by sweet consent.

3 Agreement in feeling, sympathy; harmony, accord. *arch.* **LME.**

POPE The World's great harmony, that springs From Order, Union, full Consent of things.

4 Unity of opinion, a consensus. *arch.* **E16.**

W. PALEY We are far from a perfect consent in our opinions or feelings.

†**5** Feeling, opinion. Only in **L16.**

SHAKES. *1 Hen. VI* By my consent, we'll even let them alone.

†**6** PHYSIOLOGY. A sympathetic relation between one organ and another. **E17–L18.**

consent /kənˈsɛnt/ *verb*. **ME.**
[ORIGIN Old French & mod. French *consentir* from Latin *consentire*, formed as CON- + *sentire* feel.]
▸ **I** *verb intrans.* **1** Be of the same opinion, agree (*with* a person, *that*, †*to* a doctrine etc.). *arch.* **ME.**

SHAKES. *A.Y.L.* All your writers do consent that ipse is he.

2 Express willingness, give permission, agree (*to* a proposal etc., *to do*, *that*). **ME.**

BYRON And whispering 'I will ne'er consent'—consented. E. M. FORSTER Mr. Beebe consented to run—a memorable sight.

consenting adult: who willingly takes part in a particular action, esp. a homosexual act.
†**3** Come to agreement. **LME–M17.**
†**4** Be in accord or harmony. **LME–L18.**

BACON Thinges like and consenting in qualitie.

†**5** Act or react in sympathy. Only in **M18.**
▸ **II** *verb trans.* †**6** Allow, agree to, consent to. **LME–L17.**
■ **consenter** *noun* **ME.** **consentingly** *adverb* (***a***) with consent or willing acquiescence; †(***b***) by common consent: **LME.** **consentive** *adjective* (*rare*) = CONSENTIENT **L15.**

consentaneous /kɒns(ə)nˈteɪnɪəs/ *adjective*. **L16.**
[ORIGIN from Latin *consentaneus*, from *consentire*: see CONSENT *verb*, -ANEOUS.]
1 Unanimous, done by common consent; concurrent. **L16.**
2 Accordant, suited (*to*, *with*). **E17.**
■ **consentaˈneity** *noun* consentaneous quality **L18.** **consentaneously** *adverb* **L16.** **consentaneousness** *noun* **M17.**

consentant /kənˈsɛntənt/ *adjective*. *rare*. **LME.**
[ORIGIN Old French & mod. French, pres. pple of *consentir* CONSENT *verb*: see -ANT[1].]
Consenting.

consentient /kənˈsɛnʃ(ə)nt/ *adjective*. **E17.**
[ORIGIN Latin *consentient-* pres. ppl stem of *consentire*: see CONSENT *verb*, -ENT.]
1 Agreeing, unanimous. **E17.** ▸**b** Acting together, concurrent. **M18.** ▸**c** Exhibiting or involving the body's ability to act as a unified whole in reflex response to sensory stimuli. **L19.**
2 Consenting, accordant, (*to*). **M17.**
■ **consentience** *noun* **L19.**

consequence /ˈkɒnsɪkw(ə)ns/ *noun*. **LME.**
[ORIGIN Old French & mod. French *conséquence* from Latin *consequentia*, from *consequent-* pres. ppl stem of *consequi* follow closely: see CONSECUTION, -ENCE.]
1 A thing or circumstance which follows as an effect or result from something preceding. **LME.**

J. LE CARRÉ A minor heart attack as a consequence of stress and overwork.

2 A logical result or inference. **LME.**
3 Importance, moment, weight. **M16.** ▸**b** *spec.* Importance in rank and position; social distinction. **E17.** ▸**c** *spec.* Assumed sense of importance. **L18.**

H. JAMES This defect was of no great consequence.

4 The action or condition of following as a result upon something antecedent; the relation of an effect to its cause; the following of a logical conclusion from premisses. **L16.** ▸†**b** Sequence; succession; course. **L16–E18.**

MILTON Such fatal consequence unites us three. **b** HOBBES They thought the Names.. sufficiently connected when.. placed in their natural consequence.

5 ASTROLOGY. Motion from an earlier to a later sign of the zodiac or from west to east. Now *rare* or *obsolete*. **L17.**
6 In *pl.* (usu. treated as *sing.*). A pencil-and-paper game in which a narrative is devised, usu. describing the meeting of a man and woman, and its consequences, each player contributing a part in ignorance of what has gone before. **L18.**
– PHRASES: **in consequence**, (*arch.*) **by consequence** as a result (*of*). **of consequence** (***a***) important, significant; (***b***) *arch.* as a result. †**of good consequence**, **of bad consequence**, etc., with good, bad, etc., results. **of no consequence** unimportant. **take the consequences** accept whatever results from one's choice or act, *esp.* accept punishment.
■ †**consequency** *noun* = CONSEQUENCE 1, 2, 4 **M16–E18.**

consequent /ˈkɒnsɪkw(ə)nt/ *noun*. **LME.**
[ORIGIN Old French & mod. French *conséquent*, formed as CONSEQUENT *adjective* (use as noun of pres. pple).]
†**1** = CONSEQUENCE 1. **LME–M18.**
†**2 a** = CONSEQUENCE 2. **LME–M19.** ▸**b** *spec.* The second part of a conditional proposition, dependent on the antecedent. **E17.**
†**3** A follower; a pursuer. **M16–M17.**
4 A thing which follows something else in time or order (without necessary causal connection); MATH. (now *rare*) the second of two quantities linked by some relationship or operation (e.g. a ratio). **L16.**

consequent /ˈkɒnsɪkw(ə)nt/ *adjective*. **LME.**
[ORIGIN Old French & mod. French *conséquent* from Latin *consequent-*: see CONSEQUENCE, -ENT.]
1 Following as an effect or result (*on*, *upon*, *to*), resulting. **LME.**

C

J. LONDON Reaction and exhaustion consequent upon the hard day. P. ROSE Innocence of the female nude and consequent shock when confronted with one.

2 Following as an inference or logical conclusion. LME. †**3** Following in time or order; subsequent. L16–M18. **4** Observing or characterized by logical sequence; logically consistent. M19. **5** *PHYSICAL GEOGRAPHY.* Of a stream, valley, etc.: having a course or character corresponding to the original slope of the land surface before it began to be eroded. Cf. OBSEQUENT *adjective* 1, SUBSEQUENT *adjective* 2b. L19.

– SPECIAL COLLOCATIONS: **consequent points** magnetic poles in excess of the usual pair in any magnetized body.

consequential /kɒnsɪˈkwɛnʃ(ə)l/ *adjective.* E17.

[ORIGIN from Latin *consequentia* CONSEQUENCE + -AL[1].]

1 Following, esp. as an (immediate or eventual) effect, or as a logical inference; of the nature of a consequence. E17.

S. TURNER Wars and their consequential burthens.

consequential damages, **consequential losses**: that follow or result from an act, but not directly and immediately.

2 Characterized by logical sequence or consistency. Now *rare.* M17.

COLERIDGE A consistent and strictly consequential Materialism.

3 Of consequence; important, significant. Now only of a person: having social consequence. E18. **4** Self-important. M18.

■ **consequentialism** *noun* the belief that the morality of an action is to be judged solely from its consequences M20. **consequentialist** *noun & adjective* (*a*) *noun* an advocate of consequentialism; (*b*) *adjective* pertaining to or advocating consequentialism: M20. **consequentiˈality** *noun* E19. **consequentially** *adverb* E17. **consequentialness** *noun* (*rare*) L17.

consequently /ˈkɒnsɪkw(ə)ntli/ *adverb & conjunction.* LME.

[ORIGIN from CONSEQUENTIAL + -LY[2].]

†**1** *adverb.* In following time or order; subsequently. LME–E17. †**2** *adverb.* With proper sequence or connection of thought etc.; consistently. LME–L18. **3** *adverb & conjunction.* As a consequence or result, therefore, accordingly. LME.

B. T. WASHINGTON There was no provision made in the house . . , and consequently a fire had to be built in the yard. SCOTT FITZGERALD Rosemary still thought her money was miraculously lent to her and she must consequently be very careful of it.

†**conservacy** *noun.* M16–M18.

[ORIGIN Anglo-Norman *conservacie* from Anglo-Latin *conservatia* by-form of Latin *conservatio(n-)* CONSERVATION: see -ACY.]

= CONSERVANCY.

conservancy /kənˈsəːv(ə)nsi/ *noun.* M18.

[ORIGIN Alt. of CONSERVACY: see -ANCY.]

1 A commission, (formerly) court, etc., controlling a port, river, etc.; a similar body concerned with other environmental resources. M18. **2** Official preservation of a resource, e.g. forests. M19.

conservate /ˈkɒnsəveɪt/ *verb trans. rare.* M19.

[ORIGIN Latin *conservat-* pa. ppl stem of *conservare*: see CONSERVE *verb*, -ATE[3].]

Conserve; preserve.

conservation /kɒnsəˈveɪʃ(ə)n/ *noun.* LME.

[ORIGIN Old French & mod. French, or Latin *conservatio(n-)*, from *conservat-* pa. ppl stem of *conservare*: see CONSERVE *verb*, -ATION.]

1 The action of keeping from harm, decay, loss, or waste; careful preservation. LME. ▸**b** The preservation *of* existing conditions, institutions, rights, etc. LME. ▸**c** The preservation of the environment, esp. of natural resources. E20.

c *Guardian* The conservation and environmental enhancement of the canal corridor.

2 Official charge and care of rivers, sewers, forests, etc.; conservancy. L15. **3** *PHYSICS.* (A principle stating) the invariance of the total quantity *of* energy (or any of certain other physical properties) possessed by a system of bodies not subject to external action. M19.

conservation of energy, ***conservation of mass***, ***conservation of momentum***, etc.

4 The preserving of fruit etc. L19.

– COMB.: **conservation area** an area containing noteworthy buildings etc. which is specially protected by law from undesirable changes; **conservation law**: stating the conservation (sense 3) of a particular physical property (under some or all circumstances or in certain interactions).

■ **conservational** *adjective* M19. **conservationist** *noun* a proponent or advocate of (esp. environmental) conservation L19.

conservatism /kənˈsəːvətɪz(ə)m/ *noun.* M19.

[ORIGIN from CONSERVATIVE + -ISM.]

1 (Usu. **C-**.) The doctrine and practice of Conservatives; Toryism. M19. **2** Reluctance to make changes; conservative principles in politics, theology, etc. M19.

■ **conservatist** *noun & adjective* (*rare*) (*a*) *noun* a person preferring the preservation of institutions etc. unchanged; (*b*) *adjective* conservative: M19. **conservatize** *verb trans. & intrans.* (*rare*) make or become conservative M19.

conservative /kənˈsəːvətɪv/ *adjective & noun.* LME.

[ORIGIN Late Latin *conservativus*, from Latin *conservat-*: see CONSERVATION, -ATIVE.]

▸ **A** *adjective.* **1** Characterized by a tendency to preserve or keep intact and unchanged; preservative (*of*). LME. ▸**b** *PHYSICS.* Characterized by conservation (sense 3). L19.

J. RUSKIN Jealously conservative of old things, but conservative of them as pillars, not as pinnacles.

2 (Usu. **C-**.) Of, supporting, or characteristic of the Conservative Party (see below) of Great Britain, or an analogous political party in another country. M19. **3** Characterized by caution, moderation, or reluctance to make changes; (of views, taste, etc.) avoiding extremes. M19. ▸**b** Of an estimate etc.: purposely low. E20.

N. MITFORD Being conservative by nature I was glad to see that the decoration of the room had not been changed. L. GOULD The white shirt, tie and conservative navy-blue suit. **b** *Daily Telegraph* The distances quoted are conservative.

– SPECIAL COLLOCATIONS: ***Conservative and Unionist Party***: see ***Conservative Party*** below. **Conservative Jew** an adherent of Conservative Judaism. **Conservative Judaism** a movement favouring certain non-essential adaptations or relaxations of Jewish law and tradition. **Conservative Party**, (since 1912 more fully) **Conservative and Unionist Party** a British political party which developed from the old Tory Party in the 1830s, and is generally disposed to maintain traditional institutions and promote individual enterprise. **conservative surgery**: that seeks to preserve tissues as far as possible.

▸ **B** *noun.* **1** A preserving agent or principle; a preservative. LME. **2** (Usu. **C-**.) A member or supporter of the British Conservative Party, or of an analogous party elsewhere; a Tory. In early use, a supporter of Sir Robert Peel. M19. **3** A conservative person. M19.

■ **conservatively** *adverb* M19. **conservativeness** *noun* M19. **conservativism** *noun* = CONSERVATISM M19.

conservatoire /kənˈsəːvətwɑː, *foreign* kɔ̃sɛrvatwaːr (*pl. same*)/ *noun.* L18.

[ORIGIN French from Italian CONSERVATORIO.]

An academy of music or other performing arts, esp. in France or elsewhere in Continental Europe. Cf. CONSERVATORIO, CONSERVATORIUM, CONSERVATORY *noun* 5.

conservator /*esp. in sense* 1 ˈkɒnsəveɪtə, *esp. in sense* 2 kənˈsəːvətə/ *noun.* LME.

[ORIGIN Anglo-Norman *conservatour*, Old French & mod. French *conservateur* from Latin *conservator* keeper, preserver, from *conservat-*: see CONSERVATION, -OR.]

1 A preserver, a keeper. LME. **2** An official custodian of a museum etc.; a member of a conservancy. LME.

■ **conservatorship** *noun* M17. **conˈservatrix** /-trɪks/ *noun*, pl. **-trices** /-trɪsiːz/, [Latin] a female conservator LME.

conservatoria *noun pl.* see CONSERVATORIUM.

conservatorio /kɒnsəːvəˈtɔːrɪəʊ/ *noun.* Pl. **-os.** L18.

[ORIGIN Italian, formed as CONSERVATORY *noun*.]

An (Italian or Spanish) academy of music or other performing arts. Cf. CONSERVATOIRE, CONSERVATORIUM, CONSERVATORY *noun* 5.

– NOTE: Orig. an Italian hospital or school for orphans and foundlings where a musical education was given.

conservatorium /kənsəːvəˈtɔːrɪəm/ *noun.* Pl. **-iums**, **-ia** /-ɪə/. M19.

[ORIGIN German & mod. Latin, formed as CONSERVATORY *noun*: see -ORIUM.]

An academy of music or other performing arts, esp. in Germany, Austria, or Australia. Cf. CONSERVATOIRE, CONSERVATORIO, CONSERVATORY *noun* 5.

conservatory /kənˈsəːvət(ə)ri/ *noun.* M16.

[ORIGIN Late Latin *conservatorium* use as noun of neut. of *conservatorius* adjective, from *conservat-*: see CONSERVATION, -ORY[1]. In branch II after Italian CONSERVATORIO, French CONSERVATOIRE.]

▸ **I** †**1** A thing which preserves; a preservative. M16–M17. †**2** A place where things are preserved, stored, or kept securely; a repository; a reservoir of water. E17–L18. **3** A greenhouse for tender plants; a room, esp. attached to a house, designed for the growing or displaying of plants. M17.

▸ **II** †**4** A hospital or school for orphans and foundlings. Only in 17. **5** An academy of music or other performing arts. Cf. CONSERVATOIRE, CONSERVATORIO, CONSERVATORIUM. Chiefly *N. Amer.* E19.

conservatory /kənˈsəːvət(ə)ri/ *adjective.* L16.

[ORIGIN Late Latin *conservatorius*: see CONSERVATORY *noun*, -ORY[2].]

1 Adapted to conserve; preservative. L16. **2** = CONSERVATIVE *adjective* 3. Now *rare.* E19.

conserve /kənˈsəːv, ˈkɒnsəːv/ *noun.* LME.

[ORIGIN Old French & mod. French (= Italian, Spanish, medieval Latin *conserva*) formed as CONSERVE *verb*.]

†**1** A preservative. LME–L16. †**2** A preserve; a store; a hoard. LME–M17. **3** A confectionary or (formerly) medicinal preparation of fruit etc. preserved in sugar; jam, esp. made from fresh fruit. LME.

conserve /kənˈsəːv/ *verb trans.* LME.

[ORIGIN Old French & mod. French *conserver* from Latin *conservare*, formed as CON- + *servare* keep.]

1 Keep from harm, decay, loss, or waste, esp. with a view to later use; preserve with care. LME. ▸†**b** Keep alive or flourishing. LME–L17. ▸**c** *PHYSICS.* Maintain (energy etc.) unchanged in total quantity according to a conservation law. Usu. in *pass.* L19.

EVELYN Draw them out of the ground before the frost, and conserve them in a warm place. R. DAWKINS Emperor penguins conserve heat by huddling together.

†**2** Keep (a commandment etc.); observe (a custom or rite). LME–M17. **3** Preserve (fruit etc.) in sugar or by similar means; make into a conserve. L15.

■ **conservable** *adjective* [Late Latin *conservabilis*] E17. **conserver** *noun* LME.

consider /kənˈsɪdə/ *verb.* LME.

[ORIGIN Old French & mod. French *considérer* from Latin *considerare* examine, perh. formed as CON- + *sider-*, *sidus* constellation, star.]

1 *verb trans.* Look at attentively; survey; scrutinize. *arch.* LME.

MILTON And with inspection deep Consider'd every Creature.

2 *verb intrans.* Look attentively. Long *arch.* LME.

AV *Lev.* 13:13 The Priest shall consider: and behold, if the leprosie haue couered al his flesh, he shal pronounce him cleane.

3 *verb trans.* Give mental attention to; think over, meditate or reflect on; pay heed to, take note of; weigh the merits of. LME. ▸**b** Give mental attention to the fact *that*; reflect or take note of *how*, *whether*, *who*, *why*, etc. LME.

SHAKES. *Lear* Is man no more than this? Consider him well. J. SIMMS Just before I went to Germany I had considered returning to Japan. **b** T. HARDY He paused . . to consider how they might have got there.

4 *verb intrans.* Think carefully, reflect. (Foll. by *of* (arch.), †*on*.) LME.

G. K. CHESTERTON But consider a moment; do not condemn me hastily.

†**5** *verb trans.* Estimate; reckon. LME–M16. **6** *verb trans.* Take into account; show regard for; make allowance for. LME. ▸**b** In *pa. pple* in an *absol.* clause: being taken into account. Now chiefly in ***all things considered***. LME. **7** *verb trans.* Regard in a certain light or aspect; look upon *as*; think or take *to be* (or absol.). M16. ▸**b** Be of the opinion *that*; suppose *to do*, *to have done*. M19.

A. LANG Consider yourself under arrest! N. MITFORD A determination to show people what she considered to be their proper place and keep them in it. **b** OED I consider him to have acted disgracefully. J. CONRAD She considered herself to be of French descent. D. H. LAWRENCE I consider this is really the heart of England.

†**8** *verb trans.* Recognize in a practical way; remunerate; recompense. L16–L17.

SHAKES. *Meas. for M.* You that have worn your eyes almost out in the service, you will be considered.

9 *verb trans.* Think highly of; esteem; respect. *arch.* L17.

S. JOHNSON A pamphlet . . which was . . enough considered to be both seriously and ludicrously answered.

■ **considered** *ppl adjective* (*a*) maturely reflected on, done etc. after careful thought; (*b*) *arch.* highly thought of, respected: E17. **considerer** *noun* LME. **consideringly** *adverb* thoughtfully; in a considering manner, tone, or attitude: M17.

considerable /kənˈsɪd(ə)rəb(ə)l/ *adjective, noun, & adverb.* LME.

[ORIGIN medieval Latin *considerabilis* worthy to be considered, from Latin *considerare*: see CONSIDER, -ABLE.]

▸ **A** *adjective.* †**1** That may be considered or viewed. *rare.* LME–M17. †**2** That should be considered or taken into account; notable. L16–E18. **3** Worthy of consideration or regard; of consequence. (Passing into sense 4.) E17.

W. FIELD The daughter of a considerable potter in that neighbourhood.

4 Worthy of consideration by reason of magnitude; somewhat large in amount, extent, duration, etc.; a good deal of (an abstract or (chiefly *US*) material thing). M17.

CONAN DOYLE A great wandering house, standing in a considerable park. D. L. SAYERS She evidently gave considerable thought to the subject. W. BOYD The flow of traffic was considerable.

▸ **B** *noun.* †**1** A thing to be considered; a point etc. worth considering. M–L17. **2** A fair amount or quantity (*of*), a good deal, much. *US.* L17.

W. FAULKNER Maybe a considerable of almost anything else. I. SHAW I've heard considerable about you.

▸ **C** *adverb.* = CONSIDERABLY. Now *US & dial.* **L17.**
■ **considera'bility** *noun (rare)* **M17.** **considerableness** *noun* (now *rare*) **M17.** **considerably** *adverb* †(*a*) in a way or to a degree that ought to be noticed; (*b*) to a large extent, much, a good deal: **M17.**

†**considerance** *noun.* **LME–L16.**
[ORIGIN Old French from Latin *considerantia*, from stem of *considerare*: see CONSIDER, -ANCE.]
The action or an act of considering; reflection.

SHAKES. *2 Hen. IV* After this cold considerance, sentence me.

considerate /kən'sɪd(ə)rət/ *adjective.* **L16.**
[ORIGIN Latin *consideratus* pa. pple of *considerare*: see CONSIDER, -ATE[2]. Cf. earlier INCONSIDERATE.]
1 Marked by or showing careful thought; deliberate; prudent, thoughtful. *arch.* **L16.**

J. LOCKE None of the Definitions . . are so perfect . . as to satisfy a considerate inquisitive Person. SIR W. SCOTT Foster . . paced the room twice with the same steady and considerate pace.

2 Showing consideration for the circumstances, feelings, well-being, etc., of others; thoughtful for others. **E18.**

J. G. FARRELL The Major's considerate inquiries about . . the state of her health. M. KEANE She shut the drawer carefully—she was gently considerate to all furniture.

■ **considerately** *adverb* **M16.** **considerateness** *noun* **M17.**

consideration /kənsɪdə'reɪʃ(ə)n/ *noun.* **LME.**
[ORIGIN Old French & mod. French *considération* from Latin *consideratio(n-)*, from *considerat-* pa. ppl stem of *considerare*: see CONSIDER, -ATION.]
†**1** The action of viewing with the eyes or mind; beholding. **LME–M17.**
2 The keeping of a subject before the mind; attentive thought; reflection; meditation. **LME.** ▸**b** In *pl.* Thoughts, reflections. **L15.**

M. AMIS Deciding, after mature consideration, against the hamburger.

3 The action of taking into account; the fact of being taken into account. **LME.**

M. W. MONTAGU I . . speak . . without any consideration, but that of your figure and reputation.

4 The taking into account of anything as a reason or motive; a fact or circumstance taken, or to be taken, into account. **LME.**

E. WAUGH Those with whom price is not a primary consideration. S. BELLOW Returning once more to practical considerations, he must be very careful.

5 Regard for the circumstances, feelings, comfort, etc., of another; considerateness. **LME.**

S. DELANEY She's not got a bit of consideration in her.

6 **a** *LAW.* Something given, done, or forborne in return for the promise or act of another party. **M16.** ▸**b** Something given in payment; a reward; a remuneration; a compensation. **E17.**
7 Estimation; esteem; importance; consequence. *arch.* **L16.**

LD MACAULAY A man of the first consideration.

– PHRASES: **in consideration of** in return for; on account of. **leave out of consideration** fail to make allowance for. **take into consideration** make allowance for. **under consideration** being considered. ***valuable consideration***: see VALUABLE *adjective* 1.

†**considerative** *adjective.* **LME–E19.**
[ORIGIN Old French *consideratif*, *-ive* from medieval Latin *considerativus* reflective, thoughtful; later from CONSIDERATE + -IVE.]
= CONSIDERATE.

considering /kən'sɪd(ə)rɪŋ/ *preposition, conjunction, & adverb.* **LME.**
[ORIGIN Absol. use of pres. pple or verbal noun of CONSIDER: see -ING[2], -ING[1].]
▸ **A** *preposition & conjunction.* When one considers (*that*); taking into account (the fact *that*). **LME.**

F. SMITH The Evening was pleasant, and also warm, considering we were amongst Ice. H. JAMES Considering its great fury the storm took long to expend itself.

▸ **B** *adverb.* Considering the circumstances; taking everything into account. *colloq.* **M18.**

M. R. MITFORD We went on very prosperously, *considering*; as people say of a young lady's drawing, or a Frenchman's English, or a woman's tragedy.

consigliere /kɒnslɪ'ɛːri/ *noun.* Pl. **-ri** /-ri/. **E17.**
[ORIGIN Italian, from *consiglio* counsel, advice.]
1 *POLITICS.* In Italy: a member of a council. **E17.**
2 A member of a Mafia family who serves as an adviser to the leader and resolves disputes within the family. **M20.** ▸**b** A counsellor, an adviser. *colloq.* **L20.**

consign /kən'sʌɪn/ *verb.* **LME.**
[ORIGIN French *consigner* from Latin *consignare* attest with a seal, formed as CON- + *signare* SIGN *verb.*]
†**1** *verb trans.* Mark with the sign of the cross; *spec.* confirm; dedicate *to*, *unto* thus. **LME–E18.**
†**2** *verb trans.* Attest, confirm, ratify. **LME–M19.**
3 *verb trans.* Entrust or commit to another's charge or care. **E16.** ▸**b** Deposit (money). **M16.**
†**4** *verb intrans.* Foll. by *to*: agree to, subscribe to; submit to the same terms as. *rare* (Shakes.). **L16–E17.**
5 *verb trans.* Make over as a possession, deliver formally or commit *to* a state, fate, etc. **M17.**

C. RAYNER I would have consigned them both to perdition. P. ACKROYD To escape from the academic career to which his family seemed to have consigned him.

6 *verb trans.* Deliver or transmit (goods) for sale etc. or custody; send (goods) by carrier, rail, etc., (*to*). **M17.**
■ †**consignatary** *noun* a consignee **L17–M18.** **consi'gnee** *noun* a person to whom goods are consigned **L18.** **consigner** *noun* a person who consigns **M17.** **consignor** *noun* a person who dispatches goods to another **L18.**

consignation /kɒnsɪg'neɪʃ(ə)n/ *noun.* Now *rare.* **M16.**
[ORIGIN Latin *consignatio(n-)* (in medieval Latin senses), from *consignat-* pa. ppl stem of *consignare*: see CONSIGN, -ATION.]
†**1** The action of marking with the sign of the cross. **M16–M19.**
2 The action of paying over or depositing money; a sum deposited. **M16.**
†**3** Sealing; confirmation; attestation. **E17–M19.**
†**4** (Formal) delivery; consigning *to* a state or condition. Only in **17.**
5 = CONSIGNMENT 3. **E18.**

consigne /kɔ̃siɲ/ *noun.* Pl. pronounced same. **M19.**
[ORIGIN French, from *consigner* give instructions to a sentinel.]
1 An order given to a sentinel; a password. *rare.* **M19.**
2 A left-luggage office in France. **L19.**

consignificant /kɒnsɪg'nɪfɪk(ə)nt/ *adjective. rare.* **E17.**
[ORIGIN formed as CONSIGNIFY: see -ANT[1].]
Conjointly significant; having a meaning in combination with something else.
■ Also **consignificative** *adjective (rare)* **M17.**

consignification /ˌkɒnsɪgnɪfɪ'keɪʃ(ə)n/ *noun. rare.* **E18.**
[ORIGIN medieval Latin *consignificatio(n-)*, from *consignificat-* pa. ppl stem of *consignificare*: see CONSIGNIFY, -ATION.]
Joint or conjoint signification; (a) connotation.

consignify /kɒn'sɪgnɪfʌɪ/ *verb trans. & intrans. rare.* **E17.**
[ORIGIN medieval Latin *consignificare*, from Latin CON- + *significare* SIGNIFY.]
Signify in conjunction (*with*).

consignment /kən'sʌɪnm(ə)nt/ *noun.* **M16.**
[ORIGIN from CONSIGN + -MENT.]
1 The action of sealing or dedicating with a sign. *rare.* **M16.**
2 The action or an act of handing over; committal, delivery. **M17.**
3 The action of consigning goods for sale etc. or custody. **E18.**
4 A quantity of goods consigned for sale etc. or custody. **E18.**

consilient /kɒn'sɪlɪənt/ *adjective.* **M19.**
[ORIGIN from CON- + Latin *-silient-*, *-ens* jumping (as in *resilient-*, *-ens* RESILIENT), after *concurrent*.]
Of inductions from different phenomena etc.: concurrent, agreeing.
■ **consilience** *noun* the fact or condition of being consilient **M19.**

consimilar /kɒn'sɪmɪlə/ *adjective.* Now *rare.* **M16.**
[ORIGIN from Latin *consimilis*, formed as CON- + *similis*: see SIMILAR.]
†**1** Homogeneous. **M16–M17.**
2 Entirely similar, like. **M17.**
■ **consimi'larity** *noun (rare)* mutual likeness **M17.**

consist /kən'sɪst/ *verb intrans.* **LME.**
[ORIGIN Latin *consistere* stand still, remain firm, exist, formed as CON- + *sistere* place, stand firm or still. Cf. French *consister*.]
▸ **I** **1** Foll. by *in*: ▸†**a** Exist or reside in; be located or inherent in. **LME–E19.** ▸**b** Be constituted or composed of (actions, qualities, etc.; *arch.* material things); have its essential features in. **L16.**

b S. BUTLER Moral government consists . . in rewarding the righteous, and punishing the wicked. I. MURDOCH Part of my unease about my cousin consisted in a fear that he would succeed in life and I would fail.

†**2** Exist together as compatible facts; be compatible (*with*). **M16–M19.**

J. WESLEY Costiveness cannot long consist with Health.

3 Have a settled existence; subsist, hold together, exist. *arch.* **M16.** ▸†**b** Stand firm, remain, stay; have its place. **M16–M17.**

AV *Col.* 1:17 He is before all things, and by him all things consist.

4 Be made up or composed *of.* **M16.**

C. A. LINDBERGH His education consisted largely of home study. J. SIMMS The group consisted of five string players and two singers.

†**5** Be based or rest (*up*)*on.* **M16–M17.**
6 Be consistent, be congruous, harmonize, (*with*). **M17.**

G. GROTE Appetites are to be indulged only so far as consists with some . . approved end.

▸ †**II** **7** Insist (*up*)*on. rare.* **E16–E17.**
■ †**consisting** *ppl adjective* (*a*) cohering, united; (*b*) = CONSISTENT 4: **E17–E18.**

consistence /kən'sɪst(ə)ns/ *noun.* **L16.**
[ORIGIN French *consistance*, †*-ence* or late Latin *consistentia*, from *consistent-* pres. ppl stem of *consistere*: see CONSIST, -ENCE.]
†**1** Standing or remaining still; a state of rest; a settled condition, *spec.* in the life of an organism when it is fully grown. **L16–M18.**

EVELYN I hope I have brought my affaires almost to a Consistence.

2 †**a** Matter dense enough to cohere. **L16–L18.** ▸**b** Material coherence and permanence of form; solidity sufficient to retain form. **E17.**

b T. THOMSON Cubic crystals without consistence, . . resembling a jelly.

3 = CONSISTENCY 2. **E17.**

P. V. WHITE Soup . . of a milky . . consistence.

†**4** (A) union, (a) combination. **M17–E18.**
5 = CONSISTENCY 3, 3b. **L17.**

consistency /kən'sɪst(ə)nsi/ *noun.* **L16.**
[ORIGIN from (the same root as) CONSISTENCE: see -ENCY.]
1 = CONSISTENCE 2b. **L16.**
2 The degree of firmness with which the particles of a substance cohere; degree of density, esp. of thick liquids. **M17.**
3 The quality, state, or fact of being consistent; agreement (*with* something, *of* things etc.); uniformity, regularity. **M17.** ▸**b** The agreement of parts or elements with each other, esp. as a personal attribute in life or conduct; constancy of principle etc. **E18.**

W. PALEY To question the consistency of the two records. P. V. PRICE Branded wines make consistency of quality possible. **b** R. W. EMERSON A foolish consistency is the hobgoblin of little minds.

†**4** A settled condition. **L17–E18.**

consistent /kən'sɪst(ə)nt/ *adjective & adverb.* **L16.**
[ORIGIN Latin *consistent-* pres. ppl stem of *consistere*: see CONSIST, -ENT.]
▸ **A** *adjective.* †**1** Consisting *in*, *of*, composed *of.* **L16–L17.**
†**2** Remaining still; settled, durable. Only in **17.**
†**3** Coexisting (*with*). *rare.* **M17–M18.**
†**4** Holding together as a coherent material body; firm, solid. **M17–M19.**
5 Agreeing in substance or form; congruous, compatible (*with*, †*to*), not contradictory; marked by uniformity or regularity. **M17.** ▸**b** *LOGIC.* Of an axiom system: leading to no theorems that contradict each other. **E20.** ▸**c** *STATISTICS.* Of an estimate etc.: approaching the true value of the quantity estimated more closely as the sample size is increased. **E20.**

SIR T. BROWNE An habite . . not consistent with the words of our Saviour. H. T. BUCKLE The most consistent of all combinations . . great ignorance with great arrogance. H. CECIL Since a regular backer of horses . . is usually a loser, repeated and consistent wins excite suspicion.

6 Of a person, conduct: constantly adhering to the same principles of thought or action. **M18.**

B. JOWETT Let us be consistent then, and either believe both or neither. W. S. CHURCHILL Two generations of consistent House of Commons parsimony.

▸ **B** *adverb.* Consistently. Now *rare* or *obsolete.* **M18.**
■ **consistently** *adverb* in accordance *with*; with consistency; uniformly: **E18.**

consistometer /kɒnsɪ'stɒmɪtə/ *noun.* **E20.**
[ORIGIN from CONSISTENCY + -OMETER.]
An instrument for measuring the consistency of a viscous or plastic material.

consistorial /kɒnsɪ'stɔːrɪəl/ *adjective.* **LME.**
[ORIGIN Old French & mod. French, or medieval Latin *consistorialis*, from late Latin *consistorium*: see CONSISTORY, -AL[1].]
1 Of or pertaining to a consistory. **LME.**
2 Of or pertaining to Church government by consistories; Presbyterian. **M16.**
■ **consistorially** *adverb (rare)* **E17.** †**consistorical** *adjective* = CONSISTORIAL **E17–M18.**

consistorian /kɒnsɪ'stɔːrɪən/ *adjective & noun.* **L16.**
[ORIGIN Latin *consistorianus*, from *consistorium*: see CONSISTORY, -AN.]
▸ †**A** *adjective.* = CONSISTORIAL. **L16–M17.**
▸ **B** *noun.* †**1** A settled inhabitant. *rare.* Only in **L16.**
2 A Presbyterian. *obsolete* exc. *hist.* **E17.**

consistory /kən'sɪst(ə)ri/ *noun.* **ME.**
[ORIGIN Anglo-Norman *consistorie* = Old French & mod. French *consistoire* from late Latin *consistorium*, formed as CONSIST: see -ORY[1].]
▸ †**I** **1** A place where councillors meet, a council-chamber. **ME–M18.**
†**2** A court, a company surrounding a throne. Also, a court of judgement. **ME–L17.**
3 A meeting of councillors, a council. *obsolete* exc. *hist.* or *poet.* **LME.**
▸ **II** Ecclesiastical senses.
4 (Usu. **C-**.) A bishop's court for ecclesiastical causes and offences; a diocesan court, held by the chancellor or

commissary of a diocese. (Now only in the Anglican Church.) Also ***Consistory Court***. **ME.**
5 (A meeting of) the council of the Pope and cardinals. **LME.**
6 In the Reformed Protestant Churches, a court of presbyters. **L16.**
7 In the Lutheran Church, a supervisory board of clerical officers. **L17.**

C

consociate /kɒnˈsəʊʃɪət, -sɪət/ *adjective & noun*. **LME.**
[**ORIGIN** Latin *consociatus* pa. pple, formed as **CONSOCIATE** *verb*: see **-ATE**², **-ATE**¹.]
▸ **A** *adjective*. Associated; united in fellowship. **LME.**
▸ **B** *noun*. A partner, an associate. **L16.**

consociate /kɒnˈsəʊʃɪeɪt, -səʊsɪ-/ *verb*. **L16.**
[**ORIGIN** Latin *consociat-* pa. ppl stem of *consociare*, formed as **CON-** + *sociare* to associate, from *socius* fellow: see **-ATE**³.]
1 *verb trans.* Bring into association or partnership; join in action. **L16.**
2 *verb intrans.* Enter into association or union; keep company *with*. **M17.**

consociation /kɒnsəʊʃɪˈeɪʃ(ə)n, -səʊsɪ-/ *noun*. **L16.**
[**ORIGIN** Latin *consociatio(n-)*, formed as **CONSOCIATE** *verb*: see **-ATION**.]
1 The action or fact of associating together; combination. **L16.**
2 Fellowship, companionship (*with*). **E17.**
3 An alliance or confederation, esp. of Congregational or Presbyterian churches in an area. Now *hist.* exc. *US*. **E17.** ▸**b** A council of Congregational churchmen. *US*. **L18.**
4 *ECOLOGY*. A small climax community or division of a plant association characterized by a single dominant species. **E20.**
5 A political system in which power is shared by representatives of different or antagonistic social groups. **M20.**
■ **consociational** *adjective* **L19**. **consociationalism** *noun* the principle or practice of political consociation **M20**.

consol *noun* see **CONSOLS**.

consolable /kənˈsəʊləb(ə)l/ *adjective*. **M17.**
[**ORIGIN** from **CONSOLE** *verb* + **-ABLE**. Cf. earlier **INCONSOLABLE**, **UNCONSOLABLE**.]
Able to be consoled.

consolamentum /kɒnsəʊləˈmɛntəm/ *noun*. Pl. **-ta** /-tə/. **L19.**
[**ORIGIN** mod. Latin, from Latin *consolari*: see **CONSOLE** *verb*.]
ECCLESIASTICAL HISTORY. The spiritual baptism of the Cathars.

†**consolate** *verb trans.* Pa. pple **-ated**, (earlier) **-ate**. **L15–E19.**
[**ORIGIN** Latin *consolat-*: see **CONSOLATION**, **-ATE**³.]
= **CONSOLE** *verb*.

consolatio /kɒnsəˈleɪʃɪəʊ, -ˈlɑːtɪəʊ/ *noun*. Pl. ***-iones*** /-ɪˈəʊniːz/. **M20.**
[**ORIGIN** Latin: see **CONSOLATION**.]
A thing written to expound philosophical or religious themes as comfort for the misfortunes of life.

consolation /kɒnsəˈleɪʃ(ə)n/ *noun*. **LME.**
[**ORIGIN** Old French & mod. French from Latin *consolatio(n-)*, from *consolat-* pa. ppl stem of *consolari*: see **CONSOLE** *verb*, **-ATION**.]
1 The action of consoling; alleviation of sorrow or mental distress; the state of being consoled. **LME.**
2 A fact, event, etc., that serves to console. **LME.**
– **COMB.**: **consolation prize**: given to a competitor who has just missed a main prize.

consolationes *noun* pl. of **CONSOLATIO**.

†**consolator** *noun*. **M16–M18.**
[**ORIGIN** Latin *consolator*, from *consolat-*: see **CONSOLATION**, **-OR**.]
A consoler.

consolatory /kənˈsɒlət(ə)ri, -ˈsəʊl-/ *adjective & noun*. **LME.**
[**ORIGIN** Latin *consolatorius*, formed as **CONSOLATOR**: see **-ORY**².]
▸ **A** *adjective*. Tending or intended to console. **LME.**
▸ †**B** *noun*. A consolatory speech or composition. **M–L17.**

consolatrix /kɒnsəˈleɪtrɪks/ *noun*. *rare*. Pl. **-trices** /-trɪsiːz/. **M17.**
[**ORIGIN** Late Latin, fem. of Latin **CONSOLATOR**: see **-TRIX**.]
A female consoler.

console /ˈkɒnsəʊl/ *noun*. **M17.**
[**ORIGIN** French, perh. from *consolider* consolidate.]
1 *ARCHITECTURE*. An ornamental flat-sided bracket or corbel, usu. incorporating a volute at each end. **M17.**
2 In full ***console table***. A table supported by consoles, and either fixed to a wall or free-standing. **E19.**
3 A cabinet containing the keyboards, stops, and pedals of an organ. **L19.**
4 A cabinet for audio equipment, a television set, etc. **E20.**
5 A cabinet or panel where switches, meters, and controls are grouped together. **M20.**

M. BRADBURY The booking clerk prints the tickets on a large console. *New Yorker* An enormous computer console.

console /kənˈsəʊl/ *verb trans.* **M17.**
[**ORIGIN** French *consoler* from Latin *consolari*, formed as **CON-** + *solari* soothe.]
Comfort in disappointment or distress.

J. CHEEVER He . . consoled himself with whiskey. C. FREEMAN No one wiped away the tears or consoled him.

■ **consolement** *noun* **L18**. **consoler** *noun* **M18**.

consolidate /kənˈsɒlɪdeɪt/ *verb*. Pa. pple **-ated**, (*arch.*) **-ate** /-ət/. **E16.**
[**ORIGIN** Latin *consolidat-* pa. ppl stem of *consolidare*, formed as **CON-** + *solidare* make firm or solid, from *solidus* **SOLID** *adjective*: see **-ATE**³.]
▸ **I** *verb trans.* **1** Combine (estates, laws, debts, companies, etc.) into a single whole. **E16.** ▸†**b** Unite and so heal (a wound, fracture, or rupture). **M16–L18.**
consolidated annuities the Government annuities of the UK (representing part of the national debt) which in 1751 were consolidated into a single stock, now called **CONSOLS**. **Consolidated Fund** a British government fund, formed by amalgamation in 1786, which receives the product of various taxes etc. and pays the interest on the national debt and other agreed regular charges.
2 Strengthen, give firmness to (esp. political power or an established system). **M16.**

R. NIEBUHR Religion may consolidate benevolent sentiments and lodge their force in the will. A. J. TOYNBEE The Incas came, saw, conquered, and consolidated their conquests.

3 Make (more) solid. **M17.**
▸ **II** *verb intrans.* **4** Unite solidly or compactly; become solid or firm; make one's position more secure. **E17.**
■ **consolidator** *noun* **E18**.

consolidation /kənsɒlɪˈdeɪʃ(ə)n/ *noun*. **LME.**
[**ORIGIN** Late Latin *consolidatio(n-)*, formed as **CONSOLIDATE**: see **-ATION**.]
1 The action or an act of uniting or amalgamating; combination into a single whole. **LME.**
2 The action or an act of making (more) solid or compact. **E17.**
3 (A) strengthening, esp. of power, position, or organization. **E17.**
■ **consolidationist** *noun* an advocate of federal rule in the US **M19**.

consols /ˈkɒns(ə)lz/ *noun pl.* In attrib. use & in comb. in sing. **consol**. **L18.**
[**ORIGIN** from abbreviation of *consolidated annuities* + pl. **-S**¹.]
An undated British government stock representing the consolidated annuities (see **CONSOLIDATE**) and now bearing interest at 2½ per cent. Also, Consolidated Loan stock, an undated British government stock first issued in 1926 and bearing interest at 4 per cent.

consommé /kənˈsɒmeɪ/ *noun*. **E19.**
[**ORIGIN** French, use as noun of pa. pple of *consommer* from Latin *consummare*: see **CONSUMMATE** *verb*.]
A clear, orig. meat, soup.

consonance /ˈkɒns(ə)nəns/ *noun*. **LME.**
[**ORIGIN** Old French & mod. French, or Latin *consonantia*, from *consonant-*: see **CONSONANT** *noun*, **-ANCE**.]
1 Agreement, harmony, concord. **LME.**

W. S. CHURCHILL His conversion to Christianity . . was also in consonance with his secular aims.

2 Resemblance or correspondence of sounds, now esp. consonants, in different words or syllables. **L16.**
3 (A) pleasing combination of sounds. **L16.**
4 *MUSIC*. A consonant interval. **E17.** ▸**b** The sounding of two or more notes in harmony. **L17.**
■ **consonancy** *noun* (*arch.*) = **CONSONANCE** 1, 2, 3 **LME**.

consonant /ˈkɒns(ə)nənt/ *noun*. **ME.**
[**ORIGIN** Old French from Latin *consonant-*, *consonans* (sc. *littera* letter) pres. pple of *consonare* sound together, formed as **CON-**, **SONANT**.]
1 a A letter of the alphabet that represents a consonantal sound. **ME.** ▸**b** An elementary speech sound other than a vowel, in which the airstream is at least partly obstructed, and which in forming a syllable is usu. combined with a vowel. **E17.**
b ***stop consonant***: see **STOP** *noun*² 18b.
†**2** = **CONSONANCE** 4. **LME–E18.**
– **COMB.**: **consonant shift** a systematic change in consonantal sounds during the evolution of a language.
■ **consoˈnantal** *adjective* of the nature of a consonant; pertaining to or involving a consonant or consonants: **L18**. **consonanted** *adjective* having consonants (of a specified kind) **L19**. **consoˈnantic** *adjective* (*rare*) **M19**. **consonantism** *noun* the use of consonants; the system or character of the consonants in a language or a word: **M19**.

consonant /ˈkɒns(ə)nənt/ *adjective*. **LME.**
[**ORIGIN** Old French, pres. pple of *consoner* (mod. *-nn-*), from Latin *consonare*: see **CONSONANT** *noun*, **-ANT**¹.]
1 In agreement or accordance (*with*); compatible; agreeable, accordant (*to*). **LME.** ▸†**b** Consistent, unvarying. **M16–M18.**

HENRY MORE Divine Truth will be found every-where consonant to itself. L. A. G. STRONG After as short an interval as was consonant with decency . . he married Miss Jones.

2 Harmonious; *MUSIC* constituting a concord. **L15.**
3 Of words etc.: corresponding in sound; exhibiting consonance. **M17.**
■ **consonantly** *adverb* **M16**.

consonous /ˈkɒns(ə)nəs/ *adjective*. *rare*. **M17.**
[**ORIGIN** from Latin *consonus*, formed as **CON-** + *sonus* sounding: see **-OUS**.]
Harmonious.

†**consopition** *noun*. **M17–E18.**
[**ORIGIN** Latin *consopitio(n-)*, from *consopit-* pa. ppl stem of *consopire* lull to sleep, formed as **CON-** + *sopire* (same sense): see **-ITION**.]
A lulling to sleep; a dulling of the senses.

con sordino /kɒn sɔːˈdiːnəʊ/ *adverbial & adjectival phr.* **E19.**
[**ORIGIN** Italian: see **SORDINO**.]
MUSIC. (Played) with a mute or (***con sordini*** /-iː/) mutes.

consort /ˈkɒnsɔːt/ *noun*¹. **LME.**
[**ORIGIN** French from Latin *consort-*, *consors* sharing in common, partner, formed as **CON-** + *sors* portion, lot.]
1 A partner, a companion; a colleague. Now *rare* or *obsolete* exc. as below. **LME.**
2 a A partner in marriage or sexual relations; a husband or wife, esp. of a monarch. **L16.** ▸**b** An animal's mate. **L18.**

a W. BLACKSTONE The queen of England is either queen regent, queen consort, or queen dowager. J. CLAVELL A man could have as many consorts as he wished, but only one wife at one time. *fig.*: ISAAC TAYLOR That love which is to be the consort of knowledge.

a *Prince Consort*: see **PRINCE** *noun*.
3 A ship sailing in company with another. **E17.**
■ **conˈsortion** *noun* (*arch.*) [Latin *consortio(n-)*] keeping company; alliance: **L17**. **consortism** *noun* (*rare*) symbiosis **L19**. **consortship** *noun* (now *rare*) the situation of being a consort; partnership, fellowship: **L16**.

consort /ˈkɒnsɔːt/ *noun*². **L16.**
[**ORIGIN** Partly from **CONSORT** *verb*, suggested by Latin **CONSORTIUM**; partly (branch II) early form of **CONCERT** *noun*.]
▸ **I** Connected with next.
†**1** A number consorting together; a fellowship, a partnership; a company. **L16–L18.**

J. GLANVILL Instances must be . . examined singly and in consort.

2 Accord; agreement. **L16.**

J. HILTON Conway, in whom a mystical strain ran in curious consort with scepticism.

▸ **II** †**3** Musical harmony or accord; a harmonious combination of voices or instruments. **L16–E18.**
4 A company of musicians who regularly perform together. **L16.**
†**5** = **CONCERT** *noun* 3. **L17–L18.**

consort /kənˈsɔːt/ *verb*. **L16.**
[**ORIGIN** In sense 1 from **CONSORT** *noun*¹; in other senses prob. a reinforcement of **SORT** *verb*, infl. by **CONSORT** *noun*².]
†**1** *verb trans.* Accompany; escort, attend. **L16–E17.**

SHAKES. *L.L.L.* Sweet health and fair desires consort your Grace!

2 *verb trans.* Associate in a common lot; class or bring together (*with*). **L16.**

E. BLUNDEN The men with whom I was now consorted.

3 *verb intrans.* & †*refl.* Habitually associate (*with*), esp. as a companion or a lover. **L16.**

R. W. EMERSON Men consort in camps and towns. D. CARNEGIE Fearing that he might be consorting with another woman. P. L. FERMOR I would travel on foot . . and only consort with peasants and tramps.

4 *verb intrans.* Accord, harmonize. (Foll. by *to*, *with*.) **L16.**
5 *verb trans.* & *intrans.* Musically play, sing, or sound together. *arch.* **L16.**

consortium /kənˈsɔːtɪəm/ *noun*. Pl. **-ia** /-ɪə/, **-iums**. **E19.**
[**ORIGIN** Latin, from *consors* **CONSORT** *noun*¹.]
1 Partnership, association. *rare*. **E19.**
2 *LAW*. The companionship, affection, and assistance which each spouse in a marriage is entitled to receive from the other, and for the loss of which a husband could formerly claim damages. **M19.**
3 An association of organizations or states formed for commercial or financial purposes. **L19.**

Economist A consortium of 21 state-owned and private companies commissioned by the government.

4 A group; an assortment. **M20.**

E. HUXLEY A consortium of odours in which dried and pickled fish predominate.

†**consound** *noun*. **OE–E19.**
[**ORIGIN** Old French & mod. French *consoude* from late Latin *consolida* comfrey, from Latin *consolidare* **CONSOLIDATE** *verb*.]
Any of certain herbs to which healing properties were attributed; *esp.* comfrey.

conspecific /kɒnspəˈsɪfɪk/ *adjective & noun*. **M19.**
[**ORIGIN** from **CON-** + **SPECIFIC**.]
(An organism or individual) of the same species.

†**conspectuity** *noun*. *rare* (Shakes.). Only in **E17.**
[**ORIGIN** App. joc. from Latin **CONSPECTUS** + **-ITY**.]
Faculty of sight, vision.

conspectus /kənˈspɛktəs/ *noun*. **M19.**
[**ORIGIN** Latin, from *conspect-* pa. ppl stem of *conspicere* (see **CONSPICUOUS**).]
1 A comprehensive mental survey. **M19.**
2 A summary, a synopsis. **M19.**

conspicuous /kənˈspɪkjʊəs/ *adjective*. **M16.**
[**ORIGIN** from Latin *conspicuus*, from *conspicere* look at attentively, formed as **CON-** + *specere* look (at): see **-OUS**.]
1 Clearly visible, striking to the eye. **M16.**

2 Obvious, plainly evident; attracting notice; remarkable, noteworthy. **E17.**

J. RUSSELL One provision was conspicuous . . by its absence.

3 Of expenditure etc.: lavish, with a view to enhancing one's prestige. **L19.**

■ **conspi'cuity** *noun* the state or quality of being conspicuous; ease of visibility: **E17.** **conspicuously** *adverb* **E17.** **conspicuousness** *noun* **M17.**

conspiracy /kən'spɪrəsi/ *noun.* **LME.**
[ORIGIN Anglo-Norman *conspiracie* alt. of Old French & mod. French *conspiration* from Latin *conspiratio(n-)*, from *conspirat-* pa. ppl stem of *conspirare*: see CONSPIRE, -ATION, -ACY.]

1 The action or an act of conspiring; (a) combination of people for an unlawful or a reprehensible purpose; an agreement so to combine, a plot. **LME.**
conspiracy of silence an agreement not to mention something.

2 In a neutral or good sense: combination for one purpose. *arch.* **M16.**

– COMB.: **conspiracy theory** the theory that something happens as a result of a conspiracy between interested parties; *esp.* a belief that some powerful covert agency (typically political in motivation and oppressive in intent) is responsible for an unexplained event.

■ **conspiracist** *noun & adjective* (**a**) *noun* a believer in or deviser of a conspiracy theory; (**b**) *adjective* of or relating to conspiracists or conspiracy theory: **L20.**

conspirator /kən'spɪrətə/ *noun.* **LME.**
[ORIGIN Anglo-Norman *conspiratour*, Old French & mod. French *-eur*, from Latin *conspirator*, from *conspirat-*: see CONSPIRACY, -OR.]

A person who conspires or is engaged in a conspiracy.

■ **conspirative** *adjective* conspiratorial **L19.** **conspira'torial** *adjective* pertaining to or characteristic of a conspirator or conspiracy; suggestive of a conspirator: **M19.** **conspira'torially** *adverb* **E20.** **conspiratory** *adjective* conspiratorial **E19.** **conspiratress** *noun* a female conspirator **L18.**

conspire /kən'spʌɪə/ *verb.* **LME.**
[ORIGIN Old French & mod. French *conspirer* from Latin *conspirare* agree, combine, formed as CON- + *spirare* breathe.]

1 *verb intrans.* **a** Combine secretly (*with*) for an unlawful or reprehensible purpose, esp. treason, murder, or sedition; agree secretly. (Foll. by *against*, *to do*.) **LME.** ▸**b** Combine in action or aim (*with*); cooperate by or as by intention (*to do*). **M16.**

I. MURDOCH We all conspired not to tell him.

2 *verb trans.* Plot (something unlawful, evil, or hostile). *arch.* **LME.**

†**3** *verb intrans.* Concur, agree in spirit, sentiment, etc. **M16–M18.**

■ **conspirant** *noun & adjective* (*rare*) [French] (**a**) *noun* a conspirator; (**b**) *adjective* conspiring: **E17.** **conspi'ration** *noun* (now *rare* or *obsolete*) [French] = CONSPIRACY **ME.** **conspirer** *noun* **LME.**

constable /'kʌnstəb(ə)l, 'kɒn-/ *noun.* **ME.**
[ORIGIN Old French *cunestable*, *cone-* (mod. *connétable*) repr. late Latin *comes stabuli* lit. 'count (head officer) of the stable'.]

1 *hist.* The principal officer of the household, administration, or army of a monarch or nobleman; *spec.* one of the chief officers of the French, English, or Scottish royal household. **ME.**

2 The governor or warden of a royal fortress or castle. **ME.**

3 A military officer. Long *rare.* **ME.**

4 An officer of the peace. **ME.** ▸**b** A police officer of the lowest rank. Also more fully ***police constable***. **M19.**
Chief Constable the head of the police force of a county etc. **High Constable** *hist.* the principal officer of the peace in a hundred or similar administrative area. **outrun the constable**, **overrun the constable** go too far, overstep the bounds of moderation; overspend, get into debt. **parish constable**, **petty constable** *hist.* an officer of a parish or township whose duties included being a conservator of the peace. **special constable** a person sworn in to assist the police on special occasions.

■ †**constablery** *noun* = CONSTABLEWICK **ME–M18.** **constableship** *noun* the office of constable **LME.** **constablewick** *noun* (*arch.*) (**a**) the district under a constable; (**b**) constableship: **LME.**

constabulary /kən'stabjʊləri/ *noun.* **L15.**
[ORIGIN medieval Latin *con(e)stabularia* use as noun (sc. *dignitas* rank) of fem. of *con(e)stabularius*: see CONSTABULARY *adjective*.]

1 The district under the charge of a constable. **L15.**

†**2** = CONSTABLESHIP. **E16–M18.**

3 The organized body of constables or police in an area. **M19.**

constabulary /kən'stabjʊləri/ *adjective.* **E19.**
[ORIGIN medieval Latin *con(e)stabularius*, from *con(e)stabulus* CONSTABLE: see -ARY[1].]

1 Of or pertaining to police officers, the police force, or (formerly) petty constables. **E19.**

2 Of the nature or function of constables. **M19.**

■ Also **constabular** *adjective* **M19.**

constancy /'kɒnst(ə)nsi/ *noun.* **L15.**
[ORIGIN Latin *constantia*, from *constant-*: see CONSTANT, -ANCY.]

1 The state or quality of being constant in mind; steadfastness, firmness, fortitude. **L15.**

2 Steadfastness of attachment to a person or a cause; fidelity. **M16.**

†**3** Certainty. **M–L16.**

4 The property of being invariable; unchangingness. **L16.** ▸†**b** Perseverance. *rare* (Shakes.). Only in **E17.**

5 Something permanent; a permanent arrangement. **E18.**
for a constancy as a permanent arrangement.

■ †**constance** *noun* [French] = CONSTANCY 1, 2, 4b **ME–M17.**

constant /'kɒnst(ə)nt/ *adjective & noun.* **LME.**
[ORIGIN Old French & mod. French from Latin *constant-* pres. ppl stem of *constare* stand firm, formed as CON- + *stare* stand: see -ANT[1].]

▸ **A** *adjective.* **1** Staying firm in mind or purpose; steadfast, resolute. **LME.**

MILTON The best-resolved of men, The constantest.

2 Steadfast in attachment (*to* a person or cause), faithful, true. **LME.**

POPE Tho' fortune change, his constant spouse remains. E. BOWEN She had been constant to the good resolutions made on her honeymoon.

3 Unchanging in condition, form, or magnitude; unvarying. **M16.**

†**4** **a** Permanent; always maintained. **M16–E19.** ▸**b** Continuing without intermission, incessant; unremitting; frequently occurring; (of a person) continually engaged in a particular activity. **M17.**

b MILTON A constant reader of Saint Paul's Epistles. W. LIPPMANN In the industrial revolution there is constant technical change.

b ***constant*** ATTENDANCE ***allowance***.

†**5** Confident; certain. **M16–M17.**

†**6** Not on the move, settled, steady. **L16–M18.**

▸ **B** *noun.* **1** MATH. A numerical quantity which does not vary, or is assumed not to vary; SCIENCE a number expressing a relation, property, etc., and remaining the same in all circumstances or for the same substance in the same conditions. **M19.** ▸**b** LOGIC. The name of, or a symbol representing, a particular individual, class, proposition, etc. **M20.** ▸**c** COMPUTING. = LITERAL *noun* 3. **L20.**
Avogadro constant, ***Boltzmann's constant***, ***cosmical constant***, ***cosmological constant***, ***dielectric constant***, ***gas constant***, ***Planck's constant***, ***solar constant***, ***tidal constant***, etc.

2 *fig.* A constant element or factor. **M19.**

L. DURRELL The more I knew her the less predictable she seemed; the only constant was the frantic struggle to break through the barriers.

constantan /'kɒnst(ə)ntan/ *noun.* **E20.**
[ORIGIN from CONSTANT + arbitrary *-an*.]

A copper–nickel alloy used in electrical work for its high resistance, which varies little with temperature.

Constantia /kən'stanʃə/ *noun.* **L18.**
[ORIGIN An estate near Cape Town.]

Any of the wines produced on the Constantia farms near Cape Town, South Africa, famous for their sweet dessert wines. Also ***Constantia wine***.

Constantinian /kɒnst(ə)n'tɪnɪən/ *adjective.* **M17.**
[ORIGIN from *Constantine* (see below) + -IAN.]

Of or pertaining to the Roman Emperor Constantine the Great or his period (306–37).

Constantinopolitan /kɒnˌstantɪnə'pɒlɪt(ə)n/ *adjective.* **LME.**
[ORIGIN Late Latin *Constantinopolitanus*, from *Constantinopolis* = Greek *Kōnstantinou polis* city of Constantine: see -AN.]

Of or pertaining to Constantinople (formerly Byzantium and now Istanbul in Turkey), or the Eastern Empire or Church.

constantly /'kɒnst(ə)ntli/ *adverb.* **LME.**
[ORIGIN from CONSTANT *adjective* + -LY[2].]

1 Steadfastly, faithfully. *arch.* **LME.**

†**2** Confidently. **M16–M17.**

†**3** Continuously, permanently. **M16–E17.**

4 Uniformly, regularly. **M17.**

5 Continually, incessantly. **L17.**

S. HILL Her eyes . . watered constantly. JONATHON GREEN I was constantly surrounded by all these beautiful women with no clothes on.

constatation /kɒnstə'teɪʃ(ə)n/ *noun.* **E20.**
[ORIGIN French, formed as CONSTATE: see -ATION.]

1 The process of ascertaining or verifying; something verified. **E20.**

2 A statement, an assertion. **M20.**

constate /kən'steɪt/ *verb trans. rare.* **L18.**
[ORIGIN French *constater*, from Latin *constat* 3rd person sing. pres. indic. of *constare*: see CONSTANT.]

Establish, ascertain, state.

constative /'kɒnstətɪv, kən'steɪtɪv/ *adjective & noun.* **E20.**
[ORIGIN from Latin *constat-* pa. ppl stem of *constare*, after German *konstatierend*: see CONSTANT, -IVE.]

▸ **A** *adjective.* **1** GRAMMAR. Of a use of the aorist tense: indicating that the action has taken place, rather than emphasizing its initiation or completion. **E20.**

2 Able to be true or false. **M20.**

▸ **B** *noun.* A statement able to be true or false. **M20.**

constellate /'kɒnstələt, kɒn'stɛlət/ *adjective.* **M17.**
[ORIGIN Late Latin *constellatus*, formed as CON- + *stellatus* STELLATE *adjective*.]

1 Formed into a constellation; clustered together. **M17.**

2 Studded with stars. **M19.**

constellate /'kɒnstəleɪt/ *verb.* **L16.**
[ORIGIN formed as CONSTELLATE *adjective* (see -ATE[3]), infl. by CONSTELLATION.]

†**1** *verb trans.* ASTROLOGY. ▸**a** Predict by means of the stars; cast a horoscope for; affect with or fashion under stellar influence. **L16–M19.** ▸**b** In *pass.* Be predestined (*to*) by one's stars. **M17–E19.**

2 *verb trans.* Form into a constellation or group. **M17.**

S. JOHNSON He . . must . . constellate in himself the scattered graces which shine single in other men. H. T. LANE Every immediate purpose we have is constellated with the great purpose—perfection.

3 *verb intrans.* Cluster together like stars in a constellation. **M17.**

4 *verb trans.* Adorn thickly, as with stars. **L17.**

P. L. FERMOR Miniatures and silhouettes constellate the spaces between the portraits.

constellation /kɒnstə'leɪʃ(ə)n/ *noun.* **ME.**
[ORIGIN Old French & mod. French from late Latin *constellatio(n-)*, formed as CON- + *stella* star: see -ATION.]

†**1** ASTROLOGY. The relative positions of the stars (i.e. planets), as supposed to influence events; *esp.* their positions at the time of someone's birth; character, as so influenced. **ME–M19.**

2 A group of fixed stars with a traditional imaginary outline as seen in the sky. **LME.**

3 A group or cluster, esp. of brilliant things; PSYCHOLOGY a group of associated ideas or personality components. **E17.**

R. BOYLE A Constellation of fair Ladies.

constellatory /kɒn'stɛlət(ə)ri/ *adjective. rare.* **M17.**
[ORIGIN from CONSTELLATION + -ORY[2].]

†**1** ASTROLOGY. Pertaining to constellations (sense 1) or the casting of horoscopes from them. **M17–E19.**

2 Pertaining to or of the nature of a constellation; like that of a constellation. **E19.**

consternate /'kɒnstəneɪt/ *verb trans.* **M17.**
[ORIGIN Latin *consternat-* pa. ppl stem of *consternare* lay prostrate, terrify, formed as CON- + *sternare* lay low: see -ATE[3].]

Fill with consternation; dismay. Usu. in *pass.*

consternation /kɒnstə'neɪʃ(ə)n/ *noun.* **E17.**
[ORIGIN French, or Latin *consternatio(n-)*, formed as CONSTERNATE: see -ATION.]

Amazement or dismay such that causes mental confusion.

†**constipate** *adjective.* **LME–M18.**
[ORIGIN Latin *constipatus* pa. pple, formed as CONSTIPATE *verb*: see -ATE[2].]

Constipated.

constipate /'kɒnstɪpeɪt/ *verb trans.* **M16.**
[ORIGIN Latin *constipat-* pa. ppl stem of *constipare*, formed as CON- + *stipare* press, cram: see -ATE[3].]

1 Affect (a person, the bowels) with constipation; render costive. Chiefly in *pass.* **M16.** ▸†**b** Make (body tissue) more compact; constrict (a pore or duct). **E17–M18.** ▸**c** *fig.* Hinder or obstruct abnormally. **L19.**

†**2** Crowd, pack, or press closely together; condense, thicken (a fluid). **M16–M18.**

■ **constipated** *adjective* affected with constipation, costive; characteristic of or associated with constipation: **M16.**

constipation /kɒnstɪ'peɪʃ(ə)n/ *noun.* **LME.**
[ORIGIN Old French & mod. French, or late Latin *constipatio(n-)* crowding together, (in medieval Latin) costiveness, formed as CONSTIPATE *verb*: see -ATION.]

†**1** **a** Contraction or constriction of passages or tissues of the body. **LME–M17.** ▸**b** Irregularity and difficulty in defecation. **M16.** ▸**c** *fig.* Abnormal lack of efficacy or ease. **E19.**

†**2** Compression or condensation of matter. **E17–E18.**

constituency /kən'stɪtjʊənsi/ *noun.* **M19.**
[ORIGIN from CONSTITUENT: see -ENCY.]

1 All the people entitled to vote for a particular seat or member in a public, esp. a legislative, body; the area or population represented by an elected member. **M19.**

2 A body of customers, supporters, etc. **L19.**

constituent /kən'stɪtjʊənt/ *noun & adjective.* **L15.**
[ORIGIN (Partly through French *constituant*) from Latin *constituent-* pres. ppl stem of *constituere* CONSTITUTE *verb*: see -ENT.]

▸ **A** *noun.* **1** A person who appoints another as agent or representative. **L15.**

2 A voting member or an inhabitant of a constituency. **E18.**

3 A constituent part (*of*); an element of a complex whole. **M18.**

F. NORRIS As the spot grew larger, it resolved itself into constituents.

immediate constituent: see IMMEDIATE *adjective*.

▸ **B** *adjective.* †**1** That makes a thing what it is; characteristic. **M17–M19.**

W. WHEWELL To each degree of pressure . . there is a constituent temperature corresponding.

C

C

2 That goes to make up; *esp.* that jointly constitute a whole. (Foll. by *of*.) M17.

> W. PALEY The constituent parts of water. L. MACNEICE Tone of voice or syntax or rhythm . . found . . to be not only formal but constituent of meaning.

3 That appoints or elects a representative. M18.
4 Able to frame or alter a (political) constitution. L18.

> *New York Times* Voters will elect a 60-member Constituent Assembly to write a new constitution and name an interim president.

■ **constituently** *adverb* M19.

constitute /ˈkɒnstɪtjuːt/ *verb*. Pa. pple **-tuted**, †**-tute**. LME.
[ORIGIN Latin *constitut-* pa. ppl stem of *constituere* establish, appoint, formed as CON- + *statuere* set up.]
1 *verb trans.* **a** Make up, go to form; be the constituent parts or material of. LME. ▸**b** Frame or make by combination of elements. Usu. in *pass.*, of bodily or mental constitution. L16. ▸**c** Make (a thing) what it is; determine. M19.

> **a** L. DEIGHTON The lectures and diagrams that would constitute the afternoon briefing. A. FRASER His marriageability constituted about his only ace. **b** E. F. BENSON She was so constituted that she had to object.

2 *verb trans.* (with compl.). ▸**a** Appoint (a person) to the office or post of. LME. ▸**b** Set (a person, oneself, a thing) up as. M16.

> **a** DEFOE We constituted him captain. **b** J. A. FROUDE The will of a single man . . cannot be allowed to constitute itself an irremoveable obstacle to a great national good.

†**3** *verb trans.* Set, place, (*in* a specified situation etc.). L15–L19.
4 †**a** *verb intrans.* Make laws. L15–M17. ▸**b** *verb trans.* Make, establish, (a law etc.). (Formerly foll. by subord. clause.) Now *rare* or *obsolete*. M16. ▸**c** *verb trans.* Establish (an institution etc.); give legal form to. M16.
■ **constituter** *noun* (now *rare*) L17. **constitutor** *noun* M16.

constitution /kɒnstɪˈtjuːʃ(ə)n/ *noun*. ME.
[ORIGIN Old French & mod. French, or Latin *constitutio(n-)*, formed as CONSTITUTE: see -ION.]
▸ **I 1** *hist.* A decree, an ordinance, a law, a regulation. ME.
†**2** A body of rules, customs, or laws. Cf. sense 4b. Only in ME.
3 The way in which a thing is constituted or made up; composition, make-up. M16. ▸**b** The character of the body as regards health, strength, vitality, etc. M16. ▸**c** Condition of mind; (a) disposition, (a) temperament. L16.

> SHAKES. *Twel. N.* The excellent constitution of thy leg. H. MARTINEAU That . . is the fault of the constitution of society. **b** R. LEHMANN Thanks to his excellent constitution he rallied steadily.

4 a The manner in which a state is organized, esp. as regards the location of ultimate power. E17. ▸**b** The set of fundamental principles according to which a state is constituted and governed; a body of rules prescribing the major elements of the structure and activities of any organization. M18.

> **a** H. HALLAM The original constitution of England was highly aristocratical. **b** M. PATTISON Any further change in the constitution of the University.

b ***unwritten constitution***, ***written constitution***.
▸ **II 5** The action of constituting. LME.
†**6** The action of decreeing or ordaining. LME–M17.
■ **constitutioned** *adjective* having a constitution (of a specified kind) E18.

constitutional /kɒnstɪˈtjuːʃ(ə)n(ə)l/ *adjective & noun*. L17.
[ORIGIN from CONSTITUTION + -AL¹.]
▸ **A** *adjective*. **1** Of, belonging to, or inherent in a person's constitution. L17.

> L. STEPHEN Pope's constitutional irritability.

2 Affecting a person's constitution, *spec.* beneficially. M18.
3 Forming an essential part. M18.
4 In harmony with or authorized by the constitution of a state etc. Cf. ***unconstitutional***. M18.

> W. LIPPMANN While in free societies opposition is a constitutional function, in authoritarian societies it is treason.

constitutional government, **constitutional monarchy**, **constitutional sovereign**: limited by a constitution or its forms.
5 Of, pertaining to, or dealing with the constitution of a state or states, etc. L18.
▸ **B** *noun*. **1** = CONSTITUTIONALIST *noun* 2. L18.
2 A walk taken (esp. regularly) for the sake of one's health or well-being. E19.
■ **constitutioˈnality** *noun* L18. **constitutionalize** *verb* (*a*) *verb trans.* make constitutional; (*b*) *verb intrans.* (*colloq.*) take a constitutional: M19.

constitutionalist /kɒnstɪˈtjuːʃ(ə)n(ə)lɪst/ *noun & adjective*. M18.
[ORIGIN from CONSTITUTIONAL + -IST.]
▸ **A** *noun*. **1** A person who studies or writes on the constitution of a state. M18.
2 A supporter of constitutional principles, or of a particular constitution. L18.
▸ **B** *adjective*. Of, pertaining to, or being a constitutionalist or constitutionalists. M19.
■ **constitutionalism** *noun* constitutional government; adherence to constitutional principles: M19.

constitutionally /kɒnstɪˈtjuːʃ(ə)n(ə)li/ *adverb*. M18.
[ORIGIN formed as CONSTITUTIONALIST + -LY².]
1 By virtue of one's constitution; by nature. M18.
2 In accordance with the constitution of a state etc. Cf. ***unconstitutionally***. M18.
3 As regards the constitution (of a thing or a person). M18.

constitutive /ˈkɒnstɪtjuːtɪv/ *adjective*. L16.
[ORIGIN Late Latin *constitutivus* confirmatory, defining, formed as CONSTITUTE: see -IVE.]
1 Having the power of constituting; giving formal or definite existence or expression to something. L16.

> B. BROWN The great constitutive ideas which have moulded powerfully the institutions of society. W. NOLL Constitutive equations defining the particular ideal material we wish to study.

2 = CONSTITUTIONAL *adjective* 3. E17.
3 Forming a part; constituent. M17.
4 With *of*: that constitutes. M17.
5 BIOCHEMISTRY. Designating or pertaining to an enzyme which is continuously produced in an organism rather than depending on the presence of an inducer. M20.
■ **constitutively** *adverb* M17. **constitutiveness** *noun* (*rare*) L17. ˌ**constituˈtivity** *noun* (BIOCHEMISTRY) the property of being constitutive (sense 5) M20.

constrain /kənˈstreɪn/ *verb*. ME.
[ORIGIN Old French *constraindre* (mod. *contraindre*), pres. stem *constraign-*, from Latin *constringere* bind tightly together, formed as CON- + *stringere* (see STRAIN *verb*¹).]
1 a *verb trans. & intrans.* Compel or oblige (a person; *to* or *into* a course of action, state, etc.; *to do*); urge irresistibly or by necessity. ME. ▸**b** *verb trans.* Bring about by compulsion. E17. ▸**c** *verb trans.* MECHANICS. Restrict the motion of (a body or particle) to a certain path. M19.

> **a** POPE Some rule, that guides, but not constrains. J. FULLER The season constrained them to carry on the harvest. **b** I. WATTS Sufficient testimony to constrain our assent.

†**2** *verb trans.* Force out; produce by effort or straining. LME–E18.
†**3** *verb trans.* Afflict, distress. LME–M19.
4 *verb trans.* Confine forcibly; imprison. LME. ▸**b** *fig.* Limit, keep within bounds. E17.
†**5** *verb trans.* Constrict, contract. LME–L17.
†**6** *verb trans.* Take by force; ravish. L16–L17.
■ **constrainable** *adjective* LME. **constrained** *adjective* that has been constrained; not natural; embarrassed; (earlier in UNCONSTRAINED): E16. **constrainedly** /-nɪdli/ *adverb* M16. **constrainer** *noun* (*rare*) LME.

constraint /kənˈstreɪnt/ *noun*. LME.
[ORIGIN Old French *constreinte* use as noun of fem. of pa. pple of *constraindre* (see CONSTRAIN).]
1 Coercion, compulsion. LME.

> E. A. FREEMAN How far the electors acted under constraint.

†**2** Oppression, affliction. LME–L16.
3 Restriction of liberty; something that restricts freedom of action or (MECHANICS) of motion. L16.

> M. MCCARTHY Social constraints.

4 Restricted expression of natural feelings and impulses; a constrained manner. E18.

> V. WOOLF There was always some constraint between them.

constrict /kənˈstrɪkt/ *verb trans.* M18.
[ORIGIN Latin *constrict-* pa. ppl stem of *constringere*: see CONSTRAIN.]
1 Draw together as by an encircling pressure; make more narrowly confined (*lit. & fig.*); compress. M18.
2 Cause (living tissue) to contract. M18.
■ **constricted** *adjective* drawn together or narrowed by constriction; narrow as if compressed: M18. **constrictive** *adjective* [Latin *constrictivus*] †(*a*) checking discharge from or distension of a part of the body; (*b*) pertaining to, characterized by, or causing constriction: LME.

constriction /kənˈstrɪkʃ(ə)n/ *noun*. LME.
[ORIGIN Late Latin *constrictio(n-)*, formed as CONSTRICT: see -ION.]
1 The action of making narrower or smaller as by an encircling pressure; the state of being so contracted. LME.
2 A thing which constricts or limits. M17.

> B. ELTON Boys and girls had become tired of the terrible social constrictions of political correctness.

3 A feeling of tightness in a part of the body. L18.
4 A constricted part. E19.
primary constriction: see PRIMARY *adjective*. ***secondary constriction***: see SECONDARY *adjective*.

constrictor /kənˈstrɪktə/ *noun & adjective*. E18.
[ORIGIN mod. Latin, formed as CONSTRICT + -OR.]
▸ **A** *noun*. **1** A snake that kills by compressing, *esp.* = ***BOA constrictor***. E18.
2 A constrictor muscle. M18.
▸ **B** *adjective*. ANATOMY. That draws together or narrows a part. M19.

constringe /kənˈstrɪn(d)ʒ/ *verb*. *literary*. L16.
[ORIGIN Latin *constringere*: see CONSTRAIN.]
1 *verb trans. & intrans.* Constrict (tissue): see CONSTRICT 2. L16.
2 *verb trans.* = CONSTRICT 1. Now *rare* or *obsolete*. E17.
3 *verb trans.* Cause to contract, as by cold etc. M17.

constringent /kənˈstrɪn(d)ʒ(ə)nt/ *adjective*. E17.
[ORIGIN Latin *constringent-* pres. ppl stem of *constringere*: see CONSTRAIN, -ENT.]
Causing constriction.
■ **constringency** *noun* L17.

construable /kənˈstruːəb(ə)l/ *adjective*. M17.
[ORIGIN from CONSTRUE *verb* + -ABLE.]
Able to be construed.
■ **construaˈbility** *noun* M19.

construal /kənˈstruːəl/ *noun*. M20.
[ORIGIN from CONSTRUE *verb* + -AL¹.]
An act or the action of construing; (an) interpretation.

construct /ˈkɒnstrʌkt/ *noun*. L19.
[ORIGIN from the verb.]
1 SEMITIC GRAMMAR. The construct state. L19.
2 LINGUISTICS. A group of words forming a phrase. L19.
3 a PSYCHOLOGY. An object of perception or thought constructed by combining sense impressions. L19. ▸**b** *gen.* Anything constructed, esp. by the mind; a concept. E20.

construct /ˈkɒnstrʌkt/ *adjective*. E19.
[ORIGIN from pa. pple of CONSTRUCT *verb*.]
SEMITIC GRAMMAR. Designating the state or form of a noun when it precedes another noun that has an attributive or possessive relationship to it (usu. expressible in English by *of* or *in*).

construct /kənˈstrʌkt/ *verb trans.* Pa. pple **constructed**, (*arch.*) **construct**. LME.
[ORIGIN Latin *construct-* pa. ppl stem of *construere*, formed as CON- + *struere* lay, pile, build.]
1 Make by fitting parts together; build, erect. LME. ▸**b** Form in the mind, devise. M18.

> *New Civil Engineer* The tower was constructed in the early 12th century.

†**2** Interpret, understand (in a certain way). *Scot.* E17–M18.
3 Find a geometrical construction for (a problem); draw precisely (a geometrical figure). E18.
4 GRAMMAR. Combine (words) according to grammatical rules. M19.
■ **constructible** *adjective* M19. **constructor**, †**-er** *noun* †(*a*) a person who construes or interprets; (*b*) a person who constructs: E17.

constructio ad sensum /kɒnˌstrʌktɪəʊ ad ˈsɛnsəm/ *noun phr.* L19.
[ORIGIN mod. Latin, lit. 'construction according to the sense'.]
GRAMMAR. The overriding of grammatical requirements by those of word-meaning, so that, for example, a plural verb is used with a singular collective noun.

construction /kənˈstrʌkʃ(ə)n/ *noun*. LME.
[ORIGIN Old French & mod. French from Latin *constructio(n-)*, formed as CONSTRUCT *verb*: see -ION.]
▸ **I** Construing.
1 GRAMMAR. The syntactical relationship between words in a sentence etc.; the action of arranging words in accordance with established usage so as to convey the desired sense; an instance or type of this. LME.

> M. MCCARTHY The ablative absolute as a construction in English.

pregnant construction: see PREGNANT *adjective*¹.
2 An explanation or interpretation of a text, statement, statute, etc.; an interpretation put upon conduct, facts, etc.; the (good, bad, etc.) way in which these are taken by others. L15.

> R. D. LAING The construction we put on this behaviour.

strict construction: see STRICT.
▸ **II** Constructing.
3 The action of constructing something (material or mental); the art or science of doing this. LME. ▸**b** The action or method of drawing precisely a geometrical figure or a diagram. L16.
b ***mechanical construction***: see MECHANICAL *adjective*.
4 The manner in which something is arranged; structure, disposition. L16.
5 A constructed thing; a material or mental structure. L18.
ideal construction: see IDEAL *adjective*.
– COMB.: **construction camp**, **construction railway**, etc.: used or engaged in the construction of a railway or similar undertaking.
■ **constructional** *adjective* of, pertaining to, or engaged in construction; structural, belonging to the original structure: M18. **constructionally** *adverb* L19. **constructionism** *noun* = CONSTRUCTIVISM 1 E20. **constructionist** *noun* (*a*) (with *strict* or *loose*) a person who puts a strict or a loose construction upon something, *spec.* the US Constitution; (*b*) a constructivist: M19.

constructive /kənˈstrʌktɪv/ *adjective*. M17.
[ORIGIN Late Latin *constructivus*, formed as CONSTRUCT *verb*: see -IVE.]
1 Resulting from a certain interpretation; inferred, not directly expressed; such in law though not necessarily in fact. M17.

constructive blasphemy, constructive contempt, constructive dismissal, etc. **constructive delivery** LAW delivery of goods which is deemed to have taken place, esp. in relation to secured credit transactions.
2 Of or pertaining to construction; structural. E19.
3 Tending to construct or build up something non-material; contributing helpfully, not destructive. M19.

Artist After a while . . I realised that their comments had been personal opinions, not constructive criticism.

4 Of or pertaining to constructivism. E20.
5 MATH. Of a proof: showing how an entity may in principle be constructed or arrived at in a finite number of steps. Also, accepting as valid only proofs of this kind. M20.
■ **constructively** *adverb* L17. **constructiveness** *noun* E19.

constructivism /kən'strʌktɪvɪz(ə)m/ *noun*. E20.
[ORIGIN from CONSTRUCTIVE + -ISM, after Russian *konstruktivizm*.]
1 An orig. Russian artistic movement or style which makes use of three-dimensional, usu. non-representational, arrangements of different materials. E20.
2 MATH. A view which admits as valid only constructive proofs and entities demonstrable by them. M20.
■ **constructivist** *adjective & noun* (**a**) *noun* an exponent or advocate of constructivism; (**b**) *adjective* of or pertaining to constructivism or constructivists: E20.

†**constructure** *noun*. E17–M19.
[ORIGIN Old French, or late Latin *constructura*, formed as CONSTRUCT *verb*: see -URE.]
= CONSTRUCTION II.

construe /kən'struː, 'kɒnstruː/ *noun*. Now *rare*. M19.
[ORIGIN from the verb.]
An act of grammatical construing; a verbal translation.

construe /kən'struː/ *verb*. LME.
[ORIGIN Latin *construere* CONSTRUCT *verb*, (in late Latin) construe (sense 4).]
1 *verb trans.* Give the sense of (a word, passage, legal document, etc.); expound; interpret. (Foll. by *as, into, to be*.) LME.
2 *verb trans.* Interpret, understand (an action, thing, or person) in a specified way; put a construction on. (Foll. by *as*, †*for, into, to be*, and with double obj.) LME.

D. L. SAYERS Whether the offer . . could reasonably be construed into a motive for murder.

3 *verb trans.* Deduce, infer. LME.

I. HAMILTON How little of his life . . can be construed from the poems.

4 *verb trans. & intrans.* Analyse the grammatical construction of (a sentence); translate word for word; translate orally. LME.
5 *verb trans.* Combine (a word) grammatically with or *with* others. LME.

†**constuprate** *verb trans*. M16–L17.
[ORIGIN Latin *constuprat-* pa. ppl stem of *constuprare*, formed as CON- + *stuprare* ravish, from *stuprum* defilement: see -ATE³.]
Ravish, violate.
■ †**constupration** *noun* E17–M18.

consubstantial /kɒnsəb'stanʃ(ə)l/ *adjective*. LME.
[ORIGIN ecclesiastical Latin *consubstantialis* (translating Greek *homoousios*), formed as CON- + SUBSTANTIAL.]
Of the same substance or essence (esp. in CHRISTIAN THEOLOGY of the three persons of the Trinity).
■ **consubstantialist** *noun* (CHRISTIAN THEOLOGY) a believer in the consubstantiality of the persons of the Trinity, or in the doctrine of consubstantiation M17. ˌ**consubstantiˈality** *noun* [ecclesiastical Latin *consubstantialitas*] identity of substance or essence M16. **consubstantially** *adverb* L16.

consubstantiate /kɒnsəb'stanʃɪət/ *adjective*. M17.
[ORIGIN Late Latin *consubstantiatus*, formed as CONSUBSTANTIATE *verb*: see -ATE².]
United in substance or essence.

consubstantiate /kɒnsəb'stanʃɪeɪt/ *verb*. L16.
[ORIGIN from late Latin *consubstantiat-* ppl adjective (cf. medieval Latin *consubstantiare*), formed as CON-, SUBSTANTIATE.]
1 *verb trans.* Unite in one common substance. L16.
†**2** *verb intrans.* CHRISTIAN THEOLOGY. Believe in consubstantiation. L17–E18.

consubstantiation /ˌkɒnsəbstanʃɪ'eɪʃ(ə)n, -sɪ-/ *noun*. L16.
[ORIGIN mod. Latin *consubstantiatio(n-)*, formed as CON- after *trans(s)ubstantiatio(n-)* TRANSUBSTANTIATION.]
1 CHRISTIAN THEOLOGY. (The doctrine of) the real substantial presence of Christ's body and blood together with the bread and wine in the Eucharist. L16.

MILTON The Lutheran holds Consubstantiation.

†**2** The action or an act of making consubstantial. M17–L18.
■ **consubstantiationist** *noun* (CHRISTIAN THEOLOGY) a believer in consubstantiation E19.

consuetude /'kɒnswɪtjuːd/ *noun*. LME.
[ORIGIN Old French, or Latin *consuetudo*, from *consuetus* pa. pple of *consuescere* accustom, use, formed as CON- + *suescere* become accustomed: see -TUDE.]
1 Custom, esp. as having legal force. Chiefly *Scot.* LME.
2 Familiarity; acquaintance. E19.

■ **consueˈtudinal** *adjective* customary, consuetudinary; *spec.* in GRAMMAR, designating or in a mood of Celtic languages expressing customary action: M17.

consuetudinary /kɒnswɪ'tjuːdɪnəri/ *adjective & noun*. LME.
[ORIGIN Late Latin *consuetudinarius*, formed as CONSUETUDE: see -ARY¹.]
▸ **A** *adjective*. Customary. LME.
▸ **B** *noun*. A written collection of the customs of a particular locality or body, esp. of a religious house or order. LME.

consul /'kɒns(ə)l/ *noun*. LME.
[ORIGIN Latin, rel. to *consulere* take counsel.]
1 *hist.* **a** Either of two annually elected magistrates who jointly exercised supreme authority in the Roman Republic; a holder of a corresponding title (without the function) in the Roman Empire. LME. ▸**b** Each of the three chief magistrates of the French Republic, from 1799 to 1804, the first of whom was head of state. E19.
b First Consul Napoleon Bonaparte.
2 A medieval earl or count. L15.
†**3** A member of a council. E16–M18.
†**4** A foreign official or magistrate; *spec.* a representative head of the merchants of a particular nation resident in a foreign town. E16–L18.
5 An agent appointed by a state to reside in a foreign town to protect the interests of the state's subjects and assist its commerce. M16.
consul general [GENERAL *adjective*]: of the highest status, usu. having jurisdiction over other consuls.
■ **consulage** *noun* consular charge or dues L16. **consuˈless** *noun* (*arch.*) the wife of a consul E19. **consulship** *noun* the post of consul; the term of office of a consul: M16.

consular /'kɒnsjʊlə/ *adjective & noun*. LME.
[ORIGIN Latin *consularis*, formed as CONSUL: see -AR¹.]
▸ **A** *adjective*. Of, pertaining to, or of the nature of a consul. LME.
▸ **B** *noun*. Chiefly *hist.* A person of consular rank. LME.
■ **consulary** *adjective* (now *rare* or *obsolete*) = CONSULAR *adjective* L16.

consulate /'kɒnsjʊlət/ *noun*. LME.
[ORIGIN Latin *consulatus*, formed as CONSUL: see -ATE¹.]
1 *hist.* A consular government; the period of this in France (1799–1804); the post or position of governing consuls. LME.
†**2** A body of councillors called consuls. L15–E17.
3 The post or establishment of a (modern) consul. L17.

consult /kən'sʌlt, 'kɒnsʌlt/ *noun*. M16.
[ORIGIN In sense 1 from Latin *consultum*, from *consultus* pa. pple of *consulere* CONSULT *verb*; in other senses from French *consulte* from medieval Latin *consulta* use as noun of fem. of Latin *consultus*.]
1 *hist.* A decree of the Roman senate. M16.
2 The action or an act of consulting; (a) consultation. Now *rare*. M16.
3 *hist.* A meeting for consultation; *spec.* a secret meeting for seditious purposes. M17.

consult /kən'sʌlt/ *verb*. E16.
[ORIGIN Old French & mod. French *consulter* from Latin *consultare* frequentative of *consult-* pa. ppl stem of *consulere* take counsel.]
1 *verb intrans.* Deliberate, take counsel, confer, (*with* someone; *about, upon* a matter). E16.

W. COWPER The gods all sat consulting.

†**2** *verb trans.* Confer about, deliberate upon, consider. M16–E18. ▸**b** Meditate, plan, contrive. M16–M17.

CLARENDON Many things were there consulted for the future. **b** R. EDEN They consulted to burne the shyppe.

3 *verb trans. & intrans.* (foll. by *for*, †*with*). Take into consideration, have consideration for, (the interest, feelings, good, etc., of a person or persons). M17.

ADDISON Those whose Safety I would principally consult. SOUTHEY For the general weal Consulting first.

4 *verb trans.* Ask advice of, seek counsel or a professional opinion from; refer to (a source of information); seek permission or approval from for a proposed action. M17.

A. A. MILNE You must *never* go down to the end of the town without consulting me. G. VIDAL Maximus consulted forbidden oracles. I. WALLACE He consulted his wristwatch.

consulting room: *spec.* in which a doctor examines patients.
■ **consultable** *adjective* M17. **consulˈtee** *noun* a person consulted M19. **consulter** *noun* (**a**) = CONSULTOR (b); †(**b**) = CONSULTOR (a): L16. †**consultive** *adjective* = CONSULTATIVE E17–E19. **consultor** *noun* (**a**) a person who gives advice, esp. officially; (**b**) a person who consults: E17.

consulta /kɒn'sʌltə/ *noun*. Also (earlier) †**-to**, pl. **-o(e)s**. L17.
[ORIGIN Italian, Spanish, & Portuguese, formed as CONSULT *noun*.]
A meeting of council (in Italy, Spain, or Portugal); a record of such a meeting.

consultant /kən'sʌlt(ə)nt/ *noun*. L17.
[ORIGIN Prob. from French, from Latin *consultant-* pres. ppl stem of *consultare* CONSULT *verb*: see -ANT¹.]
1 A person who consults. L17.
2 A consulting physician; *spec.* a clinician in the highest grade of the British hospital service, having independent charge of patients. L19.
3 A person who gives professional advice or services in a specialist field. L19.
■ **consultancy** *noun* the work or position of a consultant; a department of consultants: M20.

†**consultary** *adjective* var. of CONSULTORY.

consultation /kɒnsəl'teɪʃ(ə)n/ *noun*. LME.
[ORIGIN Old French & mod. French, or Latin *consultatio(n-)*, from Latin *consultat-* pa. ppl stem of *consultare* CONSULT *verb*: see -ATION.]
1 A meeting in which parties consult together, or one person consults another, *spec.* on a medical or legal matter. LME.

E. F. BENSON The two held consultation.

2 LAW (now *hist.*). A writ by which a cause removed from an ecclesiastical court to a civil court was returned to ecclesiastical jurisdiction. E16.
3 The action of consulting; deliberation. M16.

consultative /kən'sʌltətɪv/ *adjective*. L16.
[ORIGIN from CONSULT *verb* + -ATIVE.]
Of or pertaining to consultation; having the right to advise but not to decide on an issue.

consultatory /kən'sʌltət(ə)ri/ *adjective*. E17.
[ORIGIN Late Latin *consultatorius*, from *consultat-*: see CONSULTATION, -ORY².]
Pertaining to or serving for consultation; consultative.

consulting /kən'sʌltɪŋ/ *ppl adjective*. M17.
[ORIGIN from CONSULT *verb* + -ING²; in sense 2 translating French (*médicin*) *consultant* from obsolete sense of *consulter* give professional counsel.]
1 That consults, that asks advice. M17.
2 Designating a person who makes a business of giving professional advice, esp. in specialized areas to those in the same profession. E19.
consulting architect, consulting engineer, etc. **consulting physician** a physician who is consulted by colleagues or patients in special cases; a consultant.

†**consulto** *noun* see CONSULTA.

consultory /kən'sʌltəri/ *adjective*. Now *rare* or *obsolete*. Also †**-ary**. E17.
[ORIGIN from CONSULTATION + -ORY².]
= CONSULTATORY.

consumable /kən'sjuːməb(ə)l/ *adjective & noun*. M17.
[ORIGIN from CONSUME + -ABLE.]
▸ **A** *adjective*. Able to be consumed, as by fire; suitable for consumption as food. M17.
▸ **B** *noun*. An article intended for consumption, not for repeated use. Usu. in *pl.* E19.

consume /kən'sjuːm/ *verb*. LME.
[ORIGIN (Partly through French *consumer*) from Latin *consumere*, formed as CON- + *sumere* take.]
▸ **I** *verb trans.* **1 a** Destroy by or like fire or (formerly) disease; cause to vanish (*away*), as by evaporation. LME. ▸**b** *fig.* Engage the full attention or interest of (a person); engross. Chiefly as ***consumed*** *ppl adjective* (foll. by *with, by*), ***consuming*** *ppl adjective*. LME. ▸**c** In optative form in angry imprecations: damn. Long *dial.* M18.

b SCOTT FITZGERALD He was consumed with wonder at her presence. E. CALDWELL His career . . would be his consuming interest for many years. D. CAUTE I was consumed by a passion that I've recently been able to diagnose as ambition.

2 Occupy or waste (time, or a period of time). LME.

M. L. KING Most of my early evenings were consumed in this fashion.

3 Spend (money or goods), esp. wastefully. LME.
4 Use so as to destroy; take up and exhaust; use up. E16.

A. MACLEAN The *Morning Rose* consumed a great deal of fuel.

5 Eat up, drink down; devour. L16.

J. HERRIOT I had consumed several whiskies.

▸ **II** *verb intrans.* †**6** Waste away with disease or grief. LME–L17.
7 Decay, rot. E16.
8 Burn away (*lit.* & *fig.*). L16.
■ **consumingly** *adverb* so as to consume or be consumed; exceedingly: M16.

consumed /kən'sjuːmd/ *ppl adjective & adverb*. LME.
[ORIGIN from CONSUME + -ED¹.]
1 *adjective*. That has been consumed (esp. *fig.*). LME.
†**2** *adjective & adverb*. Confounded(ly), damn(ably). E18–L19.
■ **consumedly** /-mɪdli/ *adverb* †(**a**) confoundedly, damnably; (**b**) *arch.* excessively, extremely: E18.

consumer /kən'sjuːmə/ *noun*. LME.
[ORIGIN formed as CONSUMED + -ER¹.]
1 A person who or thing which squanders, destroys, or uses up. LME.
2 A user of an article or commodity, a buyer of goods or services. Opp. ***producer***. L17.
– COMB.: **consumer durable** an article for domestic use which does not need to be rapidly replaced; **consumer goods**: used in their own right, esp. domestically, not for manufacturing etc.; **consumer price index** (in the US) an index of the variation in prices for retail goods and other items; **consumer research** investigation of the wants and opinions of those who might buy a product; **consumer resistance** sales resistance from consumers.
■ **consumerism** *noun* (**a**) protection of the interests of consumers; (**b**) preoccupation with consumer goods and their acquisition: M20. **consumerist** *adjective & noun* (a person) advocating or

C

involved in the protection of consumers' interests **L20**. **consume'ristic** *adjective* **L20**.

consummate /kən'sʌmət, 'kɒnsʌmət/ *adjective* (orig. *pa. pple*). **LME**.
[**ORIGIN** Latin *consummatus* pa. pple, formed as **CONSUMMATE** *verb*: see **-ATE**².]
†**1 a** Completed; fully accomplished. **LME–M19**. ▸**b** Of a marriage: consummated. **M16–M18**.
†**2** Having in it finality. Only in **LME**.
3 Of a thing: complete, perfect. *arch.* **E16**.
4 Of the highest degree; supreme, utmost. **M16**.

P. G. WODEHOUSE A sweeping and consummate vengeance. C. HILL His consummate skill.

5 Of a person: fully accomplished; supremely skilled. **M17**.

R. FRY The prince of craftsmen, the consummate technician.

■ **consummately** *adverb* **E17**. **consummateness** *noun* (*rare*) **E20**.

consummate /'kɒnsəmeɪt, -sjʊ-/ *verb*. **M16**.
[**ORIGIN** Latin *consummat-* pa. ppl stem of *consummare*, formed as **CON-** + *summa* **SUM** *noun*, *summus* highest, supreme: see **-ATE**³.]
1 *verb trans.* Bring to completion; accomplish, fulfil, finish. **M16**.
2 *verb trans.* & (now *rare*) *intrans.* Complete (marriage) by sexual intercourse. **M16**.
3 *verb intrans.* Fulfil or perfect itself. **M19**.
■ **consummator** *noun* **L16**. **consummatory** /kən'sʌmət(ə)ri/ *adjective* = **CONSUMMATIVE**; *spec.* designating an (animal or human) action that is an end in itself: **M17**.

consummation /kɒnsə'meɪʃ(ə)n, -sjʊ-/ *noun*. **LME**.
[**ORIGIN** Old French & mod. French *consommation* or Latin *consummatio(n-)*, formed as **CONSUMMATE** *verb*: see **-ATION**.]
1 The action of consummating (esp. a marriage). **LME**.
2 A conclusion, an end (in time), *spec.* that of the world. **LME**.
3 The action of perfecting; the condition of full development; acme; a desired end or goal. **LME**.

Time The meal in preparation and its consummation at the table. F. WARNER A perfect end The consummation of a life of prayer.

consummative /'kɒnsəmeɪtɪv, kən'sʌmətɪv/ *adjective*. **L17**.
[**ORIGIN** formed as **CONSUMMATE** *verb* + **-IVE**.]
That consummates or tends to consummate.
■ **consummatively** *adverb* **E17**. **consummativeness** *noun* (*rare*) **E18**.

consumpt /kən'sʌm(p)t/ *noun*. Chiefly *Scot.* **E18**.
[**ORIGIN** Latin *consumpt-*: see **CONSUMPTION**.]
= **CONSUMPTION** 4.

consumption /kən'sʌm(p)ʃ(ə)n/ *noun*. **LME**.
[**ORIGIN** Old French & mod. French *consomption* from Latin *consumptio(n-)*, from *consumpt-* pa. ppl stem of *consumere* **CONSUME**: see **-ION**.]
1 The action or fact of consuming by use, waste, eating, etc. (see **CONSUME**). **LME**.

fig.: W. OWEN To borrow a book for Dorothy's immediate consumption.

2 Wasting of the body by disease; (formerly) a wasting disease; now *spec.*, severe pulmonary tuberculosis. **LME**.

M. GIROUARD Galloping consumption forced him to spend more .. time on the south coast.

3 Decay, wasting away, wearing out. **E16**.
4 The purchase and use of or *of* goods, material, or energy; the amount or rate of this. **M17**.
specific consumption, ***specific fuel consumption***: see **SPECIFIC** *adjective*.
■ †**consumptioner** *noun* a consumer **M17–M18**.

consumptive /kən'sʌm(p)tɪv/ *adjective* & *noun*. **M17**.
[**ORIGIN** medieval Latin *consumptivus*, from Latin *consumpt-*: see **CONSUMPTION**, **-IVE**.]
▸ **A** *adjective*. **1** Tending to consume; wasteful, destructive. **M17**.
2 Affected by or pertaining to a wasting disease; *spec.* of or pertaining to, having or tending to, pulmonary tuberculosis. **M17**.

U. BENTLEY She lay .. on the sofa, .. looking romantically consumptive.

3 Of or for economic consumption. **M19**.
▸ **B** *noun*. **1** A person with consumption. **M17**.
†**2** A destructive or corrosive agent. **L17–L18**.
■ **consumptively** *adverb* **L17**. **consumptiveness** *noun* **M18**.

contabescence /kɒntə'bɛs(ə)ns/ *noun*. Now *rare* or *obsolete*. **M17**.
[**ORIGIN** from Latin *contabescent-* pres. ppl stem of *contabescere* waste away: see **-ENCE**.]
Wasting away, atrophy; *BOTANY* suppression of pollen formation in the anthers of flowers.
■ **contabescent** *adjective* **M19**.

contact /'kɒntakt/ *noun*. **E17**.
[**ORIGIN** Latin *contactus*, from *contact-* pa. ppl stem of *contingere* touch closely, border on, formed as **CON-** + *tangere* touch. Cf. French *contact*.]
1 The state or condition of touching; an instance of touching. **E17**. ▸**b** The touching of electrical conductors to permit the flow of current; a device for effecting this; each of the conductors involved. **M19**.
b break contact, ***make contact***.
2 *MATH.* The touching of a straight line and a curve, of two curves, or of two surfaces. **M17**.
3 Meeting, communication. **E19**.

R. K. NARAYAN His lifelong contact with tough men had hardened him. V. GRISSOM I was in radio contact with .. the helicopters which were on their way to pick me up.

4 a A person who has been exposed to infection by proximity to someone suffering from an infectious disease. **E20**. ▸**b** A person who can be called upon for assistance, information, etc.; a business etc. acquaintance who may be useful. **M20**.

b J. DIDION He was a good contact. He knew a lot of things.

5 = ***contact lens*** below. Usu. in *pl.* *colloq.* **M20**.
– **PHRASES**: **come in contact with**, **come into contact with** touch, meet, come across, be brought into communication with. *SLIDING* ***contact***.
– **COMB.**: **contact breaker** a contrivance for breaking an electric circuit automatically; **contact flight**, **contact flying** navigation of an aircraft by the observation of landmarks; **contact healing** *SPIRITUALISM* the healing of illness by physical contact with a medium; **contact herbicide**: that affects a plant only when it comes into contact with it, not when it is taken up through the roots; **contact lens** a small glass or plastic lens placed on the surface of the eyeball to correct faulty vision; **contact man** a go-between; a man who carries or supplies information; **contact metamorphism** *GEOLOGY*: due to contact with or proximity to an igneous intrusion; **contact print**, **contact-printing** *PHOTOGRAPHY* a print made by, the making of prints by, passing light through a negative on to sensitized paper, glass, or film held in direct contact with the negative; **contact process** *CHEMISTRY*: for making sulphuric acid by means of the oxidation of sulphur dioxide in the presence of a solid catalyst; **contact screen** a halftone screen made on a film base; **contact sport** a sport in which the participants necessarily come into bodily contact with one another.

contact /'kɒntakt, kən'takt/ *verb*. **M19**.
[**ORIGIN** from the noun.]
1 *verb trans.* Bring into or place in contact. *rare*. **M19**.
2 *verb intrans.* Come into or be in contact (*with*). **L19**.
3 *verb trans.* Come into contact with; get in touch with. **E20**.
■ **contactable** *adjective* **M20**. **contactor** *noun* a device for making and breaking an electric circuit **E20**.

contadina /konta'di:na, kɒntə'di:nə/ *noun*. Pl. ***-ne*** /-ne, -ni/, ***-nas***. **E19**.
[**ORIGIN** Italian, fem. of **CONTADINO**.]
An Italian peasant girl or peasant woman.

contadino /konta'di:no, kɒntə'di:nəʊ/ *noun*. Pl. ***-ni*** /-ni/, ***-nos***. **M17**.
[**ORIGIN** Italian, from *contado* county, (peasant population of) agricultural area round a city: cf. **-INE**¹.]
An Italian peasant or countryman.

contagion /kən'teɪdʒ(ə)n/ *noun*. **LME**.
[**ORIGIN** Latin *contagio(n-)*, formed as **CON-** + base of *tangere* to touch: see **-ION**. Cf. French *contagion*.]
1 A contagious disease; a plague, a pestilence. *fig.* a contagious moral disease, corruption. **LME**.

M. L. KING Hate is a contagion; .. it grows and spreads as a disease.

2 Harmful contagious influence or quality (chiefly *fig.*). **LME**.

E. P. THOMPSON The tendency of the Methodists .. to keep their members apart from the contagion of the unconverted.

3 The communication of disease from body to body by direct or indirect contact. **E17**.
4 *MEDICAL HISTORY*. A substance or agent by which a contagious disease is transmitted. **E17**. ▸†**b** A poison that infects the blood. *rare* (Shakes.). Only in **E17**.
5 In a good or neutral sense: the infectious quality or influence of an emotion, action, etc. **M17**.

J. A. FROUDE The contagion of example.

■ **contagionist** *noun* (*obsolete* exc. *hist.*) a believer in the contagiousness of a particular disease or particular diseases **E19**.

contagious /kən'teɪdʒəs/ *adjective*. **LME**.
[**ORIGIN** Late Latin *contagiosus*, formed as **CONTAGION**: see **-OUS**.]
1 Communicating disease or corruption by contact. **LME**.

fig.: SOUTHEY Ere the contagious vices of the court Polluted her.

†**2** Apt to breed disease, pestilential; *gen.* harmful, noxious. **LME–L18**.

R. HAKLUYT The Winter comming .. with much contagious weather.

3 Of a disease: infectious by direct or indirect contact; communicable. **LME**.
contagious abortion brucellosis in cattle, as producing abortion.
4 Charged with the agents (as bacteria etc.) of a communicable disease. **L16**.

DEFOE Their breath, their sweat, their very clothes were contagious.

5 *fig.* Of an emotion etc.: infectious, quickly affecting others. **E17**.

CONAN DOYLE The faculty of deduction is certainly contagious, Watson ... It has enabled you to probe my secret.

■ **contagiously** *adverb* **LME**. **contagiousness** *noun* **L15**.

contagium /kən'teɪdʒɪəm/ *noun*. Pl. **-ia** /-ɪə/. **M17**.
[**ORIGIN** Latin, var. of *contagio(n-)* **CONTAGION**.]
†**1** *gen.* Contagion. Only in **M17**.
2 *spec.* = **CONTAGION** 4. **L19**.

contain /kən'teɪn/ *verb*. **ME**.
[**ORIGIN** Repr. tonic stem of Old French & mod. French *contenir* from Latin *continere*, formed as **CON-** + *tenere* hold.]
▸ **I** Have in it.
1 *verb trans.* Include as a part or the whole of its substance or content; comprise. **ME**. ▸**b** Of a measure: be equal to (so much or many of another). **LME**. ▸**c** *MATH.* Of a number: be divisible by, esp. without a remainder. Usu. in *pass.* **L16**.

J. TYNDALL The rock .. contains a good deal of iron. T. HARDY The next letter .. contained .. a statement of his position.

†**2** *verb trans.* Extend over, take up. **LME–M18**.

SWIFT A complete history .. would contain twelve large volumes in folio.

3 *verb trans.* Have inside itself, (be able to) hold within itself. **LME**.

A. URE Waggons .. containing each 53 cwts. J. BUCHAN The side pocket .. contained an old .. cigar case.

4 *verb trans.* Have (an area, a space, etc.) within its boundaries, enclose (*between*, *within*); *MATH.* form the boundary of (a geometric figure). Usu. in *pass.* **LME**.

OED The space contained between the orbits of Mars and Jupiter.

▸ **II** Restrain, control.
5 *verb trans.* Restrain, keep in check, repress, (oneself, one's emotions etc., †another). (Foll. by †*from* an action etc.) **ME**. ▸**b** *verb intrans.* Control oneself or one's emotions. Now *rare*. **E17**.

SPENSER To contayne the unruly people from a thousand evill occasions. E. BOWEN She could hardly contain herself for apprehension and pleasure. D. LESSING She made efforts to contain her feelings. **b** AV *1 Cor.* 7:9 But if they cannot conteine, let them marry.

†**6** *verb refl.* & *intrans.* Behave. **ME–L15**.
7 *verb trans.* Restrict, limit, confine. Now *esp.* keep (a hostile force, ideology, etc.) within certain boundaries; prevent from moving or extending. **LME**.

A. DAVIS The collective anger was so great that the people could not be contained. Defiant throngs pressed forward through the doors of the building. C. RYAN The assault was aimed at containing the fifteenth Army.

†**8** *verb trans.* Retain in a desired state or order. (Foll. by *in*, *within*.) **M16–M19**. ▸†**b** Keep in one's possession or control. **L16–M17**.

GIBBON That he could .. contain in obedience .. his wide-extended dominions.

■ **containable** *adjective* (earlier in **UNCONTAINABLE**) **L17**. **contained** *ppl adjective* (**a**) included, enclosed, held; (**b**) restrained, showing self-restraint, reserved (see also **SELF-CONTAINED**): **LME**. **containing** *noun* (**a**) the action of the verb; †(**b**) that which is contained; contents: **LME**. **containment** *noun* the action or fact of containing or holding; restraint; *esp.* the action of preventing a hostile force etc. from expanding into other areas: **M17**.

container /kən'teɪnə/ *noun*. **LME**.
[**ORIGIN** from **CONTAIN** + **-ER**¹.]
A person who or thing which contains something; a receptacle designed to contain some particular thing(s); *spec.* a large boxlike receptacle of standard design, used for the transportation of goods.
– **COMB.**: **container lorry**, **container ship**, **container train**: designed to carry goods stored in (large) containers.
■ **containerize** *verb trans.* pack into or transport by means of containers **M20**.

contaminate /kən'tamɪneɪt/ *verb trans.* Pa. pple & ppl adjective **-ated**, (*arch.*) **-ate** /-ət/. **LME**.
[**ORIGIN** Latin *contaminat-* pa. ppl stem of *contaminare*, from *contamen*, *-min-*, contact, pollution, from base of *tangere* touch: see **-ATE**³. Cf. **CONTAGION**.]
1 Make impure by contact or mixture; pollute, corrupt, infect. **LME**.
2 *spec.* ▸**a** Subject to contamination by radioactivity. **E20**. ▸**b** Subject to textual contamination. **E20**.
■ **contaminant** *noun* something which contaminates, a contaminating substance **M20**. **contaminative** *adjective* that contaminates **E19**. **contaminator** *noun* **E19**.

contamination /kəntamɪ'neɪʃ(ə)n/ *noun*. **LME**.
[**ORIGIN** Latin *contaminatio(n-)*, formed as **CONTAMINATE**: see **-ATION**.]
1 The action of making impure or polluting; defilement, infection. **LME**. ▸**b** *spec.* The introduction or presence of radioactivity where it is harmful or undesirable. **E20**.
2 Something which contaminates; an impurity. **E19**.
3 a The blending of two or more stories, plots, etc., into one. **L19**. ▸**b** *LINGUISTICS*. The blending of forms of similar meaning or use in order to produce a form of a new type. **L19**. ▸**c** *TEXTUAL CRITICISM*. A blending of manuscripts resulting in readings from different traditions occurring in the same (group of) manuscript(s). **E20**.

contango /kən'taŋgəʊ/ *noun & verb*. M19.
[ORIGIN Prob. arbitrary, on the analogy of Latin 1st person pres. sing. in -*o*, perh. with notion '(I) make contingent'.]
COMMERCE. ▶**A** *noun*. Pl. **-os**. A premium paid by a buyer of stock to postpone transfer to a future settling day. Cf. BACKWARDATION. M19.
– COMB.: **contango day** the eighth day before a settling day.
▶**B** *verb trans*. Pay contango on (stocks or shares). E20.

conte /kɔ̃:t/ *noun*. Pl. pronounced same. L19.
[ORIGIN French.]
A short story, as a form of literary composition; *spec*. a medieval narrative tale.
■ **conteur** /kɔ̃tœ:r (*pl. same*)/ *noun* a composer of *contes*; a narrator: M19.

Conté /'kɒnteɪ/ *adjective*. Also **c-**. M19.
[ORIGIN Nicolas Jacques *Conté* (1755–1805), French inventor.]
Designating a kind of pencil, crayon, or chalk which Conté developed.

contemn /kən'tɛm/ *verb trans*. Now chiefly *literary*. LME.
[ORIGIN Old French *contemner* or Latin *contemnere*, formed as CON- + *temnere* despise.]
Treat as of small value, view with contempt; disregard; despise, scorn.
■ **contemner**, **-or** *noun* E16. **contemningly** *adverb* (now *rare*) in a contemning or scornful manner L15.

contemper /kən'tɛmpə/ *verb trans*. Now *rare* or *obsolete*. L16.
[ORIGIN French †*contempérer* or Latin *contemperare* temper by mixing, formed as CON- + TEMPER *verb*[1].]
1 Mingle together. L16.
2 Temper, moderate, qualify. E17.
3 Adjust (*to*) by tempering. E17.

†**contemperate** *verb trans*. Pa. pple **-ated**, (earlier) **-ate**. L15–M18.
[ORIGIN Latin *contemperat-* pa. ppl stem of *contemperare*: see CONTEMPER, -ATE[3].]
= CONTEMPER.

contemperature /kən'tɛmp(ə)rətʃə/ *noun*. Now *rare* or *obsolete*. M16.
[ORIGIN formed as CONTEMPERATE after TEMPERATURE.]
The action or product of blending together; a harmonious mixture.

contemplable /kən'tɛmpləb(ə)l/ *adjective*. *rare*. E17.
[ORIGIN Latin *contemplabilis*, from *contemplari*: see CONTEMPLATE, -ABLE.]
That may be contemplated.

contemplamen /kɒntəm'pleɪmɛn/ *noun*. *rare*. L17.
[ORIGIN mod. Latin, from *contemplari*: see CONTEMPLATE.]
An object of contemplation.

contemplant /kən'tɛmpl(ə)nt/ *noun & adjective*. *rare*. E17.
[ORIGIN Latin *contemplant-* pres. ppl stem of *contemplari*: see CONTEMPLATE, -ANT[1].]
▶†**A** *noun*. A person who contemplates. Only in E17.
▶**B** *adjective*. That contemplates. L18.

contemplate /'kɒntɛmpleɪt, -təm-/ *verb*. L16.
[ORIGIN Latin *contemplat-* pa. ppl stem of *contemplari*, formed as CON- + *templum* open space for observation, temple: see -ATE[3].]
1 *verb intrans*. Meditate (†*on*), muse; be occupied in contemplation. L16.

SOUTHEY Julian was silent then, and sate contemplating. I. D'ISRAELI Too deeply occupied with their own projects to contemplate on those of others.

2 *verb trans*. Meditate on, ponder; view mentally; consider in a particular aspect, regard. L16.

S. TURNER [It] must not be contemplated as a barbarism of the country. J. LONDON He would have . . to do a thousand and one things that were awful to contemplate.

contemplate one's navel: see NAVEL 1.
3 *verb trans*. & †*intrans*. foll. by *on*. Look at with continued attention; gaze on, observe thoughtfully. E17.

J. CONRAD She continued to contemplate . . the bare and untidy garden.

4 *verb trans*. Regard as possible, expect, take into account as a contingency. L18. ▸**b** Have in view as a purpose; intend. E19.

E. F. BENSON Failure, however, she did not contemplate. **b** A. CHRISTIE We are not contemplating arresting anyone at present. B. WEBB I am . . contemplating a course of reading on music and musicians.

■ †**contemplatist** *noun* a person given to contemplation M17–M19.

contemplation /kɒntɛm'pleɪʃ(ə)n, -təm-/ *noun*. ME.
[ORIGIN Old French & mod. French from Latin *contemplatio(n-)*, formed as CONTEMPLATE: see -ATION.]
1 Religious musing; devout meditation. ME.
2 *gen*. The action of thinking about or of pondering over a thing continuously; musing, meditation. ME. ▸**b** A state or period of meditation or study. Also, a meditation expressed in writing (usu. in *pl*.). E16.

M. DE LA ROCHE Each absorbed in contemplation of his own thoughts. J. GLASSCO I sat down . . and gave myself up to contemplation.

3 The action of viewing as a possibility or as a purpose; taking into account; prospect, intention. LME. ▸†**b** Request, petition. LME–M16.
in contemplation in mind; under serious consideration.
4 The action of gazing on or looking at attentively or thoughtfully. L15.
5 (A) matter for contemplation. Now *rare*. E18.

S. JOHNSON Everything must supply you with contemplation.

contemplative /kən'tɛmplətɪv; *in senses A.2, 3 also* 'kɒntɛmpleɪtɪv, -təm-/ *adjective & noun*. ME.
[ORIGIN Old French & mod. French *contemplatif*, *-ive* or Latin *contemplativus*, formed as CONTEMPLATE: see -ATIVE.]
▶**A** *adjective*. 1 Devoted or given up to religious contemplation and prayer. Esp. in ***contemplative life*** [Latin *vita contemplativa*]. ME.
2 *gen*. Given to contemplation; meditative, thoughtful. ME.
3 Characterized by, of the nature of, or tending to contemplation. LME.

W. BLACK Smoking a contemplative cigar under the . . starlight.

▶**B** *noun*. A person devoted to meditation or religious contemplation; a person who leads the contemplative life. ME.
■ **contemplatively** *adverb* LME. **contemplativeness** *noun* M18.

contemplator /'kɒntɛmpleɪtə, -təm-/ *noun*. LME.
[ORIGIN Latin *contemplator*, formed as CONTEMPLATE: see -OR. Partly from CONTEMPLATE + -OR.]
A person who contemplates something; a person given to or engaged in contemplation.

†**contemporane** *adjective & noun*. Also **-an**. LME.
[ORIGIN formed as CONTEMPORANEOUS.]
▶**A** *adjective*. Contemporaneous (*with*). LME–L16.
▶**B** *noun*. A contemporary. M16–M18.

contemporaneity /kəntɛmp(ə)rə'ni:ɪti, -'neɪɪti/ *noun*. L18.
[ORIGIN from CONTEMPORANEOUS + -ITY. Cf. French *contemporanéité*. See also COTEMPORANEITY.]
Contemporaneous condition or state.

contemporaneous /kəntɛmpə'reɪnɪəs, kɒn-/ *adjective*. M17.
[ORIGIN from Latin *contemporaneus*, formed as CON- + *tempus*, *tempor-* time: see -OUS. See also COTEMPORANEOUS.]
1 Existing or occurring at the same time (*with*). M17.
2 Of the same historical or geological period (*with*); of the same age. M19.
■ **contemporaneously** *adverb* E19. **contemporaneousness** *noun* E19.

contemporary /kən'tɛmp(ə)r(ər)i/ *noun & adjective*. M17.
[ORIGIN medieval Latin *contemporarius*, formed as CON- + *tempus*, *tempor-* time, after Latin *contemporaneus* (see CONTEMPORANEOUS) and late Latin *contemporalis* (see CON-, TEMPORAL *adjective*[1]): see -ARY[1]. See also COTEMPORARY.]
▶**A** *adjective*. 1 Belonging to the same time; existing or occurring together in time. (Foll. by *with*, †(*un*)*to*.) M17.

M. PATTISON Writers contemporary with the events they write of. G. M. TREVELYAN The . . changes in Scottish mind and manners . . did not come to any serious collision with the . . church, such as marked contemporary movements of opinion in France.

2 Equal in age, coeval. M17.

JAMES SULLIVAN The water is as ancient as the earth, and contemporary with it.

3 Occurring at the same moment or during the same period; contemporaneous, simultaneous. M17.
4 Modern or ultra-modern in style or design. M19.

A. TATE It was often said of T. S. Eliot that his poems were *very* contemporary but that his ideas . . were all frozen in the past.

▶**B** *noun*. A person who lives at the same time as or is the same age as another or others; *transf*. a journal etc. published at the same time as another. M17.
■ **contemporarily** *adverb* (**a**) contemporaneously; (**b**) in a contemporary manner: M18. **contemporariness** *noun* M17.

contemporize /kən'tɛmpərʌɪz/ *verb trans. & intrans*. Also **-ise**. M17.
[ORIGIN from late Latin *contemporare* + -IZE.]
(Cause to) synchronize.

contempt /kən'tɛm(p)t/ *noun*. LME.
[ORIGIN Latin *contemptus*, from *contempt-* pa. ppl stem of *contemnere* CONTEMN.]
1 The action of scorning or despising; the mental attitude in which something or someone is considered as worthless or of little account. LME.

P. G. WODEHOUSE A true woman's contempt for consistency. C. P. SNOW She said it dismissively and with contempt.

beneath contempt: see BENEATH *preposition* 3.
2 The condition of being held worthless or of being despised; dishonour, disgrace. LME.
bring into contempt make despised. **fall into contempt** become despised. **have in contempt**, **hold in contempt** despise.
3 LAW. Disobedience or open disrespect to the monarch's lawful commands or to the authority of Parliament or another legislative body; (in full ***contempt of court***) disobedience or open disrespect to, or interference with the proper administration of justice by, a court of law. LME.
in contempt (**of court**) in the position of having committed contempt and not having purged this offence.
4 A scornful or disrespectful act; *esp*. an act in contempt of a court of law. L16.

J. WESLEY Our sins are so many contempts of this highest expression of his love.

†5 An object of contempt. E17–M19.

†**contempt** *verb trans*. Pa. pple **-ed**, (earlier) **contempt**. LME–E19.
[ORIGIN Latin *contempt-* (see CONTEMPT *noun*).]
= CONTEMN.

contemptible /kən'tɛm(p)tɪb(ə)l/ *adjective & noun*. LME.
[ORIGIN Old French & mod. French, or late Latin *contemptibilis*, formed as CONTEMPT *noun*: see -IBLE.]
▶**A** *adjective*. 1 Worthy only of contempt; despicable. LME.
2 Expressing contempt, full of contempt. *obsolete* exc. *dial*. L16.
▶**B** *noun*. A contemptible person or thing. *rare* exc. as below. M17.
Old Contemptibles *hist*. the British army in France in 1914 (with ref. to the German Emperor's alleged mention of a 'contemptible little army').
■ **contempti'bility** *noun* E17. **contemptibleness** *noun* L16. **contemptibly** *adverb* LME.

contemptuous /kən'tɛm(p)tjʊəs/ *adjective*. M16.
[ORIGIN medieval Latin *contemptuosus*, formed as CONTEMPT *noun*: see -UOUS.]
†1 Defying or despising law and public order. M16–L17.
2 Exciting or worthy of contempt; despicable. Now *rare*. M16.

SHAKES. *2 Hen. VI* Contemptuous base-born callet as she is.

3 Showing or full of contempt; disdainful, scornful, insolent. L16.

P. WARNER Henry . . had at first been contemptuous of Strongbow. L. O'FLAHERTY Proud, contemptuous, closed lips and an arrogant expression.

■ **contemptuously** *adverb* E16. **contemptuousness** *noun* M17.

contend /kən'tɛnd/ *verb*. LME.
[ORIGIN Old French *contendre* or Latin *contendere*, formed as CON- + *tendere* stretch, strive.]
1 *verb intrans*. Be in rivalry, compete, vie, (*with* a person, *for* a thing). LME.

HENRY FIELDING Nature and fortune . . seem to have contended which should enrich him most. W. LIPPMANN The pulling and pushing of interested groups contending for the assistance of the sovereign power.

2 *verb intrans*. Engage in conflict, fight (*with* a person, *for* a thing); strive *with* or *against* feelings, natural forces, difficulties, etc. L15.

SHAKES. *Coriol*. In ambitious strength I did Contend against thy valour. POPE Strength of Shade contends with strength of Light. D. H. LAWRENCE The only thing he had to contend with was the colliers setting snares for rabbits.

†3 *verb intrans*. Make great efforts; endeavour. L15–E19. ▸**b** Proceed with effort. L16–E17.

SWIFT Contending to excel themselves and their fellows.

4 *verb intrans*. Argue (*with*, *against*, etc.). M16.
5 *verb trans*. Maintain, assert, (*that*). M16.

H. J. LASKI The Nonjurors might with justice contend that they had right on their side.

†6 *verb trans*. Dispute (an object). *rare*. L17–L18.

SOUTHEY From his grasp Wrench the contended weapon.

■ †**contendent** *noun & adjective* (**a**) *noun* a person who contends; (**b**) *adjective* contending: M16–E19. **contender** *noun* a person who contends or is given to contention M16.

contenement /kən'tɛnɪm(ə)nt/ *noun*. *obsolete* exc. *hist*. E16.
[ORIGIN Old French, or medieval Latin *contenementum*, formed as CON- + TENEMENT.]
Land held by a feudal tenant; property necessary for the maintenance of status.
– NOTE: Used to render *contenementum* in Magna Carta, a word of which the precise meaning is uncertain.

content /'kɒntɛnt/ *noun*[1]. LME.
[ORIGIN medieval Latin *contentum*, pl. *contenta* things contained, use as noun of *contentus* pa. pple of *continere* CONTAIN.]
▶**I** 1 In *pl*. & †*sing*. What is contained (in a vessel, object, book, document, etc.). (Foll. by *of* or possess.) LME. ▸**b** In full ***table of contents***, †***table of content***. A summary of the subject matter of a book (usu. a list of the titles of chapters etc.). L15.

W. COWPER A letter ought not to be estimated by the length of it, but by the contents. J. CHEEVER She dumped the contents of her handbag onto the counter.

†2 *sing*. & in *pl*. (treated as *sing*. or *pl*.). Tenor, purport, (of a document etc.). LME–M17.

MILTON Terms of weight, Of hard contents.

3 The sum of the constituent elements of something (usu. abstract); the substance as opp. to the form; the

amount (of a specified element or material component) contained or yielded. M19. ▸**b** *PSYCHOLOGY.* [translating German *Inhalt.*] The totality of the constituents of a person's experience at any particular moment. L19. ▸**c** Information made available by a website or other electronic medium. L20.

W. D. WHITNEY The inner content or meaning of words. M. SCHORER Works [of literature] with the most satisfying content. F. HOYLE The moisture content of the air. **c** *www.corante.com* Many of them access the Internet wirelessly and are starting to pay for online content.

local content: see LOCAL *adjective*.

▸ **II 4** Containing capacity; volume; (now *rare*) area, extent. LME. ▸†**b** A portion of material or of space of a certain extent. L16–L17.

– COMB.: **content word** a word having an independent lexical meaning (as a noun, adjective, verb, etc.) as opp. to one expressing primarily a grammatical relationship (as a preposition, conjunction, auxiliary, etc.).

■ **con'tentual** *adjective* (PHILOSOPHY & PSYCHOLOGY) pertaining to or dealing with content (as opp. to form) E20.

content /kən'tɛnt/ *noun*². LME.

[ORIGIN Perh. from CONTENT *adjective* & *noun*³. Cf. Spanish, Portuguese, Italian *contento*.]

†**1** Payment, compensation for something done. *rare.* LME–M17.

2 Satisfaction, pleasure; contented state. L15.

DRYDEN In Concord and Content The Commons live, by no Divisions rent. K. MANSFIELD A look of deep content shone in her eyes.

to one's heart's content to the full extent of one's desires.

†**3** A source of satisfaction; in *pl.*, pleasures, delights. L16–E18.

†**4** Acquiescence; unquestioning acceptance. M17–M18.

POPE The sense they humbly take upon content.

5 A sweet drink, served hot or cold. *obsolete* exc. *Scot.* L17.

■ **contentful** *adjective* (now *rare*) full of content M16. **contentless** *adjective* (now *rare*) discontented E17.

content /kən'tɛnt/ *pred. adjective* & *noun*³. LME.

[ORIGIN Old French & mod. French from Latin *contentus* that is satisfied, pa. pple of *continere* (fig.) repress, restrain: cf. CONTAIN.]

▸ **A** *adjective.* **1** Desiring nothing more; satisfied (*with* what one has, *with* things as they are); contented, not unwilling *to do*, †*that*. LME.

L. URIS Abdul Kadar was content to play a waiting game. DAY LEWIS As a small child, I was content enough with the life around me. R. HARRIES I am content But I'm not happy.

2 Pleased, gratified. *arch.* exc. in ***well content***. LME.

TENNYSON So the three . . Dwelt with eternal summer, ill-content.

3 As *interjection.* Agreed! All right! *obsolete* exc. in the House of Lords expr. formal assent or (***not content***) dissent (corresp. to ***ay*** and ***no*** in the House of Commons). L16.

SHAKES. *1 Hen. VI* Content: I'll to the surgeon's.

▸ **B** *noun.* In the House of Lords: an affirmative or (***not content***) dissenting voter. E17.

content /kən'tɛnt/ *verb.* LME.

[ORIGIN Old French & mod. French *contenter* from Proto-Romance (medieval Latin) *contentare*, from *contentus*: see CONTENT *adjective* & *noun*³.]

1 *verb trans.* Satisfy; be enough for. LME. ▸**b** *refl.* Foll. by *with*, (arch.) *to do*: be satisfied or not unhappy with; accept or do no more than. LME. ▸†**c** *verb intrans.* Be content, acquiesce. LME–L16.

SHAKES. *A.Y.L.* I will content you if what pleases you contents you. E. M. FORSTER No ordinary view will content the Miss Alans. **b** S. JOHNSON Most men, when they should labour, content themselves to complain. P. G. WODEHOUSE George Pennicut contented himself with saying 'Goo!' He was a man of few words. C. MCCULLOUGH Ashamed to sit with a great plate of meat . . when the people of the country contented themselves with bread.

†**2** *verb trans.* Pay in full, reimburse, make good. LME–E19.

J. USSHER To content the workeman for his paynes. SIR W. SCOTT A certain sum of sterling money to be presently contented and paid to him.

†**3** *verb trans.* Please, gratify, delight. M16–L17.

■ **contentable** *adjective* able to be contented L16.

contentation /kɒntɛn'teɪʃ(ə)n/ *noun. arch.* LME.

[ORIGIN medieval Latin *contentatio(n-)*, from *contentat-* pa. ppl stem of *contentare*: see CONTENT *verb*, -ATION. Cf. Old French *contentacion*.]

†**1** Compensation; payment in satisfaction. Also, expiation of sin. LME–M17.

†**2** Satisfying of the conscience, allaying of doubt. L15–M17.

†**3** The action of contenting; the fact of being contented. L15–E18.

4 Contented condition. M16.

†**5** A source of satisfaction or pleasure. M16–L17.

contented /kən'tɛntɪd/ *adjective.* E16.

[ORIGIN from CONTENT *verb* + -ED¹.]

Satisfied, not displeased; not disposed to complain; willing to be content *with*; willing *to do*.

■ **contentedly** *adverb* M16. **contentedness** *noun* M17.

contention /kən'tɛnʃ(ə)n/ *noun.* LME.

[ORIGIN Old French & mod. French, or Latin *contentio(n-)*, from *content-* pa. ppl stem of *contendere*: see CONTEND, -ION.]

1 Strife, dispute, verbal controversy; a dispute or quarrel. LME.

fig.: SHAKES. *Oth.* The great contention of the sea and skies Parted our fellowship.

bone of contention: see BONE *noun*. ***draw the saw of contention***: see SAW *noun*¹.

2 Earnest exertion, endeavour. *arch.* M16.

3 Competition; (an act of) rivalry. L16.

in contention competing; in a position to win.

4 A point contended for in argument. M17.

B. MAGEE My central contention . . is that Wagner's music expresses . . repressed and highly charged contents of the psyche.

■ **contentional** *adjective* of the nature of contention E19.

contentious /kən'tɛnʃəs/ *adjective.* LME.

[ORIGIN Old French & mod. French *contentieux* from Latin *contentiosus*, from *content-*: see CONTENTION, -IOUS.]

1 Characterized by, involving, or subject to contention; disputed. LME.

GLADSTONE Forbearing to raise contentious issues.

2 Of or pertaining to differences between contending parties. L15.

contentious jurisdiction *LAW* jurisdiction over cases in which the parties seek resolution of a matter in dispute (as distinct from the formal approval of a transaction).

3 Given to contention; quarrelsome. L15.

AV *Prov.* 21:19 Better to dwell in the wildernesse, then with a contentious and an angry woman.

■ **contentiously** *adverb* M16. **contentiousness** *noun* L16.

contentive /kən'tɛntɪv/ *adjective.* Now *rare.* L17.

[ORIGIN French *contentif*, *-ive*, formed as CONTAIN + -IVE.]

That contains, having containing power.

contentment /kən'tɛntm(ə)nt/ *noun.* LME.

[ORIGIN French *contentement*, formed as CONTENT *verb*: see -MENT.]

†**1** Payment of a claim. LME–E17.

2 The action of satisfying; satisfaction. *arch.* L15.

†**3** Pleasure, delight, gratification. L16–L18.

†**4** A source of satisfaction or pleasure; a delight. L16–L17.

5 The fact, condition, or quality of being contented; tranquil happiness, contentedness. (Foll. by *with*, †*in*.) L16.

J. BEATTIE From health contentment springs. L. DE BERNIÈRES Contentment is more to be desired than happiness.

conterminal /kɒn'tə:mɪn(ə)l/ *adjective.* M17.

[ORIGIN Alt. of CONTERMINOUS with substitution of suffix -AL¹. Cf. COTERMINAL.]

= COTERMINOUS 1.

conterminate /kɒn'tə:mɪnət/ *adjective.* Now *rare.* L16.

[ORIGIN Late Latin *conterminatus* pa. pple, formed as CONTERMINOUS: see -ATE².]

= COTERMINOUS.

†**conterminate** *verb intrans.* M17–E19.

[ORIGIN Late Latin *conterminat-* pa. ppl stem of *conterminare*, formed as CONTERMINOUS: see -ATE³.]

Be conterminous in space or time; have a common limit.

conterminous /kɒn'tə:mɪnəs/ *adjective.* M17.

[ORIGIN from Latin *conterminus*, formed as CON- + TERMINUS: see -OUS. See also COTERMINOUS.]

1 Having a common boundary (*with*), adjacent (*to*). M17.

2 Meeting at their ends. M18.

3 Coextensive in space, time, or meaning. E19.

■ **conterminously** *adverb* M19. **conterminousness** *noun* E20.

†**conterraneous** *adjective.* M17–E18.

[ORIGIN from Latin *conterraneus*, formed as CON- + *terra* land: see -OUS.]

Of or belonging to the same country.

contessa /kɒn'tɛsə/ *noun.* Also (esp. in titles) **C-**. E19.

[ORIGIN Italian from medieval Latin *comitissa*: see COUNTESS.]

An Italian countess.

contest /'kɒntɛst/ *noun.* M17.

[ORIGIN from the verb, or French *conteste*, from *contester* CONTEST *verb*.]

1 A controversy; debate, argument. *arch.* M17.

EDWARD WARD He was, without Contest, As grand a Rebel as the best.

2 A struggle for victory, for an objective, etc.; conflict, strife. M17.

3 A competition; amicable contention for a prize etc. M17.

G. VIDAL They were in serious contest to determine who could spit the farthest. JAN MORRIS The Boat Race is a straight contest, start to finish.

contest /kən'tɛst/ *verb.* L16.

[ORIGIN Latin *contestari* call to witness, introduce (a suit) by calling witnesses, initiate (an action), formed as CON- + *testari* bear witness.]

†**1** *verb trans.* Swear to (a fact or statement). L16–E17.

†**2** *verb trans.* Attest. *rare.* L16–M17.

†**3** *verb trans.* Call to witness, adjure. Only in E17.

4 *verb intrans.* Strive in argument (*with*, *against*), wrangle. E17.

5 *verb intrans. gen.* Strive, contend. E17.

POPE For Forms of Government let Fools contest.

6 *verb intrans.* Contend in rivalry, compete. E17.

7 *verb trans.* Dispute by fighting; struggle or fight for. E17.

R. S. THOMAS Before Wars were contested. JOHN BROOKE Great Britain and France contested the supremacy of Western Europe.

8 *verb trans.* Debate, argue (a point etc.); call in question. M17. ▸**b** *spec.* Challenge the legality of (the result of an election). Chiefly *N. Amer.* L18.

DRYDEN A fifth Rule (which one may hope will not be contested). J. CHEEVER I'm going to declare that contract null and void, and if Murchison contests it, we'll drag him into court.

9 *verb trans.* Set in contention. *rare.* L17.

M. AYRTON Contesting the inertness of the mud against the spring in the rib.

10 *verb trans.* Contend or compete in (an election etc.) or for (a seat in Parliament etc.). E18.

■ **contestee** /kɒntɛs'ti:/ *noun* (*US*) a candidate whose election is contested L19. **contester**, **-or** *noun* a person who contests L19.

contestable /kən'tɛstəb(ə)l/ *adjective.* E18.

[ORIGIN from CONTEST *verb* + -ABLE. Cf. earlier INCONTESTABLE.]

Able to be contested; open to question or argument, disputable.

contestant /kən'tɛst(ə)nt/ *noun.* M17.

[ORIGIN French, pres. pple of *contester* CONTEST *verb*: see -ANT¹.]

A person who contests. Now usu. a person who takes part in a competition.

contestation /kɒntɛ'steɪʃ(ə)n/ *noun.* M16.

[ORIGIN Latin *contestatio(n-)*, from *contestat-* pa. ppl stem of *contestari*: see CONTEST *verb*, -ATION; partly through French.]

†**1 a** Adjuration; solemn appeal or protest. M16–E18. ▸**b** *ECCLESIASTICAL HISTORY.* In the Gallican liturgy, the prayer immediately preceding the Canon of the Mass. E18.

†**2** Confirmation by sworn testimony; solemn oath. L16–M17.

3 A disputation; controversy, argument. E17. ▸**b** An assertion contended for, a contention. L19.

4 The action of struggling against each other; conflict. E17.

5 Competition; rivalry. Latterly *Scot.* Now *rare.* E17.

†**contex** *verb trans.* Also **context**. Pa. pple **context(ed)**. M16–L18.

[ORIGIN Latin *contexere*, *context-*: see CONTEXT *noun*.]

Weave together (*lit.* & *fig.*).

context /'kɒntɛkst/ *noun.* LME.

[ORIGIN Latin *contextus*, from *context-* pa. ppl stem of *contexere* weave together, formed as CON- + *texere* weave.]

†**1** = CONTEXTURE 3. LME–M17.

†**2** = CONTEXTURE 4. M16–M17.

3 The part or parts immediately preceding or following a passage or word as determining or helping to reveal its meaning; the surrounding structure as determining the behaviour of a grammatical item, speech sound, etc. M16. ▸**b** *fig.* Ambient conditions; a set of circumstances; relation to circumstances. M19.

CONAN DOYLE That phrase 'Lion's Mane' haunted my mind. I knew that I had seen it somewhere in an unexpected context. **b** L. P. HARTLEY Applied to another context, the thought struck him unpleasantly. N. PODHORETZ Much less Marxist . . though equally given to the seeing of things in historical and social context.

out of context without relation to context and with consequently misleading implication. **b in this context** in this connection.

■ **contextless** *adjective* M20.

†**context** *verb* see CONTEX.

contextual /kən'tɛkstjʊəl/ *adjective.* E19.

[ORIGIN from CONTEXT *noun* after *textual*.]

Of or belonging to the context; depending on the context.

contextual definition: see DEFINITION 2.

■ **contextualism** *noun* (**a**) any philosophical doctrine emphasizing the importance of the context of inquiry in a particular question; (**b**) in literary criticism, the setting of a work in its cultural context: E20. **contextualist** *noun* an exponent or adherent of contextualism M20. **contextually** *adverb* E19.

contextualize /kən'tɛkstjʊəlʌɪz/ *verb trans.* Also **-ise**. M20.

[ORIGIN from CONTEXTUAL + -IZE.]

Place in or treat as part of a context; study in context.

■ **contextuali'zation** *noun* M20.

contexture /kən'tɛkstʃə/ *noun.* Now *literary.* E17.

[ORIGIN French, prob. from medieval Latin, from Latin CON- + *textura* TEXTURE *noun*.]

1 The action of weaving or linking together to form a connected whole (*lit.* & *fig.*); the fact or manner of being woven or linked together; structure, constitution. E17.

2 A mass *of* things interwoven together; a fabric (*lit.* & *fig.*). E17.

3 The putting together of words and sentences in connected composition; the construction of a text. E17.

4 A connected literary structure, a continuous text. E17.
5 = CONTEXT *noun* 3. E17.

contignation /kɒntɪɡˈneɪʃ(ə)n/ *noun. arch.* L16.
[ORIGIN Latin *contignatio(n-)*, from *contignat-* pa. ppl stem of *contignare* join together with beams, formed as CON- + *tignum* building material, piece of timber: see -ATION.]
1 A structure formed by joining timbers together, a framework; *spec.* a floor, storey, or stage so formed. L16.
2 The joining together of beams or boards; jointing. M17.

contiguity /kɒntɪˈɡjuːɪti/ *noun.* E16.
[ORIGIN Late Latin *contiguitas*, from Latin *contiguus*: see CONTIGUOUS, -ITY.]
1 Contact (*lit. & fig.*); close proximity. E16. ▸**b** PSYCHOLOGY. The proximity of ideas or impressions in place or time, as a principle of association. M18.
†**2** A contiguous thing. Only in M17.
3 A continuous mass. Now *rare*. L18.

contiguous /kənˈtɪɡjʊəs/ *adjective.* E16.
[ORIGIN from Latin *contiguus* touching together, from *contingere*: see CONTINGENT, -OUS.]
1 Neighbouring, in close proximity. E16.
> L. P. HARTLEY They occupied contiguous deck-chairs.

2 Touching, in contact; adjoining. Foll. by *to*. E17.
> S. JOHNSON An heiress whose land lies contiguous to mine.

3 Next in order, successive. E17.
> D. HARTLEY Two contiguous Moments of Time.

†**4** Continuous. Only in E18.
> DEFOE The notion of the Hills being contiguous, like a wall that had no gates.

■ †**contigual** *adjective* = CONTIGUOUS LME–M17. **contiguously** *adverb* M17. **contiguousness** *noun* M17.

continence /ˈkɒntɪnəns/ *noun.* ME.
[ORIGIN Old French & mod. French, or Latin *continentia*, from *continent-* pres. ppl stem of *continere* restrain: see CONTAIN, -ENCE.]
▸ **I 1** Self-restraint. ME.
2 *spec.* Sexual self-restraint; *esp.* complete sexual abstinence. LME.
3 The possession of normal voluntary control over excretory functions. Opp. earlier ***incontinence***. E20.
▸ †**II 4** Continuity. Only in E18.
■ **continency** *noun* (now *rare*) = CONTINENCE 1, 2 E16.

continent /ˈkɒntɪnənt/ *noun.* L15.
[ORIGIN In branches I & II from use as noun of Latin *continent-* (see CONTINENCE); branch I also infl. by the adjective. In branch III corresp. to French *continent*, Italian *continente*, repr. ellipt. use of Latin *terra continens* continuous land.]
▸ †**I 1** A person who is continent in appetites; a person under a vow of continence. L15–E18.
▸ **II 2** That which contains or holds something; *fig.* that which comprises or sums up something. Now *rare*. M16.
> G. MACDONALD Stealing from the significance of the content by the meretricious grandeur of the continent.

†**3** Containing area; capacity. Only in 17.
▸ **III 4** A continuous tract of land. *obsolete* exc. as in sense 6 below. M16. ▸†**b** Land as opp. to water; the earth. Only in L16. ▸†**c** The globe of the sun or moon. E–M17.
> P. ERONDELLE That part of New France which is one Continent with Virginia.

5 The main land, as distinguished from islands, peninsulas, etc.; mainland. Now chiefly in ***the Continent*** (***of Europe***), the mainland of Europe as distinct from the British Isles. L16.
> DEFOE It is not known whether that country be an island or the continent.

6 Any of the main continuous bodies of land (in GEOLOGY, continental crust) on the earth's surface (of which six are now recognized—Europe, Asia, Africa, N. and S. America, Australia, Antarctica). E17.
> *fig.*: CARLYLE Continents of parchment.

the Dark Continent: see DARK *adjective*.
7 US HISTORY. The colonies or states of America collectively, esp. at the time of the War of Independence. M18.

continent /ˈkɒntɪnənt/ *adjective.* LME.
[ORIGIN Latin *continent-*: see CONTINENCE, -ENT.]
▸ **I 1** Characterized by self-restraint; temperate. LME.
2 *spec.* Sexually self-restrained; chaste. LME.
†**3** Restraining, restrictive. *rare* (Shakes.). L16–E17.
> SHAKES. *Macb.* My desire all continent impediments would o'erbear That did oppose my will.

4 Capable of containing; capacious. *rare*. M19.
5 Having normal voluntary control over one's excretory functions. Opp. earlier ***incontinent***. M20.
▸ †**II 6** Continuous in space; connected *to*, *with*. LME–L17.
> R. GRAFTON The mayne and continent land of the whole worlde.

7 Continuous in duration; MEDICINE (of a fever etc.) not intermittent. E17–L18.
■ **continently** *adverb* (**a**) in moderation, chastely, temperately; †(**b**) *rare* continuously: LME.

continental /kɒntɪˈnɛnt(ə)l/ *adjective & noun.* M18.
[ORIGIN from CONTINENT *noun* + -AL[1].]
▸ **A** *adjective.* **1** Of or pertaining to a continent. M18.
2 (Often **C-**.) Belonging to or characteristic of the continent of Europe. M18.
3 US HISTORY. Of or belonging to the colonies or states of America collectively, esp. at the time of the War of Independence. L18.
– SPECIAL COLLOCATIONS: **continental breakfast** a light uncooked breakfast of coffee, rolls, etc. **continental climate**: having wide seasonal variations of temperature (characteristic of continental interiors far from the moderating influence of the sea). **Continental Congress** US HISTORY each of the three congresses held by the American colonies in revolt against British rule in 1774, 1775, and 1776 respectively. **continental crust** GEOLOGY the sialic crust which forms the earth's large land masses and the continental shelf (cf. SIAL). **continental day** a school day extending from early morning to early afternoon, as is customary in many countries of mainland Europe. **continental drift** the continuing slow movement of the continents (due to the movement of the lithospheric plates on the upper layer of the earth's mantle) which has brought them to their present positions. ***continental quilt***: see QUILT *noun* 1. **continental roast** (designating) dark-roasted coffee beans with a taste associated with mainland Europe. **continental shelf** the bed of the shallow sea area bordering a continent. **continental slope**: between the outer edge of the continental shelf and the ocean bed. **continental Sunday** Sunday as a day of recreation rather than of rest and worship. **Continental System** *hist.* Napoleon's plan to blockade England in 1806.
▸ **B** *noun.* **1** US HISTORY. ▸**a** A soldier of the continental army in the War of Independence. L18. ▸**b** A currency note of an early US issue that rapidly depreciated; *colloq.* the least possible amount. L18.
> **b** M. TWAIN He didn't give a continental for anybody.

2 A native or inhabitant of a continent, *spec.* (often **C-**) of the continent of Europe. E19.
■ **continentalist** *noun* (**a**) US HISTORY an advocate of the federation of the states after the War of Independence; (**b**) = CONTINENTAL *noun* 2: L18. **continenˈtality** *noun* (**a**) the condition of being continental; (**b**) *spec.* the properties characteristic of a continental climate: 19. **continentalize** *verb* (**a**) *verb intrans.* (*rare*) make a continental tour; (**b**) *verb trans.* make continental, impart a continental character to: M19. **continentally** *adverb* L18.

contingence /kənˈtɪndʒ(ə)ns/ *noun.* LME.
[ORIGIN formed as CONTINGENCY: see -ENCE.]
1 = CONTINGENCY 1, 5. Now *rare*. LME.
2 Touching, contact. M16.
†**3** Connection, affinity. M16–E17.

contingency /kənˈtɪndʒ(ə)nsi/ *noun.* M16.
[ORIGIN Late Latin *contingentia* in its medieval Latin sense of circumstance, contingency: see CONTINGENT, -ENCY.]
▸ **I 1 a** PHILOSOPHY. The condition of being free from necessity with regard to existence, action, etc.; openness to the effect of chance or free will. M16. ▸**b** *gen.* The quality or condition of being contingent; uncertainty of occurrence; chance. E17.
> **b** L. STERNE 'Twas a matter of contingency, which might happen or not. T. PYNCHON The War, the absolute rule of chance, their own pitiable contingency here, in its midst.

2 A thing dependent on an uncertain event. L16.
> D. ACHESON Its thoroughness in preparation left no contingencies uncovered.

3 A thing that may happen at a later time; a condition that may or may not be present in the future. E17.
> W. COBBETT All the . . ever-varying contingencies of marriage, number of children, etc.

4 A thing incident to another; an incidental expense etc. E17.
> C. V. WEDGWOOD He was compelled . . to modify his plan to meet unexpected and sometimes unwelcome contingencies. O. NASH Ready with a quip for any conversational contingency.

5 A chance occurrence; a concurrence of events, a juncture. E17.
> A. TROLLOPE Some settled contingencies to be forthcoming on their father's demise.

▸ **II 6** Close relationship or connection (*spec.* in SCOTS LAW, between processes); affinity. E17.
†**7** Touching, contact. M–L17.
– COMB.: **contingency fee** (in the US) a sum of money that a lawyer receives as a fee only if the case is won; **contingency fund**: set aside to deal with possible future or incidental expenses; **contingency plan**: to take account of a possible future event or circumstance.

contingent /kənˈtɪndʒ(ə)nt/ *adjective & noun.* LME.
[ORIGIN Latin *contingent-* pres. ppl stem of *contingere* be contiguous, be in connection or in contact, befall, formed as CON- + *tangere* to touch.]
▸ **A** *adjective* **I 1** Of uncertain occurrence; liable to happen or not. LME. ▸**b** Incidental (*to*). M18.
> GEO. ELIOT The results of confession were not contingent, they were certain.

2 PHILOSOPHY. Of a proposition etc.: that may or may not be true or false. L16. ▸**b** Dependent for its existence on something else; non-essential. E17.
> **b** H. T. BUCKLE The senses only supply what is finite and contingent. I. MURDOCH There are some parts of London which are necessary and others which are contingent.

3 Happening by chance; fortuitous. E17.
> M. BRADBURY An accident is a happening, . . a chance or a contingent event.

4 Conditional; dependent *on*, *upon*. E17.
> W. S. MAUGHAM The best opening . . was contingent on his putting in a considerable amount of capital.

†**5** Not predetermined by necessity; free. E17–L18.
> RICHARD WATSON If human actions are not Contingent, what . . of the morality of actions?

†**6** Subject to accident etc.; at the mercy of; chance. E18–M19.
7 LAW. Dependent on a foreseen possibility; provisionally liable to exist or take effect. E18.
> F. MARRYAT We are not looked upon as actual, but only contingent, inheritors of the title.

▸ **II 8** In contact, touching; tangential. Now *rare*. L16.
▸ **B** *noun.* **1** A chance occurrence; an accident. M16.
2 A thing that may or may not happen; a possibility. E17.
3 The proportion falling to a person on a division; a quota. E18.
4 Troops contributed to form part of an army etc.; *gen.* a group contributed to a larger one or having a similar origin. (The usual sense.) E18.
> I. MURDOCH The Finch contingent had tactfully not stayed to lunch. JO GRIMOND The Viking contingents going to or from the Crusade.

■ **continˈgential** *noun & adjective* (*rare*) (**a**) *noun* a non-essential; (**b**) *adjective* of a contingent nature, non-essential: M17. **contingently** *adverb* LME.

continua *noun* pl. of CONTINUUM.

continual /kənˈtɪnjʊəl/ *adjective.* ME.
[ORIGIN Old French & mod. French *continuel*, formed as CONTINUE: see -AL[1].]
1 Always happening; very frequent and without cessation; *arch.* regularly recurring. ME. ▸**b** LAW. Of a claim: formally reiterated within statutory intervals in order that it might not be deemed to be abandoned. *obsolete* exc. *hist.* E16.
> J. GALSWORTHY 'Why did she marry me?' was his continual thought. C. BROOKS Her devotion is continual whereas that of the poet is sporadic.

†**2** Perpetually existing or acting; unchanging in position. LME–M19.
> N. HAWTHORNE Beating it down with the pressure of his continual feet.

†**3** Forming a connected whole or continuous series; unbroken in expanse etc. LME–M18.
> H. SAVILE A deepe masse of continuall sea.

†**4** Of a disease: chronic, not intermittent. E16–M18.
■ **continuˈality** *noun* (*rare*) E19. **continually** *adverb* ME. **continualness** *noun* (*rare*) E17.

continuance /kənˈtɪnjʊəns/ *noun.* LME.
[ORIGIN Old French, formed as CONTINUE: see -ANCE.]
1 The action of making something continue or allowing something to continue; the maintaining or prolonging of an action, process, etc. LME.
> ADDISON His own preservation, or the continuance of his species. C. SAGAN This is a tradition worthy of continuance.

2 LAW. The adjournment of a suit or trial until a future date or for a period. Now *US*. LME.
3 The action of continuing in something; perseverance, persistence. *arch.* LME.
4 The lasting or enduring of an action, state, etc.; duration. LME.
> T. HALE Any Voyage not exceeding five or six years continuance.

5 The action or fact of remaining in or *in* a place, state, etc. LME.
> SHAKES. *1 Hen. VI* Cloy'd With long continuance in a settled place.

6 Course or length of time; a continuing period. *arch.* LME.
> R. L. STEVENSON I have . . seen him re-peruse it for a continuance of minutes.

†**7** Continuity. LME–M18.
†**8** The quality of lasting or having lasted; permanence, durability; antiquity. E16–L17.
9 = CONTINUATION 5. Now *rare* or *obsolete*. M16.

†**continuando** *noun.* Pl. **-os**. L17–M18.
[ORIGIN Latin = by continuing.]
LAW. A continuation or repetition of alleged acts, or an alleged act, of trespass; *gen.* a continuation.

continuant /kənˈtɪnjʊənt/ *adjective & noun.* E17.
[ORIGIN Partly from French, pres. pple of *continuer*; partly from Latin *continuant-* pres. ppl stem of *continuare*: see CONTINUE, -ANT[1].]
▸ **A** *adjective.* **1** Continuing, persisting in time; remaining in force. E17.

2 *PHONETICS*. Of a consonant: of which the sound can be prolonged as desired, articulated without complete obstruction of the airstream (as *f*, *n*, *r*, *s*). **L19.**
▸ **B** *noun*. **1** *PHONETICS*. A continuant consonant. **M19.**
2 *PHILOSOPHY*. A thing that retains its identity although its states and relations may be changed. **E20.**
■ †**continuantly** *adverb* **LME–L16.**

†**continuate** *adjective* (orig. *pa. pple*). **L15.**
[**ORIGIN** Latin *continuatus* pa. pple, formed as **CONTINUATION**: see **-ATE**[2].]
1 Continued; long-continued, lasting. **L15–M17.**
2 Continuous; uninterrupted. **M16–M17.**

†**continuate** *verb trans.* **L16–M19.**
[**ORIGIN** Latin *continuat-*: see **CONTINUATION**, **-ATE**[3].]
Make continuous in space or time.

continuation /kəntɪnjʊˈeɪʃ(ə)n/ *noun*. **LME.**
[**ORIGIN** Old French & mod. French from Latin *continuatio(n-)*, from *continuat-* pa. ppl stem of *continuare*: see **CONTINUE**, **-ATION**.]
†**1** The action of continuing in something; = **CONTINUANCE** 3. **LME–L15.**
†**2** Continuity in space or of substance. **LME–E18.**
3 The action or fact of remaining in a state; continuous or prolonged existence or operation. **LME.** ▸†**b** The action or fact of remaining in a place. **M–L17.**

G. B. SHAW To impose a continuation of marriage on people who have ceased to desire to be married.

4 *SCOTS LAW*. Adjournment, prorogation. Long *rare*. **LME.**
5 Something which continues another thing; an additional part or parts. **LME.**

J. GARDNER The page four continuation of a front-page story.

with continuation of days *SCOTS LAW* with allowance for the possible adjournment of the matter to a date later than that cited.
6 The carrying on or resumption of an action, course, story, etc. **L16.**
7 *STOCK EXCHANGE*. The carrying over of an account to the next settling day. **E19.**
8 In *pl*. Gaiters (as a continuation of knee breeches worn by bishops etc.); trousers (as a continuation of the waistcoat). *arch. slang*. **E19.**
– **COMB.**: **continuation day** = *contango day* s.v. **CONTANGO** *noun*; **continuation school** *hist*. a school for the additional teaching in spare time of those who had left full-time education.

continuative /kənˈtɪnjʊətɪv/ *noun & adjective*. **M16.**
[**ORIGIN** Late Latin *continuativus*, from *continuat-*: see **CONTINUATION**, **-ATIVE**.]
▸ **A** *noun*. A thing that serves to produce continuity (esp. of expression etc.) or to express continuance. **M16.**
▸ **B** *adjective*. **1** Tending or serving to continue something. **L17.**
2 Expressing continuance. **L19.**

continuator /kənˈtɪnjʊeɪtə/ *noun*. **M17.**
[**ORIGIN** from Latin *continuat-* (see **CONTINUATION**) + **-OR**. In sense 2 repr. French *continuateur*.]
1 A person who continues or maintains continuity. **M17.**
2 A person who continues work begun by another; *esp*. a person who writes a continuation of another's work. **M17.**

continue /kənˈtɪnjuː/ *verb*. **ME.**
[**ORIGIN** Old French & mod. French *continuer* from Latin *continuare* make or be continuous, from *continuus* **CONTINUOUS**. In branch III infl. by **CONTAIN**.]
▸ **I** *verb trans*. **1** Carry on, maintain, persist in, not stop, (an action, usage, etc.). **ME.**

G. BANCROFT To continue the struggle. E. HEMINGWAY Come to the Soviet Union and continue your studies there.

2 Cause to last or endure; prolong (something external to the agent); keep on in a place, a condition, etc. **LME.**

S. JOHNSON Almighty God who hast continued my life to this day. W. IRVING He was continued in his office.

3 Take up, resume, (a narrative, journey, etc.); form a prolongation of, extend; be a sequel to. **LME.** ▸**b** With direct speech as obj.: proceed or resume by saying. **E18.**

SHAKES. *2 Hen. IV* Our humble author will continue the story, with Sir John in it. D. BREWSTER If we continue backwards the rays . . they will meet at *m*. M. ARNOLD The man of intelligence was continued by successors like . . Euler. **b** J. CONRAD 'It's an official statement,' he continued.

4 *LAW*. Postpone or adjourn (legal proceedings). Chiefly *Scot. & US*. **LME.**
†**5** Connect, attach *to*. **LME–M17.**
▸ **II** *verb intrans*. **6** Persist in action or (of a person, now *rare*) in or *in* a course of action; persevere, keep on. **ME.**

SHAKES. *Macb.* I have known her continue in this a quarter of an hour. J. H. BLUNT The persecution continued with unabated rigour.

7 Remain in existence or in its present condition; last, endure. **LME.**

BROWNING Let what now exists continue. D. CARNEGIE Our friendship continued to his death.

8 Remain in or *in* a place or state. With compl., not stop being, not become other than. **LME.**

W. WHISTON The Deity would continue their friend. S. JOHNSON Your English style still continues in its purity and vigour. J. AUSTEN Frederica is made wretched by his continuing here. G. M. FRASER The weather continues fine.

9 Go on *doing*; not cease *to do*. **LME.**

LD MACAULAY He continued to offer his advice daily. W. GASS They would certainly continue growing.

10 Proceed in one's discourse, resume. **E18.**
▸ †**III 11** *verb trans*. Contain. **LME–L16.**
■ **continuable** *adjective* **L18.** **continuer** *noun* a person who or thing which continues **M16.**

continued /kənˈtɪnjuːd/ *ppl adjective*. **LME.**
[**ORIGIN** from **CONTINUE** + **-ED**[1].]
1 Carried on without cessation; constant. **LME.**
2 Extended unbroken or uninterrupted in space or time; carried on in a series or sequence. **LME.**
– **SPECIAL COLLOCATIONS**: **continued fraction** *MATH*. a fraction of infinite length whose denominator is a quantity plus a fraction, which latter fraction has a similar denominator, and so on. **continued proportionals** *MATH*. quantities belonging to a series such that the ratio between every two adjacent terms is the same. **continued story** *US* a serial story.

continuity /kɒntɪˈnjuːɪti/ *noun*. **LME.**
[**ORIGIN** Old French & mod. French *continuité* from Latin *continuitas*, from *continuare*: see **CONTINUE**, **-ITY**.]
1 The state or quality of being continuous; connectedness; unbroken succession; logical sequence. **LME.**

WELLINGTON The continuity of the frontier. J. BERGER Neither by way of his children . . nor by way of society can he find any sense of succession or continuity.

law of continuity: that all changes in nature are continuous, not abrupt. **solution of continuity** the fact or condition of being or becoming discontinuous; fracture; rupture; (orig. *MEDICINE* with ref. to injury to the body).
2 A continuous or connected whole; an unbroken course or series. **E17.**

COLERIDGE A chain that ascends in a continuity of links.

3 Uninterrupted duration. *rare*. **M17.**

D. BREWSTER The severity and continuity of his studies.

4 A detailed scenario of a film; the maintenance of consistency or of a continuous flow of action in a cinema or television sequence; (commentary etc. providing) linkage between items in a broadcast. **E20.**
– **COMB.**: **continuity girl**, **continuity man**, etc. *CINEMATOGRAPHY*: responsible for ensuring the necessary agreement of detail between different filmings.

continuo /kənˈtɪnjʊəʊ/ *noun*. Pl. **-os**. **E18.**
[**ORIGIN** Italian = continuous.]
A figured bass, a thorough bass, (= ***basso continuo*** s.v. **BASSO**); an accompaniment, usu. for keyboard, improvised from this. Also, the instrument(s) playing this part.

continuous /kənˈtɪnjʊəs/ *adjective*. **M17.**
[**ORIGIN** from Latin *continuus* uninterrupted, from *continere* hang together, formed as **CON-** + *tenere* hold: see **-OUS**.]
1 Characterized by continuity; extending in space without a break; uninterrupted in time or sequence; acting without interruption; connected. **M17.**

C. DARWIN In most cases the area inhabited by a species is continuous. B. JOWETT The power of . . continuous thought is very rare. W. STYRON A dog howls on and on . . , a continuous harsh lonely cry.

2 *GRAMMAR*. Designating an aspect or tense of the verb expressing continuing action or action in progress, or a particular form expressing this aspect or tense. **L19.**
– **SPECIAL COLLOCATIONS**: **continuous assessment** the evaluation of a student's progress based on work done throughout a course as well as or instead of by examination. **continuous creation** creation of the universe or of matter in it regarded as occurring continuously rather than in a particular event. **continuous function** *MATH*. a function whose graph is a continuous (unbroken) curve; a function such that as the value of *x* approaches a given value *a*, the value of *f*(*x*) approaches that of *f*(*a*) as a limit. **continuous stationery**: with sheets joined together and folded alternately. **continuous wave** *PHYSICS* an electromagnetic wave of constant amplitude.
■ **continuously** *adverb* **L17.** **continuousness** *noun* **E19.**

continuum /kənˈtɪnjʊəm/ *noun*. Pl. **-nua** /-njʊə/. **M17.**
[**ORIGIN** Use as noun of neut. sing. of Latin *continuus*: see **CONTINUOUS**.]
A continuous thing, quantity, or substance; a continuous series of elements passing into each other; *MATH*. the set of real numbers.

A. E. SMAILES No longer . . a . . dichotomy of town and country; rather it is an urban-rural continuum. E. FIGES This endless continuum of days.

space–time continuum: see **SPACE** *noun*.
– **COMB.**: **continuum hypothesis** *MATH*.: that there is no transfinite cardinal between the cardinal of the set of positive integers and that of the set of real numbers.

contline /ˈkɒntlʌɪn/ *noun*. **M19.**
[**ORIGIN** Perh. alt. of ***cant-line*** s.v. **CANT** *noun*[1].]
NAUTICAL. = ***cant-line*** s.v. **CANT** *noun*[1].

conto /ˈkɒntəʊ/ *noun*. *hist*. Pl. **-os**. **E17.**
[**ORIGIN** Portuguese from Latin *computus* **COUNT** *noun*[1].]
In Portugal, Brazil, etc.: a million reis; a thousand escudos or cruzeiros.

contoid /ˈkɒntɔɪd/ *adjective & noun*. **M20.**
[**ORIGIN** from *cont* contr. of **CONSONANT** *noun* + **-OID**.]
PHONETICS. (Designating or pertaining to) a speech sound of the consonantal type. Cf. **VOCOID**.

contorni *noun* pl. of **CONTORNO**.

contorniate /kɒnˈtɔːnɪət/ *adjective & noun*. **L17.**
[**ORIGIN** French, or Italian *contorniato*, from *contorniare* to surround, border, edge.]
▸ **A** *adjective*. Of a medal, coin, etc.: having a deep furrow round the disc, within the edge. **L17.**
▸ **B** *noun*. A contorniate coin or medal; *esp*. any of certain brass pieces of Nero and other Roman emperors. **E19.**

contorno /konˈtorno/ *noun*. *literary*. Pl. **-ni** /-ni/. **M18.**
[**ORIGIN** Italian = circuit, contour.]
A contour, an outline of a figure.

†**contorsion** *noun* var. of **CONTORTION**.

contort /kənˈtɔːt/ *verb trans*. **LME.**
[**ORIGIN** Latin *contort-* pa. ppl stem of *contorquere*, formed as **CON-** + *torquere* twist.]
Twist, esp. out of normal shape; distort by twisting.

R. P. JHABVALA He . . contorts himself so as to dig himself in the base of his spine. A. CARTER A face contorted by pain.

■ **contorted** *ppl adjective* (**a**) twisted, esp. out of shape, distorted; (**b**) (of petals etc.) overlapping at one margin and overlapped at the other: **E17.**

contortion /kənˈtɔːʃ(ə)n/ *noun*. Also †**-sion**. **LME.**
[**ORIGIN** Latin *contortio(n-)*, formed as **CONTORT**: see **-ION**. Cf. French *contorsion*.]
1 (An act of) twisting, esp. of the face or body; distortion by twisting or writhing. **LME.**

R. W. EMERSON The contortions of ten crucified martyrs.

2 A contorted condition, state, or form. **M17.**

W. BLACK The curious contortions of the rocks.

■ **contortionist** *noun* a person who practises contortion; *esp*. an acrobat who adopts unusual postures; *fig*. a person who contorts meanings etc. **M19.**

contortuplicate /kɒntɔːˈtjuːplɪkət/ *adjective*. **E19.**
[**ORIGIN** Latin *contortuplicatus*, from *contortus* twisted together + *-plicatus* folded: see **-ATE**[2].]
BOTANY. Twisted back upon itself.

contour /ˈkɒntʊə/ *noun & verb*. **M17.**
[**ORIGIN** French from Italian *contorno*, from *contornare* draw in outline, formed as **CON-** + *tornare* to turn.]
▸ **A** *noun*. **1** The outline of a figure, object, topographical feature, etc.; *spec*. a line separating differently coloured parts of a design etc. Freq. in *pl*. **M17.** ▸**b** Artistic quality of outline. **L18.**

R. L. STEVENSON The sides . . bulging outward with the contour of the ship. J. ANTHONY Her firm tawny body whose contours reminded me of the low-lying Tunisian hills.

2 In full ***contour line***. A line, passing through points of equal elevation (or depth) on a map, as one of a series drawn at regular height intervals; a similar but imaginary line on the ground. **M19.**

F. J. MONKHOUSE The contours are numbered on the upper side of each line, which indicates . . uphill and downhill directions, placing the figures in a row above one another.

3 *PHONETICS*. A particular level or a sequence of varying levels of pitch, tone, or stress. **M20.**
– **COMB.**: **contour-chasing** *slang* flying close to the ground following the contours of the landscape; **contour feather**: any of those that form the outline of a bird; ***contour line***: see sense 2 above; **contour map**: showing contour lines; **contour ploughing**: along lines of a constant altitude to minimize soil erosion.
▸ **B** *verb trans*. **1** Mark with contour lines. **M19.**
2 Cause (a road etc.) to follow the contours of the terrain etc.; shape so as to match a particular form. **L19.**
3 Follow the contour of. **E20.**

contourné /kɒnˈtʊəneɪ/ *adjective*. **E18.**
[**ORIGIN** French.]
HERALDRY. Turned about, towards the sinister side.

contra /ˈkɒntrə/ *adverb, preposition, & noun*. **LME.**
[**ORIGIN** Latin = against (adverb & preposition), abl. fem. of a compar. from *com*, *cum* with.]
▸ **A** *adverb*. On or to the contrary; contrariwise. Chiefly in ***pro and contra*** s.v. **PRO** *preposition* etc. **LME.**
▸ **B** *preposition*. Against. **LME.**
▸ **C** *noun*. **1** The contrary or opposite (side); an opposing factor or argument. Chiefly in ***pros and contras*** s.v. **PRO** *preposition* etc. **LME.**
PER CONTRA.
2 (Also **C-**.) [Spanish.] A counter-revolutionary in Nicaragua, *esp*. one opposing the government. Cf. **SANDINISTA**. **L20.**

contra- /ˈkɒntrə/ *prefix*.
[**ORIGIN** Latin, formed as **CONTRA**. Freq. through Italian, Spanish.]
Used in words adopted (ult.) from Latin and in English words modelled on these, with the sense 'against,

opposing, contrary', forming chiefly verbs and verbal derivs., as ***contradict***, (***contradiction***, ***contradictory***), ***contradistinguish***, ***contraindicate***, ***contravene***; in MUSIC forming the names of instruments and organ stops having a pitch of an octave below that of the instrument etc. named, as ***contrabass***, ***contrabassoon***. Not a very productive prefix in mod. English, the usual form being COUNTER-.

contraband /ˈkɒntrəband/ *noun & adjective*. L16.
[ORIGIN Spanish *contrabanda* from Italian *contrabando* (now *-bb-*), from *contra-* CONTRA- + *bando*: see BAN *noun*[1].]
▸ **A** *noun*. **1** Illegal or prohibited trade; smuggling. L16.
2 Something whose import or export is prohibited; smuggled goods. L16.
3 In full ***contraband of war***. Something forbidden to be supplied by neutrals to belligerents. M18.
4 During the American Civil War: a black slave, *esp.* a fugitive or captured slave. (From a decision of General Butler in 1861 that such slaves were contraband of war.) *US. obsolete* exc. *hist.* M19.
▸ **B** *adjective*. Forbidden to be imported or exported; concerned with smuggled goods etc.; *fig.* forbidden, illegitimate, unauthorized. M17.
– NOTE: Earlier anglicized as COUNTERBAND.
■ **contrabandist** *noun* a smuggler E19. **contrabanˈdista** *noun* [Spanish] a smuggler M19.

contraband /ˈkɒntrəband/ *verb trans. Long rare*. E17.
[ORIGIN from CONTRABAND *noun & adjective*. Cf. COUNTERBAND *verb*.]
Import (prohibited goods); smuggle. Chiefly as ***contrabanded*** *ppl adjective*.

contrabass /ˈkɒntrəbeɪs/ *noun & adjective*. E19.
[ORIGIN Italian *contrabasso* (now *-bb-*), French *contrebasse*, formed as CONTRA- + BASS *noun*[2].]
MUSIC. ▸**A** *noun*. **1** (A part within) the octave below the normal (bass) range. E19.
2 A double bass. L19.
▸ **B** *attrib.* or as *adjective*. Designating an instrument with range an octave lower than the usual type, as ***contrabass tuba***. L19.
– NOTE: Earlier anglicized as COUNTERBASS.
■ **contraˈbassist** *noun* a double bass player L19.

contrabasso /kɒntrəˈbasəʊ/ *noun*. Pl. **-bassos**, **-bassi** /-ˈbasi/. E19.
[ORIGIN Italian: see CONTRABASS.]
1 = CONTRABASS *noun* 2. E19.
2 = CONTRABASS *noun* 1. M19.

contra-bassoon /kɒntrəbəˈsuːn/ *noun*. L19.
[ORIGIN from CONTRA- + BASSOON.]
= ***double*** BASSOON.

contraception /kɒntrəˈsɛpʃ(ə)n/ *noun*. L19.
[ORIGIN from CONTRA- + CONCEPTION.]
The prevention of pregnancy from being a consequence of sexual intercourse; the use of contraceptive methods.

contraceptive /kɒntrəˈsɛptɪv/ *noun & adjective*. L19.
[ORIGIN from CONTRA- + CONCEPTIVE.]
▸ **A** *noun*. A device, drug, etc., which serves to prevent uterine conception (or implantation of the ovum) while allowing sexual intercourse. L19.
▸ **B** *adjective*. Serving to prevent pregnancy from being a consequence of sexual intercourse. E20.
■ **contraceptively** *adverb* E20.

contraconscientiously /ˌkɒntrəkɒnʃɪˈɛnʃəsli/ *adverb*. *rare*. M17.
[ORIGIN from CONTRA- + CONSCIENTIOUSLY.]
Against conscience.

contract /ˈkɒntrakt/ *noun*[1]. ME.
[ORIGIN Old French (mod. *contrat*) from Latin *contractus*, from *contract-* pa. ppl stem of *contrahere*, formed as CON- + *trahere* draw.]
1 A binding agreement between two or more parties, *spec.* one enforceable by law; as (***a***) (the earliest use) a formal agreement to marry, betrothal; (***b***) a business agreement for the supply of goods or the performance of work at a specified price or rate; (***c***) the conveyance of property. ME. ▸**b** An arrangement for someone to be killed, usu. by a hired assassin. *slang*. M20.

W. BLACKSTONE Our law considers marriage in no other light than as a civil contract. E. PEACOCK He faithfully carried out the terms of his contract.

quasi-contract, ***subcontract***, etc. ***collateral contract***: see COLLATERAL *adjective*. ***consensual contract***: see CONSENSUAL *adjective* 1. ***nude contract***: see NUDE *adjective* 2. ***privity of contract***: see PRIVITY 5. ***social contract***: see SOCIAL *adjective*. **under contract** party to a legal contract. ***yellow dog contract***: see YELLOW *adjective*.
2 A document in which an agreement is set out for signature by the parties concerned. E17.
†**3** Mutual attraction. E–M17.
4 The branch of law relating to contracts. M19.
5 The commitment to make a stated number of tricks in a hand of bridge. Also *ellipt.*, contract bridge. E20.
– COMB.: ***contract bridge***: see BRIDGE *noun*[2]; **contract killer** a hired assassin; **contract work**: done according to the terms of an agreement to supply a service, commodity, etc. (formerly often with derog. connotation).

contract /kənˈtrakt/ *ppl adjective & noun*[2]. LME.
[ORIGIN Old French, var. of *contrait* from Latin *contractus* pa. pple of *contrahere*: see CONTRACT *noun*[1].]
▸ **A** *ppl adjective*. = CONTRACTED. Now *rare* or *obsolete*. LME.
▸ **B** *noun*. †**1** A paralytic. Only in L15.
†**2** An abridgement, an epitome. Only in M17.
3 A contracted form or word; an abbreviation. *rare*. M17.

contract /kənˈtrakt, *in sense 5 also* ˈkɒntrakt/ *verb*. Pa. t. & pple **-ed**, (earlier) †**contract**. LME.
[ORIGIN Orig. pa. pple: see CONTRACT *adjective & noun*[2]. Cf. Old French & mod. French *contracter*.]
▸ **I** Agree on, make a contract.
1 *verb trans.* Formally enter into (marriage). LME. ▸**b** Engage formally, affiance. M16.

I. MURDOCH She wondered if having failed in one marriage she should hastily contract another. **b** SHAKES. *Wint. T.* But come on, Contract us fore these witnesses.

2 *verb trans. gen.* Agree on, establish by agreement, undertake mutually, enter on. Now *rare*. M16.

R. HAKLUYT We have contracted an inviolable amitie, peace and league with the aforesaid queene.

3 *verb intrans.* Enter into an agreement (*to do*, *for* an action, a thing to be done, etc.), esp. a business or legal engagement. M16.

EVELYN This Dutchman had contracted with the Genoese for all their marble. S. UNWIN Harrison . . had contracted with my uncle to write a book.

4 *verb trans.* Arrange (work) to be done by contract; let *out* by contract. L19. ▸**b** Place under contract (*for*). M20.
5 *verb intrans. & refl.* **a** Foll. by *out* (*of*): arrange for one's exemption or exclusion from (the provisions of a law etc.); decline or refuse to take part in (a scheme etc.). L19. ▸**b** Foll. by *in*(*to*): arrange for one's subjection to (the provisions of a law etc.); agree to take part in (a scheme etc.). E20.
▸ **II** **6** *verb trans.* Enter into, form (a friendship, a habit, etc.); bring on oneself; incur (a liability, debt, etc.); become infected with, catch (a disease, illness). LME.

S. PEPYS And he contract the displeasure of the world. CHESTERFIELD Contract a habit of correctness and elegance. G. GISSING He died of a cold contracted on one of his walks.

▸ **III** Draw together, narrow, shrink.
†**7** *verb trans.* Bring together, collect, concentrate. LME–L18.

B. HARRIS The king contracted formidable forces near Sedan.

8 *verb trans.* Cause to shrink, bring the parts of (a muscle etc.) together; knit (the brow); stiffen by contraction. E16.

SHAKES. *Timon* Aches contract and starve your supple joints! J. STEINBECK The house cracked loudly as the cooler night air contracted the wood.

9 *verb trans.* Reduce in extent, amount, or scope; make smaller, narrow; limit, confine. L16. ▸**b** LINGUISTICS. Shorten (a word, syllable, etc.) by combination or elision of elements. E17. ▸†**c** Abridge, summarize; *refl.* write or speak briefly. E17–M18.

S. JOHNSON Selfishness has contracted their understandings. W. LIPPMANN The economic area must be contracted to exclude competitors.

10 *verb intrans.* Become smaller in extent or volume; shorten, shrink. M17.

J. TYNDALL In passing from the solid to the liquid state, ice . . contracts. B. RUBENS His stomach contracted . . in agonizing cramps.

■ **contractable** *adjective* liable to be contracted L19. **contractant** *noun* (*rare*) a contracting party M16. **contractiˈbility** *noun* the quality of being contractible M18. **contractible** *adjective* capable of contracting, contractile M17. **contractive** *adjective* having the property of contracting; of the nature of contraction; tending to produce contraction: E17.

†**contractation** *noun*. Also **contrat-**. M16–E18.
[ORIGIN Spanish *contratación* trade, business transaction, with assim. to CONTRACT *verb*, -ATION.]
Mutual dealing, exchange.
– COMB.: **contractation-house** an exchange or treasury in Seville where contracts were made in connection with the West Indian trade.

contracted /kənˈtraktɪd/ *ppl adjective*. M16.
[ORIGIN from CONTRACT *verb* + -ED[1].]
†**1** Engaged to be married, betrothed. M16–E17.
2 Arranged by contract, established by agreement. Now *rare* exc. in ***contracted-in***, ***contracted-out***, that has contracted into, out of, a scheme etc. (see CONTRACT *verb* 5). L16.
3 Made smaller by contraction; shrunken, narrowed; condensed, concise; restricted, narrow. L16.
†**4** Collected, combined. Only in E17.
5 Incurred, acquired. M17.
■ **contractedly** *adverb* E17. **contractedness** *noun* M17.

contractee /kɒntrakˈtiː/ *noun*. L19.
[ORIGIN from CONTRACT *noun*[1] or *verb* + -EE[1].]
A person with whom a contract is made.

contractile /kənˈtraktʌɪl/ *adjective*. E18.
[ORIGIN from CONTRACT *verb* + -ILE.]
Capable of or producing contraction.

W. B. CARPENTER The contractile tissues, by which the movements of plants are produced.

contractile vacuole a vacuole in some protozoans which expels excess liquid on contraction.
■ **contracˈtility** *noun* L18.

contraction /kənˈtrakʃ(ə)n/ *noun*. LME.
[ORIGIN Old French & mod. French from Latin *contractio(n-)*, from *contract-*: see CONTRACT *noun*[1], -ION.]
▸ **I** **1** The action of contracting; the state of being contracted; decrease in extent, shortening, shrinking, narrowing; limitation; *esp.* (a) shortening of a muscle or muscles in response to a nerve impulse, generating tension in the muscle(s) and frequently producing movement. LME.

L. P. HARTLEY Not expansion but contraction of personality was what he sought.

2 **a** Abbreviation of a writing etc.; (an) abridgement; condensation, conciseness. Now *rare* or *obsolete*. L16. ▸**b** LINGUISTICS. The shortening of a word, syllable, etc. by combination or elision; a contracted form of a word etc. E18.

a A. C. SWINBURNE A poem of . . exquisite contraction and completeness.

3 The action of drawing together or back. *rare*. E17.

D. H. LAWRENCE The cattle . . ducked their heads . . in sudden contraction from her.

▸ **II** **4** The action of agreeing on or establishing by contract; *spec.* the action of contracting marriage. Now *rare*. L16.
5 The action of incurring or acquiring a debt, disease, habit, etc. L17.
– COMB.: **contraction joint** a joint in a structure (esp. of concrete) to allow for contraction of the material.
■ **contractional** *adjective* relating to or produced by contraction L19.

contractor /kənˈtraktə/ *noun*. E16.
[ORIGIN Late Latin, from *contract-* (see CONTRACT *noun*[1]) or directly from CONTRACT *verb*: see -OR.]
1 A person who enters into a contract or agreement. Now chiefly *spec.* a person or firm that undertakes work by contract, esp. for building to specified plans. E16.
2 A thing that contracts or causes contraction; *spec.* (more fully ***contractor muscle***) a contracting muscle. E17.

contractual /kənˈtraktʃʊəl/ *adjective*. M19.
[ORIGIN from Latin *contractus* CONTRACT *noun*[1] + -AL[1]. Cf. French *contractuel*.]
Pertaining to or of the nature of a contract.
■ **contractually** *adverb* E20.

contractural /kənˈtraktʃ(ə)r(ə)l/ *adjective*. E20.
[ORIGIN from CONTRACTUAL with erron. *r*.]
= CONTRACTUAL.

contracture /kənˈtraktʃə/ *noun*. M17.
[ORIGIN French, or Latin *contractura*, from (the same root as) *contract-*: see CONTRACT *noun*[1], -URE.]
MEDICINE. A condition of shortening and hardening of tissue, esp. muscles and tendons, often leading to deformity and rigidity of joints.
■ **contractured** *adjective* affected by contracture L19.

contradance *noun* var. of CONTREDANSE.

contradict /kɒntrəˈdɪkt/ *verb*. L16.
[ORIGIN Latin *contradict-* pa. ppl stem of *contradicere*, orig. *contra dicere* speak against.]
†**1** *verb trans.* Speak against; oppose in speech; forbid. L16–M18.
2 *verb trans. & intrans.* Deny a statement made by (a person); affirm the contrary of (a statement etc.). L16.
3 Of a statement, action, etc.: be contrary to, go counter to. L16.
■ **contradictable** *adjective* M19. **contradictor** *noun* L16.

contradiction /kɒntrəˈdɪkʃ(ə)n/ *noun*. LME.
[ORIGIN Old French & mod. French from Latin *contradictio(n-)*, formed as CONTRADICT: see -ION.]
1 The action of speaking against or opposing; gainsaying, opposition. LME.

STEELE There are those who pursue their own Way out of a Sourness and Spirit of Contradiction.

2 The action of declaring to be untrue or erroneous; affirming the contrary; denial. LME.

SHAKES. *Ant. & Cl.* Without contradiction I have heard that.

3 A statement containing propositions or terms which are at variance with one another; a contradictory proposition. LME. ▸**b** More fully ***contradiction in terms***. A statement, phrase, etc., which appears to be self-contradictory. E18.

HOBBES Both parts of a contradiction cannot possibly be true. **b** B. JOWETT A virtuous tyrant is a contradiction in terms.

4 A state of opposition in things compared; variance; logical inconsistency. L16.

GEO. ELIOT The contradiction between men's lives and their professed beliefs had pressed upon him.

5 A contradictory act, fact, or condition; an inconsistency. E17.

S. JOHNSON An attempt to make contradictions consistent.

6 A statement contradicting another. E18.

OED An official contradiction of the recent rumours.

7 A person or thing made up of contradictory qualities. M18.

POPE Woman's at best a contradiction still.

contradictious /kɒntrəˈdɪkʃəs/ *adjective*. E17.
[ORIGIN from CONTRADICT + -IOUS.]
†1 Characterized by contradiction; contrary. E17–M18.
2 Self-contradictory; involving a contradiction in terms. *arch.* M17.
3 Inclined to contradict; disputatious. L17.
■ **contradictiously** *adverb* E17. **contradictiousness** *noun* M17.

contradictive /kɒntrəˈdɪktɪv/ *adjective*. M17.
[ORIGIN from CONTRADICT + -IVE.]
1 Of contradictory quality or tendency. M17.
†2 = CONTRADICTIOUS 3. M–L17.
■ **contradictively** *adverb* M19. **contradictiveness** *noun* E19.

contradictory /kɒntrəˈdɪkt(ə)ri/ *noun & adjective*. LME.
[ORIGIN Late Latin *contradictorius*, formed as CONTRADICT + -ORY².]
▸ **A** *noun*. **1** *LOGIC*. A proposition, assertion, or principle that contradicts another. LME.

A. J. AYER It is impossible that a proposition and its contradictory should neither of them be true.

2 The opposite, the contrary. M19.

T. ARNOLD A place the very contradictory . . of the hill Difficulty.

▸ **B** *adjective* **1 a** Mutually opposed or inconsistent; inconsistent in itself; (of two propositions) so related that one and only one must be true. M16. ▸**b** Having the quality of contradicting; making denial. E17.

a STEELE If we sit down satisfy'd with such contradictory accounts. **b** A. TROLLOPE Two answers which were altogether distinct, and contradictory one of the other.

a contradictory terms *LOGIC*: of the form A and not-A, which admit of no intermediate. **b contradictory opposition** *LOGIC*: between contradictory propositions.

2 Of opposite character or tendency; diametrically opposed, contrary. M18.

J. BUTLER There is nothing in the human mind contradictory . . to virtue.

3 Inclined to contradict. L19.
■ **contradictorily** *adverb* (*a*) in a way that contradicts; (*b*) *LOGIC* with contradictory opposition: L16. **contradictoriness** *noun* M18.

contradistinct /kɒntrədɪˈstɪŋkt/ *adjective*. E17.
[ORIGIN from CONTRA- + DISTINCT *adjective*. Cf. COUNTERDISTINCT.]
Contradistinguished; distinct and in contrast (*to*, *from*).

contradistinction /kɒntrədɪˈstɪŋkʃ(ə)n/ *noun*. M17.
[ORIGIN from CONTRA- + DISTINCTION. Cf. earlier COUNTERDISTINCTION.]
The action of contradistinguishing; distinction by contrast or opposition.

H. A. L. FISHER A country which . . must, in contradistinction to the prevailing misery of the continent, have presented a spectacle of rare . . prosperity.

contradistinctive /kɒntrədɪˈstɪŋktɪv/ *adjective*. M17.
[ORIGIN from CONTRA- + DISTINCTIVE.]
Serving to contradistinguish. Also (*rare*), expressing contradistinction.
■ **contradistinctively** *adverb* E19.

contradistinguish /kɒntrədɪˈstɪŋgwɪʃ/ *verb trans*. E17.
[ORIGIN from CONTRA- + DISTINGUISH *verb*. Cf. COUNTERDISTINGUISH.]
Distinguish (*from* or †*to* another) by contrast or opposition.

T. JEFFERSON When the common law and statute law began to be contra-distinguished. COLERIDGE Doctrines . . which contradistinguish the religion as Christian. M. ARNOLD The development which contradistinguishes the Hellene from the barbarian.

contrafacta *noun* pl. of CONTRAFACTUM.

contrafactual /kɒntrəˈfaktʃʊəl/ *adjective*. M20.
[ORIGIN from CONTRA- + FACTUAL *adjective*.]
PHILOSOPHY. = COUNTERFACTUAL *adjective*.

contrafactum /kɒntrəˈfaktəm/ *noun*. Pl. **-ta** /-tə/. M20.
[ORIGIN mod. Latin, use as noun of neut. pa. pple of medieval Latin *contrafacere* to counterfeit: see COUNTERFEIT *adjective & noun*.]
EARLY MUSIC. A rearrangement of a vocal composition whereby the music is retained and the words altered.

contrafagotto /kɒntrəfəˈgɒtəʊ/ *noun*. Pl. **-tti** /-ti/. L19.
[ORIGIN Italian (now *-trof-*).]
= ***double*** BASSOON.

contrafissure /kɒntrəˈfɪʃə/ *noun*. Now *rare* or *obsolete*. L17.
[ORIGIN from CONTRA- + FISSURE *noun*.]
MEDICINE. A fracture (of the skull) in a part opposite to the site of the blow.

contraflexure /kɒntrəˈflɛkʃə/ *noun*. L19.
[ORIGIN from CONTRA- + FLEXURE.]
The condition of being bent or curved in opposite directions; the point or piece at which this occurs.

contraflow /ˈkɒntrəfləʊ/ *noun*. M20.
[ORIGIN from CONTRA- + FLOW *noun*¹.]
Flow in the opposite direction or in opposite directions; *esp.* (a system allowing) movement of road traffic alongside and in a direction contrary to the established or usual flow. Freq. *attrib.*

contragredient /kɒntrəˈgriːdɪənt/ *adjective*. M19.
[ORIGIN from CONTRA- + Latin *-gredient-* pres. ppl stem (in comb.) of *gradi* proceed, step: see -ENT.]
MATH. Characterized by change in an opposite sense (*to*), or in opposite senses, under equivalent substitution.

contrahent /ˈkɒntrəhənt/ *postpositive adjective & noun*. Now *rare* or *obsolete*. E16.
[ORIGIN Latin *contrahent-* pres. ppl stem of *contrahere*: see CONTRACT *verb*, -ENT.]
(A person etc.) entering into a contract.

contrail /ˈkɒntreɪl/ *noun*. M20.
[ORIGIN Contr.]
A condensation trail.

contraindicant /kɒntrəˈɪndɪk(ə)nt/ *noun*. E17.
[ORIGIN from CONTRA- + INDICANT.]
A contraindication.

contraindicate /kɔntrəˈɪndɪkeɪt/ *verb trans*. M17.
[ORIGIN from CONTRA- + INDICATE. Cf. COUNTER-INDICATE.]
Chiefly *MEDICINE*. Give indications contrary to; *esp.* act as an indication against the use of (a particular treatment etc.). Usu. in *pass.*

I. HAMILTON In the course of drug treatment alcohol would have been 'contraindicated'.

contraindication /ˌkɒntrəɪndɪˈkeɪʃ(ə)n/ *noun*. E17.
[ORIGIN from CONTRA- + INDICATION. Cf. COUNTER-INDICATION.]
A contrary indication; *esp.* a symptom, circumstance, etc., which tends to make a particular course of (remedial) action inadvisable.

contrair /ˈkɒntrɛː/ *adjective, noun, adverb, & preposition*. Chiefly & now only *Scot.* LME.
[ORIGIN Old French & mod. French *contraire*: see CONTRARY *adjective*.]
▸ **A** *adjective & noun*. (The) contrary. LME.
▸ **B** *adverb*. Contrariwise. LME.
▸ **C** *preposition*. Against, in opposition to. LME.

contralateral /kɒntrəˈlat(ə)r(ə)l/ *adjective*. L19.
[ORIGIN from CONTRA- + LATERAL *adjective*.]
MEDICINE. Belonging to or occurring on the opposite side of the body. Opp. ***ipsilateral***.

contralto /kənˈtraltəʊ/ *noun & adjective*. M18.
[ORIGIN Italian, formed as CONTRA- + ALTO: cf. COUNTER-TENOR.]
MUSIC. ▸**A** *noun*. Pl. **-os**. The lowest female voice or (formerly) highest adult male voice; a singer having such a voice; a part written for such a voice. M18.
▸ **B** *adjective*. Possessing, belonging to, or written for a contralto voice. M18.

contra mundum /ˌkɒntrə ˈmʌndəm/ *adverbial phr*. M18.
[ORIGIN Latin.]
Against the world; defying or opposing everyone.

contranatant /kɒntrəˈneɪt(ə)nt/ *adjective*. E20.
[ORIGIN from CONTRA- + NATANT *adjective*.]
Of the migration of fish: against the current. Opp. DENATANT.
■ **contranaˈtation** *noun* the act of migrating against the current E20.

contranatural /kɒntrəˈnatʃ(ə)r(ə)l/ *adjective*. M17.
[ORIGIN from CONTRA- + NATURAL *adjective*.]
Opposed to what is natural; contrary to nature.

contrapose /kɒntrəˈpəʊz/ *verb trans*. E17.
[ORIGIN from CONTRA- + POSE *verb*¹ after Latin *contraponere*. Cf. earlier COUNTERPOSE.]
1 Set in opposition or against each other. E17. ▸**b** Foll. by *to*: contrast directly with. E20.
2 *LOGIC*. Convert (a proposition) by contraposition. M19.

contraposit /kɒntrəˈpɒzɪt/ *verb trans*. L19.
[ORIGIN Back-form. from CONTRAPOSITION.]
= CONTRAPOSE 2.

contraposition /kɒntrəpəˈzɪʃ(ə)n/ *noun*. M16.
[ORIGIN Late Latin *contrapositio(n-)*, from *contraposit-* pa. ppl stem of *contraponere*, formed as CONTRA- + *ponere* to place: see -ITION. Cf. COUNTERPOSITION.]
1 *LOGIC*. The conversion of a proposition from *all A is B* to *all not-B is not-A*. M16.
2 *gen.* Opposition, antithesis, contrast. L16.

contrapositive /kɒntrəˈpɒzɪtɪv/ *noun & adjective*. M19.
[ORIGIN from Latin *contraposit-*: see CONTRAPOSITION, -IVE.]
▸ **A** *noun*. A thing characterized by contraposition; *LOGIC* a contrapositive proposition. M19.
▸ **B** *adjective*. Of, belonging to, or produced by contraposition. L19.
■ **contrapositively** *adverb* M19.

contrapposto /kontrapˈposto/ *noun*. Pl. **-ti** /-ti/. E20.
[ORIGIN Italian, pa. pple of *contrapporre* from Latin *contraponere* CONTRAPOSE.]
In the visual arts, an arrangement of a figure in which the action of the arms and shoulders contrasts as strongly as possible with that of the hips and legs; a twisting of a figure on its own axis.

contra proferentem /ˌkɒntrə prɒfəˈrɛntɛm/ *adverbial phr.* E20.
[ORIGIN Latin.]
LAW. Against the party which proposes or puts forward a contract or a condition in a contract.

contraption /kənˈtrapʃ(ə)n/ *noun*. *colloq*. E19.
[ORIGIN Perh. from CONTRIVE *verb*¹ (cf. *conceive*, *conception*), assoc. with TRAP *noun*¹.]
A strange machine; a device, a contrivance.

contrapuntal /kɒntrəˈpʌnt(ə)l/ *adjective*. M19.
[ORIGIN from Italian *contrapunto* (now *-pp-*) from medieval Latin as COUNTERPOINT *noun*¹ + -AL¹.]
MUSIC. Of, pertaining to, or of the nature of counterpoint; according to the rules of counterpoint.
■ **contrapuntally** *adverb* L19. **contrapuntist** *noun* a person skilled in counterpoint L18.

contra-remonstrant /kɒntrərɪˈmɒnstr(ə)nt/ *noun*. E17.
[ORIGIN from CONTRA- + REMONSTRANT *noun*.]
A person who remonstrates in answer or opposition to a remonstrance.
■ **contra-remonstrance** *noun* a remonstrance drawn up in answer to a previous one L17. **contra-remonstrancer** *noun* (*rare*) = CONTRA-REMONSTRANT E17.

contrarian /kənˈtrɛːrɪən/ *noun & adjective*. M20.
[ORIGIN from CONTR(ARY *adjective* + -ARIAN.]
▸ **A** *noun*. A person who takes an opposing view to the majority or who behaves in a contrary manner; *spec.* in *FINANCE*, an investor who goes against the general consensus when trading, e.g. by buying the stock of an unpopular company. M20.
▸ **B** *adjective*. Relating to or characteristic of a contrarian. L20.
■ **contrarianism** *noun* L20.

contrariant /kənˈtrɛːrɪənt/ *preposition, adjective, & noun*. LME.
[ORIGIN Old French & mod. French, pres. pple of *contrarier*: see CONTRARY *verb*, -ANT¹.]
▸ †**A** *preposition*. Acting contrary to, in opposition to. Only in LME.
▸ **B** *adjective*. **1** Opposed, repugnant, contrary *to*. M16.
2 Mutually opposed or antagonistic. M16.
†3 Unfavourable, prejudicial; adverse. M16–M17.
▸ **C** *noun*. A person who or thing which is opposed to another in purpose or nature. M17.
■ **contrariantly** *adverb* L18.

contrariety /kɒntrəˈrʌɪəti/ *noun*. LME.
[ORIGIN Old French & mod. French *contrariété* from late Latin *contrarietas*, from *contrarius*: see CONTRARY *adjective* etc., -ITY.]
1 Opposition in nature, quality, or action; contrariness; disagreement, inconsistency. LME. ▸**b** An antagonistic action or fact; a discrepancy. LME.

MILTON In the words of our Saviour there can be no contrariety. GEO. ELIOT With an odd contrariety to her former niceties she liked his rough attire. **b** W. DE LA MARE O riddle of life that is An endless war 'twixt contrarieties.

2 Opposition to one's purpose or advantage; an adversity, a mishap. LME.

SIR T. BROWNE The tempests and contrarieties of winds.

3 *LOGIC*. Contrary opposition. LME.

contrarious /kɒnˈtrɛːrɪəs/ *adjective*. *arch.* ME.
[ORIGIN Old French from medieval Latin *contrariosus*, from Latin *contrarius*: see CONTRARY *adjective* etc., -OUS.]
†1 Of opposed character or tendency, repugnant (*to*). ME–M17.
2 Mutually opposed, antagonistic; inconsistent. Now *rare* or *obsolete*. ME.
†3 Opposed in purpose, hostile. ME–M16.
4 Characterized by self-willed or refractory opposition; perverse; = CONTRARY *adjective* 3b. ME.
5 Of a thing: opposed to one's interests; adverse. ME.
■ **contrariously** *adverb* LME. **contrariousness** *noun* LME.

contrariwise /kənˈtrɛːrɪwʌɪz, ˈkɒntrərɪwʌɪz/ *adverb*. LME.
[ORIGIN from CONTRARY *adjective* + -WISE.]
1 On the other hand, on the contrary. LME.
2 In the opposite way or order; vice versa; in opposite directions; in the opposite direction; on opposite sides. LME.
3 In opposition (*to*); *esp.* with self-willed opposition, perversely. L16.

contra-rotating /kɒntrərəʊˈteɪtɪŋ/ *adjective*. M20.
[ORIGIN from CONTRA- + *rotating* pres. ppl adjective of ROTATE *verb*. Cf. COUNTERROTATE.]
Rotating in the opposite direction or in opposite directions, esp. about the same shaft.

contra-rotation /kɒntrərəʊˈteɪʃ(ə)n/ *noun.* **E18.**
[ORIGIN from CONTRA- + ROTATION.]
Rotation in an opposite direction.

contrary /ˈkɒntrəri, *in sense A.3b* kənˈtrɛːri/ *adjective, noun, adverb, & preposition.* **ME.**
[ORIGIN Anglo-Norman *contrarie*, Old French & mod. French *contraire* from Latin *contrarius*, from *contra* CONTRA: see -ARY[1]. Cf. CONTRAIR.]
▸ **A** *adjective.* **1** Opposed in nature or tendency; mutually opposed. (Foll. by *to*, †*than*, †*from*.) **ME.** ▸†**b** Different, other. **L16–L17.**

C. BEATON Artificial perfumes were contrary to her tastes. B. BETTELHEIM A passionate struggle raging between two contrary impulses.

contrary to nature: see NATURE *noun.*
2 The opposite, the other (of two things). **ME.** ▸†**b** Opposite to the proper or right thing; wrong. *rare* (Shakes.). Only in **L16.**

SPENSER All ignorant of her contrary sex.

3 Of a person, an action, etc.: ▸†**a** Actively opposed, hostile. **ME–M17.** ▸**b** Characterized by self-willed or refractory opposition, perverse; (= earlier CONTRARIOUS 4). *colloq.* **M18.**

a J. BARGRAVE In despite of the Spaniards, to whom he was much contrary. **b** J. MASEFIELD I was my folk's contrary son; I bit my father's hand right through.

4 a Of wind: impeding, unfavourable. **LME.** ▸†**b** *gen.* Of a thing: opposed to one's well-being or interests, unfavourable. **L15–M18.**

b W. WHISTON The remedies . . proved contrary to his case.

5 Opposite in position or direction. **LME.**

GOLDSMITH A quite contrary way from that in which they then marched.

– SPECIAL COLLOCATIONS & COMB.: **contrary-minded** *adjective* of the contrary opinion. **contrary opposition** LOGIC the opposition of contrary propositions and terms. **contrary proposition** LOGIC either of two propositions each of which denies every case of the other. **contrary terms** LOGIC terms which are at opposite ends of a single scale, as ***black*** and ***white***. **contrary-to-fact** *adjective* counterfactual, untrue.

▸ **B** *noun.* **1** *The* exact opposite or reverse of what has previously been mentioned. **ME.**

A. STORR An individual who, in early life, believed himself to be inadequate, is driven to . . prove the contrary.

on the contrary on the other hand, in contradistinction; far from it. **to the contrary** to the opposite effect.
2 An object, fact, quality, etc., that is the exact opposite of something else; in *pl.*, things of the same class showing the most difference. **LME.** ▸**b** PAPER-MAKING. A foreign body or any substance which resists pulping. Usu. in *pl.* **E20.**

N. PEVSNER The need for considering national character in contraries or polarities.

by contraries by direct contrast; in direct opposition to logic or expectation. **b *pernicious contrary***: see PERNICIOUS *adjective*[1].
†**3** The opposite position or side. **LME–E17.**
†**4** (An act of) opposition or hostility. **LME–M16.**
†**5** An adversary. **LME–E17.**
†**6** A denial, an opposing statement. **M16–M19.**
7 LOGIC. A contrary term or proposition. **M16.**
▸ **C** *adverb.* **1** In opposition (*to*). **LME.**

W. S. CHURCHILL The Royalist commanders . . , contrary to all previous conventions, were . . shot.

2 On the other hand, on the contrary. *arch.* **LME.**

N. CULPEPER The seed thereof contrary doth bind the belly.

3 Adversely, unfavourably. **L15.**

SHAKES. *Rom. & Jul.* What storm is this that blows so contrary?

4 In an opposite or very different way. **L16.**
†**5** In the opposite direction. **E–M17.**
▸ †**D** *preposition.* Against, contrary to. **LME–M16.**

contrary /ˈkɒntrəri, kənˈtrɛːri/ *verb.* **ME.**
[ORIGIN Old French & mod. French *contrarier* oppose, from late Latin *contrariare*, from Latin *contrarius*: see CONTRARY *adjective* etc.]
1 *verb trans.* Oppose, thwart; contradict; do what is contrary to. *obsolete* exc. *dial.* **ME.**
†**2** *verb intrans.* Act, speak, or write in opposition. **LME–L16.**

contra-seasonal /kɒntrəˈsiːz(ə)n(ə)l/ *adjective.* **M20.**
[ORIGIN from CONTRA- + SEASONAL.]
Unusual for the time of year; contrary to the seasonal norm.
■ **contra-seasonally** *adverb* **M20.**

contrast /ˈkɒntrɑːst/ *noun.* **L16.**
[ORIGIN French *contraste* from Italian *contrasto* strife, opposition, from *contrastare* withstand, strive, from medieval Latin *contrastare*: see CONTRAST *verb*.]
▸ †**I 1** Contention, strife. **L16–M18.**
▸ **II 2** In the visual arts, the juxtaposition of different forms, colours, etc., to heighten the total effect. **E18.**

M. GIROUARD Colour contrasts between brown stock bricks, red brick dressings, and white woodwork.

SIMULTANEOUS ***contrast***.
3 A thing or person having noticeably different qualities (*to*). **E18.**

I. D'ISRAELI Buckingham offered a provoking contrast to his master.

4 Comparison of things showing striking differences; (an instance of) display of opposing qualities; manifest difference. **M18.**

J. TYNDALL The contrast between the two waters was very great. ARNOLD BENNETT She was . . especially pale by contrast with the black of her . . dress. G. MAXWELL A labouring dog-paddle in amazing contrast to his smooth darting grace below water. M. DRABBLE The area attracted her strongly, in its violent seedy contrasts, its juxtaposition of the rich and the poor.

5 PSYCHOLOGY. The modification or intensification of a sensation by the juxtaposition of another (freq. opposite) sensation; *spec.* (the interaction producing) a change of the perceived appearance of an object caused by adjacent objects etc. **L19.**
6 The degree of difference between tones in a photograph, television picture, etc. **E20.**
– COMB.: **contrast medium** a substance introduced into a subject in order to improve the visibility of organs etc. during radiography.
■ **contrasty** *adjective* (esp. of a photograph, television picture, etc.) showing a high contrast **L19.**

contrast /kənˈtrɑːst/ *verb.* **L15.**
[ORIGIN In branch I from Old French *contrester* from medieval Latin *contrastare*, from Latin *contra-* CONTRA- + *stare* to stand; in branch II from French *contraster* from Italian *contrastare*, ult. from Latin (as I).]
▸ †**I 1** *verb trans. & intrans.* Withstand, fight (against); resist. **L15–L17.**
▸ **II 2** *verb trans.* **a** In the visual arts, juxtapose so as to bring out differences of form, colour, etc., and thus heighten the total effect. **L17.** ▸**b** *gen.* Set (two things, one *with* or *to* another) in opposition so as to show their differences. **E18.**

a DRYDEN Contrasted by contrary motions, the most noble parts foremost in sight. **b** THOMAS HUGHES He contrasted our hero with the few men with whom he generally lived. E. M. FORSTER Our business is not to contrast the two, but to reconcile them.

3 *verb trans.* Set off (each other) by opposition or contrast; offer or form a contrast to (usu. in *pass.*, foll. by *by*, *to*). *arch.* **L17.**

J. F. COOPER The dark foliage of the evergreens was brilliantly contrasted by the glittering whiteness of the plain. C. P. SNOW My mother's thin beak of a nose contrasted itself to Aunt Milly's bulbous one.

4 *verb intrans.* Form a contrast; show a striking difference on comparison (*with*). **E18.**

A. WILSON The deep voice . . contrasted oddly with the tiny body. J. FRAME Her sudden energy contrasted with Henry's sudden exhaustion.

contrastive /kənˈtrɑːstɪv/ *adjective.* **M19.**
[ORIGIN from CONTRAST *verb* + -IVE.]
Forming a contrast; standing in contrast (*to*); concerned with contrasts.
■ **contrastively** *adverb* **E19.** **contrastiveness** *noun* **M20.**

contra-suggestible /kɒntrəsəˈdʒɛstɪb(ə)l/ *adjective.* **E20.**
[ORIGIN from CONTRA- + SUGGESTIBLE.]
PSYCHOLOGY. Tending to respond to a suggestion by believing or doing the contrary.
■ **contra-suggestiˈbility**, **contra-suggestion** *nouns* the tendency to believe or do the contrary of what is suggested **E20.**

†**contratation** *noun* var. of CONTRACTATION.

contrate /ˈkɒntreɪt/ *adjective.* **L15.**
[ORIGIN medieval Latin, Proto-Romance *contrata* adjective: see COUNTRY.]
†**1** Opposed, contrary, adverse. *rare.* Only in **L15.**
2 ***contrate wheel***, a crown wheel, esp. in a watch mechanism. **L17.**

contratenor /ˈkɒntrətɛnə/ *noun.* **M16.**
[ORIGIN Italian *contratenore*, from *contra-* CONTRA- + TENOR *noun*[1].]
MUSIC. = COUNTER-TENOR. Now only *hist.*, a part written against the tenor in the same range.

contravallation /kɒntrəvəˈleɪʃ(ə)n/ *noun.* **L17.**
[ORIGIN French *contrevallation* or Italian *contravallazione*, from Latin *contra-* CONTRA- + *vallatio(n-)*, from late Latin *vallare* entrench, from *vallum* rampart: see WALL *noun*[1], -ATION.]
hist. A chain of redoubts and breastworks constructed by besiegers for protection against sorties of the garrison.

contravariant /kɒntrəˈvɛːrɪənt/ *noun & adjective.* **M19.**
[ORIGIN from CONTRA- + VARIANT, after *covariant*.]
MATH. ▸**A** *noun.* A contravariant quantity. **M19.**
▸ **B** *adjective.* Of a tensor etc.: such that the order of items has to be inverted for certain transformations and equations to hold (as in $F(f * g) = F(g) * F(f)$). **M20.**

contravene /kɒntrəˈviːn/ *verb.* **M16.**
[ORIGIN Late Latin *contravenire*, formed as CONTRA- + *venire* come. Cf. French *contrevenir*.]
▸ **I** *verb trans.* **1** Go counter to; infringe (a law, rule, etc.); (of a thing) conflict with. **M16.**

BURKE Either to conform to the tenour of the article, or to contravene it. D. ADAMS The band's public address system contravenes local strategic arms limitations treaties.

2 Oppose in argument; contradict, dispute, deny. **E18.**

T. H. HUXLEY Are those conclusions so firmly based that we may not contravene them?

▸ **II** *verb intrans.* †**3** Foll. by *to*: infringe; contradict. *Scot.* **L16–M17.**
■ **contravener** *noun* **M16.**

contravention /kɒntrəˈvɛnʃ(ə)n/ *noun.* **M16.**
[ORIGIN Old French & mod. French from medieval Latin *contraventio(n-)*, formed as CONTRA-, CONVENTION.]
The action of contravening; infringement.

P. G. WODEHOUSE The dealers . . in direct contravention of their professed object in life, had refused to deal.

contrayerva /kɒntrəˈjəːvə/ *noun.* **M17.**
[ORIGIN Spanish, lit. 'counter-herb', i.e. one used as an antidote, from *contra-* CONTRA- + *yerva* (now *hierba*) herb.]
(The root of) any of several tropical American plants of the genus *Dorstenia*, of the mulberry family, used medicinally (formerly against snakebites).

†**contre-approach** *noun* see COUNTER-APPROACH.

contrecoup /ˈkɔ̃trəkuː/ *noun.* **M18.**
[ORIGIN French, from *contre* against + *coup* blow.]
1 A repercussion, an adverse consequence. *rare.* **M18.**
2 MEDICINE. An injury of a part (esp. one side of the brain) resulting from a blow on the opposite side. **M19.**

contrectation /kɒntrɛkˈteɪʃ(ə)n/ *noun.* Long *rare.* **E17.**
[ORIGIN Latin *contrectatio(n-)*, from *contrectat-* pa. ppl stem of *contrectare*, formed as CON- + *tractare* to touch: see -ATION.]
Handling, touching, fingering.

contredanse /ˈkɒntrədɑːns, *foreign* kɔ̃trədɑ̃ːs (*pl. same*)/ *noun.* Also **contradance.** **E19.**
[ORIGIN French, alt. of ***COUNTRY dance*** by assoc. with *contre* against, opposite.]
A country dance, *esp.* a social dance of which quadrille is a variant; a piece of music for such a dance.

contre-jour /ˈkɔ̃ːtrəʒʊə/ *noun.* **E20.**
[ORIGIN French, from *contre* against + *jour* daylight.]
PHOTOGRAPHY. Back-lighting. Usu. ***attrib.***

contretemps /ˈkɔ̃ːtrətɒ̃ː, ˈkɒn-/ *noun.* Pl. same /-z/. **L17.**
[ORIGIN French, orig. 'motion out of time', from *contre* against + *temps* time.]
1 FENCING. Orig., a thrust made at an inopportune moment or at the same time as one's opponent makes one. Now, a feint made with the intention of inducing a counter-thrust. **L17.**
2 An unexpected or untoward occurrence, esp. of an embarrassing kind; a hitch, a mishap. **E18.** ▸**b** A disagreement, an argument, a dispute. *colloq.* **M20.**

E. M. FORSTER The son . . took every little contretemps as if it were a tragedy. **b** M. EDWARDES The Zambian President had had a particularly unpleasant contretemps with the Rhodesians.

3 DANCING. A (ballet) step danced on the offbeat. Also, an academic ballet step involving a partial crossing of the feet and a small jump from a knees-bent position. **E18.**

contribuent /kənˈtrɪbjʊənt/ *noun.* **M19.**
[ORIGIN Latin *contribuent-* pres. ppl stem of *contribuere*: see CONTRIBUTE, -ENT.]
A contributing factor or person.

contributable /kənˈtrɪbjʊtəb(ə)l/ *adjective.* **E17.**
[ORIGIN from CONTRIBUTE + -ABLE.]
1 Liable to contribute, subject to contribution. **E17.**
2 To be contributed, payable as a contribution. **E19.**

†**contributary** *adjective & noun.* **LME.**
[ORIGIN from CONTRIBUTE + -ARY[1]: cf. late Latin *contributarius* jointly taxed, CONTRIBUTORY.]
▸ **A** *adjective.* **1** Paying or liable to pay tribute etc. Of property: subject to a tax. **LME–M17.**
2 Contributing to a common stock, purpose, or result. Of a stream: tributary. **LME–E19.**
▸ **B** *noun.* A person who contributes. **L16–E17.**

contribute /kənˈtrɪbjuːt, ˈkɒntrɪbjuːt/ *verb.* **M16.**
[ORIGIN Latin *contribut-* pa. ppl stem of *contribuere*, formed as CON- + *tribuere* to grant.]
1 a *verb trans.* Supply or pay along with others to a common fund or stock (*lit. & fig.*). **M16.** ▸**b** *verb intrans.* Make a contribution. **E17.**

a S. JOHNSON Every hand is open to contribute something. **b** L. STEFFENS The local corporations contributed heavily to the Tammany campaign fund. S. BRETT Walter Proud didn't contribute to the conversation.

2 a *verb intrans.* Play a part in the achievement of a result. Foll. by *to*, *to do.* **E17.** ▸**b** *verb trans.* Provide (agency or assistance) *to* a common result or purpose. **M17.**

a J. TYNDALL If I thought his presence would in any degree contribute to my comfort. **b** L. DURRELL The high magnification . . and the heat haze . . contributed a feathery vibration to the image.

3 *verb trans. & intrans.* Supply (literary work) for publication in a magazine etc. **M19.**

contribution /kɒntrɪˈbjuːʃ(ə)n/ *noun*. LME.
[ORIGIN Old French & mod. French, or late Latin *contributio(n-)*, formed as CONTRIBUTE: see -ION.]
1 A payment imposed on a body of people, a levy, an impost; *esp.* (*hist.*) one imposed on a district by an army of occupation. Also, the action of paying such a levy. LME.

LD MACAULAY An infantry regiment.. had levied contributions on the people of that town.

lay under contribution (esp. of an army) exact an imposition from.
2 Something paid or given (voluntarily) to a common fund or stock; an action etc. which helps to bring about a result; the action of contributing. L16. ▸**b** A writing forming part of a joint literary work; *esp.* an article contributed to a magazine or newspaper. E18.

AV *Rom.* 15:26 To make a certaine contribution for the poore saincts.. in Hierusalem. B. JOWETT He makes a distinction .. which is a real contribution to the science of logic.

superannuation contribution: see SUPERANNUATION 2.
3 *LAW*. The payment by each of the parties concerned of his or her share in a common loss or liability. M17.

contributive /kənˈtrɪbjʊtɪv/ *adjective*. L16.
[ORIGIN from CONTRIBUTE + -IVE.]
That contributes; tending to contribute (*to*).

contributor /kənˈtrɪbjʊtə/ *noun*. LME.
[ORIGIN Anglo-Norman *contributour* (mod. French *-eur*), formed as CONTRIBUTIVE: see -OUR, -OR.]
†**1** A person who pays a tax or tribute. LME–M17.
2 A person or body that contributes to a common fund or stock; a person who or thing which contributes to a result. M16. ▸**b** A writer who contributes to a joint literary work; *spec.* one who writes articles for a newspaper or magazine. M18.

contributory /kənˈtrɪbjʊt(ə)ri/ *adjective* & *noun*. LME.
[ORIGIN medieval Latin *contributorius*, formed as CONTRIBUTE: see -ORY[2]. Cf. CONTRIBUTARY.]
▸ **A** *adjective*. **1** Contributing to a common fund or undertaking. LME. ▸**b** Of things: subject to a contribution or tax. L15. ▸†**c** Paying tribute to the same lord. M16–E17.
2 Contributing to a result; partly responsible. M17.

CLARENDON Contributory to our own destruction.

contributory negligence *LAW* lack of care on the part of an accident victim such as justifies a reduction in the compensation which would otherwise be payable.
3 Relating to or of the nature of contribution; *spec.* (of a pension or insurance scheme) in which the premiums are paid partly by the employee and partly by the employer. M19.
▸ **B** *noun*. **1** A person who or thing which contributes. LME.
2 *LAW*. A person who is bound, on the winding up of a company, to contribute towards the payment of its debts. M19.

†**contrist** *verb trans*. LME–E19.
[ORIGIN Old French & mod. French *contrister* from Latin *contristare*, formed as CON- + *tristis* sad.]
Make sad, distress.

contrite /ˈkɒntrʌɪt, ˈkɒntrʌɪt/ *adjective*. ME.
[ORIGIN Old French & mod. French *contrit*, *-ite* from Latin *contritus* pa. pple of *conterere*, formed as CON- + *terere* rub, grind (see TRITE *adjective*).]
1 Crushed or broken in spirit by a sense of wrongdoing; sincerely penitent; (of an action, speech, etc.) showing contrition. ME.

L. WOOLF She was miserably contrite, saying that she had no excuse. W. STYRON His manner.. became apologetic, civilized, almost contrite.

†**2** Physically bruised or crushed; abraded. M17–M18.
■ **contritely** *adverb* LME. **contriteness** *noun* (*rare*) L17.

†**contrite** *verb trans*. LME.
[ORIGIN from Latin *contrit-*: see CONTRITION.]
Chiefly as ***contrited*** *ppl adjective*.
1 Bruise, crush, abrade. LME–M18.
2 Make contrite. L15–E19.

contrition /kənˈtrɪʃ(ə)n/ *noun*. ME.
[ORIGIN Old French & mod. French from late Latin *contritio(n-)*, from *contrit-* pa. ppl stem of *conterere*: see CONTRITE *adjective*, -ION.]
†**1** The action of bruising or pounding, esp. so as to pulverize. ME–L17.
2 The condition of being distressed in mind for some fault or injury done; *spec.* complete penitence for sin (cf. ATTRITION 1). ME.

G. GREENE How easily we believe we can slide out of our guilt by a motion of contrition. R. A. KNOX Contrition must be accompanied by the desire to put things right.

contrivance /kənˈtrʌɪv(ə)ns/ *noun*. E17.
[ORIGIN from CONTRIVE *verb*[1] + -ANCE.]
1 A thing contrived as a means to an end; an expedient, a stratagem; a trick. E17. ▸**b** A device, an arrangement, an invention. Freq. *derog*. M17.

J. BUCHAN A clumsy contrivance to persuade me that I was unsuspected. **b** P. G. WODEHOUSE One of those silk contrivances .. which you tie round your waist instead of a waistcoat.

2 a The action of contriving or ingeniously bringing about; machination (in a bad sense), trickery. M17. ▸**b** Arrangement of parts according to a plan; design. L17.

a M. ELPHINSTONE He escaped.. by the contrivance of his mother. **b** T. REID The marks of good contrivance which appear in the works of God.

3 Inventive capacity. M17.
†**4** The way in which an object etc. is contrived. M17–M19.

contrive /kənˈtrʌɪv/ *verb*[1]. ME.
[ORIGIN Old French *controver* (with suffix stress), *contreuve* (with stem stress), mod. French *controuver* invent, from medieval Latin *contropare* compare, prob. formed as CON- + *tropus* TROPE.]
▸ **I** *verb trans*. **1** Plan or design with ingenuity or skill; devise, invent; (in a bad sense) plot. ME.

K. GRAHAME Scheming and planning and contriving how to get your property back. A. J. CRONIN Using sticks and a blanket, Stephen contrived a primitive shade over the cart. M. AMIS The tirade hadn't been contrived wholly for Rachel's benefit.

2 Discover (the answer to a problem etc.); find out; imagine, guess. *obsolete* exc. *dial*. LME.
3 Find a means of effecting; find a way *to do*, manage (freq. *iron.*, unintentionally or fortuitously). LME.

SHELLEY Prophecies.. Contrive their own fulfilment. H. JAMES How a place in the deepest depths of Essex.. could contrive to look so suburban. J. GALSWORTHY Somehow he must contrive to see her!

4 Bring by ingenuity *into* a position or form. Now *rare*. L16.

O. HENRY To contrive the rope into an ingenious noose-bridle.

▸ **II** *verb intrans*. †**5** Form schemes, conspire (*with*, *against*). LME–M17.

SHAKES. *Jul. Caes.* The Fates with Traitors do contrive.

6 Manage household affairs etc. resourcefully; get by (well etc.). *arch*. M18.
■ **contrivable** *adjective* able to be contrived M17. **contrived** *adjective* that has been contrived (in a particular way); obviously planned, artificial, not spontaneous: LME. **contrivement** *noun* (*arch.*) = CONTRIVANCE 1, 2, 4 L16. **contriver** *noun* a person who contrives; a skilful deviser; a (good, bad, etc.) manager: LME.

†**contrive** *verb*[2] *trans*. LME.
[ORIGIN App. irreg. from Latin *contrivi* etc. perf. of *conterere*: see CONTRITE *adjective*.]
1 Wear down, defeat (an enemy). Only in LME.
2 Pass, spend (time). M–L16.

SHAKES. *Tam. Shr.* Please ye we may contrive this afternoon, And quaff carouses to our mistress' health.

control /kənˈtrəʊl/ *noun*. Also †-**oul**. L16.
[ORIGIN from CONTROL *verb*, or French *contrôle*, from *contrôler*: see CONTROL *verb*.]
1 The act or power of directing or regulating; command, regulating influence. L16.

G. B. SHAW Any Act transferring the theatres to the control of a licensing authority. DAY LEWIS The cart.. swayed behind the ass, which Keyes.. lost all control of. M. TIPPETT This process of imagination is outside our control.

2 The action of holding in check; restraint; self-restraint; prevention of the spread of something unwanted; regulation of the numbers of an animal species etc. L16.

J. BEATTIE Lust that defies controul. D. CUSACK My God! What control! If she'd only cried. N. TINBERGEN Attempts at gull control by taking the eggs.

3 A means of restraining or regulating; a check; *spec.* a measure adopted to regulate prices, consumption of goods, etc. L16.

D. HUME The particular checks and controuls provided by the constitution.

4 A person or body that acts as a guide or check; a controller. L18. ▸**b** *SPIRITUALISM*. An agency held to direct the actions of or to convey messages through a medium. L19. ▸**c** A member of an intelligence organization who personally directs the activities of a spy; a spymaster. M20.

H. H. MILMAN He could not be a resident.. control upon the Doge. **c** B. FORBES He sat with his KGB control.., listening.. as the details of his new assignment were explained.

5 A standard of comparison for checking inferences drawn from an experiment; *spec.* a patient, specimen, etc., similar to the one(s) being investigated but not subjected to the same treatment. Freq. *attrib*. L19.
6 A device or mechanism for controlling the operation of a machine, esp. the direction, speed, etc., of an aircraft or vehicle. Usu. in *pl*. E20.

A. BLOND He took over the controls and landed the plane.

7 A military or other checkpoint; a point on a motor rallying etc. course where contestants must halt to have particulars recorded, or a section where speed is controlled. E20.
8 *CARDS*. Esp. in bridge, (possession of) a card which will enable its holder to win a trick in a given suit at a desired moment. E20.
9 *COMPUTING*. A key on a keyboard that produces an effect rather than a graphic character (such as movement of a cursor), and is usu. used in conjunction with a character key. Also more fully ***control key***. M20.
– PHRASES: ***arms control***: see ARM *noun*[2]. ***biological control***. ***birth control***: see BIRTH *noun*[1]. ***board of control***: see BOARD *noun*. ***dual control***: see DUAL *adjective*. ***locus of control***: see LOCUS *noun*[1]. **out of control** not or no longer subject to proper direction or restraint. ***quality control***: see QUALITY *noun* & *adjective*. ***remote control***: see REMOTE *adjective*. ***social control***: see SOCIAL *adjective*. ***span of control***: see SPAN *noun*[1]. ***throttle control***: see THROTTLE *noun* 2b. **under control** subject to proper direction; *fig.* in proper order.
– COMB.: **control board** (*a*) = ***control panel*** below; (*b*) a board of control; **control experiment**: used to verify another experiment, using conditions identical except in one respect; **control freak** (orig. *US*) a person who feels an obsessive need to exercise control over his or her surroundings, appearance, etc., esp. by taking command of any situation or exerting authority over others; ***control key***: see sense 9 above; **control panel** a surface on which are mounted switches, dials, etc., for the remote control of electrical or other apparatus; **control rod**: of neutron-absorbing material used to control the rate of reaction in the core of a nuclear reactor; **control room** a room in or from which an operation is controlled; **control surface** a movable surface or aerofoil used to control the aerodynamic behaviour of an aircraft etc.; ***control tower***: see TOWER *noun*[1] 3f; **control unit** a self-contained controlling device; *esp.* the element in a central processing unit which accepts and decodes instructions from the main memory and sends executive signals to other units.

control /kənˈtrəʊl/ *verb trans*. Also †-**oul**, †**comptrol**. Infl. -**ll**-. LME.
[ORIGIN Anglo-Norman *contreroller*, French †*conteroller* (now *contrôler*), from medieval Latin *contrarotulare*, from *contrarotulus* copy of a roll, from *contra* against + *rotulus* ROLL *noun*[1].]
1 a Check or verify and hence regulate (accounts etc.), orig. by comparison with a duplicate register. LME. ▸**b** *gen*. Check the accuracy of (a statement etc.). *arch*. M16.

b SIR T. MORE He shalbe sure seldome to meete any manne.. by whom hys tale might be controlled.

2 a Exercise power or influence over; dominate, regulate. L15. ▸**b** Restrain from action, hold in check (emotions etc.). Freq. *refl*. M16. ▸**c** Curb the growth or spread of. M19.

a W. S. CHURCHILL The militia must be controlled by the Lord-Lieutenants of the counties. E. L. DOCTOROW By controlling the speed of the moving belts he could control the workers' rate of production. **b** B. C. BRODIE Difficulty in controlling his temper. N. COWARD You're far too temperamental. Try to control yourself. **c** C. S. FORESTER Fire would be.. difficult to control in the sails and the rigging.

a controlled drug, **controlled substance**: restricted by law in respect of use and possession. **controlling interest** the ability of a person or group to determine the policy of a company, esp. through owning a majority of the stock.
†**3** Take to task, reprove (a person); censure, object to (a thing). E16–M18.
4 †**a** Overpower, subdue. L16–M18. ▸**b** *LAW* (now *hist.*). Overrule (a judgement etc.). E18.
5 Subject to verification by a control experiment. Chiefly as ***controlled*** *ppl adjective*. M19.
■ **controllaˈbility** *noun* the quality or condition of being (easily) controllable E20. **controllable** *adjective* able to be controlled or restrained L16.

controller /kənˈtrəʊlə/ *noun*. See also COMPTROLLER. LME.
[ORIGIN Anglo-Norman *contrerollour*, from *contreroller*: see CONTROL *verb*, -ER[2].]
1 A person who keeps a duplicate register so as to exercise a check on a treasurer or person in charge of accounts; an official appointed to supervise expenditure; a steward. (Freq. COMPTROLLER.) LME.
†**2** A (censorious) critic. M16–E17.
3 A person who or thing which controls or regulates. M16. ▸**b** A device or mechanism by means of which the operation of a machine can be regulated. L19.
quality controller: see QUALITY *noun* & *adjective*.
– COMB.: **controller-general** an official exercising overall responsibility.
■ **controllership** *noun* the office of controller L15.

controlment /kənˈtrəʊlm(ə)nt/ *noun*. *arch*. Also †**compt-**. LME.
[ORIGIN from CONTROL *verb* + -MENT.]
†**1** The checking or verifying and regulating of accounts. LME–E18.
2 Control; direction, regulation; restraint, check. L15.
†**3** Censure, reproof. M16–M17.

†**controul** *noun*, *verb* vars. of CONTROL *noun*, *verb*.

†**controverse** *noun*. E16–M17.
[ORIGIN Old French & mod. French from Latin *controversia* CONTROVERSY *noun*.]
A dispute, a controversy.

†**controverse** *verb trans*. L16–M18.
[ORIGIN Orig. as pa. ppl adjective, from French *controversé*, earlier *controvers* from Latin *controversus*: see CONTROVERSY.]
Make the subject of controversy, dispute.

controversial /kɒntrəˈvəːʃ(ə)l/ *adjective*. L16.
[ORIGIN Late Latin *controversialis*, from *controversia* CONTROVERSY *noun*: see -AL[1].]
1 Subject to controversy; forming an object of debate, disputed; *loosely* about the merits of which opinions are divided. L16.

J. WILSON As controversial a point as the authorship of Junius. C. HAMPTON If I didn't disgust at least a substantial minority, I wouldn't be controversial.

2 Of or pertaining to controversy; polemical. **M17.**

W. STUBBS The . . object of his writing was didactic rather than controversial.

3 Given to controversy; disputatious. **M17.**

■ **controversialism** *noun* controversial spirit or practice **M19.** **controversialist** *noun* a person who engages in or is skilful in controversy **M18.** **controversi'ality** *noun* controversial nature **L20.** **controversially** *adverb* **L17.**

controversion /kɒntrəˈvəːʃ(ə)n/ *noun.* **L17.**
[ORIGIN Old French from late Latin *controversio(n-)*, from Latin *controversus*: see CONTROVERSY, -ION.]
1 A turning in the opposite direction (*lit. & fig.*). **L17.**
†**2** A controversy, a dispute. **L17–M18.**
3 The action of controverting. **M18.**

controversy /ˈkɒntrəvəːsi, kənˈtrɒvəsi/ *noun & verb.* **LME.**
[ORIGIN Latin *controversia*, from *controversus* disputed, from *contro-* var. of *contra-* CONTRA- + *versus* pa. pple of *vertere* turn: see -Y[3].]
► **A** *noun.* **1** Disputation on a matter of opinion or (formerly) rival claims. **LME.**

H. E. MANNING This text has been the subject of endless controversy.

beyond controversy, **without controversy** unquestionably. ***draw the saw of controversy***: see SAW *noun*[1].

2 A (prolonged) argument or debate, *esp.* one conducted in public. **LME.**

A. TOFFLER A fierce controversy is . . raging today among biologists over the . . ethical issues arising out of eugenics.

► †**B** *verb intrans.* Engage in controversy. *rare.* **L16–M19.**

controvert /ˈkɒntrəvəːt, kɒntrəˈvəːt/ *verb.* **M16.**
[ORIGIN from Latin *contro-* in *controversus* + *vertere*: see CONTROVERSY.]
1 *verb trans.* **a** Make a subject of verbal contention; argue about, debate. **M16.** ►†**b** Dispute (a right, possession, etc.); contest (an election). **L16–M19.**

a HENRY FIELDING A point which was controverted between Mr. Thwackum and Mr. Square.

2 *verb intrans.* Engage in controversy (*with*). **M16.**
3 *verb trans.* Attempt to disprove; argue against, deny (an idea). **E17.**

A. G. GARDINER The idea . . was too foolish to be controverted.

■ **controverter** *noun* **L16.** **contro'vertible** *adjective* debatable **E17.** **controvertist** *noun* a controversialist **M17.**

contubernal /kənˈtjuːbən(ə)l/ *noun & adjective.* **E17.**
[ORIGIN Latin *contubernalis* tent-companion, formed as CON- + *taberna* hut, booth: see -AL[1]. Cf. Latin *contubernium* occupation of a tent in common.]
► **A** *noun.* An intimate companion, a comrade. **E17.**
► **B** *adjective.* Of or relating to cohabitation (as the only form of marital relationship recognized among slaves in ancient Rome). **L19.**

contumacious /kɒntjʊˈmeɪʃəs/ *adjective.* **L16.**
[ORIGIN formed as CONTUMACY: see -ACIOUS.]
1 Obstinately disobedient to authority; stubbornly perverse; *spec.* (chiefly *hist.*) wilfully disobedient to the summons or order of a court. **L16.**
†**2** Of a disease: resistant to treatment. Only in **17.**
■ **contumaciously** *adverb* **E17.** **contumaciousness** *noun* **M17.**

contumacy /ˈkɒntjʊməsi/ *noun.* **ME.**
[ORIGIN Latin *contumacia*, from *contumax*, *-ac-*, perh. formed as CON- + *tumere* swell: see -Y[3].]
1 Obstinate disobedience to authority; stubborn perverseness; *spec.* (chiefly *hist.*) wilful disobedience to the summons or order of a court. **ME.** ►**b** An act of disobedience. **E18.**
†**2** Resistance of a disease to treatment. **M16–M17.**
■ Also **contu'macity** *noun* (*rare*) **LME.**

contumelious /kɒntjʊˈmiːlɪəs/ *adjective.* **LME.**
[ORIGIN Old French *contumelieus* (mod. *-eux*) from Latin *contumeliosus*, from *contumelia*: see CONTUMELY, -OUS.]
1 Of a word, action, etc., (formerly) a person: scornfully insulting, insolent, reproachful. **LME.**

SHAKES. *1 Hen. VI* With scoffs, and scorns, and contumelious taunts. TENNYSON Curving a contumelious lip.

†**2** Shameful, ignominious. **M16–M17.**
■ **contumeliously** *adverb* **M16.** **contumeliousness** *noun* **M17.**

contumely /ˈkɒntjuːmɪli, -tjuːmli/ *noun.* **LME.**
[ORIGIN Old French *contumelie* from Latin *contumelia*, perh. formed as CON- + *tumere* swell.]
1 (An instance of) contemptuously insulting language or treatment, scornful and humiliating rudeness. **LME.**

R. GRAVES The Rhodians, seeing him deprived of . . his magisterial powers . . began to treat him . . with contumely.

2 Disgrace, ignominy. **L15.**

contund /kənˈtʌnd/ *verb trans.* **LME.**
[ORIGIN Latin *contundere*, formed as CON- + *tundere* beat, thump.]
1 Pound, beat small. Now *rare* or *obsolete.* **LME.**
2 Bruise; beat, thrash. Now only *joc.* **M17.**

†**conturbation** *noun.* **LME–E19.**
[ORIGIN Latin *conturbatio(n-)*, from *conturbat-* pa. ppl stem of *conturbare*, formed as CON- + *turbare* disturb: see -ATION.]
(A) disturbance (physical or mental).

contuse /kənˈtjuːz/ *verb trans.* **LME.**
[ORIGIN Latin *contus-* pa. ppl stem of *contundere*: see CONTUND.]
1 Injure (a part of the body) without breaking the skin; bruise. **LME.**
†**2** Pound, beat small. **M16–E17.**
■ **contusive** /-ˈtjuːsɪv/ *adjective* producing contusion; of or pertaining to contusions: **L18.**

contusion /kənˈtjuːʒ(ə)n/ *noun.* **LME.**
[ORIGIN French from Latin *contusio(n-)*, formed as CONTUSE: see -ION.]
1 Injury to the body without breaking of the skin, bruising; a bruise. **LME.**
†**2** The action of pounding or beating small. **E17–M18.**

conundrum /kəˈnʌndrəm/ *noun.* **L16.**
[ORIGIN Unknown.]
†**1** Used as a term of abuse for a person (perh. a crank or a pedant). *rare.* Only in **L16.**
†**2** A whim, a fancy. **E17–E18.**
†**3** A play on words, a pun. **M17–L18.**
4 A riddle with a punning answer; a puzzle; a hard question. **L17.**

J. GALSWORTHY The conundrum of existence remained unsolved.

5 A thing whose name one cannot recall. *Scot. rare.* **E19.**

conurbation /kɒnəːˈbeɪʃ(ə)n/ *noun.* **E20.**
[ORIGIN from CON- + Latin *urbs*, *urbis* city + -ATION.]
An aggregation of contiguous towns or urban areas forming a single community in some respects.

conure /ˈkɒnjʊə/ *noun.* **M19.**
[ORIGIN mod. Latin *Conurus* former genus name, from Greek *kōnos* CONE *noun* + *oura* tail.]
Any of numerous Central and S. American parrots belonging to the genera *Aratinga*, *Pyrrhura*, and related genera.

conus /ˈkəʊnəs/ *noun.* Pl. **-ni** /-nʌɪ/. **L19.**
[ORIGIN Latin: see CONE *noun*.]
1 ANATOMY. A structure or organ resembling a cone. **L19.**
conus arteriosus /ɑːˌtɪərɪˈəʊsəs/ [Latin = arterial] the upper and anterior part of the right ventricle of the heart. **conus medullaris** /mɛdəˈlɑːrɪs/ [Latin = medullary] the conical lower extremity of the spinal cord.
2 MEDICINE. A pale crescent-shaped or annular patch next to the optic disc resulting from atrophy of the choroid and exposure of the sclera. **L19.**

†**conusable** *adjective*, **conusance** *noun* vars. of COGNIZABLE, COGNIZANCE.

†**conusant** *adjective.* **M17–E19.**
[ORIGIN Old French (also *-is(s)ant*, *-ois(s)ant*) pres. pple of *conuistre*, *-oistre* (mod. *connaître*) from Latin *cognoscere*: see COGNITION, -ANT[1].]
= COGNIZANT.

†**conusee**, **conusor** *nouns* vars. of COGNIZEE, COGNIZOR.

convalesce /kɒnvəˈlɛs/ *verb intrans.* **L15.**
[ORIGIN Latin *convalescere*, formed as CON- + *valescere* grow strong, from *valere* be strong or well.]
Regain health after an illness, injury, etc., esp. through a period of rest or reduced activity.

Q. BELL They . . were sent off to Bath to convalesce.

convalescence /kɒnvəˈlɛs(ə)ns/ *noun.* **L15.**
[ORIGIN French from Latin *convalescentia*, formed as CONVALESCENT: see -ENCE.]
(A period of) gradual recovery after illness, injury, etc.
■ Also **convalescency** *noun* (*rare*) **M17.**

convalescent /kɒnvəˈlɛs(ə)nt/ *adjective & noun.* **M17.**
[ORIGIN Latin *convalescent-* pres. ppl stem of *convalescere*: see CONVALESCE, -ENT.]
► **A** *adjective.* **1** (Gradually) recovering from illness, injury, etc. **M17.**
2 *attrib.* Of or for persons in convalescence. **E19.** ***convalescent home***, ***convalescent hospital***, etc.
► **B** *noun.* A convalescent person. **M18.**

convalidate /kənˈvalɪdeɪt/ *verb trans. rare.* **M17.**
[ORIGIN medieval Latin *convalidat-* pa. ppl stem of *convalidare*, formed as CON- + VALIDATE.]
Strengthen, confirm; ratify, give legal effect to.
■ **convali'dation** *noun* **E16.**

convect /kənˈvɛkt/ *verb.* **L19.**
[ORIGIN Back-form. from CONVECTION.]
1 *verb trans.* Transport by convection. **L19.**
2 *verb intrans.* Be convected; undergo convection. **L20.**

convection /kənˈvɛkʃ(ə)n/ *noun.* **E17.**
[ORIGIN Late Latin *convectio(n-)*, from *convect-* pa. ppl stem of *convehere*, formed as CON- + *vehere* carry: see -ION.]
†**1** The action of carrying. *rare.* Only in **E17.**
2 (The transport of heat by) the relative movement of parts of a fluid differing in density (and usu. temperature); *spec.* in METEOROLOGY, upward motion of warmer (less dense) air or downward motion of cooler (denser) air. **M19.**
– COMB.: **convection cell** a self-contained convective zone in which upward motion of warmer fluid in the centre is balanced by downward motion of cooler fluid at the periphery.
■ **convectional** *adjective* of, pertaining to, or induced by convection; *spec.* (of rain) resulting from the condensation of water vapour carried into the upper atmosphere by convection: **L19.**

convective /kənˈvɛktɪv/ *adjective.* **M19.**
[ORIGIN from Latin *convect-*: see CONVECTION, -IVE.]
1 Having the property of conveying. **M19.**
2 Of, relating to, or resulting from convection. **M19.**
■ **convectively** *adverb* **M19.**

convector /kənˈvɛktə/ *noun.* **E20.**
[ORIGIN from CONVECTION: see -OR.]
More fully ***convector heater***. A type of heater employing convection to warm a room.

†**convell** *verb trans.* **M16.**
[ORIGIN Latin *convellere*, formed as CON- + *vellere* tear, pull, pluck.]
1 Refute completely, overthrow. **M16–E18.**
2 Tear, wrench. *rare.* **M–L17.**

convenable /ˈkɒnvɪnəb(ə)l/ *adjective*[1]. Long *rare.* Also (earlier) †**cov-**. **ME.**
[ORIGIN Anglo-Norman, Old French *covenable*, later *conv-*, from *co(n)venir* agree from Latin *convenire*: see CONVENE, -ABLE. Form in *conv-* from late Middle English.]
1 Appropriate, suitable; becoming, congruous. **ME.**
†**2** Convenient. **ME–M17.**

convenable /kənˈviːnəb(ə)l/ *adjective*[2]. **M17.**
[ORIGIN from CONVENE + -ABLE.]
Able to be convened.

convenance /kɔ̃vnɑ̃ːs/ *noun.* Pl. pronounced same. **L15.**
[ORIGIN French, from *convenir* from Latin *convenire*: see CONVENE, -ANCE.]
†**1** Agreement, concurrence. *rare.* **L15–L17.**
2 Conventional propriety or usage; in *pl.*, the proprieties. **M19.**
– NOTE: Formerly naturalized.

convene /kənˈviːn/ *verb.* **LME.**
[ORIGIN Latin *convenire* assemble, agree, suit, formed as CON- + *venire* come.]
► **I** **1** *verb intrans. & refl.* Come together, meet, assemble, esp. for a common purpose; (of things) occur together. **LME.**

D. G. ROSSETTI The murmuring courts Where the shapes of sleep convene! D. ACHESON The UN Atomic Energy Commission was convening for discussions.

2 *verb trans.* Summon (a person) before a tribunal; *esp.* (at Cambridge University) bring (a student) before a college court of discipline. **LME.**
3 *verb trans.* Cause (individuals, a collective body, an assembly) to come together; convoke. **M16.**

V. SACKVILLE-WEST More intimate parties, where only twenty guests . . were convened. A. E. STEVENSON President Eisenhower convened a White House Conference on Education.

► **II** **4** *verb intrans.* Agree, accord, harmonize. Long *rare.* **LME.**

THACKERAY Articles which the marriage-monger cannot make to convene at all, tempers . . tastes, etc.

convener /kənˈviːnə/ *noun.* Also **-or**. **M16.**
[ORIGIN from CONVENE + -ER[1], -OR.]
†**1** A person who assembles with others. **M16–M17.**
2 A person who convenes a meeting; *esp.* an official who arranges (and presides at) meetings of a committee or other body. **L17.**
■ **convenership** *noun* **L19.** **convenery** *noun* (*Scot.*) an assembly, a convention **M19.**

convenience /kənˈviːnɪəns/ *noun & adjective.* **LME.**
[ORIGIN Latin *convenientia*, formed as CONVENIENT: see -ENCE. Cf. CONVENIENCY.]
► **A** *noun.* †**1** Agreement; congruity; an agreement. (CONVENIENCY 1 recorded later.) **LME–M17.**
†**2** Suitability by nature; fitness. **LME–M18.** ►**b** Moral fitness, propriety. (Earlier CONVENIENCY 2b.) Only in **L17.**

SHAKES. *All's Well* The Duke will lay upon him all the honour That good convenience claims.

3 **a** The quality of being convenient generally; suitability. **LME.** ►**b** The quality of being personally convenient; material advantage; personal comfort; trouble-saving. (Earlier CONVENIENCY 3b.) **E18.**

a J. Q. ADAMS The convenience . . of decimal arithmetic for 'calculation'. **b** J. K. GALBRAITH We associate truth with convenience—with what most closely accords with self-interest. JO GRIMOND A . . causeway of cobbles laid for the convenience of walkers.

4 **a** A convenient state; an advantage. **E17.** ►**b** An opportune occasion. (Earlier CONVENIENCY 4b.) **L17.**

a B. PLAIN A fine convenience it was, to have water running in the kitchen.

5 A material arrangement or appliance conducive to personal comfort, ease of action, or saving of trouble; a utensil. Usu. in *pl.* (Earlier CONVENIENCY 5.) **L17.** ►**b** *spec.* A

C

conveyance. Now *rare* or *obsolete*. **L17.** ▸**c** *spec.* A privy, a lavatory. Now esp. in ***public convenience***. **M18.**

J. E. T. ROGERS Necessary conveniences for the homestead.

– PHRASES: **at one's convenience** in a way or at a time convenient to one. **at one's earliest convenience** as soon as one can. ***flag of convenience***: see FLAG *noun*⁴. LEATHERN ***convenience***. **make a convenience of** use (a person) without consideration of his or her feelings. **marriage of convenience** a marriage that is not primarily a love match and serves another purpose. MODERN ***convenience***.

▸ **B** *attrib.* or as *adjective*. Designed for convenience, that is convenient. Orig. *US*. **M20.**

convenience food pre-prepared food needing a minimum of further treatment and suitable for use whenever desired. **convenience store**: stocking a wide range of goods and remaining open outside usual shopping hours.

convenience /kən'viːnɪəns/ *verb trans.* **M17.**

[ORIGIN from the noun.]

Afford convenience to, suit; accommodate.

conveniency /kən'viːnɪənsi/ *noun.* Now *rare*. **L15.**

[ORIGIN formed as CONVENIENCE *noun*: see -ENCY.]

†**1** = CONVENIENCE *noun* 1. **L15–E18.**

†**2** = CONVENIENCE *noun* 2. **E16–M17.** ▸**b** = CONVENIENCE *noun* 2b. **L16–M17.**

3 a = CONVENIENCE *noun* 3a. **E17.** ▸**b** = CONVENIENCE *noun* 3b. **E17.**

4 †**a** = CONVENIENCE *noun* 4a. **M17–L18.** ▸**b** = CONVENIENCE *noun* 4b. **M17.**

5 = CONVENIENCE *noun* 5. **M17.**

convenient /kən'viːnɪənt/ *adjective.* **LME.**

[ORIGIN Latin *convenient-* pres. ppl stem of *convenire*: see CONVENE, -ENT.]

†**1** Foll. by *to*, *for*: in accordance with the nature of; in keeping with; befitting, becoming. **LME–L17.**

†**2** Morally suitable, proper. **LME–E18.**

AV *Eph.* 5:4 Neither filthinesse, nor foolish talking, nor iesting, which are not conuenient.

†**3** Suitable (*to* or *for* a purpose, the circumstances, etc.); appropriate, due. **LME–L18.**

SHAKES. *Mids. N. D.* Here's a marvellous convenient place for our rehearsal. J. WESLEY Many were destitute of convenient clothing.

4 Personally suitable, well-adapted to one's purpose or situation; available or occurring at a suitable moment; favourable, comfortable; trouble-free. **L15.**

E. A. FREEMAN It had once been convenient to forget, it was now equally convenient to remember. G. GISSING I thought five o'clock . . would be a convenient time. BETTY SMITH His red trousers had a convenient hole . . so that his tail could stick out.

5 Within easy reach; readily accessible; near (*to*) in space or time. *colloq.* **E19.**

THACKERAY Heretics used to be brought thither convenient for burning hard by.

▪ **conveniently** *adverb* **LME.**

convenor *noun* see CONVENER.

convent /'kɒnv(ə)nt, -vɛnt/ *noun.* Also **cov-** /'kɒv-/ (long *obsolete* exc. in names, as *Covent Garden*, London). **ME.**

[ORIGIN Anglo-Norman *covent*, Old French *convent* (mod. *couvent*), from Latin *conventus* assembly, company, from *convent-* pa. ppl stem of *convenire* CONVENE. Cf. COVIN.]

†**1** A gathering, an assembly. **ME–M17.**

†**2** A company; *spec.* (*a*) the twelve apostles; (*b*) a company of twelve (or thirteen including a superior) religious persons. **ME–M16.**

3 A religious community (usu. Christian) living together under discipline; a religious institution founded for communal living; now *esp.* such a community of or institution for women (cf. ***monastery***). **ME.**

4 The buildings or estate occupied by such a community. **LME.**

– COMB.: **convent school**: conducted by members of a convent.

▪ **con'ventical** *adjective* (*rare*) of or pertaining to a convent **M18.**

convent /kɒn'vɛnt/ *verb. obsolete* exc. *hist.* **M16.**

[ORIGIN Latin *convent-* pa. ppl stem of *convenire* CONVENE.]

1 *verb trans. & intrans.* = CONVENE *verb* I. **M16.**

†**2** *verb intrans.* Be convenient, suit. *rare* (Shakes.). Only in **E17.**

conventicle /kən'vɛntɪk(ə)l/ *noun & verb.* **LME.**

[ORIGIN Latin *conventiculum* (place of) assembly, formally dim. of *conventus* meeting: see CONVENT *noun*.]

▸ **A** *noun.* †**1** A (regular) assembly or meeting. **LME–M17.**

2 A meeting or assembly of a private, clandestine, irregular, or illegal nature. *obsolete* exc. as below. **LME.** ▸**b** *spec.* A clandestine or unlawful religious meeting, esp. (*hist.*) of Nonconformists or Dissenters in England, or of Covenanters in Scotland. **E16.**

3 A place of (irregular etc.) meeting; esp. (*hist.*, formerly *derog.*) a Nonconformist or Dissenting meeting house. **LME.**

†**4** A small convent. **M16–E17.**

– COMB.: **Conventicle Acts** *hist.*: of the reign of Charles II, suppressing religious meetings not conforming to the Church of England.

▸ †**B** *verb trans. & intrans.* Form into a conventicle; hold or frequent conventicles. **L16–E18.**

▪ †**conventicleer** *noun* = CONVENTICLER **M17–E18.** **conventicler** *noun* an attender of conventicles **LME.**

convention /kən'vɛnʃ(ə)n/ *noun.* **LME.**

[ORIGIN Old French & mod. French from Latin *conventio(n-)* meeting, covenant, from *convent-*: see CONVENT *verb*, -ION.]

▸ **I 1** An assembly or gathering of people; esp. a formal meeting for deliberation, legislation, etc. **LME.** ▸**b** *spec.* (*hist.*) A meeting of Parliament, or of the Scottish Estates, without the formal summons usually required. **M16.** ▸**c** In the US, an assembly of delegates of a political party for the purpose of nominating a candidate for the presidency, etc. **E19.**

T. DREISER There was a convention of dentists in the city.

c national convention: see NATIONAL *adjective*.

†**2** The action of coming together, meeting, or assembling; an assemblage, a union. **L15–L18.**

J. HOWELL Venice is . . a Convention of little Ilands.

†**3** The action of summoning before a person in authority. **L16–E19.**

4 The action of convening a meeting etc. **M17.**

▸ **II 5** An agreement or covenant between parties; an agreement creating legal relations. **LME.** ▸**b** *spec.* A diplomatic agreement between states, now *esp.* one less formal than a treaty. **E17.** ▸**c** *spec.* An agreement between belligerents as to the suspension of hostilities, exchange or treatment of prisoners, etc. **L18.**

Geneva Convention(s): see GENEVA *noun*¹.

6 General agreement or consent, deliberate or implicit, as to any custom, usage, behaviour, etc. **L18.** ▸**b** Accepted social behaviour, esp. if merely formal or repressively artificial. **M19.**

G. B. SHAW A man . . is by convention the master and lawgiver of the hearthstone.

7 A generally accepted rule or practice based on custom, usage, etc. **L18.** ▸**b** CARDS. A prearranged method of play or bidding, esp. in bridge, used to convey information. **M19.**

G. GREENE I may have been christened—it's a social convention isn't it? L. P. HARTLEY Bound by the moral conventions of the eighteenth century.

– COMB.: **Convention right** LAW a right protected under the European Convention on Human Rights and hence under the Human Rights Act of 1998.

▪ **conventio'neer** *noun* (orig. *US*) = CONVENTIONER **M20.** **conventioner** *noun* a member of a convention, a person who attends conventions **L17.** **conventionist** *noun* †(*a*) a party to a convention or agreement; (*b*) = CONVENTIONER: **M18.**

conventional /kən'vɛnʃ(ə)n(ə)l/ *adjective & noun.* **L15.**

[ORIGIN French *conventionnel* or late Latin *conventionalis*, formed as CONVENTION: see -AL¹.]

▸ **A** *adjective.* **1** Relating to, based on, or of the nature of a formal agreement or convention, e.g. between states. **L15.** ▸**b** CARDS. Of, pertaining to, or characterized by a convention (sense 7b) or conventions. **M19.**

2 Relating to or depending on agreed social usage, custom, etc.; arbitrarily or artificially determined. **M18.** ▸**b** Accepting social conventions; in accordance with accepted (artificial) standards or models, orthodox; lacking originality, spontaneity, or realism. **M19.** ▸**c** Of weapons, warfare, power stations, etc.: non-nuclear. **M20.**

H. BLAIR The connexion between words and ideas may . . be considered as arbitrary and conventional. **b** L. W. MEYNELL Tall poplars silhouetted . . resembling the conventional trees of a child's Noah's Ark. T. S. ELIOT I'm not a person of liberal views. I'm very conventional. A. TOFFLER It is conventional wisdom to assert that the age of the entrepreneur is dead.

3 Of, pertaining to, or of the nature of a convention or assembly. **E19.**

▸ **B** *noun.* **1** *absol.* That which is conventional. **E19.**

2 = CONVENTIONALIST 1. *rare*. **L19.**

▪ **conventionally** *adverb* **M19.**

conventionalise *verb* var. of CONVENTIONALIZE.

conventionalism /kən'vɛnʃ(ə)n(ə)lɪz(ə)m/ *noun.* **M19.**

[ORIGIN from CONVENTIONAL + -ISM.]

1 Adherence to or regard for what is conventional. **M19.**

2 An instance of mere convention, a conventional usage etc. **M19.**

3 PHILOSOPHY. A doctrine holding that a priori truths are true by virtue of linguistic convention. Also, a doctrine holding that at least some apparently empirical scientific laws are in fact postulates. **M20.**

conventionalist /kən'vɛnʃ(ə)n(ə)lɪst/ *noun.* **E19.**

[ORIGIN formed as CONVENTIONALISM + -IST.]

1 *hist.* A supporter of the French National Convention of 1792. **E19.**

2 A person who follows conventional usage etc. **M19.**

3 PHILOSOPHY. An adherent of conventionalism. **M20.**

conventionality /kənvɛnʃə'nalɪti/ *noun.* **M19.**

[ORIGIN from CONVENTIONAL + -ITY.]

1 The quality or state of being conventional. **M19.**

2 A conventional thing or practice; in *pl.*, *the* forms and usages established as fit and proper by society. **M19.**

conventionalize /kən'vɛnʃ(ə)n(ə)lʌɪz/ *verb trans.* Also **-ise**. **M19.**

[ORIGIN from CONVENTIONAL + -IZE.]

Render conventional, treat conventionally.

▪ **conventionali'zation** *noun* **L19.**

conventionary /kən'vɛnʃ(ə)n(ə)ri/ *adjective.* **E17.**

[ORIGIN medieval Latin *conventionarius*, from Latin *conventio(n-)*: see CONVENTION, -ARY¹.]

Designating or holding tenure on terms fixed by agreement rather than custom.

conventual /kən'vɛntjʊəl/ *adjective & noun.* **LME.**

[ORIGIN medieval Latin *conventualis*, from Latin *conventus* CONVENT *noun*: see -AL¹.]

▸ **A** *adjective.* **1** Of or belonging to a convent; characteristic of a convent. **LME.**

M. BEERBOHM A conventual hush in her voice.

2 (**C-**.) Designating or pertaining to the Franciscan Conventuals (see sense B.1 below). **E18.**

▸ **B** *noun.* **1** (**C-**.) A member of a branch of the Franciscans in which the friars live in large convents and follow a less strict rule. Cf. ***Observant***. **M16.**

2 A member or inmate of a convent. **E17.**

▪ **conventually** *adverb* **LME.**

converge /kən'vəːdʒ/ *verb.* **L17.**

[ORIGIN Late Latin *convergere* incline together, formed as CON- + Latin *vergere* bend, turn, incline.]

1 *verb intrans.* Tend to meet in a point; approach nearer together as if to meet or join (*on* a point). **L17.**

P. PEARCE Footsteps were coming to the house, converging on it from different directions. *fig.*: B. WEBB Our points of view are slowly converging.

2 *verb intrans.* MATH. Of an infinite series: have the property that as more terms are taken, in order from the first, their sum gets closer and closer to a definite limit. **E18.**

3 *verb trans.* Cause to approach each other or come together. **L18.**

converging lens: causing light rays to converge.

▪ **converger** *noun* a person whose thought is convergent **M20.**

convergence /kən'vəːdʒ(ə)ns/ *noun.* **E18.**

[ORIGIN from CONVERGENT: see -ENCE.]

1 The action, fact, or property of converging; tendency to come together at a point. **E18.**

2 BIOLOGY. The tendency of distinct animals and plants to evolve similar structural or physiological characteristics under similar environmental conditions. **M19.**

3 METEOROLOGY & OCEANOGRAPHY. A place where airflows or ocean currents meet, characteristically marked by upwelling (of air) or downwelling (of water). **M20.**

Antarctic convergence: see ANTARCTIC *adjective*.

▪ **convergency** *noun* convergent quality, convergence **E18.**

convergent /kən'vəːdʒ(ə)nt/ *adjective.* **E18.**

[ORIGIN Late Latin *convergent-* pres. ppl stem of *convergere*: see CONVERGE, -ENT.]

1 Converging; of or pertaining to convergence; MATH. (of an infinite series) that converges (CONVERGE 2). **E19.**

2 BIOLOGY. Characterized by or displaying evolutionary convergence (CONVERGENCE 2). **L19.**

pointwise convergent: see POINTWISE *adverb* 2.

3 PSYCHOLOGY. Of thought: tending to reach only the most rational result. Cf. DIVERGENT 2. **M20.**

conversable /kən'vəːsəb(ə)l/ *adjective.* **L16.**

[ORIGIN Obsolete French = affable etc. from medieval Latin *conversabilis*, from Latin *conversari*: see CONVERSE *verb*, -ABLE. See also CONVERSIBLE *adjective*².]

1 That may be conversed with. Now *esp.* pleasant in conversation, disposed to converse. **L16.**

2 Of or pertaining to social converse. **M17.**

▪ **conversableness** *noun* **L17.** **conversably** *adverb* **M17.**

conversance /kən'vəːs(ə)ns/ *noun.* **E17.**

[ORIGIN from CONVERSANT: see -ANCE.]

The state or quality of being conversant (*with*).

▪ Also **conversancy** *noun* **L18.**

conversant /kən'vəːs(ə)nt/ *adjective & noun.* **ME.**

[ORIGIN Old French & mod. French, pres. pple of *converser*: see CONVERSE *verb*, -ANT¹.]

▸ **A** *adjective.* †**1** Living or passing time habitually or frequently *in* or in a specified place. **ME–E19.**

T. PENNANT On marshy . . grounds, where they are conversant.

2 Associating regularly *with* (also †*in*, †*among*); on familiar terms *with*. **ME.**

STEELE I am afraid you have been very little conversant with Women.

3 Occupied or engaged *with* (also †*in*, †*among*, †*about*); having to do *with*. **LME.**

W. LILLY A meer Fisherman, or man conversant in water. C. G. B. DAUBENY Chemistry . . had . . been conversant merely with the qualities of matter.

4 Well versed or experienced *in*, familiar *with*, (a subject). **LME.**

B. EMECHETA Men who were conversant with the goings-on in world politics. M. MOORCOCK My mother . . was conversant in all forms of literature and learning.

†**5** Of a thing: well known, familiar. **LME–M17.**
▸ †**B** *noun.* A familiar acquaintance. **L16–L17.**

conversation /kɒnvəˈseɪʃ(ə)n/ *noun.* **ME.**
[ORIGIN Old French & mod. French from Latin *conversatio(n-)*, from *conversari* CONVERSE *verb*: see -ATION.]
†**1** The action of living or having one's being *in, among.* **ME–E18.**

G. STANHOPE Proneness to Idolatry, which a long Conversation in Egypt had disposed them to.

†**2** The action of consorting (*with*); intimacy. **ME–L18.**

MILTON The good and peace of wedded conversation.

3 Behaviour, mode of life. *arch.* **ME.**

AV *Ps.* 50:23 Him that ordereth his conversation aright.

4 Sexual intercourse or relations. *obsolete* exc. in ***criminal conversation*** (see CRIMINAL *adjective* 1). **LME.**
5 The informal interchange of information, ideas, etc., by spoken words; ability or proficiency in this. **L16.** ▸**b** An informal spoken interchange, a talk. **L17.**

S. JOHNSON We had *talk* enough, but no *conversation*; there was nothing *discussed*. A. POWELL Neither of the girls had much conversation. **b** J. T. STORY They . . held a long . . conversation in Italian.

make conversation converse, esp. only as a social duty.
†**6** Occupation or acquaintance *with* (an object of study etc.). **L16–E18.**
†**7** A circle of acquaintance; company. **E17–E18.**

CLARENDON His Domestick Conversation . . were all known Papists.

†**8** A social gathering, an at-home. Cf. CONVERSAZIONE. **L17–L18.**
– COMB.: **conversation card** *hist.* a card containing a sentence for use in a question-and-answer game; **conversation chair** a type of upright chair on which the occupant sits astride, facing the back; **conversation lozenge** a lozenge with an inscribed motto; **conversation piece** (*a*) a type of genre painting involving a portrait group posed in a landscape or domestic setting; (*b*) a subject serving as a topic of conversation on account of its unusualness etc.; **conversation-stopper** *colloq.* a remark etc. that admits of no reply; something outrageous or startling.
■ **conversationist** *noun* = CONVERSATIONALIST **L17.**

conversational /kɒnvəˈseɪʃ(ə)n(ə)l/ *adjective.* **L18.**
[ORIGIN from CONVERSATION + -AL[1].]
1 Of or pertaining to conversation; characteristic of or appropriate to conversation. **L18.**
2 Fond of or good at conversation. **L18.**
■ **conversationalist** *noun* a participant in conversation; a person who is good at conversation: **E19. conversationally** *adverb* **E19.**

conversative /kənˈvəːsətɪv/ *adjective. rare.* **M17.**
[ORIGIN from CONVERSE *verb* + -ATIVE.]
†**1** Of or fitted for social intercourse, sociable. Only in **M17.**
2 = CONVERSATIONAL 2. **E18.**

conversazione /ˌkɒnvəsatsɪˈəʊni/ *noun.* Pl. **-nes**, **-ni** /-ni/. **M18.**
[ORIGIN Italian = conversation.]
1 In Italy, an evening gathering for conversation and recreation. **M18.**
†**2** An at-home. **L18–E19.**
3 A social gathering for discussion of the arts, literature, etc.; an educational soirée. **L18.**

converse /ˈkɒnvəːs/ *noun*[1]. **LME.**
[ORIGIN formed as CONVERSE *adjective*[2].]
1 A form of words derived from another by the transposition of some terms; a thing or action which is the exact opposite of another; *the* opposite or contrary. **LME.**
2 MATH. A proposition whose premiss and conclusion are the conclusion and premiss of another. **L16.**
3 LOGIC. A converted proposition (CONVERT *verb* 4). **M17.**

converse /ˈkɒnvəːs/ *noun*[2]. Now *literary* or *arch.* **L15.**
[ORIGIN from the verb.]
1 Social communication, intercourse. *obsolete* exc. as passing into senses 2, 3. **L15.**
2 Informal spoken interchange of ideas etc., conversation. **L16.** ▸†**b** A conversation. **M17–L18.**

I. MURDOCH Ann was sitting . . in close converse with Douglas Swann.

3 Spiritual or mental intercourse, communion. **M17.**

W. SHENSTONE With Nature here high converse hold.

†**4** = CONVERSATION 6. **M17–E18.**
†**5** = CONVERSATION 3. **M17–E18.**
– NOTE: Orig. pronunc. the same as the verb.

converse /ˈkɒnvəːs/ *adjective*[1] & *noun*[3]. **ME.**
[ORIGIN Old French & mod. French *convers* from Latin *conversus* (use as noun of) pa. pple of *convertere* CONVERT *verb*.]
▸ †**A** *adjective.* Converted in mind or feeling. Only in **ME.**
▸ **B** *noun.* †**1** A religious convert. **LME–L15.**
2 *hist.* = CONVERSUS. **LME.**

converse /ˈkɒnvəːs/ *adjective*[2]. **L16.**
[ORIGIN Latin *conversus* turned about, transformed: see CONVERSE *adjective*[1] & *noun*[3].]
That is the opposite of something expressed or implied; reversed; contrary.
■ **conversely** /ˈkɒnvəːsli, kənˈvəːsli/ *adverb* **E19.**

converse /kənˈvəːs/ *verb.* **LME.**
[ORIGIN Old French & mod. French *converser* from Latin *conversari*, middle voice of *conversare* turn round, formed as CON- + *versare* frequentative of *vertere* turn.]
▸ **I** *verb intrans.* †**1** Live, dwell, (*in, among*). **LME–E18.**
†**2** Consort, be familiar; have sexual relations; deal, trade. Foll. by *with*. **LME–E19.**
3 Be engaged *in*; have to do, be conversant, *with*. *obsolete* exc. as *fig.* use of sense 5. **L16.**
4 Communicate, interchange ideas, (*with*). *obsolete* in *gen.* sense. **L16.**
5 Commune *with*. **L16.**
6 Engage in conversation, talk, (*with* a person, *on* or *about* a subject). **E17.**
▸ **II** *verb trans.* †**7** Associate with; talk with. **M17–E18.**
■ **converser** *noun* **L16.**

conversi *noun* pl. of CONVERSUS.

conversible /kənˈvəːsɪb(ə)l/ *adjective*[1]. *rare.* **M16.**
[ORIGIN Late Latin *conversibilis*, from *convers-*: see CONVERSION, -IBLE.]
Able to be converted or transposed.

conversible /kənˈvəːsɪb(ə)l/ *adjective*[2]. **E18.**
[ORIGIN Alt. of CONVERSABLE after -IBLE.]
= CONVERSABLE.

conversion /kənˈvəːʃ(ə)n/ *noun.* **ME.**
[ORIGIN Old French & mod. French from Latin *conversio(n-)*, from *convers-* pa. ppl stem of *convertere*: see CONVERT *verb*, -ION.]
▸ **I** Change in character, nature, etc.
1 THEOLOGY. The turning of sinners to God; a change from sinfulness to righteousness. **ME.**
2 The action of bringing a person over, or the fact of being brought over, to a particular belief or opinion, *spec.* to a religious faith. **LME.**

S. LEWIS To be picked out as a missionary within half an hour of his conversion! OED Conversion to Free Trade principles.

3 The action or an act of changing or being changed (*to* or *into* something else); (esp. structural) alteration for a different function. **LME.** ▸**b** *spec.* The structural adaptation of (part of) a building for new purposes; (a part of) a building so modified. **E20.** ▸**c** GRAMMAR. Change of the function or class of a word; zero derivation. **E20.** ▸**d** RUGBY & *N. Amer.* FOOTBALL. The action or an act of scoring immediately following a try, by kicking the ball over the crossbar from a place kick. **E20.** ▸**e** The transformation of fertile into fissile material in a nuclear reactor. **M20.**

BACON Artificiall Conuersion of Water into Ice. P. NORMAN Conversion of the High Street shop into a café.

†**4** MILITARY. The converting of files into ranks; a change of front to a flank. **L16–M19.**
▸ **II** Turning.
†**5** The action or an act of turning (*to* a particular direction) or of directing *to* some object; turning round, revolution, rotation; turning back, returning, *spec.* the solstice. **LME–E18.**
6 Transposition, inversion; *spec.* in LOGIC, (an instance of) the transposition of the subject and predicate of a proposition to form a new proposition. **M16.**
†**7** RHETORIC. = ANTISTROPHE 1. Also = APOSTROPHE *noun*[1]. **M16–M18.**
8 LAW. The action of wrongfully dealing with goods in a manner inconsistent with the true owner's rights. **E17.**

N. BACON Fraudulent conversion of Treasure-trove.

▸ **III** Change by substitution.
9 The change of moneys, stocks, units in which a quantity is expressed, etc., into others of a different kind. **M16.** ▸†**b** (A) translation into another language. **L16–M17.**
10 LAW. (An instance of) the reclassification of real property as personal, or of joint property as separate, on the basis that the law should regard that as done which ought to have been done, e.g. under a trust for sale. **L18.**
11 PSYCHIATRY. The manifestation of a mental disturbance as a physical disorder or disease. **L19.**
– COMB.: **conversion factor** (*a*) an arithmetical multiplier for converting a quantity expressed in one set of units into an equivalent expressed in another; (*b*) ECONOMICS the manufacturing cost of a product relative to the cost of raw materials; **conversion hysteria**, **conversion symptom**, etc. PSYCHIATRY: manifesting conversion (sense 11 above). **conversion van** *N. Amer.* a motor vehicle in which the area behind the driver has been converted into a living space.
■ **conversionism** *noun* preoccupation with bringing about the religious conversion of others **L19. conversionist** *noun* a person advocating or preoccupied with the religious conversion of others **L19.**

conversive /kənˈvəːsɪv/ *adjective.* **E17.**
[ORIGIN French †*conversif*, *-ive* = medieval Latin *conversivus*, from *convers-*: see CONVERSION, -IVE.]
†**1** = CONVERSE *adjective*[2]. **E–M17.**
2 Having the power or function of conversion. **M17.**
waw conversive: see WAW *noun*[3].

conversus /kənˈvəːsəs/ *noun.* Pl. **-versi** /-ˈvəːsʌɪ/. **L18.**
[ORIGIN Latin: see CONVERSE *adjective*[1] & *noun*[3].]
hist. A lay member of a monastery or convent, *esp.* one entering monastic life as a mature person.

convert /ˈkɒnvəːt/ *noun & adjective.* **M16.**
[ORIGIN from the verb, superseding and perh. infl. by synon. CONVERSE *noun*[3]. Cf. VERT *noun*[2].]
▸ **A** *noun.* A person (newly) converted to a religious faith, an opinion, a belief, etc. **M16.**
▸ †**B** *adjective.* **1** Converted to a religious faith. **E17–E19.**
2 ***convert brother***, ***convert sister***, = CONVERSUS. **M–L17.**
■ **convertism** *noun* the system or practice of making converts **E18.** †**convertist** *noun* (*a*) = CONVERT *noun*; (*b*) = CONVERTER 2: **E17–M18.**

convert /kənˈvəːt/ *verb.* **ME.**
[ORIGIN Old French & mod. French *convertir* from Proto-Romance var. of Latin *convertere* turn about, transform, formed as CON- + *vertere* turn.]
▸ **I** Turn.
†**1** *verb trans.* Give a different direction to, turn about; direct. **ME–L18.**

SHAKES. *Sonn.* The eyes . . now converted are . . and look another way. GOLDSMITH The two kings . . agreed to convert their whole attention to the rescuing Jerusalem.

†**2** *verb trans.* Cause to return; restore. **LME–M17.**
3 *verb trans.* Turn or apply *to* (another or a specific use), divert; *spec.* in LAW, appropriate illegally *to one's own use*. **LME.**
4 *verb trans.* Reverse in position, sense, or direction; invert, transpose. *obsolete* exc. LOGIC, transpose the terms of (a proposition). **LME.**
▸ **II** Change in nature etc.
5 *verb trans.* & †*intrans.* THEOLOGY. (Cause to) turn from a sinful to a righteous life. **ME.**
6 *verb trans.* & *intrans.* (Cause to) turn to and adopt a particular faith, belief, opinion, course of action, etc.; *spec.* (cause to) adopt Christianity. (Foll. by *to*.) **ME.**

C. POTOK Many . . went away converted to his way of thinking. D. CUPITT There were hopes of converting the Emperor . . and so eventually . . the whole country.

†**7** *verb trans.* & *intrans.* (Cause to) change in mental state, disposition, etc. **LME–L16.**
8 *verb trans.* Turn or change (*in*)*to* something different; change in character or function, transform. **LME.** ▸†**b** Assimilate, digest. **LME–M17.** ▸**c** *spec.* Make structural alterations in (a building). **E19.**

MILTON That . . lessens The sorrow, and converts it nigh to joy. R. HOGGART They convert an electric-kettle into a lethal weapon. A. HAILEY Night college classes . . converted young Paulsen to a graduate engineer.

9 *verb intrans.* Undergo change or transformation (*to, into*). Now *esp.* be able or designed to be changed. **M16.**

S. WEINBERG The neutrons began to convert to protons. *Sunday Telegraph* The sofa . . converts into a double bed.

10 *verb trans.* & *intrans.* FOOTBALL. Complete (a try, touchdown, etc.) by scoring a goal; score from (a penalty kick, place kick, etc.). **L19.**
▸ **III** Change by substitution.
†**11** *verb trans.* Translate (*into* another language). **M16–M17.**
12 *verb trans.* Change by substitution of something equivalent; change (moneys, stocks, etc.) into others of a different kind; express in terms of different units. **M16.** ▸**b** LAW. Reclassify from real property to personal, or from joint to separate property, on the basis that the law should regard that as done which ought to have been done. **L18.**

LYNDON B. JOHNSON To convert their dollars into gold at the official rate of $35 an ounce. D. STOREY Struggling to convert a fraction of a yard into feet and inches.

■ **converted** *ppl adjective* & *noun* (*a*) *adjective* that has been converted; (*b*) *noun pl.* the people who have been converted, as a class (***preach to the converted***: see PREACH *verb*): **L16. convertive** *adjective* (*rare*) (*a*) characterized by turning; (*b*) having the property of converting: **E17.**

convertend /ˈkɒnvətɛnd/ *noun.* **M19.**
[ORIGIN Latin *convertendus*, *-um* to be converted, gerundive of *convertere* CONVERT *verb*: see -END.]
LOGIC. The proposition as it stands before conversion (CONVERSION 6).

converter /kənˈvəːtə/ *noun.* **M16.**
[ORIGIN from CONVERT *verb* + -ER[1].]
1 A person who converts one thing into another, or who converts a thing to his or her own use. **M16.**
2 A person who makes converts. **L16.**
3 An apparatus for converting or transforming one thing into another; *spec.* (*a*) a retort lined with a heat-resistant substance in which air or oxygen can be passed through a charge of metal or ore in certain metallurgical (esp. steel-making) processes; (*b*) a device for altering the nature of an electrical current, esp. for the interconversion of alternating current and direct current or of analogue and digital data signals; (*c*) (in full ***converter***

reactor) a nuclear reactor that transforms fertile material into fissile material. M19.
BESSEMER *converter*. CATALYTIC *converter*. *rotary converter*: see ROTARY *adjective*.

convertible /kən'vəːtɪb(ə)l/ *adjective & noun*. LME.
[ORIGIN Old French & mod. French from Latin *convertibilis*, from *convertere* CONVERT *verb*: see -IBLE.]
▸ **A** *adjective*. **1** Interchangeable; (of terms) synonymous. LME. ▸**b** *LOGIC*. That may be legitimately transposed by conversion (CONVERSION 6). L16.
†**2** Able to be turned or directed. L15–M17.
3 Able to be changed (*into* or *to* something else). M16. ▸**b** Of a car: having a roof that can be folded down or removed. E20.
4 Able to be converted to a religion, belief, opinion, etc. E19.
5 Able to be turned to a particular use or purpose. E19.
6 Able to be converted by exchange; *esp*. (**a**) (of paper money) able to be converted into coin; (**b**) (of currency etc.) that may be converted into gold or US dollars; (**c**) (of a bond, stock, etc.) that may be converted into other shares, esp. ordinary shares. M19.
▸ **B** *noun*. **1** In *pl*. Interchangeable or synonymous things or terms. E17.
2 A car with a folding or removable roof. E20.
3 A convertible bond etc. M20.
■ **converti'bility** *noun* M18. **convertibly** *adverb* E18.

convertiplane /kən'vəːtɪpleɪn/ *noun*. M20.
[ORIGIN from CONVERTIBLE + AEROPLANE *noun*.]
A type of aircraft combining certain features of the helicopter with those of a conventional aeroplane.

convertite /'kɒnvətʌɪt/ *noun*. *arch*. M16.
[ORIGIN from CONVERT *noun* or *verb* + -ITE[1], after French *converti* use as noun of pa. pple of *convertir* to convert.]
1 A person converted to righteousness or approved conduct; *spec*. a reformed prostitute. M16.
2 A convert to a religion, belief, etc. L16.

convex /'kɒnvɛks, *pred. also* kɒn'vɛks/ *adjective & noun*. L16.
[ORIGIN Latin *convexus* vaulted, arched. Cf. Old French & mod. French *convexe*.]
▸ **A** *adjective*. Having an outline or surface curved like the exterior of a circle or sphere; the reverse of concave. L16.
convex lens, ***convex mirror***, etc.
▸ **B** *noun*. †**1** A convex surface or body; a vault etc. as viewed from above or (*poet*.) below. E17–L18.

MILTON This huge convex of Fire . . immures us round Ninefold.

2 The convex part of something. E18.
3 A convex lens, mirror, etc. E18.
■ **convexly** *adverb* M18. **convexness** *noun* M18.

convex /'kɒnvɛks/ *verb trans. & intrans*. L16.
[ORIGIN from the adjective.]
Make or become convex; bow or bend outwards. Orig. & chiefly as ***convexed*** *ppl adjective*.

convexity /kɒn'vɛksɪti/ *noun*. L16.
[ORIGIN Latin *convexitas*, from *convexus*: see CONVEX *adjective & noun*, -ITY. Cf. French *convexité*.]
1 The quality or condition of being convex. L16.
2 A convex curve, surface, side, or part. E17.

convexo- /kən'vɛksəʊ/ *combining form*.
[ORIGIN from CONVEX *adjective & noun* + -O-.]
Convexly, convex and —.
■ **convexo-'concave** *adjective* convex on one side and concave on the other (and thickest in the centre: cf. CONCAVO-CONVEX) L17. **convexo-'convex** *adjective* convex on both sides L19.

convey /kən'veɪ/ *verb & noun*. ME.
[ORIGIN Old French *conveier* (mod. *convoyer* CONVOY *verb*), from medieval Latin *conviare*, formed as CON- + *via* way.]
▸ **A** *verb trans*. †**1** Escort; convoy. ME–E18.
2 Lead, guide. Long *Scot. rare*. ME.
3 Take from one place to another; transport, carry. LME.

E. WAUGH They conveyed her to a nursing-home in Wimpole Street. I. MURDOCH She plucked a leaf, and conveyed it to her mouth.

4 Remove, take *away* (esp. secretly or clandestinely); make away with; *esp*. steal. *arch*. LME.

SMOLLETT Teresa . . was . . detected in the very act of conveying a piece of plate.

5 Transmit, transfer (esp. something abstract); communicate, impart (a benefit, influence, sentiment, etc.); express, carry as a meaning. LME. ▸†**b** Transfer secretly or furtively. E17–E18.

HOBBES Any influence . . but such as is conveighed . . from the Soveraign Authority. V. WOOLF Her manner conveyed an extraordinary degree of sympathy. P. G. WODEHOUSE He could convey to Ruth that he thought her a . . neglected wife. G. GREENE He seemed to be looking for words . . with which to convey his meaning.

†**6** Bring down by succession, derive; transmit to posterity, hand down. LME–M18.
†**7** Carry on (an affair, business, etc.); manage. LME–M17.

SHAKES. *Lear* I will . . convey the business as I shall find means.

8 *LAW*. Transfer by deed or legal process. L15.
9 Act as a channel, path, or medium for the movement of; conduct. M16.

DRYDEN Thro' reeden Pipes convey the Golden Flood. S. P. WOODWARD The auditory nerves convey impressions of sound.

▸ †**B** *noun*. **1** = CONVOY *noun* 2. LME–L17.
2 Conveyance. L16–E17.
■ **conveyable** *adjective* †(**a**) having the quality of conveying; (**b**) that may be conveyed: M16.

conveyance /kən'veɪəns/ *noun*. LME.
[ORIGIN from CONVEY + -ANCE.]
1 The action of carrying or transporting; transport. LME.
†**2** Conduct (*of* an affair etc.), execution; skilful or cunning management; sleight of hand. LME–E18. ▸**b** A secret or cunning device, an artifice, a trick. M16–M17.
3 a Nimble carrying off; stealing. *arch*. L15. ▸†**b** *gen*. Removal, riddance. M16–M17.
4 Transference, handing from one to another; *esp*. communication or imparting (*of* a thing, *to* a person). L15.
†**5** The conveying of meaning by words; expression; manner of expression, style. L15–L18.
6 Escorting; conduct. Long *arch. rare*. E16.
7 *LAW*. (A document effecting) the transfer of the legal title to property. E16.
innocent conveyance: see INNOCENT *adjective*.
8 A conducting or communicating channel or medium; a passage. Now only *spec*. a conducting pipe in an organ. M16.
9 The conducting or transmission of fluid, heat, electricity, etc. L16.
10 A means of transport, a vehicle. L16.

conveyancer /kən'veɪənsə/ *noun*. E17.
[ORIGIN from CONVEYANCE + -ER[1].]
1 = CONVEYER 1. E17.
2 A lawyer who prepares documents for the conveyance of property. M17.

conveyancing /kən'veɪənsɪŋ/ *noun*. L17.
[ORIGIN from CONVEYANCE + -ING[1].]
†**1** Deceitful contrivance. Only in L17.
2 (The branch of the law that deals with) the preparation of documents for the conveyance of property. E18.

conveyer /kən'veɪə/ *noun*. Also (the usual form in sense 4) **-or**. E16.
[ORIGIN from CONVEY *verb* + -ER[1], -OR.]
1 *gen*. A person who or thing which conveys something. E16.
†**2** A deft thief. M–L16.
3 A person who transfers property. M17.
4 A mechanical contrivance for conveying articles or materials during manufacture or processing; *esp*. (in full ***conveyor belt***) an endless moving belt of rubber, canvas, etc., for this purpose. E19.

fig.: G. CLARE For Grandmother this conveyor-belt production of sons must have been traumatic.

■ **conveyorize** *verb trans*. equip with a conveyor, carry out by means of a conveyor M20.

convict /'kɒnvɪkt/ *noun*. L15.
[ORIGIN from original pa. pple & ppl adjective of CONVICT *verb*, with subsequent shift of stress.]
1 *gen*. A person judicially convicted of a criminal offence. *arch*. L15.
2 *spec*. A criminal serving a sentence of imprisonment or (*hist*.) penal servitude, transportation, etc. L18.
■ **convictism** *noun* (*hist*.) the system of penal settlements for convicts; the body of convicts so treated: M19.

convict /kən'vɪkt/ *verb*. Pa. pple & ppl adjective **convicted**, (earlier, now *arch*.) **convict**. ME.
[ORIGIN Latin *convict-* pa. ppl stem of *convincere* CONVINCE.]
▸ **I** *verb trans*. **1** Prove to be guilty by judicial procedure; declare guilty by the verdict of the jury or by the decision of the judge. (Foll. by *of*, †*for*, †*to have done*.) ME. ▸**b** Prove or declare guilty of an error or reprehensible conduct. LME.

COVERDALE A convicte transgressour of the lawe. J. CONRAD A city clerk . . gets himself convicted of a common embezzlement. **b** J. MORLEY Convicted . . of want of sensibility.

†**2** = CONVINCE 3. ME–M17.
†**3** Demonstrate, prove. LME–M18.
†**4** Overcome; vanquish; conquer. LME–E17.

SHAKES. *John* A whole armado of convicted sail Is scattered and disjoin'd from fellowship.

5 Cause (a person) to admit or realize his or her sinfulness or error. E16.

B. JOWETT He is supposed to have a mission to convict men of self-conceit.

6 Disprove; refute. *arch*. M16.

G. GROTE No man shall be able to convict you in dialogue.

▸ **II** *verb intrans*. **7** Bring in a verdict of guilty, make a conviction. M19.

J. THURBER The testimony . . was, under the law, not enough to convict.

■ **convictable** *adjective* L18.

conviction /kən'vɪkʃ(ə)n/ *noun*. LME.
[ORIGIN Latin *convictio(n-)*, formed as CONVICT *verb*: see -ION.]
1 Proof of guilt by judicial procedure; (a) declaration of guilt by the verdict of the jury or by the decision of the judge; the fact or condition of being convicted of an offence. LME.

A. URE The perjury of the witnesses placed an effectual barrier against conviction. L. DURRELL Impossible to secure convictions against people unless caught *in flagrante delicto*.

summary conviction: by judge or magistrates without a jury.
†**2** Proof or detection of error; confutation; exposure. L16–E18.
3 The act of convincing someone of something. Now *rare*. M17.

JAMES SULLIVAN To require something more for the conviction of the experimentalist.

4 Awakened consciousness of sin; a feeling of one's own sinfulness. M17.
5 The condition of being convinced; strong belief on the ground of satisfactory reasons or evidence; convincing quality of expression; a settled belief or opinion. L17.

S. JOHNSON A painful conviction of his defects. O. WISTER Every good man in this world has convictions about right and wrong. F. WELDON Her lack of conviction showed through: the words on the page rang false.

carry conviction: see CARRY *verb*. ***courage of one's convictions***: see COURAGE *noun* 4.

convictive /kən'vɪktɪv/ *adjective*. E17.
[ORIGIN from CONVICT *verb* + -IVE.]
Having the power of producing conviction, convincing.
■ **convictively** *adverb* M17. **convictiveness** *noun* M17.

convictor /kən'vɪktə/ *noun*. M17.
[ORIGIN Latin = a person who lives with another, from *convict-* pa. ppl stem of *convivere*, formed as CON- + *vivere* live: see -OR.]
A person who eats at a communal table; a boarder, esp. in a Roman Catholic seminary etc.

convince /kən'vɪns/ *verb trans*. M16.
[ORIGIN Latin *convincere* convict of error, refute, formed as CON- + *vincere* overcome.]
▸ **I** †**1** Overcome; vanquish. M16–M17.

SHAKES. *Macb*. His two chamberlains Will I with wine and wassail so convince That memory . . shall be a fume.

†**2** Overcome in argument; confute. M16–E18.

MILTON Satan stood . . confuted and convinced Of his weak arguing and fallacious drift.

3 Persuade to believe firmly the truth (*of*, *that*); satisfy by argument or evidence; in *pass*., be firmly persuaded. E17. ▸**b** Prevail upon, persuade *to do*. Orig. *N. Amer*. M20.

SCOTT FITZGERALD I suspected that he was pulling my leg, but a glance . . convinced me otherwise. M. DRABBLE I couldn't convince him that I didn't care. M. AMIS Herbert . . seems pretty well convinced it will be him.

4 Bring (a person) to an awareness *of* his or her sinfulness or error. M17.
▸ †**II 5** = CONVICT *verb* 1. M16–L18.
6 Demonstrate, prove; expose in its true character; prove (a quality etc.) *of* its possessor. M16–M18.
7 Disprove; refute. M16–E17.
■ **convinced** *ppl adjective* firmly persuaded L17. **convincement** *noun* conviction E17. **convincer** *noun* M17. **convincing** *adjective* that convinces; able to convince: E17. **convincingly** *adverb* M17. **convincingness** *noun* M17.

convincible /kən'vɪnsɪb(ə)l/ *adjective*. M17.
[ORIGIN Late Latin *convincibilis*, from *convincere*: see CONVINCE, -IBLE.]
Orig., able to be convicted. Now, able to be convinced.

†**convival** *noun & adjective*. E17.
[ORIGIN Latin *convivalis*: see CONVIVIAL, -AL[1].]
▸ **A** *noun*. A guest. Only in E17.
▸ **B** *adjective*. = CONVIVIAL. M17–M18.

convive /kɔ̃viːv (*pl. same*), 'kɒnvʌɪv/ *noun*. M17.
[ORIGIN (French from) Latin *conviva*, from *convivere* live together with, formed as CON- + *vivere* live.]
A member of a company who eat together, a fellow feaster.

†**convive** *verb intrans*. *rare* (Shakes.). Only in E17.
[ORIGIN Latin *convivere*: see CONVIVE *noun*.]
Feast together.

convivial /kən'vɪvɪəl/ *adjective*. M17.
[ORIGIN Latin *convivialis*, *convivalis* (cf. CONVIVAL), from *convivium* feast, formed as CON- + *vivere* live: see -IAL.]
1 Of or befitting a feast or banquet; festive. M17.

J. CONRAD He sang his praises . . over a convivial glass.

2 Fond of feasting and good company; jovial. E18.

W. COWPER The plump convivial parson.

■ **convivialist** *noun* a person of convivial habits E19. **convivi'ality** *noun* the quality of being convivial; (the enjoyment of) festivity; convivial spirit: L18. **convivially** *adverb* E19.

convocate /'kɒnvəkeɪt/ *verb trans*. *arch*. Pa. pple & ppl adjective **-ate** /-ət/ (earlier), **-ated**. M16.
[ORIGIN Latin *convocat-* pa. ppl stem of *convocare*: see CONVOKE, -ATE[3].]
Call or summon together.

convocation /kɒnvəˈkeɪʃ(ə)n/ *noun*. LME.
[ORIGIN Latin *convocatio(n-)*, formed as CONVOCATE: see -ATION.]
1 The action of calling together or assembling by summons; the state or fact of being called together. LME.
2 *gen.* An assembly of people called together or summoned. LME.
3 A provincial assembly of the clergy. Now *spec.* a synod of the Anglican clergy of the province of Canterbury or York. LME.
4 A legislative or deliberative assembly of certain universities. E16.
†**5** The parliament of tinners in Cornwall. Cf. STANNATOR. Only in 18.
■ **convocational** *adjective* M17.

convoke /kənˈvəʊk/ *verb trans.* L16.
[ORIGIN Latin *convocare* call together, formed as CON- + *vocare* call.]
Call together; summon to assemble.

R. L. STEVENSON Where soft joys prevail, where people are convoked to pleasure. D. ACHESON That the President convoke a world-disarmament committee.

convolute /ˈkɒnvəluːt/ *adjective & noun*. L18.
[ORIGIN Latin *convolutus* pa. pple, formed as CONVOLUTE *verb*.]
► **A** *adjective*. **1** BOTANY & ZOOLOGY. Rolled longitudinally upon itself, as a leaf in the bud. L18.
2 *gen.* Convoluted. M19.
► **B** *noun*. Something of a convoluted form; a convolution. M19.

convolute /ˈkɒnvəluːt/ *verb*. *rare*. L17.
[ORIGIN Latin *convolut-*: see CONVOLUTION.]
†**1** *verb trans.* Twist or coil round (something); embrace. L17–E18.
2 *verb trans. & intrans.* Twist or wind about; coil up. (Earlier as CONVOLUTED.) E19.

convoluted /ˈkɒnvəl(j)uːtɪd/ *adjective*. L18.
[ORIGIN from CONVOLUTE *verb* + -ED¹.]
Coiled, twisted; complex, involved.

M. LASKI Elaborately convoluted fire-irons. B. CASTLE A convoluted statement of wonderful circularity.

convolution /kɒnvəˈluːʃ(ə)n/ *noun*. M16.
[ORIGIN medieval Latin *convolutio(n-)*, from Latin *convolut-* pa. ppl stem of *convolvere*: see CONVOLVE.]
1 A fold, turn, or twist (of something coiled); a complexity. M16. ▸**b** *spec.* Any of the folds of the surface of the brain. E17.
2 The action of coiling, twisting, or winding together; the condition of being convoluted. L16.
3 MATH. An integral function of two or more functions f_1, f_2, f_3, . . . of the type $\iiint f_1(x)f_2(y-x)f_3(z-y)\,dxdydz$; an analogous summation. M20.
■ **convolutional** *adjective* = CONVOLUTIONARY L19. **convolutionary** *adjective* of or pertaining to a convolution or convolutions, esp. of the brain E20.

convolve /kənˈvɒlv/ *verb*. L16.
[ORIGIN Latin *convolvere*, formed as CON- + *volvere* to roll.]
†**1** *verb trans.* Enclose in folds. L16–L18.
2 *verb trans.* Roll together; coil; twist. Freq. as ***convolved*** *ppl adjective*, convoluted. M17.
†**3** *verb trans.* In *pass.* Be contorted. M17–L18.
4 *verb intrans.* Revolve together. E19.

convolvulaceous /kənvɒlvjʊˈleɪʃəs/ *adjective*. M19.
[ORIGIN from mod. Latin *Convolvulaceae* (see below), formed as CONVOLVULUS: see -ACEOUS.]
BOTANY. Of or pertaining to the family Convolvulaceae, to which belong convolvulus and numerous other twining plants.

convolvulus /kənˈvɒlvjʊləs/ *noun*. Pl. **-luses**, **-li** /-lʌɪ, -liː/. M16.
[ORIGIN Latin = bindweed, formed as CONVOLVE.]
Any member of the large genus *Convolvulus* of twining plants (e.g. some bindweeds) with slender stems and trumpet-shaped flowers; *loosely* = BINDWEED 1.

convoy /ˈkɒnvɔɪ/ *noun*. Orig. *Scot.* E16.
[ORIGIN Old French & mod. French *convoi*, formed as CONVOY *verb*.]
†**1** Conduct (of oneself or of affairs). *Scot.* Only in 16.
2 An escort for courtesy's sake or for guidance or protection; *esp.* (**a**) a funeral train or cortège; (**b**) a group of warships escorting unarmed vessels. E16.

P. HOLLAND Heavie funerals and convoies of the dead. DRYDEN And with a convoy send him safe away.

3 The act of escorting as a courtesy or for guidance or protection; protection afforded by an escort. M16.

MILTON Through this adventurous glade . . to give him safe convoy.

4 An individual, company, supply of provisions, etc., under (protective) escort; a group of merchant ships, vehicles, etc., travelling under escort or together. L16.

A. HARDY Great merchant fleets, sailing in armed convoys. B. PLAIN A rumbling convoy of army vehicles.

5 †**a** A conducting medium, channel, way, or path. L16–M17. ▸**b** A brake for conducting a vehicle down an incline. Now *rare* or *obsolete*. M18.
†**6** A guide; a conductor. E17–E18.
– PHRASES: **in convoy** (travelling) under escort with others, as a group, together.

convoy /ˈkɒnvɔɪ/ *verb trans.* Orig. &, exc. in the usual mod. sense (4), chiefly *Scot.* LME.
[ORIGIN Old French & mod. French *convoyer* var. & mod. form of *conveier* CONVEY.]
1 Convey, carry. Now *rare*. LME.
†**2** Conduct or carry through (an affair); manage. LME–L18.
3 Escort, conduct; accompany (as a guide). *arch.* LME.
4 Escort with, or as, an armed force for protection; *esp.* (of a warship) escort merchant vessels in a convoy. L15.
†**5** Conduct or lead (a band of men); conduct or drive (a vehicle). E16–M17.
■ **convoyance** *noun* (now *rare* or *obsolete*) M16. **convoyer** *noun* L15.

convulsant /kənˈvʌls(ə)nt/ *adjective & noun*. L19.
[ORIGIN French, pres. pple of *convulser* CONVULSE.]
(A drug) that produces convulsions. Cf. ANTICONVULSANT.

convulse /kənˈvʌls/ *verb & noun*. M17.
[ORIGIN Latin *convuls-* pa. ppl stem of *convellere* pull violently, wrench, formed as CON- + *vellere* pluck, pull.]
► **A** *verb*. **1** *verb trans.* Shake violently; agitate or disturb severely. M17.

I. D'ISRAELI A revolution . . was to convulse England for many years. H. ROTH Suddenly a blind, shattering fury convulsed him.

2 *verb trans.* Affect with violent involuntary contraction of the muscles, producing contortion of the body or limbs; throw into convulsions. Usu. in *pass.* M17.
3 *verb intrans.* Become convulsed; go into convulsions. L17.

S. HILL The limbs perked and convulsed before going still again.

4 *verb trans.* Throw into a violent fit of laughter. M18.

M. HOLROYD If one caught sight of the other . . she would be convulsed with giggles.

► **B** *noun*. = CONVULSION. *rare*. E19.

convulsion /kənˈvʌlʃ(ə)n/ *noun*. M16.
[ORIGIN French, or Latin *convulsio(n-)*, formed as CONVULSE: see -ION.]
1 MEDICINE. Orig., cramp; spasms. Now, a violent involuntary contraction of the muscles producing contortion of the body or limbs. Freq. in *pl.* M16.

J. C. POWYS A person . . shaken by the convulsions of some terrible fit.

†**2** The action of wrenching; the condition of being wrenched. L16–E19.

MILTON Those two massy pillars With horrible convulsion to and fro He tugged, he shook.

3 Violent agitation or upheaval; social or political disturbance; violent natural disturbance, esp. produced by an earthquake etc. Usu. in *pl.* M17.

DISRAELI Her voice was choked with the convulsions of her passion. W. S. CHURCHILL The awful convulsions which would . . shiver into fragments the structures of the nineteenth century. E. F. BENSON The most terrific convulsion of Nature.

4 In *pl.* A violent fit of laughter. M18.
■ **convulsional** *adjective* (*rare*) of, pertaining to, or of the nature of convulsion(s) M19. **convulsionist** *noun* (*hist.*) (**a**) = CONVULSIONARY *noun*; (**b**) = CATASTROPHIST *noun*: E19.

convulsionary /kənˈvʌlʃ(ə)n(ə)ri/ *noun & adjective*. M18.
[ORIGIN from CONVULSION + -ARY¹, after French *convulsionnaire*.]
► **A** *noun*. *hist.* A member of a sect of Jansenist fanatics in France in the 18th cent., who repeatedly threw themselves into convulsions. M18.
► **B** *adjective*. **1** Pertaining to, affected with, or marked by convulsion(s). L18.
2 *hist.* Of or pertaining to the convulsionaries. E19.

convulsive /kənˈvʌlsɪv/ *adjective*. E17.
[ORIGIN from CONVULSE *verb* + -IVE. Cf. French *convulsif*.]
1 Of the nature of or characterized by convulsion(s). E17.

T. COLLINS The convulsive sobs which the girl vainly tried to repress.

2 Affected with convulsion(s). L17.
3 Producing convulsion(s). L17.

DRYDEN Convulsive rage possess'd Her trembling limbs, and heav'd her lab'ring breast.

■ **convulsively** *adverb* L18. **convulsiveness** *noun* L19.

cony /ˈkəʊni/ *noun*. Also (the usual form in HERALDRY) **coney**; (*obsolete* exc. as in sense 4b, where now the only form) **cunny** /ˈkʌni/. ME.
[ORIGIN Anglo-Norman *coning*, Old French *conin*, from Latin *cuniculus*. In senses 4a & (esp.) 4b infl. by CUNT.]
1 A rabbit. Now *arch.* & *dial.* exc. HERALDRY. ME.
2 The skin or fur of a rabbit. ME.
3 **a** A rock hyrax. (In biblical translations and allusions translating Hebrew *šāpān*.) LME. ▸**b** A pika. *N. Amer.* L19.
4 †**a** Used as a term of endearment or (later) abuse for a woman. Cf. CUNT 2. E16–L17. ▸**b** The female genitals. *coarse slang*. E17.
†**5** A dupe. Latterly only in ***cony-catcher*** below. L16–E19.
6 A sea bass, *Cephalopholis fulva*, of the tropical Atlantic. See also ***cony-fish*** below. L19.
– COMB.: †**cony-catch** *verb trans.* dupe, gull; †**cony-catcher** (**a**) a person who catches rabbits; (**b**) a person who catches dupes, a swindler; **cony-fish** *dial.* a burbot; **cony-garth** (now *dial.*) a rabbit warren; **cony-wool** the fur of the rabbit.
– NOTE: The historical pronunc. is /ˈkʌni/, but during the 19th cent. this was superseded by /ˈkəʊni/ except in, and perh. partly because of, sense 4b.

conynger /ˈkʌnɪndʒə/ *noun*. Long *obsolete* exc. *dial.* Also **conyger** /ˈkʌnɪdʒə/, **conygree** /ˈkʌnɪgriː/, & other vars. ME.
[ORIGIN Old French *con(n)iniere* var. of *con(n)il(l)iere* from medieval Latin *cunicularium*, pl. *-aria*, from Latin *cuniculus* rabbit: see -ARY¹.]
A rabbit warren.

conyza /kəˈnʌɪzə/ *noun*. LME.
[ORIGIN Latin from Greek *konuza*.]
Orig., fleabane (genus *Inula*) or a similar plant. Now, a plant of the genus *Conyza* (which formerly included *Inula* species), of the composite family.

coo /kuː/ *verb & noun*. M17.
[ORIGIN Imit.]
► **A** *verb*. 3 sing. pres. **coo(e)s**.
1 *verb intrans.* Of a pigeon: make its natural soft murmuring sound. Of a person, esp. an infant: make a sound similar to this. M17.
2 *verb intrans.* Converse caressingly or amorously. Chiefly in ***bill and coo*** s.v. BILL *verb*¹ 2b. L17.
3 *verb trans.* Utter or express by cooing. L18.
► **B** *noun*. A sound (as) of a pigeon. E18.
■ **cooer** *noun* M19. **cooingly** *adverb* in a cooing manner E19.

coo /kuː/ *interjection*. *slang*. Also **coo-er** /kuːˈɜː/. E20.
[ORIGIN Imit.]
Expr. surprise or incredulity.

cooba(h) *noun* var. of COUBA.

cooee /ˈkuːɪ, -iː/ *noun, interjection, & verb*. Chiefly *Austral.* & *NZ*. Also **cooey**. L18.
[ORIGIN Imit. of a signal used by Aborigines and copied by settlers.]
► **A** *noun & interjection*. (A call or cry) used as a signal to draw attention to the caller. L18.
within a cooee (of), **within cooee (of)** *colloq.* within hailing distance (of), within easy reach (of), near (to).
► **B** *verb intrans.* Pa. t. & pple **cooeed**. Utter this call. E19.

coo-er *interjection* see COO *interjection*.

cooey *noun, interjection, & verb* var. of COOEE.

coof /kuːf/ *noun*. *Scot.* E18.
[ORIGIN Unknown.]
A dull spiritless person.

cook /kʊk/ *noun*. OE.
[ORIGIN popular Latin *cocus* for Latin *coquus*.]
1 A person (orig. *spec.* a male) who cooks, esp. as an occupation; a person responsible for the preparation of food for the table. OE. ▸**b** *fig.* A person who falsifies or concocts something. *rare*. E17.

Proverb: Too many cooks spoil the broth.

plain cook: see PLAIN *adjective*¹ & *adverb*.
2 CHESS. An unforeseen second solution that spoils a problem, position, etc. L19.
– COMB.: **cook-general**, pl. **cooks-general**, a domestic servant who does both housework and cookery; **cook-maid** a maid who cooks or assists a cook; **cook's knife** a general-purpose kitchen knife. (See also combs. of COOK *verb*.)
■ **cookess** *noun* (*rare*) a female cook LME. **cookless** *adjective* without a cook M19.

cook /kʊk/ *verb*. LME.
[ORIGIN from the noun.]
1 *verb intrans.* Act as cook; prepare food for eating with the application of heat. LME.
2 **a** *verb trans.* Prepare for eating with the application of heat. L15. ▸**b** *verb intrans.* Of food: undergo the process of being cooked. M19. ▸**c** *verb trans. & intrans.* Prepare (opium) for use by heating. L19.
3 *verb trans.* Concoct, make *up*, invent. E17.

W. GOLDING I don't think there's a scientific explanation though . . you may cook one up.

4 *verb trans.* Falsify; alter surreptitiously to produce a desired result. *colloq.* M17.

Times The evidence about the bribes was the evidence of . . gentlemen who cooked the books.

5 *verb trans.* Ruin, spoil, defeat; *spec.* in CHESS, spoil (a problem, position, etc.) by discovering an alternative solution. M19.

H. ROBBINS You can't afford to sit still . . If you do, you're cooked.

6 *verb trans. & intrans.* Make or become radioactive. *colloq.* M20.
7 *verb intrans.* Play music with excitement or inspiration; perform or proceed well. *slang*. M20.
– PHRASES: **cook a person's goose** *slang* spoil a person's plans, cause a person's downfall. **cook on the front burner**, **cook with gas** *N. Amer. slang* be on the right lines, be on the way to rapid success. ***pressure cook***: see PRESSURE *noun*. **what's cooking?** *colloq.* what is happening? what is being planned?
– COMB.: **cookbook** a cookery book; *gen.* an instruction manual, a detailed account or list; **cook-camp** *N. Amer.* the part of a camp where the cooking is done; a building used as kitchen and eating room; **cook-chill** *verb & noun* (**a**) *verb trans.* cook and then immediately refrigerate (food) for later reheating; (**b**) *noun* the process or

C

practice of cook-chilling food; **cookhouse**, **cook-room** an outdoor or camp kitchen; a ship's galley; **cook-shack** *N. Amer.* a shack used for cooking; **cookshop** an eating house; *NZ* a sheep station's kitchen; **cook stove** *US* a cooking stove; **cooktop** a cooking unit, usu. with hot plates or burners, built into or fixed on the top of a cabinet etc.; **cookware** utensils used in cooking.
▪ **cookable** *adjective & noun* (something) that may be cooked **M19**.

cookee *noun* see **COOKIE** *noun*².

C

cooker /ˈkʊkə/ *noun*. **M19**.
[**ORIGIN** from **COOK** *verb* + **-ER**¹.]
1 A person who concocts or manipulates something. **M19**.
2 A stove or other apparatus used for cooking; a vessel in which something is cooked. **L19**.
electric cooker, ***gas cooker***, ***pressure cooker***, ***slow cooker***, etc.
3 A fruit, esp. an apple, or other eatable, which cooks well, and is better eaten cooked than raw. **L19**.
– **COMB.**: **cooker hood** a canopy or hood above a cooker for extracting smells, smoke, etc.

cookery /ˈkʊk(ə)ri/ *noun*. **LME**.
[**ORIGIN** from **COOK** *noun* or *verb* + **-ERY**.]
1 The art or practice of cooking; the preparation of food using heat. **LME**.
2 A place for cooking, a kitchen. Now *US*. **L16**.
3 The action of concocting a work, falsifying figures, etc. **E18**.
4 (An item of) cooked food. *rare*. **M18**.
– **COMB.**: **cookery book** a book of recipes and instructions for cooking.

cookie /ˈkʊki/ *noun*¹. Orig. chiefly *Scot. & N. Amer.* Also **cooky**. **E18**.
[**ORIGIN** Dutch *koekje* dim. of *koek* cake.]
1 Any of various small cakes; (orig. *N. Amer.*) a small flat sweet cake, a biscuit. In Scotland also, a plain bun. **E18**.
the way the cookie crumbles *colloq.* (chiefly *N. Amer.*) how things turn out, the unalterable state of things.
2 A woman, *esp.* an attractive girl; a person of a specified kind. *slang*. **E20**.

W. R. BURNETT He's a real tough cookie and you know it.

3 A bomb. *Air Force slang*. **M20**.
4 COMPUTING. A packet of data sent by an Internet server to a browser, which is returned by the browser each time it subsequently accesses the same server, thereby identifying the user or monitoring his or her access to the server. **L20**.
– **COMB.**: **cookie cutter** (chiefly *N. Amer.*) (***a***) a device with sharp edges for cutting dough for biscuits etc. into particular shapes; (***b***) *attrib.* denoting something mass-produced or lacking individual character; **cookie jar** a jar for biscuits etc.; *transf. & fig.* a place where good things are kept, a source of good things; **cookie-pusher** *US colloq.* a diplomat who devotes time to protocol and social engagements rather than to work, a person only superficially effective in his or her work; **cookie sheet** (chiefly *N. Amer.*) a flat metal tray on which biscuits etc. may be cooked.

cookie /ˈkʊki/ *noun*². Also (chiefly *N. Amer.*) **cookee**, **cooky**. **L18**.
[**ORIGIN** from **COOK** *noun* + **-Y**⁶, **-IE**.]
(A name for) a cook; *esp.* (*N. Amer.*) an assistant cook in a camp.

cooking /ˈkʊkɪŋ/ *verbal noun*. **M17**.
[**ORIGIN** from **COOK** *verb* + **-ING**¹.]
The action of **COOK** *verb*; the style of this. Also, food that has been cooked.

I. BANKS There was a faint smell of institutional cooking.

home cooking, ***plain cooking***, etc.
– **ATTRIB. & COMB.**: In the sense 'suitable for or used in cooking', as ***cooking apple***, ***cooking sherry***, etc. Special combs., as ***cooking range***: see **RANGE** *noun*¹; ***cooking stove*** a stove used for cooking; **cooking top** = ***cooktop*** s.v. **COOK** *verb*.

cookout /ˈkʊkaʊt/ *noun*. Also **cook-out**. **M20**.
[**ORIGIN** from **COOK** *noun*, *verb* + **OUT** *adverb*.]
A gathering at which food is cooked in the open air; a barbecue.

Cook's tour /kʊks ˈtʊə, ˈtɔː/ *noun phr.* **E20**.
[**ORIGIN** Thomas *Cook* (1808–92), English travel agent.]
A tour or journey in which many places are visited, often briefly.

cooky *noun* var. of **COOKIE** *noun*¹, *noun*².

cool /kuːl/ *noun*. **LME**.
[**ORIGIN** from the adjective.]
1 That which is cool or moderately cold; the cool part, place, time, etc. **LME**.

M. SINCLAIR Papa walked in the garden in the cool of the evening.

2 = **COOLNESS** 1. Now *rare*. **LME**.
3 Composure, relaxedness. Esp. in ***keep one's cool***, ***lose one's cool***. *slang*. **M20**.

S. BELLOW My interviewer's detachment or professional cool.

blow one's cool: see **BLOW** *verb*¹.

cool /kuːl/ *adjective*.
[**ORIGIN** Old English *cōl* = Middle Low German, Middle Dutch *kōl* (Dutch *koel*) from Germanic, from base also of **COLD** *adjective*.]
1 Moderately cold; agreeable and refreshing, in contrast with heat or cold; producing or maintaining a feeling of coolness; suggestive of coolness. **OE**.
2 Not affected by passion or emotion; undisturbed, calm. **OE**. ▸**b** Assured and unabashed where diffidence might be expected; calmly audacious in making a proposal or demand. **E19**.

D. LESSING Very cool, clear and efficient, she found . . a new flat and settled into it. **b** A. CHRISTIE Cool customer. Not giving anything away, is he? A. EDEN A deed of cool and outstanding bravery.

3 Lacking enthusiasm or warmth of interest; lacking in cordiality. **L16**.

E. GASKELL He had been friendly, though the Cranford ladies had been cool.

4 Of a sum of money: actual, no less than. (Chiefly used as an intensive.) *colloq.* **E18**.

A. SILLITOE Mam collected a cool five hundred in insurance and benefits.

5 (Esp. of jazz music) restrained or relaxed in style (opp. ***hot***); *gen.* admirably up to date, fashionable, stylish; good, excellent, pleasing. *colloq.* **L19**.

Dazed & Confused If it tells a story to me, that's cool. *New York Times* I wanted to buy my brother a really cool . . birthday present. JIM GOAD I'm wearing . . platform shoes, so I still look really cool.

– **PHRASES**: ***cool as a cucumber***: see **CUCUMBER** 2. **leave a person cool** not particularly excite or interest a person. ***play it cool***: see **PLAY** *verb*.
– **SPECIAL COLLOCATIONS & COMB.**: **cool box** an insulated box for keeping food cool. **cool chamber**: where perishable goods may be kept cool. **cool-headed** *adjective* not easily excited; calm. **cool-house** a greenhouse kept at a cool temperature. **cool store**: where perishable goods may be kept cool. **cool tankard** *arch.* a cooling drink, usu. made of wine, water, lemon juice, spices, and borage.
▪ **coolish** *adjective* somewhat cool **E18**. **coolly** /-(l)li/ *adverb* **L16**.

cool /kuːl/ *verb*.
[**ORIGIN** Old English *cōlian* = Old Saxon *cōlon*, from Germanic, from base of **COOL** *adjective*: cf. **KEEL** *verb*¹.]
1 *verb intrans.* Become less hot; *fig.* become less zealous or ardent, lose the heat of excitement or passion. Freq. foll. by *down*, *off*, (*US colloq.*) *out*. **OE**. ▸†**b** Of a thing: lose its opportuneness. *rare* (Shakes.). **L16–E17**. ▸†**c** Of the senses: become cold with fear. *rare* (Shakes.). Only in **E17**.

SCOTT FITZGERALD The rain cooled . . to a damp mist. T. MORRISON You want to calm down . . . Cool out. M. MEYER Strindberg cooled on the idea, the project lapsed.

2 *verb trans.* Make less hot; cause to lose heat; *fig.* make less zealous or ardent, diminish the intensity of (strong feeling, resolve). Also foll. by *down*, (*US colloq.*) *out*. **ME**. ▸**b** Deprive (a thing) of its opportuneness. *rare*. **E18**.

B. SPOCK Bring to a boil, . . then cool it down to body temperature. B. PLAIN The hard slick metal cooled her burning shoulders and back.

3 *verb trans.* Kill. *US slang*. **M20**.
– **PHRASES**: **cool it** *slang* calm down, relax, go more slowly. **cool one's heels** rest; be kept standing or waiting. **cool out** *slang* relax. ***keep one's breath to cool one's porridge***, ***save one's breath to cool one's porridge***: see **BREATH**.

coolabah *noun* var. of **COOLIBAH**.

coolamon /ˈkuːləmən/ *noun*. *Austral.* Also **-liman** /-lɪmən/. **M19**.
[**ORIGIN** Kamilaroi *gulaman*.]
A vessel made of wood or bark for carrying water etc.

coolant /ˈkuːl(ə)nt/ *noun*. **M20**.
[**ORIGIN** from **COOL** *verb* + **-ANT**¹, after **LUBRICANT**.]
A cooling agent; *esp.* (***a***) a liquid used to cool and lubricate a cutting tool; (***b***) a fluid for removing heat from an engine or a nuclear reactor.

cooler /ˈkuːlə/ *noun*. **L16**.
[**ORIGIN** from **COOL** *verb* + **-ER**¹.]
1 Something that cools or makes cool (*lit. & fig.*); *N. Amer.* a refrigerator, an insulated picnic box, jug, etc. **L16**. ▸**b** A cooling medicine (*arch.*); a cooling drink; a long drink, now *esp.* one containing some alcohol or for mixing with alcohol; a mixture of wine and soda water, a spritzer. **E17**.
2 A vessel in which something is cooled; *spec.* one used for cooling the wort in brewing, or for crystallizing the syrup in sugar refining. **L16**. ▸**b** Something which cools water; a place where or machine from which cool drinking water is available. *N. Amer.* **M19**.
3 A prison, a prison cell. *slang*. **L19**.

Cooley's anaemia /ˈkuːlɪz əˈniːmɪə/ *noun phr.* Also ***Cooley's anemia**. **M20**.
[**ORIGIN** Thomas B. *Cooley* (1871–1945), US paediatrician.]
MEDICINE. = ***THALASSAEMIA major***.

Coolgardie safe /kuːlˈgɑːdi seɪf/ *noun phr.* *Austral.* **E20**.
[**ORIGIN** A town in Western Australia + **SAFE** *noun*.]
A food safe made of netting and cooled by strips of fabric suspended round it with their ends in water.

coolibah /ˈkuːlɪbɑː/ *noun*. *Austral.* Also **-lab-** /-ləb-/. **L19**.
[**ORIGIN** Yuwaaliyaay (an Aboriginal language of northern New South Wales) *gulabaa*.]
More fully ***coolibah tree***. Any of various eucalypts, esp. *Eucalyptus microtheca*, which is usu. found by watercourses.

coolie /ˈkuːli/ *noun & adjective*. Also **-ly**. **L16**.
[**ORIGIN** Sense A.1 formed as **KOLI**. Sense A.2 from Hindi, Telugu *kūlī* day-labourer, prob. from Tamil, Telugu *kūli* hire; assoc. with Urdu *kulī* slave from Turkish.]
▸ **A** *noun*. **1** = **KOLI** *noun*. Now *rare* or *obsolete*. **L16**.
2 A (non-European) hired labourer or burden-carrier in India, China, and elsewhere. **M17**. ▸**b** A person from the Indian subcontinent, a person of Indian descent. *derog. & offensive*. *S. Afr.* **L19**.
▸ **B** *attrib.* or as ***adjective***. That is a coolie; of or pertaining to coolies. **E19**.
coolie hat a broad conical hat, usu. made of straw, similar to those worn in Asia by coolies.

cooliman *noun* var. of **COOLAMON**.

cooling /ˈkuːlɪŋ/ *verbal noun*. **ME**.
[**ORIGIN** from **COOL** *verb* + **-ING**¹.]
The action of **COOL** *verb*. (Foll. by *down*, *off*.)
– **COMB.**: **cooling-off period**: to allow time for reflection before committing oneself; ***cooling pond***: see **POND** *noun* 2a; **cooling tower** a tall tower for cooling hot water from an industrial process before reuse.

coolness /ˈkuːlnɪs/ *noun*. **OE**.
[**ORIGIN** from **COOL** *adjective* + **-NESS**.]
1 The condition of being or feeling moderately cold. **OE**.

Century Magazine The dewy coolness of the morning.

2 *fig.* Freedom from excitement. **M17**.
3 Lack of enthusiasm or friendly warmth. **L17**.
4 Calm and unabashed assurance. **M18**.

Argosy Coolness is as essential to the soldier as courage.

5 A relaxed or cool quality or style. **M20**.

coolth /kuːlθ/ *noun*. **M16**.
[**ORIGIN** from **COOL** *adjective* + **-TH**¹: cf. **WARMTH**.]
= **COOLNESS** 1.
– **NOTE**: Rare before **20**.

cooly *noun & adjective* var. of **COOLIE**.

coom /kuːm/ *noun*. **L16**.
[**ORIGIN** In senses 1, 2 app. a var. of **CULM** *noun*¹. In sense 3 prob. a different word.]
1 Soot. *obsolete* exc. *Scot. & N. English*. **L16**.
2 Coal dust or refuse. *obsolete* exc. *Scot. & N. English*. **E17**.
3 A black grease or dust from axles or bearings. **E18**.
▪ **coomy** *adjective* dirty with coom **E19**.

coomb /kuːm/ *noun*¹. Also **comb**.
[**ORIGIN** Old English *cumb* prob. identical with older Low German *kumb*, High German *kump(f)*, mod. Low German, High German *kumm*, mod. German *Kumme*.]
†**1** A vessel, a cup. Only in **OE**.
†**2** A brewing tub or vat. **LME–M19**.
3 A dry unit of capacity equal to four bushels. **LME**.

coomb *noun*² var. of **COMBE** *noun*.

coomb *noun*³ var. of **COMB** *noun*².

coon /kuːn/ *noun & verb*. Chiefly *N. Amer.* **M18**.
[**ORIGIN** Abbreviation of **RACCOON**.]
▸ **A** *noun*. **1** A raccoon. **M18**.
2 One of the US Whigs (1834–56), who had the raccoon as an emblem. **M19**.
3 A sly knowing person. *colloq.* **M19**.
4 A black person. *slang. offensive*. **M19**.
5 A member of any of the colourfully costumed dance troupes which parade through the streets of Cape Town during an annual New Year carnival. *S. Afr.* **E20**.
– **COMB. & PHRASES**: **a coon's age** *US slang* a long time; ***a gone coon***: see **GONE** *adjective* 1; **coon dog**, **coonhound** *US* a dog trained to hunt raccoons; **coonskin** *noun & adjective* (***a***) *noun* (a cap etc. made from) the skin of a raccoon; (***b***) *adjective* made from coonskin; **coon song** *arch.* (now considered *offensive*) (a popular song resembling) a song sung by black people.
▸ **B** *verb trans. & intrans.* Creep along (a branch etc.) clinging close like a raccoon. **M19**.

cooncan /ˈkuːnkan/ *noun*. **L19**.
[**ORIGIN** Perh. from Spanish *¿con quién?* with whom?]
A card game of Mexican origin, for two players and ancestral to (gin) rummy. Formerly also, a form of this played with two packs each with two jokers.

coonjine /ˈkuːndʒʌɪn/ *verb & noun*. *US slang*. **L19**.
[**ORIGIN** Unknown.]
▸ **A** *verb intrans. & trans.* Walk or carry in a waddling shuffling manner (orig. associated with black riverboat loaders); sing songs while doing this. **L19**.
▸ **B** *noun*. A waddling shuffling walk. **M20**.

coontie /ˈkuːnti/ *noun*. *US*. Also **-tah** /-tə/. **L18**.
[**ORIGIN** Seminole *kunti*.]
Any of several low-growing palmlike cycads of the genus *Zamia*, native to tropical and subtropical America; the arrowroot yielded by these plants.

coop /kuːp/ *noun*¹. **ME**.
[**ORIGIN** = Middle Low German, Middle Dutch *kūpe* (Dutch *kuip* tub, vat) = Old Saxon *kōpa*, Old High German *kuofa* (German *Kufe*) cask, from Latin *cupa*, medieval Latin *copa* tun, barrel.]
†**1** *gen.* A basket. Only in **ME**.
2 A wickerwork basket used in catching fish. **ME**.
3 A cage or pen for confining poultry etc. **ME**.
4 A narrow place of confinement; *slang* a prison. **L18**.

– PHRASES: **fly the coop** *N. Amer. slang* leave abruptly.

coop /kuːp/ *noun*[2]. E19.
[ORIGIN Unknown.]
A small heap of soft material, esp. manure.

coop *noun*[3] var. of COUP *noun*[2].

coop /kuːp/ *verb trans.* L16.
[ORIGIN from COOP *noun*[1].]
1 Put or confine (poultry etc.) in a coop. (Foll. by *up*.) L16.
2 Confine (a person) in an irksomely small space. Formerly also, confine (a thing or substance) within a vessel or narrow limits. Usu. foll. by *up*. L16.

P. G. WODEHOUSE He had had a boring afternoon, cooped up in his room. R. SUTCLIFF Cooped within doors all winter long.

3 Surround with a protective grating or fence. Now *rare* or *obsolete*. M17.

co-op /ˈkəʊɒp/ *noun & adjective. colloq.* M19.
[ORIGIN Abbreviation.]
= COOPERATIVE; *spec.* a cooperative society, store, or (*N. Amer.*) dwelling.

Spare Rib This press is a co-op . . so please don't ask to see the boss . . or the manager. *New Yorker* We bought a co-op overlooking the Hudson on Riverside Drive.

cooper /ˈkuːpə/ *noun & verb.* ME.
[ORIGIN Middle Dutch, Middle Low German *kūper*, formed as COOP *noun*[1]: see -ER[1].]
▸ **A** *noun.* **1** A skilled worker who makes and repairs wooden vessels formed of staves and hoops, as casks, tubs, etc. ME. ▸**b** A crew member on a ship who repairs casks etc. E17.
2 A person engaged in the trade of sampling, bottling, or retailing wine. E16.
3 A bottle basket used in wine cellars. E19.
4 A drink composed of a mixture of stout and porter, orig. drunk by the coopers in breweries. L19.
– COMB.: **cooper-shop** *arch.* a shop selling wine.
▸ **B** *verb trans.* **1** Make or repair the staves or hoops of (casks etc.); equip or secure with hoops. E18.
2 Put or stow in casks. M18.
3 Foll. by *up*: get into a presentable form. *colloq.* E19.
4 Ruin, spoil. *slang.* M19.

cooperage /ˈkuːp(ə)rɪdʒ/ *noun.* L15.
[ORIGIN from COOPER *noun* + -AGE.]
1 Cooper's work; a cooper's products. L15.
2 Money payable for a cooper's work. M17.
3 A cooper's workshop. E18.

cooperant /kəʊˈɒpər(ə)nt/ *adjective & noun.* Also **co-operant**. LME.
[ORIGIN ecclesiastical Latin *cooperant-* pres. ppl stem of *cooperari*: see COOPERATE *verb*, -ANT[1].]
▸ **A** *adjective.* Working together or for the same purpose. LME.
▸ **B** *noun.* A cooperating agent or factor. *rare.* M16.
■ **cooperancy** *noun* (*a*) the state of being cooperant; †(*b*) cooperation: M17.

cooperate /kəʊˈɒpərət/ *adjective.* Also **co-operate**. M19.
[ORIGIN from COOPERATION after *corporation*, *corporate*, etc.]
Caused to cooperate; brought into cooperation; cooperative.

cooperate /kəʊˈɒpəreɪt/ *verb intrans.* Also **co-operate**. L16.
[ORIGIN ecclesiastical Latin *cooperat-* pa. ppl stem of *cooperari*, formed as CO- + *operari* OPERATE: see -ATE[3].]
1 Of things: concur in producing an effect. L16.
2 Of people: work together for the same purpose or in the same task. Of an individual: act jointly with or *with* another (*in* a task, (*arch.*) *to* an end); participate in a joint or mutual enterprise. E17.

C. ODETS We want to make your boy famous, a millionaire, but he won't let us—won't co-operate. D. MAY The French Vichy government . . co-operated erratically with the Germans.

3 Practise economic or industrial cooperation. E19.

cooperation /kəʊˌɒpəˈreɪʃ(ə)n/ *noun.* Also **co-operation**. LME.
[ORIGIN Latin *cooperatio(n-)*, formed as COOPERATE *verb*: see -ATION. Later partly, through French *coopération*.]
1 The action of working together for the same purpose or in the same task. LME.

C. BROOKE-ROSE Structures of power . . depend on the assistance and cooperation of innumerable individuals.

2 The combination of a number of individuals in an economic activity so that all may share the benefits. E19.

H. FAWCETT The essential characteristic of cooperation is a union of capital and labour.

■ **cooperationist** *noun* a person who practises or advocates cooperation M19.

cooperative /kəʊˈɒp(ə)rətɪv/ *adjective & noun.* Also **co-operative**. E17.
[ORIGIN Late Latin *cooperativus*, formed as COOPERATE *verb*: see -IVE. Later partly, through French *coopératif*.]
▸ **A** *adjective.* **1** Working together, acting jointly; willing to cooperate; of or pertaining to cooperation. E17.

H. H. MILMAN Four great principles . . mutually cooperative. G. BROWN The Boilermakers, often accused of being troublemakers . . , proved splendidly cooperative.

2 Pertaining to economic or industrial cooperation; based on the principle of cooperation; *N. Amer.* (of a dwelling) jointly owned or leased by the occupiers. E19.
cooperative farm: in which the profits are shared by all those involved in it. **cooperative society** a union of people for the production or distribution of goods, in which the profits are shared by the members. **cooperative store** a store or shop belonging to a cooperative society, the profits being shared among the members and customers.
▸ **B** *noun.* **1** A cooperationist; a member of a cooperative society. *rare.* E19.
2 A cooperative society or store; an organization or business owned by its workers or those who use its services. L19.
3 A dwelling jointly owned or leased by the occupiers. *N. Amer.* M20.
■ **cooperatively** *adverb* M19. **cooperativeness** *noun* M17. **coopera'tivity** *noun* L20. **cooperativi'zation** *noun* the action of organizing or restructuring as a cooperative or as cooperatives M20.

cooperator /kəʊˈɒpəreɪtə/ *noun.* Also **co-operator**. LME.
[ORIGIN ecclesiastical Latin = fellow worker, formed as COOPERATE *verb*: see -OR.]
1 A person who cooperates. LME.
2 A cooperationist; a member of a cooperative society. E19.

Cooper pair /ˈkuːpə pɛː/ *noun phr.* M20.
[ORIGIN L. N. *Cooper* (b. 1930), US physicist.]
A loosely bound pair of electrons with opposite spins and moving with the same speed in opposite directions, held to be responsible for the phenomenon of superconductivity; a similar bound pair of atoms in a superfluid.

Cooper's hawk /ˈkuːpəz hɔːk/ *noun phr.* E19.
[ORIGIN William *Cooper* (1798–1864), US naturalist.]
A N. American bird of prey, *Accipiter cooperii*, resembling but smaller than the goshawk.

coopery /ˈkuːpəri/ *noun.* LME.
[ORIGIN from COOPER *noun* + -Y[3]: see -ERY.]
= COOPERAGE 1.

co-opt /kəʊˈɒpt/ *verb.* Also ***coöpt**. M17.
[ORIGIN Latin *cooptare*, formed as CO- + *optare* choose.]
1 *verb trans. & intrans.* Elect (a person) to a body by the votes of its existing members. M17.
2 *verb trans.* Absorb into a larger (esp. political) group; take over, adopt, (an idea etc.). *N. Amer.* M20.
■ **co-optable** *adjective* L20. **co-optee** *noun* a person who is co-opted M20. **co-option** *noun* the action of co-opting L19. **co-optive** *adjective* pertaining to co-option; (composed of members) chosen by co-option: L19.

co-optate /kəʊˈɒpteɪt/ *verb trans.* Now *rare.* Also ***coöp-**. E17.
[ORIGIN Latin *cooptat-* pa. ppl stem of *cooptare*: see CO-OPT, -ATE[3].]
= CO-OPT. Formerly more widely, elect, choose, admit to a body.
■ **co-optative** *adjective* = CO-OPTIVE L19.

co-optation /kəʊɒpˈteɪʃ(ə)n/ *noun.* Also ***coöp-**. M16.
[ORIGIN Latin *cooptatio(n-)*, formed as CO-OPTATE: see -ATION.]
Election into a body by the votes of its existing members. Formerly more widely, election, adoption.

coordinate /kəʊˈɔːdɪnət/ *adjective & noun.* Also **co-ordinate**, ***coör-**. M17.
[ORIGIN from CO- + Latin *ordinatus* (see ORDINATE *adjective*) after earlier SUBORDINATE *adjective*.]
▸ **A** *adjective.* **1** Of the same order; equal in rank (*with*); GRAMMAR designating each clause of a compound sentence. Opp. SUBORDINATE *adjective*. M17.
2 Involving coordination, coordinated. M18.
3 CHEMISTRY. Designating a type of covalent bond in which one atom, ion, or molecule provides both the shared electrons. E20.
4 Designating a university having separate classes or colleges for men and women students or a college, esp. for women, of such a university. *US.* E20.
▸ **B** *noun.* **1** MATH. Each of a set of two or more quantities used to define the position of a point, line, or plane, by reference to a fixed system of lines, points, etc. E19.
Cartesian coordinates, ***homogeneous coordinates***, ***polar coordinates***, ***rectangular coordinates***, ***trilinear coordinates***, etc.
2 A person or thing of the same rank as another; an equal; an equivalent; *US* a coordinate college. M19.

Publishers Weekly Kirkland College in Clinton, N.Y., the women's co-ordinate of prestigious Hamilton College for men.

3 In *pl.* Clothes matching in colour, fabric, or other features. M20.
■ **coordinately** *adverb* L17.

coordinate /kəʊˈɔːdɪneɪt/ *verb.* Also **co-or-**, ***coör-**. M17.
[ORIGIN from CO- + Latin *ordinare* (see ORDINATE *verb*), after SUBORDINATE *verb*.]
1 *verb trans.* Make coordinate or equal; place or class in the same rank or division. M17.
coordinating conjunction GRAMMAR: placed between words, phrases, clauses, or sentences of equal rank, e.g. *and*, *but*.
2 *verb trans.* Cause (things or persons) to function together or occupy their proper place as parts of an interrelated whole. M19.

D. LESSING Nothing would work if someone didn't co-ordinate things.

3 *verb intrans.* Act in the proper order for the production of a particular result. M19.
4 *verb trans. & intrans.* CHEMISTRY. Be or become linked *with* or *to* (an atom or atoms) by a coordinate bond; form a coordinate bond or coordination compound (with). E20.
■ **coordinative** *adjective* †(*a*) involving coordination; (*b*) placing in proper order, coordinating: M17. **coordinator** *noun* (*a*) a person who or thing which coordinates; (*b*) GRAMMAR a coordinating conjunction: M19.

C

coordination /kəʊˌɔːdɪˈneɪʃ(ə)n/ *noun.* Also **co-ordination**, ***coör-**. E17.
[ORIGIN Old French & mod. French, or late Latin *coordinatio(n-)*, from Latin CO- + *ordinatio(n-)* ORDINATION.]
†**1** Orderly combination. E–M17.
2 The action or result of placing in the same degree or rank. M17.
3 The action or result of placing things in due order or relation to each other; the harmonious functioning together of different interrelated parts. M19.

E. H. ERIKSON Man's . . highly specialized brain-eye-hand coordination.

4 CHEMISTRY. The formation or existence of a coordinate bond; linking by means of a coordinate bond. E20.
– COMB.: **coordination compound** CHEMISTRY: containing coordinate bonds, esp. between a central atom (usu. of a metal) and a definite number of other atoms or groups; **coordination number** CHEMISTRY (*a*) the number of atoms linked to the central atom or group in a coordination compound; (*b*) the number of ions surrounding a molecule or ion in a crystal.

coot /kuːt/ *noun*[1]. ME.
[ORIGIN Prob. of Low German origin: cf. Dutch *koet*.]
1 An aquatic bird, *Fulica atra*, belonging to the rail family, with black and dark grey plumage and the upper mandible extended backwards to form a white plate on the forehead; any other bird of the genus *Fulica*, esp. *F. americana* of N. America. ME.
as bald as a coot, ***bald coot***, ***baldicoot***: see BALD *adjective*.
2 Any of various other swimming or diving birds, *esp.* (*a*) the guillemot; (*b*) the water rail; (*c*) the moorhen. *dial.* ME.
3 A silly person; a man, a chap. *colloq.* M18.

X. HERBERT He's a good sort of coot. R. CHANDLER The widow of an old coot with whiskers.

coot /kuːt/ *noun*[2]. *Scot.* Also †**cute**. E16.
[ORIGIN Of Low German origin.]
1 The ankle joint. E16.
2 The fetlock of a horse. Now *rare.* L17.

Cootamundra /kuːtəˈmʌndrə/ *noun.* E20.
[ORIGIN A town in New South Wales, Australia.]
More fully ***Cootamundra wattle***. A small Australian tree, *Acacia baileyana*, with feathery foliage and fluffy golden flowers.

cooter /ˈkuːtə/ *noun*[1]. E19.
[ORIGIN Unknown.]
Any of several freshwater turtles of the southern US, esp. of the genus *Pseudemys*. Cf. SLIDER 4.

cooter *noun*[2] var. of COUTER.

cootie /ˈkuːti/ *noun. slang.* Also **k-**. E20.
[ORIGIN Perh. from Malay *kutu* a biting insect.]
A body louse.

cootie /kuːti/ *adjective. Scot.* Also **cooty**. L18.
[ORIGIN from COOT *noun*[2] + -Y[1].]
Of a bird: having feathered legs.

cop /kɒp/ *noun*[1]. OE.
[ORIGIN Unknown. Several different words may be represented.]
1 The top of something, esp. a hill. OE. ▸†**b** A crest on a bird's head. L15–L18.
2 A conical heap of unbound barley, hay, etc. *dial.* E16.
3 A conical ball of thread wound on a spindle in a spinning machine. L18.
4 A hedge bank; an embankment. *dial.* E19.

cop /kɒp/ *noun*[2]. Long *obsolete* exc. *dial.* LME.
[ORIGIN Abbreviation of ATTERCOP.]
A spider.

cop /kɒp/ *noun*[3]. *obsolete* exc. *dial.* L17.
[ORIGIN Unknown.]
A movable frame used to extend the surface of a farm cart for bulky loads.

cop /kɒp/ *noun*[4]. *slang.* M19.
[ORIGIN from COP *verb*[2], COPPER *noun*[2].]
1 A police officer. M19.

C. BUKOWSKI The cops caught them and threw them in jail.

cops and robbers a children's game of hiding and chasing. ***motor cop***: see MOTOR *noun & adjective*. ***silent cop***: see SILENT *adjective*.
2 A capture, an arrest. Chiefly in ***a fair cop*** s.v. FAIR *adjective*. L19.

C

3 An acquisition; a welcome chance or opportunity. Chiefly *Austral. & NZ*. L19.
4 Value or use, esp. in something acquired. Chiefly with neg. E20.

J. TORRINGTON The wages aren't much cop.

– COMB.: **cop shop** a police station.

cop /kɒp/ *verb*¹ *trans.* Now *dial.* Infl. **-pp-**. M16.
[ORIGIN from COP *noun*¹.]
Heap up; stack.

cop /kɒp/ *verb*². *slang* (orig. *dial.*). Infl. **-pp-**. E18.
[ORIGIN Prob. var. of CAP *verb*².]
1 *verb trans.* Capture, catch; get, obtain; steal. E18.

J. MILNE I trembled in the darkness until I could cop a cab to Dockhead.

cop a packet: see PACKET *noun* 3. ***cop a plea***: see PLEA *noun* 2c.
2 *verb trans.* with *it* (the usual form), *one*, & *intrans.* with *out*. Get into trouble, be punished; die. L19.
3 *verb trans.* Strike (a person). (Foll. by *one*.) L19.
4 *verb intrans.* Foll. by *out*: escape; drop out of something; evade a responsibility or decision; go back on a promise. M20.
5 *verb intrans.* Foll. by *off*: have a sexual encounter (*with* someone). L20.

copacetic /kəʊpəˈsɛtɪk, -ˈsiːt-/ *adjective*. *N. Amer. slang*. Also **-set-**. E20.
[ORIGIN Unknown.]
Excellent; in good order.

copaiba /kəʊˈpʌɪbə/ *noun*. Also **-va** /-və/. E17.
[ORIGIN Portuguese *copaíba* (whence Spanish *copaiba*) from Tupi *copaíba*, Guarani *cupaüba*.]
A balsam of aromatic odour and acrid taste obtained from S. American leguminous trees of the genus *Copaifera* and used in medicine and the arts. Formerly also, a tree yielding this.

copal /ˈkəʊp(ə)l/ *noun*. L16.
[ORIGIN Spanish from Nahuatl *copalli* incense.]
A hard translucent odoriferous resin obtained from various tropical trees and used to make a fine transparent varnish. Also ***gum copal***.

copalm /ˈkəʊpɑːm/ *noun*. L18.
[ORIGIN Louisiana French *copalme* from *palme de copal* (cf. COPAL).]
The N. American liquidambar or sweet gum tree, or its timber; a balsam (liquid storax) got from it.

coparcenary /kəʊˈpɑːs(ə)n(ə)ri/ *noun & adjective*. E16.
[ORIGIN from CO- + PARCENARY. The adjective by assoc. with -ARY¹.]
ENGLISH LAW (now *hist.*).
▸ **A** *noun*. **1** Joint heirship; the status of a coparcener. E16.
2 Co-partnership; joint ownership. L16.
▸ **B** *adjective*. Of or pertaining to coparceners. M19.
■ **coparceny** *noun* = COPARCENARY *noun* M16.

coparcener /kəʊˈpɑːs(ə)nə/ *noun*. LME.
[ORIGIN from CO- + PARCENER.]
ENGLISH LAW (now *hist.*). A person who shares equally with others in the inheritance of an undivided estate or in the rights to it.

†**copart(i)ment** *nouns* vars. of COMPARTMENT *noun*.

co-partner /kəʊˈpɑːtnə/ *noun*. LME.
[ORIGIN from CO- + PARTNER.]
A person who shares or takes part with another (*in* any activity, undertaking, etc.). Formerly = COPARCENER.
■ **co-partnership** *noun* the relationship of co-partners; a company or association of co-partners: L16. **co-partnery** *noun* (a) co-partnership L17.

copasetic *adjective* var. of COPACETIC.

†**copataine** *noun*. *rare* (Shakes.). Only in L16.
[ORIGIN Unknown.]
A sugarloaf hat.

cope /kəʊp/ *noun*¹. ME.
[ORIGIN medieval Latin *capa* var. of late Latin *cappa* CAP *noun*¹.]
†**1** A long cloak or cape worn outdoors. ME–M18.
2 ECCLESIASTICAL. A semicircular cloak of rich material worn in processions and on other, chiefly non-Eucharistic, occasions. ME.
3 *fig.* Anything likened to a cloak or canopy; *esp.* the vault of heaven, the firmament. LME.

ADDISON The dark cope of night. W. DE LA MARE Heaven's midnight cope.

under the cope of heaven *arch.* in all the world.
4 FOUNDING. The upper or outer part of a flask. M19.
– COMB.: **copestone** the top or head stone of a building; chiefly *fig.*, a finishing touch.

†**cope** *noun*². E16–L18.
[ORIGIN from COPE *verb*¹ or from Old French *co(l)p*.]
An encounter in combat.

cope /kəʊp/ *noun*³. E16.
[ORIGIN from COPE *verb*³.]
†**1** ***God's cope***, a very large sum. E–M16.
2 A bargain. Now *dial.* M16.
3 *hist.* A duty payable by Derbyshire miners for permission to raise lead ore. M17.
– COMB.: **copeman**, †**copesman** *arch.* a merchant.

cope /kəʊp/ *verb*¹. ME.
[ORIGIN Old French *co(l)per* (mod. *couper*) strike, cut, from *co(l)p* blow from medieval Latin *colpus*: see COUP *noun*¹. Cf. COUP *verb*².]
▸ **I** *verb intrans.* **1** Strike, hit; come to blows *with*; engage or meet (*together*) in battle. *arch. & dial.* ME.
2 Contend successfully *with* (an opponent, difficulty, situation, etc.); *colloq.* deal competently with one's life or situation. L16.

E. A. FREEMAN An army able to cope with the insurgents. B. PYM It wasn't as if Marcia was an invalid or unable to cope.

3 Have to do *with*; come into contact or relation *with*. *arch.* L16.
▸ †**II** *verb trans.* **4** Meet. L16–E17.
5 Match (something) *with* an equivalent. *rare* (Shakes.). Only in L16.

cope /kəʊp/ *verb*². LME.
[ORIGIN from COPE *noun*¹.]
1 *verb trans.* Supply with or dress in a cope. Chiefly as ***coped*** *ppl adjective*. LME.
2 *verb trans.* Cover with or as with a coping. E16.
3 *verb intrans. & trans.* (Cause to) slope down or hang *over* like a coping. E17.
4 *verb trans.* Cover as with a vault or canopy. E18.

cope /kəʊp/ *verb*³. LME.
[ORIGIN Middle Dutch, Middle & mod. Low German *kōpen* rel. to Old High German *koufen*, *koufōn*: see CHEAP *verb*.]
†**1** *verb trans.* Buy. LME–L16.
2 *verb trans.* Exchange, barter (*away*). Now *dial.* L16.
†**3** *verb intrans.* Make an exchange or bargain. L16–E17.

cope /kəʊp/ *verb*⁴ *trans.* L16.
[ORIGIN App. from Old French *coper* cut: see COPE *verb*¹.]
Cut or pare (the beak or talons of a hawk).

cope /kəʊp/ *verb*⁵ *trans.* Long *obsolete* exc. *dial.* E17.
[ORIGIN Unknown.]
Tie or sew up or *up* the mouth of (a ferret); stop (a person) from talking.

copek *noun* var. of KOPEK.

†**copemate** *noun*. Also **copes-**. M16.
[ORIGIN from COPE *verb*¹ + MATE *noun*², with assim. to *cope(s)man*.]
1 An adversary. M16–M17.
2 A partner, a colleague; a companion; *spec.* a lover, a spouse. L16–L17.
3 A man. *colloq.* or *derog.* L16–M18.

copen /ˈkəʊp(ə)n/ *noun*. *N. Amer.* E20.
[ORIGIN Abbreviation of *Copenhagen*, English form of Danish *København*, the capital of Denmark.]
In full ***copen blue***. A strong light blue colour.

copepod /ˈkəʊpɪpɒd/ *noun & adjective*. L19.
[ORIGIN mod. Latin *Copepoda* pl., from Greek *kōpē* handle, oar + -POD.]
▸ **A** *noun*. A crustacean of the class Copepoda, which comprises small aquatic, mostly marine, organisms without a carapace and with paddle-like feet used for swimming. L19.
▸ **B** *adjective*. Of or pertaining to a copepod or copepods. L19.
■ **coˈpepodan** *adjective* pertaining to or characteristic of copepods L19. **coˈpepodid** *adjective & noun* (a) *adjective* designating or characteristic of certain free-swimming stages in the development of some copepods, following naupliar stages; (b) *noun* a copepodid individual: E20. **coˈpepodous** *adjective* = COPEPODAN L19.

coper /ˈkəʊpə/ *noun*. M16.
[ORIGIN from COPE *verb*³ + -ER¹.]
A dealer, a merchant; *spec.* a horse-dealer.

Copernican /kəˈpəːnɪk(ə)n/ *adjective & noun*. M17.
[ORIGIN from *Copernicus* (see below) Latinized form of *Koppernigk* + -AN.]
▸ **A** *adjective*. Of or pertaining to the Polish astronomer Copernicus (1473–1543) or his theory that the planets, including the earth, revolve around the sun. M17.
▸ **B** *noun*. A person who holds the Copernican theory. M17.
■ **Copernicanism** *noun* (belief in) the Copernican theory E19.

coperta /kəˈpəːtə/ *noun*. L19.
[ORIGIN Italian = covering, from *coprire* to cover from Latin *coperire*, *cooperire* COVER *verb*².]
A transparent lead glaze given as a final glaze to some majolica.

†**copesmate** *noun* var. of COPEMATE.

cophosis /kəˈfəʊsɪs/ *noun*. Now *rare* or *obsolete*. M17.
[ORIGIN Greek *kōphōsis*, from *kōphos* deaf: cf. -OSIS.]
MEDICINE. Complete deafness.

copia /ˈkəʊpɪə/ *noun*. M16.
[ORIGIN Latin: see COPY *noun*¹.]
An abundance, a plentiful supply.
copia verborum /vəːˈbɔːrəm/ an abundance of words, a copious vocabulary.

copiability *noun*, **copiable** *adjective* vars. of COPYABILITY, COPYABLE.

copiapite /ˈkəʊpɪəpʌɪt/ *noun*. M19.
[ORIGIN from *Copiapó* a city in Chile + -ITE¹.]
MINERALOGY. A yellow, triclinic, hydrated basic sulphate of ferric and ferrous iron and often other metals, usu. occurring as loose masses of tiny tabular crystals.

copier /ˈkɒpɪə/ *noun*. L16.
[ORIGIN from COPY *verb*¹ + -ER¹.]
1 A person who makes copies of documents, works of art, etc. L16.
2 An imitator. L17.
3 A machine that produces facsimile copies of documents; a photocopier. E20.

co-pilot /ˈkəʊpʌɪlət/ *noun*. E20.
[ORIGIN from CO- + PILOT *noun*.]
A second pilot in an aircraft.

coping /ˈkəʊpɪŋ/ *noun*. M16.
[ORIGIN from COPE *verb*² + -ING¹.]
A course of masonry or tiling on the top of a wall, usu. sloping so as to deflect rain.
– COMB.: **coping saw** a very narrow saw held taut in a U-frame, similar to but longer than a fretsaw and used for cutting curves in wood; **coping stone** a stone forming part of a coping; *fig.* a pinnacle, a finishing touch.

copious /ˈkəʊpɪəs/ *adjective & adverb*. LME.
[ORIGIN Old French & mod. French *copieux* or Latin *copiosus*, from *copia*: see COPY *noun*¹, -IOUS.]
▸ **A** *adjective*. **1** Existing or produced in abundance; plentiful. LME.
2 Yielding an abundance *of*. Formerly also, having an abundant supply of or *of* something, rich *in*. LME.

J. DALRYMPLE A .. toune copious in citizenis. J. GAY Newgate's copious market. W. COWPER Copious of flow'rs. W. H. PRESCOTT More copious sources of knowledge.

3 Profuse in speech; diffuse or exuberant in style. Of a language: having a large vocabulary. LME.
†**4** Numerous, multitudinous. LME–M18.
5 Having much information. L15.

H. JAMES A copious diary.

▸ **B** *adverb*. Copiously. *arch.* L18.
■ **copiously** *adverb* LME. **copiousness** *noun* LME.

†**copist** *noun*. M16–L18.
[ORIGIN French *copiste* or its source medieval Latin *copista*, from *copiare* COPY *verb*¹: see -IST.]
= COPYIST.

copita /kəʊˈpiːtə, kɒ-/ *noun*. M19.
[ORIGIN Spanish, dim. of *copa* from popular Latin *cuppa* CUP *noun*.]
A tulip-shaped sherry glass of a type traditionally used in Spain; a glass of sherry.

coplanar /kəʊˈpleɪnə/ *adjective*. L19.
[ORIGIN from CO- + PLANAR.]
MATH. Situated or acting in the same plane.
■ **coplaˈnarity** *noun* M19.

copolymer /kəʊˈpɒlɪmə/ *noun*. M20.
[ORIGIN from CO- + POLYMER.]
CHEMISTRY. A composite polymer formed by copolymerization and composed of units of more than one kind.

copolymerization /ˌkəʊpɒlɪmərʌɪˈzeɪʃ(ə)n, kəʊˌpɒl-/ *noun*. Also **-isation**. M20.
[ORIGIN from CO- + POLYMERIZATION.]
CHEMISTRY. The polymerization together of two or more different compounds to form a polymer that contains part of each.
■ **coˈpolymerize** *verb intrans. & trans.* M20.

†**coportion** *noun*. *rare* (Spenser). Only in L16.
[ORIGIN from CO- + PORTION *noun*.]
A joint portion.

cop-out /ˈkɒpaʊt/ *noun*. *slang*. M20.
[ORIGIN from COP *verb*² + OUT *adverb*: see COP *verb*² 4.]
1 An escape, esp. from reality; a pretext, an excuse; an evasion of responsibility. M20.
2 An escapist, a drop-out. M20.

copped /ˈkɒpɪd, kɒpt/ *adjective*. OE.
[ORIGIN from COP *noun*¹ + -ED².]
▸ **I** *lit.* †**1** Polled. Only in OE.
2 Crested. Now *dial.* ME.
3 Having a peak. LME.
▸ **II** *fig.* **4** Irritable; uncooperative. Now *Scot.* LME.
5 Conceited. *dial.* M17.

†**coppel** *noun & verb* var. of CUPEL.

copper /ˈkɒpə/ *noun*¹ *& adjective*.
[ORIGIN Old English *copor*, *coper* corresp. to Middle Dutch *coper* (Dutch *koper*), Old Norse *koparr*, from Germanic (whence also Middle Low German *kopper*, Old High German *kupfar* (German *Kupfer*)), from late Latin *cuprum* from Latin *cyprium (aes)* lit. '(metal) of Cyprus', so called from its most noted ancient source.]
▸ **A** *noun*. **1** A malleable and ductile reddish metal which is a chemical element of the transition series, atomic no. 29, used esp. for electrical conductors and as the base of alloys (symbol Cu). OE.
PITCHY ***copper ore***. ***purple copper*** (***ore***): see PURPLE *adjective*. ***red copper ore***: see RED *adjective*. ***rose copper***: see ROSE *adjective*. ***ruby***

copper: see RUBY *adjective*. ***set copper***: see SET *adjective*. ***velvet copper ore***: see VELVET *noun & adjective*.
2 A copper or iron vessel for boiling water, esp. for cooking or laundry; a copper mug. E17.
3 = COPPERPLATE *noun* 2. M17.
4 A bronze or copper coin; money composed of such coins. E18.
5 Any of various reddish-orange butterflies of the genus *Lycaena* (family Lycaenidae), of which only the small copper, *L. phlaeas*, is now common in Britain. L18.
6 In *pl.* The throat. *slang*. M19.
hot coppers a throat and mouth parched through excessive drinking.
7 In *pl.* Shares in a copper-mining company. L19.
8 A ceremonial copper sheet used by N. American Indians. L19.
▸ **B** *adjective*. **1** Made of copper; *fig.* worthless. L16.
2 Of the colour of copper. L17.
– COMB. & SPECIAL COLLOCATIONS: **Copper Age** a prehistoric period when copper was used in a particular culture but not bronze; **copper beech** a kind of beech with copper-coloured leaves; **copper-belly** (*a*) = COPPERHEAD 1a; (*b*) a harmless N. American water snake, *Natrix erythrogaster*, having a red belly; **copper belt** an area of central Africa where much copper is mined; **copper-bit** a soldering iron bit made of copper; **copper-bottomed** *adjective* (esp. of a ship) having a bottom covered with copper; *fig.* thoroughly sound or reliable; **copper-captain** a sham (ship's) captain; **copper-cut** a copperplate engraving; **copper-fasten** *verb trans.* (*fig.*) make more secure, establish firmly; **copper-fastened** *adjective* (of a ship) fastened with copper bolts; **copper glance** MINERALOGY = CHALCOCITE; **copper-headed** *adjective* having a copper-coloured head; relating to a copperhead (sense 2 or 3); ***copperknob***: see ***coppernob*** below; **copper loss** loss of energy as a result of electrical resistance in the copper conductors of machinery etc.; **copper-nickel** [German *Kupfernickel*, from its resemblance to copper] MINERALOGY = NICCOLITE; **coppernob**, **copperknob** *colloq.* a red-haired person; **copper-nose** a red nose caused by disease, intemperance, etc.; ***copper pyrites***: see PYRITES 2; **copperskin** *US slang* an American Indian; ***copper*** VITRIOL.
■ **copperish** *adjective* (*rare*) somewhat coppery M17. **coppery** *adjective* resembling copper, esp. in colour; containing copper: E18.

copper /ˈkɒpə/ *noun*[2]. *slang*. M19.
[ORIGIN from COP *verb*[2] + -ER[1].]
A police officer.
come copper, **turn copper** inform on someone. ***copper's nark***: see NARK *noun* 1a.

copper /ˈkɒpə/ *verb*[1]. M16.
[ORIGIN from COPPER *noun*[1].]
1 *verb trans.* Cover or sheathe with copper. M16.
2 *verb trans.* & *intrans.* Place a copper coin on (a card) in faro to indicate a bet against it; bet against anything; place (such a bet). M19.
3 *verb trans.* Give a false colour to by means of salts of copper. L19.
■ **copperer** *noun* a person who works in copper ME.

copper /ˈkɒpə/ *verb*[2]. *slang*. L19.
[ORIGIN from COPPER *noun*[2].]
1 *verb trans.* Arrest. L19.
2 *verb trans.* & *intrans.* Inform the police (about). L19.

copperas /ˈkɒp(ə)rəs/ *noun*. LME.
[ORIGIN Old French & mod. French *couperose* from medieval Latin *cup(e)rosa* lit. 'flower of copper', ult. from late Latin *cupri-* combining form of Latin *cuprum* copper + *rosa* ROSE *noun*, after Greek *khalkanthon*.]
Ferrous sulphate heptahydrate, $FeSO_4{\cdot}7H_2O$, a green crystalline compound used in inks and pigments and in medicine. Formerly also, the sulphate of copper or zinc.
†**blue copperas** copper sulphate. **green copperas** ferrous sulphate heptahydrate. †**white copperas** zinc sulphate.
– COMB.: †**copperas-stone** marcasite.

copperhead /ˈkɒpəhɛd/ *noun*. L18.
[ORIGIN from COPPER *noun*[1] & *adjective* + HEAD *noun*.]
1 More fully ***copperhead snake***: ▸**a** A venomous but rarely fatal N. American pit viper, *Agkistrodon contortrix*. L18. ▸**b** A venomous but unaggressive Australian snake, *Denisonia superba*, of the cobra family, Elapidae. L19.
2 *hist.* In the American Civil War, a Northerner who sympathized with the South. M19.
3 An American Indian. *US*. Now *rare* or *obsolete*. M19.

copper Maori *noun phr.* var. of KOPA MAORI.

copperplate /ˈkɒpəpleɪt/ *noun & verb*. M17.
[ORIGIN from COPPER *noun*[1] + PLATE *noun*.]
▸ **A** *noun*. **1** A plate, or plates, made of copper. M17.
2 *spec.* A polished printing plate of copper on which a design is engraved or etched. M17.
3 A print made with a copperplate. M17.
4 An English style of handwriting (a kind of round hand) for which the copybooks were printed from copperplates; round neat handwriting. M18.
5 Engraving or printing done from copperplate. E19.
▸ **B** *verb trans.* Engrave on and print from a copperplate. E19.

coppersmith /ˈkɒpəsmɪθ/ *noun*. ME.
[ORIGIN from COPPER *noun*[1] + SMITH *noun*.]
1 A person who works in copper. ME.
2 The crimson-breasted barbet, *Megalaima haemacephala*, of SE Asia (so called from its metallic note). M19.

coppice /ˈkɒpɪs/ *noun & verb*. Also †**cop(p)y**. LME.
[ORIGIN Old French *copeiz*, ult. from Proto-Romance verb (whence COPE *verb*[1]) from medieval Latin *colpus*: see COUP *noun*[1]. Cf. COPSE *noun*[1] & *verb*.]
▸ **A** *noun*. A small wood of undergrowth and small trees, grown for periodic cutting. LME.
– COMB.: **coppice wood** = *copsewood* s.v. COPSE *noun*[1].
▸ **B** *verb*. **1** *verb trans.* Grow or treat as a coppice; cut down periodically. LME.
2 *verb intrans.* Of a tree: produce new shoots from a stump. L19.

copping /ˈkɒpɪŋ/ *verbal noun*. L18.
[ORIGIN from COP *noun*[1] + -ING[1].]
The formation of cops of thread.

copple /ˈkɒp(ə)l/ *noun*. Long *obsolete* exc. *dial.* in ***copple-crown***. LME.
[ORIGIN Dim. of COP *noun*[1]: see -LE[1].]
1 More fully ***copple-crown***. A crest on a bird's head, = COP *noun*[1] 1b. LME.
†**2** A small summit or piece of rising ground. *rare*. Only in E17.
■ †**coppled** *adjective* (*a*) crested; (*b*) rising conically to a point: E17–E18. †**coppling** *adjective* swelling upwards towards a summit L17–M18.

†**coppy** *noun & verb* var. of COPPICE.

copra /ˈkɒprə/ *noun*. L16.
[ORIGIN Portuguese & Spanish from Malayalam *koppara*.]
Dried coconut kernels, from which oil is obtained.

co-precipitation /ˌkəʊprɪsɪpɪˈteɪʃ(ə)n/ *noun*. M20.
[ORIGIN from CO- + PRECIPITATION.]
CHEMISTRY. The simultaneous precipitation of two or more compounds from a solution; the removal of a compound from solution by causing it to bind to a precipitate.
■ **co-preˈcipitate** *verb trans.* deposit by co-precipitation M20.

co-presence /kəʊˈprɛz(ə)ns/ *noun*. E19.
[ORIGIN from CO- + PRESENCE.]
Presence together.
■ **co-present** *adjective* E19.

copro- /ˈkɒprəʊ/ *combining form* of Greek *kopros* dung: see -O-.
■ **coproˈlalia** *noun* the use of obscene language, esp. as a symptom of mental illness or organic brain disease L19. **coprolite** *noun* [-LITE] (a piece of) fossilized dung E19. **coproˈlitic** *adjective* pertaining to or containing coprolite; of the nature of coprolite: E19. **coprolith** *noun* [-LITH] a mass of hardened faeces in the appendix or bowel; also, a coprolite: L19. **coˈprology** *noun* (the treatment of) filthy subjects in literature or art M19. **coproˈmaniac** *noun* a person with an obsession with faeces L19. **coproˈmania** *noun* an coproˈmania E20. **coproˈphagia** *noun* = COPROPHAGY E20. **coproˈphagic** *adjective* involving or engaging in the eating of dung E20. **coˈprophagous** *adjective* [-PHAGOUS] (esp. of a beetle) that eats dung E19. **coˈprophagy** *noun* the eating of dung L19. **coprophil(e)** *noun* [-PHIL] a person with coprophilia M20. **coproˈphilia** *noun* an undue interest in faeces and defecation M20. **coproˈphilic** *adjective & noun* (*a*) *adjective* of, pertaining to, or exhibiting coprophilia; (*b*) *noun* a coprophilic person: E20. **coˈprophilous** *adjective* exhibiting coprophilia; (esp. of a fungus) that grows on dung: L19. **coˈprophily** *noun* = COPROPHILIA E20. **coproˈporphyrin** *noun* any of several porphyrins present in urine and faeces, esp. in certain diseases E20. **coproˈzoic** *adjective* [Greek *zōē* life] (of an animal) living in or feeding on dung M20.

coprosma /kəˈprɒzmə/ *noun*. L19.
[ORIGIN mod. Latin *Coprosma*, formed as COPRO- + Greek *osmē* smell.]
A plant of the genus *Coprosma* (family Rubiaceae), which comprises small evergreen trees and shrubs found in Australasia.

co-prosperity /kəʊprɒˈspɛrɪti/ *noun*. M20.
[ORIGIN from CO- + PROSPERITY.]
Joint prosperity; *spec.* (*hist.*) in ***co-prosperity sphere***, the parts of eastern and SE Asia which Japan aimed to control in the Second World War and which were mostly occupied by her.

cops *noun* var. of COPSE *noun*[2].

copse /kɒps/ *noun*[1] & *verb*. L16.
[ORIGIN Syncopated from COPPICE.]
▸ **A** *noun*. **1** = COPPICE *noun*. L16.
2 Undergrowth, *esp.* the low trees and undergrowth of a copse. M18.
– COMB.: **copsewood** †(*a*) a copse; (*b*) the low trees and undergrowth of a copse.
▸ **B** *verb trans.* **1** = COPPICE *verb* 1. L16.
2 Cover with a copse. M18.
■ **copsy** *adjective* planted with copses M18.

copse /kɒps/ *noun*[2]. Long *obsolete* exc. *dial.* Also **cops**.
[ORIGIN Old English *cops*, *cosp* = Old Saxon *cosp* fetter.]
†**1** A shackle, a fetter, a manacle. OE–ME.
2 A hasp for fastening a door or gate. L15.
3 A clevis. Cf. earlier COPSOLE. L18.

copsole /ˈkɒps(ə)l/ *noun*. Long *obsolete* exc. *dial.* Also **-sil**. M16.
[ORIGIN App. from COPSE *noun*[2] + obscure 2nd elem.]
A clevis; = COPSE *noun*[2] 3.

Copt /kɒpt/ *noun & adjective*. E17.
[ORIGIN French *Copte* or mod. Latin *Cop(h)tus* from Arabic *al-ḳibṭ*, *al-ḳubṭ* Copts from Coptic *Gyptios*, from Greek *Aiguptios* Egyptian: see AL-[2].]
▸ **A** *noun*. An Egyptian not of Arab descent; a member of the Coptic Church. E17.
▸ **B** *adjective*. = COPTIC *adjective*. M17.

copter /ˈkɒptə/ *noun*. *colloq.* (chiefly *N. Amer.*). Also **'c-**. M20.
[ORIGIN Abbreviation.]
= HELICOPTER *noun*.

Coptic /ˈkɒptɪk/ *noun & adjective*. M17.
[ORIGIN from COPT + -IC.]
▸ **A** *noun*. The medieval language of Egypt, now used only in the liturgy of the Coptic Church. M17.
▸ **B** *adjective*. Of or pertaining to the Copts; designating or pertaining to the Monophysite Christian Church in Egypt. L17.

copula /ˈkɒpjʊlə/ *noun*. E17.
[ORIGIN Latin = connection, linking of words, formed as CO- + *apere* fasten: see -ULE.]
1 GRAMMAR & LOGIC. That part of a proposition which connects the subject and the predicate; the verb *be* as a mere sign of predication; a verb with a similar function. E17.
2 A connection, a link. M17.
3 ANATOMY. A part (e.g. a bone or ligament) connecting other parts. Now *rare* or *obsolete*. L17.
■ **copular** *adjective* M19.

copulate /ˈkɒpjʊleɪt/ *verb*. LME.
[ORIGIN Latin *copulat-* pa. ppl stem of *copulare* fasten together, formed as COPULA: see -ATE[3].]
†**1** *verb trans.* Join, link together. LME–E19.
2 *verb intrans.* Of a male and female: have copulation, unite sexually (*with*). E17.
■ **copulatory** *adjective* pertaining to or used for copulation M19.

copulation /kɒpjʊˈleɪʃ(ə)n/ *noun*. LME.
[ORIGIN Old French & mod. French from Latin *copulatio(n-)*, formed as COPULA: see -ATION.]
1 *gen.* The action of linking together two things or ideas; the state of being linked. Now *rare* or *obsolete*. LME.
2 The physical union of male and female (esp. animals) by means of their genitals, as in the act of procreation; sexual intercourse. L15.
3 Grammatical or logical connection. L16.

copulative /ˈkɒpjʊlətɪv/ *adjective & noun*. LME.
[ORIGIN Old French & mod. French *copulatif*, *-ive* or late Latin *copulativus*, formed as COPULATE: see -IVE.]
▸ **A** *adjective*. **1** Serving to connect, esp. (GRAMMAR) words or clauses that are joined in sense (opp. ***disjunctive***), or subject and predicate (or complement); involving such connection. LME.
2 ZOOLOGY & ANATOMY. = COPULATORY. M19.
▸ **B** *noun*. **1** GRAMMAR. A copulative conjunction or particle. M16.
†**2** In *pl.* Persons about to be joined in marriage. *joc. rare* (Shakes.). Only in L16.
■ **copulatively** *adverb* E17.

copy /ˈkɒpi/ *noun*[1] & *adjective*. ME.
[ORIGIN Old French & mod. French *copie* from Latin *copia* abundance, plenty; the medieval Latin & Proto-Romance sense 'transcript' arose from such phrs. as *copiam describendi facere* give the power (permission) of transcription).]
▸ **A** *noun* **I 1** A piece of written or printed matter that reproduces the contents of another; a transcript, *spec.* (LAW, now *hist.*) of a manorial court roll; a specimen of penmanship made in imitation of a model. ME. ▸**b** Anything (regarded as) made to reproduce the appearance of something else (a picture, personality, etc.). L16.

b D. HUME Of this impression there is a copy taken by the mind. R. CAMPBELL Lilian Bayliss . . photographed the house, and sent me a copy of it.

2 An original from which a copy is to be made; *spec.* a specimen of penmanship. L15. ▸†**b** *fig.* A pattern, an example. L16–L18.
3 **a** Matter or text prepared for printing, *spec.* the wording of an advertisement. Formerly also, a passage or manuscript of such matter. L15. ▸**b** Something which lends itself to interesting narration in a newspaper etc. M19.

a Q. BELL Repeated failures to float magazines, to produce copy on time. **b** G. B. SHAW Socialist speeches which make what the newspapers call 'good copy'.

4 Each of the written or printed specimens of a work or publication. M16.

E. J. HOWARD He picked up a copy of *Country Life*.

†**5** A copyright work; copyright. L16–L18.
†**6** = COPYHOLD *noun*. Cf. earlier B. below. E–M17.
7 A particular size of paper, now disused. E18.
▸ †**II 8** Abundance, plenty, copiousness. LME–M17.
– PHRASES: **copy of verses** a short verse composition, esp. in Greek or Latin as an exercise. †**copy of one's countenance** a mere outward show of what one would do or be; a pretence. ***Chinese copy***: see CHINESE *adjective*. ***fair copy***: see FAIR *adjective*. ***rough copy***: see ROUGH *adjective*. ***set a copy to***: see SET *verb*[1]. ***soft copy***: see SOFT *adjective*. ***top copy***: see TOP *adjective*. ***working copy***: see WORKING *noun*.
– COMB.: **copyboard** a part of a camera that holds a document ready for photographing; **copydesk** *US*: where copy is edited for printing; **copy-edit** *verb trans.* read and edit for printing; **copy editor** a person who reads and edits copy for printing; †**copy-**

money: paid to an author for his or her manuscript or copyright; **copyreader** = *copy editor* above; **copy-taster** a person who selects what is to be published; **copy typist** a person who makes typewritten transcripts of documents or recorded dictation; **copywriter** a person who writes or prepares copy, esp. advertising copy, for publication.

▸ †**B** *adjective*. = COPYHOLD *adjective*. E16–M17.

†**copy** *noun*² var. of COPPICE *noun*.

C

copy /ˈkɒpi/ *verb*¹. LME.
[ORIGIN Old French & mod. French *copier* from medieval Latin *copiare* from Latin *copia* (see COPY *noun*¹).]
1 *verb trans.* Make a copy of (a text, work of art, etc., also foll. by *out*); transcribe (*from* an original); design or produce by making a copy of something else (foll. by *from* the original). LME. ▸**b** COMPUTING. Read (data stored in one location), read the data in (a disk etc.), and reproduce in another. (Foll. by *from* one, *into*, *to* another.) M20. ▸**c** Send a copy of (a document) *to* a person etc. L20.

R. W. EMERSON The potters copied his ugly face on their stone jugs. B. HINES He copied age, address and other details from the record card.

2 *verb trans.* Imitate, follow the example of; follow in behaviour, mode, etc. M17.

T. HARDY This scheme of extinction by death was but tamely copying her rival's method.

3 *verb intrans.* Imitate or follow the example of another or others; make a copy or copies rather than create something original. (Foll. by *after*, *from*.) L17.

J. RUSKIN No painter who is worth a straw ever will copy.

– COMB.: **copycat** *noun, adjective, & verb* (*colloq.*) (**a**) *noun* an unimaginative or slavish imitator; (**b**) *attrib. adjective* characterized by or consisting in imitation; (**c**) *verb trans.* imitate unimaginatively; **copying pencil**: used for indelible writing and for duplicating by a direct-transfer process.

†**copy** *verb*² var. of COPPICE *verb*.

copyable /ˈkɒpɪəb(ə)l/ *adjective*. Also **copiable**. M18.
[ORIGIN from COPY *verb*¹ + -ABLE.]
Able to be copied.
■ **copyaˈbility** *noun* M20.

copybook /ˈkɒpɪbʊk/ *noun & adjective*. M16.
[ORIGIN from COPY *noun*¹ + BOOK *noun*.]
▸ **A** *noun*. **1** A book containing copies of accounts etc. Now *US*. M16.
2 A book containing specimens of handwriting for learners to copy. L16.
blot one's copybook: see BLOT *verb* 1.
▸ **B** *adjective*. **1** Of a conventional or trite nature. M19.
2 Accurate, exemplary. E20.

copyhold /ˈkɒpɪhəʊld/ *noun & adjective*. *hist.* LME.
[ORIGIN from COPY *noun*¹ + HOLD *noun*¹.]
▸**A** *noun*. **1** Tenure of land according to the custom of the manor to which it belonged, as recorded in transcripts of the manorial court rolls. LME.
2 An estate, land, held by copyhold. LME.
▸ **B** *adjective*. Held by copyhold; relating to or of the nature of copyhold. E16.

copyholder /ˈkɒpɪhəʊldə/ *noun*. LME.
[ORIGIN from COPY *noun*¹ + HOLDER¹.]
1 *hist.* A person who held an estate or land in copyhold. LME.
2 A clasp for holding copy while it is set or keyboarded. L19.
3 An assistant who reads copy aloud to a proofreader. L19.

copyist /ˈkɒpɪɪst/ *noun*. M17.
[ORIGIN from COPY *verb*¹ + -IST. Cf. COPIST.]
A person who copies (esp. documents) or imitates.
■ **copyism** *noun* the practice of copying, esp. slavishly, (slavish) imitation E19.

copyleft /ˈkɒpilɛft/ *noun*. L20.
[ORIGIN Punning alt. of COPYRIGHT.]
A legal agreement which allows a piece of software to be used without licence, modified, and further distributed by the user, provided that a notice to this effect is included with it. Freq. *attrib.*, as ***copyleft agreement*** etc.

copyright /ˈkɒpɪrʌɪt/ *noun & adjective*. E18.
[ORIGIN from COPY *noun*¹ + RIGHT *noun*¹.]
▸ **A** *noun*. The exclusive right, given to the originator or his or her assignee for a fixed number of years, to reproduce or perform a literary, musical, cinematic, etc., work and to authorize others to do the same. E18.
– COMB.: **copyright library**: entitled to a free copy of every book published in Britain.
▸ **B** *adjective*. Protected by copyright. L19.

copyright /ˈkɒpɪrʌɪt/ *verb trans.* E19.
[ORIGIN from the noun.]
Secure copyright for.
■ **copyrightable** *adjective* L19.

coq *noun* var. of COQUE *noun*².

coq au vin /kɒk əʊ vã/ *noun phr.* M20.
[ORIGIN French, lit. 'cock in wine'.]
Chicken cooked in wine.

coque /kɒk/ *noun*¹. E19.
[ORIGIN French = shell.]
†**1** BOTANY. = COCCUS 2. *rare*. Only in E19.
2 A loop, a looped bow. Now *spec.* a small loop of ribbon in the trimming of a woman's hat. E19.

coque /kəʊk/ *noun*². Also **coq** /kɒk/. E20.
[ORIGIN French *coq* = COCK *noun*¹.]
In full ***coque feather***. A cock's feather used in the trimming of a hat etc.

coquelicot /ˈkəʊklɪkəʊ/ *noun & adjective*. L18.
[ORIGIN French = red poppy, var. of *coquerico* cock-a-doodle-doo.]
(Of) the colour of the red poppy, a brilliant orange-red.

†**coqueluche** *noun*. E17–L19.
[ORIGIN French, of unknown origin.]
Orig., an epidemic catarrh; later, whooping cough.

coquet /kɒˈkɛt/ *noun & adjective*. L17.
[ORIGIN French, dim. of *coq* COCK *noun*¹; as adjective = forward, wanton, gallant. The noun was formerly both masc. & fem.; later the fem. became *coquette*.]
▸ **A** *noun*. **1** A man given to flirting or coquetry. L17.
†**2** = COQUETTE *noun*. L17–E19.
▸ **B** *adjective*. Coquettish. L17.

coquet /kɒˈkɛt/ *verb*. Also **-ette**. L17.
[ORIGIN French *coqueter*, formed as COQUET *noun & adjective*.]
1 *verb intrans.* & †*trans.* with *it*. Of a woman, or (formerly) a man: flirt (*with*). L17.
†**2** *verb trans.* Flirt with. Only in 18.
3 *verb intrans.* Dally, trifle, or toy (*with* a matter etc.). L18.

W. E. H. LECKY Lady Townshend . . coquetted with Methodism as with Popery.

coquetry /ˈkɒkɪtri, ˈkəʊ-/ *noun*. M17.
[ORIGIN French *coquetterie*, from *coqueter* COQUET *verb*: see -RY.]
1 a Behaviour intended to excite admiration or love in the opposite sex merely for the sake of vanity or mischief; flirtation. Formerly, attractive pertness in a woman. M17. ▸**b** A coquettish act. M18.
2 Trifling or dalliance with a cause etc. without serious interest in it. L18.

coquette /kɒˈkɛt/ *noun & adjective*. M17.
[ORIGIN French, fem. of *coquet*: see COQUET *noun & adjective*, -ETTE.]
▸ **A** *noun*. **1** A woman who trifles with men's affections; a woman given to flirting or coquetry. M17. ▸**b** ***male coquette***, = COQUET *noun* 1. Now *rare* or *obsolete*. L18.
2 A crested hummingbird of the genus *Lophornis*. M19.
▸ **B** *adjective*. = COQUET *adjective*. M18.
■ **coquettish** *adjective* like (that of) a coquette; characterized by coquetry: E18. **coquettishly** *adverb* L18. **coquettishness** *noun* L19.

coquette *verb* var. of COQUET *verb*.

coquilla nut /kəʊˈkɪl(j)ə nʌt/ *noun phr.* M19.
[ORIGIN App. Spanish or Portuguese dim. of *coca* shell from Old Spanish: see COQUINA.]
The nut of the Brazilian palm tree *Attalea funifera*, the hard shell of which is used by turners.

coquimbite /kəʊˈkɪmbʌɪt/ *noun*. M19.
[ORIGIN from *Coquimbo*, province of Chile + -ITE¹.]
A hexagonal hydrated ferric sulphate, $Fe_2(SO_4)_3 \cdot 9H_2O$, occurring as coloured crystals that dehydrate in air to a white powder.

coquina /kəʊˈkiːnə/ *noun*. M19.
[ORIGIN Spanish = shellfish, cockle, from Old Spanish *coca* from medieval Latin by-form of Latin CONCHA.]
A soft white limestone composed of broken marine shells cemented together and used for building in the W. Indies and Florida. Also ***coquina rock***, ***coquina stone***.

coquito /kəʊˈkiːtəʊ/ *noun*. Pl. **-os**. M19.
[ORIGIN Spanish, dim. of *coco* coconut.]
The Chilean wine palm, *Jubaea chilensis*, which yields palm honey and fibre. Also ***coquito palm***.

cor /kɔː/ *noun*. LME.
[ORIGIN Hebrew *kōr*.]
hist. A Hebrew measure of capacity of about 400 litres (100 gallons), = HOMER *noun*¹.

cor /kɔː/ *interjection*. *slang*. M20.
[ORIGIN Alt. of *God*.]
Expr. surprise, alarm, etc.
cor blimey = GORBLIMEY *interjection*.

cor- /kɒ, *unstressed* kə/ *prefix*.
Var. of Latin COM- before *r*. Cf. CO-, COL-, CON-.

Cor. *abbreviation*.
1 Corinthians (New Testament).
2 Corner. *US*.

†**coracine** *noun*. E17–M18.
[ORIGIN Latin *coracinus*, from Greek *korax* raven: so called from its black colour: see -INE¹.]
A fish resembling a perch, found in the River Nile.

coracle /ˈkɒrək(ə)l/ *noun*. M16.
[ORIGIN Welsh *corwg*(*l*), *cwrwgl* coracle (= Gaelic, Old Irish & mod. Irish *curach* (small) boat: cf. CURRACH).]
A small boat made of wickerwork covered with watertight material, used on lakes and rivers in Wales and Ireland.

coraco- /ˈkɒrəkəʊ/ *combining form*.
[ORIGIN from CORACOID: see -O-.]
ANATOMY. Pertaining to or connecting the coracoid and —, as ***coracohumeral***.

coracoid /ˈkɒrəkɔɪd/ *adjective & noun*. M18.
[ORIGIN mod. Latin *coracoides* from Greek *korakoeidēs* raven-like, from *korax* raven, crow: see -OID.]
ANATOMY. ▸**A** *adjective*. Designating or pertaining to a short projection of the human shoulder blade that extends towards the breastbone and resembles a crow's beak. Also, designating or pertaining to a bone in birds and reptiles homologous with this, forming the distal or ventral element of the scapular arch. M18.
▸ **B** *noun*. The coracoid process or bone. E19.
■ **coraˈcoidal** *adjective* L19.

coradgee *noun* see KORADJI.

coraggio /koˈraddʒo, kɒˈrɑːdʒəʊ/ *interjection*. E17.
[ORIGIN Italian.]
Courage! (see COURAGE *noun* 4b).

corah /ˈkɔːrə/ *noun & adjective*. E19.
[ORIGIN Hindi *korā* new, unbleached.]
▸ **A** *noun*. An Indian-pattern silk handkerchief. E19.
▸ **B** *adjective*. Of silk: undyed. L19.

coral /ˈkɒr(ə)l/ *noun & adjective*. ME.
[ORIGIN Old French (mod. *corail*) from Latin *corallum*, *-alium* from Greek *korallion*, *kouralion*.]
▸ **A** *noun* **I 1** A usu. hard calcareous substance secreted by many marine polyps as an external skeleton for support and habitation, and occurring in both single specimens and extensive accumulations; a similar substance produced by other lime-secreting marine organisms. Orig. *spec.* the red variety of this. ME.
pink coral, ***red coral***, ***white coral***, etc. ***precious coral***: see PRECIOUS *adjective*. ***soft coral***: see SOFT *adjective*. ***stony coral***: see STONY *adjective*.
2 A particular kind of coral or coral-producing polyp. L16.

D. ATTENBOROUGH The profusion of shapes and colours of the corals.

3 A piece of red coral used as an ornament etc. E17.
4 A toy of polished coral or other hard material given to teething babies. E17.
▸ **II** *transf.* & *fig.* **5** Anything bright red or (formerly) precious. ME.
6 The unimpregnated roe of the lobster (which turns red when boiled). M18.
7 In full ***coral snake***. Any of various snakes with some red colour; *esp.* any venomous elapid snake with red, black, and yellow bands. M18.
▸ **B** *adjective*. **1** Made or formed of coral. LME.
2 Of the colour of red coral. E16.
– COMB. & SPECIAL COLLOCATIONS: **coralberry** a N. American shrub (*Symphoricarpos orbiculatus*) of the honeysuckle family, with deep-red berries; **coral fern** *Austral.* any fern of the genus *Gleichenia*, the members of which form dense mats; **coral insect** = *coral polyp* below; **coral island**: formed by the accumulation of coral on a coral reef or an undersea mountain top; **coral-limestone** coralline limestone; **coral pea** any leguminous plant of the genus *Kennedia*, which comprises trailing and climbing shrubs native to Australia and bearing showy, usu. red, flowers; **coral-pink** *adjective & noun* (of) the colour of red coral; **coral-plant** †(**a**) any plant resembling coral; (**b**) a tropical American tree or large shrub, *Jatropha multifida*, of the spurge family, bearing scarlet flowers; (**c**) a Central American shrub of the genus *Russelia*, of the figwort family, *esp.* the red-flowered *R. equisetiformis*; **coral polyp** a polyp that produces coral; **coral rag** rubbly limestone composed chiefly of petrified coral; **coral-red** *noun & adjective* (of) the colour of red coral; **coral reef**: composed chiefly of coral or similar calcareous material of plant or animal origin; **coralroot** (**a**) a cruciferous woodland plant, *Cardamine* (or *Dentaria*) *bulbifera*, with scaly rhizomes and purple flowers; (**b**) (more fully ***coralroot orchid***) any member of the genus *Corallorhiza* of brown saprophytic orchids with much-branched coral-like roots, esp. *C. trifida*; ***coral snake***: see sense 7 above; **coral spot** (a disease of shrubs caused by) the fungus *Nectria cinnabarina*; **coral tree** †(**a**) branched coral; (**b**) any of numerous tropical or subtropical thorny leguminous shrubs and trees constituting the genus *Erythrina*, with showy red or orange flowers; **coral vine** = CORALLITA; **coral-wood** (**a**) a hard red cabinet wood from Central and S. America; (**b**) the SE Asian tree *Adenanthera pavonina*, which yields a red wood used in furniture; **coralwort** = *coralroot* (a) above.
■ **coralled** *adjective* covered with coral E18. **coˈralliform** *adjective* shaped like coral E19. **coraˈlligenous** *adjective* producing coral E19. **coral-like** *adjective* resembling coral; having a crustose or branching form: M19.

coral /ˈkɒr(ə)l/ *verb trans. rare*. Infl. **-ll-**, ***-l-**. M17.
[ORIGIN from CORAL *noun & adjective*.]
Make red like coral.

coraleta, **coralita** *nouns* vars. of CORALLITA.

Corallian /kɒˈralɪən/ *adjective & noun*. M19.
[ORIGIN from Latin *corallium* coral + -AN.]
▸ **A** *adjective*. Of or relating to coral; *spec.* (GEOLOGY) = OXFORDIAN *adjective* 1 (with reference to the coral-derived limestone deposits).
▸ **B** *noun*. GEOLOGY. The Oxfordian period or system. L19.

coralline /ˈkɒrəlʌɪn/ *noun*¹. M16.
[ORIGIN Italian *corallina* dim. of *corallo* CORAL *noun*.]
1 A seaweed of the genus *Corallina* (family Corallinaceae), having a calcareous jointed stem; any plant of the family

Corallinaceae, which comprises lime-secreting red algae. **M16.**
2 A marine animal, esp. a bryozoan, which lives in colonies resembling coral. **E18.**

coralline /ˈkɒrəlʌɪn/ *adjective & noun*². **M17.**
[ORIGIN French *corallin*, *-ine* or late Latin *corallinus*, from Latin *corallum* CORAL *noun*: see -INE¹.]
▶ **A** *adjective*. **1** Of the colour of red coral. **M17.**
2 Of the nature of coral; formed of or from coral. **M17.**
JOHN PHILLIPS Coralline oolite and calcareous grits.
3 Resembling coral; *spec.* (of an alga) belonging to the family Corallinaceae (see CORALLINE *noun*¹ 1). **M19.**
▶ **B** *noun*. Coral. **L18.**

corallita /kɒrəˈliːtə/ *noun*. Also **coraleta**, **-ita**. **L19.**
[ORIGIN Amer. Spanish *coralito* dim. of Spanish *coral* CORAL *noun*.]
A climbing vine, *Antigonon leptopus*, of the knotgrass family that grows in the W. Indies and as an ornamental elsewhere and has pink flowers.

corallite /ˈkɒrəlʌɪt/ *noun*. **E19.**
[ORIGIN formed as CORALLUM + -ITE¹.]
PALAEONTOLOGY. **1** A fossil coral. **E19.**
2 The cuplike skeleton of a single coral polyp. **M19.**

coralloid /ˈkɒrəlɔɪd/ *adjective & noun*. **E17.**
[ORIGIN formed as CORALLUM + -OID.]
(An organism) resembling coral.
■ **coraˈlloidal** *adjective* **M17.**

corallum /kəˈraləm/ *noun*. **M19.**
[ORIGIN Latin = CORAL *noun*.]
The calcareous skeleton of a colony of coral polyps.

coram /ˈkɔːrəm/ *preposition*. **M16.**
[ORIGIN Latin.]
The Latin for 'before, in the presence of', occurring in various phrases used in English.
coram judice /ˈjuːdɪsɪ/ [Latin *judex*, *judic-* judge] before a judge, i.e. a properly constituted or an appropriate court. ***coram nobis*** /ˈnəʊbɪs/ [Latin *nos* we] before us (the monarch), i.e. in the King's or Queen's Bench. ***coram populo*** /ˈpɒpjʊləʊ/ [Latin *populus* people] in public.

Coramine /ˈkɔːrəmiːn, ˈkɒr-/ *noun*. **E20.**
[ORIGIN from *cor-* (origin unknown) + AMINE.]
PHARMACOLOGY. (Proprietary name for) nikethamide.

cor anglais /kɔːr ˈɑːŋgleɪ, ˈɒŋgleɪ/ *noun phr*. Pl. **cors anglais** (pronounced same). **L19.**
[ORIGIN French, lit. 'English horn'.]
A musical instrument like an oboe but lower in pitch; a player of this. Also, an organ reed stop of similar quality.

coranto /kɒˈrantəʊ/ *noun*¹. *obsolete* exc. *hist*. Pl. **-os**. **M16.**
[ORIGIN Alt., by addition of Italian ending, of French COURANTE.]
= COURANTE.

coranto /kɒˈrantəʊ/ *noun*². *obsolete* exc. *hist*. Pl. **-os**. **E17.**
[ORIGIN Alt. of French *courant* or English COURANT *noun*¹ in same way as CORANTO *noun*¹.]
= COURANT *noun*¹.

corban /ˈkɔːban/ *noun*. **ME.**
[ORIGIN popular Latin from New Testament Greek *korban* from Hebrew *qorbān* offering, from *qāraḇ* approach.]
†**1** The treasury of the Temple at Jerusalem; *transf.* a church treasury. **ME–M17.**
2 An offering or sacrifice made to God by the ancient Hebrews. **LME.**

†**corbe** *noun*. *rare* (Spenser). Only in **L16.**
[ORIGIN Abbreviation.]
= CORBEL *noun* 2.

corbeau /ˈkɔːbəʊ/ *noun & adjective*. **E19.**
[ORIGIN French = crow, raven: see CORBEL.]
In the drapery trade, (of) a dark green colour verging on black.

corbeil /ˈkɔːbeɪl/ *noun*. **E18.**
[ORIGIN Old French & mod. French *corbeille* basket from late Latin *corbicula* dim. of *corbis* basket.]
†**1** A basket filled with earth and placed on a parapet to protect defending soldiers. *rare*. Only in **E18.**
2 *ARCHITECTURE*. A representation in stone of a basket of flowers. **M18.**

corbeille /kɔːˈbeɪj/ *noun*. **E19.**
[ORIGIN French: see CORBEIL.]
An elegant basket of flowers or fruit.

corbel /ˈkɔːb(ə)l/ *noun & verb*. **LME.**
[ORIGIN Old French *corbel* (mod. *corbeau*) crow, raven, corbel, dim. of *corp* from Latin *corvus* raven: see -EL².]
▶ **A** *noun*. †**1** A raven. Only in **LME.**
2 A projection of stone, timber, etc., jutting out from a wall to support weight. **LME.**
3 A short timber laid longitudinally under part of a beam to give a better bearing on the supporting wall or pier. **E18.**
– COMB.: **corbel stone** = sense 2 above; **corbel table** a projecting course resting on a series of corbels.
▶ **B** *verb intrans. & trans*. Infl. **-ll-**, ***-l-**. (Cause to) stick *out* like or on a corbel. **M19.**
■ **corbelled** *adjective* provided with corbels; fashioned as a corbel: **M19. corbelling** *noun* corbels collectively; work consisting of corbels: **M16.**

corbicula /kɔːˈbɪkjʊlə/ *noun*. **E19.**
[ORIGIN Late Latin: see CORBEIL.]
= ***pollen basket*** s.v. POLLEN *noun*.

corbie /ˈkɔːbi/ *noun*. *Scot*. **LME.**
[ORIGIN from Old French *corb* var. of *corp* (see CORBEL) + -IE.]
A raven; a carrion crow. Also ***corbie crow***.
– COMB.: **corbie gable**: having corbie steps; **corbie messenger** [after *Genesis* 8:7]: who returns too late or not at all; **corbie steps** projections in the form of steps on the sloping sides of a gable.

corbin /ˈkɔːbɪn/ *noun*. Long *obsolete* exc. in comb. **ME.**
[ORIGIN Old French formed as CORBIE: cf. Latin *corvinus* of or pertaining to a raven.]
A raven.
– COMB.: **corbin-bone** the lower end of a deer's breastbone (customarily thrown to the birds).

Corbusian /kɔːˈbjuːzɪən/ *adjective*. **M20.**
[ORIGIN from the name of the French architect Le *Corbusier* (Charles Edouard Jeanneret, 1887–1965) + -IAN.]
Pertaining to the architect Le Corbusier.

corcass /ˈkɔːkəs/ *noun*. **L18.**
[ORIGIN Irish *corcach* marsh.]
A salt marsh bordering certain Irish rivers.

corchorus /ˈkɔːk(ə)rəs/ *noun*. Now *rare* or *obsolete* exc. as a genus name. **M18.**
[ORIGIN Greek *korkhoros* blue pimpernel, jute.]
The plant kerria.

corcule /ˈkɔːkjuːl/ *noun*. Now *rare* or *obsolete*. Also **corcle** /-k(ə)l/, **corculum** /-kjʊləm/. **L18.**
[ORIGIN Latin *corculum* dim. of *cor* heart: see -ULE.]
The embryo in a plant seed.

cord /kɔːd/ *noun*¹ *& adjective*. **ME.**
[ORIGIN Old French & mod. French *corde* from Latin *chorda* from Greek *khordē* gut, string of musical instrument. Cf. CHORD *noun*².]
▶ **A** *noun*. **I** *lit*. **1** (A piece of) string or rope composed of several strands twisted or woven together; now *esp.* a thick string or light rope. **ME.** ▸**b** (A piece of) electric flex. Chiefly *N. Amer.* **L19.**
T. PYNCHON Binds his hands and feet with scarlet silk cords.
the cord *spec.* the hangman's rope. ***bungee cord***, ***light cord***, ***ripcord***, ***whipcord***, etc.
†**2** A string of a musical instrument. Cf. CHORD *noun*² 4. **ME–M19.**
3 Any structure in the body that is long, flexible, and rounded like a cord; *spec.* = UMBILICAL ***cord***. **LME.**
S. KING Clamped so tightly . . that the cords in his wrist stood out.
spermatic cord, ***spinal cord***, ***vocal cords***, etc.
4 *sing.* & (usu.) in *pl.* Stringhalt of horses. Now *rare* or *obsolete*. **E16.**
†**5** = CHORD *noun*² 2. **M–L16.**
6 A measure of cut wood, esp. firewood (usu. 128 cu. ft, approx. 3.62 cu. metres). **E17.**
7 A raised cordlike rib on cloth; ribbed cloth, *esp.* corduroy; in *pl.* (*colloq.*), corduroy trousers. **L18.**
▶ **II** *fig*. **8** A moral or emotional tie. **LME.**
R. L. STEVENSON The cords of discipline.
silver cord: see SILVER *noun & adjective*.
– COMB.: **cord-drill**: worked by a cord twisted round it and pulled to and fro; **cordgrass** any of several spartina grasses, valuable in binding coastal mudflats; **cord-ornamented** *adjective* (*ARCHAEOLOGY*) (of pottery) decorated by pressing cord into the soft clay; **cordwood** wood stacked in cords; firewood cut in standard (usu. 4-ft) lengths.
▶ **B** *attrib.* or as *adjective*. **1** Made of ribbed cloth, esp. corduroy. **M19.**
MOLLIE HARRIS He always wore thick brown cord trousers.
2 *ARCHAEOLOGY*. Of pottery: cord-ornamented. **E20.**
■ **cordless** *adjective* (of an electrical appliance) working without (fixed) connection to the mains; battery-powered: **E20. cordlike** *adjective* resembling (that of) (a) cord **E17. cordy** *adjective* (*rare*) of or like cord **E17.**

†**cord** *noun*² var. of CHORD *noun*¹.

cord /kɔːd/ *verb*¹. **LME.**
[ORIGIN from CORD *noun*¹.]
1 *verb trans*. Provide with a cord or cords. **LME.**
2 *verb trans*. Fasten or tie with cord. **L15.**
DICKENS Miss Charity called to him to come and cord her box.
3 *verb trans*. Stack (wood) in cords. **M17.**
S. SCHAMA Dead and fallen wood would be gathered and corded for fuel.
4 *verb intrans*. Of a muscle or vein: form a visible ridge on the skin; become visibly hard or taut. Cf. earlier CORDED 2b. **M20.**
M. RENAULT The vein . . corded and stood out.
■ **corder** *noun* a person who or thing which fastens with a cord or forms a cord **LME.**

cord /kɔːd/ *verb*² *trans. & intrans*. Long *Scot*. *rare*. **ME.**
[ORIGIN Aphet. Cf. CHORD *verb*.]
= ACCORD *verb*.

cordage /ˈkɔːdɪdʒ/ *noun*. **L15.**
[ORIGIN Old French & mod. French, formed as CORD *noun*¹: see -AGE.]
Cords or cordlike ridges collectively; *esp.* a ship's rigging.

†**cordal** *noun*. **LME–E19.**
[ORIGIN Old French *corda(i)l*, formed as CORD *noun*¹: see -AL¹.]
A cord, esp. of a heraldic robe.

†**cordant** *adjective*. **ME–M19.**
[ORIGIN Aphet.]
= ACCORDANT.

cordate /ˈkɔːdeɪt/ *adjective*. **M17.**
[ORIGIN Latin *cordatus* wise, in mod. Latin heart-shaped from *cor(d-)* heart: see -ATE².]
†**1** Wise, prudent. **M17–M18.**
2 *BOTANY & ZOOLOGY*. Heart-shaped; pointed at one end and rounded and indented at the other. **M18.**
■ †**cordated** *adjective* = CORDATE 2: only in **18.**

cordax *noun* var. of KORDAX.

corded /ˈkɔːdɪd/ *adjective*. **LME.**
[ORIGIN from CORD *noun*¹ + -ED².]
1 Having cords; in the form of cords. **LME.**
2 Having a ribbed appearance or texture. **M18.** ▸**b** Of part of the body: with muscles or veins forming a visible ridge on the skin. Of a muscle or vein: forming such a ridge, visibly hard or taut. **L19.**
corded ware cord-ornamented ware, esp. of a Neolithic people of Thuringia (also called ***Schnurkeramik***).

Cordelier /kɔːdɪˈlɪə/ *noun*. **LME.**
[ORIGIN Old French & mod. French, formed as CORDELLE: see -IER.]
1 A Franciscan Observant (so called from the knotted cord worn round the waist). **LME.**
2 A member of a political club of the French Revolution which met in a former convent of the Cordeliers. **M19.**

cordelière /kɔːdəlɪˈɛː/ *noun*. **M16.**
[ORIGIN French, formed as CORDELIER.]
†**1** A kind of coarse knotted work in embroidery. **M–L16.**
2 *HERALDRY*. A loosely knotted silver cord around armorial bearings of women (in Britain only occasionally, and denoting a widow). **E18.**

cordelle /kɔːˈdɛl/ *noun & verb*. **E16.**
[ORIGIN Old French & mod. French, dim. of *corde* CORD *noun*¹: see -EL².]
▶ **A** *noun*. †**1** A rope, esp. on a ship. *Scot*. **E16–E17.**
2 A ship's towing line. *N. Amer.* **E19.**
▶ **B** *verb trans. & intrans*. Give a tow (to) with a cordelle. *N. Amer.* **E19.**

cordia /ˈkɔːdɪə/ *noun*. **E19.**
[ORIGIN mod. Latin (see below), from E. *Cordus* (1486–1535) and his son V. *Cordus* (1515–44), German botanists: see -IA¹.]
Any of various (sub)tropical shrubs and trees of the genus *Cordia*, of the borage family, grown as ornamentals or for timber.

cordial /ˈkɔːdɪəl/ *adjective & noun*. **ME.**
[ORIGIN medieval Latin *cordialis*, from *cor(d-)* heart: see -IAL.]
▶ **A** *adjective*. †**1** Of or belonging to the heart. **ME–M17.**
2 Heartfelt, earnest, warm; warm and friendly without showing intimacy. **ME.**
R. W. DALE A cordial abhorrence of what is sensual. J. HILTON Sanders was very cordial and said he hoped to meet us again.
3 Stimulating, invigorating; reviving. **LME.**
▶ **B** *noun*. A medicine, food, or drink to stimulate the circulation and invigorate; a flavoured and sweetened drink. **ME.**
■ **cordially** *adverb* **LME.**

cordialise *verb* var. of CORDIALIZE.

cordiality /kɔːdɪˈalɪti/ *noun*. **E17.**
[ORIGIN from CORDIAL *adjective* + -ITY.]
Cordial quality; heartfelt warmth; warm friendliness without intimacy.

cordialize /ˈkɔːdɪəlʌɪz/ *verb*. Also **-ise**. **L18.**
[ORIGIN formed as CORDIALITY + -IZE.]
1 *verb trans*. Make into a cordial. **L18.**
2 *verb trans*. Make cordial or friendly. *rare*. **E19.**
3 *verb intrans*. Be or become cordial (*with*), be on friendly terms. Chiefly *Scot*. **M19.**

cordierite /ˈkɔːdɪərʌɪt/ *noun*. **E19.**
[ORIGIN from P. L. A. *Cordier* (1777–1861), French geologist + -ITE¹.]
MINERALOGY. An aluminium and magnesium silicate occurring in an altered state in metamorphic rocks and otherwise as blue, transparent or translucent, orthorhombic crystals which are pleochroic and have been used as gems.

cordiform /ˈkɔːdɪfɔːm/ *adjective*. **E19.**
[ORIGIN from Latin *cor(d-)* heart + -I- + -FORM.]
Heart-shaped; = CORDATE 2.

cordillera /kɔːdɪˈljɛːrə/ *noun*. **E18.**
[ORIGIN Spanish, from *cordilla* dim. of *cuerda* from Latin *chorda* CORD *noun*¹.]
Each of a series of parallel mountain ridges or chains, esp. in the Andes; an extensive belt of mountains, valleys, etc., esp. as a major continental feature.
■ **cordilleran** *adjective* **L19.**

cordiner *noun* see CORDWAINER.

C

C

cording /ˈkɔːdɪŋ/ *noun*. L16.
[ORIGIN from CORD *noun*[1], *verb*[1] + -ING[1].]
1 Cords collectively. L16.
2 The action of fastening with or hanging by a cord; the arrangement of cords in a loom. E17.

cordite /ˈkɔːdʌɪt/ *noun*. L19.
[ORIGIN from CORD *noun*[1] (from its stringlike appearance) + -ITE[1].]
A smokeless explosive used in guns, made from gun cotton, nitroglycerine, and petroleum jelly.

cordoba /ˈkɔːdəbə, -və/ *noun*. E20.
[ORIGIN from Hernández de *Córdoba* (fl. 1524), Spanish governor of Nicaragua.]
The basic monetary unit of Nicaragua, equal to 100 centavos.

cordon /ˈkɔːd(ə)n; *in sense 4 also foreign* kɔrdɔ̃ (*pl. same*)/ *noun*. LME.
[ORIGIN Italian *cordone* augm. of *corda* CORD *noun*[1] & Old French & mod. French *cordon* dim. of *corde* CORD *noun*[1]: cf. -OON.]
1 An ornamental cord or braid worn on a garment. LME.
2 FORTIFICATION. A course of stones where a parapet meets a rampart, or forming a coping on the inner wall of a ditch. L16.
3 ARCHITECTURE. A projecting band of stone on the face of a wall. E18.
4 A ribbon forming part of the insignia of an order of knighthood. E18.
5 A line or circle of troops etc. positioned to prevent passage to or from a guarded area; a system of police roadblocks. M18. ▸b A guarded line between districts affected with a disease and those unaffected, to prevent its spread. E19.
6 A fruit tree trained to grow as a single stem, usu. against a wall. L19.
■ **cordoned** *adjective* decorated with the cordon of an order M16.

cordon /ˈkɔːd(ə)n/ *verb trans*. M16.
[ORIGIN French *cordonner*, from *cordon*: see CORDON *noun*.]
†1 Ornament with a cordon. *rare*. Only in M16.
†2 Twist into a cord. *rare*. Only in E17.
3 Cut *off* or surround (as) with a cordon of police etc. L19.

cordon bleu /ˌkɔːdɔ̃ ˈbləː/ *noun & adjectival phr*. M18.
[ORIGIN French, formed as CORDON *noun* + *bleu* BLUE *adjective*.]
▸ **A** *noun phr*. Pl. **-s -s** (pronounced same).
1 (A person having) a supreme distinction; *spec*. a first-class cook. M18.
2 *hist*. A blue ribbon signifying the highest order of chivalry under the Bourbon kings. L18.
▸ **B** *adjectival phr*. Of cooking: first-class. M20.

cordon sanitaire /ˌkɔːdɔ̃ sanɪˈtɛː/ *noun phr*. Pl. **-s -s** (pronounced same). M19.
[ORIGIN French, formed as CORDON *noun* + *sanitaire* sanitary.]
= CORDON *noun* 5b.

> *fig*.: B. WARD The Allies succeeded in creating a *cordon sanitaire* of buffer-states to cut Communism off from Europe.

cordovan /ˈkɔːdəv(ə)n/ *adjective & noun*. L16.
[ORIGIN Spanish *cordován* (now *-bán*) noun, *-ano* adjective, from *Còrdova* (now *-oba*) from Latin *Corduba* Cordoba (see below).]
▸ **A** *adjective*. Of or pertaining to the city of and province of Cordoba in Spain; made of cordovan. L16.
▸ **B** *noun*. **1** A kind of pliable fine-grained leather used esp. for shoes, made orig. at Cordoba from goatskin and now from horsehide. L16.
†2 A skin of this leather. M17–E19.

Cordtex /ˈkɔːdtɛks/ *noun*. M20.
[ORIGIN from CORD *noun*[1] + TEXTILE.]
(Proprietary name for) fuse cable consisting of a core of explosive material in a plastic and textile sheath.

corduroy /ˈkɔːdərɔɪ/ *noun & adjective*. L18.
[ORIGIN Prob. from CORD *noun*[1] + DUROY.]
▸ **A** *noun*. **1** A coarse cotton velvet with thick ribbing. L18.
2 In *pl*. Corduroy trousers. *colloq*. L18.
3 A road made of logs laid together transversely; ground made up into such a road. M19.
▸ **B** *adjective*. **1** Made of corduroy. L18.
2 Having ridges and furrows like corduroy; *spec*. (of a road etc.) made of logs laid together transversely. L18.
■ **corduroyed** *adjective* wearing corduroy M19.

corduroy /ˈkɔːdərɔɪ/ *verb trans*. M19.
[ORIGIN from the noun.]
Make as a corduroy road; cross (a swamp etc.) with such a road.

cordwain /ˈkɔːdweɪn/ *noun*. *arch*. LME.
[ORIGIN Old French *cordewan*, *cordoan*, from *Cordoue* from Spanish *Córdova*: see CORDOVAN.]
= CORDOVAN *noun* 1.

> SIR W. SCOTT Shoes of Spanish cordwain fastened with silver buckles.

cordwainer /ˈkɔːdweɪnə/ *noun*. *arch*. Also (now *Scot*.) **cordiner** /ˈkɔːd(ə)nə/. ME.
[ORIGIN Anglo-Norman *cordewaner* = Old French *cordoanier* (mod. *cordonnier*), formed as CORDWAIN.]
A worker in cordwain, a shoemaker.
– NOTE: Now only in names of guilds etc.
■ **cordwainery** *noun* shoemaker's work M19. **cordwaining** *noun* = CORDWAINERY M18.

CORE *abbreviation*. *US*.
Congress of Racial Equality.

core /kɔː/ *noun*[1]. ME.
[ORIGIN Unknown.]
▸ **I 1** The hard central part of an apple, pear, quince, etc., containing the seeds. ME. ▸†**b** *fig*. Something that sticks in one's throat, something one cannot get over. LME–M17.
2 An unburnt part in the middle of a piece of coal, limestone, etc. LME.
3 The hard centre of a boil. M16.

> *fig*.: R. NORTH The Canker, or Coar, of the late Rebellion was torn out by this loyal Acknowledgment.

▸ **II 4** The innermost part or heart of anything (*lit*. & *fig*.), *spec*. of timber or of one's person. LME.

> SHAKES. *Haml*. In my heart's core, ay, in my heart of heart. WELLINGTON Our system is rotten to the core. S. BARING-GOULD A solid core of fact. P. PORTER The fire storm bit out the core of Dresden.

▸ **III** A central portion that is separated from the rest.
5 A piece cut out and removed from the middle of something, esp. the ground or the seabed. M17.
6 A central portion that is left; *spec*. (ARCHAEOLOGY) a piece of stone left as a waste product after the removal of flakes to make implements. E19.
▸ **IV 7** *gen*. A central part of different character. Chiefly *techn*. M17.
8 An internal mould filling the space to be left hollow in a casting. E18.
9 A length of soft iron forming the centre of an electromagnet or an induction coil. M19. ▸**b** Each of an array of small magnetic units in a computer whose magnetization is reversed by passing a current through a nearby wire. M20.
10 The central strand of a rope or an electric cable. M19.
11 The central part of the earth; *spec*. that within the mantle, with a radius of 3500 km (2200 miles). L19.
12 PHYSICS. The part of an atom other than the valency electrons. E20.
13 The part of a nuclear reactor that contains the fissile material. M20.
– PHRASES ETC.: ***hard core***: see HARD *adjective*. ***red core***: see RED *adjective*. ***soft-core***: see SOFT *adjective*.
– ATTRIB. & COMB.: In the sense 'central, basic, fundamental', as ***core vocabulary*** etc. Special combs., as **core area** a central geographical area in which characteristic elements are concentrated; **core curriculum** a group of basic subjects whose study is compulsory and to which optional ones may be added; **core implement**, **core tool** ARCHAEOLOGY a stone tool shaped by the removal of waste and trimming flakes from a block or nodule; **core loss** energy loss in electrical machinery by hysteresis and eddy currents in cores; **core sampler** a device for extracting a core from the seabed etc.; **core-sampling** drilling of the seabed etc. so as to extract cores as samples; ***core tool***: see ***core implement*** above.
■ **coreless** *adjective* E19.

core /kɔː/ *noun*[2]. E17.
[ORIGIN Partly var. of CHORE *noun*[1], partly anglicized spelling of CORPS.]
1 A body or company of people; *spec*. the players in a curling match, a rink. Chiefly *Scot*. E17.
2 A gang of miners working together in one shift. L18.
3 A shift in a Cornish mine. L18.

core /kɔː/ *verb trans*. LME.
[ORIGIN from CORE *noun*[1].]
1 Take out the core of. LME.
2 In *pass*. Be enshrined. E19.
3 Hollow *out* by using a core (in founding) or extracting one. L19.
■ **corer** *noun* (*a*) a device for extracting cores from fruit; (*b*) = ***core sampler*** s.v. CORE *noun*[1]: L18.

-core /kɔː/ *combining form*. L20.
[ORIGIN from *-core* in ***hardcore*** s.v. HARD *adjective, adverb, & noun*.]
Forming nouns designating extreme or intense genres of rock or dance music, as ***queercore*** etc.

coreal *noun* var. of CORIAL.

†**Corean** *noun & adjective* see KOREAN.

†**Coreis** *noun* see KOREISH.

†**Coreis(h)** *noun pl. & adjective* see KOREISH.

co-relation /kəʊrɪˈleɪʃ(ə)n/ *noun*. M19.
[ORIGIN from CO- + RELATION.]
(A) mutual relation; (a) correlation.

corelative /kəʊˈrɛlətɪv/ *adjective & noun*. Also **co-relative**. M18.
[ORIGIN from CO- + RELATIVE.]
(A) correlative.
■ **corelatively** *adverb* L19.

co-religionist /kəʊrɪˈlɪdʒ(ə)nɪst/ *noun*. Also ***corel-**. E19.
[ORIGIN from CO- + RELIGION + -IST.]
An adherent of the same religion.

corella /kəˈrɛlə/ *noun*. M19.
[ORIGIN Wiradhuri *garila*.]
The long-billed cockatoo, *Cacatua tenuirostris*, a white Australian bird that can be taught to talk.

coreopsis /kɒrɪˈɒpsɪs/ *noun*. Pl. same. M18.
[ORIGIN mod. Latin, from Greek *koris* bug + *opsis* appearance, in ref. to the shape of the seeds.]
A plant of the mostly American genus *Coreopsis*, of the composite family, comprising annuals and perennials with rayed usu. yellow flowers, some of which are grown as garden flowers.

co-respondent /kəʊrɪˈspɒnd(ə)nt/ *noun*. Also ***corespondent**. M19.
[ORIGIN from CO- + RESPONDENT.]
LAW. A person with whom a married person, esp. a married woman, is alleged to have committed adultery.
co-respondent shoes *joc*. men's two-toned shoes.

corf /kɔːf/ *noun*. Pl. **corves** /kɔːvz/. LME.
[ORIGIN Middle & mod. Low German, Middle Dutch & mod. Dutch *korf* = Old High German *chorp*, *korb* (German *Korb*), from Latin *corbis* basket.]
†1 A basket. LME–E17.
2 A large basket formerly used for conveying, hoisting, or delivering mined coal or ore; the tub which has superseded it. M17.
3 A container through which water can flow for keeping fish etc. in it alive. L17.

Corfiote /ˈkɔːfɪəʊt/ *noun & adjective*. Also **-ot** /-ət/. M19.
[ORIGIN from *Corfu* (see below) after CYPRIOT.]
(A native or inhabitant) of the Greek island of Corfu.

corgi /ˈkɔːgi/ *noun*. E20.
[ORIGIN Welsh, from *cor* dwarf + *ci* dog.]
A dog of a small short-legged breed of Welsh origin, with a head resembling that of a fox. Also ***Welsh corgi***.

coriaceous /kɒrɪˈeɪʃəs/ *adjective*. L17.
[ORIGIN from late Latin *coriaceus*, formed as CORIUM: see -ACEOUS.]
1 Resembling leather in texture or appearance; leathery. L17.
2 Made of leather. *rare*. E19.

corial /kɔːrɪˈɑːl/ *noun*. Also **-eal**. L18.
[ORIGIN Amer. Spanish from Arawak *kuljara*: cf. CURIARA.]
In Guyana, a dugout canoe with pointed ends.

coriander /kɒrɪˈandə/ *noun*. ME.
[ORIGIN Old French & mod. French *coriandre* from Latin *coriandrum* from Greek *koriannon*.]
1 An annual umbelliferous plant, *Coriandrum sativum*, native to southern Europe and Asia Minor and with aromatic fruit used for flavouring. ME.
2 = ***coriander seed*** below. Also, the leaves of coriander, as a culinary item. M16.
– COMB.: **coriander seed** (*a*) the globose fruit of coriander, *esp*. the dried ripe fruit; (*b*) *slang* (now *rare* or *obsolete*) money.

†**Corinth** *noun*. ME.
[ORIGIN Old French & mod. French *Corinthe* (Anglo-Norman *Corauntz*) from Latin *Corinthos* from Greek *Korinthos*: see CORINTHIAN.]
▸ **I 1** ***raisins of Corinth***, (orig.) ***raisins of Corauntz*** [see CURRANT], currants. ME–E17.
2 (**c-**.) See CURRANT. ME.
▸ **II 3** In *pl*. Natives or inhabitants of Corinth. LME–M17.
4 A brothel. E17–L18.

Corinthian /kəˈrɪnθɪən/ *noun & adjective*. E16.
[ORIGIN from Latin *Corinthius* from Greek *Korinthios*, from *Korinthos* Corinth (see below): see -AN.]
▸ **A** *noun*. **1** A native or inhabitant of Corinth, a city of ancient and modern Greece. In *pl*. (treated as *sing*.), either of St Paul's two Epistles to the Corinthians, books of the New Testament. E16.
†2 A wealthy man; a profligate idler; a licentious man. L16–L19.
3 A wealthy man of fashion or lover of sport. *arch*. E19.
▸ **B** *adjective*. **1** Of or pertaining to Corinth. L16.
Corinthian brass, **Corinthian bronze** an alloy produced at Corinth, much prized for ornaments, said to be of gold, silver, and copper; *fig*. effrontery, shamelessness.
2 ARCHITECTURE. Designating the lightest and most ornate of the three classical orders, characterized by bell-shaped capitals with rows of acanthus leaves giving graceful volutes and helices. E17.
3 Profligate, licentious; given to luxurious dissipation. *arch*. M17.
4 After the elegant style of the art of Corinth; too brilliant. M19.
5 Amateur (in sport). (Earlier in CORINTHIANISM.) L19.
■ **Corinthiaˈnesque** *adjective* approximating to the Corinthian architectural style M19. **Corinthianism** *noun* amateurism in sport E19. **Corinthianize** *verb intrans*. (*a*) *arch*. live licentiously; (*b*) imitate the Corinthian order of architecture: E19.

Coriolis /kɒrɪˈəʊlɪs/ *attrib. adjective*. E20.
[ORIGIN G. G. *Coriolis* (1792–1843), French engineer.]
Pertaining to or designating the effect whereby a body moving relative to a rotating frame of reference is accelerated in that frame in a direction perpendicular to its motion and to the axis of rotation.
Coriolis acceleration, ***Coriolis force***, etc.

corium /ˈkɔːrɪəm/ *noun*. **E19**.
[ORIGIN Latin = skin, hide, leather.]
1 *ENTOMOLOGY*. A hardened part at the base of the forewings of heteropteran insects, next to the clavus. **E19**.
2 = DERMIS. **M19**.
3 *hist*. A suit of leather armour composed of overlapping flaps. **M19**.

co-rival /kəʊˈrʌɪv(ə)l/ *noun & adjective*. **L17**.
[ORIGIN Partly from CO- + RIVAL *noun & adjective*, partly var. of CORRIVAL.]
(A person) who is one of two or more joint rivals.
■ **co-rivalry** *noun* **M19**.

cork /kɔːk/ *noun*[1] *& adjective*. **ME**.
[ORIGIN Dutch, Low German *kork* from Spanish *alcorque* cork soled sandal, from Arabic AL-[2] + (prob.) Hispano-Arabic *qurq*, *qorq* ult. from Latin *quercus* oak, (in some parts of Iberia) cork oak.]
▸ **A** *noun*. **1** A buoyant light-brown material that is obtained from the cork oak, being the cork (sense 1b) of that tree. **ME**. ▸**b** *BOTANY*. The material forming the outer layer of the periderm in parts of some higher plants, providing protection by its impermeability to air and water. Also called ***phellem***. **L19**.
BURNT cork.
2 A sandal, sole, or heel made of cork. Now *hist*. **LME**.
3 A piece of cork used as a float for a fishing line or a person swimming. **L15**.
4 A cylindrical or tapering stopper for a bottle, made of cork or other material. **M16**.
5 An evergreen oak, *Quercus suber*, which is native to the Mediterranean and has the distinctive property of producing more cork after some is removed. **M16**.
▸ **B** *attrib*. or as *adjective*. Made of or with cork. **E18**.
– COMB. & SPECIAL COLLOCATIONS: **cork cambium** the tissue of a plant's periderm that gives rise to cork on its outer surface and phelloderm on its inner; **cork-jacket**: made with cork, to support a person in the water; **cork lino**, **cork linoleum**: made of canvas backed with a mixture of linseed oil and ground cork; **cork oak** = sense 5 above; **cork-tipped** *adjective* (of a cigarette) having a filter of corklike material; **cork tree** (*a*) = sense 5 above; (*b*) any of several deciduous trees of eastern Asia belonging to the genus *Phellodendron* of the rue family and having corklike bark; **corkwing** a small European wrasse (*Crenilabrus melops*); **corkwood** (a tree yielding) any very light and porous wood, esp. *Leitneria floridana*, a rare deciduous shrub or tree of the south-eastern US, and the whau, *Entelea arborescens*, of New Zealand.
■ **corklike** *adjective* resembling (that of) cork **M19**.

cork /kɔːk/ *noun*[2]. **ME**.
[ORIGIN Gaelic & Old Irish & mod. Irish *corcur* (orig.) purple from Latin *purpur*.]
A purple or red dye obtained from certain lichens.

cork *noun*[3] see CALK *noun*.

cork /kɔːk/ *verb*[1] *trans*. **E16**.
[ORIGIN from CORK *noun*[1].]
†**1** Provide with a cork as a sole, float, etc. **E16–M19**.
2 Stop (a bottle etc.) with a cork. **M17**.
3 Shut *up* or confine with or as with a cork; bottle *up* (feelings). Also foll. by *down*. **M17**.
4 Blacken with burnt cork. **E19**.
■ **corked** *ppl adjective* that has been corked; (of wine) tasting of the cork, impaired by a defective cork: **E16**.

cork *verb*[2] see CALK *verb*[1].

corkage /ˈkɔːkɪdʒ/ *noun*. **M19**.
[ORIGIN from CORK *noun*[1] or *verb*[1] + -AGE.]
A charge made by a hotel or restaurant for serving a bottle of liquor, esp. one not supplied by it.

corker /ˈkɔːkə/ *noun & adjective*. **E18**.
[ORIGIN from CORK *verb*[1] + -ER[1].]
▸ **A** *noun*. **1** A person who puts corks into bottles. Formerly perh. also a person who cut cork into stoppers. **E18**.
2 Orig., something that puts an end to a matter. Now usu., a very good thing or person. *colloq*. **M19**.
▸ **B** *adjective*. Very good. *NZ colloq*. **M20**.

corking /ˈkɔːkɪŋ/ *noun*. **M17**.
[ORIGIN from CORK *noun*[1], *verb*[1] + -ING[1].]
1 The action of CORK *verb*[1]. **M17**.
2 The development or presence of a corky taste in wine. **E20**.

corking /ˈkɔːkɪŋ/ *adjective*. *colloq*. **L19**.
[ORIGIN from CORKER + -ING[2].]
Exceptionally fine, excellent, or large.
Loaded Four corking lasses . . beckon us back in.
■ **corkingly** *adverb* **E20**.

†**corking-pin** *noun*. **E18–M19**.
[ORIGIN App. from alt. of CALKIN + PIN *noun*.]
A pin of the largest size.

corkir /ˈkɔːkə/ *noun*. *Scot*. Also **k-**. **E18**.
[ORIGIN Gaelic *corcur*: see CORK *noun*[2].]
A lichen, *Lecanora tartarea*, which yields a red dye.

corks /kɔːks/ *interjection*. *slang*. **E20**.
[ORIGIN Alt. of COCK *noun*[4] or blend of this and LAWK.]
Expr. astonishment or dismay.

corkscrew /ˈkɔːkskruː/ *noun, verb, & adjective*. **E18**.
[ORIGIN from CORK *noun*[1] + SCREW *noun*[1].]
▸ **A** *noun*. **1** An instrument for drawing a cork from a bottle, comprising a steel helix with a (usu. transverse) handle. **E18**.
2 Something, esp. a curl, with a spiral twist. **M19**.
– COMB.: **corkscrew rule**: that the direction of the magnetic field produced by an electric current following a spiral path is that which a corkscrew would have if it were turned in the same way as the current.
▸ **B** *verb*. **1** *verb trans. & intrans*. Move or twist in a spiral course. **L18**.
2 *verb trans*. Get *out of* someone by devious means or with effort. **M19**.
▸ **C** *adjective*. Spirally twisted. **E19**.
THACKERAY Little corkscrew ringlets. TENNYSON Up the cork-screw stair.
■ **corkscrewy** *adjective* **L19**.

corky /ˈkɔːki/ *adjective*. **E17**.
[ORIGIN from CORK *noun*[1] + -Y[1].]
1 Light, frivolous; buoyant, lively; restive. *colloq*. **E17**.
†**2** Dry and stiff; withered. Only in **E17**.
3 *gen*. Resembling cork. **M18**.
4 Having a taste of cork; corked. **L19**.
■ **corkiness** *noun* **M19**.

Corliss /ˈkɔːlɪs/ *adjective*. **M19**.
[ORIGIN G. H. *Corliss* (1817–88), US engineer.]
MECHANICS. Designating (a steam engine employing) a kind of valve gear with an oscillatory rotary motion.

corm /kɔːm/ *noun*. **M19**.
[ORIGIN mod. Latin *cormus* from Greek *kormos* trunk of a tree with the boughs lopped off.]
An underground rounded, swollen portion of the stem of some perennial plants which develops buds, leaves, and roots and each year dries up after giving rise to new corms.
■ **cormel**, **cormlet** *nouns* a small corm growing at the side of a mature corm **E20**.

cormorant /ˈkɔːm(ə)r(ə)nt/ *noun & adjective*. **ME**.
[ORIGIN Old French *cormaran* (mod. *cormoran*) from medieval Latin *corvus marinus* sea-raven. For final *t* cf. *peasant*, *tyrant*.]
▸ **A** *noun*. **1** A large lustrous-black fish-eating waterbird, *Phalacrocorax carbo*, having a long neck and bill and found near many coasts; any bird of the same family (Phalacrocoracidae) of dark fish-eating waterbirds. **ME**.
2 *fig*. An insatiably greedy person or thing. **E16**.
▸ **B** *attrib*. or as *adjective*. Greedy; rapacious. **M16**.

corn /kɔːn/ *noun*[1].
[ORIGIN Old English *corn* = Old Frisian, Old Saxon, Old High German, Old Norse *korn*, Gothic *kaurn* from Germanic; rel. to Latin *granum* GRAIN *noun*[1].]
1 A small hard particle, as of sand or salt. Long *dial*. **OE**.
2 *spec*. The small hard seed or fruit of a plant; *esp*. a cereal seed. **OE**.
BARLEYCORN. PEPPERCORN.
3 The seed, collectively, of a cereal plant; grain; *esp*. that of the chief cereal of a district, as in England wheat, in Scotland oats. **OE**. ▸**b** More fully ***Indian corn***. Maize. Without qualifying adjective chiefly *N. Amer*. **E17**. ▸**c** More fully ***corn whiskey***. Whiskey distilled from maize. *US*. **E19**.
TENNYSON A sack of corn.
b POPCORN.
4 Cereal plants as a standing or a harvested crop. **OE**.
SHAKES. *Hen. VIII* Her foes shake like a field of beaten corn.
5 In *pl*. Cereal crops. Now *dial*. **OE**.
†**6** A single stalk or plant of a cereal. *rare*. **LME–L16**.
7 Something corny (CORNY *adjective*[1] 5), *esp*. old-fashioned or sentimental music. *colloq*. **M20**.
– PHRASES: **acknowledge the corn** admit defeat, a charge, etc. **corn in Egypt** a plentiful supply (in allusion to *Genesis* 42:2). ***corn on the cob***: see COB *noun*[1] 8. ***Indian corn***: see sense 3b above. ***lye corn***: see LYE *verb*. ***soft corn***: see SOFT *adjective*. ***sweet corn***: see SWEET *adjective & adverb*.
– COMB.: **corn baby** [alt. of KIRN *noun*[2]] = ***corn dolly*** below; **corn beef** corned beef; **corn borer** any of several moths (or their larvae) whose larvae bore into corn, *esp*. (more fully ***European corn borer***) a pyralid moth, *Ostrinia* (*Pyrausta*) *nubilalis*, of Europe and N. America, and (more fully ***south-western corn borer***) a grass moth, *Diatraea* (*Zeadiatraea*) *grandiosella* of the southern US; **corn brandy** whiskey; **cornbread** *N. Amer*. bread made of the meal of maize; **corn bunting** a brown bunting, *Miliaria calandra*, of the open countryside; **corn buttercup** a Eurasian buttercup, *Ranunculus arvensis*, similar to the meadow buttercup, formerly a common weed in cornfields in Britain; also called ***corn crowfoot***; **corn cake** *US* cornbread made in the form of flat cakes; one of these cakes; **corn chandler** a dealer in corn; **corn circle** = ***crop circle*** s.v. CROP *noun*; **corncockle**: see COCKLE *noun*[1] 1; ***corn crib***: see CRIB *noun* 8; **corn crowfoot** = ***corn buttercup*** above; **corn dance** *US* any dance connected with the sowing or harvesting of maize among N. American Indians or black Americans; **corn dodger** *US* a type of cake of cornbread; **corn dog** *N. Amer*. a hot dog covered in maize-flour batter, fried, and served on a stick; **corn dolly** [alt. of KIRN *noun*[2]] a symbolic or decorative figure made of plaited straw; **corn earworm** a moth, *Heliothis armigera* or *H. zea*, whose larvae are a major pest of cultivated plants, esp. of maize in N. America; a larva of this moth; **corn exchange** a building where corn is or used to be bought and sold; **corn-factor** a dealer in corn; **corn-fed** *adjective* fed on grain, esp. maize; *fig*. (*colloq*.) plump, well-fed; *Jazz slang* old-fashioned, trite; **cornfield**: in which corn is grown; **corn-flag** any plant of the genus *Gladiolus* (see GLADIOLUS); **cornflake** (*a*) in *pl*., a kind of breakfast cereal made from toasted and flavoured flakes of maize meal; (*b*) a flake of this cereal; **cornflour** (*a*) fine flour got from maize, used in making puddings, corn syrup and corn sugar, adhesives, etc.; (*b*) flour got from rice or other grain; **corn-ground**: on which corn is grown; **corn-house** †(*a*) a granary; (*b*) *US* = ***corn crib*** s.v. CRIB *noun* 8; **corn husk** *N. Amer*. the husk of coarse leaves enclosing an ear of maize; **corn-husker** *N. Amer*. a machine which or person who strips the husks from the ears of maize; **corn-husking** *N. Amer*. the separation of maize husks; a convivial gathering that begins with this task; **Corn Laws** laws regulating the corn trade; *esp*. those in England restricting the import of corn, repealed in 1846; **corn lily** = IXIA 2; **corn marigold** a tall annual plant of the composite family, *Chrysanthemum segetum*, with yellow flowers like daisies and occurring as a weed on cultivated land; **cornmeal** meal made from corn, *spec*. in Scotland oatmeal, in N. America, meal of maize; †**cornmonger** a dealer in corn; **corn oil**: made from the germ of maize for use as a salad and cooking oil; **corn parsley** a glaucous parsley, *Petroselinum segetum*, of chalky banks and fields; **corn-pipe** a rustic musical instrument made of a stalk of corn; ***corn pone***: see PONE *noun*[2]; **corn-pone** *adjective* (*US*) rustic, unsophisticated; **corn-popper** *N. Amer*. a device for making popcorn; ***corn poppy***: see POPPY *noun* 1; **corn-rent**: paid in corn, or determined annually by the price of corn; **corn roast** *N. Amer*. a party at which green maize is roasted and eaten; **corn rose** (*a*) = ***corn poppy*** above; (*b*) the cockle (COCKLE *noun*[1] 1, 2); **corn salad** a plant of the genus *Valerianella* in the valerian family, esp. *V. locusta* or *V. eriocarpa*, annuals grown as salad plants in Europe; **corn-shuck** *N. Amer*. = ***corn husk*** above; **corn-shucking** *N. Amer*. = ***corn-husking*** above; ***corn silk***: see SILK *noun*; **corn smut** a smut fungus, *Ustilago zeae*, that attacks maize; the disease it causes; **corn snake** a long non-venomous snake, *Elaphe guttata*, common in the US; **corn snow** *US* coarse wet snow resulting from alternate thawing and freezing; ***corn spurrey***: see SPURREY 1; **corn-stalk** (*a*) a stalk of corn; (*b*) *slang* an Australian, esp. one from New South Wales; **cornstarch** (chiefly *N. Amer*.) = ***cornflour*** (a) above; **corn sugar** *US* glucose sugar, esp. when made from cornflour; **corn syrup** *N. Amer*. glucose syrup, esp. when made from cornflour; ***corn whiskey***: see sense 3c above; **corn-worm** a moth larva or other insect destructive to grain.

corn /kɔːn/ *noun*[2]. **LME**.
[ORIGIN Anglo-Norman = Old French & mod. French *cor* from Latin *cornu* horn.]
A small, horny, usu. tender area of thickened skin, esp. on the foot, caused by undue pressure.
tread on a person's corns: see TREAD *verb*.

corn /kɔːn/ *verb*. **LME**.
[ORIGIN from CORN *noun*[1].]
▸ **I** *verb trans*. **1** †**a** Provision with corn. *rare*. Only in **LME**. ▸**b** Give (a horse) a feed of oats. *Scot*. **M18**.
2 Form (esp. gunpowder) into grains, as by sieving. **M16**.
3 Sprinkle or preserve with salt. **M16**.
4 Plant with corn; grow corn on. **M17**.
▸ **II** *verb intrans*. †**5** Become granular. **M16–L17**.
6 Of a cereal or legume: form seeds in the ear or pod. **M17**.

cornada /kɔrˈnaða, kɔːˈnɑːdə/ *noun*. Pl. **-as** /-as, -əz/. **M20**.
[ORIGIN Spanish, from *cuerno* from Latin *cornu* horn.]
The goring of a bullfighter by a bull; a wound so caused.

cornage /ˈkɔːnɪdʒ/ *noun*. **L16**.
[ORIGIN Old French, from *corn(e)* from Latin *cornu* horn: see -AGE. In medieval Latin *cornagium*.]
A feudal service, being a form of rent fixed by the number of horned cattle.
– NOTE: The term was formerly widely misunderstood, and explained as a duty to blow a horn to warn of a border incursion.

cornball /ˈkɔːnbɔːl/ *noun & adjective*. **M19**.
[ORIGIN from CORN *noun*[1] + BALL *noun*[1].]
▸ **A** *noun*. **1** A sweet consisting of a ball of popcorn and syrup. *US*. **M19**.
2 A cornball person. *slang*. **M20**.
▸ **B** *adjective*. = CORNY *adjective*[1] 5. *slang*. **M20**.

cornbrash /ˈkɔːnbraʃ/ *noun*. **E19**.
[ORIGIN from CORN *noun*[1] + BRASH *noun*[2].]
GEOLOGY. An earthy fossiliferous limestone occurring widely in England in a thin formation of Jurassic age.

corncob /ˈkɔːnkɒb/ *noun*. **L18**.
[ORIGIN from CORN *noun*[1] + COB *noun*[1].]
1 The cylindrical woody part to which the grains are attached in an ear of maize. **L18**.
2 More fully ***corncob pipe***. A tobacco pipe made from a corncob. **M19**.

corncrake /ˈkɔːnkreɪk/ *noun*. **LME**.
[ORIGIN from CORN *noun*[1] + CRAKE *noun*[1].]
A slender brown bird, *Crex crex*, of the rail family which has a harsh grating cry and lives in grassland. Also called ***landrail***, ***meadow crake***.

cornea /ˈkɔːnɪə/ *noun*. **LME**.
[ORIGIN Short for medieval Latin *cornea tela* horny web, from Latin *corneus* CORNEOUS.]
The transparent circular outer covering at the front of the eye, over the iris and pupil.
luna cornea: see LUNA 2C.
■ **corneal** *adjective* **E19**.

†**corned** *adjective*[1]. **E16–M19**.
[ORIGIN from French *corné* from Latin *corneus* CORNEOUS: see -ED[2].]
Horned; pointed.

C

corned /kɔːnd/ *adjective*². L16.
[ORIGIN from CORN *noun*¹, *verb*: see -ED², -ED¹.]
1 Granulated. L16.
2 Preserved or cured with salt. E17.
corned beef beef preserved with salt and often tinned.
3 Drunk, intoxicated. Cf. CORNY *adjective*¹ 4. *slang*. L18.
4 Bearing seeds or grains; having the seeds developed. E19.

cornel /ˈkɔːn(ə)l/ *noun*¹. Long *obsolete* exc. *dial.* LME.
[ORIGIN Old French *cornal* var. of *cornée*, *cornier* CORNER *noun*.]
A corner; an angle (of a building etc.).

cornel /ˈkɔːn(ə)l/ *noun*² & *adjective*. LME.
[ORIGIN Old French *corn(e)ille*, *cornolle* (mod. *cornouille*) from Latin *cornus*.]
▸ **A** *noun*. **1** Long only more fully ***cornel wood***. The wood of the cornelian cherry, formerly used for weapons because of its hardness. LME.
2 Either of two plants, (orig. & more fully ***cornel tree***) the cornelian cherry (*Cornus mas*), and the dogwood (*Cornus sanguinea*); any of various other plants of the genus *Cornus*, which comprises mostly deciduous shrubs and trees. M16.
3 More fully ***cornel berry***, ***cornel fruit***. The fruit of the cornelian cherry, of the size and shape of an olive. L16.
4 [translating Latin *cornus*.] A javelin made of cornel wood. *literary*. E17.
▸ **B** *adjective*. Made of cornel wood. L17.

cornelian /kɔːˈniːlɪən/ *noun*¹. E17.
[ORIGIN from CORNEL *noun*² + -IAN.]
Now only more fully ***cornelian cherry***. A European flowering shrub or small tree, *Cornus mas*, of the dogwood family which bears edible fruit and is grown as an ornamental; the fruit itself (= CORNEL *noun*² 3).

cornelian *noun*² var. of CARNELIAN.

cornemuse /ˈkɔːnəmjuːz; *foreign* kɔrnəmyːz (*pl. same*)/ *noun*. LME.
[ORIGIN Old French & mod. French, prob. from *cornemuser* play the cornemuse, from *corner* sound a horn (from *corne* horn from Latin *cornu*) + *muser* play the musette.]
An early form of bagpipe; a kind of mouth-blown bagpipe of the present day in France and Belgium.

corneo- /ˈkɔːnɪəʊ/ *combining form*.
[ORIGIN from CORNEA: see -O-.]
MEDICINE. Of or pertaining to the cornea and —, as ***corneo-iritis***.

corneous /ˈkɔːnɪəs/ *adjective*. Now *techn.* M17.
[ORIGIN from Latin *corneus*, from *cornu* horn: see -EOUS.]
Horny.

corner /ˈkɔːnə/ *noun*. ME.
[ORIGIN Anglo-Norman *corner*, Old French *cornier* from Proto-Romance from Latin *cornu* horn, tip, corner: see -ER².]
1 A place where the converging sides or edges of something meet, forming an angular projection. ME.

GOLDSMITH The corners of the mouth. J. TYNDALL The corner of a window. T. COLLINS I regarded him out of the corner of my eye. *fig.*: J. K. JEROME There are one or two corners about you that are not perfect.

Oxford corners: see OXFORD *adjective*.
2 A projecting angle or extremity, esp. where two streets meet, or a road etc. changes direction. ME. ▸**b** A triangular piece cut from the hind end of a side of bacon. L19.

Daily Mirror Youngsters . . hanging around on street corners.

cut a corner, ***cut corners***: see CUT *verb*. **just around the corner**, **just round the corner** *colloq.* close at hand; imminent. **turn the corner** pass round a corner into another street; *fig.* pass from worsening to improving, esp. in an illness.
3 The small space included between meeting sides or edges, esp. of a room. ME. ▸**b** Each of the diagonally opposite angles of a boxing or wrestling ring, where a contestant rests between rounds and is attended by a second or seconds; *transf.* a boxer's or wrestler's second(s). M19.

DAY LEWIS Dark corners or passages of the houses we occupied.

cosy corner: see COSY *adjective* 2. ***tight corner***: see TIGHT *adjective*. **drive someone into a corner**, **paint oneself into a corner** *fig.* force someone, bring oneself, into a difficult situation from which there is no escape. ***every nook and corner***: see NOOK *noun* 3b. ***puss in the corner***: see PUSS *noun*¹. **within the four corners** within the scope or extent *of*. **b *neutral corner***: see NEUTRAL *noun* & *adjective*.
4 A secluded or remote region; somewhere that readily escapes notice. ME. ▸**b** A part of anywhere, even the smallest or most secluded. E16.

JOSEPH HALL Whatever private contract may be transacted in corners betwixt the parties. B. JOWETT A dark corner of the human mind. L. P. HARTLEY This small corner of Wales. **b** H. CONWAY My friend must have seen every nook and corner in the house. J. BUCHAN No corner of the globe left unexplored.

hole-and-corner: see HOLE *noun*¹. **keep a corner** reserve a small place.
5 A distant part; a quarter *of* the earth. Formerly also, a direction. LME.

SHAKES. *Much Ado* Sits the wind in that corner? MAX-MÜLLER Carried to all the corners of the earth.

6 A landmark or surveyor's mark at the angle of a plot of land. *US*. L17.
7 A point in whist and certain other card games. M18.
8 *COMMERCE*. The speculative purchase by a syndicate of all the available supply of a stock or commodity, so as to make speculative sellers unable to meet their obligations except by coming to the syndicate on its own terms; any combination to raise prices by securing a monopoly. M19.

R. H. TAWNEY Speculators who had made a corner in wheat. *fig.*: S. BELLOW I don't have a corner on troubles. You've got your own.

9 A share in something, esp. the proceeds of a robbery. *dial.* & *slang*. L19.
stand one's corner contribute or pay for one's share.
10 In some field games, a free kick or hit after an opponent has sent the ball over his or her own goal line, taken from the nearest corner (as in soccer) or from a point on the goal line or sideline at or towards the corner (as in hockey). Also ***corner kick***, ***corner hit***. L19.

Norwich Mercury His goal-bound effort was deflected for a corner.

long corner: see LONG *adjective*¹. ***short corner***: see SHORT *adjective*.
– COMB.: **cornerback** in certain field sports, as American football, hurling, (a player in) a defensive position on the wing; **corner boy** a street rough, a loafer esp. in Ireland (cf. ***cornerman*** below); †**corner-cap** a cap with four (or three) corners, worn by divines and members of a university; †**corner-creeper** *fig.* an underhand and stealthy person; **corner cupboard**: fitted into the corner of a room; **corner flag**: marking a corner of the playing area in football, hockey, and lacrosse; **corner forward** in hurling, (a player in) an attacking position on the wing; ***corner hit***, ***corner kick***: see sense 10 above. **cornerman** (*a*) a street rough, a loafer (cf. ***corner boy*** above); (*b*) a performer at either end of a row of blackface minstrels, playing bones or tambourine and contributing comic effects; (*c*) = CORNERER; (*d*) a person whose job is to assist a boxer or wrestler at the corner between rounds; **corner shop** a shop at a street corner; any small local shop, as distinct from a supermarket etc.; **cornerstone** [after late Latin (Vulgate) *lapis angularis*] a stone forming the projecting angle of a wall; *fig.* an indispensable or essential part, a basis on which something depends; **corner throw** (*a*) in certain ball games, a free throw of the ball from a corner of the playing area; (*b*) *JUDO* = SUMI-GAESHI.
■ **cornerless** *adjective* L16. **cornerwise** *adverb* so as to form a corner; diagonally: L15. **cornery** *adjective* having many corners L16.

corner /ˈkɔːnə/ *verb*. ME.
[ORIGIN from the noun.]
1 *verb trans.* Provide with corners. Usu. in *pass.* ME.

MILTON The Imperial City . . corner'd with four white Towers.

2 *verb trans.* Place in a corner. LME.
3 *verb trans.* Drive into a corner or a place from where escape is impossible; *fig.* put into a difficult or embarrassing position. E19.

M. TWAIN The little Lady Jane turned to Tom and cornered him with this question. J. COLVILLE Our 51st Division is cornered at St. Valéry and has been ordered to surrender.

4 *verb intrans.* Abut *on* at a corner; meet at an angle. *US*. E19.

N. HAWTHORNE A pew cornering on one of the side-aisles.

5 *verb trans.* *COMMERCE*. Operate in (a stock etc.) or against (a dealer) by means of a corner; control (a market) in this way. M19.

E. WILSON His employers . . had succeeded in cornering the market and wanted to keep up the price.

6 *verb trans.* Go round (a corner) in a road, racetrack, etc. M19.
7 *verb intrans.* Go round a corner, take corners, esp. in a specified manner. E20.

Times Letting plenty of fresh air into the car, . . driving smoothly with no fast cornering or sudden braking.

■ **cornerer** *noun* a person who makes a corner in a stock or commodity M19.

cornered /ˈkɔːnəd/ *adjective*. ME.
[ORIGIN from CORNER *noun*, *verb*: see -ED², -ED¹.]
Having a corner or corners. Freq. as 2nd elem. of comb., as ***three-cornered***, ***sharp-cornered***, etc.

cornet /ˈkɔːnɪt/ *noun*¹. In sense 1 now usu. **-tt**. LME.
[ORIGIN Old French & mod. French dim. of Proto-Romance var. of Latin *cornu* horn: see -ET¹.]
▸ **I** *MUSIC* **1 a** *EARLY MUSIC*. Orig., a wind instrument made of a horn or resembling a horn. Later = CORNETTO. Also, a player of such an instrument. LME. ▸**b** Orig. †***cornet-à-piston(s)***. A valved brass instrument used chiefly in bands, similar to a trumpet but shorter and with a wider mouth; a player of this instrument. M19.
2 Any of various organ stops suggestive of a cornet(t), esp. a powerful mixture stop. M17.
▸ **II 3 a** A piece of paper rolled into a conical form and twisted at the tip, for carrying sugar, salt, etc. M16. ▸**b** A conical wafer, esp. one filled with ice cream. E20.
†**4** A farrier's instrument formerly used for blood-letting. Also ***cornet horn***. L16–M18.
5 In gold assaying, a small flat coil into which the sample is rolled after cupellation, prior to the removal of silver by nitric acid. E19.
■ **corˈnettist**, **-etist** *noun* a player of the cornet(t) L18.

cornet /ˈkɔːnɪt/ *noun*². M16.
[ORIGIN Old French & mod. French *cornette* dim. of *corne* horn, orig. collect., from Proto-Romance alt. of Latin *cornua* pl. of *cornu* horn: see -ET¹.]
1 *hist.* A kind of ladies' headdress; the large white, winged headdress formerly worn by the Sisters of Charity. M16.
†**2** The standard of a troop of cavalry. L16–M19.
3 A company of cavalry. *obsolete* exc. *hist.* L16.
4 Chiefly *hist.* The fifth commissioned officer in a troop of cavalry, who carried the colours. L16.

C. V. WEDGWOOD The King was seized by a party of soldiers under Cornet Joyce.

5 Formerly, the mounted bearer of a standard or colour. Now only *Scot.*, the chief rider and standard-bearer of a burgh at the riding of the marches. E18.
■ **cornetcy** *noun* the rank of a cornet M18.

cornett *noun* see CORNET *noun*¹.

cornetto /kɔːˈnɛtəʊ/ *noun*. Pl. **-tti** /-ti/, **-ttos**. L19.
[ORIGIN Italian, dim. of CORNO.]
EARLY MUSIC. A straight or curved wooden wind instrument with finger holes and a cup-shaped mouthpiece; a player of this instrument. Cf. CORNET *noun*¹ 1a.

cornflower /ˈkɔːnflaʊə/ *noun*. E16.
[ORIGIN from CORN *noun*¹ + FLOWER *noun*.]
1 Any of several flowers that grow in corn, esp. *Centaurea cyanus*, a tall, usu. blue, annual formerly common as a weed; a flower or flowering stem of such a plant. E16.
2 A soft purplish-blue colour. Also ***cornflower blue***. E20.

cornice /ˈkɔːnɪs/ *noun* & *verb*. Also (now *dial.*) **-ish** /-ɪʃ/. M16.
[ORIGIN French *corniche*, †*-ice*, †*-isse* from Italian *cornice*, perh. from Latin *cornix*, *cornic-* crow (cf. etym. of CORBEL) but with blending of a deriv. of Greek *korōnis* coping stone.]
▸ **A** *noun*. **1** *ARCHITECTURE*. A horizontal, usu. moulded projection crowning the outside of a building or structure; *spec.* the uppermost part of an entablature, above the frieze. M16.
2 An ornamental moulding running round the wall of a room near the ceiling; a picture rail. L17.
3 An overhanging ledge of ice or snow at the edge of a steep ridge or cliff. L19.
▸ **B** *verb trans.* Provide with a cornice; finish as with a cornice. Chiefly as ***corniced*** *ppl adjective*. M18.
■ **cornicing** *noun* work consisting of a cornice or cornices L17.

corniche /ˈkɔːnɪʃ, kɔːˈniːʃ/ *noun*. M19.
[ORIGIN French: see CORNICE.]
A road along the edge of a cliff; any coastal road with panoramic views. Also ***corniche road***.

cornicle /ˈkɔːnɪk(ə)l/ *noun*. M16.
[ORIGIN Latin *corniculum* dim. of *cornu* horn: see -CULE.]
A small projecting part of an animal; *spec.* each of a pair of erect dorsal tubules on an aphid which secrete a waxy liquid as a defence against predators.

corniculate /kɔːˈnɪkjʊlət/ *adjective*. M17.
[ORIGIN Latin *corniculatus*, formed as CORNICLE: see -ATE².]
Having horns or hornlike projections; shaped like a horn.
corniculate cartilage either of a pair of small conical lumps of elastic cartilage in the larynx articulating with the arytenoid cartilages.

cornify /ˈkɔːnɪfʌɪ/ *verb trans.* E17.
[ORIGIN from Latin *cornu* horn + -I- + -FY.]
†**1** Cuckold. Only in E17.
2 Turn (tissue) into horny material; keratinize. Chiefly as ***cornified*** *ppl adjective*. M19.
■ **cornifiˈcation** *noun* M19.

cornigerous /kɔːˈnɪdʒ(ə)rəs/ *adjective*. M17.
[ORIGIN from Latin *corniger*, formed as CORNIFY: see -GEROUS.]
Having horns; producing horny material.

cornish *noun*¹ & *verb* see CORNICE.

Cornish /ˈkɔːnɪʃ/ *adjective* & *noun*². LME.
[ORIGIN from *Corn-* in *Cornwall* (see below) + -ISH¹.]
▸ **A** *adjective*. Of or belonging to Cornwall, a county in SW England. LME.
Cornish boiler a cylindrical horizontal boiler with a single flue through its middle. ***Cornish chough***: see CHOUGH 2. **Cornish cream** clotted cream. **Cornish engine** a kind of single-acting beam engine first used in Cornwall for pumping up water. **Cornishman** a man who is a native of Cornwall. ***Cornish moneywort***: see ***moneywort*** s.v. MONEY *noun*. **Cornish pasty** a pasty containing seasoned meat and cooked vegetables.
▸ **B** *noun*. The Brittonic language formerly spoken in Cornwall. M16.

cornist /ˈkɔːnɪst/ *noun*. Now *rare* or *obsolete*. E19.
[ORIGIN French *corniste*, from *corne* horn from Latin *cornu*: see -IST.]
A horn player.

corno /ˈkɔːnəʊ/ *noun*. Pl. **corni** /-iː/. E19.
[ORIGIN Italian from Latin *cornu* horn.]
MUSIC. A horn, *esp.* a French horn.
corno da caccia /da ˈkatʃə/ [lit. 'hunting horn'] a natural horn. **corno di bassetto** /diː baˈsɛtəʊ/ (*a*) = BASSET-HORN; (*b*) a kind of

organ reed stop of 8-ft pitch. **corno inglese** /ɪŋˈgleɪzeɪ/ [lit. 'English horn'] = COR ANGLAIS.

cornopean /kɔːˈnəʊpɪən/ *noun*. M19.
[ORIGIN Obscurely from CORNET *noun*[1].]
MUSIC. **1** = CORNET *noun*[1] 1b. Now *rare* or *obsolete*. M19.
2 A kind of organ reed stop of 8-ft pitch, similar to a trumpet stop. M19.

cornrow /ˈkɔːnrəʊ/ *noun & verb*. M18.
[ORIGIN from CORN *noun*[1] + ROW *noun*[1].]
▸ **A** *noun*. **1** A row of Indian corn (maize). *N. Amer*. M18.
2 Each of a line of small braids made close to the head, as in the hairstyle of some black people (usu. in *pl.*); a hairstyle in which the head is covered in this way. L20.
▸ **B** *verb trans*. Arrange (hair) in cornrows. L20.

cornstone /ˈkɔːnstəʊn/ *noun*. E19.
[ORIGIN from CORN *noun*[1] + STONE *noun*.]
GEOLOGY. A concretionary earthy limestone characteristic of the Old and the New Red Sandstone.

cornu /ˈkɔːnjuː/ *noun*. Pl. **-ua** /-juːə/. L17.
[ORIGIN Latin = horn.]
ANATOMY. Any formation with a shape likened to a horn, as (*a*) either of the two lateral cavities of the womb, into which the Fallopian tubes pass; (*b*) each of three elongated parts of each of the lateral ventricles of the brain; (*c*) a horn-shaped process on the thyroid cartilage or certain bones (as the hyoid and the coccyx).
▪ **cornual** *adjective* L19.

Cornu- /ˈkɔːnjuː/ *combining form*. M18.
[ORIGIN from CORNUBIAN.]
Cornish and—, as **Cornu-Breton**, **Cornu-British**, *adjectives*.

cornua *noun* pl. of CORNU.

Cornubian /kɔːˈnjuːbɪən/ *adjective*. L18.
[ORIGIN from medieval Latin *Cornubia* Cornwall + -AN.]
Cornish.

cornucopia /kɔːnjʊˈkəʊpɪə/ *noun*. E16.
[ORIGIN Late Latin *cornucopia* from Latin *cornu copiae* horn of plenty (a mythical horn able to provide whatever is desired).]
1 A goat's horn depicted as a horn of plenty, overflowing with flowers, fruit, and corn; an ornamental vessel or other representation of this. E16.
2 *fig*. An overflowing stock; an abundant source. E17.

> Jo GRIMOND Archie .. was a cornucopia of agricultural and other information.

▪ **cornucopian** *adjective* pertaining to or characteristic of a cornucopia; overflowingly abundant: E17.

cornus /ˈkɔːnəs/ *noun*. M19.
[ORIGIN Latin = dogwood.]
A plant of the genus *Cornus* of the dogwood family. Cf. CORNEL *noun*[2] 2.

cornute /kɔːˈnjuːt/ *verb, noun, & adjective*. L16.
[ORIGIN Latin *cornutus* horned, from *cornu* horn.]
▸ **A** *verb trans*. Cuckold. *arch*. L16.
▸ †**B** *noun*. **1** A retort for distillation. E17–M18.
2 A cuckold. E17–E18.
▸ **C** *adjective*. = CORNUTED. *rare*. E18.
▪ †**cornutor** *noun* a man who makes cuckolds L17–M18.

cornuted /kɔːˈnjuːtɪd/ *adjective*. E17.
[ORIGIN formed as CORNUTE + -ED[1].]
1 a Having horns or hornlike projections. E17. ▸**b** Shaped like a horn. M19.
2 Cuckolded. *arch*. E17.

cornuto /kɔːˈn(j)uːtəʊ/ *noun*. Now *rare* or *obsolete*. Pl. **-os**. LME.
[ORIGIN Italian, formed as CORNUTE.]
A cuckold.

corny /ˈkɔːni/ *adjective*[1]. LME.
[ORIGIN from CORN *noun*[1] + -Y[1].]
1 Of beer: tasting strongly of malt. Long *obsolete* exc. *dial*. LME.
2 Of or pertaining to corn. L16.
3 Producing corn; having much corn, as a crop or as grains. L16.
4 Drunk, intoxicated. Cf. CORNED *adjective*[2] 3. *dial*. E19.
5 Rustic, unsophisticated; ridiculously old-fashioned; trite, banal, mawkishly sentimental. *colloq*. M20.

> *Times* One of those scenes which is so bad, so corny, it is physically painful to watch.

▪ **corniness** *noun* (*colloq*.) the quality of being corny (sense 5) M20.

corny /ˈkɔːni/ *adjective*[2]. E18.
[ORIGIN from CORN *noun*[2] + -Y[1].]
Having corns on the feet; pertaining to corns on the feet.

corocoro /kɔːrəʊˈkɔːrəʊ/ *noun*. Pl. **-os**. E17.
[ORIGIN Malay *kurakura*.]
A style of boat with outriggers used in the Malay archipelago.

corody *noun* var. of CORRODY.

corolla /kəˈrɒlə/ *noun*. L17.
[ORIGIN Latin, dim. of *corona* CROWN *noun*.]
1 A little crown. *rare*. L17.
2 The whorl of modified leaves (petals), separate or combined, that form the inner, coloured, envelope of a flower and are its most conspicuous part. M18.
– COMB.: *corolla tube*: see TUBE *noun* 10.
▪ †**corol** *noun* = COROLLA 2 M18–M19. **coroˈllaceous** *adjective* having or being a corolla L18. **corolline** *adjective* pertaining to the corolla M19.

corollary /kəˈrɒləri/ *noun & adjective*. LME.
[ORIGIN Latin *corollarium* money paid for a garland, present, gratuity, deduction, from COROLLA: see -ARY[1].]
▸ **A** *noun* **1 a** A proposition, esp. in geometry, appended to one that has already been demonstrated as following immediately from it; an immediate inference. LME. ▸**b** A practical consequence, a result. L17.

> **a** LYTTON That is scarcely a fair corollary from my remark. **b** W. LIPPMANN When advanced nations adopt collectivism, and its inevitable corollary, the self-contained economy.

†**2** An addition to a speech or composition; an appendix; a concluding or crowning part. E17–E18.
3 Something additional or surplus. E17.
†**4** A proposition, a thesis. M17–E19.
▸ **B** *adjective*. Of the nature of a corollary; appended as an inference; accompanying, supplementary; resulting. LME.

Coromandel /kɒrə(ʊ)ˈmand(ə)l/ *noun & adjective*. M19.
[ORIGIN The *Coromandel* coast, SE India.]
▸ **A** *noun*. Calamander. Also ***Coromandel ebony***, ***Coromandel wood***. M19.
▸ **B** *adjective*. Designating oriental lacquerware, esp. folding screens, having incised decorations and orig. transhipped on the Coromandel coast. L19.

corona /kəˈrəʊnə/ *noun*[1]. Pl. **-nas**, **-nae** /-niː/. OE.
[ORIGIN Latin = CROWN *noun*.]
†**1** = CROWN *noun* 1. Only in OE.
2 *ARCHITECTURE*. A part of a cornice having a broad vertical face, usu. of considerable projection, and lying below the cyma. M16.
3 a A small circle of light sometimes seen round the sun, moon, or other luminary; *esp*. one due to diffraction by water droplets, often prismatically coloured with red on the outside. Cf. HALO *noun*. M17. ▸**b** The irregularly shaped area of light seen around the moon's disc in a solar eclipse; the hot, highly rarefied, outermost gaseous envelope of the sun responsible for this; a similar envelope around other celestial objects. M19.
4 Any of various parts of the human body (as of a tooth or the penis), or of an animal's, that are likened to a crown. E18.
5 *BOTANY*. **a** An appendage on the top of certain seeds, as those of a dandelion. M18. ▸**b** The cup-shaped or trumpet-shaped outgrowth of perianth tissue in the centre of the flower of a daffodil or other narcissus. Also, the ring of filaments in the flower of the passion flower. M19.
6 A circular chandelier in a church. E19.
7 A glow around a conductor when the electric field is strong enough to ionize the air but not strong enough to cause a spark. E20.
– PHRASES: **Corona Australis** /ɒˈstreɪlɪs/ [Latin *australis* AUSTRAL *adjective*] (the name of) a small constellation of the southern hemisphere, on the edge of the Milky Way next to Sagittarius. **Corona Borealis** /bɔːrɪˈeɪlɪs/ [Latin *borealis* BOREAL] (the name of) a small constellation of the northern hemisphere, between Boötes and Hercules.

Corona /kəˈrəʊnə/ *noun*[2]. Also **c-**. L19.
[ORIGIN from (formerly proprietary) name *La Corona* (Spanish, lit. 'the crown').]
A brand of Havana cigar; a long straight-sided cigar.

coronach /ˈkɒrənək, -x/ *noun*. E16.
[ORIGIN Gaelic *corranach*, from *comh-* together + *rànach* outcry.]
†**1** An outcry of a crowd. *Scot*. E16–L17.
2 A funeral lamentation in the Scottish Highlands or Ireland. M16.

coronagraph /kəˈrəʊnəgrɑːf/ *noun*. Also **corono-**. L19.
[ORIGIN from CORONA *noun*[1] + -GRAPH.]
An instrument for observing or photographing the sun's corona, esp. other than during an eclipse.
▪ **coronaˈgraphic** *adjective* L19.

coronal /ˈkɒrən(ə)l/ *noun*. ME.
[ORIGIN App. from Anglo-Norman from *cor(o)une* CROWN *noun*. In sense 3 prob. from medieval Latin *coronalis*. Cf. CROWNAL *noun*.]
▸ **I 1** A circlet, esp. of gold or gems, for the head; a coronet. ME.
2 A wreath for the head; a garland. L16.
▸ **II** *ANATOMY*. †**3** The coronal bone (see CORONAL *adjective* 1). LME–M18.
▪ **coronalled** *adjective* bearing a coronal LME.

coronal /kəˈrəʊn(ə)l, ˈkɒr(ə)n(ə)l/ *adjective*. LME.
[ORIGIN French, or Latin (& medieval Latin) *coronalis*, from *corona* CROWN *noun*: see -AL[1]. Cf. CROWNAL *adjective*.]
1 Of or pertaining to the crown of the head. LME.
coronal bone (now *rare*) the frontal bone. **coronal plane**: dividing the body vertically into front and back halves.
†**2** Pertaining to a crown or crowning. M16–M17.
3 Of or pertaining to a corona, esp. that of the sun. M18.
4 *PHONETICS*. Designating or pertaining to speech sounds produced with the tip or blade of the tongue raised towards the hard palate. L19.

coronary /ˈkɒr(ə)n(ə)ri/ *adjective & noun*. E17.
[ORIGIN Latin *coronarius*, formed as CORONAL *adjective*: see -ARY[1].]
▸ **A** *adjective*. †**1** Suitable for use in making garlands. Only in 17.
2 Of the nature of or resembling a crown; pertaining to or forming a crown. *obsolete* exc. in ***coronary gold*** below. M17.
coronary gold [translating Latin *coronarium aurum*] *hist*. money awarded in lieu of a crown to a victorious Roman general.
3 *ANATOMY*. Pertaining to or designating blood vessels, nerves, and ligaments which encircle a part. L17.

> D. WATERSON The coronary ligament consists of the folds of peritoneum which are reflected from the liver to the diaphragm.

coronary artery either of two arteries that supply the tissues of the heart with blood. **coronary thrombosis**: occurring in a coronary artery.
4 Pertaining to or designating the second phalangeal bone of a horse's foot. M19.
▸ **B** *noun*. †**1** A plant or flower suitable for use in making garlands. Only in L17.
2 The coronary bone of a horse. M19.
3 A coronary blood vessel; a coronary thrombosis. L19.

coronate /ˈkɒr(ə)neɪt/ *verb trans*. Pa. pple **-ate** (*arch*.), **-ated**. LME.
[ORIGIN Latin *coronat-* pa. ppl stem of *coronare* CROWN *verb*[1]: see -ATE[3].]
Crown.

coronated /ˈkɒr(ə)neɪtɪd/ *ppl adjective*. L17.
[ORIGIN formed as CORONATE + -ED[1].]
BOTANY & ZOOLOGY. Having something resembling a crown.

coronation /kɒrəˈneɪʃ(ə)n/ *noun*. LME.
[ORIGIN Old French & mod. French from medieval Latin *coronatio(n-)*, formed as CORONATE: see -ATION. Cf. CROWNATION.]
1 The action or an act of crowning; *spec*. the ceremony of investing a monarch or monarch's consort with a crown as an emblem of royal status. LME.
2 *fig*. The crowning or completion *of* a work. L16.
†**3** = CARNATION *noun*[3]. Only in L16.
– ATTRIB. & COMB.: Designating articles produced to commemorate a particular coronation, as ***coronation mug***. Special combs., as **coronation chicken** a cold dish of cooked chicken served in a sauce flavoured with apricots and curry powder, created for the coronation of Queen Elizabeth II in 1953. **coronation oath**: taken by a monarch at his or her coronation. **Coronation Street** [a fictitious street in, and the title of, a television series] (characteristic of) a working-class street in the middle of an industrial city in the north of England.

†**coronel** *noun* see COLONEL *noun*.

coroner /ˈkɒr(ə)nə/ *noun*. ME.
[ORIGIN Anglo-Norman *cor(o)uner*, from *cor(o)une* CROWN *noun* (see -ER[2]), from the Latin title *custos placitorum coronae* guardian of the pleas of the crown; in medieval Latin *coronarius*, later *coronator*. Cf. CROWNER *noun*[2].]
1 Orig., an officer of the royal household responsible for safeguarding the private property of the Crown. Now, a legal officer with local or national jurisdiction who holds inquests on deaths of those who may have died by violence or accident, and also on treasure trove. ME.
coroner's jury: composed of 7–11 persons, appointed to decide an issue of fact at a coroner's inquest.
2 The chief officer of a sheading in the Isle of Man. L16.
▪ **coronership** *noun* the office of coroner LME.

coronet /ˈkɒr(ə)nɪt/ *noun & verb*. LME.
[ORIGIN Old French *coronet(t)e* dim. of *corone* CROWN *noun*: see -ET[1]. Cf. CRONET, CROWNET.]
▸ **A** *noun*. **1** A small or inferior crown, *esp*. one denoting noble or royal but not sovereign rank; a heraldic representation of this. LME.
2 A band of beautiful or precious materials worn as an ornament on the head, now esp. as part of a woman's formal dress. L16.
3 A garland of flowers for the head. L16.
OBSIDIONAL ***coronet***.
4 The lowest part of the pastern of a horse, forming a ridge round the top of the hoof. Cf. earlier CRONET 3, CROWNET 2. L17.
5 A moth, *Craniophora ligustri*, with greenish or brownish forewings. Also ***coronet moth***. E19.
6 = BUR *noun*[1] 4. L19.
▸ **B** *verb trans*. Infl. **-t-**, **-tt-**. Adorn with a coronet; confer a coronet or noble title upon. Chiefly as ***coroneted*** *ppl adjective*. M18.

coronilla /kɒrəˈnɪlə/ *noun*. L18.
[ORIGIN mod. Latin, dim. of Latin *corona* CROWN *noun*.]
Any leguminous plant of the genus *Coronilla*, comprising evergreen and deciduous shrubs and herbaceous plants bearing usu. yellow flowers in umbels.

C

C

coronis /kəˈrəʊnɪs/ *noun*. **M17**.
[**ORIGIN** Latin from Greek *korōnis* flourish at end of book or chapter.]
†**1** An end, a conclusion. *rare*. Only in **M17**.
2 *GREEK GRAMMAR*. The sign ʼ placed over a Greek vowel as a mark of contraction or crasis. **M19**.

coronium /kəˈrəʊnɪəm/ *noun*. **L19**.
[**ORIGIN** from **CORONA** *noun*[1] + **-IUM**.]
An element formerly thought to exist in the sun's corona, producing spectral lines now attributed to highly ionized atoms of other elements.

coronograph *noun* var. of **CORONAGRAPH**.

coronoid /ˈkɒr(ə)nɔɪd/ *adjective & noun*. **M18**.
[**ORIGIN** from Greek *korōnē* crow, anything hooked, coronoid process + **-OID**.]
▸ **A** *adjective*. *ANATOMY*. Pertaining to or designating projections of bone likened to a crow's beak. **M18**.
coronoid fossa a hollow immediately above the trochlea on the anterior surface of the condyle of the humerus, into which the coronoid process of the ulna fits when the arm is bent. **coronoid process** (*a*) a flattened triangular projection directed upwards and forwards on the ramus of the mandible; (*b*) a projection from the front of the upper end of the ulna, immediately below the olecranon.
▸ **B** *noun*. *ZOOLOGY*. A membrane bone in the lower jaw of certain lower vertebrates, projecting upwards behind the teeth. **L19**.

coroplast /ˈkɔːrəplast, -plɑːst/ *noun*. **L19**.
[**ORIGIN** Greek *koroplastēs*, from *korē* girl, doll: see **-PLAST**.]
ANTIQUITIES. A maker of terracotta figures.

corozo /kəˈrəʊzəʊ/ *noun*. Pl. **-os**. **M18**.
[**ORIGIN** Spanish, var. of dial. *carozo* stone or core of fruit.]
Any of several S. American palm trees, *esp*. the ivory nut palm, *Phytelephas macrocarpa*, and the American oil palm, *Corozo (Elaeis) oleifera*.
– **COMB.**: **corozo nut** the seed of *Phytelephas macrocarpa*, from which vegetable ivory is obtained.

corp /kɔːp/ *noun*. *colloq*. **E20**.
[**ORIGIN** Abbreviation.]
= **CORPORAL** *noun*[2] 1.

Corp. *abbreviation*.
1 Corporal.
2 Corporation. *N. Amer.*

corpocracy /kɔːˈpɒkrəsi/ *noun*. **L20**.
[**ORIGIN** Blend of **CORPORATE** *adjective* and **BUREAUCRACY**.]
Bureaucratic organization as manifested in large companies, esp. where a rigid hierarchical structure leads to inefficiency; a company characterized by such organization; such companies collectively.
■ ˈ**corpocrat** *noun* an executive within a corpocracy **L20**. **corpoˈcratic** *adjective* pertaining to or characteristic of corpocracy or corpocracies **L20**.

corpora *noun pl*. see **CORPUS**.

corporal /ˈkɔːp(ə)r(ə)l/ *noun*[1]. **OE**.
[**ORIGIN** Old French & mod. French, or medieval Latin *corporale* use as noun (sc. *pallium* **PALL** *noun*[1]) of neut. of *corporalis* **CORPORAL** *adjective*.]
CHRISTIAN CHURCH. †**1** A certain ancient Eucharistic vestment. **OE–M17**.
2 A (now square) cloth on which the chalice and paten are placed during the Eucharist, before the consecration; a smaller cloth placed over the chalice, a pall. **LME**.

corporal /ˈkɔːp(ə)r(ə)l/ *noun*[2]. **M16**.
[**ORIGIN** French, obsolete var. of *caporal* from Italian *caporale* (of which there appears to have been a Venetian form †*corporale*), prob. from *corpo* from Latin **CORPUS**, *corpor-* body (of troops) with assim. to Italian *capo* head: cf. **CORPORAL** *adjective*.]
1 A non-commissioned officer in the army, air force, or marines who ranks next below a sergeant. **M16**.
orderly corporal: see **ORDERLY** *adjective*. **the little Corporal** Napoleon.
2 *hist*. Orig., a petty officer on board a warship responsible for teaching the use of small arms; later (also ***ship's corporal***), a superior petty officer who attended solely to police matters under the master-at-arms. **E17**.
3 A freshwater fish, *Semotilus corporalis*, of the carp family. *US*. **L19**.
■ **corporalship** *noun* †(*a*) a body of soldiers under the command of a corporal; (*b*) the position or rank of a corporal: **L16**.

corporal /ˈkɔːp(ə)r(ə)l/ *adjective*. **LME**.
[**ORIGIN** Old French (mod. *-el*) from Latin *corporalis*, from **CORPUS**, *corpor-* body: see **-AL**[1].]
1 Of or belonging to the human body; bodily; personal. **LME**. ▸†**b** Having a body, embodied. **L15–M17**.

> **MILTON** Corporal pleasure. **S. RICHARDSON** Taking his corporal leave of her. **THACKERAY** A quite unheroic state of corporal prostration.

†**2** Of the nature of matter; physical, material. **LME–E18**.
– **SPECIAL COLLOCATIONS**: **corporal oath** *arch.*: ratified by touching a sacred object. **corporal punishment**: inflicted on the body, now esp. by flogging.
■ **corporally** *adverb* **L15**.

corporality /kɔːpəˈralɪti/ *noun*. **LME**.
[**ORIGIN** Late Latin *corporalitas*, from Latin *corporalis*: see **CORPORAL** *adjective*, **-ITY**.]
1 Material or corporeal existence; body. **LME**.
2 Embodied existence or condition. Now *rare*. **M17**.

corporas /ˈkɔːp(ə)rəs/ *noun*. **ME**.
[**ORIGIN** Old French *corporaus* (earlier *-als*) nom. sing. of *corporal* **CORPORAL** *noun*[1].]
= **CORPORAL** *noun*[1] 2.

corporate /ˈkɔːp(ə)rət/ *adjective*. **L15**.
[**ORIGIN** Latin *corporatus* pa. pple, formed as **CORPORATE** *verb*: see **-ATE**[2].]
1 Forming or being a corporation; having a legal existence distinct from that of the individuals who compose it. **L15**. ▸**b** Of or belonging to a corporation, esp. (now) an industrial corporation, or a group of people; collective, joint. **E17**.

> **b** **H. CARPENTER** Auden was not sociable at school and kept out of corporate activities. **S. BELLOW** Lawyers and corporate executives.

body corporate: see **BODY** *noun*. **corporate town**: having municipal rights. ***county corporate***: see **COUNTY** *noun*[1]. **b *corporate image***: see **IMAGE** *noun*. **corporate name**: under which a corporation engages in legal acts. **corporate raider** a person who or organization which attempts to take over companies against their wishes or interests. **corporate state**: governed by representatives not of geographical areas but of vocational corporations of the employers and employees in each industry etc.
†**2** Pertaining to or affecting the body. **L15–E17**.
†**3** Corpulent. **E16–L18**.
†**4** Having a body; material. **L16–M19**.
■ **corporately** *adverb* **L15**.

corporate /ˈkɔːpəreɪt/ *verb*. *arch*. Pa. pple **-ate(d)**. **LME**.
[**ORIGIN** Latin *corporat-* pa. ppl stem of *corporare*, from **CORPUS**, *corpor-* body: see **-ATE**[3].]
1 *verb trans. & (rare) intrans*. Unite or combine in one body; embody. **LME**.
†**2** *verb trans*. Form into a corporation, incorporate. **LME–M17**.

corporation /kɔːpəˈreɪʃ(ə)n/ *noun*. **LME**.
[**ORIGIN** Late Latin *corporatio(n-)*, formed as **CORPORATE** *verb*: see **-ATION**.]
†**1** The action or result of incorporating. **LME–M16**.
2 A body of people that has been given a legal existence distinct from the individuals who compose it; a single person with a separate legal existence; a fictitious person created by statute, royal charter, etc.; *spec*. (*a*) (more fully ***municipal corporation***) the civic authorities of a borough, town, or city; (*b*) a large industrial company. **LME**. ▸**b** An incorporated company of traders who orig. controlled their particular trade in a place. **M16**. ▸**c** A body of people. **M16**.

> **BROWNING** A thousand guilders! The Mayor looked blue; so did the Corporation too. *Encycl. Brit.* The company was liquidated and replaced by a public corporation, the British Broadcasting Corporation.

corporation aggregate: comprising more than one individual. **corporation sole**: comprising only one individual at any one time, as a king or bishop.
3 A protruding or prominent abdomen. Formerly, the body. *colloq*. **M18**.
– **COMB.**: **corporation tax**: levied on companies' profits.
■ **corporational** *adjective* **M19**.

corporatism /ˈkɔːp(ə)rətɪz(ə)m/ *noun*. **L19**.
[**ORIGIN** from **CORPORATE** *adjective* + **-ISM**.]
The principles or practice of corporate action or organization, esp. in a corporate state.
■ **corporatist** *adjective* **L19**.

corporative /ˈkɔːp(ə)rətɪv/ *adjective*. **M19**.
[**ORIGIN** formed as **CORPORATISM** + **-IVE**.]
= **CORPORATE** *adjective* 1b.
■ **corporativism** *noun* = **CORPORATISM** **M20**.

corporatize /ˈkɔːp(ə)rətʌɪz/ *verb trans*. Also **-ise**. **L20**.
[**ORIGIN** from **CORPORATE** *adjective* + **-IZE**.]
Convert (a state body) into an independent commercial company.
■ **corporatization** *noun* **M20**.

corporator /ˈkɔːp(ə)reɪtə/ *noun*. **L18**.
[**ORIGIN** Irreg. from **CORPORATION** + **-OR**.]
A member of a corporation, esp. a municipal corporation.

corporeal /kɔːˈpɔːrɪəl/ *adjective & noun*. **LME**.
[**ORIGIN** Late Latin *corporealis*, from Latin *corporeus*, from **CORPUS**, *corpor-* body: see **-AL**[1].]
▸ **A** *adjective*. **1** Of the nature of matter, material. **LME**.
2 **a** Of the nature of the body rather than the spirit; bodily; mortal. **E17**. ▸†**b** Pertaining to or affecting the body, corporal. **E18–M19**.

> **a** **J. STRYPE** Any manner of corporeal presence in the Sacrament. **D. PIPER** The full corporeal presence of that massive torso. **b** **W. HAMILTON** The infliction of corporeal punishment.

3 *LAW*. Tangible; consisting of material objects. **L17**.

> **W. BLACKSTONE** Corporeal hereditaments consist wholly of substantial and permanent objects.

▸ **B** *noun*. In *pl*. Corporeal things; *LAW* corporeal possessions. **M17**.
■ **corporealism** *noun* materialism **L17**. †**corporealist** *noun* a materialist **M17–M19**. **corporeˈality** *noun* corporeal quality or state; bodily nature: **M17**. **corporealiˈzation** *noun* the action of corporealizing **M19**. **corporealize** *verb trans*. render or represent as corporeal **L18**. **corporeally** *adverb* in a corporeal manner; bodily: **M17**. †**corporeous** *adjective* = **CORPOREAL** **E17–M19**.

corporeity /kɔːpəˈriːɪti, -ˈreɪɪti/ *noun*. **E17**.
[**ORIGIN** French *corporéité* or medieval Latin *corporeitas*, from Latin *corporeus*: see **CORPOREAL**, **-ITY**.]
1 The quality of being or having a material body. **E17**.
2 (A) bodily substance. **M17**.

> **E. H. PLUMPTRE** A subtle attenuated corporeity . . investing the soul.

3 Material or physical nature. Formerly also, relative density. **M17**.

†**corporify** *verb trans*. **M17**.
[**ORIGIN** from Latin **CORPUS**, *corpor-* body + **-FY**, perh. through French *corporifier*.]
1 Make material, *esp*. convert into liquid or solid. **M17–E18**.
2 Incorporate (itself) into a material substance. **M17–E18**.
■ †**corporification** *noun* the action or result of making material; embodiment: **M17–M19**.

corporosity /kɔːpəˈrɒsɪti/ *noun*. *US colloq*. (*joc*.). **M19**.
[**ORIGIN** formed as **CORPORIFY** + **-OSITY**.]
A person's body or bodily bulkiness.
your corporosity you (as a greeting).

corposant /ˈkɔːpəzant/ *noun*. Also **composant** /ˈkɒmp-/, **comozant** /ˈkɒməz-/. **M16**.
[**ORIGIN** Old Spanish, Portuguese, & Italian *corpo santo* holy body.]
A luminous corona sometimes seen in the air adjacent to a ship or aircraft during a storm, esp. near pointed objects such as mastheads.

corps /kɔː; *foreign* kɔːr/ *noun*. Pl. same /kɔːz, *foreign* kɔːr/. **L16**.
[**ORIGIN** French from Latin **CORPUS** body. Cf. **CORE** *noun*[2].]
1 A tactical division of an army; an organized body of troops assigned to a special duty or a particular kind of work (medical, ordnance, intelligence, etc.). (Earliest in ***corps de garde*** below.) **L16**.
2 A body of people engaged (collectively or as individuals) in a particular activity. **M18**.

> **J. B. MORTON** Tips . . given away by a corps of bookies. *Sunday Times* A 200-strong international Press corps.

3 A students' society in a German university. **L19**.
– **PHRASES**: ***corps à corps*** /a kɔːr/ in close, esp. bodily, contact. ***corps de ballet*** /də balɛ, də ˈbaleɪ/, pl. same, the company of supporting dancers in a ballet; the ballet dancers at a theatre. ***corps de garde*** /də gard, də ˈgɑːd/, pl. same, a small body of soldiers stationed on guard or as sentinels; the post they occupy, a guardroom, a guardhouse. ***corps d'élite*** /delit, deɪˈliːt/, pl. same, a select group, a body of specially picked people. ***corps de logis*** /də lɔʒi/, pl. same, [lit. 'body of dwelling'] the main (part of a) building. ***corps diplomatique*** /diplɔmatik, dɪpləməˈtiːk/, pl. ***-iques*** (pronounced same) = ***diplomatic corps*** s.v. **DIPLOMATIC** *adjective* 2. *ESPRIT* ***de corps***.
– **COMB.**: **corpsman** *US* an enlisted medical auxiliary in the army or navy.

corpse /kɔːps/ *noun & verb*. Orig. †**corps** (pl. **corps(es)**). **ME**.
[**ORIGIN** Alt. of **CORSE** *noun* after Latin *corpus*, French *corps* body. The inserted *p* was at first mute, as in French, but began to be pronounced before 1500. The final *e* was rare before 19, but then became standard, providing differentiation from **CORPS**. Cf. also **CORPUS**.]
▸ **A** *noun*. †**1** The living body of a person or animal. **ME–E18**.
2 A dead (usu. human) body. **LME**.
walking corpse: see **WALKING** *ppl adjective*.
†**3** The main portion or body *of*; a body or corpus *of* (law etc.). **LME–M17**.
4 *hist*. The endowment of an ecclesiastical or (formerly) civil office, esp. a prebend. **M16**.
– **COMB.**: **corpse candle** (*a*) a lambent flame seen in a churchyard and superstitiously believed to portend a coming death or funeral route; (*b*) a lighted candle, esp. of unbleached wax, placed beside a corpse before burial; **corpse light** = ***corpse candle*** (a) above; ***corpse-reviver***: see **REVIVER** *noun*[1] 1c.
▸ **B** *verb*. **1** *verb trans*. Kill. *slang*. **M19**.
2 *verb trans*. Confuse (an actor) in the performance of his or her part; spoil (a piece of acting) by some blunder. *slang*. **M19**.
3 *verb intrans*. Spoil a piece of acting by some blunder, as forgetting one's lines or laughing; burst out laughing at an inappropriate moment. *slang*. **L19**.
■ **corpsy** *adjective* resembling or characteristic of a corpse; cadaverous: **L19**.

corpulence /ˈkɔːpjʊl(ə)ns/ *noun*. **LME**.
[**ORIGIN** Old French & mod. French, formed as **CORPULENCY**: see **-ENCE**.]
†**1** Size or habit of body. **LME–L15**.
2 Bulk of body; excessive bulk, obesity. **M16**.

corpulency /ˈkɔːpjʊl(ə)nsi/ *noun*. **M16**.
[**ORIGIN** Latin *corpulentia*, formed as **CORPULENT**: see **-ENCY**.]
†**1** = **CORPULENCE** 1. **M16–E17**.
2 = **CORPULENCE** 2. **L16**.

corpulent /ˈkɔːpjʊl(ə)nt/ *adjective*. **LME**.
[**ORIGIN** Latin *corpulentus*, from **CORPUS** body: see **-ULENT**.]
†**1** Of the nature of a physical body; solid, dense, gross. **LME–M17**.
2 Bulky of body; fleshy, fat. **LME**.
†**3** Corporeal, material. **LME–M17**.

cor pulmonale /kɔː pʌlməˈnɑːli, -ˈeɪli/ *noun phr.* **M19.**
[**ORIGIN** from Latin *cor* heart + mod. Latin *pulmonalis*, *-e* (from Latin *pulmo(n-)* lung).]
MEDICINE. †**1** The right auricle and ventricle of the heart. Only in **M19.**
2 Disease, esp. enlargement, of the right side of the heart as a result of disease of the lungs or their blood vessels. **M20.**

corpus /ˈkɔːpəs/ *noun*. Pl. **corpora** /ˈkɔːp(ə)rə/, **corpuses**. **LME.**
[**ORIGIN** Latin = body.]
1 The body of a person or animal. Now *joc.* **LME.**
2 *ANATOMY*. Any of various masses of tissue in the body that have a distinct structure or function. Chiefly in phrs. below. **L17.**
3 A body or collection of writing, knowledge, etc.; the whole body *of* a particular category of literature etc. **E18.** ▸**b** *spec.* A body of spoken or written material on which a linguistic analysis is based. **M20.**

GLADSTONE Assaults on the corpus of Scripture. A. BEVAN The accumulated corpus of knowledge in his own particular field.

4 Principal or capital, as opp. to interest or income. *arch.* **M19.**
5 *BOTANY*. The inner layers of cells in an apical meristem, which divide mainly periclinally and contribute to volume growth. Cf. **TUNICA** *noun*[1] 2. **M20.**
– **PHRASES**: **corpus callosum** /kəˈləʊsəm/, pl. **-sa** /-sə/, [Latin, neut. of *callosus* tough] a broad band of nerve fibres joining the two hemispheres of the brain. **corpus cavernosum** /kavəˈnəʊsəm/, pl. **-sa** /-sə/, [Latin, neut. of *cavernosus* containing hollows] either of two masses of erectile tissue forming the bulk of the penis and the clitoris. **Corpus Christi** /ˈkrɪsti/, pl. **Corpus Christis** [Latin, genit. of *Christus* Christ] a holy day in parts of the Western Church in commemoration of the Holy Eucharist, observed on the first Thursday after Trinity Sunday. **corpus delicti** /dɪˈlɪktiː/ [Latin, genit. of *delictum* offence] *LAW* the facts and circumstances constituting a crime; *popularly* concrete evidence of a crime, *esp.* a corpse. **corpus juris**, **corpus iuris** /ˈdʒʊərɪs, ˈjʊə-/ [Latin, genit. of *jus* law] a body of law. **corpus juris canonici** /kəˈnɒnɪsiː/ [Latin, genit. of *canonicus* **CANONIC**] the chief collection of law in the Western Church until 1917. **corpus juris civilis** /sɪˈvɪlɪs/ [Latin: see **CIVIL**] the body of Roman civil law based on Justinian's compilation. **corpus luteum** /ˈluːtɪəm, ˈljuː-/, pl. **-tea** /-tɪə/, [Latin, neut. of *luteus* yellow] a hormone-secreting body that develops in the ovary after the ovum is discharged, degenerating after a few days unless pregnancy has begun. **corpus spongiosum** /spʌndʒɪˈəʊsəm/, pl. **-sa** /-sə/, [Latin, neut. of *spongiosus* porous] a mass of erectile tissue alongside the corpora cavernosa of the penis and terminating in the glans. **corpus striatum** /straɪˈeɪtəm/, pl. **-ta** /-tə/, [Latin, neut. of *striatus* grooved] part of the basal ganglia of the brain, comprising the caudate and lentiform nuclei. **corpus vile** /ˈvʌɪli/, pl. **-lia** /-lɪə/, [Latin, neut. of *vilis* cheap] something that can be made the object of experimentation because of no intrinsic worth.

corpuscle /ˈkɔːpʌs(ə)l/ *noun*. **M17.**
[**ORIGIN** Latin *corpusculum* dim. of **CORPUS**: see **-CULE**. Cf. **CORPUSCULE**.]
1 A minute particle of matter; an atom; a molecule. *arch.* **M17.** ▸**b** *HISTORY OF SCIENCE*. An electron. **L19.**
2 A minute structure forming a distinct part of the body; *esp.* a blood cell; an encapsulated sensory nerve ending. **M18.**
Malpighian corpuscle, ***Meissner's corpuscle***, ***Pacinian corpuscle***, ***red corpuscle***, ***white blood corpuscle***, etc.

corpuscular /kɔːˈpʌskjʊlə/ *adjective*. **M17.**
[**ORIGIN** formed as **CORPUSCLE** + **-AR**[1].]
1 Involving the idea or hypothesis of corpuscles. **M17.**
corpuscular theory *HISTORY OF SCIENCE*: that light consists of a stream of particles; also called ***emission theory***.
2 Of or pertaining to corpuscles; consisting of or being corpuscles. **L17.**
■ **corpuscuˈlarian** *adjective & noun* (**a**) *adjective* = **CORPUSCULAR** 1; (**b**) *noun* (*HISTORY OF SCIENCE*) a person who believed that matter, or light, is composed of corpuscles: **M17.**

corpuscule /kɔːˈpʌskjuːl/ *noun*. *arch.* Also (earlier) in Latin form **-culum** /-kjʊləm/, pl. **-la** /-lə/. **M17.**
[**ORIGIN** formed as **CORPUSCLE**.]
= **CORPUSCLE**.
■ **corpusculated** *adjective* = **CORPUSCULAR** 2 **M19.** **corpusculous** *adjective* = **CORPUSCULAR** 2 **L19.**

†**corrack** *noun* var. of **CURRACH**.

corrade /kəˈreɪd/ *verb trans.* **E17.**
[**ORIGIN** Latin *corradere*, formed as **COR-** + *radere* scrape.]
†**1** Scrape together (*lit.* & *fig.*). **E–M17.**
2 Wear down by scraping. Now only *GEOLOGY*, subject to corrasion. **M17.**

corral /kəˈrɑːl/ *noun & verb*. **L16.**
[**ORIGIN** Spanish & Old Portuguese *corral*, Portuguese *curral*: cf. **CRAWL** *noun*[1], **KRAAL**.]
▸ **A** *noun*. **1** An enclosure for horses, cattle, etc. Chiefly *N. Amer.* **L16.**
2 An enclosure in which to trap and capture wild animals. **M19.**
3 A defensive enclosure formed of wagons in an encampment. **M19.**
▸ **B** *verb*. Infl. **-ll-**, ***-l-**.
1 *verb trans.* & *intrans.* Form (wagons) into a corral. **M19.**
2 *verb trans.* Shut up (as) in a corral, confine. **M19.**
3 *verb trans.* Obtain, get hold of. *N. Amer. colloq.* **M19.**

corrasion /kəˈreɪʒ(ə)n/ *noun*. **E17.**
[**ORIGIN** from Latin *corras-* pa. ppl stem of *corradere*: see **CORRADE**, **-ION**.]
†**1** The action of scraping together (*fig.*). *rare*. Only in **E17.**
2 *GEOLOGY*. The local wearing away of part of the earth's surface by moving air, water, ice, etc., and matter transported by them. **L19.**

correct /kəˈrɛkt/ *adjective*. **L16.**
[**ORIGIN** French from Latin *correctus* pa. pple, formed as **CORRECT** *verb*. Cf. earlier **INCORRECT**.]
1 Free from error; accurate; in accordance with fact, truth, or reason. **L16.**

LD MACAULAY Mr. Hunt is . . quite correct in saying that [etc.]. G. GORDON Trying to open a safe without knowing the correct combination.

2 Conforming to acknowledged standards of style, manners, or behaviour; proper. **L17.**

S. JOHNSON The best and correctest authours. R. FORD The correct thing is to have the owner's name worked in on the edge. D. ABSE Rabbi Shatz in his correct black homburg.

■ **correctly** *adverb* **L17.** **correctness** *noun* **L17.**

correct /kəˈrɛkt/ *verb*. Pa. pple **corrected**, †**correct**. **ME.**
[**ORIGIN** Latin *correct-* pa. ppl stem of *corrigere*, formed as **COR-** + *regere* lead straight, direct.]
▸ **I** *verb trans.* **1** Put right (an error or fault). **ME.**

W. S. CHURCHILL Having made a mistake . . he went back and corrected it.

2 Cure (a person) *of* a fault; admonish, or point out the faults of, with a view to amendment. **ME.**

C. BURNEY Pleasure . . in seeing one of my own children corrected of all natural defects. E. BLUNDEN He corrected me for carrying an untrimmed . . stick. T. F. POWYS He always corrected himself.

3 Punish for faults of character or conduct (with a view to amendment). *arch.* **LME.**
4 Put (a thing) right; substitute what is right for the errors in; mark errors in (a proof etc.). **LME.**

E. WAUGH I sit with a blue pencil correcting history essays.

5 Remove or prevent the harmful effect of, counteract. **M16.**

D. BREWSTER Take a prism of each with such angles that they correct each other's dispersion as much as possible. J. A. FROUDE The heart . . corrects the folly of the head.

†**6** Reduce to order, reclaim from wildness. **L16–E18.**
7 Bring (the body) into a healthy state. **E17.**
8 Adjust (a numerical result or reading) to allow for departure from standard conditions. **L18.**
▸ **II** *verb intrans.* **9** Make a correction or corrections. **L15.**
■ **correctable** *adjective* able to be corrected **LME.** **correctible** *adjective* = **CORRECTABLE** **L19.**

correction /kəˈrɛkʃ(ə)n/ *noun*. **ME.**
[**ORIGIN** Old French & mod. French from Latin *correctio(n-)*, formed as **CORRECT** *verb*: see **-ION**.]
1 **a** The action of putting right or indicating errors. **ME.** ▸**b** An act or instance of emendation; that which is substituted for what is wrong, esp. in a text. **E16.**

a *Literature & Theology* Page proofs will be sent to authors for correction. **b** T. BIRCH To see the first Thoughts and subsequent Corrections of so great a Poet as Milton.

a under correction subject to correction, esp. by a higher authority.
†**2** Reproof of a person for a fault of character or conduct. (Foll. by *of* the fault.) **ME–E19.**
3 Chastisement, disciplinary punishment; *esp.* corporal punishment. *arch.* **LME.**
house of correction (**a**) *hist.* an institution where vagrants and minor offenders were confined and set to work; (**b**) (in the US) an institution for the short-term confinement of minor offenders.
4 The neutralization of anything harmful or unpleasant. **LME.**
5 Adjustment of a numerical result; the quantity added or subtracted in this. **M18.**
– **COMB.**: **correction fluid** a (usu. white) liquid that can be painted over a typed or written error leaving a blank surface on which to type or write afresh; **correction officer**, **correction official**, **corrections officer**, **corrections official** *N. Amer.* a prison officer.
■ **correctional** *adjective* of or pertaining to correction **L18.** †**correctioner** *noun* (*rare*, Shakes.) a person who administers correction: only in **L16.**

correctitude /kəˈrɛktɪtjuːd/ *noun*. **L19.**
[**ORIGIN** from **CORRECT** *adjective* + **RECTITUDE**.]
Correctness; *esp.* conscious correctness of behaviour.

corrective /kəˈrɛktɪv/ *adjective & noun*. **M16.**
[**ORIGIN** Old French & mod. French *correctif*, *-ive*, or late Latin *correctivus*, formed as **CORRECT** *verb*: see **-IVE**.]
▸ **A** *adjective*. Having the property or function of correcting or of counteracting what is harmful. **M16.**
corrective justice, ***corrective training***.
▸ **B** *noun*. **1** Something that restores to a healthy condition. **E17.**
†**2** A correction, an emendation. **L17–M18.**
3 Something that tends to counteract an evil, put right an error, etc. (Foll. by *of*, *to*.) **M18.**

H. T. BUCKLE Patriotism is a corrective of superstition. R. W. EMERSON The criticism of memory as a corrective to first impressions.

■ **correctively** *adverb* **E17.**

corrector /kəˈrɛktə/ *noun*. **LME.**
[**ORIGIN** Anglo-Norman *cor(r)ectour*, Old French & mod. French *correcteur* from Latin *corrector*, formed as **CORRECT** *verb*: see **-OR**.]
1 A person who points out errors and indicates what is right; a critic; *spec.* (also ***corrector of the press***, ***press corrector***) a proofreader. **LME.**
2 A person who exercises discipline or inflicts punishment. **LME.**
3 As an official title: a controller; a director; a religious superior. **LME.**
4 Something that provides a means of correction or prevents error. **E17.**
†**5** = **CORRECTIVE** *noun* 1. **E17–L18.**
■ **correctory** *adjective* (now *rare* or *obsolete*) of the nature of a corrector or correction **E17.** **correctress** *noun* (now *rare*) a female corrector **E17.** †**correctrice** *noun* = **CORRECTRESS** **M16–E18.**

Correggiesque /kɒˌrɛdʒɪˈɛsk/ *adjective*. **M18.**
[**ORIGIN** from *Correggio* (see below) + **-ESQUE**.]
Characteristic of, or in the style of, the Italian painter Antonio Allegri Correggio (*c* 1489–1534); consciously elegant and charming or with soft outlines, in the manner of Correggio.
■ **Correggiescity** *noun* (*rare*) Correggiesque style **M18.**

corregidor /kəˈrɛgɪdɔː/ *noun*. Pl. **corregidores** /kərɛgɪˈdɔːriːz/, **-ors**. **L16.**
[**ORIGIN** Spanish agent noun from *corregir* from Latin *corrigere* **CORRECT** *verb*.]
The chief magistrate of a Spanish town or a town in former Spanish territory.

correlate /ˈkɒrəleɪt, -rɪl-/ *noun*. **M17.**
[**ORIGIN** Prob. formed as **CORRELATE** *verb*: see **-ATE**[1].]
1 Either of two or more related things, esp. that imply or are complementary to one another. **M17.**
2 Something corresponding or analogous. **E19.**

correlate /ˈkɒrəleɪt, -rɪl-/ *verb*. **M18.**
[**ORIGIN** Back-form. from **CORRELATION**.]
1 *verb intrans.* Have a mutual relation; be correlative or correlated (*with*, *to*). **M18.**

G. GROTE Ethical obligation correlates . . with ethical right. *Scientific American* The number of nights when the aurora is seen correlates well with the number of spots on the sun.

2 *verb trans.* Bring into mutual relation; establish the likely relation between. (Foll. by *with*.) **M19.**

N. BOHR It has been possible to correlate each term with the occurrence of electron orbits of a given type.

3 *verb trans.* In *pass.* Be regularly connected or related; exhibit a correlation. **M19.**

G. GORER Class is not directly correlated with income.

■ **correˈlatable** *adjective* **L19.**

correlation /kɒrəˈleɪʃ(ə)n, -rɪ-/ *noun*. **M16.**
[**ORIGIN** medieval Latin *correlatio(n-)*, formed as **COR-** + *relatio(n-)* **RELATION**. Cf. **CO-RELATION**.]
1 Mutual close or necessary relation of two or more things; *spec.* an interdependence of variable quantities; the degree of such interdependence. **M16.**

K. PEARSON A sensible correlation . . between fertility and height in the mothers of daughters. W. LIPPMANN A real correlation of cause and effect.

2 The action of correlating. **L19.**
– **COMB.**: **correlation coefficient** a number between +1 and −1 calculated so as to represent the linear interdependence of two variables or sets of data.
■ **correlational** *adjective* of, pertaining to, or employing correlation **M20.**

correlative /kəˈrɛlətɪv/ *adjective & noun*. **M16.**
[**ORIGIN** medieval Latin *correlativus*, formed as **COR-** + late Latin *relativus* **RELATIVE**. Cf. French *corrélatif*, *-ive*; **CORELATIVE**.]
▸ **A** *adjective*. **1** Related each to the other; occurring together; analogous; *GRAMMAR* (of two words) corresponding to each other and regularly used together, (of a construction) formed with such words. (Foll. by *with*, *to*.) **M16.**

ISAAC TAYLOR Such utterances of desire, or hope, or love, as seem to suppose the existence of correlative feelings. P. G. PERRIN *Either . . . or* Correlative conjunctions.

2 Having or involving a relation such that each implies the other; mutually interdependent. (Foll. by *with*, *to*.) **L17.**

J. LOCKE Husband and wife, and such other correlative terms. G. GROTE Correlative rights and duties.

3 *MATH*. Of geometric figures, propositions, etc.: such that points in one correspond to lines (in two dimensions) or to planes (in three) in the other, and vice versa. **L19.**
▸ **B** *noun*. A correlative thing or word. **M16.**
objective correlative: see **OBJECTIVE** *adjective & noun*.
■ **correlatively** *adverb* **M17.** **correlativeness** *noun* **M18.** **correlaˈtivity** *noun* **L19.**

correption /kəˈrɛpʃ(ə)n/ *noun*. **LME.**
[**ORIGIN** Latin *correptio(n-)*, from *correpl-* pa. ppl stem of *corripere*, formed as **COR-** + *rapere* snatch: see **-ION**.]
†**1** (A) reproof. **LME–M18.**

C

2 *GRAMMAR.* Shortening in pronunciation; an instance of this. *rare.* **L19.**

correspond /kɒrɪˈspɒnd/ *verb.* **LME.**
[ORIGIN Old French & mod. French *correspondre* from medieval Latin *correspondere*, formed as COR- + Latin *respondere* RESPOND *verb*.]
▸ **I** *verb intrans.* **1** Be congruous or in harmony (*with*), be agreeable or conformable (*to*). **LME.**

R. FRY To consider.. how far the pictured past corresponds to any reality. J. BARZUN Difficulty obtaining employment corresponding to their.. talents.

2 Have a similar or analogous character, form, or function; agree in position, amount, etc. (Foll. by *to*, *with*.) **E16.**

H. J. STEPHEN Their general assembly, corresponding with our House of Commons. G. MAXWELL To transpose them until each ball and socket corresponded. *Times* Radiation of 21.1 cm wavelength, corresponding with a frequency of about 1430 megahertz.

3 Communicate (*with*) by the interchange of letters or (formerly) any other (esp. secret) means. **E17.**

DEFOE To correspond with him, by the passages of the mountains. D. BREWSTER Locke and Newton had corresponded on the prophecies of Daniel.

†**4** Respond in like manner. (Foll. by *to*, *with*.) **M17–E19.**
▸ †**II** *verb trans.* **5** Answer to, agree with, suit. **M16–L17.**
■ **corresponder** *noun* (now *rare*) a person who corresponds, a correspondent **L18.**

correspondence /kɒrɪˈspɒnd(ə)ns/ *noun.* **LME.**
[ORIGIN Old French & mod. French from medieval Latin *correspondentia*, from *correspondent-*: see CORRESPONDENT, -ENCE.]
1 Congruity, harmony, agreement; (a) similarity of character, form, or function; (an) analogy. **LME.** ▸**b** *MATH.* A relation between two sets such that each element of one is associated with a specified number of elements in the second set, and each element of the second is associated with a specified number of elements in the first. **M19.**

J. BUTLER The correspondence of actions to the nature of the agent renders them natural. E. B. PUSEY The correspondence of the punishment with the sin. F. SMYTH The gunsmith.. pointed out the points of correspondence between the bullets.

b one-to-one correspondence: in which each element of one set is associated with just one element of the second, and vice versa.

†**2** A concordant or sympathetic response. **M16–L17.**
†**3** Relations, a relationship, between persons or communities, usu. of a specified nature. **L16–M19.**

MARVELL Our ill correspondence with the French Protestants.

†**4** Dealings between individuals, esp. of a secret or illicit nature; communication for purposes of trade; an instance of this. **L16–L18.**
5 Vital or active communication; an instance of this. **E17.**

C. LAMB Sun-dials.. holding correspondence with the fountain of light.

6 Communication by letters to and fro; letters exchanged, sent, or received; an exchange of letters. **M17.**

F. NORRIS A correspondence had been maintained between the two. E. WELTY He had dispatched all his correspondence promptly.

– COMB.: **correspondence college**: that instructs by means of correspondence; **correspondence course** a course of instruction conducted by correspondence; **correspondence principle** *PHYSICS*: that in the limit the laws of quantum theory pass into those of classical physics; **correspondence school**: that instructs by means of correspondence; **correspondence theory** *PHILOSOPHY*: that the definition or criterion of truth is that true propositions correspond to the facts.
■ **correspondency** *noun* (now *rare*) = CORRESPONDENCE (now only sense 1) **L16.**

correspondent /kɒrɪˈspɒnd(ə)nt/ *adjective & noun.* **LME.**
[ORIGIN Old French & mod. French *correspondant* or medieval Latin *correspondent-* pres. ppl stem of *correspondere* CORRESPOND: see -ENT.]
▸ **A** *adjective.* **1** = CORRESPONDING 1. (Foll. by *to*, *with*.) *arch.* **LME.**

WELLINGTON The.. price has been.. increased without any correspondent improvement in the quality of the goods. J. RUSKIN Sculptural sketching, exactly correspondent to a painter's light execution of a background.

†**2** Responsive; compliant, submissive. **E17–M18.**
▸ **B** *noun.* **1** A thing that corresponds to something else. **M17.**
†**2** A person who has (esp. secret) communication with another; an accomplice. **M17–L18.**
3 a A writer of letters. **M17.** ▸**b** A person employed to contribute matter for publication in a newspaper or magazine or for broadcasting, esp. from a particular place or on a particular subject. Formerly, a contributor of letters to a periodical. **E18.**

a P. H. JOHNSON She was a poor correspondent, her letters brief and schoolgirlish.

b ***Brussels correspondent***, ***chess correspondent***, ***political correspondent***, ***special correspondent***, ***war correspondent***, etc.

4 A person with whom one has business dealings, esp. at a distance. **L17.**
■ **correspondential** /ˌkɒrɪspɒnˈdɛnʃ(ə)l/ *adjective* pertaining to correspondence or a correspondent **E19.** **correspondently** *adverb* correspondingly **L15.** **correspondentship** *noun* the post of correspondent for a newspaper etc. **M19.**

corresponding /kɒrɪˈspɒndɪŋ/ *ppl adjective.* **L16.**
[ORIGIN from CORRESPOND + -ING².]
1 That corresponds to something else; analogous, equivalent, proportional. **L16.**
2 That corresponds by letter. **M18.**
corresponding member an honorary member of a learned society who lives at a distance and has no voice in its discussions.
■ **correspondingly** *adverb* **M19.**

corresponsive /kɒrɪˈspɒnsɪv/ *adjective.* Now *rare.* **E17.**
[ORIGIN from COR- + RESPONSIVE.]
= CORRESPONDING 1.

corrida /kɔːˈriːdə, *foreign* kɔˈrriða/ *noun.* **L19.**
[ORIGIN Spanish, lit. 'course (of bulls)'.]
In full ***corrida de toros*** /də ˈtɔːrəʊz, *foreign* ðe ˈtorɔs/. A bullfight; bullfighting.

corridor /ˈkɒrɪdɔː/ *noun.* **L16.**
[ORIGIN French from Italian *corridore* alt., by assim. to *corridore* runner, of *corridoio* running place, from *correre* run from Latin *currere*.]
†**1** *FORTIFICATION.* = ***covered way*** (a) s.v. COVERED *adjective.* **L16–E18.**
2 A passage or covered way between two places. **E17.**
3 An outdoor covered way round the inside of a quadrangle or the court of a building. **M17.**
4 A long passage in a building, *esp.* one with many doors to side rooms; a similar passage in a railway carriage, with doors to the compartments. **E19.**
corridors of power places or society where covert influence is exerted in government.
5 A strip of territory that runs through that of another state and secures access to the sea or some desired part. **E20.**
6 A belt of land or a route where traffic is concentrated or to which it is confined; *spec.* = ***air corridor*** s.v. AIR *noun*¹. **E20.**

C. RYAN They were charged with holding open the corridor.. over which British armour would drive. *Economist* The area is something of a corridor for commuter traffic.

– COMB.: **corridor carriage**, **corridor coach** a railway carriage with a corridor; **corridor train**: made up of carriages with corridors.

corrie /ˈkɒri/ *noun.* Chiefly *Scot.* **M16.**
[ORIGIN Gaelic, Old Irish & mod. Irish *coire* cauldron, hollow.]
A circular hollow on a mountainside; a cirque.

Corriedale /ˈkɒrɪdeɪl/ *noun & adjective.* *NZ.* **E20.**
[ORIGIN An estate in N. Otago, NZ.]
(Designating) a sheep of a New Zealand breed yielding both wool and meat; the breed itself.

corrigendum /kɒrɪˈdʒɛndəm/ *noun.* Pl. **-da** /-də/. **E19.**
[ORIGIN Latin, neut. gerundive of *corrigere* CORRECT *verb*.]
Something requiring correction, *spec.* in a book. In *pl. esp.* errors listed with the corrections alongside.

corrigible /ˈkɒrɪdʒɪb(ə)l/ *adjective.* **LME.**
[ORIGIN French from medieval Latin *corrigibilis*, from Latin *corrigere* CORRECT *verb*: see -IBLE. Cf. earlier INCORRIGIBLE.]
†**1** Deserving punishment; punishable by law. **LME–M17.**
2 Able to be corrected; rectifiable; (of a fault or weakness) capable of improvement or reformation. **L15.**
3 Of a person: receptive to admonishment or punishment. **L16.**
†**4** Corrective. Only in **E17.**
■ **corrigiˈbility** *noun* **M18.**

corrival /kəˈrʌɪv(ə)l/ *noun & adjective.* *arch.* **L16.**
[ORIGIN French, or Latin *corrivalis*: see COR-, RIVAL *noun & adjective*. Cf. CO-RIVAL.]
▸ **A** *noun.* **1** A person who is one of two or more joint rivals, a person with rival claims; *esp.* a rival suitor. **L16.**
†**2** A person having equal rights; a partner. Only in **L16.**
▸ **B** *adjective.* Rival. **M17.**
■ †**corrivality** *noun* **L16–M17.** †**corrivalry** *noun* [cf. CO-RIVALRY] **E–M17.** †**corrivalship** *noun* the situation of a corrival **E17–M18.**

corroborant /kəˈrɒb(ə)r(ə)nt/ *adjective & noun.* **E17.**
[ORIGIN French, or Latin *corroborant-* pres. ppl stem of *corroborare*: see CORROBORATE, -ANT¹.]
▸ **A** *adjective.* Strengthening, invigorating. **E17.**
▸ **B** *noun.* **1** A corroborant agent; a tonic. **M18.**
2 A fact which corroborates a statement etc. **E19.**

corroborate /kəˈrɒbəreɪt/ *verb trans.* Pa. pple **-ated**, (long *arch.*) **-ate** /-ət/. **M16.**
[ORIGIN Latin *corroborat-* pa. ppl stem of *corroborare*, formed as COR- + *roborare* strengthen, from *robur*, *robor-* strength: see -ATE³.]
†**1** Make stronger materially. **M16–E19.**
†**2** Strengthen (the body or spirit), act on (a part) as a restorative; invigorate. **M16–E19.**
3 Strengthen (a faculty, power, etc.) or (a person) *in* a quality. *arch.* **M16.**
4 Confirm formally (a law etc.). *arch.* **M16.**

W. CRUISE For the purpose of corroborating the conveyance.

5 Support (a statement, argument, etc.) with agreeing statements; provide or be additional evidence for, confirm. **E18.**

J. TYNDALL This observation corroborates those of Professor Forbes. A. BRINK Under oath his wife corroborated his evidence.

■ **corroborator** *noun* **L17.** **corroboratory** *adjective* = CORROBORATIVE *adjective* **M17.**

corroboration /kərɒbəˈreɪʃ(ə)n/ *noun.* **LME.**
[ORIGIN French, or late Latin *corroboratio(n-)*, formed as CORROBORATE: see -ATION.]
†**1** Strengthening. **LME–E19.**
2 a Legal confirmation. *arch.* **M16.** ▸**b** Confirmation of a statement etc. by additional evidence. **M18.**
3 Something which corroborates. **M16.**

corroborative /kəˈrɒb(ə)rətɪv/ *adjective & noun.* **L16.**
[ORIGIN French *corroboratif*, *-ive*, formed as CORROBORATE: see -IVE.]
▸ **A** *adjective.* Having the quality of corroborating; *esp.* confirmatory. **L16.**
▸ †**B** *noun.* = CORROBORANT *noun* 1. **E17–E19.**
■ **corroboratively** *adverb* **M19.**

corroboree /kəˈrɒbəri/ *noun & verb.* **L18.**
[ORIGIN Dharuk *garabari*, style of dance.]
▸ **A** *noun.* **1** A night-time dance of Australian Aborigines, which may be either festive or warlike; a song or chant for this. **L18.**
2 A noisy gathering; a disturbance. **M19.**
▸ **B** *verb intrans.* Take part in a corroboree; dance. **E19.**

corrode /kəˈrəʊd/ *verb.* **LME.**
[ORIGIN Latin *corrodere*, formed as COR- + *rodere* gnaw.]
1 *verb trans.* Gradually destroy or wear away, esp. through chemical action or disease. Formerly also, (of water) erode by physical action. **LME.**

A. HIGGINS A paraffin lamp much corroded by rust. *fig.*: M. L. KING Dignity is.. corroded by poverty.

†**2** *verb trans.* Of an animal: eat into, gnaw away. **M16–M19.**
3 *verb intrans.* Cause corrosion. **E17.**

fig.: GOLDSMITH Suffering this jealousy to corrode in her breast.

4 *verb intrans.* Undergo corrosion, be corroded. **E19.**
■ **corrodaˈbility** *noun* = CORRODIBILITY **L20.** **corrodable** *adjective* = CORRODIBLE **L20.** **corrodent** *adjective & noun* (now *rare* or *obsolete*) (*a*) *adjective* corrosive; (*b*) *noun* a corrosive agent: **L16.** **corroder** *noun* a person who or thing which causes corrosion **L17.**

corrodiary /kəˈrəʊdɪəri/ *noun.* **M17.**
[ORIGIN Anglo-Norman *corrōdiārius* from Anglo-Latin *corrodium* CORRODY: see -ARY¹.]
hist. A recipient of a corrody.

corrodible /kəˈrəʊdɪb(ə)l/ *adjective.* **M17.**
[ORIGIN from CORRODE + -IBLE. Cf. CORROSIBLE.]
Able to be corroded; susceptible to corrosion.
■ **corrodiˈbility** *noun* **M18.**

corrody /ˈkɒrədi/ *noun.* Also **coro-**. **LME.**
[ORIGIN Anglo-Norman *corodie*, Anglo-Latin *corrodium* var. of *corredium*, from Old French *conrei*, *conroi* (mod. *corroi*), from *correier* CURRY *verb*¹.]
hist. Provision for maintenance, esp. as given regularly by a religious house; a pension.

corrosible /kəˈrəʊzɪb(ə)l/ *adjective.* **E18.**
[ORIGIN from Latin *corros-*: see CORROSION, -IBLE.]
= CORRODIBLE.
■ **corrosiˈbility** *noun* **L17.**

corrosion /kəˈrəʊʒ(ə)n/ *noun.* **LME.**
[ORIGIN Old French, or late Latin *corrosio(n-)*, from Latin *corros-* pa. ppl stem of *corrodere* CORRODE: see -ION.]
The action or process of corroding; the state, esp. of a metal, of having been partly altered or destroyed by slow chemical action.

fig.: S. JOHNSON Peevishness.. wears out happiness by slow corrosion.

corrosive /kəˈrəʊsɪv/ *adjective & noun.* **LME.**
[ORIGIN Old French *corosif*, *-ive* (mod. *corr-*) from medieval Latin *corrosivus*, from Latin *corros-*: see CORROSION, -IVE.]
▸ **A** *adjective.* **1** Having the property of corroding, tending to corrode. **LME.**

J. HELLER The corrosive blot of some crawling disease.

corrosive sublimate: see SUBLIMATE *noun* 1.
2 *fig.* Destructive, consuming; fretting, wearing. **LME.**

R. HOOKER A pensive and corrosive desire.

▸ **B** *noun.* **1** A drug, remedy, etc., that destroys tissue. **LME.**
2 A chemical that causes corrosion. **L15.**
■ **corrosively** *adverb* **L17.** **corrosiveness** *noun* **L16.**

corrugate /ˈkɒrʊgeɪt/ *verb.* Pa. pple **-ated**, (now chiefly *BOTANY & ZOOLOGY*) **-ate** /-ət/. **LME.**
[ORIGIN Latin *corrugat-* pa. ppl stem of *corrugare*, formed as COR- + *rugare*, from *ruga* wrinkle: see -ATE³.]
1 *verb trans.* Wrinkle (skin); mark with or bend into (usu. parallel) ridges and furrows. **LME.**

J. BUCHAN Trees.. whose roots corrugated the path. S. HILL A corrugated tin roof.

corrugated iron iron or steel sheeting bent into a uniform series of parallel ridges and hollows to give added rigidity and strength. **corrugated paper**: with parallel flutings (for added rigidity and strength) and a flat backing sheet attached on one or both sides.
2 *verb intrans.* Become corrugated. **M18.**

corrugation /kɒrəˈɡeɪʃ(ə)n/ *noun*. **E16**.
[**ORIGIN** Old French & mod. French, or medieval Latin *corrugatio(n-)*, formed as **CORRUGATE**: see **-ATION**.]
1 The action of corrugating; the state of being corrugated. **E16**.
2 A wrinkle, furrow, etc., of a corrugated surface. **E19**.
J. PACKER Poor car on the corrugations!

corrugator /ˈkɒrəɡeɪtə/ *noun*. **L18**.
[**ORIGIN** from (the same root as) **CORRUGATE** + **-OR**.]
1 *gen*. A thing which or person who causes corrugation. **L18**.
2 *spec*. Either of two muscles which contract the eyebrows in frowning. **M19**.

corrupt /kəˈrʌpt/ *adjective*. **ME**.
[**ORIGIN** Old French, or Latin *corruptus* pa. pple of *corrumpere* destroy, mar, bribe, formed as **COR-** + *rumpere* break.]
1 Depraved; infected with evil; perverted. **ME**.
H. REED Charles II came back.. with tastes as corrupt as his morals.
2 Turned from a sound into an unsound condition; infected with decay; mouldy, rotten; rotting. *arch*. **LME**.
3 Influenced by bribery; perverted from fidelity. **LME**.
BURKE A corrupt representative of a virtuous people.
corrupt practice *spec*. any of various illegal practices (as bribery, personation) in connection with elections (usu. in *pl*.).
4 a Of a language, text, etc.: unconsciously or accidentally altered from the original or correct form; containing errors or alterations; debased. **LME**. ▸**b** *ELECTRONICS & COMPUTING*. Of data or code: having had errors introduced. **L20**.
T. PYNCHON The 'Whitechapel' edition.. abounds in such corrupt and probably spurious lines.
■ **corruptly** *adverb* **LME**. **corruptness** *noun* **M16**.

corrupt /kəˈrʌpt/ *verb*. **LME**.
[**ORIGIN** from the adjective.]
▸ **I** *verb trans*. **1** Render morally unsound; destroy the moral purity or chastity of; defile. **LME**.
C. MACKENZIE Letting a rascal.. corrupt the minds of children. B. PLAIN The hidden envy that can corrupt old age.
2 Make mouldy or rotten; turn from a sound into an unsound condition; contaminate, infect. *arch*. **LME**.
W. LITHGOW The infectious air, that corrupted the blood of strangers.
3 Induce to act dishonestly or unfaithfully; bribe. **LME**.
MILTON The greatest part Of Mankind they corrupted to forsake God their Creator.
†**4** Pervert the text or sense of (a law etc.) for evil ends. **LME–E18**.
5 Mar, spoil in quality. Now *rare* or *obsolete*. **E16**.
6 a Destroy the purity of (a language) or the correctness of (a text); unconsciously or accidentally alter (a word of a language). **M17**. ▸**b** *ELECTRONICS & COMPUTING*. Introduce errors into (data or code). **M20**.
▸ **II** *verb intrans*. **7** Putrefy, rot; decompose. *arch*. **LME**.
8 Undergo moral decay; degenerate. **L16**.
9 Cause corruption; destroy moral purity. **L19**.
LD ACTON Power tends to corrupt and absolute power corrupts absolutely.
■ **corruptedly** *adverb* in a corrupted manner **E17**. **corruptedness** *noun* the state of being corrupted **M17**. **corrupter**, **-or** *noun* a person who or thing which corrupts **LME**. **corruptful** *adjective* (*rare*) fraught with corruption **L16**. **corruptless** *adjective* (*arch*.) not subject to corruption **E17**. **corruptress** *noun* (now *rare*) a female corrupter **E17**.

corruptible /kəˈrʌptɪb(ə)l/ *adjective*. **ME**.
[**ORIGIN** ecclesiastical Latin *corruptibilis*, from Latin *corrupt-*: see **CORRUPTION**, **-IBLE**.]
1 Perishable, mortal; subject to decay. **ME**.
SOUTHEY The soul Inhabits still its corruptible clay.
2 Capable of moral corruption; open to bribery. **LME**.
■ **corruptiˈbility** *noun* **LME**. **corruptibleness** *noun* **LME**. **corruptibly** *adverb* **L16**.

corruption /kəˈrʌpʃ(ə)n/ *noun*. **ME**.
[**ORIGIN** Old French & mod. French from Latin *corruptio(n-)*, from *corrupt-* pa. ppl stem of *corrumpere*: see **CORRUPT** *adjective*, **-ION**.]
1 Putrefaction; decay, esp. of a dead body. Formerly also more widely, decomposition of any kind, of organic or inorganic substances. **ME**.
2 Moral deterioration; depravity; an instance or manifestation of this. **ME**.
V. KNOX Seminaries of young ladies.. are in danger of great corruption.
3 A corrupting influence; a cause of deterioration or depravity. **ME**.
B. JOWETT The love of money is the corruption of states.
4 Perversion of a person's integrity in the performance of (esp. official or public) duty or work by bribery etc. **LME**.
HOBBES The frequent corruption and partiality of Judges.
5 Evil nature; anger, temper. Now *dial*. **LME**.
A. BRONTË I am no angel, and my corruption rises against it.
6 Decomposed or putrid matter; pus. *obsolete* exc. *dial*. **LME**.
7 The unconscious or accidental alteration of a word, text, etc., in transmission; a word or passage so altered. **L15**.
G. K. CHESTERTON Whether Notting Hill.. is a corruption of Nothing-ill.
8 (A) change for the worse of an institution, custom, etc.; a departure from a state of original purity. **M17**.
– **PHRASES**: **corruption of blood** *hist*. the effect of attainder by which the person attainted could neither inherit, retain, nor transmit land.
■ **corruptionist** *noun* a person who supports or practises corruption, esp. in public affairs **E19**.

corruptive /kəˈrʌptɪv/ *adjective*. **LME**.
[**ORIGIN** Old French & mod. French *corruptif*, *-ive* or ecclesiastical Latin *corruptivus*, from Latin *corrupt-*: see **CORRUPTION**, **-IVE**.]
1 Tending to corrupt. **LME**.
†**2** Subject or liable to corruption. **L16–L17**.
■ **corruptively** *adverb* **M17**.

†**cors** *noun* see **CORSE** *noun*.

corsac /ˈkɔːsak/ *noun*. **M19**.
[**ORIGIN** Russian *korsak* from Turki *karsak*.]
A fox, *Vulpes corsac*, of the steppes of central Asia.

corsage /kɔːˈsɑːʒ, ˈkɔːsɑːʒ/ *noun*. **LME**.
[**ORIGIN** Old French & mod. French, from *cors* (mod. **CORPS**): see **-AGE**.]
†**1** The body, the trunk; size and shape of body. **LME–M17**.
2 The bodice of a woman's dress. **E19**.
3 A posy for the front of a woman's dress. **E20**.

corsair /ˈkɔːsɛː/ *noun*. **M16**.
[**ORIGIN** French *corsaire* from medieval Latin *cursarius*, from *cursa*, *cursus* hostile inroad, plunder, a spec. use of Latin *cursus* **COURSE** *noun*[1].]
1 *hist*. **a** A privateersman of the Mediterranean, esp. the Barbary coast; a pirate. **M16**. ▸**b** A privateering ship; a pirate ship. Also ***corsair ship***. **M17**.
2 Either of two nocturnal reduviid bugs of the western and southern US, of the genus *Rasahus*, which can give a painful bite. **E20**.

cors anglais *noun phr*. pl. of **COR ANGLAIS**.

corse /kɔːs/ *noun*. Also (the only form in sense 4) †**cors**. **ME**.
[**ORIGIN** Old French *cors* (mod. **CORPS**). Cf. **CORPSE** *noun*.]
†**1** = **CORPSE** *noun* 1. **ME–L16**.
2 = **CORPSE** *noun* 2. Now *arch*. & *poet*. **ME**.
†**3** A ribbon or band serving as ground for an ornamented girdle, garter, etc. **ME–M16**.
†**4** *ARCHITECTURE*. A slender pillar surmounted by a pinnacle or figure and close to but not supporting a wall. **L15–M19**.
– **COMB.**: †**corse-present** a customary gift due to the clergy from the effects of a deceased householder.

corse /kɔːs/ *verb trans*. Long *obsolete* exc. *dial*. Also **course**. **ME**.
[**ORIGIN** Unknown. Cf. **COSS** *verb*, **SCORSE** *verb*[1].]
Barter, exchange, buy and sell, (esp. horses).
■ **corser** *noun* a dealer, a jobber; *esp*. (more fully ***horse-corser***) a horse-dealer: **LME**.

corselet /ˈkɔːslɪt/ *noun*. Also **corslet**. **L15**.
[**ORIGIN** Old French & mod. French, dim. of *cors* (mod. **CORPS**): see **-LET**.]
▸ **I 1 a** *hist*. A piece of armour covering the body, orig. from the head to the thighs, later just the upper trunk. **L15**. ▸†**b** A soldier wearing a corselet. **L16–E18**.
2 A usu. tight-fitting garment covering the trunk. **E16**.
3 = **CORSELETTE**. **M20**.
▸ **II 4** The thorax or prothorax of an insect, esp. a beetle. **M18**.

corselette /kɔːs(ə)ˈlɛt, ˈkɔːs(ə)lɛt/ *noun*. **E20**.
[**ORIGIN** from **CORSE** *noun*: see **-ETTE**.]
A foundation garment combining girdle and bra.

corset /ˈkɔːsɪt/ *noun* & *verb*. **ME**.
[**ORIGIN** Old French & mod. French, dim. of *cors* (mod. **CORPS**): see **-ET**[1].]
▸ **A** *noun*. **1** *hist*. A close-fitting laced or stiffened outer bodice or gown worn by women; a similar garment worn by men. **ME**.
2 *sing*. & in *pl*. A woman's close-fitting undergarment for giving shape and support to the figure, formerly with lacing and stiffening. **L18**.
fig.: *Listener* It imprisons the state in a bureaucratic corset designed to restrict development.
3 A close-fitting support worn because of injury, weakness, or deformity, esp. of the thorax or spine. **M19**.
▸ **B** *verb trans*. **1** Fit or provide with a corset. Chiefly as ***corseted*** *ppl adjective*, ***corseting*** *verbal noun* **M19**.
2 *fig*. Place restraints or controls on; force *into*. **M20**.
■ **corsetless** *adjective* **L19**. **corsetry** *noun* (**a**) the making or fitting of corsets; (**b**) corsets collectively: **E20**.

corsetière /ˈkɔːsɪtjɛː/ *noun*. **M19**.
[**ORIGIN** French, fem. of *corsetier*, formed as **CORSET**: see **-IER**.]
A woman who makes or fits corsets.

Corsican /ˈkɔːsɪk(ə)n/ *noun* & *adjective*. **M18**.
[**ORIGIN** from *Corsica* (see below) + **-AN**.]
▸ **A** *noun*. A native or inhabitant of Corsica, an island in the Mediterranean; the dialect of Italian spoken there. **M18**.
▸ **B** *adjective*. Of or pertaining to Corsica. **M18**.
– **PHRASES**: **Corsican pine** a tall slender pine (a subspecies of the Austrian pine *Pinus nigra*) which is native to southern Europe and has been introduced into Britain. **the Corsican**, **the Corsican ogre**, **the Corsican robber** Napoleon, who was born in Corsica.

C

†**corsie** *noun* & *adjective*. Also **corsive**. **LME**.
[**ORIGIN** Syncopated from **CORROSIVE**.]
▸ **A** *noun*. **1** = **CORROSIVE** *noun*. **LME–M17**.
2 A cause of trouble and grief, a grievance. **M16–L19**.
▸ **B** *adjective*. = **CORROSIVE** *adjective*. **L16–E17**.

corslet *noun* var. of **CORSELET**.

corsned /ˈkɔːsnɛd/ *noun*.
[**ORIGIN** Old English *cor-snǣd*, from *cor* choice, trial + *snǣd* bit, piece, from *snīdan* to cut.]
hist. A piece of bread consecrated by exorcism which in pre-Conquest times an accused person was required to swallow without harm to demonstrate his or her innocence.

Corso /ˈkɔːsəʊ/ *noun*. Also **c-**. Pl. **-os**. **L17**.
[**ORIGIN** Italian = course, main street from Latin *cursus* **COURSE** *noun*[1].]
In Italy and some other Mediterranean countries: a procession of carriages; a social promenade; a street given over to this, or where races etc. were formerly held.

Cortaillod /kɔːˈtʌɪjəʊ/ *noun* & *adjective*. **L19**.
[**ORIGIN** Place in the canton of Neuchâtel, Switzerland.]
▸ **A** *noun*. A red table wine made in the canton of Neuchâtel, Switzerland, from Pinot grapes. **L19**.
▸ **B** *adjective*. *ARCHAEOLOGY*. Designating or pertaining to an early Neolithic culture of Switzerland, represented esp. by lakeside sites. **M20**.

cortège /kɔːˈteɪʒ/ *noun*. **M17**.
[**ORIGIN** French from Italian *corteggio*, from *corteggiare* attend court, from *corte* **COURT** *noun*[1].]
A train of attendants; a procession of people, esp. mourners.

Cortes /ˈkɔːtɛs, -z/ *noun*. Pl. same. **M17**.
[**ORIGIN** Spanish & Portuguese, pl. of *corte* **COURT** *noun*[1].]
The legislative assembly of Spain or (*hist*.) Portugal or any of various medieval Spanish kingdoms.

cortex /ˈkɔːtɛks/ *noun*. Pl. **-tices** /-tɪsiːz/. **LME**.
[**ORIGIN** Latin = bark.]
1 An outer layer of a part in an animal or plant, as of the kidney or a hair; *spec*. (*ANATOMY*) the outer layer of the cerebrum, composed of folded grey matter and playing an important role in consciousness; a similar layer of the cerebellum; *BOTANY* a layer of plant tissue between the epidermis and the central vascular tissue. **LME**.
adrenal cortex: see **ADRENAL** *adjective*. ***motor cortex***: see **MOTOR** *noun* & *adjective*. ***visual cortex***: see **VISUAL** *adjective*.
†**2** *fig*. An outer shell or husk. **M17–M18**.
3 The bark of a tree, or the peel or rind of a plant, as used medicinally; *spec*. cinchona bark. **L17**.

Corti /ˈkɔːti/ *noun*. **L19**.
[**ORIGIN** A. *Corti* (1822–88), Italian histologist.]
ANATOMY. ***organ of Corti***, a sense organ on the basilar membrane of the cochlea, containing sensory hair cells.

cortical /ˈkɔːtɪk(ə)l/ *adjective*. **M17**.
[**ORIGIN** medieval Latin *corticalis*, from Latin *cortic-*, **CORTEX**: see **-AL**[1].]
1 Belonging to or forming a cortex. **M17**.
†**2** *fig*. Superficial, external. **M17–M19**.

corticated /ˈkɔːtɪkeɪtɪd/ *adjective*. **M17**.
[**ORIGIN** from Latin *corticatus* derived from bark, from *cortic-*, **CORTEX**: see **-ATE**[2], **-ED**[1].]
BOTANY & ZOOLOGY. Having a cortex; having a bark, rind, or other outer layer.
■ Also **corticate** /-eɪt, -ət/ *adjective* **M19**.

corticene /ˈkɔːtɪsiːn/ *noun*. Also **-ine**. **L19**.
[**ORIGIN** from Latin *cortic-*, **CORTEX** + **-ENE**, **-INE**[4].]
A floor-covering material made from ground cork.

cortices *noun* pl. of **CORTEX**.

cortici- /ˈkɔːtɪsi/ *combining form* of **CORTEX**: see **-I-**. Cf. **CORTICO-**.
■ **cortiˈcifugal** *adjective* = **CORTICOFUGAL** **L19**. **cortiˈcipetal** *adjective* = **CORTICOPETAL** **L19**.

corticine *noun* var. of **CORTICENE**.

cortico- /ˈkɔːtɪkəʊ/ *combining form* of **CORTEX**: see **-O-**. Used esp. with ref. to the adrenal and cerebral cortices. Cf. **CORTICI-**.
■ **corticoˈfugal** *adjective* [Latin *fugere* flee] (of a nerve fibre) originating in and running from the cerebral cortex **L19**. **corticoid** *noun* = **CORTICOSTEROID** **M20**. **corticoˈpetal** *adjective* [Latin *petere* seek] (of a nerve fibre) originating outside and running into the cerebral cortex **L19**. **corticoˈsteroid** *noun* any of the steroid hormones produced in the adrenal cortex, which are concerned with one or other of electrolyte balance, carbohydrate metabolism, anti-inflammatory activity, and sexuality; any analogous synthetic steroid: **M20**. **corticoˈsterone** *noun* [**-STERONE**] a corticosteroid, $C_{21}H_{30}O_4$, which is converted in the body to aldosterone **M20**. **corticoˈtrophic**, **-tropic** *adjective* = **ADRENOCORTICO-**

TROP(H)IC M20. cortico'trophin, -tropin noun the adrenocorticotropic hormone M20.

corticolous /kɔːˈtɪkələs/ adjective. M19.
[ORIGIN from Latin cortic-, CORTEX + -COLOUS.]
BOTANY. Of a plant, esp. a lichen: growing on bark. Cf. SAXICOLOUS.
■ Also 'corticole adjective L19.

C

cortile /korˈtiːle, kɔːˈtiːli/ noun. Pl. **-li** /-li/, **-les**. E18.
[ORIGIN Italian, deriv. of corte COURT noun[1].]
An enclosed usu. roofless and arcaded area within or attached to an Italian building.

cortina /kɔːˈtʌɪnə, -ˈtiːnə/ noun. M19.
[ORIGIN Late Latin = CURTAIN noun.]
A thin weblike structure left hanging from the cap of mushrooms etc. after the lower edge of the partial veil separates from the stalk; the partial veil itself.

cortisol /ˈkɔːtɪsɒl/ noun. M20.
[ORIGIN from CORTISONE + -OL.]
= HYDROCORTISONE.

cortisone /ˈkɔːtɪzəʊn/ noun. M20.
[ORIGIN from 17-hydroxy-11-dehydroxycorticosterone, chemical name: see CORTICOSTERONE.]
A steroid hormone, $C_{21}H_{28}O_5$, formed from hydrocortisone in the liver or made synthetically, that is used as an anti-inflammatory and anti-allergy agent.

corundum /kəˈrʌndəm/ noun. E18.
[ORIGIN Tamil kuruntam, Telugu kuruvindam.]
Aluminium oxide, Al_2O_3, a very hard mineral occurring in many rocks as hexagonal crystals of various colours (some of gem quality, as sapphires, rubies, etc.), and made synthetically for use in abrasives, refractories, and bearings.

coruscant /kɒˈrʌsk(ə)nt/ adjective. L15.
[ORIGIN Latin coruscant- pres. ppl stem of coruscare: see CORUSCATE, -ANT[1].]
Glittering, sparkling, (lit. & fig.).

coruscate /ˈkɒrəskeɪt/ verb intrans. E18.
[ORIGIN Latin coruscat- pa. ppl stem of coruscare vibrate, glitter: see -ATE[3].]
Flash; sparkle, glitter, (lit. & fig.).

D. CECIL A flight of comic fantasy, coruscating with grotesque images and . . plays on words.

coruscation /kɒrəˈskeɪʃ(ə)n/ noun. L15.
[ORIGIN Latin coruscatio(n-), formed as CORUSCATE: see -ATION.]
A quivering flash or glow of light; a display of such flashes.

L. M. MONTGOMERY Reflecting the sunlight back from its window in several little coruscations of glory.

corvée /ˈkɔːveɪ/ noun. ME.
[ORIGIN Old French & mod. French = Provençal corroada from Proto-Romance use as noun (sc. opera work) of Latin corrogata neut. pl. pa. pple of corrogare summon, formed as COR- + rogare ask.]
A day's unpaid work required of a vassal by a feudal lord; forced labour exacted as a tax, spec. that on public roads in France before 1776; fig. an unpleasant duty, an onerous task.

corver /ˈkɔːvə/ noun. E18.
[ORIGIN from CORF + -ER[1].]
A maker of corves.

corves noun pl. of CORF.

corvette /kɔːˈvɛt/ noun. M17.
[ORIGIN French, ult. dim. of Middle Dutch & mod. Dutch korf basket, kind of ship: see CORF, -ETTE.]
hist. **1** Orig., a kind of small French vessel using both oars and sail. Later, a warship with a flush deck and one tier of guns. M17.
2 An escort vessel smaller than a frigate used esp. for protecting convoys against submarines in the Second World War. M20.

corvid /ˈkɔːvɪd/ noun & adjective. M20.
[ORIGIN mod. Latin Corvidae (see below), from Latin corvus raven: see -ID[3].]
(A bird) of the passerine family Corvidae, which includes crows, jays, magpies, choughs, and ravens.

corvina /kɔːˈviːnə/ noun. L18.
[ORIGIN Spanish & Portuguese, formed as CORVINE.]
Any of several marine fishes of the family Sciaenidae, esp. an American food fish of the genus Cynoscion.

corvine /ˈkɔːvʌɪn/ adjective. M17.
[ORIGIN Latin corvinus, from corvus raven: see -INE[1].]
Of or pertaining to a raven or crow; of the crow kind.

†**corviser** noun. OE–E18.
[ORIGIN Anglo-Norman corvoiser, Old French co(u)rvoisier, from courveis leather from Latin Cordubensis of Cordoba, from Corduba: see CORDOVAN, -ER[1].]
A shoemaker; = CORDWAINER.

Corvus /ˈkɔːvəs/ noun. LME.
[ORIGIN Latin corvus raven.]
(The name of) an inconspicuous constellation of the southern hemisphere south of Virgo; the Crow, the Raven.

Corybant /ˈkɒrɪbant/ noun. Pl. **Corybants**, **Corybantes** /kɒrɪˈbantiːz/. LME.
[ORIGIN Latin Corybas, -bant- from Greek Korubas.]
GREEK HISTORY. A priest of the fertility and nature goddess Cybele, whose worship involved wild dances and ecstatic states.
■ cory'bantic, C- adjective resembling (that of) the Corybants; wild, frenzied: M17.

Corycian /kəˈrɪʃɪən, -ʃ(ə)n, -sɪən/ adjective. M16.
[ORIGIN from Latin Corycius of or belonging to Corycus or the Corycian cave from Greek Kōrukios, from Kōrukos Corycus: see -IAN.]
1 GREEK MYTHOLOGY. Designating a large cave on Mount Parnassus in Greece and the nymphs, daughters of Pleistos, supposed to live there. M16.
2 Of or pertaining to Corycus in Cilicia (now Curco in Turkey). E20.

corydalis /kəˈrɪdəlɪs/ noun. E19.
[ORIGIN mod. Latin from Greek korudallis crested lark (with allus. to the flower, likened to the bird's spur), from korus helmet: cf. LARKSPUR.]
A plant of the genus Corydalis (family Fumariaceae), comprising mostly rhizomatous or tuberous herbaceous perennials with racemose flowers. Also (with specifying word), a plant of any of several related genera.

corymb /ˈkɒrɪmb/ noun. E18.
[ORIGIN French corymbe or Latin corymbus from Greek korumbos summit, cluster of fruit or flowers.]
1 BOTANY. An inflorescence whose lower flower stalks are proportionally longer so that the flowers form a flat or slightly convex head. Formerly also, a discoidal head of a composite flower. E18.
2 A cluster of ivy berries or grapes. E18.
■ co'rymbiform adjective having the form of a corymb L19. **corymbose** adjective growing in or as a corymb; of the nature of a corymb: L18. **corymbosely** adverb M19.

corymbiferous /kɒrɪmˈbɪf(ə)rəs/ adjective. M17.
[ORIGIN from Latin corymbifer bearing clusters of berries, from corymbus: see CORYMB, -FEROUS.]
1 Bearing berries. rare (Dicts.). M17.
2 BOTANY. Bearing corymbs; belonging to an obsolete division of the family Compositae called Corymbiferae. Now rare or obsolete. L17.

corynebacterium /ˌkɒrɪnɪbakˈtɪərɪəm, kəˌrɪn-/ noun. Pl. **-ia** /-ɪə/. E20.
[ORIGIN mod. Latin, from Greek korunē club + BACTERIUM.]
A bacterium of the genus Corynebacterium of Gram-positive club-shaped rods, of which some species cause disease in plants, animals, or humans (e.g. diphtheria).

coryneform /kəˈrɪnɪfɔːm/ adjective. M20.
[ORIGIN from Greek korunē club + -FORM.]
Resembling or being a corynebacterium.

coryphaeus /kɒrɪˈfiːəs/ noun. Pl. **-phaei** /-ˈfiːʌɪ/. E17.
[ORIGIN Latin from Greek koruphaios chief, chorus-leader, from koruphē head, top.]
1 The leader of a chorus. E17.
2 The leader of a party, sect, school of thought, etc. E17.
3 A post of assistant to the Choragus that formerly existed in Oxford University. M19.

coryphée /ˈkɒrɪfeɪ/ noun. E19.
[ORIGIN French formed as CORYPHAEUS.]
A leading dancer of a corps de ballet.

coryphodon /kəˈrɪfədɒn/ noun. M19.
[ORIGIN mod. Latin, from Greek koruphē head, top + -ODON.]
A large extinct herbivorous quadruped of the fossil genus Coryphodon (order Pantodonta), which lived in late Palaeocene and early Eocene times.
■ Also co'ryphodont noun L19.

coryza /kəˈrʌɪzə/ noun. E16.
[ORIGIN Latin from Greek koruza nasal mucus, catarrh.]
(An) acute catarrhal inflammation of the nose; esp. the common cold.
■ **coryzal** adjective E20.

COS abbreviation.
Chief of Staff.

cos /kɒs/ noun[1]. Also **C-**. L17.
[ORIGIN Cos, one of the Dodecanese islands.]
In full **cos lettuce**. A variety of lettuce with long smooth leaves (orig. introduced from Cos).

cos /kɒz, -s/ noun[2]. M18.
[ORIGIN Abbreviation.]
MATH. Cosine (of).

cos /kɒz, kəz/ adverb & conjunction. dial. & colloq. Also **'cos**. E19.
[ORIGIN Alt. of 'CAUSE.]
= BECAUSE.

Cosa Nostra /ˈkəʊzə ˈnɒstrə/ noun phr. M20.
[ORIGIN Italian = our thing.]
The American branch of the Mafia.

cosaque /kɒˈzɑːk/ noun. M19.
[ORIGIN App. from French Cosaque COSSACK.]
= CRACKER 3b.

coscinomancy /ˈkɒsɪnəmansi/ noun. E17.
[ORIGIN medieval Latin coscinomantia from Greek koskinomantis, from koskinon sieve: see -MANCY.]
Divination by the turning of a sieve (held on a pair of shears etc.).

coscoroba /kɒskəˈrəʊbə/ noun. E19.
[ORIGIN mod. Latin, of unknown origin.]
In full **coscoroba swan**. A small S. American swan, Coscoroba coscoroba, with white plumage and bright pink legs and feet.

cose /kəʊz/ verb[1] intrans. colloq. M19.
[ORIGIN Back-form. from COSY adjective.]
Make oneself cosy.

cose verb[2] var. of COSS verb.

cosec /ˈkəʊsɛk/ noun. M18.
[ORIGIN Abbreviation.]
MATH. Cosecant (of).

cosecant /kəʊˈsiːk(ə)nt, -ˈsɛk-/ noun. E18.
[ORIGIN mod. Latin cosecant-: see CO-, SECANT.]
MATH. The secant of the complement of a given angle; in a right-angled triangle containing the angle, the ratio of the hypotenuse to the side opposite the angle. Abbreviation COSEC.

coset /ˈkəʊsɛt/ noun. E20.
[ORIGIN from CO- + SET noun[2].]
MATH. A subset of a group composed of all the products obtained by multiplying each element of a subgroup in turn by one particular element of the group.

cosh /kɒʃ/ noun[1] & verb. colloq. Also **k-**. M19.
[ORIGIN Unknown.]
▸ **A** noun. A heavy stick or bludgeon; a truncheon. M19.
– COMB.: **cosh boy** a youth or man who uses or carries a cosh.
▸ **B** verb trans. Strike with a cosh. L19.

fig.: J. BARNES Some writers . . sneak in at the back door and cosh the reader with a highly personal style.

■ **cosher** noun a person who uses a cosh; slang a police officer: L19.

cosh /kɒʃ, kɒˈseɪtʃ/ noun[2]. L19.
[ORIGIN from COS noun[2] + h (for hyperbolic).]
MATH. Hyperbolic cosine (of).

cosher /ˈkɒʃə/ verb[1] intrans. L16.
[ORIGIN from Irish cóisir feast.]
IRISH HISTORY. Quarter oneself as the guest of another, esp. a dependant or kinsman; live at another's expense.
■ **cosherer** noun a person who coshers or lives by coshering M17. **coshery** noun entertainment for themselves and their followers exacted by Irish chiefs from their dependants L16.

cosher /ˈkɒʃə/ verb[2] trans. M19.
[ORIGIN Unknown.]
Pamper; coddle. (Foll. by up.)

COSHH abbreviation.
Control of substances hazardous for health, a body of regulations introduced in Britain by the Health and Safety Executive in 1989 to govern the storage and use of such substances.

co-signatory /kəʊˈsɪgnət(ə)ri/ noun & adjective. Also **cosig-**. M19.
[ORIGIN from CO- + SIGNATORY.]
(A person or state) who signs a treaty, cheques, etc., jointly with another.

cosine /ˈkəʊsʌɪn/ noun. E17.
[ORIGIN from CO- + SINE noun.]
MATH. The sine of the complement of a given angle; in a right-angled triangle containing the angle, the ratio of the adjacent side to the hypotenuse. Abbreviation COS noun[2].
hyperbolic cosine a hyperbolic function defined by $y = \frac{1}{2}(e^x + e^{-x})$. LOGARITHMIC cosine.

†**cosins** noun. Only in E18.
[ORIGIN from the name of the maker.]
A kind of corset or bodice.

Coslettize /ˈkɒzlɪtʌɪz/ verb trans. Also **c-**, **-ise**. E20.
[ORIGIN from T. W. Coslett (fl. 1906), English chemist + -IZE.]
Give (iron or steel) a rustproof coating of phosphate by boiling in dilute phosphoric acid.

cosmea /ˈkɒzmɪə/ noun. E19.
[ORIGIN mod. Latin, from COSMOS noun[2]: see -A[1].]
= COSMOS noun[2].

cosmeceutical /ˌkɒzməˈs(j)uːtɪk(ə)l/ noun. L20.
[ORIGIN Blend of COSMETIC + PHARMACEUTICAL.]
A cosmetic that has or is claimed to have medicinal properties.

cosmetic /kɒzˈmɛtɪk/ noun, adjective, & verb. E17.
[ORIGIN French cosmétique from Greek kosmētikos, from kosmein arrange, adorn, from kosmos COSMOS noun[1]: see -IC.]
▸ **A** noun. **1** sing. & in pl. The art of adorning or beautifying the body. E17.
2 A preparation for use in beautifying the face, skin, or hair. M17.

▸ **B** *adjective.* **1** Able or used to beautify a person's appearance, esp. the complexion; of or pertaining to cosmetics. **M17.**
2 Of surgery: aimed at improving or modifying the appearance. Of a prosthetic device: re-creating the normal appearance. **E20.**
Observer His metal alloy legs . . are finished with cosmetic shoes.
3 *fig.* Intended merely to improve appearances; superficial. **M20.**
J. BAYLEY The alterations . . are not much more than cosmetic. *Daily Telegraph* The ferry was able to sail . . despite 'cosmetic' damage to the bows.
▸ **C** *verb trans.* Infl. **-ck-**. Treat with cosmetics; apply a cosmetic to. **L19.**
■ **cosmetical** *adjective* **M16.** **cosmetically** *adverb* **L19.** **cosmetician** /kɒzməˈtɪʃ(ə)n/ *noun* (chiefly *N. Amer.*) an expert in cosmetics, a beautician **E20.** **cosmeticize** /-sʌɪz/ *verb trans.* treat with cosmetics; *fig.* make superficially presentable: **E19.**

cosmetology /kɒzmɪˈtɒlədʒi/ *noun.* **M19.**
[ORIGIN French *cosmétologie*, formed as COSMETIC: see -OLOGY.]
†**1** A book on dress and personal hygiene. *rare.* Only in **M19.**
2 The art and practice of beautifying the face, hair, and skin; the branch of science that deals with this as a technical skill. **M20.**
■ **cosmetologist** *noun* **E20.**

cosmic /ˈkɒzmɪk/ *adjective.* **M17.**
[ORIGIN from COSMOS *noun*[1] + -IC, after French *cosmique* (from Greek *kosmikos*, from *kosmos* COSMOS *noun*[1]).]
†**1** Of this world. Only in **M17.**
2 Of or pertaining to the universe as an ordered system or totality; universal; immense, infinite. **M19.**
W. D. WHITNEY The great cosmic law of gravitation. H. NICOLSON The Civil War . . as a cosmic clash between strong men and massive principles. C. SAGAN A deep and common wish . . to have human affairs matter in the cosmic context.
3 Belonging to the universe as distinguished from the earth; extraterrestrial. **L19.**
4 Characteristic of the vast scale of the universe. **L19.**
J. TYNDALL Cosmic ranges of time.
5 [After Russian *kosmicheskiĭ.*] Of or pertaining to travel through space. **M20.**
Daily Telegraph Cosmic flights.
– SPECIAL COLLOCATIONS: **cosmic dust** minute particles of matter in or from space. ***cosmic string***: see STRING *noun* 18b. **cosmic radiation**, **cosmic rays** radiation of great energy (chiefly atomic nuclei) which originates in space and reaches the earth from all directions (also more fully ***primary cosmic radiation***); radiation that this gives rise to in the atmosphere (also more fully ***secondary cosmic radiation***).

cosmical /ˈkɒzmɪk(ə)l/ *adjective.* **M16.**
[ORIGIN formed as COSMIC: see -ICAL.]
†**1** Pertaining to the earth; geographical. *rare.* **M16–E19.**
2 ASTRONOMY. Of the rising or setting of a star: occurring at sunrise. **M16.**
3 = COSMIC 2, 3, 4. **L17.**
cosmical constant = *COSMOLOGICAL constant*.

cosmically /ˈkɒzmɪk(ə)li/ *adverb.* **M16.**
[ORIGIN from COSMIC or COSMICAL: see -ICALLY.]
1 ASTRONOMY. Coincidently with the rising of the sun. **M16.**
2 In a cosmic manner; in relation to the cosmos. **M19.**

cosmism /ˈkɒzmɪz(ə)m/ *noun.* **M19.**
[ORIGIN from COSMOS *noun*[1] + -ISM.]
The view that the universe is a self-existent, self-acting whole explicable purely in scientific terms.
■ **cosmist** *noun* a believer in cosmism **M19.**

cosmo- /ˈkɒzməʊ/ *combining form.*
[ORIGIN Greek *kosmo-* from *kosmos* COSMOS *noun*[1]: see -O-.]
Used in words adapted from Greek and in English words modelled on these, with the sense 'world, universe'.
■ **cosmoˈcentric** *adjective* centred in the cosmos **M19.** **cosmoˈchemical** *adjective* of or pertaining to cosmochemistry **M20.** **cosmoˈchemically** *adverb* from a cosmochemical point of view **M20.** **cosmoˈchemistry** *noun* the branch of science that deals with the chemical properties of stars etc. and the cosmic distribution of elements and compounds **M20.** **cosmodrome** *noun* [after AERODROME] in the countries of the former USSR, a launching site for spacecraft **M20.** **cosmogeˈnetic** *adjective* = COSMOGENIC (a) **L19.** **cosmoˈgenic** *adjective* (*a*) of or pertaining to cosmogeny; (*b*) of cosmic origin: **E20.** **cosˈmogeny** *noun* the origin or evolution of the universe **M19.** **cosmoˈrama** *noun* a peep show containing views of all parts of the world **E19.** **cosmoˈramic** *adjective* belonging to or of the nature of a cosmorama **E19.** **cosmoˈthetic** *adjective* that posits or assumes an external world **M19.**

cosmogony /kɒzˈmɒgəni/ *noun.* **L17.**
[ORIGIN Greek *kosmogonia* creation of the world, formed as COSMOS *noun*[1]: see -GONY.]
1 A theory or account of the origin of the universe; the branch of science that deals with the origin of the universe. **L17.**
C. SAGAN The Babylonian cosmogony enshrined in Genesis.
2 The creation of the universe. **M18.**
■ **cosmoˈgonic**, **cosmoˈgonical** *adjectives* **E19.** **cosmogonist** *noun* †(*a*) a person who holds that the world had a beginning in time; (*b*) a person who studies cosmogony or propounds a cosmogony: **L17.**

cosmographer /kɒzˈmɒgrəfə/ *noun.* **E16.**
[ORIGIN from late Latin *cosmographus* from Greek *kosmographos*, formed as COSMO- + -GRAPH: see -ER[1]. Cf. Old French & mod. French *cosmographe*.]
A person skilled in cosmography. Formerly also, a geographer.

cosmography /kɒzˈmɒgrəfi/ *noun.* **LME.**
[ORIGIN French *cosmographie* or late Latin *cosmographia*, from Greek *kosmographia*, formed as COSMO-: see -GRAPHY.]
1 An overall description or representation of the universe or the earth. **LME.**
2 The science which deals with the general features and disposition of the universe, including the earth. Formerly also, geography. **E16.**
■ **cosmoˈgraphic** *adjective* **E19.** **cosmoˈgraphical** *adjective* **M16.** **cosmoˈgraphically** *adverb* **M16.** **cosmographist** *noun* (*rare*) = COSMOGRAPHER **M17.**

Cosmoline /ˈkɒzmə(ʊ)liːn/ *noun.* Also **c-**. **L19.**
[ORIGIN from COSM(ETIC + -OL + -INE[5].]
(Proprietary name for) petroleum jelly.

cosmological /kɒzməˈlɒdʒɪk(ə)l/ *adjective.* **L18.**
[ORIGIN from COSMOLOGY: see -ICAL.]
Of or pertaining to cosmology.
cosmological argument: for the absolute existence of God from the contingent existence of things. **cosmological constant** an arbitrary constant in the field equations of general relativity.
■ **cosmologically** *adverb* **M19.**

cosmology /kɒzˈmɒlədʒi/ *noun.* **M17.**
[ORIGIN French *cosmologie* or mod. Latin *cosmologia*, formed as COSMO- + -LOGY.]
1 The science of the evolution and structure of the universe; a theory or postulated account of this. **M17.**
S. WEINBERG The big bang cosmology. P. DAVIES The expanding universe is now a cornerstone of cosmology.
2 The branch of philosophy or metaphysics which deals with the universe as a whole. **M18.**
■ **cosmologist** *noun* a person who studies cosmology or propounds a cosmology **L18.**

cosmonaut /ˈkɒzmənɔːt/ *noun.* **M20.**
[ORIGIN from COSMO- after *aeronaut* and Russian *kosmonavt*.]
An astronaut, *esp.* a Soviet astronaut.
■ **cosmoˈnautic**, **cosmoˈnautical** *adjectives* **M20.** **cosmoˈnautics** *noun pl.* (usu. treated as *sing.*) = ASTRONAUTICS **M20.**

cosmopolis /kɒzˈmɒp(ə)lɪs/ *noun.* **M19.**
[ORIGIN from COSMO- + -POLIS.]
A cosmopolitan city; a capital city, a world capital.

cosmopolitan /kɒzməˈpɒlɪt(ə)n/ *noun & adjective.* **M17.**
[ORIGIN from COSMOPOLITE + -AN: cf. METROPOLITAN.]
▸ **A** *noun.* **1** A person who treats the whole world as his or her country; a person with no national attachments or prejudices. **M17.**
2 A plant or animal found all over the world. **M20.**
3 A cocktail made with Cointreau, lemon vodka, cranberry juice, and lime juice. **L20.**
▸ **B** *adjective.* **1** Belonging to all or many parts of the world; not restricted to any one country or region. **M19.**
2 Free from national limitations or attachments; having characteristics suited to or arising from an experience of many countries. **M19.**
LD MACAULAY That cosmopolitan indifference to constitutions and religions. A. KOESTLER Cosmopolitan by nature and education, wherever she was she was at home.
3 Containing people from many different countries. **E20.**
■ **cosmopolitanism** *noun* (*a*) cosmopolitan character; (*b*) *hist.* (in Soviet usage) disparagement of Russian traditions and culture: **E19.** **cosmopolitanize** *verb trans.* make cosmopolitan **L19.** **cosmopolitanly** *adverb* **L19.**

cosmopolite /kɒzˈmɒpəlʌɪt/ *noun & adjective.* **E17.**
[ORIGIN French from Greek *kosmopolitēs*, formed as COSMO- + *politēs* citizen.]
▸ **A** *noun.* **1** = COSMOPOLITAN *noun* 1. **E17.**
2 = COSMOPOLITAN *noun* 2. **M19.**
▸ **B** *adjective.* = COSMOPOLITAN *adjective.* **E19.**
■ ˌ**cosmopoˈlitical** *adjective* [after *political*] relating to all states and polities **L16.** **cosmopolitism** *noun* = COSMOPOLITANISM (a) **L18.**

cosmos /ˈkɒzmɒs/ *noun*[1]. **ME.**
[ORIGIN Greek *kosmos* order, ornament, world.]
1 The universe as an ordered whole. **ME.**
2 Harmony, order. **M19.**
3 An ordered system of ideas etc. **L19.**

cosmos /ˈkɒzmɒs/ *noun*[2]. **E19.**
[ORIGIN mod. Latin, formed as COSMOS *noun*[1].]
A tropical American plant of the genus *Cosmos*, of the composite family, having flowers of various bright colours; esp. *C. bipinnatus*, an annual with single blossoms on long stems that is cultivated as a garden plant.

COSPAR /ˈkəʊspɑː/ *abbreviation.*
Committee on Space Research.

coss *noun* var. of KOS.

coss /kɒs/ *verb trans. & intrans.* Chiefly *Scot.* Also **cose** /kəʊz/. **LME.**
[ORIGIN Unknown. Cf. CORSE *verb*, SCORSE *verb*[1].]
Barter, exchange.

Cossack /ˈkɒsak/ *noun & adjective.* **L16.**
[ORIGIN Russian *kazak* (whence French *Cosaque*) from Turkic = vagabond, nomad, adventurer; later infl. by French Cf. KAZAKH.]
▸ **A** *noun.* **1** A member of a people living in southern and SW Russia, noted as horsemen from early times and formerly serving as border guards for Poland and pre-Communist Russia. **L16.**
2 A high boot. **E19.**
3 In *pl.* Baggy trousers pleated into a waistband. **E19.**
4 A police officer, *esp.* a member of a strikebreaking force. *slang.* **M19.**
▸ **B** *adjective.* Of, pertaining to, or being a Cossack or Cossacks. **E19.**
Cossack boot = sense A.2 above. **Cossack hat** a brimless hat widening towards the top. **Cossack post** *hist.* an outpost of a few mounted men under a non-commissioned officer or senior soldier. **Cossack trousers** = sense A.3 above.

cosset /ˈkɒsɪt/ *noun & verb.* **M16.**
[ORIGIN Perh. from Anglo-Norman *coscet*, *cozet* cottager formed as COTSET.]
▸ **A** *noun.* **1** A lamb brought up by hand. **M16.**
2 A petted child; a spoiled person. **L16.**
▸ **B** *verb.* **1** *verb trans.* Pamper; pet, fondle. **M17.**
2 *verb intrans.* Indulge in pampering; nestle *up*. **L19.**

†**cossic** *adjective.* **M16–M19.**
[ORIGIN Italian *cossico*, from *cosa* thing, translating Arabic *šay'* lit. 'something, thing', unknown quantity in an equation: see -IC.]
Algebraic.
■ Also †**cossical** *adjective* **L16–E19.**

cossid /ˈkɒsɪd/ *noun.* **L17.**
[ORIGIN Persian from Arabic *qāṣid* foot-messenger, courier.]
hist. In the Indian subcontinent: a running messenger.

cossie /ˈkɒzi, -s-/ *noun. slang* (chiefly *Austral.*). Also **cozzie** /-z-/. **E20.**
[ORIGIN from COS(TUME + -IE.]
A swimsuit, a pair of swimming trunks.

†**cost** *noun*[1]. **OE–L16.**
[ORIGIN Latin *costum*, COSTUS from Greek *kostos* from Arabic *qusṭ* from Sanskrit *kuṣṭha*.]
The plant costmary.
– NOTE: Survives in ***alecost*** s.v. ALE; COSTMARY.

cost /kɒst/ *noun*[2]. **ME.**
[ORIGIN Anglo-Norman *cost*, Old French *coust* (mod. *coût*), from *couster*: see COST *verb*.]
1 What must be given in order to acquire, produce, or effect something; the price (to be) paid for a thing. **ME.** ▸**b** What a thing originally cost. **L19.**
2 In *pl.* Charges, expenses; *obsolete* exc. LAW, the expenses of litigation, prosecution, or other legal transaction, *esp.* those allowed in favour of the winning party or against the losing party. **ME.**
3 Expenditure of time or labour; what is borne, lost, or suffered in accomplishing or gaining something. (Now chiefly in phrs. or with *of*.) **ME.**
†**4** Outlay, expenditure. **LME–L18.**
ADDISON No Art or Cost is omitted to make the Stay . . agreeable.
†**5** What money etc. is expended on; a costly thing. *rare.* **LME–L16.**
– PHRASES: **at all costs**, **at any cost** whatever the cost may be. **at cost** at the initial cost; at cost price. **at the cost of** at the expense of losing (something). ***bill of costs***: see BILL *noun*[3]. **cost of living** the financial outlay required for the basic necessities of life. **count the cost** consider the risks, disadvantages, or repercussions of an action. **know to one's cost** have learned by bitter experience. ***prime cost***: see PRIME *adjective*. ***social cost***: see SOCIAL *adjective*. **to a person's cost** with loss or disadvantage to him or her. ***unit cost***: see UNIT *noun*[1] & *adjective*. ***with costs***: see WITH *preposition*.
– COMB.: **cost accountant**: engaged in cost accounting; **cost accounting** the recording and review of all the costs incurred in a business, as an aid to management (***current cost accounting***: see CURRENT *adjective*); **cost-benefit analysis**, **cost-benefit study**: assessing the relation of the cost of an operation to the value of the resulting benefits; **cost centre** a part of an organization to which costs may be charged for accounting purposes; **cost clerk**: who records all the costs incurred in a business, as an aid to management; **cost-effective** *adjective* providing a satisfactory return for the outlay; **cost-of-living index**: measuring the change with time in the level of retail prices; **cost-plus** *adjective* designating or pertaining to a pricing system in which a fixed profit factor is added to the cost incurred; **cost price**: at which a merchant etc. buys; **cost-push** *noun & adjective* (caused by) increasing costs, esp. pay, rather than increasing demand as agents of inflation.
■ **costless** *adjective* without cost, free **E16.** **costlessness** *noun* an absence of any expense **M19.**

cost /kɒst/ *noun*[3]. Now *rare.* **L16.**
[ORIGIN Old French *coste* (mod. *côte*) rib from Latin *costa*.]
HERALDRY. A cottise, esp. when borne singly.

cost /kɒst/ *verb.* Pa. t. & pple **cost**, (in branch II) **costed.** **LME.**
[ORIGIN Old French *coster*, *couster* (mod. *coûter*) from Proto-Romance var. of Latin *constare* stand firm, be fixed, stand at a price, from Latin CON- + *stare* stand.]

C

C

▸ **I** *verb trans.* with adverbial obj. & *intrans.* **1** *verb trans.* Be acquired or acquirable at, be bought or maintained for, necessitate the expenditure of, (so much). Also with the person buying, spending, etc. as indirect obj. LME.

SHAKES. *Oth.* His breeches cost him but a crown.

2 *verb trans.* Necessitate or involve the expenditure of (time, trouble, etc.), loss or sacrifice of (some valued possession), suffering of (some penalty etc.). Also with the person losing, suffering, etc., as indirect obj. LME.

G. HERBERT Good words are worth much and cost little. T. H. HUXLEY His eagerness to witness the spectacle cost him his life. R. KIPLING The horses were stampeded . . and . . it cost a day and a half to get them together again.

cost an arm and a leg: see ARM *noun*[1]. **cost a person dear(ly)** involve a heavy penalty on a person.

3 *verb intrans.* Be expensive; prove costly. Also with pers. indirect obj. *colloq.* E20.

SCOTT FITZGERALD I like them but my God they cost. M. KENYON 'That call was from Chicago.' 'It must have cost him.'

▸ **II** *verb trans.* with simple obj.

4 *verb trans.* Determine the cost of producing (an article) or undertaking (a piece of work). L19.

A. N. WILSON Fox and Henderson, the Smethwick contracting firm, had costed the design to the nearest pound.

■ **costing** *verbal noun* the determination of the cost of producing or undertaking something; *sing.* & in *pl.*, the cost so arrived at: L19. **costing** *ppl adjective* costly; spiritually exhausting or expensive: E20. **costingly** *adverb* in a costly or costing way E20. **costingness** *noun* E20.

cost- *combining form* see COSTO-.

costa /ˈkɒstə/ *noun*[1]. Pl. **costae** /ˈkɒstiː/. M19.
[ORIGIN Latin.]
Chiefly BOTANY & ZOOLOGY. A rib or riblike structure; *esp.* the main vein running along the anterior edge of an insect's wing.

Costa /ˈkɒstə/ *noun*[2]. *joc.* M20.
[ORIGIN Spanish (= COAST *noun*, formed as COSTA *noun*[1]), in *Costa Brava, Costa del Sol*, etc.]
A coast: in pseudo-Spanish names of resort areas with a specified characteristic or location.
Costa Geriatrica /dʒɛrɪˈatrɪkə/: largely frequented or inhabited by elderly people.

costae *noun* pl. of COSTA *noun*[1].

costal /ˈkɒst(ə)l/ *adjective & noun.* M17.
[ORIGIN French from mod. Latin *costalis*, formed as COSTA *noun*[1]: see -AL[1].]
▸ **A** *adjective.* **1** ANATOMY. Of or pertaining to the ribs. M17.
costal pleura: see PLEURA *noun*[1] 1.
2 Chiefly BOTANY & ZOOLOGY. Pertaining to or of the nature of a costa. M19.
▸ **B** *noun.* †**1** The side. Only in M17.
2 ANATOMY & ZOOLOGY. A costal vein, muscle, plate, etc. E19.

co-star /ˈkəʊstɑː/ *noun.* Orig. *US.* E20.
[ORIGIN from CO- + STAR *noun*[1].]
A cinema or stage star appearing with one or more other stars of equal importance; an actor or actress receiving star billing with another.

co-star /ˈkəʊstɑː/ *verb.* Orig. *US.* Infl. **-rr-**. E20.
[ORIGIN from CO- + STAR *verb*.]
1 *verb intrans.* Perform as a co-star. E20.
2 *verb trans.* Include as a co-star or co-stars. E20.

costard /ˈkɒstəd, ˈkʌst-/ *noun.* ME.
[ORIGIN Anglo-Norman, from *coste* rib from Latin COSTA *noun*[1]: see -ARD. Cf. CUSTARD *noun*[2].]
1 A large ribbed kind of apple. ME.
2 The head. *joc. arch.* M16.

Costa Rican /ˌkɒstə ˈriːk(ə)n/ *adjective & noun.* M19.
[ORIGIN from *Costa Rica* (see below) + -AN.]
▸ **A** *adjective.* Of, pertaining to, or characteristic of the Central American country of Costa Rica. M19.
▸ **B** *noun.* A native or inhabitant of Costa Rica. M19.

costate /ˈkɒsteɪt/ *adjective.* E19.
[ORIGIN Latin *costatus* ribbed, formed as COSTA *noun*[1]: see -ATE[2].]
BOTANY & ZOOLOGY. Having a rib or ribs.
■ Also **costated** *adjective* M19.

co-state /ˈkəʊsteɪt/ *noun.* Also **-State**. L18.
[ORIGIN from CO- + STATE *noun*.]
A state allied with another. (Foll. by *of*.)

costean /kɒˈstiːn/ *verb & noun.* Orig. *Cornish.* Also **-een**. L18.
[ORIGIN from Cornish *cotha* to drop + *stean* tin.]
MINING. ▸**A** *verb intrans.* Sink pits through the surface soil to the underlying rock in order to establish the direction of a lode. L18.
▸ **B** *noun.* A pit sunk in costeaning; a trench cut to expose the width of a seam. Also ***costean pit***. L18.

coster /ˈkɒstə/ *noun*[1]. Long *obsolete* exc. *hist.* ME.
[ORIGIN Anglo-Norman = Old French *costier* side, something by the side, hanging, from *coste* from Latin COSTA *noun*[1]: see -ER[2].]
A hanging for a bed, the walls of a room, an altar, etc.

coster /ˈkɒstə/ *noun*[2]. *colloq.* M19.
[ORIGIN Abbreviation.]
= COSTERMONGER.
■ **costerdom** *noun* = COSTERMONGERDOM L19. **costering** *noun* = COSTERMONGERY M19.

costermonger /ˈkɒstəmʌŋgə/ *noun & adjective.* E16.
[ORIGIN from COSTARD + MONGER.]
▸ **A** *noun.* Orig., an apple-seller. Now, a person who sells fruit, vegetables, etc., from a street barrow. E16.
▸ **B** *adjective.* Base, worthless. Now *rare* or *obsolete.* L16.
■ **costermongerdom** *noun* L19. **costermongering** *noun* = COSTERMONGERY M19. **costermongery** *noun* the occupation of a costermonger M19.

costive /ˈkɒstɪv/ *adjective.* LME.
[ORIGIN Anglo-Norman, Old French *costivé* from Latin *constipatus*: see CONSTIPATE *verb*.]
1 Constipated. LME.
†**2** Tending to prevent evacuation of the bowels. M16–M17.
3 Slow or reluctant in action; niggardly; reticent. L16.

L. A. G. STRONG The parrot was still very costive in the matter of speech.

■ **costively** *adverb* M19. **costiveness** *noun* LME.

costly /ˈkɒs(t)li/ *adjective & adverb.* LME.
[ORIGIN from COST *noun*[2] + -LY[1].]
▸ **A** *adjective.* **1** That costs much; expensive; sumptuous. LME.
costly colours an obsolete card game.
2 Lavish in expenditure; extravagant. *arch.* M17.

DRYDEN To curse the Costly sex.

▸ †**B** *adverb.* In a costly manner; sumptuously. LME–E17.
■ **costliness** *noun* M16.

costmary /ˈkɒstmɛːri/ *noun.* LME.
[ORIGIN from COST *noun*[1] + (St) MARY.]
An aromatic perennial plant of the composite family, *Tanacetum balsamita*, formerly used for flavouring ale; alecost.

costo- /ˈkɒstəʊ/ *combining form.* Before a vowel **cost-**.
[ORIGIN from Latin COSTA *noun*[1]: see -O-.]
Of or pertaining to the ribs and —.
■ **costocla'vicular** *adjective* of or pertaining to the ribs and clavicle M19.

costrel /ˈkɒstr(ə)l/ *noun.* Long *obsolete* exc. *dial.* LME.
[ORIGIN Old French *costerel* flagon, prob. dim. of *costier*: see COSTER *noun*[1], -EL[2].]
A bottle for wine etc. with an ear or ears by which it may be hung from the waist; a wooden keg similarly used.

costume /ˈkɒstjuːm/ *noun & verb.* E18.
[ORIGIN French from Italian = custom, fashion, habit, from Latin *consuetudo, -din-*: see CUSTOM *noun, adjective, & adverb*.]
▸ **A** *noun.* **1** In historical and literary art: the custom and fashion proper to the time and locality in which a scene is set. E18.

J. REYNOLDS Hardly reconcileable to strict propriety, and the costume, of which Raffaele was in general a good observer.

2 The style or fashion of clothing, hair, etc., of a particular country, class, or period. E19.

H. JAMES She sought to . . make up for her diffidence of speech by a fine frankness of costume. J. MARQUAND The Chinese in their silk robes the only persons clinging to a national costume.

3 Fashion of clothing appropriate to a particular occasion or season; a garment for a particular activity. E19. ▸**b** The dress or attire worn by an actor in a play etc. L19. ▸**c** *spec.* A swimsuit. L19.

DISRAELI A Court costume. A. GRAY The costumes they would wear at the fancy-dress ball.

bathing costume, ***swimming costume***, etc.

4 A complete set of outer garments; a woman's matching jacket and skirt or dress. M19.
– COMB.: **costume drama**, **costume piece**, **costume play**: in which the actors wear historical costume. **costume jewellery** artificial jewellery worn to decorate clothes.
▸ **B** *verb trans.* Provide with or dress in a costume. Chiefly as ***costumed*** *ppl adjective.* E19.
■ **costumer** *noun* = COSTUMIER M19. **co'stumery** *noun* arrangement of costumes; costumes collectively: M19.

costumier /kɒˈstjuːmɪə/ *noun.* M19.
[ORIGIN French, from *costumer* COSTUME *verb*.]
A person who makes or deals in costumes; *esp.* a person who sells or hires out theatrical costumes and properties.

costus /ˈkɒstəs/ *noun.* L16.
[ORIGIN Latin: see COST *noun*[1].]
More fully ***costus root***. The aromatic root of the Kashmiri plant *Saussurea costus*, of the composite family, which yields an oil used in perfumery.

cosy /ˈkəʊzi/ *adjective, noun, & verb.* Orig. *Scot.* Also ***cozy**. E18.
[ORIGIN Unknown.]
▸ **A** *adjective.* **1** Of a person: comfortably sheltered, snug. E18.

N. COWARD I feel completely lost, completely bewildered . . . I don't feel any too cosy.

2 Of a place: sheltered; warm and comfortable, inviting. L18.

R. BURNS In some cozie place, They close the day.

cosy corner an upholstered seat for fitting into the corner of a room; a corner so furnished.
3 Of a person or thing: warmly intimate or friendly; *derog.* complacent, smug, unadventurous, parochial. E20.

C. P. SNOW It was mildly ironic . . to find her set on seeing him a cosy, bourgeois success. *Daily Mail* A cosy chat.

▸ **B** *noun.* **1** More fully ***tea cosy***, ***egg cosy***. A covering for keeping a teapot or a boiled egg warm. M19.
2 [Perh. suggested by French *causeuse*.] A cosy seat; *spec.* a canopied seat for two. L19.
▸ **C** *verb.* †**1** *verb intrans.* Be cosy. *dial.* Only in L19.
2 *verb trans.* Reassure; deceive to prevent suspicion or alarm. Also foll. by *along*. *colloq.* M20.

M. SHARP Her impulse . . was to cosy Mr Clark on every point.

3 *verb intrans.* Foll. by *up to*: snuggle up to; become friendly with; ingratiate oneself with. *colloq.* (chiefly *N. Amer.*). M20.
■ **cosily** *adverb* E18. **cosiness** *noun* M19.

cot /kɒt/ *noun*[1].
[ORIGIN Old English *cot* = Middle Low German, Middle Dutch, Old Norse *kot*, from Germanic base (cf. Old Norse *kytja* hovel) rel. to that of COTE *noun*[1].]
1 A (small) cottage; a humble dwelling. Now chiefly *poet.* & *literary.* OE.

F. QUARLES Poor cots are ev'n as safe as princes halls.

2 A small erection for shelter or protection; = COTE *noun*[1] 2. ME.
3 A protective covering; *spec.* a fingerstall. *obsolete* exc. *dial.* E17.
– COMB.: **cot-house** *Scot.* & *dial.* (**a**) a small cottage; *spec.* in Scotland, the house of a cottar; (**b**) an outhouse, a shed; **cotland** *hist.* a piece of land (about 5 acres, 2 hectares) attached to a peasant's cot; **cotman** *hist.* a tenant of a cot or cottage; *Scot.* a cottar; **cot-town** *Scot.* a hamlet of cot-houses.

cot /kɒt/ *noun*[2]. *dial.* ME.
[ORIGIN Anglo-Norman, perh. identical with medieval Latin *cot(t)um* bed-quilt, stuffed mattress.]
1 Wool matted together in the fleece. ME.
2 A tangled mass (of hair, weeds, etc.). M19.

cot /kɒt/ *noun*[3]. *Irish.* M16.
[ORIGIN Old Irish & mod. Irish *coite*, Gaelic *coit*.]
A small roughly made boat; a dugout.

cot /kɒt/ *noun*[4]. M17.
[ORIGIN Hindi *khāṭ* bedstead, couch, hammock.]
1 **a** A light bedstead. *Indian.* M17. ▸**b** A portable or folding bed; a camp bed. *US.* M19. ▸**c** A type of bed or wheeled stretcher used in hospitals. *US.* L19.

b R. JARRELL She just slept on the cot in her office. **c** P. GALLICO Sitting on the edge of his cot in the Brothers of Man Mission House.

2 *hist.* A canvas bed in a wooden frame suspended from deck beams, in which naval officers etc. used to sleep. M18.
3 A small bed for a child: orig., one suspended so as to swing between uprights; now, a bed with high sides to stop the child from falling out; a bed in a children's hospital. Cf. CRIB *noun* 5. E19.
– COMB.: **cot-case** a person too ill to leave bed; **cot death** a sudden unexplained death of a baby in its sleep.

cot /kɒt/ *noun*[5]. M18.
[ORIGIN Abbreviation.]
MATH. Cotangent (of).

cot /kɒt/ *verb*[1] *trans.* Infl. **-tt-**. E19.
[ORIGIN from COT *noun*[1].]
Put (a sheep) in a cote.

cot /kɒt/ *verb*[2] *trans.* & *intrans.* *dial.* Infl. **-tt-**. L19.
[ORIGIN from COT *noun*[2]. Cf. earlier COTTED *adjective*[1].]
Tangle or mat together.

cotangent /kəʊˈtandʒ(ə)nt/ *noun.* E17.
[ORIGIN from CO- + TANGENT *noun*.]
MATH. The tangent of the complement of a given angle. Abbreviation COT *noun*[5].

cotch /kɒtʃ/ *verb.* *W. Indian.* M19.
[ORIGIN Sense 1 alt. of CATCH *verb*. Sense 2 from SCOTCH *verb*[2].]
1 *verb trans.* Catch. M19.
2 **a** *verb intrans.* Stay, live; lie; rest, relax. E20. ▸**b** *verb trans.* Place or rest (a thing). M20.

cote /kəʊt/ *noun*[1].
[ORIGIN Old English *cote* corresp. to Low German *kote*, from Germanic base rel. to that of COT *noun*[1].]
1 A cottage, a cot. Now *dial.* OE.
2 A light building or enclosure for sheltering or confining animals or for storing something; *spec.* a sheepfold. Now usu. in *comb.*, as ***dovecote***, ***sheep-cote***. LME.
– COMB.: **cote-house** *Scot.* & *dial.* = **cot-house** s.v. COT *noun*[1].

cote /kəʊt/ *noun*[2]. Now *rare* or *obsolete.* L16.
[ORIGIN from COTE *verb*[1].]
The action (of a dog) of making a hare alter course by 'coting' another dog.

cote /kəʊt/ *verb*[1] *trans.* Now *rare* or *obsolete*. **M16.**
[ORIGIN Perh. from Old French *coster* proceed by the side of, follow closely, from *coste* side from Latin COSTA *noun*[1].]
1 Of either of two dogs in coursing: pass (the other dog) at an angle so as to cause the hare etc. to alter course. **M16.**
2 *transf.* & *fig.* Pass by; exceed, surpass. **M16.**

cote /kəʊt/ *verb*[2] *trans.* **M17.**
[ORIGIN from COTE *noun*[1].]
Put (an animal) in a cote.

†**cote** *verb*[3] & *noun*[3] see QUOTE *verb* & *noun*[2].

coteau /kɒˈtəʊ, *foreign* kɔto/ *noun*. *N. Amer.* Pl. **-eaus**; **-eaux** /-əʊ/. **M19.**
[ORIGIN French = slope, hillside from Old French *costel*, from *coste*: see COST *noun*[3], -EL[2].]
Any of various kinds of elevated geographical features, as a plateau, a divide between valleys, etc.

cote-hardie /ˈkəʊthɑːdiː/ *noun*. **ME.**
[ORIGIN Old French, from *cote* COAT *noun* + *hardie* bold (see HARDY *adjective*).]
hist. A medieval close-fitting sleeved tunic, worn by both sexes.

cotemporaneity /kəʊˌtɛmp(ə)rəˈniːɪti, -ˈneɪɪti/ *noun*. Now *rare*. **E19.**
[ORIGIN Alt. of CONTEMPORANEITY: see CO-.]
= CONTEMPORANEITY.

cotemporaneous /kəʊˌtɛmpəˈreɪnɪəs/ *adjective*. Now *rare*. **M19.**
[ORIGIN Alt. of CONTEMPORANEOUS: see CO-.]
= CONTEMPORANEOUS.

cotemporary /kəʊˈtɛmp(ə)rəri/ *adjective* & *noun*. Now *rare*. **M17.**
[ORIGIN Alt. of CONTEMPORARY: see CO-.]
= CONTEMPORARY.
– NOTE: Although condemned by some, during 18 *cotemporary* almost ousted *contemporary*, only to become less frequent again.

coterell /ˈkɒt(ə)r(ə)l/ *noun*. **LME.**
[ORIGIN Old French *coterel*, medieval Latin *coterellus*, dim. of Old French *cotier* COTTIER.]
FEUDAL HISTORY. = COTTAR 1.
– NOTE: Recorded from late Old English in surnames. Cf. COTSET, COTSETLA.

coterie /ˈkəʊt(ə)ri/ *noun*. **E18.**
[ORIGIN French (in Old French = tenants holding land together), ult. from Middle Low German *kote* COTE *noun*[1]: see -ERY.]
1 A small exclusive group with common interests; *esp.* a select social group. **E18.**
M. DRABBLE She found herself elected to an honorary membership of the fastest, smartest . . coterie.
2 A meeting of such a group. **E19.**

coterminal /kəʊˈtəːmɪn(ə)l/ *adjective*. Now *rare*. **M19.**
[ORIGIN from CO- + TERMINAL *adjective*. Cf. CONTERMINAL.]
= COTERMINOUS 2.

coterminous /kəʊˈtəːmɪnəs/ *adjective*. **L18.**
[ORIGIN Alt. of CONTERMINOUS: see CO-.]
1 Having a common boundary (*with*). **L18.**
2 Coextensive (*with*) in space, time, or meaning. **M19.**

coth /kɒθ/ *noun*. **L19.**
[ORIGIN from COT *noun*[5] + *h* (for hyperbolic).]
MATH. Hyperbolic cotangent (of).

cothe /kəʊð/ *noun*. Also **coath**.
[ORIGIN Old English *coþu*, *coþe*.]
†**1** Sickness; an attack of something. **OE–LME.**
2 A disease of the liver in animals, esp. sheep. *dial.* **L18.**

cothe /kəʊð/ *verb trans.* *obsolete* exc. *dial.* **LME.**
[ORIGIN from the noun.]
Give (a sheep) cothe or rot. Formerly, give any disease to.

cothurn /ˈkəʊθəːn, kəʊˈθəːn/ *noun*. Now *rare*. **E17.**
[ORIGIN French *cothurne* from Latin COTHURNUS.]
= COTHURNUS.
■ **cothurned** *adjective* wearing cothurns **L19.**

cothurnus /kəʊˈθəːnəs/ *noun*. Pl. **-ni** /-nʌɪ/. **E18.**
[ORIGIN Latin from Greek *kothornos*.]
= BUSKIN 2.
fig.: F. W. FARRAR St. Paul cannot always wear the majestic cothurnus, yet his lightest words are full of meaning.
■ **cothurnal** *adjective* of or pertaining to the cothurnus; tragic: **E17.** **cothurnate** *adjective* wearing cothurni; tragic in style: **E17.**

co-tidal /kəʊˈtʌɪd(ə)l/ *adjective*. **M19.**
[ORIGIN from CO- + TIDAL.]
Of a line: connecting places where high tide occurs at the same time. Of a chart etc.: showing such lines.

cotillion /kəˈtɪljən/ *noun* & *verb*. In senses A.1, B. also **cotillon** /kəˈtɪljən; *foreign* kɔtijɔ̃ (*pl. same*)/. **E18.**
[ORIGIN French *cotillon* petticoat, dance, dim. of *cotte* COAT *noun*.]
▸ **A** *noun*. **1** Any of several dances with elaborate steps and figures; *spec.* (*a*) an 18th-cent. French social dance based on the contredanse; (*b*) *US* a quadrille; (*c*) (in full ***German cotillion***) a complex dance in which one couple leads the other couples through a variety of figures and there is a continual change of partners. **E18.**
2 A formal ball, *esp.* one at which debutantes are presented. *US*. **L19.**
▸ **B** *verb intrans.* Dance a cotillion. **M19.**

cotinga /kəˈtɪŋgə/ *noun*. **L18.**
[ORIGIN French from Tupi *cutinga*.]
A passerine bird of the tropical American family Cotingidae or its type genus *Cotinga*, including many noted for their brilliant plumage.

cotise *noun* & *verb* var. of COTTISE.

cotoneaster /kətəʊnɪˈastə/ *noun*. **M18.**
[ORIGIN mod. Latin, from Latin *cotoneum* QUINCE + -ASTER.]
A shrub or small tree of the European and northern Asian (esp. Himalayan and Chinese) genus *Cotoneaster*, of the rose family, with small pink or white flowers and red or black berries.

cotonnade *noun* & *adjective* var. of COTTONADE.

†**cotquean** *noun*. **M16.**
[ORIGIN from COT *noun*[1] + QUEAN.]
1 The wife of a cotman. **M16–E17.**
2 A coarse scolding woman. **L16–M17.**
3 A man who occupies himself with housework and women's concerns. **L16–E19.**

co-trimoxazole /kəʊtrʌɪˈmɒksəzəʊl/ *noun*. **L20.**
[ORIGIN from CO- + TRIM(ETHOPRIM + SULPHAMETH)OXAZOLE.]
A synergistic mixture of sulphamethoxazole and trimethoprim used to treat many bacterial infections.

†**cots** *noun*. **E16–E18.**
[ORIGIN Alt. Cf. CUTS.]
God's: used in oaths and exclamations.

cotset /ˈkɒtsɛt/ *noun*.
[ORIGIN Old English *cotsǣta*, from COT *noun*[1] + *sǣta*, from var. of Germanic base of SIT *verb*. See also COSSET.]
FEUDAL HISTORY. = COTTAR 1.
– NOTE: Not recorded from ME until use as a historical term in 19. In early use chiefly Latinized. Cf. COTSETLA, COTERELL.

cotsetla /kɒtˈsɛtlə/ *noun*. Also **-setle** /-sɛt(ə)l/. **OE.**
[ORIGIN from COT *noun*[1] + Old English *-sǣtla* settler.]
FEUDAL HISTORY. = COTTAR 1.
– NOTE: Not recorded from ME until use as a historical term in 19. Cf. COTSET, COTERELL.

Cotswold /ˈkɒtswəʊld/ *noun*. **M16.**
[ORIGIN *Cotswold* Hills (see below).]
1 Used *attrib.* to designate things originally produced or found in the Cotswold Hills, a range mainly in Gloucestershire noted for their sheep pasture. **M16.**
Cotswold cheese double Gloucester cheese with chives (and onions). **Cotswold lion** *joc.* a Cotswold sheep. **Cotswold sheep** a sheep of a long-woolled breed.
2 *ellipt.* A Cotswold sheep; Cotswold cheese. **M19.**

cotta /ˈkɒtə/ *noun*. **M19.**
[ORIGIN Italian from Proto-Romance, whence also COAT *noun*.]
CHRISTIAN CHURCH. A short surplice.

cottabus /ˈkɒtəbəs/ *noun*. Also **-os**. **E19.**
[ORIGIN Latin from Greek *kottabos*.]
An amusement at drinking parties in ancient Greece, in which the dregs in one's cup had to be flicked into a metal basin so as to strike it noisily.

cottage /ˈkɒtɪdʒ/ *noun*. **LME.**
[ORIGIN Anglo-Norman *cotage*, Anglo-Latin *cotagium*, from COT *noun*[1], COTE *noun*[1]: see -AGE.]
1 A small house in the country, orig. as occupied by poorer people; any small modest house. **LME.**
cottage orné(e) /ˈɔːneɪ/ a villa in the form of a cottage with an ornate design. ***love in a cottage***: see LOVE *noun*.
†**2** A small temporary shelter. **M16–L18.**
3 **a** A private summer holiday residence. *N. Amer.* **L19.** ▸**b** A one-storey house, a bungalow. *Austral.* **L19.** ▸**c** One of a group of small detached dwelling units forming part of a larger complex, as in a hotel or institution. *N. Amer.* **M20.**
4 A public toilet used for casual homosexual encounters. *slang*. **E20.**
– COMB.: **cottage-bonnet** a woman's close-fitting straw bonnet fashionable in the early 19th cent.; **cottage cheese** a soft white cheese made from unpressed curds; **cottage hospital** a small hospital without resident medical staff; **cottage industry**: carried on partly or wholly in people's homes; **cottage loaf**: of two round masses, a smaller on top of a larger; †**cottage lecture** an address given by a clergyman in a layman's home; **cottage piano** a small upright piano; **cottage pie** a pie of minced meat and potatoes under mashed potatoes;
■ **cottaged** *adjective* †(*a*) *rare* lodged in a cottage or humble dwelling; (*b*) set with cottages: **M17.** **cottagey**, **-gy** *adjective* resembling or suggestive of a cottage **M19.** **cottaging** *noun* (*slang*) using or frequenting public toilets for homosexual sex **L20.**

cottager /ˈkɒtɪdʒə/ *noun*. **M16.**
[ORIGIN from COTTAGE + -ER[1].]
1 *gen.* A person, esp. a rural labourer, living in a cottage. **M16.**
2 *spec.* = COTTAR 2. **L18.**
3 A person with a private summer holiday residence. *N. Amer.* **L19.**

cottar /ˈkɒtə/ *noun*. Also **-er**. **LOE.**
[ORIGIN from COT *noun*[1] + -ER[1] (Scot. *-ar*): cf. medieval Latin *cotarius* COTTIER. In earliest uses perh. repr. Old French *cot(i)er* COTTIER.]
1 FEUDAL HISTORY. A villein who held a cot with an attached plot of land in return for working for his lord part of the time. (In early use chiefly in surnames. Not recorded from ME until use as a historical term in 19. Cf. COTSET, COTSETLA.) **LOE.**
2 In Scotland: a tenant occupying a farm cottage, sometimes with a small plot of land, orig. in return for labouring on the farm as required, now usu. as part of a contract of employment with the farmer. **LME.**
3 IRISH HISTORY. = COTTIER 2. **L18.**

C

cottary *noun* var. of COTTERY.

cotted /ˈkɒtɪd/ *adjective*[1]. **L18.**
[ORIGIN from COT *noun*[2] + -ED[2].]
Matted, tangled.

cotted /ˈkɒtɪd/ *adjective*[2]. **E19.**
[ORIGIN from COT *noun*[1] + -ED[2].]
Dotted or lined with cottages; cottaged.

cotter /ˈkɒtə/ *noun*[1]. **ME.**
[ORIGIN Unknown: see COTTEREL.]
In machinery etc.: a pin, wedge, or bolt which passes into a hole and holds two parts together.
– COMB.: **cotter pin** (*a*) a cotter of circular cross-section; (*b*) a split pin for keeping a cotter in place.

cotter *noun*[2] var. of COTTAR.

cotter /ˈkɒtə/ *verb*[1]. Chiefly *dial.* **L16.**
[ORIGIN Unknown: cf. COTTED *adjective*[1].]
1 *verb trans.* Cause to thicken or coagulate; *esp.* scramble (an egg). **L16.**
2 *verb trans.* & *intrans.* Form into a tangled mass; entangle, mat. **L18.**
3 *verb intrans.* Shrivel or shrink *up*. **E19.**

cotter /ˈkɒtə/ *verb*[2] *trans.* **M17.**
[ORIGIN from COTTER *noun*[1].]
Fasten (esp. a window shutter) with a cotter.

cotterel /ˈkɒt(ə)r(ə)l/ *noun*. *dial.* **LME.**
[ORIGIN Closely rel. to COTTER *noun*[1], which may be a shortened form, or the primitive of which this is a dim.]
1 A hook, crane, or bar from which a pot is hung over a fire. *dial.* **LME.**
2 = COTTER *noun*[1]. *N. English*. **L16.**

cottery /ˈkɒtəri/ *noun*. *Scot.* *obsolete* exc. *hist.* Also **-ary**. **L15.**
[ORIGIN from *cotter* COTTAR: see -ERY. Cf. COTERIE.]
A cottar's holding.

cottice *noun* & *verb* var. of COTTISE.

cottid /ˈkɒtɪd/ *noun*. **L19.**
[ORIGIN mod. Latin *Cottidae* (see below), from *Cottus* genus name: see -ID[3].]
Any acanthopterygian fish of the family Cottidae, including the sculpins and other small mostly marine fishes of the northern hemisphere.

cottier /ˈkɒtɪə/ *noun*. **ME.**
[ORIGIN Old French *cotier* (in medieval Latin *cotarius*), ult. from Germanic base of COT *noun*[1]: see -IER.]
1 Orig. = COTTAR 1. Now, a rural labourer living in a cot or cottage. **ME.**
2 IRISH HISTORY. A peasant who rented a smallholding under a system of tenure (***cottier tenure***) by which land was let annually in small portions direct to the labourers, the rent being fixed by public competition. **M19.**

cottise /ˈkɒtɪs/ *noun* & *verb*. Also **cottice**, **cotise**. **L16.**
[ORIGIN French *cotice* (earlier †*cotisse*) leather thong.]
HERALDRY. ▸**A** *noun*. A charge like the bend etc. that it runs alongside but one quarter of its width, usu. occurring in a pair, one on each side of the bend etc. (originating as a stylized leather band). **L16.**
▸ **B** *verb trans.* Border (a bend etc.) with a pair of cottises. Chiefly as ***cottised*** *ppl adjective*. **L16.**

cotton /ˈkɒt(ə)n/ *noun*[1] & *adjective*. **LME.**
[ORIGIN Old French & mod. French *coton* from Arabic *quṭn*, *quṭun*, Hispano-Arabic *quṭūn*: cf. ACTON.]
▸ **A** *noun*. **1** The soft white fibrous substance which surrounds the seeds of various plants of the tropical and subtropical genus *Gossypium*, used for making thread and cloth. **LME.** ▸**b** A similar substance found in other plants. **M16.**
2 In full ***cotton plant***. A plant of the genus *Gossypium*, of the mallow family, that yields cotton or is cultivated for cotton; such plants collectively, as a crop. **LME.**
3 **a** Cloth or fabric made from cotton; a cotton fabric or garment (usu. in *pl.*). **LME.** ▸**b** Thread spun from cotton yarn. **M19.**
†**4** The pile of fustian. Only in **L15.**
– PHRASES ETC.: ***absorbent cotton***: see ABSORBENT *adjective*. **French cotton** the floss surrounding the seeds of the mudar, *Calotropis procera*. ***gun cotton***: see GUN *noun*. ***lavender cotton***: see LAVENDER *noun*[2]. NANKEEN ***cotton***. ***silk cotton***: see SILK *noun* & *adjective*. **spit cotton** *US colloq.* spit white saliva; have a mouth parched by thirst; *fig.* be very angry. ***Upland cotton***: see UPLAND *adjective*.
– COMB.: **cotton batting** *N. Amer.* cotton wool; **cotton belt** the cotton-producing region of the southern US; **cotton-boll weevil** = *boll weevil* s.v. BOLL *noun*[1]; **cotton bush** (*a*) a cotton plant; (*b*) *Austral.* any of several low downy drought-resistant

C

shrubs, esp. *Bassia aphylla*; **cotton cake** a mass of compressed cotton-seed used as cattle feed; **cotton candy** *N. Amer.* candyfloss; **cotton famine** *hist.* the failure of the supply of cotton to the English cotton mills during the American Civil War; **cotton-fish** *Austral.* = *cotton spinner* (b) below; **cotton flannel** a strong cotton fabric with a raised nap; **cotton gin** a machine for separating cotton fibre from the seed; **cotton grass** a sedge of the genus *Eriophorum*, the fruiting heads of which bear long white cottony hairs; *esp.* (more fully ***common cotton grass***) *E. angustifolium*, characteristic of wet bogs, and (more fully ***hare's-tail cotton grass***) *E. vaginatum*, common in damp moorland; **cotton-leaf worm** the larva of a moth, *Alabama argillacea*, which feeds on the leaves of the cotton plant in America; **cotton lord** a wealthy manufacturer of cotton yarn or goods; **cotton-mouth (moccasin)** = ***water moccasin*** s.v. MOCCASIN 2; **cotton-picking** *noun & adjective* (*a*) *noun* the harvesting of cotton; *US* a social gathering to mark this occasion; (*b*) *adjective* (*N. Amer. slang*) unpleasant, damned, confounded; ***cotton plant***: see sense 2 above; **cotton plush** = ***cotton flannel*** above; **cotton-powder** an explosive made from gun cotton; **cotton rat** a rodent, *Sigmodon hispidus*, common in the southern US; **cotton-sedge** = ***cotton grass*** above; **cotton-seed** the seed of the cotton plant, from which an edible oil is obtained; **cotton spinner** (*a*) a worker who spins cotton; a cotton manufacturer; (*b*) *Austral.* a sea cucumber of the genus *Holothuria*, which shoots out long white threads (Cuvierian organs) when disturbed; **cotton stainer** an insect of the heteropteran genus *Dysdercus*, esp. *D. suturellus*, which feeds on cotton bolls and stains the fibre reddish; **cotton state** any of the states of the southern US of which cotton is or was a major product; *spec.* (with cap. initials) Alabama; **cottontail** a rabbit of the N. American genus *Sylvilagus*, most species of which have a white fluffy underside to the tail; **cotton thistle** a tall white-felted thistle, *Onopordum acanthium*, often grown in gardens; Scotch thistle; **cotton-top** (in full ***cotton-top tamarin***) a brown and cream tamarin, *Saguinus oedipus*, of northern Colombia, with a crest of white hair; **cotton tree** (*a*) any of various tropical trees (of the genera *Bombax* and *Ceiba*) producing a cottony floss; (*b*) *dial.* the wayfaring tree, *Viburnum lantana*; (*c*) the N. American plane, *Platanus occidentalis*; (*d*) = **cottonwood** (a) below; (*e*) either of two Australian trees, *Hibiscus tiliaceus* and *Cochlospermum heteronemum*; **cotton waste** waste cotton yarn, used to clean machinery etc.; **cottonweed** any of several related plants of the composite family with hoary pubescent stems and leaves, esp. *Otanthus maritimus* of maritime sands in southern and western Europe; **cottonwood** (*a*) any of various N. American poplars with cottony hairs surrounding the seeds; (*b*) a downy-leaved Australian shrub of the composite family, *Bedfordia salicina*; (*c*) *NZ* = TAUHINU 2; **cotton-worm** = ***cotton-leaf worm*** above. See also COTTON WOOL.

▸ **B** *attrib.* or as *adjective*. Made of cotton. **M16.**

■ **cottonize** *verb trans.* reduce (flax, hemp, etc.) to a short staple resembling cotton **M19.** **cottony** *adjective* resembling cotton; consisting of or covered with soft hairs like cotton (***cottony-cushion scale***, an Australian scale insect, *Icerya purchasi*, which infests citrus trees): **L16.**

†cotton *noun*[2]. **E16–M19.**

[ORIGIN Perh. from COTTON *noun*[1] *& adjective* in sense 'down, nap'.]

A coarse woollen fabric formerly made in NW England (***Manchester cotton*** and ***Kendal cotton***), and in Wales (***Welsh cotton***).

cotton /ˈkɒt(ə)n/ *verb*. **ME.**

[ORIGIN from (the same root as) COTTON *noun*[1]. Cf. French *cotonner*.]

▸ **I** *lit.* **1** Pad, wrap, or block with cotton (wool). **ME.**

†**2 a** *verb trans.* Give a nap or finish to (cloth). **L15–L16.** ▸**b** *verb intrans.* Of cloth etc.: take on a nap. **E17–E19.**

▸ **II** *fig.* **3** *verb intrans.* Prosper, succeed. *obsolete* exc. *dial.* **M16.**

4 *verb intrans.* Of a person or thing: get on well, be in harmony, (*with*, *together*). **M16.**

> C. BURY The vaulted roof of a cathedral . . did not 'cotton' with lively ideas.

5 *verb intrans.* Behave in a friendly or warm way. (Foll. by *together*, *with*.) **M17.**

> W. CONGREVE I love to see 'em hug and cotton together, like Down upon a Thistle.

6 *verb intrans.* Be drawn *to*, take a liking *to*. **E19.**

> E. BIRNEY I was workin in a store . . . Dint cotton much to the job, though.

— WITH ADVERBS IN SPECIALIZED SENSES: **cotton on** *colloq.* (*a*) take a liking *to*; (*b*) get wise (*to*), understand. **cotton up** *arch.* make friendly overtures (*to*).

■ **cottoner** *noun* a person who puts a nap on cloth **ME.**

cottonade /kɒtəˈneɪd/ *noun & adjective*. Also **cotonnade**. **E19.**

[ORIGIN French *cotonnade*, formed as COTTON *noun*[1]: see -ADE.]

(Made of) any of various coarse cotton fabrics.

Cottonian /kɒˈtəʊnɪən/ *adjective*. **E18.**

[ORIGIN from *Cotton* (see below) + -IAN.]

Of or pertaining to the English antiquary and book collector Sir Robert Cotton (1570–1631); *spec.* designating the library he formed, now in the British Library, London.

cottonocracy /kɒtəˈnɒkrəsi/ *noun*. **M19.**

[ORIGIN from COTTON *noun*[1]: see -CRACY.]

Cotton lords as a class.

Cottonopolis /kɒtəˈnɒp(ə)lɪs/ *noun*. **M19.**

[ORIGIN from COTTON *noun*[1] + -O- + -POLIS.]

The city of Manchester, in NW England, once a centre of the British cotton trade.

cotton wool /kɒt(ə)n ˈwʊl/ *noun & adjectival phr.* **LME.**

[ORIGIN from COTTON *noun*[1] + WOOL *noun*.]

▸ **A** *noun*. **1** Raw cotton as gathered from the bolls of the cotton plant. Now *US*. **LME.**

2 Raw cotton prepared for use as packing or wadding; this substance with its natural wax removed, used as a soft absorbent material. **M19.** ▸**b** *fig.* Excessive comfort or protection. **M19.**

▸ **B** *attrib.* or as *adjective*. Made of or resembling cotton wool; protected as if with cotton wool. **M17.**

■ **cotton-ˈwoolly** *adjective* resembling cotton wool **E20.**

cotwal *noun* var. of KOTWAL.

cotyledon /kɒtɪˈliːd(ə)n/ *noun*. **M16.**

[ORIGIN Latin = navelwort from Greek *kotulēdōn* cup-shaped cavity, from *kotulē* cup, socket.]

1 ANATOMY. Each of the distinct patches of villi on the fetal chorion of ruminants; each of the analogous lobes or their constituent lobules in the disc of the human placenta, each lobule containing a branching chorionic blood vessel. **M16.**

2 A succulent of the largely southern African genus *Cotyledon* or one of the European species formerly included in it, *esp.* navelwort. **E17.**

3 BOTANY. A seed leaf, a primary leaf in the embryo of a higher plant (in angiosperms borne either singly (in monocotyledons) or in pairs (in dicotyledons), in gymnosperms borne in numbers varying from 2 to 15 or more). **L18.**

■ **cotyledonary**, **cotyledonous** *adjectives* marked by the presence of cotyledons; pertaining to or of the nature of a cotyledon: **M19.**

cotyloid /ˈkɒtɪlɔɪd/ *adjective*. **M18.**

[ORIGIN from Greek *kotuloeidēs*, from *kotulē*: see COTYLEDON, -OID.]

ANATOMY. Cup-shaped; *spec.* designating the acetabulum (***cotyloid cavity***) and parts connected with it.

couac /kʊˈak/ *noun*. **L19.**

[ORIGIN French: imit.]

MUSIC. A quacking sound made by bad blowing on the clarinet, oboe, or bassoon.

couba /ˈkuːbə/ *noun*. *Austral.* Also **coo-**, **-bah**. **L19.**

[ORIGIN Wiradhuri *gubaa*.]

An acacia, *Acacia salicina*, with a drooping habit of growth.

coucal /ˈkuːk(ə)l, ˈkʊkɑːl/ *noun*. **E19.**

[ORIGIN French, said to be from *couc(ou* cuckoo + *al(ouette* lark.]

Any of numerous non-parasitic birds of the cuckoo family that belong to the genera *Centropus* and *Coua*, found in Africa, southern Asia, Australia, and Madagascar.

couch /kaʊtʃ/ *noun*[1]. **ME.**

[ORIGIN Old French & mod. French *couche*, formed as COUCH *verb*.]

1 A frame, with what is spread over it, on which to lie down; anything on which one sleeps. Now *arch.* or *literary*. **ME.**

> LD MACAULAY Hospitality could offer little more than a couch of straw.

2 The den or lair of an animal, esp. an otter. **LME.**

3 A piece of furniture for reclining or sitting on, *esp.* one with a low back and an arm at one end. **LME.** ▸**b** *spec.* The couch on which a doctor's or psychiatrist's patient reclines for examination or treatment. **M20.**

> LE ROI JONES Both of you sit on this couch where I'm sitting.

casting couch: see CASTING *noun*.

4 In malting, a layer of grain laid on the floor to germinate after steeping; the floor itself. **E17.**

5 A layer, a stratum, a bed; *esp.* a layer of paint. **M17.**

— COMB.: **couch potato** *slang* a person whose spare time is spent lounging about, esp. watching television.

couch /kaʊtʃ, kuːtʃ/ *noun*[2]. **L16.**

[ORIGIN Var. of QUITCH.]

Any of various esp. rhizomatous grasses occurring as weeds, esp. *Elymus repens*. Also (with specifying word), any of several other grasses of the genus *Elytriga*. Also ***couch grass***.

onion couch: see ONION *noun*.

■ **couchy** *adjective* full of couch grass; resembling couch grass: **L18.**

couch /kaʊtʃ/ *verb*. **ME.**

[ORIGIN Old French & mod. French *coucher* from Latin *collocare*: see COLLOCATE.]

▸ **I** Lay down flat, and related senses.

†**1** *verb trans.* Lay (things); place, set down, esp. horizontally or in layers. **ME–L18.**

> R. SURFLET An vnderstorie . . to couch your wines and cidres in.

2 *verb trans. & intrans.* Embroider with gold thread etc. laid flat on the surface. **LME.**

3 *verb trans.* Cause to lie down, lay down (a person, one's head, etc.); put to bed; *refl.* lie down. Now only of an animal and as ***couched*** *ppl adjective*, laid or lying (as) on a couch. **LME.**

> KEATS Two fair creatures, couched side by side in deepest grass. E. MUIR The tractors lie . . like dank sea-monsters couched and waiting.

†**4** *verb trans.* Cause to crouch. Chiefly as ***couched*** *ppl adjective*, prostrated, cowering. **LME–E18.**

> SHAKES. *Lucr.* Like a falcon tow'ring in the skies, Coucheth the fowl below with his wings' shade.

5 *verb trans.* In malting, spread (grain) on a floor to germinate. **M16.**

6 *verb trans.* PAPER-MAKING. Lay (a sheet of pulp) on a felt etc. to be pressed. **M18.**

▸ **II** Place, arrange.

†**7** *verb trans.* Place in a lodging. **LME–L17.**

†**8** *verb trans.* Collect *together*; include *in* a list etc. or *under* a heading. **LME–E18.**

9 *verb trans.* Put together, arrange, (words etc.); put into writing or speech; express. Now always foll. by *in* certain *terms*, *words*, etc. **E16.**

> K. M. E. MURRAY The flowery language in which he couched his eloquent speeches.

10 *verb trans.* Hide (a meaning, idea, etc.) *under*, *in*. **M16.**

> J. CAIRD Materialistic metaphors under which our spiritual conceptions are couched.

11 *verb trans.* Hide, conceal; place in concealment. Now *rare* or *obsolete*. **L16.**

▸ **III** Lower, bring down.

12 *verb trans.* **a** Lower (a spear etc.) to the position of attack; level (a gun etc.). **L15.** ▸**b** Lay down, bring down, or lower, (a part of the body etc.). **E17.**

> a T. GRAY To arms! cried Mortimer, and couch'd his quiv'ring lance.

13 *verb trans. & intrans.* SURGERY. Treat (a cataract, a patient, etc.) by displacing the opaque lens of the eye downwards into the vitreous by means of a needle. **L16.**

> *fig.*: DE QUINCEY She it was . . that first couched his eye to the sense of beauty.

▸ **IV** Lie.

14 *verb intrans.* Lie, esp. at rest or in sleep. Now chiefly of a wild animal: lie in its lair. **LME.**

> W. OWEN I have couched in exactly twelve different rooms. *fig.*: R. BROOKE Raindrops couching in cool flowers.

15 *verb intrans.* Crouch, cower, in fear, obedience, submission, etc. Formerly also, stoop under a burden. **LME.**

> J. BAILLIE Like spaniel couching to his lord.

16 *verb intrans.* Lie in ambush, lurk. **L16.**

> TENNYSON Sir Launcelot passing by Spied where he couch'd.

17 *verb intrans.* Of leaves etc.: lie in a heap for decomposition. **L18.**

■ **couching** *noun* (*a*) the action of the verb; (*b*) EMBROIDERY couched work (***surface couching***: see SURFACE *adjective*): **LME.**

couchancy /ˈkaʊtʃ(ə)nsi/ *noun*. **L17.**

[ORIGIN from COUCHANT: see -ANCY.]

LAW (now *hist.*). The fact of being couchant. Only in ***levancy and couchancy***.

couchant /ˈkaʊtʃ(ə)nt/ *adjective*. **LME.**

[ORIGIN Old French & mod. French, pres. pple of *coucher* COUCH *verb*: see -ANT[1].]

1 Esp. of an animal: lying down; couching. **LME.**

levant and couchant: see LEVANT *adjective*.

2 HERALDRY. Of an animal: lying on its belly with its head up, lodged. Usu. *postpositive*. **E16.**

†**3** Lying hidden, lurking. **M17–E18.**

couché /ˈkuːʃeɪ/ *adjective*. **M18.**

[ORIGIN French, pa. pple of *coucher* COUCH *verb*.]

HERALDRY. Of a shield: shown tilted, with the sinister corner uppermost.

couchee /ˈkuːʃeɪ; *foreign* kuʃe (*pl. same*)/ *noun*. **L17.**

[ORIGIN French *couché* var. of *coucher* lying down, going to bed, use as noun of *coucher* COUCH *verb*. Cf. LEVEE *noun*[1].]

An evening reception.

coucher /ˈkaʊtʃə/ *noun*[1]. **LME.**

[ORIGIN App. Anglo-Norman, from base of Old French & mod. French *couche*: see COUCH *noun*[1], -ER[2]. Cf. French *coucheur*.]

1 A person lying down (*rare*); *Scot.* a laggard, a coward. **LME.**

†**2 a** A large book; *esp.* a large breviary permanently on a desk in a church etc. **LME–M16.** ▸**b** More fully ***coucher-book***. A large cartulary or register. **E17–L19.**

coucher /ˈkaʊtʃə/ *noun*[2]. **M18.**

[ORIGIN from COUCH *verb* + -ER[1]: cf. French *coucheur*, *couchart*.]

PAPER-MAKING. A person who or thing which couches pulp to be pressed.

couchette /kuːˈʃɛt; *foreign* kuʃɛt (*pl. same*)/ *noun*. **E20.**

[ORIGIN French, lit. 'little bed', formed as COUCH *noun*[1]: see -ETTE.]

A (Continental) railway carriage in which the seats convert into sleeping berths; such a berth.

coudé /kuːˈdeɪ/ *adjective & noun*. **L19.**

[ORIGIN French, pa. pple of *couder* bend at right angles, from *coude* elbow from Latin *cubitum* CUBIT.]

(Of, pertaining to, or designating) a telescope in which the rays are bent to focus at a fixed point off the axis.

Couéism /ˈkuːeɪɪz(ə)m/ *noun*. **E20.**

[ORIGIN Emile *Coué* (1857–1926), French psychologist + -ISM.]

A system of psychotherapy by systematic auto-suggestion, usu. of an optimistic nature.

■ **Coué** *noun & verb* (*a*) *noun* Couéism; (*b*) *verb trans.* bring (oneself) *into* or *out of* a certain state by Couéism; produce by Couéism: E20. **Couéist** *noun* a person who practises or advocates Couéism E20. **Coué'istic** *adjective* of or pertaining to Couéism, resembling Couéism M20.

Couette /kuːˈɛt/ *noun.* M20.
[ORIGIN M. F. A. *Couette*, 19th-cent. French physicist.]
PHYSICS. Used *attrib.* with ref. to the work of Couette in hydrodynamics.
Couette flow flow of a Newtonian fluid between two parallel surfaces one of which is moving relative to the other. **Couette viscometer** a viscometer consisting of two concentric cylinders with liquid in between them, the torque on one cylinder being measured when the other is rotated.

cougar /ˈkuːɡə/ *noun.* Chiefly *N. Amer.* Also (now *rare*) **-guar** /-ɡjʊə, -ɡwə/. L18.
[ORIGIN French *couguar*, †*-gar* abbreviation from mod. Latin *cuguarcarana* from Guarani *cuguaçuarana*.]
= PUMA.

cough /kɒf/ *noun.* ME.
[ORIGIN from the verb.]
1 A tendency to cough; a disorder of the respiratory tract manifesting itself in bouts of coughing. Formerly ***the cough***. ME.

SHAKES. 2 *Hen. IV* What disease hast thou? . . A whoreson cold, sir, a cough, sir.

smoker's cough: see SMOKER. ***whooping cough***: see WHOOPING *ppl adjective*.
2 A single act of coughing; a sudden expulsion of air from the lungs with a noise produced by abrupt opening of the glottis. M18. ▸**b** The sound of a shell being fired or bursting. *colloq.* E20.

JOYCE He announced his presence by that gentle . . cough which so many have tried . . to imitate.

– COMB.: **cough candy** *N. Amer.* = ***cough sweet*** below; **cough drop** (*a*) a medicated lozenge taken to relieve a cough; (*b*) *slang* an awkward or disagreeable person or thing; **cough medicine**, **cough mixture** a medicinal concoction for the relief of a cough; **cough sweet**: medicated to relieve a cough.

cough /kɒf/ *verb.* ME.
[ORIGIN from imit. base repr. by Old English *cohhetan* shout, Middle & mod. Low German, Middle Dutch & mod. Dutch *kuchen* cough, Middle High German *küchen* breathe, exhale (German *keuchen* pant).]
1 *verb intrans.* Expel air from the lungs with a sudden effort and a noise produced by the abrupt opening of the glottis, usu. in order to remove something obstructing or irritating the air passages. ME. ▸**b** Of an engine etc.: make a noise like coughing, esp. when starting; misfire. Of a gun: fire shells. L19. ▸**c** Confess, give information. *slang.* E20.

YEATS It was but the cart-horse coughing. G. B. SHAW Pothinus coughs admonitorily. J. H. BURN The reluctance of the patient to cough and to clear his airways. **b** J. HARVEY Machines coughed and started. **c** M. PROCTER Slade would never 'cough' while there was no evidence.

2 *verb trans.* Express by coughing. LME.
3 *verb trans.* With adverbs: bring into a specified position or condition by coughing (see also below). LME.
– WITH ADVERBS IN SPECIALIZED SENSES: **cough away** bring (one's life etc.) to an end with coughing. **cough down** put down or silence (a speaker) by coughing. **cough out** = ***cough up*** (a) below. **cough up** (*a*) *verb phr. trans.* eject by coughing, say with a cough; *slang* disclose, confess, give information; (*b*) *verb phr. trans. & intrans.* (*slang*) bring out or produce (esp. money) reluctantly.
■ **cougher** *noun* a person who coughs E17. **coughing** *noun* the action of the verb; the sound of a person, engine, etc., coughing: LME.

couguar *noun* see COUGAR.

coul *noun* var. of COWL *noun*[2].

could *verb* etc.: see CAN *verb*[1].

coulee /kuːˈleɪ, ˈkuːli/ *noun.* Also **-lée**, (sense 1) ***-lie** /ˈkuːli/. E19.
[ORIGIN French *coulée* (lava) flow, from Latin *colare* filter, strain, (in Proto-Romance) flow, from *cōlum* strainer.]
1 (The bed of) an intermittent stream; a dry valley; a gulch or valley with steep sides. *N. Amer. dial.* E19.
2 GEOLOGY. A stream of molten or solidified lava. M19.

couleur /kuːˈləː/ *noun.* M19.
[ORIGIN French = COLOUR *noun*.]
In the game rouge-et-noir, the section of the table in which are placed bets, that the colour of the first card dealt will be the same as that of the winning row.

couleur de rose /kulœːr də roːz/ *noun & adjectival phr.* LME.
[ORIGIN French = rose colour.]
▸ **A** *noun phr.* Rose-colour, pink; *fig.* optimism, cheerfulness. LME.
▸ **B** *adjectival phr.* Rose-coloured, pink; *fig.* optimistic, cheerful. L18.

coulibiac /kuːlɪˈbjak/ *noun.* Also **k-**. L19.
[ORIGIN Russian *kulebyaka*.]
A Russian pie of fish or meat, cabbage, etc.

coulie *noun* see COULEE.

coulis /ˈkuli/ *noun.* M18.
[ORIGIN French, from *couler* to flow, run: cf. CULLIS *noun*[1].]
1 The juices of roasted or grilled meat; these made into a broth, jelly, or gravy; = CULLIS *noun*[1]. Also, a thick rich soup of shellfish, poultry, etc., = BISQUE *noun*[3]. M18.
2 A light thin sauce of puréed fruit or vegetables, used esp. as a garnish in nouvelle cuisine. M20.

coulisse /kuːˈliːs/ *noun.* E19.
[ORIGIN French, use as noun of fem. of *coulis* sliding: see CULLIS *noun*[2]. Cf. PORTCULLIS.]
1 THEATRICAL. Each of the side scenes of a stage; *sing.* & (usu.) in *pl.*, the space between them, the wings. E19.
2 A groove in which a sluice gate or other movable partition slides up and down. M19.
3 The body of outside dealers on the Paris Bourse; similar dealers in other stock exchanges; the place where they deal. L19.
4 A corridor; *fig.* a place of informal discussion or negotiation. E20.

couloir /ˈkuːlwɑː; *foreign* kulwaːr (*pl. same*)/ *noun.* E19.
[ORIGIN French = channel, from *couler* pour (from Latin *colare* filter) + *-oir* -ORY[1].]
A steep gully on a mountainside.

Coulomb /ˈkuːlɒm/ *noun.* In sense 2 **c-**. M19.
[ORIGIN C. A. de *Coulomb* (1736–1806), French physicist.]
PHYSICS. **1** Used *attrib.* and in *possess.* with ref. to Coulomb's work in electrostatics. M19.
Coulomb force the electrostatic force of attraction or repulsion exerted by one charged particle on another. **Coulomb interaction** the electrostatic interaction between charged particles. **Coulomb law**, **Coulomb's law**: that like charges repel and opposite charges attract, with a force proportional to the product of the charges and inversely proportional to the square of the distance between them.
2 The SI unit of electric charge; the quantity of electricity conveyed in one second by a current of one ampere. (Symbol C.) L19.
■ **cou'lombian**, **C-** *adjective* = COULOMBIC E20. **cou'lombic**, **C-** *adjective* of or pertaining to Coulomb or the force, laws, etc., named after him M20.

coulometer /kuːˈlɒmɪtə/ *noun.* E20.
[ORIGIN from COULOMB + -METER.]
An electrolytic cell for finding the amount of electricity that has flowed in electrolysis by measuring the products of the process.
■ **coulo'metric** *adjective* pertaining to or employing coulometry M20. **coulometry** *noun* the use of a coulometer; chemical analysis in which quantities are determined from the amount of electricity needed for their electrolysis: M20.

coulrophobia /ˌkɒlrəˈfəʊbɪə/ *noun. rare.* L20.
[ORIGIN from Greek *kolobatheron* stilt + -PHOBIA.]
Irrational fear of clowns.

coulter /ˈkəʊltə/ *noun.* Also ***colter.** OE.
[ORIGIN Latin *culter* knife, ploughshare.]
The vertical cutting blade fixed in front of the share in a plough.
– COMB.: **coulterneb** *dial.* the puffin (from the shape of its bill).

coumarin /ˈkuːmərɪn/ *noun.* M19.
[ORIGIN French *coumarine*, from *coumarou* from Portuguese & Spanish *cumarú* from Tupi, substance from tonka beans: see -IN[1].]
An aromatic chromone, $C_9H_6O_2$, with the smell of new-mown hay, occurring in various plants and used in perfumery etc.

coumarone /ˈkuːmərəʊn/ *noun.* Also **cum-**. L19.
[ORIGIN from COUMARIN + -ONE.]
CHEMISTRY. A colourless liquid (C_8H_6O) present in coal tar, which is related to coumarin and is used in making synthetic resins; any derivative of this.
– COMB.: **coumarone resin** any of various thermoplastic resins produced by polymerizing coumarone with indene and used esp. in the rubber and varnish industries.

council /ˈkaʊns(ə)l, -sɪl/ *noun.* OE.
[ORIGIN Anglo-Norman *cuncile*, *concilie* from Latin *concilium* assembly, meeting, formed as CON- + *calare* call, summon.]
▸ **I** An assembly.
1 An assembly of ecclesiastics (with or without laymen) convened to regulate doctrine or discipline in the Church or to settle disputes between the ecclesiastical and civil powers. OE.
diocesan council, ***ecumenical council***, ***general council***, etc.
†**2** *gen.* An assembly called together for any purpose. Only in ME.
3 An assembly or meeting for consultation or advice. ME.
Cabinet Council, ***family council***, etc.
4 In New Testament translations: (a meeting of) the Sanhedrin. LME.
▸ **II** A body of counsellors or councillors.
5 A body of people chosen as advisers on matters of state. ME.
6 The local administrative body of a village, parish, town, or larger area. LME.
city council, ***county council***, ***district council***, ***parish council***, ***regional council***, ***town council***, etc.
7 A deliberative committee sharing the administration of a society or institution. M17.
– PHRASES: ***Aulic Council***: see AULIC. ***Common Council***: see COMMON *adjective*. **council of war** (*a*) an assembly of officers of the armed services called together usu. in a special emergency; *fig.* a meeting held to discuss a plan of action; (*b*) *hist.* in some foreign countries, a permanent advisory committee on military affairs. **Great Council** *hist.* (occas.) = WITENAGEMOT; (more often) an assembly under the Norman kings of tenants-in-chief and great ecclesiastics, out of which the House of Lords developed. **in council** in consultation or deliberation in a council. **King in Council**, **Queen in Council** the Privy Council as issuing Orders in Council or receiving petitions etc. ***Nicene Council***: see NICENE *adjective* 1. ***Order in Council***: see ORDER *noun*. ***privy council***: see PRIVY *adjective*. ***Queen in Council***: see ***King in Council*** above. ***Second Vatican Council***: VATICAN *Council*. ***wages council***: see WAGE *noun*.
– COMB.: **council-board** a table at which councillors sit; councillors in session; **council-book** a book in which the acts of a council are registered; the register of Privy Counsellors; **council-chamber** a room used for council meetings; **council estate** an estate of council houses; **council-fire** a fire kindled by N. American Indians when in council; **council flat**: owned and let by a local council; **council-general** a general or common council; **council house** (*a*) a house in which a council meets; in Scotland, a town hall; (*b*) a house used by N. American Indians when in council; (*c*) a house owned and let by a local council; **council school**: supported by a town or county council; **council-table** (*a*) a council-board; †(*b*) the Privy Council; **council tax** a tax levied by local authorities (from 1993, replacing the community charge) based on the band in which the estimated capital value of a property falls.
– NOTE: Confused with COUNSEL *noun* until 16.

C

councillor /ˈkaʊns(ə)lə/ *noun.* Also ***-ilor.** LME.
[ORIGIN Alt. of COUNSELLOR by assim. to COUNCIL.]
An official member of a council.
county councillor, ***parish councillor***, etc. ***privy councillor***: see PRIVY *adjective*.
■ **councillorship** *noun* the office or position of councillor L16.

councilman /ˈkaʊns(ə)lmən, -sɪl-/ *noun.* Pl. **-men.** M17.
[ORIGIN from COUNCIL + MAN *noun*.]
A member of a council, esp. a local council, in the City of London or the US.
Common Councilman: see COMMON *adjective*.
■ **councilmanic** /-ˈmanɪk/ *adjective* M19.

councilor *noun* see COUNCILLOR.

counsel /ˈkaʊns(ə)l/ *noun.* ME.
[ORIGIN Old French *c(o)unseil* (mod. *conseil*) from Latin *consilium* consultation, plan, deliberating body, rel. to *consulere*: see CONSULT *verb*.]
▸ **I 1** (A piece of) advice, (a) direction, esp. when the result of deliberation. ME. ▸**b** THEOLOGY. Any of the advisory declarations of Christ and the Apostles, given as a means of attaining greater moral perfection. LME.

S. JOHNSON The counsels of philosophy and the injunctions of religion. SAKI Francesca . . not only sought his counsel but frequently followed it.

2 Interchange of opinions; deliberation, consultation. ME.
†**3** The ability to counsel or give advice; judgement, prudence, sagacity. ME–M17.
4 The result of deliberation; a resolution, a purpose; a plan. ME.
5 A secret purpose or opinion; a secret. Long *obsolete* exc. with *keep* (see below). ME.
▸ **II** Cf. COUNCIL.
†**6** *gen.* A body of advisers. ME–M16. ▸**b** A counsellor. LME–M17.
7 Usu. *collect. pl.* A body of legal advisers engaged in the direction or conduct of a court case. LME. ▸**b** (Pl. usu. same.) A legal adviser; a barrister, an advocate (in Scotland etc.). L17.

LD DENNING They went off to their solicitors. They saw counsel. **b** *New Statesman* Counsel is holding the photograph the wrong way up. JO GRIMOND I was briefed as junior counsel to defend a man charged with murder.

– PHRASES: **counsel of despair** an action to be taken when all else fails. **counsel of perfection** advice designed to guide one towards moral perfection (see *Matthew* 19:21); ideal but impracticable advice. †**in counsel** in private, in confidence. **keep counsel** *arch.* observe secrecy. **keep one's counsel**, **keep one's own counsel** keep one's secret; be reticent. †**keep someone's counsel** keep a secret which someone has committed to one. **King's Counsel**, **Queen's Counsel** a senior barrister appointed on the recommendation of the Lord Chancellor. ***leading counsel***: see LEADING *ppl adjective*. ***Parliamentary Counsel***: see PARLIAMENTARY *adjective*. ***purge of partial counsel***: see PURGE *verb* 4b. ***Queen's Counsel***: see ***King's Counsel*** above. **take counsel** consult (*with*).
■ **counselless** /-l-l-/ *adjective* without counsel ME.

counsel /ˈkaʊns(ə)l/ *verb.* Infl. **-ll-**, ***-l-.** ME.
[ORIGIN Old French *cons(e)illier* (mod. *conseiller*) from Latin *consiliari*, from *consilium*: see COUNSEL *noun*.]
1 *verb trans.* Give or offer counsel or counselling to (a person); advise (*to do*). ME. ▸**b** *verb intrans.* Give or offer counsel (†*to* a course or purpose). Now *rare* or *obsolete*. LME.

LYTTON Since we have thus met, I will pause to counsel you. J. MCPHEE The passenger . . counselled the pilot to stay with the principal stream in sight.

2 *verb trans.* Recommend (a plan, suggestion, etc.; *that*). ME.

E. M. FORSTER His mother . . would be pleased; she had counselled the step. M. EDWARDES Armstrong counselled that we should moderate the letter.

†3 *verb trans.* Ask counsel of, consult. ME–M16.
4 *verb intrans.* Take counsel with others, deliberate. ME.
■ **counsellable** *adjective* (*a*) willing to be counselled; (*b*) (of a thing) advisable: M16. **counse'llee** *noun* a person who receives counselling M20.

C

counselling /ˈkaʊns(ə)lɪŋ/ *verbal noun.* Also ***-eling**. ME.
[ORIGIN from COUNSEL *verb* + -ING¹.]
The action of COUNSEL *verb*; *spec.* a therapeutic procedure in which a usu. trained person adopts a supportive non-judgemental role in enabling a client to deal more effectively with psychological or emotional problems or gives advice on practical problems.

> *Listener* Some students need counselling or even psychological treatment in these testing years.

counsellor /ˈkaʊns(ə)lə/ *noun.* Also ***-elor**. ME.
[ORIGIN Old French & mod. French *conseiller* from Latin *consiliarius* (see -ARY¹), and Old French *conseillour*, Old French & mod. French *-eur* from Latin *consiliator*: see -OR.]
1 A person who gives or offers counsel; an adviser; *spec.* a person who provides counselling as a therapy. ME.
2 More fully ***counsellor-at-law***. A person whose profession is to give legal advice to clients and conduct their cases in court; a barrister, an advocate. Now chiefly *Irish & US*. LME.
3 A senior officer in the British diplomatic service, esp. in one of the larger embassies; a senior officer in the Foreign and Commonwealth Office. E20.
– PHRASES: **Counsellor of State** any of a group of people appointed to act for the British monarch during a temporary absence abroad. ***privy counsellor***: see PRIVY *adjective*.

count /kaʊnt/ *noun*¹. Also †**compt**. ME.
[ORIGIN Old French *co(u)nte* (mod. *compte* reckoning, *conte* tale) from late Latin *computus* calculation, from *computare* COMPUTE *verb*.]
1 The action of counting; a calculation. ME. ▸**b** The counting aloud of up to ten seconds by the referee when a boxer or wrestler is knocked down or otherwise unable to rise (ten seconds marking a knockout). E20.

> P. G. WODEHOUSE In actual count of time, he was no longer in his first youth. M. MOORCOCK About fifty titles, at the present count.

keep count be aware how many there have been. **lose count** fail to know how many there have been. **b out for the count** defeated, *spec.* in BOXING or WRESTLING by being unable to rise within ten seconds. **take the count** be defeated.
2 A reckoning as to money or property; a statement of moneys received and expended, an account. LME.
3 *fig.* = ACCOUNT *noun* 3. *arch.* L15.

> SHAKES. *Oth.* When we shall meet at compt This look of thine will hurl my soul from heaven.

4 The result of a numerical calculation; a sum total. L15. ▸**b** A number expressing the fineness of yarn, e.g. the length per unit mass of yarn. Also ***yarn count***. M19. ▸**c** PHYSICS. The detection of an ionizing event by a Geiger counter etc.; an event so detected. E20.

> J. A. MICHENER The count was at its maximum, around forty million. **c** *Nature* An intensity of 20 counts s^{-1}.

blood count, ***pollen count***, etc.
5 Estimation, consideration; the way of estimating; regard, notice. L15.

> E. B. BROWNING Of miserable men, he took no count.

6 In LAW, a charge in an indictment; *fig.* any of several points under discussion. L16.

> A. T. ELLIS You are entirely wrong on both counts.

– COMB.: **countline** a branded item of confectionery; **count noun** GRAMMAR a noun denoting something of which there is more than one, a countable noun, in English usu. a noun which has a plural and is used with an indefinite article (opp. ***mass noun***).

count /kaʊnt/ *noun*². Also (esp. in titles) **C-**. LME.
[ORIGIN Old French *conte* (mod. *comte*), from Latin *comes*, *comit-* companion, overseer, attendant, etc., (in late Latin) occupant of a state office, formed as COM- + *it-* pa. ppl stem of *ire* go.]
A foreign nobleman corresponding to a British earl.
Count Palatine: see PALATINE *adjective*¹.
– COMB.: **count-bishop**, **count-cardinal**: who holds both the temporal and the spiritual dignities designated.
■ **countship** *noun* the position, domain, or jurisdiction of a count E18.

count /kaʊnt/ *verb.* Also †**compt**. LME.
[ORIGIN Old French *c(o)unter* reckon, relate (mod. *compter* reckon, *conter* relate), from Latin *computare* COMPUTE *verb*.]
▸ **I** *verb trans.* **1** Find the number of, esp. by assigning successive numerals to the members of; repeat numerals in order up to (a selected number). LME. ▸**b** Foll. by *out*: (*a*) complete a count of ten seconds over (a boxer or wrestler unable to rise), adjudge to be knocked out after a count; (*b*) count while taking from a stock; (*c*) procure an adjournment of (the House of Commons) when fewer than forty members are present; (*d*) in children's games, select (a player) for a special role or dismissal by counting with the words of a rhyme etc. E19. ▸**c** Foll. by *up*: find the sum of. L19. ▸**d** Foll. by *down*: mark (time remaining before an event) by counting backwards to zero; mark the time remaining to (an event) by so counting. M20.

> ALDOUS HUXLEY 'One, two, three . . .'; the seekers . . began to count their hundred, aloud. E. BIRNEY He counted the flies on the ceiling.

be counting the days, **be counting the hours**, etc., be waiting impatiently for an event a few days, hours, etc., ahead. ***count heads***: see HEAD *noun*. ***count noses***: see NOSE *noun*. ***count one's beads***: see BEAD *noun* 2. ***count one's blessings***: see BLESSING. ***count one's chickens***: see CHICKEN *noun*¹. ***count sheep***: see SHEEP *noun*. ***count ten***, ***count up to ten***: see TEN *noun* 2.
2 (With double obj., or obj. and compl.) consider to be; regard *as*, (*arch.*) take *for*. LME.

> E. M. FORSTER I count myself a lucky person. J. BUCHAN America . . . Among her citizens I count many of my closest friends. I. MURDOCH Mor still counted Tim as one of his best friends.

3 Reckon, estimate, (at such a price, in such terms, etc.). Formerly also, esteem, value. LME.

> H. L. MENCKEN Nearly all of them count success in terms of money.

†4 Tell, relate, recount. LME–L18.
5 Include in a reckoning or plan; take into consideration. E16. ▸**b** Foll. by *in*, *out*: include, exclude, (a person) as a participant or supporter. *colloq.* M19.

> R. GRAFTON He is not counted in the number of kinges. E. ALBEE Martha hasn't been sick a day in her life, unless you count the time she spends in the rest home.

count the cost: see COST *noun*².
†6 Impute, put down to the account of. Foll. by *to*. M16–E18.
▸ **II** *verb intrans.* †**7** Take account *of*; think (much, lightly, etc.) *of*; care *for*. LME–M19.

> SHAKES. *Two Gent.* So painted, to make her fair, that no man counts of her beauty.

8 Reckon, make a reckoning. Now only in ***count without***, not take into account. LME.
9 Repeat or list numerals in order (foll. by *from* one numeral, (*up*) *to* or *down to* another); foll. by *down*: repeat numerals in descending order to zero, esp. when launching a rocket etc. Also, do arithmetic, conduct reckoning. L16.

> M. ARNOLD To count by tens is the simplest way of counting.

10 Foll. by (*up*)*on*: make the basis of one's plans; expect confidently; depend or rely on (a future contingency). M17.

> ADDISON We . . may possibly never possess what we have so foolishly counted upon.

†11 LAW. Plead in a court of law; state a plaintiff's case. Foll. by *upon*: make the basis of a plea. M17–E19.
12 With compl.: amount to, be in number. *arch.* E19.
13 Be regarded or considered *as*. M19.

> B. PYM He didn't count as an ordinary man who went out to work.

14 Be included in the reckoning (*against*, *in someone's* or *something's favour*); be important, be significant; (foll. by *for*) be worth *much*, *little*, *nothing*, etc. M19.

> THOMAS HUGHES Oxford ought to be the place . . where money should count for nothing. J. RHYS It is the small things that count.

'count /kaʊnt/ *noun. dial.* M19.
[ORIGIN Aphet.]
= ACCOUNT *noun* 4. Cf. COUNT *noun*¹ 5, ***no-'count*** s.v. NO *adjective*.

countable /ˈkaʊntəb(ə)l/ *adjective & noun.* As adjective also †**compt-**. LME.
[ORIGIN Old French *contable* (mod. *comptable*), formed as COUNT *verb*: see -ABLE.]
▸ **A** *adjective.* †**1** Answerable (*to*), accountable (*for*). LME–E19.
2 Able or fit to be counted; *spec.* in MATH., = DENUMERABLE. LME.
†3 Sensitive *to*. Only in E17.
4 GRAMMAR. Of a noun: denoting something of which there is more than one, able to form a plural or be used with an indefinite article. Cf. ***count noun*** s.v. COUNT *noun*¹. M20.
▸ **B** *noun.* GRAMMAR. A countable thing, a countable noun. E20.
■ **counta'bility** *noun* the property of being countable L20. **countably** *adverb* (MATH.) in a denumerable way E20.

countdown /ˈkaʊntdaʊn/ *noun.* M20.
[ORIGIN from COUNT *noun*¹ or *verb* + DOWN *adverb*: see COUNT *verb* 1d.]
The action or an act of counting numerals in reverse order to zero, esp. in the procedure for launching a rocket etc.; (the procedures carried out in) the period of time so marked.

> *fig.*: *Times* The count-down begins for the first Test match.

countenance /ˈkaʊnt(ə)nəns, -tɪn-/ *noun.* ME.
[ORIGIN Anglo-Norman *c(o)untenaunce*, Old French & mod. French *contenance* bearing, behaviour, mien, contents, from *contenir*: see CONTAIN, -ANCE.]
▸ **I** †**1** Bearing, demeanour; conduct. ME–E18.
†2 Appearance, aspect; mere show, pretence. ME–M19.
3 The expression on a person's face. ME. ▸**b** The face. LME.

> J. LONDON The man flung past Martin with an angry countenance. **b** P. GALLICO She . . peered up into his countenance long and searchingly.

4 Calmness of appearance, composure. ME.
†5 A sign, a gesture. LME–M16.
▸ **II** †**6** Manner towards others as expressing good or ill will. LME–M17.
7 Appearance of favour to one side; moral support. L16.

> H. JAMES He had given countenance to the reprehensible practice of gaming.

▸ †**III** **8** One's position in the world, standing; credit, repute. LME–L18.
– PHRASES: **change countenance** change expression as a result of emotion. †**for a countenance**, †**for countenance** for appearance's sake. **keep a person in countenance** keep a person from being disconcerted, esp. by a show of support. **keep one's countenance** maintain composure, *esp.* refrain from laughing. **lose countenance** become embarrassed. **out of countenance** disconcerted. **put out of countenance** disconcert.
■ **countenanced** *adjective* having a countenance (of a specified kind) L16.

countenance /ˈkaʊnt(ə)nəns, -tɪn-/ *verb.* LME.
[ORIGIN from the noun.]
▸ †**I** *verb intrans.* **1** Gesture. Only in LME.
2 Assume a particular demeanour; behave (*as if*), pretend. L15–E16.
▸ **II** *verb trans.* †**3** Face *out*, persist in maintaining; (of a thing) bear *out*, confirm. E16–E17.
4 Give approval to; sanction, permit; favour, encourage. M16.

> SHAKES. *2 Hen. IV* I beseech you, sir, to countenance William Visor . . against Clement Perkes. C. POTOK He disagreed with Reb Saunders . . but he would countenance no slander against his name.

†5 Make a show of, feign. *rare* (Spenser). Only in L16.
†6 Keep in countenance (by acting in accordance with); be in keeping with. *rare* (Shakes.). Only in E17.

> SHAKES. *Macb.* As from your graves rise up . . To countenance this horror!

■ **countenancer** *noun* a person who gives approval, support, or encouragement E17.

counter /ˈkaʊntə/ *noun*¹. Also (now only in sense 6) **compter**. ME.
[ORIGIN Anglo-Norman *count(e)our*, Old French *conteo(i)r* (mod. *comptoir*), from medieval Latin *computatorium*, from Latin *computare* COMPUTE *verb*: see -ER². Not formally distinguished in Anglo-Norman from source of COUNTER *noun*². Cf. also COMPTOIR.]
▸ **I** **1** Something used in counting or keeping count; *esp.* a small disc of metal, plastic, etc., used for keeping account or as a piece marking position etc. in a game. ME.
2 An imitation coin; a token representing a coin. Also, debased coin; *derog.* money generally; anything worthless. LME.
▸ **II** †**3** A table or desk for counting money. ME–L16.
†4 A counting house. LME–E19.
5 A banker's or money-changer's table; the table etc. in a shop on which money is counted out and across which goods are delivered; a similar structure where service is provided in a library, cafeteria, etc. L17.

> M. INNES A counter ineptly piled with *démodé* goods.

nail to the counter: see NAIL *verb*. **over the counter** (*a*) by ordinary purchase in a shop, *spec.* without prescription; (*b*) by direct transaction outside the stock exchange system. **under the counter** surreptitiously, *esp.* illegally.
▸ **III** Also **C-**.
6 The prison attached to a city court; *esp.* (the name of) any of certain prisons for debtors in London, Southwark, and elsewhere. *obsolete* exc. *hist.* LME.
†7 The office, court, or hall of justice of a mayor. L15–M18.
– COMB.: **counter-caster** *arch.* & *poet.* a person who reckons with counters, *derog.* an arithmetician; **counter-jumper** *colloq.* (*derog.*) a shop assistant; **counter lunch**: served at the counter of a public house etc.; **counterman** a man who serves at a counter.

counter /ˈkaʊntə/ *noun*². LME.
[ORIGIN Partly from Anglo-Norman *count(e)our*, Old French *conteor* from Latin *computator*, from *computare* COMPUTE *verb*: see -OR. Partly from COUNT *verb* + -ER¹. Cf. COUNTER *noun*¹, COUNTOUR.]
†1 = COUNTOUR. LME–L15.
2 A person who counts or calculates. LME.
3 An apparatus for counting; *spec.* (PHYSICS) = ***RADIATION counter***. E19.
Geiger counter, ***rev counter***, ***scintillation counter***, etc. ***kern counter***: see KERN *noun*². ***proportional counter***: see PROPORTIONAL *adjective* 2.

counter /ˈkaʊntə/ *noun*³. LME.
[ORIGIN from COUNTER-.]
1 HUNTING. The opposite direction to that taken by the game. LME.
2 The contrary, the opposite. LME.
3 MUSIC. A voice or part contrasting with (and usu. lower than) the principal melody or part. Also, a counter-tenor voice or part. LME.
4 The enclosed part of a printed or written character. L19.
5 SKATING. A figure in which the body is revolved in a direction opposite to that in which it was revolved in the previous turns. L19.

counter /ˈkaʊntə/ *noun*[4]. L15.

[ORIGIN French *contre* corresp. to Italian *contro*, use as noun of preposition, formed as CONTRA.]

1 FENCING. A circular parry. L15.

2 BOXING. A blow returned in response to the opponent's. M19.

counter /ˈkaʊntə/ *noun*[5]. E16.

[ORIGIN Uncertain: perh. rel. to COUNTER *noun*[3].]

1 The part of a horse's breast between the shoulders and under the neck. Now *rare*. E16.

2 The curved part of the stern of a ship. E17.

counter /ˈkaʊntə/ *noun*[6]. M19.

[ORIGIN Abbreviation of COUNTERFORT.]

The back part of a boot or shoe, round the heel.

counter /ˈkaʊntə/ *adjective*. L16.

[ORIGIN Independent use of COUNTER-.]

Acting in opposition; lying or tending in the opposite direction; opposed, opposite; duplicate, serving as a check.

> K. CLARK The loose swinging movement, the twist and counter twist. U. LE GUIN This idea was so counter to Shevek's habits of thinking that . . he suppressed it at once.

counter /ˈkaʊntə/ *verb*. ME.

[ORIGIN In branch I aphet. from ENCOUNTER *verb*; in branch II infl. by COUNTER-, COUNTER *noun*[4].]

► †**I 1** *verb trans. & intrans.* Meet. ME–E19.

2 *verb trans. & intrans.* (with *with*). Meet in opposition; engage in combat. ME–E19.

► **II 3** *verb trans.* Act or speak against; contradict, oppose; answer with a countermove; counterbalance. LME. ►**b** BOXING & WRESTLING. Meet (a blow, move, etc.) with or *with* a counterblow, countermove, etc. E19.

> J. C. POWYS The revolutionary ideas of the man were countered by the inflexible Toryism of the woman. **b** J. B. MORTON She countered my double-lock with a half-Nelson.

†**4** *verb intrans.* Engage in argument; retort *against*, dispute *with*. LME–L16.

5 *verb intrans.* Make a move or reply in response; respond (*with*); BOXING & WRESTLING give a counterblow, make a countermove. M19.

> J. AGATE Coming up to me and saying: 'Sir, a bone to pick with you,' and me countering with . . 'Madam, a whole skeleton!'

counter /ˈkaʊntə/ *adverb*. LME.

[ORIGIN Old French & mod. French *contre* formed as CONTRA. Due mainly to analysis of verbs etc. in COUNTER-.]

1 In the opposite direction; back again. LME.

go counter, **hunt counter**, **run counter**: in a direction opposite to that taken by the quarry.

†**2** In opposite directions to each other. Only in 17.

3 In opposition; contrary. M17.

> CARLYLE Sigismund voted clearly so, and Jobst said nothing counter.

run counter to be or act contrary to.

counter- /ˈkaʊntə/ *prefix*.

[ORIGIN Anglo-Norman *countre-*, Old French & mod. French *contre-*, formed as CONTRA-.]

A freely productive prefix forming verbs, nouns, and adjectives.

1 Forming verbs from verbs, with the senses 'against, in the opposite direction', as ***counteract***, ***counterbrace***, etc.; 'with the opposite effect, so as to rival or frustrate', as ***countercharm***, ***counterwork***, etc.; 'in response, reciprocally', as ***counterargue***, ***counterclaim***, etc.

2 Forming nouns from nouns, with the senses 'contrary, opposed (in direction or effect), reciprocal', as ***counter-attack***, ***countercurrent***, ***countermarch***, ***counter-reformation***, etc.; also 'corresponding, matching', as ***counterbalance***, ***counterfoil***, etc.; 'substitute, secondary', as ***counterdrain***, ***counterearth***, etc.; 'false', as ***counterprophet*** etc.

3 Forming adjectives from adjectives and nouns, with the senses 'contrary to, in opposition to', as ***counternatural*** etc.; 'turned in the opposite direction, placed on opposite sides', as ***counterpassant*** etc.; 'reversed, interchanged', as ***counter-coloured*** etc.

■ **counter-agency** *noun* agency in opposition (*to* something) M19. **counter-agent** *noun* = COUNTERACTIVE *noun* E19. **counter-arch** *noun & verb* (**a**) *noun* an inverted arch opposite to another arch; an arch connecting counterforts at the top; (**b**) *verb trans.* provide or support with a counter-arch: E18. **counter-ˈargue** *verb trans. & intrans.* argue against or in return M17. **counter-argument** *noun* an argument on the opposite side or against anything M19. **counter-attack** *noun & verb* (**a**) *noun* an attack (*lit. & fig.*) in reply to an attack by an enemy or opponent; (**b**) *verb trans. & intrans.* make a counter-attack (on): L19. **counter-attraction** *noun* an attraction of a contrary tendency; a rival attraction, tending to draw attention away from another M18. **counter-battery** *noun* †(**a**) a counter-attack made with artillery; (**b**) a battery raised against another: L16. **counterbid** *noun* a bid made in return, *esp.* a takeover bid made in response to another bid for the same company M20. **counter-bill** *noun* the counterpart or duplicate of a bill L16. **counterblast** *noun* an energetic declaration or action in opposition (*to*) M16. **counterblow** *noun* a blow given in return; a blow resulting from a rebound: M17. **counterbond** *noun* a bond to indemnify a person who has entered into a bond for another L16. **counter-book** *noun* a duplicate account book to serve as a check E17. **counterbuff** *noun & verb* †(**a**) *noun* a counterblow; a rebuff; an exchange of blows; (**b**) *verb trans.* (*arch.*) strike in return; meet (a blow) with another blow; rebuff: L16. †**counter-cast** *noun* (*rare*, Spenser) an antagonistic artifice: only in L16. **countercharge** *noun* a charge brought in opposition to another or against an accuser E18. **countercharge** *verb trans.* (**a**) charge with an opposing or contrary charge; †(**b**) oppose with a contrary charge: E17. **counter-charm** *noun* a counteracting charm E17. **counterˈcharm** *verb trans.* (now *rare*) neutralize the effect of (a charm), affect with an opposing charm L16. **counterclaim** *noun & verb* (**a**) *noun* a claim made to rebut a previous claim; LAW a claim made by a defendant against a plaintiff; (**b**) *verb trans. & intrans.* make a counterclaim (against); L18. **counterclaimant** *noun* a person who makes a counterclaim L19. **counterˈclockwise** *adjective & adverb* = ANTICLOCKWISE L19. **counter-ˈcoloured** *adjective* (HERALDRY) having the tinctures interchanged in opposite or corresponding parts; counterchanged: L16. †**counter-componed** *adjective* = COUNTER-COMPONY L16–E18. **counter-comˈpony** *adjective* (HERALDRY) composed of two conjoined rows of squares of alternate tinctures E17. **countercross** *verb intrans.* (*rare*) cross in contrary directions E17. **counterˈcultural** *adjective* of, pertaining to, or characteristic of a counterculture L20. **counterculture** *noun* a mode of life deliberately deviating from established social practices; a group that has adopted such a lifestyle: L20. **counterˈculturist** *noun* a person who belongs to or shows sympathy with a counterculture L20. †**countercuff** *noun* a blow given in return or to parry another L16–E18. **countercurrent** *noun & adjective* (**a**) *noun* an opposite flow or trend; (**b**) *adjective* running in the opposite direction; involving countercurrents: L16. **counterˈcurrently** *adverb* against another current M20. **countercycle** *noun* an economic change or trend stimulated by a government to mitigate or compensate for the effects of fluctuation in business or in the national economy M20. **counterˈcyclical** *adjective* of or pertaining to a countercycle, having the nature or effect of a countercycle M20. **counter-disenˈgage** *noun & verb* (FENCING) (**a**) *noun* the action of disengaging; a riposte made by this means; (**b**) *verb intrans.* disengage and make a thrust as the opponent changes the engagement: L18. **counter-disenˈgagement** *noun* = COUNTER-DISENGAGE *noun* L19. †**counterdistinct** *adjective* = CONTRADISTINCT M–L17. †**counterdistinction** *noun* = CONTRADISTINCTION: only in 17. †**counterdistinguish** *verb trans.* = CONTRADISTINGUISH E17–M18. **counter-earth** *noun* = ANTICHTHON 2 M19. **counter-elite** *noun* an elite that replaces another elite after the latter is overthrown M20. **counter-emˈbattled** *adjective* (HERALDRY) (of an ordinary) embattled on both sides with the battlements on one side opposite the indentures on the other (cf. BRETESSY) M19. **counter-eˈnamel** *verb trans.* enamel on the back as well as the front L19. **counter-ˈespionage** *noun* action directed against espionage by an enemy L19. **counter-ˈetch** *verb & noun* (**a**) *verb trans.* treat (a lithographic plate) with dilute acid to make it clean and receptive to grease; (**b**) *noun* the process of counter-etching; the acid solution used for it: E20. **counter-evidence** *noun* evidence tending to rebut other evidence M17. **counter-exˈtend** *verb trans.* (MEDICINE) exercise counter-extension on (a limb etc.) M17. **counter-extension** *noun* (MEDICINE) the action of pulling on or holding the upper part of a limb so as to oppose extension applied to the lower part M19. **counter-faller** *noun* in a spinning mule, a wire which passes between the yarns, when pressed down by the faller wire, so as to keep the tension uniform M19. **counter-fire** *noun & verb* (**a**) *noun* a fire lit deliberately in order to combat a heath or forest fire; (**b**) *verb intrans.* use a counter-fire: L19. **counterˈfleury**, **-ˈflory** *adjective* (HERALDRY) (of an ordinary) having flowers on each side set opposite each other in pairs L16. **counter-ˈflowered** *adjective* = COUNTERFLEURY L18. **counterfoil** *noun* the complementary part of a cheque, official receipt, etc., with a note of the particulars, retained by the person issuing such a document E18. **counterforce** *noun & adjective* (**a**) *noun* a force acting or maintained in opposition to another; (**b**) *adjective* based on or involving nuclear retaliation against military forces or bases: E17. **counter-goˈbony** *adjective* (HERALDRY) = COUNTER-COMPONY M19. **counter-ˈindicate** *verb trans.* = CONTRAINDICATE L19. **counter-indication** *noun* = CONTRAINDICATION M18. **counter-influence** *noun* an opposing influence M19. †**counter-influence** *verb trans.* influence in the opposite direction: only in M17. **counter-inˈsurgency** *noun* military or political action taken against revolutionaries or guerrillas M20. **counter-intelligence** *noun* activity intended to stop information from reaching the enemy, counter-espionage M20. **counter-interroˈgation** *noun* cross-examination E19. **counter-inˈtuitive** *adjective* contrary to intuition M20. **counter-ion** *noun* an ion of opposite charge associated with a substance or particle M20. **counterˈirritant** *noun* (MEDICINE) something used to produce irritation of the skin in order to counteract a more deep-seated symptom or disease; *fig.* an irritant that acts as a distraction from another: M19. **counterirriˈtation** *noun* (the use of) a counterirritant M19. **counterlath** *noun & verb* (**a**) *noun* a lath or rafter laid between two more substantial or more accurately placed ones; (**b**) *verb trans.* provide with counterlaths or counterlathing: M17. **counterlathing** *noun* laths for plastering nailed to fillets on beams or timber M19. †**counter-letter** *noun* a letter countermanding another letter E17–E19. **counter-marque** *noun* (*obsolete* exc. *hist.*) reprisals against letters of marque E16. **counter-mart** *noun* (*obsolete* exc. *hist.*) [alt.] = COUNTER-MARQUE E18. **counterˈmatch** *verb trans.* †(**a**) *rare* match (one thing) against another; (**b**) be a match for, counterbalance: L16. **countermeasure** *noun* an action taken to counteract a danger, threat, etc. E20. **countermelody** *noun* a subordinate melody accompanying a principal one M20. **countermissile** *noun* a missile designed to intercept and destroy another missile, an anti-missile missile M20. **counter-motion** *noun* (**a**) motion in the opposite direction; (**b**) a motion contrary to one already proposed: E17. **countermove** *noun & verb* (**a**) *noun* a move or action in opposition to another; (**b**) *verb intrans.* move in an opposite direction or opposite directions: M19. **countermovement** *noun* a movement in opposition, a contrary movement E19. **counteroffensive** *noun* (esp. MILITARY) an offensive action designed to allow escape from a defensive situation M20. **counter-offer** *noun* an offer made in return, esp. by a company to one making a takeover bid for it L18. **counter-opening** *noun* an opening opposite another, *esp.* a surgical one LME. †**counterpace** *noun* (**a**) *rare* a movement in a contrary direction; (**b**) a step taken against something: L16–M18. **counter-passant** *adjective* (HERALDRY) walking in opposite directions, repassant E17. **counter-passion** *noun* (**a**) a passion opposed to or the opposite of another; †(**b**) an outburst of passion against something: L16. **counter-penalty** *noun* [translating Greek *antitimēsis*] GREEK HISTORY the penalty which an accused person who had been pronounced guilty suggested in opposition to that called for by the accuser M19. **counter-plea** *noun* (LAW) an answer to a plea or request, giving arguments why it should not be admitted E16. **counterplot** *noun* a plot contrived to defeat another plot E17. **counterplot** *verb* (**a**) *verb intrans.* make a counterplot *against*; (**b**) *verb trans.* plot against, frustrate by a counterplot: L16. **counter-pole** *noun* the opposite pole M19. **counter-ˈpotent** *adjective* (HERALDRY) (of a fur) having potents of the same tincture arranged base to base as in countervair E17. **counter-pressure** *noun* opposite or contrary pressure M17. †**counter-price** *noun* [translating Greek *anti-lutron* in *1 Timothy* 2:6] a ransom L17–E18. **counter-prolifeˈration** *noun* action intended to stop an increase in the possession of nuclear weapons L20. **counterproof** *noun* †(**a**) proof to the contrary; (**b**) PRINTING an impression taken from a freshly printed image, appearing the same way round as the image on the original printing surface: E17. **counterˈprove** *verb trans.* †(**a**) disprove; (**b**) take a counterproof of: L17. **counter-question** *noun* a question put in response to another person's question M19. **counter-ˈquestioning** *noun* the asking of counter-questions M19. **counter-revoˈlution** *noun* a revolution opposed to an earlier one or reversing its results L18. **counter-revoˈlutionary** *noun & adjective* (**a**) *noun* a person who takes part in, supports, or works for a counter-revolution; (**b**) *adjective* pertaining to or of the nature of a counter-revolution: L18. **counter-rhythm** *noun* a subordinate rhythm acting as counterbalance to a main rhythm E20. **counter-ˈsalient** *adjective* (HERALDRY) (of two animals borne as charges) salient in opposite directions E17. **counter-scale** *noun* the opposite scale (of the balance) (chiefly *fig.*) M17. **counter-seˈcure** *verb trans.* (**a**) secure (a person) against the risk he or she incurs by becoming security for another; (**b**) give an additional security to: M17. **countersense** *noun* [French *contresens*] a meaning opposed to the true sense M17. **countershading** *noun* coloration (esp. of a bird or animal) in which parts normally in shadow are light and those exposed to the sky are dark L19. **countershaft** *noun* an intermediate shaft transmitting drive from one shaft to another or to an individual machine M19. **counterslope** *noun* (**a**) the opposite slope of a hill etc.; a slope in the opposite direction; (**b**) an overhanging slope: M19. **counter-spell** *noun* a spell against something; a spell to dissolve another spell: E18. **counterspy** *noun* a spy engaged in counter-espionage M20. **counterstain** *noun & verb* (**a**) *noun* an additional dye used in a microscopy specimen to produce a contrasting background to the parts of interest or to make clearer the distinction between different kinds of tissue etc.; (**b**) *verb trans. & intrans.* treat with or use a counterstain: L19. **counter-step** *noun* a step in opposition or in the opposite direction E18. **counterstroke** *noun* (**a**) a stroke given in return; (**b**) = CONTRECOUP *noun* 2: L16. **countersubject** *noun* (MUSIC) a second or subsidiary subject, esp. accompanying the subject or its answer in a fugue M19. †**countersway** *verb trans.* forcibly move or incline to the opposite side M17–E18. **counterterrorism** *noun* political or military activities designed to prevent or thwart terrorism M20. **counter-tide** *noun* a tide running against the main or usual current L16. **counter-title** *noun* (LAW) a title to property in opposition to another title E19. **countertrade** *noun* (**a**) = ANTITRADE *noun*; (**b**) international trade in which goods are exchanged instead of cash paid: E20. **countertype** *noun* †(**a**) = ANTITYPE; (**b**) a parallel, a counterpart; (**c**) an opposite type: E17. **counterˈvair** *noun* (HERALDRY) a variety of vair in which the bells or shield-shaped forms of the same tincture are placed base to base M18. **countervaˈllation** *noun* (*rare*) = CONTRAVALLATION L17. **counterˈvalue** *noun & adjective* (**a**) *noun* equivalent value; (**b**) *adjective* based on or involving nuclear retaliation against civilian targets: M17. **counterview** *noun* †(**a**) a view from opposite sides or in opposite directions; a contrasting or confronting position; (**b**) *rare* the opposite opinion: L16. **counter-walk** *noun* (now *rare* or *obsolete*) a smaller parallel path as an accessory to a main path M17.

counteract /kaʊntərˈakt/ *verb trans.* L17.

[ORIGIN from COUNTER- 1 + ACT *verb*.]

1 Hinder or defeat by contrary action; neutralize the action or effect of. L17.

> T. H. HUXLEY The weight upon the upper surface is counteracted by the upward pressure of the air on the under surface. A. STORR The therapist may be able to counteract the depressive's negative view of his own accomplishments.

†**2** Act in opposition to; oppose. E18–M19.

> J. WILLOCK I had counteracted his intentions often before, especially in going to sea . . against his inclinations.

■ **counteractant** *noun* = COUNTERACTIVE *noun* L19. **counteraction** *noun* (**a**) the action of counteracting; opposition; (**b**) a counteracting influence or force: M18. **counteractive** *adjective & noun* (**a**) *adjective* tending to counteract; (**b**) *noun* a counteracting agent or force: E19.

counter-approach /ˈkaʊnt(ə)rəprəʊtʃ/ *noun*. Also (earlier) †**contre-**. L17.

[ORIGIN French *contre-approche*, from *contre-* COUNTER- + *approche* APPROACH *noun*.]

MILITARY. A work constructed outside permanent fortifications by a besieged force, to check and command the works of the besiegers. Usu. in *pl.*

counterbalance /ˈkaʊntəbal(ə)ns/ *noun*. L16.

[ORIGIN from COUNTER- 2 + BALANCE *noun*.]

†**1** The opposite side of a balance. *rare*. Only in L16.

2 A weight used to balance another weight; *spec.* one used to balance the weight of a rotating or an ascending and descending part, so as to facilitate movement. E17.

3 *fig.* A power, influence, emotion, etc., which balances the effect of a contrary one. M17.

counterbalance /kaʊntəˈbal(ə)ns/ *verb trans.* **L16.**
[ORIGIN from COUNTER- 1 + BALANCE *verb*.]
†**1** Of a person: weigh or balance (one thing) against another. (Foll. by *to*, *with*.) **L16–E17.**
2 Of a thing: act as a counterbalance to. **E17.**
3 *fig.* Balance or cancel the effect of. **M17.**

†**counterband** *noun, adjective, & verb.* **E16.**
[ORIGIN Alt. of Spanish *contrabanda* CONTRABAND *noun*: see COUNTER-.]
▸ **A** *noun & adjective.* = CONTRABAND *noun & adjective.* **E16–E19.**
▸ **B** *verb trans.* = CONTRABAND *verb.* **M17–E18.**

counterbass /ˈkaʊntəbeɪs/ *noun.* Long *rare* or *obsolete.* Also **-base.** **L16.**
[ORIGIN from COUNTER- 2 + BASS *noun*[2] after Italian CONTRABASSO.]
MUSIC. = CONTRABASS *noun* 1.

counterbore /ˈkaʊntəbɔː/ *noun.* **L19.**
[ORIGIN from COUNTER- 2 + BORE *noun*[1].]
1 A drilled hole that has a flat-bottomed enlargement at its mouth. **L19.**
2 A drill whose bit has a uniform smaller diameter near the tip, for drilling counterbores in one operation. **L19.**

counterbore /ˈkaʊntəbɔː; *in sense 1* kaʊntəˈbɔː/ *verb.* **E17.**
[ORIGIN Sense 1 from COUNTER- 1 + BORE *verb*[1]; sense 2 from the noun.]
1 *verb intrans.* Bore in the opposite direction. Now *rare* or *obsolete.* **E17.**
2 *verb intrans. & trans.* Drill a counterbore (in). **L19.**

counterchange /ˈkaʊntətʃeɪndʒ/ *noun.* **L16.**
[ORIGIN French *contrechange* (= Italian *contraccambio*), formed as COUNTER-, CHANGE *noun*.]
1 Exchange of one thing for another. Long *rare.* **L16.** ▸†**b** Equal or equivalent return; requital. **L16–M17.**
†**2** Transposition. **L16–E17.**
3 Patterning in which a dark motif on a light ground alternates with the same motif light on a dark ground. **L19.**

counterchange /ˈkaʊntətʃeɪndʒ/ *verb.* **LME.**
[ORIGIN French *contrechanger*, formed as COUNTER-, CHANGE *verb*.]
1 *verb trans.* *HERALDRY.* Interchange the tincture of (a charge) with that of the field when the latter is of two tinctures; interchange (tinctures) in this way. Chiefly as ***counterchanged ppl adjective.*** **LME.** ▸**b** Chequer; mark *with* contrasting shades etc. **E17.**
†**2** *verb trans.* Exchange for or *for* another. **L16–M17.**
3 *verb trans.* Change to the opposite (position, state, quality); transpose. Long *rare.* **E17.**
4 *verb intrans.* Change places or parts. **M19.**

countercheck /ˈkaʊntətʃɛk/ *noun.* **M16.**
[ORIGIN from COUNTER- 2 + CHECK *noun*[1].]
1 A rebuke or reproof in reply to or in return for one given; a retort. Long *rare.* **M16.**
2 A restraint that opposes something; a check. **L16.**
3 A restraint that operates against another restraint. **M19.**

countercheck /ˈkaʊntətʃɛk/ *verb trans.* **L16.**
[ORIGIN from COUNTER- 1 + CHECK *verb*[1].]
†**1** Rebuke or reprove in return or as an expression of opposition. Only in **L16.**
2 Check or arrest by contrary action. **L16.**

counterfactual /kaʊntəˈfaktʃʊəl/ *adjective & noun.* **M20.**
[ORIGIN from COUNTER- 3 + FACTUAL *adjective*. Cf. CONTRAFACTUAL.]
PHILOSOPHY. ▸**A** *adjective.* Pertaining to or expressing what has not happened or is not the case. **M20.**
▸ **B** *noun.* A counterfactual conditional statement. **M20.**
■ **counterfactually** *adverb* contrary to fact **M20.**

†**counterfeisance** *noun.* **L16–M17.**
[ORIGIN Old French *contrefaisance*, from *contrefaire*: see COUNTERFEIT *adjective & noun*, -ANCE.]
The action of counterfeiting; deceit, fraud, imposture.

counterfeit /ˈkaʊntəfɪt, -fiːt/ *adjective & noun.* **LME.**
[ORIGIN Anglo-Norman *co(u)ntrefet*, Old French & mod. French *contrefait* pa. pple of *contrefaire* from Proto-Romance (medieval Latin) *contrafacere*, formed as CONTRA- + Latin *facere* make.]
▸ **A** *adjective* (orig. *pa. pple*).
1 Made in imitation, not genuine; made of inferior materials; forged. **LME.**

W. S. JEVONS It is difficult to make any counterfeit gold or silver. M. HOLROYD A counterfeit Van Dyck to hang in his dining-room.

2 Pretended, feigned, sham; falsely represented or representing oneself to be (what is denoted by the noun). **LME.** ▸†**b** Misrepresenting oneself, deceitful. **M16–M18.**

T. CHALMERS The counterfeit and the worthless Poor do a world of mischief to the cause of beneficence. J. H. NEWMAN I also warn you against a counterfeit earnestness.

counterfeit crank: see CRANK *noun*[3].
†**3** Made to a pattern, fashioned. **LME–M16.**
†**4** Disguised, transformed in appearance. **LME–E18.**
†**5** Misshapen, deformed. **LME–L16.**
†**6** Represented in a picture, writing, etc.; portrayed. **L16–M19.**

SHAKES. *Haml.* Look here upon this picture and on this, the counterfeit presentment of two brothers.

▸ **B** *noun.* **1** A false or spurious imitation; something not genuine; something made of inferior materials; a forgery. **LME.**

J. ARBUTHNOT He has the original deed . . the others are counterfeits. LD MACAULAY One who does not value real glory, will not value its counterfeit.

2 †**a** A representation in painting, sculpture, etc.; an image; a portrait. **LME–M19.** ▸**b** *fig.* A copy, a likeness. *arch.* **L16.**

a SHAKES. *Merch. V.* What find I here? Fair Portia's counterfeit! **b** J. D. LONG Entranced at such A counterfeit of his own filial love.

†**3** A pretender, an impostor. **L15–M18.**
†**4** A deformed person. **M–L16.**
■ **counterfeitly** *adverb* **M16.** **counterfeitness** *noun* **M16.**

counterfeit /ˈkaʊntəfɪt, -fiːt/ *verb.* **ME.**
[ORIGIN Anglo-Norman *countrefeter*, from *countrefet* pa. pple: see COUNTERFEIT *adjective & noun*.]
▸ **I** *verb trans.* **1** Imitate (an action, thing, etc.) with intent to deceive; make a fraudulent imitation of (money etc.). **ME.**

G. BERKELEY That it be felony to counterfeit the notes of this bank. K. AMIS He . . moved off counterfeiting a heavy limp.

†**2** Assume the character of (a person); pass oneself off as, impersonate. **ME–E17.**

BACON To counterfeite and personate the second sone of Edward the Fourth, supposed to be murdered.

†**3** Imitate, without intending to deceive; follow the example of (a person); copy (a fashion etc.). **ME–E17.**

JAMES I Counterfeiting the maners of others. M. WROTH Her complexion . . never was . . equald, or could be counterfeited.

4 Feign (a feeling, state, etc.). Formerly also, pretend *to be*, *that*. **LME.**

SHAKES. *A.Y.L.* Take a good heart and counterfeit to be a man. S. JOHNSON To counterfeit happiness which they do not feel.

5 Have the appearance of; resemble, be like. **LME.**

S. LEACOCK The scales of the fish counterfeit the glistening water of the brook.

6 Make in fraudulent imitation of something else; devise (something spurious) and pass it off as genuine. **LME.**

T. HERBERT He lost a Ring of Gold . . he conceals the loss, and counterfeits another like it of silver.

†**7** Make in imitation, without intending to deceive. **LME–L16.**
†**8** Represent by a picture, in writing, etc.; delineate, portray. **LME–M17.**
†**9** Put a false or deceptive appearance on; disguise, falsify; adulterate. **LME–E18.**

DEFOE I counterfeited my voice.

▸ **II** *verb intrans.* **10** Make pretence, practise deceit. Long *rare.* **LME.**

SHAKES. *Twel. N.* Are you not mad indeed, or do you but counterfeit?

■ **counterfeiter** *noun* (**a**) a maker of fraudulent imitations, *spec.* a maker of counterfeit coins; (**b**) a pretender, a dissembler; (**c**) an imitator (with no intent to deceive): **LME.**

counterfort /ˈkaʊntəfɔːt/ *noun.* **L16.**
[ORIGIN French *contrefort*, from Old French *contreforcier* prop, buttress.]
A buttress or projecting piece of masonry to support and strengthen a wall or terrace, esp. as part of a fortification.

counterglow /ˈkaʊntəgləʊ/ *noun.* **M19.**
[ORIGIN from COUNTER- 2 + GLOW *noun*, as translation of German *Gegenschein*.]
= GEGENSCHEIN.

counterguard /ˈkaʊntəgɑːd/ *noun.* **E16.**
[ORIGIN French *contregarde*, formed as COUNTER-, GUARD *noun*.]
†**1** An extra guard to act as a check on another, or as a reserve defence. **E16–M17.**
2 *FORTIFICATION.* A narrow detached rampart immediately in front of an important work to prevent it from being breached. **L16.**

countermand /kaʊntəˈmɑːnd/ *noun.* **L15.**
[ORIGIN Old French *contremand*, formed as COUNTERMAND *verb*.]
1 A command or order that revokes or annuls a previous one. **L15.**
†**2** A prohibition. **L16–L17.**
3 *LAW.* An action that has the effect of making void something previously executed. **E17.**

countermand /kaʊntəˈmɑːnd/ *verb trans.* **LME.**
[ORIGIN Old French *contremander* from medieval Latin *contramandare*, formed as CONTRA- + Latin *mandare* command.]
▸ **I** Implying the cancellation of an earlier command.
1 Command the opposite of; revoke (a command) by a contrary one. **LME.**

Q. BELL She proposed . . a second visit to the shop to countermand the order. W. GOLDING I can find no one who has the authority to countermand this singularly foolish order.

†**2** Order (a person *to do* something, or *that* something be done) in reversal of a command already issued. **LME–M16.**
3 Recall (a person, forces, etc.) by a contrary order. **LME.**

GOLDSMITH Our regiment is countermanded.

4 Stop or prohibit (what has been commanded, ordered, or allowed); cancel an order for (goods etc.). **M16.**
▸ †**II** Without the implication of branch I.
5 Go counter to or oppose the command of (a person in authority). **L16–M17.**
6 Give a command against, prohibit. **L16–M17.**
7 Control, keep under command. **L16–M17.**

C. MARLOWE And all the sea my galleys countermand.

8 Counteract; counterbalance. **M17–E18.**
■ **countermandable** *adjective* **E17.** **countermander** *noun* (now *rare*) **M17.**

countermarch /ˈkaʊntəmɑːtʃ/ *noun.* **L16.**
[ORIGIN from COUNTER- 2 + MARCH *noun*[3].]
1 A march (*lit. & fig.*) in the opposite direction. **L16.**
2 *MILITARY HISTORY.* An evolution by which a column turns to face in the opposite direction while retaining the same order, so that those at the front are finally at the rear. **M17.**
3 A march held as a demonstration opposing another march. **M20.**

countermarch /ˈkaʊntəmɑːtʃ/ *verb intrans. & trans.* **E17.**
[ORIGIN from COUNTER- 1 + MARCH *verb*[2].]
1 *MILITARY HISTORY.* (Cause to) execute a countermarch. **E17.**
2 (Cause to) march in a contrary direction; march back. **M17.**

countermark /ˈkaʊntəmɑːk/ *noun.* **E16.**
[ORIGIN French *contremarque*, formed as COUNTER-, MARQUE *noun*[2].]
An additional mark placed on something already marked, e.g. for increased security; a second watermark.

countermine /ˈkaʊntəmʌɪn/ *noun & verb.* **LME.**
[ORIGIN from COUNTER- 2 + MINE *noun*.]
▸ **A** *noun.* **1** *MILITARY.* A subterranean excavation made by defenders to intercept one made by besiegers. **LME.**
2 *fig.* A counterplot. **L16.**
▸ **B** *verb.* **1** *verb trans. & intrans.* Make a countermine (against). **L16.**
2 *verb trans.* Defeat by a counterplot. **L16.**
3 *verb intrans.* Lay mines intended to explode an enemy's mines. **L19.**
■ **counterminer** *noun* **L17.**

countermure /ˈkaʊntəmjʊə/ *noun.* **E16.**
[ORIGIN Old French & mod. French *contremur*, formed as COUNTER- + *mur* wall.]
1 A defensive wall raised inside another wall, in case of a breach in the latter. **E16.**
2 An outer wall round a city. **M16.**
3 A wall or mound raised outside a fortress to help besiegers. **M16.**
4 *fig.* A strong defence. **L16.**

countermure /ˈkaʊntəmjʊə/ *verb trans.* **LME.**
[ORIGIN French *contremurer*, formed as COUNTERMURE *noun*.]
Defend with a countermure.

counter-order /ˈkaʊntərɔːdə/ *noun.* **L18.**
[ORIGIN from COUNTER- 2 + ORDER *noun*.]
An order contrary to or reversing a previous order.

counter-order /kaʊntərˈɔːdə/ *verb trans.* **M17.**
[ORIGIN from COUNTER- 1 + ORDER *verb*.]
Give an order against, countermand.

†**counterpane** *noun*[1]. **L15.**
[ORIGIN Anglo-Norman *countrepan*, formed as COUNTER- + Old French *pan* piece, part.]
1 = COUNTERPART 2, 3, 4. **L15–L17.**
2 *LAW.* The counterpart of an indenture. **E16–L17.**

counterpane /ˈkaʊntəpeɪn/ *noun*[2]. **E17.**
[ORIGIN Alt. of COUNTERPOINT *noun*[2] by assim. to PANE *noun*[1].]
A bedspread, usu. woven in raised figures, quilted, etc.; a quilt.

counterpart /ˈkaʊntəpɑːt/ *noun.* **LME.**
[ORIGIN from COUNTER- 2 + PART *noun* after Old French & mod. French *contrepartie*.]
1 *LAW.* The opposite part of an indenture; each of two or more similar copies of a deed or lease, *esp.* one not regarded as the principal one. **LME.**
2 Either of two parts which fit and complete each other; a person or thing forming a natural complement to another. **M17.**

HAZLITT Popular fury finds its counterpart in courtly servility.

†**3** A duplicate, an exact copy. **L17–E18.**
4 A person or thing so like another as to appear a duplicate; an equivalent; a person or thing with an exactly comparable function etc., esp. at a different time or in a different context. **L17.**

W. IRVING A full-length portrait . . the very counterpart of his visitor of the preceding night. H. CARPENTER The middle-class Englishman of 1851, like his counterpart a century later.

5 *MUSIC.* A part written to accompany another. **E18.**
– COMB.: **counterpart fund** a sum of money in local currency equivalent to goods or services received from abroad.

counterpoint /ˈkaʊntəpɔɪnt/ *noun*¹ & *verb*. LME.
[ORIGIN In branch I from Old French & mod. French *contrepoint* from medieval Latin *contrapunctum*, *cantus contrapunctus* song pricked or marked opposite (i.e. to the original melody), formed as CONTRA- + medieval Latin *punctus* musical note, use as noun of Latin pa. pple of *pungere* prick. In branch II directly from COUNTER- 2 + POINT *noun*¹.]
▸ **A** *noun* **I 1** The art or practice of combining two or more musical parts in accordance with definite rules so that they are heard simultaneously as independent lines; the style of composition in which this is done; *fig.* a pleasing or effective combination of contrasting things. LME. ▸**b** A melody or part added to another in counterpoint. M16.

S. BRETT The depressing nature of his surroundings seemed, by counterpoint, to enhance his sunny mood.

quadruple counterpoint: see QUADRUPLE *adjective*. **strict counterpoint**: according to rules as an academic exercise, not as an actual composition.
2 The combination of two types of rhythm in a line of verse. L19.
▸ **II** †**3** A contrary point (in an argument). M16–E17.
4 The opposite point. Formerly, the antithesis. L16.
▸ **B** *verb*. **1** *verb intrans.* Compose or play musical counterpoint. *rare*. L19.
2 *verb trans.* Write or add a counterpoint to. L19.
3 *verb trans.* Set in contrast (*against*); emphasize by juxtaposition the contrast between. M20.

†**counterpoint** *noun*². LME–L17.
[ORIGIN Old French *contrepointe*, from alt. of medieval Latin *culcit(r)a puncta* quilted mattress, from *culcit(r)a* cushion, mattress + *puncta* fem. of *punctus* (see COUNTERPOINT *noun*¹ & *verb*).]
A quilted bedcover; a counterpane.

counterpoise /ˈkaʊntəpɔɪz/ *noun*. LME.
[ORIGIN Old French *countrepeis*, *-pois* (mod. *contrepoids*), formed as COUNTER- + POISE *noun*¹.]
1 A weight which balances another weight or establishes equilibrium against a force. LME.
2 Something of equivalent force, effect, etc., on the opposite side. LME. ▸†**b** A compensation; an equivalent. L16–E17.

T. COLLINS Deeming my birth and education a sufficient counterpoise to her wealth. **b** SHAKES. *All's Well* To whom I promise A counterpoise, if not to thy estate A balance more replete.

3 The state of being balanced; equilibrium. L16.

MILTON The pendulous round earth with ballanc't Aire In counterpoise.

4 A horizontal network of conductors connected to a transmitting aerial just above the ground to reduce losses to earth. E20.
5 A conductor or network of conductors buried in the ground and connected to an electricity pylon in order to reduce the risk of flashovers caused by lightning. M20.

counterpoise /ˈkaʊntəpɔɪz/ *verb*. LME.
[ORIGIN from tonic stem of Old French *contrepeser*, formed as COUNTER-, PEISE *verb*. Later assim. to the noun.]
1 *verb trans.* **a** Balance in power, quality, or effect; compensate for. LME. ▸**b** Balance by a weight on the opposite side or acting in opposition; counterbalance. M16.

a HENRY FIELDING A weakness which may counterpoise this merit. **b** W. HARRISON One shilling of siluer in those daies did counterpeise our common ounce.

†**2** *verb intrans.* Act as a counterbalance (*to*, *with*, *against*). LME–M16.

T. NORTON Such a bitternesse of sorrow . . as may in balaunce counterpaise with the trust of pardon.

3 *verb trans.* Bring into or keep in equilibrium. LME.
†**4** *verb trans.* & *intrans.* Consider or ponder carefully. LME–L17.
5 *verb trans.* Compare (a thing) *with* another to ascertain their relative values. L17.

SOUTHEY Who in the deceitful scales Of worldly wisdom, dare to counterpoise The right with the expedient.

counterpoison /ˈkaʊntəpɔɪz(ə)n/ *noun*. M16.
[ORIGIN French *contrepoison*, formed as COUNTER-, POISON *noun*.]
1 A medicine that counteracts the effect of a poison; an antidote (*lit.* & *fig.*). M16.
2 An opposite poison. L18.

counterpose /kaʊntəˈpəʊz/ *verb trans.* L16.
[ORIGIN from COUNTER- 1 + POSE *verb*¹, with influence of COUNTERPOISE *verb* on sense. Cf. CONTRAPOSE.]
Set against or in opposition; counterbalance.

counterposition /ˈkaʊntəpəzɪʃ(ə)n/ *noun*. L16.
[ORIGIN from COUNTER- 2 + POSITION *noun*, in sense 1 after CONTRAPOSITION.]
1 = CONTRAPOSITION 2. L16.
2 An opposite position. M19.

counterproductive /ˌkaʊntəprəˈdʌktɪv/ *adjective*. M20.
[ORIGIN from COUNTER- + PRODUCTIVE.]
Having the opposite of the desired effect; tending to act against the attainment of an objective.

Annual Register These tactics were not only useless but counterproductive.

counterpunch /ˈkaʊntəpʌn(t)ʃ/ *noun* & *verb*. L17.
[ORIGIN from COUNTER- 2 + PUNCH *noun*¹.]
▸ **A** *noun*. **1** A punch used to make a depression in the face of a type founder's punch corresponding to an enclosed non-printing part of a letter. L17.
2 A boxer's counter; a punch or an attack given in return. M20.
▸ **B** *verb*. **1** *verb trans.* Form by means of a counterpunch. L17.
2 *verb intrans.* Of a boxer etc.: make a counterpunch or counterpunches. Chiefly as ***counterpunching*** *verbal noun*. M20.
■ **counterpuncher** *noun* a defensive boxer; a person who retaliates readily or well: M20.

counter-reformation /ˈkaʊntərɛfəˌmeɪʃ(ə)n/ *noun*. Also **Counter-Reformation**. M19.
[ORIGIN from COUNTER- 2 + REFORMATION *noun*¹.]
The activity in the Roman Catholic Church in the 16th and early 17th cents. directed towards countering the effects of the Protestant Reformation.

counter-roll /ˈkaʊntərəʊl/ *noun*. *obsolete* exc. *hist.* E17.
[ORIGIN French †*contrerolle* (now *contrôle*), from medieval Latin *contrarotulus*: see CONTROL *verb*.]
A copy of a roll or document, kept for purposes of checking.
■ †**counterrollment** *noun* the making of an entry in a counter-roll: only in L16.

counterrotate /kaʊntərəʊˈteɪt/ *verb intrans.* M20.
[ORIGIN from COUNTER- 1 + ROTATE *verb*.]
Rotate in opposite directions, esp. about the same axis; (of a propeller) have blades that do this. Chiefly as ***counterrotating*** *ppl adjective* (cf. CONTRA-ROTATING).

counterscarp /ˈkaʊntəskɑːp/ *noun*. L16.
[ORIGIN French *contrescarpe* from Italian *controscarpa*, formed as CONTRA-, SCARP *noun*².]
1 The outer wall or slope of a ditch surrounding a fortification; this slope together with the glacis beyond it. L16.
2 *fig.* A means of defence; a protective barrier. E17.

counter-seal /ˈkaʊntəsiːl/ *noun* & *verb*. Now *hist.* E17.
[ORIGIN Old French *contre-seel*, formed as COUNTER-, SEAL *noun*².]
▸ **A** *noun*. A smaller seal impressed on the reverse of a main seal for further security or sanction. Also, the reverse side of a seal. E17.
▸ †**B** *verb trans.* Seal with a counter-seal. *rare* (Shakes.). Only in E17.

countersign /ˈkaʊntəsʌɪn/ *noun*. L16.
[ORIGIN French *contresigne* from Italian *contrasegno* (now *contrassegno*), formed as CONTRA- + *segno* from Latin *signum* SIGN *noun*.]
1 A sign or signal made in response to another sign; *spec.* a password given on request. L16.
2 A special sign or mark put on something for the purpose of authentication, identification, or reference. L16.

countersign /ˈkaʊntəsʌɪn/ *verb trans.* M17.
[ORIGIN French *contresigner*, formed as COUNTER-, SIGN *verb*¹.]
†**1** Mark with a countersign. Only in M17.
2 Sign (a document) near or in addition to another signature; add one's signature to (a document already signed by another). L17.

C. PEBODY The Secretary of State . . had countersigned the warrant for his arrest.

3 *fig.* Confirm, sanction, ratify. M19.
■ **counterˈsignature** *noun* an additional signature M19.

countersink /ˈkaʊntəsɪŋk/ *verb* & *noun*. L18.
[ORIGIN from COUNTER- 1 + SINK *verb*.]
▸ **A** *verb trans.* Pa. t. & pple **-sunk** /-sʌŋk/.
1 Sink the head of (a screw, bolt, etc.) in a countersink so that it does not protrude. L18.
2 Enlarge the outer part of (a drilled hole) by bevelling the edge. Cf. earlier COUNTERSUNK. M19.
▸ **B** *noun*. **1** A tool for countersinking. L18.
2 A conical enlargement of the outer part of a drilled hole for receiving the head of a screw etc. M19.

countersunk /ˈkaʊntəsʌŋk/ *noun*. L18.
[ORIGIN from pa. pple of COUNTERSINK *verb*.]
= COUNTERSINK *noun* 2.

counter-tenor /kaʊntəˈtɛnə/ *noun*. LME.
[ORIGIN Old French *contreteneur* from Italian †*contratenore*, formed as CONTRA- + *tenore* from Latin TENOR *noun*¹. Cf. CONTRATENOR.]
1 A part higher than a tenor for a man's voice; a male alto. Formerly, a man's part written against the tenor in the same range. LME.
2 A singer with a counter-tenor voice. E16.
3 A counter-tenor voice. L18.

counter-turn /ˈkaʊntətəːn/ *noun*. L16.
[ORIGIN from COUNTER- 2 + TURN *noun*. In sense 1 translating Greek *antistrophē*.]
†**1 a** PROSODY. The continued repetition of the same word at the end of successive clauses. Only in L16. ▸**b** An antistrophe. Only in M17.
2 An unexpected development in the plot of a play etc. at its climax. M17.
3 A turn in the opposite direction. M18.

countervail /kaʊntəˈveɪl/ *verb* & *noun*. LME.
[ORIGIN Anglo-Norman *countrevaloir* repr. Latin *contra valere* be of worth against: see CONTRA, VAIL *verb*¹.]
▸ **A** *verb*. †**1** *verb trans.* Be equivalent to in value. LME–M17.
2 *verb trans.* Make up for (damage, trouble, etc.), be compensation for. Formerly also, give compensation for. LME.

ADDISON It . . more than countervails all the calamities and afflictions which can possibly befal us.

3 *verb intrans.* **a** Be of equal force or weight on the contrary side; avail *against*. (Also foll. by †*with*, †*for*.) LME. ▸†**b** Be equivalent or equal; vie *with*. M–L16.

a H. A. L. FISHER Such is human nature that great calamities provoke . . countervailing efforts.

4 *verb trans.* Equal, match; be equivalent to. *arch.* M16. ▸†**b** Make an equivalent return for, reciprocate. L16–M17.
5 *verb trans.* Avail or be effective against; offset the effect of, counterbalance. M16.

Sunday Times Philby's accession to secret work did something to countervail the rather strong MI5 bias.

countervailing duty: put on imports to offset a subsidy in the exporting country or a tax on similar goods not from abroad.
†**6** *verb trans.* Act against or resist with equal physical force. L16–M17.
▸ **B** *noun*. Something which countervails; an equivalent. Now *rare* or *obsolete*. L15.

counterweigh /kaʊntəˈweɪ/ *verb*. LME.
[ORIGIN from COUNTER- 1 + WEIGH *verb*: cf. COUNTERPOISE *verb*.]
1 *verb trans.* Mentally weigh (things) against each other. Now *rare* or *obsolete*. LME.
2 *verb intrans.* Act as a counterbalance (*lit.* & *fig.*); weigh evenly (*with*, *against*). E16.
3 *verb trans.* = COUNTERBALANCE *verb* 2, 3. E19.

counterweight /ˈkaʊntəweɪt/ *noun*. L17.
[ORIGIN from COUNTER- 2 + WEIGHT *noun*.]
A counterbalancing weight.

counterwork /ˈkaʊntəwəːk/ *noun*. L16.
[ORIGIN from COUNTER- 2 + WORK *noun*.]
1 Work to counteract other work; an opposing act. L16.
2 MILITARY. A work raised in opposition to those of the enemy. M17.

counterwork /ˈkaʊntəwəːk/ *verb*. Pa. t. & pple **-worked**, (*arch.*) **-wrought** /-rɔːt/. E17.
[ORIGIN from COUNTER- 1 + WORK *verb*.]
1 *verb intrans.* Work in opposition or with contrary intent. E17.
2 *verb trans.* Work against, counteract, frustrate. E17.
■ **counterworker** *noun* a person who opposes or works in opposition M19.

countess /ˈkaʊntɪs/ *noun*. Also (esp. in titles) **C-**. ME.
[ORIGIN Old French *cuntesse*, *contesse* (mod. *comtesse*) from medieval Latin *comitissa* fem. of *comes*, *comit-*: see COUNT *noun*², -ESS¹.]
1 The wife or widow of an earl or a count; a woman holding the rank of earl or count in her own right. ME.
2 A roofing slate of a middle size. Cf. DUCHESS 4, LADY *noun* 11. E19.
■ **countess-ship** *noun* (*rare*) the quality, position, or personality of a countess E17.

counting /ˈkaʊntɪŋ/ *verbal noun* †**compt-**. LME.
[ORIGIN from COUNT *verb* + -ING¹.]
The action of COUNT *verb*.
counting of the omer: see OMER 2.
– COMB.: **counting frame** an abacus; **counting house** an office, *esp.* one where accounts are kept; **counting number** MATH. = ***natural number*** s.v. NATURAL *adjective*; **counting room** (chiefly *US*) a counting house.

countless /ˈkaʊntlɪs/ *adjective*. L17.
[ORIGIN from COUNT *noun*¹ + -LESS.]
That cannot be counted or valued; *esp.* too many to be counted.

SHAKES. *Ven. & Ad.* And one sweet kiss shall pay this countless debt. TOLKIEN They saw the torches, countless points of fiery light.

countour /ˈkaʊntə/ *noun*. Also **-tor**, **C-**. ME.
[ORIGIN Anglo-Norman *count(e)our* lawyer: see COUNTER *noun*².]
†**1** An accountant; an official who assisted in collecting or auditing the county dues. Only in ME.
2 LAW. A legal pleader; a serjeant-at-law. *obsolete* exc. *hist.* ME.

countrify /ˈkʌntrɪfʌɪ/ *verb trans.* *rare* exc. as COUNTRIFIED. Also **countryfy**. M17.
[ORIGIN from COUNTRY + -FY.]
Give characteristics of the country to; make rural or rustic. Usu. in *pass.*
■ **countrified** *ppl adjective* (**a**) having country manners and character; rustic, unsophisticated; (**b**) (of scenery) rural, of the kind seen in the country: M18.

country /ˈkʌntri/ *noun* & *adjective*. ME.
[ORIGIN Old French *cuntrée* (mod. *contrée*) from medieval Latin, Proto-Romance *contrata* use as noun (sc. *terra* land) of fem. of adjective from Latin CONTRA: see -Y⁵.]
▸ **A** *noun*. **1** An expanse of land; a region. ME. ▸**b** Land, territory; *esp.* land with distinct characteristics or associated with (the work of) a particular person. L19.

C

C

N. SHUTE A country of gracious farms on undulating hilly slopes. **b** T. KENEALLY Back again in country where the horse was futile. P. MORTIMER Constable country, of course. You care for Constable? *fig.*: A. HAILEY The trio walked deeper into computer country, past rows of . . metal and glass cabinets.

2 An area of land defined in terms of human occupation, e.g. owned by the same lord or inhabited by speakers of the same language. Formerly, a county, a barony. **ME.** ▸**b** The fox-hunting area of any one hunt. **M19.**

SIR W. SCOTT The fort . . constructed for the express purpose of bridling the country of the MacGregors.

3 The territory of a nation; a region constituting an independent state, or a province etc. which was formerly independent and is still distinct in institutions, language, etc. **ME.**

M. L. KING There were only three independent countries in . . Africa.

4 With *possess.* or *absol.* The land of one's birth, citizenship, residence, etc.; one's native land, one's homeland. **ME.**

TENNYSON If love of country move thee there at all. G. B. SHAW We call it justice . . or our duty to king and country.

5 *The* areas away from cities and conurbations; *the* part of a state outside the capital. **ME.** ▸**b** More fully ***country and western (music)***, ***country music***. Popular music of a style originating in folk music of the rural southern US in which the fiddle, guitar, and banjo were dominant instruments. **M20.**

V. WOOLF He would give up London . . and live in the country.

6 The people of a district or state; the national population, esp. as electors. Usu. ***the country***. **ME.**

AV *Gen.* 41:57 All countreys came into Egypt . . for to buy corne. T. STOPPARD The country . . looks to its elected representatives to set a moral standard.

7 *LAW.* A jury. *arch.* **ME.**

H. COX When the prisoner has . . put himself 'upon the country'.

8 In full ***country rock***. Rock enclosing a mineral deposit or an igneous intrusion. Formerly, rock pierced by lodes other than the principal one. **L17.**

9 *NAUTICAL.* A region of the sea. Now *rare* or *obsolete*. **M18.**

10 *CRICKET.* *The* outfield. *slang.* **L19.**

– PHRASES ETC.: **across country** across fields etc., not keeping to (main) roads (cf. CROSS-COUNTRY). **appeal to the country** test the opinion of the electorate by (calling) a general election. ***Black Country***: see BLACK *adjective*. ***country and western (music)***: see sense 5b above. CROSS-COUNTRY. DOWNCOUNTRY. ***free country***: see FREE *adjective*. ***God's country***, ***God's own country***: see GOD *noun*. **go to the country** = *appeal to the country* above. ***high country***: see HIGH *adjective*. ***inside country***: see INSIDE *adjective*. **line of country** a subject etc. with which a person is familiar. ***live off the country***: see LIVE *verb*. ***Low Countries***: see LOW-COUNTRY. ***Lucky Country***: see LUCKY *adjective*. ***Never Never Country***: see NEVER. ***north country***: see NORTH. ***old country***: see OLD *adjective*. ***Queen and country***: see QUEEN *noun*. ***red country***: see RED *adjective*. ***satellite country***: see SATELLITE *noun* 3a. ***serve one's country***: see SERVE *verb*[1]. SOUTH **country**. ***the old country***: see OLD *adjective*. ***third country***: see THIRD *adjective & noun*. ***town and country planning***: see TOWN *noun*. **unknown country** an unfamiliar place or topic. UP-COUNTRY. ***West Country***: see WEST *adjective*.

▸ **B** *attrib.* or as *adjective* (rarely *pred.*).

1 Of or pertaining to rural as distinct from urban districts; situated or living in the country; belonging to or characteristic of the country, esp. as contrasted with the town. **ME.**

C. H. WARREN He is country to the core—and Cotswold country at that. G. GORER In a society as urban as that of modern England, country ways represent a survival of earlier patterns.

†**2** Of the country, district, or part of the world implied; national. Usu. with possess. or demonstr. adjective. **LME–E18.**

DRYDEN Talk not of our country ladies: I declare myself for the Spanish beauties.

3 Of or belonging to India (or other foreign country) as distinguished from European. *obsolete* exc. *hist.* **L16.**

T. S. RAFFLES Since the conquest . . a very extensive trade has been carried on in country ships.

– COMB. & SPECIAL COLLOCATIONS: **country club** a sporting and social club in a rural district; **country cousin** a countrified relation or other person who is out of place in a city or among city-dwellers; **country dance** an English rural, native, or traditional dance, *esp.* one with couples face to face in long lines (cf. CONTREDANSE); **country dancing** the performing of country dances; **country folk** (*a*) = *country people* (a) below; (*b*) (*obsolete* exc. *dial.*) = *country people* (b) below; **country gentleman**: having landed property in a rural area; **country house** a substantial rural residence, *esp.* one of a country gentleman; ***country jake***: see JAKE *noun*[1]; **countrymade** *adjective* made in a rural area; *Indian* (esp. of a weapon) manufactured by an illegal cottage industry; ***country mouse***: see MOUSE *noun*; ***country music***: see sense A.5b above; **country party** a political party supporting agricultural against manufacturing, or national against sectional, interests; **country people** (*a*) people who live in the country; †(*b*) (with *possess.*) compatriots; ***country put***: see PUT *noun*[2]; **country road** †(*a*) a public road made and maintained by a country or province; (*b*) a road leading through a rural area; **country rock** (*a*) see sense A.8 above; (*b*) a blend of country and western and rock music; ***country seat***: see SEAT *noun* 11b; **countryside** (*a*) the land and scenery of the country; (*b*) (the inhabitants of) a region or regions in the country; **countrywide** *adjective* extending throughout the whole of a nation.

– NOTE: The original stress was on the final syllable.

■ **countryship** *noun* relationship based on (a common) country **E17.**

countryfy *verb* var. of COUNTRIFY.

countryman /ˈkʌntrɪmən/ *noun*. Pl. **-men**. **ME.**

[ORIGIN from COUNTRY + MAN *noun*.]

1 A man (in *pl.* also, people) of a (specified or indicated) country or district. **ME.**

North countryman: see NORTH. ***WHAT countryman?***

2 A man (in *pl.* also, people) of one's own country; a compatriot. Usu. with *possess.* **LME.**

B. JOWETT Simonides is a countryman of yours.

3 A man (in *pl.* also, people) living in the country, *esp.* one following country ways. **L16.**

A. F. DOUGLAS-HOME My father was a countryman, and a naturalist, and on the right interpretation of wind or weather depended the action of the day.

countryman's treacle (now *dial.*) (*a*) garlic, *Allium sativum*; †(*b*) rue, *Ruta graveolens*.

countrywoman /ˈkʌntrɪwʊmən/ *noun*. Pl. **-women** /-wɪmɪn/. **LME.**

[ORIGIN formed as COUNTRYMAN + WOMAN *noun*.]

1 A female compatriot. Usu. with *possess.* **LME.**

2 A woman of a (specified or indicated) country or district. **L16.**

North countrywoman: see NORTH.

3 A woman who lives in the country, *esp.* one following country ways. **L17.**

county /ˈkaʊnti/ *noun*[1] *& adjective*. **ME.**

[ORIGIN Anglo-Norman *counté*, Old French *cunté*, *conté* (mod. *comté*), from Latin *comitatus*, from *comes*, *comit-*: see COUNT *noun*[2], -Y[5].]

▸ **A** *noun*. **1** *hist.* The meeting or court held periodically under the sheriff for the transaction of shire business; a particular session of this court. **ME.**

2 The domain or territory of a count. *obsolete* exc. in ***county palatine*** s.v. PALATINE *adjective*[1]. **LME.**

3 Each of the territorial divisions of Great Britain and Ireland, long forming the chief unit for administrative, judicial, and political purposes and orig. equivalent to the English shire; *hist.* an English city or town given the status and powers of a county. **LME.** ▸**b** An administrative division in a British colony or Commonwealth country; in the US, an administrative division next in rank below a state. **L17.**

Home Counties: see HOME *adjective*. ***the Six Counties***: see SIX *adjective*. ***the Twenty-Six Counties***: see TWENTY *adjective*.

4 The people or ratepayers of a county collectively; *esp.* (members of) county families. **M17.**

– COMB.: **county borough** *hist.* a large borough ranking as a county for administrative purposes; **county clerk** *US* an elected county official responsible for local elections and maintaining public records; **county commissioner** (*a*) a Justice of the Peace on the commission of a county; (*b*) *US* an elected administrative officer of a county; **county corporate** *hist.* a city or borough ranking as an administrative county; **county council** the representative governing body of an administrative county; **county court** a court with local civil (and in some countries criminal) jurisdiction; *hist.* = sense 1 above; **county-court** *verb trans.* (*colloq.*) sue in the county court, esp. for debt; **county cricket**: between teams representing counties; **county family**: belonging to the nobility or gentry, with an ancestral seat in a particular county; **county hall** a building where county administration is carried on or (*hist.*) the county quarter sessions, assizes, etc., were held; **county library** a public library run by a county authority; **county school**: supported by a county council; **county seat** *US* the place which is the administrative centre of a county; **county town** the chief town or administrative capital of a county.

▸ **B** *adjective*. Having the social status or characteristics of county families. **E20.**

C. ISHERWOOD Mummy's bringing her up to be very county.

†**county** *noun*[2]. **M16–M19.**

[ORIGIN App. from Anglo-Norman *counte* or Old French and Italian *conte* (see COUNT *noun*[2]), with unusual retention of the final vowel, and infl. in form by COUNTY *noun*[1] *& adjective*.]

= COUNT *noun*[2].

coup /kuː; *foreign* ku (*pl. same*)/ *noun*[1]. **LME.**

[ORIGIN Old French & mod. French from medieval Latin *colpus* from Latin *colaphus* from Greek *kolaphos* blow with the fist. Reintroduced from French in 18 in branch II.]

▸ †**I** **1** A blow given or received in combat. **LME–M16.**

▸ **II** **2** A stroke or move that one makes; *esp.* a notable or strikingly successful move. **L18.** ▸**b** = COUP D'ÉTAT. **M19.** ▸**c** *hist.* Among N. American Indians: the act of touching an enemy, as a deed of bravery; the act of first touching an item of the enemy's in order to claim it. **M19.**

W. GERHARDIE I made a bold *coup* to regain my tottering prestige.

grand coup: see GRAND *adjective*[2]. ***Vienna coup***: see VIENNA 1.

3 *BILLIARDS.* The direct pocketing of the cue ball, which is a foul stroke. **L18.**

– PHRASES: ***coup d'essai*** /desɛ/ *rare.* [lit. 'stroke of trial'] a first attempt. ***coup de force*** /də fɔrs/ [lit. 'stroke of force'] a sudden violent action. ***coup de foudre*** /də fudr/ [lit. 'stroke of lightning'] a sudden unforeseen event; love at first sight. ***coup de glotte*** /də glɔt/ a glottal stop. ***coup de grâce*** /də grɑːs/ [lit. 'stroke of grace'] a blow by which a person condemned or mortally hurt is put out of his or her misery; a decisive finishing stroke. ***coup de main*** /də mɛ̃/ [lit. 'stroke of hand'] (chiefly *MILITARY*) a surprise attack. ***coup de maître*** /də mɛːtr/ a master-stroke. ***coup de poing*** /də pwɛ̃/ [lit. 'stroke of fist'] *ARCHAEOLOGY* (now *rare*) a hand axe. ***coup de soleil*** /də sɔlɛːj/ an attack of sunstroke. ***coup de théâtre*** /də teɑːtr/ a theatrical hit; a sensational or dramatically sudden action or turn of events, *spec.* in a play. ***coup de vent*** /də vɑ̃/ [lit. 'stroke of wind'] a whirlwind; a gale. ***coup d'œil*** /dœj/ [lit. 'stroke of eye'] a comprehensive glance; a general view; *MILITARY* the action or faculty of rapidly sizing up a position and estimating its advantages etc.

– COMB.: **coup stick** among N. American Indians, a stick used to touch the enemy in a coup.

coup /kuːp, kaʊp/ *noun*[2]. Now *dial.* Also **cowp**; **coop** /kuːp/. **LME.**

[ORIGIN Perh. same word as COOP *noun*[1].]

A cart or wagon with closed sides and ends for moving dung, lime, etc.

coup /kaʊp/ *noun*[3]. *Scot.* **M16.**

[ORIGIN from COUP *verb*[2].]

1 A fall; an upset. **M16.**

2 A place for emptying rubbish, a dump. **L19.**

coup /kuːp/ *verb*[1] *trans.* **ME.**

[ORIGIN French *couper*, Old French *co(l)per*: see COPE *verb*[1].]

†**1** Cut; slash. Only as ***couped ppl adjective***. Only in **ME.**

2 Chiefly *HERALDRY.* Cut clean off; depict as having an extremity cut off in a straight line. Chiefly as ***couped ppl adjective***. **E16.**

Times The bust appearing on coins will be 'couped', or cut off above the shoulders.

coup /kaʊp/ *verb*[2]. *Scot.* **LME.**

[ORIGIN Prob. same word as COPE *verb*[1].]

†**1** *verb intrans.* Strike; come to blows. Only in **LME.**

2 *verb trans.* Overturn, upset; empty out, as from a cart or wheelbarrow by tilting. **L16.**

coup the crans: see CRAN *noun*[1] 3. ***coup the creels***: see CREEL *noun*[1].

3 *verb intrans.* Be overturned or upset; fall or tumble over; capsize. **L18.**

coup-cart /ˈkaʊpkɑːt/ *noun*. Now *dial.* **ME.**

[ORIGIN Uncertain: assoc. with COUP *noun*[2], *noun*[3], or *verb*[2].]

1 = COUP *noun*[2]. **ME.**

2 A cart with a body that tips up to release the load. **M18.**

coup d'état /kuː deɪˈtɑː, *foreign* ku deta/ *noun phr.* Pl. **coups d'état** /kuːz deɪˈtɑː, *foreign* ku deta/, **coup d'états** /kuː deɪˈtɑːz/. **M17.**

[ORIGIN French, lit. 'blow of state'.]

A violent or illegal change in government. Formerly also, any sudden and decisive stroke of state policy.

coupe /kuːp/ *noun*[1]. **L19.**

[ORIGIN French = goblet from medieval Latin *cuppa*: see CUP *noun*.]

1 A shallow dish; a short-stemmed glass. **L19.**

2 A dessert of ice cream, fruit, etc., served in a glass coupe. **E20.**

coupe /kuːp/ *noun*[2]. **E20.**

[ORIGIN French = felling, formed as COUP *verb*[1].]

A periodic felling of trees; an area so cleared.

coupé /ˈkuːpeɪ/ *noun*. In sense 3b also ***coupe** /kuːp/. **E18.**

[ORIGIN French, formed as COUPÉ *adjective*. In branch II abbreviation of *carrosse coupé* lit. 'cut carriage'. Cf. earlier COUPEE.]

▸ **I** **1** Formerly = COUPEE *noun*. Now, a step in ballet in which one foot displaces another and weight is transferred to it. **E18.**

2 *FENCING.* A movement of the sword similar to a disengage, but effected by drawing the sword along and over the point of the opponent's. **L19.**

▸ **II** **3** **a** Chiefly *hist.* A four-wheeled carriage with a seat for two inside and an outside seat for the driver. **M19.** ▸**b** An enclosed two-door car with two or four seats and (now) usu. a sloping rear. **E20.**

b coupé de ville /də viːl/ [lit. 'of town'] a car in which the passenger seats are roofed and the driver's seat open or adapted to open.

4 *hist.* **a** The front or after compartment of a Continental stagecoach. **M19.** ▸**b** An end compartment in old railway carriages, with seats on one side only. **M19.**

coupé /ˈkuːpeɪ/ *adjective*. *rare.* **L16.**

[ORIGIN French, pa. pple of *couper* cut: see COUP *verb*[1].]

HERALDRY. Couped, cut off. Cf. COUP *verb*[1] 2.

coupee /kʊˈpiː, ˈkuːpi/ *noun & verb*. *obsolete* exc. *hist.* **L17.**

[ORIGIN formed as COUPÉ *noun*.]

▸ **A** *noun*. A dance step in which the dancer rests on one foot and passes the other forward or backward in a kind of salutation; a bow made while advancing. **L17.**

▸ **B** *verb intrans.* Perform a coupee; make a bow or salutation in dancing. **L17.**

coupla *adjective* see COUPLE *noun* 5.

couple /ˈkʌp(ə)l/ *noun*. **ME.**

[ORIGIN Old French *cople*, *cuple* (mod. *couple*) from Latin COPULA.]

▸ **I** A union of two; a pair.

1 A set of two people who are married or in a romantic or sexual relationship; a pair of people associated as partners in a dance etc. **ME.** ▸**b** (Pl. after numeral often same.) A pair of animals consisting of a male and a female. LME.

STEELE A very loving Couple.

happy couple: see HAPPY *adjective*.

2 Either of a pair of inclined rafters that form the main support of a roof. Usu. in *pl.* ME.

main couple: see MAIN *adjective*.

†**3** = COUPLET 1. *rare*. ME–L16.

4 a (Pl. after numeral often same.) A brace of hunting dogs; a brace of rabbits. LME. ▸**b** A ewe and her lamb. E18.

a MALORY A noyse as hit hadde ben a thyrtty couple of houndes.

5 *gen.* Two individuals (persons, animals, or things) of the same sort considered together. Also (with following quantifier) passing into *adjective*. LME. ▸**b** *ellipt.* A couple of alcoholic drinks. *colloq.* M20.

J. MCPHEE A couple of tributaries came into the river, the first from the east, the second from the west. **b** R. KEVERNE Stopped at the 'Swan' for a couple.

a couple more (*adjective & adverb*) (about) two more. **a couple of —**, **a coupla —** [repr. colloq. pronunc.: see A *preposition*[2]], (*US colloq.*) **a couple —** a pair of, (approximately) two.

6 MECHANICS. A pair of equal but opposite forces acting along parallel lines, tending to cause rotation. M19.

7 A set of two plates of different conducting materials in electrical contact, between which a voltage arises. M19.

▸ **II** That which unites two.

†**8** Union in marriage; the marriage bond; sexual union. ME–E17.

T. CORYAT To be begotten in the honest and chast couple of marriage.

9 *sing.* & (usu.) in *pl.* A brace, a leash, or joined collars for holding two hunting dogs together. LME.

go in couples, ***hunt in couples***, ***run in couples***.

†**10** GRAMMAR. A connecting word or particle, a copula. L16–E18.

■ **coupl**y *adjective* (*colloq.*) pertaining to or characteristic of a couple in a romantic or sexual relationship, esp. in being intimate or socially exclusive L20.

couple /ˈkʌp(ə)l/ *verb*. ME.

[ORIGIN Old French *copler*, *cupler* (mod. *coupler*) from Latin *copulare* COPULATE.]

▸ **I** *verb trans.* **1** *gen.* Fasten or link (two things) together or *together*; fasten or link (one thing) *to* another; join, connect. ME. ▸**b** CHEMISTRY. Cause to combine chemically with, esp. with the elimination of a simple molecule. E20.

POPE Measuring syllables and coupling rhymes. SHELLEY My young lambs coupled two by two With willow bands.

2 Join or link (abstract things), associate in thought or speech, (*together*, *with* or *to* something else). ME.

W. H. DIXON A man who coupled acts with words. SAKI Their names had naturally been coupled in the match-making gossip of the day. R. V. JONES The background of the Grenadiers coupled with seven years in the O.T.C.

†**3 a** Join in marriage or sexual union (*together*, *to*). ME–M18. ▸**b** Mate (animals); mate (one animal) *with* another. E18.

SWIFT A parson who couples all our beggars.

4 Bring (persons) together or *together* in pairs or as companions or partners; pair (one person) *with* another, attach (one person) *to* another. Formerly also, match or engage as opponents in a contest. LME.

WORDSWORTH See Latimer and Ridley in the might Of Faith stand coupled for a common flight.

5 Tie or fasten (hunting dogs) together in pairs or as a pair; pair (one dog) *with* or attach (one dog) *to* another by a leash etc. LME.

P. DRABBLE Coupling young hounds to their elders and betters.

6 Connect (one thing) *to* another for joint or coordinated operation; *esp.* connect (one group of pipes in an organ) *to* another by means of a coupler. E19.

7 Connect (railway vehicles *together*, one railway vehicle *to* another) by a coupling. M19.

C. JACKSON When her Pullman had finally been coupled between two cars of the new train. P. THEROUX The engine was being coupled to the coach.

8 Bring about a coupling between (oscillating systems, subatomic particles, etc.); in *pass.*, interact *with*, be physically or causally connected *to*. Cf. COUPLING 4. L19.

Scientific American The predatory adaptation of the lynx meant that the populations of both caribou and arctic hares were tightly coupled to the snowshoe hare population.

9 PHYSICS. Cause to pass, transfer, (*into*, *out of*). L20.

Physics Bulletin The energy is coupled out of the laser using a . . beam divider.

▸ **II** *verb intrans.* **10** = COPULATE 2. LME.

11 Come together in a pair; join with another as a companion. Formerly also, engage (*with* another) in a contest. L15.

12 Be able or intended to be coupled (*with*, *to*, etc.). M20.

Nature One arm . . couples directly into the Hersch cell.

couple-close /ˈkʌp(ə)lkləʊs/ *noun*. L16.

[ORIGIN App. from French *couple* COUPLE *noun* + *close* closed, shut.]

1 HERALDRY. Either of a pair of cottises in the form of narrow chevrons one quarter the width and often bordering an ordinary chevron. L16.

2 A pair of couples in a roof. M19.

coupled /ˈkʌp(ə)ld/ *ppl adjective*. LME.

[ORIGIN from COUPLE *verb* + -ED[1].]

1 Tied, joined, linked, or associated together in pairs. LME.

coupled columns ARCHITECTURE columns disposed in pairs close together, with wider intervals between the pairs.

2 Of a horse or other quadruped: having a specified type of conformation from the forequarters to the hindquarters, as ***short-coupled***, ***well-coupled***, etc. M17.

†**couplement** *noun*. M16.

[ORIGIN Old French, formed as COUPLE *verb*: see -MENT.]

1 The act of coupling; the fact of being coupled. M16–M18.

2 A couple, a pair. L16–E19.

coupler /ˈkʌplə/ *noun*. M16.

[ORIGIN from COUPLE *verb* + -ER[1].]

1 A person who couples, or couples things together. M16.

2 A thing that couples or links things together; *spec.* a device in an organ, harpsichord, etc., for connecting two manuals, a manual with a pedal, or two keys, so that both can be played with a single motion. M17.

3 PHOTOGRAPHY. A compound in a developer or an emulsion which combines with the products of development to form an insoluble dye, part of the image. M20.

4 In full ***acoustic coupler***. A modem which converts digital signals from a computer into audible sound signals and vice versa, so that the former can be transmitted and received over telephone lines. M20.

■ **coupleress** *noun* (*rare*) a female coupler; a procuress: M19.

couplet /ˈkʌplɪt/ *noun*. L16.

[ORIGIN Old French & mod. French, dim. of *couple* COUPLE *noun*: see -ET[1].]

1 A pair of successive lines of verse, esp. when rhyming together and of the same length. L16.

heroic couplet: see HEROIC *adjective*.

2 *gen.* A pair, a couple. E17.

3 ARCHITECTURE. A window of two lights. M19.

4 MUSIC. A duplet. L19.

■ **couple'teer** *noun* a writer of couplets; a versifier: E19.

coupling /ˈkʌplɪŋ/ *noun*. ME.

[ORIGIN from COUPLE *verb* + -ING[1].]

▸ **I** An action or state.

1 Joining in couples; (a) pairing, (a) linking. ME.

R. W. EMERSON Their realistic logic, or coupling of means to ends.

2 (An act of) sexual intercourse. LME.

I. MCEWAN One of the most desolating couplings known to copulating mankind.

3 GENETICS. More fully ***gametic coupling***. = LINKAGE 2. Now *rare*. E20.

4 PHYSICS. A mutual dependence of oscillations or oscillatory systems; an interaction, esp. by means of an electromagnetic etc. field. E20. ▸**b** A causal relationship. L20.

Scientific American The howl was caused by acoustic coupling between the transducers. B. LOVELL A magnetic coupling between the Sun and the planetary disk.

loose coupling: see LOOSE *adjective*.

▸ **II** A thing joining or joined.

5 *gen.* Something that couples things or is used to join things together. M16.

6 A transverse timber connecting a pair of inclined ones in a roof. L16.

†**7** *sing.* (usu.) in *pl.* = COUPLE *noun* 9. Only in 17.

8 A device for connecting parts of machinery, esp. in order to transmit motion; *spec.* (**a**) a device for connecting two shafts; (**b**) a link by which two railway vehicles are connected in a train. E19.

9 (The conformation of) the part of the body of a horse or other quadruped between the forequarters and the hindquarters. L19.

10 The recording on the other side or the remainder of a gramophone record; a pair of recordings on the same record. M20.

11 A pair of people in a romantic or sexual relationship, a couple. M20.

www.moviereviews.com Once upon a time, there was glamor associated with Hollywood couplings.

– COMB.: **coupling coefficient**: representing the degree of coupling between electric circuits etc.; **coupling constant** PHYSICS: representing the strength of the interaction between a particle and a field; **coupling pin**: that secures the connection between a train's carriages, a lorry's cab and trailer, etc.; **coupling reins**: that couple a pair of horses together; **coupling rod**: that connects two cranks so that they turn as one, e.g. in a steam engine.

coupon /ˈkuːpɒn/ *noun & verb*. E19.

[ORIGIN French = piece cut off, slice, from *couper* to cut: see COPE *verb*[1], -OON.]

▸ **A** *noun*. **1** A detachable portion of a stock certificate which is given up in return for a payment of interest; any detachable ticket entitling the holder to something, esp. the purchase of rationed goods. E19. ▸**b** The nominal rate of interest on a fixed-interest stock. M20.

2 A voucher issued with a product for the purchaser to exchange for cash or goods; part of a printed wrapper etc. used similarly. E20.

cigarette coupon etc.

3 Part of an advertisement which a reader can fill in and send to the advertiser for more information or as an order for goods. E20.

4 An entry form for a competition, esp. for a football pool. E20.

football coupon, ***pools coupon***, etc.

5 *hist.* A recommendation given by a party leader to a parliamentary candidate. E20.

– COMB.: **coupon bond**: on which interest is paid by coupons; **coupon-clipper** *colloq.* (**a**) *US* a person with a large number of coupon bonds; a wealthy person; (**b**) a person who cuts out and uses coupons (for discounts on goods etc.) from newspapers and magazines; **coupon-free** *adjective* obtainable without coupons.

▸ **B** *verb trans.* **1** *hist.* Give party approval to (a parliamentary candidate). E20.

2 Ration by means of coupons. M20.

■ **couponed**, **-nn-** *adjective* (**a**) having or bearing a coupon; (**b**) that has been couponed: L19.

coupure /kuːˈpjʊə/ *noun*. E18.

[ORIGIN French, from *couper* cut: see COPE *verb*[1], -URE.]

MILITARY. A ditch or trench, *esp.* one dug for defence; in FORTIFICATION, a passage cut through the glacis to facilitate sallies by the besieged.

courage /ˈkʌrɪdʒ/ *noun & verb*. ME.

[ORIGIN Old French *corage*, *curage* (mod. *courage*) from Proto-Romance, from Latin *cor* heart: see -AGE.]

▸ **A** *noun*. †**1** The heart as the seat of feeling etc.; disposition, nature. ME–M17.

†**2** What is in one's mind; purpose; desire, inclination. ME–E17.

†**3 a** Anger; pride, haughtiness; boldness. LME–E17. ▸**b** Spirit, vigour. L15–E17. ▸**c** Sexual vigour; lust. E16–E17.

4 The quality of character which shows itself in facing danger undaunted or in acting despite fear or lack of confidence. LME. ▸**b** As *interjection*. Take courage! Cheer up! L16.

R. H. HUTTON Illusions from which . . men have had the courage to break free. E. LONGFORD Ney faced the firing squad with the courage to be expected of 'the bravest of the brave'.

courage of one's convictions the courage to act in accordance with one's beliefs. **Dutch courage** *colloq.* temporary boldness induced by drinking alcohol. ***moral courage***: see MORAL *adjective*. **take one's courage in both hands** nerve oneself to a venture.

▸ †**B** *verb trans.* Encourage. LME–E17.

■ **couraged** *adjective* having courage (now only in comb., as ***high-couraged***) L15. **courageless** *adjective* (now *rare*) without courage L16.

courageous /kəˈreɪdʒəs/ *adjective*. ME.

[ORIGIN Anglo-Norman *corageous*, Old French *corageus* (mod. *courageux*), formed as COURAGE: see -OUS.]

1 Having or showing courage; brave, valiant. ME.

†**2** Eager (*to do* something). Only in ME.

†**3** Virile, vigorous, lusty. LME–L16.

■ **courageously** *adverb* LME. **courageousness** *noun* LME.

courant /kʊˈrant/ *noun*[1] *& adjective*. E17.

[ORIGIN French, pres. pple of *courir* run from Latin *currere*: see -ANT[1]. Cf. CORANTO *noun*[2].]

▸ **A** *noun*. †**1** A drawstring. Only in E17.

†**2** An express messenger or message. E17–E18.

3 A newspaper. *obsolete* exc. in titles of newspapers. E17.

▸ **B** *adjective*. HERALDRY. Of an animal: running. E18.

■ †**couranteer** *noun* a journalist E–M18.

courant *noun*[2] see COURANTE.

courante /kʊˈrɒ̃t, -rɑːnt/ *noun*. Also **-rant** /-ˈrant/. L16.

[ORIGIN French, use as noun of fem. pres. pple of *courir*: see COURANT *noun*[1] *& adjective*. Cf. CORANTO *noun*[1].]

1 A court dance of the 16th and 17th cents. characterized by glides and light hops. L16.

2 MUSIC. A piece of music for this dance; a piece of music in triple time, *esp.* one which forms a movement of a suite. L16.

†**courb** *verb intrans. & trans.* Also **curb**. LME–E19.

[ORIGIN Old French & mod. French *courber* from Latin *curvare* CURVE *verb*.]

Bend, bow.

courbette /kʊəˈbɛt/ *noun*. M17.

[ORIGIN French from Italian *corvetta*: see CURVET.]

A leap in *haute école* in which a trained horse rears up and jumps forward on the hind legs without the forelegs' touching the ground.

coureur /kuˈrœːr/ *noun*. Pl. pronounced same. E18.

[ORIGIN French = (wood-)runner.]

hist. In full **coureur de bois** /də bwa/. A woodsman, trader, etc., of French origin in Canada and the northern US.

courge /kʊədʒ/ *noun*. M19.

[ORIGIN French = GOURD from Old French *cohourde* from Latin *cucurbita*.]

A basket for holding live bait, towed behind a fishing boat.

C

courgette /kʊə'ʒɛt/ *noun*. **M20**.
[**ORIGIN** French, formed as **COURGE**: see **-ETTE**.]
A small variety of vegetable marrow. Also called ***zucchini***.

courida /kuːrɪ'dɑː/ *noun*. **E19**.
[**ORIGIN** Prob. from Carib.]
In Guyana, the black mangrove.

courier /'kʊrɪə/ *noun & verb*. **LME**.
[**ORIGIN** French †*courier* (now *courrier*) from Italian *corriere* (medieval Latin *currerius*), from *correre* to run from Latin *currere*: see **-IER**. In sense 1 from Old French *coreor* (mod. *coureur*) from Proto-Romance, from Latin *currere*.]
▸ **A** *noun*. **1** A running messenger, a messenger sent in haste; a special messenger. Also in titles of newspapers. **LME**. ▸**b** A messenger for an underground or espionage organization. **E20**.

H. KISSINGER I sent a courier to Bonn . . with personal letters to Bahr and Rush.

†**2** *MILITARY*. A light horseman acting as skirmisher or scout. **E16–E17**.
3 A person employed on a journey to make the necessary travel arrangements, now esp. to assist and guide a party of tourists. **L16**.
▸ **B** *verb trans. & intrans.* Attend or travel as a courier. **E19**.

course /kɔːs/ *noun*[1] *& adverb*. As adverb also **'course**. **ME**.
[**ORIGIN** Old French & mod. French *cours* from Latin *cursus*, from *curs*- pa. ppl stem of *currere* run; reinforced by Old French & mod. French *course* from Proto-Romance use as noun of fem. pa. pple.]
▸ **A** *noun*. **I** Action, direction, or place of running.
†**1** A run; a gallop. **ME–L17**.
2 Onward movement in a particular path, as of a celestial object, a ship, etc. **ME**.

S. JOHNSON They slackened their course.

†**3** Impetus; force. **ME–E16**.
4 The charge of combatants in a battle or tournament; a bout, an encounter. *obsolete* exc. *hist.* **ME**.
5 †**a** Running (of liquids); flow, flux. **ME–M17**. ▸**b** The faculty or opportunity of moving, flowing, etc. **LME**. ▸†**c** Circulation (of money etc.); currency. **LME–E16**.

b AV *2 Thess.* Pray for us, that the word of the Lord may have free course.

6 The ground on which a race is run; the route to be taken, with any obstacles to be negotiated, in a race (passing into sense 26). **ME**. ▸**b** More fully ***golf course***. An area of land on which golf is played. **L19**.

A. E. T. WATSON A familiar phrase on the turf is 'horses for courses' . . . The Brighton Course is very like Epsom, and horses that win at one meeting often win at the other.

racecourse, ***racing course***, etc.

7 The path taken by a moving body, a stream, etc., *esp.* the intended route of a ship or aircraft; the line of a mountain chain etc. **ME**. ▸**b** A channel in which water flows; a watercourse. **LME**. ▸**c** The direction in which a ship or aircraft is travelling. **M16**. ▸**d** In *pl.* The points of the compass. **E17**.

F. L. WRIGHT The course of the sun as it goes from east to west. **c** L. MACNEICE In sight of Stornoway harbour the captain altered his course.

8 A race. *arch.* **LME**.
9 The pursuit of game (esp. hares) with greyhounds by sight rather than scent. **LME**.
†**10** A fashionable riding or driving place. **M17–M18**.
▸ **II** *fig.* Of time, events, or action.
11 The continuous process (of time), succession (of events); progress through successive stages. **ME**. ▸†**b** Length (in time), duration. **M17–E18**.

L. STRACHEY In the ordinary course, the Queen never saw a Tory. R. P. WARREN At some time or other during the course of almost every meeting of the board. A. C. BOULT Richter's influence on the whole course of British music was immense.

12 Habitual or regular manner of procedure; custom, practice. **ME**.
13 Life viewed as a race that is run; a person's career. **LME**.

M. HANMER Where he made an end of his course.

†**14** The purport or general drift of a narrative. **M16–E18**.
†**15** Appointed order of succession. **M16–E17**.
16 A line of conduct, a person's method of proceeding. **L16**.

DISRAELI Our wisest course will be to join the cry. E. PEACOCK He had made up his mind to a certain course of action.

▸ **III** (Each member of) a consecutive series.
17 Each of the successive divisions of a meal, as soup, meat, pudding, etc. **ME**.
18 a A row, a layer. *obsolete* exc. in *BUILDING*. **LME**. ▸**b** A single horizontal row of bricks etc. in a wall. **LME**. ▸**c** *MUSIC*. A group of strings tuned to the same note and placed side by side so that they can be plucked together. **L19**. ▸**d** A row of knitted stitches. **M20**.
†**19** Any of several successive attacks, as of a disease or of the dogs in bear-baiting. **LME–E19**.
†**20 a** The time for anything which comes to each person in turn; (a person's) turn. **LME–M17**. ▸**b** Each of two or more groups of people who take turns. **L15–M17**.

a G. HAVERS Trouble and peace . . comfort and discontent, come all of them by courses.

21 In *pl.* A woman's periods. **M16**.
22 A set of things, esp. (*hist.*) candles, made or used at the same time. **M16**.
23 A planned or prescribed series of actions, esp. lessons etc. or therapeutic measures; the content of or a text for such a series of lessons. **M16**. ▸**b** *ECCLESIASTICAL*. The prescribed series of prayers for the seven canonical hours. **L16**.

GIBBON A regular course of study and exercise was judiciously instituted. P. H. NEWBY They gave him a course of drugs. *fig.*: T. DUNCAN It's a wonderful short course in human nature, being a doctor's son in a town of eight hundred.

correspondence course, ***crash course***, ***orientation course***, ***refresher course***, ***sandwich course***, etc.

24 *BELL-RINGING*. The successive shifting of the order in which a particular bell is struck; a series of changes which brings the bells back to their original order. **L17**.
25 A particular mode of rotating crops; a cycle of crop rotation. **M18**.
26 A series of fences, obstacles, etc., to be negotiated in a race, competition, or exercise; these and the ground on which they are situated (passing into sense 6). **L19**.

M. C. SELF The course is set up with a variety of jumps placed around the hall or ring.

assault course, ***obstacle course***, etc.

▸ **IV 27** A sail bent to the lowest yard on the mast of a square-rigged ship, esp. on the foremast, mainmast, or mizzenmast. **LME**.
– **PHRASES**: **a matter of course** the natural or expected thing. †**by course** (*a*) in due course; duly; (*b*) by turns, alternately. ***clerk of the course***: see **CLERK** *noun*. **course of nature** the ordinary recurring processes of nature. ***damp course***, ***damp-proof course***: see **DAMP** *noun*. ***horses for courses***: see **HORSE** *noun*. **in course** (*a*) (now *ECCLESIASTICAL*) in order, in turn; †(*b*) = ***in due course*** below; (*c*) (now *non-standard*) naturally, of course. **in course of** in the process of (construction, being constructed, etc.). **in due course** in the usual or natural order; at about the expected time. **in the course of** while *doing*; during the progress or length of (***in the course of things***, in the ordinary sequence of events). ***main course***: see **MAIN** *adjective*. ***middle course***: see **MIDDLE** *adjective*. **of course** (*a*) (now *rare* exc. in ***a matter of course*** above) customary, natural, to be expected; (*b*) in the ordinary course of things, as a natural result; (*c*) naturally, obviously; admittedly. **off course** not on course. **on course** †(*a*) in the ordinary course of things; (*b*) following the right path or direction or (*fig.*) the course that will have the desired or specified result. ***par for the course***: see **PAR** *noun*[1] 4. ***reciprocal course***: see **RECIPROCAL** *adjective*. **run its course** complete its natural development. ***shape one's course***: see **SHAPE** *verb*. ***stay the course***: see **STAY** *verb*[1]. **take its course** = ***run its course*** above. ***warn off the course***: see **WARN** *verb*[1] 7c.
– **COMB.**: **coursebook**: for use on a course of study; ***course unit***: see **UNIT** *noun*[1] 2d; **courseware** material for a training course, esp. in computing.
▸ **B** *adverb*. = ***of course*** (c) above. *colloq.* **L19**.

†**course** *noun*[2] var. of **KOS**.

course /kɔːs/ *verb*[1]. **LME**.
[**ORIGIN** from the noun.]
†**1** *verb trans.* Persecute, harass. **LME–E17**.
2 *verb intrans.* Gallop about, run, career; flow swiftly. **L15**. ▸†**b** *fig.* Run *over* or *through* a set of particulars, writings, etc. **L16–M18**.

P. LARKIN The rain courses in cart-ruts down the deep mud lane. **b** MILTON It were tedious to course through all his writings.

3 *verb trans.* Exercise, run, (a horse). **L15**.
4 *verb trans. & intrans.* Hunt (game) with hounds; *spec.* hunt (hares etc.) with greyhounds by sight rather than scent; use (greyhounds) to hunt hares in this way. **E16**.
5 *verb intrans.* Direct one's course; take a course. **M16**.
6 *verb trans. gen.* Chase, pursue; follow quickly. **L16**.
†**7** *verb trans.* Chase with blows; thrash. **L16–E17**.
†**8** *verb intrans.* Run a course (in a fight or tournament). *rare* (Spenser). Only in **L16**.
9 *verb trans.* Move swiftly over (a place) or along (a path). **E18**.
■ **coursing** *noun* the action of the verb; *spec.* the sport of hunting hares etc. with greyhounds by sight rather than scent: **E16**.

course *verb*[2] var. of **CORSE** *verb*.

course libre /kurs libr/ *noun phr.* Pl. **-s -s** (pronounced same). **M20**.
[**ORIGIN** French = free course.]
A bullfight, as in France, in which the bull is baited but not killed.

courser /'kɔːsə/ *noun*[1]. **ME**.
[**ORIGIN** Orig. repr. Old French *courseur* from Latin *cursor* **CURSOR**; later prob. from **COURSE** *verb*[1] or *noun*[1] + **-ER**[1]. In sense 4 after mod. Latin *Cursorius* genus name, lit. 'adapted to running'.]
†**1** A runner in a race. **ME–M17**.
†**2** A chaser, a pursuer. **L16–L17**.
3 A dog used for coursing; a person who goes coursing. **E17**.
4 Any of several long-legged birds of the Old World genus *Cursorius* and allied genera, related to the pratincoles, which are found in open usu. arid parts of Africa and Asia. **M18**.

courser /'kɔːsə/ *noun*[2]. **ME**.
[**ORIGIN** Old French *corsier* (mod. *coursier*) from Proto-Romance from Latin *cursus* **COURSE** *noun*[1]: see **-ER**[2].]
1 A swift horse. Formerly, a large powerful horse ridden in battle. Now *poet.* **ME**.
2 A stallion. *obsolete* exc. *Scot.* **LME**.

courses libres *noun phr.* pl. of **COURSE LIBRE**.

court /kɔːt/ *noun*[1]. **ME**.
[**ORIGIN** Anglo-Norman *curt* from Old French *cort* (mod. *cour*) from Proto-Romance from Latin *cohors*, *cohort-*: see **COHORT**.]
▸ **I** An enclosed area.
1 A clear space enclosed by walls or buildings; at Cambridge University, a college quadrangle. **ME**. ▸**b** A subdivision of a building open to the general roof. **M19**.
2 A large building or set of buildings standing in a courtyard; a large house, *hist.* a manor house. Now only in proper names. **ME**.
3 A walled or marked-off quadrangular area for playing one of certain games involving the striking of a ball, as tennis, squash, etc.; a marked-off division of such an area. **E16**.

badminton court, ***croquet court***, ***fives court***, ***squash court***, ***tennis court***, etc. ***clay court***, ***grass court***, ***hard court***, etc.

4 A confined yard opening off a street; a yard surrounded by houses and communicating with the street by an entry. **L17**.

V. WOOLF Jacob's rooms . . were in Neville's Court.

▸ **II** A princely residence or household.
5 The place where a monarch etc. lives and holds state. **ME**. ▸**b** In full ***court shoe***. A woman's light shoe with a low-cut upper and often a high heel. **L19**.

SHAKES. *A.Y.L.* Dispatch you with your safest haste, And get you from our court. LD MACAULAY The quarters of William now began to present the appearance of a court.

6 The establishment and surroundings of a monarch with his or her retinue. With or without determiner (article, possess. or demonstr. adjective, etc.). **ME**.

N. MITFORD No tiara, no necklace, what will the poor child wear at Court?

7 The monarch with his or her ministers and councillors as the ruling power. Treated as *sing.* **ME**.
8 A monarch's retinue; the body of courtiers collectively. Treated as *pl.* **ME**.

THACKERAY The king and the whole court. *fig.*: H. ACTON A life of generous affluence surrounded by a court of writers and artists.

9 Formal assembly of the monarch and his or her retinue. Chiefly in ***hold court***, ***keep court***. **ME**.

DRYDEN That sweet isle where Venus keeps her court.

10 Homage; flattering attention, courtship. Chiefly in ***pay court*** (***to***), ***make court*** (***to***). **L16**.
▸ **III** A place of law or administration.
11 (A session of) an assembly of judges or other persons acting as a tribunal legally appointed to hear and determine causes. Also more fully ***court of law***, ***court of justice***, ***court of judicature***. **ME**.
12 A place or hall in which justice is administered. With or without determiner (article, possess. or demonstr. adjective, etc.). **ME**.
13 (A meeting of) the members or the managers of a company collectively. **E16**. ▸**b** A local branch of certain friendly societies. **M19**.
– **PHRASES**: ***chancery court***: see **CHANCERY** 2b. ***civil court***: see **CIVIL** *adjective*. ***contempt of court***: see **CONTEMPT** *noun* 3. ***Court of Appeal***, ***court of appeals***: see **APPEAL** *noun* 1. ***Court of Arches***: see **ARCH** *noun*[1] 1. ***Court of Audience***: see **AUDIENCE** 2. ***Court of Augmentations***: see **AUGMENTATION** 1. ***Court of Cassation***: see **CASSATION** *noun*[1]. ***Court of Chancery***, ***court of chancery***: see **CHANCERY** 2. **Court of Claims**: in which claims, *spec.* (*US*) against the government, are adjudicated. ***court of first instance***: see **INSTANCE** *noun*. **court of inquiry** a tribunal appointed in the armed forces to investigate a matter and decide whether a court martial is called for. ***court of judicature***, ***court of justice***, ***court of law***: see sense 11 above. ***court of peculiars***: see **PECULIAR** *noun*. ***Court of Piepowders***: see **PIEPOWDER**. ***court of record***: see **RECORD** *noun*. ***Court of Request(s)***: see **REQUEST** *noun*. ***court of review***: see **REVIEW** *noun*. **Court of Rome** the papal Curia. **Court of St James's** the British monarch's court. ***Court of Session***: see **SESSION** *noun* 4b. ***Court of Star Chamber***: see **STAR** *noun*[1] *& adjective*. ***criminal court***: see **CRIMINAL** *adjective* 2. ***customary court***: see **CUSTOMARY** *adjective* 1. ***Divisional Court***: see **DIVISIONAL** 2. **General Court** a legislative assembly, *spec.* that of Massachusetts or New Hampshire. **go to court** take legal action. ***High Court***: see **HIGH** *adjective*. ***High Court of Chancery***: see **CHANCERY** 2. ***High Court of Justiciary***: see **JUSTICIARY** *noun*[2]. **High Court of Parliament** Parliament. ***higher court***: see **HIGHER** *adjective*. **hold court** *fig.* preside over one's admirers etc. ***Inn of Court***: see **INN** *noun*. ***in open court***: see **OPEN** *adjective*. ***juvenile court***: see **JUVENILE** *adjective*. ***last-court***: see **LAST** *noun*[3]. ***laugh out of court***: see **LAUGH** *verb*. ***lower court***: see **LOWER** *adjective*. ***magistrates' court***: see **MAGISTRATE** 3. ***motor court***: see **MOTOR** *noun & adjective*. ***Orphan's Court***: see **ORPHAN** *noun* 1. **out of court** (*a*) (of a plaintiff) having forfeited his or her claim to be heard; (*b*) (of a settlement) arrived at without the intervention of a court; (*c*) *fig.* not worthy of consideration.

having no claim to be considered. ***prevotal court***: see PREVOTAL *adjective*. ***rule of court***: see RULE *noun*. ***service court***: see SERVICE *noun*[1]. ***small claims court***: see SMALL *adjective*. ***spiritual court***: see SPIRITUAL *adjective* 2. ***standing rule of court***: see RULE *noun*. ***suit of court***: see SUIT *noun* 1a. ***superior court***: see SUPERIOR *adjective*. ***Supreme Court***: see SUPREME *adjective* 2. ***Supreme Court of Judicature***: see JUDICATURE. **the ball is in your court** *fig.* you must be next to act. ***the Verge of the Court***: see VERGE *noun* 9. ***ward of court***: see WARD *noun* 15a.

– COMB.: **court card** [orig. *coat card*: see COAT *noun*] a playing card other than a joker or a tarot, bearing the representation of a human figure (king, queen, jack, etc.), typically ranking above the sequence of numerals; ***Court Christian***: see CHRISTIAN *adjective*; **court circular** a daily report of the doings of the court issued to the press; **court-craft** (*a*) the art practised or required at court; (*b*) skill in the movements and positioning of a tennis player; **court cupboard** a 16th- or 17th-cent. sideboard for displaying plate etc., *esp.* one consisting of three open shelves and sometimes a small cupboard in the upper half; **court-day**: on which a (legal etc.) court is held or a prince holds court; **court dress** formal dress as worn at court; **court fool** = ***court jester*** below; **court-hand** a style of handwriting used in English courts of law until prohibited there by an act of 1731; †**court holy water** insincere flattery; **courthouse** (*a*) a building in which courts of law are held; (*b*) *US* the seat of government of a county; (*c*) *US* a building containing the main administrative offices of a county; **court jester**: kept to entertain a court; ***court leet***: see LEET *noun*[1] 1; **court-man** a (male) courtier; **court-metre** = DRÓTTKVÆTT; **court order**: given by a court of law and requiring a party to do or refrain from doing a specified act; **court party** a political party advocating the interests of the court; **court plaster** [from its former use for beauty spots by ladies at court] sticking plaster made of silk coated with isinglass; **court roll** *hist.* a record of a manorial court giving the holdings, rents, successions, etc., of the tenants; **courtroom**: in which a court of law is held; ***court shoe***: see sense 5b above; **court tennis** *N. Amer.* real tennis; **court week** *US*: during which the county court meets; **courtyard** a court (sense 1 above), *esp.* one adjacent to a house.

■ **courtlet** *noun* a small or petty court M19. **courtlike** *adjective* after the manner of court; courtly, elegant, polite: M16. **courtling** *noun* (*a*) a young or minor courtier; †(*b*) any courtier: L16.

†**court** *noun*[2]. ME–E18.
[ORIGIN Unknown.]
A kind of cart.

court /kɔːt/ *verb*. E16.
[ORIGIN After Old Italian *corteare* (mod. *corteggiare*), Old French *courtoyer* (mod. *courtiser*), from *cort* COURT *noun*[1].]
†**1** *verb intrans.* Be or reside at court. E–M16.
†**2** *verb trans.* with *it*. Act the courtier. M16–M17.
3 *verb trans.* Seek the favourable attention of, pay courteous attention to. L16.

GOLDSMITH To flatter kings, or court the great.

4 *verb trans.* Try to win the affection of, esp. with a view to marriage; woo. L16.

M. PUZO He had been courting his second wife in Spain, trying to get her to marry him. *fig.*: W. MOTHERWELL Their broad sheets court the breeze.

5 *verb intrans.* Behave amorously; conduct a courtship. L16.

R. BURNS When feather'd pairs are courting.

6 *verb trans.* Set out to gain or win (popularity etc.). L16.

E. J. HOWARD 'Are you glad I'm back?' she asked the children—hearing herself courting their approbation.

7 *verb trans.* Allure, entice (*from*, *to do*, etc.). E17.

S. JOHNSON An interval of calm sunshine courted us out to see a cave on the shore.

8 *verb trans.* Unwisely invite, incur the risk of, (inquiry, disaster, etc.). M20.

G. B. SHAW A prophet who . . courted and suffered a cruel execution. K. TYNAN A dramatist could inject a shot of colloquialism into a tragic aria without courting bathos.

■ **courter** *noun* a person who courts E17.

court baron /kɔːt'bar(ə)n/ *noun*. LME.
[ORIGIN Anglo-Norman, earlier *court de baroun* (Anglo-Latin *curia baronis*) court of the baron.]
hist. A usu. annual court for dealing with small civil disputes, consisting of the freehold tenants of a manor under the presidency of the steward.

court bouillon /kɔːt 'buːjɒn, *foreign* kur bujɔ̃/ *noun phr.* M17.
[ORIGIN French, from *court* short (formed as CURT) + BOUILLON.]
A stock made from wine, vegetables, etc., in which fish is boiled.

courteous /'kəːtjəs/ *adjective*. ME.
[ORIGIN Old French *corteis*, *curteis* (mod. *courtois*) from Proto-Romance (as COURT *noun*[1]) + *-ensis* -ESE (*-eous* replacing *-eis* in 16).]
1 Having manners such as befit the court of a prince; polite, kind, considerate, in manner or approach. ME.
†**2** Of a superior: gracious. ME–E19.
3 Of a deed, quality, etc.: appropriate to a courteous person, showing courtesy. ME.
■ **courteously** *adverb* ME. **courteousness** *noun* LME.

†**courtepy** *noun*. ME–M19.
[ORIGIN Middle Dutch *korte pie*, from *kort* (formed as CURT) + *pie* (mod. *pij*) coat, habit.]
A short coat of coarse material worn in medieval times.

courtesan /kɔːtɪ'zan/ *noun*. Also **-zan**. M16.
[ORIGIN French *courtisane* from Italian †*cortigiana* fem. of *cortigiano* courtier, from *corte* COURT *noun*[1].]
A prostitute, *esp.* one whose clients are wealthy or upper-class.
■ **courtesanship** *noun* the practice and position of a courtesan, high-class prostitution M19.

courtesy /'kəːtɪsi/ *noun & adjective*. In sense A.4 also **curtesy**. See also CURTSY *noun*. ME.
[ORIGIN Old French *curtesie*, *co(u)r-* (mod. *courtoisie*), formed as COURTEOUS: see -Y[3].]
▸ **A** *noun*. **1** Courteous behaviour; graceful politeness or consideration towards others. ME.

I. COMPTON-BURNETT She was your guest, and entitled to courtesy at your hands.

2 Courteous disposition, courteousness. Formerly also, nobleness, benevolence. ME.

A. WILSON Sir Edgar's old-world courtesy never deserts him.

3 A courteous act or expression. ME.
4 *LAW* (now *hist.*). A tenure by which a surviving husband was, provided certain conditions were satisfied, entitled to a life interest in his deceased wife's freehold property. Also ***courtesy of England***, ***courtesy of Scotland***. ME.
5 †**a** Customary expressing of respect by action or gesture, esp. to a superior. Chiefly in ***make courtesy***, ***do courtesy***. E16–M17. ▸**b** A curtsy. *arch.* L16.
†**6** A moderate quantity. (Earlier as CURTSY *noun* 1.) M16–E17.
– PHRASES: **by courtesy** by favour, not by right. **by courtesy of**, **courtesy of** with the kind permission of, through the good offices of, with thanks to. ***remember one's courtesy***: see REMEMBER 1.
– COMB.: **courtesy call** a social call made for no more specific reason than that of general courtesy; **courtesy cop** *slang* a police officer whose duty it is to persuade motorists etc. by polite firmness to drive well; **courtesy light** a light in a motor vehicle which comes on automatically when a door is opened; **courtesy title** a title of no legal validity given by social custom, *esp.* that of a peer's son or daughter.
▸ **B** *attrib.* or as *adjective*. (Supplied) free of charge, as a courtesy. Chiefly *N. Amer.* M20.

D. LODGE He tries to read a courtesy copy of *Time*.

courtesy /'kəːtɪsi/ *verb*. L16.
[ORIGIN from the noun: cf. CURTSY *verb*.]
†**1** *verb trans.* Treat with courtesy. Only in L16.
2 *verb intrans.* & (*rare*) *trans.* Curtsy (to). M17.

courtezan *noun* var. of COURTESAN.

courtier /'kɔːtɪə/ *noun*. ME.
[ORIGIN Anglo-Norman *courte(i)our*, from Old French *courtoyer*: see COURT *verb*. Ending assim. to -IER through *-e(y)er*.]
1 A person who attends or frequents a royal court. ME.
†**2** A wooer. E17–M18.
■ **courtierism** *noun* the practice or quality of a courtier M19. **courtierly** *adjective* having the characteristics of a courtier L19. **courtiership** *noun* the practice or position of a courtier M16.

courtly /'kɔːtli/ *adjective*. ME.
[ORIGIN from COURT *noun*[1] + -LY[1].]
1 Such as befits a royal court; polished, refined, markedly courteous. ME.

F. BURNEY I could but accede, though I fear with no very courtly grace.

courtly love a highly conventionalized medieval tradition of chivalric love and etiquette first developed by the troubadours of southern France (cf. AMOUR COURTOIS).
†**2** Of or pertaining to a royal court. L15–L19.
3 Given to flattery; obsequious. E17.
■ **courtliness** *noun* L15.

courtly /'kɔːtli/ *adverb*. L15.
[ORIGIN formed as COURTLY *adjective* + -LY[2].]
In courtly fashion.

court-martial /kɔːt'mɑːʃ(ə)l/ *verb trans.* Infl. **-ll-**, ***-l-**. M19.
[ORIGIN from COURT MARTIAL.]
Try by court martial.

court martial /kɔːt 'mɑːʃ(ə)l/ *noun phr.* Pl. **courts martial**, **court-martials**. Also †**court marshal**. LME.
[ORIGIN from COURT *noun*[1] + MARTIAL *adjective*, in early use freq. identified with MARSHAL *noun*[1].]
†**1** A court presided over by the Constable and Marshal of England. LME–M17.
2 A judicial court held in one of the armed forces under its disciplinary code. M16.

court of guard /kɔːt əv 'gɑːd/ *noun phr.* L16.
[ORIGIN Alt.]
hist. = CORPS ***de garde***.

courtship /'kɔːtʃɪp/ *noun*. L16.
[ORIGIN from COURT *noun*[1] + -SHIP.]
†**1** Courtliness of manners; courteous behaviour. L16–E18.
†**2** The state befitting a court or courtier; position at court, courtiership. L16–M17.
†**3** Court-craft; diplomacy, flattery, etc. L16–M18.
†**4** The activity of paying courteous attentions. L16–E18.
5 The activity or period of courting a woman with a view to marriage. L16. ▸**b** Animal behaviour that precedes and leads up to copulation. L18.

F. ASTAIRE They were married after a brief courtship.

6 The action of enticing or seeking to win over. E18.

BYRON In vain from side to side he throws His form, in courtship of repose.

couscous /'kʊskʊs, 'kuːskuːs/ *noun*[1]. Also **kouskous**, **couscoussou** /'kuːskuːsuː/. E17.
[ORIGIN French from Arabic *kuskus*, *kuskusū*, prob. of Berber origin. Cf. CUSCUS *noun*[1].]
A spicy N. African dish of crushed wheat or coarse flour steamed over broth, freq. with meat or fruit added; the granules of flour from which this dish is made.

couscous *noun*[2] var. of CUSCUS *noun*[2].

couscoussou *noun* var. of COUSCOUS *noun*[1].

cousin /'kʌz(ə)n/ *noun & adjective*. ME.
[ORIGIN Old French *cosin*, *cusin* (mod. *cousin*) from Latin *consobrinus* mother's sister's child, formed as CON- + *sobrinus* second cousin, from *soror* sister.]
▸ **A** *noun*. **1** The child of one's uncle or aunt. Also ***first cousin***. ME.
2 Any collateral relative. Formerly *esp.* a nephew or niece; now always, a relative at least as distant as a first cousin. ME.

SHAKES. *Much Ado* How now, brother! Where is my cousin, your son? W. FAULKNER Some remote maiden cousins of his mother.

†**3** *LAW*. One's next of kin; a person one was next of kin to. LME–M17.
4 (Also **C-**.) ▸**a** A title used by a monarch in formally addressing another monarch or a nobleman of the same realm. LME. ▸**b** As *voc.* Friend. Freq. with following pers. name. Now chiefly *dial.* LME.
5 *fig.* A person or thing having affinity of nature to another. LME.

B. JOWETT The Sophist is the cousin of the parasite and flatterer.

†**6** A prostitute (cf. AUNT 3). Also, a dolt. Also ***Cousin Betty***. *slang*. L16–M19.
7 A person of a kindred race or nation. M19.

J. C. JEAFFRESON Our American cousins.

– PHRASES & COMB.: ***call cousin(s)***: see CALL *verb*. ***Cousin Betty***: see sense 6 above. **cousin-in-law**, pl. **cousins-in-law**, a cousin's wife or husband; a cousin of one's wife or husband. **Cousin Jack** *slang* a Cornishman. **cousin once removed**, **cousin twice removed**, etc. (*a*) the child, grandchild, etc., of a cousin; (*b*) the cousin of a parent, grandparent, etc. ***first cousin***: see sense 1 above. ***kissing cousin***: see KISSING *ppl adjective*. ***parallel cousin***: see PARALLEL *adjective*. ***Scotch cousin***: see SCOTCH *adjective*. **second cousin**, **third cousin**, etc., a child of a parent's first, second, etc., cousin.
▸ **B** *adjective*. Kindred, related. LME.

CHAUCER The wordes moote be cosyn to the dede.

■ **cousinage** *noun* = COUSINHOOD ME. **cousi'ness** *noun* (now *rare*) a female cousin LME. **cousinhood** *noun* (*a*) the relation of being a cousin or cousins, kinship; (*b*) (a body of) cousins or kinsfolk: LME. **cousinliness** *noun* cousinly behaviour or character E20. **cousinly** *adjective* characteristic of or befitting a cousin; behaving like a cousin: E19. **cousinry** *noun* a body of cousins or kinsfolk M19. **cousinship** *noun* (*a*) kinship, cousinhood; *fig.* relationship; (*b*) action proper to a cousin: L16.

cousin /'kʌz(ə)n/ *verb trans.* M17.
[ORIGIN from the noun.]
Call cousin, claim kinship with.

cousin-german /kʌz(ə)n'dʒəːmən/ *noun*. Pl. **cousins-german**, †**cousin-germans**. ME.
[ORIGIN French *cousin germain*: see COUSIN *noun*, GERMAN *adjective*[2].]
1 = COUSIN *noun* 1. ME.
2 = COUSIN *noun* 5. M16.

couteau /kuto, 'kuːtəʊ/ *noun*. Pl. **couteaux** /kuto/, **couteaus** /'kuːtəʊz/. L17.
[ORIGIN French formed as COUTEL.]
Chiefly *hist.* A large knife used as a weapon.
couteau de chasse /kuto də ʃas, 'kuːtəʊ də ʃas/ a hunting knife.

coutel /kuː'tɛl/ *noun*. LME.
[ORIGIN Old French from Latin *cultellus* knife.]
hist. A dagger, a knife used as a weapon.

couter /'kuːtə/ *noun*. *slang*. *obsolete* exc. *hist.* Also **coo-**. M19.
[ORIGIN Perh. from Danubian Romany *cuta* gold coin.]
A sovereign (the coin).

couth /kuːθ/ *adjective* (orig. *pa. pple*) & *noun*.
[ORIGIN Old English *cūþ* pa. pple of *cunnan* CAN *verb*[1]. In sense A.7 back-form. from UNCOUTH.]
▸ **A** *adjective*. †**1** *pa. pple & adjective*. Known. OE–E17.
†**2** Of a person: well known, familiar. OE–M16.
†**3** Famous, renowned. OE–M16.
†**4** Acquainted (*with*, *of*). OE–LME.
5 Kind, agreeable. *Scot.* LME.
6 Comfortable, snug, cosy. *Scot.* M18.
7 Cultured, well-mannered, refined. L19.
▸ **B** *noun*. Good manners, refinement. M20.
■ **couthie**, **couthy** *adjective & adverb* (*Scot.*) (*a*) *adjective* kindly, agreeable; comfortable, cosy; (*b*) *adverb* genially, kindly: E18. **couthly** *adverb* (*a*) (now *Scot.*) familiarly, kindly; †(*b*) certainly, dearly: OE.

C

C

coutil /kuˈtɪl/ *noun*. M19.
[ORIGIN French from Old French *keutil*, from *keute*, *coute* mattress from Latin *culcita*: cf. QUILT *noun*.]
A strong cotton-based fabric used esp. in foundation garments.

couture /kuːˈtjʊə/ *noun*. E20.
[ORIGIN French from Old French *cousture* sewing from late Latin *consutura*, from Latin *consutus* pa. pple of *consuere* sew together, formed as CON- + *suere* sew.]
Dressmaking; (the design and making of) fashionable garments, esp. French ones.
HAUTE COUTURE. MAISON *de couture*.
▪ **couturier** /kuːˈtjʊərɪeɪ, -rɪə/ *noun* a fashion designer, *esp.* a leading French one L19. **couturière** /kuːˈtjʊərɪɛː/ *noun* a female dressmaker or couturier E19.

couvade /kuːˈvɑːd/ *noun*. M19.
[ORIGIN French, from *couver* hatch from Latin *cubare* lie: see -ADE 1.]
A custom in some cultures by which a man takes to his bed and goes through certain rituals when his wife bears a child.

couvert /kuvɛːr/ *noun*. Pl. pronounced same. M18.
[ORIGIN French: see COVERT *noun*.]
= COVER *noun*¹ 5.

couverture /ˈkuːvətjʊə/ *noun*. M20.
[ORIGIN French = covering: see COVERTURE.]
(A layer of) chocolate for coating sweets and cakes.

couvre-pied /kuvrəpje (*pl. same*)/ *noun*. Also **-pieds** /-pje/. E19.
[ORIGIN French, lit. 'cover foot', from *couvrir* COVER *verb*¹.]
A rug to cover the feet.

covalent /kəʊˈveɪl(ə)nt/ *adjective*. E20.
[ORIGIN from CO- + -VALENT.]
CHEMISTRY. Of, pertaining to, or characterized by covalency.
covalent bond: formed by the sharing of electrons, usu. in pairs by two atoms in a molecule.
▪ **covalence**, **covalency** *nouns* (the linking of atoms by) a covalent bond; the number of covalent bonds that an atom can form: E20. **covalently** *adverb* by a covalent bond M20.

covariance /kəʊˈvɛːrɪəns/ *noun*. L19.
[ORIGIN In sense 1 from COVARIANT; in sense 2 from CO- + VARIANCE.]
1 MATH. The property of being covariant; the property of a function of retaining its form when the variables are linearly transformed. L19.
2 STATISTICS. The mean value of the product of the deviations of two variates from their respective means. M20.
▪ **covariancy** *noun* covariance; covariation: L19.

covariant /kəʊˈvɛːrɪənt/ *noun & adjective*. M19.
[ORIGIN from CO- + VARIANT.]
▸ **A** *noun*. MATH. A function of the coefficients and variables of a given function which is invariant under a linear transformation except for a factor equal to a power of the determinant of the transformation; a covariant quantity. M19.
▸ **B** *adjective*. Changing in such a way that mathematical interrelations with another simultaneously changing quantity or set of quantities remain unchanged; correlated; *esp.* (MATH.) having the properties of a covariant; of or pertaining to a covariant. E20.

covariation /ˌkəʊvɛːrɪˈeɪʃ(ə)n/ *noun*. E20.
[ORIGIN from CO- + VARIATION.]
Correlated variation.
▪ **co-ˈvary** *verb intrans.* change simultaneously with something else, while preserving interrelations between the two unchanged M20.

cove /kəʊv/ *noun*¹ *& verb*.
[ORIGIN Old English *cofa* chamber = Middle Low German *cove*, Middle High German *kobe* (German *Koben*) stable, pigsty, Old Norse *kofi* hut, shed, from Germanic. Cf. CUB *noun*².]
▸ **A** *noun*. **1** A small chamber, cell, etc. Only in Old English exc. in ***cove and key*** (now *hist.*), closet or chamber and key (used in reference to the functions and rights of the mistress of a house). OE.
2 a A hollow or recess in a rock; a cave. *Scot. & N. English*. OE. ▸**b** A steep-sided recess in a mountainside. E19.
3 A sheltered recess among hills, woods, etc.; a narrow valley. LME.
M. HOWITT Small farm-houses . . in the little coves of the valleys.
4 ARCHITECTURE. A concave arch; the curved junction of a wall with the ceiling or floor. E16.
5 A sheltered recess in a coast; a small bay, creek, or inlet where boats may shelter. L16.
▸ **B** *verb*. †**1** *verb intrans. & trans.* (with *it*). Shelter in a cove. *rare*. M17–E18.
2 *verb trans.* Give an arched or vaulted form to; provide (a ceiling) with a cove. Chiefly as ***coved*** *ppl adjective*. M18.
H. SWINBURNE The mosques . . are rounded into domes and coved roofs.
▪ **covelet** *noun* a small cove L19. **coving** *noun* (*a*) an arched or vaulted piece of building; coved work; (*b*) in *pl.*, the inclined sides of a fireplace: E18.

cove /kəʊv/ *noun*². *colloq*. M16.
[ORIGIN Perh. from Romany *kova* thing, person, or rel. to COFF *verb*.]
A fellow, a chap.
J. COE He really is about as decent an uncle as any cove could possibly want.

covellite /kəʊˈvɛlʌɪt/ *noun*. M19.
[ORIGIN from N. *Covelli* (1790–1829), Italian chemist + -ITE¹.]
MINERALOGY. A blue hexagonal copper sulphide usu. occurring as massive coatings and disseminations with other copper minerals.

coven /ˈkʌv(ə)n/ *noun*. LME.
[ORIGIN Var. of COVIN.]
†**1** = COVIN I. LME–E17.
2 A company of witches who regularly meet together; *fig.* a secret or inward-looking group of associates. M17.

†**covenable** *adjective* see CONVENABLE *adjective*¹.

covenant /ˈkʌv(ə)nənt/ *noun*. ME.
[ORIGIN Old French *covenant* use as noun of pres. pple (later and mod. *convenant*) of *co(n)venir* agree from Latin *convenire* CONVENE: see -ANT¹.]
1 A mutual agreement between two or more people to do or refrain from doing certain acts; the undertaking of either party in such an agreement. ME. ▸†**b** A term of an agreement. LME–E17.
2 LAW. A formal agreement or promise of legal validity; *esp.* in ENGLISH LAW, a promise or contract under seal. ME. ▸**b** A clause of agreement contained in a deed. E17.
†**3** The matter agreed between two parties, or undertaken or promised by either; agreed wages, rent, etc. ME–M18.
4 In biblical translations and allusions, an engagement entered into by God with a person, nation, etc. ME. ▸**b** = DISPENSATION 5. E19.
MILTON And makes a Covenant never to destroy The Earth again by flood.
5 CHRISTIAN CHURCH. The engagement with God which is entered into by believers at their baptism, or admission into the Visible Church. M16.
6 SCOTTISH HISTORY. (**C-**.) An agreement signed by Presbyterians for the maintenance of their form of Church government in Scotland (***National Covenant***, 1638) and in England and Scotland (***Solemn League and Covenant***, 1643). M17.
– PHRASES: ***ark of the Covenant***: see ARK 2. **Church Covenant** the formal agreement made by the members of a Congregational church in order to constitute themselves a distinct religious society. **Covenant of Grace**, **Covenant of Works** THEOLOGY the two relations which are represented as subsisting between God and humankind, before the Fall and since the Atonement. **Day of the Covenant** *S. Afr.* a national holiday observed annually on 16 December, on which a vow made by the Voortrekkers before the battle at Blood River on that day in 1838 is honoured. **deed of covenant** a deed in which one party covenants to pay stated sums to another over a stated period of time. **land of the Covenant** the promised land, Canaan. ***National Covenant***: see sense 6 above. **New Covenant** the New Testament. **Old Covenant** the Old Testament. ***restrictive covenant***: see RESTRICTIVE *adjective* 3. ***Solemn League and Covenant***: see sense 6 above.
▪ **coveˈnantal** *adjective* of or pertaining to a covenant E19.

covenant /ˈkʌv(ə)nənt/ *verb*. ME.
[ORIGIN from the noun.]
1 *verb intrans.* Enter into a covenant (*for*, *to do*). ME.
T. ARNOLD Did you not covenant to write to me first?
2 *verb trans.* Agree formally to give or do (something); make a deed of covenant for (a sum). LME.
C. H. PEARSON She refused to pay the witch . . the sum covenanted.
3 *verb trans.* Stipulate (*that*). LME.
▪ **covenanˈtee** *noun* the person to whom a promise by covenant is made M17. **covenantor** *noun* the party who is to perform the obligation expressed in a covenant M17.

covenanted /ˈkʌv(ə)nəntɪd/ *ppl adjective*. M17.
[ORIGIN from COVENANT *verb* + -ED¹.]
1 Of a thing: agreed on, established, or secured by covenant. M17.
2 Of a person: having entered into a covenant, bound by a covenant; *spec.* in *hist.* (*a*) *Scot.* (also **C-**) having subscribed to the National Covenant or the Solemn League and Covenant; (*b*) having entered into a covenant with the East India Company or (later) the Secretary of State for India to become a regular member of the Indian Civil Service. M17.

covenanter /ˈkʌv(ə)nəntə, *in sense 2 also* kʌvəˈnantə/ *noun*. In sense 2 usu. **C-**. L16.
[ORIGIN formed as COVENANTED + -ER¹.]
1 *gen.* A person who enters into a covenant. L16.
2 SCOTTISH HISTORY. A subscriber to or adherent of the National Covenant or the Solemn League and Covenant. M17.

covent *noun* see CONVENT *noun*.

Coventry /ˈkɒv(ə)ntri, ˈkʌv-/ *noun*. L16.
[ORIGIN A city in the English Midlands.]
†**1** In full ***Coventry blue***. A kind of blue embroidery thread formerly manufactured at Coventry. L16–E17.
†**2** ***Coventry bells***, = ***Canterbury bell(s)*** s.v. CANTERBURY *noun*¹ 1. L16–L18.
3 ***send to Coventry***, refuse to associate with or speak to; ostracize. M18.

cover /ˈkʌvə/ *noun*¹. ME.
[ORIGIN from COVER *verb*² or partly a var. of COVERT *noun*.]
▸ **I** A thing which covers.
1 *gen.* A thing which is put on or which lies over something. ME.
W. BUCKLAND The alluvial cover which rests upon the rocks of this district.
†**2 a** A piece of armour; an article of clothing. ME–L18. ▸**b** More fully ***bedcover***. A cloth for putting on a bed, *spec.* a quilt; in *pl.*, bedclothes. E19.
b D. RUNYON He just pulls the covers up over his head and lies there.
3 A lid. LME.
4 The binding, wrapper, or case of a book; either of the boards forming the front and back of a book; an outer page of a magazine. L16.
5 An envelope or other wrapper for a letter; *spec.* a stamped envelope of philatelic interest. M18.
6 CRICKET. = ***cover point*** (a) s.v. COVER *verb*²; ***the covers***, cover point and extra cover point. M19.
7 TEXTILES. A design that is printed over another design in resist work. Also ***cover pattern***. L19.
8 COMMERCE. Funds adequate to cover or meet a liability or to secure against contingent loss. L19. ▸**b** Adequate insurance against loss, damage, etc.; the state of being protected by this. E20.
9 In full ***cover version***. A recording of a previously recorded song etc., *esp.* one made to take advantage of the latter's publicity or success. M20.
▸ **II** A thing which conceals.
10 A thing which serves for shelter or concealment; a shelter; a hiding place. LME. ▸**b** A disguise, a screen; *spec.* a spy's assumed identity or activity as concealment. L16. ▸**c** The partner who screens the operations of a pickpocket. E19.
J. BUCHAN There was not cover in the whole place to hide a rat. C. MILNE When a storm broke we took cover. D. BOGARDE Leaving . . under cover of night. **b** B. JOWETT Under the cover of rhetoric much higher themes are introduced. A. PRICE The precipitate withdrawal to Holland when it looked as though his cover had been blown.
11 Woodland, undergrowth, etc., that serves to shelter or conceal wild animals or game. E18. ▸**b** The vegetation covering the surface of the ground. E20.
b *Discovery* This denudation of forest cover is due to human interference.
12 Protection from attack, *esp.* that provided by a supporting force etc.; a force providing such protection. E19.
▸ **III** [French COUVERT.]
13 The utensils laid for each person's use at table; a plate, napkin, knife, fork, spoon, etc., a place setting. E17.
H. ALLEN The man . . began to lay covers for two.
– PHRASES: ***break cover***: see BREAK *verb*. ***extra cover***: see EXTRA *adjective*. **first-day cover** an envelope postmarked with the date on which its stamp was first issued. **from cover to cover** from beginning to end (of a book). ***loose cover***: see LOOSE *adjective*. ***open cover***: see OPEN *adjective*. ***paper cover***: see PAPER *noun & adjective*. **take cover** use natural or prepared shelter (against attack). **under cover to** in an envelope or other postal packet addressed to. **under separate cover** in another envelope or postal packet.
– COMB.: **cover charge** a charge for service added to that for food and drink in a restaurant; **cover crop** a usu. leguminous crop sown to protect the soil or to enrich it by being ploughed under; **cover drive** CRICKET a drive past cover point; **cover girl** a young woman whose picture appears on the front cover of a magazine; **cover glass** a slip of glass used to cover a specimen for the microscope; **cover note**: certifying the existence of a current insurance policy; **coverslip** = ***cover glass*** above; **cover story** (*a*) a fictitious life history etc. concocted as a false identity for a person; (*b*) a news story illustrated or mentioned on the front cover of a magazine; ***cover version***: see sense 9 above.

cover /ˈkəʊvə/ *noun*². Chiefly *dial.* E20.
[ORIGIN from COVE *noun*¹ + -ER¹.]
A person who lives in a cove.

cover /ˈkʌvə/ *verb*¹. Long *obsolete* exc. *dial.* Orig. †**acover**.
[ORIGIN Old English *ācofrian* corresp. to Old High German *ir-koboron* from Latin *recuperare* RECUPERATE. Aphet. Middle English to *cover* (infl. by Old French *co(u)vrer* get, acquire: cf. French *recouvrer* RECOVER *verb*¹), which became thereafter the only form.]
1 *verb trans.* Get, gain, obtain, attain. OE. ▸†**b** *verb intrans.* Get *to*, *out of*, *up*, etc. OE–L15.
†**2** *verb trans.* Recover, regain. OE–LME.
†**3** *verb trans.* Restore, relieve (a person etc.); heal (a wound). OE–E17.
4 *verb intrans.* Recover (from sickness etc.); regain health; be restored. OE.

cover /ˈkʌvə/ *verb*². ME.
[ORIGIN Old French *cuvrir*, *covrir* (mod. *couvrir*) from Latin *cooperire*, formed as CO- + *operire* to cover.]
▸ **I 1** *verb trans.* Put or lay something over or in front of (an object) so as to conceal, protect, or enclose it; put a covering or cover on (*spec.* a book). (Foll. by *with*.) ME. ▸†**b** Put a roof on or over. LME–M18. ▸**c** Put a cloth on (a table). M16.

A. B. SOYER Cover the saucepan for an instant. R. C. HUTCHINSON The winter sun had.. been covered by fresh clouds. J. THURBER He wore a cap to cover his baldness. P. MORTIMER I covered my face with my hands.

cover one's feet (in biblical translations) urinate; defecate.
2 *verb trans.* Clothe (a body); wrap or enclose (a limb etc.); enclose (a chair etc.) *in* fabric. ME.

V. WOOLF Six yards of silk will cover one body. W. PLOMER An Empire sofa.. had been newly covered in striped lavender satin. *fig.*: HENRY FIELDING He stood.. covered with confusion.

cover oneself with glory be remarkably successful.
3 *verb trans. & intrans.* Put a hat etc. on (one's head); in *pass.*, put on or wear a hat etc. ME.

SHAKES. *A.Y.L.* Good ev'n... Nay, prithee be cover'd. J. HELLER Her head was covered in a knitted cap.

4 *verb trans.* Serve as a covering to; lie or be over (an object) so as to conceal, protect, or enclose it. ME.

J. TYNDALL Pines.. covered with the freshly-fallen snow. I. MURDOCH A wet scarf covered her hair. G. GREENE One wall was almost covered by a large roller map.

5 *verb trans.* Occur here and there over the whole surface of; cause the surface of (something) to be overlain or marked (foll. by *with, in*). ME.

W. COWPER Gardens, fields and plains Were cover'd with the pest. J. R. GREEN Art and literature covered England with great buildings and busy schools. R. BROOKE The breeze moves in the trees.. And covers you with white petals. *Observer* He.. was covered in ink.

6 *verb trans.* Of a stallion, bull, etc.: copulate with. M16. ▸**b** Of a bird: sit on (eggs). E17.
7 *verb trans.* **a** In wagering, match (a coin etc.) with another of equal value. E19. ▸**b** Play a higher-ranking card on top of (a card already played). L19. ▸**c** Make a cover version of (a song etc.). M20.
▸**II 8** *verb trans. gen.* Shield; protect; shelter; be a means of defence or protection for. ME.

H. NELSON She was an American Vessel, although covered by British Papers. J. SEACOME Cannon.. to cover the Ships in the Harbour. *Granta* We moved back slowly.., covering the battalion's retreat.

9 *verb trans. gen.* Hide or screen from view; conceal, prevent the perception or discovery of. ME.

SOUTHEY Thou shalt wish The earth might cover thee. D. LODGE He forced a laugh to cover his embarrassment.

cover a person's tracks: see TRACK *noun*.
10 *verb trans.* Aim a gun at; have within firing range; command (territory etc.) from a superior position. L17. ▸**b** In TENNIS etc., have (an area) within the scope of one's play; in various team games, be responsible for defence in (an area). L19.
11 *verb trans.* Include within its application or scope; deal with, provide for. L18. ▸**b** Report on or photograph for the press; attend or investigate as a journalist. L19.

BURKE Mr. Fox's general principle fully covered all this. K. AMIS I cover the medieval angle for the History Department here. **b** P. LIVELY The paper is sending her to cover a party conference.

cover all the bases *colloq.* deal with something thoroughly.
12 *verb trans.* **a** MILITARY. Stand directly behind or in line with. L18. ▸**b** In CRICKET, stand behind (another fielder) so as to be able to stop the balls he or she misses; in various team games, mark (an opponent). M19.
13 a *verb trans.* Of a pickpocket's partner: screen the operations of (the pickpocket). E19. ▸**b** *verb trans. & intrans.* Of a medical practitioner: act for or cooperate improperly with (an unqualified practitioner). L19. ▸**c** *verb trans. & intrans.* with *for*. Stand in for (an absent colleague); take (a class) for an absent teacher. M20.
14 *verb trans.* **a** Pass over (ground); traverse (a given distance). E19. ▸**b** Extend over, be co-extensive with; occupy (a period or area). M19.

a J. BUCHAN The hill-top.. from which the eye may cover half the southern midlands. K. M. E. MURRAY In three days they covered at least fifty miles. **b** A. CARNEGIE During the period which these events cover I had made repeated journeys to Europe. D. MURPHY Letters.. covering more than twenty foolscap pages.

b ***cover much ground, cover the ground***: see GROUND *noun*.
15 *verb trans.* Be sufficient to defray (expenses), pay (a dividend etc.), or meet (a liability); compensate for (a loss or risk); protect by insurance. E19. ▸**b** *verb intrans.* Insure oneself; provide cover. L19.

Times With the dividend covered three times there is unlikely to be any danger to shareholders.

– WITH ADVERBS IN SPECIALIZED SENSES: **cover in** complete the covering of (something) by adding the upper layer or part; provide with a roof. **cover over** cover the whole surface of; overlay; cover with something that overhangs. **cover up** (*a*) *verb phr. trans.* conceal under a cover; cover over; (*b*) *verb phr. trans. & intrans.* conceal (a misdeed), assist in a deception.
– COMB.: **covering letter, covering note**: sent with an enclosure and indicating its contents; **cover point** (*a*) CRICKET (the position of) a fielder a little in front of the batsman on the off side, further from the pitch than point; (*b*) LACROSSE a player who is positioned just in front of point; **cover-shame** (*a*) something used to conceal shame; (*b*) the shrub savin (as an abortifacient); **cover-slut** an apron, a pinafore; **cover-up** (*a*) something designed to conceal a crime or restrict knowledge of misconduct; (*b*) a high-necked garment; a coverall.
■ **coverable** *adjective* able to be covered L20. **coverer** *noun* a person or thing which covers ME.

coverage /ˈkʌv(ə)rɪdʒ/ *noun*. Orig. *US*. E20.
[ORIGIN from COVER *verb*² + -AGE.]
1 The area, range, etc., that is covered; *spec.* the area or number of people reached by a particular broadcasting station or advertising medium. E20.

G. MILLERSON The longer the focal length of the lens.., the narrower its coverage.

2 The action of covering something for the press; the fact or extent of being included in news reports, broadcasts, etc.; reporting. M20.

Economist Soviet radio gave greater radio coverage to this peace congress.

coverall /ˈkʌvərɔːl/ *noun & adjective*. M19.
[ORIGIN from COVER *verb*² + ALL.]
▸**A** *noun sing.* & in *pl.* Something that covers entirely, *esp.* a full-length protective outer garment. M19.
▸**B** *adjective*. That covers entirely. L19.

coverchief /ˈkʌvətʃɪf/ *noun*. Long *obsolete* exc. *hist.* ME.
[ORIGIN Old French *cuevre-chief*, (also mod.) *couvre-chef*: see KERCHIEF.]
= KERCHIEF.

covercle /ˈkʌvək(ə)l/ *noun*. LME.
[ORIGIN Old French (mod. *couvercle*) from Latin *cooperculum*, from *cooperire* COVER *verb*².]
†**1** A cover; a lid. LME–L19.
2 BOTANY & ZOOLOGY. Any natural structure acting as a lid; an operculum. *rare*. L17.

covered /ˈkʌvəd/ *adjective*. LME.
[ORIGIN from COVER *noun*¹, *verb*²: see -ED², -ED¹.]
1 Having a cover, covering, or lid. LME.
†**2** Hidden; secret; ambiguous. LME–L16.
3 Sheltered, protected, screened. Now *rare* or *obsolete* exc. in ***covered way*** below. L15.
4 Overgrown with vegetation. Now only as 2nd elem. of comb., as ***moss-covered, weed-covered***, etc. M17.
5 Roofed or closed in overhead. M17.
covered bridge, covered market, covered wagon.
6 Wearing one's hat. M17.
– SPECIAL COLLOCATIONS: **covered way** (*a*) FORTIFICATION a strip of land beyond the outer edge of a ditch and protected by a parapet; (*b*) a path that is roofed in.

covering /ˈkʌv(ə)rɪŋ/ *noun*. ME.
[ORIGIN from COVER *verb*² + -ING¹.]
1 The action of COVER *verb*². ME.
short covering: see SHORT *adjective*.
2 Something which covers or is adapted to cover; a cover. ME. ▸†**b** *spec.* A lid. L15–M17.

coverlet /ˈkʌvəlɪt/ *noun*. Also **-lid** /-lɪd/. ME.
[ORIGIN Anglo-Norman *covrelet*, *-lit*, from *covre-* pres. stem of Old French *covrir* COVER *verb*² + *lit* bed.]
1 A bedspread; a counterpane. ME.
2 A covering of any kind; a cover. LME.

co-versed /kəʊˈvəːst/ *adjective*. Now *rare*. E18.
[ORIGIN from CO- + VERSED *adjective*.]
MATH. ***co-versed sine***, the versed sine of the complement of an angle.

covert /ˈkʌvə, ˈkʌvət/ *noun*. ME.
[ORIGIN Old French (mod. *couvert*) use as noun of masc. pa. pple of *cuvrir*, *covrir* COVER *verb*².]
1 *gen.* A covering. ME.
2 = COVER *noun*¹ 10. ME.
3 A flock or company of coots. Long *rare*. LME.
4 A place which gives shelter to wild animals or game; *esp.* a thicket. L15.
†**5** = COVERTURE 8. Chiefly in ***under covert***. M16–E18.
6 ORNITHOLOGY. More fully ***covert feather***. A feather covering the base of wing or tail feathers. Also called ***tectrix***. Usu. in *pl.* L16.
– COMB.: **covert cloth** a medium-weight fabric with a twill weave; **covert coat** a short light overcoat worn for shooting, riding, etc.; **covert coating** = *covert cloth* above; *covert feather*: see sense 6 above.

covert /ˈkʌvət, ˈkəʊvəːt/ *adjective*. ME.
[ORIGIN Old French (mod. *couvert*) pa. pple of *cuvrir*, *covrir* COVER *verb*².]
1 Covered; hidden; sheltered. Now *rare*. ME.

WORDSWORTH This covert nook reports not of his hand.

2 Secret, concealed; disguised. ME.

N. CHOMSKY Unless intervention is discreet and covert, there will be protest, disaffection.

3 Of a person: secretive, sly. ME.

SHAKES. *Rich. III* He was the covert'st shelt'red traitor That ever liv'd.

4 Of a word: of hidden or obscure meaning. Now *rare*. LME.
5 LAW. Of a woman: married (formerly as under the authority or protection of her husband). L15.
– SPECIAL COLLOCATIONS: **covert way** = *covered way* (a) s.v. COVERED. *FEME covert*. *pound covert*: see POUND *noun*² 1a.
■ **covertly** *adverb* LME. **covertness** *noun* LME.

covert-baron /ˈkʌvətbar(ə)n/ *adjective & noun*. *obsolete* exc. *hist.* E16.
[ORIGIN Anglo-Norman *couverte baroun*, orig. *coverte de barun* covered by a husband: see COVERT *adjective*, BARON.]
▸**A** *adjective*. = COVERT *adjective* 5. E16.
▸**B** *noun*. The condition of being a married woman. Chiefly in ***under covert-baron***. Cf. COVERT *noun* 5, COVERTURE 8. L16.

coverture /ˈkʌvətjʊə/ *noun*. ME.
[ORIGIN Old French (mod. *couverture*), from *covrir* COVER *verb*² or late Latin *coopertura* (from ppl stem of Latin *cooperire* COVER *verb*²): see -URE.]
†**1** A bedcover; a coverlet. ME–L17.
†**2** Clothing; a garment; a horse's trappings. ME–E17.
3 *gen.* (A) covering. Formerly also, a cover (of a dish, book, letter, etc.). LME.
4 An overhead covering; a canopy. Now *rare*. LME.
5 Protective covering; (a) shelter, (a) refuge. LME.

SPENSER Agaynst his cruell scortching heate, Where hast thou couerture?

6 Concealing covering; (a) disguise. LME. ▸**b** *fig.* Concealment; dissimulation, deceit. Now *rare*. LME.

I. BARROW Shrowded under the coverture of other Persons and Names.

†**7** A pretext, a pretence. LME–M16.
8 The legal status of a married woman (formerly as under the authority and protection of her husband); a woman's married state. Esp. in ***during the coverture***, ***under coverture***. M16.

covess /kəʊˈvɛs/ *noun*. *slang*. L18.
[ORIGIN from COVE *noun*² + -ESS¹.]
A woman, a girl.

covet /ˈkʌvɪt/ *verb*. ME.
[ORIGIN Old French *coveitier*, *cu-* (mod. *convoiter*) from Proto-Romance, from Latin *cupiditas* CUPIDITY.]
1 *verb trans.* Desire; *esp.* desire eagerly, long for. ME.

J. ARBUTHNOT They covet subacid Liquors, and abhor fat and oily things. F. BURNEY Her mind.. coveted to regain its serenity. D. HALBERSTAM He did not covet small-bore social acceptance.

2 *verb trans.* Long for (what belongs to another); desire culpably. ME.

C. JACKSON She coveted the necklace and made up her mind to own it.

†**3** *verb trans.* Desire with concupiscence; desire sexually. ME–L16.
†**4** *verb intrans.* Have inordinate or culpable, esp. sexual, desire. Foll. by *for, after, against*. LME–E16.
■ **covetable** *adjective* highly desirable ME. **coveter** *noun* a person who covets or is given to coveting LME. **covetingly** *adverb* with great longing LME.

covetise /ˈkʌvətiːs/ *noun*. Long *arch.* ME.
[ORIGIN Old French *coveitise* (mod. *convoitise*) alt. with suffix-change of *coveitié*, *covoitié* from Latin *cupiditas* CUPIDITY: see -ISE¹, -ICE¹.]
Inordinate or ardent desire; lust; *spec.* excessive desire for wealth etc.; covetousness.

covetous /ˈkʌvɪtəs/ *adjective*. ME.
[ORIGIN Old French *coveitous* (mod. *convoiteux*) from Proto-Gallo-Romance, from Latin *cupiditas* CUPIDITY: see -OUS.]
1 Having an ardent or excessive desire. Foll. by *of*, †*for*; *to do, have, be*. ME.
2 Culpably or inordinately desirous of gaining wealth or possessions; greedy, grasping; avaricious. ME.
3 Of an action: proceeding from cupidity. LME.
■ **covetously** *adverb* LME. **covetousness** *noun* †(*a*) inordinate desire (*of*); (*b*) culpable desire: L15.

covey /ˈkʌvi/ *noun*¹. ME.
[ORIGIN Old French *covée* (mod. *couvée*) use as noun of fem. pa. pple of *cover* from Latin *cubare* lie.]
1 A brood or flock of partridges (or occas. of grouse etc.); a family of partridges etc. keeping together during the first season. ME.
2 A party, group, etc., *of* persons or things. ME.

V. WOOLF Coveys of nursemaids pushed perambulators.

covey /ˈkəʊvi/ *noun*². *slang*. E19.
[ORIGIN from COVE *noun*² + -Y⁶.]
A little chap or fellow.

†**covid** *noun*. L17–E19.
[ORIGIN Portuguese *côvado* from Latin *cubitum* CUBIT.]
An Indian unit of length varying from 36 to 14 inches (approx. 91 to 36 cm).

covin /ˈkʌvɪn/ *noun*. Also **-ine**. See also COVEN. ME.
[ORIGIN Old French *covin(e)* from medieval Latin *convenium*, from Latin *convenire* CONVENE. Cf. CONVENT *noun*.]
▸**I** †**1** A number of people allied together; a company, a band. ME–E16.
2 A collusion between two or more to the prejudice of another; a secret plan or agreement. Now *rare* or *obsolete*. LME.
3 Fraud; deceit; treachery. *arch.* LME.
†**4** Secret contrivance or intent. Only in LME.

†**5** State, character. **LME–L15.**
▸ **II 6** = COVEN 2. *Scot.* **M19.**
– COMB.: **covin-tree** *Scot.* a large tree in front of a Scottish mansion where the laird met or took leave of his visitors etc.
■ **covinous** *adjective* (now *rare*) collusive; fraudulent: **L16.** **covinously** *adverb* (now *rare*) **M16.**

cow /kaʊ/ *noun*[1] *& adjective*. Pl. **cows**, (*arch.*) **kine** /kʌɪn/, (*Scot. & N. English*) **kye** /kʌɪ/.
[ORIGIN Old English *cū* = Old Frisian *kū*, Old Saxon *kō* (Dutch *koe*), Old High German *kuo*, *chuo* (German *Kuh*), Old Norse *kýr*, from Germanic, from Indo-European base also of Latin *bos*, Greek *bous*.]
▸ **A** *noun* **I 1** A domesticated female ox, esp. one that has calved (kept for milk etc.); any mature female bovine animal. **OE.** ▸**b** A domestic bovine animal (regardless of sex or age). Orig. *US*. **M19.**
2 The female of various other large animals, as the elephant, rhinoceros, whale, seal, etc. **E18.**
▸ **II 3** †**a** A faint-hearted person. **L16–E17.** ▸**b** A woman, *esp.* a coarse or unpleasant one. *slang. derog.* **L17.** ▸**c** An objectionable person, thing, or situation. *Austral. & NZ slang.* **L19.**

b C. MACKENZIE Silly cow! She ought to know better. **c** F. D. DAVISON Looking for work's a cow of a game!

– PHRASES ETC.: ***bull-and-cow***: see BULL *noun*[1] *& adjective*. ***Lucanian cow***: see LUCANIAN *adjective*. ***muley cow***: see MULEY *noun & adjective*[1]. ***sacred cow***: see SACRED *adjective*. ***Sussex cow***: see SUSSEX 1. ***the tune the cow died of***, ***the tune the old cow died of***: see TUNE *noun*. **till the cows come home** *colloq.* for an indefinitely long period.
– COMB.: **cow-baby** (*obsolete* exc. *dial.*) a childish timorous person; **cowbail** *Austral. & NZ.* [BAIL *noun*[2]] (*a*) a framework for securing the head of a cow at milking; (*b*) a cowshed; **cowbane** any of several marsh umbellifers poisonous to cattle, esp. *Cicuta virosa* of Europe and *C. maculata* and *Oxypolis rigidior* of the US; **cow-banger** *dial., & Austral. & NZ slang* a dairy farmer; a worker on a dairy farm; **cowbell** (*a*) a bell hung round a cow's neck to indicate its whereabouts; (*b*) a bell without a clapper used as a percussion instrument; **cowberry** (the red acid fruit of) an evergreen bilberry, *Vaccinium vitis-idaea*, of upland moors; red whortleberry; **cowbind** the twining plant white bryony, *Bryonia dioica*; **cowbird** *US* any of several related N. American orioles, esp. *Molothrus ater*, which associate with cattle for the insects stirred up in grazing; **cow camp** *US* an encampment of cowboys; **cowcatcher** (chiefly *N. Amer.*) an apparatus fixed in front of a locomotive to push aside cattle and other obstructions; **cow chip** *N. Amer.* a dried cowpat; **cow cocky** *Austral. & NZ slang* a dairy farmer; **cow-creamer** an antique cream jug in the form of a cow; **cowfish** (*a*) any of several small cetaceans, e.g. the manatee; (*b*) a trunkfish with hornlike spines over the eyes, esp. *Lactophrys quadricornis*; **cow flap**, **cow flop** (*a*) *dial.* the foxglove; (*b*) *dial. & US* = ***cowpat*** below; **cow-gait**, **-gate** *hist.* a pasture where a cow may be grazed; right of grazing cattle, as on common land; †**cow-gun** *nautical slang* a heavy naval gun; **cowhand** a person employed to tend or ranch cattle; **cowheel** (a dish made from) the heel of a cow or ox stewed to a jelly; **cowherd** [HERD *noun*[2]] a person who tends grazing cattle; **cowhide** *noun, adjective, & verb* (*a*) *noun* (leather made from) the hide of a cow; *US* a whip made of cowhide; (*b*) *adjective* made of cowhide; (*c*) *verb trans.* flog with a cowhide whip; **cow-hitch** NAUTICAL an improperly tied knot which slips under strain; **cow-hocked** *adjective* (of a horse or dog) having hocks that turn inwards like a cow's; **cow-horse** *US* a horse used in herding or driving cattle; **cow-house** a cowshed; **cow-hunt** *US*: for strayed cattle; **cow-keeper** a dairyman; a dairy farmer; **cow-lady** *dial.* a ladybird; **cowlick** a projecting lock of hair, esp. on the forehead; **cowman** (*a*) a cowherd; (*b*) = COWBOY *noun* 3; **cow-pad** = ***cowpat*** below; **cow parsley** a tall hedgerow umbellifer, *Anthriscus sylvestris*, with white flowers and finely cut leaves; **cow parsnip** a tall hedgerow umbellifer, *Heracleum sphondylium*, with whitish flowers and segmented leaves; hogweed; **cowpat** a roundish patch of cow dung; **cowpea** a leguminous plant, *Vigna unguiculata*, grown as fodder in southern Europe and the southern US; its seed, eaten as pulse; **cow pen** an enclosure for cows; **cow-pen** *verb trans.* pen cows on (land); **cow pie** *N. Amer. colloq.* a cowpat; **cowpoke** *N. Amer. colloq.* = COWBOY *noun* 3; **cow pony** *US*: trained for use in cattle-ranching; **cowpox** a viral disease of cows which produces vesicles on teats and udders and the virus of which is used in vaccination against smallpox; **cowpuncher** *N. Amer. colloq.* = COWBOY *noun* 3; **cow-run** a common on which cows pasture; **cow shark** a shark of the family Hexanchidae, with six or seven gill openings on either side of the head instead of the usual five; **cowshed** a shed for cows not at pasture; a milking shed; **cow-shot** *Cricket slang* a clumsy attacking shot made by hitting across the ball, usu. in the direction of midwicket; **cow-skin** *noun & verb trans.* = ***cowhide*** above; **cow-spanker** *Austral. & NZ slang* = ***cow-banger*** above; **cow-tail** †(*a*) the bushy tail of the Tibetan yak used as a fly whisk; (*b*) the coarsest grade of wool, sheared from the sheep's hind legs; **cow town** *N. Amer.* (*a*) a town that is a local centre in a cattle-raising area; (*b*) a small isolated or unsophisticated town; **cow tree** a Venezuelan tree, *Brosimum utile*, of the mulberry family, with a juice looking and tasting like cow's milk; any of several other tropical American trees with a milky juice; **cow wheat** (orig.) *Melampyrum arvense*, a Eurasian cornfield weed of the figwort family with pinkish bracts; (now) any plant of the same genus, *esp.* (more fully **common cow wheat**) *M. pratense* of woods and heaths.
▸ **B** *attrib.* or as *adjective*. Of a domesticated ox or other large animal (orig. of a calf): female. **OE.**

cow /kaʊ, kuː/ *noun*[2]. *Scot.* **L15.**
[ORIGIN from Old French *coe*, *coue* (mod. *queue*) tail, or from COW *verb*[1].]
A twig; a tufted stem of heather; a bunch of these, *esp.* a besom or a birch.

cow /kaʊ/ *noun*[3]. *Scot.* **E16.**
[ORIGIN Unknown.]
A hobgoblin; an object of terror. Cf. WORRICOW.

cow /kaʊ/ *noun*[4]. *dial.* **M18.**
[ORIGIN Var. of COWL *noun*[1].]
= COWL *noun*[1] 4.

cow /kaʊ, kəʊ/ *verb*[1] *trans. Scot.* **E16.**
[ORIGIN Var. of COLL *verb*[2]: cf. *knowe*, *pow* for *knoll*, *poll*.]
1 Crop the hair of; clip, cut short. **E16.**
2 Surpass, outdo. **M19.**

cow /kaʊ/ *verb*[2] *trans.* **L16.**
[ORIGIN Prob. from Old Norse *kúga* oppress, tyrannize over (Norwegian *kue*, Middle Swedish *kufwa*, Swedish *kuva*).]
Frighten or browbeat into humility or submission; overawe, intimidate. Freq. foll. by *into*.

C. ACHEBE He seemed the quiet type and . . a little cowed by his beautiful, bumptious wife. M. ESSLIN The individual cowed into conformism by society.

cowabunga /kaʊəˈbʌŋɡə, kɑːwə-/ *interjection. slang.* **M20.**
[ORIGIN Prob. fanciful.]
Esp. among children: expr. exhilaration, delight, or satisfaction, or as an excited call to action.

cowage /ˈkaʊɪdʒ/ *noun*. Also **cowhage**. See also COWITCH. **M17.**
[ORIGIN Hindi *kawāc*, *-āc*.]
The stinging hairs on the pods of a leguminous vine, *Mucuna pruriens*, formerly used as an antidote for intestinal worms; the plant itself; its pods.

cowan /ˈkaʊən/ *noun*. **L16.**
[ORIGIN Unknown.]
1 A drystone-waller; *derog.* a person who does a mason's work without having been apprenticed to the trade. *Scot.* **L16.**
2 A person who is not a Freemason. **E18.**

coward /ˈkaʊəd/ *noun, adjective, & verb*. **ME.**
[ORIGIN Old French *cuard* (later *couard*) from Proto-Romance var. of Latin *cauda* tail (cf. sense B.2 below): see -ARD.]
▸ **A** *noun*. A person who shows unworthy fear in the face of danger, pain, or difficulty; a person with little or no courage. **ME.**
▸ **B** *attrib.* or as *adjective*. **1** Cowardly. **ME.**

POPE The Coward-Counsels of a tim'rous Throng.

2 HERALDRY. Of a lion or other animal: having the tail drawn in between the hind legs. **E16.**
▸ †**C** *verb trans.* **1** Weaken the courage of, make afraid. **ME–L17.**
2 Call, or show to be, a coward. **M–L17.**
■ **cowardize** *verb trans.* make cowardly, daunt **E17.** **cowardness** *noun* (*obsolete* exc. *Scot.*) cowardice **LME.** †**cowardship** *noun* cowardice **ME–E17.**

cowardice /ˈkaʊədɪs/ *noun*. **ME.**
[ORIGIN Old French *couardise*, from *couard*: see COWARD, -ISE[1], -ICE[1].]
Cowardly quality; lack of courage.
moral cowardice: see MORAL *adjective*.

cowardly /ˈkaʊədli/ *adjective*. **M16.**
[ORIGIN from COWARD + -LY[1].]
1 Acting like a coward; having little or no courage. **M16.**

SHAKES. *Hen. V* The cowardly rascals that ran from the battle.

2 Characteristic of a coward; proceeding from a spirit of cowardice. **L16.**

LD MACAULAY The affront was not only brutal, but cowardly.

■ **cowardliness** *noun* **L15.**

cowardly /ˈkaʊədli/ *adverb*. **LME.**
[ORIGIN from COWARD *adjective* + -LY[2].]
In the manner of a coward; with base avoidance of danger.

cowardy /ˈkaʊədi/ *adjective. colloq.* **M19.**
[ORIGIN from COWARD *noun* + -Y[1].]
Cowardly. Esp. in the children's taunts ***cowardy custard***, ***cowardy cowardy custard*** (CUSTARD *noun*[2]).

cowboy /ˈkaʊbɔɪ/ *noun, verb, & adjective*. Esp. in sense A.1 also **cow boy**, **cow-boy**. **E17.**
[ORIGIN from COW *noun*[1] + BOY *noun*.]
▸ **A** *noun*. **1** A boy who tends cows. **E17.**
2 US HISTORY. In the War of Independence, a member of a band of pro-British marauders operating near New York. **L18.**
3 *N. Amer.* A mounted cattle-herder or rancher; *spec.* one employed to drive large herds of cattle to new pastures, ports, etc., in the days of open ranges, *c* 1865–90 (later a stock character in the genre of westerns). **M19.**
cowboys and Indians a children's game in which conflicts between cowboys and American Indians are imitated.
4 A boisterous, unruly, or aggressive young man. *slang.* **E20.**
drugstore cowboy: see DRUG *noun*[1].
5 A reckless or irresponsible motorist. *colloq.* **M20.**
6 An unqualified, unskilled, or unauthorized trader or operator. *colloq.* **L20.**
– COMB.: **cowboy boots** high-heeled, freq. richly ornamented, boots of a style worn by cowboys.
▸ **B** *verb intrans.* Work as a cowboy. *N. Amer. colloq.* **E20.**
▸ **C** *attrib.* or as *adjective*. Irresponsible, dubiously legal; providing an inferior service or product; employing sharp practices. *colloq.* **M20.**

Times A 'cowboy' carpet fitter has left a trail of complaints in South Yorkshire.

cower /ˈkaʊə/ *verb*. **ME.**
[ORIGIN Middle Low German *kūren* lie in wait (whence German *kauern*), of unknown origin.]
1 *verb intrans.* Stand or squat in a bent position; crouch, esp. for shelter or in fear. **ME.**

F. BOWEN The dog cowers at the sight of the whip. J. STEINBECK He crouched cowering against the wall.

2 *verb trans.* Lower, bend down. *rare* exc. *Scot.* **L18.**
■ **coweringly** *adverb* in the manner of a person who cowers **E19.**

cowey *adjective* var. of COWY.

cowhage *noun* var. of COWAGE.

cow-heart /ˈkaʊhɑːt/ *noun*. Now *dial.* **M18.**
[ORIGIN Alt., after COW *noun*[1], HEART *noun*.]
A coward.
■ **cow-ˈhearted** *adjective* faint-hearted, timorous, cowardly **M17.**

cowish /ˈkaʊɪʃ/ *noun*. **E19.**
[ORIGIN Prob. N. American Indian.]
An umbelliferous plant of the Oregon region, *Lomatium cous*; its edible root.

cowish /ˈkaʊɪʃ/ *adjective*. **L16.**
[ORIGIN from COW *noun*[1] + -ISH[1].]
1 Like a cow. **L16.**
†**2** Cowardly. **L16–E17.**

cowitch /ˈkaʊɪtʃ/ *noun*. **M17.**
[ORIGIN Alt. of COWAGE by assoc. with *itch*.]
= COWAGE.

cowl /kaʊl/ *noun*[1] *& verb*.
[ORIGIN Old English *cug(e)le*, *cūle*, corresp. to Middle Low German, Middle Dutch *cōghel*, Old High German *cucula*, *cugula*, *chugela* (German *Kugel*, *Kogel*), from ecclesiastical Latin *cuculla* from Latin *cucullus* hood of a cloak. In Middle English reinforced by *kuuele* from Old English *kufle* and prob. by Old French & mod. French *coule*.]
▸ **A** *noun*. **1** A hooded sleeveless garment worn by monks. Also, a full cloak with wide sleeves worn by members of Benedictine orders. **OE.**
2 The hood of such a garment. **L16.**
3 Monkhood, monasticism; a monk. **M17.**

POPE What differ more (you cry) than crown and cowl?

4 A vented covering fitted on top of a chimney or ventilation shaft to improve the draught. (Earlier as COW *noun*[4].) **E19.**
– COMB.: **cowl neck** a neck on a woman's garment that hangs in draped folds.
▸ **B** *verb trans.* **1** Clothe (as) with a monk's cowl; make a monk of. **M16.**

R. D. BLACKMORE Mountains, cowled with fog.

2 Draw over like a cowl. **E19.**

H. E. BATES A sort of black cloak . . half like the garment, cowled over the head, that nuns or nurses wear.

■ **cowled** *adjective* wearing or provided with (something resembling) a cowl **LME.**

cowl /kaʊl/ *noun*[2]. Now *arch. & dial.* Also **coul**.
[ORIGIN Old English *cyfel* app. from Old French *cuvele* from late Latin *cupella* dim. of *cupa* tub, vat.]
A tub or large vessel for water etc.; *esp.* one with two ears, for carrying by two people on a cowl staff (see below).
– COMB.: **cowl staff** a stout stick for carrying a burden, supported on the shoulders of two bearers.

cowle /kaʊl/ *noun. Indian.* **L17.**
[ORIGIN Arabic *qawl* utterance, declaration.]
A written agreement; *esp.* (a) safe conduct or amnesty.

cowling /ˈkaʊlɪŋ/ *noun*. **E20.**
[ORIGIN from COWL *noun*[1] + -ING[1].]
The removable covering over the engine etc. of an aeroplane or motor vehicle.

cowp *noun* var. of COUP *noun*[2].

Cowper's gland /ˈkaʊpəz gland/ *noun phr.* **M18.**
[ORIGIN William *Cowper* (1666–1709), English anatomist.]
= ***BULBO-URETHRAL gland***.
■ **Cowperian** /kaʊˈpɪərɪən/ *adjective* **L19.** **Cowpeˈritis** *noun* inflammation of a bulbo-urethral gland **L19.**

cowrie /ˈkaʊ(ə)ri/ *noun*. Also **cowry**. **M17.**
[ORIGIN Hindi *kauṛī*.]
1 A small gastropod, *Cypraea moneta*, of the Indian Ocean; its polished shell, formerly used as money in parts of Africa and southern Asia. Also ***money-cowrie***. **M17.**
2 (The usu. smooth glossy shell of) any gastropod of this genus or the family Cypraeidae, marked by an oval shape and narrow elongated opening. **M19.**

cowslip /ˈkaʊslɪp/ *noun*.
[ORIGIN Old English *cūslyppe*, *cūsloppe*, formed as COW *noun*[1] + SLIP *noun*[1]: cf. OXLIP, SLOP *noun*[2].]
1 A spring-flowering primula, *Primula veris*, of dry grassy banks and pastures, bearing drooping umbels of fragrant yellow flowers; (with specifying word) any of various other plants resembling this. Also, a flowering stem of such a plant. **OE.**
American cowslip any of various N. American plants bearing umbellate mostly purple or white flowers with reflexed petals

that constitute the genus *Dodecatheon*, of the primrose family; esp. *D. meadia*. **Cape cowslip** = LACHENALIA. ***Virginia cowslip***: see VIRGINIA 1. ***Virginian cowslip***: see VIRGINIAN *adjective*.
2 The marsh marigold, *Caltha palustris*. *US*. **M19**.
▪ **cowslipped** *adjective* covered with cowslips **L18**. **cowslipping** *noun* the gathering of cowslips **L19**.

cowson /ˈkaʊs(ə)n/ *noun*. *slang*. *derog*. **M20**.
[ORIGIN from COW *noun*[1] + SON *noun*[1], after *whoreson*.]
A detestable person or (occas.) thing.

J. R. ACKERLEY A cowson of a place.

cowy /ˈkaʊi/ *adjective*. Also **-ey**. **L19**.
[ORIGIN from COW *noun*[1] + -Y[1].]
Of, pertaining to, or characteristic of a cow.

cox /kɒks/ *noun*[1] & *verb*. **M19**.
[ORIGIN Abbreviation of COXSWAIN.]
▸ **A** *noun*. A coxswain, esp. of a racing boat. **M19**.
▸ **B** *verb trans*. & *intrans*. Act as the cox of (a boat); be a cox. **L19**.
▪ **coxless** *adjective* **L19**.

Cox /kɒks/ *noun*[2]. Also **Cox's** /ˈkɒksɪz/. **M19**.
[ORIGIN R. *Cox*, amateur English fruit-grower, who first raised it (1825).]
In full ***Cox's orange pippin***. A leading variety of eating apple with a red-tinged green skin.

COX /kɒks/ *noun*[3]. **L20**.
[ORIGIN Shortened from *cyclooxygenase*.]
The enzyme cyclooxygenase (freq. with distinguishing number designating the main forms, esp. in ***COX-1*** and ***COX-2***).

coxa /ˈkɒksə/ *noun*. Pl. **coxae** /ˈkɒksiː/. **LME**.
[ORIGIN Latin = hip.]
†**1** ANATOMY. The thigh; the thigh bone. Only in **LME**.
2 ANATOMY. The hip; the hip bone. *rare*. **L17**.
3 ZOOLOGY. The segment nearest the body in the leg of an insect or other arthropod. **E19**.
▪ **coxal** *adjective* **E19**. **coˈxalgia** *noun* [Greek *algos* pain] pain in the hip joint **M19**. **coˈxalgic** *adjective* pertaining to or affected with coxalgia **L19**.

coxcomb /ˈkɒkskəʊm/ *noun*. Also †**cockscomb**, †**cock's comb**. See also COCKSCOMB. **M16**.
[ORIGIN Var. of COCKSCOMB.]
1 Orig., a fool, a simpleton. Now, a conceited showy empty-headed person; a fop. **M16**.

GOLDSMITH Fond to be seen she kept a bevy Of powdered coxcombs at her levy.

2 See COCKSCOMB II.
▪ †**coxcombly** *adjective* = COXCOMBICAL **L16–E19**. **coxcombry** /-kəmri/ *noun* †(***a***) foolishness; (***b***) coxcombical quality; a coxcombical trait or act: **E17**.

coxcombical /kɒksˈkəʊmɪk(ə)l, -ˈkɒm-/ *adjective*. **E18**.
[ORIGIN from COXCOMB + -ICAL.]
Resembling, pertaining to, or characteristic of a coxcomb; foolishly conceited.
▪ **coxcombic** *adjective* = COXCOMBICAL **L18**. **coxcombiˈcality** *noun* coxcombical quality; a coxcombical act: **M18**. **coxˈcombically** *adverb* **M18**.

†**coxen** *noun*. Also **-on**. **E17–M18**.
[ORIGIN Repr. pronunc.]
= COXSWAIN.

coxopodite /kɒkˈsɒpədʌɪt/ *noun*. **L19**.
[ORIGIN from COXA + -O- + Greek *pous*, *pod-* foot + -ITE[1].]
ZOOLOGY. The segment nearest the body in the leg of an arthropod, esp. a crustacean.
▪ **coxopoˈditic** *adjective* **L19**.

Cox's *noun* see Cox *noun*[2].

Coxsackie virus /kɒkˈsaki ˌvʌɪrəs, kʊk-/ *noun phr*. Also **c-** & as one word. **M20**.
[ORIGIN *Coxsackie* in New York State, where the first cases were found.]
Any of a group of enteroviruses which cause various respiratory, neurological, and muscular diseases in humans.

coxswain /ˈkɒks(ə)n, -sweɪn/ *noun* & *verb*. Also **cockswain**. **ME**.
[ORIGIN from COCK *noun*[2] + SWAIN *noun*.]
▸ **A** *noun*. The steersman of a ship's boat, lifeboat, racing boat, etc.; the senior petty officer on board a small ship, submarine, etc. **ME**.
▸ **B** *verb trans*. & *intrans*. Act as the coxswain of (a boat); be a coxswain. **E20**.
▪ **coxswainless** *adjective* **L19**. **coxswainship** *noun* **L19**.

coxy /ˈkɒksi/ *adjective*. *dial*. & *slang*. Also **cocksy**. **E18**.
[ORIGIN from COCK *noun*[1] + -SY.]
Impudent, bumptious, cocky.
▪ **coxiness** *noun* **M19**.

coy /kɔɪ/ *noun*. Now *dial*. **E17**.
[ORIGIN Dutch *kooi*, †*koye*, a parallel development to Middle Dutch *kouwe* (Dutch dial. *kouw* cage), = Middle Low German *kaue* from Latin *cavea* CAGE *noun*. Cf. DECOY *noun*.]
1 A place for entrapping wildfowl; = DECOY *noun* 1. **E17**.
2 In full ***coy-duck***. A decoy-duck. **E17**.

coy /kɔɪ/ *adjective*. **ME**.
[ORIGIN Old French & mod. French *coi*, earlier *quei*, from Proto-Romance var. of Latin *quietus* QUIET *adjective*.]
†**1** Quiet, still. Chiefly in ***bear*** (***oneself***) ***coy***, ***hold*** (***oneself***) ***coy***, ***keep*** (***oneself***) ***coy***. **ME–M17**.
2 Displaying modest backwardness, shy; *spec*. (of a (young) woman) unresponsive to amorous advances, esp. in an affected or coquettish way. Of behaviour, a look, etc.: suggesting or marked by this quality. **LME**. ▸**b** Affecting reluctance to make a statement or give information; archly reticent. **M20**.

SHAKES. *Ven. & Ad*. 'Tis but a kiss I beg; why art thou coy?

†**3** Distant in manner, disdainful. **L15–M17**.
4 Chary or shy *of*; reluctant *to*. **L16**.
5 Of a place or thing: withdrawn from view or access; secluded. **M17**.
▪ **coyish** *adjective* (now *rare*) **M16**. **coyly** *adverb* **LME**. **coyness** *noun* **L16**.

coy /kɔɪ/ *verb*. **LME**.
[ORIGIN from COY *adjective*, or perh. orig. aphet. from ACCOY.]
†**1** *verb trans*. Calm, make quiet. **LME–M16**.
†**2** *verb trans*. Stroke or touch soothingly; caress. **LME–L17**.
†**3** *verb trans*. Coax; win over by caresses. **L15–L18**.
4 *verb intrans*. & (usu.) *trans*. with *it*. Behave coyly; affect modesty or reserve. *arch*. **L16**.
†**5** *verb intrans*. Disdain *to do*. *rare* (Shakes.). Only in **E17**.
6 *verb trans*. Disguise (affection etc.) in a coy manner. *rare*. **L19**.

Coy. *abbreviation*.
Esp. MILITARY. Company.

coydog /ˈkɔɪdɒg/ *noun*. *N. Amer*. **M20**.
[ORIGIN from COYOTE + DOG *noun*.]
A hybrid between a coyote and a wild dog.

†**coyn** *noun* see QUINCE.

coynye /ˈkɔɪn(j)i/ *noun*. Also **coignye**, **coyne** /kɔɪn/. **LME**.
[ORIGIN Irish *coinneamh*.]
IRISH HISTORY. Food and entertainment exacted by chiefs for the billeting of their attendants; a tax imposed in place of this.

coyote /ˈkɔɪəʊt, kɔɪˈəʊti/ *noun* & *verb*. Pl. same, **-s**. **M18**.
[ORIGIN Mexican Spanish from Nahuatl *coyotl*.]
▸ **A** *noun*. A small nocturnal wolflike animal, *Canis latrans*, of western N. America, noted for its mournful howling. Also called ***prairie wolf***. **M18**.
– COMB.: **coyote diggings** small lateral shafts sunk by miners in California, resembling the holes of the coyote.
▸ **B** *verb intrans*. MINING. Make a small lateral tunnel from a shaft etc. *US slang*. **M19**.

coypu /ˈkɔɪpuː/ *noun*. Also **-pou**. Pl. same, **-s**. **L18**.
[ORIGIN Mapuche.]
A S. American semi-aquatic rodent, *Myocastor coypus*, resembling a beaver, bred for its fur (nutria) and now naturalized in parts of Europe and the US.

coz /kʌz/ *noun*. *arch*. **M16**.
[ORIGIN Abbreviation.]
Cousin. (Usu. as a form of address.)

coze /kəʊz/ *noun* & *verb*. **E19**.
[ORIGIN App. from French *causer* chat, perh. assoc. with *cozy*, COSY.]
▸ **A** *noun*. A long intimate talk. **E19**.
▸ **B** *verb intrans*. Converse in a friendly way; have a long chat. **E19**.

cozen /ˈkʌz(ə)n/ *verb trans*. **L16**.
[ORIGIN Perh. from Italian †*cozzonare* act as a horsebreaker, cheat, from *cozzone* middleman, broker from Latin *cocio(n-)*, *coctio(n-)* dealer. Cf. also Old French *coçoner* act as a middleman with, ult. from same Latin source.]
1 Cheat, trick, (*of*, *out of*); trick, beguile, *into*. **L16**.
2 Deceive, mislead. **L16**.
▪ **cozenage** *noun* the practice or an act of cozening; (a) deception, (a) fraud: **L16**. **cozener** *noun* a cheat, an impostor **M16**.

cozy *adjective*, *noun*, & *verb* see COSY.

cozzie *noun* var. of COSSIE.

CP *abbreviation*.
1 *hist*. Cape Province.
2 PARTICLE PHYSICS. Charge conjugation and parity.
3 Communist Party.
4 Country Party. *Austral*.

cp. *abbreviation*.
Latin *compara* compare.

c.p. *abbreviation*.
Candlepower.

CPA *abbreviation*. *US*.
Certified public accountant.

C.Phys. *abbreviation*.
Chartered physicist.

CPI *abbreviation*. *US*.
Consumer price index.

Cpl *abbreviation*.
Corporal.

CPO *abbreviation*.
Chief Petty Officer.

CPR *abbreviation*.
Canadian Pacific Railway.

CPRE *abbreviation*.
Council for the Protection of Rural England.

cps *abbreviation*.
COMPUTING. **1** Characters per second.
2 Cycles per second.

C

CPSA *abbreviation*.
Civil and Public Services Association.

CPT *abbreviation*.
PARTICLE PHYSICS. Charge conjugation, parity, and time reversal.

CPU *abbreviation*.
Central processing unit.

CR *abbreviation*.
CHRISTIAN CHURCH. Community of the Resurrection.

Cr *symbol*.
CHEMISTRY. Chromium.

Cr. *abbreviation*.
1 Councillor.
2 Creditor.

crab /krab/ *noun*[1].
[ORIGIN Old English *krabba* = Middle & mod. Low German, Middle Dutch & mod. Dutch *krabbe*, Old Norse *krabbi* rel. to Middle Low German *krabben* CRAB *verb*[1], Old Norse *krafla* scratch.]
1 Any of numerous decapod crustaceans of the section Brachyura, which have the first pair of legs modified into pincers and can move in any direction, including sideways and backwards; *esp*. any of the edible kinds found near seashores; the flesh of any of these used as food. Also (with qualification), any of various similar crustaceans and arachnids. **OE**.
fiddler crab, ***hermit crab***, ***horseshoe crab***, ***land crab***, ***peeler crab***, ***shore crab***, ***spider crab***, ***velvet crab***, etc. **catch a crab** (in rowing) get one's oar jammed under water, as if it were being held down by a crab; also, miss the water with the stroke.
2 **a** (Usu. **C-**.) *The* constellation and zodiacal sign Cancer. **OE**. ▸**b** ***the Crab*** (***nebula***), a nebula in the constellation Taurus, the remnant of a supernova outburst observed in 1054. **M19**.
3 In full ***crab louse*** (otherwise usu. in *pl*.). A parasitic insect, *Phthirus pubis*, infesting the pubic and other hair in humans. **M16**.
4 Any of various contrivances (orig. one with claws) for hoisting or hauling heavy weights; *esp*. (***a***) a kind of capstan without a drumhead; (***b***) a portable winch; (***c***) the lifting gear of a travelling crane. **E17**.
5 In *pl*. The lowest throw in the game of hazard, two ones. Formerly also, hazard. Cf. ***crab's eyes*** (c) below, CRAPS. **M18**.
6 [After German *Krebs*.] A book returned unsold to the publisher. *colloq*. **L19**.
– COMB.: **crab-catcher** *W. Indian* a heron which feeds on crabs, *esp*. the green heron *Butorides striatus*; †**crab fish** = sense 1 above; **crabgrass** †(***a***) glasswort; (***b***) (orig. *US*) a creeping grass; esp. *Digitaria sanguinalis*, widespread as a weed in warmer parts of the world; **crab harrow** a harrow with bent teeth for breaking up deeply ploughed land; **crab hole** *Austral*. a depression in the ground attributed to the action of a land crab; ***crab louse***: see sense 3 above; ***Crab nebula***: see sense 2b above; **crab plover** a gregarious large-billed white and black crab-eating wading bird, *Dromas ardeola*, of coasts around the Indian Ocean; **crab pot** a wickerwork trap for catching crabs; **crab's eye** (***a***) a calcareous concretion from the stomach of a crayfish etc., formerly used in powdered form as an absorbent and antacid (usu. in *pl*.); (***b***) in *pl*., (the scarlet, black-tipped seeds of) the jequirity; (***c***) in *pl*., (*slang*) = sense 5 above; **crab spider** a spider of the family Thomisidae which runs sideways like a crab.
▪ **crabber** *noun*[1] a person who fishes for crabs; a boat used in crabbing: **LME**. **crablike** *adjective* & *adverb* (***a***) *adjective* resembling (that of) a crab; (***b***) *adverb* = CRABWISE *adverb*: **L16**. **crabwise** *adverb* & *adjective* (***a***) *adverb* moving sideways or backwards like a crab; (***b***) *adjective* = CRABLIKE *adjective*: **E20**.

crab /krab/ *noun*[2]. **LME**.
[ORIGIN Perh. alt. of SCRAB *noun* by assoc. with CRAB *noun*[1] or CRABBED. Sense 3 in later use back-form. from CRABBED.]
1 The wild apple, a native fruit of northern Europe, smaller than the cultivated apple and noted for its sour, astringent flavour. Also, the fruit of an ornamental crab (see sense 2 below). **LME**.
2 In full ***crab tree***. The European tree, *Malus sylvestris*, which bears the wild apple. Also, any of various small-fruited trees of the genus *Malus* grown for ornament, e.g. the Siberian crab, *M. baccata*. **LME**.
3 A sour or cross-grained person. **L16**.
– COMB.: **crab apple** = senses 1, 2 above; **crab stick** a stick made from the wood of the crab tree; *fig*. a bad-tempered person; **crab stock** a young crab tree used as a stock for grafting on; ***crab tree***: see sense 2 above.

crab /krab/ *noun*[3]. Also **carap(a)** /kəˈrap(ə)/. **M18**.
[ORIGIN from *carap*, the Antillean name from Carib = oil.]
A S. American tree, *Carapa guianensis*, of the mahogany family.
– COMB.: **crab-nut** the seed of the crab; **crab-oil** the oil obtained from crab-nuts, used in lamps and as an anthelmintic; **crabwood** the timber of the crab.

C

crab /krab/ *noun*⁴. *colloq.* L19.
[ORIGIN from CRAB *verb*¹.]
The action or an instance of finding fault or complaining; a reason for fault-finding or complaint, a grouse.

crab /krab/ *verb*¹. Infl. **-bb-**. L16.
[ORIGIN Middle & mod. Low German *krabben* rel. to CRAB *noun*¹.]
1 *verb trans. & intrans.* FALCONRY. Of hawks: scratch and fight (each other). L16.
2 *verb trans.* Obstruct the progress or success of (a scheme etc.); spoil the plans of (a person). *colloq.* E19.
C. SANDBURG You're trying to crab my act.
3 *verb trans.* Criticize, find fault with. *colloq.* M19.
R. MACAULAY It is a pity to crab all governments and everything they do.
4 *verb intrans.* Grumble, complain (*at*, *about*). *colloq.* L19.
B. TRAPIDO If you don't come he'll crab on at us about the expense.
■ **crabber** *noun*² a person who criticizes or complains E20.

crab /krab/ *verb*². Infl. **-bb-**. M17.
[ORIGIN from CRAB *noun*¹.]
1 *verb intrans.* Fish for or take crabs. Chiefly as ***crabbing*** *verbal noun* M17.
2 *verb intrans.* NAUTICAL. Drift sideways to leeward. M19.
3 *verb trans. & intrans.* AERONAUTICS. Turn (an aircraft) into the wind to offset drift. E20.
4 *verb trans. & intrans. gen.* Move (something), move oneself, sideways or obliquely like a crab. M20.

crab /krab/ *verb*³ *trans.* Infl. **-bb-**. L19.
[ORIGIN Unknown.]
In worsted finishing: wind (cloth) on a roller under tension and subject it to hot water or steam, to prevent subsequent cockling or wrinkling. Chiefly as ***crabbing*** *verbal noun*.

crabbed /ˈkrabɪd, krabd/ *adjective*. ME.
[ORIGIN Orig. from CRAB *noun*¹ (cf. DOGGED *adjective*), with ref. to the gait and habits of the crab, which suggest a cross-grained disposition: cf. Low German *krabbe* cantankerous man, *krabbig* contentious, cross-grained. Later assoc. with CRAB *noun*².]
1 Of a person: orig., objectionably perverse or wayward; later, irritable, cantankerous (passing into sense 5). ME. ▸**b** In a bad mood; cross, irritated. Orig. & chiefly *Scot.* LME. ▸†**c** Of words, facial expression, etc.: indicating irritability or anger. LME–M17.
†**2** Unpleasant to the taste, unpalatable. LME–E17.
3 †**a** Of a tree, stick, etc.: crooked, gnarled. E16–L17. ▸**b** Of weather, terrain: rough, rugged. *obsolete* exc. *dial.* L16.
4 a Of writings, an author, etc.: hard to understand or interpret; involved, intricate. M16. ▸**b** Of handwriting: hard to decipher. E17.
5 Like a crab apple; *fig.* sour-tempered, morose. M16.
■ **crabbedly** *adverb* LME. **crabbedness** *noun* LME.

crabby /ˈkrabi/ *adjective*. M16.
[ORIGIN from CRAB *noun*¹ (in sense 3, partly from CRAB *noun*²) + -Y¹.]
†**1** Crooked; perplexing. M–L16.
2 Resembling the crab (CRAB *noun*¹). Formerly *spec.*, moving obliquely. L16.
3 Bad-tempered; morose. L18.

crack /krak/ *noun*. Also †**crake**. ME.
[ORIGIN Corresp. to Middle Dutch *crak*, Old High German, German *Krach*: cf. CRACK *verb*.]
▸ **I** Of sound, & derived senses.
1 A sudden sharp loud noise (as) of something breaking or exploding, of a whip, a rifle, thunder, etc. ME.
a crack of the whip, **a fair crack of the whip** *colloq.* a (fair) chance to act, participate, or prove oneself. **crack of doom** *arch.* the thunder peal of the Day of Judgement.
2 a Formerly, a cannon shot. Now (*colloq.*), a rifle shot. LME. ▸**b** An attempt, a try. Chiefly in ***have a crack at***. *colloq.* (orig. *US*). E19. ▸**c** A sharp blow. *colloq.* M19.
b B. SCHULBERG Maybe I'll give another agency first crack at it instead.
3 a Boastful talk; an instance of this. Also, a flagrant lie. Now *dial.* LME. ▸**b** A gossip, an intimate talk; in *pl.*, items of gossip. *Scot. & N. English.* E18. ▸**c** A witty or sarcastic remark; a wisecrack. *colloq.* (orig. *US*). L19. ▸**d** Amusement provided by conversation; congenial conversation. Chiefly in ***for the crack***. Cf. CRAIC. *Irish colloq.* M20.
c J. THURBER Insinuations, reflections, or . . cracks about old boy friends . . should be avoided.
4 A short space of time, a moment. Esp. in ***in a crack***. *colloq.* E18.
crack of dawn the moment when dawn breaks.
▸ **II** Breaking or the result of it.
5 A slight opening formed by the breaking of a hard substance; a fissure. L15. ▸**b** *spec.* A gap between floorboards. *US.* E19. ▸**c** The chink left when a door etc. is not quite closed. L19.
F. A. KEMBLE Centipedes . . come out of the cracks . . of the walls.
paper over the cracks *fig.* use temporary expedients to disguise confusion or disagreement.
6 A deficiency or flaw (in an abstract thing). M16. ▸**b** A mental flaw; a mania, a craze. E17.
b STEELE The Upholsterer, whose Crack towards Politicks I have . . mentioned.
7 An incomplete break or fracture, in which the parts still cohere. L16.
8 Cracked or broken tone (as of a boy's voice at puberty). E17.
SHAKES. *Cymb.* Though now our voices Have got the mannish crack.
9 A burglary. *arch. criminals' slang.* E19.
▸ **III** Transferred or doubtfully derived senses.
†**10** A lively, boisterous boy or youth. L16–L17.
11 A sports player, horse, etc., of outstanding excellence. M17.
†**12** A disreputable woman; a prostitute. L17–L18.
13 Cocaine heated with baking powder until hard and broken into small pieces for smoking or inhaling. Orig. *US slang.* L20.
– COMB.: **crackhead** *slang* a person who habitually takes crack; **crack house** *slang* a place where crack is bought and sold.
■ **crackless** *adjective* free from cracks or flaws E17.

crack /krak/ *adjective*. *colloq.* L18.
[ORIGIN from CRACK *noun* 11.]
Pre-eminent in a particular sphere, first-class.
J. K. JEROME Crack shots, winners of Queen's prizes. P. USTINOV Soldiers of several crack regiments.

crack /krak/ *verb*. Also †**crake**.
[ORIGIN Old English *cracian* = Middle Dutch & mod. Dutch *kräken*, Old High German *krahhōn* (German *krachen*).]
▸ **I** With chief ref. to sound.
1 *verb intrans.* Of a thing breaking, of thunder, a gun, a whip, etc.: make a sudden sharp or explosive noise. OE. ▸**b** *verb trans.* Strike with a resounding blow. Now *dial.* or *colloq.* LME. ▸**c** *verb trans.* Cause (a whip etc.) to make a sharp noise. M17.
POPE Silks russle, and tough Whalebones crack. J. STEINBECK The flame cracked up among the twigs. **b** X. HERBERT Don't be cheeky or I'll crack you.
2 *verb trans.* Utter or tell, esp. suddenly or with éclat. Now only in ***crack a joke*** or with the spoken words of a joke or wisecrack as obj. ME.
T. HOCCLEVE Not a worde dar he crake. B. SCHULBERG 'Yeah,' Sammy cracked, 'you should have been there.'
3 *verb intrans.* Talk big, boast. Now *dial.* LME. ▸†**b** *verb trans.* Claim boastfully *that*, a person or thing *to be*. M16–L17.
CARLYLE My sleep was nothing to crack of.
4 *verb intrans.* Discuss the news, gossip, chat. *Scot. & N. English.* LME.
▸ **II** With chief ref. to breaking.
5 *verb trans.* Break (esp. something hard and hollow) with a sudden sharp noise. ME.
N. MOSLEY His head was like an egg that you crack and it runs over the egg cup.
6 a *verb intrans. & trans.* (Cause to) snap or break in two. *arch.* ME. ▸**b** *verb intrans. fig.* Break down, give way, yield (to torture etc.), succumb to pressure. Cf. ***crack up*** (b) below. M17.
a *fig.*: SHAKES. *Cymb.* He could not But think her bond of chastity quite crack'd. **b** N. MAILER They both cracked . . . They couldn't stop laughing.
7 a *verb intrans. & trans.* (Cause to) break without complete separation of parts. LME. ▸**b** *verb trans.* Open up fissures in. M17. ▸**c** *verb trans.* Break or crush (esp. corn) into small particles. *US.* M19.
a W. SALMON Some Colours . . will crack when they are dry. D. W. JERROLD There's four glasses broke and nine cracked.
8 *transf. & fig.* **a** *verb trans.* Damage (something abstract) so that it is no longer sound. Formerly esp. in †***crack credit***. M16. ▸**b** *verb trans.* Impair the reasoning power of. E17. ▸**c** *verb trans. & intrans.* With ref. to the voice, esp. in puberty or old age: make or become hoarse or dissonant, like a cracked bell. E17.
a ANTHONY WOOD [This] . . hath much crak'd his Reputation. **b** STEELE Lest this hard . . student should . . crack his brain with studying. **c** G. VIDAL Gallus's voice cracked with anger.
9 *verb trans.* Open and drink (a bottle of liquor). *colloq.* L16.
10 *verb trans.* Find the solution to (a problem, code, etc.). E17.
11 *verb trans.* Break into (a house, safe, etc.). *criminals' slang.* E18.
12 *verb trans.* Decompose (heavy oils) by heat or pressure so as to produce lighter hydrocarbons, such as petrol. M19.
▸ **III** Of sudden action.
13 *verb trans.* Move with a jerk or sudden movement; snatch *out*, clap *on*. M16.
14 *verb intrans.* Travel with speed; rush *along*, press *on*. Chiefly NAUTICAL exc. in ***get cracking*** below. M19.
– PHRASES: **crack a crib** *criminals' slang* burgle a house. **crack hardy**, **crack hearty** *Austral. & NZ slang* put on a show of courage in the face of misfortune or difficulty. **crack on sail** NAUTICAL hoist additional sails to increase speed. **crack the whip** *fig.* enforce one's authority. **get cracking** *colloq.* set to work briskly. ***take a sledgehammer to crack a nut***, ***use a sledgehammer to crack a nut***: see SLEDGEHAMMER *noun*.
– WITH ADVERBS IN SPECIALIZED SENSES: **crack down** *colloq.* take severe repressive measures (foll. by *on*, *upon*). **crack up** *colloq.* (*a*) extol, praise; in *pass.* (usu. in neg. contexts), be asserted in glowing terms *to be*; (*b*) collapse under strain etc., suffer a nervous breakdown; collapse with laughter.

crack /krak/ *interjection & adverb*. L17.
[ORIGIN from CRACK *noun*, *verb*.]
▸ **A** *interjection.* Repr. a cracking sound. L17.
▸ **B** *adverb.* With a crack. M18.

crack- /krak/ *combining form*. L15.
[ORIGIN Partly repr. the stem of CRACK *verb*, usu. with a following obj.; partly for CRACKED.]
1 a That cracks (the 2nd elem. of the comb.). ▸**b** That cracks.
2 Cracked.
■ **crack-brain** *colloq.* a crazy person, a crank. **crackbrained** *adjective* (*colloq.*) crazy, cranky. †**crack-halter** = ***crack-rope*** *noun* below. **crack-headed** *adjective* (*colloq.*) crazy, cranky. †**crack-hemp** = ***crack-rope*** *noun* below. **crack-jaw** *noun & adjective* (*colloq.*) (a word that is) difficult to pronounce. **crackpot** *noun & adjective* (*colloq.*) (*a*) *noun* a crazy person; an eccentric or unpractical person; (*b*) *adjective* crazy, cranky, eccentric, unpractical. †**crack-rope** *noun & adjective* (*a*) *noun* a person fit to be hanged, a gallows bird; (*b*) *adjective* fit to be hanged; roguish. **crack-voiced** *adjective* having a broken voice. **crack willow** a willow, *Salix fragilis*, with branches that break off readily.

crackajack *noun & adjective* var. of CRACKERJACK.

crackdown /ˈkrakdaʊn/ *noun*. *colloq.* M20.
[ORIGIN from ***crack down*** s.v. CRACK *verb*.]
An instance of cracking down, a taking of severe repressive measures.

cracked /krakt/ *ppl adjective*. Also †**crackt**. E16.
[ORIGIN from CRACK *verb* + -ED¹.]
1 That has cracked or been cracked; broken. E16. ▸**b** *spec.* Broken or crushed into coarse particles. Orig. *US.* M19.
SHAKES. *1 Hen. IV* We must have bloody noses and crack'd crowns. DICKENS The lips were parched and cracked in many places. R. WEST She forced her voice, and only achieved a cracked whisper.
b ***cracked corn***, ***cracked rice***, ***cracked wheat***, etc.
2 *fig.* Flawed, unsound; blemished in reputation etc. *arch.* E16.
T. DEKKER A most false and crackt Latin oration. SWIFT A cracked chambermaid.
3 Deranged, slightly mad, crazy; infatuated. Now *colloq.* E17.
D. JACOBSON He was a little cracked—it could be seen in his remote, pale eyes.
– COMB.: **cracked-pot** *noun & adjective* (*fig.*, *colloq.*) = ***crackpot*** s.v. CRACK-.
■ **crackedness** *noun* (*colloq.*) unsoundness of mind E20.

cracker /ˈkrakə/ *noun*. LME.
[ORIGIN from CRACK *verb* + -ER¹.]
1 A noisy boastful person. Also, an extravagant liar. LME. ▸**b** A flagrant lie. *colloq.* E17.
2 An instrument for cracking or crushing something, esp. (*sing.* & (usu.) in *pl.*) for cracking nuts. Also, an installation for cracking hydrocarbons. M16.
cat cracker, ***nutcracker***, etc.
3 A kind of firework that explodes with a sharp report or series of reports. L16. ▸**b** A cylindrical paper structure made so as to break with a bang when its ends are pulled, used on festive occasions, and often containing a paper hat, a motto or joke, a small toy or novelty, etc. M19.
b ***Christmas cracker***.
4 The pintail duck (so called from its alarm call). *local.* M17.
5 A thin dry biscuit. M18. ▸**b** A light crisp made of rice or tapioca flour. Usu. with specifying word. M20.
cream cracker etc. **b** ***prawn cracker***, ***shrimp cracker***, etc.
6 Orig., a frontier outlaw. Later, a 'poor white' in certain of the southern states of the US, esp. Florida and Georgia. *derog. US.* M18.
7 An attachment to the end of a whiplash, to enhance its cracking. *US, Austral., & NZ.* M19.
8 An outstandingly good person or thing. *colloq.* E20.
R. DOYLE She was a cracker alright.
– COMB.: **cracker-barrel** *noun & adjective* (*N. Amer.*) (*a*) *noun* a barrel in which crackers (biscuits) are packed; (*b*) *adjective* (of philosophy, a philosopher, etc.) homespun; **cracker-bush** an Australian tree of the spurge family, *Petalostigma glabrescens*, with a fruit that splits open with a loud report.

crackerjack /ˈkrakədʒak/ *noun & adjective*. *colloq.* (orig. *US*). Also **crackajack**. L19.
[ORIGIN Fanciful formation from CRACK *verb* or CRACKER.]
▸ **A** *noun.* **1** Something exceptionally good of its kind. Also, a very skilful person. L19.
2 A sweet made of popcorn and syrup. (Orig. a proprietary name.) E20.
▸ **B** *adjective.* Of outstanding excellence, first-rate. E20.

crackers /ˈkrakəz/ *pred. adjective*. *slang.* E20.
[ORIGIN from CRACKER *noun*: see -ER⁶. Cf. CRACKED 3.]
Crazy, mad; infatuated.

cracket *noun* see CRICKET *noun*³.

cracking /ˈkrakɪŋ/ *adjective & adverb*. LME.
[ORIGIN from CRACK *verb* + -ING².]
▸ **A** *adjective*. **1** That cracks or breaks. LME.
†**2** Bragging; boastful. E16–L17.
3 Very good or pleasing, outstanding; (of pace) very fast. *slang*. M19.

A. CARTER She'd have made a cracking dancer, if she'd put her mind to it.

▸ **B** *adverb*. Outstandingly, very. *slang*. E20.

crackle /ˈkrak(ə)l/ *noun*. L16.
[ORIGIN from the verb.]
†**1** A child's rattle. Only in L16.
2 A crackling sound. M19.

E. GLASGOW The crackle of the leaves underfoot. F. WELDON The transistor radio produced only crackle.

snap, crackle, and pop, snap, crackle, pop: see SNAP *noun*.
3 A network of fine cracks induced in the glaze of china, pottery, glass, etc., for decorative effect. Also = ***crackle-ware*** below. M19.
– COMB.: **crackle-ware** a kind of china marked by a crackle in the glaze.

crackle /ˈkrak(ə)l/ *verb*. LME.
[ORIGIN from CRACK *verb*: see -LE³.]
1 *verb intrans*. Emit a succession of slight cracking sounds. Formerly also (*derog.*), trill or quaver in singing. LME. ▸**b** *fig*. Sparkle with vigour or animation. M20.

C. HARDWICK Huge logs blazed and crackled. D. H. LAWRENCE The wind made the canvas crackle.

2 *verb trans*. Cause to emit a crackling sound; break with a crackling sound. E17.

J. STEINBECK His fingers crackled the paper in his pocket.

■ **crackled** *ppl adjective* (*a*) (of roast pork) having the skin crisp and hard (see CRACKLING 3); (*b*) (esp. of ceramics etc.) marked by many small cracks. E17. **crackly** *adjective* having a tendency to crackle M19.

crackling /ˈkraklɪŋ/ *noun*. L16.
[ORIGIN from CRACKLE *verb* + -ING¹. Cf. SCRATCHING *noun*¹.]
1 The action of CRACKLE *verb*. L16.
2 In *pl*. ▸**a** The residue of tallow-melting, used to feed dogs. L16. ▸**b** The residue of hogs' fat after the lard has been fried out. *dial. & US*. M19.
3 The crisp skin of roast pork. E18. ▸**b** Sexually attractive women collectively. Esp. in ***a bit of crackling***, ***a nice bit of crackling***. *slang, offensive*. M20.
4 Crackle-ware. L19.

cracknel /ˈkrakn(ə)l/ *noun*. LME.
[ORIGIN Alt. of Old French & mod. French *craquelin* from Middle Dutch *krākeline*, from *krāken* CRACK *verb*.]
A light crisp kind of biscuit. Also, a brittle sweet made from set melted sugar.

cracksman /ˈkraksmən/ *noun*. *criminals' slang*. Pl. **-men**. L18.
[ORIGIN from CRACK *noun* 9 + -'S¹ + MAN *noun*.]
A burglar. Also, a person who breaks open safes.

†**crackt** *ppl adjective* var. of CRACKED.

crack-up /ˈkrakʌp/ *noun*. *colloq*. E20.
[ORIGIN from *crack up* s.v. CRACK *verb*.]
An instance of cracking up, a collapse under strain etc.; a nervous breakdown.

cracky /ˈkraki/ *adjective*. L15.
[ORIGIN from CRACK *noun* or *verb* + -Y¹.]
1 Full of cracks or fissures; inclined to crack. L15.
2 Full of conversation; talkative, affable. *Scot. & N. English*. E19.
3 Cracked in the head, crazy. *colloq*. M19.
■ **crackiness** *noun* (*colloq.*) craziness M19.

cracovienne /krəkəʊvɪˈɛn/ *noun*. M19.
[ORIGIN French, fem. adjective from *Cracovie* Kraków (Cracow), a city in southern Poland.]
A lively Polish dance; a ballet dance in a Polish style. Also called ***krakowiak***.

-cracy /krəsi/ *suffix*.
[ORIGIN Repr. French *-cratie*, medieval Latin *-cratia*, Greek *-kratia* power, rule (*kratos* strength, authority).]
In or forming nouns referring to types of government or ruling class, as ***democracy***, ***aristocracy***, etc. From the *o* which regularly precedes the suffix in words of Greek origin a form *-ocracy* has been inferred which has been added to certain English words (mainly in nonce-formations), as ***meritocracy***.

cradle /ˈkreɪd(ə)l/ *noun*.
[ORIGIN Old English *cradol*, perh. from the same base as Old High German *kratto*, Middle High German, German *Kratte* basket.]
▸ **I 1** A little bed or cot for an infant, *esp*. one mounted on rockers or swinging. OE.
cradle to grave, **from cradle to grave**, **from the cradle to the grave** throughout one's whole life. **from the cradle**, **from one's cradle** from infancy (to any stage in life). See also ***cat's cradle*** s.v. CAT *noun*¹.
2 Any bed or place of repose. *poet*. ME.
3 *fig*. The place in which a thing begins or is nurtured in its earlier stage; the beginning. (Foll. by *of*.) L16.

A. BEVAN The district which was the cradle of heavy industry in Britain.

4 NAUTICAL. A bedstead for a wounded seaman. Now *rare*. E19.
▸ **II** *techn*. **5** A framework of bars, cords, rods, etc., used as a support or protection; a grating, a structure resembling a hurdle. LME.
6 A framework on which a ship or boat rests during construction or repairs or down which it is slid when launched. E16.
7 A wooden frame attached to a scythe, with a row of long curved teeth parallel to the blade, which enable the cut corn to be laid more evenly. L16.
8 MEDICINE. A framework to protect an injured limb etc. from the weight of bedclothes. E18. ▸**b** A frame placed round the neck of an animal to prevent it from biting an injury or sore. M19.
9 ENGRAVING. A chisel-like tool with a serrated edge, which is rocked to and fro over a metal plate to produce a mezzotint ground. Also called ***rocker***, ***mezzotint rocker***. L18.
10 A trough on rockers in which auriferous earth or sand is shaken in water in order to separate the gold. E19.
11 A framework on or in which a person is supported to work on the vertical face of a building, ship, etc. L19.
12 A rest or support for a telephone receiver not in use. E20.
13 CRICKET. A device used to deflect a ball thrown on it in practising short-range fielding. M20.
– COMB.: **cradleboard** among N. American Indians, a board to which an infant is strapped; **cradle cap** (*a*) a cap worn by a baby; (*b*) an area of yellowish or brownish scales that sometimes forms on the top of a baby's head; the condition of having this, seborrhoeic eczema of the scalp in a baby; **cradle Catholic** a person who has been a Roman Catholic from birth; **cradle-rocker** (*a*) any of the curved bars fitted under a child's cradle to enable it to rock; (*b*) a person who rocks a child's cradle; **cradle-roof** a roof of semi-cylindrical shape, divided into panels by wooden ribs; **cradle scythe** a scythe fitted with a cradle (sense 7); **cradle-snatch** *verb trans. & intrans*. (*slang*) have a love affair with or marry (a much younger person); **cradle-snatcher** *slang* a person who has a love affair with or marries a much younger person; **cradle song** a lullaby.

cradle /ˈkreɪd(ə)l/ *verb*. LME.
[ORIGIN from the noun.]
▸ **I** *verb trans*. **1** Lay in, or as in, a cradle; rock to sleep; hold or shelter as in a cradle. LME.

W. STYRON Her head was cradled against the inside of her arm.

2 Nurture, shelter, or rear in infancy (*lit. & fig.*). E17.
3 Mow (corn etc.) with a cradle scythe. M18.
4 *techn*. Support in or on a cradle; raise (a vessel) to a higher level by a cradle. L18.
5 Wash (auriferous earth etc.) in a miner's cradle. M19.
6 Support the back of (a picture etc.) by ribs and transverse narrow strips. L19.
7 Replace (a telephone receiver) on its cradle. M20.
▸ †**II** *verb intrans*. **8** Lie as in a cradle. *rare* (Shakes.). Only in E17.
■ **cradler** *noun* a person who or thing which cradles; formerly *esp*. a person who mows with a cradle scythe: M18.

cradling /ˈkreɪdlɪŋ/ *noun*. E19.
[ORIGIN from CRADLE *verb* + -ING¹.]
1 The action of CRADLE *verb*. E19.
2 ARCHITECTURE. A wooden or iron framework, esp. in a ceiling. E19.

craft /krɑːft/ *noun*.
[ORIGIN Old English *cræft* = Old Frisian *kraft*, Old Saxon *kraft* (Dutch *kracht*), Old High German, German *Kraft*, Old Norse *kraptr* (in sense 1 only). The transference to 'skill, art, occupation' is English only.]
▸ **I** †**1** Strength, power, force. OE–E16.
2 Skill, art; ability in planning or constructing; ingenuity, dexterity. Now chiefly as 2nd elem. of comb. OE. ▸†**b** *spec*. Occult art, magic. ME–L15. ▸†**c** Human skill; art as opp. to nature. LME–L16.
priestcraft, ***stagecraft***, ***statecraft***, ***witchcraft***, ***woodcraft***, etc.
†**3** An artifice, a device, a skilful contrivance; *spec*. a magical device. OE–M16.
4 In a bad sense: ▸†**a** A deceitful action; a trick, a fraud. OE–L17. ▸**b** Skill or art applied to deceive or overreach; guile, cunning. ME.

b J. CONRAD With her it was very difficult to distinguish between craft and innocence.

5 An art, trade, or profession requiring special skill or knowledge, esp. manual dexterity. OE. ▸**b** The members of a trade or handicraft collectively; a trade union, guild, or company of craftsmen. LME.

C. PRIEST I determined to learn country crafts: weaving, woodwork, pottery. S. SPENDER Painting is largely a craft . . whereas writing is largely cerebral.

handicraft etc. ***arts and crafts***: see ART *noun*¹. ***the gentle craft***: see GENTLE *adjective*. **b the Craft** the brotherhood of Freemasons.
†**6** Scholarship; a branch of learning, a science. ME–M16.
▸ **II** Vehicles, equipment, etc.
7 (Pl. same (*collect*., the earliest use), †**-s**.) A boat, esp. of small size; a vessel; a machine for flying in or for travelling in space. LME.

L. T. C. ROLT The water was packed with crowded, flag-bedecked craft.

aircraft, ***spacecraft***, etc. ***small craft***: see SMALL *adjective*.
8 *collect*. (usu. treated as *pl*.). Implements used in catching and killing fish. Now *rare*. L17.
– COMB.: **craft-brother** one of the same craft or trade; **craft-conscious** *adjective* aware of the value of craftsmanship; **craft guild** a guild of people of the same craft or trade; **craftsmaster** *arch*. (*a*) a person skilled in a particular craft or trade; †(*b*) a master of deceitful craft or cunning; **craftspeople** artisans; **craftsperson** an artisan; **craftswoman** a female artisan; **craft union** a trade union of people of the same skilled craft; **craftwork** work in a handicraft, (the production of) items of handicraft.
■ **craftless** *adjective* OE.

craft /krɑːft/ *verb*. ME.
[ORIGIN from the noun.]
†**1** *verb trans*. Attain, win. *rare*. Only in ME.
2 *verb trans*. Make or construct skilfully. (In isolated use before M20.) LME.

T. KENEALLY One of the prisoners, a jeweller . . had been crafting a present.

†**3** *verb intrans*. Act craftily; use one's craft or skill. E16–E17.

craftsman /ˈkrɑːftsmən/ *noun*. Also †**craftman**. Pl. **-men**. LME.
[ORIGIN from CRAFT *noun* + -'S¹ + MAN *noun*.]
1 A person who practises a handicraft; an artisan. LME.
2 A person who cultivates one of the fine arts, = ARTIST 3. L19.
3 A private soldier in the Royal Electrical and Mechanical Engineers. M20.
■ **craftsmanship** *noun* M17.

crafty /ˈkrɑːfti/ *adjective*.
[ORIGIN Old English *cræftig* = Old Saxon *kraftag*, *-ig*, Old High German *kreftig* (German *kräftig*), Old Norse *kroptugr*: see CRAFT *noun*, -Y¹.]
†**1** Strong, powerful. OE–ME.
2 Skilful, dexterous, clever, ingenious. Now *arch. & dial*. OE.

W. MORRIS His crafty hands are busy yet.

3 Cunning, artful, wily. ME.

B. HARRIS The most crafty Cheats are held the best Politicians. LD MACAULAY Had not his crafty schemes been disconcerted.

– COMB.: †**crafty-sick** *adjective* feigning sickness.
■ **craftily** *adverb* OE. **craftiness** *noun* LME.

crag /krag/ *noun*¹. Also (*Scot. & N. English*) **craig** /kreɪg/. ME.
[ORIGIN Of Celtic origin. Sense 3 prob. a different word.]
1 A steep rugged rock; a rough rock detached or projecting. ME.

A. MASON That barren . . land of crags and precipices.

crag and tail GEOLOGY a rock formation which is steeply rugged on one side and gently sloping on the other.
†**2** As a material: rock. LME–E19.
3 GEOLOGY. Deposits of shelly sand found in East Anglia; the Pliocene and Miocene strata to which these belong. M18.
– COMB.: **crag-bound**, **crag-fast** *adjectives* (of a person or animal) trapped on a crag and unable to go either up or down; **cragsman** a person accustomed to or skilled in climbing crags.

crag /krag/ *noun*². Chiefly *Scot. & N. English*. Also **craig** /kreɪg/. LME.
[ORIGIN Prob. from Low Dutch: cf. Middle Low German *krage*, Middle Dutch *crāghe*, Dutch *kraag*. Cf. SCRAG *noun*¹.]
1 The neck. LME. ▸**b** The throat. L18.
†**2** A neck of mutton or veal. LME–M18.

cragged /ˈkragɪd/ *adjective*. LME.
[ORIGIN from CRAG *noun*¹ + -ED².]
1 Rugged, rough. LME.
2 Formed into or having many crags. M16.
■ **craggedness** *noun* L16.

craggy /ˈkragi/ *adjective*. LME.
[ORIGIN from CRAG *noun*¹ + -Y¹.]
1 Having many crags; of the nature of a crag, steep and rugged. LME.
2 Of a person, a face, etc.: rough or rugged in form. M16.
3 *fig*. Hard to deal with; rough, difficult. Now *rare*. L16.
■ **cragginess** *noun* E17.

craic /krak/ *noun*. *Irish*. L20.
[ORIGIN Irish form of CRACK *noun*.]
Fun, amusement; entertaining conversation; = CRACK *noun* 3d.

craig *noun*¹, *noun*² see CRAG *noun*¹, *noun*².

craigie /ˈkreɪgi/ *noun*. *Scot. & N. English*. E18.
[ORIGIN from *craig*, CRAG *noun*² + -IE.]
= CRAG *noun*².

crake /kreɪk/ *noun*¹. Also (*Scot.*) **craik**. ME.
[ORIGIN Old Norse *krāka*, *krākr*, of imit. origin: cf. CROAK.]
1 A crow, a raven. *N. English*. ME.
2 A bird of the family Rallidae, *esp*. any of the shorter-billed kinds such as the corncrake and the members of the genus *Porzana* (cf. RAIL *noun*³). LME.
CORNCRAKE. SORA ***crake***. **spotted crake** *Porzana porzana*, a brown skulking marsh bird with a high, sharp call.
3 The harsh cry of the corncrake. M19.

†**crake** *noun*² see CRACK *noun*.

C

crake /kreɪk/ *verb*[1] *intrans.* LME.
[ORIGIN Prob. imit.]
1 Utter a harsh grating cry. LME.
2 Of a door etc.: grate harshly, creak. Now *Scot. & dial.* M17.

†**crake** *verb*[2] var. of CRACK *verb*.

crakow /ˈkrakəʊ/ *noun*. *obsolete* exc. *hist.* LME.
[ORIGIN *Cracow*, *Kraków*, or French *Cracovie*, in Poland: see CRACOVIENNE.]
A boot or shoe with a very long pointed toe, worn in the 14th cent.

cram /kram/ *verb & noun*.
[ORIGIN Old English *(ge)crammian* corresp. to Middle Low German *kremmen*, Old Norse *kremja* squeeze, pinch, from Germanic. Rel. to Dutch *krammen* cramp, clamp, Middle High German *krammen* claw.]
▸ **A** *verb*. Infl. **-mm-**.
1 *verb trans.* Fill (a space, receptacle, etc.) completely, esp. by force or compression; overfill. (Foll. by *with*.) OE.

A. J. CRONIN A large chilly basement, crammed to the ceiling with second-hand goods. J. G. FARRELL An enormous letter, crammed with confidences.

2 *verb trans.* Feed to excess (*spec.* poultry etc. to fatten them up, *with* food). ME. ▸**b** *verb intrans.* Eat greedily or to excess, stuff oneself. M16.
3 *verb trans.* Force or stuff (something) *into* a receptacle, space, etc., which it overfills, *down* someone's throat, etc. LME.

E. REVELEY Most working parents . . have to cram everything into two tightly organized days.

4 *verb trans.* Convince (a person) of a false or exaggerated statement. *slang.* L18.
5 *verb trans. & intrans.* Prepare for an examination etc. by intensive coaching or study; study (a subject) intensively for an examination etc. *colloq.* E19.

THOMAS HUGHES He had been well crammed in his science. A. S. NEILL I crammed Botany and Zoo for my degree and I know nothing about either. J. GALSWORTHY They were cramming for an important examination.

6 *verb trans.* Urge (a horse) on forcibly. *arch. slang.* E19.
▸ **B** *noun*. **1** In *pl.* Food used to fatten poultry or other livestock. *dial.* E17.
2 A dense crowd, a crush, a squeeze. *colloq.* E19.
3 The action of cramming for an examination etc.; information crammed. *colloq.* E19.
4 A lie. *slang.* M19.
– COMB.: **cram-full** *adjective* as full as cramming can make it; **cram-jam** *verb trans. & adverb* (*colloq. & dial.*) (fill) cram-full.
■ **crammable** *adjective* (of information) able to be crammed M19.

†**crambe** *noun*. M16.
[ORIGIN Latin from Greek *krambē*: usu. with ref. to *crambe repetita* (Juvenal). Cf. CRAMBLE.]
1 Cabbage (in *fig.* contexts as something distasteful repeated); distasteful repetition. Also ***crambe bis cocta*** [medieval Latin = twice cooked]. M16–M18.
2 = CRAMBO 2, 3. E17–E19.

cramble /ˈkramb(ə)l/ *verb intrans.* Long *obsolete* exc. *dial.* Also **crammle** /ˈkram(ə)l/. L16.
[ORIGIN Imit.: cf. SCRAMBLE *verb*.]
†**1** Of roots, stems, etc.: creep about, twine. Only in L16.
2 Hobble, crawl. E17.

crambo /ˈkrambəʊ/ *noun*. E17.
[ORIGIN Alt. of CRAMBE, on an Italian or Spanish model.]
†**1** A particular fashion in drinking. Only in E17.
2 A game in which one player gives a word or line of verse to which each of the others has to find a rhyme. M17.
dumb crambo a game in which one side has to guess a word chosen by the other side, after being given a word which rhymes with it, by acting in mime various words until they find it.
3 Rhyme, rhyming. *derog.* L17.
†**4** Distasteful repetition; = CRAMBE 1. L17–E18.

crammer /ˈkramə/ *noun*. M17.
[ORIGIN CRAM *verb* + -ER[1].]
1 A person who or an apparatus which crams poultry etc. M17.
2 A person who or an institution which crams pupils for an examination etc. E19.
3 A lie. *slang.* M19.

crammle *verb* var. of CRAMBLE.

cramoisy /ˈkramɔɪzi/ *adjective & noun*. *arch.* LME.
[ORIGIN Early Italian *cremesi* and Old French *crameisi* (mod. *cramoisi*) ult. from Arabic *qirmizī*, from *qirmiz* KERMES: cf. CRIMSON.]
Crimson (cloth).

cramp /kramp/ *noun*[1]. LME.
[ORIGIN Old French *crampe* from Middle Low German, Middle Dutch *krampe* = Old High German *krampfo* rel. to Old Saxon *kramp*, Old High German, German *Krampf*, uses as noun of an adjective meaning 'bent' (Old High German *krampf*, Old Norse *krappr* narrow, Old English *crampiht*). Cf. CRAMP *noun*[2], CRIMP *verb*[1].]
1 Involuntary painful contraction of a muscle or muscles, often caused by cold, a slight strain, etc.; an instance of this. LME.

E. BLISHEN A tendency to sensational cramp . . I would fall writhing to the ground, my leg muscles knotted. J. DOS PASSOS Her belly was all knotted up with a cramp.

SCRIVENER's cramp. ***writer's cramp***: see WRITER.
2 Any of various diseases of animals, *esp.* a disease affecting the wings of hawks. Now *rare.* LME.
– COMB.: **cramp-bone** the kneecap of a sheep, formerly believed to be a charm against cramp; **cramp fish** the electric ray or torpedo; **cramp-ring** a ring believed to be efficacious against cramp etc., *esp.* (*hist.*) one of those consecrated by the English monarch on Good Friday for this purpose.
■ **crampy** *adjective*[1] liable to or suffering from cramp; inducing cramp; of the nature of cramp: LME.

cramp /kramp/ *noun*[2]. LME.
[ORIGIN Middle Dutch *krampe* (whence German *Krampe*, French *crampe*) = Old Saxon *krampo*, of same ult. origin as CRAMP *noun*[1].]
1 = CRAMPON 2. *obsolete* exc. *dial.* LME.
2 = CRAMP-IRON 2. LME.
3 A portable tool or press with a movable part which can be screwed up so as to hold things together. Cf. CLAMP *noun*[1] 3. M17.
4 *fig.* A constraining force or power; a cramping restraint. E18.

H. MATTHEWS His genius was embarrassed by the cramp . . of the French literary laws.

5 A footplate of iron etc. worn on ice to secure one's grip or, if polished, to skate on. Cf. CRAMPET 3, CRAMPON 2. E19.
■ **crampy** *adjective*[2] restricting, confining M19.

cramp /kramp/ *adjective*. L17.
[ORIGIN Uncertain: perh. from CRAMP *noun*[1] or *verb*.]
1 Difficult to make out; crabbed; cramped. L17.
2 Constrained, narrow; cramping. L18.
■ **crampness** *noun* M19.

cramp /kramp/ *verb*. LME.
[ORIGIN from CRAMP *noun*[1], *noun*[2].]
▸ **I** Connected with CRAMP *noun*[1].
1 *verb trans.* Affect with cramp. Usu. in *pass.* LME.
†**2** *verb trans.* Cause (a person) to be seized with cramp. L16–L17.
▸ **II** Connected with CRAMP *noun*[1] and (esp.) CRAMP *noun*[2].
†**3** *verb trans.* Compress or squeeze with irons in punishment or torture. (Opp. *rack*.) M16–E18.
4 *verb trans.* Restrict or confine narrowly. Also foll. by *up*. E17.

ALDOUS HUXLEY He has only narrowed . . his life; and . . cramped his intellect. B. SPOCK The shoes big enough so that the toes aren't cramped. *Country Life* A car . . with a very cramped interior.

cramp a person's style restrict a person's natural behaviour, prevent a person from acting freely.
5 *verb trans. & intrans.* Deflect or turn to one side. *US.* L19.

J. DICKEY The river hooked and cramped.

▸ **III** Connected with CRAMP *noun*[2].
6 *verb trans.* Fasten or secure with a cramp or cramps. M17.
■ **cramped** *adjective* (*a*) that has been cramped; (*b*) (of handwriting) small and difficult to read: L17.

crampet /ˈkrampɪt/ *noun*. LME.
[ORIGIN App. from CRAMP *noun*[2].]
1 = CRAMP-IRON 2. LME.
2 The chape of the scabbard of a sword. L15.
3 = CRAMPON 2, formerly *esp.* one used by curlers, to enable the player to remain steady while delivering the stone; a footboard used for the same purpose. Orig. *Scot.* M17.
4 A wall hook. E20.

cramp-iron /ˈkrampʌɪən/ *noun*. M16.
[ORIGIN from CRAMP *noun*[2] + IRON *noun*.]
†**1** = CRAMPON 2. M16–L18.
2 A small metal bar with the ends bent so as to hold together two pieces of masonry, timber, etc. L16.

crampon /ˈkrampən/ *noun*. Also ***crampoon** /kramˈpuːn/. ME.
[ORIGIN Old French & mod. French from Frankish: cf. CRAMP *noun*[2].]
1 = CRAMP-IRON 2. Also, a metal bar with the end bent in the form of a hook; a grappling iron. ME.
2 A small plate of iron etc. set with spikes and fastened to the foot in order to give a better grip on ice or steep inclines. L18.

cramponny /kramˈpɒni/ *adjective*. Also **-nnée** /-neɪ/. E18.
[ORIGIN French *cramponnée*, formed as CRAMPON.]
HERALDRY. Of a cross: having a right-angled hook at the end of each limb.

crampoon *noun* see CRAMPON.

cran /kran/ *noun*[1]. *Scot.* LME.
[ORIGIN Var. of CRANE *noun*[1].]
▸ **I 1** The crane; the heron. Now *rare* or *obsolete.* LME.
2 The swift. M19.
▸ **II 3** An iron instrument to support a pot or kettle over a fire. M18.
coup the crans *fig.* have an upset, come to grief.

cran /kran/ *noun*[2]. *Scot.* L18.
[ORIGIN Gaelic *crann*, perh. identical with *crann* lot, applied to the share of fish given to each man engaged.]
A measure for fresh herrings, equal to 37½ gallons (170 litres, or about 750 fish).

cranage /ˈkreɪnɪdʒ/ *noun*. LME.
[ORIGIN from CRANE *noun*[1] + -AGE.]
(Dues paid for) the use of a crane to hoist goods.

cranberry /ˈkranb(ə)ri/ *noun*. M17.
[ORIGIN from German *Kranbeere*, Low German *kranebeere* lit. 'crane berry'.]
1 (The acid bright red fruit of) any of several Eurasian or American dwarf hardy shrubs of the genus *Vaccinium*, of the heath family, esp. *V. oxycoccos*, and the larger American *V. macrocarpon*. M17.
2 Any of various shrubs of similar appearance, the fruits of which may be used in cooking as a substitute for cranberries. M19.
bush cranberry a N. American bush, *Viburnum trilobum*, allied to the guelder rose. **native cranberry** *Austral.* (the fruit of) either of two shrubs of the epacris family, *Styphelia sapida* and *Astroloma humifusum*.
– COMB.: **cranberry bush** = ***bush cranberry*** above; **cranberry jelly**, **cranberry sauce**: made with cranberries and eaten as a relish with turkey etc; **cranberry tree** = ***bush cranberry*** above.
– NOTE: The word was orig. adopted by N. American colonists from a German source; previously the plant was known by such names as *marsh-whort*, *fen-whort*, *fen-berry*, and *moss-berry*.

crance /krans/ *noun*. M19.
[ORIGIN Perh. from Dutch *krans* garland. Cf. CRANTS.]
NAUTICAL. An iron cap on the outer end of the bowsprit, through which the jib boom passes; a boom iron.

cranch /krɑːn(t)ʃ/ *verb & noun*. Also (exc. in sense B.1) **craunch** /krɔːn(t)ʃ/. M17.
[ORIGIN Prob. imit.: cf. SCRANCH.]
▸ **A** *verb trans. & intrans.* Crunch, crush or grind noisily. M17.
▸ **B** *noun*. **1** MINING. A part of a stratum or vein left when excavating, to support the roof. M18.
2 A crunch. E19.

crane /kreɪn/ *noun*[1] & *adjective*. See also CRAN *noun*[1].
[ORIGIN Old English *cran* = Middle Low German *krān*, *krōn*, Middle Dutch *crāne* (Dutch *kraan*), Old High German *krano* (German *Kran* in sense 2), rel. to Latin *grus*, Greek *geranos*.]
▸ **A** *noun*. **1** Any of various large birds of the family Gruidae, with long legs, neck, and bill; *esp.* one of the common European species *Grus grus*, ash-grey in colour. Also (*Austral.*), the brolga. OE. ▸**b** A heron; an egret; a stork; a shag. *dial.* or *local* exc. as below. LME. ▸**c** (Usu. **C-**.) *The* constellation Grus. L17.
demoiselle crane, ***sandhill crane***, ***whooping crane***, etc. ***wattled crane***: see WATTLED 2. **b blue crane** (*a*) *Austral.* the white-faced heron, *Ardea novaehollandiae*; (*b*) *S. Afr.* = ***STANLEY crane***.
2 A machine for moving heavy weights, usu. consisting of a vertical post capable of rotation on its axis, a projecting arm or jib over which passes the chain, rope, etc., from which the load is suspended, and a barrel round which the chain or rope is wound. ME. ▸**b** Any of various similar mechanical contrivances, as (***a***) a machine for weighing goods, constructed on the principles of a crane for moving heavy loads; (***b***) an upright revolving axis with a horizontal arm for suspending a pot, kettle, etc., over the fire; (***c***) NAUTICAL in *pl.*, projecting pieces of iron, timber, etc., on board a ship, to support a boat or spar; (***d***) a moving platform for a camera. E18.
luffing crane: see LUFF *verb*. ***travelling crane***: see TRAVELLING *ppl adjective*.
3 A bent tube used to draw liquor out of a vessel; a siphon. M17.
4 More fully ***water crane***. An apparatus consisting of an elevated tank and tube, for supplying water, esp. to a locomotive. M17.
– COMB.: **crane-colour** ashy-grey; **crane-coloured** *adjective* of crane-colour; **crane-driver** a person who drives and operates a crane; **crane fly** a long-legged two-winged fly of the family Tipulidae, a daddy-long-legs; **crane line** NAUTICAL any of a set of small ropes set up to prevent the lee backstays from chafing against the yards of a square-rigged ship when running before the wind (usu. in *pl.*); **craneman** a man in charge of a crane (sense 2); **crane-neck** (chiefly *hist.*) an iron bar uniting the back and front timbers of a carriage; **crane-necked** *adjective* (*a*) (chiefly *hist.*) having a crane-neck; (*b*) (esp. of a person) having a long neck like a crane's; **cranesbill** (*a*) any of the plants constituting the genus *Geranium* (family Geraniaceae), characterized by five-petalled purple, violet, pink, etc., flowers and long-beaked fruits; (*b*) a kind of surgical forceps with long jaws.
▸ **B** *adjective*. †**1** Crane-coloured. Only in E16.
2 Cranelike, long and lanky. L17.
■ **cranelike** *adjective* resembling (that of) a crane L19.

crane /kreɪn/ *noun*[2]. Now *arch. rare.* LME.
[ORIGIN French *crâne* formed as CRANIUM.]
The skull, the cranium.

crane /kreɪn/ *verb*. L16.
[ORIGIN from CRANE *noun*[1].]
1 *verb trans.* Hoist or lower (as) with a crane or similar apparatus. L16.

SIR W. SCOTT Being safely craned up to the top of the crag.

2 *verb trans. & intrans.* Stretch (the neck, *arch.* the head) like a crane; lean or bend forward with outstretched neck.

L18. ▸**b** *verb intrans.* Of a camera mounted on a crane: alter range or direction. Usu. foll. by adverb. M20.

J. WAIN He began craning to see over people's heads. B. CHATWIN Ganders hissed and craned their necks. J. K. ROWLING She spent so much of her time craning over garden fences, spying on the neighbours.

3 *verb intrans.* In the hunting field, pull up at a hedge etc. and look over before jumping; *fig.* (*colloq.*) hesitate at a danger, difficulty, etc. E19.

BYRON He clear'd hedge, ditch, and double post, and rail, And never *craned*.

crang *noun* var. of KRENG.

crani- *combining form* see CRANIO-.

cranial /ˈkreɪnɪəl/ *adjective*. E19.
[ORIGIN from CRANIUM + -AL[1].]
Of or pertaining to the cranium.
cranial index the ratio of the width of the skull to its length, usu. expressed as a percentage. **cranial nerve** each of twelve pairs of nerves arising directly from the brain and passing through separate apertures in the cranium.

craniate /ˈkreɪnɪət/ *noun & adjective*. L19.
[ORIGIN mod. Latin *craniatus*, formed as CRANIUM: see -ATE[2].]
(An animal) having a skull or cranium.

cranio- /ˈkreɪnɪəʊ/ *combining form* of Greek *kranion* skull: see -O-. Before a vowel also **crani-**.
■ **cranio-facial** *adjective* of or pertaining to both the cranium and the face L19. **craniˈometry** *noun* the science of measuring the differences in size and shape of skulls M19. **craniˈopathy** *noun* any disease of the cranium L19. **cranioplasty** *noun* (an instance of) a surgical operation to reconstruct or alter the shape of part of the skull L19. **cranio-spinal** *adjective* of or pertaining to both the cranium and the spine L19. **craniotome** *noun* a special instrument used for (esp. obstetric) craniotomy L19. **craniˈotomy** *noun* a surgical removal of part of the skull, performed in order to operate on the brain M19.

craniology /kreɪnɪˈɒlədʒi/ *noun*. E19.
[ORIGIN from CRANIO- + -LOGY.]
†**1** Phrenology. E–M19.
2 The branch of knowledge that deals with the size, shape, and character of skulls of different races etc. M19.
■ **cranioˈlogical** *adjective* of or pertaining to craniology E19. **cranioˈlogically** *adverb* M20. **craniologist** *noun* one who practises or is versed in craniology E19.

craniopagus /kranɪˈɒpəgəs/ *noun*. Pl. **-gi** /-gʌɪ/. L19.
[ORIGIN from CRANIO- + Greek *pagos* that which is fixed.]
MEDICINE. Conjoined twins attached at the head. Now usu. *attrib.*

cranium /ˈkreɪnɪəm/ *noun*. Pl. **-ia** /-ɪə/, **-iums**. LME.
[ORIGIN medieval Latin *cranium* from Greek *kranion* skull.]
1 The bones enclosing the brain; the bones of the whole head, the skull. LME.
2 The head. *joc.* M17.

crank /kraŋk/ *noun*[1].
[ORIGIN Old English *cranc-* in *crancstæf* weaver's implement (cf. *crenčestre* female weaver), rel. to *crinčan*, parallel to *cringan* fall in battle. Cf. Middle High German, German, Dutch *krank* sick (a fig. devel. of the primary notion of something bent or crooked).]
1 A part of an axle or shaft bent at right angles, used to communicate motion or for converting reciprocal into circular motion, or vice versa. OE.
2 An elbow-shaped connection in bell-hanging. M18.
3 An elbow-shaped support or bracket. M18.
4 *hist.* A revolving disc to which a regulated pressure could be applied, turned by prisoners as a punishment. M19.
– COMB.: **crank-axle** (*a*) the driving axle of an engine or machine; (*b*) a carriage axle with the ends bent twice at a right angle to lower the body while permitting the use of large wheels; **crankcase** the case or covering in which a crankshaft is enclosed; **crankpin** a pin by which a connecting rod is attached to a crank; **crankshaft** a shaft driven by a crank; **crank-wheel** a wheel acting as a crank; *esp.* one having near its circumference a pin to which the end of a connecting rod is attached as to a crankpin.

crank /kraŋk/ *noun*[2]. M16.
[ORIGIN Prob. ult. formed as CRANK *noun*[1]; in sense 6 back-form. from CRANKY *adjective*.]
†**1** An inaccessible hole or crevice; a cranny; a chink. M16–M19.
2 A crook, a bend; a crooked path, course, or channel; *fig.* a deceit, a wile. Long *obsolete* exc. *Scot.* L16.
3 A fanciful turn of speech; a conceit. L16.

MILTON Quips, and cranks, and wanton wiles.

4 In *pl.* Slight ailments; aches. *dial.* E19.
5 An eccentric notion or action; a crotchet, a whim, a caprice. Cf. earlier CRANKUM 2. M19.

T. S. ELIOT The critic . . should endeavour to discipline his personal prejudices and cranks.

6 An eccentric person; *esp.* a person subject to a whimsical enthusiasm. Orig. *US.* M19.

L. T. C. ROLT Amateurs and cranks aired their theories. M. SHADBOLT The man beside him looks normal, no crank.

†**crank** *noun*[3]. *slang*. M16–E17.
[ORIGIN Dutch or German *krank* sick: see CRANK *noun*[1].]
In full ***counterfeit crank***. A person who feigned sickness for the purpose of begging.

crank /kraŋk/ *adjective*[1]. LME.
[ORIGIN Unknown.]
†**1** Strong, vigorous; in good condition. LME–M17.
2 Lively, brisk; cheerful; aggressively or impudently high-spirited. Now *dial.* & *US.* L15.
■ **crankly** *adverb* (now *rare*) M16.

crank /kraŋk/ *adjective*[2]. E17.
[ORIGIN Uncertain: perh. connected with CRANK *adjective*[3] or with CRANK *noun*[1].]
More fully ***crank-sided***. Of a ship: liable to capsize, esp. through being built too deep or narrow, or through having too little ballast to carry full sail.

fig.: T. MOORE Things, which . . Still serve to ballast, with convenient words, A few crank arguments for speeching lords.

■ **crankness** *noun* L16.

crank /kraŋk/ *adjective*[3]. E18.
[ORIGIN from CRANK *noun*[1] or back-form. from CRANKY *adjective*.]
1 Crooked, distorted; angularly twisted or bent. *Scot.* E18.
2 Awkward or difficult to pronounce, understand, or do. *obsolete* exc. *Scot.* E18.

SWIFT Hard, tough, crank, gutt'ral, harsh, stiff names.

3 Infirm, in poor health; weak, ailing. *dial.* E19.
4 Of machinery etc.: in a shaky condition, in poor order; working with difficulty. M19.

CARLYLE The machinery of laughter took some time to get in motion, and seemed crank and slack.

■ **crankous** *adjective* (*Scot.*) irritable, fretful L18.

crank /kraŋk/ *verb*[1] *intrans.* L16.
[ORIGIN from CRANK *noun*[2].]
Twist and turn about; move in a sharply winding course; zigzag. Now chiefly with allus. to Shakes. (see below).

SHAKES. *1 Hen. IV* See how this river comes me cranking in, And cuts me from the best of all my land . . a monstrous cantle out.

crank /kraŋk/ *verb*[2]. L18.
[ORIGIN from CRANK *noun*[1].]
1 *verb trans.* Bend at right angles; bend sharply. L18.
2 *verb trans.* Provide with a crank, attach a crank to. M19.
3 *verb trans.* Fasten with a crank. L19.
4 *verb trans.* Draw *up* by means of a crank; operate by a crank. L19.
5 *verb trans.* & *intrans.* Turn (an engine) with a crank. E20. ▸**b** *verb trans.* & *intrans.* Foll. by *up*: start (an engine of a motor vehicle) by turning a crank, *slang* increase (speed etc.) by intensive effort. E20. ▸**c** *verb intrans.* Inject narcotics. Also foll. by *up*. *slang*. L20.

J. B. PRIESTLEY The car refused to start again . . . She cranked away until she was breathless. E. WAUGH The taxi-driver . . got out of his seat and cranked up the engine.

6 *verb trans.* Foll. by *out*. Produce (something) laboriously or mechanically. *colloq.* M20.

Economist An army of researchers . . crank out worthy studies on South-East Asian co-operation.

crank /kraŋk/ *verb*[3] *intrans.* E19.
[ORIGIN App. imit.]
Make a jarring or grating sound.

crankle /ˈkraŋk(ə)l/ *noun*. L16.
[ORIGIN from the verb or from CRANK *noun*[1], *noun*[2] + -LE[1]. Cf. CRINKLE-CRANKLE.]
A bend, a twist; an angular prominence.

crankle /ˈkraŋk(ə)l/ *verb*. L16.
[ORIGIN Frequentative of CRANK *verb*[1]: see -LE[3].]
1 *verb intrans.* Bend in and out; wind; follow a zigzag course. L16.
†**2** *verb trans.* Cause to follow a zigzag course; wrinkle (a surface). L16–E18.

crankum /ˈkraŋkəm/ *noun*. M17.
[ORIGIN Fanciful formation from CRANK *noun*[2].]
†**1** In *pl.* = CRINKUM. Only in M17.
2 = CRANK *noun*[2] 5. Cf. CRINKUM-CRANKUM. E19.

cranky /ˈkraŋki/ *adjective*. L18.
[ORIGIN Perh. orig. from CRANK *noun*[3]; also infl. by assoc. with CRANK *noun*[2]: see -Y[1].]
1 Sickly; in poor health; ailing. *dial.* L18.
2 Awkward; difficult to please; bad-tempered. E19.

M. FRENCH The baby . . was cranky and hungry.

3 Subject to whims; odd, eccentric. M19.

R. MACAULAY It's shockingly cranky, anyway, all this Morris craze of yours. E. P. THOMPSON William Blake seems no longer the cranky untutored genius.

4 Out of order; working badly; shaky. M19.
5 Crooked; full of crannies. M19.

W. S. LANDOR No curling dell, no cranky nook.

6 = CRANK *adjective*[2]. M19.
■ **crankily** *adverb* M19. **crankiness** *noun* M19.

crannog /ˈkranəg/ *noun*. E17.
[ORIGIN Irish *crannóg*, Gaelic *crannag* timber structure, from *crann* tree, beam.]
An ancient fortified dwelling constructed in a lake or marsh in Scotland or Ireland.

cranny /ˈkrani/ *noun*[1] & *verb*. LME.
[ORIGIN Old French *crané* (see -Y[5]) pa. pple of verb (implied by *craneüre* notch) from Old French & mod. French *cran*, from popular Latin *crena* incision, notch.]
▸ **A** *noun*. A small narrow opening or hole; a chink, a crevice, a crack. LME.
every nook and cranny: see NOOK *noun* 3b.
▸ **B** *verb intrans.* †**1** Open in crannies or chinks. LME–E17.
2 Penetrate into crannies. *rare.* E19.
■ **crannied** *adjective* (*a*) having crannies; (*b*) *rare* formed like a cranny: LME.

cranny /ˈkrani/ *noun*[2]. M17.
[ORIGIN Unknown.]
A rod of iron etc. used in forming the necks of glass bottles.

cranreuch /ˈkranrəx/ *noun*. *Scot.* L17.
[ORIGIN from Gaelic *crann* tree + *reodhadh* freezing.]
(A) hoar frost.

crants /krants/ *noun*. *obsolete* exc. *hist.* Pl. same. M16.
[ORIGIN Dutch *krans*, German *Kranz* garland, wreath: cf. CRANCE.]
†**1** A form of candleholder. *Scot.* M–L16.
2 A garland, a chaplet, a wreath. L16.

†**crany** *noun*. E16–M18.
[ORIGIN Alt.]
= CRANIUM.

crap /krap/ *noun*[1] & *adjective*. LME.
[ORIGIN Corresp. to Dutch *krappe* rel. to *krappen* pluck off, cut off. Cf. Old French *crappe* siftings, Anglo-Latin *crappa* chaff.]
▸ **A** *noun*. †**1** The husk of grain; chaff. LME–L15.
2 Any of various plants, *esp.* buckwheat or a weed growing among corn, as darnel, charlock, etc. *dial.* LME.
3 a *sing.* & (usu.) in *pl.* The residue formed in boiling, melting, or rendering fat; crackling. *dial.* L15. ▸**b** The dregs of beer etc. *dial.* M19.
†**4** A scrap. Only in 16.
5 Money. *slang* or *dial.* L17.
6 Faeces; an act of defecation. Also, rubbish, nonsense; something worthless, inferior, or offensive. *coarse slang.* L19.

T. ROETHKE I'm writing a lot of inane crap. J. T. FARRELL One who hadn't backed down or taken any crap.

▸ **B** *attrib.* or as *adjective*. Worthless, rubbish, useless. *slang.* Cf. CRAPPY *adjective*. M20.

M. HODKINSON When David first started he was totally crap. He couldn't sing and he couldn't write songs. A. WARNER She's a crap dancer.

– COMB.: **crap-artist** *coarse slang* a liar, a boaster, an exaggerator.

†**crap** *noun*[2]. E18–E19.
[ORIGIN Dutch *krap*.]
Madder.

crap /krap/ *noun*[3]. *arch. slang.* E19.
[ORIGIN Dutch *krap* cramp, clamp.]
The gallows.

crap *noun*[4] see CRAPS.

crap /krap/ *verb*[1] *trans. arch. slang.* Infl. **-pp-**. L18.
[ORIGIN from CRAP *noun*[3].]
Hang (on the gallows). Usu. in *pass.*

crap /krap/ *verb*[2]. *coarse slang.* Infl. **-pp-**. M19.
[ORIGIN from CRAP *noun*[1]. In sense 4 perh. from or infl. by CRAPS.]
1 *verb intrans.* Defecate. M19.
2 *verb trans.* & *intrans.* Lie, boast, or exaggerate (to); act deceitfully (to). M20.
3 *verb intrans.* Mess or fool *around* (*with*). *US.* M20.
4 *verb intrans.* Foll. by *out*: be unsuccessful; withdraw from a game etc. *US.* M20.

crapaud /ˈkrapəʊ/ *noun*. ME.
[ORIGIN Old French *crapau(l)t* (mod. *crapaud*), medieval Latin *crapaldus*.]
†**1** A toad. ME–M17.
†**2** More fully ***crapaud-stone***. A toadstone. LME–L16.
3 An edible bullfrog, *Leptodactylus pentadactylus*, of S. and Central America. M20.
– NOTE: See also *JOHNNY Crapaud*.

crapaudine /ˈkrapədiːn, krapəˈdiːn/ *noun*. LME.
[ORIGIN Old French & mod. French from medieval Latin *crapaudinus*, *-ina*, formed as CRAPAUD: see -INE[1].]
1 = TOADSTONE *noun*[1]. Long *obsolete* exc. *hist.* LME.
2 An ulcer on the coronet of a horse. M18.

crape /kreɪp/ *noun & adjective*. E16.
[ORIGIN French CRÊPE *noun*.]
▸ **A** *noun*. **1** Transparent but dull black gauze with a crimped surface, esp. for mourning dress; a band of this, esp. worn round a hat etc. as a sign of mourning. Formerly also, a piece of crape worn as a mask. E16.
2 A kind of thin worsted used for clerical dress; *transf.* a clergyman. *obsolete* exc. *hist.* L17.
▸ **B** *attrib.* or as *adjective*. Made of crape. M16.

– **SPECIAL COLLOCATIONS & COMB.**: **crape fern** a New Zealand fern, *Leptopteris superba*, with tall dark-green plumes. **crape hair** artificial hair for an actor's false beard etc. **crape myrtle** a Chinese ornamental shrub, *Lagerstroemia indica*, of the purple loosestrife family, with pink, white, or purplish crinkled petals.
■ **crapy** *adjective* (*a*) resembling crape; (*b*) of crape, clothed in crape: **M19**.

crape /kreɪp/ *verb trans.* **E18**.
[**ORIGIN** from the noun. For sense 1 cf. French *crêper*, **CRÊPE** *verb*.]
†**1** Crimp, make wrinkled or crinkled; curl (hair). **E18–E19**.
2 Cover, clothe, or drape with crape. **E19**.

crapola /kraˈpəʊlə/ *noun. N. Amer. slang.* **M20**.
[**ORIGIN** from **CRAP** *noun*[1] + **-OLA**.]
Material of poor quality, rubbish; nonsense.

crapper /ˈkrapə/ *noun. coarse slang.* **M20**.
[**ORIGIN** from **CRAP** *verb*[2] + **-ER**[1].]
A water closet, a lavatory.

crappie /ˈkrapi/ *noun.* Also **croppie** /ˈkrɒpi/. **M19**.
[**ORIGIN** Unknown.]
A N. American freshwater sunfish of the genus *Pomoxis*, *esp.* (in full ***white crappie***) *P. annularis* and (in full ***black crappie***) *P. nigromaculatus*.

crappit-head /ˈkrapɪthɛd/ *noun. Scot.* **E19**.
[**ORIGIN** Cf. Dutch *krappen* cram.]
The head of a haddock stuffed with the roe, oatmeal, suet, and spices.

crappy /ˈkrapi/ *adjective. coarse slang.* **M19**.
[**ORIGIN** from **CRAP** *noun*[1] + **-Y**[1].]
Rubbishy; disgusting.

craps /kraps/ *noun. N. Amer.* Also (usual in comb.) **crap**. **E19**.
[**ORIGIN** App. alt. of *crabs*: cf. **CRAB** *noun*[1] 5.]
1 A game of chance played with two dice. **E19**.
shoot craps play craps.
2 A losing throw of 2, 3, or 12 in craps. **L19**.
– **COMB.**: **crap game** a game of craps; **crapshooter** a player at craps; **crapshooting** playing at craps.

crapulence /ˈkrapjʊl(ə)ns/ *noun.* **E18**.
[**ORIGIN** from **CRAPULENT**: see **-ENCE**.]
1 Sickness or indisposition resulting from intemperance in drinking or eating. **E18**.
2 Intemperance, esp. in drinking. **E19**.
■ †**crapulency** *noun* (*rare*) = **CRAPULENCE** 2: only in **M17**.

crapulent /ˈkrapjʊl(ə)nt/ *adjective.* **M17**.
[**ORIGIN** Late Latin *crapulentus* very drunk, from Latin *crapula* inebriation from Greek *kraipalē* drunken headache: see **-ULENT**.]
1 Of or pertaining to crapulence; suffering from the effects of intemperance. **M17**.
2 Given to intemperance. **L19**.

crapulous /ˈkrapjʊləs/ *adjective.* **M16**.
[**ORIGIN** Late Latin *crapulosus*, from Latin *crapula*: see **CRAPULENT**, **-ULOUS**.]
1 Characterized by intemperance; debauched. **M16**.
2 Suffering from the effects of intemperance in drinking; resulting from drunkenness. **M18**.
■ **crapuˈlosity** *noun* inclination to drunkenness or gluttony **M16**. **crapulousness** *noun* **M19**.

craquelure /ˈkrakljʊə, *foreign* kraklyːr/ *noun.* **E20**.
[**ORIGIN** French.]
A network of small cracks in the pigment or varnish on the surface of a painting.

crare *noun* var. of **CRAYER**.

crases *noun* pl. of **CRASIS**.

crash /kraʃ/ *noun*[1] & *adjective*[1]. **E16**.
[**ORIGIN** from the verb.]
▸ **A** *noun.* †**1** A bout of revelry, fighting, etc.; a short spell, a spurt. **E16–M18**.
2 A sudden loud noise as of a violent collision or of shattering; the sound of thunder, loud music, etc.; violent percussion or breakage. **L16**.

> POPE The whole forest in one crash descends. J. CHEEVER The crash of the sea outside. A. AYCKBOURN A distant crash of colliding vehicles.

3 *HUNTING.* The outcry made by hounds when they find the game. **L18**.
4 *fig.* A sudden ruin, failure, or collapse, esp. of a financial undertaking or of a computer system. **L18**.

> J. W. KRUTCH A depression by comparison with which that following the crash of 1929 would seem like boom time.

5 A violent impact or fall; *esp.* the collision of a vehicle or aircraft with another, with a fixed object, or with land or water; (the wreckage at) the scene of such a collision. **E20**.

> *Daily Telegraph* 70 feared dead in rail crash.

– **COMB.**: **crash barrier**: along a carriageway, racetrack, etc., to stop out-of-control vehicles; **crash cymbal**: suspended by a cord and struck with a drumstick; **crash-dive** *noun & verb* (*a*) *noun* a sudden dive made by a submarine in an emergency; a dive by an aircraft ending in a crash; (*b*) *verb intrans.* make a crash-dive; **crash-halt** a sudden stop by a vehicle; **crash helmet**: worn, esp. by motorcyclists, to protect the head in case of a crash; **crash-helmeted** *adjective* wearing a crash helmet; **crash-land** *verb intrans.* make a crash-landing; **crash-landing** a landing by an aircraft with a crash, usu. without lowering the undercarriage; **crash pad** *slang* a place to sleep, esp. in an emergency; **crash-stop** = *crash-halt* above; **crash-tackle** *verb & noun* (*FOOTBALL*) (*a*) *verb trans. & intrans.* tackle vigorously; (*b*) *noun* a vigorous tackle; **crash team** (in a hospital) a team of medical practitioners that stands by to resuscitate patients who have suffered cardiac or respiratory failure.
▸ **B** *attrib.* or as *adjective.* Done rapidly, intensively, or urgently. **M20**.
crash course, ***crash diet***, ***crash programme***, etc.
■ **crashworthiness** *noun* the quality in an aircraft or motor vehicle that increases its safety in the event of a crash **M20**. **crashworthy** *adjective* relatively well able to withstand a crash **M20**.

crash /kraʃ/ *noun*[2] & *adjective*[2]. **E19**.
[**ORIGIN** Russian *krashenina* dyed coarse linen.]
(Made of) a coarse plain fabric of linen etc.

crash /kraʃ/ *verb & adverb.* **LME**.
[**ORIGIN** Imit., perh. partly suggested by *craze* and *dash*.]
▸ **A** *verb.* **I** *verb intrans.* **1** Break into pieces with a crash, shatter noisily; make a crash; move or go with a crash (usu. with adverb or adverbial phr.). **LME**.

> W. OWEN Your guns may crash around me. I'll not hear. I. MURDOCH The glass crashed into pieces on the floor. D. M. THOMAS She heard them crashing through the undergrowth, close behind her.

†**2** Make a grating or gnashing noise; gnash. **LME–L16**.
3 Collide violently with an obstacle etc.; run violently *into*; (of an aircraft) fall violently on to land or sea. **E20**.

> *Daily Telegraph* A car crashed into a bus stop queue.

4 *fig.* Be ruined, esp. financially; fail, come to grief; *colloq.* be heavily defeated. **E20**. ▸**b** Of a computer system: suddenly fail or stop working. **L20**. ▸**c** Of a patient: suffer a cardiac arrest. Chiefly *N. Amer.* **L20**.

> T. S. ELIOT I must give up the *Criterion* before my health crashes. CLIVE JAMES On the day after Lionel's flatwarming party the stock market crashed. *Sun* US Open champion Pete Sampras also crashed out, to an unknown American.
> **b** *www.fictionpress.com* My computer crashed and it's all my brother's fault.

crash and burn *N. Amer. colloq.* come to grief or fail spectacularly.
5 Go *in*, *into* without authorization, invitation, etc. *colloq.* **E20**.

> D. RUNYON He hears rumours of the party, and just crashes in.

6 Go to bed, go to sleep. Also foll. by *out*. *slang.* **M20**.

> *It* You can only crash here one night.

▸ **II** *verb trans.* **7** Break into pieces with a crash; shatter, smash. Now *rare.* **LME**.

> POPE Full on his Ankle dropt the pond'rous Stone, Burst the strong Nerves, and crash'd the solid Bone.

†**8** Gnash (the teeth); crush with the teeth. **M16–M18**.
9 Throw or drive with a crash; cause (a vehicle etc.) to crash. **M19**.

> S. O'FAOLÁIN He could . . see the bigger of the two crash his fist into the face of the other. V. SCANNELL The one Who . . crashed his bike Doing a ton.

10 Enter or pass without authorization; intrude at (a party) without an invitation. *colloq.* **E20**.

> R. FULLER I hope you'll forgive me crashing your excellent party.

crash the gate gatecrash.
▸ **B** *adverb.* With a crash. **M18**.

> THOMAS HUGHES Crash went the slight deal boards.

■ **crasher** *noun* (*a*) a thing which crashes or makes a crash; a loud, percussive blow; (*b*) a person who intrudes uninvited at a party, a gatecrasher: **M19**. **crashing** *ppl adjective* (*a*) that crashes; (*b*) *colloq.* overwhelming (esp. in ***crashing bore***): **L16**. **crashingly** *adverb* (*colloq.*) overwhelmingly (esp. boring) **L20**.

crasis /ˈkreɪsɪs/ *noun.* Pl. **crases** /ˈkreɪsiːz/. **M16**.
[**ORIGIN** Greek *krasis* mixture, combination.]
†**1** The blending of the constituents or humours of an animal body etc., either as a permanent characteristic or as constituting a particular state of health. **M16–M19**.
2 A mixture, a combination. *rare.* **L17**.
3 *GREEK GRAMMAR.* The contraction of two adjacent vowels into one long vowel or diphthong, esp. at the end of one word and beginning of the next. **M19**.

crass /kras/ *adjective.* **L15**.
[**ORIGIN** Latin *crassus* solid, thick, fat.]
1 Coarse, thick, dense, gross, (in physical constitution or texture). Now *rare.* **L15**.
2 Grossly stupid, dull, or insensitive. **M17**.

> GEO. ELIOT Crass minds . . whose reflective scales could only weigh things in the lump. R. A. KNOX There is such a thing, you see, as crass ignorance. U. BENTLEY My action now struck me as crass and blundering.

■ **crassly** *adverb* **M17**. **crassness** *noun* **M16**.

crassitude /ˈkrasɪtjuːd/ *noun.* **LME**.
[**ORIGIN** Latin *crassitudo*, formed as **CRASS**: see **-TUDE**.]
†**1** Thickness of dimension. **LME–E18**.
†**2** Thickness of consistency; coarseness of physical constitution. **E17–E19**.
3 Gross stupidity, dullness, or insensitivity; an instance of this. **L17**.

crassula /ˈkrasjʊlə/ *noun.* Pl. **-lae** /-liː/, **-las**. **LME**.
[**ORIGIN** medieval Latin, dim. of Latin *crassus* thick: see **-ULE**.]
1 Orig., any of certain kinds of stonecrop, *esp.* orpine, *Sedum telephium*. Now, any of numerous succulent herbaceous plants and shrubs constituting the related, chiefly southern African, genus *Crassula*, some of which are grown as house plants. **LME**.
2 *BOTANY.* A thickening between the pits of gymnosperm tracheids, made up of primary wall and intercellular material. **M20**.

-crat /krat/ *suffix.*
[**ORIGIN** Repr. French *-crate*, from adjectives in *-cratique*, formed as **-CRACY**.]
In or forming nouns with the sense 'a supporter or member of a **-CRACY**', as *aristocrat*, *plutocrat*, etc.
■ **-cratic**, **-critical** *suffixes* in or forming adjectives.

cratch /kratʃ/ *noun*[1]. **ME**.
[**ORIGIN** Old French *creche* (mod. **CRÈCHE**) from Proto-Romance from Germanic base also of **CRIB** *noun*.]
1 A rack for feeding animals out of doors; (now *dial.*) a manger. **ME**.
2 A wooden grating; a sparred frame or rack. *dial.* **LME**.

cratch /kratʃ/ *verb & noun*[2]. *obsolete* exc. *dial.* **ME**.
[**ORIGIN** Uncertain: its meaning associates it with Middle Low German, Middle Dutch *kratsen*, Old High German *krazzōn* (German *kratzen*), Old Swedish *kratta* to scratch.]
▸ †**A** *verb.* **1** *verb trans. & intrans.* Scratch. **ME–M16**.
2 *verb trans.* Snatch (as) with claws; grab. **LME–L16**.
▸ **B** *noun.* †**1** Scratching, an itch. Only in **ME**.
2 In *pl.* A sore condition of the feet of horses or sheep; scratches (see **SCRATCH** *noun* 2a). **E16**.

crate /kreɪt/ *noun & verb.* **LME**.
[**ORIGIN** Perh. from Dutch *krat* tailboard of a wagon, †box of a coach, of unknown origin; sense 1 appears in Anglo-Latin as *crata*.]
▸ **A** *noun.* †**1** A hurdle. **LME–E16**.
2 A large wickerwork basket or hamper for carrying crockery, glass, etc.; any openwork, wood-framed, or partitioned case or basket for carrying fragile goods. **LME**.
3 An (old) aeroplane or other vehicle. *slang.* **E20**.
▸ **B** *verb trans.* Pack in a crate. **L19**.
– **COMB.**: **crateman** *arch.* a hawker of pottery.
■ **crateful** *noun* as many as a crate will hold **L19**.

crater /ˈkreɪtə/ *noun & verb.* **E17**.
[**ORIGIN** Latin from Greek *kratēr* bowl, mixing vessel.]
▸ **A** *noun* **I 1** A bowl- or funnel-shaped hollow forming the mouth of a volcano. **E17**.
2 A bowl-shaped cavity, esp. one made by the explosion of a mine, shell, or bomb. **M19**. ▸**b** *spec.* A cavity (usu. with a raised rim) on the moon, a planet, etc., formed by the impact of a meteorite or larger celestial body. **M19**.
▸ **II 3** (Usu. **C-**.) (The name of) an inconspicuous constellation of the southern hemisphere, between Hydra and Virgo; the Cup. **M17**.
4 *GREEK ANTIQUITIES.* A large wide-mouthed bowl in which wine was mixed with water. **M18**.
– **COMB.**: **crater lake** a lake formed by the collection of water in the crater of an inactive volcano.
▸ **B** *verb.* **1** *verb intrans.* Yield inwards to form a crater. *rare.* **L19**.
2 *verb trans.* Form a crater in, esp. by an explosive. **E20**.
■ **crateral** *adjective* pertaining to or resembling a (volcanic) crater **M19**. **crateriform** *adjective* shaped like a (volcanic) crater; *BOTANY* bowl-shaped: **M19**. **craterlet** *noun* a small crater, esp. on the moon **L19**. **crater-like** *adjective* resembling (that of) a crater **M19**. **craterous** *adjective* (*a*) crater-like; (*b*) having many craters: **M19**.

craton /ˈkratɒn/ *noun.* **M20**.
[**ORIGIN** Alt. of **KRATOGEN**.]
GEOLOGY. A large stable block of the earth's crust that has resisted deformation over a geologically long period; a shield. Also called ***kratogen***.
■ **craˈtonic** *adjective* **M20**.

craunch *verb & noun* see **CRANCH**.

†**cravant** *adjective, noun, & verb* see **CRAVEN**.

cravat /krəˈvat/ *noun & verb.* **M17**.
[**ORIGIN** French *cravate* appellative use of *Cravate* from German *Krabat(e)*, (dial.) *Krawat* from Croatian *Hrvat* **CROAT**.]
▸ **A** *noun.* A neckerchief, a necktie, a scarf tied round the neck; orig., a scarf of lace, linen, etc., tied in a bow with flowing ends, worn by men and women; now usu., a neckerchief or loosely fastened broad necktie, worn by men. **M17**.
▸ **B** *verb.* Infl. **-tt-**.
1 *verb trans.* Provide or cover with a cravat. **E19**.
2 *verb intrans.* Put on a cravat. **E19**.

crave /kreɪv/ *verb & noun.*
[**ORIGIN** Old English *crafian* from Germanic, rel. to Old Norse *krǫf* a request, *krefja*.]
▸ **A** *verb.* **I** *verb trans.* **1** Demand, esp. as a legal right; claim as one's own or one's due. Long *dial. rare* exc. *Scot.* **OE**. ▸†**b** Summon, prosecute. **OE–ME**.
2 Ask earnestly, courteously, or humbly for (a thing), *to do*, *that* something be done, (foll. by *of*, *from* the person

asked); beg (a person, *for*, *to do*, †a thing). ME. ▸**b** *spec.* Ask (a debtor) for payment. *Scot.* LME. ▸**c** Beg to know. L16.

SHAKES. *Rom. & Jul.* Madam, your mother craves a word with you. DRYDEN I must crave leave to tell you. J. HACKET The Keeper craved to be heard. SIR W. SCOTT The crown, says he, canna be craved to prove a positive. T. H. WHITE I crave the privilege of being the very first . . to address you with it. **c** SMOLLETT He craved my name.

3 Long for, desire earnestly. LME.

POPE If, when the more you drink, the more you crave, You tell the Doctor. W. C. WILLIAMS Lonesome creatures craving affection, not only craving it, but actively going out to get it. I. MURDOCH What I now abjectly craved was to see Palmer.

4 Require, call for. *arch.* M16.

SHAKES. *Rich. II* His designs crave haste.

▸ **II** *verb intrans.* **5** Beg (*for*); long *for*, yearn (*for*, *after*). ME.

H. T. BUCKLE They taught the men of their generation to crave after the unseen. ALDOUS HUXLEY Being obsessed with time and our egos, we are for ever craving and worrying. P. BROOK He confuses a sort of intellectual satisfaction with the true experience for which he craves.

▸ **B** *noun.* **1** SCOTS LAW. A demand or claim addressed to a court. E18.

2 A craving. M19.

■ **craver** *noun* ME. **craving** *noun* the action of the verb; an instance of this; a strong desire, an intense longing: ME. **cravingly** *adverb* in a craving manner E17.

craven /ˈkreɪv(ə)n/ *adjective, noun, & verb.* Also (earlier) †**cravant**. ME.

[ORIGIN Perh. from Anglo-Norman abbreviation of Old French *cravanté* overcome, vanquished, pa. pple of *cravanter* crush, overwhelm, from Proto-Romance, from Latin *crepant-* pres. ppl stem of *crepare* rattle, burst; later assim. to pa. pples in -EN⁶.]

▸ **A** *adjective* †**1 a** Vanquished, defeated. Only in ME. ▸**b** ***cry craven***, acknowledge defeat, surrender. *arch.* M17.

2 Cowardly, abjectly pusillanimous. LME. ▸†**b** *spec.* Of a cock: unwilling to fight. L16–M17.

SIR W. SCOTT The poor craven bridegroom said never a word. SAKI To turn back would seem rather craven.

▸ **B** *noun.* **1** A confessed or acknowledged coward. L16.

2 A cock that is unwilling to fight. Long *arch.* L16.

▸ **C** *verb trans.* Make craven. E17.

SHAKES. *Cymb.* Against self-slaughter There is a prohibition so divine That cravens my weak hand.

■ **cravenly** *adverb* E17. **cravenness** /-n-n-/ *noun* (*rare*) M19.

craw /krɔː/ *noun*[1]. LME.

[ORIGIN from or cogn. with Middle Low German *krage* (whence Icelandic *kragi*), Middle Dutch *crāghe* (Dutch *kraag*) neck, throat, gullet = Middle High German *krage* (German *Kragen*), of unknown origin. The limitation of sense is peculiar to English.]

1 The crop of birds or insects. LME.

stick in one's craw *fig.* be unacceptable.

2 *transf.* The stomach (of humans or animals) *joc.* or *derog.* E16.

craw *noun*[2] & *adjective*, *noun*[3], *verb* see CROW *noun*[1] & *adjective*, *noun*[2], *verb*.

craw-craw /ˈkrɔːkrɔː/ *noun.* Also **kraw-kraw**. L18.

[ORIGIN App. from Dutch *kraauwen* to scratch.]

In W. Africa: a skin disease with itching due to nematode infestation.

crawdad /ˈkrɔːdad/ *noun. N. Amer.* E20.

[ORIGIN Fanciful alt. of CRAWFISH.]

A freshwater crayfish.

crawfish *noun & verb* see CRAYFISH.

crawk /krɔːk/ *verb intrans. & noun.* M19.

[ORIGIN Imit.]

(A) squawk, (a) croak.

crawl /krɔːl/ *noun*[1]. M17.

[ORIGIN Portuguese *curral*: cf. CORRAL *noun*, KRAAL *noun*.]

1 In the W. Indies, an enclosure or building for keeping hogs. M17.

2 An enclosure in water, or a tank or reservoir, for holding live turtles, fish, sponges, etc. L17.

3 = KRAAL *noun* 1. *arch.* L18.

crawl /krɔːl/ *noun*[2]. E19.

[ORIGIN from the verb.]

1 The action or an act of crawling; a slow rate of movement. E19. ▸**b** In full ***pub crawl***, (arch.) ***gin-crawl***. A journey taking in several pubs or drinking places, with one or more drinks at each. *colloq.* L19.

P. LEACH A real crawl, moving along deliberately with his tummy right off the floor, is very unusual before six months. S. KING Time slowed to an inchworm's crawl.

2 A high-speed swimming stroke with alternate overhand arm movements and rapid kicks of the legs. Also ***crawl stroke***. E20.

crawl /krɔːl/ *verb.* ME.

[ORIGIN Unknown: cf. Swedish *kravla*, Danish *kravle*.]

▸ **I** *verb intrans.* **1** Move slowly, dragging the body along close to the ground etc., as a child on hands and knees, a short-limbed reptile or quadruped, a snake, worm, or other limbless creature, etc. Cf. CREEP *verb* 1. ME.

J. GAY Slow crawl'd the snail. R. C. HUTCHINSON My grandson, nearly a year old, . . had hardly tried to crawl yet. M. ESSLIN A mythical universe peopled by lonely creatures crawling through the mud on their bellies.

2 Of ground etc.: be covered or swarming *with* crawling things; be filled *with*. ME.

I. HAY Country districts crawling with troops. W. STEVENS The place is crawling with books.

3 Walk or move along with a slow or laborious motion. LME. ▸**b** Move stealthily, sneakingly, or abjectly. E17. ▸**c** Behave abjectly or ingratiatingly (*to*). *colloq.* L19.

SHAKES. *Mids. N. D.* I can no further crawl. N. MAILER Southbound traffic whose drivers were crawling by at five miles an hour. S. BRETT Time crawled by. **b** SHAKES. *Hen. VIII* Cranmer . . Hath crawl'd into the favour of the King. **c** A. SACHS I don't actually crawl to them but I am so eager to win their approval.

crawling peg ECONOMICS a system whereby the exchange rate can be frequently and marginally adjusted. ***kerb-crawling***: see KERB *noun*. **pub-crawl** *verb intrans.* engage in a pub crawl (CRAWL *noun*[2] 1b).

4 Of a plant: spread over a surface with extending stems or branches. Cf. CREEP *verb* 4. M17.

MILTON A green mantling vine That crawls along the side of yon small hill.

5 Feel a creepy sensation. Cf. CREEP *verb* 5. L19.

make a person's flesh crawl: see FLESH *noun*.

6 Swim with a crawl stroke. E20.

▸ **II** *verb trans.* **7** Crawl on or over. *rare.* M17.

■ **crawlingly** *adverb* in a crawling manner L17. **crawly** *adjective* having or suggestive of the sensation of insects etc. crawling on one's skin, creepy; (see also CREEPY-*crawly*): M19.

crawler /ˈkrɔːlə/ *noun.* E17.

[ORIGIN from CRAWL *verb* + -ER[1].]

1 A person or creature that crawls along the ground etc. E17.

night crawler: see NIGHT *noun*.

2 An idler, a loafer. *Austral. arch.* E19.

3 A slow-moving domestic animal. *Austral. & NZ arch.* M19.

4 A cab or cab-driver moving slowly along the streets in search of a fare; (a driver of) any slow-moving vehicle. M19.

kerb-crawler: see KERB *noun*.

5 An abject or obsequious person, a sycophant. L19.

6 *sing.* & (usu.) in *pl.* A baby's overall for crawling in. L19.

7 In full ***crawler tractor***. A tractor moving on an endless chain. E20.

8 COMPUTING. More fully ***web crawler***. A program that searches the World Wide Web, typically in order to create an index of data. L20.

cray /kreɪ/ *noun.* Chiefly *Austral. & NZ.* E20.

[ORIGIN Abbreviation.]

= CRAYFISH *noun* 1, 2.

crayer /krɛː/ *noun.* Also **crare**. ME.

[ORIGIN Old French *crayer* etc., in medieval Latin *craiera*, *creiera*.]

hist. A small trading vessel.

crayfish /ˈkreɪfɪʃ/ *noun & verb.* Also **craw-** /ˈkrɔː-/ (see below); (earlier) †**crevice** & other vars. ME.

[ORIGIN Old French *crevice*, *-is* from Frankish corresp. to Old High German *krebiz* (German *Krebs*) CRAB *noun*[1]; 2nd syll. assim. to FISH *noun*[1].]

▸ **A** *noun.* Pl. same, **-es** /-ɪz/.

1 Any of various long-bodied freshwater decapod crustaceans of the infraorder Astacidea. ME.

2 (Often *craw-*.) Orig., any large, esp. edible, crustacean; a lobster, (formerly) a crab. Now *spec.* a spiny lobster. LME.

3 (*craw-*.) A political renegade. *US colloq.* M19.

▸ **B** *verb intrans.* **1** Fish for crayfish. Chiefly as ***crayfishing*** *verbal noun*. M19.

2 (*craw-*.) Retreat, back *out*. *US colloq.* M19.

3 Move like a crayfish; *fig.* act in a cowardly or scheming manner. *Austral.* L19.

crayon /ˈkreɪən/ *noun & verb.* M17.

[ORIGIN French, from *craie* from Latin *creta* chalk, clay: see -OON.]

▸ **A** *noun.* **1** A small stick or pencil of charcoal or chalk, wax, etc., coloured with pigment, for drawing. M17. ▸**b** ***in crayon(s)***, drawn with a crayon or crayons. M17.

2 A drawing made with a crayon or crayons. M17.

▸ **B** *verb trans.* **1** Draw with a crayon or crayons. M17.

2 *fig.* Sketch (*out*), rough *out*. M18.

craze /kreɪz/ *noun.* L16.

[ORIGIN from the verb.]

†**1** A crack, a breach, a flaw; an infirmity. L16–E19.

2 An insane fancy, a mania, a crazy condition. E19.

3 A temporary enthusiasm. L19.

G. SWIFT There's a craze at the moment for films with heroes who are actually admired because they are half robots. B. GUEST African sculpture . . was the latest craze of the avant-garde.

craze /kreɪz/ *verb.* LME.

[ORIGIN Perh. from Old Norse (cf. Swedish *krasa* crunch, *kras* in phr. *gå i kras* fly into pieces, *slå i kras* dash to pieces).]

▸ **I** *verb trans.* **1** Break in pieces, shatter; bruise, damage. LME–E19.

2 Crack; *spec.* produce small cracks on (pottery glaze etc.). LME.

A. R. AMMONS Mesquite roots crazed the stone.

3 Impair in physical health, make infirm. Usu. in *pass.* *arch.* L15.

MILTON Till length of years And sedentary numbness craze my limbs.

4 Impair in intellect, make insane. Usu. in *pass.* L15.

SHAKES. *Lear* The grief hath craz'd my wits.

5 *fig.* Impair; ruin financially. Usu. in *pass.* Long *arch.* M16.

▸ **II** *verb intrans.* †**6** Be broken, shattered, or bruised; suffer damage. LME–M19.

†**7** Become infirm or diseased. *rare.* Only in M17.

8 Go mad, become crazy. E19.

9 Of pottery glaze etc.: develop small cracks. M19.

■ **crazed** *adjective* that has been crazed; insane, crazy: LME.

crazia /ˈkrɑːtsɪə/ *noun.* Pl. **-ie** /-ɪeɪ/. L18.

[ORIGIN Italian from German *Kreuzer* KREUTZER.]

An ancient Tuscan copper coin, the twelfth part of a lira.

crazy /ˈkreɪzi/ *adjective, noun, & adverb.* E16.

[ORIGIN from CRAZE *verb* or *noun* + -Y[1].]

▸ **A** *adjective.* †**1** Infirm, ailing, sickly. E16–L19.

SHAKES. *1 Hen. VI* Some better place, Fitter for sickness and for crazy age.

2 Full of cracks or flaws; (esp. of a ship or a building) shaky, unsound. L16. ▸**b** Of paving, a quilt, etc.: made of irregular pieces fitted together. L19.

ADAM SMITH The house is crazy . . and will not stand very long. QUILLER-COUCH A crazy, rusty blunderbuss hung over the fire-place.

3 Of a person, action, etc.: insane, mad; absurd. E17. ▸**b** Extremely enthusiastic (*about*). *colloq.* E19. ▸**c** Unrestrained, exciting, excellent. *slang* (orig. *US*). E20.

J. BRAINE As they say in the films, I'm just a crazy mixed-up kid.

(*as*) ***crazy as a loon***: see LOON *noun*[2]. ***crazy as a two-bob watch***: see WATCH *noun*. **crazy like a fox**, **crazy as a fox** *colloq.* (orig. *US*) very cunning or shrewd. **like crazy** *colloq.* (orig. *US*) like mad. **b crazy about**, **crazy for** *spec.* infatuated with, in love with.

– SPECIAL COLLOCATIONS & COMB.: **crazy ant** an ant with fast or erratic movement, *esp.* the tropical ant *Prenolepsis longicornus*. **crazy bone** *US* the funny bone. **crazy-pave** *verb trans.* cover with crazy paving.

▸ **B** *noun.* A mad or eccentric person. *colloq.* M19.

▸ **C** *adverb.* Extremely, excessively. *slang* (chiefly *US*). L19.

■ **crazily** *adverb* M17. **craziness** *noun* E17.

CRC *abbreviation.*

Camera-ready copy.

creagh /krɛk, -x/ *noun.* Chiefly *Scot. & Irish. obsolete* exc. *hist.* Also **creach**. E19.

[ORIGIN Gaelic & Irish *creach* plunder.]

1 A foray. E19.

2 Booty; prey. E19.

creaght /kreɪt, krɛxt/ *noun & verb.* Chiefly *Irish. obsolete* exc. *hist.* L16.

[ORIGIN Irish *caeraigheacht*, from *caera* sheep.]

▸ **A** *noun.* A nomadic herd of cattle, freq. including the drovers. L16.

▸ **B** *verb intrans.* Take cattle from place to place to graze. E17.

creak /kriːk/ *verb & noun.* ME.

[ORIGIN Imit.: cf. CRAKE *verb*[1], CROAK *verb*.]

▸ **A** *verb.* **1** *verb intrans.* Of a crow, rook, goose, etc.: utter a harsh cry. Long *rare.* ME.

2 *verb intrans.* Speak in a strident or querulous tone. *obsolete* exc. as passing into sense 3. LME.

3 *verb intrans.* Make a harsh squeaking or grating sound. L16. ▸**b** Move with a creak or creaks. M19.

TOLKIEN The pine-trees . . creaking and cracking in the wind. **b** J. G. WHITTIER A single hay-cart down the dusty road Creaks slowly.

creaking gate *fig.* a chronic invalid (likely to outlive others more healthy).

4 *verb trans.* Cause to make a creak or creaks. E17.

SHAKES. *All's Well* Creaking my shoes on the plain masonry.

▸ **B** *noun.* A strident noise, as of an ungreased hinge etc.; a harsh squeak. E17.

J. STEINBECK He heard the creak of the leather of the saddle. S. HEANEY The treble Creak of her voice like the pump's handle.

■ **creakily** *adverb* in a creaky manner; with a creaky sound: E20. **creakingly** *adverb* = CREAKILY M19. **creaky** *adjective* characterized by creaking; apt to creak: M19.

cream /kriːm/ *noun*[1]. *obsolete* exc. *hist.* ME.

[ORIGIN Old French *cresme* (mod. *chrême*) from ecclesiastical Latin *chrisma* unction: see CHRISM *noun*.]

= CHRISM *noun*.

cream /kriːm/ *noun*[2] & *adjective.* ME.

[ORIGIN Old French *creme*, *craime*, *cresme* (mod. *crème* fem.) repr. blending of late Latin *cramum*, *crama* (perh. of Gaulish origin) with ecclesiastical Latin *chrisma* CHRISM *noun*.]

C

C

▸ **A** *noun*. **1** The part of milk with high fat content, which collects at the top of the milk and which by churning is made into butter. ME.
clotted cream, Cornish cream, dairy cream, Devonshire cream, double cream, full cream, half cream, single cream, sour cream, whipping cream, etc.
2 A fancy dish or pudding of which cream is an ingredient, or which has the appearance and consistency of cream. LME. ▸**b** More fully ***cream sherry***. A full-bodied sweet sherry. L19. ▸**c** A sweet or biscuit with a creamy filling. M20.
3 *The* most excellent element or part; *the* most outstanding group of people within a larger group; *the* quintessence. L16.

R. DAVIES The successful Parisian entertainer, drawing the cream of society to his little theatre. S. BRILL These auto and steel pensions are the cream of the crop.

4 The part of a liquid that gathers at the top; a head of scum, froth, etc. (Implied earlier in CREAM *verb* 1a.) M17. ▸**b** The liquid rich in droplets or particles of the dispersed phase that forms a separate (esp. upper) layer in an emulsion or suspension when it is allowed to stand or is centrifuged. E20.
5 A creamlike preparation used cosmetically or medicinally. E18.

GOLDSMITH In vain she tries her paste and creams To smooth her face or hide its seams.

6 *ellipt.* Cream colour; a cream-coloured horse, rabbit, etc. L18.
– PHRASES: **burnt cream** = *crème brûlée* s.v. CRÈME 1. **cold cream**: see COLD *adjective*. **cream of chicken (soup)**, **cream of tomato (soup)**, etc., a chicken etc. soup made with cream or milk. **cream of tartar** purified and crystallized potassium bitartrate, used in medicine etc.; ***cream of tartar fruit*** (Austral.), the fruit of the baobab; ***cream of tartar tree*** (Austral.), the baobab. ***night cream***: see NIGHT *noun*. ***peaches and cream***: see PEACH *noun*[1]. ***Swiss cream***. ***vanishing cream***: see VANISH *verb*. ***violet cream***: see VIOLET *noun*.
– COMB.: **cream bun**, **cream cake**: filled with cream; **cream cheese** a soft rich kind of cheese made of unskimmed milk and cream; a cheese of this kind; **cream colour** the colour of the cream of milk, a yellowish white; **cream-coloured** *adjective* of cream colour, yellowish white; **cream cracker** a crisp unsweetened biscuit; **cream-crackered** *adjective* [rhyming slang for KNACKERED] *slang* very tired; **cream-cups** a Californian and Mexican plant of the poppy family, *Platystemon californicus*, with yellow or cream-coloured flowers; **cream horn** a pastry shaped like a horn and filled with cream and jam; **cream ice** (an) ice cream; **cream nut** a Brazil nut; **cream puff** (*a*) a puff pastry filled with cream; (*b*) an unimportant person or thing; (*c*) an effeminate person; a male homosexual; **cream sauce**: made with cream or milk; ***cream sherry***: see sense 2b above; **cream soda** a carbonated drink of vanilla-flavoured soda water; **cream soup**: made with cream or milk; **cream tea** an afternoon tea which includes bread or scones with jam and (clotted) cream; **creamware** earthenware of a rich cream colour.
▸ **B** *adjective*. Cream-coloured; yellowish-white. M19.
■ **creamlike** *adjective* resembling (that of) cream M19.

cream /kriːm/ *verb*. LME.
[ORIGIN from CREAM *noun*[2].]
1 *verb intrans.* **a** Of a liquid: form a scum or frothy layer on the surface; foam. LME. ▸**b** Of milk: form cream. L16. ▸**c** Of an emulsion or suspension: form cream, separate into cream and another layer. E20.
2 *verb trans.* Separate as cream; take the best or any specified part of; gather as the cream. Usu. foll. by *off*. E17.

A. BEVAN The industrialists . . were not prepared to allow any substantial part of their profits to be creamed off for welfare expenditure. *Times Educ. Suppl.* Creaming is another potential problem: do the magnet schools attract the most able staff and pupils to the detriment of other schools in the area?

3 *verb trans.* Skim the cream from the surface of (milk). E18.
4 *verb trans.* Make or flavour with cream; prepare (fish, chicken, etc.) in a cream sauce. Chiefly as ***creamed ppl adjective***. M18.
5 *verb trans.* & *intrans.* Add cream to (tea, coffee, etc.). E19.
6 *verb trans.* **a** Cause or allow (milk, an emulsion or suspension) to form cream. L19. ▸**b** Work (butter and sugar, mashed potatoes and milk, etc.) into a creamy consistency. L19. ▸**c** Defeat heavily; ruin, wreck. *colloq.* (orig. *US*). E20.

b D. CANFIELD You put the silver around, while I cream the potatoes.

7 *verb trans.* Treat (the skin) with a cosmetic cream. E20.

creamer /ˈkriːmə/ *noun*. M19.
[ORIGIN from CREAM *verb* + -ER[1].]
1 A flat dish for skimming the cream off milk; a machine for separating cream. M19.
2 A jug for cream. Orig. *US*. L19.
3 A cream or milk substitute for adding to coffee, tea, etc. L20.

creamery /ˈkriːm(ə)ri/ *noun*. M19.
[ORIGIN from CREAM *noun*[2] + -ERY, through French *crémerie*.]
1 A shop where milk, cream, butter, etc., are sold. M19.
2 A butter factory. L19.
– COMB.: **creamery butter** factory-made butter as distinguished from that made at a private dairy.

creamometer /kriːˈmɒmɪtə/ *noun*. L19.
[ORIGIN formed as CREAMERY + -OMETER, after LACTOMETER.]
An instrument for measuring the percentage of cream in a sample of milk.

creamy /ˈkriːmi/ *adjective*. LME.
[ORIGIN from CREAM *noun*[2] + -Y[1].]
1 Containing (much) cream. LME.
2 Resembling cream; soft and rich; of a soft or rich cream colour. E17.
■ **creamily** *adverb* with a creamy tint or surface; in a creamy or smooth manner: E20. **creaminess** *noun* L17.

creance /ˈkriːəns/ *noun*. ME.
[ORIGIN Old French & mod. French *créance* from medieval Latin *credentia*, from Latin *credere* believe: see -ANCE. Cf. CREDENCE.]
†**1** The mental action or condition of believing; faith. ME–E17. ▸**b** The thing believed; one's faith; a creed. LME–M17.
†**2** Credit (personal and commercial); reputation; trust. ME–L15.
3 FALCONRY. A long fine cord attached to a hawk's leash to prevent escape during training; a line used to confine the game at which a hawk is flown. L15.

crease /kriːs/ *noun*[1] & *verb*. L16.
[ORIGIN Prob. var. of CREST *noun* (formerly also with long vowel): cf. Old French *cresté* wrinkled, furrowed.]
▸ **A** *noun*. **1** A line or mark produced on the surface of anything by folding or pressing; a fold; a wrinkle; a ridge. L16.

M. E. BRADDON Never mind the creases in that blue frock. J. GALSWORTHY Very well dressed, with special creases down their evening trousers. T. KENEALLY His cheeks folded themselves . . into creases of apparent contentment.

2 ARCHITECTURE. A curved or ridge tile. E18.
3 CRICKET. A line defining the legitimate position of bowler and batsman. M18. ▸**b** In ice hockey and lacrosse, the area marked out in front of the goal. L19.
bowling-crease. ***popping crease***. ***return crease***: see RETURN *noun*.
▸ **B** *verb*. **1** *verb trans.* Make a crease or creases in or on the surface of; wrinkle; fold in a crease; *fig.* (*slang*) convulse with laughter, amuse highly, (usu. foll. by *up*). L16.

G. A. BIRMINGHAM Major Kent . . creased his trousers and dressed for dinner every night. F. HERBERT A smile creased his mouth.

2 *verb trans.* Stun (a horse etc.) by a grazing shot in the ridge of the neck. E19. ▸**b** Stun (a person); graze with a bullet; kill; exhaust physically. *slang* (orig. *US*). E20.
3 *verb intrans.* Become creased; fall into creases; *fig.* (*slang*) be convulsed with laughter, be highly amused, (usu. foll. by *up*). L19.

OED A material that is apt to crease. B. CHATWIN He creased with laughter, and clung to his stomach as if he were never going to stop.

■ **creased** *adjective* having a crease or creases, wrinkled, folded in a crease M16. **creaser** *noun* a person who or thing which creases L19. **creasy** *adjective* full of creases M19.

crease *noun*[2] var. of KRIS.

create /kriːˈeɪt/ *adjective* (orig. *pa. pple*). *arch.* LME.
[ORIGIN Latin *creatus* pa. pple, formed as CREATE *verb*: see -ATE[2].]
Created.

create /kriːˈeɪt/ *verb*. LME.
[ORIGIN Latin *creat-* pa. ppl stem of *creare* bring forth, produce: see -ATE[3]. Earliest as pa. pple *created*, an extension (see -ED[1]) of CREATE *adjective*.]
1 *verb trans.* Of a divine agent: bring into being; *esp.* form out of nothing. Also with obj. & compl. LME.

MAX-MÜLLER And the gods consulted a second time how to create beings that should adore them. F. HALL God created man a moral creature.

2 *verb trans.* Invest (a person) with (a rank, title, etc.). LME.

R. GRAFTON He created two Dukes. W. S. CHURCHILL He was created Earl of Marlborough.

3 *verb trans.* Make, form, or constitute for the first time or afresh; bring into legal existence; invent. (Implied earlier in CREATION 2.) L16.

W. CRUISE The word heirs is not necessary to create a fee simple. R. LYND He . . wished to create an Irish civilization that would be as acceptable ultimately to the old Unionists as to the Nationalists. J. FOWLES These characters I create never existed outside my own mind.

4 *verb trans.* Cause, occasion, produce, give rise to, (a condition, set of circumstances, etc.). L16.

L. NAMIER They accepted a measure which under normal conditions would have created an uproar. C. RAYNER Her gown belled and lifted, . . creating a waft of air.

5 *verb trans.* Of an actor: be the first to represent (a role) and so give it its character. L19.

S. BRETT You dare to offer me the job of understudy to a part I CREATED!

6 *verb trans.* Design (a costume, dress, etc.); design and execute a scheme of interior decoration for (a room etc.). E20.

J. BUCHAN If ever I . . had a house of my own, I would create just such a room. *Daily Telegraph* A brown mixture tweed suit . . created by Schiaparelli.

7 *verb intrans.* Make a fuss, complain loudly, (*about*). *slang*. E20.

K. FARRELL If my old man doesn't get 'is bit of fish at one . . he'll create.

■ **creatable** *adjective* L17.

creatine /ˈkriːətiːn/ *noun*. M19.
[ORIGIN Irreg. from Greek *kreas* (stem *kreo-*) flesh + -INE[5].]
BIOCHEMISTRY. A guanidine derivative, $C_4H_9N_3O_2$, present in living animal tissue, esp. muscle.

creatinine /krɪˈatɪniːn/ *noun*. M19.
[ORIGIN from CREATINE + -INE[5].]
BIOCHEMISTRY. An alicyclic compound, $C_4H_7N_3O$, which is produced by metabolism of creatine and excreted in the urine.

creation /kriːˈeɪʃ(ə)n/ *noun*. LME.
[ORIGIN Old French & mod. French *création* from Latin *creatio(n-)*, formed as CREATE *verb*: see -ION.]
1 The action of a divine agency in creating something, esp. the world; the fact of being created by divine agency. LME. ▸**b** *The* creating of the world; *the* beginning of the world, as a point in time. L16.

b M. INNES For the first time since the creation every continent and every sea was under fire.

2 *gen.* The action of making, forming, producing, or constituting for the first time or afresh; invention; causation, production. LME.

C. LYELL The creation of a new lake, the engulphing of a city, or the raising of a new island. E. LONGFORD The creation of the Metropolitan Police force was in every sense the child of Peel's foresight and labour. P. DAVIES The big bang represents the creation of the physical universe.

continuous creation.
3 The action of investing with a title, dignity, or function. LME.
4 That which divine agency has created; the created world; creatures collectively. E17.

K. AMIS Hell . . Is eternal banishment from God And from the whole of his creation.

beat creation, **lick creation**, **whip creation** *US colloq.* surpass everything. ***lords of creation***, ***lords of the creation***: see LORD *noun*.
5 An original (esp. imaginative) production of human intelligence or power. E17. ▸**b** *spec.* The first representation by an actor of a dramatic character or role; a dramatic character as portrayed by a particular actor. L19. ▸**c** A costume, dress, etc., as the work of its designer. L19.

J. GALSWORTHY Those stripey, streaky creations of Monet's.

– COMB.: **creation science** the interpretation of scientific knowledge according to belief in the literal truth of the Bible, esp. as regards the origins of matter, life, and humanity.
■ **creational** *adjective* (*rare*) M17. **creationism** *noun* a system or theory of creation; *spec.* (*a*) the theory that God creates a soul for every human being at conception or birth (opp. ***traducianism***); (*b*) the theory which attributes the origin of matter, biological species, etc., to a special creation (opp. ***evolutionism***); *esp.* = CREATION ***science***: M19. **creationist** *noun* an adherent of creationism M19.

creative /kriːˈeɪtɪv/ *adjective*. L15.
[ORIGIN from CREATE *verb* + -IVE: cf. Old French *creatif*, *-ive*, medieval Latin *creativus*.]
1 Having the quality of creating; able to create; of or pertaining to creation; *spec.* inventive, imaginative, showing imagination as well as routine skill; intended to stimulate the imagination. L15.
creative art, ***creative artist***, ***creative literature***, ***creative writer***, ***creative writing***, etc. **creative accountancy**, **creative accounting** *colloq.* modification of accounts to achieve a desired end; falsification of accounts that is misleading though not illegal.
2 Productive *of*. E19.

H. MARTINEAU Laws and customs cannot be creative of virtue: they may encourage and help to preserve it; but they cannot originate it.

■ **creatively** *adverb* M19. **creativeness** *noun* E19. **creaˈtivity** *noun* creative power or faculty; ability to create: L19.

creator /kriːˈeɪtə/ *noun*. ME.
[ORIGIN Old French & mod. French *creatour*, *-tur* (now *créateur*) from Latin *creator*, formed as CREATE *verb*: see -OR.]
1 The divine agent creating from nothing, God. ME.

AV *Eccles.* 12:1 Remember now thy Creatour in the dayes of thy youth.

2 *gen.* A person who or thing which creates or gives origin to something. L16. ▸**b** A person who creates a dramatic character or role. L19. ▸**c** A person who creates or designs a costume etc. E20.

MILTON Custom was the creator of prelaty.

■ **creatorship** *noun* M19. **creatress** *noun* a female creator L16. **creatrix** /-trɪks/ *noun*, pl. **-trices** /-trɪsiːz/, [Latin] = CREATRESS L16.

creature /ˈkriːtʃə/ *noun*. See also CRITTER. ME.
[ORIGIN Old French & mod. French *créature* from late Latin *creatura*, formed as CREATE *verb*: see -URE.]
1 *gen.* A created thing; a created being. ME. ▸†**b** The created universe; creation. ME–E17. ▸**c** A material comfort, a thing that promotes well-being. Also ***good creature***. *arch.* E17.

W. COWPER The first boat or canoe that was ever formed . . was a more perfect creature in its kind than a balloon at present.

c the creature *colloq.* intoxicating liquor, *esp.* whisky.
2 An animate being; an animal (often as distinct from a human being). ME. ▸**b** *spec.* A farm animal; in *pl.*, cattle. *US dial.* M17.

D. ATTENBOROUGH Several creatures . . quite unlike any other animals that we know, living or fossil.

3 A human being, a person. Freq. with specifying word of admiration, contempt, patronage, etc. ME.

SHAKES. *Rich. III* There is no creature loves me. STEELE Decent Dresses being often affected by the Creatures of the Town. E. BLISHEN This woman was a charming creature.

4 A person who owes his or her fortune to, and remains subservient to, another; a puppet. L16.

LD MACAULAY The corporations were filled with his creatures.

5 A result or product *of*. M17.

E. G. WHITE If we are creatures of circumstance, we shall surely fail of perfecting Christian characters. W. MAXWELL We were both creatures of the period . . heavy-businessman-father-and-the-oversensitive-artistic-son.

creature of habit a person whose behaviour is guided by habit.
– COMB.: ***creature comforts***: see COMFORT *noun* 5.
■ **creatural** *adjective* pertaining to creatures; of the nature of a creature: M17. **creaturehood** *noun* the condition of a creature L19. **creatureliness** *noun* creaturely state or quality M19. **creaturely** *adjective* creatural; characteristic of a creature: M17. **creatureship** *noun* the state or condition of a creature M17.

creave *verb* see CREE.

crebrity /ˈkriːbrɪti/ *noun*. *rare*. M17.
[ORIGIN Latin *crebritas*, from *creber* frequent: see -ITY.]
Frequency.

crèche /krɛʃ, kreɪʃ/ *noun*. L18.
[ORIGIN French: see CRATCH *noun*[1].]
1 A model of the infant Jesus in the manger with attending figures, often displayed at Christmas. L18.
2 A day nursery for infants and young children. M19.

cred /krɛd/ *noun*[1]. *slang*. L20.
[ORIGIN Abbreviation: earliest in ***street cred*** s.v. STREET *noun*.]
= CREDIBILITY *noun*.

cred /krɛd/ *noun*[2]. *slang*. L20.
[ORIGIN Abbreviation.]
Credit on goods, services, etc.

credal /ˈkriːd(ə)l/ *adjective*. Also **creedal**. M19.
[ORIGIN from CREED *noun* + -AL[1], spelling with single *e* after Latin *credere* etc.]
Of or pertaining to a creed; characterized by a creed.

credence /ˈkriːd(ə)ns/ *noun*. ME.
[ORIGIN Old French & mod. French *crédence* from medieval Latin *credentia*, from Latin *credent-* pres. ppl stem of *credere* believe: see -ENCE.]
1 Belief, acceptance as true. ME.

H. JAMES This programme seemed almost too agreeable for credence. J. CHEEVER An evangelical credence in the romance and sorcery of business success.

attach credence to, **give credence to** believe.
2 Trustworthiness; credit, repute. *obsolete* exc. in ***letter of credence***, a letter of recommendation or introduction, esp. of an ambassador. ME. ▸†**b** A document providing credentials; a message entrusted to an embassy etc. LME–L18.
†**3** Trust, confidence *in*, reliance *on* (a person, authority, etc.). LME–M16.
†**4** Safekeeping, charge, care. L15–L16.
†**5 a** = CREDENZA. M16–M19. ▸**b** ECCLESIASTICAL. In full ***credence shelf***, ***credence table***, etc. A small side table, shelf, or niche for the Eucharistic elements before consecration. E19.
■ **credent** *adjective* (*rare*) (*a*) believing, trustful; †(*b*) having credit or repute; credible: L16.

credenda /krɪˈdɛndə/ *noun pl.* M17.
[ORIGIN Latin, neut. pl. of gerundive of *credere* believe.]
Things to be believed; matters of faith.

credential /krɪˈdɛnʃ(ə)l/ *adjective & noun*. LME.
[ORIGIN medieval Latin *credentialis*, from *credentia* CREDENCE: see -AL[1], -IAL.]
▸ **A** *adjective*. Recommending or entitling to credit or confidence. *rare*. LME.
▸ **B** *noun*. A letter of recommendation or introduction, esp. of an ambassador; an indication of trustworthiness or achievement. Usu. in *pl.* M17.

F. BURNEY The whole ceremony of delivering his credentials to the King in state. J. B. MOZLEY The superiority of the virtues is no credential to the motive. W. C. WILLIAMS I was approached by a young chap at my office door who showed me his credentials. J. C. RANSOM They scarcely had the credentials to judge of such matters.

■ **credentialled**, **-ialed** *adjective* having credentials L19.

credenza /krɪˈdɛnzə/ *noun*. L19.
[ORIGIN Italian from medieval Latin *credentia*: see CREDENCE.]
A sideboard, a cupboard, a buffet.

credibility /krɛdɪˈbɪlɪti/ *noun*. M16.
[ORIGIN medieval Latin *credibilitas*, formed as CREDIBLE: see -ITY.]
The quality of being credible; good reputation.
– COMB.: **credibility gap** a disparity between facts and what is said or written about them, esp. officially.

credible /ˈkrɛdɪb(ə)l/ *adjective*. LME.
[ORIGIN Latin *credibilis*, from *credere* believe: see -IBLE.]
1 Believable; worthy of belief or support. LME. ▸**b** Of a threat etc.: convincing. M20.

W. SEWEL Which I noted down from the mouth of credible persons. J. A. FROUDE When the falsehood ceased to be credible the system which was based upon it collapsed.

†**2** Ready, willing, or inclined to believe. LME–L17.
†**3** Creditable, reputable. M17–E18.
■ **credibleness** *noun* = CREDIBILITY L16. **credibly** *adverb* LME.

credit /ˈkrɛdɪt/ *noun*. M16.
[ORIGIN French *crédit* from Italian *credito* or Latin *creditum* use as noun of neut. pa. pple of *credere* believe, put trust in.]
1 Belief, faith, trust. M16. ▸†**b** Something believed; a report. *rare* (Shakes.). Only in E17.

GIBBON Charges like these may seem to deserve some degree of credit.

†**2** Trustworthiness, credibility; authority (on which testimony is accepted). M16–M19.

T. FULLER I dare take it on the credit of an excellent witness. D. HUME The abstract philosophy of Cicero has lost its credit.

3 Reputation. Now *spec.* good reputation, good name. M16.

W. COWPER John Gilpin was a citizen of credit and renown.

4 Power derived from character or reputation, personal influence. M16.

W. H. PRESCOTT Granvelle . . was not slow to perceive his loss of credit with the regent.

†**5** Safekeeping, charge, care. M16–M17.
6 Trust in a person's ability and intention to pay at a later time for goods, services, etc., supplied; consent or opportunity for deferring payment; the length of time for which payment may be deferred. M16. ▸**b** Reputation for solvency and honesty. L16.

DEFOE He buys his wool . . at two or three months' credit. S. UNWIN The good lady in the shop, evidently feeling that as a regular customer I was entitled to credit, . . said I could pay the halfpenny the next time. **b** SHAKES. *Merch. V.* Try what my credit can in Venice do.

7 A source of commendation or honour *to*; something creditable. L16.

DICKENS You are a credit to the school. M. DRABBLE Her name could be a credit and not a shame.

8 Acknowledgement of merit (*for*, *of* an action etc.); honour. E17. ▸**b** In full ***pass-with-credit***. A grade above 'pass' in an examination. E20.

N. O. BROWN The credit for recognizing the central importance of the excremental theme in Swift belongs to Aldous Huxley. G. F. KENNAN These ventures . . were serious mistakes. They reflected no credit on the governments that sent them.

9 A sum at a person's disposal in the books of a bank etc.; a note, bill, etc., acting as security against a loan etc. E17.
10 The acknowledgement of payment by entry in an account; (a sum entered on) the credit side (see below) of an account. Opp. DEBIT *noun* 2. M18.
11 A certificate or other acknowledgement of a student's completion of (part of) a course of study; a unit of study for completion of which such official acknowledgement is given. Chiefly *N. Amer.* E20.
12 An acknowledgement of a contributor's services to a film, broadcast programme, etc. Usu. in *pl.* E20.
– PHRASES: **do credit to** enhance the reputation of, reflect well on. **get credit for** be given credit for. **give a person credit for** enter (a sum) to a person's credit; *fig.* ascribe (usu. a good quality or achievement) to a person, acknowledge in a person's favour. **give credit to** (*a*) believe (a story etc.); (*b*) allow to have goods or services on credit. **letter of credit** †(*a*) = ***letter of credence*** s.v. CREDENCE 2; (*b*) an order authorizing a person to draw money from the writer's correspondent in another place; a letter from an importer's bank guaranteeing payment to the exporter for specified goods. ***line of credit***: see LINE *noun*[2]. **on credit** with payment to be made at a later time by agreement. ***postwar credit***: see POSTWAR *adjective*. ***revolving credit***: see REVOLVING *adjective*. ***social credit***: see SOCIAL *adjective*. ***Social Credit League***: see SOCIAL *adjective*. ***Social Credit Party***: see SOCIAL *adjective*. **to a person's credit** on the credit side of a person's account; *fig.* to a person's advantage, in a person's favour. **vote of credit** the voting by Parliament of a sum on account in anticipation of the annual estimates.
– COMB.: **credit account** an account to which goods and services may be charged on credit; **credit card** a card issued by a bank, business, etc., authorizing the acquisition of goods and services on credit; **credit insurance** insurance against bad debts; **credit note** a written acknowledgement of a sum credited, as for goods returned; **credit rating** an estimate of a person's ability and intention to pay his or her debts in due course; **credit sale**: of goods or services charged to a credit account; **credit side** the side or column of an account, conventionally the right-hand side, in which credits are entered; **credit squeeze** the restriction of financial credit facilities through banks etc.; **credit title** a credit (sense 12) at the beginning or end of a cinema or television film; **credit transfer** a method of payment by which a sum is transferred from one person's bank account to another's; **credit union** a non-profit-making money cooperative whose members can borrow from pooled savings at low interest rates.
■ **creditworthiness** *noun* the extent to which a person, firm, etc., is creditworthy M20. **creditworthy** *adjective* (*a*) (now *rare*) trustworthy; (*b*) qualified to receive commercial credit: M16.

C

credit /ˈkrɛdɪt/ *verb*. M16.
[ORIGIN from the noun or from Latin *credere* (see CREDIT *noun*).]
1 *verb trans.* & †*intrans.* with *to*. Believe; put faith in. M16.

L. DURRELL An absurdity so patent that I could hardly credit it. C. P. SNOW I found it impossible to credit that I had much will.

†**2** *verb trans.* Supply with goods etc. on credit. M16–M19.
†**3** *verb trans.* Entrust (a person) *with*, (a thing) *to*. L16–M18.
4 *verb trans.* Bring into credit or estimation; do credit to. Now *rare*. L16.

S. PALMER Smatterers in science . . neither instruct the company, nor credit themselves.

5 *verb trans.* Enter a sum on the credit side of (an account) or of the account of (a person), (foll. by *with* the sum); enter (a sum) on the credit side of an account (foll. by *to* the account, the person whose account is credited). L17. ▸**b** *fig.* Ascribe (usu. a good quality or achievement) *to*; ascribe a good quality, achievement, etc., to (a person: foll. by *with* the quality etc.). M19.

b H. L. MENCKEN Very little of the extraordinary progress of medicine . . is to be credited to the family doctor. L. TRILLING Hegel . . credits him with great wit.

creditable /ˈkrɛdɪtəb(ə)l/ *adjective*. E16.
[ORIGIN from CREDIT *noun* or *verb* + -ABLE.]
†**1** Credible. E16–E19.
2 That brings credit or honour (*to*). M17. ▸†**b** Respectable, decent. L17–M19.

Select Tim . . came a creditable second in his heat.

†**3** Qualified to receive commercial credit, creditworthy. L18–E19.
4 Able to be ascribed *to*. E20.
■ **creditaˈbility** *noun* L19. **creditableness** *noun* M17. **creditably** *adverb* L17.

Créditiste /krɛdɪˈtiːst/ *noun & adjective*. M20.
[ORIGIN French.]
(An adherent) of the Quebec wing of the Social Credit Party in Canada.

creditor /ˈkrɛdɪtə/ *noun*. LME.
[ORIGIN Anglo-Norman *creditour*, Old French & mod. French *créditeur* from Latin *creditor*, from *credit-* pa. ppl stem of *credere*: see CREDIT *noun*, -OR.]
▸ **I 1** A person who gives credit for money or goods; a person to whom a debt is owing. LME.
2 The credit side of an account. Formerly also, a sum entered in this. M16.
▸ †**II 3** A person who stands surety. LME–E16.
■ **creditress** *noun* (now *rare*) a female creditor E17. **creditrix** /-trɪks/ *noun* (now *rare*), pl. **-trices** /-trɪsiːz/, [Latin] = CREDITRESS E17.

credo /ˈkriːdəʊ, ˈkreɪ-/ *noun*. Pl. **-os**. ME.
[ORIGIN Latin *credo* I believe. Cf. CREED *noun*.]
1 The Apostles' Creed, the Nicene Creed, (from their first word). Now *esp.* a musical setting of the Nicene Creed. ME.
2 *gen.* A creed, a set of opinions or principles. L16.

credulity /krɪˈdjuːlɪti/ *noun*. LME.
[ORIGIN Old French & mod. French *crédulité* from Latin *credulitas*, from *credulus*: see CREDULOUS, -ITY.]
Orig., belief, faith, readiness to believe. Now *spec.* (an) overreadiness to believe, (a) disposition to believe on weak or insufficient grounds.
■ ˈ**credulence** *noun* (*rare*) credulity M17.

credulous /ˈkrɛdjʊləs/ *adjective*. L16.
[ORIGIN from Latin *credulus*, from *credere* believe: see -ULOUS.]
1 Disposed to believe. Now *spec.* disposed to believe too readily. (Foll. by *of*.) L16.
2 Of behaviour etc.: characterized by or showing credulity. M17.
■ **credulously** *adverb* M17. **credulousness** *noun* L16.

Cree /kriː/ *noun & adjective*. Also (earlier) †**Cris**. M18.
[ORIGIN Canad. French *Cris* abbreviation of earlier *C(h)ristinaux* from Algonquian (now *kinistino:*).]
▸ **A** *noun*. Pl. **-s**, same.
1 A member of an Algonquian people of central N. America. M18.
2 The language of this people. E19.
▸ **B** *attrib.* or as *adjective*. Of or pertaining to the Cree or their language. M18.

cree /kriː/ *verb*. Chiefly *dial.* Also **creave**, **creeve**, /kriːv/. LME.
[ORIGIN Old French & mod. French *crever* burst, split from Latin *crepare* crackle, crack.]
†**1** *verb intrans.* Burst, split. Only in LME.
2 *verb trans.* Soften (grain) by boiling. E17.
3 *verb trans.* Pound into a soft mass. E19.
4 *verb intrans.* Become soft or pulpy by soaking or boiling. M19.

creed /kriːd/ *noun*. OE.
[ORIGIN formed as CREDO.]
1 A brief formal summary of Christian doctrine, *esp.* each of those known as the (Apostles') Creed, the Athanasian Creed, and the Nicene Creed. OE.
Apostles' Creed: see APOSTLE. ***Athanasian Creed***: see ATHANASIAN *adjective*. ***Nicene Creed***: see NICENE *adjective* 2. **the Creed** *spec.* the Apostles' Creed.
2 A repetition of the Creed as an act of devotion, esp. as part of the Mass. LME.
3 A system of religious belief. M16.
> JOHN BROOKE The history and doctrines of Christianity according to the creed of the Church of England.

4 A set of opinions or principles on any subject; *esp.* a political philosophy. E17.
> R. W. EMERSON The cynical creed . . of the market. G. STEINER Communism . . is a creed penetrated . . by a sense of the values of intellect and art.

5 Belief or confidence *in*; an article of faith. *rare*. E19.
■ **creedless** *adjective* without a creed M19. **creedlessness** *noun* M19.

creed /kriːd/ *verb trans. & intrans.* Long *obsolete* exc. *dial.* E17.
[ORIGIN Latin *credere*, after CREED *noun*.]
Believe.

creedal *adjective* var. of CREDAL.

creek /kriːk/ *noun*[1]. Also **crick** /krɪk/. ME.
[ORIGIN Old Norse *kriki* chink, nook, or Old French & mod. French *crique* from Old Norse. Perh. partly also from Middle Dutch *krēke* (Dutch *kreek* creek, bay).]
▸**I** **1** An inlet on a sea coast or in the tidal estuary of a river. ME.
2 A small port or harbour; an inlet within the limits of a haven or port. L15.
3 A short arm of a river. L16.
4 A tributary of a river; a stream, a brook. *N. Amer., Austral., & NZ.* E17.
5 *transf.* A valley extending from a plain into a highland area. M17.
▸**II** †**6** A cleft in the face of a rock etc. Also, the cleft between the buttocks. ME–M17.
†**7** A trick, an artifice, a contrivance. LME–E17.
8 A narrow or winding passage; an out-of-the-way corner, a nook. *obsolete* exc. *dial.* L16.
†**9** A bend, a turning, a winding. L16–L17.
– PHRASES ETC.: ***fly-up-the-creek***: see FLY *verb*. ***up shit creek***: see SHIT *noun*. **up the creek** *slang* (*a*) in a tight corner, in trouble; *spec.* pregnant; (*b*) crazy, eccentric.
■ **creeklet** *noun* a little creek L16. **creeky** *adjective* full of creeks M16.

creek /kriːk/ *noun*[2]. *obsolete* exc. *Scot.* M16.
[ORIGIN Corresp. to early mod. Dutch *kriecke*, from earlier Dutch *kriecken*, *krieckelen*, mod. Dutch *krieken*, break or burst through as the daylight. See also SKREEK.]
Dawn; break *of* day.

Creek /kriːk/ *noun*[3] *& adjective*. E18.
[ORIGIN from CREEK *noun*[1].]
▸**A** *noun*. Pl. **-s**, same.
1 A member of a N. American Indian confederacy of the Muskogee and some other peoples; a member of the Muskogee. E18.
2 The Muskogean language of the Muskogee. L19.
▸**B** *attrib.* or as *adjective*. Of or pertaining to the Muskogee or their language, or the confederacy including the Muskogee. E18.

creel /kriːl/ *noun*[1] *& verb*. Orig. *N. English*. ME.
[ORIGIN Unknown.]
▸**A** *noun*. **1** A large wicker basket, now esp. for fish. ME. ▸**b** An angler's fishing basket. E19.
2 A trap made of wickerwork for catching fish, lobsters, etc. LME.
– PHRASES: **coup the creels** *Scot.* fall head over heels; meet with a mishap. **in a creel** *Scot.* in a state of temporary mental aberration.
▸**B** *verb trans.* **1** Put into a creel. E16.
2 In certain marriage customs in Scotland: make (a newly married man) go through some ceremony with a creel. L18.
■ **creelful** *noun* as much as a creel will hold E19.

creel /kriːl/ *noun*[2]. L18.
[ORIGIN Perh. same word as CREEL *noun*[1] *& verb*.]
1 *gen.* A framework, a rack. L18.
2 A frame for holding bobbins in a spinning machine. M19.
■ **creeler** *noun* a person who attends to a creel in a spinning machine. M19.

creep /kriːp/ *noun*. L15.
[ORIGIN from the verb.]
1 The action or an act of creeping; slow and stealthy motion. L15.
the creep *slang* stealthy robbery.
2 **a** A gradual bulging of or a bulge in the floor in a coalmine, owing to pressure on the pillars. E19. ▸**b** GEOLOGY. The gradual (esp. downhill) movement of soil, disintegrated rock, etc., owing to gravity, atmospheric changes, etc. Also, the gradual displacement of strata or the earth's crust by expansion, contraction, compression, etc. L19. ▸**c** METALLURGY. Gradual change of shape under stress. E20.
3 **a** An enclosure with a small entrance for animals; *spec.* a feeding enclosure with an entrance admitting only young animals. E19. ▸**b** A low arch under a railway embankment, road, etc.; an opening in a hedge etc. for an animal to pass through. L19.
4 A shivering or shuddering sensation, esp. caused by dread or revulsion. Chiefly in ***the creeps***. *colloq.* E19.
> M. MITCHELL The live oaks with their waving curtains of grey moss gave Scarlett the creeps.

5 A dislikeable, tiresome, or fawning person. *slang* (orig. *US*). L19.
> N. WHITTAKER A couple of days previously she'd been kerb-crawled by a creep in a Cortina.

6 A sneak thief. *slang*. E20.
– NOTE: Rare before 19.

creep /kriːp/ *verb*. Pa. t. & pple **crept** /krɛpt/.
[ORIGIN Old English *crēopan* = Old Frisian *kriapa*, Old Saxon *criopan*, Old Norse *krjūpa*, from Germanic.]
▸**I** *verb intrans.* **1** Move dragging the body close to the ground, as a person on all fours, a short-limbed reptile or quadruped, (formerly) a snake, worm, or other limbless creature, etc. Cf. CRAWL *verb* 1. OE.
> T. HERBERT Land Tortoyses so great that they will creepe with two mens burthens. DAY LEWIS A hole in the hedge . . through which I must creep if I was to play with the neighbour's children.

†**creep to the Cross** advance towards the crucifix on one's knees or prone, in the Roman Catholic service on Good Friday.
2 Move timidly, slowly, softly, or stealthily. ME.
> SHAKES. *A.Y.L.* The whining school-boy . . creeping like snail Unwillingly to school. J. G. WHITTIER The mists crept upwards. B. PYM She grew cold at last and crept back to bed.

3 *fig.* Advance by imperceptible degrees, develop gradually; insinuate oneself *into*; come *in*, *up*, etc., unobserved. ME. ▸**b** Proceed or exist abjectly; behave timidly, diffidently, or unambitiously. L16.
> B. JOWETT The licence of which you speak very easily creeps in. E. WELTY A sudden alert, tantalized look would creep over the little man's face. **b** POPE Wit that can creep, and Pride that licks the dust.

4 (Of a plant) spread over or along a surface with extending stems or branches; extend like a creeping plant. LME.
> A. P. STANLEY Vineyards creep along the ancient terraces.

gill-creep-by-ground: see GILL *noun*[1].
5 Of a person: shiver or shudder with dread, revulsion, etc.; feel as if things were creeping over one's skin. Of the flesh or skin: feel as if things were creeping over it, through dread, revulsion, etc. LME.
make a person's flesh creep: see FLESH *noun*.
6 Drag a river, the seabed, etc., with a creeper. L18.
7 Of a mine floor, soil, metal, etc.: undergo creep (see CREEP *noun* 2). M19.
8 Of a liquid: cover a surface as a thin film. L19.
9 Commit robbery with stealth. *slang*. E20.
▸**II** *verb trans.* †**10** Advance towards (the Cross) on one's knees or prone. L15–L16.
11 Creep along or over. *rare*. M17.
12 Foll. by *in*: introduce or increase gradually or imperceptibly. M20.
– COMB.: **creep-hole** a hole through which a person creeps; a hole into which an animal etc. creeps; **creep-joint** *US slang* (*a*) a gambling game that shifts location each night; (*b*) a brothel or other seedy place of resort, esp. where patrons are robbed; **creep-mouse** *noun & adjective* (*a*) *noun* pretending to be a mouse in playing with a small child; (*b*) *adjective* furtive, timid, shy.
■ **creepage** *noun* gradual movement; *spec.* leakage of electricity: E20.

creeper /ˈkriːpə/ *noun*. OE.
[ORIGIN from CREEP *verb* + -ER[1].]
1 A person who creeps (*lit.* & *fig.*). OE. ▸**b** A trainee tea planter, esp. in Sri Lanka. Now *arch.* or *hist.* L19.
> *New Yorker* Though Brian was clever enough at his books he was no swot or creeper.

2 A creature that creeps. LME. ▸**b** A bird that climbs up trees, over bushes, etc. Formerly *spec.* the treecreeper. M17.
b *brown creeper*, *honeycreeper*, *treecreeper*, *wallcreeper*, *woodcreeper*.
3 **a** A grapnel, *spec.* one used for dragging a river, the seabed, etc. LME. ▸**b** A small iron firedog. Now *dial.* or *hist.* M16.
4 A plant that creeps along the ground, up a wall, etc. E17.
caustic creeper: see CAUSTIC *adjective* 1. ***Rangoon creeper***. ***Virginia creeper***: see VIRGINIA 1. ***Virginian creeper***: see VIRGINIAN *adjective*.
5 CRICKET etc. A bowled ball that travels low along the ground, a daisy-cutter. M19.
6 In *pl.* Soft-soled shoes (also ***brothel creepers***). *slang*. E20.
■ **creepered** *adjective* covered with a creeping plant, esp. Virginia creeper L19.

creepie /ˈkriːpi/ *noun*. *Scot.* & *dial.* M17.
[ORIGIN from CREEP *verb* + -IE, -Y[6].]
A low stool.

creeping /ˈkriːpɪŋ/ *ppl adjective*. OE.
[ORIGIN from CREEP *verb* + -ING[2].]
That creeps.
creeping barrage a curtain of gunfire moving ahead of advancing troops. **creeping buttercup** a common buttercup, *Ranunculus repens*, with strong spreading stems which root at nodes. **creeping Jenny** a trailing loosestrife, *Lysimachia nummularia*, with yellow flowers in the axils of glossy paired roundish leaves; also called ***moneywort***. **creeping Jesus** *slang* an abject or hypocritical person. ***creeping palsy***: see PALSY *noun*[1] 1. **creeping paralysis** locomotor ataxia. ***creeping soft-grass***: see SOFT *adjective*. ***creeping thistle***: see THISTLE *noun* 1.
■ **creepingly** *adverb* M16.

creepy /ˈkriːpi/ *adjective*. L18.
[ORIGIN from CREEP *verb* or *noun* + -Y[1].]
1 Characterized by creeping, given to creeping. L18.
2 Having or producing a creeping of the flesh; eerie, uncanny. M19.
> A. TROLLOPE It is dark and cold and what I call creepy. T. PYNCHON Women avoid him . . . he's creepy.

– COMB.: **creepy-crawly** *adjective & noun* (*a*) *adjective* that creeps and crawls; sneaking, servile; (of feelings etc.) eerie, uncanny; (*b*) *noun* a creature that creeps and crawls, an insect.

creese *noun* var. of KRIS.

creesh /kriːʃ/ *noun & verb*. *Scot.* Also **creish**. LME.
[ORIGIN Old French *craisse* = *graisse* from Latin *crassa* thick, fat; cf. GREASE *noun*.]
▸**A** *noun*. **1** Grease, fat. LME.
2 A smart blow. L18.
▸**B** *verb trans.* Grease. L15.
■ **creeshy** *adjective* greasy M16.

creeve *verb* see CREE.

creish *noun & verb* var. of CREESH.

crema /ˈkreɪmə/ *noun*. L20.
[ORIGIN Italian, lit. 'cream'.]
A frothy film that forms on the top of freshly made espresso coffee.

crémaillère /kremɑjɛːr/ *noun*. Pl. pronounced same. E19.
[ORIGIN French, formerly *cramaillère*, from *cramail* pot-hanger, chimney-hook.]
FORTIFICATION. A zigzag or indented inside line of a parapet.

cremains /krɪˈmeɪnz/ *noun pl.* Chiefly *N. Amer.* M20.
[ORIGIN Blend of *cremated* and *remains*.]
The ashes of a cremated person.

cremaster /krɪˈmastə/ *noun*. L17.
[ORIGIN Greek *kremastēr*, from *krema-* hang.]
1 ANATOMY. The muscle of the spermatic cord, by which the testicle can be partially raised. L17.
2 ENTOMOLOGY. The tip of the abdomen of the pupa of an insect, serving as an anchorage point. L19.
■ **cremasˈteric** *adjective* of or pertaining to the cremaster (muscle) L19.

cremate /krɪˈmeɪt/ *verb trans.* L19.
[ORIGIN Latin *cremat-* pa. ppl stem of *cremare* burn, or back-form. from CREMATION: see -ATE[3].]
Consume (a corpse) by fire, burn.
■ **cremator** *noun* a person who cremates corpses etc.; a crematory furnace: L19.

cremation /krɪˈmeɪʃ(ə)n/ *noun*. E17.
[ORIGIN Latin *crematio(n-)*, formed as CREMATE: see -ATION.]
The action of cremating; *spec.* the burning of a corpse as a means of disposing of it instead of burial; an instance of this.
■ **cremationist** *noun* an advocate of cremation L19.

crematorium /krɛməˈtɔːrɪəm/ *noun*. Pl. **-ria** /-rɪə/, **-riums**. L19.
[ORIGIN mod. Latin, formed as CREMATE: see -ORIUM.]
A place for cremating corpses.

crematory /ˈkrɛmət(ə)ri/ *adjective & noun*. L19.
[ORIGIN from CREMATE *verb* + -ORY[1], -ORY[2].]
▸**A** *adjective*. Of or pertaining to cremation. L19.
▸**B** *noun*. = CREMATORIUM. Now chiefly *N. Amer.* L19.

crème /krɛm (*pl. same*); kreɪm/ *noun*. E19.
[ORIGIN French = CREAM *noun*[2].]
1 Cream; a cream, a custard. Used esp. in names of desserts and liqueurs (see below). E19.
crème anglaise /ɑ̃ˈgleɪz/ [French = English] a rich egg custard. **crème brûlée** /bryle, ˈbruːleɪ/ [French = burnt] a cream or custard dessert topped with caramelized sugar. **crème caramel** /karamɛl, ˈkarəmɛl/ a custard dessert made with whipped cream and eggs and topped with caramel. **crème *Chantilly*** /ʃɑ̃tiji, ʃanˈtɪli/ whipped cream sweetened and flavoured with vanilla. **crème de cacao** /də kakao, kəˈkɑːəʊ/ a chocolate-flavoured liqueur. **crème de menthe** /də mɑ̃ːt, ˈmɑːnt, ˈmɒnθ/ a

peppermint-flavoured liqueur. ***crème de noyau*** /də nwajo, ˈnwʌɪəʊ/ an almond-flavoured liqueur. **crème fraiche** /ˈfrɛʃ/ [French = fresh] a type of thick cream made from double cream with the addition of buttermilk, sour cream, or yogurt. ***crème renversée*** /rɑ̃vɛrse, ˈrɛnvəːseɪ/ [French = inverted] a custard turned out of a mould.

2 ***crème de la crème*** /də la, lɑː/, the pick of society; the elite. **M19.**

P. SCANLAN There's a marina around here somewhere, where the *crème de la crème* of the Mediterranean park their yachts.

3 (Usu. **creme**.) A substance, esp. a cosmetic product, with a thick, creamy consistency. **E20.**

cremini /krəˈmiːni/ *noun*. Pl. same. **L20.**
[ORIGIN Italian.]
A brown variety of mushroom, *Agaricus bisporus*, eaten before the cap has opened and fully matured.

Cremnitz white /ˈkrɛmnɪts ˈwʌɪt/ *noun phr.* Also **K-**. **L19.**
[ORIGIN from German *Kremnitz*, (formerly also) *C-*, Kremnica, a town in Slovakia + WHITE *noun*.]
A white lead pigment used as a paint base.

cremnophobia /krɛmnəˈfəʊbɪə/ *noun*. **E20.**
[ORIGIN from Greek *krēmnos* overhanging cliff + -O- + -PHOBIA.]
Irrational fear of precipices or steep places.

cremona /krɪˈməʊnə/ *noun*[1]. **M17.**
[ORIGIN Alt. of KRUMMHORN.]
= CROMORNE, KRUMMHORN 2.

Cremona /krɪˈməʊnə/ *adjective & noun*[2]. **L17.**
[ORIGIN A town in Lombardy.]
(Designating) an old Italian violin of fine quality, *spec.* one made in Cremona in the 17th and early 18th cents.

cremor /ˈkrɛmə/ *noun*. Now *rare*. **E17.**
[ORIGIN Latin: erron. assoc. with French CRÈME.]
A thick juice or liquid; a broth. Also, a scum gathering on the top of a liquid.

crenate /ˈkriːneɪt/ *adjective*. **L18.**
[ORIGIN mod. Latin *crenatus*, from popular Latin *crena* (in late gloss) notch, incision, of unknown origin: see -ATE[2].]
BOTANY, ZOOLOGY, etc. = CRENATED.
■ **creˈnation** *noun* a crenated formation, a crenature; crenated condition: **M19.** **crenature** /ˈkrɛnətjʊə, ˈkriː-/ *noun* a rounded tooth or denticulation on the margin of a leaf etc. **E19.**

crenated /ˈkriːneɪtɪd/ *adjective*. **L17.**
[ORIGIN formed as CRENATE + -ED[1].]
BOTANY, ZOOLOGY, etc. Having a notched edge or rounded teeth; finely scalloped.

crenel /ˈkrɛn(ə)l/ *noun*. Also **crenelle** /krɪˈnɛl/. **L15.**
[ORIGIN Old French (mod. *créneau*) from Proto-Gallo-Romance dim. of popular Latin *crena* (see CRENATE). Cf. KERNEL *noun*[2].]
Each of the open spaces or indentations in a battlemented parapet, orig. used for shooting through etc.; an embrasure. In *pl.*, battlements.

crenel /ˈkrɛn(ə)l/ *verb trans.* Infl. **-l(l)-**. **L17.**
[ORIGIN Old French & mod. French *créneler*, formed as CRENEL *noun* Cf. KERNEL *verb*[2].]
Indent the edge of; crenellate. Chiefly as ***crenelled*** *ppl adjective*.

crenellate /ˈkrɛn(ə)leɪt/ *verb trans.* Also **-elate**. **E19.**
[ORIGIN formed as CRENEL *noun* + -ATE[3].]
Provide with battlements or embrasures.
■ **creneˈllation** *noun* the action of crenellating; the condition of being crenellated; a battlement: **M19.**

crenelle *noun* see CRENEL *noun*.

crenellé /ˈkrɛnəli/ *adjective*. Also **-lly**. **L16.**
[ORIGIN French *crénelé* pa. pple of *créneler*: see CRENEL *verb*.]
HERALDRY. Having battlements, or indentations similar to battlements.

crenulate /ˈkrɛnjʊleɪt/ *adjective*. **L18.**
[ORIGIN mod. Latin *crenulatus*, from *crenula* dim. of *crena*: see CRENATE, -ATE[2].]
1 BOTANY & ZOOLOGY. Of a leaf, a shell, etc.: minutely crenate; finely scalloped. **L18.**
2 PHYSICAL GEOGRAPHY. Of a shoreline: having many small irregular bays due to the erosion of rock of varying hardness. **E20.**
■ **crenulated** *adjective* = CRENULATE 1 **E19.** **crenuˈlation** *noun* a crenulated formation **M19.**

creodont /ˈkriːədɒnt/ *noun & adjective*. **L19.**
[ORIGIN mod. Latin *Creodonta* (see below), from Greek *kreas* flesh + -ODONT.]
PALAEONTOLOGY. A member of, of or pertaining to, the order Creodonta of extinct carnivorous mammals, from the Palaeocene, Eocene, and Oligocene epochs.

creole /ˈkriːəʊl/ *noun & adjective*. Also (esp. in strict use of sense A.1 & corresp. uses of the adjective) **C-**. **E17.**
[ORIGIN French *créole*, earlier *criole* from Spanish *criollo* prob. from Portuguese *crioulo* black person born in Brazil, home-born slave, from *criar* nurse, breed from Latin *creare* CREATE *verb*.]
▸ **A** *noun*. **1** A descendant of European settlers or (occas.) of black slaves, in the W. Indies or Central or S. America; a descendant of French settlers in the southern US, esp. Louisiana. Also *loosely*, a person of mixed European and black descent. **E17.**
2 A former pidgin language that has developed into the sole or native language of a community. **L19.**
– PHRASES: *SCOTCHMAN hugging a Creole*.
▸ **B** *adjective*. **1** That is a creole; of, pertaining to, or characteristic of a creole or creoles. **M18.**

V. S. NAIPAUL Old creole woman from 42 owe six dollars. E. L. ORTIZ Serve with . . any creole soup. *Scientific American* Creole languages throughout the world exhibit the same uniformity and even the same grammatical structures that are observed in Hawaii.

2 Of an animal or plant: bred or grown in the W. Indies etc. but not of indigenous origin; of local origin or production. **M18.**
■ **creˈolian** *noun & adjective* (now *rare*) = CREOLE *noun* 1, *adjective* 1 **L17.** **creolism** *noun* (now *rare*) creole descent **L18.** **creolist** *noun* an expert in or student of creole languages **M20.** **creoˈlistics** *noun* the branch of linguistics that deals with creole languages **L20.**

creolize /ˈkriːəʊlʌɪz, ˈkrɪ-/ *verb*. Also **-ise**. **E19.**
[ORIGIN from CREOLE + -IZE.]
1 *verb intrans.* Relax in an elegant fashion in a warm climate. *rare*. **E19.**
2 *verb trans.* Naturalize in the W. Indies, Central or S. America or Louisiana. **M19.**
3 *verb trans.* Make (a language) into a creole. **L19.**
■ **creoliˈzation** *noun* the action or process of creolizing someone or something; the process by which a pidgin language develops into a creole: **L19.**

creophagous /krɪˈɒfəgəs/ *adjective*. Also **k-**. **L19.**
[ORIGIN Greek *kreophagos*, from *kreas* flesh: see -PHAGOUS.]
Flesh-eating, carnivorous.
■ **creophagy** /-dʒi/ *noun* the eating of flesh **L19.**

creosol /ˈkriːəsɒl/ *noun*. **M19.**
[ORIGIN from CREOS(OTE + -OL.]
CHEMISTRY. A colourless liquid phenolic ether, $C_8H_{10}O_2$, forming the chief constituent of wood-tar creosote.

creosote /ˈkriːəsəʊt/ *noun & verb*. **M19.**
[ORIGIN German *Kreosote*, from Greek *kreo-* combining form of *kreas* flesh + *sōtēr* saviour, *sōteria* safety, intended to mean 'flesh-saving', with ref. to its antiseptic properties.]
▸ **A** *noun*. **1** A colourless oily liquid distilled from wood tar, having powerful antiseptic properties. **M19.**
2 More fully ***creosote oil***. A dark brown oil distilled from coal tar and used as a wood preservative. **M19.**
▸ **B** *verb trans.* Treat (wood etc.) with creosote. **M19.**

crêpe /kreɪp/ *noun & adjective*. Also **crepe**. See also CRAPE *noun & adjective*. **L18.**
[ORIGIN French, earlier †*crespe*, use as noun of Old French *crespe* curled, frizzed from Latin *crispus* curled. Cf. CRISP *noun, adjective*.]
▸ **A** *noun*. **1** A fine cotton or gauzelike fabric with a crinkled surface. **L18.**
China crêpe, **crêpe de Chine** /də ˈʃiːn/ a fine crêpe of silk or a similar fabric. ***romaine crêpe***: see ROMAINE 2.
2 = ***crêpe rubber*** below. **E20.**
3 A very thin pancake. **E20.**
crêpe Suzette /suːˈzɛt/ a thin dessert pancake served in a spirit or liqueur.
▸ **B** *attrib.* or as *adjective*. Made of crêpe; resembling crêpe. **L18.**
crêpe paper thin crinkled paper resembling crêpe. **crêpe rubber** a type of raw rubber rolled into thin sheets with a corrugated surface, used for shoe soles etc. **crêpe sole** a layer of crêpe rubber forming the underside of a shoe. ***pale crêpe rubber***: see PALE *adjective*.
■ **crêpey**, **-py** *adjective* resembling crêpe **L19.**

crêpe /kreɪp/ *verb trans.* **E19.**
[ORIGIN French *crêper*.]
Crimp, frizz (hair). Cf. CRAPE *verb* 1.
■ **crêpé** /-pi/ *ppl adjective* (of the hair) crimped, frizzed **E19.** **crêping** *verbal noun* (***a***) crimping or frizzing of hair; (***b***) production of crêpe rubber or crêpe paper: **L19.**

crêpeline /ˈkreɪpəliːn/ *noun*. Also **-oline**. **L19.**
[ORIGIN French, dim. of CRÊPE *noun*.]
A thin light dress material made of silk or silk and wool.

crêperie /ˈkreɪpəri, ˈkrɛp-/ *noun*. Also **crepe-**. **L20.**
[ORIGIN French.]
A small restaurant (esp. in France) in which crêpes are served.

crepine /ˈkrɛpiːn/ *noun*. *obsolete* exc. *hist.* Also **crespin(e)** /ˈkrɛspiːn, -ɪn/. **M16.**
[ORIGIN Old French *crespine* (mod. *crépine*), from *crespe*: see CRÊPE *noun & adjective*.]
A ladies' net or caul for the hair; a ruffled part of a hood. Also, a frill or fringe for a bed, dais, etc.

crépinette /kreɪpɪˈnɛt/ *noun*. **L19.**
[ORIGIN French, dim. of *crépine* caul: see -ETTE.]
A kind of flat sausage consisting of minced meat and savoury stuffing wrapped in pieces of pork caul.

crepitate /ˈkrɛpɪteɪt/ *verb intrans.* **E17.**
[ORIGIN Latin *crepitat-* pa. ppl stem of *crepitare* crackle, from *crepare* rattle: see -ATE[3].]
†**1** Break wind. **E17–M18.**
2 ENTOMOLOGY. Of a (bombardier) beetle: eject a pungent fluid with a sudden sharp report. **E19.**
3 Make a crackling sound; MEDICINE (of the lungs) make the sound of crepitation (sense 2). **M19.**
■ **crepitant** *adjective* crackling, crepitating **E19.**

crepitation /krɛpɪˈteɪʃ(ə)n/ *noun*. **M17.**
[ORIGIN French *crépitation* or late Latin *crepitatio(n-)*, formed as CREPITATE: see -ATION.]
1 A crackling or sharp rattling sound. **M17.**
2 MEDICINE. A crackling sound in the lungs heard on auscultation, arising in the alveoli during inhalation, often a symptom of lung disease. Also, crepitus caused by bone. **M19.**

crepitus /ˈkrɛpɪtəs/ *noun*. **E19.**
[ORIGIN Latin, from *crepare* rattle etc.]
MEDICINE. **1** A crackling sound or sensation caused by friction between bone and cartilage or between the fractured parts of a bone. Also, crepitation in breathing. **E19.**
2 The breaking of wind. *rare*. **E19.**
■ **crepitous** *adjective* of the nature of or such as to produce crepitus **M19.**

crêpoline *noun* var. of CRÊPELINE.

crépon /ˈkreɪpɒn/ *noun & adjective*. **L19.**
[ORIGIN French, formed as CRÊPE *noun & adjective*: see -OON.]
(Made of) a fabric resembling crêpe, but heavier.

crept *verb pa. t. & pple* of CREEP *verb*.

crepuscle *noun* see CREPUSCULUM.

crepuscular /krɪˈpʌskjʊlə, krɛ-/ *adjective*. **M17.**
[ORIGIN from CREPUSCULUM + -AR[1]: cf. French *crépusculaire*.]
1 Resembling the twilight of morning or evening; dim, indistinct; not yet fully enlightened. **M17.**

J. L. MOTLEY The state of crepuscular civilization to which they have reached.

2 Of or pertaining to twilight. **M18.**
3 ZOOLOGY. Appearing or active by evening twilight. **E19.**

crepusculum /krɪˈpʌskjʊləm, krɛ-/ *noun*. Also anglicized as **crepuscle** /ˈkrɛpʌs(ə)l/, **crepuscule** /ˈkrɛpəskjuːl/. **LME.**
[ORIGIN Latin, rel. to *creper* dusky, dark.]
The period of half-dark at the beginning or end of the day; twilight, dusk.
■ **crepusculine** *adjective* (*rare*) of or pertaining to twilight, dusky **M16.** **crepusculous** *adjective* = CREPUSCULAR 1 **M17.**

Cres. *abbreviation*[1].
Crescent.

cres. *abbreviation*[2]. Also **cresc.**
MUSIC. Crescendo.

†**crescence** *noun*. **L15–M18.**
[ORIGIN Latin *crescentia*: see CRESCENT *noun*, -ENCE.]
Growth; (an) increase.

crescendo /krɪˈʃɛndəʊ/ *adverb, adjective, noun, & verb*. **L18.**
[ORIGIN Italian, pres. pple of *crescere* to increase from Latin *crescere* grow.]
▸ **A** *adverb & adjective*. MUSIC. (A direction:) with a gradual increase in loudness. **L18.**
▸ **B** *noun*. Pl. **-dos**, **-di** /-di/.
1 MUSIC. A gradual increase in loudness; a passage (to be) played or sung with such an increase. **L18.**
2 A progressive increase in force or effect; a progress towards a climax. **L18.**

J. B. PRIESTLEY The shock . . coming at the end of a long crescendo of excitement, cut the last binding thread of self-control.

3 A climax. **E20.**

P. G. WODEHOUSE The babble at the bar had risen to a sudden crescendo.

▸ **C** *verb intrans.* Increase gradually in loudness or intensity. **E20.**

crescent /ˈkrɛs(ə)nt/ *noun*. See also CROISSANT. **LME.**
[ORIGIN Anglo-Norman *cressaunt*, Old French *creissant* (mod. *croissant*) from Latin *crescent-* pres. ppl stem of *crescere* grow: see -ENT. In 17 assim. to Latin.]
1 The waxing moon during the period between new moon and full. **LME.**
2 The convexo-concave figure of the waxing or waning moon during the first or last quarter, esp. when very new or very old. **LME.**

SHELLEY The moon's argentine crescent hung In the dark dome of heaven.

3 A representation of this phase of the moon, esp. (***a***) as an ornament; (***b***) HERALDRY as a charge or a cadence mark for a second son in England; (***c***) as a badge or emblem adopted by the Turks, and hence Muslims in general, as a military and religious symbol (analogous to the Christian cross); *fig.* (**C-**) *the* Muslim religion, esp. as a political force (formerly) *the* Ottoman Empire. **LME.**
4 *gen.* Anything of the shape of the new or old moon; a crescent-shaped figure. **L17.**

T. BEWICK The breast [of a bird] is distinguished by a crescent of pure white. R. WEST Sandy hair which curved across the front of her head in a high hollow crescent.

5 *spec.* A street or terrace of houses built in a crescent shape or arc. **M18.**
6 *spec.* A croissant. Chiefly *N. Amer.* **L19.**
– PHRASES: ***Fertile Crescent***: see FERTILE *adjective* 1. ***olive crescent***: see OLIVE *noun*[1] & *adjective*. ***Red Crescent***: see RED *adjective*. ***Turkish crescent***: see TURKISH *adjective*.
■ **crescenˈtade** *noun* [after *crusade*] (now *rare* or *obsolete*) (***a***) a religious war waged under the Turkish flag; (***b***) a holy war for Islam: **M19.**

C

crescented *adjective* formed as a crescent or new moon **E19.** **crescentic** /krɪˈsɛntɪk/ *adjective* crescent-shaped **M19.** **crescentric** /krɪˈsɛntrɪk/ *adjective* (*rare*) = CRESCENTIC **M19.**

crescent /ˈkrɛs(ə)nt/ *adjective.* **L16.**
[ORIGIN Latin *crescent-* pres. ppl stem of *crescere* grow: see CRESCENT *noun*, -ENT.]
1 Growing, increasing, developing, esp. as or like the moon's figure. **L16.**

SHAKES. *Ant. & Cl.* My powers are crescent, and my auguring hope Says it will come to th' full.

2 Shaped like the new or old moon; convexo-concave. **E17.**

W. H. RUSSELL New Orleans is called the 'crescent city' in consequence of its being built on a curve of the river. *Scientific American* Two fine pictures of crescent Mars.

crescent roll a croissant.

crescive /ˈkrɛsɪv/ *adjective.* **M16.**
[ORIGIN from Latin *crescere* grow + -IVE.]
Growing.

cresol /ˈkriːsɒl/ *noun.* **M19.**
[ORIGIN from *cres-* for CREOSOTE + -OL.]
CHEMISTRY. Each of three isomeric crystalline phenols (*ortho-*, *meta-*, and *para-*methylphenol), $(CH_3)C_6H_4OH$, present in coal tar creosote and used as disinfectants.

crespin(e) *noun* see CREPINE.

cress /krɛs/ *noun.*
[ORIGIN Old English *cressa*, *cresse*, *cærse*, *cerse* = Middle Low German *kerse*, Middle Dutch *kersse*, *korsse* (Dutch *kers*), Old High German *kresso*, *kressa* (German *Kresse*), from West Germanic.]
sing. & (now *rare*) in *pl.* Any of various plants belonging to Cruciferae or occas. other families, usu. with pungent edible leaves; *esp.* = ***garden cress*** s.v. GARDEN *noun*.
Indian cress, ***Pará cress***, ***pennycress***, ***rock cress***, ***swine cress***, ***watercress***, etc. ***mustard and cress***: see MUSTARD *noun*.
– NOTE: Until **19** usu. in pl.

cresset /ˈkrɛsɪt/ *noun.* **LME.**
[ORIGIN Old French *cresset*, *craisset*, from *craisse* var. of *graisse* oil, GREASE *noun*: see -ET[1].]
hist. A metal vessel, usu. mounted on a pole, for holding oil, coal, etc., to be burnt for light.

fig.: SIR W. SCOTT The moon . . hung her dim dull cresset in the heavens.

– COMB.: †**cresset-light** a blazing cresset; the light of a cresset; a beacon light.

cresson /krɛsɔ̃/ *noun.* **M17.**
[ORIGIN French = CRESS.]
†**1** In *pl.* Cress. *rare.* Only in **M17.**
2 A shade of green resembling that of watercress. **L19.**

crest /krɛst/ *noun.* **ME.**
[ORIGIN Old French *creste* (mod. *crête*) from Latin *crista* tuft, plume.]
1 An erect plume of feathers, horsehair, etc., fixed to the top of a helmet or headdress; any ornament worn similarly as a cognizance. **ME.** ▸**b** (The apex of) a helmet. **ME.**

T. H. WHITE Many were vain enough to have these armorial crests . . but Sir Lancelot always contented himself with a bare helmet. **b** MILTON On his crest Sat horror plum'd.

2 A comb, tuft of feathers, etc., on a bird's or animal's head. **LME.**

E. T. GILLIARD The cockatoos . . differ from other parrots in having the crest erectile and usually greatly elongated.

3 *HERALDRY.* A figure or device, often a representation of an animal or bird, placed on a wreath, coronet, etc., and borne above the shield and on the helmet in a coat of arms or used separately as a cognizance on seals, plate, notepaper, etc. **LME.** ▸**b** *ARCHERY.* A coloured identifying pattern below the fletching of an arrow. **E20.**

SHAKES. *Tam. Shr.* What is your crest—a coxcomb?

4 The head, summit, or top of or *of* anything, esp. a hill or mountain. **LME.**

fig.: V. SACKVILLE-WEST Her relations with Sebastian would seem to have reached the crest of their perfection.

5 *ARCHITECTURE.* The finishing of stone, metal, etc., which surmounts a roof ridge, wall, etc. **LME.**
6 An elevated ridge; *spec.* (***a***) the ridge of a mountain, pass, bank, etc.; (***b***) *FORTIFICATION* the top line of a parapet or slope; (***c***) a baulk or ridge in a field between two furrows; (***d***) the curling foamy top of a wave; the peak of a wave. **LME.**

I. MURDOCH The sea is agitated, very dark blue with white crests.

on the crest of the wave *fig.* at the most favourable moment in one's progress.

7 The ridge of the neck of a horse, dog, lion, etc.; an animal's mane. **L16.**
8 A raised ridge on the surface of any object; *esp.* (*ANATOMY*) a ridge running along the surface of a bone. **L16.**
frontal crest, ***occipital crest***, ***parietal crest***, ***sagittal crest***, etc. ***neural crest***: see NEURAL *adjective* 1.
– COMB.: **crestfallen** *adjective* (***a***) with drooping crest; *fig.* dejected, abashed; (***b***) (of a horse) having the ridge of the neck hanging to one side; **crest-line** (***a***) a series of ridges; (***b***) the skyline of a ridge.

■ **cresting** *noun* (***a***) *ARCHITECTURE* an ornamental ridging to a wall or roof; (***b***) ornamental edging on a chair, settee, etc.: **M19.** **crestless** *adjective* **L16.**

crest /krɛst/ *verb.* **LME.**
[ORIGIN from the noun.]
1 *verb trans.* Provide with a crest. **LME.**
2 *verb trans.* Mark with long streaks (with allus. to the streaming hair of a crest). *rare.* **L16.**
3 *verb trans.* Serve as a crest to, top, crown. **E17.**

SOUTHEY Broad battlements Crested the bulwark.

4 *verb intrans.* Erect one's crest; raise oneself proudly. *obsolete* exc. *dial.* **E18.**
5 *verb trans.* Reach the crest or summit of (a hill, wave, etc.). **M19.**

J. H. NEWMAN In this inquisitive age, when the Alps are crested, and seas fathomed.

6 *verb intrans.* (Of a wave) form or rise into a crest; *gen.* peak. **M19.**

S. KING The boy's temperature had crested at a giddy one hundred and five degrees.

crested /ˈkrɛstɪd/ *adjective.* **LME.**
[ORIGIN from CREST *noun*, *verb*: see -ED[2], -ED[1].]
1 Wearing or having a crest; *spec.* designating plants and animals distinguished by a crest. **LME.**

D. H. LAWRENCE The bird lifted its crested head. E. WAUGH A fat order for crested note-paper.

crested argus, ***crested dogstail***, ***crested kingfisher***, ***crested penguin***, etc. **crested newt** a large newt, *Triturus cristatus*, the male of which has a tall crest along its back and tail in the breeding season, and which is found from Britain to central Asia. **crested tit** a small tit, *Parus cristatus*, which has a short crest and is found in coniferous forests from western Europe to the Urals. **great crested grebe** a large grebe, *Podiceps cristatus*, which has a black crest and chestnut and black ear ruffs, and is found in many areas of the Old World.
2 *HERALDRY.* Esp. of a bird: having a crest of a different (specified) tincture from that of the body. **L16.**
†**3** Having raised lines or striae; ribbed. **L16–M19.**
4 Having a raised ridge. **M19.**

Creswellian /krɛzˈwɛlɪən/ *adjective & noun.* **E20.**
[ORIGIN from *Creswell* Crags in Derbyshire (where the phase is well represented) + -IAN.]
ARCHAEOLOGY. ▸**A** *adjective.* Designating or pertaining to a cultural period of the late Palaeolithic in NW Europe, esp. Britain, roughly contemporary with the later part of Magdalenian. **E20.**
▸**B** *ellipt.* as *noun.* The Creswellian period. **M20.**

cresyl /ˈkriːsʌɪl, -sɪl/ *noun.* **M19.**
[ORIGIN from CRES(OL + -YL.]
CHEMISTRY. Each of three isomeric radicals, $CH_3C_6H_4O\cdot$, derived from the cresols. Usu. in *comb.*
■ **cresylic** *adjective* of cresyl; ***cresylic acid***, a mixture of cresols and other phenols distilled from coal tar: **M19.**

cretaceous /krɪˈteɪʃəs/ *adjective & noun.* In *GEOLOGY* usu. **C-**. **L17.**
[ORIGIN from Latin *cretaceus*, from *creta* chalk: see -ACEOUS.]
▸**A** *adjective.* **1** Of the nature of chalk; chalky. **L17.**
2 *GEOLOGY.* Designating or pertaining to the last period of the Mesozoic era, following the Jurassic and preceding the Tertiary, in which many chalk deposits were formed and flowering plants first appeared. **M19.**
▸**B** *noun.* *GEOLOGY.* The Cretaceous period; the system of rocks dating from this time. **M19.**
■ **cretaceously** *adverb* **M19.**

Cretan /ˈkriːt(ə)n/ *adjective & noun.* **L16.**
[ORIGIN Latin *Cretanus*, from *Creta* from Greek *Krētē* Crete: see -AN.]
▸**A** *adjective.* Of or belonging to the island of Crete in the eastern Mediterranean (at one time supposed to contain many liars). **L16.**
▸**B** *noun.* A native or inhabitant of Crete. **L16.**

T. HARDY He was perfectly truthful towards men, but to women lied like a Cretan.

cretic /ˈkriːtɪk/ *adjective & noun.* **L16.**
[ORIGIN Latin *creticus* from Greek *krētikos*, from *Krētē*: see CRETAN, -IC.]
CLASSICAL PROSODY. (Designating) a metrical foot consisting of one short syllable between two long. Cf. AMPHIMACER.

cretin /ˈkrɛtɪn/ *noun.* **L18.**
[ORIGIN French *crétin* from Swiss French *creitin*, *crestin* from Latin *Christianus*: see CHRISTIAN *adjective*.]
1 *MEDICINE* (*arch.*). A person afflicted with cretinism. **L18.**
2 A fool; a person who behaves stupidly. **L19.**
■ **cretinism** *noun* the condition of a cretin; *MEDICINE* (*arch.*) mental disability, deficient growth, and coarseness of the skin and facial features due to congenital lack of thyroid hormone: **E19.** **cretinize** *verb trans.* reduce to cretinism **M19.** **cretinoid** *adjective* resembling a cretin or cretinism **L19.** **cretinous** *adjective* pertaining to or characteristic of a cretin; of the nature of cretinism: **M19.**

cretize /ˈkriːtʌɪz/ *verb intrans.* Now *rare* or *obsolete*. Also **-ise**. **M17.**
[ORIGIN Greek *krētizein*, from *Krētē* Crete.]
Behave in a manner attributed to Cretans, lie.

cretonne /krɛˈtɒn, ˈkrɛtɒn/ *noun.* **L19.**
[ORIGIN French, of unknown origin.]
A strong unglazed fabric printed on one or both sides with a (usu. large floral) pattern, used for chair covers, curtains, etc.

Creutzfeldt–Jakob disease /krɔɪtsfɛltˈjakɒb dɪˌziːz/ *noun phr.* **L20.**
[ORIGIN from H. G. *Creuzfeldt* (1885–1964) + A. M. *Jakob* (1884–1931), German neurologists.]
A usu. fatal disease in which there is degeneration of nerve cells in the brain, causing mental, physical, and sensory disturbances such as dementia and seizures. (Abbreviation ***CJD***.)
(**new**) **variant Creutzfeldt–Jakob disease** a similar disease which may affect younger people and is believed to be causally related to bovine spongiform encephalopathy (BSE); abbreviation ***nvCJD***, ***vCJD***.

crevasse /krɪˈvas/ *noun.* **E19.**
[ORIGIN French (Old French *crevace*): see CREVICE *noun*[1].]
1 A (usu. deep) fissure or chasm in the ice of a glacier; *transf.* a deep crack or chasm. **E19.**
2 A breach in the bank or levee of a river, canal, etc. *US.* **E19.**

crevasse /krɪˈvas/ *verb.* **M19.**
[ORIGIN French *crevasser*, formed as CREVASSE *noun*.]
1 *verb trans.* Fissure with crevasses. Chiefly as ***crevassed*** *ppl adjective*. **M19.**
2 *verb intrans.* Form crevasses. Chiefly as ***crevassing*** *verbal noun*. **M19.**

crève /krɛv/ *noun.* **L19.**
[ORIGIN Abbreviation.]
= CRÈVECOEUR.

crèvecoeur /ˈkrɛvkəː/ *noun.* **M19.**
[ORIGIN French, lit. 'split heart' (from the shape of the comb).]
A variety (usu. black) of the domestic fowl, of French origin.

crevette /krəˈvɛt/ *noun.* **L19.**
[ORIGIN French = shrimp.]
1 A deep shade of pink. **L19.**
2 A shrimp or prawn, esp. as an item on a menu. **E20.**

crevice /ˈkrɛvɪs/ *noun*[1]. **ME.**
[ORIGIN Old French *crevace* (mod. CREVASSE *noun*), from *crever* to burst, split from Latin *crepare* rattle, crack, break with a crash.]
1 An opening produced by a crack, esp. in rock, a building, etc.; a cleft; a fissure; a chink. **ME.**

J. BALDWIN Dirt was in every corner, angle, crevice of the monstrous stove.

2 *spec.* *MINING.* A fissure in which a deposit of ore or metal is found. **M19.**
■ **creviced** *adjective* **M16.** **crevicing** *noun* (*N. Amer.*) the working of a crevice or crevices for ore or metal **M19.**

†**crevice** *noun*[2] see CRAYFISH.

crew /kruː/ *noun*[1]. **LME.**
[ORIGIN Old French *creüe* (mod. *crue*) increase, use as noun of fem. pa. pple of *croistre* (mod. *croître*) from Latin *crescere* grow, increase.]
▸**I** *gen.* †**1** An augmentation or reinforcement of a military force; a company of soldiers. **LME–L16.**
2 Any organized armed band. **L16.**

W. GILPIN Those crews of outlawed banditti, who . . plundered the country.

3 A number of people associated together; a company. **L16.** ▸**b** An assemblage of animals or things. **E17.**

MILTON Mirth, admit me of thy crew.

4 A number of people classed together; a set, a gang, a mob. **L16.**

J. GALSWORTHY He was not of 'that catch-penny crew,' new paid off.

▸**II** *spec.* **5** A squad of workers under an overseer; an organized unit of workers. **L17.**
6 A squad of sailors on a warship under the direction of a petty officer or with some particular duty. **L17.**
7 A body of people manning a ship, boat, aircraft, spacecraft, train, etc.; such people other than the officers. Also, a person single-handedly manning a yacht etc. **L17.**

N. SHUTE Besides her eleven officers she carried a crew of about seventy petty officers and enlisted men.

8 A team of people concerned with the technical aspects or a specified technical aspect of making a film, recording, etc. **M20.**
camera crew, ***film crew***, ***sound crew***, etc.
– COMB.: **crew cut** a closely cropped style of haircut for men and boys (app. first adopted by boat crews at Harvard and Yale Universities); **crew-cut** *adjective* (of hair) closely cropped all over; (of a person) having a crew cut; **crewman** a member of a crew; **crew neck** (orig. *US*) a round neckline, esp. of a sweater, fitting closely to the throat as on vests worn by oarsmen.

crew *noun*[2] var. of CRUE.

crew /kruː/ *verb*[1]. **M20.**
[ORIGIN from CREW *noun*[1].]
1 *verb intrans.* Act as (a member of) a crew (*for*). **M20.**

F. CHICHESTER Martin had crewed for me in a number of races.

2 *verb trans.* Act as (a member) of the crew of; supply crew for. **M20.**

crew *verb*[2] see CROW *verb*.

crewel /ˈkruːəl/ *noun & adjective*. **L15.**
[ORIGIN Unknown.]
▸ **A** *noun*. **1** A thin loosely twisted worsted yarn, used esp. for tapestry and embroidery. **L15.**
2 = ***crewel work***, sense B.2 below. **L19.**
▸ **B** *attrib.* or as *adjective*. **1** *gen.* Made of or with crewel. *obsolete* exc. *dial.* **M16.**
2 ***crewel work***, (embroidery with) a design worked in worsted on a ground of linen or cloth. **M19.**
3 Of or pertaining to crewel work; for use in crewel work; embroidered with crewel work. **L19.**
■ **crewelist** *noun* a person who works crewel work **L19.**

crewels /ˈkruːəlz/ *noun pl.* *Scot.* Long *arch.* **L16.**
[ORIGIN French *écrouelles*.]
Scrofula.

criard /kriaːr/ *adjective*. Also (French fem.) ***criarde*** /kriaːrd/. **M19.**
[ORIGIN French.]
Shrill; garish.

crib /krɪb/ *noun*.
[ORIGIN Old English *crib(b)* = Old Frisian *cribbe*, Old Saxon *kribbia* (Dutch *krib(be)*, Old High German *krippa* (German *Krippe*). In branch III from the verb.]
▸ **I 1** A barred receptacle for fodder etc.; a manger, *esp.* that in which the infant Jesus was said to be laid. **OE.** ▸**b** A model of the manger scene at Bethlehem. **L19.**
2 A stall in a cowshed. Now *dial.* **ME.**

AV *Prov.* 14:4 Where no Oxen are, the crib is cleane.

†**3** A wickerwork basket, pannier, etc.; a hop-picker's bin. **LME–M19.**
4 A small house, a cabin, in NZ *spec.* at the seaside, a holiday resort, etc.; a hovel; a narrow room; *fig.* a confined space. **L16.** ▸**b** A house, an apartment; *spec.* a public house, a saloon; a brothel. *slang.* **M19.**

SHAKES. 2 *Hen. IV* Why rather, sleep, liest thou in smoky cribs . . Than in the perfum'd chambers of the great. *fig.*: A. H. CLOUGH The world . . Whithersoever we turn, still is the same narrow crib.

b *crack a crib*: see CRACK *verb*.
5 A small bed for a child, with barred or latticed sides; also occas., a cradle. Cf. COT *noun*[4] 3. **M17.**
6 Food, provisions; a light meal or snack. Now chiefly *Austral. & NZ.* **M17.**
7 A rack used in salt-making for drying salt after boiling. Now *rare* or *obsolete*. **L17.**
8 In full ***corn crib***. A bin or ventilated building for storing maize. *US.* **L17.** ▸**b** A storage bin or receptacle for other commodities, tools, etc. **M19.**
9 A framework of bars or spars for strengthening, support, etc. **L17.** ▸**b** *spec.* A small raft of boards etc. *N. Amer.* **L18.** ▸**c** Heavy crossed timbers used in foundations in loose soil, to support a pier, to form a dam, etc., (also more fully ***cribwork***); a structure of such timbers. **E19.** ▸**d** A framework lining the shaft of a mine. **M19.**
▸ **II 10** In the game of cribbage, the set of cards given to the dealer by himself or herself and each other player; *colloq.* the game of cribbage. **L17.**
▸ **III 11** A translated version for (esp. illegitimate) use by students. *colloq.* **E19.**
12 A plagiarism; a translation taken from a crib. *colloq.* **M19.**
– COMB.: **crib-biter** a horse given to crib-biting; *fig.* a grumbler; **crib-biting** a horse's habit of seizing a manger, door, or projection in the teeth and at the same time noisily drawing in breath; ***cribwork***: see sense 9c above.

crib /krɪb/ *verb*. Infl. **-bb-**. **LME.**
[ORIGIN from the noun.]
†**1** *verb intrans.* Feed from a crib. *rare*. Only in **LME.**
2 *verb trans.* Shut up (as) in a crib; confine in a small space; hamper. **E17.** ▸**b** Place (maize etc.) in a crib. *US.* **E18.**

SHAKES. *Macb.* I am cabin'd, cribb'd, confin'd, bound in.

3 *verb trans.* Provide with a crib or cribs. **M17.**
4 *verb trans.* Pilfer, purloin, steal; appropriate furtively (a small part of something). *colloq.* **M18.**
5 *verb trans. & intrans.* Copy (a passage, a translation, etc.) unfairly or without acknowledgement; plagiarize. *colloq.* **L18.**

A. S. NEILL There has been no real authority on education, and I do not know of any book from which I can crib. A. S. BYATT An essay . . clearly largely cribbed from C. S. Lewis.

6 *verb intrans.* Of a horse: engage in crib-biting. **M19.** ▸**b** *fig.* Complain, grumble. *colloq.* **E20.**

cribbage /ˈkrɪbɪdʒ/ *noun*. **M17.**
[ORIGIN Uncertain: cf. CRIB *noun* 10.]
1 A card game for two, three, or four players, played with a complete pack and a board with pegs and holes for scoring, in which the dealer scores also from the cards given to him or her as discards from each player's hand. **M17.**
2 The action of cribbing; something cribbed. *rare*. **M19.**
– COMB.: **cribbage-board**: for scoring at cribbage; **cribbage-faced** *adjective* (*arch.*) pockmarked.

cribble /ˈkrɪb(ə)l/ *noun*. Now *rare* or *obsolete*. **LME.**
[ORIGIN Old French & mod. French *crible* from popular Latin var. of Latin *cribrum* sieve.]
†**1** Bran, coarse meal, etc., remaining in a sieve after the fine flour has been sifted out; *spec.* a particular quality of coarse meal. **LME–E18.**
2 A sieve. **M16.**
– COMB.: †**cribble bread**: made of this particular quality of coarse meal.

cribellum /krɪˈbɛləm/ *noun*. Pl. **-lla** /-lə/. **L19.**
[ORIGIN Late Latin, dim. of *cribrum* sieve: see -ELLUM.]
ZOOLOGY. An additional spinning organ, having numerous fine pores, situated in front of the spinnerets in certain spiders.
■ **ˈcribellate** *adjective* having a cribellum **E20.** **ˈcribellated** *adjective* = CRIBELLATE *adjective* **E20.**

criblé /krible/ *noun & adjective*. **L19.**
[ORIGIN French, formed as CRIBBLE.]
(Designating) a type of engraving with small punctures or depressions on a wood or metal ground. See also MANIÈRE CRIBLÉE.

cribo /ˈkriːbəʊ, ˈkrʌɪbəʊ/ *noun*. Pl. **-os**. **L19.**
[ORIGIN Unknown.]
= ***indigo snake*** s.v. INDIGO *noun*.

cribriform /ˈkrɪbrɪfɔːm/ *adjective*. **M18.**
[ORIGIN from Latin *cribrum* sieve + -I- + -FORM.]
ANATOMY & BOTANY. Having numerous small holes; perforated like a sieve.
cribriform plate the part of the ethmoid bone which forms the roof of the nasal cavity and is traversed by the olfactory nerves.

cribrose /krʌɪˈbrəʊs/ *adjective*. **M19.**
[ORIGIN from Latin *cribrum* sieve: see -OSE[1].]
Chiefly BOTANY & ANATOMY. Perforated like a sieve.
■ Also †**cribrous** *adjective* **L17–E18.**

Crichton /ˈkrʌɪt(ə)n/ *noun*. **E19.**
[ORIGIN James *Crichton* of Clunie (1560–85?), a Scottish prodigy of intellectual and knightly accomplishments.]
More fully ***Admirable Crichton***. A person who excels in all kinds of studies and pursuits; a person noted for supreme competence.

crick /krɪk/ *noun*[1]. **LME.**
[ORIGIN Unknown.]
A sudden painful stiffness of the muscles in the neck, back, etc.

crick *noun*[2] var. of CREEK *noun*[1].

crick /krɪk/ *verb*[1] *intrans.* **E17.**
[ORIGIN Imit.: cf. French *criquer*, *cric* interjection. Cf. CRICKET *noun*[1].]
Make a sharp abrupt chirping sound, as a grasshopper.

crick /krɪk/ *verb*[2] *trans.* **M19.**
[ORIGIN from CRICK *noun*[1].]
Produce a crick in (the neck etc.).

crick-crack /ˈkrɪkkrak/ *noun & interjection*. **M16.**
[ORIGIN Redupl. of CRACK *noun*. Cf. French *cric crac*, Dutch *krikkrakken* crackle.]
(Repr.) a repeated sharp, explosive, or light cracking noise.

cricket /ˈkrɪkɪt/ *noun*[1]. **ME.**
[ORIGIN Old French & mod. French *criquet* †grasshopper, cricket, from *criquer* crackle, of imit. origin: cf. Middle Dutch & mod. Dutch *krekel* cricket, from imit. base.]
Any of various jumping, chirping orthopterous insects of the family Gryllidae; *esp.* (more fully ***house-cricket***) *Acheta domestica*, formerly a familiar insect living indoors near fireplaces, ovens, etc., or (more fully ***field-cricket***) *Gryllus campestris*, found in meadows etc. Also (with specifying word), any of various other insects related to or resembling the crickets.

J. G. HOLLAND Mullens had become as cheerful and lively as a cricket.

BALM-CRICKET. **bush cricket** any of various mainly arboreal grasshoppers of the family Tettigoniidae, having very long antennae; also called ***long-horned grasshopper***. **mole-cricket** any large nocturnal burrowing orthopteran of the family Gryllotalpidae; esp. *Gryllotalpa gryllotalpa*. ***MORMON cricket***.
– COMB.: **cricket-frog** a small N. American tree frog of the genus *Acris*, noted for its clicking call; **cricket-teal** *dial.* the garganey.

cricket /ˈkrɪkɪt/ *noun*[2] & *verb*. **L16.**
[ORIGIN Unknown.]
▸ **A** *noun*. An open-air game played with ball, bats, and wickets between two sides now usu. of eleven players each, the object being to score more runs than the opposition; the playing of this game. **L16.**
– PHRASES: **not cricket** *colloq.* infringing the codes of fair play between honourable opponents in any sphere. ***French cricket***: see FRENCH *adjective*. ***snob-cricket***: see SNOB *noun*[2].
– COMB.: **cricket bag** a long bag for carrying a cricketer's bat etc.; **cricket bat** a bat used in cricket; ***cricket-bat willow***, a glabrescent variety of white willow, *Salix alba* var. *caerulea*, which provides the best wood for cricket bats.
▸ **B** *verb intrans.* Play cricket. **L17.**
– NOTE: Many changes have been made in the character of the game since the 17th cent., when the bats were like hockey sticks, the wicket consisted of two stumps with one long bail, and the ball was trundled along the ground.
■ **crickeˈtana** *noun pl.* publications or other items concerning or associated with cricket **M19.** **cricketer** *noun* a person who plays cricket **M18.**

cricket /ˈkrɪkɪt/ *noun*[3]. Now *dial.* Also (*N. English*) **cracket** /ˈkrakɪt/. **M17.**
[ORIGIN Unknown.]
A low wooden stool; a footstool.

crickey *interjection* var. of CRIKEY.

crickle-crackle /ˈkrɪk(ə)l krak(ə)l/ *noun*. *rare*. **M17.**
[ORIGIN Redupl. of CRACKLE *noun*: cf. CRICK-CRACK.]
A repeated crackling.

crico- /ˈkrʌɪkəʊ/ *combining form*.
[ORIGIN Greek *kriko-* combining form of *krikos* = *kirkos* ring: see -O-.]
ANATOMY. Of or pertaining to the cricoid cartilage.
■ **cricoˈthyroid** *adjective* of or pertaining to the cricoid and thyroid cartilages **M19.**

cricoid /ˈkrʌɪkɔɪd/ *adjective & noun*. **M18.**
[ORIGIN mod. Latin *cricoides* ring-shaped from Greek *krikoeidēs*, from *krikos* ring: see CRICO-, -OID.]
ANATOMY. ▸ **A** *adjective*. Designating, of or pertaining to, the cartilage which forms the lower and back part of the larynx. **M18.**
▸ **B** *noun*. The cricoid cartilage of the larynx. **M19.**
■ †**cricoidal** *adjective* = CRICOID *adjective*: only in **L17.**

cri de cœur /kri də kœːr/ *noun phr.* Pl. ***cris de cœur*** (pronounced same). **E20.**
[ORIGIN French = cry of or from the heart.]
An appeal in distress.

cried *verb pa. t. & pple* of CRY *verb*.

crier /ˈkrʌɪə/ *noun*. **LME.**
[ORIGIN Anglo-Norman *criour*, Old French *criere*, nom. of *crieur*, from *crier*: see CRY *verb*, -OUR, -ER[2].]
1 A person who cries. **LME.**
2 *spec.* ▸**a** An officer who makes public announcements in a court of justice or (more fully ***common crier***, ***town crier***) in a town. **LME.** ▸**b** A person who cries goods for sale. Now *arch.* or *hist.* **M16.**

crikey /ˈkrʌɪki/ *interjection*. *slang*. Also **crickey** /ˈkrɪki/. **M19.**
[ORIGIN Alt. of CHRIST.]
Expr. astonishment.

crim /krɪm/ *noun*. *slang* (chiefly *Austral.*). **E20.**
[ORIGIN Abbreviation.]
A criminal.

T. WINTON He was unshaven and looked like a crim.

†**crimble** *verb & noun* var. of CRUMBLE.

crim. con. /krɪm ˈkɒn/ *noun*. *arch. colloq.* **L18.**
[ORIGIN Abbreviation.]
= ***criminal conversation*** s.v. CRIMINAL *adjective*.

crime /krʌɪm/ *noun*. **ME.**
[ORIGIN Old French & mod. French *crime*, †*crimne* from Latin *crimen* judgement, accusation, offence, from reduced base of *cernere* decide, give judgement.]
1 Sinfulness, wickedness; wrongdoing, sin. *arch.* **ME.**

MILTON One next himself in power, and next in crime.

2 An act or omission constituting an offence (usu. a grave one) against an individual or the state and punishable by law. Also, a soldier's offence against regulations. **LME.** ▸**b** *gen.* An evil or harmful act; a grave offence; *colloq.* a shameful act. **E16.**

B. SPOCK Stealing is a serious crime. **b** P. BAILEY It's no crime, looking one's age.

3 Such acts collectively; violation of law. **LME.**

GOLDSMITH I was imprisoned, though a stranger to crime.

†**4** Charge, accusation; matter of accusation. **LME–M17.**
– PHRASES ETC.: **crime of passion** = CRIME PASSIONNEL. ***perfect crime***: see PERFECT *adjective*. ***scene-of-crime***, ***scenes-of-crime***, ***the scene of the crime***: see SCENE.
– COMB.: **crimebuster** *slang* a person engaged in crimebusting; **crimebusting** *slang* the defeating of organized crime, the detection and arrest of criminals; **crime sheet** MILITARY a record of offences; **crime wave** a sudden brief increase in the number of crimes committed; **crime writer** an author who writes about real or fictional (usu. violent) crimes.
■ **crimeful** *adjective* (now *rare*) full of crime, criminal **L16.** **crimeless** *adjective* free from crime, innocent **M16.**

crime /krʌɪm/ *verb trans.* **LME.**
[ORIGIN from the noun.]
Now chiefly MILITARY. Charge with or convict of an offence.

Crimean /krʌɪˈmɪən/ *adjective*. **M19.**
[ORIGIN from *Crimea* (see below) + -AN.]
Of, pertaining to, or characteristic of the Crimea, a peninsula between the Sea of Azov and the Black Sea.
Crimean Gothic an East Germanic language, supposedly a dialect or descendant of Gothic, which continued to be used in the Crimea down to the 16th cent. **Crimean shirt**: of a type worn by workers in the Australian and New Zealand bush. **the Crimean War**: between Russia and Turkey (supported by her allies, including Britain and France), 1854–6, chiefly fought in the Crimea.

crime passionnel /krim pasjənɛl/ *noun phr.* Pl. **-s -s** (pronounced same). **E20.**
[ORIGIN French.]
A crime, esp. murder, due to sexual jealousy.

crimes /krʌɪmz/ *interjection. slang.* L19.
[ORIGIN Alt. of CRIMINE.]
Expr. astonishment.

crimes passionnels *noun phr.* pl. of CRIME PASSIONNEL.

criminal /ˈkrɪmɪn(ə)l/ *adjective & noun.* LME.
[ORIGIN Late Latin *criminalis* from Latin *crimin-*, *crimen* CRIME *noun*: see -AL¹.]
▶ **A** *adjective.* **1** Of the nature of or involving a crime punishable by law; *gen.* of the nature of a grave offence, wicked; *colloq.* deplorable. LME.
G. K. CHESTERTON That kind of thing is really criminal; it's against the public good. *Offshore* It would have been criminal to spend each moment . . waiting on the beach in a country which has so much to explore.
criminal conversation (now *arch.* or *hist.*) adultery. **criminal libel** the offence of making a malicious defamatory statement in a permanent form.
2 Relating to crime or its punishment. LME.
GIBBON They no longer possessed the administration of criminal justice.
criminal code a system of jurisprudence to be applied in criminal cases. **criminal court**: having jurisdiction over criminal prosecutions. **criminal law**: concerned with the punishment of offenders, opp. ***civil law***. **criminal lawyer**: whose practice lies in the criminal courts. ***criminal record***: see RECORD *noun* 4b.
3 Guilty of a crime or grave offence. L15.
I. MURDOCH He felt alien, almost criminal, hoping that no one would notice him.
▶ **B** *noun.* **1** A person guilty or convicted of a crime. E17. ***common criminal***: see COMMON *adjective*.
†**2** A person accused of a crime. M–L17.
DRYDEN Was ever criminal forbid to plead?
■ **criminalism** *noun* the state or practice of a criminal L19. **criminalist** *noun* an expert in criminal law M17. **criminally** *adverb* (*a*) according to criminal law; (*b*) in a criminal manner, so as to constitute crime: E16. **criminalness** *noun* (long *rare*) criminality M17. **criminaloid** *noun* a person with a tendency towards crime, a first or occasional offender, as opp. to a habitual criminal L19.

criminalistic /ˌkrɪmɪnəˈlɪstɪk/ *adjective.* E20.
[ORIGIN from CRIMINAL + -ISTIC.]
Of or pertaining to criminals or their habits; tending towards criminality.

criminalistics /ˌkrɪmɪnəˈlɪstɪks/ *noun.* E20.
[ORIGIN formed as CRIMINALISTIC: see -ICS. Cf. German *Kriminalistik*.]
The use of the physical sciences in investigating crimes.

criminality /krɪmɪˈnalɪti/ *noun.* E17.
[ORIGIN French *criminalité* from medieval Latin *criminalitas*, formed as CRIMINAL: see -ITY.]
The quality or fact of being criminal.

criminate /ˈkrɪmɪneɪt/ *verb trans.* M17.
[ORIGIN Latin *criminat-* pa. ppl stem of *criminare*, from *crimin-*, *crimen* CRIME *noun*: see -ATE³.]
1 Charge with crime; represent as criminal. M17.
2 Prove guilty of crime; incriminate. Now *rare*. M17.
3 Censure (a thing or action) as criminal; blame severely, condemn. M17.
■ **crimiˈnation** *noun* the action or an act of criminating; (a) severe accusation or censure: L16. **criminative** *adjective* tending to or involving crimination, accusatory M18. **criminator** *noun* a person who criminates, an accuser LME. **criminatory** *adjective* criminative L16.

crimine /ˈkrɪmɪni/ *interjection. arch. slang.* Also **-iny**. L17.
[ORIGIN Alt. of CHRIST.]
Expr. astonishment.

criminogenic /ˌkrɪmɪnəˈdʒɛnɪk/ *adjective.* E20.
[ORIGIN from CRIMIN(AL *adjective* + -O- + -GENIC.]
Causing crime or criminal behaviour.

criminology /krɪmɪˈnɒlədʒi/ *noun.* L19.
[ORIGIN from Latin *crimin-*, *crimen* CRIME *noun* + -OLOGY.]
The branch of knowledge that deals with crime.
■ **criminoˈlogical** *adjective* L19. **criminologist** *noun* M19.

criminous /ˈkrɪmɪnəs/ *adjective.* LME.
[ORIGIN Anglo-Norman *criminous*, Old French *crimineux*, from Latin *criminosus*, from *crimin-*, *crimen* CRIME *noun*: see -OUS.]
1 Of the nature of a crime; marked by crime or grave offence; criminal. Long *rare*. LME.
†**2** Accusing of crime; involving crimination. LME–M17.
3 Of a person: guilty of crime. Now only in ***criminous clerk***, a member of the clergy guilty of a crime. *arch.* M16.
■ **criminously** *adverb* E17. **criminousness** *noun* M17.

criminy *interjection* var. of CRIMINE.

crimmer *noun* var. of KRIMMER.

crimp /krɪmp/ *noun*¹. M17.
[ORIGIN Unknown.]
†**1** Used as a term of abuse or reproach. *rare*. Only in M17.
†**2** An agent or contractor for unloading coal ships. L17–L18.
3 *hist.* An agent whose business was to entrap men for service in the army, navy, etc., esp. by decoying or pressing them. Also *transf.* & *fig.* (*arch.*) a deceptive or coercive agent. M18.
■ **crimpage** *noun* (*hist.*) a payment made to a crimp for his services M18.

crimp /krɪmp/ *noun*². M17.
[ORIGIN from CRIMP *verb*¹. Sense 1 may be a different word.]
1 *hist.* A particular card game, perh. a gambling game involving turning up the corner of a card on which a bet was placed. M17.
†**2** ***be in the crimps***, be well dressed. Only in L17.
3 A curl, a wave, esp. made in the hair with a hot iron etc. or occurring naturally in a sheep's fleece (usu. in *pl.*); a crease, a pleat, a fold. M19. ▸**b** The wavy condition of a sheep's fleece. M19.
L. M. ALCOTT It's too wet. Shouldn't have a crimp left if I went out such a day as this. C. SANDBURG Respectable people With the right crimp in their napkins.
put a crimp in *fig.* (*N. Amer. slang*) thwart, interfere with.

crimp /krɪmp/ *adjective. arch.* L16.
[ORIGIN App. connected with CRIMP *verb*¹: cf. Middle High German *krimpf* crooked, curved. See also CRUMP *adjective*².]
1 Friable, brittle; crisp. L16.
2 Of hair, feathers, etc.: crimped, artificially curled. M18.

crimp /krɪmp/ *verb*¹.
[ORIGIN Old English *gecrympan*: cf. Middle & mod. Low German, Middle Dutch & mod. Dutch *krimpen* shrink, wrinkle, shrivel = Old High German *krimphan* (Middle High German *krimpfen*).]
1 *verb trans.* Compress into pleats or folds; frill; make waves or curls in (esp. hair, with a hot iron etc.); make narrow wrinkles or flutings in; corrugate. (*rare* before 18.) OE.
†**2** *verb intrans.* Be compressed, pinched, or indented. *rare*. Only in LME.
3 *verb trans.* Cause (the flesh of fish) to contract and become firm by gashing or cutting it before rigor mortis has set in; *transf.* slash, gash. L17.
4 *verb trans.* Bend or mould (leather) into shape for the uppers of boots, a saddle, etc. L19.

crimp /krɪmp/ *verb*² *trans.* E19.
[ORIGIN from CRIMP *noun*¹.]
hist. Entrap for service in the army, navy, etc.

crimper /ˈkrɪmpə/ *noun*¹. E19.
[ORIGIN from CRIMP *verb*¹ + -ER¹.]
1 A person who crimps fish, hair, etc.; *slang* a hairdresser. E19.
2 Any of various devices or machines for crimping cloth, hair, leather, metal, etc. L19.

crimper /ˈkrɪmpə/ *noun*². M19.
[ORIGIN from CRIMP *verb*² + -ER¹.]
hist. = CRIMP *noun*¹ 2.

crimple /ˈkrɪmp(ə)l/ *noun.* Now *dial.* & *US*. LME.
[ORIGIN Rel. to CRIMPLE *verb*. Cf. also CRUMPLE *noun*.]
A crease, a wrinkle, a narrow fold, a crinkle.

crimple /ˈkrɪmp(ə)l/ *verb.* Long *dial.* LME.
[ORIGIN Perh. a dim. & iterative of CRIMP *verb*¹: see -LE³.]
1 *verb intrans.* (Esp. of the legs) be or become incurved or drawn together; be lame, limp, hobble. LME.
2 *verb intrans.* & *trans.* Wrinkle, crinkle, curl. LME.

Crimplene /ˈkrɪmpliːn/ *noun.* Also **c-**. M20.
[ORIGIN Prob. from CRIMP *noun*² + TERY)LENE.]
(Proprietary name for) a synthetic yarn and fabric with good resistance to creasing.

crimpy /ˈkrɪmpi/ *adjective.* L19.
[ORIGIN from CRIMP *noun*² or *verb*¹ + -Y¹.]
Having a crimped appearance; frizzy, curly.

crimson /ˈkrɪmz(ə)n/ *adjective, noun, & verb.* LME.
[ORIGIN Old Spanish *cremesín*, French †*cramoisin*, & other Proto-Romance forms, all ult. from Arabic *qirmizī*, from *qirmiz* KERMES. Cf. CRAMOISY.]
▶ **A** *adjective.* **1** Of a rich deep-red colour inclining to purple. LME.
J. RHYS His face crimson with heat.
crimson clover a red-flowered clover, *Trifolium incarnatum*, formerly grown for fodder.
2 *fig.* Sanguinary. *arch.* L17.
J. S. BLACKIE The crimson crime, the basest in the book.
▶ **B** *noun.* **1** Crimson colour or pigment; a shade of this. LME.
†**2** Crimson cloth. LME–E17.
▶ **C** *verb.* **1** *verb trans.* Make crimson. E17.
J. BUCHAN The sun crimsoned the distant olive-green forests.
2 *verb intrans.* Become crimson, blush. E19.
H. JAMES I felt myself crimson and I covered my face with my hands.
■ **crimsony** *adjective* somewhat crimson, resembling crimson M19.

crin /krɪn, *foreign* krɛ̃/ *noun & adjective.* E20.
[ORIGIN French (Old French CRINE *noun*) = horsehair.]
(Of) a fabric wholly or partly from horsehair.

crinal /ˈkrʌɪn(ə)l/ *adjective.* M17.
[ORIGIN Latin *crinalis*, from *crinis* hair: see -AL¹.]
Of or pertaining to the hair.

crine /krʌɪn/ *noun.* E17.
[ORIGIN Old French (mod. CRIN) = hair of the head, mane, or its source Latin *crinis* hair.]
1 Hair; a head of hair. *rare*. E17.
2 Each of the small, hairlike feathers which grow around the cere of a hawk. Usu. in *pl.* L19.

crine /krʌɪn/ *verb intrans. & trans. Scot.* E16.
[ORIGIN App. from Gaelic *crìon* wither.]
Shrivel, wither; contract through dryness, heat, etc.

crined /krʌɪnd/ *adjective.* L16.
[ORIGIN from (the same root as) CRINE *noun* + -ED².]
HERALDRY. Having the hair or mane of a different (specified) tincture from the body; maned.

crinet /krɪˈnɛt/ *noun.* L15.
[ORIGIN formed as CRINE *noun* or CRIN + -ET¹.]
†**1** = CRINE *noun* 2. Usu. in *pl.* L15–L18.
2 = CRINIÈRE. *obsolete* exc. *hist.* L16.

cringe /krɪn(d)ʒ/ *noun.* L16.
[ORIGIN from the verb.]
An act of servile or fawning deference; cringing.
THACKERAY Performing cringes and congees like a court-chamberlain. THOMAS HUGHES Alternative fits of swagger & cringe.

cringe /krɪn(d)ʒ/ *verb.* ME.
[ORIGIN Corresp. to Old English *cringan*, *crinċan* yield, fall in battle, Old Frisian *krenza*, Dutch *krengen* heel over, and rel. to Old Norse *krangr* weak, frail, *kranga* creep along, Middle Low German, Dutch, Middle High German *krenken* weaken, injure, Old Frisian, Middle & mod. Low German, Middle High German, German *krank* sick, ill, slight (cf. CRANK *noun*¹).]
▶ **I** *verb intrans.* **1** Contract the muscles of the body involuntarily; shrink; cower. ME.
L. M. MONTGOMERY Bridges that made Anne's flesh cringe with . . fear. J. STEINBECK The dogs cringed to the ground and whined piteously. D. LODGE Some of the things I'm supposed to say . . make me cringe with embarrassment.
cringe-making *adjective* (*colloq.*) = CRINGEWORTHY.
2 Bow timorously or servilely (*to*). L16.
T. T. LYNCH You should bow to most people, but cringe to nobody.
3 Behave obsequiously (*to*). E17.
LD MACAULAY To teach the people to cringe and the prince to domineer.
▶ **II** *verb trans.* †**4** Draw in or contract (part of the body); distort (the neck, face, etc.). L16–M17.
SHAKES. *Ant. & Cl.* Till like a boy you see him cringe his face And whine aloud.
†**5** Cringe to (a person); usher cringingly. E17–E19.
BYRON Hence, and bow and cringe him here!
■ **cringeling** *noun* (*rare*) a cringing creature L17. **cringer** *noun* a person who cringes, an obsequious or servile person L16. **cringeworthy** *adjective* (*colloq.*) causing feelings of embarrassment or awkwardness L20. **cringing** *adjective* that cringes; obsequious, servile: L16. **cringingly** *adverb* M19. **cringingness** *noun* L17.

cringle /ˈkrɪŋg(ə)l/ *noun & verb.* E17.
[ORIGIN Low German *kringel* dim. of *kring* circle, ring: cf. CRANK *noun*¹, CRANKLE *noun, verb*, CRINKLE *noun, verb*.]
▶ **A** *noun.* **1** NAUTICAL. A ring or eye of rope containing a thimble for another rope to pass through. E17. ▸**b** A rope or wire for fastening a gate etc. *dial.* L18.
2 A crinkle. *dial.* E19.
▶ **B** *verb trans.* Fasten (*up*) with a cringle. *dial.* E17.

crinière /krɪˈnjɛː/ *noun.* Also †**-ier**. L16.
[ORIGIN French = mane, formed as CRINE *noun*, CRIN.]
Chiefly *hist.* A protective covering for the neck and throat of a warhorse. Also called ***crinet***.

crinigerous /krɪˈnɪdʒ(ə)rəs/ *adjective.* M17.
[ORIGIN from Latin *crinis* hair + -GEROUS.]
Having or bearing hair.

crinite /ˈkrʌɪnʌɪt/ *adjective.* L16.
[ORIGIN Latin *crinitus* pa. pple of *crinire* cover or provide with hair, from *crinis* hair: see -ITE². Cf. Old French *crinité*.]
Hairy; having a hairlike appendage or hairy tufts.

crinkle /ˈkrɪŋk(ə)l/ *noun.* L16.
[ORIGIN Prob. from the verb, but app. earlier (Middle English) in place names. Cf. CRINGLE.]
A twist, a bend, a wrinkle, a ripple, esp. in a line or surface. Formerly also, a circle.
– COMB.: **crinkle-cut** *adjective* (of chipped potatoes) machine-cut with regularly ridged surfaces.
■ **crinkliness** *noun* crinkly condition E20. **crinkly** *adjective* full of crinkles; characterized by crinkling sounds: E19.

crinkle /ˈkrɪŋk(ə)l/ *verb.* LME.
[ORIGIN Frequent. from base of Old English *crinċan* (see CRINGE *verb*) + -LE³.]
1 *verb intrans.* Form twists or bends; contract into wrinkles or ripples. LME.
T. C. WOLFE Huge crinkled lettuces. P. V. WHITE Her face would . . crinkle under the influence of impatience or anger.
2 *verb intrans.* Cringe; *fig.* recede from one's purpose. *obsolete* exc. *dial.* E17.

3 *verb trans.* Twist, bend; wrinkle; ripple; crimp (the hair). **E19.**

G. GREENE An expression of glee crinkled the man's face. W. BOYD The fishponds . . were . . crinkled by a breeze.

4 *verb intrans.* Make sharp rustling or crackling sounds. **M19.**

crinkle-crankle /ˈkrɪŋk(ə)lkraŋk(ə)l/ *noun, adjective, & adverb.* Chiefly *dial.* **L16.**
[ORIGIN Redupl. of CRANKLE *noun*, partly after CRINKLE *noun*. Cf. CRINKUM-CRANKUM.]
▸ **A** *noun.* A zigzag; something zigzag. **L16.**
▸ **B** *adjective & adverb.* (Twisting) in and out; zigzag. **M19.**

†**crinkum** *noun. slang.* Also **grincome**. **E17–L19.**
[ORIGIN Unknown.]
sing. & (usu.) in *pl.* Venereal disease; syphilis.

crinkum-crankum /krɪŋkəmˈkraŋkəm/ *noun & adjective.* **M17.**
[ORIGIN Fanciful redupl. of CRANK *noun*[1], *noun*[2]: cf. CRANKUM, CRINKLE-CRANKLE.]
▸ **A** *noun.* An intricate or convoluted thing; an elaborate device. Also, a crooked course (*lit.* & *fig.*), deviousness. **M17.**
▸ **B** *adjective.* Intricate, convoluted, elaborate. **L18.**

crinoid /ˈkrʌɪnɔɪd/ *noun & adjective.* **M19.**
[ORIGIN Greek *krinoeidēs* adjective, lily-like, from *krinon* lily: see -OID.]
▸ **A** *noun.* Any echinoderm of the class Crinoidea, members of which are characterized by cup-shaped bodies and usu. branched arms, and include sea-lilies, feather stars, and many fossil forms. **M19.**
▸ **B** *adjective.* Of or pertaining to the Crinoidea. **M19.**
■ **criˈnoidal** *adjective* of or pertaining to crinoids **M19.**

crinoline /ˈkrɪn(ə)lɪn/ *noun & adjective.* **M19.**
[ORIGIN French, irreg. from Latin *crinis* hair (French CRIN) + *linum* thread (French *lin* flax).]
▸ **A** *noun.* **1** A stiff fabric made of horsehair and cotton or linen thread, used for linings, hats, etc., and formerly for skirts and to expand a petticoat. **M19.**
2 *hist.* A stiff petticoat, orig. of this fabric, worn under a skirt to support or distend it; hence, a hooped petticoat. **M19.**
3 *hist.* A netting fitted round warships as a defence against torpedoes. **L19.**
▸ **B** *attrib.* or as *adjective.* Made of crinoline. **M19.**
■ **crinolined** *adjective* wearing (a) crinoline **M19.**

crinosity /krʌɪˈnɒsɪti/ *noun. rare.* **M17.**
[ORIGIN from Latin *crinis* hair: see -OSITY.]
Hairiness.

crio- /ˈkriːəʊ/ *combining form* of Greek *krios* ram: see -O-.
■ **criosphinx** *noun* a sphinx having a ram's head **M19.**

criollo /krɪˈɒləʊ/ *noun & adjective.* Also **C-**. Pl. of noun **-os**. **L19.**
[ORIGIN Spanish = native to the locality: see CREOLE.]
1 (Designating or pertaining to) a native of Spanish South or Central America, esp. one of pure Spanish descent. **L19.**
2 (Designating) a cacao tree of a variety producing thin-shelled beans of high quality. **E20.**
3 (Designating) any of various South or Central American breeds of domestic animal, *esp.* a small horse bred from South American and Arab stock, or cattle of Spanish ancestry. **M20.**

crip /krɪp/ *noun. N. Amer. slang (offensive).* **E20.**
[ORIGIN Abbreviation of CRIPPLE *noun & adjective.*]
A disabled person.

cripes /krʌɪps/ *interjection. slang.* **E20.**
[ORIGIN Alt. of CHRIST.]
Expr. astonishment.

cripple /ˈkrɪp(ə)l/ *noun & adjective.*
[ORIGIN Old English (Northumbrian) *crypel* = Old Low German *krupil*, & Old English *crēopel* = Middle Low German, Middle Dutch *krēpel*, from Germanic: cogn. with CREEP *verb.*]
▸ **A** *noun* **I 1** A person (permanently) impaired in movement by an injury or defect, *esp.* one unable to walk normally. Now regarded as *offensive.* **OE.**

D. MURPHY My mother returned . . as a complete cripple, unable to walk from the sitting-room to the downstairs lavatory, or to wash or dress herself, or to brush her hair.

2 *transf.* & *fig.* **a** A sixpence. Cf. BENDER 4. *arch. slang.* **L18.** ▸**b** A maimed or lamed animal or bird, esp. a game bird. **M19.** ▸**c** A person (permanently) impaired or deficient in some other way, specified or understood. **E20.** ▸**d** A vehicle, ship, etc., that is unfit to proceed or for service. **E20.**

c Times There would still be the emotional and psychological cripples among our children.

3 *sing.* & in *pl.* A crippling disease of cattle. *dial.* & *Austral.* **L19.**
▸ **II 4** A low opening in a wall. Chiefly in proper name ***Cripplegate***. **ME.**
5 A swamp or low-lying tract of land overgrown with trees or shrubs. *US.* **L17.**
▸ **B** *adjective.* Crippled. *obsolete* exc. *dial.* **ME.**

SHAKES. *Hen. V* And chide the cripple tardy-gaited night Who like a foul and ugly witch doth limp So tediously away.

■ **crippledom**, **cripplehood** *nouns* the condition of being a cripple **M19.**

cripple /ˈkrɪp(ə)l/ *verb.* **ME.**
[ORIGIN from the noun.]
1 *verb trans.* Cause (a person) to become unable to walk or move properly. **ME.** ▸**b** *transf.* & *fig.* Disable, impair; have a severe adverse effect on. **L17.**

G. GREENE A local farmer who had been crippled as a boy, losing his right arm in an accident. **b** L. OLIPHANT The trade . . is crippled by the difficulty of transport. A. TOFFLER Lack of an education will cripple a child's chance in the world of tomorrow.

2 *verb intrans.* Hobble; walk lamely. Now chiefly *Scot.* **ME.**
■ **crippled** *adjective* unable to walk, move, or (*transf.*) operate properly (now regarded as *offensive* when used of persons) **ME.** **crippler** *noun* (**a**) a person who or thing which cripples; (**b**) *slang* something astonishingly good: **M17.** **crippling** *adjective* (**a**) that cripples; (**b**) *slang* astonishingly good: **L16.** **cripplingly** *adverb* so as to cripple or disable; to a crippling extent: **L19.**

†**Cris** *noun & adjective* see CREE.

cris de cœur *noun phr.* pl. of CRI DE CŒUR.

crise /kriːz/ *noun.* Pl. pronounced same. **LME.**
[ORIGIN French.]
= CRISIS.
crise de conscience /də kɔ̃sjɑ̃ːs/ a crisis of conscience. ***crise de nerfs*** /də nɛːr/ [= of nerves] a fit of hysterics.
– NOTE: Formerly fully naturalized.

crisis /ˈkrʌɪsɪs/ *noun.* Pl. **crises** /ˈkrʌɪsiːz/, (*rare*) **crisises**. **LME.**
[ORIGIN Medical Latin from Greek *krisis* decision, judgement, event, issue, turning point of a disease, from *krinein* decide.]
1 The turning point of a disease. **LME.**
†**2** ASTROLOGY. A conjunction of the planets determining the issue of a disease or a critical point in the course of events. **L16–M17.**
3 *gen.* A turning point, a vitally important or decisive stage; a time of trouble, danger, or suspense in politics, commerce, etc., or in personal life. **E17.**

J. GALSWORTHY When his son-in-law . . had that financial crisis, due to speculation in Oil Shares, James made himself ill worrying over it. E. ROOSEVELT The threat of war was just over the horizon and no one else had the prestige and the knowledge to carry on through a crisis. M. HOLROYD She coped with crises ranging from burst hot-water bottles to outbreaks of measles. J. CRITCHLEY What the alienists call 'a crisis of identity'.

mid-life crisis: see MID-LIFE *adjective.*
†**4** A judgement, a decision. **E17–E18.**
†**5** A criterion; a token. **E–M17.**
– COMB.: **crisis management** the action or practice of taking managerial action only when a crisis has developed.

crisp /krɪsp/ *noun.* **ME.**
[ORIGIN App. from the adjective: cf. CRAPE *noun & adjective*, CRÊPE *noun & adjective.*]
†**1** A light fabric like crêpe; a head covering or veil made of this. **ME–E17.**
†**2** A crisp kind of pastry. Only in **LME.**
†**3** A curl (of hair); *esp.* a short or close curl. **M–L17.**
4 The crackling of roast pork. Now *dial.* **L17.**
5 A thing overdone by roasting etc. Orig. *US.* **M19.**
burn to a crisp make inedible or useless by burning.
6 More fully ***potato crisp***. A thin fried slice of potato eaten as a snack. Usu. in *pl.* Cf. CHIP *noun* 3. **E20.**
7 A crisp piece of pastry or chocolate. **L20.**

crisp /krɪsp/ *adjective.* **OE.**
[ORIGIN Latin *crispus* curled. Branch II may result from symbolic interpretation of the sound of the word.]
▸ **I 1** Of hair: curly; now *esp.* stiff and closely curling, frizzy. Also, having such hair. **OE.**
†**2** Of fabric: crinkly, like crêpe. Only in **ME.**
3 *gen.* Having a crinkled or rippled surface. *arch.* **LME.**
4 BOTANY. Having a crinkled or wavy edge, crispate. **M18.**
▸ **II 5** Hard or firm but fragile; brittle. **M16.**

J. M. NEALE When the snow lay round about, Deep and crisp and even. F. KING As crisp as a dead leaf.

crispbread a thin crisp biscuit of crushed rye etc.
6 *transf.* & *fig.* Stiff, not limp; neat, clearly defined; decisive in manner, brisk. **E19.**

WILKIE COLLINS Such a crisp touch on the piano. T. DREISER A gift . . for making crisp and cynical remarks. S. J. PERELMAN Her crisp white nurse's uniform. P. V. PRICE The crisp, almost bitterly dry white wine. A. N. WILSON The crisp creases of his trouser knees.

7 Of the air, of a day as regards atmosphere, etc.: frosty; bracing. **M19.**
■ **crispen** *verb trans.* & *intrans.* make or become (more) crisp **M20.** **crispish** *adjective* somewhat crisp **M20.** **crisply** *adverb* **E19.** **crispness** *noun* **LME.**

crisp /krɪsp/ *verb.* **ME.**
[ORIGIN from the adjective. Cf. Latin *crispare.*]
1 *verb trans.* Crimp, crinkle. **ME.**
2 *verb intrans.* Curl in short stiff folds or waves. **E16.**
3 *verb trans.* Make crisp (CRISP *adjective* II). **E17.**
4 *verb intrans.* Become crisp (CRISP *adjective* II). **E19.**
■ **crisper** *noun* a person who or thing which crisps or curls; *esp.* a container or compartment in a refrigerator for keeping salads etc. crisp and fresh: **M19.**

crispate /ˈkrɪspeɪt/ *adjective.* **M19.**
[ORIGIN Latin *crispatus* pa. pple of *crispare* curl: see -ATE[2].]
Crisped; *spec.* in BOTANY & ZOOLOGY, having a crinkled or wavy edge.

crispation /krɪˈspeɪʃ(ə)n/ *noun.* Now *rare.* **E17.**
[ORIGIN from Latin *crispat-* pa. ppl stem of *crispare* curl: see -ATION.]
1 (A) curled condition; curliness; (an) undulation. **E17.**
2 A slight contraction of a muscle etc. or of the skin, as in gooseflesh. **E18.**

crispature /ˈkrɪspətjʊə/ *noun. rare.* **M18.**
[ORIGIN formed as CRISPATION: see -URE.]
(A) crisp or curled condition.

Crispin /ˈkrɪspɪn/ *noun. arch.* Also **c-**. **E18.**
[ORIGIN Patron saint of shoemakers.]
(A name given to) a shoemaker.

crispy /ˈkrɪspi/ *adjective.* **LME.**
[ORIGIN from CRISP *adjective* + -Y[1].]
1 Curly, wavy, crinkly. **LME.**

W. MORRIS His crispy hair of gold.

2 Crisp, brittle; brisk. **E17.**

B. W. ALDISS They ate chow mein, sweet and sour pork and crispy noodles.

■ **crispiness** *noun* **M17.**

criss /krɪs/ *adjective. W. Indian.* **L20.**
[ORIGIN Alt. of CRISP *adjective.*]
Smart or fashionable.

criss-cross /ˈkrɪskrɒs/ *noun, adjective, & adverb.* Also **crisscross**. **E17.**
[ORIGIN Reduced form of CHRIST-CROSS, latterly treated as redupl. of CROSS *noun.*]
▸ **A** *noun.* **1** = CHRIST-CROSS. Now *arch.* & *dial.* exc. *hist.* **E17.**
2 A crossing of lines, currents, etc.; a network of crossing lines. **L19.**
3 The state of being at cross purposes. **E20.**
▸ **B** *adjective.* In crossing lines; marked by crossings or intersections. **M19.**
▸ **C** *adverb.* Crosswise; at cross purposes. **L19.**

criss-cross /ˈkrɪskrɒs/ *verb trans. & intrans.* Also **crisscross**. **E19.**
[ORIGIN from CRISS-CROSS *noun, adjective, & adverb.*]
Mark or work with a criss-cross pattern; move crosswise; cross or intersect repeatedly.

B. HINES Hundreds of knife cuts had criss-crossed the surface into tiny geometrical figures. E. CRISPIN Power-lines . . criss-crossing one another at all angles. S. SONTAG The metaphoric uses of TB and cancer crisscross and overlap.

crissum /ˈkrɪs(ə)m/ *noun.* **L19.**
[ORIGIN mod. Latin, from *crissare* move the haunches.]
ORNITHOLOGY. The region of the vent of a bird, including the under-tail coverts.
■ **crissal** *adjective* of or pertaining to the crissum; ***crissal thrasher***, a brown N. & Central American thrasher, *Toxostoma dorsale*, with rufous under-tail coverts: **L19.**

crista /ˈkrɪstə/ *noun.* Pl. **-stae** /-stiː/. **M19.**
[ORIGIN Latin: see CREST *noun.*]
Chiefly ANATOMY & ZOOLOGY. A ridge, a crest.

cristate /ˈkrɪsteɪt/ *adjective.* **M17.**
[ORIGIN Latin *cristatus*, formed as CRISTA: see -ATE[2].]
Chiefly ANATOMY & ZOOLOGY. Crested; having the form of a crest or ridge.
■ Also **cristated** *adjective* (now *rare*) **E18.**

cristobalite /krɪˈstəʊbəlʌɪt/ *noun.* **L19.**
[ORIGIN from Cerro San *Cristóbal*, a locality in Mexico: see -ITE[1].]
MINERALOGY. A variety of silica of which there is a stable high-temperature cubic form and a metastable low-temperature tetragonal form, and which occurs as massive deposits (e.g. in opal) and as small usu. octahedral crystals.

crit /krɪt/ *noun. colloq.* Also **crit.** (point). **M18.**
[ORIGIN Abbreviation.]
†**1** A critic. Only in **M18.**
2 (Literary, textual, etc.) criticism; a critique. **E20.**
lit. crit.: see LIT. *adjective.*
3 Critical mass. **M20.**

criteria *noun* pl. of CRITERION.

criteriology /krʌɪˌtɪərɪˈɒlədʒi/ *noun.* **L19.**
[ORIGIN from CRITERION: see -OLOGY.]
The study or analysis of criteria; the branch of logic that deals with criteria.
■ **criterioˈlogical** *adjective* pertaining to criteriology; dealing with criteria: **M20.** **criterioˈlogically** *adverb* **M20.**

criterion /krʌɪˈtɪərɪən/ *noun.* Occas. (Latinized) **-ium** /-ɪəm/. Pl. **-ia** /-ɪə/. **E17.**
[ORIGIN Greek *kritērion* means of judging, test, from *kritēs* judge.]
1 A principle, standard, or test by which a thing is judged, assessed, or identified. **E17.**

A. BEVAN Medical treatment and care . . should be made available to rich and poor alike in accordance with medical need and by no other criterion. J. L. AUSTIN Hoping to find a criterion to distinguish statements from performatives.

Rayleigh criterion, ***Rayleigh's criterion***: see RAYLEIGH. ***Richardson criterion***, ***Richardson's criterion***: see RICHARDSON *noun*[2] 1.

†**2** A (supposed) organ or faculty of judging. M–L17.

■ **criterial** *adjective* M20.

— NOTE: Throughout 17 freq. in Greek characters, but also transliterated from M17. *Criteria* is often taken to be the sing. form.

C

criterium /krʌɪˈtɪərɪəm/ *noun*. Pl. **-s**. M17.
[ORIGIN Latinized form of Greek *kritērion* CRITERION.]
1 = CRITERION. *rare*. M17.
2 A one-day bicycle race involving repeated circuits of a course that usu. consists of closed-off roads. L20.

crithomancy /ˈkrɪθəmansi/ *noun*. M17.
[ORIGIN from Greek *krithē* barleycorn + -O- + -MANCY.]
Divination by meal strewn over animals sacrificed.

critic /ˈkrɪtɪk/ *noun*[1]. L16.
[ORIGIN Latin *criticus* from Greek *kritikos*, use as noun of adjective from *kritēs* judge: see -IC.]
1 A person who pronounces judgement; *esp.* a censurer. L16.
2 A judge or writer on the qualities of literary or artistic works; a professional reviewer of books, musical or dramatic performances, etc.; a person skilled in textual criticism. E17.
drama critic, ***literary critic***, ***music critic***, ***television critic***, etc. ***New Critic***: see NEW *adjective*.
■ **criticling** *noun* = CRITICASTER M18.

†**critic** *noun*[2] see CRITIQUE *noun*.

critic /ˈkrɪtɪk/ *adjective*. Now *rare*. LME.
[ORIGIN French *critique*, from late Latin *criticus*, formed as CRITIC *noun*[1].]
†**1** = CRITICAL 1, 2. LME–E17.
†**2** = CRITICAL 4. L16–M17.
3 = CRITICAL 5. E17.

†**critic** *verb*. Infl. **-ck-**. E17.
[ORIGIN French *critiquer*, formed as CRITIQUE *noun*.]
1 *verb intrans*. Play the critic. Only in 17.
2 *verb trans*. Criticize; censure. L17–M18.

critical /ˈkrɪtɪk(ə)l/ *adjective*. M16.
[ORIGIN from late Latin *criticus* (see CRITIC *adjective*) + -AL[1].]
▸ **I 1** Of or pertaining to the crisis of a disease; determining the issue of a disease. M16.
2 Of, pertaining to, or constituting a crisis; of decisive importance, crucial; involving risk or suspense; *spec.* (of a person) extremely ill and at risk of death. E17.

H. MACMILLAN We made a serious error, at a critical moment when France was already nervous and uncertain. H. KISSINGER Their need for American grain was critical. A. HAILEY They were vulnerable, critical installations and could take weeks to repair or replace completely. J. D. PISTONE She was in intensive care, in critical condition, attached to machines and tubes.

3 MATH. & PHYSICS. Constituting or relating to a point of transition from one state etc. to another. M19. ▸**b** Of a nuclear reactor etc.: maintaining a self-sustaining chain reaction. M20.
▸ **II 4** Given to judging, esp. unfavourably; fault-finding, censorious. L16.

SHAKES. *Oth*. I am nothing if not critical. W. GOLDING She was severe and very critical of my playing.

5 Skilful at or engaged in criticism, esp. of literature or art; providing textual criticism. L16. ▸**b** Belonging to criticism. M18.

J. M. MURRY These two finely critical minds—in their separate provinces the finest critical minds we have in England to-day. A. WILSON A critical edition of the text of *Lamia*.

†**6** Involving careful judgement or observation; nice, exact, punctual. M17–M19.

— SPECIAL COLLOCATIONS & PHRASES: **critical angle** the angle of incidence at which a ray of light must strike an interface with a less dense medium so as to be refracted parallel to the interface. ***critical apparatus***: see APPARATUS 2c. **critical damping** PHYSICS damping just sufficient to prevent oscillations. **critical legal studies** an approach to jurisprudence expressing a broadly Marxist critique of legal theory but also drawing on philosophy, politics, and semiotics. **critical mass** the mass of a body of fissile material of critical size (see below). **critical path** a sequence of stages determining the minimum time needed for the execution of an entire project. **critical point** a set of conditions of temperature, pressure, and density at which a liquid and its vapour become indistinguishable. **critical pressure** the pressure required to liquefy a gas at its critical temperature. **critical size** the minimum size of a body of a given fissile material which is capable of sustaining a nuclear chain reaction. **critical temperature**: above which a gas cannot be liquefied by pressure. **critical volume** the volume of unit mass of a gas or vapour at its critical temperature and pressure. **go critical** (of a nuclear reactor etc.) begin to sustain a nuclear chain reaction. ***New Critical***: see NEW *adjective*.

■ **critiˈcality** *noun* the state or quality of being critical; *esp.* the condition of sustaining a nuclear chain reaction: M18. **critically** *adverb* M17. **criticalness** *noun* M17.

criticaster /krɪtɪˈkastə, ˈkrɪtɪkastə/ *noun*. L17.
[ORIGIN from CRITIC *noun*[1] + -ASTER.]
A petty or inferior critic.

criticise *verb* var. of CRITICIZE.

criticism /ˈkrɪtɪsɪz(ə)m/ *noun*. E17.
[ORIGIN from (the same root as) CRITIC *noun*[1] + -ISM.]
1 The expression of disapproval on the basis of perceived faults or mistakes; fault-finding, censure; an act of criticizing. E17.

Daily Mail Being exposed to ridicule and unfair criticism. HOWARD GARDNER His criticisms of Milton as overly intellectual.

†**2** A nicety, a subtlety; a quibble. Only in 17.
3 The analysis and judgement of the merits and faults of a literary or artistic work; a critical analysis, article, etc. M17. ▸**b** The art or practice of estimating the qualities and character of literary or artistic works; the work of a critic. L17.
textual criticism: dealing with and seeking the correct reading of a text, esp. a manuscript text, of an author. **the higher criticism**: dealing with the origin, character, etc., of texts, esp. of biblical writings. **the lower criticism** the textual criticism of the Bible. **b** ***literary criticism***: see LITERARY *adjective*. ***New Criticism***: see NEW *adjective*. ***practical criticism***: see PRACTICAL *adjective*.
4 The critical philosophy of Kant (based on critical examination of the faculty of knowledge). Now *rare* or *obsolete*. M19.
■ **criticist** *noun* an adherent of the critical philosophy of Kant L19.

criticize /ˈkrɪtɪsʌɪz/ *verb*. Also **-ise**. M17.
[ORIGIN formed as CRITICISM + -IZE.]
1 *verb intrans*. Pass judgement, esp. unfavourably; find fault, be censorious. (Foll. by †(*up*)*on*.) M17.

MILTON His Criticizing about the sound of Prayers.

2 *verb trans*. Discuss critically. M17.

BOLINGBROKE The verses I sent you are very bad . . you would do them too much honour, if you criticized them. J. KOSINSKI Each of them would criticize the others and himself, giving praise where due, pointing out shortcomings.

3 *verb trans*. Censure; find fault with. E18.

SWIFT To criticise his gait, and ridicule his dress. E. LONGFORD His wife was criticizing him for not giving enough to charity.

■ **criticizable** *adjective* M19. **criticizer** *noun* L17.

critico- /ˈkrɪtɪkəʊ/ *combining form*. E19.
[ORIGIN After Greek *kritiko-*, from *kritikos*: see CRITIC *noun*[1], -O-.]
Critically, critical and —, as ***critico-historical***, ***critico-theological***, etc.

critique /krɪˈtiːk/ *noun*. Orig. †**critic**. M17.
[ORIGIN French, ult. from Greek *kritikē* (sc. *tekhnē*) the critical art, criticism.]
1 Criticism; *esp.* the art of criticism. M17.

R. BENTLEY I do not expect from our Editors much sagacity in way of Critic.

2 A criticism; *esp.* a critical analysis, article, or essay. M17.

G. STEINER The student and the person interested in the current of literature reads reviews and critiques of books rather than the books themselves. E. FROMM Marx's whole critique of capitalism and his vision of socialism.

critique /krɪˈtiːk/ *verb trans*. M18.
[ORIGIN from the noun.]
Discuss critically; write a critique of; make a critical assessment of.

critter /ˈkrɪtə/ *noun*. *dial*. & *joc*. Also **-ur**. E19.
[ORIGIN Var. of CREATURE.]
A creature, *esp.* an ox, cow, or horse; *derog.* a person.

crivvens /ˈkrɪv(ə)nz/ *interjection*. *slang*. E20.
[ORIGIN Alt. of CHRIST, perh. after *heavens!*]
Expr. astonishment or horror.

crizzle /ˈkrɪz(ə)l/ *verb trans*. & *intrans*. Now *dial*. E17.
[ORIGIN Perh. dim. of CRAZE *verb*: see -LE[3].]
(Cause to) become rough on the surface, as glass etc. by scaling, or water beginning to freeze.

cro /krəʊ/ *noun*[1]. Pl. **-oes**. LME.
[ORIGIN Old Irish *cró* wound, violent death, Gaelic *cró* blood.]
CELTIC HISTORY. Compensation payable for the killing of a man, according to his rank.

†**cro** *noun*[2] var. of CRUE.

croak /krəʊk/ *verb* & *noun*. ME.
[ORIGIN Imit. Cf. Old English *crakettan*.]
▸ **A** *verb*. **1** *verb intrans*. Of a frog or raven: make its characteristic deep harsh sound. ME.
2 *verb intrans*. Of a person: speak in a hoarse manner; *fig.* talk dismally or despondently. Formerly also, groan, cry. LME.
†**3** *verb intrans*. Of the stomach or bowels: rumble. M16–L18.
4 *verb trans*. Say or proclaim with a croak or dismally. E17.
5 *verb intrans*. Die. *slang*. E19.
6 *verb trans*. Kill; murder. *slang*. E19.
▸ **B** *noun*. A deep harsh sound made by a frog or raven; a sound likened to this. M16.

A. ALVAREZ His throat was raw and tender and the words came out in a formless croak.

■ **croaky** *adjective* like a croak; hoarse: M19.

croaker /ˈkrəʊkə/ *noun*. E17.
[ORIGIN from CROAK + -ER[1].]
1 A person or animal that croaks; *spec.* any fish of the family Sciaenidae (= DRUM *noun*[1] 3b). E17.
2 A person who talks dismally or despondently; a prophet of evil. E17.
3 A doctor, *esp.* a prison doctor. *slang* (chiefly *US*). M19.

Croat /ˈkrəʊat/ *noun* & *adjective*. M17.
[ORIGIN mod. Latin *Croatae* pl. from Croatian *Hrvat*.]
▸ **A** *noun*. = CROATIAN *noun*; *hist.* a soldier of a French cavalry regiment composed mainly of Croatians. M17.
▸ **B** *adjective*. = CROATIAN *adjective*. E19.

Croatian /krəʊˈeɪʃɪən, -ʃ(ə)n/ *noun* & *adjective*. M16.
[ORIGIN from mod. Latin *Croatia*, from *Croatae*: see CROAT, -IAN.]
▸ **A** *noun*. A native or inhabitant of Croatia, one of the Balkan states; the Slavonic language of Croatia, almost identical to Serbian but written in the Roman alphabet. M16.
▸ **B** *adjective*. Of or pertaining to Croatia, its people, or its language. E17.

croc /krɒk/ *noun*. L19.
[ORIGIN Abbreviation.]
= CROCODILE *noun* 1, 4.
mock croc imitation crocodile skin.

crocard *noun* var. of CROCKARD.

crocean /ˈkrəʊsɪən/ *adjective*[1]. *rare*. E17.
[ORIGIN from Latin *croceus*, formed as CROCUS *noun*[1]: see -AN.]
Of the colour of saffron.
■ Also **croceate** *adjective* M19.

Crocean /ˈkrəʊtʃɪən, ˈkrəʊsɪən/ *adjective*[2]. Also **-ian**. E20.
[ORIGIN from *Croce* (see below) + -AN, -IAN.]
Of, pertaining to, or characteristic of the Italian philosopher and statesman Benedetto Croce (1866–1952) or his idealistic 'philosophy of the spirit'.

croche /krəʊtʃ/ *noun*. L16.
[ORIGIN French, cogn. with Old French & mod. French *croc* hook from Old Norse *krókr*: cf. CROOK *noun*.]
One of the knobs at the top of a stag's horn.

crochet /ˈkrəʊʃeɪ, -ʃi/ *noun* & *verb*. M19.
[ORIGIN French, dim. of *croc* with *-ch-* from *crochié*, *crochu* hooked: see CROCHE, -ET[1].]
▸ **A** *noun*. A kind of knitting done using a single hooked needle to form intertwined loops; knitted material made in this way. M19.
— COMB.: **crochet hook** the needle used in crochet work.
▸ **B** *verb*. **1** *verb trans*. Make in crochet. L19.
2 *verb intrans*. Do crochet work. L19.

croci *noun pl*. see CROCUS *noun*[1].

Crocian *adjective* var. of CROCEAN *adjective*[2].

crocidolite /krə(ʊ)ˈsɪdəlʌɪt/ *noun*. M19.
[ORIGIN from Greek *krokis*, *-id-* nap of woollen cloth + -O- + -LITE.]
A blue or green fibrous variety of riebeckite mined as a source of asbestos which is strong but has low heat resistance.

crocin /ˈkrəʊsɪn/ *noun*. M19.
[ORIGIN from Latin *crocus* (see CROCUS *noun*[1]) + -IN[1].]
A yellowish carotenoid glycosidic pigment, $C_{44}H_{64}O_{24}$, which is the colouring matter in saffron and some other kinds of crocus.

crock /krɒk/ *noun*[1].
[ORIGIN Old English *croc*, *crocca* rel. to synon. Old Norse *krukka* and prob. to Old English *crōg* small vessel (= Old High German *kruog*, German *Krug*), *crūce* pitcher (= Old Saxon *krūka*, Dutch *kruik*, Middle High German *kruche*).]
1 An earthenware vessel. OE.
2 A metal pot. *dial*. L15.
3 A broken piece of earthenware, *esp.* one used for covering the hole in a flowerpot. M19.

crock /krɒk/ *noun*[2]. LME.
[ORIGIN Perh. of Flemish origin, but appropriate words have a different vowel, as Middle Dutch *kraecke* (Dutch *krak*), Flemish *krake*; presumably rel. to CRACK *verb*.]
1 An old ewe. *Scot*. LME.
2 An old broken-down horse. L19.
3 A weak or debilitated person; a hypochondriac. *colloq*. L19.
4 An old worn-out vehicle, ship, etc. *slang*. E20.

crock /krɒk/ *noun*[3]. *obsolete* exc. *dial*. M17.
[ORIGIN Unknown.]
Dirt; a smut.

crock *noun*[4] see CRUCK.

crock /krɒk/ *verb*[1] *trans*. Now *dial*. L16.
[ORIGIN from CROCK *noun*[1].]
Put away (as) in a crock.

crock /krɒk/ *verb*[2]. M17.
[ORIGIN from CROCK *noun*[3].]
1 *verb trans*. Make dirty or grimy. M17.
2 *verb intrans*. Of a coloured article: impart its colour to something else. Of a colour or dye: transfer to something else. M19.

crock /krɒk/ *verb*³. *colloq.* M19.
[ORIGIN from CROCK *noun*².]
1 *verb intrans.* Become feeble or decrepit; break down. Also foll. by *up.* M19.
2 *verb trans.* Injure, damage. Also foll. by *up.* L19.
Times I had 'crocked' my knee at hockey.

crockard /ˈkrɒkɑːd/ *noun.* Also **crocard**. ME.
[ORIGIN Anglo-Norman from Old French *crocard*.]
One of various base coins of foreign origin current in the reign of Edward I.

crocked /krɒkt/ *adjective. slang.* E20.
[ORIGIN Perh. from CROCK *verb*³ + -ED¹.]
Intoxicated.

†**crocker** *noun.* ME–E18.
[ORIGIN from CROCK *noun*¹ + -ER¹.]
A potter.

crockery /ˈkrɒk(ə)ri/ *noun.* E18.
[ORIGIN from CROCKER: see -ERY.]
Earthenware vessels, esp. for household use; pottery. Also ***crockery-ware***.

crocket /ˈkrɒkɪt/ *noun.* ME.
[ORIGIN Old Northern French, var. of Old French & mod. French *crochet* CROTCHET *noun*¹.]
†**1** A curl of some kind. Only in ME.
2 In Gothic architecture, each of a series of small projecting decorative features (usu. buds or leaves) on the sides of a pinnacle, gable, etc. L17.
3 = CROCHE. L19.
■ **crocketed** *adjective* having crockets E19.

Crockford /ˈkrɒkfəd/ *noun.* L19.
[ORIGIN Named after John *Crockford* (1823–65), the first publisher of the book.]
In full ***Crockford's Clerical Directory***. A reference book for the clergy and the Church of England, first issued in 1860.

crocodile /ˈkrɒkədʌɪl/ *noun, adjective, & verb.* ME.
[ORIGIN Old French *cocodrille* (mod. *crocodile*) from medieval Latin *cocodrillus* for Latin *crocodilus* from Greek *krokodilos*. Refashioned after Latin & Greek, 16–17.]
▸ **A** *noun* **1 a** Any of a group of tropical and subtropical reptiles (sometimes treated as a family, Crocodylidae) related to alligators; any crocodilian. ME. ▸**b** The skin of the crocodile (or alligator). E20.
Nile crocodile: see NILE 1. ***Nilotic crocodile***: see NILOTIC *adjective* 1.
2 *fig.* A person who makes a show of sorrow hypocritically or for a malicious purpose (as the crocodile was said to do in fable). L16.
3 A sophism in which an opponent is presented with a choice in the form of a question, but either of the two contrary answers leads to his or her defeat. E18.
4 A long line of children etc. walking together; a long procession of moving objects close together. *colloq.* L19.
– COMB.: **crocodile bird** the Egyptian black-headed plover, *Pluvianus aegyptius* (family Glareolidae), which eats insects parasitic on crocodiles; **crocodile clip** a metal spring clip with long serrated jaws, used for making temporary electrical connections.
▸ **B** *attrib.* or as *adjective.* Feigned; hypocritical. M16.
G. S. FABER A crocodile affectation of clemency.
crocodile tears false or affected sorrow.
▸ **C** *verb intrans.* Walk in a crocodile. L19.
■ **crocodiling** *noun* = ALLIGATORING M20.

crocodilian /krɒkəˈdɪlɪən/ *adjective & noun.* M17.
[ORIGIN from Latin *crocodilus* (see CROCODILE) + -IAN.]
▸ **A** *adjective.* †**1** Treacherous; that feigns sorrow. Only in M17.
2 Pertaining to or being a crocodilian. M19.
▸ **B** *noun.* A reptile of the group including crocodiles and alligators; *spec.* one of the order Crocodylia, which also includes the caimans, the gharials, and numerous extinct animals, all large lizard-like semi-aquatic carnivores with a long tail and snout and a covering of horny and bony plates. M19.

crocoite /ˈkrəʊkəʊʌɪt/ *noun.* M19.
[ORIGIN Orig. French *crocoïse* from Greek *krokoeis* saffron-coloured, from *krokos* (see CROCOSMIA); alt. to *crocoisite*, then to *crocoite*: see -ITE¹.]
MINERALOGY. Lead chromate occurring as bright orange monoclinic crystals. Also called ***red lead ore***.

crocosmia /krə(ʊ)ˈkɒzmɪə/ *noun.* L20.
[ORIGIN mod. Latin (see below), from Greek *krokos* saffron.]
A plant of the genus *Crocosmia* (family Iridaceae), which includes montbretia.

crocus /ˈkrəʊkəs/ *noun*¹. Pl. **-es**, (in sense 1) **-i** /-ʌɪ/. LME.
[ORIGIN Latin from Greek *krokos* of Semitic origin: cf. Hebrew *karkōm*, Arabic *kurkum*.]
1 A plant of the genus *Crocus*, of the iris family, which comprises small plants with corms and single bright (often yellow or purple) flowers that usu. appear in spring. LME. ▸**b** ***autumn crocus***, an autumn-flowering plant of the genus *Colchicum*, *esp.* meadow saffron, *C. autumnale*. E19.
2 Saffron. LME.
3 Ferric oxide obtained as a reddish or purplish powder by calcination of ferrous sulphate and used for polishing metal; any of various red or yellow powders obtained from metals by calcination. M17.
4 A quack doctor. *slang.* L18.
– PHRASES: **autumn crocus** (*a*) a crocus of SW Europe, *Crocus nudiflorus*, with flowers appearing before the leaves, which is naturalized locally in England; (*b*) see sense 1b above. ***saffron crocus***: see SAFFRON *noun* 1.

crocus /ˈkrəʊkəs/ *noun*² & *adjective.* Now *US & W. Indian dial.* L17.
[ORIGIN Uncertain: perh. the same word as CROCUS *noun*¹.]
(Made of) a coarse heavy cloth used esp. for making bags and (formerly) cheap clothing.
V. S. REID I see my bro' take a crocus bag with him to the beach.

croeso /ˈkrɔɪsɔː/ *interjection. Welsh.* L20.
[ORIGIN Welsh.]
Welcome!

Croesus /ˈkriːsəs/ *noun.* M17.
[ORIGIN Latin form of the name of a king of Lydia (in Greek *Kroisos*) in the 6th cent. BC who was famous for his wealth.]
A very rich person.

croft /krɒft/ *noun*¹. OE.
[ORIGIN Unknown.]
A piece of enclosed land used for tillage or pasturage; *esp.* a plot of arable land attached to a house. Also, a smallholding worked by a tenant; *esp.* one in the Highlands and Islands of Scotland comprising a plot of arable land attached to a house and a right of pasturage in common with others.
toft and croft: see TOFT *noun*¹ 1.
■ **crofting** *noun* the system of land tenure by crofters; a crofter's holding: L16.

croft /krɒft/ *noun*². *rare.* L15.
[ORIGIN Middle Dutch *crofte* (Middle Low German *kruft*) cave, hole from medieval Latin *crupta* from Latin *crypta* CRYPT.]
A crypt; a cavern. See also UNDERCROFT.

crofter /ˈkrɒftə/ *noun.* L18.
[ORIGIN from CROFT *noun*¹ + -ER¹.]
A person who rents and cultivates a croft, esp. in the Highlands and Islands of Scotland.
– NOTE: Recorded ME as a surname, which may be the same word.

Crohn's disease /ˈkrəʊnz dɪˌziːz/ *noun phr.* M20.
[ORIGIN B. B. *Crohn* (1884–1983), US pathologist.]
A chronic inflammatory disease of the gastrointestinal tract, esp. the colon and ileum, causing ulcers and fistulae.

†**croisade**, **croisado** *nouns* see CRUSADE *noun.*

†**croises** *noun pl.* E17–M19.
[ORIGIN French *croisés* pl. of *croisé* use as noun of pa. pple of *croiser* cross from Old French *cruisier*, *croisier* from ecclesiastical Latin *cruciare*, from Latin *cruc-*, *crux* cross.]
Crusaders.

croisette /krwɒˈzɛt/ *noun.* L17.
[ORIGIN French, dim. of *croix* CROSS *noun.*]
A small cross.

croissant /ˈkrwasɒŋ/ *noun.* L16.
[ORIGIN French: see CRESCENT *noun.*]
†**1** Var. of CRESCENT *noun* 1–4. L16–L17.
2 A French flaky pastry roll in the shape of a crescent. L19.

Croix de Guerre /krwɑ də gɛːr/ *noun phr.* Pl. same. E20.
[ORIGIN French, lit. 'cross of war'.]
A French medal instituted in 1915 for individual gallantry in war.

cro'jack *noun* var. of CROSS-JACK.

Crokerism /ˈkrəʊkərɪz(ə)m/ *noun.* M19.
[ORIGIN from *Croker* (see below) + -ISM.]
hist. The political principles of J. W. Croker (1780–1857), Conservative opponent of the Reform Bill.

Cro-Magnon /krəʊˈmanjɔ̃, -ˈmagnən/ *adjective & noun.* M19.
[ORIGIN A hill near Les Eyzies, Dordogne department, France, containing a cave in which the skeletons were found.]
▸ **A** *adjective.* Pertaining to or designating an individual of the type represented by certain skeletons found in 1868 in upper Palaeolithic deposits, belonging to tall people with long skulls and short wide faces who were of physically modern type; pertaining to or designating any example of physically modern human of the early upper Palaeolithic of western Europe. M19.
▸ **B** *noun.* A Cro-Magnon human. M20.

cromb *noun & verb* var. of CROME.

crombec /ˈkrɒmbɛk/ *noun.* E20.
[ORIGIN French, from Dutch *krom* crooked + *bek* beak.]
Any African warbler of the genus *Sylvietta*.

crome /krəʊm, kruːm/ *noun & verb.* Now *dial.* Also **cromb**. LME.
[ORIGIN Repr. an Old English word rel. to CRUM *adjective*.]
▸ **A** *noun.* A hook, a crook. Formerly also, a claw, a talon. LME.
▸ **B** *verb trans.* Seize or draw with a crook. M16.

Cromerian /krəʊˈmɪərɪən/ *adjective & noun.* E20.
[ORIGIN from *Cromer* (see below) + -IAN.]
▸ **A** *adjective.* **1** GEOLOGY & PALAEONTOLOGY. Designating or pertaining to a series of estuarine and freshwater deposits rich in fossils which outcrop at Cromer, Norfolk, and the interglacial or stratigraphic stage in the Middle Pleistocene when they were formed. Also, designating or pertaining to a much longer period in the Early and Middle Pleistocene that includes this interglacial as a warm period. E20.
2 ARCHAEOLOGY. Designating or pertaining to a supposed culture formerly thought to be represented by remains that were found in Pliocene deposits near Cromer but are no longer thought to be artefacts. E20.
▸ **B** *noun.* **1** ARCHAEOLOGY. A person of the Cromerian culture. E20.
2 GEOLOGY. The Cromerian interglacial or its deposits. M20.

cromlech /ˈkrɒmlɛk/ *noun.* L17.
[ORIGIN Welsh, from *crom* fem. of *crwm* bowed, arched + *llech* (flat) stone, LECH *noun*¹.]
A dolmen; any megalithic chamber-tomb.

cromoglycate /krəʊməˈglʌɪseɪt/ *noun.* M20.
[ORIGIN from alt. of CHROMO(NE + GLYC(EROL + -ATE¹.]
PHARMACOLOGY. A drug whose sodium salt is inhaled to prevent asthmatic attacks and allergic reactions.

cromorne /krəʊˈmɔːn/ *noun.* E18.
[ORIGIN French from German KRUMMHORN.]
An organ reed stop, usu. of 8-ft pitch, suggestive of a krummhorn or (later) a clarinet in sound; = CREMONA *noun*¹, KRUMMHORN 2.

Cromwell /ˈkrɒmwɛl/ *noun.* M19.
[ORIGIN Oliver *Cromwell*: see CROMWELLIAN, CROMWELLIAN *adjective* 1.]
1 In full ***Cromwell chair***. A dining chair with a square seat and slightly sloping back, both being stuffed and covered with leather. M19.
2 In full ***Cromwell shoe***. A shoe with a large buckle or bow. L19.

Cromwellian /krɒmˈwɛlɪən/ *adjective & noun.* M17.
[ORIGIN from *Cromwell* (see below) + -IAN.]
▸ **A** *adjective.* **1** Of, pertaining to, or characteristic of Oliver Cromwell (1599–1658), English soldier, statesman, and Puritan leader of the Parliamentary forces in the English Civil War and Lord Protector 1653–8. M17.
2 Designating a Cromwell chair. E20.
▸ **B** *noun.* A supporter of Cromwell; one of the English settlers in Ireland following Cromwell's defeat of the Irish and the Act of Settlement of 1652; a descendant of such a settler. L17.

crone /krəʊn/ *noun.* LME.
[ORIGIN Prob. Middle Dutch *croonje*, *caroonje* carcass, old ewe from Old Northern French *caroigne* (mod. French *charogne*) CARRION, cantankerous or mischievous woman. Sense 1 perh. directly from Old Northern French.]
1 a A withered old woman. LME. ▸**b** A worn-out old man. *rare.* M17.
2 An old ewe. Also ***crone sheep***. M16.

†**cronet** *noun.* E16.
[ORIGIN Syncopated from CORONET. Cf. CROWNET.]
1 A head of a tilting spear, usu. with three or four short spreading points. E16–M18.
2 = CORONET *noun* 1, 2. M16–E17.
3 = CORONET *noun* 4. E17–E18.

Cronian /ˈkrəʊnɪən/ *adjective. rare.* E17.
[ORIGIN from Greek *Kronios* belonging to Kronos (Saturn) + -AN.]
Designating the frozen sea of the north.
MILTON Two Polar Winds blowing adverse upon the Cronian sea.

cronk /krɒŋk/ *adjective. Austral. colloq.* L19.
[ORIGIN Cf. CRANK *adjective*³.]
(Of a racehorse) unfit to run, run dishonestly; *gen.* unsound; fraudulent.

crony /ˈkrəʊni/ *noun & verb.* Also †**ch-**. M17.
[ORIGIN from Greek *khronios* long-lasting, long-continued, from *khronos* time. Orig. university slang, the Greek word being perverted to the sense 'contemporary'.]
▸ **A** *noun.* An intimate friend or associate. M17.
ARNOLD BENNETT The two were regular cronies for about a couple of months. E. HEATH The beer cellar where Hitler and his cronies had first met.
▸ **B** *verb intrans.* Associate (*with*) as a crony. E19.
■ **cronyism** *noun* friendship, fondness for the company of cronies; *US* the appointment of friends to political posts without due regard to their qualifications: M19.

croo *noun* var. of CRUE.

crood /kruːd/ *verb intrans. Scot.* E16.
[ORIGIN Imit.]
= CROODLE *verb*².

croodle /ˈkruːd(ə)l/ *verb*¹ *intrans. dial.* L18.
[ORIGIN Unknown.]
Crouch down; draw oneself together, as for warmth; nestle; cling close *to* a person.

C

croodle /ˈkruːd(ə)l/ *verb^{2} intrans.* E19.
[ORIGIN from CROOD + -LE^{3}.]
Coo like a dove.

crook /krʊk/ *noun & adjective.* ME.
[ORIGIN Old Norse *krókr* hook, barb, peg, bend, corner (Swedish *krok*, Danish *krog*).]
▸ **A** *noun* **I 1** An implement, weapon, or tool of hooked form; a hook. ME.
R. S. SURTEES Crooks, from whence used to dangle . . legs of . . mutton.
2 A shepherd's staff, one end of which is hooked for catching a sheep's leg. LME.
3 The pastoral staff of a bishop etc., shaped like a shepherd's crook. LME.
4 A sharply curved part or appendage of anything. LME.
M. SINCLAIR With a dead child in the crook of her arm.
5 A curve, a bend, e.g. of a river. LME.
6 A small piece of ground; an odd corner. LME.
†**7** TYPOGRAPHY. A bracket, a parenthesis. L16–M18.
8 A crooked or incurved piece of timber; *spec.* = CRUCK. E19.
9 A curved piece of tubing which can be fitted to a wind instrument to change its pitch. Cf. SHANK *noun* 4g. M19.
▸ **II** †**10** A trick, an artifice, a wile. ME–L16.
11 A professional criminal; a swindler or dishonest person. *colloq.* L19.
▸ **III 12** An act of crooking or bending something. ME.
– PHRASES: ***by hook or by crook***: see HOOK *noun*. **crook in one's lot** *Scot.* something untoward or distressing; a trial, an affliction. **on the crook** *slang* dishonestly.
▸ **B** *adjective.* **1** Crooked (*lit.* & esp. *fig.*). Now chiefly *Austral. & NZ.* E16.
B. CRONIN The crook business man is in a decided minority.
2 Of a thing or situation: bad; unpleasant; unsatisfactory. *Austral. & NZ.* L19.
D. IRELAND Things were crook at Tallarook.
3 Annoyed; angry. (Foll. by *on, at.*) *Austral. & NZ.* E20.
P. V. WHITE His mum went crook, and swore.
4 Out of sorts; injured. *Austral. & NZ.* E20.
X. HERBERT He's got a crook heart.
– COMB.: **crookback** (*a*) a hunchback; †(*b*) a crooked back; **crookbacked** *adjective* hunchbacked; **crookneck** *N. Amer.* a squash with a recurved neck.
▪ **crookdom** *noun* the realm of crooks E20. **crookery** *noun* the state of being a crook; the dealings of crooks; the world of crooks: E20. **crookish** *adjective* characteristic or suggestive of crooks or crooked dealings E20.

crook /krʊk/ *verb.* ME.
[ORIGIN from the noun.]
1 *verb trans.* Make into a curved or angular form; bend. ME. **crook one's elbow**, **crook one's little finger** *slang* drink alcohol, esp. to excess.
2 *verb intrans.* Be or become crooked in form. ME.
3 *verb intrans.* Bow as a sign of reverence or humility. Now *rare* or *obsolete*. ME.
4 *verb trans.* POLO. Interpose one's stick in front of (an opponent's). L19.

crooked /ˈkrʊkɪd; *in sense A.5 usu.* krʊkt/ *adjective & adverb.* ME.
[ORIGIN from CROOK *noun* + -ED^{2}, prob. after Old Norse *krókóttr* crooked, cunning.]
▸ **A** *adjective.* **1** Bent from a straight form; twisted, awry. ME.
O. HENRY His smile became crooked.
2 Of a person: deformed; bowed with age. ME. ▸†**b** Of a horse: broken down, old and decrepit. ME–L17.
3 *fig.* Not straightforward; deviating from uprightness of character or conduct; dishonest; corrupt. ME.
M. PUZO A crooked police official.
4 Dishonestly come by; stolen. *colloq.* M19.
5 = CROOK *adjective* 3. (Foll. by *on.*) *Austral. & NZ slang.* M20.
– COMB.: **crooked-necked squash** *US* = *crookneck* s.v. CROOK *noun*.
▸ **B** *adverb.* In or into a crooked position. M16.
K. A. PORTER A young officer with his cap knocked crooked.
▪ **crookedly** *adverb* LME. **crookedness** *noun* (*a*) the quality or state of being crooked; (*b*) a crooked part; a crooked act: LME.

crooken /ˈkrʊk(ə)n/ *verb trans.* Now *dial.* M16.
[ORIGIN Irreg. from CROOK *verb* + -EN^{5}.]
Make crooked; bend.

Crookes /krʊks/ *noun.* L19.
[ORIGIN See below.]
Used **attrib.** and in **possess.** with ref. to the inventions and observations of the English physicist Sir William Crookes (1832–1919).
Crookes dark space, **Crookes's dark space**: between the negative glow and the cathode of a low-pressure discharge tube. **Crookes glass**, **Crookes lens**, **Crookes's glass**, **Crookes's lens**: made so as to absorb ultraviolet light. **Crookes radiometer**, **Crookes's radiometer** an evacuated globe containing four vanes which have one side blackened and jointly spin when heat radiation impinges on them. **Crookes space**, **Crookes's space** = *Crookes dark space* above. **Crookes tube**, **Crookes's tube** a highly evacuated electron tube in which stratified electric discharges can be produced.

croon /kruːn/ *verb & noun.* L15.
[ORIGIN Middle Low German, Middle Dutch *krōnen* lament, groan (Dutch *kreunen*), of imit. origin.]
▸ **A** *verb.* **1** *verb intrans.* Make a low murmuring sound; *esp.* sing a popular sentimental song in a low smooth voice. L15.
2 *verb intrans.* Make a continued loud, deep sound; bellow; boom. *Scot. & N. English.* E16.
3 *verb trans.* Sing or say in a low murmuring voice; *esp.* sing (a popular sentimental song) in a low smooth voice. L16.
Fortune Rudy Vallée crooning I'm a Dreamer. C. ISHERWOOD 'Poor little Mummy, . . little Muttchen,' he crooned.
▸ **B** *noun.* **1** A loud, deep sound. *Scot. & N. English.* E16.
2 A low murmuring sound. E18.
▪ **crooningly** *adverb* in a crooning manner E20.

crooner /ˈkruːnə/ *noun.* E18.
[ORIGIN from CROON *verb* + -ER^{1}.]
1 The grey gurnard, *Eutrigla gurnardus* (from the noise it makes when landed). *Scot.* E18.
2 A person who croons; *spec.* a person who sings in a crooning style. L19.

croove *noun* var. of CRUIVE.

crop /krɒp/ *noun.*
[ORIGIN Old English *crop* corresp. to Middle Low German, Middle Dutch *kropp*, Old High German, German *Kropf*, Old Norse *kroppr*; further relations uncertain.]
▸ **I 1 a** A pouchlike enlargement of the gullet of many birds in which food is stored and prepared for digestion; an analogous organ in insects and some other animals. OE. ▸**b** *transf. & fig.* The stomach; the throat. Now *dial.* ME.
2 The head of a flower, herb, etc., esp. as picked for use; an ear of corn. Now *dial.* OE.
3 The top of a tree; a topmost branch. Now *dial.* ME.
4 The upper part of a whip or (now *Scot.*) a fishing rod; the whole stock of a whip; *spec.* (more fully ***riding crop***, ***hunting crop***) a short whipstock with a loop instead of or as well as a lash. LME.
5 ARCHITECTURE. The foliate part of a finial. L15.
6 *gen.* The top of anything material. *Scot.* E16.
▸ **II 7** [From sense 2.] The annual produce of cultivated plants, esp. the cereals, whether in the field or gathered. ME.
JOSEPH HALL The Husbandman looks not for a crop in the wild desart. J. H. B. PEEL Is the crop really ready?
8 The yield of any natural product in a particular season or locality; a plant etc. which is periodically harvested. LME.
POPE Fields waving high with heavy crops. G. B. SHAW Their first crop of potatoes. W. FAULKNER Cotton is a speculator's crop.
9 The entire tanned hide of an animal. LME.
10 A quantity produced or appearing, esp. at one time. L16.
G. B. SHAW The world's crop of infamy. M. MCCARTHY This new crop of girls was far less idealistic . . than their mothers.
▸ **III** [from the verb.]
11 A joint of or *of* meat; a piece cut off anything. LME.
12 An earmark made by cutting off part of the ear, esp. of an animal. M17.
13 An outcrop of rock. E18.
14 A conspicuously short haircut. L18.
– PHRASES: ***Eton crop***: see ETON 5. ***green crop***: see GREEN *adjective*. ***lop and crop***: see LOP *noun*^{2} 1. ***main crop***: see MAIN *adjective*. ***neck and crop***: see NECK *noun*^{1}. ***sour crop***: see SOUR *adjective*. ***standing crop***: see STANDING *adjective*.
– COMB.: **crop circle** a circular area in a field of standing crops (esp. wheat or another cereal) in which the stalks have been flattened to the ground, usu. in concentric rings; **crop dusting** the spraying of crops with powdered insecticide etc. from the air; †**crop-ear** (an animal or person with) an ear that has been cropped; **crop-eared** *adjective* (*a*) having the ears cropped; (*b*) *arch.* having the hair cut short and close to the head so that the ears are conspicuous, in a style favoured by Puritan supporters of Parliament in the English Civil War (cf. PRICK-EARED 2); **crop-full** *adjective* having a full crop or stomach (*lit. & fig.*); ***crop husbandry***: see HUSBANDRY *noun* 2; **cropland** land used for growing crops; **crop-mark** a local variation in the colour or growth of a crop, esp. when seen from the air, caused by a varying depth of soil (used to detect the presence of buried archaeological features); **crop-over** the end of the sugar cane harvest on a W. Indian plantation; the accompanying celebration; **crop-sick** *adjective* (now *dial.*) having an upset stomach, esp. through overindulgence.

†**crop** *adjective.* M17–E19.
[ORIGIN from the noun.]
Having the ears or hair cropped.

crop /krɒp/ *verb.* Infl. **-pp-**. Pa. t. & pple **cropped**, (*arch.*) **cropt**. ME.
[ORIGIN from the noun.]
1 *verb trans.* Remove the top or terminal parts of (a plant); pick (a flower or fruit). ME.
2 *verb trans. & intrans.* Of an animal: bite off the top of (grass etc.) in feeding. LME.
E. GLASGOW The stony hillside where sheep were cropping. W. DE LA MARE His horse moved, cropping the dark turf.
3 *verb trans.* Cut off short (*lit. & fig.*); cut short the ears of (a person or animal) or the hair of (a person, a head); trim the pages of (a book); cut off or mask unwanted areas of (a photograph etc.). E16.
CARLYLE By the hundred and the thousand, men's lives are cropt. A. J. CRONIN A beard, cropped close on cheek and chin. *Vogue* Cropped black top.
4 *verb trans.* Reap, harvest; cull (animals). E17.
Nature The cropping of whales.
5 *verb intrans.* Bear or yield a crop. E17.
6 *verb trans.* Raise a crop on; sow or plant with a crop. E17. ▸**b** *verb intrans.* Grow crops; work as a farmer. *US.* M19.
L. MACNEICE They won't crop their farms regularly.
SHARECROP *noun & verb*.
7 *verb intrans.* GEOLOGY. Of a stratum etc.: appear at the surface. Usu. foll. by *out* or *up*. M17.
8 *verb intrans.* Foll. by *up*: occur unexpectedly or incidentally. M19.
J. GALSWORTHY That nonsense of the separate room had cropped up again!
9 *verb intrans.* Foll. by *out*: come out or disclose itself incidentally. M19.

cropper /ˈkrɒpə/ *noun*^{1}. ME.
[ORIGIN from CROP *verb* or *noun* + -ER^{1}.]
▸ **I 1** A person who or thing which crops or trims; *spec.* a shearing machine or implement for cutting metal; a person who uses one. ME.
2 A person who raises a crop. L16.
sharecropper: see SHARE *noun*^{2}.
3 A plant which yields a crop of a specified kind or in a specified way. M19.
▸ **II 4** A pigeon of a breed that is able greatly to puff up its crop; a pouter-pigeon. M17.

cropper /ˈkrɒpə/ *noun*^{2}. *colloq.* M19.
[ORIGIN Perh. from ***neck and crop*** s.v. NECK *noun*^{1}.]
A heavy fall; *fig.* a severe misfortune, personal failure, etc.
come a cropper fall heavily; be ruined, suffer sudden misfortune.

Cropper /ˈkrɒpə/ *noun*^{3}. Also **c-**. L19.
[ORIGIN H. S. *Cropper*, English manufacturer.]
A kind of small treadle platen printing machine.

croppie *noun* var. of CRAPPIE.

croppy /ˈkrɒpi/ *noun.* L18.
[ORIGIN from CROP *noun* + -Y^{1}.]
hist. A person who has his or her hair cut short; *spec.* (*a*) (also ***croppy-boy***) one of the Irish rebels of 1798, who showed their sympathy with the French Revolution in this way; (*b*) *Austral.* an escaped convict.

cropt *verb pa. t. & pple*: see CROP *verb*.

croquembouche /krɒkɒmˈbuːʃ/ *noun.* L19.
[ORIGIN French, alt. of *croque en (la) bouche*, lit. '(that) crunches in the mouth', in ref. to the crispy caramel coating.]
A decorative dessert consisting of choux pastry and crystallized fruit or other confectionery items arranged in a cone and held together by a caramel sauce.

croque-monsieur /krɒkməˈsjəː/ *noun.* M20.
[ORIGIN French, lit. 'bite (a) man'.]
A fried or grilled cheese and ham sandwich.

croquet /ˈkrəʊkeɪ, -ki/ *noun & verb.* M19.
[ORIGIN Uncertain: perh. from northern French var. of French CROCHET.]
▸ **A** *noun.* **1** A game played on a lawn in which mallets are used to drive wooden etc. balls in a particular order through hoops fixed in the ground. M19.
2 The act of croqueting another ball. L19.
▸ **B** *verb trans. & intrans.* Drive away (the ball of an opponent) or the ball of (an opponent), after hitting it with one's own, by placing the two in contact and striking one's own with the mallet. M19.

croquette /krɒˈkɛt/ *noun.* E18.
[ORIGIN French, from *croquer* to crunch: see -ETTE.]
A small ball or roll of vegetable, minced meat, or fish (to be) fried in breadcrumbs.

croquis /krɔki, krəʊˈkiː/ *noun.* Pl. same /-i, -iːz/. E19.
[ORIGIN French, from *croquer* to sketch.]
A rough draft; a sketch.

crore /krɔː/ *noun.* Pl. same, **-s**. E17.
[ORIGIN Hindi *k(a)ror* from Sanskrit *koṭi*.]
In the Indian subcontinent: ten million, a hundred lakhs. (Foll. by *of*.)
Bangladesh Times Lakhs and crores of people. F. A. MEHTA Capital equipment exported . . was under a crore of rupees. *Nature* The 1976–77 budget on oil exploration at Rupees 42 crores (42 million dollars).

crosier *noun* var. of CROZIER.

cross /krɒs/ *noun*. See also CROSS-. LOE.
[ORIGIN Old Norse *kross* from Old Irish *cros* (corresp. to Gaelic *crois*, Welsh *croes*) from late Latin var. of Latin CRUX, *cruc-*, whence also Old French *croiz*, *crois* (mod. *croix*).]
► **I 1** A monument consisting of or surmounted by an upright and a short transverse piece, symbolizing the Cross of Jesus (sense 3 below). LOE. ▸**b** A marketplace; a market. Now *dial.* L16.
2 A tall upright stake usu. with a transverse beam, to which a person was fastened as a mode of execution in the ancient world. ME.
Calvary cross, ***cross Calvary***: see CALVARY 1. ***holy cross***: see HOLY *adjective*. ***St Cross***: see SAINT *noun & adjective*.
3 *spec.* (Also **C-**.) The particular structure on which Jesus was crucified. ME.
Invention of the Cross: see INVENTION *noun*. ***St Cross***: see SAINT *noun & adjective*. ***Station of the Cross***: see STATION *noun* 10. ***the Way of the Cross***: see WAY *noun*.
4 CHRISTIAN CHURCH. A devotional and liturgical act in which a hand or digit traces the shape of a cross on the body of oneself or another, usu. on the forehead or by touching in turn the forehead, chest, each shoulder, and the chest again. Now usu. ***sign of the cross***. ME.
5 A model of a cross (sense 2 above) as a religious emblem in a church, an ornament worn round the neck, etc. ME.

A. WILSON A small opal cross on her ample bosom.

creep to the cross: see CREEP *verb* 1.
6 A staff surmounted by a cross and carried in religious processions, esp. as an archbishop's emblem of office. ME.
7 a (Also **C-**.) The Christian religion. ME. ▸**b** CHRISTIAN CHURCH. (Also **C-**.) The atonement accomplished by Christ through his Crucifixion and death. LME.
8 An affliction seen as to be borne with Christian patience; any source of personal trouble or vexation. ME.

ALDOUS HUXLEY We all have our cross to bear. J. CARY My father was . . a cross and burden to his family.

9 A more or less elaborate representation of a cross on a surface, as a religious symbol. ME.
10 A figure of a cross stamped on one side of a coin; a coin bearing such a figure; any coin. *arch.* ME.
cross and pile, **cross or pile** (**a**) *arch.* the obverse and (or) reverse of a coin; a coin; money; †(**b**) (usu. with *cast*, *throw*, etc.) a toss-up (*lit.* & *fig.*).
11 A mark or figure consisting of two short lines cutting one another, usu. at right angles; any object seen as having a similar shape. LME.

EVELYN The body of the Church formes a Crosse. D. STOREY Examining the marks, the ticks, the crosses.

long cross: see LONG *adjective*[1]. ***noughts and crosses***: see NOUGHT *pronoun & noun* 4.
12 A stylized representation of a cross used as a heraldic device. LME. ▸**b** An order of knighthood or a decoration for valour having a cross as its emblem; the emblem itself; a recipient of such an honour. L17.
Celtic cross, ***Greek cross***, ***Latin cross***, ***Lorraine cross***, ***Maltese cross***, ***St Andrew's cross***, ***St Anthony cross***, ***St George's cross***, ***tau cross***, ***Teutonic cross***, etc. **b** ***Distinguished Flying Cross***, ***George Cross***, ***Iron Cross***, ***Military Cross***, ***Victoria Cross***, etc. **Grand Cross** the highest degree of any of certain orders of knighthood having a cross-shaped decoration.
13 ***the Cross*** (more fully ***the Southern Cross***), (the name of) a small but conspicuous constellation of the southern hemisphere, lying in the Milky Way near Centaurus and having a cross- or kite-shaped group of four bright stars pointing approximately north–south. M16.
14 A surveyor's instrument having two sights at right angles to one another. M17.
► **II** †**15 a** A crossed position. Chiefly in ***on cross*** (surviving as ACROSS *adverb*). LME–M17. ▸**b** ***the cross***, the diagonal across the warp of a material, the bias. Chiefly in ***on the cross*** after verbs like ***cut***. L19.
16 A place where two lines or routes cross each other. M16.
17 An instance of being thwarted, a disappointment. L16.

W. H. DIXON Anne was suffering from a cross in love.

18 An intermixture of animal breeds or of plant varieties or species; an animal or plant so produced, a hybrid. M18. ▸**b** A thing or person intermediate in character or appearance *between* two different things or persons. L18.

b R. S. SURTEES A cross between a military dandy and a squire. G. MAXWELL The studio came to look like a cross between a monkey-house and a furniture repository.

FIRST ***cross***. ***reciprocal cross***: see RECIPROCAL *adjective*.
19 a ***the cross***, dishonest or fraudulent practices; criminal activities. *slang.* E19. ▸**b** A fraudulent deed or arrangement. *slang.* E19.
a on the cross dishonest(ly), criminal(ly).
20 A transverse movement; THEATRICAL a movement from one side of the stage to the other; a blow in boxing that crosses the opponent's lead; a cross-pass. M19.

J. DEMPSEY The right cross, deadliest of all counterpunches.

— NOTE: In Old English only in place names.
■ **crossless** *adjective* L15.

cross /krɒs/ *adjective*. See also CROSS-. E16.
[ORIGIN Partly attrib. use of the noun, partly ellipt. use of CROSS *adverb*.]
1 Lying across; extending from side to side; transverse; (of a cricket bat) held slanting. E16. ▸**b** Of a wind: blowing across one's course. Of a sea: running across the direction of the wind; composed of two sets of waves crossing each other. E17.

fig.: DISRAELI How many cross issues baffle the parties. **b** DICKENS In the cross-swell of two steamers.

2 Contrary, opposed, (*to*). Now usu. *attrib.* M16.
3 Adverse, unfavourable; not in accord with one's desire. M16.

T. DEKKER Such crosse fortune! DEFOE We had but a cross voyage.

4 *attrib.* Involving interchange or reciprocal action. L16.
†**5** Inclined to quarrel or disagree; perverse. L16–M19.
6 Annoyed, bad-tempered, (*at*, *with*, †*to*); expressing or showing annoyance or ill temper. M17.

J. AUSTEN I have never had a cross word from him. A. J. CRONIN He was cross with her for being out of sorts.

7 Dishonest; dishonestly come by. *slang.* E19.
8 Of an animal or plant: crossbred; hybrid. L19.
■ **crossly** *adverb* L16. **crossness** *noun* L16.

cross /krɒs/ *verb*. ME.
[ORIGIN from CROSS *noun*.]
1 *verb trans.* Make the sign of the cross on or over (esp. oneself, as an act of devotion or reverence or to invoke divine protection). ME.
2 *verb trans.* Draw a line or lines across; (usu. foll. by *off*, *out*) cancel in this way. LME.

THACKERAY I have . . crossed the t's and dotted the i's. E. BOWEN Hermione . . crossed off the days on her calendar.

3 *verb trans.* Of a line etc.: intersect; lie or pass across. LME. ▸**b** *verb intrans.* Intersect, lie or pass across each other. L17. ▸**c** *verb trans.* Bestride (a horse). M18.

b A. MASON A pair of stout sticks had been thrust into the ground slantwise so that they crossed near the top.

4 *verb trans.* Place crosswise (*with*); set (things) across one another; place (one thing) *over* another. L15.

M. KEANE They crossed and uncrossed their legs clumsily. S. PLATH I sat . . and crossed my right ankle over my left knee.

5 a *verb intrans.* Pass (*over*) from one side or end to or *to* the other. L15. ▸**b** *verb trans.* Pass over (a line, boundary, etc.); go or travel across (a region etc.). L16. ▸**c** *verb trans.* Of a thing: extend across. L16. ▸**d** *verb trans.* Carry or take (something) across. E19. ▸**e** *verb trans.* & *intrans.* FOOTBALL etc. Pass (the ball) across the pitch, esp. from a wing to the centre. M20.

a R. ADAMS We will cross to the further side of the river. T. STOPPARD French enters and crosses to his place. C. P. SNOW They had to cross, to the island in the middle of the road. **b** H. JAMES If he crossed that threshold. J. CONRAD I crossed the landing to my sitting-room. N. COWARD If we crossed Siberia by train. **c** O. HENRY A little river . . crossed by a hundred little bridges.

6 *verb trans.* **a** Thwart; resist the wishes of; oppose (a plan etc.). M16. ▸†**b** Contradict; contravene. L16–M18. ▸†**c** Debar *from*. *rare.* L16–M17.

C. WILSON When crossed, he had an explosive temper.

7 a *verb trans.* Meet in one's way, esp. adversely. *arch.* L16. ▸**b** *verb trans.* & †*intrans.* (with *on*, *upon*). Come across, encounter. Now *rare.* L17.
8 a *verb trans.* Meet and pass; pass in an opposite direction; (of a letter etc.) be on its way at the same time as (one to the sender from the recipient). L18. ▸**b** *verb intrans.* (Of a letter etc.) be on its way at the same time as one to the sender from the recipient (foll. by *with*); (of letters etc. between two people) be on their way at the same time. L18.

a C. LAMB Now and then a solitary gardening man would cross me. K. M. E. MURRAY His letter crossed an apology from Wheatley. **b** DICKENS This letter will cross with your second.

9 *verb trans.* Breed (an animal or plant) with or *with* one of a different breed, variety, etc.; modify by this means. L18.
10 *verb trans.* Act dishonestly towards (a person) or in (a matter). *slang.* E19.
— PHRASES, & WITH ADVERBS IN SPECIALIZED SENSES: **cross a cheque** draw or print two parallel lines across a cheque, so that it has to be paid into a bank account. **cross a person's hand (with silver)**, **cross a person's palm (with silver)** give a person a coin as payment for fortune-telling (orig. describing a cross with it in the palm). ***cross my heart (and hope to die)***: see HEART *noun*. ***cross one's bridge when one comes to it***: see BRIDGE *noun*[1] 1. **cross one's face** appear briefly in one's expression. **cross one's fingers** crook one finger over another to bring good luck. **cross one's heart** make the sign of the cross over one's heart in attestation of sincerity. **cross one's mind** come suddenly into one's thoughts. **cross one's path** meet, esp. so as to obstruct or thwart; pass across one's path in front of one. **cross over** (**a**) BIOLOGY (of chromosome segments) undergo crossing over (CROSSING ***over***); (**b**) *euphem.* die; (see also senses 4, 5a above). **cross swords** *fig.* have a fight, controversy, or overt rivalry, (*with*). ***cross the floor***: see FLOOR *noun*. ***cross the T***: see T, T 2. ***cross the t's***: see T, T 1. **cross wires** accidentally connect telephone circuits so that one call is heard with another; *fig.* have a misunderstanding; (usu. in *pass.*). **get one's wires crossed** = *cross wires* above. **keep one's fingers crossed** keep one finger over another to bring good luck; be in suspenseful hope (*that*).
■ **crossable** *adjective* M19. **crosser** *noun* M16.

cross /krɒs/ *preposition & adverb*. See also CROSS-. M16.
[ORIGIN Aphet. from ACROSS.]
► **A** *preposition*. = ACROSS *preposition* 1, 2, 3. Now *dial.* or *poet.* exc. as CROSS-. M16.
► **B** *adverb*. †**1** = ACROSS *adverb* 2. L16–L18.
†**2** In a contrary way *to*. E17–M18.
3 = ACROSS *adverb* 3. Now *rare*. E17.

C

cross- /krɒs/ *combining form*.
[ORIGIN Repr. CROSS *noun*, *adjective*, *preposition & adverb*.]
In combs. in various relations and with various senses, as 'a cross', 'transverse(ly)', 'in opposition', 'across'. (In some a hyphen is optional, others are customarily written as two words or as one.)
■ **cross-accent** *noun* (MUSIC) a syncopated accent, syncopation M20. **cross-action** *noun* a legal action brought on the same subject by a defendant against a plaintiff or another defendant M19. †**cross-aisle** *noun* (an arm of) a transept LME–L18. **cross-beak** *noun* = CROSSBILL *noun* L17. **cross-beam** *noun* a transverse beam L15. **cross-bearer** *noun* a person who carries or wears a cross; *esp.* one who carries an archbishop's cross before him in procession: M16. **cross-bearings** *noun pl.* (NAUTICAL) bearings of two or more objects from one point, or of one object from two or more points, which enable the single position to be found given the others E19. **cross-'bedding** *noun* (GEOLOGY) layering within a stratum and at an angle to the main bedding plane L19. **cross bench** *noun* each of the benches in the House of Lords where peers sit who have no party allegiance (usu. in *pl.*) M19. **cross-'bencher** *noun* a member of either House of Parliament who sits on the cross benches or asserts his or her independence of party allegiance L19. **crossbones** *noun pl.* a figure of two crossed thigh bones as an emblem of death (usu. under the figure of a skull: see ***skull and crossbones*** s.v. SKULL *noun*[1]) L18. **cross-border** *adjective* (**a**) that forms a border across a fabric etc.; (**b**) passing, occurring, or performed across a border between two countries etc.: L19. **cross bun** *noun phr.* (usu. more fully ***hot cross bun***): marked with a cross, traditionally for eating on Good Friday M18. **cross-'buttock** *noun & verb* (**a**) *noun* a throw in which a wrestler throws an opponent head first over his or her hip; (**b**) *verb trans.* throw in this way: E18. **cross-'buttocker** *noun* (a wrestler who uses) a cross-buttock E19. **cross-channel** *adjective* passing or situated across a channel, esp. the English Channel L19. **cross-co'nnect** *verb trans.* connect (each of a set of wires etc.) to a non-corresponding wire etc. in another set L19. **cross-contami'nation** *noun* contamination of one substance or object with bacteria or other micro-organisms from another M20. **cross-co'nnection** *noun* a cross-connected arrangement L19. **cross-corner** *noun* a diagonally opposite corner of a quadrilateral; ***at cross-corners with*** (fig.), directly contrary to: E19. **cross-corre'lation** *noun* a correlation between two different series of measurements etc. E20. **cross-'country** *adjective*, *adverb*, & *noun* (**a**) *adjective & adverb* (going, leading, or taking place) across fields etc. rather than along (main) roads; (of a flight) involving landing at a point distant from the take-off point and the practice of air navigation; (**b**) *noun* a cross-country run, flight, etc.; cross-country running, skiing, etc.: M18. **cross-court** *adjective* (of a stroke in tennis etc.) hit diagonally across the court E20. **cross-cousin** *noun* either of two cousins who are children of a brother and sister L19. **cross crosslet** *noun phr.* a Greek cross in which each limb is crossed L15. **cross-'cultural** *adjective* pertaining to or involving different cultures or comparison between them M20. **cross-'culturally** *adverb* in cross-cultural terms M20. **cross-current** *noun* (**a**) a current in a river or sea which flows across another; (**b**) *fig.* a process or tendency which is in conflict with another: L16. **cross-'date** *verb trans.* (ARCHAEOLOGY) date by correlation with the chronology of another culture, site, etc. M20. **cross-division** *noun* (an instance of) division of a group according to more than one principle, producing problems of classification E19. **cross-'dress** *verb intrans.* wear clothes of members of the opposite sex L20. **cross-'dresser** *noun* a transvestite L20. **cross-exami'nation** *noun* a spell of, or the action of, cross-examining E19. **cross-e'xamine** *verb trans.* examine with minute and persistent questioning; (of a barrister etc.) question (a witness for the other side) in order to weaken evidence previously given or elicit evidence favourable to the barrister's own side: M17. **cross-eyed** *adjective* having one or both eyes turned inwards in a squint L18. **cross-fade** *verb & noun* (BROADCASTING) (**a**) *verb intrans.* fade out one sound while fading in another; (**b**) *noun* an act of cross-fading: M20. **cross-'fenced** *adjective* (*US*) having additional fencing inside a fenced enclosure L20. **cross-fertili'zation** *noun* fertilization in which the fusing gametes come from different individuals; *fig.* the fruitful interchange of ideas, information, etc.: M19. **cross-'fertilize** *verb* (**a**) *verb trans.* fertilize with gametes from another individual of the same species; cross-pollinate; *fig.* help or promote by interchange of ideas, information, etc.; (**b**) *verb intrans.* employ cross-fertilization (*lit.* & *fig.*): M19. **cross-fingering** *noun* on a woodwind instrument, a method or the action of changing a note by a semitone by uncovering one hole part of the way along the instrument and covering up one or more of the holes nearer the open end; an instance of this: L19. **crossfire** *noun* lines of gunfire crossing one another from different positions; *fig.* (danger due to) attacks from different quarters: M19. †**cross-fixed** *adjective* crucified E17–M19. **crossflow** *noun* a type of engine cylinder head where the intake ports are on the opposite side of the engine from the exhaust ports L20. **cross fox** *noun phr.* = ***patch fox*** s.v. PATCH *noun*[1] M19. **cross-'garnet** *noun* a hinge composed of a short vertical piece fastened to a door frame and a longer horizontal one fastened to the face of the door M17. **cross-'gartered** *adjective* (*hist.*) having garters crossed on the legs L16. **cross-'gartering** *noun* (*hist.*) the wearing of garters crossed on the legs E17. **cross-'grained** *adjective & adverb* (**a**) *adjective* (of wood) having a grain that deviates from the longitudinal direction; *fig.* difficult to deal with, perverse; (**b**) *adverb* across the grain (*lit.* & *fig.*): M17. **cross-'grainedness** *noun* perversity, irritability M17. **cross guard** *noun* a guard on a sword, dagger, etc., consist-

ing of a short transverse bar M19. **cross hair** *noun* = CROSS-WIRE L19. **cross-'handed** *adjective & adverb* (*a*) *adjective* having the hands crossed; (of a boat) rowed with hands crossed; (*b*) *adverb* with the hands crossed: M19. **cross-handled** *adjective* having a handle in the form of a cross E19. **cross-hatch** *verb trans.* engrave with two sets of parallel lines crossing each other; shade in this way; mark with crossing lines: E19. **cross-'index** *verb trans.* index under another heading as a cross-reference L19. **cross-in'fection** *noun* transfer of infection, esp. to a hospital patient with a different infection etc. M20. **cross-keys** *noun pl.* two keys depicted in the form of an X, as in the papal arms M16. **cross-kick** *verb & noun* (*a*) *verb intrans.* kick a football across the field; (*b*) *noun* a kick across a football field: E20. **cross-legged** *adverb & adjective* (*a*) *adverb* with the legs crossed at the ankles and bent outwards; (*b*) *adjective* lying with one leg laid over the other; sitting cross-legged: M16. **cross-license** *verb trans.* give a licence to use (patented or copyright material) in return for a similar licence M20. **cross light** *noun* a light which crosses another and illuminates parts which the other leaves in shade M19. **cross-line** *noun* (*a*) a line drawn across another; (*b*) a fishing line stretched across a stream with many hooks attached: LME. **cross-link** *noun & verb* (CHEMISTRY) (*a*) *noun* a bond, atom, or short chain of atoms that connects two long chains in a polymer molecule etc.; (*b*) *verb trans. & intrans.* form a cross-link (with): M20. **cross-'linkage** *noun* (CHEMISTRY) a cross-link M20. **cross-'lots** *adverb* (*N. Amer. dial.*) by a short cut E19. **cross-member** *noun* a structural member across the width of a motor-vehicle chassis E20. **cross-multiplication** *noun* a method of multiplying together quantities given in feet and inches, etc., without reducing them to one denomination; also called ***duodecimals***: E18. **cross-'party** *adjective* involving or pertaining to two or more political parties E20. **cross-pass** *noun* a pass across a football etc. field E20. **crosspatch** *noun* a bad-tempered person L17. **cross-path** *noun* a path that crosses between two roads or points M16. **cross-peen**, **pein** *adjective* (of a hammer) having a peen that lies crossways to the length of the shaft L19. **crosspiece** *noun* a transverse component of a structure etc. E17. **cross-plough**, (*N. Amer. & arch.*) **-plow** *verb trans.* plough (a field etc.) across the furrows of a previous ploughing M17. **cross-ply** *adjective & noun* (designating) a tyre in which successive layers of fabric have their cords running diagonally, crossways to each other M20. **cross-point** *noun* †(*a*) some kind of dance step; (*b*) a compass point between two of the cardinal points: L16. **cross-'pollinate** *verb trans.* (BOTANY) subject to cross-pollination E20. **cross-polli'nation** *noun* the pollination of one plant with pollen from another plant L19. **cross-'post** *verb trans.* (*a*) move (an employee) to a different department or industry; (*b*) send (a message) to more than one Internet newsgroup simultaneously: L20. **cross-'posting** *noun* a move to a different department or industry M20. **cross product** *noun phr.* = ***vector product*** s.v. VECTOR *noun* M20. **cross-pro'mote** *verb trans.* market by cross-promotion L20. **cross-pro'motion** *noun* cooperative marketing by two or more companies of one another's products L20. **cross 'purpose** *noun phr.* conflicting purpose: in *pl.* (treated as *sing.*), a parlour game involving mismatched questions and answers; ***at cross purposes***, with a misunderstanding of each other's meaning or intention: M17. **cross-'question** *noun & verb* (*a*) *noun* a question put by way of cross-examination; (*b*) *verb trans.* interrogate with questions that tend to check previous answers; cross-examine: L17. **cross-re'act** *verb intrans.* take part in a cross reaction M20. **cross re'action** *noun* the reaction of an antibody with an antigen other than the one which gave rise to it M20. **cross-'reading** *noun* a reading continued across adjacent columns of a newspaper etc. so as to produce a comic effect L18. **cross-re'fer** *verb intrans. & trans.* refer from or *from* one place in a book or list to or *to* another; provide with a cross-reference: L19. **cross-'reference** *noun & verb* (*a*) *noun* a reference to another place in a book, list, etc., where the same subject or word is treated; (*b*) *verb trans.* provide with a cross-reference; refer *to* another place by means of a cross-reference: M19. **cross-rhythm** *noun* simultaneous use of more than one rhythm; an instance of this: E20. †**cross-row** *noun* the alphabet; = ***Christ-cross-row*** s.v. CHRIST-CROSS 2: E16–L17. **cross-ruff** *noun & verb* (*a*) *noun* an obsolete card game; a sequence of play in bridge etc. in which partners alternately trump each other's leads; (*b*) *verb trans. & intrans.* play (in) a cross-ruff: L16. **cross-saddle** *noun & adverb* (*a*) *noun* a saddle on which the rider sits astride; (*b*) *adverb* astride a saddle: L19. **cross-sea** *noun*: running across the wind, or having two sets of waves crossing M19. **cross-sectoral** *adjective* from or involving more than one sector M20. **cross-sell** *verb trans.* sell (a different product or service) to an existing customer L20. **cross slide** *noun phr.* a sliding part on a lathe or planing machine which is supported by the saddle and carries the tool in a direction at right angles to the bed of the machine L19. **cross-springer** *noun* (ARCHITECTURE) a rib that extends diagonally in vaulting E19. **cross-staff** *noun* (*a*) *arch.* an archbishop's cross; a bishop's crook; (*b*) *hist.* an instrument formerly used for finding the altitude of the sun: LME. **cross stitch** *noun & verb* (*a*) *noun* a stitch formed of two stitches that make a cross; needlework characterized by such stitches; (*b*) *verb trans.* sew or embroider with cross stitches: M17. **cross-street** *noun* a street crossing another or connecting two streets M17. **cross-'subsidize** *verb trans.* subsidize out of the profits of another business or activity M20. **cross-'subsidy** *noun* the financing of losses arising from one business or activity out of profits from another, which may be deliberately increased for the purpose M20. **crosstalk** *noun* unwanted transfer of signals from one circuit, channel, etc., to another; *fig.* repartee; conversation: L19. **cross tie** *noun* a transverse connecting piece, *esp.* (*N. Amer.*) a railway sleeper E19. **cross-tongue** *noun* a slip of wood with the grain running crossways, used to strengthen a joint L19. **cross-town** *adjective & adverb* (*N. Amer.*) (that goes or leads) across a town L19. **'cross-train** *verb trans. & intrans.* (*a*) *verb trans.* train to perform a new skill or job, esp. one which complements a person's existing employment; (*b*) *verb intrans.* train in several different sports in order to improve fitness and performance in one's main sport: L20. **cross-trainers** training shoes suitable for a range of sporting activities L20. **crosstree** *noun* (*a*) in *pl.*, a pair of horizontal struts attached to a mast, esp. athwartships to spread the rigging or support a top; (***jack crosstree***: see JACK *noun*[1]); (*b*) *poet.* = CROSS *noun* 3: E17. **cross-vault**, **cross-vaulting** *nouns* (ARCHITECTURE): formed by the intersection of two or more vaults M19. **cross-'voting** *noun* voting for a party not one's own or for more than one party L19. **crosswalk** *noun* (*a*) a path or walk that crosses another; (*b*) *N. Amer. & Austral.* a pedestrian crossing: M18. **cross-wind** *noun* a wind blowing across one's course E20. **cross-wire** *noun* a fine wire at the focus of an optical instrument, crossing the field of view, to aid in positioning or measuring M19. **crossword** *noun* (more fully ***crossword puzzle***) a puzzle in which words crossing one another, usu. horizontally and vertically in a chequered pattern of squares, have to be filled in from clues provided E20. **crosswort** *noun* any of various plants with leaves arranged in a cross, or whorl of four, esp. *Cruciata laevipes*, a straggling hedgerow plant of the madder family L16.

crossbar /ˈkrɒsbɑː/ *noun.* M16.
[ORIGIN from CROSS- + BAR *noun*[1].]
1 A bar fixed across something, esp. a bicycle frame or a goal. M16.
2 A transverse line or stripe. L16.
†**3** = ***bend sinister*** s.v. BEND *noun*[2] 2. M17–M18.

crossbar /ˈkrɒsbɑː/ *verb trans.* Infl. **-rr-**. L16.
[ORIGIN Partly from CROSS- + BAR *verb*, partly from CROSSBAR *noun*.]
1 Mark crosswise (*with*); draw bars or stripes across. L16.
2 Put or fix a bar or bars across. E17.

crossbill /ˈkrɒsbɪl/ *noun.* L17.
[ORIGIN from CROSS- + BILL *noun*[2].]
Any bird of the genus *Loxia* of the finch family, occurring widely in the northern hemisphere and having mandibles that cross one another when the bill is closed.

cross-bill /ˈkrɒsbɪl/ *noun.* M17.
[ORIGIN from CROSS- + BILL *noun*[3].]
hist. A bill filed in the Court of Chancery by a defendant against the plaintiff or other defendants in the same suit.

†**crossbite** *verb & noun.* M16.
[ORIGIN from CROSS- + BITE *verb*.]
▸ **A** *verb trans.* Pa. t. **-bit**, pa. pple **-bit(ten)**.
1 Cheat in return; dupe, deceive. M16–M19.
2 Censure bitingly or bitterly. L16–M18.
▸ **B** *noun.* A swindle; a deception. L16–E18.

crossbow /ˈkrɒsbəʊ/ *noun.* LME.
[ORIGIN from CROSS- + BOW *noun*[1].]
1 An orig. medieval weapon for propelling missiles with great force, comprising a bow, usu. of metal, fixed to the end of a wooden stock that has a groove to hold the missile, a trigger to release it, and often a crank for drawing the cord tight. LME.
2 A man armed with a crossbow. Usu. in *pl.* L15.
– COMB.: **crossbowman** = sense 2 above.

crossbred /ˈkrɒsbrɛd/ *ppl adjective & noun.* M19.
[ORIGIN from CROSS- + BRED *ppl adjective*.]
▸ **A** *ppl adjective.* Bred from parents of different breeds or varieties; (of wool) obtained from a crossbred sheep. M19.
▸ **B** *noun.* A crossbred animal; wool from a crossbred sheep. L19.

crossbreed /ˈkrɒsbriːd/ *noun.* L18.
[ORIGIN from CROSS- + BREED *noun*.]
A breed produced by crossing; an individual of such a breed.

crossbreed /ˈkrɒsbriːd/ *verb trans.* Pa. t. & pple **-bred** /-brɛd/. L17.
[ORIGIN from CROSS- + BREED *verb*.]
Produce or modify by crossing different breeds, varieties, etc.

cross-check /ˈkrɒstʃɛk/ *noun.* M20.
[ORIGIN from CROSS- + CHECK *noun*[1].]
A method or act of cross-checking.

cross-check /ˈkrɒstʃɛk/ *verb trans.* M20.
[ORIGIN from CROSS- + CHECK *verb*[1].]
1 In ice hockey and lacrosse, obstruct (an opponent) with the use of the length of one's stick. M20.
2 Check by reference to additional sources, calculations, etc. M20.

cross-cut /ˈkrɒskʌt/ *noun.* L18.
[ORIGIN from CROSS- + CUT *noun*[2].]
1 MINING. A cutting made across the course of a vein or the general direction of the workings. L18.
2 A direct route going diagonally or transversely across. E19.
3 A cross-cut saw. M19.
4 A cross-section, a representative sample. M20.

cross-cut /ˈkrɒskʌt/ *adjective.* M17.
[ORIGIN Partly from the verb; partly from CROSS- + CUT *ppl adjective*.]
1 Designed for cutting across. M17.
cross-cut saw: having a handle at each end for two people to cut across the grain of timber.
2 Cut across; having transverse cuts. M19.

cross-cut /ˈkrɒskʌt/ *verb.* Infl. **-tt-**. Pa. t. & pple **-cut**. L16.
[ORIGIN from CROSS- + CUT *verb*.]
1 *verb trans.* Cut transversely. L16.
2 *verb trans. & intrans.* CINEMATOGRAPHY. Switch back and forth between (two or more sequences) in editing a film; alternate (one sequence) with another; employ this technique. M20.

crosse /krɒs/ *noun.* M19.
[ORIGIN French *crosse*, Old French *croce* bishop's crook: see CROZIER.]
The stick used in lacrosse, having a curved L-shaped or triangular frame at one end with a piece of netting in the angle.

cross head /ˈkrɒshɛd/ *noun & verb.* E19.
[ORIGIN from CROSS- + HEAD *noun*.]
▸ **A** *noun.* **1** A block at the end of a piston rod of a steam engine which slides between straight guides and communicates motion to an attached connecting rod. E19.
2 Any transverse structure at the top of a machine etc. M19.
3 A heading printed across a column or page within the text of an article. L19.
▸ **B** *verb trans.* Provide with a printed cross head (sense 3 above). L19.
■ **cross heading** *noun* = CROSS HEAD *noun* 3 L19.

crossing /ˈkrɒsɪŋ/ *noun.* LME.
[ORIGIN from CROSS *verb* + -ING[1].]
1 The action or an act of making or marking with the sign of the cross; the action or an act of drawing lines across; striking *off* or *out* by drawing lines across. LME.
2 The action or an act of passing, lying, or placing across; the action or an act of passing in an opposite direction. LME.
3 The action or an act of thwarting; an act of resistance or opposition. L16.
4 Dishonest practice. *rare.* L16.
5 **a** A place at which a river or road is crossed; *esp.* a designated part of a road where crossing is facilitated. M17. ▸**b** The intersection of two roads, two railway lines, etc., or of one with another. L17. ▸**c** The part of a cruciform church where the transepts cross the nave. M19.
a pedestrian crossing, ***pelican crossing***, ***zebra crossing***, etc. **b** ***grade crossing***: see GRADE *noun*. ***level crossing***: see LEVEL *adjective*.
6 The action or an instance of crossbreeding. M19.

C. SAGAN Such crossings are about as reasonable as the mating of a man and a petunia.

– COMB.: **crossing over** BIOLOGY the exchange of chromosome segments between paired homologous chromosomes, resulting in a mixture of parental characters in offspring; **crossing sweeper** *hist.* a person who sweeps a street crossing.

cross-jack /ˈkrɒsdʒak, ˈkrɒdʒɪk/ *noun.* Also **cro'jack**. E17.
[ORIGIN from CROSS- + JACK *noun*[3].]
A sail bent to the lower yard of a mizzenmast of a square-rigged ship; (in full ***cross-jack yard***) such a yard.

crosslet /ˈkrɒslɪt/ *noun.* LME.
[ORIGIN from CROSS *noun* + -LET, after Anglo-Norman *croiselete*; cf. Old French *croisete* (mod. *croissete*).]
1 HERALDRY. A small cross. LME.
CROSS CROSSLET.
2 A small object in the form of a cross. LME.
■ **crossleted** *adjective* decorated with a crosslet or crosslets E19.

crossopterygian /ˌkrɒsɒptəˈrɪdʒɪən/ *adjective & noun.* Also **C-**. M19.
[ORIGIN from mod. Latin *Crossopterygii*, *-ia* (from Greek *krossos* tassel, (in pl.) fringe + *pterux*, *pterug-* fin + -IA[2]) + -AN.]
▸ **A** *adjective.* Of, pertaining to, or designating a group of mostly extinct bony fish with fleshy lobed fins and a cranium divided into two parts, from which amphibians and other land vertebrates are thought to have evolved. M19.
▸ **B** *noun.* A crossopterygian fish. M19.

crossover /ˈkrɒsəʊvə/ *noun & adjective.* L18.
[ORIGIN from *cross over* s.v. CROSS *verb*.]
▸ **A** *noun.* **1** (A) fabric having the design running across from selvedge to selvedge instead of lengthways. L18.
2 A wrap worn round the shoulders and crossed in front. M19.
3 A short length of track joining two adjacent lines of a railway or tramway. L19.
4 The action or process of crossing over; an instance of this, *esp.* (BIOLOGY) an individual with a genetic character produced by crossing over; a chromatid resulting from crossing over. E20. ▸**b** The process by which a piece of recorded music gains popularity (unexpectedly or through marketing) with an audience outside that usual for its particular genre or style; a song or record gaining such popularity. L20.
▸ **B** *adjective.* That crosses over; characterized by crossing over; having a part that crosses over. L19.
crossover distortion ELECTRONICS: occurring where a signal changes from positive to negative or vice versa. **crossover network** a filter in a loudspeaker unit that divides the signal and delivers different parts to bass and treble speakers etc. **crossover vote**, **crossover voter**, **crossover voting** *US*: switching support from the expected political party or candidate to another.

crossroad /ˈkrɒsrəʊd/ *noun & adjective.* E18.
[ORIGIN from CROSS- + ROAD *noun*.]
▸ **A** *noun.* **1** A road crossing another; a road joining two main roads; a byroad. E18.
2 *sing.* & (usu.) in *pl.* treated as *sing.* A place where two roads cross; *fig.* a situation in which two courses of action or two lines of development diverge; a critical turning point in life, a career, etc. L18.
dirty work at the crossroads: see DIRTY *adjective*.
▸ **B** *adjective.* Passing by crossroads; situated at a crossroads; *fig.* (*US*) small, cheap. L18.

cross-section /krɒs'sɛkʃ(ə)n/ *noun & verb.* M19.
[ORIGIN from CROSS- + SECTION *noun.*]
▸**A** *noun.* **1** A cut made through an object or substance, esp. through its narrow dimension; a surface exposed in this way; the area the surface has or would have; a diagram representing what such a cut would reveal. M19.
2 *fig.* A typical or representative sample, group, etc. E20.
E. GRIERSON The jury, a fair cross-section of the community.
3 PHYSICS. A numerical quantity, expressed as an area, representing the likelihood that a particle will undergo a specified interaction with another particle. E20.
▸**B** *verb trans.* Make a cross-section of; cut into a cross-section. L19.
■ **cross-sectional** *adjective* L19.

crossway /'krɒsweɪ/ *noun.* ME.
[ORIGIN from CROSS- + WAY *noun.*]
1 *sing.* & in *pl.* (treated as *sing.* or *pl.*). A place where two roads or paths cross. ME.
2 = CROSSROAD 1. L15.

crossway /'krɒsweɪ/ *adverb & adjective.* LME.
[ORIGIN from CROSS- + -WAY.]
▸**A** *adverb.* = CROSSWISE *adverb.* LME.
▸**B** *adjective.* Placed or running across; transverse. E19.

crossways /'krɒsweɪz/ *adjective & adverb.* ME.
[ORIGIN from CROSS- + -WAYS.]
▸†**A** *adjective.* = CROSSWAY *adjective.* Only in ME.
▸**B** *adverb.* = CROSSWISE *adverb.* LME.

crosswise /'krɒswʌɪz/ *adverb & adjective.* LME.
[ORIGIN from CROSS- + -WISE.]
▸**A** *adverb.* **1** In the form of a cross. LME.
S. JOHNSON A church built crosswise.
2 Transversely, across. L16.
F. L. WRIGHT A tremendous spaciousness . . cut up crosswise or lengthwise.
▸**B** *adjective.* = CROSSWAY *adjective.* E20.

Crostarie /krɒs'tɑːri/ *noun. Scot.* L17.
[ORIGIN Gaelic *cros-tàraidh*, *-tàra* cross of gathering.]
= *FIERY cross.*

crostini /krɒ'stiːni/ *noun pl.* M20.
[ORIGIN Italian, pl. of *crostino* 'little crust'.]
Small pieces of toasted or fried bread served with a topping as a starter or canapé.

crotal /'krɒt(ə)l/ *noun*[1] *& adjective.* Also **crottle**. M18.
[ORIGIN Gaelic, Irish.]
(Of the golden-brown colour of) any dye-producing lichen.

crotal /'krəʊt(ə)l/ *noun*[2]. L18.
[ORIGIN Latin CROTALUM or French CROTALE.]
A usu. small bell or rattle that wholly encloses the pellet that sounds it.

crotala *noun* pl. of CROTALUM.

crotale /'krəʊt(ə)l/ *noun.* M20.
[ORIGIN French from Latin CROTALUM.]
A small tuned cymbal; a kind of castanet or clapper; a crotalum.

crotaline /'krəʊt(ə)lʌɪn/ *adjective & noun.* M19.
[ORIGIN mod. Latin *Crotalinae* (see below), from *Crotalus*, name of the genus that includes rattlesnakes, formed as CROTALUM: see -INE[1].]
▸**A** *adjective.* Of, pertaining to, or designating the viperid subfamily Crotalinae, which comprises the pit vipers and rattlesnakes. Cf. VIPERINE *adjective* 3b. M19.
▸**B** *noun.* A snake of this subfamily. Cf. VIPERINE *noun.* L19.

crotalum /'krɒt(ə)l(ə)m, 'krəʊ-/ *noun.* Pl. **-la** /-lə/. M18.
[ORIGIN Latin from Greek *krotalon.*]
An ancient clapper or castanet whose two halves were struck together with the finger and thumb.

crotch /krɒtʃ/ *noun.* M16.
[ORIGIN Perh. ult. rel. to Old French *croche* crozier, CROOK *noun*, but partly var. of CRUTCH *noun.*]
†**1** A fork used in agriculture or the garden. M–L16.
†**2** = CRUTCH *noun* 1. M–L16.
3 A support in the form of a stake or rod with a forked end. L16.
4 A fork of a tree or bough. L16.
5 The place where the legs join the trunk (of the human body or a garment). L16.
6 A fork of a river or road. Chiefly *US.* L17.
7 NAUTICAL. = CRUTCH *noun* 4. M18.
■ **crotched** *adjective* (now *US*) forked L16. **crotchless** *adjective* (of a garment) having a hole cut so as to leave the genitals uncovered L20.

crotchet /'krɒtʃɪt/ *noun*[1]. ME.
[ORIGIN Old French & mod. French *crochet* dim. of *croc* hook: see -ET[1].]
1 A hook, as an instrument or implement, or (formerly) an ornamental fastener. ME. ▸**b** A hooklike organ or process. L17.
2 ARCHITECTURE. = CROCKET 2. LME.
3 MUSIC. The symbol for a note lasting half as long as a minim and twice as long as a quaver, having a solid black head and a straight stem with no hook; a note of this length. LME.
4 A whimsical fancy; a perverse belief or preference, usu. about a trivial matter. L16.
5 A fanciful literary, artistic, or mechanical device. E17.
6 TYPOGRAPHY. A square bracket. *obsolete* exc. *hist.* L17.
■ **crotche'teer** *noun* a person with a crotchet, *esp.* one who obtrudes his or her crotchets in politics etc. E19. **crotchetiness** *noun* crotchety character M19. **crotchety** *adjective* peevish, given to crotchets; of the nature of a crotchet: E19.

†**crotchet** *noun*[2]. M17–L18.
[ORIGIN from CROTCH + -ET[1].]
= CROTCH 3.

crotchet /'krɒtʃɪt/ *verb.* Long *rare.* L16.
[ORIGIN from CROTCHET *noun*[1].]
†**1** *verb trans. & intrans.* MUSIC. Break up (a longer note) into crotchets. L16–E17.
†**2** *verb trans.* Affect with crotchets or whimsical fancies. *rare.* Only in E17.
3 *verb trans.* ARCHITECTURE. Ornament with crockets. L19.

crotey /'krəʊti/ *verb & noun.* Long *arch.* LME.
[ORIGIN App. from an Anglo-Norman & Old French verb from Old French *crote* (mod. *crotte*) dung.]
▸**A** *verb intrans. & trans.* Of a hare etc.: void (excrement). LME.
▸**B** *noun.* In *pl.* = CROTTELS. LME.

croton /'krəʊt(ə)n/ *noun*[1]. M18.
[ORIGIN Greek *krotōn* sheep tick (which the seeds of the croton, sense 1, resemble).]
1 Any plant of the genus *Croton* of the spurge family, comprising strong-scented tropical and subtropical herbs, shrubs, and trees, several of which yield economically important products (as cascarilla, croton oil). M18.
2 Any plant of the genus *Codiaeum* of the spurge family, comprising evergreen shrubs and trees from Asia; esp. *Codiaeum variegatum*, cultivated as a pot plant for its brilliant glossy leaves. L19.
– COMB.: **croton oil** an evil-smelling oil from the seeds of the E. Indian tree *Croton tiglium*, formerly used as a violent purgative.

Croton /'krəʊt(ə)n/ *noun*[2]. *US.* M19.
[ORIGIN A river near New York.]
1 In full ***Croton water***. Water, esp. (orig.) water from the Croton River, utilized from 1842 to supply New York. M19.
2 ***Croton bug***, = ***German cockroach*** s.v. GERMAN *adjective*[1]. M19.

crottels /'krɒt(ə)lz/ *noun pl.* L16.
[ORIGIN App. dim. of Old French *crot(t)e*: see CROTEY, -EL[2].]
The globular lumps of dung from hares etc.

crottin /'krɒtɛ̃/ *noun.* L20.
[ORIGIN French, lit. 'piece of horse dung'.]
A small round goat's cheese.

crottle *noun & adjective* var. of CROTAL *noun*[1] *& adjective.*

crouch /kraʊtʃ/ *noun*[1]. Long *obsolete* exc. *hist.*
[ORIGIN Old English *crūc* from Latin *cruc-*, CRUX.]
A cross. Latterly only in ***Crouchmas***, the festival of the Invention of the Cross, formerly observed on 3 May.

crouch /kraʊtʃ/ *verb & noun*[2]. LME.
[ORIGIN Perh. from Old French *crochir* be bent, from *croche* (see CROTCH).]
▸**A** *verb.* **1** *verb intrans.* Of a person: stand (or sit) low with the legs bent close to the body, as for concealment or shelter or in fear; formerly also, bend low in reverence. Of an animal: stand low with bent legs and tense body, in fear or readiness to spring. LME.
OED To *cower* concerns chiefly the head and shoulders: to *crouch* affects the body as a whole. S. BECKETT He crouched over the fire trying to get warm.
crouched burial ARCHAEOLOGY: with the body in a crouching posture, usu. on its side.
2 *verb intrans.* Behave submissively or fawningly. E16.
SIR W. SCOTT I crouch to no one—obey no one.
3 *verb trans.* Bend (the knee, one's head, etc.), esp. in a cringing way. E18.
▸**B** *noun.* **1** An act of crouching. L16.
2 A crouching posture used at the start of a race. E20.
– COMB.: **crouchback** *noun & adjective* (*obsolete* exc. *hist.*) (**a**) *noun* (a person who has) a hunched back; (**b**) *adjective* hunchbacked; **crouch start** = sense 2 above.
■ **crouchant** *adjective* crouching L16. **croucher** *noun* L16. **crouchingly** *adverb* in a crouching manner M19.

†**crouched** *adjective* see CRUTCHED *adjective*[1].

Crouch ware /'kraʊtʃ wɛː/ *noun phr.* L18.
[ORIGIN Unknown.]
Brownish salt-glazed stoneware made in Staffordshire in the early 17th cent.

croup /kruːp/ *noun*[1]. ME.
[ORIGIN Old French & mod. French *croupe* from Proto-Romance from Germanic base rel. to CROP *noun.*]
The rump, the hindquarters, esp. of a horse or other beast of burden.

croup /kruːp/ *noun*[2]. M18.
[ORIGIN from the verb.]
A harsh brassy painful cough with difficult breathing (and often stridor) in a child with severe laryngitis; any respiratory infection with this symptom.
■ **croupal**, **croupous**, **croupy** *adjectives* characteristic of or accompanied by croup; affected with croup: M19.

croup /kruːp/ *verb intrans. obsolete* exc. *dial.* E16.
[ORIGIN Imit.]
Give a hoarse cry; croak.

croupade /krʊ'peɪd/ *noun.* M17.
[ORIGIN French from Italian *groppata* (with assim. to French *croupe* CROUP *noun*[1]), from Italian *groppa* croup.]
HORSEMANSHIP. A single leap with the hind legs brought up under the belly. Also, a high kick with the hind legs with forelegs on the ground.

croupier /'kruːpɪə, -pɪeɪ/ *noun.* E18.
[ORIGIN French (orig. a person who rides behind on the croup), formed as CROUP *noun*[1]: cf. -IER.]
†**1** A person who stands behind a gambler to give support and advice. Only in E18.
2 A person who rakes in and pays out the money or tokens at a gaming table. M18.
3 An assistant chairman sitting at the lower end of the table at a public dinner. L18.

†**croupon** *noun.* LME–L18.
[ORIGIN Old French & mod. French, formed as CROUP *noun*[1]: see -OON.]
A croup; a person's buttocks; the hinder part of something; a crupper.

crouse /kruːs/ *adjective & adverb. Scot. & N. English.* ME.
[ORIGIN Prob. from Low German or Old Frisian; agrees in form with Low German, Middle Low German, Middle High German *krus* (German *kraus*) crisp, and in sense with Dutch *kroes* (from Low German) cross, annoyed, German *kraus* sullen.]
▸**A** *adjective.* **1** Touchy, overcritical. Formerly also, angry. ME.
2 Bold; forward, cocky; conceited. ME.
3 In good spirits; vivacious, lively; jolly. LME.
4 Cosy, comfortable. E19.
▸**B** *adverb.* Boldly, confidently; vivaciously. LME.
■ **crousely** *adverb* (*Scot.*) L16.

croustade /krʊ'stɑːd/ *noun.* M19.
[ORIGIN French, from Old French *crouste* (mod. CROÛTE) or Italian *crostata* tart (from *crosta* crust).]
A crisp piece of bread or pastry hollowed to receive a savoury filling.

croûte /krut/ *noun.* Pl. pronounced same. E20.
[ORIGIN French: see CRUST *noun.*]
A crisp piece of toasted or fried bread; a crouton. See also EN CROÛTE.

crouton /'kruːtɒn; krutɔ̃ (*pl. same*)/ *noun.* Also **croûton**. E19.
[ORIGIN French *croûton*, from CROÛTE.]
A small piece of toasted or fried bread served with soup or as a garnish.

crove *noun* var. of CRUIVE.

crow /krəʊ/ *noun*[1] *& adjective.* Also (*Scot. & N. English*) **craw** /krɔː, krɑː/.
[ORIGIN Old English *crāwe* corresp. to Old Saxon *krāia* (Dutch *kraai*), Old High German *krāwa*, *krāja*, *krā* (German *Krähe*), from West Germanic base of CROW *verb.*]
▸**A** *noun* **I 1** Any of various large, mostly glossy black passerine birds of the genus *Corvus* (family Corvidae), e.g. a rook, raven, or jackdaw; *esp.* (**a**) (more fully ***carrion crow***) a uniformly black bird, *Corvus corone*, of western Europe and parts of Asia; (**b**) (more fully ***hooded crow***) a subspecies of *Corvus corone* having a grey mantle and underparts, found in northern and eastern Europe and parts of Asia; (**c**) (more fully ***American crow***) the common crow of N. America, *Corvus brachyrhynchos*. Also, any bird of the family Corvidae (e.g. a magpie, chough, or jay), *esp.* a large black one. OE. ▸**b** (Usu. **C-**.) *The* constellation Corvus. M17.
Clark's crow, ***hooded crow***, ***pied crow***, ***rain crow***, ***saddleback crow***, etc. **a crow to pick**, **a crow to pluck**, **a crow to pull** something disagreeable to settle or a fault to find *with* someone. **as the crow flies** in a straight line. ***eat crow***: see EAT *verb*. ***starve the crows***: see STARVE *verb* 5. **stone the crows** expr. surprise or disgust. ***wattled crow***: see WATTLED 2. **white crow** *fig.* a rare thing or event.
2 An iron bar with a curved, usu. beaklike, end for use as a lever. Now usu. ***crowbar***. LME.
3 A grappling hook. *obsolete* exc. *hist.* M16.
4 A kind of door knocker. *obsolete* exc. *hist.* L16.
5 A person who pitches sheaves to a stacker. *NZ colloq.* L19.
6 A girl or woman, *esp.* one who is old or ugly. Also ***old crow***. *slang.* E20.
▸**II 7** (**C-**.) Pl. **-s**, same. A member of a N. American Indian people formerly occupying a region south of the Yellowstone River, Montana, and subsequently a reservation in that state; the Siouan language of this people. E19.
– COMB.: **crowbait** an old horse; old horses; **crowbar**: see sense 2 above; **crowberry** [prob. translating German *Krähenbeere*] (the usu. black flavourless berry of) a low heathlike evergreen shrub of the genus *Empetrum* (family Empetraceae); (the berry of) a small evergreen shrub of the genus *Corema* of the same family; **crow-bill** a forceps for extracting bullets etc. from wounds;

C

crow-blackbird *US* a grackle of the genus *Quiscalus*; **crow-boy**: employed to scare crows away from farmland; **croweater** *Austral. slang* a South Australian; **crow-flower** any of various wild flowers, *esp.* the buttercup; **crow garlic** a common wild garlic, *Allium vineale*; **crow-hop** *verb & noun* (*a*) *verb intrans.* hop like a crow with both feet at the same time; *US* (of a horse) jump with an arched back and stiffened legs; (*b*) *noun* a crow-hopping action; **crow quill** a quill from a crow's wing, used for fine writing; a small fine pen for map drawing etc.; **crow's nest** a lookout platform high up a ship's mast etc.; **crow step** a step of a corbie gable; **crowstepped** *adjective* having corbie steps; **crow-toe** *arch. & dial.* any of various wild flowers, *esp.* (*a*) a bluebell, (*b*) a buttercup (cf. CROWFOOT 1).

▸ **B** *adjective*. **1** MINING. Of ore, rock, etc.: of poor or impure quality. *Scot. & N. English*. L18.

2 (**C-**.) Of or pertaining to the Crows or their language. E19.

crow /krəʊ/ *noun*². Also (*Scot. & N. English*) **craw** /krɔː, krɑː/. ME.
[ORIGIN from CROW *verb*.]
A cry (as) of a crow; the joyful cry of a baby.

crow /krəʊ/ *noun*³. M17.
[ORIGIN Rel. to Middle High German (*ge*)*kroese*, *kroes* (German *Gekröse* mesentery, calf's pluck, goose's giblets), Middle Dutch *croos*, Dutch *kroost* entrails, giblets.]
The mesentery of an animal.

crow /krəʊ/ *verb intrans*. Also (*Scot. & N. English*) **craw** /krɔː, krɑː/. Pa. t. **-ed**, (esp. sense 1) **crew** /kruː/.
[ORIGIN Old English *crāwan*, corresp. to Old High German *krāen* (German *krähen*), from West Germanic verb of imit. origin.]
1 Of a cock: utter its characteristic loud shrill cry. OE.
2 Express gleeful triumph; exult loudly or prominently (*over*); swagger, boast. LME.

A. S. NEILL A public accusation might make him crow and show off what a tough guy he was. CLIVE JAMES Nor is there any reason to crow about things going wrong.

3 Give an inarticulate joyful cry. L16.

R. C. HUTCHINSON He was not one who smiled often or who crowed as other babies do.

crowd /kraʊd/ *noun*¹. ME.
[ORIGIN Welsh CRWTH.]
1 = CRWTH. *obsolete* exc. *hist*. ME.
2 A fiddle. Now *dial*. E17.

crowd /kraʊd/ *noun*². M16.
[ORIGIN from CROWD *verb*¹.]
1 A number of people gathered together so as to press upon or impede each other; any large group of people in one place, *esp.* an audience, a mass of spectators. M16. ▸**b** A group of actors representing a crowd. L19.

Independent A tear-gas grenade is highly effective at dispersing a crowd. *Chicago Tribune* They spoke before a crowd of thousands.

2 *sing.* & in *pl.* A large number *of* people or things considered collectively. E17.

J. B. PRIESTLEY The first to be swept away were the crowds of middle-men.

3 *The* multitude, *the* masses. L17.

T. GRAY Far from the madding crowd's ignoble strife.

4 A set of associates; a set, a lot. *colloq*. M19.

J. P. DONLEAVY The theatrical crowd he knocked around with.

– PHRASES: **crowd of sail** an unusual number of sails hoisted for speed. **follow the crowd** conform with the majority. **will pass in a crowd**, **would pass in a crowd** is not conspicuously below the average, esp. in appearance.

– COMB.: **crowd-pleaser**, **crowd-pleasing** *colloq.* (an event, person, or performance) having great popular appeal; **crowd-puller** *colloq.* an event, person, or thing which attracts a large audience or mass of spectators; **crowd-surf** *colloq.* be passed over the heads of the audience at a rock concert, esp. after having jumped from the stage.

crowd /kraʊd/ *verb*¹.
[ORIGIN Old English *crūdan* corresp. to Middle Low German, Middle Dutch *kruden* (Dutch *kruien* push in a wheelbarrow).]
†**1** *verb intrans.* Exert pressure. OE–ME.
2 *verb intrans.* Press on, hurry, (orig. of a ship or its crew). Now *US colloq*. OE.
3 *verb trans.* Press, push, formerly esp. in a barrow. Now *US & dial*. ME.

O. HENRY Then official duties crowded the matter from his mind.

4 *verb intrans.* Push one's way into a confined space or through a crowd. Now *rare*. LME.
5 *verb intrans.* Congregate closely so as to press upon one another; come or go (*in*, *round*, *upon*, etc.) in a crowd; flock, throng. LME.

M. SPARK The girls crowded around each other. D. MAHON Everyone Crowds to the window.

6 *verb trans.* Cram (things) *in* or *into* a small space or a short time; compress; pack closely together. L16.

LD MACAULAY The experience of years is crowded into hours.

7 *verb trans.* Press closely about; hamper by pressure of numbers; come aggressively or uncomfortably close to (a person). E17.

E. J. BANFIELD Don't crowd a fellow. Go to a rock of your own. G. BOYCOTT We crowded him with as many men as we could get near the bat.

8 *verb trans.* Fill as a crowd does, occupy densely; cram *with*, fill to excess or encumbrance *with*. E17.

A. S. NEILL The poems that crowd the average school-book. H. MACMILLAN Four days . . crowded with colour and even excitement.

9 *verb trans.* Approach (a specified age) closely. *US colloq*. M20.

– PHRASES, & WITH ADVERBS IN SPECIALIZED SENSES: **crowd on sail**, **crowd sail** hoist a large number of sails for speed. **crowd out** †(*a*) force out by pressure of a crowd; (*b*) exclude by crowding. **crowd the mourners** *US colloq.* exert undue pressure, hurry in an unseemly manner.

– NOTE: Rare before 17.

■ **crowdedness** *noun* a crowded state E19.

†**crowd** *verb*² *intrans*. ME–M18.
[ORIGIN Imit.]
Crow, croak, screech.

crowd /kraʊd/ *verb*³ *intrans. obsolete* exc. *dial*. LME.
[ORIGIN from CROWD *noun*¹.]
Play a fiddle or (formerly) a crwth.

crowder /ˈkraʊdə/ *noun*¹. ME.
[ORIGIN from CROWD *noun*¹ or *verb*³ + -ER¹.]
A player on a crwth; *dial.* a fiddler.

crowder /ˈkraʊdə/ *noun*². L16.
[ORIGIN from CROWD *verb*¹ + -ER¹.]
A person who crowds; a member of a crowd.

crowdie /ˈkraʊdi/ *noun*¹. *Scot. & N. English*. Also **-y**. E16.
[ORIGIN Unknown.]
Meal and water stirred into a thick gruel; porridge.

crowdie /ˈkraʊdi, *Scot. also* ˈkrʌdi/ *noun*². Also **-y**. E19.
[ORIGIN from CRUD *noun* + -IE.]
Soft cheese made from or with buttermilk or sour milk, orig. in Scotland.

crowdy *noun*¹, *noun*² vars. of CROWDIE *noun*¹, *noun*².

crowfoot /ˈkrəʊfʊt/ *noun*. Pl. **-feet** /-fiːt/, in sense 1 usu. **-foots**. LME.
[ORIGIN from CROW *noun*¹ + FOOT *noun*.]
1 Any of various wild flowers, *esp.* a buttercup or other member of the genus *Ranunculus*. LME.
corn crowfoot: see CORN *noun*¹. ***water crowfoot***: see WATER *noun*.
2 NAUTICAL. A number of short lines spreading from a single eye or block. L16.
3 = CROW'S FOOT 1. E17.
4 MILITARY. A caltrop. L17.
■ **crow-ˈfooted** *adjective* (*a*) *Scot.* having crow steps; (*b*) having crow's feet about the eyes: E19.

†**crowl** *verb intrans*. E16–E18.
[ORIGIN Imit.]
Of the stomach or bowels: rumble.

crown /kraʊn/ *noun*. ME.
[ORIGIN Anglo-Norman *corune*, Old French *corone* (mod. *couronne*) from Latin *corona* wreath, chaplet from Greek *korōnē* something bent (*korōnis* crown). Cf. CORONA.]
▸ **I 1** An ornamental object worn on the head by a monarch as a symbol of sovereignty and usu. made of or adorned with precious metals and jewels. ME.

J. MASEFIELD The Kings go by with jewelled crowns. AV *Matt.* 27:29 When they had platted a crowne of thornes, they put it vpon his head.

2 A (freq. idealized or imaginary) wreath or circlet worn on the head for personal adornment or as a mark of honour or victory; *transf. & fig.* any honourable distinction or reward given as a mark of honour or victory, a championship. ME.

G. B. SHAW You shall have a laurel crown of gold. Superb fighter. *Guardian* The Venezuelan . . will defend his World Boxing Association crown.

3 A chief adornment; a culminating attribute, event, etc. LME.

H. KELLER What I consider my crown of success is the happiness and pleasure that my victory has brought dear Teacher.

4 The authority symbolized by a crown; a monarch's rule or sovereignty. LME.

JOHN BROOKE The Crown suffered from the conflict between King and heir apparent.

5 ***the Crown***, the monarch in his or her official character; the supreme governing power under a monarchical constitution. L16.

L. STRACHEY The Crown intended to act independently of the Prime Minister.

DEMESNE ***of the Crown***.
▸ **II** Something having a figure of a crown.
6 An ornament, figure, or sign (esp. of an inn) having the shape of a crown or depicting a crown. ME.

S. PEPYS To the Crown . . and there supped. T. PARKER To be a sergeant major and have a crown on my sleeve.

7 Any of various coins, orig. bearing the figure of a crown; *esp.* an English or British coin of the value of 5 shillings or (now) 25 pence; a krona, krone, or koruna of some other European countries. LME.
8 (Usu. **C-**.) (More fully ***Northern Crown***) *the* constellation Corona Borealis; (more fully ***Southern Crown***) *the* constellation Corona Australis. M16.
9 A size of paper orig. watermarked with a crown (now usu. 15 × 20 inches, 381 × 508 mm). E18.
▸ **III** Something with the circular form of a crown or wreath.
†**10** A cleric's tonsure. ME–M16.
11 = CORONA 3a. M16.
12 In full ***crown glass***. Lead-free glass made from alkali-lime silicates, used as an optical glass of low dispersion and formerly for windows (orig. made in circular sheets by blowing and whirling). E18.
13 = CORONA 6. M19.
▸ **IV** The top of something.
14 The top of the head; the head itself. ME.
15 The top of a hat or cap. L15.
16 The rounded summit of a mountain, hill, or mound. L16.
17 The leafy head of a tree or shrub. L16. ▸**b** The cluster of leaves on the top of a pineapple. L17.
18 The highest, central part of an arch or arched surface, e.g. a road with a camber; the surface of a crown green. M17.
19 The flattened or rounded roof of a tent or building. E18.
20 The top, with the ear or canons, of a bell. M18.
21 The part of a tooth which projects from the gums; an artificial structure made to cover or replace this. E19.
22 The part of a root or tuber from which the stem arises; the underground bud of a herbaceous perennial. M19.
23 The part of an anchor where the shank meets the arms. M19.
24 The part of a cut gem above the girdle. L19.

– COMB. & PHRASES: **Crown Agents** a body orig. appointed by the British Government to act as commercial and financial agents in Britain for the colonies, but now offering a similar service to foreign governments and international bodies; **crown and anchor** a gambling game played with three dice each bearing a crown, an anchor, and the four card suits, and played on a board similarly marked; **crown bowler** a player of crown bowls; **crown bowling**, **crown bowls**: played on a crown green; **crown cap** a cork-lined metal cap which is crimped on to a bottle top; **Crown Colony** a British colony in which the Crown has some power of legislation or appointment; **crown cork** = ***crown cap*** above; **crown court** (*a*) *hist.* the court in which the criminal business of an assize was dealt with; (*b*) (with cap. initials) a court of criminal jurisdiction in England and Wales which replaced in 1971 the assizes and quarter sessions and sits in various towns; **Crown Derby** china made at Derby after *c* 1784 with a crown as an additional mark; **crown ether** CHEMISTRY a polyether with a large molecule that is approximately flat and circular and selectively binds metal ions; **crown fire** a forest fire that spreads from treetop to treetop; **crown gall** a bacterial disease of many plants, marked by galls on the roots and lower stem; ***crown glass***: see sense 12 above; **crown graft** a graft in which scions are inserted between the inner bark and the sapwood; **crown green** a bowling green which rises to the centre; **crown imperial** BOTANY a fritillary, *Fritillaria imperialis*, native to northern India, Pakistan, Iran, and Afghanistan, having a cluster of leaves and bell-like flowers at the top of a tall, largely bare stem; **Crown jewels** jewels forming part of royal regalia or associated with a royal house; *transf. & fig.* the most beautiful feature or possession, the most valuable asset; *slang* a man's genitals; **Crown land** land belonging to the British Crown or (in parts of the Commonwealth) the Government; **crown lens**: made of crown glass and usu. forming one component of an achromatic lens; **Crown Office** (*a*) an office of the King's or Queen's Bench (now the King's or Queen's Bench Division of the High Court) dealing with criminal and ministerial business; (*b*) part of the Central Office of the High Court (orig. an office of Chancery concerned with the sealing of certain documents); **crown of thorns (starfish)** a starfish, *Acanthaster planci*, which has spines on its upper surface and feeds on coral polyps; **crown piece** = sense 7 above; **Crown prince** [translating German *Kronprinz*, etc.] a male heir apparent to a throne; a non-reigning head of a royal house; *fig.* a likely successor in any office; **Crown princess** the wife of a crown prince; a female heir to a throne; **Crown privilege** the right of the Crown and Ministers acting on its behalf to withhold a document from court on the grounds that it is in the public interest to do so; ***Crown Prosecution Service***: see PROSECUTION 5; **crown roast** a roast of pork, lamb, or veal consisting of rib pieces arranged in a circle like a crown; **crown rot** a fungus disease of rhubarb; **crown rust** a rust affecting cereals and other grasses; **crown saw**: having teeth on the edge of a hollow cylinder; **crown vetch** a trailing plant, *Coronilla varia*, of the bean family, that has pink and white flowers, native to Europe and used for ground cover in the US; **crown-wearing** *hist.* a ceremonial appearance of a medieval monarch with his crown and regalia; **crown wheel** a gearwheel with teeth parallel to its axis, *esp.* one in the differential of a motor vehicle; ***French crown***: see FRENCH *adjective*.; ***jewel in the crown***: see JEWEL *noun* 2; ***Minister of the Crown***: see MINISTER *noun* 3a; ***naval crown***; ***obsidional crown***: see OBSIDIONAL; ***Pleas of the Crown***: see PLEA *noun*; ***triple crown***: see TRIPLE *adjective & adverb*; ***veneer crown***: see VENEER *noun* 5; ***wear a crown***: see WEAR *verb*¹.
■ **crownless** *adjective* E19. **crownlet** *noun* a little crown E19.

crown /kraʊn/ *verb*¹. ME.
[ORIGIN Anglo-Norman *coruner*, Old French *coroner* (mod. *couronner*) from Latin *coronare*, from *corona* CROWN *noun*.]
▸ **I** *verb trans.* **1** Place a crown or wreath on the head of. ME.

2 a Invest with a regal crown; officially give (a person) the dignity of a monarch etc. Also with the title as compl. ME. ▸**b** Endow with honour, dignity, plenty, or other desirable thing. Now *poet.* M16.

a E. PERRONET To crown Him Lord of All. *fig.*: AV *Ps.* 8:5 Thou . . hast crowned him with glory and honour. **b** AV *Ecclus* 19:5 He that resisteth pleasures, crowneth his life.

3 Surmount (something) *with*; occupy the top of; form a crowning ornament to. LME. ▸**b** Cover as a crown does, constitute a crown for. E17.

T. RICKMAN The walls are crowned by a parapet. E. WAUGH A brimless top-hat crowned his venerable head. S. PLATH Doctor Gordon's private hospital crowned a grassy rise. *Adweek (US)* One Florida bar is serving a shot of pepper vodka spiked with horseradish and crowned with either a clam or an oyster.

4 Fill to overflowing. L16.
5 Put the finishing touch to, complete worthily. L16.

W. IRVING A bottle of wine to crown the repast.

crown all end with something that confirms and surpasses everything previous, esp. bad luck.

6 Bring to or bless with a successful outcome; be the happy fruit of. E17.

E. PEACOCK Success did not immediately crown his efforts.

7 Adorn the surface of (something) *with* what is beautiful, rich, or splendid. L17.
8 Hit (a person) on the head. *colloq.* M18.
9 DRAUGHTS. Make (a piece) a king by placing another on top of it. M19.
10 DENTISTRY. Protect the remains of (a tooth) by fixing an artificial crown on to it. L19.
▸**II** *verb intrans.* **11** Rise to a rounded summit, arch. M18.
12 MEDICINE. Of a baby's head in labour: fully appear in the vaginal opening prior to emerging, without receding between contractions. M20.

crown /kraʊn/ *verb*² *trans. obsolete* exc. *dial.* E17.
[ORIGIN from CROWNER *noun*².]
Hold a coroner's inquest on.

crownal /ˈkraʊn(ə)l/ *noun. arch.* E16.
[ORIGIN By-form of CORONAL *noun*.]
= CORONAL *noun* 1, 2.

crownal /ˈkraʊn(ə)l/ *adjective. rare.* M16.
[ORIGIN By-form of CORONAL *adjective*.]
= CORONAL *adjective*.

crownation /kraʊˈneɪʃ(ə)n, kruː-/ *noun. obsolete* exc. *dial.* M16.
[ORIGIN By-form of CORONATION with assim. to *crown*.]
= CORONATION 1.

crowned /kraʊnd/ *adjective.* ME.
[ORIGIN from CROWN *noun*, *verb*¹: see -ED², -ED¹.]
1 That has been crowned. ME.
crowned head a king, a queen.
2 Surmounted by a crown; headed by a monarch. LME.
†**3** Consummate, perfect; sovereign. LME–M17.
4 Brimming, abundant, bounteous. Long *rare.* E17.
5 Having a crown or top (of a specified description); crested. M17.
crowned crane either of two African cranes of the genus *Balearica*, with prominent crests, *B. pavonina* of central Africa and *B. regulorum* of southern Africa; also called ***Kavirondo crane***. **crowned pigeon** each of three large pigeons with ornate crests, of the genus *Goura*, native to New Guinea and adjacent islands; also called ***goura*** (***Victoria crowned pigeon***: see VICTORIA 6).

crowner /ˈkraʊnə/ *noun*¹. LME.
[ORIGIN from CROWN *verb*¹ + -ER¹.]
1 A person who crowns someone or something. LME.
2 A thing that crowns all. *US.* E19.
3 A fall in which the head is struck. M19.

crowner /ˈkraʊnə, ˈkruː-/ *noun*². Now *arch.* & *dial.* LME.
[ORIGIN By-form of CORONER with assim. to *crown*.]
1 = CORONER 1. LME.
2 A commander of troops from a county, a colonel. *Scot. obsolete* exc. *hist.* L16.

†**crownet** *noun.* LME.
[ORIGIN By-form of CORONET *noun*, CRONET.]
1 = CORONET *noun* 1, 2. LME–M19.
2 = CORONET *noun* 4. E17–E18.

crowning /ˈkraʊnɪŋ/ *adjective.* E17.
[ORIGIN from CROWN *verb*¹ + -ING².]
1 That crowns, that bestows a crown. *rare.* E17.
2 Forming the crown or acme; consummating; highest, most perfect. M17.
crowning glory the most beautiful feature or possession, the greatest achievement; *spec.* a woman's hair.

crow's foot /ˈkrəʊzfʊt/ *noun.* Also **crowsfoot**. Pl. **-feet** /-fiːt/. LME.
[ORIGIN from CROW *noun*¹ + -'S¹ + FOOT *noun*.]
1 A small wrinkle at the outer corner of the eye. Usu. in *pl.* LME.
†**2** NAUTICAL. = CROWFOOT 2. E17–E19.
3 MILITARY. A caltrop, = CROWFOOT 4. M17.
4 In *pl.* Numerous small creases or wrinkles in a fabric. M20.

■ **crow's-footed** *adjective* having crow's feet about the eyes M19.

†**croy** *noun* var. of CRUE.

croze /krəʊz/ *noun.* E17.
[ORIGIN Perh. from French *creux*, *creuse*, Old French *crues*, *cros* hollow.]
1 A groove in the end of a stave of a cask to receive the edge of the head. E17.
2 A cooper's tool for making such grooves. M19.

croze /krəʊz/ *verb trans.* M19.
[ORIGIN from CROZE *noun* or French *creuser*, Old French *croser* hollow out, formed as CROZE *noun*.]
Make a croze in.

crozier /ˈkrəʊzɪə, -ʒə/ *noun.* Also **-s-**. ME.
[ORIGIN Partly from Old French *croisier* (medieval Latin *cruciarius*) cross-bearer, from *crois* CROSS *noun*; partly from Old French *crocier*, *crossier* bearer of a bishop's crook, from *croce* (mod. *crosse*) from Germanic base also of CRUTCH *noun*: see -IER.]
▸**I 1** A person who bears a processional cross in front of an archbishop. Now *hist.* ME.
†**2** The bearer of a bishop's crook. LME–M16.
3 = CROOK *noun* 3. E16.
4 An archbishop's processional cross. E18.
▸**II** †**5** The constellation of the Southern Cross; in *pl.*, its four chief stars. M16–E18.
6 The curled tip of a young fern. L19.
■ **croziered** *adjective* E18.

CRT *abbreviation.*
Cathode-ray tube.

cru /kry (*pl. same*), kruː/ *noun* & *adjective.* Also **crû**. E19.
[ORIGIN French, from *crû* pa. pple of *croître* grow.]
(The grade or quality of wine produced in) a French vineyard or wine-producing region; (designating) French wine of a specified quality.

P. V. PRICE Just below the classed growths come the *crus bourgeois* . . then the *crus artisans*.

cru classé /klase, ˈklaseɪ/, pl. **-s -s** (pronounced same) [= classified] = ***classed growth*** s.v. CLASS *verb* 3. ***grand cru*** /grɑ̃, grand/ (pl. ***grands crus*** /grɑ̃ kry/, ***grand crus*** /grand ˈkruːz/) [= great] (designating) a wine of superior quality. PREMIER CRU.

crub /krʌb/ *noun.* Long *obsolete* exc. *dial.* M16.
[ORIGIN Metath. var.]
= CURB *noun*.

crubeen /krʊˈbiːn, ˈkruːbiːn/ *noun. Irish.* M19.
[ORIGIN Irish *crúibín* dim. of *crúb* claw, hoof, paw.]
The foot of an animal; *esp.* a (cooked) pig's trotter.

cruces *noun pl.* see CRUX.

cruche /kruːʃ/ *noun.* M19.
[ORIGIN French = pitcher.]
= CRUSE.

crucial /ˈkruːʃ(ə)l/ *adjective.* E18.
[ORIGIN French, from Latin *cruc-*, *crux* cross: see -IAL. In sense 2 from *instantia crucis* (Bacon) crucial instance.]
1 Chiefly ANATOMY. Of the form of a cross, cruciate. Now *rare.* E18.
2 That finally decides between hypotheses; relating or leading to decision between hypotheses; decisive; critical; *colloq.* very important. M19. ▸**b** Excellent. *slang.* L20.

J. MARTINEAU Crucial experiments for the verification . . of his theory. DAY LEWIS The most crucial and agonising decisions I have been faced with have arisen from personal relationships. G. GORDON Did it encourage their secretaries and junior executives to feel they belonged to some crucial organization?

■ **cruciˈality** *noun* M20. **crucially** *adverb* L19. **crucialness** *noun* L20.

crucian /ˈkruːʃ(ə)n/ *noun.* M18.
[ORIGIN from alt. of Low German *karus(s)e*, *karutze* (German *Karausche*) ult. formed as CORACINE: see -AN.]
More fully ***crucian carp***. A European cyprinid fish, *Carassius carassius*, with an olive green or reddish-brown back, paler sides, and bright reddish-bronze fins.

†**cruciat** *noun* see CRUSADE *noun*.

cruciate /ˈkruːʃɪət, -eɪt/ *noun* & *adjective.* L17.
[ORIGIN medieval Latin *cruciatus*, from Latin *cruc-*, *crux* cross: see -ATE².]
ANATOMY, BOTANY, & ZOOLOGY. ▸**A** *noun.* †**1** A cross-shaped incision. Only in L17.
2 A cruciate ligament. L20.
▸**B** *adjective.* Cross-shaped; in the form of a cross. E19.
cruciate ligament either of two ligaments in the knee joint which cross each other and connect the femur and tibia.

cruciate /ˈkruːʃɪeɪt/ *verb trans. arch.* Pa. pple †**-ate** (earlier), **-ated**. LME.
[ORIGIN Orig. pa. pple, from Latin *cruciatus* pa. pple of *cruciare* torture, from *cruc-*, *crux* cross: see -ATE³. Sense 2 is from ecclesiastical Latin.]
1 Torture; torment; excruciate. LME.
†**2** Crucify. M16–M17.

cruciation /kruːʃɪˈeɪʃ(ə)n/ *noun.* Long *rare.* LME.
[ORIGIN Old French, or ecclesiastical Latin *cruciatio(n-)*, formed as CRUCIATE *verb*: see -ATION.]
Torture; torment.

crucible /ˈkruːsɪb(ə)l/ *noun* & *verb.* LME.
[ORIGIN medieval Latin *crucibulum* night lamp, crucible, from Latin *cruc-*, *crux* cross.]
▸**A** *noun.* **1** A pot, usu. of earthenware, for melting metals etc. LME. ▸**b** A hollow or basin for collecting molten metal etc. at the bottom of a furnace. M19.
2 *fig.* A place or occasion of severe test or trial. M17.
▸**B** *verb trans.* Put into or melt in a crucible. *rare.* L18.

crucifer /ˈkruːsɪfə/ *noun.* M16.
[ORIGIN Christian Latin, from Latin *cruc-*, *crux* cross: see -FER.]
1 ECCLESIASTICAL. A cross-bearer in processions. M16.
2 BOTANY. A cruciferous plant. M19.

cruciferous /kruːˈsɪf(ə)rəs/ *adjective.* M17.
[ORIGIN formed as CRUCIFER + -OUS.]
1 Bearing, wearing, or adorned with a cross. M17.
2 BOTANY. Of, pertaining to, or characteristic of the family Cruciferae, which comprises plants having flowers with four equal petals arranged crosswise (as cabbage, mustard, cress, stock, etc.). M19.

crucified /ˈkruːsɪfʌɪd/ *adjective* & *noun.* ME.
[ORIGIN from CRUCIFY + -ED¹.]
▸**A** *adjective.* That has been crucified; nailed or otherwise fastened to a cross. ME.
▸**B** *noun.* ***the Crucified***, Jesus Christ. M16.

crucifix /ˈkruːsɪfɪks/ *noun.* ME.
[ORIGIN Old French & mod. French from ecclesiastical Latin *crucifixus* from Latin *cruci fixus* fixed to a cross: cf. CRUCIFY.]
†**1** ***the crucifix***, Jesus on the Cross. ME–M17.
2 A model, figure, or image of (Jesus on) the Cross. ME.
3 GYMNASTICS. A position in exercises on parallel rings, in which the body is held rigid with arms stretched horizontally. M20.

crucifixion /kruːsɪˈfɪkʃ(ə)n/ *noun.* LME.
[ORIGIN ecclesiastical Latin *crucifixio(n-)*, from *crucifix-* pa. ppl stem of *crucifigere* CRUCIFY: see -ION.]
1 The action or an act of crucifying or putting to death on a cross; *spec.* (**C-**) the crucifying of Jesus. LME. ▸**b** A picture or other representation of the Crucifixion of Jesus. M19.
2 The action or an act of crucifying or mortifying passions, sins, the flesh, etc. E18.

cruciform /ˈkruːsɪfɔːm/ *adjective.* M17.
[ORIGIN from Latin *cruc-*, *crux* cross + -I- + -FORM.]
Cross-shaped; in the form of a cross.

A. W. CLAPHAM These . . churches . . show a highly developed plan which is sometimes cruciform.

crucify /ˈkruːsɪfʌɪ/ *verb trans.* ME.
[ORIGIN Old French & mod. French *crucifier* from Proto-Romance alt. of ecclesiastical Latin *crucifigere*, from Latin *cruci figere* fix to a cross: see CRUX, FIX *verb*.]
1 Put to death by nailing or otherwise fastening to a cross (an ancient mode of capital punishment, considered by the Greeks and Romans to be especially ignominious). ME.
2 Mortify, destroy the power of, (passions, sins, the flesh, etc.). ME.
3 Cause extreme mental or (now less commonly) physical pain to; torment; persecute. E17.

H. ROBBINS Somebody has to be held up before the stockholders and crucified so that they can say: 'See, it was all his fault. He was to blame!' *Listener* He would be severely beaten up, then subjected to some crucifying punishment and, if that did not teach him, very probably executed.

■ **crucifier** *noun* ME.

cruciverbalist /kruːsɪˈvəːb(ə)lɪst/ *noun.* L20.
[ORIGIN from Latin *crucis*, *crux* cross + *verbum* word: see VERBALIST.]
An enthusiast for crossword puzzles; a compiler or solver of crossword puzzles.

cruck /krʌk/ *noun.* Also (now *dial.*) **crock** /krɒk/. L16.
[ORIGIN Prob. var. of CROOK *noun*.]
Either of a pair of curved timbers, forming with other pairs the framework of a house.

crud /krʌd/ *noun.* Also (*US slang*) **crut** /krʌt/. LME.
[ORIGIN Earlier form of CURD *noun*.]
▸**I 1** See CURD *noun.* LME.
▸**II 2** Filth, excrement; undesirable foreign matter; *fig.* nonsense, rubbish. *colloq.* (orig. *US*). M20.
3 Disease, *esp.* venereal or skin disease; any horrible disease. *slang* (orig. *US military slang*). M20.
4 A despicable or undesirable person or thing. *slang* (orig. *US*). M20.

crud *verb* see CURD *verb*.

crudded *adjective* see CURDED.

cruddle *verb* see CURDLE *verb*.

cruddy /ˈkrʌdi/ *adjective.* LME.
[ORIGIN Earlier form of CURDY *adjective*.]
1 See CURDY *adjective.* LME.
2 Filthy, dirty; unpleasant, unsavoury. *slang* (orig. *US*). M20.

crude /kruːd/ *adjective* & *noun.* LME.
[ORIGIN Latin *crudus* raw, rough, cruel.]
▸**A** *adjective* **I 1** In the natural or raw state; not changed by any process or preparation; not manufactured, refined, tempered, etc. LME. ▸†**b** *spec.* Of food: uncooked.

M16–L18. ▸**c** Designating the insoluble fibre left when vegetable matter is boiled alternately in dilute acids and alkalis, corresponding roughly to its indigestible part. L19.

G. RAWLINSON Sometimes the crude and the burnt brick were used in alternate layers.

crude oil (an) unrefined petroleum. ***crude turpentine***: see TURPENTINE *noun* 1.

2 Of bodily humours, secretions, etc.: not pure, unnatural, morbid. Of food in the stomach: undigested, not fully digested. *arch.* LME. ▸†**b** Characterized by or affected with indigestion. Only in 17.

3 Of fruit: unripe; sour. *arch.* M16.

4 Of a disease etc.: in an early or undeveloped stage. Now *rare* or *obsolete*. M17.

▸ **II** *fig.* **5** Not completely thought out or worked up; lacking finish or maturity of treatment; roughly or inexpertly planned, executed, or made. E17.

DISRAELI The crude opinions of an unpractised man. J. M. MURRY A fair example of Keats' poetry at the beginning of the four years—crude and naïve, but spontaneous in feeling. C. G. SELIGMAN Their dwellings are crude semi-circular shelters of branches.

6 Rude, blunt, rough; unrefined; lacking subtlety or sophistication; unmitigated; brutally plain; characterized by coarseness of thought, feeling, action, or character. M17.

R. LYND The humour was crude; but it went home to the honest Victorian heart. C. BROWN I knew I was kind of crude, right off the streets of Harlem. ANNE STEVENSON Windless gardens / walled to protect eccentric vegetation / from a crude climate.

7 GRAMMAR. (Of a word) uninflected; being or forming the base or stem which undergoes inflection. Now *rare* or *obsolete*. E19.

8 STATISTICS. Unadjusted; not corrected by reference to modifying circumstances. L19.

▸ **B** *noun*. (A) crude oil. L19.

■ **crudely** *adverb* M17. **crudeness** *noun* M16.

†crudelity *noun*. LME–E18.
[ORIGIN Old French *crudelitie* or Latin *crudelitas* CRUELTY.]
= CRUELTY.

crudify /ˈkruːdɪfʌɪ/ *verb trans*. L19.
[ORIGIN from CRUDE *adjective* + -FY.]
Make (more) crude.
■ **crudifiˈcation** *noun* E20.

crudités /ˈkruːdɪteɪ, *foreign* krydite/ *noun pl*. M20.
[ORIGIN French: see CRUDITY.]
Mixed raw vegetables as an hors d'oeuvre.

crudity /ˈkruːdɪti/ *noun*. LME.
[ORIGIN Old French & mod. French *crudité* or Latin *cruditas*, from *crudus*: see CRUDE, -ITY.]
▸ **I 1** Impurity, unnaturalness, or morbidity of bodily humours, secretions, etc.; in *pl.*, impure etc. bodily humours. Also, the state of being undigested or indigestible in the stomach; undigested or indigestible matter; indigestion. *arch.* LME.

2 The state or quality of being raw, unprocessed, unrefined, untempered, etc., or (*arch.*) unripe or sour; an instance of this; in *pl.* also, raw or (*arch.*) unripe products or substances. E17.

3 The early or undeveloped stage of a disease etc. Now *rare* or *obsolete*. E18.

▸ **II** *fig.* **4** A crude idea, statement, literary work, etc.; the state or quality of being crude in planning, execution, thought, expression, action, etc. M17.

ADDISON This Author, in the last of his Crudities, has amassed together a Heap of Quotations. G. B. SHAW Beside themselves by the crudity of his notions of government.

crue /kruː/ *noun*. *Scot. & dial.* Also **crew**, **croo**, **†cro(y)**. ME.
[ORIGIN Gaelic *crò*, Irish *cró* sheepfold, pen.]
1 = CRUIVE 1. ME.
2 A dam or other structure to protect a riverbank. *Scot.* E16.
3 = CRUIVE 2, 3. M16.

cruel /krʊəl/ *adjective, noun, adverb, & verb*. ME.
[ORIGIN Old French & mod. French from Latin *crudelis* rel. to *crudus*: see CRUDE.]
▸ **A** *adjective*. Compar. **-l(l)er**, superl. **-l(l)est**.
1 Disposed to inflict suffering; having or showing indifference to or pleasure in another's pain; merciless; pitiless; hard-hearted. ME.

S. JOHNSON The meanest and cruelest of human beings. H. JAMES It was cruel to bewilder her. E. O'BRIEN I could feel her cruel eyes on me.

2 Painful; distressing; *colloq.* difficult to bear, hard. ME.

SWIFT I have got a cruel cold, and staid within all this day. A. N. WILSON She had died . . with cruel and unannounced suddenness.

†3 Fierce; savage. ME–L17.
†4 Severe; strict; rigorous. ME–L17.
▸ **B** *absol.* as *noun*. A cruel person. Now *arch. & poet.* LME.

POPE Canst thou, oh cruel, unconcerned survey Thy lost Ulysses on this signal day?

▸ **C** *adverb*. Cruelly; distressingly; exceedingly, very. *obsolete* exc. *dial.* L16.
▸ **D** *verb trans.* Infl. **-l(l)-**. Spoil; destroy all chance of success with. *Austral. slang.* L19.
■ **cruellie** *noun* (*colloq.*) a cruel joke, remark, comment, etc. M20. **cruelly** *adverb* in a cruel manner; to a cruel degree; excessively: ME. **cruelness** *noun* (*rare*) ME.

cruelty /ˈkrʊəlti/ *noun*. ME.
[ORIGIN Old French *crualté* (mod. *cruauté*) from Proto-Romance var. of Latin *crudelitas*, from *crudelis*: see CRUEL, -ITY.]
1 The quality of being cruel, disposition to inflict suffering, delight in or indifference to another's pain, mercilessness, pitilessness, hard-heartedness, esp. as exhibited in action. Also, an instance of this. ME.
mental cruelty: see MENTAL *adjective*[1]. ***Theatre of Cruelty***: see THEATRE *noun*.
†2 Severity (of pain); strictness; rigour. ME–M17.
– COMB.: **cruelty man** *colloq.* an officer of the National Society for the Prevention of Cruelty to Children, the Royal Society for the Prevention of Cruelty to Animals, or a similar organization.

†cruentous *adjective*. *rare*. M17–L19.
[ORIGIN from Latin *cruentus* bloody + -OUS.]
Bloody, mixed with blood.

cruet /ˈkruːɪt/ *noun*. ME.
[ORIGIN Anglo-Norman dim. of Old French *crue* from Old Saxon *krūka* (Dutch *kruik*) = Old English *crūce*, Middle High German *krūche* (German *Krauche*) rel. to CROCK *noun*[1].]
1 ECCLESIASTICAL. A small vessel to hold wine or water for use in the celebration of the Eucharist etc. ME.
2 Formerly, any small bottle or vial for liquids. Now *spec.* a small stoppered glass bottle etc. for vinegar, oil, etc., for the table; (in extended use) a caster for holding salt, pepper, etc. (usu. in *pl.*, such casters with or without a vinegar bottle etc.); also, (in full ***cruet-stand***) a stand for cruets. LME.

T. PYNCHON Tall cruets of pale banana syrup to pour oozing over banana waffles.

cruise /kruːz/ *noun*. E18.
[ORIGIN from the verb.]
1 A voyage in which a ship sails to and fro over a particular region, esp. for the protection of shipping or for pleasure; a sail for pleasure with no particular destination or calling at a series of places. E18.
2 *transf.* A similar journey by land or air; a journey, or part of a journey, at cruising speed. M18.
3 FORESTRY. A survey or estimate of the amount of timber in a particular area. Chiefly *US*. E20.
4 In full ***cruise missile***. A low-flying missile carrying a warhead, which is guided continuously to its target by computer. M20.
– COMB.: **cruise control** (a device providing) the facility for maintaining a motor vehicle at a predetermined constant speed without use of the accelerator pedal; **cruise liner** a liner designed for holiday cruises; ***cruise missile***: see sense 4 above; **cruise ship** = ***cruise liner*** above; **cruiseway** an inland waterway intended chiefly for pleasure cruising; **cruisewear** clothes suitable for wearing on a holiday cruise.

cruise /kruːz/ *verb*. M17.
[ORIGIN Prob. from Dutch *kruisen* to cross, from *kruis* CROSS *noun*.]
1 *verb intrans. & trans.* Sail to and fro (over), esp. for the protection of shipping or for pleasure; sail for pleasure making for no particular place or calling at a series of places. M17.

J. CONRAD The *Amelia* was cruising off the peninsula. *Nature* He cruised the waters of Newfoundland and Northern Labrador in a small sailboat and in a kayak . . on vacations with his family.

2 *verb intrans. & trans. transf.* Walk or travel about making for no particular place or calling at a series of places (in); *esp.* (of a vehicle or driver) drive around at random, esp. slowly when patrolling, looking for passengers, etc.; walk or drive around looking for amusement, a sexual partner, etc. L17.

A. HAILEY She continued to cruise the district in her sports convertible. H. CARPENTER The habit of 'cruising'—picking up boys for casual sex. *Times* As the taxi drivers cruise Islamic streets, they listen to cassettes of the latest American disco hits.

3 *verb intrans. & trans.* FORESTRY. Search (forest land) for saleable timber; search for (such timber). (Earlier in CRUISER 2.) Chiefly *US*. E20.
4 *verb intrans.* (Of an aircraft, motor vehicle, etc.) travel comfortably and economically at less than top speed; *transf. & fig.* move at a comfortable speed, progress easily. E20.

C. A. LINDBERGH If the *Spirit of St. Louis* can cruise at 1750 r.p.m. with this load, I have *more* than enough fuel to reach Paris. *Which?* Even on motorways they will cruise happily at 70 mph. *Times* Prideaux Boy cruised up to the leaders on the home turn.

– COMB.: **cruising radius**, **cruising range** the maximum distance that the fuel capacity of a ship or aircraft will allow it to travel and return at cruising speed; **cruising speed** the best economic travelling speed for a ship, aircraft, or vehicle.

cruiser /ˈkruːzə/ *noun*. L17.
[ORIGIN Dutch *kruiser*, from *kruisen*: see CRUISE *verb*.]
1 A ship that cruises, formerly *esp.* a privateer. Now, a high-speed warship less heavily armed than a battleship. L17. ▸**b** A yacht constructed or adapted for cruising; a motor vessel designed for pleasure cruises. L19.
battlecruiser: see BATTLE *noun*. **b *cabin cruiser***: see CABIN *noun*. ***THROUGH-DECK cruiser***.
2 FORESTRY. **a** A person who searches forest land for saleable timber. Chiefly *US*. L19. ▸**b** A long-legged boot of a type worn by cruisers for timber. *US*. E20.
3 In some science fiction: an aircraft, a spacecraft. E20.
4 A police patrol car. *N. Amer.* E20.
5 A person who walks or drives around looking for amusement, a sexual partner, etc. E20.
6 A person sailing on a pleasure cruise. M20.
– COMB.: **cruiserweight** (of) a boxing weight, equivalent to light heavyweight; (a boxer) of this weight.

cruisie *noun* var. of CRUSIE.

cruiskeen /ˈkruːʃkiːn/ *noun*. *Irish*. M19.
[ORIGIN Irish *crúiscín*.]
A small jug.

cruive /kruːv/ *noun*. Orig. & chiefly *Scot.* Also **croove**; **crove** /krəʊv/. ME.
[ORIGIN Prob. from CRUE with parasitic *v*, but cf. CORF.]
1 A coop of wickerwork or spars placed in tideways etc. to trap salmon or other fish. ME.
2 A hovel, a hut, a cabin. *Scot.* L15.
3 A pen for livestock; *esp.* a pigsty. *Scot.* L16.

†crull *adjective*. Only in ME.
[ORIGIN Middle Dutch *krul* rel. to Middle Low German *krus* crisp, curly.]
Curly.

†crulled *adjective* see CURLED.

cruller /ˈkrʌlə/ *noun*. *N. Amer.* E19.
[ORIGIN Dutch *kruller*, from *krullen* to curl.]
A small cake made of dough containing eggs, butter, sugar, etc., twisted or curled and deep-fried until crisp.

crum *noun*[1] & *verb*[1] see CRUMB *noun & verb*[1].

crum *noun*[2] see CRUMBS.

crum /krʌm/ *adjective & verb*[2] *trans.* Long *obsolete* exc. *Scot. & N. English*. Infl. **-mm-**. Also **crumb**.
[ORIGIN Old English *crumb* = Old Frisian, Old Saxon *krumb*, Old High German *krump*, *krumb-* (German *krumm*), from West Germanic var. of base of CRAMP *noun*[1].]
(Make) crooked or curved.

crumb /krʌm/ *noun & verb*[1]. Also (earlier, now *rare*) **crum** (verb infl. **-mm-**).
[ORIGIN Old English *cruma* = Middle Dutch *crūme* (Dutch *kruim*), Middle Low German, Middle Dutch *crōme*, Middle High German, German *Krume*. The parasitic *b* appears in 16: cf. *dumb*, *thumb*.]
▸ **A** *noun*. **1** A small particle; *esp.* a small fragment of bread, cake, etc., such as breaks off by rubbing etc. OE. ▸**b** In soil, a more or less spheroidal compound particle. Cf. ***crumb structure*** below. E20. ▸**c** In rayon manufacture, a particle of cellulose. E20.

J. FOWLES He brings me food, but I have touched *not one crumb*.

gather up one's crumbs, **pick up one's crumbs** (*obsolete* exc. *dial.*) recover strength or health; improve in condition.
2 The soft inner part of (a loaf, roll, or slice of) bread. LME.
3 *fig.* A very small particle or portion of something abstract; an atom; a scrap. (Foll. by *of*.) M16.

T. D'URFEY To beg Some Crumbs of Comfort.

4 A body louse. *US slang*. M19. ▸**b** A lousy or filthy person; an objectionable, worthless, or insignificant person. *slang* (orig. *US*). E20.

b H. M. RIDEOUT A couple of crumbs want to kill you.

– COMB.: **crumb-bum** *slang* = sense 4b above; **crumb structure** the (porous) structure or condition of soil when its particles are largely aggregated into crumbs (sense 1b).
▸ **B** *verb*. **1** *verb trans.* Break into crumbs or small fragments. LME.

H. JAMES The way he crumbed up his bread.

†2 *verb intrans.* Fall into crumbs; crumble. M16–E19.
3 *verb trans.* Thicken or cover with crumbs. L16.

BUNYAN A Dish of Milk well Crumbed.

■ **crumblet** *noun* (*rare*) a little crumb E17.

crumb *adjective & verb*[2] var. of CRUM *adjective & verb*[2].

crumble /ˈkrʌmb(ə)l/ *verb & noun*. Also **†crim-**. LME.
[ORIGIN Prob. repr. an Old English verb, ult. from same Germanic base as CRUMB *noun*: see -LE[3].]
▸ **A** *verb trans. & intrans.* Break or fall into crumbs, particles, or fragments, (*lit.* & *fig.*); disintegrate; (cause to) go to pieces. LME.

EVELYN Marbles with their deepest inscriptions crumble away. D. C. PEATTIE The termites live on the Joshua tree, . . crumbling the fortress from within. G. SWIFT My father did not crumble at my mother's death.

the way the cookie crumbles: see COOKIE *noun*[1] 1.
▸ **B** *noun*. **1** A crumb, a particle, a fragment. *rare*. L16.

2 Crumbly or crumbled substance. *rare* in *gen.* sense. M19.
3 Flour, fat, and sugar etc. mixed to a crumbly consistency, usu. topping cooked fruit; a dish of this. M20.
■ **crumbling** *noun* (*a*) the action of the verb; (*b*) in *pl.*, crumbled particles, debris: M17.

crumbly /ˈkrʌmbli/ *adjective & noun*. As noun also **crumblie**. E16.
[ORIGIN Orig. from CRUMB *noun* + -LY¹; later from CRUMBLE *verb* + -Y¹.]
▸ **A** *adjective*. †**1** Consisting of crumbs; crumbed. E16–E17.
2 Liable to crumble, friable. M18.
▸ **B** *noun*. A person considered very old or senile, esp. by teenagers. Cf. WRINKLY *noun*. *slang* (*derog.*). L20.
■ **crumbliness** *noun* E19.

crumbs /krʌmz/ *noun & interjection*. Also **crums**; (as noun) **crum**. L19.
[ORIGIN Alt. of CHRIST.]
▸ **A** *noun*. ***by crumbs***, = sense B. below. L19.
▸ **B** *interjection*. Expr. astonishment, consternation, or dismay. L19.

crumby /ˈkrʌmi/ *adjective*. Also (earlier, now freq. in sense 4) **crummy**. M16.
[ORIGIN from CRUMB *noun* + -Y¹.]
†**1** Crumbly. M16–E18.
2 **a** Of the nature of the crumb of bread. L16. ▸**b** Full of crumbs; scattered or covered with crumbs. M18.
3 Plump; comely; rich. *arch. slang*. E18.
4 Inferior, shoddy, of poor quality; filthy, dirty, untidy. *colloq.* M19.

Variety A crummy flat on the top floor of an abandoned building. N. WHITTAKER It turned out to be just another crummy job.

■ **crumbiness**, **crumminess** *nouns* M20.

crumen /ˈkruːmɛn/ *noun*. L19.
[ORIGIN Latin *crumena* purse.]
ZOOLOGY. The suborbital gland in certain deer and antelopes, which secretes a waxy substance.

crumhorn *noun* var. of KRUMMHORN.

crummie /ˈkrʌmi/ *noun*. *Scot. & N. English*. Also **-y**. E18.
[ORIGIN from CRUM *adjective* + -IE, -Y⁶.]
A cow with crooked horns; (a name for) any cow.

crummy /ˈkrʌmi/ *noun*¹. *N. Amer. slang*. E20.
[ORIGIN from CRUMBY *adjective*.]
= CABOOSE 3. Also, an old or converted vehicle for transporting workmen etc.

crummy *noun*² var. of CRUMMIE.

crummy *adjective* see CRUMBY.

†**crump** *noun*¹. M17.
[ORIGIN from CRUMP *adjective*¹.]
1 A hump on the back. *rare*. Only in M17.
2 A humpbacked person. L17–M18.

crump /krʌmp/ *noun*². M19.
[ORIGIN from CRUMP *verb*².]
1 A hard abrupt hit. *colloq. & dial.* M19.
2 (The sound of) the explosion of a heavy shell or bomb; a shell or bomb that explodes heavily. *military slang*. E20.
3 A violent burst in the floor, walls, or ceiling of a mine. E20.

crump /krʌmp/ *adjective*¹. *obsolete* exc. *dial.*
[ORIGIN Old English *crump* (= Old High German *krumpf*) by-form, prob. intensive, of *crumb* CRUM *adjective*.]
Esp. of the body: crooked.

crump /krʌmp/ *adjective*². *Scot. & N. English*. L18.
[ORIGIN By-form of CRIMP *adjective*.]
= CRIMP *adjective* 1.

crump /krʌmp/ *verb*¹ *intrans. & trans. obsolete* exc. *dial.* ME.
[ORIGIN from CRUMP *adjective*¹. Cf. CRIMP *verb*¹.]
Bend into a curve; crook; curl up.

crump /krʌmp/ *verb*². M17.
[ORIGIN Imit.]
1 *verb trans. & intrans.* Esp. of a horse or pig: eat with a muffled crunch. M17.
2 *verb intrans.* Of snow, snow-covered ground: crunch dully under the feet. L18.
3 *verb trans. & intrans.* Chiefly CRICKET. Strike hard and abruptly. L19.
4 *military slang*. **a** *verb trans. & intrans.* Bombard with or fire heavy shells or bombs. E20. ▸**b** *verb intrans.* Explode with a crump. E20.
■ **crumper** *noun* (*colloq. & dial.*) a large heavy person or thing; a large specimen of its kind: M19.

crumpet /ˈkrʌmpɪt/ *noun*. L17.
[ORIGIN Uncertain: perh. connected with *crumb* CRUM *verb*².]
†**1** A thin griddle cake. L17–M19.
2 A soft cake made with flour and yeast and cooked on a griddle or other hot surface, now usu. of a type intended for toasting and eating with butter etc. M18.
3 The head. Esp. in ***barmy in the crumpet***, ***barmy on the crumpet***, wrong in the head, mad. *slang*. L19.
4 ***old crumpet***: used as a familiar form of address. *slang*. E20.
5 Sexually attractive women collectively; sexual intercourse with a woman. *colloq.* M20.
bit of crumpet, **piece of crumpet** a (desirable) woman.

crumple /ˈkrʌmp(ə)l/ *noun*. L16.
[ORIGIN from the verb. Cf. CRIMPLE *noun*.]
A crushed fold, a wrinkle.

†**crumple** *adjective* (*attrib.*). ME–M19.
[ORIGIN from the verb.]
Crumpled. Usu. in *comb.*, as ***crumple-horned*** *adjective*.

crumple /ˈkrʌmp(ə)l/ *verb*. ME.
[ORIGIN from CRUMP *verb*¹ or *adjective*¹ + -LE³. Cf. CRIMPLE *verb*.]
▸ **I** *verb trans.* **1** Make crooked, bend together, contort, now esp. by crushing. ME.
2 Crush into irregular creases; crush together or *up* into a creased state; ruffle, wrinkle, crinkle. M16.

LYTTON Don't crumple that scarf. M. SHADBOLT To crumple the page into a ball and throw it away.

3 *fig.* Cause to collapse or give way; deprive of strength or energy. Also foll. by *up*. M19.

R. KIPLING For the sickness gets in as the liquor dies out, An' it crumples the young British soldier.

▸ **II** *verb intrans.* **4** Shrivel up or *up*; become crooked or bent together, now esp. by crushing; become creased, wrinkle, crinkle. LME.
5 *fig.* Collapse, give way; lose strength or energy. Also foll. by *up*. L19.
– COMB.: **crumple zone** an area of a motor vehicle designed to crumple and absorb impact.
■ **crumpled** *adjective* that has been crumpled; *spec.* (of the horns of cattle) bent spirally, curly: ME. **crumpler** *noun* (*a*) a person who or thing which causes crumpling; (*b*) a fall by a horse and rider in which both are doubled up: M19. **crumply** *adjective* M19.

crums *noun & interjection* var. of CRUMBS.

crunch /krʌn(t)ʃ/ *noun & adjective*. M19.
[ORIGIN from the verb.]
▸ **A** *noun*. **1** An act or the action of crunching; a crunching sound. M19.

E. K. KANE Listening to the half-yielding crunch of the ice. S. W. BAKER The hippo . . killed him by one crunch.

2 A crisis; a crucial moment; a decisive event; a showdown. Also, the main problem, a sticking point. M20.

W. S. CHURCHILL At the crunch he was sure he could count on his influence. J. I. M. STEWART Wouldn't Tony, in a crunch, do as you tell him? *Irish Times* The real crunch—a problem which can be solved only through pragmatic global politics.

when it comes to the crunch, **when the crunch comes** when it comes to the point, in a showdown.
▸ **B** *attrib.* or as *adjective*. Critical, decisive, crucial. L20.

G. BOYCOTT The crunch period was approaching fast; at lunch there were only eleven overs to go before the new ball was due. R. D. LAING The first, decisive, crunch decision.

crunch /krʌn(t)ʃ/ *verb*. E19.
[ORIGIN Var. of CRANCH *verb* with assim. to *munch*, *crush*.]
1 *verb trans. & intrans.* Crush with the teeth, esp. noisily; chew or bite with a crushing noise. E19.

H. WILLIAMSON She ate her prey, holding it in her fore-paws and crunching with her head on one side. L. GOULD He reads the paper and crunches his toast.

number-crunch: see NUMBER *noun*.
2 *verb intrans.* Make or move with a crunching sound; be crushed or ground under foot etc. with a crunching sound. E19.

D. WELCH The cinders crunched under our feet. W. PLOMER We crunched over the gravel path into the chapel. P. V. WHITE The car was crunching on the drive.

3 *verb trans.* Cause to make a crunching sound; crush or grind under foot etc. with a crunching sound. M19.

C. BRONTË A sound of heavy wheels crunching a stony road. T. KENEALLY His feet crunched the stiff frost.

■ **cruncher** *noun* (*a*) *slang* a crucial question, a sticking point, a decisive blow; (*b*) see ***number cruncher*** s.v. NUMBER *noun*: M20. **crunchiness** *noun* the quality of being crunchy L19. **crunchingly** *adverb* in a crunching manner, with a crunching action or sound M19. **crunchy** *adjective* fit for crunching or being crunched, crisp E20.

crunk /krʌŋk/ *adjective*² *& noun*. L20.
[ORIGIN perh. alt. pa. pple. of CRANK *verb*² or a blend of CRAZY + DRUNK *adjective & noun*.]
▸ **A** *adjective*. Very excited or full of energy, esp. as a result of listening to music. *slang* (orig. *US*). L20.
▸ **B** *noun*. A type of hip hop or rap music characterized by repeated shouted catchphrases. E21.

crunk /krʌŋk/ *verb & noun*¹. Long *obsolete* exc. *dial.* M16.
[ORIGIN Cf. Icelandic *krúnka* to croak.]
▸ **A** *verb intrans.* Of a bird: utter a hoarse harsh cry. M16.
▸ **B** *noun*. The harsh cry of a bird; a croak. M19.

crunkle /ˈkrʌŋk(ə)l/ *verb*¹ *trans.* Chiefly *N. English*. LME.
[ORIGIN Parallel to CRINKLE *verb*.]
Wrinkle, rumple, crinkle. Chiefly as ***crunkled*** *ppl adjective*.

crunkle /ˈkrʌŋk(ə)l/ *verb*² *intrans.* L19.
[ORIGIN Imit.]
Make a harsh dry sound as by grinding the jaws, etc.

crunode /ˈkruːnəʊd/ *noun*. L19.
[ORIGIN Irreg. from Latin *crux* cross + NODE.]
MATH. A point on a curve where it intersects itself; a node with two real tangents.
■ **cruˈnodal** *adjective* L19.

crunt /krʌnt/ *noun & verb*. *Scot.* L18.
[ORIGIN Prob. imit.: cf. CRUMP *noun*², *verb*².]
▸ **A** *noun*. A blow on the head. L18.
▸ **B** *verb trans.* Strike on the head. E20.

cruor /ˈkruːɔː/ *noun*. Now *rare* or *obsolete*. M17.
[ORIGIN Latin.]
Coagulated blood, gore.

crupper /ˈkrʌpə/ *noun & verb*. ME.
[ORIGIN Anglo-Norman *cropere*, Old French *cropiere* (mod. *croupière*), from Proto-Romance, from base of CROUP *noun*¹: see -ER².]
▸ **A** *noun*. **1** A strap buckled to the back of a saddle and looped under the horse's tail, to prevent the saddle from slipping forward. ME.
2 *transf.* The hindquarters of a horse. L16. ▸**b** A person's buttocks. Chiefly *joc.* L16.
3 *hist.* A piece of armour covering the hindquarters of a horse. M17.
4 NAUTICAL. More fully ***crupper-chain***. A chain to secure a jib boom down in its saddle. M19.
▸ **B** *verb trans.* Equip with a crupper, put a crupper on. Chiefly as ***cruppered*** *ppl adjective*. L18.

crura *noun* pl. of CRUS.

crural /ˈkrʊər(ə)l/ *adjective*. L16.
[ORIGIN French, or Latin *cruralis*, from *crus*, *crur-* leg: see -AL¹.]
ANATOMY. Of or pertaining to the leg, *spec.* that part between the knee and ankle. Also, of or pertaining to the crura cerebri.

crus /krʌs/ *noun*. Pl. **crura** /ˈkrʊərə/. E18.
[ORIGIN Latin: see CRURAL.]
1 ANATOMY. The leg or hind limb; *spec.* the part from the knee to the ankle, the shank. E18.
2 Any of various elongated processes or parts of a structure occurring in pairs; *esp.* (in full ***crus cerebri*** /ˈsɛrɪbrʌɪ/ [= of the brain]) either of two symmetrical nerve tracts of the midbrain linking the pons and the cerebral hemispheres. E18.

crusade /kruːˈseɪd/ *noun*. Also (earlier) †**crois-**, †**-ado** (pl. **-o(e)s**), (earliest, in senses 1, 2) †**cruciat**, & other vars. Also (esp. in sense 1) **C-**. LME.
[ORIGIN In early use from medieval Latin *cruciata*, from Latin *cruc-*, *crux* cross; later (16) partly from French *croisade* alt. of *croisée* (from *crois* CROSS *noun*) by assim. to Spanish, partly from Spanish *cruzada* (from *cruz* CROSS *noun*): see -ADE, -ADO.]
1 A war or expedition instigated by the Church for alleged religious ends; *spec.* (*hist.*) any of several Christian military expeditions made in the 11th, 12th, and 13th cents. to recover Jerusalem and the Holy Land from the Muslims (freq. in *pl.*). LME.

R. W. EMERSON The power of the religious sentiment . . inspired the crusades.

†**2** A papal bull authorizing a crusade. LME–L18.
3 *hist.* In the Spanish kingdoms, a levy of money, originally intended to finance expeditions against the Moors, afterwards diverted to other purposes. L16.
†**4** The symbol of the cross, the badge worn by crusaders. E17–E18.
5 A vigorous movement or enterprise against poverty or a similar social evil; a personal campaign undertaken for a particular cause. L18.

P. MORTIMER God and my grandfather headed the crusade for compulsory education in Melksham.

crusade /kruːˈseɪd/ *verb intrans.* M18.
[ORIGIN from the noun.]
Engage in a crusade.

crusader /kruːˈseɪdə/ *noun*. Also (*hist.*) **C-**. M18.
[ORIGIN from CRUSADE *noun* or *verb* + -ER¹.]
A person who engages in a crusade.

crusado *noun*¹ see CRUZADO.

†**crusado** *noun*² see CRUSADE *noun*.

cruse /kruːz/ *noun*. *arch.*
[ORIGIN Old English *crūse* = Middle High German *krūse* (German *Krause*), Old Norse *krús*; reinforced in Middle English by Middle & mod. Low German *krūs*.]
A small earthenware pot or jar; a drinking vessel. Also *fig.* (with allus. to *1 Kings* 17:16), a seemingly slight resource which is in fact not readily exhausted (more fully ***widow's cruse***).

THACKERAY He had dipped ungenerously into a generous mother's purse, basely . . spilt her little cruse.

crush /krʌʃ/ *noun*. ME.
[ORIGIN from the verb.]
†**1** The noise of violent percussion; clashing; a crash. Only in ME.

C

2 An act of crushing; violent compression or pressure that bruises, breaks down, injures, or destroys; destruction by crushing. L16.

ADDISON The wrecks of matter, and the crush of worlds. *fig.*: S. JOHNSON A heavy crush of disaster.

3 A bruise or injury caused by crushing. Now *rare* or *obsolete*. E17.

4 The crowding together of a number of things; a crowded mass, esp. of people. E19. ▸**b** A crowded social gathering. *colloq.* M19. ▸**c** A group of people; *spec.* a body or unit of troops, a regiment. *slang.* E20.

DICKENS A crush of carts and chairs and coaches. **b** LD MACAULAY I fell in with her at Lady Grey's great crush.

5 In full ***crush pen***. A fenced passage with one narrow end for handling cattle, sheep, etc. M19.

6 (A person who is the object of) an infatuation. *slang.* L19.

M. LASKI The pupil with a crush who would . . give unstinting doglike devotion.

have a crush on, **get a crush on**, etc., be, become, infatuated with.

7 CROQUET. In full ***crush stroke***. A foul stroke made when a mallet touches a ball that is in contact with a peg or hoop other than in playing it away. E20.

8 A drink made from the juice of crushed fruit. E20.

– COMB.: **crush bar** a place in a theatre, opera house, etc., for the audience to buy drinks in the intervals; **crush barrier** a (temporary) barrier for restraining a crowd; **crush-hat** a soft hat which can be crushed flat; *spec.* a hat constructed with a spring so as to collapse, an opera hat; ***crush pen***: see sense 5 above; **crush-room** *arch.* a room or area in a theatre, opera house, etc., for the audience to walk about during the intervals; ***crush stroke***: see sense 7 above.

crush /krʌʃ/ *verb.* ME.

[ORIGIN Anglo-Norman *crussir*, *corussier*, Old French *croissir*, *cruissir* gnash (the teeth), crash, crack, from Proto-Romance: ult. origin unknown.]

▸**I 1** *verb trans.* Compress forcibly so as to break, bruise, injure, or destroy. ME. ▸**b** Crumple or crease (a fabric, dress, etc.) by pressure or rough handling; give (a fabric etc.) a crumpled or crinkled finish (chiefly as ***crushed ppl adjective***). L19.

T. HERBERT Some . . cast themselves in the way and are crusht to death. L. LEE A man . . crushed a glass like a nut between his hands. **b** OED Her bonnet and dress were all crushed. *Belfast Telegraph* Crushed velvet for curtains.

2 *verb trans.* Bruise, pound, break down into small pieces; reduce to powder, pulp, etc., by pressure. LME.

M. DONOVAN The apples had . . been well crushed and pressed.

3 *verb trans.* Press or squeeze forcibly (*against*, *into*, *out of*, *through*, etc.); force out or *out* by pressing or squeezing. L16.

SHAKES. *1 Hen. IV* To crush our old limbs in ungentle steel. R. CHANDLER She bent to crush out her cigarette. R. ELLISON I was crushed against a huge woman. R. BRADBURY Wine was being crushed from under the grape-blooded feet of dancing vintners' daughters.

4 *verb trans. fig.* Break down the strength or power of; extinguish, stamp *out* (actions, feelings, etc.); subdue, overwhelm. L16.

GIBBON His enemies were crushed by his valour. E. J. HOWARD While she was with him, she was able to crush these feelings of guilt. C. HAMPTON The urban guerrilla movement was said to be crushed and finished.

5 *verb trans.* Drink, quaff, (a glass of wine, pot of ale, etc.). *arch.* L16.

SIR W. SCOTT You shall crush a cup of wine to the health of the Fathers of the city.

6 *verb intrans.* Become crushed. M18.

G. MACDONALD I heard hailstones crush between my feet and the soft grass.

7 *verb intrans.* Advance or make one's way by pressing, squeezing, pushing, etc. M18.

J. T. FARRELL He arose, crushed out to the aisle, walked to the exit.

8 *verb intrans.* CROQUET. Touch with a mallet a ball that is in contact with a peg or hoop other than in playing it away (constituting a foul stroke). Chiefly as ***crushing verbal noun*** & ***ppl adjective***. L19.

crushing stroke = CRUSH *noun* 7.

▸**†II 9** *verb trans. & intrans.* Dash together with the sound of violent percussion; clash, crash. Chiefly as ***crushing verbal noun***. Only in LME.

■ **crushable** *adjective* able to be crushed, esp. without damage (earlier in UNCRUSHABLE) M19. **crushing** *ppl adjective* that crushes; *esp.* overwhelming: L16. **crushingly** *adverb* E19.

crusher /ˈkrʌʃə/ *noun.* L16.

[ORIGIN from CRUSH *verb* + -ER¹.]

1 A person or thing which crushes or compresses forcibly. L16.

Daily Telegraph The cars were dropped into the crusher complete with tyres, engines, seats and instruments.

2 An overwhelming person, thing, or event; a crushing blow or retort. *colloq.* M19.

THACKERAY She is a crusher, ain't she now? C. DICKSON That's where he had a very bad bit of luck, a crusher, the thing that did for him.

3 A police officer. *slang.* M19. ▸**b** A ship's corporal; a regulating petty officer. *nautical slang.* E20.

crusie /ˈkruːzi/ *noun. Scot.* Also **cruisie**. E16.

[ORIGIN Perh. repr. French *creuset* crucible.]

A small lamp with a handle, burning oil or tallow (also ***crusie lamp***). Also, a type of triangular candlestick.

crusily /ˈkruːsɪli/ *adjective.* Also **-lly**. L16.

[ORIGIN Old French *crusillé* var. of *croisillé*, from Old French & mod. French *croisille* dim. of *croix* CROSS *noun*: see -Y⁵.]

HERALDRY. Of a shield or charge: strewn with cross crosslets rather than crosses.

Crusoe /ˈkruːsəʊ/ *verb & noun.* L19.

[ORIGIN See ROBINSON CRUSOE.]

▸**A** *verb intrans.* Live as a castaway; live a solitary open-air life. Chiefly as ***Crusoeing verbal noun***. L19.

▸**B** *noun.* A castaway; an independent and resourceful person isolated from others (physically or intellectually etc.); = ROBINSON CRUSOE *noun*. E20.

crust /krʌst/ *noun.* ME.

[ORIGIN Old French *crouste* (mod. CROÛTE) from Latin *crusta* rind, shell, encrustation.]

1 The hard outer part of (a loaf, roll, or slice of) bread; a portion of this; a hard dry scrap of bread; a piece of bread as a meagre means of sustenance; *slang* (chiefly *Austral.* & *NZ*) a livelihood, a living. ME.

KEATS Love in a hut, with water and a crust, Is—Love, forgive us!—cinders, ashes, dust. E. DE MAUNY 'What do you do for a crust?' 'I work on a newspaper.' S. BRETT Anchovy paste sandwiches with the crusts cut off.

2 The pastry forming the covering of a pie. LME.

3 A hard dry formation on the skin covering a burn, ulcer, etc., or caused by a skin disease; a scab. LME.

H. JOLLY This treatment clears the scalp . . although crusts may reappear.

4 A more or less hard coating or deposit on the surface of anything; an encrustation; a deposit on the sides of a bottle, thrown by some ports and other wines; a harder layer over soft snow. LME.

P. CAREY A dry crust of spittle marked the corners of her mouth. J. GRIGSON The cream takes 1½ hours to form its crust.

5 A plank cut from the outside of a tree trunk. Long *obsolete* exc. *dial.* L15.

6 Orig., the upper surface or layer of the ground. Now GEOLOGY, the outer rocky portion of the earth (*spec.* those parts above the Mohorovičić discontinuity), the moon, a planet, etc. M16.

7 A crusty person. Long *arch.* L16.

8 The hard external covering of an animal (esp. a crustacean) or plant; a shell, a husk. Now *rare* or *obsolete*. E17.

9 *fig.* A deceptive outward appearance; a superficial hardness of demeanour etc.; *slang* impudence, effrontery (cf. RIND *noun*¹ 3c). M17.

F. W. ROBERTSON Break through the crust of his selfishness. P. G. WODEHOUSE The blighter had the cold, cynical crust to look me in the eyeball without a blink.

10 In leather manufacture, the state of skins when tanned but not yet dyed or coloured. Chiefly in ***in the crust***. L17.

– PHRASES: ***continental crust***: see CONTINENTAL *adjective*. ***oceanic crust***. ***upper crust***: see UPPER *adjective*.

■ **crustless** *adjective* E20.

crust /krʌst/ *verb.* LME.

[ORIGIN from the noun.]

1 *verb intrans.* Form or become covered with a crust. LME.

T. PYNCHON Blood darkened and crusting at the lesion in his neck.

2 *verb trans.* Cover (as) with a crust; form into a crust. M16.

WILKIE COLLINS The dirt of half a century, crusted on the glass. J. A. FROUDE The truth had been crusted over with fictions. C. MCCULLERS A thin coat of ice crusted the puddles.

3 *verb trans.* Hunt (deer etc.) on the crust of snow. *N. Amer.* M19.

crusta /ˈkrʌstə/ *noun.* Pl. **crustae** /ˈkrʌstiː/. E19.

[ORIGIN Latin: see CRUST *noun*.]

1 Chiefly ANATOMY & MEDICINE. A hard outer layer, rind, shell, or encrustation. E19.

crusta petrosa /pɛˈtrəʊsə/ [= hard, like rock] the cement of a tooth.

2 ANTIQUITIES. A thin plate of embossed metal etc. inlaid on a vessel, wall, or other object. M19.

crustacean /krʌˈsteɪʃ(ə)n/ *noun & adjective.* M19.

[ORIGIN from mod. Latin *Crustacea* (see below), use as noun of neut. pl. of *crustaceus* adjective: see CRUSTACEOUS, -AN.]

ZOOLOGY. ▸**A** *noun.* Any member of the large class Crustacea of mainly aquatic, hard-shelled arthropods including the crab, lobster, shrimp, woodlouse, etc. M19.

▸**B** *adjective.* Of or pertaining to the Crustacea. M19.

crustaceology /krʌˌsteɪʃɪˈɒlədʒi/ *noun.* E19.

[ORIGIN formed as CRUSTACEAN + -OLOGY.]

The branch of zoology that deals with the Crustacea.

■ **crustaceoˈlogical** *adjective* E19. **crustaceologist** *noun* M19.

crustaceous /krʌˈsteɪʃəs/ *adjective.* M17.

[ORIGIN from mod. Latin *crustaceus*, from Latin *crusta* CRUST *noun*: see -ACEOUS.]

1 Pertaining to or of the nature of a crust or hard integument; (of a lichen) crustose. M17.

2 Of an animal: having a hard integument. M17.

3 ZOOLOGY. Of, pertaining to, or resembling the Crustacea; crustacean. M17.

†crustade *noun* see CUSTARD *noun*¹.

crustal /ˈkrʌst(ə)l/ *adjective.* M19.

[ORIGIN from Latin *crusta* CRUST *noun* + -AL¹.]

Of or pertaining to a crust, esp. that of the earth, moon, etc.

†crustarde *noun* see CUSTARD *noun*¹.

crustate /ˈkrʌsteɪt/ *adjective.* M17.

[ORIGIN Latin *crustatus*, from *crusta* CRUST *noun*: see -ATE².]

Crusted, crustaceous.

■ **crustated** *adjective* = CRUSTATE L18. **cruˈstation** *noun* the formation of a crust; an encrustation: M17.

crusted /ˈkrʌstɪd/ *adjective.* LME.

[ORIGIN from CRUST *noun* or *verb*: see -ED², -ED¹.]

Having a crust; (of wine, esp. port) having deposited a crust; *fig.* antiquated, venerable.

T. HARDY Fine old crusted characters who had a decided taste for living without worry.

crustie *noun* var. of CRUSTY *noun*.

crustose /krʌˈstəʊs/ *adjective.* L19.

[ORIGIN Latin *crustosus*, from *crusta* CRUST *noun*: see -OSE¹.]

Of the nature of a crust; crustaceous. Of a lichen: having a thin thallus which adheres closely to the substrate like a crust.

crusty /ˈkrʌsti/ *adjective & noun.* LME.

[ORIGIN from CRUST *noun* + -Y¹.]

▸**A** *adjective.* **1** Resembling a crust, hard; having a crisp crust. Of wine, esp. port: crusted. LME.

M. R. MITFORD His loaves, which are crusty, and his temper, which is not.

2 *fig.* Of a person, disposition, etc.: short-tempered, irritable; curt. L16.

▸**B** *noun.* Also **crustie**. A homeless or vagrant young person who has a shabby appearance and rejects conventional values. *colloq.* L20.

JANE OWEN The crusties drinking special brew stagger along the towpath.

■ **crustily** *adverb* L16. **crustiness** *noun* E17.

crut *noun* see CRUD *noun*.

crutch /krʌtʃ/ *noun.*

[ORIGIN Old English *cryć(ċ)* = Old Saxon *krukka* (Dutch *kruk*), Old High German *krucka* (German *Krücke*), Old Norse *krykkja*, from Germanic. Rel. to CROOK *noun*. See also CROTCH *noun*.]

▸**I 1** A staff to support a lame or infirm person in standing or walking, now usu. with a crosspiece at the top to fit under the armpit, or a curved rest to take the weight on the forearm. Freq. in ***pair of crutches***. OE.

A. HAILEY Some walking with the aid of canes, a few on crutches.

walk on crutches: see WALK *verb*¹.

2 Orig., the raised part of a saddle in front and rear. Now, the forking front of a saddle tree, which supports the pommel; also, a forked rest for the leg in a side saddle. E17.

3 A support or prop with a forked or concave top. Cf. CROTCH *noun* 3. M17.

CAPT. COOK The hunters fix their crutches in the ground, on which they rest their firelocks.

4 NAUTICAL. Any of various forked contrivances in a ship or boat, as (***a***) a support for a boom, mast, spar, etc., when not in use, (***b***) a rowlock. In *pl.* also, crooked timbers or bands of iron etc. bolted to the sternpost and the sides of a vessel. M18.

5 = CROTCH *noun* 5. M18.

S. RAVEN I hope . . your bloody cousin gets hit in the crutch by a cricket ball.

6 In a mechanical clock, a fork at the end of the arm hanging down from the axis of the anchor escapement, which supports the pendulum rod. M18.

7 a A handle of a tool etc. with a crossbar. M19. ▸**b** An implement consisting of a shaft and crosspiece, used in dipping sheep. (Implied earlier in CRUTCH *verb* 3.) Chiefly *Austral.* & *NZ*. E20.

▸**II 8** *fig.* A person or thing which provides support against faltering. L16.

crutch /krʌtʃ/ *verb.* M17.

[ORIGIN from the noun.]

1 *verb trans.* Support as with a crutch or crutches; prop *up*, sustain. M17.

DRYDEN Two fools that crutch their feeble sense on verse. G. W. THORNBURY Old crippled buildings . . crutched up with posts and logs.

2 *verb intrans. & trans.* with *it*, *one's way*. Go on crutches, limp. **E19.**

Dirt Bike Using a stick he found on the ground, he crutched his way over to it.

3 *verb trans.* Push (a sheep) into a dip with a crutch. Chiefly *Austral. & NZ.* **L19.**
4 *verb trans.* Clip the wool or hair from the hindquarters of (a sheep, dog, etc.). Chiefly *Austral. & NZ.* **E20.**

crutched /ˈkrʌtʃɪd/ *adjective*¹. Also (earlier) †**crouched**; **C-**. **L16.**
[ORIGIN from CROUCH *noun*¹ + -ED², after Latin *cruciferi*, *sanctae crucis*.]
Chiefly *hist.* Designating a friar of any of various religious congregations noted for their bearing or wearing a cross.

crutched /krʌtʃt/ *adjective*². **E18.**
[ORIGIN from CRUTCH *noun* + -ED².]
Having a crutch; resembling a crutch.

crux /krʌks/ *noun*. Pl. **cruxes** /ˈkrʌksɪz/; **cruces** /ˈkruːsiːz/. **M17.**
[ORIGIN Latin = CROSS *noun*.]
1 (A representation of) a cross. Chiefly in ***crux ansata*** /anˈseɪtə/, pl. ***cruces ansatae*** /-tiː/ [= with a handle] = ANKH. **M17.**
2 A difficult matter, a puzzle; the decisive point at issue; the central point. **E18.**

E. DOWDEN The consideration of a textual crux in itself sharpens the wits. L. MACNEICE The crux of the story is the great gulf separating the people of the sea from human beings.

3 (Usu. **C-**.) (The name of) the constellation of the Southern Cross (see CROSS *noun* 13). **M19.**

cruzado /kruːˈzɑːdəʊ/ *noun*. In sense 1 also (earlier) **crusado** /kruːˈseɪdəʊ/. Pl. **-os**. **M16.**
[ORIGIN Portuguese, use as noun of adjective = bearing a cross.]
1 *hist.* Any of various Portuguese gold or silver coins bearing the figure of a cross. **M16.**
2 The principal monetary unit of Brazil between 1988 and 1990, equal to 1000 cruzeiros. **L20.**

cruzeiro /kruːˈzɛːrəʊ/ *noun*. Pl. **-os**. **E20.**
[ORIGIN Portuguese, lit. 'large cross'.]
A monetary unit of Brazil, formerly the basic unit superseding the milreis, later equal to one-thousandth of a cruzado, now the basic unit, equal to one hundred centavos.

crwth /kruːθ/ *noun*. **M19.**
[ORIGIN Welsh: cf. Gaelic *cruit* harp, violin, Irish *cruit* small harp, Old Irish *crot* harp, cithara. Adopted earlier as CROWD *noun*¹.]
An old Celtic musical instrument with three, or later six, strings which was held against the chest and played by bowing and plucking.

cry /krʌɪ/ *noun*. **ME.**
[ORIGIN Old French & mod. French *cri*: Proto-Romance formed as the verb.]
1 A loud inarticulate sound made by a person to express grief, pain, or other strong emotion. Also, the making of such a sound. **ME.**

J. GOWER With such weping and with such cry Forth . . he goth. M. ARNOLD We shall not meet [our doom] . . With women's tears and weak complaining cries. TENNYSON In one blind cry of passion and of pain. D. DU MAURIER She saw the Christmas tree . . and gave a cry of pleasure.

2 A loud excited utterance of words; a shout. Formerly also, shouting, calling out. **ME.** ▸†**b** Clamour, tumultuous noise. **ME–E16.**

POPE With the hunter's cry the grove resounds.

3 A loud importunate call; an appeal (*for* mercy, help, etc.). **ME.**

AV *Prov.* 21:13 Whoso stoppeth his eares at the cry of the poore. M. BRAGG The miners' cry for the Eight-Hour Day had grown into a practicable demand.

4 A summons (orig. formal). Now only *Scot.* **ME.**
5 a *gen.* A loud public announcement; a proclamation, an edict. Long *obsolete* exc. *hist.* **ME.** ▸**b** In *pl.* The proclamation of marriage-banns: cf. CRY *verb* 4e. Long *obsolete* exc. *Scot.* **ME.** ▸**c** A public complaint or outcry against a wrong. *obsolete* exc. in HUE AND CRY. **ME.** ▸**d** A proclamation of goods or business in the streets; a street vendor's special call. **M17.**

a LD BERNERS Kyng yuoryn made a crye thorow all the cyte that euery man sholde be armed.

6 a Public report or rumour. **ME.** ▸**b** The public voice as expressing approval or condemnation. Hence, an opinion generally expressed. **E17.**

a SHAKES. *Oth.* Faith, the cry goes that you marry her. **b** STEELE Then the Cry would be, Images were put up for the . . ignorant People to worship. E. LONGFORD There is a general cry throughout France against the occupation.

7 The loud natural utterance of an animal, bird, etc., *esp.* the distinctive call of one. **ME.** ▸**b** *spec.* The yelping of hounds giving chase. **LME.**

N. TINBERGEN The clear, . . resounding cries of the Herring Gulls.

†**8 a** A company or troop of people, esp. soldiers. In later use *derog.* and infl. by sense 8b. **ME–M17.** ▸**b** A pack of hounds. **L16.**

a SHAKES. *Haml.* Would not this . . get me a fellowship in a cry of players, sir?

9 A word or phrase shouted to encourage or rally people, esp. soldiers in battle; a watchword. **M16.** ▸**b** *spec.* A political or electioneering slogan or rallying cry. **L18.**

W. MORRIS Ho, friends, and ye that follow, cry my cry! **b** D. BREWSTER The Tory election cry . . was 'the Church in danger'.

battle cry, ***rallying cry***, ***war cry***, etc.

10 A fit of weeping. *colloq.* **E19.**
11 The creaking noise made by tin when bent. **L19.**
– PHRASES: **a far cry** (chiefly *fig.*) a very long distance (*from*, *to*). **a good cry** *colloq.* a prolonged or violent fit of weeping that relieves the feelings. **cry from the heart** a *cri de cœur*. **great cry and little wool**, **much cry and little wool** (the proverbial result of shearing pigs) a lot of fuss with little effect, a lot of fuss about nothing. **in full cry** in hot pursuit. †**out of all cry**, †**out of cry** excessively. **within cry of** within calling distance of.

cry /krʌɪ/ *verb*. Pa. t. & pple **cried** /krʌɪd/. **ME.**
[ORIGIN Old French & mod. French *crier* from Latin *quiritare* raise a public outcry (lit. 'call on the *Quirites* or Roman citizens for help').]
1 *verb trans.* Ask for earnestly or in a loud voice. *arch.* **ME.** ▸†**b** Call for, demand, require. **E17–L18.**

CAXTON Whan they repente . . and crye their god mercy. DEFOE The Portuguese cry quarter. W. IRVING 'I cry your mercy,' said I, 'for mistaking your age.' **b** SOUTHEY The innocent blood cried vengeance.

cry craven: see CRAVEN *adjective* 1b. ***cry halves***: see HALF *noun*.

2 *verb intrans.* Call out or *out* in a loud voice, esp. in seeking mercy, help, etc., or in expressing emotion. (Foll. by *to*, †*unto*, †(*up*)*on* a person addressed, *for* a person or thing desired, *to do* a thing desired, (arch.) *against* a cause of complaint.) **ME.** ▸**b** *fig.* Of a thing: call *for*, suggest strongly the need *for*. **ME.**

SPENSER The damned ghosts . . with sharp shrilling shrieks do bootlesse cry. SHAKES. *Wint. T.* How he cried to me for help. D. G. ROSSETTI She is cried upon In all the prayers my heart puts up. E. O'NEILL I . . cried to be buried with her. **b** C. THIRLWALL Injuries and insults . . which cried aloud for vengeance.

be crying out for be asking urgently for, be in urgent need of. ***cry a person mercy***: see MERCY *noun*. **cry for the moon** ask for what is unattainable, ask the impossible. **for crying out loud!** *colloq.*: expr. exasperation, impatience, or surprise.

3 *verb trans.* Utter (esp. specified words) in a loud voice. **ME.**

R. RAYMOND Where so many voices cry encouragement, it is well that one should speak warning. E. M. FORSTER 'The field's cut!' Helen cried excitedly.

cry aim: see AIM *noun* 3. ***cry cupboard***: see CUPBOARD *noun* 4. ***cry harrow***: see HARROW *interjection*. ***cry havoc***: see HAVOC *noun*. ***cry quits***: see QUITS *adjective*. ***cry roast meat***: see ROAST *adjective*. ***cry shame on***, ***cry shame upon***: see SHAME *noun*. ***cry uncle***: see UNCLE *noun*. ***cry wolf (too often)***: see WOLF *noun*.

4 *verb trans.* Announce publicly in a loud voice; proclaim. **ME.** ▸**b** Of a street vendor or auctioneer: announce (a sale, goods for sale). **LME.** ▸**c** Give oral notice of (things lost or found). Now *arch.* or *hist.* **L16.** ▸†**d** Extol; = ***cry up*** below. Only in **E17.** ▸**e** Proclaim the marriage banns of. Now *Scot. & US dial.* **L18.**

TENNYSON She sent a herald forth, And bade him cry, with sound of trumpet, all The hard condition. **b** W. H. AUDEN A pedlar still, . . I no longer cry my wares.

b ***cry stinking fish***: see STINKING *adjective*.

5 *verb intrans.* Utter inarticulate exclamations of distress; wail. **ME.** ▸**b** *verb intrans. & trans.* With little or no idea of sound: weep, shed (tears). (Foll. by *for* a person or thing desired.) **M16.** ▸**c** *verb refl.* Bring oneself into a specified state by weeping. **E17.** ▸**d** *verb trans.* ***cry one's eyes out***, weep bitterly; ***cry one's heart out***, cry violently or exhaustingly, cry to an extreme degree. **E18.**

SHAKES. *Much Ado* If you hear a child cry in the night, you must call to the nurse. **b** C. KINGSLEY He . . cried salt tears from sheer disappointment. E. WAUGH The boy took out a handkerchief and began to cry quietly.

b ***a shoulder to cry on***: see SHOULDER *noun*. ***cry all the way to the bank***: see BANK *noun*³ 3. ***cry on a person's shoulder***: see SHOULDER *noun*. ***cry over spilt milk***: see MILK *noun*. ***give something to cry about***, ***give something to cry for***: see GIVE *verb*. **c** ***cry oneself to sleep*** etc.

6 *verb intrans.* Of an animal, bird, etc.: utter a loud (esp. distinctive) call. Of a hound: yelp as when giving chase. **ME.**

W. FULKE Frogs crying . . forewarne us of a tempest. BYRON Hark, hark! the sea-birds cry!

– WITH ADVERBS IN SPECIALIZED SENSES: **cry back** (in hunting) go back on one's tracks; revert to an ancestral type. **cry down** (*a*) proclaim unlawful or forbidden; publicly disclaim responsibility for; disparage, decry; †(*b*) overcome or silence by louder or more vehement crying out. **cry off** excuse oneself from a commitment, decline to keep a promise. †**cry out** be in childbirth. **cry up** proclaim the merits of, extol.

crybaby /ˈkrʌɪbeɪbi/ *noun & verb*. *colloq.* **M19.**
[ORIGIN from CRY *noun* or *verb* + BABY *noun*.]
▸ **A** *noun*. A person easily reduced to childish tears. **M19.**
▸ **B** *verb intrans.* Behave like a crybaby; be easily reduced to childish tears or complaints. *US.* **E20.**

crying /ˈkrʌɪɪŋ/ *adjective*. **LME.**
[ORIGIN from CRY *verb* + -ING².]
1 That cries. **LME.**
2 *fig.* Of a problem, an evil, etc.: that calls for notice or urgent action; flagrant. **E17.**

DAY LEWIS Some crying need for self-protection. F. DHONDY It was nothing less than a crying shame for a workers' government to treat the workers so.

■ **cryingly** *adverb* **E19.**

cryo- /ˈkrʌɪəʊ/ *combining form*. Also (occas.) **kryo-**.
[ORIGIN from Greek *kruos* frost, icy cold: see -O-.]
Used in SCIENCE with the sense 'of, involving, or producing very low temperatures'.
■ **cryobiˈology** *noun* the biology of organisms, tissues, etc., cooled to temperatures below those at which they normally function **M20.** **cryogen** *noun* (CHEMISTRY) a substance used to induce very low temperatures; a freezing mixture: **L19.** **cryoˈglobulin** *noun* (BIOCHEMISTRY) any of a group of proteins which occur in the blood in certain disorders and may be precipitated when cooled outside the body **M20.** **cryopreˈcipitate** *noun* a substance precipitated by controlled freezing; *spec.* an extract rich in a haemostatic factor obtained as a residue when frozen blood plasma is thawed: **L20.** **cryopreserve** *verb trans.* subject to cryopreservation **L20.** **cryopreserˈvation** *noun* the cooling of living matter to below the freezing point of water in order to prolong its life **L20.** **cryoprobe** *noun* an ultra-cooled probe employed in cryosurgery **M20.** **cryoproˈtectant** *noun* an agent used for cryoprotection **L20.** **cryoproˈtection** *noun* protection against damage caused by freezing temperatures **M20.** **cryopump** *noun* a vacuum pump which uses a liquefied gas such as helium to freeze out the gases in a volume **M20.** **cryosphere** *noun* the permanently frozen part of the earth's surface **M20.** **cryostat** *noun* (*a*) an apparatus for maintaining a very low steady temperature; (*b*) a cold chamber in which frozen tissue is divided with a microtome; the microtome itself: **E20.** **cryoˈsurgery** *noun* surgery using local application of intense cold usu. in order to freeze and destroy unwanted tissue **M20.** **cryoˈtherapy** *noun* the use of extreme cold in the treatment of disease **M20.** **cryoturˈbation** *noun* physical disturbance to the soil caused by freezing (and thawing) of water in the soil **M20.**

cryoconite /krʌɪəˈkəʊnʌɪt/ *noun*. Also (earlier) †**k-**. **L20.**
[ORIGIN from CRYO- + Greek *konis* dust + -ITE¹.]
A powdery material of aeolian origin forming layered deposits in holes in glaciers, ice sheets, etc.

cryogenic /krʌɪə(ʊ)ˈdʒɛnɪk/ *adjective*. **E20.**
[ORIGIN from CRYO- + -GENIC.]
Of or pertaining to the production of very low temperatures and their effects.
■ **cryogenically** *adverb* by cryogenic means **M20.** **cryoˈgenics** *noun* the branch of physics and technology that deals with the production of very low temperatures and their effects **M20.**

cryolite /ˈkrʌɪəlʌɪt/ *noun*. **E19.**
[ORIGIN from CRYO- + -LITE: named from large deposits in Greenland.]
MINERALOGY. A monoclinic fluoride of sodium and aluminium which occurs usu. as white or colourless massive deposits and is used as a flux in the electrolytic smelting of aluminium.

cryonics /krʌɪˈɒnɪks/ *noun*. **M20.**
[ORIGIN Contr. of CRYOGENICS.]
The practice or technique of deep-freezing the bodies of those who have died of an incurable disease, in the hope that some cure for it will be discovered in the future.
■ **cryonic** *adjective* **M20.** **cryonically** *adverb* **L20.** **cryonicist** /-sɪst/ *noun* **L20.**

cryophorus /krʌɪˈɒf(ə)rəs/ *noun*. **E19.**
[ORIGIN mod. Latin, formed as CRYO- + Greek *-phoros*: see -PHORE.]
An instrument for illustrating the freezing of water by evaporation.

cryoscopy /krʌɪˈɒskəpi/ *noun*. **E20.**
[ORIGIN from CRYO- + -SCOPY.]
The determination of the freezing point of liquids, esp. (in medical diagnosis) that of blood or urine compared with distilled water; CHEMISTRY the measurement of the lowering of the freezing point of a liquid by a substance dissolved in it (used in the calculation of molecular weight).
■ **cryoˈscopic** *adjective* of or pertaining to cryoscopy **E20.** **cryoˈscopically** *adverb* **E20.**

crypt /krɪpt/ *noun*. **LME.**
[ORIGIN Latin *crypta* from Greek *kruptē* vault, use as noun of fem. of *kruptos* hidden.]
†**1** A grotto, a cavern. Only in **LME.**
†**2** An underground passage or tunnel. Only in **M17.**
3 An underground chamber or vault; *spec.* one under a church, used as a burial place etc. **L18.**
4 *transf. & fig.* A recess, a secret hiding place. **M19.**
5 ANATOMY. A small tubular gland, pit, or recess. **M19.**
crypt of LIEBERKÜHN.
■ **cryptal** *adjective* **M19.**

crypt- *combining form* see CRYPTO-.

C

crypta /ˈkrɪptə/ *noun*. Now *rare*. Pl. **-tae** /-tiː/. M16.
[ORIGIN Latin: see CRYPT.]
†**1** = CRYPT 1, 2, 3. M16–E18.
2 = CRYPT 5. M19.

cryptanalysis /krɪptəˈnalɪsɪs/ *noun*. Orig. *US*. E20.
[ORIGIN from CRYPT- + ANALYSIS.]
The practice or art of solving cryptograms by analysis; code-breaking.
■ **crypˈtanalyst** *noun* an expert in cryptanalysis E20. **cryptanaˈlytic**, **cryptanaˈlytical** *adjectives* of or pertaining to cryptanalysis M20.

cryptand /ˈkrɪptand/ *noun*. L20.
[ORIGIN from CRYPTO- + -AND.]
CHEMISTRY. A bicyclic compound whose molecule contains a cavity able to hold metal cations. Cf. CRYPTATE.

cryptate /ˈkrɪpteɪt/ *noun*. M20.
[ORIGIN formed as CRYPTAND + -ATE[1].]
CHEMISTRY. An organometallic complex in which a metal cation is held inside a cryptand.

cryptic /ˈkrɪptɪk/ *noun & adjective*. E17.
[ORIGIN Late Latin *crypticus* from Greek *kruptikos*, from *kruptē*: see CRYPT, -IC.]
▸ **A** *noun*. †**1** A secret method. Only in E17.
2 A cryptogrammic puzzle. M20.
▸ **B** *adjective*. **1** Secret, mystical; mysterious; obscure in meaning; enigmatic. E17. ▸**b** Of a crossword (clue): indicating the answer(s) in a way that is not straightforward. M20.

F. W. CROFTS 'It just shows. You never know'; with which rather cryptic remark the interview closed. C. S. LEWIS That cryptic knight who comes and goes we know not whence or whither. J. T. STORY Covered in cryptic figures and names, like a code.

2 ZOOLOGY. Of markings, coloration, etc.: serving to camouflage an animal etc. in its natural environment. L19.
■ **cryptical** *adjective* = CRYPTIC *adjective* 1 E17. **cryptically** *adverb* L17.

cryptid /ˈkrɪptɪd/ *noun*. L20.
[ORIGIN from CRYPTO- + -ID *suffix*[3].]
An animal whose existence or survival is disputed or unsubstantiated, e.g. the yeti.

crypto /ˈkrɪptəʊ/ *noun*. *colloq*. Pl. **-os**. M20.
[ORIGIN Use of CRYPTO- as separate word.]
A person who secretly supports a political group; *spec*. a crypto-Communist.

crypto- /ˈkrɪptəʊ/ *combining form*. Before a vowel or *h* also **crypt-**.
[ORIGIN Greek *kruptos* hidden: see -O-.]
Forming words, mostly scientific terms, modelled on Greek compounds, with the sense 'concealed, secret, not visible to the naked eye', as ***cryptogram***, ***cryptobranchiate***. Hence as a freely productive elem. forming nouns and adjectives with the sense 'unavowed(ly), not overt(ly)', as ***crypto-Communist***, ***crypto-Fascist***, ***crypto-Semite***.
■ **cryptobiosis** /-bʌɪˈəʊsɪs/ *noun* (BIOLOGY) a state of existence in which metabolic activity is reduced to an undetectable level without disappearing altogether M20. **cryptobiˈotic** *adjective* †(*a*) designating primitive organisms presumed to have existed in earlier geological periods but to have left no trace of their existence; (*b*) = CRYPTOZOIC 1; (*c*) pertaining to or in a state of cryptobiosis: E20. **cryptoˈbranchiate** *adjective* (esp. of certain divisions of crustaceans, gastropods, etc.) having the gills concealed L19. **crypto-ˈCalvinist** *noun* in 16th-cent. Germany, a Lutheran suspected of harbouring Calvinist sympathies; a Philippist: M18. **cryptoˈcrystalline** *adjective* crystalline, but so finely structured that its crystals are not visible even under a microscope M19. **cryptoˈgenic** *adjective* (of a disease) of obscure or uncertain origin E20. **cryptolect** *noun* a secret or coded language L20. **cryptophyte** *noun* †(*a*) a cryptogam; (*b*) a plant that bears perennating buds below the surface of the ground: M19. **crypˈtorchid** *noun & adjective* (MEDICINE) (a person) suffering from or exhibiting cryptorchidism L19. **crypˈtorchidism** *noun* (MEDICINE) a condition in which one or both of the testes fail to descend into the scrotum M19. **cryptovolˈcanic** *adjective* (GEOLOGY) (of a structure) that is, or is presumed to be, of volcanic origin although exposed material does not afford direct evidence of volcanic activity E20. **cryptozooˈlogical** *adjective* of or pertaining to cryptozoology M20. **cryptozoˈologist** *noun* an expert in or student of cryptozoology M20. **cryptozoˈology** *noun* the search for and study of creatures (e.g. the Loch Ness monster) whose supposed existence is evidenced by tradition, unsubstantiated reports, etc. M20. **cryptozoon** /-ˈzəʊɒn/ *noun*, pl. **-zoa** /-ˈzəʊə/, (*a*) GEOLOGY a reef-forming Cambrian fossil, thought to derive from algae; (*b*) ZOOLOGY (in *pl.*) cryptozoic organisms: L19.

cryptococcosis /ˌkrɪptəʊkəˈkəʊsɪs/ *noun*. Pl. **-ccoses** /-ˈkəʊsiːz/. M20.
[ORIGIN from mod. Latin *Cryptococcus* (see below) + -OSIS.]
MEDICINE. Infestation with a yeastlike fungus, *Cryptococcus neoformans*, usu. attacking the lungs and central nervous system. Also called ***torulosis***.
■ **cryptoˈcoccal** *adjective* of or pertaining to *Cryptococcus* or cryptococcosis L20.

cryptogam /ˈkrɪptəʊgam/ *noun*. M19.
[ORIGIN French *cryptogame* from mod. Latin *cryptogamae* (sc. *plantae*) fem. pl. of *cryptogamus* adjective, formed as CRYPTO- + Greek *gamos* marriage: so called because the means of reproduction was not apparent.]
Any plant of the Linnaean division Cryptogamia (now disused), which embraced all non-flowering plants, as ferns, mosses, algae, fungi, etc. (opp. PHANEROGAM). Now *rare* exc. as ***vascular cryptogam***, any plant of the group that includes ferns and their allies (e.g. horsetails and clubmosses), which resemble flowering plants in possessing a vascular system.
■ **cryptoˈgamic** *noun & adjective* (*a*) *noun* a cryptogam; (*b*) *adjective* belonging to the Cryptogamia: E19. **crypˈtogamist** *noun* a botanist specializing in cryptogams M19. **crypˈtogamous** *adjective* = CRYPTOGAMIC *adjective* L18.

cryptogram /ˈkrɪptəgram/ *noun*. L19.
[ORIGIN from CRYPTO- + -GRAM.]
Something written in cipher; a coded message.
■ **cryptoˈgrammic**, **cryptogrammˈatic**, **cryptogrammˈatical** *adjectives* of, pertaining to, or of the nature of a cryptogram L19. **cryptoˈgrammatist** *noun* a person who encodes or decodes messages L19. **cryptoˈgrammist** *noun* = CRYPTOGRAMMATIST E20.

cryptograph /ˈkrɪptəgrɑːf/ *noun*. M19.
[ORIGIN from CRYPTO- + -GRAPH.]
1 A cryptogram. M19.
2 A device for encoding or decoding messages. L19.

cryptography /krɪpˈtɒgrəfi/ *noun*. M17.
[ORIGIN mod. Latin *cryptographia*: see CRYPTO-, -GRAPHY.]
1 The practice or art of encoding messages. M17.
2 Cryptanalysis. M20.
■ **crypˈtographer** *noun* a person who encodes messages M17. **cryptoˈgraphic** *adjective* of, pertaining to, or of the nature of cryptography E19. **crypˈtographist** *noun* a cryptographer M19.

cryptology /krɪpˈtɒlədʒi/ *noun*. M17.
[ORIGIN from CRYPTO- + -LOGY.]
1 Secret speech or communication; mysterious or enigmatic language. M17.
2 The practice or art of encoding and decoding messages; the knowledge of codes. M20.

cryptomeria /krɪptə(ʊ)ˈmɪərɪə/ *noun*. M19.
[ORIGIN mod. Latin, formed as CRYPTO- + Greek *meros* part (because the seeds are concealed by scales).]
(The wood of) an ornamental evergreen tree *Cryptomeria japonica*, allied to the cypresses, native to Japan and China. Also called ***Japan cedar***, ***Japanese cedar***, ***sugi***.

cryptonym /ˈkrɪptənɪm/ *noun*. L19.
[ORIGIN from CRYPTO- + -NYM.]
A secret name, a code name.
■ **cryptonymous** /krɪpˈtɒnɪməs/ *adjective* whose name is secret, of the nature of a cryptonym L19.

cryptoporticus /krɪptə(ʊ)ˈpɔːtɪkəs/ *noun*. L17.
[ORIGIN Latin, formed as CRYPTO- + *porticus* gallery.]
CLASSICAL ARCHITECTURE. An enclosed gallery having side walls with openings instead of columns. Also, a covered or subterranean passage.

cryptosporidium /ˌkrɪptə(ʊ)spɒˈrɪdɪəm/ *noun*. Pl. **-dia**. E20.
[ORIGIN mod. Latin (see below), formed as CRYPTO- + SPORIDIUM.]
A protozoan of the parasitic coccidian genus *Cryptosporidium*, which includes many species which occur in the intestinal tract of vertebrates where they sometimes cause disease.
■ **cryptosporidiˈosis** *noun* disease caused by infection with cryptosporidia L20.

cryptozoic /krɪptə(ʊ)ˈzəʊɪk/ *adjective & noun*. L19.
[ORIGIN from CRYPTO- + -ZOIC.]
▸ **A** *adjective*. **1** ZOOLOGY. Of a small invertebrate: living hidden in the leaf litter or soil. Opp. PHANEROZOIC *adjective* 1. L19.
2 GEOLOGY. Usu. **C-**. Precambrian, esp. as marked by a dearth of fossil remains. E20.
▸ **B** *noun*. GEOLOGY. The Cryptozoic period. M20.

crystal /ˈkrɪst(ə)l/ *noun & adjective*. Also †**chr-**. LOE.
[ORIGIN Old French & mod. French *cristal* from Latin *crystallum* from Greek *krustallos* ice.]
▸ **A** *noun*. †**1** (Clear) ice. (A literalism of translation.) LOE–M16.
2 A mineral clear and transparent like ice; *esp*. a form of quartz having these qualities (now more fully ***rock crystal***: see ROCK *noun*[1]). LOE. ▸**b** Pure clear water. *poet*. L16. **(*as*) *clear as crystal***. MIXED ***crystal***. ***twin crystal***: see TWIN *noun* 5.
3 A piece of rock crystal or a similar mineral; *esp*. a crystal ball (see below). LME. ▸**b** An eye. Usu. in *pl*. *poet*. L16.

JAMES I The Seer looks into a Chrystal or Berryl, wherein he will see the answer.

4 CHEMISTRY & MINERALOGY. An aggregation of atoms or molecules of a substance with an ordered internal structure and the external form of a solid enclosed by symmetrically arranged plane faces; a solid with a regular arrangement of atoms etc. E17. ▸**b** Used in old names of chemical salts of crystalline form. Usu. in *pl*. *arch*. M17.

D. PAGE Granite is composed of crystals of felspar, quartz and mica.

crystal form: see FORM *noun* 1d. ***liquid crystal***: see LIQUID *adjective & noun*. ***plastic crystal***: see PLASTIC *adjective & noun*[3]. **b *crystals of tartar*** etc.

5 [Ellipt. for ***crystal glass*** below.] A highly transparent form of glass, flint glass; *loosely* fine cut glass. Hence, glass vessels etc. of this material. M17. ▸**b** A vessel etc. made of this glass; *spec*. the glass over the face of a watch. M17.

A. LURIE The stainless-steel tableware . . , the utility glassware . . had been replaced with silver and crystal.

6 A crystalline piece of a semiconductor used in electronic devices as a detector, rectifier, etc. E20.
▸ **B** *attrib*. or as *adjective*. **1** Made of crystal. LME.
2 Like crystal; clear as crystal. LME.

G. DURRELL Peering . . through a fathom of crystal water at the sea bottom.

– COMB. & SPECIAL COLLOCATIONS: **crystal axis** each of the three directions chosen to define the edges of the unit cell of a crystal; **crystal ball** a globe-shaped piece of rock crystal, used in crystal-gazing; **crystal-clear** *adjective* completely clear, transparent, unclouded, (*lit. & fig.*); **crystal class** CRYSTALLOGRAPHY any of the 32 possible classes into which crystals can be divided on the basis of the particular combination of symmetry elements that they possess; **crystal-gazer** a person who engages in crystal-gazing; a clairvoyant; **crystal-gazing** concentrating one's gaze on a crystal to see images forecasting the future or representing distant events; *fig*. unfounded speculation about the future; **crystal glass** [German *Krystallglas*] = sense 5 above; **crystal healing** the use of the supposed healing powers of crystals in alternative medicine; **crystal lattice** the space lattice underlying the arrangement of atoms or molecules in a crystal; also, the arrangements of points occupied by the atoms or molecules or of the atoms or molecules themselves; **crystal meth** *slang* the drug methamphetamine in a crystalline form; **crystal set** *hist*. a primitive form of radio receiving set using a crystal touching a metal wire as the rectifier; **crystal therapy** = ***crystal healing*** above; **crystal violet** an aniline dye used as a microscopical stain and as an antiseptic in the treatment of skin infections.
■ **cryˈstallic** *adjective* (*rare*) (*a*) of, pertaining to, or like crystal; (*b*) of or pertaining to crystals or their formation: M17. **crystaˈlliferous** *adjective* containing or yielding crystals L19. **cryˈstalliform** *adjective* having a crystalline form L18. **crystal-like** *adjective* L19.

crystal /ˈkrɪst(ə)l/ *verb trans*. Also †**chr-**. Infl. **-ll-**, ***-l-**. L17.
[ORIGIN from the noun.]
Convert into crystal, crystallize.

crystallin /ˈkrɪst(ə)lɪn/ *noun*. M19.
[ORIGIN from Latin *crystallum* CRYSTAL *noun* + -IN[1].]
BIOCHEMISTRY. Any of various globulins contained in the lens of the eye.

crystalline /ˈkrɪst(ə)lʌɪn/, *poet*. *also* krɪˈstalɪn/ *adjective & noun*. Also †**chr-**. ME.
[ORIGIN Old French & mod. French *cristallin* from Latin *crystallinus* from Greek *krustallinos*, from *krustallos*: see CRYSTAL *noun & adjective*, -INE[2].]
▸ **A** *adjective*. **1** Clear and transparent like crystal; *fig*. perfectly clear to the understanding. ME.

T. GRAY She eyes the clear chrystalline well. J. BUCHAN There was a crystalline sharpness of outline in the remotest hills.

crystalline heaven, **crystalline sphere(s)** *hist*. a sphere (or two spheres) postulated by medieval astronomers between the primum mobile and the firmament. †**crystalline humour** the substance of the lens of the eye. ***crystalline lens***: see LENS *noun* 2a.
2 Made or consisting of crystal. E16.
3 Having the form or structure of a crystal; composed of crystals. E17. ▸**b** Of or pertaining to crystals and their formation. *rare*. M19.
▸ **B** *noun*. **1** *hist*. The crystalline heaven (see sense A.1 above). LME.
2 The crystalline lens or (formerly) humour of the eye. LME.
3 Rock crystal; a crystal, a crystalline rock. *rare*. M16.
■ **crystaˈllinity** *noun* crystalline quality; degree of crystallization: L19.

crystallisation *noun*, **crystallise** *verb* vars. of CRYSTALLIZATION, CRYSTALLIZE.

crystallite /ˈkrɪst(ə)lʌɪt/ *noun*. E19.
[ORIGIN from CRYSTAL *noun & adjective* + -ITE[1].]
†**1** Volcanic rock in a crystalline state after fusion and slow cooling. E–M19.
2 A minute body, lacking definite crystalline form, found in glassy volcanic rocks etc.; an incipient crystal. Formerly also = MICROLITE. L19. ▸**b** An individual crystal or grain in a metal or other polycrystalline substance. E20. ▸**c** A region within a volume of cellulose or other polymer with a degree of structural ordering as in a crystal. Also called ***micelle***. E20.
■ **crystaˈllitic** *adjective* (of the nature) of a crystallite; consisting of or containing crystallites: M19.

crystallization /krɪst(ə)lʌɪˈzeɪʃ(ə)n/ *noun*. Also ***-aliz-**, **-isation**. M17.
[ORIGIN from CRYSTALLIZE + -ATION.]
1 The action or process of crystallizing (*lit. & fig.*). M17.

H. J. LASKI The age which saw the crystallization of the party-system.

water of crystallization water forming an essential part in the structure of some crystals, esp. hydrated salts.
2 A product of crystallizing, a crystallized formation, (*lit. & fig.*). L17.

W. IRVING Salt springs . . forming beautiful crystallizations.

crystallize /ˈkrɪst(ə)lʌɪz/ *verb.* Also ***-alize**, **-ise**. L16.
[ORIGIN from CRYSTAL *noun* & *adjective* + -IZE.]
†**1** *verb trans.* Convert into crystal or ice. L16–L18.
2 *verb trans.* & *intrans.* (Cause to) become crystalline in form or structure. M17.
crystallize out separate in the form of crystals from a solution. *crystallized* VERDIGRIS.
3 *fig.* **a** *verb trans.* Give a definite or permanent shape to (something vague or unformed). M17. ▸**b** *verb intrans.* Assume a definite or permanent shape. E19.

a G. MURRAY The writers who have most . . revelation about them do not crystallize their revelation into formulae. **b** J. MCCARTHY This vague impression crystallised into a conviction. J. LONDON Just as my style is taking form, crystallizing.

4 *verb trans.* Preserve (fruit, ginger, etc.) by impregnating and coating with crystals of sugar. Chiefly as ***crystallized*** *ppl adjective.* L19.
■ **crystallizable** *adjective* capable of crystallizing or being crystallized L18. **crystallizer** *noun* a person who or an apparatus which crystallizes E17.

crystallo- /ˈkrɪst(ə)ləʊ/ *combining form* of Greek *krustallos* CRYSTAL *noun*: see -O-.
■ **crystallo'blastic** *adjective* (GEOLOGY) (of rock texture) characteristic of or produced by recrystallization in a metamorphic process E20. **crystallo-ceramie** /-ˈsɛrəmi/ *noun* the technique of embedding decorative ceramic objects in clear glass, esp. in paperweights; objects made by this technique: E19. **crystallomancy** *noun* divination by means of a crystal E17.

crystallogenesis /krɪst(ə)ləʊˈdʒɛnɪsɪs/ *noun.* L19.
[ORIGIN from CRYSTALLO- + -GENESIS.]
The formation of crystals, esp. as a branch of study in science.
■ **crystallogenic** *adjective* leading to the formation of crystals M19. **crysta'llogeny** *noun* crystallogenesis M19.

crystallography /krɪstəˈlɒɡrəfi/ *noun.* E19.
[ORIGIN from CRYSTALLO- + -GRAPHY.]
The scientific study of the structure and properties of crystals and their classification.
X-RAY crystallography.
■ **crystallographer** *noun* E19. **crystallo'graphic**, **crystallo'graphical** *adjectives* of or pertaining to crystallography or to crystals scientifically considered E19. **crystallo'graphically** *adverb* with regard to or by means of crystallography M19.

crystalloid /ˈkrɪst(ə)lɔɪd/ *noun* & *adjective.* Now *rare.* LME.
[ORIGIN from CRYSTAL *noun* & *adjective* + -OID.]
▸ **A** *noun.* †**1** The substance of the lens of the eye. Only in LME.
2 CHEMISTRY. A crystalline substance, capable of dissolving in water and, when dissolved, of diffusing through a membrane. M19.
3 BOTANY. A crystal-like granule formed by the precipitation of protein, found in seeds and other storage organs. L19.
▸ **B** *adjective.* Of crystalline form; pertaining to or of the nature of a crystalloid. M19.
■ **crysta'lloidal** *adjective* = CRYSTALLOID *adjective* M19.

CS *abbreviation.*
1 Chartered surveyor.
2 Civil Service.
3 Court of Session.

Cs *symbol.*
CHEMISTRY. Caesium.

CS /siːˈɛs/ *noun.* M20.
[ORIGIN B. B. Corson (1896–1987) & R. W. Stoughton (1906–57), US chemists.]
In full ***CS gas***. An irritant compound used in finely divided form for riot control etc.

c/s *abbreviation.*
Cycles per second.

CSA *abbreviation.*
Child Support Agency.

csardas /ˈtʃɑːdɑːʃ, ˈzɑːdəs/ *noun.* Also **cz-**. Pl. same. M19.
[ORIGIN Hungarian *csárdás*, from *csárda* inn.]
A Hungarian dance usu. having a slow start and a rapid wild finish, with many turns and leaps; a piece of music for this dance.

CSC *abbreviation.*
1 Civil Service Commission.
2 Conspicuous Service Cross.

CSE *abbreviation.*
hist. Certificate of Secondary Education.

C-section /ˈsiːsɛkʃ(ə)n/ *noun. N. Amer.* M20.
[ORIGIN Abbreviation.]
A Caesarean section.

CSF *abbreviation.*
MEDICINE. Cerebrospinal fluid.

CSI *abbreviation.*
Companion of (the Order of) the Star of India.

CSIRO *abbreviation.*
Commonwealth Scientific and Industrial Research Organization.

CSM *abbreviation.*
Company Sergeant Major.

C sol fa *noun* var. of CESOLFA.

CST *abbreviation. N. Amer.*
Central Standard Time.

CSU *abbreviation.*
Civil Service Union.

CT *abbreviation*[1].
1 MEDICINE. Computed (or computerized) tomography (cf. CAT).
2 Connecticut.

Ct *abbreviation*[2].
1 Count.
2 Court.

ct *abbreviation*[3].
1 Carat.
2 Cent.

CTC *abbreviation.*
1 City Technology College.
2 Cyclists' Touring Club.

ctenidium /tɪˈnɪdɪəm/ *noun.* Pl. **-dia** /-dɪə/. L19.
[ORIGIN mod. Latin from Greek *ktenidion* dim. of *kteis*, *kten-* comb.]
ZOOLOGY. Each of the respiratory organs or gills in a mollusc, consisting of an axis with a row of projecting filaments; a row of spines like a comb in some insects.
■ **ctenidial** *adjective* L19.

ctenoid /ˈtiːnɔɪd/ *noun* & *adjective.* M19.
[ORIGIN from Greek *kteis*, *kten-* comb + -OID.]
▸ **A** *noun.* A member of a former order of fishes comprising those with ctenoid scales. Now *rare* or *obsolete.* M19.
▸ **B** *adjective.* Of the scales of certain fishes: having marginal projections like the teeth of a comb. Of a fish: having such scales. L19.

ctenophore /ˈtiːnəfɔː, ˈtɛn-/ *noun.* L19.
[ORIGIN from mod. Latin *ctenophorus*, formed as CTENOID: see -PHORE.]
ZOOLOGY. Any animal of the phylum Ctenophora, comprising pelagic marine creatures resembling jellyfish and moving by means of stiff cilia borne on comblike plates. Also called ***comb jelly***.
■ **cte'nophoral** *adjective* of or pertaining to the Ctenophora or a ctenophore M19. **cte'nophoran** *adjective* & *noun* (**a**) *adjective* = CTENOPHORAL; (**b**) *noun* = CTENOPHORE: L19. **cteno'phoric** *adjective* = CTENOPHORAL L19.

C2C *abbreviation.*
Consumer-to-consumer, designating transactions conducted via the Internet between consumers.

CTS *abbreviation.*
Carpal tunnel syndrome.

CU *abbreviation.*
Cambridge University.

Cu *symbol.*
[ORIGIN from Latin *cuprum*.]
CHEMISTRY. Copper.

cu. *abbreviation.*
Cubic.

cuadrilla /kwadˈriʎa, kwɒdˈriːljə/ *noun.* Pl. **-as** /-as, -əz/. M19.
[ORIGIN Spanish: see QUADRILLE *noun*[2].]
A company of people; *esp.* a matador's team.

cuartel /kwarˈtel, kwɔːˈtɛl/ *noun.* Pl. **-es** /-ɛs, -ɪz/. M19.
[ORIGIN Spanish, from *cuarta* quarter from *cuarto* fourth from Latin *quartus*.]
A military barracks in Spain and Spanish-speaking countries.

cuatro *noun* var. of QUATRO.

cub /kʌb/ *noun*[1] & *verb*[1]. M16.
[ORIGIN Unknown.]
▸ **A** *noun.* **1** A young fox. M16.
2 A young bear, wolf, lion, tiger, etc.; a young whale. L16.
3 An awkward unpolished youth. E17. ▸**b** An apprentice, a beginner; *spec.* (in full ***cub reporter***) a young or inexperienced newspaper reporter. M19.

THACKERAY He thinks it necessary to be civil to the young cub.

b attrib.: ***cub engineer***, ***cub pilot***, etc.
4 (**C-**.) More fully ***Cub Scout*** (formerly ***Wolf Cub***). A member of the junior branch of the Scout Association. E20.
▸ **B** *verb.* Infl. **-bb-**.
1 *verb trans.* & *intrans.* Give birth to (a cub or cubs). M18.
2 *verb intrans.* Hunt fox cubs. L19.
■ **cubhood** *noun* the state or period of being a cub M19.

cub /kʌb/ *noun*[2] & *verb*[2]. Now *dial.* M16.
[ORIGIN Prob. from Low German: cf. East Frisian *kübbing*, *kübben* in same sense, Low German *kübbing*, *kübje* shed or lean-to for cattle. Cf. COVE *noun*[1].]
▸ **A** *noun.* A stall, pen, or shed for cattle; a coop, a hutch. Also, a crib for fodder. M16.
▸ **B** *verb trans.* Infl. **-bb-**. Coop *up.* E17.

cubage /ˈkjuːbɪdʒ/ *noun.* M19.
[ORIGIN from CUBE *noun*[1] or *verb* + -AGE.]
Cubature; cubic content.

Cuba libre /ˈkjuːbə ˈliːbreɪ/ *noun phr.* Pl. **Cuba libres**. L19.
[ORIGIN Amer. Spanish = free Cuba (a toast during the Cuban War of Independence, 1895–8).]
A long drink usu. containing lime juice and rum.

Cuban /ˈkjuːbən/ *adjective* & *noun.* L16.
[ORIGIN from *Cuba* (see below) + -AN.]
(A native or inhabitant) of Cuba, an island in the W. Indies.
Cuban heel a broad straight-fronted moderately high shoe heel.

cubature /ˈkjuːbətjʊə/ *noun.* L17.
[ORIGIN from CUBE *verb* after QUADRATURE.]
The determination of the cubic content of a solid.

cubbish /ˈkʌbɪʃ/ *adjective.* E19.
[ORIGIN from CUB *noun*[1] + -ISH[1].]
Resembling a cub; awkward, unpolished.
■ **cubbishly** *adverb* L19. **cubbishness** *noun* E19.

cubby /ˈkʌbi/ *noun.* M17.
[ORIGIN Rel. to CUB *noun*[2].]
1 A straw basket. *Scot.* M17.
2 In full ***cubbyhole***. A small closet, a confined space, *esp.* one used for storage. E19.
3 An enclosure containing bait and a hidden trap for animals. *N. Amer.* E20.
– COMB.: ***cubbyhole***: see sense 2 above; **cubby house** something that children playing pretend is a house; *esp.* a toy house.

cube /kjuːb/ *noun*[1] & *adjective.* M16.
[ORIGIN Old French & mod. French, or its source Latin *cubus* from Greek *kubos*.]
▸ **A** *noun.* **1** A solid contained by six equal squares; a regular hexahedron. M16. ▸**b** A block of something so or similarly shaped; a cubical object. E17.
b ***ice cube***, ***sugar cube***, etc. **cube farm** (chiefly *US*) a large office divided into cubicles for individual workers. ***double cube***: see DOUBLE *adjective* & *adverb*. NECKER CUBE. RUBIK'S CUBE.
2 MATH. The product obtained by multiplying a number by the square of that number; the third power *of* a quantity. M16.
3 An extremely conventional or conservative person. (Cf. ***square***.) *slang.* M20.
▸ **B** *adjective.* **1** = CUBIC *adjective* 1, 2. Now chiefly in ***cube root*** below, ***cube sugar***. L16.

R. P. WARREN He took all the cube sugar that was in the bowl.

cube root that number of which the given number is the cube.
2 Following a measurement: of the form of a cube with edges of the stated length. E18.

J. D. DANA Some of these were six feet cube.

cube /ˈkuːbeɪ, ˈkjuː-/ *noun*[2]. Also **cubé**. E20.
[ORIGIN Amer. Spanish *cubé*.]
Any of various S. American shrubby leguminous plants of the genus *Lonchocarpus* with roots containing the insecticide rotenone; (an extract from) the roots of such a plant.

cube /kjuːb/ *verb trans.* L16.
[ORIGIN from the noun.]
1 MATH. Raise (a number) to the third power; find the cube of. L16.
2 Determine the cubic content of. M17.
3 Cut into small cubes; dice. M20.
■ **cuber** *noun* a machine for cutting meat etc. into cubes M20.

cubeb /ˈkjuːbɛb/ *noun.* ME.
[ORIGIN Old French & mod. French *cubèbe*, †*quibibe* (medieval Latin *cubeba*, *quibiba*) from Hispano-Arabic *kubēba* for Arabic *kubāba*.]
The pungent berry of a SE Asian shrub of the pepper family, *Piper cubeba*, used in medicine (esp. crushed in medicated cigarettes) and cookery. Usu. in *pl.*

cubic /ˈkjuːbɪk/ *adjective* & *noun.* L15.
[ORIGIN Old French & mod. French *cubique* or its source Latin *cubicus* from Greek *kubikos*, from *kubos* CUBE *noun*[1]: see -IC.]
▸ **A** *adjective.* **1** MATH. Relating to or involving a third power but no higher one; of three dimensions; of the third degree. L15.
***cubic* RESIDUE.**
2 = CUBICAL 2. M16. ▸**b** Belonging to or being a crystal system in which there are three crystallographic axes equal in length and mutually perpendicular. L19.
cubic nitre sodium nitrate.
3 Of three dimensions; solid; *esp.* designating a volume equal to that of a cube whose edge is a specified unit of length. M17.
cubic centimetre, ***cubic foot***, etc.
▸ **B** *noun.* MATH.
†**1** = CUBE *noun*[1] 2. Only in L15.
2 A cubic expression, equation, or curve. L18.

cubica /ˈkjuːbɪkə/ *noun* & *adjective.* M19.
[ORIGIN Spanish.]
(Of) a fine worsted fabric, similar to shalloon.

C

cubical /ˈkjuːbɪk(ə)l/ *adjective*. L15.
[ORIGIN from CUBIC + -AL¹.]
1 = CUBIC *adjective* 1. Now *rare*. L15.
2 Having the shape or form of a cube. L16.
3 = CUBIC *adjective* 3. L16.
■ **cubically** *adverb* L15. **cubicalness** *noun* (*rare*) E18.

cubicle /ˈkjuːbɪk(ə)l/ *noun*. LME.
[ORIGIN Latin *cubiculum*, from *cubare* recline: see -CULE.]
†**1** A bedroom. LME–E16.
2 A small individual sleeping compartment. M19.
3 Any small partitioned space to accommodate one or two people, e.g. containing a shower or toilet. E20.
4 A chamber or compartment to hold switchgear. E20.
■ **cuˈbicular** *noun & adjective* †(*a*) *noun* (chiefly *Scot.*) an attendant in a bedroom; a chamberlain; (*b*) *adjective* of or belonging to a bedroom: LME.

cubiculum /kjuːˈbɪkjʊləm/ *noun*. Pl. **-la** /-lə/. M19.
[ORIGIN Latin: see CUBICLE.]
A sleeping chamber (now *joc.*); ARCHITECTURE a chapel or oratory attached to a church.
■ Also †**cubiculo** *noun* (*rare*, Shakes.): only in E17.

cubiform /ˈkjuːbɪfɔːm/ *adjective*. M18.
[ORIGIN from Latin *cubus* CUBE *noun*¹ + -I- + -FORM.]
Having the form of a cube.

cubism /ˈkjuːbɪz(ə)m/ *noun*. Also **C-**. E20.
[ORIGIN French *cubisme*, formed as CUBE *noun*¹: see -ISM.]
An artistic movement begun by Picasso and Braque in which perspective with a single viewpoint was abandoned and use was made of, initially, simple geometric shapes or interlocking semi-transparent planes and, later, solid objects stuck on the canvas.
■ **cubist** *noun & adjective* (*a*) *noun* a practitioner or adherent of cubism; (*b*) *adjective* of or pertaining to cubists or cubism: E20. **cuˈbistic** *adjective* somewhat cubist, in a style resembling that of cubism E20. **cuˈbistically** *adverb* E20.

cubit /ˈkjuːbɪt/ *noun*. ME.
[ORIGIN Latin *cubitum* elbow, forearm, cubit.]
1 *hist.* A unit of length approximately equal to the length of the forearm. ME.
†**2** The forearm; the ulna. LME–M19.
3 The analogous part of the forelimb of a bird or quadruped. Now *rare*. E18.

cubital /ˈkjuːbɪt(ə)l/ *adjective*. LME.
[ORIGIN Latin *cubitalis*, from *cubitus* CUBIT: see -AL¹.]
1 *hist.* Of the length of a cubit. LME.
2 ANATOMY. Pertaining to the elbow or (formerly) the forearm or ulna. LME.
3 Of or pertaining to the cubitus or the cubit of an animal, esp. an insect. E19.

cubitus /ˈkjuːbɪtəs/ *noun*. E19.
[ORIGIN Latin: see CUBIT.]
ENTOMOLOGY. †**1** The fourth joint in the first pair of legs in an insect. Only in E19.
2 The fifth longitudinal vein from the anterior edge of an insect's wing. L19.
■ **cubito-** *combining form* [see -O-] of the cubitus and —: L19.

cuboctahedron /ˌkjuːbɒktəˈhiːdr(ə)n, -ˈhɛd-/ *noun*. Also **cubo-octa-** /ˌkjuːbəʊɒktə-/. Pl. **-dra** /-drə/, **-drons**. M19.
[ORIGIN from CUBE *noun*¹ + -O- + OCTAHEDRON.]
A solid of fourteen faces formed by cutting off the corners of a cube so as to add eight equilateral triangular faces corresponding to those of an octahedron.
■ **cuboctahedral** *adjective* E19.

cuboid /ˈkjuːbɔɪd/ *adjective & noun*. E19.
[ORIGIN mod. Latin *cuboides* from Greek *kuboeidēs*, from *kubos* CUBE *noun*¹: see -OID.]
▸ **A** *adjective*. Resembling or approximating to a cube in form, cuboidal. E19.
cuboid bone, a squat bone on the outer side of the foot, next to the fourth and fifth metatarsals.
▸ **B** *noun*. **1** The cuboid bone. M19.
2 A solid with six faces that are rectangular but not all equal; an object with a cuboid shape. L19.
■ **cuˈboidal** *adjective* resembling or approximating to a cube in form; ANATOMY of or pertaining to the cuboid bone; (of epithelium) composed of cuboidal cells: E19.

cuck /kʌk/ *verb*¹ *intrans. obsolete* exc. *hist.* in comb. LME.
[ORIGIN Of Scandinavian origin: cf. Icelandic *kúka* defecate, *kúkur* excrement.]
Defecate.
– COMB.: **cucking stool** *hist.*, †**cuck stool** a chair in which disorderly women etc. were punished by ducking or exposure to public ridicule.

cuck /kʊk/ *verb*² *intrans*. L17.
[ORIGIN Back-form. from CUCKOO.]
= CUCKOO *verb* 1.

cuckold /ˈkʌk(ə)ld/ *noun & verb*. LOE.
[ORIGIN Old Northern French var. of Old French *cucuault*, from *cucu* CUCKOO + *-ald*, *-aud*, *-ault* pejorative suffix.]
▸ **A** *noun*. A man whose wife is adulterous. *derog.* LOE.
▸ **B** *verb trans*. Make a cuckold of. L16.
■ †**cuckoldly** *adjective* = CUCKOLDY L16–M18. **cuckoldom** *noun* (*a*) the state or position of a cuckold; †(*b*) = CUCKOLDRY (a): L16. **cuckoldry** *noun* (*a*) the action of making a cuckold of a man; †(*b*) = CUCKOLDOM (a): E16. **cuckoldy** *adjective* (*arch.*) having the character or qualities of a cuckold (freq. as a general term of abuse) E17.

cuckoo /ˈkʊkuː/ *noun, interjection, adjective, & verb*. ME.
[ORIGIN Old French *cucu* (mod. *coucou*) of imit. origin: cf. Latin *cuculus*, Greek *kokkux*. Superseded Old English *ġēac* GOWK.]
▸ **A** *noun*. **1** A migratory Eurasian grey or brown speckled bird, *Cuculus canorus*, which leaves its eggs in the nests of other birds and has a distinctive cry, the first hearing of which is regarded as a harbinger of spring. ME. ▸**b** Any bird of the cosmopolitan family Cuculidae, including cuckoos, the roadrunner, and the anis. L18.

SPENSER The merry Cuckow, messenger of Spring.

b chestnut-bellied cuckoo a large brownish cuckoo of Jamaica, *Hyetornis pluvialis*; also called ***hunter***, ***old man***. EMERALD ***cuckoo***. KLAAS'S CUCKOO. SHINING ***cuckoo***.
2 Also *interjection*. (Repr.) the call of the cuckoo; an imitation of this. ME.
3 A person who behaves like a cuckoo; *spec.* (*slang*) a silly person. L16.

O. W. HOLMES We Americans are all cuckoos,—we make our homes in the nests of other birds. J. K. JEROME Give us a hand here, can't you, you cuckoo; standing there like a stuffed mummy.

cuckoo in the nest an unwanted intruder.
– COMB.: **cuckoo-bud** *dial.* any of various plants (in Shakes. perh. a buttercup); **cuckoo clock**: in which the hours are sounded by an imitation of the cuckoo's call (often with an imitation cuckoo appearing); **cuckooflower** any of various spring wild flowers, esp. *Cardamine pratensis*, a cruciferous plant with small pink flowers (also called ***lady's smock***); **cuckoo land** = ***cloud cuckoo land*** s.v. CLOUD *noun*; ***cuckoo roller***: see ROLLER *noun*²; **cuckoo scab** *Austral.* & *NZ* a skin disease of sheep; **cuckoo-shrike** any of various tropical Old World passerines of the family Campephagidae, which resemble shrikes; **cuckoo's mate** the wryneck; **cuckoo's meat** = ***wood sorrel*** s.v. WOOD *noun*¹; **cuckoo spit**, **cuckoo spittle** a frothy secretion exuded on plants by larvae of insects of the family Cercopidae (froghoppers or spittle bugs); **cuckoo wasp** any wasp of the family Chrysididae, which includes solitary wasps of a metallic blue or green colour which lay eggs in the nests of other wasps and bees; **cuckoo wrasse** a nest-building European wrasse, *Labrus mixtus*.
▸ **B** *adjective*. **1** Of or pertaining to the cuckoo; resembling the cuckoo and its uniformly repeated call. Usu. *attrib.* E17.

A. HELPS Tired of hearing this cuckoo exclamation.

2 Crazy; foolish. *slang*. E20.

M. GILBERT She must be cuckoo.

▸ **C** *verb*. **1** *verb intrans*. Utter the call of the cuckoo. E17.
2 *verb trans*. Repeat incessantly and without variation. M17.

cuckoo pint /ˈkʊkuːpʌɪnt, -pɪnt/ *noun*. Earlier †**-pintle**. LME.
[ORIGIN from CUCKOO + PINT(LE, with ref. to the shape of the spadix.]
The wild arum, *Arum maculatum*.

cuckquean /ˈkʌkwiːn/ *noun & verb*. Long *rare*. M16.
[ORIGIN from CUCK(OLD + QUEAN.]
▸ **A** *noun*. A woman whose husband is adulterous. M16.
▸ †**B** *verb trans*. Make a cuckquean of. L16–M17.

cucujo *noun* var. of CUCUY.

cuculiform /kəˈkjuːlɪfɔːm/ *adjective*. L19.
[ORIGIN mod. Latin *Cuculiformes*, from Latin *cuculus* cuckoo + -FORM.]
ORNITHOLOGY. Belonging or pertaining to the order Cuculiformes, which comprises the cuckoo family (Cuculidae) and the turaco family (Musophagidae).

cucullate /ˈkjuːkʌleɪt, kjʊˈkʌlət/ *adjective*. L18.
[ORIGIN Late Latin *cucullatus*, from *cucullus* hood: see -ATE².]
BOTANY & ZOOLOGY. Shaped like a hood or cowl.
■ **cucullately** *adverb* M19.

cucullated /ˈkjuːkʌleɪtɪd/ *adjective*. M17.
[ORIGIN formed as CUCULLATE + -ED¹.]
1 BOTANY & ZOOLOGY. Cucullate. M17.
2 Wearing a hood, cowled. M18.

cucumber /ˈkjuːkʌmbə/ *noun*. LME.
[ORIGIN Latin *cucumis*, *cucumer-*, whence Old French *cocombre* (mod. *concombre*) to which the English word was assim.]
1 A trailing vine of the gourd family, *Cucumis sativus* native to southern Asia, whose fruit is the cucumber (sense 2). LME.
2 The long fleshy fruit of this plant, usu. eaten sliced in salads or sandwiches, or pickled when young (see GHERKIN). LME.
cool as a cucumber perfectly cool or self-possessed.
3 Any of various related or similar plants or their fruits. M16.
squirting cucumber a plant of the gourd family, *Ecballium elaterium*, whose fruit when ripe expels its seeds and pulp with force.
4 ***sea cucumber***, a holothurian; formerly, some shellfish mentioned by Pliny. E17.
5 In full ***cucumber tree***. Any of several American magnolias, esp. *Magnolia acuminata*, with small cucumber-shaped fruit. *US*. L18.
– COMB.: **cucumber beetle** *N. Amer.* any of several beetles which attack cucumbers, corn, and other plants; **cucumber mosaic** a virus disease of cucurbits spread by cucumber beetles and aphids and causing mottling and stunting; **cucumber tree** (*a*) a tropical Asian tree of the oxalis family, *Averrhoa bilimbi*, with edible astringent cucumber-shaped fruit; (*b*) see sense 5 above.

cucumiform /kjʊˈkjuːmɪfɔːm/ *adjective*. M19.
[ORIGIN from Latin *cucumis* cucumber + -FORM.]
Of the shape of a cucumber.

cucurbit /kjʊˈkəːbɪt/ *noun*. LME.
[ORIGIN Old French & mod. French *cucurbite* from Latin *cucurbita*.]
1 A plant of the gourd family, Cucurbitaceae. Formerly, a gourd. LME.
2 A vessel or retort (orig. gourd-shaped) for chemical or alchemical use. *obsolete* exc. *hist.* LME.

cucurbitaceous /kjʊˌkəːbɪˈteɪʃ(ə)s/ *adjective*. E19.
[ORIGIN from mod. Latin *Cucurbitaceae* (see below), from Latin *cucurbita* gourd: see -ACEOUS.]
BOTANY. Of or pertaining to the family Cucurbitaceae, which comprises trailing or climbing plants with fleshy fruits, as the gourd, melon, pumpkin, cucumber, etc.

cucuy /kəˈkuːi/ *noun*. Also **cucujo** /kəˈkuːjəʊ/, pl. **-os**, & other vars. L16.
[ORIGIN Spanish *cucuyo* from Haitian creole.]
A luminous W. Indian click beetle, *Pyrophorus noctilucus*.

cud /kʌd/ *noun & verb*.
[ORIGIN Old English *cudu*, earlier *cwudu*, *cwidu* = Old High German *quiti*, *kuti* glue (German *Kitt* cement, putty).]
▸ **A** *noun*. **1** The partly digested food which a ruminating animal brings back into its mouth from its first stomach for further chewing. OE.
2 Any substance used by a person to keep in the mouth and chew. (Cf. QUID *noun*³.) Now *dial.* OE.
– PHRASES: **chew the cud** *fig.* reflect meditatively, ruminate.
▸ **B** *verb*. Infl. **-dd-**.
1 *verb trans*. Chew as cud; ruminate upon. *rare*. M16.
2 *verb intrans*. Of an animal: chew the cud. M20.

cudbear /ˈkʌdbɛː/ *noun*. M18.
[ORIGIN Alt. of *Cuthbert* by Cuthbert Gordon, 18th-cent. Scot. chemist who patented the powder: cf. CUDDY *noun*².]
A purple or violet powder used for dyeing, prepared from various lichens, esp. *Ochrolechia tartarea*. Also, this lichen.

†**cudden** *noun*¹. L17–M19.
[ORIGIN Unknown.]
A fool, a dolt.

cudden *noun*² var. of CUDDING.

cuddie *noun* var. of CUDDY *noun*³.

cuddikie *noun* see CUDEIGH.

cudding /ˈkʌdɪŋ/ *noun*. Chiefly *Scot.* Also **-din**, **-den**. L17.
[ORIGIN Gaelic *cudainn*: cf. CUDDY *noun*³.]
1 = CHAR *noun*³. Now *rare* or *obsolete*. L17.
2 = CUDDY *noun*³. M19.

cuddle /ˈkʌd(ə)l/ *verb & noun*. E16.
[ORIGIN Perh. from COUTH + -LE³.]
▸ **A** *verb*. **1** *verb trans*. Hold in an affectionate embrace, hug and fondle. E16.
2 *verb intrans*. Settle close and snug to another or together. (Foll. by *up*.) E18.
3 *verb intrans.* & *refl.* Curl oneself *up* in preparing to sleep; lie down to sleep. E19.
▸ **B** *noun*. An affectionate hug, a close embrace. E19.
– NOTE: Rare before 18.
■ **cuddleable** *adjective* (*colloq.*) = CUDDLY (b) E20. **cuddlesome** *adjective* = CUDDLY (b) L19. **cuddly** *adjective* (*a*) given to cuddling; (*b*) that invites cuddling; *spec.* (of a toy) padded or spongy and covered in soft fabric: M19.

cuddy /ˈkʌdi/ *noun*¹. M17.
[ORIGIN Prob. from early mod. Dutch *kajute*, *kaiuyte* (now *kajuit* whence French *cajute*) from Old French & mod. French *cahute* shanty, of unknown origin.]
1 NAUTICAL. A room or cabin in a ship; *esp.* (*a*) one where the captain and passengers eat; (*b*) a shelter or locker in the bow of a small boat. M17.
2 *gen.* A small room, closet, or cupboard. L18.

cuddy /ˈkʌdi/ *noun*². E18.
[ORIGIN Perh. a use of *Cuddy*, pet form of male forename *Cuthbert*: cf. NEDDY *noun*.]
1 A donkey. Chiefly *Scot.* E18. ▸**b** A stupid person, an ass. Chiefly *Scot.* M19. ▸**c** A (small) horse. Chiefly *N. English* & *Austral.* L19.
2 A lever mounted on a tripod for lifting stones etc. M19.
– PHRASES: ***Scotch cuddy***: see SCOTCH *adjective*.

cuddy /ˈkʌdi/ *noun*³. *Scot.* Also **cuddie**. L18.
[ORIGIN Gaelic *cudaig*: cf. CUDDING.]
The coalfish, *esp.* a young one.

†**cuddy** *noun*⁴ var. of next.

cudeigh /ˈkʌdɪx/ *noun*. Also **cuddikie** /ˈkʌdɪki/, †**cuddy**. LME.
[ORIGIN Repr. Old Irish & mod. Irish & Gaelic *cuid oidhche* (*cuid* share, part, meal, *oidhche* night).]
1 *hist.* In Scotland and Ireland, a supper and night's entertainment formerly due to a lord from his tenant; a rent or present in lieu of this. LME.
†**2** *transf.* A gift, a bribe; a premium on a loan. *Scot.* E18–E19.

cudgel /ˈkʌdʒ(ə)l/ *noun & verb*.
[ORIGIN Old English *cycgel*, of unknown origin.]
▸ **A** *noun*. **1** A short thick stick used as a weapon; a club. OE.
take up the cudgels *fig*. engage in a vigorous debate (*for* etc.).
2 In *pl*. The use of cudgels; the art of combat with cudgels. M17.

ADDISON They learned to Box and play at Cudgels.

– COMB.: **cudgel-play**, **cudgel-playing** = sense 2 above.
▸ **B** *verb*. Infl. **-ll-**, ***-l-**.
1 *verb trans*. Beat (as) with a cudgel. L16.
cudgel one's brains: see BRAIN *noun*.
2 *verb intrans*. Wield a cudgel or cudgels. Chiefly as ***cudgelling*** *verbal noun*. L18.
■ **cudgeller** *noun* L16.

cudgerie /ˈkʌdʒəri/ *noun*. *Austral*. L19.
[ORIGIN Bandjalang *gajari*.]
Any of several Australian trees, *spec*. the southern silver ash, *Flindersia scholtiana*, an evergreen rainforest timber tree (family Rutaceae).

†**cuds** *noun*. L16–M17.
[ORIGIN Alt.]
God's: used in oaths and exclamations.
■ Also †**cudso** *noun*: only in E18.

cudweed /ˈkʌdwiːd/ *noun*. M16.
[ORIGIN from CUD *noun* + WEED *noun*[1].]
Any of various erect herbaceous plants of the composite family, esp. of the genera *Gnaphalium* and *Filago*, with hairy or downy foliage.

cudwort /ˈkʌdwəːt/ *noun*. M16.
[ORIGIN from CUD *noun* + WORT *noun*[1].]
= CUDWEED.

†**cue** *noun*[1]. LME.
[ORIGIN Repr. pronunc. of Q.]
1 The sum of half a farthing, formerly denoted in college accounts by the letter q (for Latin *quadrans* quarter). LME–E17.
2 A particular small quantity of bread, beer, etc. *Univ. slang*. E17–M19.

cue /kjuː/ *noun*[2]. M16.
[ORIGIN Unknown.]
▸ **I 1 a** THEATRICAL. A particular word or phrase in a play etc. which serves as a signal to another actor to enter or begin a speech. M16. ▸**b** MUSIC. In an orchestral or vocal score, a short passage from another part written in small notes as a signal to a performer of an approaching entry. L19. ▸**c** CINEMATOGRAPHY & BROADCASTING. A prearranged signal for action to begin or end; *spec*. a mark on a film serving as a signal for a film editor or projectionist. M20.

a M. RENAULT An actor who dries up on the crucial cue for which the scene is waiting.

2 An indication or hint of when or how to speak, behave, etc. M16.

E. F. BENSON Lucia had not been thinking of this . . but she picked up her cue instantaneously.

3 The part assigned to one to play; the proper course to take. L16.
4 PSYCHOLOGY. A feature of a perception or of something perceived that is used as an aid in the brain's interpretation of the perception. E20.
5 A facility for playing a tape recording during a fast forward wind, so that it can be stopped when a particular recording is reached. L20.
▸ **II 6** A mood, a disposition, a frame of mind. Now *rare*. M16.
– PHRASES: **cue and review** a tape-recording cue facility combined with a similar one for fast rewind. **on cue** (as if) in response to a signal; at the correct moment. **take one's cue from** follow the example or advice of.
– COMB.: **cue bid** *noun & verb intrans*. (BRIDGE) (make) an artificial bid, inviting a particular response from one's partner, for exploratory or informative purposes; **cue card**: held beside a camera for an announcer to read from while looking into the camera.

cue /kjuː/ *noun*[3]. M18.
[ORIGIN Var. of QUEUE *noun*.]
1 A long plait of hair worn hanging down behind, a pigtail. M18.
2 The long straight tapering rod with which the white ball is struck in billiards, snooker, etc. M18.
– COMB.: **cue ball** the white ball which is to be struck with the cue in billiards, snooker, etc.
■ **cueist** *noun* a player of billiards, snooker, etc.; a person skilled in the use of a cue: L19.

cue /kjuː/ *noun*[4]. *colloq*. E20.
[ORIGIN Abbreviation: cf. CUKE.]
= CUCUMBER 2.

cue /kjuː/ *verb*[1] *trans*. Now *rare*. L18.
[ORIGIN from CUE *noun*[3]. Cf. QUEUE *verb*.]
Form or twist (the hair) into a cue.

cue /kjuː/ *verb*[2] *trans*. E20.
[ORIGIN from CUE *noun*[2].]
Provide with a cue or signal; lead *in* by means of a cue.

A. COOKE Cued by my mention of some of the great names, he went off into a bout of marvellous total recall.

cueca /ˈkwɛkə/ *noun*. E20.
[ORIGIN Amer. Spanish from ZAMACUECA.]
A lively S. American dance. Also called ***marinera***.

cue-owl /ˈkjuːaʊl/ *noun*. *rare*. M19.
[ORIGIN Italian *chiù*, *ciù*, from the sound of its cry.]
The European scops owl, *Otus scops*.

cuesta /ˈkwɛstə/ *noun*. E19.
[ORIGIN Spanish = slope from Latin *costa*: see COAST *noun*.]
Orig. (*US dial*.), a steep slope that terminates a gently sloping plain; a plain in this configuration. Now (GEOGRAPHY), a ridge with a gentle slope on one side and a steep one on the other, a scarp and dip.

cuff /kʌf/ *noun*[1]. LME.
[ORIGIN Unknown.]
1 A mitten, a glove. Long *obsolete* exc. *Canad. dial*. LME.
2 A distinctive part at the end of a long sleeve, consisting of the sleeve itself turned back or a band of material sewn on; a separate band of linen worn round the wrist. L15. ▸**b** A turn-up on a trouser leg. Chiefly *N. Amer*. E20.
3 A handcuff. Usu. in *pl*. M17.
4 An inflatable bag which is wound round a limb when blood pressure is measured. E20.
– PHRASES: ***French cuff***: see FRENCH *adjective*. **off the cuff** *colloq*. extempore, without preparation. **on the cuff** *colloq*. (**a**) *US* on credit; (**b**) *NZ* beyond what is appropriate or conventional. ***shoot one's cuffs***: see SHOOT *verb*.
– COMB.: **cufflink** a device which goes through two buttonholes in a cuff to hold its two sides together.
■ **cuffless** *adjective* L19.

cuff /kʌf/ *noun*[2]. M16.
[ORIGIN from CUFF *verb*[2].]
A blow, *esp*. one given with the open hand.

W. C. WILLIAMS He was my boss and many a time he gave me a cuff over the ears.

go to cuffs, **fall to cuffs** (now *rare*) come to blows, start fighting.

cuff /kʌf/ *noun*[3]. *slang*. *derog*. E17.
[ORIGIN Unknown: cf. CUFFIN.]
An old man, *esp*. a miserly one.

cuff /kʌf/ *noun*[4]. Chiefly *Scot*. M18.
[ORIGIN Unknown: cf. SCUFF *noun*[2], SCRUFF *noun*[2].]
The nape *of* the neck.

Cuff /kʌf/ *noun*[5]. *US colloq*. Now *rare* & considered *derog*. M18.
[ORIGIN Abbreviation.]
= CUFFEE.

cuff /kʌf/ *verb*[1] *trans*. E16.
[ORIGIN from CUFF *noun*[1].]
1 Provide with a cuff or cuffs. Chiefly as ***cuffed*** *ppl adjective*. E16.

Daily Telegraph Flannel trousers, deeply cuffed.

2 Handcuff. *rare*. L17.
■ **cuffing** *verbal noun* (**a**) the action of the verb; (**b**) the pathological accumulation of lymphocytes etc. in a ring within a blood vessel: L17.

cuff /kʌf/ *verb*[2]. M16.
[ORIGIN Perh. imit.: cf. German slang *kuffen* thrash, Swedish *kuffa* thrust, push.]
1 *verb trans*. Strike, esp. with the open hand; buffet. M16.

B. CHATWIN She cuffed him when he tried to make love to her. W. GOLDING The wind . . did not clear the sky but cuffed the air this way and that.

2 *verb intrans*. Deal or exchange blows; scuffle. E17.
3 *verb trans*. Discuss, talk *over*, (a tale, a matter); tell (a tale). *dial*. M18.
■ **cuffer** *noun* (**a**) *arch*. a person who cuffs; a fighter; (**b**) *dial. & slang* a yarn, a story: M17.

Cuffee /ˈkʌfi/ *noun*. *US colloq*. Now *rare* & *offensive*. Also **Cuffy**, **c-**. E18.
[ORIGIN Personal name formerly common among black people.]
1 (A nickname for) a black person. E18.
2 A black bear. E19.

cuffin /ˈkʌfɪn/ *noun*. *criminals' slang*. M16.
[ORIGIN Unknown: cf. CHUFF *noun*[1].]
= COVE *noun*[2].

Cuffy *noun* var. of CUFFEE.

Cufic *adjective* var. of KUFIC.

cufuffle *noun* var. of KERFUFFLE.

cui bono /kwiː ˈbɒnəʊ, kuːi ˈbəʊnəʊ/ *interjection (interrog.)*, *adjectival phr.*, & *noun phr*. E17.
[ORIGIN Latin = to whom (is it) a benefit?]
▸ **A** *interjection (interrog.)*. What is the purpose (of)? Who stands to gain (and so might be responsible)? E17.
▸ **B** *adjectival phr*. Of or pertaining to the question ***cui bono?*** M18.
▸ **C** *noun phr*. The question ***cui bono?*** M19.

cuirass /kwɪˈras/ *noun & verb*. Also †**curats**. LME.
[ORIGIN Old French *cuirace*, later *curas*, *-ace* (mod. *cuirasse*), from alt. (after Old French & mod. French *cuir* leather) of Proto-Romance use as noun of fem. of Latin *coriaceus* adjective, from *corium* leather: see -ACEOUS.]
▸ **A** *noun*. **1** *sing*. & in *pl*. A piece of armour for the body (orig. of leather); *spec*. a piece reaching down to the waist, and consisting of a breastplate and a backplate, buckled or otherwise fastened together. In *sing*. occas., the breastplate alone. LME.
2 = BUCKLER *noun* 3. E17.
3 The armour plating of a ship etc. M19.
4 A close-fitting sleeveless bodice, often stiffened with metal trimmings or embroidery, formerly worn by women. L19.
5 In full ***cuirass respirator***. A respirator which encloses the trunk but not the limbs. M20.
▸ **B** *verb trans*. Cover or protect (as) with a cuirass. M19.
■ **cuirassed** *adjective* provided with cuirasses; protected (as if) by a cuirass: E18.

C

cuirassier /kwɪrəˈsiːə/ *noun*. M16.
[ORIGIN French, formed as CUIRASS: see -IER.]
A cavalry soldier wearing a cuirass.

cuir-bouilli /kwɪəˈbuːlji, *foreign* kɥirbuji/ *noun*. Long *obsolete* exc. *hist*. LME.
[ORIGIN French = boiled leather.]
Leather boiled or soaked in hot water and, when soft, moulded into any required form, which it retains on becoming dry and hard (formerly often used for armour).

cuir-ciselé /kwɪəˈsiːzleɪ, *foreign* kɥirsizle/ *adjective*. M20.
[ORIGIN French = engraved leather.]
(Of a design on a leather binding) cut in relief with a pointed tool; having such a design.

Cuisenaire /kwiːzəˈnɛː/ *noun*. M20.
[ORIGIN Georges *Cuisenaire* (c 1891–1976), Belgian educationalist.]
Cuisenaire rod, each of a set of wooden rods, of different length and colour according to the number they represent, used in teaching children about numbers.
– NOTE: *Cuisenaire* is a proprietary name.

cuish *noun* var. of CUISSE.

cuisine /kwɪˈziːn/ *noun*. L18.
[ORIGIN French = kitchen from Latin *coquina*, *cocina*, from *coquere* to cook: cf. KITCHEN.]
A culinary establishment; cookery as an art, esp. as characteristic of a particular country or establishment.
batterie de cuisine: see BATTERIE 2. **cuisine bourgeoise** /ˈbʊəʒwɑːz/ [middle-class] plain (French) home cooking. NOUVELLE CUISINE.
■ **cuisinier** *noun* a (French) cook M19.

cuisse /kwɪs/ *noun*. Also **cuish** /kwɪʃ/. ME.
[ORIGIN Orig. in pl. from Old French *cuiss(i)eus* pl. of *cuissel* from late Latin *coxale*, from *coxa* hip.]
In *pl*., armour for protecting the front of the thighs; *sing*. a thigh-piece.

†**cuit** *adjective & noun*. Also **cute**. LME–M18.
[ORIGIN French (from Latin *coctus*), pa. pple of *cuire* from Latin *coquere* cook, boil.]
(A wine, liquor, etc.) made thicker by boiling down, and sweetened.

cuiter /ˈkuːtə/ *verb trans*. *Scot*. L17.
[ORIGIN Unknown.]
Attend to (a person) with kindly assiduity.

cuittle /ˈkuːt(ə)l/ *verb trans*. *Scot*. M16.
[ORIGIN Unknown.]
1 Curry (favour); wheedle, coax. M16.
2 Tickle. L18.

cuivré /ˈkiːvreɪ, *foreign* kɥivre/ *adverb & noun*. M20.
[ORIGIN French, pa. pple of *cuivrer* play with a brassy tone, from *cuivre* COPPER *noun*[1] from late Latin *cuprum*.]
MUSIC. (With) a harsh strident tone (in a brass instrument).

cuke /kjuːk/ *noun*. *colloq*. (chiefly *N. Amer*.). E20.
[ORIGIN Abbreviation: cf. CUE *noun*[4].]
= CUCUMBER *noun* 2.

culbut /ˈkʌlbət/ *verb intrans. & trans*. *rare*. L17.
[ORIGIN French *culbuter*, from *cul* buttocks + *buter* BUTT *verb*[1].]
Overturn backwards; drive back in disorder.

culch /kʌltʃ/ *noun*. *local & US*. Also **cultch**. M17.
[ORIGIN Unknown. Cf. SCULCH.]
1 The mass of stones, old shells, etc., of which an oyster bed is formed. M17.
2 *gen*. Rubbish, refuse. M18.
■ **culching** *noun* the practice of strewing an oyster bed with culch L19.

culchie /ˈkʌl(t)ʃi/ *noun & adjective*. *Irish colloq*. (freq. *derog*.). Also **-shie** /-ʃi/. M20.
[ORIGIN Perh. alt. of 1st part of *Kiltimagh*, a country town in County Mayo, Ireland.]
▸ **A** *noun*. A country bumpkin; a provincial or rustic person. M20.
▸ **B** *attrib*. or as *adjective*. Of, pertaining to, or characteristic of a culchie, provincial, rustic. L20.

Culdee /ˈkʌldiː/ *noun & adjective*. LME.
[ORIGIN medieval Latin *culdeus* alt. (after Latin *cultor Dei* worshipper of God) of *Kel(e)deus*, from Old Irish *cēle Dé*, *céile Dé* anchorite, lit. 'client of God' (*Dé* genit. of *Día* god).]
▸ **A** *noun*. A member of an ancient Scoto-Irish religious order, found from the 8th cent. onwards. LME.
▸ **B** *adjective*. Of or pertaining to the Culdees. L19.

C

■ **Cul'dean** *adjective* E19.

cul-de-lampe /kydlɑ̃:p/ *noun*. Pl. **culs-de-lampe** (pronounced same). E18.
[ORIGIN French, lit. 'bottom of lamp'.]
1 ARCHITECTURE. An ornamental support or pendant of inverted conical form. E18.
2 TYPOGRAPHY. An ornament, often based on an inverted conical form, placed at the end of a passage of text. Now *rare*. E19.

cul-de-sac /'kʌldəsak, kʊldə'sak/ *noun*. Pl. **culs-de-sac** (pronounced same), **cul-de-sacs**. M18.
[ORIGIN French = sack-bottom.]
1 ANATOMY. A vessel, tube, sac, etc., open only at one end; the closed end of such a vessel. M18.
2 A street, passage, etc., closed at one end; a blind alley; MILITARY a position in which an army is hemmed in on all sides except behind. L18.

culdoscopy /kʌl'dɒskəpi/ *noun*. M20.
[ORIGIN from CUL-DE-SAC + -O- + -SCOPY.]
MEDICINE. Visual examination of a woman's pelvic viscera by means of an endoscope passed through the vaginal wall.
■ **'culdoscope** *noun* an endoscope designed for this M20.

-cule /kju:l/ *suffix*.
[ORIGIN Repr. French *-cule* from Latin *-culus*, *-cula*, *-culum*, dim. suffix: cf. -CLE, -UNCLE.]
Forming (orig. dim.) nouns, as ***molecule***, ***crepuscule***, etc. The Latin endings *-culus*, *-cula*, *-culum*, are retained in some (esp. technical) words from Latin.

culet /'kʌlɪt/ *noun*[1]. *obsolete* exc. *hist*. M16.
[ORIGIN Old French *cueillete* from medieval Latin *collecta* sum collected.]
A sum collected from all those who are obliged to pay it; an assessment, a rate.

culet /'kju:lɪt/ *noun*[2]. Also (earlier) **collet** /'kɒlɪt/. L17.
[ORIGIN French, dim. of *cul* bottom: see -ET[1].]
1 The horizontal base of a diamond, formed by the blunting of a point, when the stone is cut as a brilliant. L17.
2 A piece of armour for protecting the hinder part of the body below the waist. M19.

culex /'kju:lɛks/ *noun*. In sense 2 also **C-**. Pl. **-lices** /-lɪsi:z/. L15.
[ORIGIN Latin = gnat.]
†**1** A gnat. Only in L15.
2 Any mosquito of the genus *Culex*, which includes the common house mosquito. Also more fully ***culex mosquito***. E19.

†**culgee** *noun*. *Indian*. M17.
[ORIGIN Urdu from Persian *kalgī*.]
1 A rich figured silk used for turbans, gowns, etc. M17–M18.
2 A jewelled plume on a turban. E18–M19.

culici- /'kju:lɪsi/ *combining form* of Latin *culic-*, CULEX: see -I-. Also **culi-**.
■ **culici'cidal** *adjective* pertaining to or being a culicicide L19. **culicicide** *noun* [-CIDE] an insecticide for destroying mosquitoes E20. **culi'cidal** *adjective* = CULICICIDAL L19. **culicide** *noun* = CULICICIDE *noun* E20. **culicifuge** *noun* [-FUGE] a substance applied to the body or to clothing in order to keep mosquitoes away L19.

culicine /'kju:lɪsi:n/ *noun & adjective*. E20.
[ORIGIN mod. Latin *Culicini*, *-nae*, from Latin *culic-*, CULEX: see -INE[1].]
ENTOMOLOGY. (Pertaining to or designating) a mosquito of a group that contains the genus *Culex* but not *Anopheles*.

culinary /'kʌlɪn(ə)ri/ *adjective*. M17.
[ORIGIN Latin *culinarius*, from *culina* kitchen: see -ARY[1].]
1 Of or pertaining to a kitchen or cookery. M17.
2 Of a vegetable etc.: fit for cooking. M18.
■ **culi'narian** *adjective* (*rare*) of or pertaining to a kitchen E17. **culinarily** *adverb* (*rare*) M19.

cull /kʌl/ *noun*[1] *& adjective*. E17.
[ORIGIN from CULL *verb*[1].]
▸ **A** *noun*. **1** An act of culling; a selection; *spec*. the process of selecting and killing surplus or inferior animals from a flock etc. E17.

> *Times Lit. Suppl.* A list of the words and phrases I'd found . . showing an average daily cull from an intelligent newspaper. *Guardian* A cull of 375 seals is to be allowed . . this summer.

2 An animal selected in a cull; *spec*. an inferior farm animal. L18.
3 *sing*. & in *pl*. Inferior or refuse timber. Chiefly *N. Amer*. E19.
4 *gen*. In *pl*. Items picked out as surplus or inferior. Chiefly *dial*. L19.
▸ **B** *attrib*. or as *adjective*. Selected in a cull; rejected as surplus or inferior. L18.

cull /kʌl/ *noun*[2]. *slang & dial*. L17.
[ORIGIN Perh. from CULLY.]
= CULLY.

cull /kʌl/ *verb*[1]. ME.
[ORIGIN Old French *coillier*, (also mod.) *cueiller* from Proto-Romance from Latin *colligere* COLLECT *verb*.]
1 *verb trans*. Choose from a fairly large number; pick, select. (Foll. by *from*, (arch.) *out*.) ME. ▸**b** *verb trans. & intrans*. Select (livestock etc.) according to quality; select from a flock and kill (surplus or inferior animals etc.); *N. Amer*. remove (timber) as inferior. E19.

> G. CRABBE Words aptly culled, and meanings well exprest. H. CARPENTER His wide general knowledge, culled from his father's library. **b** *transf*.: T. KENEALLY The limpers, the coughers, were culled at the beginning of each stage and executed.

2 *verb trans*. Gather, pick, (flowers, fruit, etc.). M17.
3 *verb trans*. Subject (something containing or consisting of many items) to a process of selection. E18.
■ **culler** *noun* a person who culls or selects (esp. inferior or surplus items) LME.

cull *verb*[2] var. of COLL *verb*[1].

cullender *noun & verb* var. of COLANDER.

Cullen skink /ˌkʌlən 'skɪŋk/ *noun*. M20.
[ORIGIN from *Cullen*, a village in NE Scotland + SKINK *noun*[2].]
A Scottish soup made from smoked haddock, potatoes, onions, and milk.

cullet /'kʌlɪt/ *noun*. E19.
[ORIGIN Var. & extension of use of COLLET *noun*[1] 4.]
Broken or scrap glass which is melted down for reuse.

†**cullible** *adjective*. Only in E19.
[ORIGIN from CULL *noun*[2], CULLY + -IBLE. No corresp. verb *cull* is recorded.]
Easily made a fool of; gullible.
■ †**cullibility** *noun* gullibility E18–M19.

culling /'kʌlɪŋ/ *noun*. LME.
[ORIGIN from CULL *verb*[1] + -ING[1].]
1 The action of selecting or picking out; *spec*. the selective killing of surplus or inferior animals. LME.
2 An item picked out; *spec*. an old or inferior animal taken out from a flock. Freq. in *pl*. E17.

cullion /'kʌljən/ *noun*. LME.
[ORIGIN Old French *coillon* (mod. *couillon*) from Proto-Romance, from Latin *coleus*, *culleus* bag, testicle from Greek *koleos* sheath.]
1 A testicle. Now *rare*. LME.
2 A base despicable person. *arch*. L16.
3 In *pl*. An orchid. Now *rare*. E17.
■ †**cullionly** *adjective* contemptible, base E17–E19.

cullis /'kʌlɪs/ *noun*[1]. Now *rare*. LME.
[ORIGIN Old French *coleïz* (mod. *coulis*) use as noun of adjective from Proto-Romance, from Latin *colare* strain, flow (whence French *couler*).]
A strong broth of meat, fowl, etc., boiled and strained.

cullis /'kʌlɪs/ *noun*[2]. M19.
[ORIGIN French COULISSE.]
ARCHITECTURE. A grooved timber, a gutter, a channel.

cully /'kʌli/ *noun & verb*. *slang*. M17.
[ORIGIN Unknown.]
▸ **A** *noun*. **1** A person who is cheated or imposed upon; a dupe; a simpleton. Now *rare*. M17.
2 A man; a mate, a pal. L17.
▸ †**B** *verb trans*. Make a fool of, cheat, take in. L17–M19.

culm /kʌlm/ *noun*[1]. ME.
[ORIGIN Prob. rel. to COAL *noun*.]
1 Soot, smut. *obsolete* exc. *Scot*. ME.
2 Coal dust, slack, esp. of anthracite. E17.
3 Anthracite. M18.
4 GEOLOGY. (Also **C-**.) The material of a set of Carboniferous strata (***the Culm Measures***) in SW England, mostly shale and limestone with occasional thin coal seams. Also, this set of strata. M19.

†**culm** *noun*[2]. *rare*. L16–E19.
[ORIGIN Abbreviation of CULMEN.]
The summit, the culminating point.

culm /kʌlm/ *noun*[3]. M17.
[ORIGIN Latin *culmus*.]
BOTANY. The stem of a plant; *esp*. the jointed stem of grasses and sedges.

culmen /'kʌlmɛn/ *noun*. M17.
[ORIGIN Latin, contr. of *columen* top, summit, etc.]
1 The top, the summit; *fig*. the acme, the culminating point. M17.
2 The upper ridge of a bird's bill. M19.
3 ANATOMY. An anterior part of the vermis of the cerebellum bounded by deep fissures. E19.

culmiferous /kʌl'mɪf(ə)rəs/ *adjective*[1]. E18.
[ORIGIN from CULM *noun*[3] + -FEROUS.]
BOTANY. Having a jointed hollow stalk, like grasses.

culmiferous /kʌl'mɪf(ə)rəs/ *adjective*[2]. M19.
[ORIGIN from CULM *noun*[1] + -FEROUS.]
GEOLOGY. Containing or producing culm.

culminant /'kʌlmɪnənt/ *adjective*. E17.
[ORIGIN Late Latin *culminant-* pres. ppl stem of *culminare*: see CULMINATE, -ANT[1].]
1 (Of a celestial object) at its greatest altitude, on the meridian; *gen*. at its greatest height. E17.
2 Forming the highest point; topmost. M19.

culminate /'kʌlmɪneɪt/ *verb*. M17.
[ORIGIN Late Latin *culminat-* pa. ppl stem of *culminare* exalt, extol, from *culmen*, *-min-* summit: see -ATE[3].]
1 *verb intrans*. Of a celestial object: reach its greatest altitude, be on the meridian. M17.
2 *verb intrans*. *gen*. Reach its highest point; rise to an apex or summit. (Foll. by *in*.) M17.

> O. SITWELL Almost every hill culminates in a tower.

3 *verb intrans*. Reach its climax or point of highest development. (Foll. by *in*.) M17.

> H. J. LASKI The speculative mania which culminated in the South Sea Bubble. HENRY MILLER Did my life really lead up to this culminating moment? *Nature* The warm period in the present century has culminated.

4 *verb trans*. Bring to a climax; form the summit or climax of, crown. (*rare* before L19.) M17.

> *New Scientist* Feynman and . . Gell-Mann, whose work culminated a period of feverish experimental and theoretical development.

culmination /kʌlmɪ'neɪʃ(ə)n/ *noun*. M17.
[ORIGIN from CULMINATE: see -ATION.]
1 The attainment by a celestial object of its highest altitude; the act of reaching the meridian. M17.
2 The attainment of the highest or climactic point; that in which something culminates, the crown, the consummation, (*of*). M17.

> *Sunday Times* Fat Tuesday is the culmination of two weeks of celebrations.

3 GEOLOGY. **a** A part of a fold, esp. a nappe, where the strata were at their highest before they were eroded. E20. ▸**b** A locally highest part in a fold system which rises and falls in axial as well as transverse directions; a high point between two saddles. M20.

culotte /kju:'lɒt, *foreign* kylɔt/ *noun*. Pl. pronounced same. M19.
[ORIGIN French = knee breeches. Cf. SANS-CULOTTE.]
1 Knee breeches. *rare*. M19.
2 *sing*. & (usu.) in *pl*. A woman's garment that hangs like a skirt but has separate legs, as in trousers; a divided skirt. E20.
3 A fringe of soft hair on the back of the forelegs of some dogs. E20.

culpa /'kʌlpə/ *noun*. M19.
[ORIGIN Latin: see CULPABLE.]
LAW. Neglect resulting in damage, negligence.

culpable /'kʌlpəb(ə)l/ *adjective & noun*. ME.
[ORIGIN Old French & mod. French *coupable* from Latin *culpabilis*, from *culpare* to blame, from *culpa* fault, blame: see -ABLE.]
▸ **A** *adjective*. **1** Guilty (*of*, †*in* an offence), criminal; deserving punishment. Now *rare* or *obsolete*. ME.

> G. P. R. JAMES The greatest crime of which a man could render himself culpable.

culpable homicide SCOTS LAW homicide not amounting to murder.
†**2** Foll. by *of*: deserving, liable to, (punishment, judgement, etc.). LME–E17.
3 Deserving censure; blameworthy. L16.

> HOBBES What circumstances make an action laudable, or culpable.

▸ †**B** *noun*. A guilty person, a culprit. ME–M18.
■ **culpa'bility** *noun* L17. **culpableness** *noun* LME. **culpably** *adverb* in a culpable manner, to a culpable degree M17.

culpose /kʌl'pəʊs/ *adjective*. M19.
[ORIGIN from Latin *culpa* fault + -OSE[1], after *dolose*.]
ROMAN LAW. Characterized by (criminal) negligence.

culprit /'kʌlprɪt/ *noun*. L17.
[ORIGIN Perh. from misinterpretation as a form of address of written abbreviation *cul. prist* for Anglo-Norman *Culpable: prest d'averrer notre bille* '(You are) guilty: (we are) ready to aver our indictment'. In sense 3 infl. by Latin *culpa* fault.]
1 LAW. A person arraigned for high treason or felony. Only in the formula ***Culprit, how will you be tried?***, said by the clerk to a prisoner who has pleaded not guilty. Long *obsolete* exc. *hist*. L17.
2 A person accused of a criminal offence. E18.

> M. PRIOR An author is in the condition of a culprit: the public are his judges.

3 A person who is guilty of an offence; a person responsible for a fault. M18.

> L. URIS We will find the culprit and he will tell us where he has planted the bomb.

culrach /'kʌlreɪx/ *noun*. *obsolete* exc. *hist*. Also **-reach**. LME.
[ORIGIN App. from Gaelic *cùl* back + *ràth(an)* surety.]
SCOTS LAW. A surety given to a court when a case is removed from its jurisdiction to that of another court.

culs-de-lampe *noun* pl. of CUL-DE-LAMPE.

culs-de-sac *noun pl*. see CUL-DE-SAC.

culshie *noun & adjective* var. of CULCHIE.

cult /kʌlt/ *noun & adjective*. E17.
[ORIGIN French *culte* or its source Latin *cultus* worship, from *colere* inhabit, cultivate, protect, honour with worship.]
▸ **A** *noun*. †**1** Worship; reverential homage rendered to a divine being. Only in 17.

EVELYN God, abolishing the cult of Gentile idols.

2 A system of religious worship, esp. as expressed in ceremonies, ritual, etc. **L17.**

K. CLARK The cult of the Virgin. G. VIDAL Like a priest of a pagan cult he began to perform the ritual of arranging plates.

3 Devotion or homage paid to a person or thing; *esp.* a fashionable enthusiasm; *derog.* a transient fad of an in-group. **E18.**

M. GIROUARD The cult of aestheticism was brought to England . . by Swinburne and Walter Pater.

▸**B** *attrib.* or as *adjective*. That is the object of a cult; involving or involved in a cult; cultic. **E20.**

Punch There has been a small cult-following for West. *Listener* One of the stars . . has become an unlikely cult hero.

cultch *noun* var. of CULCH.

cultic /ˈkʌltɪk/ *adjective*. **L19.**
[ORIGIN from CULT *noun* + -IC, perh. after German *kultisch*.]
Of or pertaining to a (religious) cult.
■ **cultically** *adverb* **M20.**

cultigen /ˈkʌltɪdʒ(ə)n/ *noun*. **E20.**
[ORIGIN from *cultivated* pa. pple of CULTIVATE + -GEN.]
A plant species or variety known only in cultivation, *esp.* one with no known wild ancestor.

cultish /ˈkʌltɪʃ/ *adjective*. **E20.**
[ORIGIN from CULT *noun* + -ISH[1].]
Of the nature of, resembling, or belonging to a cult, esp. one regarded as eccentric or unorthodox.

Daily Telegraph Her kind of clowning . . seems to exercise a cultish appeal.

■ **cultishness** *noun* **M20.**

cultism /ˈkʌltɪz(ə)m/ *noun*[1]. **L19.**
[ORIGIN Spanish *cultismo*, from *culto* polished, ult. from Latin *cultus* pa. pple of *colere*: see CULT, -ISM.]
= GONGORISM.
■ **cultist** *noun*[1] = GONGORIST **M19.**

cultism /ˈkʌltɪz(ə)m/ *noun*[2]. **M20.**
[ORIGIN from CULT *noun* + -ISM.]
The principle, system, or practice of a cult or cultic activity.
■ **cultist** *noun*[2] a devotee of a cult **M20.** **culˈtistic** *adjective* **E20.**

cultivable /ˈkʌltɪvəb(ə)l/ *adjective*. **L17.**
[ORIGIN Old French & mod. French, from *cultiver* CULTIVATE *verb*: see -ABLE. Earlier in UNCULTIVABLE.]
Able to be cultivated.
■ **cultivaˈbility** *noun* **L19.**

cultivar /ˈkʌltɪvɑː/ *noun*. **E20.**
[ORIGIN from CULTIVATE + VAR(IETY).]
A plant variety that has arisen in cultivation.

cultivate /ˈkʌltɪveɪt/ *verb trans.* **M17.**
[ORIGIN medieval Latin *cultivat-* pa. ppl stem of *cultivare* (cf. Old French & mod. French *cultiver*), from *cultivus* in *cultiva terra* arable land (cf. Old French *terres cultives*), from Latin *cult-* pa. ppl stem of *colere*: see CULT, -IVE, -ATE[3].]
▸**I** *lit.* **1** Prepare and use (soil) for crops; bring (land) into a state of cultivation. **M17.** ▸**b** Break up (ground) with a cultivator. **M19.**
2 Give attention to (a plant) to promote growth, improve fertility, etc.; produce or raise by agriculture or horticulture. **L17.** ▸**b** = CULTURE *verb* 2. **L19.**

C. PRIEST The previous owners had cultivated fruit and vegetables, but everything was now overgrown.

▸**II** *fig.* **3** Promote the growth of, devote oneself to the development of, (an art, sentiment, faculty, etc.); foster. **M17.**

A. S. NEILL I try hard to cultivate their sense of humour and their imagination.

4 *spec.* Foster (another person's friendship, good opinion, etc.) in relation to oneself. **L17.** ▸**b** Pay attention to (a person); seek to win the favour or friendship of; court. **E18.**

S. RICHARDSON He was more solicitous to cultivate her mamma's good opinion, than hers. **b** D. L. SAYERS Bunter has been cultivating Hannah Westlock almost to breach of promise point.

5 Improve and develop (a person, his or her mind, manners, etc.) by education or training. Freq. as ***cultivated*** *ppl adjective*. **L17.**
6 Pay attention to, practise, cherish, (a sentiment, skill, pursuit, etc.), esp. with the object of acquiring it or improving oneself in it. **M18.**

J. BUCHAN That air of brisk competence which shy women often cultivate in self-defence.

– PHRASES: **cultivate one's garden** *fig.* attend to one's own affairs.
■ **cultivataˈbility** *noun* (*rare*) the quality of being cultivable **L19.** **cultivatable** *adjective* cultivable **M19.**

cultivation /kʌltɪˈveɪʃ(ə)n/ *noun*. **L17.**
[ORIGIN French, from *cultiver*: see CULTIVATE, -ATION.]
1 The action of cultivating (*lit.* & *fig.*). **L17.** ▸**b** = CULTURE *noun* 3. **L19.**

DEFOE I saw several Sugar Canes, but wild, and for want of Cultivation, imperfect. JAS. HARRIS The cultivation of every liberal accomplishment. C. W. DILKE The amount of land under cultivation.

shifting cultivation: see SHIFTING *adjective* 1.

2 The state of being cultivated, esp. in mind or manners; refinement. **M19.**

J. GROSS Reviewers . . assumed an imposing degree of cultivation among their readers.

3 A culture of bacteria etc. **L19.**
– COMB.: **cultivation bank**, **cultivation ridge**, **cultivation terrace** ARCHAEOLOGY a steplike feature formed naturally or artificially on a cultivated hillside.

cultivator /ˈkʌltɪveɪtə/ *noun*. **M17.**
[ORIGIN from CULTIVATE + -OR, prob. after French *cultivateur*.]
1 A person who cultivates something (*lit.* & *fig.*). **M17.**
2 An implement or machine for breaking up the ground and uprooting weeds. **M18.**

cultrate /ˈkʌltrət/ *adjective*. **M19.**
[ORIGIN Latin *cultratus*, from *culter* knife: see -ATE[2].]
ZOOLOGY & BOTANY. Shaped like a knife; sharp-edged.
■ **culˈtrated** *adjective* = CULTRATE **L18.** **cultriform** *adjective* [-FORM] = CULTRATE **E19.**

culturable /ˈkʌltʃ(ə)rəb(ə)l/ *adjective*. **L18.**
[ORIGIN from CULTURE *verb* + -ABLE.]
Able to be cultured or cultivated (*lit.* & *fig.*); cultivable.

Lancet Culturable acid-fast microorganisms.

cultural /ˈkʌltʃ(ə)r(ə)l/ *adjective*. **M19.**
[ORIGIN from Latin *cultura* tillage + -AL[1].]
1 Of or pertaining to cultivation, esp. of the mind, manners, etc. **M19.**
2 Of or pertaining to culture in a society or civilization. **L19.**
cultural ANTHROPOLOGY. **cultural attaché** an embassy official whose function is to promote cultural relations between his own country and that to which he is accredited. ***cultural*** RELATIVISM. **Cultural Revolution** an extreme reform movement in China, 1966–76, which sought to combat revisionism by the restoration of pure Maoist doctrine.
3 Of or pertaining to the culture of micro-organisms, tissues, etc. **E20.**
■ **culturally** *adverb* **L19.**

culturati /ˌkʌltʃəˈrɑːti/ *noun pl.* **M20.**
[ORIGIN Blend of CULTURE *noun* and LITERATI.]
Well-educated people who appreciate the arts.

culture /ˈkʌltʃə/ *noun*. **ME.**
[ORIGIN French, or its source Latin *cultura*, from *cult-*: see CULTIVATE, -URE.]
▸**I** †**1** A cultivated field or piece of land. **ME–M18.**
2 The action or practice of cultivating the soil; tillage. **LME.**
3 The action or practice of cultivating a crop or raising certain animals (as fish, oysters, bees); the production of silk. **E17.** ▸**b** The action or process of causing bacteria, tissue, etc., to grow in prepared media; a growth of cells or spores so obtained. **L19.**

F. FITZGERALD Their method of rice culture was far superior to any other in SE Asia. **b** F. SMYTH He worked in a cancer research centre, managed to smuggle out a cancer culture.

b ***pure culture***: see PURE *adjective*.

▸**II 4** The cultivation or development of the mind, manners, etc.; improvement by education and training. **E16.**

R. W. DALE The Jewish system was intended for the culture of the religious life.

physical culture: see PHYSICAL *adjective*.

5 Refinement of mind, tastes, and manners; artistic and intellectual development; the artistic and intellectual side of civilization. **E19.**

M. ARNOLD The great men of culture. E. SHINWELL Of what use is culture to a labourer?

6 A particular form, stage, or type of intellectual development or civilization in a society; a society or group characterized by its distinctive customs, achievements, products, outlook, etc. **M19.**

P. DAVIES Such diverse cultures as the Sumerians and the N. American Indians. D. ATTENBOROUGH A community having shared skills and knowledge, shared ways of doing things—in short, a culture.

the two cultures literature and science, as disciplines that tend to be mutually incompatible or hostile.

7 The distinctive customs, achievements, products, outlook, etc., of a society or group; the way of life of a society or group. **L19.**
material culture the physical objects which give evidence of the type of culture developed by a society or group. ***pop culture***, ***street culture***, etc.
– COMB.: **culture-bound** *adjective* restricted in character, outlook, etc., by belonging to a particular culture; **culture pearl** a cultured pearl; **culture shock**: experienced by a person who finds himself or herself in a notably unfamiliar or uncongenial cultural environment; **culture vulture** *joc.* a person who devotes much time and effort to acquiring culture; **culture war** a conflict between groups with different ideals, beliefs, philosophies, etc.
■ **culturist** *noun* (**a**) a person engaged in the culture of crops etc. (***physical culturist***: see PHYSICAL *adjective*); (**b**) an advocate of culture: **E19.** **cultureless** *adjective* uncultivated (*lit.* & *fig.*); lacking culture: **E19.**

culture /ˈkʌltʃə/ *verb trans.* **E16.**
[ORIGIN French †*culturer* or medieval Latin *culturare*, formed as CULTURE *noun*.]
1 Subject to culture; cultivate (*lit.* & *fig.*). Now *rare* exc. as CULTURED. **E16.**
2 Maintain (bacteria etc.) in artificial conditions that promote growth. **E20.**

-culture /ˈkʌltʃə/ *suffix*.
[ORIGIN from AGRICULTURE.]
Forming nouns denoting the raising or breeding of a certain kind of organism, or in a certain kind of environment, as ***apiculture***, ***aquaculture***, ***aviculture***.

cultured /ˈkʌltʃəd/ *adjective*. **M18.**
[ORIGIN from CULTURE *noun*, *verb*: see -ED[2], -ED[1].]
1 Of ground, a plant, etc.: subjected to or produced by cultivation. Chiefly *poet.* **M18.**
2 Improved by education and training; possessed of culture; refined, cultivated. **L18.**

C. FREEMAN For all her cultured background Sara had lived in poverty.

3 Caused to develop by artificial means or in an artificial nutrient medium. **E20.**

Nature Experiments with nuclei from cultured tadpole cells.

cultured pearl: formed by an oyster after the insertion of a suitable foreign body.

culturology /kʌltʃəˈrɒlədʒi/ *noun*. **M20.**
[ORIGIN German *Kulturologie*, from *Kultur* culture + *-ologie* -OLOGY.]
The science or study of culture or cultures as a branch of anthropology.
■ **culturoˈlogical** *adjective* **M20.** **culturologist** *noun* **M20.**

cultus /ˈkʌltəs/ *noun*. **M17.**
[ORIGIN Latin, from pa. ppl stem of *colere*: see CULT.]
†**1** = CULT *noun* 1. *rare*. Only in **M17.**
2 A system of religious worship or ritual; a cult. **M19.**

cultus-cod /ˈkʌltəskɒd/ *noun*. *N. Amer.* Pl. same. **L19.**
[ORIGIN from Chinook Jargon *cultus* good-for-nothing, from Lower Chinook *kə̆ltas* in vain, + COD *noun*[3].]
= ***lingcod*** s.v. LING *noun*[1].

-culum, **-culus** *suffixes* see -CULE.

culver /ˈkʌlvə/ *noun*. Now *poet.* & *dial.*
[ORIGIN Old English *cul(u)fre*, *culfer* from Latin *columbula* dim. of *columba* dove, pigeon.]
A pigeon, *esp.* the woodpigeon.

culverin /ˈkʌlv(ə)rɪn/ *noun*. **L15.**
[ORIGIN Old French & mod. French *coulevrine* (cf. medieval Latin *colubrina*, *colo-*, Italian *colubrina*), from *couleuvre* snake from Proto-Romance from Latin *colubra*, *coluber* snake: see -INE[1].]
hist. **1** A kind of handgun. **L15.**
2 A large cannon long in proportion to its bore. **E16.**
■ **culveriˈneer** *noun* a soldier armed with or in charge of a culverin **E16.**

culverkeys /ˈkʌlvəkiːz/. *noun*. Now *dial.* In branch I also **-key** /-kiː/. **E17.**
[ORIGIN from CULVER + KEY *noun*[1].]
▸**I 1** The wild hyacinth. **E17.**
2 The cowslip. **M18.**
▸**II 3** The seed pods of the ash. **L18.**

culvert /ˈkʌlvət/ *noun* & *verb*. **L18.**
[ORIGIN Unknown.]
▸**A** *noun*. **1** An enclosed channel or conduit for carrying a stream under an embankment, road, etc. **L18.**
2 A conduit for electric cables. **L19.**
▸**B** *verb trans.* Provide or lay with culverts; enclose in a culvert. **L19.**

culvertage /ˈkʌlvətɪdʒ/ *noun*. **E17.**
[ORIGIN Old French, from *culvert* villein from medieval Latin *collibertus* freed serf, in classical Latin fellow freedman, formed as COL- + *libertus* freedman: see -AGE.]
hist. The state or condition of a villein; degradation to the position of a villein.

cum /kʌm/ *preposition*. **LME.**
[ORIGIN Latin = with.]
1 Combined with: used in names of combined parishes. **LME.**
Chorlton-cum-Hardy, ***Stow-cum-Quy***, etc.
2 With: chiefly in Latin phrs. and English ones imitating them. **L16.**
cum dividend (with ref. to share prices) with a dividend about to be paid. **cum grano (salis)** /ˌɡrɑːnəʊ ˈsɑːlɪs/ [Latin] with a grain of salt, with reservations. **cum laude** /ˈlɔːdi, ˈlaʊdeɪ/ (chiefly *N. Amer.*) [Latin = praise] (a degree, diploma, etc.) with distinction, with honours. MAGNA CUM LAUDE. SUMMA CUM LAUDE.
3 And also: denoting a dual or combined nature or function. **L19.**

R. KIPLING Motor-bike-*cum*-side-car trips. K. CROSSLEY-HOLLAND He was the poet cum priest cum doctor.

C

C

cumacean /kjʊˈmeɪʃ(ə)n/ *adjective & noun.* Also **C-**. L19.
[ORIGIN from mod. Latin *Cumacea* (see below), from *Cuma* genus name from Greek *kuma*: see CYMA, -ACEAN.]
ZOOLOGY. ▸**A** *adjective.* Of or pertaining to the Cumacea, an order of small sessile-eyed marine crustaceans resembling prawns and living in mud or sand. L19.
▸**B** *noun.* A cumacean animal. L19.

Cumaean /kjʊˈmiːən/ *adjective & noun.* M18.
[ORIGIN from *Cumae* (Latin *Cumae*, Greek *Kumē*) (see below) + -AN.]
▸**A** *adjective.* Of or pertaining to Cumae, an ancient city on the Italian coast near Naples; *spec.* designating the Sibyl of Virgil's *Aeneid*, who had her seat nearby. M18.
▸**B** *noun.* A native or inhabitant of Cumae. M20.

Cuman /ˈkjuːmən/ *noun & adjective.* Also **K-**. Pl. of noun **-s**, same, (earliest) †**Cumani**. L16.
[ORIGIN medieval Latin *Cumani* pl., perh. ult. from the River *Kuma* in the northern Caucasus.]
= KIPCHAK.
■ Also **Cuˈmanian** *noun & adjective* M19.

cumarone *noun* var. of COUMARONE.

Cumb. *abbreviation.*
Cumberland (former English county).

cumbent /ˈkʌmbənt/ *adjective.* M17.
[ORIGIN Latin *-cumbent-* pres. ppl stem of *-cumbere* (only in compounds, as *recumbere* etc.) lie down, nasalized stem corresp. to *cubare* lie: see -ENT.]
Esp. of a statue: lying down, reclining.

cumber /ˈkʌmbə/ *noun.* ME.
[ORIGIN from the verb or aphet. from ENCUMBER *noun*.]
†**1** Overthrow, destruction, rout. Only in ME.
2 A thing which cumbers, an encumbrance; a hindrance, an obstruction; a burden (*lit. & fig.*). LME.

A. UTTLEY Hay chambers . . with their cumber of past days . . parts of spinning-wheels, giant presses, cheese-stones.

3 Trouble, distress; embarrassment, inconvenience. Now *arch. rare.* E16.
4 The action or quality of encumbering; the fact of being encumbered; hindrance, obstruction. M16.

J. RUSKIN Of other prefatory matter . . the reader shall be spared the cumber.

5 Pressure of business; in *pl.*, affairs that occupy and trouble one. Now *rare* or *obsolete.* M17.
■ **cumberless** *adjective* M16.

cumber /ˈkʌmbə/ *verb trans.* ME.
[ORIGIN Prob. aphet. from ACCUMBER, ENCUMBER *verb*.]
†**1** Overwhelm, overthrow, destroy. ME–L16.
2 Benumb; stiffen with cold. Chiefly as ***cumbered*** *ppl adjective. obsolete* exc. *Scot.* ME.
3 Incommode, bother. Formerly also, harass, distress, trouble. ME.

AV *Luke* 10:40 But Martha was cumbred about much seruing.

†**4** Perplex, puzzle. LME–E17.
5 Hamper, hinder; get or be in the way of (a person, a person's movement, etc.). LME.

BROWNING Body shall cumber Soul-flight no more. C. S. FORESTER They were cumbered with greatcoats and swords.

6 Occupy obstructively or inconveniently; burden, load. LME.

G. A. BIRMINGHAM Out-of-date theological books . . were cumbering my over-full shelves. *fig.*: D. CECIL Cumbered with the permanent care of a mentally afflicted sister.

– COMB.: **cumber-ground** *arch.* a person or thing which uselessly occupies the ground; an unprofitable occupant of a position.
■ **cumberer** *noun* a person who or thing which cumbers LME. **cumberment** *noun* †(*a*) the state of being cumbered; (*b*) (now *rare* or *obsolete*) an encumbrance: ME.

Cumberland /ˈkʌmbələnd/ *noun.* M17.
[ORIGIN A former English county, now part of Cumbria.]
1 Used *attrib.* to designate things originating in or associated with Cumberland. M17.
Cumberland ham: cured separately from the rest of the carcass. **Cumberland pig** a lop-eared white pig of a breed now extinct. **Cumberland sauce** a piquant sauce served esp. as a relish with cold meat. **Cumberland sausage** a type of coarse-grained sausage traditionally made in a continuous strip from which the amount required is cut off.
2 More fully ***Cumberland and Westmorland***. A style of wrestling in which the wrestlers stand chest to chest and clasp hands, the first to break hold or to touch the ground other than with the feet being the loser. E19.

cumbersome /ˈkʌmbəs(ə)m/ *adjective.* LME.
[ORIGIN from CUMBER *verb* + -SOME[1].]
†**1** Of a place or way: presenting obstruction, difficult to pass through. LME–L17.
2 Causing trouble or annoyance; full of trouble; wearisome, oppressive. Now *rare* or *obsolete.* E16.
3 Inconvenient in size, weight, or shape; unwieldy, clumsy to handle. L16.

J. G. FARRELL The cat . . had become too big and cumbersome to remain on her lap.

4 *fig.* Involving effort but serving no purpose; needlessly complicated or indirect. M17.

HENRY MORE Cumbersome Ceremonies. D. LESSING Government had become so enormous, so cumbersome, so ridden with bureaucracy.

■ **cumbersomely** *adverb* L17. **cumbersomeness** *noun* L16.

cumbia /ˈkʊmbɪə/ *noun.* M20.
[ORIGIN Colombian Spanish, perh. from Spanish *cumbé* the name of a dance and the tune to which it was performed.]
A form of dance music originating from Colombia; a dance resembling the fandango which is performed to this music.

cumble /ˈkʌmb(ə)l/ *verb trans. & (rare) intrans. obsolete* exc. *dial.* ME.
[ORIGIN Old French & mod. French *combler* load etc. from Latin *cumulare*: see CUMULATE *verb*.]
Deprive or become deprived of strength or power; *esp.* stiffen with cold.

cumbly /ˈkʌmli/ *noun.* Also **cumly**. L17.
[ORIGIN Hindi *kamlī* from Sanskrit *kambala*.]
In the Indian subcontinent: a blanket, a coarse woollen cloth.

†**cumbrance** *noun.* ME.
[ORIGIN from CUMBER *verb* + -ANCE.]
1 The action of cumbering; the state of being cumbered. ME–M17.
2 A source of trouble or annoyance. LME–M17.
3 An encumbrance. M–L17.

Cumbrian /ˈkʌmbrɪən/ *adjective & noun.* M18.
[ORIGIN from medieval Latin *Cumbria*, from Welsh *Cymry* Welshmen or Brittonic word meaning 'compatriots': see -AN.]
▸**A** *adjective.* Of, pertaining to, or native to the ancient British kingdom of Cumbria, or the modern English county of Cumbria (formerly Cumberland and Westmorland), or the area of NW England that was anciently Cumbria, esp. the former county of Cumberland or the Lake District. M18.
▸**B** *noun.* A Cumbrian person. L18.

Cumbric /ˈkʌmbrɪk/ *noun & adjective.* M20.
[ORIGIN formed as CUMBRIAN + -IC.]
(Of) the Celtic language of the ancient British kingdom of Cumbria.

cumbrous /ˈkʌmbrəs/ *adjective.* LME.
[ORIGIN from CUMBER *noun* + -OUS.]
†**1** = CUMBERSOME 1. LME–M19.
†**2** = CUMBERSOME 2. LME–M17.
3 = CUMBERSOME 3. LME.
4 = CUMBERSOME 4. M18.
■ **cumbrously** *adverb* LME. **cumbrousness** *noun* M16.

cumdach /ˈkuːdɑːx/ *noun.* L19.
[ORIGIN Irish *cumhdach*.]
IRISH HISTORY. An ornamented casket for keeping manuscript books.

cumec /ˈkjuːmɛk/ *noun.* M20.
[ORIGIN from cubic metres per second.]
A cubic metre per second, as a unit of rate of flow of water.

cumene /ˈkjuːmiːn/ *noun.* M19.
[ORIGIN from Latin *cuminum* CUMIN + -ENE.]
Any of a group of isomeric derivatives, C_9H_{12}, of benzene; *spec.* $C_6H_5CH(CH_3)_2$, a liquid made from propylene and benzene and used in making phenol and acetone.

cumin /ˈkʌmɪn/ *noun.* Also **-mm-**.
[ORIGIN Old English *cymen* from Latin *cuminum* from Greek *kuminon*, of Semitic origin: cf. Hebrew *kammōn*, Arabic *kammūn*. Superseded in Middle English by forms from Old French *cumin*, *comin* from Latin.]
1 An umbelliferous plant, *Cuminum cyminum*, similar to fennel and native to the Mediterranean; the small aromatic fruit of this, used in curry powders etc. and as a source of oil. OE.
2 With specifying word: any of various similar plants. L16.
black cumin fennel flower, *Nigella sativa*, a Mediterranean plant of the buttercup family whose seeds are used for seasoning. **sweet cumin** the anise, *Pimpinella anisum*.

cumly *noun* var. of CUMBLY.

cummer /ˈkʌmə/ *noun. Scot.* Also **kimmer** /ˈkɪmə/. ME.
[ORIGIN Old French & mod. French *commère* from ecclesiastical Latin *commater*, *-tr-*, formed as COM- + *mater* MOTHER *noun*[1].]
1 A godmother. ME.
2 A female companion or close friend. E16.
3 A woman; *spec.* a young girl; a witch; a midwife. M18.

cummerbund /ˈkʌməbʌnd/ *noun.* E17.
[ORIGIN Urdu *kamar-band* loincloth, waistband from Persian, from *kamar* waist, loins + Persian & Urdu *-bandī* a tie, a band.]
A wide sash worn round the waist.

cummin *noun* var. of CUMIN.

cummingtonite /ˈkʌmɪŋtənʌɪt/ *noun.* E19.
[ORIGIN from *Cummington*, Massachusetts, US + -ITE[1].]
MINERALOGY. A magnesium iron silicate of the amphibole group occurring as brownish fibrous crystals in some metamorphic rocks.

cumquat *noun* var. of KUMQUAT.

cumshaw /ˈkʌmʃɔː/ *noun.* E19.
[ORIGIN Chinese dial. *gǎmsiā*, (Mandarin) *gǎnxiè* (phr. used by beggars), from *gǎn* be grateful + *xiè* thank.]
In China: a gratuity, a tip.

cumulate /ˈkjuːmjʊlət/ *adjective & noun.* M16.
[ORIGIN Latin *cumulatus* pa. pple, formed as CUMULATE *verb*: see -ATE[2].]
▸**A** *adjective.* Heaped up, massed. M16.
▸**B** *noun.* An igneous rock that was formed by particles in a magma settling to the bottom. M20.
■ **cumulately** *adverb* (*rare*) M19.

cumulate /ˈkjuːmjʊleɪt/ *verb.* M16.
[ORIGIN Latin *cumulat-* pa. ppl stem of *cumulare*, from *cumulus* a heap: see -ATE[3].]
1 *verb trans. & (rare) intrans.* Gather in a heap; heap up; accumulate. M16.
2 *verb trans.* Combine *with* something additional. M17.
▸**b** Combine (successive lists, e.g. of books) into a single comprehensive list, esp. at regular intervals. E20.

E. EDWARDS Allowed him to cumulate the councillorship with the corregidorship.

3 *verb trans.* Put the finishing touches to, crown, culminate. *arch.* M17.

MARVELL To cumulate all this happiness, they had this new Law against the Fanaticks.

■ **cumulated** *adjective* that has been cumulated; (of cloud) formed into cumuli; CHEMISTRY involving two double bonds attached to the same carbon atom: M17.

cumulation /kjuːmjʊˈleɪʃ(ə)n/ *noun.* E17.
[ORIGIN Late Latin *cumulatio(n-)*, formed as CUMULATE *verb*: see -ATION.]
1 The action of heaping up; a mass, a heap; accumulation. Chiefly *fig.* E17.
†**2** The taking of higher and lower university degrees together. Cf. ACCUMULATION 3. Only in M17.
3 (A list obtained by) the process of cumulating lists of book titles. E20.

cumulative /ˈkjuːmjʊlətɪv/ *adjective.* E17.
[ORIGIN from CUMULATE *verb* + -IVE. Cf. French *cumulatif*, *-ive*.]
†**1** Such as is formed by accumulation (rather than organic growth). Only in E17.

BACON As for knowledge which man receiveth by teaching, it is cumulative and not original.

2 Formed by or arising from accumulation; increasing in quantity or effect by successive additions. M17. ▸**b** Of a statistical function: concerned with all the values of a variate up to and (usually) including the one specified. M20.

H. KISSINGER The cumulative total of Americans killed in action since 1961 . . stood at over 31,000. R. HAYMAN The cumulative effect of working six hours a day for six days a week.

3 LAW (now *hist.*). Of jurisdiction: shared. M17.
4 Tending to accumulate. L19.
– SPECIAL COLLOCATIONS: **cumulative error**: increasing, or not decreasing, as more observations are taken into account. **cumulative preference share**: entitling the holder to an annual dividend which, if it cannot be paid in any year, accrues until it can. **cumulative vote**, **cumulative voting**: in which each voter has as many votes as there are candidates and may give all to any one of them.
■ **cumulatively** *adverb* M17. **cumulativeness** *noun* L19.

cumulet /ˈkjuːmjʊlɪt/ *noun.* L19.
[ORIGIN from CUMULUS + *-et* of unknown origin.]
A high-flying variety of the domestic pigeon.

cumuliform /ˈkjuːmjʊlɪfɔːm/ *adjective.* L19.
[ORIGIN from CUMULUS + -I- + -FORM.]
METEOROLOGY. Of cloud etc.: developed in a predominantly vertical direction.

cumulo- /ˈkjuːmjʊləʊ/ *combining form* of CUMULUS: see -O-.
■ **cumuloˈnimbus** *noun* (METEOROLOGY) a cloud or cloud type resembling cumulus but towering and massive, often with the top spread out like an anvil L19. **cumuloˈstratus** *noun* (METEOROLOGY) = STRATOCUMULUS E19.

cumulous /ˈkjuːmjʊləs/ *adjective.* E19.
[ORIGIN from CUMULUS + -OUS.]
Of the nature of or resembling a cumulus cloud or cumuli.

M. PEAKE Dense and cumulous smoke.

cumulus /ˈkjuːmjʊləs/ *noun.* Pl. **-li** /-lʌɪ, -liː/. M17.
[ORIGIN Latin.]
1 A heap, a pile; an accumulation; the conical top of a heap. M17.
2 METEOROLOGY. (A cloud type consisting of) rounded masses of cloud heaped on each other and having a horizontal base at usu. a low altitude. Also ***cumulus cloud***. E19.

W. BOYD Great ranges of purple cumulus loomed in the sky.

3 ANATOMY. (The material of) a mass of follicular cells surrounding an oocyte in an ovarian follicle. Also ***cumulus oophorus***. M19.

cun *verb*[1] see CON *verb*[1].

†**cun** *verb*[2] var. of CON *verb*[2].

Cuna *noun & adjective* var. of KUNA *noun*[1] & *adjective*.

cunabulum /kjʊˈnabjʊləm/ *noun. rare.* Pl. **-la** /-lə/. L18.
[ORIGIN from Latin *cunabula* neut. pl., from *cunae* cradle: see -ULE. Cf. INCUNABULUM.]
A cradle (*lit.* & *fig.*); in *pl.*, the place where something began or was nurtured.

Cunarder /kjuːˈnɑːdə/ *noun.* M19.
[ORIGIN from *Cunard* (see below) + -ER[1].]
A ship belonging to the Cunard Line, founded by Sir Samuel Cunard (1787–1865) as the first regular steamship line for transatlantic passenger traffic.

cunctation /kʌŋ(k)ˈteɪʃ(ə)n/ *noun.* L16.
[ORIGIN Latin *cunctatio(n-)*, from *cunctat-* pa. ppl stem of *cunctari* delay: see -ATION.]
The action or an instance of delaying; tardy action.
■ **cunctatious** *adjective* (*rare*) prone to delay M19. ˈ**cunctative** *adjective* (*rare*) = CUNCTATIOUS E17.

cunctator /kʌŋ(k)ˈteɪtə/ *noun.* E17.
[ORIGIN Latin, from *cunctat-*: see CUNCTATION, -OR.]
A person who acts tardily, a delayer.
– NOTE: Generally used with reference to Q. Fabius Maximus Cunctator, Roman general in the war against Hannibal.
■ ˈ**cunctatory** *adjective* (*rare*) disposed to delay M19.

cunctipotent /kʌŋ(k)ˈtɪpət(ə)nt/ *adjective. rare.* L15.
[ORIGIN Late Latin *cunctipotent-*, *-ens*, from *cunctus* all, after classical Latin *omnipotens* OMNIPOTENT *adjective*.]
Omnipotent.

†**cund** *verb* var. of COND.

cundurango /kʌndʊˈraŋɡəʊ/ *noun.* Also **con-** /kɒn-/. Pl. **-os.** L19.
[ORIGIN Spanish, from Quechua *cuntur* CONDOR + *anku* nerve, tendon.]
A S. American climbing plant, *Marsdenia cundurango*, an extract of the bark of which has been used therapeutically; its bark.

cuneal /ˈkjuːnɪəl/ *adjective.* Now *rare* or *obsolete*. L16.
[ORIGIN medieval or mod. Latin *cunealis*, from classical Latin *cuneus* wedge: see -AL[1].]
Wedge-shaped.

cuneate /ˈkjuːnɪət/ *adjective.* E19.
[ORIGIN from Latin *cuneus* wedge + -ATE[2]: cf. *caudate*.]
Wedge-shaped; (of a leaf, petal, etc., or its base) triangular with the narrow end at the point of attachment.
■ **cuneated** *adjective* = CUNEATE E18. **cuneˈatic** *adjective* = CUNEATE M19.

cuneiform /ˈkjuːnɪfɔːm, -nɪf-/ *adjective* & *noun.* Also **-nif-** /-nɪf-/. L17.
[ORIGIN French *cunéiforme* or mod. Latin *cuneiformis*, from Latin *cuneus* wedge: see -FORM.]
▸ **A** *adjective.* **1** Having the form of a wedge; wedge-shaped. L17.
cuneiform bone each of three bones in the tarsus that articulate with a bone of the metatarsus in front and with the navicular bone behind.
2 Designating or pertaining to (inscriptions composed of) writing in wedge-shaped impressed strokes, usu. in clay, in ancient inscriptions of Assyria, Persia, etc. E19.
▸ **B** *noun.* **1** ANATOMY. A cuneiform bone. M19.
2 Cuneiform writing. M19.
■ **cuneiformist** *noun* a specialist or expert in cuneiform L19.

cunet *noun* var. of CUNIT.

cunette /kjʊˈnɛt/ *noun.* L17.
[ORIGIN French from Italian *cunetta* ditch.]
FORTIFICATION. A trench along the middle of a dry ditch or moat, serving as a drain or obstacle etc.

cuniculus /kjʊˈnɪkjʊləs/ *noun.* Pl. **-li** /-lʌɪ, -liː/. M17.
[ORIGIN Latin = rabbit, underground passage.]
An underground passage or mine; *spec.* (ARCHAEOLOGY) an underground drain of preclassical times in Italy.
■ **cunicular** *adjective* †(**a**) living underground; (**b**) of or pertaining to cuniculi: M18.

cuniform *adjective* & *noun* var. of CUNEIFORM.

cu-nim /kjuːˈnɪm/ *noun. colloq.* Also **-nimb** /-ˈnɪmb/. M20.
[ORIGIN Abbreviation.]
Cumulonimbus; a cumulonimbus cloud.

cunit /ˈkjuːnɪt/ *noun.* Also **-et** /-ət/. M20.
[ORIGIN from C (= a hundred) + UNIT *noun*[1].]
A unit of stacked wood equal to 100 cu. ft (approx. 2.83 cu. metres).

cunjee *noun* var. of CUNJIE.

cunjevoi /ˈkʌndʒɪvɔɪ/ *noun.* In sense 2 also **-boi** /-bɔɪ/. M19.
[ORIGIN Prob. from Bandjalang.]
1 A tall Australian plant (*Alocasia macrorrhiza*) of the arum family whose corms were formerly cooked as food. M19.
2 A kind of sea squirt found on Australian reefs and rocks and used as bait. E20.

cunjie /ˈkʌndʒi/ *noun. Austral. colloq.* Also **-jee.** M20.
[ORIGIN Abbreviation of CUNJEVOI.]
= CUNJEVOI 2.

cunner /ˈkʌnə/ *noun.* Also **conner** /ˈkɒnə/. E17.
[ORIGIN Perh. assoc. with CONDER 1.]
Either of two wrasses, *Crenilabrus melops* of the Mediterranean and eastern Atlantic and *Tautogolabrus adspersus* of the Atlantic coast of N. America.

cunnilingus /kʌnɪˈlɪŋɡəs/ *noun.* L19.
[ORIGIN Latin = a person who licks the vulva, from *cunnus* female external genitals + *lingere* to lick.]
Stimulation of a woman's genitals with the tongue.
■ **cunnilingue** /ˈkʌnɪlɪŋ/ *noun* & *verb* (**a**) *noun* a person who performs cunnilingus; (**b**) *verb trans.* & *intrans.* perform cunnilingus (on): L19.

cunning /ˈkʌnɪŋ/ *noun.* ME.
[ORIGIN Perh. from Old Norse *kunnandi* knowledge, accomplishments, from *kunna* know (see CAN *verb*[1]), but may be verbal noun from CUN *verb*[1].]
†**1** Knowledge; learning, erudition. ME–M17.
†**2** The capacity or faculty of knowing; wit, wisdom, intelligence. ME–M16.
3 Knowledge how to do something; skill, dexterity. *arch.* ME.

AV *Ps.* 137:5 Let my right hand forget her cunning.

†**4** An art, a craft; a branch of knowledge; *esp.* occult art, magic. LME–L16.
5 Skill in deceit or evasion; selfish cleverness or insight. LME.

R. GRAVES To pride themselves on their cunning in avoiding detection.

cunning /ˈkʌnɪŋ/ *adjective.* ME.
[ORIGIN Old Norse *kunnandi* knowing, pres. pple of *kunna*: see CUNNING *noun*.]
†**1** Learned; knowledgeable (*in* a subject). ME–M17.
2 Possessing practical knowledge or skill; dexterous. *arch.* ME. ▸**b** Ingenious, skilfully contrived or executed. LME.

b P. BARRY A cunning little camera.

3 Possessing magical knowledge or skill. Only in ***cunning man***, ***cunning woman***. *obsolete* exc. *hist.* L16.
4 Skilled in deceit or evasion; artful, crafty; exhibiting or characterized by craftiness. L16.

DICKENS His black eyes were restless, sly, and cunning.

5 Possessing keen intelligence or wit; clever. Now *rare.* L17.
6 Attractively quaint; charming; picturesque. *N. Amer.* M19.
■ **cunningly** *adverb* LME. **cunningness** *noun* LME.

cunny *noun* see CONY.

cunt /kʌnt/ *noun. coarse slang.* ME.
[ORIGIN Corresp. to Old Norse *kunta* (Norwegian, Swedish dial. *kunta*, Danish dial. *kunte*), Old Frisian, Middle Low German, Middle Dutch *kunte*, from Germanic.]
1 The female genitals, the vulva. ME.
2 A very unpleasant or stupid person. E20.
– NOTE: One of the most taboo words in English. It was not included in the original *Oxford English Dictionary*, and until recently rarely appeared in print; it is still often referred to in a euphemistic way, e.g. *the C-word*.

CUP *abbreviation.*
Cambridge University Press.

cup /kʌp/ *noun.* OE.
[ORIGIN popular Latin *cuppa*, prob. from Latin *cupa* tub.]
1 A small open vessel, usu. hemispherical or nearly so, with or without a handle or handles, used for drinking from; now *spec.* a single-handled one with matching saucer for certain hot drinks (***coffee cup***, ***teacup***, etc.). Also, the bowl of a more ornamental drinking vessel that has a stem or a lid. OE. ▸**b** *fig.* Something to be endured or enjoyed; fate, (esp. unhappy) experience. ME.

b A. SEEGER We drained deeper the deep cup of life.

between cup and lip, **betwixt cup and lip**, **twixt cup and lip** while something is on the point of being achieved. ***cup of assay***: see ASSAY *noun* 5. ***cup of estate***: see ESTATE *noun* 4. ***cup of tea*** *fig.* (*colloq.*) a person of a specified kind; ***different cup of tea***, a quite different situation etc.; ***one's cup of tea***, what interests or suits one. ***loving cup***: see LOVING *ppl adjective*. ***mazer cup***: see MAZER 2. ***paper cup***: see PAPER *noun* & *adjective*. ***TREMBLEUSE cup***. ***TUMBLER-cup***. ***VINCENNES cup***.
2 *spec.* ▸**a** CHRISTIAN CHURCH. = CHALICE 2. ME. ▸**b** An ornamental vessel, typically of silver and comprising a bowl with a stem and base, that is offered as a prize in a competitive event. M17.

b A. E. HOUSMAN The still-defended challenge-cup.

3 A cup with the drink it contains; the contents of a cup; a cupful. LME. ▸**b** CHRISTIAN CHURCH. The wine administered at the Eucharist. L16. ▸**c** Wine, beer, cider, or fruit juice to which other ingredients have been added for flavouring, usu. served chilled from a bowl or jug; a drink of this. L18. ▸**d** COOKERY. A standard measure of capacity equal to half a US pint (0.237 litre, 8.33 British fluid ounces). Chiefly *N. Amer.* M19.

C. THIRLWALL A cup of poison had been prepared for him. C. M. YONGE All ready for tea! . . Won't you . . have a cup, Amy? **c** R. MACAULAY A glassful of hock cup, full of fruit and vegetables.

kiss the cup: see KISS *verb*.
4 In *pl.* & †*sing.* The drinking of intoxicating liquor; drunken revelry. Usu. & now only in ***in one's cups***, while intoxicated, (formerly) while drinking. LME.
5 SURGERY. A vessel used for cupping. Also, a vessel to receive a measured amount of blood (usu. 4 ounces) in blood-letting. Now *hist.* LME.
6 A natural structure in a plant or animal having the form of a cup or bowl, e.g. the calyx of a flower, the corona of a narcissus flower, the cupule of an acorn, the socket of a bone. LME.

W. SHENSTONE The cowslip's golden cup.

buttercup etc. ***Indian cup***: see INDIAN *adjective*. ***NEPTUNE'S cup***. ***optic cup***: see OPTIC *adjective*. ***PAINTED cup***.
7 (Usu. **C-**.) *The* constellation Crater. M16.
8 In *pl.* One of the four suits in packs of playing cards in Italy, Spain, and Spanish-speaking countries, and in tarot packs. E19.
9 A rounded cavity, small hollow, or depression in the ground; *spec.* †(**a**) a small deep depression forming a hazard on a golf course; (**b**) (the liner of) each of the holes into which a golf ball is played. E19.
10 A manufactured article resembling a cup or bowl. M19. ▸**b** The part of a bra that contains or supports one breast. M20.

b K. KESEY Did she wear a B cup, he wondered, or a C cup.

grease cup: see GREASE *noun*.
– COMB.: **cup-and-ball** *hist.* a toy consisting of a cup at the end of a stem to which a ball is attached by a string, the object being to toss the ball and catch it in the cup or on the spike end of the stem; the game played with this; = BILBOQUET 2; **cup-and-cone** *adjective* designating a metal fracture in which one surface consists of a raised rim enclosing a flat central portion into which the other surface fits; **cup-and-ring** *adjective* (ARCHAEOLOGY) designating marks cut in megalithic monuments consisting of a circular depression surrounded by concentric rings; **cupbearer** a person who serves wine, esp. as an officer of a royal or noble household; **cupcake** a cake baked in a small open container or from ingredients measured in cupfuls; **Cup Final** the final match in a competition for a (football etc.) cup; **cup fungus** any of various ascomycetous fungi in which the spore-producing layer develops as the lining of a shallow cup; **cup grease** a lubricating grease for use in grease cups; **cup hook**: for screwing into a cupboard etc. and hanging cups and mugs on; **cup lichen** a lichen, *Cladonia pyxidata*, with cup-shaped processes arising from the thallus; **cup-marked** *adjective* (ARCHAEOLOGY) designating megalithic monuments marked with a circular depression; **cup-moss** = ***cup lichen*** above; **cup-mushroom** = ***cup fungus*** above; **cup shake** = ***ring shake*** s.v. RING *noun*[1]; ***cup tie***: see TIE *noun*[1] 5b; **cup-tied** (of a soccer player) ineligible to play for one's club in a cup tie as a result of having played for another club earlier in the competition.
■ **cupful** *noun* as much as a cup will hold; *spec.* (*N. Amer.*) an 8-fluid-ounce measure in cookery: ME. **cuplike** *adjective* resembling a cup, esp. in shape; deeply concave: M19.

cup /kʌp/ *verb.* Infl. **-pp-**. LME.
[ORIGIN from the noun.]
1 *verb trans. hist.* Apply a cupping glass to; bleed (a person) by means of a cupping glass placed over an incision in a vein. LME.
†**2** *verb trans.* Supply with liquor; make drunk, intoxicate. *rare.* Only in E17.
3 *verb trans.* Receive, place, or hold as in a cup; place the curved hand round. M19.

R. WEST Aunt Lily had an elbow on the table and cupped her chin in one hand.

4 *verb intrans.* Form a cup; be or become cup-shaped. M19.
5 *verb trans.* Make concave or cup-shaped; form into a cup. E20.

X. FIELDING The despatcher . . cupped his hand to my ear.

cupboard /ˈkʌbəd/ *noun* & *verb.* LME.
[ORIGIN from CUP *noun* + BOARD *noun*.]
▸ **A** *noun.* **1** A table on which to display cups and plates etc.; a sideboard. *obsolete* exc. in ***court cupboard*** s.v. COURT *noun*[1]. LME.
†**2** A set of vessels for the table. E16–L17.
3 A recess or piece of furniture with a door and usu. shelves for storing crockery, provisions, or other small items. M16.
skeleton in the cupboard: see SKELETON *noun*.
4 Food, provisions, etc. Chiefly in ***cry cupboard***, crave for food. Now *rare* or *obsolete*. L17.
– COMB.: **cupboard love**: simulated for the sake of what one can get by it.
▸ **B** *verb trans.* Place or keep (as) in a cupboard. *rare.* E17.

cupel /ˈkjuːp(ə)l/ *noun* & *verb.* Also †**coppel**. E17.
[ORIGIN French *coupelle* dim. of *coupe* CUP *noun*: see -EL[2].]
▸ **A** *noun.* A shallow vessel made of a heat-resistant material which absorbs impurities when gold or silver is melted in it. E17.

fig.: DISRAELI Money is to be the cupel of their worth.

▸ **B** *verb trans.* Infl. **-ll-**, *-**l-**. Assay or refine in a cupel; subject to cupellation. M17.
■ **cupeˈllation** *noun* assaying or refining using a cupel; separation of silver from lead in this way: L17.

cupferron /ˈkʌpfɛrən, ˈkjuːp-/ *noun.* E20.
[ORIGIN German, from Latin *cuprum* copper + *ferrum* iron + *-on*.]
CHEMISTRY. A compound, $C_6H_5N(NO)ONH_4$, used as a quantitative precipitant for iron, titanium, zirconium, and certain other metals and formerly as a reagent for copper.

Cupid /ˈkjuːpɪd/ *noun*. LME.
[ORIGIN Latin *Cupido* personification of *cupido* desire, love, from *cupere* to desire.]
The Roman god of love, son of Mercury and Venus (represented as a beautiful naked winged boy with a bow and arrows); (also **c-**) a representation of the god; a beautiful young boy.
Cupid's bow (the upper edge of) the upper lip etc. shaped like the double-curved bow carried by Cupid. **Cupid's dart** (*a*) the conquering power of love; (*b*) in *pl.*, rutilated quartz; (*c*) a herbaceous perennial of the composite family, *Catananche caerulea*, with blue or white flowers.

cupidity /kjuːˈpɪdɪti/ *noun*. LME.
[ORIGIN French *cupidité* or its source Latin *cupiditas*, from Latin *cupidus* eagerly desirous, from *cupere* to desire: see -ID[1], -ITY.]
1 Inordinate desire to appropriate another's wealth or possessions; greed for gain. LME.
> W. GOLDING She had a variety of. . brilliant hair-ribbons; and I . . desired them with hopeless cupidity.

2 *gen.* Inordinate longing or lust; covetousness; an ardent desire. *arch.* M16.
> COLERIDGE The cupidity for dissipation and sensual pleasure.

Cupidon /ˈkjuːpɪdɒn; *foreign* kypidɔ̃ (*pl. same*)/ *noun*. Chiefly *poet*. Also **c-**. E19.
[ORIGIN French = CUPID.]
A beautiful youth; a cupid, an Adonis.

cupidone /ˈkjuːpɪdəʊn/ *noun*. M19.
[ORIGIN French = CUPIDON.]
= ***Cupid's dart*** (c) s.v. CUPID.

cupie *noun* var. of KEWPIE.

cupola /ˈkjuːpələ/ *noun*. M16.
[ORIGIN Italian from late Latin *cupula* small cask or vault, dim of *cupa* cask.]
1 A rounded vault or dome forming the roof of (part of) a building; *spec.* a small rounded dome forming or adorning a roof; the ceiling of a dome. M16. ▸**b** Something likened to such a dome. M17.
2 A tall usu. cylindrical furnace, open at the top and tapped at the bottom, for melting metal that is to be cast. Also ***cupola furnace***. E18.
3 *ANATOMY.* The small dome-shaped end of the cochlear duct. E19.
4 A revolving dome for protecting mounted guns on a warship etc. M19.
5 *GEOLOGY.* A small dome-shaped projection on the top of a larger igneous intrusion. E20.
■ **cupola'd**, **cupolaed** *adjectives* provided with a cupola E16.

cuppa /ˈkʌpə/ *noun*. *colloq*. Also **cupper**. M20.
[ORIGIN Repr. *cup of* as spoken.]
A cup of tea (or coffee).

cupped /kʌpt/ *adjective*. L18.
[ORIGIN from CUP *noun* or *verb*: see -ED[2], -ED[1].]
1 Shaped like a cup; having a rounded depression or hollow. L18.
2 Lying as if in a cup. L19.

cupper /ˈkʌpə/ *noun*[1]. ME.
[ORIGIN formed as CUPPED: see -ER[1].]
†**1** A cup-maker; a cup-bearer. ME–M17.
2 *hist.* A person who performed the surgical operation of cupping. E19.

cupper /ˈkʌpə/ *noun*[2]. *slang*. E20.
[ORIGIN from CUP *noun* + -ER[6].]
A series of intercollegiate matches played in competition for a cup at Oxford University. Usu. in *pl.*

cupper *noun*[3] var. of CUPPA.

cupping /ˈkʌpɪŋ/ *noun*. LME.
[ORIGIN from CUP *noun* or *verb* + -ING[1].]
1 *hist.* A procedure for drawing blood by applying a heated cup to the scarified skin. Also ***wet cupping***. LME. ▸**b** A similar procedure without scarification, as a counterirritant. Also ***dry cupping***. M18. ▸**c** In Chinese medicine: a therapy in which heated glass cups are applied to the skin along the meridians of the body. M20.
2 The drinking of intoxicating liquor; a drinking bout. E17.
3 The formation of a concavity; the assumption of a curved or hollow shape. L19.
4 The process of forming a depression in sheet metal by forcing a plunger into it when it is placed over a die. E20.
5 Cuppiness in metal; the flaws present in cuppy wire. E20.
– COMB.: **cupping glass** a wide-mouthed glass vessel for use in cupping (sense 1); **cupping test**: of the ductility of metal by means of cupping.

cuppy /ˈkʌpi/ *adjective*. L19.
[ORIGIN from CUP *noun* + -Y[1].]
1 Cup-shaped; concave, hollow. L19.
2 Of ground: full of shallow depressions. Of (the position of) a golf ball: in such a depression. L19.
3 Of drawn metal, esp. wire: having internal cavities liable to lead to a cup-and-cone fracture. E20.
■ **cuppiness** *noun* the state or condition (of metal) of being cuppy E20.

cupr- *combining form* see CUPRO-.

cuprammonium /kjuːprəˈməʊnɪəm/ *noun*. M19.
[ORIGIN from CUPPY + AMMONIUM.]
A complex ion of copper and ammonia, $Cu(NH_3)_4^{++}$, solutions of which dissolve cellulose.
– COMB.: **cuprammonium rayon**: made from cellulose dissolved in cuprammonium solution.
■ **cuprammonia** *noun* liquid containing cuprammonium ions M19.

cuprea bark /ˈkjuːprɪə bɑːk/ *noun phr.* L19.
[ORIGIN from late Latin *cuprea* fem. of *cupreus* CUPREOUS + BARK *noun*[2].]
The coppery-red bark of a S. American tree of the madder family, *Remijia pedunculata* (and *R. purdieana*), a source of quinine.

cupreous /ˈkjuːprɪəs/ *adjective*. M17.
[ORIGIN from late Latin *cupreus*, formed as CUPRIC: see -OUS.]
1 Of the nature of copper; containing or consisting of copper. M17.
2 Looking like copper; copper-coloured. E19.

cupric /ˈkjuːprɪk/ *adjective*. L18.
[ORIGIN from late Latin *cuprum* COPPER *noun*[1] + -IC.]
CHEMISTRY. Of copper in the divalent state.
■ **cuprate** *noun* a salt containing divalent copper M19.

cupriferous /kjuːˈprɪf(ə)rəs/ *adjective*. L18.
[ORIGIN formed as CUPRIC + -FEROUS.]
Yielding or containing copper.

cuprite /ˈkjuːprʌɪt/ *noun*. M19.
[ORIGIN formed as CUPRO- + -ITE[1].]
Native cuprous oxide, a red cubic mineral important as an ore of copper.

cupro /ˈkuːprəʊ/ *noun*. L20.
[ORIGIN from CUPR(AMMONIUM + -O.]
(A fabric made from) a heavy, silky synthetic fibre spun from a liquid produced by dissolving cotton fibres or cellulose in a solution of cuprammonium salts.

cupro- /ˈkjuːprəʊ/ *combining form* of late Latin *cuprum* COPPER *noun*[1]: see -O-. Before a vowel **cupr-**.
■ **cupro-'nickel** *noun* an alloy of copper and nickel, esp. in the proportions 3:1 as used in the 'silver' coinage of the UK E20.

cuprous /ˈkjuːprəs/ *adjective*. M17.
[ORIGIN Partly (orig.) from late Latin *cuprum* COPPER *noun*[1], partly from CUPRIC: see -OUS.]
Cupreous; *CHEMISTRY* of copper in the monovalent state.

cupule /ˈkjuːpjuːl/ *noun*. Also **-ula** /-jʊlə/. LME.
[ORIGIN Late Latin *cupula*: see CUPOLA. Cf. French *cupule*.]
1 *BOTANY.* A cuplike structure associated with the reproductive parts of certain plants; *spec.* (*a*) the woody involucre partly enclosing an acorn; (*b*) the case at the base of a kernel or grain on a corncob. LME.
2 *ZOOLOGY & ANATOMY.* A small cup-shaped organ, as the sucker of a cuttlefish etc.; *esp.* (as *cupula*) one of the gelatinous masses into which sensory hairs protrude in a semicircular canal of the ear. E19.
3 A small cup-shaped depression on a surface. L19.
■ **cupular** *adjective* shaped like a cupule L19. **cupulate** *adjective* cupular; having a cupule: M19.

cur /kəː/ *noun*. ME.
[ORIGIN Prob. orig. in *cur-dog*, perh. from Old Norse *kurr* grumbling, *kurra* murmur.]
1 Orig., a dog. Now *spec.* a worthless, low-bred, or snappish dog. Also ***cur-dog***. ME.
> C. CONNOLLY I feel like a cringing cur kicked about in a crowd.

2 A despicable, low-born, or cowardly man. E16.
†**3** Either of two fishes, the red gurnard (*Aspitrigla cuculus*) and the bullhead (*Cottus gobio*). Also ***cur fish***. L16–M18.
4 The goldeneye, *Bucephala clangula*. *dial.* E17.
■ **curship** *noun* (*rare*) (with possess. adjective, as ***your curship*** etc.) a mock title of respect M17.

curable /ˈkjʊərəb(ə)l/ *adjective*. LME.
[ORIGIN Old French & mod. French, or its source late Latin *curabilis*, from *curare* CURE *verb*: see -ABLE.]
1 Able to be cured; remediable (*lit.* & *fig.*). LME.
†**2** Able to cure; curative. L15–E17.
■ **cura'bility** *noun* LME. †**curableness** *noun* M17–E18.

curaçao /kjʊərəˈsəʊ/ *noun*. Also **-oa**, **C-**. Pl. **-s**. E19.
[ORIGIN *Curaçao*, a Caribbean island of the Lesser Antilles producing oranges used in the flavouring.]
A sweet liqueur of spirits flavoured with the peel of bitter oranges.

curacy /ˈkjʊərəsi/ *noun*. LME.
[ORIGIN from CURATE *noun*: see -ACY.]
The office or position of curate; *hist.* the benefice of a perpetual curate.

curandero /kuranˈdero/ *noun*. Pl. **-os** /-ɔs/. Fem. ***-dera*** /-ˈdera/. M20.
[ORIGIN Spanish, from *curar* to cure from Latin *curare*.]
In Spain and Latin America: a healer who uses folk remedies.

curare /kjʊˈrɑːri/ *noun*. L18.
[ORIGIN (Spanish & Portuguese from) Carib word repr. also by WOURALI.]
A resinous bitter substance obtained from the bark and stems of various tropical and subtropical S. American plants of the genus *Strychnos*, esp. the vine *S. toxifera*, and from the similar *Chondrodendron tomentosum*, which paralyses the motor nerves and was formerly used as an arrow poison by S. American Indians and in surgery etc. to relax the muscles.
> *fig.*: P. ACKROYD The lethargy of the will, the curare that annihilates the nervous elements of thought and motion.

■ **'curarine** *noun* an alkaloid obtained from curare (now replaced in medicine by tubocurarine) M19. **curari'zation** *noun* the action or process of curarizing; the state of being curarized: L19. **'curarize** *verb trans.* administer curare to; produce temporary paralysis in by the administration of curarine or a drug with similar action: L19.

curassow /ˈkjʊərəsəʊ/ *noun*. L17.
[ORIGIN Alt. of *Curaçao*: see CURAÇAO.]
Any of various gallinaceous birds of the family Cracidae similar to turkeys, native to Central and S. America; *esp.* (also ***black curassow***) *Crax alector*, with greenish-black plumage.
helmeted curassow a Venezuelan curassow, *Crax pauxi*, which has a large casque at the base of the bill; also called ***pauxi***.

†**curat** *noun*. M16–E17.
[ORIGIN Back-form from *curats* var. of CUIRASS.]
sing. & in *pl.* = CUIRASS.

curatage /ˈkjʊərətɪdʒ/ *noun*. M18.
[ORIGIN from CURATE *noun* + -AGE.]
†**1** The post of guardian; the provision of guardians. Only in M18.
2 A residence provided for a curate. L19.

curate /ˈkjʊərət/ *noun*. ME.
[ORIGIN medieval Latin *curatus* a person who has a cure or charge (of a parish), from *cura*: see CURE *noun*[1], -ATE[1].]
▸**I** A person holding a spiritual charge.
1 *gen.* An ecclesiastical or spiritual pastor. *arch.* ME.
2 A member of the clergy engaged as a paid assistant or deputy to an incumbent in the Church of England or in the Roman Catholic Church in Ireland. M16.
3 The priest of a Roman Catholic parish in Continental Europe. M17.
▸**II** A person holding a temporal charge.
†**4** A curator; an overseer. LME–M17.
5 In Ireland: an assistant to a person selling spirits etc.; a bartender. E20.
– PHRASES & COMB.: **curate-in-charge**: appointed to take charge of an Anglican parish during the incapacity or suspension of the incumbent. **curate's comfort**, **curate's friend** a cake stand with two or more tiers. ***perpetual curate***: see PERPETUAL *adjective*.
■ †**curateship** *noun* the post or position of curate, a curacy L16–M19. **cu'ratic**, **cu'ratical** *adjectives* L19.

curate /kjʊ(ə)ˈreɪt/ *verb*[1] *trans.* E18.
[ORIGIN Back-form. from CURATOR.]
†**1** *verb intrans.* Provide a record of curation. *rare*. Only in E18.
2 *verb trans.* Act as the curator of (a museum, exhibits, etc.); look after and preserve. L19.
3 *verb intrans.* Perform the duties of a curator; store and preserve exhibits etc. Chiefly as ***curating*** *verbal noun*. E20.

curate /ˈkjʊərət/ *verb*[2] *intrans.* M19.
[ORIGIN from the noun.]
Act as curate.

curate's egg /ˈkjʊərətz ɛg/ *noun phr.* E20.
[ORIGIN from an 1895 cartoon in *Punch* magazine depicting a meek curate who, given a stale egg at the bishop's table, assures his host that 'parts of it are excellent'.]
A thing of very mixed character, partly good and partly bad.
> *Vox* A bit of a curate's egg, picking moments from Mould's two . . solo albums.

curation /kjʊ(ə)ˈreɪʃ(ə)n/ *noun*. LME.
[ORIGIN Old French *curacion* from Latin *curatio(n-)*, from *curat-*: see CURATOR, -ATION.]
†**1** Healing, cure. LME–L17.
2 Guardianship, esp. of a collection of preserved or exhibited items. M18.

curative /ˈkjʊərətɪv/ *adjective* & *noun*. LME.
[ORIGIN French *curatif*, *-ive* from medieval Latin *curativus*, from Latin *curat-*: see CURATOR, -ATIVE.]
▸**A** *adjective*. **1** Of or pertaining to the curing of disease, healing of wounds, etc. LME.
2 Able or tending to cure; *fig.* remedial, corrective. M17.
▸**B** *noun*. A curative agent. M19.
■ **curatively** *adverb* M19. **curativeness** *noun* L19.

curator /kjʊ(ə)ˈreɪtə; *in branch I also* ˈkjʊərətə/ *noun*. LME.
[ORIGIN Partly from Old French & mod. French *curateur*, partly from its source Latin *curator*, from *curat-* pa. ppl stem of *curare*: see CURE *verb*, -OR.]
▸**I** Senses derived through French.
†**1** = CURATE *noun* 1. Only in LME.
2 Now chiefly *SCOTS LAW*. A person appointed as guardian of a minor or other person legally incapable of conducting his or her own affairs. LME.

▸ **II** Senses directly from Latin.
3 A person in charge, a manager, a steward. **M17.**
4 The officer in charge of a museum, library, or other collection; a keeper, a custodian. **M17.**
5 In some universities, a board member or official with responsibility for overseeing property or for choosing professors. **L17.**
6 Any of various public officers under the Roman Empire. **E18.**
▪ **cura'torial** *adjective* **M18.** **cu'ratorship** *noun* the post or position of a curator **L16.** **'curatory** *noun* curatorship; guardianship: **LME.**

curatory /ˈkjʊərət(ə)ri/ *adjective*. **LME.**
[**ORIGIN** Latin *curatorius*, from *curator*: see **CURATOR**, **-ORY**². In mod. use referred to *cūrāre* **CURE** *verb*.]
Curative.

curatrix /kjʊ(ə)ˈreɪtrɪks/ *noun*. Pl. **-trices** /-trɪsiːz/, **-trixes**. **L16.**
[**ORIGIN** Late Latin, fem. of Latin **CURATOR**: see **-TRIX**.]
A female curator or guardian.

†**curats** *noun* var. of **CUIRASS**.

curb /kəːb/ *noun*. See also **KERB** *noun*. **L15.**
[**ORIGIN** Prob. from **CURB** *verb*². Cf. **CRUB**.]
▸ **I 1** A chain or strap passing under the lower jaw of a horse and attached to the bit, used chiefly as a check. **L15.**

W. HOLTBY The big horse pulled at the curb.

2 *fig.* Anything that curbs or restrains; a check, a restraint. **E17.**

Time Italy has imposed curbs on Japanese motorcycles.

▸ **II** Senses corresp. to French *courbe* curve.
3 A hard swelling on a horse's leg; the disease characterized by this. **E16.**
4 A curve, an arc. *obsolete* exc. *dial.* **E17.**
5 A mould or template for marking out curved work. **L18.**
▸ **III** An enclosing (orig. curved) framework or border.
6 A frame round the top of a well or a brewer's copper; the frame of a trapdoor or skylight. **E16.**
7 A raised margin or edging, as a fender round a hearth. **M18.**
8 An edging of stone etc. to a pavement or raised path; = **KERB** *noun* 3. Now *N. Amer.* **L18.**
9 A circular ring or plate round the edge of a dome or other circular structure; the base of a well. (Earlier as **KERB** *noun* 2.) **E19.**
– **COMB.**: **curb bit**, **curb bridle**: fitted with a curb; **curb chain**: acting as a horse's curb; **curb-plate** the curb of a dome or a well; the horizontal timber where the upper and lower slopes of a curb roof meet; **curb roof**: of which each face has two slopes, the lower one being the steeper; **curb service** *N. Amer.* service by a shop etc. to customers in cars at the street kerb; **curbstone** = ***kerbstone*** s.v. **KERB** *noun*.
▪ **curbed** *adjective* having a curb; *fig.* checked, restrained: **L16.** **curbless** *adjective* (*rare*) without curb or restraint **E19.**

curb /kəːb/ *verb*¹ *trans.* See also **KERB** *verb*. **M16.**
[**ORIGIN** from the noun.]
1 Put a curb on (a horse); check or restrain by means of a curb. **M16.**
2 *fig.* Restrain; keep in check. (Foll. by †*of*, †*from*.) **L16.**

J. BERGER If we curb the power of monarchy and rely upon parliamentary government. A. HAILEY Nim curbed a sharp reply.

3 = **KERB** *verb*. Now *N. Amer.* **M19.**
▪ **curber** *noun* a person who or thing which restrains **E17.**

†**curb** *verb*² var. of **COURB**.

curby /ˈkəːbi/ *adjective*. **M19.**
[**ORIGIN** from **CURB** *noun* + **-Y**¹.]
Of a horse's leg: liable to be affected with curb.
▪ **curbily** *adverb* **L19.**

curch /kəːtʃ/ *noun*. *Scot.* **LME.**
[**ORIGIN** Erron. sing. repr. Old French *cuevrechés* pl. of *couvrechef*: see **COVERCHIEF**. Cf. **KERCH** *noun*¹.]
A woman's head covering or kerchief.

curculio /kəːˈkjuːlɪəʊ/ *noun*. Pl. **-os**. **M18.**
[**ORIGIN** Latin = corn weevil.]
Any of various beetles of the family Curculionidae, comprising the weevils.

curcuma /ˈkəːkjʊmə/ *noun*. **LME.**
[**ORIGIN** medieval Latin from Arabic *kurkum* (Persian *karkam*) from Sanskrit *kuṅkuma* saffron.]
Turmeric (the substance and the plant).

curd /kəːd/ *noun*. Also (earlier, now *dial.*) **crud** /krʌd/. **LME.**
[**ORIGIN** Unknown. Cf. **CRUD** *noun*.]
1 The coagulated substance formed (naturally or artificially) by the action of acids or rennet on milk, and made into cheese or eaten as food; a mass of this. Often in *pl.* **LME.**

Nursery rhyme: Little Miss Muffet Sat on a tuffet Eating some curds and whey.

2 Any similar substance, as a conserve. **LME.** ▸**b** The edible head of such brassicas as cauliflower and broccoli. **M18.** ▸**c** The fatty substance found between the flakes of flesh in boiled salmon. **E19.**
lemon curd, ***lime curd***, etc.
– **COMB.**: **curd cheese** soft cheese made from unfermented curds; **curd soap** a white soap made of tallow and soda.
▪ **curdlike** *adjective* resembling curds **M17.**

curd /kəːd/ *verb*. Also (earlier, now *dial.*) **crud** /krʌd/, infl. **-dd-**. **LME.**
[**ORIGIN** from the noun.]
1 *verb trans.* & *intrans.* Make into or become curd; coagulate; congeal. **LME.**
†**2** *verb trans.* Curdle (blood). *rare* (Shakes.). Only in **E17.**

curded /ˈkəːdɪd/ *adjective*. Also (earlier, now *dial.*) **crudded** /ˈkrʌdɪd/. **LME.**
[**ORIGIN** from **CURD** *noun*, *verb*: see **-ED**², **-ED**¹.]
1 Formed into (something like) curd; congealed. **LME.**
2 Having curd or a curd. **LME.**

curdle /ˈkəːd(ə)l/ *noun*. *rare*. **L16.**
[**ORIGIN** from the verb.]
The act or product of curdling; a curd.

curdle /ˈkəːd(ə)l/ *verb trans.* & *intrans.* Also (earlier, now *dial.*) **cruddle** /ˈkrʌd(ə)l/. **L16.**
[**ORIGIN** Frequentative of **CURD** *verb*: see **-LE**³.]
Turn into curd or a soft semi-solid substance resembling it; form curd (in); coagulate, congeal.

fig.: E. BOWEN Mist, at freezing-point, curdled under the headlights.

curdle someone's blood horrify or terrify someone.
▪ **curdler** *noun* something which causes curdling; *spec.* a story etc. that curdles the blood: **M19.** **curdly** *adjective* apt to curdle; of a curdled nature: **L17.**

curdy /ˈkəːdi/ *adjective*. Also (earlier, now *dial.*) **cruddy** /ˈkrʌdi/. **LME.**
[**ORIGIN** from **CURD** *noun* + **-Y**¹. Cf. **CRUDDY**.]
1 Full of curdlike coagulations; curdlike in consistency or appearance. **LME.**
2 Full of curd or curds. **E16.**

SPENSER His cruell woundes with cruddy bloud congeald.

▪ **curdiness** *noun* **E19.**

†**curdy** *verb trans.* *rare* (Shakes.). Only in **E17.**
[**ORIGIN** from the adjective.]
Make curdlike; congeal.

cure /kjʊə/ *noun*¹. **ME.**
[**ORIGIN** Old French & mod. French from Latin *cura* care.]
▸ **I** †**1** Care, heed, concern; anxiety. **ME–E17.**
†**2** Care committed to a person, responsibility; a duty, an office. **ME–M17.**
3 *ECCLESIASTICAL.* **a** More fully ***cure of souls***. The spiritual charge or oversight of parishioners etc. **ME.** ▸**b** A parish; the people under the charge of a priest; a sphere of spiritual ministry. **L15.**
†**4** Medical treatment. **LME–E18.**
5 Successful medical treatment; the action or process of healing a sick person, an illness, etc.; a thing that does this, a remedy. **LME.**

E. S. TURNER Physical cures happen at Lourdes and the phenomenon cannot be ignored. T. S. ELIOT Tried to impose upon me Your own diagnosis, and prescribe your own cure.

miracle cure: see **MIRACLE** *noun*.
6 a A particular method or course of medical treatment. **M19.** ▸**b** A period of residence at a health resort, under medical regimen, in order to restore or benefit one's health. **L19.**

a A. FLINT In order to carry out . . the 'milk-cure', . . milk . . should be taken largely. **b** W. S. MAUGHAM The cure at Montecatini had not done him the good he expected.

a rest cure: see **REST** *noun*¹.
▸ **II 7** The curing or preserving of fish, pork, etc.; a catch of fish so treated. **M18.**
8 The process of curing rubber or plastic; the degree of hardness produced. **E20.**
▪ **cureless** *adjective* incurable, irremediable **M16.** **curelessly** *adverb* **M19.**

cure /kjʊə/ *noun*². *slang*. **M19.**
[**ORIGIN** Abbreviation of **CURIOSITY**, with play on **CURE** *noun*¹: cf. **CURIO**.]
An odd person; a funny fellow.

cure /kjʊə/ *verb*. **LME.**
[**ORIGIN** Old French & mod. French *curer* take care of, clean from Latin *curare* care for, cure.]
†**1** *verb trans.* & *intrans.* Take care (of); take trouble; care (for). **LME–E17.**
†**2** *verb trans.* & *intrans.* Take charge of the spiritual interests of (a parish etc.). **LME–L16.**
†**3** *verb trans.* Treat surgically or medically. **LME–L16.**
4 *verb trans.* Restore to health, relieve *of* an illness, an evil. **LME.**

G. STEIN He tried to cure the boy of his bad ways and make him honest.

5 *verb trans.* Heal (an illness, a wound); remedy, remove, (an evil). **LME.**

J. FREEMAN The pain that never the new years may cure. B. SPOCK Dehydration fever . . can always be cured immediately by giving fluid.

6 *verb intrans.* Effect a cure. Freq. in ***kill or cure*** s.v. **KILL** *verb*². **L16.**
†**7** *verb intrans.* Be cured, get well again. *rare*. **L16–L18.**
8 *verb trans.* Prepare for keeping by salting, drying, etc.; preserve (meat, fish, tobacco, etc.). **E17.**

D. L. SAYERS A farmer who cured his own bacon.

9 *verb intrans.* Undergo preservation by salting etc. **M17.**
10 *verb trans.* Vulcanize (rubber); change physical properties of, esp. harden, (plastic) chemically during manufacture; harden (concrete). **M19.**
11 *verb intrans.* Undergo vulcanization; harden, set. **E20.**

G. BOYCOTT Cement which has cured too quickly.

12 *verb intrans.* Stay at a health resort in order to follow a health-improving regimen. **E20.**
▪ **curer** *noun* (**a**) a person who or thing which cures illness etc.; (**b**) a person whose occupation is to cure fish etc.: **L16.** **curist** *noun* = **CURER** (a) (only as 2nd elem. of comb., as ***mind-curist*** etc.) **L19.**

curé /kyre/ *noun*. Pl. pronounced same. **M17.**
[**ORIGIN** French from medieval Latin *curatus*: see **CURATE** *noun*.]
A parish priest in France and French-speaking countries.

cure-all /ˈkjʊərɔːl/ *noun*. **L18.**
[**ORIGIN** from **CURE** *verb* + **ALL**.]
A universal remedy, a panacea. Formerly, a plant with healing properties.

Curetonian /kjʊəˈtəʊnɪən/ *adjective* & *noun*. **M19.**
[**ORIGIN** from *Cureton* (see below) + **-IAN**.]
(Designating) the Syriac version of the Gospels discovered and edited by the Revd William Cureton (1808–64).

curettage /kjʊəˈrɛtɪdʒ, kjʊərɪˈtɑːʒ/ *noun*. **L19.**
[**ORIGIN** French, formed as **CURETTE**: see **-AGE**.]
SURGERY. The scraping or cleaning of an internal surface of an organ or body cavity with a curette; a common operation on the womb which consists of this (see ***dilatation and curettage*** s.v. **DILATATION** 1).

curette /kjʊəˈrɛt/ *noun* & *verb*. **M18.**
[**ORIGIN** French, formed as **CURE** *verb*: see **-ETTE**.]
SURGERY. ▸**A** *noun*. A small instrument resembling a scoop used to remove material by a scraping action, esp. from the womb. **M18.**
▸ **B** *verb trans.* & *intrans.* Scrape or clean with a curette. **L19.**
▪ **curettement** *noun* (*rare*) curettage **E20.** **curetting** *noun* (**a**) use of a curette; (**b**) in *pl.*, material removed with a curette: **L19.**

curf /kəːf/ *noun*. **M19.**
[**ORIGIN** Alt. of **CARF**.]
A cherty limestone found in one of the strata of Portland stone.

curfew /ˈkəːfjuː/ *noun*. **ME.**
[**ORIGIN** Anglo-Norman *coeverfu*, Old French *cuevrefeu* (mod. *couvrefeu*), from tonic stem of *cuvrir* **COVER** *verb*¹ + *feu* fire.]
▸ **I 1** A regulation, widespread in medieval Europe, by which fires had to be covered or extinguished at a fixed hour each evening, indicated by the ringing of a bell; (also ***curfew-bell***) the bell itself; the time of its ringing; the practice of ringing a bell at a fixed hour each evening (for any purpose). **ME.** ▸†**b** The ringing of a bell at a fixed hour each morning. **L16–E18.**

C. LYELL At nine o'clock, a . . curfew tolls . . after which no coloured man is permitted to be abroad.

2 A regulation forbidding people to be out of doors (at all, or occas. except under specified conditions) between certain hours, usu. of the night; the time of effectiveness of such a regulation; *transf.* (the time of effectiveness of) any restriction on movement at night. **L19.**

K. AMIS The unbreakable midnight curfew her father had put on her evenings out till she was turned eighteen. G. GREENE The curfew had been lifted.

▸ **II 3** A cover for a fire. Now *rare*. **E17.**

curfuffle *noun* var. of **KERFUFFLE**.

curfuffle /kəˈfʌf(ə)l/ *verb trans.* *Scot.* **L16.**
[**ORIGIN** from (perh.) Gaelic *car* twist, bend, turn about + **FUFFLE**. Cf. **KERFUFFLE**.]
Disorder; ruffle.

curia /ˈkjʊərɪə/ *noun*. Pl. **-iae** /-ɪiː/, **-ias**. **E17.**
[**ORIGIN** Latin.]
1 Each of the ten divisions into which each of the three tribes of ancient Rome was divided; a similar division in another ancient city; the senate of an ancient Italian town, as distinguished from that of Rome. **E17.**
2 A court of justice, counsel, or administration, esp. of the Roman Catholic Church or (*hist.*) under the feudal system. **E18.**
3 (**C-**.) *The* Vatican tribunals, congregations, and other institutions through which the Pope directs the work of the Roman Catholic Church; *the* government departments of the Vatican. **M19.**

curial /ˈkjʊərɪəl/ *noun* & *adjective*. **LME.**
[**ORIGIN** French *curiale* noun, *curial(e)* adjective, from Latin *curialis*, formed as **CURIA**: see **-AL**¹.]
▸ **A** *noun*. †**1** A courtier. Only in **LME.**
2 *hist.* A member of an ancient Roman or Italian curia. **L17.**

C

▸ **B** *adjective*. †**1** Courtly. L15–M16.
2 Of or pertaining to a curia. L17.
■ **curialism** *noun* a curial or courtly system, *esp.* Vaticanism L19. **curialist** *noun* a member or supporter of the papal Curia M19. **curia'listic** *adjective* of or pertaining to curialists or curialism L19.

C

†**curiality** *noun*. LME–M19.
[ORIGIN Old French *curialité*, medieval Latin *curialitas*, from *curialis* CURIAL.]
What pertains to a court; courtliness; courtesy, favour.

curiara /kuːrɪ'ɑːrə/ *noun*. E20.
[ORIGIN Amer. Spanish from Carib *culiala*: cf. CORIAL.]
In Venezuela and Colombia: a dugout canoe.

curiate /'kjʊərɪət/ *adjective*. M16.
[ORIGIN Latin *curiatus*, formed as CURIA: see -ATE².]
Of or pertaining to the Roman curiae.

curie /'kjʊəri/ *noun*. In sense 2 usu. **C-**. E20.
[ORIGIN Pierre (1859–1906) and Marie (1867–1934) *Curie*, co-discoverers of radium.]
PHYSICS. **1** A unit of radioactivity equal to 3.7×10^{10} disintegrations per second; a quantity of radioactive material with this activity. Formerly, a quantity of a decay product of radium in radioactive equilibrium with 1 gram of radium. E20.
2 ***Curie point***, ***Curie temperature***, a temperature at which the type of magnetism or electrical behaviour exhibited by a substance changes, *spec.* that at which a substance loses its ferromagnetism on being heated and becomes paramagnetic. E20.

curing /'kjʊərɪŋ/ *verbal noun*. LME.
[ORIGIN from CURE *verb* + -ING¹.]
1 Healing, cure. Now *rare*. LME.
2 The process of preparing fish etc. for preservation by salting, drying, etc. L17.
3 The process of curing rubber etc. M19.

curio /'kjʊərɪəʊ/ *noun*. Pl. **-os**. M19.
[ORIGIN Abbreviation of CURIOSITY: cf. CURE *noun*².]
An *objet d'art*, souvenir, etc., valued as a curiosity or a rarity; an unusual person.

curiologic /kjʊərɪə'lɒdʒɪk/ *adjective & noun*. Also †**cyrio-**. M17.
[ORIGIN Irreg. from Greek *kuriologikos* speaking literally, opp. *sumbolikos* symbolic.]
▸ **A** *adjective*. Designating or pertaining to that form of hieroglyphic writing in which objects are represented by pictures. M17.
▸ **B** *noun*. In *pl.* (treated as *sing.*). Representation by picture-writing. E19.
■ **curiological** *adjective* E19. **curiologically** *adverb* M18.

curiosa /kjʊərɪ'əʊsə/ *noun pl.* L19.
[ORIGIN Latin, neut. pl. of *curiosus*: see CURIOUS.]
Curiosities, oddities; *spec.* erotic or pornographic books.

curiosa felicitas /kjʊərɪ,əʊsə fə'lɪsɪtɑːs/ *noun phr.* M18.
[ORIGIN Latin, lit. 'careful felicity'.]
A studied appropriateness of expression.

curiosity /kjʊərɪ'ɒsɪti/ *noun*. LME.
[ORIGIN Old French *curiouseté* (mod. *curiosité*) from Latin *curiositas*, from *curiosus*: see CURIOUS, -ITY.]
▸ **I** As a personal attribute.
†**1** Carefulness; scrupulousness; fastidiousness. LME–M18.
†**2** Skill, cleverness, ingenuity. LME–M18.
3 a Inquisitiveness about matters that do not concern one. Formerly also, any undue or inquisitive desire to know or learn. LME. ▸**b** A desire or inclination to know or learn about something, esp. what is novel or strange. E17.

> **a** L. DURRELL I spied upon her . . from curiosity to know what she might be doing or thinking. **b** D. MORRIS Our curiosity, our inquisitiveness, urges us on to investigate all natural phenomena.

†**4** A fancy, a whim; a hobby. E17–E18.
†**5** Scientific or artistic interest; connoisseurship. M17–E19.
▸ **II** As a quality of things.
†**6** Careful or elaborate workmanship; delicacy or elegance of construction. LME–E19.
7 The quality of being interesting on account of novelty or strangeness. L16.
▸ **III** A matter or thing embodying this quality.
†**8** A subtle or abstruse matter of investigation; a nicety. LME–E18.

> DONNE Troubling the peace of the Church, with . . inextricable curiosities.

†**9** A matter receiving undue attention; a vanity. LME–E18.
†**10** A curious detail or trait. M17–M18.
11 A curious, rare, or strange object. M17.

> H. JAMES He had been to China and brought home a collection of curiosities.

curioso /kjʊərɪ'əʊzəʊ/ *noun*. *arch.* Pl. **-si** /-si/, **-sos**. M17.
[ORIGIN Italian.]
Orig., a person with a keen interest in matters of science and art. Later, a connoisseur.

curious /'kjʊərɪəs/ *adjective & adverb*. ME.
[ORIGIN Old French *curios* (mod. *curieux*) from Latin *curiosus* careful, assiduous, inquisitive, from *cura* care: see CURE *noun*¹, -OUS.]
▸ **A** *adjective*. **I** As a subjective quality of people.
1 Having a wish to see or to know; eager to learn, esp. about what does not concern one; inquisitive. ME.

> F. NORRIS Annixter, curious for details, forbore, nevertheless, to question.

†**2** Careful, attentive, solicitous. LME–L18.
3 Having high standards; fastidious, particular; cautious. *obsolete* exc. *dial.* LME.
†**4** Skilful, clever, ingenious. LME–M19.

> HOR. WALPOLE That neat and curious painter Vander Heyden.

†**5** Having expertise as a connoisseur or virtuoso. L16–M19.
†**6** Accurate in observation or investigation; (of the eye etc.) sharp, perceptive. L16–E19.
▸ **II** As an objective quality of things etc.
†**7 a** Of an inappropriately searching nature; abstruse, subtle; occult. ME–M18. ▸**b** Of an investigation etc.: characterized by special care; meticulous. Now *rare*. E16. ▸†**c** Very accurate, exact, precise. E17–E19.

> **b** DISRAELI A subject which demands the most curious investigation. **c** J. SELDEN Your curious learning and judgment. R. HOOKE The most curious Mathematical Instruments.

†**8 a** Elaborately or carefully made or prepared. LME–M19. ▸**b** Performed with or requiring skill. L17–L18.
†**9** Exquisite, excellent, fine. LME–E19.

> S. PEPYS A very calm, curious morning.

†**10** Interesting, noteworthy. LME–E19.

> J. RICHARDSON Statues, Intaglias, and the like Curious Works of Art. J. REYNOLDS It is curious to observe, that [etc.].

11 Deserving or arousing curiosity; somewhat surprising; strange, queer. E18.

> R. CAMPBELL Father had some very curious cranky habits mostly concerned with the telephone. E. ROOSEVELT She was not exactly a hunchback, but she had a curious figure.

curiouser and curiouser more and more curious; increasingly strange.
12 Of an action etc.: prompted by curiosity. M19.

> DICKENS She stole a curious look at my face.

13 *euphem.* Erotic; pornographic. L19.

> I. MONTAGU The bookseller's catalogue labelled 'Erotica' or 'Curious'.

– COMB.: **curious-minded** *adjective* having an inquisitive or a strange mind.
▸ †**B** *adverb*. Curiously. LME–M18.
■ **curiously** *adverb* ME. **curiousness** *noun* LME.

curium /'kjʊərɪəm/ *noun*. M20.
[ORIGIN formed as CURIE + -IUM.]
A radioactive metallic chemical element of the actinide series, atomic no. 96, which is produced artificially (symbol Cm).

curl /kəːl/ *noun*. L16.
[ORIGIN from the verb.]
1 A lock of hair of a spiral or coiled form. L16. ▸**b** The state (of hair) of being curled. M19.

> SHAKES. *Haml.* Hyperion's curls, the front of Jove himself.

MONTAGUE *curl*. **b in curl** (of hair) curled. **out of curl** (of hair) having become straight (***go out of curl*** fig., lose one's drive or energy).
2 Anything of a spiral or incurved shape; a coil. E17.

> E. BOWEN The steamer's smoke hung in curls on the clear air.

3 A ripple or wave on water. M17. ▸**b** The curved top of a wave about to break. M20.

> **b** P. O'BRIAN He saw the vast breaking wave with the *Waakzaamheid* broadside on in its curl.

4 The action or an act of curling, esp. by a cricket ball or a bowler. L18.
curl of the lip a curving of the upper lip, expressive of scorn or disgust.
5 A disease of plants in which the shoots or leaves are curled up and imperfectly developed. L18.
6 MATH. The vector product of the operator ∇ (see DEL) and any given vector. L19.
– COMB.: **curl-paper** a piece of paper with which hair is twisted into a curl; **curl-pate** *arch.* (a person with) a curly head; **curl-pated** *adjective* (*arch.*) curly-haired.
■ **curlless** /-l-l-/ *adjective* M19.

curl /kəːl/ *verb*. LME.
[ORIGIN Orig. pa. pple, from (the same root as) CURLED. See also QUERL.]
1 *verb trans.* Bend round or twist into curls or a spiral shape. LME. ▸**b** Ripple, make waves on, (water). L16.

> **b** POPE Soft zephyrs curling the wide, watery main.

2 *verb intrans.* Of hair, a fleece: form curls, be susceptible to curling. M16.
†**3** *verb trans.* Curl the hair of. Cf. CURLED 2. L16–M17.
4 *verb intrans.* Adopt an incurved form or posture. Freq. foll. by *up*. M17. ▸**b** Foll. by *up*: collapse, lose energy. *slang*. L19. ▸**c** Shrink or writhe with shame, horror, etc. Freq. foll. by *up*. E20. ▸**d** *verb intrans.* Foll. by *up*: settle oneself cosily. M20.

> W. GASS I wanted to curl up, face to my thighs. **c** P. G. WODEHOUSE I'm going to . . look him in the eye . . and watch him curl up at the edges. **d** R. JARRELL I'll bet *you've* often curled up in a window-seat with *Little Women*.

5 *verb intrans.* Move in spiral convolutions or undulations. E18.

> J. FOWLES The breeze . . sent little waves curling . . along the shingle.

6 *verb intrans.* Play at curling. *Scot.* E18.
7 CRICKET. **a** *verb intrans.* Of a ball: turn in after pitching; turn in its flight before pitching. M19. ▸**b** *verb trans.* Of a bowler: cause (the ball) to swing in the air. E20.
– PHRASES & COMB.: **curl a person's hair** *fig.* (*colloq.*) horrify or shock a person. **curl one's lip**, **curl the lip** curve the upper lip slightly on one side, as an expression of scorn or disgust. **curl the mo** *verb & adjective* (*Austral. slang*) [MO *noun*²] (**a**) *verb* succeed brilliantly, win; (**b**) *adjective* (with hyphens), excellent, outstanding. **make a person's hair curl** = ***curl a person's hair*** above. **want to curl up and die** wish to escape from a highly embarrassing situation; feel mortified.
■ **curlingly** *adverb* in a curling manner E17.

curled /kəːld/ *adjective*. Orig. †**crulled**. LME.
[ORIGIN Earliest use from CRULL *adjective*, later from CURL *noun*, *verb*: see -ED², -ED¹. Metathesized form also late Middle English.]
1 Formed into curls; having a spiral or wavy form. LME.
curled kale: see KALE 1. ***curled-leaved mallow***, ***curled mallow***: see MALLOW.
2 Having the hair in curls. L16.
3 Of potatoes: affected with curl. L18.
4 Of wood, esp. maple: having a wavy or curly grain. L18.

curler /'kəːlə/ *noun*. M17.
[ORIGIN from CURL *verb* + -ER¹.]
1 A player at the game of curling. (Earlier than the verb.) M17.
2 A person who or thing which produces curls; *spec.* a clasp, roller, etc., used to curl the hair. M18.

curlew /'kəːl(j)uː/ *noun*. ME.
[ORIGIN Old French & mod. French *courlieu* var. of *courlis*, orig. imit. of the bird's cry, but prob. assim. to Old French *courliu* courier, messenger, from *courre* run + *lieu* place.]
1 Any bird of the genus *Numenius*, comprising waders with long slender downcurved bills; *esp.* one of the common European species *N. arquata*. Cf. ***stone curlew*** s.v. STONE *noun, adjective, & adverb*. ME.
Eskimo curlew: see ESKIMO *adjective*. ***Hudsonian curlew***. ***Jack curlew***: see JACK *noun*¹. ***slender-billed curlew***: see SLENDER *adjective*.
†**2** [translating Latin *coturnix*, Greek *ortux*.] In biblical translations and allusions: a quail. ME–E16.

curlicue /'kəːlɪkjuː/ *noun & verb*. Also **curly-**. M19.
[ORIGIN from CURLY + CUE *noun*¹ or *noun*².]
▸ **A** *noun*. A fantastic curl or twist; *US* a caper. M19.
▸ **B** *verb trans. & intrans.* Bend elaborately or fantastically. M19.

curlie-wurlie *noun* see CURLY-WURLY.

curling /'kəːlɪŋ/ *noun*. LME.
[ORIGIN from CURL *verb* + -ING¹.]
1 The action of CURL *verb*; a curl, an undulation. LME.
2 A game played on ice in Scotland and elsewhere, in which large circular stones are slid along a defined area (the ***rink***) towards a mark (the ***tee***). (Earlier than the corresponding sense of the verb.) M17.
– COMB.: **curling iron**, **curling pin**: used for curling the hair; **curling rink** (a building containing) an area of ice prepared and marked for the game of curling; **curling stone**: used in playing curling (now a large polished circular stone with an iron handle on top); **curling tongs** metal tongs which are heated and around which strands of hair are wound to put a curl in them.

curly /'kəːli/ *adjective*. L18.
[ORIGIN from CURL *noun* + -Y¹.]
1 Of hair: having curls, in curls. L18.
2 Of a curled form; wavy. L18.
3 Having curly hair. E19.
4 = CURLED 4. E20.
– PHRASES: ***curly kale***: see KALE 1. ***Lincolnshire Curly-Coat***, ***Lincolnshire Curly-Coated***: see LINCOLNSHIRE. ***get by the short and curlies***, ***have by the short and curlies***: see SHORT *adjective*.
■ **curliness** *noun* E19.

curlycue *noun & verb* var. of CURLICUE.

curly-wurly /kəːlɪ'wəːli/ *noun & adjective*. *colloq.* As noun also **curlie-wurlie**. L18.
[ORIGIN Redupl. of CURLY.]
▸ **A** *noun*. A fantastically curling ornament. L18.
▸ **B** *adjective*. Twisting and curling. M19.

curmudgeon /kəː'mʌdʒ(ə)n/ *noun*. L16.
[ORIGIN Unknown.]
Orig., a mean-spirited or miserly person. Now usu., a gruff, irritable, or cantankerous (esp. elderly) man.
■ **curmudgeonly** *adjective* miserly, niggardly; gruff, irritable, cantankerous: L16.

curmurring /kə'mʌrɪŋ/ *noun*. *Scot.* L18.
[ORIGIN Imit.]
A low rumbling, growling, or murmuring sound.

curn /kəːn/ *noun. N. English.* Long only *Scot.* ME.
[ORIGIN Perh. rel. to KERN *noun*[2].]
†1 In *pl.* Grain. Only in ME.
2 A grain. LME.
3 A small quantity; a few. E17.
■ **curny** *adjective* granular E19.

curple /ˈkəːp(ə)l/ *noun. Scot.* Now *rare.* L15.
[ORIGIN Var. of CRUPPER *noun* with metathesis & dissimilation of /r/ to /l/.]
1 A crupper for a horse etc. L15.
2 The buttocks. L18.

curr /kəː/ *verb & noun.* LME.
[ORIGIN Imit.]
▸ **A** *verb intrans.* Make a low murmuring sound; coo; purr. LME.
▸ **B** *noun.* A curring sound. M19.

currach /ˈkʌrə(x)/ *noun.* Also **-agh**, †**corrack**. LME.
[ORIGIN Irish, Gaelic *curach* small boat: cf. CORACLE.]
In Ireland and Scotland: a small boat made of slats or laths covered with watertight material (formerly hide, now usu. tarred canvas).

curragh /ˈkʌrə(x)/ *noun*[1]. M17.
[ORIGIN Irish *currach* marsh, Manx *curragh* moor, bog, fen.]
In Ireland and the Isle of Man: (a piece of) marshy waste ground.
the Curragh a level stretch of open ground in Co. Kildare, Ireland, famous for its racecourse and military camp.

curragh *noun*[2] var. of CURRACH.

currajong *noun* var. of KURRAJONG.

currance *noun* var. of CURRENCE.

currant /ˈkʌr(ə)nt/ *noun.* Also †**corinth**. E16.
[ORIGIN Abbreviation of *raisins of Corauntz* from Anglo-Norman *raisins de Corauntz* for Old French & mod. French *raisins de Corinthe* lit. 'grapes of Corinth' (their original place of export): see CORINTH.]
1 A dried fruit of a dwarf seedless variety of grape grown in the eastern Mediterranean region, used in cookery. E16.
2 The small round edible berry of certain shrubs of the genus *Ribes.* L16.
3 A shrub producing this berry or (usu. edible) fruit resembling it (also ***currant bush***); any shrub of the genus *Ribes.* M17.
– PHRASES: BLACKCURRANT. **flowering currant** a N. American shrub, *Ribes sanguineum*, grown for its conspicuous crimson flowers; also (*US*) a yellow-flowered currant, *R. aureum.* **Indian currant** = *coralberry* s.v. CORAL *noun & adjective.* REDCURRANT. **white currant** (the whitish berry of) a cultivar of the redcurrant, *Ribes rubrum.*
– COMB.: **currant borer** *US*, **currant clearwing** a black and yellow clearwing, *Ramosia tipuliformis*; its larva, which bores into the canes of currant bushes; **currant jelly** a preserve made from the strained juice of boiled currants heated and mixed with sugar; **currant tomato** a tomato with tiny fruits, *Lycopersicon pimpinellifolium.*

currawong /ˈkʌrəwɒŋ/ *noun. Austral.* E20.
[ORIGIN Prob. from Yagara (an Australian Aboriginal language of SE Queensland) *garrawan* or perh. from Dharuk *gurawarun.*]
Any of various large woodland songbirds of the Australian genus *Strepera*, similar to the magpie.

†**currence** *noun.* Also **-ance**. L16.
[ORIGIN formed as CURRENCY: see -ENCE.]
1 = CURRENCY 1. Only in L16.
2 = CURRENCY 2, 5. M17–M19.

currency /ˈkʌr(ə)nsi/ *noun & adjective.* M17.
[ORIGIN from CURRENT *adjective*: see -ENCY.]
▸ **A** *noun.* **1** The fact or condition of flowing; a current, a stream. *rare.* M17.
2 The fact or quality of being in circulation as a medium of exchange. L17.
3 The money or other commodity which is in circulation as a medium of exchange. E18. ▸**b** *spec.* A medium of exchange which differs in value from that used for official reckoning, e.g. local money formerly used in British colonies (usu. contrasted with ***sterling***); *fig.* (*Austral.*) a native-born Australian. *arch.* M18.

G. BOYCOTT Having surrendered all our local currency . . we had no money to buy food or a drink.

hard currency: see HARD *adjective.* ***managed currency***: see MANAGED 2. ***postal currency***: see POSTAL *adjective.* ***reserve currency***: see RESERVE *noun & adjective.* ***soft currency***: see SOFT *adjective.*
4 The course *of* time; the time during which something runs its course. E18.

J. R. McCULLOCH During the entire currency of the lease.

5 The fact or quality of being generally accepted; prevalence (of an idea, report, etc.). E18.

G. F. KENNAN The . . prejudiced views about Russian Communism that were beginning to find currency in Western officialdom. N. PODHORETZ When I was in college, the term WASP had not yet come into currency.

– COMB.: **currency note** a note issued as a medium of exchange, *esp.* one of the £1 and 10s. notes first issued by the Treasury during the First World War.
▸ **B** *attrib.* or as *adjective.* Native-born Australian. *arch.* E19.

Landfall She spoke the King's English like a currency lass.

current /ˈkʌr(ə)nt/ *noun.* LME.
[ORIGIN Old French *corant* (mod. *courant*) use as noun of the pres. pple: see CURRENT *adjective.*]
1 Something which flows; *spec.* a portion of a body of water, air, etc., moving in a definite direction. LME.

N. CALDER The Gulf Stream, the warm current that runs . . across the Atlantic.

Japan current, ***Japanese current***, ***Labrador current***, etc.
2 The flow of a river etc. M16.

W. IRVING A river with high banks and deep rapid current.

3 The slope given to a gutter, roof, etc., to enable water to run off. L16.
4 The course of time or of events. L16.

T. CHALMERS The whole current of my restless and ever-changing history.

5 Course or progress in a defined direction; tendency, drift, (of events, opinions, etc.). L16.

K. CLARK All the intellectual currents of the time. L. P. HARTLEY Did she . . think that a new experience . . could change the current of an author's work?

6 (A) flow of electricity; the rate of this, measured as quantity of charge per second. M18. ▸**b** PARTICLE PHYSICS. A transfer or exchange of a subatomic particle, esp. as mediating an interaction between other particles. M20.

fig.: M. M. KAYE He saw her exchange a brief glance with Ash, and . . it seemed . . that an invisible current leapt between them.

alternating current, ***direct current***. ***dark current***: see DARK *adjective.* ***TOWNSEND current***.
– COMB.: **current bedding** GEOLOGY: with a direction produced by a current of water or air at the time of deposition.
■ **currentless** *adjective* M19.

current /ˈkʌr(ə)nt/ *adjective.* ME.
[ORIGIN Old French *corant* (mod. *courant*) pres. pple of *courre* (mod. *courir*) from Latin *currere* to run; spelling assim. to Latin: see -ENT, -ANT[1].]
1 Running; flowing. Now *rare.* ME. ▸**b** Running easily and swiftly; flowing smoothly. Now *rare.* L15.
2 **a** Of money: in circulation, in general use as a medium of exchange. L15. ▸†**b** Genuine, authentic. L16–M18.
3 Generally reported or known; prevalent; generally accepted, established by common consent, (passing into sense 4). M16.

DRYDEN A word which is not current English. W. C. WILLIAMS A story current in Paris at the time.

4 (Of time) now passing, in progress; belonging to the current period of time. E17.

DICKENS We must call the current number for that date the Christmas number.

– SPECIAL COLLOCATIONS & PHRASES: ***current account***, ***account current***: see ACCOUNT *noun.* **current affairs**, **current events** matters of public interest in progress. **current asset** COMMERCE an asset in the form of cash or expected to be converted into it, e.g. stock. **current cost accounting** a method of accounting in which assets are valued on the basis of their current replacement cost and increases in their value as a result of inflation are excluded from calculations of profit. **go current**, **pass current**, †**go for current**, †**pass for current** be generally accepted as true or genuine.
■ **currently** *adverb* LME. **currentness** *noun* (now *rare*) L16.

currente calamo /kʌˌrɛnteɪ ˈkaləməʊ/ *adverbial phr.* L18.
[ORIGIN mod. Latin, lit. 'with the pen running on'.]
Extempore; without deliberation or hesitation.

curricle /ˈkʌrɪk(ə)l/ *noun.* LME.
[ORIGIN Latin CURRICULUM.]
†1 The running or course of one continuous thing or several consecutive things. LME–E18.
2 Chiefly *hist.* A light open two-wheeled carriage, usually drawn by two horses abreast. M18.

curricula *noun* pl. of CURRICULUM.

curricular /kʌˈrɪkjʊlə/ *adjective.* L18.
[ORIGIN from (the same root as) CURRICULUM + -AR[1].]
1 Of or pertaining to driving or carriages. *rare.* L18.
2 Of or pertaining to a curriculum. E20.

curriculum /kʌˈrɪkjʊləm/ *noun.* Pl. **-la** /-lə/, **-lums**. E19.
[ORIGIN Latin = running, course, race-chariot, from *currere* to run.]
A course of study at a school, university, etc.; the subjects making up such a course.
national curriculum: see NATIONAL *adjective.*

curriculum vitae /kʌˌrɪkjʊləm ˈviːtʌɪ, ˈvʌitiː/ *noun phr.* Pl. **curricula vitae** /kʌˈrɪkjʊlə/. E20.
[ORIGIN formed as CURRICULUM + Latin *vitae* of life.]
A brief account of one's life or career, esp. as required in an application for employment.

†**currie** *noun* var. of CURRY *noun*[1].

currier /ˈkʌrɪə/ *noun*[1]. LME.
[ORIGIN Old French *corier* from Latin *coriarius*, from *corium* leather: see -ER[2]. In sense 2 from CURRY *verb*[1] + -ER[1].]
1 A person who curries tanned leather. LME.
2 A person who curries horses etc. M16.

†**currier** *noun*[2]. M16–M19.
[ORIGIN Unknown.]
A firearm of the same calibre and strength as the harquebus, but with a longer barrel.

currish /ˈkəːrɪʃ/ *adjective.* L15.
[ORIGIN from CUR + -ISH[1].]
1 Like a cur in nature; snappish, quarrelsome; mean-spirited, base. L15.
2 Relating to or resembling a cur(-dog). M16.
■ **currishly** *adverb* E16. **currishness** *noun* LME.

†**curry** *noun*[1]. Also **currie**. E16–M19.
[ORIGIN French *curée*, earlier Old French *cuirée*; gen. referred to *cuir* leather: see -Y[5], QUARRY *noun*[1].]
The parts of an animal killed in hunting that were given to the hounds; the cutting up and disembowelling of the game.

curry /ˈkʌri/ *noun*[2]. L16.
[ORIGIN Tamil *kaṟi.*]
(A dish of) meat, fish, vegetables, etc., cooked with a mixture of strong spices and turmeric; (in full ***curry powder***) a mixture of strong spices and turmeric used in making such a dish.
give a person curry *Austral. & NZ slang* abuse, reprove, express anger at, a person. ***Madras curry***, ***vindaloo curry***, etc.
– COMB.: **curry leaf** the leaf of a shrub or small tree, *Murraya koenigii* (family Rutaceae), native to India and Sri Lanka, used in Indian cooking; **curry paste**, **curry sauce**: made with curry powder; ***curry powder***: see above.

curry /ˈkʌri/ *verb*[1]. ME.
[ORIGIN Old French *correier* (mod. *courroyer*) arrange, equip, curry (a horse) from Proto-Romance, from Latin CON- + Germanic base of READY *adjective.*]
1 *verb trans.* Groom (a horse etc.) with a curry comb. ME. ▸**b** Dress (the hair); dress the hair of. L16.
†**curry favel** [lit. 'the fallow or chestnut horse': see FAVEL] use insincere flattery etc. to gain personal advantage.
2 *verb trans.* Treat (tanned leather) by soaking, scraping, beating, etc., to improve its properties. LME.
3 *verb trans.* Beat, thrash, (a person). LME.
†4 *verb intrans. & trans.* Employ flattery (with). LME–M19.
5 *verb trans.* ***curry favour*** [alt. of *curry favel* above], seek to win favour or ingratiate oneself (*with* a person) by flattery etc. E16. ▸†**b** Seek to win (goodwill, friends, etc.) by flattery etc. L16–E19.

G. VIDAL 'I was a close follower in the first few years,' I said, currying favor. **b** COLERIDGE Currying pardon for his last liberalism by charging . . himself with the guilt of falsehood.

curry /ˈkʌri/ *verb*[2] *trans.* M19.
[ORIGIN from CURRY *noun*[2].]
Flavour or prepare with curry or curry powder.

curry comb /ˈkʌrɪkəʊm/ *noun & verb.* L16.
[ORIGIN from CURRY *verb*[1] + COMB *noun*[1].]
▸ **A** *noun.* A toothed instrument used for getting coarse dirt out of the coat of a horse etc. or for cleaning brushes for a horse etc. L16.
▸ **B** *verb trans.* Rub down or groom with a curry comb. E18.

curse /kəːs/ *noun.* See also CUSS *noun.* OE.
[ORIGIN Unknown.]
1 An utterance of God, or of a person invoking God, consigning or intending to consign a person or thing to destruction, divine vengeance, misery, etc.; *spec.* a formal ecclesiastical censure, a sentence of excommunication. OE.
2 A profane oath; an imprecation. OE.

SHAKES. *Mids. N. D.* I give him curses, yet he gives me love.

3 An evil supposedly inflicted by divine or supernatural power in response to an imprecation or as retributive punishment. ME. ▸**b** A thing which blights or blasts; a bane. L16. ▸**c** ***the curse***, menstruation. *colloq.* M20.

H. B. STOWE This is God's curse on slavery! **b** W. BUCHAN Many people look upon the necessity . . of earning . . bread by labour, as a curse.

4 Something that is cursed; an accursed person or thing. LME. ▸**b** An annoying, wretched, or despicable person. L18.
5 In *pl.* as *interjection.* Expr. strong annoyance. L19.
– PHRASES: **Curse of Scotland** the nine of diamonds in a pack of cards. ***not care a tinker's curse***, ***not worth a tinker's curse***: see TINKER *noun.* **under a curse** feeling or liable to the effects of a curse.
■ **curseful** *adjective* (*rare*) fraught with curses LME.

curse /kəːs/ *verb.* Pa. pple **cursed**, (now *rare*) **curst**. See also CUSS *verb.* OE.
[ORIGIN from the noun. Cf. ACCURSE.]
1 *verb trans.* Utter against (a person or thing) words intended to consign their object to destruction, divine vengeance, misery, etc.; anathematize, excommunicate. OE.
2 *verb trans.* Speak impiously against (fate, God, etc.); blaspheme. OE.
3 *verb trans.* Pour maledictions upon; swear at. ME. ▸**b** In subjunct. with no subj. expressed: damn, confound. M18.

HUGH WALPOLE He cursed Foster for a meddling, cantankerous fanatic. C. FREEMAN The rain that she had been cursing . . now seemed like a blessing. **b** L. STERNE Curse the fellow . . . I am undone for this bout.

4 *verb intrans.* Utter curses; swear in anger or irritation. **ME.**

A. MACLEAN Morris Schaffer . . cursed fluently as . . a cup of scalding coffee emptied itself over his thigh.

5 *verb trans.* Afflict with or *with* an evil regarded as the result of divine wrath or malignant fate. Usu. in *pass.* **LME.**

B. EMECHETA Leprosy was a disease with which the goddess . . cursed anyone who dared to flout one of the town's traditions. A. KOESTLER The serpent . . was cursed . . to walk on its belly.

■ **curser** *noun* **ME.**

cursed /ˈkəːsɪd, kəːst/ *adjective & adverb.* Also (usual in sense 4) **curst** /kəːst/. See also CUSSED. **ME.**
[ORIGIN pa. pple of CURSE *verb*: see -ED¹. Cf. ACCURSED.]
▸ **A** *adjective.* **1** Under a curse. **ME.**
2 Deserving or bringing a curse or misery; heinously wicked; execrable, detestable. **ME.**
3 Damned, confounded. **LME.**

SWIFT I have cut my thumb with this cursed knife.

4 Malignant; perversely disagreeable or cross. Long *obsolete* exc. *dial.* & as CUSSED. **LME.**
†**5** Fierce, savage, vicious. **LME–L18.**
▸ **B** *adverb.* Damnably; very. **E18.**
■ **cursedly** *adverb* **LME.** **cursedness** *noun* **ME.**

†**cursh** *noun* var. of QURSH.

cursillo /kurˈsiʎo; kʊəˈsiːjəʊ, -ˈsiːljəʊ/ *noun.* Pl. **-os** /-ɒs, -əʊz/. **M20.**
[ORIGIN Spanish, lit. 'little course'.]
A short course of study etc., *spec.* of intensive religious studies and exercises, orig. for Roman Catholics in Spain.
■ ***cursillista*** /kursiˈʎista, kʊəsiːˈ(l)jɪstə/ *noun* a person who has participated in a *cursillo* **M20.**

cursitor /ˈkəːsɪtə/ *noun.* **E16.**
[ORIGIN Legal Anglo-Norman *coursetour* from medieval Latin *cursitor*, from *cursus* COURSE *noun*¹.]
1 Each of twenty-four officers of the Court of Chancery who until 1835 made out all the common or routine writs for their respective counties. *obsolete* exc. *hist.* **E16.**
†**2** A tramp or vagrant. **M16–E18.**
†**3** A courier. **L16–M17.**
– COMB.: **Cursitor Baron** a baron of the former Court of Exchequer appointed for fiscal rather than legal expertise.

cursive /ˈkəːsɪv/ *adjective & noun.* **L18.**
[ORIGIN medieval Latin *cursivus*, from Latin *curs-* pa. ppl stem of *currere* to run: see -IVE.]
▸ **A** *adjective.* Designating writing, esp. in ancient manuscripts, in which the pen etc. is not raised after each character; written in this style, in a running hand. **L18.**
▸ **B** *noun.* A manuscript in cursive writing. **M19.**
■ **cursively** *adverb* (*rare*) †(**a**) in continuous succession; (**b**) in cursive writing: **E17.** **cursiveness** *noun* (*rare*) cursive quality **E19.**

cursor /ˈkəːsə/ *noun.* **ME.**
[ORIGIN Latin = runner, from *curs-*: see CURSIVE, -OR.]
†**1** A runner, a running messenger. **ME–M17.**
2 A part of a mathematical or surveying instrument which can be slid back and forwards; *spec.* the transparent slide with a fine line with which the readings on a slide rule are taken. **L16.**
3 A movable visual marker forming part of a VDU display, showing where the next character to be keyed will appear. **M20.**

†**cursorary** *adjective. rare* (Shakes.). Only in **E17.**
[ORIGIN formed as CURSOR + -ARY¹.]
= CURSORY 1.

cursorial /kəːˈsɔːrɪəl/ *adjective.* **M19.**
[ORIGIN formed as CURSORY + -AL¹.]
ZOOLOGY. Having limbs adapted for running.

cursory /ˈkəːs(ə)ri/ *adjective.* **E17.**
[ORIGIN Latin *cursorius*, formed as CURSOR: see -ORY².]
1 Passing rapidly over a thing or subject; hasty, hurried; superficial. **E17.**

T. HARDY Since he could not call at her father's . . cursory encounters . . were what the acquaintance would have to feed on. E. F. BENSON The whole place, as could be seen at the most cursory glance, had been laid out with skill and care.

†**2** Travelling. *rare.* **E–M17.**
3 *hist.* Designating informal lectures at medieval universities given, esp. by bachelors, in addition to the prescribed lectures by authorized teachers. **M19.**
■ **cursorily** *adverb* hastily, superficially **E17.** **cursoriness** *noun* **E18.**

curst *adjective* see CURSED.

curst *verb pa. pple*: see CURSE *verb.*

cursus /ˈkəːsəs/ *noun.* Pl. same, **-uses. M18.**
[ORIGIN Latin = course, from *currere* to run.]
1 *ARCHAEOLOGY.* A Neolithic structure consisting of a long straight avenue, usu. closed at the ends, formed by two earthen banks with a ditch on the outer side of each. **M18.**
2 A stated order of daily prayer or worship. **M19.**
3 One of the cadences which mark the ends of sentences and phrases, esp. in Greek and Latin prose; the use of such cadences in accordance with definite rules. **E20.**
4 In full ***cursus honorum*** /ɒˈnɔːrəm/ [= of honours]. An established hierarchy of positions through which a person may be promoted. **E20.**

curt /kəːt/ *adjective.* **LME.**
[ORIGIN Latin *curtus* cut short, mutilated, abridged.]
1 Short, shortened. *arch.* **LME.**
2 Of words, manner, etc.: concise, terse; discourteously brief. **M17.**

C. P. SNOW Pictures drawn by himself of what, from the curt descriptions, he imagined the saga heroes to have looked like. D. DU MAURIER I barely answered him, and he must have thought me curt.

■ **curtly** *adverb* **M17.** **curtness** *noun* **M18.**

curtail /kəːˈteɪl/ *verb trans.* **L15.**
[ORIGIN from CURTAL, from 16 assoc. with *tail* and perh. later with French *tailler* to cut.]
1 Shorten in length, duration, extent, or amount; abridge, reduce. **L15.**

A. J. AYER The freedom of expression . . may have to be curtailed when it threatens the security of the state. I. MURDOCH My account is curtailed, but omits nothing of substance.

2 Deprive *of.* **L16.**

SHAKES. *Rich. III* I—that am curtail'd of this fair proportion.

3 Cut short the tail of. Now *rare* or *obsolete.* **L16.**
■ **curtailer** *noun* a person who curtails **E18.** **curtailment** *noun* **L18.**

curtail-step /kəːteɪlˈstɛp/ *noun.* **M18.**
[ORIGIN Origin of 1st elem. unkn.]
The lowest step of a stair with the outer end carried round in a semicircle or scroll.

curtain /ˈkəːt(ə)n/ *noun.* **ME.**
[ORIGIN Old French *cortine* (mod. *courtine*) from late Latin *cortina* (Vulgate), rendering Greek *aulaia*, from *aulē* court (= Latin *cohort-, cort-*).]
1 A piece of cloth or other material suspended by the top so as to form a screen, and usu. able to be moved sideways or upwards. **ME.**

W. S. MAUGHAM Heavy lace curtains over the window shut out the light.

draw the curtain(s), **pull the curtain(s)** draw the curtain(s) back so as to reveal, or forward so as to cover, what is behind.
2 Something (material or abstract) that covers, conceals, divides, or hangs like a curtain. **LME.**

C. M. YONGE Her lilac-spotted bonnet . . with a huge curtain serving for a tippet. J. CHEEVER They sat . . in the shelter of the dense foliage, watching the moving curtain of rain.

bamboo curtain: see BAMBOO *noun.*
3 More fully ***curtain wall***. The plain wall of a fortification, connecting two towers etc.; a plain enclosing wall not supporting a roof. **M16.**
4 A screen which is lowered to separate the stage of a theatre from the auditorium (raised at the start of the action and lowered at the end). **L16.**
behind the curtain behind the scenes, away from public view. ***iron curtain***: see IRON *noun & adjective.* ***safety curtain***: see SAFETY *noun & adjective.*
5 *THEATRICAL.* **a** In full ***curtain call***. An audience's summons to a performer or performers to take a bow after the curtain has fallen. **L19.** ▸**b** The fall of the curtain at the end of a scene etc.; a finale; in *pl.* (*slang*), the end, *esp.* a final downfall. **L19.**

a L. MACNEICE The music stopped, the dancers took their curtain. **b** P. KAVANAGH We will wait and watch the tragedy to the last curtain. B. SCHULBERG In court it looks like curtains for her.

6 In *pl.* A wrinkled effect resembling a draped curtain on a painted surface etc. *colloq.* **E20.**
7 In full ***curtain of fire*** etc. A concentration of gunfire etc. serving to create a barrier. **E20.**

T. HORSLEY We . . began our glide through the curtain of lead towards the inner harbour.

– COMB.: ***curtain call***: see sense 5a above; **curtain fire** gunfire forming a curtain; **curtain hook**: used to fasten a curtain to a curtain rail; **curtain lecture** a wife's private reproof to her husband (orig. behind bed curtains); **curtain line** *THEATRICAL* the last line of a play, act, or scene; **curtain rail**: from which a curtain is suspended esp. by means of sliding hooks; **curtain-raiser** a short opening piece performed before the principal play; *fig.* any preliminary event; **curtain ring**: used to fasten a curtain to the rail or rod; **curtain rod**: from which a curtain is suspended by means of sliding rings; **curtain-up** the beginning of a stage performance; ***curtain wall***: see sense 3 above.
■ **curtainless** *adjective* **L18.**

curtain /ˈkəːt(ə)n/ *verb trans.* **ME.**
[ORIGIN from the noun.]
Provide, cover, surround, screen, or shut *off* (as) with a curtain or curtains.

curtal /ˈkəːt(ə)l/ *noun & adjective.* **L15.**
[ORIGIN French *courtault*, *-auld* (now *courtaud*), from *court* short (ult. formed as CURT) + pejorative suffix *-ault*.]
▸ **A** *noun.* **1** A kind of short-barrelled cannon. *obsolete* exc. *hist.* **L15.**
2 A horse or other animal with its tail docked; anything cut short. Now *rare* or *obsolete.* **E16.**
†**3** A criminal wearing a short cloak. *slang.* **M16–E18.**
4 *MUSIC.* An early form of bassoon. **L16.**
▸ **B** *adjective.* †**1** Shortened, short; abridged, curtailed; brief. **L16–M17.**
†**2** Of an animal: with a docked tail. **L16–M17.**
3 ***curtal friar***, a friar with a short gown. *arch.* **E17.**

curtal-axe /ˈkəːt(ə)laks/ *noun. obsolete* exc. *hist.* Also ***-ax**, (earlier) †**curtelace. M16.**
[ORIGIN Alt. of CUTLASS by assim. to CURTAL and AXE *noun*¹.]
A cutlass; a heavy slashing sword.

Curtana /kəːˈtɑːnə, -ˈteɪnə/ *noun.* **ME.**
[ORIGIN Anglo-Latin *curtana* fem. (sc. *spatha* sword) from Anglo-Norman *curtain*, Old French *cortain*, name of Roland's sword, so called because it had broken at the point when thrust into a block of steel, from *cort* CURT.]
The unpointed sword borne before the British monarch at the Coronation, emblematically considered the sword of mercy.

curtate /ˈkəːteɪt/ *adjective.* **L17.**
[ORIGIN Latin *curtatus* pa. pple, formed as CURTATION: see -ATE².]
1 *GEOMETRY & ASTRONOMY.* Shortened by being projected on to a plane. **L17.**
2 *ECONOMICS & STATISTICS.* Calculated for the number of full years in a period, excluding any odd fraction of a year. **L19.**

curtation /kəːˈteɪʃ(ə)n/ *noun.* **L16.**
[ORIGIN from Latin *curtat-* pa. ppl stem of *curtare*, from *curtus*: see CURT, -ATION.]
†**1** *ALCHEMY.* The shorter process for transmuting base metals into gold. **L16–L17.**
2 *ASTRONOMY.* The difference between the actual and the curtate distance. Now *rare* or *obsolete.* **E18.**

†**curtaxe** *noun. rare* (Spenser). Only in **L16.**
[ORIGIN Alt.]
= CURTAL-AXE.

†**curtelace** *noun* see CURTAL-AXE.

curtesy *noun* see COURTESY *noun.*

curtilage /ˈkəːt(ɪ)lɪdʒ/ *noun.* **ME.**
[ORIGIN Anglo-Norman = Old French *co(u)rtillage*, from *co(u)rtil* small court, kitchen garden, from *cort* COURT *noun*¹: see -AGE.]
A small court, yard, or piece of ground attached to a house and forming one enclosure with it.

curtsy /ˈkəːtsi/ *noun & verb.* Also **-sey. E16.**
[ORIGIN Syncopated from COURTESY *noun.*]
▸ **A** *noun.* †**1** = COURTESY *noun* 6. Only in **16.**
†**2** = COURTESY *noun* 5a. **M–L16.**
†**3** = COURTESY *noun* 1, 2, 3. **L16–M17.**
4 A gesture of deferential respect. Now *spec.* a woman's or girl's salutation made by lowering the body and bending the knees. Freq. in ***drop a curtsy***, ***make a curtsy***. **L16.**
▸ **B** *verb intrans.* & (*rare*) *trans.* Make a curtsy (to). **M16.**

curucui /kʊərʊˈkuːiː/ *noun.* **L17.**
[ORIGIN Repr. Tupi *surucuá*, of imit. origin.]
The blue-crowned trogon, *Trogon curucui*, native to S. America.

curule /ˈkjʊəruːl/ *adjective.* **M16.**
[ORIGIN Latin *curulis*, from *currus* chariot, from *currere* to run.]
hist. Designating a seat inlaid with ivory and shaped like a camp stool with curved legs, used by the highest magistrates of ancient Rome; (of a magistrate etc.) entitled to sit on such a seat; *gen.* of high civic dignity.

curvaceous /kəːˈveɪʃəs/ *adjective.* **M20.**
[ORIGIN from CURVE *noun* + -ACEOUS.]
Having many, or conspicuous, curves; *esp.* (of a woman or a woman's figure) shapely.

H. HOBSON Sharon; lissome and curvaceous in a revealing leopard-spotted bikini. D. PIPER The grand generalizing and curvaceous amplitude of the baroque.

■ **curvaceously** *adverb* **M20.** **curvaceousness** *noun* **M20.**

curvant /ˈkəːv(ə)nt/ *adjective. rare.* **L15.**
[ORIGIN Latin *curvant-* pres. ppl stem of *curvare* CURVE *verb.*]
Curving.

curvated /kəːˈveɪtɪd/ *adjective. rare.* **E18.**
[ORIGIN from Latin *curvat-* (see CURVATURE) + -ED¹.]
Curved; of a curved form.

curvation /kəːˈveɪʃ(ə)n/ *noun.* **LME.**
[ORIGIN Latin *curvatio(n-)*, from *curvat-*: see CURVATURE, -ATION.]
Curvature; a curving motion.

curvature /ˈkəːvətʃə/ *noun.* **LME.**
[ORIGIN Old French from Latin *curvatura*, from *curvat-* pa. ppl stem of *curvare* CURVE *verb*: see -URE.]
1 The action of curving or bending; the fact or manner of being curved; curved form. **LME.** ▸**b** *spec.* in *SCIENCE.* (The degree of) the deviation of a curve from a straight line,

or of a curved surface from a plane; an analogous property of a space of three or more dimensions. **E18.**

J. CHEEVER A tall man with an astonishing . . curvature of the spine.

b centre of curvature, radius of curvature: those of the circle which passes through a curve at a given point and has the same tangent and curvature at that point.

2 A curved portion of anything; a curve. **LME.**

curve /kəːv/ *adjective & noun*. **LME.**
[ORIGIN Latin *curvus* bent, curved.]
▶ **A** *adjective*. Curved. Now *rare* or *obsolete* exc. as passing into attrib. use of the noun. **LME.**
▶ **B** *noun*. **1** A line of which no part is straight. **L17.** ▸**b** A (straight or curved) line showing how one quantity varies with another, e.g. time; a graph. **M19.**

b *Listener* The population curve has slowed down.

geodesic curve, Jordan curve, loxodromic curve, etc.
b ***characteristic curve, J-curve***, etc.

2 A curved form, outline, etc.; a curved thing or part; *spec.* the curving line of a woman's figure (usu. in *pl.*). **E18.**

P. G. WODEHOUSE I can remember the days . . when every other girl you met . . had as many curves as a Scenic Railway. P. THEROUX The track was perfectly straight—not a curve in it anywhere.

3 A template used for drawing curved lines. Also ***French curve***. **L19.**
4 BASEBALL. In full ***curve ball***. A ball which deviates from the path it would otherwise take, because of spin put on it by the pitcher. **L19.**
5 A parenthesis, a round bracket. *US*. **E20.**
– COMB.: ***curve ball***: see sense 4 above; **curve-fitting** the finding of (the equation of) the curve which most closely represents the points on a graph.
■ **curveless** *adjective* **E19**. **curvesome** *adjective* (of a woman or a woman's figure) shapely **M20.**

curve /kəːv/ *verb*. **LME.**
[ORIGIN Latin *curvare*, formed as CURVE *adjective & noun*.]
1 *verb trans.* Bend or shape so as to form a curve. **LME.** ▸**b** BASEBALL. Throw (a ball) so that it is a curve ball. **L19.**
2 *verb intrans.* Have or take a curved form or path. **L16.**
■ **curvedly** *adverb* (*rare*) in a curved manner **L19**. **curvedness** *noun* (*rare*) curvature **L17**. **curvingly** *adverb* in a curving manner **E20.**

curvet /kəːˈvɛt/ *noun & verb*. **L16.**
[ORIGIN Italian *corvetta* dim. of *corva*, early form of *curva* curve, from Latin *curva* fem. of *curvus* bent, curved.]
▶ **A** *noun*. A horse's leaping or frisking motion; *spec.* = COURBETTE. **L16.**
▶ **B** *verb intrans.* Infl. **-t(t)-**. (Of a horse or rider) perform a curvet; *gen.* leap (about), frisk. **L16.**

P. G. WODEHOUSE He curveted past me into the sitting room.

curvi- /ˈkəːvi/ *combining form*. **M19.**
[ORIGIN from Latin *curvus* bent, curved + -I-.]
Having or consisting of (a) curved (what the second elem. denotes), as ***curvidentate, curviform***.

curvilineal /kəːvɪˈlɪnɪəl/ *adjective*. **M17.**
[ORIGIN from CURVI- after RECTILINEAL.]
= CURVILINEAR.

curvilinear /kəːvɪˈlɪnɪə/ *adjective*. **E18.**
[ORIGIN formed as CURVILINEAL after RECTILINEAR.]
Consisting of or contained by a curved line or lines; of the form of a curved line; ARCHITECTURE designating a style of Decorated tracery characterized by ornate ogee curves with a continuous flow from curve to curve.
■ **ˌcurvilineˈarity** *noun* **M19**. **curvilinearly** *adverb* **E19.**

curvity /ˈkəːvɪti/ *noun*. Now *rare* or *obsolete*. **LME.**
[ORIGIN French *curvité* or late Latin *curvitas*, from Latin *curvus* bent, curved: see -ITY.]
Curvature; a curve; *fig.* crookedness of conduct or character.

curvous /ˈkəːvəs/ *adjective*. *rare*. **L17.**
[ORIGIN from CURVE *noun* + -OUS.]
Curved; crooked.

curvy /ˈkəːvi/ *adjective*. **E20.**
[ORIGIN from CURVE *noun* + -Y[1].]
Having a curve or curves; full of curves.
■ **curviness** *noun* **L20.**

cuscus /ˈkʊskʊs/ *noun*[1]. **L16.**
[ORIGIN Arabic *kuskus*: see COUSCOUS *noun*[1].]
The grain of African millet, an article of food in Africa and Asia.

cuscus /ˈkʌskʌs/ *noun*[2]. Also **couscous** /ˈkuːskuːs/. **M17.**
[ORIGIN French *couscous* from Dutch *koeskoes* from native Moluccas name.]
Any of several phalangers of the genus *Phalanger* and related genera, native to New Guinea and N. Australia.

cuscus /ˈkʌskʌs/ *noun*[3]. Also **khus-khus**. **E19.**
[ORIGIN Urdu & Persian *ḳaskas*.]
(The sweet-scented root of) a grass, *Vetiveria zizanioides*, used in the Indian subcontinent to make fans and screens.

cusec /ˈkjuːsɛk/ *noun*. **E20.**
[ORIGIN Abbreviation of *cubic foot per second*.]
A unit of flow of rivers etc. equal to one cubic foot per second.

cush /kʊʃ/ *noun*. *colloq.* **L19.**
[ORIGIN Abbreviation of CUSHION *noun*.]
A cushion, *esp.* that of a billiard table.

cushat /ˈkʌʃət/ *noun*. Chiefly *Scot.* & *N. English*. **OE.**
[ORIGIN Unknown. Cf. QUEEST.]
The woodpigeon.

cushaw /kʊˈʃɔː, ˈkuːʃɔː/ *noun*. *US*. **L16.**
[ORIGIN Unknown.]
A winter curved-necked squash (crookneck); a variety of this.

cush-cush /ˈkʊʃkʊʃ/ *noun*. **L19.**
[ORIGIN Perh. ult. of African origin.]
A yam, *Dioscorea trifida*, native to S. America and cultivated for its edible tubers.

Cushing /ˈkʊʃɪŋ/ *noun*. **M20.**
[ORIGIN Harvey W. *Cushing* (1869–1939), US surgeon, who described the condition.]
MEDICINE. **1** ***Cushing's syndrome***, a syndrome of hypertension, obesity, metabolic disorders, etc., caused by overproduction of hormones by the adrenal cortex. **M20.**
2 ***Cushing's disease***, Cushing's syndrome accompanied and caused by a tumour of the pituitary gland. **M20.**
■ **Cushingoid**, **c-** *adjective* similar to (that of) Cushing's syndrome; resembling a patient with Cushing's syndrome: **L20.**

cushion /ˈkʊʃ(ə)n/ *noun*. **ME.**
[ORIGIN Old French *co(i)ssin*, *cu(i)ssin*, (also mod.) *coussin*, from Proto-Gallo-Romance form ult. from Latin *coxa* hip, thigh.]
1 A mass of soft or yielding material, esp. stuffed into a bag of cloth, silk, etc., used to give support or comfort to the body in sitting, reclining, or kneeling. **ME.** ▸**b** A similar item for supporting a book in a pulpit. **E17.** ▸**c** The seat of a judge or ruler. **M17.**
2 An object resembling a cushion; *spec.* (**a**) a small soft pad for sticking pins in to keep them ready for use, a pincushion; (**b**) *hist.* a bustle; (**c**) a pad worn by women under the hair; (**d**) a sweet in the shape of a cushion. **L16.**
3 a The fleshy part of the buttock of a horse, pig, etc. **E18.** ▸**b** The frog of a horse's hoof; the coronet just above the hoof. **L19.**
4 A thing acting as a cushion, esp. by providing protection or support; *spec.* (**a**) (BILLIARDS & SNOOKER etc.) the sides of the table from which the balls rebound; (**b**) the steam left in the cylinder of a steam engine as a buffer to the piston; (**c**) the body of air supporting a hovercraft etc. **L18.**
5 A dense compact mass of foliage. **L19.**
– PHRASES: ***lady's cushion***: see LADY *noun & adjective*. ***ride cushions, ride the cushions***: see RIDE *verb*. ***squab cushion***: see SQUAB *noun* 2b. ***thump a cushion***: see THUMP *verb* 1a.
– COMB.: **cushion capital** ARCHITECTURE: resembling a cushion pressed down by a weight; **cushion-dance** *hist.* a ring dance formerly danced at weddings, in which women and men alternately knelt on a cushion to be kissed; **cushion star** any of various small short-armed starfish, esp. of the genera *Asterina* and *Porania*; **cushion stitch** a flat embroidery stitch used to fill in backgrounds; **cushion-thumper** *colloq.* a violent preacher; an evangelist.
■ **cushionless** *adjective* **M19**. **cushion-like** *adverb & adjective* (**a**) *adverb* in the manner of a cushion; (**b**) *adjective* resembling a cushion: **M17**. **cushiony** *adjective* **M19.**

cushion /ˈkʊʃ(ə)n/ *verb trans.* **M18.**
[ORIGIN from the noun.]
1 Rest, seat, set, (a person or thing) on or against a cushion; prop *up* with cushions. **M18.**
2 Provide or protect (as) with a cushion or cushions; mitigate the effects of (as) with a cushion. **E19.**

Listener Action . . to cushion the economy against a recession. H. FAST She looked for a role instead, always cushioning her defeats with Martin Spizer's promises.

3 Suppress quietly. **E19.**

C. BRONTË There my courage failed: I preferred to cushion the matter.

4 Form into a cushion of steam or air. **L19.**
5 BILLIARDS & SNOOKER etc. Leave, place, or rebound (a ball) against the cushion. Now *rare*. **L19.**

cushioned /ˈkʊʃ(ə)nd/ *adjective*. **M18.**
[ORIGIN from CUSHION *noun*, *verb*: see -ED[2], -ED[1].]
1 In the form of a cushion; cushion-shaped. **M18.**
2 Provided with a cushion or cushions. **L18.**
3 Seated on or supported by a cushion; *fig.* protected from harm or adverse effects. **E19.**

Cushite /ˈkʊʃʌɪt/ *noun & adjective*. Also **K-**. **M19.**
[ORIGIN from *Cush*, an ancient country in the Nile valley + -ITE[1].]
▶ **A** *noun*. **1** A member of an ancient people of E. Africa, south of Egypt. **M19.**
2 Cushitic. **M20.**
▶ **B** *adjective*. Of or pertaining to this people. **M19.**

Cushitic /kʊˈʃɪtɪk/ *adjective & noun*. Also **K-**. **E20.**
[ORIGIN from CUSHITE + -IC.]
(Designating, of, or pertaining to) an Afro-Asiatic language family of NE Africa.

cushla-machree /ˌkʊʃləməˈkriː/ *noun*. *Irish*. **E19.**
[ORIGIN from Irish *cuisle* pulse + *mo* my + *chroidhe* heart: see ACUSHLA, MACHREE. Cf. MACUSHLA.]
As a form of address: my dear, darling.

cushty /ˈkʊʃti/ *adjective*. *slang*. **E20.**
[ORIGIN from Romany *kushto*, *kushti* good, perh. influenced by CUSHY.]
Very good or pleasing (freq. as a general term of approval).

J. SULLIVAN Don't worry about it, everything is gonna be cushty.

C

cushy /ˈkʊʃi/ *adjective*. *colloq.* (orig. *Indian*). **E20.**
[ORIGIN Urdu *ḵušī* pleasure, from Persian *ḵuš*.]
Of a post, task, etc.: easy, comfortable, esp. more so than might be expected.

N. WHITTAKER All in all he had it cushy. C. DIVAKARUNI Pretty soon she'll land a cushy teaching job and start bringing in a fat paycheck.

■ **cushiness** *noun* **M20.**

cusimanse *noun* var. of KUSIMANSE.

cusk /kʌsk/ *noun*. *US*. **E17.**
[ORIGIN Unknown: cf. TORSK.]
1 The burbot. *rare*. **E17.**
2 The torsk. **L19.**
– COMB.: **cusk-eel** any of a group of mostly small marine eel-like fishes of the family Ophidiidae.

cusp /kʌsp/ *noun*. **L16.**
[ORIGIN Latin *cuspis*, *-id-* point, apex.]
1 ASTROLOGY. The initial point or entrance of a house. **L16.**
2 *gen.* An apex, a pointed end or tip, *spec.* that of a canine tooth or a leaf. **M17.**
3 Each of the pointed ends of the crescent moon, the partly eclipsed sun, etc. **L17.**
4 GEOMETRY. A point at which two branches of a curve come together and share a common tangent, as if a point describing the curve had its motion reversed there. **M18.**
5 ARCHITECTURE. A projecting point between adjacent small arcs in Gothic tracery, arches, etc. **E19.**
■ **cuspate** *adjective* cusp-shaped **L19**. **cuspated** *adjective* (ARCHITECTURE) cuspidated **M19**. **cusped** *adjective* having a cusp or cusps **E19**. **cusping** *noun* (ARCHITECTURE) cusp-shaped stonework; a cusp-shaped part of a window etc.: **M19.**

cusparia /kʌˈspɛːrɪə/ *noun*. **L19.**
[ORIGIN mod. Latin *Cusparia* genus name from Amer. Spanish from Galibi *cuspare*.]
More fully ***cusparia bark***. = ANGOSTURA ***bark***.

cuspid /ˈkʌspɪd/ *noun*. **M18.**
[ORIGIN Latin *cuspid-*: see CUSP, -ID[2].]
1 GEOMETRY. = CUSP 4. **M18.**
2 A cusped tooth. **L19.**

cuspidal /ˈkʌspɪd(ə)l/ *adjective*. **M17.**
[ORIGIN formed as CUSPID + -AL[1].]
†**1** Belonging to the apex (of a cone). Only in **M17.**
2 Of a tooth: cuspidate. **M19.**
3 GEOMETRY. Having, relating to, or being a cusp. **L19.**

cuspidate /ˈkʌspɪdət, -deɪt/ *adjective*. **L17.**
[ORIGIN mod. Latin *cuspidatus*, from *cuspidat-* pa. ppl stem of *cuspidare* provide with a point, from *cuspid-*: see CUSP, -ATE[2].]
Having a cusp or a sharp point; *spec.* (**a**) (of a leaf) tapering to a rigid point; (**b**) designating a canine tooth.

cuspidated /ˈkʌspɪdeɪtɪd/ *adjective*. **M17.**
[ORIGIN formed as CUSPIDATE + -ED[1].]
Having a cusp or cusps.

cuspidation /kʌspɪˈdeɪʃ(ə)n/ *noun*. **M19.**
[ORIGIN from Latin *cuspidat-*: see CUSPIDATED, -ATION.]
ARCHITECTURE. Ornamentation with cusps; cusps collectively.

cuspides *noun* pl. of CUSPIS.

cuspidor /ˈkʌspɪdɔː/ *noun*. Chiefly *N. Amer.* **M18.**
[ORIGIN Portuguese = spitter, from *cuspir* to spit from Latin *conspuere*: see -OR.]
A spittoon.

cuspis /ˈkʌspɪs/ *noun*. Now *rare*. Pl. **cuspides** /-pɪdiːz/. **M17.**
[ORIGIN Latin: see CUSP.]
= CUSP 2.

cuss /kʌs/ *noun*. *colloq.* (orig. *US*). **L18.**
[ORIGIN Var. of CURSE *noun*. Sense 1 later often regarded as abbreviation of CUSTOMER.]
1 A person, a creature; *esp.* a detestable, perverse, or obstinate one. **L18.**

P. LIVELY I am going to need you, though I will never let on, being the obstinate cuss that I am.

2 A curse; a profane oath. **M19.**
tinker's cuss: see TINKER *noun*.
– COMB.: **cuss word** a swear word.

cuss /kʌs/ *verb trans. & intrans.* *colloq.* (orig. *US*). **E19.**
[ORIGIN Var. of CURSE *verb*.]
Curse, swear (at).
cuss a person out *US* silence, intimidate, or subdue a person by swearing at him or her.

cussed /ˈkʌsɪd/ *adjective*. *colloq.* (orig. *US*). **M19.**
[ORIGIN Var. of CURSED.]
Cursed; detestable; *esp.* perversely disagreeable or cross, obstinate, pig-headed (cf. CURSED 4).
■ **cussedly** *adverb* **M19**. **cussedness** *noun* **M19.**

C

custard /ˈkʌstəd/ *noun*[1]. Also (earlier) †**crusta(r)de**. ME.
[ORIGIN from Old French *crouste* CRUST *noun*: see -ADE. Forms without -*r*- also LME.]
Orig., a kind of open pie containing meat or fruit covered with broth or milk, thickened with eggs, sweetened, and spiced. Now, a sauce made of heated sweetened milk with cornflour or egg, etc.; (an) egg custard.
– COMB.: **custard apple** the fruit of any of several trees of the genus *Annona* (family Annonaceae), characterized by sweet yellow pulp, esp. the bullock's heart, *A. reticulata*, and sweetsop, *A. squamosa*; (also ***custard-apple tree***) a tree bearing such a fruit; **custard marrow** a variety of summer squash, *Cucurbita pepo* var. *melopepo*, having round flattened fruits scalloped at the edges; also called ***simlin***; **custard pie** *noun & adjective* (**a**) *noun* an open pie with a filling of cold thick custard; *fig.* slapstick comedy (in which such pies are commonly used as missiles); (**b**) *adjective* slapstick; **custard powder** a preparation of cornflour etc. for making custard.
■ **custardy** *adjective* L19.

custard /ˈkʌstəd/ *noun*[2]. *colloq. derog.* M19.
[ORIGIN Alt. of COSTARD.]
A person. Only in the children's taunt ***cowardy custard*** or ***cowardy cowardy custard***.

custock *noun* var. of CASTOCK.

custode /kʌˈstəʊdi, *foreign* kuˈstɔde/ *noun*. Pl. **-di** /-di/. M19.
[ORIGIN Italian from Latin *custos*, *-od-*.]
A person who has the custody of something; a guardian; a custodian.

custodee /kʌstəˈdiː/ *noun*. E19.
[ORIGIN from Latin *custod-* (see CUSTODY) or CUSTODY: see -EE[1].]
A person entrusted with the custody of anything.

custodes *noun* pl. of CUSTOS.

custodi *noun* pl. of CUSTODE.

custodial /kʌˈstəʊdɪəl/ *adjective & noun*. L18.
[ORIGIN from Latin *custodia* CUSTODY + -AL[1].]
▸ **A** *adjective*. Relating to custody or guardianship; of or pertaining to imprisonment or forcible institutionalization. L18.

H. H. GODDARD Those .. technically called *imbeciles*, also require more or less custodial care. T. BERGER While I was on my lunch .. the custodial staff watched the door for me. *Guardian* The first person to be given a custodial sentence under the Health and Safety Act.

▸ **B** *noun*. ECCLESIASTICAL. A receptacle for sacred objects. M19.

custodiam /kʌˈstəʊdɪəm/ *noun*. *obsolete* exc. *hist.* M16.
[ORIGIN Latin, accus. sing. of *custodia* CUSTODY (from the wording of the grant).]
LAW. A three-year grant by the exchequer of lands etc. in possession of the Crown.

custodian /kʌˈstəʊdɪən/ *noun*. L18.
[ORIGIN from CUSTODY + -AN, after *guardian*.]
1 A person who has custody; a guardian, a keeper, esp. of a public building. L18.
2 SPORT. A goalkeeper or wicketkeeper. Chiefly *joc.* E20.
■ **custodianship** *noun* M19.

custodier /kʌˈstəʊdɪə/ *noun*. Now *Scot.* L15.
[ORIGIN formed as CUSTODY + -ER[1].]
A custodian.

custody /ˈkʌstədi/ *noun*. LME.
[ORIGIN Latin *custodia*, from *custos*, *-od-* guardian: see -Y[3].]
1 Safe-keeping; protection; care; guardianship. LME.

T. CAPOTE He was returned to the custody of his father. D. LESSING Enough to prevent him from divorcing her and gaining custody of Tommy.

2 Imprisonment. L15.
protective custody: see PROTECTIVE *adjective*. ***remand in custody***: see REMAND *verb* 1b. **take into custody** arrest.

custom /ˈkʌstəm/ *noun, adjective, & adverb*. ME.
[ORIGIN Anglo-Norman *custume*, *-ume*, Old French *co(u)stume* (mod. *coutume*), from alt. of Latin *consuetudo*, *-din-*, from *consuescere* become accustomed, formed as CON- + *suescere* become accustomed.]
▸ **A** *noun*. **1** A habitual or usual practice; a common way of behaving; usage, fashion, habit. ME. ▸**b** LAW. An established usage which by long continuance has acquired the force of a law or right. ME. ▸**c** The practising of something habitually; the fact of being or becoming accustomed. E16.

N. MITFORD The English custom which keeps the men in the dining-room after dinner. R. HOGGART Individuals .. who are not paid but by custom are supplied with drinks. I. FLEMING It was his custom, when unpleasant things had to be said, to sweeten his breath. **b** W. BLACKSTONE The will of the lord was to be interpreted by the custom of the manor. **c** J. INGELOW Custom makes all things easy.

†**custom of women** menstruation. ***old Spanish custom***: see SPANISH *adjective*.
2 A customary service, rent, or due paid to a lord or ruler. *obsolete* exc. *hist.* ME.
3 Orig., duty levied by a lord or local authority on commodities on their way to market, *esp.* that levied in the name of the monarch on imports and exports. Now, in *pl.*, such duty levied by a government on imports, the area at a port etc. where goods are examined for this purpose. LME.
Customs the official department that levies customs duties.
4 The practice of habitually giving business to any particular shop etc.; regular business; regular customers. L16.

P. G. WODEHOUSE The head waiter came up and suggested that we should take our custom elsewhere.

– COMB.: **custom house** an office (esp. in a port) at which customs are collected or administered; **customs union** a group of states with an agreed common tariff and usu. free trade with each other.
▸ **B** *adjective*. Made or done to order for individual customers; (of a place or person) specializing in such work. Chiefly *N. Amer.* exc. in ***custom car*** below. M19.

T. STERLING He had designed the murder for one woman and no other. It was a perfect custom fit. H. HORWOOD We do a lot of custom sawing .. —cutting logs that people bring to us.

– SPECIAL COLLOCATIONS: **custom car**: built or modified to the owner's design. **custom clothes** etc. (chiefly *N. Amer.*): made to the customer's order.
▸ **C** *adverb*. In response to individual requirements; for an individual customer. Only in comb. with following verb or pa. pple. Chiefly *N. Amer.* exc. in ***custom-built***, ***custom-made***. M20.

M. MCLUHAN Custom-make your own book by simply Xeroxing a chapter from this one, a chapter from that one. *Offshore Engineer* We'll custom-install a compact Total Cementing Concept system for your platform.

custom /ˈkʌstəm/ *verb*. LME.
[ORIGIN Old French *costumer*, from *costume*: see CUSTOM *noun, adjective, & adverb*.]
1 *verb trans.* Make customary or usual; practise habitually. *obsolete* exc. as ***customed*** *pa. pple.* LME.
2 *verb trans.* & (*rare*) *intrans.* Accustom, habituate, (oneself or another); in *pass.*, be accustomed (*to do* something). *arch.* LME.

E. SMITHER The eyes of a nightbird customed to the splash of the sea.

†**3** *verb trans.* Pay duty or toll on; pass through a custom house. L15–E18.
4 *verb trans.* Bestow one's custom on; frequent as a customer. Now *rare*. L16.

customable /ˈkʌstəməb(ə)l/ *adjective & adverb*. ME.
[ORIGIN Anglo-Norman *custumable*, Old French *cost-*, formed as CUSTOM *noun*: see -ABLE.]
▸ **A** *adjective*. †**1** Customary, usual. ME–M17.
†**2** Of a person: accustomed (*to*); wont (*to do*); (with agent noun) habitual. ME–L16.

R. PECOCK King Saul was a wickid customable synner.

3 Liable to duty, dutiable. *rare*. LME.
▸ †**B** *adverb*. Customarily; habitually. ME–M17.
■ †**customableness** *noun* LME–M18. **customably** *adverb* (now *dial.*) customarily; habitually, usually: ME.

customal *noun* var. of CUSTUMAL.

customary /ˈkʌstəm(ə)ri/ *noun*. Also **custu-** /ˈkʌstjʊ-/. LME.
[ORIGIN medieval Latin *custumarius* use as noun of the adjective: see CUSTOMARY *adjective*.]
1 The customs of a country etc. collectively, esp. as set down in a book or legal document. LME.
2 ECCLESIASTICAL. = CONSUETUDINARY *noun*. L19.

customary /ˈkʌstəm(ə)ri/ *adjective*. E16.
[ORIGIN medieval Latin *custumarius*, from *custuma* from Anglo-Norman *custume*: see CUSTOM *noun*, -ARY[1].]
1 LAW (now *hist.*). Subject to or held by customs (CUSTOM *noun* 2), esp. of a manor. E16.

J. WILKINSON If any customarie tenant or copiholder hold two parcels of land by herriot service.

customary court a manorial court which exercised jurisdiction over the copyhold tenants and administered the customary law of the manor.
2 LAW. Established by custom, based on custom, (rather than common law or statute). L16.

Encycl. Brit. The origin of international customary law is frequently found in earlier treaty clauses .. subsequently .. taken for granted.

3 According to custom; commonly done etc.; usual. E17.

G. SANTAYANA Anxious talk had kept them up for a full hour beyond their customary bed-time. R. P. GRAVES During their fourth year at St John's, it was customary for men to live in lodgings.

■ **customarily** *adverb* E17. **customariness** *noun* M17.

customer /ˈkʌstəmə/ *noun*. LME.
[ORIGIN Orig. from Anglo-Norman *custumer* or medieval Latin *custumarius*; in some senses newly from CUSTOM *noun*: see -ER[1].]
†**1** A person who acquires ownership by long use or possession. Only in LME.
†**2** A person who collects customs, a customs officer. LME–L19.
3 A person who makes a purchase or gives business, esp. habitually to any particular seller or establishment. LME.

P. THEROUX Everyone in Colón looks unemployed, even the shopkeepers: not a customer in sight.

customer-facing providing customer service, dealing with customers.
†**4** A person with whom one has dealings; an associate, a companion. LME–E17. ▸**b** A prostitute. *rare* (Shakes.). Only in E17.
5 a A person of a specified character to deal with. *colloq.* L16. ▸**b** A fox that affords good sport in the field. M19.
a awkward customer, ***cool customer***, ***queer customer***, ***ugly customer***, etc.
†**6** = CUSTUMAL *noun*. E17–L18.

customize /ˈkʌstəmʌɪz/ *verb trans.* Orig. *US*. Also **-ise**. M19.
[ORIGIN from CUSTOM *noun* + -IZE.]
Make or modify to order or according to individual requirements.
■ **customizable** *adjective* M20. **customiˈzation** *noun* L20. **customizer** *noun* M20.

custos /ˈkʌstɒs/ *noun*. Pl. **custodes** /kʌˈstəʊdiːz/, (orig.) †**-oses**. LME.
[ORIGIN Latin.]
A keeper, a guardian, a custodian. Now chiefly in titles from mod. Latin.
custos rotulorum /rəʊtjʊˈlɔːrəm/ [Latin = keeper of the rolls] the principal Justice of the Peace of a county, who has nominal custody of the records of the commission of the peace.

custrel /ˈkʌstr(ə)l/ *noun*. Also **coistrel** /ˈkɔɪstr(ə)l/. L15.
[ORIGIN In sense 1 corresp. in meaning to Old French *coustillier*, *-illeur* soldier armed with a *coustille* (a double-edged sword); sense 2 (not in French) perh. infl. by CUSTRON.]
1 *hist.* An attendant on a knight or man-at-arms. L15.
2 As a term of reproach: fool or low-born man. Now *rare* (chiefly *Scot.*). E16.

custron /ˈkʌstr(ə)n/ *noun*. Now *Scot.* ME.
[ORIGIN Old French *coistron*, nom. *cuistre* scullion, from popular Latin *coquistro*, *-on-* shopkeeper.]
A scullion; a low-born person.

custumal /ˈkʌstjʊm(ə)l/ *noun*. Also **-tom-** /-təm-/. L16.
[ORIGIN medieval Latin *custumale* customs-book, neut. of *custumalis*, from *custuma* = Old French *co(u)stume* CUSTOM *noun*: see -AL[1].]
LAW. A written collection of the customs of a city etc.

custumary *noun* var. of CUSTOMARY *noun*.

cut /kʌt/ *noun*[1]. *obsolete* exc. *dial.* ME.
[ORIGIN Perh. from the verb (as CUT *noun*[2]).]
1 A lot that is drawn. Chiefly in ***draw cuts*** (orig. †***draw cut***, †***lay cut***), cast lots by the chance drawing of sticks, straws, etc., of unequal length. ME.
†**2** A person's lot, fate, etc.; fate or fortune as a ruler of events. ME–M17.

cut /kʌt/ *noun*[2]. LME.
[ORIGIN from the verb.]
▸ **I** A result of cutting.
1 A piece (esp. of meat or cloth) cut off; *spec.* each of the joints of meat into which a butcher divides a carcass; *Scot.* & *N. English* a certain quantity of yarn; *N. Amer.* a quantity of timber etc. harvested; *N. Amer.* (a large thick snack of) a slice of meat (*obsolete* exc. in ***cold cuts***: see COLD *adjective*). LME. ▸**b** A part of a field cut or for cutting at one time. *US*. M18. ▸**c** A number of sheep or cattle taken out of a flock or herd. *US*, *Austral.*, & *NZ*. L19. ▸**d** *fig.* A share of profits or takings; commission. *slang*. E20.

M. EDGEWORTH Mary spun nine cuts a day. E. DAVID Recipes for the cheaper cuts of meat.

2 A long narrow opening in a surface, esp. the skin, made by something sharp; an incision; a gash. M16.

J. STEINBECK A long deep cut in his chin .., a deep bleeding slash. J. HOOKER Stones with red marks like cuts of a rusty axe.

SPEEDY *cut*.
3 An incision made in the edge of a garment etc. for ornament. M16.
4 a A passage cut or dug out; a new channel made for a river; a railway cutting. M16. ▸**b** A natural narrow opening or passage by water; a channel, a strait; a creek, an inlet. *obsolete* exc. *dial.* L16.
5 A design engraved on a block of wood (formerly also copper or steel) for printing; an electrotype; an illustration made with such a block etc. M17.
WOODCUT.
6 A gramophone record or recording; a version of a film after editing. M20.
lateral cut: see LATERAL *adjective*. ***rough cut***: see ROUGH *adjective*.
▸ **II** An act of cutting.
7 An act or utterance that wounds the feelings; a blow, a shock. M16.

R. BOLTON A most cruel cut to a troubled conscience.

8 A stroke or blow given with a sharp-edged instrument, as a knife, sword, etc.; FENCING a stroke given with the edge of the weapon as distinguished from the point; an act of cutting a person's hair, a haircut, (cf. sense 18 below). L16. ▸**b** A sharp stroke with a whip, cane, etc. See also ***uppercut*** (a) s.v. UPPER *adjective*. E18.

T. H. WHITE Waving his blade and trying to get a cut at him. **b** A. BRINK He tried to protest against Jonathan's sentence of six cuts . . . By that time the flogging had . . been administered.

cut and thrust the use of both the edge and the point of one's sword while fighting; *fig.* lively interchange of argument etc. ***second cut***: see SECOND *adjective*. **b the cuts** *Austral. & NZ slang, hist.* the strap or cane, as a child's punishment.

9 The act of cutting a pack of cards; the card obtained by cutting. **L16.**

10 The excision or omission of part of a play, film, book, etc. **E17.**

make the cut *GOLF* equal or better a required score, thus avoiding elimination from the last two rounds of a four-round tournament.

11 A step in which a dancer cuts (CUT *verb* 29). **L17.**

12 A deliberate refusal to recognize or acknowledge another person. *colloq.* **L18.**

13 An act of absenting oneself from a class etc. Chiefly *US*. **M19.**

14 A stroke made by cutting in cricket, tennis, etc. **M19.**

late cut: see LATE *adjective*. ***square cut***: see SQUARE *adjective*.

15 A reduction in price, rate of pay, service offered, etc. Also, a temporary cessation of the availability of electricity, gas, water, or telephone communication. **L19.**

power cut etc.

16 *CINEMATOGRAPHY*. An immediate transition from one scene to another. **M20.**

▸ **III** A thing that cuts.

17 A passage, course, or way straight across, esp. as contrasted with a longer way round. Now chiefly *US* exc. in ***short cut*** below. **L16.**

A. FONBLANQUE The cut across the fields is shut up. E. BOWEN Crossing . . Oxford Street, they took a cut through Mayfair.

near cut (now *Scot.*), **short cut** a shorter route to a place than the usual or expected (*lit. & fig.*).

▸ **IV** A style of cutting.

18 The way something is cut; fashion, style, (of clothes, hair, etc.); *spec.* (freq. with specifying word) a hairstyle created by cutting, a haircut. **L16.**

S. BELLOW The German cut of his overcoat. *fig.*: J. CARLYLE These Londoners are all of the cut of this woman.

crew cut, ***urchin cut***, etc. **a cut above** noticeably superior to. ***the cut of a person's jib***: see JIB *noun*[1].

– COMB.: **cutline** (*a*) *RACKETS* the line above which a served ball must strike the wall; (*b*) a caption to an illustration.

†**cut** *noun*[3]. **L15.**

[ORIGIN from pa. pple of CUT *verb*.]

1 Used as a term of abuse. **L15–E19.**

2 A labouring horse; a gelding. **E16–E17.**

cut /kʌt/ *ppl adjective*. **LME.**

[ORIGIN from CUT *verb*.]

1 That has been cut. **LME.** ▸**b** Of a garment: having the edges etc. indented or slashed for ornament or as a fashion. **LME.**

Farmers Weekly Extensive pot plant and cut flower nurseries.

clean-cut, ***clear-cut***, etc. **cut and dried** *fig.* completely decided, prearranged; (of ideas etc.) ready-made, without freshness or originality. ***fine-cut***: see FINE *adverb*. ***single-cut***: see SINGLE *adjective & adverb*.

2 Drunk. *slang.* **L17.**

– SPECIAL COLLOCATIONS & COMB.: **cut glass** *noun & adjective* (*a*) *noun* glass that has been ornamented by having patterns cut into it by grinding and polishing; (*b*) *adjective* made of cut glass; *fig.* characterized by (excessively) careful enunciation. **cut loaf** a sliced loaf. **cut lunch** *Austral. & NZ* a packed lunch. **cut paper**: cut into a desired shape, usually for decorative purposes. **cut-price**, **cut-rate** *adjectives* selling or sold at a reduced price. **cut splice** *NAUTICAL* two ropes spliced together to form an eye. **cut-under** *US* a horse-drawn vehicle with part of the body cut away to allow the front wheels to turn underneath it.

cut /kʌt/ *verb*. Infl. **-tt-**. Pa. t. & pple **cut**. See also CUT, CUTTED *ppl adjectives*. **ME.**

[ORIGIN Rel. to Norwegian *kutte*, Icelandic *kuta* cut with a little knife, *kuti* little blunt knife. Prob. already in Old English.]

▸ **I** Make an incision (in, through, etc.).

1 *verb trans.* Penetrate or wound with a sharp-edged thing; make an incision in. **ME.** ▸**b** *fig.* Wound the feelings of (a person), hurt deeply. Chiefly in ***cut to the heart***, ***cut to the quick***. **ME.**

N. MOSLEY The edge of the pipe cut his mouth, which bled. *fig.*: ADDISON Tormenting thought! it cuts into my soul. **b** F. BURNEY He says something so painful that it cuts us to the soul.

2 *verb trans.* Divide with a knife or other sharp-edged instrument into two or more pieces; sever (string, cord, etc.); carve (meat); slice (a loaf, a cake). **ME.**

I. MURDOCH Julius . . began to cut it straight across into narrow black strips.

3 *verb trans. & intrans.* Divide (what grows) with an edged instrument in order to take the part detached; hew (timber), mow (grass), etc.; divide the stalk of and gather (a flower). **ME.** ▸**b** *verb trans.* Cut the crop on (land). **L18.**

fig.: J. GATHORNE-HARDY By war and legislation, the wealth of the upper classes had been effectively cut into.

†**4** *verb trans.* Break up, reduce, or dissolve the viscidity of (a liquid, phlegm, etc.). **LME–M18.**

5 *verb intrans.* Make an incision; be capable of making an incision. **LME.**

EVELYN Cut close to the stem. *fig.*: G. HERBERT The tongue is not steel, yet it cuts.

6 a *verb intrans.* Be or become cut; admit of being cut (esp. with a good, bad, etc., result). **M16.** ▸**b** *verb trans.* Of land etc.: yield as a crop. **M18.**

OED The cloth does not cut to advantage.

7 *verb trans.* Make a narrow opening through (a dyke etc.), breach the bank of (a canal), esp. to permit the escape of water. **L16.**

8 *verb trans. & intrans.* Strike sharply with a whip, cane, etc. Of a whip etc.: cause a painful blow. **E17.**

9 *verb trans.* In full ***cut open***. Separate the leaves of (a book) by cutting the folds of the sheets. **L18.**

10 *verb intrans. FENCING.* Attempt a cut at an opponent. **M19.**

▸ **II** Separate, shorten, etc., by cutting.

11 *verb trans.* **a** Separate or remove by cutting; sever from the main body; remove (lines etc.) from a text; *COMPUTING* remove (information, esp. text) for placing elsewhere (cf. PASTE *verb* 1b). (Foll. by *from* or other preposition, adverbial compl.) **ME.** ▸†**b** Cut off, isolate, *from*. **L16–L18.**

P. THOMAS We were obliged . . to cut the Raft adrift. P. THOMPSON Halfpenny-worths of bread cut off the loaf.

12 *verb trans.* Shorten or reduce by cutting off a portion; trim, prune. **ME.**

J. BUCHAN The lawn was . . cut with a scythe instead of a mower. N. FREELING His hair needed cutting.

13 *verb trans. fig.* Curtail, abridge; shorten (a text etc.) by omitting part; reduce (a price, wage, service, etc.); cancel, abolish, (a service etc.); stop (one's talking). **LME.**

Observer We didn't cut the fares; the voters did. *Times* British Telecom . . denied suggestions that 15,000 jobs might be cut.

14 *verb trans.* Reduce the intensity of (a colour etc.); *esp.* dilute or adulterate (alcohol, a drug, etc.). Chiefly *N. Amer.* **M19.**

G. VIDAL He did not cut his wine with water.

15 *verb trans.* Outdo, beat, surpass. Chiefly *US*. **L19.**

16 *verb trans. & intrans. CINEMATOGRAPHY.* Edit (a film); make an immediate transition *to* another shot. **E20.**

N. KNEALE Cut—to the excavation.

17 *verb trans. & intrans.* (Cause to) cease running or operating. **M20.**

H. ROBBINS The motors cut and died away.

▸ **III** Make by cutting.

18 *verb trans.* Make or form by cutting, engraving, carving, etc. **ME.** ▸**b** Make a sound recording of, esp. on a gramophone record; make (a sound recording). **M20.**

W. S. MAUGHAM The clever dressmaker had cut her frock to conceal youthful plumpness. J. BUCHAN I cut a walking-stick of hazel. A. CARTER The key gleamed as freshly as if it had just been cut. *transf.*: S. C. HALL His features were finely cut.

19 *verb trans.* Make by excavation or digging; make (one's way) thus (*lit. & fig.*). **L16.**

LD MACAULAY He cut his way gallantly through them. A. H. MARKHAM Cutting a road through the hummocks.

20 *verb trans.* Perform, execute, (an action, gesture, or display, esp. of a striking or surprising kind). **E17.**

W. IRVING Two of us . . saw a fellow . . cutting queer antics.

▸ **IV** Pass through as in cutting.

21 *verb trans. & intrans.* Divide, separate, intersect, run into or *through*, (by virtue of position rather than motion). **LME.**

J. G. WHITTIER Yon spire . . That cuts the evening sky. I. TODHUNTER If two straight lines cut one another.

22 *verb intrans.* Cross (*over*), pass straight *through*, *across*, esp. as a shorter way. **M16.**

S. BARSTOW We cut across the grass to the shelter.

23 *verb trans. & intrans.* Move sharply through or *through* (the air, water); cleave. Chiefly *literary*. **L16.**

24 a *verb intrans.* Run away or *away*, make *off*, escape; move sharply or suddenly. Now *colloq.* **L16.** ▸**b** *verb trans.* Of a vehicle: move sharply in front of (another); pass recklessly or illegally. **M20.**

THOMAS HUGHES We all cut up-stairs after the Doctor. E. NESBIT You'll be late for your grub! . . Then cut along home.

25 *verb trans. & intrans.* Come across, hit upon (a path, trail, etc.). Chiefly *US*. **L19.**

▸ **V** Contextual, ellipt., & techn. uses.

26 a *verb trans.* Castrate. **LME.** ▸**b** *verb trans. & intrans.* Operate (on) to remove a stone. *arch.* **M16.** ▸**c** *verb trans.* Circumcise. *rare.* **M17.**

†**27** *verb intrans. & trans.* Speak, talk, say. *slang.* **E16–E19.**

28 *verb trans. & intrans.* Divide (a pack of cards) by lifting the upper half (or thereabouts) and either revealing one of the cards at the join to determine at random a dealer, trump suit, seating position, etc., or placing the upper half face down for the lower half to be replaced on it, to conceal the identity of the last card dealt; select (a card) by cutting a pack. **M16.**

29 *verb intrans.* Execute a dance movement by springing from the ground and twiddling the feet one in front of the other alternately. Now *hist.* **E17.**

30 *verb intrans.* Of a horse: strike and bruise the inside of the fetlock with the shoe or hoof of the opposite foot. **M17.**

31 a *verb trans.* Renounce (an acquaintance); refuse to recognize or acknowledge (a person) on meeting or passing. **M17.** ▸†**b** *verb intrans.* Break off acquaintance or connection (*with*). **L18–E19.** ▸**c** *verb trans.* Absent oneself from, choose not to attend. **L18.**

c E. BOWEN Next day, Sunday, she cut chapel.

32 *verb trans.* Have (a tooth) appear through the gum. **L17.**

33 *verb intrans. NAUTICAL.* Cut the cable in order to get quickly under way. **E18.**

34 *verb intrans. & trans.* **a** *CRICKET.* (Of a ball) turn sharply after pitching; (of a bowler) make (a ball) do this. **E19.** ▸**b** *CRICKET.* Hit (a ball) with the bat nearly horizontal, esp. (backward of) square on the offside. **M19.** ▸**c** Slice (a golf ball). **L19.** ▸**d** *CROQUET.* Drive (a ball) away obliquely by a stroke from another ball. **L19.**

– PHRASES: **cut a caper**, **cut capers** move friskily, *arch.* dance; (see also *cut up capers* below). **cut a corner** take the shortest course around a corner, esp. on the wrong side of the road; *fig.* do a piece of work hastily and shoddily; (***cut a corner off***: see *cut off a corner* below). ***cut a dash***: see DASH *noun*[1]. ***cut a figure***: see FIGURE *noun*. ***cut a long story short***: see SHORT *adjective*. **cut and run** (*a*) *NAUTICAL* cut the cable and make sail without waiting to weigh anchor; (*b*) *colloq.* hurry off, run away. **cut a person dead** completely refuse to recognize him or her. ***cut a person some slack***: see SLACK *noun*[3]. ***cut a rug***: see RUG *noun*[2]. **cut a shine** *colloq.* = *cut a dash* s.v. DASH *noun*[1]; (see also *cut up shines* below). ***cut a splash***: see SPLASH *noun*[1] 3. ***cut a swathe***, ***cut a wide swathe***: see SWATHE *noun*[2]. **cut both ways** have good and bad effect; (of an argument) support both sides. ***cut capers***: see *cut a caper* above. **cut corners** *fig.* do something perfunctorily to save time or money. ***cut each other's throats***: see THROAT *noun*. **cut ice** *slang* have influence or importance, achieve something (chiefly in neg. contexts). **cut it** *colloq.* succeed; come up to expectations, meet requirements (cf. ***cut the mustard*** s.v. MUSTARD *noun*). ***cut it fine***: see FINE *adjective*. ***cut loose***: see LOOSE *adjective*. ***cut one's coat according to one's cloth***: see CLOTH *noun* 4. **cut one's eye teeth** acquire experience, attain worldly wisdom. **cut one's losses** abandon a losing speculation in good time. ***cut one's lucky***: see LUCKY *noun*[2]. ***cut one's own throat***: see THROAT *noun*. **cut one's stick** *slang* make off. **cut one's teeth on** *fig.* acquire experience from. ***cut open***: see sense 9 above. ***cut out work for a person***: see WORK *noun*. ***cut short***: see SHORT *adverb*. ***cut the cackle***: see CACKLE *noun* 2. ***cut the comb of***: see COMB *noun*[1] 4. ***cut the GORDIAN knot***. ***cut the grass from under a person's feet***: see GRASS *noun*. ***cut the ground from under a person's feet***: see GROUND *noun*. ***cut the mustard***: see MUSTARD *noun*. ***cut the painter***: see PAINTER *noun*[2]. ***cut the rug***: see RUG *noun*[2]. ***cut the throat of***: see THROAT *noun*. **cut to pieces** destroy (a military division etc.) by inflicting heavy losses. **cut to the chase** [orig. lit. in film-making, meaning 'cut to a more interesting part of a film, such as a chase sequence'] *slang* get to the point; get on with it. ***have one's work cut out***: see WORK *noun*. ***rotary cutting***: see ROTARY *adjective*. ***that one could cut with a knife***: see KNIFE *noun*.

– WITH ADVERBS & PREPOSITIONS IN SPECIALIZED SENSES: **cut back** (*a*) *verb phr. trans.* shorten, prune, (a branch etc.); (*b*) *verb phr. trans. & intrans.* reduce (expenditure, production, etc.), curtail; economize; (*c*) *verb phr. intrans. & trans.* (*CINEMATOGRAPHY*) repeat part of a previous scene, esp. for dramatic effect; return (so far) in doing this. **cut down** (*a*) *verb phr. trans.* bring or throw down by cutting; (*b*) *verb phr. trans.* kill by the sword or disease; (*c*) *verb phr. trans.* = sense 15 above; (*d*) *verb phr. trans. & intrans.* curtail, abridge; reduce consumption or expenses; ***cut down to size***: see SIZE *noun*[1] 6b. **cut in** (*a*) *verb phr. intrans.* come in abruptly (*between*); interpose in conversation; (*b*) *verb phr. intrans.* join in a card game by taking the place of a player who cuts out; (*c*) *verb phr. intrans.* take a dance partner from another; (*d*) *verb phr. intrans.* obstruct the path of a vehicle one has just overtaken by returning to one's own side of the road too soon; (*e*) *verb phr. trans.* (*slang*) give a share of profits etc. to (a person); (*f*) *verb phr. trans. & intrans.* incorporate into a film sequence; switch into an electric circuit; (of a motor etc.) begin operating. **cut off** (*a*) remove or detach (as) by cutting (***cut off one's nose to spite one's face***: see NOSE *noun*); (*b*) bring to an abrupt end or (esp. early) death; (*c*) intercept (a supply, communication); stop the availability of (electricity, gas, water, or telephone communication); break the telephone connection of (a caller) during a call; (*d*) conceal from view; exclude *from* access, influence, etc.; (*e*) ***cut off a corner***, ***cut a corner off***, take a short cut that saves going round it; (*f*) ***cut off with a shilling***, disinherit (bequeathing a trivial sum to demonstrate that the disinheritance was intentional). **cut out** (*a*) *verb phr. trans.* take out by cutting; omit (part of a text etc.); *colloq.* stop (an action) (usu. *imper.* in ***cut it out***); (*b*) *verb phr. trans.* (*NAUTICAL*) surprise and carry off (a ship) by getting between it and the shore; (*c*) *verb phr. trans.* (chiefly *US*) separate (an animal) from the herd; (*d*) *verb phr. trans.* = sense 15 above; (*e*) *verb phr. trans.* fashion or shape (esp. a garment) by cutting; *fig.* make suitable *for* a particular purpose (usu. in *pass.*); ***have one's work cut out***: see WORK *noun*; (*f*) *verb phr. intrans.* & †*trans.* leave, or exclude from, a card game after an unfavourable card has been cut; (*g*) *verb phr. trans. & intrans.* disconnect from an electric circuit; (of a motor etc.) cease operating; (*h*) *verb phr. intrans.* (*Austral. & NZ*) finish shearing or some other activity. **cut up** (*a*) *verb phr. trans.* cut in pieces; divide by cutting; *fig.* destroy utterly, mar irretrievably; criticize severely; (*b*) *verb phr. intrans.* (*slang*, of a deceased person) turn out (well etc.), as to the amount of fortune left; (*c*) *verb phr. trans.* distress (greatly); (usu. in *pass.*); (*d*) *verb phr. trans.* root up by cutting; (*e*) *verb phr. intrans. & trans.* (*N. Amer. colloq.*) show off; behave (in a specified way), esp. badly;

C

cut up capers, *cut up shines*, behave in a mischievous or frolicsome way; (*f*) *verb phr. trans.* **cut up rough** (*colloq.*), behave in a quarrelsome, aggressive, or unruly way; (*g*) *adjectival phr.* (*colloq.*) (of a person) very distressed.

– COMB.: **cut-and-come-again** *noun & adjective* (allowing) the act or faculty of helping oneself as often as one likes, abundance; **cut-and-cover** (*a*) *US* a mode of ploughing whereby the furrow slice is turned over on an unploughed strip; (*b*) a method of building a tunnel by making a cutting which is then lined and covered in; **cut-and-fill** the process or result of removing material from a place and depositing it nearby; **cutgrass** any grass of the genus *Leersia* of Europe and N. America, with tiny hooks on the blades able to cut the skin; **cut moth** = *cutworm* (b) below; **cutworm** (*a*) a caterpillar that eats young shoots near ground level, *esp.* that of the turnip moth; (*b*) any of various noctuid moths with such caterpillars.

C

cutaneous /kjuːˈteɪnɪəs/ *adjective*. L16.
[ORIGIN from mod. Latin *cutaneus* (from Latin *cutis* skin): see -ANEOUS.]
Of, pertaining to, or affecting the skin.

cutaway /ˈkʌtəweɪ/ *adjective & noun*. M19.
[ORIGIN from CUT *ppl adjective* + AWAY *adverb*.]
▸ **A** *adjective*. **1** Of a coat: having the skirt cut back from the waist. M19.
2 Of a diagram etc.: with some parts of the object omitted, to reveal the interior. M20.
3 CINEMATOGRAPHY. Designating a shot filmed separately from the shot to which it is subsequently joined in editing. M20.
▸ **B** *noun*. **1** A cutaway coat. M19.
2 CINEMATOGRAPHY. A cutaway shot. M20.

cutback /ˈkʌtbak/ *noun*. L19.
[ORIGIN from *cut back* (inf. & pa. pple): see CUT *verb*.]
1 A plant which has been pruned hard. L19.
2 CINEMATOGRAPHY. A scene which is a return to a previous action. E20.
3 A reduction in expenditure, production, etc. M20.

cutch /kʌtʃ/ *noun*. M18.
[ORIGIN Malay *kachu*.]
= CATECHU.

cutcha *adjective & noun* var. of KUTCHA.

cutcherry /kʌˈtʃɛri/ *noun*. Also **cutchery** /ˈkʌtʃəri/. E17.
[ORIGIN Hindi *kacahrī*, *kacerī*.]
In the Indian subcontinent: an office; a courthouse.

†**cute** *noun*[1] var. of COOT *noun*[2].

†**cute** *noun*[2] var. of CUIT *noun*.

cute /kjuːt/ *adjective*[1]. *colloq.* E18.
[ORIGIN Aphet. from ACUTE.]
1 Clever, keen-witted, shrewd; ingenious. E18.
2 Attractive, pretty; quaint, fascinating. E19.

P. MORTIMER She's ever so cute—blue eyes.

■ **cutely** *adverb* M18. **cuteness** *noun* M18.

†**cute** *adjective*[2] var. of CUIT *adjective*.

cutesy /ˈkjuːtsi/ *adjective*. M20.
[ORIGIN from CUTE *adjective*[1] + -SY.]
Dainty or quaint to an affected degree.

cutey *noun* var. of CUTIE.

Cuthbert /ˈkʌθbət/ *noun*. L17.
[ORIGIN Male forename: in senses 1 & 2 from St *Cuthbert* (c 635–87), bishop of Lindisfarne.]
1 *Cuthbert's beads*, *St Cuthbert's beads*, detached and perforated joints of fossil crinoids found along the Northumbrian coast. L17.
2 *Cuthbert duck*, *St Cuthbert's duck*, the eider duck, which breeds in the Farne Islands. L17.
3 A man who deliberately avoids military service; *esp.* in the First World War, one who did so by securing a post in a Government office or the Civil Service; a conscientious objector. *slang. derog.* E20.

cuticle /ˈkjuːtɪk(ə)l/ *noun*. L15.
[ORIGIN Latin *cuticula* dim. of *cutis* skin: see -CULE.]
1 Orig., a membrane of the body. Now *spec.* the epidermis. L15. ▸**b** The area of dead skin at the base of a fingernail or toenail. E20.
2 Any of various outer layers in a plant or animal, *esp.* a non-cellular protective film covering the epidermis in a plant or insect. M17.
†**3** A thin film formed on the surface of a liquid; a thin coating left by the evaporation of brine etc. M17–E18.

cuticula /kjuːˈtɪkjʊlə/ *noun*. E17.
[ORIGIN formed as CUTICLE.]
The cuticle of an insect or (formerly) the skin.

cuticular /kjuːˈtɪkjʊlə/ *adjective*. L16.
[ORIGIN formed as CUTICLE + -AR[1].]
Of or pertaining to a cuticle, resembling a cuticle.
■ **cuticulariˈzation** *noun* the process or result of cuticularizing L19. **cuticularize** *verb trans.* change into a cuticle; cover with cutin: L19.

cutie /ˈkjuːti/ *noun*. *slang*. Also **cutey**. M18.
[ORIGIN from CUTE *adjective*[1] + -IE.]
A cute person; *esp.* an attractive young woman.

cutikin /ˈkuːtɪkɪn/ *noun*. *Scot.* E19.
[ORIGIN from COOT *noun*[2] + -KIN.]
A gaiter, a spat.

cutin /ˈkjuːtɪn/ *noun*. M19.
[ORIGIN from CUTIS + -IN[1].]
BOTANY. A hydrophobic substance in the cuticle of plants, consisting of highly polymerized esters of fatty acids.
■ **cutiniˈzation** *noun* the process or result of cutinizing L19. **cutinize** *verb trans.* change into cutin, impregnate with cutin L19.

cut-in /ˈkʌtɪn/ *noun & adjective*. L19.
[ORIGIN from *cut in* (inf. & pa. pple): see CUT *verb*.]
▸ **A** *noun*. **1** An act of cutting in. L19.
2 Something that is cut in, *esp.* an interposed scene in a film. E20.
3 A device for completing an electric circuit, esp. automatically. E20.
▸ **B** *adjective*. Designating something that is cut in. L19.

cutis /ˈkjuːtɪs/ *noun*. E17.
[ORIGIN Latin = skin.]
MEDICINE. The skin; the dermis. Now chiefly with following Latin adjectives, forming the names of skin conditions. ***cutis laxa***, ***cutis marmorata***.

cutlass /ˈkʌtləs/ *noun*. L16.
[ORIGIN French *coutelas* from Proto-Romance, from Latin *cultellus* (see CUTLER) + augm. suffix *-aceum*: cf. CURTAL-AXE.]
A short sword with a flat slightly curved blade, *esp.* that with which sailors were formerly armed; a machete.
– COMB.: **cutlassfish** any of various long slender marine fishes of the family Trichiuridae, with long jaws and sharp teeth; esp. *Trichiurus lepturus*, a silvery-coloured fish of the Atlantic, caught for food in the tropics.

cutler /ˈkʌtlə/ *noun*. ME.
[ORIGIN Old French & mod. French *coutelier*, from Old French *coutel* (mod. *couteau*) knife from Latin *cultellus* dim. of *culter* COULTER: see -ER[2].]
A person who makes, deals in, or repairs knives, forks, and similar utensils.

cutlery /ˈkʌtləri/ *noun*. ME.
[ORIGIN Old French & mod. French *coutellerie*, formed as CUTLER: see -ERY.]
The craft or trade of a cutler; *collect.* knives and other wares made or sold by cutlers, *esp.* knives, forks, and spoons for use at table.

cutlet /ˈkʌtlɪt/ *noun*. E18.
[ORIGIN French *côtelette*, formerly *costelette* dim. of *coste* (now *côte*) rib from Latin *costa*: see -EL[2], -ETTE. Assim. to CUT *noun*[2], -LET.]
A neck chop of mutton or lamb; a small piece of veal etc. for frying; a similarly shaped cake of minced meat etc.
Maintenon cutlet: see MAINTENON 1. **nut cutlet** a cutlet-shaped savoury cake of chopped nuts and other ingredients.

cutling /ˈkʌtlɪŋ/ *noun*. Long *obsolete* exc. *dial.* M17.
[ORIGIN from CUTLER, CUTLERY + -ING[1]. Cf. also CUTTLE *noun*[2].]
The business or occupation of a cutler; the making of cutlery.

cutlings /ˈkʌtlɪŋz/ *noun pl.* Long *obsolete* exc. *dial.* L17.
[ORIGIN Unknown.]
Husked oat grains; coarse oatmeal.

cut-off /ˈkʌtɒf/ *noun & adjective*. M17.
[ORIGIN from *cut off* (pa. pple & inf.): see CUT *verb*.]
▸ **A** *noun*. **1** A portion or quantity cut off. M17. ▸**b** An oxbow lake. L19.

Scientific American Cutoffs discarded during the manufacture of new cotton goods.

2 An artificial channel cut to shorten the course of a river or to join two bodies of water. L18.
3 A shorter section of a river where it has cut across the neck of a bend; *US* a bayou. E19.
4 A land route which serves as a short cut. E19.
5 (A device for producing) an interruption or cessation of flow; an instance of being cut off or cut short. M19. ▸**b** ELECTRICITY. A sudden drop in amplification or responsiveness at a certain frequency. M20.

fig.: G. B. SHAW His death . . seems to me a complete cut-off.

6 In *pl.* Shorts, *esp.* ones made by cutting short a pair of jeans. Chiefly *N. Amer.* L20.
▸ **B** *adjective*. **1** That is cut off; *spec.* isolated; remote. E19.

J. F. FIXX Cut-off jeans.

2 That cuts off; that stops a flow. M19.
3 That constitutes a limit. E20.

R. QUIRK We take this level as our cut-off point in choosing samples of English for inclusion.

■ **cut-ˈoffness** *noun* E20.

cut-out /ˈkʌtaʊt/ *adjective & noun*. L18.
[ORIGIN from *cut out* (pa. pple & inf.): see CUT *verb*.]
▸ **A** *adjective*. Made by cutting out; of or pertaining to a piece cut out. L18.
▸ **B** *noun*. **1** A space or outline where something has been cut out. M19.

Practical Wireless Cut-outs are provided for the only two connections which must pass beneath them.

2 A device for automatically breaking an electric circuit under certain circumstances. L19.

Which? All the kettles we tested have a safety cut-out.

3 An act of separating animals from a herd. *US.* L19.
4 The end of shearing; the end of shearing a particular group. *Austral. & NZ.* L19.
5 Something that is cut out or intended for cutting out; *spec.* a preprinted figure that can be cut out of paper or card; THEATRICAL a flat piece of board painted to simulate scenery etc. E20.

fig.: W. GOLDING It reveals Philip to me as a person in three D, as more than a cut-out.

6 A middleman, an intermediary, esp. in espionage. *slang.* M20.
– COMB.: **cut-out box** *US* a fuse box.

cut-over /ˈkʌtəʊvə/ *noun & adjective*. L19.
[ORIGIN from *cut over* (inf. & pa. pple): see CUT *verb*.]
▸ **A** *noun*. FENCING. An offensive disengage executed over the opponent's blade. L19.
▸ **B** *adjective*. Of land etc.: having had the saleable timber felled and removed. L19.

cutpurse /ˈkʌtpəːs/ *noun*. *arch.* LME.
[ORIGIN from CUT *verb* + PURSE *noun*.]
A person who stole by cutting purses from the girdles from which they were suspended; a pickpocket, a thief.

†**cuts** *noun*. L17–E18.
[ORIGIN Alt. Cf. COTS.]
God's: used in oaths and exclamations.

cuttable /ˈkʌtəb(ə)l/ *adjective*. LME.
[ORIGIN from CUT *verb* + -ABLE.]
Able to be cut.

cuttanee /ˈkʌtəniː/ *noun*. E17.
[ORIGIN Urdu *katānī* from Arabic *kattān* flax, linen.]
hist. A type of cloth of silk, cotton, or both, usu. striped and sometimes decorated, imported from India or Malaya and used esp. for quilts and upholstery.

cutted /ˈkʌtɪd/ *ppl adjective*. Long *obsolete* exc. *dial.* LME.
[ORIGIN from CUT *verb* + -ED[1].]
1 = CUT *ppl adjective* 1. LME.
†**2** Wearing a short skirt or cloak. LME–E17.
3 Curt, testy. Cf. CUTTY *adjective* 2. M16.

cuttee /kʌˈtiː/ *noun*. E19.
[ORIGIN from CUT *verb* + -EE[1].]
A person who is cut socially.

cutter /ˈkʌtə/ *noun*. ME.
[ORIGIN from CUT *verb* + -ER[1]. Branch III perh. a different word.]
▸ **I** A person who cuts.
1 *gen.* A person who cuts (*lit.* & *fig.*); (with specifying word) a person who shapes etc. things by cutting. Also with adverbs, as ***cutter-in***, ***cutter-out***. ME.

J. PYCROFT A good cutter at the wicket. C. E. MULFORD The cutters-out rode after some calf.

2 *spec.* **a** A person who cuts hair. LME. ▸**b** A person who castrates animals. Now *dial.* M16. ▸**c** Orig., a tailor. Now, a person in a tailoring establishment who takes measurements and cuts the cloth. L16. ▸**d** A person who cuts or edits film. E20.
3 A person over-ready to use a weapon; a bully; a cut-throat, a highway robber. *arch.* M16.
▸ **II** A thing.
4 An implement or tool that cuts; the cutting part of a machine. M17.

A. ALVAREZ The younger man mangled his cigar's sleek end with the cutter.

attrib.: ***cutter-bar***, ***cutter-head***, etc.

5 MINING. A crack or fissure intersecting the lines of stratification; the cleavage of slate (usu. in *pl.*). *dial.* M18.
6 A fine kind of brick which can be sawn and rubbed smooth, formerly used esp. for arches. M19.
7 A pig heavier than a porker but lighter than a baconer. E20.
8 An animal yielding an inferior grade of meat. E20.
9 CRICKET. A ball that turns sharply after pitching. M20.
▸ **III 10** A ship's boat fitted for rowing and sailing, and used for carrying light stores, passengers, etc. M18.
11 Orig., a small fore-and-aft rigged boat with one mast, more than one headsail, and a running bowsprit, formerly used esp. as a fast auxiliary. Now also, a sailing yacht with one mainsail and two foresails; a light pilot or patrol vessel. M18.
12 A light horse-drawn sleigh. *N. Amer.* E19.
– PHRASES: ***laver cutter***: see LAVER *noun*[3]. ***off-cutter***: see OFF *preposition & adjective*. ***rotary cutter***: see ROTARY *adjective*. ***silage cutter***: see SILAGE *noun*. ***top cutter***: see TOP *adjective*.

cutthroat /ˈkʌtθrəʊt/ *noun & adjective*. Also **cut-throat**. M16.
[ORIGIN from CUT *verb* + THROAT *noun*.]
▸ **A** *noun*. **1** An assassin, a murderer; a violent criminal. M16.
†**2** A kind of firearm. *Scot.* M16–M17.
†**3** A lantern, *esp.* one whose light could be completely obscured. M17–E19.
4 Any of several games of chance; *esp.* (more fully ***cutthroat bridge***, ***cutthroat poker***, etc.) a card game for

three or more players in which players score individually and not in partnership. **E19.**
5 The mustang grape. Also ***cutthroat grape***. **L19.**
6 In full ***cutthroat finch***, ***cutthroat weaver***. A small African bird, *Amadina fasciata*, of the waxbill family, the male of which has a red mark round the throat. **L19.**
7 In full ***cutthroat trout***. A N. American trout, *Salmo clarki*, that has red markings under its jaw and is a game and food fish in the US. **L19.**
8 In full ***cutthroat razor***. A razor with a long blade fixed in a handle, as opp. to a safety razor. **M20.**
▸ **B** *attrib.* or as *adjective*. Reminiscent of or suitable for an assassin; (of competition) merciless, intense. **M16.**

W. SHEED The cutthroat worlds of business and politics.

cutting /ˈkʌtɪŋ/ *noun*. **ME.**
[ORIGIN from CUT *verb* + -ING[1].]
1 The action of CUT *verb*. Also with adverbs, as ***cutting out***, ***cutting up***, etc. **ME.**
rotary cutting: see ROTARY *adjective*.
2 A piece cut off; *esp.* a shred etc. made in preparing or trimming an object for use. Also, a quantity of timber etc. suitable for cutting. **ME.** ▸**b** A small shoot, branch, etc., cut off a plant for use in propagation. **L17.** ▸**c** A paragraph or short article cut from a newspaper etc. Also ***newspaper cutting***, ***press cutting***. **M19.**
†**3** An intersection of two lines; a portion of a line between two intersections. **L16–E18.**
4 A figure, representation, etc., produced by cutting; a carving etc. **L18.**
5 A large gully or trench made through higher ground so that a road etc. can pass through with little change of slope. **M19.**
6 In *pl.* Low-grade fragments of ore, esp. when mixed with better quality; small fragments produced by a coal-cutting machine or brought up in rock drilling. **L19.**
– COMB.: **cutting compound** an abrasive substance used to smooth and blend paintwork on a motor vehicle; **cutting edge** *noun & adjective* (**a**) *noun* an edge that cuts; *fig.* the factor with most implications, the most significant factor; the forefront of a movement etc.; (**b**) *adjective* pioneering, innovative; **cutting horse** *US*: trained in separating cattle from a herd; **cutting-out scissors** large scissors for cutting patterns from fabric; **cutting room** a room where the cutting of material, meat, etc., is carried out, *esp.* (CINEMATOGRAPHY) where film is cut and edited.

cutting /ˈkʌtɪŋ/ *adjective*. **LME.**
[ORIGIN from CUT *verb* + -ING[2].]
1 That cuts. **LME.**

H. MARTINEAU You don't know . . what a cutting wind it is.

cutting grass (**a**) any of several grasses or sedges of Australia and New Zealand with sharp-edged leaves or stems, esp. *Gahnia psittacorum*; (**b**) = ***cane rat*** s.v. CANE *noun*[1].
2 *fig.* Acutely wounding to the mind, sensibilities, etc.; sharp, hurtful. **L16.**

C. BRONTË He can say the driest, most cutting things in the quietest of tones.

†**3** Violent, swaggering; that is a cutthroat or bully. **L16–L17.**
■ **cuttingly** *adverb* **L16.**

cuttle /ˈkʌt(ə)l/ *noun*[1].
[ORIGIN Old English *cudele*, corresp. to Old Low Frankish *cudele*, Norwegian dial. *kaule*, from base of COD *noun*[1], with allus. to its ink bag.]
= CUTTLEFISH.
– COMB.: **cuttlebone** the thick light shell inside a cuttlefish, now crushed for use as a dietary supplement for cage birds.

†**cuttle** *noun*[2]. **M16–L17.**
[ORIGIN App. from Old French *coutel* (mod. *couteau*): see CUTLER.]
A knife; a cutter.

cuttle /ˈkʌt(ə)l/ *verb intrans. rare. obsolete* exc. *dial.* **LME.**
[ORIGIN Unknown.]
Whisper; talk privately and confidentially.

cuttlefish /ˈkʌt(ə)lfɪʃ/ *noun*. Pl. **-es** /-ɪz/, (usu.) same. **L16.**
[ORIGIN from CUTTLE *noun*[1] + FISH *noun*[1].]
Any of various marine cephalopods of the genus *Sepia* or order Sepioidea, having an elongated body with an undulating lateral fin, ten arms, a cuttlebone, and the habit of ejecting a black fluid when alarmed; *loosely* a squid, an octopus.

cuttoe /ˈkʌtəʊ/ *noun*. Chiefly *US*. Also **-o**, pl. **-o(e)s**. **M17.**
[ORIGIN French COUTEAU.]
= COUTEAU.

cutty /ˈkʌti/ *adjective & noun*. **M17.**
[ORIGIN from *cut* pa. pple of CUT *verb* + -Y[6].]
▸ **A** *adjective*. **1** Cut short; exceptionally short. *Scot. & N. English.* **M17.**

R. BURNS Her cutty sark, o' Paisley harn . . In longitude tho' sorely scanty.

cutty stool *Scot.* a low stool; *esp.* (*hist.*) a particular seat in a church on which offenders had to sit, to be publicly rebuked during divine service.
2 Testy, short-tempered. Cf. CUTTED 3. *Scot. & N. English.* **E19.**
3 Capable of cutting, sharp. Chiefly *NZ* in ***cutty grass*** below. **E20.**
cutty grass *NZ* = ***cutting grass*** (a) s.v. CUTTING *adjective*.
▸ **B** *noun*. **1** A short pipe; *Scot.* a short spoon. **M18.**
2 A wren. *Scot. & dial.* **L18.**
3 A short stumpy young woman; (also *joc.*) a short-tempered or naughty woman or girl. *Scot.* **E19.**

cut-up /ˈkʌtʌp/ *noun & adjective*. **L18.**
[ORIGIN from *cut up* (inf. & pa. pple): see CUT *verb*.]
▸ **A** *noun*. **1** A distressing event, a deep loss. **L18.**
2 a A practical joke; an event at which there is much fooling around. *rare*. Chiefly *N. Amer.* **M19.** ▸**b** A person who plays the fool; a boisterous person. Chiefly *N. Amer.* **L19.**
3 An article of hosiery made from one of a series of pieces cut from a long length rather than being knitted fully fashioned. **M19.**
▸ **B** *adjective*. That has been or is cut up. **L19.**

cutwater /ˈkʌtwɔːtə/ *noun*. **M17.**
[ORIGIN from CUT *verb* + WATER *noun*.]
1 a The forward curve of a ship's stem, the part that divides the water. **M17.** ▸**b** A wedge-shaped end of the pier of a bridge, serving to divide the current, break up ice, etc. **L18.**
2 The black skimmer, *Rhynchops nigra*, of N. America. *US.* **M18.**

cutwithe /ˈkʌtwɪð/ *noun*. *obsolete* exc. *dial.* Also **-withy** /-wɪði/. **M16.**
[ORIGIN from CUT *ppl adjective* + WITHE *noun*.]
A bar etc. at the front of a plough or harrow to which the gear of a draught animal may be attached.

cutwork /ˈkʌtwəːk/ *noun*. **LME.**
[ORIGIN from CUT *ppl adjective* + WORK *noun*.]
1 Garments or embroidery with the edges cut into elaborate shapes, as a medieval fashion; embroidery or lace with parts cut out and the edges oversewn or filled with needlework designs; appliqué work in which the pattern is cut out and sewn on. **LME.**
2 *gen.* Work produced by cutting or carving. **M17.**
†**3** Flower beds cut in the turf so as to form elaborate patterns. **L17.**

cuvée /kjuːˈveɪ, *foreign* kyve (*pl. same*)/ *noun*. **M19.**
[ORIGIN French = vatful, from *cuve* from Latin *cupa* cask, vat.]
The contents of a vat of wine; a particular blend or batch of wine.

cuvette /kjuːˈvɛt/ *noun*. **L17.**
[ORIGIN French, dim. of *cuve*: see CUVÉE, -ETTE.]
1 FORTIFICATION. = CUNETTE. **L17.**
2 A shallow vessel for holding liquid; a transparent vessel with flat sides for holding a spectrophotometric sample etc. **E18.**
3 A large clay basin or crucible used in making plate glass. **M19.**
4 GEOLOGY. A basin in which sedimentation is occurring or has occurred. **E20.**

Cuvierian /kjuːˈvɪərɪən/ *adjective*. **M19.**
[ORIGIN from *Cuvier* (see below) + -IAN.]
Of, pertaining to, or named after the French naturalist Georges Cuvier (1769–1832); characteristic of his methods or system of classification.

CV *abbreviation*. Also **c.v.**
Curriculum vitae.

cv. *abbreviation*.
Cultivated variety; cultivar.

CVO *abbreviation*.
Commander of the Royal Victorian Order.

CVS *abbreviation*.
MEDICINE. Chorionic villus sampling.

CW *abbreviation*.
1 Chemical warfare, chemical weapons.
2 Continuous wave.

Cwlth *abbreviation*.
Commonwealth.

cwm /kʊm/ *noun*. **M19.**
[ORIGIN Welsh = COMBE.]
A bowl-shaped valley or hollow in (Welsh) mountains; PHYSICAL GEOGRAPHY = CIRQUE *noun* 3.

c.w.o. *abbreviation*.
Cash with order.

CWS *abbreviation*.
Cooperative Wholesale Society.

cwt *abbreviation*.
[ORIGIN *c* from Latin *centum* hundred.]
Hundredweight.

cwtch /kʊtʃ/ *noun*. *Welsh.* **L20.**
[ORIGIN Welsh, from *cwts* couch, recess: rel. to COUCH[1].]
1 A cupboard or cubbyhole. **L20.**
2 A cuddle or hug. **L20.**

-cy /sɪ/ *suffix*.
[ORIGIN Repr. Latin *-cia*, *-tia*, Greek *-k(e)ia*, *-t(e)ia*: see -Y[3].]
Forming nouns of state or quality (orig. and esp. in forms such as -ACY, -ANCY, -CRACY, -ENCY, -MANCY), as ***bankruptcy***, ***captaincy***, ***chaplaincy***, ***idiocy***, ***normalcy***, etc.

cyan /ˈsʌɪən/ *noun & adjective*. **L19.**
[ORIGIN Greek *kuan(e)os* dark blue.]
(Of) a greenish-blue colour. Also more fully ***cyan-blue***.

cyan- *combining form* see CYANO-.

cyanamide /sʌɪˈanəmʌɪd/ *noun*. **M19.**
[ORIGIN from CYAN + AMIDE.]
CHEMISTRY. Cyanogen amide, a weakly acidic crystalline solid, CN_2H_2, or a salt of this, esp. (in full ***calcium cyanamide***) that of calcium, $CaCN_2$, used as a fertilizer.
– COMB.: **cyanamide process**: for making calcium cyanamide by the action of nitrogen on calcium carbide at high temperature.

cyanate /ˈsʌɪəneɪt/ *noun*. **M19.**
[ORIGIN from CYANIC + -ATE[1].]
CHEMISTRY. A salt or ester of isocyanic acid, containing the ion NCO^- or one of the groups ·N=CO and ·OC≡N (= ISOCYANATE), or of the hypothetical cyanic acid HONC.

cyanelle /sʌɪəˈnɛl/ *noun*. **M20.**
[ORIGIN from CYAN-: see -EL[2].]
BOTANY. A blue-green alga in symbiosis within a protozoan.

cyaneous /sʌɪˈeɪnɪəs/ *adjective*. *rare*. **L17.**
[ORIGIN from Latin *cyaneus* from Greek *kuaneos*: see CYAN, -OUS.]
Deep blue, azure.

cyanic /sʌɪˈanɪk/ *adjective*. **E19.**
[ORIGIN from CYAN- + -IC.]
1 CHEMISTRY. Of cyanogen; ***cyanic acid***, a colourless, volatile, strongly acidic liquid, unstable above 0°C, HN=C=O (= ***ISOCYANIC acid***); *esp.* the hypothetical isomer of this, HO·CN. **E19.**
2 Blue, azure. *rare*. **M19.**

cyanicide /sʌɪˈanɪsʌɪd/ *noun*. **L19.**
[ORIGIN from CYANIDE + -CIDE.]
Any substance present in a metal ore which reacts detrimentally with the cyanide used in a metal extraction process.

cyanide /ˈsʌɪənʌɪd/ *noun & verb*. **E19.**
[ORIGIN from CYAN- + -IDE.]
▸ **A** *noun*. CHEMISTRY. A salt or ester of hydrocyanic acid, containing the group ·CN or the ion CN^- (in ORGANIC CHEMISTRY = NITRILE); such a salt as the type of a powerful poison; the sodium, calcium, or other salt used in the extraction of gold, silver, or other metals from their ores. **E19.**
▸ **B** *verb trans.* **1** Treat (ores of gold, silver, etc.) with cyanide solution in order to form a soluble complex with the metal, as part of an extraction process. **L19.**
2 Case-harden (steel etc.) by immersion in a molten cyanide. **E20.**
■ **cyaniˈdation** *noun* (metal extraction involving) the treatment of ores with cyanides **L19.**

cyanin /ˈsʌɪənɪn/ *noun*. **M19.**
[ORIGIN from CYAN- + -IN[1].]
CHEMISTRY. A violet anthocyanin present as a pigment in many flowers, e.g. cornflower, dahlia, violet.
■ **cyanidin** /sʌɪˈanɪdɪn/ *noun* the aglycone of cyanin (usu. isolated as the chloride $C_{15}H_{11}O_6Cl$) **E20.**

cyanine /ˈsʌɪəniːn/ *noun*. **L19.**
[ORIGIN formed as CYANIN + -INE[5].]
1 In full ***cyanine dye***. Any of a large class of synthetic dyestuffs having a molecular structure typically containing two heteroaromatic ring systems joined by one or more carbon atoms. **L19.**
2 A blue pigment that is a mixture of cobalt blue and Prussian blue. **L19.**
– COMB.: **cyanine blue** (**a**) a blue cyanine dye; (**b**) = sense 2 above; ***cyanine dye***: see sense 1 above.

cyanite *noun* var. of KYANITE.

cyano- /ˈsʌɪənəʊ/ *combining form*. Before a vowel or *h* **cyan-**.
[ORIGIN Greek *kuan(e)os* dark blue: see -O-.]
Dark blue; CHEMISTRY cyanogen, cyanide.
■ **cyanoˈacrylate** *noun* a substance of a class forming exceptionally strong adhesives **M20.** **cyanobacˈterium** *noun*, pl. **-ria** /-rɪə/, a blue-green alga **L20.** **cyanoˈchroite** *noun* [Greek *khroia* colour] MINERALOGY a monoclinic hydrated sulphate of copper and potassium occurring as blue tabular crystals or crystalline crusts **M19.** **cyanocoˈbalamin** *noun* (BIOCHEMISTRY) a form of vitamin B_{12} containing a cyanide group bonded to the central cobalt atom of the cobalamin molecule **M20.** **cyanolabe** *noun* [Greek *lab-* base of *lambanein* take] PHYSIOLOGY a blue-sensitive pigment in the cones of the retina **M20.** **cyanometer** /sʌɪəˈnɒmɪtə/ *noun* an instrument for measuring the blueness of the sky **E19.** **cyanometry** /sʌɪəˈnɒmɪtri/ *noun* the measurement of the blueness of the sky **L19.** **cyanophilous** /sʌɪəˈnɒfɪləs/ *adjective* (BIOLOGY) readily stained by blue and green dyes **L19.** **cyanoˈphycin** *noun* (BIOCHEMISTRY) a polypeptide that is the principal constituent of the food storage granules of most cyanobacteria **L19.** **cyanophyte** *noun* (BOTANY) a blue-green alga **M20.** **cyanophytic** /-ˈfɪtɪk/ *adjective* (BOTANY) of or pertaining to a cyanophyte or the cyanophytes **M20.** **cyanotrichite** /-ˈtrɪkʌɪt/ *noun* [Greek *trikh-*, *thrix* hair] MINERALOGY an orthorhombic hydrated basic sulphate of copper and aluminium, occurring as blue fibrous crystals **M19.** **cyaˈnurate** *noun* (CHEMISTRY) a salt or ester of cyanuric acid **M19.** †**cyanuret** *noun* =

CYANIDE *noun* E–M19. **cya'nuric** *adjective* (CHEMISTRY) designating polymers of cyanogen; ***cyanuric acid***, a colourless crystalline tribasic heterocyclic acid, $C_3H_3O_3N_3$, obtained by dry distillation of urea: M19.

cyanogen /sʌɪ'anədʒ(ə)n/ *noun.* E19.
[ORIGIN French *cyanogène*, formed as CYANO- + -GEN, as being related chemically to Prussian blue.]
CHEMISTRY. A colourless flammable highly toxic gas, $(CN)_2$, chemically one of the pseudohalogens.

cyanogenic /sʌɪənə'dʒɛnɪk/ *adjective.* M20.
[ORIGIN from CYANO- + -GENIC.]
BIOCHEMISTRY. Capable of producing (hydrogen) cyanide; containing a cyanogen group in the molecule.
■ **cyanogenesis** *noun* cyanogenic property M20. **cyanoge'netic** *adjective* = CYANOGENIC E20.

cyanohydrin /sʌɪənə(ʊ)'hʌɪdrɪn/ *noun.* E20.
[ORIGIN from CYANO- + HYDRO- + -IN[1].]
CHEMISTRY. Any organic compound containing a carbon atom linked to both a cyanide group and a hydroxyl group.

cyanosis /sʌɪə'nəʊsɪs/ *noun.* Pl. **-noses** /-'nəʊsiːz/. M19.
[ORIGIN mod. Latin from Greek *kuanōsis* blueness, formed as CYAN- + -OSIS.]
MEDICINE. A blue discoloration of the skin due to deficient oxygenation of the blood.
■ **'cyanosed** *adjective* affected with cyanosis M19. **cyanotic** /-'nɒtɪk/ *adjective* pertaining to, of the nature of, or affected with cyanosis M19.

cyathi *noun* pl. of CYATHUS.

cyathiform /sʌɪ'aθɪfɔːm/ *adjective.* L18.
[ORIGIN from CYATHIUM + -I- + -FORM.]
Chiefly BOTANY. Shaped like a cup widened at the rim.

cyathium /sʌɪ'aθɪəm/ *noun.* Pl. **-ia** /-ɪə/. L19.
[ORIGIN mod. Latin, from Greek *kuathion* dim. of *kuathos* CYATHUS.]
BOTANY. The characteristic inflorescence of the spurges (genus *Euphorbia*), consisting of a cup-shaped involucre of fused bracts enclosing several greatly reduced male flowers and a single female flower; the involucre forming part of such an inflorescence.

cyathus /'sʌɪəθəs/ *noun.* Pl. **-thi** /-θʌɪ/. LME.
[ORIGIN Latin from Greek *kuathos*.]
CLASSICAL ANTIQUITIES. A cup or ladle used for drawing wine from a bowl. Also, a wine glass as a measure of volume (usu. about 50 ml.).

cyber /'sʌɪbə/ *adjective.* L20.
[ORIGIN Independent use of CYBER-.]
Of, relating to, or characteristic of the culture of computers, information technology, the Internet, and virtual reality.

D. HECHT Maybe Gus had some image of himself as a sort of Cyber Batman.

cyber- /'sʌɪbə/ *combining form.*
[ORIGIN Shortened from CYBERNETIC, CYBERSPACE, etc.]
Forming words relating to (the culture of) computers, information technology, the Internet, and virtual reality, or denoting futuristic concepts.
■ **cybercafe** *noun* a cafe in which customers may use computer terminals to access the Internet L20. **cybercrime** *noun* criminal activities carried out by means of computers or the Internet. L20. **cybernaut** *noun* (*a*) a robot; a cyborg; (*b*) a computer user or programmer; an (expert or habitual) user of the Internet: M20. **cybersex** *noun* (*a*) sexual arousal or activity using computer technology, *spec.* by wearing virtual reality equipment or by exchanging messages with another person via the Internet; (*b*) pornographic or sexually explicit material available on the Internet: L20. **cybershop** (*a*) *noun* a website through which goods may be purchased; (*b*) *verb intrans.* browse through and buy products over the Internet: L20. **cybersquatting** *noun* the practice of registering names, esp. well-known company or brand names, as Internet domains, in the hope of reselling them at a profit L20. **cyberstalking** *noun* the repeated use of electronic communications to harass or frighten someone, e.g. by sending threatening emails L20. **cyberterrorism** *noun* the politically motivated use of computers to cause severe disruption or widespread fear L20. **cyberwar** *noun* the use of computers to disrupt the activities of an enemy country, esp. the deliberate attacking of communication systems L20.

cybernation /sʌɪbə'neɪʃ(ə)n/ *noun.* M20.
[ORIGIN from CYBERNETICS + -ATION.]
Control of processes, communities, etc., by machines.
■ **'cybernate** *verb trans.* place under machine control (usu. in *pass.*) M20.

cybernetics /sʌɪbə'nɛtɪks/ *noun.* M20.
[ORIGIN from Greek *kubernētēs* steersman, from *kubernan* to steer: see -ICS.]
The science of systems of control and communications in living organisms and machines.
■ **cybernetic** *adjective* of or pertaining to cybernetics M20. **cybernetician** /-nɪ'tɪʃ(ə)n/, **cyberneticist** /-sɪst/ *nouns* an expert in cybernetics M20.

cyberphobia /sʌɪbə'fəʊbɪə/ *noun.* L20.
[ORIGIN from CYBER- + -PHOBIA.]
Fear of or anxiety about computing or technology; reluctance to engage with computers, esp. (in later use) the Internet.
■ **'cyberphobe** *noun* L20. **cyberphobic** *adjective* L20.

cyberpunk /'sʌɪbəpʌŋk/ *noun.* L20.
[ORIGIN from CYBER- + PUNK *noun*[2].]
Science fiction featuring punk styles and attitudes.

cyberspace /'sʌɪbəspeɪs/ *noun.* L20.
[ORIGIN from CYBER- + SPACE *noun*.]
The notional environment within which electronic communication occurs, esp. when represented as the inside of a computer system; space perceived as such by an observer but generated by a computer system and having no real existence; the space of virtual reality.

cyborg /'sʌɪbɔːg/ *noun.* M20.
[ORIGIN Blend of CYBERNETIC *adjective* and ORGANISM.]
A person whose physical tolerances or capabilities are extended beyond normal human limitations by a machine etc.; an integrated man–machine system.

cybotaxis /sʌɪbə'taksɪs/ *noun.* E20.
[ORIGIN from Greek *kubos* CUBE *noun*[1] + -TAXIS.]
PHYSICS. The arrangement of molecules in a liquid in transitory aggregates each having approximately crystalline structure.
■ **cybotactic** *adjective* of, pertaining to, or exhibiting cybotaxis E20.

cybrid /'sʌɪbrɪd/ *noun.* L20.
[ORIGIN Blend of CYTOPLASMIC and HYBRID.]
MICROBIOLOGY. A hybrid cell produced artificially by the fusion of two cells, one of which lacks a nucleus.

cycad /'sʌɪkad/ *noun.* M19.
[ORIGIN from mod. Latin *Cycas* genus name, from supposed Greek *kukas*, scribal error for *koïkas* accus. pl. of *koïx* Egyptian doum palm: see -AD[1].]
An evergreen palmlike gymnospermous plant of the order Cycadales (including many fossil forms), and esp. of the genus *Cycas*, some members of which yield sago.
■ **cy'cadean** *adjective* of, pertaining to, or resembling (that of) a cycad M19. **cy'cadeoid** *adjective & noun* (of, pertaining to, or designating) a cycadophyte of the extinct Mesozoic order Bennettitales (or Cycadeoidales) M19. **cyca'daceous** *adjective* of or pertaining to a cycad or the cycads, or the family Cycadaceae M19. **cycadophyte** *noun* a plant of the group Cycadophyta, which includes cycads and related fossil forms M20.

Cycladic /sɪ'kladɪk, sʌɪ-/ *adjective.* E20.
[ORIGIN from Latin *Cyclades* (see below) from Greek *Kuklades* (*nēsoi* islands), from *kuklos* circle: see -IC.]
Of or pertaining to the Cyclades, a group of Greek islands in the Aegean Sea; *spec.* designating or pertaining to the prehistoric civilization of these islands.

cyclamate /'sɪkləmeɪt, 'sʌɪk-/ *noun.* M20.
[ORIGIN Contr. of *cyclohexylsulphamate*.]
CHEMISTRY. Any salt of cyclohexylsulphamic acid, C_6H_{11}·$NHSO_3H$; *esp.* the sodium or calcium salt used as an artificial sweetening agent.

cyclamen /'sɪkləmən/ *noun.* M16.
[ORIGIN medieval Latin from Latin *cyclaminos*, *-on* from Greek *kuklaminos*, perh. from *kuklos* circle, with ref. to the bulbous roots of the plant.]
1 Any of various plants of the Eurasian genus *Cyclamen*, of the primrose family, usu. with reflexed twisted petals and including several kinds cultivated as pot plants. M16.
2 A pink colour characteristic of some cyclamen flowers. E20.

cyclas /'sɪkləs/ *noun.* M19.
[ORIGIN Latin from Greek *kuklas* a woman's garment with a border all round it.]
hist. A close-fitting tunic; *spec.* a surcoat made shorter in front than behind and worn over armour.

cycle /'sʌɪk(ə)l/ *noun.* LME.
[ORIGIN French, or late Latin *cyclus* from Greek *kuklos* circle: in sense 5 an abbreviation.]
1 A recurrent period of definite duration; a period in which a certain series of events or phenomena is completed, usu. as part of a repeating succession of similar periods; *loosely* an age. LME.

TENNYSON Better fifty years of Europe than a cycle of Cathay. CONAN DOYLE If the cycle of nine days holds good then we shall have the Professor at his worst to-night.

lunar cycle, ***Metonic cycle***, ***Sothic cycle***, ***Victorian cycle***, etc.
2 A circle or orbit in the heavens. *arch.* M17.
3 A recurrent round or course of events or phenomena; a series of successive events through which something runs to completion. M17. ▸**b** *spec.* (chiefly SCIENCE). A recurring series of successive operations, reactions, or states, e.g. in the working of an internal-combustion engine, in the alternation of an electric current or a wave, or in the metabolism of an organism. Also (*ellipt.*), a cycle per second (= HERTZ 2). M19. ▸**c** LINGUISTICS. More fully ***transformational cycle***. (The application of) a set of transformational rules operating successively at each level of structure. M20.

SHELLEY Or hadst thou waited the full cycle, when Thy spirit should have filled its crescent sphere. E. WILSON He seems to have imagined history as a series of repetitive cycles. L. D. STAMP As the cycle of erosion progresses . . the surface is reduced to a monotonous level . . plain. D. LODGE An almost unbroken cycle of grants, fellowships, leaves of absence and alcoholic cures.

vicious cycle: see VICIOUS *adjective*. **b** ***carbon cycle***, ***Carnot's cycle***, ***Krebs cycle***, ***life cycle***, ***menstrual cycle***, ***open cycle***, ***Otto cycle***, ***Rankine cycle***, ***Stirling cycle***, ***thermal cycle***, ***tricarboxylic acid cycle***, etc.
4 A complete set or series; *spec.* a series of poems, songs (more fully ***song cycle***), etc., composed round a central event or idea. M17.

R. MACAULAY The Arthurian cycle, the cycle of Charlemagne, . . the cycle of Christ—these are the European folk tales which filled the Middle Ages. A. C. BOULT Our last pre-war memory is Toscanini's Beethoven Cycle.

5 A bicycle, tricycle, or similar machine. L19.
motorcycle, ***pedal cycle***, etc.
– COMB.: **cycle clip** = BICYCLE ***clip***; **cycle track**, **cycleway**: reserved for cyclists.

cycle /'sʌɪk(ə)l/ *verb intrans.* M19.
[ORIGIN from the noun.]
1 Move in or pass through cycles; complete a cycle. M19.
2 Ride a cycle (*spec.* a bicycle). L19.
cycling lizard = RACEHORSE ***lizard***.
■ **cycler** *noun* = CYCLIST 2 L19. **cycling** *verbal noun* the action of the verb; *spec.* the riding of bicycles as a sport or recreation L19.

cycli *noun* pl. of CYCLUS.

cyclian /'sʌɪklɪən/ *adjective. rare.* L17.
[ORIGIN from Greek *kuklios* circular, cyclic + -AN.]
= CYCLIC (esp. sense 3b).

cyclic /'sʌɪklɪk, 'sɪk-/ *adjective.* L18.
[ORIGIN French *cyclique* or Latin *cyclicus* or Greek *kuklikos*: see CYCLE *noun*, -IC.]
1 Of, pertaining to, or of the nature of a cycle; moving or recurring in cycles. L18.

U. LE GUIN The whole universe is a cyclic process, an oscillation of expansion and contraction, without any before or after.

2 Of or belonging to a cycle of legends, poems, etc. E19.

SHELLEY Episodes of that cyclic poem written by Time upon the memories of men.

3 GREEK PROSODY. Of a dactyl or anapaest: occupying in scansion only three time units instead of four. M19.
4 MATH. Of or pertaining to a circle or other closed curve; (of a polygon) having all its vertices lying on a circle. M19. ▸**b** Of a group: having the property that each element of the group can be expressed as a power of one particular element. L19.
5 BOTANY. Of a flower: having its parts arranged in whorls. L19.
6 CHEMISTRY. Having a molecular structure containing one or more closed rings of atoms. L19.
■ **cyclicity** /sʌɪ'klɪsɪti/ *noun* L20.

cyclical /'sʌɪklɪk(ə)l/ *adjective.* E19.
[ORIGIN formed as CYCLIC + -AL[1].]
= CYCLIC (esp. sense 1).
■ **cyclically** *adverb* L19.

cyclin /'sʌɪklɪn/ *noun.* L20.
[ORIGIN from CYCLE *noun* + -IN[1].]
BIOCHEMISTRY. Any of several proteins which are involved in regulating cell division.

cyclise *verb* var. of CYCLIZE.

cyclist /'sʌɪklɪst/ *noun.* M19.
[ORIGIN from CYCLE *noun* + -IST.]
1 A person who recognizes cycles in the course of phenomena etc. *rare.* M19.
2 A person who rides a cycle (without specification usu. a bicycle), esp. habitually. L19.
motor cyclist: see MOTOR *noun & adjective*. ***trick cyclist***: see TRICK *adjective*.

cyclitis /sɪ'klʌɪtɪs/ *noun.* M19.
[ORIGIN from Greek *kuklos* circle + -ITIS.]
MEDICINE. Inflammation of the ciliary body of the eye.

cyclize /'sʌɪklʌɪz/ *verb trans. & intrans.* Also **-ise**. M20.
[ORIGIN from CYCLIC + -IZE.]
CHEMISTRY. (Cause to) undergo a reaction which results in the formation of a closed ring of atoms.
■ **cycli'zation** *noun* E20.

cyclo- /'sʌɪkləʊ/ *combining form.*
[ORIGIN from Greek *kuklos* circle, or directly from CYCLE *noun*, CYCLIC: see -O-.]
1 Forming nouns and adjectives with the sense 'circular, cyclic, of circles or cycles'.
2 CHEMISTRY. Prefixed to names of hydrocarbons to form names of cyclic hydrocarbons with rings of corresponding numbers of carbon atoms (as ***cyclobutane***, ***cyclopentadiene***, ***cyclopentane***, etc.), or used more generally with the sense 'involving cyclic compounds'.
3 With the sense 'of bicycles or cycling'.
■ **cycloa'ddition** *noun* an addition reaction in which a cyclic molecule is formed M20. **cyclo'alkane** *noun* (CHEMISTRY) = CYCLOPARAFFIN M20. **cyclo-cross** *noun* cross-country racing on bicycles M20. **cyclo'dextrin** *noun* (CHEMISTRY) a compound whose molecule is a ring of six to eight cyclic hexoses linked end to end M20. **cyclodi'alysis** *noun*, pl. **-lyses** /-lɪsiːz/, MEDICINE an operation for relieving glaucoma by surgically detaching the ciliary body of the eye from the sclera E20. **cyclogiro** *noun*, pl. **-os**, a rotor aircraft obtaining lift from aerofoils rotating about a horizontal axis M20. **cyclograph** *noun* an instrument for tracing circular arcs E19. **cyclo'hexane** *noun* a colourless liquid cycloparaffin, C_6H_{12}, obtained in petroleum or by hydrogenating benzene, and widely used as a solvent L19. **cyclomor'phosis** *noun*, pl. **-phoses**

/-ˈfəʊsiːz/, (BIOLOGY) a seasonal change in form undergone by some planktonic organisms E20. **cyclo'paraffin** *noun* any saturated cyclic hydrocarbon E20. **cyclo'phosphamide** *noun* [from PHOSPH- + AMIDE] PHARMACOLOGY a white crystalline synthetic compound, $C_7H_{15}Cl_2N_2O_2P$, used as a cytotoxic drug in the treatment of tumours and some kinds of leukaemia M20. **cyclo'plegia** *noun* (MEDICINE) paralysis of the ciliary muscle of the eye E20. **cyclo'plegic** *adjective & noun* (*a*) *adjective* pertaining to or producing cycloplegia; (*b*) *noun* a substance that produces cycloplegia: E20. **cyclo'propane** *noun* (CHEMISTRY) a flammable gaseous hydrocarbon, C_3H_6, used chiefly as an anaesthetic M20. **cyclo'rrhaphous** *adjective* [Greek *rhaphē* seam] ENTOMOLOGY of or pertaining to the very large suborder Cyclorrhapha of dipteran insects characterized by the emergence of the adult from the puparium through a circular split L19. **cyclo'sporin** *noun* [mod. Latin *polysporum* (see below) + -IN[1]] (more fully ***cyclosporin A***) a cyclic oligopeptide produced by the fungus *Trichoderma polysporum* and used as an immunosuppressive drug to prevent the rejection of grafts and transplants L20. **cyclostrophic** /-ˈstrəʊfɪk, -ˈstrɒfɪk/ *adjective* (METEOROLOGY) designating the force acting on a wind as a consequence of the curvature of its path; (of a wind) dominated by such forces: E20. **cyclothem** *noun* [Greek *thema* something laid down, THEME] GEOLOGY a sedimentary deposit whose structure shows evidence of a cyclic process of deposition M20.

cycloid /ˈsʌɪklɔɪd/ *noun & adjective*. M17.
[ORIGIN from Greek *kukloeidēs* adjective, circular: see CYCLE *noun*, -OID.]
▸ **A** *noun*. **1** MATH. A curve traced by a point on the circumference of a circle (or occas. in some other fixed relation to it) as the circle rolls along a straight line. M17.
2 PSYCHIATRY. = CYCLOTHYMIC *noun*. E20.
▸ **B** *adjective*. **1** ZOOLOGY. Designating fish scales of approximately circular form with concentric striations; having such scales. M19.
2 PSYCHIATRY. = CYCLOTHYMIC *adjective*. E20.
■ **cy'cloidal** *adjective* (MATH.) of, pertaining to, or of the form of a cycloid (CYCLOID *noun* 1) E18.

cyclometer /sʌɪˈklɒmɪtə/ *noun*. M17.
[ORIGIN from CYCLO- + -METER.]
†**1** A person concerned with measuring the circle. *rare*. Only in M17.
2 An instrument for measuring arcs of circles. E19.
3 An apparatus attached to the wheel of a cycle for measuring the distance travelled. L19.
■ **cyclometry** *noun* the measurement of circles; squaring the circle: M17.

Cyclon *noun* var. of ZYKLON.

cyclone /ˈsʌɪkləʊn/ *noun*. M19.
[ORIGIN Prob. from Greek *kuklōma* wheel, coil of a snake, from *kuklos* circle: the change of *m* to *n* is unexpl.]
1 A storm or atmospheric disturbance involving circular motion of winds. *obsolete* in *gen.* sense. M19. ▸**b** = ***tropical cyclone*** s.v. TROPICAL *adjective* 3a. M19. ▸**c** METEOROLOGY. A pressure system characterized by a low central barometric pressure and an anticlockwise (northern hemisphere) or clockwise (southern hemisphere) circulation; a depression. M19.
2 A centrifugal machine for separating solids. Freq. *attrib.* L19.
– COMB.: **cyclone cellar** *US*: intended to give shelter during a cyclone (in the US).
■ **cyclonic** /sʌɪˈklɒnɪk/ *adjective* of, pertaining to, of the nature of, or characteristic of a cyclone M19. **cy'clonically** *adverb* L19.

cyclonite /ˈsʌɪklənʌɪt/ *noun*. E20.
[ORIGIN from CYCLO- + NITRO- (as elems. of alternative chemical name), with ending assim. to -ITE[1].]
A kind of high explosive, chemically 1,3,5-trinitrohexahydro-1,3,5-triazine, $(N(NO_2)CH_2)_3$. Also called ***hexogen***, ***RDX***.

Cyclop *noun* see CYCLOPS.

cyclopaedia *noun* var. of CYCLOPEDIA.

Cyclopean /sʌɪkləˈpiːən, -ˈkləʊpɪən/ *adjective*. Also **Cyclopian** /*usu.* sʌɪˈkləʊpɪən/, **c-**. L16.
[ORIGIN from Latin *Cyclopeus*, *-pius* from Greek *Kuklōpios*, from *Kuklōps* CYCLOPS: see -EAN, -IAN.]
1 Belonging to or resembling the Cyclopes; monstrous, huge. L16.
2 Of (esp. ancient) masonry: made with massive irregular or crudely shaped blocks. E19.

cyclopedia /sʌɪkləˈpiːdɪə/ *noun*. Also **-paedia**. E17.
[ORIGIN Abbreviation.]
†**1** = ENCYCLOPEDIA 1. Only in 17.
2 = ENCYCLOPEDIA 2. E18.
■ **cyclopedic** *adjective* M19.

cyclopentadiene /ˌsʌɪkləʊpɛntəˈdʌɪiːn/ *noun*. L19.
[ORIGIN from CYCLO- + PENTA- + DI- *prefix*[2] + -ENE.]
A liquid unsaturated cyclic hydrocarbon formed as a by-product of the cracking of petroleum, used in the manufacture of synthetic resins and in organic syntheses. Also, a substituted derivative of this.

Cyclopes *noun pl.* see CYCLOPS.

cyclopia /sʌɪˈkləʊpɪə/ *noun*. M19.
[ORIGIN from CYCLOPS + -IA[1].]
ZOOLOGY & MEDICINE. The fusion of two eyes into one central eye (whether as a normal condition or a malformation).

Cyclopian *adjective* see CYCLOPEAN.

Cyclopic /sʌɪˈklɒpɪk/ *adjective*. *rare*. M17.
[ORIGIN Greek *Kuklōpikos*, from *Kuklōps* CYCLOPS: see -IC.]
Cyclopean; monstrous.
■ †**Cyclopical** *adjective* L16–M17.

cyclopoid /ˈsʌɪkləpɔɪd/ *adjective & noun*. M19.
[ORIGIN from mod. Latin CYCLOPS + -OID.]
ZOOLOGY. A member of, belonging to or resembling, the order Cyclopoida of copepods, typified by the cyclopes.

Cyclops /ˈsʌɪklɒps/ *noun*. In sense 2 usu. **c-**. Pl. **Cyclopes** /sʌɪˈkləʊpiːz/, same, (sense 1) **-ses**. In sense 1 also (*rare*) **-op**, pl. **-ops**. LME.
[ORIGIN Latin *Cyclops* from Greek *Kuklōps* lit. 'round-eyed', from *kuklos* circle + *ōps* eye.]
1 GREEK MYTHOLOGY. A member of a race of one-eyed giants who forged thunderbolts for Zeus. LME.
2 A free-swimming copepod of the genus *Cyclops*, characterized by having a single centrally placed eye. M19.

cyclorama /sʌɪkləˈrɑːmə/ *noun*. M19.
[ORIGIN from CYCLO- after *panorama* etc.]
1 A panoramic scene arranged on the inside of a cylindrical surface, to be viewed by a central spectator. M19.
2 THEATRICAL. A large (curved) backcloth or wall at the rear of a stage for displaying a background, esp. of the sky. E20.

cyclosis /sʌɪˈkləʊsɪs/ *noun*. M19.
[ORIGIN Greek *kuklōsis* encirclement.]
1 BIOLOGY. Circulatory motion, e.g. of cytoplasm within a cell. M19.
2 PHYSICS etc. The existence of cycles; cyclic behaviour. L19.

cyclostome /ˈsʌɪkləstəʊm/ *noun*. M19.
[ORIGIN from CYCLO- + Greek *stoma* mouth.]
A fish of the former taxon Cyclostomata (now incorporated in Agnatha: cf. AGNATHAN), which includes primitive forms (the lampreys and hagfishes) having a round sucking mouth.
■ **cyclo'stomatous** *adjective* M19.

cyclostyle /ˈsʌɪkləstʌɪl/ *noun & verb*. L19.
[ORIGIN from CYCLO- + STYLE *noun*.]
▸ **A** *noun*. An apparatus for printing copies of writing by means of a stencil plate, orig. one cut with a pen bearing a small toothed wheel which perforated sheets of waxed paper. L19.
▸ **B** *verb trans.* Print or copy using a cyclostyle. L19.

cyclothymia /sʌɪkləˈθʌɪmɪə/ *noun*. E20.
[ORIGIN from CYCLO- + Greek *thumos* mind, temper + -IA[1].]
PSYCHIATRY. Behaviour characterized by an alternation of mood between depression and elation; manic-depressive behaviour.
■ **cyclothyme**, **cyclo'thymic** *adjectives & nouns* (*a*) *adjective* of, pertaining to, or exhibiting cyclothymia; manic-depressive; (*b*) *noun* a person with cyclothymia: E20.

cyclotomy /sʌɪˈklɒtəmi/ *noun*. L19.
[ORIGIN from CYCLO- + -TOMY.]
1 MATH. The division of a circle into a given number of equal parts. L19.
2 Surgical cutting of the ciliary muscle of the eye; an instance of this. L19.
■ **cyclo'tomic** *adjective* (MATH.) of or pertaining to cyclotomy L19.

cyclotron /ˈsʌɪklətrɒn/ *noun*. M20.
[ORIGIN from CYCLO- + -TRON.]
PHYSICS. An apparatus for accelerating with an electric field charged atomic particles revolving in a magnetic field.

cyclus /ˈsʌɪkləs/ *noun*. Pl. **-li** /-lʌɪ, -liː/. E19.
[ORIGIN Latin.]
A cycle of myths, poems, songs, etc.

cyder *noun* see CIDER.

cydippe /sʌɪˈdɪpi/ *noun*. M19.
[ORIGIN mod. Latin (see below) from Greek *Kudippē*, a Nereid.]
A ctenophore of the genus *Pleurobrachia* (formerly *Cydippe*).
■ **cydippid** *noun & adjective* (a larval ctenophore) resembling an adult of the order Cydippida L19.

cygnet /ˈsɪɡnɪt/ *noun*. LME.
[ORIGIN from Old French *ci(g)ne* (mod. *cygne*) or its ult. source Latin *cycnus*, *cyg-* swan from Greek *kuknos*: see -ET[1].]
A young swan.

Cygnus /ˈsɪɡnəs/ *noun*. M16.
[ORIGIN Latin *cygnus* swan: see CYGNET.]
(The name of) a large constellation of the northern hemisphere, in the Milky Way between Hercules and Pegasus; the Swan.

cylices *noun pl.* see KYLIX.

cylinder /ˈsɪlɪndə/ *noun*. L16.
[ORIGIN Latin *cylindrus* from Greek *kulindros* roller, from *kulindein* to roll.]
▸ **I 1** A solid geometrical figure generated by a straight line fixed in direction and describing with one of its points a closed curve, esp. a circle (in which case the figure is a ***circular cylinder***, its ends being parallel circles). L16.
scalene cylinder: see SCALENE *adjective* 1.
2 A (solid or hollow) body, object, or part having this shape, exemplified by a roller, straight tree trunk, pencil, etc. L16.
VASCULAR *cylinder*.
▸ **II** *spec.* **3** A chamber in which a fluid exerts pressure on a piston or analogous part, e.g. in a steam or internal-combustion engine. L17.
fire on all cylinders, **function on all cylinders**, etc., *fig.* work at full power.
4 A metal roller used in printing. M18.
5 WATCHMAKING. The cylindrical recess, cut away to allow the passage of the escape wheel, on the verge of the balance in a particular kind of escapement (called ***cylinder escapement***). M18.
6 A hollow barrel-shaped object of baked clay, covered with cuneiform script and buried under the foundations of a Babylonian or Assyrian temple; a small stone of similar shape used in antiquity as a seal. M19.
7 *hist.* A cylindrical phonograph record. L19.
8 A cylindrical container for liquefied gas etc. E20.
– COMB.: **cylinder bore** a cylinder-bored gun; **cylinder-bored** *adjective* having an unrifled bore of uniform diameter; ***cylinder escapement***: see sense 5 above; **cylinder head** the end cover of a cylinder in an internal-combustion engine, against which the piston compresses the cylinder contents; **cylinder lock**: having the keyhole and tumbler mechanism contained in a cylinder; **cylinder oil**: of a kind suitable for lubricating steam engine valves and pistons; **cylinder press** a printing machine in which the printing surface is carried on a flat bed and pressure is applied by a revolving cylinder; **cylinder saw** a crown saw.
■ **cylindered** *adjective* having a cylinder or cylinders (of a specified number or kind) L19.

cylindraceous /sɪlɪnˈdreɪʃəs/ *adjective*. L17.
[ORIGIN from CYLINDER + -ACEOUS.]
= CYLINDRICAL 1.

cylindric /sɪˈlɪndrɪk/ *adjective*. L17.
[ORIGIN mod. Latin *cylindricus* from Greek *kulindrikos*, from *kulindros* CYLINDER: see -IC.]
Cylindrical.
■ **cylindricity** /sɪlɪnˈdrɪsɪti/ *noun* M19.

cylindrical /sɪˈlɪndrɪk(ə)l/ *adjective*. M17.
[ORIGIN formed as CYLINDRIC + -AL[1].]
1 Shaped like a cylinder. M17.
2 Of or pertaining to a cylinder. M17.
cylindrical projection a map projection in which part of a spherical surface is projected on to a cylinder which is then unrolled into a plane.
■ **cylindrically** *adverb* M17. **cylindricalness** *noun* E18.

cylindriform /sɪˈlɪndrɪfɔːm/ *adjective*. L19.
[ORIGIN from Latin *cylindrus* CYLINDER + -I- + -FORM.]
= CYLINDRICAL 1.

cylindrite /sɪˈlɪndrʌɪt/ *noun*. L19.
[ORIGIN from Greek *kulindros* CYLINDER + -ITE[1].]
MINERALOGY. A blackish-grey metallic sulphide of lead, antimony, and tin, occurring usu. as cylindrical masses.

cylindro- /sɪˈlɪndrəʊ/ *combining form* of Greek *kulindros* CYLINDER: see -O-.
■ **cylindro-'conical** *adjective* of cylindrical form with one end conical M19. **cylindro-co'noidal** *adjective* of cylindrical form with one end conoidal L19.

cylindroid /ˈsɪlɪndrɔɪd/ *noun & adjective*. M17.
[ORIGIN from CYLINDRO- + -OID.]
▸ **A** *noun*. A figure or body resembling a cylinder; a cylinder of elliptical section. M17.
▸ **B** *adjective*. Resembling a cylinder in shape; somewhat cylindrical. M19.
■ **cylin'droidal** *adjective* (*a*) of the form of a cylindroid; (*b*) = CYLINDROID *adjective*: M19.

cylindroma /sɪlɪnˈdrəʊmə/ *noun*. Pl. **-mas**, **-mata** /-mətə/. L19.
[ORIGIN from CYLINDRO- + -OMA.]
MEDICINE. A cutaneous or dermal tumour having a cylindrical structure.

cylix *noun* var. of KYLIX.

cyma /ˈsʌɪmə/ *noun*. M16.
[ORIGIN mod. Latin from Greek *kuma* billow, wave, wavy moulding, from *kuein* become pregnant.]
1 ARCHITECTURE. An ogee moulding of a cornice. M16.
cyma recta /ˈrɛktə/ [= straight]: having the concave part of the curve uppermost. **cyma reversa** /rɪˈvəːsə/ [= reversed]: having the convex part of the curve uppermost.
2 BOTANY. = CYME *noun* 2. E18.
■ **cymagraph** *noun* an instrument for tracing the contours of mouldings M19.

†**cymaise** *noun*. M17–M18.
[ORIGIN French formed as CYMATIUM.]
ARCHITECTURE. = CYMA 1.

cymar *noun* var. of SIMAR.

cymatium /sɪˈmatɪəm, -ˈmeɪʃəm/ *noun*. Pl. **-tia** /-tɪə, -ʃə/. M16.
[ORIGIN Latin = ogee, Ionic volute from Greek *kumation* dim. of *kuma* CYMA.]
ARCHITECTURE. = CYMA 1.

cymbal /ˈsɪmb(ə)l/ *noun & verb*. OE.
[ORIGIN Latin *cymbalum* from Greek *kumbalon*, from *kumbē* cup, hollow vessel. Readopted in Middle English from Old French & mod. French *cymbale* from Latin.]
▸ **A** *noun*. A musical instrument consisting of a concave plate of brass or bronze, which is struck against another

or with a stick etc. to produce a ringing or clashing sound. Formerly also *loosely*, any of various other percussion instruments. OE.

ride cymbal: see RIDE *noun* 4c. *top cymbal*: see TOP *adjective*.

▸ **B** *verb intrans. & trans.* Infl. **-l(l)-**. Play on cymbals. *rare.* LME.

■ **cymbalist** *noun* a cymbal player M17.

cymbalo /ˈsɪmbələʊ/ *noun.* Pl. **-os.** L19.
[ORIGIN Italian *cembalo*, *cim-* from Latin *cymbalum* CYMBAL *noun.* Cf. CIMBALOM.]
A dulcimer.

cymbidium /sɪmˈbɪdɪəm/ *noun.* E19.
[ORIGIN mod. Latin (see below), from Greek *kumbē* cup: so called from a hollow recess in the flower-lip.]
An epiphytic orchid of the large tropical Asian and Australasian genus *Cymbidium*.

cymbiform /ˈsɪmbɪfɔːm/ *adjective.* E19.
[ORIGIN from Latin *cymba* boat + -I- + -FORM.]
Boat-shaped.

cyme /sʌɪm/ *noun.* In sense 1 also †**cime.** E18.
[ORIGIN French *cyme*, *cime* summit, top from popular form of Latin CYMA.]
†**1** The unopened head of a plant. *rare.* Only in E18.
2 *BOTANY.* An inflorescence (freq. forming a more or less flat head) in which the primary axis bears a single flower which develops first, flowers of secondary and higher order axes developing successively later. Cf. RACEME. L18.
■ **cymose** *adjective* of the nature of a cyme; bearing or arranged in cymes: E19.

cymene /ˈsʌɪmiːn/ *noun.* M19.
[ORIGIN from Greek *kuminon* CUMIN + -ENE.]
CHEMISTRY. Each of three isomeric liquid aromatic hydrocarbons, 1-methyl-2-isopropylbenzene, 1-methyl-3-isopropylbenzene, and 1-methyl-4-isopropylbenzene, $C_{10}H_{14}$, one or more of which are present in oil of cumin and other volatile oils.

cymling *noun* see SIMLIN.

cymoid /ˈsʌɪmɔɪd/ *adjective.* E19.
[ORIGIN from CYMA + -OID.]
Resembling a cyma or a cyme.

cymophane /ˈsʌɪməfeɪn/ *noun.* E19.
[ORIGIN from Greek *kumo-* *kuma* CYMA + *-phanēs* showing.]
Chrysoberyl, now *spec.* of a chatoyant variety used for gems.

cymotrichous /sʌɪˈmɒtrɪkəs/ *adjective.* E20.
[ORIGIN formed as CYMOPHANE + -TRICH + -OUS.]
ANTHROPOLOGY. Having wavy hair; (of hair) wavy.
■ **cymotrichy** *noun* the state or condition of having wavy hair E20.

Cymraeg /kʌmˈrʌɪɡ/ *noun.* L18.
[ORIGIN Welsh.]
The Welsh language.

Cymric /ˈkʌmrɪk/ *adjective.* M19.
[ORIGIN from Welsh *Cymru* Wales, *Cymry* the Welsh + -IC.]
Welsh.

†**cynanche** *noun.* M16–M19.
[ORIGIN Late Latin from Greek *kunagkhē* canine quinsy, sore throat, from *kun-*, *kuōn* dog + *agkhein* to throttle: cf. QUINSY.]
Quinsy or a similar inflammatory complaint.

cynanthropy /sɪˈnanθrəpi/ *noun. rare.* L16.
[ORIGIN French †*cynanthropie* (after *lycanthropie* LYCANTHROPY) from Greek *kun-*, *kuōn* dog. Cf. Greek *kunanthrōpos*.]
A form of madness in which a person believes himself or herself to be a dog and behaves accordingly.

cyne- /ˈkɪnə, *foreign* ˈkynə/ *combining form.* Long *obsolete* exc. *hist.* OE.
[ORIGIN Cf. KING *noun.*]
Royal: occurring in certain Old English compounds retained by historians.
cynebót [BOOT *noun*[1]] compensation paid to the people for the murder of the king.

cynegetics /sɪnɪˈdʒɛtɪks/ *noun pl. rare.* M17.
[ORIGIN from Greek *kunēgetikos* adjective, from *kunēgetēs* hunter, from *kun-*, *kuōn* dog + *hēgetēs* leader: see -ICS.]
The chase, hunting.
■ **cynegetic** *adjective* relating to the chase E18.

cynghanedd /kəŋˈhɑːnɛð/ *noun.* M19.
[ORIGIN Welsh.]
An intricate system of alliteration and rhyme in Welsh poetry.

cynic /ˈsɪnɪk/ *noun & adjective.* M16.
[ORIGIN Latin *cynicus* adjective from Greek *kunikos* lit. 'doglike, churlish', prob. from *Kunosarges* gymnasium where Antisthenes taught, but assoc. with *kun-*, *kuōn* dog: see -IC.]
▸ **A** *noun.* **1** (**C-**.) Any of a sect of ancient-Greek philosophers founded by Antisthenes (a pupil of Socrates), who had an ostentatious contempt for ease and pleasure. M16.
2 A cynical person; one who sarcastically doubts or despises human sincerity and merit. L16.

> G. MEREDITH Cynics are only happy in making the world as barren to others as they have made it for themselves.

▸ **B** *adjective* **1 a** = CYNICAL *adjective* 1. L16. ▸**b** (**C-**.) Belonging to or characteristic of the sect of Cynics. M17.
2 Of or suggesting a dog; canicular. *rare.* E17.
■ **cynicism** /-sɪz(ə)m/ *noun* (*a*) (**C-**) the philosophy of the Cynics; (*b*) cynical disposition or quality: L17. **cynism** *noun* (*rare*) [French *cynisme*] = CYNICISM M19.

cynical /ˈsɪnɪk(ə)l/ *adjective.* L16.
[ORIGIN formed as CYNIC + -AL[1].]
1 Resembling or characteristic of the Cynic philosophers; distrustful or incredulous of human goodness and sincerity; sceptical and mocking. L16.

> R. WEST We were experts in disillusion, we had learned to be cynical about fresh starts. S. NAIPAUL One is led to the cynical conclusion that most had been opposed to the draft rather than to the war itself; passionately dedicated to saving their own skins.

2 Of dogs, canine. Chiefly *joc. rare.* E17.
■ **cynically** *adverb* E17.

cyno- /ˈsʌɪnəʊ, ˈsɪnəʊ/ *combining form* of Greek *kun-*, *kuōn* dog: see -O-.
■ **cynoˈlogical** *adjective* of or pertaining to cynology E20. **cyˈnology** *noun* the branch of science that deals with dogs L19. **cynoˈphobia** *noun* irrational fear of dogs L19.

cynocephalus /sʌɪnəˈsɛf(ə)ləs, sɪn-/ *noun.* Pl. **-li** /-lʌɪ, -liː/. ME.
[ORIGIN Latin from Greek *kunokephalos* adjective = dog-headed, formed as CYNO- + *kephalē* head.]
1 A member of a fabled race of men with dogs' heads. ME.
2 A baboon or other primate having a doglike head. *obsolete* exc. as mod. Latin name of a genus of Asian flying lemurs. E17.
■ **cynocephalous** *adjective* dog-headed M19.

cynodont /ˈsʌɪnədɒnt/ *noun & adjective.* L19.
[ORIGIN from CYNO- + -ODONT. Cf. earlier DICYNODONT.]
PALAEONTOLOGY. ▸**A** *noun.* A Triassic mammal-like reptile with well developed specialized teeth. L19.
▸ **B** *adjective.* Designating or pertaining to a cynodont. L19.

cynosure /ˈsɪnəzjʊə, ˈsʌɪn-, -sjʊə/ *noun.* L16.
[ORIGIN French, or Latin *Cynosura* from Greek *kunosoura* from *kunos* genit. sing. of *kuōn* dog + *oura* tail.]
1 (**C-**.) *The* constellation Ursa Minor, or *the* Pole Star which it contains. Now *rare* or *obsolete.* L16.
2 A thing which serves for guidance or direction. *arch.* L16.

> JOSEPH HALL For the guidance of our either caution or liberty . . the onely Cynosure is our Charity.

3 A thing which or person who is the centre of attraction or admiration. E17.

> CARLYLE The fair young Queen . . the cynosure of all eyes. M. MEYER Rome . . . the cynosure of contemporary writers and artists.

Cynthia /ˈsɪnθɪə/ *noun. poet.* L16.
[ORIGIN Latin, a name of the goddess Diana, born on Mount Cynthus in Delos: see -IA[1].]
The moon personified as a goddess.

cyperus /sʌɪˈpɪərəs, ˈsʌɪpərəs/ *noun.* LME.
[ORIGIN Latin from Greek *kupeiros*, *kuperos* an aromatic marsh-plant.]
A sedge of the genus *Cyperus* (family Cyperaceae); *esp.* (English) galingale.
■ **cyperaceous** /sʌɪpəˈreɪʃəs/ *adjective* of or pertaining to the family Cyperaceae M19.

cyphel /ˈsʌɪf(ə)l/ *noun.* LME.
[ORIGIN App. from Greek *kuphella* the hollows of the ears.]
Orig., the houseleek, *Sempervivum tectorum*. Now (more fully ***mossy cyphel***), a cushion-forming alpine plant, *Minuartia sedoides*, of the pink family, with sessile apetalous flowers.

cypher *noun, verb* vars. of CIPHER *noun, verb.*

cypherpunk /ˈsʌɪfəpʌŋk/ *noun.* L20.
[ORIGIN from CIPHER *noun* + PUNK *noun*[2], after *cyberpunk*.]
A person who uses encryption when accessing a computer network in order to ensure privacy, esp. from government authorities.

cyphonism /ˈsʌɪfənɪz(ə)m/ *noun.* E18.
[ORIGIN Greek *kuphōnismos*, from *kuphōn* crooked piece of wood, from *kuphos* bent: see -ISM.]
GREEK HISTORY. Punishment of offenders by means of a wooden pillory fastened to the neck.

†**cyphosis** *noun* see KYPHOSIS.

cypraea /sʌɪˈpriːə/ *noun.* E19.
[ORIGIN mod. Latin (see below), from *Cypria*, a name of Venus.]
A gastropod of the large genus *Cypraea*; a cowrie.

cy pres /siː preɪ/ *adverbial & adjectival phr.* E19.
[ORIGIN Anglo-Norman = French *si près* as near (as).]
LAW. Esp. in the context of gifts for charitable purposes: as near as possible (to the intentions of a testator or donor when these cannot be precisely followed).

cypress /ˈsʌɪprəs/ *noun*[1]. ME.
[ORIGIN Old French *cipres* (mod. *cyprès*) from late Latin *cypressus* from Greek *kuparissos*, of alien origin; spelling later assim. to Latin.]
1 An evergreen coniferous tree of the Eurasian and N. American genus *Cupressus* having flattened shoots with scalelike leaves; *esp.* (also ***Italian cypress***) *C. sempervirens*, a tall, often fastigiate, tree native to southern Europe and the Middle East, with dark foliage and hard durable wood. Also ***cypress tree***. ME. ▸**b** With specifying word: any of numerous trees or shrubs related to or resembling the true cypresses. M16. ▸**c** Foliage of *C. sempervirens* regarded or used as a symbol of mourning. L16.

> G. DURRELL An admonishing finger of black cypress against the sky. **c** TENNYSON That remorseless iron hour Made cypress of her orange flower. *attrib.*: O. WILDE The quenched-out torch, the lonely cypress-gloom.

b African cypress a conifer of the African genus *Widdringtonia*. **bald cypress** *Taxodium distichum*, a N. American conifer of water margins, often with exposed root buttresses. **false cypress** a conifer of the N. American and Asian genus *Chamaecyparis*, closely related to *Cupressus*. **LAWSON'S CYPRESS. *Monterey cypress***: see MONTEREY 1. ***Nootka cypress***: see NOOTKA *adjective* 1. ***Sitka cypress***. **summer cypress** = BELVEDERE 2. **swamp cypress** = ***bald cypress*** above.
2 The wood of any of these trees. ME.
– COMB.: **cypress-knee** an exposed root buttress of bald cypress; **cypress pine** a small Australian conifer of the genus *Callitris*; **cypress spurge** a European spurge, *Euphorbia cyparissias* (freq. cultivated), with numerous pale green linear leaves, suggesting a miniature conifer; **cypress vine** a tropical American climbing plant with scarlet flowers, *Ipomoea quamoclit*, of the bindweed family.

cypress /ˈsʌɪprəs/ *noun*[2]. Now *rare* or *obsolete.* LME.
[ORIGIN Alt. of CYPERUS, app. confused with CYPRESS *noun*[1].]
(English) galingale.

cypress /ˈsʌɪprəs/ *noun*[3] *& adjective.* Now *rare* or *obsolete.* LME.
[ORIGIN Anglo-Norman *cipres*, *cypres* from Old French *Cipre*, *Cypre* (mod. *Chypre*) the island of Cyprus.]
▸ **A** *noun.* A textile fabric originally brought from Cyprus; *spec.* (a piece of) a light transparent material of silk and hair resembling crape, formerly often worn (as crape) in mourning. LME.
▸ **B** *attrib.* or as *adjective.* Made of or resembling this fabric. M16.

Cyprian /ˈsɪprɪən/ *adjective & noun.* L16.
[ORIGIN from Latin *Cyprius* of Cyprus (see CYPRIOT) + -AN.]
▸ **A** *adjective.* Of or pertaining to Cyprus. Formerly often *transf.*, of prostitutes, licentious (from the ancient fame of Cyprus for the worship of Aphrodite or Venus). L16.
▸ **B** *noun.* A Cypriot. Formerly also, a promiscuous person or a prostitute. L16.

Cyprianic /sɪprɪˈanɪk/ *adjective.* L17.
[ORIGIN mod. Latin *Cyprianicus*, from *Cyprianus* (see below): see -IC.]
Of, pertaining to, or characteristic of St Cyprian (Thascius Caecilius Cyprianus), Bishop of Carthage, martyred AD 258.

cyprides *noun* pl. of CYPRIS.

cyprinodont /sɪˈprʌɪnədɒnt/ *noun & adjective.* M19.
[ORIGIN formed as CYPRINOID + -ODONT.]
▸ **A** *noun.* A member of the family Cyprinodontidae of small tropical and warm-temperate freshwater fishes. M19.
▸ **B** *adjective.* Of, pertaining to, or designating this family. L19.

cyprinoid /ˈsɪprɪnɔɪd/ *adjective & noun.* M19.
[ORIGIN from Latin *cyprinus* carp from Greek *kuprinos* + -OID.]
▸ **A** *adjective.* Resembling or related to the carp; belonging to the large superfamily Cyprinoidea, which includes Cyprinidae (see below) and several other families. M19.
▸ **B** *noun.* A cyprinoid fish. M19.
■ **cyprinid** *noun & adjective* (*a*) *noun* a fish of the family Cyprinidae, which includes the carps and minnows; (*b*) *adjective* of, pertaining to, or designating this family: L19. **cypˈriniform** *noun & adjective* (*a*) *noun* a fish of the order Cypriniformes, which includes the carps, loaches, and suckers; (*b*) *adjective* of or pertaining to this order; carplike: L19.

Cypriot /ˈsɪprɪət/ *noun & adjective.* Also **-ote** /-əʊt/. L16.
[ORIGIN Greek *Kupriōtēs*, from *Kupros* Cyprus. Cf. CYPRIAN.]
▸ **A** *noun.* **1** A native or inhabitant of Cyprus, an island in the eastern Mediterranean; a person descended from inhabitants of Cyprus. L16.
2 The (ancient or modern) Greek dialect of Cyprus. L19.
▸ **B** *adjective.* Of or pertaining to Cyprus or Cypriots. L19.
Greek Cypriot, **Turkish Cypriot**: of Greek, Turkish, extraction.

cypripedium /sɪprɪˈpiːdɪəm/ *noun.* L18.
[ORIGIN mod. Latin (see below), from Greek *Kupris* Aphrodite + *pedilon* slipper.]
An orchid of the genus *Cypripedium*, to which the lady's slipper orchids belong.

cypris /ˈsʌɪprɪs/ *noun.* Pl. **-ides** /-ɪdiːz/. M19.
[ORIGIN mod. Latin (see below) from Greek *Kupris* Aphrodite.]
A freshwater ostracod of the genus *Cypris*. Also, a cirripede larva at a stage (following the ***nauplius***) in which it acquires a shell like that of a *Cypris* ostracod and becomes anchored to a rock etc.

cypsela /ˈsɪpsɪlə/ *noun.* Pl. **-lae** /-liː/. L19.
[ORIGIN mod. Latin from Greek *kupselē* hollow vessel, chest, etc.]
BOTANY. An achene with the calyx attached, as in plants of the composite family.

Cyrenaic /sʌɪrɪˈneɪɪk/ *noun & adjective. hist.* L16.
[ORIGIN Latin *Cyrenaicus* from Greek *Kurēnaikos*, from *Kurēnē* Cyrene, an ancient Greek colony in N. Africa.]
▸**A** *noun.* A philosopher belonging to a hedonistic school founded by Aristippus of Cyrene during the 4th cent. BC. L16.

▸ **B** *adjective.* Designating or belonging to this school. **M17.**

Cyrenaican /sʌɪrɪˈneɪɪk(ə)n/ *adjective & noun.* **E17.**
[**ORIGIN** formed as **CYRENAIC** + **-AN.**]
▸ **A** *adjective.* Of or pertaining to Cyrenaica, a region of N. Africa (now part of Libya), or its people. **E17.**
▸ **B** *noun.* A native or inhabitant of Cyrenaica. **M20.**

Cyrenian /sʌɪˈriːnɪən/ *adjective & noun.* As adjective also **-ean. E17.**
[**ORIGIN** from Latin *Cyrene* Cyrene (see **CYRENAIC**) + **-IAN, -EAN.** In senses A.2, B. from Simon of Cyrene (*Matthew* 27:32 etc.), helper of Jesus on the road to Calvary.]
▸ **A** *adjective.* **1** = **CYRENAIC** *adjective.* **E17.**
2 Designating or pertaining to an organization for helping the destitute. **L20.**
▸ **B** *noun.* A member of the Cyrenian organization; a helper of the destitute. **L20.**

Cyrillic /sɪˈrɪlɪk/ *adjective & noun.* **E19.**
[**ORIGIN** from St *Cyril* (826–69), apostle of the Slavs, author of the Glagolitic alphabet (from which Cyrillic was later derived): see **-IC.**]
(Designating, written in, or pertaining to) an alphabet or script used in writing Old Church Slavonic and some modern Slavonic languages (e.g. Russian, Bulgarian, Serbian).

†**cyriologic** *adjective* var. of **CURIOLOGIC.**

cyrto- /ˈsəːtəʊ/ *combining form* of Greek *kurtos* curved: see **-O-.**
■ **cyrtolite** *noun* (*MINERALOGY*) a variety of zircon containing uranium and rare earth elements and freq. having convex crystal faces **M19.** **cyrˈtometer** *noun* an instrument for measuring or recording curves of the body **L19.**

†**cyssors** *noun pl.* var. of **SCISSORS.**

cyst /sɪst/ *noun.* **E18.**
[**ORIGIN** Late Latin **CYSTIS.**]
1 A thin-walled hollow organ or cavity in an animal or plant, containing a liquid secretion; a sac, a vesicle, a bladder. **E18.**
2 *MEDICINE.* A sac or cavity of abnormal character, containing fluid; a structure enclosing a larva of a parasitic worm etc. **E18.**
MEIBOMIAN **cyst.** *NEURENTERIC* **cyst.**
3 A cell or cavity enclosing reproductive bodies, an embryo, etc. **M19.**
■ **cystlike** *adjective* resembling (that of) a cyst **M19.**

cyst- /sɪst/ *combining form* of Greek *kustis* bladder, cyst, used before a vowel. Cf. **CYSTI-, CYSTO-.**
■ **cyˈstalgia** *noun* (*MEDICINE*) pain in the urinary bladder **L19.** **cyˈstectomy** *noun* (an instance of) surgical removal of a cyst or (usu.) of the urinary bladder **L19.**

cysteine /ˈsɪstiːɪn, -tɪɪn, -teɪn, -tiːn/ *noun.* Also **-ein. L19.**
[**ORIGIN** from **CYSTINE** + **-EINE.**]
BIOCHEMISTRY. A sulphur-containing amino acid, HS $\cdot CH_2CH(NH_2)COOH$, which occurs in proteins, notably keratins, often in the form of cystine. Cf. **CYSTINE.**
– **NOTE:** Increasingly pronounced as a disyllable (cf. *protein*), leading to confusion with **CYSTINE.**

†**cystes** *noun* pl. of **CYSTIS.**

cysti- /ˈsɪsti/ *combining form* of Greek *kustis* bladder, cyst. Cf. **CYST-, CYSTO-.**
■ **cystiform** *adjective* of the form of a bladder or cyst **M19.**

cystic /ˈsɪstɪk/ *adjective.* **M17.**
[**ORIGIN** French *cystique* or mod. Latin *cysticus*: see **CYSTIS, -IC.**]
1 Pertaining to or connected with the gall bladder. **M17.**
cystic artery, cystic duct, etc.
2 *MEDICINE.* Of the nature of a cyst; characterized by the formation of cysts; containing cysts. **E18.**
cystic **FIBROSIS.**
3 Of or pertaining to the urinary bladder. **E19.**
4 Enclosed in a cyst. **M19.**

cysticercus /sɪstɪˈsəːkəs/ *noun.* Pl. **-ci** /-sʌɪ/. **M19.**
[**ORIGIN** mod. Latin (orig. the name of a supposed genus), formed as **CYSTI-** + Greek *kerkos* tail.]
ZOOLOGY. A larval tapeworm, esp. of the family Taeniidae, at a stage in which the scolex is invaginated, typically found as a cyst in the muscle tissue of the host.
■ **cysticercoid** *adjective & noun* (pertaining to, resembling, or of the nature of) a cysticercus **M19.**

cystid /ˈsɪstɪd/ *noun.* **M19.**
[**ORIGIN** from **CYSTIS** + **-ID**[3].]
PALAEONTOLOGY. A cystoid.
■ Also **cyˈstidean** *noun* **M19.**

cystidium /sɪˈstɪdɪəm/ *noun.* Pl. **-dia** /-dɪə/. **M19.**
[**ORIGIN** mod. Latin, from Greek *kustis* **CYST**: see **-IDIUM.**]
BOTANY. A sterile body projecting from the spore-bearing surface of a basidiomycete.

cystine /ˈsɪstiːn, -tɪn/ *noun.* **M19.**
[**ORIGIN** from Greek *kustis* bladder + **-INE**[5]: orig. isolated from urinary calculi.]
BIOCHEMISTRY. A base, $C_6H_{12}N_2O_4S_2$, which is in effect an oxidized dimer of cysteine (with which it is readily interconvertible), and is the form in which cysteine often occurs in organic tissue.
■ **cystiˈnosis** *noun,* pl. **-noses** /-ˈnəʊsiːz/, *MEDICINE* an inherited metabolic disorder resulting in the accumulation of cystine in the body **M20.** **cystinotic** /-ˈnɒt-/ *adjective* exhibiting cystinosis, containing excessive amounts of cystine **M20.** **cystiˈnuria** *noun* (*MEDICINE*) the abnormal presence of cystine in the urine, usu. as a result of an inherited disorder of amino-acid metabolism **M19.**

†**cystis** *noun.* Pl. **cystes. M16–M18.**
[**ORIGIN** Late Latin from Greek *kustis* bladder.]
A cyst.

cystitis /sɪˈstʌɪtɪs/ *noun.* **L18.**
[**ORIGIN** from **CYST-** + **-ITIS.**]
MEDICINE. Inflammation of the urinary bladder.

cysto- /ˈsɪstəʊ/ *combining form* of Greek *kustē* = *kustis* bladder, cyst: see **-O-.** Cf. **CYST-, CYSTI-.**
■ **cystocarp** *noun* (*BOTANY*) the fruiting body of the gametophyte in some algae of the subclass Florideae **L19.** **cystocele** *noun* (*MEDICINE*) (an instance of) prolapse of the base of the urinary bladder in women **E19.** **cystolith** *noun* (*BOTANY*) a hard mineralized ingrowth of the wall of cells in the epidermis of certain plants **M19.** **cystometer** /sɪˈstɒmɪtə/ *noun* an instrument for measuring the internal pressure and volume of the urinary bladder **E20.** **cystometry** /sɪˈstɒmɪtri/ *noun* measurement of the internal pressure and volume of the urinary bladder **M20.** **cystoscope** *noun* an instrument for internal examination of the urinary bladder **L19.** **cyˈstoscopy** *noun* examination of the urinary bladder with a cystoscope **E20.** **cyˈstostomy** *noun* (an instance of) the surgical formation of a (semi-)permanent artificial opening in the urinary bladder **E20.** **cyˈstotomy** *noun* (an instance of) surgical incision into the urinary bladder **L19.**

cystoid /ˈsɪstɔɪd/ *adjective & noun.* **L19.**
[**ORIGIN** from Greek *kustis* bladder + **-OID.**]
1 *MEDICINE.* (Of the nature of) a cyst. *rare.* **L19.**
2 *PALAEONTOLOGY.* A member of, of or pertaining to, the order Cystoidea of fossil echinoderms. **L19.**

cytase /ˈsʌɪteɪz/ *noun.* **L19.**
[**ORIGIN** from **CYTO-** + **-ASE.**]
BIOCHEMISTRY. An enzyme, present in some plant seeds, capable of hydrolysing the hemicellulose constituents of cell walls of plants.

cytaster /ˈsʌɪtastə/ *noun.* **L19.**
[**ORIGIN** from **CYTO-** + **ASTER.**]
BIOLOGY. A star-shaped structure formed in the cytoplasm of a cell prior to the onset of cell division. Cf. **ASTER** *noun* 3.

-cyte /sʌɪt/ *suffix.*
[**ORIGIN** from Greek *kutos* receptacle.]
Forming nouns denoting (usu. mature) cells, as ***erythrocyte.*** Cf. **-BLAST.**

Cytherean /sɪθəˈriːən/ *noun & adjective.* **M18.**
[**ORIGIN** from Latin *Cytherea*, a name of Venus, from *Cythēra* Kithira, an Ionian island: see **-AN.**]
▸ **A** *noun.* A votaress of Venus; a temple prostitute. **M18.**
▸ **B** *adjective.* Of or pertaining to Venus (goddess or planet). **M19.**

cytidine /ˈsʌɪtɪdiːn/ *noun.* **E20.**
[**ORIGIN** from **CYTO-** + **-IDINE.**]
BIOCHEMISTRY. A nucleoside composed of cytosine combined with ribose, a constituent of RNA and coenzymes.

cytidylic /sʌɪtɪˈdɪlɪk/ *adjective.* **M20.**
[**ORIGIN** from **CYTIDINE** + **-YL** + **-IC.**]
BIOCHEMISTRY. ***cytidylic acid***, a nucleotide composed of a phosphoric acid ester of cytidine, present in most DNA and RNA.

cytisine /ˈsɪtɪsiːn/ *noun.* **M19.**
[**ORIGIN** from **CYTISUS** + **-INE**[5].]
CHEMISTRY. A poisonous alkaloid, $C_{11}H_{14}N_2O$, present in laburnum and numerous other leguminous plants.

cytisus /ˈsɪtɪsəs/ *noun.* **M16.**
[**ORIGIN** Latin from Greek *kutisos.*]
Orig., a shrubby plant mentioned by classical writers; *spec.* a southern European medick, *Medicago arborea.* Now, any of a large genus of leguminous shrubs, mostly native to southern Europe, including some brooms and (formerly) laburnum.

cyto- /ˈsʌɪtəʊ/ *combining form* of Greek *kutos* receptacle: see **-O-.** Freely used in *BIOLOGY* etc. to form nouns and adjectives with the sense 'of a cell or cells'.
■ **cytoarchitecˈtonic** *adjective* (*MEDICINE*) pertaining to the arrangement of cells in a tissue; *spec.* designating numbered areas of the cerebral cortex which are characterized by the arrangement of their cells and are each associated with particular functions: **E20.** **cytoarchitecˈtonics** *noun* (treated as *sing.* or *pl.*) *MEDICINE* the cytoarchitectonic properties of something; the field of study that deals with these: **M20.** **cytoarchiˈtectural** *adjective* (*MEDICINE*) = **CYTOARCHITECTONIC M20.** **cytoarchiˈtecturally** *adverb* (*MEDICINE*) from a cytoarchitectonic point of view **M20.** **cytoˈarchitecture** *noun* (*MEDICINE*) = **CYTOARCHITECTONICS M20.** **cytoˈcentrifuge** *noun* a centrifuge used for depositing cells suspended in a liquid on a slide for microscopic examination **M20.** **cytochalasin** /-kəˈleɪsɪn/ *noun* [Greek *khalasis* dislocation] any of several fungal metabolites used in research for their property of interfering with cell processes **M20.** **cytoˈchemical** *adjective* of or pertaining to cytochemistry **M20.** **cytoˈchemistry** *noun* the chemistry of living cells, esp. as studied microscopically **E20.** **cytochrome** *noun* any of various compounds consisting of haem bonded to a protein, which function as electron transfer agents in many biochemical reactions, esp. in cellular respiration **E20.** **cytoˈcidal** *adjective* that kills living cells **E20.** **cyˈtogamy** *noun* †(**a**) fusion of cells; (**b**) simultaneous autogamy of two individual protozoans in contact, with no exchange of material between them: **E20.** **cytokine** *noun* any of a variety of proteins which carry signals locally between cells **L20.** **cytokiˈnesis** *noun* the division of a cell's cytoplasm into two parts at the end of mitosis or meiosis **L19.** **cytokinin** /-ˈkʌɪnɪn/ *noun* (*BIOCHEMISTRY*) = **KININ** 2 **M20.** **cyˈtolysis** *noun* dissolution or disruption of cells, esp. by an external agent **E20.** **cytoˈlytic** *adjective* pertaining to or bringing about cytolysis **E20.** **cytoˈmegalic** *adjective* (*MEDICINE*) characterized by enlarged cells; *spec.* designating a disease caused by a cytomegalovirus: **M20.** **cytoˈmegalovirus** *noun* (*MEDICINE*) a kind of herpesvirus which usually produces very mild symptoms in an infected person but may cause severe neurological damage in people with weakened immune systems and in the newborn (abbreviation ***CMV***) **M20.** **cytomorˈphosis** *noun* the series of morphological changes undergone by a cell during its existence **E20.** **cytoˈpathic**, **cytopathoˈgenic** *adjectives* of, pertaining to, or producing damage to living cells **M20.** **cytopaˈthology** *noun* the pathology of cells; the branch of science that deals with cells as affected by disease: **M20.** **cytoˈphilic** *adjective* having an affinity for living cells; *spec.* designating antibodies which attach themselves to cells other than at the cells' specific combining sites: **E20.** **cytoplast** *noun* the body or unit of protoplasm contained in a cell **L19.** **cytoˈskeletal** *adjective* of or pertaining to a cytoskeleton **M20.** **cytoskeleton** *noun* a network of protein filaments and tubules in the cytoplasm of many eukaryotic cells that contributes to their shape and coherence **M20.** **cytosol** *noun* the aqueous component of cytoplasm **M20.** **cytoˈsolic** *adjective* of or pertaining to cytosol **L20.** **cytotaˈxonomy** *noun* taxonomy based on cytological (and esp. cytogenetic) study **M20.** **cytoˈtoxic** *adjective* toxic to cells **E20.** **cytoˈtoxin** *noun* a substance toxic to cells **E20.** **cytotropic** /-ˈtrəʊpɪk, -ˈtrɒpɪk/ *adjective* exhibiting cytotropism; having an affinity for cells: **M20.** **cytotropism** /-ˈtrəʊp-/ *noun* the tendency of cells to move towards or (***negative cytotropism***) away from each other **E20.**

cytogenetics /ˌsʌɪtəʊdʒəˈnɛtɪks/ *noun.* **M20.**
[**ORIGIN** from **CYTO-** + **GENETICS.**]
BIOLOGY. The branch of science that deals with the behaviour and properties of chromosomes.
■ **cytogenetic** *adjective* †(**a**) of or pertaining to cell generation; (**b**) of or pertaining to cytogenetics: **L19.** **cytogenetical** *adjective* = **CYTOGENETIC** (b) **M20.** **cytogenetically** *adverb* **M20.** **cytogeneticist** /-sɪst/ *noun* **M20.**

cytoid /ˈsʌɪtɔɪd/ *adjective.* **L19.**
[**ORIGIN** formed as **CYTOGENETICS** + **-OID.**]
Resembling a living cell.

cytology /sʌɪˈtɒlədʒi/ *noun.* **L19.**
[**ORIGIN** formed as **CYTOGENETICS** + **-LOGY.**]
The science of the structure and functions of the cells of organisms.
■ **cytoˈlogic** *adjective* (chiefly *US*) = **CYTOLOGICAL M20.** **cytoˈlogical** *adjective* of or pertaining to cytology **L19.** **cytoˈlogically** *adverb* **E20.** **cytologist** *noun* **L19.**

cytophotometry /ˌsʌɪtəʊfəˈtɒmɪtri/ *noun.* **M20.**
[**ORIGIN** formed as **CYTOGENETICS** + **PHOTOMETRY.**]
BIOLOGY. The investigation of the contents of cells by measuring the light they allow through after staining.
■ **cytophoˈtometer** *noun* a photometer for use in cytophotometry **M20.** **cytophotoˈmetric** *adjective* **M20.** **cytophotoˈmetrically** *adverb* by means of cytophotometry **L20.**

cytoplasm /ˈsʌɪtəplaz(ə)m/ *noun.* **L19.**
[**ORIGIN** formed as **CYTOGENETICS** + **PLASMA.**]
BIOLOGY. The material contained within a cell, other than the nucleus.
■ **cytoˈplasmic** *adjective* of, pertaining to, or of the nature of cytoplasm **L19.**

cytosine /ˈsʌɪtəsiːn/ *noun.* **L19.**
[**ORIGIN** formed as **CYTOGENETICS** + **-OSE**[2] + **-INE**[5].]
BIOCHEMISTRY. A derivative of pyrimidine which is one of the bases of nucleic acids, paired with guanine in double-stranded DNA; 2-oxy-4-aminopyrimidine, $C_4H_5N_3O$.

cyul /kiːl/ *noun.* **E17.**
[**ORIGIN** Anglo-Latin *cyula* from Old English *cēol, ciol* **KEEL** *noun*[2].]
hist. A N. European sailing vessel or war galley of the period before the Norman Conquest.

czar *noun* var. of **TSAR.**

czardas *noun* var. of **CSARDAS.**

czarevich *noun* var. of **TSAREVICH.**

czarevna *noun* var. of **TSAREVNA.**

czarina *noun* var. of **TSARINA.**

czaritsa *noun* var. of **TSARITSA.**

Czech /tʃɛk/ *noun & adjective.* **E19.**
[**ORIGIN** Polish spelling of Czech *Čech* noun (cf. Czech *Čechy* Bohemia, *český* adjective, Bohemian).]
▸ **A** *noun.* **1** A native or inhabitant of the Czech Republic or (*hist.*) Czechoslovakia. **E19.**
2 The Slavonic language of the Czech Republic. **L19.**
▸ **B** *attrib.* or as *adjective.* Of or pertaining to the Czechs or their language. **E19.**

Czechoslovak /tʃɛkəʊˈsləʊvak/ *noun & adjective.* **E20.**
[**ORIGIN** formed as **CZECHOSLOVAKIAN**, after **SLOVAK.**]
= **CZECHOSLOVAKIAN.**

Czechoslovakian /ˌtʃɛkə(ʊ)sləˈvakɪən/ *noun & adjective.* **E20.**
[**ORIGIN** from *Czechoslovakia* (see below) + **-AN.**]
▸ **A** *noun.* A native or inhabitant of Czechoslovakia, a former state in central Europe comprising most of the territories of Bohemia, Moravia, and Slovakia. Also *loosely*, the Czech or Slovak language. **E20.**
▸ **B** *adjective.* Of or pertaining to Czechoslovakia or its peoples. **E20.**

Dd

D, d /diː/.
The fourth letter of the modern English alphabet and of the ancient Roman one, corresp. to Greek *delta*, Hebrew *daleth*. The sound normally represented by the letter is a voiced alveolar plosive consonant. Pl. **D's, Ds**. See also DEE *noun*.
▸**I 1** The letter and its sound.
2 The shape of the letter. ▸**b** BILLIARDS etc. The semicircle marked on the table in the baulk area, with its diameter part of the baulk line, from which a player must play after retrieving the cue ball by hand.
D-lock a D-shaped mechanism used to secure a parked bicycle or motorcycle, consisting of a U-shaped bar and crosspiece of solid metal. **D-ring** a D-shaped metal ring through which a strap etc. can pass. **D-shaped** *adjective* having a shape or a cross-section like the capital letter D.
▸**II** Symbolical uses.
3 Used to denote serial order; applied e.g. to the fourth group or section, sheet of a book, etc.
4 MUSIC. (Cap. D.) The second note of the diatonic scale of C major. Also, the scale of a composition with D as its keynote.
5 The fourth hypothetical person or example.
6 MATH. (Usu. italic *d*.) In calculus, used before variables to indicate a derivative, e.g. in *dy/dx*, the derivative of *y* with respect to *x*.
7 (Usu. cap. D.) Designating the fourth-highest class (of academic marks, population as regards affluence, etc.).
8 The roman numeral for 500. [Understood to be half of CIƆ, earlier form of M = 1,000.]
9 CHEMISTRY. Orig. italic *d*, now only as a small capital D: applied to (a compound having) a configuration about an asymmetric carbon atom analogous to that of an arbitrarily chosen compound (now D-glyceraldehyde for organic compounds). Also, as D(+), D(−), further denoting respectively dextro- or laevorotation of polarized light by the compound. [Extended use of *d* = dextrorotatory.]
10 ***D-layer***, the lowest stratum of the ionosphere.
▸**III 11** Abbrevs.: **D.** = (US) Democrat; Distinguished (in decorations); Doctor (in academic degrees). **D** = defence (in ***D notice***, an official request to British news editors not to publish items on specified subjects, for reasons of security); (CHEMISTRY) deuterium; dimension, dimensional, (esp. in ***3-D***, three-dimensions, -dimensional). **d.** = (*colloq.*) damn (*adjective & adverb*), damned; daughter; day; (*colloq.*) decent (esp. in ***jolly d.***); delete; departs; depth; deputy; died; (in former British currency) [Latin] *denarius*, *-rii* penny, pence. **d** = (as *prefix*) deci-; (CHEMISTRY) (as *prefix*) dextrorotatory (cf. sense 9 above); (PHYSICS & CHEMISTRY) diffuse: orig. designating one of the four main series (S, P, D, F) of lines in atomic spectra, now more frequently applied to electronic orbitals, states, etc., possessing two units of angular momentum (as ***d-electron***, ***d-orbital***, etc.); (PARTICLE PHYSICS) a quark flavour associated with a charge of −⅓ (cf. DOWN *adjective* 5).

'd *verb* see HAVE *verb*, WILL *verb*[1].

-d, -'d *suffixes* see -ED[1], -ED[2].

DA *abbreviation*[1].
1 Deposit account.
2 District Attorney. *US*.

da *abbreviation*[2].
(As *prefix*) deca-.

da /dɑː/ *noun*. *dial. & nursery*. M19.
[ORIGIN Abbreviation of DADA *noun*[1].]
Father. Cf. DAD *noun*[1], DADA *noun*[1].

d.a. *abbreviation*.
Duck's arse (haircut: see DUCK *noun*[1]).

D/A *abbreviation*.
COMPUTING. Digital to analogue.

DAB *abbreviation*.
Digital audio broadcasting.

dab /dab/ *noun*[1]. ME.
[ORIGIN from the verb.]
▸**I 1** A slight or undecided blow; a tap, a peck, a jab; *fig.* a slight or casual effort. ME.

> SMOLLETT Giving us several dabs with its beak. DICKENS Making two dabs at him in the air with her needle.

2 A gentle blow or tap with a soft substance; a brief application of a sponge, handkerchief, etc., to a surface without rubbing. M18.
3 A blob of some soft or moist substance dabbed or dropped on something; a small amount, a smear. M18. ▸**b** In *pl.* Fingerprints. *slang*. E20.

> WILL ROGERS I had . . half way decided to get a little dab of some kind of stock. E. WAUGH The clownish dabs of rouge high on the cheekbones. B. PYM Purple jelly with a dab of synthetic cream.

▸**II 4** A wet or dirty cloth or garment. *obsolete* exc. *dial.* E18.
5 An unfortunate or unkempt person; a small child. *obsolete* exc. *dial.* M18.

dab /dab/ *noun*[2]. LME.
[ORIGIN Unknown.]
Any of several small coastal flatfishes of the family Pleuronectidae; spec. *Limanda limanda*, common in British waters. Also, the flesh of these as food.

dab /dab/ *noun*[3]. *colloq.* L17.
[ORIGIN Unknown.]
An expert, one who is skilful or adept (*at*, occas. *in*). Also ***dab hand***.

dab /dab/ *verb*. Infl. **-bb-**. ME.
[ORIGIN Imit. Cf. DABBLE, DIB *verb*.]
1 *verb trans.* Strike lightly or undecidedly, hit feebly, pat, peck. ME.
2 *verb trans.* Press briefly with a cloth, sponge, etc., without rubbing; apply (a substance) in this manner. Also, daub, plaster. L16.

> J. TYNDALL I dip my brush . . . and dab it against the paper. V. WOOLF She walked about the room, dabbing her wet cheeks with a towel. L. LEE The porridge was dabbed on our plates from a . . spoon.

3 *verb trans.* Put down roughly or carelessly. Now *dial.* L18.
4 *verb intrans.* Aim a light or hesitant blow *at*; press gently *at*. Orig. *Scot.* E19.

> OED If you go near the nest, the hen will dab at you. F. TUOHY Mrs. Peverill drank some tea and dabbed at her mouth with a handkerchief.

■ **dabber** *noun* a person or thing which dabs; *spec.* a rounded pad used by printers etc. to apply ink, colour, etc., to a surface: L18.

dab /dab/ *adverb*. E17.
[ORIGIN from the verb.]
With a dab, abruptly; *colloq.* exactly, squarely.

dabble /ˈdab(ə)l/ *verb*. M16.
[ORIGIN Dutch †*dabbelen*, or from DAB *verb* + -LE[3].]
1 *verb trans.* Moisten or soil by sprinkling, splashing, or dipping into water or other liquid; move, splash (the hands, feet, etc.) in water etc. M16.

> T. TROLLOPE I dabbled a handkerchief in a neighbouring fountain. M. MITCHELL She . . dabbled her burning feet in the cool water.

2 *verb intrans.* Move the feet, hands, bill, etc., in shallow water; paddle. E17.

> WORDSWORTH Where the duck dabbles 'mid the rustling sedge.

dabbling duck any of the tribe Anatini of mostly freshwater ducks that habitually feed in shallow water by dabbling or upending, exemplified by the mallard, teal, shoveler, etc.
3 *verb intrans.* Engage *in* or work *at* a pursuit in a desultory manner. E17. ▸**b** Meddle, interfere. *obsolete* exc. *dial.* M17.

> D. L. SAYERS The idle rich gentleman who dabbles in detection.

■ **dabbler** *noun* a person or thing which dabbles; a dilettante: E17.

dabby /ˈdabi/ *adjective*. Now *dial.* L16.
[ORIGIN from DAB *noun*[1] + -Y[1].]
Damp, moist; (of clothes) wet and clinging.

dabchick /ˈdabtʃɪk/ *noun*. Also (*obsolete* exc. *dial.*) **dob-** /ˈdɒb-/, **dop-** /ˈdɒp-/, & other vars. M16.
[ORIGIN from *dab-* perh. rel. to 2nd elem. of DIVE-DAP (cogn. with DEEP *adjective*, DIP *verb*, DOP *verb*) + CHICK *noun*[1].]
The little grebe, *Tachybaptus ruficollis*; *US* the pied-billed grebe, *Podilymbus podiceps*. Also (*dial.*), the moorhen.

Dabitis /ˈdabɪtɪs/ *noun*. L16.
[ORIGIN Latin = you will give, taken as a mnemonic, A indicating a universal affirmative proposition and I a particular affirmative proposition.]
LOGIC. An indirect mood of the first syllogistic figure, in which the major premiss is universal and affirmative and the minor premiss and conclusion are particular and affirmative.

daboia /dəˈbɔɪə/ *noun*. L19.
[ORIGIN Hindi *daboyā* lit. 'lurker', from *dabnā* lurk.]
= RUSSELL'S VIPER.

dabster /ˈdabstə/ *noun*. E18.
[ORIGIN from DAB *noun*[3] or *noun*[1] + -STER.]
1 A person skilled at something, an expert. Chiefly *dial.* E18.
2 An incompetent or careless worker, a person who dabbles. L19.

da capo /dɑː ˈkɑːpəʊ/ *adverbial phr.* E18.
[ORIGIN Italian = from the beginning.]
MUSIC. A direction: repeat from the beginning.

dace /deɪs/ *noun*. Also †**darse**. Pl. same. LME.
[ORIGIN Old French *dars* nom. of *dart* dace (= DART *noun*). For loss of *r* cf. BASS *noun*[1]. Cf. DARE *noun*[1].]
A European freshwater cyprinoid fish, *Leuciscus leuciscus*; *US* any of several small cyprinoid fishes.

dacha /ˈdatʃə/ *noun*. Also **datcha**. M19.
[ORIGIN Russian = grant of land.]
In Russia: a small country house or villa.

dachs /daks/ *noun*. *colloq.* Pl. same. L19.
[ORIGIN Abbreviation.]
= DACHSHUND.

dachshund /ˈdakshʊnd, -s(ə)nd/ *noun*. L19.
[ORIGIN German = badger-dog.]
An animal of a German breed of dog with short legs and a long body, orig. used to hunt badgers.

Dacian /ˈdeɪʃ(ə)n, -sjən/ *noun & adjective*. L16.
[ORIGIN from *Dacia* (see below) + -AN.]
▸**A** *noun*. A native or inhabitant of Dacia, an ancient Roman province containing the Carpathian Mountains and Transylvania; the language of this region, a Thracian dialect. L16.
▸**B** *adjective*. Of or pertaining to Dacia, its people, or their language. L18.

dacite /ˈdeɪsʌɪt/ *noun*. L18.
[ORIGIN formed as DACIAN + -ITE[1].]
GEOLOGY. A volcanic rock resembling andesite but containing free quartz.
■ **dacitic** /-ˈsɪtɪk/ *adjective* of the nature of or containing dacite M20.

dacker /ˈdakə/ *verb*. *Scot. & N. English*. Also **daiker** /ˈdeɪkə/. L16.
[ORIGIN Unknown: perh. two words. In branch II cf. Middle Flemish *daeckeren*.]
▸**I 1** *verb trans. & intrans.* Search, ransack; search for or *for*. L16.
▸**II 2** *verb intrans.* Waver, totter, stagger; saunter; work irregularly, potter. M17.

dacoit /dəˈkɔɪt/ *noun & verb*. L18.
[ORIGIN Hindi *ḍakait*, from *ḍākā* gang-robbery.]
▸**A** *noun*. A member of an Indian or Myanmar (Burmese) band of armed robbers. L18.
▸**B** *verb trans. & intrans.* Plunder as a dacoit. L19.
■ **dacoity** *noun* [Hindi *ḍakaitī*] (an act of) robbery with violence committed by dacoits E19.

Dacron /ˈdakrɒn, ˈdeɪ-/ *noun*. Also **d-**. M20.
[ORIGIN Invented name: cf. NYLON.]
(Proprietary name for) polyethylene terephthalate used as a textile fabric.
– NOTE: Another proprietary name for this substance is TERYLENE.

dacryo- /ˈdakrɪəʊ/ *combining form* of Greek *dakruon* tear: see -O-.
Used in MEDICINE.
■ **dacryoadeˈnalgia** *noun* pain in a lacrimal gland M19. **dacryoadeˈnitis** *noun* inflammation of a lacrimal gland M19. **dacryocyˈstitis** *noun* inflammation of a tear-sac M19.

dacryon /ˈdakrɪɒn/ *noun*. L19.
[ORIGIN Greek *dakruon* tear.]
ANATOMY. In the cranium, the point of juncture of the lacrimal and frontal bones with the frontal process of the maxilla.

dactyl /ˈdaktɪl/ *noun*. LME.
[ORIGIN Latin *dactylus* from Greek *daktulos* finger, date, dactyl (from its three joints).]
1 PROSODY. A metrical foot consisting of one long syllable followed by two short syllables, or, in English etc., of one stressed syllable followed by two unstressed syllables; a verse composed of or containing such feet. LME.

> J. GALSWORTHY 'This young Bösinney' (he made the word a dactyl in opposition to general usage of a short o) 'has got nothing.'

†**2** A date (fruit). LME–M17.
3 A terminal part of a jointed claw, limb, etc.; *rare* a digit. L19.

dactylic /dakˈtɪlɪk/ *adjective & noun*. L16.
[ORIGIN Latin *dactylicus* from Greek *daktulikos*, from *daktulos*: see DACTYL, -IC.]
PROSODY. ▸**A** *adjective*. Composed of or containing dactyls; of or pertaining to a dactyl or dactyls. L16.
dactylic hexameter: see HEXAMETER.
▸**B** *noun*. A dactylic verse or line. Usu. in *pl.* L18.

■ **dactylically** *adverb* L19.

dactylio- /dak'tɪlɪəʊ/ *combining form* of Greek *daktulios* ring: see -O-.

■ **dactyliomancy** *noun* divination by means of a finger ring E17.

dactylo- /'daktɪləʊ/ *combining form* of Greek *daktulos* finger: see -O-.

■ **dactylogram** *noun* a fingerprint E20. **dactylographer** /-'lɒgrəfə/ *noun* (*a*) a person who takes or studies fingerprints; (*b*) *rare* a typist: E20. **dactylology** /-'lɒlədʒi/ *noun* the art of communicating by signs made with the fingers M17. **dactylopodite** /-'lɒpədʌɪt/ *noun* (ZOOLOGY) the terminal joint of a crustacean limb L19. **dactyloscopy** /-'lɒskəpi/ *noun* the examination of fingerprints E20. **dactylo'zooid** *noun* (ZOOLOGY) a mouthless cylindrical zooid in some hydrozoans L19.

dad /dad/ *noun*[1]. M16.
[ORIGIN Perh. imit. of infants' first speech: cf. DADA *noun*[1], DADDY.]
1 Father. Freq. as a form of address or reference. *colloq.* M16.

HELEN FIELDING I'm really looking forward to Daniel meeting my dad.

2 Used as a form of address to a man other than one's father. *slang* (esp. JAZZ). M20.

dad /dad/ *noun*[2] & *interjection. colloq.* (now chiefly *US*). L17.
[ORIGIN Alt.: cf. DOD *noun*[3] & *interjection*.]
God: used in oaths and exclamations.

dad /dad/ *verb* & *noun*[3]. *Scot.* & *N. English.* Also **daud**. L16.
[ORIGIN Imit.: cf. DOD *verb*[2].]
▸ **A** *verb trans.* Infl. **dadd-**. Knock, beat; shake with knocking or beating. L16.
▸ **B** *noun.* **1** A knock, a thump. E18.
2 A large piece, a lump. L18.

dada /'dadə/ *noun*[1]. *colloq.* (*nursery*). L17.
[ORIGIN formed as DAD *noun*[1].]
Father.

D. BOLGER Waiting for dada to put out the gas lamp in his room.

Dada /'dɑːdɑː/ *noun*[2] & *adjective.* Also **d-**. E20.
[ORIGIN French, title of a review first appearing at Zürich in 1916, lit. 'hobby horse'.]
(Of, pertaining to, or designating) an international movement in art and literature about 1915–20, which repudiated conventions and reason and intended to shock.
■ **Dadaism** *noun* the theory or practice of Dada E20. **Dadaist** *noun* & *adjective* (*a*) *noun* an adherent or practitioner of Dada; (*b*) *adjective* of or pertaining to Dadaism or Dadaists: E20.

†**da-da** *interjection. nursery* & *colloq.* L17–M18.
[ORIGIN Unknown: cf. TA-TA.]
Goodbye.

dadah /'dɑːdɑː/ *noun.* L20.
[ORIGIN Malay = medicine, drugs.]
In Malaysia: illegal drugs.

dadder /'dadə/ *verb intrans.* Long *obsolete* exc. *dial.* LME.
[ORIGIN from obscure 1st elem. + -ER[5]. Cf. DADE, DODDER *verb*, DIDDER *verb*, DITHER *verb*.]
Quake, tremble.

daddle /'dad(ə)l/ *noun. dial.* L18.
[ORIGIN Unknown.]
The hand, the fist.

daddle /'dad(ə)l/ *verb intrans. dial.* Also (*Scot.* & *N. English*) **daidle** /'deɪd(ə)l/. L18.
[ORIGIN from 1st elem. of DADDER + -LE[3]. Cf. DAWDLE *verb*, DODDLE *verb*.]
Walk unsteadily, like a small child; dawdle.

daddy /'dadi/ *noun.* E16.
[ORIGIN formed as DAD *noun*[1] + -Y[6]. Cf. also DADA *noun*[1].]
1 Father. Freq. as a form of address or reference. *colloq.* E16.

O. NASH Are we there yet, Daddy? Z. SMITH He's just found out he's going to be a daddy.

2 A man; a man in charge; (*US*, chiefly JAZZ) a husband, a woman's lover. Also **daddy-o**. Chiefly *voc. slang.* M19.

B. BEHAN He was the daddy of the wing and what he claimed was his.

sugar daddy: see SUGAR *noun*.
3 The doyen *of*; a superlative example *of. colloq.* E20.

M. FRANKLIN I never felt such a daddy of a thirst on me before.

– COMB.: **daddy-long-legs** *colloq.* (*a*) a crane fly; (*b*) (chiefly *US*) a long-legged spider, a harvestman.

dade /deɪd/ *verb trans.* Long *obsolete* exc. *dial.* L16.
[ORIGIN 1st elem. of DADDER.]
Lead and support (a person who totters, esp. a child learning to walk).

dado /'deɪdəʊ/ *noun.* Pl. **-os**. M17.
[ORIGIN Italian = die, cube, from Latin *datum*: see DIE *noun*[1].]
ARCHITECTURE. **1** The plain portion of a pedestal between the base and the cornice. Cf. DIE *noun*[1] 3. M17.
2 The lower part of an interior wall when faced or coloured differently from the upper part. L18.
– COMB.: **dado rail** a moulding round the wall of a room to protect it from damage by furniture pushed against it.

dae *verb* see DO *verb*.

daedal /'diːd(ə)l/ *noun. rare.* Also **ded-**. M17.
[ORIGIN Latin *Daedalus*: see DAEDALIAN.]
1 A skilful or ingenious artificer like Daedalus. M17.
2 A maze, a labyrinth. L17.

daedal /'diːd(ə)l/ *adjective. literary.* Also **ded-**. L16.
[ORIGIN Latin *daedalus* from Greek *daidalos* skilful, variegated.]
1 Skilful, inventive, ingenious. L16.
2 Of the earth etc.: rich in natural wonders; variously adorned. L16.
3 Complex, intricate; like a maze. M17.

Daedalian /dɪ'deɪlɪən/ *adjective.* Also **Ded-**, **-ean**. L16.
[ORIGIN Sense 1 formed as DAEDAL *adjective*; sense 2 from Latin *Daedaleus*, Greek *daidaleos*, from *Daedalus* (Greek *Daidalos*), legendary builder of the Cretan labyrinth, and maker of wings for himself and Icarus: see -IAN, -EAN.]
†**1** = DAEDAL *adjective* 2. Only in L16.
2 In the manner of Daedalus; ingenious, intricate, labyrinthine. E17.

Daedalic /'diːdəlɪk/ *adjective.* Also **Ded-**. M20.
[ORIGIN formed as DAEDAL *adjective* + -IC.]
ARCHAEOLOGY. Designating or pertaining to a Greek (chiefly Dorian) sculptural style of the 7th cent. BC.

daemon *noun*[1]. Also **daimon**. M16.
[ORIGIN Greek *daimōn*: see DEMON *noun*[1].]
1 GREEK MYTHOLOGY. A divinity or supernatural being of a nature between gods and humans, = DEMON *noun*[1] 3. M16.

SHAKES. *Ant. & Cl.* Antony . . Thy dæmon . . is Noble, courageous, high, unmatchable.

2 An inner or attendant spirit or inspiring force, = DEMON *noun*[1] 2. E17.

J. BRYANT Subordinate daemons, which they supposed to be emanations and derivatives from their chief Deity.

3 arch. var. of DEMON *noun*[1]. M18.
■ **daemonic** /-məʊnɪk, -mɒnɪk/ *adjective* L18.

daemon /'diːmən/ *noun*[2]. Also **demon**. L20.
[ORIGIN Perh. from *d(isk) a(nd) e(xecution) mon(itor)* or from *de(vice) mon(itor)*, or merely a transf. use of DEMON *noun*[1].]
COMPUTING. A background process that handles requests for services such as print spooling and file transfers, and is dormant when not required.

daemonic *adjective*, **daemonism** *noun*, etc., see DEMONIC, DEMONISM, etc.

dafadar /dʌfə'dɑː/ *noun. obsolete* exc. *hist.* Also **duff-**. E19.
[ORIGIN Persian & Urdu *daf'adār*.]
A non-commissioned officer in the British Indian army or police.

daff /daf/ *noun*[1]. Now *N. English.* ME.
[ORIGIN Uncertain: cf. DAFT.]
A person deficient in sense or spirit; a simpleton; a coward.

daff /daf/ *noun*[2]. *colloq.* E20.
[ORIGIN Abbreviation.]
= DAFFODIL 2.

daff /daf/ *verb*[1]. M16.
[ORIGIN from DAFF *noun*[1].]
1 *verb intrans.* Play the fool. Chiefly *Scot.* M16.
2 *verb trans.* Daunt. *N. English.* L17.

daff /dɑːf/ *verb*[2] *trans. arch.* L16.
[ORIGIN Var. of DOFF.]
†**1** Put off (as clothes); divest oneself of. *rare* (Shakes.). L16–E17.
2 Put or turn aside; waive. L16. ▸†**b** Put off (with an excuse etc.). *rare* (Shakes.). Only in E17.

SHAKES. *1 Hen. IV* The . . Prince of Wales, And his comrades that daff'd the world aside And bid it pass.

daffadowndilly /dafədaʊn'dɪli/ *noun.* Chiefly *dial.* & *joc.* L16.
[ORIGIN Playful extension of DAFFODIL: cf. DAFFODILLY.]
= DAFFODIL 2.

daffle /'daf(ə)l/ *verb intrans. dial.* & *colloq.* L18.
[ORIGIN from DAFF *verb*[1] + -LE[3].]
Become silly; act stupidly; falter.

daffodil /'dafədɪl/ *noun.* M16.
[ORIGIN Alt. of AFFODILL. The initial *d* is unexpl.]
†**1** = ASPHODEL. M16–E17.
2 A narcissus, *esp.* one with yellow flowers; *spec.* a western European plant, *Narcissus pseudonarcissus*, native in woods etc. and widely cultivated, having a bright yellow corona as long as the perianth segments (cf. NARCISSUS 1); a flower or flowering stem of such a plant, esp. as the Welsh national emblem. M16.
3 The colour of the daffodil; (bright) yellow. Freq. *attrib.* M19.
■ **daffodilly** *noun* (*poet.* & *dial.*) = DAFFODIL 1, 2 M16.

Daffy /'dafi/ *noun*[1]. *arch.* Also **d-**. L17.
[ORIGIN Thomas *Daffy* (d. 1680), English clergyman.]
In full ***Daffy's elixir***. Orig., a medicine given to infants to which gin was commonly added. Later (*slang*), gin itself.

daffy /'dafi/ *noun*[2]. *colloq.* (orig. *dial.*). L18.
[ORIGIN Abbreviation of DAFFODILLY.]
= DAFFODIL 2.

daffy /'dafi/ *adjective. dial.* & *slang.* L19.
[ORIGIN from DAFF *noun*[1] or *verb*[1] + -Y[1].]
Silly; mildly eccentric.

F. KIDMAN 'Don't be silly sweetheart,' Hester said, in a fond daffy voice.

daft /dɑːft/ *adjective.* See also DEFT.
[ORIGIN Old English *gedæfte* from Germanic, from stem also of Gothic *gadaban* become, be fitting.]
†**1** Mild, meek, humble. OE–ME.
2 Silly; lacking in intelligence; stupid; reckless, wild. ME.

D. LODGE This was not . . quite such a daft development as it seems on first consideration.

daft as a brush: see BRUSH *noun*[2] 3.
3 Of unsound mind; crazy. LME.

T. ARNOLD I hope you will not think I ought to . . adjourn to the next asylum for daft people.

4 Madly frolicsome; giddy. *Scot.* L16.

SIR W. SCOTT Ay, ay—they were daft days thae—but they were a' vanity and waur.

■ **daftie** *noun* (*colloq.*) a daft person L19. **daftly** *adverb* E18. **daftness** *noun* M16.

dag /dag/ *noun*[1]. LME.
[ORIGIN Unknown: cf. TAG *noun*[1].]
†**1** A pendent pointed portion of something; a pointed ornamental division made in the lower edge of a garment. LME–E17.
†**2** = AGLET *noun* 1, 2. LME–E17.
3 In full ***dag-lock***. A lock of wool clotted with dung about the hind legs of a sheep. Usu. in *pl.* Now chiefly *Austral.* & *NZ.* E17.
rattle one's dags *Austral.* & *NZ slang* hurry up.
4 a An extraordinary person; a character; a tough but amusing person. *Austral.* & *NZ slang.* L19. ▸**b** An extraordinary or amusing situation or event. *NZ slang.* M20.
5 A socially inept or awkward person, esp. one who is staid or unfashionable; also as a general term of abuse. *Austral. slang.* M20.
– COMB.: **dag-boy** etc.: employed to remove dags from wool or sheep; ***dag-lock***: see sense 3 above.
■ **daggy** *adjective* (*a*) (chiefly *Austral.* & *NZ*) (of a sheep or wool) clotted with dags; (*b*) (*Austral. slang*) unfashionable, awkward, unattractive: L19.

dag /dag/ *noun*[2]. LME.
[ORIGIN Old French & mod. French *dague* lit. 'long dagger', from Provençal or Italian *daga*.]
1 A metal pin, bolt, etc.; a pointed implement. LME.
2 The simple straight pointed horn of a young stag. M19.

dag /dag/ *noun*[3]. Orig. *Scot. obsolete* exc. *hist.* M16.
[ORIGIN Gaelic, of unknown origin.]
A kind of heavy pistol or handgun.

dag /dag/ *verb*[1]. Infl. **-gg-**. LME.
[ORIGIN Rel. to or from DAG *noun*[1].]
1 *verb trans.* Cut the edge of (a garment) into jags; slash. Long *rare.* LME.
2 *verb trans.* Clog with dirt; bemire. Now *dial.* L15. ▸**b** *verb intrans.* Trail in the dirt or wet. *dial.* M19.
3 *verb trans.* Cut the dags from (sheep). Chiefly *Austral.* & *NZ.* E18.

†**dag** *verb*[2] *trans.* Infl. **-gg-**. LME–E19.
[ORIGIN Rel. to Old French & mod. French *dague* DAG *noun*[2].]
Pierce or stab (as) with a pointed weapon.

dageraad /'dagərɑːd/ *noun. S. Afr.* Also **daggerhead** /'dagəhɛd/. M19.
[ORIGIN Afrikaans from Dutch = daybreak (from its colour).]
A brilliantly coloured marine fish, *Chrysoblephus cristiceps*, of the family Sparidae.

dagesh /'dɑːgɛʃ/ *noun* & *verb.* M16.
[ORIGIN Hebrew *dāgēš*.]
HEBREW GRAMMAR. ▸**A** *noun.* A point or dot placed within a Hebrew letter, denoting either that it is doubled or that it is not aspirated. M16.
▸ **B** *verb trans.* Mark with a dagesh. M18.

Dagestan /dɑːgə'stɑːn/ *noun.* Also **-gh-**. E20.
[ORIGIN A district of the eastern Caucasus.]
In full ***Dagestan rug***. A rug with a geometric design, handwoven in Dagestan.

dagga /'dagə/ *noun*[1]. *S. Afr.* L17.
[ORIGIN Afrikaans from Nama *daχa*.]
Cannabis used as a narcotic; any indigenous plant of the genus *Leonotis* which is similarly used (also ***wild dagga***).

dagga /'dɑːgə/ *noun*[2]. *S. Afr.* L19.
[ORIGIN Zulu, Xhosa *udaka* mud, clay, mortar.]
A kind of mortar made of mud and cow dung, often combined with ox blood.

dagger /'dagə/ *noun*[1] & *verb.* LME.
[ORIGIN Perh. from DAG *verb*[2] + -ER[1], infl. by Old French & mod. French *dague* (see DAG *noun*[2]).]
▸ **A** *noun.* **1** A short stabbing weapon with a pointed and edged blade. LME. ▸**b** Something that wounds grievously. L16.

D

D

2 Chiefly *NAUTICAL*. A piece of wood standing upright or aslant. Also = ***dogshore*** s.v. DOG *noun*. **M17.**
3 *TYPOGRAPHY*. A mark resembling a dagger (†); an obelisk. **E18.**
4 Any of a number of noctuid moths chiefly of the genus *Apatele* with a dark marking in the shape of a dagger on the forewings. **M19.**
– PHRASES: **at daggers drawn** on the point of fighting, in bitter enmity, (*with*). **double dagger** a mark like a dagger but with a second crosspiece near the foot (‡). **look daggers** stare angrily (*at* a person). ***Spanish dagger***: see SPANISH *adjective*. †**speak daggers** speak angrily or woundingly. ***wooden dagger***: see WOODEN *adjective*.
– COMB.: **daggerboard** *NAUTICAL* a sliding centreboard; **dagger plant** a yucca, *Y. aloifolia*, having sharp-edged and pointed leaves.
▸ **B** *verb trans.* Stab with a dagger. **M16.**
■ **daggered** *adjective* armed with a dagger **LME.**

dagger /ˈdaɡə/ *noun*[2]. *Austral. & NZ.* **L19.**
[ORIGIN from DAG *noun*[1] + -ER[1].]
1 A person who removes dags from wool. **L19.**
2 In *pl.* Hand shears. **L19.**

daggerhead *noun* var. of DAGERAAD.

daggett /ˈdaɡɪt/ *noun*. **M19.**
[ORIGIN Russian *dëgot'* tar.]
A dark oil obtained by distilling birch bark, used in the preparation of Russia leather.

daggle /ˈdaɡ(ə)l/ *verb*. Now chiefly *dial.* **M16.**
[ORIGIN Frequentative of DAG *verb*[1]: see -LE[3].]
1 *verb trans.* Orig., clog with wet mud; wet and soil (a garment etc.) by trailing through mud etc. Later, wet by splashing etc. **M16.**
2 *verb trans. & intrans.* Drag or trail about (through mud etc.). **L17.**
– COMB.: **daggle-tail** *noun* = DRAGGLE-TAIL *noun*; **daggle-tailed** *adjective* = DRAGGLE-TAILED.
■ **daggly** *adjective* (esp. of the weather) wet **L18.**

Daghestan *noun* var. of DAGESTAN.

dago /ˈdeɪɡəʊ/ *noun*. *slang* (*derog. & offensive*). Orig. *US*. Pl. **-o(e)s. M19.**
[ORIGIN Alt. of Spanish DIEGO.]
1 A Spaniard; a Portuguese; an Italian; any foreigner. **M19.**
2 The Spanish language; the Italian language. **E20.**
– COMB.: **dago red** *US* cheap red wine, esp. from Italy.

dagoba /ˈdɑːɡəʊbə/ *noun*. **E19.**
[ORIGIN Sinhalese *dāgaba* from Pali *dhātu-gabbha* receptacle for relics.]
A stupa or dome-shaped structure containing Buddhist relics.

Dagon /ˈdeɪɡɒn/ *noun*. **LME.**
[ORIGIN Latin from Greek *Dagōn* from Hebrew *dāgōn*, perh. from *dāgān* corn, but derived by folk etym. from *dāg* fish.]
The national god of the ancient Philistines, prob. a corn god, but later represented with the head, chest, and arms of a man, and the tail of a fish.

Daguerrean /dəˈɡɛrɪən/ *adjective*. Also **-eian. M19.**
[ORIGIN from *Daguerre* (see DAGUERREOTYPE) + -AN.]
Pertaining to Daguerre or the daguerreotype. Also (now *rare* or *obsolete*), photographic.

daguerreotype /dəˈɡɛrə(ʊ)taɪp/ *noun & verb*. Also **-rro-. M19.**
[ORIGIN French *daguerréotype*, from Louis-Jacques-Mandé *Daguerre* (1789–1851), the inventor: see -O-, -TYPE.]
▸ **A** *noun*. (A photograph taken by) an early photographic process using an iodine-sensitized silver(ed) plate and mercury vapour. **M19.**
▸ **B** *verb trans.* Photograph by the daguerreotype process. **M19.**

Dagwood /ˈdaɡwʊd/ *noun*. *N. Amer.* **L20.**
[ORIGIN *Dagwood* Bumstead, comic-strip character who makes and eats such sandwiches.]
In full ***Dagwood sandwich***. A thick sandwich filled with mixed meats and cheeses with a variety of seasonings and dressings.

dah /dɑː/ *noun*[1]. Also **dao** /daʊ/. **M19.**
[ORIGIN Burmese.]
A short heavy sword, used also as a knife, esp. in Myanmar (Burma).

dah /dɑː/ *noun*[2]. **M20.**
[ORIGIN Imit.]
= DASH *noun*[1] 2c.

dahabeeyah /dɑːhəˈbiːjə/ *noun*. Also **-biah. M19.**
[ORIGIN Arabic *dahabīya* = golden (*sc.* boat), orig. the gilded state barge of the Muslim rulers of Egypt.]
A large sailing boat, used on the Nile.

dahlia /ˈdeɪlɪə/ *noun*. **E19.**
[ORIGIN from Andreas *Dahl* (1751–89), Swedish botanist + -IA[1].]
1 Any of various Central American plants of the genus *Dahlia*, of the composite family, many of which (esp. *D. pinnata*) are cultivated for their many-coloured single or double flowers. **E19.**
blue dahlia: see BLUE *adjective*.
2 A shade of red. **M19.**

Dahoman /dəˈhəʊmən/ *noun & adjective*. *hist.* Also **-mean** /-mɪən/. **L18.**
[ORIGIN from *Dahomey* (see below) or the tribal name *Dahomeh* + -AN.]
▸**A** *noun*. A member of the people of the former W. African kingdom of Dahomey, or of the modern state of Dahomey (now called Benin), occupying much of the former territory. **L18.**
▸ **B** *adjective*. Of or pertaining to Dahomey, its people, or their language. **L18.**

dai /dʌɪ, ˈdɑːi/ *noun*. **L18.**
[ORIGIN Urdu *dāī*, from Persian *dāyah*.]
In the Indian subcontinent and Iran: a nurse, wet nurse, or midwife.

daidle *verb* see DADDLE *verb*.

daiker *noun* var. of DAKER.

Dáil /dɔɪl/ *noun*. **E20.**
[ORIGIN Irish *Dáil (Éireann)* assembly (of Ireland).]
In full ***Dáil Éireann*** /ˈɛːr(ə)n/. The lower house of the Parliament of the Republic of Ireland.

daily /ˈdeɪli/ *adjective & noun*. **LME.**
[ORIGIN from DAY *noun* + -LY[1]: cf. Old English *-dæġlic*.]
▸ **A** *adjective*. Of or belonging to each day; produced, occurring, or working on every day or weekday. **LME.**

T. HEARNE A Daily paper comes out call'd The Spectator.

daily bread: see BREAD *noun*[1]. ***daily dozen***: see DOZEN *noun* 1.
▸ **B** *noun*. **1** A daily newspaper. **M19.**
2 Daily bread; food; livelihood. *rare*. **E20.**
3 A domestic cleaner or charwoman who comes in daily. **M20.**
4 In *pl.* The first prints from cinematographic takes, made rapidly for film producers or editors; the rushes. **M20.**
■ **dailiness** *noun* daily quality or occurrence; humdrum routine: **L16.**

daily /ˈdeɪli/ *adverb*. **LME.**
[ORIGIN from DAY *noun* + -LY[2].]
Every day or weekday; day-by-day; constantly.

W. HUTTON Three-quarters of a million contracts are bought and sold daily.

daimio *noun* var. of DAIMYO.

daimon /ˈdʌɪməʊn/ *noun* var. of DAEMON *noun*[1].

daimyo /ˈdʌɪmɪəʊ, -mjəʊ/ *noun*. Also **-io**. Pl. **-os. E18.**
[ORIGIN Japanese, from *dai* great + *myō* name.]
In feudal Japan, any of the chief land-owning nobles, vassals of the shogun.

†**daint** *adjective & noun*. **L16–M17.**
[ORIGIN Abbreviation.]
= DAINTY *adjective*, *noun*.
■ †**daintly** *adverb* **M–L16.**

dainteth /ˈdeɪntɪθ/ *noun*. Long *obsolete* exc. *Scot.* Now *rare*. Also **-ith. ME.**
[ORIGIN Old French *deintiet* older form of *deintié* DAINTY *noun*.]
= DAINTY *noun*.

daintify /ˈdeɪntɪfʌɪ/ *verb trans.* **L18.**
[ORIGIN from DAINTY *adjective* + -FY.]
Make dainty.

daintihood /ˈdeɪntɪhʊd/ *noun*. *rare*. **L18.**
[ORIGIN from DAINTY *adjective* + -HOOD.]
Daintiness.

daintily /ˈdeɪntɪli/ *adverb*. **ME.**
[ORIGIN from DAINTY *adjective* + -LY[2].]
†**1** Excellently; finely; handsomely; delightfully. **ME–M17.**
2 In a dainty manner; delicately; nicely; elegantly; deftly. **LME.**

SHAKES. *Tit. A.* Why, there they are, both baked in this pie, Whereof their mother daintily hath fed. J. L. WATEN Our piebald mare . . trotted easily and daintily.

†**3** Rarely; sparingly. **L15–L16.**

daintiness /ˈdeɪntɪnɪs/ *noun*. **M16.**
[ORIGIN from DAINTY *adjective* + -NESS.]
1 The quality of being fine, handsome, delightful etc. Now only of food: choiceness. **M16.**
2 Niceness; fastidiousness; delicacy. **M16.**
3 Elegance; neatness; deftness. **L16.**

daintith *noun* var. of DAINTETH.

dainty /ˈdeɪnti/ *noun*. **ME.**
[ORIGIN Anglo-Norman *dainté*, Old French *daintié*, *deintié* from Latin *dignitas* worthiness, worth, beauty, from *dignus* worthy: see -TY[1].]
▸ **I** †**1** Estimation, regard; affection. **ME–E16.**
†**2** Choice quality, sumptuousness. Only in **ME.**
†**3** Liking *to do* or *see* something; delight. **ME–E16.**
†**4** Fastidiousness. Only in **L16.**
▸ **II 5** Something choice or pleasing, *esp.* something pleasing to the palate, a delicacy. **ME.**

dainty /ˈdeɪnti/ *adjective & adverb*. **ME.**
[ORIGIN from DAINTY *noun*.]
▸ **A** *adjective*. **1** Handsome; choice; delightful. Now chiefly *dial.* **ME.**

CHAUCER Full many a deynte hors hadde he in stable.

2 Pleasing to the palate. **LME.**

MILTON The daintiest dishes shall be serv'd up last.

3 (Now the predominant sense.) Of delicate beauty; small and graceful. **LME.**
†**4** Precious; rare; scarce. **LME–L17.**
5 Of a person: having delicate tastes or sensitivities; fastidious, particular; (over)nice. **M16.**

SHAKES. *Macb.* And let us not be dainty of leave-taking, But shift away. R. L. STEVENSON I was surprised to find them so dainty in their notions.

▸ **B** *adverb*. Daintily. *rare*. **E17.**

daiquiri /ˈdʌɪkɪri, ˈdak-/ *noun*. **E20.**
[ORIGIN *Daiquiri*, a rum-producing district in Cuba.]
A cocktail containing rum and lime juice.

dairi /ˈdʌɪri/ *noun*. *arch.* **E17.**
[ORIGIN Japanese = (palace of the) emperor, from *dai* inside + *ri* within.]
The emperor of Japan.

dairy /ˈdɛːri/ *noun & verb*. **ME.**
[ORIGIN from DEY *noun*[1] + -ERY, -RY.]
▸ **A** *noun*. **1** A room or building for keeping milk and cream and making butter, cheese, etc.; a shop for milk etc.; a company that distributes milk etc.; *NZ* a local shop selling groceries (including milk) and other goods. **ME.**
2 A dairy farm; that department of a farm or farming which is concerned with the production of milk etc. **ME.**
– COMB.: **dairy cattle**, **dairy cow**, etc.: kept for milk production; **dairy cream** real cream made from milk; **dairy factory** (chiefly *NZ*): for making butter and cheese; **dairy farm**, **dairy farming**: concerned largely with the keeping of cows for milk production; **dairy-free** *adjective* containing no milk product; **dairymaid** a woman employed in a dairy; **dairyman** (***a***) a man employed in a dairy or in dairy farming; (***b***) a man who deals in dairy products; **dairy products** milk and its derivatives (cream, butter, cheese, etc.).
▸ **B** *verb*. **1** *verb intrans.* Keep a dairy farm; produce milk and dairy products. Chiefly as ***dairying*** *verbal noun*. **M17.**
2 *verb trans.* Keep or feed (cows) for milk. *rare*. **L18.**

dais /ˈdeɪɪs, deɪs/ *noun*. Also (*Scot.*) **deas** /*also* diːs/. **ME.**
[ORIGIN Old French *deis* (mod. *dais*) from medieval Latin DISCUS table.]
†**1** A raised table in a hall, at which distinguished persons sat at feasts etc.; the high table. **ME–L16.**
2 The raised platform in a hall etc. for the high table, seats of honour, throne, etc. **ME.** ▸**b** *gen.* A raised platform. **M19.**
chamber of dais: see CHAMBER *noun* 1.
3 A seat; a bench; a settle. *Scot. & N. English.* **ME.**
– NOTE: In sense 2 largely obsolete for several centuries until revived by historical and antiquarian writers *c* 1800, with the disyllabic pronunciation.

daisy /ˈdeɪzi/ *noun*, *adjective*, *& verb*.
[ORIGIN Old English *dæġes ēage* day's eye, the disc of the flower being revealed in the morning.]
▸ **A** *noun*. **1** A small European wild and garden plant of the composite family, *Bellis perennis*, with a flower of yellow disc and white rays (also ***common daisy***). Also, a flower head or flowering stem of this plant; a flower head resembling that of the daisy. **OE.**
fresh as a daisy: see FRESH *adjective*. **pushing up the daisies** *slang* dead and buried.
2 (A flowering stem of) any of various similar plants. Usu. with specifying word. **LME.**
African daisy, ***Michaelmas daisy***, ***moon-daisy***, ***ox-eye daisy***, ***Shasta daisy***, etc.
3 A first-rate person or thing. (Earlier as sense B.2.) *US slang*. **M19.**
– COMB.: **daisy bush** a shrub of the Australasian genus *Olearia*, of the composite family; **daisy chain** *noun & verb* (***a***) *noun* a string of daisies with the stems threaded together; *fig.* a linked series of persons or things; (***b***) *verb intrans. & trans.* form into a linked series; **daisy-cutter** (***a***) a horse that steps low in trotting; (***b***) (*CRICKET* etc.) a bowled ball that travels low along the ground (cf. CREEPER 5); (***c***) an immensely powerful aerial thermobaric bomb; **daisy roots** *rhyming slang* boots; **daisy tree** = ***daisy bush*** above; **daisy wheel** a circular element in some electric printers, typewriters, etc., which carries the type on radiating spokes.
▸ **B** *attrib.* or as *adjective*. **1** Resembling a daisy. **E17.**
2 First-rate, excellent. *slang* (chiefly *US*). **M18.**

E. WALLACE I'll introduce you to the daisiest night club in town.

▸ **C** *verb trans.* Cover or adorn with daisies. Chiefly as ***daisied*** *ppl adjective*. **E17.**
■ **daisy-like** *adjective* resembling (that of) a daisy **L19.**

dak /dɑːk, dɔːk/ *noun*. Also **dawk. E18.**
[ORIGIN Hindi *ḍāk*.]
In the Indian subcontinent: orig., post or transport by relays; now, postal service, delivery of letters, mail.
– COMB.: **dak bungalow** a travellers' resting house, orig. one on a dak route.

Dak. *abbreviation*.
Dakota.

daker /ˈdeɪkə/ *noun*. Also **daiker. LME.**
[ORIGIN Old French *dacre*, *dakere*, medieval Latin *dacra* var. of *dicra*: see DICKER *noun*[1].]
hist. = DICKER *noun*[1] 1.

daker-hen /ˈdeɪkəhɛn/ *noun. dial.* M16.
[ORIGIN Unknown.]
The corncrake.

dakhma /ˈdɑːkmə/ *noun.* M19.
[ORIGIN Persian.]
= *tower of silence* s.v. TOWER *noun*[1].

Dakin /ˈdeɪkɪn/ *noun.* E20.
[ORIGIN H. D. *Dakin* (1880–1952), Brit. chemist.]
MEDICINE. ***Dakin's fluid, Dakin's solution***, an antiseptic solution of sodium hypochlorite.

Dakota /dəˈkəʊtə/ *noun & adjective.* E19.
[ORIGIN Dakota *Dakhóta* lit. 'allies'.]
▸ **A** *noun.* Pl. same, **-s**.
1 A member of a N. American Indian people inhabiting the upper Mississippi and Missouri river valleys. Also called ***Sioux***. E19.
2 The Siouan language of this people. M19.
▸ **B** *attrib.* or as *adjective.* Of or pertaining to the Dakota or their language. E19.

Dakotan /dəˈkəʊt(ə)n/ *noun & adjective.* L19.
[ORIGIN from *Dakota* (see below) formed as DAKOTA: see -AN.]
(A native or inhabitant) of the former US territory of Dakota or the states of North and South Dakota into which it is now organized.

dal *noun* /dɑːl/ *noun.* Also **dhal**. L17.
[ORIGIN Hindi *dāl*.]
Split pulses (esp. the seed of the pigeon pea, *Cajanus cajan*), a common foodstuff in the Indian subcontinent.

Dalai Lama /dalʌɪ ˈlɑːmə/ *noun phr.* L17.
[ORIGIN Mongolian *dalai* ocean + LAMA *noun*.]
The chief lama of the dominant Tibetan Buddhist order, widely regarded as the spiritual leader of the Tibetan people.

dalang /dəˈlaŋ/ *noun.* E19.
[ORIGIN Malay, Javanese.]
The performer who recites the story and manipulates the puppets in Indonesian and Malaysian puppet theatre.

dalasi /dɑːˈlɑːsiː/ *noun.* Pl. same, **-s**. L20.
[ORIGIN Name of a previous local coin.]
The basic monetary unit of The Gambia, equal to 100 butut.

Dalcroze /dalˈkrəʊz/ *adjective & noun.* E20.
[ORIGIN Émile Jaques-*Dalcroze* (1865–1950), Swiss music teacher and composer.]
(Designating or pertaining to) eurhythmics as developed by Dalcroze.

dale /deɪl/ *noun*[1].
[ORIGIN Old English *dæl* corresp. to Old Frisian *del*, Old Saxon (Dutch) *dal*, Old High German *tal* (German *Tal*), Old Norse *dalr*, Gothic *dal(s)*, from Germanic.]
1 A valley, esp. in N. England. In literary English chiefly *poet.* OE.
> TENNYSON Till over down and over dale All night the shining vapour sail.

dale and down: see DOWN *noun*[1] 2. ***hill and dale, up hill and down dale***: see HILL *noun*.
†**2** A hole in the ground, a hollow. OE–L15.
– COMB.: **dales folk**, **dalesman**, etc.: inhabiting dales in N. England.

dale /deɪl/ *noun*[2]. Now *rare* or *obsolete*. E17.
[ORIGIN Prob. from French *dalle* conduit, tube, etc. from Old Norse *dæla* bilge-water conduit; cf. Low German, Dutch *daal* in same sense.]
A conduit for carrying off water from a (ship's) pump.

dale *noun*[3] see DOLE *noun*[1].

Dalecarlian /dɑːlɪˈkɑːlɪən/ *noun & adjective.* M19.
[ORIGIN from *Dalecarlia* (see below) + -AN.]
(A native or inhabitant) of Dalecarlia (now more usually called Dalarna), a province of central Sweden.

dalek /ˈdɑːlɛk/ *noun.* M20.
[ORIGIN Invented word.]
An alien machine-organism appearing in the BBC television science-fiction series *Doctor Who*; *gen.* a ruthless automaton, a robot.

Daliesque /dɑːlɪˈɛsk/ *adjective.* M20.
[ORIGIN from *Dalí* (see below) + -ESQUE.]
Resembling or characteristic of the work of the Spanish painter Salvador Dalí (1904–89), esp. in the use of partly abstract improbable juxtapositions; surrealistic.

†**Dalilah** *noun* var. of DELILAH.

Dalit /ˈdɑːlɪt/ *noun.* L20.
[ORIGIN Hindi, = oppressed, from Sanskrit *dalita*.]
In India: a member of the lowest caste, a Harijan.

dalle /dal/ *noun.* Pl. pronounced same. E18.
[ORIGIN French from Low Dutch, rel. to DEAL *noun*[2].]
A flat slab of stone, marble, or terracotta, used for flooring, esp. of an ornamental kind.
■ **dallage** /dalaːʒ/ *noun* flooring with *dalles* M19.

dalles /dalz/ *noun pl. US.* L18.
[ORIGIN French, pl. of *dalle* conduit, tube, etc. Cf. DALE *noun*[2].]
In the western US, rapids where a river is compressed into long narrow troughlike channels.

dalliance /ˈdalɪəns/ *noun.* ME.
[ORIGIN from DALLY *verb* + -ANCE.]
†**1** Talk, chat; conversation. ME–L15.
†**2** Waste of time in trifling; idle delay. LME–L16.
> SHAKES. *Com. Err.* My business cannot brook this dalliance.

3 Amorous toying, (an) idle flirtation. LME.
> POPE The lewd dalliance of the queen of love. A. FRASER Did their summer dalliance have more serious consequences than either intended?

4 Idle or frivolous action; trifling (*with* a matter). M16.
> W. H. PRESCOTT He continued to live in idle dalliance.

Dally /ˈdali/ *noun & adjective. NZ colloq.* M20.
[ORIGIN Abbreviation.]
(A) Dalmatian.

dally /ˈdali/ *verb.* ME.
[ORIGIN Old French *dalier* to converse, chat (frequent in Anglo-Norman), of unknown origin.]
†**1** *verb intrans.* Talk or converse lightly or idly; chat. Only in ME.
2 *verb intrans.* Amuse oneself with a person or thing; toy; sport, flirt, trifle, *with*. LME.
> V. SACKVILLE-WEST He liked to dally with pretty and sycophantic women. C. CONNOLLY After dallying with the Church, he plunged into the world of letters.

3 *verb intrans.* Idle, linger, delay. M16.
> V. WOOLF Hugh Whitbread ruminated, dallying there in front of the shop window.

†**4** *verb trans.* Put off or defer by trifling. L16–E19.
5 *verb trans.* Fritter *away* (time, opportunity, etc.). L17.
■ **dallier** *noun* M16.

Dalmatian /dalˈmeɪʃ(ə)n/ *noun & adjective.* L16.
[ORIGIN from *Dalmatia* (see below) + -AN.]
▸ **A** *noun.* **1** A native or inhabitant of Dalmatia, a region on the Adriatic coast of Croatia. L16.
2 A dog of a breed characterized by its short-haired white coat with many dark spots, formerly used as a carriage dog. E19.
3 A Romance language formerly spoken by natives of Dalmatia. E20.
▸ **B** *adjective.* Of or pertaining to Dalmatia or its inhabitants. E17.
Dalmatian dog = sense A.2 above.

dalmatic /dalˈmatɪk/ *noun & adjective.* Also **D-**. LME.
[ORIGIN Old French & mod. French *dalmatique* or Latin *dalmatica* use as noun (sc. *vestis* robe, made of Dalmatian wool) of *Dalmaticus* of Dalmatia: see DALMATIAN, -IC.]
(Designating) a wide-sleeved ecclesiastical vestment with two stripes, worn by deacons and bishops on certain occasions, or a similar robe worn by monarchs and emperors esp. at coronations.

Dalradian /dalˈreɪdɪən/ *adjective.* L19.
[ORIGIN from *Dalrad-*, altered form of *Dalriada* an ancient kingdom of Scotland and N. Ireland + -IAN.]
GEOLOGY. Designating or pertaining to a series of metamorphosed sedimentary and volcanic rocks of early Cambrian age found in a belt extending from the west coast of Ireland to the southern highlands of Scotland.

dal segno /dal ˈsemjəʊ/ *adverbial phr.* L19.
[ORIGIN Italian = from the sign.]
MUSIC. A direction: go back to the point indicated by the sign (not the beginning). Cf. AL SEGNO.

dalt /dɔːlt/ *noun. Scot.* Also **dault**. L18.
[ORIGIN Gaelic *dalta*.]
A foster-child.

dalton /ˈdɔːlt(ə)n/ *noun.* M20.
[ORIGIN John *Dalton* (see DALTONIAN).]
CHEMISTRY. = ***atomic mass unit***: chiefly used in expressing the molecular weight of proteins.

Daltonian /dɔːlˈtəʊnɪən/ *adjective & noun.* E19.
[ORIGIN from John *Dalton* (1766–1844), English chemist and sufferer from colour blindness: -IAN.]
▸ **A** *adjective.* Relating to Dalton or the atomic theory first enunciated by him. E19.
▸ **B** *noun.* A person affected with daltonism (see DALTONISM). M19.

daltonism /ˈdɔːlt(ə)nɪz(ə)m/ *noun.* M19.
[ORIGIN French *daltonisme*, formed as DALTONIAN + -ISM.]
Colour blindness; *esp.* protanopia.

Dalton plan /dɔːlt(ə)n plan/ *noun phr.* E20.
[ORIGIN *Dalton*, Massachusetts, US, location of the first school to use the plan.]
A system of education in which pupils are made responsible for the completion of assignments over fairly long periods.
■ **Daltonize** *verb trans.* manage or arrange by the Dalton plan E20.

dam /dam/ *noun*[1]. ME.
[ORIGIN Middle & mod. Low German, Middle Dutch & mod. Dutch = Old Frisian (also *dom*), Middle High German *tam* (German *Damm* from Low German), from a base repr. also by Old English *for)demman*, Old Frisian *demmen*, Gothic *faur)dammjan* dam up, close up, of unknown origin.]
1 A barrier constructed to hold back water and raise its level, so as to form a reservoir or prevent flooding. ME. ▸**b** In full ***beaver dam***. A barrier constructed in a stream by beavers. M17. ▸**c** A causeway through fens. E19.
mill dam: see MILL *noun*[1]. ***water over the dam***: see WATER *noun*.
2 A body of water confined by a barrier or embankment. Now *local.* ME.
3 An area of flat land from which water has been drained. *local.* E17.
4 A partition or enclosure for excluding or confining fluids. E18. ▸**b** *spec.* In full ***rubber dam***. A rubber sheet used to keep saliva from the teeth during dental operations. Chiefly *N. Amer.* L19.
cofferdam: see COFFER *noun*.
– COMB.: **dam-head** *Scot.* a weir on a river for diverting the water into a mill race.

dam /dam/ *noun*[2]. ME.
[ORIGIN Alt. of DAME.]
†**1** = DAME I. Only in ME.
2 A (human) mother. Now *derog.* ME.
3 A female parent (of animals, now usu. quadrupeds). Correl. to ***sire***. (Earlier as DAME 11). LME.

dam /dam/ *noun*[3]. Chiefly *Scot.* L16.
[ORIGIN French DAME lady, a piece in draughts (*jeu de dames*).]
Each of the pieces in the game of draughts. Now only in *pl.*, the game of draughts.

dam /dɑːm/ *noun*[4]. *obsolete* exc. *hist.* L18.
[ORIGIN Hindi *dām*.]
An Indian copper coin of the value of one-fortieth of a rupee.

dam /dam/ *verb trans.* Infl. **-mm-**. LME.
[ORIGIN from DAM *noun*[1], repl. Old English compound verb *fordemman*.]
Confine with a dam; block *up*, hold *back*, obstruct, (*lit.* & *fig.*).
> W. C. WILLIAMS The complete damming up of all my creative capacities. R. BRAUTIGAN The boards dammed up the creek enough to form a huge bathtub there.

dam(') *adjective & adverb* var. of DAMN *adjective & adverb*.

†**dama** *noun*[1] see TAMMAR.

Dama *noun*[2] see DAMARA.

damage /ˈdamɪdʒ/ *noun.* ME.
[ORIGIN Old French (mod. *dommage*), from *dam*, *damme* loss, damage, prejudice from Latin *damnum* loss, hurt: see DAMN *verb*, -AGE.]
1 Loss or detriment to one's property, reputation, etc. *arch.* ME.
> CHAUCER As moche to oure damage as to oure profit.

2 Harm done to a thing or (less usually, chiefly *joc.*) person; *esp.* physical injury impairing value or usefulness. LME.
> DEFOE She was leaky, and had damage in her hold. S. WEIGHELL In our industry we have the power to cause enormous damage to the economy.

collateral damage: see COLLATERAL *adjective*. VACCINE ***damage***.
†**3** A disadvantage, an inconvenience; a misfortune. LME–E18.
> T. SHELTON The Damage is . . that I have no money here about me.

4 *LAW* †*sing.* & (now) in *pl.* A sum of money claimed or awarded in compensation for loss or injury. LME.
> W. LIPPMANN An injured workman should not have to sue, but should receive damages according to a definite schedule.

consequential damages: see CONSEQUENTIAL *adjective* 1. ***exemplary damages***: see EXEMPLARY *adjective* 4. ***with damages***: see WITH *preposition*. ***vindictive damages***: see VINDICTIVE 1.
5 Cost, expense. Esp. in ***what's the damage?*** how much is there to pay? *slang.* M18.
> BYRON I must pay the damage, and will thank you to tell me the amount of the engraving.

– COMB.: **damage control** action taken to alleviate the effects of damage after an accident etc.; the taking of such action; **damage limitation** action taken to limit the effects of damage after a hostile attack, accident, error, etc.; the taking of such action.

damage /ˈdamɪdʒ/ *verb trans.* ME.
[ORIGIN Old French *damagier*, formed as DAMAGE *noun*.]
Injure (a thing) so as to diminish its value or usefulness; cause harm (now rarely physically) to (a person), *esp.* detract from the reputation of.
> A. LURIE Charlie didn't kill himself, after all, . . didn't even damage much furniture. G. GREENE They would like to disrupt us, damage morale and hurt us with the Americans. M. AMIS I feel strangely protective of little Martin here: . . I would hate to damage him, or see him damaged.

damaged goods merchandise which has deteriorated in quality. VACCINE-***damaged***.

■ **damageable** *adjective* †(*a*) causing loss or injury; (*b*) liable to be damaged: L15. **damagement** *noun* (*rare*) [Old French] the action of damaging; the fact of being damaged: E17. **damagingly** *adverb* so as to cause damage, hurtfully M19.

damage feasant /damɪdʒˈfiːz(ə)nt/ *adjective & noun*. L16.
[ORIGIN Old French *damage fesant* (mod. *dommage faisant*) doing damage.]
ENGLISH LAW. (Causing or involving) damage done on a person's land by animals or goods of another, which would justify the landowner in distraining them until compensated.

daman /ˈdamən/ *noun*. M18.
[ORIGIN Arabic *damān ʾisrāʾīl* lit. 'lamb of Israel'.]
The rock hyrax.

Damara /ˈdɑːmərə, ˈdam-/ *noun*. Also **Dama** /ˈdɑːmə/. Pl. **-s**, same. E19.
[ORIGIN Nama.]
More fully ***Hill Damara***, ***Berg Damara***, ***Mountain Damara***. A member of a people of the mountainous parts of SW Africa, who have adopted the Nama language.

Damascene /ˈdaməsiːn, daməˈsiːn/ *noun & adjective*. See also DAMSON. LME.
[ORIGIN Latin *Damascenus* from Greek *Damaskēnos*, from *Damaskos* Damascus, from Semitic name (Hebrew *dammeśeq*, Arabic *dimašq*, *dimišq*).]
▸ **A** *noun*. **1** A native or inhabitant of the city of Damascus in Syria. LME.
2 (Usu. **d-**.) (An item of) damascened work; a pattern characteristic of damascened work. Formerly also, the fabric damask. L15.
▸ **B** *adjective*. **1** Of or pertaining to the city of Damascus. M16.
2 (Usu. **d-**.) Of or pertaining to the damascening of metal or the fabric damask. M16.

damascene /ˈdaməsiːn, daməˈsiːn/ *verb trans*. M19.
[ORIGIN from the adjective Cf. earlier DAMASKEEN *verb*.]
1 Ornament (metal, a metal object) with inlaid designs in gold or silver; inlay (a design) thus. M19.
2 Produce or ornament (steel, a blade, etc.) with the watered pattern produced in welding. M19.
■ **damascener** *noun* a person who damascenes metal M19.

Damascus /dəˈmaskəs/ *adjective*. Orig. in Italian form †**Damasco**. E17.
[ORIGIN attrib. use of name of city of Damascus, from Latin from Greek *Damaskos*: see DAMASCENE *noun & adjective*.]
hist. Designating (objects of) damask steel.

damask /ˈdaməsk/ *noun & adjective*. LME.
[ORIGIN Latin DAMASCUS, prob. through Anglo-Norman. Cf. French *damas*.]
▸ **A** *noun*. **1** A richly figured woven material (orig. of silk) with a pattern visible on either side, orig. produced at Damascus. Also, a twilled table linen with woven designs shown by reflection of light. LME.
2 The colour of the damask rose (see below); velvety pink or light red, esp. as the colour of a woman's complexion. L16.

> KEATS She . . Blush'd a live damask.

3 Damask steel (see below); the wavy pattern characteristic of this. E17.
▸ **B** *adjective*. **1** (Originally) made at or associated with Damascus. LME.
2 Of the colour of the damask rose; blushing. L16.
3 Made of the fabric damask. E17.
4 Made of or characteristic of damask steel. E17.
– SPECIAL COLLOCATIONS: **damask rose** a rose of an old sweet-scented species, *Rosa damascena*, grown esp. to make attar. **damask steel** *hist*. steel made at Damascus, or in the manner employed there, with a characteristic wavy surface pattern resulting from the method of repeated heating and hammering together of strips of steel and iron. **damask violet** = *DAME'S violet*. **damask work** damascened work.

damask /ˈdaməsk/ *verb trans*. M16.
[ORIGIN from the noun.]
Freq. as ***damasked*** *pa. pple & ppl adjective*.
1 Weave with richly figured designs. M16.
2 = DAMASCENE *verb*. L16.
3 Cause to have the colour of a damask rose. *poet*. L16.

> SHAKES. *Sonn*. I have seen roses damask'd . . But no such roses see I in her cheeks.

4 Ornament with an intricate or variegated pattern. E17.

> MILTON On the soft downie Bank damaskt with flours.

5 Deface or destroy by stamping or marking with lines or figures. L17.
†**6** Warm (wine). *slang*. L17–L18.

damaskeen /daməˈskiːn/ *verb trans*. Also **-squine**. L16.
[ORIGIN French *damasquiner*, from *damasquin(e)* from Italian *damaschino*, from *Damasco* Damascus.]
= DAMASCENE *verb*.

dame /deɪm/ *noun*. ME.
[ORIGIN Old French & mod. French, earlier †*damme* from Latin *domina* fem. corresp. to *dominus* lord. Cf. DAM *noun*[2], DAN *noun*[1], DOM *noun*[1], DON *noun*[1].]
▸ **I 1** A female ruler or head. *obsolete* in *gen*. sense. ME.

> MILTON Sovran of Creatures, universal Dame.

†**2** A form of address: my lady, madam. (Orig. the fem. corresp. to *sire*, later applied only to women of lower rank.) ME–E18.
3 (Used as a title preceding the name of) a woman of rank, formerly *spec*., the wife or widow of a knight or baronet, now *spec*. a woman Knight Commander or holder of Grand Cross in the Order of the Bath, the Order of the British Empire, the Royal Victorian Order, or the Order of St Michael and St George. ME. ▸**b** Used as a title preceding the name of an abstraction personified as a woman, as ***Dame Fortune***, ***Dame Nature***, etc. ME.
4 (Used before the surname of) the mistress of a household, an elderly matron, or a housewife. Now *arch. & dial*. ME.

> SHAKES. *Wint. T*. This day she was . . Both dame and servant; welcom'd all; serv'd all.

5 (Used as a title preceding the name of) the superior of a nunnery, an abbess, prioress, etc.; *spec*. (as a formal title of) a Benedictine nun who has made her solemn profession. LME.
6 A woman, a lady. Now *arch., poet., joc.*, or *slang* (chiefly *N. Amer.*). M16.

> W. H. AUDEN If you pass up a dame, you've yourself to blame.

7 *hist*. (Used before the surname of) the mistress of a children's school. M17.
8 At Eton College: one of a class of women (at one time also men) who keep boarding houses for oppidans but are not attached to the teaching staff. M18.
9 A comic character in modern pantomime, that of a middle-aged woman, traditionally played by a man. E20.
▸ †**II 10** = DAM *noun*[2] 2. ME–E19.
11 = DAM *noun*[2] 3. ME–E18.
– COMB.: **dame school** *hist*. a primary school of a kind kept by elderly women; **dame's violet** a cruciferous plant, *Hesperis matronalis*, with pale lilac flowers which have no scent until evening.

dame de compagnie /dam də kɔ̃paɲi/ *noun phr*. Pl. ***dames de compagnie*** (pronounced same). L18.
[ORIGIN French, lit. 'lady of company'.]
A paid female companion.

dame d'honneur /dam dɔnœːr/ *noun phr*. Pl. ***dames d'honneur*** (pronounced same). E19.
[ORIGIN French, lit. 'lady of honour'.]
A maid of honour, a lady-in-waiting.

dames de compagnie, ***dames d'honneur*** *noun phrs*. pls. of DAME DE COMPAGNIE, DAME D'HONNEUR.

damfool /ˈdamfuːl/ *adjective & noun*. *colloq*. Also **damn-fool**. L19.
[ORIGIN from DAMN *adjective* + FOOL *noun*[1].]
(A person who is) thoroughly foolish or stupid.
■ **damˈfoolery** *noun* E20. **damˈfoolishness** *noun* L19.

damiana /ˌdeɪmɪˈɑːnə/ *noun*. L19.
[ORIGIN Amer. Spanish.]
A small shrub, *Turnera diffusa*, of tropical America, whose leaves are used in herbal medicine and to produce a liqueur.

dammar /ˈdamə/ *noun*. Also **-er**. L17.
[ORIGIN Malay *damar* resin.]
Any of various resins used to make varnish etc. obtained from eastern Asian and Australasian conifers, esp. of the genera *Agathis* (cf. KAURI) or *Shorea* (cf. SAL *noun*[2]). Also (in full ***dammar-pine***, ***dammar-tree***), a tree yielding this.

damme /ˈdami/ *interjection & noun*. *arch*. E17.
[ORIGIN Alt.]
Damn me!; this oath, or (formerly) a person using this or similar oaths.

dammer *noun* var. of DAMMAR.

dammit /ˈdamɪt/ *interjection*. M19.
[ORIGIN Alt.]
Damn it!
as — as dammit very — indeed.

damn /dam/ *noun*. E17.
[ORIGIN from the verb.]
1 An utterance of the word 'damn'; an oath, an imprecation. E17.

> R. B. SHERIDAN The best terms will grow obsolete. Damns have had their day.

2 A negligible amount (in ***not care a damn***, ***not give a damn***, ***not worth a damn***, etc.). *colloq*. M18.

> LD MACAULAY How they settle the matter I care not . . one twopenny damn.

not care a tinker's damn, ***not worth a tinker's damn***: see TINKER *noun* 1.

damn /dam/ *adjective & adverb*. *colloq*. Also **dam**, **dam(n)'**. L18.
[ORIGIN Abbreviation.]
= DAMNED.

> E. WALLACE It's none of your dam' business. N. COWARD We . . intended to damn well get on with it. DOUGLAS STUART You one of those damn' Yankee reporters?

a damn sight a great deal (*better*, *more*, etc.). ***damn all***: see ALL *pronoun & noun* 3. ***damn-fool***: see DAMFOOL.

damn /dam/ *verb*. ME.
[ORIGIN Old French *dampner*, (also mod.) *damner* from Latin *dam(p)nare* (orig.) inflict loss upon, from *damnum* loss, damage, expenditure.]
†**1** *verb trans*. Pronounce to be guilty; condemn judicially, sentence, (*to* a penalty or fate). ME–L19.
2 *verb trans*. Pronounce to be bad, a failure, etc.; censure, denounce; condemn esp. by public expression of disapproval. ME.

> W. GODWIN We should [not] totally damn a man's character for a few faults. W. S. CHURCHILL The Fabian Society . . damned all revolutionary theory and set about the propagation of a practical Socialist doctrine.

damn with faint praise commend so feebly as to imply disapproval.
3 *verb trans*. (Of God) condemn to eternal punishment; doom to hell; cause the damnation or condemnation of; be the ruin of. Also (*colloq*.) in imprecations, freq. in imper. or optative form (for ***God damn*** — etc.), expr. anger, hatred, contempt, irritation, etc. ME. ▸**b** *verb intrans*. as *interjection*. Expr. anger, irritation, displeased surprise or realization, etc. Cf. DAMNATION *noun* 3. M20.

> DICKENS I will see them d—d before I make any further alteration. T. F. POWYS He . . damned the gate to Hell because it would not open. G. GORER It may not be necessary to believe that any soul is permanently damned. E. WAUGH No one is damned except by his own deliberate act. **b** N. BALCHIN I shall have to let go of the other wrench. Damn and blast.

damn your eyes!, **damn my eyes!**, etc., *arch*.: expr. contempt etc. **I'll be damned**: expr. astonishment etc. **I'm damned if I —**, **I'll be damned if I —** I certainly do not —, I will not —.
4 *verb intrans. & trans*. Say 'damn' (at), swear (at), curse. E17.

> G. B. SHAW I don't mind your damning and blasting . . but there is a certain word I must ask you not to use.

■ **damner** *noun* LME. **damningly** *adverb* so as to damn or condemn, to a damning degree E18.

damna *noun* pl. of DAMNUM.

damnable /ˈdamnəb(ə)l/ *adjective & adverb*. ME.
[ORIGIN Old French *dampnable*, (also mod.) *damnable* from Latin *dam(p)nabilis*, from *dam(p)nare*: see DAMN *verb*, -ABLE.]
▸ **A** *adjective*. **1** Subject to divine condemnation; deserving damnation. ME.

> SMOLLETT Those enthusiasts who look upon every schism from the established articles of faith as damnable.

2 Worthy of condemnation, reprehensible, detestable; accursed, confounded. LME.

> T. HEARNE This is a damnable Shame. J. HAWKES What was admirable when it concerned only the transport of the finest materials to build the greatest buildings has become damnable when dictated by commercial expediency.

▸ †**B** *adverb*. Damnably, extremely. E17–E18.
■ **damnaˈbility** *noun* M16. **damnably** *adverb* †(*a*) so as to deserve or incur damnation; (*b*) in a damnable way, to a damnable extent; reprehensibly, detestably, confoundedly, extremely: LME.

damnation /damˈneɪʃ(ə)n/ *noun, adjective, & adverb*. ME.
[ORIGIN Old French *dampnation*, (also mod.) *damnation* from Latin *dam(p)natio(n-)*, from *dam(p)nat-* pa. ppl stem of *dam(p)nare*: see DAMN *verb*, -ATION. See also DEMNITION.]
▸ **A** *noun*. **1** The action of condemning, the fact of being condemned; condemnation. ME.

> H. SIDDONS The fatal cough, well known to authors as the sure forerunner of dramatic damnation.

2 *THEOLOGY*. Condemnation to eternal punishment in hell; perdition; the cause of such condemnation. ME.

> SHAKES. *Merch. V*. 'Twere damnation To think so base a thought.

3 As *interjection*. Expr. anger, irritation, displeased surprise or realization, etc. Cf. DAMN *verb* 3b. E17.
▸ **B** *adjective & adverb*. = DAMNED *adjective* 4 & *adverb*. *colloq*. M18.

> F. MARRYAT The damned Frenchman and his damnation horse.

damnatory /ˈdamnət(ə)ri/ *adjective*. L17.
[ORIGIN Latin *damnatorius*, from *damnat-*: see DAMNATION, -ORY[2].]
1 Conveying or causing censure or condemnation. L17.
2 *THEOLOGY*. Conveying a sentence of damnation in hell; incurring damnation. M18.

damned /damd, *poet. also* ˈdamnɪd/ *adjective, noun, & adverb*. LME.
[ORIGIN from DAMN *verb* + -ED[1].]
▸ **A** *adjective*. †**1** Doomed, condemned, sentenced. LME–E19.

> C. LAMB The reveries of the cell-damned murderer.

2 *THEOLOGY*. Condemned to eternal punishment; consigned to hell. LME.
3 Deserving damnation, worthy of a curse. *obsolete* exc. as passing into senses 2, 4. M16.
4 Accursed, damnable; confounded, infernal. (Formerly freq. printed *d—*, *d—d*; abbreviation *d*.) *colloq*. L16.

> H. B. FEARON There was 'nothing in America but d—d Yankees and rogues'. THACKERAY You would be a d— fool not to take the place. CONAN DOYLE Many people . . would think that this insistence had reached the point of damned impertinence.

▸ **B** *noun*. **1** *absol*. as *noun pl. The* souls in hell. E16.
2 ***one's damnedest***, one's utmost, *esp*. one's very best effort. M19.
▸ **C** *adverb*. Damnably; extremely. *colloq*. M18.

damn-fool *adjective & noun* var. of DAMFOOL.

damnify /ˈdamnɪfʌɪ/ *verb trans*. E16.
[ORIGIN Old French *damnefier*, *dam(p)nifier* from Latin *damnificare* injure, condemn, from Latin *damnificus* hurtful, from *damnum*: see DAMN *verb*, -FY.]
1 Cause loss or inconvenience to; hurt (financially, in reputation, etc.). Now *rare* (chiefly LAW). E16.
2 Injure or damage physically. *obsolete* exc. *dial*. M16.
†**3** Destroy. Only in 17.
■ **damnifiˈcation** *noun* E17.

damnosa hereditas /damˌnəʊsə hɪˈrɛdɪtas/ *noun phr*. M19.
[ORIGIN Latin = inheritance that causes loss.]
An inheritance, tradition, etc., bringing more burden than profit.

damnum /ˈdamnəm/ *noun*. Pl. **-na** /-nə/. E19.
[ORIGIN Latin = hurt, harm, damage.]
LAW. A loss, a wrong.

Damocles /ˈdaməkliːz/ *noun*. M18.
[ORIGIN Latin from Greek *Damoklēs*, of a flatterer whom Dionysius of Syracuse (4th cent. BC) feasted while a sword hung by a hair above him.]
sword of Damocles, ***Damocles sword***, ***Damocles's sword***, an imminent danger, a constant threat, esp. in the midst of prosperity.
■ **Damoˈclesian** *adjective* L19.

damoiseau /ˈdamɪzəʊ, *foreign* damwazo/ *noun*. Long *arch*. Pl. **-eaux** /-əʊz, *foreign* -o/. L15.
[ORIGIN French, later form of Old French *damoisel* masc., corresp. to fem. *damoiselle* (mod. *demoiselle*): see DAMSEL.]
A young man of gentle birth, not yet a knight.

damosel, **damozel** *nouns* see DAMSEL.

damp /damp/ *noun*. ME.
[ORIGIN Middle & mod. Low German = vapour, steam, smoke (so in mod. Dutch) = Old & mod. High German *dampf* steam, from West Germanic.]
▸ **I 1** A noxious exhalation; now *spec*. (usu. with specifying word) a harmful vapour or gas occurring in a coalmine. ME.
afterdamp, ***black damp***, ***choke-damp***, ***firedamp***, etc.
†**2** A visible vapour; fog, mist. E17–E19.
3 Moisture in the air, on a surface, or diffused through a solid; (a state or period of) slight wetness or high humidity. (The ordinary current sense.) E18.

T. S. SURR We keep fires in all the rooms by turns, so that no damp has come to the tapestry. LONGFELLOW Amid the chills and damps Of the vast plain where death encamps.

rising damp: see RISING *adjective*.
▸ **II** †**4** A dazed condition, a stupor. M16–E18.

ADDISON I felt a general Damp and a Faintness all over me.

5 A check, a discouragement. L16.

BURKE Those accidents that cast an occasional damp upon trade.

6 A state of dejection; a depression, a chill. E17.

W. H. PRESCOTT This news struck a damp into the hearts of the Castilians.

– COMB.: **damp course** a layer of damp-proof material laid in a wall near ground level to keep moisture from rising; **damp-proof** *adjective & verb trans*. (make) impervious to damp; ***damp-proof course*** = ***damp course*** above.
■ **dampy** *adjective* †(*a*) vaporous, foggy; (*b*) somewhat damp: E17.

damp /damp/ *adjective*. L16.
[ORIGIN from the noun.]
†**1** Affected with or showing stupefaction or depression. L16–M19.

MILTON With looks Down cast and damp.

†**2** Of the nature of or pertaining to a noxious exhalation. M17–M18.
3 Slightly wet, moist; permeated with moisture. E18.

G. BERKELEY A cold, damp, sordid habitation, in the midst of a bleak country. N. COWARD I'm still damp from the bath. J. C. POWYS Damp odours . . of dew-soaked grasses and river mud.

damp-dry *verb trans*. dry to the state of being only damp. ***damp squib***: see SQUIB *noun* 1.
■ **damply** *adverb* L19. **dampness** *noun* M17.

damp /damp/ *verb*. LME.
[ORIGIN from the noun.]
1 *verb trans*. Stifle, choke, extinguish, dull. LME. ▸**†b** Benumb, daze (the faculties etc.). L16–E18. ▸**c** PHYSICS & MUSIC. Stop or reduce the vibration of (a string or other oscillating body); impose or act as a resisting influence on (an oscillation or vibration) so that it is progressively reduced in amplitude or stopped. M19.

BACON All shutting in of Air . . dampeth the Sound.

damp down heap (a fire, furnace, etc.) with ashes etc. to retard combustion. **c** CRITICAL ***damping***.
2 *verb trans*. Depress, discourage, check (zeal, hopes, etc.). M16.

J. CLARE Sorrow damps my lays. P. G. WODEHOUSE It kind of damps you to come to a place where the youngest member is about eighty-seven. L. DURRELL They tempered her enthusiasm without damping it.

3 *verb trans*. Moisten. E17.
4 *verb intrans*. Foll. by *off*: (of a plant) die from fungal attack in damp conditions. M19.

dampen /ˈdamp(ə)n/ *verb*. M16.
[ORIGIN from DAMP *adjective* or *verb* + -EN[5].]
1 *verb trans*. Dull, depress, discourage. M16.

J. K. ROWLING Even the endless rain that had replaced the snow couldn't dampen his spirits.

2 *verb intrans*. Become dull, depressed, or damp. L17.
3 *verb trans*. Make damp, moisten. E19.
4 = DAMP *verb* 1C. L19.
■ **dampener** *noun* a thing that dampens; US a contrivance for moistening linen etc.: L19.

damper /ˈdampə/ *noun*. M18.
[ORIGIN from DAMP *verb* + -ER[1].]
1 A person who or thing which damps or depresses the spirits. M18.

HOR. WALPOLE Sussex is a great damper of curiosity. B. BAINBRIDGE A room so lofty and so full of draughts as to put the damper on any occasion.

2 a A contrivance in a piano for damping or stopping the vibrations of the strings. Also, the mute of a horn etc. L18. ▸**b** Any device for damping mechanical or other vibrations; *spec*. (*a*) a shock absorber on a motor vehicle; (*b*) a conductor serving to reduce hunting in an electric motor or generator. M19.
3 A movable metal plate in a flue or chimney, used to control the combustion by regulating the draught. L18.
4 Something which takes the edge off appetite. L18.
5 An unleavened cake made of flour and water and baked in hot ashes. Chiefly *Austral*. & *NZ*. E19.

K. GRENVILLE The damper was burned from being cooked too fast.

6 A device for dampening or moistening. E19.
– COMB.: **damper pedal** = ***sustaining pedal*** (a) s.v. SUSTAINING.

dampish /ˈdampɪʃ/ *adjective*. L16.
[ORIGIN Orig. from DAMP *noun* + -ISH[1]; later treated as from DAMP *adjective*.]
†**1** Vaporous, foggy, misty. L16–M17.
2 Somewhat damp or moist. M17.
■ **dampishly** *adverb* E17. **dampishness** *noun* E17.

damsel /ˈdamz(ə)l/ *noun*. In sense 1 also **damosel**, **-ozel**, /daməˈzɛl/. ME.
[ORIGIN Old French *dameisele*, *damisele* (mod. *demoiselle*), alt. (after *dame*) of *danzele*, *donsele* from Proto-Gallo-Romance dim. of Latin *domina* lady: see DAME. Cf. DAMOISEAU.]
1 A young unmarried woman, orig. one of noble birth. Now *arch*., *literary*, or *joc*. ME. ▸**b** *spec*. A maid-in-waiting. Now *arch*. & *literary*. ME.

P. G. WODEHOUSE In the Middle Ages . . practically everybody whose technical rating was that of Damsel was in distress and only too willing to waive the formalities in return for services rendered.

2 [Cf. 1 *Kings* 1:1–4.] A hot iron for warming a bed. *obsolete* exc. *hist*. E18.
3 A projection on the spindle of a millstone for shaking the shoot of the hopper. L19.
– COMB.: **damselfish** any of numerous brightly coloured tropical marine fishes of the family Pomacentridae; **damselfly** any slender insect of the suborder Zygoptera (order Odonata), like a dragonfly but with wings of equal length folded over the body when resting.

damson /ˈdamz(ə)n/ *noun & adjective*. Orig. †**damascene**. LME.
[ORIGIN Latin *damascenum* (*prunum* plum) of Damascus: cf. DAMASCENE *noun & adjective*.]
▸ **A** *noun*. A small dark-purple plum borne by the tree *Prunus domestica* subsp. *insititia*. Also, the tree itself. LME.
– COMB.: **damson cheese** a solid preserve of damsons and sugar; **damson plum** (*a*) the damson or (usu.) a larger plum resembling it; (*b*) (the edible purple fruit of) a neotropical tree, *Chrysophyllum oliviforme*, of the sapodilla family.
▸ **B** *adjective*. Of a dark-purple or purplish-brown colour. M17.

dan /dan/ *noun*[1]. Long *arch*. ME.
[ORIGIN Old French, also *dam* (mod. *dom*) from Latin *dominus* master, lord: cf. DOM *noun*[1], DON *noun*[1].]
Used as an honourable title preceding a name: master, sir.

SPENSER Dan Chaucer, well of English undefyld.

dan /dan/ *noun*[2]. L17.
[ORIGIN Unknown.]
A small buoy, used as a marker in deep-sea fishing or in minesweeping. Also ***dan buoy***.

Dan /dan/ *noun*[3]. M18.
[ORIGIN A town in the territory of Dan, one of the twelve tribes of Israel, taken to represent the northern limit of Israelite settlement in biblical times, as Beersheba was taken to represent the southern limit (*Judges* 20:1 etc.).]
from Dan to Beersheba, over the whole extent, to the furthest extremity.

dan /dan/ *noun*[4]. M20.
[ORIGIN Japanese.]
Each of the (numbered) grades of the advanced level of proficiency in judo, karate, etc. (also ***dan grade***); a person who has reached (a specified grade of) this level. Cf. KYU.

Dan. *abbreviation*.
Daniel (in the Bible).

Danaert /ˈdanət/ *noun*. Also **dannert**. M20.
[ORIGIN Its 20th-cent. German inventor.]
In full ***Danaert wire***. Spring steel wire, usually barbed and in a spiral form, used in defensive warfare.

danaid /ˈdaneɪɪd/ *noun & adjective*. L19.
[ORIGIN formed as DANAINE + -ID[3].]
ENTOMOLOGY. = DANAINE.

danaine /ˈdaneɪʌɪn/ *noun & adjective*. L19.
[ORIGIN from mod. Latin *Danainae* (see below), from *Danaus* genus name: see -INE[1].]
ENTOMOLOGY. ▸ **A** *noun*. A butterfly of the family Danaidae or Danainae, exemplified by the monarch or milkweed. L19.
▸ **B** *adjective*. Of or belonging to this family. L19.

danaite /ˈdɑːnəʌɪt, ˈdeɪn-/ *noun*. M19.
[ORIGIN from J. Freeman *Dana* (1793–1827), US chemist + -ITE[1].]
MINERALOGY. A cobaltiferous variety of arsenopyrite.

Danakil /ˈdanəkɪl, dəˈnɑːk(ə)l/ *noun & adjective*. Also **Dankali** /daŋˈkɑːli/. L19.
[ORIGIN Arabic *danāqil* pl. of *danqalī*.]
▸ **A** *noun*. A member of a widely spread Hamitic people of Djibouti and NE Ethiopia; the Cushitic language of this people. Also called ***Afar***. L19.
▸ **B** *adjective*. Of or pertaining to this people, their language, or their lands. E20.

danalite /ˈdeɪnəlʌɪt, ˈdɑːn-/ *noun*. M19.
[ORIGIN from James D. *Dana* (1813–95), US mineralogist + -LITE.]
MINERALOGY. A cubic silicate and sulphide of beryllium and iron, crystallizing in the cubic system and usu. occurring as reddish octahedra.

danburite /ˈdanbjʊrʌɪt/ *noun*. M19.
[ORIGIN from *Danbury*, Connecticut, US + -ITE[1].]
MINERALOGY. An orthorhombic calcium borosilicate, usu. occurring as colourless, yellow, or brownish prisms.

dance /dɑːns/ *noun*. ME.
[ORIGIN Old French *dance*, (also mod.) *danse*, formed as DANCE *verb*.]
1 The action or an act of dancing; a single round or turn of dancing; the art or practice of dancing. ME.
2 An arrangement of steps and movements constituting a specific form of dancing, often given a particular name. LME. ▸**b** A musical composition for dancing to or in a rhythm suitable for dancing to. E16.
ballroom dance, ***barn dance***, ***clog dance***, ***country dance***, ***Highland dance***, ***morris dance***, ***square dance***, ***sword dance***, ***tap dance***, ***war dance***, etc.
3 A social gathering for the purpose of dancing. LME.

B. A. STAPLES Yvonne told my mother she was going to a dance.

dinner dance, ***tea dance***, etc.
4 *fig*. A course of action, a proceeding; a game. Now only in set phrs. below. LME.
5 A genre of popular music which is largely or wholly synthesized and has a repetitive beat with few or no lyrics. L20.

Guardian The blurring of the line between dance and rock.

– PHRASES: **begin the dance** *fig*. take the lead in a course of action. ***dance macabre***: see MACABRE *noun*. **Dance of Death** an allegorical representation of Death leading people of all conditions in the dance to the grave, popular in the Middle Ages; = DANSE MACABRE. ***dance of macabre***: see MACABRE *adjective*. **lead a person a dance**, **lead a person a merry dance** cause a person a lot of trouble esp. by leading him or her on a lengthy pointless course. **lead the dance** = ***begin the dance*** above. ***song and dance***: see SONG *noun*[1]. ***St Vitus's dance***, ***St Vitus' dance***: see SAINT *noun & adjective*. ***waggle dance***: see WAGGLE *noun*.
– COMB.: **dance band** a band that plays music (suitable) for dancing to; **dance card** a card bearing the names of a woman's prospective partners at a dance; **dance drama** a drama in which all the action is expressed by dancing; **dance floor** a usu. uncarpeted area of flooring reserved for dancing; **dancehall** (*a*) a place where public dances are held; (*b*) an uptempo style of dance music derived from reggae; **dance hostess** (*a*) a woman who holds a dance at her house etc.; (*b*) a woman dancing partner (see ***dancing partner*** (b) s.v. DANCING *verbal noun*); **dance-house** (chiefly US) a dancehall; **dance programme** a dance card.

dance /dɑːns/ *verb*. ME.
[ORIGIN Old French *dancer*, (also mod.) *danser* from Proto-Romance, of unknown origin.]
1 *verb intrans*. Move with rhythmical steps, leaps, glides, and other gestures, usually in time to a musical accompaniment, alone or with a partner or set. ME. ▸**b** Of an animal: perform, after training, simple rhythmic movements. M16.
2 *verb intrans*. Of a person or animal: leap, spring, move up and down, from excitement or strong emotion. Of the heart, blood, etc.: move in a lively way. LME.

D

TENNYSON Yniol's heart Danced in his bosom, seeing better days.

3 *verb trans.* Perform (dance steps); perform the steps and movements of (a particular dance). LME.

R. DAVIES Makes you want to grab someone and dance ring-a-ring-o-roses.

4 *verb trans.* Move or toss up and down with a dancing jerky motion; dandle. LME.

R. P. JHABVALA She . . picked up the child and danced her up and down in her arms.

5 *verb intrans.* Of an insect, inanimate thing, etc.: bob up and down, move about, esp. in the air or on the surface of water. M16.

C. P. SNOW The midges were dancing over the water. A. HIGGINS She saw firelight dancing on the kitchen walls and over the ceiling.

6 *verb trans.* Lead in a dance, cause to dance; remove, put bring, etc., *off, away, to*, etc., by dancing. M17.

R. BOLT You'd dance him to the Tower—You'd dance him to the block! A. MASON The music danced him, on and on, towards its consummation.

– PHRASES: *dance* ATTENDANCE (*on*). *dance a person off his or her legs*: see LEG *noun*. †**dance barefoot** *fig.* (of an elder daughter) remain single while a younger daughter is married. **dance to a person's tune**, **dance to a person's pipe**, **dance after a person's tune**, **dance after a person's pipe**, etc., follow a person's lead, do as a person demands. **dance upon nothing** *arch.* be hanged.

■ **danceable** *adjective* (*colloq.*) suitable for dancing; fit to dance with: M19. **dancey** *adjective* (*colloq.*) (of a person) inclined to dance; (of music) suitable for dancing to: E20.

dancer /ˈdɑːnsə/ *noun*. LME.
[ORIGIN from DANCE *verb* + -ER¹.]
1 A person who dances; *spec.* a person who dances professionally in public. LME.
ballet dancer, clog dancer, morris dancer, tap dancer, etc.
2 In *pl.* Stairs. *arch. slang*. L17.
3 In *pl.* More fully ***merry dancers***. The aurora borealis. Chiefly *Scot.* E18.
4 In *pl.* A sect of Christian visionaries who arose in 1374 in Flanders and were noted for their wild dancing. M18.
5 A housebreaker, *esp.* one who enters through the roof of a building. *arch. slang*. M19.
■ **danceress** *noun* (long *rare*) LME.

dancercise /ˈdɑːnsəsʌɪz/ *noun*. Also **-ize**. M20.
[ORIGIN from DANCE *noun* + EXERCISE *noun*.]
Dancing performed as physical exercise.

dancette /dɑːnˈsɛt/ *noun*. E19.
[ORIGIN Inferred from DANCETTÉ.]
ARCHITECTURE. A zigzag or chevron moulding.

dancetté /ˈdɑːnsəti/ *adjective*. Also **-tty**. E17.
[ORIGIN Alt. of French *danché, denché*, earlier †*dansié* from late Latin adjective, from Latin *dens, dent-* tooth.]
HERALDRY. Having (esp. three) large, deep indentations.

dancing /ˈdɑːnsɪŋ/ *verbal noun*. ME.
[ORIGIN from DANCE *verb* + -ING¹.]
The action of DANCE *verb*; style of this; *rare* an act or instance of dancing.
ballroom dancing, clog dancing, disco dancing, morris dancing, tap dancing, etc.
– COMB.: **dancing master**, **dancing mistress** a teacher of dancing; **dancing partner** (*a*) a person with whom one dances; (*b*) an expert dancer engaged to act as teacher or partner as required; **dancing school** a school for instruction in dancing.

dancing /ˈdɑːnsɪŋ/ *ppl adjective*. M16.
[ORIGIN from DANCE *verb* + -ING².]
That dances.
dancing DERVISH. **dancing girl** a female professional dancer, esp. a member of a group.
■ **dancingly** *adverb* M17.

D and C *abbreviation*. Also **D & C**.
MEDICINE. Dilatation and curettage.

dandelion /ˈdandɪlʌɪən/ *noun*. LME.
[ORIGIN French *dent-de-lion*, rendering medieval Latin *dens leonis* lion's tooth: so called from the toothed leaves.]
Any of numerous composite plants constituting the genus *Taraxacum*, which are characteristic of grassland and have heads of bright yellow ligulate florets, stems containing a milky juice, and leaves in a basal rosette; a flower or flowering stem of this plant. Also (*Austral.*), Capeweed, *Cryptostemma candulaceum*.
– COMB.: **dandelion clock** = CLOCK *noun*¹ 5; **dandelion coffee** (a drink prepared from) dried dandelion roots; **dandelion greens** *N. Amer.* fresh dandelion leaves used as a green food or herb.

dander /ˈdandə/ *noun*¹. *Scot.* L18.
[ORIGIN Unknown.]
A calcined cinder from a forge etc.

dander /ˈdandə/ *noun*². L18.
[ORIGIN Rel. to DANDRUFF.]
Dandruff, scurf, esp. as found in the hair of animals.

dander /ˈdandə/ *noun*³. *colloq.* (orig. *US*). M19.
[ORIGIN Unknown.]
Temper, anger, indignation.
get one's dander up become angry.

dander /ˈdandə/ *verb* & *noun*⁴. *Scot.* & *N. English*. Also **daun(d)er** /ˈdɔːn(d)ə/. L16.
[ORIGIN Frequent. (see -ER⁵), perh. rel. to DADDER, DADDLE *verb*, etc.]
▸ **A** *verb intrans.* **1** Stroll, saunter; walk aimlessly. L16.
2 Talk incoherently, ramble; make a trembling sound, vibrate. E18.
▸ **B** *noun*. A stroll, a saunter. E19.

dandiacal /danˈdʌɪək(ə)l/ *adjective*. M19.
[ORIGIN from DANDY *noun*² after *hypochondriacal* etc.]
Dandyish, dandified.

Dandie /ˈdandi/ *noun*. L19.
[ORIGIN Abbreviation.]
= DANDIE DINMONT.

Dandie Dinmont /dandɪ ˈdɪnmənt/ *noun*. E19.
[ORIGIN A character in Sir Walter Scott's novel *Guy Mannering*.]
(A dog of) a breed of terrier from the Scottish borders, with short legs, a long body, and a rough coat.

dandify /ˈdandɪfʌɪ/ *verb trans. colloq.* E19.
[ORIGIN from DANDY *noun*² + -FY.]
Make like a dandy; smarten up. Freq. as ***dandified*** *ppl adjective*.
■ **dandifiˈcation** *noun* the act of dandifying; a dandified ornament: E19.

dandilly /ˈdandɪli/ *noun* & *adjective*. *Scot.* E16.
[ORIGIN App. a deriv. of DANDLE *verb*.]
▸ **A** *noun*. A pet, a darling. E16.
▸ **B** *adjective*. Petted, spoiled. M18.

dandiprat /ˈdandɪprat/ *noun*. *arch.* Also **dandy-**. E16.
[ORIGIN Unknown.]
†**1** A small 16th-cent. coin, worth three halfpence. E16–M17.
2 A small, insignificant, or contemptible fellow; a young boy, an urchin. M16.

dandiya raas /ˈdandɪə ˌrɑːs/ *noun*. M20.
[ORIGIN Gujarati, from *dandiya* sticks and *raas* dance.]
A type of traditional Gujarati stick dance. Also, a festival featuring such dances.

dandizette /dandɪˈzɛt/ *noun*. Also **dandy-**. Now *rare*. E19.
[ORIGIN from DANDY *noun*², after French *grisette* etc.: see -ETTE.]
A female dandy.

dandle /ˈdand(ə)l/ *verb*. M16.
[ORIGIN Unknown.]
1 *verb trans.* Move (a child etc.) lightly up and down in the arms or on the knee; *gen.* move lightly up and down. M16.

S. BECKETT Perhaps she had dandled me on her knees while I was still in swaddling clothes. G. HOUGH An apple tree Dandled its fruit.

2 †**a** *verb trans.* Trifle, play, or toy with. M16–M17. ▸**b** *verb intrans.* Play or toy (*with*). *rare*. E19.
3 *verb trans.* Make much of, pet, pamper. M16.
■ **dandler** *noun* L16. **dandling** *noun* (*obsolete* exc. *dial.*) a dandled child, a darling E17.

dandruff /ˈdandrʌf/ *noun*. Also (now *rare*) **-iff** /-ɪf/. M16.
[ORIGIN 1st elem. obscure, 2nd perh. identical with ROVE *noun*².]
Dead skin in small scales entangled in the hair, esp. when excessive as in seborrhoea.
■ **dandruffy** *adjective* like dandruff, having much dandruff M19.

dandy /ˈdandi/ *noun*¹. L17.
[ORIGIN Hindi *ḍā̃ḍī*, from *ḍā̃ḍ* staff, oar.]
1 *hist.* A boatman on the Ganges. L17.
2 In the Indian subcontinent, a type of litter, carried by two men. L19.

dandy /ˈdandi/ *noun*². L18.
[ORIGIN Perh. abbreviation of JACK-A-DANDY, the last elem. of which may be identical with *Dandy*, pet form of male forename *Andrew*.]
1 A man whose style of dress is ostentatiously elegant or fashionable; a fop, a beau. L18.

R. FRY An exquisite and refined intellectual dandy living in a society of elegant frivolity. S. GIBBONS Mr. Neck was a great dandy, who usually changed his button-hole twice a day.

2 A very good thing of its kind; *the* best. *colloq.* L18.

J. RUNCIMAN The barque looked a real dandy.

3 A bantam fowl. *dial.* E19.
4 NAUTICAL. A sloop or cutter with a jigger-mast right aft, on which a mizzen-lugsail is set. M19.
5 In full ***dandy roll, dandy roller***. A wire roller used to compress the fibres of a partly formed web of paper, which also simultaneously imparts the watermark. M19.
– COMB.: **dandy brush** a stiff brush used for cleaning horses; **dandy cart** (now *rare*) a kind of spring cart; **dandyfunk** NAUTICAL hard tack soaked in water and baked with fat and molasses; **dandy horse** *hist.* an early form of bicycle, in which the rider achieved propulsion by pushing the ground with each foot alternately; **dandy line** a weighted fishing line with crosspieces at short intervals, each of which has a hook on either end; ***dandy roll, dandy roller***: see sense 5 above.
■ **dandydom** *noun* M19. **dandyish** *adjective* like a dandy, foppish E19. **dandyishly** *adverb* M19. **dandyism** *noun* E19.

dandy /ˈdandi/ *noun*³. E19.
[ORIGIN W. Indian alt. of DENGUE.]
More fully ***dandy-fever***. Dengue.

dandy /ˈdandi/ *adjective* & *adverb*. L18.
[ORIGIN from DANDY *noun*².]
▸ **A** *adjective*. **1** Splendid, first-rate; very good of its kind. *colloq.* (orig. *US*). L18.

R. LARDNER She plays a dandy game of bridge, lots better than her husband.

fine and dandy: see FINE *adjective*.
2 Of, belonging to, or characteristic of a dandy or dandies; affectedly neat, trim, or smart. E19.
▸ **B** *adverb*. Finely, splendidly. *N. Amer. colloq.* E20.

dandyprat *noun* var. of DANDIPRAT.

dandyzette *noun* var. of DANDIZETTE.

Dane /deɪn/ *noun*.
[ORIGIN Old English *Dene* (repr. in *Denmark*), superseded in Middle English by forms from Old Norse *Danir* pl. (late Latin *Dani*).]
1 A native or inhabitant of Denmark, a Scandinavian country between the North Sea and the Baltic; orig. & *hist.*, any Norse invader of England between the 9th and 11th cents. OE.
2 More fully ***Great Dane***. (An animal of) a large, powerful, short-haired breed of dog, between the mastiff and the greyhound in type. L18.
– COMB.: **Dane gun** a primitive gun of a kind orig. introduced to western and southern Africa by Danish traders; **Danes' blood**, **daneweed** (now *rare*) danewort; **danewort** [so called because orig. supposed to spring up where Danish blood was spilt in battle] a herbaceous elder, *Sambucus ebulus*.

Danebrog *noun* var. of DANNEBROG.

Danegeld /ˈdeɪngɛld/ *noun*. Also (now *rare*) **-gelt** /-gɛlt/. LOE.
[ORIGIN from Old Norse genit. of *Danir* (pl.) Danes + *gjald* payment, tribute (cf. GELD noun); = Old Danish *Danegjeld*.]
1 ENGLISH HISTORY. An annual tax, imposed orig. (it is believed) to provide funds for the protection of England against the Danes (but often identified with the tribute exacted by the Danes in the late 10th century), and continued as a land tax. LOE.
2 A sum of money paid or demanded in order to ensure safety against a more powerful enemy; protection money. E20.

dane-hole *noun* var. of DENE-HOLE.

Danelaw /ˈdeɪnlɔː/ *noun*.
[ORIGIN Late Old English *Dena lagu* Danes' law.]
hist. **1** The Danish law formerly in force over that part of England which was occupied by Danes from the 9th to the 11th cents. LOE.
2 *The* part of northern and eastern England over which this law prevailed. M19.

dang /daŋ/ *verb*¹ & *noun*. *colloq.* L18.
[ORIGIN Euphem. alt.]
▸ **A** *verb trans.* = DAMN *verb* 3. L18.
▸ **B** *noun*. = DAMN *noun*. E20.

dang *verb*² see DING *verb*¹.

dangdut /ˈdaŋdʌt/ *noun*. L20.
[ORIGIN Indonesian, imit. of the sound of a drum beat. Cf. Javanese *dang* a musical beat.]
In Indonesia: a style of popular music which combines Arab and Malay folk elements with contemporary international music styles.

danger /ˈdeɪn(d)ʒə/ *noun*. ME.
[ORIGIN Anglo-Norman *da(u)nger*, Old French *dangier* (mod. *danger*) from Proto-Romance, from Latin *domnus, dominus* lord, master: see -ER².]
†**1** Power of a lord or master, jurisdiction; power to harm or injure. ME–M19. ▸†**b** Liability (to loss, punishment, etc.). LME–L17.

fig.: SHAKES. *Haml.* Keep you . . Out of the shot and danger of desire.

in a person's danger at the mercy of or under obligation to a person.
†**2** Difficulty (made or raised); reluctance; chariness. ME–E16.
†**3** Mischief, harm, damage. LME–L16.
4 Liability or exposure to harm or injury; risk, peril. Also, an instance or cause of this; an unwelcome possibility *that*. LME. ▸**b** The position or indication of a railway signal directing stoppage or caution. M19.

TOLKIEN The desire to eat hobbits, had seemed the chief danger in Gollum. M. DRABBLE I sensed danger on every side.

in danger of likely to incur, do, etc. **out of danger** unlikely to die of a present illness or injury.
– COMB.: **danger angle** NAUTICAL the angle enclosed by lines drawn from two known points to the point marking the limit of safe approach for a vessel to a danger to navigation; **danger line** a real or imaginary line marking the division between safety and danger; **danger list** a (notional) list of patients (in a hospital) whose lives are in danger (chiefly in ***on the danger list***, dangerously ill); **danger man** someone perceived as posing a particular threat (in sport etc.); **danger money** a payment made beyond basic wages for dangerous work; **danger signal** an indicator of impending danger, *esp.*, on a railway, a red light or a semaphore signal in the 'on' position.
■ †**dangerful** *adjective* dangerous E16–E19. **dangerless** *adjective* (now *rare*) without danger LME. **dangersome** *adjective* (*obsolete* exc. *dial.*) dangerous M16.

danger /ˈdeɪn(d)ʒə/ *verb trans.* Now *rare.* LME.
[ORIGIN Old French *dangerer*, from *dangier*: see DANGER *noun*.]
†1 Render liable. LME–M17.
2 Expose to danger; endanger, imperil, risk. L15.
†3 Harm, injure. M16–E17.

dangerous /ˈdeɪn(d)ʒ(ə)rəs/ *adjective.* ME.
[ORIGIN Anglo-Norman *da(u)ngerous*, Old French *dangereus* (mod. *-eux*), formed as DANGER *noun*: see -OUS.]
†1 Difficult to deal with or to please; arrogant; uncooperative; fastidious. ME–L16. ▸b Cautious, reserved, chary (*of*). LME–M17.
2 Fraught with or causing danger; involving risk; perilous, hazardous; unsafe. LME.

Drive Since December the charges of dangerous driving and causing death by dangerous driving have been abolished. A. THWAITE The dangerous possibility that she might grow up to resemble her mother.

dangerous drug a powerful drug, *esp.* one that can cause addiction.
†3 Hurtful, harmful. M–L16.
4 Extremely ill; at risk (of death) from an illness or injury. Now *dial.* & *US colloq.* E17.
■ **dangerously** *adverb* in a dangerous manner; to a dangerous degree: L16. **dangerousness** *noun* M16.

dangle /ˈdaŋg(ə)l/ *adjective & noun.* E17.
[ORIGIN from the verb.]
▸ **A** *adjective.* Dangling. *rare.* E17.
▸ **B** *noun.* The act of dangling; something that dangles. M18.

dangle /ˈdaŋg(ə)l/ *verb.* L16.
[ORIGIN Imit.: cf. Northern Frisian *dangeln*, Swedish *dangla*, Danish *dangle*, parallel to Icelandic, Swedish *dingla*, Danish *dingle*. See -LE[3].]
1 *verb intrans.* Hang loosely, swaying to and fro. L16. ▸b *spec.* Hang from the gallows, be hanged. L17.

F. L. WRIGHT When sitting on the high chairs . . their short legs would dangle. M. FRAYN A cigarette dangled permanently from her lips.

2 *verb trans.* Make (a thing) hang loosely and sway to and fro; hold suspended loosely; keep (hopes etc.) hanging uncertainly or as a temptation. E17.

C. SANDBURG He dangles herring before prospective customers.

3 *verb intrans.* Hang *after*, hover, as an unofficial follower, aspirant lover, etc. *arch.* E17.

LD MACAULAY Heirs of noble houses . . dangling after actresses.

■ **danglement** *noun* dangling M19. **dangler** *noun* (*a*) something that dangles, a dangling object or part; (*b*) *arch.* a hanger-on, a dallying follower: E18. **dangling** *ppl adjective* (*a*) that dangles; (*b*) GRAMMAR lacking a proper grammatical connection; ***dangling participle***, a participle in an absolute clause or phrase whose subject is omitted, with possible ambiguity: L16. **dangly** *adjective* loosely hanging and swaying L19.

Danic /ˈdeɪnɪk/ *adjective. rare.* E17.
[ORIGIN medieval Latin *Danicus*, from *Dania* Denmark: see -IC.]
Danish.

Daniel /ˈdanj(ə)l/ *noun.* L16.
[ORIGIN The prophet *Daniel*, introduced as a shrewd judge in the apocryphal Book of Susanna.]
An upright judge; a person of infallible wisdom.
– NOTE: First recorded in Shakes.

Daniell /ˈdanj(ə)l/ *noun.* M19.
[ORIGIN John F. *Daniell* (1790–1845), English physicist.]
PHYSICS. 1 In full ***Daniell battery***, ***Daniell cell***, ***Daniell's battery***, ***Daniell's cell***. An electrochemical cell having an amalgamated zinc cathode standing in dilute sulphuric acid and a copper anode in a solution of copper sulphate, the electrolytes being in contact usu. through a porous pot or plate. M19.
2 ***Daniell's hygrometer***, a hygrometer in which the cooling is produced by the forced evaporation of ether. M19.

danio /ˈdeɪnɪəʊ/ *noun.* Pl. **-os**. E19.
[ORIGIN mod. Latin genus name.]
A freshwater fish of the cyprinid genera *Danio* or *Brachydanio*, which occur in the Indian subcontinent and SE Asia and include some popular aquarium fishes.

Danish /ˈdeɪnɪʃ/ *adjective & noun.*
[ORIGIN Old English *Denisċ* = Old Norse *Danskr*, from Germanic, superseded by forms from Anglo-Norman *danes*, Old French *daneis* (mod. *danois*) from medieval Latin *Danensis* from late Latin *Dani* Danes. Later assim. to adjectives in -ISH[1].]
▸ **A** *adjective.* Of or pertaining to Denmark in Scandinavia, the Danes, or their language. OE.
Danish axe *hist.* a kind of battleaxe with a very long blade. **Danish blue (cheese)** a soft white cheese from Denmark, with blue mould veins. **Danish dog** the Great Dane. **Danish modern** a plain, simple style of furniture made of light-coloured wood. **Danish oil** a mixture of tung oil, other vegetable oils, and chemicals to quicken drying, used to treat wood. **Danish pastry** a rich cake of leavened pastry topped with icing, nuts, etc., sometimes with a filling.
▸ **B** *noun.* 1 The North Germanic language of Denmark. LME.
2 A Danish pastry. *colloq.* M20.
■ **Danishry** *noun* (*obsolete* exc. *hist.*) the people of Danish descent (in Britain) LME.

Danism /ˈdeɪnɪz(ə)m/ *noun.* M19.
[ORIGIN from DANE + -ISM.]
A Danish idiom or expression. Also (*rare*), favour towards Denmark.

Danite /ˈdanʌɪt/ *noun.* M16.
[ORIGIN from *Dan* one of the twelve sons of the patriarch Jacob + -ITE[1].]
hist. 1 A member of the Hebrew tribe founded by Dan. M16.
2 A member of an alleged secret order of Mormons, supposed to have arisen in the early days of the sect to act as spies and suppress disaffection. M19.

dank /daŋk/ *verb, adjective, & noun.* ME.
[ORIGIN Prob. of Scandinavian origin: cf. Swedish *dank* marshy spot, Old Norse *døkk* pit, pool.]
▸ **A** *verb trans.* (Esp. of rain, mist, etc.) wet, damp, moisten; dampen (the spirits). *obsolete* exc. *dial.* ME.
▸ **B** *adjective.* 1 Wet, watery; oozy. (Now esp. of ground, marshes, etc.) LME.

R. COBB A big Victorian house . . with a dank, dripping, overgrown garden.

2 Unpleasantly or unwholesomely damp and cold. L16. ▸b Growing in damp places. E19.

O. NASH I do not like the foggy fall . . The dank, rheumatic air. B. PLAIN The house smelled dank and musty. **b** SHELLEY Dock, and henbane, and hemlock dank.

▸ †**C** *noun.* Wetness, damp; a wet place, a pool, a marsh. LME–M17.
■ **dankish** *adjective* M16. **dankly** *adverb* E19. **dankness** *noun* L16. **danky** *adjective* somewhat dank, dampish M16.

Dankali *noun & adjective* var. of DANAKIL.

†**danna** *noun* see DUNNY *noun*.

Dannebrog /ˈdanəbrɒg/ *noun.* Also **Dane-**. E18.
[ORIGIN Danish, from *Danne-*, *Dane-* Danish + *brog* breech, cloth.]
The Danish national flag.
order of Dannebrog, **Dannebrog order**: a Danish order of knighthood.

dannert *noun* var. of DANAERT.

Dano- /ˈdeɪnəʊ/ *combining form.*
[ORIGIN from Latin *Danus* DANISH + -O-.]
Danish and —, Denmark or the Danes in connection with —.
■ **Dano-Norwegian** *adjective & noun* (designating or pertaining to) the Danish language as modified and used in Norway after its separation from Denmark L19.

danse du ventre /dɑ̃ːs dy vɑ̃ːtr/ *noun phr.* Pl. ***danses du ventre*** (pronounced same). L19.
[ORIGIN French.]
A belly dance.

danse macabre /dɑ̃ːs makɑːbr, -ka-/ *noun phr.* Pl. **-s -s** (pronounced same). L19.
[ORIGIN French. Earlier anglicized as *dance (of) macabre*: see MACABRE.]
The Dance of Death; a musical piece or passage representing or suggestive of this.

danses du ventre, ***danses macabres*** *noun phrs.* pls. of DANSE DU VENTRE, DANSE MACABRE.

danseur /dɑ̃sœːr/ *noun.* Pl. pronounced same. E19.
[ORIGIN French, from *danser* (see DANCE *verb*) + *-eur* -OR.]
A male ballet dancer.
danseur noble /nɔbl/ the partner of a ballerina. PREMIER DANSEUR.

danseuse /dɑ̃søːz/ *noun.* Pl. pronounced same. E19.
[ORIGIN French.]
A female dancer; a ballerina.
PREMIÈRE DANSEUSE.

†**Dansk** *adjective.* M16–E17.
[ORIGIN Danish, Swedish *Dansk*, Icelandic *Danskur*.]
= DANISH *adjective*
■ †**Dansker** *noun* (*rare*, Shakes.) a Dane: only in E17.

dante /ˈdanti/ *noun.* Also **-ta** /-tə/. E17.
[ORIGIN Spanish *ante*, *dante* elk, buffalo, *danta* tapir; Italian *dante*; ult. from Arabic *lamṭ* North African oryx.]
The American tapir.

Dantean /ˈdantɪən, danˈtiːən/ *adjective & noun.* L18.
[ORIGIN from *Dante* (see below) + -AN, -EAN.]
▸ **A** *adjective.* Of or pertaining to the Italian poet Dante Alighieri (1265–1321) or his writing; in the style of or reminiscent of Dante's works. L18.
▸ **B** *noun.* An admirer or student of Dante or his writing. M19.
■ **Danˈtesque** *adjective* in the style of or reminiscent of Dante's works E19.

danthonia /danˈθəʊnɪə/ *noun.* E20.
[ORIGIN mod. Latin, from Étienne *Danthoine*, 19th-cent. French botanist: see -IA[1].]
Any of various tufted pasture grasses of the large genus *Danthonia*, chiefly of Australia and New Zealand. Also called ***wallaby-grass***.

Dantonist /ˈdantənɪst/ *noun.* M19.
[ORIGIN from *Danton* (see below) + -IST.]
A follower of Georges Jacques Danton (1759–94), one of the leaders in the French Revolution.

†**Dantzig** *adjective* var. of DANZIG.

Danubian /daˈnjuːbɪən/ *adjective.* M19.
[ORIGIN from medieval Latin *Danubius*, *Danuvius* from Greek *Danoubios* + -IAN.]
Of, pertaining to, or bordering on the River Danube, which rises in the Black Forest in SW Germany and flows into the Black Sea; of or pertaining to the prehistoric cultures of the surrounding region.

Danzig /ˈdanzɪg/ *adjective.* Now *arch.* or *hist.* Also †**-tzig**. L16.
[ORIGIN A city (now *Gdańsk*) in Poland.]
Of Danzig or its region (formerly *esp.* designating timber or beer).

D

Dao, **Daoism** *nouns* vars. of TAO, TAOISM.

dap /dap/ *noun.* M19.
[ORIGIN from the verb. Sense 3 perh. a different word.]
1 The bounce of a ball; the skip of a stone on water. *dial.* M19.
2 In fishing: a bait made to bob lightly on the surface. E20.
3 A rubber-soled shoe; a sports shoe, a plimsoll. *slang.* E20.

dap /dap/ *verb.* Infl. **-pp-**. M17.
[ORIGIN App. parallel to DAB *verb*, the final *p* expressing a lighter touch. Cf. also DOP *verb*.]
1 *verb intrans.* Fish by making the bait bob lightly on the water. M17.

J. BUCHAN He had gone off . . to dap for trout in the park lake.

2 *verb trans.* Use as bait in this mode of fishing. M17.
3 *verb intrans.* Rebound, bounce; hop or skip like a stone across water. M19.
4 *verb intrans.* Dip lightly or suddenly into water. L19.

dapatical /dəˈpatɪk(ə)l/ *adjective. rare.* E17.
[ORIGIN from late Latin *dapaticus*, from Latin *daps* feast + -AL[1].]
Sumptuous, costly.

daphne /ˈdafni/ *noun.* LME.
[ORIGIN Greek *daphnē* laurel, bay tree, *Daphnē* a nymph who escaped Apollo's advances by being changed into a laurel.]
Orig., a laurel or bay tree. Now, a flowering shrub of the genus *Daphne*, of the mezereon family; *esp.* spurge laurel, *D. laureola*.
– COMB.: **daphne heath** *Austral.* any of various flowering shrubs of the genus *Brachyloma*, of the epacris family.

Daphnean /ˈdafnɪən/ *adjective.* L16.
[ORIGIN from Latin *Daphnaeus*, from Greek *Daphnaios*, formed as DAPHNE: see -EAN.]
†1 Of laurel. Only in L16.
2 Pertaining to or characteristic of the nymph Daphne (see DAPHNE); pertaining to or showing maidenly timidity or modesty. E17.

daphnia /ˈdafnɪə/ *noun.* Pl. same. M19.
[ORIGIN mod. Latin (see below), formed as DAPHNE: see -IA[1].]
A freshwater cladoceran of the genus *Daphnia*; a water flea.

daphnin /ˈdafnɪn/ *noun.* E19.
[ORIGIN from mod. Latin *Daphne* genus name formed as DAPHNE: see -IN[1].]
CHEMISTRY. A bitter glycoside occurring in some shrubs of the genus *Daphne*.
■ **daphnetin** /ˈdafnɪtɪn/ *noun* a yellow crystalline compound, 7,8-dihydroxycoumarin, $C_9H_6O_4$, the aglycone of daphnin M19.

dapifer /ˈdapɪfə/ *noun. obsolete* exc. *hist.* M17.
[ORIGIN Late Latin, from *daps*, *dap-* food, feast: see -FER.]
A person who brings food to the table; the steward in a monarch's or noble's household.

dapper /ˈdapə/ *adjective.* LME.
[ORIGIN Middle Low German, Middle Dutch = heavy, powerful, strong, stout (Dutch = bold, valiant) = Old High German *tapfar* heavy, weighty, firm (late Middle High German, German *tapfer* brave), Old Norse *dapr* sad, dreary.]
1 Neat, trim, smart in dress or appearance. LME.

ANTHONY WOOD Mounting my dapper nagg, Pegasus. A. N. WILSON Those walks . . with her father, in those days rather dapper, with yellow kid gloves, and an Inverness cape.

2 *spec.* Of a small person, esp. a man; smart in movements etc., active, sprightly. E17.

R. W. EMERSON We are dapper little busybodies, and run this way and that superserviceably.

■ **dapperling** *noun* a little dapper fellow E17. **dapperly** *adverb* LME. **dapperness** *noun* M16.

dapple /ˈdap(ə)l/ *noun.* L16.
[ORIGIN from DAPPLED or DAPPLE *adjective*.]
1 Each of many roundish patches of colour or shade on a surface. Usu. in *pl.* L16.

J. R. LOWELL To watch the dapples of sunlight on the grass.

2 Dappled condition or effect; mottled marking. L16.

G. MAXWELL The dapple of changing cloud shadow upon the shoulders of the hills.

3 An animal, esp. a horse, with a dappled coat. M17.

dapple /ˈdap(ə)l/ *adjective.* L15.
[ORIGIN from DAPPLED. Perh. earlier in DAPPLE GREY.]
Dappled.

dapple /ˈdap(ə)l/ *verb*. L16.
[ORIGIN from DAPPLED.]
1 *verb trans.* Variegate with rounded spots or patches of colour or shade. L16.
SHAKES. *Much Ado* The gentle day . . Dapples the drowsy east with spots of grey.
2 *verb intrans.* Become dappled. L17.
BYRON Methought that mist of dawning gray Would never dapple into day.

dappled /ˈdap(ə)ld/ *adjective*. LME.
[ORIGIN Uncertain: perh. from Old Norse *depill* spot (cf. Norwegian *dape* puddle). Cf. DAPPLE GREY.]
Marked with spots or patches of a different colour or shade; speckled, mottled.
J. RUSKIN Beeches cast their dappled shade. J. C. OATES His lovely gray-and-white dappled Shetland pony.
– COMB.: **dappled-grey** *adjective & noun* = next.

dapple grey /dap(ə)l ˈgreɪ/ *adjectival & noun phr.* LME.
[ORIGIN Perh. from *dappled-grey* (see DAPPLED) or alt. of an unattested comb. *apple-grey* (cf. Old Norse *apalgrár*, Old High German *aphelgrāo* (German *apfelgrau*), Dutch *appelgrauw*, = French *pommelé* dapple grey).]
▶ **A** *adjectival phr.* Of a horse: grey variegated with spots or patches of a darker shade. LME.
▶ **B** *noun phr.* A horse of this colour. LME.

daps /daps/ *noun pl. obsolete* exc. *dial.* L16.
[ORIGIN Unknown.]
1 Ways, modes of action. L16.
2 Likeness, image in ways or appearance. M18.

dapsone /ˈdapsəʊn/ *noun*. M20.
[ORIGIN from *di*(*para-aminophenyl*)*sulphone* (alternative systematic name).]
PHARMACOLOGY. A crystalline bacteriostatic compound, bis(4-aminophenyl)sulphone, $(H_2NC_6H_4)_2SO_2$, used esp. in the treatment of leprosy.

Darapti /dəˈrapti/ *noun*. M16.
[ORIGIN A mnemonic of scholastic philosophers, first used in medieval Latin, A indicating a universal affirmative proposition and I a particular affirmative proposition.]
LOGIC. The first valid mood of the third syllogistic figure, in which a particular affirmative conclusion is drawn from two universal affirmative premisses.

darbuka /dɑːˈbʊkə/ *noun*. L19.
[ORIGIN Arabic *darabukka*, perh. from *darba* to strike.]
A kind of goblet-shaped hand drum originating in various Middle Eastern and North African countries.

Darby /ˈdɑːbi/ *noun*. L16.
[ORIGIN A personal surname, perh. in some cases repr. the usual pronunc. of the English city *Derby*.]
▶ **I 1 a** ***Darby's bands***, ***Father Darby's bands***, some rigid form of band for debtors. Long *obsolete* exc. *hist.* L16. ▸**b** (Usu. **d-**.) In *pl.* Handcuffs; (formerly) fetters. *slang*. L17.
†**2** Ready cash. *slang*. L17–L18.
3 A kind of plasterer's float, usu. with two handles. E19.
4 In full ***Darby kelly***, also ***Darby kel***. = BELLY *noun* 2, 4. *rhyming slang*. E20.
▶ **II 5** [Perh. from characters in a poem published in 1735 in the *Gentleman's Magazine*.] ***Darby and Joan***, a devoted old married couple. L18.
– COMB.: **Darby and Joan club**: for elderly people.

Darbyite /ˈdɑːbɪʌɪt/ *noun*. M19.
[ORIGIN from John *Darby* (1800–82), founder of the sect + -ITE[1].]
A member of the Plymouth Brethren, *spec.* of the Exclusive Brethren.

darcy /ˈdɑːsi/ *noun*. Pl. **-cies**, **-cys**. M20.
[ORIGIN H. P. G. *Darcy* (1803–58), French hydrologist and waterworks inspector.]
PHYSICS. A cgs unit of permeability to fluid flow, being the permeability of a medium that allows a flow of 1 cubic centimetre per second of 1 centipoise viscosity under a pressure gradient of 1 atmosphere/centimetre.

Dard /dɑːd/ *noun & adjective*. M19.
[ORIGIN Dard.]
▶ **A** *noun*. A member of any of several peoples inhabiting eastern Afghanistan, northern Pakistan, and Kashmir; (any of) a group of Indic languages spoken by these peoples. M19.
▶ **B** *attrib.* or as *adjective*. Of or pertaining to these peoples or (any of) their languages. L19.
■ **Dardic** *adjective & noun* (**a**) *adjective* = DARD *adjective*; (**b**) *noun* any Dard language: E20.

Dardan /ˈdɑːd(ə)n/ *adjective & noun*. *rare*. E17.
[ORIGIN Latin *Dardanus*.]
(A) Trojan.
■ Also **Dardanian** /-ˈdeɪnɪən/ *adjective* L16.

†**dare** *noun*[1]. L15–M18.
[ORIGIN A sing. from †*darse* var. of DACE.]
= DACE.

dare /dɛː/ *noun*[2]. Now *colloq.* L16.
[ORIGIN from DARE *verb*[1].]
1 An act of defiance; a challenge. L16.
BUNYAN Sin is the dare of God's justice. LYNDON B. JOHNSON I wanted to see if I could keep up this arduous task. In a way, I made myself a dare.
2 Boldness. *rare*. L16.
SHAKES. *1 Hen. IV* It lends . . A larger dare to our great enterprise.

dare /dɛː/ *noun*[3]. M19.
[ORIGIN from DARE *verb*[2].]
A contrivance for catching larks by fascinating them.

dare /dɛː/ *verb*[1]. 3 sing. pres. usu. **dare** before expressed or implied inf. without *to*; otherwise **dares**. Pa. t. in this context occas. **dare**; otherwise **dared**; (now *arch. & dial.*) **durst** /dəːst/. Pa. pple **dared**. Informal abbreviated forms: **daren't** /dɛːnt/ = *dare not*; **durstn't** /ˈdəːs(ə)nt/ = *durst not*.
[ORIGIN Old English *durran*, pres. *dearr*, *durron*, pa. *dorste*, a preterite-pres. verb, corresp. to Old Frisian *dūra*, Old Saxon *gidurran*, Old High German *giturran*, Gothic *gadaursan*, from Germanic bases from Indo-European, whence Sanskrit *dhṛṣ-*, Greek *tharsein* be bold.]
▶ **I** *verb intrans.* **1** Have sufficient courage or impudence; be so bold (as). (Foll. by (*to*) *do*.) OE.
AV *John* 21:12 None of the disciples durst aske him, Who art thou? W. IRVING No one would dare to desert. J. BUCHAN He would have gone himself, but he dared not. G. VIDAL I don't dare mention his name to my family.
I dare say, (*colloq.*) **I daresay** I am prepared to believe, I do not deny, it is very likely. **I dare swear** I feel sure that. ***I dare*** UNDERTAKE.
2 *ellipt.* Dare to go, venture. *poet.* LME.
DRYDEN Nor dare beyond the Reed.
▶ **II** *verb trans.* **3** Challenge, defy, (a person). (Foll. by *to* an action, *to do*.) L16.
F. MARRYAT You wish to dare me to it—well, I won't be dared to anything. DYLAN THOMAS Gomer Owen kissed her when she wasn't looking because he was dared. P. GOODMAN He promptly dared the others to jump off the roof.
4 Venture to meet or be exposed to, meet defiantly; have enough courage for (an action), venture on. E17.
SWIFT Should some sourer mongrel dare too near an approach. JAS. HOGG To . . dare In his dark home the sullen bear. G. A. WAGNER Against his will he'd dared A dreadful danger.
■ **darer** *noun* E17.

dare /dɛː/ *verb*[2]. *obsolete* exc. *dial.*
[ORIGIN Old English *darian* from stem also of Middle Dutch and Low German *bedaren* appease, calm, Flemish *verdaren* amaze.]
†**1** *verb intrans.* Lie hidden, lurk. OE–LME.
2 *verb intrans.* Lie motionless, crouch, esp. in fear; tremble with fear. ME.
†**3** *verb intrans.* Gaze fixedly; stare in amazement or terror. ME–M16.
4 *verb trans.* Daze; fascinate. M16.
5 *verb trans.* Daunt, terrify, paralyse with fear. E17.

dare-all /ˈdɛːrɔːl/ *noun & adjective*. M19.
[ORIGIN DARE *verb*[1] + ALL *pronoun*.]
▶ **A** *noun*. A person who or thing which defies all adversity. Also, a weatherproof covering. *rare*. M19.
▶ **B** *adjective*. Bold, reckless. E20.

daredevil /ˈdɛːdɛv(ə)l/ *noun & adjective*. L18.
[ORIGIN from DARE *verb*[1] + DEVIL *noun*.]
(A person who is) recklessly daring.
CONAN DOYLE He is about the most daredevil rider in England. D. JACOBSON A team of French dare-devils turning their cars over and over.
■ **daredevilry** *noun* reckless daring M19.

†**dareful** *adjective*. *rare*. Only in E17.
[ORIGIN from DARE *noun*[2] or *verb*[1] + -FUL.]
Full of daring or defiance.

darg /dɑːg/ *noun*. *Scot.*, *N. English*, & *Austral.* Also †**dark**, (earliest) †**dawark**. LME.
[ORIGIN Syncopated from *daywork*.]
1 A day's work; a particular amount of work, a task. LME.
2 The result or product of a day's work. L15.
– NOTE: Mod. form recorded from M16.

dargah /ˈdɑːgə/ *noun*. Also **durgah** /ˈdəːgə/. L18.
[ORIGIN Persian *dargāh* royal court.]
The tomb or shrine of a Muslim saint.

daric /ˈdarɪk/ *noun*. M16.
[ORIGIN Greek *Dareikos* (sc. *statēr* stater): see -IC.]
hist. A gold coin of ancient Persia, named from the first King Darius. Also, a silver Persian coin of similar design.

Darii /ˈdɛːrɪʌɪ/ *noun*. M16.
[ORIGIN A mnemonic of scholastic philosophers, first used in medieval Latin, A indicating a universal affirmative proposition and I a particular affirmative proposition.]
LOGIC. The third valid mood of the first syllogistic figure, in which a particular affirmative conclusion is drawn from a universal major premiss and a particular affirmative minor premiss.

daring /ˈdɛːrɪŋ/ *noun*. E17.
[ORIGIN from DARE *verb*[1] + -ING[1].]
The action of DARE *verb*[1]; adventurous courage, boldness, audacity.

daring /ˈdɛːrɪŋ/ *adjective*. L16.
[ORIGIN from DARE *verb*[1] + -ING[2].]
Bold, adventurous, audacious; unconventional.
B. PYM I wonder what could possibly be regarded as too daring to publish nowadays. G. SWIFT Dad was involved in a succession of daring operations in France.
■ **daringly** *adverb* E17. **daringness** *noun* E17.

dariole /ˈdarɪəʊl/ *noun*. LME.
[ORIGIN Old French & mod. French.]
1 An individual sweet or savoury dish of various kinds; now *spec.* one made in a dariole mould. LME.
2 In full ***dariole mould***. A small metal mould shaped like a flowerpot and used for making such a dish. M19.

Darjeeling /dɑːˈdʒiːlɪŋ/ *noun*. L19.
[ORIGIN A town and district in West Bengal.]
In full ***Darjeeling tea***. A high-quality tea grown in the mountainous regions of northern India.

dark /dɑːk/ *noun*[1]. ME.
[ORIGIN from the adjective.]
1 The absence of light, darkness; a dark time or place; night, nightfall. ME.
DEFOE The Darks of Hell. J. RHYS I . . stayed away till dark. A. LURIE I couldn't see his face in the dark.
after dark at night. **dark of the moon** the time when there is no moonlight. **leap in the dark**, **shot in the dark** *fig.* an action of which the outcome cannot be foreseen. **whistle in the dark** keep up one's courage, esp. by a show of confidence.
2 Obscurity; secrecy; ignorance. E17.
be in the dark, **keep in the dark** be, keep, in a state of ignorance about some matter.
3 A dark colour or shade; *esp.* a part of a painting in shadow. L17.
J. ROSENBERG Rembrandt's light becomes most selective and evocative, through its peculiar interpenetration with the darks.
– COMB.: **dark adaptation** adjustment of the eye to low intensity of light; **dark-adapted** *adjective* (of the eye) adjusted to low intensity of light; **darkfall** dusk, nightfall.
■ **darksome** *adjective* (now chiefly *poet.*) somewhat dark (*lit. & fig.*); gloomy, sombre, obscure: M16.

†**dark** *noun*[2] var. of DARG.

dark /dɑːk/ *adjective*.
[ORIGIN Old English *deorc*, prob. from Germanic base; perh. rel. to Old High German *tarnjan* (German *tarnen*) conceal.]
▶ **I** *lit.* **1** Devoid of or deficient in light; unilluminated. OE.
O. HENRY The alley was dark except for one patch of light. SCOTT FITZGERALD It was a dark night with no moon.
†**keep a person dark** keep a person confined in a darkened room (as the insane were formerly kept).
2 Reflecting or transmitting little light; gloomy, sombre. OE.
J. CONRAD A . . vision of dark peaks. S. SPENDER Dusk drops a dark cloak.
3 Of colour, an object, etc.: approaching black in hue; having intensity or depth of colour. LME. ▸**b** Of a person, or the complexion: having brown or black hair or skin, not blonde. LME.
SOUTHEY Her dark hair floating on the morning gale. SIR W. SCOTT The bound of dark-brown doe. **b** P. S. BUCK She had always been a dark woman, her skin ruddy and brown.
▶ **II** *fig.* **4** Devoid of moral or spiritual light; evil, wicked, sinister; foul, atrocious. OE.
C. V. WEDGWOOD Colonel Harrison . . had assured the King that nothing dark or underhand would be done to him. I. MURDOCH A man destined by dark forces to commit a murder for which he had no will.
5 Gloomy, dismal, sullen, sad. OE. ▸**b** Of facial expression: clouded with anger or dislike, frowning. L16.
J. STEINBECK They're a dark people with a gift for suffering way past their deserving. **b** A. LURIE The dark spiteful glance of . . your enemy.
6 Obscure in meaning; indistinct. LME.
L. STRACHEY The issue grew doubtful and more dark.
7 Partially or totally blind. *obsolete* exc. *dial.* LME.
8 Unenlightened, uninformed, ignorant. LME.
MILTON What in me is dark Illumine, what is low raise and support.
9 Hidden from view or knowledge; concealed, secret. E17. ▸**b** Of a person: reticent, secretive. L17.
DICKENS He hid himself . . kept himself dark. **b** POPE And Lyttelton a dark, designing knave.
keep something dark *colloq.* keep something secret.
10 Of whom or of which little is known. M19.
11 In *superl.* Of part of a region (orig. of Africa): most remote, inaccessible, and uncivilized. Now chiefly *joc.* L19.
H. M. STANLEY Through Darkest Africa. C. S. COOPER They shunted him off to darkest Somerset.
12 PHONETICS. Velarized, retracted; *spec.* designating the velarized, as opp. to the 'clear' or palatalized, lateral consonant (/ɫ/). L19.

13 Of a theatre etc.: closed, not in use. **E20**.
– SPECIAL COLLOCATIONS & COMB.: **Dark Age** (*a*) the period between the end of the Bronze Age and the beginning of the historical period in Greece and other Aegean countries; (*b*) = ***Dark Ages*** (a) below. **Dark Ages** (*a*) the Medieval period, now usu. the earlier part, between the fall of Rome and the appearance of vernacular documents; *transf.* an unenlightened or ignorant period; an age of which little is known; *joc.* an obscure or little-regarded period before the present; (*b*) = ***Dark Age*** (a) above. **dark arches (moth)** a noctuid moth, *Apamea monoglypha*, with highly variable brown or black wing coloration. **dark chocolate** = PLAIN CHOCOLATE. **dark current** the electric current flowing in a photoelectric device when no radiation is incident on it. **dark days**: of adversity. **dark glasses** spectacles with tinted lenses. **dark horse** a racehorse whose form is little known; *fig.* a person, esp. a competitor, about whom little is known. **dark lantern**: with means for concealing its light. **dark lines** (in a spectrum) absorption lines. **dark matter** ASTRONOMY matter whose existence is postulated to account for the dynamical behaviour of galaxies, but which has not been detected (***cold dark matter***: in the form of exotic weakly interacting particles; ***hot dark matter***: in the form of high-energy randomly moving particles soon after the Big Bang). **darknet** COMPUTING a computer network with restricted access that is used chiefly for illegal peer-to-peer file sharing. **dark night (of the soul)** a period of spiritual aridity suffered by a mystic etc., *transf.* a period of anguish or despair. **darkroom**: from which all actinic rays, such as daylight, have been excluded, for photographic developing etc. **the dark side** (in the *Star Wars* films) a state of mind in which the Force works for evil purposes rather than good; *transf.* evil, an evil enemy or opposing force. **dark space** any of several non-luminous areas in a vacuum tube traversed by an electric discharge. **the Dark Continent** Africa, esp. in the time before it was fully explored by Europeans.
■ **darkful** *adjective* (*rare*) full of darkness **OE**. **darkish** *adjective* **LME**. **darkly** *adverb* **OE**.

dark /dɑːk/ *verb*. **OE**.
[ORIGIN from the adjective.]
1 *verb trans. & intrans.* Make or become dark, darken. *obsolete* exc. *dial.* **OE**.
2 *verb intrans.* Lie concealed, lurk. Now only (*dial.*), listen furtively, eavesdrop. **ME**.
3 *verb trans. fig.* Obscure, dim, sully. Now *rare* or *obsolete*. **LME**.
– NOTE: Largely superseded by DARKEN.

darken /ˈdɑːk(ə)n/ *verb*. **ME**.
[ORIGIN from DARK *adjective* + -EN[5].]
1 *verb trans. & intrans.* Make or become devoid of or deficient in light. **ME**.
MILTON When Night darkens the Streets. E. BOWEN Day darkened over the Channel, the skyline vanished.
2 *verb trans. fig.* Cast a shadow over; cloud, tarnish; eclipse. **LME**. ▸**b** *verb intrans.* Become gloomy or sad; cloud with anger. **M18**.
SHAKES. *Coriol.* And you are dark'ned in this action, sir, Even by your own. S. C. HALL Domestic affliction . . darkened the later years of his life. **b** SIR W. SCOTT His displeasure seemed to increase, his brow darkened.
darken a person's door(s) make a visit, esp. an unwelcome one (usu. in neg. contexts).
3 *verb trans. & intrans.* Make or become blind or dim-sighted. Now chiefly *fig.* **M16**.
AV *Ps.* 69:23 Let their eyes be darkened, that they see not.
4 *verb trans. & intrans.* Make or become obscure in meaning or intelligibility. **M16**.
AV *Job* 38:2 Who is this that darkeneth counsel by words without knowledge? LYTTON The vision darkens from me.
5 *verb trans. & intrans.* Make or become darker in hue or colour. **E18**.

darkey, **darkie** *nouns* vars. of DARKY.

darkle /ˈdɑːk(ə)l/ *verb*. **E19**.
[ORIGIN Back-form. from DARKLING.]
1 *verb intrans.* Become dark or gloomy. **E19**.
2 *verb intrans.* Appear dimly or indistinctly. **E19**.
3 *verb trans.* Make obscure, darken. **L19**.

darkling /ˈdɑːklɪŋ/ *adverb, adjective, & noun*. **LME**.
[ORIGIN from DARK *noun*[1] + -LING[2].]
▸ **A** *adverb*. In the dark. **LME**.
▸ **B** *adjective*. **1** Being or taking place in the dark. **M18**.
2 Characterized by darkness or obscurity. **M18**.
– SPECIAL COLLOCATIONS: **darkling beetle** = TENEBRIONID *noun*.
▸ **C** *noun*. The dark. **E20**.
■ Also **darklings** *adverb* (*rare*) **M17**.

darkmans /ˈdɑːkmənz/ *noun. slang*. Now *rare* or *obsolete*. **M16**.
[ORIGIN from DARK *adjective*: for 2nd elem. cf. LIGHTMANS, TOGEMANS.]
The night.

darkness /ˈdɑːknɪs/ *noun*. **OE**.
[ORIGIN from DARK *adjective* + -NESS.]
1 Partial or total absence of light. **OE**.
2 *fig.* Lack of spiritual or intellectual light; wickedness, evil; ignorance. **ME**. ▸**b** Death. **LME**.
ADDISON The Darkness and Superstition of later Ages.
Prince of Darkness Satan, the Devil.
3 The quality of being dark in hue or colour. **LME**.
4 Blindness, dimness of sight. Now chiefly *poet.* **LME**.
TENNYSON His eyes . . Were shrivell'd into darkness in his head.
5 Unhappiness, distress, gloom. **LME**.
SHELLEY The darkness of deepest dismay.
6 Secrecy, mystery; obscurity. **LME**.

darky /ˈdɑːki/ *noun. slang*. Also **-key**, **-kie**. **L18**.
[ORIGIN from DARK *adjective* + -Y[6].]
1 The night, darkness. **L18**.
2 A black person. *colloq.* (*offensive*). **L18**.
3 A dark lantern. *arch.* **E19**.

darl /dɑːl/ *noun. colloq.* (chiefly *Austral.*). **M20**.
[ORIGIN Abbreviation.]
= DARLING *noun*[1].

darling /ˈdɑːlɪŋ/ *noun*[1] *& adjective*. Also †**dear-**. **OE**.
[ORIGIN from DEAR *adjective*[1], *noun* + -LING[1].]
▸ **A** *noun*. **1** A person who is dearly loved. Freq. as a form of address. **OE**.
TENNYSON Answer, darling, answer, no. M. GEE Then he would kiss her and call her his darling.
2 A favourite, a pet; an object of indulgent affection. **OE**.
H. ROBBINS Mark was the columnists' darling He was always good for an item. Q. BELL A nervous, delicate boy, his mother's darling.
3 A lovable person, an endearing creature. **L18**.
▸ **B** *adjective*. **1** Best-loved, dearest, favourite. **L16**.
COLERIDGE His [the devil's] darling sin Is pride that apes humility.
2 Lovable; (in affected use) sweetly pretty or charming. **E19**.
QUEEN VICTORIA Short clothes with darling little stockings and . . pink satin shoes—really too darling!

Darling /ˈdɑːlɪŋ/ *noun*[2]. **M19**.
[ORIGIN A river in western New South Wales, Australia.]
Used *attrib.* to designate things associated with the area of the River Darling, esp. in names of plants growing there.
Darling clover sweet fenugreek, *Trigonella suavissima*, a fragrant herb growing along watercourses. **Darling lily** a bulbous plant of the amaryllis family, *Crinum flaccidum*, with large white or pink flowers. **Darling pea** either of two leguminous plants of the genus *Swainsona*, *S. galegifolia* and *S. greyana*, with flowers which are poisonous to sheep; also called ***poison-bush***. **Darling shower** *local* a dust storm.

darling /ˈdɑːlɪŋ/ *verb trans*. **L19**.
[ORIGIN from DARLING *noun*[1].]
Address as 'darling'.
T. RATTIGAN Wonderful the way you stage people darling each other.

darlint /ˈdɑːlɪnt/ *noun & adjective. dial. & joc.* **L19**.
[ORIGIN Alt.]
= DARLING *noun*[1] *& adjective*.

darmstadtium /dɑːmˈstatɪəm/ *noun*. **E21**.
[ORIGIN named after the city of *Darmstadt* in Germany, where it was discovered, + -IUM.]
A radioactive transuranic chemical element, atomic number 110, which is produced artificially (symbol Ds).

darn /dɑːn/ *noun*[1]. **E18**.
[ORIGIN from DARN *verb*[1].]
A place in a garment repaired by darning.

darn /dɑːn/ *noun*[2], *adjective, & adverb. slang* (orig. *US*). Also ***dern**, ***durn**, /dəːn/. **L18**.
[ORIGIN Euphem. alt.]
= DAMN *noun, adjective & adverb*.
■ **darˈnation** *noun, adjective, & adverb* = DAMNATION *noun* 3, *adjective & adverb* **L18**.

darn /dɑːn/ *verb*[1]. **E17**.
[ORIGIN Perh. from DERN *verb*[1]: cf. Middle Dutch *dernen* stop holes in (a dyke).]
1 *verb trans. & intrans.* Mend (a garment, fabric, esp. knitted material) by filling in the damaged area with interwoven yarn. **E17**.
2 *verb trans.* Ornament or embroider with darning stitch. **L19**.
darned net net embroidered so as to resemble lace.

darn /dɑːn/ *verb*[2] *trans. slang* (orig. *US*). Also ***dern**, ***durn**, /dəːn/. **L18**.
[ORIGIN Alt. of DAMN *verb*.]
In imprecations, freq. in imper. or optative form: damn.
■ **darned** *ppl adjective & adverb* = DAMNED *adjective* 4 & *adverb* **E19**.

darn *verb*[3] var. of DERN *verb*[1].

darnel /ˈdɑːn(ə)l/ *noun*. **ME**.
[ORIGIN Uncertain: cf. French (Walloon) *darnelle* (in standard French *ivraie*).]
A grass of the genus *Lolium*; esp. *L. temulentum*, formerly common as a weed in cornfields in Europe and Asia.
fig.: H. BARROW [Satan] sowing his darnel of errors and tares of discord among them.
red darnel: see RED *adjective*.

darner /ˈdɑːnə/ *noun*. **E17**.
[ORIGIN from DARN *verb*[1] + -ER[1].]
1 A person who repairs garments, fabric, etc., by darning. **E17**.
2 A darning machine. Also, a tool used in darning; a darning needle, a darning egg. **L19**.

darning /ˈdɑːnɪŋ/ *noun*. **E17**.
[ORIGIN from DARN *verb*[1] + -ING[1].]
1 The action of DARN *verb*[1]; mending fabric using interwoven stitches. **E17**. ▸**b** (Embroidering with) darning stitch. **L19**.
2 Articles darned or to be darned. **L19**.
– COMB.: **darning ball**, **darning egg**, **darning last** a curved piece of wood or other smooth hard material used to stretch and support material being darned; **darning cotton**: of a kind suitable for darning with; ***darning egg***, ***darning last***: see ***darning ball*** above; **darning machine**: for repairing garments, fabric, etc., by darning; **darning needle** a long thick needle with a large eye, suitable for darning with (***devil's darning needle***: see DEVIL *noun*); **darning stitch** a large running stitch as used in darning; **darning wool**: of a kind suitable for darning with.

D

daroga /dəˈrəʊɡə/ *noun*. **M17**.
[ORIGIN Persian & Urdu *dārōgā*.]
In the Indian subcontinent: orig., a governor or chief officer, a head of police or excise; now, a police sub-inspector.

DARPA /ˈdɑːpə/ *abbreviation*. *US*.
Defense Advanced Research Projects Agency.

†**darrein** *adjective*. **E16–M19**.
[ORIGIN Anglo-Norman, Old French *derrein*, *darrein*, whence Old French *derrenier*, (also mod.) *dernier* last.]
LAW. Last, ultimate, final; = DERNIER.

†**darse** *noun* var. of DACE.

darshan /ˈdɑːʃən/ *noun*. **E20**.
[ORIGIN Hindi pronunc. of Sanskrit *darśana* sight, seeing, from *dṛś-* to see.]
In the Indian subcontinent etc.: the opportunity or occasion of seeing a holy person or the image of a deity.

dart /dɑːt/ *noun*. **ME**.
[ORIGIN Old French (mod. *dard*), accus. of *darz*, *dars*, from Frankish = spear, lance, repr. by Old English *daroþ*, Old High German *tart*, Old Norse *darraðr*; in senses 2 and 4 from the verb.]
1 A small pointed missile shot or thrown as a weapon; *poet.* an arrow. **ME**. ▸**b** A small pointed missile, usu. with a feather or plastic flight, thrown at a target in a game; in *pl.*, the indoor game played with such missiles and a circular target. **E20**.
transf. & fig.: W. M. PRAED The lightning's vivid dart. E. BLUNDEN Shrapnel shells, uncoiling their . . smoke downwards while their white-hot darts scoured the acre below.
Cupid's dart. ***heart and dart***: see HEART *noun*.
†**2** In full ***dart-snake***, ***dart-serpent***. A snake or snakelike lizard with characteristic darting movements. **L16–M19**.
3 An animal organ resembling a dart in shape or function; *spec.* (*a*) (now only *poet.*) the sting of a venomous insect etc.; (*b*) a calcareous pointed organ in some gastropods forming part of the reproductive system. **M17**.
4 An act of darting; a sudden rapid movement. **E18**.
A. TROLLOPE She . . prepared herself for a dart at the door.
5 In full ***dart-moth***. Any of a large group of noctuid moths, most having dart-shaped markings on their wings. **E19**.
6 A plan, a scheme; a good idea; a fancy; a favourite. *slang* (chiefly *Austral.*). Now *rare*. **M19**.
7 DRESSMAKING. A stitched tapered tuck for shaping a garment. **L19**.
– COMB.: **dartboard** a circular target with numbered sectors used in the game of darts; **dartman** a soldier armed with darts; ***dart-moth***: see sense 5 above; **dart-sac** a hollow organ in some gastropods, secreting the reproductive dart; ***dart-serpent***, ***dart-snake***: see sense 2 above.

dart /dɑːt/ *verb*. **LME**.
[ORIGIN from the noun Cf. French *darder*.]
1 *verb trans.* Pierce with a dart or other pointed weapon. Now *rare*. **LME**.
2 *verb intrans.* (now *rare*) *& trans.* Throw or shoot (a dart or similar missile). **M16**.
3 *verb trans.* Send out suddenly and rapidly, make a rapid movement with; cast (a glance etc.) quickly and keenly. **L16**.
F. HERBERT The old eyes darted a hard glance at Jessica. R. P. JHABVALA He darted the tip of his tongue over his lips.
4 *verb intrans.* Move like a dart, swiftly and suddenly; start rapidly in some direction; make rapid changes of direction. **E17**.
V. WOOLF The firelight darting and making the room red. W. S. MAUGHAM His restless eyes darted here and there like a hare trying to escape a pursuer. E. MANNIN Lizards darted up and down the trunks of the palms.

†**dartars** *noun*. **L16–M18**.
[ORIGIN French DARTRE.]
A kind of scab on the chin of sheep.

darter /ˈdɑːtə/ *noun*. **M16**.
[ORIGIN from DART *verb* + -ER[1].]
▸ **I** **1** A person who throws or shoots darts. Now usu. *hist.* **M16**.
2 A person who or thing which darts or moves swiftly. **E19**.

D

▸ **II** †**3** = DART *noun* 2. E17–E19.
4 Any of a number of long-necked fish-eating birds of the genus *Anhinga*, esp. of any of the Old World species. Cf. ANHINGA. L18.
5 Any of numerous small quick-moving N. American percid fishes belonging to the genus *Etheostoma* and related genera. M19.
6 In full ***darter dragonfly***. A dragonfly that darts to and fro from a particular perch when flying; *spec.* = LIBELLULID. M20.

Dartford warbler /dɑːtfəd 'wɔːblə/ *noun phr.* L18.
[ORIGIN *Dartford* in Kent, England, near where the bird was first seen.]
A small dark warbler, *Sylvia undata*, of Europe and N. Africa.

dartle /'dɑːt(ə)l/ *verb trans. & intrans. rare.* M19.
[ORIGIN Dim. & iterative of DART *verb*: see -LE³.]
Dart or shoot out repeatedly.

Dartmoor /'dɑːtmʊə, -mɔː/ *noun.* M19.
[ORIGIN A moorland plateau in Devon, England.]
1 In full ***Dartmoor pony***. (An animal of) a breed of small shaggy pony native to Dartmoor. M19.
2 In full ***Dartmoor sheep***. (An animal of) a hardy variety of sheep bred on Dartmoor. M19.

dartos /'dɑːtɒs/ *noun.* M17.
[ORIGIN Greek = flayed.]
ANATOMY. The muscle of the scrotal skin.
■ **dartoid** *adjective* of the nature of, resembling, or pertaining to the dartos L19.

dartre /'dɑːtə/ *noun.* Now *rare* or *obsolete*. E19.
[ORIGIN French from medieval Latin *derbita*, of Gaulish origin.]
A skin ailment or scab, *esp.* herpes. Cf. DARTARS.
■ **dartrous** *adjective* M19.

Darwin /'dɑːwɪn/ *noun.* L19.
[ORIGIN Charles *Darwin*: see DARWINIAN.]
1 In full ***Darwin tulip***. A tall late-flowering type of tulip with self-coloured flowers rectangular in outline in their lower part. L19.
2 ***Darwin's finch***, any of a diverse group of related buntings of the Galapagos Islands adapted to a wide range of ecological niches and used by Darwin to illustrate speciation. Usu. in *pl.* M20.
3 (**d-**.) A unit of rate of change in evolution, corresponding to variation by a factor *e* (= 2.718.) in one million years. M20.

Darwinian /dɑː'wɪnɪən/ *adjective & noun.* L18.
[ORIGIN from *Darwin*, a family name (sense 1 Erasmus, sense 2 his grandson Charles) + -IAN.]
▸ **A** *adjective.* **1** Of or pertaining to the English physician, naturalist, and poet Erasmus Darwin (1731–1802), his speculations, or his poetical style. L18.
2 Of or pertaining to the English naturalist Charles Robert Darwin (1809–82) or his views, esp. his theory of the evolution of species. (The predominant sense.) M19.
Darwinian tubercle ANATOMY a small projection on the edge of the human ear, present in the fetus and sometimes persisting in the adult, hypothesized to be a vestige of the pointed ear of primates.
▸ **B** *noun.* A follower of Erasmus or (more commonly) Charles Darwin; an adherent of Charles Darwin's theory of evolution. E19.
■ **Darwinianism** *noun* = DARWINISM E19.

Darwinism /'dɑːwɪnɪz(ə)m/ *noun.* M19.
[ORIGIN formed as DARWINIAN + -ISM.]
1 The doctrines or hypotheses of Erasmus Darwin. *rare.* M19.
2 The biological theories of Charles Darwin concerning the evolution of species, etc. M19.
■ **Darwinist** *noun* L19. **Darwi'nistic** *adjective* L19.

Darwinize /'dɑːwɪnʌɪz/ *verb.* Also **-ise**. L19.
[ORIGIN formed as DARWINISM + -IZE.]
1 *verb intrans.* Speculate after the manner of Erasmus or Charles Darwin. L19.
2 *verb trans.* Affect or influence by Darwinian theories of evolution. E20.

das /das, dɑːs/ *noun.* Pl. same, **dassen** /-s(ə)n/. L15.
[ORIGIN Dutch = German *Dachs*: cf. DASSIE.]
†**1** A badger. Only in L15.
2 A rock hyrax, *Procavia capensis*, = DASSIE 1. *S. Afr.* L18.

Dasein /'dɑːzaɪn/ *noun.* M19.
[ORIGIN German, from *dasein* exist, from *da* there + *sein* be.]
PHILOSOPHY. In Hegelian terms, existence, determinate being; in existentialism, human existence, the being of a person in the world.

dash /daʃ/ *noun*¹. LME.
[ORIGIN from DASH *verb*¹.]
1 A violent blow, stroke, impact, or collision. LME.

fig.: SHAKES. *1 Hen. VI* She takes upon her bravely at first dash.

2 A stroke or line (usu. short and straight) made with or as with a pen etc., esp. (**a**) drawn through writing for erasure, (**b**) forming part of a character or used as a flourish, (**c**) marking a parenthetic clause, break in sense, omission, substitution, etc., or separating distinct portions of matter. M16. ▸**b** MUSIC. A short vertical mark (ˈ) placed above or beneath a note to indicate that it is to be performed staccato, esp. more so than when marked with a dot (see DOT *noun*¹ 4b). M19. ▸**c** The longer of the two signals (the other being the dot) which in various combinations make up the letters of the Morse alphabet. M19.
swung dash.
3 A hasty stroke of the pen. L16.
†**4** A sudden blow; affliction; discouragement. L16–M18.
5 A splash, splashing; the sound of water striking or being struck. L16.

W. COWPER Music not unlike The dash of Ocean on his winding shore.

6 A small quantity (*of* something) mingled with something else; a slight admixture or infusion; a tinge. L16.

E. BLUNDEN He went off, leaving a dash of bitterness in my mild draught of content.

7 A small portion (of colour etc.) thrown on a surface; a splash of colour; something laid roughly on a surface. E18.

J. T. BENT Syra is almost entirely a white town, relieved now and again by a dash of yellow wash.

pebble-dash: see PEBBLE *noun*.
8 A showy appearance; showy behaviour. Chiefly in ***cut a dash*** below. E18.
9 (Capacity for) vigorous and spirited action. L18.

WELLINGTON The affair . . was occasioned . . by the imprudence of the officer, and the dash and eagerness of the men.

10 The dasher of a churn. L18.
11 A sudden impetuous movement; a rush; a sudden vigorous attack. E19.

G. STEIN She made a rapid dash out of the door.

12 A race run in one heat; a sprint. Chiefly *N. Amer.* M19.
13 = DASHBOARD 1. M19.
– PHRASES: **cut a dash** make a brilliant show. **do one's dash** *Austral. & NZ colloq.* become played out. **have a dash at** *colloq.* make an attempt at. **make a dash for** try to reach by quickness, rush towards.
– COMB.: **dashlight** a light on the dashboard of a motor vehicle.

dash /daʃ/ *noun*². Also †**dashee**. E17.
[ORIGIN (Guinean *dashee* from) Portuguese *das* ult. from Latin DATA.]
In W. Africa, a gift or commission; *slang* a bribe.

dash /daʃ/ *verb*¹. ME.
[ORIGIN Prob. of imit. origin: an appropriate base is repr. by Swedish *daska*, Danish *daske* beat, but no older Scandinavian forms are recorded.]
▸ **I** *verb trans.* **1** Strike with violence so as to shatter, smash; strike violently against. ME.

SHAKES. *Temp.* A brave vessel . . Dash'd all to pieces! S. HAZZARD Refinement was a frail construction continually dashed by waves of a raw . . humanity.

2 Knock, drive, throw, or thrust (*away*, *down*, *out*, etc.) with violence; fling, impel with destructive contact *against* or *into* something. ME.

SIR W. SCOTT Dashing from him the snake which was about to sting him. A. J. CRONIN He . . seized a vase . . and dashed it hard upon the floor. V. ACKLAND The rain drops dashed themselves against . . the windscreen.

3 Splash or splatter *with* mud etc. Also, put *out* by splashing water on (a fire). LME.

DICKENS Rows of fire-buckets for dashing out a conflagration. TENNYSON Deep tulips dash'd with fiery dew.

4 *fig.* Destroy, frustrate, (now esp. a person's hopes etc.). E16.

V. WOOLF I . . dashed my pleasure by losing my Roman brooch. J. BUCHAN Years . . of zeal and hope not yet dashed by failure.

5 Depress; daunt; confound, abash. M16.

SHAKES. *Oth.* I see this hath a little dash'd your spirits.

6 Qualify *with* some (freq. inferior) admixture; dilute, mix. M16.

C. J. LEVER Dash the lemonade with a little maraschino.

7 a Draw a dash through. Now *rare* or *obsolete*. M16. ▸**b** Mark with a dash; underline. L18.
8 Write or sketch rapidly without premeditation. Usu. foll. by *off* or *down*. E18.

K. TYNAN Like watching a series of lightning water-colours, dashed off by a master.

9 In mild imprecations, freq. in imper. or optative form: damn. E19.

DICKENS Dash it, Tony . . you really ought to be careful.

▸ **II** *verb intrans.* **10** Move, fall, or throw itself with violence; come *against* etc. with violent collision. ME.

E. PEACOCK The full force of the Atlantic is dashing on the cliffs.

11 Rush with impetuosity or spirit; move about, ride, run, etc., in a great hurry. ME.

J. STEINBECK Jack-rabbits . . dashed away in long jolting steps. J. RABAN I had . . lost most of my eagerness to dash headlong into new places.

12 Make a display; cut a dash. L18.

T. S. SURR That blade dashes most confoundedly . . he is a princely fellow, to be sure.

■ **dashed** *adjective & adverb* (**a**) *adjective* that has been dashed; *euphem.* damned; (**b**) *adverb* confoundedly: M17. **dashy** *adjective* (*colloq.*) given to cutting a dash E19.

dash /daʃ/ *verb*² *trans.* Also †**dashee**. E18.
[ORIGIN from DASH *noun*².]
In W. Africa, give as a gift or commission; *slang* bribe.

dash /daʃ/ *adverb.* L17.
[ORIGIN from DASH *verb*¹.]
With a dash. See also SLAPDASH *adverb*.

dashboard /'daʃbɔːd/ *noun.* M19.
[ORIGIN from DASH *verb*¹ or *noun*¹ + BOARD *noun*.]
1 a A board of wood or leather in the front of a carriage to keep out mud. M19. ▸**b** A panel beneath the windscreen of a motor vehicle, in an aircraft, etc., containing instruments and controls. E20.
2 ARCHITECTURE. A sloping board to carry off rainwater from the face of a wall. L19.

†**dashee** *noun, verb* vars. of DASH *noun*², *verb*².

dasheen /da'ʃiːn/ *noun.* Orig. *W. Indian*. L19.
[ORIGIN Unknown.]
A cultivated variety of taro.

dasher /'daʃə/ *noun.* L18.
[ORIGIN from DASH *verb*¹ + -ER¹.]
1 A person who or thing which dashes; *colloq.* a person who cuts a dash, a stylish person; *Austral.* a daring gambler. L18.
2 A contrivance for agitating cream in a churn. M19.
3 = DASHBOARD 1. *US*. M19.

Dashera *noun* var. of DUSSEHRA.

dashi /'daʃi/ *noun.* M20.
[ORIGIN Japanese, shortened from *dashi-jiru*, from *dashi* to draw, extract + *jiru* juice, broth.]
Cooking stock made from dried bonito and seaweed, used in Japanese cookery.

dashiki /'dɑːʃɪki/ *noun.* M20.
[ORIGIN Prob. from Yoruba from Hausa: cf. Krio *da(n)shiki*.]
A loose brightly coloured shirt or tunic, orig. from W. Africa.

dashing /'daʃɪŋ/ *noun.* LME.
[ORIGIN from DASH *verb*¹ + -ING¹.]
1 The action of DASH *verb*¹. LME.
2 = DASH *noun*¹ 7. L16.
pebble-dashing: see PEBBLE *noun*.

dashing /'daʃɪŋ/ *adjective.* LME.
[ORIGIN from DASH *verb*¹ + -ING².]
1 That dashes. LME.
2 Spirited, lively, impetuous. L18.
3 Given to cutting a dash, stylish. L18.
– SPECIAL COLLOCATIONS: **Dashing White Sergeant** a lively country dance performed in sets of three.
■ **dashingly** *adverb* E19. **dashingness** *noun* M20.

dashpot /'daʃpɒt/ *noun.* M19.
[ORIGIN from DASH *verb*¹ + POT *noun*¹.]
A hydraulic device for damping shock or vibration, a hydraulic buffer.

†**dasje** *noun* var. of DASSIE.

dassen *noun pl.* see DAS.

Dassera *noun* var. of DUSSEHRA.

dassie /'dasi/ *noun. S. Afr.* Also †**dasje**. L18.
[ORIGIN Afrikaans from Dutch *dasje* dim. of DAS *noun*.]
1 A rock hyrax, *Procavia capensis*, = DAS *noun* 2. L18.
2 A sparid coastal fish, *Diplodus sargus*, with a black tail-spot; the blacktail. M19.

dassievanger /'dasɪfaŋə, -vaŋə, *foreign* 'dasifaŋər/ *noun. S. Afr.* M19.
[ORIGIN Afrikaans, formed as DASSIE + *vanger* catcher.]
An eagle; *esp.* Verreaux's eagle, *Aquila verreauxii*.

dastard /'dastəd, 'dɑː-/ *noun, adjective, & verb.* LME.
[ORIGIN Prob. from *dazed* pa. pple & ppl adjective of DAZE *verb* + -ARD, infl. by DOTARD *noun*¹ & *adjective*¹.]
▸ **A** *noun.* †**1** A dullard; a stupid person. LME–M16.
2 A mean, base, or despicable coward, *esp.* one who does malicious acts in a skulking way. L15.
▸ **B** *adjective.* = DASTARDLY. L15.
▸ †**C** *verb trans.* = DASTARDIZE. L16–M17.
■ †**dastardice** *noun* = DASTARDY L16–M18. **dastardize** *verb trans.* (now *rare*) make a dastard of, cow M17. **dastardy** *noun* (*arch.*) base or mean cowardice, dastardliness L16.

dastardly /'dastədli, 'dɑː-/ *adjective.* M16.
[ORIGIN from DASTARD + -LY¹.]
†**1** Dull, stupid. Only in M16.
2 Resembling or characteristic of a dastard; showing mean or despicable cowardice. L16.
■ **dastardliness** *noun* M16.

dastur /də'stʊə/ *noun*¹. Also **destour**. M17.
[ORIGIN Persian *dastūr*, from Old Persian *dastōbār* prime minister, Zoroastrian high priest.]
A chief priest of the Parsees.

dastur /də'stʊə/ *noun*². Also **dustoor**. L17.
[ORIGIN Urdu *dastūr* from Persian.]
In the Indian subcontinent: custom, usage. Also = DASTURI.

dasturi /də'stʊəri/ *noun*. Also **dustoory**. E17.
[ORIGIN Urdu *dastūrī*, formed as DASTUR *noun*².]
In the Indian subcontinent: a customary fee, a perquisite.

dasylirion /dasɪ'lɪrɪən/ *noun*. M19.
[ORIGIN mod. Latin, from Greek *dasus* thick + *leirion* lily.]
Any plant of the genus *Dasylirion* of the lily family, comprising plants of Mexico and the south-western US which have white bell-shaped flowers and are often cultivated as greenhouse evergreens.

dasypygal /dasɪ'pʌɪg(ə)l/ *adjective*. L19.
[ORIGIN from Greek *dasupugos*, from *dasus* hairy + *pugē* buttocks: see -AL¹.]
ZOOLOGY. Having hairy buttocks.

dasyure /'dasɪjʊə/ *noun*. M19.
[ORIGIN French from mod. Latin *dasyurus*, from Greek *dasus* rough, hairy + *oura* tail.]
Any of a number of carnivorous arboreal catlike marsupials of the genus *Dasyurus*, native to Australia and New Guinea.
URSINE *dasyure*.

DAT *abbreviation*.
Digital audio tape.

dat /dat/ *demonstr. pronoun, adjective, adverb, & conjunction. black English & dial.* L17.
[ORIGIN Repr. a pronunc.]
= THAT.

data /'deɪtə/ *noun*. M17.
[ORIGIN Latin, pl. of DATUM.]
▸ **I** *pl. & collect. sing.* **1** Things given or granted; things known or assumed as facts, and made the basis of reasoning or calculation. M17.

E. F. BENSON She had to make the best plans on the data that were hers.

2 Facts, esp. numerical facts, collected together for reference or information. L19.

B. LOVELL These data confirmed . . that the surface of Venus must have a high temperature.

3 The quantities, characters, or symbols on which operations are performed by computers and other automatic equipment, and which may be stored and transmitted in the form of electrical signals, records on magnetic, optical, or mechanical recording media, etc. M20.

Computer Weekly They have done little to analyse and interpret this data.

▸ **II** *sing.* **4** A piece of information, a statistic. *rare*. E19.
– COMB.: **databank** a place where data are stored in large amounts; **database** an organized store of data for computer processing; ***data capture***: see CAPTURE *noun* 6; **datacom(s)**, **data communications** the use of communication networks and devices to transmit digital information; **data entry** the process or operation of inputting data to a computer system; **dataglove** a device worn like a glove and containing sensors linked to a representation of a hand in a computer display, allowing the manual manipulation of images in virtual reality; **data link** a telecommunications link over which data are transmitted; ***datalogger***: see LOGGER *noun*¹ 2; **data mining** the practice of examining large pre-existing databases in order to generate new information; **data processing** the performance by automatic means of any operations on empirical data, such as classifying or analysing them; **data processor** a machine for data processing; **data protection** the legal regulation of access to data stored in computers; **data retrieval** the obtaining of data stored on a computer system; **data sheet** a leaflet containing a summary of useful information on a subject; **data stream** = STREAM *noun* 5e; **data structure** the way data are organized in a computer, in so far as it affects the use or modification of the data; **data terminal**: at which a person can enter data into a computer-based system or receive data from one; **data type** a particular kind of data item, as defined by the values it can take or the operations that can be performed on it; **data warehouse** a large store of data accumulated from a wide range of sources within a company and used to guide management decisions.
– NOTE: Historically and in specialized scientific fields *data* is treated as a pl. in English, taking a pl. verb. In modern non-scientific use, however, it is often treated as a mass noun, like e.g. *information*, and takes a sing. verb.

datal /'deɪt(ə)l/ *adjective*¹. M19.
[ORIGIN from DATE *noun*² + -AL¹.]
Containing or including the date (as of a charter). Also (*rare*), chronological.

datal *adjective*² var. of DAY-TALE.

datary /'deɪt(ə)ri/ *noun*. E16.
[ORIGIN medieval Latin *datarius*, *-ria*, from *datum* DATE *noun*²: see -ARY¹.]
1 An officer of the papal court, charged with the duty of registering and dating all documents issued by the Pope, and of representing the Pope in matters relating to grants, dispensations, etc. E16.
2 The function or office of dating papal documents etc. E17.

dataveillance /deɪtə'veɪl(ə)ns/ *noun*. L20.
[ORIGIN Blend of DATA and SURVEILLANCE.]
The monitoring of private information about a person or group from their online activities.

datcha *noun* var. of DACHA.

date /deɪt/ *noun*¹. ME.
[ORIGIN Old French (mod. *datte*) from Latin *dactylus* from Greek *daktulos* finger, toe, date (see DACTYL); so called from the finger-like leaf-shape.]
1 The fruit of the date palm (see below), an oblong one-seeded drupe with sweet pulp, growing in clusters. ME. ▸**b** More fully ***soppy date***. A foolish, comic, or sentimental person. *colloq*. E20.
2 More fully ***date palm***. A palm tree of the genus *Phoenix*; esp. *P. dactylifera*, source of most commercially grown dates, native to northern Africa and western Asia. LME.
– COMB.: ***date palm***: see sense 2 above; **date plum** (the fruit of) any of several kinds of persimmon, esp. *Diospyros kaki* and *D. virginiana*.

date /deɪt/ *noun*². ME.
[ORIGIN Old French & mod. French from medieval Latin *data* use as noun of fem. of *datus* pa. pple of *dare* give. Derived from the Latin formula used in dating letters, e.g. *Data (sc. epistola) Romae*, '(letter) given at Rome'.]
1 The day of the month; the day of the month, the month, or the year of an event; the time or period at which something happened or the time at which something is to happen. ME. ▸**b** A statement in a document, letter, book, or inscription, of the time (and often place) of execution, writing, publication, etc. LME.

GOLDSMITH Not far remov'd the date, When commerce proudly flourish'd through the state. E. WAUGH A date was fixed for the wedding. A. BURGESS 714 to 768, if you want his dates.

2 Term of life or existence; season; duration. ME.

MILTON Ages of endless date Founded in righteousness.

3 The period to which something old belongs; the age (of a thing or person). LME.

E. A. FREEMAN Rich in antiquities of Roman date.

4 The limit or end of a period of time or of the duration of something. *arch*. LME.

W. COWPER All has its date below; the fatal hour Was registered in Heaven ere time began.

5 a An appointment or engagement at a particular time (esp. with a person of the opposite sex); a social activity engaged in by two people. *colloq*. L19. ▸**b** The person with whom such an appointment is made. *colloq*. (orig. *US*). E20. ▸**c** A theatrical, musical, etc., engagement or performance; a place where such a performance is given (esp. as part of a tour). *colloq*. E20.

a E. BOWEN He won't be in for supper. He's got a date. **b** J. D. SALINGER There were about a million girls . . waiting for their dates to show up. **c** P. G. WODEHOUSE He proposed to teach it a few simple tricks and get it dates on television.

– PHRASES: ***bear date***: see BEAR *verb*¹. ***blind date***: see BLIND *adjective*. ***double date***: see DOUBLE *adjective & adverb*. **out of date** old-fashioned; obsolete. ***sell-by-date***: see SELL *verb*. **to date** to the present time or moment; until now. ***up to date***: see UP *adverb*¹. ***up-to-date***: see UP *adverb*¹. ***use-by date***: see USE *verb*.
– COMB.: **date-cancel** *verb trans.* cancel by a written or stamped date; **date letter** a letter stamped on gold or silver plate, pottery, etc., denoting the year of manufacture; **date line** (*a*) (with cap. initials) an internationally recognized line from the North to the South Pole, partly along meridian 180 degrees from Greenwich, east and west of which the date differs; (*b*) a line in a newspaper at the head of a dispatch, special article, etc., giving the date (and usu. place) of writing; **date-lined** *adjective* (of an article etc.) having a (specified) date line; **date mark** a mark showing the date; *spec.* = ***date letter*** above; **date rape**: of a girl or woman by a person she is dating or with whom she is on a date; **date stamp** *noun & verb* (*a*) *noun* (the impression made by) an adjustable rubber stamp etc. used to record the date of delivery, receipt, etc., of a letter, parcel, bill, etc.; (*b*) *verb trans.* (with hyphen) mark with a date stamp.

date /deɪt/ *verb*. LME.
[ORIGIN from DATE *noun*².]
1 *verb trans.* Mark with a date. LME.

J. AUSTEN The letter . . was dated from Rosings at eight o'clock in the morning.

2 *verb trans.* Fix or ascertain the date or time of; reckon as beginning *from*; reckon chronologically. LME. ▸**b** *verb intrans.* Count the time; reckon. M18. ▸**c** *verb trans. & intrans.* Mark as or bear evidence of being of a certain date; make, be, or become outdated. *colloq*. L19. ▸**d** *verb trans.* Assign *to* a specified date. E20.

N. PODHORETZ Several short passages . . that the student was expected to date within ten years or so. **c** H. BELLOC All the middle and early Victorians are already dating—except Macaulay. M. MCCARTHY It was wiser not to use slang because it dated you so quickly. **d** E. T. LEEDS This find can be dated by coins to about A.D. 290.

3 *verb trans.* Put an end or period to; assign a duration to. Long *rare*. L16.
4 *verb intrans.* Assign itself or be assigned to a particular time; have its origin *from*. E19.

E. K. KANE The house dated back as far as the days of Matthew Stach. J. L. WATEN Father's affection for Ginger dated from this encounter.

date back to have existed since.
5 *verb intrans.* Bear date; be written or addressed *from* (a specified place). M19.

D. G. ROSSETTI Dante's sonnet probably dates from Ravenna.

6 *verb trans. & intrans.* Make or have a date (with); *esp.* do so regularly, go out with (a person). Also foll. by *up*. *colloq*. (orig. *US*). E20.

J. D. SALINGER She was dating this terrible guy. O. SACKS She never dated . . variously maintaining that she despised, hated, or feared the other sex.

■ **datable**, **dateable** *adjective* M19. **dated** *adjective* (*a*) marked or assigned with a date; (*b*) *colloq*. outdated, old-fashioned; (*c*) (long *rare*) having a fixed term: L16. **dater** *noun* E17.

dateless /'deɪtlɪs/ *adjective*. L16.
[ORIGIN from DATE *noun*² + -LESS.]
1 Having no limit or fixed term; endless; not likely to become out of date. L16.
2 Not bearing a date, undated. Also, timeless. M17.
3 Crazed; insensible; foolish. Chiefly *dial*. L17.
4 Indefinitely ancient, immemorial. L18.
■ **datelessly** *adverb* M20. **datelessness** *noun* M17.

dating /'deɪtɪŋ/ *verbal noun*. L17.
[ORIGIN from DATE *verb* + -ING¹.]
1 *gen*. The action of DATE *verb*. L17.
2 (A particular technique used in) the determination of the age of a rock, fossil, archaeological specimen, etc. E20.
carbon dating, ***potassium–argon dating***, ***radiocarbon dating***, ***rubidium–strontium dating***, ***tree-ring dating***, etc.
3 The act or practice of making dates (DATE *noun*² 5), esp. regularly. *colloq*. M20.
– COMB.: **dating agency** a service which arranges introductions for people seeking romantic partners with similar interests.

dation /'deɪʃ(ə)n/ *noun*. Long *obsolete* exc. LAW. M17.
[ORIGIN Old French & mod. French, or Latin *datio(n-)*, from *dat-* pa. ppl stem of *dare* give: see -ION.]
The action of giving or conferring; that which is given.

Datisi /də'tʌɪsʌɪ/ *noun*. M16.
[ORIGIN A mnemonic of scholastic philosophers, first used in medieval Latin, A indicating a universal affirmative proposition, and I a particular affirmative proposition.]
LOGIC. A valid mood of the third syllogistic figure, in which a universal affirmative major premiss and a particular affirmative minor yield a particular affirmative conclusion.

dative /'deɪtɪv/ *adjective & noun*. LME.
[ORIGIN Latin *dativus* of giving, from *dat-* pa. ppl stem of *dare* give: see -IVE. In grammar (sc. *casus*) translating Greek (*ptōsis*) *dotikē* (see CASE *noun*¹).]
▸ **A** *adjective*. **1** GRAMMAR. Designating, being in, or pertaining to a case in inflected languages expressing the indirect object or recipient (equivalent to modern English *to* or *for* with the noun etc.). LME.
dative absolute in some inflected languages, a construction resembling the Latin ablative absolute, in which a noun and participle in the dative case form an adverbial clause of time, cause, or coexistence.
2 LAW. In a person's gift; (of an office etc.) removable, temporary; *Scot.* given by a magistrate etc., not by disposition of law. L15.
executor dative: named by a court, not by a testator.
†**3** Of the nature of a gift; conferred or bestowed as a gift. L16–M17.
▸ **B** *noun*. GRAMMAR. The dative case; a word, form, etc., in the dative case. LME.
■ **datival** /də'tʌɪv(ə)l/ *adjective* E19. **datively** *adverb* M19.

dato *noun* var. of DATUK.

datok *noun* var. of DATUK.

datolite /'datəlʌɪt/ *noun*. E19.
[ORIGIN from Greek *dateisthai* to divide + -O- + -LITE.]
MINERALOGY. A monoclinic hydrated basic silicate of boron and calcium, occurring as glassy prisms (colourless when pure).

dattock /'datək/ *noun*. L19.
[ORIGIN Cf. Krio, Wolof *dita*.]
(The hard wood, resembling mahogany, of) a W. African leguminous tree, *Detarium senegalense*.

datuk /'dɑːtək/ *noun*. Also **-ok**, **dato** /'dɑːtəʊ/ (pl. **-os**), **datu** /'dɑːtuː/. M19.
[ORIGIN Malay *dato'*, *datok* elder (as a term of address and a title) (in Indonesian *datuk*), and Tagalog *datò* ruler.]
A landowner or chief in northern Borneo, the Philippines, and some adjacent areas.

datum /'deɪtəm/ *noun sing*. Pl. DATA. M18.
[ORIGIN Latin, neut. pa. pple of *dare* give.]
A thing given or granted; a thing known or assumed as a fact, and made the basis of reasoning or calculation; a fixed starting point for a series of measurements etc.
datum line, ***datum point***, etc. ORDNANCE ***datum***. ***sense datum***: see SENSE *noun*.

D

datura /də'tjʊərə/ *noun*. **L16**.
[**ORIGIN** mod. Latin (see below) from Hindi *dhatūrā*. Cf. **DEWTRY**.]
Any of various plants of the genus *Datura* (all containing toxic or narcotic alkaloids), of the nightshade family; *esp.* the thorn apple, *D. stramonium*.
▪ **daturine** *noun* = **ATROPINE M19**.

daub /dɔːb/ *noun*. **LME**.
[**ORIGIN** from the verb.]
1 Material for daubing; plaster, clay, etc., for surface-coating, esp. mixed with straw and applied to laths or wattles to make walls. **LME**.
wattle and daub: see **WATTLE** *noun*[1] 1.
2 An act or instance of daubing. **M17**.
3 A patch or smear of some moist substance. **M18**.
A. BURGESS Sandwiches with a raw onion and a daub of mustard.
4 A coarsely executed painting. **M18**.
W. COWPER That he discerns The difference of a Guido from a daub.
▪ **daubster** *noun* a crude or inartistic painter, a dauber **L19**. **dauby** *adjective* of the nature of (a) daub **M17**.

daub /dɔːb/ *verb*. **LME**.
[**ORIGIN** Old French *dauber* from Latin *dealbare* whiten, whitewash, plaster, from *de-* **DE-** 1 + *albus* white.]
▶ **I** *verb trans.* **1** Coat or cover *with* plaster, mortar, clay, etc., esp. in building walls. **LME**.
2 Cover or coat *with* a moist, sticky, greasy, or dirty substance; smear; soil, stain. **LME**.
R. SUTCLIFF Their bodies daubed with strange designs in woad and madder. *fig.*: W. COWPER I would not be a king to be . . daubed with undiscerning praise.
†**3** *fig.* Cover or conceal with a plausible exterior; whitewash, gloss over. **M16–L18**.
S. FIELDING The painted canvas is most innocent; but the daubed hypocrite most criminal.
4 Smear or lay on (a moist or sticky substance, plaster, etc.); apply (paint) crudely. (Foll. by *on*.) **L16**.
R. MACAULAY She's quite clever at drawing, and daubs on her paint rather amusingly.
5 Cover with tasteless finery. *obsolete* exc. *dial.* **L16**.
6 Paint crudely or inartistically. **M17**.
DRYDEN A lame, imperfect piece, rudely daubed over with . . too much haste.
▶ **II** *verb intrans.* **7** Apply a plaster etc. coating; paint crudely or inartistically. **E16**.
A. TROLLOPE He . . daubed away briskly at the background.
8 *fig.* Put on a false show; dissemble, flatter. *obsolete* exc. *dial.* **E17**.
†**9** Practise bribery. **M17–L18**.
▪ **daubing** *noun* (*a*) the action of the verb; (*b*) = **DAUB** *noun*: **LME**.

daube /dəʊb, *foreign* doːb (*pl. same*)/ *noun*. **E18**.
[**ORIGIN** French.]
A braised meat (usu. beef) stew with wine, spices, etc.
À LA daube. **EN DAUBE**.

Daubenton's bat /'dɔːbəntənz bat, dəʊbã'tɔ̃z/ *noun phr.* **L19**.
[**ORIGIN** from Jean Marie *Daubenton* (1716–?1800), French naturalist + **BAT** *noun*[3].]
A small Eurasian bat, *Myotis daubentoni*.

dauber /'dɔːbə/ *noun*. **ME**.
[**ORIGIN** Anglo-Norman *daubour*, *-ber*, or directly from **DAUB** *verb* + **-ER**[1].]
1 A person who builds with daub, a plasterer. *obsolete* exc. *hist.* **ME**.
2 A crude or inartistic painter. **M17**.
3 = ***mud-dauber*** (a) s.v. **MUD** *noun*[1]. Chiefly *US*. **M19**.
▪ **daubery** *noun* the practice of daubing; the work of a dauber: **M16**.

daubréeite /dəʊ'breɪʌɪt/ *noun*. **L19**.
[**ORIGIN** from Gabriel Auguste *Daubrée* (1814–96), French mineralogist + **-ITE**[1].]
MINERALOGY. A tetragonal basic oxychloride of bismuth, colourless when pure, occurring as massive or scaly secondary deposits.

daubréelite /dəʊ'breɪlʌɪt/ *noun*. **L19**.
[**ORIGIN** formed as **DAUBRÉEITE** + **-LITE**.]
MINERALOGY. A cubic sulphide of chromium and iron occurring in iron meteorites.

daud *verb* & *noun* var. of **DAD** *verb* & *noun*[3].

daughter /'dɔːtə/ *noun* & *adjective*.
[**ORIGIN** Old English *dohtor* = Old Frisian *dochter*, Old Saxon *dohtar* (Dutch *dochter*), Old High German *tohter* (German *Tochter*), Old Norse *dóttir*, Gothic *dauhtar*, from Germanic from Indo-European, whence also Sanskrit *duhitr*, Greek *thugatēr*.]
▶ **A** *noun*. **1** A female human being in relation to either or both of her parents. Also, a female offspring of an animal. **OE**.
SHAKES. *Lear* The dear father would with his daughter speak.
2 A female descendant; a female member of a family, nation, etc. Also, a woman who is the spiritual or intellectual product *of* a specified person or thing. **OE**.
J. WESLEY A daughter of affliction came to see me. TENNYSON A daughter of our meadows.
3 a Used as a term of affectionate address to a woman or girl, by an older or superior person. *arch.* **OE**. ▸**b** A young woman. *arch.* **LME**.
a AV *Matt.* 9:22 But Iesus . . said, Daughter, bee of good comfort, thy faith hath made thee whole.
4 A thing (usu. personified as female) as the product, reflex, or dependant of something else. **ME**. ▸**b** *PHYSICS.* A nuclide formed by the disintegration of another. **M20**.
WORDSWORTH Stern Daughter of the Voice of God! O Duty! OED Carthage the famous daughter of Tyre.
– **PHRASES**: ***daughter of Eve***: see **EVE** *noun*[1]. **Daughters of the American Revolution**: a patriotic American women's society. **Duke of Exeter's daughter** an instrument of torture supposedly invented by a Duke of Exeter. ***GUNNER's daughter***.
▶ **B** *attrib.* or as *adjective*. (Freq. with hyphen.) That is a daughter (esp. *fig.*). **E17**.
Word The passive could have existed in Proto-Indo-European, rather than in its daughter languages.
– **SPECIAL COLLOCATIONS & COMB.**: **daughter atom** = sense 4b above. **daughterboard** a printed circuit board which contains subsidiary components of a microcomputer etc. and which may be connected to a motherboard. **daughter cell** *BIOLOGY* a cell formed by division or budding etc. of another. **daughter element** = sense 4b above. **daughter-in-law**, pl. **daughters-in-law**, (*a*) the wife of one's son; †(*b*) a stepdaughter.
▪ **daughterhood** *noun* (*a*) the condition of being a daughter; (*b*) daughters collectively: **M19**. **daughterless** *adjective* **LME**.

daughterly /'dɔːtəli/ *adjective*. **M16**.
[**ORIGIN** from **DAUGHTER** + **-LY**[1].]
Such as becomes a daughter; filial.
▪ **daughterliness** *noun* **M17**.

Daulian /'dɔːlıən/ *adjective*. *literary*. **L19**.
[**ORIGIN** from mod. Latin *Daulias* nightingale from Greek, lit. 'woman of Daulis', Procne, who in Greek mythol. was changed into a nightingale: see **-AN**.]
Daulian bird, the nightingale.

dault *noun* var. of **DALT**.

dauncy /'dɔːnsi/ *adjective*. *US* & *dial.* **M19**.
[**ORIGIN** Var. of **DONSIE**.]
Sickly; delicate.

daun(d)er *verb* & *noun* var. of **DANDER** *verb* & *noun*[4].

daunomycin /dɔːnəʊ'mʌɪsın/ *noun*. **M20**.
[**ORIGIN** from *Daunia*, a former region of southern Italy, + **-O-** + **-MYCIN**.]
PHARMACOLOGY. = **DAUNORUBICIN**.

daunorubicin /dɔːnəʊ'ruːbısın/ *noun*. **M20**.
[**ORIGIN** formed as **DAUNOMYCIN** + *-rubi-* red (cf. **RUBICUND**).]
PHARMACOLOGY. An antibiotic used to treat various forms of cancer.

daunt /dɔːnt/ *verb* & *noun*. **ME**.
[**ORIGIN** Anglo-Norman *daunter*, Old French *danter*, var. of *donter* (mod. *dompter*) from Latin *domitare* frequentative of *domare* to tame.]
▶ **A** *verb trans.* **I** †**1** Overcome, subdue; control; quell. **ME–E18**.
2 Discourage, dispirit, intimidate. **ME**.
W. PLOMER I had felt a little daunted by the extreme modishness of her clothes and by her poise. R. MACAULAY Such barriers to religion, which daunt those not brought up to them.
3 Tame, break in (an animal). Long *obsolete* exc. *dial.* **LME**.
4 Daze, stupefy. *obsolete* exc. *dial.* **L16**.
5 Press (salted herring) into the barrel with a daunt. Chiefly *Scot.* **E18**.
▶ †**II 6** Dandle, fondle. Cf. **DAUT**. **ME–L15**.
▶ **B** *noun*. **1** The act of daunting; intimidation; a check. Now *Scot.* & *dial.* **LME**.
2 A wooden disc used to press down herring in barrels. Chiefly *Scot.* **M19**.
▪ **daunter** *noun* **E16**. **daunton** *verb trans.* (*Scot.*) daunt **M16**.

dauntless /'dɔːntlıs/ *adjective*. **L16**.
[**ORIGIN** from **DAUNT** + **-LESS**.]
Not to be daunted; bold, intrepid; persevering.
▪ **dauntlessly** *adverb* **E19**. **dauntlessness** *noun* **M18**.

dauphin /'dɔːfın, 'dəʊfã/ *noun* & *adjective*. Also **D-**. **LME**.
[**ORIGIN** French (Old French *daulphin*: see **DOLPHIN**), family name of the lords of Viennois or Dauphiné. Cf. also **DELPHIN**.]
▶ **A** *noun*. **1** *hist.* (The title of) the eldest son of the King of France, from 1349 to 1830. **LME**.
†**2** A dolphin. *rare*. Only in **L16**.
▶ †**B** *attrib.* or as *adjective*. = **DELPHIN** *adjective*. Only in **E18**.
▪ **dauphinate** *noun* (*hist.*) the rule or jurisdiction of a dauphin (cf. earlier **DOLPHINATE**) **L19**. **dauphiness** /'dɔːfınıs/ *noun* (*hist.*) the wife of a dauphin (cf. earlier **DOLPHINESS**) **L17**.

dauphinois /dəʊfı'nwɑː/ *adjective*. Also **dauphinoise** /dəʊfı'nwɑːz/. **E20**.
[**ORIGIN** French, lit. 'from the province of Dauphiné'.]
Of potatoes or other vegetables: sliced and cooked in milk, typically with a topping of cheese.

daut /dɔːt/ *verb trans.* *Scot.* Also **dawt**. **E16**.
[**ORIGIN** Unknown. Cf. **DAUNT** *verb* 6.]
Pet, fondle, make much of.

daven /'dɑːv(ə)n/ *verb intrans.* **M20**.
[**ORIGIN** Yiddish *davnen*.]
JUDAISM. Recite the prescribed liturgical prayers.

davenport /'dav(ə)npɔːt/ *noun*[1]. Also **devon-** /'dɛv(ə)n-/. **M19**.
[**ORIGIN** Prob. from Capt. *Davenport*, for whom early examples were made in late 18th cent.]
1 A kind of escritoire fitted with drawers and a hinged writing slab. **M19**.
2 A large sofa. *US*. **M20**.

Davenport /'dav(ə)npɔːt/ *noun*[2]. **M19**.
[**ORIGIN** See below.]
More fully ***Davenport china***, ***Davenport porcelain***, ***Davenport ware***, etc. A kind of earthenware made by the Davenport family firm at Longport, Staffordshire, England, between 1793 and 1882.

Davidic /deɪ'vıdık, də-/ *adjective*. **M19**.
[**ORIGIN** from *David* (see below) + **-IC**.]
Of or pertaining to David (d. *c* 970 BC), king of Judah and later of all Israel, traditionally regarded as author of the Psalms.
▪ Also **Davidical** *adjective* **E19**.

Davis /'deɪvıs/ *noun*. **M20**.
[**ORIGIN** Sir Robert H. *Davis* (1870–1965), English inventor.]
Used *attrib.* to designate a breathing apparatus designed to enable a person to escape from a submerged submarine.

davit /'davıt, 'deıv-/ *noun*. **L15**.
[**ORIGIN** Anglo-Norman, Old French *daviot*, later *daviet* (mod. *davier*), dim. of *Davi* David.]
A (curved) crane mounted on a ship for hoisting objects inboard or outboard; orig. one mounted at the bow for use in hoisting the anchor. Now freq. either of a pair of cranes used for suspending or lowering a ship's boat.

davy /'deıvi/ *noun*[1]. *slang*. **M18**.
[**ORIGIN** Abbreviation.]
An affidavit.

Davy /'deıvi/ *noun*[2]. **E19**.
[**ORIGIN** Sir Humphry *Davy* (1778–1828), English chemist.]
In full ***Davy lamp***. A miners' safety lamp invented by Davy, in which the flame is surrounded with wire gauze so as to prevent its transmission to explosive gases outside the lamp.

Davy Jones /deıvı 'dʒəʊnz/ *noun*. *nautical slang*. **E18**.
[**ORIGIN** Unknown.]
The evil spirit of the sea. Chiefly in ***Davy Jones's locker***, the deep, esp. as the grave of those who perish at sea.

daw /dɔː/ *noun*. **LME**.
[**ORIGIN** Rel. to Old High German *tāha* (German dial. *Tach*), beside Middle High German *dāhele*, *tāle* (German *Dohle*): prob. already in Old English. Cf. **CADDOW** *noun*[1].]
1 = **JACKDAW**. **LME**.
2 A simpleton; a lazy person; a slattern. **LME**.

daw /dɔː/ *adjective*. **M19**.
[**ORIGIN** Unknown.]
Of a pale primrose colour, as the eyes of certain gamefowl.

daw /dɔː/ *verb*. *obsolete* exc. *Scot.*
[**ORIGIN** Old English *dagian*, corresp. to Middle Dutch *daghen*, Dutch, Low German *dagen*, Old High German *tagēn* (German *tagen*), from West Germanic base of **DAY** *noun*.]
1 *verb intrans.* Dawn. **OE**.
†**2** *verb intrans.* & *trans.* Waken, revive. **ME–L17**.

†**dawark** *noun* see **DARG**.

dawdle /'dɔːd(ə)l/ *verb* & *noun*. **M17**.
[**ORIGIN** Prob. of dial. origin. Cf. **DADDLE** *verb*, **DODDLE** *verb*.]
▶ **A** *verb*. **1** *verb intrans.* Idle, waste time; loiter, dally. **M17**.
HENRY MILLER The breakfast . . was the one ceremony of the day over which she dawdled and lingered. *fig.*: D. MORRIS While our reproductive systems raced ahead, our brain-growth dawdled behind.
2 *verb trans.* Waste, fritter *away* (time etc.). **M18**.
▶ **B** *noun*. A person who dawdles; an act of dawdling. **M18**.
▪ **dawdler** *noun* **E19**.

dawg /dɔːg/ *noun*. *dial.* & *joc.* **L19**.
[**ORIGIN** Repr. a pronunc.]
= **DOG** *noun*.

dawing /'dɔːıŋ/ *noun*. *obsolete* exc. *Scot.* **OE**.
[**ORIGIN** from **DAW** *verb* + **-ING**[1].]
Dawn, daybreak.

dawk *noun* var. of **DAK**.

dawn /dɔːn/ *noun*. **L16**.
[**ORIGIN** from the verb.]
1 The first appearance of light in the sky before sunrise; daybreak. **L16**.
crack of dawn: see **CRACK** *noun* 4. ***false dawn***: see **FALSE** *adjective*.
2 *fig.* The beginning, rise, or first appearance *of* something; an incipient gleam *of*. **M17**.
S. JOHNSON From the dawn of manhood to its decline. C. LAMB You could see the first dawn of an idea stealing slowly over his countenance.

– COMB.: **dawn chorus** the early-morning singing of birds; **dawn man** an extinct primitive human; formerly *esp.* Piltdown man; **dawn raid** (*a*) a surprise attack at dawn; (*b*) *Stock Exchange slang* a swift operation early in trading whereby a broker buys for a client a markedly increased holding in a company; ***dawn redwood***: see REDWOOD *noun*[1] 2.

dawn /dɔːn/ *verb intrans.* L15.
[ORIGIN Back-form. from DAWNING, largely repl. DAW *verb*.]
1 Of the morning, the day, etc.: begin to grow light. L15.
J. BARTH I saw him more clearly as the day dawned.
2 Begin to brighten (as) with the light of dawn. M17.
TENNYSON I waited underneath the dawning hills.
3 *fig.* Begin to appear or develop; become visible or evident. E18. ▸**b** Of ideas, facts, etc.: begin to become evident to the mind, be perceived. Usu. foll. by *on*, *upon* a person. M19.
LD MACAULAY In the year 1685 . . his fame . . was only dawning. H. L. MENCKEN It was not until skepticism arose in the world that genuine intelligence dawned. **b** D. LODGE The awful truth dawned upon him: Radio One was like this all the time. C. WILSON It dawned on him that the alchemists were talking in symbols. H. CARPENTER The realisation had dawned that the apparent triumphs of the Industrial Revolution had produced widespread misery.

dawning /ˈdɔːnɪŋ/ *noun.* ME.
[ORIGIN Alt. of DAWING after Scandinavian (Old Swedish *daghning*, Swedish, Danish *dagning*).]
1 The beginning of daylight; daybreak, dawn; *transf.* the east. Now chiefly *poet.* ME.
C. KINGSLEY Oh sing, and wake the dawning.
2 *fig.* The first gleam, the appearance, the beginning, (*of* something). E17.
W. H. PRESCOTT The dawnings of a literary culture.

dawt *verb* var. of DAUT.

DAX *abbreviation.*
Deutsche Aktienindex, the German stock exchange.

day /deɪ/ *noun.*
[ORIGIN Old English *dæg* = Old Frisian *dei*, Old Saxon (Dutch) *dag*, Old High German *tac* (German *Tag*), Old Norse *dagr*, Gothic *dags*, from Germanic.]
▸ **I** (The time of) sunlight.
1 The time during which the sun is above the horizon; the interval of light between two nights; the interval betweeen the usual times of getting up in the morning and going to bed at night. OE.
N. CARPENTER The longest day is equall to the longest night. S. KING The day was overcast and drippy.
2 Daybreak, dawn. Now *rare* or *obsolete*. ME.
H. NELSON This morning at day we fell in with a Spanish . . Ship.
3 Daylight, the light of day. ME.
DEFOE It was broad day.
4 Any of the perpendicular divisions or lights of a mullioned window. *arch.* LME.
5 *MINING.* The surface of the ground over a mine. M17.
▸ **II** As a unit of time.
6 The time for one rotation of the earth on its axis; the period of twenty-four hours as a unit of time, esp. from midnight to midnight. Also (*ASTRONOMY*), a single rotation of a planet in relation to its primary. OE. ▸**b** A day of notable eventfulness etc. *colloq.* E20.
D. BREWSTER We may regard the length of the day as one of the most unchangeable elements in the system of the world. R. S. THOMAS So the days will drift into months. P. CHEYNEY Life is what you make it. Rome wasn't built in a day. **b** E. HEMINGWAY I say. We have had a day . . I must have been blind [drunk].
7 This period of time, esp. the civil day, treated as a point or unit of time, a particular date, etc. OE.
DAY LEWIS I was born next day—April 27th, 1904.
▸ **III** A specified or appointed day.
8 A specific period of twenty-four hours, the whole or part of which is assigned to some particular purpose, observance, or action; the date of a specified festival etc. (freq. with specifying word(s)). OE. ▸**b** The period of time in each day, established by law or usage, during which work is customarily done; a working day. M19.
J. CHEEVER The day of the flower show. **b** R. TANGYE A great agitation . . in favour of a nine hours' day. M. MCCARTHY A little light chatter about her day in the store.
Ascension Day, ***birthday***, ***Boxing Day***, ***Christmas Day***, ***Father's Day***, ***holiday***, ***Labour Day***, ***Lady Day***, ***May Day***, ***New Year's Day***, ***pay day***, ***St Andrew's Day***, ***St Swithin's Day***, ***washday***, ***wedding day***, ***workday***, etc.
9 A date agreed on; a day for a regular event, as being at home for guests, seeing patients at a clinic, etc. ME.
DRYDEN Or if my debtors do not keep their day. MRS H. WARD We found she was in town, and went on her 'day'.
10 The day of a battle or contest; (victory in) a battle. L15.
T. TUSSER The battell is fought, thou hast gotten the daye. J. MCCRAE These . . died not knowing how the day had gone.
▸ **IV** A space of time, a period.
11 *sing.* & in *pl.* The time during which something exists or takes place; a period, a time, an era; *the* current period. Also (with possess. pers. noun or pronoun) the period of a person's rule, activity, career, or life; one's lifetime; time of action, period of power or influence. OE.
DRYDEN I at Naples pass my peaceful Days. M. L. KING The Hitlers and the Mussolinis have their day, and for a period they may wield great power. J. C. OATES A popular tune of the day. *Proverb*: Every dog has his day.
12 Time allowed in which to be ready for something, esp. payment; delay, respite; credit. Long *rare*. LME.
13 A space of time (freq. of a defined extent). *obsolete* exc. *Scot.* LME.
– PHRASES: ***a good day's work***: see WORK *noun*. **all day (long)**, **all the day (long)** throughout the day, from daybreak to nightfall. **all in a day's work**, **all in the day's work** part of the normal routine, a matter of course. ***an eight days***: see EIGHT *adjective*. **any day** at any time, under any conditions. ***as clear as day***: see CLEAR *adjective*. **astronomical day** = *solar day* below. **at the end of the day** in the final reckoning. **better days** times of greater prosperity. ***break of day***: see BREAK *noun* 4. **call it a day** decide that one has worked at a task long enough, cease working (for the day, for the present, or finally); be satisfied with what one has done. ***carry the day***: see CARRY *verb*. **civil day**: as used for time reckoning in ordinary affairs. **day after day** each day as a sequel to the preceding one, esp. in an unvarying sequence. **day and night**: throughout these or in both alike. **day by day** on each successive day, daily without ceasing. ***day in, day out***: see IN *adverb*. ***Day of Atonement***: see ATONEMENT. **day off** a day away from work, school, etc. ***Day of Judgement***: see JUDGEMENT. ***day of*** RECKONING. **day of rest** *spec.* the Sabbath. ***day of retribution***: see RETRIBUTION 2. ***day of the Covenant***: see COVENANT *noun*. ***day of the week***: see WEEK *noun*. ***day of truce***: see TRUCE *noun*. **day out** a day away from home etc., an excursion. ***days of grace***: see GRACE *noun*. **day-to-day** continuous(ly), routine(ly). ***dish of the day***: see DISH *noun* 3a. ***dog days***: see DOG *noun*. ***dominical day***: see DOMINICAL *adjective* 1. ***eight days***: see EIGHT *adjective*. ***Ember day***: see EMBER *adjective*. **end one's days** pass the last part of one's life, die. ***equinoctial day***: see EQUINOCTIAL *adjective*. ***evil day(s)***: see EVIL *adjective*. ***eye of day***: see EYE *noun*. ***fifth day***: see FIFTH *adjective*. ***FIRST day***. ***FOURTH day***. **from day to day** continuously or without interruption from one day to another. **have had its day** be of no further use or effect. ***high day***: see HIGH *adjective*. **if he's a day**, **if she's a day**, etc., at least (a particular age etc.). **in this day and age** at the present time, the way things are at the present. ***Judgement Day***: see JUDGEMENT. ***last day(s)***: see LAST *adjective*. **late in the day** *fig.* late in the proceedings; *esp.* so late as to be of doubtful use. ***light of day***: see LIGHT *noun*. ***Lord's day***: see LORD *noun*. ***lunar day***: see LUNAR *adjective*. ***make a day of it***: see MAKE *verb*. ***make a person's day***: see MAKE *verb*. ***mean solar day***: see MEAN *adjective*[2]. **natural day** (*a*) = sense 1 above; (*b*) = sense 6 above (the usual sense). **night and day** = *day and night* above. **not one's day** a day when things go badly for one. **of a day** transitory, ephemeral. **one day** on some unspecified day, past or future. ***one fine day***, ***one of these fine days***: see FINE *adjective*. **one of these days** before long. **one of those days** a day of misfortune. **on one's day** at the time of one's best achievement etc., when at one's best. ***open day***: see OPEN *adjective*. ***order of the day***: see ORDER *noun*. ***red-letter day***: see RED *adjective*. ***SALAD days***. ***second day***: see SECOND *adjective*. ***SIDEREAL day***. ***solar day***: see SOLAR *adjective*[1]. ***some day***: see SOMEDAY *adverb*. **that will be the day** that will be worth waiting for, *iron.* that will never happen. **these days** *adverb* nowadays, at present. **The Day** [translating German DER TAG] a day expected to be marked by an important event, esp. a military conflict or victory. ***the Lord's day***: see LORD *noun*. ***the other day***: see OTHER *adjective*. ***the tother day***: see TOTHER *adjective*. ***this day MONTH***. **those were the days** (particular) past times were good or *iron.* bad (in comparison with the present). ***time of day***: see TIME *noun*. ***to one's dying day***: see DYING *adjective*[1]. ***tother day***: see TOTHER *adjective*. **to this day** at the present time as in the past, still, yet. ***twelfth day***: see TWELFTH *adjective*. ***until one's dying day***: see DYING *adjective*[1]. ***VARNISHING day***. ***wait the day***: see WAIT *verb*. ***win the day***: see WIN *verb*[1]. ***with continuation of days***: see CONTINUATION 5. ***WORKING day***. See also WEEKDAY.
– COMB.: **daybed** a bed for daytime sleep or rest; a sofa, a couch; **day blindness** = HEMERALOPIA; **daybook** (*a*) *arch.* a journal, a diary; formerly also, a nautical logbook; (*b*) an account book in which esp. sale transactions are entered at once for later transfer to a ledger; **day boy** a schoolboy who attends a boarding school but lives at home; **daybreak** dawn, the first light of day; **day care** the supervision of young children during the day, esp. while a parent or guardian is at work; **day centre** a place providing social, recreational, or other facilities for elderly or disabled persons during the day; **day-dawn** *poet.* daybreak; **day flower** any of various plants of the genus *Commelina* of the spiderwort family, having short-lived flowers usually blue in colour; **dayfly** a mayfly, living only a few hours or days; **day girl** a schoolgirl who attends a boarding school but lives at home; **day labour** work performed as a daily task, daily labour; labour hired by the day; **day labourer**: hired by the day; **day letter** *US HISTORY* a low-priority telegram sent by day; **day lily** any of various plants of the genus *Hemerocallis* of the lily family, with yellow, reddish, or purplish flowers lasting only for a day; **daylong** *adjective & adverb* (lasting) for a whole day; **daymare** [after *nightmare*] a frightening or oppressive trance or hallucinatory condition experienced while awake; **day nursery** (*a*) a room for children in the daytime; (*b*) a place where young children are looked after while a parent or guardian is at work; **day owl** an owl that hunts by day, *esp.* the short-eared owl; **daypack** a small rucksack; **day-peep** *arch.* earliest dawn; **day release** a system of allowing employees days off work to follow educational courses; **day return** (a ticket) at a reduced rate for a journey made both ways in one day; **day room** a room used by day only; *esp.* a common living room at a boarding school, a common room for inmates of a hospital, etc.; †**day rule** a rule or order which permitted a prisoner to go beyond the confines of prison for one day; **daysack** = *daypack* above; **day school** a school attended daily during the week, esp. as opp. to boarding school; **day shift** a shift worked during the daylight hours, as opp. to the night shift; **daysman** (*a*) *arch.* an arbitrator, a mediator; (*b*) a day labourer; **dayspring** *arch. & poet.* dawn; **day star** (*a*) the morning star; (*b*) (chiefly *poet.*) the sun; **daytime** the time of daylight; **day trader** a person employed in day trading; **day trading** a form of share dealing in which individuals buy and sell shares over the Internet over a period of a single day's trading, with the intention of profiting from small price fluctuations; **daywork** (*a*) (*obsolete* exc. *dial.*) a day's work; †(*b*) the amount of land able to be ploughed in a day; (*c*) work paid for according to the time worked.
■ **dayless** *adjective* †(*a*) without redress, resource, or result; (*b*) *poet.* devoid of daylight, dark: LME.

†**day** *verb.* ME.
[ORIGIN Branch I var. of DAW *verb* assim. to DAY *noun*; branch II from DAY *noun*.]
▸ **I** *verb intrans.* **1** Dawn. ME–M16.
▸ **II** *verb trans.* **2** Submit (a matter) to arbitration, decide by arbitration. LME–E17.
3 *year and day*, subject to a statutory period of a year and a day. E16–E17.
4 Measure by the day; provide with days. E17–M19.

Dayak /ˈdʌɪak/ *noun & adjective.* Also **Dyak**. M19.
[ORIGIN Malay = up-country.]
▸ **A** *noun.* A member of a group of aboriginal peoples inhabiting parts of Borneo and Sarawak; the language of these peoples. M19.
▸ **B** *attrib.* or as *adjective.* Of or pertaining to these peoples or their language. M19.
Sea Dayak = IBAN.

dayan /daˈjɑːn/ *noun.* Pl. **-im** /-ɪm/, **-s**. L19.
[ORIGIN Hebrew *dayyān*, from *dān* to judge.]
A religious judge in a Jewish community.

daydream /ˈdeɪdriːm/ *noun & verb.* M17.
[ORIGIN from DAY *noun* + DREAM *noun*[2].]
▸ **A** *noun.* A fancy or reverie (esp. of happiness) indulged in while awake; a fantasy, a castle in the air. M17.
▸ **B** *verb.* **1** *verb intrans.* Indulge in a daydream; become lost in one's imaginings. E19.
2 *verb trans.* Imagine in a daydream; transport (oneself) imaginatively in a daydream. L19.
■ **daydreamer** *noun* a person who daydreams, esp. habitually M19.

Day-Glo /ˈdeɪgləʊ/ *noun & adjective.* Also **dayglo** & other vars. M20.
[ORIGIN from DAY *noun* + GLOW *noun*.]
▸ **A** *noun.* (Proprietary name for) fluorescent paint or other colouring material. M20.
▸ **B** *adjective.* Coloured (as) with Day-Glo; (of colour) vivid, luminous, fluorescent. M20.

daylight /ˈdeɪlʌɪt/ *noun.* ME.
[ORIGIN from DAY *noun* + LIGHT *noun*.]
1 The light of day. Also *fig.*, the full light of knowledge and observation; openness, publicity. ME.
burn daylight: see BURN *verb* 8b. **let daylight into** *slang* make a hole in, stab, shoot. **see daylight** *fig.* understand what was previously puzzling.
2 The time of daylight, the daytime; *spec.* dawn. ME.
3 In *pl.* The vital organs. Formerly also, the eyes. *slang.* M18.
beat the living daylights out of, **scare the living daylights out of**, etc., beat, scare, etc., severely.
4 A clear visible interval, as between boats in a race, the rim and contents of a wine glass, a rider and the saddle, etc. E19.
– COMB.: ***daylight robbery***: see ROBBERY *noun* 3; **daylight-saving** the use of modified time to give longer evening daylight esp. in summer, by making clocks show a later time.

days /deɪz/ *adverb.* Now *colloq.* & *US*. OE.
[ORIGIN from DAY *noun* + -S[3], later identified with -S[1]. Cf. NIGHTS *adverb*.]
During the day, by day.

day-tale /ˈdeɪteɪl/ *adjective.* Chiefly *dial.* Also **da(y)tal** /ˈdeɪt(ə)l/. M16.
[ORIGIN from DAY *noun* + TALE *noun* reckoning etc.]
Designating work, wages, a worker, etc., reckoned, paid, or engaged by the day.

daze /deɪz/ *noun.* L17.
[ORIGIN from the verb.]
†**1** Mica. L17–L18.
2 A dazed condition (*lit. & fig.*); (a state of) stupefaction or bewilderment. E19.
DAY LEWIS In a daze of pure satisfaction. D. BAGLEY Conscious but in a daze, hardly aware of what was happening.

daze /deɪz/ *verb.* ME.
[ORIGIN Orig. in pa. pple from Old Norse *dasaðr* weary or exhausted from cold or exertion. Cf. Old Norse *dasask* (verb refl.) become exhausted, *dasi* lazy fellow, Swedish *dasa* lie idle.]
▸ **I** *verb trans.* **1** Stupefy, bewilder (a person), as by a blow on the head, drink, etc.; stun, confuse. Freq. as ***dazed ppl adjective***. ME.
G. MACDONALD She looked dazed, perhaps from the effects of her fall. D. MURPHY I was so dazed with joy that I could hardly speak.
2 Benumb, blight, or destroy with cold. *Scot. & N. English.* ME.
3 Confound or bewilder (the vision) by excessive light or brilliance; dazzle (*lit. & fig.*). Chiefly *poet.* E16.

D

TENNYSON The sudden light Dazed me half-blind.

▸ **II** *verb intrans.* †**4** Be or become stupefied or bewildered; be benumbed with cold; remain inactive or torpid. **ME–E16.**
†**5** Be or become dazzled; gaze stupidly. **LME–M17.**
6 Of meat, bread, etc.: become spoiled by being cooked at the wrong temperature. Of wood etc.: become rotten or spoiled from dampness etc. Chiefly as ***dazed*** *ppl adjective. Scot. & N. English.* **L17.**
■ **dazedly** /-zɪdli/ *adverb* in a dazed manner **LME.** **dazedness** *noun* the state or condition of being dazed **LME.** **dazy** *adjective* (*rare*) in a dazed condition **E16.**

D

dazibao /ˈdɑːdzəbaʊ/ *noun.* Pl. same. **M20.**
[ORIGIN Chinese *dàzìbào*, from *dà* big + *zì* character + *bào* newspaper, poster.]
In the People's Republic of China, a wall poster written in large characters expressing an (esp. political) opinion.

dazzle /ˈdaz(ə)l/ *verb & noun.* **L15.**
[ORIGIN from DAZE *verb* + -LE³.]
▸ **A** *verb.* **1** *verb intrans.* Of the eyes: lose the faculty of steady vision, esp. from gazing at too bright a light. *arch.* **L15.**

J. WEBSTER Cover her face; mine eyes dazzle.

2 *verb trans.* Confuse or dim (the sight, eye, etc.), bewilder (a person), with an excess of light, intricate motion, an incalculable number, etc. **E16.**

B. PYM She opened her eyes but was . . too dazzled by the sun to be able to see.

3 *verb trans. & intrans.* Delude or surprise (the mind, a person) by a brilliant or showy display or prospect; confuse or impress *by* or *with* brilliance etc.; temporarily overcome (a person's judgement etc.) in this way. **M16.**

L. STEPHEN Pope seems to have been dazzled by the amazing vivacity of the man. M. ARNOLD A style to dazzle, to gain admirers everywhere.

4 *verb trans.* Outshine, dim, eclipse, (chiefly *fig.*). *rare.* **L16.**

N. HAWTHORNE This church was dazzled out of sight by the Cathedral.

▸ **B** *noun.* **1** A dazzled state or condition. *rare.* **E17.**
2 An act of dazzling; a brightness, glitter, etc., that dazzles the vision; a bright confusing light. **M17.**

A. MASON The dazzle of armour too bright to look at in the sun. *fig.*: J. RUSKIN Amidst the tumult and the dazzle of their busy life.

3 More fully ***dazzle paint***. Paint patterned on a ship to deceive an enemy about its type or course. **E20.**
– COMB.: ***dazzle paint***: see sense 3 above; **dazzle-painted** *adjective*, **dazzle-painting** camouflaged, camouflaging, by dazzle paint.
■ **dazzlement** *noun* (*a*) the act of dazzling; a cause of dazzling; (*b*) a dazzled condition: **M17.** **dazzler** *noun* (see also BOBBY-DAZZLER) **L18.** **dazzling** *ppl adjective* †(*a*) that is or becomes dazzled; (*b*) that dazzles the eyes, mind, etc.; bright, brilliant, or splendid to a degree that dazzles: **L16.** **dazzlingly** *adverb* **E17.**

dB *abbreviation.*
Decibel(s).

Db *symbol.*
CHEMISTRY. Dubnium.

DBE *abbreviation.*
Dame Commander (of the Order) of the British Empire.

DBMS *abbreviation.*
COMPUTING. Database management system.

DBS *abbreviation.*
Direct-broadcast satellite, direct broadcasting by satellite.

dbx /diːbiːˈɛks/ *noun.* **L20.**
[ORIGIN from *db* = decibel + *x* = expander.]
(Proprietary name for) a device designed to increase the dynamic range of reproduced sound.

DC *abbreviation.*
1 MUSIC. Da capo.
2 (Also **d.c.**) Direct current (cf. AC, AC/DC).
3 District Commissioner.
4 District of Columbia.

DCB *abbreviation.*
Dame Commander (of the Order) of the Bath.

DCC *abbreviation.*
Digital compact cassette.

DCL *abbreviation.*
Doctor of Civil Law.

DCM *abbreviation.*
Distinguished Conduct Medal.

DCMG *abbreviation.*
Dame Commander (of the Order) of St Michael and St George.

DCVO *abbreviation.*
Dame Commander of the Royal Victorian Order.

DD *abbreviation.*
Doctor of Divinity.

D-Day /ˈdiːdeɪ/ *noun.* **E20.**
[ORIGIN from D for *day* + DAY *noun*.]
1 The day on which a particular (esp. military) operation is scheduled to begin; *spec.* (an anniversary of) 6 June 1944, when Allied forces invaded German-occupied northern France. **E20.**
2 The day of conversion of a country to decimal currency (in Britain, 15 February 1971). **M20.**

DDC *abbreviation.* Also **ddC**.
PHARMACOLOGY. Dideoxycytidine, a synthetic drug which inhibits the replication of HIV and is used in the treatment of Aids, especially in combination with zidovudine.

DDoS *abbreviation.*
COMPUTING. Distributed denial of service, denoting the intentional paralysing of a computer network by flooding it with data sent simultaneously from many individual computers.

DDR *abbreviation.*
hist. German *Deutsche Demokratische Republik* German Democratic Republic.

DDT *abbreviation.*
Dichlorodiphenyltrichloroethane, a chlorinated hydrocarbon ($CCl_3CH(C_6H_4Cl)_2$) used as an insecticide (now banned in many countries).

DE *abbreviation.*
Delaware.

de- /diː, dɪ/ *prefix.*
[ORIGIN from or after Latin *de-* from *de* adverb & preposition, = off, from. In privative sense 3 partly through French *dé-* from Old French *des-* from Latin *dis-*, treated as identical with Latin *de-* (cf. DIS-).]
1 In verbs (with derivs.) of Latin origin with the senses 'down, down from, down to', as ***depend***, ***depress***, etc., 'off, away, aside', as ***decline***, ***deduce***, ***desist***, etc., 'completely, thoroughly', as ***declaim***, ***denude***, ***derelict***, etc., 'to exhaustion', as ***deliquesce*** etc., or in a bad sense, as ***deceive***, ***deride***, ***detest***, etc.
2 In or after late Latin with the sense 'repeatedly, over again', as ***decomposite***, ***decompound***, etc. ▸**b** In adjectives with the sense 'formed from (what is denoted by the root noun)', as ***de-adjectival***, ***denominal***, ***deverbal***, etc.
3 With privative sense (denoting removal or reversal), in verbs from Latin, as ***decorticate*** etc., from French, as ***debauch***, ***defrock***, etc., and as a freely productive prefix, forming verbs (with derivs.) from verbs, as ***de-acidify***, ***decentralize***, ***decentralization***, ***de-escalate***, ***depressurize***, ***desegregate***, etc., or from nouns, as ***defuse***, ***de-ice***, ***delouse***, ***detrain***, etc.

DEA *abbreviation. US.*
Drug Enforcement Administration.

deaccession /diːəkˈsɛʃ(ə)n/ *verb & noun.* **L20.**
[ORIGIN from DE- 3 + ACCESSION *verb*.]
▸ **A** *verb trans. & intrans.* Officially remove (an item) from the listed holdings of a library, museum, etc., esp. for sale or disposal. **L20.**
▸ **B** *noun.* The action or process of deaccessioning items; a deaccessioned item. **L20.**

deacon /ˈdiːk(ə)n/ *noun.* Also (esp. as a title) **D-**. **OE.**
[ORIGIN ecclesiastical Latin *diaconus* from Greek *diakonos* servant, (in ecclesiastical Greek) Christian minister.]
▸ **I** CHRISTIAN CHURCH **1 a** In the early Church, an appointed minister of charity (see *Acts* 6:1–6). **OE.** ▸**b** In the episcopal Churches, a member of the third order of the ministry, ranking below bishops and priests and having the functions of assisting the priest in divine service (esp. the celebration of the Eucharist), parish work, etc. **OE.** ▸**c** In Nonconformist Churches, an officer appointed or elected to attend to secular matters affecting the congregation. **M16.**
b cardinal deacon: see CARDINAL *adjective* 3.
†**2** A set of Eucharistic garments worn by a deacon. **LME–M16.**
▸ **II** †**3** = LEVITE *noun* 1. **OE–LME.**
4 The president of an incorporated craft or trade in any town; a master craftsman, a thoroughly capable man. *Scot.* **LME.**
5 A junior officer in a Masonic lodge. **L18.**
6 (The hide of) a very young or aborted calf. *US colloq.* **L19.**
– COMB.: **deacon seat** *N. Amer.* a long seat in a log cabin, cut from a single log.
■ **deaconate** *noun* (*a*) deaconship; (*b*) a body of deacons: **L19.** **deaconhood** *noun* (*rare*) = DEACONATE **LME.** **deaconship** *noun* the position or office of deacon **LME.**

deacon /ˈdiːk(ə)n/ *verb trans.* **M19.**
[ORIGIN from the noun.]
1 Read aloud (a hymn etc.) one or two lines at a time, before it is sung. Freq. foll. by *off*. *US colloq.* **M19.**
2 Pack (fruit etc.) with the finest specimens on top; *gen.* alter so as to deceive, display deceptively. *US colloq.* **M19.**
3 Admit to the office of deacon. **L20.**

deaconess /diːkəˈnɛs, ˈdiːk(ə)nɪs/ *noun.* Also (esp. as a title) **D-**. **LME.**
[ORIGIN from DEACON *noun* + -ESS¹, after Latin *diaconissa*.]
CHRISTIAN CHURCH **1 a** In the early Church, a woman performing diaconal duties among other women. **LME.** ▸**b** In some modern Churches, a woman with functions analogous to those of a deacon. **E17.**
2 (**D-**.) A member of any of several Protestant orders of women, with educational and charitable aims. **M19.**
3 A deacon's wife. *rare.* **M19.**

deaconry /ˈdiːk(ə)nri/ *noun.* **L15.**
[ORIGIN formed as DEACONESS + -RY.]
1 The position or office of deacon; deaconship. **L15.**
2 A body of deacons. **L17.**
3 ROMAN CATHOLIC CHURCH. A chapel or charitable institution, in the charge of a cardinal deacon. **L17.**

deactivate /diːˈaktɪveɪt/ *verb trans.* **M20.**
[ORIGIN from DE- 3 + ACTIVATE *verb*.]
Render inactive; make less (chemically) reactive.
■ **deactiˈvation** *noun* **E20.** **deactivator** *noun* a substance which deactivates (chemically) **M20.**

dead /dɛd/ *noun*¹. **OE.**
[ORIGIN from the adjective.]
1 A dead person. Chiefly *collect.*, those or all who have died. **OE.**

I. MURDOCH The dead are the victims of the living. J. C. OATES Even the dead were washed out of their graves.

dead's part SCOTS LAW the part of an estate whose disposal is decidable by the testator or by the law of intestacy. **from the dead** from among those who are dead, from a state of death. **on the dead** *US slang* in dead earnest, honestly. ***walking dead***: see WALKING *ppl adjective*.
2 The dead period *of* a particular time, season, etc. **M16.**

W. S. CHURCHILL Driven in dead of winter along the mountain roads covered with snow.

3 MINING. In *pl.* Earth or rock containing no ore. **M17.**

dead *noun*² see DEATH.

dead /dɛd/ *adjective & adverb.*
[ORIGIN Old English *dēad* = Old Frisian *dād*, Old French *dōd* (Dutch *dood*), Old High German *tōt* (German *tot*), Old Norse *dauðr*, Gothic *dauþs*, from Germanic, from pa. pple of ult. base of DIE *verb*¹.]
▸ **A** *adjective* **I 1** That has ceased to live; deprived of life. **OE.**

DEFOE He was shot dead. S. JOHNSON Macbean . . is dead of a suppression of urine. DAY LEWIS A semi-circle of drive . . littered with dead leaves.

2 Having lost sensation or vitality; benumbed, insensible. Also *hyperbol.*, exhausted, drained of strength, worn out. **ME.**

OED She fell on the floor in a dead faint. A. HIGGINS My feet have gone dead on me.

3 Foll. by *to*: completely insensible or unresponsive to; unappreciative of; hardened against. Also, as good as dead in a particular respect or capacity; *spec.* legally cut off from all civil rights. **ME.**

N. BACON He that is in a monastery is dead to all worldly affairs. SHELLEY Sensual, and vile; Dead to all love. *Washington Post* Rome . . dismissed as culturally dead.

4 Devoid of living organisms; barren, infertile. **ME.**

HENRY MILLER The arid surface of dead planets.

5 Lacking spiritual life or energy. **LME.**

W. COWPER He lives, who lives to God alone, And all are dead beside.

6 Not endowed with life; inanimate; inert. **LME.**

ADDISON There are some living creatures which are raised but just above dead matter.

†**7** Causing death; deadly, mortal. **LME–E17.**

SHAKES. *Wint. T.* Though full of our displeasure, yet we free thee From the dead blow of it.

8 [Partly attrib. use of DEAD *noun*¹.] Of, pertaining or relating to a dead person, animal, etc., or a death. Also, (of a hedge or fence) made of dead plants etc. **L15.**

W. COMBE What the medical people call a dead case . . a consultation . . to discover the disorder of which their patient died.

9 No longer in use or existence; obsolete; past; *esp.* (of a language etc.) no longer spoken. **L16.**

TENNYSON My doubts are dead. J. IRVING Old East Norse is a dead language.

▸ **II 10** Without vigour or animation, lifeless. **OE.** ▸**b** Of a racehorse: not intended to win, fraudulently run to prevent its winning. *slang.* **M19.**

L. HUTCHINSON A bare dead description. R. W. EMERSON Active intellect and dead conservatism.

11 Without motion, unmoving; still, standing; (of a mechanical part) not designed to move independently. **OE.**

I. Walton From the dead, still water, into the sharp streames and the gravel. O. G. Gregory The dead pulley is fixed to the axis and turns with it.

12 Without active force or practical effect; ineffectual, inoperative. **ME.**

J. H. Newman So earnest for a dead ordinance.

13 Without commercial, social, or intellectual activity; marked by inactivity, dull; (of capital, stock, etc.) lying unutilized, unprofitable, unsaleable. **ME.**

Robert Knox And now caps were become a very dead commodity. J. A. Froude It was the dead season; but there were a few persons still in London.

14 Deprived of or wanting a vital or characteristic quality; extinguished, extinct; spent, burnt-out; flat, dull, lustreless. **ME.** ▸**b** Of an electric circuit, conductor, etc.: not carrying or transmitting a current; not connected. Of a microphone, telephone, etc.: not transmitting sounds. **E20.**

Evelyn It will not ferment . . and then the Cider will be dead, flat, and soure. Dryden The dead colour of her face. Hartley Coleridge The crackling embers on the hearth are dead. **b** I. Murdoch There was a big electric torch, but the battery was dead.

15 Of sound: muffled, without resonance, dull. Of a room etc.: allowing minimal acoustic reverberation. **LME.**

16 Characterized by absence of physical motion or sound; profoundly quiet or still. Of ground etc.: lacking resilience or springiness; *military slang* naturally sheltered from a line of fire. Of a house (*slang*): uninhabited. **M16.**

Shakes. *Meas. for M.* 'Tis now dead midnight.

17 Characterized by complete and abrupt cessation of motion, action, or speech. **M17.**

Dickens The answer spoilt his joke, and brought him to a dead stop.

18 *Games.* Of the ball: not in play, (temporarily) inactive. Also (*Golf*), so close to a hole that the putt is deemed to be unmissable. **M17.**

B. Johnston A ball does *not* become dead when it strikes an umpire.

19 *Architecture.* Lacking its ostensible purpose; false, blind; inoperative. **E19.**

R. Forsyth A . . bridge . . the dead arches of which have been fitted up as a town-hall.

▸**III 20** Unrelieved, unbroken; profound, deep; (of the state of the tide) lowest; (of pull, strain, etc.) applied to its utmost against an unmoving body. **M16.**

D. Livingstone I crossed it at dead low-water. Tennyson We heard In the dead hush the papers . . Rustle. J. R. Lowell To reduce all mankind to a dead level of mediocrity.

21 Absolute, complete, entire, thorough, downright; unerring, certain, sure; exact. **L16.**

R. Sharrock Till the seed . . be come to a full and dead ripenesse. Sir W. Scott This is a dead secret. Thackeray He is a dead hand at piquet.

22 Of an expense etc.: unrelieved, complete, utter. Of an outlay: unproductive, without returns. **E18.**

W. Cobbett Those colonies are a dead expense to us.

– Phrases: **dead and gone**, **dead and buried** *rhet.* in one's grave, deceased; *fig.* past, over. **dead as a doornail** quite dead. **dead as mutton** quite dead. **dead as a dodo**, **dead as the dodo** extinct, entirely obsolete. **dead from the neck up** *colloq.* brainless, stupid, doltish. **dead to the wide** *slang* (**a**) = ***dead to the world*** below; (**b**) totally exhausted. **dead to the world** unconscious, fast asleep. ***lay dead***: see lay *verb*[1]. ***the dead ring*** (*of*): see ring *noun*[2]. ***top dead centre***: see top *adjective*. **wouldn't be seen dead in**, **wouldn't be seen dead with** *colloq.* shall have nothing to do with, refuse to wear etc.

– Special Collocations & Comb.: **dead-alive**, **dead-and-alive** alive without animation, dull, spiritless, monotonous. **dead-ball line** *Rugby* a line behind the goal line beyond which the ball is considered out of play. **dead bat** *Cricket* a bat held loosely so that the ball strikes it and immediately falls to the ground. ***dead body***: see body *noun*. **dead cat bounce** *Stock Exchange* a temporary recovery in share prices after a substantial fall, caused by speculators buying in order to cover their positions. **dead-born** *adjective* (chiefly *dial.*) born dead. **dead centre** (**a**) the exact centre; (**b**) = ***dead point*** below; (**c**) in a lathe, the centre which does not revolve. ***dead cert***: see cert *noun*. **dead colour** the first or preparatory layer of colour in a painting. **dead-colour** *verb trans.* paint in dead colour. †**dead-doing** *adjective* killing, murderous. ***dead duck***: see duck *noun*[1]. **deadeye** *Nautical* a round flat three-holed block for extending shrouds. **deadfall** (chiefly *N. Amer.*) (**a**) a trap with a falling weight to kill an animal, a snare (*lit.* & *fig.*); (**b**) a tangled mass of fallen trees etc.; (**c**) a disreputable drinking or gambling place. **dead-fire** a corposant, taken as a presage of death. ***dead giveaway***: see giveaway *noun* 2. **dead hand** (**a**) [translation] = mortmain; (**b**) posthumous control, *esp.* an undesirable persisting posthumous influence. **dead-hearted** *adjective* callous, insensible. **dead heat** a race in which two or more competitors finish exactly level. **dead-heat** *verb intrans.* run a dead heat (*with* another competitor). **dead horse** *fig.* something no longer of use, something it is pointless to attempt to revive, (***flog a dead horse***, waste energy on something unalterable). **dead house** *arch. colloq.* a mortuary. **dead leg** an injury caused by a numbing blow with the knee to a person's upper leg. **dead letter** (**a**) a writing etc. taken literally without reference to its spirit or intention, and so useless or ineffective; (**b**) a law no longer observed, a disused practice; (**c**) an unclaimed or undelivered letter. **dead letter box** a place where (esp. secret) messages can be left and collected without the sender and recipient meeting. **dead lift** (**a**) a lift made without mechanical assistance or other advantage; an exertion of the utmost strength to lift or move something (esp. beyond one's strength); (**b**) (now *arch.* & *dial.*) an extremity, a hopeless case (chiefly in ***at a dead lift***). **deadlight** (**a**) *Nautical* a strong shutter fixed inside or outside a porthole etc. to keep out water in a storm; (**b**) *Scot.* = ***corpse candle*** (a) s.v. corpse *noun*. **deadline** (**a**) a line, constituting a piece of tackle etc., that does not move or run; (**b**) a line beyond which it is not permitted or possible to go; (**c**) a time limit, *esp.* the time by which an article etc. scheduled for publication must be completed. **dead load** a load of constant and invariable weight. **dead loss** (**a**) a complete and unrelieved (financial) loss; (**b**) *colloq.* a useless or contemptible person or thing. **dead march** a slow solemn march for a funeral etc., a funeral march. **dead-melt** *verb trans.* keep (a metal) at a melting temperature until it is perfectly fluid and no more gas is evolved. **dead-nettle** any of various labiate plants of the genus *Lamium* and allied genera, with leaves like those of stinging nettles but without stinging hairs; *esp.* (**a**) (more fully ***red dead-nettle***) *L. purpureum*, a European weed with pinkish-purple flowers; (**b**) (more fully ***white dead-nettle***) *L. album*, a Eurasian hedge plant with large white flowers; (**c**) ***yellow dead-nettle*** = ***yellow archangel*** s.v. archangel 2. †**dead palsy**: producing complete insensibility or immobility of the affected part. **dead pay** [cf. French *morte-paye*] †(**a**) (a soldier etc. receiving) pay continued after active service has ceased; (**b**) *hist.* a soldier etc. actually dead or discharged but for whom nevertheless pay is claimed; pay drawn in this way. **dead point** the position of a crank in direct line with the connecting rod and not exerting torque. **dead reckoning** estimation of the position of a ship, aeroplane, etc., by log, compass, etc., when observations are impossible. **deadrise** *Nautical* the vertical distance between a line horizontal to the keel of a boat and its chine. ***dead set***: see set *noun*[1] 4, 5. **dead shot** an unerring marksman. ***dead soldier***: see soldier *noun*. **dead-stick landing**: of an aircraft with the engine(s) stopped. **dead stock**, **deadstock** (**a**) (as two words) commercially inactive or unproductive stock, capital, etc.; (**b**) (as one word) farm machinery etc. (as opp. ***livestock***). **dead time** *Physics* the period after the recording of a pulse etc. when a detector is unable to record another. **dead-tongue** (chiefly *dial.*) a poisonous umbellifer, hemlock water dropwort, *Oenanthe crocata*. **dead water** (**a**) the neap tide; (**b**) water without any current, still water; (**c**) *Nautical* the eddy water just behind the stern of a ship under way. **dead weight** (**a**) a heavy unrelieved weight or burden; an inert mass; (**b**) the weight of cargo, fuel, crew, and passengers carried by a ship etc.; (**c**) *fig.* a debt not covered by assets; (**d**) the weight of an animal after it has been slaughtered and prepared as a carcass. **dead well**: sunk to a porous stratum to carry off surface or refuse water. **dead white** (**a**) flat or lustreless white; (**b**) pure white. **dead white European male**, **dead white male** *colloq.* a writer, philosopher, etc., whose importance and talents may have been exaggerated by virtue of his belonging to a historically dominant gender and ethnic group (abbreviation ***DWEM***, ***DWM***). **dead wood** (**a**) wood no longer alive; *fig.* a person or persons, a thing or things, regarded as useless or unprofitable; (**b**) *Nautical* solid blocks of timber fastened just above the keel at each end of a ship, to strengthen her structure. **dead work** (**a**) unproductive work (in mining etc.); †(**b**) = ***upper works*** (a) s.v. upper *adjective*. **dead zone** (**a**) a place or period in which nothing happens or in which no life exists; (**b**) a place where it is not possible to receive a mobile phone or radio signal.

▸**B** *adverb.* **1** To a degree suggesting death; with extreme inactivity, stillness, etc.; profoundly; to extremity. **LME.**

J. Carlyle Whether I fainted, or suddenly fell dead-asleep.

dead drunk so drunk as to be insensible or immobile.

2 Utterly, entirely, absolutely, quite, exactly. Now *colloq.* **L16.**

W. F. Hook One horse . . which soon became dead lame. R. Cobb The train came in dead on time. Sloan Wilson You're just like the others—dead ordinary.

dead broke, ***dead certain***, ***dead right***, ***dead sure***, etc. **dead on** exactly right. ***dead to rights***: see right *noun*[1].

3 Directly, straight. **E19.**

J. Conrad It loomed up dead to leeward.

dead against directly opposed or opposite to (*lit.* & *fig.*).

4 With an abrupt cessation of motion or action. **M19.**

E. Pound Don't make each line stop dead at the end.

■ **deadish** *adjective* (now *rare*) **LME.** **deadness** *noun* **L16.**

dead /dɛd/ *verb.* **OE.**

[Origin from the adjective. Superseded by deaden.]

▸**I** *verb intrans.* †**1** = deaden 5. **OE–M17.**

▸**II** *verb trans.* **2** Cause to die, kill. Now *nursery & joc.* **LME.**

†**3** = deaden 3. **LME–L17.**

†**4** = deaden 1. **E17–M18.**

†**5** = deaden 2. Only in **17.**

dead beat /ˈdɛdbiːt, *as pred. adjective* dɛdˈbiːt/ *adjective phr., noun, & verb.* **E19.**

[Origin from dead *adverb* + beat *ppl adjective*.]

▸**A** *adjective.* **1** Completely exhausted; at the end of one's resources. *colloq.* **E19.**

2 Of an escapement etc.: without recoil. **L19.**

▸**B** *noun.* (**deadbeat**.) A worthless sponging idler, a loafer (orig. *US*); a man down on his luck. *colloq.* (orig. *Austral.*). **M19.**

▸**C** *verb.* (**dead-beat**.) *colloq. rare.*

1 *verb trans.* Exhaust, wear out. **M19.**

2 *verb trans. & intrans.* Sponge (on), cheat. **L19.**

■ **dead-'beaten** *adjective* exhausted **L19.**

deaden /ˈdɛd(ə)n/ *verb.* **M17.**

[Origin from dead *adjective* + -en[5]. Superseding dead *verb*.]

▸**I** *verb trans.* **1** Deprive of some effective physical quality, as flavour, lustre, sharpness, etc.; make (sound) dull or indistinct. **M17.** ▸**b** Make impervious to sound. **E20.**

E. Bowen Grass which had seeded between the cobbles . . deadened her steps.

2 Destroy or reduce the energy of (motion). **M17.**

3 Deprive of vitality, force, etc.; dull, benumb; make dead or insensible *to*. **L17.**

A. S. Neill A bairn does like the dramatic; prosiness deadens its wee soul at once. M. Shadbolt He was given injections to deaden pain.

D

4 Deprive (tissue etc.) of life, kill; *spec.* (*US*) kill (trees), clear (ground) of trees, by ringbarking. **L18.**

▸**II** *verb intrans.* **5** Become dead; *esp.* lose vitality, vigour, brightness, feeling, etc. **E18.**

Southey The dash Of the out-breakers deaden'd.

■ **deadener** *noun* **M19.** **deadeningly** *adverb* in a deadening manner, so as to deaden **M20.**

dead end /dɛd ˈɛnd/; *as attrib. adjective* ˈdɛd ɛnd/ *noun, adjective, & verb.* **L19.**

[Origin from dead *adjective* + end *noun*.]

▸**A** *noun.* The closed end of a passage etc., a cul-de-sac; *fig.* a job, policy, course of action, etc., with no prospects of advancement. **L19.**

▸**B** *adjective.* Closed at the end, leading nowhere; *fig.* having no possibilities for advancement, promotion, etc. **L19.**

dead-end kid a young slum-dwelling tough, a juvenile delinquent.

▸**C** *verb trans. & intrans.* (with hyphen.) Bring or come to a dead end. **E20.**

deadhead /ˈdɛdhɛd/ *noun & verb.* Also **dead-head**. **L16.**

[Origin from dead *adjective* + head *noun*.]

▸**A** *noun.* †**1** = caput mortuum. **L16–E18.**

2 A disposable or unmoving mechanical part. **M19.**

3 A non-paying theatregoer, passenger, etc. *colloq.* (orig. *US*). **M19.** ▸**b** An empty train, vehicle, etc. *US colloq.* **M20.**

4 A useless or unenterprising person; one who contributes nothing to an activity etc., a hanger-on. *colloq.* **L19.**

5 In full ***deadhead log***. A sunken or submerged log. *N. Amer.* **E20.**

6 A faded flower head, esp. when still attached to the plant. **M20.**

▸**B** *verb.* **1** *verb trans. & intrans.* Enter or admit to a theatre etc. without payment; (allow to) travel free. *US colloq.* **M19.**

2 *verb intrans. & trans.* Drive or travel in (a train, vehicle, etc.) with no passengers or cargo. *colloq.* (orig. *US*). **E20.**

3 *verb trans.* Remove a dead flower or flowers from (a plant). **M20.**

de-adjectival /ˌdiːadʒɛkˈtʌɪv(ə)l/ *adjective.* **M20.**

[Origin from de- 2 + adjectival.]

Grammar. Derived from an adjective.

deadlock /ˈdɛdlɒk/ *noun & verb.* **L18.**

[Origin from dead *adjective* + lock *noun*[2].]

▸**A** *noun.* **1** A condition or situation in which no progress or activity is possible; a complete standstill; lack of progress due to irreconcilable disagreement or equal opposing forces. **L18.**

2 A lock which opens and shuts only with a key (as opp. to a spring lock); occas., a padlock. **M19.**

▸**B** *verb trans. & intrans.* Bring or come to a state of deadlock. **L19.**

■ **deadlocked** *adjective* (of negotiation, conflict, etc.) in which no progress is possible **L19.**

deadly /ˈdɛdli/ *adjective.* **OE.**

[Origin from dead *adjective* + -ly[1].]

▸†**I 1** Subject to death, mortal. **OE–M19.**

2 In danger of death; of or belonging to death. **ME–E17.**

▸**II 3** Causing fatal injury or serious damage; mortal; poisonous, venomous, pestilential. **OE.**

J. Beattie Tho' Fortune aim her deadliest blow. Tolkien To wield his sword with left hand more deadly than his right had been.

deadly nightshade.

4 *Christian Theology.* Of sin: entailing damnation, mortal (as opp. ***venial***), *esp.* designating each of the seven chief or cardinal sins. **ME.**

5 Aiming or involving an aim to kill or destroy; implacable; internecine. **ME.** ▸**b** Of aim: extremely accurate. **E20.**

G. F. Kennan A deadly, implacable, snakelike enmity. **b** D. Brown Pistol outstretched, taking deadly aim at Langdon's chest.

6 Resembling or suggestive of death; deathlike, esp. in unconsciousness or physical prostration; (of darkness, gloom, silence, etc.) intense; *colloq.* dreary. **ME.**

Shakes. *Com. Err.* I know it by their pale and deadly looks.

7 Excessive, intense. *colloq.* **M17.**

Carlyle Why such deadly haste to make money?

8 Very good; excellent. *Irish, Austral., & NZ colloq.* **M20.**

■ **deadlily** *adverb* (*rare*) **E17.** **deadliness** *noun* **ME.**

deadly /ˈdɛdli/ *adverb*. OE.
[ORIGIN from DEAD *adjective* + -LY².]
†**1** In a way that causes death; mortally, fatally; *THEOLOGY* in a way entailing damnation. OE–E19.
†**2** Implacably, to the death. ME–M17.
3 In a manner resembling or suggesting death; as if dead. ME.
J. CONRAD Being so deadly white . . like a horrible . . invalid.
4 Extremely, excessively. *colloq.* L16.
M. KEANE A deadly dull display of barometers.
5 In a dead manner; like a dead thing. *rare.* L16.

D

dead man /dɛd ˈman/ *noun phr.* Pl. **dead men** /ˈmɛn/. Also (now *rare*) **deadman** /ˈdɛdman/, pl. **deadmen**. OE.
[ORIGIN from DEAD *adjective* + MAN *noun*.]
▸ **I** *lit.* **1** A man who is dead. OE.
▸ **II** *transf.* & *fig.* **2** In *pl.* Empty liquor bottles. *slang.* L17.
†**3** A loaf charged to a customer but never delivered. *slang.* M18–L19.
†**4** A dummy at whist etc. Only in L18.
5 *NAUTICAL.* In *pl.* Reef or gasket ends left dangling when a sail is furled. E19.
6 Any of various objects buried in or secured to the ground for the purpose of providing anchorage or leverage. M19.
7 A scarecrow. *dial.* M19.
– PHRASES: **dead man's bells**, **dead men's bells** *Scot.* the foxglove. †**dead man's eye** = *deadeye* s.v. DEAD *adjective* etc. **dead man's fingers**, **dead men's fingers** (*a*) any of various orchids, *esp.* the early purple orchid; (*b*) a soft coral, *Alcyonium digitata*; (*c*) the divisions of the gills in a crab or lobster. **dead man's hand** (*a*) = *dead man's fingers* (a), (b) above; (*b*) the male fern, *Dryopteris filix-mas*. **dead man's handle**, **dead man's pedal**, etc., a control in an electric train etc. which acts as a safety device by automatically cutting off the current if released; an emergency brake in a motor lorry etc. **dead man's thumb** (*a*) the early purple orchid; (*b*) = *dead man's fingers* (b) above. ***dead men's bells***, ***dead men's fingers***: see *dead man's bells*, *dead man's fingers* above. ***dead men's shoes***: see SHOE *noun*.

deadpan /ˈdɛdpan/ *adjective, noun, adverb, & verb*. Also (esp. as noun) **dead pan**. E20.
[ORIGIN from DEAD *adjective* + PAN *noun*¹.]
▸ **A** *adjective*. Expressionless, impassive, unemotional; detached, impersonal. E20.
I. BAIRD Matt's eyes lost their cold deadpan look. *Listener* The Baron's marvellously deadpan tall tales.
▸ **B** *noun*. (A person with) a deadpan expression; a deadpan demeanour or style. M20.
▸ **C** *adverb*. With a deadpan face; in a deadpan manner. M20.
▸ **D** *verb trans. & intrans.* Infl. **-nn-**. Speak, perform, behave, etc., with a deadpan face or in a deadpan manner. M20.

Dead Sea /dɛd ˈsiː/ *noun phr.* ME.
[ORIGIN from DEAD *adjective* + SEA *noun*, translating Latin *mare mortuum*, Greek *hē nekra thalassa*.]
The inland sea into which the River Jordan flows, which has no outlet and is noted for its bitter, saline waters and arid surroundings; *gen.* (**d- s-**) any sea considered to be devoid of life.
– COMB.: **Dead Sea apple**, **Dead Sea fruit** (*a*) a legendary fruit, of attractive appearance, which dissolved into smoke and ashes when held; (*b*) either of two plants with showy fruit, *Solanum sodomeum*, an African nightshade naturalized in the Mediterranean region, and a mudar, *Calotropis procera*; the fruit of either of these plants; (*c*) *fig.* any outwardly desirable object which on attainment turns out to be worthless; any hollow disappointing thing; **Dead Sea Scrolls** a collection of ancient Jewish scrolls and fragments discovered in caves in the area of Qumran, a region on the NW shore of the Dead Sea, between 1947 and 1956.

de-aerate /diːˈɛːreɪt/ *verb trans.* L18.
[ORIGIN from DE- 3 + AERATE.]
Remove air from.
■ **de-aeˈration** *noun* M19.

deaf /dɛf/ *adjective & noun*.
[ORIGIN Old English *dēaf* = Old Frisian *dāf*, Old Saxon *dōf* (Dutch *doof*), Old High German *toup* (German *taub*), Old Norse *daufr*, Gothic *daufs*, *daubs*, from Germanic, from Indo-European base repr. also by Greek *tuphlos* blind.]
▸ **A** *adjective*. **1** Without hearing; defective in the sense of hearing. OE. ▸**b** Insensitive to certain kinds of sound, musical rhythm, harmony, etc. Foll. by *to* or in *comb.*, as ***tone-deaf*** etc. L18.
SIR W. SCOTT Lady Suffolk is a little deaf. E. LONGFORD He was to be stone deaf in the left ear for life. *fig.*: SHELLEY Have its deaf waves not heard my agony?
(*as*) ***deaf as an adder***, (*as*) ***deaf as a beetle***, (*as*) ***deaf as a post***, etc.
2 Lacking its essential quality or characteristic; hollow, barren; insipid. Now chiefly *dial.* OE.
3 Not giving ear *to*; unwilling to hear or pay attention *to*; unresponsive, uncompliant. ME.
J. L. WATEN Although their voices floated out into the kitchen I was deaf to them.
fall on deaf ears be ignored. **turn a deaf ear (to)** pretend not to hear, be unresponsive (to an appeal etc.).
†**4** Of a sound: so dull as to be hardly or indistinctly heard; muffled. E17–E18.
▸ **B** *absol.* as *noun*. A deaf person. Long only *collect. pl.*, the class of deaf people. OE.
– SPECIAL COLLOCATIONS & COMB.: **deaf adder** (*a*) the slow-worm; (*b*) *US* a hognose snake. **deaf aid** a hearing aid. **deaf and dumb** able neither to hear nor to speak (see note s.v. DUMB adjective). **deaf-nettle** *dial.* a dead-nettle. **deaf nut** a nut with no kernel; *fig.* something hollow or worthless.
■ **deafish** *adjective* E17. **deafly** *adverb* (*a*) without hearing (*lit.* & *fig.*); (*b*) dully, indistinctly: ME. **deafness** *noun* OE.

deaf /dɛf/ *verb trans.* Now *arch.* & *dial.* LME.
[ORIGIN from the adjective: cf. earlier DEAVE. Superseded by DEAFEN.]
1 = DEAFEN 1. LME.
2 = DEAFEN 2. M17.

deafen /ˈdɛf(ə)n/ *verb trans.* L16.
[ORIGIN from DEAF *adjective* + -EN⁵. Superseding DEAF *verb*.]
1 Make deaf; deprive of hearing by noise, temporarily or permanently. L16.
M. W. MONTAGU Hunting horns . . that almost deafen the Company.
deafening silence *iron.* a conspicuous or significant failure to comment on a matter or otherwise respond.
2 Make (a sound) inaudible; drown *by* a louder sound. E19.
3 *BUILDING.* Make (a floor etc.) soundproof. Now chiefly *Scot.* E19.
■ **deafened** *adjective & noun* (*a*) *adjective* that has been made deaf (now esp. permanently); (*b*) *noun* the class of deafened people: E17. **deafeningly** *adverb* so as to deafen M19.

deafferent /diːˈaf(ə)r(ə)nt/ *verb trans.* E20.
[ORIGIN from DE- 3 + AFFERENT *adjective*.]
BIOLOGY & MEDICINE. Interrupt or destroy the afferent connections of (nerve cells); deprive of afferent connection with the central nervous system.
■ **deafferenˈtation** *noun* M20.

de-afforest /diːəˈfɒrɪst/ *verb trans.* M17.
[ORIGIN medieval Latin *deafforestare*, formed as DE- 1, AFFOREST. Cf. DEFOREST, DISAFFOREST, DISFOREST.]
hist. = DISAFFOREST 1.
■ **de-afforeˈstation** *noun* M17.

deaf mute /dɛf ˈmjuːt/ *noun & adjectival phr.* Now regarded as *offensive*. Also (esp. as adjective) **deaf-mute**. M19.
[ORIGIN from DEAF *adjective* + MUTE *adjective* & *noun*² after French *sourd-muet*.]
▸ **A** *noun phr.* A person who is both deaf and unable to speak. M19.
▸ **B** *adjective*. Both deaf and unable to speak. M19.
■ **deaf-ˈmutism** *noun* M19.

deal /diːl/ *noun*¹.
[ORIGIN Old English *dǣl* = Old Frisian, Old Saxon *dēl* (Dutch *deel*), Old High German, German *Teil*, Gothic *dails*, from Germanic base also of DOLE *noun*¹.]
†**1** A part or division of a whole; a portion, section. OE–M18.
AV *Num.* 15:9 A meate offering of three tenth deales of flowre.
EVERYDEAL, HALFENDEAL, SOMEDEAL.
2 A portion allowed to anyone; a share. Now *dial.* OE.
3 A (specified, now usu. *great* or *good*) quantity, amount, or number (*of*). Also (*colloq.*) *absol.*, a considerable quantity, a lot, much. In adverbial phrs.: to a specified degree or extent. OE.
J. RAY So vast a deal of room, that 40,000 people may shelter . . in it. K. GRAHAME In the winter time the Rat slept a great deal. J. GALSWORTHY A deal of mortals in this world, and not enough imagination to go round! J. G. COZZENS Quite a good deal younger than her husband. R. MACAULAY I have a great deal to say to you, my child.

deal /diːl/ *noun*². ME.
[ORIGIN Middle Low German, Middle Dutch *dele* plank, floor (Dutch *deel* plank), corresp. to Old High German *dil*, *dilo*, *dillo*, *dilla* (German *Diele* floorboard, floor), Old Norse *þilja*, Old English *þille*, from Germanic.]
1 A piece of sawn timber (now always fir or pine wood) of standard size; a plank or board of fir or pine; timber in such planks or boards. Also more fully ***deal board***. ME.
2 Fir or pine timber. E17.
attrib.: S. HEANEY The deal table where he wrote.
red deal the wood of the Scots pine, *Pinus sylvestris*. **white deal** the wood of the Norway spruce, *Picea abies*, or of the silver fir, *Abies alba*. **yellow deal** = *red deal* above.
– COMB.: ***deal board***: see sense 1 above; **dealfish** a N. Atlantic fish, *Trachipterus arcticus*, belonging to the ribbonfish family Trachipteridae, with laterally compressed body (likened to a deal).

deal /diːl/ *noun*³. L15.
[ORIGIN from the verb.]
†**1** Dealings, intercourse. *Scot.* L15–L16.
2 The distribution of cards to players before a round of play; a player's turn for this; the round of play following this; the set of hands dealt to players. E17.
3 An act of trading or of buying or selling; a business transaction, a bargain, an arrangement; *esp.* a private or secret arrangement entered into by parties for their mutual benefit. *colloq.* M19.
H. F. PRINGLE Deals and counterdeals between Tammany and anti-Tammany Democrats. P. G. WODEHOUSE If you don't wish to meet my terms, the deal is off. J. DIDION It was kind of a Swiss Family Robinson deal down there.
a fair deal equitable treatment, honest dealing. **a raw deal**, **a rough deal** harsh or unfair treatment. ***a square deal***: see SQUARE *adjective*. ***big deal!***: see BIG *adjective*. ***new deal***: see NEW *adjective*.
– COMB.: **deal-breaker** (in business and politics) a factor or issue which, if unresolved during negotiations, would cause one party to withdraw from a deal.

deal /diːl/ *verb*. Pa. t. & pple **dealt** /dɛlt/.
[ORIGIN Old English *dǣlan* = Old Frisian *dēla*, Old Saxon *dēljan* (Dutch *deelen*), Old High German, German *teilen*, Old Norse *deila*, Gothic *dailjan*, from Germanic, from base of DEAL *noun*¹.]
▸ **I** †**1** *verb trans.* Divide. OE–L16.
CAXTON This kyngdome of Northumberland was first deled in two prouynces.
†**2** *verb trans.* & (*rare*) *intrans.* Separate, part (*from*). OE–LME.
†**3** *verb trans.* Divide (property etc.) in due shares, portion out; share *with* another or others. OE–M16.
COVERDALE *Josh.* 8:2 Ye shal deale amonge you their spoyle & catell.
4 *verb trans.* Distribute, give out (gifts etc.) among a number of recipients; (*esp.* of Providence etc.) deliver as share or deserts (*to* a person). Freq. foll. by *out*. OE.
M. ARNOLD Has thou yet dealt him, O life, thy full measure? K. AMIS A woman in a corner sweet-shop . . who had dealt out the lollies . . to the school kids.
5 *verb trans.* Cause to be received, administer, deliver (esp. a blow (*lit.* & *fig.*)). ME.
DRYDEN By fits he deals his fiery bolts about. E. BOWEN You dealt us a knock, you know. You gave us a fright.
6 *verb trans. & intrans.* Distribute (cards) to the players in a game or round; give a player (such or so many cards) in dealing. E16. ▸**b** *verb trans.* Include (a person) *in* those to whom cards are dealt; *fig.* include (someone) *in* an undertaking, give (a person) a share or part. *colloq.* (orig. *US*). M20.
C. COTTON He that deals hath the advantage of this game. *transf.*: M. AMIS I picked up the stack of mail . . and dealt myself one off the bottom. **b** W. GARNER If they won't deal us in we may end up having to steal it.
▸ **II** †**7** *verb intrans.* Engage *with* in conflict; contend. OE–E18.
MILTON Brutish that contest and foule, When Reason hath to deal with force.
†**8** *verb intrans.* Take part *in*, share or participate *in* or *with*, partake *of*. OE–L15.
9 *verb intrans.* Have to do, have dealings *with* (esp. with neg.); *arch.* negotiate, treat *with*, esp. in an underhand or secret way; do business, trade *with* a person, *in* goods etc., (*lit.* & *fig.*). ME.
JONSON Now have they dealt with my pothecary to poison me. I. WATTS True Logic is not that noisy thing that deals all in dispute and wrangling. E. A. FREEMAN One of the charges . . was that of dealing with a familiar spirit. W. H. AUDEN War is but a kind of trading: Instead of cheese, it deals in lead.
10 *verb intrans.* Foll. by *with*: be concerned with (a thing) in any way; busy or occupy oneself with, esp. with a view to discussion or refutation. Also, take (esp. punitive or corrective) measures regarding, cope with, handle (a difficult person, situation, etc.). ME.
LD MACAULAY A power more than sufficient to deal with Protector and Parliament together. B. PYM His notes dealt almost entirely with religion. F. WELDON The way to deal with Hilda was to agree with what she said, while believing none of it.
11 *verb intrans.* Foll. by *with* or *by*: behave towards, treat (a person etc.) (in a specified way). Also *absol.*, act towards people generally (in a specified way), conduct oneself. ME.
EARL OF CHATHAM If we would deal fairly by ourselves. SWIFT They had better give up now, if she will not deal openly.
†**12** *verb intrans.* Take action, act, proceed (*in* a matter). ME–M17.
SHAKES. *Much Ado* Do not you meddle; let me deal in this.
13 *verb intrans.* Set to work, practise (*up*)*on*. *arch. rare.* L16.
SHAKES. *Rich. III* Two deep enemies . . Are they that I would have thee deal upon.
– PHRASES: ***wheel and deal***: see WHEEL *verb*.
■ **dealable** *adjective* (*rare*) able to be dealt *with*; suitable for dealing: M17.

dealbate /diːˈalbət/ *adjective*. *rare.* LME.
[ORIGIN Latin *dealbatus* pa. pple of *dealbare*: see DEALBATION, -ATE².]
Presenting a white appearance; whitened.

dealbation /diːalˈbeɪʃ(ə)n/ *noun*. LME.
[ORIGIN Latin *dealbatio(n-)*, from *dealbat-* pa. ppl stem of *dealbare*: see DAUB *verb*, -ATION.]
The action of whitening; blanching, bleaching.

de-alcoholize /diːˈalkəhɒlʌɪz/ *verb trans.* Also **-ise**. M19.
[ORIGIN from DE- 3 + ALCOHOL *noun* + -IZE.]
Remove the alcohol from (wine etc.). Chiefly as ***de-alcoholized*** *ppl adjective.*

dealer /ˈdiːlə/ *noun.* OE.
[ORIGIN from DEAL *verb* + -ER¹.]
1 A person who divides, distributes, or delivers something; *spec.* the player dealing at cards. OE.
2 A person who has dealings *with* another or others, *in* an affair, etc.; an agent, a negotiator. Now chiefly as *transf.* use of sense 4. OE.

DEFOE A sorcerer . . or dealer with the Devil. SWIFT Small dealers in wit and learning.

3 A person who acts (in a specified way) in relation to others. Now usu. in *comb.*, as below. M16.
double-dealer: see DOUBLE *adjective & adverb*. ***plain dealer***: see PLAIN *adjective¹ & adverb*.
4 A person or (in *pl.*) firm dealing in merchandise, a trader; *spec.* one buying and selling articles of a particular commodity. L16.
antique-dealer, ***horse-dealer***, ***money-dealer***, etc.
5 A jobber on a stock exchange. See also ***BROKER-dealer***. E18.
■ **dealership** *noun* the position, business, etc., of a dealer; an authorized trading establishment: E20.

dealign /diːəˈlʌɪn/ *verb intrans.* L20.
[ORIGIN from DE- 3 + ALIGN.]
Of a voter: withdraw allegiance from a political party.

dealing /ˈdiːlɪŋ/ *noun.* LME.
[ORIGIN formed as DEAL *verb* + -ING¹.]
1 Division, distribution, delivering (of gifts, blows, cards, etc.); sharing *out*. LME.
2 *sing.* & (now usu.) in *pl.* Friendly or business communication (*with*); personal connection or association (*with*). LME.

J. SULLIVAN I will admit I have suffered some misfortunes in my business dealings of late. M. MEDVED Shady dealings with the Mafia.

3 *sing.* & in *pl.* Mode of acting towards others, treatment of others; conduct, behaviour. (Foll. by *with* the person(s) towards whom the behaviour is directed.) L15.
plain dealing: see PLAIN *adjective¹ & adverb*.
4 *sing.* & in *pl.* Trading, trafficking; buying and selling, esp. of a particular commodity. M17.

dealkylation /ˌdiːalkɪˈleɪʃ(ə)n/ *noun.* E20.
[ORIGIN from DE- 3 + ALKYLATION.]
CHEMISTRY. The removal of an alkyl group from a compound.
■ **deˈalkylate** *verb trans.* remove an alkyl group from M20.

dealt *verb. pa. t. & pple* of DEAL *verb*.

deambulation /dɪˌambjʊˈleɪʃ(ə)n/ *noun.* E16.
[ORIGIN Latin *deambulatio(n-)*, from *deambulat-* pa. ppl stem of *deambulare* walk about, formed as DE- 1 + AMBULATION.]
The action of walking about; a walk.
■ **deˈambulate** *verb intrans.* (*rare*) E17.

deambulatory /dɪˈambjʊlət(ə)ri/ *noun & adjective.* LME.
[ORIGIN medieval Latin *deambulatorium* noun, *-orius* adjective, from *deambulat-*: see DEAMBULATION, -ORY¹, -ORY².]
▸ **A** *noun.* A place to walk in for exercise; *esp.* a covered walk or cloister. LME.
▸ **B** *adjective.* Walking about; peripatetic. E17.

deaminate /dɪˈamɪneɪt/ *verb trans.* E20.
[ORIGIN from DE- 3 + AMINE + -ATE³.]
CHEMISTRY. Remove an amino group or groups from.
■ **deamiˈnation** *noun* E20.

dean /diːn/ *noun¹*. Also (esp. as a title) **D-**. ME.
[ORIGIN Anglo-Norman *de(e)n*, Old French *d(e)ien* (mod. *doyen*), from late Latin *decanus* chief of a group of ten, from Latin *decem* ten, after *primanus* member of the first legion, perh. infl. by Greek *deka* ten.]
▸ **I** CHRISTIAN CHURCH. **1** The head of the chapter of a cathedral or a collegiate church. ME.
2 More fully ***rural dean***, ***area dean***. A member of the clergy exercising supervision (under the bishop or archdeacon) over a group of parochial clergy within a division of an archdeaconry. ME. ▸**b** More generally, a member of the clergy invested with a specified charge and having a particular jurisdiction. M17.
b ***Dean of peculiars***: see PECULIAR *noun*. ***Dean of the Arches***: see ARCH *noun¹* 1.
3 *hist.* [translating ecclesiastical Latin *decanus*.] The head of ten monks in a monastery. LME.
▸ **II** *gen.* †**4** A head, chief, or commander of a division of ten. LME–L15.
5 *hist.* More fully ***Dean of guild***. An officer of a medieval guild who summoned members to attend meetings etc. Also (*Scot.*), the head of the guild or merchant company of a royal burgh, latterly usu. a member of the town council. LME.
6 The leader or senior member of any body; a doyen. LME.
Dean of Faculty the president of the Faculty of Advocates in Scotland. **Dean of the Sacred College** the senior member of the Sacred College, usu. the oldest of the Cardinal Bishops, who presides in the consistory in the absence of the Pope.
7 The head of a university faculty or department, or of a medical school. Also (*N. Amer.*), the registrar or secretary of a university or college faculty. E16.
dean's list *N. Amer.* a list of students receiving special recognition from the dean of a college or university for academic excellence.
8 In a college or university (esp. Oxford or Cambridge), a fellow, or each of a number of fellows (formerly and still sometimes resident) with disciplinary and advisory functions. L16.
junior dean, ***senior dean***, etc.
■ **deaness** *noun* (**a**) CHRISTIAN CHURCH a woman who is head of a female chapter; (**b**) *joc.* the wife of a dean: M18. **deanship** *noun* the office, position, or rank of a dean; *joc.* (***his Deanship*** etc.) used as the title of a dean: M16.

dean *noun²* var. of DENE *noun¹*.

deaner /ˈdiːnə/ *noun. slang* (chiefly *Austral. & NZ*). *obsolete* exc. *hist.* Also **deener**. M19.
[ORIGIN Prob. ult. from DENARIUS, DENIER *noun²*.]
A shilling.

deanery /ˈdiːnəri/ *noun.* LME.
[ORIGIN from DEAN *noun¹* + -ERY, after Anglo-Norman *denrie*.]
1 The position or office of a dean. LME.
2 The group of parishes presided over by a rural dean. Formerly also, the jurisdiction of a dean. LME.
3 The official residence of a dean. L16.

de-anglicize /diːˈaŋglɪsʌɪz/ *verb trans.* Also **-ise**. L19.
[ORIGIN from DE- 3 + ANGLICIZE.]
Remove English characteristics or influence from.
■ **de-angliciˈzation** *noun* E20.

dear /dɪə/ *adjective¹*, *noun*, & *interjection*.
[ORIGIN Old English *dēore*, (West Saxon) *dīere* = Old Frisian *diore*, Old Saxon *diuri* (Dutch *dier* beloved, *duur* high-priced), Old High German *tiuri* distinguished, worthy, costly (German *teuer*), Old Norse *dýrr*, from Germanic.]
▸ **A** *adjective.* †**1** Glorious, noble, honourable, worthy. OE–E17.

SHAKES. *1 Hen. IV* Dear men Of estimation and command in arms.

2 Regarded with esteem and affection; beloved; loved, cherished; precious *to*. Freq. used in speech in addressing a person (sometimes as a merely polite or iron. form), and as part of the polite introduction (or occas. subscription) of a letter, esp. in a formula denoting the degree of formality involved. OE. ▸**b** Affectionate, loving, fond. Now *rare* exc. as passing into sense 2c. L16. ▸**c** Lovable, endearing, sweet. *colloq.* M18.

T. WYATT Therewith all sweetly did me kiss And softly said, 'Dear heart how like you this?' JER. TAYLOR I am . . Dear Sir, your obliged and most affectionate friend and servant J. Taylor. D. H. LAWRENCE My dear Lady Ottoline,—I arrived home safely. E. WAUGH No, no, dear boy. You are to lunch with Jo. J. D. SALINGER The kind of information that will be very, very dear to your heart. W. VAN T. CLARK As if I were an old, dear friend she was worried about. **b** I. WALTON Sir Henry Wotton, a dear lover of this Art. J. KEBLE My dear love to — and —.

†**3** Highly esteemed; high in worth or value; valuable; important. OE–E17.

SHAKES. *Sonn.* And with old woes new wail my dear time's waste.

4 High in price or charge made, absolutely or in relation to value; costly, expensive. OE. ▸**b** Having or charging high prices. ME. ▸**c** Of money: available on loan only at a high rate of interest. L19.

T. FULLER The dearest town in England for fuel. D. DU MAURIER Any stuff like this is dear, but it will last for years.

5 Heartfelt; earnest. L16.

G. B. SHAW My father-in-law's dearest wish was to be a teacher and a preacher.

— PHRASES: **be dear of** be kind or thoughtful of (a person, *to do* something). **Dear John (letter)** *colloq.* a letter from a woman to an absent fiancé, husband, etc., notifying him of the end of their relationship and her attachment to another man. **for dear life** as though life itself were at stake. **hold dear** regard with affection, value highly.
▸ **B** *noun.* **1** (With or, as a form of address, also without possess.) a person dear to one; a dear one, a darling, a lovable or endearing person. Cf. DEAREST 3. ME.

SPENSER From that day forth Duessa was his deare. M. EDGEWORTH 'Really, my dear', answered she, 'I can't say.' R. MACAULAY Aunt Stanley was a great dear; treated one always as a friend. K. AMIS The two things are completely different, dear. B. PYM I don't grudge the old dears a lunch.

2 ***dear knows***, ***the dear knows*** = ***God knows*** s.v. KNOW *verb*. E19.
▸ **C** *interjection.* Expr. surprise, distress, sympathy, regret, etc. L17.
dear, dear! I am sorry, concerned, etc. **dear me!**, **oh dear!** I am shocked, surprised, disappointed, etc.

dear /dɪə/ *adjective². arch.* OE.
[ORIGIN Unknown.]
†**1** Brave, strenuous, hardy. Only in OE.
2 Hard, severe, grievous; fell, dire. OE.

SHAKES. *Sonn.* Made lame by Fortune's dearest spite. SHELLEY Now I forget them at my dearest need.

†**3** Difficult. Only in ME.

dear /dɪə/ *verb trans.* LME.
[ORIGIN from DEAR *adjective¹*.]
†**1** Make dear or expensive; raise the price of. *Scot.* Only in LME.
2 Endear. *rare.* E17.
3 Make a fuss *over* a person. *rare.* L18.
4 Address as 'dear'. E19.

F. MARRYAT Don't dear *me*, Sir Hurricane, I am not one of *your* dears.

dear /dɪə/ *adverb.*
[ORIGIN Old English *dīore*, *dēore* = Old High German *tiuro* (German *teuer*).]
1 At a high price; at great cost. OE.

P. GALLICO Buy cheap and sell dear.

cost a person dear: see COST *verb* 2. **dear-bought** bought at a high price, obtained at great cost.
2 Fondly, earnestly, dearly. *arch.* ME.

SHAKES. *Rom. & Jul.* Rosaline, that thou didst love so dear.

dearborn /ˈdɪəbɔːn/ *noun. US.* E19.
[ORIGIN Prob. from Gen. Henry *Dearborn* (1751–1829).]
A kind of light four-wheeled wagon.

dearest /ˈdɪərɪst/ *noun.* LME.
[ORIGIN Superl. of DEAR *adjective¹* used absol.]
†**1** *The* most noble or worthy people. Only in LME.
†**2** *The* highest price offered. Only in LME.
3 With, or as a form of address, also without possess.: the person(s) most dear to one, dearest one. Cf. DEAR *noun*. L16.

H. MARTINEAU Do not exhaust yourself at once, dearest.

nearest and dearest: see NEAR *adjective*.

dearie /ˈdɪəri/ *noun, adjective, & interjection.* Also **deary**. L17.
[ORIGIN Dim. of. DEAR *adjective¹*, *noun*, *& interjection*: see -IE, -Y⁶.]
▸ **A** *noun.* Chiefly as a form of address, with or without possess.: little dear, darling. L17.
▸ **B** *adjective.* Attractively small, tiny. *dial.* L17.
▸ **C** *interjection.* Expr. sorrow, dismay, etc. Chiefly in ***dearie me!***, dear me, alas. L18.

†**dearling** *noun & adjective* var. of DARLING *noun¹ & adjective*.

dearly /ˈdɪəli/ *adverb.*
[ORIGIN Old English *dēorlīce* = Old Saxon *diurlīco*, Old High German *tiurlīhho*, formed as DEAR *adjective¹* + -LY².]
†**1** In a precious, worthy, or excellent manner; finely, richly. OE–E17.
2 As one who is held dear; affectionately, fondly. Now usu. modifying *love*, *like*, etc. ME.

MILTON His dearly-lovèd mate.

3 Earnestly, in a heartfelt manner; keenly. Now usu. in a weakened sense: very much, greatly. ME.

SHAKES. *A.Y.L.* My father hated his father dearly. A. PRICE He would dearly have liked a pint now himself.

4 At a high price, at great cost, (freq. *fig.*). L15.

E. K. KANE All the dearly-earned documents of the expedition. B. PYM I valued my independence very dearly.

cost a person dearly: see COST *verb* 2.

dearness /ˈdɪənɪs/ *noun.* ME.
[ORIGIN from DEAR *adjective¹* + -NESS.]
1 The quality of being held dear. Also, intimacy, (mutual) affection, fondness. ME. ▸†**b** An expression or token of affection. M17–E18.

G. BURNET The dearness that was between them, was now turned . . to . . enmity. I. GURNEY The dearness of common things, Beechwood, tea, plate shelves.

2 The quality of being dear in price; expensiveness, costliness. M16.

dearth /dəːθ/ *noun & verb.* ME.
[ORIGIN from DEAR *adjective¹* + -TH¹. Cf. Old Saxon *diur(i)þa*, Old High German *tiurida*, *diurida*, Old Norse *dýrð*.]
▸ **A** *noun.* **1** Scarcity and dearness of food; formerly, a famine. ME.

GIBBON The fertility of Egypt supplied the dearth of Arabia. J. UPDIKE In this time of crisis and dearth, our human resources must be conserved.

2 A scarcity *of* anything; a practical deficiency; want or lack *of* a quality. ME.

W. JAMES The veriest lack and dearth of your imagination. K. TYNAN Nor is there a dearth of English actors; the land is alive with them.

3 Costliness, high price. *obsolete* exc. *Scot.* E17.
▸ **B** *verb trans.* Make dear in price; cause a dearth of. Long *obsolete* exc. *Scot.* LME.

deary *noun, adjective, & interjection* var. of DEARIE.

deas *noun* see DAIS.

deasil /ˈdɛs(ə)l, ˈdjɛʃ(ə)l/ *adverb & noun.* Chiefly *Scot.* Also **deisal**, & other vars. L18.
[ORIGIN Gaelic *deiseil*.]
▸ **A** *adverb.* In the direction of the sun's apparent course (considered as lucky), clockwise. L18.

D

▸ **B** *noun.* Movement in a clockwise direction, esp. round a particular object. **L18.**

death /dɛθ/ *noun.* Also (*obsolete* exc. *Scot.*) **dead** /dɛd/, (*Scot.*) **deid** /diːd/.

[**ORIGIN** Old English *dēaþ* = Old Frisian *dāth*, Old Saxon *dōþ* (Dutch *dood*), Old High German *tōd* (German *Tod*), Old Norse *dauðr*, Gothic *dauþus*, from Germanic base ult. also of **DIE** *verb*[1]: see **-TH**[1].]

1 The act or fact of dying; the end of life; the final and irreversible cessation of the vital functions of an animal or plant. **OE.** ▸**b** An instance of a person's dying. **E18.** ▸**c** Cessation of life in a particular part or tissue. **E19.**

J. R. SEELEY The Greek did not believe death to be annihilation. DAY LEWIS My mother's untimely death. C. V. WEDGWOOD The hideous death designed by the law for traitors. *personified*: MILTON Over them triumphant Death his Dart Shook; but delaid to strike. TENNYSON Into the jaws of Death . . Rode the six hundred.

2 The state of being dead; the state or condition of being without life, animation, or activity. **OE.**

OED His eyes were closed in death.

3 *transf.* & *fig.* **a** The lack or loss of spiritual life; the loss or deprivation of particular rights, privileges, etc. (chiefly in ***civil death*** below). **OE.** ▸**b** The ceasing to be, extinction, or annihilation of something. **LME.**

a TINDALE *Rom.* 8:6 To be carnally mynded, is deeth. **b** SHELLEY From the lamp's death to the morning ray.

4 A cause or occasion of death; something that kills or renders liable to death; an offence punishable by death (*for* a person *to do* something); *poet.* a deadly weapon, poison, etc. **OE.**

POPE The clam'rous lapwings feel the leaden death. GOLDSMITH A school would be his death.

5 A general mortality caused by an epidemic disease; plague, pestilence. Now chiefly in ***Black Death*** (see **BLACK** *adjective*). **LME.**

R. HOLINSHED A great death of the pestilence reigned in London.

†**6** *HUNTING.* A note sounded on the horn at the death of the quarry; the mort. **LME–M18.**

7 Bloodshed, slaughter, murder. *arch.* **E17.**

BACON Not to suffer a man of death to live.

8 As *interjection*. Expr. vehement anger, surprise, etc. Cf. **'SDEATH.** *arch.* **E17.**

SHAKES. *Oth.* Death and damnation! O!

— PHRASES: **a fate worse than death** *arch.* (*euphem.* or *joc.*) being raped; seduction. **as sure as death** *colloq.* quite certain(ly). **at death's door** in imminent danger of or very close to death through illness etc. **be death on** *slang* be skilful at killing (prey etc.) or dealing with. **be the death of** cause the death of (freq. *hyperbol.*). ***Black Death***: see **BLACK** *adjective*. ***brain death***: see **BRAIN** *noun*. **catch one's death (of cold)** *colloq.* contract a fatal chill etc. (usu. *hyperbol.*). **civil death** the loss of a citizen's privileges through outlawry, banishment, etc. ***clinical death***: see **CLINICAL** 1. ***Dance of Death***: see **DANCE** *noun*. ***die the death***: see **DIE** *verb*[1]. **do to death** (*a*) *arch.* kill; (*b*) *fig.* overdo, repeat too frequently. **everlasting death** damnation. ***flog to death***: see **FLOG** *verb*. **in at the death** present in the hunting field etc. when the quarry is killed; *gen.* present at the ending of any enterprise. **like death warmed up** *slang* notably ill or exhausted in appearance. **like grim death** with all one's strength. ***living death***: see **LIVING** *adjective*. **put to death** kill, *esp.* execute. ***sudden death***: see **SUDDEN** *adjective*. ***the gate of death***, ***the gates of death***: see **GATE** *noun*[1]. ***the kiss of death***: see **KISS** *noun*. ***the valley of the shadow of death***, ***the shadow of death***: see **SHADOW** *noun*. **to death** (*a*) so as to kill or be killed, esp. in a specified way, as ***burn to death***, ***stone to death***, etc. (see also ***do to death***, ***put to death*** above); fatally, mortally; (*b*) *fig.* utterly, at or beyond the point of endurance, to excess, (as ***scared to death***, ***sick to death***, ***tickled to death***, ***tired to death***; see also ***worked to death*** below). **to the death** = ***to death*** above: now only *lit.*, (*fight*, *pursue*, etc.) until death results. ***Wall of Death***: see **WALL** *noun*[1]. ***white death***: see **WHITE** *adjective*. **worked to death** *fig.* hackneyed. **worse than death** *arch.* = ***a fate worse than death*** above.

— COMB.: **death adder** (*a*) *dial.* the deaf adder; (*b*) any of various venomous elapid snakes of the genus *Acanthophis*; *esp.* a thick-bodied Australian snake, *A. antarcticus*; **deathbed** †(*a*) the grave; (*b*) the bed etc. on which a person died or will die (***deathbed repentance*** etc., a last-minute change of conduct or policy); **death bell** a passing bell; **death bird** a carrion bird, a bird associated with or presaging death; **death blow** a blow etc. that causes death (*lit.* & *fig.*); **death cap** the poisonous toadstool *Amanita phalloides*; **death cell** a condemned cell, a cell occupied by a prisoner condemned to death; **death certificate** an official document stating the time, place, cause, etc., of a person's death; **death cup** = ***death cap*** above; **death day** (the anniversary of) the day of a person's death; **death-dealing** *adjective* lethal; **death duties**, **death duty** *hist.* & *colloq.* tax levied on a dead person's estate; **death-fire** = ***corpse candle*** (a) s.v. **CORPSE** *noun*; **death futures** *US colloq.* life insurance policies of terminally ill people, purchased by a third party at less than their mature value as a form of short-term investment: cf. ***viatical settlement***; **death grant** a statutory payment towards funeral expenses made by the state to the appropriate relative of a dead person; **death-head** = ***death's head*** (a) below; **death house** (*a*) a place where someone has died; (*b*) *US* a group of death cells; **death-in-life** life that lacks any satisfaction or purpose, living death; **death knell** the tolling of a bell to mark a person's death; *fig.* an event etc. that heralds the end of something; **death mask** a cast taken of a dead person's face; **death metal** a form of heavy metal music with lyrics preoccupied with death, suffering, and destruction; **death-or-glory** *adjective* brave to the point of foolhardiness, dashing, reckless (***Death-or-Glory Boys***, in the British army, the 17th Regiment of Lancers); **death penalty** *the* penalty of death, capital punishment; **death-place** the place where a person died or will die; **death rate** the ratio of the number of deaths to the population, usu. calculated per thousand of population per year; **death rattle** a rattling sound in a dying person's throat; **death ray** a ray (imaginary or actual) capable of killing; **death roll** a list or the number of those killed in an accident, a battle, an epidemic, etc.; **death row** *US colloq.* the area of a prison where prisoners under sentence of death are confined; †**death's face** = ***death's head*** (a) below; **death's head** (*a*) (a figure or representation of) a skull, esp. as an emblem of mortality; (*b*) ***death's head hawkmoth***, ***death's head moth***, a large dark hawkmoth, *Acherontia atropos*, having pale markings on the back of the thorax resembling a skull; **death-sick** *adjective* mortally ill; **deathsman** *arch.* an executioner; **death song** [cf. German *Todesgesang*, *Totengesang*] a song sung immediately prior to one's death or the death of another, or to commemorate the dead; **death-stricken**, **death-struck** *adjectives* (*arch.*) subject to a mortal illness, wound, etc.; **death tax** *US* = ***death duty*** above; **death throe(s)** the final violent anguish, struggle, etc., of a dying person or animal or *fig.* of a custom, practice, etc., coming to an end; **death toll** = ***death roll*** above; **death trap** an unsuspectedly unhealthy or dangerous place, structure, etc.; **death warrant** a warrant for the execution of a convicted person; *fig.* any action etc. which signals the abolition or end of a custom, practice, etc.; **death watch** (*a*) any of various insects making a sound like a watch ticking, once supposed to portend death; *spec.* (in full ***death watch beetle***) a beetle, *Xestobium rufovillosum*, whose larvae bore in old wood and are notably destructive to house timbers, furniture, etc.; (*b*) a vigil kept beside a dying person; **death wish** [translating German *Todeswunsch*] a wish, esp. an unconscious wish, for the death of oneself or another; **death wound** a mortal wound.

■ **deathlike** *adjective* †(*a*) deadly, fatal; (*b*) resembling death: **M16.** **deathling** *noun* (*rare*) a person subject to death, a mortal **L16.**

deathful /ˈdɛθfʊl, -f(ə)l/ *adjective.* **ME.**

[**ORIGIN** from **DEATH** + **-FUL.**]

1 Fatal, destructive, deadly. **ME.**

2 Subject to death, mortal. *arch. rare.* **E17.**

3 Having the appearance of death, deathly. **M17.**

■ **deathfully** *adverb* **E19.** **deathfulness** *noun* **M17.**

deathless /ˈdɛθlɪs/ *adjective.* **L16.**

[**ORIGIN** from **DEATH** + **-LESS.**]

Not subject to death; immortal, undying, unending.

E. A. FREEMAN The deathless name of Godwine. I. MURDOCH Zeus deplores the sight of deathless beings involved in the pointless horrors of morality. Q. CRISP My jumbled speech would be translated into deathless prose.

■ **deathlessly** *adverb* **M19.** **deathlessness** *noun* **L17.**

deathly /ˈdɛθli/ *adjective.*

[**ORIGIN** Old English *dēaþlīc* (= Old High German *tōdlīh*), formed as **DEATH** + **-LY**[1].]

1 Subject to death, mortal. Long *rare.* **OE.**

2 Causing death, fatal, deadly. *arch.* **ME.**

3 Of the nature of or resembling death; deathlike; gloomy, pale, etc., as death. **ME.**

P. D. JAMES Without a word, Lorrimer, deathly pale, turned on his heels.

4 Of or pertaining to death. *poet.* **M19.**

■ **deathliness** *noun* **ME.**

deathly /ˈdɛθli/ *adverb.* **ME.**

[**ORIGIN** In early use from **DEATH** + **-LY**[2], later from the adjective.]

†**1** In a way causing or tending to death. Only in **ME.**

2 To a degree resembling or suggestive of death. **L19.**

deathward /ˈdɛθwəd/ *adverb* & *adjective.* **LME.**

[**ORIGIN** from **DEATH** + **-WARD.**]

▸ **A** *adverb.* Orig. (arch.) ***to deathward***, †***to one's deathward***. In the direction of death, towards death. **LME.**

▸ **B** *adjective.* Tending or moving towards death. **M19.**

■ Also **deathwards** *adverb* **E19.**

deathy /ˈdɛθi/ *adverb* & *adjective.* *arch.* or *poet.* **L18.**

[**ORIGIN** from **DEATH** + **-Y**[1].]

▸ **A** *adverb.* To a degree resembling or suggestive of death, deathly. **L18.**

▸ **B** *adjective.* Of the nature or character of death, deathly. **E19.**

■ **deathiness** *noun* **E19.**

deaurate /dɪˈɔːrət/ *adjective.* Now *rare* or *obsolete.* **LME.**

[**ORIGIN** Late Latin *deauratus* pa. pple, formed as **DEAURATE** *verb*: see **-ATE**[2].]

Gilded, golden.

deaurate /dɪˈɔːreɪt/ *verb trans.* Now *rare* or *obsolete.* **M16.**

[**ORIGIN** Late Latin *deaurat-* pa. ppl stem of *deaurare* gild, from Latin *aurum* gold: see **-ATE**[3].]

Gild over, make golden. Chiefly as ***deaurated*** *ppl adjective.*

■ **deau'ration** *noun* **M17.**

deave /diːv/ *verb.* Now *Scot.* & *N. English.*

[**ORIGIN** Old English *-dēafian*, formed as **DEAF** *adjective*. Cf. **DEAF** *verb.*]

†**1** *verb intrans.* Become deaf. *rare.* **OE–LME.**

2 *verb trans.* Deafen; stun, worry, or confuse with din or talk. **ME.**

deb /dɛb/ *noun.* *colloq.* **E20.**

[**ORIGIN** Abbreviation.]

= **DEBUTANTE** 2.

debs' delight, **deb's delight** an eligible young man in fashionable society.

†**debacchation** *noun.* **M17–M18.**

[**ORIGIN** Late Latin *debacchatio(n-)*, from Latin *debacchat-* pa. ppl stem of *debacchari* rave as a bacchanal, from *de-* **DE-** 1 + *bacchari*, from *Bacchus* god of wine: see **-ATION.**]

Noisy or drunken raving; a drunken revel.

debacle /deɪˈbɑːk(ə)l, dɪ-/ *noun.* Also **débâcle.** **E19.**

[**ORIGIN** French *débâcle*, from *débâcler* unbar, from *dé-* **DE-** 3 + *bâcler* to bar.]

1 A breaking up of ice in a river; a sudden flood or rush of water carrying along debris. **E19.**

2 A sudden and ignominious failure or defeat; a fiasco, a disaster. **M19.**

L. URIS The British suffered one debacle after another. Dunkirk! Crete! Greece! J. GROSS The extent to which Liberal attitudes survived the debacle of the party as such.

debag /diːˈbag/ *verb trans.* *slang.* Infl. **-gg-.** **E20.**

[**ORIGIN** from **DE-** 3 + **BAG** *noun.*]

Remove the trousers from, as a punishment or joke.

deballast /diːˈbaləst/ *verb trans.* **M20.**

[**ORIGIN** from **DE-** 3 + **BALLAST** *noun* & *verb.*]

Remove ballast from (a ship etc.).

debamboozle /diːbamˈbuːz(ə)l/ *verb trans.* *colloq.* **E20.**

[**ORIGIN** from **DE-** 3 + **BAMBOOZLE.**]

Undeceive, enlighten, disabuse.

debar /dɪˈbɑː/ *verb trans.* Infl. **-rr-.** **LME.**

[**ORIGIN** French *débarrer*, Old French *desbarrer*, from *des-* **DE-** 3 + *barrer* to bar.]

1 Exclude, shut out *from* (†*of*) a place or condition; prevent *from doing*; deprive of. **LME.**

SHAKES. *Sonn.* I . . that am debarr'd the benefit of rest. A. STORR This disability need not debar a man from being a conscientious and valuable priest.

2 Prohibit, obstruct, prevent (an action etc.). **L15.**

T. SPENCER The dore when it is shut, debarres all entrance.

■ **debarment** *noun* the act of debarring, the fact of being debarred **M17.**

debarbarize /diːˈbɑːbərʌɪz/ *verb trans.* Also **-ise.** **E19.**

[**ORIGIN** from **DE-** 3 + **BARBARIZE.**]

Free from barbarous character, make not barbarous.

debark /diːˈbɑːk/ *verb*[1] *trans.* & *intrans.* **M17.**

[**ORIGIN** French *débarquer*, from *dé-* **DE-** 3 + *barque* **BARK** *noun*[3].]

= **DISEMBARK.**

debark /diːˈbɑːk/ *verb*[2] *trans.* **M18.**

[**ORIGIN** from **DE-** 3 + **BARK** *noun*[2].]

Strip (a tree etc.) of its bark.

debark /diːˈbɑːk/ *verb*[3] *trans.* **M20.**

[**ORIGIN** from **DE-** 3 + **BARK** *noun*[1].]

Deprive (a dog) of the ability to bark.

debarkation /diːbɑːˈkeɪʃ(ə)n/ *noun.* **M18.**

[**ORIGIN** from **DEBARK** *verb*[1] + **-ATION.**]

The action of disembarking; *esp.* the unloading of troops, supplies, or equipment from a ship or aircraft.

debarrass /dɪˈbarəs/ *verb trans.* Now *rare.* **L18.**

[**ORIGIN** French *débarrasser*, from *dé-* **DE-** 3 + (*em*)*barrasser* **EMBARRASS.**]

= **DISEMBARRASS.**

debase /dɪˈbeɪs/ *verb trans.* **M16.**

[**ORIGIN** from **DE-** 1 + **BASE** *noun*[1], *verb.* Cf. **ABASE.**]

†**1** Lower in position or rank, humiliate. **M16–E19.**

†**2** Decry, belittle, depreciate. **M16–M18.**

3 Lower in quality, value, or character, corrupt; adulterate; degrade. **L16.** ▸**b** *spec.* Decrease the value of (coinage) by alloying etc. **E17.**

S. JOHNSON Words which convey ideas of dignity . . are in time debased. I. MURDOCH They simply resented their stepfather . . as a debased version of human existence.

■ **debasedness** *noun* the quality or condition of being debased **E18.** **debasement** *noun* (*a*) the action or process of debasing; debased condition; †(*b*) abasement: **L16.** **debaser** *noun* **E17.**

débat /deba/ *noun.* Pl. pronounced same. **L19.**

[**ORIGIN** French = **DEBATE** *noun.*]

A poetic discussion between persons, personifications, or abstractions, on a question of morality, politics, or love, common in medieval European literature.

debatable /dɪˈbeɪtəb(ə)l/ *adjective.* Also **debateable.** **LME.**

[**ORIGIN** Old French, from *debatre*, or Anglo-Latin *debatabilis*, formed as **DEBATE** *verb* + **-ABLE.**]

1 Open to question or argument, controversial. **LME.**

2 Of or pertaining to land or territory on the border of two countries and claimed by each, *spec.* (*hist.*) designating the tract between the Rivers Esk and Sark on the border between England and Scotland. **LME.**

debate /dɪˈbeɪt/ *noun.* **ME.**

[**ORIGIN** Old French *debat* (mod. *débat*), formed as **DEBATE** *verb.*]

1 Strife, dissension, quarrelling, (formerly) fighting; a quarrel. Long *arch.* **ME.**

2 Contention in argument, (a) discussion; *esp.* (a) formal discussion of a matter in a legislature or public assembly. **LME.** ▸**b** = **DÉBAT.** **M19.**

J. COLVILLE Big debate on Finland this evening, during which the P.M. won great personal success. J. HERRIOT It was a matter of debate whether she was a widow or separated.

full-dress debate: see FULL *adjective*.

debate /dɪˈbeɪt/ *verb*. LME.
[ORIGIN Old French *debatre* (mod. *débattre*) from Proto-Romance, from Latin *dis-* (cf. DE- 3) + *battere* to fight.]
1 *verb †intrans. & trans.* Contend, fight (over), quarrel (about). *arch.* LME.

SPENSER Well could he tourney, and in lists debate. DRYDEN The boys and Latian youth debate The martial prizes on the dusty plain.

2 *verb trans. & intrans.* Argue, discuss, esp. formally in a public assembly etc.; take part in debate (about). LME.

TOLKIEN They debated long on what was to be done. B. LOVELL The existence of extragalactic systems had been debated for centuries.

debating club, **debating society**: whose members meet for debating. **debating point** a minor point open to argument, esp. one used to gain advantage in debate.
3 *verb trans. & intrans.* Consider in one's mind, deliberate (on), ponder. LME.

W. MORRIS Debating in her mind of this and that. HARPER LEE I was debating whether to stand there or run.

†**4** *verb trans.* Defend, fight for. *Scot.* L15–E17.
■ †**debatement** *noun* the act of debating; discussion, contention, strife: M16–M17. **debater** *noun* a person who debates, or is skilled in debate. LME.

debateable *adjective* var. of DEBATABLE.

debauch /dɪˈbɔːtʃ/ *noun*. Now chiefly *literary*. E17.
[ORIGIN French *débauche*, formed as DEBAUCH *verb*.]
1 A bout of excessive indulgence in sensual pleasures; a binge. E17.

S. PEPYS My head akeing all day from last night's debauch.

2 The habit or practice of sensual indulgence. L17.

J. S. BLACKIE All debauch is incipient suicide.

3 *transf. & fig.* An excess. L17.

G. ORWELL An enormous debauch of work.

4 A debauchee. Long *obsolete* exc. *dial.* L17.

debauch /dɪˈbɔːtʃ/ *verb*. Now chiefly *literary*. Also †**debosh**. L16.
[ORIGIN French *débaucher*, Old French *desbaucher*, from *des-* DE- 3 + elem. of unknown origin.]
▸ **I** *verb trans.* †**1** Turn away, entice, or seduce from allegiance or duty. (Foll. by *from* a leader etc., *to* an action etc.) L16–E19.

JAS. MILL To betray their master and debauch his army.

2 Pervert from virtue or morality, corrupt, deprave, esp. by intemperance or sensual indulgence. L16. ▸**b** Seduce (a woman) from chastity. E18.

J. TILLOTSON To debauch himself by intemperance and brutish sensuality.

†**3** Damage in reputation, disparage. E–M17.
4 Deprave, vitiate, (the senses, judgement, etc.). M17.

SIR W. SCOTT They debauch the spirit of the ignorant and credulous with mystical trash.

▸ **II** *verb intrans.* **5** Indulge riotously or to excess in sensual pleasures. Now *rare* or *obsolete*. E17.
■ **debaucher** *noun* E17.

debauched /dɪˈbɔːtʃt/ *adjective*. Now chiefly *literary*. Also (*arch.*) **deboshed** /dɪˈbɒʃt/. L16.
[ORIGIN from DEBAUCH *verb* + -ED[1].]
That has been debauched; dissolute, licentious.
■ **debauchedly** *adverb* (now *rare*) M17. **debauchedness** *noun* (now *rare*) E17.

debauchee /dɪbɔːˈtʃiː, -ˈʃiː/ *noun*. Now chiefly *literary*. M17.
[ORIGIN French *débauché* pa. pple of *débaucher*: see DEBAUCH *verb*, -EE[1].]
A person addicted to sensual indulgence; an excessively sensual person.

debauchery /dɪˈbɔːtʃ(ə)ri/ *noun*. Now chiefly *literary*. E17.
[ORIGIN from DEBAUCH *verb* + -ERY.]
1 Excessive indulgence in sensual pleasures; immorality, licentiousness. E17.
†**2** Seduction from duty or virtue; corruption. E18–M19.

debby /ˈdɛbi/ *noun*. *colloq.* E20.
[ORIGIN from DEB *noun* + -Y[6].]
= DEBUTANTE 2.

debby /ˈdɛbi/ *adjective*. *colloq.* M20.
[ORIGIN from DEB *noun* + -Y[1].]
Of, pertaining to, or characteristic of a debutante or fashionable society.

debeak /diːˈbiːk/ *verb trans.* M20.
[ORIGIN from DE- 3 + BEAK *noun*[1].]
Remove the upper part of the beak of (a bird) to prevent cannibalism etc.

debel /dɪˈbɛl/ *verb trans.* Now *rare* or *obsolete*. Infl. **-ll-**. LME.
[ORIGIN Latin *debellare*, from *de-* DE- 1 + *bellare* wage war, from *bellum* war.]
Subdue in battle, conquer, vanquish.
■ †**debellation** *noun* conquest, subjugation LME–M19.

de bene esse /diː ˌbɛni ˈɛsi; deɪ/ *adverbial phr.* E17.
[ORIGIN Latin = of well-being.]
LAW. As conditionally allowed for the present.

debenture /dɪˈbɛntʃə/ *noun*. LME.
[ORIGIN Latin *debentur* are owing or due, 3rd person pl. pres. indic. pass. of *debere* owe, occurring as the first word of a certificate of indebtedness: final syll. assim. to -URE.]
1 A voucher issued in the royal household or by government enabling the recipient to claim the sum due for goods or services rendered. *arch.* LME. ▸**b** A certificate authorizing the repayment of import duty on goods which are re-exported. M17.
†**2** *gen.* An acknowledgement of indebtedness (*lit. & fig.*). L16–L17.
†**3** A certificate of a loan made to the government. E18–E19.
4 A sealed bond issued by a corporation or company in respect of a long-term (esp. fixed-interest) loan, the principal of which, in Britain, constitutes a charge on the assets of the company. M19.
– COMB.: **debenture bond** = sense 4 above; **debenture stock** company stock comprising debentures, with only the interest secured.
■ **debentured** *adjective* having or secured by a debenture. E19.

debile /ˈdiːbʌɪl/ *adjective*. *arch.* M16.
[ORIGIN French *débile* or Latin *debilis*.]
Weak, debilitated.

debilitate /dɪˈbɪlɪteɪt/ *verb trans.* M16.
[ORIGIN Latin *debilitat-* pa. ppl stem of *debilitare* weaken, from *debilitas*: see DEBILITY, -ATE[3].]
Weaken, enfeeble.

A. BROOKNER Emerging slowly from some debilitating illness.

■ **debilitative** *adjective* causing debilitation, tending to debilitate L17.

debilitation /dɪˌbɪlɪˈteɪʃ(ə)n/ *noun*. LME.
[ORIGIN French *débilitation* or its source Latin *debilitatio(n-)*, formed as DEBILITATE: see -ATION.]
The action of debilitating, weakening; a debilitated condition.

debility /dɪˈbɪlɪti/ *noun*. LME.
[ORIGIN Old French & mod. French *débilité* from Latin *debilitas*, from *debilis* weak: see -ITY.]
1 Weakness, infirmity, lack of strength or vitality; feebleness of purpose etc. LME.
2 An instance of weakness. M16.

debit /ˈdɛbɪt/ *noun*. LME.
[ORIGIN Sense 1 from Latin *debitum* DEBT *noun*; sense 2 from French *débit*.]
†**1** A debt. LME–E17.
2 The acknowledgement of a sum owing by entry in an account; (a sum entered on) the debit side (see below) of an account. Opp. CREDIT *noun* 10. L18.
direct debit: see DIRECT *adjective*.
– COMB.: **debit card**: giving the holder access (through a computer terminal) to an account in order to transfer funds to another's account when making a purchase etc.; **debit side** the side or column of an account, conventionally the left-hand side, in which debits are entered.

debit /ˈdɛbɪt/ *verb*[1] *trans.* L17.
[ORIGIN from the noun.]
Enter a sum on the debit side of (an account) or of the account of (a person), (foll. by *with* the sum); enter (a sum) on the debit side of an account (foll. by *against* or *to* the account, the person whose account is debited).
■ **debitable** *adjective* L19.

debit /ˈdɛbɪt/ *verb*[2] *trans.* L19.
[ORIGIN French *débiter*: see DEBITAGE.]
Put into circulation, spread (news etc.).

debitage /dɛbɪˈtɑːʒ/ *noun*. M20.
[ORIGIN French *débitage* cutting of stone.]
ARCHAEOLOGY. Waste material produced in the making of prehistoric stone implements.

debiteuse /dɛbɪˈtjuːz, -ˈtɜːz/ *noun*. E20.
[ORIGIN French *débiteuse* a device that dispenses or discharges some substance, fem. of *débiteur*, from *débiter* retail, dispense.]
GLASS-MAKING. A troughlike heat-resistant object which floats on the molten glass in the Fourcault process, and has a slit through which the sheet glass is drawn.

†**debitor** *noun*. L15.
[ORIGIN Old French (learned var. of *det(t)or*) from Latin *debitor*: see DEBTOR.]
1 = DEBTOR 1. L15–L18.
2 = DEBTOR 2. M16–M17.
■ †**debitrice** *noun* a female debtor LME–E18.

deblazon /dɪˈbleɪz(ə)n/ *verb trans.* Long *rare*. E17.
[ORIGIN from DE- 1 + BLAZON *verb*.]
= BLAZON *verb*.

deblur /diːˈbləː/ *verb trans.* Infl. **-rr-**. M20.
[ORIGIN from DE- 3 + BLUR *noun*.]
Clarify (an image), remove blur from, bring into focus.

†**deboise** *verb trans.* Pa. pple **deboist**. E17–E18.
[ORIGIN By-form.]
= DEBAUCH *verb* I. Chiefly as ***deboist*** *pa. ppl adjective*.

debonair /dɛbəˈnɛː/ *adjective & noun*. Also **-nn-**, **-aire**. ME.
[ORIGIN Old French *debonaire* (mod. *débonnaire*), from *de bon aire* of good disposition.]
▸ **A** *adjective*. †**1** Of a gentle disposition, meek, gracious, courteous. ME–L17.

SPENSER Was neuer Prince so meeke and debonaire.

2 Pleasant in manner, affable, urbane; cheerful, carefree, unembarrassed. E18.

F. ASTAIRE The carefree, the best-dressed, the debonair Astaire!

▸ †**B** *noun*. **1** A courteous being or person. Only in LME.
2 Debonair character or disposition. LME–M18.
■ **debonairly** *adverb* LME. **debonairness** *noun* LME. †**debonairty**, **-arity** *noun* debonair character or disposition ME–L17.

D

debord /dɪˈbɔːd/ *verb intrans.* Now *rare* or *obsolete*. L16.
[ORIGIN French *déborder*, from *dé-* DE- 3 + *bord* edge, border.]
Of a body of water: go beyond its margins, overflow.

†**debosh** *verb* var. of DEBAUCH *verb*.

deboshed *ppl adjective* see DEBAUCHED.

debouch /dɪˈbaʊtʃ, -ˈbuːʃ/ *verb*. M18.
[ORIGIN French *déboucher*, from *dé-* DE- 3 + *bouche* mouth, after synon. Italian *sboccare*.]
1 *verb intrans.* (Orig. *MILITARY*, of troops etc.) emerge from a narrow or confined place into open ground; issue (as) from a mouth or outlet (*into*, *on*). M18.

A. PRICE The Parliamentary battle-line began to debouch from the trees. M. M. KAYE Here another spring debouched from the rocks above.

2 *verb trans.* Lead into open ground; provide an outlet for; pour forth. M18.

J. CHEEVER An enormous samovar . . debouched forty men in Cossack uniform singing.

■ **debouchment** *noun* E19.

débouché /debuʃe/ *noun*. Pl. pronounced same. M18.
[ORIGIN French, formed as DEBOUCH.]
An opening where troops etc. (may) debouch; *gen.* an outlet.

debouchure /dɪbʊˈʃʊə/ *noun*. M19.
[ORIGIN Alt. of EMBOUCHURE after DEBOUCH. The sense is not French.]
The mouth or outlet of a river etc.

debridement /deɪˈbriːdmɑ̃, dɪˈbriːdm(ə)nt/ *noun*. Also **dé-**. M19.
[ORIGIN French = unbridling.]
MEDICINE. The removal of damaged tissue or foreign matter from a wound etc.
■ **debride** *verb trans.* [back-form.] subject to debridement M20.

debrief /diːˈbriːf/ *verb trans.* M20.
[ORIGIN from DE- 3 + BRIEF *verb* 3.]
Question (a person) about a completed mission, undertaking, etc.

Life He went to the debriefing shed and made a routine report on the . . bombing mission.

debris /ˈdɛbriː, ˈdeɪbriː/ *noun*. Also **dé-**. E18.
[ORIGIN French *débris*, from †*débriser* break down or up, from *dé-* DE- 3 + *briser* break.]
The remains of anything broken down or destroyed (orig. *fig.*, of institutions, states, etc.); fragments, wreckage, ruins; accumulated waste matter; *GEOLOGY* fragmentary material accumulated from the breakdown of rocks etc.

A. GEIKIE The sandstone cliffs . . are battered down and their debris carried out to sea. C. CONNOLLY A writer has to construct his shell, like the caddis worm, from the débris of the past. R. SUTCLIFF The wells were choked with the debris of thirty autumns.

de Broglie /də ˈbrəʊli, də ˈbrɒgli/ *adjectival phr.* E20.
[ORIGIN Louis Victor *de Broglie* (1892–1987), French physicist.]
PHYSICS. Designating the wave(length) representing or accounting for the wavelike properties of a material particle in wave mechanics.

debruise /dɪˈbruːz/ *verb trans.* ME.
[ORIGIN Old French *debruisier*, *debrisier*, from *dé-* DE- 3 + *bruisier*, *brisier* (mod. *briser*) break.]
†**1** Break down, smash in pieces. ME–E17.
2 *HERALDRY.* Cross and partially hide (a charge, esp. an animal) with an ordinary which extends over the field. Chiefly as ***debruised*** *ppl a.* M16.

debt /dɛt/ *noun*. ME.
[ORIGIN Old French & mod. French *dette* from Proto-Romance use as fem. noun of pl. of Latin *debitum* neut. pple of *debere* owe; *-b-* introduced 16 after French †*debte*.]
1 Something owed or due; something (as money, goods, or service) which one person is under an obligation to pay or render to another. ME. ▸**b** *spec.* In biblical translations and allusions: an offence requiring atonement, a sin. ME.

B. T. WASHINGTON It was my greatest ambition . . to save money enough with which to pay this debt. **b** AV *Matt.* 6:12 And forgiue vs our debts, as we forgiue our debters.

2 A liability or obligation to pay or render something; the condition of being so liable or obligated. ME.

AV He hath for euer bound the Church vnto him, in a debt of speciall remembrance and thankefulnesse. C. A. LINDBERGH I left France with a debt of gratitude which . . I shall always remember. T. S. ELIOT She's always in debt. *Proverb*: Out of debt, out of danger.

†**3** (One's) duty. Chiefly *Scot.* ME–L16.

– PHRASES: ***bad debt***: see BAD *adjective*. **debt of honour** a debt that is not legally enforceable, *esp.* a gambling debt. **debt of nature**, **debt to nature** (the necessity of) death. **floating debt**: payable on demand or at a certain time. ***good debt***: see GOOD *adjective*. **in debt to someone**, **in someone's debt** owing something to someone. **national debt** the total of all a state's borrowings. **small debt**: of a limited amount, for which summary jurisdiction is provided in a county or (*Scot.*) sheriff's court.

– COMB.: **debt collector** a person whose business it is to collect debts on behalf of creditors; **debt-slave** a person kept in slavery until a debt is paid; **debt swap** (more fully ***debt-for-nature swap***) a transaction in which a foreign exchange debt owed by a developing country is transferred to another organization on the condition that the country uses local currency for a designated purpose, usually environmental protection.

■ **debtless** *adjective* LME.

†**debt** *adjective*. ME–E17.
[ORIGIN Prob. from the noun.]
Owed, owing.

SHAKES. *Haml.* To pay ourselves what to ourselves is debt.

†**debted** *ppl adjective*. LME–E17.
[ORIGIN Perh. aphet. from INDEBTED.]
Owed; (of a person) indebted.

debtee /dɛˈtiː/ *noun*. M16.
[ORIGIN from DEBTOR: see -EE[1].]
A person to whom a debt is owed; a creditor.

debtor /ˈdɛtə/ *noun*. ME.
[ORIGIN Old French *det(t)or*, -*our* from Latin *debitor*, from *debit-* pa. ppl stem of *debere* owe: see -OR.]
1 A person who is indebted to another; one who owes money or an obligation or duty. ME. ▸**b** In biblical translations and allusions: a person who has offended or sinned against another. ME.
2 (An entry on) the debit side of an account. Cf. earlier DEBITOR 2. E18.

debug /diːˈbʌg/ *verb trans*. Infl. **-gg-**. M20.
[ORIGIN from DE- 3 + BUG *noun*[2].]
1 Delouse. M20.
2 Remove the faults from (a machine, system, computer program, etc.). M20.
3 Remove concealed microphones, wiretaps, etc., from. M20.
■ **debugger** *noun* a person who or thing which debugs; *esp.* a computer program which detects, prevents, or corrects programming errors: M20.

debunk /diːˈbʌŋk/ *verb trans*. *colloq.*, orig. *US*. E20.
[ORIGIN from DE- 3 + BUNK *noun*[3].]
Expose the false claims or pretensions of; reduce the inflated reputation of (a person, institution, idea, etc.), esp. by ridicule.
■ **debunker** *noun* E20.

deburr /diːˈbɜː/ *verb trans*. Also **debur**, infl. **-rr-**. M20.
[ORIGIN from DE- 3 + BURR *noun*[4].]
Neaten and smooth the rough edges or ridges of (an object, esp. one made of metal).

†**deburse** *verb trans*. Chiefly *Scot.* LME–L18.
[ORIGIN French *débourser*: see DISBURSE.]
= DISBURSE *verb* 1.

debus /diːˈbʌs/ *verb trans. & intrans. colloq.* (chiefly MILITARY). Infl. **-ss-**. E20.
[ORIGIN from DE- 3 + BUS *noun* 3.]
Unload or alight from a motor vehicle or vehicles.

Debussyan /dəˈbuːsɪən, -ˈb(j)uːs-/ *adjective & noun*. E20.
[ORIGIN from *Debussy* (see below) + -AN.]
▸ **A** *adjective*. Of or pertaining to the French composer Achille-Claude Debussy (1862–1918), his music, or his style of composition. E20.
▸ **B** *noun*. An interpreter, student, or admirer of Debussy or his music. M20.
■ **Debussyˈesque** *adjective* resembling the style of Debussy M20.

debut /ˈdeɪb(j)uː, ˈdɛ-; deɪˈbjuː, dɛˈbjuː/ *noun*. Also **dé-**. M18.
[ORIGIN French *début*, from *débuter* lead off.]
Entry into society; the first appearance in public of a performer etc.

BYRON The début Of embryo actors, to the Drama new.

make one's debut appear or perform in public for the first time.

debut /ˈdeɪb(j)uː, ˈdɛ-/ *verb intrans*. Also **dé-**. L18.
[ORIGIN Partly from French *débuter* lead off, partly from DÉBUT *noun*.]
Make one's debut; appear or perform in public for the first time.

debutant /ˈdɛbjʊtɒ̃, ˈdeɪ-/ *noun*. Also **dé-**. E19.
[ORIGIN French *débutant*, pres. pple of *débuter* lead off: see -ANT[1].]
A male person making his debut.

debutante /ˈdɛbjʊtɑːnt, ˈdeɪ-/ *noun*. Also **dé-**. E19.
[ORIGIN French *débutante*, fem. of *débutant*: see DEBUTANT.]
1 A female performer etc. making her debut. E19.
2 A young woman making her social debut; *loosely* a young woman in fashionable society. Cf. DEB, DEBBY *noun*. E19.

Debye /dəˈbʌɪ/ *noun*. In sense 2 usu. **d-**. E20.
[ORIGIN Peter J. W. *Debye* (1884–1966), Dutch physicist.]
PHYSICS **I 1** Used *attrib.* and in *comb.* to designate concepts and methods arising out of Debye's work. E20.
Debye–Scherrer method /ˈʃɛrə/ [Paul H. *Scherrer* (1890–1969), Swiss physicist]: for obtaining X-ray diffraction patterns of powdered crystalline samples. **Debye temperature** a temperature used to characterize crystalline solids in Debye's theory of specific heats, corresponding to excitation of all lattice vibrations of the maximum allowed frequency.
▸**II 2** A unit of electric dipole moment (esp. used for molecular moments) equal to 3.336×10^{-30} coulomb metre. Also ***Debye unit***. M20.

Dec. *abbreviation*[1].
December.

dec. *abbreviation*[2].
1 Deceased.
2 CRICKET. Declared.

deca- /ˈdɛkə/ *combining form*. Before a vowel **dec-**.
[ORIGIN Greek *deka* ten.]
Used with the sense 'having ten, tenfold'; *spec.* in names of units of measurement, used to denote a factor of ten, as ***decagram***, ***decalitre***, ***decametre***, etc. Abbreviation ***da***.
■ **decagynous** /dɪˈkadʒɪnəs/ *adjective* (BOTANY) having ten pistils M19. **decahydroˈnaphthalene** *noun* (CHEMISTRY) a colourless liquid hydrocarbon, $C_{10}H_{18}$, used esp. as a solvent in the paint industry; = DECALIN: L19. **decamer** *noun* (CHEMISTRY) a compound whose molecule is composed of ten molecules of monomer M20. **decaˈmeric** *adjective* (CHEMISTRY) of the nature of a decamer, consisting of a decamer or decamers M20. **decaˈmetric** *adjective* (of radio waves) having a wavelength of 10 to 100 metres M20. **decandrous** /dɪˈkandrəs/ *adjective* (BOTANY) having ten stamens E19. **decangular** /dɪˈkaŋgjʊlə/ *adjective* having ten angles, decagonal E19. **decaˈpeptide** *noun* (BIOCHEMISTRY) any peptide composed of ten amino-acid residues E20. **decaˈphyllous** *adjective* (BOTANY) having ten leaves L18. **decaploid** *adjective* [-PLOID] BIOLOGY having ten homologous sets of chromosome E20.

decachord /ˈdɛkəkɔːd/ *noun*. Also **-cord**. LME.
[ORIGIN Late Latin *decachordus* adjective, *decachordus*, -*um* noun, from Greek *dekakhordos* ten-stringed, formed as DECA- + *khordē* string (see CORD *noun*[1]).]
A musical instrument, esp. a psaltery, having ten strings.

decad /ˈdɛkad/ *noun*[1]. E17.
[ORIGIN Late Latin *decad-*, -*as* from Greek *dekas*, from *deka* ten: see -AD[1].]
The number ten, as the perfect number of the Pythagoreans.

decad *noun*[2] see DECADE.

decadal /ˈdɛkəd(ə)l/ *adjective*. M18.
[ORIGIN formed as DECAD *noun*[1] + -AL[1].]
Of or relating to the number ten; belonging to a decade.

decadary /ˈdɛkəd(ə)ri/ *adjective*. E19.
[ORIGIN Alt. of French *décadaire* (formed as DECADE) after -ARY[1].]
FRENCH HISTORY. Of or pertaining to a decade of ten days.

decade /ˈdɛkeɪd, dɪˈkeɪd/ *noun*. Also (now *rare*) **-ad** /ˈdɛkəd/. LME.
[ORIGIN Old French & mod. French *décade* from late Latin *decas*, *decad-*: see DECAD *noun*[1].]
1 Each of ten books or parts of a single literary work. LME.

LD MACAULAY As hopelessly lost as the second decade of Livy.

2 A group or series of ten; *spec.* each of the five divisions of each chapter of the rosary. L16.
3 (The predominant sense.) A period of ten years. E17. ▸**b** FRENCH HISTORY. A period of ten days, substituted for a week in the French Republican calendar of 1793. L18.

M. L. KING The decade of 1955 to 1965 with its constructive elements misled us.

4 (A range of quantities spanning) a power of ten. Freq. used ***attrib.*** to denote sets of resistors or other electrical components providing values of resistance ranging from one to ten times a base value. E20.

decadence /ˈdɛkəd(ə)ns/ *noun*. M16.
[ORIGIN French *décadence* from medieval Latin *decadentia*, from *decadent-* pres. ppl stem of Proto-Romance verb whence also DECAY *verb*: see -ENCE.]
The process of falling away or declining (from a state of excellence, vitality, prosperity, etc.); decadent condition; decay, deterioration, *spec.* of a particular period in art, literature, etc., after a culmination.

GOLDSMITH Some pathetic exclamation on the decadence of taste and genius. E. M. FORSTER I have no profession . . . It is another example of my decadence.

decadency /ˈdɛkəd(ə)nsi/ *noun*. M17.
[ORIGIN formed as DECADENCE: see -ENCY.]
Decaying condition; decadence.

decadent /ˈdɛkəd(ə)nt/ *adjective & noun*. M19.
[ORIGIN French *décadent*, formed as DECADENCE: see -ENT.]
▸ **A** *adjective*. **1** Declining, decaying (from a condition of excellence, vitality, prosperity, etc.); characteristic of decadence, self-indulgent. M19.

G. ORWELL Our civilization is decadent, and our language . . must . . share in the general collapse.

2 Designating or belonging to a period of (artistic) decadence; *spec.* = AESTHETIC *adjective* 4. L19.
▸ **B** *noun*. A decadent person; *spec.* an adherent of a decadent movement in art, literature, etc. L19.
■ **decadentism** *noun* the qualities or spirit of a decadent movement in art, literature, etc.; decadent behaviour or characteristics. L19. **decadently** *adverb* L19.

decadic /dɪˈkadɪk/ *adjective*. M19.
[ORIGIN Greek *dekadikos*, from *dekas*, *dekad-*: see DECAD *noun*[1], -IC.]
Belonging to or designating the system of counting by tens; denary.

Decaf /ˈdiːkaf/ *noun*. Also **d-**. M20.
[ORIGIN Abbreviation.]
(Proprietary name for) decaffeinated coffee; a drink made with this.

decaffeinate /diːˈkafɪneɪt/ *verb trans*. M20.
[ORIGIN from DE- 3 + CAFFEINE + -ATE[3].]
Remove the caffeine from, reduce the quantity of caffeine in (coffee etc.). Chiefly as ***decaffeinated*** *ppl adjective*.
■ **decaffeiniˈzation** *noun* the process of decaffeinating coffee etc. E20.

decagon /ˈdɛkəg(ə)n/ *noun*. M17.
[ORIGIN medieval Latin *decagonum* from Greek *dekagōnon*, from *deka-* DECA- + *-gōnos* -GON.]
A plane figure with ten straight sides and ten angles.
■ **decagonal** /dɪˈkagən(ə)l/ *adjective* having the form of a decagon; having ten sides: L16.

decahedron /dɛkəˈhiːdr(ə)n, -ˈhɛd-/ *noun*. Pl. **-dra** /-drə/, **-drons**. E19.
[ORIGIN from DECA- + -HEDRON.]
GEOMETRY. A solid figure or object with ten plane faces.
■ **decahedral** *adjective* having the form of a decahedron; having ten faces: E19.

decal /ˈdiːkal/ *noun*. Chiefly *N. Amer.* M20.
[ORIGIN Abbreviation of DECALCOMANIA.]
A picture etc. prepared on special paper for durable transfer on to glass, china, plastic models, etc.

decalage /ˈdiːkəlɑːʒ/ *noun*. E20.
[ORIGIN French *décalage* displacement, from *décaler* displace.]
AERONAUTICS. The difference in the angle of incidence between two aerofoils on an aeroplane.

decalcify /diːˈkalsɪfʌɪ/ *verb trans*. M19.
[ORIGIN from DE- 3 + CALCIFY.]
Deprive (bone etc.) of calcium compounds. Chiefly as ***decalcified*** *ppl adjective*.
■ **decalcifiˈcation** *noun* M19.

decalcomania /dɪˌkalkəˈmeɪnɪə/ *noun*. M19.
[ORIGIN French *décalcomanie*, from *décalquer* transfer a tracing + *-manie* -MANIA.]
The process of transferring pictures etc. from specially prepared paper on to surfaces of glass, china, etc.

decalescence /diːkəˈlɛs(ə)ns/ *noun*. L19.
[ORIGIN from DE- 3 + CALESCENCE.]
METALLURGY. The absorption of heat by a metal, without a corresponding increase in temperature, when the metal is heated through a critical point.
■ **decalescent** *adjective* E20.

decalin /ˈdɛkəlɪn/ *noun*. Also **dek-**, (US proprietary name) **D-**. E20.
[ORIGIN from DECA- + *-l-* + -IN[1].]
CHEMISTRY. = DECAHYDRONAPHTHALENE.

Decalogue /ˈdɛkəlɒg/ *noun*. Also **d-**. LME.
[ORIGIN French *décalogue* or ecclesiastical Latin *decalogus* from Greek *dekalogos*, orig. fem. adjective (sc. *biblos* book), after *hoi deka logoi* the Ten Commandments (Septuagint), from *deka* ten + *logos* saying, speech: see -LOGUE.]
The Ten Commandments collectively as a body of law.
■ **Decalogist** /dɪˈkalədʒɪst/ *noun* (*rare*) a person who expounds the Decalogue M17.

†**decalvation** *noun*. LME–M18.
[ORIGIN Latin *decalvatio(n-)*, from *decalvare* make bald, from *de-* DE- 1 + *calvus* bald: see -ATION.]
Removal of hair, making bald.

decamp /dɪˈkamp/ *verb intrans*. L17.
[ORIGIN French *décamper*, from *dé-* DE- 3 + *camp* CAMP *noun*[2]. Cf. earlier DISCAMP.]
1 Orig. MILITARY. Break up or leave a camp; remove from a camping place. L17.

WELLINGTON We found on our arrival that the armies of both chiefs had decamped.

2 Go away promptly or suddenly; take oneself off. M18.

O. MANNING The Minister had decamped to Switzerland with the Ministry funds.

■ **decampment** *noun* [French *décampement*] the breaking up of a camp; (a) prompt departure: L17.

decan /ˈdɛk(ə)n/ *noun*. **OE**.
[**ORIGIN** Late Latin *decanus*: see **DEAN** *noun*[1].]
†**1** A chief or ruler of ten, = **DEAN** *noun*[1] 4. **OE–M16**.
†**2** = **DEAN** *noun*[1] I. **LME–M16**.
3 *ASTROLOGY*. Each of the three divisions of a zodiacal sign, extending over ten degrees; the ruler of such a division. **L16**.

decanal /dɪˈkeɪn(ə)l, ˈdɛk(ə)n(ə)l/ *adjective*. **E18**.
[**ORIGIN** medieval Latin *decanalis*, formed as **DECAN**: see **-AL**[1].]
1 Of or pertaining to a dean or deanery. **E18**.
2 Designating or pertaining to the south side of the choir of a church, on which the dean usually sits. Cf. **CANTORIAL**. **L18**.
■ **decanally** *adverb* (*rare*) **L19**.

decanate /ˈdɛk(ə)neɪt/ *noun*. **M17**.
[**ORIGIN** medieval Latin *decanatus*, formed as **DECAN**: see **-ATE**[1].]
ASTROLOGY. Each of the three divisions (of ten degrees) of a zodiacal sign.

decane /ˈdɛkeɪn/ *noun*. **L18**.
[**ORIGIN** from **DECA-** + **-ANE**.]
CHEMISTRY. Any of a series of saturated hydrocarbons (alkanes) with the formula $C_{10}H_{22}$; *spec.* (also *n-decane*) the unbranched isomer, $CH_3(CH)_8CH_3$.

decani /dɪˈkeɪnʌɪ/ *adjective*. **M18**.
[**ORIGIN** Latin, genit. of *decanus* **DEAN** *noun*[1].]
= **DECANAL** 2; *MUSIC* to be sung by the decanal side in antiphonal singing (cf. **CANTORIS**).

decant /dɪˈkant/ *verb trans*. **M17**.
[**ORIGIN** medieval Latin *decanthare* (whence also French *décanter*), from Latin *de-* **DE-** 1 + *canthus* angular lip of a jug from Greek *kanthos* corner of the eye.]
1 Pour off (a liquid or solution) by gently inclining the vessel so as not to disturb sediment. **M17**.
2 Pour (wine etc.) from a bottle into a decanter; *loosely* pour into a drinking vessel. **M18**.
3 Empty out; move or transfer as if by pouring. *colloq.* **M18**.

F. WELDON The bus broke down and we were all . . decanted into another.

decantation /diːkanˈteɪʃ(ə)n/ *noun*. **M17**.
[**ORIGIN** French *décantation* or medieval Latin *decanthatio(n-)*, formed as **DECANT**: see **-ATION**.]
The action of decanting, esp. of pouring off liquid from sediment.

decanter /dɪˈkantə/ *noun*. **E18**.
[**ORIGIN** from **DECANT** + **-ER**[1].]
1 A vessel used for decanting or receiving decanted liquors; *spec.* a bottle of clear or cut glass, with a stopper, from which wine etc. is served. **E18**.

M. ALLINGHAM He . . shot a hopeless glance at the whisky decanter.

2 A person who decants. Only in Dicts. **M18**.

decapacitate /diːkəˈpasɪteɪt/ *verb trans*. **M20**.
[**ORIGIN** from **DE-** + **CAPACITATE**.]
PHYSIOLOGY. Remove the effect of capacitation from; deprive (a spermatozoon) of the ability to penetrate an ovum. Usu. in *pass.*
■ **decapaciˈtation** *noun* **M20**.

decapitalize /diːˈkapɪt(ə)lʌɪz/ *verb trans*. Also **-ise**. **L19**.
[**ORIGIN** from **DE-** 3 + **CAPITAL** *noun*[2] + **-IZE**.]
1 Reduce from the rank of capital city. *rare*. **L19**.
2 Reduce the capital assets of. **M20**.
■ **decapitaliˈzation** *noun* **L19**.

decapitate /dɪˈkapɪteɪt/ *verb trans*. **E17**.
[**ORIGIN** Late Latin *decapitat-* pa. ppl stem of *decapitare*, from *de-* **DE-** 3 + *caput*, *capit-* head: see **-ATE**[3].]
1 Cut off the head of, behead; cut the top or end from (a thing). **E17**.

C. CHAPLIN He had cut his throat, almost decapitating himself. C. CONRAN Skin the tomatoes, then decapitate them with a saw-bladed knife.

2 Dismiss abruptly from office. *US*. **M19**.
■ **decapitator** *noun* a person or thing which decapitates **E19**.

decapitation /dɪˌkapɪˈteɪʃ(ə)n/ *noun*. **M17**.
[**ORIGIN** French *décapitation* or medieval Latin *decapitatio(n-)*, formed as **DECAPITATE** (see **-ATION**), or from **DECAPITATE** on the analogy of similar pairs.]
1 The action of beheading a person or cutting the top or end from a thing; the fact of being so decapitated. **M17**.
2 Summary dismissal from office. *US*. **M19**.

decapod /ˈdɛkəpɒd/ *noun & adjective*. **E19**.
[**ORIGIN** French *décapode* from mod. Latin *Decapoda* (see below), use as noun of neut. pl. adjective, formed as **DECA-** + **-POD**.]
▸ **A** *noun*. **1** *ZOOLOGY*. A crustacean of the order Decapoda, members of which have ten feet or legs, and which includes the lobster, crab, shrimp, etc. Also, a cephalopod of the sub-order Decapoda, members of which have ten tentacles, as the cuttlefish and squid. **E19**.
2 A steam locomotive with ten driving wheels. Chiefly *US*. **L19**.
▸ **B** *adjective*. *ZOOLOGY*. Of or pertaining to the (crustacean or cephalopod) Decapoda. **E19**.
■ **deˈcapodan** *adjective* = **DECAPOD** *adjective* **M19**.

decapsulate /diːˈkapsjʊleɪt/ *verb trans*. **E20**.
[**ORIGIN** from **DE-** 3 + **CAPSULE** *noun* + **-ATE**[3].]
(Surgically) remove the capsule of.
■ **decapsuˈlation** *noun* **E20**.

decarbonate /diːˈkɑːb(ə)neɪt/ *verb trans*. **M19**.
[**ORIGIN** from **DE-** 3 + **CARBON** *noun* + **-ATE**[3]. Cf. French *décarbonater*.]
Remove carbon or carbon compounds from.

decarbonize /diːˈkɑːb(ə)nʌɪz/ *verb trans*. Also **-ise**. **E19**.
[**ORIGIN** from **DE-** 3 + **CARBON** *noun* + **-IZE**.]
Remove carbon or carbon compounds from; *spec.* remove carbon deposits from (an internal-combustion engine).
■ **decarboniˈzation** *noun* **M19**.

decarboxylate /diːkɑːˈbɒksɪleɪt/ *verb*. **E20**.
[**ORIGIN** from **DE-** 3 + **CARBOXYL** + **-ATE**[3].]
CHEMISTRY. **1** *verb trans*. Remove a carboxyl group from (a molecule). **E20**.
2 *verb intrans*. Lose a carboxyl group; undergo decarboxylation. **M20**.
■ **decarboxylase** *noun* an enzyme that promotes the decarboxylation of a molecule **M20**. **decarboxyˈlation** *noun* the removal of a carboxyl group from a molecule **E20**.

decarburize /diːˈkɑːbjʊrʌɪz/ *verb trans*. Also **-ise**. **M19**.
[**ORIGIN** from **DE-** 3 + **CARBURIZE**, after French *décarburer*.]
Chiefly *METALLURGY*. Remove carbon from.
■ **decarburiˈzation** *noun* **M19**.

decarch /ˈdɛkɑːk/ *noun*. Also **dek-**. **M17**.
[**ORIGIN** Greek *dekarkhēs*, *-os* decurion, from *deka* ten + *arkhos* leader.]
GREEK HISTORY. Each of a ruling body of ten.

decarchy /ˈdɛkɑːki/ *noun*. Also **dek-**. **M17**.
[**ORIGIN** Greek *dekarkhia*, formed as **DECARCH**: see **-Y**[3].]
GREEK HISTORY. A ruling body of ten.

decartelization /diːˌkɑːtɛlʌɪˈzeɪʃ(ə)n/ *noun*. Also **-ll-**, **-isation**. **M20**.
[**ORIGIN** from **DE-** 3 + **CARTELIZATION**.]
Abolition of a system of trade cartels.

decastyle /ˈdɛkəstʌɪl/ *adjective & noun*. **E18**.
[**ORIGIN** Greek *dekastulos* having ten columns, from Greek *deka* ten + *stulos* column. Cf. French *décastyle*.]
ARCHITECTURE. ▸ **A** *adjective*. Having ten columns (in front). **E18**.
▸ **B** *noun*. A building with ten columns in front; a portico etc. of ten columns. **E18**.

decasualize /diːˈkaʒjʊəlʌɪz, -zj-/ *verb trans*. Also **-ise**. **L19**.
[**ORIGIN** from **DE-** 3 + **CASUAL** *adjective* + **-IZE**.]
Do away with the casual employment of (labour) by introducing permanent jobs.
■ **decasualiˈzation** *noun* the abolition of casual labour **L19**.

decasyllabic /dɛkəsɪˈlabɪk/ *adjective & noun*. **L18**.
[**ORIGIN** from **DECA-** + **SYLLABIC**. Cf. French *décasyllabique*.]
PROSODY. ▸ **A** *adjective*. Consisting of ten syllables. **L18**.
▸ **B** *noun*. A line of ten syllables. **L19**.
■ Also **ˈdecasyllable** *adjective & noun* **M19**.

decathlon /dɪˈkaθlɒn, -lən/ *noun*. **E20**.
[**ORIGIN** from **DECA-** + Greek *athlon* contest.]
An athletic or sporting contest in which competitors engage in ten different events.
■ **decathlete** *noun* a competitor in the decathlon **M20**.

decatize /ˈdɛkətʌɪz/ *verb trans*. Also **-ise**. **E20**.
[**ORIGIN** from French *décatir* sponge or steam (cloth) + **-IZE**.]
Give lustre to (cloth) by means of the action of steam.

decaudate /diːˈkɔːdeɪt/ *verb trans*. *rare*. **M19**.
[**ORIGIN** from **DE-** 3 + Latin *cauda* tail + **-ATE**[3].]
Remove the tail(s) from.
■ **decauˈdation** *noun* **L19**.

Decauville /dəˈkəʊvɪl/ *adjective & noun*. **L19**.
[**ORIGIN** P. *Decauville* (1846–1922), French engineer.]
(Designating or pertaining to) a type of narrow-gauge railway invented by Decauville.

decay /dɪˈkeɪ/ *noun*. **LME**.
[**ORIGIN** from the verb.]
1 The process of departing from a thriving condition; progressive decline. Also, the condition of having declined. **LME**. ▸†**b** Downfall; *poet.* fall, death. **LME–E18**.

AV *Lev.* 25:35 If thy brother bee waxen poore, and fallen in decay with thee. R. G. COLLINGWOOD The decay of our civilization, . . a break-down of social structures and . . a drying-up of the emotional springs of life.

2 Material deterioration, dilapidation, falling apart; ruinous condition. **E16**. ▸†**b** In *pl.* Ruins, debris. **L16–L18**.

BACON It is a reverend thing to see an ancient castle or building not in decay. J. STEINBECK Over the whole lot a spirit of decay, of mold and rust.

†**3** A cause of decline or deterioration. **M16–L17**.
4 Mental or physical decline (through illness or old age). **L16**. ▸†**b** A wasting disease; consumption. **E18–E19**.

J. FRAME She accepted age with its gradual decay of faculties and energies as an autumnal dignity.

5 The rotting or decomposition of organic tissue; decomposed tissue. **L16**.

J. BRAINE There was a speck of decay on one of her upper incisors.

6 Decrease in quantity etc. Now chiefly *PHYSICS*, a gradual decrease in the magnitude of a physical quantity, esp. in the intensity of radioactivity or in the amplitude of an oscillation. Also, the spontaneous change of a substance, nucleus, etc., into another by radioactivity. **M17**.

J. A. FLEMING Frictional resistance causes decay in the amplitude of the oscillations by dissipating their energy as heat. J. B. PRIESTLEY These gentlefolk watch the decay of their incomes and keep open house for young male relatives on leave from the East. N. CALDER Decay of uranium produces . . lead.

D

decay /dɪˈkeɪ/ *verb*. **L15**.
[**ORIGIN** Old French *decair* by-form of *decaoir* var. of *dechaoir*, *decheoir* (mod. *déchoir*) from Proto-Romance var. of Latin *decidere*, from *de-* **DE-** 1 + *cadere* to fall.]
▸ **I** *verb intrans*. **1** Deteriorate, decline in quality, prosperity, etc. **L15**.

SIR W. SCOTT Ancient . . families . . decayed . . into the humble vale of life. JOHN GLOAG Impoverished widows and spinsters of the middle classes . . were officially described as 'decayed gentlewomen'.

2 Fall into physical ruin or disrepair; waste away, fall apart; rot. **L15**.

J. CONRAD His new but already decaying house. C. PRIEST The . . heap that would . . decay into . . compost.

3 Decrease in quantity or magnitude; dwindle. Now chiefly *PHYSICS*, undergo gradual decrease in the magnitude of a physical quantity. **L15**. ▸**b** *spec.* Of radioactivity: gradually decrease in intensity. Of a radioactive substance, nucleus, etc.: spontaneously change into one or more different substances, particles, etc. **E20**.

C. SAGAN The orbits of artificial satellites are decaying all the time . . . They are . . slowed by collisions with the . . atmosphere. **b** D. R. HOFSTADTER A photon . . can decay . . into an electron-positron pair.

4 Lose one's health and strength of body or mind; decline through age. **M16**.

POPE But since, alas! frail beauty must decay.

▸ **II** *verb trans*. **5** Cause to fall off or decline in quality, prosperity, number, etc.; ruin physically, dilapidate. Now *rare*. **E16**. ▸**b** Destroy by decomposition, make rotten. **E17**.

M. BERESFORD The Bishop . . faced with an accusation of decaying three houses.

6 Cause to fail in health, strength, etc. Now *rare*. **M16**.

ADDISON Almost every thing which corrupts the soul decays the body.

■ **decayable** *adjective* able or liable to decay **E17**. **decayer** *noun* a person who or thing which causes decay **M16**.

decease /dɪˈsiːs/ *noun*. Chiefly *formal* or *LAW*. **ME**.
[**ORIGIN** Old French & mod. French *décès* from Latin *decessus* departure, death, from pa. ppl stem of *decedere* go away, depart, from *de-* **DE-** 1 + *cedere* go.]
Departure from life, death.

decease /dɪˈsiːs/ *verb intrans*. **LME**.
[**ORIGIN** from the noun.]
1 Depart from life; die. **LME**.
2 *fig.* Come to an end, perish; cease. **M16**.

deceased /dɪˈsiːst/ *adjective & noun*. **L15**.
[**ORIGIN** from **DECEASE** *verb* + **-ED**[1].]
▸ **A** *adjective*. Dead; *esp.* lately dead; belonging to a dead person. **L15**.
▸ **B** *noun*. A (recently) dead person; *collect.* (*rare*) dead persons, *the* dead. **E17**.

decedent /dɪˈsiːd(ə)nt/ *noun*. **L16**.
[**ORIGIN** Latin *decedent-* pres. ppl stem of *decedere* die: see **DECEASE** *noun*, **-ENT**.]
Now chiefly *US LAW*. A deceased person. Formerly also, a person retiring from office.

deceit /dɪˈsiːt/ *noun*. **ME**.
[**ORIGIN** Old French, use as noun of pa. pple (from Latin *deceptus*) of *deceveir* **DECEIVE**.]
1 The action or practice of deceiving; concealment or misrepresentation of the truth in order to mislead; deception, fraud, cheating. **ME**.

MILTON By violence? no . . But by deceit and lies.

2 An instance of deception; a device intended to deceive; a trick, a wile, a stratagem. **ME**.
3 Disposition or tendency to deceive or mislead; deceitfulness. **ME**.

deceitful /dɪˈsiːtfʊl, -f(ə)l/ *adjective*. **LME**.
[**ORIGIN** from **DECEIT** + **-FUL**.]
Full of deceit; given to deceiving; misleading, false; deceptive.
■ **deceitfully** *adverb* **LME**. **deceitfulness** *noun* **LME**.

deceivable /dɪˈsiːvəb(ə)l/ *adjective*. **ME**.
[**ORIGIN** Old French & mod. French *décevable*, from *décevoir*: see **DECEIVE**, **-ABLE**.]
1 Capable of deceiving; tending to deceive. *arch.* **ME**.
2 Able or liable to be deceived. Now *rare*. **M17**.

D

■ **deceivableness** *noun* LME. **deceivably** *adverb* (*arch.*) deceitfully, fraudulently, falsely LME.

deceive /dɪˈsiːv/ *verb*. ME.
[ORIGIN Old French *deceivre*, *deçoivre* from Latin *decipere*, from *de-* DE- 1 + *capere* take, seize; or from *deceiv-* tonic stem of *deceveir* (mod. *décevoir*) from Proto-Romance alt. of Latin *decipere*.]
†**1** *verb trans.* Trap or overcome by trickery; take unawares by craft or guile; lead astray. ME–L18.

MILTON Th'infernal Serpent.. whose guile.. deceived The mother of mankind.

2 *verb trans.* Cause to believe what is false; delude, take in; *refl.* & in *pass.*, allow oneself to be misled, be mistaken, err. ME. ▸**b** *verb intrans.* Use deceit, act deceitfully. ME.

J. CONRAD Cosmopolitan enough not to be deceived by London's topographical mysteries. I. MURDOCH Mor had never deceived his wife, except for.. one or two lies about his health. **b** SIR W. SCOTT Ah, what a tangled web we weave, When first we practise to deceive!

3 *verb trans.* Be or prove false to, betray. Now chiefly *fig.*, disappoint (hopes etc.). ME.

JAS. MILL Never was expectation more completely deceived.

†**4** *verb trans.* Cheat, defraud; deprive of by deception. (Foll. by *of*.) ME–M18.
†**5** *verb trans.* Beguile (time etc.). L16–M19.
■ **deceiver** *noun* a person or thing which deceives or cheats; a cheat, an impostor: LME. **deceivingly** *adverb* so as to deceive, deceptively LME.

decelerate /diːˈsɛləreɪt/ *verb*. L19.
[ORIGIN from DE- 3 + AC)CELERATE.]
1 *verb trans.* Diminish the speed of; cause to go slower, retard. L19.
2 *verb intrans.* Move more slowly, slow down. E20.
■ **deceleˈration** *noun* L19. **decelerator** *noun* a device for reducing speed E20. **deceleˈrometer** *noun* an instrument for measuring the deceleration of a moving body E20.

decem- /ˈdɛsəm/ *combining form*.
[ORIGIN Latin = ten.]
Ten, tenfold.
■ ˌ**decemnoveˈnarian** *noun* (*rare*) a man or woman of the 19th century M19. **decempedal** /dɪˈsɛmpɪd(ə)l/ *adjective* (*rare*) †(**a**) ten feet in length; (**b**) having ten feet: M17.

December /dɪˈsɛmbə/ *noun*. ME.
[ORIGIN Old French & mod. French *décembre* from Latin *december*, from *decem* ten: orig. the tenth month of the Roman year. The meaning of *-ber* is unkn. (cf. *September* etc.).]
The twelfth and last month of the year in the Gregorian calendar. Also *fig.*, with allusion to December's being the month in which the winter solstice occurs in the northern hemisphere.
– COMB.: **December moth** a winter-flying lasiocampid moth, *Poecilocampa populi*.

Decembrist /dɪˈsɛmbrɪst/ *noun*. L19.
[ORIGIN from DECEMBER + -IST: cf. DEKABRIST.]
hist. A participant in an uprising which took place in St Petersburg, Russia, in December 1825, on the accession of Tsar Nicholas I.

decemvir /dɪˈsɛmvə/ *noun*. LME.
[ORIGIN Latin, sing. of *decemviri*, orig. *decem viri* ten men.]
1 A council or ruling body of ten. Orig. & *esp.* (ROMAN HISTORY) either of two bodies of magistrates appointed in 451 and 450 BC respectively to draw up a code of laws, who were in the meantime entrusted with the supreme government of Rome. LME.
2 A member of such a body. E18.
■ **decemviral** *adjective* of or pertaining to decemvirs E17. **decemvirate** *noun* the position or government of decemvirs; a body of decemvirs: E17.

decenary *noun* var. of DECENNARY *noun*[1].

†**decence** *noun*. Also **dé-**. L16–M19.
[ORIGIN Old French & mod. French *décence* formed as DECENCY: see -ENCE.]
= DECENCY.

decency /ˈdiːs(ə)nsi/ *noun*. M16.
[ORIGIN Latin *decentia*, from *decent-*: see DECENT, -Y[3], -ENCY.]
▸**I** †**1** Appropriateness or fitness to the circumstances of the case; seemliness; what is appropriate. M16–M18.

I. WATTS The great Design of Prudence.. is to determine and manage every Affair with Decency.

†**2** Orderly condition of civil or social life. M17–E18.
3 Propriety of behaviour or demeanour; conformity, behaviour that conforms, to recognized standards of good taste, modesty, or decorum; *esp.* avoidance of impropriety, obscenity, or immorality. M17.

WORDSWORTH Many.. there are Who live a life of virtuous decency. K. AMIS Why hadn't they had the decency to ask him if he'd like to join in?

4 Respectability. M18.
▸**II 5** In *pl.* The requirements of decorum or respectable behaviour. M17.

LD MACAULAY Careless of the decencies.. expected from a man so highly distinguished.

6 An essential of a respectable lifestyle. Usu. in *pl.* L18.

H. SIDGWICK It was not easy to distinguish decencies and comforts on the one hand and luxuries on the other.

decener /ˈdɛs(ə)nə/ *noun*. Also **deciner**. LME.
[ORIGIN formed as DECENNARY *noun*[1]: see -ER[2]. Cf. DOZENER.]
1 *hist.* The head of a tithing; a member of a tithing. LME.
†**2** A commander of ten soldiers. M16–E17.

decennary /dɪˈsɛn(ə)ri/ *noun*[1]. Also **decenary**. M17.
[ORIGIN medieval Latin *decenarius*, *decennarius*, from *decena*, *decenna* tithing: see -ARY[1].]
hist. A tithing.

decennary /dɪˈsɛn(ə)ri/ *noun*[2] & *adjective*. E19.
[ORIGIN from Latin DECENNIUM + -ARY[1].]
▸**A** *noun*. A period of ten years; a decennium. E19.
▸**B** *adjective*. Decennial. M19.

decennia *noun pl.* see DECENNIUM.

decenniad /dɪˈsɛnɪad/ *noun*. M19.
[ORIGIN formed as DECENNIAL + -AD[1].]
= DECENNIUM.

decennial /dɪˈsɛnɪəl/ *adjective* & *noun*. M17.
[ORIGIN from Latin DECENNIUM + -AL[1].]
▸**A** *adjective*. Of or pertaining to a period of ten years; lasting ten years; occurring every ten years; (of a person) holding office for ten years. M17.
▸**B** *noun*. (The celebration of) a decennial anniversary. *US*. L19.
■ †**decennal** *adjective* = DECENNIAL *adjective* M17–E18. **decennially** *adverb* L19.

decennium /dɪˈsɛnɪəm/ *noun*. Pl. **-ia** /-ɪə/, **-iums**. L17.
[ORIGIN Latin, from *decennis*, from *decem* ten + *annus* year.]
A period of ten years, a decade.

decent /ˈdiːs(ə)nt/ *adjective*. M16.
[ORIGIN French *décent* or Latin *decent-* pres. ppl stem of *decere* be fitting: see -ENT.]
1 Suitable or appropriate to the circumstances of the case; fitting. M16. ▸†**b** Appropriate with regard to rank or dignity. M16–L18.

A. LURIE A victor must show decent modesty and reserve.

2 Conforming to recognized standards of propriety, good taste, modesty, or decorum; avoiding impropriety, obscenity, or immorality. M16. ▸**b** Sufficiently clothed to see visitors; not in a state of undress. *colloq.* M20.

S. O'CASEY I always think th' kilts is hardly decent. R. MACAULAY To grow into a decent, civilized young woman.

†**3** Handsome, comely. E17–E18.
4 In keeping with one's position or circumstances; respectable. E18.
5 Tolerable, passable, good enough. E18.

J. KEROUAC If only I had enough money to raise a decent lawyer.

6 Of a person: kind, pleasant; obliging, generous; reasonable. *colloq.* E20.

R. LEHMANN This is a ripping place, and they're being jolly decent to us.

■ **decentish** *adjective* E19. **decently** *adverb* M16. **decentness** *noun* (*obsolete* exc. *dial.*) decency M16.

decenter *verb* see DECENTRE.

decentralize /diːˈsɛntrəlʌɪz/ *verb trans.* Also **-ise**. M19.
[ORIGIN from DE- 3 + CENTRALIZE.]
Do away with centralization of; confer local government on; distribute (administrative powers etc.) among local centres.
■ **decentralist** *noun* an advocate of decentralization E20. **decentraliˈzation** *noun* M19. **decentralizer** *noun* = DECENTRALIST L19.

decentre /diːˈsɛntə/ *verb trans.* Also *-**ter**. L19.
[ORIGIN from DE- 3 + CENTRE *noun* or *verb*.]
1 Remove the centre from. L19.
2 Chiefly OPTICS. Place out of centre; render (a lens) eccentric. L19.
■ **decenˈtration** *noun* L19.

deceptible /dɪˈsɛptɪb(ə)l/ *adjective*. *rare*. M17.
[ORIGIN French †*déceptible* or medieval Latin *deceptibilis*, from *decept-*: see DECEPTION, -IBLE.]
Apt to be deceived.
■ **decepti'bility** *noun* M17.

deception /dɪˈsɛpʃ(ə)n/ *noun*. LME.
[ORIGIN Old French & mod. French *déception* or late Latin *deceptio(n-)*, from Latin *decept-* pa. ppl stem of *decipere*: see DECEIVE, -ION.]
1 The action of deceiving or cheating; deceived condition. LME.
2 Something which deceives; a piece of trickery. L18.

deceptious /dɪˈsɛpʃəs/ *adjective*. Now *rare*. E17.
[ORIGIN Old French *deceptieus* or late Latin *deceptiosus*, from *decept-*: see DECEPTION, -IOUS.]
That tends to deceive, cheat, or mislead.

deceptive /dɪˈsɛptɪv/ *adjective*. E17.
[ORIGIN Old French *deceptif*, *-ive* or late Latin *deceptivus*, from *decept-*: see DECEPTION, -IVE.]
Apt or tending to deceive; giving a false impression; easily mistaken for something else or as having a different quality.

J. M. MURRY Keats' letters have a deceptive spontaneity which invites the mind to pass over them.. without pausing to penetrate below the surface. N. COWARD It was probably an optical illusion. This half light is very deceptive.

■ **deceptiveness** *noun* M19.

deceptively /dɪˈsɛptɪvli/ *adverb*. E19.
[ORIGIN from DECEPTIVE + -LY *suffix*[2].]
In such a way as to deceive: *spec.* (**a**) to a lesser extent than appears the case; (**b**) to a greater extent than appears the case.

T. MACKINTOSH-SMITH The method of building is deceptively simple. *Kildare Nationalist (online ed.)* A fine family residence extending to offer a deceptively spacious home.

– NOTE: The meaning can be ambiguous when the word is used before an adjective.

decerebrate /diːˈsɛrɪbrət/ *adjective*. L19.
[ORIGIN from DE- 3 + CEREBRUM + -ATE[2].]
Having had the cerebrum removed or the brainstem severed below the midbrain; resulting from decerebration.
■ **decereˈbration** *noun* the removal of the cerebrum; the cutting of the brainstem below the midbrain: E20.

decern /dɪˈsəːn/ *verb*. LME.
[ORIGIN Old French & mod. French *décerner* from Latin *decernere* decide, pronounce a decision, from *de-* DE- 1 + *cernere* separate, sift. Conf. with DISCERN.]
▸**I** †**1** *verb trans.* Decide, determine. LME–E17.
2 *verb trans.* & *intrans.* Decree by judicial sentence. Now only SCOTS LAW. LME.
▸†**II** See DISCERN.
■ **decerniture** *noun* (SCOTS LAW) the action of decerning; a decree of a Scottish court: M17.

†**decernment** *noun* var. of DISCERNMENT.

†**decerp** *verb trans.* Pa. t. & pple **decerped**, **-pt**. M16–L17.
[ORIGIN Latin *decerpere* pluck off, from *de-* DE- 1 + *carpere* pluck: cf. DISCERP.]
Tear or pluck off or out; sever, excerpt, (*from*).

decertify /diːˈsəːtɪfʌɪ/ *verb trans.* E20.
[ORIGIN from DE- 3 + CERTIFY.]
Remove a certificate or certification (esp. one of insanity) from.
■ **decertifiˈcation** *noun* M20.

decession /dɪˈsɛʃ(ə)n/ *noun*. Long *rare* or *obsolete*. LME.
[ORIGIN Latin *decessio(n-)*, from *decess-* pa. ppl stem of *decedere* depart, from *de-* DE- 1 + *cedere* go: see -ION. Cf. Old French *decession*.]
Departure, (a) secession; (a) diminution (opp. ***accession***).

de-Christianize /diːˈkrɪstʃənʌɪz, -tɪən-/ *verb trans.* Also **-ise**. M19.
[ORIGIN from DE- 3 + CHRISTIANIZE.]
Deprive of Christian character; make no longer Christian.

deci- /ˈdɛsi/ *combining form*.
[ORIGIN Abbreviation of Latin *decimus* tenth: see -I-.]
Used in names of units of measurement to denote a factor of one-tenth, as ***decibel***, ***decigram***, ***decilitre***, ***decimetre***, etc. Abbreviation ***d***.

Decian /ˈdiːsɪən/ *adjective*. L17.
[ORIGIN from *Decius* (see below) + -AN.]
Of or pertaining to the Roman Emperor Decius or his reign (249–51); *esp.* designating the persecution of Christians which occurred under Decius.

decibel /ˈdɛsɪbɛl/ *noun*. E20.
[ORIGIN from DECI- + BEL *noun*[1].]
A logarithmic unit (one-tenth of a bel, abbreviation ***dB***) used to express the ratio between two levels of sound intensity, electrical power, etc., one of which is usu. a (stated or understood) reference level; *loosely* a degree of noise.

decidable /dɪˈsʌɪdəb(ə)l/ *adjective*. L16.
[ORIGIN from DECIDE + -ABLE.]
1 Able to be decided. L16.
2 MATH. & LOGIC. Able to be proved within a formal system of axioms. M20.
■ **decidaˈbility** *noun* M20.

decide /dɪˈsʌɪd/ *verb*. LME.
[ORIGIN French *décider* or Latin *decidere* cut off, determine, from *de-* DE- 1 + *caedere* cut.]
1 *verb trans.* Settle (a question, dispute, etc.) by finding in favour of one side; bring to a settlement, resolve; influence decisively the outcome of (a contest etc.). LME. ▸**b** *verb intrans.* Settle a question in dispute, pronounce judgement. (Foll. by *between*, *in favour of*, *against*.) M18. ▸**c** *verb trans.* Determine on as a settlement, pronounce in judgement. M19.

POPE Deeds must decide our Fate. CONAN DOYLE The fight [a boxing match].. will.. be decided upon points. G. B. SHAW The only evidence that can decide a case of malpractice is expert evidence. **b** SMOLLETT Let heaven decide Between me and my foes. **c** F. MARRYAT What you decide shall be irrevocable.

2 *verb trans.* Bring (a person) to a determination or resolution (*against*, *in favour of*, *to do*). E18.

E. M. FORSTER Quite a little thing decided me to speak to you. V. S. REID Something which decided him against interfering.

3 a *verb trans.* Come to a determination or resolution *that, to do, whether.* **M19.** ▸**b** *verb intrans.* Come to a determination or resolution (*against, in favour of,* (*up*)*on*). **M19.**

a I. MURDOCH He wondered if he should call out . . but decided not to. J. WAIN She could not decide whether or not to shorten the skirt. O. MANNING Why had she suddenly decided she must see Flora? **b** C. S. FORESTER He had already decided on the next move. D. FRASER The Japanese had decided against invasion of Australia.

decided /dɪˈsʌɪdɪd/ *adjective.* **M18.**
[ORIGIN from DECIDE + -ED[1]. Cf. earlier UNDECIDED.]
1 Unhesitating, resolute, determined, = DECISIVE 2. **M18.**

A. ALISON He found them vacillating, he left them decided. P. LARKIN She drove them along in an ungainly but decided way.

2 Settled, certain; distinct, pronounced, noticeable; (of an opinion etc.) clearly formed, definite. Cf. DECISIVE 3. **M18.**

C. DARWIN Habit also has a decided influence. S. UNWIN He . . had decided views about the husbands his daughters ought to accept.

■ **decidedly** *adverb* (*a*) definitely, in a manner that precludes all doubt; (*b*) resolutely, unwaveringly: **L18.** **decidedness** *noun* **E19.**

decider /dɪˈsʌɪdə/ *noun.* **L16.**
[ORIGIN from DECIDE + -ER[1].]
1 A person who or thing which decides a dispute, question, etc. **L16.**
2 *spec.* A final match, race, etc., in a series, which will decide the outcome. **L19.**

decidua /dɪˈsɪdjʊə/ *noun.* **L18.**
[ORIGIN mod. Latin *decidua* (sc. *membrana*), use as noun of fem. sing. of Latin *deciduus* DECIDUOUS: so called as being discarded at parturition.]
ANATOMY. The thick layer of modified endometrium which lines the uterus during pregnancy in certain mammals, including humans.
■ **decidual** *adjective* of or pertaining to the decidua **M19.** **deciduate** *adjective* possessing a decidua; of the nature of a decidua: **M19.**

deciduoma /dɪˌsɪdjʊˈəʊmə/ *noun.* Pl. **-mas**, **-mata** /-mətə/. **L19.**
[ORIGIN from DECIDUA + -OMA.]
MEDICINE. An intrauterine tumour composed of retained decidual tissue.
†**deciduoma malignum** [Latin = malignant] = *chorion-epithelioma* s.v. CHORION.

deciduous /dɪˈsɪdjʊəs/ *adjective.* **M17.**
[ORIGIN from Latin *deciduus*, from *decidere* fall down or off, from *de-* DE- 1 + *cadere* fall: see -UOUS.]
†**1** Falling down; sinking. *rare.* **M17–L18.**
2 Of the leaves of a tree or shrub: shed each year at the end of the period of growth. Of a tree or shrub: that sheds its leaves in this way. Opp. EVERGREEN *adjective* 1. **L17.**
3 *gen.* Of a part of a plant or animal: normally discarded at a particular time or stage of growth (opp. PERSISTENT); (of an insect) that sheds its wings after copulation. **L17.** ▸**b** = DECIDUAL. **E19.**

T. PENNANT Upright branched horns, annually deciduous.

deciduous tooth = *milk tooth* s.v. MILK *noun*.
4 *fig.* Transitory, fleeting. **E19.**
■ **deciduously** *adverb* **M19.** **deciduousness** *noun* **E18.**

decile /ˈdɛsʌɪl/ *noun & adjective.* **L17.**
[ORIGIN Corresp. to French *décile*, prob. from medieval Latin deriv. of Latin *decem* ten. Cf. French *sextil* SEXTILE, -ILE.]
1 *adjective & noun.* ASTROLOGY. (Designating) the aspect of two planets which are one-tenth of a circle (36 degrees) apart in the sky. **L17.**
2 *noun.* STATISTICS. Each of the nine values of a variate which divide a frequency distribution into ten equal groups; each of the ten groups thus formed. **L19.**

decillion /dɪˈsɪljən/ *noun.* **L18.**
[ORIGIN from DECI- after *million*, *billion*, etc.]
Orig. (esp. in the UK), the tenth power of a million (10^{60}). Now usu. (orig. *US*), the eleventh power of a thousand (10^{33}). Also *loosely*, an enormous number.
■ **decillionth** *adjective & noun* **M19.**

decima /ˈdɛsɪmə/ *noun. rare.* **M17.**
[ORIGIN Latin, for *decima pars* tenth part.]
A tenth part; a tax of one-tenth, a tithe.

decimal /ˈdɛsɪm(ə)l/ *adjective & noun.* **E17.**
[ORIGIN mod. Latin *decimalis*, from Latin *decimus* tenth, from *decem* ten: see -AL[1].]
▸ **A** *adjective.* **1** Relating to tenth parts or to the number ten; reckoning or proceeding by tens or tenths. **E17.**
2 Designating, of, or pertaining to a system of coinage or currency, weights and measures, etc., in which the smaller units are related to the principal units as powers of ten. **M19.**
go decimal adopt decimal currency.
– SPECIAL COLLOCATIONS: **decimal arithmetic** (*a*) arithmetic in which arabic numerals are used; (*b*) the arithmetic of decimal fractions. **decimal classification** a library classification using numbers decimally arranged for its notation; *spec.* the Dewey system. **decimal fraction** a fraction in which the denominator (not expressed) is a power of ten and the numerator appears as a series of figures written after a decimal point, which according to their position represent tenths, hundredths, etc. **decimal place** the position of a digit to the right of the decimal point. **decimal point** a dot before the numerator in a decimal fraction. **decimal system** (*a*) the numerical system based on 10, in which numbers are expressed by the digits 0 to 9; (*b*) a system of weights, measures, etc., in which each denomination is 10 times the one before it; (*c*) = *decimal classification* above.
▸ **B** *noun.* A decimal fraction; in *pl.* freq., the arithmetic of such fractions. **M17.**
recurring decimal: see RECUR *verb*.
■ **decimalism** *noun* a decimal system or theory **M19.** **decimalist** *noun* an advocate of a decimal system of coinage or currency, weights and measures, etc. **M19.** **decimally** *adverb* by tens or tenths; into tenths; as a decimal: **L17.**

decimalize /ˈdɛsɪm(ə)lʌɪz/ *verb trans.* Also **-ise**. **M19.**
[ORIGIN from DECIMAL + -IZE.]
Express as a decimal; convert to a decimal system (of coinage or currency, weights and measures, etc.).
■ **decimaliˈzation** *noun* **M19.**

decimate /ˈdɛsɪmeɪt/ *verb trans.* **L16.**
[ORIGIN Latin *decimat-* pa. ppl stem of *decimare*, from *decimus*: see DECIMAL, -ATE[3].]
1 *hist.* Select by lot and execute one in every ten of, esp. as a punishment in the Roman legions. **L16.**
2 *gen.* Kill, destroy, or remove a large proportion of (orig. one in ten of); cause heavy losses or fatalities in. **M17.**

R. LEHMANN All my parents' friends, all my friends' brothers were getting killed. Our circle was decimated. V. CRONIN Plague decimated Moscow in 1771.

†**3** Subject to a tithe or tax of one-tenth. **M17–M19.**
– NOTE: The predominant modern meaning is 'kill, destroy, or remove a large proportion of'. This prob. stems from a misunderstanding of sense 1 as 'execute nine out of ten of'.
■ **decimator**, **-er** *noun* †(*a*) a person who exacts tithes; (*b*) a person who or thing which decimates a body of people, etc. **L17.**

decimation /dɛsɪˈmeɪʃ(ə)n/ *noun.* **LME.**
[ORIGIN Late Latin *decimatio(n-)*, formed as DECIMATE: see -ATION.]
1 *hist.* (The exaction or payment of) a tithe or tax of one-tenth; *esp.* the tax imposed by Cromwell on Royalists in 1655. **LME.**
2 *hist.* The selection by lot and execution of one man in every ten (see DECIMATE *verb* 1). **L16.**
3 *gen.* The killing or removal of one in ten; *loosely* destruction of a large proportion, infliction of heavy losses or fatalities. **L17.**

decimetre /ˈdɛsɪmiːtə/ *noun.* Also *-**meter**. **L18.**
[ORIGIN from DECI- + METRE *noun*[2].]
One-tenth of a metre, equal to 3.937 inches.

decimo-sexto /ˌdɛsɪməʊˈsɛkstəʊ/ *noun.* Now *rare* or *obsolete*. Pl. **-os**. **L16.**
[ORIGIN For Latin *sexto decimo* abl. sing. of *sextus decimus* sixteenth, orig. in phr. *in sexto decimo*.]
= SEXTODECIMO.

deciner *noun* var. of DECENER.

decinormal /dɛsɪˈnɔːm(ə)l/ *adjective.* **M19.**
[ORIGIN from DECI- + NORMAL *adjective*.]
CHEMISTRY. Of a solution: having a concentration one-tenth of that of a normal solution (i.e. containing one-tenth of a gram-equivalent of solute per litre of solution).

decipher /dɪˈsʌɪfə/ *verb & noun.* Also **decypher**. **E16.**
[ORIGIN from DE- 3 + CIPHER *verb*, after French *déchiffrer*.]
▸ **A** *verb trans.* †**1** Find out, discover; detect, make out. **E16–M18.**

SHAKES. *Tit. A.* You are both decipher'd . . For villains.

†**2** Reveal, make clear (by signs or actions), give the key to. **E16–L18.**

T. HOLCROFT Each man has his favorite gesture which might decypher his whole character.

3 Convert to plain text (something in cipher); decode. **M16.**
†**4** Portray, describe, delineate. **M16–M18.**

P. HOLLAND First I will discipher the medicinable vertues of trees.

†**5** Express in disguised or symbolic form. **L16–E18.**

C. COTTON I am the very man deciphered in his book under the name of Venator.

6 *transf.* & *fig.* Succeed in reading or interpreting (hieroglyphics, ill-formed or obliterated characters, etc.); discover the meaning of (something obscure or perplexing). **E17.**

N. FRYE Blake's prophecies . . may need interpretation, but not deciphering. A. BRINK The postmark was too indistinct for him to decipher.

▸ **B** *noun.* A deciphered message. **M16.**
■ **decipherable** *adjective* **E17.** **decipherer** *noun* **L16.** **decipherment** *noun* **M19.**

decision /dɪˈsɪʒ(ə)n/ *noun.* **LME.**
[ORIGIN Old French & mod. French *décision* or Latin *decisio(n-)*, from *decis-* pa. ppl stem of *decidere* DECIDE: see -ION.]
1 The action of deciding a contest, dispute, etc.; settlement, a final (formal) judgement or verdict. **LME.** ▸**b** BOXING. The awarding of a fight, in the absence of a knockout, to the boxer with the most points. **L19.**

G. B. SHAW The two umpires shall then elect a referee, whose decision shall be final. *New Society* They appealed the juvenile court decision.

b *split decision*: see SPLIT *adjective*.
2 Determined character; firmness, resolve. **L18.**

R. W. EMERSON On the English face are combined decision and nerve.

3 The action of coming to a determination or resolution with regard to any point or course of action; a resolution or conclusion arrived at. **M19.**

C. DARWIN I have not been hasty in coming to a decision. S. BELLOW A breath of relief at my decision to surrender. P. FITZGERALD Decision is torment for anyone with imagination.

– COMB.: **decision problem** MATH. & LOGIC the problem of finding a way to decide whether a formula or class of formulas is true or provable within a given system of axioms; **decision theory** MATH. & LOGIC the mathematical study of strategies for optimal decision-making between options involving different risks or expectations of gain or loss.
■ **decisional** *adjective* of or relating to (a) decision **L19.**

decisive /dɪˈsʌɪsɪv/ *adjective.* **E17.**
[ORIGIN French *décisif*, *-ive* from medieval Latin *decisivus*, from *decis-*: see DECISION, -IVE.]
1 That finally decides or determines a question, the outcome of a contest, etc.; conclusive. **E17.**

A. KOESTLER The decisive argument his friends had used to convince him. D. FRASER Midway . . one of the decisive battles of the war.

2 Unhesitating, resolute, determined; = DECIDED 1. **M18.**

J. C. POWYS The decisive gesture of a strong man showing off before a weak girl.

3 Pronounced, unmistakable; undisputed. Cf. DECIDED 2. **L18.**

L. STEPHEN A decisive superiority over its rivals. W. S. CHURCHILL A decisive electoral victory.

■ **decisively** *adverb* **M17.** **decisiveness** *noun* **E18.**

decivilize /diːˈsɪvɪlʌɪz/ *verb trans.* Also **-ise**. **M19.**
[ORIGIN from DE- 3 + CIVILIZE.]
Divest of civilization, make uncivilized.
■ **deciviliˈzation** *noun* **L19.**

deck /dɛk/ *noun*[1]. **LME.**
[ORIGIN Middle Dutch *dec* roof, covering, cloak, from Germanic base of THATCH *noun*. The Naut. sense appears to be an English development.]
▸ **I** A covering, surface, or floor.
†**1** A material, as canvas, used to form a covering, esp. on a ship; the covering itself. **LME–E18.**
2 A platform, usu. of wooden planks or metal covered with planks, extending across (part of) a ship, covering in the area below and acting as a floor for the area above. **L15.**
boat-deck, *flight deck*, *half-deck*, *hurricane deck*, *lower deck*, *main deck*, *middle deck*, *orlop deck*, *poop deck*, *promenade deck*, *quarterdeck*, *upper deck*, etc. **below deck(s)** in(to) the space under the main deck. *between decks*: see BETWEEN *adverb*. *clear the decks*: see CLEAR *verb* 8. **on deck** (*a*) not below deck; (*b*) *fig.* (orig. *US*) on hand, ready for action.
3 Any surface area used to stand or move on; a floor or platform, e.g. of a pier; a floor or compartment of a bus etc.; a platform for sunbathing. **M19.** ▸**b** The roof of a railway carriage. *US*. **M19.** ▸**c** An aeroplane wing, *esp.* a wing of a biplane. *colloq.* **M19.** ▸**d** The ground; the floor. *slang* (orig. AERONAUTICS). **E20.**

Times Multi-deck car parks with direct access to the stores. I. SHAW Randolph was sitting on the deck in front of the house. B. BAINBRIDGE When the No. 13 bus came, Ann sat on the top deck at the front.

d *hit the deck*: see HIT *verb*.
▸ **II 4** A pack of cards. Now chiefly *N. Amer.* **L16.** ▸†**b** A pile of things laid flat on each other. Only in **17.** ▸**c** A small package of narcotics. *US slang*. **E20.**
cold deck: see COLD *adjective*. *stack the deck*: see STACK *verb* 3.
5 A line or group of lines in a newspaper etc. heading differentiated from the others typographically, e.g. by size. **E20.**
6 A unit comprising the playing and recording mechanisms for sound or video tapes; a similar unit for playing records, compact discs, etc. **M20.**
cassette deck, *record deck*, *tape deck*, etc.
– COMB.: **deck beam** a strong transverse beam supporting the deck of a ship; **deck cargo**: stowed on the deck of a ship; **deckchair** an adjustable folding chair, used on passenger ships' decks and elsewhere; **deck class** a grade of accommodation on a ship entitling a passenger to deck space only; **deckhand** a person employed on the deck of a ship to clean, do odd jobs, etc.; **deckhead** the underside of the deck of a ship; **deckhouse** a room erected on the deck of a ship; **deck passenger** a passenger on a ship who has no cabin; **deck quoits** a game played, chiefly on ships, by throwing a rope quoit over a peg; **deck shoe** a flat canvas or leather shoe with a rubber sole, orig. intended to be worn on the deck of a ship; **deck tennis** a game played, esp. on ships, by tossing a quoit etc. to and fro over a net.

deck /dɛk/ *noun*². *colloq.* (orig. *Indian*). **M19.**
[**ORIGIN** Hindi *dekh* familiar imper. of *dekhnā* see, look at.]
= DEKKO *noun*.

deck /dɛk/ *verb trans.* **LME.**
[**ORIGIN** Middle Dutch & mod. Dutch *dekken* cover = Old English *þeććan* cover, roof over, THATCH *verb*, or from DECK *noun*¹.]
†**1** Cover, clothe; fit out, equip. **LME–M17.**
2 Cover or clothe in a rich or ornamental style; array, adorn. Freq. foll. by *out*. **E16.**

J. CLARE Daisies deck the green. A. MOOREHEAD Houses . . decked with garlands and flowers. E. REVELEY Here he was all decked out in . . his Super-suede jacket, his silk shirt and Countess Mara tie.

3 Provide with a deck; cover (as) with a deck. **E17.**

R. GRAVES Fast . . galleys, all decked in as a protection to the oarsmen.

4 Knock to the ground, floor. Chiefly *N. Amer., Austral., & NZ.* **M20.**

Y. BOLAND Belle decked him for trying to stop her from driving home under the influence.

decked /ˈdɛkt/ *adjective*. **L15.**
[**ORIGIN** from DECK *verb*, *noun*¹: see -ED¹, -ED².]
1 Arrayed, adorned; that has been decked out. **L15.**
2 Having a deck or decks; *esp.* as 2nd elem. of comb., having a specified number or kind of decks. **M18.**
double-decked, ***single-decked***, ***three-decked***, ***two-decked***, etc.

decker /ˈdɛkə/ *noun*¹. **M16.**
[**ORIGIN** from DECK *verb* + -ER¹.]
A person who arrays, adorns, or decks out someone or something.

decker /ˈdɛkə/ *noun*² *& adjective*. **L18.**
[**ORIGIN** from DECK *noun*¹ + -ER¹.]
1 *noun & adjective*. As 2nd elem. of comb.: (a ship, bus, etc.) having a specified number or kind of decks or layers. **L18.**
double-decker, ***single-decker***, etc. (*bus, ship*, etc.). ***flush-decker***, ***three-decker***, ***two-decker***, etc. (*ship* etc.).
2 *noun*. A deckhand; a deck passenger. *nautical slang*. **E19.**

deckie /ˈdɛki/ *noun*. *nautical slang*. Also **-y**. **E20.**
[**ORIGIN** from DECK *noun*¹ + -IE, -Y⁶.]
A deckhand.

decking /ˈdɛkɪŋ/ *noun*. **M16.**
[**ORIGIN** from DECK *verb*, *noun*¹ + -ING¹.]
1 The action of DECK *verb*; adornment, ornamentation. **M16.**
2 The material of the deck(s) of a ship etc. **L16.**

deckle /ˈdɛk(ə)l/ *noun*. **M18.**
[**ORIGIN** German *Deckel* dim. of *Decke* covering; cf. -LE¹.]
PAPER-MAKING. A device which confines the pulp and so limits the size of a sheet of paper, consisting of either a frame on the mould used in hand paper-making, or (in full ***deckle strap***) a continuous belt on either side of the wire on a machine.
– COMB.: **deckle edge** the rough uncut edge of a sheet of paper, formed by the deckle; **deckle-edged** *adjective* having a deckle edge, as handmade paper; ***deckle strap***: see above.
■ **deckled** *adjective* formed by a deckle; deckle-edged: **E20.**

decky *noun* var. of DECKIE.

declaim /dɪˈkleɪm/ *verb*. **LME.**
[**ORIGIN** French *déclamer* or Latin *declamare*, from *de-* DE- 1 + *clamare* CLAIM *verb*.]
1 *verb intrans. & trans.* Speak aloud or recite with studied rhetorical expression; practise speaking or reciting (a passage). **LME.**

R. W. EMERSON Wordsworth . . reciting to me . . like a schoolboy declaiming. E. F. BENSON Declaiming a particularly unchristian psalm which called down many curses on her enemies.

2 *verb intrans.* Deliver an impassioned (rather than reasoned) speech; inveigh *against*. **L16.**

L. STERNE Let him declaim as pompously as he chooses upon the subject. R. L. STEVENSON Declaiming . . against the greed and dishonesty of landlords.

■ **declaimer** *noun* **LME.**

declamation /dɛkləˈmeɪʃ(ə)n/ *noun*. **LME.**
[**ORIGIN** French *déclamation* or Latin *declamatio(n-)*, from *declamat-* pa. ppl stem of *declamare*: see DECLAIM, -ATION.]
1 A rhetorical exercise or address; a set speech. **LME.**
2 The action or art of speaking or reciting with studied rhetorical emphasis. **M16.**
3 An impassioned or emotional speech; a harangue. **L16.**
4 Speaking in an impassioned manner; emotional denunciation. **E17.**

†**declamator** *noun*. **LME–E18.**
[**ORIGIN** Latin, from *declamat-*: see DECLAMATION, -OR.]
A declaimer.

declamatory /dɪˈklamət(ə)ri/ *adjective*. **L16.**
[**ORIGIN** Latin *declamatorius*, formed as DECLAMATOR: see -ORY².]
Of or pertaining to rhetorical declaiming; of the nature of or characterized by declamation.
■ **declamatorily** *adverb* **L19.** **declamatoriness** *noun* **M19.**

declarable /dɪˈklɛːrəb(ə)l/ *adjective*. **M17.**
[**ORIGIN** from DECLARE + -ABLE.]
Able to be declared.

declarant /dɪˈklɛːr(ə)nt/ *noun*. **L17.**
[**ORIGIN** French *déclarant* pres. pple of *déclarer* DECLARE: see -ANT¹.]
Chiefly *LAW*. A person who makes a declaration.

declaration /dɛkləˈreɪʃ(ə)n/ *noun*. **LME.**
[**ORIGIN** Latin *declaratio(n-)*, from *declarat-* pa. ppl stem of *declarare* DECLARE: see -ATION.]
†**1** The action of explaining or making clear; elucidation. **LME–M17.**
2 †**a** The setting forth of a topic; exposition. **LME–M17.** ▸**b** *spec.* A statement or confession of love; a proposal of marriage. *arch.* **M18.**
3 The action of setting forth, stating, or announcing publicly, formally, or explicitly; a positive statement, an emphatic or solemn assertion. **LME.**

HOBBES If he dye . . without declaration of his Heyre. J. AUSTEN Marianne's declaration that the day would be lastingly fair.

4 A proclamation or formal public statement, usu. embodied in a document, public act, etc. **LME.**

LYNDON B. JOHNSON We sought widespread support for a declaration affirming the right of innocent passage through the Gulf of Aqaba.

Declaration of Independence (the document embodying) the public act by which the American Continental Congress, on 4 July 1776, declared the N. American colonies to be free and independent of Great Britain. ***Declaration of Indulgence***: see INDULGENCE *noun*. **declaration of peace** a formal proclamation announcing the end of hostilities. ***Declaration of Rights***: see RIGHT *noun*¹. **declaration of the poll** the public official announcement of the numbers of votes for each candidate in an election. **declaration of war** a formal proclamation by one state announcing the commencement of hostilities against another.

5 *LAW*. A formal affirmation or statement, usu. made in writing; *esp.* (***a***) an affirmation made in lieu of an oath; (***b***) a formal statement of a party's rights made by a court, esp. in cases involving the government or other public agency and in cases involving personal (e.g. marital) status. **L15.**
6 *CARDS*. An announcement of a score, combination held, trump suit, etc.; *spec.* in *BRIDGE*, the final bid of the auction, nominating the contract. **M19.**
7 *CRICKET*. The voluntary closing of an innings by the team batting. **E20.**
8 *COMPUTING*. A definition of a data item etc. to be used in a program. **M20.**

declarative /dɪˈklarətɪv/ *noun & adjective*. **LME.**
[**ORIGIN** Old French & mod. French *déclaratif*, *-ive* or Latin *declarativus* adjective, from *declarat-*: see DECLARATION, -ATIVE.]
▸ **A** *noun*. A declaratory statement, or act; a declarative sentence. **LME.**
▸ **B** *adjective*. †**1** Making clear or evident; (of a person) forthcoming. **M16–L18.**
2 Characterized by making a declaration; of the nature of a declaration; *GRAMMAR* (of a sentence) that takes the form of a simple statement. **E17.**
3 *COMPUTING*. Designating high-level programming languages of a kind that can be used to solve problems without requiring the programmer to specify an exact procedure to be followed. **L20.**
■ **declaratively** *adverb* **E17.**

declarator /dɪˈklarətə/ *noun*. **E16.**
[**ORIGIN** Repr. French *déclaratoire* adjective, formed as DECLARATORY.]
SCOTS LAW. An action whereby a legal right or status is declared, but nothing further is done. Also more fully ***action of declarator***.

declaratory /dɪˈklarət(ə)ri/ *adjective & noun*. **LME.**
[**ORIGIN** medieval Latin *declaratorius*, from Latin *declarator* declarer, from *declarat-*: see DECLARATION, -ORY².]
▸ **A** *adjective*. Having the nature or form of a declaration; explanatory; affirmatory; (of a statute etc.) that explains what the existing law is. **LME.**
▸ †**B** *noun*. A declaration, an explanation. **LME–L17.**

declare /dɪˈklɛː/ *verb*. **ME.**
[**ORIGIN** Latin *declarare* make clear, from *de-* DE- 1 + *clarare*, from *clarus* clear. Cf. French *déclarer*.]
†**1 a** *verb trans. & intrans.* with *of*. Relate, recount (facts, a matter, etc.); tell of. **ME–E18.** ▸**b** *verb trans.* Explain, make clear, elucidate. **LME–L17.**
2 *verb trans.* Make known or state publicly, formally, or explicitly; affirm, assert; proclaim; (in weakened sense) say, announce. **ME.** ▸**b** With compl.: proclaim or assert (a person etc.) to be (something). **M16.**

E. BOWEN Lewis declared it was hot . . and went out to order Edward a drink. K. VONNEGUT The charter . . declared . . that the presidency . . was to be inherited. **b** G. F. KENNAN Men . . who had been declared physically unfit for service.

declare war formally announce the commencement of hostilities (*on, against*). **well, I declare**, **well, I do declare** *colloq.*: expr. incredulity, surprise, or vexation.

3 *verb refl.* Make known one's opinions, intentions, etc.; reveal one's (or *fig.* its own) true nature, identity, etc.; (with compl.) reveal oneself to be. **LME.** ▸**b** *verb refl. & intrans.* Announce oneself to be *against, for, in favour of*, etc., a person, action, etc. **M17.** ▸†**c** *verb intrans.* Announce oneself to be a candidate *for*, make a bid *for*. **M17–M18.** ▸**d** *verb refl.* Confess one's love, propose marriage, (*to*). *arch.* **M19.**

J. CONRAD His vocation for the sea had declared itself. LYNDON B. JOHNSON Wallace . . had declared himself a candidate for President. **d** M. E. BRADDON He must either declare himself, or . . go away.

4 *verb trans.* Of a thing: manifest, show, prove. (Passing into *fig.* use of sense 2.) **LME.**

SIR W. SCOTT Nor track nor pathway might declare That human foot frequented there.

5 *verb intrans.* Make a legal declaration (see DECLARATION 5). **E16.**
6 *verb trans.* Acknowledge by legal or formal statement; *spec.* acknowledge possession of (goods liable to duty, taxable income, etc.). **L17.**

A. LOOS I put the unset diamonds in my handbag so I did not have to declare them at the customs.

7 *verb intrans.* Foll. by *off*: break off an engagement, practice, etc.; back out, withdraw. *arch. colloq.* **M18.**
8 *verb intrans. & trans. HORSE-RACING*. Withdraw from a race. **M19.**
9 *verb trans. CARDS*. Announce or nominate by a declaration (see DECLARATION 6). **M19.**
10 *verb trans. & intrans. CRICKET*. Close (an innings) voluntarily before the usual ten wickets have fallen. **L19.**
■ **declared** *ppl adjective* that has been declared; avowed, made known; (of a person) admitted, professed: **LME.** **declaredly** /-rɪdli/ *adverb* professedly, avowedly **M17.** **declarer** *noun* a person who or thing which declares; *spec.* in *BRIDGE*, the player who first bids the suit of the contract and who therefore plays both his or her own and the exposed hands: **LME.**

declass /diːˈklɑːs/ *verb trans.* **L19.**
[**ORIGIN** French *déclasser*, from *dé-* DE- 3 + *classer* CLASS *verb*: cf. DÉCLASSÉ.]
Remove or degrade from one's class.

déclassé /deɪˈklaseɪ, *foreign* deklase (*pl. same*)/ *adjective & noun*. Fem. **-ée**. **L19.**
[**ORIGIN** French, pa. pple of *déclasser*: see DECLASS.]
(A person who is) reduced or degraded in social class or status.

declassify /diːˈklasɪfʌɪ/ *verb trans.* **M19.**
[**ORIGIN** from DE- 3 + CLASSIFY.]
Remove from a classification; *spec.* cease to designate (information etc.) as secret.
■ **declassifiable** *adjective* **M20.** **declassifiˈcation** *noun* **M20.**

declaw /diːˈklɔː/ *verb trans.* **M20.**
[**ORIGIN** from DE- + CLAW *noun*.]
Remove the claws from (an animal, esp. a cat); *fig.* make harmless or less threatening.

declension /dɪˈklɛnʃ(ə)n/ *noun*. **LME.**
[**ORIGIN** Old French & mod. French *déclinaison*, from *décliner* DECLINE *verb*, alt. after Latin *declinatio(n-)* DECLINATION.]
1 *GRAMMAR*. The variation of form or inflection of a noun, adjective, or pronoun so as to constitute its different cases, numbers, and genders; each of the classes into which nouns are divided on the basis of these forms or inflections; the action of declining or of setting out in order the different forms of a noun etc. **LME.**
2 Inclination from the vertical or horizontal position. Now only *fig.*, moral deviation, falling away from a standard etc., apostasy. Now *arch.* or *literary*. **L16.**
3 Deterioration, decay; a condition of decline. Now *arch.* or *literary*. **E17.**
4 The action of declining or refusing politely. *rare*. **E19.**
■ **declensional** *adjective* of or belonging to (grammatical) declension **M19.**

de Clerambault's syndrome /də ˈklɛrəmbəʊz ˌsɪndrəʊm/ *noun phr.* **M20.**
[**ORIGIN** from the name of the French psychiatrist Gatin *de Clérambault* (1872–1934), who first described the syndrome in 1921.]
A delusion in which a person (usu. a woman) believes that another person (esp. one of higher social or professional status) is in love with them; erotomania.

declericalize /diːˈklɛrɪk(ə)lʌɪz/ *verb trans.* Also **-ise**. **L19.**
[**ORIGIN** from DE- 3 + CLERICAL + -IZE.]
Free from clerical influence or character.
■ **declericaliˈzation** *noun* **L19.**

declinable /dɪˈklʌɪnəb(ə)l/ *adjective*. **LME.**
[**ORIGIN** Old French & mod. French *déclinable* or late Latin *declinabilis*, from *declinare* DECLINE *verb*: see -ABLE.]
†**1** Liable to deteriorate. Only in **LME.**
2 *GRAMMAR*. Able to be declined; having inflections for case, number, or gender. **M16.**

declinate /ˈdɛklɪnət/ *adjective*. **E19.**
[**ORIGIN** Latin *declinatus* pa. pple of *declinare* DECLINE *verb*: see -ATE².]
BOTANY. Inclined forwards or downwards.
■ Also †**declinated** *adjective*: only in **M18.**

declination /dɛklɪˈneɪʃ(ə)n/ *noun*. **LME.**
[**ORIGIN** Latin *declinatio(n-)*, from *declinat-* pa. ppl stem of *declinare* DECLINE *verb*: see -ATION.]
1 Inclination from the vertical or horizontal position; downward bend or turn. **LME.** ▸†**b** Turning aside, (moral) deviation, falling away from a standard etc. **M16–E19.**

†**2** Sinking, descent; *fig.* deterioration, decline, decay. LME–L18.
†**3** GRAMMAR. = DECLENSION 1. LME–M18.
4 **a** ASTRONOMY. Angular distance from the celestial equator (corresp. to terrestrial latitude). LME. ▸†**b** SURVEYING. The deviation of a given vertical plane from the prime vertical or from the meridian. L16–M18. ▸**c** The angular deviation of a compass needle, orig. from the horizontal (= DIP *noun* 3), now from the true north and south line. Cf. VARIATION 8. M17.
5 Non-acceptance; polite refusal. Now *US*. E17.
– COMB.: **declination axis** the axis of an equatorial telescope which is at right angles to the polar axis and about which the telescope is turned in order to alter the declination of the object being viewed; **declination circle** a graduated circle on an equatorial telescope, on which declination is marked.
■ **declinational** *adjective* L19.

†**declinator** *adjective & noun*. L15–E19.
[ORIGIN medieval Latin *declinatorius*: see DECLINATORY, -OR. Cf. DECLINATURE.]
SCOTS LAW. (Constituting, in ***exception declinator***) a declinature.

declinatory /dɪˈklʌɪnət(ə)ri/ *adjective & noun*. L17.
[ORIGIN medieval Latin *declinatorius*, from *declinat-*: see DECLINATION, -ORY². Cf. Old French & mod. French *déclinatoire*.]
▸ **A** *adjective*. Expressing refusal. Chiefly LAW (now *hist.*), designating a plea claiming exemption from the court's jurisdiction. L17.
▸ **B** *noun*. A declinatory plea. Now *hist.* L17.

declinature /dɪˈklʌɪnətjʊə/ *noun*. M17.
[ORIGIN Alt. of DECLINATOR: see -URE.]
1 SCOTS LAW. A formal refusal to admit the jurisdiction of a judge or court; refusal of a judge to accept jurisdiction in a case. M17.
2 Courteous refusal. M19.

decline /dɪˈklʌɪn/ *noun*. ME.
[ORIGIN from (the same root as) the verb. Cf. Old French & mod. French *déclin*.]
1 The process of declining or sinking; (a) gradual loss of vigour or excellence; falling off, decay, diminution, deterioration. ME. ▸**b** A wasting disease, *esp.* tuberculosis. *arch.* L18. ▸**c** A fall in price or value. L19.

J. ROSENBERG It is only in the . . year of Rembrandt's death that we detect some decline in the artist's expressive power. J. G. FARRELL The Turf, which had fallen into a decline in recent years had revived wonderfully.

on the decline in a declining state.
2 The sinking of the sun towards its setting; the latter part of the course of the day, life, etc. LME.

STEELE A Gentleman who according to his Years should be in the Decline of his Life.

3 A downward incline, a slope. *rare*. M16.

decline /dɪˈklʌɪn/ *verb*. LME.
[ORIGIN Old French & mod. French *décliner* from Latin *declinare*, from *de-* DE- 1 + *clinare* to bend.]
▸ **I** *verb intrans.* †**1** Turn aside; deviate; turn away. LME–M19.
†**2** Have astronomical or magnetic declination. LME–E18.
†**3** *fig.* Turn aside in conduct; fall away *from* rectitude, duty, etc. LME–M18.

AV *Ps.* 119:157 Yet doe I not decline from thy testimonies.

†**4** *fig.* Lean or incline *to*. LME–L17.

P. HOLLAND That purple luster . . declineth . . to the color of wine.

5 Slope downwards. LME.

E. J. HOWARD The sloping lawn declined from the house.

6 Bend down, bow down, droop. LME.

T. HARDY Declining from his sitting position.

†**7** Descend. *rare*. LME–E17.
8 Of the sun etc.: descend towards setting. Of the day, one's life, etc.: draw towards its close. LME.

R. WOODHOUSE As the Moon, having passed the meridian, declines.

9 Fall off in vigour or vitality; decay, diminish; deteriorate. LME.

R. L. STEVENSON England has already declined, since she has lost the States. J. CONRAD His voice declined to a mere sleepy murmur. H. A. L. FISHER The government which began in a blaze of glory steadily declined in strength.

declining years old age.
10 Fall morally or in dignity. Now only *literary* (after Shakes.). LME.

SHAKES. *Haml.* What a falling off was there, from me . . to decline Upon a wretch whose natural gifts were poor To those of mine.

11 (Politely) refuse an invitation, offer, request, etc. (Cf. sense 13b below.) L19.

JOYCE She pressed me to take some cream crackers . . but I declined.

▸ **II** *verb trans.* †**12** Avert; deflect, turn aside (*from*, *to*). LME–M18.

S. JOHNSON To decline the pressure of resistless arguments.

13 †**a** Turn aside from; avoid, shun. LME–M18. ▸**b** Turn away from out of unwillingness; not consent to engage in or practise, not agree to *doing*; refuse, esp. politely (an invitation, request, offer, etc., or *to do*). M17. ▸**c** Give up (a practice). Long *rare*. L17. ▸**d** CHESS. Refuse to take a piece or pawn offered in (a gambit). M19.

b T. JEFFERSON I decline all newspaper controversy. CARLYLE I declined satisfying his curiosity. A. CARNEGIE He declined an interest in the firm which would have made him a millionaire. P. G. WODEHOUSE I decline to give in to this absurd suggestion. A. GUINNESS She . . offered me a glass of sherry, which I declined.

b decline with thanks refuse graciously; *iron.* reject scornfully.
14 SCOTS LAW. Refuse or formally object to the jurisdiction of (a judge or court). LME.
15 GRAMMAR. Inflect (a noun, adjective, or pronoun) through any different cases, numbers, or genders; recite the cases etc. of in order; *loosely* conjugate. LME. ▸†**b** Recite formally or in a definite order. L16–E17.
16 Bend down, bow down. LME.

SOUTHEY He sate with folded arms and head declined Upon his breast.

†**17** Lower, degrade. LME–L18.
†**18** Undervalue, disparage. E16–M17.
19 Cause to slope downwards, incline. L16.
■ **decliner** *noun* a person who or thing which declines E17.

declinometer /dɛklɪˈnɒmɪtə/ *noun*. M19.
[ORIGIN from DECLINATION + -OMETER.]
An instrument for measuring astronomical or magnetic declination.

declive /dɪˈklʌɪv/ *noun*. L19.
[ORIGIN formed as DECLIVE *adjective*.]
ANATOMY. An area of the upper surface of the vermis of the cerebellum posterior to the culmen.

declive /dɪˈklʌɪv/ *adjective*. Long *rare* or *obsolete*. M17.
[ORIGIN French *déclive* from Latin *declivis* sloping downward, from *de-* DE- 1 + *clivus* slope.]
Sloping downwards.

declivitous /dɪˈklɪvɪtəs/ *adjective*. L18.
[ORIGIN from DECLIVITY + -OUS.]
Having a (considerable) declivity; steep.
■ **declivitously** *adverb* L19.

declivity /dɪˈklɪvɪti/ *noun*. E17.
[ORIGIN Latin *declivitas*, from *declivis* sloping down: see DECLIVE *adjective*, -ITY.]
1 Downward slope, inclination. E17.
2 A downward slope, sloping ground. L17.

declivous /dɪˈklʌɪvəs/ *adjective*. L17.
[ORIGIN from Latin *declivus* rare var. of *declivis*: see DECLIVE *adjective*, -OUS.]
Sloping downwards, slanting.

declutch /diːˈklʌtʃ/ *verb intrans.* E20.
[ORIGIN from DE- 3 + CLUTCH *noun*¹.]
Disengage the clutch of a motor vehicle.
double-declutch: see DOUBLE *adjective & adverb*.

declutter /diːˈklʌtə/ *verb trans.* M20.
[ORIGIN from DE- 3 + CLUTTER *verb*.]
Remove superfluous or unnecessary articles from (a thing, esp. a house).

Independent There's no better time to declutter the home than the . . New Year.

deco /ˈdɛkəʊ/ *noun*. M20.
[ORIGIN Abbreviation of French (*art*) *décoratif* decorative (art).]
In full ***art deco***. A decorative artistic style of the 1920s and 1930s, characterized by modernist and streamlined design.

decoct /dɪˈkɒkt/ *verb trans.* Pa. pple **-ed**, (earlier) †**decoct**. LME.
[ORIGIN Latin *decoct-* pa. ppl stem of *decoquere* boil down, from *de-* DE- 1 + *coquere* COOK *verb*.]
†**1** Prepare (food) by boiling, cook; heat up as in cooking. LME–M17.
†**2** Mature or prepare (a mineral, metal) by heat (according to old notions). L15–M17.
3 Boil in water etc. so as to concentrate or to extract the essence of; prepare a decoction of. M16.
†**4** Boil down, concentrate; *fig.* consume. M16–L17.
†**5** Digest in the stomach. M16–E17.

decoction /dɪˈkɒkʃ(ə)n/ *noun*. LME.
[ORIGIN Old French & mod. French *décoction* or late Latin *decoctio(n-)*, formed as DECOCT: see -ION.]
1 Concentration of, or extraction of the essence of, a substance by boiling in water etc. LME.

T. THOMSON Catechu . . is . . obtained by decoction and evaporation from a species of mimosa.

2 A liquid essence made by boiling; an (esp. medicinal) extract. LME.

G. BERKELEY A decoction of briar-roots for the bloody flux.

†**3** Maturation or preparation of a mineral or ore by heat (according to old notions). LME–L17.
†**4** Digestion of food. M16–M17.
†**5** Reduction, boiling down, (*lit. & fig.*). L16–M17.

decode /diːˈkəʊd/ *verb trans.* L19.
[ORIGIN from DE- 3 + CODE *noun* or *verb*.]
Decipher, interpret, translate (a coded message); analyse (a coded audio etc. signal).
■ **decoder** *noun* a person who or thing which decodes; *spec.* a device for analysing stereophonic signals and feeding separate amplifier channels: E20.

decohere /diːkə(ʊ)ˈhɪə/ *verb trans. & intrans.* *obsolete* exc. *hist.* E20.
[ORIGIN from DE- 3 + COHERE.]
ELECTRONICS. Restore (a coherer), be restored, to its normal condition of sensitivity.
■ **decoherer** *noun* a device for decohering a coherer L19.

decoke /diːˈkəʊk/, *as* noun *freq.* ˈdiːkəʊk/ *verb & noun*. *colloq.* E20.
[ORIGIN from DE- 3 + COKE *noun*¹.]
▸ **A** *verb trans.* Decarbonize (an internal-combustion engine). E20.
▸ **B** *noun*. The action of decarbonizing an engine. M20.

decollate /dɪˈkɒleɪt, ˈdɛkəleɪt/ *verb*¹ *trans.* Pa. pple **-ated**, (earlier, long *arch. rare*) **-ate** /-ət/. LME.
[ORIGIN Orig. pa. pple, from Latin *decollatus* pa. pple of *decollare* behead, from *de-* DE- 3 + *collum* neck: see -ATE³.]
1 Behead. LME.
2 CONCHOLOGY. In *pass.* of a shell: be broken off near the apex. Freq. as ***decollated*** *pa. ppl adjective*. M19.
■ **decollator** *noun*¹ a person who or thing which decollates; a decapitator: M19.

decollate /diːkəˈleɪt/ *verb*² *trans. & intrans.* M20.
[ORIGIN from DE- 3 + COLLATE.]
Separate (sheets of paper, esp. of continuous stationery) mechanically into different piles.
■ **decollator** *noun*² a machine for decollating stationery L20.

decollation /dɪkəˈleɪʃ(ə)n/ *noun*. LME.
[ORIGIN Old French & mod. French *décollation* or late Latin *decollatio(n-)*, from *decollat-*: see DECOLLATE *verb*¹, -ATION.]
The action of beheading; the state of being beheaded; truncation; SURGERY severance of the head of a fetus.

décollement /deɪˈkɒlmɔ̃, *foreign* dekɔlmɑ̃/ *noun*. M19.
[ORIGIN French, from *décoller* unstick, disengage: see -MENT.]
1 MEDICINE. The process of separating organs or tissues from surrounding parts; the state of being thus separated. M19.
2 GEOLOGY. The sliding (and subsequent deformation) of strata over those beneath; a boundary separating deformed strata from underlying strata which are not (similarly) deformed. E20.

décolletage /ˌdeɪkɒlɪˈtɑːʒ, deɪˈkɒltɑːʒ, *foreign* dekɔltaːʒ/ *noun*. L19.
[ORIGIN French, from *décolleter*: see DÉCOLLETÉ, -AGE.]
The low-cut neckline of a woman's garment. Also, exposure of the neck and shoulders by such a neckline.

décolleté /deɪˈkɒlteɪ, *foreign* dekɔlte/ *adjective*. Also **-ée**. M19.
[ORIGIN French (fem. *-ée*), from *décolleter* expose the neck, from *dé-* DE- 3 + *collet* collar of a dress etc.]
Of a (woman's) garment: having a low-cut neckline. Of a woman: wearing a low-necked garment. Also *fig.*, daring, slightly improper.

Listener Her décolleté dresses and décolleté past.

decolonization /ˌdiːkɒlənʌɪˈzeɪʃ(ə)n/ *noun*. Also **-isation**. M20.
[ORIGIN from DE- 3 + COLONIZATION.]
The withdrawal of a state from its former colonies, leaving them independent; the acquisition of independence by a former colony.

decolor *verb*, **decolorant** *noun & adjective* see DECOLOUR, DECOLOURANT.

decoloration /diːˌkʌləˈreɪʃ(ə)n, ˌdiːkʌl-/ *noun*. Also **-lour-**. E17.
[ORIGIN French *décoloration* from Latin *decoloratio(n-)*, from *decolorat-* pa. ppl stem of *decolorare* DECOLOUR: see -ATION.]
†**1** Discoloration, staining. E17–E18.
2 Loss or removal of colour, decolorizing. M17.

decolorize /diːˈkʌlərʌɪz/ *verb*. Also **-colour-**; **-ise**. M19.
[ORIGIN from DE- 3 + COLORIZE.]
1 *verb trans.* Remove colour from, make colourless or pale. M19.
2 *verb intrans.* Lose colour, become colourless or pale. E20.
■ **decoloriˈzation** *noun* M19.

decolour /diːˈkʌlə/ *verb trans.* Also ***-or**. LME.
[ORIGIN French *décolorer* or Latin *decolorare*, from *de-* DE- 3 + *colorare* to colour.]
†**1** Discolour, stain. LME–M17.
2 = DECOLORIZE 1. M19.

decolourant /diːˈkʌlər(ə)nt/ *noun & adjective*. Also ***-lor-**. M19.
[ORIGIN French *décolorant*, from *décolorer*: see DECOLOUR, -ANT¹.]
▸ **A** *noun*. A decolorizing agent. M19.
▸ **B** *adjective*. Able to decolorize, decolorizing. L19.

decolouration *noun* var. of DECOLORATION.

D

decommission /diːkəˈmɪʃ(ə)n/ *verb trans.* E20.
[ORIGIN from DE- 3 + COMMISSION *verb*.]
Take (a ship, installation, etc.) out of service.

decommunize /diːˈkɒmjʊnʌɪz/ *verb trans.* Also **-ise**. L20.
[ORIGIN from DE- 3 + COMMUNIZE.]
Remove the features of Communism from; reverse the communization of.
■ **decommuniˈzation** *noun* L20.

decompensation /ˌdiːkɒmp(ə)nˈseɪʃ(ə)n/ *noun*. E20.
[ORIGIN from DE- 3 + COMPENSATION.]
MEDICINE. (A condition of) failure of compensation (COMPENSATION 1b); *esp.* inability of the heart to maintain circulation after a period of compensation.
■ **deˈcompensated** *adjective* associated with or exhibiting decompensation M20.

decompile /diːkəmˈpʌɪl/ *verb trans.* L20.
[ORIGIN from DE- 3 + COMPILE *verb*.]
COMPUTING. Produce source code from (compiled code).
■ **decompilation** *noun* L20.

decomplement /diːˈkɒmplɪm(ə)nt/ *verb trans.* M20.
[ORIGIN from DE- 3 + COMPLEMENT *noun*.]
IMMUNOLOGY. Inactivate the complement in (blood serum, an animal).
■ **decomplemenˈtation** *noun* the process or result of inactivating serum complement M20.

decomplex /ˈdiːkɒmplɛks/ *adjective*. M18.
[ORIGIN from DE- 2 + COMPLEX *adjective*.]
Repeatedly complex; made up of complex parts.

decomposable /diːkəmˈpəʊzəb(ə)l/ *adjective*. L18.
[ORIGIN from DECOMPOSE + -ABLE.]
Able to be decomposed or separated into its constituent elements.
■ **decomposaˈbility** *noun* M19.

decompose /diːkəmˈpəʊz/ *verb*. M18.
[ORIGIN French *décomposer*, from *dé-* DE- 3 + *composer* COMPOSE.]
1 *verb trans.* Break down or separate into its component elements or simpler constituents. M18.

D. BREWSTER We have . . by absorption decomposed green light into yellow and blue.

2 *verb intrans.* Undergo (esp. chemical) decomposition; break down, decay, rot. L18.

T. H. HUXLEY Soon after death the softer parts of organized bodies begin to decompose. *fig.*: S. H. BEER Insofar as deference has collapsed, class has decomposed.

decomposible /diːkəmˈpəʊzɪb(ə)l/ *adjective*. E19.
[ORIGIN from DECOMPOSE + -IBLE.]
= DECOMPOSABLE.
■ **decomposiˈbility** *noun* L19.

decomposite /diːˈkɒmpəzɪt/ *noun & adjective*. E17.
[ORIGIN Late Latin *decompositus* (for Greek *parasunthetos*), from *de-* DE- 2 + *compositus* COMPOSITE *adjective & noun*.]
= DECOMPOUND *noun & adjective*.

decomposition /ˌdiːkɒmpəˈzɪʃ(ə)n/ *noun*. M17.
[ORIGIN Branch I formed as DECOMPOSITE + -ION; branch II from French *décomposition*, formed as DECOMPOSE + -ITION.]
► †**I 1** Compounding of things already composite, decompounding. M–L17.
► **II 2** The action or process of separating or resolving something into its component elements or simpler constituents. M18.
3 *spec.* The natural breaking down of (organic) matter into simpler substances; rotting, decay, disintegration, putrescence; decayed condition. L18.

J. LUBBOCK The bones were in such a state of decomposition, that the ribs and vertebrae crumbled into dust. *fig.*: M. MUGGERIDGE The whole decaying social structure, the stench of whose decomposition was so strongly in my nostrils.

double decomposition: see DOUBLE *adjective & adverb*.

decompound /ˈdiːkɒmpaʊnd/ *noun & adjective*. E17.
[ORIGIN from DE- 2 + COMPOUND *adjective* or *noun*[1].]
(A word, substance, etc.) made up of elements that are themselves compound; (something) repeatedly compound.

decompound /diːkəmˈpaʊnd/ *verb*. LME.
[ORIGIN from DE- 2 (sense 1), 3 (sense 2) + COMPOUND *verb*.]
1 *verb trans.* Compound further, form by adding to or combining compounds. Freq. as ***decompounded*** *ppl adjective*, consisting of compound constituents. LME.
2 *verb intrans. & trans.* Decompose. M18.

decompress /diːkəmˈprɛs/ *verb*. E20.
[ORIGIN from DE- 3 + COMPRESS *verb*.]
1 *verb trans. & intrans.* Subject to or undergo decompression. E20.
2 *verb trans.* COMPUTING. Restore (a previously compressed file or digital signal) to its original state. M20.

P. CORNWELL A graphic file had been attached, and I downloaded and decompressed it.

3 *verb intrans.* Calm down and relax. *US colloq.* M20.

P. OUELLETTE Michael . . sits for a minute to decompress before starting home.

■ **decompressive** *adjective* of, pertaining to, or producing decompression E20. **decompressor** *noun* a device for reducing compression E20.

decompression /diːkəmˈprɛʃ(ə)n/ *noun*. E20.
[ORIGIN from DE- 3 + COMPRESSION.]
1 The process of relieving or reducing pressure; *spec.* (***a***) the returning of a subject experiencing increased pressure, e.g. a deep-sea diver, to atmospheric pressure, usu. gradually under controlled conditions; (***b***) (sudden) reduction of air pressure in an aircraft etc. to the ambient external pressure; (***c***) surgical relief of excessive internal pressure in a part of the body. E20.
2 COMPUTING. The expansion or restoration of files or digital signals that have previously been compressed. M20.
– COMB.: **decompression chamber**: in which pressure can be maintained either above atmospheric, esp. in order to decompress a diver etc. gradually, or below atmospheric, e.g. to subject an organism to reduced pressure; **decompression sickness** a condition which results from too rapid decompression (and consequent formation of nitrogen bubbles in the tissues) and may involve pain in the joints (the bends (BEND *noun*[3])), numbness, nausea, paralysis, etc.

deconcentrate /diːˈkɒns(ə)ntreɪt/ *verb trans.* L19.
[ORIGIN from DE- 3 + CONCENTRATE *verb*.]
Reverse or reduce the concentration of; decentralize.
■ **deconcenˈtration** *noun* L19.

decondition /diːk(ə)nˈdɪʃ(ə)n/ *verb trans.* M20.
[ORIGIN from DE- 3 + CONDITION *verb*.]
Undo the results of conditioning in (a person, animal, etc.); remove or reverse the conditioned reflexes of.

deconflict /diːkənˈflɪkt/ *verb trans.* Orig. *US*. L20.
[ORIGIN from DE- 3 + CONFLICT *verb* or *noun*.]
MILITARY. Reduce the risk of collision in (an area) by separating the flight paths of one's own aircraft or airborne weaponry.
■ **deconfliction** *noun* L20.

decongest /diːk(ə)nˈdʒɛst/ *verb trans.* M20.
[ORIGIN Back-form. from DECONGESTION.]
Relieve the congestion of; *esp.* ease the flow of traffic etc. in or through (a place).

decongestant /diːk(ə)nˈdʒɛst(ə)nt/ *noun & adjective*. M20.
[ORIGIN from DE- 3 + CONGEST *verb* + -ANT[1].]
► **A** *noun.* A decongestive agent; *spec.* a substance which relieves nasal congestion. M20.
► **B** *adjective.* That relieves (esp. nasal) congestion. M20.

decongestion /diːk(ə)nˈdʒɛstʃ(ə)n/ *noun*. E20.
[ORIGIN from DE- 3 + CONGESTION.]
The reduction or relief of congestion.

decongestive /diːk(ə)nˈdʒɛstɪv/ *adjective*. E20.
[ORIGIN from DECONGESTION + -IVE.]
That reduces or relieves congestion.

deconsecrate /diːˈkɒnsɪkreɪt/ *verb trans.* L19.
[ORIGIN from DE- 3 + CONSECRATE *verb*.]
Undo the consecration of; transfer (a church etc.) to secular use; secularize.
■ **deconseˈcration** *noun* M19.

deconstruction /diːk(ə)nˈstrʌkʃ(ə)n/ *noun*. L19.
[ORIGIN from DE- 3 + CONSTRUCTION.]
1 The reverse of construction; taking to pieces. *rare*. L19.
2 A strategy of critical analysis of (esp. philosophical and literary) language and texts which emphasizes features exposing unquestioned assumptions and inconsistencies; a deconstructionist analysis. L20.
■ **deconstruct** *verb trans.* subject to deconstruction L19. **deconstructible** *adjective* able to be deconstructed, amenable to deconstruction L20. **deconstructionism** *noun* the theory or practice of deconstruction L20. **deconstructionist** *noun & adjective* (***a***) *noun* an adherent or practitioner of deconstruction; (***b***) *adjective* of or pertaining to deconstruction or deconstructionists: L20. **deconstructor** *noun* a practitioner of deconstruction L20.

decontaminate /diːk(ə)nˈtamɪneɪt/ *verb trans.* M20.
[ORIGIN from DE- 3 + CONTAMINATE *verb*.]
Remove contamination from; *esp.* free from (the risk of) contamination by infectious disease, harmful chemicals, radioactivity, etc.
■ **decontamiˈnation** *noun* M20.

decontextualize /diːk(ə)nˈtɛkstjʊəlʌɪz/ *verb trans.* Also **-ise**. L20.
[ORIGIN from DE- 3 + CONTEXTUALIZE.]
Study or treat in isolation from its context.
■ **decontextualiˈzation** *noun* L20.

decontrol /diːk(ə)nˈtrəʊl/ *noun & verb*. E20.
[ORIGIN from DE- 3 + CONTROL *noun* or *verb*.]
► **A** *noun.* The removal of (esp. governmental) control or restrictions. E20.
► **B** *verb trans.* Infl. **-ll-**. Release from (esp. governmental) controls; remove restrictions on. E20.

deconvolution /ˌdiːkɒnvəˈluːʃ(ə)n/ *noun*. L20.
[ORIGIN from DE- 3 + CONVOLUTION.]
The action or process of deconvolving something.

deconvolve /diːk(ə)nˈvɒlv/ *verb trans.* L20.
[ORIGIN from DE- 3 + CONVOLVE.]
MATH. & PHYSICS. Resolve (a function) into the functions of which it is a convolution; *gen.* resolve into constituent elements. Also, obtain by resolving thus.

decor /ˈdeɪkɔː/ *noun*. Also **dé-**. L19.
[ORIGIN French *décor*, from *décorer* DECORATE *verb*.]
1 The scenery and furnishings of a theatre stage; the set. L19.
2 (The overall effect of) the decoration and furnishings of a room, building, etc. E20.

N. MAILER The grey, green and beige décor of their living room.

decorament /ˈdɛkərəm(ə)nt/ *noun*. *rare*. E18.
[ORIGIN Late Latin *decoramentum*, from *decorare* DECORATE *verb*: see -MENT.]
(A) decoration, (an) ornament.

decorate /ˈdɛkərət/ *ppl adjective* (orig. *pa. pple*). Long *arch.* LME.
[ORIGIN Latin *decoratus* pa. pple of *decorare*: see DECORATE *verb*, -ATE[2].]
Adorned, decorated; ornate.

decorate /ˈdɛkəreɪt/ *verb trans.* M16.
[ORIGIN from DECORATE *adjective* or Latin *decorat-* pa. ppl stem of *decorare* beautify, from *decus*, *decor-* embellishment: see -ATE[3].]
1 Embellish; grace, honour. Now *rare* or *obsolete*. M16.

J. A. FROUDE War and plunder were decorated by poetry as the honourable occupation of heroic natures.

2 Provide with adornments, add colour or ornament to; make (a house etc.) more attractive with paint, wallpaper, etc.; serve as adornment to. L18.

E. PEACOCK The old armour which decorated its walls. J. H. PARKER The custom of decorating churches with flowers. M. GIROUARD Rooms were decorated in a wide variety of tertiary colours.

3 Invest (a person) with a military or other decoration, medal, etc. Usu. in *pass.* E19.

G. ORWELL So far from being decorated, he had been censured for showing cowardice in the battle.

■ **decorated** *adjective* (***a***) that has been decorated; (***b***) (**D-**) designating or displaying the architectural style of the second stage of English Gothic (14th cent.), characterized by increasing use of decoration, and geometrical, curvilinear, and reticulated tracery: E17.

decoration /dɛkəˈreɪʃ(ə)n/ *noun*. LME.
[ORIGIN Old French & mod. French *décoration* or late Latin *decoratio(n-)*, from *decorat-*: see DECORATE *verb*, -ATION.]
1 The action of decorating; the fact or condition of being decorated; ornateness. LME.

S. JOHNSON She . . applied all her care to the decoration of her person.

2 A thing that adorns; an ornament. In *pl.*, temporary ornaments (bunting, lights, paper chains, etc.) put up on festive occasions. L16.

R. HOGGART Pin-ups used to be, and still are, standard decoration for servicemen's billets. E. MANNIN The dress was black and very plain, its sole decoration an Egyptian collarette of gold and coral.

3 A medal, cross, etc., conferred and worn as an honour. E19.
– COMB.: **Decoration Day** *US* = *Memorial Day* s.v. MEMORIAL *noun*.

decorative /ˈdɛk(ə)rətɪv/ *adjective*. LME.
[ORIGIN Isolated early use from Old French & mod. French *décoratif*, *-ive*; later (L18) from DECORATE *verb*: see -ATIVE.]
Pertaining to or of the nature of decoration; ornamental.

J. WYNDHAM The finger-nails . . showed a length more decorative than practical.

decorative arts: see ART *noun*[1].
■ **decoratively** *adverb* L19. **decorativeness** *noun* M19.

decorator /ˈdɛkəreɪtə/ *noun*. M18.
[ORIGIN from DECORATE *verb* + -OR.]
A person who decorates; *spec.* (freq. more fully ***painter and decorator***) one whose business is the decoration of buildings with paint, wallpaper, etc.

decore /dɪˈkɔː/ *verb trans.* Long *obsolete* exc. *Scot.* LME.
[ORIGIN Old French & mod. French *décorer* from Latin *decorare* DECORATE *verb*.]
Decorate, adorn, embellish.
■ **decorement** *noun* [Old French] an ornament, an embellishment L16.

decorous /ˈdɛk(ə)rəs/ *adjective*. M17.
[ORIGIN from Latin *decorus* + -OUS.]
†**1** Appropriate, seemly. M–L17.
2 Characterized by decorum; not violating good taste or propriety; dignified and decent. L17.

J. I. M. STEWART Junior Ministers . . probably keep more . . decorous company than writers do. I. MCEWAN Their greetings were intimate yet restrained, decorous.

– NOTE: Pronunc. after Latin with stress on 2nd syll. was formerly common but is now old-fashioned.
■ **decorously** *adverb* in a decorous manner; with decorum: E19. **decorousness** *noun* L17.

decorticate /diːˈkɔːtɪkeɪt/ *verb trans.* E17.
[ORIGIN Latin *decorticat-* pa. ppl stem of *decorticare*, from *de-* DE- 3 + *cortex*, *cortic-* bark: see -ATE[3].]
Remove the peel, husk, bark, or outer layer from; subject to decortication. Freq. as ***decorticated*** *ppl adjective*.
■ **decorticator** *noun* a person who or thing which decorticates; a device for decorticating: L19.

decortication /dɪˌkɔːtɪˈkeɪʃ(ə)n/ *noun*. **E17**.
[**ORIGIN** Latin *decorticatio(n-)*, formed as **DECORTICATE**: see **-ATION**.]
The removal of the peel, bark, or other outer layer from something; *spec*. surgical removal of the cortex of the brain or other organ, esp. the cutting of the brainstem above the midbrain.

decorum /dɪˈkɔːrəm/ *noun*. **M16**.
[**ORIGIN** Latin, use as noun of neut. sing. of *decorus* seemly.]
▸ **I 1** Suitability of artistic or literary style to the subject; congruity, unity. **M16**.

> T. HEARNE Neither is a just Decorum always observ'd, for he sometimes makes Blockheads and Barbarians talk like Philosophers.

2 Suitability to the dignity or circumstances of a person or occasion. *arch*. **L16**.

> SHAKES. *Ant. & Cl.* Majesty, to keep decorum, must No less beg than a kingdom.

3 Propriety of behaviour or demeanour; seemliness; etiquette. **L16**.

> J. AUSTEN His sense of decorum is strict. D. CECIL He could not . . trust himself to behave with proper decorum during the ceremony.

▸ **II** †**4** Beauty arising from congruity, order, or harmony; orderliness. **L16–E18**.
5 †**a** An appropriate act. **E17–E18**. ▸**b** A particular usage required by politeness or decency. Usu. in *pl*. Now *rare*. **E17**.

> **b** GOLDSMITH No decorums could restrain the impatience of his blushing mistress to be forgiven.

découpage /dekupaːʒ/ *noun*. Pl. pronounced same. **M20**.
[**ORIGIN** French, from *découper* cut up or out.]
1 The decoration of a surface with cut-out paper patterns or illustrations; an object so decorated. **M20**.
2 *CINEMATOGRAPHY*. The cutting or editing of a film. **M20**.

decouple /diːˈkʌp(ə)l/ *verb*. **E17**.
[**ORIGIN** Orig. from French *découpler*; later from **DE-** 3 + **COUPLE** *verb*.]
1 *verb trans*. Uncouple. *rare* in *lit*. sense. **E17**.
2 *verb trans*. Make separate or independent (*from*); *esp*. in *PHYSICS*, make the coupling between oscillators, systems, etc. so weak that there is little transfer of energy between them. **M20**. ▸**b** Muffle the sound or shock of (a nuclear explosion) by causing it to take place in an underground cavity. **M20**.

> *Times* If we want to bring interest rates down we have to decouple the pound from the dollar.

3 *verb intrans*. Become decoupled; *esp*. in *PHYSICS*, cease to interact (so that thermal equilibrium is no longer maintained), become differentiated. **M20**.

decoy /ˈdiːkɔɪ, dɪˈkɔɪ/ *noun*. **E17**.
[**ORIGIN** Perh. from Dutch *de kooi* the decoy: see **COY** *noun*.]
1 A pond from which net-covered channels lead, into which ducks or other wildfowl can be enticed for capture. **E17**.
2 A bird or animal, or an imitation of one, used to attract others. Also *fig*., a person or thing employed to entice or deceive others into capture, danger, error, etc.; a swindler's confederate; a tempter; a bait, an enticement. Cf. earlier **DECOY-DUCK**. **M17**.

> J. BUCHAN She would be the decoy . . to get Karolides out of the care of his guards.

– **COMB.**: **DECOY-DUCK**; **decoy ship**: used to decoy enemy vessels.

decoy /ˈdiːkɔɪ, dɪˈkɔɪ/ *verb trans*. **M16**.
[**ORIGIN** Prob. from the noun, but in isolated Scot. use earlier.]
Entice (an animal) into a trap, esp. with the aid of another animal. Also *fig*., lure, tempt, entice, ensnare, (a person etc.). (Foll. by *into*, *out of*, *from* a place, situation, action, etc., or adverb.)

> H. MARTINEAU They would not be decoyed away by a false alarm. W. IRVING A black horse . . being decoyed under a tree by a tame mare.

decoy-duck /ˈdiːkɔɪdʌk, dɪˈkɔɪ-/ *noun*. **E17**.
[**ORIGIN** from **DECOY** *noun* + **DUCK** *noun*[1], translating Dutch *kooieend*.]
A tame or imitation duck used to decoy others; *fig*. a person who entices others into danger or mischief. Cf. **DECOY** *noun* 2.

decrease /ˈdiːkriːs, dɪˈkriːs/ *noun*. **LME**.
[**ORIGIN** Old French *de(s)creis*, from stem of *de(s)creistre*: see **DECREASE** *verb*.]
1 The process of growing less; diminution; an amount by which something is decreased. **LME**.
†**2** The waning of the moon. **E17–M18**.

decrease /dɪˈkriːs, ˈdiːkriːs/ *verb intrans. & trans*. **LME**.
[**ORIGIN** Old French *de(s)creiss-* pres. stem of *de(s)creistre* (mod. *décroître*) from Proto-Romance var. of Latin *decrescere*, from *de-* **DE-** 1 + *crescere* grow.]
(Cause to) grow less; lessen; diminish.

> A. SILLITOE The bruise was still visible . . though the swelling had decreased. J. G. FARRELL Decreasing the chances of his proposal being accepted.

■ **decreasingly** *adverb* to a decreasing extent **E19**.

decreation /diːkriˈeɪʃ(ə)n/ *noun*. **M17**.
[**ORIGIN** from **DE-** 3 + **CREATION**.]
The undoing of creation; annihilation.

decree /dɪˈkriː/ *noun*. **ME**.
[**ORIGIN** Old French *decré* var. of *decret* from Latin *decretum* use as noun of neut. of *decretus* pa. pple of *decernere* **DECERN**.]
1 An edict or law of an ecclesiastical council, settling some disputed point of doctrine or discipline; in *pl*. = **DECRETAL**. **ME**.
2 An ordinance or edict set forth by the civil or other authority; an authoritative decision having the force of law. **LME**.

> SHAKES. *Merch. V.* There is no force in the decrees of Venice. *Times* In France the matter . . is being decided . . by presidential decree.

3 A judicial decision; *spec*. (*a*) *ENGLISH LAW* the judgement of a court of divorce or (*hist*.) equity, probate, or admiralty; (*b*) *SCOTS LAW* a final judgement or sentence of a civil court, whereby the question at issue is decided (earlier as **DECREET** *noun* 1b). **LME**.
decree absolute *ENGLISH LAW* a court's final order legally ending a marriage, enabling either party to remarry. **decree nisi** /ˈnʌɪsʌɪ/ [**NISI**] *ENGLISH LAW* an order by a court stating the date on which a marriage will end unless a good reason not to grant a divorce is produced.
4 The will, as shown by events, of God, or of providence, nature, etc., personified. **L16**.

> T. KEN Her Conscience tells her God's Decree . . made her free.

decree /dɪˈkriː/ *verb*. Pa. t. & pple **decreed**. **LME**.
[**ORIGIN** from the noun.]
1 *verb trans*. Command by decree; order, appoint, or assign authoritatively. **LME**. ▸**b** Of God, or providence, nature, etc., personified: ordain. **L16**.

> R. GRAVES The Senate had decreed an arch in Livia's memory. **b** SHAKES. *Twel. N.* Fate, show thy force: . . What is decreed must be.

2 *verb trans. & intrans*. Decide, determine, or resolve authoritatively (*that*, (arch.) *to do*). **LME**.

> HOBBES Whatsoever that Assembly shall Decree. HENRY FIELDING Here we decreed to rest and dine. JO GRIMOND The Organisation and Methods division decreed that every office must have a Budget.

3 *verb trans. & intrans*. *LAW*. Pronounce (as) judgement in a cause. Formerly, pronounce judgement on. **M16**.

> M. L. KING The Court decreed an end to the old Plessey decision of 1896.

■ **decreer** *noun* a person who or body etc. which decrees **E17**.

decreet /dɪˈkriːt/ *noun*. *arch*. Long only *Scot*. **LME**.
[**ORIGIN** Old French & mod. French *décret* or Latin *decretum* **DECREE** *noun*.]
1 †**a** *gen*. A decree. **LME–E17**. ▸**b** *SCOTS LAW*. A final judgement or sentence of a civil court, whereby the question at issue is decided. **L15**.
†**2** A determination, a resolve. **LME–L16**.

decreet /dɪˈkriːt/ *verb trans. & intrans*. *arch*. *obsolete* exc. *Scot*. **LME**.
[**ORIGIN** from the noun or French *décréter*, formed as the noun.]
Decree; *esp*. pronounce (as) a legal judgement.

decrement /ˈdɛkrɪm(ə)nt/ *noun*. **L16**.
[**ORIGIN** Latin *decrementum*, from *decre-* stem of *decrescere* **DECREASE** *verb*: see **-MENT**.]
1 At Oxford University, an amount deducted from a scholar's endowment for college expenses. Long *obsolete* exc. *hist*. **L16**.
2 The process or fact of growing (gradually) less; an instance of this; decrease, diminution, loss, waste. **E17**. ▸**b** Chiefly *HERALDRY*. The waning of the moon. **E17**.
3 A quantity lost by diminution or waste: a negative increment. **M17**. ▸**b** In full ***decrement of life***. The annual decrease in a given set of people by death. **M18**. ▸**c** *PHYSICS*. The ratio (often expressed logarithmically, freq. ***logarithmic decrement***) of the amplitudes in successive cycles of a damped oscillation. **L19**.

decreolize /diːˈkriːə(ʊ)lʌɪz, -ˈkrɪ-/ *verb trans*. Also **-ise**. **M20**.
[**ORIGIN** from **DE-** 3 + **CREOLIZE**.]
Cause (a language) to lose creole characteristics. Usu. in *pass*.
■ **decreoliˈzation** *noun* **L20**.

decrepit /dɪˈkrɛpɪt/ *adjective*. Also †**-id**. **LME**.
[**ORIGIN** Latin *decrepitus* (partly through French *décrépit*), from *de-* **DE-** 1 + *crepitus* pa. pple of *crepare* to rattle, creak.]
Worn out; enfeebled with age and infirmity: dilapidated.

> DRYDEN How can you be so good to an old decrepid man? D. MURPHY The dwelling itself was so irreparably decrepit that no modern squatter would stay there overnight.

■ **decrepitly** *adverb* **M19**. †**decrepitness** *noun* = **DECREPITUDE** **E17–E18**.

decrepitate /dɪˈkrɛpɪteɪt/ *verb*. **M17**.
[**ORIGIN** from **DE-** 1 + Latin *crepitat-* pa. ppl stem of *crepitare* crackle: see **-ATE**[3].]
1 *verb trans*. Heat (a crystalline substance) until crackling ceases. **M17**.
2 *verb intrans*. Crackle and disintegrate on heating. **L17**.
■ **decrepiˈtation** *noun* **M17**.

decrepitude /dɪˈkrɛpɪtjuːd/ *noun*. **L16**.
[**ORIGIN** Old French & mod. French *décrépitude*, from Latin *decrepitus*: see **DECREPIT**, **-TUDE**.]
The state of being decrepit; feebleness and decay, esp. due to old age.
■ Also †**decrepity** *noun* **L16–E17**.

decrescendo /diːkrɪˈʃɛndəʊ/ *adverb, adjective, noun, & verb intrans*. Pl. of noun **-os**. **E19**.
[**ORIGIN** Italian, pres. pple of *decrescere* **DECREASE** *verb*.]
= **DIMINUENDO**.

decrescent /dɪˈkrɛs(ə)nt/ *adjective & noun*. **E17**.
[**ORIGIN** Latin *decrescent-* pres. ppl stem of *decrescere* **DECREASE** *verb*: see **-ENT**.]
▸ **A** *adjective*. Decreasing; growing gradually less. Esp. of the moon: waning (in *HERALDRY* depicted with the horns directed to the sinister side). Cf. **INCRESCENT**. **E17**.
▸ **B** *noun*. The waning or decrescent moon. **E17**.

decreta *noun* pl. of **DECRETUM**.

decretal /dɪˈkriːt(ə)l/ *noun & adjective*. **ME**.
[**ORIGIN** Late Latin *decretale* (whence also Old French & mod. French *décrétale*), use as noun of neut. sing. of *decretalis* adjective (whence the English adjective), from Latin *decret-* pa. ppl stem of *decernere* **DECERN**: see **-AL**[1].]
▸ **A** *noun*. **1** *ECCLESIASTICAL*. A papal decree or decretal epistle; a document issued by a pope determining some point of doctrine or ecclesiastical law; in *pl*., the collection of such decrees forming part of the canon law. **ME**.
2 *gen*. A decree; an ordinance. **L16**.
▸ **B** *adjective*. **1** Pertaining to, of the nature of, or containing, a decree or decrees (esp. papal). **L15**.
†**2** Esp. of God's laws: imperative, inviolable. Also, decisive, definitive. Only in **17**.
■ †**decretaline** *adjective* of or pertaining to the decretals **E17–E18**. **decretalist** *noun* (*a*) a holder of the Calvinistic doctrine of the decrees of God; (*b*) = **DECRETIST**: **E18**. **decretally** *adverb* in a decretal way; by way of decree: **E17**.

decretion /dɪˈkriːʃ(ə)n/ *noun*. Long *rare*. **M17**.
[**ORIGIN** from Latin *decret-* pa. ppl stem of *decrescere* **DECREASE** *verb* + **-ION**. Cf. **ACCRETION**.]
Decrease.

decretist /dɪˈkriːtɪst/ *noun*. **LME**.
[**ORIGIN** medieval Latin *decretista*, from *decretum* **DECREE** *noun* + *-ista* **-IST**.]
A person versed in (esp. papal) decretals.

decretive /dɪˈkriːtɪv/ *adjective*. **E17**.
[**ORIGIN** from Latin *decret-* pa. ppl stem of *decernere* **DECERN** + **-IVE**.]
Of the nature of, involving, or relating to a decree.

decretorial /diːkrɪˈtɔːrɪəl/ *adjective*. **L16**.
[**ORIGIN** from Latin *decretorius* **DECRETORY** + **-AL**[1].]
†**1** = **DECRETORY** 1. **L16–M17**.
2 = **DECRETIVE**. **L18**.

decretory /dɪˈkriːt(ə)ri/ *adjective*. Now *rare* or *obsolete*. **L16**.
[**ORIGIN** Latin *decretorius*, from *decret-* pa. ppl stem of *decernere* determine: see **DECERN**, **DECREE** *noun*, **-ORY**[2].]
1 Determinative, critical; *spec*. pertaining to or decisive of the final outcome of a disease etc. **L16**.
†**2** = **DECRETIVE**. **M17–E19**.

decretum /dɪˈkriːtəm/ *noun*. Pl. ***-ta*** /-tə/. **E17**.
[**ORIGIN** Latin.]
A decree.

†**decrew** *verb intrans*. *rare* (Spenser). Only in **L16**.
[**ORIGIN** French *décru* pa. pple of *décroître* **DECREASE** *verb*.]
Decrease, wane.

decrial /dɪˈkrʌɪəl/ *noun*. *rare*. **E18**.
[**ORIGIN** from **DECRY** + **-AL**[1].]
An act of decrying; open disparagement.

decrier /dɪˈkrʌɪə/ *noun*. **L17**.
[**ORIGIN** from **DECRY** + **-ER**[1].]
A person who decries.

decriminalize /diːˈkrɪmɪn(ə)lʌɪz/ *verb trans*. Also **-ise**. **M20**.
[**ORIGIN** from **DE-** 3 + **CRIMINAL** + **-IZE**.]
1 Reform through psychiatric treatment. *rare*. **M20**.
2 Make, or treat as, no longer criminal; legalize (esp. a drug, or its possession or use). **L20**.
■ **decriminaliˈzation** *noun* **M20**.

decrown /diːˈkraʊn/ *verb trans*. Now *rare* or *obsolete*. **E17**.
[**ORIGIN** from **DE-** 3 + **CROWN** *noun*.]
Deprive (a monarch etc.) of the crown.

decry /dɪˈkrʌɪ/ *verb & noun*. **E17**.
[**ORIGIN** from **DE-** 1 + **CRY** *verb*, after French *décrier* cry down. Cf. **DESCRY** *verb*[1].]
▸ **A** *verb trans*. **1** Chiefly *hist*. Denounce, suppress, or depreciate (coins etc.) by proclamation. **E17**.

> W. BLACKSTONE The king may . . decry . . any coin of the kingdom, and make it no longer current.

2 Cry out against; disparage openly; belittle. **M17**.

> O. SITWELL There were some who had even decried Britain's War Effort.

▸ **B** *noun*. The decrying of money etc. *rare*. **L17**.

D

D

decrypt /ˈdiːkrɪpt/ *noun.* **M20.**
[**ORIGIN** from the verb.]
A deciphered cryptogram.

decrypt /diːˈkrɪpt/ *verb trans.* **M20.**
[**ORIGIN** from **DE-** 3 + *crypt-* as in *cryptogram* etc.]
Decipher (a cryptogram) with or without knowledge of the key.
■ **decryption** *noun* **M20.**

decubitus /dɪˈkjuːbɪtəs/ *noun.* **L19.**
[**ORIGIN** mod. Latin, from Latin *decumbere* lie down, after *accubitus* reclining at table, etc. Earlier in French.]
MEDICINE. Manner or posture of lying; the recumbent position.
■ **decubital** *adjective* pertaining to or resulting from decubitus **L19.**

decuman /ˈdɛkjʊmən/ *adjective.* **M17.**
[**ORIGIN** Latin *decumanus* var. of *decimanus* of or belonging to the tenth part or tenth cohort, (by metonymy) large, from *decimus*: see **DECIMAL.**]
1 Esp. of a wave: very large, immense. **M17.**

F. W. FARRAR Amid the decuman billows of modern scepticism.

2 *ROMAN HISTORY.* Of or belonging to the tenth cohort. **E19.**
decuman gate the main gate of the camp where the tenth cohort was quartered.

decumbency /dɪˈkʌmb(ə)nsi/ *noun.* **M17.**
[**ORIGIN** from **DECUMBENT**: see **-ENCY.**]
1 Lying down; decumbent position or posture. **M17.**
2 The action of taking to one's bed. **M17.**
■ Also **decumbence** *noun* **M17.**

decumbent /dɪˈkʌmb(ə)nt/ *noun & adjective.* **E17.**
[**ORIGIN** Latin *decumbent-* pres. ppl stem of *decumbere* lie down, from *de-* **DE-** 1 + *-cumbere*: see **CUMBENT.**]
▸ †**A** *noun.* A person lying (ill) in bed. Only in **17.**
▸ **B** *adjective.* **1** Lying down; reclining. Now *rare* or *obsolete.* **M17.** ▸†**b** Lying in bed through illness. **L17–M18.**
2 a *BOTANY.* Of a plant, shoot, etc.: lying or trailing on the ground (with the extremity ascending). **L18.** ▸**b** *ZOOLOGY.* Of hairs or bristles: lying flat on the surface of the body. **E19.**

decumbiture /dɪˈkʌmbɪtʃə/ *noun.* Now *rare* or *obsolete.* **M17.**
[**ORIGIN** Irreg. from Latin *decumbere* (see **DECUMBENT**) + **-URE.**]
1 The act or time of taking to one's bed in an illness; *ASTROLOGY* a horoscope made for the time at which this happens, affording prognostication of the outcome. **M17.**
2 Lying down, *spec.* as an invalid in bed. **L17.**

decuple /ˈdɛkjʊp(ə)l/ *noun & adjective.* **LME.**
[**ORIGIN** Late Latin *decuplus* adjective, *decuplum* noun, from *decem* ten.]
▸ **A** *noun.* A tenfold amount; a number or quantity ten times another. **LME.**
▸ **B** *adjective.* Tenfold. **E16.**
■ **decuplet** *noun* a set of ten things of the same kind **L19.**

decuple /ˈdɛkjʊp(ə)l/ *verb trans. & intrans.* **L17.**
[**ORIGIN** Late Latin *decuplare*, from *decuplus*: see **DECUPLE** *noun & adjective.*]
Multiply or increase tenfold.
■ Also **decuplate** *verb trans. & intrans.* **L17.**

decurion /dɪˈkjʊərɪən/ *noun.* **LME.**
[**ORIGIN** Latin *decurio(n-)*, from *decuria* (see **DECURY**) after *centurio(n-)* **CENTURION.**]
1 *ROMAN HISTORY.* A cavalry officer in command of a company of ten horse. Also *gen.*, a captain of ten men. **LME.**
2 *ROMAN HISTORY.* A member of the senate of a colony or municipal town; a town councillor. **LME.**
3 A member of the great council in Italian cities and towns. **M17.**
■ **decurionate** *noun* the office of a decurion **M19.**

decurrence /dɪˈkʌr(ə)ns/ *noun.* **M17.**
[**ORIGIN** from **DECURRENT** + **-ENCE.**]
†**1** The state or act of running down; lapse (of time). **M–L17.**
2 *BOTANY.* The condition of being decurrent. **M19.**
■ **decurrency** *noun* **M17.**

decurrent /dɪˈkʌr(ə)nt/ *adjective.* **LME.**
[**ORIGIN** Latin *decurrent-* pres. ppl stem of *decurrere* run down, from *de-* **DE-** 1 + *currere* run: see **-ENT.**]
†**1** Running down. Only in **LME.**
2 *BOTANY.* Of a leaf etc.: extending down the stem below the point of attachment. **M18.**
■ **decurrently** *adverb* **E19.**

†**decursion** *noun.* **LME.**
[**ORIGIN** Latin *decursio(n-)*, from *decurs-* pa. ppl stem of *decurrere*: see **DECURRENT, -ION.**]
1 Downward course; lapse (of time). **LME–L17.**
2 *ANTIQUITIES.* A marching of soldiers etc.; a solemn procession around a funeral pyre. **E17–E18.**

decursive /dɪˈkəːsɪv/ *adjective.* **L18.**
[**ORIGIN** mod. Latin *decursivus*, from *decurs-*: see **DECURSION, -IVE.**]
BOTANY. = **DECURRENT** 2.
■ **decursively** *adverb* **E19.**

†**decurtate** *verb trans.* Pa. pple & ppl adjective **-ate(d).** **L16–M19.**
[**ORIGIN** Latin *decurtat-* pa. ppl stem of *decurtare* cut short, abridge, from *de-* **DE-** 1 + *curtare* shorten: see **-ATE**[3].]
Cut short, shorten, abridge.

†**decurtation** *noun.* **LME–E18.**
[**ORIGIN** Latin *decurtatio(n-)*, formed as **DECURTATE**: see **-ATION.**]
The action or an act of cutting short, shortening, or abridging.

decurved /dɪˈkəːvd/ *adjective.* **M19.**
[**ORIGIN** from **DE-** 1 + **CURVE** *verb* + **-ED**[1].]
Curving or bending downwards.

decury /ˈdɛkjʊri/ *noun.* **M16.**
[**ORIGIN** Latin *decuria*, from *decem*, after *centuria* **CENTURY.**]
ROMAN HISTORY. A division, company, or body of ten.

decus /ˈdiːkəs/ *noun. slang. obsolete* exc. *hist.* **L17.**
[**ORIGIN** Latin *decus et tutamen* ornament and safeguard, inscribed on the rim.]
A crown piece.

decussate /dɪˈkʌsət/ *adjective.* **E19.**
[**ORIGIN** Latin *decussatus*, formed as **DECUSSATE** *verb*: see **-ATE**[2].]
1 Having the form of an X; X-shaped. **E19.**
2 *BOTANY.* (Bearing leaves etc.) arranged oppositely in pairs, each pair being at right angles to the pair below. **M19.**
■ **decussately** *adverb* **M19.**

decussate /dɪˈkʌseɪt, ˈdɛkəseɪt/ *verb trans. & intrans.* **M17.**
[**ORIGIN** Latin *decussat-* pa. ppl stem of *decussare* divide crosswise, from *decussis* the numeral 10, coin worth 10 asses, intersection of lines crosswise (X), from *decem* ten: see **AS** *noun*, **-ATE**[3].]
Arrange or be arranged in decussate form; (cause to) intersect.
■ **decussated** *ppl adjective* (**a**) formed with crossing lines like an X; intersected; having decussations; (**b**) *RHETORIC* = **CHIASTIC**: **M17.**

decussation /dɪkəˈseɪʃ(ə)n, dɛkə-/ *noun.* **M17.**
[**ORIGIN** Latin *decussatio(n-)*, from *decussat-*: see **DECUSSATE** *verb*, **-ATION.**]
1 Crossing of lines, rays, fibres, etc., so as to form a figure like an X; intersection. **M17.**
2 *RHETORIC.* = **CHIASMUS** 2. **M19.**

decyl /ˈdɪsʌɪl, -sɪl/ *noun.* **M19.**
[**ORIGIN** from Greek *deka* ten + **-YL.**]
CHEMISTRY. Any of the series of monovalent radicals $C_{10}H_{21}$·, obtained from the decanes. Usu. in *comb.*

decypher *verb & noun* see **DECIPHER.**

dedal *noun, adjective* vars. of **DAEDAL** *noun, adjective.*

Dedalean, **Dedalian** *adjectives* vars. of **DAEDALIAN.**

Dedalic *adjective* var. of **DAEDALIC.**

dedans /dəˈdɑ̃/ *noun.* **E18.**
[**ORIGIN** French = inside, interior.]
REAL TENNIS. The open gallery at the end of the service side of the court; the spectators watching a match (from this area).

dedecorate /dɪˈdɛkəreɪt/ *verb trans.* **E17.**
[**ORIGIN** Sense 1 from Latin *dedecorat-* pa. ppl stem of *dedecorare* dishonour, from *dedecus, dedecor-* disgrace: see **-ATE**[3]; sense 2 from **DE-** 3 + **DECORATE** *verb.*]
†**1** Dishonour. Only in **E17.**
2 Disfigure. **E19.**

dedendum /dɪˈdɛndəm/ *noun.* **E20.**
[**ORIGIN** Latin, neut. gerundive of *dedere* give up, surrender.]
MECHANICS. The radial distance from the pitch circle of a cogwheel, wormwheel, etc., to the bottoms of the tooth spaces or grooves.

dedentition /diːdɛnˈtɪʃ(ə)n/ *noun.* **M17.**
[**ORIGIN** from **DE-** 3 + **DENTITION.**]
PHYSIOLOGY. The shedding of the (deciduous) teeth.

dedicant /ˈdɛdɪk(ə)nt/ *noun.* **L19.**
[**ORIGIN** from Latin *dedicant-* pres. ppl stem of *dedicare*: see **DEDICATE** *adjective*, **-ANT**[1].]
A person who dedicates or is dedicated (*to*).

dedicate /ˈdɛdɪkət, -eɪt/ *adjective* (orig. *pa. pple*). *arch.* **LME.**
[**ORIGIN** Latin *dedicatus* pa. pple of *dedicare* proclaim, devote, consecrate, from *de-* **DE-** 1 + *dic-* say: see **-ATE**[2].]
Dedicated.

dedicate /ˈdɛdɪkeɪt/ *verb trans.* **LME.**
[**ORIGIN** Latin *dedicat-* pa. ppl stem of *dedicare*, after **DEDICATE** *adjective* or **DEDICATION**: see **-ATE**[3].]
1 Devote with solemn rites *to* a god, saint, or sacred use; consecrate, set apart (a church etc.), esp. without certain forms necessary for legally consecrating ground or buildings. **LME.**

A. RIDLER Can we say Mass to dedicate our bombs? K. CLARK The great Romanesque churches were dedicated to the saints whose relics they contained.

2 Introduce (a book, piece of music, or other artistic work) with words (usu. written therein) addressed *to* a friend, patron, etc., as a mark of honour, regard, or gratitude. **E16.** ▸†**b** Address (a letter etc.) *to*. **L17–L18.**

YEATS A subtle book which I cannot praise as I would, because it has been dedicated to me.

3 Give up earnestly or wholly *to* a special purpose, cause, etc. **M16.**

I. WALTON When you . . dedicate a day or two to this Recreation. N. MOSLEY She knew he would not force her, since they were both people dedicated to non-violence. E. WELTY Irene . . had dedicated her life to Sylvia, sparing herself nothing.

4 Formally or legally devote (land) for the use of the general public or for a particular purpose (*spec.* forestry: cf. **DEDICATED** 1b). **M19.**
■ **dedicaˈtee** *noun* a person to whom something is dedicated **M18.** **dedicative** *adjective* having the attribute of dedicating **M17.** **dedicator** *noun* a person who dedicates, *esp.* one who inscribes a book to a friend, patron, etc. **L16.**

dedicated /ˈdɛdɪkeɪtɪd/ *adjective.* **L16.**
[**ORIGIN** from **DEDICATE** *verb* + **-ED**[1].]
1 *gen.* That has been dedicated. **L16.** ▸**b** Of private woodland: managed for timber production according to an approved plan and with financial assistance from the forestry authority. **M20.**
2 Of a person: devoted to his or her aims or vocation; single-mindedly loyal and conscientious. **M20.**

I. MURDOCH One of those dedicated single women on whom society so much depends. J. CHEEVER Francis had been a dedicated boy scout when he was young.

3 Designed and used exclusively for a particular purpose or by a particular user. **M20.**

Broadcast Consumer demand for a dedicated children's television service. *Which Computer?* A 16-bit processor with its own 32 KB of dedicated RAM.

dedication /dɛdɪˈkeɪʃ(ə)n/ *noun.* **LME.**
[**ORIGIN** Old French & mod. French *dédication* or Latin *dedicatio(n-)*, formed as **DEDICATED**: see **-ATION.**]
1 The action of dedicating, or the fact of being dedicated, to God, a saint, sacred purposes, etc. **LME.** ▸**b** A service or form of words by which something is dedicated. **LME.**
2 The action of dedicating a book, artistic work, etc.; a dedicatory inscription. **L16.**
3 The action of dedicating oneself to a particular purpose, cause, etc. **E17.** ▸**b** The quality of being dedicated in aims, vocation, etc. (see **DEDICATED** 2). **M20.**

B. JOWETT The dedication of himself to the improvement of his fellow-citizens. **b** W. HUTTON Jenny . . navigated the book through to publication against tough deadlines with great dedication.

4 Formal or legal giving over of land etc. to public or other use. **E19.**

dedicatory /ˈdɛdɪkət(ə)ri, ˈdɛdɪkeɪt-, -ˈkeɪt(ə)ri/ *adjective & noun.* **M16.**
[**ORIGIN** from late Latin *dedicator*, from *dedicat-*: see **DEDICATE** *verb*, **-OR, -ORY**[2]. Cf. French *dédicatoire.*]
▸ **A** *adjective.* That has the attribute of dedicating; serving to dedicate something. **M16.**
▸ †**B** *noun.* A dedicatory inscription or address. **L16–L17.**
■ **dedicatorily** *adverb* **E19.**

dedifferentiate /ˌdiːdɪfəˈrɛnʃɪeɪt/ *verb intrans.* **E20.**
[**ORIGIN** from **DE-** 3 + **DIFFERENTIATE** *verb.*]
BIOLOGY. Of a cell, tissue, etc.: undergo a reversal of differentiation, lose specialized characteristics.
■ **dedifferentiˈation** *noun* **E20.**

†**dedignation** *noun.* **LME–E18.**
[**ORIGIN** Old French from Latin *dedignatio(n-)*, from *dedignat-* pa. ppl stem of *dedignari* **DISDAIN** *verb*: see **-ATION.**]
Disdain, contempt.

dedimus /ˈdɛdɪməs/ *noun.* **LME.**
[**ORIGIN** Latin *dedimus potestatem* we have given the power, used in the wording of the writ.]
LAW. In full ***dedimus potestatem*** /pɒtɪˈsteɪtəm, -ˈstɑː-/. A writ empowering a private person to do some act in place of a judge.

dedition /dɪˈdɪʃ(ə)n/ *noun.* Now *rare* or *obsolete.* **E16.**
[**ORIGIN** Old French *dedicion* or Latin *deditio(n-)*, from *dedit-* pa. ppl stem of *dedere* give up, from *de-* **DE-** 1 + *dare* give: see **-ION.**]
Yielding, surrender.

dedolent /ˈdɛdəl(ə)nt/ *adjective.* Long *rare.* **M17.**
[**ORIGIN** Latin *dedolent-* pres. ppl stem of *dedolere*, from *de-* **DE-** 3 + *dolere* grieve: see **-ENT.**]
That feels sorrow no more; insensible, callous.

dedolomitization /ˌdiːdɒləmɪtʌɪˈzeɪʃ(ə)n/ *noun.* Also **-isation.** **E20.**
[**ORIGIN** from **DE-** 3 + **DOLOMITIZATION.**]
GEOLOGY. Conversion of dolomite into rock of another kind; *esp.* loss of magnesium from dolomite (leaving calcite).
■ **deˈdolomitize** *verb trans.* cause to undergo dedolomitization **E20.**

deduce /dɪˈdjuːs/ *verb trans.* **LME.**
[**ORIGIN** Latin *deducere*, from *de-* **DE-** 1 + *ducere* to lead.]
1 Lead, bring, convey. *arch.* **LME.** ▸†**b** Divert. **M16–M17.** ▸**c** *ROMAN HISTORY.* Found (a colony). **E17.**
2 Infer, draw as a logical conclusion (*from* something already known or assumed); derive by a process of reasoning. **LME.**

SIR T. MORE Ye case once graunted, ye deduce your conclusion very surelye. N. MARSH From that . . I deduce that you are a painter in oils. S. WEINBERG The existence of the antielectron was first deduced theoretically by . . Dirac.

3 Draw from its source, derive; trace the origin of, show to be derived (*from*). *arch.* L15.

J. USSHER They deduced themselves from the Athenians. F. W. FARRAR The attempt to prove that all languages were deduced from the Hebrew.

4 Orig., conduct (a process), deal with (a matter). Later, trace the course of, go through in sequence. *arch.* L15.

GIBBON The general design of this work will not permit us . . to deduce the various fortunes of his private life.

†**5** Deduct, subtract. L15–E19.
†**6** Reduce to a different form. L16–M18.
■ †**deducement** *noun* the act of deducing; a deduction: E17–E19.

deducible /dɪˈdjuːsɪb(ə)l/ *adjective & noun*. E17.
[ORIGIN from DEDUCE + -IBLE.]
(An inference, conclusion, etc.) able to be deduced.
■ **deduciˈbility** *noun* M19. **deducibleness** *noun* E18.

deduct /dɪˈdʌkt/ *verb trans.* LME.
[ORIGIN Latin *deduct-* pa. ppl stem of *deducere* DEDUCE.]
1 Subtract (*from*), take away (an amount, portion, etc.). LME.

T. S. ELIOT I wish him to deduct twenty-five dollars from the next payment.

†**2** = DEDUCE 3, 4. M16–M17.
†**3** = DEDUCE 1. M16–E17.
4 = DEDUCE 2. Now *rare*. M16.
■ **deductable** *adjective* = DEDUCTIBLE *adjective* L19.

deductible /dɪˈdʌktɪb(ə)l/ *adjective & noun*. M19.
[ORIGIN from DEDUCT + -IBLE.]
▸ **A** *adjective*. That can or may be deducted; *spec.* (in full ***tax-deductible***) that may be deducted from one's tax or taxable income. M19.
▸ **B** *noun*. A proportion of the risk which must be borne by the holder of an insurance policy. Orig. *US*. E20.

deduction /dɪˈdʌkʃ(ə)n/ *noun*. LME.
[ORIGIN Old French & mod. French *déduction* or Latin *deductio(n-)*, formed as DEDUCTIBLE: see -ION.]
1 Subtraction, taking away; an amount subtracted. LME.

Times A $2,500 tax deduction.

2 An act of leading forth or away. *rare*. LME. ▸**b** ROMAN HISTORY. The founding of a colony. L17.
3 The process of deducing a conclusion from what is known or assumed; inference from the general to the particular (cf. ***induction***); an inference, a conclusion. L15.

DENNIS POTTER I'm impressed with your astonishing powers of deduction.

†**4** The action of setting down in order; a detailed account. M16–E19.
†**5** Derivation. E17–M19.

deductive /dɪˈdʌktɪv/ *adjective*. M17.
[ORIGIN medieval Latin *deductivus*, formed as DEDUCT *verb*: see -IVE.]
Of or pertaining to deduction; of the nature of or characterized by deduction; reasoning from the general to the particular (cf. ***inductive***).
■ **deductively** *adverb* M17. **deductivism** *noun* belief in the superiority of, or preference for, deductive over inductive methods of reasoning E20. **deductivist** *noun & adjective* (*a*) an adherent of deductivism; (*b*) of or pertaining to deductivists or deductivism: M20.

deductory /dɪˈdʌkt(ə)ri/ *adjective*. *rare*. E17.
[ORIGIN Latin *deductorius*, from *deductor* agent noun from *deducere* DEDUCE: see -ORY[2].]
†**1** LAW. Having the effect of bringing a matter before a court. Only in E17.
2 = DEDUCTIVE. M17.

dee /diː/ *noun & verb*. L18.
[ORIGIN Repr. pronunc. of *D*, *d* as the letter's name.]
▸ **A** *noun*. **1** The letter D, d; a D-shaped object, *esp.* an iron or steel loop for connecting parts of a harness or for fastening articles to a saddle. L18. ▸**b** PHYSICS. Either of two hollow semicircular electrodes used to accelerate particles in a cyclotron. E20.
2 A detective. *slang*. L19.
▸ **B** *verb trans.* Pa. t. & pple **deed**. *euphem.* = DAMN *verb* 4. Chiefly as ***deed***, damned. M19.

deed /diːd/ *noun & verb*.
[ORIGIN Old English *dēd*, (West Saxon) *dǣd* = Old Frisian *dēd(e)*, Old Saxon *dād* (Dutch *daad*), Old High German *tāt* (German *Tat*), Old Norse *dáð*, Gothic *-deþs*, from Germanic, ult. from Indo-European base of DO *verb*.]
▸ **A** *noun*. **1** A thing done by a responsible agent; an act. OE. ▸**b** A brave, skilful, or conspicuous act; a feat. OE. ▸†**c** A thing to be done, a contemplated task; duty. ME–L16.

SHAKES. *Jul. Caes.* They that have done this deed are honourable. **b** TENNYSON Arthur yet had done no deed of arms. C. CAUDWELL Deeds of outstanding individual heroism.

take the will for the deed: see WILL *noun*[1].

2 Action, performance; actual fact. (Freq. contrasted with **word**.) OE. ▸**b** *collect.* Doings; ado, to-do. *dial.* E16.

J. RUSKIN The strength of Hercules is for deed not misdeed.

in deed in action, in practice, in actual fact; earlier also in all senses of INDEED. **in very deed** *arch.* in undoubted effect or fact, in truth.

3 LAW. A written or printed instrument signed (and in English law formerly sealed and delivered) by the disposer, effecting some legal disposition such as the transfer of property or the creation of a contract. ME.

B. TARKINGTON His father had never given Mabel a deed to her house.

deed of association: see ASSOCIATION 1. ***deed of covenant***: see COVENANT *noun*. ***deed of gift***: see GIFT *noun* 2. **deed of variation**, **deed of family arrangement** a deed by which the beneficiary under a will settlement or an intestacy redirects the gift to some other person. ***title deed***: see TITLE *noun*.
– COMB.: **deed box** a strongbox for keeping deeds and other documents; **deed poll** [POLL *adjective*; so called because the paper is polled or cut even, not indented] ENGLISH LAW a deed made and executed by one party only, esp. to formalize a change of a person's name.
▸ **B** *verb trans.* Convey or transfer by legal deed. *US*. E19.
■ **deedful** *adjective* full of deeds, active, effective E17. **deedless** *adjective* without action or deeds; performing no deeds, inactive: L16.

deed /diːd/ *adverb*. Also **'deed**. Now chiefly *Scot.* M16.
[ORIGIN Aphet.]
= INDEED.

deedy /ˈdiːdi/ *adjective*. *dial. & colloq.* LME.
[ORIGIN from DEED *noun* + -Y[1].]
Active, industrious; effective, handy; earnest, serious.
■ **deedily** *adverb* E19.

deejay /diːˈdʒeɪ, ˈdiːdʒeɪ/ *noun*. *slang* (orig. *US*). M20.
[ORIGIN Repr. pronunc. of abbreviation DJ.]
A disc jockey.

Deely-bobber /ˈdiːlɪbɒbə/ *noun*. Also **Deelie-**, **d-**. M20.
[ORIGIN Fanciful.]
1 (US proprietary name for) a construction toy comprising a number of interlinking building blocks. M20.
2 (US proprietary name for) a piece of novelty headgear consisting of a pair of ornaments, e.g. balls, attached like antennae by springs or wires to a headband. L20.

deem /diːm/ *verb & noun*.
[ORIGIN Old English *dēman* = Old Frisian *dēma*, Old Saxon *dōmian* (Dutch *doemen*), Old High German *tuomen*, Old Norse *dœma*, Gothic *domjan*, from Germanic base of DOOM *noun*[1].]
▸ **A** *verb* **1** †**a** *verb trans. & intrans.* Act as judge (with respect to); sit in judgement (on), pronounce judgement (on). OE–E17. ▸**b** *verb trans.* Administer (law). *arch.* LME.

J. SKENE Thou Judge be ware, for as ye deme, ze sall be demed.

†**2** *verb trans.* Sentence, condemn (*to*, *to do*); censure. OE–E17.
†**3** *verb trans.* Decree; decide; award. OE–E17.
†**4** *verb trans.* Announce; tell, say. *poet.* OE–M16.
5 *verb trans. &* (now *rare*) *intrans.* Believe, consider, judge, or count to be or *to be*; believe etc. *that*, (a person or thing) *to do*, *to have done*. OE.

POPE He too, I deem, implores the power divine. T. HARDY When she deemed . . that she had carried the alarm far enough, she . . dragged herself back again. J. G. FARRELL The major had . . deemed it best to say nothing. J. BARZUN To accomplish what he deemed his mission.

†**6** Form a judgement or opinion of or *of*; distinguish (between). ME–L16.
7 *verb intrans.* Expect, hope *to do*. *rare*. ME.
8 *verb intrans.* Think in a specified way *of*. LME.

SIR W. SCOTT Where the ties of affection were highly deemed of.

9 †**a** *verb trans.* Think of as existing; imagine, suspect. LME–L16. ▸**b** *verb intrans.* Foll. by *of*: think of, imagine. *poet. rare*. E19.

b BYRON Something unearthly which they deem not of.

▸ †**B** *noun*. Judgement, opinion, surmise. LME–M17.
■ **deemer** *noun* †(*a*) a judge; (*b*) *gen.* a person who deems: OE.

de-emphasis /diːˈɛmfəsɪs/ *noun*. Pl. **-phases** /-fəsiːz/. M20.
[ORIGIN from DE- 3 + EMPHASIS.]
A lessening or removal of emphasis; *spec.* the reversal of pre-emphasis in an audio signal by attenuating higher frequencies, so as to restore tonal balance on reproduction.

de-emphasize /diːˈɛmfəsʌɪz/ *verb trans.* Also **-ise**. M20.
[ORIGIN from DE- 3 + EMPHASIZE.]
Remove emphasis from, reduce emphasis on.

deemster /ˈdiːmstə/ *noun*. ME.
[ORIGIN from DEEM + -STER. Cf. DEMPSTER, DOOMSTER.]
1 *gen.* A judge. *arch.* ME.
2 (The title of) either of the two justices of the Isle of Man. E17.

deener *noun* var. of DEANER.

de-energize /diːˈɛnədʒʌɪz/ *verb trans. & intrans.* Also **-ise**. L19.
[ORIGIN from DE- 3 + ENERGIZE.]
Disconnect or be disconnected from a power supply; (cause to) undergo loss of electrical power.

deep /diːp/ *noun*.
[ORIGIN Old English *dēop* neut. of *dēop* adjective: see DEEP *adjective*.]
†**1** Depth, deepness *rare*. OE–M17.
2 A deep part of the sea, a lake, or river. Freq. in *pl.*, deep water, a deep place. OE.

CARLYLE Some silent . . mountain-pool, into whose black deeps you fear to gaze.

3 *sing.* & †in *pl.* *The* ocean; *the* deep sea. *poet. & rhet.* OE. ▸**b** *The* depths or abyss of space. L16.

Book of Common Prayer We therefore commit his body to the Deep. POPE The monstrous wonders of the deeps. **b** SHAKES. 1 *Hen. IV* I can call spirits from the vasty deep.

rapture of the deep, ***raptures of the deep***: see RAPTURE *noun*.

4 A deep place in the earth; a cavity, an abyss, a pit. LME.
5 The remote central part. *rare*. LME.
6 A mysterious region of thought or feeling. *poet. & rhet.* LME.

K. HULME The rock of desolation, and the deep of despair.

7 The middle *of* winter or night, when the cold, dark, etc., are at their most intense. M16.
8 NAUTICAL. An estimated fathom on a sounding line between marked depths. Cf. earlier DIP *noun* 4a. M19.
9 CRICKET. The deep field. E20.

deep /diːp/ *adjective*.
[ORIGIN Old English *dēop* = Old Frisian *diāp*, Old Saxon *diop*, *diap* (Dutch *diep*), Old High German *tiuf* (German *tief*), Old Norse *djúpr*, Gothic *diups* from Germanic, from base repr. also by DIP *verb*.]
▸ **I** *lit.* **1** Having great, or a specified, extension downward from the top. OE.

I. MURDOCH He feared the deep crevasses down which a man might slide. J. C. OATES It was fairly shallow in parts, and as deep as . . fifteen feet in others.

between the Devil and the deep* (*blue*) *sea: see DEVIL *noun*.

2 Having great, or a specified, extension inward from the surface or edge. OE. ▸**b** *pred.* After a number: in that number of ranks one behind the other. (Passing into adverb.) L17.

SHELLEY When birds die In the deep forests. D. H. LAWRENCE He had a deep cut across his thumb. **b** C. THIRLWALL The Thebans . . stood five-and-twenty deep.

3 Going or placed far, or a specified distance, down, back, or inwards; sunk *in*; (of a ship) low in the water. OE. ▸**b** *spec.* In CRICKET, distant from the batsman; in FOOTBALL & HOCKEY etc., distant from the front line of one's team. M19.

DRYDEN The frozen Earth lyes buried there . . seven Cubits deep in Snow. J. RHYS Standing knee deep in the river.

†**4** Covered with a depth of mud, sand, etc. LME–E19.

SMOLLETT Three hundred miles through deep roads.

5 Of a physical action etc.: extending to or coming from a depth. L15.

H. S. MERRIMAN She . . swept him a deep curtsey. J. STEINBECK Lee lifted the bottle . . and took a deep hot drink. R. P. WARREN He gulped a full, deep, exquisite breath.

▸ **II** *fig.* **6** Of an oath, sin, etc.: solemn; grave. Now *rare* or *obsolete*. OE.

MILTON A deep and serious verity.

7 Penetrating far into a subject; hard to fathom; profound, not superficial. OE.

DAY LEWIS He preaches such deep sermons Lily can't make head or tail of them.

8 That affects one profoundly; rooted in one's innermost feelings. ME.

I. MURDOCH He felt a deep need to explain this.

9 Having profound knowledge, learning, or insight. ME.

R. HOLINSHED A deepe clerke, and one that read much.

10 Cunning, subtle, secretive. Now *slang*. ME.

DICKENS You're a deep one, Mr. Pip.

11 Of a condition, quality, state, etc.: intense, profound, extreme. LME.

T. HARDY Little Abraham was aroused from his deep sleep. J. CONRAD A . . deserted street in deep shadow.

12 Of colour etc.: intense, vivid. LME.

R. HOOKE All manner of Blues, from the faintest to the deepest.

13 Of sound etc.: low in pitch; full-toned, resonant; not shrill. LME.

J. D. SALINGER I made my voice quite deep so that she wouldn't suspect my age.

14 Of an agent: who does (what is expressed by the noun) profoundly. E16.

M. ARNOLD Shakspeare was no deep reader.

15 *pred.* Involved or immersed greatly or to a specified degree (*in*). (Passing into adverb.) M16.

R. KIPLING He was deep in meditation, mechanically clicking his rosary.

16 Of an action etc.: mentally absorbing. L16.

E. W. LANE He passed the next night in deep study.

17 Involving heavy expense or liability. Now *rare*. L16.

SWIFT That ruinous practice of deep gaming.

D

18 *pred.* After a number: having that number of engagements or obligations. (Passing into adverb.) **E20.**

> H. JAMES Mrs Guy . . was always engaged ten parties deep.

– SPECIAL COLLOCATIONS & COMB. (see also s.v. DEEP *adverb*): **deep-bodied** *adjective* (of a fish etc.) having a body which is much deeper dorsoventrally than it is wide. **deep breathing** the act of breathing deeply esp. as a form of physical exercise. **deep-discount** *adjective* (**a**) denoting financial securities carrying a low rate of interest and issued at a discount to their redemption value, so mainly providing capital gain rather than income; (**b**) *N. Amer.* heavily discounted, greatly reduced in price. **deep-dish pie** (orig. *US*) a pie without pastry on the bottom, baked in a deep dish. **deep end** the deeper end of a swimming pool (***go in off the deep end, go off the deep end, go in at the deep end***, give way to emotion or anger; ***in at the deep end***, into a difficult situation without preparation). **deep field** CRICKET that part of the field near the boundary, esp. behind the bowler. **deep kiss**: involving contact between partners' tongues. **deep litter** a deep layer of litter used in poultry houses etc. **deep mourning**: expressed by dressing completely in black. **deep-mouthed** *adjective* (esp. of a dog) having a deep voice. **deep sea** the deeper parts of the sea, at a distance from the shore (***deep-sea fishing***: involving prolonged periods at sea; ***deep-sea lead***, ***deep-sea line***, a lead and line used for soundings in deep water). †**deep-sinker** *Austral.* (a drink served in) a glass of the largest size. **deep six** *slang* burial, death, esp. at sea; *the* grave. **deep-six** *verb trans.* (*slang*) bury or lose at sea or in water, dispose of irretrievably. **Deep South** the southernmost parts of the US, *esp.* those states adjacent to the Gulf of Mexico. **deep space** the regions of space that are either outside the earth's atmosphere or beyond the solar system. **deep structure** LINGUISTICS in transformational grammar, (the representation of) the fundamental abstract grammatical or semantic relationships of the elements of a phrase or sentence (opp. ***surface structure***). **deep tank** a section of a ship's hold used to store liquid. **deep therapy** curative treatment with short-wave X-rays of high penetrating power. **deep throat** [orig. applied to an anonymous informant in the Watergate scandal, from the name of a pornographic film (1972)] (the name of) a person who supplies anonymously information about covert or illegal action within an organization. **deep-vein thrombosis** thrombosis in a vein lying deep below the skin, especially in the legs (cf. ***ECONOMY-class syndrome***). **deep water(s)** *fig.* trouble, difficulty (usu. ***in deep water, into deep water***). **deep X-ray therapy** = ***deep therapy*** above.

■ **deepish** *adjective* L19. **deepmost** *adjective* (*rare*) deepest E19.

deep /diːp/ *verb.* Long *rare.*

[ORIGIN Old English *dīepan*, *dȳpan* = Old Frisian *diūpa* (Dutch *diepen*), Middle High German *tiefen*, *tiufen*, Gothic *gadiupjan*, formed as DEEP *adjective*. Cf. DEEPEN.]

†**1** *verb trans.* = DEEPEN 1. OE–E17.

†**2** *verb trans.* Plunge or immerse deeply (*lit.* & *fig.*). LME–L16.

3 *verb intrans.* = DEEPEN 2. L16.

deep /diːp/ *adverb.*

[ORIGIN Old English *dīope*, *dēope*, formed as DEEP *adjective*.]

1 Deeply; far down, in, on, or back; *fig.* profoundly, intensely, seriously, heavily. OE.

> W. H. DIXON The three men sat up deep into the night. T. WILLIAMS Dusk settles deeper. L. DEIGHTON Her eyes were . . sunk deep into her face. *Proverb*: Still waters run deep.

drink deep: see DRINK *verb*.

2 CRICKET. In the deep field. M19.

– COMB.: **deep-down** *adjective* & *adverb* far down, very deep(ly); **deep drawing** the process of shaping a sheet or strip of metal by forcing it through a die while cold; **deep-drawn** *adjective* (**a**) drawn from the depths; (**b**) produced by or suitable for deep drawing; **deep-dyed** *adjective* (*fig.*) thoroughgoing; inveterate; **deep-etch**, **deep-etching** a photo-engraving process in which the lithographic plate is slightly etched; †**deep-fet**, †**deep-fetched** *adjectives* from far below the surface; far-fetched; **deep-fried** *adjective* (of food) fried in fat or oil of sufficient depth to cover it; **deep-frying** the frying of food in enough fat or oil to cover it completely; **deep-laid** *adjective* planned with great cunning; secret and elaborate; **deep-milking** the production of a good yield of milk; **deep-mined** *adjective* (of coal etc.) obtained far below the surface of the ground (as opp. *opencast*); **deep-read** *adjective* (*arch.*) skilled by extensive reading, erudite; **deep-rooted** *adjective* (esp. of a belief etc.) deeply rooted or implanted; **deep-seated** *adjective* (esp. of disease, emotion, etc.) sited or originating far below the surface, deeply rooted; **deep-set** *adjective* (esp. of the eyes) deeply set.

deepen /ˈdiːp(ə)n/ *verb.* L16.

[ORIGIN from DEEP *adjective* + -EN⁵, superseding DEEP *verb*.]

1 *verb trans.* Make deep or deeper. L16.

> J. STOW He . . heightened the ditches, deepened the trenches. S. KING The religious business began to deepen its hold on her.

2 *verb intrans.* Become deep or deeper. L17.

> J. GALSWORTHY The sky that had been blue . . deepened . . to the bloom of purple grapes. A. S. BYATT The snow was still deepening and the roads . . were blocked.

■ **deepener** *noun* a person who or thing which deepens something E19. **deepeningly** *adverb* so as to become deeper, in a deepening manner M19.

deepest /ˈdiːpɪst/ *noun. arch.* & *poet.* LME.

[ORIGIN Superl. of DEEP *adjective* used absol.: see -EST¹.]

The deepest part *of*.

deep-freeze /diːpˈfriːz, *as* noun *also* ˈdiːpfriːz/ *noun* & *verb.* In sense A.1 also (US proprietary name) **Deepfreeze**. M20.

[ORIGIN from DEEP *adjective* + FREEZE *noun*¹.]

▸**A** *noun.* **1** A refrigerator etc. in which food can be quickly frozen and stored for long periods at a very low temperature. M20.

2 Cold storage; *fig.* suspension of activity, suspended animation. M20.

▸**B** *verb trans.* Infl. as FREEZE *verb*; pa. t. **-froze** /-ˈfrəʊz/, pa. pple usu. **-frozen** /-ˈfrəʊz(ə)n/. Freeze and store in a deep-freeze; preserve as by refrigeration. Freq. as ***deep-frozen*** *ppl adjective*. M20.

■ **deep-freezer** *noun* = DEEP-FREEZE *noun* 1 M20.

deepie /ˈdiːpi/ *noun. colloq.* M20.

[ORIGIN from DEEP *adjective* + -IE, after *talkie* etc.]

A three-dimensional cinematographic or television film.

deeping /ˈdiːpɪŋ/ *noun.* E17.

[ORIGIN from DEEP *verb* or *adjective* + -ING¹.]

A fathom-deep section of a fishing net.

deeply /ˈdiːpli/ *adverb.* OE.

[ORIGIN from DEEP *adjective* + -LY².]

1 With profound thought, insight, knowledge, etc.; thoroughly. OE. ▸**b** With profound cunning or subtlety. L16.

> B. JOWETT I should like to consider the matter a little more deeply. **b** SHAKES. *Tam. Shr.* Both dissemble deeply their affections.

†**2** Solemnly. ME–L17.

3 Gravely, seriously, heavily. LME.

> J. A. FROUDE The archbishop had committed himself so deeply that he could not afford to wait.

4 With intense feeling, emotion, etc.; in a high degree, extremely. LME.

> D. H. LAWRENCE He despised it deeply and bitterly. E. WAUGH Air Force jokes are deeply depressing.

5 To a great depth; far down, back, or inwards. LME.

> J. TYNDALL The glacier was deeply fissured. E. BOWEN Woods . . go back deeply behind the ruin. H. SECOMBE He bowed deeply, a theatrical gesture.

6 With complete absorption of the faculties. M17.

> G. GREENE In a few minutes he was deeply asleep.

7 With deep colour. L17.

> J. BUCHAN She . . blushed deeply.

8 With a deep voice or sound. L19.

deepness /ˈdiːpnɪs/ *noun.* Now *rare.* OE.

[ORIGIN from DEEP *adjective* + -NESS. Largely superseded by DEPTH.]

1 Depth of thoughts, feelings, qualities, etc.; profundity, intensity, seriousness. OE.

†**2** A deep place; a deep part of the sea. OE–M16.

3 Physical depth; (considerable) extension downwards, inwards, or from front to back. ME.

deepsome /ˈdiːps(ə)m/ *adjective. poet. rare.* E17.

[ORIGIN from DEEP *adjective* or *noun* + -SOME¹.]

Having depth; more or less deep.

deer /dɪə/ *noun.* Pl. same, (*rare*) **-s**.

[ORIGIN Old English *dēor* = Old Frisian *diār*, Old Saxon *dior* (Dutch *dier*), Old High German *tior* (German *Tier*), Old Norse *dýr*, Gothic (dat. pl.) *diuzam*, from Germanic from Indo-European, orig. 'breathing creature'.]

1 An animal, a beast, *esp.* a quadruped. Long *obsolete* exc. in ***small deer*** (arch.), small creatures collectively, *fig.* insignificant things. OE.

2 Any ruminant quadruped of the family Cervidae, distinguished in the male by the presence of deciduous branching horns or antlers and in the young by the presence of spots, or of the related families Tragulidae and Moschidae (both lacking horns). OE.

fallow deer, moose deer, mouse deer, musk deer, red deer, reindeer, roe deer, rusa deer, sika deer, Virginian deer, etc.

– COMB.: **deer-ball** an underground fruiting body of a fungus of the genus *Elaphomyces*; **deerberry** (the fruit of) any of various N. American shrubs, esp. *Vaccinium caesium* or *V. stamineum*; **deer-brush** a shrub, *Ceanothus integerrimus*, of the south-western US; **deer-coloured** *adjective* (now *rare*) tawny red; **deer-culler** *NZ* a professional shooter of deer; **deer fly** any of various flies which infest deer, *esp.* one of the tabanid genus *Chrysops*; ***deer-forest***: see FOREST *noun* 2b; **deergrass**, (*N. English*) **deer hair** a small moorland clubrush, *Trichophorum cespitosum*; **deer-horn** (**a**) (the material of) a deer's antler; (**b**) *US* a large mussel, *Tritigonia verrucosa*, the shell of which is used to make buttons etc.; **deerhound** a dog used for hunting deer, a staghound; *esp.* a large rough-haired greyhound; **deer lick** a spring or damp spot impregnated with salt etc., where deer come to lick; **deer mouse** any mouse of the large N. and Central American genus *Peromyscus*; esp. *P. maniculatus*, which is common throughout N. America; **deer park** a park in which deer are kept; **deer's hair** *N. English* = ***deergrass*** above; **deerskin** *adjective* & *noun* (made from) the skin of a deer; **deerstalker** (**a**) a hunter who stalks deer; (**b**) a cloth cap peaked in front and behind, with earflaps which are usually tied up on the top; **deer-stealer** *arch.* a poacher who kills and steals deer; **deer-track** the track of a deer; a path made by deer.

■ **deerlet** *noun* a small deer; *spec.* a chevrotain: L19. **deerlike** *adjective* resembling (that of) a deer M19.

de-escalate /diːˈɛskəleɪt/ *verb.* M20.

[ORIGIN from DE- 3 + ESCALATE.]

1 *verb trans.* Reduce the level or intensity of; reverse the escalation of (a crisis, war, etc.). M20.

2 *verb intrans.* Become less intense. M20.

■ **de-escaˈlation** *noun* M20.

deeshy /ˈdiːʃi/ *adjective. Irish.* E19.

[ORIGIN Unknown.]

Tiny; insignificant.

de-ethicize /diːˈɛθɪsʌɪz/ *verb trans.* Also **-ise**. L19.

[ORIGIN from DE- 3 + ETHICIZE.]

Deprive of its ethical character; separate from ethics.

deevy /ˈdiːvi/ *adjective. colloq.* Now *rare.* E20.

[ORIGIN Affected alt. of DIVVY *adjective*¹.]

Divine, delightful.

de-excite /diːɪkˈsʌɪt/ *verb trans.* M20.

[ORIGIN from DE- 3 + EXCITE *verb*.]

PHYSICS. Cause (an atom etc.) to undergo a transition from an excited state to a lower or ground state.

■ **de-exciˈtation** *noun* M20.

deface /dɪˈfeɪs/ *verb trans.* ME.

[ORIGIN Old French & mod. French †*défacer*, earlier *deffacer*, for Old French *desfacier*, from *des-* DE- 3 + FACE *noun*.]

1 Spoil the surface or appearance of, disfigure, mar. ME.

> P. BAYNE Every religion . . will be more or less defaced by error. C. PRIEST Walls defaced with spray-can graffiti.

2 Destroy, demolish. Long *arch.* ME.

3 Blot out, obliterate, efface (writing etc.). ME.

> M. R. MITFORD The beginning of this letter is irreparably defaced.

†**4** Destroy the reputation of, discredit. LME–M17.

†**5** Outshine, put in the shade. Also, outface, abash. M16–L18.

■ **defacement** *noun* the action of defacing; defaced condition; a disfigurement: M16. **defacer** *noun* a person who or thing which defaces M16.

de facto /deɪ ˈfaktəʊ, diː/ *adverbial & adjectival phr.* E17.

[ORIGIN Latin = of fact.]

(Existing, held, etc.) in fact, in reality; in actual existence, force, or possession, whether by right or not. Opp. ***de jure***.

defaecate *adjective, verb* see DEFECATE *adjective, verb*.

defaecation *noun* var. of DEFECATION.

defaillance /dɪˈfeɪl(ə)ns/ *noun.* Also ***défaillance*** /defajɑ̃s/. E17.

[ORIGIN French *défaillance*, from Old French & mod. French *défaillir* fail from Proto-Romance, formed as DE- 1 + FAIL *verb*: see -ANCE.]

Weakness, shortcoming, failure.

defalcate /ˈdiːfalkeɪt/ *verb.* M16.

[ORIGIN medieval Latin *defalcat-* pa. ppl stem of *defalcare*, from *de-* DE- 1 + Latin *falx*, *falc-* sickle, scythe: see -ATE³.]

†**1** *verb trans.* Subtract (a part) from a whole, deduct. M16–E19.

†**2** *verb trans.* Reduce, curtail. L17–E19.

3 *verb intrans.* Commit defalcations, misappropriate property in one's charge. M19.

■ ˈ**defalcator** *noun* a person who misappropriates funds etc. E19.

defalcation /diːfalˈkeɪʃ(ə)n/ *noun.* LME.

[ORIGIN medieval Latin *defalcatio(n-)*, formed as DEFALCATE: see -ATION.]

†**1** The action of cutting off or subtracting; a deduction. LME–M19.

†**2** Reduction of a whole by taking away a part, *spec.* of an account etc. by an amount set against it. L15–M19.

3 Diminution suffered or sustained. *arch.* M17.

4 Falling away, defection; shortcoming, failure. M18.

5 (An act of) misappropriation of money or other property by a person to whom it is entrusted; *sing.* & (usu.) in *pl.*, an amount misappropriated. M19.

defalk /dɪˈfɔːlk/ *verb.* Now *rare* or *obsolete*. LME.

[ORIGIN Old French & mod. French *défalquer* or medieval Latin *defalcare*: see DEFALCATE.]

†**1** *verb trans.* Reduce by deductions. LME–M18.

2 *verb trans.* Subtract; *spec.* deduct (a sum) from an account etc. LME.

†**3** *verb intrans.* Make a deduction; take away *from*. LME–M18.

defamation /dɛfəˈmeɪʃ(ə)n, diː-/ *noun.* ME.

[ORIGIN Old French & mod. French *diffamation* from late Latin *diffamatio(n-)*, from Latin *diffamat-* pa. ppl stem of *diffamare*: see DEFAME *verb*, -ATION.]

†**1** The bringing of dishonour upon someone; disgrace, shame. ME–E18.

2 The action, or an act of defaming; the fact of being defamed; LAW the offence of bringing a person into undeserved disrepute by making false statements (whether written or spoken); libel, slander. LME.

defamatory /dɪˈfamət(ə)ri/ *adjective.* LME.

[ORIGIN medieval Latin *diffamatorius*, from Latin *diffamat-*: see DEFAMATION, -ORY². Cf. Old French & mod. French *diffamatoire*.]

1 Of the nature of or characterized by defamation; tending to defame. LME.

2 (Habitually) employing defamation. M18.

defame /dɪˈfeɪm/ *noun.* Long *rare.* LME.

[ORIGIN Old French *deffame* (usu. *desfame*, *diff-*), from *deffamer*, *diffamer*: see DEFAME *verb*.]

Disgrace, infamy; defamation, slander.

defame /dɪˈfeɪm/ *verb trans.* ME.

[ORIGIN Old French *diffamer*, also *desf-*, *def(f)-*, from Latin *diffamare* spread about as an evil report, from *dis-* DIF-, DE- 3 + *fama* FAME *noun*.]

1 Bring dishonour on; shame, disgrace. *arch.* ME.

> TENNYSON The grand old name of gentleman, Defamed by every charlatan.

2 Attack the good reputation of, speak ill of; slander, libel. ME.

MILTON Hypocrites . . Defaming as impure what God declares Pure.

†**3** Cause to be suspected of an offence; accuse. Usu. foll. by *of*. ME–E19.

SIR W. SCOTT Rebecca . . is, by many . . circumstances, defamed of sorcery.

■ **defamer** *noun* ME.

defamed /dɪˈfeɪmd/ *ppl adjective*. LME.
[ORIGIN from DEFAME *verb* + -ED[1]. Sense 3 after French *diffamé*.]
†**1** Disgraced, dishonoured, infamous. LME–M17.
2 Attacked in reputation; slandered, libelled. L17.
3 *HERALDRY*. Of a lion or other animal: without its tail. M19.

defamiliarize /diːfəˈmɪljərʌɪz/ *verb trans*. Also **-ise**. L20.
[ORIGIN from DE- 3 + FAMILIARIZE.]
Render unfamiliar, esp. as a formalist technique.
■ **defamiliariˈzation** *noun* [translating Russian *ostranenie* making strange] L20.

defamous /ˈdɛfəməs/ *adjective*. Long *rare*. LME.
[ORIGIN from DEFAME *noun* + -OUS.]
†**1** Infamous, disgraceful. LME–M16.
2 Defamatory. LME.

defang /diːˈfaŋ/ *verb trans*. M20.
[ORIGIN from DE- 3 + FANG *noun*.]
Extract the fangs of (a snake etc.); *fig.* render harmless.

defat /diːˈfat/ *verb trans*. Infl. **-tt-**. E20.
[ORIGIN from DE- 3 + FAT *noun*[2].]
Remove fat or fats from.

defatigable /dɪˈfatɪgəb(ə)l/ *adjective*. M17.
[ORIGIN Orig. (obsolete from E18) from DE- 1 + FATIGABLE. Later (M20) back-form. from INDEFATIGABLE.]
Easily wearied, apt to tire.

E. WAUGH Then they lost interest. I did too. I was always the most defatigable of hacks.

defatigation /dɪˌfatɪˈgeɪʃ(ə)n/ *noun*. Long *rare*. E16.
[ORIGIN Latin *defatigatio(n-)*, from *defatigat-* pa. ppl stem of *defatigare* weary, exhaust, from *de-* DE- 1 + *fatigare*: see FATIGUE *verb*, -ATION.]
The action of tiring out; a state of exhaustion; fatigue.

default /dɪˈfɔːlt/ *noun & adjective*. ME.
[ORIGIN Partly from Old French *défaute*, from *défaillir* (see DEFAILLANCE) on the model of *faute* FAULT *noun*, *faillir* FAIL *verb*; partly from Old French & mod. French *défaut* back-form. from *défaute*.]
▸ **A** *noun*. **1** Lack; absence or scarcity of. Now only in ***in default of*** below. ME.
2 An imperfection, a defect, a blemish, (latterly only in character or abstract things). *arch.* ME.

SWIFT My own excellencies and other men's defaults.

3 Failure to act or perform adequately (by a person or, formerly, a thing); failure to compete in or finish a contest; failure to fulfil a legal requirement, esp. to appear in court on the appointed day. ME. ▸†**b** *HUNTING*. Failure to follow the scent. ME–M18. ▸†**c** An error, a mistake. LME–E19.

J. AGEE Some failure of the soul or default of the heart.

4 Failure to meet (now esp. financial) obligations; negligence; an instance of this. ME.

H. FAST The bank took it over on a mortgage default.

5 A preselected option adopted by a computer etc. when no other is specified by the user. M20.
– PHRASES: **by default** because of absence or failure to act. **go by default** incur judgement by default; fail or be overlooked because of negligence etc. **in default** guilty of default. **in default of** if or since (a thing) is lacking. **judgement by default** judgement awarded to the plaintiff on the defendant's failing to plead. **make default** fail to appear in court.
▸ **B** *attrib.* or as *adjective*. **1** Dealing with or relating to a (legal or financial) default. L19.
2 Adopted by a computer etc. if no other command is given. M20.

default /dɪˈfɔːlt/ *verb*. ME.
[ORIGIN from the noun; partly suggested by Old French & mod. French *défaut* 3 pres. indic. of *défaillir*: see DEFAILLANCE.]
1 *verb intrans*. Be lacking or deficient. Long *rare*. ME.
†**2** *verb intrans*. Fail in strength, faint. LME–E17.
3 *verb trans*. Put in default; *LAW* declare in default and enter judgement against (a party). LME.
4 *verb intrans*. Fail to fulfil an obligation (now esp. financial) or engagement (also foll. by *on* an obligation etc.); fail to appear in court or take part in a contest; lose a case etc. by default. L16.

J. GROSS When it came to it the other contributors defaulted, so he took on the job single-handed.

5 *verb trans*. Fail to fulfil (an obligation); lose by default; fail to make payment of. M17.

T. C. WOLFE When her boarders defaulted payments she seized their belongings. *New Yorker* Let's go . . and have a nice beer and default the fourth set.

defaulter /dɪˈfɔːltə/ *noun*. M17.
[ORIGIN from DEFAULT *verb* + -ER[1].]
1 A person etc. who is guilty of default, *esp.* one who fails to fulfil a legal or financial obligation. M17.
2 A serviceman or servicewoman guilty of a military offence. E19.

defeasance /dɪˈfiːz(ə)ns/ *noun*. LME.
[ORIGIN Old French *defesance*, from *defesant* pres. pple of *de(s)faire* (mod. *défaire*) undo, from *des-*, *dé-* DE- 3 + *faire* do: see -ANCE.]
1 *LAW*. **a** A condition which, if fulfilled, renders an agreement or instrument null and void; a document setting out such a condition. LME. ▸**b** Annulment; rendering null and void. L16.
†**2** Discharge from an obligation. *Scot.* LME–M16.
3 Defeat, undoing. *arch.* L16.

defease /dɪˈfiːz/ *verb trans*. L15.
[ORIGIN Back-form. from DEFEASANCE and DEFEASIBLE.]
†**1** Discharge from an obligation; deduct from a charge etc. *Scot.* L15–M17.
2 Undo, destroy. *rare*. E17.

defeasible /dɪˈfiːzɪb(ə)l/ *adjective*. ME.
[ORIGIN Anglo-Norman, from stem of Old French *defesant*: see DEFEASANCE, -IBLE, FEASIBLE.]
Able to be (legally) defeated or annulled; liable to forfeiture.
■ **defeasiˈbility** *noun* L19. **defeasibleness** *noun* (*rare*) E17.

defeat /dɪˈfiːt/ *noun*. M16.
[ORIGIN from the verb: cf. French *défaite*.]
1 The action of gaining victory in a battle, competition, vote, etc.; the state or an instance of being vanquished or overcome. M16.

J. R. GREEN The defeat of the Armada. J. HELLER It was check mate, match, and defeat from the opening move.

†**2** Undoing, ruin; an act of destruction. L16–M17.

SHAKES. *Much Ado* If you . . Have . . made defeat of her virginity.

3 Frustration of plans etc.; the action of bringing to nothing; *LAW* annulment. L16.

EVELYN My defeat of correspondence at Rome.

defeat /dɪˈfiːt/ *verb trans*. LME.
[ORIGIN Anglo-Norman *defeter*, from *defet*, Old French *deffait*, *desfait* pa. pple of *desfaire* (mod. *défaire*) from medieval Latin *disfacere* undo, from Latin *dis-* DE- 3 + *facere* make.]
†**1** Undo, do away with, destroy. LME–M17.

SHAKES. *Oth.* His unkindness may defeat my life.

2 *LAW*. Annul. LME.
†**3** Disfigure, deface, spoil. LME–E17.
4 Cause to fail, frustrate (a plan etc.), baffle. L15.

SHAKES. *Haml.* My stronger guilt defeats my strong intent.

5 Gain victory over in battle, competition, matter decided by voting, etc.; vanquish, overcome. M16.

J. G. FARRELL England had been defeated in the first test match. *fig.*: SHELLEY She Who loved me did with absent looks defeat Despair.

†**6** Do out *of*, cheat, disappoint; deprive *of*, dispossess. M16–M19.
■ **defeater** *noun* M19. †**defeatment** *noun* L16–M18.

defeatism /dɪˈfiːtɪz(ə)m/ *noun*. E20.
[ORIGIN French *défaitisme*, from *défaite* DEFEAT *noun*: see -ISM.]
Conduct or thinking encouraging the expectation or acceptance of defeat; disposition to accept defeat.
■ **defeatist** *noun & adjective* [French *défaitiste*] (a person) advocating defeatism or tending to accept defeat E20.

defeature /dɪˈfiːtʃə/ *noun & verb*. *arch.* L16.
[ORIGIN Old French *deffaiture*, *desfaiture* destruction, disguise, from *desfaire*: see DEFEAT *verb*, -URE. In sense A.2 assoc. with FEATURE *noun* (cf. DISFEATURE).]
▸ **A** *noun* †**1** **a** Undoing, ruin. L16–E17. ▸**b** Defeat. L16–M19.
2 (A) disfigurement, a marring of features. L16.

SHAKES. *Com. Err.* Careful hours with time's deformed hand Have written strange defeatures in my face.

▸ **B** *verb trans*. Disfigure. L18.

†**defecate** *adjective*. Also **-faec-**. LME–M18.
[ORIGIN Latin *defaecatus* pa. pple, formed as DEFECATE *verb*: see -ATE[2].]
Purified from dregs, clear; (esp. spiritually) pure.

defecate /ˈdɛfɪkeɪt, ˈdiːf-/ *verb*. Also **-faec-**. L15.
[ORIGIN Latin *defaecat-* pa. ppl stem of *defaecare*, from *de-* DE- 3 + *faex*, pl. *faeces* dregs: see FAECES, -ATE[3].]
1 *verb trans*. Clear from dregs or impurities; purify, clarify, refine, (*lit.* & *fig.*). Now *rare*. L15.

fig.: S. JOHNSON To defecate and clear my mind by brisker motions.

2 *verb trans*. Remove in purifying; purge away, void as excrement. Now *rare*. L15.
3 *verb intrans*. Discharge faeces from the bowels. M19.
■ **defecated** *ppl adjective* (now *rare*) purified (esp. spiritually), clarified; (of evil) unmitigated: E17. **defecator** *noun* a person who or thing which defecates; *spec.* in sugar manufacture, an apparatus in which sugar solutions are purified: M19.

defecation /dɛfɪˈkeɪʃ(ə)n, diːf-/ *noun*. Also **-faec-**. E17.
[ORIGIN Latin *defaecatio(n-)*, formed as DEFECATE *verb*: see -ATION.]
1 Purification from dregs; clarification, refinement. Now chiefly *techn.* E17.
2 Discharging of faeces from the bowels. M19.

defect /ˈdiːfɛkt, dɪˈfɛkt/ *noun*. LME.
[ORIGIN Latin *defectus*, from *defect-* pa. ppl stem of *deficere* leave, desert, fail, from *de-* DE- 3 + *facere* make, do. Partly through Old French *defect* deficiency.]
1 The absence of something essential to completeness; a lack, a deficiency. LME.

J. MORLEY The excess of scepticism and the defect of enthusiasm.

in defect wanting, deficient. **in defect of** for want of.
2 A shortcoming, a failing; a fault, an imperfection. (The usual sense.) LME. ▸**b** *PHYSICS*. An irregularity in a crystal lattice, such as a vacant site, interstitial atom, etc. M20.

H. JAMES She . . accused herself of no end of defects. *Punch* Should any mechanical defect ever occur, we promise to repair or replace your pen.

the defects of a person's qualities those faults which often accompany a person's particular virtues.
†**3** Imperfection, faultiness. M16–L18.
†**4** A falling away; defection. M16–L18.
†**5** Failure of the sun, moon, etc., to shine; an eclipse. Only in 17.
6 A quantity or amount by which something falls short of a given quantity etc. M17.
mass defect: see MASS *noun*[2] & *adjective*.

defect /dɪˈfɛkt/ *verb*. L16.
[ORIGIN Latin *defect-*: see DEFECT *noun*.]
†**1** *verb intrans*. Fail, fall short, become deficient. L16–L17.
2 *verb intrans*. Fall away in allegiance (*from*); desert; *esp.* desert to or *to* a country with an opposing ideology. L16.

L. DEIGHTON Your wife defected . . . Your wife is working for the bloody Russkies.

3 *verb trans*. Cause to desert. Long *rare*. M17.

defectible /dɪˈfɛktɪb(ə)l/ *adjective*. Now *rare*. E17.
[ORIGIN Late Latin *defectibilis*, formed as DEFECT *verb*: see -IBLE.]
Liable to fail or fall short.
■ **defectiˈbility** *noun* E17.

defection /dɪˈfɛkʃ(ə)n/ *noun*. M16.
[ORIGIN Latin *defectio(n-)*, from *defect-*: see DEFECT *noun*, -ION.]
1 The action or fact of failing or becoming defective; a failure. *arch.* M16. ▸**b** Imperfection, defectiveness; a defect. *obsolete* exc. *Scot.* L16.

C. BRONTË I underwent . . miserable defections of hope.

2 Desertion of one's party, cause, etc., esp. in order to join the opposition; the leaving of one's country to settle in a country with an opposing ideology. M16.

D. FRASER The defection of her Italian Ally would pose grave problems for Germany.

3 A falling away from faith, duty, or principles; backsliding. *arch.* M16.

J. PRIESTLEY The times of defection and idolatry.

defective /dɪˈfɛktɪv/ *adjective & noun*. ME.
[ORIGIN Old French & mod. French *défectif*, *-ive*, or late Latin *defectivus*, from *defect-*: see DEFECT *noun*, -IVE.]
▸ **A** *adjective*. **1** Having a defect or defects; imperfect, incomplete (in some respect); faulty. ME. ▸**b** Deficient or lacking *in* (†*of*). LME. ▸**c** *spec.* Of a person: having a mental disability. Also more fully ***mentally defective***. Now *offensive*. L19.

J. TYNDALL My defective French pronunciation. G. GREENE A defective gutter which emptied itself like a tap.

†**2** At fault; guilty of negligence, error, or wrongdoing. LME–L17.
3 Lacking for completion; missing. *arch.* L15.

CARLYLE I wish you had a Fortunatus hat; it is the only thing defective in your outfit.

4 *GRAMMAR*. Lacking one or more of the forms, inflections, or uses normal for the part of speech. L15.
▸ **B** *noun*. †**1** A thing lacking. Only in L15.
2 A person who is inadequate or disabled; *spec.* (more fully ***mental defective***) a person who has a mental disability. Now *offensive*. L16.
3 *GRAMMAR*. A word lacking one or more of the forms, inflections, or uses normal for the part of speech. L16.
■ **defectively** *adverb* E17. **defectiveness** *noun* E17.

defector /dɪˈfɛktə/ *noun*. M17.
[ORIGIN Latin *defector*, formed as DEFECT *noun*: see -OR.]
A person who defects; one who changes sides or who deserts (cf. DEFECT *verb* 2).

†**defectuous** *adjective*. M16–E18.
[ORIGIN medieval Latin *defectuosus*, from *defectus* DEFECT *noun*: see -UOUS. Cf. Old French & mod. French *défectueux*.]
Defective, faulty, imperfect.

†**defedation** *noun*. Also **defoed-**. M17–L18.
[ORIGIN French †*défédation* or medieval Latin *defoedatio(n-)*, from *defoedat-* pa. ppl stem of late Latin *defoedare* defile, from *de-* DE- 1 + *foedare*, from *foedus* foul.]

D

D

The action of making impure, pollution; a contamination.

defeminize /diːˈfɛmɪnʌɪz/ *verb trans.* Also **-ise**. E20.
[ORIGIN from DE- 3 + FEMINIZE.]
Deprive of femininity; make less feminine.
■ **defemini'zation** *noun* E20.

defence /dɪˈfɛns/ *noun.* Also ***defense**. ME.
[ORIGIN Old French *defens(e)* (mod. *défense*) from late Latin use as nouns of *defensum*, *defensa* neut. and fem. pa. pples of *defendere*: see DEFEND.]
▸ **I 1** Prohibition. *obsolete* exc. as below. ME.
in defence (of fish or waters) prohibited from being taken or fished in.
†**2** The action of warding off. LME–L16.
▸ **II 3** *gen.* The action of guarding from attack; resistance against attack; protection. ME. ▸†**b** The faculty or capacity of defending; strength against attack. L15–M17.

A. RADCLIFFE What are your weapons of defence? *Proverb*: Attack is the best form of defence. **b** SPENSER A man of great defence.

civil defence: see CIVIL *adjective*. **defence in depth** a system of defence with successive areas of resistance. **line of defence** (*a*) MILITARY a line representing the course of a projectile fired from a curtain wall to defend a bastion; (*b*) a line or series of points at which an enemy is resisted (*lit.* & *fig.*). SELF-DEFENCE.
4 A means of resisting attack; a defensive force; the military resources of a country; in *pl.*, fortifications, defensive installations. ME.

AV *Ps.* 94:22 The Lord is my defence. C. RYAN His real fear was that German armour . . would break through his meagre defences. *Rolling Stone* His immune system, the body's defense against illness. *attrib.*: C. R. ATTLEE The Government are thinking . . of having a Defence Minister.

5 Defending, supporting, or maintaining by argument; justification, vindication; an argument, speech, or writing used to this end. LME.

B. JOWETT Socrates prefaces his defence by resuming the attack. H. JAMES Will you hear me abused without opening your lips in my defence?

6 (The science or art of) defending oneself; self-defence. *arch.* E17.
7 CHESS. A move or series of moves played with the object of countering an opponent's attack. Also, any opening or opening variation initiated by Black. E17.
French defence, ***Indian defence***, ***Nimzowitsch defence***, ***Sicilian defence***, etc.
8 SPORTS & GAMES. An attempt to resist an opponent's attack; play, moves, or tactics aimed at such resistance; (the function of) those members of a team whose principal responsibility is to resist attacks; CRICKET batting, the batsmen, (opp. to bowling, the bowlers). E19. ▸**b** A reigning champion's attempt to retain a title. M20.
9 PSYCHOANALYSIS. Avoidance of conscious conflict or anxiety by repression, compensation, projection, or other (unconscious) mechanism; a mechanism for this (= ***defence mechanism*** (b) below). E20.
▸ **III** (Orig. from branch I, later also from II.)
10 LAW. A defendant's denial of the truth of allegations made against him or her; a pleading in answer to a claim; the case against an allegation or claim; an issue of law or fact that could relieve a defendant of liability. Also, the person(s) defending the accused. LME.

A. PATON The defence will be that the shot was fired in fear and not to kill. *Rolling Stone* The defense had argued insanity.

– COMB.: **defence bond**: issued by a government borrowing money for military defence; **defenceman** in ice hockey and lacrosse, a player in a defensive position; **defence mechanism** (*a*) a process by which an organism reacts against pathogens, predators, etc.; (*b*) PSYCHOANALYSIS a usu. unconscious mental process avoiding conscious conflict or anxiety.
■ **defenceless** *adjective* (*a*) without defence; unprotected; †(*b*) affording no defence or protection: M16. **defencelessly** *adverb* E19. **defencelessness** *noun* E18.

defence /dɪˈfɛns/ *verb trans.* Also **defense**. LME.
[ORIGIN from the noun.]
1 Defend, protect; provide with defences, fortify. Long *rare* in *gen.* sense. LME.
2 SPORTS & GAMES. Attempt to resist the attack of (an opponent); attempt to resist (an attack). *N. Amer.* M20.

Montreal Star We did a pretty poor job of defensing him and even when we played good defence against him it didn't seem to help.

defend /dɪˈfɛnd/ *verb.* ME.
[ORIGIN Old French & mod. French *défendre* from Latin *defendere* ward off, protect, from *de-* DE- 1 + *-fendere* (as in *offendere* OFFEND).]
▸ **I** †**1** *verb trans.* Ward off, avert. ME–E19.
†**2** *verb trans.* Prevent, hinder; keep *from* doing something. ME–M17.
3 *verb trans.* Prohibit, forbid. *arch.* ME.
▸ **II 4** *verb trans.* Ward off an attack on; fight for the safety of; protect from or against assault or injury; keep safe. ME. ▸**b** SPORTS & GAMES. Protect (a wicket etc.) from the ball; resist an attack on (a goal etc.). M18.

P. HOLLAND Trees . . defended and clad with thick leaued branches. F. FITZGERALD Defending the airport against enemy attack.

5 *verb trans.* Uphold by argument, vindicate; speak or write in favour of. ME. ▸†**b** Maintain (a contested statement); contend (*that*). L15–E17.

J. PRIESTLEY I am far from pretending . . to defend this passage of Irenæus.

6 *verb intrans.* Resist an attack; put up a defence. M16.

Toronto Sun Champion Hulla Hogan defending against Randy (Macho Man) Savage. *Guardian* Mabbutt . . proved his all-round qualities . . by defending well and heading England's first goal.

▸ **III** (Orig. from branch I, later also from II.)
7 *verb trans.* & *intrans.* LAW. Deny the truth of (an allegation against oneself); present a defence of (oneself, one's cause); represent (a defendant) as legal counsel. LME.

L. STEFFENS He was defended by three attorneys of high repute in criminal jurisprudence.

– PHRASES: **God defend**, **heaven defend** *arch.* may God or heaven forbid or prevent it.
■ **defendable** *adjective* LME.

defendant /dɪˈfɛnd(ə)nt/ *adjective* & *noun.* ME.
[ORIGIN Old French & mod. French *défendant* pres. pple of *défendre*: see DEFEND, -ANT[1].]
▸ **A** *adjective* **1** †**a** *pres. pple.* Defending. Only in ME. ▸**b** Defending oneself, or an opinion, cause, etc., against attack; opposing the plaintiff's plea in a suit at law. LME.
†**2** Defensive. *rare.* Only in L16.
▸ **B** *noun.* †**1** The challenged party in a wager of battle. LME–E19.
2 A person or body sued or accused in a court of law. LME.
3 A defender against hostile attack; a protector. Now *rare.* LME.
†**4** = DEFENDER 3. E–M17.

defender /dɪˈfɛndə/ *noun.* ME.
[ORIGIN Anglo-Norman *defendour*, Old French *defendeor*, formed as DEFEND + -ER[2].]
1 A person who defends or wards off an attack; a protector. ME. ▸**b** IRISH HISTORY (**D-**.) A member of a society of Roman Catholics formed in the late 18th cent. to resist the Orangemen. L18.
2 Chiefly SCOTS LAW. = DEFENDANT *noun* 2. LME.
3 A person who defends by argument; one who speaks or writes in defence of a person, cause, or opinion. E16.
Defender of the Faith: a title of English monarchs since Henry VIII, who received it from Pope Leo X as a reward for writing against Luther. ***public defender***: see PUBLIC *adjective* & *noun*.
4 SPORTS & GAMES. A player who defends, one whose principal responsibility is to resist attacks. Also, a reigning champion who defends a title. M18.
left defender: see LEFT *adjective*. ***right defender***: see RIGHT *adjective*.
■ **Defenderism** *noun* (IRISH HISTORY) the principles or policy of the Defenders L18. **defendress** *noun* (now *rare*) [French *défenderesse*] a female defender LME.

defenestration /ˌdiːfɛnɪˈstreɪʃ(ə)n/ *noun.* E17.
[ORIGIN mod. Latin *defenestratio(n-)*, from *de-* DE- 1 + *fenestra* window: see -ATION.]
The action of throwing a thing or (usu.) a person out of a window.
– NOTE: Chiefly in *the Defenestration of Prague*, an incident in 1618 which precipitated the Thirty Years War.
■ **de'fenestrate** *verb trans.* E17.

†**defensative** *adjective* & *noun.* Also **-itive**. L16.
[ORIGIN Extended form of DEFENSIVE (cf. *preventive*, *-ative*): see -ATIVE.]
▸ **A** *adjective.* **1** Able to be defended. Only in L16.
2 Defensive, protective; of the nature of a defence. E17–E18.
▸ **B** *noun.* = DEFENSIVE *noun* 1. L16–L18.

defense *noun*, *verb* see DEFENCE *noun*, *verb*.

defensible /dɪˈfɛnsɪb(ə)l/ *adjective.* ME.
[ORIGIN Late Latin *defensibilis*, from *defens-* pa. ppl stem of *defendere* DEFEND: see -IBLE.]
†**1** Of a weapon, armour, fortified place, etc.: (capable of) affording defence; defensive. ME–E19.
2 Able to be defended; easily defended; justifiable. LME.
†**3** In a state of defence; secure. L16–L18.
■ **defensi'bility** *noun* M19. **defensibleness** *noun* L17. **defensibly** *adverb* LME.

defension /dɪˈfɛnʃ(ə)n/ *noun.* LME.
[ORIGIN Latin *defensio(n-)*, from *defens-*: see DEFENSIBLE, -ION. Cf. Old French *defension*.]
†**1** Protection; vindication. LME–M16.
2 The formal defence of a thesis as an academic exercise, esp. in Roman Catholic colleges. M16.

defensist /dɪˈfɛnsɪst/ *noun.* E20.
[ORIGIN from DEFENSE *noun* + -IST.]
RUSSIAN HISTORY. A person who advocated a continuation of the First World War by Russia against Germany, in preference to the conclusion of a separate peace.

†**defensitive** *noun* & *adjective* var. of DEFENSATIVE.

defensive /dɪˈfɛnsɪv/ *adjective* & *noun.* LME.
[ORIGIN Old French & mod. French *défensif*, *-ive* from medieval Latin *defensivus*, from *defens-*: see DEFENSIBLE, -IVE.]
▸ **A** *adjective.* **1** Serving or intended for defence, protective; having the function of or aimed at resisting an opponent's attack. LME. ▸**b** CRICKET. Of batting: cautious, having the protection of the wicket as the chief consideration. L19.

SHAKES. *Rich. II* As a moat defensive to a house. F. BURNEY I was obliged to resolve upon a defensive conduct in future. W. CAMP As a tackler and defensive player . . he was exceptional. J. CONRAD The perfect stillness . . made her raise her eyes . . with a hard, defensive expression. K. CLARK Grim defensive houses strong enough to withstand party feuds. J. LEHANE The primary emphasis in defensive play is to prevent the offensive player from doing what he wants to do.

defensive end AMER. FOOTBALL (the position of) a defensive winger who lines up close to the tackle.
2 Of the nature of a defence or vindication (*of*). E17.

H. BROUGHTON Two little workes defensive of our Redemption.

3 Of or pertaining to defence. M17.

S. AUSTIN Their position was entirely a defensive one.

▸ **B** *noun.* †**1** Something that serves to defend or protect; *esp.* a medicine, dressing, etc., serving to prevent injury or infection. LME–E18.
2 A state or position of defence. Chiefly in ***on the defensive***. E17.

SWIFT The French army acts now wholly on the defensive.

■ **defensively** *adverb* in a defensive manner; as regards defence: M16. **defensiveness** *noun* E17.

defensor /dɪˈfɛnsə/ *noun.* LME.
[ORIGIN Anglo-Norman *defensour*, Old French *defenseor* (mod. *-eur*) from Latin *defensor*, from *defens-*: see DEFENSIBLE, -OR.]
†**1** A defender. LME–L17.
2 ROMAN HISTORY. In the later period of the empire, a provincial magistrate whose duty was to afford protection against oppression by a governor. LME.

defensory /dɪˈfɛns(ə)ri/ *noun* & *adjective.* LME.
[ORIGIN Late Latin *defensorius* adjective, from *defensor*: see DEFENSOR, -ORY[1], -ORY[2].]
▸ †**A** *noun.* A defence. LME–L17.
▸ **B** *adjective.* Serving or intended for defence, defensive. M16.

defer /dɪˈfəː/ *verb*[1]. Infl. **-rr-**. Also †**differ**. LME.
[ORIGIN Old French & mod. French *différer* defer, differ: see DIFFER *verb*.]
†**1** *verb trans.* Put on one side. Only in LME.
2 *verb trans.* Put off (an action or procedure, an event, matter, or question, †a person) to some later time; delay, postpone, (a thing, *doing*, †*to do*). LME. ▸**b** Relegate to a later part of a work. M16. ▸**c** Postpone the date of military call-up of (a person). *US.* M20.

AV *Prov.* 13:12 Hope deferred maketh the heart sicke. J. USSHER Neither did he long defer to put those Jews to death. J. LONDON Her first proposal would have to be deferred to a more propitious time. A. J. CRONIN He made up his mind to defer the more exacting examinations until another time.

deferred annuity: that does not begin immediately. **deferred payment** payment by instalments. **deferred share**: on which no dividend is payable until after a certain lapse of time, or until all the dividend on ordinary and preference shares has been paid.
†**3** *verb trans.* Waste (time etc.) in delay. LME–M17.

SHAKES. *1 Hen. VI* Defer no time, delays have dangerous ends.

4 *verb intrans.* Procrastinate, delay. LME.

E. YOUNG Be wise to-day; 'tis madness to defer.

■ **deferment** *noun* a putting off; postponement: E17. **deferral** *noun* = DEFERMENT L19. **deferrer** *noun* M16.

defer /dɪˈfəː/ *verb*[2]. Infl. **-rr-**. LME.
[ORIGIN Old French & mod. French *déférer* from Latin *deferre* carry away, refer (a matter), from *de-* DE- 1 + *ferre* bear, carry.]
†**1** *verb intrans.* Submit oneself *to*. *Scot.* LME–L15.
†**2** *verb trans.* Submit (a matter *to* a person etc.) for determination or judgement; refer. L15–L17.
†**3** *verb trans.* Offer, proffer, tender; esp. in LAW, offer for acceptance. M16–M19.
4 *verb intrans.* Submit or make concessions in opinion or action (*to* a person etc.); pay deference *to*. L17.

V. SACKVILLE-WEST Everybody must defer She, and she alone, must decide. S. BELLOW He deferred to his brother's opinion.

deference /ˈdɛf(ə)r(ə)ns/ *noun.* M17.
[ORIGIN French *déférence*, formed as DEFER *verb*[2]; see -ENCE.]
1 Submission to or compliance with the acknowledged superior claims, skill, judgement, or other qualities, of another. M17.

I. D'ISRAELI Charles often yielded a strange deference to minds inferior to his own.

2 Courteous regard; the manifestation of a disposition to yield to the claims or wishes of another. M17.

EARL OF CHATHAM Their age and learning . . entitle them to all deference. I. COLEGATE The two footmen standing . . with just the right mixture of deference and shared pleasure in the guests' surprise.

– PHRASES: **in deference to** out of respect for the authority or wishes of.

deferent /ˈdɛf(ə)r(ə)nt/ *noun & adjective*[1]. LME.
[ORIGIN French *déférent* or (Astron.) its source, medieval Latin *deferent-*, *-ens*, use as noun of pres. pple of *deferre*: see DEFER *verb*[2], -ENT.]
▸ **A** *noun*. **1** HISTORY OF SCIENCE. In the Ptolemaic system: the circular orbit of the centre of the epicycle in which a planet was thought to move. LME.
2 A carrying or conducting agent; *spec.* (ANATOMY) a deferent duct (see sense B.2 below). Now *rare* or *obsolete*. E17.
▸ **B** *adjective*. †**1** Of or pertaining to the deferent in the Ptolemaic system. Only in LME.
2 Carrying or conveying to a particular destination; *spec.* (ANATOMY) designating or pertaining to a duct for conveying fluids, e.g. the vas deferens. Now *rare* or *obsolete*. E17.

deferent /ˈdɛf(ə)r(ə)nt/ *adjective*[2]. E19.
[ORIGIN from DEFER *verb*[2] and DEFERENCE: see -ENT.]
Showing deference, deferential.

deferential /dɛfəˈrɛnʃ(ə)l/ *adjective*[1]. E19.
[ORIGIN from DEFERENCE + -IAL, after *prudence*, *prudential*, etc.]
Characterized by or showing deference, respectful.
▪ **deferentiˈality** *noun* L19. **deferentially** *adverb* M19.

deferential /dɛfəˈrɛnʃ(ə)l/ *adjective*[2]. Now *rare* or *obsolete*. L19.
[ORIGIN French *déférentiel*, from *déférent* DEFERENT *adjective*[1].]
ANATOMY. Serving to convey; pertaining to a deferent duct (see DEFERENT *adjective*[1] 2).

defervescence /diːfəˈvɛs(ə)ns/ *noun*. E18.
[ORIGIN from Latin *defervescent-* pres. ppl stem of *defervescere* cease boiling, etc., from *de-* DE- 3 + *fervescere* inceptive verb from *fervere* be hot: see -ENCE.]
1 Cooling down. Only in Dicts. E18.
2 MEDICINE. (The period of) the decrease of bodily temperature accompanying the abatement of fever. M19.
▪ Also †**defervescency** *noun* M–L17.

deffo /ˈdɛfəʊ/ *interjection*. *colloq.* L20.
[ORIGIN Abbreviation.]
Definitely, certainly.

defial /dɪˈfʌɪəl/ *noun*. *rare*. LME.
[ORIGIN Old French *defiaille*, from *défier* defy; in mod. use directly from DEFY *verb*: see -AL[1].]
= DEFIANCE.

defiance /dɪˈfʌɪəns/ *noun*. ME.
[ORIGIN Old French & mod. French *défiance* (now only = distrust), from *défier* DEFY *verb*: see -ANCE.]
†**1** Renunciation of allegiance or friendship, rejection; (a) declaration of hostility. ME–M17.
2 A challenge to a fight or contest, or to uphold an assertion etc. Now *rare* or *obsolete*. ME.

SHAKES. *Rich. II* Shall we . . send Defiance to the traitor, and so die?

3 The act of defying; open or daring resistance to authority or an opposing force. E18.

J. SHARP This open and scandalous violation and defiance of his most sacred fundamental laws. R. MAY When parents say 'Don't' he often must scream defiance at them.

— PHRASES: †**at defiance** in enmity or hostility. ***cartel of defiance***: see CARTEL 1. **in defiance of** with open disregard of.

defiant /dɪˈfʌɪənt/ *adjective*. L16.
[ORIGIN from French *défiant*, or directly from DEFIANCE: see -ANT[1].]
Showing open resistance or defiance.
— NOTE: Rare before M19.
▪ **defiantly** *adverb* M19. **defiantness** *noun* (*rare*) L19.

defibrillation /ˌdiːfɪbrɪˈleɪʃ(ə)n/ *noun*. M20.
[ORIGIN from DE- 3 + FIBRILLATION.]
MEDICINE. The stopping of fibrillation of the heart (by administering a controlled electric shock).
▪ **deˈfibrillate** *verb trans.* stop the fibrillation of M20. **deˈfibrillator** *noun* an apparatus used to control heart fibrillation M20.

defibrinate /diːˈfʌɪbrɪneɪt/ *verb trans.* M19.
[ORIGIN from DE- 3 + FIBRIN + -ATE[3].]
MEDICINE. Remove fibrin from (blood).
▪ **defibriˈnation** *noun* the process of removing fibrin from blood; the state of being deficient in fibrin: L19.

†**deficience** *noun*. LME–M19.
[ORIGIN formed as DEFICIENCY: see -ENCE.]
= DEFICIENCY.

deficiency /dɪˈfɪʃ(ə)nsi/ *noun*. M17.
[ORIGIN from DEFICIENT: see -ENCY.]
1 The quality or state of being deficient; (the amount of) a shortfall; something lacking, a defect. M17.

J. H. NEWMAN Where art has to supply the deficiencies of nature. H. CECIL Mrs Poulter was very short of gin and had to make up the deficiency with water. P. PARISH In children vitamin C deficiency may delay bone growth.

mental deficiency *arch.* the condition of having a mental disability.
2 GENETICS. The loss of a segment from a chromosome; the segment lost. E20.
— COMB.: **deficiency disease**: caused by the lack of a vitamin or other essential substance in the diet; **deficiency payment**: paid to producers by Government to ensure a guaranteed minimum price.

deficient /dɪˈfɪʃ(ə)nt/ *adjective & noun*. L16.
[ORIGIN Latin *deficient-* pres. ppl stem of *deficere* undo, leave, fail, from *de-* DE- 3 + *facere* make, do: see -ENT.]
▸ **A** *adjective*. †**1** Theol. ***deficient cause***, that failure or deficiency which causes some result or state. Cf. ***efficient cause***. L16–L17.
†**2** Failing, fainting. E–M17.
3 Incomplete, lacking (*in*) something, defective. E17. ▸**b** MATH. Of a number: that exceeds the sum of its divisors. Opp. ABUNDANT *adjective* 3. E18.

P. G. WODEHOUSE I am not deficient in an appreciation of the humorous. T. HEGGEN A competent metallurgist, but his knowledge of explosives was deficient.

mentally deficient (now *offensive*) having a mental disability.
4 Insufficient in quantity, force, etc.; inadequate. M17.

R. W. EMERSON Uniformly polite, but with deficient sympathy.

▸ **B** *noun*. †**1** A deficiency. M–L17.
2 †**a** A deficient thing; a defaulter. M17–E18. ▸**b** A person who has a mental disability. Now *offensive*. E20.
▪ **deficiently** *adverb* E18.

deficit /ˈdɛfɪsɪt, ˈdiː-/ *noun*. L18.
[ORIGIN French *déficit*, from Latin 3rd person sing. pres. indic. of *deficere*: see DEFICIENT.]
(The amount of) a deficiency, esp. of money; an excess of expenditure or liabilities over income or assets.
— COMB.: **deficit financing** the financing of deficit spending; **deficit spending** Government spending, in excess of revenue, of funds raised by borrowing, not by taxation.

de fide /diː ˈfʌɪdi/ *adjectival phr.* M17.
[ORIGIN Latin = of faith.]
To be accepted as an article of faith.

defier /dɪˈfʌɪə/ *noun*. L16.
[ORIGIN from DEFY *verb* + -ER[1].]
A person who defies.

†**defiguration** *noun*. L16–M19.
[ORIGIN from medieval Latin *defigurat-* pa. ppl stem of *defigurare* disfigure, from *de-* DE- 3 + *figurare* FIGURE *verb*: see -ATION. Cf. French *défiguration*.]
(A) disfigurement.

defilade /dɛfɪˈleɪd/ *verb & noun*. E19.
[ORIGIN from French *défiler* + -ADE. Cf. ENFILADE.]
▸ **A** *verb trans.* Shield (a position, troops, etc.) from observation or (enfilading) fire by utilizing natural obstacles or erecting fortifications. E19.
▸ **B** *noun*. The action of defilading; protection of troops etc. from enemy observation or fire; an obstacle or fortification giving protection. M19.

defile /dɪˈfʌɪl, ˈdiːfʌɪl/ *noun*. Also †**defilé(e)**. L17.
[ORIGIN French *défilé* use as noun of pa. pple of *défiler* DEFILE *verb*[2].]
1 A narrow way through which troops can only march in file; a gorge, a narrow mountain pass. L17.
2 The action of marching in single file or in narrow columns; a march in file. M19.

defile /dɪˈfʌɪl/ *verb*[1]. LME.
[ORIGIN Alt. of DEFOUL after BEFILE.]
▸ **I** *verb trans.* **1** Make physically dirty or foul; soil, pollute. LME.

H. LATIMER An evyll birde that defiles hys own nest.

2 Corrupt morally, taint, sully. LME.

AV *Mark* 7:20 That which commeth out of the man, that defileth the man.

3 Violate the chastity of; deflower, debauch. LME.

M. PRIOR The husband murder'd, and the wife defil'd.

4 Desecrate, profane; make unfit for ritual or ceremonial use. LME.

F. M. CRAWFORD It is a criminal offence . . for a non-Hindu person to defile the food of even the lowest caste man.

†**5** Defame, dishonour. LME–E18.

SHAKES. *Mids. N. D.* He is defil'd That draws a sword on thee.

▸ **II** *verb intrans.* †**6** Cause defilement, drop excrement. M–L16.

SHAKES. *1 Hen. IV* This pitch, as ancient writers do report, doth defile.

†**7** Become foul. Only in L17.
▪ **defilement** *noun* the act of defiling; the state of being defiled; a thing which defiles: L16. **defiler** *noun* LME.

defile /dɪˈfʌɪl/ *verb*[2] *intrans.* E18.
[ORIGIN French *défiler*, from *dé-* DE- 3 + *file* FILE *noun*[2].]
March in single file or in narrow columns.

definable /dɪˈfʌɪnəb(ə)l/ *adjective*. M17.
[ORIGIN from DEFINE + ABLE *adjective*.]
Able to be defined.
▪ **definaˈbility** *noun* M19. **definably** *adverb* E19.

define /dɪˈfʌɪn/ *verb*. LME.
[ORIGIN Old French *definer* from Proto-Romance var. of Latin *definire* (whence French *définir*), from *de-* DE- 1 + *finire* FINISH *verb*.]
▸ **I** *verb trans.* †**1** Bring to an end; settle. LME–L17.

I. BARROW A more ready way to define Controversies.

2 Determine or indicate the boundary or extent of. LME. ▸**b** Delineate, make distinct in outline or form. Freq. *refl.* E19.

S. HEANEY Machine-gun posts defined a real stockade. **b** MRS H. WARD The slender figure suddenly defined itself against the road.

†**3** State precisely; declare. LME–M17.
4 Set out precisely, describe or explain the nature, properties, scope, or essential qualities of (a thing or concept). LME. ▸**b** Interpret or state precisely the meaning of (a word or phrase). M16.

J. BUCHAN He . . defines the problems which he leaves for later . . philosophers to solve. **b** BOSWELL A lady once asked him how he came to define *Pastern* 'the *knee* of a horse'.

5 *verb trans.* Determine, prescribe, fix precisely, specify. L15.

GIBBON Two or three years were loosely defined for the term of my absence.

†**6** Restrict, confine. E16–M17.
7 Establish the character or essence of, characterize. M17.

M. AMIS A serious Fauntleroy defined by his frill shirt and pageboy collar.

8 Separate by definition, distinguish *from*. *rare*. E19.
▸ **II** *verb intrans.* †**9** Decide, pass judgement. LME–E17.
†**10** Make a precise statement. LME–E17.
11 Frame a description or definition. L16.

BURKE When we define we seem in danger of circumscribing nature within the bounds of our own notions.

— PHRASES: **define one's position** state one's position clearly.
▪ **defined** *adjective* having a definite or specified outline or form; clearly marked, definite: E18. **definement** *noun* (*rare*) (a) definition, (a) description. E17. **definer** *noun* a person who or thing which defines L16.

definiendum /dɪˌfɪnɪˈɛndəm/ *noun*. Pl. **-da** /-də/. L19.
[ORIGIN Latin *definiendum* neut. gerundive of *definire*: see DEFINE.]
The word or phrase which is (to be) defined; the word or symbol being introduced by definition into a system.

definiens /dɪˈfɪnɪɛnz/ *noun*. Pl. **definientia** /dɪfɪnɪˈɛntɪə, -ˈɛnʃɪə/. L19.
[ORIGIN medieval Latin *definiens* pres. pple of *definire*: see DEFINE.]
The defining part of a definition, the word or phrase that states the meaning; the verbal or symbolic expression to which a definiendum is declared to be equivalent.

definite /ˈdɛfɪnɪt/ *adjective & noun*. M16.
[ORIGIN Latin *definitus* pa. pple of *definire*: see DEFINE *verb*, -ITE[2].]
▸ **A** *adjective*. **1** Having fixed limits or form; determinate, certain, precise, specific; (of a person) decided, sure in opinion, statement, etc. M16.

E. BOWEN The eyebrows were lightly marked but their structure was definite. A. THWAITE He should not begin any translations without some definite promise from a publisher.

2 GRAMMAR. Designating the article (demonstrative adjective or similar element) which is principally used to indicate a defined or particularized individual (viz. in English *the*); in German etc., designating an adjective inflection used after such an article, or an adjective with such a form. E18.
— SPECIAL COLLOCATIONS & PHRASES: **definite description** PHILOSOPHY a denoting phrase introduced by the definite article or equivalent. **definite inflorescence** BOTANY = CYME *noun* 2. **definite integral** MATH. an integral taken between specified upper and lower limits of the independent variable and calculated as the difference between the values of the integral at these limits. ***past definite***: see PAST *noun*.
▸ **B** *noun*. Something which is definite; *spec.* in GRAMMAR, a noun denoting a definite thing or object. M16.
▪ **definitely** *adverb* (*a*) in a definite manner, with certainty; (*b*) (*colloq.*, as an emphatic affirmative) certainly, yes (***definitely not***, no): L16. **definiteness** *noun* E18.

definition /dɛfɪˈnɪʃ(ə)n/ *noun*. Also (earlier) †**diff-**. LME.
[ORIGIN Old French & mod. French *définition* (Old French also *diff-*) from Latin *definitio(n-)*, from *definit-* pa. ppl stem of *definire*: see DEFINE, -ITION.]
1 The action of settling a controversy etc., (a) decision; *spec.* a formal decision of an ecclesiastical authority. Now *rare* or *obsolete*. LME.
2 A precise statement of the nature, properties, scope, or essential qualities of a thing; an explanation of a concept etc.; a statement or formal explanation of the meaning of a word or phrase. LME.

S. JOHNSON It has been found hard to describe man by an adequate definition. N. PODHORETZ Cardinal Newman's definition of a gentleman as a person who could be at ease in any company. R. SCRUTON It is a limp definition of conservatism to describe it as the desire to conserve.

contextual definition, **definition in use**: in which the signification of an expression, symbol, etc., is defined implicitly by its context or use. ***nominal definition***: see NOMINAL *adjective*.
3 The action of defining the nature of a thing or the meaning of a word. E17.

R. G. COLLINGWOOD Definition necessarily means defining one thing in terms of something else.

by definition self-evidently, axiomatically.
4 Precision, clarity, exactitude. M19.

D

W. SANSOM That her eyes were shadowed with illness or trouble he could with definition say.

5 The action of making, or the state of being made, visually clear and distinct; the capacity of a lens etc. to make an image distinct to the eye; the degree of clarity of a photograph, television picture, or other image. **M19.**

S. NEWCOMB The definition of this telescope is very fine. M. INNES Shadows that were losing definition and merging.

■ **definitional** *adjective* of, pertaining to, or of the nature of a definition **M19. definitionally** *adverb* **M20.**

D

definitive /dɪˈfɪnɪtɪv/ *adjective & noun.* Also (earlier) †**diff-**. **LME.**

[ORIGIN Old French & mod. French *définitif* (Old French also *diff-*) from Latin *definitivus* pa. pple of *definire*: see DEFINE, -IVE.]

▸ **A** *adjective.* **1** Having the function or character of finality; decisive, conclusive, final; definite, fixed, finally settled, unconditional. **LME.** ▸†**b** Of a person: definite, decided. **E17–M18.** ▸**c** Of a literary or artistic work etc.: setting a standard; authoritative, reliable, complete. **L19.**

LD MACAULAY A jury had pronounced: the verdict was definitive. S. NEWCOMB A definitive orbit of the comet. E. BOWEN This evening's fiasco has been definitive: I think it better our acquaintance should close. **c** D. MACDONALD Here is the definitive work, and I hope it will become a model for future scholarly biographies. L. DEIGHTON Some of his performances remained definitive ones.

definitive host BIOLOGY: of the adult or sexually reproductive form of a parasite.

†**2** METAPHYSICS. Having a definite position but not occupying space. **E16–E18.**

3 Serving to define or specify; GRAMMAR specifying the individual referred to. **M18.**

W. TAYLOR To preserve a name of sect, which ought to be simply definitive, from sliding into a term of reproach.

4 Serving to define visually. *rare.* **E19.**

5 PHILATELY. Of a postage stamp: forming the regular or standard issue (i.e. not special or commemorative). **E20.**

▸ **B** *noun.* †**1** A definitive judgement or sentence. **L16–E19.**

†**2** GRAMMAR. A definitive word; an article, a demonstrative. **M18–E19.**

3 PHILATELY. A definitive postage stamp. **E20.**

■ **definitively** *adverb* **E16. definitiveness** *noun* **E18.**

definitor /dɪˈfɪnɪtə, dɛfɪˈnʌɪtə/ *noun.* **L15.**

[ORIGIN Late Latin *definitor* a person who determines, (in medieval Latin) definitor, from *definit-*: see DEFINITION, -OR.]

1 ROMAN CATHOLIC CHURCH. An officer of the chapter in certain monastic orders responsible for rulings on disciplinary matters. **L15.**

†**2** A kind of surveying instrument. **M17–L18.**

definitory /dɪˈfɪnɪt(ə)ri/ *noun.* **L17.**

[ORIGIN formed as DEFINITOR: see -ORY[1].]

ROMAN CATHOLIC CHURCH. A body or council of definitors.

definitory /dɪˈfɪnɪt(ə)ri/ *adjective.* **E20.**

[ORIGIN from Latin *definit-* (see DEFINITION) + -ORY[2].]

Relating or belonging to definition.

definitude /dɪˈfɪnɪtjuːd/ *noun.* **M19.**

[ORIGIN from DEFINITE after *infinite*, *infinitude*: see -TUDE. Cf. earlier INDEFINITUDE.]

The quality of being definite; precision.

definitum /dɛfɪˈnʌɪtəm/ *noun.* Pl. **-ta** /-tə/. **E17.**

[ORIGIN Latin *definitum* thing defined, neut. of pa. pple of *definire* DEFINE.]

LOGIC. The thing or expression which a definition defines.

deflagrate /ˈdɛfləgreɪt/ *verb trans. & intrans.* **E18.**

[ORIGIN Latin *deflagrat-* pa. ppl stem of *deflagrare* burn up, from *de-* DE- 1 + *flagrare* burn: see -ATE[3].]

Chiefly CHEMISTRY. (Cause to) burst into flames and burn away rapidly.

deflagrating spoon a long-handled metal spoon used for holding small quantities of materials that deflagrate.

■ **deflagrator** *noun* an apparatus for producing deflagration **E19.**

deflagration /dɛfləˈgreɪʃ(ə)n/ *noun.* **E17.**

[ORIGIN Latin *deflagratio(n-)*, formed as DEFLAGRATE: see -ATION.]

†**1** The rapid burning away of anything in a destructive fire. **E17–M19.**

2 Chiefly CHEMISTRY. The action of deflagrating; rapid combustion accompanied by flame. **M17.**

deflate /dɪˈfleɪt/ *verb.* **L19.**

[ORIGIN from DE- 3 + *-flate* of INFLATE *verb.*]

1 *verb trans.* Release the air or gas from (something inflated). **L19.** ▸**b** *verb intrans.* Of an inflated object: go down, become emptied of the inflating air or gas. **E20.**

H. JAMES The train the cyclist takes when his tyre's deflated.

2 *verb trans.* Reduce the size or importance of; depreciate, debunk; cause to lose conceitedness or confidence. **E20.** ▸**b** *verb intrans.* Lose one's spirit, confidence, etc.; climb down. **E20.**

H. G. WELLS My disposition to deflate the reputation of Marx. N. COWARD There's nothing more deflating than telling someone some exciting news and discovering that they already know it. E. REVELEY Adrian's bitchiness had entirely deflated her sense of well-being.

3 *verb trans.* ECONOMICS. Reduce the inflation of (a currency). **E20.** ▸**b** *verb intrans.* Pursue a policy of deflation. Also, become reduced by deflation. **E20.**

■ **deflater, -or** *noun* a person who or thing which deflates **L19.**

deflation /dɪˈfleɪʃ(ə)n/ *noun.* **L16.**

[ORIGIN Branch I (ult.) from Latin *deflat-* ppl stem of *deflare* blow away, from *de-* DE- 1 + *flare* to blow; sense 2 through German *Deflation*. Branch II from DEFLATE: see -ATION.]

▸ **I** †**1** The loss or release of heat from within an object. Only in **L16.**

2 GEOGRAPHY. The removal of particles of rock, sand, etc., by the wind. **L19.**

▸ **II 3** The release of air from something inflated. **L19.**

4 ECONOMICS. A policy or process of reducing economic activity and the inflation of currency. Opp. ***inflation***. **E20.**

5 Reduction in importance, reputation, confidence, etc.; disparagement. **M20.**

■ **deflationary** *adjective* of, pertaining to, or tending to (esp. economic) deflation **E20. deflationist** *noun & adjective* (**a**) *noun* an advocate of a policy of deflation; (**b**) *adjective* of or pertaining to deflationists; deflationary: **E20.**

deflect /dɪˈflɛkt/ *verb.* **M16.**

[ORIGIN Latin *deflectere* bend aside, from *de-* DE- 1 + *flectere* to bend.]

1 *verb trans.* Bend or turn aside from a straight course; cause to deviate (*from*); change the direction of. (*lit. & fig.*) **M16.**

H. READ He was deflected from this intention by the unexpected appearance of a figure. O. MANNING Quintin did nothing to deflect or direct enquiries. J. D. SALINGER Almost anything could deflect a marble from going straight to its mark.

2 *verb intrans.* Change direction; deviate from its or one's course. **E17.**

R. H. ELLIOT Then deflecting a little to their right, they got on a long ridge of grassy hill. C. POTOK It hit the finger section of my glove, deflected off, . . and knocked me down.

3 *verb trans.* Turn to something other than its natural quality or use. Now *rare* or *obsolete*. **E17.**

T. KEN To greatest Good deflected greatest ill.

4 *verb trans.* Bend or curve downwards. Chiefly (BOTANY & ZOOLOGY) as ***deflected*** *ppl adjective* = DEFLEXED. **M17.**

■ **deflective** *adjective* having the quality of deflecting **E19.**

deflection /dɪˈflɛkʃ(ə)n/ *noun.* Also **deflexion**. **E17.**

[ORIGIN Late Latin *deflexio(n-)*, from Latin *deflex-* pa. ppl stem of *deflectere* DEFLECT: see -ION. Cf. French *déflexion* (also †*déflection*).]

1 The action of turning, or state of being turned, from a straight line or course; the amount of such deviation; a lateral turn or deviation. **E17.**

BACON A digression and deflexion from the ordinary course of generations. C. MERIVALE The great deflection of the coast southward from Cape Wrath.

2 The turning of a word or phrase aside from its actual form, application, or use. *arch.* **E17.**

3 The action of bending something downwards; downcurved condition; a downward bend or curve. **M17.**

J. S. FOSTER Excessive deflection of beams and buckling of columns must be avoided.

4 (The extent of) the movement of an instrument's pointer away from its zero. **M17.**

deflectometer /diflɛkˈtɒmɪtə/ *noun.* **M19.**

[ORIGIN from DEFLECT *verb* + -OMETER.]

An instrument for measuring the deflection or deformation of an object under stress.

deflector /dɪˈflɛktə/ *noun.* **M19.**

[ORIGIN from DEFLECT + -OR.]

A device that deflects; *esp.* a plate or diaphragm that deflects a current of air etc.

deflex /dɪˈflɛks/ *adjective.* *rare.* **L18.**

[ORIGIN Latin *deflexus* pa. pple of *deflectere* DEFLECT.]

= DEFLEXED.

deflexed /dɪˈflɛkst/ *adjective.* **E19.**

[ORIGIN from DEFLEX + -ED[1].]

BOTANY & ZOOLOGY. Bent or curving downwards.

deflexion *noun* var. of DEFLECTION.

deflexure /dɪˈflɛkʃə, -sjə/ *noun.* *rare.* **M17.**

[ORIGIN from Latin *deflex-*: see DEFLECTION, -URE.]

(A) deflection.

deflocculate /diːˈflɒkjʊleɪt/ *verb trans. & intrans.* **E20.**

[ORIGIN from DE- 3 + FLOCCULATE *verb.*]

(Cause to) undergo deflocculation.

■ **deflocculant** *noun* a deflocculating agent **M20. defloccuˈlation** *noun* the process by which floccules in a liquid break up into fine particles, producing a dispersion **E20.**

defloration /diːflɔːˈreɪʃ(ə)n/ *noun.* **LME.**

[ORIGIN Old French & mod. French *défloration* or late Latin *defloratio(n-)*, from *deflorat-* pa. ppl stem of *deflorare*: see DEFLOWER, -ATION.]

1 The action of deflowering a virgin. **LME.**

Observer A rather perfunctory defloration in a Scarborough hotel.

2 A selection of choice passages from a book; the selecting of such passages. **LME.**

T. CARTE The Historia Britonum out of which . . he made those deflorations.

deflower /diːˈflaʊə/ *verb trans.* **LME.**

[ORIGIN Old French *deflourer*, earlier *de(s)flo(u)rer* (mod. *déflorer*) from Proto-Romance var. of late Latin *deflorare*, from *de-* DE- 3 + *flos*, *flor-* FLOWER *noun.*]

1 Deprive (a woman) of her virginity; violate, ravish. **LME.** ▸**b** *fig.* Ravage, desecrate, spoil. **L15.**

S. RUSHDIE The . . headmistress . . refused to concede that the wretch might have been deflowered upon her antiseptic premises. **b** J. R. LOWELL A sanctuary which telegraph or telephone had not deflowered.

†**2** Select or abstract the finest parts from (a book etc.). **LME–L18.**

3 Deprive or strip of flowers. **M17.**

KEATS Garlands . . From vales deflower'd.

■ **deflowerer** *noun* **M16.**

defluent /ˈdɛflʊənt/ *adjective & noun.* *rare.* **M17.**

[ORIGIN Latin *defluent-* pres. ppl stem of *defluere* flow down, from *de-* DE- 1 + *fluere* flow: see -ENT.]

(A stream etc.) that flows down or away.

■ **defluence** *noun* a flowing down or away **L17.** †**defluency** *noun* = DEFLUENCE: only in **M17.** †**defluous** *adjective* flowing down, falling **E18–E19.**

defluvium /dɪˈfluːvɪəm/ *noun.* **E19.**

[ORIGIN Latin = loss by flowing or falling away.]

MEDICINE. A complete shedding of hair, fingernails, or another part, as a result of disease.

defluvium capillorum /kapɪˈlɔːrəm/ [mod. Latin = of the hair] shedding of hair, alopecia.

†**deflux** *noun.* **L16–E18.**

[ORIGIN Latin *defluxus*, from *deflux-* pa. ppl stem of *defluere*: see DEFLUENT.]

= DEFLUXION.

defluxion /dɪˈflʌkʃ(ə)n/ *noun.* **M16.**

[ORIGIN French *défluxion* or late Latin *defluxio(n-)*, from *deflux-*: see DEFLUX, -ION.]

†**1** A flowing or running down; a shedding. **M16–M19.** ▸**b** Something that flows or runs down; an emanation. Only in **17.**

2 *spec.* MEDICINE. A flow or running esp. from the nose or eyes; catarrh, phlegm. *obsolete* exc. *Scot.* **L16.**

defocus /diːˈfəʊkəs/ *verb trans. & intrans.* Infl. **-s-, -ss-**. **M20.**

[ORIGIN from DE- 3 + FOCUS *verb.*]

Put or go out of focus.

†**defoedation** *noun* var. of DEFEDATION.

†**defoil** *verb* var. of DEFOUL.

defoliate /diːˈfəʊlɪeɪt/ *verb trans.* **L18.**

[ORIGIN Late Latin *defoliat-* pa. ppl stem of *defoliare*, from *de-* DE- 3 + *folium* leaf: see -ATE[3].]

Remove the leaves from; cause the defoliation of, esp. as a military tactic.

■ **defoliant** *noun* a chemical used to cause defoliation **M20. defoliator** *noun* a thing that defoliates; *spec.* an insect which strips trees of their leaves: **L19.**

defoliation /dɪˌfəʊlɪˈeɪʃ(ə)n/ *noun.* **M17.**

[ORIGIN formed as DEFOLIATE: see -ATION.]

1 Loss or shedding of leaves. **M17.**

2 Deliberate destruction of foliage (for military purposes). **M20.**

deforce /dɪˈfɔːs/ *verb trans.* **LME.**

[ORIGIN Anglo-Norman *deforcer*, Old French *deforcier*, from *des-* DE- 3 + *forcier*, *forcer* FORCE *verb*[1]. Cf. ENFORCE *verb* etc.]

1 LAW. Keep by force (*from* the rightful owner); withhold wrongfully. **LME.** ▸**b** Deprive forcibly (*of* rightful property); deprive wrongfully. **LME.**

2 SCOTS LAW. Forcibly prevent (a legal officer) from carrying out an official duty. **LME.**

†**3** Rape. *Scot.* **LME–E17.**

■ **deforcement** *noun* **L15. deforcer** *noun* **LME.**

deforciant /dɪˈfɔːsɪənt/ *noun.* **LME.**

[ORIGIN Anglo-Norman *deforceant* pres. pple of *deforcer*: see DEFORCE, -ANT[1].]

LAW. A person who deforces another of property.

deforest /diːˈfɒrɪst/ *verb trans.* **M16.**

[ORIGIN from DE- 3 + FOREST *noun*. Cf. DE-AFFOREST, DISAFFOREST, DISFOREST.]

1 *hist.* = DISAFFOREST 1. **M16.**

2 = DISFOREST 2. **L19.**

■ **deforeˈstation** *noun* **L19.**

deform /dɪˈfɔːm/ *adjective.* *arch.* **LME.**

[ORIGIN Latin *deformis*, from *de-* DE- 3 + *forma* shape. Cf. DIFFORM.]

Deformed; hideous.

MILTON Sight so deform what heart of rock could long Drie-ey'd behold?

■ †**deformly** *adverb* **L17–M18.**

deform /dɪˈfɔːm/ *verb.* **LME.**

[ORIGIN Old French *difformer*, *de(s)former* (mod. *difformer*, *déformer*) from medieval Latin *difformare*, Latin *deformare*, formed as DIS-, DE- 3 + *forma* FORM *noun.*]

1 *verb trans.* Mar the beauty or excellence of; disfigure, deface. **LME.**

N. HAWTHORNE The square . . had mean little huts, deforming its ample space.

2 *verb trans.* Spoil the form or shape of; misshape. LME.

SHAKES. *Rich. III* Cheated of feature by dissembling nature, Deform'd, unfinish'd.

3 *verb trans.* Chiefly SCIENCE. Alter the form or configuration of. LME.

D. CAMERON A tendency for the wind to deform the balloon.

4 *verb intrans.* Chiefly SCIENCE. Undergo deformation. (*rare* before M20.) M18.

Which? If the driver hits the wheel this bracket deforms, absorbing some of the force.

■ **deformer** *noun* L15.

deformable /dɪˈfɔːməb(ə)l/ *adjective.* LME.
[ORIGIN from DEFORM *verb* + -ABLE.]
†**1** Deformed, disfigured. LME–L17.
2 Able to be deformed. L19.
■ **deforma'bility** *noun* L19.

deformation /diːfɔːˈmeɪʃ(ə)n/ *noun.* LME.
[ORIGIN Old French & mod. French *déformation* or Latin *deformatio(n-)* (medieval Latin *diff-*), from *deformat-* pa. ppl stem of *deformare*: see DEFORM *verb*, -ATION.]
1 The action or result of marring the appearance, beauty, or excellence of; disfigurement, defacement. LME.

I. WATTS The deformations and disgraces of time.

2 Alteration of form for the worse; the action or result of misshaping. M16. ▸**b** An altered form of a word, used esp. to avoid overt blasphemy or profanity (as ***dad***, ***od***, etc., for ***God***). L19.

R. WHATELY A most extensive ecclesiastical reformation (or deformation, as it may turn out).

3 Chiefly SCIENCE. Change in shape, configuration, or structure (*of*); the extent of this; an altered structure etc. M19.

A. CAYLEY Two skew surfaces . . deformations of each other. *Scientific American* These . . fracture zones resulted from some massive deformation of the earth's crust.

ELASTIC ***deformation***. ***plastic deformation***: see PLASTIC *adjective* & *noun*[3].
■ **deformational** *adjective* of or pertaining to deformation E20.

deformed /dɪˈfɔːmd/ *adjective.* LME.
[ORIGIN from DEFORM *verb* + -ED[1].]
†**1** Marred in appearance, defaced. LME–E18.
2 Misshapen, distorted. Now chiefly of a person: misshapen in body or limb. LME.

J. MARQUAND His left hand was badly deformed from some wound and was minus three fingers.

†**3** Shapeless, formless. M16–L17.
4 Perverted; morally repugnant. M16.
5 Chiefly SCIENCE. That has undergone deformation. L20.
■ **deformedly** /dɪˈfɔːmɪdli, -mdli/ *adverb* (now *rare*) L16.

deformity /dɪˈfɔːmɪti/ *noun*[1]. Also †**diff-**. LME.
[ORIGIN Old French *deformité* (*deff-*, *desf-*) from Latin *deformitas*, from *deformis* misshapen: see DEFORM *adjective*, -ITY.]
1 The quality or condition of being deformed; disfigurement; (esp. bodily) misshapenness. LME.

SHAKES. *Rich. III* To spy my shadow in the sun And descant on mine own deformity. HOR. WALPOLE Beautifull Gothic architecture was engrafted on Saxon deformity.

2 An instance or kind of disfigurement or malformation, esp. of the body. LME. ▸**b** A deformed being or thing. L17.

E. P. THOMPSON Tailors had a characteristic deformity of the shoulders and chest.

3 (An instance of) moral disfigurement or crookedness. LME.

T. NORTON The corruption and deformitie of our nature. LD MACAULAY Cromwell had tried to correct the deformities of the representative system.

†**deformity** *noun*[2] var. of DIFFORMITY *noun*[1].

†**defoul** *verb trans.* Also **defoil**. ME.
[ORIGIN Old French *defouler*, *defuler*, from *dé-* DE- 1 + *fouler* to tread: see FOIL *verb*[1], FULL *verb*[1]. Cf. DEFILE *verb*[1].]
1 Trample down; break, crush. ME–L16. ▸**b** *fig.* Oppress; maltreat, abuse. ME–M16.
2 Deflower, debauch. ME–L16.
3 Violate (a law, holy place, etc.); desecrate. ME–E17.
4 Make filthy or dirty; pollute; *fig.* defile, corrupt. ME–E17.

defrag /diːˈfrag/ *verb trans.* L20.
[ORIGIN Abbreviation.]
= DEFRAGMENT.

defragment /diːfragˈmɛnt/ *verb trans.* L20.
[ORIGIN from DE- 3 + FRAGMENT *verb*.]
COMPUTING. Of software: reduce the fragmentation of (a file) by concatenating parts stored in separate locations on a disk.
■ **defragmen'tation** *noun* L20. **defragmenter** *noun* L20.

deframe /diːˈfreɪm/ *verb trans.* E20.
[ORIGIN from DE- 3 + FRAME *verb*.]
Remove the frame from (a picture).

defraud /dɪˈfrɔːd/ *verb & noun.* LME.
[ORIGIN Old French *defrauder* or Latin *defraudare*, from *de-* DE- 1 + *fraudare* to cheat, from *fraus*, *fraud-* FRAUD.]
▸ **A** *verb.* **1** *verb trans.* Take or withhold rightful property, status, etc., from (a person) by fraud; deprive wrongfully, cheat. (Foll. by *of*.) LME.

E. KIRKE We who defraud four million citizens of their rights. E. F. BENSON All three . . considered that they and theirs had been positively defrauded. *Daily Mirror* The scrounger who defrauded the country of £36,000.

2 *verb intrans.* Act with or employ fraud. LME.

AV *Mark* 10:19 Doe not beare false witnesse, Defraud not.

▸ †**B** *noun.* = DEFRAUDATION. LME–E19.
■ **defrauder** *noun* LME. **defraudment** *noun* the action or an act of defrauding M17.

defraudation /diːfrɔːˈdeɪʃ(ə)n/ *noun.* LME.
[ORIGIN Old French, or late Latin *defraudatio(n-)*, from Latin *defraudat-* pa. ppl stem of *defraudare*: see DEFRAUD, -ATION.]
(An act of) fraudulent deprivation of property or rights; cheating.

defray /dɪˈfreɪ/ *verb trans.* LME.
[ORIGIN French *défrayer*, from *dé-* DE- 3 + †*frai*, †*frait* (usu. pl. *frais*, †*fres*) expenses, cost, from medieval Latin *fredum*, *-us*, fine for breach of the peace.]
†**1** Pay out, spend (money). LME–E17.
†**2** Pay the expenses of (a person), reimburse; entertain free of charge. L16–M19.

P. SIDNEY Defraying the mariners with a ring bestowed upon them.

3 Pay for; meet the expense of. Now *arch. rare.* L16.

C. BARKER The estate of the defunct member was not sufficient to defray his funeral.

4 Pay (the expense or cost of something); meet, settle. L16.

E. A. FREEMAN The payment was defrayed out of the spoils.

■ **defrayable** *adjective* liable to be defrayed L19. **defrayal** *noun* the action of defraying, defrayment E19. **defrayer** *noun* L16. **defrayment** *noun* the action or fact of defraying; payment (of expenses etc.): M16.

defreeze /diːˈfriːz/ *verb trans.* E20.
[ORIGIN from DE- 3 + FREEZE *verb*.]
= DEFROST.

defrock /diːˈfrɒk/ *verb trans.* E17.
[ORIGIN French *défroquer*, from *dé-* DE- 3 + *froc* FROCK.]
Deprive of priestly frock or ecclesiastical rank; unfrock.

defrost /diːˈfrɒst/ *verb.* L19.
[ORIGIN from DE- 3 + FROST *noun*.]
1 *verb trans.* Unfreeze, remove the frost from (frozen food, the interior of a refrigerator, a windscreen, etc.). L19.
2 *verb intrans.* Become unfrozen. M20.
■ **defroster** *noun* a device for defrosting, esp. one preventing the formation of ice on a windscreen E20.

deft /dɛft/ *adjective.* ME.
[ORIGIN Var. of DAFT.]
†**1** = DAFT 1. *rare.* Only in ME.
2 Clever or neat in action; skilful, dexterous. LME.

M. FRAYN By a deft manoeuvre Riddle got herself appointed to a Procedure Committee. J. G. FARRELL Matthews was deft and experienced at removing ladies' garments.

3 Tidy, trim, neat; pretty. *obsolete* exc. *dial.* L16.
4 Quiet; gentle. *obsolete* exc. *dial.* M18.
■ **deftly** *adverb* LME. **deftness** *noun* E17.

defterdar /dɛftəˈdɑː/ *noun.* Also †**t-** & other vars. L16.
[ORIGIN Turkish from Persian *daftardār*, from *daftar* DUFTER + *-dār* holding, holder.]
A Turkish finance officer or treasurer; *esp.* a provincial accountant-general.

defunct /dɪˈfʌŋ(k)t/ *adjective & noun.* M16.
[ORIGIN Latin *defunctus* pa. pple of *defungi* discharge, perform, finish, from *de-* DE- 3 + *fungi* perform. Cf. Old French & mod. French *défunt*.]
▸ **A** *adjective.* **1** Dead, deceased. M16.

A. S. BYATT Mrs Daisy Wapshott would part with her defunct husband's inherited treasure.

2 No longer in use or in existence; out of fashion. M18.

A. POWELL A Ninetyish aestheticism . . was by no means defunct in Oxford of those days. A. WEST A reporter from the now defunct *Evening Star*.

▸ **B** *noun. The* deceased, *the* dead. M16.
■ **defunctive** *adjective* pertaining to dying; becoming defunct: E17. **defunctness** *noun* L19.

defunction /dɪˈfʌŋ(k)ʃ(ə)n/ *noun. rare.* L16.
[ORIGIN Late Latin *defunctio(n-)*, from *defunct-* ppl. stem of *defungi*: see DEFUNCT, -ION.]
Dying, (a) death.

defuse /diːˈfjuːz/ *verb trans.* M20.
[ORIGIN from DE- 3 + FUSE *noun*[1].]
1 Remove the fuse from (an explosive). M20.
2 *fig.* Reduce the likelihood of trouble arising from (a crisis etc.). M20.

A. T. ELLIS She knocked over a cup in her haste to defuse this touchy situation.

defusion /dɪˈfjuːʒ(ə)n/ *noun.* E20.
[ORIGIN from DE- 3 + FUSION, translating German *Entmischung* separation.]
PSYCHIATRY. A reversal of the normal fusion of (*spec.* life and death) instincts.

defy /dɪˈfʌɪ/ *noun.* Now chiefly *US.* L16.
[ORIGIN French *défi*, from *défier*: see DEFY *verb*. In recent use perh. directly from the verb.]
(A) declaration of defiance; a challenge to fight.

DRYDEN The challenger with fierce defie His trumpet sounds.

defy /dɪˈfʌɪ/ *verb.* ME.
[ORIGIN Old French & mod. French *défier* (earlier *des-*, *def-*) from Proto-Romance, from Latin *dis-* (see DE-) + *fidus* faithful, rel. to *fides* FAITH.]
1 *verb trans.* Renounce faith or allegiance to; declare hostilities or war against. *obsolete* exc. *hist.* ME.
2 *verb trans.* Challenge to or to combat or battle. *arch.* ME.

MILTON Th' infernal Serpent . . Who durst defie th' Omnipotent to Arms.

†**3** *verb trans.* Reject, renounce, disdain, revolt at. ME–E18.

J. GAY The mastiff . . Whose honest jaws the bribe defy'd.

†**4** *verb intrans.* Show lack of faith; have distrust *of*. LME–E17.
5 *verb trans.* Challenge the power of; resist openly, refuse to obey. LME. ▸**b** Of a thing: resist completely, present insuperable obstacles to. E18.

ISAIAH BERLIN Mill likes dissent, . . those who defy the establishment. M. EDWARDES The fear that employees would . . defy union instructions. **b** C. PATMORE Beauty which defies analysis. E. WAUGH A . . warmth which defied the gathering blizzard.

6 *verb trans.* Challenge *to do* something which the challenger believes cannot be done. L17.

C. DARWIN I defy any one at first sight to be sure that it is not a fish leaping for sport. P. P. READ A hard look, as if defying him to say that he disapproved of her scheme.

deg. *abbreviation.*
Degree(s).

dégagé /degaʒe, deɪˈgɑːʒeɪ/ *adjective.* Fem. **-ée**. L17.
[ORIGIN French, pa. ppl adjective of *dégager* set free, from *dé-* DE- 3 after *engager* ENGAGE *verb*.]
Unconstrained, relaxed; detached, unconcerned.

C. CHAPLIN To offset my embarrassment I assumed a dégagé manner.

degas /diːˈgas/ *verb trans.* Infl. **-ss-**. E20.
[ORIGIN from DE- 3 + GAS *noun*[1].]
Remove unwanted gas from.
■ **degasifi'cation** *noun* the process of degassing E20. **degasify** *verb trans.* = DEGAS E20.

de Gaullism *noun*, **de Gaullist** *adjective* & *noun* see GAULLISM, GAULLIST.

degauss /diːˈgaʊs/ *verb trans.* M20.
[ORIGIN from DE- 3 + GAUSS.]
Neutralize the magnetic field of (a ship esp. as a protection against magnetic mines) by encircling it with a conductor carrying electric current; remove unwanted magnetism from (esp. a television receiver) by this or other means.

degeneracy /dɪˈdʒɛn(ə)rəsi/ *noun.* M17.
[ORIGIN from DEGENERATE *adjective* & *noun*: see -ACY.]
1 The condition, quality, or property of being degenerate. M17.

ADDISON Nature in its utmost Corruption and Degeneracy. P. W. ATKINS A distortion of the molecule that removes the degeneracy of the electronic states.

2 An instance of being degenerate; a degenerate thing or state. *rare* exc. PHYSICS (cf. DEGENERATE *adjective* 4). L17.

degenerate /dɪˈdʒɛn(ə)rət/ *adjective & noun.* L15.
[ORIGIN Latin *degeneratus* pa. pple, formed as DEGENERATE *verb*: see -ATE[2].]
▸ **A** *adjective* (orig. *pa. pple*).
1 Degenerated; having lost the qualities that are normal and desirable or proper to the kind; having fallen from excellence; debased, degraded; that has reverted to a lower type; in BIOLOGY, having a simpler structure or a lower degree of activity. L15.

J. A. FROUDE The degenerate representatives of a once noble institution. J. RABAN A . . yellow, vulpine bitch—a degenerate descendant of the Saluki family.

degenerate code BIOCHEMISTRY a genetic code in which each amino acid is encoded by several different triplets.

2 Characterized by degeneration. M17.

POPE Such men as live in these degenerate days.

3 MATH. Relating to or denoting an example of a particular type of equation, curve, or other entity that is equivalent to a simpler type, often occurring when a variable or parameter is set to zero. L19.

4 PHYSICS. Of a quantized or oscillating system: having two or more states with the same energy. Of a state or states: equal in energy (with one or more others). Of particles: occupying degenerate states. E20. ▸**b** Of matter: so compressed (as in some stars) that electrons or other particles occupy degenerate energy levels and exert pressure (resisting further compression) through quantum effects. Hence, consisting of such matter. M20.

P. W. ATKINS The three *np*-orbitals of any free atom constitute a triply degenerate set of [wave] functions.

▶ **B** *noun.* A degenerate person or animal; *esp.* someone considered to be of debased mentality or character. M16.

W. J. H. SPROTT The deplorable Jukes family, their dismal record of defectives and degenerates.

■ **degenerately** *adverb* M17. **degenerateness** *noun* M17.

D

degenerate /dɪˈdʒɛnəreɪt/ *verb.* M16.
[ORIGIN Latin *degenerat-* pa. ppl stem of *degenerare* depart from its race or kind, from *degener* debased, ignoble, from *de-* DE- 1 + *genus, gener-* kind: see -ATE³.]
▶ **I** *verb intrans.* **1** Lose the qualities that are normal and desirable or appropriate to the kind or type; revert to a lower type; deteriorate physically, mentally, or morally; gradually change *into* something inferior; in BIOLOGY, change to a simpler structure or a less active form. M16.

T. TAYLOR When men degenerate, and by sinne put off the nature of man. J. K. JEROME We never ought to allow our instincts of justice to degenerate into mere vindictiveness. H. G. WELLS A complicated metaphysical digression that began badly and degenerated towards the end. I. MURDOCH A road which degenerated into a farm track.

2 Show a decline or degeneration *from* an antecedent or standard. Now *rare* or *obsolete.* M16.

POPE How the son degenerates from the sire.

†**3** Be or become altered (without implying debasement); change, differ. M16–E17.

R. HAKLUYT Some . . followed Courses degenerating from the Voyage before pretended.

▶ **II** *verb trans.* **4** Cause to deteriorate; debase, degrade. M17.

A. BRONTË How completely his past life has degenerated his once noble constitution.

degeneration /dɪˌdʒɛnəˈreɪʃ(ə)n/ *noun.* L15.
[ORIGIN French *dégénération* or late Latin *degeneratio(n-)*, formed as DEGENERATE *verb*: see -ATION.]
1 The condition of having degenerated or being degenerate; degeneracy. L15.
2 The process of degenerating; change or reversion to an inferior type or state; decay, decline; in BIOLOGY, change to a simpler structure or less active form. L16. ▸**b** MEDICINE & BIOLOGY. (A particular kind of) deterioration in the structure or function of a cell or tissue. M19.
b *fatty degeneration, hyaline degeneration, Nissl degeneration,* etc.
†**3** That which has degenerated; a degenerate form. M17–M18.
■ **degenerationism** *noun* (*hist.*) the belief that all humankind was once civilized and that primitive peoples have degenerated from this state M20. **degenerationist** *noun & adjective* (*hist.*) (*a*) *noun* an adherent of degenerationism; (*b*) *adjective* of or pertaining to degenerationism or degenerationists: L19.

degenerative /dɪˈdʒɛn(ə)rətɪv/ *adjective.* M19.
[ORIGIN formed as DEGENERATE *verb* + -ATIVE.]
Of the nature of, tending to, or associated with degeneration.
degenerative disease: characterized by progressive, often irreversible, deterioration of tissue or loss of function.

degenerescence /dɪˌdʒɛnəˈrɛs(ə)ns/ *noun.* M19.
[ORIGIN French *dégénérescence*, from *dégénérer* to degenerate: see -ESCENT, -ENCE.]
Tendency to degenerate; the process of degeneration.

†**degenerous** *adjective.* L16–E19.
[ORIGIN from Latin *degener* (see DEGENERATE *verb*) + -OUS, after GENEROUS.]
Unworthy of one's ancestry or kind; degenerate; characterized by degeneration.

deglaciation /ˌdiːgleɪsɪˈeɪʃ(ə)n, -glas-/ *noun.* L19.
[ORIGIN from DE- 3 + GLACIATION.]
GEOLOGY. The disappearance of ice from a previously glaciated region.

deglamorize /diːˈglamərʌɪz/ *verb trans.* Also **-our-**, **-ise**. M20.
[ORIGIN from DE- 3 + GLAMORIZE *verb.*]
Deprive of glamour.
■ **deglamoriˈzation** *noun* M20.

deglaze /diːˈgleɪz/ *verb trans.* L19.
[ORIGIN from DE- 3 + GLAZE *noun.* In sense 2 after French *déglacer.*]
1 Remove the glaze from, give a dull or matt surface to. L19.
2 Dilute the meat sediments in (a pan) in order to make a gravy or sauce. M20.

deglute /dɪˈgluːt/ *verb trans. & intrans. rare.* L16.
[ORIGIN Latin *deglut(t)ire* swallow down, from *de-* DE- 1 + *glut(t)ire* swallow.]
Swallow (food etc.).

deglutinate /dɪˈgluːtɪneɪt/ *verb trans.* E17.
[ORIGIN Latin *deglutinat-* pa. ppl stem of *deglutinare* unglue, from *de-* DE- 3 + *glutinare* to glue: see -ATE³.]
†**1** Unglue; loosen or separate (things glued together). E17–E18.
2 Extract the gluten from (a cereal, esp. wheat). L19.
■ **deglutiˈnation** *noun* †(*a*) ungluing; (*b*) removal of gluten: E17.

deglutition /diːgluːˈtɪʃ(ə)n/ *noun. arch.* exc. MEDICINE. M17.
[ORIGIN French *déglutition* or mod. Latin *deglutitio(n-)*, from *deglutit-* pa. ppl stem of *deglut(t)ire*: see DEGLUTE, -ITION.]
The action of swallowing.
■ **deglutitious** *adjective* (*rare*) of or pertaining to swallowing E19. **deglutitory** *adjective* (*rare*) having the function of swallowing; pertaining to swallowing: M19.

†**degorge** *verb trans.* E16–E18.
[ORIGIN French *dégorger* (Old French *des-*), from *dé-* DE- 3 + *gorge* GORGE *noun*¹.]
= DISGORGE.

degradation /dɛgrəˈdeɪʃ(ə)n/ *noun*¹. M16.
[ORIGIN Old French & mod. French *dégradation* or ecclesiastical Latin *degradatio(n-)*, from *degradat-* pa. ppl stem of *degradare*: see DEGRADE *verb*, -ATION.]
1 Deposition from some office, rank, or position of honour, as a punishment. M16.
2 Lowering in character or quality; moral or intellectual debasement. L17.

B. C. BRODIE Nothing can tend more to every kind of . . degradation than the vice of gin-drinking. P. H. GIBBS War . . was the degradation of all civilized ideals.

3 (Action leading to) lowering in social position, status, or estimation; humiliation. M18.

H. MARTINEAU They would complain of the degradation of obtaining their food by rendering service. D. WELCH I hated to be fed. It seemed the final degradation.

4 Reduction in strength, amount, or other measurable property. M18.

Engineering The picture degradation normally experienced between successive generations of facsimile pictures.

5 The wearing down and disintegration of material, esp. GEOLOGY, of rock, strata, etc., by erosion etc. L18.

JOHN PHILLIPS The chalk . . yields rather easily to degradation.

6 Reduction to an inferior type, or to a simpler or more rudimentary structure. M19. ▸**b** *spec.* (Natural or artificial) conversion of matter to simpler substances; chemical breakdown. L19. ▸**c** PHYSICS. Conversion of energy to a form less able to be transformed. L19.

c F. HOYLE Levelling-up of the energy distribution within a system is often referred to as 'degradation', or more technically as an increase of . . entropy.

■ **degradational** *adjective* of, pertaining to, or characterized by (esp. structural) degradation M19.

degradation /diːgrəˈdeɪʃ(ə)n/ *noun*². E18.
[ORIGIN French *dégradation* from Italian *digradazione*, from *digradare* come down by degrees. Cf. GRADATION.]
The gradual lessening in intensity of colour or light in a painting, *esp.* that which gives the effect of distance.

degradative /dɪˈgreɪdətɪv/ *adjective.* M20.
[ORIGIN from DEGRADE *verb* + -ATIVE.]
Causing (esp. structural) degradation.

degrade /dɪˈgreɪd/ *noun.* E20.
[ORIGIN from the verb.]
A defective piece of timber; the production of defects in timber that lower its quality.

degrade /dɪˈgreɪd/ *verb.* LME.
[ORIGIN Old French & mod. French *dégrader* from ecclesiastical Latin *degradare*, from *de-* DE- 1 + *gradus* rank, degree. Cf. DISGRADE.]
▶ **I** *verb trans.* **1** Reduce to lower rank, depose from a position of honour; *spec.* deprive formally of rank, office, degree, or ecclesiastical orders, as a punishment. (Foll. by *from.*) LME.

J. PRIESTLEY A priest could not be degraded but by eight bishops. J. H. NEWMAN The man . . was degraded from his high estate.

2 Lower in estimation; bring into dishonour or contempt. LME.

P. G. WODEHOUSE You're degrading yourself by sponging on him.

3 Lower in character or quality, debase. M17.

B. MAGEE They degraded art to the level of entertainment.

4 Chiefly GEOLOGY. Wear down and cause to disintegrate. E19.
5 Reduce in strength, amount, or some other measurable property. M19. ▸**b** *spec.* Reduce or tone down in colour (cf. DEGRADATION *noun*²). M19.

R. COBDEN He proposed to degrade prices instead of aiming to sustain them.

6 Reduce to an inferior type; make simpler or more rudimentary in structure. M19. ▸**b** PHYSICS. Reduce (energy) to a less convertible form. L19. ▸**c** Convert to simpler substances; break down chemically. M20.

G. ROLLESTON Annelids degraded by the special habit of parasitism.

▶ **II** *verb intrans.* **7** Undergo degradation, esp. in type or structure; degenerate; break down chemically. L18.

TENNYSON Throned races may degrade. *New Scientist* Atrazine and other herbicides . . are made to degrade quickly.

8 OXFORD & CAMBRIDGE UNIVS. Orig., defer taking one's honours examination for one year beyond the statutory time. Now, take an examination for a degree lower than one's standing or lower than that for which one originally entered. E19.
■ **degradaˈbility** *noun* susceptibility to (chemical or biological) degradation M20. **degradable** *adjective* able to be degraded; *spec.* susceptible to chemical or biological degradation (cf. BIODEGRADABLE): M19. **degrader** *noun* M18. **degrading** *ppl adjective* that degrades; *esp.* that lowers in dignity or debases: L17. **degradingly** *adverb* so as to degrade; to a degrading extent: E18.

degraded /dɪˈgreɪdɪd/ *adjective*¹. L15.
[ORIGIN from DEGRADE *verb* + -ED¹.]
That has been degraded; showing degradation, debased.

degraded /dɪˈgreɪdɪd/ *adjective*². M16.
[ORIGIN from DE- 1 + Latin *gradus* step + -ED².]
HERALDRY. Of a cross: set on steps or degrees.

†**degraduate** *verb trans.* E17–M19.
[ORIGIN from DE- 3 + GRADUATE *verb.*]
Degrade from a position or dignity.
■ †**degraduation** *noun* (*rare*): only in L16.

degranulate /diːˈgranjʊleɪt/ *verb.* M20.
[ORIGIN from DE- 3 + GRANULATE *verb.*]
MEDICINE. **1** *verb trans.* Remove granules or granularity from, cause the degranulation of. M20.
2 *verb intrans.* Lose granules or granularity, undergo degranulation. M20.
■ **degranuˈlation** *noun* M20.

degras /ˈdɛgrəs, *foreign* degrɑ/ *noun.* Also **dé-**. L19.
[ORIGIN French *dégras*, from *dégraisser* remove grease from.]
1 A dark wax or grease obtained when fish oils are rubbed into hides and recovered, used in the dressing of leather; a preparation containing this or synthesized in imitation of it; moellon. L19.
2 Wool grease, wool fat; a crude mixture of wax and fats obtained by scouring wool or treating it with organic solvents. *US.* L19.

degrease /diːˈgriːs/ *verb trans.* L19.
[ORIGIN from DE- 3 + GREASE *noun.*]
Remove grease or fat from.

degree /dɪˈgriː/ *noun.* ME.
[ORIGIN Old French & mod. French *degré* from Proto-Romance, from Latin *de-* DE- 1 + *gradus* step, GRADE *noun.*]
▶ **I 1 a** A step, *esp.* each of a flight of steps; a rung of a ladder. *obsolete* exc. HERALDRY. ME. ▸**b** A thing placed like a step in a series; a row, a tier. E17.

a SHAKES. *Jul. Caes.* Scorning the base degrees By which he did ascend.

2 A step in direct genealogical descent; in *pl.*, the number of steps from a common ancestor by which is determined the closeness of the relation of collateral descendants. ME.

H. JAMES A . . poor relation, of distant degree. T. H. WHITE I am . . near cousin to Joseph of Arimathea—and you . . are but the eighth degree from . . Jesus Christ.

3 A stage or position in a social or official scale; a class, rank, grade, station, etc. ME.

T. GUNN I served / all degrees and both sexes.

4 Relative state or condition; manner, way, respect. ME.

O. W. HOLMES A simple evening party in the smallest village is just as admirable in its degree.

5 A step or stage in a process or scale. Esp. in ***by degrees*** below. ME.

DRYDEN To go unknown is the next degree to going invisible.

6 A stage in intensity or amount; the relative intensity, extent, or amount of a quality, attribute, or action. LME.

LONGFELLOW I have the faculty of abstraction to a wonderful degree. W. S. CHURCHILL Pitt was able to bring a degree of order into this chaos. ISAIAH BERLIN The ordinary run of men are blind in varying degrees to that which truly shapes their lives.

▶ **II 7** A stage of proficiency in an art, craft, course of study, etc.; *spec.* an academic rank conferred by a university or college as a mark of proficiency in scholarship; LAW (now *rare*) the status of barrister. LME. ▸**b** Any of the ranks of Freemasonry. LME.

I. MURDOCH Ann was reading for a degree in English.

8 GRAMMAR. Each of the three stages (see POSITIVE, COMPARATIVE, SUPERLATIVE *adjectives*) in the comparison of an adjective or adverb. LME.
9 A unit of measurement of angles or circular arcs, and hence of latitude, longitude, etc., equal to the 90th part of a right angle or the 360th part of the circumference of a circle (symbol °). LME. ▸**b** A position on the earth's surface as measured by degrees; latitude, longitude. M17.

F. HOYLE A plane with a slope of 10 degrees to the horizontal. **b** S. BUTLER He knew the Seat of Paradise, Could tell in what Degree it lies.

10 *MUSIC.* Each of the successive notes of a scale (esp. the diatonic scale); the interval between any two of these; each of the successive lines and spaces on the stave. **L17.**
11 A legal grade of crime or criminality; *spec.* in *US Law*, either of two grades of murder (*murder in the first degree* or *first-degree murder*, *murder in the second degree* or *second-degree murder*). **L17.**
12 *PHYSICS.* A unit in a scale of temperature, hardness, etc., (symbol ° or deg, or omitted where the letter indicating the scale being used serves as the symbol). **E18.**

J. C. OATES Midday temperatures as high as 105 degrees.

degree absolute, ***degree Celsius***, ***degree centigrade***, ***degree Fahrenheit***, ***degree Kelvin***, ***degree Rankine***, etc.

13 *MATH.* The rank of an equation or expression (or a curve etc. representing it) as determined by the highest power of the unknown or variable quantity, or the highest dimensions of the terms which it contains. **M18.**

M. KLINE The methods of solving the second, third, and fourth degree equations were quite different.

14 Each of a number of grades, usu. three (*first*, *second*, *third*), used to classify burns according to their severity. **M19.**

– PHRASES: ***advanced degree***: see ADVANCED 2. **by degrees** by successive stages, little by little, gradually. ***degree of comparison***: see COMPARISON 4. ***degree of FREEDOM***. ***degrees of cold***: see COLD *noun*. ***first degree***: see FIRST *adjective, adverb, & noun*. **forbidden degrees** = ***prohibited degrees*** below. **honorary degree** an academic degree awarded as a recognition of distinction or a tribute of honour. ***Levitical degrees***: see LEVITICAL *adjective*. **prohibited degrees** the number of steps of consanguinity or affinity within which marriage is not allowed. ***second degree***: see SECOND *adjective*. ***Song of Degrees***: see SONG *noun*[1]. ***third degree***: see THIRD *adjective*. **to a degree** (***a***) to a considerable extent (now *rare*); (***b***) to some extent. **to the last degree** to the utmost measure.

– COMB.: **degree day** (***a***) a day on which academic degrees are formally awarded; (***b***) (orig. *US*) a unit used to determine the heating requirements of buildings, representing a fall of one degree below a specified average outdoor temperature for one day.

■ **degreeless** *adjective* without a degree or degrees **E19.**

degree /dɪˈɡriː/ *verb trans.* Pa. t. & pple **degreed**. **LME.**
[ORIGIN from the noun.]
Chiefly as ***degreed*** *ppl adjective.*
†**1** Advance or change by degrees. **LME–M17.**
2 Confer an academic degree on. **M16.**

Guardian Much-degreed ladies.

degression /dɪˈɡrɛʃ(ə)n/ *noun.* **L15.**
[ORIGIN Latin *degressio(n-)* going down, from *degress-*: see DEGRESSIVE, -ION.]
†**1** Stepping down, descent. Only in **L15.**
2 Stepwise reduction, esp. of taxation. **L19.**

degressive /dɪˈɡrɛsɪv/ *adjective.* **E20.**
[ORIGIN from Latin *degress-* pa. ppl stem of *degredi* descend + -IVE.]
Characterized by stepwise reduction, esp. (***a***) in levels of taxation, (***b***) in the length of a book's bibliographical description in different contexts.

dégringolade /degrɛ̃ɡɔlad/ *noun.* Pl. pronounced same. **L19.**
[ORIGIN French, from *dégringoler* descend rapidly.]
A rapid descent or deterioration; decadence.

degu /ˈdeɪɡuː/ *noun.* **M19.**
[ORIGIN Amer. Spanish from S. Amer. Indian *deuñ*.]
Any of several S. American rodents of the family Octodontidae, *spec.* one of the genus *Octodon*, similar to cavies.

degum /diːˈɡʌm/ *verb trans.* Infl. **-mm-**. **L19.**
[ORIGIN from DE- 3 + GUM *noun*[2].]
Deprive of gum; *spec.* deglutinate (silk) as part of processing.

degust /dɪˈɡʌst/ *verb trans. & intrans.* **E17.**
[ORIGIN Latin *degustare*, from *de-* DE- 1 + *gustare* to taste; in mod. use from French *déguster*.]
Taste, savour, (food etc.).

degustate /dɪˈɡʌsteɪt/ *verb trans. rare.* **L16.**
[ORIGIN Latin *degustat-* pa. ppl stem of *degustare*: see DEGUST, -ATE[3].]
Taste, savour.

degustation /diːɡʌˈsteɪʃ(ə)n/ *noun.* **M17.**
[ORIGIN Latin *degustatio(n-)*, formed as DEGUSTATE: see -ATION.]
The action or an act of tasting or savouring.

degut /diːˈɡʌt/ *verb trans.* Infl. **-tt-**. **M20.**
[ORIGIN from DE- 3 + GUT *noun*.]
Remove the guts, contents, or essential elements of.

dehair /diːˈhɛː/ *verb trans.* **E20.**
[ORIGIN from DE- 3 + HAIR *noun*.]
Remove the hair from (a skin), unhair.

de haut en bas /də o ɑ̃ bɑ/ *adverbial phr.* **L17.**
[ORIGIN French = from above to below.]
In a condescending or superior manner.

dehisce /dɪˈhɪs/ *verb intrans.* **M17.**
[ORIGIN Latin *dehiscere*, from *de-* DE- 1 + *hiscere* inceptive of *hiare* to gape. Cf. HIATUS.]
Gape, open out (chiefly *ANATOMY & PHYSIOLOGY*); in *BOTANY*, (of a seed vessel etc.) burst open.

dehiscence /dɪˈhɪs(ə)ns/ *noun.* **E19.**
[ORIGIN mod. Latin *dehiscentia*, from Latin *dehiscent-* pres. ppl stem of *dehiscere*: see DEHISCE, -ENCE.]
Gaping, opening by divergence of parts (chiefly *ANATOMY & PHYSIOLOGY*); in *BOTANY*, the bursting open of seed vessels etc. in order to discharge their mature contents.
■ **dehiscent** *adjective* gaping open; *BOTANY* (of a seed vessel etc.) bursting open when ripe: **M17.**

dehonestate /diːˈɒnɪsteɪt/ *verb trans. rare.* **M17.**
[ORIGIN Latin *dehonestat-* pa. ppl stem of *dehonestare* to dishonour, from *de-* DE- 3 + *honestus* honest: see -ATE[3].]
Dishonour; disparage.
■ **dehoneˈstation** *noun* [Latin *dehonestatio(n-)*] **LME.**

dehorn /diːˈhɔːn/ *verb trans.* **L19.**
[ORIGIN from DE- 3 + HORN *noun*.]
1 Deprive (an animal) of horns. **L19.**
2 Saw off the end or the protruding branches of (a log etc.); prune heavily. **E20.**
■ **dehorner** *noun* a person who dehorns; an instrument for dehorning animals: **L19.**

dehors /dəɔːr, dəˈhɔː/ *preposition.* **E18.**
[ORIGIN Old French preposition, mod. French adverb and noun.]
LAW. Outside of; not within the scope of.

dehort /dɪˈhɔːt/ *verb.* Now *rare.* **M16.**
[ORIGIN Latin *dehortari* dissuade, from *de-* DE- 1 + *hortari* exhort.]
1 *verb trans. & intrans.* Use exhortation to dissuade (a person). Now only foll. by *from* a course of action etc. **M16.**

J. WHITGIFT Christ doth not here dehort from bearing rule . . but from seeking rule. SOUTHEY Croker dehorts me from visiting Ireland.

†**2** *verb trans.* Advise strongly against (a course of action etc.). **M–L17.**

DONNE I am far from dehorting those fixed Devotions.

■ **dehorter** *noun* **L16.**

dehortation /diːhɔːˈteɪʃ(ə)n/ *noun.* Now *rare.* **E16.**
[ORIGIN Latin *dehortatio(n-)*, from *dehortat-* pa. ppl stem of *dehortari*: see DEHORT, -ATION.]
(An) exhortation intended to dissuade, earnest dissuasion (*from*).
■ **dehortative** /dɪˈhɔːtətɪv/ *adjective & noun* (***a***) *adjective* dehortatory; (***b***) *noun* an address or argument designed to dissuade: **E17.** **dehortatory** /dɪˈhɔːtət(ə)ri/ *adjective* characterized by dehortation; intended to dissuade: **L16.**

Dehua /deɪˈhwɑː/ *adjective & noun.* Also **Tê-hua** /teɪˈhwɑː/. **E20.**
[ORIGIN Place of origin in Fujian province, SE China.]
(Designating) a white glazed Chinese porcelain, esp. of the Ming period (= ***blanc de chine*** s.v. BLANC *noun* 4).

dehumanize /diːˈhjuːmənʌɪz/ *verb trans.* Also **-ise**. **E19.**
[ORIGIN from DE- 3 + HUMANIZE.]
Deprive of human attributes; make impersonal or machine-like.
■ **dehumaniˈzation** *noun* **M19.**

dehumidify /diːhjuːˈmɪdɪfʌɪ/ *verb trans.* **M20.**
[ORIGIN from DE- 3 + HUMIDIFY.]
Reduce the humidity of; remove moisture from.
■ **dehumidifiˈcation** *noun* **M20.** **dehumidifier** *noun* a device or substance for dehumidification **E20.**

dehydr- *combining form* see DEHYDRO-.

dehydrase /dɪˈhʌɪdreɪz/ *noun.* **E20.**
[ORIGIN from DEHYDRO- + -ASE.]
BIOCHEMISTRY. **1** = DEHYDROGENASE. **E20.**
2 = DEHYDRATASE. **M20.**

dehydratase /diːˈhʌɪdrəteɪz/ *noun.* **M20.**
[ORIGIN from DEHYDRATE + -ASE.]
BIOCHEMISTRY. Any enzyme catalysing the removal of a molecule of water from a substrate.

dehydrate /diːhʌɪˈdreɪt, diːˈhʌɪdreɪt/ *verb.* **L19.**
[ORIGIN from DE- 3 + Greek *hudr-*, *hudōr* water + -ATE[3].]
1 *verb trans.* Deprive of water, make dry; make (esp. the body) deficient in water; remove water from (esp. a food, in order to preserve it and reduce its bulk); in *CHEMISTRY*, remove the elements of water from. Freq. as ***dehydrated*** *ppl adjective.* **L19.**

L. GOULD Regular lunches . . instead of dehydrated plastic steaks. *fig.*: *Times* A series of rather dehydrated arguments between . . intellectual types.

2 *verb intrans.* Lose water as a constituent. **L19.**
■ **dehyˈdration** *noun* the action of dehydrating; the condition of being dehydrated: **M19.**

dehydro- /diːˈhʌɪdrəʊ/ *combining form.* Before a vowel also **dehydr-**.
[ORIGIN from DE- 3 + HYDRO-.]
Used in *CHEMISTRY* with the senses 'that has lost hydrogen', 'that has lost (the elements of) water'.
■ **dehydroaˈcetic**, **dehydracetic** *adjective*: ***dehydroacetic acid***, ***dehydracetic acid***, a crystalline cyclic compound, $C_8H_8O_4$, obtained esp. by heating ethyl acetoacetate **L19.** **dehydroaˈscorbic** *adjective*: ***dehydroascorbic acid***, a metabolic oxidation product, $C_6H_6O_6$, of ascorbic acid **M20.** **dehydrochoˈlesterol** *noun* a provitamin, $C_{27}H_{44}O$, which on ultraviolet irradiation (in skin tissue) is converted to vitamin D_3 **M20.**

dehydrogenase /diːhʌɪˈdrɒdʒəneɪz/ *noun.* **E20.**
[ORIGIN formed as DEHYDROGENATE + -ASE.]
BIOCHEMISTRY. An enzyme which abstracts a hydrogen atom or hydrogen atoms from a substrate.

dehydrogenate /diːhʌɪˈdrɒdʒəneɪt/ *verb trans.* **M19.**
[ORIGIN from DE- 3 + HYDROGEN + -ATE[3].]
CHEMISTRY. Remove one or more hydrogen atoms from (a compound).
■ **dehydrogeˈnation** *noun* **M19.**

dehydrogenize /diːhʌɪˈdrɒdʒənʌɪz/ *verb trans.* Now *rare.* Also **-ise**. **M19.**
[ORIGIN formed as DEHYDROGENATE + -IZE.]
= DEHYDROGENATE.
■ **dehydrogeniˈzation** *noun* **L19.**

de-ice /diːˈʌɪs/ *verb trans.* **M20.**
[ORIGIN from DE- 3 + ICE *noun*.]
Remove ice from, prevent the formation of ice on, (an aeroplane, windscreen, etc.).
■ **de-icer** *noun* a device or substance for de-icing (esp. windscreens) **M20.**

deicide /ˈdiːɪsʌɪd, ˈdeɪɪ-/ *noun.* **E17.**
[ORIGIN ecclesiastical Latin *deicida* killer of a god, or directly from Latin *deus*, *dei-* god: see -CIDE. Cf. French *déicide*.]
1 The killing of a god. **E17.**
2 The killer of a god. **M17.**
■ **deicidal** *adjective* of or pertaining to deicide; god-killing: **M19.**

deictic /ˈdʌɪktɪk/ *adjective & noun.* **E19.**
[ORIGIN Greek *deiktikos*, from *deiktos* verbal adjective of *deiknunai* to show: see -IC. Cf. DEIXIS.]
▸ **A** *adjective.* **1** *LOGIC.* Designating or pertaining to reasoning which proves directly. Cf. ELENCTIC. **E19.**
2 *LINGUISTICS.* Serving to relate that which is spoken of to the spatial and temporal context of the utterance; *spec.* demonstrative. **L19.**
▸ **B** *noun.* A deictic word, form, or expression. **M20.**
■ †**deictical** *adjective* = DEICTIC *adjective* 1: only in **M17.** **deictically** *adverb* (***a***) with direct indication; (***b***) with regard to deixis: **M17.**

deid *noun* see DEATH.

deific /diːˈɪfɪk, deɪ-/ *adjective.* **L15.**
[ORIGIN Old French & mod. French *déifique* or ecclesiastical Latin *deificus*, from Latin *deus* god + *-ficus* -FIC.]
Deifying, making divine; *loosely* divine, godlike.

deification /ˌdiːɪfɪˈkeɪʃ(ə)n, ˌdeɪɪ-/ *noun.* **LME.**
[ORIGIN ecclesiastical Latin *deificatio(n-)*, from *deificat-* pa. ppl stem of *deificare*: see DEIFY, -ATION.]
1 The action of deifying; deified condition; a deified embodiment. **LME.**
2 *THEOLOGY.* The action or process of becoming a sharer in the divine nature. **L17.**
■ **deificatory** *adjective* (*rare*) serving to deify; pertaining to deification: **E17.**

deiform /ˈdiːɪfɔːm, ˈdeɪɪ-/ *adjective.* **M17.**
[ORIGIN medieval Latin *deiformis*, from Latin *deus* god: see -FORM.]
1 Having the form of a god. **M17.**
2 Godlike in nature or character; holy, divine. **M17.**
■ **deiˈformity** *noun* **M17.**

deify /ˈdiːɪfʌɪ, ˈdeɪɪ-/ *verb trans.* **ME.**
[ORIGIN Old French & mod. French *déifier* from ecclesiastical Latin *deificare*, from Latin *deus* god: see -FY.]
1 Render godlike in character, spirit, or quality. **ME.**

T. HERBERT No vertue more deified a Prince then Clemencie.

2 Make a god of; exalt to the position of a god; enrol among the gods. **LME.**

M. L. KING Nontheistic humanism, a philosophy that deifies man by affirming that humanity is God.

3 Treat as a god; worship. **L16.**

S. SMILES It is possible to over-estimate success to the extent of almost deifying it.

■ **deifier** *noun* (*rare*) **M18.**

deign /deɪn/ *verb.* **ME.**
[ORIGIN Old French *degnier*, *deigner*, (also mod.) *daigner* from Latin *dignare*, *-ari* deem worthy, from *dignus* worthy.]
1 *verb intrans.* Think it worthy of oneself, see fit, condescend, *to do*. **ME.**

H. BELLOC Hardly deigning to reply to your timid sentences. D. ABSE Lunch-time arrived and still no driver deigned to stop for us.

2 *verb trans.* Condescend to give or grant (an answer etc.). Usu. with neg. *arch.* **L16.** ▸†**b** Condescend to accept or take. **L16–M17.**

M. C. CLARKE The spirit stalks away, deigning no reply. **b** SHAKES. *Ant. & Cl.* Thy palate then did deign The roughest berry on the rudest hedge.

†**3** Treat as worthy *of*; dignify *with*. **L16–M17.**

Dei gratia /deɪiː ˈɡrɑːtɪə, diːʌɪ ˈɡreɪʃə/ *adverbial phr.* **E17.**
[ORIGIN Latin.]
By the grace of God.

D

D

deil /diːl/ *noun. Scot.* LME.
[ORIGIN Var. of DEVIL *noun*.]
1 The Devil, esp. according to popular conception. LME. ***deil a haet, deil haet***: see HAET.
2 A mischievously energetic or troublesome person, = DEVIL *noun* 4b. L18.

de-index /diːˈɪndɛks/ *verb trans.* L20.
[ORIGIN from DE- 3 + INDEX *verb*.]
Cancel the indexation of (pensions or other benefits).
▪ **de-indeˈxation** *noun* L20.

deindustrialize /diːɪnˈdʌstrɪəlʌɪz/ *verb trans.* Also **-ise**. L19.
[ORIGIN from DE- 3 + INDUSTRIALIZE.]
Make less or no longer industrial; reduce the industrial capacity of.
▪ **deindustrialiˈzation** *noun* M20.

deinonychus /dʌɪˈnɒnɪkəs/ *noun.* M20.
[ORIGIN mod. Latin (see below), from Greek *deinos* terrible + *onux*, *onukh-* claw.]
A dromaeosaurid dinosaur of the genus *Deinonychus*, growing up to 3.3 m (11 ft) in length and having a slashing claw on each hind foot.

deinothere /ˈdʌɪnə(ʊ)θɪə/ *noun.* Also †**dino-**. M19.
[ORIGIN from mod. Latin *Deinotherium* (see below), from Greek *deinos* terrible + *thērion* wild animal.]
PALAEONTOLOGY. An extinct proboscidean mammal of the genus *Deinotherium*, known from fossil remains of Lower Miocene to Upper Pleistocene age.

de-institutionalize /ˌdiːɪnstɪˈtjuːʃ(ə)n(ə)lʌɪz/ *verb trans.* Chiefly *N. Amer.* Also **-ise**. M20.
[ORIGIN from DE- 3 + INSTITUTIONALIZE.]
Remove from a mental etc. institution; free from the effects of a long period spent in an institution. Chiefly as ***de-institutionalized*** *ppl adjective.*
▪ **de-institutionaliˈzation** *noun* L20.

deionize /diːˈʌɪənʌɪz/ *verb trans.* Also **-ise**. E20.
[ORIGIN from DE- 3 + IONIZE.]
Remove the ions or ionic constituents from (water etc.).
▪ **deioniˈzation** *noun* E20. **deionizer** *noun* an apparatus for removing ions from water etc. M20.

Deipara /diːˈɪpərə, deɪˈɪp-/ *noun. rare.* M17.
[ORIGIN Late Latin, from *deus* + *-parus*, *-a* bearing (see -PAROUS): a Latin equiv. of Greek *theotokos*.]
Mother of God (as a title of the Virgin Mary).
▪ **deiparous** *adjective* being the mother of God M17.

deipnosophist /dʌɪpˈnɒsəfɪst/ *noun.* E17.
[ORIGIN Greek *deipnosophistēs*, used in pl. as title of a work by Atheneus (3rd cent. AD), describing long discussions at a banquet, from *deipnon* dinner + *sophistēs* wise man.]
A person skilled in the art of dining and table talk.

deisal *adverb & noun* var. of DEASIL.

deism /ˈdiːɪz(ə)m, ˈdeɪɪ-/ *noun.* L17.
[ORIGIN from Latin *deus* god + -ISM, after DEIST. Cf. French *déisme*.]
The doctrine or belief of deists; belief in one God who created but does not intervene in the universe; natural religion. Cf. ATHEISM, THEISM *noun*[1].

deist /ˈdiːɪst, ˈdeɪɪ-/ *noun.* E17.
[ORIGIN French *déiste*, from Latin *deus* god + *-iste* -IST.]
Orig., a person who believes in God or gods (opp. ***atheist***). Now, a person who believes in one God who created but does not intervene in the universe. Cf. THEIST.
▪ **deˈistic** *adjective* of the nature of or pertaining to deists or deism L18. **deˈistical** *adjective* = DEISTIC M18. **deˈistically** *adverb* L19.

Deiters /ˈdʌɪtəz/ *noun.* M19.
[ORIGIN Otto Friedrich Carl *Deiters* (1834–63), German anatomist.]
ANATOMY. **1** ***cells of Deiters***, ***Deiters' cells***, supporting cells alternating with the outer hair cells in the organ of Corti. M19.
2 ***nucleus of Deiters***, ***Deiters' nucleus***, the lateral vestibular nucleus in the brain. L19.

deity /ˈdiːɪti, ˈdeɪɪ-/ *noun.* Also **D-**. ME.
[ORIGIN Old French & mod. French *déité* from ecclesiastical Latin *deitas*, rendering Greek *theotēs*, from *theos* god: see -TY[1].]
1 The divine nature of God; divinity. ME.

> *Daily Telegraph* The Christian Church must maintain its historic faith in the deity of Christ.

2 The estate or rank of a god; divine status; godship. LME.

> E. B. BROWNING All the false gods with a cry Rendered up their deity.

3 A divine being; a god. LME.

> W. S. CHURCHILL John Nicholson . . the liberator of Delhi, was even worshipped by some Punjabis as a deity. *fig.*: SHAKES. *L.L.L.* The liver-vein, which makes flesh a deity.

4 Chiefly THEOLOGY. (Usu. **D-**.) A supreme being as creator of the universe; ***the Deity***, the supreme being, God. L16.

> E. B. PUSEY Men spoke of 'the Deity' . . and . . had lost sight of the Personal God.

▪ **deityship** *noun* the status or personality of a deity L17.

deixis /ˈdʌɪksɪs/ *noun.* M20.
[ORIGIN Greek = reference, from *deiknunai* to show. Cf. DEICTIC.]
The function or use of a deictic word, form, or expression.

déjà entendu /deʒa ɑ̃tɑ̃dy, ˈdeɪʒɑː ɒ̃tɒ̃ˈduː/ *noun phr.* M20.
[ORIGIN French = already heard, after DÉJÀ VU.]
A feeling (correct or illusory) that one has already heard or understood the words, music, etc., currently under attention.

déjà lu /deʒa ly, deɪʒɑː ˈluː/ *noun phr.* M20.
[ORIGIN French = already read, after DÉJÀ VU.]
A feeling that one may have read the present passage, or one very like it, before.

déjà vu /deɪʒɑː ˈvuː, *foreign* deʒa vy/ *noun phr.* E20.
[ORIGIN French = already seen.]
1 PSYCHOLOGY. The illusory feeling of having already experienced the present moment or situation. E20.
2 The (correct) impression that something similar has been previously experienced. M20.

> *Times* Walking into the company must have given him a sense of déjà vu.

deject /dɪˈdʒɛkt/ *adjective* (orig. *pa. pple*). *arch.* LME.
[ORIGIN Latin *dejectus* pa. pple, formed as DEJECT *verb*.]
1 Cast down, overthrown; lowered in fortune or character; debased. LME. ▸†**b** ASTROLOGY. Of a planet: that has lost its influence. LME–L16.
2 Downcast, dispirited. E16.
▪ †**dejectly** *adverb* E17–M18.

deject /dɪˈdʒɛkt/ *verb trans.* LME.
[ORIGIN Latin *deject-* pa. ppl stem of *dejicere* throw down, from *de-* DE- 1 + *jacere* to throw.]
1 Cast down; overthrow. *arch.* LME. ▸**b** Bend down, allow to droop. *arch.* E17. ▸**c** Lower (the eyes). *arch.* E17.
†**2** Cast down from high estate or dignity; humble, abase. LME–L17.
3 Dishearten, dispirit; make sad or gloomy. LME.

> S. JOHNSON Nothing dejects a trader like the interruption of his profits.

†**4** Dismiss, reject. M16–M17.
†**5** Weaken; lessen. L16–L17.

dejected /dɪˈdʒɛktɪd/ *adjective.* L16.
[ORIGIN from DEJECT *verb* + -ED[1].]
1 Low-spirited, downcast, depressed. L16.

> W. COWPER I am cheerful on paper sometimes, when I am absolutely the most dejected of all creatures. B. BAINBRIDGE His manner still continued dejected and depressed.

2 Lowered; allowed to droop; cast down, overthrown. *arch.* E17.

> POPE With humble mien and with dejected eyes. R. HEBER The mute swain . . With . . dejected head. H. JAMES Looking at her dejected pillar.

†**3** Abased, humbled, lowly. E17–E18.

> SHAKES. *Lear* The lowest and most dejected thing of fortune.

▪ **dejectedly** *adverb* E17. **dejectedness** *noun* E17.

dejection /dɪˈdʒɛkʃ(ə)n/ *noun.* LME.
[ORIGIN Latin *dejectio(n-)*, formed as DEJECT *verb*: see -ION.]
1 Depression of spirits; a dejected state, low spirits. LME.

> BOSWELL That miserable dejection of spirits to which he was constitutionally subject. F. PARKMAN A deep dejection fell upon them. A. J. CRONIN That pit of dejection into which . . he would plummet.

†**2** A lowering in fortunes, condition, quality, etc.; abasement; humiliation. LME–M17. ▸†**b** ASTROLOGY. The state (of a planet) of having lost its influence. LME–E18.
3 *lit.* The action of casting down; the fact of being cast down. *arch.* L15.

> J. RUSKIN A hole . . for the convenient dejection of hot sand and lead.

4 MEDICINE. Defecation; in *pl.*, faeces. Now *rare* or *obsolete*. E17.
5 Weakening, diminution, esp. of bodily strength. Now *rare* or *obsolete*. M17.

†**dejeune** *noun.* Also **dejune**. M17–M19.
[ORIGIN French dial. *déjun*: see DISJUNE.]
= DÉJEUNER 1.

déjeuner /deʒœne (*pl. same*), ˈdeɪʒəneɪ/ *noun.* Also †**-né**. L18.
[ORIGIN French, use as noun of inf. = break one's fast: see DISJUNE.]
1 A morning meal (early or late) in France or elsewhere; breakfast or (usu.) lunch. See also ***petit déjeuner*** s.v. PETIT *adjective*[2]. L18.
2 A set of cups, saucers, plates, etc., for serving breakfast, breakfast service. L18.

de jour *adjectival phr.* see DU JOUR.

†**dejune** *noun* var. of DEJEUNE.

de jure /diː ˈdʒʊəri, deɪ ˈjʊəreɪ/ *adverbial & adjectival phr.* M16.
[ORIGIN Latin = of law.]
(Existing, held, etc.) rightfully, according to law (freq. as opp. to ***de facto***).

Dekabrist /ˈdɛkəbrɪst/ *noun.* L19.
[ORIGIN Russian *dekabrist*, from *dekabr'* December.]
hist. = DECEMBRIST.

dekalin *noun* var. of DECALIN.

dekarch, **dekarchy** *nouns* vars. of DECARCH, DECARCHY.

deke /diːk/ *noun & verb. N. Amer.* M20.
[ORIGIN Abbreviation of DECOY *noun*.]
▸ **A** *noun.* ICE HOCKEY. A deceptive movement or feint that causes an opponent to move out of position. M20.
▸ **B** *verb.* **1** *verb trans.* ICE HOCKEY. Pass (an opponent) by making a deceptive movement. M20.

> *Sports Illustrated* Jackson deked Steinbach into thinking he was going to catch the ball.

2 *verb intrans.* Move or go quickly. *colloq.* L20.

dekink /diːˈkɪŋk/ *verb trans.* M20.
[ORIGIN from DE- 3 + KINK *noun*[2].]
Remove kinks from.

dekko /ˈdɛkəʊ/ *noun & verb. slang* (orig. *military slang*). L19.
[ORIGIN Hindi *dekho* polite imper. of *dekhnā* to look. Cf. DECK *noun*[2].]
▸ **A** *noun.* Pl. **-os**. A look. L19.

> K. TYNAN Once I'd grabbed hold of the script and taken a good dekko at it, my worst fears were confirmed.

▸ **B** *verb trans. & intrans.* Look (at). L19.

del /dɛl/ *noun.* E20.
[ORIGIN Abbreviation of DELTA, from the operator's being represented by an inverted capital delta.]
MATH. The symbolic differential operator ∇, defined as $\mathbf{i}\,\partial/\partial x + \mathbf{j}\,\partial/\partial y + \mathbf{k}\,\partial/\partial z$, where **i**, **j**, and **k** are vectors directed respectively along the Cartesian axes *x*, *y*, and *z*. Also called ***nabla***.

Del. *abbreviation.*
Delaware.

delabialize /diːˈleɪbɪəlʌɪz/ *verb trans.* Also **-ise**. L19.
[ORIGIN from DE- 3 + LABIALIZE.]
PHONETICS. Pronounce without lip-rounding; deprive of labial character.
▪ **delabialiˈzation** *noun* E20.

†**delacrimation** *noun.* Also **-cry-**. E17–L19.
[ORIGIN Latin *delacrimatio(n-)*, formed as DE- 1 + LACHRYMATION.]
(Excessive) lachrymation.

delafossite /dɛləˈfɒsʌɪt/ *noun.* L19.
[ORIGIN from Gabriel *Delafosse* (1796–1878), French mineralogist + -ITE[1].]
MINERALOGY. A black hexagonal oxide of iron and copper occurring usu. as tabular crystals or as botryoidal crusts.

delaine /dəˈleɪn/ *noun.* M19.
[ORIGIN Abbreviation.]
= ***MOUSSELINE-de-laine***.

delaminate /diːˈlamɪneɪt/ *verb intrans.* L19.
[ORIGIN from DE- 1 + Latin *lamina* thin plate, layer + -ATE[3].]
Split into separate layers.
▪ **delamiˈnation** *noun* L19.

delapse /dɪˈlaps/ *verb intrans.* Now *rare* or *obsolete*. M16.
[ORIGIN Latin *delaps-* pa. ppl stem of *delabi*, from *de-* DE- 1 + *labi* slip, fall.]
Fall or slip down, sink, (*lit.* & *fig.*).

Delasol /diːlɑːˈsɒl/ *noun. obsolete* exc. *hist.* Also **D la sol**. E17.
[ORIGIN formed as DELASOLRE.]
MEDIEVAL MUSIC. The note D in Guido d'Arezzo's 6th and 7th hexachords, where it was sung to the syllables *la* or *sol*. Cf. ALAMIRE, BEMI, CESOLFA, etc.

Delasolre /ˌdiːlɑːsɒlˈreɪ/ *noun. obsolete* exc. *hist.* Also **D la sol re**. LME.
[ORIGIN from D as a pitch letter + *la*, *sol*, and *re* designating tones in the solmization of Guido d'Arezzo (c 990–1050).]
MEDIEVAL MUSIC. The note D in Guido d'Arezzo's 3rd, 4th, and 5th hexachords, where it was sung to the syllables *la*, *sol*, or *re*. Cf. ALAMIRE, BEMI, CESOLFA, etc.

délassement /delasmɑ̃/ *noun.* Pl. pronounced same. E19.
[ORIGIN French, from *délasser* relax, from *dé-* DE- 3 + *las* weary: see -MENT.]
(A) relaxation.

delate /dɪˈleɪt/ *verb trans. arch.* L15.
[ORIGIN Latin *delat-* stem of functional pa. pple of *deferre*: see DEFER *verb*[2], -ATE[3].]
†**1** Hand down or over; refer (a matter, *to* a person). L15–M19.
2 Relate, report, (esp. an offence). L15.
3 Accuse, impeach; denounce to a tribunal, esp. (*hist.*) that of the Scottish civil and ecclesiastical courts. E16.
†**4** = DEFER *verb*[2] 3. M16–L19.
†**5** Carry down or away, convey. L16–E17.

delation /dɪˈleɪʃ(ə)n/ *noun. arch.* M16.
[ORIGIN Latin *delatio(n-)*, from *delat-*: see DELATE, -ATION.]
1 The action of informing against someone; (an) accusation, (a) denunciation, criminal information. M16.
†**2** Conveyance (to a place); transmission. L16–E17.
†**3** Handing down, transference. L17–L19.

delator /dɪˈleɪtə/ *noun. arch.* LME.
[ORIGIN Latin *delator*, from *delat-*: see DELATE, -OR.]
An informer, a secret or professional accuser.

Delaware /ˈdɛləwɛː/ *noun & adjective.* E18.
[ORIGIN River *Delaware* (see below).]
▸ **A** *noun.* Pl. **-s**, same.
1 A member of an Algonquian people formerly inhabiting the Delaware river basin in the north-eastern US. E18.

2 Either or both of the two languages of this people. **E19.** ▸**B** *attrib.* or as *adjective*. Of or pertaining to the Delawares or their languages. **E18.**

Delawarean /dɛlə'wɛːrɪən/ *noun.* **E20.**
[ORIGIN from *Delaware* (see below) + -AN.]
A native or inhabitant of Delaware, a state of the US.
▪ Also **Delawarian** *noun* **M20.**

delay /dɪ'leɪ/ *noun.* **ME.**
[ORIGIN Old French & mod. French *délai*, formed as DELAY *verb*[1].]
1 The action or process of delaying; procrastination; lingering; putting off. **ME.**

SHAKES. *Haml.* For who would bear . . the law's delay. C. S. FORESTER What the hell's all this delay for, Mr Hornblower? D'you want us to miss the tide?

without delay, **without any delay**, **without further delay** immediately, at once.
2 Hindrance to progress; (a period of) time lost by inaction or inability to proceed. **M18.** ▸**b** *spec.* The time interval between the propagation of an electrical signal and its reception. **M20.**

B. JOWETT There will be a delay of a day.

– COMB.: **delay line** a device producing a desired delay in the transmission of an electrical signal.

delay /dɪ'leɪ/ *verb*[1]. **ME.**
[ORIGIN Old French *delayer* var. of *deslaier*, presumably from *des-* DE-3 + *laier* leave.]
1 *verb trans.* Put off to a later time; postpone, defer, (a thing, *doing*, (arch.) *to do*). **ME.** ▸†**b** Put (a person) off, keep (a person) waiting. **LME–M18.**

POPE Th' unprofitable moments . . That . . still delay Life's instant business to a future day. TENNYSON As the tender ash delays To clothe herself, when all the woods are green. A. C. BOULT Mozart had works complete in his head, and delayed writing them down until the last possible minute.

2 *verb trans.* Impede the progress of, make late, hinder. **LME.**

STEELE Joy and Grief can hasten and delay Time. R. C. HUTCHINSON I thought the snow might delay the train. I. MURDOCH I had been delayed by the strike.

3 *verb intrans.* Loiter, be late; wait; (now *poet.*) tarry in a place. **LME.**

SHAKES. *1 Hen. IV* Advantage feeds him fat while men delay. W. C. BRYANT Wind of the sunny south! oh still delay, in the gay woods. P. KAVANAGH Eusebius was delaying up the road till the priest went away.

▪ **delayer** *noun* **E16.**

†**delay** *verb*[2]. **ME.**
[ORIGIN French *délayer*, in Old French *desleier* from Proto-Romance, from Latin *dis-* DIS- 2 + *ligare* bind. Cf. ALLAY *verb*[1].]
1 *verb intrans.* Of the sight: grow dim. Only in **ME.**
2 *verb trans.* Mitigate, assuage, alleviate. **LME–E17.**
3 *verb trans.* Weaken by admixture, dilute, qualify; debase (coin). **L15–E17.**

delayed /dɪ'leɪd/ *adjective.* **M16.**
[ORIGIN from DELAY *verb*[1] + -ED[1].]
1 That has been delayed; retarded, deferred, held back. **M16.**
2 *spec.* NUCLEAR PHYSICS. Of a particle: emitted by one of the products of fission or other decay process. Cf. ***prompt***. **M20.**
– COMB.: **delayed-action** *adjective* operating, designed to operate, after a predetermined interval of time.

delayering /diː'leɪərɪŋ/ *noun.* **L20.**
[ORIGIN from DE- 3 + LAYERING.]
The action or process of reducing the number of levels in the hierarchy of employees in an organization.
▪ **delayer** *verb trans.* **L20.**

del credere /dɛl 'kreɪdəri, -'krɛd-/ *adjectival, adverbial, & noun phr.* **L18.**
[ORIGIN Italian = of belief, of trust.]
COMMERCE. (Subject or relating to) a selling agent's guarantee, for which a commission is charged, that the buyer is solvent.

dele /'diːli/ *verb & noun.* **E18.**
[ORIGIN Latin, 2nd person sing. pres. imper. act. of *delere* DELETE.]
▸**A** *verb trans.* Pres. pple & verbal noun **deleing**. Delete, or mark for deletion, from typeset material. **E18.**

RICHARD MORRIS The comma after ape should be deled.

▸**B** *noun.* A proofreaders' sign (esp. ₰) indicating matter to be deleted. **E18.**

delect /dɪ'lɛkt/ *verb.* Long *rare.* **LME.**
[ORIGIN Latin *delectare*: see DELECTABLE. Cf. Old French *delecter*.]
†**1** *verb trans.* Ease the pain of. Only in **LME.**
2 *verb trans. & intrans.* = DELIGHT *verb.* **M16.**

delectable /dɪ'lɛktəb(ə)l/ *adjective.* **LME.**
[ORIGIN Old French & mod. French *délectable* from Latin *delectabilis*, from *delectare* to delight: see -ABLE.]
Very pleasing, delightful; (of food or drink) delicious; *colloq.* (of a person) very attractive.

MILTON Trees of God, Delectable both to behold and taste. W. BOYD Every biting insect saw her as a delectable target. C. DEXTER He . . was starting out on a new conquest—the delectable Lucy Downes.

▪ **delecta'bility** *noun* **LME.** **delectableness** *noun* **E16.** **delectably** *adverb* **LME.**

delectate /'diːlɛkteɪt, dɪ'lɛkteɪt/ *verb trans.* Now *rare.* **E19.**
[ORIGIN Latin *delectat-*: see DELECTATION, -ATE[3].]
Delight.

delectation /diːlɛk'teɪʃ(ə)n/ *noun.* **LME.**
[ORIGIN Old French & mod. French *délectation* from Latin *delectatio(n-)*, from *delectat-* pa. ppl stem of *delectare* delight: see -ATION.]
The action of delighting; pleasure, entertainment.

J. CAREY Bogus suffering, put on a stage for the delectation of a crowd, offended his reason.

delectus /dɪ'lɛktəs/ *noun.* **E19.**
[ORIGIN Latin, use as noun of pa. pple of *deligere* pick out, select, from *de-* DE- 1 + *legere* choose.]
A selection of (esp. Latin or Greek) passages for translation.

delectus personae /dɪˌlɛktəs pɔː'səʊniː/ *noun phr.* **M18.**
[ORIGIN Latin, lit. 'choice of a person'.]
LAW (now *hist.*). The right of each partner in a firm, party to a contract, etc., to choose or be satisfied with any person subsequently admitted to partnership etc.

delegable /'dɛlɪgəb(ə)l/ *adjective.* **M17.**
[ORIGIN from Latin *delegare*: see DELEGATE *verb*, -ABLE.]
Able to be delegated.

delegacy /'dɛlɪgəsi/ *noun.* **LME.**
[ORIGIN from DELEGATE *noun* after *prelate*, *prelacy*: see -ACY.]
1 The action or system of delegating; the state of being delegated; appointment as a delegate; delegated authority. **LME.**
2 A body or committee of delegates. **L15.**

delegant /'dɛlɪg(ə)nt/ *noun.* **E17.**
[ORIGIN Latin *delegant-* pres. ppl stem of *delegare*: see DELEGATE *verb*, -ANT[1].]
Chiefly LAW (now *hist.*). A person who delegates.

delegate /'dɛlɪgət/ *noun.* **LME.**
[ORIGIN Latin *delegatus* use as noun of pa. pple of *delegare*: see DELEGATE *verb*, -ATE[2].]
1 A person deputed or authorized to act for or represent another or others; a deputy, a member of a deputation; *esp.* a person chosen or elected to represent others at a meeting, conference, etc. **LME.**

E. MELLOR He [the priest] claims simply to stand as delegate of heaven. E. LONGFORD The Paris peace conference had opened . . with Wellington and Castlereagh as British delegates.

House of Delegates in the US, the lower house of the legislature in Virginia, West Virginia, and Maryland. ***walking delegate***: see WALKING *ppl adjective*.
2 A commissioner appointed by the Crown to hear appeals from ecclesiastical courts. *obsolete* exc. *hist.* **M16.**
3 At Oxford University, a member of any of various permanent committees entrusted with some branch of University business. **E17.**
4 A non-voting representative of a territory in the US Congress. **L18.**
▪ **delegateship** *noun* the position or office of a delegate **M19.**

delegate /'dɛlɪgeɪt/ *verb trans.* Pa. pple & ppl adjective **-ated**, (earliest form, long *arch.*) **-ate** /-ət/. **LME.**
[ORIGIN Latin *delegat-* pa. ppl stem of *delegare*, from *de-* DE- 1 + *legare* send on a commission: see -ATE[3].]
1 Send or commission (a person) to act as a deputy or representative; depute. **LME.**

S. UNWIN It was the elder boy's duty to decide what tools . . were needed and to delegate the small boys to fetch them.

†**2** *loosely.* Assign, deliver, convey. **LME–L18.**
3 Assign or entrust (a duty, authority, etc.) to another as agent or deputy. **L15.**

BOLINGBROKE The Peers have an inherent, the Commons a delegated Right. T. JEFFERSON Those bodies . . to whom the people have delegated the powers of legislation.

4 LAW (now *hist.*). Assign (a person who is a debtor to oneself) to a creditor as debtor in one's place. **E19.**
▪ **delega'tee** *noun* (chiefly LAW, now *hist.*) a person to whom something or someone is delegated **L19.** **delegator** *noun* a person who delegates **L19.**

delegation /dɛlɪ'geɪʃ(ə)n/ *noun.* **E17.**
[ORIGIN Latin *delegatio(n-)*, formed as DELEGATE *verb*: see -ATION.]
1 The action of delegating, the fact of being delegated; entrusting of authority to a representative. **E17.**

H. EVANS [Gerald] Long commanded by orderly delegation; he had an acute sense of hierarchy.

2 A commission given to a delegate; delegated power. **E17.**

J. LOCKE When . . others usurp the place, who have no such authority or delegation.

3 LAW (now *hist.*). Assignment of a debtor by his or her creditor to a creditor of the latter. **E18.**
4 A delegated body; a number of people chosen to act as representatives; a deputation. **L18.**

R. P. GRAVES Mrs Pankhurst led a delegation to Parliament to present a petition to the Prime Minister.

delegatory /'dɛlɪgət(ə)ri/ *adjective.* **L16.**
[ORIGIN Latin *delegatorius*, from *delegat-*: see DELEGATE *verb*, -ORY[2].]
†**1** Of a person: holding delegated authority. Only in **L16.**
2 Of, relating to, or of the nature of delegation or delegated power. **E17.**

D

delegitimize /diːlɪ'dʒɪtɪmʌɪz/ *verb trans.* Also **-ise**. **M20.**
[ORIGIN from DE- 3 + LEGITIMIZE.]
Withdraw legitimate status from.
▪ **delegitimi'zation** *noun* **L20.**

delete /dɪ'liːt/ *verb trans.* Pa. pple **-d**, (earlier) †**delete**. **LME.**
[ORIGIN Latin *delet-* pa. ppl stem of *delere* blot out, efface.]
†**1** Destroy, annihilate, do away with. **LME–M19.**
2 Cross out, cancel, remove, or erase (a character, letter, word, passage, etc.); make no longer effective by removal from a printed etc. record. **M16.** ▸**b** Remove (an item, esp. a recording) from a catalogue, so that it is no longer offered for sale. **M20.**

H. BEVERIDGE The peerage would be granted if the censure were deleted. H. ARENDT They deleted from Jewish prayerbooks the visions of an ultimate restoration of Zion. *fig.*: T. REID So imprinted as not to be deleted by time.

3 GENETICS. In *pass.* Be lost from a chromosome. **E20.**

deleterious /dɛlɪ'tɪərɪəs/ *adjective.* **M17.**
[ORIGIN from medieval Latin *deleterius* from Greek *dēlētērios* noxious: see -OUS.]
Detrimental to life or health, noxious, harmful; mentally or morally damaging.

BYRON 'Tis pity wine should be so deleterious, For tea and coffee leave us much more serious. R. W. EMERSON Politics is a deleterious profession.

▪ †**deleterial** *adjective* = DELETERIOUS: only in **17.** **deleteriously** *adverb* **L19.** **deleteriousness** *noun* **E19.** †**deletery** *adjective* = DELETERIOUS **L16–L17.**

deletion /dɪ'liːʃ(ə)n/ *noun.* **L15.**
[ORIGIN Latin *deletio(n-)*, from *delet-* pa. ppl stem of *delere* DELETE: see -ION.]
1 The action of obliterating or destroying; annihilation, destruction. *arch.* **L15.**
2 The action of deleting written or printed matter; the fact of being deleted; a deleted passage etc., an erasure. **L16.** ▸**b** The action of deleting an item, esp. a recording, from a catalogue; the item deleted. **M20.**
3 GENETICS. = DEFICIENCY 2. **E20.**

delf /dɛlf/ *noun*[1]. *obsolete* exc. *dial.* Also **-ph**.
[ORIGIN Old English *dælf*, *(ge)delf*, formed as DELVE *verb*.]
1 An excavation; a pit, ditch, quarry, etc.; a drainage canal (in the fens). **OE.**
2 A cut turf, a sod. *Scot.* **E16.**
3 A spade thrust. **E17.**
†**4** A bed of earth or a mineral that is or can be dug into. **E17–E18.**

†**delf** *noun*[2] & *adjective* var. of next.

delft /dɛlft/ *noun & adjective.* Also †**delf**, **delph** /dɛlf/. **L17.**
[ORIGIN from *Delf*, now *Delft*, a town in the Netherlands.]
▸**A** *noun.* **1** A kind of tin-glazed earthenware, usu. having blue decoration on a white ground, orig. made in Delft. **L17.**
2 (**delph**.) Plates, dishes, etc.; crockery. *Irish.* **M18.**
▸**B** *adjective.* Designating earthenware from Delft. **M18.**

Delhi belly /dɛli 'bɛli/ *noun phr. slang.* **M20.**
[ORIGIN *Delhi*, capital of India.]
An upset stomach accompanied by diarrhoea, esp. as suffered by visitors to India.

deli /'dɛli/ *noun. colloq.* (orig. *US*). **M20.**
[ORIGIN Abbreviation.]
= DELICATESSEN (esp. sense 2); in Australia, a small shop open long hours selling perishable goods, newspapers, etc.

Delian /'diːlɪən/ *adjective*[1]. **L16.**
[ORIGIN from Latin *Delius*, Greek *Dēlios* Delos (see below) + -AN.]
Of or pertaining to Delos, a Greek island in the Cyclades, or its inhabitants.
Delian League a confederacy of ancient Greek states under Athens, formed in 478 BC to oppose the Persians. **Delian problem**: of finding geometrically the side of a cube having twice the volume of a given cube (from the Delian oracle's pronouncement that a plague in Athens would cease if the cubical altar to Apollo were doubled in size).

Delian /'diːlɪən/ *adjective*[2] & *noun.* **M20.**
[ORIGIN from *Delius* (see below) + -AN.]
▸**A** *adjective.* Of or pertaining to the English composer Frederick Delius (1862–1934), his music, or his style of composition. **M20.**
▸**B** *noun.* An interpreter, student, or admirer of Delius or his music. **M20.**

†delibation *noun*. M17–L18.
[ORIGIN Latin *delibatio(n-)*, from *delibare* take a little of, taste, from *de-* DE- 1 + *libare* to taste: see -ATION.]
A portion extracted; a taste or slight knowledge *of* something.

†deliber *verb*. LME.
[ORIGIN French *délibérer* or Latin *deliberare*: see DELIBERATE *verb*.]
1 *verb intrans*. = DELIBERATE *verb* 1. LME–L15.
2 *verb intrans*. & (in *pass*.) *verb trans*. = DELIBERATE *verb* 2. LME–L16.
3 *verb trans*. = DELIBERATE *verb* 3. Only in M16.

deliberant /dɪˈlɪb(ə)r(ə)nt/ *noun*. *rare*. L17.
[ORIGIN Latin *deliberant-* pres. ppl stem of *deliberare*: see DELIBERATE *verb*, -ANT[1].]
A person who deliberates.

deliberate /dɪˈlɪb(ə)rət/ *adjective*. LME.
[ORIGIN Latin *deliberatus* pa. pple, formed as DELIBERATE *verb*: see -ATE[2].]
1 Carefully thought out, studied; intentional, done on purpose. LME.
L. P. HARTLEY The silence which had become habitual to her, unless she made a deliberate effort to break it. R. D. LAING Contrived, deliberate, cynical lies.
2 Firm, unhurried, purposeful; careful, not rash or hasty. L16.
J. R. GREEN Striving to be deliberate in speech. J. STEINBECK Abra moved with firm and deliberate steps.
■ **deliberately** *adverb* L15. **deliberateness** *noun* E17.

deliberate /dɪˈlɪbəreɪt/ *verb*. M16.
[ORIGIN Latin *deliberat-* pa. ppl stem of *deliberare*, from *de-* DE- 1 + *librare* weigh, from *libra* scales: see -ATE[3]. Cf. earlier DELIBER.]
1 *verb intrans*. Think carefully, pause for consideration, ponder; confer, take counsel together. Foll. by *about*, *on*, *upon*, †*of*. M16.
J. A. FROUDE The future relations of the two countries could now be deliberated on with a hope of settlement. W. S. MAUGHAM I deliberated a long time about buying it. B. PYM He deliberated for a moment then walked into a pew.
†**2** *verb intrans*. & (in *pass*.) *verb trans*. Resolve, determine (*to do*). M16–M17.
3 *verb trans*. Think over, confer about, deliberate on. Now usu. with obj. clause M16.
C. TOURNEUR To deliberate The cause or author of this accident. W. ROBERTSON She deliberated . . how she might overcome the regent's scruples.
■ **deliberator** *noun* [Latin] a person who deliberates. L18.

deliberation /dɪˌlɪbəˈreɪʃ(ə)n/ *noun*. LME.
[ORIGIN Old French *deliberacion* (later and mod. *délibération*), from Latin *deliberatio(n-)*, from *deliberat-*: see DELIBERATE *verb*, -ATION.]
▸ **I 1** The action of deliberating; careful consideration, weighing up with a view to decision. LME.
J. UPDIKE The answer came after maddening deliberation 'No'.
2 *spec*. Consideration and discussion of a question by a legislative assembly, committee, etc.; debate; an instance of this (freq. in *pl*.). LME.
P. LARKIN The chairman of the . . panel . . has risen to announce the result of its deliberations.
†**3** A resolution, a determination; a plan, an intention. M16–E18.
▸ **II 4** The quality of acting with careful thought; avoidance of precipitancy; deliberateness of action; absence of hurry; slowness in action or movement. LME.
S. WILLIAMS The chiefs consulted with great deliberation. F. RAPHAEL Susan served the meal with a slow deliberation which emphasized the trouble she had taken with it. C. PRIEST Raising and lowering my feet with the deliberation of a shackled man.

deliberative /dɪˈlɪb(ə)rətɪv/ *adjective*. L15.
[ORIGIN French *délibératif*, *-ive*, or Latin *deliberativus*, from *deliberat-*: see DELIBERATE *verb*, -ATIVE.]
1 Characterized by deliberation. L15.
2 Concerned with or having the function of deliberating. M16.
3 GRAMMAR. Expressing deliberation or doubt. M19.
■ **deliberatively** *adverb* M17. **deliberativeness** *noun* M17.

delible /ˈdɛlɪb(ə)l/ *adjective*. E17.
[ORIGIN Latin *delebilis*, from *delere*: see DELETE, -IBLE and cf. INDELIBLE, UNDELIBLE.]
Able to be deleted or effaced.

delicacy /ˈdɛlɪkəsi/ *noun*. LME.
[ORIGIN from DELICATE + -ACY.]
▸ **I** The quality of being delicate.
†**1** Addiction to pleasure or sensuous delights; voluptuousness, luxuriousness. LME–M18.
†**2** Luxury, indulgence. LME–E18. ▸**b** Gratification, pleasure. LME–M17.
†**3** The quality of being delightful or delicious; beauty, daintiness, pleasantness. LME–M17.
†**4** Fastidiousness. LME–L18.
5 Exquisite fineness of texture, substance, finish, etc.; graceful slightness, tender beauty. L16.
J. R. GREEN She would play with her rings that her courtiers might note the delicacy of her hands.
6 Weakliness of constitution or health; susceptibility to disease or injury. M17.
7 Fineness of skill, expression, touch, etc. L17.
8 Sensitivity of perception, feeling, observation, etc.; (of an instrument) sensitiveness, precision. E18.
LD MACAULAY His principles would be relaxed, and the delicacy of his sense of right and wrong impaired.
9 Avoidance of what is immodest or offensive; careful regard for the feelings of others. E18.
STEELE A false Delicacy is Affectation, not Politeness. S. LEWIS They coughed politely . . they blew their noses with a delicacy altogether optimistic and refined.
10 The quality or condition of requiring careful and skilful handling. L18.
BURKE Our concerns in India were matters of delicacy. J. GALSWORTHY When June determined on anything, delicacy became a somewhat minor consideration.
▸ **II 11** A thing which gives delight. Now *esp*. a choice or dainty item of food. LME.
P. PEARCE A tea-table laden with delicacies for him alone.
12 A delicate trait, observance, or attention. E18.
STEELE The . . Delicacies that attend the Passion towards them [women] in elegant Minds.
13 A nicety, a refinement. L18.
E. A. FREEMAN The grammatical delicacies of the written language.

delicate /ˈdɛlɪkət/ *adjective* & *noun*. LME.
[ORIGIN Old French & mod. French *délicat* or Latin *delicatus*, of unknown origin: see -ATE[2].]
▸ **A** *adjective*. **1** Delightful, pleasant, charming, lovely, nice. Now only of food: dainty and palatable. LME.
EVELYN Haerlem is a very delicate town. G. WHITE The sun broke out into a warm delicate day. M. PATTISON Not to take delight in delicate meats.
†**2** Characterized by sensuous delight; luxurious, voluptuous; (of a person) given to pleasure or luxury. LME–M18.
†**3** Self-indulgent, indolent. LME–E17.
†**4** Fastidious, particular. LME–L18.
†**5** Not robust; effeminate. LME–L17.
SHAKES. *Haml*. Witness this army . . Led by a delicate and tender prince.
6 Of weakly constitution; liable to illness or injury; not strong. LME. ▸**b** Fragile; easily spoiled or damaged. M16.
V. WOOLF I am supposed . . to be too delicate to go with them, since I get so easily tired and am then sick. **b** K. ISHIGURO The teacup . . was of the same delicate material.
in a delicate condition: see CONDITION *noun* 8.
7 Fine in texture, finish, quality, workmanship, etc.; exquisitely shaped or constructed; slight, slender, soft. LME. ▸**b** Soft or subdued in colour. E19.
E. WAUGH A delicate pair of gold manicure scissors. J. HARVEY It was a fine face with delicate edges and corners. **b** D. H. LAWRENCE Looking at the water, I perceived a delicate flush from the west.
8 Having finely developed perception, feeling, appreciation, etc.; (of a person or instrument) sensitive. M16.
T. HEGGEN Ensign Pulver's feet were enormous and he was delicate about them. G. ORWELL You could not control the beating of your heart, and the telescreen was quite delicate enough to pick it up.
9 Finely skilful. L16. ▸†**b** Characterized by skilful action. L16–L17.
SHAKES. *Oth*. So delicate with her needle.
10 Sensitive to propriety, modesty, or the feelings of others; avoiding what is offensive or immodest. M17.
L. STERNE We were both too delicate to communicate what we felt to each other upon the occasion.
11 So slight as to be hard to appreciate; subtle. L17.
A. BAIN Discrimination of the most delicate differences.
12 Requiring careful and skilful handling; ticklish. M18.
S. NAIPAUL The subject is a delicate one and I do not pursue it. E. REVELEY The whole thing will take some pretty delicate manoeuvering.
▸ **B** *noun*. †**1** A person with luxurious or fastidious tastes. LME–E18.
2 A luxury, a delight; *esp*. a choice item of food. Now *rare* or *obsolete*. LME.
■ **delicately** *adverb* LME. **delicateness** *noun* M16.

délicatesse /delikatɛs/ *noun*. L17.
[ORIGIN French, from *délicat* delicate.]
Delicacy.

delicatessen /ˌdɛlɪkəˈtɛs(ə)n/ *noun*. Orig. *US*. L19.
[ORIGIN German *Delikatessen* pl. or Dutch *delicatessen* pl., formed as DÉLICATESSE.]
1 Cooked meats, cheeses, and unusual or foreign prepared foods. L19.
2 A shop, or shop counter or department, selling delicatessen. M20.

†delice *noun*. ME.
[ORIGIN Old French & mod. French *délice* masc., *délices* fem. pl., from Latin *delicium* neut. sing., *deliciae* fem. pl.]
1 Delight, pleasure; *esp*. sensual or worldly pleasure. ME–L17.
2 A delight; a delicacy. ME–M19.

delicious /dɪˈlɪʃəs/ *adjective* & *noun*. ME.
[ORIGIN Old French (mod. *délicieux*) from late Latin *deliciosus*, from Latin *delicia*, pl. *deliciae*: see DELICE, -OUS.]
▸ **A** *adjective*. **1** Highly delightful; giving great pleasure or enjoyment; intensely amusing. ME.
C. KINGSLEY A delicious joke it would have been. ARNOLD BENNETT A delicious wave of joy and of satisfaction animated him.
2 Highly pleasing to the bodily senses, esp. to those of taste or smell. ME.
V. WOOLF These delicious mouthfuls of roast duck. B. PYM The delicious fragrance of shrubs. I. MURDOCH He paraded his delicious fiancée in theatre foyers.
†**3** Characterized by or addicted to sensuous indulgence. ME–L17.
▸ **B** *noun*. (Also D-.) A variety of eating apple of N. American origin. E20.
Golden Delicious: see GOLDEN *adjective*. ***Red Delicious***: see RED *adjective*.
■ **deliciously** *adverb* ME. **deliciousness** *noun* LME.

delict /dɪˈlɪkt, ˈdiːlɪkt/ *noun*. *arch*. LME.
[ORIGIN Latin *delictum* use as noun of *delictus* pa. pple of *delinquere*: see DELINQUENT.]
A violation of law; an offence.
in flagrant delict = IN FLAGRANTE DELICTO.
■ **deˈlictual** *adjective* (*rare*) of or belonging to a delict L19.

deligation /dɛlɪˈgeɪʃ(ə)n/ *noun*. Now *rare* or *obsolete*. M17.
[ORIGIN from DE- 1 + LIGATION.]
MEDICINE. †**1** Bandaging; a bandage. M17–M19.
2 The tying of an artery etc. with a ligature. M19.

delight /dɪˈlʌɪt/ *noun*. ME.
[ORIGIN Old French *delit*, from stem of *delitier* from Latin *delectare* to allure, charm, frequentative of *delicere*. The spelling with *-gh-* on the analogy of native words like *light* dates from 16.]
1 The fact or condition of being delighted; pleasure, joy, or gratification felt in a high degree. ME.
COLERIDGE He gazed! he thrilled with deep delight! B. JOWETT The branch of knowledge . . in which he takes the greatest delight.
2 A thing which or person who causes great pleasure or joy, a source of delight. ME.
LD MACAULAY The poetry and eloquence of Greece had been the delight of Raleigh. K. A. PORTER She enjoyed Freytag's good looks, he was a delight to her eyes. L. BLUE There are many other delights in a Polish kitchen. *New Scientist* The mammalogist's delight—faecal analysis.
debs' delight, ***deb's delight***: see DEB. ***hell's delight***: see HELL *noun*. ***lady's delight***: see LADY *noun* & *adjective*.
3 The quality of delighting; delightfulness. Now *poet*. ME.
WORDSWORTH She was a Phantom of delight.
4 ***Turkish delight***, †***lumps of delight***, a sweet made of boiled syrup and cornflour coated with powdered sugar. M19.
■ **delightless** *adjective* not giving delight L16.

delight /dɪˈlʌɪt/ *verb*. ME.
[ORIGIN Old French *delitier*: see DELIGHT *noun*.]
1 *verb trans*. Give great pleasure or enjoyment to; please highly. Freq. in *pass*. (foll. by *with*, *at*, †*in*, *to do*). ME. ▸**b** *verb intrans*. Give great pleasure, cause delight. L19.
W. CATHER She laughed as if the idea . . delighted her. A. MASON More than pleased: he had been delighted. **b** G. F. ATHERTON There had been much to delight and awe.
2 *verb intrans*. & (*arch*.) *refl*. Be highly pleased (*to do*, *with*), take great pleasure (*in*). ME.
AV *Ps*. 119:16 I will delight my selfe in thy statutes. J. MORLEY The kind of man whom this system delights to honour. G. M. TREVELYAN Ever since the days of Burns . . the English have delighted in Scottish tradition and story.
†**3** *verb trans*. Enjoy greatly, delight in. LME–E17.
■ **delighter** *noun* a person who takes delight (*in*) L16. **delightingly** *adverb* with delight E17.

delightable /dɪˈlʌɪtəb(ə)l/ *adjective*. Long *rare*. ME.
[ORIGIN Orig. from Old French *delitable*, from *delitier*: see DELIGHT *noun*, -ABLE; later directly from DELIGHT *noun* or *verb*.]
Causing delight, delightful.

delighted /dɪˈlʌɪtɪd/ *adjective*. E17.
[ORIGIN from DELIGHT *noun*, *verb*: see -ED[2], -ED[1].]
†**1** Causing delight; delightful. E17–M18.
SHAKES. *Oth*. If virtue no delighted beauty lack.
2 Filled with delight, highly pleased or gratified. L17.
M. SPARK He laughed in a delighted way.
■ **delightedly** *adverb* E19.

delightful /dɪˈlʌɪtfʊl, -f(ə)l/ *adjective*. LME.
[ORIGIN from DELIGHT *noun* + -FUL.]
1 Causing delight; highly pleasing, charming. LME.
†2 Experiencing delight; delighted. L16–L17.
■ **delightfully** *adverb* L16. **delightfulness** *noun* L16.

delightsome /dɪˈlʌɪts(ə)m/ *adjective*. Now *literary*. E16.
[ORIGIN from DELIGHT *noun* + -SOME[1].]
Delightful.
■ **delightsomely** *adverb* L16. **delightsomeness** *noun* L16.

delignification /ˌdiːlɪgnɪfɪˈkeɪʃ(ə)n/ *noun*. E20.
[ORIGIN from DE- 3 + LIGNIN + -FICATION.]
The removal of lignin from woody tissue.
■ **deˈlignify** *verb trans.* subject to delignification (chiefly as *delignified ppl adjective*) M20.

Delilah /dɪˈlʌɪlə/ *noun*. Also †**Dal-**. L16.
[ORIGIN The woman who betrayed Samson to the Philistines (*Judges* 16).]
A temptress, a seductive and treacherous woman.

delimit /dɪˈlɪmɪt/ *verb trans.* M19.
[ORIGIN French *délimiter* from Latin *delimitare*, from *de-* DE- 1 + *limitare*: see LIMIT *verb*.]
Mark or determine the limits of; define the territorial boundary of.
■ **delimitate** *verb trans.* = DELIMIT L19. **delimitative** *adjective* having the function of delimiting L19. **delimiter** *noun* (COMPUTING) a character etc. used to indicate the beginning or end of a group of characters or a field M20.

delimitation /dɪˌlɪmɪˈteɪʃ(ə)n/ *noun*. M19.
[ORIGIN French *délimitation* from Latin *delimitatio(n-)*, from *delimitat-* pa. ppl stem of *delimitare*: see DELIMIT, -ATION.]
The action of delimiting; determination of a limit or boundary, esp. of the frontier of a territory.

†**deline** *verb trans.* L16–M18.
[ORIGIN Latin *delineare*: see DELINEATE *verb*.]
= DELINEATE *verb*.

delineable /dɪˈlɪnɪəb(ə)l/ *adjective*. *rare*. M17.
[ORIGIN formed as DELINE + -ABLE.]
Able to be delineated.

delineate /dɪˈlɪnɪət/ *ppl adjective*. Now *arch.* or *poet.* L16.
[ORIGIN Latin *delineatus* pa. pple, formed as DELINEATE *verb*: see -ATE[2].]
Delineated; traced out, portrayed, described.

delineate /dɪˈlɪnɪeɪt/ *verb trans.* M16.
[ORIGIN Latin *delineat-* pa. ppl stem of *delineare* outline, sketch out, from *de-* DE- 1 + *lineare* draw lines, from *linea* LINE *noun*[2]: see -ATE[3].]
1 Trace out by lines, trace or serve as the outline of. M16.
> F. R. WILSON The exact position is delineated on the plan. S. SPENDER Straight mouldings delineate tall windows.

2 Represent by drawing, portray; draw in fine detail. L16.
> G. GROTE If . . lions could paint, they would delineate their gods in form like themselves.

3 Sketch out, outline (something to be constructed, a scheme, etc.). E17.
> MARVELL Not willing . . to deliniate his whole proposall.

4 *fig.* Describe or portray in words; express. E17.
> M. FRAYN Every well-formed smile . . seemed to delineate an intolerable sadness. H. ACTON A tendency to identify herself with the characters she delineated.

■ **delineative** *adjective* pertaining to delineation; serving to delineate: M19. **delineator** *noun* (*a*) a person who delineates; (*b*) an instrument for tracing outlines: L18.

delineation /dɪˌlɪnɪˈeɪʃ(ə)n/ *noun*. L16.
[ORIGIN Late Latin *delineatio(n-)*, formed as DELINEATE *verb*: see -ATION.]
1 The action of tracing out something by lines; a drawing, a diagram, a figure. L16. ▸**b** Pictorial representation; a drawing, a portrait. L16.
2 The action of outlining something to be constructed or established; a sketch, a plan, a rough draft. L16.
3 The action of portraying in words; description, expression. L16.
> *Times Literary Supplement* His delineation of the differences between 'non-didactic' and 'didactic' teaching.

delink /diːˈlɪŋk/ *verb trans.* M20.
[ORIGIN from DE- 3 + LINK *verb*[1].]
Separate (something, esp. orig. the currency of a nation) from something else.

†**delinquence** *noun*. L17–M19.
[ORIGIN formed as DELINQUENT: see -ENCE.]
The fact of being a delinquent; (a) culpable failure in duty.

delinquency /dɪˈlɪŋkw(ə)nsi/ *noun*. M17.
[ORIGIN ecclesiastical Latin *delinquentia*, formed as DELINQUENT: see -ENCY.]
1 The quality of being a delinquent; failure in or violation of duty; delinquent behaviour. M17.
juvenile delinquency: see JUVENILE *adjective*.
2 A delinquent act; a failing, a misdeed, an offence. Usu. in *pl.* M17.

delinquent /dɪˈlɪŋkwənt/ *noun & adjective*. L15.
[ORIGIN Latin *delinquent-* pres. ppl stem of *delinquere* be at fault, offend, from *de-* DE- 1 + *linquere* leave: see -ENT.]
▸ **A** *noun*. 1 A person who fails in duty or obligation; an offender; now *esp.* a young offender. L15.
> STEELE Where Crimes are enormous, the Delinquent deserves little Pity. I. MURDOCH Had he turned out a problem child, perhaps a delinquent.

juvenile delinquent: see JUVENILE *adjective*.
2 *hist.* (A name given by the parliamentarians to) a person who helped Charles I and Charles II to make war between 1642 and 1660. M17.
▸ **B** *adjective*. 1 Failing in or neglectful of a duty or obligation; guilty of a misdeed or offence. E17.
> P. HOLLAND Having offended or being delinquent in any duetie.

2 Of or pertaining to a delinquent or delinquents. M17.
> I. MCEWAN Raymond, in his earlier, delinquent days had fed glass splinters to the pigeons.

†**deliquate** *verb*. M17.
[ORIGIN from DE- 3 + LIQUATE *verb*.]
1 *verb intrans.* Deliquesce. M17–E19.
2 *verb trans.* Dissolve, melt down. Only in L17.

deliquesce /dɛlɪˈkwɛs/ *verb intrans.* M18.
[ORIGIN Latin *deliquescere* melt away, dissolve, from *de-* DE- 1 + *liquescere* inceptive of *liquere* be liquid: see -ESCE.]
1 CHEMISTRY. Become liquid by absorbing moisture from the air, as certain salts do. M18.
2 BIOLOGY. Esp. of fungi: become liquid after maturity, or in the course of decay. M19.
3 *gen.* Melt away, dissolve. Chiefly *fig.* M19.

deliquescence /dɛlɪˈkwɛs(ə)ns/ *noun*. M18.
[ORIGIN formed as DELIQUESCENT: see -ESCENCE.]
The process of deliquescing; the property of being deliquescent; liquid produced in deliquescing.
■ Also **deliquescency** *noun* (*rare*) M18.

deliquescent /dɛlɪˈkwɛs(ə)nt/ *adjective*. L18.
[ORIGIN Latin *deliquescent-* pres. ppl stem of *deliquescere*: see DELIQUESCE, -ESCENT.]
1 CHEMISTRY. That deliquesces; having the property of dissolving in moisture absorbed from the air. L18.
2 *gen.* Turning to liquid, melting away (chiefly *fig.*); *joc.* dissolving in perspiration. M19. ▸**b** Esp. of fungi: turning to liquid in the process of maturity or decay. L19.
> J. BRAINE A middle-aged woman . . with black dyed hair and a sort of deliquescent distinction.

3 Of a tree, trunk, etc.: dissolving into ramifications, repeatedly branching. M19.

†**deliquiate** *verb intrans.* M18–M19.
[ORIGIN Irreg. from Latin *deliquare* (= DELIQUATE) or from DELIQUIUM *noun*[2].]
= DELIQUESCE *verb* 1.

deliquium /dɪˈlɪkwɪəm/ *noun*[1]. *arch.* E17.
[ORIGIN Latin *deliquium* failure, want, (in medieval Latin) offence, transgression, from *delinquere*: see DELINQUENT.]
1 Failure of the vital powers, a swoon. E17.
†2 A failure of light, an eclipse. M–L17.
3 (Confused with next.) A melting away; the state of having melted. Chiefly *fig.* E18.

†**deliquium** *noun*[2]. E17–E19.
[ORIGIN from DELIQUATE after *effluvium* etc.]
CHEMISTRY. = DELIQUESCENCE.

delirament /dɪˈlɪrəm(ə)nt/ *noun*. *rare*. LME.
[ORIGIN Latin *deliramentum*, from *delirare*: see DELIRIUM, -MENT.]
Raving, frenzy; a craze.

†**delirancy** *noun*. M17–M18.
[ORIGIN from Latin *delirare* (see DELIRIUM) + -ANCY.]
Raving, madness.

deliration /dɛlɪˈreɪʃ(ə)n/ *noun*. E17.
[ORIGIN Latin *deliratio(n-)*, from *delirat-* pa. ppl stem of *delirare*: see DELIRIUM, -ATION.]
Delirium, mental aberration, madness; absurdity; an attack of this.

delire /dɪˈlɪə/ *verb intrans.* Long *obsolete* exc. *Scot.* LME.
[ORIGIN Latin *delirare*: see DELIRIUM. Cf. French *délirer*.]
Go astray, err, esp. in reason; wander in mind, go mad, rave.
> R. BURNS Gotten fright, An' liv'd an' di'd deleerit.

deliriant /dɪˈlɪrɪənt/ *adjective & noun*. L19.
[ORIGIN from DELIRIUM + -ANT[1].]
(A drug) having the power to produce delirium.

deliriate /dɪˈlɪrɪeɪt/ *verb trans.* *rare*. M17.
[ORIGIN formed as DELIRIANT + -ATE[3].]
Make delirious.

delirious /dɪˈlɪrɪəs/ *adjective*. L16.
[ORIGIN formed as DELIRIUM + -OUS.]
1 (Of an action etc.) belonging to or characteristic of delirium; betraying delirium or ecstasy. L16.
> BYRON How the giant element From rock to rock leaps with delirious bound. W. B. CARPENTER The delirious ravings of Intoxication or of Fever.

2 (Of a person) affected with delirium; temporarily or apparently mad, raving; wildly excited, ecstatic. E18.
> J. GALSWORTHY The young man seemed quite delirious about her. J. FRAME They thought he was drunk . . until they realized he was delirious with pneumonia.

■ **deliriously** *adverb* E19. **deliriousness** *noun* L18.

delirium /dɪˈlɪrɪəm/ *noun*. Pl. **-iums**, **-ia** /-ɪə/. M16.
[ORIGIN Latin *delirium*, from *delirare* deviate, be deranged, from *de-* DE- 1 + *lira* ridge between furrows.]
1 A disordered state of the mind resulting from disease, intoxication, etc., characterized by incoherent speech, hallucinations, restlessness, and often extreme excitement. M16.
delirium tremens /ˈtriːmɛnz, trɛ-/ [Latin = trembling delirium] delirium with tremors and terrifying delusions, occurring esp. as a withdrawal symptom in chronic alcoholism.
2 Great excitement; ecstasy, rapturous frenzy. M17.
> W. IRVING He . . danced in a delirium of joy, until he upset the canoe.

†**delirous** *adjective*. M17–E18.
[ORIGIN from Latin *delirus*, formed as DELIRIUM: see -OUS.]
Delirious, raving.

delish /dɪˈlɪʃ/ *adjective*. *colloq.* E20.
[ORIGIN Abbreviation.]
Delicious.
> A. CARTER Cyn would do us a couple of lamb chops, a bit of liver and bacon . . . Delish.

delist /diːˈlɪst/ *verb trans.* M20.
[ORIGIN from DE- 3 + LIST *noun*[3].]
Remove from a list, *esp.* (*a*) remove (a security) from the official register of a stock exchange; (*b*) remove (a product) from the list of those sold by a particular retailer.

delitescent /dɛlɪˈtɛs(ə)nt/ *adjective*. Now *rare*. L17.
[ORIGIN Latin *delitescent-* pres. ppl stem of *delitescere* hide away, lurk, from *de-* DE- 1 + *latescere*, inceptive of *latere* lie hid: see -ESCENT.]
Lying hidden, concealed; latent.
■ **delitescence** *noun* L18. **delitescency** *noun* L17.

deliver /dɪˈlɪvə/ *adjective*. Long *arch.* ME.
[ORIGIN Old French *de(s)livre*, from *delivrer*: see DELIVER *verb*.]
Free of encumbrance; agile, nimble, active; mentally quick, lively.
■ **deliverly** *adverb* LME. **deliverness** *noun* LME.

deliver /dɪˈlɪvə/ *verb*. ME.
[ORIGIN Old French & mod. French *délivrer* from Proto-Gallo-Romance, from Latin *de-* DE- 1 + *liberare* LIBERATE *verb*.]
▸ **I** *verb trans.* 1 Save, rescue, set free, (*from*, †*of*). ME. ▸**b** POTTERY & FOUNDING. Release from the mould. M19.
> AV *1 Sam.* 17:37 The Lord . . will deliver me out of the hand of this Philistine. T. HARDY A mood of disgust . . from which he was only delivered by . . abandoning these studies.

2 Free, rid, divest, (*of*, *from*). *arch.* ME. ▸**b** Unload (a ship, container, etc.). L18.
> W. LITHGOW The vertue to deliuer a woman from her paine in child-birth.

deliver a jail *hist.*: clear it of prisoners in order to bring them to trial at the assizes.
3 Assist (a woman, *occas.* a female animal) in giving birth; assist at the birth of (a child, offspring); give birth to. Freq. (earlier) in *pass.*, give birth (foll. by *of* a child, offspring), be born. ME.
> SHAKES. *Wint. T.* She is, something before her time, deliver'd. S. PLATH Will . . had to deliver eight babies before he could graduate. G. BOURNE The majority of women will deliver their heaviest child when they are about 35. B. TRAPIDO The baby . . could not be delivered without forceps. *fig.*: B. JOWETT I have been delivered of an infinite variety of speeches about virtue before now.

4 *refl.* Disburden oneself *of* what is in one's mind; speak, discourse. ME.
> L. VAN DER POST Theologians . . delivering themselves of resounding solemnities.

5 Give up entirely, give over; surrender, yield, abandon, resign. Freq. foll. by *up*, *over*. ME. ▸**b** *refl.* Devote oneself *to*. *rare*. M16.
> SHAKES. *Rich. II* See them delivered over To execution and the hand of death. M. PATTISON When premiers deliver up their portfolios. A. MASON God would deliver their enemies into their hand. **b** M. BRADBURY Howard delivers himself to the task of persuasion.

6 Hand over to another's possession or keeping, transfer; *esp.* bring and hand over (a letter, a parcel, ordered goods, etc.) to the proper recipient or address; present, render (an account etc.). ME. ▸**b** LAW. Formally hand over (a thing, formerly esp. a sealed deed to the grantee). L16.
> W. H. PRESCOTT A message which he must deliver in person. B. MALAMUD He delivered the prisoner first to Secret Police Headquarters. *fig.*: G. GREER The marriage bargain offers what cannot be delivered if it is thought to offer emotional security.

deliver the goods *fig.* carry out one's part of an agreement, do what is expected of one.

7 Give out in words; utter, recite; pronounce (judgement etc.). LME.

J. AGATE Good criticisms . . tellingly delivered. W. S. CHURCHILL Scarcely literate enough to deliver a decent sermon. M. MCCARTHY They had never heard 'their marriage is not lawful' delivered with such emphasis.

†**8** Communicate, make known; describe, report, set forth. LME–E19.

SHAKES. *Wint. T.* I . . heard the old shepherd deliver the manner how he found it.

D

9 Launch, aim, send forth (a blow, an attack, etc.); cast, throw, project (a missile, ball, etc.); produce, supply. Also with indirect obj. L16.

T. MEDWIN In delivering his harpoon he lost his balance. I. MURDOCH She . . brought the brush into play, delivering me a sharp jab on the ankle. I. T. BOTHAM You can't decide how you're going to play a ball before it's delivered. *Dirt Bike* The six-speed gearbox . . delivers almost 50 miles per gallon.

► **II** *verb intrans.* **10** Give birth; hand something over; distribute mail, goods, etc., to the proper recipients or addresses; speak, pronounce; CRICKET bowl a ball. LME. ▸**b** *spec.* Provide what is expected or what one has promised. (Foll. by *on* a pledge etc.) Orig. *US.* M20.

J. ROBINSON They first delivered on civil affairs: afterwards the discourse turned on war. SIR W. SCOTT Are we commanded to stand and deliver on the King's highway? OED The postman who delivers in that part of the town. M. BRADBURY Mrs Macintosh, when she did deliver, delivered in bulk, and had twins. **b** S. BRILL Fitzsimmons was trying to deliver on one of the reforms he had promised the government.

11 POTTERY & FOUNDING. Come free from the mould. L18.

■ **deliverable** *adjective & noun* (*a*) *adjective* able to be delivered; (*b*) *noun* a thing able to be delivered, esp. at an agreed stage in the development of a product (usu. in *pl.*): M18.

deliverance /dɪˈlɪv(ə)r(ə)ns/ *noun.* ME.

[ORIGIN Old French & mod. French *délivrance*, formed as DELIVER *verb*: see -ANCE.]

1 The act of setting free, the fact of being set free; liberation, release, rescue. ME.

HOBBES Our deliverance from the bondage of sin. W. C. WILLIAMS A sense of thanksgiving for her miraculous deliverance.

2 The action of giving up, or of handing over or transferring, surrender; = DELIVERY 2, 3. Long *obsolete* exc. LAW (see below). ME.

writ of second deliverance LAW (now *hist.*) a writ for redelivery to the owner of goods distrained or unlawfully taken.

†**3** The bringing forth of offspring; = DELIVERY 4. LME–M17.

†**4 a** The delivery of words, utterance, enunciation; the action of stating something, declaration, narration. LME–E17. ▸**b** A (formal or authoritative) utterance. M19.

b J. S. MILL The recorded deliverances of the Founder of Christianity.

5 LAW (chiefly *Scot.*). Judgement delivered, verdict; a judicial or administrative order. LME.

deliverer /dɪˈlɪv(ə)rə/ *noun.* ME.

[ORIGIN Old French *delivrere*, formed as DELIVER *verb*: see -ER².]

1 A person or being who sets free or releases; a rescuer, a saviour. ME.

Great Deliverer: see GREAT *adjective*.

2 A person who hands over, transfers, or commits something to another; one who delivers letters, parcels, ordered goods, etc. LME.

3 A person or being who utters, enunciates, or recites, something; one who pronounces judgement etc. L16.

■ **deliveress** *noun* (*rare*) a female deliverer M17.

delivery /dɪˈlɪv(ə)ri/ *noun.* LME.

[ORIGIN Anglo-Norman *delivree* use as noun of fem. pa. pple of *delivrer*: see DELIVER *verb*, -Y³. Sense 6 is assoc. with DELIVER *adjective*.]

1 a *hist.* ***jail-delivery***, the action of clearing a jail of prisoners in order to bring them to trial at an assize; the application of the judicial process to the prisoners in a jail. LME. ▸**b** The action of setting free; deliverance. Now *rare*. L15.

2 The action of giving up possession *of*, surrender. LME.

3 The action of handing over something to another; *esp.* a (scheduled) performance of the action of delivering letters, goods, etc. LME. ▸**b** LAW. A formal handing over or transfer, esp. of a deed to the grantee or a third party. L16.

DICKENS It [a letter] will be here by the two o'clock delivery.

4 The act of giving birth, or assisting at a birth; parturition, childbirth. L16.

5 The uttering of words, a speech, a pronouncement; the manner of enunciating speech, song, etc. L16. ▸†**b** Setting forth in words; narration, statement. L16–M17.

JAS. MILL Four days were occupied in the delivery of the speech. A. POWELL This delivery made his words . . appear to protest.

†**6** (Free) use of the limbs; bodily activity, bearing. L16–E19.

H. WOTTON The duke had the neater limbs, and freer delivery.

7 The sending forth or delivering of a missile, a blow, etc.; the throwing or bowling of a ball etc.; the action shown in doing this. Also, discharge, provision, supply. E18.

J. FINGLETON Bailey . . played 'doggo' to 388 deliveries. *Scientific American* Dissatisfaction with the delivery of medical care in the U.S.

– PHRASES: ***cash on delivery***: see CASH *noun*¹. ***constructive delivery***: see CONSTRUCTIVE *adjective* 1. ***special delivery***: see SPECIAL *adjective*. ***symbolic delivery***: see SYMBOLIC *adjective*. ***symbolical delivery***: see SYMBOLICAL *adjective*. **take delivery of** receive after ordering.

– COMB.: **delivery room** a specially equipped hospital room in which births take place; **delivery van**, **delivery vehicle**, etc.: for making deliveries of goods.

dell /dɛl/ *noun*¹.

[ORIGIN Old English *dell* = Middle Low German, Middle Dutch *delle* (Dutch *del*), Middle High German *telle* (German dial. *Telle*), from Germanic, from base also of DALE *noun*¹.]

1 A small valley or natural hollow, usu. wooded. OE.

†**2** A deep hole, a pit. LME–L18.

dell /dɛl/ *noun*². *arch. slang.* M16.

[ORIGIN Unknown.]

A young woman.

Della Cruscan /dɛlə ˈkrʌskən/ *adjective & noun.* E19.

[ORIGIN from Italian (*Accademia*) *della Crusca* (Academy) of the bran (with ref. to 'sifting'): see -AN.]

► **A** *adjective.* Of, pertaining to, or characteristic of the Accademia della Crusca, established at Florence in 1582 with the main purpose of purifying the Italian language. Also, designating, belonging to, or characteristic of an artificial school of English poetry of the late 18th cent. E19.

► **B** *noun.* A member of the Accademia della Crusca or of the Della Cruscan school. E19.

■ **Della Cruscanism** *noun* (*rare*) the principles or practices of Della Cruscans L18.

Della Robbia /dɛlə ˈrɒbɪə/ *noun.* L18.

[ORIGIN A family of 15th-cent. Italian painters & sculptors.]

In full ***Della Robbia ware*** etc. Enamelled terracotta ware made by Luca Della Robbia and his successors; any similar ware.

delocalize /diːˈləʊk(ə)lʌɪz/ *verb trans.* Also **-ise**. M19.

[ORIGIN from DE- 3 + LOCALIZE.]

Detach or remove from its place, not limit to a particular location; CHEMISTRY in *pass.* (of electrons) be shared among more than two atoms in a molecule.

■ **delocaliˈzation** *noun* L19.

delope /dɪˈləʊp/ *verb intrans.* M19.

[ORIGIN Unknown.]

Of a duellist: deliberately fire into the air.

– NOTE: Popularized in the historical novels of Georgette Heyer (1902–74).

delouse /diːˈlaʊs/ *verb trans.* E20.

[ORIGIN from DE- 3 + LOUSE *noun*.]

Rid of lice; *fig.* rid of undesirable things.

delph *noun*¹ see DELF *noun*¹.

delph *noun*² *& adjective* var. of DELFT.

Delphi /ˈdɛlfi, -fʌɪ/ *noun.* M20.

[ORIGIN formed as DELPHIC.]

In full ***Delphi method***, ***Delphi technique***, etc. A technique of using questionnaires to arrive at consensual judgements, decisions, etc.

Delphian /ˈdɛlfɪən/ *adjective.* L16.

[ORIGIN formed as DELPHIC + -AN.]

= DELPHIC.

Delphic /ˈdɛlfɪk/ *adjective.* L16.

[ORIGIN from *Delphi* (see below) + -IC.]

Of or relating to Delphi, a town of Phocis in ancient Greece, esp. as the site of a sanctuary and oracle of Apollo; resembling or characteristic of the oracle of Delphi; (of an utterance etc.) obscure, ambiguous, enigmatic.

Times Mr Begin maintained a Delphic silence about his intentions.

■ **delphically** *adverb* in a manner characteristic of the Delphic oracle; enigmatically, obscurely, prophetically: E20.

delphin /ˈdɛlfɪn/ *noun & adjective.* ME.

[ORIGIN Latin *delphin*, *-inus*: see DOLPHIN. Cf. also DAUPHIN.]

► †**A** *noun.* **1** = DOLPHIN 1. ME–M17.

2 The dauphin. Only in LME.

► **B** *adjective.* (**D-**.) [Latin phr. *ad usum Delphini*.] Designating or pertaining to an edition of Latin classics prepared 'for the use of the dauphin', son of Louis XIV of France. Cf. earlier DAUPHIN *adjective*. L18.

delphinidin /dɛlˈfɪnɪdɪn/ *noun.* E20.

[ORIGIN from DELPHINIUM + -IDIN.]

CHEMISTRY. An anthocyanidin, $C_{15}H_{11}O_7Cl$, found combined as glycosides in many plant pigments.

delphinine /ˈdɛlfɪniːn/ *noun.* L19.

[ORIGIN from DELPHINIUM + -INE⁵.]

CHEMISTRY. A poisonous alkaloid obtained from the seeds of stavesacre, *Delphinium staphisagria*.

delphinium /dɛlˈfɪnɪəm/ *noun.* E17.

[ORIGIN mod. Latin (see below) from Greek *delphinion* larkspur, from DELPHIN (from the shape of the spur).]

Any of numerous plants with spurred flowers constituting (or formerly included in) the genus *Delphinium*, of the buttercup family; *esp.* any of certain perennials, hybrids of *D. elatum*, grown for their long spikes of blue, purple, or white flowers (cf. LARKSPUR). Also, a flower or flowering stem of such a plant.

delphinoid /ˈdɛlfɪnɔɪd/ *adjective & noun.* L19.

[ORIGIN Greek *delphinoeidēs*, from *delphin* DOLPHIN: see -OID.]

ZOOLOGY. ► **A** *adjective.* Of the nature of a dolphin; related to the dolphins; belonging to the division Delphinoidea, which includes the dolphins, killer whales, and porpoises. L19.

► **B** *noun.* A delphinoid mammal; a member of Delphinoidea. L19.

Delphinus /dɛlˈfʌɪnəs/ *noun.* L17.

[ORIGIN Latin *delphinus*: see DOLPHIN.]

(The name of) a small constellation of the northern hemisphere near Cygnus; the Dolphin.

delta /ˈdɛltə/ *noun.* ME.

[ORIGIN Latin from Greek.]

1 The fourth letter (Δ, δ) of the Greek alphabet. ME.

delta-v, **delta-vee** [from the use of δ as a mathematical symbol denoting variation + *v* for *velocity*] rate of change of velocity; acceleration.

2 A tract of alluvial land, often more or less triangular in shape, enclosed or traversed by the diverging mouths of a river; orig. (***the Delta***) *spec.* that of the River Nile. M16.

3 A triangle; a triangular area or formation. Usu. *attrib.*: (*a*) (ELECTRONICS) ***delta connection*** etc., a closed arrangement (represented by a triangle) of three-phase windings in series, each of the three wires of the circuit being connected to a junction of two windings; (*b*) ***delta wing***, a triangular swept-back wing of an aircraft. M17.

4 Denoting the fourth in a numerical sequence: ▸**a** *attrib.* SCIENCE. Freq. written δ. (*a*) ASTRONOMY (preceding the genitive of the Latin name of the constellation): the fourth brightest star in a constellation; (*b*) ***delta rays***, rays of low penetrative power consisting of slow electrons released from atoms by other particles (esp. alpha rays); (*c*) ***delta rhythm***, ***delta waves***, slow electrical activity of the unconscious brain, consisting of deep oscillations having a frequency of 0.5 to 3 hertz. L18. ▸**b** A fourth-class or poor mark in an examination etc. E20.

b delta plus, **delta minus** rather better, worse, than the average fourth class.

deltaic /dɛlˈteɪɪk/ *adjective.* M19.

[ORIGIN from DELTA + -IC.]

Of, pertaining to, or forming a (river) delta; of the nature of a delta.

deltidium /dɛlˈtɪdɪəm/ *noun.* Pl. **-dia** /-dɪə/. M19.

[ORIGIN mod. Latin, dim. of Greek DELTA: see -IDIUM.]

ZOOLOGY. A plate covering the triangular space between the beak and the hinge in certain brachiopods.

deltiology /dɛltɪˈɒlədʒi/ *noun.* M20.

[ORIGIN from Greek *deltion* dim. of *deltos* writing tablet: see -OLOGY.]

The hobby of collecting postcards.

■ **deltiologist** *noun* a person who collects postcards M20.

deltoid /ˈdɛltɔɪd/ *adjective & noun.* M18.

[ORIGIN French *deltoïde* or mod. Latin *deltoides* from Greek *deltoeidēs*, from DELTA: see -OID.]

► **A** *adjective.* **1** Like the Greek letter delta (Δ) in shape; triangular. M18. ▸**b** ANATOMY. Designating or pertaining to the large muscle of triangular shape covering the shoulder joint. M18.

2 Of the nature of a (river) delta. M19.

► **B** *noun.* **1** The deltoid muscle. M18.

2 A deltoid moth. M19.

■ **deltoidal** *adjective* M19.

delucidate *verb* var. of DILUCIDATE.

delude /dɪˈluːd, -ˈljuːd/ *verb trans.* LME.

[ORIGIN Latin *deludere* play false, mock, from *de-* DE- 1 + *ludere* play, from *ludus* play, game.]

†**1** Play with under the pretence of seriousness; cheat the hopes of; mock. LME–E18.

2 Cause to accept foolishly a false or mistaken belief; deceive, beguile; impose upon with false impressions. LME.

TINDALE *Acts* 8:11 With Sorcery he had deluded their wittes. D. H. LAWRENCE I don't delude myself that I shall find an elixir of life in Dresden. G. M. TREVELYAN This cheerful picture . . must not delude us into imagining that England was already the land of improved agriculture.

†**3** Frustrate the purpose of; evade, elude. LME–L17.

■ **deluder** *noun* L16.

deluge /ˈdɛljuːdʒ/ *noun & verb.* LME.

[ORIGIN Old French & mod. French *déluge*, alt., after popular formations in *-uge*, of earlier *diluve*, *delouve* from Latin DILUVIUM.]

► **A** *noun.* A great flood or inundation (*lit.* & *fig.*); a torrent, a heavy downpour. LME.

J. L. MOTLEY The memorable deluge . . out of which the Zuyder Zee was born. W. BLACK This deluge of rhetoric. C. MCCULLOUGH Not a gentle downpour but a steady, roaring deluge which went on and on.

the Deluge Noah's flood (*Genesis* 6–8).

▸ **B** *verb trans.* Flood, inundate, (*lit. & fig.*). **L16.**

W. IRVING The kingdom was deluged with pamphlets.

■ **deluginous** /dɪˈljuːdʒɪnəs/ *adjective* [after *ferruginous* etc.] like a deluge **M19.**

delusion /dɪˈluːʒ(ə)n, -ˈljuː-/ *noun.* **LME.**
[ORIGIN Late Latin *delusio(n-)*, from *delus-* pa. ppl stem of *deludere*: see DELUDE, -ION.]
1 The action of deluding or of being deluded; the state of being deluded. **LME.**

SIR T. MORE Thinges . . done by the deuill for our delusion.

2 A false impression or opinion, esp. as a symptom of mental illness. **M16.**

C. GEIKIE The poor fellow was only labouring under a delusion. R. D. LAING A common paranoid delusion is that there is a plot directed against the self.

delusions of grandeur an exaggerated estimation of one's own status or personality; megalomania.
■ **delusional** *adjective* of the nature of or characterized by delusion **L19.**

delusive /dɪˈluːsɪv, -ˈljuː-/ *adjective.* **E17.**
[ORIGIN formed as DELUSION + -IVE.]
Tending to delude; of the nature of a delusion; deceptive, unreal, disappointing.
■ **delusively** *adverb* **M17.** **delusiveness** *noun* **M17.**

delusory /dɪˈluːs(ə)ri, -ˈljuː-; -z-/ *adjective.* **L15.**
[ORIGIN Late Latin *delusorius*, from *delus-*: see DELUSION, -ORY[2].]
Delusive.

delustre /diːˈlʌstə/ *verb trans.* Also *-ter. **E20.**
[ORIGIN from DE- 3 + LUSTRE *noun*[1].]
Remove lustre or sheen from (a textile).

de luxe /dɪ ˈlʌks, ˈlʊks, də/ *adjectival phr.* **E19.**
[ORIGIN French = of luxury.]
Luxurious, sumptuous; of a superior kind.
POULE-de-luxe.

delve /dɛlv/ *noun.* **L16.**
[ORIGIN Partly alt. of DELF *noun*[1], partly from the verb.]
1 Something that has been delved; an excavation, a pit. Also, a hollow, a wrinkle. Now *literary.* **L16.**
2 An act of delving. **M19.**

delve /dɛlv/ *verb.*
[ORIGIN Old English *delfan* = Old Frisian *delva*, Old Saxon *bi-delban* (Dutch *delven*), Old High German *bi-telban*, from West Germanic.]
▸ **I** *verb trans.* **1** Dig, turn up with a spade; make by digging, excavate; burrow. Now *literary* exc. *Scot. & N. English.* **OE.**

TOLKIEN Dwarves . . had delved for themselves great halls and mansions . . in the . . Ered Luin. *fig.*: SHAKES. *Sonn.* Time . . delves the parallels in beauty's brow.

2 Dig *up* or *out*, exhume. Also, put in by digging, bury. Now *arch. & dial.* **OE.**

N. HAWTHORNE Minerals, delved . . out of the hearts of the mountains.

3 †**a** Penetrate (as) by digging. Only in **ME.** ▸**b** Dent, indent. *dial.* **L18.**
▸ **II** *verb intrans.* **4** Labour with a spade, dig. Now *literary* exc. *Scot. & N. English.* **OE.** ▸**b** *transf.* Reach, dig with the hand, *in* or *into* a container etc. **M20.**

Proverb: When Adam delved and Eve span, who was then the gentleman? **b** A. PRICE Stocker delved into his brief-case. 'There's another cutting here.'

5 *fig.* Search, esp. painstakingly; research in documents etc.; investigate, make enquiry. (Foll. by *in*, *into*.) **LME.**

G. SAINTSBURY He never delves beneath the surface for hidden wealth of suggestion.

6 Work hard, slave. *dial. & slang.* **M19.**

L. M. ALCOTT Delve like slaves.

7 Of a slope, road, etc.: make a sudden dip or descent. **M19.**
■ **delver** *noun* a person who delves **OE.**

dem /dɛm/ *noun. colloq.* **M20.**
[ORIGIN Abbreviation of DEMONSTRATION. Cf. DEMO *noun*[2].]
= DEMONSTRATION 3; *esp.* a practical display of a piece of equipment etc.

dem /dɛm/ *pronoun & demonstr. adjective. black English.* **M19.**
[ORIGIN Repr. a pronunc.]
= THEM.

dem /dɛm/ *verb trans. & intrans. arch.* Infl. **-mm-**. Also (earlier) **demn.** **ME.**
[ORIGIN Repr. alt. pronunc.]
= DAMN *verb*, esp. as an imprecation.

BARONESS ORCZY That demmed elusive Pimpernel.

Dem. *abbreviation. US.*
Democrat.

demagnetize /diːˈmagnɪtʌɪz/ *verb trans.* Also **-ise.** **M19.**
[ORIGIN from DE- 3 + MAGNETIZE.]
Remove the magnetization of; deprive of magnetic properties.
■ **demagnetiˈzation** *noun* **M19.** **demagnetizer** *noun* **L20.**

demagnify /diːˈmagnɪfʌɪ/ *verb trans. & intrans.* **M20.**
[ORIGIN from DE- 3 + MAGNIFY.]
Reduce the degree of magnification of (the image in an electron microscope etc.).
■ **demagnifiˈcation** *noun* **M20.**

demagogic /dɛməˈgɒgɪk, -ˈgɒdʒɪk/ *adjective.* **M19.**
[ORIGIN Greek *dēmagōgikos*, from *dēmagōgos* DEMAGOGUE: see -IC.]
Of, pertaining to, or of the nature of a demagogue.
■ **demagogical** *adjective* **M18.**

demagogue /ˈdɛməgɒg/ *noun & verb.* **M17.**
[ORIGIN Greek *dēmagōgos*, from *dēmos* people + *agōgos* leading, from *agein* to lead. Cf. French *démagogue*.]
▸ **A** *noun.* **1** In ancient Greece etc., a leader or orator who espoused the cause of the common people. **M17.**
2 A leader or orator who appeals to popular desires or prejudices to further personal interests, a rabble-rouser. **M17.**
▸ **B** *verb.* Chiefly *US.*
1 *verb intrans.* Behave like a demagogue. (*rare* before **M19.**) **M17.**
2 *verb trans.* Deal with (a matter) in the manner of a demagogue. **L19.**
■ **demagogism** *noun* = DEMAGOGY 1, 2 **E19.** **demagoguery** *noun* = DEMAGOGY 1, 2 **M19.**

demagogy /ˈdɛməgɒgi, -gɒdʒi/ *noun.* **M17.**
[ORIGIN Greek *dēmagōgia*, formed as DEMAGOGUE: see -Y[3].]
1 The actions, principles, or qualities of a demagogue. **M17.**
2 The rule of demagogues. **M19.**
3 A body of demagogues. **L19.**

demand /dɪˈmɑːnd/ *noun.* **ME.**
[ORIGIN Old French & mod. French *demande*, formed as DEMAND *verb*.]
1 An authoritative or peremptory request or claim; *transf.* something demanded. **ME.**

W. ROBERTSON Henry's extravagant demands had been received at Madrid with that neglect which they deserved. *fig.*: S. BUTLER Compassion is . . a demand of nature, to relieve the unhappy.

2 A question, a request. *arch.* **ME.**
3 *LAW.* A legal claim, esp. to property; the action of making a legal claim. **LME.**
4 The action of demanding; requesting or claiming peremptorily or authoritatively. **E17.**

SHAKES. *Haml.* He shall . . to England For the demand of our neglected tribute.

5 A call for a commodity or service on the part of consumers; *ECONOMICS* the desire and ability of consumers to purchase goods or services (correl. to ***supply***). **E18.**

B. T. WASHINGTON There was a demand for bricks in the general market. J. B. PRIESTLEY A large number of . . excellent skilled workmen . . who might as well be crossbow-men . . for all the demand there is for their services.

6 An urgent or pressing requirement; need actively expressing itself. Freq. in *pl.* **L18.**

T. COLLINS His private fortune is fully sufficient for all demands even of good society. M. GORDON One of those women who make impossible demands on everyone.

– PHRASES: ***final demand***: see FINAL *adjective.* **in demand** sought after, generally desired. **on demand** as soon as or whenever requested. ***supply and demand***: see SUPPLY *noun.*
– COMB.: **demand curve** a graph showing how the demand for a commodity or service varies with some other factor, esp. price; **demand deposit** *US* a bank account from which funds may be drawn on demand; **demand draft** a draft payable on demand; **demand-driven** *adjective* (*ECONOMICS*) caused or affected by consumer demand; **demand feeding**: of a baby when it cries, not according to a timetable; **demand-led** *adjective* (*ECONOMICS*) determined by consumer demand; **demand note** (***a***) a request for payment; (***b***) *US* = ***demand draft*** above.

demand /dɪˈmɑːnd/ *verb.* **LME.**
[ORIGIN Old French & mod. French *demander* from Latin *demandare* hand over, entrust, (in medieval Latin) demand, request, from *de-* DE- 1 + *mandare* to commission, order.]
▸ **I** *verb trans.* **1** Ask for (a thing) imperiously, urgently, or authoritatively; ask peremptorily (*that*, *to do*); claim as of right. **LME.**

GOLDSMITH Two ruffians . . demanded to speak with the king. L. RITCHIE To demand that the bones . . should be returned to their care. W. S. CHURCHILL The Crown claimed ownership . . and demanded a licence fee.

2 *LAW.* Formally claim (esp. realty) as the rightful owner. **LME.**
†**3** Ask (a person) formally or authoritatively to inform one (*of*, *how*, etc.). **LME–E18.**
4 Ask authoritatively or brusquely to know; insist on being told. Freq. with direct speech as obj. **L15.**

SHAKES. *Lucr.* They . . demanded the cause of her sorrow. J. STEINBECK 'What's funny about it?' George demanded defensively.

†**5** Ask (a person) *for*; require (a person) *to do*. **E17–L18.**
6 Ask to see (a person); require to appear, summon. **M17.**
7 Of a thing: require, need. **E18.**

J. B. PRIESTLEY Fellows capable of working day and night . . when the occasion demanded it. C. S. FORESTER The temperament that demands immediate action in the face of a crisis.

▸ **II** *verb intrans.* **8** Ask, inquire, make inquiry *of* (†*at*) a person etc. *arch.* **LME.**

AV *Luke* 3:14 And the soldiers likewise demanded of him, saying, And what shall we do?

9 Make a demand (†*for*), ask authoritatively. **E16.**

SHAKES. *All's Well* Our French lack language to deny, If they demand.

■ **demandable** *adjective* that may be demanded or claimed **LME.** **demander** *noun* **LME.** **demanding** *adjective* that demands; hard to satisfy, exacting, difficult: **L19.**

demandant /dɪˈmɑːnd(ə)nt/ *noun.* **L15.**
[ORIGIN Anglo-Norman, use as noun of pres. pple of Old French & mod. French *demander*: see DEMAND *verb*, -ANT[1].]
1 *LAW.* A claimant, esp. in a real action. **L15.**
2 A person who makes a demand or claim. **L16.**
3 A person who questions or interrogates. **M17.**

demantoid /dɪˈmantɔɪd/ *noun.* **L19.**
[ORIGIN German, from *Demant* diamond.]
A lustrous green gem variety of andradite garnet.

demarcate /ˈdiːmɑːkeɪt/ *verb trans.* **E19.**
[ORIGIN Back-form. from DEMARCATION: see -ATE[3].]
Mark out or determine the boundaries or limits of; separate or distinguish *from*.
■ **demarcator** *noun* **L19.**

demarcation /diːmɑːˈkeɪʃ(ə)n/ *noun.* Also **-k-.** **E18.**
[ORIGIN Spanish *demarcación* (Portuguese *demarcação*) from *demarcar* mark out the bounds of, from *de-* DE- 1 + *marcar* MARK *verb*: see -ATION.]
The action of marking the boundary or limits of something; delimitation, separation; a dividing line (*lit. & fig.*). Orig. in ***line of demarcation*** below.

B. MAGEE Their chief aim was to find a criterion of demarcation between sense and nonsense.

line of demarcation a dividing line; orig. *spec.* that dividing the New World between the Spanish and the Portuguese, decreed by Pope Alexander VI in 1493.
– COMB.: **demarcation dispute** an industrial dispute concerning the separation of kinds of work considered by trade unions to belong to particular trades.

demarcative /dɪˈmɑːkətɪv/ *adjective.* **M20.**
[ORIGIN from DEMARCATION: see -ATIVE.]
Chiefly *LINGUISTICS.* Of, pertaining to, or characterized by demarcation; serving to demarcate words etc.

demarch /ˈdiːmɑːk/ *noun.* **M17.**
[ORIGIN Latin *demarchus* from Greek *dēmarkhos*, from *dēmos* people + *arkhos* leader.]
In ancient Greece, the chief magistrate of an Attic deme. In modern Greece, the mayor of a commune.

démarche /demarʃ (*pl. same*), deɪˈmɑːʃ/ *noun.* **M17.**
[ORIGIN French, from *démarcher* take steps, from *dé-* DE- 1 + *marcher* MARCH *verb*[2].]
A step, a proceeding; *esp.* a diplomatic action or initiative.

demark /diːˈmɑːk/ *verb trans.* **M19.**
[ORIGIN from DEMARCATION after MARK *verb*.]
= DEMARCATE.

demarkation *noun* var. of DEMARCATION.

dematerialize /diːməˈtɪərɪəlʌɪz/ *verb.* Also **-ise.** **L19.**
[ORIGIN from DE- 3 + MATERIALIZE.]
1 *verb trans.* Deprive of material character or qualities. **L19.**
2 *verb intrans.* Lose material qualities; cease to have material existence; *fig.* disappear, vanish. **L19.**

Listener Nuclear particles behave in embarrassingly paranormal ways, materialising and dematerialising.

■ **dematerialiˈzation** *noun* **L19.**

deme /diːm/ *noun.* **M19.**
[ORIGIN Greek *dēmos* DEMOS.]
1 A township of ancient Attica; an administrative division in modern Greece. **M19.**
2 *BIOLOGY.* A group of taxonomically similar animals or plants forming a distinct local population. **M20.**

†**demean** *noun.* **LME.**
[ORIGIN from DEMEAN *verb*[1].]
1 Bearing, behaviour, demeanour. **LME–M18.**
2 Treatment (of others). *rare* (Spenser). Only in **L16.**

demean /dɪˈmiːn/ *verb*[1] *trans.* **ME.**
[ORIGIN Old French & mod. French *démener* lead, exercise, practise, *se démener* behave, from Proto-Romance, from Latin *de-* DE- 1 + *minare* drive (animals), (orig.) drive on with threats, from Latin *minari* threaten.]
†**1** Conduct, manage, control, handle. **ME–M17.**
2 *refl.* Behave, conduct oneself (in a specified way). **ME.**

N. HAWTHORNE The Prince Borghese certainly demeans himself like a kind and liberal gentleman.

3 Deal with (a person) in a particular way; *esp.* treat badly. *obsolete* exc. *Scot.* **LME.**

D

SPENSER That mighty man did her demeane With all the evill termes . . That he could make.

†**4** Express, exhibit (an emotion etc.). LME–E17.

demean /dɪˈmiːn/ *verb*² *trans.* E17.
[ORIGIN from DE- 1 + MEAN *adjective*¹, after *debase*.]
Lower in dignity or status, humble, (esp. oneself).

W. BLACK Could a girl so far demean herself as to ask for love? M. BRADBURY That demeans them into something trivial.

■ **demeaning** *ppl adjective* that demeans; beneath one's dignity: L19.

D

demeanour /dɪˈmiːnə/ *noun.* Also ***-or.** L15.
[ORIGIN from DEMEAN *verb*¹, prob. by assoc. with †*havour* HAVIOUR: see -OUR.]
1 Conduct, way of acting, behaviour, esp. towards others. Formerly also, an action (cf. MISDEMEANOUR). Now *rare.* L15.
2 Bearing, mien, outward manner. L15.

E. WAUGH Curiosity and resentment contended for mastery in Troutbeck's demeanour. A. HIGGINS Trying to assume a calmness of demeanour which she did not feel.

démêlé /demele/ *noun.* Pl. pronounced same. M17.
[ORIGIN French = quarrel, contest.]
A debate, a contention, a quarrel.

†**demember** *verb trans. Scot.* LME–E18.
[ORIGIN French *démembrer* or medieval Latin *demembrare*: see DEMEMBRATION.]
= DISMEMBER.

demembration /diːmɛmˈbreɪʃ(ə)n/ *noun. obsolete* exc. *hist.* L16.
[ORIGIN medieval Latin *demembratio(n-)*, from *demembrat-* pa. ppl stem of *demembrare* var. of *dismembrare* dismember: see DISMEMBRATION, -ATION.]
Chiefly SCOTS LAW. The cutting off of a limb; dismemberment.

déménagement /demenaʒmɑ̃/ *noun.* L19.
[ORIGIN French.]
The removal of household possessions from one place to another; moving house.

demency /ˈdɛm(ə)nsi/ *noun.* Long *rare.* E16.
[ORIGIN formed as DEMENTIA: see -ENCY.]
Madness, dementia, loss of mental faculties.

dement /dɪˈmɛnt/ *adjective & noun.* L15.
[ORIGIN French *dément* or Latin *demens*: see DEMENT *verb*.]
▶ **A** *adjective.* Demented, insane. Long *rare.* L15.
▶ **B** *noun.* A person affected with dementia. L19.

dement /dɪˈmɛnt/ *verb trans.* M16.
[ORIGIN Old French *dementer* or late Latin *dementare*, from *demens*, *-ment-* insane, from *de-* DE- 3 + *mens*, *ment-* mind.]
Send out of one's mind, drive mad.
■ **demen'tation** *noun* [medieval Latin *dementatio(n-)*] the act of dementing; the state or fact of being demented: E17.

dementate /dɪˈmɛnteɪt/ *verb trans.* Now *rare* or *obsolete.* E17.
[ORIGIN Latin *dementat-* pa. ppl stem of *dementare*: see DEMENT *verb*, -ATE³.]
= DEMENT *verb.*

demented /dɪˈmɛntɪd/ *adjective.* M17.
[ORIGIN from DEMENT *verb* + -ED¹.]
1 Out of one's mind; crazy, mad. M17.
2 MEDICINE. Suffering from dementia. L19.
■ **dementedly** *adverb* L19. **dementedness** *noun* L19.

démenti /demɑ̃ti/ *noun.* Pl. pronounced same. L16.
[ORIGIN French, from *démentir* contradict, from *dé-* DE- 3 + *mentir* to lie.]
A contradiction, a denial; now *esp.* an official denial of a published statement.

dementia /dɪˈmɛnʃə/ *noun.* L18.
[ORIGIN Latin, from *demens*: see DEMENT *verb*, -IA¹.]
1 PSYCHIATRY. Chronic mental and emotional deterioration caused by organic brain disease; a form or case of this. L18.
dementia praecox /ˈpriːkɒks/ *noun* (now *arch.* or *hist.*) [Latin *praecox* precocious] = SCHIZOPHRENIA. ***senile dementia***: see SENILE *adjective* 1.
2 Madness, folly. L19.

demerara /dɛməˈrɛːrə, -ˈrɑːrə/ *noun.* Also **D-.** M19.
[ORIGIN *Demerara* (see below).]
In full ***demerara sugar***. A light-brown raw cane sugar orig. and chiefly from the Demerara region of Guyana.

demerger /diːˈməːdʒə/ *noun.* M20.
[ORIGIN from DE- 3 + MERGER.]
The dissolution of a merger between companies etc.

demerit /diːˈmɛrɪt/ *noun.* LME.
[ORIGIN Old French *de(s)merite* or Latin *demeritum*, from *demerit-* pa. ppl stem of *demereri* merit, deserve, from *de-* DE- 1, 3 + *mereri* MERIT *verb*.]
1 A quality that deserves reward or gratitude, merit, worth. Freq. in *pl.* Long *arch. rare.* LME. ▶†**b** A meritorious or deserving act. M16–M17.

J. GAY Envy not the demerits of those who are most conspicuously distinguished.

2 Quality or conduct deserving censure; lack of merit, a defect. LME. ▶†**b** A blameworthy act, a sin, an offence. LME–M17.

S. RICHARDSON God teach me humility, and to know my own demerit! J. K. GALBRAITH They . . oppose the expenditure not on the merits of the service but on the demerits of the tax system.

†**3** That which is deserved, one's desert; *esp.* punishment. E17–E18.

A. CADE Ahab . . had quickly his demerits, being destroyed.

4 In full ***demerit mark***. A mark awarded against an offender, esp. in a school or the armed forces or for traffic offences. Chiefly *N. Amer.* E20.

M. J. BRUCCOLI He accumulated conduct demerits and did poorly in his studies.

demerit /diːˈmɛrɪt/ *verb.* LME.
[ORIGIN Latin *demerit-* (see DEMERIT *noun*); partly after French *démériter*.]
†**1** Merit, deserve, be worthy of, earn. LME–E18.
2 *verb trans.* †**a** Take away the merit of, disparage. L16–M17. ▶**b** Give a demerit mark to. *US.* L19.
†**3** *verb intrans.* Incur or deserve disapproval or blame. E17–M18.
4 *verb trans.* Fail to merit; deserve to lose or be without. *arch.* M17.
■ **demeri'torious** *adjective* blameworthy, sinful LME.

Demerol /ˈdɛmərɒl/ *noun.* M20.
[ORIGIN Unknown.]
PHARMACOLOGY. (Proprietary name for) pethidine.

demersal /dɪˈməːs(ə)l/ *adjective.* L19.
[ORIGIN from Latin *demersus* pa. pple of *demergere* submerge, sink, from *de-* DE- 1 + *mergere* plunge, dip: see -AL¹.]
(Of fish etc.) living near the bottom of the sea; (of fish eggs) deposited at or sinking to the seabed.

demerse /dɪˈməːs/ *verb trans. arch.* LME.
[ORIGIN Latin *demers-* pa. ppl stem of *demergere*: see DEMERSAL.]
Immerse, submerge.
■ **demersion** *noun* (now *rare* or *obsolete*) [Latin *demersio(n-)*] L17.

demesmerize /diːˈmɛzmərʌɪz/ *verb trans.* Also **-ise.** M19.
[ORIGIN from DE- 3 + MESMERIZE.]
Bring out of a hypnotic state.

demesne /dɪˈmeɪn, dɪˈmiːn/ *noun & adjective.* ME.
[ORIGIN Anglo-Norman, Old French *demeine*, later Anglo-Norman *demesne*, use as noun of adjective = of or belonging to a lord, from Latin *dominicus* of a lord or master, from *dominus* lord. Cf. DOMAIN.]
▶ **A** *noun.* **1** LAW (now *hist.*). The possession of real property as one's own. ME. ▶†**b** *gen.* Possession; dominion, power. ME–M18.
2 a The land or territory subject to a ruler: sovereign territory; a realm, domain. *arch.* ME. ▶**b** *sing.* & (freq.) in *pl.* Landed property, estates. L16.
3 a *hist.* Land held and worked by the owner for the maintenance of his or her own household, i.e. not let to a subordinate tenant. LME. ▶**b** The land immediately adjacent to a manor house etc. retained by the owner for his or her own use; the park, home farm, etc. M16.
4 A district, a region; the territory or sphere *of*. *arch.* or *poet.* L16.

L. G. GIBBON William . . gave to him all the wide parish as his demesne.

– PHRASES: **ancient demesne** (tenure of) land recorded in Domesday Book as belonging to the Crown. **demesne of the Crown** the Crown Lands. **hold in demesne** occupy as the owner, not sublet to a tenant or tenants. **in one's demesne as of fee** in one's possession as an inherited estate. **royal demesne** = ***demesne of the Crown*** above.
▶ **B** *attrib.* or as *adjective.* Of, pertaining to, or constituting a demesne. LME.
■ **demesnial** *adjective* = DEMESNE *adjective* M19.

demethylate /diːˈmɛθɪleɪt/ *verb trans.* M20.
[ORIGIN from DE- 3 + METHYLATE *verb*.]
CHEMISTRY. Remove a methyl group from (a molecule).
■ **demethy'lation** *noun* E20.

Demetian /dɪˈmiːʃ(ə)n/ *adjective.* Also **Di-.** M18.
[ORIGIN from *Demetia*, *Dimetia* (see below) + -AN.]
Of or pertaining to an area in SW Wales (once the ancient kingdom of Demetia and now the county of Dyfed), its inhabitants, or the dialect of English spoken there.

demi *adjective & noun* see DEMY.

demi- /ˈdɛmi/ *prefix.*
[ORIGIN from French *demi* from medieval Latin *dimedius* half, for Latin *dimidius*. Cf. DEMY.]
Used in words adopted from French and in English formations with the senses 'half, half-sized, partial(ly), curtailed, inferior', forming nouns from nouns, as ***demigod***, ***demilune***, ***demi-monde***, ***demisemiquaver***, etc., or, less commonly, adjectives from adjectives and verbs from verbs. Prevalent in some subjects with much vocabulary of French origin, as heraldry, costume, armour, fortification, etc., but as a living prefix almost completely displaced by SEMI-.
■ **demi-'bastion** *noun* (FORTIFICATION) a half-bastion comprising one flank and one front L17. **demi-'cannon** *noun* (*hist.*) a cannon of about 6½ inches (16.5 cm) bore M16. †**demicastor** *noun* (a hat made from) inferior beaver's fur or a mixture of beaver's and other fur M17–E18. **demi-circle** *noun* (now *rare*) a semicircle M17. **demi-'culverin** *noun* (*hist.*) a cannon of about 4½ inches (11.4 cm) bore L16. **demi-devil** *noun* a half-devil E17. **demi-gorge** *noun* (FORTIFICATION) the length of half of the gorge or entrance of a bastion, measured from either point where the bastion joins the curtain to the point of intersection of the lines of the adjacent curtains E18. **demi-hag**, **demi-hake** *noun* (*hist.*) a small hackbut M16. †**demi-isle** *noun* a peninsula E17–L18. **demi-lion** *noun* (HERALDRY) a figure of a lion cut off below the waist E17. †**demi-puppet** *noun* (*rare*, Shakes.) a half-sized or dwarf puppet: only in E17. †**demi-tint** *noun* (PAINTING) a half tint M18–E19. **demi-toilette**, **-toilet** *noun* (now *rare*) half evening (or dinner) dress, not full dress E19. **demi-volte** *noun* (HORSEMANSHIP) a 180-degree turn pivoting on the horse's quarters M17.

demi-caractère /ˌdɛmɪkarəkˈtɛː, *foreign* dəmikaraktɛːr (*pl. same*)/ *noun & adjective.* L18.
[ORIGIN French, lit. 'half character'.]
BALLET. ▶**A** *noun.* A dance retaining the form of the character dance but executed with steps based on the classical technique. Also, a dancer of demi-caractères. L18.
▶ **B** *adjective.* Of, pertaining to, or designating dancing of this kind. E19.

demi-glace /ˈdɛmɪglas/ *noun.* E20.
[ORIGIN French, lit. 'half-glaze'.]
COOKERY. In full ***demi-glace sauce***. A meat stock from which the liquid has been partially evaporated.

demigod /ˈdɛmɪgɒd/ *noun.* M16.
[ORIGIN from DEMI- + GOD *noun*, translating Latin *semideus*.]
In MYTHOLOGY, a partly divine being: the offspring of a god and a mortal, a mortal raised to divine rank, or an inferior deity; *gen.*, a person who has godlike powers. Cf. SEMIGOD.
■ **demigoddess** *noun* (*rare*) a female demigod E17.

†**demigration** *noun.* E17–M18.
[ORIGIN Latin *demigratio(n-)*, from *demigrat-* pa. ppl stem of *demigrare*, from *de-* DE- 1 + *migrare* MIGRATE: see -ATION.]
Removing oneself to another place; migration.

demijohn /ˈdɛmɪdʒɒn/ *noun.* M18.
[ORIGIN Prob. alt. of French *dame-jeanne* 'Lady Jane', assim. to DEMI- and JOHN.]
A bulging narrow-necked bottle holding from 3 to 10 gallons (13.6 to 45.5 litres), usu. cased in wicker and with one or two wicker handles.

demi-lance /ˈdɛmɪlɑːns/ *noun. obsolete* exc. *hist.* L15.
[ORIGIN French †*demie lance* lit. 'half lance'.]
1 A lance with a short shaft, chiefly used in the 15th and 16th cents. L15.
2 A light horseman armed with a demi-lance. M16.
■ **demi-lancer** *noun* = DEMI-LANCE 2 M16.

demilitarize /diːˈmɪlɪtərʌɪz/ *verb trans.* Also **-ise.** L19.
[ORIGIN from DE- 3 + MILITARIZE.]
Remove the military organization or forces from (a frontier, zone, etc.); place (a state) under an obligation not to maintain armed forces.
■ **demilitari'zation** *noun* L19.

demilune /ˈdɛmɪluːn/ *noun & adjective.* E18.
[ORIGIN French *demi-lune* lit. 'half-moon'. Cf. SEMILUNE.]
▶ **A** *noun.* **1** FORTIFICATION. An outwork resembling a bastion, with a crescent-shaped gorge. E18.
2 A half-moon, a crescent; a crescent-shaped body. M18.
▶ **B** *adjective.* Crescent-shaped, semilunar. L19.

demi-mondaine /dəmimɔ̃dɛn (*pl. same*), ˌdɛmɪmɒnˈdeɪn/ *noun.* L19.
[ORIGIN French, formed as DEMI-MONDE.]
A woman of the demi-monde.

demi-monde /ˌdɛmɪˈmɒnd, *foreign* dəmimɔ̃d/ *noun.* M19.
[ORIGIN French, lit. 'half world'.]
The class of women of doubtful reputation and social standing; *transf.* any social group regarded as behaving with doubtful propriety or legality.

demineralize /diːˈmɪn(ə)r(ə)lʌɪz/ *verb trans.* Also **-ise.** M20.
[ORIGIN from DE- 3 + MINERALIZE.]
Remove the salts from (seawater etc.).
■ **demineral'ization** *noun* (**a**) an abnormal loss of salts from the body; (**b**) the removal of salts from seawater etc.: E20. **demineralizer** *noun* an apparatus or installation for demineralization M20.

de minimis /deɪˈmɪnɪmiːs/ *adjective.* L16.
[ORIGIN from Latin *de minimis non curat lex* the law is not concerned with trivial matters.]
LAW. Too minor or trivial to merit consideration by the law.

demi-ostage /dɛmɪˈɒstɪdʒ/ *noun.* Long *obsolete* exc. *hist.* Also **-ostade** /-stəd/. E16.
[ORIGIN Old French *demie ostade*, from *demi(e)* DEMI- + *ostade* worsted.]
A cloth, half-worsted half-linen; linsey-woolsey.

demiourgos *noun* see DEMIURGE.

demi-pension /dəmipɑ̃sjɔ̃/ *noun.* M20.
[ORIGIN French.]
In France etc.: (the price of) bed, breakfast, and one other meal at a hotel etc.; half board.

demi-pique /ˈdɛmɪpiːk/ *noun & adjective*. L17.
[ORIGIN from DEMI- + alt. of PEAK *noun*¹. (Not connected with French *demi-pique* half-pike.)]
hist. (Designating) a saddle having a peak of about half the height of that of the older war saddle.
■ **demi-piqued** *adjective* M18.

demirep /ˈdɛmɪrɛp/ *noun*. *arch.* M18.
[ORIGIN from DEMI- + abbreviation of REPUTABLE. Cf. REP *noun*².]
A woman of doubtful reputation, esp. as regards chastity.

demi-saison /dəmisɛzɔ̃/ *adjective*. M18.
[ORIGIN French, lit. 'half season'.]
Of a style of fashion: intermediate between that of the past and that of the coming season.

demise /dɪˈmʌɪz/ *noun & verb*. LME.
[ORIGIN Anglo-Norman, use as noun of fem. pa. pple of Old French *de(s)mettre* (mod. *démettre*) dismiss, (refl.) resign, abdicate.]
▸ **A** *noun* **1 a** LAW. Conveyance or transfer of an estate by will or lease; an instance of this. LME. ▸**b** Transference of sovereignty, as by the death or deposition of the sovereign. Chiefly in ***demise of the crown***. M17.
2 A death which occasions such transference; *gen.* death; downfall, disappearance, final fate. M16.

S. RICHARDSON Her father's considerable estate, on his demise . . went with the name. GLADSTONE The Odyssey does not bring us to the demise of Odusseus. C. BEATON The war of 1914–18 had hastened the demise of the tightly swathed skirt.

▸ **B** *verb*. **1** *verb trans.* LAW. Convey or grant (an estate) by will or lease. LME. ▸**b** Transmit (a title etc., esp. sovereignty) by death or abdication. L17.

b G. B. SMITH He . . recommended the Convention to declare that James II had voluntarily demised the crown.

†**2** *verb trans.* **a** Let go; dismiss. M16–E17. ▸**b** Pass on, impart. L16–M17.

b SHAKES. *Rich. III* What Honour Canst thou demise to any child of mine?

3 *verb intrans.* Decease, die; pass on the crown (by death). *rare.* E18.
■ **demisable** *adjective* M17.

demi-sec /dɛmɪˈsɛk; *foreign* dəmisɛk/ *adjective*. M20.
[ORIGIN French, lit. 'half-dry'.]
Of wine: medium dry.

demi-semi- /ˈdɛmɪsɛmi/ *prefix*. Also as adjective **demi-semi**. E19.
[ORIGIN from DEMI- + SEMI-, after DEMISEMIQUAVER.]
Half half-, quarter-. Usu. *derog.*, insignificant, inadequate. Cf. SEMI-DEMI-.

demisemiquaver /ˈdɛmɪsɛmɪˌkweɪvə/ *noun*. E18.
[ORIGIN from DEMI- + SEMIQUAVER.]
MUSIC. A note of half the value of a semiquaver, represented as a quaver with three hooks.

demiss /dɪˈmɪs/ *adjective*. L16.
[ORIGIN Latin *demissus* let down, dejected, pa. pple of *demittere* DEMIT *verb*¹.]
1 Submissive, humble; abject, base. *arch.* L16.
†**2** Hanging down; *esp.* (of the head or countenance) downcast. L16–L17.
■ †**demissive** *adjective* = DEMISS E17–M18. **demissness** *noun* (*arch.*) E17.

demission /dɪˈmɪʃ(ə)n/ *noun*¹. M16.
[ORIGIN French *démission*, Old French *desmission*, corresponding to medieval Latin var. of Latin *dimissio(n-)* DIMISSION.]
1 Resignation, relinquishment, abdication. M16.

T. CARTE Apply to his Majesty for a demission of his charge. G. HUNTINGTON I was sent to a post abroad. But I am at liberty to give my demission.

2 Sending away, dismissal. *rare.* E19.

demission /dɪˈmɪʃ(ə)n/ *noun*². M17.
[ORIGIN Latin *demissio(n-)*, from *demiss-* pa. ppl stem of *demittere*: see DEMIT *verb*¹, -ION.]
1 Abasement, degradation. Now *rare.* M17.
†**2** Dejection, depression. M17–E18.
†**3** Lowering; bending down. E–M18.

†**demissory** *noun & adjective* var. of DIMISSORY.

demist /diːˈmɪst/ *verb trans.* M20.
[ORIGIN from DE- 3 + MIST *noun*¹.]
Clear the mist from (a windscreen etc.).
■ **demister** *noun* a device for demisting a windscreen etc. M20.

demit /dɪˈmɪt/ *verb*¹ *trans.* Also †**di-**. Infl. **-tt-**. LME.
[ORIGIN Latin *demittere* let or send down, from *de-* DE- 1 + *mittere* send.]
†**1** Abase, humble (oneself). LME–L17.
2 Send, put, or let down; lower. E17.

demit /dɪˈmɪt/ *verb*². Chiefly *Scot.* Infl. **-tt-**. E16.
[ORIGIN French *démettre*, Old French *desmettre*, from *des-*, *dé-* DE- 3 + *mettre*, taking the place of Latin *dimittere*: see DIMIT *verb*¹, DISMISS *verb*.]
1 *verb trans.* Let go, send away, dismiss. *arch.* E16.
†**2** *verb trans.* Put away, part with. M16–L17.
3 *verb trans. & intrans.* Resign; abdicate. M16.
†**4** *verb trans.* Send out. L17–M18.
†**5** *verb trans.* Convey by lease. Only in L18.

demitasse /ˈdɛmɪtas; *foreign* dəmitɑs (*pl. same*)/ *noun*. M19.
[ORIGIN French, lit. 'half-cup'.]
(The contents of) a small coffee cup.

demiurge /ˈdiːmɪəːdʒ, ˈdɛm-/ *noun*. Also in Greek form **demiourgos** /diːmɪˈaʊəgɒs/, pl. **-goi** /-gɔɪ/, & (earliest) Latin form **demiurgus** /diːmɪˈəːgəs/, pl. **-gi** /-dʒʌɪ/. E17.
[ORIGIN ecclesiastical Latin *demiurgus* from Greek *dēmiourgos* craftsman, artisan, from *dēmios* public (formed as DEMOS) + *-ergos* working.]
1 GREEK HISTORY. A magistrate in certain Greek states and in the Achaean League. E17.
2 (Also **D-**.) In Platonic philosophy, the fashioner of the world. In Gnosticism etc., the being subordinate to the supreme being, who is responsible for the existence of the world. L17.
■ **demiˈurgic** *adjective* of or pertaining to the demiurge or the work of the demiurge; creative: L17. †**demiurgical** *adjective* = DEMIURGIC E17–L18. **demiˈurgically** *adverb* E19.

demi-vierge /dəmivjɛrʒ/ *noun*. Pl. pronounced same. E20.
[ORIGIN French, lit. 'half-virgin', from *Les demi-vierges* (1874), a novel by M. Prévost.]
A woman who behaves licentiously while remaining a virgin.

demn *verb* var. of DEM *verb*.

demnition /dɛmˈnɪʃ(ə)n/ *noun, adjective, & adverb*. Chiefly *US*. M19.
[ORIGIN Repr. alt. pronunc.]
= DAMNATION *noun* 3, *adjective & adverb*.

Demo /ˈdɛməʊ/ *noun*¹. *US colloq.* Pl. **-os**. L18.
[ORIGIN Abbreviation.]
= DEMOCRAT *noun* 2.

demo /ˈdɛməʊ/ *noun*². *colloq.* Pl. **-os**. E20.
[ORIGIN Abbreviation of DEMONSTRATION. Cf. DEM *noun*.]
▸ **A** *noun*. **1** = DEMONSTRATION 6. E20.
2 A practical demonstration of the capabilities of a piece of equipment, computer software, group of musicians, etc.; a piece of equipment, software, a recording, etc., displayed or distributed for this purpose. M20.
attrib.: ***demo disc***, ***demo tape***, etc.
▸ **B** *verb trans.* Give a practical demonstration of; *esp.* record (a song etc.) or display (an item of esp. computing equipment) for demonstration purposes. L20.

demob /diːˈmɒb/ *verb & noun*. *colloq.* E20.
[ORIGIN Abbreviation.]
▸ **A** *verb trans.* Infl. **-bb-**. = DEMOBILIZE. E20.
▸ **B** *noun*. = DEMOBILIZATION. M20.
– COMB.: **demob suit** a suit issued to a serviceman on demobilization.

demobilize /diːˈməʊbɪlʌɪz/ *verb trans.* Also **-ise**. L19.
[ORIGIN French *démobiliser*, formed as DE- 3 + MOBILIZE.]
Release from a mobilized state or from service in the armed forces; disband (troops etc.).
■ **demobiliˈzation** *noun* the action of demobilizing, the disbanding of troops etc. M19.

democracy /dɪˈmɒkrəsi/ *noun*. L16.
[ORIGIN Old French & mod. French *démocratie* from late Latin *democratia* from Greek *dēmokratia*, formed as DEMOS + -CRACY.]
1 Government by the people; a form of government in which the power resides in the people and is exercised by them either directly or by means of elected representatives; a form of society which favours equal rights, the ignoring of hereditary class distinctions, and tolerance of minority views. L16.

G. M. TREVELYAN An age of transition from aristocracy to democracy, from authority to mass-judgement. B. CASTLE The Labour Party . . rank and file were ready to defend the unions to death as a vital expression of democracy.

2 A state or community in which the power of government resides in or is exercised by the people. L16.

C. S. LEWIS All nations, those we call democracies as well as dictatorships.

3 That class of people which has no hereditary or special rank or privilege; the common people. Now *rare.* M17.
4 (**D-**.) The Democratic Party of the US; its principles or members. *US.* E19.

democrat /ˈdɛməkrat/ *noun & adjective*. L18.
[ORIGIN French *démocrate*, formed as DEMOCRACY after *aristocrate* ARISTOCRAT.]
▸ **A** *noun*. **1** An adherent or advocate of democracy; orig. (now *hist.*), an opponent of the aristocrats in the French Revolution of 1790. L18.

H. ARENDT A true democrat, he wanted to liberate an oppressed people and not bestow privileges upon individuals.

2 (**D-**.) A member of the Democratic Party of the US, or more widely, of any political party styled 'Democratic'. L18.
Christian Democrat, ***Social Democrat***, etc.
3 More fully ***democrat wagon***. A light wagon seating two or more people and usu. drawn by two horses. *N. Amer.* (now *hist.*). L19.

B. BROOKER There were buggies and democrats drawn up at the stores.

▸ **B** *adjective*. Democratic. *rare.* L18.

democratic /dɛməˈkratɪk/ *adjective & noun*. E17.
[ORIGIN Old French & mod. French *démocratique* from medieval Latin *democraticus* from Greek *dēmokratikos*, from *dēmokratia* DEMOCRACY: see -IC.]
▸ **A** *adjective*. **1** Of the nature of or characterized by democracy; advocating or upholding democracy; *gen.* favouring social equality. E17.

A. S. NEILL Summerhill is a self-governing school, democratic in form. D. BOGARDE He rather wished the General was not so damned democratic, and had not insisted on sharing everyone's discomfort. *fig.*: *Nature* All the . . neutrinos would interact equally, the neutral current being 'democratic' in neutrino types.

2 (**D-**.) Of or pertaining to a political party styled 'Democratic', *spec.* the US Democratic Party (see below). E19.
Christian Democratic, ***Social Democratic***, etc. **Democratic Party** one of the two main US political parties (the other being *Republican*) which generally supports international commitment and broad social reform.
▸ **B** *noun*. = DEMOCRAT *noun*. *rare.* M17.
■ **democratical** *adjective & noun* (**a**) *adjective* = DEMOCRATIC *adjective* 1; †(**b**) *noun* = DEMOCRAT *noun* 1: L16. **democratically** *adverb* E17.

democratise *verb* var. of DEMOCRATIZE.

democratism /dɪˈmɒkrətɪz(ə)m/ *noun*. L18.
[ORIGIN from DEMOCRAT + -ISM.]
Democracy as a principle or system.

democratize /dɪˈmɒkrətʌɪz/ *verb*. Also **-ise**. L18.
[ORIGIN French *démocratiser*, formed as DEMOCRAT, DEMOCRACY: see -IZE.]
1 *verb trans.* Make democratic; give a democratic character to. L18.
2 *verb intrans.* Become democratic. *rare.* M19.
■ **democratiˈzation** *noun* M19. **democratizer** *noun* L19.

Democritean /dɪˌmɒkrɪˈtiːən/ *adjective*. M19.
[ORIGIN from Latin *Democriteus* (Greek *Dēmokriteios*) + -AN.]
Of, pertaining to, or after the style of the Greek philosopher Democritus (5th cent. BC), or of his theories.
■ Also †**Democritial** *adjective*: only in E17. **Demoˈcritic** *adjective* M17. †**Democritical** *adjective* M17–E18.

démodé /demɔde, deɪˈməʊdeɪ/ *adjective*. L19.
[ORIGIN French, pa. pple of *démoder* send or go out of fashion, from *dé-* DE- 3 + *mode* fashion.]
Out of fashion, unfashionable.

demodectic /diːməˈdɛktɪk/ *adjective*. Also (earlier) **-decic** /-ˈdiːsɪk/. L19.
[ORIGIN from mod. Latin *Demodex* (see below) from Greek *dēmos* fat + *dēx* woodworm, + -IC.]
VETERINARY MEDICINE. Of, pertaining to, or caused by parasitic mites of the genus *Demodex*.

demoded /diːˈməʊdɪd/ *adjective*. L19.
[ORIGIN from DÉMODÉ + -ED¹.]
= DÉMODÉ.

demodulation /ˌdiːmɒdjʊˈleɪʃ(ə)n/ *noun*. E20.
[ORIGIN from DE- 3 + MODULATION.]
The process of extracting a modulating signal from the carrier wave.
■ **deˈmodulate** *verb trans.* extract (a modulating signal) from its carrier; separate a modulating signal from: M20. **deˈmodulator** *noun* a device or circuit used to effect demodulation E20.

Demogorgon /diːməˈgɔːg(ə)n/ *noun*. L16.
[ORIGIN Late Latin, perh. a disguised oriental name.]
MYTHOLOGY. (The name of) a mysterious and terrible infernal god.

demographic /dɛməˈgrafɪk, diː-/ *adjective & noun*. L19.
[ORIGIN from DEMOGRAPHY: see -GRAPHIC.]
▸ **A** *adjective*. Of or pertaining to demography. L19.
▸ **B** *noun*. **1** In *pl.* Demographic statistics; (usu. treated as *sing.*) the branch of knowledge that deals with these. M20.
2 A particular sector of a population, as defined by age, income, ethnic origin, etc. L20.

Music Week Virgin Radio . . targets the 30-year-old-plus demographic.

■ **demographical** *adjective* = DEMOGRAPHIC *adjective* E20. **demographically** *adverb* E20.

demography /dɪˈmɒgrəfi/ *noun*. L19.
[ORIGIN from Greek *dēmos* people + -OGRAPHY.]
The branch of knowledge that deals with human populations; *esp.* the statistical analysis of births, deaths, migrations, disease, etc., as illustrating the conditions of life in communities. Also, the composition of a particular human population.
■ **demographer** *noun* L19.

demoi *noun* pl. of DEMOS.

demoiselle /dɛmwɑːˈzɛl/ *noun*. E16.
[ORIGIN French: see DAMSEL.]
1 A young lady, a girl. *arch.* E16.
2 A Eurasian and N. African crane, *Anthropoides virgo*, with elongated black breast feathers and white neck plumes. Now usu. more fully ***demoiselle crane***. L17.
3 A dragonfly or (*esp.*) a damselfly. M19.
4 A damselfish. L19.

demolish /dɪˈmɒlɪʃ/ *verb trans.* M16.
[ORIGIN Old French & mod. French *démoliss-* lengthened stem of *démolir* from Latin *demoliri*, from *de-* DE- 3 + *moliri* construct, from *moles* mass: see MOLE *noun*³, -ISH².]

D

D

1 Destroy (a building etc.) by violent disintegration of its fabric; pull or throw down. M16.

G. ORWELL The bomb had demolished a group of houses. A. N. WILSON The City Council wanted to demolish a derelict church . . to make way for . . a Leisure Park.

2 Overthrow (an institution); refute (a theory); make an end of. E17.

New Statesman [The authors] demolish the myth that Labour owed its 1974 victory to public . . approval of its radical promises.

3 Eat up quickly and entirely. *joc.* M18.

J. BEERBOHM He demolished the whole side of a young guanacho at one sitting.

■ **demolishable** *adjective* L18. **demolisher** *noun* E17. **demolishment** *noun* (now *rare*) = DEMOLITION E17.

demolition /dɛməˈlɪʃ(ə)n, diː-/ *noun*. M16.

[ORIGIN Old French & mod. French *démolition* from Latin *demolitio(n-)*, from *demolit-* pa. ppl stem of *demoliri*: see DEMOLISH, -ITION.]

1 Destruction, overthrow. Chiefly *fig.* use of sense 2. M16. **2** The action of demolishing a building etc.; the fact or state of being demolished. E17. **3** In *pl.* Demolished remains, ruins. Long *rare*. M17.

– COMB.: **demolition ball** a large metal ball which, hung from a crane, may be swung against a building to demolish it; **demolition derby** (orig. *US*) a competition in which cars are driven so as to collide; **demolition order**: issued by a local authority for the pulling down of a building or buildings.

■ **demolitionist** *noun* a person who aims at or advocates demolition M19.

demon /ˈdiːmən/ *noun*¹. Also (*arch.*) **dae-**. ME.

[ORIGIN medieval Latin *demon*, Latin *daemon* from Greek *daimōn* divinity, genius. Cf. Old French & mod. French *démon*. Also (in sense 1) repr. Latin *daemonium*, Greek dim. *daimonion*. Cf. DAIMON.]

1 An evil spirit; a malignant being of superhuman nature. ME. ▸**b** Esp. in biblical translations and allusions: an evil or unclean spirit possessing or actuating a demoniac; a heathen god or idol. E18.

T. WRIGHT The three special characteristics of mediæval demons were horns, hoofs . . and tails.

2 An attendant or indwelling spirit, one's genius; = DAEMON *noun* 2. LME.

3 GREEK MYTHOLOGY. A being of a nature between that of gods and men; the soul of a deceased person regarded as an inferior divinity; = DAEMON *noun* 1. M16.

4 A person, or personified animal or thing, of a malignant or terrible nature or of a hideous appearance. E17.

CARLYLE The Tartar Khan, with his shaggy demons of the wilderness.

5 *fig.* An evil passion or agency, now *esp.* alcoholic drink, regarded as a spirit or devil. E18.

JOYCE Had her father only avoided the clutches of the demon drink.

6 A person of superhuman or diabolical energy, skill, etc.; an action etc. exhibiting superhuman or diabolical energy, skill, etc. L19.

a demon for work etc. a person who works etc. strenuously. ***Maxwell's demon***: see MAXWELL.

7 CARDS. A form of patience (also ***demon patience***); *esp.* (also ***racing demon***) a competitive version of this using several packs. L19.

– COMB.: **demon bowler** CRICKET a particularly successful bowler in a match or series; ***demon patience***: see sense 7 above.

■ **demoness** *noun* a female demon M17. **demonish** *adjective* (*rare*) demonic M19.

demon /ˈdiːmən/ *noun*². *Austral. slang*. L19.

[ORIGIN App. from Van *Diemen*'s Land, an early name for Tasmania, after DEMON *noun*¹.]

1 A police officer; a detective. L19. **2** A bushranger; a convict. E20.

demon *noun*³ var. of DAEMON *noun*².

demonetize /diːˈmʌnɪtʌɪz, -mɒn-/ *verb trans.* Also **-ise**. M19.

[ORIGIN French *démonétiser*, from *dé-* DE- 3 + Latin *moneta* MONEY *noun*: see -IZE. Cf. MONETIZE.]

Deprive of standard monetary value; withdraw (gold etc.) from use as money.

■ **demonetiˈzation** *noun* M19.

demoniac /dɪˈməʊnɪak/ *adjective & noun*. LME.

[ORIGIN Old French & mod. French *démoniaque* from ecclesiastical Latin *daemoniacus*, from *daemonium*: see DEMON *noun*¹, -AC.]

▸ **A** *adjective*. **1** Possessed by a demon or an evil spirit. LME. ▸**b** Of or pertaining to possession by evil spirits. L17. **2** Of or pertaining to demons. M17. **3** Befitting a demon, devilish. E19. **4** = DEMONIC 2. M19.

▸ **B** *noun*. A person possessed by a demon or evil spirit. LME.

■ **demoniacal** /diːməˈnʌɪək(ə)l, dɛm-/ *adjective* = DEMONIAC *adjective* 1, 2, 3 E17. **demoniacally** /diːməˈnʌɪək(ə)li/ *adverb* E19.

demonian /dɪˈməʊnɪən/ *adjective*. L17.

[ORIGIN from Latin *daemonium*: see DEMON *noun*¹, -AN.]

Of, relating to, or of the nature of a demon or demons.

■ **demonial** *adjective* (*rare*) [Old French] = DEMONIAN L17. **demonianism** *noun* (the doctrine of) demoniacal possession M18.

demonic /dɪˈmɒnɪk/ *adjective*. Also (esp. in sense 2) **dae-**. M17.

[ORIGIN Late Latin *daemonicus* from Greek *daimonikos*, from *daimon*: see DEMON *noun*¹, -IC.]

1 Of, belonging to, or of the nature of an evil spirit; devilish. M17. **2** Relating to, of the nature of, or having supernatural power or genius. L18.

■ **demonical** *adjective* (**a**) = DEMONIC 1; (**b**) = DEMONIAC *adjective* 1: L15. **demonically** *adverb* in a manner befitting a demon; superhumanly: E20.

demonise *verb* var. of DEMONIZE.

demonism /ˈdiːmənɪz(ə)m/ *noun*. Also **dae-**. L17.

[ORIGIN from DEMON *noun*¹ + -ISM.]

Belief in the evil power of demons; worship of demons; the doctrine of demons.

■ **demonist** *noun* a believer in or worshipper of demons M17.

demonize /ˈdiːmənʌɪz/ *verb trans.* Also **-ise**. L18.

[ORIGIN from DEMON *noun*¹ + -IZE.]

1 Make into or like a demon; represent as a demon. L18. **2** Subject to demonic influence. M19.

■ **demoniˈzation** *noun* the action of making into or like a demon L18.

demono- /ˈdiːmənəʊ/ *combining form*.

[ORIGIN Repr. Greek *daimono-* combining form of *daimon* DEMON *noun*¹: see -O-.]

Of or relating to demons.

■ **demoˈnocracy** *noun* the rule of demons M18. **demoˈnographer** *noun* a writer on demons M18. **demoˈnolatrous** *adjective* of, pertaining to, of the nature of, or practising demon-worship M19. **demoˈnolatry** *noun* demon-worship M17. **demonoˈmania** *noun* a mental illness in which the patient believes himself or herself possessed by an evil spirit M19. **demonoˈmaniac** *adjective* a person suffering from demonomania M19.

demonology /diːməˈnɒlədʒi/ *noun*. Also †**dae-**. L16.

[ORIGIN from DEMONO- + -LOGY.]

The branch of knowledge that deals with demons or with beliefs about demons; a treatise on demons.

■ **demonoˈlogical** *adjective* concerned with demonology E19. **demonoˈlogically** *adverb* M19. **demonologist** *noun* a person versed in demonology L17.

demonopolize /diːməˈnɒpəlʌɪz/ *verb trans.* Also **-ise**. L19.

[ORIGIN from DE- 3 + MONOPOLIZE.]

Destroy the monopoly of; make no longer a monopoly.

■ **demonopoliˈzation** *noun* L20.

demonstrable /dɪˈmɒnstrəb(ə)l, ˈdɛmən-/ *adjective*. LME.

[ORIGIN Latin *demonstrabilis*, from *demonstrare*: see DEMONSTRATE *verb*, -ABLE.]

1 Able to be shown or made evident. Formerly also occas., evident. LME. **2** Able to be proved conclusively. LME.

■ **demonstraˈbility** *noun* the quality or condition of being demonstrable E19. **demonstrableness** *noun* L17. **demonstrably** *adverb* so as to be demonstrable; by demonstration: M17.

†**demonstrance** *noun*. LME.

[ORIGIN Old French, from *demonstrer* from Latin *demonstrare*: see DEMONSTRATE *verb*, -ANCE.]

1 A pointing out, a sign; indication. LME–E18. **2** Demonstration, proof. LME–M17.

†**demonstrate** *adjective* (*pa. pple*). E16.

[ORIGIN Latin *demonstratus* pa. pple, formed as DEMONSTRATE *verb*: see -ATE².]

1 Evident. E16–M17. **2** Demonstrated. L16–E18.

demonstrate /ˈdɛmənstreɪt/ *verb*. M16.

[ORIGIN Latin *demonstrat-* pa. ppl stem of *demonstrare*, from *de-* DE- 1 + *monstrare* to show: see -ATE³.]

†**1** *verb trans.* Point out, indicate; set out. M16–L17.

2 *verb trans.* Make known by outward indications; manifest, show; show evidence of (feelings etc.). L16.

WELLINGTON His Highness has demonstrated the most implicit confidence in the protection of the British power. H. CARPENTER Nobody's appearance actually demonstrates their spiritual character.

3 *verb trans.* Establish by logical reasoning or argument, or by practical proof; prove beyond doubt, prove the existence or reality of. L16.

SIR T. BROWNE Archimedes demonstrates . . that the proportion of the Diameter unto the Circumference is as 7 almost unto 22. S. SASSOON I had been ambitious of winning races because that had seemed a . . way of demonstrating my equality with my contemporaries. D. LESSING She might have deduced it all for herself without waiting to have it demonstrated.

4 *verb trans.* Describe and explain with the help of examples or specimens, or by experiments; display, explain, and implement the working functions of (a piece of equipment, etc.). L17. ▸**b** *verb intrans.* Teach or act as a demonstrator. M19.

C. P. SNOW I demonstrated the principle of the leg-glance. J. KEROUAC The idea was to get invited . . to a dinner party and then leap up and start demonstrating the pressure cooker.

5 *verb intrans.* Make a military demonstration. E19.

6 *verb intrans.* Make or take part in a public protest etc. (*against*, *in support of*, etc.). L19.

A. J. P. TAYLOR Select bands of unemployed . . marched on London, where they demonstrated to little purpose.

demonstration /dɛmənˈstreɪʃ(ə)n/ *noun*. LME.

[ORIGIN Old French *demonstracion* (later *-tion*) or Latin *demonstratio(n-)*, formed as DEMONSTRATE *verb*: see -ATION.]

1 †**a** The action of pointing out, indicating, or making known. Also, a sign, an indication. LME–L17. ▸**b** A manifestation or outward display of or *of* feeling, a quality, etc. M16.

b R. L. STEVENSON He dares not be comical; his fun must escape from him unprepared, and . . be unaccompanied by any physical demonstration. E. TEMPLETON She was not given to demonstrations of motherly fondness in company.

2 The action or process of making evident by reasoning; establishing beyond doubt by argument, deduction, or practical proof; (with *pl.*) a logical argument which proves an asserted conclusion. LME. ▸**b** Something which serves as proof or evidence; a proof. LME.

L. T. C. ROLT Left to the engineer to prove the theorist wrong by practical demonstration.

3 A practical exhibition or explanation of something by experiment or example, esp. in scientific instruction, in order to teach or inform; a practical display of a piece of equipment etc. to show how it works and its capacity. E19.

J. MARQUAND What followed gave me a first hand demonstration . . of how news travels in Peking. R. WARNER Some demonstrations of the latest type of machine-guns. *attrib.*: *Which Micro?* A demonstration tape that explains the MSX system.

4 ROMAN LAW. The statement of the alleged facts on which the plaintiff's case is founded. M19.

5 A show of military force or of offensive movement. M19.

H. P. BROUGHAM The Barons having, by an armed demonstration, compelled the King to allow the appointment.

6 An exhibition of public opinion on a political or other question, usually taking the form of a mass meeting or procession. M19.

Sunday Times Protest demonstrations against the Government's Industrial Relations Bill. M. RICHLER It was the largest demonstration since the war and many who had come to protest were astonishingly young.

■ **demonstrational** *adjective* M19. **demonstrationist** *noun* a person who takes part in a demonstration L19.

demonstrative /dɪˈmɒnstrətɪv/ *adjective & noun*. LME.

[ORIGIN Old French & mod. French *démonstratif*, *-ive* from Latin *demonstrativus*, formed as DEMONSTRATE *verb*: see -ATIVE.]

▸ **A** *adjective*. **1** Having the function or quality of demonstrating; making evident or manifest; illustrative; serving as conclusive evidence (*of*). LME.

G. CHALMERS These military works . . are equally demonstrative of their skill. F. BOWEN Logic, as it proceeds from axiomatic principles, . . is a purely demonstrative science.

2 GRAMMAR. Esp. of a pronoun or adjective: indicating the person or thing referred to. (Earlier in sense B. below.) E16.

I. WATT There are 9 'thats'—only two of them demonstrative and the rest relative pronouns.

3 RHETORIC. Describing with praise or censure. Now *rare* or *obsolete*. M16.

4 Provable by demonstration. E17.

5 Given to or characterized by open expression of feelings etc. E19.

J. SIMMS Sumi had always been a demonstrative child; she sprang at us and hugged us.

6 That teaches or informs by practical display and description. *rare*. E19.

▸ **B** *noun*. GRAMMAR. A demonstrative pronoun or adjective. LME.

■ **demonstratively** *adverb* L16. **demonstrativeness** *noun* M17.

demonstrator /ˈdɛmənstreɪtə/ *noun*. E17.

[ORIGIN Latin, formed as DEMONSTRATE *verb*: see -OR. Partly after French *démonstrateur*.]

1 A person who or thing which demonstrates, points out, or proves. E17.

2 *spec.* ▸**a** A person who teaches by demonstration, esp. in a laboratory etc.; one who explains the workings of a piece of equipment etc. to prospective customers. L17. ▸**b** A piece of equipment used for demonstration; a motor vehicle in which a prospective customer may take a test drive. M20.

C. ISHERWOOD An overalled woman demonstrator was exhibiting the merits of a patent coffee-strainer.

3 A person who takes part in a public demonstration. L19.

H. KISSINGER Antiwar demonstrators had marched against him continually since he became President.

■ **demonstratorship** *noun* the position or post of a scientific demonstrator M19. **demonstratory** /dɪˈmɒnstrət(ə)ri/ *adjective* that has the property of demonstrating E18.

demoralize /dɪˈmɒrəlʌɪz/ *verb trans.* Also **-ise**. L18.
[ORIGIN French *démoraliser* (from *dé-* DE- 3 + *moral* MORAL *adjective*), a word of the French Revolution: see -IZE.]
1 Corrupt the morals or moral principles of; deprave. *arch.* L18.
SOUTHEY To debase, demoralize, and debilitate human nature.
2 Lower or destroy the morale or confidence of; dishearten. M19.
J. R. GREEN The long series of English victories had . . demoralized the French soldiery.
■ **demoraliˈzation** *noun* the action of demoralizing; a demoralized condition: L18. **demoralizer** *noun* L19. **demoralizingly** *adverb* E20.

De Morgan /də ˈmɔːg(ə)n/ *noun.* E20.
[ORIGIN Augustus *De Morgan* (1806–71), English mathematician.]
MATH. & LOGIC. Used in *possess.* to designate two laws of propositional calculus: (*a*) the negation of a conjunction is equivalent to the alternation of the negations of the conjoined expressions; (*b*) the negation of an alternation is equivalent to the conjunction of the negations of the alternated expressions; (symbolically: ∼(p∧q) ≡ ∼p∨∼q; ∼(p∨q) ≡ ∼p∧∼q).

demos /ˈdiːmɒs/ *noun.* Pl. **-moi** /-mɔɪ/. E17.
[ORIGIN Greek *dēmos*.]
1 A district of ancient Attica, Greece; a deme. *rare.* E17.
2 (**D-**.) The common people of an ancient Greek state; (a personification of) the populace, esp. in a democracy. M19.

Demosthenean /dɪˌmɒsθəˈniːən, dɛmɒsˈθiːnɪən/ *adjective.* Also **-ian**. M18.
[ORIGIN from Greek *Dēmosthenēs* (see below): see -EAN, -IAN.]
Of, pertaining to, or resembling the Athenian statesman and orator Demosthenes (384–322 BC) or his style of oratory.
■ Also **Demosthenic** /dɛmɒsˈθɛnɪk/ *adjective* E19.

demote /diːˈməʊt/ *verb trans.* L19.
[ORIGIN from DE- 3 + PROMOTE *verb*.]
Reduce to a lower rank or class.
JOHN BROOKE He was first elevated to the leadership of the House of Commons and then summarily demoted to make way for Fox.

demotic /dɪˈmɒtɪk/ *adjective & noun.* E19.
[ORIGIN Greek *dēmotikos* popular, from *dēmotēs* one of the people, formed as DEMOS: see -OT[2], -IC.]
▸ **A** *adjective* **1 a** Designating or pertaining to the popular simplified form of Egyptian hieroglyphic script. Opp. ***hieratic***. E19. ▸**b** Designating or pertaining to a form of modern Greek based on popular speech. E20.
2 *gen.* Of or pertaining to the common people; popular, vulgar. M19.
Listener Advertising has . . to use simple, forceful, easily understandable words—'demotic' language. M. STOTT Perhaps . . we shall, like the Chinese, have some kind of demotic English and some kind of Mandarin?
▸ **B** *noun.* Demotic language; demotic script. E20.
■ **demoticist** /-sɪst/ *noun* a student of demotic script E20.

demotion /diːˈməʊʃ(ə)n/ *noun.* E20.
[ORIGIN from DEMOTE after *promotion*.]
The action of demoting; reduction to a lower rank or class.

demotivate /diːˈməʊtɪveɪt/ *verb trans.* L20.
[ORIGIN from DE- 3 + MOTIVATE.]
Reduce the motivation of; make less strongly motivated.
■ **demotiˈvation** *noun* L20.

demount /diːˈmaʊnt/ *verb.* M16.
[ORIGIN Orig. from French *démonter* (cf. DISMOUNT *verb*); in recent use formed as DEMOUNTABLE.]
†**1** *verb intrans.* Dismount. Also, admit of unmounting. *Scot.* M–L16.
2 *verb trans.* Remove from its mounting; unmount; dismantle (for later reassembly). Cf. DEMOUNTABLE. Orig. *Scot.* L16.
3 *verb intrans.* Descend. *rare.* M19.
– NOTE: In sense 2 not recorded 18–19; reintroduced in 20 after *demountable*.

demountable /diːˈmaʊntəb(ə)l/ *adjective.* E20.
[ORIGIN from DE- 3 + MOUNT *noun*[2] + -ABLE, prob. after French *démontable*.]
Able to be dismantled or removed from its mounting (and readily reassembled or repositioned).
■ **demountaˈbility** *noun* M20.

dempster /ˈdɛm(p)stə/ *noun.* ME.
[ORIGIN formed as DEEMSTER with shortening of vowel of first syll.]
1 A judge. Long *obsolete* exc. *Scot.* ME.
2 In Scotland: an officer of the court who pronounced sentence as directed by the judge, and often also acted as public executioner. *obsolete* exc. *hist.* LME.

demulce /dɪˈmʌls/ *verb trans.* Now *rare* or *obsolete.* M16.
[ORIGIN Latin *demulcere*: see DEMULCENT.]
Soothe, mollify; soften, make gentle.

demulcent /dɪˈmʌls(ə)nt/ *adjective & noun.* M18.
[ORIGIN Latin *demulcent-* pres. ppl stem of *demulcere* stroke caressingly, from *de-* DE- 1 + *mulcere* stroke, appease: see -ENT.]
▸ **A** *adjective.* Soothing, mollifying; allaying irritation. M18.
▸ **B** *noun.* MEDICINE. A substance giving protection from or relieving (physical) irritation. M18.

demur /dɪˈməː/ *noun.* ME.
[ORIGIN Old French & mod. French *demeure*, from *demeurer*: see DEMUR *verb*.]
†**1** Delay, waiting; procrastination. Also, residence, stay. ME–E18.
2 †**a** LAW. = DEMURRER *noun*[1] 1. M16–E18. ▸**b** The action of demurring or objecting; an objection. Freq. in ***without demur***, ***with no demur***. M17.
b P. L. FERMOR Warming to the scheme after initial demur.
†**3** Hesitation, pause; a state of indecision. L16–E19.

demur /dɪˈməː/ *verb.* Infl. **-rr-**. ME.
[ORIGIN Old French *demo(u)rer*, (also mod.) *demeurer*, delay, linger, wait from Proto-Romance var. of Latin *demorari*, from *de-* DE- 1 + *morari* tarry, delay.]
†**1** *verb intrans. & trans.* (Cause to) linger, tarry, or delay. ME–L17.
2 *verb intrans.* **a** LAW. Enter a demurrer. E17. ▸**b** *gen.* Raise scruples or objections; take exception *to* or *at*. M17. ▸**c** *verb trans.* Object to. *rare.* E19.
b A. MACLAREN We can afford to recognise the fact, though we demur to the inference. F. WELDON Butt and Sons at first demurred, but then conceded.
†**3** *verb intrans.* Hesitate, pause in uncertainty. M17–E19. ▸†**b** *verb trans.* Hesitate about. *rare.* M17–M18.

demure /dɪˈmjʊə/ *adjective & verb.* LME.
[ORIGIN Perh. from Anglo-Norman *demuré*, Old French *demo(u)ré* pa. pple of *demo(u)rer* (see DEMUR *verb*), infl. by Old French *mur*, *meür* (mod. *mûr*) grave, from Latin *maturus* ripe, MATURE *adjective*.]
▸ **A** *adjective.* †**1** Calm, settled, still. Only in LME.
2 Orig., sober, grave, composed. Later also, affectedly or artificially quiet and serious; coy; decorous. LME.
MILTON Come, pensive Nun, devout and pure, Sober, steadfast and demure. J. FOWLES Theirs was an age when the favoured feminine look was the demure, the obedient, the shy.
▸ †**B** *verb.* **1** *verb intrans.* Look demurely. *rare* (Shakes.). Only in E17.
2 *verb trans.* Make demure. E–M17.
■ **demurely** *adverb* LME. **demureness** *noun* E16. **demurity** *noun* (*rare*) demure quality; (an embodiment of) demureness: L15.

demurrable /dɪˈməːrəb(ə)l/ *adjective.* E19.
[ORIGIN from DEMUR *verb* or *noun* + -ABLE.]
Chiefly LAW. Able to be demurred to; open to objection.

demurrage /dɪˈmʌrɪdʒ/ *noun.* M17.
[ORIGIN Old French *demo(u)rage*, formed as DEMUR *verb*: see -AGE. In sense 2 from DEMUR *noun* or *verb* + -AGE.]
†**1** Procrastination; delay, waiting; detention. M17–E19.
2 Failure to load or discharge a chartered ship within the time agreed with the owner; the rate or amount payable to the owner by the charterer in respect of such failure. M17. ▸**b** (A charge for) the similar retention of railway trucks or other goods. M19.

demurral /dɪˈməːr(ə)l/ *noun. rare.* E19.
[ORIGIN from DEMUR *verb* + -AL[1].]
The action of demurring; demur.

demurrant /dɪˈmʌr(ə)nt/ *adjective & noun.* LME.
[ORIGIN Old French *demo(u)rant*, formed as DEMUR *verb*: see -ANT[1].]
▸ **A** *adjective.* **1** Staying, dwelling, resident. Long *arch. rare.* LME.
†**2** Demurring, hesitating, putting off. *rare.* M17–M19.
▸ **B** *noun.* Chiefly LAW. A person who demurs or puts in a demurrer. E19.

demurrer /dɪˈmʌrə/ *noun*[1]. E16.
[ORIGIN Anglo-Norman, use as noun of inf. = Old French *demo(u)rer*: see DEMUR *verb*, -ER[4].]
1 LAW. An objection to the relevance of an opponent's point even if granted, which stays the action until relevance is settled. E16. ▸**b** *gen.* An objection. L16.
†**2** A state of hesitation, a pause. E16–M17.

demurrer /dɪˈməːrə/ *noun*[2]. E18.
[ORIGIN from DEMUR *verb* + -ER[1].]
A person who demurs.

demutualize /diːˈmjuːtʃʊəlʌɪz, -tjʊə-/ *verb trans.* Also **-ise**. L20.
[ORIGIN from DE- 3 + MUTUALIZE.]
Change (a building society etc.) from a mutual organization to one of a different kind.
■ **demutualiˈzation** *noun* L20.

demy /ˈdɛmi, *in senses A.2, B.3* dɪˈmʌɪ/ *adjective & noun.* Also (now *rare* or *obsolete*) **demi**. LME.
[ORIGIN from DEMI- or its source, French *demi*.]
▸ **A** *adjective.* **1** Half, half-sized, diminutive. Now *rare* or *obsolete*. LME.
2 Designating, of, or pertaining to any of various sizes of paper, now *spec.* that measuring 564 × 444 mm (approx. 22.2 × 17.5 inches) or (*Austral.*) 216 × 138 mm (approx. 8.5 × 5.4 inches). M16.
▸ **B** *noun.* †**1** A Scottish coin of varying value, orig. a half-mark. LME–L16.
2 A foundation scholar at Magdalen College, Oxford (orig. having an allowance half that of a Fellow). L15.
3 Demy paper. E18.
■ **demyship** *noun* a scholarship at Magdalen College, Oxford M16.

demyelinate /diːˈmʌɪəlɪneɪt/ *verb trans.* M20.
[ORIGIN from DE- 3 + MYELIN + -ATE[3].]
MEDICINE. Remove or destroy the myelin of (nerve tissue etc.). Chiefly as ***demyelinated***, ***demyelinating*** *ppl adjectives.*
■ **demyeliˈnation** *noun* M20.

demystify /diːˈmɪstɪfʌɪ/ *verb trans.* M20.
[ORIGIN from DE- 3 + MYSTIFY.]
Remove the mystery from; clarify, simplify, explain.
■ **demystifiˈcation** *noun* M20.

demythicize /diːˈmɪθɪsʌɪz/ *verb trans.* Also **-ise**. M20.
[ORIGIN from DE- 3 + MYTHICIZE.]
Remove the attribution of a mythical character to (a legend, etc.); demythologize.
■ **demythiciˈzation** *noun* M20.

demythologize /diːmɪˈθɒlədʒʌɪz/ *verb trans.* Also **-ise**. M20.
[ORIGIN from DE- 3 + MYTHOLOGIZE.]
Remove the mythical elements from (a legend, cult, etc.); *spec.* in THEOLOGY, reinterpret the mythological elements of (the Bible).
■ **demythologiˈzation** *noun* M20.

D

den /dɛn/ *noun*[1].
[ORIGIN Old English *denn* corresp. to Middle Low German, Middle Dutch *denne* low ground (Western Flemish *den* threshing floor), Old High German *tenni* (German *Tenne*) floor, threshing floor, from Germanic. Rel. to DENE *noun*[1].]
1 The lair or habitation of a wild animal. OE. ▸**b** A subdivision of a Cub Scout pack. *US.* M20.
beard the lion in his den: see BEARD *verb* 1.
2 A place of retreat or concealment; a resort of criminals etc. ME. ▸**b** A small cramped (esp. squalid) room or house; a small private room set aside for a person's work, hobbies, etc. L18. ▸**c** In children's games: a sanctuary, 'home'. L19.
SIR W. SCOTT The Cavern, where . . A giant made his den of old. *Times* A search for the forger's den and printing equipment was continuing. **b** E. PEACOCK The filthy den where her mother lived. A. BOYLE A rented house complete with . . a small den . . used as a combined study and photographic darkroom.
den of thieves, ***den of vice***, ***gambling den***, ***opium den***, etc.
3 A hollow place, a cavern. *obsolete* exc. as coinciding with above. ME. ▸†**b** ANATOMY. A cavity. LME–L17.
BUNYAN I lighted on a certain place, Where was a Denn; And I laid me down . . to sleep.
4 A deep hollow between hills, usu. wooded; a dingle. *Scot.* M16.
R. BURNS Auld Coila's . . dens and dells.
– COMB.: **den mother** the woman leader of a Cub Scout den or *transf.* of any group.
– NOTE: Sense 4 may be represented earlier in place names.

den *noun*[2] var. of DENE *noun*[2].

den /dɛn/ *verb.* Infl. **-nn-**. ME.
[ORIGIN from DEN *noun*[1].]
1 *verb trans.* Ensconce or hide (oneself) in a den. In *pass.*, be ensconced in a den. ME.
2 *verb intrans.* Live in, hide oneself in, or retreat into a den. E17.
den up *US colloq.* retire into a den for the winter.

denar /ˈdiːnə, dɪˈnɑː, dɪˈnɛː/ *noun.* M16.
[ORIGIN Anglo-Norman *dener* = Old French & mod. French DENIER *noun*[2]. Cf. DINAR.]
1 *hist.* Any of various coins, as the Roman denarius, the Spanish dinero, the Middle Eastern dinar. M16.
2 The basic monetary unit of the Republic of Macedonia. L20.

denarius /dɪˈnɛːrɪəs, dɪˈnɑːrɪəs/ *noun.* Pl. **-rii** /-rɪʌɪ, -rɪiː/. LME.
[ORIGIN Latin (ellipt. for *denarius nummus* coin containing ten [asses]), from *deni* by tens, distrib. of *decem* ten. Cf DENIER *noun*[2], DENAR.]
hist. **1** An ancient Roman silver coin, orig. of the value of ten asses. Also occas., an English or British penny (as the origin of the abbreviation *d.* in £ s. d. etc.). LME.
2 A unit of weight equal to that of a Roman silver denarius. LME.
3 More fully ***golden denarius***. An ancient Roman gold coin worth 25 silver denarii. M17.

denary /ˈdiːn(ə)ri/ *adjective.* M19.
[ORIGIN Latin *denarius* containing ten: see DENARIUS.]
Having ten as the basis of reckoning, decimal.

denatant /diːˈneɪt(ə)nt/ *adjective.* E20.
[ORIGIN from DE- 1 + NATANT.]
Of the migration of fish: in the same direction as the current. Opp. CONTRANATANT.
■ **denaˈtation** *noun* the act of migrating with the current E20.

denationalize /diːˈnaʃ(ə)n(ə)lʌɪz/ *verb trans.* Also **-ise**. E19.
[ORIGIN French *dénationaliser* (from *dé-* DE- 3 + *nationaliser* NATIONALIZE), a word of the French Revolution: see -IZE.]
1 Deprive (a person etc.) of nationality; deprive (a country, people, etc.) of national identity or characteristics. E19.
2 Make (an institution etc.) no longer national; destroy the association of (an institution etc.) with the whole, or a particular, nation. M19.
3 Transfer (an industry etc.) from national to private ownership. E20.
■ **denationaliˈzation** *noun* E19.

D

denaturalize /diːˈnatʃ(ə)rəlʌɪz/ *verb trans.* Also **-ise**. E19.
[ORIGIN from DE- 3 + NATURALIZE.]
1 Change the nature or properties of, make unnatural; occas., make (alcohol etc.) unfit for drinking. E19.
2 Deprive (a person, esp. oneself) of citizenship. E19.
■ **denaturaliˈzation** *noun* E19. **denaturalizer** *noun* a person who or thing which denaturalizes M19.

denature /diːˈneɪtʃə/ *verb*. L17.
[ORIGIN French *dénaturer*, Old French *des-*, from *des-*, *dé-* DE- 3 + as NATURE *noun*.]
1 *verb trans.* Make unnatural. L17.

R. G. COLLINGWOOD Artistic motives are genuinely present, but denatured by subordination to a non-artistic end.

2 *verb trans.* Change the nature or properties of; *esp.* make (alcohol etc.) unfit for consumption. L19.
3 *spec.* BIOCHEMISTRY. ▸**a** *verb trans.* Cause denaturation (see below) of (a macromolecule), e.g. by heat or acid. E20. ▸**b** *verb intrans.* Of a macromolecule: undergo denaturation. M20.
■ **denaturant** *noun* a substance added to alcohol etc. as a denaturing agent E20. **denatuˈration** *noun* the action of denaturing; *spec.* (BIOCHEMISTRY) alteration of the properties of a macromolecule or macromolecular aggregate by disruption of its conformation: L19.

denaturize /diːˈneɪtʃərʌɪz/ *verb trans.* Also **-ise**. L19.
[ORIGIN from DE- 3 + NATURE *noun* + -IZE.]
=DENATURE *verb* 2.
■ **denaturiˈzation** *noun* M20.

†**denay** *noun*, *verb* vars. of DENY *noun*, *verb*.

denazify /diːˈnɑːtsɪfʌɪ/ *verb trans.* M20.
[ORIGIN from DE- 3 + NAZI + -FY.]
Chiefly *hist.* Remove from, declare (esp. judicially) to be free from, Nazi allegiance or influence; remove Nazis from (official positions etc.).
■ **denazifiˈcation** *noun* M20.

dendriform /ˈdɛndrɪfɔːm/ *adjective*. M19.
[ORIGIN formed as Greek *dendron* tree + -I- + -FORM.]
Of the form of a tree; branching, arborescent.

dendrimer /ˈdɛndrɪmə/ *noun*. L20.
[ORIGIN formed as DENDRIFORM + -MER.]
CHEMISTRY. A synthetic polymer whose molecule has a branching, tree-like structure.

dendrite /ˈdɛndrʌɪt/ *noun*. E18.
[ORIGIN French, from Greek *dendritēs* adjective, pertaining to a tree, from *dendron* tree: see -ITE[1].]
1 (A stone, mineral, etc., bearing) a natural treelike or mosslike marking. E18.
2 A branching crystalline growth. L19.
3 ANATOMY. Any of the branched processes of a nerve cell, through which impulses are received by the cell. L19.

dendritic /dɛnˈdrɪtɪk/ *adjective*. L18.
[ORIGIN from DENDRITE + -IC.]
1 Of the nature of or pertaining to a dendrite; of a branching form; arborescent, treelike. L18.
2 Having arborescent markings. E19.
■ **dendritical** *adjective* = DENDRITIC *adjective* E19. **dendritically** *adverb* L19.

dendro- /ˈdɛndrəʊ/ *combining form* of Greek *dendron* tree: see -O-.
■ **dendrocliˈmatic** *adjective* of or pertaining to dendroclimatology M20. **dendroclimaˈtology** *noun* the branch of science that deals with obtaining information about past climates by examining growth rings in (ancient) timber M20. **dendrogram** *noun* (BIOLOGY) a branched diagram representing the relationship between taxa M20. **denˈdrometer** *noun* an instrument for measuring the size of trees M19. **dendrophil(e)** *noun* a lover of trees L19.

dendrochronology /ˌdɛndrəʊkrəˈnɒlədʒi/ *noun*. E20.
[ORIGIN from DENDRO- + CHRONOLOGY.]
The science of dating events and environmental variations by means of the comparative study of the growth rings in (ancient) timber.
■ **dendrochronoˈlogical** *adjective* pertaining to, involving, or obtained by the use of dendrochronology M20. **dendrochronoˈlogically** *adverb* M20. **dendrochronologist** *noun* M20.

dendroid /ˈdɛndrɔɪd/ *adjective* & *noun*. M19.
[ORIGIN from DENDRO- + -OID.]
▸ **A** *adjective*. Tree-shaped, arborescent, dendritic; *spec.* (PALAEONTOLOGY) designating or pertaining to graptolites of the order Dendroidea, which form much-branched colonies. M19.
▸ **B** *noun*. PALAEONTOLOGY. A dendroid graptolite. E20.

dendrology /dɛnˈdrɒlədʒi/ *noun*. E18.
[ORIGIN from DENDRO- + -LOGY.]
The branch of science that deals with trees.
■ **dendroˈlogic** *adjective* (*rare*) E19. **dendroˈlogical** *adjective* L19. **dendrologist** *noun* E19.

dendron /ˈdɛndrɒn/ *noun*. L19.
[ORIGIN from DENDRITE + *-on* as in *axon* etc.]
ANATOMY. = DENDRITE 3.

dene /diːn/ *noun*[1]. Also **dean**.
[ORIGIN Old English *denu* from Germanic. Rel. to DEN *noun*[1].]
A valley; now usu. *spec.*, the deep narrow wooded valley of a rivulet.

dene /diːn/ *noun*[2]. Also **den** /dɛn/. ME.
[ORIGIN Perh. rel. to Low German (whence German) *düne*, Dutch *duin* DUNE.]
A bare sandy tract by the sea; a low sandhill.

denegation /dɛnɪˈgeɪʃ(ə)n/ *noun*. L15.
[ORIGIN French *dénégation* from late Latin *denegatio(n-)*, from *de-* DE- 1 + *negare*: see -ATION.]
†**1** Refusal of what is asked. L15–M17.
2 Denial, contradiction. M19.
■ **denegatory** *adjective* (*rare*) contradictory E19.

dene-hole /ˈdiːnhəʊl/ *noun*. Also **dane-** /ˈdeɪn-/. M18.
[ORIGIN Uncertain: perh. from DANE + HOLE *noun*[1]. Assoc. by later archaeologists with DENE *noun*[2] and DEN *noun*[1].]
ARCHAEOLOGY. An ancient excavation of a kind found in chalk formations in England and France, consisting of a narrow shaft sunk down to the chalk, and there widening out into one or more chambers.

denervate /diːˈnəːveɪt/ *verb trans.* E20.
[ORIGIN from DE- 3 + NERVATE *verb*.]
MEDICINE. Remove or cut off the nerve supply from (an organ etc.).
■ **denerˈvation** *noun* E20.

dengue /ˈdɛŋgi/ *noun*. Also **denga** /ˈdɛŋgə/. E19.
[ORIGIN W. Indian Spanish, from Kiswahili *denga*, *dinga* (in full *kidingapopo*), identified with Spanish *dengue* fastidiousness, prudery, with ref. to the stiffness of the neck and shoulders caused by the disease.]
A debilitating tropical viral disease which is transmitted to humans by the mosquito *Aedes aegypti*, and is characterized by an eruptive fever and severe pain esp. in the joints and muscles. Also ***dengue fever***.

deni /ˈdɛniː/ *noun*. L20.
[ORIGIN Macedonian, from DENAR.]
A monetary unit of the Republic of Macedonia, equal to one-hundredth of a denar.

deniable /dɪˈnʌɪəb(ə)l/ *adjective*. M16.
[ORIGIN from DENY *verb* + -ABLE.]
That can be denied.
■ **deniaˈbility** *noun* E19.

denial /dɪˈnʌɪ(ə)l/ *noun*. E16.
[ORIGIN from DENY *verb* + -AL[1].]
1 The act of saying 'no'; refusal of something asked or desired. E16.

SHAKES. *Tam. Shr.* Neuer make denial; I must and will have Katherine to my wife.

2 A statement or assertion that something is untrue or untenable; contradiction; refusal to acknowledge the existence or reality of a thing. L16.

B. JOWETT The denial of abstract ideas is the destruction of the mind.

3 (A) disavowal, disowning; *esp.* refusal to acknowledge a person as leader etc. L16.

AV *John* 18 Peters deniall.

4 LAW. The opposing by a defendant of a charge etc. made against him or her. E18.
5 A drawback, disadvantage. *dial.* M18.
6 BRIDGE. A bid intended to show weakness in response to one's partner's bid. E20.

denier /dɪˈnʌɪə/ *noun*[1]. LME.
[ORIGIN from DENY *verb* + -ER[1].]
A person who denies.

denier /ˈdɛnɪə/ *noun*[2]. LME.
[ORIGIN Old French & mod. French from Latin DENARIUS.]
1 *hist.* A French coin of little value (equal to one-twelfth of a sou) which was withdrawn from use in the 19th cent.; (the type of) a very small sum. LME.

SHAKES. *Rich. III* My dukedom to a beggarly denier.

†**2** = DENARIUS 2. M16–E18.
†**3** = DENARIUS 1. L16–E17.
4 Orig., a unit of weight used for silk, equal to 1/24 oz (1.181 gram). Now, a unit of fineness of yarn equal to the weight in grams of 9,000 metres of it. M19.

denigrate /ˈdɛnɪgreɪt/ *verb trans.* LME.
[ORIGIN Latin *denigrat-* pa. ppl stem of *denigrare*, from *de-* DE- 1 + *nigrare* blacken, from *niger* black: see -ATE[3].]
1 Make black or dark in colour. Now *rare* or *obsolete*. LME.
2 Blacken the reputation of (a person etc.); defame, decry. E16.

G. F. FIENNES Whether, if I called Judas . . a not too good apostle, I was denigrating the profession of apostle. P. ACKROYD He was not . . happy with his journalistic productions and tended to denigrate them . . to his friends.

■ **denigrator** *noun* a person who or thing which denigrates someone or something M17. **denigratory** /dɛnɪˈgreɪt(ə)ri, ˈdɛnɪgrət-/ *adjective* defamatory M20.

denigration /dɛnɪˈgreɪʃ(ə)n/ *noun*. LME.
[ORIGIN Latin *denigratio(n-)*, formed as DENIGRATE: see -ATION.]
1 The action or process of blackening or darkening in colour. Now *rare* or *obsolete*. LME.
2 Blackening of reputation or character; defamation. LME.

dénigrement /denigrəmɑ̃/ *noun*. L19.
[ORIGIN French.]
Blackening of character, denigration.

denim /ˈdɛnɪm/ *noun* & *adjective*. Orig. †**serge denim**. L17.
[ORIGIN *serge denim* from French *serge de Nîmes* serge of Nîmes (a city in southern France).]
▸ **A** *noun*. Orig., a kind of serge. Now, a twilled hard-wearing cotton fabric (freq. blue) used for overalls, jeans, etc. In *pl.*, overalls or jeans made of denim. L17.
▸ **B** *adjective*. Made of denim. E18.

denitrate /diːˈnʌɪtreɪt/ *verb trans.* M19.
[ORIGIN from DE- 3 + NITRATE.]
Remove nitrates from.
■ **deniˈtration** *noun* E19.

denitrify /diːˈnʌɪtrɪfʌɪ/ *verb trans.* L19.
[ORIGIN from DE- 3 + NITRIFY.]
Remove nitrates or nitrites from; *esp.* (of bacteria) remove nitrates etc. from (soil) by chemical reduction, ultimately to gaseous nitrogen.
■ **denitrifiˈcation** *noun* L19.

denizate /ˈdɛnɪzeɪt/ *verb trans.* E17.
[ORIGIN Anglo-Latin *denizat-* pa. ppl stem of *denizare*, *denizatio(n-)*, from DENIZEN *noun* & *adjective*: see -ATE[3].]
LAW (now *hist.*). Make a denizen; naturalize.
■ **deniˈzation** *noun* E17.

†**denize** *verb trans.* L16–E18.
[ORIGIN from DENIZEN *noun* & *adjective*, prob. repr. an Anglo-Norman form.]
Make a denizen; naturalize.

denizen /ˈdɛnɪz(ə)n/ *noun* & *adjective*. LME.
[ORIGIN Anglo-Norman *deinzein* (from Old French *deinz* within from late Latin *de intus* from within + *-ein* from Latin *-aneus*), assim. to *citizen*.]
▸ **A** *noun*. **1** A person who lives within a country, as opp. to a foreigner who lives outside its boundaries; *gen.* an inhabitant, an occupant, a citizen (*of* a place). LME.

G. P. R. JAMES The towns . . and their laborious denizens. H. CARPENTER Salmon, Lobster, and many smaller denizens of sea and river-bed.

2 A person who lives in a country but is not native-born; a foreigner admitted to residence and allowed certain rights. E16. ▸**b** A person admitted to or given the freedom of a particular group; one who, though not a native, is at home in a particular place. M16. ▸**c** A foreign word, animal, plant, etc., which has become naturalized. L16.

I. D'ISRAELI Charles seemed ambitious of making English denizens of every man of genius in Europe. **b** H. REED He was a denizen . . of Alpine regions, and of Greek and Italian plains.

▸ **B** *attrib.* or as *adjective*. That has the entitlements of or is a denizen. L15.
■ **denizenship** *noun* the position or status of a denizen E17.

denizen /ˈdɛnɪz(ə)n/ *verb trans.* M16.
[ORIGIN from the noun.]
Make a denizen; naturalize.

SOUTHEY The cholera is not a passing evil. It is denizened among us.

Denmark /ˈdɛnmɑːk/ *noun*. L18.
[ORIGIN A country in Scandinavia: see DANE.]
1 ***Denmark satin***, a kind of worsted used esp. to make women's shoes. *obsolete* exc. *hist.* L18.
2 ***Denmark Street*** [a London street], the world of composers and publishers of popular music, Tin Pan Alley. M20.

denn /dɛn/ *noun*. M20.
[ORIGIN Revival of Old English (Kentish), surviving as *-den* in place names e.g. *Tenterden*, perh. = DEN *noun*[1]. Cf. Middle Dutch *dann* forest, haunt of wild beasts.]
hist. A woodland pasture (in SE England), esp. for swine.

†**dennage** *noun* see DUNNAGE.

dennebol /ˈdɛnəbɒl/ *noun*. *S. Afr.* E20.
[ORIGIN Afrikaans, from *denne (boom)* pine (tree) + *bol* ball, bulb.]
A fir cone.

dennet /ˈdɛnɪt/ *noun*. E19.
[ORIGIN Perh. from a surname.]
Chiefly *hist.* A light open two-wheeled carriage, similar to a gig, popular in Britain in the early 19th cent.

denominable /dɪˈnɒmɪnəb(ə)l/ *adjective.* **M17.**
[ORIGIN medieval Latin *denominabilis*, from Latin *denominare* DENOMINATE: see -ABLE.]
Able to be denominated or named.

denominal /dɪˈnɒmɪn(ə)l/ *noun & adjective.* **M20.**
[ORIGIN from DE- 2 + NOMINAL.]
GRAMMAR. = DENOMINATIVE *noun*, *adjective* 2.

denominate /dɪˈnɒmɪneɪt/ *verb trans.* Pa. pple **-ated**, (orig.) †**-ate**. **LME.**
[ORIGIN Latin *denominat-* pa. ppl stem of *denominare*, from *de-* DE- 1 + *nominare* to name: see -ATE[3].]
1 Give a name to; name, call, (orig. *from* or *after* something). **LME.**

R. H. MOTTRAM That standard compost that . . before nine . . was denominated 'coffee', . . before or after noon 'soup', until the end of the day, when . . it became 'tea'.

2 Of a thing: give (something) its name or character, characterize; make what it is. Now *rare*. **L16.**

J. BENTHAM That . . acquaintance with the . . classics which denominates a man a good scholar.

†**3** Denote. Only in **18.**

denomination /dɪˌnɒmɪˈneɪʃ(ə)n/ *noun.* **LME.**
[ORIGIN Old French *denominacion* (later & mod. *-tion*) or Latin *denominatio(n-)*, formed as DENOMINATE: see -ATION.]
1 The action of naming (*from* or *after*); giving a name to, calling by a name. **LME.**
2 A characteristic name given to a thing or class of things; a designation, a title. **LME.**

SIR W. SCOTT Gypsies, jockies, or cairds . . by all these denominations such banditti were known.

3 A class of one kind of unit in any system of numbers, weights, money, etc., distinguished by a specific name. **L15.**

M. MCCARTHY Her . . boxes held Stamps of various denominations. D. BAGLEY A bank-note of large denomination.

4 A class, sort, or kind distinguished by a specific name. **M17.**

A. HAMILTON Good Cotton Cloth of several Qualities and Denominations.

5 A body of people classed together under the one name; *spec.* a religious sect or body with distinctive name and organization. **M17.**

M. L. KING Within American Protestantism there are more than two hundred and fifty denominations.

denominational /dɪˌnɒmɪˈneɪʃ(ə)n(ə)l/ *adjective.* **M19.**
[ORIGIN from DENOMINATION + -AL[1].]
Belonging to or of the nature of a denomination; (esp. of education, a school, etc.) sectarian.
■ **denominationalism** *noun* adherence to denominational principles or a denominational system (of education) **M19.** **denominationalize** *verb trans.* make denominational **M19.** **denominationally** *adverb* **M19.**

denominative /dɪˈnɒmɪnətɪv/ *noun & adjective.* **L16.**
[ORIGIN Late Latin *denominativus* adjective, from *denominat-*: see DENOMINATE, -ATIVE.]
▸ **A** *noun.* GRAMMAR. A word formed or derived from a noun. **L16.**
▸ **B** *adjective.* **1** That gives a name to something; *esp.* (of a word or term) having the function of naming or describing. **L16.**
2 GRAMMAR. Formed or derived from a noun. **L18.**
■ **denominatively** *adverb* **M16.**

denominator /dɪˈnɒmɪneɪtə/ *noun.* **M16.**
[ORIGIN French *dénominateur* or medieval Latin *denominator*, from *denominat-*: see DENOMINATE, -OR.]
1 The number written below the line in a vulgar fraction, which gives the denomination or value of the parts into which the integer is divided; the divisor in an algebraic fraction. (Correl. to ***numerator***.) **M16.**
common denominator a common multiple of the denominators of several fractions; *fig.* something common to or characteristic of a number of things, people, etc.; (***least common denominator***, ***lowest common denominator***, the lowest such multiple or common characteristic).
2 A person who or thing which gives a name to something. Now *rare*. **L16.**

de nos jours /də no ʒuːr/ *postpositive adjectival phr.* **E20.**
[ORIGIN French = of our days.]
Of the present time; contemporary.

denotata *noun* pl. of DENOTATUM.

denotation /diːnə(ʊ)ˈteɪʃ(ə)n/ *noun.* **M16.**
[ORIGIN French *dénotation* or Latin *denotatio(n-)*, from *denotat-* pa. ppl stem of *denotare*: see DENOTE, -ATION.]
1 The action of denoting; expression by marks, signs, or symbols; indication. **M16.** ▸**b** A mark etc. denoting a thing; a sign. **M17.**
2 The meaning or signification of a term, as distinct from its implications or connotations. **E17.**
3 A term used to describe something; a designation. **M17.**
4 LOGIC. The object or range of objects which a word denotes; extension. **M19.**
■ **denotational** *adjective* **M20.**

denotative /dɪˈnəʊtətɪv, ˈdiːnə(ʊ)teɪtɪv/ *adjective & noun.* **E17.**
[ORIGIN from Latin *denotat-*: see DENOTATION, -ATIVE.]
▸ **A** *adjective.* Having the quality of denoting; designating, indicative. **E17.**
▸ **B** *noun.* A denotative term. **M20.**
■ **denotatively** *adverb* **M19.**

denotatum /diːnəʊˈteɪtəm, -ˈtɑːt-/ *noun.* Pl. **-tata** /-ˈteɪtə, -ˈtɑːtə/. **M20.**
[ORIGIN Latin, neut. pa. pple of *denotare* DENOTE.]
PHILOSOPHY. The thing denoted by an expression; *esp.* an existent object of reference. Cf. DESIGNATUM.

denote /dɪˈnəʊt/ *verb trans.* **L16.**
[ORIGIN Old French & mod. French *dénoter* or Latin *denotare*, from *de-* DE- 1 + *notare* NOTE *verb*[1].]
1 Mark out; distinguish by a mark or sign. **L16.**
2 Indicate; be an outward or visible sign of. **L16.** ▸**b** Give to understand; make known. **M17.**

OED A falling barometer denotes an approaching storm. J. MARQUAND I was reminded again that the smile of a Japanese does not necessarily denote humour. **b** SMOLLETT Thou hast enough Denoted thy concern.

†**3** Note down; describe. Only in **17.**
4 Signify; be a symbol for or a name of. **M17.** ▸**b** Express *by* a symbol. **L19.**

B. RUSSELL No sentence can be made up without at least one word which denotes a universal. **b** M. KLINE These fields . . have four sides, which we shall denote by *a*, *b*, *c*, *d*.

5 Designate; have as a meaning or name; be predicated of. (Freq. as opp. ***connote***.) **M19.**

H. SPENCER We can do no more than ignore the connotation of the words, and attend only to the things they avowedly denote. R. FRY Some other word to denote what we now call art.

■ **denotable** *adjective* able to be denoted or marked **L17.** **denotement** *noun* (*a*) the fact of denoting; (*b*) a token, a sign: **E17.** **denotive** *adjective* serving to denote **M19.**

denouement /deɪˈnuːmɒ̃, -mɒŋ/ *noun.* Also **dé-**. **M18.**
[ORIGIN French, from *dénouer* (earlier *des-*) untie, from *des-*, *dé-* DE- 3 + *nouer* to knot.]
The unravelling of the complications of a plot, or of a confused situation or mystery; the final resolution of a play, novel, or other narrative.

denounce /dɪˈnaʊns/ *verb trans.* **ME.**
[ORIGIN Old French *dénoncier* (mod. *dénoncer*) from Latin *denuntiare* give official information, from *de-* DE- 1 + *nuntiare* make known, report.]
1 Give official information of; proclaim, announce. Now *arch. rare*. **ME.** ▸†**b** Of a thing: indicate, portend, presage. **L16–M18.**

AV *Deut.* 30:18 I denounce unto you this day, that ye shall surely perish. J. STRYPE He was solemnly denounced excommunicate.

2 Proclaim or pronounce (a person) to be (cursed, a rebel, etc.); publicly declare (a person or thing) to be wicked or evil, accuse publicly, openly inveigh against. **ME.** ▸†**b** Proclaim (*as*) *king*, *emperor*, etc. **L15–E17.**

W. S. CHURCHILL General Weyler's policy of herding civilians into concentration camps . . was vehemently denounced. B. MOORE The Bishop . . denounced Hartmann as a false priest.

3 Make known (an offender) to the authorities; inform against. **L15.**

J. AYLIFFE Archdeacons . . shall . . denounce such of them as are negligent . . to the Bishop.

4 Announce as a threat or warning. *arch.* **L16.**

W. IRVING Captain Wyeth . . had heard the Crows denounce vengeance on them, for having murdered two of their warriors.

5 Give formal notice of the termination of (a treaty, armistice, etc.). **M19.**
■ **denouncement** *noun* the action of denouncing; (a) denunciation: **M16.** **denouncer** *noun* **LME.**

de nouveau /də nuvo/ *adverbial phr.* **L18.**
[ORIGIN French = from new.]
Afresh, starting again from the beginning.

de novo /deɪ ˈnəʊvəʊ, diː/ *adverbial phr.* **E17.**
[ORIGIN Latin = from new.]
= DE NOUVEAU.

†**densation** *noun.* **E17–E18.**
[ORIGIN Latin *densatio(n-)*, from *densat-* pa. ppl stem of *densare* make thick, from *densus*: see DENSE, -ATION.]
Thickening, condensation.

dense /dɛns/ *adjective.* **LME.**
[ORIGIN French, or Latin *densus* thick, dense, crowded.]
1 Closely compacted in substance; thick, compact; having a high density. **LME.** ▸**b** With the constituent parts closely crowded together; closely set. **L18.**

R. J. SULLIVAN It pervades all bodies, dense as well as rare. H. KELLER A dense fog, when it seemed as if a tangible white darkness shut you in. F. HOYLE Seawater that has lost its heat in melting icebergs is very dense and plunges to the very bottom of the ocean. **b** F. MARRYAT The crowd . . was so dense that it was hardly possible to move. P. THEROUX The jungle . . was so dense no light showed through it.

2 *fig.* Profound, intense; impenetrable. **M18.** ▸**b** Crass, stupid. **E19.**

B. FRANKLIN Six weeks of the densest happiness I have met with. P. SCOTT Such dense blackness of skin. **b** E. F. BENSON The stuffy girls were not so dense as not to perceive her opinion of them.

3 PHOTOGRAPHY. Of high density (DENSITY 4). **L19.**
■ **densely** *adverb* **E19.** **densen** *verb trans. & intrans.* (*rare*) make or become (more) dense **M19.** **denseness** *noun* **M17.**

Denshire *noun & verb* see DEVONSHIRE.

densify /ˈdɛnsɪfʌɪ/ *verb trans.* **E19.**
[ORIGIN from DENSE + -I- + -FY.]
Make (more) dense.

densimeter /dɛnˈsɪmɪtə/ *noun.* **M19.**
[ORIGIN from Latin *densus* DENSE + -IMETER. Cf. DENSOMETER.]
An instrument for measuring density, esp. of liquids.

D

densitometer /dɛnsɪˈtɒmɪtə/ *noun.* **E20.**
[ORIGIN from DENSITY + -OMETER.]
An instrument for measuring photographic density.
■ **densito'metric** *adjective* **E20.** **densitometry** *noun* **E20.**

density /ˈdɛnsɪti/ *noun.* **E17.**
[ORIGIN French *densité* or Latin *densitas*, from *densus*: see DENSE, -ITY.]
1 The quality or condition of being closely compacted in substance; closeness of texture or consistency. **E17.**

fig.: W. J. BATE In all of these works are the same weight and density of meaning.

2 PHYSICS. The degree of consistency of a body or substance measured by the quantity of mass in unit volume. **M17.** ▸**b** Any of various physical properties defined as a quantity (of electric charge, particles, energy, etc.) per unit (physical or mathematical) extent. Usu. with specifying word. **L19.**

R. V. JONES This gives a mean density for the rocket of about four times that of water. **b** H. M. ROSENBERG The density of states will be used to describe the number of atomic oscillators per unit energy . . range.

b ***charge density***, ***electron density***, etc. ***optical density***: see OPTICAL *adjective*. ***vapour density***: see VAPOUR *noun*.
3 The degree of aggregation; a crowded state; *spec.* in any population, the average number of individuals per spatial unit. **M19.**

N. HAWTHORNE Stems, supporting a cloud-like density of boughs. E. F. SCHUMACHER The United States could accommodate more than half the world population before it attained a density equal to that of the United Kingdom.

4 PHOTOGRAPHY. (A measure of) the opacity of the image produced (i.e. the amount of silver deposited) in a photographic emulsion under given conditions. **L19.**
5 *fig.* Stupidity, crassness. **L19.**
6 COMPUTING. = ***packing density*** s.v. PACKING *noun*[1]. **M20.**

densometer /dɛnˈsɒmɪtə/ *noun.* **L19.**
[ORIGIN from Latin *densus* DENSE + -OMETER.]
= DENSIMETER.

dent /dɛnt/ *noun*[1]. **ME.**
[ORIGIN Var. of DINT *noun*; in sense 3 prob. from DENT *verb*. Cf. DUNT *noun*.]
1 †**a** A stroke or blow, *esp.* one given with a weapon; = DINT *noun* 1. **ME–E17.** ▸**b** A clap of thunder. Long *obsolete* exc. *dial.* **ME.**
†**2** Dealing of blows; vigorous wielding of a weapon; force of attack. **LME–L16.**
3 A hollow or impression in a surface, as made by a blow with a sharp or edged instrument; an indentation. **M16.** ▸**b** *fig.* A (detrimental) reducing effect or reduction. **M20.**

GEO. ELIOT Dents and disfigurements in an old family tankard. J. CARY The lower cottages in a dip or dent on the hillside. **b** *Times* There is going to be a dent in our profits.

dent /dɛnt/ *noun*[2]. **M16.**
[ORIGIN French = tooth.]
1 A toothlike notch in the edge of something. Now only in NEEDLEWORK, a pointed or square design cut as a decorative edging to the hem of a dress etc. **M16.**

DRYDEN His [a cock's] comb . . In dents embattl'd like a castle-wall.

2 A tooth-shaped projection, esp. in a clothmakers' card, a gearwheel, etc.; *spec.* in weaving, = SPLIT *noun* 2b. **E18.**

dent /dɛnt/ *adjective & noun*[3]. **LME.**
[ORIGIN Abbreviation of *dented* pa. pple of DENT *verb*.]
▸ **A** *adjective.* †**1** Embossed. Only in **LME.**
†**2** HERALDRY. Indented. Only in **E17.**
3 Designating a variety of Indian corn (maize) having a dent or depression in each kernel. *US.* **M19.**
▸ **B** *noun.* Dent corn. *US.* **M19.**

dent /dɛnt/ *verb.* **LME.**
[ORIGIN Prob. aphet. from INDENT *verb*[2].]
1 *verb trans.* Make a dent in, as with a blow on a surface; mark with a dent or dents; indent. **LME.** ▸**b** *fig.* Have an (esp. adverse) effect on; damage. **M20.**

M. E. BRADDON Armour . . battered and dented at Cressy. R. MACAULAY The sun beat hotly on the asphalt, making it soft, so that one could dent it with one's heels. **b** *Listener* Lack of candour . . has further dented public faith in Downing Street statements.

2 *verb trans.* Imprint, impress. **LME.**

3 *verb intrans.* Sink *in*, so as to make or dent; become indented. L15.

K. KESEY The head dented into the pillow.

dental /ˈdɛnt(ə)l/ *adjective & noun*. L16.
[ORIGIN Late Latin *dentalis*, from Latin *dens*, *dent-* tooth: see -AL[1].]
▸ **A** *adjective*. **1** Of or pertaining to a tooth, the teeth, or dentistry; of the nature of a tooth. L16.
2 PHONETICS. Of a consonant: articulated with the tip of the tongue against the upper front teeth as English *th* /θ, ð/, French *d*, *n*, *t*; = ALVEOLAR *adjective*. L16.
– SPECIAL COLLOCATIONS: ***dental floss***: see FLOSS *noun*[2] 3. **dental formula**: expressing the number and kinds of teeth possessed by a mammal (usu. written in the form of a 'fraction' with the upper and lower lines describing the upper and lower jaws respectively). **dental hygienist** an ancillary dental worker specializing in oral hygiene, scaling and polishing of teeth, etc. **dental mechanic** a person who makes and repairs artificial teeth. **dental nurse** a nurse who assists a dentist. ***dental*** PLAQUE. **dental surgeon** a dentist. **dental technician** = ***dental mechanic*** above.
▸ **B** *noun*. **1** PHONETICS. A dental consonant. L17.
†**2** A tooth shell. L17–E18.
†**3** = DENTEX. M18–M19.
4 ARCHITECTURE. = DENTIL. M18.
■ **denˈtality** *noun* (PHONETICS) dental quality L19. **dentaliˈzation** *noun* (PHONETICS) the action of dentalizing; the state of being dentalized: L19. **dentalize** *verb trans.* (PHONETICS) make dental, change into a dental sound M19. **dentally** *adverb* M20.

dentalium /dɛnˈteɪlɪəm/ *noun*. Pl. **-lia** /-lɪə/. M19.
[ORIGIN mod. Latin (see below), from late Latin *dentalis*: see DENTAL.]
A tusk shell (*spec.* of the genus *Dentalium*), freq. used as an ornament or as currency by primitive peoples.

dentaria /dɛnˈtɛːrɪə/ *noun*. E19.
[ORIGIN mod. Latin (see below), fem. sing. of late Latin *dentarius*: see DENTARY.]
Any cruciferous plant of the genus *Dentaria* (now freq. included in the genus *Cardamine*), characterized by toothlike scales on the roots, e.g. coralroot, pepper-root.

dentary /ˈdɛnt(ə)ri/ *adjective & noun*. M19.
[ORIGIN Late Latin *dentarius*, from Latin *dens*, *dent-* tooth: see -ARY[1]. Cf. French *dentaire*.]
ANATOMY & ZOOLOGY. ▸**A** *adjective*. Of or connected with the teeth. M19.
dentary bone = sense B. below.
▸ **B** *noun*. The bone of the lower jaw which bears the teeth (in mammals, the single bone of the lower jaw). M19.

dentate /ˈdɛnteɪt/ *adjective*. LME.
[ORIGIN Latin *dentatus*, from *dens*, *dent-* tooth: see -ATE[2].]
Chiefly ZOOLOGY & BOTANY. Toothed; having toothlike projections or notches along the edge; *spec.* (of a leaf etc.) having sharp outwardly directed teeth.
■ **dentated** *adjective* = DENTATE M18. **denˈtation** *noun* the condition or fact of being dentate E19.

-dentate /dɛnteɪt/ *suffix*.
[ORIGIN formed as DENTATE.]
Forming adjectives with the senses (***a***) ZOOLOGY & BOTANY having teeth or toothlike projections of the specified number or kind, (***b***) CHEMISTRY forming the specified number of bonds with another atom, esp. as a ligand; as ***bidentate***, ***curvidentate***, ***duplicato-dentate***, ***polydentate***.

dented /ˈdɛntɪd/ *adjective*. LME.
[ORIGIN from DENT *noun*[1], *noun*[2], *verb*: see -ED[2], -ED[1].]
1 Having a dent or dents; bent inward, incurved (now only by a blow etc.). LME.

A. TYLER They had reached his car, a dented gray Chevy.

2 Indented, notched; toothed. LME.

dentellated /ˈdɛntɪleɪtɪd/ *adjective*. Also **-elated**. L18.
[ORIGIN formed as DENTELLE, after French *dentelé*: see -ATE[2], -ED[1].]
Having small notches or teeth; finely indented.

dentelle /dɛnˈtɛl; *foreign* dɑ̃tɛl (*pl. same*)/ *noun*. M19.
[ORIGIN French, from *dent* tooth + *-elle* -EL[2].]
1 (A piece of) lace. M19.
2 BOOKBINDING. An ornamental tooling resembling lace edging. Usu. *attrib.* L19.

†**dentello** *noun* see DENTIL.

dentex /ˈdɛntɛks/ *noun*. Pl. same. M19.
[ORIGIN mod. Latin (see below) from Latin *dentex*, *-tix* a kind of marine fish.]
A sea bream of the genus *Dentex*; spec. *D. dentex* of the Mediterranean and N. African Atlantic coast.

denti- /ˈdɛnti/ *combining form* of Latin *dens*, *dent-* tooth, *dentes* teeth: see -I-.
■ **dentiform** *adjective* of the form of or resembling a tooth; tooth-shaped: E18. **denˈtigerous** *adjective* bearing teeth; (of a cyst) surrounding an unerupted tooth: M19. **dentiˈlingual** *adjective & noun* (PHONETICS) (a consonant, sound, etc.) formed by the teeth and tongue L19.

Denticare /ˈdɛntɪkɛː/ *noun*. Chiefly *N. Amer.* Also **d-**. M20.
[ORIGIN from DENTAL *adjective* + CARE *noun*, after MEDICARE.]
Dental care; a scheme providing this, esp. sponsored by a state (US proprietary) or province.

denticle /ˈdɛntɪk(ə)l/ *noun*. LME.
[ORIGIN Latin *denticulus*: see DENTICULE.]
1 Chiefly ZOOLOGY. A small tooth or toothlike projection. In early use *spec.* a pointer on the rete of the astrolabe. LME.
2 ARCHITECTURE. = DENTIL 1. Now *rare*. L17.

denticular /dɛnˈtɪkjʊlə/ *adjective*. M19.
[ORIGIN formed as DENTICULE + -AR[1].]
1 ARCHITECTURE. Characterized by dentils. M19.
2 Resembling or of the nature of a small tooth. L19.

denticulate /dɛnˈtɪkjʊlət/ *adjective*. M17.
[ORIGIN Latin *denticulatus*, formed as DENTICULE: see -ATE[2].]
Having small teeth or toothlike projections; finely toothed.
■ **denticulated** *adjective* (***a***) = DENTICULATE; (***b***) ARCHITECTURE = DENTICULAR 1: M17. **denticuˈlation** *noun* the condition of being denticulate or finely toothed; an instance of this; a small indentation or projection: L17.

denticule /ˈdɛntɪkjuːl/ *noun*. M16.
[ORIGIN Latin *denticulus* dim. of *dens*, *dent-* tooth: see -CULE.]
ARCHITECTURE. That member of the entablature in which the dentils are cut.

dentifrice /ˈdɛntɪfrɪs/ *noun*. LME.
[ORIGIN French from Latin *dentifricium*, from *dens*, *dent-* tooth (cf. DENTI-) + *fricare* to rub.]
A powder, paste, or other preparation for cleaning the teeth.

dentil /ˈdɛntɪl/ *noun & adjective*. Also (earlier) in Italian form †**-tello**, pl. **-telli**. L16.
[ORIGIN (Italian *dentello* or) French †*dentille* (now *dentelle*) fem. dim. of *dent* tooth, from Latin *dens*, *dent-*.]
ARCHITECTURE. ▸**A** *noun*. **1** Each of the small rectangular blocks resembling teeth, under the bed-moulding of the cornice in the Ionic, Corinthian, Composite, and sometimes Doric, orders. L16.
†**2** = DENTICULE. E18–E19.
▸ **B** *attrib.* or as *adjective*. Consisting of or containing dentils; resembling (a series of) dentils. M18.

dentine /ˈdɛntiːn/ *noun*. Also ***-tin** /-tɪn/. M19.
[ORIGIN from Latin *dens*, *dent-* tooth + -INE[4].]
The hard dense tissue forming the chief constituent of teeth.
■ **dentinal** /-tɪn(ə)l/ *adjective* pertaining to or of the nature of dentine M19.

dentiscalp /ˈdɛntɪskalp/ *noun*. Now *rare* or *obsolete*. M17.
[ORIGIN Latin *dentiscalpium* toothpick, formed as DENTI- + *scalpere* scrape.]
A toothpick, a tooth-scraper.

dentist /ˈdɛntɪst/ *noun*. M18.
[ORIGIN French *dentiste*, from *dent* tooth: see -IST.]
A person whose profession it is to diagnose and treat diseases, injuries, and malformations of the teeth, jaws, and mouth, extract teeth, insert artificial ones, etc.
■ **denˈtistical** *adjective* (*rare*) of, pertaining to, or of the nature of a dentist E19. **dentistry** *noun* the profession or practice of a dentist M19.

dentition /dɛnˈtɪʃ(ə)n/ *noun*. L16.
[ORIGIN Latin *dentitio(n-)*, from *dentit-* pa. ppl stem of *dentire* teethe, from *dens*, *dent-* tooth: see -ITION.]
1 The production or cutting of teeth; teething. L16.
2 The characteristic arrangement, kind, and number of teeth in a particular species at a particular age. M19.

denture /ˈdɛntʃə/ *noun*[1]. Long *obsolete* exc. *dial.* LME.
[ORIGIN Aphet.]
An indenture.

denture /ˈdɛntʃə/ *noun*[2]. *rare*. L17.
[ORIGIN from DENT *verb* + -URE.]
An indentation, indent.

denture /ˈdɛntʃə/ *noun*[3]. L19.
[ORIGIN French, from *dent* tooth: see -URE.]
sing. & (usu.) in *pl.* A set of (esp. artificial) teeth.
■ **denturist** *noun* a maker of artificial dentures M20.

denuclearize /diːˈnjuːklɪərʌɪz/ *verb trans.* Also **-ise**. M20.
[ORIGIN from DE- 3 + NUCLEAR *adjective* + -IZE.]
Deprive of nuclear weapons; remove nuclear weapons from.
■ **denucleariˈzation** *noun* M20.

denudate /dɪˈnjuːdeɪt/ *verb trans.* Pa. pple **-ated**, (orig.) †**-ate**. LME.
[ORIGIN Latin *denudat-* pa. ppl stem of *denudare*: see DENUDE, -ATE[3].]
Strip naked or bare; denude.

denudation /diːnjʊˈdeɪʃ(ə)n/ *noun*. LME.
[ORIGIN Late (eccl.) Latin *denudatio(n-)* uncovering, laying bare, as DENUDATE: see -ATION.]
1 The action of making bare; a stripping off of clothing or covering; denuded condition. LME.

fig.: DONNE The Denudation of your Souls and your Sins by a humble confession.

2 The action of divesting or depriving (*of*). M17.
3 GEOLOGY. The laying bare of an underlying rock or formation through the erosion of what lies above it. E19.

C. DARWIN The enormous power of denudation which the sea possesses.

■ **denudational** *adjective* of or pertaining to (geological) denudation E20. **deˈnudative** *adjective* having the property of denuding; causing (geological) denudation: L19.

denude /dɪˈnjuːd/ *verb*. LME.
[ORIGIN Latin *denudare*, from *de-* DE- 1 + *nudare* to bare, from *nudus* nude.]
1 *verb trans.* Make naked or bare; strip *of* clothing or covering. LME. ▸**b** *fig.* Strip, divest, deprive, (*of* any possession, attribute, etc.). L15. ▸**c** GEOLOGY. Of a natural agency: expose (a rock or formation) by the removal of overlying material. M19.

D. H. LAWRENCE The park was denuded of its timber. **b** A. BURGESS That wicked boy has denuded the larder of practically everything. W. S. CHURCHILL The Island he had left denuded of troops. **c** A. R. WALLACE Rapidly denuded by rain and rivers.

2 *verb intrans.* Divest oneself of a legal right etc. L17.

denumerable /dɪˈnjuːm(ə)rəb(ə)l/ *adjective*. E20.
[ORIGIN from late Latin *denumerare*: see DENUMERATION, -ABLE.]
MATH. Finite or countably infinite, enumerable; *spec.* able to be counted by one-to-one correspondence with the infinite set of all positive integers.
■ **denumeraˈbility** *noun* M20. **denumerably** *adverb* M20.

denumeration /dɪˌnjuːməˈreɪʃ(ə)n/ *noun*. Now *rare*. E17.
[ORIGIN from late Latin *denumerare*, from *de-* DE- 1 + *numerare* count out, enumerate: see -ATION.]
1 Enumeration; reckoning. E17.
2 LAW (now *hist.*). An immediate payment of money. E18.

denunciate /dɪˈnʌnsɪeɪt, -ʃɪ-/ *verb trans. & intrans.* L16.
[ORIGIN medieval Latin *denunciat-* for Latin *denuntiat-* pa. ppl stem of *denuntiare*: see DENOUNCE, -ATE[3].]
Denounce; inveigh openly (against).
■ **denunciative** *adjective* denunciatory E17.

denunciation /dɪˌnʌnsɪˈeɪʃ(ə)n/ *noun*. LME.
[ORIGIN Old French & mod. French *dénonciation* or Latin *denunciatio(n-)*, formed as DENUNCIATE: see -ATION.]
1 *gen.* (A) public announcement; (a) proclamation, declaration. *arch.* LME.

W. BLACKSTONE Why . . a denunciation of war ought always to precede the actual commencement of hostilities.

2 An accusation before a public prosecutor; a charge. LME.
3 (A) warning, (a) threatening announcement. M16.

W. WHISTON The prophet . . by the denunciation of miseries, weakened the alacrity of the multitude.

†**4** SCOTS LAW. The action or an act of denouncing a person as a rebel or outlaw. L16–L19.
5 (A) public condemnation, (an) invective. M19.

M. MEYER Kierkegaard's denunciation of state religion. G. PRIESTLAND Many proposals for action are little more than gestures of denunciation.

6 The action or an act of denouncing a treaty. L19.

denunciator /dɪˈnʌnsɪeɪtə, -ʃɪ-/ *noun*. L15.
[ORIGIN French *dénonciateur* or Latin *denunciator*, formed as DENUNCIATE: see -OR.]
A person who denounces or utters denunciations. Formerly, in CIVIL LAW, one who lodges a charge or complaint against another.
■ **denunciatory** *adjective* of or pertaining to denunciation; characterized by denouncing: E18.

denutrition /diːnjʊˈtrɪʃ(ə)n/ *noun*. Now *rare* or *obsolete*. M19.
[ORIGIN from DE- 3 + NUTRITION.]
MEDICINE. Degeneration of tissue arising from lack of nutrition. Also, treatment by deprivation of nourishment.

Denver boot /ˈdɛnvə buːt/ *noun phr.* *N. Amer.* M20.
[ORIGIN from the name of *Denver*, a city in Colorado, USA.]
A wheel clamp.

†**deny** *noun*. Also **denay**. LME.
[ORIGIN French *déni*, Old French *desni*, from stem of *dénier* DENY *verb*.]
1 (A) refusal of what is asked, offered, etc. LME–E17.
2 (A) contradiction of a statement; negation. M16–E17.

deny /dɪˈnʌɪ/ *verb trans.* Also †**denay**. ME.
[ORIGIN Old French *deni-* tonic stem of *deneier*, *denoier*, later (also mod.) *dénier*, from Latin *denegare*, from *de-* DE- 1 + *negare* say no, refuse.]
1 Contradict (a statement or allegation); declare to be untrue or untenable. ME.

HENRY FIELDING Jones could not deny the charge. W. CRUISE I beg leave to deny this to be law. S. BELLOW My client denies that he struck him. R. P. JHABVALA We have, I can't deny, had a lot of trouble with him.

2 LOGIC. Assert the contradictory of (a proposition). LME.
3 Refuse to admit the truth of (a doctrine etc.); refuse to admit the existence or reality of. LME.

ROBERT BURTON Many deny Witches at all. G. BERKELEY They who deny the Freedom and Immortality of the soul in effect deny its being.

4 Refuse to recognize or acknowledge (a person or thing) as having a certain character or certain claims; disown, disavow, repudiate. LME.

R. L. STEVENSON A man must not deny his manifest abilities, for that is to evade his obligations.

5 Withhold (a thing requested, claimed, or desired); refuse to give or grant. (Foll. by *to* a person, or with indirect obj.) LME. ▸**b** Refuse access to (a person sought). M17.

I. D'ISRAELI All the consolations of fame were denied him during his life. V. NABOKOV To bring that coffee to her, and then deny it until she had done her morning duty. *fig.*: J. BUTLER The known course of human things . . denies to virtue its full scope. **b** R. B. SHERIDAN He is . . in the house, though the servants are ordered to deny him.

6 Refuse the request or demand of (a person). Formerly also, reject (a candidate). LME. ▸†**b** Refuse admittance to (a visitor). L16–M18.

T. HARDY Don't refuse me, . . I shall think it hard if you deny me.

7 Refuse *to be* or *do*. *obsolete* exc. *Scot.* LME.
8 Refuse permission to or for; forbid (*to do*, *the doing of*). Now *rare*. LME.

SHAKES. *Tit. A.* One thing more, That womanhood denies my tongue to tell.

†**9** Refuse to take or accept. LME–E18.
10 *refl.* Refrain from the gratification of desire; be abstinent. LME.

W. S. MAUGHAM My mother . . denied herself so that I shouldn't go hungry.

■ **denyingly** *adverb* in a way that denies or refuses LME.

deobstruct /diːəbˈstrʌkt/ *verb trans.* M17.
[ORIGIN from DE- 3 + OBSTRUCT. Cf. medieval Latin *deobstruere*.]
Clear of obstruction; unblock.

†**deobstruent** *noun & adjective.* L17–M19.
[ORIGIN from DE- 3 + OBSTRUENT.]
(A medicine or substance) that clears obstructions by opening the natural passages or pores of the body.

deoch an doris /dɒx (ə)n ˈdɒrɪs, dɒk/ *noun phr. Scot. & Irish.* Also **doch an doris**. L17.
[ORIGIN Gaelic *deoch an doruis*, Irish *deoch an dorais* a drink at the door.]
A drink taken at parting, a stirrup cup.

deoculate /diːˈɒkjʊleɪt/ *verb trans. rare.* E17.
[ORIGIN from DE- 3 + Latin *oculus* eye + -ATE[3].]
Blind; put out the eyes of. Usu. in *pass.*

deodand /ˈdiːə(ʊ)dand/ *noun.* E16.
[ORIGIN Law French *deodande* from Anglo-Latin *deodanda*, *-um*, from Latin *Deo dandum* thing to be given to God (*Deus* god, *dare* give).]
Something to be given to God; *spec.* (LAW, now *hist.*) a thing forfeited to the Crown for a religious or charitable use, as having caused a human death; *loosely* a sum forfeited as the value of a deodand.

deodar /ˈdiːə(ʊ)dɑː/ *noun.* E19.
[ORIGIN Hindi *deodār* from Sanskrit *devadāru*.]
A cedar, *Cedrus deodara*, native to the Himalayas, which is used as a source of timber in the Indian subcontinent and is also planted as an ornamental elsewhere.

deodorant /dɪˈəʊd(ə)r(ə)nt/ *noun.* M19.
[ORIGIN formed as DEODORIZE + -ANT[1].]
A substance that removes or conceals unwanted odours; *esp.* a preparation applied to the skin to inhibit the odour of perspiration.

deodorize /dɪˈəʊdərʌɪz/ *verb trans.* Also **-ise**. M19.
[ORIGIN from DE- 3 + Latin *odor* ODOUR + -IZE.]
Destroy the odour of; remove or conceal the (unpleasant) odour of.
■ **deodoriˈzation** *noun* M19. **deodorizer** *noun* something that deodorizes, a deodorant M19.

Deo gratias /deɪəʊ ˈgrɑːtɪəs, ˈgrɑːʃɪəs/ *interjection.* L16.
[ORIGIN Latin = (we give) thanks to God.]
Thanks be to God.

deontic /dɪˈɒntɪk/ *noun & adjective.* M19.
[ORIGIN formed as DEONTOLOGY + -IC.]
▸ **A** *noun.* PHILOSOPHY. In *pl.* (treated as *sing.*). The branch of philosophy that deals with duty or obligations. M19.
▸ **B** *adjective.* PHILOSOPHY & LINGUISTICS. Of or relating to duty or obligation, or its linguistic expression. M20.

deontology /diːɒnˈtɒlədʒi/ *noun.* E19.
[ORIGIN from Greek *deont-* pres. ppl stem of *dei* it is right + -OLOGY.]
The science of duty or moral obligation; ethics.
■ **deontoˈlogical** *adjective* M19. **deontologist** *noun* M19.

deoperculate /diːə(ʊ)ˈpəːkjʊlət/ *adjective.* M17.
[ORIGIN from DE- 3 + OPERCULATE.]
†**1** Uncovered. *rare.* Only in M17.
2 BOTANY. Having shed the operculum; having an operculum that does not separate from the capsule. M19.

†**deoppilate** *verb trans. & intrans.* E17–E18.
[ORIGIN from DE- 3 + OPPILATE.]
MEDICINE. Remove an obstruction or obstructions (from).
■ †**deoppilation** *noun* the removal of obstructions M17–M19. †**deoppilative** *adjective & noun* (a medicine or drug) tending to remove obstructions E17–E18.

de-orbit /diːˈɔːbɪt/ *verb & noun.* M20.
[ORIGIN from DE- 3 + ORBIT *noun* or *verb*.]
▸ **A** *verb trans. & intrans.* (Cause to) leave or move out of orbit around the earth or other body. M20.
▸ **B** *noun.* A spacecraft's moving out of orbit. M20.

deordination /dɪˌɔːdɪˈneɪʃ(ə)n/ *noun.* Now *rare* or *obsolete.* L15.
[ORIGIN Late Latin *deordinatio(n-)*, from Latin *de-* DE- 3 + *ordinatio(n-)* ORDINATION.]
(A) departure from or violation of (esp. moral) order; disorder.

†**deosculation** *noun.* M17–L18.
[ORIGIN from Latin *deosculat-* pa. ppl stem of *deosculari* kiss warmly: see DE- 1, OSCULATION.]
(An act of) kissing.

Deo volente /ˌdeɪəʊ vɒˈlɛnteɪ/ *adverbial phr.* M18.
[ORIGIN Latin.]
God willing; if nothing prevents it.

deoxidate /diːˈɒksɪdeɪt/ *verb trans.* L18.
[ORIGIN from DE- 3 + OXIDATE.]
CHEMISTRY. = DEOXIDIZE.
■ **deoxiˈdation** *noun* L18.

deoxidize /diːˈɒksɪdʌɪz/ *verb trans.* Also **-ise**. L18.
[ORIGIN from DE- 3 + OXIDIZE.]
CHEMISTRY. Remove (esp. combined) oxygen from; reduce. Cf. DEOXIDATE, DEOXYGENATE.
■ **deoxidizer** *noun* a deoxidizing agent M19.

deoxy- /diːˈɒksi/ *combining form.* Also **desoxy-** /dɛˈsɒksi/.
[ORIGIN from DE- 3 + OXY-.]
Used in CHEMISTRY with the senses 'that has lost oxygen', 'that has fewer oxygen atoms'.
■ **deoxyˌcorticoˈsterone** *noun* (BIOCHEMISTRY) a corticosteroid hormone, $C_{21}H_{30}O_3$, involved in regulating the salt and water balance M20. **deoxyˈribose** *noun* (BIOCHEMISTRY) any of the isomeric sugars ($C_5H_{10}O_4$) derived from ribose by replacement of a hydroxyl group by a hydrogen atom; *spec.* (more fully *2-deoxyribose*) that isomer present in DNA: M20.

deoxygenate /diːˈɒksɪdʒəneɪt/ *verb trans.* L19.
[ORIGIN from DE- 3 + OXYGENATE.]
Remove (esp. free) oxygen from. Cf. DEOXIDATE, DEOXIDIZE.
■ **deoxygeˈnation** *noun* E19.

deoxyribonucleic /diːˌɒksɪrʌɪbəʊnjuːˈkleɪɪk, -ˈkliːɪk; -ˈnjuː-/ *adjective.* Also **desoxy-** /dɛˌsɒksɪ-/. M20.
[ORIGIN from DEOXYRIBOSE + NUCLEIC.]
BIOCHEMISTRY. ***deoxyribonucleic acid***, = DNA.
■ **deoxyribonuclease** *noun* = DNASE M20. **deoxyribonucleotide** *noun* a nucleotide containing deoxyribose M20.

dep. *abbreviation.*
1 Departs.
2 Deputy.

depaint /dɪˈpeɪnt/ *verb trans.* Long *arch. rare.* Pa. pple (earlier, *arch.*) **depaint**, **-ed**. ME.
[ORIGIN Orig. pa. pple, from Old French & mod. French *dépeint* pa. pple of *dépeindre* from Latin *depingere*: see DE- 1, PAINT *verb*. Cf. DEPEINCT, DEPICT.]
1 Represent in colours; paint; depict; delineate. Freq. in *pass.* ME.
2 Paint or decorate (as) with painted figures; paint or colour (a surface). Usu. in *pass.* ME.
3 Portray in words. Also foll. by *out*, *forth*. LME.
†**4** Stain. LME–E17.

depalatalization /diːˌpalət(ə)lʌɪˈzeɪʃ(ə)n/ *noun.* Also **-isation**. M20.
[ORIGIN from DE- 3 + PALATALIZATION.]
PHONETICS. Loss of palatalization.

depark /diːˈpɑːk/ *verb trans.* M16.
[ORIGIN from DE- 3 + PARK *noun*. Cf. French *déparquer* (earlier †*des-*).]
= DISPARK.

†**depart** *noun.* ME.
[ORIGIN Partly from Old French & mod. French *départ*, formed as DEPART *verb*; partly from DEPART *verb*.]
1 The act of departing, departure; parting; death. ME–M19.
2 CHEMISTRY. The separation of one substance from another. LME–M18.

depart /dɪˈpɑːt/ *verb.* ME.
[ORIGIN Old French & mod. French *départir* from Proto-Romance var. of Latin *dispertire* divide: see DE- 3, PART *verb*.]
▸ **I** Divide or part.
†**1** *verb trans. & intrans.* Separate into two or more parts. ME–L18.
†**2** *verb trans.* Divide or part among persons etc.; distribute; occas., impart, bestow. ME–M17. ▸**b** *verb intrans.* Share or partake (*in* a thing, *with* a person). LME–M16.
†**3** *verb trans.* Sunder; separate *from* another (*lit. & fig.*). ME–L17. ▸**b** *verb intrans.* Separate, make separation. LME–L15. ▸**c** *verb intrans.* CHEMISTRY. Separate a metal from an alloy or solution. E–M18.

CAXTON That god hath ioyned man may not departe.

†**4** *verb trans.* Break off or dissolve (a connection etc.). LME–L16. ▸**b** *verb intrans.* Of a connection etc.: be broken off or dissolved. LME–E16.

MALORY Ye departed the loue bitwene me and my wyf.

▸ **II** Go apart or away.
†**5** *verb intrans.* Part or separate from each other; take leave of each other. ME–M17.
6 *verb intrans.* Go away (*from*); take one's leave; (esp. of public transport) set out, start, leave, (*for*). Now chiefly *formal* or *literary*. ME. ▸†**b** Go away *to*, *into*; make one's way. LME–E17. ▸**c** Leave this world, decease, die, pass away. Now chiefly as DEPARTED *adjective* 3. E16.

A. E. HOUSMAN And watch them depart on the way. *Observer* The train about to depart from platform one. **b** AV *Matt.* 2:12 They departed into their owne countrey another way.

7 *verb trans.* Go away from, leave, forsake. Now chiefly in ***depart this life*** below. ME.

T. KEIGHTLEY The clergy were ordered to depart the kingdom.

8 *verb intrans.* Diverge, deviate, withdraw, desist, (*from* a course of action etc.). LME.

HOBBES A design to depart from the worship of God. H. L. MENCKEN Their speculations tend . . to depart from the field of true science. J. ADAMSON One matinee performance at which they had departed from the script.

†**9** *verb trans.* Send away, dismiss. L15–E17.
– PHRASES: **depart from life**, **depart from this life**, **depart this life** (now chiefly *formal* or *literary*) die. †**depart with** part with, give up, give away.
■ †**departable**, **-ible** *adjective* LME–M18.

departed /dɪˈpɑːtɪd/ *adjective & noun.* LME.
[ORIGIN from DEPART *verb* + -ED[1].]
▸ **A** *adjective.* †**1** Divided into parts. Only in LME.
†**2** Separated, parted; cut off from the main body, schismatic. LME–M17.
3 That has departed by death; deceased. E16.

ADDISON Magicians, Demons, and departed Spirits.

4 Past, bygone. M16.

JOHN SAUNDERS Antiquity and departed greatness.

▸ **B** *absol.* as *noun.* A deceased person; *pl.* deceased people as a class, *the* dead. E18.

E. LONGFORD If the living Albert kept Queen Victoria and Disraeli apart, the dear departed brought them together.

département *noun* see DEPARTMENT.

departer /dɪˈpɑːtə/ *noun*[1]. LME.
[ORIGIN from DEPART *verb* + -ER[1]. In sense 2 perh. from French †*départeur* (Old French *departeōr*).]
†**1** A divider, a distributor; a discerner. Only in LME.
2 A person who departs or goes away. Formerly also, a seceder. L16.

†**departer** *noun*[2]. E16–M18.
[ORIGIN Use as noun of Anglo-Norman inf. *departer* = Old French & mod. French *départir* DEPART *verb*: see -ER[4].]
= DEPARTURE *noun* 2.

department /dɪˈpɑːtm(ə)nt/ *noun.* In sense 4 also ***département*** /departəmɑ̃ (*pl. same*)/. LME.
[ORIGIN Old French & mod. French *département*, formed as DEPART *verb*: see -MENT.]
†**1** Division, partition, distribution. *rare.* LME–L17.
†**2** Departure; separation; leave-taking, withdrawal; decease. L15–L17.
3 A separate part of a complex whole or organized system, a branch, *esp.* of municipal or state administration, of a university, school, or college, or of a shop; *loosely*, an area of (specialist) activity. M18.

C. ISHERWOOD To find my way through departments of underwear, outfitting, . . sport and cutlery. H. BELLOC Lombroso's own department of charlatanry was to attack Christian morals.

4 An administrative district in France and some other countries. L18.
– COMB.: **department store** a large shop supplying many kinds of goods from various departments.

departmental /diːpɑːtˈmɛnt(ə)l/ *adjective.* L18.
[ORIGIN from DEPARTMENT + -AL[1].]
Of or pertaining to a department.
departmental store = *DEPARTMENT store*.
■ **departmentalism** *noun* adherence to departmental methods or structure M19. **departmentaliˈzation** *noun* division into departments M19. **departmentalize** *verb trans.* divide into departments L19. **departmentally** *adverb* L19.

departure /dɪˈpɑːtʃə/ *noun.* LME.
[ORIGIN Old French *departeüre*, formed as DEPART *verb*: see -URE.]
1 The action of going away; *arch.* decease, death. LME.

S. JOHNSON The loss of our friends . . impresses . . upon us the necessity of our own departure. SAKI The farewell dinner . . in honour of her son's departure.

2 LAW. A change in pleading from the ground taken by the same party in an earlier plea. L15.
†**3** Separation, severance, parting. Also, a boundary separating two areas, a division. E16–E18.
4 The action of setting out or starting on a journey; *esp.* the (scheduled) starting of a train, aeroplane, or public transport vehicle; the starting or setting out on a course of action or thought. M16.

OED The Booking Office is open 15 minutes before the departure of each train. J. BARZUN The free public high school of 1900 was a bold departure.

new departure a fresh start, the beginning of a new course of procedure.

D

5 *NAUTICAL.* The amount of a ship's change of longitude. Also, the bearing of an object on the coast, taken at the start of a voyage, from which the dead reckoning begins. **M17.**
6 Withdrawal, divergence, deviation, (*from* a path, course, or standard). **L17.**

H. J. S. MAINE Partial and local departures from the Brehon Law were common all over Ancient Ireland.

7 In full ***departure lounge***. An area in an airport in which passengers wait immediately prior to boarding. **M20.**

D

depascent /dɪˈpas(ə)nt/ *adjective. rare.* **M17.**
[ORIGIN Latin *depascent-* pres. ppl stem of *depascere* eat up, consume, from *de-* DE- 1 + *pascere* feed, pasture: see -ENT.]
Consuming.

depasture /diːˈpɑːstʃə, -tjə/ *verb.* **E16.**
[ORIGIN from DE- 1 + PASTURE *verb*.]
1 *verb trans.* Of cattle: consume the produce of (land) by grazing on it; use for pasturage. **E16.**
2 *verb intrans.* Of cattle: graze. **M16.**
3 *verb trans.* Put (cattle) to graze; pasture, feed, (cattle). **E18.**
4 *verb trans.* Of land: give pasturage to (cattle). **E19.**
■ **depasturage** *noun* the consumption of pasture by grazing animals; the right of pasture: **M18.**

†**depatriate** *verb intrans.* **L17–L18.**
[ORIGIN medieval Latin *depatriat-* pa. ppl stem of *depatriare* (also *dis-*) leave home, from Latin *de-* DE- 3 + *patria* fatherland: see -ATE[3].]
Leave or renounce one's native country; expatriate oneself.

depauperate /dɪˈpɔːp(ə)rət/ *adjective.* **LME.**
[ORIGIN medieval Latin *depauperatus* pa. pple, formed as DEPAUPERATE *verb*: see -ATE[2].]
1 *gen.* Made poor, impoverished. Long *obsolete* exc. *Scot. rare.* **LME.**
2 Chiefly *BOTANY & ZOOLOGY.* Imperfectly developed, stunted; (of a flora or fauna) lacking in numbers or variety of species. **M19.**

depauperate /dɪˈpɔːpəreɪt/ *verb trans.* **M16.**
[ORIGIN medieval Latin *depauperat-* pa. ppl stem of *depauperare*, from Latin *de-* DE- 1 + *pauperare* make poor, from *pauper* poor: see -ATE[3].]
Make poor, impoverish; reduce in quality, vigour, or capacity.
■ **depauperated** *adjective* = DEPAUPERATE *adjective* **M17.** **depaupeˈration** *noun* [medieval Latin *depauperatio(n-)*] **M17.**

depauperize /diːˈpɔːpərʌɪz/ *verb*[1] *trans.* Also **-ise**. **M19.**
[ORIGIN from DE- 3 + PAUPERIZE.]
= DISPAUPERIZE.

depauperize /dɪˈpɔːpərʌɪz/ *verb*[2] *trans. rare.* **L19.**
[ORIGIN from DE- 1 + PAUPERIZE, after Latin *depauperare*: see DEPAUPERATE *verb*.]
Depauperate, pauperize.
■ **depauperiˈzation** *noun* **M19.**

dépaysé /depeize/ *adjective.* Fem. ***-ée***. **E20.**
[ORIGIN French = (removed) from one's own country.]
Removed from one's habitual surroundings.

†**depeinct** *verb trans.* Also **depinct**. **L16–L17.**
[ORIGIN Intermediate forms between DEPAINT and DEPICT: cf. Old French *depeinct*, Italian *depinto*.]
= DEPICT.

depel /dɪˈpɛl/ *verb trans.* Long *rare.* Also **-ll**. Infl. **-ll-**. **M16.**
[ORIGIN Latin *depellere* drive out, from *de-* DE- 1 + *pellere* drive.]
Drive away, expel.

†**depencil** *verb trans.* Infl. **-l(l)-**. **L16–M18.**
[ORIGIN from DE- 1 + PENCIL *verb*.]
Write with a pencil or a brush, inscribe, depict.

depend /dɪˈpɛnd/ *verb intrans.* **LME.**
[ORIGIN Old French & mod. French *dépendre* from Proto-Romance var. of Latin *dependere*, from *de-* DE- 1 + *pendere*: cf. PEND *verb*[3].]
1 Hang down, be suspended *from*. Now *literary.* **LME.**

R. LEHMANN From one hand depended a meagre trail of botanical specimens.

†**2** Wait in suspense or expectation *on*, *upon*. **LME–E18.**

DRYDEN The hearer on the speaker's mouth depends.

3 Be in suspense, be undetermined; be waiting for settlement; be pending. Chiefly as ***depending*** *ppl adjective.* **LME.**

T. HUTCHINSON Whilst these disputes . . were depending, the . . Indians made attacks.

4 Be attached, as a result or consequence is to its condition or cause; be contingent, be conditioned. Foll. by (*up*)*on*, †*of*, (colloq.) *interrog. clause*, or *absol.* **LME.**

SLOAN WILSON The broadcasting company's decision might depend on the recommendation Dick gave him. K. LAFFAN Depends how you look at it, sir. R. HAYMAN Depending on whether you viewed it from the plain . . or from the woods, the castle presented different aspects. *Observer* Whether there is inside information . . or not, depends.

that depends the question can only be answered conditionally.
5 Foll. by (*up*)*on*, †*of*: belong to or be connected with as something subordinate; be grammatically dependent on. **LME.**

T. FULLER Hereupon a story depends.

6 Rely in mind, reckon, or count confidently *on* or *upon*. **E16.** ▸**b** Be sure or confident *that*. *arch. colloq.* **E18.**

K. A. PORTER The kind of man a girl may depend on to be a gentleman in whatever circumstances. A. PRICE I'll have a damn good try . . . You can depend on that. **b** J. C. MORISON We may depend that a swift blight would have shrivelled his labours.

7 Foll. by *on*, *upon*: rest entirely on for maintenance, support, or other requirement; be obliged to use; be unable to do without. **M16.**

A. E. STEVENSON We depend on our forests for vast and constantly increasing supplies of . . essential timber products. D. BAGLEY I always depend on my intuition and it rarely lets me down. P. FITZGERALD It was quite wrong to come to depend too much upon one's children.

†**8** Impend. *rare.* **E17–E18.**
■ **depender** *noun* †(*a*) *rare* a protector, a supporter; †(*b*) (chiefly *Scot.*) a dependant; (*c*) *rare* a person who depends or relies *on* something: **L15.**

dependable /dɪˈpɛndəb(ə)l/ *adjective.* **M18.**
[ORIGIN from DEPEND + -ABLE.]
Able to be depended on; trustworthy, reliable.
■ **dependaˈbility** *noun* **E20.** **dependableness** *noun* **M19.** **dependably** *adverb* **M19.**

dependance *noun* see DEPENDENCE *noun*.

dependancy *noun* see DEPENDENCY.

dependant /dɪˈpɛnd(ə)nt/ *noun.* Also **-ent**. **LME.**
[ORIGIN French *dépendant* pres. pple of *dépendre*: see DEPEND, -ANT[1], -ENT.]
†**1** Something subordinately attached, belonging to, or connected with, something else; a dependency. **LME–M19.**
2 A person who depends on another for maintenance or position; a retainer, a servant, a subordinate. **L16.**

dependence /dɪˈpɛnd(ə)ns/ *noun.* Also **-ance**. **LME.**
[ORIGIN Old French & mod. French *dépendance*, formed as DEPEND: see -ANCE, -ENCE.]
†**1** The action of hanging down; something that hangs down. *rare.* **LME–L17.**
2 The relation of having existence hanging upon, or conditioned by, the existence of something else; the fact of depending *on* another thing or person; the state or condition of being dependent. **LME.**

J. TYNDALL The chain of dependence which runs throughout creation. N. CHOMSKY The dependence of the American economy on Third World resources.

3 = DEPENDENCY 4. Now *rare.* **M16.**

E. HEMINGWAY It had been a dependence of the Grand Hotel—but now it was its own hotel.

4 †**a** A quarrel or affair of honour awaiting settlement. **L16–E19.** ▸**b** The condition of waiting for settlement, now esp. for the resolution of a legal action. **E17.**
5 The condition of a dependant; inability to do without someone or something; subjection, subordination. **E17.**

J. MORTIMER Sudden freedom, growing up, the end of dependence.

6 The condition of waiting in faith or expectation; reliance, confident trust. **E17.** ▸**b** An object of confidence or trust; something (to be) relied on. Now *rare* or *obsolete.* **M18.**

B. JOWETT Living . . in dependence on the will of God.

dependency /dɪˈpɛnd(ə)nsi/ *noun.* Also ***-ancy**. **L16.**
[ORIGIN formed as DEPENDENCE: see -ANCY, -ENCY.]
1 = DEPENDENCE 2. **L16.**

SHAKES. *Meas. for M.* The oddest frame of sense, such a dependency of thing on thing, As e'er I heard.

2 = DEPENDENCE 5. **L16.**

A. STORR Every child, if it is to become an adult in its own right, has to escape from dependency. *Times* Self-generated and minus any dependency on government gratuities.

†**3** = DEPENDENCE 6. **L16–E17.**
4 A dependent or subordinate thing; *esp.* a country or province controlled by another. Formerly also, a body of dependants, a household establishment. **E17.**

G. MURRAY An Empire, in which Athens . . dictated the foreign policy, while the dependencies paid tribute for their protection.

†**5** = DEPENDENCE 4a. **E17–E19.**

dependent *noun* var. of DEPENDANT *noun*.

dependent /dɪˈpɛnd(ə)nt/ *adjective.* **LME.**
[ORIGIN formed as DEPENDANT *noun*.]
1 Hanging down, pendent. **LME.**

J. MORSE A regular rock, from the upper part of which are dependent many excrescences.

2 Contingent on or determined or conditioned by something else. (Foll. by *on*, *upon*.) **LME.**

H. POWER Effects dependent upon the same . . Causes.

dependent variable *MATH.*: having a value depending on that of another variable.
3 Resting entirely on someone or something for maintenance, support, or other requirement; obliged to use something; unable to do without someone or something, esp. a drug; maintained at another's cost. (Foll. by *on*, *upon*.) **LME.**

DAY LEWIS Trustfully dependent upon the grown-ups.

4 Subordinate, subject; *GRAMMAR* (of a grammatical unit) in a subordinate relation to another grammatical unit. (Foll. by *on*, *upon*.) **E17.**

ISAAC TAYLOR The temper of mind which is proper to a dependant and subordinate agent.

■ **dependently** *adverb* **M17.**

depeople /dɪˈpiːp(ə)l/ *verb trans. arch.* **E17.**
[ORIGIN French *dépeupler*, from *dé-* DE- 3 + *peuple* PEOPLE *noun*. Cf. DISPEOPLE.]
Depopulate.

†**deperdit** *adjective & noun.* Also **-ite**. **E17.**
[ORIGIN Latin *deperditus* pa. pple of *deperdere* destroy, ruin, from *de-* DE- 1 + *perdere* destroy, lose.]
▸ **A** *adjective.* Lost, abandoned. **E–M17.**
▸ **B** *noun.* Something lost or perished. Only in **E19.**

deperdition /diːpəːˈdɪʃ(ə)n/ *noun.* Now *rare* or *obsolete.* **E17.**
[ORIGIN French *déperdition*, formed as DEPERDIT: see -ITION.]
Loss, waste, destruction by wasting away.

deperition /dɛpəˈrɪʃ(ə)n/ *noun. rare.* **L18.**
[ORIGIN from DE- 1 + Latin *perire* perish + -ITION, perh. after DEPERDITION.]
Perishing, complete wasting away.

deperm /diːˈpəːm/ *verb trans.* **M20.**
[ORIGIN from DE- 3 + abbreviation of *permanent (magnetism)*.]
Demagnetize (a ship).

depersonalize /diːˈpəːs(ə)n(ə)lʌɪz/ *verb trans.* Also **-ise**. **M19.**
[ORIGIN from DE- 3 + PERSONALIZE.]
Deprive of personality; make impersonal.
■ **depersonaliˈzation** *noun* the action of depersonalizing; the fact of being depersonalized; *PSYCHIATRY* a pathological state in which one's thoughts and feelings seem unreal or not to belong to oneself: **E20.**

depetal /diːˈpɛt(ə)l/ *verb trans.* Infl. **-ll-**, ***-l-**. **M20.**
[ORIGIN from DE- 3 + PETAL.]
Remove the petals from.

dephlegmate /dɪˈflɛgmeɪt/ *verb trans. obsolete* exc. *hist.* **M17.**
[ORIGIN from Latin *de-* DE- 3 + *phlegma* PHLEGM: see -ATE[3].]
CHEMISTRY. Free from phlegm or watery matter, rectify.
■ **dephlegˈmation** *noun* **M17.** ˈ**dephlegmator** *noun* an apparatus for dephlegmation **E19.**

dephlogisticate /diːfləˈdʒɪstɪkeɪt/ *verb trans.* **L18.**
[ORIGIN from DE- 3 + PHLOGISTICATE.]
1 *CHEMISTRY* (now *hist.*). Deprive of 'phlogiston'. **L18.**
dephlogisticated air oxygen (orig. so analysed).
†**2** Relieve of inflammation. **M–L19.**
■ **dephlogistiˈcation** *noun* **L18.**

dephosphorize /diːˈfɒsfərʌɪz/ *verb trans.* Also **-ise**. **L19.**
[ORIGIN from DE- 3 + PHOSPHORIZE.]
Free (esp. steel) from phosphorus.
■ **dephosphoriˈzation** *noun* **L19.**

dephosphorylate /diːfɒsˈfɒrɪleɪt/ *verb trans.* **E20.**
[ORIGIN from DE- 3 + PHOSPHORYLATE *verb*.]
CHEMISTRY. Remove a phosphate group from (a compound), esp. (*BIOCHEMISTRY*) enzymatically.
■ **dephosphoryˈlation** *noun* **M20.**

depict /dɪˈpɪkt/ *verb trans.* **LME.**
[ORIGIN Latin *depict-* pa. ppl stem of *depingere* portray, from *de-* DE- 1 + *pingere* paint. Cf. DEPAINT, DEPEINCT.]
1 Portray or represent (as if) in colours or in drawing, painting, or sculpture. **LME.**

D. LODGE The stained-glass windows . . that depict Scenes from the life of Our Lady. B. PYM Faded sepia photographs depicting groups of country people.

2 Portray or represent in words; describe graphically. **M18.**

JOHN BROOKE King George has been depicted as a neurotic and unstable character. M. ESSLIN Plays depicting a . . brutal nightmare world.

■ **depicter**, **-or** *noun* **M19.** **depiction** *noun* [Latin *depictio(n-)*] the action of depicting; painted representation; graphic description: **L17.** **depictive** *adjective* having the quality or function of depicting **E19.**

depicture /dɪˈpɪktʃə/ *noun.* **E16.**
[ORIGIN formed as DEPICT + -URE.]
(A) depiction.

depicture /dɪˈpɪktʃə/ *verb trans.* **L16.**
[ORIGIN from DE- 1 + PICTURE *verb*.]
1 = DEPICT. **L16.**
2 Picture to one's own mind; imagine. **L18.**
■ **depicturement** *noun* **M19.**

depigment /diːˈpɪgm(ə)nt/ *verb trans.* **E20.**
[ORIGIN from DE- 3 + PIGMENT *noun*.]
Deprive of pigment; reduce the pigmentation of. Chiefly as ***depigmented*** *ppl adjective.*
■ ˌ**depigmenˈtation** *noun* loss or deficiency of pigment **L19.**

depilate /ˈdɛpɪleɪt/ *verb trans.* M16.
[ORIGIN Latin *depilat-* pa. ppl stem of *depilare*, from *de-* DE- 1 + *pilare* deprive of hair, from *pilus* hair: see -ATE[3].]
Remove the hair from.

depilation /dɛpɪˈleɪʃ(ə)n/ *noun*. LME.
[ORIGIN Latin *depilatio(n-)*, formed as DEPILATE: see -ATION.]
1 The action or an act of stripping of hair; the condition of being without hair. LME.
†**2** (An act of) pillage. Only in 17.

depilatory /dɪˈpɪlət(ə)ri/ *adjective & noun*. E17.
[ORIGIN Latin *depilatorius*, formed as DEPILATE: see -ORY[2].]
► **A** *adjective*. Having the property of removing hair. E17.
► **B** *noun*. A depilatory agent or substance. E17.

depilous /ˈdɛpɪləs/ *adjective*. M17.
[ORIGIN from Latin *depilis*, from *de-* DE- 1 + *pilus* hair: see -OUS.]
Deprived of hair; without hair.

†**depinct** *verb* var. of DEPEINCT.

deplace /dɪˈpleɪs/ *verb trans. rare*. M19.
[ORIGIN French *déplacer*, from *dé-* DE- 3 + *placer* to place.]
= DISPLACE.

deplane /diːˈpleɪn/ *verb*. E20.
[ORIGIN from DE- 3 + PLANE *noun*[4].]
1 *verb intrans*. Disembark from an aeroplane. E20.
2 *verb trans*. Remove from an aeroplane. M20.

deplete /dɪˈpliːt/ *adjective*. L19.
[ORIGIN Latin *depletus* pa. pple of *deplere*: see DEPLETE *verb*.]
Emptied out, exhausted (*of* contents).

deplete /dɪˈpliːt/ *verb*. E19.
[ORIGIN Latin *deplet-* pa. ppl stem of *deplere* empty out, from *de-* DE- 3 + base of *plenus* full.]
1 *verb trans. & intrans.* MEDICINE (now *rare* or *obsolete*). Empty or relieve (the bodily system, blood vessels) when overcharged, as by bleeding or purgatives. E19.
2 *verb trans*. Deprive of contents or stocks; empty out, exhaust; reduce the numbers or quantity of. M19.

A. E. STEVENSON As . . higher grade . . mineral resources are depleted, the costs of extraction . . go up. A. FRASER This royal family had recently been depleted by two deaths. V. ACKLAND I was feeling utterly depleted and drained.

depleted uranium uranium from which most of the fissile isotope uranium-235 has been removed, used esp. in very dense alloys for armour-piercing shells.
■ **depleter** *noun* M19. **depletive**, **depletory** *adjectives* (MEDICINE) characterized by or causing depletion M19.

depletion /dɪˈpliːʃ(ə)n/ *noun*. M17.
[ORIGIN French *déplétion* or late Latin *depletio(n-)* (earlier *depletura*) blood-letting, formed as DEPLETE *verb*: see -ION.]
1 The action of depleting; the condition of being depleted; the emptying of contents; exhaustion; an instance of this. M17.

J. M. KEYNES The depletion of the surplus stocks will have an offsetting effect on the amount by which investment increases. T. WILLIAMS He holds the bottle to the light to observe its depletion.

2 MEDICINE. The emptying or relieving of overfilled organs or cavities in the body. Now *rare* or *obsolete*. M18.
– COMB.: **depletion allowance** *US* a tax concession allowable to a company whose normal business activities (esp. oil extraction) reduce the value of its own assets.

deplorable /dɪˈplɔːrəb(ə)l/ *adjective*. E17.
[ORIGIN French *déplorable* or late Latin *deplorabilis*, from *deplorare*: see DEPLORE, -ABLE.]
To be deplored, lamentable, regrettable, wretched. Now usu., objectionable, scandalous, exceedingly bad.

W. ROBERTSON The people beheld the deplorable situation of their sovereign with insensibility. P. G. WODEHOUSE Odd . . how often the noblest girls had these deplorable brothers. L. MACNEICE He often writes badly—most of his verse is deplorable.

■ **deploraˈbility** *noun* M19. **deplorableness** *noun* M17. **deplorably** *adverb* M17.

deploration /diːplɔːˈreɪʃ(ə)n/ *noun*. Now *rare*. L15.
[ORIGIN Latin *deploratio(n-)*, from *deplorat-* pa. ppl stem of *deplorare*: see DEPLORE, -ATION.]
The action of deploring; (a) lamentation.

deplore /dɪˈplɔː/ *verb*. M16.
[ORIGIN Old French & mod. French *déplorer* or Italian *deplorare* from Latin *deplorare*, from *de-* DE- 1 + *plorare* wail, bewail.]
1 *verb trans*. Weep for, bewail, lament; grieve over, regret deeply. Now usu., regard as scandalous, feel or express strong disapproval of. M16. ►†**b** Give up as hopeless. *rare*. M16–E18. ►†**c** Tell with grief. *rare* (Shakes.). Only in E17.

H. F. CARY He . . must aye deplore With unavailing penitence his crime. D. MURPHY Twice a week Mrs Mansfield called to drink tea . . and deplore the appalling inroads being made by democracy on good manners. **b** W. CONGREVE A true Poetick State we had deplor'd.

†**2** *verb intrans*. Lament, mourn. M17–L18.
■ **deplorer** *noun* L17. **deploringly** *adverb* in a deploring manner M19.

deploy /dɪˈplɔɪ/ *verb & noun*. L15.
[ORIGIN French *déployer* from Latin *displicare* unfold (later also, explain), also late Latin *deplicare* unfold, explain, from *de-*, *dis-* (see DE-) + *plicare* fold.]
► **A** *verb*. †**1** *verb trans*. Unfold, display. Only in L15.
2 *verb trans*. **a** MILITARY. Spread out (troops etc.) to form an extended line instead of a column; bring (armaments, men, etc.) into position for action. L18. ►**b** *gen*. Bring into or position for effective action, make good use of. M19.

a E. HEATH We . . deployed our guns on the hills close to Caen. D. FRASER The 18th Division was already deployed in Picardy. **b** E. BOWEN He was an excellent match, and . . the cream of the young lady visitors . . must have been deployed for him. M. HUNTER The form of writing that best deploys his particular talent. H. WILSON The arguments he will be deploying.

3 *verb intrans*. Chiefly MILITARY. (Of troops etc.) spread out in line; take up positions for action. L18.

R. GRAVES John's men . . could not deploy, because of the narrowness of the defile.

► **B** *noun*. MILITARY. The action or an act of deploying someone or something. L18.
■ **deployable** *adjective* M20. **deployment** *noun* the action or an act of deploying someone or something; a force etc. deployed: L18.

deplumate /dɪˈpluːmət/ *adjective*. *rare*. LME.
[ORIGIN medieval Latin *deplumatus* pa. pple of *deplumare*: see DEPLUME, -ATE[2].]
Stripped of feathers, deplumed.
■ Also **deplumated** *adjective* E18.

deplumation /diːplʊˈmeɪʃ(ə)n/ *noun*. E17.
[ORIGIN French *déplumation*, or from DEPLUME + -ATION.]
The action of depluming; the condition of being deplumed; loss of feathers; *fig*. loss of honour, wealth, etc.

deplume /dɪˈpluːm/ *verb trans*. LME.
[ORIGIN French *déplumer*, Old French *desplumer* or medieval Latin *deplumare*, from Latin *de-* DE- 3 + *plumare* PLUME *verb*.]
1 Strip (a bird etc.) of feathers; pluck the feathers off. LME.
2 *fig*. Strip or deprive of honour, ornament, wealth, etc. M17.

depoeticize /diːpəʊˈɛtɪsʌɪz/ *verb trans*. Also **-ise**. E19.
[ORIGIN from DE- 3 + POETICIZE.]
Deprive of poetic character.
■ Also **deˈpoetize** *verb trans*. M19.

depolarize /diːˈpəʊlərʌɪz/ *verb trans*. Also **-ise**. E19.
[ORIGIN from DE- 3 + POLARIZE.]
Chiefly PHYSICS. Reduce or remove the polarization or polarity of.
■ **depolariˈzation** *noun* E19. **depolarizer** *noun* a device for depolarizing light etc. M19.

depolish /diːˈpɒlɪʃ/ *verb trans*. L19.
[ORIGIN from DE- 3 + POLISH *verb* or *noun*[1].]
Remove the polish from; deprive of polish.

depoliticize /diːpəˈlɪtɪsʌɪz/ *verb trans*. Also **-ise**. M20.
[ORIGIN from DE- 3 + POLITICIZE.]
Make non-political; remove from political activity or influence.
■ **depoliticiˈzation** *noun* E20.

depollute /diːpəˈluːt, -ˈljuːt/ *verb trans*. M20.
[ORIGIN from DE- 3 + POLLUTE *verb*.]
Cleanse of (environmental) pollution.

depolymerize /diːˈpɒlɪmərʌɪz/ *verb trans. & intrans.* Also **-ise**. L19.
[ORIGIN from DE- 3 + POLYMERIZE.]
CHEMISTRY. (Cause to) break down into monomers or other smaller units.
■ **depolymeriˈzation** *noun* L19.

depone /dɪˈpəʊn/ *verb*. Chiefly *Scot*. LME.
[ORIGIN Latin *deponere* lay aside, put down, (in medieval Latin) testify, from *de-* DE- 1 + *ponere* to place.]
1 *verb trans. & intrans*. State, declare, or testify on oath in court; depose. (Foll. by *that*, *to*.) LME.
†**2** *verb trans*. Lay down (a burden, an office). M16–M19.
■ †**deponer** *noun* a person who depones, a deponent (DEPONENT *noun* 2) M16–M18.

deponent /dɪˈpəʊnənt/ *adjective & noun*. LME.
[ORIGIN Latin *deponent-* pres. ppl stem of *deponere*: see DEPONE, -ENT.]
► **A** *adjective*. GRAMMAR. Of a verb: passive (in Latin) or middle (in Greek) in form, but active in sense. LME.
► **B** *noun*. **1** A deponent verb. M16.
2 A person who makes a deposition under oath; a person who gives written testimony or makes an affidavit for use in court etc. M16.
– NOTE: Deponent verbs were so called from the notion that they had laid aside a passive sense. In fact they were orig. reflexive.

depopularize /diːˈpɒpjʊlərʌɪz/ *verb trans*. Also **-ise**. M19.
[ORIGIN from DE- 3 + POPULARIZE.]
Deprive of popularity; make unpopular.

depopulate /diːˈpɒpjʊlət/ *ppl adjective* (orig. *pa. pple*). Now *arch*. or *poet*. M16.
[ORIGIN Latin *depopulatus* pa. pple, formed as DEPOPULATE *verb*: see -ATE[2].]
Laid waste; deprived (wholly or partly) of inhabitants.

depopulate /diːˈpɒpjʊleɪt/ *verb*. M16.
[ORIGIN Latin *depopulat-* pa. ppl stem of *depopulare*, *-ari* ravage, from *de-* DE- 1 + *populare*, *-ari* (from *populus* people) lay waste, (in medieval Latin) depopulate: see -ATE[3].]
†**1** *verb trans*. Ravage, plunder, lay waste. M16–L17.
†**2** *verb trans*. Reduce or lessen the number of; thin out. M16–L18.
3 *verb trans*. Reduce the population of; deprive (wholly or partially) of inhabitants. L16. ►**b** *verb intrans*. Become less populous. M18.

J. CHILD The late Plague, which did much depopulate this Kingdom. F. SPENCE Forests and valleys were . . depopulated of game.

†**4** *verb trans*. Destroy, cut off. L16–M17.
■ **depopulator** *noun* [Latin] †(**a**) a devastator; (**b**) a person or agent that reduces the population of a district etc.: LME.

D

depopulation /diːˌpɒpjʊˈleɪʃ(ə)n/ *noun*. LME.
[ORIGIN Late Latin *depopulatio(n-)*, formed as DEPOPULATE *verb*: see -ATION.]
†**1** Laying waste, devastation, ravaging. LME–E19.
2 Reduction of population; the action or process of depriving of inhabitants; an instance of this. LME. ►**b** Depopulated condition. M17.

†**deport** *noun*. L15.
[ORIGIN Old French *de(s)port* diversion, pleasure, etc., formed as DEPORT *verb*[1] or DISPORT *verb*.]
1 = DISPORT *noun*. Only in L15.
2 Behaviour, deportment. L15–M18.

deport /dɪˈpɔːt/ *verb*[1]. L15.
[ORIGIN Old French *deporter*, from *de-* DE- 1 + *porter* carry, PORT *verb*[1].]
†**1** *verb trans*. Bear with; treat with consideration. *rare*. Only in L15.
†**2** *verb intrans. & refl*. Abstain, forbear. L15–E17.
3 *refl*. Bear or conduct oneself (in a specified manner). Now *rare*. L16.

deport /dɪˈpɔːt/ *verb*[2] *trans*. M17.
[ORIGIN French *déporter* from Latin *deportare* from *de-* DE- 1 + *portare* carry.]
Carry away, remove; *esp*. remove into exile, banish, expel from a country.

A. BRINK Undesirable immigrant. Promptly deported.

■ **deportable** *adjective* liable to or punishable by deportation L19. **deportee** /diːpɔːˈtiː/ *noun* a person who is or has been deported L19.

deportation /diːpɔːˈteɪʃ(ə)n/ *noun*. L16.
[ORIGIN Late Latin *deportatio(n-)*, from Latin *deportat-* pa. ppl stem of *deportare*: see DEPORT *verb*[2], -ATION.]
The action of carrying away; *esp*. (an instance of) forcible removal of a person from a country, banishment.

deportment /dɪˈpɔːtm(ə)nt/ *noun*. E17.
[ORIGIN Old French & mod. French *déportement*, formed as DEPORT *verb*[1]: see -MENT.]
1 *sing*. & (formerly) in *pl*. Manner of conducting oneself; general behaviour. Now chiefly *N. Amer*. E17.

P. MCGILLIGAN She had stiffed him too many times with her unprofessional deportment.

2 The way a person stands and walks, esp. as an element of etiquette. M17.

J. GALSWORTHY Swithin drew his heels together, his deportment ever admirable.

deposal /dɪˈpəʊz(ə)l/ *noun*. LME.
[ORIGIN Prob. from Anglo-Norman *deposaille*, formed as DEPOSE: see -AL[1].]
= DEPOSITION 2.

depose /dɪˈpəʊz/ *verb*. ME.
[ORIGIN Old French & mod. French *déposer*, based on Latin *deponere* (see DEPONE *verb*) but re-formed after Latin pa. pple *depositus* and Old French & mod. French *poser*: see POSE *verb*[1].]
1 *verb trans*. Remove from office or authority; *esp*. dethrone. ME.

P. USTINOV The boyars promptly deposed Vassili, and left the throne empty for a while.

2 *verb trans*. Lay down, put down, deposit. *arch*. LME. ►†**b** *verb trans*. Lay aside, remove, overcome, (a feeling, quality, etc.). LME–L17. ►†**c** Place for safe keeping; entrust. L16–M18.
†**3** *verb trans*. Take away, deprive someone of (authority etc.); remove (a burden or obligation). LME–L17.
4 *verb trans. & intrans*. Bear witness, testify, (to); affirm; *spec*. attest by or make a written deposition (see DEPOSITION 1). LME.

BROWNING And what discretion proved, I find deposed At Vire, confirmed by his own words. R. K. NARAYAN The railway staff are going to depose against me. W. GOLDING Augustus deposed before an ecclesiastical court that Miss Chudleigh had never been his wife.

5 *verb trans*. Examine (a deponent) on oath; cite as a witness. M16.
■ **deposable** *adjective* able or liable to be deposed M17. **deposer** *noun* a person who deposes L16.

deposit /dɪˈpɒzɪt/ *noun*. L16.
[ORIGIN Latin *depositum* use as noun of neut. pa. pple of *deponere*: see DEPONE.]
1 The state of being deposited or placed in safe keeping. Freq. in ***on deposit***, ***upon deposit***, †***in deposit***. L16.

D

2 Something stored or entrusted to a person for safe keeping. M17. ▸**b** A sum of money placed in an account with a bank, building society, etc., usu. at interest. M18. ▸**c** A sum of money or other security required and laid down as a pledge for the fulfilment of a contract, the return of something hired, etc., or as the first instalment of payment, and often refundable at the end of the transaction; the purchaser's own contribution to the purchase price of a property being bought with a mortgage loan. M18. ▸**d** *spec.* A sum paid on nomination by each of the candidates in a parliamentary election in the UK, which is refunded if the candidate receives more than a specified percentage of the votes cast. E20.

> **d** *Times* In 1951 no Liberals ran—they probably needed to convalesce after losing deposits.

3 A depository, a depot. Chiefly *US*. E18. **4** The act of depositing; *SCOTS LAW* a contract whereby goods are transferred from one person to another for safe keeping but must be returned on demand. L18. **5** A layer of matter that has collected, a natural accumulation of a substance. L18.

> E. M. FORSTER Over everything there lay a deposit of heavy white dust. N. CALDER Rich deposits of metal have accumulated.

– COMB.: ***deposit account***: see ACCOUNT *noun*.

deposit /dɪˈpɒzɪt/ *verb*. E17.
[ORIGIN French †*dépositer* or medieval Latin *depositare* from Latin *depositum*: see DEPOSIT *noun*.]
1 *verb trans.* Pay or give (esp. money) to another as a pledge for the fulfilment of a contract etc., or as the first instalment of a payment. E17. **2** *verb trans.* Place in a repository or in someone's charge, for safe keeping; *spec.* place (money) in a bank, building society, etc., usu. at interest. M17.

> B. TRAPIDO He . . deposited one million lire in my bank account.

†**3** *verb trans. fig.* Lay aside, give up. M17–E19. **4** *verb trans.* Put, place, or set down; lay (an egg). L17.

> H. JAMES He . . deposited his big tea-cup upon the table. F. TUOHY A taxi was depositing the last drunks outside the doors of the apartment buildings.

5 *verb trans.* Of a natural agent: form or lay down as a deposit. Freq. in *pass.* L17. ▸**b** *verb intrans.* Form a natural deposit, settle. *rare*. M19.

> D. L. SAYERS If a person takes arsenic, a certain proportion . . will be deposited in the skin, nails, and hair. F. TUOHY The stream had deposited centuries of rich dark soil.

■ **depositable** *adjective* E17. **deposiˈtee** *noun* a person with whom something is deposited L17.

depositary /dɪˈpɒzɪt(ə)ri/ *noun*. E17.
[ORIGIN Late Latin *depositarius*, from Latin *deposit-* pa. ppl stem of *deponere*: see DEPONE, -ARY¹. Cf. French *dépositaire*.]
1 A person or body receiving something in trust; a trustee. E17.

> C. BRONTË I have never been the depositary of her plans and secrets.

2 = DEPOSITORY 2. L18.

depositary /dɪˈpɒzɪt(ə)ri/ *adjective*. *rare*. M19.
[ORIGIN from DEPOSIT *noun* + -ARY¹.]
1 Chiefly *GEOLOGY*. Belonging to or of the nature of a deposit. M19. **2** Receiving deposits. L19.

†**depositate** *verb trans*. E17–L18.
[ORIGIN medieval Latin *depositat-* pa. ppl stem of *depositare*: see DEPOSIT *verb*, -ATE³.]
Deposit.

depositation /dɪˌpɒzɪˈteɪʃ(ə)n/ *noun*. Chiefly *Scot.* E17.
[ORIGIN from medieval Latin *depositare* (see DEPOSIT *verb*) + -ATION.]
= DEPOSIT *noun* 4.

deposition /dɛpəˈzɪʃ(ə)n, diː-/ *noun*. LME.
[ORIGIN Old French & mod. French *déposition* from Latin *depositio(n-)*, from *deposit-* pa. ppl stem of *deponere*: see DEPONE, -ION.]
1 The giving of testimony on oath in court; the testimony so given; *spec.* a sworn written statement that may be read out in court as a substitute for the production of the witness. LME.

> *fig.*: T. MALLON Our diaries . . can be our depositions.

2 The action of deposing from a position of power or authority; dethronement; degradation. LME.

> C. V. WEDGWOOD The removal of King Charles by deposition or by death.

3 The action of depositing, laying down, or putting in a position of rest; interment, *spec.* the laying of a saint's body and relics in a new resting place. LME. **4** (A representation of) the taking down of the body of Jesus from the Cross. M16. †**5** The action of laying aside or giving up something. Chiefly *fig.* L16–M18. **6** The placing of something in a repository, account, etc., or in someone's charge for safe keeping; a deposit. Now *rare*. L16. **7** The process of depositing by natural agency. L18. ▸**b** A natural deposit or accumulation. L18.

> D. ATTENBOROUGH Rocks are not built up by deposition but broken down by erosion.

■ **depositional** *adjective* of, pertaining to, or resulting from (geological) deposition E20.

depositor /dɪˈpɒzɪtə/ *noun*. L16.
[ORIGIN from DEPOSIT *verb* + -OR.]
†**1** A person who makes a legal deposition. Only in L16. **2** A person who places something in the charge of another; *spec.* a person who places money in an account at a bank, building society, etc. E17.

depository /dɪˈpɒzɪt(ə)ri/ *noun*. M17.
[ORIGIN medieval Latin *depositorium*, from Latin *deposit-* pa. ppl stem of *deponere*: see DEPONE, -ORY¹.]
1 = DEPOSITARY *noun* 1. M17. **2** A storehouse, a repository. M18.

> H. AINSWORTH The Jewel Tower . . the depository of the Regalia.

†**depositum** *noun*. L16.
[ORIGIN formed as DEPOSIT *noun*.]
1 Something given as a pledge or entrusted to another for safe keeping; *spec.* (*fig.*) the faith or doctrine which is committed to the keeping of the Church. L16–L18. **2** = DEPOSITORY 2. M17–L18.

depositure /dɪˈpɒzɪtjə/ *noun*. *rare*. M17.
[ORIGIN from Latin *deposit-* (see DEPOSITION) + -URE.]
= DEPOSITION 3.

depot /ˈdɛpəʊ/ *noun*. Also (now *rare*) **depôt**. L18.
[ORIGIN French *dépôt*, Old French *depost* from Latin *depositum*: see DEPOSIT *noun*.]
1 †**a** The action or an act of depositing. *rare*. L18–M19. ▸**b** A deposit, a collection, a store. Now *spec.* (*transf.* from sense 4 below) a localized accumulation of a substance in the body. M19.

> **b** P. PARISH It takes several days for the depot of the drug to accumulate, so high starter doses are normally given.

2 A military establishment at which stores are deposited, recruits or other troops assembled, or, formerly, prisoners of war confined; *esp.* a regimental headquarters. L18.

> T. PARKER The letter . . told me to report to the depot at Bassingbourne.

3 A place where goods etc. are deposited or stored, often for later dispatch; a storehouse, an emporium. L18. ▸**b** A place where vehicles, locomotives, etc., are housed and maintained and from which they are dispatched for service; *N. Amer.* a railway or bus station. M19.

> G. G. SCOTT The church was used as the coal depôt for the castle. R. H. TAWNEY The Portuguese Government made it [Antwerp] in 1503 the depôt of the Eastern spice trade. **b** L. T. C. ROLT Midnight after the last electric train has gone to its depot.

4 A site in the body at which a particular substance naturally concentrates or is deposited. E20.

> *attrib.*: *Lancet* Daily injections . . were replaced by a single intramuscular depot injection.

– COMB.: **depot battalion**, **depot company**: remaining behind at headquarters when the rest of the regiment is on foreign service; **depot ship**: acting as a depot, for small warships, fishing vessels, naval forces, etc.

†**depravate** *verb trans.* Pa. pple **-ated**, (earlier) **-ate**. E16–M19.
[ORIGIN Latin *depravat-*: see DEPRAVATION, -ATE³.]
= DEPRAVE.

depravation /dɛprəˈveɪʃ(ə)n/ *noun*. E16.
[ORIGIN Latin *depravatio(n-)*, from *depravat-* pa. ppl stem of *depravare*: see DEPRAVE, -ATION.]
†**1** Vilification, defamation, detraction. E16–E17.

> SHAKES. *Tr. & Cr.* Stubborn critics, apt . . For depravation.

2 The action or fact of making or becoming depraved; degeneration (esp. moral), corruption. M16. ▸†**b** Vitiation or corruption of a text etc. M16–M19. ▸†**c** Physical degeneration of an organ etc. M17–M19.

> A. COWLEY The total Loss of Reason is less deplorable than the total Depravation of it.

3 The condition of being depraved; an instance of depravity. L16.

> R. TAYLOR A sense of the depravation of our nature, or of original sin which is in us.

deprave /dɪˈpreɪv/ *verb*. LME.
[ORIGIN Old French & mod. French *dépraver* or Latin *depravare*, from *de-* DE- 1 + *pravus* crooked, perverse, wrong.]
▸ **I 1** *verb trans. & intrans.* Vilify, defame, disparage; speak ill (of). Now *rare*. LME.

> MILTON Unjustly thou deprav'st it with the name Of Servitude. BYRON Behold the host! delighting to deprave, Who track the steps of Glory to the grave.

2 *verb trans.* †**a** Misconstrue, misrepresent; pervert the meaning or intention of. LME–E18. ▸**b** Vitiate, corrupt, (a text, word, etc.). Now *rare*. LME. ▸†**c** Debase (coin), fraudulently alter, falsify, (a seal etc.). L16–M18. **3** *verb trans. & intrans.* Corrupt in moral character or habits. L15.

> J. FOWLES Prostitutes . . were explicable as creatures so depraved that they overcame their . . disgust at the carnal in their lust for money. C. HAMPTON Peevishly complaining about the tendency of modern literature to deprave and corrupt.

4 *verb trans. gen.* Make bad, deteriorate, impair. Now *rare*. M16.

> S. JOHNSON The loss of teeth may deprave the voice of a singer.

▸ †**II** [By confusion.]
5 *verb trans.* Deprive. L16–M18.
■ **depravedly** /-vɪdli, -vdli/ *adverb* in a depraved manner M17. **depravedness** *noun* E17. **depravement** *noun* depravation; (a) perversion, corruption: M17. **depraver** *noun* M16.

depravity /dɪˈpravɪti/ *noun*. M17.
[ORIGIN Alt. of PRAVITY after DEPRAVE.]
1 Moral corruption, wickedness; *THEOLOGY* the innate corruption of human nature due to original sin. M17.

> J. MACKINTOSH The winding approaches of temptation, the slippery path to depravity. T. S. ELIOT He's a fiend in feline shape, a monster of depravity.

†**2** *gen.* Deteriorated quality; a defect. M17–M18. **3** A depraved act or practice. M17.

> R. L. STEVENSON Combining in one person the depravities of . . two civilisations.

deprecate /ˈdɛprɪkeɪt/ *verb trans*. E17.
[ORIGIN Latin *deprecat-* pa. ppl stem of *deprecari*, from *de-* DE- 1 + *precari* pray: see -ATE³.]
1 Pray against (evil); try to avert by prayer. *arch.* E17.

> H. MARTINEAU The rest of the nation were at church, deprecating God's judgments.

†**2** Entreat, beseech, (a person). E17–E19. **3** Plead or protest against; express disapproval of or an earnest wish against. M17.

> F. A. G. OUSELEY Such a method of proceeding is greatly to be deprecated. H. KISSINGER He deprecated an interim settlement, claiming that Egypt would reject it.

†**4** Invoke (evil). M–L18. **5** = DEPRECIATE 1. L19.

> M. FRAYN Trying to shrink into himself, as if to deprecate . . his authority and to become as other men.

■ **deprecatingly** *adverb* so as to deprecate M19. **deprecator** *noun* [Latin] a person who deprecates something or someone M17.

deprecation /dɛprɪˈkeɪʃ(ə)n/ *noun*. LME.
[ORIGIN Latin *deprecatio(n-)*, formed as DEPRECATE: see -ATION.]
1 A prayer, *spec.* one to ward off evil, disaster, etc. *arch.* LME. **2** (An) expression of disapproval; (expression of) a wish that something may be averted. E17.

> S. JOHNSON The censures of criticism, which, however, I shall not endeavour to soften by a formal deprecation. DICKENS A tone of gentle deprecation.

†**3** An imprecation. *rare*. M17–E19. **4** [By assoc.] = DEPRECIATION 2. Orig. & chiefly in ***self-deprecation***. E20.

> A. FRASER Rather peculiar-looking, as he himself was the first to admit, with typical self-deprecation.

deprecative /ˈdɛprɪkətɪv/ *adjective*. LME.
[ORIGIN French *déprécatif* from Latin *deprecativus*, formed as DEPRECATE: see -ATIVE.]
That deprecates, deprecatory; of or pertaining to deprecation.
■ **deprecatively** *adverb* M17.

deprecatory /ˈdɛprɪkət(ə)ri, -keɪt-/ *adjective*. L16.
[ORIGIN Late Latin *deprecatorius*, from Latin *deprecator* deprecator, formed as DEPRECATE: see -ORY².]
1 Trying to avert evil by prayer. *arch.* L16.

> DONNE All his Prayer . . is but Deprecatory, he does not pray that God will forbeare him.

2 Expressing disapproval or a wish that something may be averted; deprecating anticipated unpleasantness or disapproval. E18.

> GEO. ELIOT 'Oh', said Rosamund, with a slight deprecatory laugh, 'I was only going to say that we sometimes have dancing.'

■ **deprecatorily** *adverb* L19.

depreciate /dɪˈpriːʃɪeɪt, -sɪeɪt/ *verb*. LME.
[ORIGIN Late Latin *depreciat-* pa. ppl stem of *depretiare* (medieval Latin *deprec-*), from *de-* DE- 1 + *pretium* price: see -ATE³.]
1 *verb trans.* Disparage, belittle, underrate. LME. ▸**b** *verb intrans.* Be disparaging; detract *from*. E18.

> R. ELLMANN Before this Wilde depreciated pity as a motive in art; now he embraced it.

2 *verb trans.* Lower the value of; *esp.* lower the market price of, reduce the purchasing power of (money). M17.

> J. GALSWORTHY A Sanatorium would depreciate the neighbourhood, and he should certainly sign the petition . . against it.

3 *verb intrans.* Fall in value. M18.

E. WILSON The value of the paper money had depreciated almost to zero.

■ **depreciatingly** *adverb* disparagingly M19. **depreciative** /dɪˈpriːʃətɪv, -ʃɪətɪv/ *adjective* depreciatory M19. **depreciator** *noun* a person who depreciates or causes depreciation L18. **depreciatory** /dɪˈpriːʃət(ə)ri, -ʃɪət(ə)ri/ *adjective* tending to depreciate; disparaging: E19.

depreciation /dɪˌpriːʃɪˈeɪʃ(ə)n, -sɪˈeɪ-/ *noun*. M18.
[ORIGIN from DEPRECIATE + -ATION.]
1 The action or process of lowering in value; *esp.* (a) fall in the exchange value of currency etc. M18. ▸**b** (An allowance made in balance sheets etc. for) loss of value due to wear and tear. M19.
2 The action of speaking slightly of someone or something; disparagement, belittlement. L18.

depredate /ˈdɛprɪdeɪt/ *verb*. Now *rare* or *obsolete*. E17.
[ORIGIN Latin *depraedat-*: see DEPREDATION, -ATE³.]
1 *verb trans.* Prey on, pillage, consume. E17.
2 *verb intrans.* Make depredations (*on*). L18.

depredation /dɛprɪˈdeɪʃ(ə)n/ *noun*. L15.
[ORIGIN French *déprédation* from late Latin *depraedatio(n-)*, from *depraedat-* pa. ppl stem of *depraedari*, from *de-* DE- 1 + *praedari* to plunder: see -ATION.]
1 The action of plundering, pillaging, or despoiling; an instance of robbery or pillage; in *pl.*, ravages. L15. ▸**b** *SCOTS LAW*. The (capital) offence of stealing cattle by armed force. *obsolete* exc. *hist.* L18.

A. FRASER The beautiful stained glass . . had not survived the depredations of the Parliamentary troops. A. BROOKNER War and depredation may have raged up and down the coast.

2 *fig.* †**a** Destructive waste, consumption (*of*). E–M17. ▸**b** In *pl.* Harmful effects of natural agents, destructive operations. M17.

b A. T. ELLIS Tying up some Michaelmas daisies against the depredations of the wind.

depredator /ˈdɛprɪdeɪtə/ *noun*. E17.
[ORIGIN Late Latin *depraedator*, formed as DEPREDATE: see -OR.]
A person who or agent which makes depredations; a despoiler, a pillager.
■ **depredatory** /dɪˈprɛdət(ə)ri, ˈdɛprɪdeɪt(ə)ri/ *adjective* characterized by depredation; plundering, ravaging: M17.

†**deprehend** *verb trans.* LME.
[ORIGIN Latin *deprehendere*, from *de-* DE- 1 + *prehendere* seize.]
1 Take by surprise; catch in the act. LME–L17. ▸**b** Seize, capture, arrest. M16–M19.
2 Detect, discover; perceive, understand. LME–L17.

depress /dɪˈprɛs/ *verb trans.* LME.
[ORIGIN Old French *depresser* from late Latin *depressare* frequentative of Latin *depress-* pa. ppl stem of *deprimere* press down, from *de-* DE- 1 + *premere* press.]
†**1** Overcome, subjugate, vanquish. LME–L17.
2 Bring into a lower position physically; press or push down. LME.

C. MILNE The steel balls . . were trapped in grooves until you depressed a . . plunger. F. HOYLE The weight of the ice-age glaciers depressed the whole Scandinavian area.

3 Bring down in fortune or status; humble, debase. Also, keep down, oppress. Now *rare* or *obsolete*. LME. ▸†**b** Depreciate, disparage. M16–L18.

MILTON Depressing . . their King . . to the condition of a Captive. W. PENN Therefore depress Vice and cherish Virtue.

4 Lessen the energy, force, or intensity of; reduce in activity or degree, weaken. LME. ▸**b** Lower (a musical note, the voice, etc.) in pitch. M16. ▸**c** Decrease in economic activity; lower in market value or price. L19.

STEELE Wine . . raises the Imagination, and depresses Judgment. P. PARISH Any drug which depresses brain function may produce dependence. **c** *Times* The Falklands news depressed BATs a further 8 p.

5 Dispirit, deject, sadden; cause to feel depression. LME.

A. EDEN What depressed me most was that I could see no hope of improvement ahead.

■ **depressible** *adjective* able to be depressed. M19. **depressing** *adjective* that depresses, causing depression; *esp.* dispiriting: L18. **depressingly** *adverb* M19. **depressingness** *noun* E20.

depressant /dɪˈprɛs(ə)nt/ *adjective & noun*. L19.
[ORIGIN from DEPRESS + -ANT¹.]
1 *MEDICINE*. (An agent) that lowers functional or nervous activity; (a) sedative. L19.
2 (An influence which is) depressing or dispiriting. L19.
3 In flotation separation of ores etc., (an agent) that causes sinking of certain components. M20.

depressed /dɪˈprɛst/ *ppl adjective*. LME.
[ORIGIN from DEPRESS + -ED¹.]
†**1** *ASTROLOGY*. Of a planet: in its least influential position. Only in LME.
2 Having a flattened or hollowed form, such as would result from downward pressure. L16.
3 Pressed down; put or kept down by force or pressure. E17.
4 Brought low in fortune or status; oppressed; socially or economically deprived. E17. ▸**b** Lowered in energy, force, intensity, amount, or degree; weakened. M19.

R. CRITCHFIELD Britain's most depressed city.

5 Lowered in physical position, sunken; lower than the general surface. M17.
6 Dejected, dispirited; suffering from depression. L18.

M. GILBERT I continue to be depressed about the future.

– SPECIAL COLLOCATIONS: **depressed area** an area of economic depression. **depressed class(es)** (in the Indian subcontinent) the lowest caste(s). **depressed fracture** a fracture of the skull involving displacement of bone inward from the normal cranial contour.
■ **depressedly** /dɪˈprɛstli, -ˈprɛsɪdli/ *adverb* M18.

depression /dɪˈprɛʃ(ə)n/ *noun*. LME.
[ORIGIN Old French & mod. French *dépression* or Latin *depressio(n-)*, from *depress-*: see DEPRESS, -ION.]
1 *ASTRONOMY* etc. Angular distance below the horizon or a horizontal plane. LME.
2 Defeat, suppression; degradation. Now *rare* or *obsolete*. LME.
3 Dejection, melancholy, low spirits. LME. ▸**b** *MEDICINE*. A pathological state of excessive melancholy, characterized by a mood of hopelessness, with feelings of inadequacy, and sometimes physical symptoms. E20.

GEO. ELIOT In a state of deep depression, overmastered by those distasteful miserable memories. **b** G. PRIESTLAND Depression . . has little to do with the perfectly normal experience of 'feeling a bit depressed'.

4 Lowering in physical position, sinking; the action of pressing down; the fact or condition of being pressed down. M17.
5 A sunken place on the ground or other surface; a hollow. M17.

D. NOBBS The depression left in the upholstery by her recently-departed bottom.

6 (A) reduction in quality, vigour, amount, activity, etc.; *spec.* (a) severe and prolonged decline in economic activity, a slump. L18. ▸**b** Lowering of pitch of the voice, a note, etc. M19.

J. D. MACDONALD A whole world on the slide into depression.

the Depression the financial and industrial slump of 1929 and subsequent years.

7 An atmospheric region or weather system marked by relatively low barometric pressure; = CYCLONE 1C. L19.

depressive /dɪˈprɛsɪv/ *adjective & noun*. E17.
[ORIGIN French *dépressif*, *-ive* or medieval Latin *depressivus*, from *depress-*: see DEPRESS, -IVE.]
▸ **A** *adjective*. Tending to produce, involving, or characterized by depression, esp. of the spirits; dispiriting, melancholy; *MEDICINE* involving, marked by, or suffering from pathological depression. E17.
▸ **B** *noun*. *MEDICINE*. A person suffering from depression. M20. *manic-depressive*: see MANIC.
■ **depressively** *adverb* M17. **depressiveness** *noun* M19.

depressor /dɪˈprɛsə/ *noun*. E17.
[ORIGIN Latin *depressor*, from *depress-*: see DEPRESS, -OR.]
1 A person who or thing which depresses. E17.
2 *ANATOMY*. A muscle which pulls down the part to which it is attached. Also ***depressor muscle***. E17.
3 A surgical instrument for pressing down some organ etc. L19.

†**depressure** *noun*. E17–L18.
[ORIGIN from Latin *depress-*: see DEPRESS, -URE.]
The action or an instance of depressing; (a) depression.

depressurize /diːˈprɛʃərʌɪz/ *verb trans.* Also **-ise**. M20.
[ORIGIN from DE- 3 + PRESSURIZE.]
Cause an appreciable drop of air or gas pressure in (a container, compartment, etc.), esp. to the pressure prevailing in the surroundings.

depriment /ˈdɛprɪm(ə)nt/ *noun & adjective*. *rare*. E17.
[ORIGIN Latin *depriment-* pres. pple of *deprimere*: see DEPRESS, -ENT.]
(Something) that depresses.

deprival /dɪˈprʌɪv(ə)l/ *noun*. E17.
[ORIGIN from DEPRIVE + -AL¹.]
The act of depriving, deprivation.

deprivation /dɛprɪˈveɪʃ(ə)n/ *noun*. LME.
[ORIGIN medieval (eccl.) Latin *deprivatio(n-)*, from *deprivat-* pa. ppl stem of *deprivare*: see DEPRIVE, -ATION.]
1 Removal from office or position, esp. of a member of the clergy from a benefice or preferment. LME.
2 *gen.* The action of depriving; the fact of being deprived; loss *of* something enjoyed or desired; a deprived condition, (a) hardship. M16.
■ **deprivative** /dɪˈprɪvətɪv/ *adjective* of, pertaining to, or characterized by deprivation E18.

deprive /dɪˈprʌɪv/ *verb trans.* ME.
[ORIGIN Old French *depriver* from medieval (eccl.) Latin *deprivare*, from *de-* DE- 1 + *privare* deprive.]
▸ **I** Dispossess, debar. Foll. by *of*, (now *rare*) *from*; also (now *rare*) with double obj. (cf. branch II below).
1 Divest, strip, dispossess (a person etc.) of a possession. ME.

SLOAN WILSON A fire engine, deprived of its siren. ISAIAH BERLIN To coerce a man is to deprive him of freedom.

2 Divest of (esp. ecclesiastical) office; depose. ME.

H. HALLAM Archbishop Bancroft deprived a considerable number of puritan clergymen.

3 Deny (a person) the future possession or enjoyment of something; debar from a right etc. LME.

AV *Isa.* 38:10 I am depriued of the residue of my yeeres. HOBBES Deprived from all possibility to acquire . . necessaries. R. PRICE Both saving and depriving them further speech.

▸ †**II 4** Take away, remove (a possession). ME–M17.
■ **deprivable** *adjective* liable to be deprived L16. **deprived** *adjective* subject to deprivation, dispossessed; now *esp.* underprivileged, poor, (of a child) lacking a normal home life: M16. †**deprivement** *noun* (a) deprivation M17–E18. **depriver** *noun* LME.

D

de profundis /deɪ prəˈfʊndɪs/ *noun & adverbial phr.* LME.
[ORIGIN Latin = from the depths, the initial words of Psalm 130 (129).]
▸ **A** *noun phr.* A psalm of penitence; *spec.* Psalm 130 (129 in the Vulgate); *gen.* a cry of appeal from the depths (of sorrow, humiliation, etc.). LME.
▸ **B** *adverbial phr.* Out of the depths (of sorrow etc.). LME.

deprogramme /diːˈprəʊgram/ *verb trans.* Also ***-gram**. L20.
[ORIGIN from DE- 3 + PROGRAMME *verb*.]
Release (a person) from apparent brainwashing by systematic indoctrination.

deproletarianize /ˌdiːprəʊlɪˈtɛːrɪənʌɪz/ *verb trans.* Also **-ise**. M20.
[ORIGIN from DE- 3 + PROLETARIANIZE.]
Cause to lose proletarian character or qualities.
■ **deproletariani'zation** *noun* M20.

deproteinize /diːˈprəʊtiːnʌɪz/ *verb trans.* Also **-ise**. M20.
[ORIGIN from DE- 3 + PROTEIN + -IZE.]
Remove the protein from, esp. as a measure in chemical purification.
■ **deproteini'zation** *noun* M20.

deprovincialize /diːprəˈvɪnʃ(ə)lʌɪz/ *verb trans.* Also **-ise**. M19.
[ORIGIN from DE- 3 + PROVINCIALIZE.]
Remove provincial elements or character from; make broader in outlook etc.

depside /ˈdɛpsʌɪd/ *noun*. E20.
[ORIGIN from Greek *depsein* make supple, tan + -IDE.]
CHEMISTRY. Any of a class of naturally occurring phenols, found esp. in lichens, which include some tannins and have two or more phenolic groups joined by ester linkages in the molecule.
■ **depsidone** /-sɪdəʊn/ *noun* any depside derivative in which the phenolic rings are joined also by ether linkages M20.

Dept *abbreviation*.
Department.

Deptford pink /dɛtfəd ˈpɪŋk/ *noun phr.* M17.
[ORIGIN *Deptford*, a district of SE London, formerly a village.]
A rare wild pink of dry banks, *Dianthus armeria*, with clusters of rose-red flowers.

depth /dɛpθ/ *noun*. LME.
[ORIGIN from DEEP *adjective* + -TH¹, after *long*: *length* etc. Largely superseding earlier DEEPNESS.]
▸ **I 1** Extent or distance from the top downwards, from the surface or edge inwards or from front to back; a particular measurement of this. LME. ▸**b** *MILITARY*. The distance from front to rear of a body of soldiers etc., as measured by the number of ranks. M17.

B. GOOGE Trenches of a cubite in depth. J. UPDIKE They swim in the icy water . . at a depth no greater than their height.

2 Intensity or profundity of a feeling, moral quality, or state. LME.

J. WESLEY The Depth of sympathetic Woe!

3 The quality of having considerable extension downwards, inwards, or from front to back. E16.

TINDALE *Matt.* 13:5 Because it had no depth of earth.

4 a Abstruseness of (subjects of) thought; complexity. L16. ▸**b** Intellectual penetration, sagacity, insight. E17.

a C. MARLOWE Settle thy studies, Faustus, and begin To sound the depth of that thou wilt profess. **b** T. HEARNE A man of extraordinary Depth. A. S. BYATT Boys before the age of self-consciousness . . could give . . depths they were unconscious of to lines they didn't understand.

5 Intensity of physical qualities or conditions, as silence, darkness, colour, etc. E17.

DRYDEN All seeking the noise in the depth of silence. D. LESSING Her smart new coat flaring jade, emerald, dark green, as she moved through varying depths of light.

▸ **II 6** A deep body of water; a deep part of the sea, or of any body of water. Usu. in *pl.* LME. ▸†**b** = DEEP *noun* 3. LME–E17.

E. LANGLEY The blue lake chanted in its blue and white depths. C. SAGAN Organisms now live from the top of Mount Everest to the deepest portions of the abyssal depths.

7 A deep, remote, or inmost part (*of*). Freq. in *pl.* LME.

POPE Some safer world, in depth of woods embrac'd. V. WOOLF How did she manage these things in the depths of the country?

8 *fig.* A deep, mysterious, unfathomable, etc., region of or *of* thought, feeling, character, etc. Freq. in *pl.* LME.

AV *Ps.* 130:1 Out of the depths have I cried unto thee, O Lord. E. WAUGH Depths of confusion you didn't know existed. B. BAINBRIDGE Nina wasn't the sort to like lovable men. Perhaps Douglas had hidden depths.

9 A deep place in the earth etc.; the lowest part of a pit, cavity, etc. Formerly also, a valley. E16.

POPE A monster, horrible and fell, Begot by furies in the depths of hell. J. B. PRIESTLEY Moaning for a doctor from the depths of the armchair into which he'd collapsed.

10 A vast or unfathomable space (*of*). Usu. in *pl.* E17.

LONGFELLOW Measureless depths of air around.

11 The deepest, harshest, or most intense period. E17.

E. BOLTON Though it were the depth of Winter. R. BROOKE Fish (fly-replete, in depth of June . .).

– PHRASES: *defence in depth*: see DEFENCE noun 3. *depth of field*: see FIELD noun. *depth of focus*: see FOCUS noun. **in depth** profound(ly), comprehensive(ly); penetrating(ly). **out of one's depth** in water too deep to stand in; *fig.* beyond one's capacities or understanding. *rapture of the depths*, *raptures of the depths*: see RAPTURE noun.

– COMB.: **depth bomb**, **depth charge** a bomb that explodes under water at a preset depth, used for attacking a submerged submarine etc.; **depth-finder** a device for measuring the depth of the sea etc., esp. using echo-sounding; **depth psychology** psychology seeking to explain behaviour in terms of the unconscious; psychoanalysis intended to reveal hidden motives etc.; **depth-recorder** a recording depth-finder.

■ **depthen** *verb trans.* (*rare*) = DEEPEN 1 L16. **depthless** *adjective* (*a*) unfathomable; abyssal; (*b*) shallow, superficial: E17.

depurate /dɪˈpjʊəreɪt, ˈdɛpjʊreɪt/ *verb trans.* E17.
[ORIGIN medieval Latin *depurat-* pa. ppl stem of *depurare*, from *de-* DE- 1 + *purare* purify, from *purus* pure: see -ATE³.]
Make free from impurities; subject to depuration.
■ **depurative** *adjective & noun* [medieval Latin *depurativus*] (an agent) that purifies L17. ˈ**depurator** *noun* an agent or apparatus that purifies M19. **deˈpuratory** *adjective* = DEPURATIVE L17.

depuration /dɛpjʊˈreɪʃ(ə)n/ *noun.* E17.
[ORIGIN formed as DEPURATE + -ATION.]
Purification, refining; *esp.* the process of keeping shellfish etc. in clean water for a period so as to free them of undesirable substances.

depure /dɪˈpjʊə/ *verb trans.* Long *arch. rare.* LME.
[ORIGIN Old French & mod. French *dépurer* or medieval Latin *depurare*: see DEPURATE.]
= DEPURATE.

deputable /dɪˈpjuːtəb(ə)l, ˈdɛpjʊ-/ *adjective.* E17.
[ORIGIN from DEPUTE *verb* + -ABLE.]
Able to be deputed, suitable for deputing.

deputation /dɛpjʊˈteɪʃ(ə)n/ *noun.* LME.
[ORIGIN Late Latin *deputatio(n-)*, from Latin *deputat-* pa. ppl stem of *deputare*: see DEPUTE *verb*, -ATION.]
†**1** *gen.* Appointment, assignment to an office, function, etc. LME–M17. ▸**b** An appointment by the lord of a manor to the office and rights of a gamekeeper. *obsolete* exc. *hist.* M18.

b S. WALPOLE Country gentlemen who were desirous of doing a neighbour a good turn were in the habit of giving him a 'deputation' as a gamekeeper.

2 *spec.* Appointment to act on behalf of another or others; delegation. M16.
3 A document conveying an appointment; a commission, a warrant. *obsolete* exc. *hist.* E17.
4 A body of people, or a single person, appointed to represent another or others, usu. on a particular mission. M17.

T. STOPPARD Inspecting the toilets like a deputation from the Water Board. P. USTINOV They sent the Tsar a deputation which repeated their demands for urgent constitutional reforms.

deputative /ˈdɛpjʊtətɪv/ *adjective.* M17.
[ORIGIN Late Latin *deputativus*, from *deputat-*: see DEPUTATION, -ATIVE.]
Characterized by deputation; of the nature of a deputy or deputation.
■ **deputatively** *adverb* M17.

deputator /ˈdɛpjʊteɪtə/ *noun. rare.* M17.
[ORIGIN from Latin *deputat-*: see DEPUTATION, -OR.]
A person who deputes another to act for him or her.

depute /ˈdɛpjuːt/ *adjective* (orig. *pa. pple*) & *noun.* Now only *Scot.* LME.
[ORIGIN Old French & mod. French *député* pa. pple of *députer* DEPUTE *verb* (repr. late Latin *deputatus*). Cf. DEPUTY.]
▸ **A** *adjective.* †**1** *pa. pple.* Deputed; imputed; appointed, assigned. LME–E17.
2 *adjective.* Appointed or acting as deputy, *spec.* in certain legal offices. Freq. *postpositive.* LME.
▸ **B** *noun.* A person deputed; a deputy. LME.

depute /dɪˈpjuːt/ *verb trans.* LME.
[ORIGIN Partly from Old French & mod. French *députer* from Latin *deputare* destine, assign, from *de-* DE- 1 + *putare* consider; partly based on DEPUTE *noun.*]
†**1** Appoint, assign, or ordain to or for a particular office, purpose, or function. LME–L17.
2 Appoint as a substitute, representative, or deputy. LME.

SHAKES. *Oth.* To depute Cassio in Othello's place. A. JOHN The Princess . . deputing me to see them into their train, sent us off in her car.

†**3** Impute, ascribe, attribute. LME–L16.
†**4** Consign, deliver over. LME–L15.
5 Commit (a task, authority, etc.) to or *to* a deputy or substitute. L15.

DEFOE The Devil may depute such and such powers and privileges to his confederates.

deputize /ˈdɛpjʊtʌɪz/ *verb.* Also **-ise**. M18.
[ORIGIN from DEPUTY + -IZE.]
1 *verb trans.* Appoint as a deputy. Chiefly *US.* M18.
2 *verb intrans.* Act as a deputy or understudy (*for*). M19.

deputy /ˈdɛpjʊti/ *noun, adjective, & verb.* LME.
[ORIGIN Var. of DEPUTE *noun*, with final syll. of the French retained: see -Y⁵.]
▸ **A** *noun.* **1** A person appointed or delegated to act or to exercise authority for another or others; a substitute, a lieutenant. LME. ▸**b** LAW. A person authorized to exercise disinterestedly the whole or a part of an office on behalf of the office-holder. LME.

H. P. BROUGHAM The lesser barons were called to send deputies, instead of attending personally.

by deputy by another person in one's stead, by proxy.
2 *spec.* ▸**a** A person deputed to exercise authority on behalf of the sovereign (power); a Lord or a Deputy Lieutenant (of Ireland), a viceroy, a proconsul. *obsolete* exc. *hist.* LME. ▸**b** In the City of London, a person who acts instead of an alderman in the absence of the latter. M16. ▸**c** An overseer responsible for safety in a coalmine. M19.
3 A member of a legislative assembly, *spec.* of a Chamber of Deputies (see below). E17.
Chamber of Deputies the lower house of Parliament of the French Third Republic, of Italy, and some other countries.
▸ **B** *attrib.* or as *adjective.* Deputed; acting or appointed to act instead of another or others. L15.
deputy lieutenant the deputy of the Lord Lieutenant of a county.
▸ **C** *verb trans.* Appoint or send as deputy. *rare.* E17.
■ **deputyship** *noun* the position or the term of office of a deputy L16.

dequeue /diːˈkjuː/ *verb trans.* COMPUTING. L20.
[ORIGIN from DE- 3 + QUEUE *noun.*]
Remove (an item of data awaiting processing) from a queue of such items.

deracialize /diːˈreɪʃəlʌɪz/ *verb trans.* Also **-ise**. L19.
[ORIGIN from DE- 3 + RACIAL + -IZE.]
Remove racial characteristics or features from.
■ **deracialiˈzation** *noun* M20.

deracinate /dɪˈrasɪneɪt/ *verb trans. literary.* L16.
[ORIGIN from French *déraciner* (Old French *des-*), from *dé-* DE- 3 + *racine* root: see -ATE³.]
Tear up by the roots (*lit. & fig.*), eradicate.
■ **deraciˈnation** *noun* E19.

déraciné /derasine (*pl. same*), deɪˈrasɪneɪ/ *adjective & noun.* Fem. **-ée**. E20.
[ORIGIN French = uprooted, pa. ppl adjective of *déraciner*: see DERACINATE.]
▸ **A** *adjective.* Uprooted from one's environment; displaced geographically or socially. E20.
▸ **B** *noun.* A *déraciné* person. E20.

deraign /dɪˈreɪn/ *verb¹ trans. obsolete* exc. *hist.* ME.
[ORIGIN Anglo-Norman *derainer*, *dereiner*, Old French *deraisnier*, *dereis-* from Proto-Romance, from Latin *de-* DE- 1 + *ratio(n-)* account, REASON *noun¹*.]
1 LAW. Prove, justify, or vindicate (a claim etc.), esp. by wager of battle; dispute (the claim of another) thus. ME.
2 Maintain a claim to; claim the possession of, esp. by wager of battle. ME.
3 Decide (a claim or dispute) by judicial argument or by wager of battle; determine. ME.
4 a *deraign battle*, *deraign combat*, etc., maintain a wager of battle or single combat in vindication of a claim, right, etc. Also (*pseudo-arch.*), do battle; order, arrange a battle. LME. ▸†**b** Dispose in battle array; order. *pseudo-arch.* L16–E18.

deraign /dɪˈreɪn/ *verb² trans.* E16.
[ORIGIN Old French *desregner* var. of *desrengier* (mod. *déranger*) put out of ranks, DERANGE.]
†**1** Put into disorder; derange. E16–E18.
2 In *pass.* Be discharged from (religious) orders. *obsolete* exc. *hist.* L16.

deraignment /dɪˈreɪnm(ə)nt/ *noun¹. obsolete* exc. *hist.* M16.
[ORIGIN Old French *desrenement*, from *desregner*: see DERAIGN *verb²*, -MENT.]
The action of DERAIGN *verb²*; discharge from religious orders.

deraignment /dɪˈreɪnm(ə)nt/ *noun². obsolete* exc. *hist.* E18.
[ORIGIN Old French *desraisnement*, *derainement*, from *desraisnier*: see DERAIGN *verb¹*, -MENT.]
The action of DERAIGN *verb¹*; vindication of a claim etc., esp. by wager of battle.

derail /dɪˈreɪl/ *verb.* M19.
[ORIGIN French *dérailler*, from *dé-* DE- 3 + *rail* RAIL *noun²*.]
1 *verb trans.* Cause (a train etc.) to run off the rails. M19.

fig.: H. CRANE Passions of this kind completely derail me from anything creative for days.

2 *verb intrans.* Leave the rails. M19.
■ **derailment** *noun* the fact or an instance of a train's leaving the rails. M19.

derailleur /dɪˈreɪlə, -ljə/ *noun.* E20.
[ORIGIN French *dérailleur*, formed as DERAIL + *-eur* -OR.]
A bicycle gear in which the ratio is changed by switching the line of the chain (while pedalling) so that it jumps to a different sprocket.

derange /dɪˈreɪn(d)ʒ/ *verb trans.* L18.
[ORIGIN French *déranger* (Old French *desrengier*, *desregner* DERAIGN *verb²*), from *dé-*, *des-* DE- 3 + *rang* RANK *noun.*]
1 Disturb or destroy the arrangement of; throw into confusion; disorder, disarrange. L18.

LD MACAULAY This letter deranged all the projects of James.

2 Disturb the normal state, working, or operation of; cause to act irregularly. L18.

B. C. BRODIE Habits . . which tend in any degree to derange the animal functions, should be scrupulously avoided. D. H. LAWRENCE Time was all deranged.

3 Make insane; drive mad. Freq. as ***deranged*** *ppl adjective.* L18.

E. CALDWELL He had been killed by a deranged person. P. ROSE The eldest child was quite deranged with joy and suffered convulsions.

4 Intrude on, interrupt. M19.

R. L. STEVENSON I am sorry to have deranged you for so small a matter.

derangement /dɪˈreɪn(d)ʒm(ə)nt/ *noun.* M18.
[ORIGIN French *dérangement*, formed as DERANGE: see -MENT.]
The act of deranging; the fact or an instance of being deranged; disorder; insanity.

derate /diːˈreɪt/ *verb trans. & intrans.* E20.
[ORIGIN from DE- 3 + RATE *noun¹*.]
Diminish or remove part or all of the burden of rates (from).

deration /diːˈraʃ(ə)n/ *verb trans.* E20.
[ORIGIN from DE- 3 + RATION.]
Free (a commodity) from rationing, make no longer rationed.

derationalize /diːˈraʃ(ə)n(ə)lʌɪz/ *verb trans.* Also **-ise**. L19.
[ORIGIN from DE- 3 + RATIONALIZE.]
Deprive of reason.
■ **derationaliˈzation** *noun* M20.

deratization /diːˌratʌɪˈzeɪʃ(ə)n/ *noun.* Also **-isation**. E20.
[ORIGIN from DE- 3 + RAT *noun¹* + -IZATION.]
The expulsion or extermination of rats from a property, vessel, etc.

deray /dɪˈreɪ/ *noun.* Long *obsolete* exc. *Scot. arch.* ME.
[ORIGIN Anglo-Norman *derai*, Old French *desrai*, from Anglo-Norman *deraier*, Old French *desreer*, from Proto-Romance, from Latin DIS- + Germanic base also in ARRAY *verb.*]
1 Disorder, disturbance, tumult, confusion. ME.
†**2** Violence, molestation. ME–M16.
3 Disorderly mirth and revelry. LME.

Derby /ˈdɑːbi; *dial.* & *US* ˈdəːbi/ *noun.* Also (esp. in senses 2b, 3, 4), **d-**. E17.
[ORIGIN A city and county (see also DERBYSHIRE) in the north midlands of England, and an earldom named from the county. See also DARBY.]
1 Used *attrib.* to designate things made in or associated with Derby. E17. ▸**b** In full ***Derby cheese***. A hard pressed cheese made from skimmed milk, chiefly in Derbyshire. E19. ▸**c** In full ***Derby porcelain***. A variety of porcelain made at Derby; *spec.* a soft-paste porcelain made from *c* 1750. M19.
Lord Derby: see LORD noun. **b** *sage Derby*: see SAGE *noun¹*. **c** *Crown Derby*: see CROWN noun.
2 (Often **d-**.) A flat horse race (founded in 1780 by the twelfth Earl of Derby) run annually at Epsom, England. Also, any of various equivalent races elsewhere. M19. ▸**b** An important game or contest; *spec.* (freq. ***local derby***) a sports match between two teams from the same area. E20.

b *attrib.*: *Times* The derby match at home to Chelsea on Saturday.

Derby Day: on which the Derby is run. *donkey Derby*: see DONKEY. *Kentucky Derby*: see KENTUCKY. *roller Derby*: see ROLLER *noun¹*. **b** *demolition derby*: see DEMOLITION.
3 In full ***Derby hat***. A bowler hat. *N. Amer.* L19.
4 Orig., a kind of sporting boot having no stiffening and a very low heel. Now, a low-heeled shoe. E20.

5 ***Derby scheme***, in the First World War, a recruiting scheme initiated by the seventeenth Earl of Derby. **E20.**

Derbyshire /ˈdɑːbɪʃə/ *noun.* **L18.**
[**ORIGIN** An English county: see **DERBY**, **SHIRE** *noun*.]
1 ***Derbyshire spar***, fluorspar. **L18.**
2 ***Derbyshire neck***, goitre, formerly endemic in parts of Derbyshire. **E19.**
3 In full ***Derbyshire cheese***. = **DERBY** 1b. **E20.**

†**der-doing** *ppl adjective. pseudo-arch. rare* (Spenser). Only in **L16.**
[**ORIGIN** App. after **DERRING-DO**.]
Doing daring deeds.

†**dere** *noun.* **OE–E19.**
[**ORIGIN** Old English *daru* = Old High German *tara*, from West Germanic; later from or assim. to the verb.]
Harm, injury. Esp. in ***do a person dere***.

dere /dɪə/ *verb.* Long *obsolete* exc. *Scot.* & *N. English.*
[**ORIGIN** Old English *derian* = Old Frisian *dera*, Old Saxon *derian*, from West Germanic, from base of **DERE** *noun*.]
†**1** *verb trans.* Hurt, harm, injure. **OE–E17.** ▸**b** *verb intrans.* Do harm. **OE–LME.**
2 *verb trans.* Trouble, grieve, vex, incommode. **ME.**

derealize /diːˈrɪəlʌɪz/ *verb trans.* Also **-ise**. **L19.**
[**ORIGIN** from **DE-** 3 + **REALIZE** *verb*.]
PHILOSOPHY. Deprive of reality, make unreal.

derecho /dɪˈreɪtʃəʊ/ *noun. US.* Pl. **-os**. **L19.**
[**ORIGIN** Spanish, = direct, straight.]
A storm system that moves rapidly across a great distance and is characterized by damaging winds which can devastate an area several miles wide.

derecognition /ˌdiːrɛkəgˈnɪʃ(ə)n/ *noun.* **M20.**
[**ORIGIN** from **DE-** 3 + **RECOGNITION**.]
The withdrawal of official recognition; *esp.* withdrawal of political recognition by one state from another.
■ **deˈrecognize** *verb trans.* withdraw recognition from **M20.**

deregister /diːˈrɛdʒɪstə/ *verb trans.* **E20.**
[**ORIGIN** from **DE-** 3 + **REGISTER** *noun*[1].]
Remove from a register.
■ **deregisˈtration** *noun* **E20.**

deregulate /diːˈrɛgjʊleɪt/ *verb trans.* **M20.**
[**ORIGIN** from **DE-** 3 + **REGULATE**.]
Free from regulation, esp. tariff restriction; decontrol.
■ **dereguˈlation** *noun* **M20.** **dereguˈlatory** *adjective* **L20.**

derelict /ˈdɛrəlɪkt/ *adjective & noun.* **M17.**
[**ORIGIN** Latin *derelictus* pa. pple of *derelinquere* forsake wholly, abandon, from *de-* **DE-** 1 + *relinquere* leave, forsake.]
▸ **A** *adjective.* **1** Forsaken, abandoned by the owner, occupier, etc.; (of a ship) abandoned at sea; (esp. of property) dilapidated, decrepit, neglected. **M17.**

J. WYNDHAM A few derelict cars . . stood about on the roads. I. MURDOCH He loved its derelict splendours, the huge ornate neglected mansions of a vanished bourgeoisie.

derelict land *LAW* land left dry by the recession of the sea etc.
2 Remiss or negligent in the performance of one's duty. Chiefly *N. Amer.* **M19.**

N. BAWDEN If . . you yourself have been derelict in your duty.

▸ **B** *noun.* **1** A piece of property abandoned by the owner, occupier, etc.; a ship abandoned at sea. **L17.**
2 A forsaken person; *esp.* a person abandoned or disregarded by society, a vagrant, a social outcast. **E18.**

BROWNING Misuse me, your derelict. A. MILLER Derelicts and old men lounge here to watch the strangers go by.

3 A person who is negligent or remiss in the performance of his or her duty. *N. Amer.* **L19.**

dereliction /dɛrəˈlɪkʃ(ə)n/ *noun.* **L16.**
[**ORIGIN** Latin *derelictio(n-)*, from *derelict-* pa. ppl stem of *derelinquere*: see **DERELICT**, **-ION**.]
1 The state of being abandoned or forsaken; dilapidation, neglect. **L16.**

J. HARVEY The dereliction of a breakfast-table . . bobbing with orange-peels, ribboned with bacon-rind, cluttered with jams and marmalades.

2 The act of deliberate abandonment. Now *rare* exc. *LAW*, of a chattel or movable. **E17.** ▸**b** *LAW.* The leaving behind of dry land by the retreat of the sea; the land thus left. **M18.**

GIBBON This wise dereliction of obsolete, vexatious, and unprofitable claims.

†**3** Failure, cessation; *esp.* sudden failure of the bodily or mental powers. **M17–L18.**
4 Reprehensible abandonment; wilful neglect. Chiefly in ***dereliction of duty***. **L18.** ▸**b** Failure in duty; shortcoming. **E19.**

BURKE A dereliction of every opinion and principle that I have held. J. GALSWORTHY So grave a dereliction of all duty, both human and divine. **b** W. STYRON I was guilty of a grave dereliction.

†**derelinquish** *verb trans.* **E17–M19.**
[**ORIGIN** from **DE-** 1 + **RELINQUISH**, after Latin *derelinquere*: see **DERELICT**.]
Relinquish utterly, abandon.

derepress /diːrɪˈprɛs/ *verb trans.* **M20.**
[**ORIGIN** from **DE-** 3 + **REPRESS** *verb*.]
Make no longer repressed or inhibited; activate; *spec.* (**BIOCHEMISTRY**), activate from an inoperative or latent state by interfering with the action of a repressor.
■ **derepression** *noun* **M20.**

derequisition /ˌdiːrɛkwɪˈzɪʃ(ə)n/ *verb trans.* **M20.**
[**ORIGIN** from **DE-** 3 + **REQUISITION** *verb*.]
Return after requisitioning.

derestrict /diːrɪˈstrɪkt/ *verb trans.* **M20.**
[**ORIGIN** from **DE-** 3 + **RESTRICT** *verb*.]
Remove restrictions from.
■ **derestricted** *ppl adjective* free from restrictions; *spec.* (of a road) not subject to a special speed limit on traffic: **M20.** **derestriction** *noun* **M20.**

deride /dɪˈrʌɪd/ *verb.* **M16.**
[**ORIGIN** Latin *deridere*, from *de-* **DE-** 1 + *ridere* laugh (at).]
1 *verb trans.* Laugh contemptuously or scornfully at; treat with scorn; mock. **M16.**

J. K. JEROME They stood there, shouting ribaldry at him, deriding him, mocking him, jeering at him. F. SPALDING The public derided Post-Impressionism.

†**2** *verb intrans.* Laugh contemptuously or scornfully. Only in **17.**
■ **derider** *noun* **M16.** **deridingly** *adverb* in a deriding manner **L16.**

de rigueur /də rɪˈgəː, *foreign* də rigœːr/ *pred. adjectival phr.* **M19.**
[**ORIGIN** French, lit. 'of strictness'.]
Required by custom or etiquette.

derisible /dɪˈrɪzɪb(ə)l/ *adjective.* **M17.**
[**ORIGIN** Late Latin *derisibilis*, from *deris-*: see **DERISION**, **-IBLE**. In mod. use from **DERISION**, on the analogy of *vision*, *visible*.]
To be derided; worthy of derision.

derision /dɪˈrɪʒ(ə)n/ *noun.* **LME.**
[**ORIGIN** Old French & mod. French *dérision* from late Latin *derisio(n-)*, from *deris-* pa. ppl stem of *deridere* **DERIDE**: see **-ION**.]
1 The action of deriding; ridicule, mockery. **LME.** ▸**b** An instance of this. *rare.* **M16.**

J. GLASSCO Every attempt I made to write was greeted with derision.

be in derision (now *rare*) be a laughing stock. **bring into derision** mock, make a laughing stock of. **have in derision**, **hold in derision** *arch.* mock, treat with scorn.
2 An object of ridicule; a laughing stock. Now *rare* exc. *Scot.* **M16.**

derisive /dɪˈrʌɪsɪv, -z-/ *adjective.* **M17.**
[**ORIGIN** from (the same root as) **DERISION** + **-IVE**, after *decision*, *decisive*.]
1 Scoffing, mocking. **M17.**

T. HARDY A low gurgle of derisive laughter followed the words. J. HELLER Curt, derisive tongue and . . knowing, cynical eyes.

2 = **DERISORY** 2. **L19.**
■ **derisively** *adverb* **M17.** **derisiveness** *noun* **M19.**

derisory /dɪˈrʌɪs(ə)ri, -z-/ *adjective.* **E17.**
[**ORIGIN** Late Latin *derisorius*, from *deris-*: see **DERISION**, **-ORY**[2].]
1 = **DERISIVE** 1. **E17.**
2 So small or unimportant as to be ridiculous; laughably inadequate. **E20.**

S. UNWIN What would appear to them a derisory sum might be of importance to a poet. *Oxford Times* Both rejected the present rate offer as 'derisory'.

derivable /dɪˈrʌɪvəb(ə)l/ *adjective.* **M17.**
[**ORIGIN** from **DERIVE** + **-ABLE**.]
Able to be derived (*from*).
■ **derivaˈbility** *noun* **M19.**

derival /dɪˈrʌɪv(ə)l/ *noun. rare.* **L16.**
[**ORIGIN** from **DERIVE** + **-AL**[1].]
A derived form; derivation.

derivate /ˈdɛrɪvət, -eɪt/ *ppl adjective & noun.* **LME.**
[**ORIGIN** Latin *derivat-* pa. ppl stem of *derivare*: see **DERIVE**, **-ATE**[2].]
▸ **A** *ppl adjective.* Derived. Now *rare.* **LME.**
▸ **B** *noun.* Something derived, a derivative; *esp.* a product obtained chemically from a raw material. **LME.**
■ **derivately** *adverb* (*rare*) **M17.**

derivation /dɛrɪˈveɪʃ(ə)n/ *noun.* **LME.**
[**ORIGIN** French *dérivation* or Latin *derivatio(n-)*, formed as **DERIVATE**: see **-ATION**.]
†**1** The action or process of leading or carrying a current of water etc. *from* a source, *to* another part; diversion; *spec.* in **MEDICINE**, the drawing off of pus, blood, etc., from a diseased part of the body. **LME–L19.**

J. RAY Plenty of Vessels for the derivation of Air to all their Parts.

2 Formation of a word from an earlier word, base, or root. **LME.** ▸**b** The tracing of a word from or back to its root or roots; a statement of this. **L16.**
3 Extraction, origin, descent. **L15.**

SHAKES. *Hen. V* As good a man as yourself, both in the disciplines of war and in the derivation of my birth.

†**4** Transmission; communication. **L16–L17.**
5 The action of obtaining, drawing, or deducing from a source. **M17.**

E. A. FREEMAN There was no real derivation of English law from Normandy. D. R. HOFSTADTER The derivation of a theorem is an explicit . . demonstration of how to produce that theorem according to the rules of the formal system.

6 A derived product; a derivative. Now *rare.* **M17.**

MILTON The Father is the whole substance, . . the Son a derivation, and portion of the whole.

■ **derivational** *adjective* **M19.** **derivationally** *adverb* **L19.** **derivationist** *noun* a person concerned with derivation **L19.**

derivative /dɪˈrɪvətɪv/ *adjective & noun.* **LME.**
[**ORIGIN** French *dérivatif* from Latin *derivativus* pa. pple of *derivare*: see **DERIVE**, **-ATIVE**.]
▸ **A** *adjective.* †**1** Having the effect of transferring or conveying. Chiefly **MEDICINE**, having the power to draw off fluid from a diseased part of the body. **LME–L19.**
2 Derived or obtained from another; coming from a source; not original. **M16.** ▸**b** Formed or originating from another word, base, or root. **M16.** ▸**c** *LAW.* Secondary, subordinate. **L18.** ▸**d** *GEOLOGY.* Derived from older rocks; (of a fossil) occurring at a site other than the one where it was formed. **L19.** ▸**e** *FINANCE.* Of a financial product: having a value deriving from an underlying variable asset. **L20.**

STEELE They can only gain a secondary and derivative kind of Fame. T. GUNN I am . . a rather derivative poet. I learn what I can from whom I can.

c derivative action *US Law* an action brought by a shareholder in order to enforce a legal right of the corporation.
▸ **B** *noun.* **1** A word derived from another word, base, or root by a process of word formation; a word which is not a root. **LME.**

J. H. BURTON The use of a Greek derivative gives notice that you are scientific.

2 *gen.* Something derived; a thing flowing, proceeding, or originating from another. **L16.**

J. BRYANT Subordinate dæmons, . . emanations and derivatives from their chief Deity. A. STORR Some dreams . . are certainly derivatives of the patient's early childhood.

3 *MATH.* An expression (obtained by differentiation of a function) which represents the instantaneous rate of change of the function with respect to an independent variable. **M19.**
first derivative, **second derivative**, **third derivative**, etc.: obtained by differentiating a function once, twice, three times, etc. ***partial derivative***: see **PARTIAL** *adjective*.
4 *CHEMISTRY.* A compound obtained from another by substitution or other simple process. **M19.**
†**5** *MEDICINE.* A method or agent that produces derivation (**DERIVATION** 1). Only in **M19.**
6 *FINANCE.* An arrangement or instrument (such as a future, option, or warrant) whose value derives from and is dependent on the value of an underlying asset. **L20.**
■ **derivatively** *adverb* **M17.** **derivativeness** *noun* **M17.**

derivatize /dɪˈrɪvətʌɪz/ *verb trans.* Also **-ise**. **M20.**
[**ORIGIN** from *derivat-* (in **DERIVATIVE**) + **-IZE**.]
CHEMISTRY. Convert (a compound) into a derivative.
■ **derivatiˈzation** *noun* **M20.**

derive /dɪˈrʌɪv/ *verb.* **LME.**
[**ORIGIN** Old French & mod. French *dériver* or Latin *derivare*, from *de-* **DE-** 1 + *rivus* brook, stream.]
▸ **I** *verb trans.* †**1** Conduct (water or another fluid) *from* a source etc. *to* or *into* a channel etc.; draw or convey through a channel; draw off, drain; *spec.* in **MEDICINE**, divert (pus etc.) to another part of the body. **LME–E19.** ▸**b** Carry, lead, (a channel of any kind). **M16–L18.**
†**2** Bring, turn, direct; bring down. **L15–E19.**
3 Obtain, get, draw, (a thing *from* a source). Freq. in *pass.*, arise, be descended, be formed, originate *from*; (of a word) be formed *from* an earlier word, base, or root. **E16.** ▸**b** Trace, obtain (ancestry, origin, pedigree, etc.). **L16.** ▸**c** *CHEMISTRY.* Obtain (a compound) from another by substitution or other simple process. **M19.**

SHAKES. *1 Hen. VI* By my mother I derived am from Lionel Duke of Clarence. J. CONRAD Stevie did not seem to derive any personal gratification from what he had done. R. MACAULAY If they could derive advantage from betraying you, betray you they would. J. BARTH Tambo and Bones . . played the instruments from which their names are derived. **b** T. HERBERT The Mountains of the Moone . . whence seven-mouthed Nyle, derives his Origen.

derived fossils *GEOLOGY*: occurring in rocks other than those to which they are native.
4 Obtain by reasoning; gather, deduce. **E16.**

J. R. GREEN It is difficult . . to derive any knowledge of Shakspere's inner history from the Sonnets. *Scientific American* In order to derive Einstein's result.

†**5** Pass on, transmit, convey from one to another; hand *down.* **M16–M19.**
6 Trace or show the origin, derivation, or pedigree of; state (a thing) to have originated *from*; *esp.* trace the origin of (a word) from its etymological source. **M16.**

HENRY FIELDING An action which malice itself could not have derived from an evil motive. S. JOHNSON That etymologist . . who can seriously derive dream from drama.

7 *refl.* Originate; come or descend *from*. **M17.**

D

J. LOCKE Experience; in that all our Knowledge is founded, and from that it ultimately derives itself.

▸ **II** *verb intrans.* **8** Flow, come, arise, originate, *from*, (occas.) *out of* (a source). LME. ▸**b** Of a word: originate, come as a derivative (*from* a root etc.). L18.

A. W. KINGLAKE There was an authority not deriving from the Queen or the Parliament. G. GREENE As a story the American picture derives from Hawthorne not Kingsley. K. VONNEGUT His family's wealth derived from the discovery . . of . . buried pirate treasure.

9 Descend, pass on, come (*to* a receiver etc.). Now *rare*. M16.

D

M. PATTISON Puritanism . . derives to this country directly from Geneva.

■ **deriver** *noun* E17.

derm /dəːm/ *noun*. Now *rare* or *obsolete*. M19.
[ORIGIN formed as DERMA. Cf. French *derme*.]
ANATOMY. = DERMIS.

derma /ˈdəːmə/ *noun*. Now *rare* or *obsolete*. E18.
[ORIGIN mod. Latin from Greek = skin.]
= DERMIS.

dermabrasion /dəːməˈbreɪʒ(ə)n/ *noun*. M20.
[ORIGIN from Greek DERMA + ABRASION.]
The surgical removal of superficial layers of skin with a rapidly revolving abrasive tool.

dermal /ˈdəːm(ə)l/ *adjective*. E19.
[ORIGIN formed as DERMABRASION + -AL[1].]
1 Of or pertaining to the skin or (esp.) the dermis. E19.
2 *BOTANY*. Epidermal. L19.

dermapteran /dəːˈmaptərən/ *noun & adjective*. L19.
[ORIGIN from mod. Latin *Dermaptera* (see below), from Greek DERMA + *pteron* wing.]
ENTOMOLOGY. ▸**A** *noun*. An insect of the order Dermaptera, comprising the earwigs. L19.
▸ **B** *adjective*. Of or belonging to Dermaptera. L19.
■ Also **dermapterous** *adjective* L19.

dermat- *combining form* see DERMATO-.

dermatitis /dəːməˈtʌɪtɪs/ *noun*. L19.
[ORIGIN formed as DERMATO- + -ITIS.]
MEDICINE. Inflammation of the skin, usu. of known or specified causation. Cf. ECZEMA.

dermato- /ˈdəːmətəʊ/ *combining form* of Greek *derma*, *-mat-* skin, hide, leather: see -O-. Before a vowel also **dermat-**. Cf. DERMO-.
■ **derˈmatogen** *noun* (*BOTANY*) in the histogen theory, a supposed outermost layer of the apical meristem, which develops into the epidermis (cf. PERIBLEM, PLEROME) L19. **dermatoˈgraphia** *noun* = DERMOGRAPHISM L19. **dermaˈtographism** *noun* = DERMOGRAPHISM E20. **dermatomyˈcosis** *noun*, pl. **-ˈcoses**, *MEDICINE* (a) ringworm infestation, tinea L19. **dermatomyoˈsitis** *noun* (*MEDICINE*) inflammation of the skin and underlying muscles, with erythema and oedema, often associated with internal cancer L19. **dermatoplasty** *noun* (an instance of) the surgical replacement of damaged or destroyed skin, as by plastic surgery or skin grafting L19. **dermaˈtoptic** *adjective* (*ZOOLOGY*) characterized by or relating to the ability of skin to perceive light L19.

dermatoglyphics /dəːmətəʊˈglɪfɪks/ *noun pl.* (usu. treated as *sing.*). E20.
[ORIGIN from DERMATO- + Greek *gluphikos* GLYPHIC + -S[1].]
The branch of science that deals with skin patterns (e.g. fingerprints), esp. of the hands and feet; in *pl.*, superficial features of the skin.
■ **dermatoglyphic** *adjective* E20. **dermatoglyphically** *adverb* M20.

dermatology /dəːməˈtɒlədʒi/ *noun*. E19.
[ORIGIN formed as DERMATOGLYPHICS + -LOGY.]
The branch of science that deals with the skin, esp. its disorders. Formerly also, a treatise on the skin.
■ **dermatoˈlogic** *adjective* L19. **dermatoˈlogical** *adjective* L19. **dermatologist** *noun* M19.

dermatome /ˈdəːmətəʊm/ *noun*. L19.
[ORIGIN formed as DERMATOGLYPHICS + -TOME.]
1 *SURGERY*. A device for removing an intact layer of skin. L19.
2 *EMBRYOLOGY*. The lateral wall of a somite, regarded as the origin of the connective tissue of the skin. E20.
3 *ANATOMY*. An area of the skin supplied by nerves from a single spinal root. E20.

dermatophyte /ˈdəːmətə(ʊ)fʌɪt/ *noun*. L19.
[ORIGIN formed as DERMATOGLYPHICS + -PHYTE.]
A pathogenic fungus that grows on skin, mucous membranes, hair, nails, feathers, etc.
■ **dermatophytic** /-ˈfɪtɪk/ *adjective* L19. **dermatophyˈtosis** *noun*, pl. **-toses** /-ˈtəʊsiːz/, a disease caused by a dermatophyte L19.

dermatosis /dəːməˈtəʊsɪs/ *noun*. Pl. **-toses** /-ˈtəʊsiːz/. M19.
[ORIGIN formed as DERMATOGLYPHICS + -OSIS.]
MEDICINE. Any (esp. non-inflammatory) disease of the skin.

dermestid /dəːˈmɛstɪd/ *noun & adjective*. L19.
[ORIGIN mod. Latin *Dermestidae* (see below), from *Dermestes* genus name, irreg. from Greek DERMA + *esthiein* eat: see -ID[3].]
ENTOMOLOGY. ▸**A** *noun*. Any of numerous small beetles of the family Dermestidae, many members of which are destructive (esp. as larvae) to hides, skin, fur, wool, and other animal substances. L19.
▸ **B** *adjective*. Of, pertaining to, or designating this family. L19.

dermis /ˈdəːmɪs/ *noun*. M19.
[ORIGIN mod. Latin, after EPIDERMIS.]
ANATOMY. The skin; *spec.* the layer of leathery collagenous tissue, sometimes referred to as the 'true skin', which lies beneath the epidermis and forms the bulk of the thickness of the skin.

dermo- /ˈdəːməʊ/ *combining form*.
[ORIGIN Repr. Greek *dermo-* abbreviation of DERMATO-.]
= DERMATO- (which has largely replaced *dermo-* as a living formative).
■ **dermoˈgraphia** *noun* = DERMOGRAPHISM E20. **derˈmographism** *noun* (*MEDICINE*) an allergic condition of the skin in which applied pressure, as by lines being drawn, produces persistent raised marks or weals L19.

dermoid /ˈdəːmɔɪd/ *adjective & noun*. E19.
[ORIGIN from DERMA + -OID.]
▸ **A** *adjective*. Of the skin; skinlike. E19.
dermoid cyst *MEDICINE* a teratoma containing epidermis, hair follicles, and sebaceous glands, derived from residual embryonic cells.
▸ **B** *noun*. *MEDICINE*. A dermoid cyst. L19.

dermopteran /dəːˈmɒptərən/ *noun & adjective*. E20.
[ORIGIN from mod. Latin *Dermoptera* (see below), formed as DERMO- + Greek *pteron* wing: see -AN.]
ZOOLOGY. ▸**A** *noun*. A mammal of the order Dermoptera which comprises the colugos or flying lemurs. E20.
▸ **B** *adjective*. Of or belonging to Dermoptera. E20.

dern *noun*[1], *adjective*[1], *& adverb* see DARN *noun*[2], *adjective*, *& adverb*.

dern /dəːn/ *adjective*[2] *& noun*[2]. *obsolete* exc. *Scot. & dial.*
[ORIGIN Old English *derne*, *dierne* = Old Frisian *dern*, Old Saxon *derni*, Old High German *tarni*, from West Germanic.]
▸ **A** *adjective*. †**1** Kept concealed or secret; deceitful, secretive, sly. OE–L16.
2 Of a place: not generally known, private. *arch.* OE.
†**3** Deep, intense. LME–L16.
4 Dark, dreary, sombre; wild, desolate. *arch.* L15.
▸ **B** *noun*. †**1** A secret. OE–ME.
†**2** A secret place. ME–E18.
3 Secrecy, concealment; darkness, obscurity. *arch.* ME.
■ †**dernly** *adverb* ME–E17.

dern /dəːn/ *verb*[1]. *obsolete* exc. *Scot. & dial.* Also **darn** /dɑːn/.
[ORIGIN Old English *diernan* = Old Saxon *dernian*, Old High German *tarnen*, from West Germanic, from base of DERN *adjective*[2] *& noun*[2].]
1 *verb trans.* Hide, conceal. OE.
2 *verb intrans. & refl.* Seek concealment, hide oneself. L16.
3 *verb trans.* Cause to hide. L16.

dern *verb*[2] see DARN *verb*[2].

dernier /dɛrnje, ˈdəːnjeɪ/ *adjective*. E17.
[ORIGIN French from Old French *derrenier*, from *derrein*: see DARREIN.]
Last, ultimate, final. Now only as below.
dernier cri /kri, kriː/, ***le dernier cri*** /lə/ [French, lit. '(the) last cry'] the very latest fashion. ***dernier mot*** /mo, məʊ/ the last word. ***dernier ressort*** /rəsɔːr, rəˈsɔː/, †***dernier resort*** a last refuge; orig., the last court of appeal.
– NOTE: Formerly fully naturalized.

derogate /ˈdɛrəgət/ *ppl adjective* (orig. *pa. pple*). Now *rare*. LME.
[ORIGIN Latin *derogatus* pa. pple, formed as DEROGATE *verb*: see -ATE[2].]
†**1** Abrogated in part, lessened in authority etc. LME–M16.
2 Debased. E17.
■ †**derogately** *adverb* (*rare*, Shakes.): only in E17.

derogate /ˈdɛrəgeɪt/ *verb*. LME.
[ORIGIN Latin *derogat-* pa. ppl stem of *derogare*, from *de-* DE- 1 + *rogare* ask, question, propose (a law): see -ATE[3].]
†**1** *verb trans.* Repeal or abrogate in part (a law etc.); destroy or impair the force, effect, or authority of. LME–L17.
2 *verb trans.* Detract from; disparage, depreciate. LME.

M. EDELMAN We learn to . . derogate the conventional speech of the working class . . as . . sloppy and impoverished.

3 *verb trans.* Take away (something *from* a thing) so as to lessen or impair it. *arch.* E16.
4 *verb intrans.* Take away something *from*; detract *from*. M16.

LD BRAIN It will not . . derogate from Harvey's uniqueness to compare him with . . Sherrington.

5 *verb intrans.* Degenerate; deviate *from* correct behaviour etc. E17.

S. BECKETT Should you . . feel like derogating from the general to the particular, remember I am here.

■ **derogator** *noun* L16.

derogation /dɛrəˈgeɪʃ(ə)n/ *noun*. LME.
[ORIGIN French *dérogation* or Latin *derogatio(n-)* (only in sense 'partial abrogation of a law'), formed as DEROGATE *verb*: see -ATION.]
1 The lessening or impairment of the power or authority *of*; detraction *from*. LME.

T. CARTE Papal usurpations, to the derogation of the crown.

2 The action of lowering in value or estimation; disparagement, depreciation. LME.

ADDISON He had heard the Plaintiff speak in derogation of the Portuguese.

3 The exemption from or relaxation of a rule or law. L15.
4 Falling off in rank or character; degeneration, debasement. M19.

G. A. SALA Men . . who shudder at the derogation and degradation of the Northern American clergy.

derogative /dɪˈrɒgətɪv/ *adjective*. L15.
[ORIGIN French †*derogatif*, *-ive* or late Latin *derogativus*, formed as DEROGATE *verb*: see -ATIVE.]
Tending to derogation, derogatory.
■ **derogatively** *adverb* L19.

derogatory /dɪˈrɒgət(ə)ri/ *adjective*. E16.
[ORIGIN Late Latin *derogatorius*, formed as DEROGATE *verb*: see -ORY[2].]
1 Tending to detract from authority, rights, etc.; impairing in force or effect. Foll. by *from*, *to*, †*of*. E16.

H. COX This Act was annulled as derogatory to the King's just rights.

2 Lowering in honour or estimation; unsuited to one's dignity or position; depreciatory, disrespectful, disparaging. L16.

H. G. WELLS In secret she invented derogatory names for him; 'Old Uncle Nose-up . . ' for example.

■ **derogatorily** *adverb* E17. **derogatoriness** *noun* E18.

derout /dɪˈraʊt/ *noun*. *arch.* M17.
[ORIGIN French *déroute*, formed as DEROUT *verb*.]
An utter defeat, a rout.

derout /dɪˈraʊt/ *verb trans. arch.* M17.
[ORIGIN French *dérouter*, Old French *des-*, from *dé-* DE- 3 + *route* ROUT *noun*[3].]
Put completely to flight.

derrick /ˈdɛrɪk/ *noun*. E17.
[ORIGIN *Derrick*, the surname of a noted London hangman fl. 1600.]
†**1** (D-.) A hangman; hanging; the gallows. E17–L18.
2 A contrivance for hoisting or moving heavy weights: ▸†**a** *NAUTICAL*. A tackle used at the outer quarter of the mizzenmast. M–L18. ▸**b** A spar or boom set up obliquely, with its head steadied by guys, and fitted with tackle, orig. used on board ship. M18. ▸**c** A kind of crane with a jib or adjustable arm pivoted to the foot of the central post, deck, or floor. M19.
3 A framework erected over an oil well or similar boring, to support the drilling apparatus. M19.
■ **derricking** *noun* hoisting or moving heavy weights by a derrick L19. **derricking** *adjective* operating as or like a derrick E20.

derrière /dɛrɪˈɛː; dɛrjɛːr (*pl. same*)/ *noun*. *colloq.* L18.
[ORIGIN French = behind.]
The buttocks; = BEHIND *noun* 1.

derring-do /dɛrɪŋˈduː/ *noun*. *pseudo-arch.* L16.
[ORIGIN Misconstruction (by Spenser and others) of late Middle English *dorryng do(n)* daring to do, orig. in Chaucer, copied by Lydgate & misprinted in 16th-cent. eds. as *derrynge do*.]
Daring action or feats, heroic courage.

SIR W. SCOTT Singular . . if there be two who can do a deed of such derring-do.

■ **derring-doer** *noun* (*rare*) a performer of daring feats L16.

derringer /ˈdɛrɪndʒə/ *noun*. *N. Amer.* M19.
[ORIGIN Henry *Deringer* (1786–1868), US gunsmith.]
A small pistol with large bore.

derris /ˈdɛrɪs/ *noun*. M19.
[ORIGIN mod. Latin (see below) from Greek = leather covering (referring to the pod).]
1 Any of various tall tropical leguminous climbing plants of the genus *Derris*. Also called ***tuba***. M19.
2 The powdered tuberous root of any of such plants (or of other genera containing rotenone), orig. used in Malaya to stupefy fish, now in general use as an insecticide. L19.

derry /ˈdɛri/ *interjection & noun*. M16.
[ORIGIN Unknown. Sense 3 may be a different word.]
▸ **I** *interjection & noun*. **1** Used as a meaningless word in the refrains of popular songs. Also ***derry down***. Cf. DOWN *noun*[3] *& interjection* 1a. M16.
▸ **II** *noun*. **2** A ballad, a set of verses. *rare*. M19.
3 [App. from *derry down*.] A tendency to disapprove of someone or something; a dislike, a prejudice, a grudge; = DOWN *noun*[3] 4. *Austral. & NZ.* L19.

DOUGLAS STUART And warfare, that's another thing Peter has a derry on.

der Tag /der ˈtaːk/ *noun phr.* E20.
[ORIGIN German.]
= ***The Day*** s.v. DAY *noun*.

dertrum /ˈdəːtrəm/ *noun*. L19.
[ORIGIN mod. Latin from Greek *dertron* beak.]
ORNITHOLOGY. The extremity of the upper bill of a bird's beak.

derv /dəːv/ *noun*. M20.
[ORIGIN Acronym, from *d*iesel-*e*ngined *r*oad *v*ehicle.]
Diesel fuel for road vehicles.

dervish /ˈdəːvɪʃ/ *noun*. L16.
[ORIGIN Turkish *derviş* from Persian *darvīš* poor, a religious mendicant.]
A Muslim (*spec.* Sufi) religious man who has taken vows of poverty and austerity; *spec.* (more fully ***dancing dervish***, ***whirling dervish***, ***howling dervish***, etc.) one whose order includes the practice of dancing etc. as a spiritual exercise.

J. R. ACKERLEY They instituted fun and games and whirled about together like dervishes.

DES *abbreviation*.
1 COMPUTING. Data encryption standard.
2 *hist.* Department of Education and Science.

desacralize /diːˈsakrəlʌɪz/ *verb trans.* Also **-ise**. E20.
[ORIGIN from DE- 3 + SACRAL *adjective*[2] + -IZE.]
Ritually remove a taboo from; make less sacred.
■ **desacraliˈzation** *noun* E20.

desai /ˈdɛsʌɪ/ *noun*. L17.
[ORIGIN Marathi *deśāī*.]
hist. In India, a revenue official or petty chief.

desalinate /diːˈsalɪneɪt/ *verb trans.* M20.
[ORIGIN from DE- 3 + SALINE *noun* + -ATE[3].]
Remove the salt from (esp. seawater).
■ **desaliˈnation** *noun* M20.

desalt /diːˈsɔːlt, -ˈsɒlt/ *verb trans.* E20.
[ORIGIN from DE- 3 + SALT *noun*[1].]
Remove salt or salts from.

desaparecido /ˌdesapareˈsiðo/ *noun*. Pl. **-os** /-ɔs/. L20.
[ORIGIN Spanish = (one who has) disappeared.]
A person who disappeared in Argentina during the period of military rule between 1976 and 1983, presumed killed by members of the armed services or the police.

desaturate /diːˈsatʃʊreɪt, -tjʊr-/ *verb trans.* E20.
[ORIGIN from DE- 3 + SATURATE *verb*.]
Cause to become unsaturated, make less saturated.
■ **desatuˈration** *noun* E20.

désaxé /dezakse/ *adjective & adverb*. E20.
[ORIGIN French.]
Of the crankshaft of an engine: (set) out of line with the centre of the cylinder.

descale /diːˈskeɪl/ *verb trans.* M20.
[ORIGIN from DE- 3 + SCALE *noun*[3].]
Remove scale from.
■ **descaler** *noun* a substance or device for removing scale M20.

descamisado /ˌdeskamiˈsaðo, dɛsˌkamɪˈsɑːdəʊ/ *noun*. Pl. **-os** /-ɔs, -əʊz/. M19.
[ORIGIN Spanish = shirtless. Cf. *sans-culotte*.]
An extreme liberal in the Spanish Revolutionary War of 1820–3; *transf.* a revolutionary.

descant /ˈdɛskant/ *noun*. Also **di-** /ˈdɪ-/. LME.
[ORIGIN Old French *deschant* (mod. *déchant*) from medieval Latin *discantus* part-song, refrain, formed as DIS- 1 + *cantus* song.]
▸ **I** MUSIC. **1** A melodious accompaniment to a simple theme sung or played above it. LME.

E. FIGES Her high voice sounded in a thin piping descant above the rest.

2 The soprano or highest part of the score in part-singing. M16.

M. AMIS I was a *soprano*, a *first* soprano, often taking descants, in the choir.

3 Musical composition, harmony; a harmonized composition. M16.
4 A melodious song. *arch.* or *poet.* L16.

W. C. BRYANT I hear the wood-thrush piping one mellow descant more.

5 An instrumental prelude consisting of variations on a given theme. M17.
▸ **II** *transf.* **6** (A) discourse on a theme or subject; an observation, a criticism, a remark. *arch.* L16.

ADDISON After this short descant on the uncertainty of our English weather.

†**7** (A) variation from that which is typical or customary. M17–E18.

T. FULLER Running, Leaping, and Dancing, the descants on the plain song of walking.

descant /dɪˈskant, dɛ-/ *verb intrans.* Also **dis-**. LME.
[ORIGIN Prob. from the noun: so Old French *deschanter* (mod. *déchanter*).]
1 Sing harmoniously (*arch.*); play or sing a descant. LME.
2 Make remarks or observations; comment or talk at length *on* or *upon* a theme, esp. in praise. E16.

SHAKES. *Rich. III* To spy my shadow in the sun And descant on mine own deformity. J. GALSWORTHY On this theme he descanted for half an hour.

■ **descanter** *noun* LME.

descend /dɪˈsɛnd/ *verb*. ME.
[ORIGIN Old French & mod. French *descendre* from Latin *descendere*, from *de-* DE- 1 + *scandere* to climb.]
▸ **I** *verb intrans.* **1** Go down, come down; fall, sink; be lowered. ME. ▸**b** Of a planet, zodiacal sign, etc.: move away from the zenith, *esp.* go below the horizon; move southwards. LME. ▸**c** Alight from a conveyance. L15. ▸†**d** Withdraw *into* oneself for meditation. L16–L17.

J. HAYWARD I passed to the Nile descending on it at my leasure to the sea. J. FORBES The shades of evening began to descend. P. KAVANAGH A couple of crows descended from the parched sky and landed in Tarry's plot of turnips. **b** MILTON The setting Sun Slowly descended. **c** J. BUCHAN A big . . car, from which a man in a raincoat had descended.

2 Proceed or go on to what follows, esp. from the general to the particular. ME.

LD MACAULAY Historians rarely descend to those details from which alone the real state of a community can be collected.

3 Slope or extend downwards. LME.

D. H. LAWRENCE A flight of stone steps descended into the depths of the water itself. TOLKIEN He could see the heads of the trees descending in ranks towards the plain.

4 Of sound: fall in pitch, go down the scale. LME. ▸**b** Come or go down in any scale; proceed from superior to inferior. E17.
5 Condescend, lower oneself, stoop, (*to do*). LME.

S. JOHNSON I have seldom descended to the arts by which favour is obtained.

6 Fall violently upon, attack. LME. ▸**b** Foll. by *on*, *upon*: make an inconvenient, unexpected, or unwelcome visit. E20.

b ALDOUS HUXLEY I have . . staying with me in Balliol young Robert Nichols, who descended on me for a day or two.

7 Come of, derive *from* a progenitor or predecessor; *fig.* derive from, originate. Now usu. in *pass.* LME.

SHAKES. *A.Y.L.* Thou shouldst have better pleas'd me with this deed, Hadst thou descended from another house. DAY LEWIS Her mother . . was directly descended from Oliver Goldsmith's uncle.

8 Be transmitted by inheritance; pass by heredity, pass to an heir. LME.

W. GOUGE The Crowne and Kingdome by just and unquestionable title descended on her. STEELE The eternal Mark of having had a wicked Ancestor descends to his Posterity.

▸ **II** *verb trans.* †**9** Bring or send down. L15–L17.
10 Go or come down, climb down; move downstream along (a river etc.). E17.

T. HARDY He descended the stone stairs to a lower story of the castle.

descendable *adjective* see DESCENDIBLE.

descendance /dɪˈsɛnd(ə)ns/ *noun*. Now *rare*. Also **-ence**. L16.
[ORIGIN Old French & mod. French, or medieval Latin *descendentia*, *descendent-* pres. ppl stem of *descendere*: see DESCEND, -ANCE, -ENCE.]
The action or fact of descending from a particular ancestor or origin.
■ **descendancy**, **-ency** *noun* E17.

descendant /dɪˈsɛnd(ə)nt/ *adjective & noun*. Also (now *rare*) **-ent**. LME.
[ORIGIN Old French & mod. French, pres. pple of *descendre*: see DESCEND, -ANT[1], -ENT.]
▸ **A** *adjective* **1** *a* HERALDRY. Descending towards the base of the shield. Now *rare* or *obsolete*. LME. ▸**b** Of a planet etc.: moving away from the zenith; ASTROLOGY moving towards or just sinking below the western horizon. L16. ▸**c** *gen.* Descending; coming or going down. *rare*. L16.
2 Deriving or descending from an ancestor. L16.
▸ **B** *noun*. **1** A person, animal, plant, or thing descended or derived from an ancestor or predecessor; issue, offspring. E17.

C. DARWIN The existing forms of life are the descendants by true generation of pre-existing forms. F. W. FARRAR The Gothic language . . has left no direct descendants. O. MANNING A last descendant of one of the Greek Phanariot families that had ruled and exploited Rumania under the Turks. D. DONOGHUE The IRA's claim to be the only true descendants of our Republican martyrs.

2 ASTROLOGY (formerly also ASTRONOMY). The part of the heavens just descending below the horizon; the point at which the western horizon intersects the ecliptic. L17.

descendence *noun* var. of DESCENDANCE.

descendent *adjective & noun* see DESCENDANT.

descendental /dɪsɛnˈdɛnt(ə)l/ *adjective*. *rare*. M19.
[ORIGIN from DESCENDANT after *transcendental*.]
That descends to matter of fact; realistic.

E. P. WHIPPLE With his brain full of transcendental morality, and his heart full of descendental appetites.

†**descender** *noun*[1]. LAW. LME–M18.
[ORIGIN Anglo-Norman, use as noun of infinitive = Old French & mod. French *descendre*: see DESCEND, -ER[4].]
Descent, right of succession.

descender /dɪˈsɛndə/ *noun*[2]. M17.
[ORIGIN from DESCEND + -ER[1].]
1 A person who or thing which descends. M17.
2 TYPOGRAPHY & PALAEOGRAPHY. A descending letter; a part or stroke projecting below the baseline. E19.

descendible /dɪˈsɛndɪb(ə)l/ *adjective*. Also **-able**. L15.
[ORIGIN Old French *descendable*, formed as DESCEND: see -ABLE, -IBLE.]
1 Able to be inherited. L15.
2 Able to be descended; down which a person may go. *rare*. M18.

descending /dɪˈsɛndɪŋ/ *noun*. LME.
[ORIGIN from DESCEND + -ING[1].]
1 The action of DESCEND; descent, going down. LME.
†**2** A downward slope: extension downwards. L15–E17.
†**3** Parentage, lineage. *rare* (Shakes.). Only in E17.
– COMB.: **descending node** ASTRONOMY the point at which the moon's or a planet's orbit crosses the ecliptic from north to south.

descending /dɪˈsɛndɪŋ/ *ppl adjective*. L16.
[ORIGIN from DESCEND + -ING[2].]
1 Moving downwards, coming down; directed or extended downwards. L16.
descending colon ANATOMY the part of the large intestine which passes downwards on the left side of the abdomen towards the rectum. **descending letter** TYPOGRAPHY & PALAEOGRAPHY a letter with a part or stroke projecting below the baseline.
2 Proceeding to what is lower in position or value, or later in order; falling in pitch, stress, etc. L16.

descension /dɪˈsɛnʃ(ə)n/ *noun*. Now *rare*. LME.
[ORIGIN Old French from Latin *descensio(n-)*, from *descens-* pa. ppl stem of *descendere*: see DESCEND, -ION.]
1 The action of descending, descent. LME.
†**2** Descent from an ancestor, lineage. LME–L16.
†**3** A fall in dignity or status. LME–L17.
†**4** A method of distillation in which the vapour was made to distil downwards. LME–M17.
5 ASTRONOMY & ASTROLOGY. The descending of a celestial object; a measure of this. M16.
■ **descensional** *adjective* (*rare*) E18.

descensive /dɪˈsɛnsɪv/ *adjective*. LME.
[ORIGIN from Latin *descens-* (see DESCENSION) + -IVE.]
Characterized by or producing downward movement, falling.

descent /dɪˈsɛnt/ *noun*. ME.
[ORIGIN Old French & mod. French *descente*, from *descendre* DESCEND after *attente*, *vente* from *attendre*, *vendre*.]
1 The fact of descending or being descended from an ancestor or predecessor; derivation, origin. ME.

J. YEOWELL A chieftain of imperial descent. J. FISKE The descent of the genus *equus* from a five-toed mammal not larger than a pig.

2 †**a** A line of descent, lineage, race, stock. ME–E17. ▸†**b** A descendant; offspring, issue. L15–M17. ▸**c** A generation. E16.

b G. CHAPMAN She went Up to the chamber, where the fair descent Of great Alcinous slept. **c** J. RAY Such as can prove their Gentility for three or four Descents.

3 LAW. The passing of (real) property by inheritance, esp. in the event of intestacy. ME. ▸**b** The transmission of titles, privileges, etc., or characteristics by inheritance. LME.
4 The action or an act of descending; downward movement. LME. ▸**b** *spec.* The action or an act of climbing or travelling down a mountain, slope, stair, etc. E17. ▸†**c** = DESCENSION 4. M17–E18.

J. KEILL The great resistance they met with in their descent through the Air. S. KITZINGER The intense and thrilling sensations of the descent of the baby's head. *Washington Post* The 85-ton Skylab, whose slow descent from orbit threatened to bring it crashing to earth.

the Descent *spec.* the descent of Christ into hell.
5 A downward slope. L16. ▸†**b** The lowest part. *rare* (Shakes.). Only in E17. ▸**c** A means of descending, a way leading downwards. M17.

New York Times The variety of terrain that makes this descent so much fun for skiers.

6 A fall in any scale; *fig.* a decline to a lower state or condition. L16. ▸†**b** A lower stage; a degree below. L16–E18.

MILTON Oh, foul descent! that I, who erst contended With gods to sit in the highest, am now constrained Into a Beast.

method of steepest descent(s): see STEEP *adjective*.
7 A sudden attack or invasion. E17.

J. R. GREEN A daring descent of the English forces upon Cadiz.

– COMB.: **descent group** ANTHROPOLOGY a unit of social organization based on common descent.

descloizite /deɪˈklɔɪzʌɪt/ *noun*. M19.
[ORIGIN from Alfred *Des Cloizeaux* (1817–97), French mineralogist + -ITE[1].]
MINERALOGY. An orthorhombic basic vanadate of zinc, copper, and lead occurring chiefly as a secondary mineral encrusting ores of its constituent metals.

descramble /diːˈskramb(ə)l/ *verb trans.* M20.
[ORIGIN from DE- 3 + SCRAMBLE *verb*.]
Convert or restore (a signal) to intelligible form by applying the reverse of the scrambling process; recover an original signal from (a scrambled signal). Cf. UNSCRAMBLE.
■ **descrambler** *noun* = UNSCRAMBLER L20.

D

describable /dɪˈskrʌɪbəb(ə)l/ *adjective.* **E19.**
[ORIGIN from DESCRIBE + -ABLE. Earlier in INDESCRIBABLE.]
Able to be described.

describe /dɪˈskrʌɪb/ *verb trans.* **LME.**
[ORIGIN Latin *describere* write down, copy, from *de-* DE- 1 + *scribere* write. Cf. earlier DESCRIVE *verb*.]
▸ **I 1** Portray in words, recite the characteristics of, give a detailed or graphic account of. Foll. by *as*: assert to be, call. **LME.**

G. SAINTSBURY In a much sounder sense than that in which .. Matthew Arnold described it as being so, the eighteenth century was to be the Age of Prose. P. ACKROYD He describes .. the routines of bourgeois life—flannel suits, the cakes and tea. S. NAIPAUL It was impossible for her to describe the beauty of the river; .. to convey its peacefulness.

†**2** Enter in a register, enrol. **L15–M17.** ▸**b** Write down, transcribe, copy out. **E–M17.**
3 Trace the outline of (a geometrical figure etc.), mark out, draw. **L15.** ▸**b** Trace by motion; move in (a specified line). **M16.**

DRYDEN With chalk I first describe a circle here. **b** J. MCPHEE The sun describes a horseshoe around the margins of the sky.

4 Portray visually, make a likeness of, picture. Now *rare* or *obsolete*. **E16.** ▸†**b** Of a thing: stand for or represent visually. **M17–L18.**
5 Mark off, divide. *rare*. **M16.**
▸ **II** After confusion of DESCRIVE, DESCRY *verb*[2], and DESCRY *verb*[1].
6 Descry, perceive. Now *rare*. **L16.**

MILTON I describ'd his way Bent all on speed, and markt his Aerie Gate.

■ **describer** *noun* **M16.**

descrier /dɪˈskrʌɪə/ *noun.* **L16.**
[ORIGIN from DESCRY *verb*[1] + -ER[1].]
A person who descries or discovers something.

descript /dɪˈskrɪpt/ *ppl adjective.* Now *rare* or *obsolete*. **M17.**
[ORIGIN Latin *descriptus* pa. pple of *describere* DESCRIBE.]
Described, apportioned; inscribed, engraved.

descripta *noun* pl. of DESCRIPTUM.

description /dɪˈskrɪpʃ(ə)n/ *noun.* **LME.**
[ORIGIN Old French & mod. French from Latin *descriptio(n-)*, from *descript-* pa. ppl stem of *describere*: see DESCRIBE, -ION.]
1 A detailed account of a person, thing, scene, or event; a verbal portrait. **LME.** ▸**b** The action of describing someone or something verbally; verbal representation or portraiture. **LME.** ▸**c** *LOGIC*. A definition by non-essential attributes. **E17.**

H. JAMES He had been to places that people had written books about, and they were not a bit like the descriptions.

definite description: see DEFINITE *adjective*. **b knowledge by description** *PHILOSOPHY* knowledge or understanding not based on direct experience.
†**2** The action of writing down or inscribing; an inscription. **LME–L18.** ▸**b** Registration, enrolment. **LME–E17.**
3 †**a** A particular design; individual characteristics. **LME–M16.** ▸**b** The combination of attributes which defines a particular class or type; the type or variety defined, a sort, a kind, a class. **L16.**

b D. G. MITCHELL The man must be a roué of the worst description. B. MOORE That's the first flying machine of any description that has ever landed on Muck.

†**4** Pictorial representation. *rare*. **E–M17.**
5 The action of drawing a geometrical figure. **M17.** ▸**b** The action of tracing or passing along a particular course. **E18.**
■ **descriptionist** *noun* a person who professes to give a description, *spec.* one who avoids evaluation or explanation **E19.**

descriptive /dɪˈskrɪptɪv/ *adjective.* **M18.**
[ORIGIN Late Latin *descriptivus*, from *descript-*: see DESCRIPTION, -IVE.]
1 Serving or seeking to describe; characterized by description. **M18.**
descriptive geometry: concerned with the description of surfaces, figures, solids, etc., esp. by means of projection on to planes.
2 Consisting of or concerned with description of observable things or qualities; not expressing feelings or valuations. **M19.** ▸**b** *LINGUISTICS*. Describing a language as it is, avoiding comparison or prescription. **E20.**
3 *GRAMMAR*. Of an adjective etc.: assigning a quality rather than restricting the application of the expression modified. **E20.**
■ **descriptively** *adverb* **L18.** **descriptiveness** *noun* **M19.**

descriptivism /dɪˈskrɪptɪvɪz(ə)m/ *noun.* **M20.**
[ORIGIN from DESCRIPTIVE + -ISM.]
1 *PHILOSOPHY*. The doctrine that the meanings of ethical or aesthetic terms and statements are purely descriptive rather than prescriptive, evaluative, or emotive. **M20.**
2 *LINGUISTICS*. The practice or advocacy of descriptive linguistics. **M20.**
■ **descriptivist** *noun & adjective* (**a**) *noun* an adherent or advocate of descriptivism; (**b**) *adjective* of or pertaining to descriptivism or descriptivists: **M20.**

descriptor /dɪˈskrɪptə/ *noun.* **M20.**
[ORIGIN Latin = describer, from *descript-*: see DESCRIPTION, -OR.]
An element or term that has the function of describing, identifying, or indexing.

descriptum /dɪˈskrɪptəm/ *noun.* Pl. **-ta** /-tə/. **M20.**
[ORIGIN Latin *descriptum* neut. pa. pple of *describere* DESCRIBE.]
PHILOSOPHY. The object of a description; the object to which a descriptor refers.

descrive /dɪˈskrʌɪv/ *verb trans. obsolete* exc. *Scot.* **ME.**
[ORIGIN Old French *descrivre* (mod. *décrire*) from Latin *describere* DESCRIBE. Through DESCRY *verb*[2] conf. with DESCRY *verb*[1].]
▸ **I 1** = DESCRIBE 1. **ME.**
†**2** = DESCRIBE 2. **ME–L15.**
†**3** = DESCRIBE 3, 4, 5. **LME–M16.**
▸ †**II 4** Descry, perceive. **ME–L16.**

†**descry** *noun.* **LME**
[ORIGIN from DESCRY *verb*[1].]
1 A war cry. Only in **LME.**
2 Perception from a distance. Only in **E17.**

descry /dɪˈskrʌɪ/ *verb*[1] *trans.* **ME.**
[ORIGIN Old French *descrier* (mod. *décrier*) cry (down), publish. In branch I assoc. with DECRY *verb*. Cf. DECRY *verb*.]
▸ †**I 1** Disclose, reveal (a secret); betray. **ME–L17.**
2 Challenge to fight; taunt. **ME–L15.**
3 Announce, declare, make known. **LME–M17.**
4 Denounce, disparage. **LME–L17.**
▸ **II 5** Catch sight of, esp. from a distance; espy. **ME.**

JO GRIMOND A detour so that his passengers may descry them [seals] reclining like bananas on the rocks.

6 Discover by observation; find out, perceive. **LME.**

B. MAGEE One has to go on reading for several pages before beginning to descry .. what it is he is saying. A. STORR Their readiness to descry hostility where none exists.

†**7** Investigate, explore. **L16–M18.**

†**descry** *verb*[2] *trans.* **ME–E17.**
[ORIGIN Partly from Old French *descrire*, partly phonet. reduction of DESCRIVE.]
= DESCRIBE I.

desecrate /ˈdɛsɪkreɪt/ *verb trans.* **L17.**
[ORIGIN from DE- 3 + stem of *consecrate* (Latin *desecrare* or *desacrare* meant 'consecrate').]
1 Remove or violate the sacred nature of, profane; *fig.* spoil or treat with contempt (something venerated or admired). **L17.**

E. B. PUSEY The .. vessels of the Temple .. were desecrated by being employed in idol-worship. P. KAVANAGH He couldn't imagine any person with an artistic sense permitting such gross vulgarity to desecrate the hall of their house.

2 Dismiss from holy orders. *arch.* **L17.**
3 Dedicate or devote *to* evil. **E19.**

J. STEPHEN Particular spots .. were desecrated to Satan.

■ **desecration** *noun* the action of desecrating; a desecrated state: **E18.** **desecrative** *adjective* calculated or tending to desecrate **M19.** **desecrator** *noun* **L19.**

deseed /diːˈsiːd/ *verb trans.* **M20.**
[ORIGIN from DE- 3 + SEED *noun*.]
Remove the seed(s) from.

desegregate /diːˈsɛɡrɪɡeɪt/ *verb trans.* **M20.**
[ORIGIN from DE- 3 + SEGREGATE *verb*.]
Remove from segregation; *esp.* (orig. *US*) abolish racial segregation in (schools etc.) or of (persons etc.).
■ **desegre'gation** *noun* **M20.**

desensitize /diːˈsɛnsɪtʌɪz/ *verb trans.* Also **-ise**. **E20.**
[ORIGIN from DE- 3 + SENSITIZE.]
Reduce or eliminate the sensitivity of (*spec.* film, a lithographic plate, etc., to light, a person or animal to an allergen, a person to a neurosis, phobia, etc.).
■ **desensiti'zation** *noun* **E20.** **desensitizer** *noun* a desensitizing agent **M20.**

desert /dɪˈzəːt/ *noun*[1]. **ME.**
[ORIGIN Old French, from *deservir* DESERVE.]
1 Deserving, being worthy of reward or punishment. **ME.** ▸**b** Merit, excellence, worth. **LME.**
2 An action or quality deserving reward or punishment. Usu. in *pl.* **LME.**
3 Due reward or punishment, something deserved. Freq. in ***get one's deserts, have one's deserts, meet with one's deserts***, etc. **LME.**

desert /ˈdɛzət/ *noun*[2]. **ME.**
[ORIGIN Old French & mod. French *désert* from late Latin (Vulgate) *desertum* use as noun of neut. of *desertus* left waste, pa. pple of *deserere* leave, forsake.]
An uncultivated, sparsely inhabited tract of land, a wilderness. Now *spec.* a waterless and treeless region.

SHAKES. *A.Y.L.* In this desert inaccessible, Under the shade of melancholy boughs. R. P. JHABVALA Hot winds whistle columns of dust out of the desert into the town. *fig.*: *Daily Express* Once they move out of a town centre, others will follow, leaving a desert. *New Statesman* Far too many children have died in a desert of apathy.

ship of the desert: see SHIP *noun* 5.
– COMB. (cf. next): **desert boot** a suede etc. boot reaching to or just above the ankle and usu. with a thick ridged sole; **desert ironwood** (the wood of) a small leguminous tree, *Olneya tesota*, of arid parts of south-western N. America, with purplish flowers, very tough wood, and seeds formerly eaten locally; also called *palo de hierro*; **desert island** a remote and presumably uninhabited island; **desert lark** any of several larks of the genus *Ammomanes*, found from N. and W. Africa to the Middle East and India; **desert lemon**, **desert lime** *Austral.* = KUMQUAT 2; **desert oak** *Austral.* a casuarina, *C. decaisneana*; **desert pavement** *GEOLOGY* in arid regions, a surface layer of closely packed or cemented pebbles, rock fragments, etc., from which fine material has been removed by the wind; **desert rat** *colloq.* a soldier of the 7th British armoured division (with a jerboa as its badge) in the N. African desert campaign of 1941–2; **desert rose** a flower-like aggregate of tabular crystals of a mineral, occurring in arid areas, a rock rose; **desert varnish** a dark hard film of oxides formed on exposed rock surfaces in arid regions.
■ **desertic** /dɪˈzəːtɪk/ *adjective* characteristic of a desert; desolate: **M20.**

desert /ˈdɛzət/ *adjective.* **ME.**
[ORIGIN Old French & mod. French *désert* from Latin *desertus* pa. pple: see DESERT *noun*[2]. Now treated as attrib. use DESERT *noun*[2].]
1 Uninhabited, desolate, lonely. **ME.** ▸**b** Of the nature of a desert; uncultivated, barren. **LME.**
2 Deserted, forsaken, abandoned. *arch.* **LME.**
– NOTE: Orig., & archaically in **18** & **19**, stressed on 2nd syll.
■ **desertness** *noun* barren desolation **LME.**

desert /dɪˈzəːt/ *verb.* **LME.**
[ORIGIN French *déserter* from late Latin *desertare*, from Latin *desertus*: see DESERT *noun*[2].]
1 *verb trans.* Give up, relinquish, leave. **LME.**

POPE His slacken'd hand deserts the lance it bore. J. HAWKES St. Kilda, .. where men clung tenaciously for a time, but which .. they have now deserted.

2 *SCOTS LAW*. **a** *verb trans.* Cease to pursue (an action, summons, etc.). Formerly also, adjourn (Parliament). **L15.** ▸**b** *verb intrans.* Cease to have legal force; become inoperative. **M16.**
a desert the diet abandon criminal proceedings, finally or temporarily.
3 *verb trans.* Forsake, abandon, (a person or thing having a claim upon one). **M17.** ▸**b** Abandon or give up *to* something. *arch.* **M17.** ▸**c** Of a power or faculty: fail (someone). **M17.**

J. GALSWORTHY Deserting his wife and child and running away with that foreign governess. P. ROTH Louis deserts basic training and .. goes to hide out from the Korean War in a slum somewhere. **b** W. S. LANDOR Gracious God! Desert me to my sufferings, but sustain My faith in Thee! **c** C. CHAPLIN Mother obeyed like a child; .. her will seemed to have deserted her.

4 *verb intrans.* Run away from or forsake one's duty, post, or party, esp. from service in the armed forces. **L17.**

F. FITZGERALD Its soldiers deserted in droves to escape their enemy or to rejoin their families.

■ **deserted** *ppl adjective* Forsaken, abandoned, left desolate **E17.** **desertedness** *noun* **E19.**

deserter /dɪˈzəːtə/ *noun.* **M17.**
[ORIGIN from DESERT *verb* + -ER[1], after French *déserteur*.]
1 A person who deserts someone or something. **M17.**
2 *spec.* A member of the armed forces who deserts. **M17.**

desertification /dɛˌzəːtɪfɪˈkeɪʃ(ə)n/ *noun.* **L20.**
[ORIGIN from DESERT *noun*[2]: see -FICATION.]
The process by which fertile land becomes desert.
■ **de'sertify** *verb trans.* make desert, cause desertification of **L20.**

desertion /dɪˈzəːʃ(ə)n/ *noun.* **LME.**
[ORIGIN Old French & mod. French *désertion* from late Latin *desertio(n-)*, from *desert-* pa. ppl stem of *deserere*: see DESERT *noun*[2], -ION.]
1 The action of deserting, forsaking, or abandoning. **LME.** ▸**b** *LAW*. Wilful abandonment of one's duty or obligations, esp. (**a**) to service in the armed forces, (**b**) to live with one's spouse. **E18.**
2 The state of being deserted or abandoned. **M16.**

desertization /dɛzətʌɪˈzeɪʃ(ə)n/ *noun.* Also **-isation**. **M20.**
[ORIGIN from DESERT *noun*[2] + -IZATION.]
= DESERTIFICATION.

desertless /dɪˈzəːtlɪs/ *adjective.* **M16.**
[ORIGIN from DESERT *noun*[1] + -LESS.]
†**1** Unmerited, undeserved. **M16–M17.**
2 Without merit, undeserving. **E17.**

deserve /dɪˈzəːv/ *verb.* **ME.**
[ORIGIN Old French *deservir* (mod. *desservir*), from Latin *deservire* serve zealously or well, from *de-* DE- 1 + *servire* SERVE *verb*[1].]
†**1** *verb trans.* Earn or become worthy of (reward, punishment, etc.); secure by service or actions, gain, win. **ME–L18.**
2 *verb trans.* Be entitled to, *to do*; be worthy to have; be a justifiable cause of. **ME.**

P. DEHN We had suffered too little To deserve all the flowers, the kisses, the wine and the thanks. O. MANNING I don't know what I've done to deserve a daughter like you. H. L. MENCKEN They are really citizens of mark, whose opinions .. deserve to be heard and attended to. F. WARNER What crime can so deserve such pain?

3 *verb intrans.* Be or (formerly) become entitled; be worthy to be *well* or *ill* treated at the hands *of*. **ME.**

THACKERAY Deputies who had deserved well of their country. B. JOWETT Slaves ought to be punished as they deserve.

†4 *verb trans. & intrans.* foll. by *to, for.* Be of service to, treat or serve well. LME–M17.

†5 *verb trans.* Give in return for service rendered; requite. LME–E17.

■ **deserver** *noun* LME.

deserved /dɪˈzəːvd/ *ppl adjective.* M16.
[ORIGIN from DESERVE + -ED¹.]
1 Rightfully earned, merited. M16.
†2 Meritorious, worthy. *rare* (Shakes.). Only in E17.
■ **deservedly** /-vɪdli/ *adverb* according to desert or merit; rightfully, worthily: M16. **deservedness** /-vɪdnɪs/ *noun* worthiness, desert; excellence: E17.

deserving /dɪˈzəːvɪŋ/ *noun.* ME.
[ORIGIN formed as DESERVED + -ING¹.]
The action of DESERVE *verb*; desert, merit; *arch.* something deserved.

deserving /dɪˈzəːvɪŋ/ *adjective.* M16.
[ORIGIN formed as DESERVED + -ING².]
Meritorious, worthy. Foll. by *of*: showing conduct or qualities which ought to be given (praise, censure, etc.).

LD MACAULAY Delinquents . . deserving of exemplary punishment. F. WELDON She was deserving, so would never get what she deserved. R. C. A. WHITE Victorian notions of identifying those who are 'the deserving poor'.

■ **deservingly** *adverb* M16. **deservingness** *noun* M17.

desex /diːˈsɛks/ *verb trans.* E20.
[ORIGIN from DE- 3 + SEX *noun.*]
Castrate, spay; deprive of distinctive sexual qualities; remove or minimize the sexual appeal of.

desexualize /diːˈsɛkʃʊəlʌɪz/ *verb trans.* Also **-ise**. L19.
[ORIGIN from DE- 3 + SEXUAL + -IZE.]
Deprive of sex, sexuality, or sexual qualities.

déshabillé /ˌdeɪzaˈbiːjeɪ, *foreign* dezabije/ *noun.* Also anglicized as **dishabille** /dɪsəˈbiːl/. L17.
[ORIGIN French, use as noun of pa. pple of *déshabiller* undress, from *des-* DIS- 2 + *habiller* to dress.]
1 The state of being casually or only partially dressed. Freq. in EN DÉSHABILLÉ, *in dishabille.* L17.

M. MITCHELL He was . . unshaven and without a cravat but somehow jaunty despite his dishabille. L. EDEL The actress in her state of confused déshabille backstage.

2 A garment or costume of a casual or informal style. L17.

desi /ˈdeɪsi, ˈdɛsi/ *adjective & noun. Indian.* L19.
[ORIGIN Hindi *desī* from Sanskrit *deśa* country, land.]
▸ **A** *adjective.* Local, indigenous; *derog.* rustic, unsophisticated; (of music, dance, etc.) belonging to the folk tradition. L19.
▸ **B** *noun.* A person of Indian, Pakistani, or Bangladeshi birth or descent who lives abroad. E20.

desiccant /ˈdɛsɪk(ə)nt/ *noun & adjective.* L17.
[ORIGIN Latin *desiccant-* pres. ppl stem of *desiccare*: see DESICCATE *verb*, -ANT¹.]
▸ **A** *noun.* A drying or desiccating agent. L17.
▸ **B** *adjective.* Serving to desiccate. L18.

desiccate /ˈdɛsɪkeɪt/ *ppl adjective & noun.* LME.
[ORIGIN from Latin *desiccatus* pa. pple, formed as DESICCATE *verb*: see -ATE².]
▸ **A** *ppl adjective.* Desiccated, dried. *arch.* LME.
▸ **B** *noun.* A desiccated substance or product. E20.

desiccate /ˈdɛsɪkeɪt/ *verb.* L16.
[ORIGIN Latin *desiccat-* pa. ppl stem of *desiccare*, from *de-* DE- 1 + *siccare* make dry, from *siccus* dry: see -ATE³.]
1 *verb trans.* Remove the moisture from, dry up, (now esp. foodstuffs for preservation); *fig.* deprive of energy or feeling, make impersonal. Freq. as **desiccated** *ppl adjective.* L16.

BACON Wine helpeth to digest and desiccate the moisture. R. H. TAWNEY Piety imprisoned in a shrivelled mass of desiccated formulae. J. GRIGSON Whip the cream and fold it in, with a good tablespoon of desiccated coconut. B. BAINBRIDGE So desiccated by age that a smile might have broken her into little pieces.

2 *verb intrans.* Become dry, dry up. *rare.* L17.

Nature The lake is now desiccating.

– NOTE: Formerly stressed on 2nd syll.

desiccation /dɛsɪˈkeɪʃ(ə)n/ *noun.* LME.
[ORIGIN Latin *desiccatio(n-)*, formed as DESICCATE *verb*: see -ATION.]
The action of desiccating; the condition of being desiccated.

desiccative /ˈdɛsɪkətɪv/ *adjective & noun.* LME.
[ORIGIN Late Latin *desiccativus*, formed as DESICCATE *verb*: see -ATIVE.]
▸ **A** *adjective.* Having the tendency or quality of drying up. LME.
▸ **B** *noun.* A drying agent, a desiccant. Now *rare* or *obsolete.* LME.

desiccator /ˈdɛsɪkeɪtə/ *noun.* M19.
[ORIGIN from DESICCATE *verb* + -OR.]
An apparatus or device for desiccating a substance; *spec.* (CHEMISTRY) an apparatus containing a drying agent for removing moisture from specimens.

desiccatory /dɛˈsɪkət(ə)ri/ *adjective.* L18.
[ORIGIN formed as DESICCATOR + -ORY².]
Desiccative, drying.

desiderata *noun* pl. of DESIDERATUM.

desiderate /dɪˈzɪdərət, -ˈsɪd-/ *adjective & noun.* Long *arch. rare.* M17.
[ORIGIN Latin *desideratus* pa. pple, formed as DESIDERATE *verb*: see -ATE².]
▸ **A** *adjective.* Desired; desirable. M17.
▸ †**B** *noun.* Something desired; a desideratum. M–L17.

desiderate /dɪˈzɪdəreɪt, -ˈsɪd-/ *verb trans.* M17.
[ORIGIN Latin *desiderat-* pa. ppl stem of *desiderare* desire, perh. from *de-* DE- 1 + *sider-* star: see -ATE³.]
Feel the lack of, regret the absence of, long for, desire.

desideration /dɪˌzɪdəˈreɪʃ(ə)n, -ˌsɪd-/ *noun.* L15.
[ORIGIN Latin *desideratio(n-)*, formed as DESIDERATE *verb*: see -ATION.]
1 The action of desiderating, desire. L15.
2 A thing desired, a desideratum. *rare.* M19.

desiderative /dɪˈzɪdərətɪv, -ˈsɪd-/ *adjective & noun.* M16.
[ORIGIN Late Latin *desiderativus*, formed as DESIDERATE *verb*: see -ATIVE.]
▸ **A** *adjective.* 1 GRAMMAR. Pertaining to or designating a verb formed from another to express a desire of doing the act denoted. M16.
2 *gen.* Having, expressing, or pertaining to desire. M17.
▸ **B** *noun.* GRAMMAR. A desiderative verb, verbal form, or conjugation. M18.

desideratum /dɪˌzɪdəˈrɑːtəm, -ˈreɪtəm; -ˌsɪd-/ *noun.* Pl. **-ta** /-tə/. M17.
[ORIGIN Latin, use as noun of neut. sing. of pa. pple of *desiderare* DESIDERATE *verb.*]
A thing for which desire is felt; a thing lacked and wanted, a requirement.

desiderium /dɛzɪˈdɪərɪəm, -sɪ-/ *noun.* Pl. ***-ia*** /-ɪə/. E18.
[ORIGIN Latin, from *desiderare* DESIDERATE *verb.*]
A desire or longing, esp. for something once possessed; a sense of loss.

†**desidiose** *adjective.* E18–E19.
[ORIGIN Latin *desidiosus* slothful, from *desidia* sitting idle, from *desidere* sit about, sit idle, from *de-* DE- 1 + *sedere* sit: see -OSE¹.]
Idle, indolent, slothful, sluggish.

desight /dɪˈsʌɪt/ *noun.* Now *rare* or *obsolete.* M19.
[ORIGIN Prob. var. of DISSIGHT, alt. after DE-.]
An unsightly object, an eyesore.

design /dɪˈzʌɪn/ *noun.* M16.
[ORIGIN French †*desseing* (now *dessein, dessin*), from *desseigner, dessi(g)ner* from Italian *disegnare* from Latin *designare* DESIGNATE *verb.*]
1 A plan or scheme conceived in the mind; a project. M16. ▸**b** A plan or purpose of attack (*up*)*on* a person or thing. Now freq. in *pl.*, a plot or intention to gain possession of something or to attract someone. L17. ▸**c** The action or fact of planning or plotting; *esp.* hypocritical scheming. E18.

LD MACAULAY Grey . . had concurred in the design of insurrection. B. RUBENS She sat on the bench directly in front of his desk, not with any design, but because, unlike the others, it was empty. **b** J. LOCKE A sedate, settled design upon another man's life. H. READ The Klee drawings . . are addressed to an intelligent public; they have a design on us. M. MOORCOCK Esmé clutched my arm so tightly and listened so attentively that I began to suspect she had designs on me. **c** B. TAYLOR 'Twas all deceit and lying, false design.

2 A purpose, an intention, an aim. L16. ▸**b** Purpose, intention. Chiefly in ***by design***, †***on design***, †***upon design***, on purpose, deliberately. E17.

B. HARRIS They who ask relief, have one design: and he who gives it another. C. S. FORESTER It is my design to eliminate all possibility of collusion. **b** J. A. MICHENER The younger braves . . had gone partly by accident, partly by design, well into the mountains.

3 An end in view, a goal. E17.

M. W. MONTAGU Happiness is the natural design of all the world.

4 A preliminary sketch; a plan or pattern from which a picture, building, machine, etc., may be made. M17.

K. CLARK In 1801 Telford did a design of London Bridge, a single span of iron.

5 An idea as executed, the combination of elements in the finished work; an artistic device, a pattern. M17.

D. WILSON A silver bracelet of rare and most artistic design. I. COLEGATE Cushions embroidered by his mother in vaguely ecclesiastical designs.

6 The action or art of planning and creating in accordance with appropriate functional or aesthetic criteria; the selection and arrangement of artistic or functional elements making up a work of art, machine, or other object. M17.

TENNYSON What a lovely shell . . With delicate spire and whorl, How exquisitely minute, A miracle of design. R. DAWKINS Like a fashion in women's clothes, or in American car design. *Daily Telegraph* Independent school heads are mainly responsible for the design of a major new examination.

argument from design *the* argument that the complexity of the universe and the adaptation of means to ends are evidence of an intelligent Creator.
■ **designful** *adjective* full of design; intentional: L17. **designless** *adjective* void of design, purposeless M17.

design /dɪˈzʌɪn/ *verb.* LME.
[ORIGIN Partly from Latin *designare* DESIGNATE *verb*, partly from French *désigner* from Latin.]
▸ **I** †**1** *verb trans.* = DESIGNATE *verb* 2. LME–M17.
2 *verb trans.* = DESIGNATE *verb* 4. *arch.* LME.

SOUTHEY The plains . . ere long to be design'd Castille.

†3 *verb trans.* = DESIGNATE *verb* 3. L16–M17.

T. WARMSTRY Designing forth unto us the place whither hee is ascended.

4 *verb trans.* (Cf. DESIGNATE *verb* 1.) ▸†**a** Appoint to an office or function; nominate. L16–E18. ▸**b** Devote *to* a fate or purpose. *obsolete* exc. as passing into sense 9. L16.

b B. G. GERBIER The Duke . . designed in his Will ten Thousand Gilders . . to . . alter what he had Built amisse.

†5 *verb trans.* Assign (something *to* a person); grant, give. L16–L19.
6 *verb trans.* Set (a thing) apart *for* (†*to*, †*on*) a person. (Passing into sense 9.) M17.
▸ **II 7 a** *verb trans.* Plan and execute (a structure, work of art, etc.); fashion, shape; make a preliminary sketch for (a work of art etc.); make drawings and plans for the construction or production of (a building, machine, garment, etc.). LME. ▸**b** *verb trans. gen.* Draw, sketch; outline, delineate. Now *rare* or *obsolete.* M17. ▸**c** *verb intrans.* Be a designer of works of art, buildings, machines, garments, etc. M17.

a J. FERGUSSON The Roman bridges were designed on the same grand scale as their aqueducts. G. B. SHAW To snatch moments from his painting and sculpture to design some wonderful dresses for us. D. CARNEGIE The car was so designed that it could be operated entirely by hand. **b** EVELYN The prospect was so tempting that I designed it with my crayon. **c** J. RUSKIN A painter designs when he chooses some things, refuses others, and arranges all.

8 *verb trans.* Form a plan or scheme of; contrive. M16.

W. FAULKNER We had long ago designed marriage for him.

9 *verb trans.* Intend, purpose, (something, *as, to be, to do, doing, that*); create or intend *for* a specific purpose. E17. ▸**b** *verb trans.* in *pass.* & *intrans.* Intend to start on a journey or course, set out or be bound *for. arch.* M17.

S. BUTLER How does the Devil know What 'twas that I design'd to do? DEFOE I did not design you should have heard. G. ORWELL Political language . . is designed to make lies sound truthful and murder respectable. NEB *Eph.* 2:10 Good deeds for which God has designed us. I. MURDOCH An air of self-righteousness which was clearly designed as a provocation.

10 *verb trans.* Have in view, contemplate. L17.

designable /ˈdɛzɪgnəb(ə)l/ *adjective*¹. M17.
[ORIGIN from Latin *designare* (see DESIGNATE *verb*) + -ABLE.]
Distinguishable, identifiable.

designable /dɪˈzʌɪnəb(ə)l/ *adjective*². L19.
[ORIGIN from DESIGN *verb* + -ABLE.]
Able to be designed.

designata *noun* pl. of DESIGNATUM.

designate /ˈdɛzɪgnət/ *ppl adjective* (orig. *pa. pple*). LME.
[ORIGIN Latin *designatus* pa. pple, formed as DESIGNATE *verb*: see -ATE².]
†1 *pa. pple.* Indicated, manifested. Only in LME.
2 *postpositive adjective.* Appointed to office but not yet installed. M17.

B. WEBB The twenty Ministers designate . . went to Buckingham Palace to be sworn in.

designate /ˈdɛzɪgneɪt/ *verb trans.* L18.
[ORIGIN Latin *designat-* pa. ppl stem of *designare*, from *de-* DE- 1 + *signare* SIGN *verb*: see -ATE³. Cf. earlier DESIGN *verb* I.]
1 Appoint to an office or function, nominate; destine or devote to a fate or purpose. (Foll. by *as, for, to.*) L18.

F. D. MAURICE Josiah . . was designated to his task before his birth. D. FRASER Brooke was . . designated to succeed Wavell as Commander-in-Chief.

designated hitter BASEBALL a non-fielding player named before the start of a game to bat instead of the pitcher anywhere in the batting order.
2 Serve as a name for, stand for, signify, be descriptive of. E19.

R. L. STEVENSON It was odd to hear them, throughout the voyage, use shore words to designate portions of the vessel. J. GASKELL The Borough Orphanage . . (Children's Welfare they preferred you to designate it).

3 Point out, indicate, specify. E19.

W. S. LANDOR Her hair flew loosely behind her, designating that she was in haste. J. MARQUAND If you will be so kind as to drop me at the point I designate. *Which Computer?* The word processing keys can be designated as function keys.

4 Call by a name or distinctive term; name, identify, describe, characterize (*as*). E19.

D

D

■ **designative** *adjective* serving to designate something E17. **designator** *noun* (*rare*) E18. **designatory** *adjective* of or pertaining to a designator or designation, designative E18. **designee** *noun* (*US*) a person designated E20.

designation /dɛzɪɡˈneɪʃ(ə)n/ *noun*. LME.
[ORIGIN Old French & mod. French *désignation* or Latin *designatio(n-)*, formed as DESIGNATE *verb*: see -ATION.]
1 The action of marking or pointing out; indication by words or signs. LME.
2 The action or an act of setting aside for or devoting to a particular purpose; *SCOTS LAW* the setting apart of manses or glebes for the clergy. Now *arch.* or *hist.* L16.
3 The action of appointing or nominating a person to office; the fact of being nominated. E17. ▸†**b** The appointment of a thing; the summoning of an assembly. M17–L18.
†**4** The quality of being marked out or fitted for a particular employment; a vocation; suitability. M17–L18.
†**5** Purpose, intention, design. M17–M18.
6 A distinctive mark or indication. M17.
7 A descriptive name, an appellation; *LAW* a statement of profession, residence, etc., added for purposes of identification to a person's name. E19.

Time The Empty Quarter, an appropriate designation for a trackless region.

designatum /dɛsɪɡˈnɑːtəm, -ˈneɪtəm; -z-/ *noun*. Pl. **-ta** /-tə/. M20.
[ORIGIN Latin *designatum* neut. pa. pple of *designare* DESIGNATE *verb*.]
The object or class of objects designated by a sign. Cf. DENOTATUM.

designed /dɪˈzʌɪnd/ *ppl adjective*. L16.
[ORIGIN from DESIGN *verb* + -ED[1].]
1 Planned, intended. L16.
†**2** Designated. E17–M18.
3 Fashioned according to a design. L19.
■ **designedly** /-nɪdli/ *adverb* On purpose, intentionally M17.

designer /dɪˈzʌɪnə/ *noun & adjective*. M17.
[ORIGIN from DESIGN *verb* + -ER[1].]
▸ **A** *noun*. **1** A schemer, an intriguer. M17.
2 A person who prepares designs for a work of art, machine, or other object for construction or manufacture. M17.

J. S. FOSTER The separation existing between designer and constructor.

dress designer, *fashion designer*, *interior designer*, etc.
3 *gen.* A person who designs or plans. L17.
▸ **B** *attrib.* or as *adjective*. Bearing the name or label of a famous (fashion) designer; designed for a specific purpose, esp. to be fashionable. L20.

E. JONG All gotten up in designer clothes.

designer baby a baby whose genetic make-up has been selected in order to eradicate a particular defect, or to ensure that a particular gene is present. **designer drug** a drug synthesized to mimic a legally restricted or prohibited drug without being subject to such restriction.

designing /dɪˈzʌɪnɪŋ/ *ppl adjective*. L17.
[ORIGIN from DESIGN *verb* + -ING[2].]
1 Scheming, crafty, artful. L17.
2 Characterized by constructive forethought. L17.
■ **designingly** *adverb* L17.

designment /dɪˈzʌɪnm(ə)nt/ *noun*. Long *arch. rare*. L16.
[ORIGIN from DESIGN *verb* + -MENT.]
†**1** Appointment or nomination to office; consignment to a fate. L16–M18.
2 Planning, designing; an enterprise, an undertaking, a design. L16.
†**3** Artistic representation; an outline or sketch, an original design. L16–E18.
†**4** Indication by sign or token. Only in 17.

desilver /diːˈsɪlvə/ *verb trans*. M19.
[ORIGIN from DE- 3 + SILVER *noun*.]
Remove silver from.

desilverize /diːˈsɪlvərʌɪz/ *verb trans*. Also **-ise**. M19.
[ORIGIN from DE- 3 + SILVER *noun & adjective* + -IZE.]
Extract the silver from (lead etc.).
■ **desilveriˈzation** *noun* L19.

desinence /ˈdɛsɪnəns/ *noun*. L16.
[ORIGIN French *désinence* from medieval Latin *desinentia*, from *desinent-* pres. ppl stem of *desinere* leave off, close: see -ENCE.]
Termination, close; *GRAMMAR* a suffix, an ending of a word.
■ **desiˈnential** *adjective* pertaining to or of the nature of a desinence E19.

desipience /dɪˈsɪpɪəns/ *noun*. M17.
[ORIGIN Latin *desipientia*, from *desipere* be foolish: see -ENCE.]
Folly; silliness.
■ **desipiency** *noun* (*rare*) = DESIPIENCE L17. **desipient** *adjective* (*rare*) foolish, silly E18.

desirable /dɪˈzʌɪərəb(ə)l/ *adjective & noun*. LME.
[ORIGIN Old French & mod. French *désirable*, from *désirer*, after Latin *desiderabilis*: see DESIRE *verb*, -ABLE.]
▸ **A** *adjective*. Worth having or wishing for; causing desire; to be desired. LME.

G. B. SHAW It is not desirable that they should rule the world. C. S. FORESTER The more desirable the man—the richer, the handsomer, the more influential—the fiercer was the competition.

▸ **B** *noun*. A desirable person or thing. M17.
■ **desiraˈbility** *noun* (*a*) the quality of being desirable; (*b*) *rare* a desirable thing: E19. **desirableness** *noun* M17. **desirably** *adverb* E19.

desire /dɪˈzʌɪə/ *noun*. ME.
[ORIGIN Old French & mod. French *désir*, formed as DESIRE *verb*.]
1 The fact or condition of desiring; the feeling that one would derive pleasure or satisfaction from possessing or attaining something; a longing. ME.

E. W. LANE The elder King felt a strong desire to see his brother. J. BARZUN The democrat's conscious desire is philanthropic; he wants love to prevail. V. S. PRITCHETT Frustrated in his desire for larger premises.

2 *spec.* Sexual appetite; lust. ME.

S. W. BAKER The flesh of the crocodile is . . supposed to promote desire.

3 An expressed wish, a request. *arch.* LME.

J. BISCHOFF I . . send, at your desire, a general list of articles.

4 Something desired or longed for. LME.

W. DAMPIER We steered off . . expecting a Sea-Breez at E.N.E., and the third day had our desire. STEELE Farewel my Terentia, my Heart's Desire.

■ **desireful** *adjective* †(*a*) desirable; (*b*) full of desire, desirous: LME. **desireless** *adjective* E17. **desirelessness** *noun* M20.

desire /dɪˈzʌɪə/ *verb*. ME.
[ORIGIN Old French & mod. French *désirer* from Latin *desiderare* DESIDERATE *verb*.]
▸ **I** *verb trans.* **1** Long for, want earnestly (a thing, (a person) *to do*, *that*). ME. ▸**b** Feel sexual desire for, lust after. LME. ▸**c** Feel the loss of, miss. Now *rare* or *obsolete*. M16.

TENNYSON You desire your child to live. S. LEWIS A man who desired to lease a store-building. A. SILLITOE I would like for him only what I desire for myself.

leave much to be desired, *leave something to be desired*: see LEAVE *verb*[1].
†**2** Of a thing: require, demand. LME–E17.

SPENSER A doleful case desires a dolefull song.

3 Express a wish for, ask for, request, (a thing (*of* a person), *to do*, *that*). LME. ▸†**b** Request to know or be told. *rare*. L15–E18.

S. PEPYS My song . . which he has often desired of me. EARL OF CHATHAM If you are forced to desire farther information . . do it with proper apologies. SIR W. SCOTT He alighted at the . . Convent, and desired to see the Duke.

†**4** Request the presence or attendance of, invite (*to* a place or course of action). LME–M17.

SHAKES. *L.L.L.* But shall we dance, if they desire us to't?

5 Express a wish to (a person), entreat, command. Foll. by *to do*, *that*, †*of* the thing desired. *arch.* L15.

SHELLEY Go desire Lady Jane She place my lute. E. M. FORSTER Mrs Wilcox had desired her . . to forward the enclosed.

▸ **II** *verb intrans.* **6** Feel desire, have a desire. LME.

AV *Prov.* 13:4 The soule of the sluggard desireth, and hath nothing.

■ **desired** *ppl adjective* †(*a*) affected with desire, desirous; (*b*) wished for, longed for: ME. **desiredness** *noun* the condition of being desired M19. **desiringly** *adverb* with desire, longingly L15.

Desiree /dɪˈzɪəreɪ/ *noun*. L20.
[ORIGIN Unknown.]
A potato of a pink-skinned variety with yellow waxy flesh.

desirous /dɪˈzʌɪərəs/ *adjective*. ME.
[ORIGIN Anglo-Norman = Old French *desireus* (mod. *désireux*) from Proto-Romance, from Latin *desiderare* DESIDERATE *verb*: see -OUS.]
1 Having desire, wishful, wanting. Usu. foll. by *of*, *that*, *to do*. ME.

MILTON From dance to sweet repast they turn Desirous. T. HARDY Each of the lovers was desirous that the marriage should be kept as private as possible. G. B. SHAW Men and women are equally qualified or equally desirous to legislate, to govern. P. ACKROYD Desirous of fame and yet unsure how to claim it.

†**2** Of the nature of, characterized by, or expressing desire; covetous. LME–M17.
†**3** Full of (esp. martial) spirit, ardent. LME–L15.
†**4** Desirable. LME–E18.
■ **desirously** *adverb* (*a*) with desire, longingly; †(*b*) willingly, readily: LME. **desirousness** *noun* (now *rare*) M16.

desist /dɪˈzɪst, dɪˈsɪst/ *verb*. LME.
[ORIGIN Old French & mod. French *désister* from Latin *desistere*, from *de-* DE- 1 + *sistere* redupl. of *stare* to stand.]
1 *verb intrans.* Cease (*from*, †*in*, †*to do*); stop, forbear. LME. ▸**b** Refrain, abstain, (*from*). M20.

M. LEITCH He'd had to desist from smashing things because of the noise. **b** R. SHAW He wanted to cry out . . , but desisted because he felt he didn't have the right.

†**2** *verb trans.* Discontinue. E16–L18.
■ **desistance**, **-ence** *noun* cessation, discontinuation M17.

desition /dɪˈsɪʃ(ə)n/ *noun*. *rare*. E17.
[ORIGIN Late Latin *desitio(n-)*, from *desit-* pa. ppl stem of *desinere* cease: see -ITION.]
(A) termination or cessation of being; ending.

desize /diːˈsʌɪz/ *verb trans*. M20.
[ORIGIN from DE- 3 + SIZE *noun*[2].]
Remove size from (textiles).

desk /dɛsk/ *noun*. LME.
[ORIGIN medieval Latin *desca*, prob. based on Provençal *desc(a)* basket or Italian *desco* table, butcher's block, from Latin DISCUS discus, (Vulgate) dish, disc (of a sundial). Cf. DISH *noun*.]
1 An article of furniture (sometimes portable), having a flat or sloping surface serving as a rest for books, paper, etc., for reading or writing at and freq. also as a repository for writing materials etc. LME.
reading desk, *roll-top desk*, *school desk*, *writing desk*, etc.
2 In a place of worship, a sloping board or rest on which books used in the service are laid. Hence, a choir stall; *Scot.* a seat or pew; (chiefly *US*) a minister's stall, a pulpit. LME.
litany desk, *prayer desk*.
†**3** A shelf or case for books. M16–E18.
4 The function or office of the occupant(s) of a desk, esp. in a church or office; clerical work. L16.

T. DWIGHT He [a professor of divinity] educated between forty and fifty for the desk.

5 (In full *music desk*) a music stand, esp. as shared by two players in an orchestra; the player(s) at a desk. M19.

Gramophone It seems as though only a couple of desks are playing.

6 A (specified) section of an organization; *esp.* a section of a newspaper office dealing with a specified topic or (*US*) with editorial work. E20.

E. NEWBY The Foreign Office . . I was interviewed by a representative of the Asian Desk.

7 A counter for a cashier, hotel receptionist, etc.; the person(s) on duty in reception etc. M20.

P. BAIR Ask the desk to ring through to Miss Jackson's room.

– COMB.: **desk-bound** *adjective* obliged to remain working at a desk; **desk diary** a diary of a size and nature suited to use on a desk, esp. in an office for recording engagements etc.; **desk dictionary** a one-volume dictionary of middle size, suited to use on a desk for general reference; **desk job** a job based at a desk, esp. as opp. to one in active military service; **desk jockey** *N. Amer. colloq.* a person who works at a desk, an office worker; **desk lamp** a reading lamp suited to use on a desk; **desk-man** †(*a*) a clergyman; (*b*) a person who works at a desk, a white-collar worker; *spec.* a journalist who works mainly at a desk; **desk sergeant** *US* a sergeant in administrative charge of a police station.

deskill /diːˈskɪl/ *verb trans*. M20.
[ORIGIN from DE- 3 + SKILL *noun*.]
Reduce the level of skill required to carry out (a job); make the skills of (a worker) obsolete.

desktop /ˈdɛsktɒp/ *noun & adjective*. Also **desk-top**, **desk top**. E20.
[ORIGIN from DESK + TOP *noun*[1].]
▸ **A** *noun*. **1** The working surface of a desk. E20.
2 A desktop computer. *colloq.* L20.
3 *COMPUTING*. The working area of a computer screen viewed as a representation of the top of a desk, used with icons resembling familiar office equipment. L20.
▸ **B** *attrib.* or as *adjective*. Of a size and nature suitable for use on a desk; *esp.* designating or pertaining to a microcomputer suitable for use on an ordinary desk. Also, able to be undertaken from a desk. M20.
desktop publishing the production of high-quality printed matter using a desktop computer and a laser printer.

desman /ˈdɛsmən/ *noun*. L18.
[ORIGIN French & German from Swedish *desman-råtta* muskrat, from *desman* musk.]
Either of two semi-aquatic insectivorous shrewlike mammals of the mole family Talpidae, *Desmana moschata* of Russia, and *Galemys pyrenaicus* of the Pyrenees.

desmid /ˈdɛsmɪd/ *noun*. M19.
[ORIGIN mod. Latin *Desmidium* genus name, as if from dim. of Greek *desmos* band, chain: see -IDIUM.]
Any member of the family Desmidiaceae of freshwater microscopic unicellular green algae, often found united in chains or masses.

desmo- /ˈdɛsməʊ/ *combining form* of Greek *desmos* bond, chain: see -O-.
■ **desmognathous** /dɛsˈmɒɡnəθəs/ *adjective* (*ORNITHOLOGY*) designating or displaying a palatal structure in which the maxillopalatine bones meet each other in the median line M19. **desmosome** *noun* (*CYTOLOGY*) an area of a cell surface by which it is bound to another cell; a pair of such areas: M20.

desmoid /ˈdɛsmɔɪd/ *adjective*. M19.
[ORIGIN from Greek *desmos* bond or *desmē* bundle: see -OID.]
Fibrous, ligamentous; *esp.* (*MEDICINE*) designating a benign fibromatous and collagenous tumour of (esp. abdominal) muscle.

désoeuvré /dezœvre/ *adjective*. M18.
[ORIGIN French.]
Unoccupied; languidly idle.

desolate /ˈdɛs(ə)lət/ *adjective & noun*. LME.
[ORIGIN Latin *desolatus* pa. pple, formed as DESOLATE *verb*: see -ATE[2].]
▸ **A** *adjective*. **1** Left alone, lonely; lacking joy or comfort, forlorn, wretched. LME.

V. WOOLF To stand, like a desolate sea-bird, alone. P. P. READ Never in his life before had he felt so desolate—abandoned by everyone who had ever loved him.

2 Uninhabited, deserted; ruinous, neglected; barren, dreary. LME.

G. BERKELEY Roads untrodden, fields untilled, houses desolate. A. PATON The red desolate hills, where the earth had torn away like flesh. J. BRAINE It was only a small theatre but suddenly it seemed big and echoing and desolate.

†**3** Destitute or deprived *of*. LME–E18.
†**4** Lacking virtue; evil; dissolute. LME–L18.
▸ **B** *noun*. A desolate place or person. Long *rare*. LME.

SOUTHEY Travelling the trackless desolate.

■ **desolately** *adverb* M16. **desolateness** *noun* E17.

desolate /ˈdɛsəleɪt/ *verb trans*. LME.
[ORIGIN Latin *desolat-* pa. ppl stem of *desolare* abandon, from *de-* DE- 1 + *solus* alone: see -ATE[3].]
1 Deprive of inhabitants, depopulate; devastate, lay waste; make barren; spoil by neglect. LME.

DEFOE Would quite desolate the island, and starve them. C. LYELL As if the city had been desolated by the plague.

2 Leave alone or friendless, forsake; make wretched; overwhelm with misery. M16.

G. B. SHAW Agreeable surprises instead of desolating disappointments.

■ **desolater** *noun* M17. **desolatingly** *adverb* in a manner or to an extent that desolates or saddens L19. **desolative** *adjective* (*rare*) tending to desolate L16. **desolator** *noun* L18.

desolation /dɛsəˈleɪʃ(ə)n/ *noun*. LME.
[ORIGIN Late Latin *desolatio(n-)*, formed as DESOLATE *verb*: see -ATION.]
1 The action or an act of laying waste or rendering uninhabitable a land etc.; devastation. LME.

T. PENNANT The general desolation of the place by the Danes.

2 The condition of being naturally or by external agency unfit for habitation; waste or ruined state; dreary barrenness. LME. ▸**b** A desolate place; a dreary waste or ruin. E17.

N. MONSARRAT Along the deserted road, under the cruel moonlight which revealed only dust and desolation.

3 Deprivation of comfort; wretchedness; grief; solitariness, loneliness; a feeling of wretchedness or loneliness. LME.

SHAKES. *L.L.L.* You have liv'd in desolation here, Unseen, unvisited. W. HOLTBY There was upon his face a desolation so haggard . . she hardly recognised him.

Desolre /diːsɒlˈreɪ/ *noun*. *obsolete* exc. *hist*. Also **D sol re**. LME.
[ORIGIN from *D* as a pitch letter + *sol*, *re* designating tones in the solmization of Guido d'Arezzo (c 990–1050).]
MEDIEVAL MUSIC. The note D in Guido d'Arezzo's 1st and 2nd hexachords, where it was sung to the syllables *sol* and *re* respectively. Cf. ARE *noun*[1], BEFA, CEFAUT, etc.

de son tort /də sɔ̃ tɔːr/ *postpositive adjectival phr*. L17.
[ORIGIN French = of his wrong.]
LAW. Acting as executor or trustee without authorization and accordingly liable as such.

desophisticate /diːsəˈfɪstɪkeɪt/ *verb trans*. M19.
[ORIGIN from DE- 3 + SOPHISTICATE *verb*.]
Remove sophistication from; render unsophisticated.
■ **desophistiˈcation** *noun* M19.

desorb /diːˈsɔːb/ *verb*. E20.
[ORIGIN Back-form. from DESORPTION.]
PHYSICAL CHEMISTRY. **1** *verb trans*. Remove (a substance etc.) from a surface upon which it is adsorbed. E20.
2 *verb intrans*. Of a substance: leave a surface upon which it is adsorbed. M20.

desorption /diːˈsɔːpʃ(ə)n/ *noun*. E20.
[ORIGIN from DE- 3 + ADSORPTION.]
PHYSICAL CHEMISTRY. The release of a substance from a surface on which it is adsorbed, or from solution in a liquid phase.

desoxy- *combining form* see DEOXY-.

desoxyribonucleic *adjective* see DEOXYRIBONUCLEIC.

despair /dɪˈspɛː/ *noun*. ME.
[ORIGIN Anglo-Norman var. of Old French *desespeir* (mod. *désespoir*).]
1 Complete loss or absence of hope; (a feeling of) hopelessness. ME.

R. P. WARREN A sadness overcame him, more than sadness, a despair. M. L. KING Revolution, though born of despair, cannot long be sustained by despair. *personified*: W. COWPER Hollow-eyed Abstinence, and lean Despair.

counsel of despair: see COUNSEL *noun* 1. **in despair** in a despairing state, affected by a feeling of hopelessness.
2 A cause of hopelessness; a thing about which there is no hope. E17.

SHAKES. *Macb.* Strangely-visited people, All swoln and ulcerous . . The mere despair of surgery, he cures. SHELLEY Those faultless productions, whose very fragments, are the despair of modern art.

■ **despairful** *adjective* full of despair, desperate L16. **despairfully** *adverb* E17.

despair /dɪˈspɛː/ *verb*. ME.
[ORIGIN Old French *despeir-* tonic stem of *desperer* from Latin *desperare* to despair (of), from *de-* DE- 1 + *sperare* to hope, from *speres* old pl. of *spes* hope.]
1 *verb intrans*. & †*refl*. Lose or give up hope; be without hope. (Foll. by *of*, †*to do*.) ME.

M. W. MONTAGU His life was despaired of. L. DURRELL We carried her disease backwards and forwards over Europe . . until I began to despair. M. MOORCOCK Herr Lustgarten was beginning . . to despair of teaching me more.

†**2** *verb trans*. Deprive of hope, cast into despair. *rare*. LME–E17.
†**3** *verb trans*. Lose or give up hope of, be without hope of. LME–L18.
■ **despaired** *ppl adjective* (**a**) (long *obsolete* exc. *US dial.*) in despair, hopeless, desperate; (**b**) that is despaired *of* (or †of): ME. **despairer** *noun* a person who despairs E17. **despairingly** *adverb* in a despairing manner M17. **despairingness** *noun* (*rare*) the condition of being despairing E18.

despan *verb pa. t.*: see DESPIN.

despatch *noun, verb* vars. of DISPATCH *noun, verb*.

despecialize /diːˈspɛʃ(ə)lʌɪz/ *verb trans*. Also **-ise**. L19.
[ORIGIN from DE- 3 + SPECIALIZE.]
Make less specialized or more general.
■ **despecialiˈzation** *noun* L19.

†**despect** *noun*. LME–M19.
[ORIGIN Latin *despectus*: see DESPITE *noun*.]
(A cause of) contempt.

†**desperacy** *noun*. E17–E19.
[ORIGIN from DESPERATE *adjective*: see -ACY.]
Desperation.

desperado /dɛspəˈrɑːdəʊ/ *noun*. Pl. **-oes**, ***-os**. E17.
[ORIGIN Refashioning of DESPERATE *noun* after Spanish: see -ADO 1.]
†**1** = DESPERATE *noun* 1. E17–E18.
2 A desperate or reckless person, esp. a criminal. M17.

D. CARNEGIE The two-gun desperado was one of the most dangerous criminals ever encountered in the history of New York.

■ **desperadoism** *noun* the action or qualities of a desperado L19.

desperate /ˈdɛsp(ə)rət/ *noun*. M16.
[ORIGIN from the adjective.]
1 A person in despair; a wretch. Now *rare*. M16.
†**2** = DESPERADO *noun* 2. E17–E18.

desperate /ˈdɛsp(ə)rət/ *adjective & adverb*. LME.
[ORIGIN Latin *desperatus* pa. pple of *desperare*: see DESPAIR *verb*.]
▸ **A** *adjective* **I** **1** In despair, despairing (*of*). *arch*. LME.

SHAKES. *Two Gent.* I am desperate of obtaining her.

2 Given up as hopeless. Now chiefly of a debt: not recoverable. LME.
3 Leaving little or no room for hope; extremely grave or dangerous. L15. ▸†**b** Of an undertaking etc.: hopeless of accomplishment. M17–L19.

SWIFT Younger brothers of obscure families, and others of desperate fortunes. J. M. MURRY His suffering from Tom's desperate illness. N. MONSARRAT The food situation on the island had now become so desperate that it had overtaken even the bombing as the worst misery of their lives.

4 Expressive or indicative of despair. M16.

DISRAELI He was answered only with desperate sobs.

▸ **II** **5** Driven to desperation, reckless from despair; heedless of danger; violent, lawless. L15. ▸†**b** Utterly careless *of*. *rare*. Only in E17. ▸**c** Having an extreme need or great anxiety *for*, *to do*. M20.

J. BUCHAN The party who wish to upset the republic are pretty desperate fellows. C. S. FORESTER 'Put it down, d'ye hear?' said Hornblower, desperate with worry. **c** M. MOORCOCK I was desperate to talk my way clear of this terrible man. *Daily Telegraph* A university graduate so desperate for work that he travels 240 miles a day.

6 **a** Outrageous, extravagant; shocking. M16. ▸**b** Extremely bad; extreme, excessive, awful. E17.

b POPE Concluding all were desp'rate sots and fools, Who durst depart from Aristotle's rules. DAY LEWIS We did not go in for a desperate amount of washing. M. BINCHY Wasn't it desperate the way things never come singly.

7 Characterized by the recklessness, violence, or resolution of despair; undertaken in desperation as a last resort; staking all on a small chance. L16. ▸†**b** Involving serious risk. L16–M17.

MILTON His look denounc'd Desperate revenge, and Battel dangerous To less than Gods. LD MACAULAY A desperate conflict against overwhelming odds.

▸ **B** *adverb*. Desperately. M17.

DICKENS It's a desperate sharp night for a young lady to be out in.

desperate /ˈdɛsp(ə)reɪt/ *verb trans*. *rare*. E19.
[ORIGIN from the adjective, after verbs in -ATE[3].]
Make desperate.

desperately /ˈdɛsp(ə)rətli/ *adverb*. L15.
[ORIGIN from DESPERATE *adjective* + -LY[1].]
1 In despair or (now esp.) desperation; recklessly; with the energy or violence of despair. L15.

W. CATHER A shivering gray kitten, . . clinging desperately to the wood with her claws. JOYCE (Wrings her hands slowly, moaning desperately) O Sacred Heart of Jesus, have mercy on him!

2 To a desperate degree; so as to leave little or no room for hope; extremely, excessively, awfully. L16.

AV *Jer.* 17:9 The heart is deceitfull aboue all things, and desperately wicked. G. B. SHAW An enthusiast and a desperately hard worker. E. L. DOCTOROW So desperately in love she could no longer see properly. *Sunday Express* His son Greg, desperately ill with cancer.

desperateness /ˈdɛsp(ə)rətnɪs/ *noun*. M16.
[ORIGIN formed as DESPERATELY + -NESS.]
1 = DESPERATION 2. M16.
†**2** = DESPERATION 1. L16–M17.
3 The state or quality of leaving little or no room for hope; extreme gravity. L16.

desperation /dɛspəˈreɪʃ(ə)n/ *noun*. LME.
[ORIGIN Old French from Latin *desperatio(n-)*, from *desperat-* pa. ppl stem of *desperare*: see DESPAIR *verb*, -ATION.]
1 The action of despairing (*of*); the condition of having utterly lost hope; despair. Now *rare*. LME.
2 Despair leading to recklessness, or recklessness arising from despair; extreme need or great anxiety *for*, *to do*. M16.

despicable /dɪˈspɪkəb(ə)l, ˈdɛspɪk-/ *adjective*. M16.
[ORIGIN Late Latin *despicabilis*, from *despicari* look down upon, from *de-* DE- 1 + base cogn. with *specere* look: see -ABLE.]
1 Deserving to be despised; vile, morally contemptible. M16.
†**2** Miserable, wretched. M17–E18.
†**3** Contemptuous. M17–L18.
■ **despicaˈbility** *noun* E19. **despicableness** *noun* M17. **despicably** *adverb* M17.

†**despight** *noun, preposition, verb* vars. of DESPITE *noun* etc.

†**despightful** *adjective* var. of DESPITEFUL.

despin /diːˈspɪn/ *verb trans*. Infl. **-nn-**; pa. t. **-spun** /-ˈspʌn/, **-span** /-ˈspan/, pa. pple **-spun**. M20.
[ORIGIN from DE- 3 + SPIN *verb*.]
Counteract the spinning motion of; prevent from spinning.

despiritualize /diːˈspɪrɪtjʊəlʌɪz/ *verb trans*. Also **-ise**. M19.
[ORIGIN from DE- 3 + SPIRITUALIZE.]
Deprive of spiritual character.
■ **despiritualiˈzation** *noun* L19.

despisable /dɪˈspʌɪzəb(ə)l/ *adjective*. Now *rare*. ME.
[ORIGIN Old French, from *despis-* stem of *despire* DESPISE *verb*: see -ABLE.]
Despicable.

despise /dɪˈspʌɪz/ *noun*. Long *rare*. LME.
[ORIGIN Prob. from Old French *despiz*, -*s* nom. of *despit* DESPITE *noun*, but taking the form of an English deriv. of DESPISE *verb*.]
Contempt, scorn.

despise /dɪˈspʌɪz/ *verb*. ME.
[ORIGIN Old French *despis-* pres. stem of Old French *despire*, from Latin *despicere*, from *de-* DE- 1 + *specere* look.]
1 *verb trans*. Regard as inferior or worthless; feel contempt for. ME. ▸**b** Scorn or disdain *to do*, *that*. Long *rare*. LME.

D. RUNYON He hates and despises cheaters at cards, or dice. E. FERBER One of the vaqueros who still despised the jeep or Ford as a means of locomotion. **b** E. B. WHITE I despise to go anywhere.

†**2** *verb intrans*. Look down (*up*)*on*, *up*, *above*. Only in ME.
†**3** *verb trans*. Treat with contempt; disregard. ME–M17.
■ **despisal** *noun* the act of despising; contempt: M17. **despisement** *noun* (*arch.*) contempt, scorn E17. **despiser** *noun* ME. **despisingly** *adverb* scornfully, contemptuously L16.

despite /dɪˈspʌɪt/ *noun*. *arch*. Also †**despight**. ME.
[ORIGIN Old French *despit* (mod. *dépit*) from Latin *despectus* looking down (on), from *despect-* pa. ppl stem of *despicere*: see DESPISE *verb*.]
1 Contempt, scorn, disdain. ME.
2 Contemptuous treatment or behaviour; outrage, injury. ME.
†**3** Disregard of opposition, defiance. (Foll. by *to*.) ME–E18.
4 Indignation, anger, *esp*. such as arises from offended pride or vexation; the bearing of a grudge; ill will, spite. ME.
5 An act demonstrating contempt, hatred, or malice; an outrage. Usu. in *pl*. ME.
– PHRASES: **in despite of** (*arch*. also with *possess*. of noun or pronoun) = DESPITE *preposition*.

despite /dɪˈspʌɪt/ *verb*. *arch*. Also †**despight**. LME.
[ORIGIN Old French *despiter* (mod. *dépiter*) from Latin *despectare* frequentative of *despicere*: see DESPISE *verb*.]
1 *verb trans*. Show contempt for, treat with contempt. LME.
†**2** *verb trans*. Provoke to anger; spite. M16–M17.
†**3** *verb intrans*. Show contempt or ill will. M16–M18.

D

despite /dɪˈspʌɪt/ *preposition.* Also †**despight**. LME.
[ORIGIN Abbreviation of ***in despite of*** s.v. DESPITE *noun*.]
Notwithstanding, in spite of or (*arch.*) *of*. Formerly also, in contempt of, in defiance of.

KEATS His Voice leapt out, despite of godlike curb. M. ROBERTS Despite the sunshine, the air is chilly.

despiteful /dɪˈspʌɪtfʊl, -f(ə)l/ *adjective. arch.* Also †**despight-**. LME.
[ORIGIN from DESPITE *noun* + -FUL.]
1 Contemptuous, scornful, disdainful. LME.
2 Malicious, spiteful; cruel. LME.
■ **despitefully** *adverb* LME. **despitefulness** *noun* M16.

despiteous /dɪˈspɪtɪəs/ *adjective.* Orig. †**-itous**. See also DISPITEOUS. ME.
[ORIGIN Anglo-Norman *despitous*, Old French *despitos* (mod. *dépiteux*); alt. of late Middle English after PITEOUS.]
1 Full of contempt, or ill will; opprobrious, insulting. *arch.* ME.
2 = DISPITEOUS 2. ME.
■ **despiteously**, †**-itously** *adverb* ME.

despoil /dɪˈspɔɪl/ *noun. arch.* L15.
[ORIGIN Old French *despoille*, formed as DESPOIL *verb*.]
1 The action of despoiling. L15.
†**2** A thing or things plundered, spoil. L15–E17.

despoil /dɪˈspɔɪl/ *verb trans.* Now *literary.* ME.
[ORIGIN Old French *despoill(i)er*, *despuillier* (mod. *dépouiller*) from Latin *despoliare*, from *de-* DE- 1 + *spolia* (see SPOIL *noun*).]
1 Strip of some possession(s) by violence; plunder, rob (*lit.* & *fig.*) (Foll. by *of* the possession(s).) ME.

GIBBON The cities of Greece and Asia were despoiled of their most valuable ornaments. DICKENS The coach . . despoiled by highway-men. H. JAMES Her ruling passion had in a manner despoiled her of her humanity.

†**2** *spec.* Strip of clothes or armour; undress (oneself, another). (Foll. by *of* the clothing etc.) ME–E18.
†**3** Make useless, spoil, destroy. LME–L17.
†**4** Carry off as spoil, remove forcibly, steal. L15–E17.
■ **despoiler** *noun* LME. **despoilment** *noun* = DESPOLIATION E19.

despoliation /dɪˌspəʊlɪˈeɪʃ(ə)n/ *noun.* Now *literary.* L16.
[ORIGIN Late Latin *despoliatio(n-)*, from Latin *despoliat-* pa. ppl stem of *despoliare*: see DESPOIL *verb*, -ATION.]
The action of despoiling; the condition of being despoiled.

despond /dɪˈspɒnd/ *verb & noun.* M17.
[ORIGIN Latin *despondere* give up, resign, abandon, from *de-* DE- 1 + *spondere* promise.]
▸ **A** *verb intrans.* Lose heart or hope; become dejected. (Foll. by *of*.) M17.
▸ **B** *noun.* Despondency. Orig. & chiefly in ***Slough of Despond***, (a bog in Bunyan's *Pilgrim's Progress* representing) a state of despondency. *arch.* L17.
■ **desponder** *noun* (*rare*) L17. **despondingly** *adverb* in a desponding manner, dejectedly M17.

despondency /dɪˈspɒnd(ə)nsi/ *noun.* M17.
[ORIGIN formed as DESPOND + -ENCY.]
Dejection resulting from loss of heart or hope.
■ Also **despondence** *noun* L17.

despondent /dɪˈspɒnd(ə)nt/ *adjective.* L17.
[ORIGIN formed as DESPOND + -ENT.]
1 Characterized by despondency. L17.
2 Expressive of despondency. M19.
■ **despondently** *adverb* L17.

despot /ˈdɛspɒt/ *noun.* M16.
[ORIGIN French *despote*, earlier †*despot* from medieval Latin *despota* from Greek *despotēs* master, lord (orig. applied to a god and to the absolute ruler of a non-free people).]
1 *hist.* **a** A petty Christian ruler dependent on or tributary to the Turks after the Turkish conquest of Constantinople. M16. ▸**b** (Used as a form of address to) a Byzantine emperor or prince of the imperial house. E17.
2 An absolute ruler; a tyrant, an oppressor. L18.
3 A bishop or patriarch of the Eastern Orthodox Church. E19.
■ **despotat**, **-ate** *noun* (*hist.*) the dominion of a Greek despot under the Turks M19. **despotize** *verb intrans.* rule as a despot, act despotically L18.

despotic /dɛˈspɒtɪk/ *adjective.* M17.
[ORIGIN French *despotique* from Greek *despotikos*, from *despotēs*: see DESPOT, -IC.]
Of, pertaining to, or of the nature of a despot; arbitrary, tyrannical.

L. DEIGHTON She became too old and sick to continue her despotic reign.

■ †**despotical** *adjective* = DESPOTIC E17–M19. **despotically** *adverb* L17.

despotism /ˈdɛspətɪz(ə)m/ *noun.* E18.
[ORIGIN French *despotisme*, formed as DESPOT: see -ISM.]
1 The rule of a despot; despotic government; the exercise of absolute political authority. E18.

BURKE The simplest form of government is despotism, where all the inferior orbs of government are moved merely by the will of the Supreme.

2 Absolute power or control. L18.

R. SCRUTON The authority, the responsibility, and the despotism of parenthood.

3 A political system under the control of a despot; a despotic state; an arbitrary government. M19.

V. S. PRITCHETT From despotisms like the Soviet Union the only voices that tell one anything are the voices of private life.

■ **despotist** *noun* an advocate of despotism L18.

despumate /dɪˈspjuːmeɪt, ˈdɛspjʊ-/ *verb.* M17.
[ORIGIN Latin *despumat-* pa. ppl stem of *despumare* skim (off), from *de-* DE- 1 + *spuma* foam, froth, scum: see -ATE³. Cf. DESPUME.]
1 *verb trans.* Skim; clarify (a liquid) by removing the scum from its surface. M17.
2 *verb intrans.* Of a liquid: become clarified by casting off the scum. M18.
■ **despuˈmation** *noun* (*a*) the removal of froth or scum from a liquid; the condition of being freed from scum; (*b*) *arch.* the expulsion of impure matter from the fluids of the body; the despumated matter: E17.

†**despume** *verb trans.* LME–M18.
[ORIGIN from Latin *despumare* (see DESPUMATE) or French *despumer* from Latin.]
= DESPUMATE 1.

despun *verb pa. t. & pple*: see DESPIN.

desquamate /ˈdɛskwəmeɪt/ *verb.* E18.
[ORIGIN Latin *desquamat-* pa. ppl stem of *desquamare* scale (off), from *de-* DE- 1 + *squama* scale: see -ATE³.]
†**1** *verb trans.* Remove the scales from, take the surface layer off, peel. E–M18.
2 *verb intrans.* Come off in the form of scales; flake off. E19.
■ **desquamative** /dɪˈskwamətɪv/ *adjective* characterized by desquamation M19. **desquamatory** /dɪˈskwamət(ə)ri/ *adjective & noun* (*a*) *adjective* of or pertaining to desquamation; (*b*) *noun* a desquamatory implement: M17.

desquamation /dɛskwəˈmeɪʃ(ə)n/ *noun.* M16.
[ORIGIN formed as DESQUAMATE: see -ATION.]
1 A cast-off scale of skin etc.; something which has desquamated. *rare.* M16.
2 The action or fact of desquamating; *spec.* the shedding of the outer layer of the skin. E17.

des res /ˈdɛz rɛz/ *noun phr.* L20.
[ORIGIN Abbreviation: cf. RES *noun*².]
(In advertisements & *iron.*) A desirable residence.

†**dess** *noun.* M–L16.
[ORIGIN Old French *deis* DAIS.]
A desk.

SPENSER Ne ever once did looke up from her desse.

dessert /dɪˈzəːt/ *noun.* M16.
[ORIGIN French, use as noun of pa. pple of *desservir* clear the table, from *des-* DIS- 1 + *servir* SERVE *verb*¹.]
A course of fruit, nuts, sweets, etc., served at the end of a meal. Also, (orig. *US*) a pudding or sweet course.
– ATTRIB. & COMB.: In the sense 'for the serving or eating of dessert', as ***dessert fork***, ***dessert knife***, ***dessert plate***, ***dessert service***, etc.; in the sense 'suitable for serving for dessert', as ***dessert apple***, ***dessert pear***, etc. Special combs., as **dessertspoon** (*a*) a spoon intermediate in size between a tablespoon and a teaspoon; (*b*) a dessertspoonful; **dessertspoonful** the amount a dessertspoon will hold (a recognized measure for medicine, culinary ingredients, etc.); **dessert wine** a wine suitable for drinking with dessert, *esp.* a still, sweet, sometimes fortified, wine.

dessiatine /ˈdɛsjətiːn, -ʃj-/ *noun.* Also **desyatin** & other vars. L18.
[ORIGIN Russian *desyatina* lit. 'tithe'.]
A Russian measure of land, equivalent to about 1.1 hectares or 2.7 acres.

dessous /dəsu/ *noun.* Pl. same. M18.
[ORIGIN French = lower part, (in pl.) underwear.]
1 ***dessous des cartes*** /de kart/ ['of the cards'], the underside of playing cards when dealt face down; *fig.* a secret kept in reserve, an unknown factor. M18.
2 (Women's) underwear. E20.

destabilize /diːˈsteɪbɪlʌɪz, -b(ə)l-/ *verb trans.* Also **-ise**. E20.
[ORIGIN from DE- 3 + STABILIZE.]
Deprive of stability, make unstable; *spec.* make (a country or area) politically unstable, undermine (a foreign government).
■ **destabiliˈzation** *noun* L20.

destain /diːˈsteɪn/ *verb trans.* M20.
[ORIGIN from DE- 3 + STAIN *noun*.]
Remove stain from; *spec.* in BIOLOGY & CHEMISTRY, selectively remove stain from (a substrate, specimen for microscopy, etc.) after it has previously been stained.

de-Stalinize /diːˈstɑːlɪnʌɪz/ *verb trans. & intrans.* Also **-ise**. M20.
[ORIGIN from DE- 3 + *Stalin*: see STALINISM.]
Chiefly *hist.* Remove or counteract the influence of Stalin or Stalinism (on); remove traces of Stalin or Stalinism (from).
■ **de-Staliniˈzation** *noun* M20.

De Stijl /də ˈstʌɪl/ *noun & adjective.* M20.
[ORIGIN Dutch = the style (see below).]
(Of, pertaining to, characteristic of, or designating) a movement in art and architecture associated with the Dutch periodical *De Stijl* (1917–32), founded by Theo van Doesburg and Piet Mondrian, and devoted to the principles of neoplasticism.

destinal /ˈdɛstɪn(ə)l/ *adjective.* LME.
[ORIGIN from French *destin* (masc.) Old French *destine* (fem.), from *destiner* DESTINE: see -AL¹.]
Of, pertaining to, or according to destiny or fate.
– NOTE: In isolated use before 20.

destinate /ˈdɛstɪneɪt/ *verb trans.* Now *rare.* Pa. pple & ppl adjective †**-ate** (earlier), **-ated**. LME.
[ORIGIN Latin *destinat-*: see DESTINATION, -ATE³.]
= DESTINE.

destination /dɛstɪˈneɪʃ(ə)n/ *noun.* LME.
[ORIGIN Old French & mod. French, or Latin *destinatio(n-)*, from *destinat-* pa. ppl stem of *destinare*: see DESTINE, -ATION.]
▸ **I 1** The action of appointing or intending a person or thing for a particular end or purpose; the fact of being so appointed or intended. Now *rare.* LME.
2 The end or purpose for which a person or thing is destined. M17.
3 The fact of being destined or bound for a particular place. Chiefly in ***place of destination*** etc. (= sense 4 below). L18.
4 The place to which a person or thing is going, the intended end of a journey. E19.

K. M. E. MURRAY After a much delayed railway journey they reached their destination nearly eleven hours after leaving Oxford.

▸ **II 5** SCOTS LAW. The nomination by the testator of successors to heritable or movable property in a certain order; the series of heirs so nominated. E18.

destine /ˈdɛstɪn/ *verb trans.* ME.
[ORIGIN Old French & mod. French *destiner* from Latin *destinare* make firm, establish, from *de-* DE- 1 + causative deriv. of *stare* STAND *verb*.]
1 Foreordain, predetermine, decree. Now usu. in *pass.*, be fated, turn out (by hindsight) *to be* or *do*. ME.

R. FRY An event . . which was destined to change ultimately the face of things.

2 Ordain, appoint. *obsolete* exc. as passing into sense 1. LME.
3 Set apart *for* or devote *to* a particular purpose, activity, etc.; intend *for*, *to do*. Usu. in *pass.* M16.

H. READ He was well educated, and destined for the diplomatic service.

4 In *pass.* Be bound or intended *for* a place, be going *to* or *from* a place. L18.

S. UNWIN Many cases of books destined for Japan had been detained and opened. *Times* Traffic . . destined to and from the South-east.

destiny /ˈdɛstɪni/ *noun.* Also (esp. when personified) **D-**. ME.
[ORIGIN Old French & mod. French *destinée* from Proto-Romance use as noun of Latin *destinata* fem. pa. pple of *destinare*: see DESTINE, -Y⁵.]
1 The predetermined course of events; that which is destined to happen; the fate of a particular person, country, etc.; the ultimate condition; a person's lot in life. ME.

H. REED That battle which settled the destiny of Saxon independence. E. O'NEILL You are fully competent to direct the destiny of this company. P. TILLICH In every act of moral self-affirmation man contributes to the fulfilment of his destiny. *Guardian* Secure in their Biblical faith that their deeds are part of a divinely ordained destiny. J. CHEEVER She was the woman life meant him to have; she was his destiny.

manifest destiny: see MANIFEST *adjective*.
2 The power or agency that (supposedly) predetermines events, invincible necessity, (freq. personified or as a goddess); in *pl.*, the three Fates of mythology. LME.
man of destiny: see MAN *noun*.

destiny /ˈdɛstɪni/ *verb trans.* Long *rare.* LME.
[ORIGIN from the noun.]
Ordain or predict the destiny of.

destitute /ˈdɛstɪtjuːt/ *adjective & noun.* LME.
[ORIGIN Latin *destitutus* forsaken, pa. pple of *destituere*, from *de-* DE- 1 + *statuere* set up, place.]
▸ **A** *adjective* **1** †**a** Of a place: abandoned, deserted. LME–L16. ▸**b** Of a person: left friendless or helpless, forlorn. *obsolete* exc. as passing into sense 1c. E16. ▸**c** Without resources or (formerly) some particular resource; without means of subsistence; in great need of food, shelter, etc. (Before 18 often an implication of uses of sense 1b.) E16.
2 †**a** Deprived or bereft *of* (something formerly possessed). LME–E17. ▸**b** Devoid *of* (something desirable). L15.
▸ **B** *noun.* A destitute person. M18.
■ **destitutely** *adverb* (*rare*) M16. **destituteness** *noun* M17.

destitute /ˈdɛstɪtjuːt/ *verb trans.* Now *rare.* LME.
[ORIGIN Partly from DESTITUTE *adjective & noun*, partly repr. Latin *destituere* (see DESTITUTE *adjective & noun*).]
1 Deprive or divest *of*; make destitute. LME.
†**2** Forsake, desert, abandon. M16–L17.
3 Lay waste, ruin. M16.
†**4** Frustrate, disappoint, defeat. M16–E17.
5 Deprive of office, depose. L16.

destitution /dɛstɪˈtjuːʃ(ə)n/ *noun*. LME.
[ORIGIN Old French & mod. French from Latin *destitutio(n-)*, from *destitut-* pa. ppl stem of *destituere*: see DESTITUTE *adjective*, -ION.]
1 The state of being deprived or devoid *of* something; deprivation, want. LME. ▸**b** *spec.* Extreme poverty, great need of food, shelter, etc. E17.
2 Deprivation of office; discharge, dismissal. Long *rare*. L15.

destock /diːˈstɒk/ *verb intrans.* M20.
[ORIGIN from DE- 3 + STOCK *noun*[1].]
Reduce the quantity or number of stock held. Chiefly as ***destocking*** *verbal noun*

destool /diːˈstuːl/ *verb trans.* E20.
[ORIGIN from DE- 3 + STOOL *noun*.]
In W. Africa: remove (a tribal chief) from authority, depose.
■ **destoolment** *noun* E20.

destour *noun* var. of DASTUR *noun*[1].

de-stress /diːˈstrɛs/ *verb*. M20.
[ORIGIN from DE- 3 + STRESS *verb*[1].]
1 *verb trans.* Remove stress from or reduce stress in. M20.
2 *verb intrans.* Relax, unwind. L20.

destrier /ˈdɛstrɪə, dɛˈstriːə/ *noun*. Now *arch.* or *hist.* Also **destrer** /ˈdɛstrə/. ME.
[ORIGIN Anglo-Norman *destrer*, Old French *destrier*, from Proto-Romance, from Latin *dext(e)ra*, formed as DEXTER (being led by the right hand of a squire).]
A medieval knight's warhorse, a charger.

destroy /dɪˈstrɔɪ/ *verb trans.* ME.
[ORIGIN Old French *destruire* (mod. *détruire*) from Proto-Romance alt. of Latin *destruere*, from *de-* DE- 1 + *struere* pile up.]
1 Pull or break down, demolish; smash to pieces, shatter. ME.

M. MEYER The castle . . had been largely destroyed by a fire. H. KISSINGER An Egyptian . . missile destroyed an Israeli reconnaissance plane.

†**2** Lay waste, ravage; reduce (a person) to poverty. ME–E17.
3 Ruin completely, make utterly useless, spoil. ME. ▸**b** Ruin financially, professionally, or in reputation; deprive of power or prestige; defeat or discredit utterly. L18.

J. FORBES The long drought and extreme heat have destroyed their vegetables. J. B. PRIESTLEY Building on the old sites, instead of going outside, . . and there destroying a good piece of country. **b** H. WILSON The great events that ended the careers of Asquith and Lloyd George, and almost destroyed Baldwin.

4 Deprive of life, kill; wipe out, annihilate. ME. ▸**b** Kill (a sick or unwanted animal) humanely. M19.

R. J. SULLIVAN A deluge . . covered the whole coasts, and destroyed the greatest part of the inhabitants. J. STEINBECK Maybe Kino has cut off his own head and destroyed himself. **b** DAY LEWIS The soldiers had been ordered . . to destroy their pets before they sailed away.

5 Put an end to or do away with (something abstract, a condition, institution, etc.). ME. ▸**b** *LAW*. Nullify, invalidate. E19.

J. HAWKES The trees drove out the game herds . . and so destroyed the livelihood of the hunters. G. VIDAL The applause came, destroying the silence.

6 Counteract or neutralize the effect of; make ineffective. E18.
– PHRASES: **destroying angel** (*a*) = DANITE 2; (*b*) a highly poisonous mushroom of the genus *Amanita*, spec. *A. virosa*.
■ **destroyable** *adjective* LME. **destroyingly** *adverb* as a destroyer, destructively E19.

destroyer /dɪsˈtrɔɪə/ *noun*. LME.
[ORIGIN from DESTROY + -ER[1].]
1 A person who or thing which destroys. LME.
2 *spec.* A fast warship of a type designed to protect other ships by attacking submarines etc. with guns and torpedoes. L19.
– COMB. & PHRASES: **destroyer-escort** (chiefly *US*) a small destroyer (warship); **destroyer leader** *US* a large destroyer (warship); ***torpedo-boat destroyer***, ***torpedo destroyer***: see TORPEDO *noun*.

destruct /dɪˈstrʌkt/ *verb* & *noun*. M17.
[ORIGIN Latin *destruct-*: see DESTRUCTION.]
▸ **A** *verb trans.* †**1** *gen.* Destroy. Only in M17.
2 *spec.* Bring about the deliberate destruction of (one's own rocket, missile, etc.). See also SELF-DESTRUCT *verb*. M20.
▸ **B** *noun*. The action of deliberately destroying one's own rocket, missile, etc. M20.

destructful /dɪˈstrʌktfʊl, -f(ə)l/ *adjective*. M17.
[ORIGIN formed as DESTRUCT + -FUL.]
Destructive.

destructible /dɪˈstrʌktɪb(ə)l/ *adjective*. M18.
[ORIGIN French, or late Latin *destructibilis*, from *destruct-*: see DESTRUCTION, -IBLE. Earlier in INDESTRUCTIBLE.]
Able or liable to be destroyed.
■ **destructiˈbility** *noun* M18.

destruction /dɪˈstrʌkʃ(ə)n/ *noun*. ME.
[ORIGIN Old French & mod. French from Latin *destructio(n-)*, from *destruct-* pa. ppl stem of *destruere*: see DESTROY, -ION.]
1 The action of destroying; demolition, devastation, slaughter. ME.

Listener How can we stand by and do nothing to prevent the destruction of the world?

2 The fact or condition of being destroyed; ruin. ME.

M. MITCHELL Despite all Frank had told her about the town burning to the ground, she had never really visualized complete destruction.

3 A means of destroying; a cause of ruin. LME.

H. MARTINEAU The deplorable mistake which was likely to prove the destruction of the whole family.

■ **destructional** *adjective* of or pertaining to destruction; formed by destructive agencies, *spec.* by denudation: E20.

destructionist /dɪˈstrʌkʃ(ə)nɪst/ *noun*. E19.
[ORIGIN from DESTRUCTION + -IST.]
1 *THEOLOGY*. A person who believes in the final annihilation of the wicked. E19.
2 An advocate of a policy of destruction, esp. of an existing social system. Chiefly *derog.* M19.

destructive /dɪˈstrʌktɪv/ *adjective* & *noun*. L15.
[ORIGIN Old French & mod. French *destructif*, *-ive* from late Latin *destructivus*, from *destruct-*: see DESTRUCTION, -IVE.]
▸ **A** *adjective*. Destroying, tending to destroy; deadly *to*, causing destruction *of*; refuting or disparaging without amending, merely negative, not constructive. L15.

STEELE Vice is in itself destructive of Pleasure. O. MANNING It's the greatest destructive force in the world, poverty. *Financial Times* A rag-bag of constructive and destructive criticism, of praise and outright damnation.

destructive distillation: see DISTILLATION 2.
▸ **B** *noun*. **1** Something destructive; an agent or means of destruction. M17.
2 = DESTRUCTIONIST 2. Chiefly *derog.* M19.
■ **destructively** *adverb* M17. **destructiveness** *noun* M17.

destructor /dɪˈstrʌktə/ *noun*. L17.
[ORIGIN Latin, from *destruct-*: see DESTRUCTION, -OR.]
1 A person who or thing which destroys (= DESTROYER 1). L17.
2 *spec.* A furnace for burning refuse, an incinerator. L19.

destructure /diːˈstrʌktʃə/ *verb trans.* M20.
[ORIGIN from DE- 3 + STRUCTURE *noun*.]
Destroy or dismantle the structure of, deprive of structure.
■ **destructuˈration** *noun* L20.

desudation /diːsjʊˈdeɪʃ(ə)n/ *noun*. *rare*. LME.
[ORIGIN Late Latin *desudatio(n-)*, from Latin *desudat-* pa. ppl stem of *desudare* sweat greatly: see -ATION.]
MEDICINE. Profuse sweating.

desuetude /dɪˈsjuːɪtjuːd, ˈdɛswɪ-/ *noun*. E17.
[ORIGIN French *désuétude* or its source Latin *desuetudo*, from *desuet-* pa. ppl stem of *desuescere* become unaccustomed, from *de-* DE- 1 + *suescere* be accustomed: see -TUDE. Cf. earlier DISSUETUDE.]
†**1** The action of discontinuing something; discontinuance *of*, protracted cessation *from*. E17–E18.
2 A state of disuse; the action of passing into disuse. M17.

C. R. ATTLEE Old English words and phrases, long since fallen into desuetude. C. LAMB The gradual desuetude of old observances.

desulfurate, **desulfurize** *verbs*, etc.: see DESULPHURATE etc.

desulphurate /diːˈsʌlfəreɪt/ *verb trans.* Also (*US* & *CHEMISTRY*) **-sulfur-**. L18.
[ORIGIN from DE- 3 + SULPHURATE.]
= DESULPHURIZE.
■ **desulphuˈration** *noun* M18.

desulphurize /diːˈsʌlfərʌɪz/ *verb trans.* Also **-ise**, (*US* & *CHEMISTRY*) **-sulfur-**. M19.
[ORIGIN from DE- 3 + SULPHURIZE.]
Make free from sulphur; remove sulphur or its compounds from.
■ **desulphuriˈzation** *noun* M19. **desulphurizer** *noun* an apparatus for desulphurizing M19.

desultorious /dɛs(ə)lˈtɔːrɪəs/ *adjective*. Now *rare* or *obsolete*. M17.
[ORIGIN formed as DESULTORY + -OUS.]
= DESULTORY 1.

desultory /ˈdɛs(ə)lt(ə)ri, -z-/ *adjective*. L16.
[ORIGIN Latin *desultorius* pertaining to a vaulter, superficial, from *desultor*, from *desult-* pa. ppl stem of *desilire* leap down, from *de-* DE- 1 + *salire* leap: see -ORY[2].]
1 Skipping about or jumping from one thing to another (*lit.* & *fig.*); pursuing an irregular or erratic course (*lit.* & *fig.*); going constantly from one subject to another; digressive; lacking a fixed plan or purpose, unmethodical; occurring irregularly, intermittent. L16.

R. BENTLEY Persons of a light and desultory temper, that skip about, and are blown with every wind, as Grasshoppers are. G. WHITE I shot at it but it was so desultory that I missed my aim. T. C. WOLFE He found desultory employment as a soda-jerker, or as a delivery boy. I. WALLACE The rest of the short afternoon . . had been lost to . . napping, reading, and desultory chatter about the children, the new position that was in the offing, the utopia that was possible after that. R. TRAVERS The search out west, desultory as it was compared with the scouring of the Blue Mountains. A. GUINNESS He pushed the tagliatelli around his plate in a desultory way, indifferent to the gaieties of the Piazza Navona.

2 Occurring randomly in isolation; occasional, disconnected. E18.

R. L'ESTRANGE 'Tis not for a desultory thought to attone for a lewd course of life. J. GALSWORTHY Nothing to stare at but . . desultory Colonials charging up and down.

■ **desultorily** *adverb* M17. **desultoriness** *noun* M17.

desuperheat /diːˈsuːpəhiːt/ *verb trans.* M20.
[ORIGIN from DE- 3 + SUPERHEAT *verb*.]
Reduce the degree of superheat of (steam).
■ **desuperheater** *noun* an apparatus for desuperheating steam M20.

desyatin *noun* var. of DESSIATINE.

desynchronize /diːˈsɪŋkrənʌɪz/ *verb trans.* Also **-ise**. L19.
[ORIGIN from DE- 3 + SYNCHRONIZE.]
Remove the synchronization from, put out of step or phase.

desynonymize /diːsɪˈnɒnɪmʌɪz/ *verb*. Also **-ise**. E19.
[ORIGIN from DE- 3 + SYNONYM + -IZE.]
1 *verb trans.* End the synonymy of, differentiate in meaning (synonymous words). E19.
2 *verb intrans.* Cease to be synonymous. M19.
■ **desynonymiˈzation** *noun* M19.

Det. *abbreviation*.
Detective.

detach /dɪˈtatʃ/ *verb*. L16.
[ORIGIN French *détacher*, earlier †*destacher*, from *des-* DIS- 1 + stem of *attacher* ATTACH.]
†**1** *verb trans.* Discharge (a gun). Only in L16.
2 Unfasten and remove, disconnect, disunite, separate, (*from*). L17.

J. AGATE I found I was holding a velvet geranium which . . had become detached from Mrs Pat's headgear. S. KAUFFMANN Russell was able to detach a bit of his mind from what Norris was saying and consider Florence. B. MOORE Three monks detached themselves from the larger group.

3 *verb trans.* *MILITARY*. Separate and send off (a part from a main body) for a particular purpose, send on a separate mission. L17.
4 *verb intrans.* Disengage, withdraw, separate oneself. M19.

Scientific American As the bubbles form and expand they detach from their moorings and rise to the surface. *Navy News* H.M.S. Herald detached from the survey ground and headed for Bandar Abbas.

■ **detachaˈbility** *noun* the quality of being detachable E19. **detachable** *adjective* able to be detached E19.

detached /dɪˈtatʃt/ *adjective*. E18.
[ORIGIN from DETACH + -ED[1].]
1 Disconnected, separate(d), standing apart, (*from*); *spec.* (*a*) (of a building, esp. a house) not joined to any other (cf. SEMI-DETACHED); (*b*) (of the retina) separated from the sclera (a condition causing partial or total blindness). E18.

A. J. P. TAYLOR A new ministry of fuel and power, detached from the board of trade, was set up. S. HILL He would buy a better house than this, detached perhaps, not a terrace.

2 Characterized by emotional detachment; aloof, objective. E20.

J. F. KENNEDY The protection of her Navy had enabled Britain to take a detached view of events in Europe. S. MIDDLETON Now Fisher grew detached, immersed in his own thoughts.

■ **detachedly** *adverb* L18. **detachedness** *noun* M18.

detachment /dɪˈtatʃm(ə)nt/ *noun*. M17.
[ORIGIN French *détachement*, formed as DETACH: see -MENT.]
1 *gen.* The action of detaching; the state of being detached, absence of connection, separation, (*from*). M17.

R. FRY The complete detachment of the artistic vision from the values imposed on vision by everyday life.

2 *MILITARY*. The separation of a number of troops, ships, etc., from the main body for a particular purpose; the action of sending on a separate mission. L17.

DEFOE The army, after so many detachments, was not above nineteen thousand men.

3 A part of a military unit dispatched from the main body; *transf.* any portion of a large body separately employed. L17.

J. REED Detachments of the two regiments . . had . . been surrounded by Cossacks. A. JOHN A detachment of American tourists would appear.

Voluntary Aid Detachment: see VOLUNTARY *adjective*.
4 A condition of spiritual separation from the world; aloofness from or *from* surroundings and circumstances;

D

D

freedom from or indifference to worldly concerns, emotional commitments, etc.; impartiality, objectivity. L18.

B. PYM To observe their joys and sorrows with detachment as if one were watching a film or a play. P. LIVELY One of those medium-sized market towns that give an impression of slight detachment from the present.

detail /ˈdiːteɪl/ *noun*. E17.
[ORIGIN French *détail*, formed as DETAIL *verb*.]
1 The treatment of a matter item by item; attention to particulars; small or minor items or events collectively. E17.

DAY LEWIS The vividness and detail of the author's recollections. L. VAN DER POST Self-contained . . even to such detail as a snake-bite outfit. N. FREELING The characteristic feminine memory for detail.

2 A meticulous account or description of particulars. *arch.* L17.
3 *MILITARY*. The distribution of the orders of the day; a written list of orders, a roster. E18. ▸**b** The assignment of a small party for a particular duty; a small detachment for a particular duty; the duty assigned. L18.

b B. MALAMUD Had the cell searched by a detail of five guards. S. BELLOW I didn't often get the toilet detail; he had too many important tasks for me.

4 A particular; a small part of a whole; a minor or unimportant item or circumstance. L18.

W. S. MAUGHAM You give the reader broad indications and leave him to fill in the details. R. K. NARAYAN He asked details of our various movements.

5 *spec.* A small part of a work of art, esp. considered in isolation; a minor feature or decoration in a building, picture, etc.; the items, particulars, or parts of a building or work of art considered collectively; the manner of treating these. E19. ▸**b** In full ***detail drawing***. An architect's or designer's separate large drawing of a small part of a building, machine, etc.; a working drawing. E19.

P. NICHOLSON The detail of both sculpture and masonry on the building.

– PHRASES: **in detail** (*a*) item by item, minutely, (also ***in great detail***, ***in much detail***); (*b*) *MILITARY* by the engagement of small portions of a force one after the other. **go into detail** deal with a thing in its individual particulars. **war of detail** a war carried on in detail rather than by general engagements.
– COMB.: ***detail drawing***: see sense 5b above; **detail man** *US* a company's representative whose job is to sell (esp. new) drugs to doctors, pharmacists, etc.

detail /ˈdiːteɪl/ *verb trans.* M17.
[ORIGIN French *détailler*, from *dé-* DE- 1 + *tailler* cut in pieces.]
1 Relate or describe minutely; give particulars of, itemize. M17.

G. W. KNIGHT It is unnecessary to detail more than a few of the numerous references to darkness. J. ARCHER The story of the probable break-up of Nethercote and Company was detailed on the financial pages.

2 Orig. *MILITARY*. Assign to a specific duty. E18.

B. GUTTERIDGE Sentries were detailed and posted. MALCOLM X Some were detailed as ushers, who seated the people by designated sections. JO GRIMOND My sisters had been detailed to look after me in London.

■ **detailed** *ppl adjective* having much detail; related or described minutely; paying attention to detail: M18. **detailer** *noun* L18. **detailing** *verbal noun* (*a*) the action of the verb; (*b*) (the treatment of) detail in a work of art, building, design, etc.: M19.

†**detain** *noun*. *rare* (Spenser). Only in L16.
[ORIGIN from the verb.]
Detention.

detain /dɪˈteɪn/ *verb trans.* LME.
[ORIGIN Repr. tonic stem of Old French & mod. French *détenir*, from Proto-Romance var. of Latin *detinere*, from *de-* DE- 1 + *tenere* hold.]
†**1** In *pass.* Be afflicted *with* sickness or infirmity. LME–M17.
2 Place or keep in confinement; keep as a prisoner, esp. without charge. L15.

R. MACAULAY They would be conducted to London by the escort, and detained there for questioning. ANTHONY SMITH About twenty thousand people are compulsorily detained in psychiatric and special hospitals.

3 Withhold, retain; *esp.* keep back what is due or claimed. Now *rare* or *obsolete*. M16.
4 Keep in a certain place or condition; hold. *obsolete* exc. as passing into sense 5. M16.
5 Keep from proceeding; hold back, delay, stop. M16. ▸†**b** Restrain from action. Only in 17.

W. COBBETT I was detained . . partly by the rain, and partly by company that I liked very much. S. BELLOW Leventhal did not halt until Allbee detained him, stepping in his way.

■ **detainable** *adjective* able to be detained E19. **detainingly** *adverb* so as to detain a person M19. **detainment** *noun* (an instance of) detention L16.

detainee /diteɪˈniː, diː-/ *noun*. E20.
[ORIGIN from DETAIN *verb* + -EE[1].]
A person detained in custody, esp. on political grounds.

detainer /dɪˈteɪnə/ *noun*[1]. M16.
[ORIGIN formed as DETAINEE + -ER[1].]
A person who or thing which detains.

detainer /dɪˈteɪnə/ *noun*[2]. E17.
[ORIGIN Anglo-Norman *detener* use as noun of inf. = Old French & mod. French *détenir*: see DETAIN *verb*, -ER[4].]
LAW. **1** The action of withholding or keeping; *spec.* the (wrongful) retention of goods taken from the owner for distraint etc. E17.
forcible detainer the unlawful possession or retention of land by (the threat of) violence.
2 The detaining of a person, esp. in custody or confinement. Now *arch.* or *hist.* L17.
3 An order authorizing the continued detention of a person in custody who would otherwise be released. M19.

detangle /diːˈtaŋɡl/ *verb trans.* L20.
[ORIGIN from DE- 3 + TANGLE *verb*.]
Remove tangles from (hair).
■ **detangler** *noun* (*a*) a comb or other instrument used to remove tangles from hair; (*b*) a substance which eases the removal of tangles from hair, such as a conditioner: L20.

detant *noun* see DETENT.

detassel /diːˈtas(ə)l/ *verb trans. US*. L19.
[ORIGIN from DE- 3 + TASSEL *noun*[1].]
Remove the tassels from (maize).

detect /dɪˈtɛkt/ *verb*. Pa. pple & ppl adjective †**detect**, **-ed**. LME.
[ORIGIN Latin *detect-* pa. ppl stem of *detegere*, from *de-* DE- 3 + *tegere* cover.]
†**1** *verb trans.* Uncover, expose, display. LME–M18.
†**2** *verb trans.* Disclose information about; inform against, accuse; give (a person) away. LME–E19.
3 *verb trans.* Discover the real (esp. hidden or disguised) character of; discover *in doing*, †*to be*. Formerly also, discover in the act *of*. L16.

J. BENTHAM You have detected a baker in selling short weight.

4 *verb trans.* Discover the presence, existence, or fact of (something apt to elude notice); use an instrument to discover or observe (a signal, radiation, etc.). M18. ▸**b** Investigate or discover as a detective. E20.

G. GREENE A new finger-print stunt, . . by which they could detect the print even when the hand had been gloved. I. MURDOCH Through the leaves she detected the flash of a white shirt. B. LOVELL Scientists . . succeeded in detecting the radio emission from the planet.

5 *verb intrans.* Be engaged in detective work; act as a detective. E20.
■ **detectaˈbility** *noun* the state of being detectable, ability to be detected E19. **detectable** *adjective* able to be detected M17. **detectably** *adverb* in a way that can be detected, to a detectable degree L19. **detectiˈbility** *noun* = DETECTABILITY L20. **detectible** *adjective* = DETECTABLE M19.

detecter *noun* see DETECTOR.

detection /dɪˈtɛkʃ(ə)n/ *noun*. L15.
[ORIGIN Late Latin *detectio(n-)*, formed as DETECT: see -ION.]
†**1** Exposure, revelation of what is concealed; accusation. L15–E18.
2 The finding out or discovery of what is unknown, hidden, or disguised; detective work. E17.

S. JOHNSON It is easy for the author of a lie, however malignant, to escape detection. E. RUTHERFORD The detection of a minute quantity of neon. D. L. SAYERS A 'talk' on 'Detection in Fact and Fiction'.

3 *ELECTRICITY*. Extraction of a desired signal; demodulation. E20.
■ **detectional** *adjective* M20.

detective /dɪˈtɛktɪv/ *adjective & noun*. M19.
[ORIGIN from DETECT + -IVE, after *elect*, *elective*, etc.]
▸ **A** *adjective*. **1** Of, pertaining to, or employed in the investigation of things apt to elude notice or deliberately concealed, esp. of crimes; having the character or function of detection. M19.

GEO. ELIOT Vexed by the detective wisdom of critics. G. B. SHAW Divorces and executions and the detective operations that lead up to them.

2 [attrib. use of the noun] Describing crime and the detection of criminals. L19.
detective fiction, ***detective novel***, ***detective novelist***, ***detective story***, etc.
▸ **B** *noun*. A police officer or other person whose occupation it is to investigate crimes by eliciting evidence, information, etc.; a person engaged in detective work; the position or rank of a police detective. M19.

B. JOWETT The criminal turned detective is wonderfully suspicious and cautious. W. SAFIRE Phrase detectives the world over are searching for the origins of 'the social safety net'. *Daily Telegraph* Detectives in the original investigation protested at meeting 'a wall of silence' from potential witnesses.

private detective: see PRIVATE *adjective*.
– COMB.: **detective inspector**, **detective sergeant**, etc.: a police detective with the specified rank.
■ **detectival** *adjective* of or pertaining to detective work E20.

detector /dɪˈtɛktə/ *noun*. Also (now *rare*) **-er**. M16.
[ORIGIN from DETECT *verb* + -OR, -ER[1].]
†**1** A person who or thing which discloses information; an accuser, an informer. M16–M18.
2 A person who finds out things which are apt to elude notice. E17.

J. S. MILL The keenest detector of the errors of his predecessors.

3 An instrument or device which detects something liable to elude notice or indicates something out of the ordinary; a device for the detection or demodulation of electric signals. M19.

N. SHUTE The detector on his periscope head indicated a high level of radioactivity. R. V. JONES Whether I could develop an air-borne infra-red detector so that it could be mounted on a nightfighter and thus detect bombers.

lie detector, ***metal detector***, etc.
■ **detectorist** *noun* a person who uses a metal detector for a hobby. L20.

detemporalize /diːˈtɛmp(ə)r(ə)lʌɪz/ *verb trans.* Also **-ise**. E20.
[ORIGIN from DE- 3 + TEMPORALIZE.]
Make timeless in character; detach from a particular time.

†**detenebrate** *verb trans.* M17–E18.
[ORIGIN from DE- 3 + Latin *tenebra* darkness + -ATE[3].]
Free from darkness or obscurity.

detension /diːˈtɛnʃ(ə)n/ *verb & noun*. M20.
[ORIGIN from DE- 3 + TENSION *noun*.]
▸ **A** *verb trans.* Remove or reduce the tension from. M20.
▸ **B** *noun*. A removal or reduction of tension or anxiety; a relaxation. M20.

detent /dɪˈtɛnt/ *noun*. In sense 3 also **detant** /dɪˈtant/. L17.
[ORIGIN French *détente*, Old French *destente*, from *destendre* (mod. *détendre*) slacken, from *des-* DIS- 2 + *tendre* stretch. In English assoc. with Latin *detent-* pa. ppl stem of *detinere* DETAIN *verb*, whence branch II.]
▸ **I 1** In clocks and watches, a catch which regulates striking. L17.
2 Any stop or catch in a machine which prevents a motion until released. M19.
3 In a gunlock, a small piece designed to prevent the sere from catching in the half-cock notch in the tumbler. L19.
▸ **II 4** Restraint, inhibition. E20.

détente /deɪˈtɑ̃ːt, -tɒ̃t, -tɑːnt, -tɒnt/ *noun*. E20.
[ORIGIN French = loosening, relaxation: see DETENT.]
The easing of strained relations, esp. between states.

detention /dɪˈtɛnʃ(ə)n/ *noun*. LME.
[ORIGIN French *détention* or late Latin *detentio(n-)*, from *detent-* pa. ppl stem of *detinere* DETAIN *verb*: see -ION.]
1 The retention or withholding of what is due or claimed. LME.

SHAKES. *Timon* The detention of long-since-due debts.

2 Now chiefly *LAW*. Holding in one's possession or control; retention. LME.
3 The action of arresting or confining, the state of imprisonment or confinement, now *esp.* of a military or political offender. L16. ▸**b** The punishment of being kept in school after hours; an instance of this. L19.

LYTTON Offering twenty guineas reward for his detention. H. ARENDT In totalitarian countries all places of detention ruled by the police are made to be veritable holes of oblivion.

4 Hindrance to progress; compulsory delay. E17.
– ATTRIB. & COMB.: In the sense 'where people are held in detention', as ***detention barrack***, ***detention camp***, etc. Special combs., as **detention centre** an institution for the short-term detention of illegal immigrants, refugees, people awaiting trial or sentence, or (formerly in the UK) young offenders.

détenu /deɪtəˈnuː; *foreign* detny (*pl. same*)/ *noun*. Also **de-**. Now chiefly *Indian*. E19.
[ORIGIN French, use as noun of pa. pple of *détenir* DETAIN *verb*.]
A person held in custody, a detainee.

deter /dɪˈtəː/ *verb trans.* Infl. **-rr-**. M16.
[ORIGIN Latin *deterrere*, from *de-* DE- 1 + *terrere* frighten.]
1 Restrain or discourage (*from* acting or proceeding) by fear, doubt, dislike of effort or trouble, or consideration of consequences. M16.

J. L. WATEN I wanted to join in the laughter but Father's face deterred me. S. NAIPAUL No threat would deter them from producing it and delivering it free of charge.

2 Inhibit, prevent. M20.

Scientific American This tactic could deter torpedo attack.

■ **determent** *noun* the action or fact of deterring; a deterring circumstance: M17. **deterrable** *adjective* (chiefly *US Law*) that may be deterred from a course of action, esp. by fear of legal punishment M20.

deterge /dɪˈtəːdʒ/ *verb trans.* E17.
[ORIGIN French *déterger* or Latin *detergere*, from *de-* DE- 1 + *tergere* wipe.]
Cleanse (formerly esp. *MEDICINE*, of pus or other morbid matter); wash off or out.

detergency /dɪˈtəːdʒ(ə)nsi/ *noun*. E18.
[ORIGIN formed as DETERGENT: see -ENCY.]
1 Detergent quality. E18.
2 The process of cleansing a solid by means of a liquid; the action of a detergent. M20.

detergent /dɪˈtəːdʒ(ə)nt/ *adjective & noun*. E17.
[ORIGIN Latin *detergent-* pres. ppl stem of *detergere*: see DETERGE, -ENT.]
▸ **A** *adjective*. Cleansing; having the properties of a detergent. E17.
▸ **B** *noun*. A cleansing agent. Now *esp.* a synthetic substance mixable with water which resembles soap in its cleansing properties but does not combine with the salts present esp. in hard water; also, an oil-soluble substance which holds dirt in suspension in lubricating oils. L17.

deteriorate /dɪˈtɪərɪəreɪt/ *verb*. Pa. pple & ppl adjective †**-ate** (earlier), **-ated**. L16.
[ORIGIN Late Latin *deteriorat-* pa. ppl stem of *deteriorare*, from *deterior* worse: see -ATE³.]
1 *verb trans.* Make worse; lower in character or excellence. L16.
H. L. MENCKEN The accompanying hooey pollutes and deteriorates their mind.
2 *verb intrans.* Become worse; become impaired in quality or value; degenerate. L17.
D. ADAMS What had started out as excellent entertainment had .. deteriorated into mere abuse. P. ROSE His health deteriorated so badly that the East India Company gave him a medical leave.
■ **deteriorative** *adjective* causing or tending to deterioration E19. **deteriorator** *noun* M19.

deterioration /dɪˌtɪərɪəˈreɪʃ(ə)n/ *noun*. M17.
[ORIGIN French *détérioration* from late Latin *deterioratio(n-)*, formed as DETERIORATE: see -ATION.]
The process of growing or making worse; a deteriorated condition.
A. WEST My father was as well aware of his deterioration as anyone, and he did not enjoy the progressive stages of his decline.
■ **deteriorationist** *noun* a person who holds that deterioration, not progress, is the order of things E19.

determa /dɪˈtəːmə/ *noun*. M18.
[ORIGIN Prob. from Guyanese name.]
The hard reddish timber of a tropical American tree of the laurel family, *Ocotea rubra*; = ***red* LOURO**.

determinable /dɪˈtəːmɪnəb(ə)l/ *adjective & noun*. LME.
[ORIGIN Orig. from Old French (= fixed, determinate) from late Latin *determinabilis* finite, from *determinare*: see DETERMINE, -ABLE. Later from DETERMINE + -ABLE.]
▸ **A** *adjective*. †**1** Fixed, definite. LME–M17.
2 Able to be authoritatively decided, definitely fixed, or definitely ascertained. LME.
R. HOOKER Affairs .. which were not determinable one way or other by the Scripture. G. GROTE Whether Sidon or Tyre was the most ancient, seems not determinable.
3 Liable to come to an end; terminable. Chiefly LAW (of a lease etc.). L16.
▸ **B** *noun*. PHILOSOPHY. Something which can be more precisely specified; *spec.* a general term or concept under which several specific terms or concepts fall. L19.
■ **determinaˈbility** *noun* E19. **determinableness** *noun* E18. **determinably** *adverb* in a determinable manner; to a determinable degree: LME.

determinacy /dɪˈtəːmɪnəsi/ *noun*. L19.
[ORIGIN from DETERMINATE *adjective*: see -ACY. Cf. earlier INDETERMINACY.]
Determinateness, definiteness.

determinandum /dɪˌtəːmɪˈnandəm/ *noun*. Pl. **-da** /-də/. E20.
[ORIGIN Latin *determinandum* use as noun of neut. gerundive of *determinare* DETERMINE.]
LOGIC & GRAMMAR. A part of a proposition or expression which is to be qualified or limited by thought or by another part of the expression. Cf. DETERMINANS, DETERMINATUM.

determinans /dɪˈtəːmɪnanz/ *noun*. Pl. **-nantia** /-ˈnantɪə, -ʃɪə/. E20.
[ORIGIN Latin *determinans* use as noun of pres. pple of *determinare* DETERMINE.]
LOGIC & GRAMMAR. A qualifying or limiting part of a proposition or expression. Cf. DETERMINANDUM, DETERMINATUM.

determinant /dɪˈtəːmɪnənt/ *adjective & noun*. E17.
[ORIGIN Latin *determinant-* pres. ppl stem of *determinare* DETERMINE: see -ANT¹. As noun partly translating Latin *determinans*: see DETERMINANS.]
▸ **A** *adjective*. Determining; that determines; determinative. E17.
▸ **B** *noun*. **1** A determining factor or agent; a ruling or conditioning element. L17. ▸**b** GRAMMAR. A limiting or qualifying word or expression. M19. ▸**c** LOGIC. Each of the elements in a conjunction (CONJUNCTION 7). L19.
G. GORER Area .. seems to be much less of a determinant than age and poverty. A. STORR The events of early childhood as determinants of later personality and problems.
2 *hist.* = DETERMINER *noun*² 2. M19.
3 MATH. A square matrix (usu. represented with a vertical line at each side) which has a numerical or algebraic value obtained by adding and subtracting products of the elements of the matrix according to certain rules; a quantity obtained from or represented by a square matrix in this way. M19.
4 BIOLOGY. A gene or other factor which determines the character and development of a cell or group of cells in an organism. L19.
antigenic determinant = EPITOPE.
■ **determiˈnantal** *adjective* (MATH.) relating to, consisting of, or expressed as a determinant M19.

determinantia *noun* pl. of DETERMINANS.

determinata *noun* pl. of DETERMINATUM.

determinate /dɪˈtəːmɪnət/ *adjective*. LME.
[ORIGIN Latin *determinatus* pa. pple, formed as DETERMINATE *verb*: see -ATE².]
1 Definitely bounded or limited; clearly defined; distinct; finite. LME. ▸**b** MATH. Having a fixed value or magnitude. E18.
G. BERKELEY The clear and determinate meaning of my words.
2 Settled, fixed, established. LME.
J. S. MILL A determinate order of precedence among them.
3 Finally determined upon or decided; definitive. M16.
Times One of the determinate reasons for the decision.
4 Fixed in mind or purpose; resolved, resolute. M16.
S. JOHNSON A Tory so ardent and determinate that he did not willingly consort with men of different opinions.
†**5** Intended. L16–E17.
SHAKES. *Twel. N.* My determinate voyage is mere extravagancy.
■ **determinately** *adverb* L15. **determinateness** *noun* M17.

†**determinate** *verb trans. & intrans.* Pa. pple & ppl adjective **-ate** (earlier), **-ated**. LME–L19.
[ORIGIN Latin *determinat-* pa. ppl stem of *determinare* DETERMINE: see -ATE³.]
= DETERMINE.

determination /dɪˌtəːmɪˈneɪʃ(ə)n/ *noun*. LME
[ORIGIN Old French & mod. French *détermination* from Latin *determinatio(n-)*, formed as DETERMINATE *verb*: see -ATION.]
1 The settlement of a suit or controversy by the authoritative decision of a judge or arbiter; a settlement or decision so made, an authoritative opinion. LME. ▸†**b** The settlement of a question by reasoning or argument. LME–L16. ▸**c** The discussion and resolving of a question or the upholding of a thesis in a scholastic disputation; *spec.* (performance in) a university exercise consisting of a series of disputations, qualifying a bachelor of arts to proceed to a master's degree. *obsolete* exc. *hist.* M17.
ADDISON They were neither of them dissatisfied with the Knight's Determination. B. JOWETT In the determination of this question the identity of virtue and knowledge is found to be involved.
2 A bringing or coming to an end; a termination. *arch.* in *gen.* sense. L15. ▸**b** LAW. The cessation of an estate or interest of any kind. L15.
W. STUBBS The war continued .. seeming year by year further removed from a determination.
3 The action of coming to a decision; the result of this; a fixed intention. L15.
P. FITZGERALD Her courage .. was only a determination to survive.
4 The action of definitely locating, identifying, or establishing the nature of something; exact ascertainment (*of*); a fact established, a conclusion or solution reached. L16.
W. WHEWELL Generally founded on astronomical determinations.
5 The action of determining bounds or fixing limits; delimitation, definition. L16. ▸**b** LOGIC. The process of making a notion more specific by the addition of attributes. Also, a determining attribute. M17.
HOBBES The Circumscription of a thing, is .. the Determination, or Defining of its Place.
6 A tendency to move or flow in a fixed direction; a determining bias. *arch.* M17.
R. L. STEVENSON Some determination of blood to the head.
7 The definite direction or motivation of the mind or will towards an object or end. Now *rare*. L17.
8 Resoluteness, determinedness; fixity of intention. E19.
DAY LEWIS The set of the lips suggests a certain inward firmness, a quality of determination.

determinative /dɪˈtəːmɪnətɪv/ *adjective & noun*. M17.
[ORIGIN French *déterminatif*, *-ive* or late Latin *determinativus*, formed as DETERMINATE *verb*: see -IVE.]
▸ **A** *adjective*. Characterized by determining something; serving to determine something; decisive; limiting, distinguishing, identifying. M17.
▸ **B** *noun*. A thing which determines something; *spec.* a sign (in hieroglyphic writing) or a morpheme indicating the semantic classification of a word. M19.
■ **determinatively** *adverb* in a determinative manner, to a determinative degree; definitely, decisively: E17. **determinativeness** *noun* E19.

determinator /dɪˈtəːmɪneɪtə/ *noun*. M16.
[ORIGIN Late Latin *determinator*, formed as DETERMINATE *verb*: see -OR.]
A person who or thing which determines something; a determiner.

determinatum /dɪˌtəːmɪˈnɑːtəm, -ˈneɪtəm/ *noun*. Pl. **-ta** /-tə/. E20.
[ORIGIN Latin *determinatum* use as noun of neut. pa. pple of *determinare* DETERMINE.]
LOGIC & GRAMMAR. A part of a proposition or expression that has been qualified or limited. Cf. DETERMINANDUM, DETERMINANS.

determine /dɪˈtəːmɪn/ *verb*. LME.
[ORIGIN Old French & mod. French *déterminer* from Latin *determinare* bound, limit, fix from *de-* DE- 1 + *terminare* TERMINATE *verb*.]
▸ **I** Put an end to; come to an end.
1 *verb trans.* Now chiefly LAW. Bring to an end, esp. through judicial decision; conclude. LME.
W. STUBBS The death of Edward III determined the crisis.
2 *verb intrans.* Now chiefly LAW. Come to an end; cease to exist or be, esp. through judicial decision. LME. ▸†**b** End *in* (a conclusion, result, etc.). E17–L19.
W. CRUISE The estate of Martin did not determine by his death. **b** R. SOUTH But that which begins in vanity, must needs determine in vexation of spirit.
3 *verb trans.* Bound, limit. Now only *spec.* (**a**) LOGIC limit by adding differentia; (**b**) GRAMMAR limit the application or reference of (a noun). LME. ▸†**b** Limit *to*, restrict *to*. LME–L17.
4 *verb trans.* Settle or decide (a dispute, controversy, etc., or a sentence, conclusion, issue, etc.) as a judge or arbiter. Foll. by simple obj., subord. clause with *that*, *what*, *whether*, etc. LME. ▸**b** *verb intrans.* Discuss and resolve a question or uphold a thesis in a scholastic disputation; *spec.* perform in the university exercise of determination (see DETERMINATION 1c). *obsolete* exc. *hist.* L16.
H. H. MILMAN The Dean presided in all causes .. and determined them. B. JOWETT The law will determine all our various duties towards relatives. A. E. STEVENSON Our entire military establishment must be re-examined to determine how we can best build and keep the forces we need for our national security.
b determining bachelor = DETERMINER *noun*² 2.
5 *verb intrans.* Come to a judicial decision; make or give a decision about something. (Formerly foll. by *of*, *on*.) Cf. sense 13 below. LME.
S. JOHNSON The general inability of man to determine rightly concerning his own.
†**6** *verb trans.* Lay down authoritatively; pronounce, declare. LME–M17.
7 *verb trans.* Settle or fix beforehand (now esp. a date); ordain, decree. LME.
†**8** *verb trans.* Conclude from reasoning or investigation, deduce, (a person or thing *to be*, *that*). L15–E19.
9 *verb trans.* Fix or decide causally, condition as a cause or antecedent, be a deciding or the decisive factor in; decide on, select, choose. M17.
H. T. LANE The way the mother deals with the child determines its future character. B. WEBB It was MacDonald who alone determined who should be in his cabinet. C. BLACKWOOD None of her reactions seemed to be determined by external events.
10 *verb trans.* Definitely locate, identify, or establish the nature of; ascertain exactly. M17. ▸**b** GEOMETRY. Fix or define the position of. M19.
C. IVES What it is that inspires an art effort is not easily determined. B. GUEST Middle-class Americans are just as eager as the English to determine one's social position.
▸ **II** Direct to an end.
11 *verb trans.* Give an aim or direction to; direct; impel *to*. *arch.* LME. ▸**b** *verb intrans.* Take its course, tend *to* (a particular end). *arch.* M17.
W. CULLEN Animals are determined to take in aliment by the appetites of hunger and thirst. T. R. MALTHUS Thus determining a greater quantity of capital to this particular employment.
†**12** *verb refl.* Bring oneself to a decision or resolve (*to do*). LME–E18.
13 *verb intrans.* Come to a decision *that*; resolve *to do*, *on doing*, *on* a course of action. Cf. sense 5 above. E16.
J. A. FROUDE The bishops .. determined on a further appeal to the pope. G. VIDAL I determined to defer my attack on Paul's methods until a safer time.
14 *verb trans.* Decide the course of (a person); bring to a decision or resolution (*to do*). L17.
E. DOWDEN Credit .. for having determined Shelley to travel abroad.

D

D

determined /dɪˈtəːmɪnd/ *adjective*. LME.
[ORIGIN from DETERMINE + -ED[1].]
1 *gen.* That has been determined. LME.
2 a Resolved *that, to do, on doing, on* a course of action. E16. ▸**b** Resolute; showing determination; characterized by determination. E17.

a G. GREENE He was determined that it should have a superficial legality. O. MANNING She's determined to be an independent, wage-earning woman. D. JACOBSON He was already grimly and irrevocably determined on a course of action. **b** T. HARDY Her determined negative deterred his scrupulous heart. E. O'NEILL A brutal, determined-looking man of forty.

3 Decided or resolved on, settled. M16.
■ **determinedly** *adverb* M16. **determinedness** *noun* M18.

determiner /dɪˈtəːmɪnə/ *noun*[1]. *obsolete* exc. *hist.* LME.
[ORIGIN Anglo-Norman, use as noun of inf. = Old French & mod. French *déterminer*: see DETERMINE, -ER[4].]
LAW. The final determining of a judge or court. Chiefly in ***OYER and determiner***, OYER ***determiner***.

determiner /dɪˈtəːmɪnə/ *noun*[2]. M16.
[ORIGIN from DETERMINE *verb* + -ER[1].]
1 *gen.* A person who or thing which determines or decides something. M16.
2 A (successful) candidate in the university exercise of determination (see DETERMINATION 1c). *obsolete* exc. *hist.* L16.
3 BIOLOGY. = DETERMINANT *noun* 4. *arch.* E20.
4 GRAMMAR. A modifying word which limits the application or reference of the noun modified, in English being one of a class including articles and other definite and indefinite adjectives, and demonstrative, quantifying, and possessive adjectives, or in other analyses some subset of these, all of which precede any descriptive adjective. Cf. PREDETERMINER. M20.

determinism /dɪˈtəːmɪnɪz(ə)m/ *noun*. L18.
[ORIGIN from DETERMINE + -ISM.]
1 The doctrine that human action is necessarily determined by motives regarded as external forces acting on the will. L18.
2 The doctrine that everything that happens is determined by a necessary chain of causation. L19.

determinist /dɪˈtəːmɪnɪst/ *adjective & noun*. M19.
[ORIGIN formed as DETERMINISM + -IST.]
▸ **A** *adjective*. Of or pertaining to determinism; adhering to determinism. M19.
▸ **B** *noun*. An adherent of determinism. L19.
■ **determiˈnistic** *adjective* L19. **determiˈnistically** *adverb* L19.

deterrent /dɪˈtɛr(ə)nt/ *adjective & noun*. E19.
[ORIGIN Latin *deterrent-* pres. ppl stem of *deterrere* DETER: see -ENT.]
▸ **A** *adjective*. That deters; tending to deter. E19.
▸ **B** *noun*. A thing that deters; *esp.* a nuclear weapon the possession of which by a state or alliance is intended to deter any attack from an opposing power. E19.

Observer Britain should also be prepared to give up her independent deterrent and stop the manufacture of nuclear weapons.

■ **deterrence** *noun* the action of deterring or preventing by fear M19.

deterritorialization /ˌdiːtɛrɪˌtɔːrɪəlʌɪˈzeɪʃ(ə)n/ *noun*. Also **-isation**. M20.
[ORIGIN from DE- 3 + TERRITORIALIZATION.]
The severance of social, political, or cultural practices from their native places and populations.

detersion /dɪˈtəːʃ(ə)n/ *noun*. Now *rare*. E17.
[ORIGIN Late Latin *detersio(n-)*, from *deters-* pa. ppl stem of *detergere*: see DETERGE, -ION.]
The action or an act of cleansing (formerly esp. MEDICINE, of pus or other morbid matter).

detersive /dɪˈtəːsɪv/ *adjective & noun*. L16.
[ORIGIN French *détersif, -ive*, from Latin *deters-*: see DETERSION, -IVE.]
▸ **A** *adjective*. Cleansing, having the power to cleanse, (formerly esp. MEDICINE, of pus or other morbid matter). L16.
▸ **B** *noun*. A cleansing or detersive agent. M17.

detest /dɪˈtɛst/ *verb*. L15.
[ORIGIN Latin *detestari* denounce, renounce, from *de-* DE- 1 + *testari* bear witness, call to witness, from *testis* witness. Perh. partly back-form. from DETESTATION.]
▸ **I 1** *verb trans.* Hate or dislike intensely; abhor, abominate. L15.

D. ACHESON Perón was a fascist and a dictator detested by all good men. W. STYRON She detested New York subway trains for their grime and their noise.

†**2** *verb trans.* Curse, calling God to witness; denounce, execrate. M16–M18.
▸ †**II 3** *verb trans. & intrans.* Attest, protest, testify. M16–E17.
■ **detester** *noun* E17.

detestable /dɪˈtɛstəb(ə)l/ *adjective*. LME.
[ORIGIN Old French & mod. French *détestable* or Latin *detestabilis*, formed as DETEST: see -ABLE.]
Intensely hateful or odious; execrable, abominable.
■ **detestaˈbility** *noun* M19. **detestableness** *noun* E17. **detestably** *adverb* M16.

detestation /diːtɛˈsteɪʃ(ə)n/ *noun*. LME.
[ORIGIN Old French & mod. French *détestation* from Latin *detestatio(n-)*, from *detestat-* pa. ppl stem of *detestari* DETEST: see -ATION.]
†**1** Public or formal execration (*of*). LME–L17.
2 Intense dislike or hatred; abhorrence. LME.
3 A detested person or thing. E18.

dethrone /diːˈθrəʊn, dɪ-/ *verb trans.* E17.
[ORIGIN from DE- 3 + THRONE *noun*.]
Remove from a throne (*lit. & fig.*), depose; end the supremacy or dominant influence of.

J. BARZUN Dewey's effect on schooling was to dethrone subject matter and replace it by techniques. *Times* The dethroned world champion.

■ **dethronement** *noun* E18. **dethroner** *noun* M17.

detin /diːˈtɪn/ *verb trans.* Infl. **-nn-**. E20.
[ORIGIN from DE- 3 + TIN *noun*.]
Remove the tin from (tin plate).

detinue /ˈdɛtɪnjuː/ *noun*. LME.
[ORIGIN Old French *detenue* use as noun of fem. pa. pple of *detenir* DETAIN *verb*, assim. to Latin *detinere*.]
LAW. The wrongful detention of a personal chattel; (in full ***action of detinue***) an action against this.

detonate /ˈdɛtəneɪt/ *verb*. E18.
[ORIGIN Latin *detonat-* pa. ppl stem of *detonare*, from *de-* DE- 1 + *tonare* to thunder: see -ATE[3]. Partly back-form. from DETONATION.]
1 *verb intrans.* Undergo detonation. E18.
2 *verb trans.* Cause to detonate. E19.
■ **detonative** *adjective* having the property of detonating L19.

detonation /dɛtəˈneɪʃ(ə)n/ *noun*. L17.
[ORIGIN French *détonation*, from *détoner* from Latin *detonare*: see DETONATE, -ATION.]
1 (The sudden loud noise accompanying) an explosive chemical reaction whose gaseous products expand supersonically; explosion with loud report. L17. ▸**b** Rapid premature combustion of the fuel in an internal-combustion engine, causing pinking. E20.
2 The action of causing a substance, bomb, etc., to explode. E18.
3 *gen.* A sudden loud noise; *fig.* a sudden outburst of feeling. M19.

detonator /ˈdɛtəneɪtə/ *noun*. E19.
[ORIGIN from DETONATE + -OR.]
†**1** A gun fired by means of a percussion cap. E–M19.
2 A contrivance for detonating, esp. as part of a bomb, shell, etc. L19.
3 A railway fog signal consisting of an explosive device designed to be placed on a rail and set off by a train passing over it. L19.

†**detonize** *verb intrans. & trans.* Also **-ise**. M18–E19.
[ORIGIN from French *détoner* (see DETONATION) + -IZE.]
= DETONATE.

detorsion /dɪˈtɔːʃ(ə)n/ *noun*. In sense 1 also **-tion**. L16.
[ORIGIN from Latin *detors-, detort-* pa. ppl stem of *detorquere*, from *de-* DE- 1 + *torquere* twist: see -ION. Sense 2 perh. from DE- 3 + TORSION *noun*.]
1 Twisting, (a) distortion; *esp.* (a) perversion of meaning. Now *rare* or *obsolete*. L16.
2 ZOOLOGY. Evolutionary reversion of gastropods to a primitive linear anatomical organization, involving reversal of a 180 degrees torsion displayed by their immediate ancestors. E20.

†**detort** *verb trans.* M16–E19.
[ORIGIN Latin *detort-*: see DETORSION.]
Turn aside from its purpose; twist, pervert, esp. in meaning; derive by distortion.

detortion *noun* see DETORSION.

detour /ˈdiːtʊə/ *noun & verb*. Also **dé-** /ˈdeɪ-/. M18.
[ORIGIN French *détour* change of direction, from *détourner* turn away.]
▸ **A** *noun*. A deviation from one's route, a roundabout way; a digression. M18.

E. O'NEILL They make wide detours to avoid the spot where he stands. G. SARTON The best anatomists . . did not find the truth except after many detours.

▸ **B** *verb*. **1** *verb intrans.* Make a detour. M19.

D. ALDIS Mary detoured to pick up her bag from the table.

2 *verb trans.* Send by a detour. E20.

LADY BIRD JOHNSON The storm detoured him to Pittsburgh.

3 *verb trans.* Make a detour round, bypass. M20.

J. HERSEY A railroad line that detoured the city in a wide semicircle.

detox /ˈdiːtɒks/ *noun*. *colloq.* (chiefly *US*). L20.
[ORIGIN Abbreviation.]
= DETOXIFICATION. Also, a detoxification centre.

detox /diːˈtɒks/ *verb*. *colloq.* L20.
[ORIGIN Abbreviation of DETOXIFY.]
1 *verb trans.* Modify (a motor vehicle or engine) to remove or limit the emission of toxic fumes. L20.
2 *verb trans.* Subject (an alcoholic, drug addict, etc.) to detoxification. Chiefly *US*. L20.
3 *verb intrans.* Subject oneself to detoxification. Chiefly *US*. L20.

detoxicate /diːˈtɒksɪkeɪt/ *verb trans.* M19.
[ORIGIN from DE- 3 + Latin *toxicum* poison, after *intoxicate*.]
= DETOXIFY.
■ **detoxiˈcation** *noun* = DETOXIFICATION E20.

detoxification /diːˌtɒksɪfɪˈkeɪʃ(ə)n/ *noun*. E20.
[ORIGIN formed as DETOXICATE: see -FICATION.]
The action of detoxifying, esp. an alcoholic or drug addict; the state of being detoxified.
– COMB.: **detoxification centre** a (usu. residential) centre for the treatment of alcoholism or drug addiction.

detoxify /diːˈtɒksɪfʌɪ/ *verb trans.* E20.
[ORIGIN formed as DETOXICATE + -FY.]
Remove poison from; free from poisonous qualities.

detract /dɪˈtrakt/ *verb*. LME.
[ORIGIN Latin *detract-* pa. ppl stem of *detrahere*, from *de-* DE- 1 + *trahere* draw.]
▸ **I 1** *verb trans.* Take away, subtract, deduct, (now esp. much, something, or other indef. obj.). (Foll. by *from* a whole, †a possessor). LME.

SHAKES. *1 Hen. VI* Shall I . . Detract so much from that prerogative As to be call'd but viceroy of the whole.

2 *verb trans.* Take away from the reputation or estimation of, disparage, belittle. Now *rare*. LME.
3 *verb intrans.* Foll. by *from*: take something away from, diminish; reduce the credit due to; disparage, belittle, (something abstract, †something material). L16. ▸†**b** *verb intrans.* Speak disparagingly. L16–L18.

E. J. HOWARD Her eyes were her only good feature, said her mother, and proceeded to dress her in every shade of inferior blue which detracted from them. M. MEYER The follies of Hedin's age do not detract from the achievements of his saner years. B. PYM The view of the neglected garden next door would detract from the elegance of the occasion.

▸ †**II 4** *verb trans. & intrans.* Draw away or aside, withdraw, divert. M16–E19.
5 *verb trans. & intrans.* Protract (time); delay. M16–M17.
▸ †**III 6** *verb trans.* Draw back from, refuse; relinquish. L16–E17.
■ **detracˈtation** *noun* (*rare*) = DETRACTION LME. **detractingly** *adverb* so as to detract, disparagingly L16.

detracter *noun* see DETRACTOR.

detraction /dɪˈtrakʃ(ə)n/ *noun*. ME.
[ORIGIN Old French & mod. French *détraction* from Latin *detractio(n-)*, formed as DETRACT: see -ION.]
1 The action of detracting from a person's merit or reputation; disparagement, belittlement; calumny, slander. ME.

ADDISON Females addicted to Censoriousness and Detraction.

2 *gen.* A taking away, subtraction, deduction. Also, a part to be detracted. Now only *from* merit, reputation, etc. E16.

N. PINKNEY There is one heavy detraction . . from the excellence of the . . climate.

†**3** Prolonging, delay. L16–M17.

detractive /dɪˈtraktɪv/ *adjective*. L15.
[ORIGIN Old French *detractif, -ive* or medieval Latin *detractivus*, formed as DETRACT: see -IVE.]
1 Conveying, of the nature of, or given to, detraction. L15.
2 Tending to detract *from*. M17.
■ **detractively** *adverb* L19. **detractiveness** *noun* E18.

detractor /dɪˈtraktə/ *noun*. Also **-er**. LME.
[ORIGIN Anglo-Norman *detractour*, Old French & mod. French *détracteur* or Latin *detractor*, formed as DETRACT, -OR.]
A person who detracts from another's merit or reputation; a disparager, a belittler.
■ **detractory** *adjective* [Latin *detractorius*] = DETRACTIVE L16. **detractress** *noun* (*rare*) a female detractor E18.

detrain /diːˈtreɪn/ *verb trans. & intrans.* L19.
[ORIGIN from DE- 3 + TRAIN *noun*[1].]
Discharge or alight from a railway train.
■ **detrainment** *noun* L19.

détraqué /detrake/ *adjective & noun*. Fem. ***-ée***. E20.
[ORIGIN French, pa. ppl adjective of *détraquer* put out of order, derange.]
▸ **A** *adjective*. Deranged; crazy; psychopathic. E20.
▸ **B** *noun*. Pl. pronounced same. A deranged person, a psychopath. E20.

detribalize /diːˈtrʌɪb(ə)lʌɪz/ *verb trans.* Also **-ise**. E20.
[ORIGIN from DE- 3 + TRIBAL + -IZE.]
Make (a person) no longer a member of a tribe; remove the tribal social structure from.
■ **detribaliˈzation** *noun* E20.

detriment /ˈdɛtrɪm(ə)nt/ *noun & verb*. LME.
[ORIGIN Old French & mod. French *détriment* or Latin *detrimentum*, from *detri-* preterite stem of *deterere* wear away, from *de-* DE- 1 + *terere* rub: see -MENT.]
▸ **A** *noun*. **1** Loss sustained by or damage done to a person or thing; an instance of this. LME.

J. S. MILL The luxury of doing as they like without detriment to their estimation. E. JONES Overpraising young girls, to the detriment of their later character.

2 A cause of loss or damage; something detrimental. E16.
3 *HERALDRY.* Eclipse, esp. of the moon. E17.
4 *ASTROLOGY.* The position or (weak) condition of a planet when in the sign opposite its house. E17.
5 In *pl.* Charges made by certain colleges or societies on their members. L17.
▸ **B** *verb trans.* Cause loss or damage to. Now *rare.* E17.

detrimental /dɛtrɪˈmɛnt(ə)l/ *adjective & noun.* L16.
[ORIGIN from DETRIMENT + -AL[1].]
▸ **A** *adjective.* Causing loss or damage; prejudicial, harmful. (Foll. by *to.*) L16.
▸ **B** *noun.* A person who or thing which is prejudicial or damaging; *esp.* (*arch. slang*) a younger son of the aristocracy, an ineligible suitor. M19.
■ **detrimentally** *adverb* L19.

detrital /dɪˈtrʌɪt(ə)l/ *adjective.* M19.
[ORIGIN from DETRITUS + -AL[1].]
Of, pertaining to, or of the nature of detritus.

detrited /dɪˈtrʌɪtɪd/ *adjective.* L17.
[ORIGIN from Latin *detritus* DETRITUS + -ED[1].]
Worn down; formed as detritus.

detrition /dɪˈtrɪʃ(ə)n/ *noun.* L17.
[ORIGIN medieval Latin *detritio(n-)*, from *detri-*: see DETRIMENT, -ITION.]
The action of wearing away by rubbing.

detritivore /dɪˈtrɪtɪvɔː/ *noun.* M20.
[ORIGIN from DETRITUS + -VORE.]
ZOOLOGY. An animal which feeds on dead organic material, especially plant detritus.
■ **detritivorous** /ˌdɛtrɪˈtɪv(ə)rəs/ *adjective* M20.

detritus /dɪˈtrʌɪtəs/ *noun.* L18.
[ORIGIN Latin *detritus* rubbing away, from *detri-*: see DETRIMENT. In sense 2 after French *détritus*.]
†**1** Wearing away by rubbing; disintegration. L18–E19.
2 Matter produced by detrition; *esp.* material eroded or washed away, as gravel, sand, silt, etc. E19.
3 Debris of any kind. M19.

> S. BRETT The detritus of coffee-cups, publicity photographs and handouts that littered her desk.

■ **detritic** /dɪˈtrɪtɪk/ *adjective* (*rare*) = DETRITAL M19.

de trop /də tro, ˈtrəʊ/ *adjectival phr.* M18.
[ORIGIN French, lit. 'excessive'.]
Not wanted, unwelcome, in the way.

detrude /dɪˈtruːd/ *verb trans.* LME.
[ORIGIN Latin *detrudere*, from *de-* DE- 1 + *trudere* thrust.]
1 Thrust or push down; formerly also, subdue, defeat. LME.
2 Thrust out or away, expel. M16.

detruncate /diːˈtrʌŋkeɪt/ *verb trans.* E17.
[ORIGIN Latin *detruncat-* pa. ppl stem of *detruncare*, from *de-* DE- 1 + *truncare*: see TRUNCATE *verb*.]
Shorten by lopping off a part; cut short.
■ **detrunˈcation** *noun* [Latin *detruncatio(n-)*] the action of cutting off or short; the state of being cut short: E17.

detrusion /dɪˈtruːʒ(ə)n/ *noun.* E17.
[ORIGIN Late Latin *detrusio(n-)*, from *detrus-* pa. ppl stem of *detrudere* DETRUDE: see -ION.]
The action of thrusting down or away.

detrusor /dɪˈtruːsə/ *noun.* M18.
[ORIGIN mod. Latin, from Latin *detrus-*: see DETRUSION, -OR.]
ANATOMY. In full ***detrusor muscle***. The muscular layer of the wall of the bladder.

detumescence /diːtjʊˈmɛs(ə)ns/ *noun.* L17.
[ORIGIN from Latin *detumescere* subside from swelling, from *de-* DE- 3 + *tumescere* swell: see -ENCE.]
Subsidence from swelling, or (*fig.*) from tumult; subsidence of the penis or clitoris from erection.

detune /diːˈtjuːn/ *verb trans.* E20.
[ORIGIN from DE- 3 + TUNE *verb*.]
1 Alter or adjust (an oscillatory system) so that its resonant frequency no longer coincides with the frequency of some other oscillation with which it interacts. E20.
2 Reduce the performance or efficiency of (a motor vehicle or engine) by adjustment. M20.

detur /ˈdiːtə/ *noun.* L18.
[ORIGIN Latin = let there be given, the first word of the accompanying inscription.]
Any of several prizes of books given annually at Harvard University.

†**deturn** *verb trans.* LME–M18.
[ORIGIN French *détourner* (Old French *destorner*), from *dé-*, *des-* DE- 3 + *tourner* TURN *verb*.]
Turn away or aside.

deturpate /dɪˈtəːpeɪt/ *verb trans. & intrans.* Now *rare.* E17.
[ORIGIN Latin *deturpat-* pa. ppl stem of *deturpare* make unsightly: see -ATE[3].]
Make or become vile or base.
■ **deturˈpation** *noun* debasement, defilement; an instance of this: L15.

deuce /djuːs/ *noun*[1]. L15.
[ORIGIN Old French *deus* (mod. *deux*) from Latin *duos* two.]
1 The two on a die or in a pack of cards; a throw of two at dice. L15.
2 *TENNIS.* The state of the score (40 points all, or, in real tennis, five or more games all) at which either side must gain two consecutive points or games to win. L16.
3 (A sum of) twopence (*arch.*), two pounds, or two dollars; a two-dollar bill. *slang.* L17.
– COMB.: **deuce-ace** *arch.* a throw of two and one at dice; a poor throw, bad luck; **deuce set** in real tennis, a set in which the score reaches five games all; **deuce game** (*a*) in real tennis, a game which levels the score at more than five games each side; (*b*) in lawn tennis, a game in which the score reaches 40 points all.

deuce /djuːs/ *noun*[2]. *colloq.* M17.
[ORIGIN Low German *duus* = German *Daus*, prob. ult. identical with DEUCE *noun*[1], a throw of two (aces) at dice being the worst possible.]
Misfortune, mischief; the Devil. Freq. in exclamatory or imprecatory phrs. (in which *devil* can always be substituted) expr. surprise, incredulity, impatience, displeasure, dismay, or negation, or merely emphatic.

> SWIFT The deuce he is! married to that vengeance! R. BURNS The deuce of the matter is this: . . his salary is reduced. P. V. WHITE Dear me, if these educated young ladies are not the deuce. G. HEYER Why the deuce does she want to make Evelyn's acquaintance?

a deuce of a —, **the deuce of a —** a very bad or very remarkable —. **the deuce to pay** trouble to be expected.

deuced /ˈdjuːsɪd, djuːst/ *adjective & adverb. arch. colloq.* L18.
[ORIGIN from DEUCE *noun*[2] + -ED[2].]
Damned, devilish(ly).
■ **deucedly** /ˈdjuːsɪdli/ *adverb* E19.

deus absconditus /ˌdeɪəs abˈskɒndɪtəs, ˌdiːəs/ *noun phr.* M20.
[ORIGIN Latin = hidden god: cf. *Isaiah* 45:15.]
A god who is hidden from human perception.

†**deusan** *noun.* Also **-z-**. L16–L19.
[ORIGIN French *deux ans* two years: so called from its lasting quality.]
= ***apple-john*** s.v. APPLE.

deus ex machina /ˌdeɪəs ɛks ˈmakɪnə, ˌdiːəs/ *noun phr.* L17.
[ORIGIN mod. Latin, translating Greek *theos ek mēkhanēs* lit. 'god from the machinery' (a kind of crane by which characters, usu. gods, were lowered or swung round into view in Greek theatre).]
A power, event, or person arriving in the nick of time to solve a difficulty; a providential (often rather contrived) interposition, esp. in a novel or play.

deut- *combining form* see DEUTO-.

Deut. *abbreviation.*
Deuteronomy (in the Bible).

deutan /ˈdjuːtan/ *noun & adjective.* M20.
[ORIGIN from *deut(er)an* in DEUTERANOMALY, DEUTERANOPIA.]
OPHTHALMOLOGY. (A person) exhibiting deuteranomaly or deuteranopia.

deuter- *combining form* see DEUTERO-.

deuteragonist /djuːtəˈragənɪst/ *noun.* M19.
[ORIGIN Greek *deuteragōnistēs*, formed as DEUTERO-, AGONIST.]
The person of next importance to the protagonist in a drama.

deuteranomaly /djuːt(ə)rəˈnɒməli/ *noun.* M20.
[ORIGIN from DEUTERO- (green being regarded as the 2nd component of colour vision) + ANOMALY.]
OPHTHALMOLOGY. Anamolous trichromatism involving reduced sensitivity to green; partial deuteranopia. Cf. DEUTERANOPIA, PROTANOMALY.
■ **deuteranomal** *noun* a person exhibiting deuteranomaly E20. **deuteranomalous** *adjective* of, pertaining to, or exhibiting deuteranomaly M20.

deuteranopia /djuːt(ə)rəˈnəʊpɪə/ *noun.* E20.
[ORIGIN formed as DEUTERANOMALY + AN-[5] + -OPIA.]
OPHTHALMOLOGY. Colour blindness (esp. dichromatism) involving insensitivity to green; green-blindness. Cf. DEUTERANOMALY, PROTANOPIA.
■ **ˈdeuteranope** *noun* a deuteranopic individual E20. **deuteranopic** *adjective* of, pertaining to, or exhibiting deuteranopia M20.

deuterate /ˈdjuːtəreɪt/ *verb trans.* Also **deuteriate** /djuːˈtɪərɪeɪt/. M20.
[ORIGIN from DEUTERIUM + -ATE[3].]
CHEMISTRY. Replace ordinary hydrogen in (a substance) by deuterium. Freq. as ***deuterated*** *ppl adjective.*
■ **deuteˈration** *noun* M20.

deuteric /ˈdjuːtərɪk/ *adjective.* E20.
[ORIGIN from DEUTERO- + -IC.]
GEOLOGY. Designating, pertaining to, or resulting from alteration of the minerals of an igneous rock during the later stages of consolidation.

deuterium /djuːˈtɪərɪəm/ *noun.* M20.
[ORIGIN from Greek *deuteros* second + -IUM.]
CHEMISTRY. A naturally occurring isotope of hydrogen with about double the mass of the commonest isotope, differing from it in having a neutron as well as a proton in the nucleus (symbol ^2H or D). Also called ***heavy hydrogen***.
■ **ˈdeuteride** *noun* a binary compound of deuterium with a metal or radical M20.

deutero- /ˈdjuːtərəʊ/ *combining form.* Before a vowel also **deuter-**.
[ORIGIN Greek, from *deuteros* second: see -O-.]
Forming words with the sense 'second, secondary'. Also (*CHEMISTRY*), forming names of deuterated compounds.
■ **deuterocaˈnonical** *adjective* of, pertaining to, or constituting a second or secondary canon (of sacred books) L17. **deuteroˈchloroform** *noun* deuterated chloroform, $CDCl_3$, used as a solvent in NMR spectroscopy M20. **Deutero-Iˈsaiah** *noun* the supposed later author of *Isaiah* 40–55 M19. **deuteˈromerite** *noun* (*ZOOLOGY*) = DEUTOMERITE L19. **deuterostome** *noun* (*ZOOLOGY*) a metazoan organism whose mouth develops from a secondary embryonic opening, as a vertebrate, an echinoderm M20.

deuterogamy /djuːtəˈrɒgəmi/ *noun.* M17.
[ORIGIN Greek *deuterogamia*, formed as DEUTERO- + -GAMY.]
1 Marriage after the death or divorce of a first spouse. M17.
2 *BOTANY.* Fertilization occurring other than by simple fusion of gametes. L19.
■ **deuterogamist** *noun* a person who practises or upholds deuterogamy M18.

deuteron /ˈdjuːtərɒn/ *noun.* M20.
[ORIGIN from Greek *deuteros* second + -ON, after PROTON.]
PHYSICS. The nucleus of an atom of deuterium.

deuto- /ˈdjuːtəʊ/ *combining form.* Before a vowel **deut-**.
[ORIGIN Abbreviation of DEUTERO-.]
Forming words with the sense 'second, secondary'.
■ **deuˈtomerite** *noun* (*ZOOLOGY*) the posterior division of the body in gregarine protozoans, which contains the nucleus (cf. PROTOMERITE) E20. **deuˈtoxide** *noun* (*CHEMISTRY, arch.*) the second in a series of oxides of an element E19.

Deutschmark /ˈdɔɪtʃmɑːk/ *noun.* Also **Deutschemark**. M20.
[ORIGIN German *Deutsche Mark* = German mark (MARK *noun*[2]).]
The basic monetary unit of Germany until the introduction of the euro in 2002, equal to 100 pfennigs; a coin of this value. Abbreviation ***DM***, ***D-mark***.

deutzia /ˈdjuːtsɪə, ˈdɔɪt-/ *noun.* M19.
[ORIGIN mod. Latin, from Johann van der *Deutz*, 18th-cent. Dutch patron of botany: see -IA[1].]
Any shrub of the Asian and Central American genus *Deutzia*, which belongs to the saxifrage family and includes many ornamentals, usu. with white flowers.

†**deuzan** *noun* var. of DEUSAN.

deva /ˈdeɪvə/ *noun.* E19.
[ORIGIN Sanskrit = god, (orig.) shining one.]
Any of a class of deities in Vedic mythology; any of the lower-level gods in Hinduism and Buddhism.

devadasi /deɪvəˈdɑːsi/ *noun.* E19.
[ORIGIN Sanskrit *devadāsī* lit. 'female servant of a god' (cf. DEVA).]
A hereditary female dancer in a Hindu temple.

devall /dɪˈvɔːl/ *verb & noun.* LME.
[ORIGIN Old French & mod. French *dévaler* descend, from Proto-Romance, from Latin *de-* DE- 1 down + *vallis* valley. Cf. AVALE.]
▸ **A** *verb intrans.* †**1** Move or slope downwards. LME–M17.
2 Cease, leave off. *Scot. & N. English.* M16.
▸ **B** *noun.* **1** A slope. *Scot.* L17.
2 A stop, a cessation. *Scot.* E19.

devalorize /diːˈvalərʌɪz/ *verb trans.* Also **-ise**. E20.
[ORIGIN French *dévaloriser*, from *dé-* DE- 3 + *valoriser* VALORIZE.]
= DEVALUE.
■ **devaloriˈzation** *noun* E20.

devaluate /diːˈvaljʊeɪt/ *verb trans.* L19.
[ORIGIN from DE- 3 + VALUE *noun* + -ATE[3].]
= DEVALUE.

devaluation /diːˌvaljʊˈeɪʃ(ə)n/ *noun.* E20.
[ORIGIN from DEVALUATE or DEVALUE: see -ATION.]
The action or an act of devaluing something or someone; the fact of being devalued.
■ **devaluationist** *noun* an advocate or supporter of devaluation (of a currency) M20.

devalue /diːˈvaljuː/ *verb trans.* E20.
[ORIGIN from DE- 3 + VALUE *noun*.]
Reduce or annul the value of; deprive of value; *spec.* reduce the official value of (a currency) relative to gold or another currency.

> LYNDON B. JOHNSON The British government had decided to devalue the pound from $2.80 to $2.40. M. SARTON Men still do rather consistently undervalue or devalue women's powers. W. BOYD The reek of corn beer on his breath tended to devalue his protestations of innocence.

Devanagari /deɪvəˈnɑːg(ə)ri, dɛv-/ *adjective & noun.* L18.
[ORIGIN Sanskrit, from *deva* god + *nāgarī* NAGARI (an earlier name of the script).]
(Designating) the principal script used for Sanskrit, Hindi, and other Indian languages.

devance /dɪˈvɑːns/ *verb trans. arch.* L15.
[ORIGIN Old French & mod. French *devancer*, from *devant* before, in front.]
Anticipate, forestall, outstrip.
– NOTE: Became obsolete in 17 but reused in 19.

devast /dɪˈvɑːst, ˈdɛvəst/ *verb trans.* M16.
[ORIGIN French *dévaster* from Latin *devastare*: see DEVASTATE.]
Devastate.
■ **devaster** *noun* (*rare*) L18.

devastate /ˈdɛvəsteɪt/ *verb trans.* M17.
[ORIGIN Latin *devastat-* pa. ppl stem of *devastare*, from *de-* DE- 1 + *vastare* lay waste: see -ATE³.]
Lay waste, ravage; make desolate or wretched.

P. H. GIBBS France would have to rebuild all the areas devastated by war. P. ROSE She probably died of heart disease. Dickens was devastated.

– NOTE: Rare before 19.
■ **devastating** *ppl adjective* that devastates; very effective, overwhelming: M17. **devastatingly** *adverb* E20. **devastative** *adjective* having the quality of devastating, ravaging E19. **devastator** *noun* E19.

devastation /dɛvəˈsteɪʃ(ə)n/ *noun*. LME.
[ORIGIN French *dévastation* or late Latin *devastatio(n-)*, formed as DEVASTATE: see -ATION.]
1 The action of devastating; the fact or state of being devastated. LME.
2 *LAW*. (An instance of) waste of the property of a deceased person by an executor or administrator. L17.

devastavit /diːvəˈsteɪvɪt/ *noun*. M17.
[ORIGIN Latin = he has wasted.]
LAW. A writ against an executor or administrator for devastation (see DEVASTATION 2); the offence of devastation.

devein /diːˈveɪn/ *verb trans.* M20.
[ORIGIN from DE- 3 + VEIN *noun*.]
Remove the vein(s) of; *spec.* remove the dorsal vein of (a shrimp or prawn).

devel /ˈdɛv(ə)l/ *noun & verb. Scot.* L18.
[ORIGIN Unknown.]
▸ **A** *noun*. A stunning blow. L18.
▸ **B** *verb trans.* Infl. **-ll-**. Strike with a stunning blow. E19.

develop /dɪˈvɛləp/ *verb*. Also (now *rare*) **-ope**. M17.
[ORIGIN Old French & mod. French *développer* (also *desveloper* DISVELOP) from Proto-Romance, from Latin DIS- + base repr. also by Old French *voloper* envelop, Provençal *volopar*, Italian *viluppare* wrap up: ult. origin unknown.]
▸ **I** *verb trans.* **1** Unfold, unroll; unfurl (a banner). Now *arch.* exc. *HERALDRY*. M17. ▸**b** *MATH*. Convert (a curved surface) conceptually into a plane figure, as if by unrolling. M19.
2 Uncover, reveal, (something abstract or †material); make known, bring to light; discover, detect, find out. Now *US*. M18.
3 Unfold more fully; bring out all that is potentially contained in; bring out from a latent to an active or visible state; make fuller, more elaborate or systematic, or bigger; cause to grow or mature, evolve, (*from*, *out of*); cause to come into existence or operation; display in operation; begin to exhibit or suffer from. M18. ▸**b** *CHESS*. Bring (a piece) into position for effective use. M19. ▸**c** *MATH*. Expand (a function etc.) in the form of a series. Cf. earlier DEVELOPABLE 1a, DEVELOPMENT 4. L19. ▸**d** *MUSIC*. Subject (a theme etc.) to development (DEVELOPMENT 7). L19. ▸**e** Convert (land) to new use, so as to realize its potentialities; construct buildings etc. on (land). L19.

A. HENFREY In the Banyan tree adventitious roots are frequently developed on the outstretched woody branches. R. G. COLLINGWOOD Expounding and developing the doctrines in a series of books. D. CUSACK Teach them whatever you like, so long as it develops their character. G. VIDAL She had in recent years developed a most alarming habit. L. DEIGHTON The thick muscular legs were developed in his teens by sixty-eight-kilometre weekend cycle rides. R. L. FOX The Greeks had been slow to develop advanced siege equipment. R. P. JHABVALA In Kashmir the girl had developed dysentery. G. BOYCOTT You have to . . develop the skill through constant practice.

4 *refl.* Come gradually into existence, operation, or a visible state. L18.
5 Process (photographic film etc.) chemically so as to make visible the image(s) contained in it; convert (a photographic image) into visible form by processing. M19.
▸ **II** *verb intrans.* **6** Grow, mature, (*into*); make progress; come gradually into existence or operation; exhibit itself; become fuller, more elaborate or systematic, or bigger. M19.

H. T. LANE As the child develops so the complication and variety of its toys should increase. L. A. G. STRONG A small seaside town which had neither expanded nor developed for close on fifty years. S. SPENDER He wrote his novels without in the least knowing how the story would develop. R. K. NARAYAN A smirk developed into a chuckle.

7 Come to light, become known. *US*. M19.

developable /dɪˈvɛləpəb(ə)l/ *adjective*. E19.
[ORIGIN from DEVELOP + -ABLE.]
1 *MATH*. **a** Able to be expanded as a series. E19. ▸**b** Of a curved surface: able to be (conceptually) unrolled into a plane. M19.
2 *gen.* Able to be developed. E19.
3 Able to be developed photographically. L19.

developed /dɪˈvɛləpt/ *ppl adjective*. M17.
[ORIGIN formed as DEVELOPABLE + -ED¹.]
That has been developed; grown, mature; (of a country etc.) economically advanced, industrialized.

W. S. CHURCHILL The far more fruitful and developed land in the West. A. GRAY She . . was called Big June to distinguish her from the less developed girls she sat among. *Marxism Today* The harsh conflict of interests between the developed and developing world.

developement *noun* see DEVELOPMENT.

developer /dɪˈvɛləpə/ *noun*. M19.
[ORIGIN from DEVELOP + -ER¹.]
1 A person who or thing which develops something. M19. ▸**b** *spec.* A chemical agent for developing photographs. M19. ▸**c** A person who develops land; a speculative builder. E20.

F. D. MAURICE Developers of a certain set of theories about gods, men, and nature. *Woman* The world's most successful bustline developer.

2 A person who develops or matures at a specified time or speed, as ***late developer***, ***slow developer***, etc. M20.

F. J. SCHONELL The doctrine that dull children are frequently slow developers.

developing /dɪˈvɛləpɪŋ/ *ppl adjective*. L19.
[ORIGIN formed as DEVELOPER + -ING².]
In the process of development; (of a country etc.) becoming economically more advanced, becoming industrialized.

Which? A lot of clothing and some textiles can be made much more cheaply in developing countries than in Western Europe and North America.

development /dɪˈvɛləpm(ə)nt/ *noun*. Also (now *rare*) **develope-**. M18.
[ORIGIN formed as DEVELOPER + -MENT, after French *développement*.]
▸ **I** *gen.* **1** The action or process of developing; evolution, growth, maturation; an instance of this; a gradual unfolding, a fuller working out. M18.

GLADSTONE Essential to the entire development of my case. E. B. TYLOR Stages of development or evolution, each the outcome of previous history. G. B. SHAW The scarcity of labor in America . . has led to a development of machinery there. JOYCE An arrest of embryonic development at some stage antecedent to the human. B. RUSSELL Organic life, we are told, has developed gradually from the protozoon to the philosopher, and this development, we are assured, is indubitably an advance. A. J. P. TAYLOR Their hope was for the recovery of old industries, not the development of new ones.

research and development: see RESEARCH *noun*¹ 3.
2 A developed form or product; a result of developing; a change in a course of action or events or in conditions; a stage of advancement; an addition, an elaboration. M18.

L. STERNE A map . . with many other pieces and developements of this work will be added to the end of the twentieth volume. J. H. NEWMAN The butterfly is the development . . of the grub. E. F. SCHUMACHER Many of these small units . . provide society with most of the really fruitful new developments. D. FRASER The next development which dominated military thinking was the threat from the considerable increases made in air power.

3 The state of being developed; a developed condition, a full-grown state. M19.

H. L. MANSEL His disciple . . has carried the doctrine to its fullest development.

▸ **II** *spec.* **4** The action of unrolling something. *obsolete* exc. *MATH.*, the action of developing (DEVELOP 1b) a curved surface. E19.
5 The action of developing a photograph. M19.
6 *CHESS*. The action or an act of bringing pieces into a position for effective use; the disposition of pieces at an early stage of a game. M19.
7 *MUSIC*. Elaboration of a theme by modification of melody, harmony, rhythm, etc., esp. in the second section of a sonata movement; a passage or section with such elaboration. L19.
8 The action of developing land etc. so as to realize its potentialities; speculative building; a developed site, *esp.* a new housing estate. L19.

P. NASH All those courageous enemies of 'development' to whom we owe what is left of England. *Home Finder* The small development—of just 23 detached homes—is attractively laid out to give a 'village' atmosphere.

ribbon development: see RIBBON *noun*.
9 Economic advancement or industrialization of a country etc. not previously developed. E20.

Daedalus All African countries lack sufficient managerial, administrative, and technical skills to undertake the massive task of development contemplated at independence.

separate development: see SEPARATE *adjective*.
– COMB.: **development area**: where new industries etc. are actively encouraged in order to counteract unemployment.

developmental /dɪˌvɛləpˈmɛnt(ə)l/ *adjective*. M19.
[ORIGIN from DEVELOPMENT + -AL¹.]
Of or pertaining to development; incidental to growth; evolutionary; subject to or in process of development.

P. LEACH Your child's developmental clock has told him that it is time to stop being a baby. T. KENEALLY The munitions section was so far developmental.

developmental delay the condition of a child being less developed mentally or physically than is normal for its age.
■ **developmentalism** *noun* belief in a theory of development; evolutionism: M20. **developmentalist** *noun* a believer in a theory of development; an evolutionist: M19. **developmentally** *adverb* in relation or reference to development M19.

développé /devlɔpe/ *noun*. Pl. pronounced same. E20.
[ORIGIN French, use as noun of pa. pple of *développer* DEVELOP.]
A ballet movement in which one leg is raised and then fully extended.

Devensian /dɪˈvɛnzɪən/ *adjective & noun*. M20.
[ORIGIN from Latin *Devenses* dwellers near the River Dee (*Deva*), on the border between England and Wales, + -IAN.]
GEOLOGY. (Designating or pertaining to) the most recent Pleistocene glaciation in Britain, identified with the Weichselian of northern Europe (and perhaps the Würm of the Alps).

deverbal /diːˈvəːb(ə)l/ *noun & adjective*. M20.
[ORIGIN from DE- 2 + VERB + -AL¹.]
GRAMMAR. (A word) formed on or derived from a verb.

deverbative /diːˈvəːbətɪv/ *noun & adjective*. E20.
[ORIGIN from DE- 2 + VERB + -ATIVE, after *denominative*.]
GRAMMAR. = DEVERBAL.

devest /dɪˈvɛst/ *verb trans. arch.* M16.
[ORIGIN Old French *de(s)vester*, *devestir*, from *des-* DIS- 1 + Latin *vestire* clothe, from *vestis* garment.]
†**1** = DIVEST 1, 2. M16–E19.
2 *LAW*. = DIVEST 3. L16. ▸†**b** Dispossess (a person) of some right, authority, etc., with which he or she has been invested. M17–E19.
■ **devesture** *noun* (*rare*) the action of devesting M17.

deviable /ˈdiːvɪəb(ə)l/ *adjective*. E20.
[ORIGIN from late Latin *deviare* (see DEVIATE *verb*): see -ABLE.]
Able to be deviated, deflectable.
■ **deviaˈbility** *noun* E20.

deviance /ˈdiːvɪəns/ *noun*. M20.
[ORIGIN from DEVIANT *adjective*: see -ANCE.]
The state or quality of being deviant; (an instance of) deviant behaviour or characteristics.
■ **deviancy** *noun* M20.

deviant /ˈdiːvɪənt/ *adjective & noun*. LME.
[ORIGIN Late Latin *deviant-* pres. ppl stem of *deviare*: see DEVIATE *verb*, -ANT¹.]
▸ **A** *adjective*. Deviating, divergent, esp. from normal social or sexual standards or behaviour. LME.
▸ **B** *noun*. A person who or thing which deviates from the normal, esp. from normal social or sexual standards or behaviour. E20.
– NOTE: Rare before 20.

deviate /ˈdiːvɪət/ *adjective & noun*. M16.
[ORIGIN Late Latin *deviatus* pa. pple, formed as DEVIATE *verb*: see -ATE². In mod. use after the verb.]
▸ **A** *adjective*. †**1** Turned out of the way, remote. M16–M17.
2 = DEVIANT *adjective*. M20.
▸ **B** *noun*. **1** = DEVIANT *noun*. E20.
2 *STATISTICS*. The value of a variate measured from some standard point of distribution, usu. the mean, and usu. expressed in terms of the standard deviation of the distribution. E20.

deviate /ˈdiːvɪeɪt/ *verb*. M17.
[ORIGIN Late Latin *deviat-* pa. ppl stem of *deviare*, from Latin *de-* DE- 1 + *via* way: see -ATE³.]
1 *verb intrans.* Turn out of the way, turn aside, swerve, (*lit.* & *fig.*); diverge, digress, differ. (Foll. by *from*.) M17.

T. HARDY He has not . . deviated one hair's breadth from the course he laid down. N. SHUTE He deviated fifty yards towards it. A. POWELL A most devoted wife . . never deviating in admiration of her husband. C. P. SNOW The summer weather . . hadn't deviated for four months.

2 *verb trans.* Cause to turn aside or swerve, deflect, change the direction of, (*lit.* & *fig.*). (Foll. by *from*.) Now chiefly as ***deviated*** *ppl adjective*, not straight, oblique, deviant. M17.
■ **deviative** /-ətɪv/ *adjective* causing deviation, tending to deviate L19.

deviation /diːvɪˈeɪʃ(ə)n/ *noun*. LME.
[ORIGIN Old French & mod. French *déviation* from medieval Latin *deviatio(n-)*, formed as DEVIATE *verb*: see -ATION.]
1 Divergence from a course, method, rule, or norm; an instance of this. (Foll. by *from*.) LME. ▸**b** *spec.* (An instance of) divergence from a moral or sexual norm. E17. ▸**c** (An instance of) divergence from the political doctrine or practices of a government or party, esp. a Communist party. M20.
2 The action or an act of swerving or changing direction. M17.
3 Divergence from the straight line, mean, or standard; variation; the amount of this. L17. ▸**b** *spec.* (The amount of) deflection of the needle of a compass due to local magnetism, esp. of the iron etc. in a ship. E19. ▸**c** *STATISTICS*. The amount by which a single measurement differs from the mean. M19.
conjugate deviation: see CONJUGATE *adjective*. **c mean deviation** the mean of the absolute deviations. **standard deviation** the square root of the mean of the squares of the deviations.
■ **deviationism** *noun* political deviation, a tendency to depart from (esp. Communist) party doctrine or practices: M20.

deviationist *noun & adjective* (*a*) *noun* a person who departs from (esp. Communist) party doctrine or practices; (*b*) *adjective* of or pertaining to deviationism or deviationists: M20.

deviator /ˈdiːvɪeɪtə/ *noun*. M17.
[ORIGIN from DEVIATE *verb* + -OR.]
1 A person who or thing which deviates. M17.
2 MATH. The non-isotropic component of a tensor, esp. a stress tensor. M20.
■ **deviatoric** /diːvɪəˈtɒrɪk/ *adjective* (MATH.) of, associated with, or represented by a deviator M20.

device /dɪˈvʌɪs/ *noun*. Also †**devise**. See also DEVISE *noun*. ME.
[ORIGIN Old French *devis* (masc.), *-ise* (fem.) from Proto-Romance derivs. of Latin *divis-* pa. ppl stem of *dividere* DIVIDE *verb*.]
▸ **I 1** Intent, desire; will, pleasure; an inclination, a fancy. Long only in ***leave to one's own devices*** etc. (passing into sense 2). ME. ▸†**b** An order, a request. ME–M16. ▸†**c** Opinion, notion; advice. LME–L16.
2 An arrangement, a plan, a scheme; an (ingenious) expedient; a stratagem, a trick. ME.

B. TRAPIDO Aggression is the device I have for surviving the pain of Roger's presence. J. BARNES As for coincidences in books—there's something cheap and sentimental about the device.

3 A thing designed for a particular function or adapted for a purpose; an invention, a contrivance, *esp*. a (simple) mechanical contrivance. LME. ▸**b** An explosive contrivance, *esp*. a nuclear bomb. M20.

K. CLARK The architect has used the device known as flying buttresses. G. VIDAL Various offices, equipped with all the latest communication devices. *Daily Express* America had exploded 18 devices since last August.

4 A literary composition; *esp*. a dramatic entertainment, a masque. *arch*. LME. ▸**b** A conceit, a witticism; a witty composition. *arch*. L16.
5 An artistic design, a drawing, a figure. LME. ▸**b** *spec*. An emblematic or heraldic design, a cognizance, an emblem; a motto. LME.

b LONGFELLOW A banner with the strange device, 'Excelsior!' W. H. AUDEN The tyrant's device: *Whatever Is Possible Is Necessary*.

6 a The action of devising or planning; inventive faculty, ingenuity. Now *arch*. *rare*. LME. ▸**b** The manner in which a thing is devised; make, look. *arch*. LME.

b H. ALLEN The tweaking nose of the largest rabbit was a miracle of rare device.

†**7** Familiar conversation, chat. L15–E17.
▸ †**II** See DEVISE *noun*.
■ **deviceful** *adjective* (now *rare*) full of or characterized by invention, ingenious L16. **deviceless** *adjective* M19.

devil /ˈdɛv(ə)l/ *noun*. Also (esp. in sense 1) **D-**. See also DEIL.
[ORIGIN Old English *dēofol* = Old Frisian *diovel*, Old Saxon *diubul*, *-al* (Dutch *duivel*), Old High German *tiufal* (German *Teufel*), Old Norse *djǫfull*, from Christian Latin *diabolus* from Greek *diabolos* (in the Septuagint rendering Hebrew *Śāṭān* SATAN) lit. 'accuser, slanderer', from *diaballein* slander, traduce, from *dia-* across + *ballein* throw.]
1 In Jewish and Christian theology, *the* supreme spirit of evil, the tempter and spiritual enemy of humankind, the adversary of God, popularly believed to appear in various forms, esp. in that of a man with horns, cloven hoofs, and a forked tail; Satan. Freq. in exclamatory or imprecatory phrs. expr. surprise, incredulity, impatience, displeasure, dismay, or negation, or merely emphatic (cf. DEUCE *noun*², DIABLE *interjection*). OE.

T. HERBERT Black as the devill, and as treacherous. BYRON And wonders why the devil he got heirs. BROWNING The devil appears himself, Armed and accoutred, horns and hoofs and tail! R. W. EMERSON 'That is W,' said the teacher. 'The Devil!' exclaimed the boy, 'is that W?' J. E. HOPKINS Wesley could not see why the devil should have all the good tunes. NEB *Matt*. 4:1 Jesus was then led away . . into the wilderness, to be tempted by the devil. J. GORES Who the devil do you think gave it to me? *Proverbs*: Devil take the hindmost (a motto of selfish competition). Give the devil his due. Needs must when the devil drives. Talk of the devil (and he is bound to appear) (said when someone arrives just after being mentioned). The devil can quote Scripture for his own ends. The devil finds work for idle hands to do. The devil is not so black as he is painted. The devil looks after his own.

2 A demon; *esp*. (in biblical translations and allusions) a heathen god or idol; an evil spirit supposed to possess a demoniac. OE.

MILTON Devils to adore for deities. A. MASON A celebrated exorcist was several times accused of casting out devils by the power of Beelzebub.

3 A malignant being of angelic or superhuman nature or powers; *esp*. a follower of Satan, one of the fallen spirits described as rebelling against God and having the chief function of tormenting and tempting humankind, a fiend. Also, a malignant god. OE.

C. S. LEWIS Screaming out that devils were tearing him and that he was . . falling down into Hell.

4 A human being of diabolical character or qualities; an exceptionally cruel or wicked person. OE. ▸**b** A provoking or troublesome person; a mischievously energetic, clever, self-willed, or reckless person. E17. ▸**c** A luckless or wretched person. Chiefly in ***poor devil***. L17. ▸**d** A vicious or unmanageable animal. M19.

SHAKES. *Oth*. Thou dost belie her, and thou art a devil. AV *John* 6:70 Haue not I chosen you twelue, and one of you is a deuill? **b** R. B. SHERIDAN An ill-tempered little devil! She'll be in a passion all her life. S. MIDDLETON He was a devil for pushing his nose into an argument. **c** G. GREENE The poor devils are burnt alive. **d** T. MEDWIN He was the fastest trotter in the cantonment, but a restless devil.

5 Any of various animals or birds associated in character or appearance with the devil; *spec*. †(*a*) the coot; (*b*) ***sea devil***, = ***devilfish*** below; (*c*) (more fully ***Tasmanian devil***) a carnivorous nocturnal marsupial, *Sarcophilus harrisii*, native to Australia (now only Tasmania); (*d*) ***Indian devil*** (*N. Amer.*), the puma; also, the wolverine; (*e*) *dial*. the swift. Usu. with specifying word. L16.
6 The personification of evil and undesirable qualities by which a human being may be possessed or actuated. E17. ▸**b** Fighting spirit; dash or energy in attack; 'go'. L18.

H. BROADHURST The devil of short-sighted greed is powerful enough if left alone. **b** BARONESS ORCZY He seemed to have the very devil in his fingers, and the coach seemed to fly along the road.

7 A person employed in a subordinate position to work under the direction of or for a particular person; *spec*. (*a*) *hist*. (more fully ***printer's devil***) an errand boy or junior assistant in a printing office; (*b*) a junior legal counsel working for a principal; (*c*) a literary hack doing what his or her employer takes the credit and payment for. L17.
8 *pred*. *The* worst that can happen, *the* worst possible person or thing. L17.

SIR W. SCOTT To be cross-examined by those who have seen the true thing is the devil. V. WOOLF Audiences were the devil O to write a play without an audience.

9 A kind of exploding firework; a squib, a cracker. M18.
10 A highly seasoned, peppery dish of broiled or fried meat; peppery seasoning for meat. L18.
11 Any of various instruments or mechanical devices associated (more or less obviously) with the Devil, esp. one fitted with sharp teeth or spikes, or for tearing or other destructive work. M19.
12 A moving sand-spout, a sandstorm; (in full ***dust devil***) a dust storm, a whirlwind. M19.
13 NAUTICAL. The seam in the upper deck planking next to a ship's waterways. Also, the seam between the garboard strake and the keel. Now *arch*. or *hist*. L19.
– PHRASES: **a devil of a** — an extreme —, a terrible —, a very difficult or unusual —. **between the devil and the deep (blue) sea** in a dilemma, forced to choose one of two unwelcome possibilities. ***blue devil***: see BLUE *adjective*. ***Cartesian devil***: see CARTESIAN *adjective*. **devil a bit**, **devil a one**, etc., not at all, not even one, etc. ***devil's own luck***: see LUCK *noun*. ***dust devil***: see sense 12 above. **go to the devil** be damned, take a ruinous course; freq. *imper*., go away at once. ***hold a candle to the Devil***: see HOLD *verb*. ***Indian devil***: see sense 5 above. ***limb of the Devil***: see LIMB *noun*¹. **play the devil with** cause severe damage to or trouble for. ***printer's devil***: see sense 7 above. ***raise the devil***: see RAISE *verb*. ***red devil***: see RED *adjective*. ***sea devil***: see sense 5 above. ***sell one's soul to the devil***, ***sell oneself to the devil***: see SELL *verb*. ***Tasmanian devil***: see sense 5 above. **the devil to do**, **the devil and all to do** *arch*. much ado, much trouble and turmoil. †**the devil on two sticks** = DIABOLO. **the devil's own** — an exceptional or extreme instance of —. ***the devil's job***, ***the devil's own job***: see JOB *noun*¹. **the devil to pay** extreme trouble or difficulty concerning a particular circumstance or obligation. ***the world, the flesh, and the devil***: see FLESH *noun*. ***thorny devil***: see THORNY 1.
– COMB.: **devil bird** (*a*) *dial*. the swift; (*b*) in Sri Lanka, the brown wood owl, *Strix leptogrammatica*; **devil dance** a ritual dance performed for the invocation, propitiation, or exorcism of spirits; **devil dancer** a performer of a devil dance; **devil-devil** *Austral*. (*a*) in folklore, a devil, an evil spirit; (*b*) = GILGAI; **devil-dodger** *arch*. *joc*. a preacher, a ranter; a person who tries to secure salvation by attending the services of more than one religious denomination; **devilfish** any of various fishes of supposedly devilish appearance or reputation, *spec*. (*a*) the anglerfish; (*b*) *N. Amer*. the manta; **devil-in-a-bush** love-in-a-mist, *Nigella damascena*; **devil-may-care** *adjective & noun* (*a*) *adjective* reckless, rollicking; (*b*) *noun* a reckless or rollicking person or attitude; **devil-on-the-coals** *Austral*. & *NZ slang* a small damper hastily baked in hot ashes; **devil's advocate** [translating Latin *advocatus diaboli*] the official whose function is to put the case against beatification or canonization by the Roman Catholic Church; *transf*. a person who provokes argument or discussion by supporting the opposite side or by pointing out the weaknesses of his or her own case; **devil's bit** [from the supposedly 'bitten-off' root shape] (*a*) (more fully ***devil's bit scabious***) a bluish-flowered scabious, *Succisa pratensis*, of damp pastures; (*b*) *US* a plant of the lily family, *Chamaelirium luteum*, bearing spikelike racemes of white flowers; also called ***blazing star***; **devil's bones** *arch*. dice; **devil's books** *arch*. playing cards (= ***devil's picture books*** below); **devil's claw** any of various plants whose seed pods have claw-like hooks, esp. of the genera *Harpagophytum* (southern Africa and Madagascar, used in herbal medicine), and *Proboscidea* (America), both in the family Pedaliaceae; **devil's club** *N. Amer*. a prickly shrub of the aralia family, *Oplopanax horridus* of western N. America; **devil's coach horse** a large predatory rove beetle, *Ocypus olens*, which habitually raises its tail when alarmed; **devil's darning needle** a dragonfly or damselfly; **devil's dirt** asafoetida (= ***devil's dung*** below); ***devil's dozen***: see DOZEN *noun*; **devil's dung** asafoetida (= ***devil's dirt*** above); **devil's dust** the flock to which old cloth is reduced by a mechanical devil, shoddy; **devil's food cake** (chiefly *N. Amer*.) a rich chocolate cake; **devil's grip** *colloq*. pleurodynia, esp. as a symptom of Bornholm disease; **devil's guts** (*a*) *dial*. dodder; (*b*) *Austral*. any parasitic climbing plant of the genus *Cassytha* of the laurel family; ***devil's limb***: see LIMB *noun*¹; ***devil's matins***: see MATIN *noun* 2; **devil's milk** *dial*. any of various plants, esp. spurges, with acrid milky juice; **devils on horseback** (*a*) = ***angels on horseback*** s.v. ANGEL; (*b*) a similar dish of prune or plum in bacon; **devil's needle** = ***devil's darning needle*** above; **devil's paintbrush** *N. Amer*. a naturalized European hawkweed, *Pilosella aurantiaca*, with orange flower heads and black-haired involucres; ***devil's paternoster***: see PATERNOSTER 1c; **devil's picture books** *arch*. playing cards (= ***devil's books*** above); ***devil's tattoo***: see TATTOO *noun*¹ 2; **devil's twine** = ***devil's guts*** (b) above; **devil-wood** *US* a tree of the olive family, *Osmanthus americanus*, a native of US swamps (also called ***American olive***); the hard wood of this tree; **devil-worship** the worship or cult of a devil or the Devil, Satanism; **devil-worshipper** a person who practises devil-worship.
■ **devildom** *noun* (*a*) the dominion or rule of a devil or the Devil, exercise of diabolic power; (*b*) the domain of the Devil, the condition of devils: L17. **deviless** *noun* (now *rare*) a female devil L17. **devilet** *noun* (*a*) a little devil; (*b*) *dial*. the swift: L18. **devilhead** *noun* (long *arch*. *rare*) devilhood ME. **devilhood** *noun* the condition and estate of a devil or the Devil E17. **deviling** *noun* (*a*) a young devil, an imp, a mischievous little creature; (*b*) *dial*. the swift, the pied wagtail: L16. **devilism** *noun* a system of action or conduct appropriate to a devil, devilish quality M17. **devilize** *verb* (*a*) *verb trans*. make a devil of, make devilish in character; †(*b*) *verb intrans*. play the devil, act as a devil: E17. **devilkin** *noun* a little devil, an imp M18. **devil-like** *adjective & adverb* diabolical(ly) L15. **devilship** *noun* (*a*) (chiefly *joc*. as a title) a person having the status of a devil; (*b*) the condition or quality of a devil; the position or office of devil: ME.

devil /ˈdɛv(ə)l/ *verb*. Infl. **-ll-**, *****-l-**. L16.
[ORIGIN from the noun.]
†**1** *verb trans*. (Foll. by *it*) play the devil; play the devil with. L16–M17.
2 *verb trans*. Cook with peppery condiments. E19.
3 *verb trans*. Worry (a person) excessively; harass, annoy, tease. *colloq*. (chiefly *US*). E19.
4 *verb intrans*. Work as a lawyer's or author's devil (*for* a principal). M19.
5 Tear to pieces, break up, score, scratch, esp. with a devil (DEVIL *noun* 11). L19.

devilish /ˈdɛv(ə)lɪʃ/ *adjective & adverb*. LME.
[ORIGIN formed as DEVIL *verb* + -ISH¹.]
▸ **A** *adjective*. **1** Like the Devil or a devil; wicked, fiendish. LME.

BROWNING We pronounce Count Guido devilish and damnable.

2 Characteristic or worthy of the Devil; diabolical; damnable; execrable. LME.

W. GOUGE The matchlesse, mercilesse, devilish, and damnable gun-powder-treason.

3 Of or belonging to the Devil. E16.

J. H. BURTON So skilled in devilish arts of magic.

4 Violent, terrible; extremely bad; enormous, excessive. *arch*. *colloq*. M17.

THACKERAY She has a devilish deal more than ten thousand pounds.

▸ **B** *adverb*. Excessively, exceedingly; very. *arch*. *colloq*. E17.

P. H. GIBBS I'm devilish glad to be home again.

■ **devilishly** *adverb* in a devilish manner; *arch*. *colloq*. excessively, exceedingly, very: E16. **devilishness** *noun* M16.

devilment /ˈdɛv(ə)lm(ə)nt/ *noun*. L18.
[ORIGIN formed as DEVIL *verb* + -MENT.]
1 Action befitting a devil; mischief, wild spirits, reckless daring. L18.
2 A devilled dish of food. *rare*. L18.
3 A devilish device or invention, a devilish or strange phenomenon. L19.

devilry /ˈdɛv(ə)lri/ *noun*. LME.
[ORIGIN formed as DEVIL *verb* + -RY.]
†**1** A demon; a demoniacal possession. LME–L15.
2 Black magic; dealing with the Devil; diabolical art. LME.
3 Devilish action or conduct; (an act of) extreme wickedness. L15. ▸**b** Reckless mischief or daring. M19.

J. BUCHAN Some old devilry of the heathen has lingered in that place. **b** I. RANKIN That was a bit naughty of me, wasn't it? . . That was my spot of devilry for the night.

4 The Devil and his works. M16.
5 A system of devils, demonology. M19.
6 *collect*. A company of devils. M19.

deviltry /ˈdɛv(ə)ltri/ *noun*. L18.
[ORIGIN from DEVILRY after *harlotry* etc.]
= DEVILRY.

devious /ˈdiːvɪəs/ *adjective & adverb*. L16.
[ORIGIN from Latin *devius*, from *de-* DE- 1 + *via* way: see -OUS.]
▸ **A** *adjective*. **1** Lying out of the way; remote, sequestered. Now *rare*. L16.

E. K. KANE These devious and untrodden ice-fields.

2 Pursuing an indirect or winding course; circuitous, rambling; deviating from the straight way, erring; subtly cunning, wily, unscrupulous, dishonest. E17.

D

J. R. LOWELL A shoal of devious minnows wheel from where a pike Lurks balanced. C. V. WEDGWOOD To evade them they had travelled . . by devious ways, thus greatly lengthening the journey. W. GOLDING I should . . have to be subtle, devious, diplomatic. P. LARKIN The devious ways of practical politics.

▸ **B** *adverb.* With an indirect or winding course, circuitously. Now *rare.* L18.

C. BRONTË I sought the Continent, and went devious through all its lands.

▪ **deviously** *adverb* M18. **deviousness** *noun* E18.

devirginate /diːˈvəːdʒɪneɪt/ *verb trans.* Long *rare.* Pa. pple & ppl adjective †**-ate** (earlier), **-ated**. LME.
[ORIGIN Orig. pa. pple, from Latin *devirginatus* pa. pple of *devirginare*, from *de-* DE- 3 + *virgo*, *virgin-* virgin: see -ATE², -ATE³.]
Deprive of virginity.
▪ **devirgiˈnation** *noun* E17.

devisable /dɪˈvʌɪzəb(ə)l/ *adjective.* LME.
[ORIGIN Anglo-Norman (in Old French = dividable), formed as DEVISE *verb*; in sense 2 from DEVISE *verb*: see -ABLE.]
1 LAW. That can be devised by will. LME.
2 Contrivable. E17.

devise /dɪˈvʌɪz/ *noun.* Also †**device**. ME.
[ORIGIN Var. of DEVICE, from Old French *devise* fem.]
▸ †**I 1** See DEVICE I. ME.
▸ **II 2** LAW. The action of devising real estate by will; (a clause containing) a testamentary disposition of land. Also more widely, the action of bequeathing, a bequest. LME.

devise /dɪˈvʌɪz/ *verb.* ME.
[ORIGIN Old French & mod. French *deviser* from Proto-Romance, from Latin *divis-* pa. ppl stem of *dividere* DIVIDE *verb*.]
†**1** *verb trans.* Divide; distribute; distinguish. ME–L15.
†**2** *verb trans.* Consider, look at attentively, examine; meditate on; decide; conceive, imagine, guess. Foll. by simple obj. or obj. clause ME–E19.
3 *verb trans.* Plan, contrive, (something (now usu. abstract), *how*, †*that*, †*to do*); invent, create. ME. ▸**b** *verb trans.* Plan in a secret, underhand, or artful way, plot, (something, †*to do*); feign (something, †*that*); forge. *arch.* ME. ▸**c** *verb intrans.* Make plans, scheme. Formerly also, pretend. LME.

MILTON How suttly to detain thee I devise. W. S. MAUGHAM She could devise some means to persuade him. **b** W. COWPER Devising . . calamity to Troy.

†**4** *verb trans.* Accomplish, achieve, manage (something, *to do*). ME–L16.
†**5** *verb trans.* Recount, relate, describe. ME–L16. ▸**b** *verb intrans.* Give an account; confer, talk, (*of*). LME–L19.
†**6** *verb trans.* Appoint, direct. LME–E17.
7 *verb trans.* LAW. Assign (land) by will. Also more widely, bequeath. LME.
▪ **devisement** *noun* (*rare*) †(**a**) a description, an account; (**b**) the action of devising; a device: LME.

devisee /dɪvʌɪˈziː/ *noun.* M16.
[ORIGIN from DEVISE *verb* + -EE¹.]
LAW. A person to whom property is devised by will.

deviser /dɪˈvʌɪzə/ *noun.* L15.
[ORIGIN Alt. of DEVISOR: see -ER¹.]
A person who devises; a contriver, a planner, an inventor.

devisor /dɪˈvʌɪzɔː, dɪvʌɪˈzɔː/ *noun.* LME.
[ORIGIN Anglo-Norman *devisour*, Old French *deviseor*, formed as DEVISE *verb*.]
1 = DEVISER. Now *rare.* LME.
2 LAW. A person who devises property by will. M16.

devitalize /diːˈvʌɪt(ə)lʌɪz/ *verb trans.* Also **-ise**. E19.
[ORIGIN from DE- 3 + VITALIZE.]
Deprive of vitality or vital qualities; reduce the vitality of.
▪ **devitaliˈzation** *noun* L19.

devitrify /diːˈvɪtrɪfʌɪ/ *verb trans.* M19.
[ORIGIN from DE- 3 + VITRIFY.]
Deprive of vitreous qualities; make (glass or vitreous rock) hard, opaque, and crystalline.
▪ **devitrifiˈcation** *noun* M19.

devocalize /diːˈvəʊk(ə)lʌɪz/ *verb trans.* Also **-ise**. L19.
[ORIGIN from DE- 3 + VOCALIZE.]
PHONETICS. = DEVOICE.

devoice /diːˈvɔɪs/ *verb trans.* M20.
[ORIGIN from DE- 3 + VOICE *verb*.]
PHONETICS. Make (a vowel or voiced consonant) voiceless.

devoid /dɪˈvɔɪd/ *adjective.* LME.
[ORIGIN Orig. pa. pple of DEVOID *verb*.]
1 Foll. by *of*: quite lacking or free from, empty of. LME.

W. G. PALGRAVE A very simple style of dress, devoid of ornament or pretension. E. WAUGH The room, though spacious, was almost devoid of furniture. I. WALLACE Her . . face was devoid of any makeup except at the lips.

†**2** *absol.* Void, empty. *rare.* Only in L16.

SPENSER When I awoke, and found her place devoyd.

devoid /dɪˈvɔɪd/ *verb trans.* Long *rare.* Pa. pple & ppl adjective †**devoid** (cf. prec.), **devoided**. ME.
[ORIGIN Old French *devoidier*, *devuidier* (mod. *dévider*), from *de-* DE- 3 + *voider*, *vuider* VOID *verb*. In isolated mod. use back-form. from DEVOID *adjective*.]
†**1** Cast out, expel, discharge; withdraw *oneself*. ME–M16.
†**2** Vacate, leave. LME–M16.
3 Empty *of*, free *of*, divest *of*. LME.
†**4** Avoid, shun. LME–M16.

devoir /dəˈvwɑː/ *noun. arch.* ME.
[ORIGIN Anglo-Norman *dever*, Old French *deveir* (mod. *devoir*) from Latin *debere* owe. Cf. ENDEAVOUR.]
1 Duty; a dutiful act. Chiefly in ***do one's devoir***. ME.
†**2** One's best or utmost, an effort. LME–L17.
put oneself in devoir [after French *se mettre en devoir* do one's utmost.]
†**3** (A) service due or rendered. LME–M18.
4 An act of civility. Usu. in *pl.*, courteous or formal attentions. LME.

A. SEAGER He paid his devoirs to his hostess and went . . into the dining room.

†**5** In *pl.* Moneys due, dues. LME–M17.
– NOTE: The mod. French spelling was introduced in 15 and the pronunc. was subsequently conformed to it.

devolatilize /diːˈvɒlətɪlʌɪz/ *verb trans.* Also **-ise**. M19.
[ORIGIN from DE- 3 + VOLATILIZE.]
Remove volatile components from, make no longer volatile.
▪ **devolatiliˈzation** *noun* E20.

devolute /ˈdiːvəluːt, ˈdɛv-/ *verb trans.* M16.
[ORIGIN Latin *devolut-* pa. ppl stem of *devolvere* DEVOLVE.]
Transfer by devolution.

devolution /diːvəˈluːʃ(ə)n, dɛv-/ *noun.* L15.
[ORIGIN Late Latin *devolutio(n-)* (in medieval Latin sense), formed as DEVOLUTE: see -ION.]
1 The transference of an unexercised right to the ultimate owner; transference by default. L15. ▸†**b** The passing of jurisdiction on appeal. L16–E18.
2 a Descent by natural, legal, or due succession; the action of passing something on to a successor. M16. ▸**b** The deputing or delegation of work or authority; *esp.* the transfer of some powers by central government to a local or regional administration. M18.

a DONNE Now for the riches themselves . . he may have them by devolution from his parents. **b** B. RUSSELL There should be devolution of the powers of the State to various kinds of bodies. *Guardian* The demand for devolution . . was conceded . . to stem the threatening tide of nationalism.

3 a The action of rolling down; descent with a rolling motion. *arch.* E17. ▸**b** The rolling or passing of time; descent through a series of stages. M17. ▸**c** (In contrast to ***evolution***.) Degeneration. *rare.* L19.

b C. N. MANLOVE Devolution into ignorance and slavedom. **c** *Daily Telegraph* Instead of the survival of the fittest, we encourage the survival of the stupidest: devolution.

▪ **devolutionary** *adjective* of, pertaining to, or characterized by devolution L19. **devolutionist** *noun & adjective* (**a**) *noun* a believer in or advocate of (political) devolution; (**b**) *adjective* of or pertaining to devolutionists; tending towards devolution: E20.

devolve /dɪˈvɒlv/ *verb.* LME.
[ORIGIN Latin *devolvere*, from *de-* DE- 1 + *volvere* to roll.]
▸ **I** *verb trans.* **1** Cause to descend with a rolling motion, roll down. Also, unroll, unfurl. *arch.* LME. ▸†**b** Overturn, overthrow. LME–M17. ▸**c** Cause to pass down by the revolution of time (*into* a state or condition); cause to descend through a series of stages. *arch.* M16.

DE QUINCEY Where little England . . now devolves so quietly to the sea her sweet pastoral rivulets.

2 †**a** Transfer (a right) to the ultimate owner, esp. through the failure or forfeiture of the holder. (Foll. by *to*, *unto*.) L15–M19. ▸**b** Cause to descend by natural, legal, or due succession; pass on by inheritance. (Foll. by *to*, (arch.) *unto*.) M16. ▸†**c** Cause to fall or alight *on* or *upon* an object; throw *on* or *upon* a resource. E17–E18.

b S. JOHNSON Students . . can seldom add more than some small particle of knowledge, to the hereditary stock devolved to them from ancient times.

3 Cause (a charge or responsibility) to fall *on* or *upon* a deputy; delegate (work or authority); *spec.* transfer (power) to a lower level, esp. from central government to local or regional administration. M17.

H. A. L. FISHER The territorial lord, upon whom . . the exercise of political power is in fact devolved. *Marxism Today* 50% of Scots favouring a devolved assembly and 30% of Scots wanting a separate parliament.

▸ **II** *verb intrans.* **4 a** Pass or fall *to* another, esp. through the failure or forfeiture of the holder; pass by default *to*. M16. ▸**b** Pass by natural, legal, or due succession (*to*). E17. ▸**c** Fall as a charge or responsibility *on* or *upon*. M18.

b M. HUNTER Succession to the ruling rights devolved through the eldest daughter of a line. J. BARNES It was brought back . . by a roving cousin, and has devolved to me from my sister. **c** E. BOWEN So few having this gift, she felt it devolved on her to use it. T. BENN The peerage that devolved on me as his heir when Father died.

5 a Pass by the revolution of time *to* or *into* a state or condition; descend through a series of stages, degenerate, (*into*). L16. ▸**b** Roll or flow down (*from*); unroll, unfurl. *arch.* M17.

a DE QUINCEY Four separate movements through which this impassioned tale devolves. J. BEE A gentleman and scholar devolving into the buffoon . . is an unseemly sight. **b** SMOLLETT Devolving from thy parent lake, A charming maze thy waters make. E. BLUNDEN The earth heaved up to a great height in solid crags and clods, with devolving clouds of dust.

▪ **devolvement** *noun* M19.

Devon /ˈdɛv(ə)n/ *noun.* M19.
[ORIGIN A county in SW England: see DEVONSHIRE.]
1 Used *attrib.* to designate things found in, originating from, or associated with Devon. M19.
2 (An animal of) a breed of red beef cattle. M19.
3 ANGLING. A type of artificial lure. E20.

Devonian /dɛˈvəʊnɪən, dɪ-/ *adjective & noun.* E17.
[ORIGIN from medieval Latin *Devonia*, from *Devon(shire)*: see DEVONSHIRE, -AN, -IAN.]
▸ **A** *adjective.* **1** Of or pertaining to Devon(shire). E17.
2 GEOLOGY. Designating or pertaining to the fourth period of the Palaeozoic era, following the Silurian and preceding the Carboniferous. M19.
▸ **B** *noun.* **1** The dialect of Devon(shire). *rare.* M17.
2 A native or inhabitant of Devon(shire). L19.
3 GEOLOGY. The Devonian period; the system of rocks dating from this time. L19.

devonport *noun* var. of DAVENPORT *noun*¹.

Devonshire /ˈdɛv(ə)nʃə/ *noun & verb.* Also (repr. local pronunc.) **Denshire** /ˈdɛnʃə/; (as verb) **d-**. E17.
[ORIGIN A county (Old English *Defenascir*) in SW England: cf. DEVON.]
▸ **A** *noun.* **1** Used *attrib.* to designate things found in, originating from, or associated with Devonshire (now Devon). E17.
Devonshire cream clotted cream. **Devonshire slipper** a type of stirrup iron.
2 The dialect of Devonshire; = DEVONIAN *noun* 1. M19.
▸ **B** *verb trans. & intrans.* Clear or improve (land) by burning turf, stubble, etc. Now *arch.* or *hist.* E17.

devoré /dəˈvɔːreɪ/ *noun.* L20.
[ORIGIN French, lit. 'devoured'.]
A velvet fabric with a pattern formed by burning the pile away with acid.

dévot /devo (*pl. same*), deɪˈvəʊ/ *noun.* Fem. **-ote** /-ɔt (*pl. same*), -ɒt/. E18.
[ORIGIN French, use as noun of adjective: see DEVOUT.]
A devotee; a devout person.

†**devota** *noun* see DEVOTO.

devote /dɪˈvəʊt/ *adjective & noun. arch.* ME.
[ORIGIN Partly var. of DEVOUT, partly directly from Latin *devotus*.]
▸ **A** *adjective.* **1** = DEVOUT *adjective* 1. ME.
2 Devoted, dedicated, (*to*). LME.
▸ †**B** *noun.* A devotee. M17–E18.

devote /dɪˈvəʊt/ *verb trans.* L16.
[ORIGIN Latin *devot-* pa. ppl stem of *devovere*, from *de-* DE- 1 + *vovere* vow.]
1 Dedicate formally, consecrate, (*to*). L16.

W. LAW All Christians are by their Baptism devoted to God.

2 Apply or give up zealously or exclusively *to*. E17.

L. M. MONTGOMERY Jane says she will devote her whole life to teaching, and never, never, marry. R. G. COLLINGWOOD I learnt to devote my time more and more to music. H. L. MENCKEN Even more than Cato the Censor he devoted himself wholeheartedly to arousing fears and fomenting hatred. G. F. KENNAN *Pravda* devoted the first four and a half pages of its six-page issue exclusively to a single document. E. ROOSEVELT The begum had devoted herself to trying to carry out his plans.

3 Consign to destruction; invoke a curse on. (Earlier as DEVOTED 3.) *arch.* M17.

GIBBON The hostile army was devoted with dire execrations to the gods of war and . . thunder.

▪ **devotement** *noun* an act of devoting; devotion, dedication: E17.

†**devoté** *noun.* E18–E19.
[ORIGIN Pseudo-Fr. alt. of DEVOTE *noun* or DEVOTEE.]
A devotee.

dévote *noun* see DÉVOT.

devoted /dɪˈvəʊtɪd/ *adjective.* L16.
[ORIGIN from DEVOTE *verb* + -ED¹.]
1 Vowed; dedicated; consecrated. L16.
2 Characterized by devotion; zealously or exclusively attached (*to*); given up *to*. L16.

V. BRITTAIN Several wards exclusively devoted to head wounds and eye cases. R. PARK The girl was selflessly devoted to her father. K. A. PORTER The most devoted married pair. S. NAIPAUL Together with about one hundred and fifty of his most devoted disciples, he had migrated West.

3 Consigned to evil or destruction; cursed; doomed. *arch.* E17.
■ **devotedly** *adverb* E19. **devotedness** *noun* M17.

devotee /dɛvəʊ'tiː/ *noun*. M17.
[ORIGIN from DEVOTE *verb* + -EE[1].]
1 *gen.* A person who is zealously devoted *to* a cause, pursuit, etc.; a votary (*of*), an enthusiast (*of*). M17.

R. F. BURTON As fanatical a devotee of vegetarianism.

2 *spec.* A person characterized by religious devotion esp. of an extreme or superstitious kind. L17.

SHERWOOD ANDERSON The devotee going swiftly through decade after decade of his rosary.

devotion /dɪ'vəʊʃ(ə)n/ *noun*. ME.
[ORIGIN Old French & mod. French *dévotion* or Latin *devotio(n-)*, formed as DEVOTE *verb*: see -ION.]
1 The fact or quality of being devoted to divine worship or service; reverence, devoutness. (Foll. by *to*, *towards* a god etc.) ME. ▸†**b** A devout feeling or impulse. ME–E17.

LD MACAULAY The austere devotion which . . gave to his court the aspect of a monastery.

2 Religious observance, divine worship; a form of prayer or worship directed to a special object or for private use; in *pl.* & †*sing.*, prayers (and meditation), private worship. ME.

JOYCE She believed steadily in the Sacred Heart as the most generally useful of all Catholic devotions. G. SANTAYANA Modest and scattered worshippers . . intent each on his own devotions.

3 a The fact or quality of being devoted to a person, cause, pursuit, etc.; earnest application; zealous or exclusive attachment. ME. ▸**b** Zealous or exclusive application *to* a use or purpose. M19.

a R. L. STEVENSON Perpetual devotion to what a man calls his business, is only to be sustained by perpetual neglect of many other things. H. ACTON Her family loyalty was too intense to be hidden, and strong political dissent could not weaken her devotion. **b** J. W. KRUTCH The devotion of every foot of ground to immediately productive purposes.

4 The action of setting apart for a sacred purpose; solemn dedication, consecration. E16.

W. J. LOFTIE The inscription records the devotion of some town or place to a divinity.

†**5** An oblation; alms. M16–M17.
†**6** Devoted service, personal disposal. Chiefly in ***at the devotion of***, entirely devoted to (a person). M16–M19.
†**7** An end to which someone or something is devoted; a purpose, an intent. L16–M17.
■ **devotionary** *adjective* (now *rare*) = DEVOTIONAL M17. **devotionist** *noun* (now *rare*) a person who professes or practises devotion M17.

devotional /dɪ'vəʊʃ(ə)n(ə)l/ *adjective*. M17.
[ORIGIN from DEVOTION + -AL[1].]
Pertaining to, of the nature of, or characterized by (esp. religious) devotion.
■ **devotionalism** *noun* devotional behaviour or belief M19. **devotionalist** *noun* a person given to devotion M18. **devotionally** *adverb* M17.

†**devoto** *noun*. Pl. **-o(e)s**. Fem. **-ta**. L16–E18.
[ORIGIN Italian & Spanish from Latin *devotus*: see DEVOUT.]
A devotee.

devour /dɪ'vaʊə/ *verb trans*. ME.
[ORIGIN Old French *devour-* tonic stem of *devorer* from Latin *devorare*, from *de-* DE- 1 + *vorare* swallow.]
1 Swallow or eat up greedily or voraciously, eat like a beast. ME.

J. G. FARRELL There was no sign of the dead mouse. Presumably it had been devoured by the cats. K. CROSSLEY-HOLLAND Thor felt hungry. He devoured an entire ox, and . . eight salmon.

2 Of an inanimate agency or, formerly, a person: consume destructively; waste, destroy; engulf. ME.

G. CRABBE The ocean roar Whose greedy waves devour the lessening shore. W. STUBBS Whom the sword spared famine and pestilence devoured. R. H. MORRIESON We heard the . . crackle of flame devouring the ancient timber. M. SARTON A day of small agitations . . that devoured my peace.

3 Absorb the attention of, engross. Usu. in *pass.* E16.

L. M. MONTGOMERY Anne was devoured by secret regret.

4 Take in greedily the sense or appearance of; study or look at avidly. L16.

C. MCKAY The . . bold-eyed boys . . Devoured her shape with eager, passionate gaze. I. MURDOCH He . . had been devouring books of every kind in an insatiable hunger for knowledge.

5 Traverse (a distance, road, etc.) rapidly. L16.

SHAKES. *2 Hen. IV* He seem'd in running to devour the way, Staying no longer question. P. CAREY The Cadillac devoured the miles.

■ **devourable** *adjective* E17. **devourer** *noun* LME. **devouringly** *adverb* voraciously, so as to devour M16. **devourment** *noun* the action of devouring E19.

devout /dɪ'vaʊt/ *adjective* & *noun*. ME.
[ORIGIN Old French & mod. French *dévot* from Latin *devotus* pa. pple of *devovere* DEVOTE *verb*. See also DEVOTE *adjective* & *noun* and cf. DÉVOT, DEVOTO.]
▸ **A** *adjective*. **1** Devoted to divine worship or service, earnestly religious, pious; showing religious devotion, reverential. ME.

M. SPARK The devout Moslems . . who surge in their thousands to Mecca. I. MURDOCH He . . formed a strong attachment to Saint Brigid . . and went on devout pilgrimages upon her tracks.

2 Deeply respectful; devoted, dedicated, (*to*). Formerly also, eager *to*. *arch.* LME.

HUGH WALPOLE Young, handsome, . . and the most devout of lovers.

3 *gen.* Earnest, sincere, hearty, genuine. (Earlier as DEVOUTLY 3.) E19.

L. M. MONTGOMERY 'Thanks be to goodness . . ,' breathed Marilla in devout relief.

▸ †**B** *noun*. A devotee. E17–E18.
■ **devoutness** *noun* LME.

devoutly /dɪ'vaʊtli/ *adverb*. ME.
[ORIGIN from DEVOUT + -LY[2].]
1 With religious devotion, piously, reverentially. ME.
†**2** Intently, carefully. LME–L15.
3 *gen.* Earnestly, sincerely, heartily, genuinely. E17.

†**devove** *verb trans*. M16–E19.
[ORIGIN Latin *devovere*: see DEVOTE *verb*.]
Devote.

DEW *abbreviation*.
Distant early warning.

dew /djuː/ *noun*.
[ORIGIN Old English *dēaw* = Old Frisian *dāw*, Old Saxon *dau* (Dutch *dauw*), Old High German *tou* (German *Tau*), Old Norse *dǫgg* (genit. *dǫggvar*), from Germanic.]
1 The moisture deposited in minute drops on any cool surface by the condensation of atmospheric vapour between evening and morning. OE.

WORDSWORTH The dew was falling fast, the stars began to blink. LYTTON Arch and blooming faces bowed down to bathe in the May dew. M. SHADBOLT The paddocks glittered with dew under the cool early sun.

2 *fig.* Something likened to dew as coming with refreshing power or with gentleness, or as characteristic of the morning. ME.

SHELLEY Sleep, that healing dew of heaven. LONGFELLOW Having the dew of his youth, and the beauty thereof.

3 Moisture, a liquid, esp. when formed in minute drops or glistening; *esp.* (**a**) tears; (**b**) sweat. ME.

SOUTHEY The dews of death Stood on his livid cheek. SIR W. SCOTT Those poor eyes that stream'd with dew.

mountain dew: see MOUNTAIN.

4 An exudation or surface deposit on a plant etc. (Earlier in MILDEW.) Now *rare* exc. in HONEYDEW, MILDEW. M16.
– COMB.: †**dew-beater** (**a**) an early pioneer; (**b**) in *pl.* (*slang*), feet; **dewberry** (**a**) (the fruit of) a trailing European bramble, *Rubus caesius*, the berries of which are covered with a bluish bloom; any of several low-growing N. American brambles, esp. *Rubus flagellaris*; (**b**) *obsolete* exc. *dial.* a gooseberry; **dewbow** an arch resembling a rainbow, occurring on a dew-covered surface; **dew cup** *Scot.* the plant lady's mantle; **dewdrop** a drop of dew; something resembling a drop of dew; **dewdropped** *adjective* covered or glistening with dew; **dewfall** the deposition of dew; the time when this begins; **dew point** METEOROLOGY the atmospheric temperature (dependent on pressure and humidity) below which dew is deposited, i.e., at which the pressure of atmospheric water vapour becomes equal to saturation vapour pressure; **dew pond** a shallow (usu. artificial) pond (maintained largely by precipitation) situated on downs where there is no adequate groundwater supply; **dew rake** a rake for removing grass or stubble; **dew-ret** *verb trans.* ret or macerate (flax, hemp, etc.) by prolonged exposure to atmospheric moisture instead of by steeping in water (opp. ***water-ret***); **dew snail** (now *dial.*) a slug; **dew worm** †(**a**) ringworm; (**b**) an earthworm.
■ **dewless** *adjective* E17.

dew /djuː/ *verb*. ME.
[ORIGIN Corresp. to Old High German *touwōn* (German *tauen*), Old Norse *dǫggva*, from Germanic, from base of DEW *noun*. Prob. already in Old English.]
†**1** *verb intrans.* Give or produce dew; *impers.* in ***it dews***, ***it is dewing***, etc., dew falls, dew is falling, etc. ME–E18.
2 *verb trans.* Wet with or as with dew; moisten; steep. ME.

SIR W. SCOTT Fairy strains of music fall, Every sense in slumber dewing. J. G. COZZENS Heat and whisky had dewed his face with sweat.

Dewali *noun* var. of DIWALI.

dewan /dɪ'wɑːn/ *noun*. Also **di-**. L17.
[ORIGIN Urdu from Persian *dīwān* DIVAN, in sense 'fiscal register'. Cf. DOUANE.]
hist. A chief treasury official, finance minister, or prime minister in some Indian states.

dewani /dɪ'wɑːni/ *noun*. Also **di-**. L18.
[ORIGIN Urdu from Persian *dīwānī* from *dīwān*: see DEWAN.]
hist. The function or office of dewan; the right of revenue collection in some Indian states.

Dewar /'djuːə/ *noun*. L19.
[ORIGIN Sir James *Dewar* (1842–1923), Brit. physicist & chemist.]
1 (Also **d-**.) In full ***Dewar vessel***, ***Dewar flask***, etc. A double-walled flask with an evacuated interspace for preventing the transfer of heat into or from the inner container. L19.
2 CHEMISTRY. Used ***attrib.*** of structures for the benzene molecule which were postulated by Dewar and are of higher energy and lower symmetry than the Kekulé structure. E20.

dewater /diː'wɔːtə/ *verb trans*. E20.
[ORIGIN from DE- 3 + WATER *noun*.]
Remove water from.

dew claw /'djuːklɔː/ *noun*. L16.
[ORIGIN App. from DEW *noun* + CLAW *noun*[1].]
1 The rudimentary inner toe or hallux sometimes present in dogs. L16.
2 Either of the side toes forming the false hoof of even-toed ungulates, e.g. deer. L16.
■ **dew-clawed** *adjective* having dew claws L16.

Dewey /'djuːi/ *noun*. L19.
[ORIGIN from Melvil *Dewey* (1851–1931), US librarian.]
Used ***attrib.*** to designate a library classification using three-figure numbers from 000 to 999 to cover the major branches of knowledge, any further subdivisions being made by adding figures after the decimal point.

De-Witt /də'wɪt/ *verb trans*. Long *obsolete* exc. *hist.* L17.
[ORIGIN from John and Cornelius *De Witt*, Dutch statesmen murdered by a mob in 1672.]
Lynch.

dewlap /'djuːlap/ *noun*. ME.
[ORIGIN from DEW *noun* + LAP *noun*[1], perh. after Old Norse (Old Danish *doglæp*).]
The fold of loose skin hanging from the neck of cattle; *transf.* a similar feature of another animal, bird, or man.
■ **dewlapped** *adjective* having a dewlap LME.

deworm /diː'wəːm/ *verb trans*. M20.
[ORIGIN from DE- 3 + WORM *noun*.]
Rid (an animal etc.) of worms.

†**dewtry** *noun*. L16–E18.
[ORIGIN from cognates of Hindi *dhatūrā* DATURA, as Marathi *dhutrā*, *dhotrā*.]
Any of several Indian plants of the genus *Datura* (family Solanaceae), esp. the thorn apple, *D. stramonium*; a stupefying drug or drink prepared from such a plant.

dewy /'djuːi/ *adjective*. OE.
[ORIGIN from DEW *noun* + -Y[1].]
1 Characterized by the presence of dew; covered or wet with dew. OE. ▸**b** Affected by the presence of dew. Chiefly *poet.* E18. ▸**c** Consisting of dew. *poet.* E19.

MILTON From Noon to dewy Eve. **b** SOUTHEY O'er the landscape spread The dewy light. **c** T. HOOD The buds were hung with dewy beads.

2 Of the nature or quality of dew, moist; resembling dew; *poet.* suggestive of dew in gentleness, refreshing power, etc. OE. ▸**b** Moistened as with dew. L16. ▸**c** Innocently trusting, naively sentimental. M20.

SHAKES. *Rich. III* These dewy tears. W. COWPER Awaking from thy dewy slumbers. **c** *Times* The dewy ingenue from *Stage Struck*.

– COMB.: **dewy-eyed** *adjective* (**a**) with moist eyes, affected to tears; (**b**) = sense 2c above.
■ **dewily** *adverb* after the manner of dew E19. **dewiness** *noun* E17.

dexamethasone /dɛksə'mɛθəsəʊn, -zəʊn/ *noun*. M20.
[ORIGIN from *dexa-* (blend of HEXA- and DECA-) + METHYL + *-a-* + CORTISONE.]
PHARMACOLOGY. A synthetic corticosteroid, $C_{22}H_{29}FO_5$, which is used esp. as an anti-inflammatory agent.

dexamphetamine /dɛksam'fɛtəmiːn, -ɪn/ *noun*. M20.
[ORIGIN from DEXTRO- + AMPHETAMINE.]
PHARMACOLOGY. The pharmacologically more active dextrorotatory isomer of amphetamine.

Dexedrine /'dɛksədriːn, -ɪn/ *noun*. Also **d-**. M20.
[ORIGIN Prob. from DEXTRO- after *Benzedrine*.]
(Proprietary name for) dexamphetamine sulphate; a tablet of this.

dexie *noun* var. of DEXY.

Dexter /'dɛkstə/ *noun*. Also **d-**. L19.
[ORIGIN Said to be from a Mr *Dexter*, credited with establishing the breed.]
In full ***Dexter Kerry***. (An animal of) a small hardy breed of Irish cattle originating from the Kerry breed.

dexter /'dɛkstə/ *adjective*. M16.
[ORIGIN Latin, from base repr. also by Greek *dexios*.]
1 Of or on the right-hand side of a person or thing, esp. (HERALDRY, opp. ***sinister***) of a shield etc., (i.e. to an observer's left). M16. ▸†**b** Of an omen: seen or heard on the right-hand side, hence auspicious. M17–E18.
†**2** Dexterous. E–M17.

†**dexterious** *adjective*. **L16–M17**.
[**ORIGIN** from Latin DEXTER + -IOUS.]
= DEXTEROUS.
■ †**dexteriously** *adverb* **E–M17**.

dexterity /dɛkˈstɛrɪti/ *noun*. **E16**.
[**ORIGIN** French *dextérité* from Latin *dexteritas*, formed as DEXTER *adjective*: see -ITY.]
1 Mental adroitness or skill, cleverness. **E16**.
A. POWELL Stringham's dexterity at imitating the manner. Q. BELL Not the slightest dexterity in the use of language.
2 Manual or manipulative skill or adroitness; good physical coordination. **M16**.
R. L. STEVENSON Under the left shoulder he carried a crutch, which he managed with wonderful dexterity. M. BARING A famous pianist played some elaborate fantasies which showed off the dexterity of his fingers. A. CARTER The manual dexterity of an assembler of precision instruments.
3 A skilful, adroit, or clever act. Usu. in *pl.* **L16**.
C. BURT A consistent tendency.. to undertake new dexterities with the left hand.
4 Right-handedness, the using of the right hand. *rare*. **L19**.

dexterous /ˈdɛkst(ə)rəs/ *adjective*. Also **dextrous** /ˈdɛkstrəs/. **E17**.
[**ORIGIN** from Latin DEXTER + -OUS. Cf. earlier DEXTERIOUS.]
▸ **I** Of a person.
1 Having mental adroitness or skill, clever; contriving. **E17**.
SOUTHEY She was devout in religion,.. dextrous in business.
2 Having manual or manipulative skill or adroitness, deft of hand; having good physical coordination. **M17**.
A. WILSON Marie-Hélène, so dexterous with her needle as a rule, pricked her finger.
3 = DEXTRAL *adjective* 3. **L19**.
▸ **II** Of a thing or action.
4 Done with or characterized by dexterity. **E17**.
W. H. AUDEN His dextrous handling of a wrap.
■ **dexterously** *adverb* **E17**. **dexterousness** *noun* **E17**.

dextral /ˈdɛkstr(ə)l/ *adjective & noun*. **M17**.
[**ORIGIN** medieval Latin *dextralis* from Latin *dextra* right hand: see -AL¹.]
▸ **A** *adjective*. **1** Situated on the right-hand side; of or pertaining to the right hand or the right-hand side. **M17**.
2 *CONCHOLOGY*. Of a spiral shell: having the whorls ascending from left to right (of the observer). **M19**.
3 Of a person: (predominantly) right-handed. **E20**.
4 *GEOLOGY*. Of, pertaining to, or designating a strike-slip fault in which the motion of the block on the further side of the fault from an observer is towards the left. **M20**.
▸ **B** *noun*. A (predominantly) right-handed person. **E20**.
– NOTE: Opp. SINISTRAL.
■ **dextrality** /dɛkˈstralɪti/ *noun* right-handedness, use by preference of the right hand **M17**. **dextrally** *adverb* in a dextral manner or direction, to the right **L19**.

dextran /ˈdɛkstran/ *noun*. **L19**.
[**ORIGIN** from DEXTRO- + -AN.]
1 *CHEMISTRY*. A carbohydrate gum produced by the fermentation of some sugars and other organic materials. **L19**.
2 *MEDICINE*. A solution containing degraded, partially hydrolysed dextran, used as a substitute for blood plasma. **M20**.

dextrin /ˈdɛkstrɪn/ *noun*. **M19**.
[**ORIGIN** from DEXTRO- + -IN¹.]
A carbohydrate gum formed by enzymic or other hydrolysis of starch and used as an adhesive, thickening agent, etc.

dextro- /ˈdɛkstrəʊ/ *combining form*.
[**ORIGIN** from Latin *dexter*, *dextra* right + -O-.]
Turning or turned to the right; *CHEMISTRY* dextrorotatory. Opp. LAEVO-.
■ **dextroˈcardia** *noun* a congenital abnormality in which the disposition of the heart is reversed so that it occupies a mirror image of its normal position **L19**. **dextrotartaric** *adjective*: ***dextrotartaric acid***, the dextrorotatory (and predominant naturally occurring) form of tartaric acid **L19**. **dextroˈtartrate** *noun* a dextrorotatory tartrate **M19**.

dextrorotatory /dɛkstrəʊˈrəʊtət(ə)ri/ *adjective*. **L19**.
[**ORIGIN** from DEXTRO- + ROTATORY.]
CHEMISTRY. Having or relating to the property (possessed by some compounds) of rotating the plane of polarized light to the right, i.e. clockwise when viewed in the opposite direction to that of propagation. Opp. LAEVOROTATORY.
■ **dextroroˈtation** *noun* (the property of) rotating the plane of polarized light in this direction **L19**.

dextrorse /ˈdɛkstrɔːs/ *adjective*. **M19**.
[**ORIGIN** Latin *dextrorsum*, *dextrorsus*.]
Turned or spiralling upwards towards the right; dextral.
■ Also **dexˈtrorsal** *adjective* **E19**.

dextrose /ˈdɛkstrəʊz, -s/ *noun*. **M19**.
[**ORIGIN** formed as DEXTRO- + -OSE².]
CHEMISTRY. The dextrorotatory (and predominant naturally occurring) form of glucose. Cf. LAEVULOSE.

dextrous *adjective* var. of DEXTEROUS.

dexy /ˈdɛksi/ *noun*. *slang*. Also **dexie**. **M20**.
[**ORIGIN** Abbreviation.]
(A tablet of) Dexedrine.

dey /deɪ/ *noun*¹. *obsolete* exc. *dial*.
[**ORIGIN** Old English *dǣge* = Old Norse *deigja* female servant, from base meaning 'kneader'. Cf. DAIRY, LADY *noun*.]
A woman or (occas.) a man in charge of a dairy. Formerly also *gen*., a female servant.
– COMB.: **dey-house** a dairy; **dey-woman** a dairymaid, a woman in charge of a dairy.

dey /deɪ/ *noun*². Also (esp. in titles) **D-**. **M17**.
[**ORIGIN** French from Turkish *dayı* maternal uncle, used also as a courtesy title.]
(The title of) any of the supreme rulers of Algiers, 1710–1830, orig. the commanding officers of the janissaries of Algiers under the Ottoman Empire. Also, (the title of) the local ruler of Tunis or Tripoli under nominal Ottoman suzerainty.
■ **deyship** *noun* the position or dignity of a dey **E18**.

dezincification /diːˌzɪŋkɪfɪˈkeɪʃ(ə)n/ *noun*. **L19**.
[**ORIGIN** from DE- 3 + ZINC *noun* + -I- + -FICATION.]
METALLURGY. Removal or loss of zinc from an alloy.
■ **deˈzincify** *verb trans*. **L19**.

DF *abbreviation*.
1 Latin *Defensor Fidei* Defender of the Faith.
2 Direction-finder, -finding.

DFC *abbreviation*.
Distinguished Flying Cross.

DFM *abbreviation*.
Distinguished Flying Medal.

DG *abbreviation*.
1 Latin *Dei gratia* by the grace of God; *Deo gratias* thanks to God.
2 Director general.

dghaisa /ˈdʌɪsə/ *noun*. Also **-ajsa**. **L19**.
[**ORIGIN** Maltese.]
A boat resembling a gondola, used in Malta.

DH *abbreviation*.
BASEBALL. Designated hitter.

dha /dɑː/ *noun*. Also **dhar**. **E19**.
[**ORIGIN** Burmese.]
A Myanmar (Burmese) unit of length, between 3.5 and 4 m (approx. 11 ft 6 inches and 13 ft 1½ inches).

dhak /dɑːk/ *noun*. **E19**.
[**ORIGIN** Hindi *ḍhāk*, *dhāk*.]
A leguminous tree of eastern India and Myanmar (Burma), *Butea monosperma*, with showy orange or red flowers. Also ***dhak tree***.

dhal *noun* var. of DAL.

dhaman /ˈdɑːmən/ *noun*. Also **-min**. **L19**.
[**ORIGIN** Hindi *dhāman*, *dhāmin*.]
1 An Indian rat snake, *Ptyas mucosus*. **L19**.
2 (The tough elastic wood of) an Indian tree of the genus *Grewia* (family Tiliaceae), esp. *G. tiliifolia*. **L19**.

dhamma /ˈdɑːmə, ˈdʌmə/ *noun*. **E20**.
[**ORIGIN** Pali formed as DHARMA.]
Esp. among Theravada Buddhists, = DHARMA.

dhan /dɑːn/ *noun*. **E19**.
[**ORIGIN** Hindi *dhān* rice plant, unhusked rice from Sanskrit *dhānya*.]
In the Indian subcontinent: rice in the husk.

dhand /dand/ *noun*. **M19**.
[**ORIGIN** Sindhi.]
A lake or swamp in Sind, formerly in India, now a province in Pakistan.

dhania /ˈdanɪə/ *noun*. **E20**.
[**ORIGIN** Hindi *dhaniyā*.]
In Indian cookery: coriander.

dhansak /ˈdʌnsɑːk/ *noun*. **L20**.
[**ORIGIN** Gujarati.]
An Indian dish of meat or vegetables cooked with lentils and coriander.

dhar *noun* var. of DHA *noun*.

dharma /ˈdɑːmə, ˈdəːmə/ *noun*. **L18**.
[**ORIGIN** Sanskrit = something established, decree, custom. Cf. DHAMMA.]
In *HINDUISM*: social or caste custom, right behaviour, law; justice, virtue; natural or essential state or function, nature. In *BUDDHISM*: universal truth or law, esp. as proclaimed by Buddha.
– COMB.: **dharmashastra** a Hindu law book; **dharmasutra** an early Vedic collection of rules of life for priests.

dharmashala /ˈdɑːməʃɑːlə/ *noun*. Also ***dharmsala*** /ˈdɑːmsɑːlə/, ***dharamshala*** /ˈdɑːrəmʃɑːlə/. **E19**.
[**ORIGIN** Repr. Hindi pronunc. of Sanskrit *dharmaśālā*, from *dharma* (see DHARMA) + *śālā* house.]
In the Indian subcontinent: a building devoted to religious or charitable purposes, *esp*. a rest house for travellers.

dharna /ˈdəːnə, -ɑː/ *noun*. Also **dhurna**. **L18**.
[**ORIGIN** Hindi *dharnā* placing, act of sitting in restraint.]
In the Indian subcontinent: a mode of compelling payment or compliance, by sitting at the debtor's or offender's door without eating until the demand is complied with. Chiefly in ***sit dharna***, ***sit in dharna***.

Dharuk /ˈdʌrʊk/ *noun*. **E20**.
[**ORIGIN** Dharuk.]
An Aboriginal language of the area around Sydney, Australia.

DHEA *abbreviation*.
The hormone dehydropiandrosterone.

dhikr *noun* var. of ZIKR.

dhobey *noun* var. of DOBEY.

dhobi /ˈdəʊbi/ *noun*. Also **-by**, **-bie**. **M19**.
[**ORIGIN** Hindi *dhobī*, from *dhob* washing.]
A washerman or washerwoman in the Indian subcontinent.
– COMB.: **dhobi itch** *colloq*. ringworm infestation of the groin or armpit, or contagious dermatitis, in tropical climates.

dhol /dəʊl/ *noun*. **M19**.
[**ORIGIN** Hindi pronunc. of Sanskrit *dhola*.]
A large barrel-shaped or cylindrical drum, usu. with two heads, used in the Indian subcontinent.

dholak /ˈdəʊlək/ *noun*. Also **-uk**. **M19**.
[**ORIGIN** Hindi *ḍholak*, formed as DHOL + dim. suffix *-ak*.]
A medium-sized drum used in the Indian subcontinent.

dhole /dəʊl/ *noun*. Pl. **-s**, same. **E19**.
[**ORIGIN** Unknown.]
The Asiatic wild dog, *Cuon alpinus*, native to the Indian subcontinent, China, and SE Asia.

dholuk *noun* var. of DHOLAK.

dhoney /ˈdəʊni/ *noun*. Also **doney**. **L16**.
[**ORIGIN** Telugu *doni*; cf. Persian *dōnī* a yacht, and TONI.]
A small sailing vessel of southern India.

dhoon *noun* var. of DUN *noun*⁴.

dhoti /ˈdəʊti/ *noun*. Also **dhootie** /ˈduːti/. **E17**.
[**ORIGIN** Hindi *dhotī*.]
A garment worn by male Hindus in the Indian subcontinent, consisting of a piece of material tied around the waist and extending to cover most of the legs.

dhow /daʊ/ *noun*. Also **dow**. **L18**.
[**ORIGIN** Arabic *dāwa*, prob. rel. to Marathi *dāw*.]
A lateen-rigged sailing vessel of the Arabian Sea, with one or two masts. Formerly also *loosely*, an Arab slaver or other vessel.

dhrupad /ˈdruːpəd/ *noun*. **L19**.
[**ORIGIN** Sanskrit *dhrupada* kind of dance.]
A classical form of northern Indian vocal music, usu. sung in a slow tempo, consisting of a prelude and four sections developing various parts of the raga.

DHSS *abbreviation*.
hist. Department of Health and Social Security.

DHTML *abbreviation*.
COMPUTING. Dynamic HTML.

dhurna *noun* var. of DHARNA.

dhurra *noun* var. of DURRA.

dhurrie /ˈdʌri/ *noun*. Also **dhurry**, **du-**. **L19**.
[**ORIGIN** Hindi *darī*.]
A large piece of heavy cotton cloth used, orig. in the Indian subcontinent, as a carpet and also as a sofa cover, curtain, etc.

dhu stone /ˈdjuː stəʊn, ˈdʒuː/ *noun phr*. **L19**.
[**ORIGIN** from Welsh *du* black + STONE *noun*.]
A type of dolerite found in the Clee Hills, Shropshire.

dhyal /dʌɪˈɑːl/ *noun*. **M19**.
[**ORIGIN** Hindi *dahiyal*, *dahel*. Cf. earlier DIAL-BIRD.]
In the Indian subcontinent, = ***MAGPIE-robin***.

dhyana /dɪˈɑːnə/ *noun*. **M19**.
[**ORIGIN** Sanskrit *dhyāna*.]
HINDUISM & BUDDHISM. Profound meditation; the penultimate stage of yoga.

DI *abbreviation*.
1 Defence Intelligence.
2 Direct injection.

di- /dɪ, dʌɪ/ *prefix*¹ (not productive).
Repr. Latin *di-* the reduced form of *dis-* DIS- used before *b*, *d*, *g* (usually), *j* (sometimes), *l*, *m*, *n*, *r*, *s* + consonant, and *v*. In late Latin *di-* was sometimes changed back to the full form *dis-*: hence ***dismiss***, ***disrupt***.

di- /dʌɪ, dɪ/ *prefix*².
[**ORIGIN** Greek, from *dis* (adverb) twice.]
Used (**a**) in words of Greek origin or in English formations modelled on them, with the sense 'twice, doubly', as ***dilemma***, ***diphthong***, ***dicotyledon***; (**b**) as a productive suffix used in chemical names to indicate the presence of two atoms of an element or two similar radicals, as ***dioxide***, ***dichromate***, sometimes replacing two atoms of hydrogen, as ***dinitrobenzene***.

di- /dʌɪ/ *prefix*[3].
The form of DIA-[1] used before a vowel or (sometimes) *h*.

dia- /dʌɪə/ *prefix*[1]. See also DI-[3].
[ORIGIN Greek, from *dia* (preposition) through.]
Used in words of Greek origin, and in English formations modelled on them, with the senses 'through', as ***diaphanous***, 'across' as ***diameter***, 'transversely' as ***diaheliotropic***, 'apart' as ***diaeresis***.

dia- /dʌɪə/ *prefix*[2].
[ORIGIN Repr. Greek *dia* (see DIA-[1]) in phrases such as *dia kōdeiōn*, *dia tessarōn*, treated in Latin as single words (*diacodion*, *diatessaron*), sometimes with Latinized ending (*diachylum*).]
Used in names, mostly *obsolete*, of compound medicines, with the sense 'made or consisting of'.

dia. *abbreviation*.
Diameter.

diabase /ˈdʌɪəbeɪs/ *noun*. M19.
[ORIGIN French, irreg. as if for *di-* (DI-[2]) + *base*, 'rock with two bases'; later perh. assoc. with Greek *diabasis* transition.]
PETROGRAPHY. Orig. = DIORITE. Later (in the UK), an altered or (formerly) pre-Tertiary dolerite; (in the US) any dolerite.
■ **diaˈbasic** *adjective* pertaining to or of the nature of diabase L19.

diabetes /dʌɪəˈbiːtiːz/ *noun*. M16.
[ORIGIN Latin from Greek *diabētēs* lit. 'siphon', from *diabainō* go through.]
Either of two metabolic disorders marked by the production of excessive quantities of urine, (*a*) (more fully ***diabetes mellitus*** /mɪˈlʌɪtəs/ [Latin *mellitus* sweet]) one in which the pancreas secretes insufficient insulin and the body in consequence fails to metabolize glucose, leading to loss of energy and accumulation of glucose in the blood and urine; (*b*) ***diabetes insipidus*** /ɪnˈsɪpɪdəs/ [Latin *insipidus* INSIPID], a rare disorder of the pituitary gland caused by deficiency of vasopressin.
bronze diabetes: see BRONZE *noun & adjective*. ***bronzed diabetes***: see BRONZE *verb* 2.
■ †**diabete** *noun* = DIABETES LME–M17. ˌ**diabetoˈgenic** *adjective* producing or produced by diabetes (mellitus) E20.

diabetic /dʌɪəˈbɛtɪk/ *adjective & noun*. L18.
[ORIGIN French *diabétique*, from *diabète* DIABETES + *-ique* -IC.]
▸ **A** *adjective*. Of, pertaining to, or suffering from diabetes (mellitus); (of a food product) made with a low sugar content for the benefit of diabetics. L18.
▸ **B** *noun*. A person affected with diabetes (mellitus). M19.
■ Also **diabetical** *adjective* (long *rare*) E17.

diable /djɑːbl/ *interjection & noun*. L16.
[ORIGIN French from ecclesiastical Latin *diabolus* DEVIL *noun*.]
▸ **A** *interjection*. Expr. impatience, amazement, dismay, etc. L16.
▸ **B** *noun*. ***le diable***, = DIABOLO. Now *rare* or *obsolete*. M19.

diable au corps /djɑːbl o kɔːr/ *noun phr*. Pl. ***diables au corps*** (pronounced same). L19.
[ORIGIN French, lit. 'devil in the body'.]
Restless energy; a spirit of devilry.

diablerie /dɪˈɑːbləri/ *noun*. Also **-ery**. M18.
[ORIGIN French, from DIABLE: see -ERY.]
1 Dealings with the Devil; sorcery, witchcraft. M18. ▸**b** *fig*. Mischievous fun, devilment. M19.
2 The mythology or lore of devils; a description or representation of devils. E19.
3 The realm of devils. M19.

diables au corps *noun phr*. pl. of DIABLE AU CORPS.

diablotin /dɪˈablə(ʊ)tɪn; *foreign* djablɔtɛ̃ (*pl. same*)/ *noun*. E19.
[ORIGIN French, dim. of DIABLE.]
1 A little devil, an imp. E19.
2 In Trinidad, the oilbird, *Steatornis caripensis*. E19.
3 The black-capped petrel, *Pterodroma hasitata*, a rare bird which breeds in the mountains of several W. Indian islands. L19.

diabolic /dʌɪəˈbɒlɪk/ *adjective & noun*. LME.
[ORIGIN (Old French & mod. French *diabolique* from) ecclesiastical Latin *diabolicus*, from *diabolus* DEVIL *noun*: see -IC.]
▸ **A** *adjective*. **1** Of, pertaining to, or deriving from the Devil or devils; of or pertaining to witchcraft. LME.
2 Having the qualities of the Devil or a devil; inhumanly cruel or wicked, fiendish. L15.
3 Resembling a devil in appearance. M19.
▸ †**B** *noun*. An agent or follower of the Devil. E16–M17.

diabolical /dʌɪəˈbɒlɪk(ə)l/ *adjective & noun*. E16.
[ORIGIN formed as DIABOLIC + -AL[1].]
▸ **A** *adjective*. **1** = DIABOLIC *adjective* 1. E16.

HOBBES Hee was commonly thought a Magician, and his Art Diabolicall.

2 = DIABOLIC *adjective* 2. M16. ▸**b** (In weakened sense.) Outrageous, disgraceful; disgracefully bad or defective. *slang*. M20.

R. A. FREEMAN This crime was planned with the most diabolical cleverness. **b** *Listener* A parody piece . . which took diabolical liberties with Eurovision song contests. S. TOWNSEND Asked our postman about communications between Tunisia and England. He said they were 'diabolical'.

3 = DIABOLIC *adjective* 3. M18.
▸ †**B** *noun*. = DIABOLIC *noun*. M16–E19.

■ **diabolically** *adverb* (*a*) fiendishly, very wickedly; (*b*) *slang* shockingly, excruciatingly; exceedingly: L16. **diabolicalness** *noun* E18.

diabolify /dʌɪəˈbɒlɪfʌɪ/ *verb trans*. M17.
[ORIGIN from ecclesiastical Latin *diabolus* or Greek *diabolos* DEVIL *noun* + -I- + -FY.]
Make a devil of, represent as a devil.

diabolise *verb* var. of DIABOLIZE.

diabolism /dʌɪˈabəlɪz(ə)m/ *noun*. E17.
[ORIGIN from ecclesiastical Latin *diabolus* or Greek *diabolos* DEVIL *noun* + -ISM.]
1 Dealings with the Devil or evil spirits; witchcraft, sorcery. E17.
2 Belief in or worship of the Devil. M17.
3 Devilish or atrociously wicked conduct. L17.
4 The character or nature of a devil. M18.
■ **diabolist** *noun* a person who believes in or seeks to deal with the Devil L19.

diabolize /dʌɪˈabəlʌɪz/ *verb trans*. Also **-ise**. E18.
[ORIGIN formed as DIABOLISM + -IZE.]
1 Convert into a devil, render diabolical, represent as a devil. E18.
2 Subject to demonic influence. E19.
■ **diaboliˈzation** *noun* L19.

diabolo /dɪˈabələʊ, dʌɪ-/ *noun*. Pl. **-os**. E20.
[ORIGIN Italian from ecclesiastical Latin *diabolus* DEVIL *noun*.]
A game in which a two-headed top is thrown up and caught on a string stretched between two sticks; the top used in this game.
– NOTE: Earlier called ***le diable*** (see DIABLE *noun*); also ***the devil on two sticks***.

Diabolonian /dʌɪˌabəˈləʊnɪən/ *noun*. Also **d-**. L17.
[ORIGIN from ecclesiastical Latin *diabolus* DEVIL *noun* after *Babylonian* etc.]
A member of the host of Diabolus (the Devil) in Bunyan's *Holy War*; a follower of the Devil.

diacatholicon /dʌɪəkəˈθɒlɪk(ə)n/ *noun*. Long *rare*. LME.
[ORIGIN Old French & medieval Latin, repr. Greek *dia katholikōn* made of general ingredients: see DIA-[2].]
Orig., a kind of laxative electuary. Hence, a universal remedy.

diacaustic /dʌɪəˈkɔːstɪk/ *adjective & noun*. E18.
[ORIGIN from DIA-[1] + Greek *kaustikos* burning: see CAUSTIC.]
PHYSICS. ▸**A** *adjective*. Of a curve or surface: formed by the intersection of rays of light refracted from a curved surface. E18.
▸ **B** *noun*. A diacaustic curve or surface. Cf. CATACAUSTIC. E18.

diacetate /dʌɪˈasɪteɪt/ *noun*. E19.
[ORIGIN from DI-[2] + ACETATE.]
CHEMISTRY. A salt or ester containing two acetic acid radicals, $CH_3COO\cdot$.

diacetic /dʌɪəˈsiːtɪk/ *adjective*. L19.
[ORIGIN from DI-[2] + ACETIC.]
CHEMISTRY. ***diacetic acid***, = ACETOACETIC ***acid***.

diacetylmorphine /dʌɪˌasɪtʌɪlˈmɔːfiːn/ *noun*. L19.
[ORIGIN from DI-[2] + ACETYL + MORPHINE *noun*.]
CHEMISTRY. An acetyl derivative of morphine, more commonly called heroin. Cf. DIAMORPHINE.

diachronic /dʌɪəˈkrɒnɪk/ *adjective*. M19.
[ORIGIN from DIA-[1] + Greek *khronos* time + -IC.]
†**1** Lasting through existing time. *rare*. Only in M19.
2 Concerned with or pertaining to the historical development of a language, culture, etc. Opp. ***synchronic***. E20.
■ **diachronically** *adverb* in a diachronic manner, with regard to historical development M20. **diachroˈnistic** *adjective* = DIACHRONIC 2 M20. **diachroˈnistically** *adverb* = DIACHRONICALLY M20. **diˈachrony** *noun* the historical development of a language etc. M20.

diachronism /dʌɪˈakrənɪz(ə)m/ *noun*. E20.
[ORIGIN formed as DIACHRONIC + -ISM.]
GEOLOGY. The occurrence of a geological feature in different palaeontological zones; the property of being diachronous.

diachronous /dʌɪˈakrənəs/ *adjective*. E20.
[ORIGIN formed as DIACHRONIC + -OUS.]
1 GEOLOGY. Not of a uniform geological age throughout; exhibiting diachronism. E20.
2 = DIACHRONIC 2. M20.

diachylon /dʌɪˈakɪlɒn/ *noun*. *obsolete* exc. *hist*. Also **-chylum** /-kɪləm/, **-culum** /-kjʊləm/. ME.
[ORIGIN Old French *diaculon*, *-chilon* from Latin *diachylon* repr. Greek *dia khulōn* composed of juices: see DIA-[2], CHYLE.]
Orig., an ointment or salve made of vegetable juices. Later, a plaster with a medication made by boiling together litharge (lead oxide), olive oil, and water.

diacid /dʌɪˈasɪd/ *adjective*. M19.
[ORIGIN from DI-[2] + ACID *noun*.]
CHEMISTRY. Of a base etc.: (composed of molecules) able to combine with two monovalent acid radicals.

diaclinal /dʌɪəˈklʌɪn(ə)l/ *adjective*. L19.
[ORIGIN from DIA-[1] + Greek *klinein* to lean, slope + -AL[1].]
GEOLOGY. Of a valley, river, etc.: crossing a fold; passing through an anticline or syncline.

†**diacodium** *noun*. Also **-ion**. LME–E19.
[ORIGIN medieval Latin, repr. Greek *dia kōdeiōn* (a preparation) made from poppy heads: see DIA-[2].]
A syrup prepared from poppy heads, used as an opiate.

diaconal /dʌɪˈakən(ə)l/ *adjective*. E17.
[ORIGIN ecclesiastical Latin *diaconalis*, from *diaconus* DEACON *noun*: see -AL[1].]
Of or pertaining to a deacon.

D

diaconate /dʌɪˈakəneɪt, -ət/ *noun*. E18.
[ORIGIN ecclesiastical Latin *diaconatus*, from *diaconus*: see DIACONAL, -ATE[1].]
1 The position or office of deacon. E18.
2 The period during which a person is a deacon. L19.
3 A body of deacons. L19.

diaconicon /dʌɪəˈkɒnɪkɒn/ *noun*. Also in Latin form **-cum** /-kəm/. Pl. **-ca** /-kə/. E18.
[ORIGIN Greek *diakonikon* neut. adjective, from *diakonos* DEACON *noun*: see -IC.]
CHRISTIAN CHURCH. The part of an Orthodox church south of the sanctuary where vestments and sacred vessels are kept.

diacoustics /dʌɪəˈkuːstɪks/ *noun pl*. (usu. treated as *sing*.). Now *rare* or *obsolete*. L17.
[ORIGIN from DI-[3] + ACOUSTICS.]
The science of refracted sound. Cf. CATACOUSTICS.

diacritic /dʌɪəˈkrɪtɪk/ *adjective & noun*. L17.
[ORIGIN Greek *diakritikos*, from *diakrinein* distinguish, from *krinein* separate: see DIA-[1].]
▸ **A** *adjective*. Of a mark or sign: serving to distinguish different values or sounds of the same letter, as in é, è, ë, ē, etc. L17.
▸ **B** *noun*. A diacritic mark. M19.

diacritical /dʌɪəˈkrɪtɪk(ə)l/ *noun & adjective*. L17.
[ORIGIN formed as DIACRITIC + -AL[1].]
▸ †**A** *noun*. = DIACRITIC *noun*. Only in L17.
▸ **B** *adjective*. **1** = DIACRITIC *adjective*. M18.
2 Having the ability to distinguish, discerning. M19.

diacritically /dʌɪəˈkrɪtɪk(ə)li/ *adverb*. E19.
[ORIGIN from DIACRITIC *adjective* or DIACRITICAL *adjective*: see -ICALLY.]
With diacritic marks.

diactinic /dʌɪakˈtɪnɪk/ *adjective*. M19.
[ORIGIN from DI-[3] + ACTINIC.]
Transparent to actinic light.

diaculum *noun* see DIACHYLON.

diadelphous /dʌɪəˈdɛlfəs/ *adjective*. E19.
[ORIGIN from DI-[2] + Greek *adelphos* brother + -OUS.]
BOTANY. Of stamens: united by the filaments so as to form two groups. Of a plant: having the stamens so united.

diadem /ˈdʌɪədɛm/ *noun & verb*. ME.
[ORIGIN Old French & mod. French *diadème* from Latin *diadema* from Greek = regal headband of the Persian kings, from *diadein* bind round.]
▸ **A** *noun*. **1** Something worn on the head as a symbol of honour, esp. royalty; a crown. Now chiefly *poet. & rhet*. ME. ▸**b** *spec*. A wreath of leaves or flowers worn round the head. M16. ▸**c** *spec*. A headband, plain or jewelled, worn by or in imitation of Eastern monarchs. L16.

E. PERRONET Bring forth the royal diadem And crown him Lord of all.

2 Royal or imperial power, sovereignty. ME.
3 Something conferring dignity; a crowning glory. E16.

JOHN NEAL The name of Yankee was a reproach here; it was a diadem there.

4 An adornment on the top of something. L18.

BYRON Mont Blanc is the monarch of mountains . . With a diadem of snow.

– COMB.: **diadem monkey** = SAMANGO; **diadem spider** the garden spider, *Araneus diadematus*, which spins orb webs.
▸ **B** *verb trans*. Adorn (as) with a diadem. LME.

W. JONES Every stalk is diadem'd with flowers.

diademed monkey = SAMANGO.
■ **diademated** *adjective* (now *rare* or *obsolete*) wearing a diadem E18.

diadic *adjective & noun* var. of DYADIC.

diaeresis /dʌɪˈɪərɪsɪs, -ˈɛr-/ *noun*. Also *****dieresis**. Pl. **-eses** /-ɪsiːz/. L16.
[ORIGIN Latin from Greek *diairesis* noun of action from *diairein* take apart, divide, formed as DIA-[1] + *hairein* take.]
1 The division of one syllable into two, esp. by the resolution of a diphthong into two simple vowels. L16.
2 The sign ¨ placed over a vowel to indicate that it is pronounced separately, as in *Brontë*, *naïve*. E17.
3 PROSODY. A break in a line where the end of a foot coincides with the end of a word. M19.

■ **diaeretic** /dʌɪəˈrɛtɪk/ *adjective* (now *rare*) of or pertaining to diaeresis M17.

diagenesis /dʌɪəˈdʒɛnɪsɪs/ *noun*. L19.
[ORIGIN from DIA-[1] + -GENESIS.]
GEOLOGY. The physical and chemical changes (other than metamorphism) undergone by a sediment after deposition; the recombination of the constituents of a mineral to form a new mineral.
■ **diageˈnetic** *adjective* involving or of the nature of diagenesis; produced by diagenesis: L19. **diageˈnetically** *adverb* M20.

diageotropic /ˌdʌɪədʒiːəˈtrɒpɪk, -ˈtrəʊp-/ *adjective*. L19.
[ORIGIN from DIA-[1] + GEOTROPIC.]
BOTANY. Pertaining to or characterized by a tendency to grow horizontally.
■ **diageotropism** *noun* L19.

diaglyphic /dʌɪəˈglɪfɪk/ *adjective*. *rare*. M19.
[ORIGIN from Greek *diagluphein* carve in intaglio + -IC.]
Of the nature of an intaglio; engraved.

diagnose /ˈdʌɪəgnəʊz, -ˈnəʊz/ *verb*. M19.
[ORIGIN Back-form. from DIAGNOSIS.]
1 *verb trans. & intrans.* Make a diagnosis of, infer the presence of (a particular disease etc.) from symptoms. M19.
2 *verb trans.* Ascertain the condition of (a person etc.) by diagnosis. E20.
■ **diagˈnosable** *adjective* L19.

diagnosis /dʌɪəgˈnəʊsɪs/ *noun*. Pl. **-noses** /-ˈnəʊsiːz/. L17.
[ORIGIN mod. Latin *diagnosis* from Greek, from *diagignōskein* distinguish, discern, formed as DIA-[1] + *gignōskein* KNOW *verb*.]
1 The process of determining the nature of a disease etc.; the identification of a disease from a patient's symptoms etc.; a formal statement of this. L17. ▸**b** *transf. & fig.* (A conclusion from) analysis; the ascertainment of the cause of a mechanical fault etc. M19.
differential diagnosis: see DIFFERENTIAL *adjective* 2.
2 *TAXONOMY*. The distinctive characterization of a species etc. M19.

diagnostic /dʌɪəgˈnɒstɪk/ *adjective & noun*. E17.
[ORIGIN Greek *diagnōstikos* able to distinguish, *hē diagnōstikē* (sc. *tekhnē*) the art of distinguishing diseases: see DIAGNOSIS, -IC.]
▸ **A** *adjective*. **1** Of or pertaining to diagnosis. E17.
2 Of use in diagnosis; characteristic, distinctive. M17.

> D. ATTENBOROUGH The diagnostic character of having not one but two pairs of antennae.

3 *COMPUTING*. Of a program or a routine within one: designed to identify program errors or system faults and to give information about them. M20.
▸ **B** *noun*. **1** A diagnosis. Now *rare* exc. in *pl.*, the art of diagnosis. E17.
PLASMA ***diagnostics***.
2 A distinctive symptom or characteristic; a specific trait. M17.
3 *COMPUTING*. An output that helps a user to identify an error or malfunction; a facility or routine for producing such an output. Usu. in *pl.* M20.
■ **diagnostically** *adverb* M17. **diagnosticate** *verb trans.* diagnose M19. **diagnoˈstician** *noun* a person skilled in diagnosis; a person who makes a diagnosis: M19.

diagonal /dʌɪˈag(ə)n(ə)l/ *adjective & noun*. M16.
[ORIGIN Latin *diagonalis* from Greek *diagōnios* from angle to angle, formed as DIA-[1] + *gōnia* angle: see -AL[1]. Cf. Old French & mod. French *diagonal*.]
▸ **A** *adjective*. **1** (Of a line) joining two non-adjacent vertices of a figure or solid; extending between opposite corners or edges of something. M16.
2 Having an oblique direction; slanting. M16.

> J. ROSENBERG The diagonal shadow cast by the nose.

3 Marked with diagonal or oblique lines; having some part situated obliquely. L17.

> H. N. MOSELEY A wide patch of diagonal ornamentation upon the abdomen.

diagonal cloth = DIAGONAL *noun* 3. **diagonal matrix** *MATH.*: having non-zero elements only in the diagonal running from the upper left to the lower right.
▸ **B** *noun*. **1** A diagonal line. L16.
2 An oblique part of something. M19.
3 A twilled fabric with the ridges running diagonally. M19.
■ **diagonalizable** *adjective* (*MATH.*) able to be diagonalized M20. **diagonaliˈzation** *noun* (*MATH.*) the process of diagonalizing M20. **diagonalize** *verb* (*a*) *verb intrans.* (*rare*) move obliquely; (*b*) *verb trans.* (*MATH.*) transform into a diagonal matrix: L19. **diagonally** *adverb* in a diagonal direction; obliquely, slantwise: LME.

diagram /ˈdʌɪəgram/ *noun & verb*. E17.
[ORIGIN Latin *diagramma* from Greek, from *diagraphein* mark out by lines, formed as DIA-[1] + *graphein* write: see -GRAM.]
▸ **A** *noun*. **1** A sketch or figure showing the features of an object needed for exposition, rather than its actual appearance. E17.
floral diagram: see FLORAL *adjective*. ***tree diagram***: see TREE *noun* 5b. ***vowel diagram***: see VOWEL *noun*.
2 A figure composed of lines serving to illustrate or prove a theorem etc. in geometry or logic. M17.
3 A figure (e.g. a graph or a histogram) representing a series of related numerical quantities. M19.
INDICATOR ***diagram***.
▸ **B** *verb trans.* Infl. **-mm-**, ***-m-**. Represent by or in a diagram; *fig.* give an outline or summary of. Chiefly *US*. M19.
■ **diagraˈmmatic** *adjective* M19. **diagraˈmmatically** *adverb* M19.

diagrammatize /dʌɪəˈgramətʌɪz/ *verb trans.* Also **-ise**. L19.
[ORIGIN from Greek *diagrammat-* stem of *diagramma* DIAGRAM + -IZE.]
Put into diagrammatic form; represent by a diagram.

diagraph /ˈdʌɪəgrɑːf/ *noun*. E18.
[ORIGIN Branch I from Greek *diagraphē*, formed as DIA-[1], -GRAPH. Branch II from French *diagraphe*, from stem of Greek *diagraphein* (see DIAGRAM).]
▸ **I** †**1** A description. *rare*. Only in E18.
2 A diagram in logic. *rare*. M19.
▸ **II 3** An instrument for mechanically drawing projections or making copies, consisting of a pen governed by cords and pulleys which in turn are controlled by a pointer. Now *rare*. M19.
4 A combined protractor and scale for plotting. L19.
■ **diaˈgraphic** *adjective* (now *rare*) of or pertaining to drawing or graphic representation M17. †**diagraphical** *adjective* = DIAGRAPHIC: only in E17.

diagrid /ˈdʌɪəgrɪd/ *noun*. M20.
[ORIGIN from DIAGONAL *adjective* + GRID *noun*.]
A supporting structure of diagonally intersecting ribs of metal, concrete, etc.

diagrydium /dʌɪəˈgrɪdɪəm/ *noun*. LME.
[ORIGIN Late Latin, alt. of Greek *dakrudion* a kind of scammony, dim. of *dakru* a tear.]
A preparation of scammony, formerly used in pharmacy.

diaheliotropic /ˌdʌɪəhiːlɪəˈtrɒpɪk, -ˈtrəʊp-/ *adjective*. L19.
[ORIGIN from DIA-[1] + HELIOTROPIC.]
BOTANY. Pertaining to or characterized by a tendency to grow transversely to incident light.
■ **diaheliotropism** *noun* L19.

diakinesis /dʌɪəkʌɪˈniːsɪs/ *noun*. E20.
[ORIGIN from DIA-[1] + Greek *kinēsis* motion.]
CYTOLOGY. The last stage of the prophase of the first meiotic division, just before the disappearance of the nuclear membrane.

dial /dʌɪ(ə)l/ *noun*[1] & *verb*. ME.
[ORIGIN medieval Latin *diale* dial of a clock, use as noun of neut. of adjective implied by *dialiter* daily, from Latin *dies* day: see -AL[1]. Cf. Old French *dial* wheel in a clock that completes one turn daily.]
▸ **A** *noun* **1** †**a** A mariner's compass. ME–M17. ▸**b** A miner's compass for underground surveying. M17.
2 An instrument for telling the time of day by means of the shadow cast by a pointer on a graduated surface; *esp.* a sundial. LME.
horizontal dial, ***nocturnal dial***, ***vertical dial***, etc. ***moon-dial***: see MOON *noun*. ***sundial***: see SUN *noun*[1].
†**3** A timepiece or chronometer of any kind; a clock, a watch. LME–L17.
4 The face of a clock or watch, marked to show the hours etc. LME.
5 A circular plate or face with numbered markings on it from which can be read a measurement etc. indicated by a pointer; any device in which a moving element shows the numerical value of something, *esp.* one on a radio showing the frequency to which it is tuned. M18. ▸**b** A circular plate on a telephone with numbers etc. and a disc with finger holes which is rotated for each digit of a number being called. L19.

> M. LOWRY Hugh . . turned the radio dial back and forth, trying to get San Antonio. J. HAWKES Rows of knobs, dials with needles all set at zero.

6 A person's face. *slang*. E19.

> T. WINTON There he was again, Frederick Michael Scully. The same square dial and strong teeth.

7 A lapidary's instrument for holding a gem during cutting and polishing. L19.
▸ **B** *verb*. Infl. **-ll-**, ***-l-**.
1 *verb intrans. & trans.* Survey using a miner's dial. M17.
2 *verb trans.* Measure or indicate (as) with a dial. E19.
3 *verb intrans. & trans.* Operate the dial (or the keys) of a telephone; do this for (a digit or series of digits); call (a number, a person, etc.) by this means to establish telephonic connection. E20.

> G. GREENE I was just going to dial Inquiries. W. DE LA MARE Dial 999, and gain . . Safety from fire, police and ambulance.

dial-a-: used to prefix a noun to form adjectives and nouns denoting something that can be provided or ordered by telephone. **dial up** operate a telephone dial or keypad; gain access to (a computer etc.) over a telephone line in this way; ring up.
– COMB. (mainly from the noun): **dial-plate** the faceplate of a dial; *esp.* that of a clock or watch, marked with the hours; **dial telephone**: operated by means of a dial; **dial tone** *N. Amer.* = *DIALLING* **tone**; **dial-up** *adjective* pertaining to or designating a data transmission link that uses the public telephone system, access to it being gained by dialling.

dial /ˈdʌɪəl/ *noun*[2]. E20.
[ORIGIN from di*allylbarbituric* acid.]
PHARMACOLOGY. A preparation of diallylbarbituric acid, used as a sedative.

dial-bird /ˈdʌɪəlbəːd/ *noun*. M18.
[ORIGIN from Hindi *dahiyal*, *dahel* (see DHYAL) after DIAL *noun*[1]: see BIRD *noun*.]
In the Indian subcontinent, = *MAGPIE-robin*.

dialect /ˈdʌɪəlɛkt/ *noun*. M16.
[ORIGIN French *dialecte* or Latin *dialectus*, from Greek *dialektos* discourse, way of speaking, from *dialegesthai* converse with, discourse, formed as DIA-[1] + *legein* speak.]
†**1** = DIALECTIC *noun* 1. M16–M18.
2 A manner of speaking, language, speech; *esp.* one peculiar to or characteristic of a particular person or class; idiom. L16.

> JOHN CLARKE The Lawyer's Dialect. JOHN FOSTER The theological dialect. G. ORWELL The political dialects to be found in pamphlets, leading articles, . . and the speeches of Under-Secretaries.

3 A form of speech peculiar to a district; a variety of a language with non-standard vocabulary, pronunciation, or idioms; any language in relation to the language family to which it belongs. L16.

> DAY LEWIS Hardly understanding a word he said because of his thick East-Anglian dialect.

eye-dialect: see EYE *noun*.
4 *COMPUTING*. A particular version of a programming language. M20.
– COMB.: **dialect geography** the study of local differences within a speech area.
■ **diaˈlectal** *adjective* belonging to or of the nature of a dialect M19. **diaˈlectally** *adverb* M19.

dialectic /dʌɪəˈlɛktɪk/ *noun*. LME.
[ORIGIN Old French & mod. French *dialectique* or its source Latin *dialectica* from Greek *dialektikē* use as noun (sc. *tekhnē* art) of fem. of *dialektikos* pertaining to discourse, from *dialektos*: see DIALECT, -IC. Pl. after Latin *dialectica* treated as neut. pl.]
▸ **I** *sing.* & in *pl.* (treated as *sing.* or *pl.*).
1 The art of critically investigating the truth of opinions; logical disputation or argument. Formerly, logic as applied to rhetorical reasoning. LME.
2 The philosophy of metaphysical contradictions and their solutions, esp. in the thought of Kant and Hegel; the world process seen as a continuing unification of opposites; the existence or action of opposing forces or tendencies in society etc. L18.

> *Listener* Dialectics is indeed the grammar of Marxist thinking.

▸ **II 3** A dialectic philosopher; a critical enquirer after truth; a logical disputant. M17.

dialectic /dʌɪəˈlɛktɪk/ *adjective*. M17.
[ORIGIN Latin *dialecticus* from Greek *dialektikos*: see DIALECTIC *noun*. In branch II from DIALECT + -IC.]
▸ **I 1** Of, pertaining to, or of the nature of logical disputation. M17.
2 Fond of or practising logical disputation. M19.
▸ **II 3** = DIALECTAL. Now *rare*. E19.
■ **dialecticism** /-sɪz(ə)m/ *noun* (*a*) *rare* the tendency or influence of dialects; (*b*) dialectic philosophy or practice: L19.

dialectical /dʌɪəˈlɛktɪk(ə)l/ *noun & adjective*. E16.
[ORIGIN formed as DIALECTIC *adjective* + -ICAL.]
▸ †**A** *noun*. = DIALECTIC *noun* 1. Only in E16.
▸ **B** *adjective* **I 1** = DIALECTIC *adjective* 1. M16.

> J. C. RANSOM His understanding is intuitive rather than dialectical.

2 Of or pertaining to dialectic as a philosophy. L18.
dialectical materialism the Marxist theory of political and historical events as due to the conflict of social forces caused by humans' material needs and interpretable as a series of contradictions and their solutions.
▸ **II 3** = DIALECTAL. M18.
■ **dialectically** *adverb* (*a*) by means of dialectic, logically; (*b*) as regards dialect, dialectally: L16.

dialectician /dʌɪəlɛkˈtɪʃ(ə)n/ *noun*. M16.
[ORIGIN French *dialecticien*, formed as DIALECTIC *adjective*: see -ICIAN.]
1 A person skilled in disputation; a logician. M16.
2 A student of dialects. M19.

dialectology /dʌɪəlɛkˈtɒlədʒi/ *noun*. L19.
[ORIGIN from DIALECT + -OLOGY.]
The branch of linguistics that deals with dialects.
■ **ˌdialectoˈlogical** *adjective* L19. **dialectologist** *noun* L19.

dialer *noun* see DIALLER.

dialing *verbal noun* see DIALLING.

dialist /ˈdʌɪəlɪst/ *noun*. Also **-ll-**. M17.
[ORIGIN from DIAL *noun*[1] + -IST.]
A maker of dials; a person who uses a dial.

diallage /*in sense 1* dʌɪˈaləgi, -dʒi; *in sense 2* ˈdʌɪəlɪdʒ/ *noun*. E18.
[ORIGIN Greek *diallagē* interchange, from *diallassein* to interchange, formed as DIA-[1] + *allassein* to change, from *allos* other.]
1 A rhetorical figure by means of which arguments, after being considered from various points of view, are all brought to bear upon one point. E18.
2 *MINERALOGY*. A green, brown, or grey monoclinic pyroxene (usu. a variety of augite or diopside) with a metallic lustre and occurring in lamellar or foliated masses. E19.

dialler /ˈdʌɪələ/ *noun*. Also ***dialer**. **M18.**
[ORIGIN from DIAL *noun*[1] & *verb* + -ER[1].]
1 A person who surveys mines etc. by using a dial. **M18.**
2 A device for dialling telephone numbers automatically. **M20.**

dialling /ˈdʌɪəlɪŋ/ *verbal noun*. Also ***dialing**. **L16.**
[ORIGIN from DIAL *noun*[1] & *verb* + -ING[1].]
1 The art of constructing dials. **L16.**
2 The use of a compass in underground surveying. **L17.**
3 The action of using the dial (or keys) of a telephone. **M20.**
direct dialling: see DIRECT *adjective*.
– COMB.: **dialling code** the sequence of numbers dialled to connect a telephone to the exchange of the telephone being called; **dialling tone**: produced by a telephone when a caller may start to dial.

diallist *noun* var. of DIALIST.

diallyl /dʌɪˈalʌɪl, -lɪl/ *adjective & noun*. **M19.**
[ORIGIN from DI-[2] + ALLYL.]
CHEMISTRY. ▸**A** *adjective*. (Composed of molecules) containing two allyl groups. **M19.**
▸**B** *noun*. A liquid diallyl compound, $(CH_2CHCH_2\cdot)_2$; hexa-1,5-diene. **L19.**

dialog *noun & verb* see DIALOGUE.

dialogical /dʌɪəˈlɒdʒɪk(ə)l/ *adjective*. **E17.**
[ORIGIN Late Latin *dialogicos* from Greek *dialogikos*, from *dialogos*: see DIALOGUE, -ICAL.]
Of, pertaining to, or of the nature of dialogue.
■ **dialogic** *adjective* = DIALOGICAL **M19.** **dialogically** *adverb* **M18.** **diaˈlogician** *noun* = DIALOGIST 1 **M20.**

dialogise *verb* var. of DIALOGIZE.

dialogism /dʌɪˈalədʒɪz(ə)m/ *noun*. **M16.**
[ORIGIN Late Latin *dialogismos* from Greek, from *dialogizesthai* DIALOGIZE: see -ISM.]
1 *RHETORIC*. The discussion of a subject under the form of a dialogue. **M16.**
2 A conversational phrase or speech; a spoken or written dialogue. **E17.**

dialogist /dʌɪˈalədʒɪst/ *noun*. **M17.**
[ORIGIN Late Latin *dialogista* from Greek *dialogistēs*, from *dialogos*: see DIALOGUE, -IST.]
1 A writer of dialogue(s). **M17.**
2 A participant in a dialogue. **L17.**
■ **dialoˈgistic** *adjective* having the nature or form of dialogue; taking part in a dialogue, argumentative: **L17.** **dialoˈgistical** *adjective* (*rare*) dialogistic **E18.** **dialoˈgistically** *adverb* **M17.**

dialogize /dʌɪˈalədʒʌɪz/ *verb intrans*. Also **-ise**. **E17.**
[ORIGIN Greek *dialogizesthai* converse, debate, from *dialogos*: see DIALOGUE, -IZE. Cf. earlier DIALOGUIZE.]
Converse, carry on a dialogue (*with*).

dialogue /ˈdʌɪəlɒg/ *noun & verb*. **ME.**
[ORIGIN Old French *dialoge* (mod. *dialogue*) from Latin *dialogus* from Greek *dialogos* conversation, discourse, from *dialegesthai*: see DIALECT.]
▸**A** *noun*. Also ***-log**.
1 A literary work in conversational form; this kind of composition; the conversational part of a novel etc. **ME.**

M. H. ABRAMS The philosopher in the Platonic dialogues . . operates with three categories. A. ROAD A script writer has to tell his story through dialogue.

2 A conversation between two or more people; verbal interchange of thought, discussion. **LME.**

J. FRAME He . . conducted a dialogue with his reason.

3 Discussion or diplomatic contact between representatives of two nations or blocs; the exchange of proposals, valuable or constructive communication between different groups. **M20.**

H. KISSINGER In the nuclear age we cannot be without dialogue with Moscow.

– PHRASES & COMB.: **dialogue box** *COMPUTING* a small area on screen, usually temporarily displayed, in which the user is prompted to provide information or select commands. **dialogue of the deaf** a discussion in which the parties are unresponsive to what the others say.
▸**B** *verb*. **1** *verb trans*. Express in the form of a dialogue; provide (a story etc.) with dialogue. **L16.**
2 *verb intrans*. Take part in a dialogue (*with*). **E17.**
■ **dialoguer** *noun* = DIALOGIST **L19.** **dialoguist** *noun* = DIALOGIST 1 **M18.** **dialoguize** *verb intrans*. (long *rare*) = DIALOGIZE **L16.**

dialysate /dʌɪˈalɪzeɪt/ *noun*. Also ***-lyz-**. **L19.**
[ORIGIN from DIALYSIS, DIALYSE + -ATE[2].]
The part of a mixture which passes through the membrane in dialysis; the solution so obtained. Formerly, the part that does not pass through the membrane.

dialyse /ˈdʌɪəlʌɪz/ *verb*. Also ***-lyze**. **M19.**
[ORIGIN from DIALYSIS after *analyse*.]
1 *verb trans*. Subject to dialysis; obtain by means of dialysis. **M19.**
2 *verb intrans*. Pass through a membrane in dialysis. **E20.**
■ **dialysable** *adjective* able to dialyse or to be separated by dialysis **L19.** **dialyser** *noun* an apparatus for carrying out dialysis, *esp.* an artificial kidney **M19.**

dialysis /dʌɪˈalɪsɪs/ *noun*. Pl. **-lyses** /-lɪsiːz/. **M16.**
[ORIGIN Latin from Greek *dialusis*, from *dialuein* part asunder, formed as DIA-[1] + *luein* set free.]
†**1** *RHETORIC*. A statement of disjunctive propositions. **M–L16.**
†**2** = DIAERESIS 1, 2. **E18–E19.**
3 A process in which solutes are selectively removed from a solution as a result of their different abilities to pass through a semipermeable membrane; the use of such a process to purify the blood, e.g. of a person without adequately functioning kidneys; an occasion of undergoing this. **M19.**
renal dialysis: see RENAL *adjective*.
■ **diaˈlytic** *adjective* **M19.**

dialyzate *noun* see DIALYSATE.

dialyze *verb* see DIALYSE.

diamagnet /dʌɪəˈmagnɪt/ *noun*. **M19.**
[ORIGIN Back-form. from DIAMAGNETIC.]
= DIAMAGNETIC *noun*.

diamagnetic /dʌɪəmagˈnɛtɪk/ *noun & adjective*. **M19.**
[ORIGIN from DIA-[1] + MAGNETIC.]
▸**A** *noun*. A body or substance that exhibits diamagnetism. **M19.**
▸**B** *adjective*. **1** Of a substance or object: having a small negative magnetic susceptibility; magnetizing in a direction opposite to that of an applied magnetic field and repelled by a magnet. **M19.**
2 Of or pertaining to diamagnetism or diamagnetic substances. **M19.**
■ **diamagnetically** *adverb* in a diamagnetic manner; as regards diamagnetism: **M19.**

diamagnetism /dʌɪəˈmagnɪtɪz(ə)m/ *noun*. **M19.**
[ORIGIN from DIA-[1] + MAGNETISM, after DIAMAGNETIC.]
Diamagnetic phenomena; the property of being diamagnetic.

diamanté /dɪəˈmɒnteɪ; *foreign* djamɑ̃te (pl. of noun same)/ *adjective & noun*. **E20.**
[ORIGIN French, pa. pple of *diamanter* set with diamonds, from *diamant* DIAMOND *noun*.]
(Material) given a sparkling effect by means of artificial gems, powdered crystal, etc.

diamantiferous /dʌɪəmənˈtɪf(ə)rəs/ *adjective*. **L19.**
[ORIGIN French *diamantifère*, from *diamant* DIAMOND *noun*: see -I-, -FEROUS.]
= DIAMONDIFEROUS.

diamantine /dʌɪəˈmantɪn, -iːn/ *adjective & noun*. **M16.**
[ORIGIN French *diamantin*, from *diamant* DIAMOND *noun*: see -INE[1].]
▸**A** *adjective*. †**1** Hard as diamond, adamantine. **M16–M17.**
2 Consisting of or of the nature of diamond; containing diamonds. **E17.**
▸**B** *noun*. Powdered boron used as an abrasive. **L19.**

diameter /dʌɪˈamɪtə/ *noun*. **LME.**
[ORIGIN Old French & mod. French *diamètre* from Latin *diametrus*, *-os* from Greek *diametros* (sc. *grammē* line) diagonal, diameter, formed as DIA-[1] + *metron* measure: see -METER.]
1 A straight line passing through the centre of a circle or sphere and ending at the circumference or surface; *MATH*. a similar line through the centre of a conic or a quadric surface; a straight line joining the midpoints of a set of parallel chords of any curve. **LME.**
conjugate diameter: see CONJUGATE *adjective*.
2 The transverse measurement of any geometrical figure or body, esp. of a circle, cylinder, or sphere; *ARCHITECTURE* the transverse measurement of a column at its base, taken as a unit of measurement for the proportions of an order. **LME.** ▸**b** A unit used in expressing the number of times a linear dimension is enlarged by a microscope, in a photograph, etc. **M19.**

b F. O'BRIEN The castor of a bed-leg, magnified to roughly 118 diameters.

in diameter as measured along a diameter.
†**3** The diametrical or direct opposite; contrariety, contradiction. **L16–M17.**
4 The whole extent *of* any region, from one side or end to the other. **E17.**

diametral /dʌɪˈamɪtr(ə)l/ *adjective*. **LME.**
[ORIGIN Old French & mod. French *diamétral* from late Latin *diametralis*, from *diametrus*: see DIAMETER, -AL[1].]
1 Of or pertaining to a diameter; containing or being a diameter. **LME.** ▸†**b** Forming, or situated in, a straight line. **LME–M17.**
†**2** = DIAMETRICAL 2. **E17–M18.**
■ **diametrally** *adverb* (**a**) = DIAMETRICALLY (b); †(**b**) = DIAMETRICALLY (a): **LME.**

diametrical /dʌɪəˈmɛtrɪk(ə)l/ *adjective*. **M16.**
[ORIGIN from Greek *diametrikos*, from *diametros* DIAMETER: see -IC.]
1 = DIAMETRAL 1. **M16.**
2 Of opposition, difference, etc.: entire, complete. **E17.**
†**3** Completely opposed in nature or result. **M17–M18.**
■ **diametric** *adjective* = DIAMETRICAL **E19.** **diametrically** *adverb* (**a**) in the way of direct or complete opposition; directly, completely; (**b**) in the manner or direction of a diameter: **M17.**

diamide /dʌɪˈeɪmʌɪd, -ˈam-; ˈdʌɪəmʌɪd/ *noun*. **M19.**
[ORIGIN from DI-[2] + AMIDE.]
CHEMISTRY. A compound whose molecule contains two amido groups.

diamidine /dʌɪˈamɪdiːn/ *noun*. **M20.**
[ORIGIN from DI-[2] + AMIDINE *noun*[2].]
CHEMISTRY. A compound having a structure based on two amidine groups (usu. joined by a chain of carbon atoms and/or two benzene rings).

diamine /dʌɪˈeɪmiːn, -ˈam-; ˈdʌɪəmiːn/ *noun*. **M19.**
[ORIGIN from DI-[2] + AMINE.]
CHEMISTRY. A compound whose molecule contains two amino groups, esp. when joined to radicals other than acid radicals.

diamond /ˈdʌɪəmənd/ *noun & adjective*. **ME.**
[ORIGIN Old French & mod. French *diamant* from medieval Latin *diamas*, *diamant-* alt. of Latin *adamas* ADAMANT. In sense A.7 from Dutch *diamant*.]
▸**A** *noun*. **1** A usu. colourless or lightly tinted precious stone of great brilliance, hardness, and value, occurring chiefly in alluvial deposits; the allotrope of carbon of which it consists (the hardest naturally occurring substance), used also for cutting and abrading. **ME.** ▸**b** Any crystal or crystalline mineral resembling the diamond in brilliance, *esp.* rock crystal. Usu. with name etc. denoting place of origin. **L16.**
b *Bristol diamond*, *Cornish diamond*, *Quebec diamond*, etc.
†**2** Any substance of extreme hardness; adamant. **LME–M17.**
3 A thing or person of great worth; a person of brilliant attainments etc. **LME.**

G. F. NEWMAN He was betraying a diamond like John Tully to the filth.

4 A rhombus placed with its diagonals horizontal and vertical. Formerly, a solid of octahedral or rhombohedral form. **L15.** ▸**b** *CARDS*. A red rhombus on the face of a playing card. In *pl.* (occas. treated as *sing.*), one of the four suits into which a pack of playing cards is divided, distinguished by such markings; *sing.* a card of this suit. **L16.** ▸**c** *BASEBALL*. The area formed by the four bases; the entire field. **L19.**

b E. LINKLATER Four hearts and a diamond in her hand.

5 *HERALDRY*. The tincture gules in the fanciful blazon of arms of peers. Long *obsolete* exc. *hist.* **L16.**
6 A tool with a small diamond for cutting glass. **L17.**
7 A former small size of type equal to about 4½ points. **L18.**
8 A glittering particle or point. **E19.**

EDWARD THOMAS The great diamonds Of rain on the grassblades.

9 In *pl.* Shares in companies that mine diamonds. **E20.**
10 (The emblem of) one of the highest international awards for gliding. **M20.**
– PHRASES: **black diamond** (**a**) a dark-coloured diamond; (**b**) in *pl.*, coal. **diamond cut diamond** (a situation in which) wit or cunning meets its match. **diamond in the rough** = *rough diamond* s.v. ROUGH *adjective*. *rose diamond*: see ROSE *noun*. *rough diamond*: see ROUGH *adjective*. *table diamond*: see TABLE *noun*.
▸**B** *attrib.* or as *adjective*. **1** Made or consisting of diamond. **M16.** ▸†**b** Hard as diamond; adamantine. **L16–M17.**
2 Of the shape of a diamond, rhombic; forming a design consisting of diamonds. **L16.** ▸**b** Having a surface cut into facets. **E18.**
3 Set with a diamond or diamonds. **E17.**
– COMB. & SPECIAL COLLOCATIONS: **diamond-bird** *Austral.* a pardalote; **diamond-cement**: used in setting diamonds; **diamond crossing** a place where two railway lines cross obliquely without communicating; **diamond-cut** *adjective* (**a**) cut into the shape of a diamond; (**b**) cut with facets like a diamond; **diamond-drill**: set with diamonds for boring any hard substance; **diamond-field** a tract of land yielding diamonds; **diamond frame** a bicycle frame having a diamond shape; **diamond jubilee** the 60th (or 75th) anniversary of a monarch's accession, etc.; **diamond pane** a small diamond-shaped windowpane set in lead (usu. in *pl.*); **diamond-point** (**a**) a diamond-tipped stylus used in engraving; (**b**) a point at a diamond crossing (usu. in *pl.*); **diamond rattlesnake** = *DIAMONDBACK rattlesnake*; **diamond ring effect** *ASTRONOMY* a phenomenon visible at the edge of a total solar eclipse, when the reappearing edge of the sun resembles a diamond ring; **diamond-shaped** *adjective* of the shape of a diamond, rhombic; **diamond snake** any of various snakes with diamond-shaped markings, *esp.* a variety of the Australian python, *Python spilotes*, with yellow markings; **Diamond State** *US* Delaware; **diamond stitch** an embroidery stitch producing a diamond pattern; **diamond wedding** the 60th (or 75th) anniversary of a wedding; **diamond willow** *N. Amer.* (timber from) a willow with a diaper pattern in the bark and wood from leaf scars.
■ **diamondize** *verb trans*. bedeck (as) with diamonds **L16.** **diamond-like** *adjective* resembling (that of) a diamond **M16.** **diamondwise** *adverb* in the manner or form of a diamond **M16.**

diamond /ˈdʌɪəmənd/ *verb trans*. **M18.**
[ORIGIN from the noun.]
Adorn (as) with diamonds.

diamondback /ˈdʌɪəməndbak/ *noun & adjective*. **E19.**
[ORIGIN from DIAMOND *noun* & *adjective* + BACK *noun*[1].]
▸**A** *noun*. A diamondback terrapin, rattlesnake, etc. (see below). **E19.**
▸**B** *adjective*. Having a back with diamond-shaped markings on it. **L19.**

diamondback moth a small grey plutellid moth, *Plutella maculipennis*, which is a pest of vegetables and ornamental plants. **diamondback rattlesnake**, **diamondback rattler** either of two N. American rattlesnakes, *Crotalus adamanteus* or *C. atrox*. ***diamondback terrapin***: see TERRAPIN *noun*[1] 1.
■ **diamondbacked** *adjective* L19.

diamonded /ˈdʌɪəmәndɪd/ *adjective*. M17.
[ORIGIN from DIAMOND *noun, verb*: see -ED[2], -ED[1].]
1 Marked or covered with diamond shapes; having such a shape. M17.
2 Adorned (as) with diamonds; wearing diamonds. M19.

D

diamondiferous /dʌɪəmənˈdɪf(ə)rəs/ *adjective*. L19.
[ORIGIN from DIAMOND *noun* + -I- + -FEROUS.]
Yielding diamonds.

diamorphine /dʌɪəˈmɔːfiːn/ *noun*. E20.
[ORIGIN Abbreviation.]
= DIACETYLMORPHINE.

†**dian** *noun*[1]. Also **diana**. L16–L17.
[ORIGIN French *diane* from Spanish *diana* reveille, from *dia* day.]
A trumpet call or drum roll at early morning, reveille.

MARVELL The bee through these known allies hums Beating the dian with its drums.

Dian *noun*[2] see DIANA *noun*[1].

Diana /dʌɪˈanə/ *noun*[1]. Also **Dian** /ˈdʌɪən/; (sense 3) **diana**. LME.
[ORIGIN Latin, the Roman moon goddess and patron of virginity and hunting, whence also Old French & mod. French *Diane*.]
1 The moon. *poet*. LME.
2 A young woman with the chastity or hunting skill of the goddess Diana. L18.
3 More fully ***Diana monkey***. A tropical W. African tree monkey, *Cercopithecus diana*, with a crescentic white mark on its forehead. E19.
– PHRASES: ***tree of Diana***: see TREE *noun*.

†**diana** *noun*[2] var. of DIAN *noun*[1].

diandrous /dʌɪˈandrəs/ *adjective*. L18.
[ORIGIN from DI-[2] + Greek *anēr*, *andr-* man + -OUS.]
1 BOTANY. Having two stamens. L18.
2 ZOOLOGY. Having two male mates. L19.
■ **diandry** *noun* (BIOLOGY) fertilization in which two sets of chromosomes are contributed by a sperm or sperms M20.

Dianetics /dʌɪəˈnɛtɪks/ *noun*. Also **d-**. M20.
[ORIGIN formed as DIANOETIC: see -ICS.]
A system developed by the American writer L. Ron Hubbard (1911–86) which has as its aim the relief of psychosomatic disorder by a process of cleansing the mind of harmful mental images.
■ **dianetic** *adjective* M20.

dianoetic /dʌɪənəʊˈɛtɪk/ *adjective*. L17.
[ORIGIN Greek *dianoētikos*, from *dianoeisthai* think, formed as DIA-[1] + *noein* think, suppose: see NOETIC.]
PHILOSOPHY. Of or pertaining to thought; intellectual.
■ †**dianoetical** *adjective* = DIANOETIC L16–L17. **dianoetically** *adverb* E19.

dianthus /dʌɪˈanθəs/ *noun*. L18.
[ORIGIN from Greek *Dios* of Zeus + *anthos* flower.]
A plant of the genus *Dianthus*, of the pink family, which besides pinks includes other fragrant plants with pink or reddish flowers.

diapalma /dʌɪəˈpalmə/ *noun*. Now *rare* or *obsolete*. M17.
[ORIGIN medieval Latin, formed as DIA-[2] + Latin *palma* PALM *noun*[1].]
A desiccating plaster composed originally of palm oil, litharge, and zinc sulphate.

diapase *noun* see DIAPASON.

diapasm /ˈdʌɪəpaz(ə)m/ *noun*. *arch*. L16.
[ORIGIN Latin *diapasma* from Greek, from *diapassein* sprinkle over.]
A scented powder for sprinkling over the person.

diapason /dʌɪəˈpeɪs(ə)n, -z-/ *noun & verb*. Also (*poet*.) **diapase** /ˈdʌɪəpeɪz/. LME.
[ORIGIN Latin *diapason* from Greek *diapasōn*, i.e. *dia pasōn* (*khordōn*) through all (notes).]
▸ **A** *noun*. **1** The interval of an octave; the consonance of two notes an octave apart; a part in music producing such a consonance. Now *rare* & chiefly *hist*. LME. ▸†**b** *fig*. Complete harmony or agreement. L16–L18.

BACON The true Coincidence of Tones into Diapasons.

2 a The combination of notes or parts in a harmonious whole; a melody; *esp*. a swelling sound; a grand burst of harmony; a rich, deep burst of sound. E16. ▸**b** The whole range of notes in the scale; the compass of a voice or musical instrument. L17. ▸**c** Range, spectrum, scope. M19.

a H. M. STANLEY A deep and melodious diapason of musical voices. R. H. BARHAM Full many an Aldermanic nose Rolled its loud diapason after dinner. **c** A. HELPS In marriage the whole diapason of joy and sorrow is sounded.

3 Either of two foundation stops in an organ (***open diapason***, ***stopped diapason***), of which the open diapason gives the sound most characteristic of an organ; any of various other stops with flue pipes giving a similar quality of tone. E16.

4 A fixed standard of musical pitch, *spec*. 435 Hz (now superseded). M19.
▸ **B** *verb trans. & intrans*. Resound sonorously. E17.

diapause /ˈdʌɪəpɔːz/ *noun & verb*. L19.
[ORIGIN from DIA-[1] + PAUSE *noun*.]
BIOLOGY. ▸**A** *noun*. A period of retarded or suspended development. L19.
▸ **B** *verb intrans*. Undergo or be in diapause. Chiefly as ***diapausing*** *ppl adjective*. M20.

diapedesis /dʌɪəpəˈdiːsɪs/ *noun*. E17.
[ORIGIN mod. Latin from Greek, ult. formed as DIA-[1] + *pēdan* leap, throb.]
MEDICINE. The passage of red blood cells through the apparently intact walls of the capillaries, as in acute inflammation.

diapente /dʌɪəˈpɛnti/ *noun*. Now *rare* & chiefly *hist*. LME.
[ORIGIN Old French from late Latin, from Greek *dia pente* composed of five: see DIA-[2]. Cf. DIAPASON.]
1 MUSIC. The interval of a fifth. LME.
2 a A medicine composed of five ingredients. E17. ▸†**b** A drink made of five ingredients; punch. L17–M18.

diaper /ˈdʌɪəpə/ *noun & adjective*. ME.
[ORIGIN Old French *dia(s)pre* from medieval Latin *diasprum* from medieval Greek *diaspros* adjective, formed as DIA-[1] + *aspros* white.]
▸ **A** *noun*. **1** A kind of textile, since the 15th cent. a linen or cotton material woven so that it consists of a pattern of small diamonds, each filled with some device. ME.
2 A towel, napkin, etc., of this material; (now chiefly *N. Amer.*) a baby's nappy (orig. made of diaper). L16.
3 A geometrical or ornamental design in which a panel, shield, etc., is covered by diamonds; any space-filling geometrical pattern. M17.
▸ **B** *adjective*. **1** (Made) of diaper. LME.
2 Having a pattern of diamonds, diapered. LME.
■ **diapery** *noun* (*rare*) †(***a***) diaper; (***b***) = DIAPERING (b): LME.

diaper /ˈdʌɪəpə/ *verb trans*. LME.
[ORIGIN from DIAPER *noun & adjective*: cf. Old French & mod. French *diaprer*, *diapré* diapered.]
▸**I 1** Decorate with a small uniform pattern, esp. of diamonds. LME.
2 Adorn with diversely coloured details; variegate. L16.
▸**II 3** Change the nappy of (a baby). *N. Amer*. M20.
■ **diapering** *noun* (***a***) the action of the verb; (***b***) diapered decoration or patterns: LME.

diaphane /ˈdʌɪəfeɪn/ *adjective & noun*. M16.
[ORIGIN Old French & mod. French from medieval Latin *diaphanus* DIAPHANOUS.]
▸ †**A** *adjective*. Transparent; diaphanous. M16–E19.
▸ **B** *noun*. **1** A transparent body or substance. M19.
2 A light figured silk fabric. L19.
■ **diaphaˈneity** *noun* transparency M17. †**diaphanity** *noun* = DIAPHANEITY L15–M17.

diaphanie /dɪˈafəni/ *noun*. M19.
[ORIGIN French, formed as DIAPHANE.]
A process for imitating painted or stained glass by means of coloured paper.

diaphanous /dʌɪˈaf(ə)nəs/ *adjective*. E17.
[ORIGIN medieval Latin *diaphanus* from Greek *diaphanēs*, formed as DIA-[1] + *phainein*, *phan-* to show: see -OUS.]
Transparent; translucent; *esp*. (of a fabric etc.) so light and insubstantial as to be almost transparent.

J. CONRAD Mist.. draping the.. shores in diaphanous folds. *Premiere* A diaphanous black cape.

■ **diaphanously** *adverb* L17.

diaphone /ˈdʌɪəfəʊn/ *noun*. E20.
[ORIGIN from DIA-[1] + -PHONE, PHONE *noun*[1].]
1 A low-pitched fog signal operated by compressed air, characterized by the 'grunt' which ends each note. E20.
2 LINGUISTICS. = DIAPHONEME. M20.

diaphoneme /ˈdʌɪəˌfəʊniːm/ *noun*. M20.
[ORIGIN from DIA-[1] + PHONEME.]
LINGUISTICS. A phonemic unit of a language comprising a set of systematically corresponding forms from all its dialects. Also, each dialectal variant of such a set.
■ **diaphoˈnemic** *adjective* M20. **diaphoˈnemically** *adverb* M20.

diaphonic /dʌɪəˈfɒnɪk/ *adjective*. L18.
[ORIGIN In sense 1 from DIAPHONICS: see -IC. In sense 2 formed as DIAPHONY. In sense 3 from DIAPHONE.]
†**1** Of or pertaining to diaphonics. *rare*. L18–M19.
2 Of or pertaining to diaphony. E19.
3 LINGUISTICS. Of or pertaining to a diaphone. M20.
■ **diaphonically** *adverb* (LINGUISTICS) M20.

†**diaphonics** *noun pl*. L17–E18.
[ORIGIN from DIA-[1] + Greek *phōnē* sound + -ICS.]
= DIACOUSTICS.

diaphony /dʌɪˈaf(ə)ni/ *noun*. M17.
[ORIGIN Late Latin *diaphonia* dissonance from Greek, from *diaphōnos* dissonant, formed as DIA-[1]: see -PHONY.]
1 (A) dissonance. *rare*. M17.
2 EARLY MUSIC. Two-part polyphony. M19.

diaphorase /dʌɪˈafəreɪz/ *noun*. M20.
[ORIGIN from Greek *diaphoros* different + -ASE.]
BIOCHEMISTRY. A flavoprotein enzyme able to oxidize a reduced form of NAD.

diaphoresis /dʌɪəfəˈriːsɪs/ *noun*. L17.
[ORIGIN Late Latin from Greek, from *diaphorein* carry away, dissipate by sweating, formed as DIA-[1] + *phorein* carry.]
MEDICINE. Sweating, *esp*. artificially induced sweating.
■ **diaphoretic** /-ˈrɛtɪk/ *adjective & noun* (an agent) that induces or promotes sweating LME.

diaphototropic /ˌdʌɪəfəʊtəˈtrɒpɪk, -ˈtrəʊp-/ *adjective*. E20.
[ORIGIN from DIA-[1] + PHOTOTROPIC *adjective*.]
BOTANY. = DIAHELIOTROPIC.
■ **diaphototropism** *noun* E20.

diaphragm /ˈdʌɪəfram/ *noun & verb*. LME.
[ORIGIN Late Latin *diaphragma* from Greek, formed as DIA-[1] + *phragma* fence.]
▸ **A** *noun*. **1** The muscular sheet which in mammals separates the thoracic and abdominal cavities and whose contraction leads to expansion of the lungs in respiration. LME.
2 ZOOLOGY. A septum separating successive chambers of a shell. M17.
3 BOTANY. A layer of cells forming a partition in plant tissue. M17.
4 An opaque disc or plate with a central hole for restricting the light entering an optical instrument; *esp*. one in a camera that enables the effective aperture to be varied. M17.
iris diaphragm.
5 A taut flexible membrane, esp. in various mechanical and acoustic devices. M19.

G. J. KING Microphones.. must have some sort of diaphragm or element which responds to the sound wave.

6 A thin bowl-shaped piece of rubber or plastic made to be inserted into the vagina and over the cervix as a contraceptive. M20.
▸ **B** *verb trans*. Provide (esp. a lens) with a diaphragm; subject (light) to the effect of a diaphragm. M17.
diaphragm down reduce the aperture of (a lens) with a diaphragm.
■ **diaphragmatic** /-fragˈmatɪk/ *adjective* of or pertaining to a diaphragm, of the nature of a diaphragm M17. **diaphragˈmatically** *adverb* by means of the diaphragm or a diaphragm L19.

diaphthoresis /dʌɪafθəˈriːsɪs/ *noun*. Pl **-reses** /-ˈriːsiːz/. M20.
[ORIGIN from Greek *diaphtheirein* destroy utterly, after nouns in *-oresis*.]
PETROGRAPHY. Retrograde metamorphism.

diaphysis /dʌɪˈafɪsɪs/ *noun*. Pl. **-physes** /-fɪsiːz/. M19.
[ORIGIN Greek *diaphusis* growing through, formed as DIA-[1] + *phusis* growth.]
ANATOMY. The shaft or central part of a long bone; *spec*. the part ossified from the main centre of ossification.

diapir /ˈdʌɪəpɪə/ *noun*. E20.
[ORIGIN from Greek *diapeirainein* pierce through, formed as DIA-[1] + *peirainein*, from *peran* pierce.]
GEOLOGY. An anticline in which a core of rock has moved upward to pierce the overlying strata.
■ **diapiric** /-ˈpɪrɪk/ *adjective* of or pertaining to a diapir; having a structure characterized by an upward protruding body of rock, sediment, etc.: M20. **diaˈpirically** *adverb* in the manner of a diapir, with local upwelling M20. **diapirism** *noun* diapiric activity; a localized upward motion of rock, sediment, etc.: M20.

diapophysis /dʌɪəˈpɒfɪsɪs/ *noun*. Pl. **-physes** /-fɪsiːz/. M19.
[ORIGIN from DIA-[1] + APOPHYSIS.]
ANATOMY & ZOOLOGY. Each of a pair of transverse processes on the superior or dorsal side of a vertebra.

diaporesis /dʌɪəpəˈriːsɪs/ *noun*. L17.
[ORIGIN mod. Latin from Greek = being at a loss.]
A rhetorical figure in which the speaker professes to be uncertain which of two or more courses, statements, etc., to adopt.

diapositive /dʌɪəˈpɒzɪtɪv/ *noun*. L19.
[ORIGIN from DIA-[1] + POSITIVE *noun*.]
A positive photographic slide or transparency.

†**diapre** *adjective*. M16–E18.
[ORIGIN French *diapré* pa. pple of *diaprer* to diaper, from Old French *diapre* DIAPER *noun*.]
HERALDRY. Diapered.

diapsid /dʌɪˈapsɪd/ *adjective & noun*. E20.
[ORIGIN mod. Latin *Diapsida*, from DI-[2] + Greek *(h)apsid-*, *(h)apsis* arch.]
ZOOLOGY. (Pertaining to or designating) a reptile whose skull has two pairs of temporal arches.

diarch /ˈdʌɪɑːk/ *adjective*. L19.
[ORIGIN from DI-[2] + Greek *arkhē* origin.]
BOTANY. Of the primary xylem of the root: arising from two distinct points of origin. Of a root: having such xylem.

diarchy /ˈdʌɪɑːki/ *noun*. Also **dy-**. M19.
[ORIGIN from DI-[2] after *monarchy*.]
A mode of joint government by two; government by two independent authorities; *spec*. the system of provincial government in India from 1921 to 1937.
■ **diˈarchal**, **diˈarchial**, **diˈarchic** *adjectives* E20.

diarial /dʌɪˈɛːrɪəl/ *adjective*. M19.
[ORIGIN from Latin *diarium* DIARY *noun* + -AL[1] or from DIARY *noun* + -IAL.]
Of, pertaining to, or of the nature of a diary or journal.

diarian /dʌɪ'ɛːrɪən/ *adjective*. Now *rare* or *obsolete*. **L18.**
[**ORIGIN** formed as **DIARIAL** + **-AN**, **-IAN**.]
= **DIARIAL**. Formerly also, journalistic.

diarise *verb* var. of **DIARIZE**.

diarist /'dʌɪərɪst/ *noun*. **E19.**
[**ORIGIN** from **DIARY** *noun* + **-IST**.]
The author of a diary; a person who keeps a diary.
■ **dia'ristic** *adjective* of the style of a diarist; of the nature of a diary: **L19.**

diarize /'dʌɪərʌɪz/ *verb*. Also **-ise**. **L18.**
[**ORIGIN** from **DIARY** *noun* + **-IZE**.]
1 *verb intrans*. Keep a diary, write in a diary. **L18.**
2 *verb trans*. Record in a diary. **L19.**

diarrhoea /dʌɪə'rɪə/ *noun*. Also ***-rrhea**. **LME.**
[**ORIGIN** Late Latin from Greek *diarrhoia*, from *diarrhein* flow through, formed as **DIA-**[1]: see **-RRHOEA**.]
A condition of excessively frequent and loose bowel movements. Also, watery or semi-liquid faeces characteristic of this condition.

fig.: **HOR. WALPOLE** He . . was troubled with a diarrhoea of words.

verbal diarrhoea: see **VERBAL** *adjective* 2.
■ **diarrhoeal** *adjective* of, pertaining to, or affected with diarrhoea; of the nature of or characterized by diarrhoea: **M17.** **diarrhoeic** *adjective* = **DIARRHOEAL** **L19.**

diarthrosis /dʌɪɑː'θrəʊsɪs/ *noun*. Pl. **-throses** /-'θrəʊsiːz/. **L16.**
[**ORIGIN** Greek *diarthrōsis*, formed as **DI-**[3], **ARTHROSIS**.]
ANATOMY. Any articulation that allows one bone to move freely against another; a freely movable joint.
■ **diarthrodial** *adjective* **M19.**

diary /'dʌɪəri/ *noun*. **L16.**
[**ORIGIN** Latin *diarium* journal, diary, (in pl.) daily allowance, from *dies* day: see **-ARY**[1]. In sense 3 ellipt. for *diary fever*.]
1 A daily record of events, transactions, thoughts, etc., esp. ones involving the writer. **L16.**

D. FRASER He began to keep . . a private diary of his thoughts and experiences.

2 A book in which to keep such a record, usu. having dates printed in it; a book or calendar with daily memoranda, esp. for people with a particular interest; a person's list of forthcoming engagements. **E17.**
DESK ***diary***.
†**3** A fever or other illness lasting only for a day. **M–L17.**

diary /'dʌɪəri/ *adjective*. Now *rare* or *obsolete*. **L16.**
[**ORIGIN** medieval Latin *diarius* daily, from Latin *dies* day: see **-ARY**[1].]
†**1** Daily. **L16–E17.**
2 Lasting for one day; short-lived. Esp. in ***diary fever***. **E17.**

diasceuast, **diascevast** *nouns* vars. of **DIASKEUAST**.

diascope /'dʌɪəskəʊp/ *noun*. **M20.**
[**ORIGIN** from **DIA-**[1] + **-SCOPE**.]
A projector for use with transparencies.
■ **dia'scopic** *adjective* **E20.**

†**diascordium** *noun*. **E17–E19.**
[**ORIGIN** mod. Latin, from Greek *dia scordiōn*: see **DIA-**[2], **SCORDIUM**.]
A medicine made from the dried leaves of various herbs.

diaskeuast /dʌɪə'skjuːast/ *noun*. Also **-sceuast**, **-scevast** /-'siːvast/. **E19.**
[**ORIGIN** Greek *diaskeuastēs* reviser of a poem, interpolator, from *diaskeuazein* edit, formed as **DIA-**[1] + *skeuazein* make ready.]
A reviser; *esp*. a person who made one of the old recensions of Greek writings.

diaspora /dʌɪ'asp(ə)rə/ *noun*. Also **D-**. **L19.**
[**ORIGIN** Greek, from *diaspeirein* disperse, formed as **DIA-**[1] + *speirein* sow, scatter.]
The dispersion of Jews among the Gentile nations; all those Jews who live outside the biblical land of Israel; (the situation of) any body of people living outside their traditional homeland.
– **NOTE**: The term originated in *Deuteronomy* 28:25 (Septuagint).
■ **diasporic** *adjective* **L19.**

diaspore /'dʌɪəspɔː/ *noun*. **E19.**
[**ORIGIN** Greek *diaspora* (the mineral was so named because of its decrepitation): see **DIASPORA**.]
1 *MINERALOGY*. Native aluminium hydrogen oxide, $HAlO_2$, occurring esp. in bauxite and clay as transparent or translucent orthorhombic crystals of various colours. **E19.**
2 *BOTANY*. A spore, seed, or other structure that functions in plant dispersal; a propagule. **M20.**

diastaltic /dʌɪə'staltɪk/ *adjective*. **L17.**
[**ORIGIN** Greek *diastaltikos* serving to distinguish or expand, from *diastellein*: see **DIASTOLE** *noun*.]
1 Of ancient Greek music: tending to exalt the mind, exhilarating; contrasted with **SYSTALTIC** *adjective* 2. *rare*. **L17.**
2 *PHYSIOLOGY*. Reflex. Now *rare*. **M19.**

diastase /'dʌɪəsteɪz/ *noun*. **M19.**
[**ORIGIN** formed as **DIASTASIS**. Cf. **-ASE**.]
BIOCHEMISTRY. An amylase, *esp*. one that hydrolyses starch to maltose and is present in seeds and the pancreas.
■ **dia'static** *adjective* pertaining to or of the nature of diastase **L19.** **dia'statically** *adverb* as diastase **L19.**

diastasis /dʌɪə'steɪsɪs/ *noun*. Pl. **-ases** /-eɪsiːz/. Now *rare*. **E18.**
[**ORIGIN** mod. Latin from Greek = separation, formed as **DIA-**[1] + *stasis* placing.]
MEDICINE. Separation of two parts of a bone without fracture, esp. of an epiphysis from a long bone.

diastem /'dʌɪəstɛm/ *noun*. **L17.**
[**ORIGIN** Greek *diastēma*: see **DIASTEMA**.]
1 In ancient Greek music, an interval, *esp*. one forming a single degree of the scale. **L17.**
2 *GEOLOGY*. A period when there was a temporary halt to deposition; a non-sequence. **E20.**

diastema /dʌɪə'stiːmə/ *noun*. Pl. **-mata** /-mətə/. **LME.**
[**ORIGIN** Late Latin *diastema* from Greek, = space between.]
1 = **DIASTEM** 1. **LME.**
2 *ZOOLOGY & ANATOMY*. A gap separating teeth of one kind from those of another, found in most mammals except humans. **M19.**
■ **diaste'matic** *adjective* **M17.**

diaster /dʌɪ'astə/ *noun*. **L19.**
[**ORIGIN** from **DI-**[2] + **ASTER**.]
CYTOLOGY. The stage in mitosis when the chromosomes are in two groups near the poles of the spindle, prior to forming daughter nuclei. Formerly, the pattern of the chromosomes at this stage.
■ **diastral** *adjective* **L19.**

diastereoisomer /ˌdʌɪəstɛrɪəʊ'ʌɪsəmə/ *noun*. **M20.**
[**ORIGIN** from **DIA-**[1] + **STEREOISOMER**.]
CHEMISTRY. Either of a pair of stereoisomeric compounds that are not mirror images of one another.
■ **diaˌstereoiso'meric** *adjective* **E20.**

diastole /dʌɪ'astəli/ *noun*. **L16.**
[**ORIGIN** Late Latin from Greek = separation, expansion, dilatation, from *diastellein*, formed as **DIA-**[1] + *stellein* put, place.]
1 *PHYSIOLOGY*. The phase of the heartbeat when the heart relaxes, dilates, and fills with blood. Formerly also, the expansion of the lungs in breathing. Opp. **SYSTOLE**. **L16.**

fig.: **GEO. ELIOT** There must be a systole and diastole in all inquiry.

2 *CLASSICAL PROSODY*. The lengthening of a naturally short syllable. **L16.**
3 *GREEK GRAMMAR*. A mark (originally semicircular) used to indicate the separation of words, still occas. used in the form of a comma to distinguish a few confusable words. **E18.**
■ **dia'stolic** *adjective* **L17.**

diastrophism /dʌɪ'astrəfɪz(ə)m/ *noun*. **L19.**
[**ORIGIN** from Greek *diastrophē* distortion, dislocation, ult. formed as **DIA-**[1] + *strephein* to turn: see **-ISM**.]
The disturbances and dislocations of the earth's crust which have produced the major inequalities of its surface.
■ **diastrophic** /-'strəʊfɪk, -'strɒfɪk/ *adjective* **L19.**

diastyle /'dʌɪəstʌɪl/ *adjective & noun*. Also (earlier) †**-stylos**. **M16.**
[**ORIGIN** Partly from Latin *diastylos* from Greek *diastulos* having a space between the columns; partly from Greek *diastulion* intercolumnar space; both ult. formed as **DIA-**[1] + *stulos* column.]
ARCHITECTURE. (A colonnade etc.) having a distance between columns equal to three (or four) diameters (in the Doric order 2¾); (a distance between columns) equal to this number of diameters.

diasyrm /'dʌɪəsəːm/ *noun*. Also (earlier) †**-syrmus**. **M16.**
[**ORIGIN** Late Latin *diasyrmus* from Greek *diasurmos* disparagement.]
A rhetorical figure expressing disparagement or ridicule.

diasystem /'dʌɪəsɪstəm/ *noun*. **M20.**
[**ORIGIN** from **DIA-**[1] + **SYSTEM**.]
LINGUISTICS. A linguistic macro system constructed by treating phonological variants between dialects as part of a continuum of variation.
■ **diasy'stemic** *adjective* **L20.**

diatessaron /dʌɪə'tɛsərən/ *noun*. **LME.**
[**ORIGIN** Late Latin, from Greek *dia tessarōn* composed of four: see **DIA-**[2].]
1 *MUSIC*. The interval of a fourth. Now *rare* & chiefly *hist*. **LME.**
2 A medicine composed of four ingredients. Now *rare* & chiefly *hist*. **LME.**
3 An arrangement of the four Gospels as one narrative. **L16.**

diathermacy /dʌɪə'θəːməsi/ *noun*. **M19.**
[**ORIGIN** French *diathermasie* from Greek *diathermasia* a warming through, formed as **DIA-**[1] + *thermasia* heat, with assim. to **-ACY**.]
= **DIATHERMANCY** 2.

diathermal /dʌɪə'θəːm(ə)l/ *adjective*. **M19.**
[**ORIGIN** from **DIA-**[1] + **THERMAL** *adjective*.]
= **DIATHERMANOUS**.

diathermancy /dʌɪə'θəːm(ə)nsi/ *noun*. **M19.**
[**ORIGIN** French *diathermansie*, formed as **DIA-**[1] + Greek *thermansis* heating, with assim. to **-ANCY**.]
†**1** The property of radiant heat of comprising radiation with different wavelengths and refrangibilities. Only in **M19.**
2 The property of being diathermanous. **M19.**

diathermaneity /ˌdʌɪəθəːmə'niːəti/ *noun*. *rare*. **M19.**
[**ORIGIN** French *diathermanéité*, from *diathermane* (see **DIATHERMANOUS**) after *diaphanéité* **DIAPHANEITY**.]
= **DIATHERMANCY** 2.

diathermanous /dʌɪə'θəːmənəs/ *adjective*. **M19.**
[**ORIGIN** French *diathermane*, formed as **DIA-**[1] + Greek *thermē*, *thermon* heat after **DIAPHANE**: see **-OUS**.]
Transparent to infrared radiation.

diathermic /dʌɪə'θəːmɪk/ *adjective*. **M19.**
[**ORIGIN** French *diathermique*, formed as **DIA-**[1] + Greek *thermē*, *thermon* heat: see **-IC**.]
1 = **DIATHERMANOUS**. **M19.**
2 Of or pertaining to diathermy. **E20.**
■ **diathermically** *adverb* by means of a diathermic current **E20.** **diathermous** *adjective* = **DIATHERMANOUS** **M19.**

diathermy /'dʌɪəθəːmi/ *noun*. **E20.**
[**ORIGIN** from **DIA-**[1] + Greek *thermos* heat + **-Y**[3].]
MEDICINE. The generation of heat inside the body by passing high-frequency electric currents through it using external electrodes.
medical diathermy: in which the tissues are merely warmed. **surgical diathermy**: in which there is local cauterization etc.

diathesis /dʌɪ'aθəsɪs/ *noun*. Pl. **-eses** /-əsiːz/. **M17.**
[**ORIGIN** mod. Latin from Greek = disposition, from *diatithenai* arrange.]
1 *MEDICINE*. A constitutional predisposition to a particular disease or condition; constitution. **M17.**

fig.: **H. J. S. MAINE** The intellectual diathesis of the modern world.

2 *LINGUISTICS*. The voice of a verb. **M20.**
■ **dia'thetic** *adjective* **M19.** **dia'thetically** *adverb* **L19.**

diatom /'dʌɪətəm/ *noun*. **M19.**
[**ORIGIN** mod. Latin *Diatoma* genus name, from Greek *diatomos* (adjective) cut in two, from *diatemnein* to cut through.]
A microscopic unicellular alga that has a rigid siliceous cell wall and occurs esp. as plankton and as a fossil in diatomaceous earth.
■ **diatomaceous** /-'meɪʃəs/ *adjective* (*a*) of or pertaining to diatoms; (*b*) consisting of or formed from the fossil remains of diatoms (***diatomaceous earth***, a soft friable porous material used esp. for filters and insulation): **M19.**

diatomic /dʌɪə'tɒmɪk/ *adjective & noun*. **M19.**
[**ORIGIN** from **DI-**[2] + **ATOMIC**.]
CHEMISTRY. ▶**A** *adjective*. Consisting of two atoms. Also, dibasic, divalent. **M19.**
▶**B** *noun*. A diatomic compound. **M20.**

diatomite /dʌɪ'atəmʌɪt/ *noun*. **L19.**
[**ORIGIN** from **DIATOM** + **-ITE**[1].]
Diatomaceous earth; a sedimentary rock resembling chert, formed by the consolidation of this.

diatonic /dʌɪə'tɒnɪk/ *adjective*. **E17.**
[**ORIGIN** Old French & mod. French *diatonique* or late Latin *diatonicus*, from Greek *diatonikos* at intervals of a tone, formed as **DIA-**[1] + *tonos* **TONE** *noun*: see **-IC**.]
MUSIC. **1** *hist*. Designating (ancient Greek music based on) a tetrachord divided into two tones and a lower semitone. **E17.**
2 Using only the notes proper to one key without chromatic alteration; based on a scale with five tones and two separated semitones. **L17.**

G. MEREDITH Crossjay's voice ran up and down a diatonic scale. **A. HOPKINS** Diatonic notes are those which 'belong' to a particular scale. **C. IVES** The first movement . . is primarily diatonic.

■ **diatonically** *adverb* **E18.** **diatonicism** /-sɪz(ə)m/ *noun* (an instance of) the use of diatonic tonality **M20.** **di'atonism** *noun* = **DIATONICISM** **E20.**

diatreme /'dʌɪətriːm/ *noun*. **E20.**
[**ORIGIN** from **DIA-**[1] + Greek *trēma* perforation.]
GEOLOGY. A long vertical pipe or plug formed when gas-filled magma forced its way up through rock.

diatribe /'dʌɪətrʌɪb/ *noun*. **L16.**
[**ORIGIN** French from Latin *diatriba* learned discussion from Greek *diatribē* spending of time, discourse, formed as **DIA-**[1] + *tribein* rub.]
1 A discourse, a disquisition. *arch*. **L16.**
2 A dissertation or discourse directed against a particular person or work; a piece of bitter criticism; scolding, denunciation. **E19.**

C. KINGSLEY A rambling, bitter diatribe on the wrongs and sufferings of the labourers. **H. JAMES** Diatribes against the British middle-class.

■ **diatribist** *noun* a person who writes or utters a diatribe **M17.**

diaulos /dʌɪ'ɔːləs/ *noun*. **E18.**
[**ORIGIN** Greek, formed as **DI-**[2] + *aulos* pipe.]
GREEK ANTIQUITIES. A double course in which the racers rounded a goal and returned to the starting point.

diazepam /dʌɪ'azɪpam, -'eɪz-/ *noun*. **M20.**
[**ORIGIN** from **BENZO)DIAZEP(INE** + **AM(IDE)**.]
PHARMACOLOGY. A tranquillizer of the benzodiazepine group, $C_{16}H_{13}N_2OCl$, used esp. as an anti-anxiety agent, hypnotic, and muscle relaxant.
– **NOTE**: A proprietary name for this drug is **VALIUM**.

D

D

diazeuctic /dʌɪəˈzjuːktɪk/ *adjective*. L17.
[ORIGIN Greek *diazeuktikos* disjunctive, ult. from *zeugnunai* to join: see DIA-¹.]
In ancient Greek music, designating a tone separating two tetrachords, and tetrachords so separated.

diazine /ˈdʌɪəziːn/ *noun*. E20.
[ORIGIN from DI-² + AZINE.]
CHEMISTRY. Any compound whose molecule contains a six-membered ring of four carbon and two nitrogen atoms; *spec.* each of the three simplest such compounds (pyrazine, pyridazine, and pyrimidine).

diazinon /dʌɪˈazɪnɒn/ *noun*. M20.
[ORIGIN from DIAZINE + *-on* of unknown origin.]
An organophosphorus insecticide derived from pyrimidine.

diazo /dʌɪˈazəʊ, -ˈeɪzəʊ/ *adjective & noun*. M20.
[ORIGIN Abbreviation of DIAZOTYPE.]
▸ **A** *adjective*. Designating or pertaining to a process which employs the effect of light on material sensitized with a diazonium compound. M20.
▸ **B** *noun*. Pl. **-os**. (A copy made by) the diazo process. M20.

diazo- /dʌɪˈazəʊ, -ˈeɪzəʊ/ *combining form*. Also as attrib. adjective **diazo** (cf. prec.).
[ORIGIN from DI-² + AZO-.]
CHEMISTRY. Indicating the presence of two nitrogen atoms, now *spec.* the group ·N=N· joined to one carbon atom. Cf. AZO-, DIAZONIUM.
■ **diazo'methane** *noun* a poisonous yellow gas, CH_2N_2, used as a methylating agent L19.

diazoma /dʌɪəˈzəʊmə/ *noun*. Pl. **-mata** /-mətə/. E18.
[ORIGIN Latin from Greek = girdle, partition, etc.]
1 A semicircular passage in the auditorium of an ancient Greek theatre, parallel to its outer border and about halfway up the tiers of steps. E18.
†**2** ANATOMY. The diaphragm. E18–L19.

diazonium /dʌɪəˈzəʊnɪəm/ *noun*. L19.
[ORIGIN from DIAZO- + -ONIUM.]
CHEMISTRY. The monovalent ion $·N_2^+$ when attached to a carbon atom in an organic (usu. aromatic) compound. Usu. in *comb.*

diazotize /dʌɪˈazətʌɪz, -ˈeɪz-/ *verb trans.* Also **-ise**. L19.
[ORIGIN from DIAZO- + -IZE, after AZOTE.]
CHEMISTRY. Convert (esp. an aromatic amine) into a diazo or diazonium compound or group, e.g. in dye manufacture.
■ **diazotizable** *adjective* L19. **diazoti'zation** *noun* L19.

diazotype /dʌɪˈazəʊtʌɪp, -ˈeɪz-/ *noun*. L19.
[ORIGIN from DIAZO- + -TYPE.]
A diazo copying or colouring process.

dib *noun* var. of DUB *noun*¹.

dib /dɪb/ *verb*. Infl. **-bb-**. E17.
[ORIGIN Alt. of DAB *verb*.]
1 *verb trans. & intrans.* Dab lightly, tap. E17.
2 *verb intrans.* Dap for fish. L17.
3 *verb trans. & intrans.* = DIBBLE *verb*¹ 1, 2. *dial.* M18.
■ **dibber** *noun* = DIBBLE *noun* M18.

dibasic /dʌɪˈbeɪsɪk/ *adjective*. M19.
[ORIGIN from DI-² + BASIC *adjective*.]
CHEMISTRY. Of an acid: having two replaceable hydrogen atoms. Formerly also, divalent.
■ **dibasicity** /dʌɪbeɪˈsɪsɪti/ *noun* dibasic quality L19.

dibatag /ˈdɪbətag/ *noun*. L19.
[ORIGIN Somali.]
An antelope, *Ammodorcas clarkei*, with recurved horns, found in Somalia and eastern Ethiopia.

dibble /ˈdɪb(ə)l/ *noun & verb*¹. LME.
[ORIGIN App. connected with DIB *verb*: see -LE¹.]
▸ **A** *noun*. A pointed instrument for making holes in the ground for bulbs etc. LME.
▸ **B** *verb*. **1** *verb trans.* Make a hole in (the soil) with or as with a dibble; sow or plant by this means. (Foll. by *in*.) M16.
2 *verb intrans.* Use a dibble; make holes in the soil. L18.
■ **dibbler** *noun* (**a**) a person who dibbles; (**b**) an agricultural implement for dibbling; (**c**) a marsupial mouse, *Antechinus apicalis*, of Australia: E19.

dibble /ˈdɪb(ə)l/ *verb*² *intrans.* E17.
[ORIGIN Perh. alt. of DABBLE *verb* or from DIB *verb* + -LE³.]
†**1** = DABBLE *verb* 2. Only in E17.
2 = DIB *verb* 2. M17.

dibbuk *noun* var. of DYBBUK.

dibenzanthracene /dʌɪbɛnˈzanθrəsiːn/ *noun*. E20.
[ORIGIN from DI-² + BENZ- + ANTHRACENE.]
CHEMISTRY. Any of various isomeric anthracene derivatives with five fused rings in the molecule and the formula $C_{22}H_{14}$; *spec.* one that occurs in coal tar and tobacco smoke and is carcinogenic.

diborane /dʌɪˈbɔːreɪn/ *noun*. E20.
[ORIGIN from DI-² + BORANE.]
CHEMISTRY. A borane containing two boron atoms; *spec.* B_2H_6, a poisonous gas.

dibranchiate /dʌɪˈbraŋkɪət/ *adjective & noun*. M19.
[ORIGIN mod. Latin *dibranchiata*, from DI-² + Greek *bragkhia* gills: see -ATE².]
(Designating or pertaining to) a cephalopod with one pair of gills, sometimes placed in a group Dibranchiata comprising all living cephalopods except the pearly nautilus.

dibs /dɪbz/ *noun*¹ *pl.* M18.
[ORIGIN Prob. from DIBSTONES.]
1 A children's game played with pebbles or sheep's knuckle bones; the pebbles or bones so used. Cf. JACK *noun*¹ 15b. M18.
2 Money. *slang*. E19.

dibs /dɪbz/ *noun*². M18.
[ORIGIN Arabic, prob. rel. to Hebrew *dĕbaš* honey.]
A thick sweet syrup made in Middle Eastern countries by boiling down the juice of ripe grapes.

dibs /dɪbz/ *interjection & noun*³. *N. Amer.* M20.
[ORIGIN Prob. rel. to DUBS *interjection & noun*¹.]
(Demanding) a first claim or option. (Foll. by *on*.)

> E. EAGER You always get dibs on first 'cause you're the oldest.

dibstones /ˈdɪbstəʊnz/ *noun pl.* L17.
[ORIGIN from DIB *verb* (prob.) + STONE *noun* + -S¹.]
= DIBS *noun*¹ 1.

dicacity /dɪˈkasɪti/ *noun*. *literary*. L16.
[ORIGIN Latin *dicacitas* raillery, from *dicac-*, *dicax* sarcastic, from *dicstem* of *dicere* speak: see -ITY.]
Raillery, banter; talkativeness.

dicarboxylic /ˌdʌɪkɑːbɒkˈsɪlɪk/ *adjective*. L19.
[ORIGIN from DI-² + CARBOXYLIC.]
CHEMISTRY. Having two carboxyl groups in the molecule.

dicast /ˈdɪkast/ *noun*. Also **dik-**. E19.
[ORIGIN Greek *dikastēs* judge, juryman, from *dikazein* judge, from *dikē* judgement.]
GREEK HISTORY. Each of the 6,000 citizens selected annually in ancient Athens to try cases in the courts.
■ **dicasterion** /dɪkaˈstɪərɪən/ *noun*, pl. **-ria** /-rɪə/, = DICASTERY M17. **di'castery** *noun* any of the courts in which the dicasts sat; the court or body of dicasts: M19. **di'castic** *adjective* of or pertaining to a dicast or dicasts M19.

dicatalectic /ˌdʌɪkatəˈlɛktɪk/ *adjective*. L19.
[ORIGIN from DI-² + CATALECTIC *adjective*.]
PROSODY. A metrical line lacking a syllable both in the middle and at the end.

dice /dʌɪs/ *noun*. ME.
[ORIGIN Old French & mod. French *dés*: see DIE *noun*¹.]
▸ **I** *pl.* **1** Pl. of DIE *noun*¹. ME.

> E. O'NEILL It is not gambling when I know the dice are loaded in my favor.

2 A game or games played with dice. ME.
▸ **II** *sing.* **3** A small cube whose six faces are marked with from one to six spots, thrown and used in games of chance; a die. LME.

> E. HAYWOOD Never to touch a card or throw a dice again. *fig.*: T. D'URFEY The uncertain Dice of Fate thus far runs well.

†**4** = DIE *noun*¹ 2. LME–M16.
– PHRASES: **in the dice** liable or destined to be. LIAR **dice**. **no dice** *colloq.* (there is) no chance of success, cooperation, etc. **poker dice**: see POKER *noun*³.
– COMB.: **dice box** a box from which dice are thrown.
– NOTE: Historically, *dice* is the pl. of *die*, but in modern standard English *dice* is both the sing. and the pl., and *die* is less common.

dice /dʌɪs/ *verb*. LME.
[ORIGIN from DICE *noun*.]
▸ **I** **1** *verb trans.* COOKERY. Cut into small cubes. LME.
2 *verb trans.* Chequer, mark with squares. M17.
▸ **II** **3** *verb intrans.* Play or gamble with dice. LME.
dice with death take great risks.
4 *verb trans.* Gamble *away* at dice. M16.
5 *verb trans.* Reject, throw away; leave alone. *Austral. slang*. M20.

> F. HARDY No bastard puts my daughter in the family way then dices her . . and gets away with it.

6 *verb intrans.* Drive (as if) in a race (*with*). M20.

> A. ALVAREZ Two cars in a hurry, he thought, young fools dicing home after a party.

■ **dicer** *noun* a person who plays or gambles with dice LME.

dicentra /dʌɪˈsɛntrə/ *noun*. M19.
[ORIGIN mod. Latin from Greek *dikentros*, formed as DI-² + *kentron* (see CENTRE *noun*).]
Any plant of the genus *Dicentra*, of the fumitory family, which includes herbaceous perennials with drooping racemose flowers, e.g. bleeding heart.

dicentric /dʌɪˈsɛntrɪk/ *adjective & noun*. M20.
[ORIGIN from DI-² + -CENTRIC.]
(A chromosome etc.) having two centromeres.

dicey /ˈdʌɪsi/ *adjective*. *slang*. M20.
[ORIGIN from DICE *noun* + -Y¹.]
Risky; unreliable, uncertain.

> A. BLOND Fishermen and canners whose tenure is extremely dicey.

dich- *combining form* see DICHO-.

dichasium /dʌɪˈkeɪzɪəm/ *noun*. Pl. **-sia** /-zɪə/. L19.
[ORIGIN from Greek *dikhasis* division, from *dikhazein* divide, from *dikha* apart, + -IUM.]
BOTANY. A cyme in which each flowering branch gives rise to two more branches symmetrically placed, so that there is symmetry about a median plane.

dichlamydeous /dʌɪkləˈmɪdɪəs/ *adjective*. M19.
[ORIGIN from DI-² + Greek *khlamus*, *khlamud-* cloak + -EOUS.]
Of a flower: having both a calyx and a corolla.

dichloride /dʌɪˈklɔːrʌɪd/ *noun*. E19.
[ORIGIN from DI-² + CHLORIDE.]
A compound with two chlorine atoms in its molecule. Formerly, a compound with one chlorine atom and two of another element.

dichlorodifluoromethane
/dʌɪˌklɔːrəʊdʌɪˌflʊərəʊˈmiːθeɪn/ *noun*. M20.
[ORIGIN from DI-² + CHLORO-² + DI-² + FLUORO- + METHANE.]
An easily liquefied gas, CCl_2F_2, used as an aerosol propellant and a refrigerant.

dichlorvos /dʌɪˈklɔːvɒs/ *noun*. M20.
[ORIGIN from DI-², CHLOR-¹, V(INYL, PH)OS(PHATE *noun*, elems. of the systematic name (see below).]
A pale yellow liquid organophosphorus compound used as an insecticide and veterinary anthelmintic: 2,2-dichlorovinyl dimethyl phosphate, $(CH_3O)_2PO_2CHCCl_2$.

dicho- /ˈdʌɪkəʊ/ *combining form*. Before a vowel also **dich-**.
[ORIGIN Greek *dikho-*, from *dikha* in two, apart.]
Apart, in two; separately.
■ **dichogamous** /dʌɪˈkɒgəməs/ *adjective* [Greek *gamos* marriage] designating a flower in which male and female reproductive organs mature at different times, so that self-fertilization is prevented (cf. HOMOGAMOUS 2) M19. **di'chogamy** *noun* the condition of being dichogamous M19.

dichoptic /dʌɪˈkɒptɪk/ *adjective*. L19.
[ORIGIN from DICHO- + OPTIC *adjective*.]
1 ENTOMOLOGY. Of the eyes: widely separated. Of an insect: having such eyes. L19.
2 Involving or pertaining to the presentation of different (not merely stereoscopic) images to the two eyes. M20.
■ **dichoptically** *adverb* M20.

dichoree /dʌɪkəˈriː/ *noun*. E19.
[ORIGIN French *dichorée* from Latin *dichoreus* from Greek *dikhoreios*, formed as DI-² + *khoreios* CHOREE.]
PROSODY. A foot consisting of two trochees.

dichotic /dʌɪˈkɒtɪk/ *adjective*. M20.
[ORIGIN from DICHO- + Greek *ous*, *ōt-* ear + -IC.]
Involving or pertaining to the presentation of different auditory signals to the two ears.

†**dichotomia** *noun* see DICHOTOMY.

dichotomic /dʌɪkɒˈtɒmɪk/ *adjective*. L19.
[ORIGIN from DICHOTOMY + -IC.]
Involving dichotomy, dichotomous.
■ **dichotomically** *adverb* L19.

dichotomise *verb* var. of DICHOTOMIZE.

dichotomist /dʌɪˈkɒtəmɪst, dɪ-/ *noun*. L16.
[ORIGIN formed as DICHOTOMIZE + -IST.]
A person who dichotomizes something.

dichotomize /dʌɪˈkɒtəmʌɪz, dɪ-/ *verb*. Also **-ise**. E17.
[ORIGIN from DICHOTOMY + -IZE.]
1 *verb trans.* Divide into two (esp. sharply defined) parts, esp. in a classification. E17.
2 *verb intrans.* Divide or branch successively into two, esp. sharply. M19.
■ **dichotomi'zation** *noun* M20. **dichotomized** *ppl adjective* divided into two; *spec.* (of the moon) with exactly half the disc illuminated: E18.

dichotomous /dʌɪˈkɒtəməs, dɪ-/ *adjective*. L17.
[ORIGIN from late Latin *dichotomos* from Greek *dikhotomos*, formed as DICHO- + *temnein* to cut: see -OUS.]
Exhibiting or characterized by dichotomy; *spec.* in BOTANY, (of branching) in which the axis is divided into two branches (cf. POLYTOMOUS).
■ **dichotomously** *adverb* E19.

dichotomy /dʌɪˈkɒtəmi, dɪ-/ *noun*. Also (earlier) in Latin form †**-tomia**. L16.
[ORIGIN mod. Latin *dichotomia* from Greek *dikhotomia* division in two: see DICHO-, -TOMY.]
1 Division (esp. sharply defined) into two classes, parts, etc. L16. ▸**b** A sharp or paradoxical contrast. M20.

> **b** M. AMIS The coffee-table featured . . Shakespeare texts and a copy of *Time Out*—an intriguing dichotomy.

2 ASTRONOMY. The phase of the moon etc. at which exactly half the disc appears illuminated. M17.
3 BOTANY & ZOOLOGY. Repeated bifurcation of a plant etc. Cf. POLYTOMY. E18.

dichroiscope *noun* var. of DICHROSCOPE.

dichroism /dʌɪˈkrəʊɪz(ə)m/ *noun*. E19.
[ORIGIN from Greek *dikhroos* two-coloured, formed as DI-² + *khrōs* colour: see -ISM.]
The property of certain substances of absorbing light to a different extent according to the direction from which it

comes or its direction or state of polarization; the property of having a different colour when viewed from a different direction.
■ **dichroic** *adjective* exhibiting or pertaining to dichroism M19.

dichroite /dʌɪˈkrəʊʌɪt/ *noun*. E19.
[ORIGIN formed as DICHROISM + -ITE[1].]
MINERALOGY. = CORDIERITE.
■ **dichroˈitic** *adjective* = DICHROIC M19.

dichromasy /dʌɪˈkrəʊməsi/ *noun*. E20.
[ORIGIN from DI-[2] + -CHROMASY.]
Dichromatic colour vision.

dichromat /ˈdʌɪkrəmat/ *noun*. Also **-ate** /-eɪt/. E20.
[ORIGIN Back-form. from DICHROMATIC.]
A person with dichromatism.

dichromate /dʌɪˈkrəʊmeɪt/ *noun*[1]. M19.
[ORIGIN from DI-[2] + CHROMATE.]
CHEMISTRY. A usu. red or orange salt containing the ion $Cr_2O_7^{2-}$.

dichromate *noun*[2] var. of DICHROMAT.

dichromatic /dʌɪkrə(ʊ)ˈmatɪk/ *adjective & noun*. M19.
[ORIGIN from DI-[2] + CHROMATIC.]
► **A** *adjective*. **1** Having two colours; *spec.* (of an animal etc.) occurring with two different kinds of colouring, independently of age or sex. M19.
2 Having or designating a form of colour blindness in which the range of colours seen is limited to those produced by two primary colours, rather than the usual three. L19.
► **B** *noun*. = DICHROMAT *noun*. L19.
■ **diˈchromatism** *noun* the quality or fact of being dichromatic L19.

dichromic /dʌɪˈkrəʊmɪk/ *adjective*. M19.
[ORIGIN from Greek *dikhrōmos*, formed as DI-[2] + *khrōma* colour: see -IC.]
= DICHROMATIC *adjective* 2.

dichroscope /ˈdʌɪkrəskəʊp/ *noun*. Also **dichroi-** /dʌɪˈkrəʊɪ-/. M19.
[ORIGIN from DICHROISM + -SCOPE.]
An instrument for observing or measuring dichroism.

Dick /dɪk/ *noun*[1]. In sense 2 **d-**. M16.
[ORIGIN Male forename, playful alt. of *Ric-* from Anglo-Norman *Ricard*, Latin *Ricardus*, whence *Richard* (of which it is used as a familiar abbreviation).]
1 A man, a fellow; a lad. Freq. with qualifying adjective. M16.
clever Dick: see CLEVER *adjective*. *spotted dick*: see SPOTTED. *Tom, Dick, and Harry*: see TOM *noun*[1].
2 The penis. *coarse slang*. L18.
– COMB.: **dickhead** *slang* a stupid person; **dickwad** *slang* (a term of abuse for) a contemptible person.

dick /dɪk/ *noun*[2]. *slang*. M19.
[ORIGIN Abbreviation of DECLARATION.]
take one's dick, declare solemnly, affirm, (*that*).

dick /dɪk/ *noun*[3]. *slang*. E20.
[ORIGIN Perh. abbreviation of DETECTIVE or from obsolete slang *dick* look, from Romany.]
A detective; a police officer.

dickcissel /dɪkˈsɪs(ə)l, ˈdɪks-/ *noun*. L19.
[ORIGIN Imit. of its cry.]
A migratory songbird, *Spiza americana*, of N. and Central America, like a house sparrow but with a yellow breast.

dicken /ˈdɪk(ə)n/ *interjection*. *Austral. & NZ slang*. Also **-in**, **-on**. L19.
[ORIGIN Alt. of DICKENS.]
Expr. disgust or disbelief. (Foll. by *on*.)

D. M. DAVIN Dicken on that for a joke.

dickens /ˈdɪkɪnz/ *noun*. *colloq*. L16.
[ORIGIN Prob. from the surname *Dickens*.]
The Devil, the deuce. Chiefly in exclamatory phrases.

L. ARMSTRONG Everybody . . was frantic as the dickens. B. BRYSON Whoever was the person behind Stonehenge was one dickens of a motivator.

play the dickens cause mischief. **the dickens!**, **what the dickens!**, etc.: expr. astonishment, irritation, etc.

Dickensian /dɪˈkɛnzɪən/ *adjective & noun*. L19.
[ORIGIN from *Dickens* (see below) + -IAN.]
► **A** *adjective*. Of or pertaining to the English novelist Charles Dickens (1812–70) or his writing; similar to or suggestive of the situations or social conditions portrayed in his novels. L19.

Economist Employees busy making school satchels in allegedly Dickensian conditions.

► **B** *noun*. An admirer or student of Dickens or his writing. E20.
■ **Dickensiˈana** *noun pl.* [-ANA] publications or other items concerning or associated with Dickens L19. **Dickensianly** *adverb* L20. ˈ**Dickensy** *adjective* = DICKENSIAN *adjective* M19.

dicker /ˈdɪkə/ *noun*[1]. ME.
[ORIGIN Corresp. to Middle Low German *dēker*, Middle High German *techer*, (also mod.) *decher*, from West Germanic from Latin *decuria* group of ten, from *decem* ten + *vir* man. Prob. already in Old English.]
1 *hist.* A quantity, esp. of hides, numbering ten. (Foll. by *of*.) ME.
†**2** A considerable number, a lot. L16–L17.

dicker /ˈdɪkə/ *noun*[2]. Orig. *US*. E19.
[ORIGIN from the verb.]
Barter; articles exchanged in barter; a deal.

dicker /ˈdɪkə/ *verb*. Orig. *US*. E19.
[ORIGIN Uncertain: perh. from DICKER *noun*[1].]
1 *verb intrans.* Trade by barter; haggle. E19.

S. BELLOW She . . dickered with the photographer, . . trying to beat down his price.

2 *verb trans.* Barter, exchange. M19.
3 *verb intrans.* Vacillate, dither; hesitate. M20.

B. PEARSON Henderson, though he dickered, usually came round to the majority opinion.

dickey, **dickie** *nouns* vars. of DICKY *noun*.

dickin, **dickon** *interjections* vars. of DICKEN.

dicky /ˈdɪki/ *noun*. Also **-ey**, **-ie**. M18.
[ORIGIN Prob. several different words: app. partly from name *Dicky*, formed as DICK *noun*[1] + -Y[6].]
1 An underpetticoat. *obsolete* exc. *dial.* M18.
2 A donkey, *spec.* a male one. *colloq.* L18.
3 In full ***dicky bird***: ▸**a** A small bird. *colloq.* L18. ▸**b** A word. *rhyming slang*. E20.

b D. FRANCIS We won't get a dicky bird out of him.

4 a A false shirt front. *colloq.* E19. ▸**b** A shirt collar. *US colloq.* M19.
5 Also ***dicky seat***. ▸**a** Chiefly *hist.* A seat at the front of a horse-drawn carriage for the driver; a seat at the rear for servants or a guard. E19. ▸**b** An outside folding seat at the back of a motor vehicle. E20.
6 The boot of a car. *Indian*. M20.

R. BOND The two bottles that Kapoor had hidden in the dickey had been found and removed.

– COMB.: ***dicky bird***: see sense 3 above; **dicky bow** *colloq.* a bow tie; ***dicky seat***: see sense 5 above.

dicky /ˈdɪki/ *adjective*. L18.
[ORIGIN Uncertain: perh. from *Dick* (see DICK *noun*[1]) in proverbial phr. *as queer etc. as Dick's hatband*.]
1 Almost over; near death, defeat etc. Chiefly in ***all dicky with***, ***dicky with***, ***dicky up with***, all up with (a person etc.). *dial.* L18.
2 Unsound, shaky. *slang*. E19.

D. STOREY A doctor's note about a dicky heart.

diclinous /dʌɪˈklʌɪnəs, ˈdʌɪklɪnəs/ *adjective*. E19.
[ORIGIN from mod. Latin *diclines* noun pl., formed as DI-[2] + Greek *klinē* bed: see -OUS.]
BOTANY. Of a flower or flowering plant: having stamens and pistils in separate flowers.
■ **diclinism** *noun* diclinous condition L19.

dicondylian /dʌɪkɒnˈdɪlɪən/ *adjective*. L19.
[ORIGIN from Greek *dikondulos*, formed as DI-[2] + *kondulos*: see CONDYLE, -IAN.]
ZOOLOGY. Of a skull: having two occipital condyles.

dicot /ˈdʌɪkɒt/ *noun*. L19.
[ORIGIN Abbreviation.]
= DICOTYLEDON.

dicotyledon /ˌdʌɪkɒtɪˈliːd(ə)n/ *noun*. E18.
[ORIGIN mod. Latin *dicotyledones* pl., formed as DI-[2] + COTYLEDON.]
BOTANY. A flowering plant having two cotyledons; a member of either of the two groups (Dicotyledoneae or Dicotyledones) into which flowering plants are classified. Cf. MONOCOTYLEDON.
■ **dicotyledonous** *adjective* L18.

dicoumarin /dʌɪˈkuːmərɪn/ *noun*. L19.
[ORIGIN from DI-[2] + COUMARIN.]
CHEMISTRY. Orig., any compound with a basic structure of two joined coumarin molecules. Now *spec.* = DICOUMAROL.

dicoumarol /dʌɪˈkuːmərɒl/ *noun*. M20.
[ORIGIN from DICOUMARIN + -OL.]
CHEMISTRY & PHARMACOLOGY. A derivative, $C_{19}H_{12}O_6$, of coumarin used as an anti-coagulant. Cf. DICOUMARIN.

dicrotic /dʌɪˈkrɒtɪk/ *adjective*. E19.
[ORIGIN from Greek *dikrotos* double-beating + -IC.]
1 Of the pulse: having a detectable double beat owing to an exaggerated dicrotic wave (see sense 2). E19.
2 Designating a usu. small transient increase in pressure during the overall decreasing pressure of a heartbeat, and a notch representing this in a sphygmogram. M19.
■ ˈ**dicrotism** *noun* M19.

dict /dɪkt/ *noun*. Now *rare* or *obsolete*. LME.
[ORIGIN Old French (mod. *dit*) or its source Latin *dictum* use as noun of neut. pa. pple of *dicere* say.]
A saying, a maxim.

dict /dɪkt/ *verb trans*. Now *rare* or *obsolete*. E17.
[ORIGIN Latin *dictare* DICTATE *verb*.]
Put into words; dictate.

dicta *noun pl.* see DICTUM.

dictamen /dɪkˈteɪmɛn/ *noun*. Now *rare* or *obsolete*. Pl. **-mina** /-mɪnə/. L15.
[ORIGIN Late Latin, from *dictare* DICTATE *verb*.]
A dictate, a pronouncement.

dictamnus /dɪkˈtamnəs/ *noun*. M16.
[ORIGIN Latin: see DITTANY.]
= FRAXINELLA. Also = DITTANY 1.

Dictaphone /ˈdɪktəfəʊn/ *noun*. Also **d-**. E20.
[ORIGIN from DICTATE *verb*, DICTATION + -PHONE.]
(Proprietary name for) a machine that records speech and will subsequently reproduce it for transcription etc.

dictate /ˈdɪkteɪt/ *noun*. L16.
[ORIGIN Latin *dictatum* use as noun of neut. pa. pple of *dictare* DICTATE *verb*.]
1 An authoritative instruction (esp. *of* reason, conscience, nature, etc.). Usu. in *pl.* L16.

S. JOHNSON I could not receive such dictates without horror. P. G. WODEHOUSE Follow the dictates of your heart. V. S. REID The dictates of His Gracious Majesty, King George III.

2 A dictated utterance. Now *rare* or *obsolete*. E17.
†**3** An authoritative pronouncement, a dictum. E17–E18.
†**4** A current saying, a maxim. M–L17.

dictate /dɪkˈteɪt/ *verb*. L16.
[ORIGIN Latin *dictat-* pa. ppl stem of *dictare* frequentative of *dicere* say: see -ATE[3].]
1 *verb trans. & intrans.* Express in words which are to be written down; say or read aloud (matter to be transcribed, *to* a writer or recording machine). L16.
2 *verb trans.* Prescribe, lay down authoritatively (terms, things to be done, etc.); require as an imperative. E17.

R. TRAVERS Prudence should have dictated a quiet and withdrawn residence.

3 *verb intrans.* Lay down the law, give orders. M17.
■ ˈ**dictative** *adjective* of the nature of prescription or command L18.

dictation /dɪkˈteɪʃ(ə)n/ *noun*. M17.
[ORIGIN Late Latin *dictatio(n-)*, formed as DICTATE *verb*: see -ATION.]
1 Authoritative utterance or prescription. M17. ▸**b** The exercise of dictatorship. M19.

DISRAELI The terms were at his own dictation.

2 The act of dictating (for transcription). E18.
3 A dictated utterance. M19.

R. LOWELL Taking Ford's dictation on Samuel Butler in longhand.

– COMB.: **dictation speed** a rate of speech suitable for dictation.

dictator /dɪkˈteɪtə/ *noun*. LME.
[ORIGIN Latin, formed as DICTATE *verb*: see -OR.]
1 ROMAN HISTORY. A chief magistrate with absolute power who was appointed in an emergency. LME.
2 An absolute ruler, usu. temporary or irregular, of a state; *esp.* one who suppresses or succeeds a democratic government. L16.

LYNDON B. JOHNSON The Dominicans had lived for thirty years under the iron-fisted rule of dictator Leonidas Trujillo.

3 A person exercising absolute authority of any kind or in any sphere; a domineering person. E17.

SWIFT The dictators of behaviour, dress, and politeness.

4 A person who gives dictation to a writer or recording machine. E17.
■ **dictatorate** *noun* the position of a dictator M19. **dictatorship** *noun* the position of a dictator; a state ruled by a dictator; absolute authority in any sphere: M16.

dictatorial /dɪktəˈtɔːrɪəl/ *adjective*. E18.
[ORIGIN from Latin *dictatorius*, formed as DICTATOR + -AL[1].]
Of, pertaining to, or proper to a dictator; imperious, overbearing.

R. L. STEVENSON He rose . . to almost dictatorial authority in the State.

■ **dictatorially** *adverb* L18. **dictatorialness** *noun* L19. †**dictatorian** *adjective* = DICTATORIAL M17–E18. ˈ**dictatory** *adjective* = DICTATORIAL M17. ˈ**dictatorily** *adverb* = DICTATORIALLY L18.

dictatress /dɪkˈteɪtrɪs/ *noun*. L18.
[ORIGIN from DICTATOR + -ESS[1].]
A female dictator.
■ Also **dictatrix** /-trɪks/ *noun*, pl. **-trices** /-trɪsiːz/, E17.

dictature /dɪkˈteɪtʃə/ *noun*. M16.
[ORIGIN Latin *dictatura*, formed as DICTATE *verb*: see -URE.]
1 = DICTATORSHIP. M16.
2 A collective body of dictators. M18.

diction /ˈdɪkʃ(ə)n/ *noun*. M16.
[ORIGIN Old French & mod. French, or Latin *dictio(n-)* saying, mode of expression, (later) word, from *dict-* pa. ppl stem of *dicere* say.]
†**1** A word. M16–L17.
†**2** A phrase; a locution. M16–E18.
†**3** Speech; verbal description. L16–E17.
4 The choice of words and phrases in speech or writing; the manner of enunciation in speaking, singing, etc. L17.

W. H. AUDEN To clothe my fiction in up-to-date diction, The contemporary jargon of Pride.

Wardour-street diction: see WARDOUR STREET 1.

D

D

dictionary /ˈdɪkʃ(ə)n(ə)ri/ *noun*. E16.
[ORIGIN medieval Latin *dictionarium* (sc. *manuale* MANUAL *noun*) and *dictionarius* (sc. *liber* book), from Latin *dictio(n-)*: see DICTION, -ARY[1].]
▸ **I 1 a** A book explaining or translating, usu. in alphabetical order, words of a language or languages, giving their pronunciation, spelling, meaning, part of speech, and etymology, or one or some of these. E16. ▸†**b** The vocabulary or whole list of words used or admitted by someone. L16–E18. ▸**c** An ordered list stored in and used by a computer; *esp.* a list of words acceptable to a word processor. M20.
***a** abridged **dictionary**, children's **dictionary**, **dictionary** of Americanisms, pronouncing **dictionary**, slang **dictionary**, unabridged **dictionary**,* etc. **have swallowed the dictionary** use long and recondite words.
2 A book of information or reference on any subject in which the entries are arranged alphabetically. M17.
***biographical dictionary**, **dictionary** of the Bible, **dictionary** of proverbs*, etc.
▸ **II** *fig.* **3** A person or thing regarded as a repository of knowledge, convenient for consultation. E17.

Dictograph /ˈdɪktəɡrɑːf/ *noun*. Also **d-**. E20.
[ORIGIN formed as DICTAPHONE + -O- + -GRAPH, after *phonograph*.]
(Proprietary name for) a telephonic instrument which reproduces in one room the sounds made in another.

dictum /ˈdɪktəm/ *noun*. Pl. **-ta** /-tə/, **-tums**. L16.
[ORIGIN Latin: see DICT *noun*.]
1 A saying, an utterance; *esp.* one that claims some authority, a pronouncement. L16.
P. ACKROYD A lover of allusive quotation (particularly from the *dicta* of Sherlock Holmes).
2 LAW. An expression of opinion by a judge which is not essential to the decision and so has no binding authority as precedent. See also OBITER DICTUM. L18.
3 A common saying; a maxim. E19.
J. S. MILL The *dictum* that truth always triumphs.

dicty /ˈdɪkti/ *adjective*. *US slang*. E20.
[ORIGIN Unknown.]
Conceited, snobbish; elegant, stylish, high-class.

dictyosome /ˈdɪktɪə(ʊ)səʊm/ *noun*. L19.
[ORIGIN from Greek *diktuon* net + -SOME[3].]
BIOLOGY. Any of the discrete bodies forming the Golgi apparatus in some cells.

dictyostele /ˈdɪktɪə(ʊ)stiːl/ *noun*. E20.
[ORIGIN from Greek *diktuon* net + STELE.]
BOTANY. A stele, typical of many ferns, in which the vascular tissue is in separate strands; *esp.* one in which the phloem and xylem are arranged concentrically in each strand.
■ **dictyoˈstelic** *adjective* M20.

dicynodont /dʌɪˈsɪnədɒnt/ *noun & adjective*. M19.
[ORIGIN mod. Latin *Dicynodontia* (see below), from DI-[2] + CYNO- + -ODONT.]
PALAEONTOLOGY. ▸**A** *noun*. A fossil reptile with no teeth except for two in the upper jaw; a member of the suborder Dicynodontia of mammal-like therapsid reptiles. M19.
▸ **B** *adjective*. Designating or pertaining to a dicynodont. L19.

did *verb* see DO *verb*.

didache /ˈdɪdəkiː/ *noun*. In sense 1 **D-**. L19.
[ORIGIN Greek *didakhē* teaching.]
1 *the Didache*, a short early Christian manual. L19.
2 The instructional element in early Christianity, as contrasted with the kerygma. M20.

didactic /dɪˈdaktɪk, dʌɪ-/ *adjective & noun*. M17.
[ORIGIN Greek *didaktikos*, from *didak-* stem of *didaskein* teach: see -IC. In English perh. after French *didactique*.]
▸ **A** *adjective*. Having the character or manner of a teacher; intended to instruct; having instruction as an ulterior purpose. M17.
T. F. DIBDIN The dullest of all possible didactic and moral poetry. A. HAILEY Letting Harry London get to the point in his own didactic way.
▸ **B** *noun*. †**1** A didactic author or treatise. M17–M19.
2 In *pl.* (treated as *sing.* or *pl.*). The art of teaching. M19.
■ **didactical** *adjective* (*rare*) = DIDACTIC *adjective* E17. **didactically** *adverb* E17. **didacticism** /-sɪz(ə)m/ *noun* the practice or quality of being didactic M19. **didactive** *adjective* = DIDACTIC *adjective* E18.

didactyl /dʌɪˈdaktɪl/ *adjective*. E19.
[ORIGIN from DI-[2] + Greek *daktulos* finger.]
ZOOLOGY. Characterized by or having two fingers or toes.
■ Also **didactylous** *adjective* E19.

didakai *noun* var. of DIDICOI.

didapper /ˈdʌɪdapə/ *noun*. LME.
[ORIGIN Prob. formed as DIVE-DAP.]
A small diving bird; a little grebe.
fig.: R. CARPENTER Thou art a Didapper peering vp and downe in a moment.

didascalic /dɪdəˈskalɪk/ *adjective*. E17.
[ORIGIN Latin *didascalicus* from Greek *didaskalikos* instructive, from *didaskalos* teacher, from *didaskein* teach: see -IC.]
Pertaining to a teacher; didactic.

didder /ˈdɪdə/ *verb intrans*. *obsolete* exc. *dial*. See also DITHER *verb*. LME.
[ORIGIN Rel. to DADDER, DODDER *verb*.]
Tremble, shake, shiver.
■ **diddery** *adjective* M19.

diddicoy *noun* var. of DIDICOI.

diddle /ˈdɪd(ə)l/ *verb*[1]. M17.
[ORIGIN App. parallel to DIDDER: cf. DADDLE *verb*.]
†**1** *verb intrans*. = DADDLE *verb*. Only in M17.
2 *verb intrans*. Jerk from side to side; play the violin; dance a jig. *Scot. & dial*. E18.
3 *verb trans. & intrans*. Copulate (with); masturbate. *slang*. L19.

diddle /ˈdɪd(ə)l/ *verb*[2]. *colloq*. E19.
[ORIGIN Uncertain: perh. back-form. from DIDDLER, or identical with DIDDLE *verb*[1].]
1 *verb trans*. Cheat, swindle (*out of*). E19.
2 *verb trans*. Ruin; kill. Now *rare* or *obsolete*. E19.
3 a *verb trans*. Pass (time) idly, trifle *away*. E19. ▸**b** *verb intrans*. Idle, potter, loaf (*about*, *around*); play *around*. E19.
b H. NICOLSON I rather diddle about in the morning.

diddle- /ˈdɪd(ə)l/ *combining form* of DIDDLE *verb*[1] or *verb*[2].
■ **diddle-diddle** *noun & interjection* (repr.) the sound of a fiddle; the action of playing a fiddle: E16. **diddledum** *noun* a trifling thing L16.

diddler /ˈdɪdlə/ *noun*. *colloq*. E19.
[ORIGIN from DIDDLE *verb*[2] + -ER[1] or from the name of Jeremy *Diddler* in J. Kenney's play *Raising the Wind* (1803).]
A mean swindler, a cheat.

diddly /ˈdɪdli/ *noun*. *N. Amer. slang*. Also **diddley**, **diddly-squat** /ˌdɪdlɪˈskwɒt/. L20.
[ORIGIN Alt. of DOODLY-SQUAT.]
Nothing at all; (following a neg.) anything; = DOODLY-SQUAT.
W. GRADY I still haven't heard diddly from him. WALTER STEWART She knew diddley-squat about the theatre.

diddums /ˈdɪdəmz/ *interjection & noun*. L19.
[ORIGIN from *did 'em*, i.e. 'did they' (sc. 'tease you' etc.) + -S[1].]
(A form of address to young children and *joc*. to adults) expr. commiseration or endearment.
J. ELLIOT She's quite happy. Aren't you, diddums? N. HORNBY 'He told me to shut up,' said Lindsey. 'Diddums,' said Ellie.

diddy /ˈdɪdi/ *noun*. *slang & dial*. L18.
[ORIGIN Alt. of TITTY *noun*[2]; sense 2 may be rel. to the adjective.]
1 A woman's breast or nipple; an animal's teat. L18.
2 A fool. *Scot*. L20.

diddy /ˈdɪdi/ *adjective*. *slang & dial*. M20.
[ORIGIN Prob. a corrupt. of LITTLE *adjective*.]
Little, tiny.

didelphid /dʌɪˈdɛlfɪd/ *noun & adjective*. L19.
[ORIGIN mod. Latin *Didelphidae* (see below), from DI-[2] + Greek *delphus* womb: see -ID[3].]
ZOOLOGY. (Of, pertaining to, or designating) a marsupial of the family Didelphidae, containing the opossums, or (formerly) any marsupial.

didgeridoo /dɪdʒ(ə)rɪˈduː/ *noun*. Also **-dj-**, **-du**. E20.
[ORIGIN Imit.]
A long tubular wooden musical instrument of the Australian Aborigines which is blown to produce a resonant sound.

didicoi /ˈdɪdɪkɔɪ/ *noun*. *slang & dial*. Also **didakai**, **diddicoy**, & other vars. M19.
[ORIGIN Perh. alt. of Romany *dik akei* look here.]
A Gypsy; an itinerant tinker.

didjeridoo, **didjeridu** *nouns* vars. of DIDGERIDOO.

didn't *verb* see DO *verb*.

dido /ˈdʌɪdəʊ/ *noun*. *dial. & US slang*. Pl. **-o(e)s**. E19.
[ORIGIN Unknown.]
A prank, an antic; a disturbance, a row. Freq. in ***to cut didoes***.

didrachm /ˈdʌɪdram/ *noun*. M16.
[ORIGIN Late Latin *didrachma*, *didrachmon* from Greek *didrakhmon*, formed as DI-[2] + DRACHMA.]
An ancient Greek silver coin worth two drachmas.

didric, **didrik** *nouns* vars. of DIEDERIK.

didst *verb* see DO *verb*.

didy /ˈdʌɪdi/ *noun*. *US colloq*. E20.
[ORIGIN Childish form of DIAPER *noun*: see -Y[6].]
A baby's nappy.

didymis /ˈdɪdɪmɪs/ *noun*. Long *rare*. Pl. **-mes** /-miːz/. Also (earlier) †**dyndym(e)**, **-my**. LME.
[ORIGIN Abbreviation of Greek *epididumis* EPIDIDYMIS.]
= EPIDIDYMIS.

didymium /dɪˈdɪmɪəm/ *noun*. M19.
[ORIGIN from Greek *didumos* twin (adjective) + -IUM.]
A naturally occurring mixture of neodymium and praseodymium, used to colour glass for optical filters.
– NOTE: Orig. regarded as an element.

didymous /ˈdɪdɪməs/ *adjective*. L18.
[ORIGIN from French *didyme* (formed as DIDYMIUM) + -OUS.]
BOTANY & ZOOLOGY. Growing in pairs, twin.

didynamous /dʌɪˈdɪnəməs, dɪ-/ *adjective*. L18.
[ORIGIN from DI-[2] + Greek *dunamis* power + -OUS.]
BOTANY. Having or designating stamens arranged in two pairs, each of unequal length.

die /dʌɪ/ *noun*[1]. Pl. in branch I **dice** /dʌɪs/ (see also DICE *noun*); in branch II **dies**. ME.
[ORIGIN Old French & mod. French *dé*, pl. *dés*, from Latin DATUM.]
▸ **I 1** A small cube whose six faces are marked with from one to six spots, used in games of chance by being thrown from a box, the hand, etc., the score being decided from the uppermost face; a cube with different markings, or a solid with a different number of faces, used in the same way. ME. ▸**b** *fig*. Chance, luck. L16.
HAZLITT Dependent on the turn of a die, on the tossing up of a halfpenny. **b** SPENSER His harder fortune was to fall Under my speare; such is the dye of warre.
2 A small cubical segment, esp. of meat etc. for cooking. Usu. in *pl*. LME.
E. RAFFALD Turnips and carrots cut in dice.
▸ **II 3** A cubical block; ARCHITECTURE = DADO 1. M17.
4 An engraved stamp for impressing a design on some softer material as in coining, striking a medal, embossing paper, etc. L17.
5 Any of various devices for shaping bulk material; *esp.* (***a***) an internally threaded hollow tool for cutting a screw thread; (***b***) a part into which a punch is driven; (***c***) a block with a hole through which material is extruded; (***d***) a hollow mould into which material is forced prior to solidification. E19.
6 A toy. *Scot*. E19.
– PHRASES: **as straight as a die**, **as true as a die** (of a person) entirely honest or loyal. **the die is cast** the decisive or irrevocable step is taken.
– COMB.: **die-cast** *verb trans*. cast in a mould; **die-casting** the casting of hot metal or plastic in a mould; an article so made; **die-link** NUMISMATICS the relationship established between coins struck from the same die; **die-sinker** an engraver of dies; **die-stamping** embossing paper etc. with a die.
– NOTE: In modern standard English the singular *die* (rather than *dice*) is uncommon in senses 1 & 2. *Dice* is used for both the singular and the plural.

†**die** *noun*[2] var. of DYE *noun*.

die /dʌɪ/ *verb*[1] *intrans*. Pa. t. & pple **died** /dʌɪd/; pres. pple **dying** /ˈdʌɪɪŋ/. ME.
[ORIGIN Old Norse *deyja* (= Old Saxon *dōian*, Old High German *touwen*), from Germanic base also of DEAD *adjective & adverb*. Corresp. verb perh. already in Old English, reinforced from Old Norse.]
▸ **I** Of animate or sentient things.
1 Of a person or animal: lose life, cease to live, suffer death; expire. Freq. with prepositional phr. denoting the cause or manner of death. ME. ▸**b** THEOLOGY. Suffer spiritual death; perish everlastingly. ME.
R. CAMPBELL She died only the other day at the age of about a hundred and ten. J. FOWLES Four sons, two of whom died in the First World War. **b** NEB *John* 11:26 No one who is alive and has faith shall ever die.
***die** of illness, **die** of hunger, **die** by violence, **die** by the sword, **die** by one's own hand, **die** from a wound, **die** through neglect, **die** on the scaffold, **die** at the stake, **die** in battle, **die** for a friend, **die** for a cause, **die** in poverty.*
2 Of a plant, living tissue, etc.: lose the vital force; cease to be alive. LME.
SHELLEY The pale flowers are dying. *Nature* After death of the brain, other organs and tissues die at different times.
3 Suffer the pains or dangers of death; face death. LME.
AV 1 *Cor*. 15:31 I protest by your rejoicing which I have in Christ Jesus our Lord, I die daily.
4 Experience great suffering; languish; be consumed with longing *for*, desire greatly *to do*. L16.
G. ALLEN The pretty American's dying to see you.
5 Become exhausted *with* laughing; be overcome with embarrassment, boredom, etc. (Also foll. by *of*.) L16.
M. WILMOT I thought I should have died, when Lady Grace told him *audibly* he had turned over *two leaves*. P. SCOTT I am dying of thirst.
6 Have an orgasm. (Freq. a secondary sense in fig. uses of sense 1.) L16.
POPE Who only hoped upon his foe to die.
7 Of a person's heart: apparently stop beating, as in a faint. E17.
▸ **II** *transf*. **8** Come to an end, cease to exist; pass out of memory or knowledge. Of a flame etc.: go out. Of an engine: stop running. ME.
C. A. LINDBERGH The engine sputtered and died. E. WAUGH The secret had died with him.
9 Of a substance: lose its characteristic quality; become inactive or flat. E17.

10 Pass by dying *into* something else; change *into* something at death or termination; ARCHITECTURE merge *into*, terminate gradually *in* or *against*. M17.

TENNYSON The twilight died into the dark.

11 Pass gradually away, esp. out of hearing or sight; fade away. E18.

S. BECKETT A single confused sound, . . swelling, dying. P. BARKER Elaine . . started to say something else, but the words died on her lips.

– PHRASES ETC.: **die a — death** meet a death of the specified kind. **die game** die fighting, not yielding to weakness or cowardice. **die hard** (*a*) die painfully or only after a hard struggle; †(*b*) die obdurate or impenitent. **die in harness** die while in a job, die before retirement. **die in one's bed** die of natural causes. **die in one's boots**, (*arch.*) **die in one's shoes** = ***die with one's boots on*** below. **die in the last ditch** die desperately defending something, die fighting to the last extremity. ***die like a dog***: see DOG *noun*. **die on someone** (*a*) die in the presence or charge of someone; (*b*) cease to be of use or interest to someone. **die the death** (*arch.* or *joc.*) be put to death; (of a performer, performance, etc.) be received very badly, be a failure. **die with one's boots on**, **die with one's shoes on** die a violent death. ***do or die***: see DO *verb*. **hope I may die**, **wish I may die**, **hope to die** *colloq.*: said to vouch for the truth of an assertion. ***lie down and die***: see LIE *verb*[1]. **never say die** refuse to give in, keep your courage up. **to die for** *colloq.* (as if) worth dying for; extremely good or highly desirable. ***the tune the cow died of***, ***the tune the old cow died of***: see TUNE *noun*. ***wish I may die***: see ***hope I may die*** above. ***wish to curl up and die***: see CURL *verb*.

– WITH ADVERBS IN SPECIALIZED SENSES: **die away** (*a*) diminish gradually in force, activity, etc., cease or disappear by degrees; (*b*) (*arch.* or *poet.*) pass slowly from life, swoon; (*c*) ARCHITECTURE merge gradually into an adjacent structure. **die back** (of the shoot of a plant etc.) die from the tip towards the root. **die down** (*a*) subside by natural degrees into a quieter state; (*b*) (of a plant) die above ground but stay alive below, as an annual occurrence. **die off** (*a*) be removed one by one by death, lose members by successive deaths; (*b*) (of a sound etc.) = ***die away*** (a) above. **die out** become extinct, gradually cease to be.

– COMB.: **die-away** *adjective* having a languishing or affectedly feeble manner; **dieback** the progressive dying back of a shrub or tree shoot owing to disease or unfavourable conditions; **die-in** *colloq.* a demonstration in which people lie down as if dead; **die-off** a period in which a significant proportion of a population dies naturally, usually within a short time.

die /dʌɪ/ *verb*[2] *trans.* Pres. pple & verbal noun **dieing**. E18.
[ORIGIN from DIE *noun*[1].]
Provide with a die; shape using a die.

†**die** *verb*[3] var. of DYE *verb*.

diecious *adjective* see DIOECIOUS.

diederik /ˈdiːdərɪk/ *noun*. *S. Afr.* Also **didric**, **-ik**, /ˈdɪdrɪk/, **diedrik** /ˈdiːdrɪk/. L18.
[ORIGIN Imit.]
A small African cuckoo, *Chrysococcyx caprius*.

diegesis /dʌɪəˈdʒiːsɪs/ *noun*. Pl. **-geses** /-ˈdʒiːsiːz/. E19.
[ORIGIN Greek *diēgēsis* narrative. In mod. use partly from French *diégèse* from Greek.]
A narrative, a report of action, a plot, now esp. in a cinema or television film.
■ **diegetic** /dʌɪˈdʒɛtɪk/ *adjective* L20.

†**Diego** *noun*. Pl. **-os**. E17.
[ORIGIN Spanish = James (name of the patron saint of Spain).]
1 A Spaniard. Cf. DAGO 1. Only in 17.
2 A Spanish sword; a sword of the Spanish type. E18–M19.

diehard /ˈdʌɪhɑːd/ *noun* & *adjective*. M19.
[ORIGIN from *die hard* s.v. DIE *verb*[1].]
▸ **A** *noun*. **1** A person who resists to the last. M19.
the Diehards *slang* (in the British army) the 4th Battalion The Queen's Regiment (orig. the 57th Regiment of Foot).
2 A resolute opponent of change; a very conservative person. E20.
3 A Scotch terrier. E20.
▸ **B** *adjective*. Resisting to the last; staunchly opposing change. L19.
■ **die-hardism** *noun* E20.

diel /ˈdiːəl/ *noun* & *adjective*. M20.
[ORIGIN Irreg. from Latin *dies* day + -AL[1].]
BIOLOGY. A period of 24 hours. Now chiefly *attrib.* or as *adjective*, relating to or denoting such a period.

dieldrin /ˈdiːldrɪn/ *noun*. M20.
[ORIGIN from O. *Diels* (1876–1954), German chemist + ALDRIN.]
An insecticide consisting of an epoxide, $C_{12}H_8Cl_6O$, of aldrin.

dielectric /dʌɪɪˈlɛktrɪk/ *noun* & *adjective*. M19.
[ORIGIN from DI-[3] + ELECTRIC.]
PHYSICS. ▸ **A** *noun*. A substance which does not allow the passage of an electric current through it. M19.
▸ **B** *adjective*. **1** Pertaining to or involving a dielectric, or the transmission of electric force without an electric current. M19.
dielectric constant permittivity. **dielectric heating**: by means of a high-frequency electric field which produces heating throughout the substance of a dielectric.
2 That is a dielectric; non-conducting. L19.
■ **dielectrically** *adverb* L19.

dielectrophoresis /dʌɪˌlɛktrəfəˈriːsɪs/ *noun*. M20.
[ORIGIN Blend of DIELECTRIC *noun* and ELECTROPHORESIS.]
The migration of uncharged particles towards a maximum of the electric field.

Diels–Alder reaction /diːlzˈɔːldə rɪˌakʃ(ə)n/ *noun phr*. M20.
[ORIGIN formed as DIELDRIN + K. *Alder* (1902–58), German chemist.]
CHEMISTRY. The addition of a conjugated diene to a compound with a double or triple bond so as to form a six-membered ring.

dielytra /dʌɪˈɛlɪtrə/ *noun*. Now *rare*. M19.
[ORIGIN mod. Latin, from DI-[2] + Greek *elutron* sheath.]
A plant of a former genus called *Dielytra*, now included in *Dicentra* (see DICENTRA).

diencephalon /dʌɪɛnˈsɛf(ə)lɒn/ *noun*. L19.
[ORIGIN from DI-[3] + Greek *egkephalos* brain.]
ANATOMY. The caudal part of the forebrain, consisting of the epithalamus, thalamus, hypothalamus, and ventral thalamus and the third ventricle. Cf. TELENCEPHALON.
■ ˌ**dience'phalic** *adjective* L19.

diene /ˈdʌɪiːn/ *noun*. E20.
[ORIGIN from DI-[2] + -ENE.]
CHEMISTRY. Any organic compound containing two double bonds between carbon atoms.

dieresis *noun* see DIAERESIS.

diervilla /ˈdɪəvɪlə/ *noun*. E19.
[ORIGIN mod. Latin, from *Dierville*, French surgeon and discoverer of the plant, *c* 1700 + -A[1].]
Any of various deciduous flowering shrubs of the honeysuckle family, most of which are now placed in the genus *Weigela* leaving a few in *Diervilla*.

dies /ˈdiːeɪz, LAW ˈdʌɪiːz/ *noun*. Pl. same. L17.
[ORIGIN Latin.]
A day. Only in (chiefly legal) phrs.: see below.
Dies Irae /ˌdiːeɪz ˈɪərʌɪ, ˈɪəreɪ/ [Latin = day of wrath] a 13th-cent. Latin sequence formerly obligatory in a requiem mass in the Roman Catholic Church. ***dies non*** /dʌɪiːz ˈnɒn/ LAW = ***dies non juridicus*** below. ***dies non juridicus*** /ˌdʌɪiːz nɒn dʒʊəˈrɪdɪkəs/, pl. ***juridici*** /-dɪsʌɪ/, [lit. 'day not (judicial)'] LAW a day on which no legal business is done; a day that does not count or cannot be used for a particular purpose.

diesel /ˈdiːz(ə)l/ *noun*. Also **D-**. L19.
[ORIGIN R. *Diesel* (1858–1913), German engineer.]
1 In full ***diesel engine***. An internal-combustion engine in which indrawn air is compressed so as to heat it sufficiently to ignite the fuel that subsequently enters the cylinder. L19.
2 A vehicle with a diesel engine. E20.
3 Fuel for diesel engines; diesel oil. L20.
– COMB.: **diesel-electric** *adjective* & *noun* (an engine, locomotive, etc.) driven by electric motors powered by current from a generator which is driven by a diesel engine; ***diesel engine***: see sense 1 above; **diesel oil** a petroleum fraction used as fuel in diesel engines.
■ **dieseli'zation** *noun* the process of dieselizing M20. **dieselize** *verb trans.* equip with a diesel engine or with diesel-electric locomotives M20.

diesis /ˈdʌɪɪsɪs/ *noun*. Pl. **-eses** /-ɪsiːz/. LME.
[ORIGIN Latin from Greek = quarter-tone, from *diienai* send through, formed as DI-[3] + *ienai* send.]
1 MUSIC. An interval equal to the difference between an octave and four minor thirds (***greater diesis***) or three major thirds (***lesser diesis***); *hist.* any of various intervals smaller than a tone, *esp.* a quarter-tone. LME.
2 TYPOGRAPHY. The double dagger. E18.

diestrum, **diestrus** *nouns* see DIOESTRUS.

diet /ˈdʌɪət/ *noun*[1]. ME.
[ORIGIN Old French & mod. French *diète* from Latin *diaeta* from Greek *diaita* course of life.]
1 Food; *esp.* one's habitual food. Freq. with specifying word. ME.

M. W. MONTAGU Herbs or roots . . and plain dry bread. That is their lenten diet.

†**2** A manner of life; a way of living or thinking. LME–M17.
3 A manner of sustenance, as regards the kind of food eaten. LME.

M. PYKE Agricultural people living on a mainly vegetarian diet. R. HOGGART A balanced diet.

4 A prescribed course of food, restricted in kind or limited in quantity, *esp.* one used to control one's weight; (a) restricted provision or intake of food. LME.

S. JOHNSON To preach diet and abstinence to his patients. A. POWELL His wife kept him on a diet. *fig.*: *Guardian* It will provide a diet of feature films, sport, serials, talk shows and quizzes.

5 Board. Formerly also, an allowance or provision of food. *obsolete* exc. *hist.* *dial.* LME.

SHAKES. *1 Hen. IV* You owe money here . . for your diet and by-drinkings.

6 An allowance for the expenses of living. Long *obsolete* exc. *hist.* L15.
– COMB.: **diet-bread** special bread prepared for invalids etc.; **diet-drink**: prescribed and prepared for medicinal etc. purposes; **diet-sheet** a paper showing the daily diet prescribed for an individual patient etc.

diet /ˈdʌɪət/ *noun*[2]. LME
[ORIGIN medieval Latin *dieta* day's journey, allowance, work, wages, assoc. with Latin *dies* day. In senses 1 & 2 cf. Old French & mod. French *journée*.]
†**1** A day's journey; an excursion. Chiefly *Scot.* LME–M17.
2 A meeting formally arranged for discussion or transaction of national or international business; a conference, a congress. LME. ▸**b** *spec.* The regular meeting of the estates of a realm or confederation; *esp.* any of various foreign legislative assemblies, e.g. the former German *Reichstag*. M16.

b H. A. L. FISHER Luther was summoned to Worms to attend upon the young Emperor and his first Diet.

3 A session or sitting of a court etc. on an appointed day; a single session of any assembly occupying (a part of) one day. *Scot.* L15.
desert the diet: see DESERT *verb* 2a.
4 An appointed date or time; *spec.* the day on which a party in a legal case is cited to appear in court. *Scot.* M16.
5 The metal scraped or cut from gold and silver assayed day by day at the Mint, and retained for the purpose of trial. E18.

diet /ˈdʌɪət/ *verb*. LME.
[ORIGIN from DIET *noun*[1], after Old French *dieter*, medieval Latin *diaetare*.]
▸ **I** *verb trans.* **1** Feed, esp. in a particular way or with specified food. LME.

fig.: SHAKES. *Cymb.* Thou art all the comfort The gods will diet me with.

2 Regulate or restrict the habitual food of (a person) in nature and quantity for a particular purpose, esp. treatment or punishment. LME.

R. LOWELL His newly dieted figure was vitally trim.

3 Provide with daily meals; board. Now *rare* or *obsolete*. M17.
▸ **II** *verb intrans.* **4** Take one's habitual food, meals, etc.; feed *on*. *arch.* M16.
5 Board (*with* a person, *at*, *in* a house etc.). Now *rare* or *obsolete*. L16.
6 Eat according to set rules; restrict the amount or kind of food one eats, now esp. to control one's weight. M17.

A. NEWMAN My wife used to diet.

■ **dieter** *noun* L16.

dietary /ˈdʌɪət(ə)ri/ *noun* & *adjective*. LME.
[ORIGIN medieval Latin *dietarium*, from Latin *diaeta*, *dieta*: see DIET *noun*[1], -ARY[1].]
▸ **A** *noun*. **1** A diet; a book etc. prescribing a diet. LME.

L. MUMFORD New food crops . . enriched the dietary of Europe.

2 A regulated allowance of food in a hospital, prison, etc. M19.
▸ **B** *adjective*. Of or pertaining to (a) diet or a dietary. E17.

dietetic /dʌɪəˈtɛtɪk/ *noun* & *adjective*. M16.
[ORIGIN Latin *diaeteticus* from Greek *diaitētikos*, from *diaita*: see DIET *noun*[1], -IC.]
▸ **A** *noun*. MEDICINE. *sing.* & (usu.) in *pl.* (treated as *sing.* or *pl.*). The application of the principles of nutrition to the choice and use of diet. M16.
▸ **B** *adjective*. Of or pertaining to diet or dietetics. L16.
■ †**dietical** *adjective* = DIETETIC *adjective* E17–E19. **dietetically** *adverb* M19.

diether /dʌɪˈiːθə/ *noun*. M20.
[ORIGIN from DI-[2] + ETHER *noun*[1].]
CHEMISTRY. Any compound whose molecule contains two oxygen atoms each linked as in an ether.

diethyl /dʌɪˈiːθʌɪl, -ˈɛθɪl/ *adjective*. M19.
[ORIGIN from DI-[2] + ETHYL.]
CHEMISTRY. Having two ethyl groups in the molecule.
diethyl ether = ETHER *noun*[1] 4a.
■ **diethylamide** /-ˈɛmʌɪd/ *noun* a compound in which the group $\cdot N(C_2H_5)_2$ replaces a hydrogen atom or a hydroxyl group M20; **diethylstil'boestrol**, **-bes-** *noun* = STILBOESTROL 2 M20.

dietic /dʌɪˈɛtɪk/ *noun* & *adjective*. M17.
[ORIGIN from DIET *noun*[1] + -IC.]
▸ †**A** *noun*. A dietetic article or application. Only in M17.
▸ **B** *adjective*. = DIETETIC *adjective*. E18.
■ Also †**dietical** *adjective*: only in M17.

dietine /ˈdʌɪətiːn/ *noun*. M17.
[ORIGIN French *diétine* dim. of *diète* DIET *noun*[2]: see -INE[4].]
A subordinate diet (DIET *noun*[2]); *spec.* (*hist.*) a Polish provincial diet which elected deputies for the national diet.

dietist /ˈdʌɪətɪst/ *noun*. E17.
[ORIGIN from DIET *noun*[1] + -IST.]
A dietitian.

dietitian /dʌɪəˈtɪʃ(ə)n/ *noun*. Also **-ician**. M19.
[ORIGIN from DIET *noun*[1] + *-itian* irreg. form of -ICIAN.]
A person who is skilled in or practises dietetics.

Dietl's crisis /ˈdiːt(ə)lz krʌɪsɪs/ *noun phr*. L19.
[ORIGIN from J. *Dietl* (1804–78), physician of Kraków, Poland + CRISIS.]
MEDICINE. An acute renal pain often accompanied by vomiting and abdominal distension. Freq. in *pl.*

D

Dieu et mon droit /djəː eɪ mɔ̃ 'drwɑː/ *noun phr.* **E17.**
[ORIGIN French.]
God and my right (the motto of the British monarch).

dif *noun & adjective* see DIFF.

dif- /dɪf/ *prefix* (not productive).
Assim. form of Latin DIS- before *f*.

diff /dɪf/ *noun & adjective. colloq.* In senses A.1, B. also **dif**. **L19.**
[ORIGIN Abbreviation.]
▸ **A** *noun*. **1** = DIFFERENCE *noun*. **L19.**
2 = DIFFERENTIAL *noun* 3. **M20.**
▸ **B** *adjective*. = DIFFERENT *adjective*. **E20.**

diffarreation /dɪˌfarɪ'eɪʃ(ə)n/ *noun*. **E17.**
[ORIGIN Latin *diffareatio(n-)*, formed as DIF- + *farreum* spelt-cake: see -ATION.]
ROMAN HISTORY. The dissolution of a marriage solemnized by confarreation.

differ /'dɪfə/ *noun. Scot. & N. English.* **M16.**
[ORIGIN from DIFFER *verb*.]
= DIFFERENCE *noun*.

differ /'dɪfə/ *verb*. See also DEFER *verb*[1]. **LME.**
[ORIGIN Old French & mod. French *différer* differ, (also) defer, from Latin *differre*, from DIF- + *ferre* carry.]
▸ †**I 1** See DEFER *verb*[1]. **LME.**
▸ **II 2** *verb trans.* Separate from each other in qualities; make dissimilar, different, or distinct; cause to vary; differentiate (one thing *from* another). Now *rare*. **LME.**

W. FAULKNER That thin clear quenchless lucidity which alone differed him from this bear.

3 *verb intrans.* Be of a variant or contrasting nature or inclination; be unlike, distinct, or various. (Foll. by *from*.) **LME.**

G. GREENE If we had believed in sin, our behaviour would hardly have differed. H. L. MENCKEN If they differ from the rest it is only in the superior impudence and shamelessness of their false pretenses. I. ASIMOV The varying patterns in wall and floor covering and the differing designs in tableware.

4 *verb intrans.* Be at variance; hold opposed or contrasting views on a subject; disagree. (Foll. by *from*, *with*.) **M16.**

J. H. NEWMAN She may . . differ from me in opinion. C. IVES Geniuses . . differ as to *what* is beautiful and *what* is ugly . . but they all agree that beauty is better than ugliness.

agree to differ: see AGREE *verb* 10.
†**5** *verb intrans.* Express disagreement; dispute; quarrel (*with*). **E17–M18.**

difference /'dɪf(ə)r(ə)ns/ *noun & verb*. **ME.**
[ORIGIN Old French & mod. French *différence* from Latin *differentia*, from *different-*: see DIFFERENT, -ENCE.]
▸ **A** *noun*. **1** The condition, quality, or fact of being not the same in quality or nature; dissimilarity; non-identity. **ME.**

G. BURNET In all this Diversity there is no real difference. J. BARZUN The difference between a scientist and an inventor.

2 An instance of unlikeness; a respect in which things differ. **LME.**

S. SPENDER The differences between us remained more striking than the resemblances. J. B. PRIESTLEY The chief difference in the congregation was that there were fewer young people in it.

3 The quantity by which amounts differ; the remainder left after subtraction. **LME.** ▸**b** *spec.* The amount of increase or decrease in the price of stocks or shares between certain dates. **E18.**
4 A divergence or disagreement in opinion; a dispute; a quarrel. **LME.**

K. AMIS Buckmaster and the chauffeur were having a little difference about something.

5 A mark, device, or characteristic feature. Now *rare* or *obsolete* exc. HERALDRY, an alteration made in a coat of arms to distinguish branches or members of the same family. **LME.** ▸**b** LOGIC. A characteristic distinguishing a species from others of the same genus. **M16.**

SHAKES. *Haml.* An absolute gentleman, full of most excellent differences.

6 A distinction regarded as conceived by a person rather than existing in the objects. Now only in ***make a difference between*** below. **LME.**

E. STILLINGFLEET To make them more capable of putting a difference between truth and falsehood.

†**7** A division, a class, a kind. **M16–L17.**
– PHRASES: ***a distinction without a difference***: see DISTINCTION 2. †**at difference** at variance. **make a difference between** treat differently. **make all the difference** be the deciding factor; be very significant. ***same difference***: see SAME *adjective*. **split the difference** take the average of two proposed amounts. **with a difference** in a special way.
▸ **B** *verb*. †**1** *verb intrans.* Be different, differ. *rare*. Only in **L15.**
2 *verb trans.* †**a** *gen.* Make different, alter, vary. **L15–L17.** ▸**b** HERALDRY. Make an alteration in or addition to (a coat of arms) in order to distinguish branches or members of the same family. **E18.**
3 *verb trans.* Cause or constitute a difference in; differentiate, distinguish (one thing *from* another). Freq. in *pass.* **L16.**

E. B. TYLOR Theologic change which differences the Jew of the Rabbinical books from the Jew of the Pentateuch.

4 *verb trans.* Perceive or mark the difference in or between; make a distinction between. (Foll. by *from*.) Now *rare*. **L16.**

G. CHAPMAN I have remov'd those erring mists . . That thou may'st difference Gods from men.

†**5** *verb intrans.* Perceive or mark the difference (*between*). **M–L17.**
6 MATH. Find the difference or (formerly) the derivative of. Now *rare* or *obsolete*. **L17.**

†**differency** *noun*. **E17–E19.**
[ORIGIN Latin *differentia*: see DIFFERENT, -ENCY.]
= DIFFERENCE *noun*.

different /'dɪf(ə)r(ə)nt/ *adjective, noun, & adverb*. **LME.**
[ORIGIN Old French & mod. French *different* from Latin *different-* pres. ppl stem of *differre*: see DIFFER *verb*, -ENT.]
▸ **A** *adjective*. **1** Having divergent characters or qualities; having dissimilar or distinguishing attributes; unlike; of other form, nature, or quality. (Foll. by *from*, *to*, *than*, †*against*, †*with*.) **LME.**

I. MCEWAN A resigned smile of welcome, markedly different from his usual boisterous style. J. BRAINE Each wall was in a different shade of green.

same but different: see SAME *adjective*.
2 Distinct, separate, other. **M17.**

TOLKIEN He poured them out two full bowls from a stone jar; but from a different jar.

3 Out of the ordinary, unusual, special. *colloq.* **E20.**
▸ **B** *noun*. †**1** = DIFFERENCE *noun* 4. **L15–E17.**
2 Something different; a contrary, an opposite. *rare*. **L16.**
▸ **C** *adverb*. Differently. Chiefly *joc.* or *dial.* **M18.**
– NOTE: *Different from* is now regarded as the standard construction, and is the commonest. *Different to* and *different than* are often regarded as incorrect, though used by many well-known writers since 17; *different than* is now almost exclusively used in North American English, where *different to* is rare.
■ **differently** *adverb* in a different manner, to a different degree; diversely; ***differently abled*** (*euphem.*), disabled: **LME. differentness** *noun* the quality of being different **E18.**

differentia /dɪfə'rɛnʃɪə/ *noun*. Pl. **-iae** /-ɪiː/. **L17.**
[ORIGIN Latin: see DIFFERENCE *noun*.]
A distinguishing mark or characteristic, *esp.* (LOGIC) that distinguishing a species from others of the same genus.

differentiable /dɪfə'rɛnʃɪəb(ə)l/ *adjective*. **M19.**
[ORIGIN from DIFFERENTIATE *verb* + -ABLE, after *deprecate*, *deprecable*, *depreciate*, *depreciable*, etc.]
Able to be differentiated.
■ **differentia'bility** *noun* **E20.**

differential /dɪfə'rɛnʃ(ə)l/ *adjective & noun*. **M17.**
[ORIGIN medieval Latin *differentialis*, from Latin DIFFERENTIA: see -AL[1].]
▸ **A** *adjective*. **1** Of or relating to difference or diversity; exhibiting or depending on a difference; varying according to circumstances. **M17.**

J. E. T. ROGERS Differential duties in favour of colonial timber.

2 Constituting or pertaining to a specific difference; distinctive, special. **M17.**

DE QUINCEY Every case in the law courts . . presents some one differential feature peculiar to itself.

differential diagnosis the process of differentiating between two similar diseases etc.
3 MATH. Relating to infinitesimal differences. **E18.**
differential calculus: see CALCULUS 1. **differential coefficient** = DERIVATIVE *noun* 3. **differential equation**: involving derivatives.
4 PHYSICS & MECHANICS. Pertaining to, exhibiting, or involving the difference between two or more physical quantities. **M18.**
differential gear: enabling power to be divided between two axles in line with one another and able to rotate at different speeds, as when a vehicle corners.
▸ **B** *noun*. **1** MATH. ▸**a** The infinitesimal difference between two successive values of a variable; either of the two quantities whose ratio constitutes a differential coefficient. **E18.** ▸†**b** A logarithmic tangent. **E18–M19.**
2 An amount by which a basic charge or payment is varied; a difference between the wages of different categories of worker or between the prices of similar products etc. from different companies. **L19.**
3 A differential gear. **E20.**
■ **differentially** *adverb* (*a*) distinctively, specially; (*b*) in relation to the difference between two measurable quantities; in two different directions: **M17.**

differentiate /dɪfə'rɛnʃɪeɪt/ *verb & noun*. **E19.**
[ORIGIN medieval Latin *differentiat-* pa. ppl stem of *differentiare*, from Latin DIFFERENTIA: see -ATE[3].]
▸ **A** *verb*. **1** *verb trans.* MATH. Obtain the derivative or differential of. **E19.**
2 *verb trans.* Constitute a difference in, of, or between; serve to make different *from*. **M19.**

A. WILSON The famous private life that's supposed to differentiate him from other public servants.

3 *verb trans.* Make different in the process of growth or development. Usu. in *pass.* **M19.**

W. B. CARPENTER 'Protoplasm' or living jelly, which is not yet differentiated into 'organs'. M. K. POPE In Late Latin it was the tonic vowel that was differentiated if juxtaposed to a final flexional vowel that was homophonous.

4 *verb intrans.* Become differentiated or specialized. **L19.**
5 *verb trans. & intrans.* Observe, ascertain, or recognize the difference (in or between); distinguish, discriminate, (between). **L19.**

J. JASTROW One important use of child study is to differentiate between functions that in the adult have become merged. T. E. HULME They first began to be differentiated by the German writers on aesthetics in the eighteenth century.

▸ **B** *noun*. A rock produced by the differentiation of a magma. **E20.**
■ **differentiatedness** *noun* the property of being differentiated **M20. differentiator** *noun* a person who or thing which differentiates **L19.**

differentiation /ˌdɪfərɛnʃɪ'eɪʃ(ə)n/ *noun*. **E19.**
[ORIGIN from DIFFERENTIATE: see -ATION.]
The action or process of differentiating.

R. BARTHOLOW A careful differentiation of the causes. A. R. WALLACE Long continued isolation would often lead to the differentiation of the species. P. TILLICH Not conformity but differentiation is the end of the ways of God.

difficile /'dɪfɪsiːl, *foreign* difisil/ *adjective*. **LME.**
[ORIGIN French from Latin *difficilis*, from DIF- + *facilis* easy.]
†**1** = DIFFICULT *adjective* 1. **LME–L17.**
†**2** = DIFFICULT *adjective* 3. **L15–M17.**
3 = DIFFICULT *adjective* 2. **M16.**

R. BROOKE These Oxford people are so damn difficile.

■ **diffi'cileness** *noun* **E17.**

difficilior lectio /dɪfɪ'kɪlɪɔː ˌlɛktɪəʊ/ *noun phr.* Pl. **difficiliores lectiones** /dɪfɪkɪlɪ'ɔːreɪz lɛktɪˌəʊneɪz/. **E20.**
[ORIGIN Latin, from the maxim *difficilior lectio potior* the harder reading is to be preferred. See also LECTIO DIFFICILIOR.]
TEXTUAL CRITICISM. The more difficult or unexpected of two variant readings and therefore the one that is less likely to be a copyist's error; (the principle of) giving preference to such a reading.

difficult /'dɪfɪk(ə)lt/ *adjective*. **LME.**
[ORIGIN Back-form. from DIFFICULTY *noun*. Cf. DIFFICILIOR LECTIO.]
1 Requiring physical or mental effort or skill; occasioning or attended with trouble. (Foll. by *to do*, *of*, *in*.) **LME.**

WORDSWORTH Knowledge . . is difficult to gain. J. L. MOTLEY It is difficult to imagine a more universal disaster. J. CONRAD Some harbours . . are made difficult of access by . . sunken rocks. *Daily Mirror* Help to see him through the difficult weeks ahead.

2 Of a person: not easy to get on with; unaccommodating, stubborn, argumentative; *arch.* hard to satisfy, fastidious. **E16.**

S. BELLOW He . . became quarrelsome once again, difficult, touchy, exaggerating, illogical, overly familiar.

3 Hard to understand; puzzling, obscure. **M16.**

H. T. BUCKLE One of the most difficult of our poets.

■ **difficultly** *adverb* with difficulty; obscurely: **M16. difficultness** *noun* difficulty; perversity: **M16.**

difficult /'dɪfɪk(ə)lt/ *verb trans.* **LME.**
[ORIGIN French †*difficulter* from medieval Latin *difficultare*, formed as DIFFICULTY *noun*.]
†**1** Impede, render difficult to accomplish. **LME–E19.**
2 Put in a difficulty, perplex, embarrass (a person). Usu. in *pass.* Chiefly *Scot.* **L17.**
■ †**difficultate** *verb trans.* (*rare*) = DIFFICULT *verb* 1 **E17–E19.**

difficulty /'dɪfɪk(ə)ltɪ/ *noun*. **LME.**
[ORIGIN Latin *difficultas*, formed as DIF- + *facultas*: see FACULTY *noun*. Also infl. by French *difficulté*.]
1 The quality, fact, or condition of requiring effort or skill. **LME.**

J. THURBER Peifer twisted around on the sofa, slowly and with difficulty.

2 Reluctance, unwillingness; an objection. *obsolete* exc. in ***make a difficulty*** etc. below. **LME.**

F. VERE Her Majesty . . with some difficulty (as her manner was) granted the men to be levied.

3 Something difficult; a hindrance; an obscure point. **LME.**

R. MACAULAY The jeep . . solved all our transport difficulties.

4 Perplexing character, obscurity. **E16.**

YEATS A book whose difficulty had offended indolence.

5 *sing.* & in *pl.* A condition in which action or progress is difficult, *esp.* a shortage of money. **E18.**

S. SMILES A serious difficulty occurred between him and his wife on this very point. *Times* One of America's biggest banks . . was in difficulties.

– PHRASES: **make a difficulty**, **make difficulties**, †**make difficulty** show reluctance, be unaccommodating.

diffidation /dɪfɪˈdeɪʃ(ə)n/ *noun. arch.* **M18.**
[**ORIGIN** medieval Latin *diffidatio(n-)*, from *diffidare* renounce an alliance, from Proto-Romance, whence also **DEFY** *verb*: see **-ATION**.]
The dissolution of a relationship of trust or allegiance; declaration of hostilities.

diffide /dɪˈfʌɪd/ *verb intrans.* Now *rare.* **M16.**
[**ORIGIN** Latin *diffidere*, formed as **DIF-** + *fidere* trust.]
Lack confidence (*in*).

diffidence /ˈdɪfɪd(ə)ns/ *noun.* **LME.**
[**ORIGIN** French †*diffidence* or its source Latin *diffidentia*, formed as **DIFFIDENT**: see **-ENCE**.]
1 Lack of confidence; distrust, (a) doubt. Now *rare* or *obsolete.* **LME.**
2 Lack of confidence in one's abilities or worth; self-mistrust; (a feeling of) shyness. **E17.**

W. C. WILLIAMS I feel a certain diffidence about attempting to speak of the book at all.

■ Also **diffidency** *noun* (long *rare*) **E17.**

diffident /ˈdɪfɪd(ə)nt/ *adjective.* **LME.**
[**ORIGIN** Latin *diffident-* pres. ppl stem of *diffidere*: see **DIFFIDE** *verb*, **-ENT**.]
1 Lacking confidence or trust (*in*); distrustful, mistrustful (*of*). Now *rare.* **LME.**
2 Lacking self-confidence; timid in one's dealings with others. **E18.**
■ **diffidently** *adverb* **E17.**

†**diffinition** *noun* see **DEFINITION**.

†**diffinitive** *adjective & noun*: see **DEFINITIVE**.

†**difflation** *noun.* **M16–M18.**
[**ORIGIN** from Latin *difflat-* pa. ppl stem of *difflare*, formed as **DIF-** + *flare* blow: see **-ATION**.]
Dispersion by blowing.

diffluence /ˈdɪflʊəns/ *noun.* **M17.**
[**ORIGIN** from (the same root as) **DIFFLUENT**: see **-ENCE**.]
1 The action or fact of flowing apart; dispersion by flowing. **M17.**

G. E. HUTCHINSON The western end of Windermere suggests glacial diffluence.

2 Dissolution into a liquid state; deliquescence. **M19.**

diffluent /ˈdɪflʊənt/ *adjective.* **E17.**
[**ORIGIN** Latin *diffluent-* pres. ppl stem of *diffluere* flow apart or away, formed as **DIF-** + *fluere* flow: see **-ENT**.]
Characterized by or exhibiting diffluence.

†**difform** *adjective.* **M16.**
[**ORIGIN** Old French & mod. French *difforme* or medieval Latin *difformis* from Latin *deformis*: see **DIF-**, **DEFORM** *adjective*.]
1 Of diverse forms; differing in shape. **M16–L17.**
2 Irregular in shape; without regularity of parts. **E17–M19.**

†**difformity** *noun*[1]. Also **deform-**. **M16.**
[**ORIGIN** French *difformité* or medieval Latin *difformitas*, from *difformis*: see **DIFFORM**, **-ITY**.]
1 Difference or diversity of form; absence of uniformity between things. **M16–M19.**
2 Divergence in form (*from*); lack of conformity (*with* or *to* a standard). **M16–L17.**

†**difformity** *noun*[2] var. of **DEFORMITY** *noun*[1].

diffract /dɪˈfrakt/ *verb trans.* **E19.**
[**ORIGIN** Latin *diffract-*: see **DIFFRACTION**.]
Cause (light etc.) to undergo diffraction.

fig.: CARLYLE Some obscure distorted image of right . . diffracted, exaggerated, in the wonderfullest way.

■ **diffractive** *adjective* tending to diffract **E19.** **diffractively** *adverb* by diffraction **L19.** **diffractogram** *noun* a photograph etc. of a diffraction pattern **M20.** **diffracˈtometer** *noun* an instrument for measuring diffraction, esp. of X-rays in crystallography **E20.** **diffracˈtometry** *noun* the measurement of diffraction; the use of a diffractometer: **M20.**

diffraction /dɪˈfrakʃ(ə)n/ *noun.* **L17.**
[**ORIGIN** French, or mod. Latin *diffractio(n-)*, from Latin *diffract-* pa. ppl stem of *diffringere* break in pieces, formed as **DIF-** + *frangere* break: see **-ION**.]
The breaking up of a beam of light into a transverse series of dark and light bands or coloured spectra by the edge of an opaque body or a narrow aperture; an analogous phenomenon with other waves; the spreading of waves of any kind by the edge of an obstacle.
– **COMB.**: **diffraction grating** a plate of glass or polished metal ruled with very close equidistant parallel lines, producing a spectrum by diffraction and subsequent interference of the transmitted or reflected light. **diffraction pattern** the pattern formed by light, X-rays, etc., after diffraction, esp. by a crystal.

diffusable /dɪˈfjuːzəb(ə)l/ *adjective.* **L18.**
[**ORIGIN** formed as **DIFFUSATE** + **-ABLE**.]
= **DIFFUSIBLE**.

diffusant /dɪˈfjuːz(ə)nt/ *noun.* **M20.**
[**ORIGIN** formed as **DIFFUSATE** + **-ANT**[1].]
A substance which diffuses through another.

diffusate /dɪˈfjuːzeɪt/ *noun.* **M19.**
[**ORIGIN** from **DIFFUSE** *verb* + **-ATE**[1].]
A substance which has diffused through a membrane or barrier; a dialysate.

diffuse /dɪˈfjuːs/ *adjective.* **LME.**
[**ORIGIN** French *diffus* or Latin *diffusus* extensive, pa. pple of *diffundere* pour out, formed as **DIF-** + *fundere* pour.]
†**1** Confused, perplexed; vague, obscure, doubtful. **LME–E17.**
2 Of style, a writer, etc.: not concise; wordy, verbose. **LME.**
3 Widespread, dispersed; *spec.* (of light, disease, etc.) not localized or concentrated. **L15.**

S. JOHNSON The pomp of wide margin and diffuse typography.

■ **diffusely** *adverb* **LME.** **diffuseness** *noun* the quality of being diffuse, esp. in speech or writing **L15.**

diffuse /dɪˈfjuːz/ *verb.* **LME.**
[**ORIGIN** Latin *diffus-* pa. ppl stem of *diffundere*: see **DIFFUSE** *adjective*.]
▸**I** **1** *verb trans. & intrans.* Spread abroad or pour forth as from a centre of dispersion; spread widely over an area or through a region. **LME.**

T. KEN Love . . will all diffuse in Extacy. D. MASSON A heartless man does not diffuse geniality and kindness around him. L. DEIGHTON The moonlight . . was diffused by the thin cloud.

†**2** *verb trans.* Pour out like a fluid, shed. **L16–M18.**

SHAKES. *Temp.* Who, with thy saffron wings, upon my flow'rs Diffusest honey drops.

3 *verb trans.* Extend or stretch out (the body, limbs, etc.) freely. *arch.* or *poet.* **L17.**
4 *SCIENCE.* **a** *verb trans.* Cause to pass or intermingle by diffusion. **E19.** ▸**b** *verb intrans.* Of a fluid or individual atoms etc.: undergo diffusion, pass by diffusion. **M19.**

a D. ATTENBOROUGH Species appeared which could fill their air-bags by diffusing gas into them from the blood.

▸†**II** **5** *verb trans.* Make confused, obscure, or indistinct. Chiefly as ***diffused*** *ppl adjective.* **M16–E17.**
■ **diffusedly** *adverb* †(*a*) confusedly, obscurely; (*b*) with diffusion, interpenetration, etc.; †(*c*) with prolixity of language: **M16.** **diffusedness** *noun* the quality of being widely dispersed **E17.** **diffuser** *noun* a person who or thing which diffuses; *esp.* (*a*) a device for diffusing light; (*b*) a duct for broadening an airflow and reducing its speed: **L17.**

diffusible /dɪˈfjuːzɪb(ə)l/ *adjective.* **L18.**
[**ORIGIN** from **DIFFUSE** *verb* + **-IBLE**. Cf. **DIFFUSABLE**.]
Capable of diffusing or of being diffused; *spec.* (of fluids etc.) able to intermingle by diffusion.
■ **diffusiˈbility** *noun* **E19.**

diffusion /dɪˈfjuːʒ(ə)n/ *noun.* **LME.**
[**ORIGIN** Latin *diffusio(n-)*, from *diffus-*: see **DIFFUSE** *verb*, **-ION**.]
†**1** The action of pouring out or forth; outpouring, effusion. Chiefly *fig.* **LME–M17.**
2 The action or result of spreading abroad; wide and general distribution; the state of not being localized. **L16.**

H. E. BATES The coppery diffusion of light filtering down through crowds of turning leaves.

3 *fig.* Dispersion, dissemination, (of knowledge, fame, etc.); *ANTHROPOLOGY* the spread of elements of culture etc. from one region or people to another. **M18.**

B. C. BRODIE The effect which the general diffusion of knowledge produces on society.

4 Copiousness of language; prolixity. **L18.**
5 *SCIENCE.* The spontaneous intermingling of fluids by the natural random motion of their particles; the spread of a single fluid in this way. **E19.**
– **COMB.**: **diffusion line**, **diffusion range** a range of relatively inexpensive ready-to-wear garments produced for the mass market by a fashion designer.
■ **diffusional** *adjective* pertaining to or involving diffusion **M20.** **diffusionism** *noun* the theory that all or most cultural similarities are due to diffusion **E20.** **diffusionist** *adjective & noun* (*a*) *adjective* of or pertaining to diffusionism; (*b*) *noun* an advocate of diffusionism: **L19.**

diffusive /dɪˈfjuːsɪv/ *adjective.* **E17.**
[**ORIGIN** medieval Latin *diffusivus*, formed as **DIFFUSE** *verb*: see **-IVE**.]
1 Having the quality of diffusing; characterized by diffusion (*lit. & fig.*). **E17.**
†**2** Of a body of people: consisting of members in their individual capacity rather than a collective or representative one. **M17–E18.**
3 = **DIFFUSE** *adjective* 2. **L17.**
■ **diffusively** *adverb* **E17.** **diffusiveness** *noun* **M17.**

diffusivity /dɪfjuːˈsɪvɪti/ *noun.* **L19.**
[**ORIGIN** from **DIFFUSIVE** + **-ITY**.]
Diffusibility; *spec.* = ***thermal diffusivity*** s.v. **THERMAL** *adjective.*

dig /dɪɡ/ *noun*[1]. **L17.**
[**ORIGIN** from **DIG** *verb*.]
1 A tool for digging. *dial.* **L17.**
2 A thrust, a sharp poke, as with the elbow etc. **E19.** ▸**b** *fig.* A remark directed against a person. **M19.**

b *Today* Graham was not happy about that and had a dig at me in the press.

3 A diligent or plodding student. *US slang.* **M19.**
4 An act or spell of digging; a depth or quantity to be dug. **L19.** ▸**b** (An expedition for the purpose of) an archaeological excavation. *colloq.* **L19.**
5 In *pl.* Lodgings. *colloq.* **L19.**

Independent Sharing digs is stressful.

dig /dɪɡ/ *noun*[2]. *Austral. & NZ colloq.* **E20.**
[**ORIGIN** Abbreviation.]
= **DIGGER** 4.

dig /dɪɡ/ *verb.* Infl. **-gg-**. Pa. t. & pple **dug** /dʌɡ/, (*arch. & dial.*) **digged**. **ME.**
[**ORIGIN** Perh. from Old English *dīc* **DITCH** *noun* & already in Old English.]
1 *verb intrans.* Make a hole in, excavate, or turn up the ground etc. with a spade, pick, hands, claws, snout, etc. **ME.** ▸**b** *verb intrans.* Make archaeological investigations. **E20.**

J. BUCHAN An old stationmaster was digging in his garden. **b** T. E. LAWRENCE I would like to dig in the Persian gulf.

2 *verb trans.* Penetrate and turn (the ground etc.) with a spade etc.; *esp.* break up and turn (the soil) to prepare it for cultivation. **LME.** ▸**b** *verb trans.* Excavate archaeologically. **M18.**

D. LESSING Ground . . was being dug for new gardens.

3 *verb trans.* Make (a hole, mine, etc.) by digging. **LME.**
dig a pit for *fig.* try to entrap. ***dig the grave of***: see **GRAVE** *noun*[1].
4 **a** *verb trans.* Obtain or extract by digging. (Foll. by *from*, *out of*.) **LME.** ▸**b** *verb intrans.* Study a subject closely. Chiefly *US.* **E19.** ▸**c** *verb intrans.* Understand. *slang.* **M20.** ▸**d** *verb trans.* Appreciate, enjoy; understand; look at or listen to (something to be enjoyed). *slang.* **M20.**

a DAY LEWIS Keyes, the gardener, was digging potatoes. **b** L. M. ALCOTT Laurie 'dug' to some purpose that year. **d** D. MACDONALD The women's magazine is such an ancient and essential form of journalism that even the English dig it.

†**5** *verb trans.* Put *in* or *into* the ground by digging; bury. **M16–M17.**

J. PALSGRAVE I wyll dygge this dogge in to the grounde somewhere for feare of stynkyng.

6 *verb trans.* Thrust or force *in* or *into.* **M16.**

D. WELCH He grasped me tightly and dug his fingers into my flesh.

7 *verb intrans.* Penetrate or make one's way *into* or *through* (as) by digging; make an excavation *under.* **M16.**
8 *verb trans.* Spur (a horse) vigorously; give (a person) a sharp thrust or nudge. **M16.**
9 *verb intrans.* Have lodgings. *colloq.* **E20.**
– **WITH ADVERBS IN SPECIALIZED SENSES**: **dig down** (*a*) cause to fall by digging; (*b*) lower or remove by digging; (*c*) *N. Amer. colloq.* pay money from one's own pocket. **dig in** (*a*) mix (something) with the soil by digging; (*b*) cause to penetrate, drive in deeply, (***dig in one's heels***, ***dig in one's toes***, keep resolutely or obstinately to one's decision, opinion, etc.); (*c*) establish one's position; prepare a defensive trench or pit; *CRICKET* consolidate one's position as a batsman; (*d*) *dial. & N. Amer. colloq.* set to work earnestly and energetically; (*e*) *colloq.* begin eating, esp. heartily. **dig out** (*a*) extract or remove by digging; *fig.* obtain or get out by search or effort; (*b*) form by excavation; (*c*) *US colloq.* depart. **dig up** (*a*) take or get out of the ground by digging; (now *colloq.*) obtain, find, search out; (***dig up the tomahawk***: see **TOMAHAWK** *noun*); (*b*) break up or open by digging, excavate; (*c*) break up and loosen the soil of (fallow land).

Digambara /diːˈɡʌmbərə/ *noun.* **E19.**
[**ORIGIN** Sanskrit *Digāmbara* lit. 'sky-clad'.]
A member of one of the two principal sects of Jainism, ascetic members of which traditionally wear no clothes and renounce all property. Cf. **SVETAMBARA**.

digamma /dʌɪˈɡamə/ *noun.* **L17.**
[**ORIGIN** Latin from Greek, from *di-* **DI-**[2], **GAMMA** (from the shape of the letter).]
The sixth letter (Ϝ, ϝ) of the original Greek alphabet, probably equivalent to W, later disused.
■ **digammated** *adjective* spelled with or having the digamma **E19.**

digamy /ˈdɪɡəmi/ *noun.* **E17.**
[**ORIGIN** Late Latin *digamia* from Greek, from *digamos* married to two people, formed as **DI-**[2] + **-GAMY**.]
1 The state of having married again after the death or divorce of the first spouse. **E17.**
†**2** = **BIGAMY** 1. **M17–M18.**
■ **digamist** *noun* a person who has entered into digamy **M17.** **digamous** *adjective* **M19.**

digastric /dʌɪˈɡastrɪk/ *noun & adjective.* **L17.**
[**ORIGIN** mod. Latin *digastricus*, formed as **DI-**[2] + Greek *gastēr* belly: see **-IC**.]
ANATOMY. ▸**A** *noun.* A mandibular muscle that assists in opening the jaw. **L17.**
▸**B** *adjective.* **1** Of a muscle: having two thick fleshy parts with a tendon between. **E18.**
2 Of or pertaining to the digastric muscle of the jaw. **M19.**

Digby /ˈdɪɡbi/ *noun.* **E19.**
[**ORIGIN** See below.]
In full ***Digby chick***, ***Digby chicken***. A dried or cured herring of a type caught at Digby, Nova Scotia.

D

D

digenean /dʌɪdʒɪˈniːən, dʌɪˈdʒɛniən/ *noun & adjective*. M20.
[ORIGIN from mod. Latin *Digenea* (see below), formed as DI-² + Greek *genea* race, generation: see -AN.]
ZOOLOGY. ▸**A** *noun*. A trematode fluke of the subclass Digenea, which comprises endoparasitic species with a complex life cycle involving two to four hosts; a digenetic fluke. M20.
▸**B** *adjective*. Of or pertaining to the digeneans. M20.

digenesis /dʌɪˈdʒɛnɪsɪs/ *noun*. L19.
[ORIGIN from DI-² + -GENESIS.]
= *ALTERNATION* **of generations**.
■ **digeˈnetic** *adjective* (*a*) pertaining to or characterized by digenesis; (*b*) designating a parasite which has a life cycle involving more than one host; digenean: L19.

digenite /ˈdɪdʒənʌɪt/ *noun*. M19.
[ORIGIN from Greek *digenēs* of doubtful kind + -ITE¹.]
MINERALOGY. A blue to black cubic copper sulphide occurring in copper ores.

digerati /dɪdʒəˈrɑːti/ *noun pl*. L20.
[ORIGIN Blend of DIGITAL *adjective* and LITERATI.]
People with expertise or professional involvement in information technology.

†**digerent** *adjective & noun*. *rare*. L15.
[ORIGIN Latin *digerent-*, pres. ppl stem of *digerere*: see DIGEST *verb*, -ENT.]
▸**A** *adjective*. Digesting. L15–M18.
▸**B** *noun*. A medicine etc. that promotes suppuration. M18–M19.

digest /ˈdʌɪdʒɛst/ *noun*. LME.
[ORIGIN Latin *digesta* matters methodically arranged, neut. pl. of *digestus* pa. pple of *digerere* divide, distribute, dissolve, digest, from *di-* DI-¹ + *gerere* bear, carry.]
†**1** = DIGESTION 1, 2. LME–M18.
2 LAW. **a** The writings of Roman jurists collected and condensed by order of Justinian. Usu. ***the Digest***. LME. ▸**b** An abstract of some body of law, systematically arranged. L16.
3 A digested collection of statements; a methodically arranged compendium or summary of information. M16. ▸**b** *spec*. A periodical composed chiefly of condensed versions of pieces previously published elsewhere. E20.

H. G. WELLS We have to make a digest now of all that stuff and keep it up-to-date. **b** J. CANNAN Mad ideas they'd got from medical articles in Digests.

4 A substance obtained by digestion with heat etc. E20.

digest /dɪˈdʒɛst, dʌɪ-/ *verb*. LME.
[ORIGIN Latin *digest-* pa. ppl stem of *digerere*: see DIGEST *noun*.]
1 *verb trans. & intrans*. Assimilate (food) in the stomach and bowels or otherwise into the bodily system. LME. ▸**b** *verb trans*. Cause or promote the digestion of (food). L15. ▸**c** *verb intrans*. Of food: undergo digestion. L16.

C. DARWIN Several leaves caught successively three insects each, but most of them were not able to digest the third fly.

2 *verb trans*. **a** Settle and arrange methodically in the mind; consider, ponder. LME. ▸**b** Comprehend and assimilate mentally; obtain mental nourishment from. M16.

a JOSEPH HALL When the kyng had long digested and studied on this matter. **b** D. BOGARDE There shouldn't, he reasoned, having digested his Intelligence Reports, be much . . opposition.

3 *verb trans*. Arrange methodically; reduce to a systematic or convenient form; classify. L15.

SWIFT I have had no manner of Time to digest it into Order, or correct the Stile.

†**4** *verb trans*. **a** Disperse; dissipate. E16–E18. ▸**b** Divide and dispose, distribute. L16–L17.
5 *verb trans*. Bear without resistance; brook; endure. M16. ▸**b** Get over the effects of. *arch*. L16.

W. IRVING This wanton attack . . is too much even for me to digest!

†**6** *verb trans. & intrans*. Mature (a tumour); (cause to) suppurate. M16–M18.
7 *verb intrans. & trans*. Treat (a substance) with heat and usu. moisture or chemicals in order to decompose it, extract soluble constituents, etc. L16.
†**8** *verb trans*. Mature or bring to a state of perfection, esp. by the action of heat. E17–E18.
■ **digestant** *noun* something taken to promote digestion L19. **digestedly** *adverb* in a digested or well-arranged manner E17. **digester** *noun* a person who or thing which digests; *esp*. (*a*) a person or organism that digests food in a specified manner; (*b*) a vessel in which substances are digested: L15.

digestible /dɪˈdʒɛstɪb(ə)l, dʌɪ-/ *adjective*. LME.
[ORIGIN Old French & mod. French from Latin *digestibilis*, formed as DIGEST *verb*: see -IBLE.]
Able to be digested; easily digested.
■ **digestiˈbility** *noun* M18. **digestibleness** *noun* M17. **digestibly** *adverb* L19.

digestif /diʒɛstif (*pl. same*), dʌɪˈdʒɛstɪf/ *noun*. E20.
[ORIGIN French: see DIGESTIVE.]
Something which promotes good digestion, esp. a drink taken after a meal.

digestion /dɪˈdʒɛstʃ(ə)n, dʌɪ-/ *noun*. LME.
[ORIGIN Old French & mod. French from Latin *digestio(n-)*, formed as DIGEST *verb*: see -ION.]
1 The process by which ingested food is broken down in the body into forms that may be readily assimilated. Also (MEDICINE), the enzymic breakdown of bodily tissue in various disease states. LME.

SHAKES. *Rich. II* Things sweet to taste prove in digestion sour.

2 The power or faculty of digesting food; the ability to assimilate food without discomfort. LME.

ARNOLD BENNETT The children feared goose for their father, whose digestion was usually unequal to this particular bird.

†**3** The process of maturing an ulcer or wound; disposition to healthy suppuration. LME–M19.
4 The process of digesting a substance by heat, solvent, etc. Formerly also, susceptibility to the action of heat; a product of (gentle) heating. LME.
†**5** The action of methodizing and reducing to order; the result of this, a digest. M16–L18.
6 Mental assimilation or absorption of concepts etc. E17.

T. FULLER He had a great appetite to learning, and a quick digestion.

7 The action of bearing without resistance; endurance. Now *rare* or *obsolete*. M17.

L. STERNE The silent digestion of one wrong provokes a second.

digestive /dɪˈdʒɛstɪv, dʌɪ-/ *adjective & noun*. LME.
[ORIGIN Old French & mod. French *digestif*, *-ive* or its source Latin *digestivus*, formed as DIGEST *verb*: see -IVE.]
▸**A** *adjective*. **1** Having the function of digesting food; engaged in or pertaining to the digestion of food. LME.
digestive gland ZOOLOGY = HEPATOPANCREAS.
2 (Supposedly) promoting or aiding the digestion of food; digestible. LME. ▸**b** *spec*. Designating a type of semi-sweet wholemeal biscuit. L19.
3 Pertaining to or promoting chemical digestion. M17.
▸**B** *noun*. **1** Something which promotes good digestion. LME. ▸**b** *spec*. A digestive biscuit. M20.
2 An ointment etc. which promotes healthy suppuration in an ulcer or wound. Now *rare* or *obsolete*. M16.
■ **digestively** *adverb* in a way that promotes digestion; with regard to digestion: E17. **digestiveness** *noun* E18.

digestivo /dɪdʒesˈtiːvəʊ/ *noun*. Pl. ***-vi*** /-vi/. L20.
[ORIGIN Italian, from *digerire* to digest.]
A drink taken after a meal to promote digestion; a digestif.

†**digestory** *adjective & noun*. E17.
[ORIGIN Late Latin *digestorius*, formed as DIGEST *verb*: see -ORY².]
▸**A** *adjective*. = DIGESTIVE *adjective* 3. Only in E17.
▸**B** *noun*. A vessel or organ of digestion. L17–M18.

digger /ˈdɪgə/ *noun*. LME.
[ORIGIN from DIG *verb* + -ER¹.]
1 *gen*. A person who or animal which digs. LME. ▸**b** A miner, *esp*. one who searches for gold. M16. ▸**c** ENGLISH HISTORY. A member of a short-lived 17th-cent. radical Puritan group which believed in communal ownership of land and began cultivating commons. M17. ▸**d** A N. American Indian of any of several tribes who subsisted chiefly on roots. M19. ▸**e** A person who digs for archaeological purposes. E20.
2 (A part of) a tool or machine for digging. L17.
3 More fully ***digger wasp***. A wasp that burrows in the soil; *esp*. any of several usu. solitary wasps of the superfamily Sphecoidea. M19.
4 An Australian or New Zealander, esp. a private soldier. Freq. as a form of address: mate, pal. *colloq*. E20.
– COMB.: **digger's delight** *Austral*. a speedwell, *Veronica perfoliata*, supposed to indicate the presence of gold; ***digger wasp***: see sense 3 above.

digging /ˈdɪgɪŋ/ *noun*. LME.
[ORIGIN from DIG *verb* + -ING¹.]
1 The action of DIG *verb*; an instance of this. LME.
double digging: see DOUBLE *adjective & adverb*.
2 In *pl*. Materials dug out. M16.
3 *sing*. & (usu.) in *pl*. (treated as *sing*. or *pl*.). A place where digging is carried on; *esp*. a mine or goldfield. M16. ▸**b** *sing*. & (usu.) in *pl*. Archaeological excavation; the site of such an excavation. E20.
POOR MAN's diggings.
4 In *pl*. Lodgings. *colloq*. M19.
– COMB.: **digging stick** a primitive digging implement consisting of a pointed stick, sometimes weighted by a stone.

dight /dʌɪt/ *verb trans*. Pa. pple **dight**.
[ORIGIN Old English *dihtan* = Middle Low German, Middle Dutch *dichten* compose, contrive (Dutch *dichten* invent, compose), Old High German *tihtōn*, *dihtōn* (German *dichten*) write, compose verses, Old Norse *dikta* compose in Latin, invent, contrive, from Latin *dictare* appoint, prescribe, dictate, (in medieval Latin) write, compose.]
▸**I** Direct, ordain, dispose of, deal with.
†**1** Direct, give directions to. Only in OE.
†**2** Appoint, ordain, (a fate etc.). OE–M16.
†**3** Keep in order, manage, govern. ME–E16.
†**4** Deal with, use, (in some manner); *esp*. maltreat. ME–M17. ▸**b** Have sexual relations with. Only in LME.
†**5** Place, put; remove. ME–M16. ▸**b** Put into a specified state, esp. to death; cause (death). ME–E19.
▸**II** Compose, make.
†**6** Compose (with words); set down in writing. OE–LME.
†**7** Construct, make. ME–E17.
†**8** Perform, do. ME–L16.
▸**III** Put in order, make ready.
†**9** Put in order, arrange. ME–L15.
10 Equip, fit out (*with*). Now usu. in *pass. arch*. ME.
11 Clothe, array, adorn. Now usu. in *pass. arch. & poet*. ME. ▸†**b** Dress (a wound). LME–M16. ▸**c** Put on (armour etc.). L16. ▸**d** Dirty, befoul. *dial*. M17.

MILTON Storied windows richly dight, Casting a dim religious light. H. MACDIARMID All the changes in which the hawthorn is dight.

†**12** Make (a person, esp. oneself) ready (*to do*). ME–L16. ▸**b** Direct (oneself), make (one's way); go. ME–L16.
13 Make ready for use or a purpose; prepare. *poet*. ME. ▸**b** Winnow (corn). *Scot. & N. English*. L15. ▸**c** Wipe clean or dry. *Scot. & N. English*. E16.

W. MORRIS This Queen of the many wooers dights the wedding for us.

14 Repair, put right. Now *dial*. ME.
†**15** Cultivate, dress, (crops, land, etc.). LME–M16.
▸†**IV** **16** Lift. *rare* (Spenser). Only in L16.
■ **dighter** *noun* (now *dial*.) OE.

digicam /ˈdɪdʒɪkam/ *noun*. L20.
[ORIGIN from DIGI(TAL + CAM *noun*².]
(Proprietary name for) a digital camera.

digit /ˈdɪdʒɪt/ *noun*. LME.
[ORIGIN Latin *digitus* finger, toe.]
1 MATH. Each of the ten arabic numerals from 0 to 9, esp. when part of a number. LME.

M. AMIS I dialled seven digits.

BINARY digit. ***parity digit***: see PARITY *noun*¹. ***significant digit***: see SIGNIFICANT *adjective* 1c.
2 ASTRONOMY. The twelfth part of the diameter of the sun or moon, esp. as a measure of the magnitude of an eclipse. L16.
3 A finger, a toe, (now *joc*. exc. ANATOMY). Also ZOOLOGY, an analogous structure at the end of the limbs of many higher vertebrates. M17.
4 A finger's breadth as a unit of length; ¾ inch. M17.

digital /ˈdɪdʒɪt(ə)l/ *noun & adjective*. LME.
[ORIGIN Latin *digitalis*, formed as DIGIT: see -AL¹.]
▸**A** *noun*. †**1** = DIGIT 1. Only in LME.
2 A finger. *joc*. M19.
▸**B** *adjective*. **1** Of or pertaining to a digit (DIGIT 1) or digits; now *spec*. designating a computer which operates on data in the form of digits or similar discrete elements. (*rare* before M20.) L15. ▸**b** Of a clock or watch: showing the time by means of displayed digits rather than hands or a pointer. M20.
2 Of or pertaining to a finger or fingers; ANATOMY resembling a finger or the hollow impression made by one. M17.
3 Pertaining to or using signals or information represented by discrete values of a physical quantity such as voltage or magnetic polarization. Opp. ANALOGUE. M20. ▸**b** Designating or pertaining to a recording in which the original signal is represented by the spacing between pulses rather than by a wave. M20.

Times Digital channels . . are eating into the terrestrial channels' dominance.

4 Involving or pertaining to the use of computer technology. L20.

Scientific American Digital manipulation of news photographs can become a novel form of spin doctoring. *Independent* The digital music industry is growing at a phenomenal rate.

– SPECIAL COLLOCATIONS: **digital cash** money which may be transferred electronically from one party to another during a transaction; *spec*. (*a*) money held on a rechargeable card from which funds may be deducted at point-of-sale terminals; (*b*) money held in an electronic account which can be debited when buying goods and services on the Internet. **digital clock**: showing the time by means of displayed digits rather than hands on a dial. **digital compact cassette** a format for tape cassettes similar to ordinary audio cassettes but with digital rather than analogue recording. **digital divide** the gulf between those who have ready access to computers and the Internet and those who do not. ***digital root***: see ROOT *noun*¹. **digital signature** COMPUTING a digital code (generated and authenticated by public key encryption) which is attached to an electronically transmitted document to verify its contents and the sender's identity. **digital versatile disc**, **digital video disc** a type of compact disc with enlarged data storage capacity, which can store both video and audio data and was introduced as a replacement for videotape (abbreviation ***DVD***). ***digital watch*** see ***digital clock*** above.
■ **digitally** *adverb* (*a*) by means of or with respect to the fingers; (*b*) by means of digits; in digital form: M17.

digitalis /dɪdʒɪˈteɪlɪs/ *noun*. E17.
[ORIGIN mod. Latin, use as noun (sc. *herba* plant) of Latin *digitalis* pertaining to the finger, after German *Fingerhut* thimble, foxglove.]
1 The foxglove. E17.

2 A preparation of dried foxglove leaves used as a drug, esp. to stimulate the heart; a glycoside or mixture of glycosides present in this. L18.
■ **digitalin** *noun* the pharmacologically active constituent(s) of the foxglove M19.

digitalize /ˈdɪdʒɪt(ə)lʌɪz/ *verb*¹ *trans.* Also **-ise**. E20.
[ORIGIN from DIGITALIS + -IZE.]
MEDICINE. Administer digitalis to; produce a physiological response in (a subject) by this means.
■ **digitaliˈzation** *noun*¹ L19.

digitalize /ˈdɪdʒɪt(ə)lʌɪz/ *verb*² *trans.* Also **-ise**. M20.
[ORIGIN from DIGITAL + -IZE.]
= DIGITIZE 2.
■ **digitaliˈzation** *noun*² M20.

digitate /ˈdɪdʒɪtət, -eɪt/ *adjective*. M17.
[ORIGIN Latin *digitatus*, formed as DIGIT: see -ATE².]
1 *ZOOLOGY.* Having separate fingers or toes. M17.
2 *BOTANY & ZOOLOGY.* Divided into parts resembling fingers; having deep radiating divisions. M18.
■ **digitately** *adverb* M19.

digitate /ˈdɪdʒɪteɪt/ *verb*. M17.
[ORIGIN medieval Latin *digitat-* pa. ppl stem of *digitare* point at, indicate, formed as DIGIT: see -ATE³.]
†**1** *verb trans.* Indicate. *rare.* Only in M17.
2 *verb intrans.* Become divided into finger-like parts. M18.
■ **digiˈtation** *noun* †(*a*) the action of touching or pointing with the finger; (*b*) the condition of being digitate; (*c*) a finger-like process or division: M17.

digitated /ˈdɪdʒɪteɪtɪd/ *adjective*. M17.
[ORIGIN formed as DIGITATE *adjective* + -ED¹.]
BOTANY & ZOOLOGY. = DIGITATE *adjective*.

digiti- /ˈdɪdʒɪti/ *combining form* of Latin *digitus* DIGIT: see -I-.
■ **digitiform** *adjective* like a finger M19. **digitigrade** *adjective & noun* [Latin *-gradus* walking] *ZOOLOGY* (*a*) *adjective* walking on the digits, the heels not touching the ground, like a dog or cat; designating or adapted for such a manner of walking; not plantigrade; (*b*) *noun* a digitigrade animal: M19.

digitize /ˈdɪdʒɪtʌɪz/ *verb trans.* Also **-ise**. L17.
[ORIGIN from DIGIT *noun* + -IZE.]
1 Manipulate, point at, or count with the fingers. *rare.* L17.
2 Convert (a varying quantity) into a sequence of digits; represent in digital form. M20.
■ **digitiˈzation** *noun* M20. **digitizer** *noun* (*a*) *rare* a person who digitizes; (*b*) a device that converts analogue signals etc. to digital ones: M18.

digitorium /dɪdʒɪˈtɔːrɪəm/ *noun*. L19.
[ORIGIN formed as DIGITIZE + -ORIUM.]
A small portable silent keyboard on which a pianist etc. can exercise the fingers.

digitoxin /dɪdʒɪˈtɒksɪn/ *noun*. L19.
[ORIGIN from DIGITALIS + TOXIN.]
A potentially poisonous steroid glycoside, $C_{41}H_{64}O_{13}$, that is present in the foxglove etc. and is used like digoxin.

digladiation /dʌɪˌgladɪˈeɪʃ(ə)n/ *noun*. Now *rare* or *obsolete*. L16.
[ORIGIN from Latin *digladiat-* pa. ppl stem of *digladiari* contend fiercely, formed as DI-¹ + *gladius* sword: see -ATION.]
1 Hand-to-hand fighting, a hand-to-hand fight, esp. with swords. L16.
2 *fig.* Bickering; (an) argument. L16.

diglossia /dʌɪˈglɒsɪə/ *noun*. M20.
[ORIGIN from Greek *diglōssos* bilingual (formed as DI-² + *glōssa* tongue) + -IA¹, after French *diglossie*.]
LINGUISTICS. The systematic use by a community of two different languages or varieties or dialects of a language in different situations.
■ **diglossic** *adjective* M20.

diglot /ˈdʌɪglɒt/ *adjective & noun*. Also **-tt**. L19.
[ORIGIN Greek *diglōttos*, formed as DI-² + *glōtta* tongue.]
▸ **A** *adjective*. Using two languages; containing a text in two languages. L19.
▸ **B** *noun*. A diglot book. L19.
■ **diˈglottic** *adjective* speaking two languages M19. **diglottism** *noun* the use of (words derived from) two languages L19.

diglyph /ˈdʌɪglɪf/ *noun*. E18.
[ORIGIN Greek *digluphos* doubly indented, formed as DI-² + *gluphein* carve.]
ARCHITECTURE. An ornamental projecting face or tablet with two vertical grooves.

†**dignation** *noun*. LME–M18.
[ORIGIN Latin *dignatio(n-)*, from *dignat-* pa. ppl stem of *dignare*, *-ari* think worthy, DEIGN: see -ATION.]
The act of treating someone as worthy; (a) favour shown, (an) honour conferred.

dignified /ˈdɪgnɪfʌɪd/ *adjective*. L17.
[ORIGIN from DIGNIFY + -ED¹.]
†**1** Ranking as a dignitary, esp. an ecclesiastical one. L17–M19.
2 Invested with dignity; exalted. M18.
3 Marked by dignity; having self-respect without haughtiness; stately. E19.

L. M. MONTGOMERY Mrs. Allan is too old to dance and sing and . . it wouldn't be dignified in a minister's wife.

■ **dignifiedly** *adverb* E19.

dignify /ˈdɪgnɪfʌɪ/ *verb trans.* LME.
[ORIGIN French †*dignifier* (Old French *dignefier*) from late Latin *dignificare*, from Latin *dignus* worthy: see -FY.]
1 Add dignity or honour to; render illustrious or majestic. LME. ▸**b** Represent as worthy; give a high-sounding name to. E17.

POPE No Turbots dignify my boards. R. GRAVES A Royal Duke, with no campaigning medals To dignify his orders. **b** P. G. WODEHOUSE He made his way to the small apartment dignified by the name of library.

†**2** Confer a title or honour upon. L16–E18.
■ **dignifier** *noun* E17.

dignitary /ˈdɪgnɪt(ə)ri/ *noun & adjective*. L17.
[ORIGIN from DIGNITY after *propriety*, *proprietary*: see -ARY¹.]
▸ **A** *noun*. A person holding an official position of some status, esp. in the Church. L17.

E. HEATH The Governor's garden party . . the military band playing, local dignitaries there to meet us.

▸ **B** *adjective*. Pertaining to or invested with a dignity, esp. an ecclesiastical one. E18.

dignity /ˈdɪgnɪti/ *noun*. ME.
[ORIGIN Old French *digneté*, (also mod.) *dignité* from Latin *dignitas*, from *dignus* worthy: see -ITY.]
▸ **I** **1** The quality of being worthy or honourable; true worth, excellence. ME.

T. JEFFERSON I recollect no work of any dignity which has been lately published. *Economist* Steel workers . . prayed with the Pope . . while he spoke of the dignity of labour.

2 Honourable or high estate; degree of estimation, rank. ME. ▸**b** *collect.* Persons of high rank. M16.

A. STORR Concepts . . which cannot yet be awarded the dignity of a scientific hypothesis.

beneath one's dignity unfitting for one to do.
3 An honourable office, rank, or title; an official position. ME.

GIBBON He . . distributed the civil and military dignities among his favourites and followers.

4 A person who holds a high or official position, a dignitary. ME.
5 Elevated manner; fit stateliness. M17.

J. H. NEWMAN He preserved in his domestic arrangements the dignity of a literary and public man. G. A. BIRMINGHAM Tommy is a very lovable dog . . entirely lacking in dignity of figure or pose.

stand on one's dignity insist on respectful treatment.
▸ **II** **6** *ASTROLOGY.* A situation in which a planet's influence is heightened, either by its zodiacal position or by its aspects with other planets. LME.

digonal /ˈdɪgən(ə)l, dʌɪˈgəʊn(ə)l/ *adjective*. L19.
[ORIGIN from DI-² + Greek *gōnia* angle + -AL¹.]
CRYSTALLOGRAPHY. Designating an axis of twofold symmetry.

digoxin /dɪˈdʒɒksɪn/ *noun*. M20.
[ORIGIN Contr. of DIG(IT)OXIN.]
A poisonous steroid glycoside, $C_{41}H_{64}O_{14}$, that is present in the foxglove etc. and is used to treat irregularities of heart rhythm.

digram /ˈdʌɪgram/ *noun*. M17.
[ORIGIN from DI-² + -GRAM.]
A group or word of two letters.

digraph /ˈdʌɪgrɑːf/ *noun*¹. L18.
[ORIGIN from DI-² + -GRAPH.]
A group of two letters representing one sound.
■ **diˈgraphic** *adjective* (*a*) pertaining to or of the nature of a digraph; (*b*) written in two different characters or alphabets: L19.

digraph /ˈdʌɪgrɑːf/ *noun*². M20.
[ORIGIN from *directed graph*: see DIRECT *verb*, GRAPH *noun*¹.]
MATH. A network of lines in which each line has a direction; a set of elements together with ordered pairs of the elements.

digress /dʌɪˈgrɛs/ *verb intrans.* E16.
[ORIGIN Latin *digress-* pa. ppl stem of *digredi*, from *di-* DI-¹ + *gradi* proceed, step, from *gradus* a step.]
†**1** Deviate *from* an allegiance, standard, course of action, etc. E16–E17.
2 Depart from the main or the intended subject in speech or writing, esp. temporarily. E16.

P. ACKROYD But I digress into matters which no longer concern me.

3 Go aside from or *from* one's course; deviate; stray. M16.

C. LAMB I digress into Soho, to explore a bookstall.

†**4** Infringe a law or moral standard. M16–M17.
■ **digresser** *noun* M17. **digressingly** *adverb* by way of digression M19.

digression /dʌɪˈgrɛʃ(ə)n/ *noun*. LME.
[ORIGIN Old French & mod. French, or its source Latin *digressio(n-)*, formed as DIGRESS: see -ION.]
1 Deviation from the main or intended subject in speech or writing, esp. temporarily; an instance of this. LME.

D. JACOBSON I was speaking, then, before that last digression, about the rheumy frustrations and resentments that afflicted me.

2 The action of turning aside from a course. Now *rare*. LME.

J. RAY We made a digression to S. Marino.

†**3** Infringement of a law or moral standard. E16–E17.

SHAKES. *Lucr.* Then my digression is so vile, so base, That it will live engraven in my face.

4 *ASTRONOMY* etc. Deviation from a particular line or a mean position. M17.
■ **digressional** *adjective* pertaining to or characterized by digression. L18. **digressionary** *adjective* of the nature of a digression M18.

D

digressive /dʌɪˈgrɛsɪv/ *adjective*. E17.
[ORIGIN Late Latin *digressivus*, formed as DIGRESS: see -IVE.]
Characterized by or given to digression; of the nature of (a) digression.
■ **digressively** *adverb* M18. **digressiveness** *noun* L19.

diguanide /dʌɪˈgwɑːnʌɪd/ *noun*. E20.
[ORIGIN from DI-² + GUANID(IN)E.]
CHEMISTRY. = BIGUANIDE, DIGUANIDINE.

diguanidine /dʌɪˈgwɑːnɪdiːn/ *noun*. L19.
[ORIGIN from DI-² + GUANIDINE.]
CHEMISTRY. Any compound containing two guanidine radicals, $\cdot NH{\cdot}C(NH)(NH_2)$. Formerly also, the compound biguanide.

digue /dig (*pl. same*), diːg/ *noun*. E16.
[ORIGIN French from Old French (also *dique*) from Flemish, Dutch *dijk* DYKE *noun*¹.]
A dyke (DYKE *noun*¹ 8) in the Netherlands, Flanders, or France.

digyny /dʌɪˈdʒʌɪni/ *noun*. M20.
[ORIGIN from DI-² + Greek *gunē* woman + -Y³.]
BIOLOGY. Fertilization in which two sets of chromosomes are contributed by an ovum or ova.
■ **digynic** *adjective* L20.

dihedral /dʌɪˈhiːdr(ə)l/ *adjective & noun*. L18.
[ORIGIN from DI-² + -HEDRAL.]
▸ **A** *adjective*. **1** Having or contained by two planes or plane faces (e.g. of a crystal). L18.
2 Having or being an angle made by aircraft wings with one another, esp. when less than 180 degrees. E20.
▸ **B** *noun*. A dihedral angle or inclination. E20.

dihexagonal /dʌɪhɛkˈsag(ə)n(ə)l/ *adjective*. M19.
[ORIGIN from DI-² + HEXAGONAL.]
CRYSTALLOGRAPHY. (Of a prism or pyramid of the hexagonal system) such that a horizontal cross-section has 12 angles, alternate ones being equal; of or pertaining to a crystal of this kind.

dihybrid /dʌɪˈhʌɪbrɪd/ *noun & adjective*. E20.
[ORIGIN from DI-² + HYBRID.]
GENETICS. ▸**A** *noun*. A hybrid that is heterozygous at two genetic loci. E20.
▸ **B** *adjective*. Of, pertaining to, or being a dihybrid. E20.
■ **dihybridism** *noun* E20.

dihydr- *combining form* see DIHYDRO-.

dihydrate /dʌɪˈhʌɪdreɪt/ *noun*. E20.
[ORIGIN from DI-² + HYDRATE *noun*.]
CHEMISTRY. A hydrate containing two moles of water per mole of the compound.

dihydric /dʌɪˈhʌɪdrɪk/ *adjective*. L19.
[ORIGIN from DI-² + HYDRIC *adjective*¹.]
CHEMISTRY. Containing two hydroxyl groups or (formerly) two hydrogen atoms in the molecule.

dihydro- /dʌɪˈhʌɪdrəʊ/ *combining form*. Before a vowel also **dihydr-**.
[ORIGIN from DI-² + HYDRO-.]
CHEMISTRY. Containing two atoms of hydrogen in the molecule.
■ **dihydrotesˈtosterone** *noun* the compound into which testosterone is converted in tissue where it exerts its hormonal effect M20.

dihydroxy- /dʌɪhʌɪˈdrɒksi/ *combining form*.
[ORIGIN from DI-² + HYDROXY-.]
CHEMISTRY. Containing two hydroxyl groups in the molecule.
■ **dihydroxyˈacetone** *noun* a strongly reducing isomer, $(CH_2OH)CO$, of glyceraldehyde used in lotions for colouring the skin in sunlight L19.

diiamb /dʌɪˈʌɪam(b)/ *noun*. M18.
[ORIGIN Late Latin *diiambus* from Greek *diambos*, from *di-* DI-² + *iambos* IAMBUS.]
PROSODY. A metrical foot consisting of two iambs.

dijudicate /dʌɪˈdʒuːdɪkeɪt/ *verb intrans. & trans.* Now *rare*. E17.
[ORIGIN Latin *dijudicat-*: see DIJUDICATION, -ATE³.]
Pass judgement (on or between).

dijudication /ˌdʌɪdʒuːdɪˈkeɪʃ(ə)n/ *noun*. Now *rare*. M16.
[ORIGIN Latin *dijudicatio(n-)*, from *dijudicat-* pa. ppl stem of *dijudicare* judge, determine, from *di-* DI-¹ + *judicare* to judge: see -ATION.]
1 The action or faculty of judging between matters; discernment, discrimination. M16.

D

2 The pronouncing of a judgement. E17.

dika /ˈdiːkə/ *noun*. M19.
[ORIGIN Mpongwe *odika* condiment.]
(The fruit or seed of) the wild mango, *Irvingia gabonensis*, a W. African tree. Also, dika bread.
– COMB.: **dika bread** a paste prepared from dika seeds, which is a staple of some African peoples; **dika fat**, **dika oil** a fatty substance expressed from dika seeds.

dikaryon /dʌɪˈkarɪən/ *noun*. E20.
[ORIGIN from DI-² + Greek *karuon* nut.]
BIOLOGY. A pair of unfused haploid nuclei of opposite mating type in a cell or spore which divide simultaneously when the cell divides; a dikaryotic cell, mycelium, etc.
■ **dikaryˈotic** *adjective* containing a dikaryon; composed of dikaryons: M20.

dik-dik /ˈdɪkdɪk/ *noun*. L19.
[ORIGIN E. African name, of imit. origin.]
Any of several very small African antelopes constituting the genus *Madoqua*.

dike *noun*¹, *noun*², *verb*¹ vars. of DYKE *noun*¹, *noun*², *verb*.

dike /dʌɪk/ *verb*² *intrans*. *US colloq*. M19.
[ORIGIN Uncertain: perh. alt. of DECK *verb*.]
Dress stylishly or with elegance. Usu. foll. by *out*.

dike-grave *noun* var. of DYKE-GRAVE.

diketone /dʌɪˈkiːtəʊn/ *noun*. L19.
[ORIGIN from DI-² + KETONE.]
CHEMISTRY. Any compound with two carbonyl groups each attached to two carbon atoms.

dikh /dɪk/ *noun*. *Indian*. L19.
[ORIGIN Urdu *dikk* troubled, vexed.]
Trouble, worry, vexation.

dikkop /ˈdɪkəp/ *noun*. *S. Afr*. M19.
[ORIGIN Afrikaans, from *dik* thick + *kop* head.]
1 Any of certain African stone curlews, esp. *Burhinus vermiculatus* or *B. capensis*. M19.
2 A form of the disease bluetongue. L19.

diktat /ˈdɪktat/ *noun*. M20.
[ORIGIN German, formed as DICTATE *noun*.]
1 A severe settlement, esp. one imposed by a victorious nation on a defeated one. M20.
2 A dictate; a categorical assertion. M20.

dilacerate /dɪˈlasəreɪt, dʌɪ-/ *verb trans*. Pa. pple & ppl adjective **-ated**, (earlier) †**-ate**. LME.
[ORIGIN Orig. pa. pple, from Latin *dilaceratus* pa. pple of *dilacerare*, from *di-* DI-¹ + *lacerare* tear, lacerate: see -ATE², -ATE³.]
Tear apart; tear in pieces.
■ **dilaceˈration** *noun* LME.

dilambdodont /dʌɪˈlamdədɒnt/ *adjective*. L19.
[ORIGIN from DI-² + LAMBDA + -ODONT.]
ZOOLOGY. Having molar teeth with two transverse pointed ridges.

Dilantin /dʌɪˈlantɪn/ *noun*. M20.
[ORIGIN from DI-² + -*l*- + HYD)ANT(O)IN *noun*.]
(US proprietary name for) phenytoin.

dilapidate /dɪˈlapɪdeɪt/ *verb*. Pa. pple & ppl adjective **-ated**, †**-ate**. E16.
[ORIGIN Latin *dilapidat-* pa. ppl stem of *dilapidare*, from *di-* DI-¹ + *lapis*, *lapid-* stone: see -ATE³.]
1 *verb trans*. Waste, squander, (a benefice or estate). E16.
2 *verb trans*. Bring (a building etc.) into a state of decay, disrepair, or partial ruin. Chiefly as ***dilapidated*** *ppl adjective*. L16.

> J. RUSKIN A large and dilapidated pair of woman's shoes. J. STEINBECK The sagging dilapidated porch. E. MANNIN Dilapidated taxis. *Practical Householder* You can bring new life to dilapidated and neglected woods.

3 *verb intrans*. Become dilapidated; fall into ruin, decay, or disrepair. E18.

> S. JOHNSON The church of Elgin . . was . . shamefully suffered to dilapidate by deliberate robbery and frigid indifference.

■ **dilapidator** *noun* L16.

dilapidation /dɪˌlapɪˈdeɪʃ(ə)n/ *noun*. LME.
[ORIGIN Late Latin *dilapidatio(n-)*, formed as DILAPIDATE: see -ATION.]
1 Squandering; wasteful expenditure. LME.

> T. R. MALTHUS The dilapidation of the national resources.

2 The action of pulling down, allowing to decay, or in any way impairing (orig. *spec*. ecclesiastical) property. LME. ▸**b** In *pl*. A sum charged to an incumbent or tenant against wear and tear during occupation of premises. M16.
3 The process of falling into decay; the condition of being in ruins or disrepair. LME.

> F. WELDON The neighbours complained about the dilapidation and the weeds in the garden.

4 The falling of stones or masses of rock from mountains or cliffs by natural agency. L18.

dilatant /dʌɪˈleɪt(ə)nt, dɪ-/ *adjective*. M19.
[ORIGIN from DILATE *verb*² + -ANT¹.]
Dilating; expansive; *esp*. exhibiting dilatancy.
■ **dilatancy** *noun* the property of increasing in volume when subjected to pressure or deformed L19.

dilatate /ˈdʌɪlətət/ *adjective*. *rare*. LME.
[ORIGIN Latin *dilatatus* pa. pple of *dilatare*: see DILATE *verb*², -ATE².]
Dilated.

dilatation /dʌɪleɪˈteɪʃ(ə)n, dɪ-, -lə-/ *noun*. LME.
[ORIGIN Old French from late Latin *dilatatio(n-)*, from Latin *dilatat-* pa. ppl stem of *dilatare*: see DILATE *verb*², -ATION.]
1 Chiefly *SCIENCE*. ▸**a** The action or process of dilating; the condition of being dilated; expansion, enlargement. LME. ▸**b** A dilated form; a dilated part of any structure. M19.
dilatation and curettage *MEDICINE* an operation involving dilatation of the cervix and curettage of the uterus, carried out to arrest irregular menstrual bleeding, to terminate a pregnancy, to diagnose certain uterine diseases, etc.
2 The action or practice of dilating on a subject; expatiation, enlargement. LME.
3 The spreading abroad (of abstract things); dissemination. *arch*. LME.
■ **dilatational** *adjective* of or pertaining to dilatation L19. **ˈdilatative** *adjective* (now *rare*) of the nature of or tending to dilatation E18.

dilatator /ˈdʌɪləteɪtə/ *noun*. Now *rare*. E17.
[ORIGIN Late Latin, from Latin *dilatat-*: see DILATATION, -OR.]
= DILATOR.

dilate /dʌɪˈleɪt/ *adjective*. *arch*. L15.
[ORIGIN Latin *dilatus* pa. pple of *differre* DEFER *verb*¹, but used in sense of *dilatatus* DILATATE *adjective*: see -ATE².]
Dilated; widely extended or expanded.

†**dilate** *verb*¹ *trans*. LME–M17.
[ORIGIN Old French *dilater* from late Latin *dilatare* frequentative of Latin *differre* DEFER *verb*¹. Cf. DILATORY.]
Delay, defer; protract, prolong.
– NOTE: During currency prob. identified with DILATE *verb*².

dilate /dʌɪˈleɪt, dɪ-/ *verb*². LME.
[ORIGIN Old French & mod. French *dilater* from Latin *dilatare* spread out, from *di-* DI-¹ + *latus* wide.]
1 *verb trans*. Make wider or larger; expand, amplify, enlarge. LME.
†**2** *verb trans*. Spread abroad; extend, disseminate, disperse. LME–E18.
†**3** *verb trans*. Relate at length; enlarge upon. LME–E19.
4 *verb intrans*. Discourse or write at large (*on*, *upon*). M16.

> E. CRISPIN The Major dilated on Sal's unusual competence as a watchdog.

5 *verb intrans*. Become wider or larger; spread out, expand. M17.

> E. FIGES Her eyes . . dilated with some deep, dark, inward vision.

■ **dilatable** *adjective* able to be dilated, expandable E17. **dilataˈbility** *noun* the ability to be dilated, expansibility L17. **dilative** *adjective* †(**a**) serving to diffuse or disperse food; (**b**) having the property of dilating or expanding: E16.

dilater /dʌɪˈleɪtə, dɪ-/ *noun*. Now *rare*. E17.
[ORIGIN from DILATE *verb*² + -ER¹.]
1 *gen*. A person who or thing which dilates something. E17.
2 *SURGERY*. = DILATOR 1. M17.
3 *ANATOMY*. = DILATOR 2. L17.

†**dilation** *noun*¹. LME–M17.
[ORIGIN Old French *dilacion* (later †*dilation*) from Latin *dilatio(n)-*, from *dilat-*: see DILATORY, -ION.]
(A) delay, (a) postponement, procrastination.

dilation /dʌɪˈleɪʃ(ə)n/ *noun*². LME.
[ORIGIN Irreg. from DILATE *verb*² as if containing -ATE³: see -ATION.]
= DILATATION.

dilatometer /dʌɪləˈtɒmɪtə/ *noun*. L19.
[ORIGIN from DILATE *verb*² + -OMETER.]
An instrument for measuring the expansion of a liquid.
■ **dilatoˈmetric** *adjective* L19. **dilatometry** *noun* E20.

dilator /dʌɪˈleɪtə, dɪ-/ *noun*. L17.
[ORIGIN from DILATE *verb*² + -OR. Cf. earlier DILATER.]
1 *SURGERY*. An instrument for dilating an opening or cavity in the body. L17.
2 *ANATOMY*. A muscle that dilates an organ. M18.

dilatory /ˈdɪlət(ə)ri/ *adjective & noun*. LME.
[ORIGIN Late Latin *dilatorius* delaying, from Latin *dilator* delayer, from *dilat-* pa. ppl stem of *differre* DEFER *verb*¹: see -ORY².]
▸ **A** *adjective*. **1** Tending to cause delay; having the purpose of gaining time. LME.
dilatory plea *LAW*: put in for the sake of delay.
2 Given to or characterized by delay; slow, tardy. E17.

> J. A. FROUDE His political advisers were impatient of these dilatory movements. C. C. TRENCH His ruling passion was . . the bustle of business, but he was as dilatory in despatching it as he was eager to engage in it.

▸ **B** *noun*. *LAW*. A dilatory plea. LME.
■ **dilatorily** *adverb* E18. **dilatoriness** *noun* L17.

dildo /ˈdɪldəʊ/ *noun*. Pl. **-o(e)s**. L16.
[ORIGIN Unknown.]
1 A penis; *esp*. an artificial erect penis used for sexual pleasure. Also (*slang*), a stupid or despicable person. L16.
2 Used in refrains as a meaningless word. E17.
3 More fully ***dildo tree***. Any of several W. Indian cacti with tall ribbed cylindrical stems, esp. *Cereus peruvianus* and *Lemaireocereus hystrix*. L17.

†**dilection** *noun*. LME.
[ORIGIN Old French & mod. French, or ecclesiastical Latin *dilectio(n-)* (Christian) love, from Latin *dilect-* pa. ppl stem of *diligere* esteem highly, love: cf. DILIGENT.]
1 Love, affection; *esp*. spiritual or Christian love. LME–L17.
2 Choice, esp. (*THEOLOGY*) as exercised by God, election. LME–M17.
3 Beloved (as an honorific title). E18–M19.

dilemma /dɪˈlɛmə, dʌɪ-/ *noun & verb*. E16.
[ORIGIN Latin from Greek *dilēmma*, formed as DI-² + *lēmma* assumption, premiss.]
▸ **A** *noun*. **1** In *RHETORIC*, a form of argument involving an opponent in choice between two (or more) alternatives, both equally unfavourable. In *LOGIC*, a syllogism with two conditional major premisses and a disjunctive minor premiss. E16.
2 A choice between two (or several) alternatives which are equally unfavourable; a position of doubt or perplexity; a difficult situation or problem. L16.

> B. BAINBRIDGE He walked thoughtfully back . . , pondering on how he would extricate himself from this dilemma in a dignified manner. D. BOGARDE Three corridors . . . 'Dilemma Left, right or center?'

on the horns of a dilemma: see HORN *noun*. ***PRISONER'S dilemma***.
▸ **B** *verb trans*. Place in a dilemma. *rare*. M17.
■ **dileˈmmatic** *adjective* M19. †**dilemmatical** *adjective* M–L17. **dileˈmmatically** *adverb* M17.

dilettante /dɪlɪˈtanti/ *noun & adjective*. Pl. **-ti** /-ti/, **-tes**. M18.
[ORIGIN Italian, use as noun of verbal adjective from *dilettare* from Latin *delectare* DELIGHT *noun*.]
▸ **A** *noun*. A lover of the fine arts; a person who cultivates the arts as an amateur; a person who takes an interest in a subject merely as a pastime and without serious study, a dabbler. M18.

> T. BALOGH Mr. Churchill . . refused to trust the dilettantes at the Treasury.

▸ **B** *adjective*. Of, pertaining to, or characteristic of a dilettante; amateur. M18.
■ **dilettant** /ˈdɪlɪtɑːnt/ *adjective & noun* = DILETTANTE M19. **dilettantish** *adjective* L19. **dilettantism** *noun* the practice or action of a dilettante, amateur dabbling; the character of dilettanti: E19. **dilettantist** *adjective* characterized by dilettantism M19.

diligence /ˈdɪlɪdʒ(ə)ns/ *noun*¹. ME.
[ORIGIN Old French & mod. French from Latin *diligentia*, from *diligent-*: see DILIGENT, -ENCE.]
†**1** Careful attention; heedfulness, caution. ME–L18.
2 The quality of being diligent; industry, assiduity. LME. ▸†**b** An act of diligence; in *pl*., labours, exertions. LME–M17. ▸†**c** A diligent person. *rare* (Shakes.). Only in E17.
†**3** Speed, dispatch, haste. L15–L18.
4 *SCOTS LAW*. The legal process by which payments are enforced, debts recovered, etc. Also, a warrant issued by a court to enforce the attendance of witnesses or the production of documents. M16.
5 *LAW*. The attention and care required in a given situation. E17.
due diligence: see DUE *adjective* 2.

diligence /ˈdɪlɪdʒ(ə)ns; *foreign* diliʒɑ̃ːs (*pl. same*)/ *noun*². L17.
[ORIGIN French, abbreviation of *carrosse de diligence* 'coach of speed'.]
hist. A public stagecoach, esp. in France.

diligent /ˈdɪlɪdʒ(ə)nt/ *adjective & adverb*. ME.
[ORIGIN Old French & mod. French from Latin *diligent-*, *-ens* assiduous, attentive, pres. pple of *diligere* esteem highly, love, choose, take delight in, formed as DI-¹ + *legere* choose: see -ENT.]
▸ **A** *adjective*. **1** Of a person: steady in application; assiduous, industrious; attentive to one's duties. ME.

> F. TUOHY Although he complains of his courses he is a very diligent boy.

2 Of an action: steadily applied; prosecuted with activity and perseverance. LME.
†**3** Attentive; heedful, careful. LME–M18.
▸ †**B** *adverb*. Diligently. L15–L16.
■ **diligently** *adverb* ME.

dilithium /dʌɪˈlɪθɪəm/ *noun*. M20.
[ORIGIN Invented word.]
A fictitious crystalline substance used as a source of power for spacecraft in the US science-fiction television programme *Star Trek*.

dill /dɪl/ *noun*¹.
[ORIGIN Old English *dile* & *dyle*, respectively = Old Saxon *dilli* (Dutch *dille*), Old High German *tilli*, *dilli* (German *Dill* from Low German), & Middle Dutch *dulle*, Middle High German *tülle*, Old Norse *dylla*: ult. origin unknown.]
An umbelliferous annual plant, *Anethum graveolens*, with scented seeds and leaves and small yellow flowers; the seeds or leaves of this plant used as a flavouring.
– COMB.: **dill pickle** a pickled cucumber, gherkin, etc., flavoured with dill; **dill water** an extract distilled from dill and used to relieve flatulence.

dill /dɪl/ *noun*^{2}. *Austral. & NZ slang*. **M20**.
[**ORIGIN** App. back-form. from **DILLY** *adjective*^{1}.]
A fool, a simpleton.

dilligrout /ˈdɪlɪɡraʊt/ *noun*. **M17**.
[**ORIGIN** Unknown.]
hist. A kind of pottage which was offered to the British monarch on coronation day by the lord of the manor of Addington, Surrey (now part of London).

dilling /ˈdɪlɪŋ/ *noun*. Now *dial.* **L16**.
[**ORIGIN** Unknown.]
Formerly, as a term of endearment: darling; the youngest of a family. Now *dial.*, the weakling of a litter.

dilly /ˈdɪli/ *noun*^{1}. **L18**.
[**ORIGIN** Abbreviation of **DILIGENCE** *noun*^{2}.]
†**1** = **DILIGENCE** *noun*^{2}. *colloq.* **L18–L19**.
2 Any of various carts, trucks, etc., used in agriculture and industrial operations. *dial.* **M19**.

dilly /ˈdɪli/ *noun*^{2}. *Austral.* **M19**.
[**ORIGIN** Yagara (an Australian Aboriginal language of SE Queensland) *dili*.]
In full ***dilly bag***. A small bag or basket (formerly of plaited grass etc.) for carrying food etc.

dilly /ˈdɪli/ *noun*^{3}. *slang* (orig. *US*). **M20**.
[**ORIGIN** from **DILLY** *adjective*^{2}.]
A delightful or remarkable person or thing; an outstanding example (*of*). Freq. *iron.*

S. KING Manhattan's final traffic jam had been a dilly.

dilly /ˈdɪli/ *adjective*^{1}. *dial. & colloq.* (chiefly *Austral. & NZ*). **L19**.
[**ORIGIN** Perh. from **DAFT** *adjective* + **SILLY** *adjective*.]
Foolish, stupid; eccentric, queer.

dilly /ˈdɪli/ *adjective*^{2}. *colloq.* **L19**.
[**ORIGIN** from 1st syll. of **DELIGHTFUL**, **DELICIOUS** + **-Y**^{6}.]
Delightful, delicious.

dilly /ˈdɪli/ *interjection & noun*^{4}. *colloq. & dial.* **M19**.
[**ORIGIN** Unknown.]
(Used as a call to) a duck.

dilly-dally /ˈdɪlɪdali/ *noun & verb*. *colloq.* **E17**.
[**ORIGIN** Redupl. of **DALLY**.]
▶ †**A** *noun*. Trifling hesitancy, dilly-dallying. Only in **17**.
▶ **B** *verb intrans.* Vacillate; dawdle, loiter. **M18**.

K. GRENVILLE Other boats dilly-dallied in Broken Bay for gentle seas.

■ **dilly-ˈdallier** *noun* **L19**.

dilogy /ˈdɪlədʒi, ˈdʌɪ-/ *noun*. **M17**.
[**ORIGIN** Latin *dilogia* from Greek, from *dilogos*, formed as **DI-**^{2} + *logos* saying, speech: see **-LOGY**.]
RHETORIC. (An) ambiguity.

dilophosaurus /dʌɪˌləʊfə(ʊ)ˈsɔːrəs/ *noun*. **L20**.
[**ORIGIN** mod. Latin (see below), from Greek *dilophos* two-crested + *sauros* -**SAUR**.]
A large carnivorous theropod dinosaur of the early Jurassic genus *Dilophosaurus*, which was bipedal and had a crest on the top of the skull composed of two bony ridges.

dilruba /dɪlˈruːbə/ *noun*. **E20**
[**ORIGIN** Hindi *dilrubā* = robber of the heart.]
An Indian musical instrument with a long neck, three or four strings played with a bow, and several sympathetic strings.

dilse *noun* see **DULSE**.

dilucid /dʌɪˈluːsɪd/ *adjective*. *obsolete* exc. *poet.* **M17**.
[**ORIGIN** Latin *dilucidus* clear, bright, from *dilucere*, from *di-* **DI-**^{1} + *lucere* shine.]
Clear to the sight; lucid, plain.
■ †**dilucidity** *noun* lucidity: only in **E17**.

dilucidate /dɪˈluːsɪdeɪt/ *verb trans.* Long *rare*. Also **de-**. **M16**.
[**ORIGIN** Late Latin *dilucidat-* pa. ppl stem of *dilucidare* make clear, formed as **DILUCID**: see **-ATE**^{3}.]
Elucidate.
■ †**dilucidation** *noun* **E17–M18**.

diluent /ˈdɪljʊənt/ *noun & adjective*. **E18**.
[**ORIGIN** Latin *diluent-* pres. ppl stem of *diluere*: see **DILUTE** *verb*, **-ENT**.]
▶ **A** *noun*. **1** A medicine used to increase the proportion of water in the blood and other body fluids. Now *rare* or *obsolete*. **E18**.
2 *gen.* Something which dilutes, dissolves, or makes more fluid. **L18**.
▶ **B** *adjective*. Diluting; serving to attenuate or weaken by the addition of water etc. **M18**.

dilute /dʌɪˈl(j)uːt, dɪ-/ *adjective*. **E17**.
[**ORIGIN** Latin *dilutus* pa. pple, formed as **DILUTE** *verb*.]
1 Weak, paltry. *obsolete* exc. as *fig.* use of sense 2. **E17**.
2 Watered down; (of a solution) containing a high proportion of solvent. **M17**.
■ **diluteness** *noun* **M17**.

dilute /dʌɪˈl(j)uːt, dɪ-/ *verb trans.* **M16**.
[**ORIGIN** Latin *dilut-* pa. ppl stem of *diluere* wash away, dissolve from *di-* **DI-**^{1} + *-luere* combining form of *lavare* to wash.]
1 Weaken; take away the strength or force of, esp. by addition. **M16**.

E. BOWEN Sunset mists diluted the moon. R. CONQUEST Diluting brilliant essence With seepage of other minds.

2 Diminish the brilliance or strength of (colour). **M17**.
3 Make (a liquid) thinner, weaker, or less concentrated by adding water or other solvent; make (a gas) less concentrated by admixture. **L17**.
■ **dilutable** *adjective* able to be diluted; intended to be diluted before use: **L20**. **dilutedly** *adverb* in a diluted or weakened manner **M19**. **diluˈtee** *noun* an unskilled or semi-skilled worker who takes a place hitherto occupied by a skilled worker **E20**. **diluter** *noun* something which or someone who dilutes; *spec.* (**a**) a diluent; (**b**) a device for automatically obtaining any desired dilution of a sample: **E18**. **dilutive** *adjective* tending to dilute; characterized by dilution: **E17**.

dilution /dʌɪˈl(j)uːʃ(ə)n, dɪ-/ *noun*. **M17**.
[**ORIGIN** from **DILUTE** *verb* + **-ION**.]
1 The action of diluting. **M17**. ▸**b** The substitution of unskilled or semi-skilled workers for skilled ones. **E20**.
2 Dilute condition; the degree to which a solution has been diluted. **E19**.

ANTHONY HUXLEY This eelworm-killer is effective at a dilution of one part in five million.

3 Something in a dilute condition. **M19**.
■ **dilutional** *adjective* involving or characterized by dilution, esp. (*MEDICINE*) as a result of increased blood plasma **M20**.

diluvial /dʌɪˈl(j)uːvɪəl, dɪ-/ *adjective*. **M17**.
[**ORIGIN** Late Latin *diluvialis*, from *diluvium*: see **DILUVIUM**, **-AL**^{1}.]
1 Of or pertaining to a deluge, esp. Noah's Flood. **M17**.
2 *GEOLOGY.* Produced by or resulting from a supposed general deluge, or periods of catastrophic action of water; of, pertaining to, or being diluvium. **E19**.
diluvial theory: postulating a general deluge or catastrophic flood as an explanation of geological features.
■ **diluvialist** *noun* an advocate of a diluvial theory **E19**.

diluvian /dʌɪˈl(j)uːvɪən, dɪ-/ *adjective*. **M17**.
[**ORIGIN** formed as **DILUVIAL** + **-AN**.]
= **DILUVIAL 1**.
■ **diluvianism** *noun* belief in a past universal deluge; belief in a diluvial theory: **E19**.

diluvium /dʌɪˈl(j)uːvɪəm, dɪ-/ *noun*. Pl. **-ia** /-ɪə/. **E19**.
[**ORIGIN** Latin, from *diluere*: see **DILUTE** *verb*.]
GEOLOGY. (A deposit of) superficial material formerly attributed to a universal deluge but now to glacial action; drift.

dim /dɪm/ *adjective, noun, & adverb*.
[**ORIGIN** Old English *dim(m)* = Old Frisian *dim*, Old Norse *dimmr* rel. to synon. Old High German *timbar* (Middle High German, mod. dial. *timmer*), Old Swedish *dimber*, Old Irish *dem* black, dark.]
▶ **A** *adjective*. Compar. & superl. **-mm-**.
1 Of a light or illuminated object: faintly luminous, not shining brightly or clearly; somewhat dark, shadowy. **OE**.

J. RHYS Her room was dim, with a shaded candle by the bed. W. GOLDING Even in that dim light I could see she was shivering.

2 Not clear to the sight; obscured by distance etc., scarcely visible; misty, indistinct. **OE**. ▸**b** *fig.* Not clear to the understanding; indistinctly apprehended; obscure. **ME**.

D. H. LAWRENCE The dim smoke wavering up the chimney. R. BROOKE That fills The soul with longing for dim hills And faint horizons. **b** A. EDEN The Boer war . . was a dim memory. SIAN EVANS He felt a dim desire, which, as his thoughts lingered, grew in urgency.

3 Of colour, or an object in respect of its colour: not bright; dull, lustreless. **ME**.

R. L. STEVENSON All retired and shady spots Where prosper dim forget-me-nots.

4 Of a person or eyes: not seeing clearly. Of sight: poor. **ME**. ▸**b** *fig.* Dull of apprehension; *colloq.* not intellectually bright, somewhat stupid. **ME**.
take a dim view of *colloq.* regard with disfavour or pessimism.
5 Of sound, esp. the voice: indistinct, muffled. **ME**.
– **COMB.**: **dim-sighted** *adjective* having dim sight; unperceptive; **dimwit** *colloq.* a stupid person; **dim-witted** *adjective* (*colloq.*) stupid, dull; **dim-wittedness** the fact or quality of being a dimwit.
▶ **B** *noun*. Dimness; obscurity; dusk. **LME**.
▶ **C** *adverb*. Compar. & superl. **-mm-**. Dimly. **LME**.
■ **dimly** *adverb* in a dim manner; obscurely; faintly: **ME**. **dimmish** *adjective* **L15**. **dimmy** *adjective* (somewhat) dim **LME**. **dimness** *noun* **OE**.

dim /dɪm/ *verb*. Infl. **-mm-**. **OE**.
[**ORIGIN** from the adjective.]
1 *verb trans.* Make (more) dim, obscure; render indistinct; becloud (the eyes). **OE**.

J. BUCHAN Memories of which time has not dimmed the rapture. R. CHURCH This drab khaki which had dimmed the British army since the Boer War.

dim out reduce the brightness of (lights); subject to a dim-out (see below).
2 *verb intrans.* Become (more) dim; lose brightness, clarity, or distinctness. **ME**.
– **COMB.**: **dim-out** a reduction in the brightness or use of lights, esp. in wartime; a gradual dimming of lights in a theatre, cinema, etc.

dim. *abbreviation*.
Diminuendo.

Dimaris /ˈdɪmərɪs/ *noun*. **E19**.
[**ORIGIN** A mnemonic of scholastic philosophers first used in medieval Latin, I indicating a particular affirmative proposition and A a universal affirmative proposition.]
LOGIC. The third mood of the fourth syllogistic figure, in which a particular affirmative conclusion is drawn from a particular affirmative major and a universal affirmative minor premiss.

dimble /ˈdɪmb(ə)l/ *noun*. *obsolete* exc. *dial.* **L16**.
[**ORIGIN** Perh. connected with **DIM** *adjective* or **DINGLE** *noun*.]
A deep and shady dell, a dingle.

D

dime /dʌɪm/ *noun*. Also †**disme**. **LME**.
[**ORIGIN** Old French *dime*, †*disme*, from Latin *decima* use as noun (sc. *pars* part) of fem. of *decimus* tenth.]
1 A tenth part; a tithe. *obsolete* exc. *hist.* **LME**.
2 A coin worth a tenth of a dollar (10 cents); in *pl.* also (*colloq.*), money. *N. Amer.* **L18**.
a dime a dozen commonplace. **drop a dime on**, **drop the dime on** *N. Amer. slang* inform on.
– **COMB.**: **dime bag** *N. Amer. slang* a specified amount of an illegal drug, packaged and sold for a fixed price; **dime novel** *N. Amer.* a cheap sensational novel; **dime store** *N. Amer.* (**a**) a shop selling cheap merchandise (orig. one where the maximum price was a dime); (**b**) *attrib.* cheap and inferior.

dime /dʌɪm/ *verb trans.* *US slang*. **L20**.
[**ORIGIN** from ***drop a dime on*** s.v. **DIME** *noun*.]
Inform on (a person) to the police.

P. CORNWELL Even if someone out there dimed Mitch, you don't send in a hit man like Matos.

dimension /dɪˈmɛnʃ(ə)n, dʌɪ-/ *noun & verb*. **LME**.
[**ORIGIN** French from Latin *dimensio(n-)*, from *dimens-* pa. ppl stem of *dimetiri* measure out, from *di-* **DI-**^{1} + *metiri* measure.]
▶ **A** *noun*. **1** Measurable spatial extent of any kind, as length, breadth, area, volume. Now usu. in *pl.* **LME**. ▸†**b** Duration. **LME–L17**. ▸**c** The magnitude or scale of an abstract thing. **M17**.

K. TYNAN Shrinking before our eyes to the dimensions of a pickled walnut. **c** G. F. KENNAN Soviet trade never quite achieved, . . between the two wars, the dimensions of prewar Russian trade.

of large dimensions etc., of large etc. size.
2 A mode of linear extension of which there are three in space, two on a flat surface, etc., and which corresponds to one of a set of coordinates specifying the position of a point; *MATH.* such a coordinate. **LME**. ▸**b** *MATH.* Any of a number of quantities in a product, esp. of unknowns. **M16**. ▸**c** *SCIENCE.* The power to which any fundamental quantity or unit is raised in a product defining a derived quantity or unit; in *pl.*, the product itself. **M19**. ▸**d** An attribute or status that may be seen as inhering in or characterizing an abstract thing; an aspect. **E20**.

R. A. KNOX How do we get our notion of solid objects, when we can only see in two dimensions? **b** OED x^3, x^2y, xyz are each of three dimensions. **d** A. O. J. COCKSHUT The religious dimension . . would have given coherence and deeper meaning to the . . scraps of virtue displayed by Flora. *Listener* Atomic bombs . . brought a new dimension of destruction and horror to warfare.

FOURTH ***dimension***.
†**3** The action of measuring, measurement. **M16–L18**. ▸**b** *MUSIC.* The division of a longer note into shorter ones; in *pl.*, measured strains. **L16–M17**.
†**4** Measurable form; in *pl.*, material parts, as of the body. **L16–M17**.
– **COMB.**: **dimension line**: showing, usu. with arrowheads, the parts or lines to which the figured dimensions refer in a plan etc.
▶ **B** *verb trans.* **1** Measure, reduce to measurement. *rare*. **M18**.
2 Mark the dimensions on (a plan etc.). Cf. earlier **DIMENSIONED** 3. **E20**.

dimensional /dɪˈmɛnʃ(ə)n(ə)l, dʌɪ-/ *adjective*. **E19**.
[**ORIGIN** from **DIMENSION** + **-AL**^{1}.]
1 Of or pertaining to dimension or magnitude. **E19**. ▸**b** Of, pertaining to, or involving dimensions of units or physical qualities. **L19**.
b dimensional analysis: using the fact that quantities added to or equated with each other must have the same dimensions to make inferences about the relations between quantities and units.
2 Having a specified number of dimensions. **L19**.

H. MOORE The child learning to see, first distinguishes only two-dimensional shape.

■ **dimensioˈnality** *noun* dimensional quality; the fact of having (so many) dimensions: **M16**. **dimensionally** *adverb* as regards dimensions **L19**.

dimensioned /dɪˈmɛnʃ(ə)nd, dʌɪ-/ *adjective*. **M16**.
[**ORIGIN** from **DIMENSION** *noun*, *verb*: see **-ED**^{2}, **-ED**^{1}.]
†**1** Having material extent. Only in **M16**.
2 Having a particular size or set of measurements. **E18**.

BETTY SMITH An aircraft dimensioned like a coffin.

3 Of a plan etc.: having dimensions and distances marked on it. **L19**.
4 Having a specified number of dimensions. Usu. in *comb.* **L19**.

dimensionless /dɪˈmɛnʃ(ə)nləs, dʌɪ-/ *adjective*. M17.
[ORIGIN from DIMENSION *noun* + -LESS.]
1 Having no spatial extent; extremely minute. M17.
2 Measureless, immense. E19.
3 Having none of the three dimensions of space. M19. ▸**b** Of a physical quantity or its unit: having no dimensions; of the nature of a pure number, with a value independent of the choice of other units. E20.

dimensive /dɪˈmɛnsɪv, dʌɪ-/ *adjective*. M16.
[ORIGIN medieval Latin *dimensivus*, from Latin *dimens-*: see DIMENSION, -IVE.]
†**1** Having or related to spatial extension. M16–L17.
†**2** Serving to measure or trace out the dimensions of something. L16–E17.
3 Of or pertaining to dimension or magnitude. *rare*. M19.

dimensurator /dɪˈmɛnsjʊreɪtə, dʌɪ-/ *noun*. *obsolete* exc. *hist*. L17.
[ORIGIN from DI-[1] + MENSURATE *verb* + -OR.]
A surveyor's measuring instrument.

dimer /ˈdʌɪmə/ *noun*. E20.
[ORIGIN from DI-[2] + -MER.]
CHEMISTRY. A compound having twice the number of each atom in its molecule as another compound; *esp.* one in which two identical molecules or radicals are joined together.
■ **dimeriˈzation** *noun* formation of or conversion into a dimer M20. **dimerize** *verb trans. & intrans.* (cause to) be converted into a dimer M19.

dimeric /dʌɪˈmɛrɪk/ *adjective*. L19.
[ORIGIN In sense 1 from Greek *dimerēs* bipartite, in sense 2 from DIMER: see -IC.]
1 ZOOLOGY. Having a right and a left side. *rare*. L19.
2 CHEMISTRY. Of the nature of a dimer, consisting of a dimer or dimers. E20.

dimerous /ˈdɪm(ə)rəs/ *adjective*. E19.
[ORIGIN from mod. Latin *dimerus* from Greek *dimerēs*: see DIMERIC, -OUS.]
BOTANY & ENTOMOLOGY. Having two parts or members, *spec.* in a whorl.

dimeter /ˈdɪmɪtə/ *noun*. L16.
[ORIGIN Late Latin *dimeter*, noun, *dimetrus* adjective & noun, from Greek *dimetros* of two measures, formed as DI-[2] + *metron* measure.]
PROSODY. A line of two measures.

dimethyl /dʌɪˈmiːθʌɪl, -ˈmɛθɪl/ *adjective & noun*. M19.
[ORIGIN from DI-[2] + METHYL.]
CHEMISTRY. ▸**A** *adjective*. Having two methyl groups in the molecule. M19.
▸**B** *noun*. = ETHANE. Now *rare* or *obsolete*. L19.

Dimetian *adjective* var. of DEMETIAN.

†**dimetient** *noun & adjective*. L16.
[ORIGIN Latin *dimetient-* pres. ppl stem of *dimetiri*: see DIMENSION, -ENT.]
▸**A** *noun*. A diameter. L16–E18.
▸**B** *adjective*. **1** *dimetient line*, a diameter. E17–E18.
2 Expressing the dimension. Only in M19.

dimetrodon /dʌɪˈmiːtrədɒn/ *noun*. L19.
[ORIGIN mod. Latin (see below), formed as DI-[2] + Greek *metron* measure + -ODON.]
A large fossil carnivorous mammal-like reptile of the genus *Dimetrodon*, with long spines on its back supporting a sail-like crest, occurring in the Permian period.

dimication /dɪmɪˈkeɪʃ(ə)n/ *noun*. Now *rare*. E17.
[ORIGIN Latin *dimicatio(n-)*, from *dimicat-* pa. ppl stem of *dimicare* fight: see -ATION.]
Fighting; contention; a fight.

dimidiate /dɪˈmɪdɪət/ *adjective*. M18.
[ORIGIN Latin *dimidiatus* pa. pple, formed as DIMIDIATE *verb*: see -ATE[2].]
Divided into two; BOTANY & ZOOLOGY having one half different from the other, esp. in size or sex.
■ **dimidiately** *adverb* M19.

dimidiate /dɪˈmɪdɪeɪt/ *verb trans*. L16.
[ORIGIN Latin *dimidiat-* pa. ppl stem of *dimidiare* halve, from *dimidium* half, from *di-* DI-[1] + MEDIUM: see -ATE[3].]
1 HERALDRY. Represent only half of (a bearing or coat of arms), esp. in one half of a shield divided per pale; combine (one coat) *with* another in this way. L16.
2 *gen.* Divide in half, reduce to a half. E17.
■ **dimidiˈation** *noun* the action of halving, the condition of being halved; *spec.* (HERALDRY) the combination of two coats of arms by juxtaposing the dexter half of one and the sinister half of the other: LME.

diminish /dɪˈmɪnɪʃ/ *verb*. LME.
[ORIGIN Blend of DIMINUE and MINISH.]
▸**I** *verb trans*. **1** Make smaller or less (in fact or in appearance). LME.

L. DURRELL Nor were our follies diminished by these warnings.

2 Lessen the power, reputation, or self-esteem of (a person); belittle, depreciate. LME.

MILTON Impiously they thought Thee to diminish.

†**3** Subtract, remove, (*from*). E16–E17.
†**4** Deprive in part *of*. Usu. in *pass.* M16–M18.
5 ARCHITECTURE. Make (a column etc.) taper. M16.
▸**II** *verb intrans*. **6** Become less or smaller; decrease. E16.

G. GREENE They climbed up . . and the sound of the others diminished below them.

†**7** Foll. by *from*: make less; detract from. M17–E19.
– PHRASES: **diminishing glass** an instrument through which an object appears smaller than when viewed by the naked eye. **diminishing mirror** a convex mirror giving a smaller image. **law of diminishing returns** ECONOMICS the principle that as expenditure etc. increases each further increase produces a proportionately smaller return.
■ **diminishable** *adjective* able to be diminished (earlier in UNDIMINISHABLE) L18. **diminishableness** *noun* the property of being diminishable L19. **diminisher** *noun* (*rare*) a person who or thing which diminishes E17. **diminishingly** *adverb* †(**a**) disparagingly; (**b**) decreasingly: L17. **diminishment** *noun* (a) diminution, (a) lessening M16.

diminished /dɪˈmɪnɪʃt/ *ppl adjective*. E17.
[ORIGIN from DIMINISH + -ED[1].]
1 That has been diminished; reduced. E17.

MILTON O thou [sun] . . at whose sight all the Starrs Hide their diminisht heads. ALDOUS HUXLEY Bernard had to slink back, diminished, to his rooms.

diminished responsibility ENGLISH LAW a mental condition insufficient to amount to legal insanity but impairing the defendant's responsibility and justifying a conviction for manslaughter rather than murder.
2 MUSIC. Of an interval: less by a semitone than the corresponding minor or perfect interval. Of a chord: containing such an interval. Opp. AUGMENTED 2. E18.

†**diminue** *verb trans. & intrans*. LME–M16.
[ORIGIN Old French & mod. French *diminuer* from medieval Latin *diminuere* from Latin *deminuere* lessen, *diminuere* break up small, from *de-* DE- 1, *di-* DI-[1] + *minuere*: see MINUTE *adjective*.]
Diminish; speak disparagingly (of).

diminuendo /dɪˌmɪnjʊˈɛndəʊ/ *noun, verb, adverb, & adjective*. L18.
[ORIGIN Italian = diminishing, pres. pple of *diminuire* from Latin *deminuere*: see DIMINUE.]
MUSIC. ▸**A** *noun*. Pl. **-dos, -di** /-di/. A gradual decrease in loudness; a passage (to be) played or sung with such a decrease. L18.
▸**B** *verb intrans*. Become quieter; grow less. L18.
▸**C** *adverb & adjective*. A direction: with a gradual decrease in loudness. E19.

†**diminute** *adjective*. LME–M18.
[ORIGIN Latin *diminutus* pa. pple, formed as DIMINUTE *verb*.]
Diminished; incomplete.
■ †**diminutely** *adverb* LME–M18.

diminute /dɪˈmɪnjuːt/ *verb trans*. *rare*. LME.
[ORIGIN Latin *diminut-* pa. ppl stem of *diminuere*: see DIMINUE.]
= DIMINISH 2.

diminution /dɪmɪˈnjuːʃ(ə)n/ *noun*. ME.
[ORIGIN Old French & mod. French from Latin *diminutio(n-)*, formed as DIMINUTE *verb*: see -ION.]
†**1** Representation of something as less than it is. ME–M17.
2 The action of making or becoming less; reduction; lessening. LME.

Harper's Magazine There are complaints of a notable diminution in church attendance. G. JONES The diminution of Roman power.

†**3** Partial deprivation, curtailment. LME–L17.
†**4** Lessening of honour or reputation. L16–M18.
5 MUSIC. The repetition of a subject (esp. in fugues) in notes half or a quarter of the length of those of the original. L16.
6 LAW (now *hist.*). The absence of a correct certification of a record sent up from a lower court to a higher one. M17.
7 ARCHITECTURE. The tapering of a column etc.; the extent of this. E18.
8 CYTOLOGY. The loss or expulsion of chromosomal elements from the nuclei of embryonic cells that develop into somatic cells. E20.

diminutive /dɪˈmɪnjʊtɪv/ *adjective & noun*. LME.
[ORIGIN Old French & mod. French *diminutif*, *-ive* from late Latin *diminutivus*, formed as DIMINUTE *verb*: see -IVE.]
▸**A** *adjective*. **1** GRAMMAR. Expressing diminution in size or status; (of a word) denoting something small of its kind, hence something regarded with affection, familiarity, or contempt (as English ***lassie***, ***ringlet***, ***princeling***); (of an affix, esp. a suffix) added to the radical to form a diminutive word. LME.

L. BLOOMFIELD Some have the diminutive suffix [-ij], as *Peggy*, *Maggie* for *Margaret*, *Fanny* for *Frances*.

2 Small; remarkably small, tiny. L16.

SHAKES. *Macb.* The poor wren, The most diminutive of birds.

†**3** Disparaging, depreciative. M17–L18.
†**4** Making less or smaller. L17–E18.
▸**B** *noun*. **1** A diminutive word or affix. LME.
2 HERALDRY. One of the smaller ordinaries corresponding in form and position to the larger, but of less width. L16.
3 A diminutive thing or person; a small form *of* something. E17.
■ **diminutival** /dɪˌmɪnjʊˈtʌɪv(ə)l/ *adjective & noun* (GRAMMAR) = DIMINUTIVE *adjective* 1, *noun* 1 M19. **diminutively** *adverb* E17. **diminutiveness** *noun* E18.

†**dimiss** *verb*. LME–E18.
[ORIGIN Latin *dimiss-*: see DISMISS *verb*.]
= DISMISS *verb*.

†**dimission** *noun*. LME.
[ORIGIN Latin *dimissio(n-)*, formed as DIMISS: see -ION.]
1 = DEMISSION *noun*[1] 1. LME–M16.
2 = DEMISSION *noun*[1] 2. LME–E19.

dimissory /ˈdɪmɪs(ə)ri/ *noun & adjective*. Also †**dem-**. LME.
[ORIGIN Late Latin *dimissorius* (in *litterae dimissoriae*), formed as DIMISS, -ORY[2].]
▸†**A** *noun*. In *pl.* = ***letters dimissory***. LME–E18.
▸**B** *adjective*. **1** Pertaining to leave-taking; valedictory. Long *rare*. L16.
2 ***letters dimissory***, ***dimissory letter***, a letter or licence from a bishop etc. authorizing the bearer as a candidate for ordination by another bishop. L16.

†**dimit** *verb*[1] *trans*. Infl. **-tt-**. LME.
[ORIGIN Latin *dimittere*: see DISMISS *verb*. Cf. DEMIT *verb*[2].]
1 Send away, dismiss. LME–E18.
2 Convey by lease. L15–E17.
3 Lay aside, give up, resign. M16–L17.

†**dimit** *verb*[2] var. of DEMIT *verb*[1].

dimity /ˈdɪmɪti/ *noun*. LME.
[ORIGIN Italian *dimito* or medieval Latin *dimitum* from Greek *dimitos*, formed as DI-[2] + *mitos* thread of the warp; the origin of the final *-y* is unkn.]
A stout cotton fabric woven with raised stripes or motifs.

DIMM *abbreviation*.
COMPUTING. Dual in-line memory module.

dimmer /ˈdɪmə/ *noun*. E19.
[ORIGIN from DIM *verb* + -ER[1].]
A person who or thing which makes something dim; *esp.* a control for reducing the brightness of a light.

dimmer /ˈdɪmə/ *verb intrans*. L19.
[ORIGIN from DIM *verb* + -ER[5].]
Appear dimly, faintly, or indistinctly. (Foll. by *up*.)

dimorphemic /dʌɪmɔːˈfiːmɪk/ *adjective*. M20.
[ORIGIN from DI-[2] + MORPHEMIC.]
LINGUISTICS. = BIMORPHEMIC.

dimorphic /dʌɪˈmɔːfɪk/ *adjective*. M19.
[ORIGIN from Greek *dimorphos*, formed as DI-[2] + *morphē* form: see -IC.]
Existing or occurring in two distinct forms, *spec.* (**a**) (BOTANY & ZOOLOGY) in the same plant or species, (**b**) (MINERALOGY) of the same crystalline substance.
■ **dimorphism** *noun* M19. **dimorphous** *adjective* = DIMORPHIC M19.

dimorphotheca /ˌdʌɪmɔːfəˈθiːkə/ *noun*. M19.
[ORIGIN mod. Latin, formed as DIMORPHIC + THECA.]
A southern African plant of the genus *Dimorphotheca*, of the composite family, grown elsewhere as a half-hardy garden annual.

dimple /ˈdɪmp(ə)l/ *noun & verb*. LME.
[ORIGIN Corresp. to Old High German *tumphilo* (Middle High German *tümpfel*, German *Tümpel*) deep place in water, from Germanic, perh. a nasalized form of base of DEEP *adjective*; prob. already in Old English. Cf. DUMP *noun*[3].]
▸**A** *noun*. **1** A small hollow or dent in the surface of part of the human body, esp. in the cheeks or chin. LME.
2 Any slight depression in the surface of something. M17.

SOUTHEY The gentle waters gently part In dimples round the prow. S. B. FLEXNER The modern golf ball has 360 dimples.

▸**B** *verb*. **1** *verb trans*. Mark (as) with dimples. L16.

B. HARTE Leaden rain . . dimpling like shot the sluggish pools.

2 *verb intrans*. Break into or form dimples or ripples. E17.

TENNYSON Low knolls That dimpling died into each other. K. MANSFIELD Suddenly his face dimpled; it broke into a wide, toothless smile.

■ **dimpled** *adjective* marked (as) with dimples L16. **dimply** *adjective* full of or characterized by dimples E18.

dimps /dɪmps/ *noun*. *dial.* L17.
[ORIGIN Perh. from DIM *noun*, or dial. var. of *dumps* pl. of DUMP *noun*[1].]
Dusk, twilight.

dimpsey *noun, adjective* vars. of DIMPSY *noun, adjective*.

dimpsy /ˈdɪmpsi/ *noun*. *dial. & colloq.* Also **-ey**. L19.
[ORIGIN from DIMPS + -Y[6].]
Dusk, twilight; = DIMPS.

dimpsy /ˈdɪmpsi/ *adjective*. *dial. & colloq.* Also **-ey**. L19.
[ORIGIN formed as DIMPSY *noun* + -Y[1].]
Dusky, dim.

dim sum /dɪm ˈsʌm/ *noun phr.* Also **dim sim** /dɪm ˈsɪm/ & other vars. Pl. same, **-s**. M20.
[ORIGIN Chinese (Cantonese) *tim sam*, from *tim* dot + *sam* heart.]
A Chinese snack consisting of different hot savoury pastries.

DIN /*freq.* dɪn/ *abbreviation*.
German *Deutsche Industrie-Norm* German industrial standard.

din /dɪn/ *noun.*
[ORIGIN Old English *dyne*, *dynn* = Old High German *tuni*, Old Norse *dynr*, from Germanic.]
A loud noise; *esp.* a continuous confused distracting noise.
G. HUNTINGTON The muffled din of the station grew acuter whenever the door was opened.
■ **dinful** *adjective* noisy L19.

din /dɪn/ *verb.* Infl. **-nn-**.
[ORIGIN Old English *dynian* = Old Saxon *dunian*, Middle High German *tünen* roar, rumble, Old Norse *dynja* come rumbling down, from Germanic base of DIN *noun*.]
▸ **I** *verb intrans.* †**1** Of a place etc.: resound with noise. OE–E16.
2 Make a din; give out or be a loud confused sound. ME.
V. WOOLF A familiar sound shook and trembled—increased—fairly dinned in their ears.
▸ **II** *verb trans.* **3** Assail with clamour or persistent noise. L17.
R. C. SINGLETON With never-ceasing words On this and that side is the hero dinned.
4 Repeat continually so as to weary; *esp.* get (a lesson etc.) *into* a person by continual repetition. Cf. DING *verb*² 1a. E18.
R. RENDELL Ever since I was eighteen I've had it dinned into me I mustn't drink.

dinanderie /dinɑ̃dri/ *noun.* M19.
[ORIGIN French, from *Dinant* (formerly *Dinand*), a town near Liège, Belgium + *-erie* -ERY.]
Domestic and other utensils of brass (freq. embossed) made in late medieval times in and around Dinant; ornamental brassware from other parts, including India and the eastern Mediterranean region.

Dinantian /dɪˈnanʃɪən/ *adjective & noun.* E20.
[ORIGIN French *dinantien*, from *Dinant* (see DINANDERIE) + -IAN.]
GEOLOGY. (Of, pertaining to, or designating) the Lower Carboniferous in Europe or the rocks dating from this time.

dinar /ˈdiːnɑː/ *noun.* M17.
[ORIGIN Arabic, Persian *dīnār*, Turkish, Serbian and Croatian *dinar* from late Greek *dēnarion* from Latin DENARIUS.]
1 Any of various coins formerly used in the East, *esp.* a gold mohur. M17.
2 The basic monetary unit of Serbia and neighbouring states (and formerly of Yugoslavia), equal to 100 paras. L19.
3 The basic monetary unit of Algeria, Bahrain, Iraq, Jordan, Kuwait, Libya, Tunisia, and (formerly) South Yemen, equal to 100 centimes in Algeria, 1,000 fils in Bahrain, Iraq, Jordan, Kuwait, and (formerly) South Yemen, 1,000 dirhams in Libya, and 1,000 millimes in Tunisia; a monetary unit of Iran, equal to one-hundredth of a rial. M20.

Dinaric /dɪˈnarɪk/ *adjective.* M19.
[ORIGIN from *Dinara*, a mountain in Dalmatia + -IC.]
Pertaining to or designating a mountain range extending south-easterly along the eastern side of the Adriatic.

din-dins /ˈdɪndɪnz/ *noun. colloq.* Also **-din** /-dɪn/. L19.
[ORIGIN Childish or joc. redupl. of DINNER *noun*.]
Dinner.

dindle /ˈdɪnd(ə)l/ *verb & noun.* Now *Scot. & N. English.* LME.
[ORIGIN Prob. imit.: cf. DINGLE *verb*, TINGLE *verb*, TINKLE *verb*.]
▸ **A** *verb.* **1** *verb intrans.* Make a ringing sound or one that causes vibration. LME.
2 *verb intrans. & trans.* (Cause to) tremble or vibrate, esp. with sound. LME.
W. H. AUDEN While war-horns dindled the heavens.
3 *verb intrans.* Tingle as with cold or pain. L15.
▸ **B** *noun.* A vibration; a tingling sensation. E19.

dine /dʌɪn/ *noun. obsolete* exc. *dial.* LME.
[ORIGIN from the verb.]
(A) dinner; dinner time.

dine /dʌɪn/ *verb.* ME.
[ORIGIN Old French *disner* (mod. *dîner*) prob. from *desjuner*, *desjëuner* break fast: see DISJUNE.]
1 *verb intrans.* Have dinner. Foll. by *on* (what is eaten), *off* (a stock or supply). ME.
J. BETJEMAN Lunching with poets, dining late with peers.
2 *verb trans.* Give dinner to. Of a room etc.: accommodate for dining purposes. LME.
– PHRASES: **dine out** dine away from home. **dine out on** be invited to dinner on the strength of (one's knowledge of an interesting event, etc.). **dine with Duke Humphrey** *arch.* go without dinner. ***wine and dine***: see WINE *verb*.

diner /ˈdʌɪnə/ *noun.* E19.
[ORIGIN from DINE *verb* + -ER¹.]
1 A person who dines; a dinner guest. E19.
2 A railway dining car. Orig. *US.* M19.
3 A cheap roadside restaurant, orig. one built to resemble a railway dining car. *N. Amer.* M20.
4 A dining room, *esp.* a small one. M20.
kitchen-diner: see KITCHEN *noun*.
– COMB.: **diner-out** (pl. **diners-out**) a person who often dines out, *esp.* one much in demand as a dinner guest for his or her social qualities.

dinero /dɪˈnɛːrəʊ/ *noun.* Pl. **-os**. L17.
[ORIGIN Spanish = coin, money from Latin *denarius* DENARIUS.]
1 *hist.* A monetary unit in Spain and Peru, now disused. L17.
2 Money. *US slang.* M19.

dinette /dʌɪˈnɛt/ *noun.* M20.
[ORIGIN Irreg. from DINE *verb* + -ETTE.]
1 A small room or area of a room set aside for meals, as in a kitchen or caravan. M20.
2 A set of furniture for a dinette. M20.

ding /dɪŋ/ *noun*¹. ME.
[ORIGIN from DING *verb*¹.]
1 A blow, a knock; a push. Now *Scot. & dial.* ME.
2 A dent; a small damaged area. *colloq.* M20.

ding /dɪŋ/ *noun*². M18.
[ORIGIN from the interjection.]
A ringing metallic sound; *gen.* a din.

ding /dɪŋ/ *noun*³. *Austral. slang. derog.* M20.
[ORIGIN Abbreviation of DINGBAT.]
An Italian or other European immigrant to Australia.

ding /dɪŋ/ *noun*⁴. *Austral. slang.* M20.
[ORIGIN Prob. from WINGDING.]
A wild party, a celebration.

ding /dɪŋ/ *verb*¹. Pa. t. **dinged**, (*Scot. & N. English*) **dang** /daŋ/; pa. pple **dinged**, (*Scot. & N. English*) **dung** /dʌŋ/. ME.
[ORIGIN Prob. of Scandinavian origin: cf. Old Norse *dengja* to hammer, whet a scythe, Old Swedish *dängia*, Danish *dænge* beat, bang.]
1 *verb intrans.* Deal heavy blows; knock, hammer. Usu. foll. by *on*, *at*. *arch.* ME.
JOYCE Costello dinged with his fist upon the board.
2 *verb trans.* Strike with heavy blows or forcefully; beat, thrash; put a dent in. Now *Scot. & US colloq.* ME. ▸**b** *fig.* Overcome or surpass, beat. Now *Scot.* E18.
HENRY MORE The rider fiercely dings His horse with iron heel.
3 *verb trans.* Knock, throw, or drive with violence in some direction. *arch.* ME.
ding down overthrow, demolish.
4 *verb intrans.* †**a** Propel oneself forcefully, press, drive; fling oneself about; throw oneself or fall (*down*) heavily. LME–E18. ▸**b** Of rain, snow, etc.: beat down heavily and without intermission. Usu. foll. by *down*, *on*. *Scot.* E16.
5 *verb trans.* Throw away, discard; reject; *spec.* get rid of (something incriminating). *slang.* M18. ▸**b** Give up, abandon, (an enterprise). Esp. in ***ding it***. *Austral. slang.* L19.
6 In mild imprecations, freq. in imper. or optative form: damn. *dial. & US colloq.* E19.
GEO. ELIOT Ding me if I remember a sample to match her.

ding /dɪŋ/ *verb*². M16.
[ORIGIN Imit., but in sense 1 infl. by DING *verb*¹ and DIN *verb*.]
1 a *verb trans.* Din *into* a person. M16. ▸**b** *verb intrans.* Speak with wearisome persistence, esp. reprovingly. L16.
2 *verb intrans.* Make a sound like metal heavily struck; ring like a bell struck once. Also redupl. E19.
DICKENS Sledge hammers were dinging upon iron all day long. J. HERRIOT The bell ding-dinged and the tram began to move.

ding /dɪŋ/ *interjection.* L16.
[ORIGIN Imit.: cf. DING *verb*².]
Repr. the ringing sound of a heavy bell, or of metal when struck.

ding-a-ling /ˈdɪŋəlɪŋ/ *noun & adjective.* Also **dingaling**. L19.
[ORIGIN Imit.: cf. DING *interjection*, *noun*².]
▸ **A** *noun.* **1** The sound of a bell. L19.
2 A person who acts strangely, orig. as a result of long imprisonment; an eccentric; a fool. *N. Amer. slang.* M20.
▸ **B** *adjective.* Foolish, stupid. *N. Amer. slang.* L20.

Ding an sich /dɪŋ an zɪç/ *noun phr.* M19.
[ORIGIN German = thing in itself.]
PHILOSOPHY. A thing as it really is, apart from human observation or experience of it; = NOUMENON.

dingbat /ˈdɪŋbat/ *noun. slang.* M19.
[ORIGIN Uncertain: perh. from DING *verb*¹ + BAT *noun*¹; cf. also DINGUS. In sense 4 prob. assoc. with BAT *noun*³, BATS *adjective*.]
1 Any of various vaguely specified objects, *esp.* (**a**) anything used as a missile; (**b**) (a piece of) money; (**c**) a gadget, a contraption; a 'thingummy'. *US.* M19.
C R. BLOUNT There is a lot of great stuff in that warehouse—dingbats going back to Chester A. Arthur.
2 A tramp or vagrant. *US.* E20.
3 A stupid or foolish person. Chiefly *N. Amer., Austral., & NZ.* E20.
I. BANKS An upper class dingbat who just happened to be married to his sister.
4 Madness; a drunken delusion. *Austral. & NZ.* E20.
give a person the dingbats make a person nervous. **have the dingbats** be crazy, be suffering from delirium tremens.
5 An army batman. *Austral.* E20.
6 A typographical device other than a letter or numeral (e.g. an asterisk), used for ornament etc. *US.* E20.

dingbats /ˈdɪŋbats/ *pred. adjective. Austral. & NZ slang.* M20.
[ORIGIN from pl. of DINGBAT.]
Crazy, eccentric; suffering from delirium tremens.

ding-dong /ˈdɪŋdɒŋ, dɪŋˈdɒŋ/ *interjection, adverb, noun, adjective, & verb.* Also **dingdong**. M16.
[ORIGIN Imit.]
▸ **A** *interjection & adverb.* **1** Repr. the sound of a bell. M16.
2 *adverb.* With zeal and vigour. L17.
M. R. MITFORD I shall set to work at the 'Heiress' ding-dong.
▸ **B** *noun.* **1** The sound of a bell when individual strokes are heard rather than a continuous ring; a bell etc. that gives such a sound, *esp.* a device for sounding the quarter hours by a single stroke on each of two bells of different pitch; a jingle of rhyme. M16.
2 A heated argument, a quarrel. *colloq.* E20.
H. BELLOC A ding-dong of assertion and counter-assertion.
3 A noisy party. *colloq.* M20.
▸ **C** *adjective.* **1** Of or pertaining to the sound of bells or the jingle of rhyme. E17.
2 Of a fight or dispute: in which prospective victory swings between one side and the other; hotly contested. *colloq.* M19.
▸ **D** *verb intrans.* Ring as or like a bell; *fig.* speak with wearying repetition. M17.

dinge /dɪn(d)ʒ/ *noun*¹. E17.
[ORIGIN Unknown: rel. to DINGE *verb*¹.]
A depression in the surface of something, caused by a blow; a dint.

dinge /dɪn(d)ʒ/ *noun*². *dial. & colloq.* E19.
[ORIGIN from DINGE *verb*² or back-form. from DINGY *adjective*.]
Dinginess, drabness; darkness. Formerly, a dark night.
J. R. ACKERLEY The dust and dinge of the cluttered house.

dinge /dɪn(d)ʒ/ *noun*³ *& adjective. US slang. offensive.* M19.
[ORIGIN from DINGY *adjective*.]
▸ **A** *noun.* A black person M19.
▸ **B** *adjective.* Of or pertaining to black people or their jazz-playing. M19.

dinge /dɪn(d)ʒ/ *verb*¹ *trans.* Orig. *dial.* E17.
[ORIGIN Unknown: goes with DINGE *noun*¹.]
Make an impression in the surface of; dent, dint; damage.

dinge /dɪn(d)ʒ/ *verb*² *trans. dial. & colloq.* E19.
[ORIGIN from DINGY *adjective*.]
Make dingy.

dinger /ˈdɪŋə/ *noun.* L18.
[ORIGIN from DING *verb*¹ + -ER¹.]
1 A thief who throws away identifiable objects to avoid detection (cf. DING *verb*¹ 5). *criminals' slang.* Now *rare* or *obsolete.* L18.
2 Something outstanding of its kind; a 'humdinger'. *slang* (chiefly *US*) *& dial.* L19.
J. STEINBECK Been a dinger of a crop.

dinges *noun* var. of DINGUS.

dinghy /ˈdɪŋgi/ *noun.* E19.
[ORIGIN Hindi *ḍiṅgī*, *ḍeṅgī*. Spelt *-gh-* in English to indicate the hard *g*.]
1 A rowing boat used on the rivers of the Indian subcontinent. E19.
2 Any small boat; *spec.* (**a**) one carried on a warship or merchant vessel; the tender of a yacht; (**b**) a small pleasure boat or racing boat; (**c**) an inflatable life raft, esp. one carried on an aircraft. E19.

dingle /ˈdɪŋg(ə)l/ *noun.* ME.
[ORIGIN Uncertain: perh. a doublet of DIMBLE.]
†**1** A deep abyss. Only in ME.
2 A deep hollow or dell, *esp.* (chiefly *literary*) one shaded by trees. Also (*dial.*) a cleft between hills. M17.
SOUTHEY Seek some sequestered dingle's coolest shade.
– COMB.: **dingle-bird** = ***bell miner*** s.v. BELL *noun*¹.
■ **dingly** *adjective* of the nature of a dingle, having many dingles M19.

dingle /ˈdɪŋg(ə)l/ *verb.* L16.
[ORIGIN Prob. imit.: cf. DINDLE *verb*, TINGLE *verb*, TINKLE *verb*.]
1 *verb intrans. & trans.* (Cause to) tingle. L16.
2 *verb intrans.* Ring like a bell, tinkle. E19.
3 *verb intrans.* Vibrate with sound. M19.

dingleberry /ˈdɪŋg(ə)lbɛri/ *noun. US.* M20.
[ORIGIN from unkn. 1st elem. + BERRY *noun*¹.]
1 A deciduous cranberry, *Vaccinium erythrocarpum*, of the south-eastern US. M20.
2 A particle of faecal matter attached to anal hair. Usu. in *pl. slang.* M20.
3 A foolish or stupid person. *colloq.* M20.

D

dingle-dangle /dɪŋɡ(ə)l'daŋɡ(ə)l/ *adverb, noun, verb, & adjective.* **L16.**
[ORIGIN Redupl. of DANGLE *adjective & noun, verb.*]
▸ **A** *adverb.* In a dangling fashion; hanging loosely. **L16.**
▸ **B** *noun.* A swinging to and fro; an ornament etc. that dangles. **E17.**
▸ **C** *verb intrans.* Dangle loosely. **M17.**
▸ **D** *adjective.* Swinging loosely to and fro, dangling. **L17.**

dingo /'dɪŋɡəʊ/ *noun & verb.* **L18.**
[ORIGIN Dharuk *din-gu.*]
▸ **A** *noun.* Pl. **-oes.**
1 The wild or semi-domesticated dog of mainland Australia, *Canis dingo.* **L18.**
2 A treacherous, cowardly, or despicable person. *Austral. slang.* **M19.**

V. PALMER I'd be a hell of a dingo . . if I didn't help you now.

▸ **B** *verb. Austral. slang.*
1 *verb intrans.* Behave in a contemptible way. **M20.** **dingo on a person** let a person down.
2 *verb trans.* Shirk, back out of. **M20.**

dingus /'dɪŋɡəs/ *noun. colloq.* Also **dinges.** **L19.**
[ORIGIN from Dutch *ding* thing.]
A gadget, a contraption; a 'thingummy'.

dingy /'dɪn(d)ʒi/ *adjective.* **M18.**
[ORIGIN Perh. ult. referrable to Old English *dynġe* dung, manured land, from DUNG *noun*: see -Y[1].]
1 Dirty, soiled. *dial.* **M18.**
2 Disagreeably devoid of brightness or freshness of colour, esp. from grime or neglect; drab, dirty-looking. In *BOTANY & ZOOLOGY* (formerly *gen.*), of a naturally sombre colour. **M18.**

DISRAELI Its plumage of a dingy, yellowish white. W. GERHARDIE A bare and dingy room in a . . shabby hostel. *fig.*: H. JAMES She's not for a dingy little man of letters; she's for . . the bright rich world.

dingy skipper a Eurasian skipper, *Erynnis tages*, which has grey-brown wings with dark markings.
■ **dingily** *adverb* **E19.** **dinginess** *noun* **E19.**

dining /'dʌɪnɪŋ/ *verbal noun.* **LME.**
[ORIGIN from DINE *verb* + -ING[1].]
The action of DINE *verb*; a dinner.
– COMB.: **dining car** a railway carriage in which meals are served on the journey; **dining chair** an upright chair used at a dining table; **dining room** a room in a house etc. set aside for the principal meals; **dining table** a table on which meals are served in a dining room etc.

dink /dɪŋk/ *noun*[1]. *Austral. slang.* **M20.**
[ORIGIN Unknown.]
A ride on the handlebar of a bicycle.

dink /dɪŋk/ *noun*[2]. *US.* **M20.**
[ORIGIN Imit.]
A drop shot in tennis.

dink /dɪŋk/ *noun*[3]. *US slang. derog.* **M20.**
[ORIGIN Unknown.]
A Vietnamese.

dink /dɪŋk/ *noun*[4]. *colloq.* Also **DINK.** **L20.**
[ORIGIN Acronym, from *d*ouble *i*ncome, *n*o *k*ids.]
Either partner of a (usu. professional) married couple without children, both of whom have an income from work.

dink /dɪŋk/ *adjective*[1]. *Scot. & N. English.* **E16.**
[ORIGIN Unknown.]
Finely dressed, trim, spruce.
■ **dinkly** *adverb* **L18.**

dink /dɪŋk/ *adjective*[2] *& adverb. Austral. & NZ colloq.* **E20.**
[ORIGIN Abbreviation.]
= DINKUM *adjective & adverb.* Esp. in ***fair dink.***

dink /dɪŋk/ *verb*[1] *trans. Scot.* **E19.**
[ORIGIN from DINK *adjective*[1].]
Dress (esp. oneself) finely, adorn.

dink /dɪŋk/ *verb*[2] *trans. Austral. slang.* **M20.**
[ORIGIN from DINK *noun*[1].]
Give a ride on the handlebar of a bicycle to.

dink /dɪŋk/ *verb*[3] *intrans.* Chiefly *US.* **M20.**
[ORIGIN from DINK *noun*[2].]
In tennis, volleyball, and other games with a net: execute a drop shot that falls just beyond the net.

Dinka /'dɪŋkə/ *noun & adjective.* **M19.**
[ORIGIN from African name *Jieng* people.]
▸ **A** *noun.* Pl. **-s,** same.
1 A member of a Sudanese people of the Nile basin. **M19.**
2 The language of this people. **L19.**
▸ **B** *adjective.* Of or pertaining to the Dinkas or Dinka. **M19.**

dinkel /'dɪŋk(ə)l/ *noun.* Also **D-.** **M19.**
[ORIGIN German.]
= SPELT *noun*[1].

dinkey *noun* var. of DINKY *noun*[1].

dinki-di *adjective* var. of DINKY-DIE.

dinkie *noun* var. of DINKY *noun*[2].

dinkie *adjective* var. of DINKY *adjective.*

dinkum /'dɪŋkəm/ *noun, adjective, & adverb.* **L19.**
[ORIGIN Unknown.]
▸ **A** *noun.* **1** (Hard) work; one's due share of a task. *dial.* (formerly also *Austral. colloq.*). **L19.**

R. BOLDREWOOD It took us an hour's hard dinkum to get near the peak.

2 = ***dinkum oil*** below. *Austral. & NZ colloq.* **E20.**
†**3** (**D-**) An Australian or New Zealander, *esp.* one who fought in the First World War. *Austral. & NZ colloq.* Only in **E20.**
▸ **B** *adjective & adverb.* In full ***fair dinkum*** (also ***square dinkum, straight dinkum***). Genuine(ly), authentic(ally); honest(ly), straightforward(ly); *interrog.* really? you aren't having me on? *Austral. & NZ colloq.* **L19.**

Weekly Dispatch Real dinkum Australians . . knew . . that wombats can't fly. N. MARSH Give you a pain in the neck, dinkum, she would. F. CLUNE The Simpson Desert . . is the only fair-dinkum desert in Australia. A. WRIGHT It's like a story out of a book . . but it's dinkum.

dinkum oil the honest truth, reliable information.

dinky /'dɪŋki/ *noun*[1]. Also **-key.** **M19.**
[ORIGIN from DINKY *adjective.* In sense 'small boat' perh. alt. of DINGHY.]
A small contrivance; *spec.* a small boat or locomotive.

dinky /'dɪŋki/ *noun*[2]. *colloq.* Also **-ie.** **L20.**
[ORIGIN from (the same root as) DINK *noun*[4] + -Y[6], -IE.]
= DINK *noun*[4].

dinky /'dɪŋki/ *adjective.* Also **-kie.** **L18.**
[ORIGIN from DINK *adjective*[1] + -Y[1].]
1 Small and neat; dainty, cute. *dial. & colloq.* (esp. *Scot. & N. Amer.*). **L18.**

W. H. AUDEN In a dinky straw hat. D. WELCH Dinky lattice panes.

Dinky car, **Dinky Toy** (proprietary name for) a die-cast miniature motor vehicle.
2 Trifling, insignificant, unimpressive. *N. Amer. colloq.* **L19.**

H. CRANE In a dinky stuffy apartment.

dinky-die /dɪŋkɪ'dʌɪ/ *adjective. Austral. & NZ slang.* Also **dinki-, -di.** **E20.**
[ORIGIN from DINKUM + -Y[1] with a nonsensical addition.]
= DINKUM *adjective.*

dinmont /'dɪnm(ə)nt/ *noun. Scot. & N. English.* **ME.**
[ORIGIN Uncertain: 2nd elem. perh. Scot. form of MONTH.]
A wether between the first and second shearing.

dinna *verb* see DO *verb.*

dinner /'dɪnə/ *noun.* **ME.**
[ORIGIN Old French *di(s)ner* (mod. *dîner*) use as noun of inf.: see DINE *verb.*]
The main meal of the day, eaten either about midday or in the evening; a formal meal of several courses, *spec.* one held publicly to honour a person, mark an occasion, etc.

DAY LEWIS Sunday dinner was a joint, two veg. and pudding affair, far superior to our weekday lunches or evening meals. G. B. SHAW Speeches made by my uncle at charitable dinners.

done like a dinner *Austral. slang* (*NZ* **done like a dog's dinner**) utterly defeated. ***eat dinners***: see EAT *verb.* **have had more — than a person has had hot dinners** *colloq.*: used hyperbol. to indicate a person's wide experience of a given activity or phenomenon. ***like a dog's dinner***: see DOG *noun.* *WORKING dinner.*
– COMB.: **dinner bell**: rung to announce dinner; **dinner dance** a dinner followed by dancing; **dinner jacket** a man's short usu. black dress coat without tails, worn with a black tie for evening functions; **dinner lady** a woman employed to serve midday meals in a school; **dinner pail** *US* a pail in which a labourer's or schoolchild's dinner is carried and kept warm (***hand in one's dinner pail, pass in one's dinner pail, turn in one's dinner pail*** (*slang*), die); **dinner service** a set of matching plates, dishes, etc., for serving dinner; **dinner suit** a man's suit consisting of a dinner jacket and trousers, worn with a bow tie at a dinner or other formal occasion; **dinner table** a dining table; **dinner theatre** *N. Amer.* a theatre in which a meal is included in the price of a ticket; **dinner time**: when dinner is customarily eaten; **dinner wagon** a trolley with tiers for holding dishes etc., for service in a dining room; **dinnerware** *N. Amer.* dishes, utensils, and glassware used at table; tableware.
■ **dinnerless** *adjective* **M17.** **dinnery** *adjective* (*rare*) **M19.**

dinner /'dɪnə/ *verb.* **M18.**
[ORIGIN from the noun.]
1 *verb intrans. & trans.* (with *it*). Have dinner, dine. **M18.**
2 *verb trans.* Entertain to dinner; provide with dinner. **E19.**

dinoflagellate /dʌɪnə(ʊ)'fladʒəleɪt/ *adjective & noun.* **L19.**
[ORIGIN mod. Latin *Dinoflagellata*, from Greek *dinos* a whirling + Latin FLAGELLUM: see -ATE[2].]
BIOLOGY. ▸ **A** *adjective.* Designating or pertaining to a dinoflagellate. **L19.**
▸ **B** *noun.* Any of a group of unicellular mostly pigmented aquatic (esp. marine) organisms with two flagella, variously classed as algae and as protozoa. **E20.**

dinosaur /'dʌɪnəsɔː/ *noun.* **M19.**
[ORIGIN mod. Latin *dinosaurus*, from Greek *deinos* fearsome + -SAUR.]
An extinct terrestrial reptile, freq. of gigantic size, of a group which was dominant in Mesozoic times, some having pelvic girdles like lizards (order Saurischia) and others like birds (order Ornithischia); *fig.* something that has not adapted to changing circumstances, a clumsy survival from earlier times.
■ **dino'saurian** *adjective & noun* (*a*) *adjective* of or pertaining to a dinosaur or the dinosaurs; (*b*) *noun* a dinosaur: **M19.**

†**dinothere** *noun* var. of DEINOTHERE.

dinsome /'dɪns(ə)m/ *adjective. Scot.* **E18.**
[ORIGIN from DIN *noun* + -SOME[1].]
Full of din, noisy.

dint /dɪnt/ *noun.*
[ORIGIN Old English *dynt*, reinforced in Middle English by related Old Norse *dyntr* (*dyttr*), *dynta*: cf. DENT *noun*[1], DUNT.]
†**1** A stroke or blow; *esp.* one given with a weapon. **OE–M19.**
▸†**b** A stroke of thunder. **ME–E19.**
2 The dealing of blows; force of attack or impact (*lit. & fig.*); violence, attack, force. Now *rare* or *obsolete* exc. in ***by dint of***, through (constant) application of (a remedy etc.), by means of, by force of. **ME.**

SHAKES. *Jul. Caes.* You weep, and I perceive you feel The dint of pity. SMOLLETT By dint of cross-examination, I found he was not at all satisfied. J. MCPHEE Do the Alaskan natives, by dint of aboriginal use . . have special claim to Alaskan land?

†**by dint of sword** by force of arms. †**under the dint of**, †**within the dint of** within the range of (something harmful).
3 An impression made in a surface (as) by a blow or by pressure; an indentation; *fig.* an effect, an impression produced. **L16.**

V. WOOLF A little dint sharpened between his brows. W. S. CHURCHILL A hardy . . race which . . had . . made a deep dint upon the politics of England.

■ **dintless** *adjective* producing or showing no dint **M16.**

dint /dɪnt/ *verb.* **ME.**
[ORIGIN from the noun.]
†**1** *verb trans.* Strike, beat. **ME–M17.**
2 *verb* †*intrans. & trans.* Make a dint or impression in (or †*in*). **LME.**

J. M. NEALE In his master's steps he trod, Where the snow lay dinted.

3 *verb trans.* Drive in (as) with pressure. (Foll. by *into.*) **L16.**

DRYDEN Deep dinted wrinkles.

diocesan /dʌɪ'ɒsɪs(ə)n/ *adjective & noun.* **LME.**
[ORIGIN French *diocésain* from medieval Latin *diocesanus*, late Latin *dioecesanus*, from Latin *dioecesis* DIOCESE: see -AN.]
ECCLESIASTICAL. ▸ **A** *adjective.* Of or pertaining to a diocese. **LME.**
▸ **B** *noun.* **1** The bishop of a diocese. **LME.**
2 One of the clergy or people of a diocese. Now *rare.* **E16.**

diocese /'dʌɪəsɪs/ *noun.* **ME.**
[ORIGIN Old French *diocise* (mod. *diocèse*) from late Latin *diocesis* for Latin *dioecesis* governor's jurisdiction, district, (Eccl.) diocese, from Greek *dioikēsis* administration, government, (Eccl.) diocese, from *dioikein* keep house, administer, formed as DI-[3] + *oikos* house.]
1 *ECCLESIASTICAL.* The region over which a bishop has jurisdiction and pastoral charge subject only to an archbishop or metropolitan. **ME.**
2 A division of a country under a governor; *spec.* each of the twelve units (consisting of several provinces) into which the Roman Empire was divided from the time of Diocletian. *obsolete* exc. *hist.* **L15.**

†**diocesian** *adjective & noun.* **E17–E18.**
[ORIGIN medieval Latin *diocesianus*, from late Latin *diocesis* DIOCESE: see -IAN.]
= DIOCESAN *adjective & noun.*

dioch /'dʌɪək/ *noun.* Also **diock.** **L19.**
[ORIGIN Perh. from African name.]
Any of various African weaver birds of the genus *Quelea.*

dioctahedral /ˌdʌɪɒktə'hiːdr(ə)l/ *adjective.* **E19.**
[ORIGIN from DI-[2] + OCTAHEDRAL.]
1 *CRYSTALLOGRAPHY.* Bounded by sixteen planes, i.e. in the form of an octahedral prism with tetrahedral summits. *rare.* **E19.**
2 *MINERALOGY.* Having or designating a crystal structure in which there are two metal ions for each octahedron of hydroxyl or oxygen ions. **M20.**

diode /'dʌɪəʊd/ *adjective & noun.* **L19.**
[ORIGIN from DI-[2] + Greek *hodos* way.]
▸ †**A** *adjective.* Of a telegraph system: in which two messages can be transmitted simultaneously along one line, either in the same or in opposite directions. Only in **L19.**
▸ **B** *noun. ELECTRONICS.*
1 A thermionic valve with two electrodes (a cathode and an anode). **E20.**
2 A semiconductor rectifier with two terminals. **M20.** ***Gunn diode, junction diode, photodiode, Schottky diode,*** etc.

diodon /'dʌɪədɒn/ *noun.* **L18.**
[ORIGIN from DI-[2] + -ODON.]
A tropical globefish of the genus *Diodon*, in which each jaw has, instead of teeth, an undivided enamel beak.

dioecious /dʌɪ'iːʃəs/ *adjective.* Also ***diec-.** **M18.**
[ORIGIN from mod. Latin *Dioecia*, a class in Linnaeus's sexual system (formed as DI-[2] + Greek *oikos* house) + -OUS.]
1 *BOTANY.* Bearing male and female flowers on different plants. Also, (of a cryptogam) having male and female organs in different plants. **M18.**

2 ZOOLOGY. Having male and female reproductive organs in separate individuals. E19.
■ **dioeciously** *adverb* L19. **dioeciousness** *noun* L19. **dioecism** /-sɪz(ə)m/ *noun* dioecious state L19. **dioecy** /-si/ *noun* dioecism M20.

dioestrus /dʌɪˈiːstrəs/ *noun*. Also **-trum** /-trəm/, ***diest-** /dʌɪˈɛst-/. E20.
[ORIGIN from DI-² + OESTRUS.]
A relatively short interval of sexual quiescence or inactivity in an animal between recurrent periods of oestrus.
■ **dioestrous** *adjective* E20.

Diogenes /dʌɪˈɒdʒɪniːz/ *noun*. L16.
[ORIGIN See below.]
A person, esp. one of pointedly ascetic or unsociable behaviour, who is likened to Diogenes (*c* 400–*c* 325 BC), a Greek Cynic philosopher reputed to have shown his contempt for the comforts of civilization by living in a tub.
– COMB.: **Diogenes-crab** a W. Indian hermit crab, *Coenobita diogenes*, which lives in the empty shell of a snail.
■ **Diogenic** /-ˈdʒɛnɪk/ *adjective* pertaining to or resembling Diogenes M19. **Diogenical** /-ˈdʒɛnɪk(ə)l/ *adjective* = DIOGENIC L16.

diogenite /dʌɪˈɒdʒɪnʌɪt/ *noun*. L19.
[ORIGIN from Greek *Diogenēs* descended from Zeus + -ITE¹.]
Any of a group of achondritic meteorites consisting largely of hypersthene and bronzite.

diol /ˈdʌɪɒl/ *noun*. E20.
[ORIGIN from DI-² + -OL.]
CHEMISTRY. A compound whose molecule contains two hydroxyl groups, esp. attached to different carbon atoms.

-dione /ˈdɪəʊn/ *suffix*.
[ORIGIN from DI-² + -ONE.]
CHEMISTRY. Forming the names of compounds containing two carbonyl groups, as ***menadione***.

†**dionise** *noun*. Also in medieval Latin form **dionysia**. LME–M19.
[ORIGIN Old French from medieval Latin *dionysia* from Latin *dionysias* from Greek *dionūsias*, from *Dionūsos*: see DIONYSIAN.]
A precious stone credited by medieval writers with warding off drunkenness when ground and added to water.

Dionysiac /dʌɪəˈnɪzɪak/ *noun & adjective*. Also **d-**. E19.
[ORIGIN Late Latin *Dionysiacus* from Greek *Dionūsiakos*, from *Dionūsos*: see DIONYSIAN, -AC.]
▸ **A** *noun*. In *pl*. The festivals of Dionysus held at various times of the year in ancient Greece. E19.
▸ **B** *adjective*. = DIONYSIAN *adjective* 1. M19.

W. A. PERCY The gowns . . insist on hanging from the . . shoulders with something of a Dionysiac abandon.

■ **Dionysiacal** /dʌɪənɪˈzʌɪək(ə)l/ *adjective* = DIONYSIAC *adjective* M19. **Dionysiacally** /-ˈzʌɪək-/ *adverb* E19. **Dionysic** /-ˈnʌɪsɪk/ *adjective* = DIONYSIAC *adjective* M19.

Dionysian /dʌɪəˈnɪzɪən/ *adjective & noun*. E17.
[ORIGIN from Latin *Dionysius* from Greek *Dionūsios* adjective, also as personal name, from *Dionūsos* Dionysus (see below): see -AN, -IAN.]
▸ **A** *adjective*. **1** Of or pertaining to Dionysus, the Greek god of fruitful vegetation, wine, etc., whose cult was frequently marked by ecstatic rites; sensual, abandoned; (of character, literary work, etc.) inspired by instinct and emotion (opp. ***Apollonian***). E17.
2 Pertaining to or characteristic of the Elder or Younger Dionysius, tyrants of Syracuse notorious for cruelty. E17.
3 Pertaining to the abbot Dionysius the Little (fl. 6th cent.) or the system of dating events from the birth of Jesus which he suggested. M17.
Dionysian period [said to have been introduced by Dionysius for calculating the date of Easter] = LUNISOLAR ***period***.
▸ **B** *noun*. A worshipper or follower of Dionysus; a person of Dionysian character. E20.

Diophantine /dʌɪəˈfantʌɪn/ *adjective*. E18.
[ORIGIN from *Diophantus* of Alexandria (fl. 3rd cent. AD), mathematician + -INE¹.]
MATH. Pertaining to the solution of indeterminate equations and the restriction of variables to integral values; designating a polynomial equation with integral coefficients for which integral solutions are required.

diopside /dʌɪˈɒpsʌɪd/ *noun*. E19.
[ORIGIN French, irreg. formed as DI-² + Greek *opsis* aspect; later interpreted as from Greek *diopsis* a view through.]
MINERALOGY. A monoclinic silicate of calcium and magnesium of the pyroxene group, occurring as white to pale green transparent to translucent crystals.
■ **diopˈsidic** *adjective* M20.

dioptase /dʌɪˈɒpteɪz/ *noun*. E19.
[ORIGIN French, irreg. from Greek *dioptos* transparent, formed as DI-³ + *optos* visible.]
MINERALOGY. A hexagonal hydrated silicate of copper occurring as green transparent to translucent crystals.

diopter /dʌɪˈɒptə/ *noun*. Also **-tra** /-trə/, pl. **-trae** /-triː/. In sense 3 usu. **dioptre**. L16.
[ORIGIN French *dioptre* from Latin *dioptra* from Greek.]
1 = ALIDADE. L16.
2 An ancient optical instrument for measuring angles, altitudes, etc. E17.
3 A unit for expressing the power of a lens, equal to the reciprocal of its focal length in metres. L19.

dioptric /dʌɪˈɒptrɪk/ *adjective & noun*. M17.
[ORIGIN Greek *dioptrikos* relating to the use of the dioptra: see DIOPTER, -IC.]
▸ **A** *adjective*. †**1** Pertaining to or being a diopter. M–L17.
2 Of a lens etc.: serving as a medium for sight; assisting vision by refraction. M17.
3 Pertaining to or employing refraction. L17.
†**4** Able to be seen through. E–M19.
▸ **B** *noun*. In *pl*. (treated as *sing*.). The branch of optics that deals with refraction. M17.
■ **dioptrical** *adjective* E17. **dioptrically** *adverb* by means of refraction M18.

diorama /dʌɪəˈrɑːmə/ *noun*. E19.
[ORIGIN French, formed as DIA-¹ after PANORAMA.]
1 A scenic painting, viewed through a peephole, in which changes in lighting, colour, etc., are used to suggest different times of day, changes in weather, etc.; a building in which such paintings are exhibited. E19.

fig.: R. C. HUTCHINSON This continuous twilight, the diorama of roofs and gables ranging on livid smoke.

2 A small-scale tableau in which three-dimensional figures are shown against a painted background; a museum display of an animal etc. in its natural setting; a scale model of an architectural project in its surroundings. E20.
3 CINEMATOGRAPHY. A small-scale set used in place of a full-scale one for special effects, animation, etc. M20.
■ **dioramic** /-ˈramɪk/ *adjective* M19.

diorite /ˈdʌɪərʌɪt/ *noun*. E19.
[ORIGIN French, irreg. from Greek *diorizein* distinguish, formed as DI-³ + *orizein* limit: see -ITE¹.]
GEOLOGY. Any of a class of coarse-grained intermediate plutonic rocks consisting essentially of plagioclase feldspar and hornblende or other mafic minerals.
■ **dioritic** /-ˈrɪtɪk/ *adjective* M19.

diorthosis /dʌɪɔːˈθəʊsɪs/ *noun*. *arch*. Pl. **-thoses** /-ˈθəʊsiːz/. E18.
[ORIGIN Greek *diorthōsis*, formed as DI-³ + *orthos* straight: see -OSIS.]
The act of putting straight or in order; an agent that accomplishes this.
■ **diorthotic** /-ˈθɒtɪk/ *adjective* M19.

Dioscuric /dʌɪəˈskjʊərɪk/ *adjective*. Also **d-**. E20.
[ORIGIN from Greek *Dioskouroi* (from *Dios* genit. of *Zeus* + *kouros*, *koros* boy, son) + -IC.]
Pertaining to or resembling the legend of the twin sons of Zeus, Castor and Pollux.

diosgenin /dʌɪˈɒsdʒənɪn/ *noun*. M20.
[ORIGIN German, from mod. Latin *Dios(corea* type genus of the yam family (from *Dioscorides* Greek physician of the 1st cent. AD) + GENIN.]
CHEMISTRY. A sapogenin, $C_{27}H_{42}O_3$, obtained from Mexican yams of the genus *Dioscorea* and used in the preparation of steroid hormones.

diosma /dʌɪˈɒzmə/ *noun*. E19.
[ORIGIN mod. Latin, from Greek *dios* divine + *ozmē* odour.]
BOTANY. Any of various heathlike shrubs of the rue family belonging to the Southern African genus *Diosma* or formerly included in it, noted for their strong balsamic smell.

diota /dʌɪˈəʊtə/ *noun*. Pl. ***-tae*** /-tiː/. M19.
[ORIGIN Latin from Greek *diōtē* two-eared, formed as DI-² + *ous*, *ōt-* ear.]
CLASSICAL ANTIQUITIES. A two-handled vessel; *spec*. an amphora.

†**dioti** *noun*. M17–M18.
[ORIGIN Greek, from *dia (touto) hoti* for the reason that.]
A 'wherefore', a reason. Cf. HOTI.

diotic /dʌɪˈɒtɪk/ *adjective*. M20.
[ORIGIN from DI-² + Greek *ous*, *ōt-* ear + -IC.]
Involving or pertaining to the presentation of the same auditory signal to both ears.
■ **diotically** *adverb* M20.

Diotrephes /dʌɪˈɒtrəfiːz/ *noun*. M17.
[ORIGIN A man named in *3 John* 9.]
A person who loves pre-eminence among others, esp. in a congregation.
■ **Diotrephesian** /-ˈfiːzjən, -ʒ(ə)n/, **Diotrephian** /-ˈtrɛf-/, **Diotrephic** /-ˈtrɛf-/ *adjectives* of the nature of a Diotrephes M19.

dioxane /dʌɪˈɒkseɪn/ *noun*. Also **-an** /-ən/. E20.
[ORIGIN from DI-² + OX- + -AN, -ANE.]
A saturated cyclic diether, $C_4H_8O_2$, that is a toxic flammable liquid used as a solvent; any derivative of this.

dioxide /dʌɪˈɒksʌɪd/ *noun*. M19.
[ORIGIN from DI-² + OXIDE.]
CHEMISTRY. Any oxide containing two atoms of oxygen in its molecule or empirical formula.

dioxin /dʌɪˈɒksɪn/ *noun*. E20.
[ORIGIN from DI-² + OX- + -IN¹.]
1 CHEMISTRY. Each of three unsaturated cyclic compounds, $C_4H_6O_2$ and $C_4H_4O_2$. *rare*. E20.
2 Any derivative of such a compound, *esp*. tetrachlorodibenzoparadioxin. L20.

DIP *abbreviation*.
1 COMPUTING. Document image processing.
2 ELECTRONICS. Dual in-line package.

dip /dɪp/ *noun*. L16.
[ORIGIN from the verb.]
1 An act of dipping; *spec*. (*colloq*.) a bathe in the sea etc. L16. ▸**b** A minor fall in value or magnitude. L19.

J. GRANT A half-hour's 'dip' into some circulating-library book. TENNYSON Ev'n to the last dip of the vanishing sail She watch'd it. R. BRAUTIGAN She caught twenty fish with one dip. H. CARPENTER They take an early morning dip in an icy stream. **b** *Daily Telegraph* A £122 million dip in profits from Imperial Chemical Industries.

2 A downward slope of a surface; *esp*. in MINING & GEOLOGY, the angle made by a stratum etc. with the horizontal. L17. ▸**b** MINING. In full ***dip-head***. A passage driven downwards, esp. in the direction of dip. L19.
3 The angle made with the horizontal at any point by the earth's magnetic field. E18.
†**4** **a** = DEEP *noun* 8. M18–M19. ▸**b** Depth or amount of submergence, e.g. of a vessel. L18.
5 ASTRONOMY & SURVEYING. The apparent depression of the horizon due to the observer's elevation and the curvature of the earth. L18.
6 A hollow to which the surrounding high ground dips. L18.

S. HILL You can't see our farmhouse, it lies in the dip beyond the beeches there.

7 In full ***dip candle***. A candle made by repeatedly dipping a wick into tallow. E19.
8 **a** A substance into which food may be dipped before eating, *esp*. (***a***) fat and juice left after the cooking of meat; (***b***) a savoury sauce. E19. ▸**b** A boiled dumpling. Usu. in *pl*. *Austral. slang*. M19.

a M. BRADBURY A bowl of tomatoes and a cheese dip, into which they started popping the tomatoes.

9 A quantity of liquid taken up by dipping. M19.

S. WARREN His pen . . with a fresh dip of ink in it.

10 Crude turpentine. M19.
11 A pickpocket. *slang*. M19.
12 PROSODY. An unstressed element in a line of alliterative verse. L19.
13 A liquid into which something is dipped for treatment, *esp*. one for killing vermin on sheep, horses, etc.; a vat or tank for this purpose. L19.
sheep dip etc.
14 A receptacle from which a hidden prize may be obtained by dipping. E20.
lucky dip: see LUCKY *adjective*.
– COMB. (partly from the verb stem): ***dip candle***: see sense 7 above; ***dip-head***: see sense 2b above; **dip circle** a graduated vertical circle with a dipping needle; **dip-dye** *verb trans*. immerse (a yarn or fabric) in a special solution in order to colour it; **dip needle** = ***dipping needle*** s.v. DIP *verb* 9; **dip-net** *noun & verb* (***a***) *noun* a small fishing net with a long handle; (***b***) *verb trans*. catch using a dip-net; **dip pen**: that has to be dipped in ink; **dip slope** a usu. gentle slope of the land that approximately follows that of the underlying strata; **dipstick** (***a***) a rod for dipping into liquid, esp. oil in a motor vehicle, to find its depth; (***b***) *coarse slang* the penis; (***c***) *slang* a stupid or contemptible person; **dip switch**: for dipping headlights.

dip /dɪp/ *verb*. Infl. **-pp-**. Pa. t. & pple **dipped**, †**dipt**.
[ORIGIN Old English *dyppan* from Germanic base repr. also by DEEP *adjective*.]
▸ **I** *verb trans*. **1** Put or let down for a moment *in* or *into* (a liquid); immerse partially and briefly. OE. ▸**b** Immerse in a colouring solution, dye; imbue something with (a colour) by dipping. *poet*. M17. ▸**c** Make (a candle) by repeatedly immersing a wick in hot tallow. E18. ▸**d** Immerse (a sheep, horse, etc.) in a bath of vermin-killing liquid. E19.

H. READ He dipped his hand into the stream, right up to his sensitive wrist. **b** MILTON With . . colours dipt in Heav'n.

2 Baptize by dipping or immersing. Now usu. *derog*. OE.
3 Take (liquid, grain, etc.) out of a body of it by dipping with a scoop etc. (Foll. by *up*.) E17. ▸**b** Take (snuff) by dipping something into it and rubbing it on the gums. *US*. M19. ▸**c** Pick the pocket of. *slang*. E20.

P. S. BUCK This cauldron he filled partly full of water, dipping it with a half-gourd from an earthen jar.

4 *fig*. †**a** Implicate, involve, (*in* any affair). E17–L18. ▸**b** Involve in debt; mortgage; pawn. *colloq*. M17.

a HOR. WALPOLE Having been deeply dipped in the iniquities of the South Sea. **b** DRYDEN Never dip thy Lands.

5 Suffuse with moisture. *arch*. M17.

MILTON A cold shuddering dew Dips me all o'er.

6 Lower or let down for a moment, as if dipping in a liquid; *spec*. lower and then raise (a flag, an aircraft's wing in flight, etc.) in salute or (a sail) in tacking. L18. ▸**b** Lower (headlight beams), lower beams of (headlights), to avoid dazzling oncoming motorists. E20.
▸ **II** *verb intrans*. **7** Plunge down a little into water or other liquid and quickly emerge. Foll. by *in*, *into*, *under*. LME.

W. C. SMITH Slowly the muffled oars dip in the tide.

8 Sink or drop as if into water; extend downward a little way. LME. ▸**b** Fall a little in value or magnitude, esp. temporarily. M20.

E. BOWEN Gulls dipped over the lawn in a series of white flashes. TOLKIEN The Sun dipped and vanished. **b** *Broadcast* This week's figures . . show . . its audience share dipping to just under 41%.

9 Have a downward inclination, slope downwards. M17.

W. SCORESBY In this hemisphere, the north end of the [magnetic] needle dips. E. GARRETT You have no idea how the road dips.

D

dipping needle a magnetic needle mounted so as to be capable of moving in a vertical plane about its centre of gravity, and thus indicating by its dip the direction of the earth's magnetic field;

10 Put one's hand, a ladle, etc., into water, a receptacle, etc., to take something out. (Foll. by *into*.) L17. ▸**b** Pick pockets. *slang*. E19. ▸**c** Dip snuff. *US*. M19. ▸**d** Dip the headlights of a vehicle. E20.

A. HIGGINS She had a shiny black reticule . . into which she was continually dipping for cigarettes.

11 Look cursorily *into* a subject, book, etc. L17.

J. AGATE The only book of Proust's into which I have not dipped at one time or another.

12 Go deeply *into* a matter. M18.
13 = DAP *verb* 1. L18.

— PHRASES: **dip into one's savings**, **dip into one's reserves**, etc.: spend part of one's savings etc. ***dip one's toe in*** (***the water***), ***dip one's toes in*** (***the water***): see TOE *noun*. **dip one's wick** *coarse slang* (of a man) have sexual intercourse. **dip out** *Austral. & NZ slang* lose an opportunity or advantage, be unsuccessful.

■ **dipping** *noun* (*a*) the action of the verb; (*b*) a liquid into which things are dipped: LME.

Dip. *abbreviation*.
Diploma.

Dip.Ed. *abbreviation*.
Diploma in Education.

dipeptide /dʌɪˈpɛptʌɪd/ *noun*. E20.
[ORIGIN from DI-² + PEPTONE + -IDE.]
CHEMISTRY. Any peptide containing two amino-acid residues in its molecule.
■ **dipeptidase** /-ɪdeɪz/ *noun* an enzyme which hydrolyses a dipeptide but not higher peptides E20.

diphasic /dʌɪˈfeɪzɪk/ *adjective*. L19.
[ORIGIN from DI-² + PHASIC.]
Characterized by having two phases; occurring in or consisting of two phases.

Dip.H.E. *abbreviation*.
Diploma of Higher Education.

diphen- /ˈdʌɪfɛn/ *combining form*.
[ORIGIN from DI-² + PHEN-.]
CHEMISTRY & PHARMACOLOGY. Denoting the presence of two phenyl groups.
■ **diphenˈhydramine** *noun* an antihistamine compound used for the symptomatic relief of allergies M20. **dipheˈnoxylate** *noun* a pethidine derivative used to treat diarrhoea and colitis M20.

diphenyl /dʌɪˈfiːnʌɪl, -ˈfɛnɪl/ *noun*. L19.
[ORIGIN from DI-² + PHENYL.]
= BIPHENYL.

diphenyl- /dʌɪˈfiːnʌɪl, -ˈfɛnɪl/ *combining form*.
[ORIGIN from DIPHENYL.]
CHEMISTRY. = DIPHEN-.
■ **diphenyˈlamine** *noun* a crystalline compound, $(C_6H_5)_2NH$, used in making azo dyes and as an insecticide and larvicide M19. **diphenylhyˈdantoin** *noun* = PHENYTOIN M20.

diphonemic /dʌɪfə(ʊ)ˈniːmɪk/ *adjective*. M20.
[ORIGIN from DI-² + PHONEMIC.]
Of a speech sound: able to be assigned to either of two phonemes.

diphosphopyridine nucleotide /dʌɪˌfɒsfəˈpɪrɪdiːn ˈnjuːklɪətʌɪd/ *noun phr*. M20.
[ORIGIN from DI-² + PHOSPHO- + PYRIDINE + NUCLEOTIDE.]
BIOCHEMISTRY. The coenzyme NAD.

diphtheria /dɪfˈθɪərɪə, dɪp-/ *noun*. M19.
[ORIGIN mod. Latin, from French *diphthérie*, substituted by P. Bretonneau for his earlier *diphthérite*: see DIPHTHERITIS, -IA¹.]
An acute contagious bacterial disease characterized by the inflammation of a mucous membrane, esp. in the throat, the formation of a false membrane, and the production of potentially fatal toxins affecting the heart and nerves.
■ **diphtherial**, **diphtherian** (now *rare*), **diphtheric** /-ˈθɛrɪk/ *adjectives* L19.

diphtheritic /dɪfθəˈrɪtɪk/ *adjective*. M19.
[ORIGIN from DIPHTHERITIS: see -ITIC.]
Of the nature of or pertaining to diphtheria; affected with diphtheria.

diphtheritis /dɪfθəˈrʌɪtɪs/ *noun*. Now *rare* or *obsolete*. E19.
[ORIGIN French *diphthérite* (now *diphthérie*: see DIPHTHERIA), from Greek *diphthera* or *diphtheris* skin, hide + *-ite* -ITIS.]
= DIPHTHERIA.

diphtheroid /ˈdɪfθərɔɪd/ *adjective & noun*. M19.
[ORIGIN from DIPHTHERIA, DIPHTHERITIS + -OID.]
▸ **A** *adjective*. Resembling diphtheria or the bacterium that causes it. M19.
▸ **B** *noun*. A bacterium which resembles the one causing diphtheria but is not pathogenic, *esp*. one of the genus *Corynebacterium*. E20.

diphthong /ˈdɪfθɒŋ, ˈdɪp-/ *noun & verb*. LME.
[ORIGIN French *diphtongue* from Latin *diphthongus* from Greek *diphthoggos*, formed as DI-² + *phthoggos* voice, sound.]
▸ **A** *noun*. **1** A union of two vowels pronounced in one syllable. LME.
falling diphthong: with more stress on the first vowel than on the second. **rising diphthong**: with more stress on the second vowel than on the first.
2 A sequence of two vowel characters representing a single sound or a diphthong (sense 1), a vocalic digraph. M16.
3 A ligature of the Roman alphabet. L16.
▸ **B** *verb trans*. Sound as or make into a diphthong. M19.
■ **diphˈthongal** *adjective* of, pertaining to, or of the nature of a diphthong M18. **diphˈthongally** *adverb* M19. **diphˈthongic** *adjective* = DIPHTHONGAL M19. **diphthongiˈzation** *noun* the changing of a simple vowel into a diphthong L19. **diphthongize** *verb trans. & intrans.* turn into or form a diphthong M19.

diphy- /ˈdɪfi/ *combining form*.
[ORIGIN Greek *diphu-* from *diphuēs*, from DI-² + *phuein* generate.]
Of double form, double, bipartite.
■ **diphycercal** /-ˈsəːk(ə)l/ *adjective* [Greek *kerkos* tail] designating a fish's tail in which the vertebral column continues straight to the tip and the dorsal and ventral parts are approximately alike; having such a tail: M19. **diphyodont** *adjective & noun* [Greek *odont-*, tooth] (pertaining to or designating) an animal in which one set of teeth is replaced by another in the course of its development (cf. MONOPHYODONT) M19.

diphyletic /dʌɪfʌɪˈlɛtɪk/ *adjective*. E20.
[ORIGIN from DI-² + PHYLETIC *adjective*.]
TAXONOMY. Having evolved from two sets of ancestors; (of a classification) implying such an origin.

diphyllous /dʌɪˈfɪləs/ *adjective*. L18.
[ORIGIN mod. Latin *diphyllus* (from Greek DI-² + *phullon* leaf) + -OUS.]
BOTANY. Having two leaves (or sepals).

dipl- *combining form* see DIPLO-.

diplegia /dʌɪˈpliːdʒə/ *noun*. L19.
[ORIGIN from DI-² after HEMIPLEGIA, PARAPLEGIA.]
MEDICINE. Paralysis of corresponding parts on both sides of the body, usu. affecting the legs more severely than the arms.

dipleidoscope /dɪˈplʌɪdəskəʊp/ *noun*. M19.
[ORIGIN from Greek *diploos* double + *eidos* form, image + -SCOPE.]
An optical instrument for determining the meridian transit of a celestial object from the coincidence of two images formed by reflection in a hollow triangular prism.

diplex /ˈdʌɪplɛks/ *adjective*. L19.
[ORIGIN Alt. of DUPLEX *adjective* after DI-².]
TELECOMMUNICATIONS. Pertaining to or designating the transmission or reception of two signals simultaneously in the same direction over one channel or with one aerial. Cf. DUPLEX *adjective* 2.
■ **diplexer** *noun* a device which enables two transmitters to operate simultaneously using the same aerial M20.

diplo- /ˈdɪpləʊ/ *combining form*. Before a vowel **dipl-**.
[ORIGIN Greek, from *diploos*, *diplous* double; also repr. DIPLOID: see -O-.]
Double; diploidal.
■ **diplaˈcusis** *noun* [Greek *akousis* hearing] the hearing of two different notes when only one is sounded L19. **diplobaˈcillus** *noun*, pl. **-cilli**, a bacillus that occurs predominantly in pairs E20. **diploˈblastic** *adjective* [-BLAST] ZOOLOGY having ectoderm and endoderm but no mesoderm, as in coelenterates L19. **diploˈcoccal** *adjective* (BACTERIOLOGY) of, pertaining to, or caused by a diplococcus E20. **diploˈcoccus** *noun*, pl. **-cocci** /-ˈkɒk(s)ʌɪ, -k(s)iː/, BACTERIOLOGY a coccus that occurs predominantly in pairs, as a pneumococcus L19. **diplograph** *noun* an instrument for writing with two pens etc. simultaneously L19. **diploˈgraphic** *adjective* of or pertaining to writing double E19. **diploˈgraphical** *adjective* = DIPLOGRAPHIC M18. **diploˈhedral** *adjective* = DIPLOIDAL L19. **diploˈhedron** *noun*, pl. **-dra**, **-drons**, CRYSTALLOGRAPHY = DIPLOID *noun* 1 L19. **diploˈnema** *noun* [-NEMA] CYTOLOGY = DIPLOTENE E20. **diplophase** *noun* (BIOLOGY) the phase in a life cycle when cell nuclei are diploid E20. **diplopod** *noun & adjective* (ZOOLOGY) (*a*) *noun* any animal of the arthropod class (or subclass or order) Diplopoda, characterized by two pairs of legs on each segment; a millipede; (*b*) *adjective* of, pertaining to, or designating a diplopod or the Diplopoda: M19. **diploˈstemonous** *adjective* [Greek *stēmōn* warp (for *stēma* stamen)] BOTANY having the stamens in two series (the outer opposite the sepals, the inner opposite the petals) or (formerly) twice as many as the petals M19. **diploˈstemony** *noun* (BOTANY) diplostemonous condition L19. **diplotene** *noun* [-TENE] CYTOLOGY the stage of the prophase of the first meiotic division that follows pachytene, when the tetrads begin to separate into two pairs of chromatids E20.

diplodocus /dɪˈplɒdəkəs/ *noun*. Also **D-**. L19.
[ORIGIN mod. Latin, from Greek DIPLO- + *dokos* beam.]
Any Jurassic sauropod dinosaur of the genus *Diplodocus*, which comprises gigantic herbivorous animals with long necks.

diploe /ˈdɪpləʊiː/ *noun*. L16.
[ORIGIN Greek *diploē* doubling, from *diploos* double.]
Light cancellous bony tissue between the hard dense inner and outer layers of the skull.

diploid /ˈdɪplɔɪd/ *noun & adjective*. L19.
[ORIGIN from DIPLO- + -OID, (senses A.2, B.) ID *noun*².]
▸ **A** *noun*. **1** CRYSTALLOGRAPHY. A cubic form with twelve pairs of similar quadrilateral faces. L19.
2 BIOLOGY. A diploid cell or organism. E20.
▸ **B** *adjective*. BIOLOGY. (Of a cell) containing two homologous sets of chromosomes, one from each parent; (of an individual) composed of diploid cells. E20.
diploid number the number of chromosomes in the body cells of an organism.
■ **diˈploidal** *adjective* (CRYSTALLOGRAPHY) of, pertaining to, or designating a cubic crystal class containing the diploid and the pyritohedron M20. **diploidy** *noun* (BIOLOGY) diploid condition E20.

diploidion /dɪpləʊˈɪdɪən/ *noun*. M19.
[ORIGIN Greek, dim. of *diplois*, *diploid-* double cloak.]
A chiton or tunic worn by women in ancient Greece, with the part above the waist double and the outer fold hanging loose.

diploma /dɪˈpləʊmə/ *noun & verb*. M17.
[ORIGIN Latin *diploma*, *diplomat-* from Greek = folded paper, from *diploun* make double, fold, from *diploos* double.]
▸ **A** *noun*. Pl. **-mas**, (*rare*) **-mata** /-mətə/.
1 A state paper, an official document; a charter; in *pl.*, historical or literary muniments. M17.
2 A document conferring some honour, privilege, or licence; a certificate of a university, college, or (*N. Amer.*) school degree or qualification; such a degree or qualification. M17.
▸ **B** *verb trans*. Pa. t. & pple **-aed**, **-a'd**. Award a diploma to. Chiefly as ***diplomaed***, ***diploma'd*** *ppl adjective*. M19.
■ **ˈdiplomate** *noun* [-ATE¹] a person who holds a diploma L19. †**diplomate** *verb trans*. [-ATE³] invest with a degree, privilege, or title by diploma M17–M18.

diplomacy /dɪˈpləʊməsi/ *noun*. L18.
[ORIGIN French *diplomatie*, from *diplomatique* DIPLOMATIC after *aristocratie* ARISTOCRACY: see -ACY.]
1 The management of international relations by negotiation; the method by which these relations are managed by ambassadors etc.; skill in such affairs. L18.
†**2** The diplomatic body. L18–M19.
3 Adroitness in personal relations; tact. M19.

diplomat /ˈdɪpləmat/ *noun*. E19.
[ORIGIN French *diplomate* back-form. from *diplomatique* DIPLOMATIC after *aristocrate* ARISTOCRAT.]
A person engaged in diplomacy, esp. accredited to a court or seat of government; an adroit negotiator.
■ **diplomaˈtese** *noun* (*colloq.*) language regarded as typical of diplomats L20.

diplomatic /dɪpləˈmatɪk/ *adjective & noun*. E18.
[ORIGIN (French *diplomatique* based on) mod. Latin *diplomaticus*, from Latin *diploma* DIPLOMA: see -IC.]
▸ **A** *adjective*. **1** Of or pertaining to official or original documents, charters, or manuscripts; textual. E18.
diplomatic copy, **diplomatic edition**: exactly reproducing an original.
2 Of or pertaining to the management of international relations; of or belonging to diplomacy. L18.

H. MACMILLAN Diplomatic relations were re-established at the level of chargé d'affaires.

diplomatic bag: that contains official mail from an embassy etc. **diplomatic corps** the body of ambassadors and their staff attached to a court or seat of government. **diplomatic immunity** immunity from legal action possessed by virtue of belonging to the diplomatic mission of a foreign state. **diplomatic service** the branch of the public service which is concerned with the official representation of a country abroad.
3 Skilled in negotiations or relations of any kind; tactful; (of a statement etc.) uncandid, subtle. E19.

H. JAMES I'm diplomatic and calculating—I don't show him how bad I am.

▸ **B** *noun*. **1** A diplomat. L18.
2 *sing.* & in *pl.* (treated as *sing.*). The diplomatic art; diplomacy. L18.

W. TAYLOR Our ministers are not great in diplomatics.

3 *sing.* & in *pl.* The palaeographic and critical study of old documents. E19.

W. A. PANTIN These administrative records . . have an archaeology or a diplomatic of their own.

■ **diplomatical** *adjective* = DIPLOMATIC *adjective* 1, 2 L18. **diplomatically** *adverb* M19.

diplomatise *verb* var. of DIPLOMATIZE.

diplomatist /dɪˈpləʊmətɪst/ *noun*. E19.
[ORIGIN from French *diplomate* DIPLOMAT or Latin *diplomat-* (see DIPLOMA) + -IST.]
A diplomat.

diplomatize /dɪˈpləʊmətʌɪz/ *verb*. Also **-ise**. L17.
[ORIGIN In branch I from Latin *diplomat-* (see DIPLOMA), in branch II from DIPLOMAT: see -IZE.]
▸ **I 1** *verb trans*. Invest with a diploma. *rare*. L17.
▸ **II 2** *verb intrans*. Act or serve as a diplomat; use diplomatic arts or skill. E19.

3 *verb trans.* Act as a diplomat towards or in connection with. **M19.**

diplont /ˈdɪplɒnt/ *noun.* **E20.**
[ORIGIN from DIPL- + -ONT.]
BIOLOGY. An organism which is diploid throughout its life cycle except for the gametes.

diplopia /dɪˈpləʊpɪə/ *noun.* **E19.**
[ORIGIN from DIPLO- + -OPIA.]
MEDICINE. Double vision.
■ **diplopic** /-ˈplɒp-/ *adjective* **L19.**

dipnoan /ˈdɪpnəʊən/ *noun & adjective.* **L19.**
[ORIGIN from mod. Latin *Dipnoi* pl. (see below), from Greek *dipnoos* with two breathing apertures, formed as DI-[2] + *pnoē* breathing: see -AN.]
▸ **A** *noun.* A fish of the (mostly extinct) order or subclass Dipnoi, characterized by a lung or lungs as well as gills; a lungfish. **L19.**
▸ **B** *adjective.* Of, pertaining to, or designating a dipnoan. **L19.**
■ Also **dipnoid** *noun & adjective* **L19.**

dipody /ˈdɪpədi/ *noun.* **M19.**
[ORIGIN Late Latin *dipodia* from Greek, from *dipous*, *dipod-* two-footed, formed as DI-[2] + *pous* foot: see -Y[3].]
PROSODY. A double foot; two feet making one measure.
■ Also **dipodia** /dʌɪˈpəʊdɪə/ *noun* **E19.**

dipolar /dʌɪˈpəʊlə/ *adjective.* **M19.**
[ORIGIN from DI-[2] + POLAR *adjective.*]
SCIENCE. Of or pertaining to two poles; having two poles.

dipole /ˈdʌɪpəʊl/ *noun.* **E20.**
[ORIGIN from DI-[2] + POLE *noun*[2].]
1 SCIENCE. A pair of equal and opposite electric charges or magnetic poles, esp. close together; a molecule etc. with such a pair. **E20.**
2 An aerial composed of two equal straight rods mounted in line with one another and having an electrical connection to its centre; *spec.* such an aerial half a wavelength long overall. **E20.**
– COMB.: **dipole moment** the product of the separation of the charges etc. of a dipole and the magnitude of each.

Dippel's oil /ˈdɪp(ə)lz ɔɪl/ *noun phr.* **E19.**
[ORIGIN J. C. *Dippel* (1672–1734), German alchemist.]
More fully ***Dippel's animal oil***. Bone-oil.

dipper /ˈdɪpə/ *noun.* **LME.**
[ORIGIN from DIP *verb* + -ER[1].]
1 Any of several stocky short-tailed songbirds constituting the genus *Cinclus* and family Cinclidae, which habitually bob up and down, frequent fast-flowing streams, and swim and walk under water to feed; *esp.* the Eurasian *C. cinclus* and the N. American *C. mexicanus*; also called ***water ouzel***. Formerly also, any of several freshwater diving birds. **LME.**
2 A person who dips; *spec.* one who immerses something in a fluid. **E17.** ▸**b** A pickpocket. *slang.* **L19.**

> W. IRVING A lounger in the Bodleian library, and a great dipper into books.

3 A person who uses immersion in baptism, *esp.* an Anabaptist or Baptist. **E17.**
4 a A utensil for dipping up water etc.; *spec.* a pan with a long handle. **L18.** ▸**b** In full ***dipper dredge***. A dredging boat with a single bucket at the end of an arm. **L19.** ▸**c** (The scoop of) an excavator. **E20.**
5 a [from the similarity of its shape to the utensil] (**D-**.) (In full ***Big Dipper***, ***Great Dipper***) the Plough, in Ursa Major. ***Little Dipper***, a pattern of stars in Ursa Minor. *N. Amer.* **M19.** ▸**b** ***big dipper***, a switchback in a fairground or place of amusement. **M20.**
6 A receptacle for oil, varnish, etc., attached to a palette. **M19.**
7 A vat or tank in which sheep dip is used. **L19.**
8 A means of dipping a vehicle's headlights. **E20.**
– COMB.: **dipper gourd** a gourd used as a dipper; a form of the Old World tropical vine *Lagenaria siceraria* which bears such gourds.
■ **dipperful** *noun* (*US*) as much as a dipper will hold **M19.**

dippy /ˈdɪpi/ *adjective. slang.* **E20.**
[ORIGIN Unknown.]
Crazy (*about*, *over*); mad.

diprotodont /dʌɪˈprəʊtə(ʊ)dɒnt/ *noun & adjective.* **L19.**
[ORIGIN from DI-[2] + PROTO- + -ODONT.]
▸ **A** *noun.* A huge extinct Australian marsupial with two incisors in the lower jaw. **L19.**
▸ **B** *adjective.* Of, pertaining to, or designating such an animal. **L19.**
■ Also **diprotodon** *noun* **M19.**

dipsas /ˈdɪpsas/ *noun.* Pl. **dipsades** /ˈdɪpsədiːz/. **LME.**
[ORIGIN Latin from Greek, orig. adjective = causing thirst, from *dipsa* thirst.]
A mythical serpent whose bite produced a raging thirst.

dipshit /ˈdɪpʃɪt/ *noun. coarse slang.* **L20.**
[ORIGIN Perh. a blend of *dippy* and *shit*.]
A stupid or inept person; an idiot.

dipso /ˈdɪpsəʊ/ *adjective & noun. colloq.* **L19.**
[ORIGIN Abbreviation.]
▸ **A** *adjective.* = DIPSOMANIACAL. **L19.**
▸ **B** *noun.* Pl. **-os**. = DIPSOMANIAC. **E20.**

dipsomania /dɪpsə(ʊ)ˈmeɪnɪə/ *noun.* Also **dyp-**. **M19.**
[ORIGIN from Greek *dipso-* combining form (see -O-) of *dipsa* thirst + -MANIA.]
A morbid paroxysmal craving for alcohol; alcoholism. Also, persistent drunkenness.
■ **dipsomaniac** *noun* a person with dipsomania **M19.** **dipsomaˈniacal** *adjective* pertaining to or suffering from dipsomania **M19.**

Dip.Tech. *abbreviation.*
Diploma in Technology.

Diptera /ˈdɪpt(ə)rə/ *noun pl.* **M18.**
[ORIGIN mod. Latin from Greek, from *dipteros* two-winged, formed as DI-[2] + *pteron* wing: see -A[3].]
(Members of) a large order of two-winged insects including flies, gnats, mosquitoes, etc.
■ **dipterist** *noun* a person who studies Diptera **L19.** **dipteroˈlogical** *adjective* of or pertaining to the study of Diptera **L19.** **dipteˈrologist** *noun* = DIPTERIST **L19.**

dipteral /ˈdɪpt(ə)r(ə)l/ *adjective.* **E19.**
[ORIGIN from Latin *dipteros*, from Greek (see DIPTERA), + -AL[1].]
ARCHITECTURE. Having a double peristyle.

dipteran /ˈdɪpt(ə)r(ə)n/ *noun & adjective.* **M19.**
[ORIGIN from DIPTERA + -AN.]
▸ **A** *noun.* An insect belonging to the Diptera. **M19.**
▸ **B** *adjective.* Of or pertaining to the Diptera. **M20.**

dipterocarp /ˈdɪpt(ə)rə(ʊ)kɑːp/ *noun & adjective.* Also **D-**. **L19.**
[ORIGIN mod. Latin *Dipterocarpus*, from Greek *dipteros* (see DIPTERA) + *karpos* fruit.]
▸ **A** *noun.* A tree of the mostly SE Asian family Dipterocarpaceae, comprising resinous timber trees such as meranti. **L19.**
▸ **B** *adjective.* = DIPTEROCARPOUS. **E20.**
■ **dipteroˈcarpous** *adjective* pertaining to or designating the dipterocarps **L19.**

dipterous /ˈdɪpt(ə)rəs/ *adjective.* **L18.**
[ORIGIN from DIPTERA + -OUS.]
ENTOMOLOGY. Having two wings; of or pertaining to the Diptera.

diptote /ˈdɪptəʊt/ *noun & adjective.* **E17.**
[ORIGIN Late Latin *diptota* from Greek, neut. pl. of *diptōtos*, formed as DI-[2] + *ptōtos* falling (*ptōsis* case). Cf. TRIPTOTE.]
GRAMMAR. (A noun) having only two cases.

diptych /ˈdɪptɪk/ *noun.* **E17.**
[ORIGIN Late Latin *diptycha* from late Greek *diptukha* pair of writing tablets, neut. pl. of Greek *diptukhos* folded in two, formed as DI-[2] + *ptukhē* fold.]
1 Something folded so as to have two leaves, *esp.* an ancient hinged writing tablet, with waxed inner surfaces for writing on with a stylus. **E17.**
2 ECCLESIASTICAL HISTORY. In *pl.* Tablets recording a list of the living and the dead who were prayed for at the Eucharist; the names themselves; the intercessions in the course of which they were introduced. **M17.**
3 An altarpiece or painting composed of two leaves which close like a book. **M19.**
■ **diptychous** *adjective* of, pertaining to, or of the nature of a diptych **L19.**

dipylon /ˈdɪpɪlɒn/ *noun & adjective.* Also (earlier) †**-lum**. **M19.**
[ORIGIN (Latin from) Greek *dipulon* neut. of *dipulos* double-gated, formed as DI-[2] + *pulē* gate.]
GREEK ARCHAEOLOGY. ▸**A** *noun.* A double gateway in which the two gates are placed side by side; *spec.* (**D-**) a gateway on the north-west side of Athens. **M19.**
▸ **B** *adjective.* Designating or pertaining to the Dipylon of Athens; *spec.* designating or pertaining to a style of Greek pottery found during excavations near this site, or the designs found on such pottery. **L19.**

dipyramidal /dʌɪpɪˈramɪd(ə)l/ *adjective.* **M20.**
[ORIGIN from DI-[2] + PYRAMIDAL.]
= BIPYRAMIDAL.
■ **diˈpyramid** *noun* = BIPYRAMID **M20.**

dipyridamole /dʌɪpɪˈrɪdəməʊl/ *noun.* **M20.**
[ORIGIN from DI-[2] + PYR(IMIDINE + PIPER)ID(INE + AM(INO- + -OL.]
A drug used as a coronary vasodilator in angina pectoris and to reduce platelet aggregation and hence the chance of thrombosis.

diquark /ˈdʌɪkwɔːk, -kwɑːk/ *noun.* **M20.**
[ORIGIN from DI-[2] + QUARK *noun*[2].]
PHYSICS. A pair of quarks bound together.

diquat /ˈdʌɪkwɒt/ *noun.* **M20.**
[ORIGIN from DI-[2] + QUATERNARY.]
(The cation of) a quaternary compound, $C_{12}H_{12}N_2Br_2$, used as a contact herbicide and desiccant.

dir- /dɪr/ *prefix* (not productive).
Var. of Latin DIS- before vowels.

diram /ˈdɪərəm/ *noun.* **L20.**
[ORIGIN Tajik.]
A monetary unit of Tajikistan, equal to one-hundredth of a somoni.

Dircaean /dəːˈsiːən/ *adjective. literary.* **E17.**
[ORIGIN from Latin *Dircaeus* from *Dirce*, Greek *Dirkē* + -AN.]
Of or pertaining to the fountain of Dirce in Boeotia, ancient Greece; *fig.* poetic, Pindaric.
the Dircaean swan [translating Latin *Dircaeus cygnus* (Horace)] the Greek poet Pindar.

dirdum /ˈdəːdəm/ *noun. Scot. & N. English.* **LME.**
[ORIGIN Uncertain: cf. Gaelic *d(i)urdan* anger, snarling, Irish *deardan* storm, tempest.]
1 Uproar; a tumultuous noise or din. **LME.**
2 An outcry; a strong rebuke; blame. **E18.**

dire /ˈdʌɪə/ *adjective.* **M16.**
[ORIGIN Latin *dirus* fearful, threatening evil.]
1 Dreadful, calamitous, terrible; ominous; *colloq.* urgent, desperate. **M16.**

> MILTON All monstrous, all prodigious things . . Gorgons and Hydra's and Chimera's dire. C. BRONTË Forced by dire necessity.

dire wolf a large extinct wolf of the Pleistocene epoch, *Canis dirus*, which preyed on large mammals.
2 Very bad, awful; unpleasant. **E20.**

> B. PYM The dire state of fiction publishing. E. O'NEILL I didn't say anything so dire, did I.

■ **direly** *adverb* **E17.** **direness** *noun* **E17.**

D

direct /dɪˈrɛkt, dʌɪ-/ *noun.* **E17.**
[ORIGIN App. from DIRECT *verb.*]
1 A direction, an instruction. Long *rare.* **E17.**
2 MUSIC. A sign placed on the stave at the end of a page or line to indicate the position of the next note. **L17.**

direct /dɪˈrɛkt, dʌɪ-/ *adjective & adverb.* **LME.**
[ORIGIN formed as DIRECT *verb.*]
▸ **A** *adjective.* **1** Straight, undeviating in course, not circuitous or crooked. **LME.** ▸**b** Of ancestry or a descendant: proceeding in or derived from a continuous succession from parent to offspring. **M16.** ▸**c** LOGIC. Proceeding immediately from consequent to antecedent, from cause to effect, etc. **E19.**

> M. MITCHELL Instead of continuing the direct assault, he swung his army in a wide circle.

2 a ASTRONOMY. Of (the motion of) a planet etc.: proceeding from west to east, not retrograde. **LME.** ▸**b** MATH. & MUSIC. Following the simple or natural order; not inverse or inverted. **L16.**
3 Going straight to the point; without circumlocution or ambiguity; straightforward, esp. in manner or conduct; frank. **M16.**

> R. KIPLING This was at once a gross insult and a direct lie. J. IRVING A flat, direct introduction explaining why he had not tried to put the epic in verse.

4 Perpendicular to a given surface; not oblique. **M16.**
5 Existing or occurring without intermediaries or intervention; immediate, uninterrupted. **L16.**

> T. HARDY Almost every . . effect in that woodland place had hitherto been the direct result of the regular terrestrial roll. A. BEVAN Before the Industrial Revolution, man's relations with physical nature were immediate and direct. L. DURRELL This gave him direct access to the affections and understanding of our . . friends.

6 Of an electric current: that flows in one direction only, without reversal of polarity. Hence, associated with or producing such a current. Cf. ALTERNATING 2. **L19.**
– SPECIAL COLLOCATIONS: **direct action**: done as the most immediately effective way of achieving an object. **direct address** COMPUTING: specifying the location of data to be used as an operand. **direct debit** the automatic debiting of a bank account at the request of a creditor. **direct deposit** *N. Amer.* the electronic transfer of money from one bank account to another. **direct dialling**: of a telephone number by the caller, without making use of an operator. **direct drilling** AGRICULTURE: of seed into unprepared soil. **direct-drive** *adjective* (of a turntable etc.) driven directly by the motor, without an intervening belt. **direct dye**: not needing a mordant. **direct grant**: of money paid directly to a school by the Government as opp. to a local authority (***direct-grant school***, a school which observes agreed conditions regarding the admission of pupils etc. while in receipt of such a grant). **direct hit** striking the target directly (not as the result of a ricochet etc.). **direct injection** (in internal-combustion engines) the use of a pump to spray fuel directly into the cylinder at high pressure; **direct labour**: (**a**) involved in production rather than administration, maintenance, etc.; (**b**) employed by the authority commissioning the work, not by a contractor. **direct mail** advertising sent unsolicited through the post to prospective customers. **direct mailing** the sending of direct mail. **direct marketing** the selling of products or services directly to the public, e.g. by mail order or telephone selling, rather than through retailers. **direct method** the teaching of a foreign language in that tongue, without the use of the student's native language or the study of formal grammar. **direct object** GRAMMAR the primary object of the action of a verb. **direct opposite** that which is entirely or exactly opposite. **direct oration** GRAMMAR = ***direct speech*** below. **direct proportion** the relation between quantities whose ratio is constant. **direct question** a question on a specific matter requiring a definite answer; GRAMMAR a question in direct speech, a question that is a main clause. **direct ray** a ray of light proceeding without reflection or refraction. **direct rule** rule by a central government without devolution. **direct speech** GRAMMAR words quoted as actually spoken, not modified in person, tense, etc., by being reported (= ORATIO RECTA). **direct tax**: levied on the person who bears the ultimate burden of the tax, e.g. income tax but not value added tax. **direct taxation**: by a direct tax.
▸ **B** *adverb.* Directly. **LME.**

> W. S. MAUGHAM I'm not going to Bertha, I'm going to Craddock direct.

■ **directness** *noun* **L16.**

D

direct /dɪˈrɛkt, dʌɪ-/ *verb*. Pa. pple **directed**, (earlier) †**direct**. LME.
[ORIGIN Latin *directus* pa. pple of *dirigere*, *derigere* straighten, direct, guide from *di-* DI-¹, DE- 1 + *regere* put straight, rule.]
1 *verb trans.* Formerly, send (a letter etc.) especially *to* someone. Now, write on the outside of (a letter etc.) a name and address for delivery (*to* a recipient). LME. ▸†**b** *verb trans.* Dedicate (a book etc.) *to*. LME–E17. ▸**c** *verb intrans.* Write *to* a person (*at* an address). E18.

LD HOUGHTON Lady Ellesmere's letter missed me altogether, although directed as I desired. **c** DICKENS You may direct to me . . at 18 York Place.

2 *verb trans.* Address (spoken words) *to* someone. *arch.* LME. ▸†**b** Give (an injunction, command, etc.) *to*. LME–M17.

HOBBES To whom the Speech is directed.

3 *verb trans.* Cause to move in or take a specified direction; turn towards a specified destination or target; aim (a missile, a remark, etc.) *at* or *against*; turn *to* an aim or purpose. LME. ▸**b** Inform or guide (a person) as to the way; show or tell (a person) the way (*to*). E17.

J. R. GREEN The efforts of the French monarchy had been directed to the conquest of Italy. B. JOWETT Everybody's eyes were directed towards him. G. GREENE He directed at her his whole technique of appeasement. D. BARNES The doctor . . directed his steps back to the café. **b** J. B. PRIESTLEY A turning at the bottom of this main street directed me to the Playhouse. J. RATHBONE Rubin now directed me firmly up the wide stairs.

4 *verb trans.* Regulate the course of; guide with advice. LME. ▸**b** *verb trans.* Conduct (a musical performance). L19. ▸**c** *verb trans. & intrans.* Supervise and control the acting of (a film, play, etc.); guide and train (an actor) in performing a role. E20.

SHAKES. *Merch. V.* Some god direct my judgment!

5 *verb trans.* Keep in proper order; control, govern the actions or movements of. E16.

D. DU MAURIER Something other than blind emotion directed her actions. F. ASTAIRE A lone M.P. in the middle of the cross streets, directing traffic.

6 **a** *verb trans.* Give authoritative instructions to; order (a person) *to do*, (a thing) *to be done*; order the performance of. M16. ▸**b** *verb intrans.* Give instructions; command *that*. M17.

a W. LITHGOW He made fast the door as he was directed. **b** H. WILSON The ability of the prime minister to direct that such and such an issue shall go straight to Cabinet.

■ **directable** *adjective* able to be directed L19. **directedness** *noun* the quality of being directed E20. **direcˈtee** *noun* a person who is directed or under direction E20.

direction /dɪˈrɛkʃ(ə)n, dʌɪ-/ *noun*. LME.
[ORIGIN French, or its source Latin *directio(n-)*, from *direct-* pa. ppl stem of *dirigere*: see DIRECT *verb*, -ION.]
1 The action or function of directing; guidance, instruction; management. LME.

SHAKES. *Oth.* A soldier fit to stand by Caesar And give direction. GEO. ELIOT She felt the need of direction even in small things. D. FRASER The Chiefs of Staff Committee was concerned with the overall direction of war.

†**2** Arrangement, order. LME–M16.
3 An instruction on what to do, how to proceed, or where to go. Usu. in *pl.* LME.

GOLDSMITH Provide him with proper directions for finding me in London.

4 The action of addressing a letter, parcel, etc.; the (name and) address on an envelope etc. Formerly also, the dedication of a book etc. E16.
†**5** Capacity for directing; administrative faculty. L16–M17.

SHAKES. *Rich. III* Call for some men of sound direction.

6 The course taken by something in relation to the point towards which it is moving; the line towards anything in its relation to a given line; a point to or from which a person moves, turns, etc. M17. ▸**b** *fig.* The course of development of thought, effort, or action; a distinct tendency or trend; linear or consistent progress. M18.

J. BUCHAN Making farther from London in the direction of some western port. N. MOSLEY She appeared to be seen from two directions at once. **b** B. JOWETT New directions of enquiry. *Times* Gold shares lacked direction with the bullion price virtually unchanged.

7 = DIRECTORATE. *arch.* E18.
– PHRASES: **sense of direction** the ability to know without guidance towards which place one is walking etc. ***stage direction***: see STAGE *noun*.
– COMB.: **direction-finder** a device for direction-finding; **direction-finding** the process of finding the direction from which radio waves are coming; **direction-indicator** a device showing the direction in which the driver is about to turn a motor vehicle.
■ **directional** *adjective* (**a**) pertaining to the giving or taking of directions; (**b**) of or pertaining to direction in space, esp. of radio transmission within a narrow angle; (of a well) drilled at an angle to the vertical; (**c**) relating to, influencing, or exemplifying the latest trends in fashion: E17. **directioˈnality** *noun* directional quality; maintenance of direction: M20. **directionally** *adverb* L19. **directionless** *adjective* lacking aim or direction M19. **directionlessness** *noun* M20.

directive /dɪˈrɛktɪv, dʌɪ-/ *noun*. M17.
[ORIGIN medieval Latin *directivum* use as noun of neut. of *directivus*: see DIRECTIVE *adjective*.]
Something which directs; *spec.* a general instruction for procedure or action given to a subordinate.

H. KISSINGER The ABM directive went the way of many other Presidential instructions to the Defense Department.

– NOTE: Rare before E20.

directive /dɪˈrɛktɪv, dʌɪ-/ *adjective*. LME.
[ORIGIN medieval Latin *directivus*, from Latin *direct-* pa. ppl stem of *dirigere*: see DIRECT *verb*, -IVE. Cf. Old French & mod. French *directif*, *-ive*.]
1 Having the quality, function, or power of directing; serving to direct. LME.

J. S. MILL Utility or Happiness, considered as the directive rule of human conduct. J. C. MAXWELL The directive action of the earth's magnetism on the compass needle. A. STORR Those who are directive by nature.

†**2** Subject to direction. *rare* (Shakes.). Only in E17.
■ **directively** *adverb* in a directive manner; so as to direct or guide: M17. **directiveness** *noun* E18. **direcˈtivity** *noun* (**a**) the quality or state of being directed by a vital force or by God; (**b**) the property or degree of being directional: E20.

directly /dɪˈrɛktli, dʌɪ-/ *adverb & conjunction*. LME.
[ORIGIN from DIRECT *adjective* + -LY².]
▸ **A** *adverb*. **1** In a straight line; without deviation; MATH. linearly. LME.

L. HELLMAN I went directly to Paris. DAY LEWIS Her mother . . was directly descended from Oliver Goldsmith's uncle.

2 Straightforwardly; plainly; pointedly. LME.

BURKE I asked him his opinion directly, and without management.

3 Completely, absolutely; exactly. LME.

J. M. COETZEE A clap burst directly over him and it began to pour.

4 Without an intermediary; by a direct process. E16.

B. PYM She did not like to approach me directly.

5 At right angles to a surface, not obliquely. M16.

V. WOOLF The rain poured down more directly and powerfully as the wind fell.

6 At once, immediately; presently, in a little while. E17.

V. WOOLF She went off directly after tea. I. MURDOCH I'll be back directly.

▸ **B** *conjunction*. As soon as, the moment after. L18.

G. GREENE He realized how childish he sounded directly he had spoken.

Directoire /dɪˈrɛktwɑː; *foreign* dirɛktwaːr (pl. of noun same)/ *noun & adjective*. L18.
[ORIGIN Fr, formed as DIRECTORY *noun*.]
▸ **A** *noun*. *hist.* The French Directory. L18.
▸ **B** *adjective*. Also **d-**. Of, pertaining to, or resembling an extravagant style of fashion, decorative art, etc., prevalent at the time of the Directory and characterized esp. by an imitation of Greek and Roman modes. L19.
Directoire knickers women's knee-length knickers with elastic or bands at the waist and knee.

director /dɪˈrɛktə, dʌɪ-/ *noun*. LME.
[ORIGIN Anglo-Norman *directour* from late Latin *director*, from Latin *direct-* pa. ppl stem of *dirigere*: see DIRECT *verb*, -OR.]
1 A person who or thing which directs, governs, or guides; a manager, a superintendent. LME.
director general the chief administrator of a project etc. ***Director of Public Prosecutions***: see PROSECUTION *noun* 5.
2 A member of the board that manages the affairs of a company. M17.
3 A person who or thing which causes something to take a particular direction; SURGERY an instrument for guiding the course of the knife etc. when an incision is made. M17.
4 ECCLESIASTICAL. A spiritual adviser. M17.
5 A person who directs a theatre or cinema production. E20.
director's cut a version of a film that reflects the director's original intentions, released after the first studio version.
■ **directorate** *noun* (**a**) = DIRECTORSHIP; (**b**) management by directors; (**c**) a board of directors: M19. **direcˈtorial** *adjective* (**a**) of, pertaining to, or of the nature of a director or direction; (**b**) of or pertaining to a body of directors; (also **D-**) belonging to the French Directory: L18. **direcˈtorially** *adverb* M19. **directorship** *noun* the position or office of a director E18.

directory /dɪˈrɛkt(ə)ri, dʌɪ-/ *noun*. LME.
[ORIGIN Late Latin *directorium* use as noun of neut. sing. of *directorius*: see DIRECTORY *adjective*, -ORY¹.]
1 Something that serves to direct; a guide; a book of rules or directions, *esp.* one for the conduct of public or private worship, an ordinal. LME. ▸**b** A book containing an alphabetical or classified list of the people in some category, e.g. telephone subscribers or clergy, with information about them. M18. ▸**c** A computer file listing information about a set of other files or of programs etc. M20.
b telephone directory etc.
†**2** A surgical director. L17–M18.
3 A body of directors; *spec.* in *hist.* (also **D-**) the executive of five people in power in revolutionary France, 1795–9. L18.
– COMB.: **directory enquiries** a service which telephone callers may ring to find the number of a subscriber.

directory /dɪˈrɛkt(ə)ri, dʌɪ-/ *adjective*. LME.
[ORIGIN Late Latin *directorius*, from *director* DIRECTOR: see -ORY².]
Serving or tending to direct; guiding; *spec.* designating (any part of) a statute which is advisory rather than mandatory in effect.

directress /dɪˈrɛktrəs, dʌɪ-/ *noun*. E17.
[ORIGIN from DIRECTOR + -ESS¹.]
A female director. Formerly also, a governess.

directrice /dɪˈrɛktriːs/ *noun*. M17.
[ORIGIN French, formed as DIRECTRIX.]
= DIRECTRESS.

directrix /dɪˈrɛktrɪks, dʌɪ-/ *noun*. Pl. **-trices** /-trɪsiːz/. E16.
[ORIGIN medieval Latin, fem. of late Latin DIRECTOR: see -TRIX.]
1 = DIRECTRESS. E16.
2 GEOMETRY. A fixed line with reference to which a curve or surface is defined; *spec.* the straight line the distance of which from any point on a conic bears a constant ratio to the distance of the same point from the focus. E18.

direful /ˈdʌɪəf(ə)l, -fʊl/ *adjective*. *literary*. L16.
[ORIGIN Irreg. from DIRE *adjective* + -FUL.]
Presaging dire consequences; dreadful, terrible.
■ **direfully** *adverb* L18. **direfulness** *noun* M17.

dirempt /dɪˈrɛm(p)t/ *verb trans.* Long *rare*. Pa. t. & pple †**dirempt**, **dirempted**. M16.
[ORIGIN Latin *dirempt-* pa. ppl stem of *dirimere*, from *dir-* DIS- 1 + *emere* take.]
Separate, divide; break off.
■ **diremption** *noun* (now *rare*) forcible separation, esp. of man and wife; removal: L16.

†**direption** *noun*. L15.
[ORIGIN Latin *direptio(n-)*, from *dirept-* pa. ppl stem of *diripere* tear asunder, lay waste, from *di-* DI-¹ + *rapere* tear away: see -ION.]
1 The action or an act of snatching away or dragging apart violently. L15–L17.
2 The sacking or pillaging of a town etc. E16–E19.

dirge /dəːdʒ/ *noun & verb*. Also (noun, earlier) †**dirige**. ME.
[ORIGIN Latin *dirige* imper. of. *dirigere* DIRECT *verb*, first word of the antiphon *Dirige, Domine, Deus meus, in conspectu tuo viam meam* (Ps. 5:8) formerly in the Office of the Dead.]
▸ **A** *noun*. **1** ROMAN CATHOLIC CHURCH. The Office of the Dead, *esp.* the morning office. *arch.* ME.
2 A song of mourning sung at a funeral etc. or in commemoration of the dead; a slow mournful song; a lament. E16.
3 A funeral feast, a wake. *Scot.* M17.
▸ **B** *verb*. **1** *verb trans.* Sing a dirge over, commit with a dirge. *rare*. M19.
2 *verb trans. & intrans.* Sing (as) a dirge. L19.
■ **dirgeful** *adjective* full of lamentation, mournful L18.

dirham /ˈdɪərəm/ *noun*. Also **-hem**. L18.
[ORIGIN Arabic from Greek *drachmē* (see DRACHMA).]
A monetary unit of Morocco (now the basic unit), Libya, the United Arab Emirates (the basic unit), Qatar, and formerly some other Middle Eastern countries, equal to 100 centimes in Morocco, one-thousandth of a dinar in Libya, 100 fils in the United Arab Emirates, and one-hundredth of a riyal in Qatar. Formerly also, an Arabian unit of weight.

†**dirige** *noun* see DIRGE.

†**dirigent** *adjective & noun*. E17–M19.
[ORIGIN Latin *dirigent-* pres. ppl stem of *dirigere* DIRECT *verb*: see -ENT.]
(Something) that directs or guides.

dirigible /ˈdɪrɪdʒɪb(ə)l/ *adjective & noun*. L16.
[ORIGIN from Latin *dirigere* DIRECT *verb* + -IBLE.]
▸ **A** *adjective*. Able to be directed, *spec.* in respect of motion. L16.
▸ **B** *noun*. A dirigible balloon or airship. L19.
■ **dirigiˈbility** *noun* the quality of being dirigible, controllability L19.

dirigisme /diriʒism/ *noun*. Also **dirigism** /ˈdɪrɪdʒɪz(ə)m/. M20.
[ORIGIN French, from *diriger* from Latin *dirigere* DIRECT *verb*: see -ISM.]
The policy of state direction and control in economic and social matters.
■ ***dirigiste*** /diriʒist/ *adjective* of or pertaining to *dirigisme* M20.

diriment /ˈdɪrɪm(ə)nt/ *adjective*. M19.
[ORIGIN Latin *diriment-* pres. ppl stem of *dirimere*: see DIREMPT *verb*, -ENT.]
That renders absolutely void; nullifying.
diriment impediment: making a marriage null and void from the first.

dirk /dəːk/ *noun & verb*. Also (earlier) †**durk**. M16.
[ORIGIN Unknown.]
▸ **A** *noun*. A kind of short dagger, *esp.* that of a Scottish Highlander. M16.
▸ **B** *verb trans.* Stab with a dirk. L16.

dirl /dəːl/ *verb & noun*. *Scot. & N. English*. E16.
[ORIGIN Alt. of THIRL *verb*^{1}.]
▸ **A** *verb*. **1** *verb trans.* Pierce, thrill; cause to tingle, esp. by a sharp blow. E16.
2 *verb intrans.* Vibrate, esp. in response to a blow, a sound, etc.; tingle. E18.
3 *verb intrans.* Produce a vibrating sound; ring. E19.
▸ **B** *noun*. A thrill, a vibration; a tremulous sound. L18.

dirndl /ˈdəːnd(ə)l/ *noun*. M20.
[ORIGIN German dial., dim. of *Dirne* girl.]
1 A dress in the style of Alpine peasant costume with a bodice and full skirt. M20.
2 More fully ***dirndl skirt***. A full skirt with a tight waistband. M20.

dirt /dəːt/ *noun & verb*. ME.
[ORIGIN Old Norse *drit* excrement, corresp. to Middle Dutch *drēte* (Dutch *dreet*), rel. to the verbs Old English *gedrītan* = Old Norse *drīta*, Middle Dutch *drīten* (Dutch *drijten*).]
▸ **A** *noun*. **1** Excrement, faeces. ME.
2 Unclean matter that soils, filth; *esp.* mud, mire. ME.
3 *fig.* Something worthless or (*US, Austral., & NZ slang*) mean; scurrilous information, scandal; a despicable person. ME.

SHAKES. *Haml.* Spacious in the possession of dirt. L. G. GIBBON The dirt of gentry sat and ate up your rents but you were as good as they were. L. ALTHER What's the point of having grown children if they won't tell you the dirt?

4 Dirtiness, foulness, uncleanness, (*lit. & fig.*); meanness, sordidness. E17.
5 Earth, soil. L17.
6 MINING etc. Useless material, *esp.* that from which an ore or other useful substance is separated. L18.
7 Bad weather. *dial.* M19.
8 Firedamp. M19.
– PHRASES: **do dirt to** *slang* harm or injure maliciously. **eat dirt** (***a***) accept insults or humiliation; (***b***) *US* make a humiliating confession. ***kiss the dirt***: see KISS *verb*. ***pay-dirt***: see PAY-. **treat like dirt**: as worthless or contemptible.
– COMB.: **dirtbag** *US colloq.* a very unkempt or unpleasant person; **dirt bike** a motorcycle designed for unmade roads and scrambling across difficult terrain; **dirt cheap** *adjective & adverb* very cheap; **dirt-eating** a disease characterized by a morbid craving to eat earth; **dirt farmer** *US*: who farms his own land himself; **dirt money**: paid to workmen handling dirty materials or working in dirty conditions; **dirt-pie** a mud pie; **dirt road** (chiefly *N. Amer. & Austral.*) an unmade road, with only the natural surface; **dirt track** a course made of rolled cinders, brick dust, etc., for motorcycle racing etc., or of earth for flat-racing; **dirt wagon** *US* a dustcart.
▸ **B** *verb trans.* Make dirty, soil. *arch.* L16.
■ **dirtless** *adjective* E17.

dirty /ˈdəːti/ *adjective, noun, & adverb*. LME.
[ORIGIN from DIRT *noun* + -Y^{1}.]
▸ **A** *adjective*. **1** Soiled with dirt, unclean. LME. ▸**b** That makes a person or thing dirty or unclean. L18. ▸**c** Of a nuclear weapon: producing a lot of fallout. *colloq.* M20.

H. JOLLY His nappy may be dirty at every feed.

2 a Morally unclean or impure; obscene, pornographic; titillating; pertaining to or characterized by illicit sexual pleasure. E16. ▸**b** Bringing dishonour, base, corrupt; (of money etc.) earned by dishonourable or corrupt means. L17.

a A. SILLITOE Sniping was a dirty weapon like poison gas or liquid fire. P. MOYES You and Veronica were going off for . . a dirty week-end. **b** A. F. DOUGLAS-HOME Politics was a dirty business.

3 Containing or mixed with dirt. M16.
4 Disgusting, repulsive, hateful. E17.

D. H. LAWRENCE You are only dirty foreigners.

5 (Of weather) rough, squally, wet and windy; marked by such weather. M17.

J. RABAN Just another sort of reef to steer one's way round on dirty nights.

6 Of colour: tinged with what destroys purity or clearness; inclining to a brownish or greyish colour. M17.
7 Of a shape or movement: not smooth, irregular. *colloq.* E20.

C. GASKIN They said it was a very *dirty* fracture.

8 Of jazz or popular music: having a slurred, rasping, or distorted tone. E20.
– SPECIAL COLLOCATIONS & PHRASES: **dirty Allan** *Scot. dial.* the Arctic skua, *Stercorarius parasiticus*. **dirty bomb** a conventional bomb that contains radioactive material. **dirty dog** *slang* a despicable or untrustworthy person. **dirty end of the stick** *colloq.* the difficult or unpleasant part in a situation. **dirty look** *colloq.* a look of disapproval, anger, or disgust. **dirty money** = ***dirt money*** s.v. DIRT *noun* (see also sense 2b above). **dirty old man** *colloq.* a man who is regarded as having sexual interests inappropriate to his advanced years. **dirty rice** a Cajun dish consisting of white rice cooked with onions, peppers, chicken livers, and herbs. **dirty trick** a mean or despicable act; in *pl.* (*slang*), intelligence operations, underhand activity aimed at discrediting a political opponent. **dirty word** an obscene word; *fig.* a word denoting a concept regarded as discreditable. **dirty work** (***a***) work in doing which a person gets physically dirty; (***b***) unpleasant, dishonourable, or illicit work; freq. in ***do one's own dirty work***, ***do a person's dirty work for him or her***. **dirty work at the crossroads** dishonourable, illicit, or underhand behaviour.
▸ **B** *absol.* as *noun*. ***do the dirty***, play a mean trick (*on* a person). *colloq.* E20.
▸ **C** *adverb*. **1** Very, exceedingly. *slang*. E20.

K. AMIS A dirty great Baronial doorway.

2 Dirtily. M20.
fight dirty, ***play dirty***, ***talk dirty***, etc.
■ **dirtily** *adverb* L16. **dirtiness** *noun* M16. **dirtyish** *adjective* E19.

dirty /ˈdəːti/ *verb*. L16.
[ORIGIN from the adjective.]
1 *verb trans.* Make dirty, soil. (Foll. by *up*.) L16.
2 *verb intrans.* Become dirty. M19.

J. CARLYLE Dark blue morocco . . which won't dirty in a hurry.

dis /dɪs/ *adjective & verb*^{1}. *colloq.* Also **diss**. E20.
[ORIGIN Abbreviation of DISCONNECTED.]
▸ **A** *adjective*. Broken, not working; *fig.* weak in the head. E20.
▸ **B** *verb trans.* Infl. **-ss-**. Break, damage. M20.

dis /dɪs/ *verb*^{2} & *noun*^{1}. *slang*. L19.
[ORIGIN Abbreviation.]
PRINTING. ▸**A** *verb trans.* Infl. **-ss-**. = DISTRIBUTE 5. L19.
▸ **B** *noun*. Type that is ready for distribution. L19.

dis /dɪs/ *verb*^{3} & *noun*^{2}. *slang* (orig. *US black English*). Also **-ss**. L20.
[ORIGIN Abbreviation of DISRESPECT *verb & noun*.]
▸ **A** *verb trans.* Infl. **-ss-**. Act or speak in a disrespectful way towards. L20.

DAVID MITCHELL She said if you keep dissing her on the show she'll file a suit for stress.

▸ **B** *noun*. Disrespectful talk. L20.

dis- /dɪs/ *prefix*.
[ORIGIN Repr. Old French *des-*, *dis-* (mod. *dés-*, *dé-*, *dis-*) or its source Latin *dis-* 'two ways, in two', rel. to BIS-, BI- (= Greek *dis-*, DI-^{2}), from Latin *duo* two, appearing before *p*, *t*, *c*, *q*, and *s* (see also DI-^{1}, DIF-, DIR-). Occas. repr. late Latin *dis-* for Latin *de-* DE- 1.]
1 In words adopted from French and Latin with the sense 'apart, away, asunder, abroad', as ***discern***, ***disperse***, ***disquisition***, ***dissident***, ***distant***, ***distinguish***, ***distraction***, etc. ▸**b** Occas. in words with the senses 'between' and 'separate, singly', as ***discept*** etc.
2 In words adopted from French and Latin with privative force, as ***disadvantage***, ***disagree***, ***disease***, ***disgrace***, ***displease***, ***dissuade***, etc. Also as a freely productive prefix with privative force (occas. replacing earlier *mis-*, as in ***dislike***) forming (***a***) verbs from verbs (with their derivative nouns, adjectives, etc.) with the sense 'reverse, undo', as ***disestablish***, ***disown***, etc.; (***b***) verbs from nouns with the senses 'strip of, free, rid of', as ***disfrock***, ***dispeople***, etc., 'deprive of the character, title, etc. of', as ***disbishop***, ***dischurch***, etc., 'expel from', as ***disbar***, ***disbench***, etc., 'undo, spoil', as ***discomplexion***; (***c***) verbs from adjectives with the sense 'undo, reverse the quality denoted', as ***disable*** etc.; (***d***) nouns from nouns with the sense 'the absence or opposite of the state, quality, etc., in question', as in ***dishonour*** etc.; (***e***) adjectives from adjectives with negative force, as ***dishonest*** etc.
3 In words adopted from French and Latin with intensive force 'utterly' with words already implying reversal or removal, as ***disannul***, ***disturb***, etc., and occas. in words formed in English after these, as ***disembowel***, ***disgruntled***, etc.
■ **disacˈcept** *verb trans.* (*rare*) refuse acceptance to M17. †**disacceptance** *noun* refusal to accept, non-acceptance M17–E18. **disaˈccommodate** *verb trans.* (now *rare* or *obsolete*) put to inconvenience, incommode E17. **disaccommoˈdation** *noun* (now *rare* or *obsolete*) the action of inconveniencing; (a) lack of suitability or agreement: E17. †**disadjust** *verb trans.* (*rare*) unsettle, disturb E17–M18. †**disadorn** *verb trans.* (*rare*) deprive of adornment: L16–E18. **disaˈffiliate** *verb trans. & intrans.* cancel affiliation (of) L19. **disaffiliˈation** *noun* the action of disaffiliating E20. **disaˈllegiance** *noun* (*rare*) absence or withdrawal of allegiance M17. **disaˈlly** *verb trans.* (*poet. rare*) free from alliance or union L17. **disaˈmenity** *noun* a disadvantage, an unpleasant feature, (of a place etc.) E20. **disaˈnalogy** *noun* (a) lack of analogy, (a) dissimilarity E17. †**disangelical** *adjective* not angelical, the reverse of angelical: L17–M18. **disaˈnoint** *verb trans.* annul the anointing or consecration of M17. †**disappendant**, **-ent** *adjective* (LAW) not appendant M17–M18. **disappliˈcation** *noun* the act or result of making inapplicable L20. **disaˈpply** *verb trans.* treat (a condition etc.) as not applying L20. **disapproˈbation** *noun* disapproval M17. **disˈapprobative** *adjective* = DISAPPROBATORY E19. **disapproˈbatory** *adjective* characterized by or expressing disapproval E19. **disaˈrrange** *verb trans.* bring into disorder, make untidy M18. **disaˈrrangement** *noun* the action or result of disarranging M18. **disarˈticulate** *verb* (***a***) *verb trans.* separate joint from joint, make disjointed; (***b***) *verb intrans.* become disjointed, lose structural cohesion: M19. **disarticuˈlation** *noun* the action or result of disarticulating M19. †**disattention** *noun* lack of attention, neglect E17–M18. **disˈbalance** *noun & verb* (***a***) *noun* an imbalance; (***b***) *verb trans.* disturb the balance of: M19. **disˈbenefit** *noun* a drawback, an undesirable feature or consequence L20. **disˈbody** *verb trans.* = DISEMBODY M17. **disˈbrain** *verb trans.* remove the brain from M17. **disˈbud** *verb trans.* remove the buds of; deprive of (superfluous) buds: E18. **disˈcage** *verb trans.* let out as from a cage M17. †**discamp** *verb* [after Italian *scampare*] (***a***) *verb intrans.* decamp; (***b***) *verb trans.* decamp from; force to decamp: L16–L17. **disˈcandy** *verb intrans.* (*arch.*) melt; *fig.* melt away E17. **disˈcanonize** *verb trans.* †(***a***) exclude from the canon; (***b***) cancel the canonization of: E17. **discaˈpacitate** *verb trans.* (*rare*) deprive of capacity, incapacitate M17. **disˈcase** *verb* (*arch.*) (***a***) *verb trans.* unsheathe; (***b***) *verb trans. & intrans.* undress; divest *of*: L16. **disˈclass** *verb trans.* cut off from a social class L19. **disˈclimax** *noun* (ECOLOGY) a climax community in which the natural climax is modified by human interference, grazing, or other disturbances M20. **disˈcloister** *verb trans.* release from seclusion M17. **discoˈhere** *verb intrans.* cease to cohere L19. **disˈcommonize** *verb trans.* = DISCOMMON 2 L19. †**disconfidence** *noun* (*rare*) lack or absence of confidence E17–L18. **disconˈfirm** *verb trans.* (tend to) disprove (a hypothesis etc.); suggest the falsity of: M20. **disconˈfirmable** *adjective* able to be shown to be false or unlikely M20. **disconfirˈmation** *noun* the process or result of disconfirming M20. **disconˈfirmatory** *adjective* serving to disconfirm M20. **disconˈgruity** *noun* (now *rare* or *obsolete*) (a) lack of congruity; (a) disagreement, (an) inconsistency: E17. **disconˈsider** *verb trans.* (*rare*) bring into disrepute, discredit L19. **disconsideˈration** *noun* (*rare*) the action of discrediting; the fact of being discredited, disrepute: L19. †**disconsonant** *adjective* not consonant, out of agreement; discordant: M17–E19. †**discourt** *verb trans.* dismiss from court L16–M19. †**discovenant** *verb trans.* break covenant with, exclude from a covenant M17–M19. **discredence** *noun* (*rare*) disbelief LME. **discredibility** *noun* (*rare*) lack or absence of credibility E19. **diseˈconomy** *noun* (a factor causing) a disproportionately large increase in costs arising from an increase in the size of an organization M20. **disˈedge** *verb trans.* take the edge off, blunt E17. **disˈeducate** *verb trans.* undo or pervert the education of L19. †**dis-element** *verb trans.* put (something) out of its element E17–E18. **disemˈbed** *verb trans.* free from being embedded L19. **disemˈbellish** *verb trans.* deprive of embellishment or adornment E17. **disemˈbosom** *verb* (***a***) *verb trans.* cast out or separate from the bosom; reveal; (***b***) *verb refl. & intrans.* disclose what is in one's inmost thoughts, unburden oneself: M18. †**disembrace** *verb trans.* refrain or withdraw from embracing; undo the embraces of: M17–L18. **disemˈploy** *verb trans.* cease to employ, dismiss from employment E17. **disemˈployment** *noun* (*rare*) absence or withdrawal of employment M17. **disemˈpower** *verb trans.* deprive of power conferred M18. **diseˈnable** *verb trans.* make unable or incapable; disable: E17. **disenˈjoy** *verb trans.* get no enjoyment from, dislike E20. **diseˈnnoble** *verb trans.* deprive of nobility; make ignoble: M17. †**disenrol** *verb trans.* (*rare*) remove (a name) from a roll or list M17–M19. **disenˈslave** *verb trans.* (now *rare*) set free from enslavement M17. **disenˈtrammel** *verb trans.* free from entanglement M19. **disenˈtrance** *verb trans.* bring out of or wake from a trance M17. **disenˈtwine** *verb trans.* free from being entwined, disentangle E19. **diseˈquality** *noun* (long *rare*) (an) inequality; (a) disparity: E17. †**disespouse** *verb trans.* (*rare*, Milton) undo the marriage or betrothal of: only in M17. **disˈfaith** *noun* lack of faith; unfaithfulness: L19. **disˈflesh** *verb trans.* (*arch.*) deprive of or free from the flesh E17. **disˈfrock** *verb trans.* unfrock M19. **disˈgarland** *verb trans.* divest of a garland or garlands E17. **disˈgarrison** *verb trans.* (*arch.*) deprive of a garrison L16. †**disgout** *verb trans.* (*rare*) free or relieve from gout E17–M18. **disˈgulf** *verb trans.* eject or discharge (as) from a gulf M17. **dishaˈbilitate** *verb trans.* (now *rare* or *obsolete*) make incapable; *spec.* (SCOTS LAW, now *hist.*) subject to dishabilitation: M17. **dishabiliˈtation** *noun* (SCOTS LAW, now *hist.*) disqualification from the inheritance, possession, or transmission of land M17. **dishaˈbituate** *verb trans.* make unaccustomed M19. **dishalluciˈnation** *noun* a freeing from hallucination, disillusion L19. †**dishaunt** *verb trans.* (chiefly *Scot.*) cease to attend (esp. a church or church service) L16–E19. **disˈhoard** *verb trans.* release from a hoard E20. **disˈhome** *verb trans.* deprive of or eject from a home L19. **disˈhorn** *verb trans.* remove the horns from L16. **disˈhorse** *verb trans.* cause to dismount from a horse M19. **disˈhumanize** *verb trans.* deprive of human attributes, dehumanize M19. †**dishumour** *noun* ill humour: only in 18. **disiˈmagine** *verb trans.* cease to imagine; imagine not to exist: M17. **disiˈmmure** *verb trans.* set free from confining walls; liberate: E17. **disimˈpale** *verb trans.* disengage from a spike E20. **disimˈpassioned** *adjective* freed from passion; dispassionate: M19. **disimˈperialism** *noun* renunciation of imperial possessions M20. †**disimplicate** *verb trans.* free from implication or involvement M17–M18. **disimˈprison** *verb trans.* release from imprisonment E17. **disimˈprisonment** *noun* the action of disimprisoning M17. **disimˈprove** *verb trans.* & (*rare*) *intrans.* make or become worse M17. **disimˈprovement** *noun* (a) deterioration, worsening M17. **disinˈcarcerate** *verb trans.* = DISIMPRISON M17. **disincarceˈration** *noun* = DISIMPRISONMENT M19. **disinˈcarnate** *adjective* disembodied, not incarnate L19. **disinˈcarnate** *verb trans.* = DISEMBODY 1 L19. **disinˈcorporate** *verb trans.* make no longer a corporate body L17. **disincorpoˈration** *noun* the action of disincorporating a town etc. L18. **disindiˈvidualize** *verb trans.* divest of individuality M19. **disinˈfest** *verb trans.* rid of infesting insects, vermin, etc. E20. **disinfesˈtation** *noun* the process of disinfesting E20. †**disinhabit** *verb trans.* rid of inhabitants M16–E19. **disinˈhibit** *verb* (***a***) *verb intrans.* (*rare*) reduce or remove inhibition; (***b***) *verb trans.* release from inhibition; make less inhibited: E20. **disinhiˈbition** *noun* the suppression of an inhibition; the state of not being inhibited: E20. **disinˈhibitory** *adjective* tending to cause, or characterized by, disinhibition M20. **disinˈhume** *verb trans.* exhume E19. **disinsectiˈzation** *noun* the removal of insects M20. **disinˈsectize** *verb trans.* remove insects from (esp. an aircraft) M20. **disinˈtegrity** *noun* (now *rare*) lack of entireness; disintegrated condition: L18. **disinˈvent** *verb trans.* undo the invention of M19. **disinˈvolve** *verb trans.* free from an involved condition, disentangle E17. †**diskindness** *noun* (an) unkindness; unfriendliness: L16–M18. **disˈleaf**, **-ˈleave** *verb trans.* strip of leaves L16. **disˈlikelihood** *noun* (*rare*) improbability E19. **disˈlimb** *verb trans.* cut off the limbs of; tear limb from limb: M17. **disˈlink** *verb trans.* unlink, uncouple, separate, (things that are linked) E17. **disˈload** *verb trans. & intrans.* unload, disburden M16. **disˈlustre** *verb* (***a***) *verb trans.* deprive of lustre; dim, sully; (***b***) *verb intrans.* lose its lustre: M17. **disˈmarble** *verb trans.* free from marble or the appearance of marble M19. **disˈmast** *verb trans.* deprive of masts, break the mast(s) of M18. **disˈnest** *verb trans.* (*rare*) remove (as) from a nest; empty (a nest) *of*: L16. **disobˈstruct** *verb trans.* (now *rare*) free from obstruction E17. **disoccuˈpation** *noun* lack of occupation M19. **disˈoccupy** *verb trans.* cease to occupy, vacate L19. **disorˈganic** *adjective* having no organization or systematic arrangement M19. †**disoxidate** *verb trans.* deoxygenate: only in E19. †**disoxygenate** *verb trans.* deoxygenate E–M19. **disˈparish** *verb trans.* (***a***) deprive of the status of a parish; (***b***) deprive of a parish; eject from a parish: L16. **disˈpauper** *verb trans.* (*hist.*) deprive of the legal status of a pauper M17. **disˈpauperize** *verb trans.* free from a state of pauperism; *hist.* relieve (a community etc.) of responsibility for paupers:

D

D

M19. **dis'peace** *noun* (chiefly *Scot.*) the absence or reverse of peace; disquiet; dissension: E19. **dis'petal** *verb trans.* strip of petals M19. **displume** *verb* †(*a*) *verb intrans.* (of a bird) moult; (*b*) *verb trans.* = DEPLUME: L15. **dis'pope** *verb trans.* deprive of the popedom M17. **dis'privilege** *verb trans.* deprive of privilege E17. †**disprofess** *verb trans.* (*rare*, Spenser) renounce the profession of: only in L16. †**disproperty** *verb trans.* (*rare*, Shakes.) deprive of property, dispossess: only in E17. **dis'realize** *verb trans.* (*rare*) divest of reality, idealize L19. **disreco'mmend** *verb trans.* (*rare*) cause to be unfavourably regarded, give a recommendation against L17. **disrecommen'dation** *noun* something that causes a person or thing to be unfavourably regarded M18. **disre'late** *verb trans.* remove the connection between M17. †**disrest** *noun* disquiet, unrest M16–E18. †**disrest** *verb trans.* (*a*) remove from a place of rest; (*b*) deprive of rest, disturb: L17–M18. **dis'reverence** *verb trans.* (*arch.*) treat with irreverence; deprive of reverence: E16. **dis'roof** *verb trans.* unroof M19. **dis'save** *verb intrans.* spend more than one's income, by drawing on savings or realizing capital M20. **dis'sceptre** *verb trans.* deprive of the sceptre or of kingly authority L16. **dis'seat** *verb trans.* unseat; remove from where it is situated: E17. **dis'sepulchred** *adjective* (*rare*) disentombed M17. **dis'shadow** *verb trans.* (*rare*) free from shadow or shade E17. **dis'sheathe** *verb trans.* & †*intrans.* (*rare*) draw or (formerly) be drawn out of a sheath E17. †**disshiver** *verb* (*a*) *verb trans.* shiver in pieces, shatter; (*b*) *verb intrans.* become shattered: L16–M17. **dis'shroud** *verb trans.* (*rare*) strip of a shroud; *fig.* reveal, expose: L16. **dis'sight** *noun* an unsightly object, an eyesore E18. **dis'sightly** *adjective* (*rare*) unsightly L18. **dis'soul** *verb trans.* (*rare*) take away the soul from E17. **dis'sunder** *verb trans.* (*arch.*) sever, divide L16. **dis'sympathy** *noun* (*rare*) absence of sympathy M19. **dis'tenant** *verb trans.* (*rare*) deprive of a tenant L16. **dis'tune** *verb trans.* put out of tune LME. **dis'turnpike** *verb trans.* free (a road) of turnpikes L19. **dis'uniform** *adjective* without uniformity L17. **disuni'formity** *noun* absence of uniformity E18. **dis'unify** *verb trans.* undo or prevent the unity of L19. **disu'tility** *noun* harmfulness; a factor that tends to nullify the utility of something; a drawback: L19. †**disveil** *verb trans.* remove a veil from; unveil, unmask: L16–M19. †**disvest** *verb trans.* divest, strip; undress: E17–M18. †**disvouch** *verb trans.* (*rare*) = DISAVOW L15–E17. **disvulnera'bility** *noun* the faculty of recovering from injuries exceptionally quickly L19. **dis'warren** *verb trans.* deprive of the character of a warren; make no longer a warren: M17. **dis'wig** *verb trans.* deprive of a wig L18. **dis'wood** *verb trans.* deprive of wood or trees E17.

disa /'dʌɪsə/ *noun*. M19.
[ORIGIN mod. Latin: ult. origin unknown.]
Any of various terrestrial orchids of the genus *Disa*, native to southern Africa and Madagascar and with dark green leaves.

disability /dɪsə'bɪlɪti/ *noun*. L16.
[ORIGIN from DIS- 2 + ABILITY.]
1 Lack of ability (*to do* something); inability, incapacity. Now *rare*. L16.
2 Shortage of money. E17.
3 An instance of lacking ability; now *spec.* a physical or mental condition (usu. permanent) that limits a person's movements, activities, or senses. E17.

> T. S. ELIOT My physical disabilities . . would not disqualify me. *Daily Telegraph* Stroke is the single most common cause of disability.

4 Incapacity recognized or created by the law; legal disqualification. M17.

disable /dɪs'eɪb(ə)l/ *verb trans.* LME.
[ORIGIN from DIS- 2 + ABLE *adjective*.]
1 Disqualify legally; pronounce legally incapable. (Foll. by *from doing*, †*to do*.) LME.
2 Make incapable of action or use; deprive of physical or mental ability, esp. through injury or disease. L15.

> R. D. HAMPDEN Men are disabled from understanding what they have been taught to condemn. *Scientific American* A car that is disabled or illegally parked.

3 Pronounce incapable; disparage, belittle. Now *rare* or *obsolete*. E16.

> SHAKES. *A.Y.L.* Farewell, Monsieur Traveller . . , disable all the benefits of your own country, be out of love with your nativity.

†**4** Make or pronounce of no validity. M16–L17.
■ **disablement** *noun* the action of disabling; the state or fact of being disabled: L15. **disableness** *noun* (*arch.*) inability, incapacity; disabled state: E17.

disabled /dɪs'eɪb(ə)ld/ *adjective* & *noun*. LME.
[ORIGIN from DISABLE + -ED[1].]
▶ **A** *adjective*. **1** Legally disqualified. Now *rare* or *obsolete*. LME.
2 Made incapable of action or use; *esp.* (of a person) possessing a disability. M17. ▸**b** For the use of people with physical disabilities. L20.

> *Times* A bold experiment to treat disabled and able-bodied competitors as equals. **b** *Interior Design* Disabled toilets and access to the refreshment areas are also necessary.

▶ **B** *absol.* as *noun pl. The* people who are disabled, as a class. E20.
– NOTE: Since M20 the standard adjective in referring to people with physical or mental disabilities. Note, however, that use as a pl. noun (as in *the needs of the disabled*) is sometimes regarded as dehumanizing and is best avoided.

disablist /dɪs'eɪblɪst/ *adjective*. L20.
[ORIGIN from DISABLED + -IST, after *racist*.]
Practising or displaying discrimination against disabled people.

disabuse /dɪsə'bjuːz/ *verb* & *noun*. E17.
[ORIGIN from DIS- 2 + ABUSE *noun*.]
▶ **A** *verb trans.* **1** Rid *of* illusion, a mistaken conception, etc.; undeceive, disillusion. E17.

> H. A. L. FISHER If Justinian expected to extend to the north African littoral a Roman peace he was soon disabused. P. ACKROYD I do not disabuse them of this charming notion.

2 Mar, spoil, misuse. *Scot.* E17.
▶ †**B** *noun*. An act of disabusing; the fact of being disabused. E17–E18.

disaccharide /dʌɪ'sakərʌɪd/ *noun*. L19.
[ORIGIN from DI-[2] + SACCHARIDE.]
CHEMISTRY. Any sugar that consists of two monosaccharide residues linked together.
■ **disaccharase**, **disaccharidase** *nouns* an enzyme which hydrolyses a disaccharide M20.

disaccord /dɪsə'kɔːd/ *noun*. M16.
[ORIGIN from DIS- 2 + ACCORD *noun*: cf. Old French & mod. French *désaccord*.]
Disagreement, variance; lack of accord.

disaccord /dɪsə'kɔːd/ *verb intrans.* LME.
[ORIGIN French *désaccorder*, formed as DIS- 2, ACCORD *verb*.]
Disagree; be at variance.
■ **disaccordance** *noun* (*rare*) disagreement, variance LME. **disaccordant** *adjective* (*rare*) discordant, at variance L15.

disaccustom /dɪsə'kʌstəm/ *verb trans.* L15.
[ORIGIN Old French *desaco(u)stumer* (mod. *désaccoutumer*), formed as DIS- 2, ACCUSTOM *verb*.]
1 Cause (a thing) to cease to be customary; break off (a habit or practice). *arch.* L15.
2 Cause (a person) to lose a habit; make unaccustomed (*to*, †*from*). M16.

disacknowledge /dɪsək'nɒlɪdʒ/ *verb trans.* L16.
[ORIGIN from DIS- 2 + ACKNOWLEDGE *verb*.]
Refuse to acknowledge, disown.
■ **disacknowledgement** *noun* M17.

disacquaint /dɪsə'kweɪnt/ *verb trans.* Now *rare* or *obsolete*. M16.
[ORIGIN from DIS- 2 + ACQUAINT *verb*.]
Estrange, make unfamiliar.
■ **disa'cquaintance** *noun* lack of acquaintance L16.

†**disadvance** *verb trans.* LME–M17.
[ORIGIN Old French *desavancer* repel, push back, formed as DIS- 2, ADVANCE *verb*.]
Check the advance of; draw back, lower; *fig.* hinder from progress, lower the status of.

> SPENSER That forced him his shield to disadvaunce.

disadvantage /dɪsəd'vɑːntɪdʒ/ *noun* & *verb*. LME.
[ORIGIN Old French & mod. French *désavantage*, from DIS- 2, ADVANTAGE *noun*.]
▶ **A** *noun*. **1** Lack of advantage; an unfavourable condition or circumstance. LME.

> R. ELLMANN Lewes must have appeared to disadvantage beside this taller, handsomer . . , younger banker.

2 Loss of or injury to credit, reputation, or interest. LME.

> STEELE I . . never speak Things to any Man's Disadvantage.

▶ **B** *verb trans.* Place at a disadvantage; affect unfavourably. M16.

> *Daily Telegraph* His colour, always disadvantaging him, has damaged his native spontaneity.

■ **disadvantaged** *ppl adjective* & *noun* (*the* people who are) placed at a disadvantage, now esp. in relation to social opportunities E17.

disadvantageous /ˌdɪsadv(ə)n'teɪdʒəs/ *adjective*. E17.
[ORIGIN from DIS- 2 + ADVANTAGEOUS, perh. after French *désavantageux*.]
1 Involving disadvantage; unfavourable, prejudicial. E17.
2 Tending to the discredit of a person or thing; disparaging, derogatory. M17.
■ **disadvantageously** *adverb* E17. **disadvantageousness** *noun* E18.

†**disadventure** *noun*. LME–M17.
[ORIGIN Old French *desaventure*, formed as DIS- 2, ADVENTURE *noun*.]
(A) mishap, (a) misfortune.
■ †**disadventurous** *adjective* unfortunate, disastrous L16–E18.

disadvise /dɪsəd'vʌɪz/ *verb trans.* M17.
[ORIGIN from DIS- 2 + ADVISE.]
1 Advise against (an action, course, etc.). M17.
2 Dissuade (a person) *from*. L17.

disaffect /dɪsə'fɛkt/ *verb trans.* E17.
[ORIGIN from DIS- 2 + AFFECT *verb*[1].]
1 Have no affection for; dislike, regard with aversion. *arch.* E17.

> J. SHIRLEY Unless you disaffect his person.

2 Alienate, estrange; make unfriendly or less friendly; *spec.* make discontented with a constituted authority, as the Government, one's employer, etc. M17.

> G. F. KENNAN The Communists . . set about trying to disaffect these men from their loyalty to their own governments.

■ **disaffected** *ppl adjective* that has been disaffected; unfriendly; discontent, *spec.* with a constituted authority, as the Government, one's employer, etc.: M17.

disaffection /dɪsə'fɛkʃ(ə)n/ *noun*. E17.
[ORIGIN Partly from DIS- 2 + AFFECTION *noun*; partly from DISAFFECT *verb* after AFFECTION *noun*: see -ION.]
1 Lack or alienation of affection; estrangement; (a) dissatisfaction; *spec.* discontentment with a constituted authority, as the Government, one's employer, etc. E17.
†**2** Bodily disorder or indisposition. M17–M18.

disaffirm /dɪsə'fəːm/ *verb trans.* M16.
[ORIGIN from DIS- 2 + AFFIRM.]
Contradict, deny; *spec.* in *LAW*, reverse (a previous decision), repudiate (a settlement).
■ **disaffirmance** *noun* the action of disaffirming; annulment, repudiation: E17. **disaffir'mation** *noun* = DISAFFIRMANCE M19.

disafforest /dɪsə'fɒrɪst/ *verb trans.* LME.
[ORIGIN Anglo-Latin *disafforestare*, formed as DIS- 2, AFFOREST. Cf. DE-AFFOREST, DEFOREST, DISFOREST.]
1 *hist.* Free from the operation of forest laws; reduce from the legal status of forest to that of ordinary land. LME.
2 = DISFOREST 2. *rare*. M19.
■ **disaffore'station** *noun* the action or result of disafforesting land etc. L16. **disafforestment** *noun* = DISAFFORESTATION L19.

disaggregate /dɪs'agrɪgeɪt/ *verb trans.* E19.
[ORIGIN from DIS- 2 + AGGREGATE *verb*.]
Separate into component parts; cease to treat as aggregated.
■ **disaggre'gation** *noun* E19.

disagree /dɪsə'griː/ *verb intrans.* Pa. t. & pple **-agreed**. L15.
[ORIGIN Old French & mod. French *désagréer*, formed as DIS- 2, AGREE.]
1 Differ in nature, be unlike; not correspond. (Foll. by *with*, †*to*, †*from*.) L15.

> A. B. DAVIDSON The other numerals are nouns, and disagree in gender with the words they enumerate.

2 Refuse to accord or agree (to a proposal etc.); withhold assent. (Foll. by *to*, *with*, †*from*.) L15.

> GLADSTONE I beg now to move that the House disagree with the Lords' amendment.

3 Differ in opinion. (Foll. by *with*, (now *rare*) *from*.) M16.

> POPE Who shall decide when Doctors disagree?

AGREE to disagree.
4 Be at variance, quarrel, fall out. M16.

> S. HAYWARD Children of the same family ought not to disagree.

5 Of food, climate, etc.: be unsuited to a person's constitution, cause discomfort or illness. Foll. by *with*. M16.
■ **disagreer** *noun* (*rare*) E17.

disagreeable /dɪsə'griːəb(ə)l/ *adjective* & *noun*. LME.
[ORIGIN Old French & mod. French *désagréable*, formed as DIS- 2, AGREEABLE *adjective*.]
▶ **A** *adjective*. †**1** Not in agreement; characterized by difference; incongruous; discordant. (Foll. by *to*, *with*.) LME–M18.
2 Not to one's taste or liking; unpleasant, offensive. L17.

> J. JOHNSTON Pale mauve, a colour I normally find quite disagreeable.

3 Bad-tempered, unamiable, surly. E18.
4 Feeling discomfort, uneasy. Chiefly *US*. E19.
▶ **B** *noun*. A disagreeable thing or experience. Usu. in *pl.* L18.

> D. CECIL Hankering after life on earth, even after its disagreeables.

■ **disagreea'bility** *noun* L18. **disagreeableness** *noun* L16. **disagreeably** *adverb* L17.

disagreement /dɪsə'griːm(ə)nt/ *noun*. L15.
[ORIGIN from DISAGREE after AGREEMENT.]
1 (A) refusal to accord or agree; the withholding of assent. L15.
2 (A) difference of opinion; a quarrel; dissension. L16.

> T. WALL Disagreement in matters of faith causeth enmity. A. SAYLE Trotsky's disagreements with Stalin over the theory of Socialism.

3 (A) difference in nature, (an) unlikeness, (a) lack of correspondence. L16.
4 Unsuitableness to a person's constitution. E18.

disallow /dɪsə'laʊ/ *verb*. LME.
[ORIGIN Old French *desalouer*, formed as DIS- 2, ALLOW *verb*.]
†**1** *verb trans.* Blame; refuse to praise. LME–M17.
†**2** *verb trans.* & *intrans.* foll. by *of*. Disown. LME–M17.
3 *verb trans.* Treat as invalid; refuse to accept (a claim, suggestion, etc.). LME.

> E. WAUGH No. 13 . . cut across country . . . This lap has therefore been disallowed by the judges.

4 *verb trans.* & †*intrans.* foll. by *of*. Refuse to permit or sanction; prohibit; prevent. L15.

> O. SACKS Violent stiffness . . disallowed even passive movement.

■ **disallowable** *adjective* not to be permitted or sanctioned LME. **disallowance** *noun* (*a*) the action or result of disallowing; †(*b*) *MUSIC* an irregularity: M16.

disambiguate /dɪsam'bɪgjʊeɪt/ *verb trans.* M20.
[ORIGIN from DIS- 2 + AMBIGU(OUS + -ATE³.]
Remove ambiguity from.
■ ˌ**disambigu'ation** *noun* (the result of) the removal of ambiguity E19.

Disamis /'dɪsəmɪs/ *noun.* M16.
[ORIGIN A mnemonic of scholastic philosophers first used in medieval Latin, A indicating a universal affirmative proposition and I a particular affirmative proposition.]
LOGIC. The second mood of the third syllogistic figure, in which a particular affirmative conclusion is drawn from a particular affirmative major and a universal affirmative minor premiss.

disanchor /dɪs'aŋkə/ *verb.* Now *rare.* LME.
[ORIGIN Old French *desancrer*, formed as DIS- 2, ANCHOR *verb*.]
1 *verb intrans.* Weigh anchor, leave an anchorage. LME.
2 *verb trans.* Release (a ship) from anchorage; weigh the anchor of. L15.

disanimate /dɪs'anɪmeɪt/ *verb trans.* L16.
[ORIGIN from DIS- 2 + ANIMATE *verb*, prob. after French *désanimer*.]
Deprive of life, spirit, vigour, or animation.
■ **disani'mation** *noun* M17.

disannex /dɪsə'nɛks/ *verb trans.* LME.
[ORIGIN Old French *desannexer*, formed as DIS- 2, ANNEX *verb*.]
End the annexation of (land etc.); disjoin.
■ ˌ**disanne'xation** *noun* L19.

disannul /dɪsə'nʌl/ *verb trans.* Infl. **-ll-**. L15.
[ORIGIN from DIS- 3 + ANNUL.]
1 Cancel, annul. L15.
†**2** Deprive (a person) *of* an attribute etc. by annulment; *fig.* do out *of*. Also foll. by *from*. M16–E17.
■ **disannulment** *noun* E17.

disapparel /dɪsə'par(ə)l/ *verb trans.* & †*intrans.* Now *rare.* Infl. **-ll-**, *-**l-**. L16.
[ORIGIN from DIS- 2 + APPAREL *verb*.]
Undress.

disappear /dɪsə'pɪə/ *verb.* LME.
[ORIGIN from DIS- 2 + APPEAR *verb* after French *disparaître*.]
1 *verb intrans.* Cease to appear or be visible; pass from sight, vanish; gradually cease to be distinguishable. LME.

> JOYCE He disappears into . . the pork butcher's. L. DEIGHTON The giant planes climbed into the darkness and disappeared.

2 *verb intrans.* Cease to be present, go away; pass from existence; go, leaving no trace; be lost. M17. ▸**b** *euphem.* Be abducted, esp. for political reasons, and typically detained or killed, such that one's fate is unknown. M20.

> J. BUCHAN I would disappear early on the Sunday morning and return late at night. H. L. MENCKEN The idea of restitution seems to have disappeared from our criminal law.

3 *verb trans.* Cause to disappear. L19. ▸**b** *colloq.* Abduct and secretly kill or detain (someone), esp. for political reasons. L20.
– PHRASES: **do a disappearing trick**, **do a disappearing act**, **do the disappearing trick**, **do the disappearing act** *colloq.* disappear suddenly or unexpectedly.
■ **disappearance** *noun* the action or an act of disappearing E18. **disappearer** *noun* a person who disappears L19.

disappoint /dɪsə'pɔɪnt/ *verb* & *noun.* LME.
[ORIGIN Old French & mod. French *désappointer*, formed as DIS- 2, APPOINT *verb*.]
▸ **A** *verb.* **1** *verb trans.* Reverse the appointment of; deprive of an office, position, or possession. Now *rare.* LME.

> BYRON He would keep it Till duly disappointed or dismiss'd.

2 *verb trans.* Frustrate or fail to fulfil the desire or expectation of (a person). Freq. in *pass.* (foll. by *in*, *with*, †*of*). L15. ▸**b** *verb intrans.* Cause disappointment, be disappointing. M19.

> J. P. HENNESSY Trollope . . had been disappointed in his expectations of promotion. **b** G. GREENE One knows what to expect and Mr Cagney seldom disappoints.

agreeably disappointed agreeably surprised by something better than one expected it to be.
†**3** *verb trans.* Break off (what has been appointed); fail to keep (an engagement). M16–M17.

> JOSEPH HALL So as to put off and disappoint the day which he had set.

4 *verb trans.* Prevent the realization or fulfilment of (a plan, purpose, etc.); frustrate (a hope). L16.

> G. B. SHAW It would certainly disappoint the main hope of its advocates.

†**5** *verb trans.* Equip or prepare improperly. L16–M17.

> SHAKES. *Haml.* Cut off even in the blossoms of my sin, Unhous'led, disappointed, unanel'd.

†**6** *verb trans.* Undo, destroy, overthrow. E17–E18.

> STEELE They endeavour to disappoint the good works of the most learned . . of men.

▸ †**B** *noun.* = DISAPPOINTMENT. M17–M19.
■ **disappointedly** *adverb* in a disappointed way or tone L19. **disappointingly** *adverb* (*a*) in a disappointing way; (*b*) (modifying a sentence) it is disappointing that: L19.

disappointment /dɪsə'pɔɪntm(ə)nt/ *noun.* E17.
[ORIGIN from DISAPPOINT + -MENT.]
1 (An instance of) the frustration or non-fulfilment of desire or expectation. E17.

> J. TYNDALL Severe labour and frequent disappointment. M. MEYER It was a bitter disappointment to Strindberg . . to find himself treated . . as a servant.

2 Dejection or distress caused by this. M18.

> SCOTT FITZGERALD 'It's not exactly a *police* dog,' said the man with disappointment in his voice.

3 A person who or thing which disappoints. M18.

> W. COWPER One who has been a disappointment and a vexation to them.

disappropriate /dɪsə'prəʊprɪeɪt/ *verb trans.* Pa. pple & ppl adjective **-ated**, (earlier) †**-ate**. E17.
[ORIGIN medieval Latin *disappropriat-* pa. ppl stem of *disappropriare*, formed as DIS- 2 + Latin *appropriare* APPROPRIATE *verb*.]
Dissolve the appropriation of (a property etc.).
■ ˌ**disappropri'ation** *noun* the action of disappropriating M17.

disapprove /dɪsə'pruːv/ *verb.* L15.
[ORIGIN from DIS- 2 + APPROVE *verb*².]
†**1** *verb trans.* Prove to be untrue or wrong; disprove. L15–L18.
2 *verb trans.* Have or express an unfavourable opinion of. M17.

> M. TREVOR He disapproved this impatience.

3 *verb intrans.* Have or express an unfavourable opinion (*of*). E18.

> H. JAMES She disapproved of clamorous children. C. P. SNOW He disapproved intensely.

■ **disapprovable** *adjective* deserving disapproval M17. **disapproval** *noun* the act or fact of disapproving, possession or expression of an unfavourable opinion (*of*) M17. **disapprover** *noun* L18. **disapprovingly** *adverb* in a disapproving manner M19.

disard *noun* var. of DIZZARD.

disarm /dɪs'ɑːm/ *verb* & *noun.* LME.
[ORIGIN Old French & mod. French *désarmer*, formed as DIS- 2, ARM *verb*¹.]
▸ **A** *verb.* **I** *verb trans.* **1** Deprive (a person) of a weapon or (*arch.*) armour; force a weapon from the hand of (an opponent). (Foll. by *of*.) LME.

> G. GREENE Unless you give me your revolver I shall call the crew to disarm you.

2 *fig.* Deprive (anger etc.) of the power to injure or intimidate; allay the hostility or suspicions of (a person). LME.

> J. G. COZZENS Accustomed to disarm some of their critics by cheerfully agreeing with them. M. KEANE Her unquestioning confidence in love . . had disarmed him of any unkindness towards her. H. GUNTRIP His aggression was disarmed when he discovered that she really understood him.

3 Remove or dismantle the defences of (a city, ship, etc.); deprive (an animal) of its organs of attack and defence; remove the fuse of (a bomb). E17.
▸ **II** *verb intrans.* **4** Divest oneself of weapons or (*arch.*) armour. L16.
5 Of a nation etc.: reduce or abandon its state of military preparedness for war; renounce the use of (esp. nuclear) weapons. M18.

> A. J. AUGARDE Most governments refuse to disarm until their 'enemies' disarm.

▸ **B** *noun.* Chiefly FENCING. The action of disarming or forcing a weapon from the hand of an opponent. E19.
■ **disarmer** *noun* (*a*) a person who disarms; (*b*) a person who advocates or campaigns for (esp. nuclear) disarmament: M17. **disarming** *ppl adjective* that disarms a person; charmingly persuasive, winsome: M19. **disarmingly** *adverb* E20.

disarmament /dɪs'ɑːməm(ə)nt/ *noun.* L18.
[ORIGIN from DISARM + -MENT, after ARMAMENT and French *désarmement*.]
The action of disarming; *esp.* the reduction or abandonment of a state of military preparedness for war; the renunciation of specified weapons, by a nation.
NUCLEAR *disarmament*. *unilateral disarmament*: see UNILATERAL 2a.

disarray /dɪsə'reɪ/ *noun.* LME.
[ORIGIN Anglo-Norman *dissairay*, Old French *desaroi* (mod. *désarroi*), formed as DIS- 2, ARRAY *noun*.]
1 The state of being out of any regular order; disorder, confusion. LME.

> E. FIGES Sitting . . with her hair in disarray. *Times* This is the second year that the meeting has ended in disarray.

2 Imperfect or incorrect dress. *arch.* L16.

disarray /dɪsə'reɪ/ *verb trans.* LME.
[ORIGIN from DIS- 2 + ARRAY *verb*, perh. after Old French *desare(i)er*, *desaroier*, from *desaroi*: see DISARRAY *noun*.]
1 Throw into disorder or confusion; make untidy. LME.
2 Undress; strip (*of* clothing, any adjunct). L15.

> SHELLEY My song, its pinions disarrayed of might, drooped.

disassemble /dɪsə'sɛmb(ə)l/ *verb.* E17.
[ORIGIN from DIS- 2 + ASSEMBLE.]
†**1** *verb trans.* Separate, scatter, disperse. *rare.* Only in E17.
2 *verb trans.* Take (a machine etc.) to pieces, dismantle. E20.
3 *verb intrans.* Undergo disassembly; separate into constituent elements. M20.
■ **disassemblage** *noun* = DISASSEMBLY L20. **disassembler** *noun* (COMPUTING) a program for converting machine code into assembly language L20. **disassembly** *noun* the action of disassembling M20.

disassociate /dɪsə'səʊʃɪeɪt, -sɪ-/ *verb trans.* E17.
[ORIGIN from DIS- 2 + ASSOCIATE *verb*.]
= DISSOCIATE 1. (Foll. by *from*.)

> *Times* Efforts to disassociate their country from the attempt to murder the Pope.

■ ˌ**disassoci'ation** *noun* the action of disassociating; the fact of being disassociated; dissociation: L19.

D

disaster /dɪ'zɑːstə/ *noun* & *verb.* L16.
[ORIGIN French *désastre* or its source Italian *disastro*, from *dis-* DIS- 2 + *astro* star (from Latin *astrum*). Cf. *ill-starred*.]
▸ **A** *noun.* **1** (A) sudden or great misfortune; an event of ruinous or distressing nature, a calamity; complete failure. L16.

> D. FRASER Disaster always brought out the best in Churchill. *Daily Telegraph* The Houghton Main colliery disaster in which five miners died.

†**2** An unfavourable aspect of a star or planet. E–M17.
– COMB.: **disaster area**: in which a major disaster has recently occurred; **disaster movie** *colloq.* a film whose plot centres on a major disaster such as a fire, air crash, etc.
▸ **B** *verb trans.* Bring disaster on; ruin; cause serious injury to. Usu. in *pass.* Now *rare.* L16.

disastrous /dɪ'zɑːstrəs/ *adjective.* L16.
[ORIGIN French *désastreux* from Italian *disastroso*, from *disastro* DISASTER: see -OUS.]
†**1** Struck by or subject to disaster; ill-fated; unlucky. L16–E19.

> J. MARSTON He prov'd alwaies desastrous in love.

2 Presaging disaster, ill-omened; unpropitious. *arch.* E17.
3 Of the nature of a disaster, calamitous; attended with disaster. E17.

> M. EDWARDES A mass exodus of dealers would have been as disastrous as a major strike.

■ **disastrously** *adverb* E17.

disattire /dɪsə'tʌɪə/ *verb trans.* Long *rare.* L15.
[ORIGIN from DIS- 2 + ATTIRE *verb*.]
Undress.

disauthorize /dɪs'ɔːθərʌɪz/ *verb trans.* Long *rare.* Also **-ise**. M16.
[ORIGIN from DIS- 2 + AUTHORIZE.]
Strip of authority; make or treat as of no authority.

disavail /dɪsə'veɪl/ *verb trans.* & †*intrans.* Now *rare* or *obsolete*. LME.
[ORIGIN from DIS- 2 + AVAIL *verb*.]
Be disadvantageous or harmful (to).

disavow /dɪsə'vaʊ/ *verb trans.* LME.
[ORIGIN Old French & mod. French *désavouer*, formed as DIS- 2 + AVOW *verb*¹.]
1 Disclaim knowledge of, responsibility for, or approval of; disown, repudiate. LME.

> P. ACKROYD He was later to disavow the book, and never allowed any part to be reprinted.

†**2** Refuse to admit or acknowledge as true or valid; deny. E–M17.
†**3** Refuse to accept or *to do*. E–M17.
■ **disavowable** *adjective* liable or able to be disavowed L19. **disavowal** *noun* the action of disavowing, repudiation, (a) denial M18.

disband /dɪs'band/ *verb.* L16.
[ORIGIN French †*desbander* (now *dé-*), from *des-* DIS- 2, BAND *noun*³.]
▸ **I** *verb trans.* **1** Break up the organization of (a band or company); dissolve and dismiss from service (a military force etc.). L16. ▸†**b** Discharge from a band or company. Only in 17.
†**2** Let loose; turn out; send away. E17–L18.
†**3** Break up the coherence of, disintegrate. L17–L18.
▸ **II** *verb intrans.* **4** Break up as a body of soldiers or an organization; cease to be a band or company; break rank, disperse; leave military service. L16.

> J. SPEED The rest disbanded, turned their backes, and fled toward the desert.

†**5** Disintegrate; separate *from* a group. M–L17.
■ **disbandment** *noun* E18.

disbar /dɪs'bɑː/ *verb*¹ *trans.* Infl. **-rr-**. M16.
[ORIGIN from DIS- 1 + BAR *verb*.]
Exclude; prevent; = DEBAR.
– NOTE: Recorded again M20 after being obsolete since L16.

disbar /dɪs'bɑː/ *verb*² *trans.* Infl. **-rr-**. M17.
[ORIGIN from DIS- 2 + BAR *noun*¹.]
Expel from the bar; deprive (a lawyer) of legal status and privileges.
■ **disbarment** *noun* M19.

†**disbark** *verb*¹ *trans.* & *intrans.* M16–M19.
[ORIGIN French †*desbarquer* (now *dé-*: cf. DEBARK *verb*¹), formed as DIS- 2 + *barque* BARK *noun*³.]
= DISEMBARK.

disbark /dɪsˈbɑːk/ *verb*² *trans.* L16.
[ORIGIN from DIS- 2 + BARK *noun*².]
= DEBARK *verb*².

disbelief /dɪsbɪˈliːf/ *noun.* L17.
[ORIGIN from DIS- 2 + BELIEF. Superseded *misbelief.*]
The action or an act of disbelieving; mental rejection of a statement; positive unbelief.

W. E. H. LECKY A disbelief in ghosts. A. MACLEAN I stared at Judith Haynes in disbelief.

suspend disbelief: see SUSPEND 4.

disbelieve /dɪsbɪˈliːv/ *verb.* M17.
[ORIGIN from DIS- 2 + BELIEVE. Superseded *misbelieve.*]
1 *verb trans.* Refuse to believe (a person, statement, etc.). M17.

H. HALLAM To disbelieve such a contemporary witness as Sir Thomas More. W. S. CHURCHILL His warning was disbelieved.

2 *verb intrans.* Be a sceptic; have no belief or faith *in*. M18.

SOUTHEY It is not possible to hear and disbelieve. G. B. SHAW To disbelieve in marriage is easy.

■ **disbeliever** *noun* M17.

disbench /dɪsˈbɛn(t)ʃ/ *verb trans.* E17.
[ORIGIN from DIS- 2 + BENCH *noun*.]
†**1** Unseat. *rare* (Shakes.). Only in E17.
2 Deprive of the status of a bencher. L19.

disboard /dɪsˈbɔːd/ *verb intrans. rare.* E17.
[ORIGIN Old French *desborder* (mod. *dé-*), from *des-* DIS- 2 + *bord* BOARD *noun*.]
= DISEMBARK.

disbowel /dɪsˈbaʊəl/ *verb trans.* Infl. **-ll-**, ***-l-**. LME.
[ORIGIN from DIS- 2 + BOWEL *noun*.]
= DISEMBOWEL.

disbranch /dɪsˈbrɑːn(t)ʃ/ *verb trans.* L16.
[ORIGIN from DIS- 2 + BRANCH *noun*.]
1 Cut or break off the branches of. L16.
2 Cut or break off; sever. E17.

disburden /dɪsˈbəːd(ə)n/ *verb.* Also (*arch.*) **-burthen** /-ˈbəːð(ə)n/. M16.
[ORIGIN from DIS- 2 + BURDEN *noun*.]
1 *verb trans.* Remove a burden from; relieve of a burden. M16.

GEO. ELIOT The need . . to disburden her mind. P. DE VRIES A case I simply could not seem to close, drop, resolve, or otherwise disburden myself of.

2 *verb trans.* Get rid of (a burden); discharge, unload. L16.

J. PORY This small river . . disburdeneth it selfe into the sea not farre from the city. ADDISON Lucia, disburden all thy cares on me.

3 *verb intrans.* Discharge its load. M17.
■ **disburdenment** *noun* E19.

disburse /dɪsˈbəːs/ *verb & noun.* M16.
[ORIGIN Old French *desbourser* (mod. *débourser*), formed as DIS- 2, BURSE. Cf. DEBURSE.]
▸ **A** *verb.* **1** *verb trans.* Pay out (money). M16.
2 *verb trans.* Pay money to meet (an expense or cost), defray. M16.
†**3** *verb trans.* Give out or away. L16–L17.
4 *verb intrans.* Pay money. E17.
▸ †**B** *noun.* = DISBURSEMENT. E17–L18.
■ **disbursal** *noun* = DISBURSEMENT L16. **disbursement** *noun* the action or an act of disbursing; (an amount of) money paid out: L16. **disburser** *noun* E17.

disburthen *verb* see DISBURDEN.

disc /dɪsk/ *noun.* Also (*US & COMPUTING* now the usual form) **disk**. M17.
[ORIGIN French *disque* or its source Latin DISCUS.]
1 The seemingly flat round form that the sun, moon, and other celestial objects present to the eye; any similar round luminous shape. M17.
2 = DISCUS 1. *obsolete* exc. *hist.* E18.
3 A flat circular object thin in relation to its diameter. E18. ▸**b** A sound or video recording in the form of a disc; a gramophone record or compact disc. L19. ▸**c** *COMPUTING.* A data-storage device in the form of a disc with a prepared, usu. magnetizable, surface. M20.

G. GROTE Whether the earth was a disk or a sphere. B. MALAMUD A peephole at eye level covered by a metal disc.

4 *BOTANY & ZOOLOGY.* A roundish flattened part in a plant or animal; *spec.* (in a composite flower head with two types of floret) the inner, closely packed, tubular florets round which the outer, ligulate florets (ray) are arranged. E18. ▸**b** *ANATOMY.* The layer of cartilage and pulp between successive vertebrae. L19.
– PHRASES ETC.: ***black disc***: see BLACK *adjective*. ***compact disc***: see COMPACT *adjective* 1. *FLOPPY* ***disk***. ***hard disk***: see HARD *adjective*. ***imaginal disc***: see IMAGINAL *adjective*². ***minifloppy disk***: see MINI. ***optic disc***: see OPTIC *adjective*. ***optical disk***: see OPTICAL *adjective*. **slipped disc** an intervertebral disc that has become displaced or prolapsed and can cause pain, weakness, or paralysis by pressure on nerves or the spinal cord. ***videodisc***: see VIDEO *adjective & noun*.
– COMB.: **disc brake**: that uses disc-shaped friction surfaces; **disc camera**: in which the images are formed on a disc, not on a roll of film; **disc floret** any of the tubular florets forming the disc in certain composite plants (see sense 4 above); **disc harrow**: with concave cutting discs at an oblique angle; **disc jockey** a person who introduces and plays recorded music on a radio programme etc.; **disc parking** a system in which parked vehicles must display a disc showing time of arrival or latest permitted time of departure; **disk drive** *COMPUTING* a device with a read/write head and means for rotating a disk or disk pack; **disk emulator** *COMPUTING* a program that enables part of a memory to be used as if it were a disk; **disk pack** *COMPUTING* an assembly of disks on a common spindle inside a removable protective cover; **disc wheel** a bicycle wheel with a central disc in place of spokes.
■ **discless** *adjective* M19. **disclike** *adjective* resembling a disc, disc-shaped L19.

disc /dɪsk/ *verb trans. & intrans.* Chiefly *US & NZ*. Also **disk**. L19.
[ORIGIN from the noun.]
Cultivate with a disc harrow or similar implement.

discal /ˈdɪsk(ə)l/ *adjective.* M19.
[ORIGIN from Latin DISCUS + -AL¹.]
Of, pertaining to, or of the nature of, a disc; discoid.

discalceate /dɪsˈkalsɪət/ *adjective & noun.* M17.
[ORIGIN Latin *discalceatus*, formed as DIS- 2 + *calceatus* pa. pple of *calceare* to shoe, from *calceus* shoe: see -ATE².]
▸ **A** *adjective.* Barefoot; wearing sandals as the only footwear. M17.
▸ **B** *noun.* A discalceate friar or nun. Now *rare* or *obsolete*. M17.

discalceate /dɪsˈkalsɪeɪt/ *verb trans. & intrans.* E17.
[ORIGIN Late Latin *discalceat-* pa. ppl stem of *discalceare*, formed as DIS- 2 + Latin *calceare*: see DISCALCEATE *adjective & noun*, -ATE³.]
Take off the shoes (of). Chiefly as ***discalceated*** *ppl adjective.*

discalced /dɪsˈkalst/ *adjective.* M17.
[ORIGIN from *discalceated* (see DISCALCEATE *verb*) after French *déchaux*.]
= DISCALCEATE *adjective*.

discant *noun, verb* vars. of DESCANT *noun, verb*.

discard /ˈdɪskɑːd/ *noun.* M18.
[ORIGIN from the verb.]
1 *CARDS.* The action or an act of discarding a card; a discarded card. M18.
ruff and discard: see RUFF *noun*² 3.
2 *gen.* **a** The act of rejecting, abandoning, or discharging. L18. ▸**b** A rejected, abandoned, or discharged person or thing. L19.
a into the discard, **to the discard** into oblivion or disuse.

discard /dɪˈskɑːd/ *verb.* L16.
[ORIGIN from DIS- 2 + CARD *noun*², after French †*de(s)carter*.]
1 *verb trans. & intrans. CARDS.* Throw out or reject (a card) from a hand. Also, play (a card) from a remaining suit when not following suit or trumping. L16.
2 *verb trans.* Cast aside; reject; abandon; give up. L16.

E. TAYLOR Things she had eagerly collected not very long ago and would soon discard.

3 *verb trans.* Dismiss from employment, service, or office; discharge. L16.

SWIFT My man . . is a sad dog; and the minute I come to Ireland I will discard him.

■ **discardable** *adjective* L20. **discarder** *noun* L19. **discardment** *noun* (*rare*) abandonment M19.

discarnate /dɪsˈkɑːnət/ *adjective.* LME.
[ORIGIN from DIS- 2 + Latin *caro*, *carn-* flesh, or late Latin *carnatus* fleshy: see -ATE².]
†**1** Stripped of flesh. *rare.* LME–M17.
2 Separated from the flesh or the body; disembodied. L19.
■ **discarˈnation** *noun* E20.

discectomy /dɪsˈkɛktəmi/ *noun.* Also ***disk-**. L20.
[ORIGIN from DISC *noun* + -ECTOMY.]
Surgical removal of (part of) an intervertebral disc; an instance of this.

discept /dɪˈsɛpt/ *verb intrans. rare.* M17.
[ORIGIN Latin *disceptare*, formed as DIS- 1 + *captare* try to catch.]
Dispute, debate; express disagreement.

disceptation /dɪsɛpˈteɪʃ(ə)n/ *noun. arch.* LME.
[ORIGIN Old French, or its source Latin *disceptatio(n-)*, from *disceptat-* pa. ppl stem of *disceptare*: see DISCEPT, -ATION.]
(A) disputation, (a) debate.

discern /dɪˈsəːn/ *verb.* Also †**decern**. LME.
[ORIGIN Old French & mod. French *discerner* from Latin *discernere*, formed as DIS- 1 + *cernere* to separate. Conf. with DECERN.]
†**1** *verb trans.* Mark as separate or distinct; distinguish. LME–M17.
2 *verb intrans.* Perceive or recognize the difference or distinction *between*. *arch.* LME.
3 *verb trans. &* (now *rare*) *intrans.* Distinguish (one thing or fact) by the intellect; recognize or perceive distinctly. LME. ▸**b** *verb intrans.* Have cognizance, judge *of*. Now *rare* or *obsolete*. E17.

S. BELLOW I had learned to discern the real Kitty. A. N. WILSON Fiona had instantly discerned that he had been lying to her.

4 *verb trans. &* (*rare*) *intrans.* Distinguish by the sight (or another sense); make out by looking. LME.

A. WILSON Meg, as November fogs thickened . . could not discern the outlines of the Cathedral.

5 *verb trans.* Recognize; distinguish or separate mentally. *arch.* L15.

J. RUSKIN Not having yet the taste to discern good Gothic from bad.

■ **discerner** *noun* E16. **discerning** *adjective* that discerns; showing discernment, *esp.* having quick or true insight: L16. **discerningly** *adverb* with discernment M17.

discernible /dɪˈsəːnɪb(ə)l/ *adjective.* Also (earlier) **-able**. M16.
[ORIGIN from DISCERN + -ABLE; later conformed to Latin *discernibilis*: see -IBLE.]
1 Able to be discerned; perceptible. M16.
†**2** Distinguishable (*from* something else). Only in 17.
■ **discernibleness** *noun* E18. **discernibly** *adverb* M17.

discernment /dɪˈsəːnm(ə)nt/ *noun.* Also †**decern-**. L16.
[ORIGIN from DISCERN + -MENT.]
†**1** The act of distinguishing; a distinction. L16–M17.
2 The faculty of discerning, discrimination; keenness of intellectual perception; insight. L16.
3 The act of discerning; intellectual perception. L17.

B. JOWETT The savage . . has a quicker discernment of the track than the civilized man.

discerp /dɪˈsəːp/ *verb trans.* Now *rare*. Pa. t. & pple **discerped**, **-pt**. LME.
[ORIGIN Latin *discerpere*, formed as DIS- 1 + *carpere* pick, pluck, etc.]
1 Tear or pluck to pieces. LME.
2 Tear or pluck off or out; sever (*from*). Cf. earlier DECERP. M17.

†**discerpible** *adjective.* M17–E18.
[ORIGIN from DISCERP + -IBLE.]
= DISCERPTIBLE.
– NOTE: Survived longer (–M19) in INDISCERPIBLE.
■ †**discerpibility** *noun* L17–E18.

discerptible /dɪˈsəːptɪb(ə)l/ *adjective. literary.* M18.
[ORIGIN from Latin *discerpt-* pa. ppl stem of *discerpere* (see DISCERP) + -IBLE.]
Able to be plucked apart or divided into parts; not indestructibly one.
■ **discerptiˈbility** *noun* M18.

discerption /dɪˈsəːpʃ(ə)n/ *noun.* Now *rare*. M17.
[ORIGIN Late Latin *discerptio(n-)*, formed as DISCERPTIBLE: see -ION.]
1 The action of pulling to pieces; fragmentation. M17.
2 The action of tearing off, severance; a portion torn off or severed. L17.

discette *noun* var. of DISKETTE.

discharge /ˈdɪstʃɑːdʒ, dɪsˈtʃɑːdʒ/ *noun.* LME.
[ORIGIN from the verb.]
1 The act of freeing from obligation, liability, or restraint; exoneration from accusation or blame; release from a responsibility or position, or from service; release from custody; dismissal from office or employment. LME. ▸**b** Something that frees from obligation; a certificate of this; a receipt. LME.

b DEFOE I sent for a notary, and caused him to draw up a general release or discharge.

DISHONOURABLE ***discharge***. *HONOURABLE* ***discharge***. ***undesirable discharge***: see UNDESIRABLE *adjective*.
2 The act of freeing from or removing a load; unloading (*of* a ship etc.); removal (*of* a cargo etc.). L16.
3 The act of firing a weapon or missile, letting fly an arrow, etc. L16.
4 Fulfilment, execution, (of an obligation, duty, etc.). L16.

L. TRILLING He charges women not to interfere with men in the discharge of their cultural duty.

5 The act of settling a monetary liability; payment. E17.

T. JEFFERSON The discharge of the debt . . is vital to the destinies of our government.

6 The act of sending or pouring out; ejection; (the rate or amount of) emission. E17. ▸**b** That which is emitted, esp. from a wound etc. L17. ▸**c** The release of a quantity of electricity from a charged object; a flow of electricity through the air or other gas, esp. when accompanied by luminosity. M18. ▸**d** The place where a river enters the sea or a lake. L18.

SHAKES. *A.Y.L.* The wretched animal heav'd forth such groans That their discharge did stretch his leathern coat Almost to bursting. **c** *fig.*: A. STORR Whether there is, in animals or humans, an internal accumulation of aggressive tension which needs periodic discharge.

c *TOWNSEND* ***discharge***.
7 Formerly, the act of sending away. Now only in *LAW*, dismissal or reversal of a court order. L17.
8 *ARCHITECTURE.* The relieving of some part of weight or pressure; a structure for effecting this. E18.
9 The process of removing the colour from a fabric; a mixture used for this. M19.
– COMB.: **discharge lamp**, **discharge tube**: producing light by means of an electric discharge.

discharge /dɪsˈtʃɑːdʒ/ *verb.* ME.
[ORIGIN Old French *descharger* (mod. *dé-*) from late Latin *discar(r)icare* unload, from Latin DIS- 2 + late Latin *car(ri)care*: see CHARGE *verb*.]

▸ **I** With the person or thing relieved as (notional) obj.
1 *verb trans.* Relieve *of* (an obligation etc.); exonerate; release *from*; relieve (a bankrupt) of residual liability. **ME.** ▸†**b** Relieve (oneself) of an obligation by fulfilling it. **L16–E18.**

SHAKES. *Much Ado* I discharge thee of thy prisoner.

2 a *verb trans. & intrans.* Unload (a ship etc.); relieve of a load; disburden. **LME.** ▸**b** *verb trans.* Rid, deprive, (*of*). Now *rare*. **LME.** ▸**c** *verb trans.* Disburden (oneself) by speech. **E16.** ▸**d** *verb trans. & intrans.* Eject a projectile from (a weapon), fire (a weapon). **M16.** ▸**e** *verb trans. & intrans.* Release an electric charge (from). **M18.**

c E. BOWEN He could not discharge himself of what he had come out to say.

3 *verb trans.* Command not to do something; prohibit, forbid. *obsolete* exc. *dial.* **LME.**
4 *verb trans.* Relieve of a responsibility or position; release from service; dismiss from office or employment. **LME.**

EVELYN Being.. discovered to be a rampant Socinian, he was discharged of employment.

†**5** *verb trans.* Clear of a charge or accusation; acquit. **LME–M18.**
6 *verb trans.* Dismiss (a person charged with an offence); release from custody. **M16.** ▸**b** Send away; let go. **M16.**

A. PATON The guilt of the second and third accused is not established, and they will be accordingly discharged. **b** B. BAINBRIDGE Pamela was discharged from hospital.

7 *verb trans.* ARCHITECTURE. Relieve (some part) of pressure by distributing it over adjacent parts. **M17.**
▸ **II** With the thing removed as (notional) obj.
8 *verb trans.* Acquit oneself of (an obligation) by fulfilment or performance; pay (a debt etc.). **LME.** ▸†**b** Pay for (an item); settle with (a creditor). **M16–M19.** ▸†**c** Account for, explain. *rare* (Spenser). Only in **L16.**
9 *verb trans.* Remove or have removed (a cargo or load). **L15.** ▸**b** *verb trans. & intrans.* Let fly (a missile, blow, etc.); fire (a shot). **E16.** ▸**c** *verb trans. & intrans.* (Allow to) escape or flow out; pour forth, emit; (of a river) empty (itself), flow *into*. **E17.**

c SHAKES. *Macb.* Infected minds To their deaf pillows will discharge their secrets. ANTHONY HUXLEY Oil is discharged all over the oceans.. by ships cleaning out tanks.

10 *verb trans.* †**a** Remove, abolish, (an obligation, institution, liability, etc.). **E16–L18.** ▸**b** LAW. Cancel, annul, (a court order). **L18.**
11 *verb trans.* Acquit oneself of, perform, (an obligation, office, function, etc.). **M16.**
12 a *verb trans.* Remove (dye) *from* a textile etc.; pattern (a textile) by removing parts of the ground colour. **E18.** ▸**b** *verb intrans.* Of ink, dye, etc.: be washed out, run when wet. **L19.**
■ **dischargeable** *adjective* **LME.** **dischar'gee** *noun* a person who has been discharged **L19.** **discharger** *noun* a person who or thing which discharges; *spec.* an apparatus for producing an electric discharge: **M16.**

discharm /dɪsˈtʃɑːm/ *verb intrans. & trans. rare.* **L15.**
[ORIGIN Old French *de(s)charmer*, from *des-* DIS- 2 + *charmer* CHARM *verb*[1].]
Undo, or free from the influence of, a charm.

†**dischurch** *verb trans.* **E17.**
[ORIGIN from DIS- 2 + CHURCH *noun*.]
1 Deprive of the character of a church. **E17–L19.**
2 Exclude from the Church. **M–L17.**

disci- /ˈdɪsi, ˈdɪski/ *combining form* of Latin DISCUS: see -I-.
■ **disciform** *adjective* disc-shaped, discoidal **M19.** **di'scigerous** *adjective* (BOTANY) bearing a disc or discs **L19.**

†**discide** *verb trans.* **L15–L17.**
[ORIGIN Latin *discidere*, formed as DIS- 1 + *caedere* to cut.]
Cut in pieces; cut off or away.

SPENSER Her lying tongue was in two parts divided.. And as her tongue so was her hart discided.

discinct /dɪˈsɪŋkt/ *adjective. rare.* **M17.**
[ORIGIN Latin *discinctus* pa. pple of *discingere* undo the belt or girdle of.]
Not (tightly) girt; *fig.* unconfined.

disciple /dɪˈsʌɪp(ə)l/ *noun.* **OE.**
[ORIGIN Latin *discipulus* learner, from *discere* learn; reinforced in Middle English by Old French *deciple*.]
1 One of the personal followers of Jesus during his life; *spec.* one of the twelve Apostles. **OE.** ▸**b** In the New Testament, any early believer in Christ. Hence, in later religious use, a professed Christian. **LME.**

AV *John* 20:20 Then were the disciples glad, when they saw the Lord.

b Disciples (of Christ) a Protestant denomination, found chiefly in the US, which rejects creeds and regards the Bible as the only basis of faith.

2 *gen.* A personal follower of a religious or other teacher. **OE.**

L. TRILLING Alfred Adler was.. an early disciple of Freud's who broke away from his master.

3 A follower of another person's example or doctrine; an adherent of a leader in thought, art, or conduct. **ME.**

P. H. GIBBS She became a disciple of his liberal creed. G. S. FRASER In his clear, direct way of writing more a disciple of Jonson than of Donne.

4 A student, a pupil. Now *arch.* or *joc.* **ME.**
■ **disciplehood** *noun* (now *rare*) = DISCIPLESHIP **LME.** **discipleship** *noun* the status of being a disciple **M16.**

disciple /dɪˈsʌɪp(ə)l/ *verb trans.* **L16.**
[ORIGIN from the noun.]
1 Train, educate. Long *rare.* **L16.**

SPENSER Fraile youth is oft to follie led.. That better were in vertues discipled.

2 Make a disciple of; *spec.* convert to Christianity. *arch.* **E17.**
†**3** Subject to discipline or chastisement. **E17–E19.**

disciplinable /ˈdɪsɪplɪnəb(ə)l, dɪsɪˈplɪn-/ *adjective.* **LME.**
[ORIGIN Late Latin *disciplinabilis* to be learned by teaching, from *disciplinare* instruct: see DISCIPLINE *verb*, -ABLE.]
1 Amenable to instruction or training. **LME.**
2 Subject or liable to disciplinary action. **L19.**

disciplinal /ˈdɪsɪplɪn(ə)l, dɪsɪˈplʌɪn(ə)l/ *adjective.* **E17.**
[ORIGIN In sense 1, from late Latin *disciplinalis*; in sense 2, from DISCIPLINE *noun* + -AL[1].]
†**1** = DISCIPLINABLE 1. Only in **E17.**
2 Belonging to or of the nature of discipline. **M19.**

J. G. FITCH Disciplinal problems of a boarding-school.

disciplinant /ˈdɪsɪplɪnənt/ *noun.* **E17.**
[ORIGIN Spanish *disciplinantes* (pl.) or Italian *disciplinanti* (pl.), from medieval Latin *disciplinare* DISCIPLINE *verb*: see -ANT[1].]
ECCLESIASTICAL HISTORY. A member of a Spanish order of flagellants.

disciplinarian /ˌdɪsɪplɪˈnɛːrɪən/ *noun & adjective.* In ECCLESIASTICAL HISTORY **D-.** **L16.**
[ORIGIN formed as DISCIPLINARY + -AN: see -ARIAN.]
▸ **A** *noun.* **1** ECCLESIASTICAL HISTORY. An Elizabethan Puritan who supported the Genevan or Presbyterian ecclesiastical polity. **L16.**
2 A person who maintains or advocates (strict) discipline in an army, school, etc. **M17.**

H. MELVILLE Three of these officers.. were strict disciplinarians.

▸ **B** *adjective.* **1** ECCLESIASTICAL HISTORY. Of or belonging to the Disciplinarians (see sense A.1 above). **L16.**
2 Pertaining to discipline; disciplinary. **M17.**
■ **disciplinarianism** *noun* the principles and practice of a disciplinarian **M19.**

disciplinary /ˈdɪsɪplɪn(ə)ri, dɪsɪˈplɪn-/ *adjective.* **L15.**
[ORIGIN medieval Latin *disciplinarius*, from Latin *disciplina*: see DISCIPLINE *noun*, -ARY[1].]
1 Relating to ecclesiastical discipline (DISCIPLINE *noun* 6); formerly *spec.*, = DISCIPLINARIAN *adjective* 1. **L15.**
2 Pertaining to the acquisition of learning. **L15.**
3 Pertaining to, promoting, or enforcing disciplined behaviour. **L16.**

G. B. SHAW He [a private soldier] is taught his proper place by appropriate disciplinary measures. *Daily Mirror* The Test and County Cricket Board's disciplinary committee.

■ **disciplinarily** *adverb* (*rare*) **E18.**

disciplinatory /ˈdɪsɪplɪˌneɪt(ə)ri, dɪsɪˈplɪnət(ə)ri/ *adjective.* **M19.**
[ORIGIN medieval Latin *disciplinatorius*, from Latin *disciplinat-* pa. ppl stem of *disciplinare* DISCIPLINE *verb*: see -ORY[2].]
Tending to promote discipline.

discipline /ˈdɪsɪplɪn/ *noun.* **ME.**
[ORIGIN Old French & mod. French from Latin *disciplina*, from *discipulus* DISCIPLE *noun*.]
1 Chastisement or correction undergone as a penance, self-mortification. Also, a beating or similar punishment. **ME.** ▸**b** A scourge or whip, esp. as an instrument of penance. **E17.**

J. SERGEANT If any be found unchast, she receives three Disciplines or scourgings.

2 †**a** Instruction given to pupils or disciples; teaching, education. **LME–E17.** ▸**b** A particular course of discipleship or corpus of doctrines. *rare.* **M17.**
b Discipline of the Secret the practice ascribed to the early Church of excluding catechumens and pagans from certain doctrines and rites.
3 A branch of learning or scholarly instruction. **LME.**

Lancet Disciplines such as biochemistry and immunology.

4 Instruction fitting one to perform an activity; training. Freq. *fig.*, moral progress brought about by adversity etc. **LME.** ▸**b** *spec.* Training in military exercises etc.; drill. Formerly, knowledge of military tactics; the art of war. **LME.** ▸†**c** Medical treatment, regimen. *rare.* **M18–E19.**
5 Controlled and orderly behaviour resulting from training. **E16.** ▸**b** The system of order and strict obedience to rules enforced among pupils, soldiers, or others under authority; a particular instance of this. **M17.**

H. H. KITCHENER It will be your duty.. to set an example of discipline and perfect steadiness under fire. **b** F. MARRYAT A flagrant.. violation of discipline. M. PATTISON The inmates.. were submitted to an almost monastic discipline. M. EDWARDES Taking the company as a whole discipline was lax.

6 The system by which a Church maintains order and exercises control over its members. **M16.** ▸**b** The system by which the practices of a Church (as opp. to its doctrines) are regulated; *spec.* (ECCLESIASTICAL HISTORY) the Calvinist polity, adopted by the Presbyterians and Puritans. **M16.**

discipline /ˈdɪsɪplɪn/ *verb trans.* **ME.**
[ORIGIN Old French & mod. French *discipliner* or late Latin *disciplinare*, from Latin *disciplina* DISCIPLINE *noun*.]
1 Scourge or flog as a penance or in self-mortification; *gen.* thrash, chastise. **ME.**

SHAKES. *Coriol.* Has he disciplin'd Aufidius soundly?

2 Give instruction to, educate, train. Now *rare.* **LME.**
3 Train in habits of obedience, bring under control; *spec.* drill (troops). **L16.**

C. BRONTË Suppose you were no longer a girl well reared and disciplined, but a boy indulged from childhood. A. J. P. TAYLOR An alliance of men with widely differing views, not a disciplined army.

4 Subject (esp. a member of a Church or other organization) to formal rebuke, loss of privileges, etc., for an offence. **E19.**

New York Times If McEnroe was not harshly disciplined by tennis officials for his disruptive antics.

■ **discipliner** *noun* **LME.**

discipular /dɪˈsɪpjʊlə/ *adjective.* **M19.**
[ORIGIN from Latin *discipulus* DISCIPLE *noun* + -AR[1].]
Of, belonging to, or of the nature of a disciple.

discission /dɪˈsɪʃ(ə)n/ *noun.* **M17.**
[ORIGIN Late Latin *discissio(n-)*, from Latin *disciss-* pa. ppl stem of *discindere* split in two, formed as DIS- 1 + *scindere* cleave, tear.]
An act of tearing or cutting apart. Now only SURGERY, an incision, esp. into the lens of the eye in a case of cataract.

disclaim /dɪsˈkleɪm/ *noun.* Now *rare.* **LME.**
[ORIGIN Anglo-Norman *disclaime*, from *disclamer*: see DISCLAIM *verb*.]
A (formal) denial or repudiation of a claim.

disclaim /dɪsˈkleɪm/ *verb.* **LME.**
[ORIGIN Anglo-Norman *desclaim-* tonic stem of *desclamer*, *dis-* (Anglo-Latin *disclamare*), from *des-* DIS- 1 + *clamer* CLAIM *verb*.]
▸ **I** *verb intrans.* **1** LAW. Renounce one's claim to something; repudiate another's claim; make a formal disclaimer. (Foll. by †*in* the thing disclaimed, †*from* or †*out of* the claim of the other party.) **LME.**
†**2** Renounce all part *in*; express one's withdrawal or dissent *from*. **M16–M17.**

JONSON The sourer sort Of shepherds now disclaim in all such sport.

†**3** Cry out or declaim *against*. **E17–M18.**
▸ **II** *verb trans.* **4** Renounce all (legal) claim to. **LME.** ▸**b** Relinquish (part of a patent) by a disclaimer (DISCLAIMER *noun*[1] 1b). **M19.**
5 Deny one's possession of or connection with; disown, disavow. **L16.** ▸†**b** Refuse to acknowledge (a person) to be (so and so). **L16–L17.**

T. HEYWOOD Sir, shee's yours, Or I disclaime her ever. I. D'ISRAELI The real author.. obliged him afterwards to disclaim the work in print. D. HAMMETT He.. disclaimed any knowledge of his client's whereabouts. **b** I. WALTON To perswade him.. to disclaim himself a Member of the Church of England.

†**6** Attack the pretensions of. **L16–M17.**
†**7** Decline, refuse, *to do.* **L16–E19.**
8 Refuse to admit (something claimed by another); reject the authority of. **M17.** ▸**b** HERALDRY. Declare to have no right to bear a coat of arms. **M17.**

GIBBON The troops.. disclaimed the command of their superiors.

■ **disclaimant** *noun* (LAW) a person who disclaims (esp. part of a patent specification) **L19.**

disclaimer /dɪsˈkleɪmə/ *noun*[1]. **LME.**
[ORIGIN Anglo-Norman *disclaimer* inf. used as noun: see DISCLAIM *verb*, -ER[4].]
1 LAW. The action or an act of repudiating another's claim or renouncing one's own; refusal to accept a trust etc. **LME.** ▸**b** An alteration by which a patentee amends specification so as to relinquish part of his or her claim to an invention. **M19.**
2 *gen.* A denial of a claim, pretension, etc.; a disavowal. **L18.**

E. WAUGH The Bishop.. believes I am a secret envoy from the Pope and laughs away all my disclaimers as modesty and guile.

3 HERALDRY. An announcement by heralds of people not entitled to armorial bearings. **M19.**

disclaimer /dɪsˈkleɪmə/ *noun*[2]. **E18.**
[ORIGIN from DISCLAIM *verb* + -ER[1].]
A person who disclaims or renounces something.

D

disclamation /dɪsklə'meɪʃ(ə)n/ *noun*. M16.
[ORIGIN medieval Latin *disclamatio(n-)*, from *disclamat-* pa. ppl stem of *disclamare*: see DISCLAIM *verb*, -ATION.]
1 *SCOTS LAW*. A feudal tenant's disavowal of a person as a superior. M16.
2 *gen.* Repudiation; a disclaimer. E17.

†**disclose** *noun*. M16–M18.
[ORIGIN from the verb.]
The act of disclosing; (a) disclosure.

disclose /dɪs'kləʊz/ *verb*. LME.
[ORIGIN Old French *desclos-* pres. stem of *desclore* from Proto-Gallo-Romance, from Latin DIS- 2 + *claudere* CLOSE *verb*.]
†1 *verb trans. & intrans.* Open up (something closed or folded up); unclose, unfold. LME–E18.
B. GOOGE It [a rosebud] discloseth it selfe and spreadeth abroad.
2 *verb trans.* Remove the cover from; expose to view. LME. ▸b Hatch (a young bird etc., *fig.* mischief). Now *rare* or *obsolete*. LME.
H. JAMES The .. portal remained ajar, disclosing possible vistas. W. BOYD Small sharp teeth disclosed by a mouth continually parted in a smile.
3 *verb trans.* Make known, reveal. LME.
H. ADAMS The Normans .. disclose most unexpected qualities. E. WAUGH Inquiries .. disclosed that a young lady .. had appeared in the booking office early that afternoon.
†4 *verb intrans.* Come to light. L15–M18.
■ **disclosed** *ppl adjective* (*a*) that has been disclosed; (*b*) *HERALDRY* (of a non-predacious bird) depicted with wings outspread: L15. **discloser** *noun* M16. **disclosing** *ppl adjective* (*a*) that discloses; (*b*) *DENTISTRY* (of a tablet, solution, etc.) revealing, by means of a special dye, any plaque on the teeth: E17.

disclosure /dɪs'kləʊʒə/ *noun*. L16.
[ORIGIN from DISCLOSE *verb* + -URE, after *closure*.]
1 The action or an act of making known or visible. L16.
J. I. M. STEWART There had still been no public disclosure of the state of the tower.
2 The hatching of young from the egg; the liberation of an insect from the pupa. Now *rare* or *obsolete*. M17.
3 That which is disclosed; a revelation. E19.

disco /'dɪskəʊ/ *noun & verb*. M20.
[ORIGIN Abbreviation of DISCOTHÈQUE.]
▸ **A** *noun*. Pl. **-os**.
1 A place or event at which recorded pop music is played for dancing. M20.
2 More fully ***disco music***. Pop music of the kind played at discos, with a heavy bass beat. L20.
▸ **B** *verb intrans.* Dance at a disco or in the style characteristic of discos. L20.

discobolus /dɪ'skɒbələs/ *noun*. Pl. **-li** /-lʌɪ, -liː/. E18.
[ORIGIN Latin from Greek *diskobolos*, formed as DISCUS + *-bolos* throwing, from *ballein* to throw.]
CLASSICAL HISTORY. A discus-thrower; a statue representing one in action.

discography /dɪ'skɒgrəfi/ *noun*. M20.
[ORIGIN from DISC *noun* + -OGRAPHY.]
A catalogue of sound recordings; *esp.* a compilation of the recordings of a particular artist or composer.
■ **discographer** *noun* M20. **disco'graphical** *adjective* M20.

discoid /'dɪskɔɪd/ *adjective & noun*. L18.
[ORIGIN Greek *diskoeidēs*, from *diskos*: see DISCUS, -OID.]
▸ **A** *adjective*. Disc-shaped; *BOTANY* (of a plant of the composite family) bearing flowers consisting of a disc without rays. L18.
▸ **B** *noun*. A disc-shaped structure. E19.
■ **di'scoidal** *adjective* discoid E18.

discolor *noun, verb* see DISCOLOUR *noun, verb*.

discolorate /dɪs'kʌləreɪt/ *verb trans. rare*. Also **-lour-**. M17.
[ORIGIN medieval Latin *discolorat-*: see DISCOLORATION, -ATE³.]
= DISCOLOUR *verb* 1.

discoloration /dɪsˌkʌlə'reɪʃ(ə)n, ˌdɪsk-/ *noun*. Also **-lour-**. M17.
[ORIGIN French (now *décoloration*), or medieval Latin *discoloratio(n-)*, from *discolorat-* pa. ppl stem of *discolorare* DISCOLOUR *verb*: see -ATION.]
1 The action of discolouring; the state of being discoloured; alteration or loss of colour. M17.
2 A discoloured marking etc., a stain. L17.

discolour /dɪs'kʌlə/ *noun*. Now *rare*. Also ***-color**. LME.
[ORIGIN from DIS- 2 + COLOUR *noun*.]
= DISCOLORATION.

discolour /dɪs'kʌlə/ *verb*. Also ***-color**. LME.
[ORIGIN In senses 1 & 2 from Old French *descolorer* or medieval Latin *discolorare*, from Latin *colorare* COLOUR *verb*; in sense 3 from Latin *discolor* adjective, from *color* COLOUR *noun*: see DIS- 2, 3.]
1 *verb trans.* Change or spoil the colour of; *esp.* make duller or dingier; stain, tarnish. LME.
fig.: R. L. STEVENSON We had each of us some whimsy .. which discoloured all experience to its own shade.
2 *verb intrans.* Become discoloured; lose or change colour. LME.
†3 *verb trans.* Cause to be of various colours. Chiefly as ***discoloured*** *ppl adjective*. L15–M17.
■ **discolourment** *noun* the action or result of discolouring, discoloration. E19.

discolourate *verb* **discolouration** *noun* vars. of DISCOLORATE, DISCOLORATION.

discombobulate /dɪskəm'bɒbjʊleɪt/ *verb trans. N. Amer. slang*. Also **-boberate** /-'bɒbəreɪt/ & other vars. M19.
[ORIGIN Prob. alt. of *discompose* or *discomfit*.]
Disturb, upset, disconcert.
■ ˌ**discombobu'lation** *noun* M19.

discomfit /dɪs'kʌmfɪt/ *verb & noun*. ME.
[ORIGIN Old French *desconfit* pa. pple of *desconfire* (mod. *déconfire*) from Proto-Romance, from Latin DIS- 2 + *conficere* put together, destroy, consume, formed as CON- + *facere* do.]
▸ **A** *verb trans.* **1** Defeat in battle; beat, rout. *arch.* ME.
2 Baffle, thwart, defeat the plans, hopes, or purposes of; throw into confusion, disconcert, embarrass. LME.
R. SHARROCK Not impeded by those wants that usually discomfit private persons in such enquiries. W. STYRON He seemed flustered, discomfited.
▸ †**B** *noun*. Discomfiture. ME–M19.
■ **discomfiter** *noun* E16.

discomfiture /dɪs'kʌmfɪtʃə/ *noun*. ME.
[ORIGIN Old French *desconfiture* (mod. *déconfiture*), formed as DISCOMFIT; see -URE.]
1 Complete defeat in battle, rout. *arch.* ME.
SHAKES. *1 Hen. VI* Sad tidings .. Of loss, of slaughter, and discomfiture.
2 Defeat or frustration of plans, hopes, or purposes; utter disappointment; confusion, embarrassment. LME.
D. WELCH Laughing to cover up my discomfiture.

discomfort /dɪs'kʌmfət/ *noun*. LME.
[ORIGIN Old French *desconfort* (mod. *dé-*), formed as DISCOMFORT *verb*.]
†1 Loss or deprivation of courage; discouragement, disheartenment. LME–M16.
†2 Absence or deprivation of comfort, pleasure, or gladness; distress, grief, sorrow; annoyance. Also, something that causes this. LME–M19.
LONGFELLOW Thus did that poor soul wander in want and cheerless discomfort.
3 Uneasiness of body or mind; lack of comfort (*lit.* & *fig.*). Also, something which makes one uncomfortable, an inconvenience, a hardship. M19.
E. BAKKER Her towering over him added to his discomfort. P. THEROUX The journey was not worth this discomfort.

discomfort /dɪs'kʌmfət/ *verb trans.* ME.
[ORIGIN Old French *desconforter* (mod. *dé-*), formed as DIS- 2, COMFORT *verb*.]
▸ **I** †1 Deprive of courage or strength of mind; dishearten, dismay. ME–E18.
2 Deprive of comfort, pleasure, or gladness; distress, sadden; make unhappy. *arch.* ME.
3 Make uneasy or uncomfortable in mind or body. M19.
▸ **II 4** = DISCOMFIT *verb*. LME.
■ **discomforter** *noun* E19.

discomfortable /dɪs'kʌmf(ə)təb(ə)l/ *adjective*. Now *rare*. LME.
[ORIGIN Old French *desconfortable*, formed as DISCOMFORT *verb*: see -ABLE.]
1 Causing discouragement, distress, annoyance, etc.; destructive of comfort, pleasure, or happiness. LME.
R. L. STEVENSON Singing was their refuge from discomfortable thoughts.
†2 Marked by an absence of comfort or happiness; miserable. E16–E17.
3 Lacking in material comfort; causing physical discomfort. E17.
4 Of a person: feeling uncomfortable, uneasy. *rare*. M19.
■ **discomfortableness** *noun* L16. **discomfortably** *adverb* E17.

discomforture /dɪs'kʌmfətʃə/ *noun*. *rare*. LME.
[ORIGIN from DISCOMFORT *verb* + -URE, after DISCOMFITURE.]
Distress; (a) discomfort. Also, discomfiture.

discommend /dɪskə'mɛnd/ *verb*. LME.
[ORIGIN from DIS- 2 + COMMEND *verb*.]
1 *verb trans. & intrans.* Find fault (with), express disapproval (of). LME.
2 *verb trans.* Speak dissuasively of; advise against the use etc. of. M16.
3 *verb trans.* Cause to be received or looked on unfavourably. Now *rare* or *obsolete*. L16.
■ **discommendable** *adjective* (*a*) worthy of censure; †(*b*) not to be recommended: E16. **disˌcommen'dation** *noun* the action or an act of discommending L16.

discommodate /dɪs'kɒmədeɪt/ *verb trans.* Long *rare*. E17.
[ORIGIN Prob. alt. of INCOMMODATE.]
Inconvenience, incommode.

discommode /dɪskə'məʊd/ *verb trans.* E18.
[ORIGIN French †*discommoder* var. of *incommoder* INCOMMODE *verb*: see DIS- 2.]
Put to inconvenience; disturb, trouble.

discommodious /dɪskə'məʊdɪəs/ *adjective*. Long *rare*. M16.
[ORIGIN from DIS- 2 + COMMODIOUS.]
Causing trouble or inconvenience; disadvantageous, troublesome.
■ **discommodiously** *adverb* M17. **discommodiousness** *noun* L16.

discommodity /dɪskə'mɒdɪti/ *noun*. E16.
[ORIGIN from DIS- 2 + COMMODITY, perh. infl. by INCOMMODITY.]
1 The quality of being unsuitable or inconvenient. E16.
2 A disadvantage, an inconvenience. M16.

discommon /dɪs'kɒmən/ *verb trans.* LME.
[ORIGIN from DIS- 2 + COMMON *noun, adjective*: cf. also COMMON *verb*.]
†1 Cut off from membership of a community; disfranchise; excommunicate. LME–M17.
2 In the universities of Oxford and Cambridge: deprive (a tradesman) of the right to deal with undergraduates. Now *hist.* M16.
3 Deprive of the right of common; deprive (land) of the status of a common, enclose. L16.

discommons /dɪs'kɒmənz/ *verb trans.* Now *hist.* M19.
[ORIGIN from DIS- 2 + COMMONS *noun pl.*]
1 Deprive (an undergraduate) of commons. M19.
2 = DISCOMMON 2. M19.

discommune /dɪs'kɒmjuːn/ *verb trans.* L16.
[ORIGIN from DIS- 2 + COMMUNE *verb* or *noun*¹, after medieval Latin *discommunicare*.]
1 = DISCOMMON 1. Long *rare*. L16.
2 = DISCOMMON 2. Now *hist.* L17.

discompose /dɪskəm'pəʊz/ *verb trans.* L15.
[ORIGIN from DIS- 2+ COMPOSE.]
1 Disturb the composure of; ruffle, agitate. L15.
J. SMEATON Not a breath of wind discomposed the surface of the water.
2 Disturb the order or arrangement of; throw into confusion. Now *rare* or *obsolete*. E17.
MILTON Unwak'ned Eve With Tresses discompos'd.
†3 Make ill or indisposed. Chiefly as ***discomposed*** *ppl adjective*. L17–E18.
■ **discomposedly** /-zɪdli/ *adverb* in a discomposed manner E17. **discomposedness** /-zɪdnɪs/ *noun* disturbed state, disquietude L17. **discomposingly** *adverb* in a way that discomposes L19.

discomposure /dɪskəm'pəʊʒə/ *noun*. E17.
[ORIGIN from DISCOMPOSE after COMPOSURE.]
1 Disorder, confusion; disarrangement. Now *rare* or *obsolete*. E17.
MILTON The Prelates .. put all things into a foule discomposure.
†2 Indisposition, ill health. M17–M18.
3 Disturbance of mind or feelings; agitation, perturbation. M17.
LD MACAULAY A series of sermons was preached .. by Popish divines, to the great discomposure of zealous churchmen.

†**disconcert** *noun*. *rare*. M17–M19.
[ORIGIN from DIS- 2+ CONCERT *noun*.]
Lack of agreement or concerted action, disunity in action; an instance of this.

disconcert /dɪskən'səːt/ *verb*. L17.
[ORIGIN French *desconcerter* (now *dé-*), formed as DIS- 2, CONCERT *verb*.]
1 *verb trans.* Upset the progress or action of; spoil plans for, defeat expectations of. L17.
LD MACAULAY The scheme was .. completely disconcerted by the course which the civil war took.
2 *verb trans.* Disturb the self-possession of; ruffle, fluster. E18. ▸b *verb intrans.* Disturb self-possession, be upsetting. Chiefly as ***disconcerting*** *ppl adjective*. E19.
B. PYM He was disconcerted to find that he had lost his place. b *Smart Set* A baffling reserve, a poise that disconcerted. Q. BELL She could do disconcerting things—calmly throw a pair of scissors into the fire.
■ **disconcertedly** *adverb* in a disconcerted manner M19. **disconcertingly** *adverb* in a manner that disconcerts one L19. **disconcertion** *noun* = DISCONCERTMENT L18. **disconcertment** *noun* the action of disconcerting; the state of being disconcerted: M19.

disconformable /dɪskən'fɔːməb(ə)l/ *adjective*. L16.
[ORIGIN from DIS- 2 + CONFORMABLE.]
†1 *gen.* Not conformable. L16–E19.
2 *GEOLOGY*. Containing or constituting a disconformity. E20.

disconformity /dɪskən'fɔːmɪti/ *noun*. L16.
[ORIGIN from DIS- 2 + CONFORMITY.]
1 Complete lack of agreement or correspondence; nonconformity. (Foll. by *to*, *with*.) L16.
2 *GEOLOGY*. An unconformity in which the strata above and below are more or less parallel, the lower set having been eroded but not deformed. E20.

disconnect /dɪskə'nɛkt/ *verb & noun*. L18.
[ORIGIN from DIS- 2 + CONNECT.]
▸ **A** *verb trans.* **1** Break the connection of or between; *spec.* terminate the connection of (a device, household, etc.) to an electricity etc. supply or a telephone network. (Foll. by *from*, †*with*.) L18.

T. HOOD It was impossible to disconnect him with old clothes and oranges. G. SWIFT I disconnect the television, carry it out to the car.

†**2** Separate into individual components, fragment. (Cf. DISCONNECTED *adjective* 2.) L18–E19.

▸ **B** *noun*. **1** An instance of disconnecting or being disconnected. M20.

Science There is a disconnect in the system.

2 A lack of understanding, agreement, or connection; a discrepancy. L20.

Guardian (online ed.) There is a disconnect between broad public opinion and legislative action.

■ **disconnectable** *adjective* M20. **disconnecter**, **-or** *noun* a device for breaking a connection L19.

disconnected /dɪskəˈnɛktɪd/ *ppl adjective*. L18.
[ORIGIN from DISCONNECT + -ED[1].]
1 Having no connection (*with*); detached (*from*); separated. L18.

HANNAH MORE The chronology being reduced to disconnected dates, instead of presenting an unbroken series.

2 Having constituent parts badly connected; (of speech, a speaker, etc.) incoherent, rambling. L19.
■ **disconnectedly** *adverb* M19. **disconnectedness** *noun* L19.

disconnection /dɪskəˈnɛkʃ(ə)n/ *noun*. Also (earlier) **-connexion**. M18.
[ORIGIN from DISCONNECT after *connection*.]
The state or fact of being disconnected; lack of connection, disconnectedness; the action of disconnecting.

disconsolate /dɪsˈkɒns(ə)lət/ *adjective & verb*. LME.
[ORIGIN medieval Latin *disconsolatus*, from Latin DIS- 2 + *consolatus* pa. pple of *consolari* CONSOLE *verb*.]
▸ **A** *adjective*. **1** Without consolation or comfort; forlorn, inconsolable; unhappy, disappointed. LME.

C. C. TRENCH The death of the Queen . . was a sad blow to Caroline, who had to return disconsolate to Anspach.

2 Of a place, thing, etc.: causing or showing a complete lack of comfort; cheerless, miserable. LME.

DEFOE A desolate, disconsolate wilderness. O. MANNING She made a disconsolate little gesture.

▸ †**B** *verb trans*. Make disconsolate; deprive of consolation. M16–M18.
■ **disconsolately** *adverb* M17. **disconsolateness** *noun* M17. **disconsoˈlation** *noun* disconsolate condition L16. †**disconsolatory** *adjective* (*rare*) that makes disconsolate, saddening M17–E19.

discontent /dɪskənˈtɛnt/ *noun*[1]. L16.
[ORIGIN from DIS- 2 + CONTENT *noun*[1].]
1 Lack of content; a feeling of dissatisfaction. L16. ▸†**b** Annoyance, displeasure. Only in 17.
2 A feeling of discontent. L16.
†**3** A cause of discontent, a grievance. E–M17.
■ **discontentful** *adjective* (*arch.*) E17.

discontent /dɪskənˈtɛnt/ *adjective & noun*[2]. Now *rare*. LME.
[ORIGIN from DIS- 2 + CONTENT *adjective*: cf. French †*descontent*.]
▸ **A** *adjective*. **1** Discontented; dissatisfied. LME.

Times Non-Christian groups in Britain which are discontent with state schooling.

†**2** Displeased, annoyed. L15–M17.
▸ **B** *noun*[2]. A discontented person, a malcontent. L16.

discontent /dɪskənˈtɛnt/ *verb trans*. L15.
[ORIGIN from DIS- 2 + CONTENT *verb*: cf. French †*descontenter*.]
1 Displease, annoy. Now *rare*. L15.
2 Deprive of contentment; make dissatisfied; unsettle through frustration, disappointment, etc. Chiefly as ***discontented*** *ppl adjective*. E16.
■ †**discontentation** *noun* = DISCONTENT *noun*[1] 1, 3 M16–M18. **discontentedly** *adverb* in a discontented manner L16. **discontentedness** *noun* discontent, dissatisfaction L16. **discontentment** *noun* (*a*) = DISCONTENT *noun*[1] 1, 2; †(*b*) = DISCONTENT *noun*[1] 3: L16.

discontinuance /dɪskənˈtɪnjʊəns/ *noun*. LME.
[ORIGIN Anglo-Norman *discontinuaunce*, Old French *-ance*, formed as DISCONTINUE: see -ANCE.]
1 The action of discontinuing; temporary or permanent interruption; cessation. LME. ▸**b** The interruption or cessation of a lawsuit by the plaintiff. M16.
2 LAW. The loss of the right of possession or entry by an heir to an estate following its wrongful alienation by a deceased tenant. Now *hist*. LME.
†**3** Temporary absence from a place, *spec*. one's home. Only in 17.

discontinuation /ˌdɪskəntɪnjʊˈeɪʃ(ə)n/ *noun*. E17.
[ORIGIN Old French & mod. French from medieval Latin *discontinuatio(n-)*, from *discontinuat-* pa. ppl stem of *discontinuare*: see DISCONTINUE, -ATION.]
= DISCONTINUANCE 1.

discontinue /dɪskənˈtɪnjuː/ *verb*. LME.
[ORIGIN Old French & mod. French *discontinuer* from medieval Latin *discontinuare*, from Latin DIS- 2 + *continuare* CONTINUE *verb*.]
▸ **I** *verb trans*. †**1** Break the continuity of; interrupt, disrupt, sunder. LME–L18.

J. RAY This bank of earth . . is discontinued by seven . . breaks or apertures.

2 Cause to cease existing or being done, put a stop to; cease from (an action or habit); stop taking (a periodical) or paying (a subscription). Formerly also in LAW, dismiss or abandon (a suit). LME.

M. SPARK Freddy decided to discontinue the lessons with Abdul.

†**3** LAW. Alienate (land etc.) so as to cause discontinuance. LME–E19.
†**4** Cease to frequent, occupy, or inhabit. L15–M17.

SHAKES. *Much Ado* I must discontinue your company.

▸ **II** *verb intrans*. **5** Cease to continue; cease, stop. LME.

J. BARET To discontinue a while from labour.

†**6** Be absent (*from*); cease to reside. Only in 17.

AV *Jer*. 17:4 Thou . . shalt discontinue from thine heritage that I gave thee.

■ **discontinuˈee** *noun* (*hist.*) a person to whom an estate was alienated in a case of discontinuance L16. **discontinuer** *noun* (*a*) a person who discontinues something; (*b*) *spec*. an absentee: L16. **discontinuor** *noun* (*hist.*) the tenant whose alienation of an estate caused a discontinuance L18.

discontinuity /ˌdɪskɒntɪˈnjuːɪti/ *noun*. L16.
[ORIGIN medieval Latin *discontinuitas*, formed as DISCONTINUOUS: see -ITY.]
1 The quality or state of being discontinuous; lack of continuity; interrupted condition. L16.
2 A break in continuity; an abrupt change in value; MATH. a point at which a function is discontinuous or undefined. L18.
discontinuity layer a layer of seawater etc. in which the temperature changes rapidly with depth.

discontinuous /dɪskənˈtɪnjʊəs/ *adjective*. M17.
[ORIGIN medieval Latin *discontinuus*, formed as DIS- 2, CONTINUOUS: cf. French *discontinu*.]
†**1** Producing discontinuity; breaking continuity between parts; gaping. M17–E18.

MILTON The griding sword with discontinuous wound Pass'd through him.

2 Not continuous in space or time; characterized by lack of continuity; having interstices or breaks; interrupted, intermittent. E18.

A. LURIE Are we persuading our readers to divide their lives into ever smaller, discontinuous bits?

discontinuous function MATH. that has one or more discontinuities (cf. ***continuous***).
■ **discontinuously** *adverb* in a discontinuous manner, without continuity M19. **discontinuousness** *noun* discontinuous condition, lack of continuity M19.

disconvenience /dɪskənˈviːnɪəns/ *noun & verb*. Now *dial*. LME.
[ORIGIN from DIS- 2 + CONVENIENCE *noun*, or alt. of INCONVENIENCE *noun*.]
▸ **A** *noun*. †**1** Lack of agreement or correspondence; incongruity, inconsistency. LME.
†**2** Unfitness, unsuitability, impropriety. LME–L16.
3 (A) disadvantage; (an) inconvenience. M16.
▸ **B** *verb trans*. Inconvenience. E19.

disconvenient /dɪskənˈviːnɪənt/ *adjective*. Now *dial*. LME.
[ORIGIN from DIS- 2 + CONVENIENT, or alt. of INCONVENIENT.]
†**1** Not in accordance (*with*); incongruous; unsuitable. LME–M17.
2 Inconvenient, disadvantageous. LME.

discophile /ˈdɪskəfʌɪl/ *noun*. Also **-phil** /-fɪl/. M20.
[ORIGIN from DISC *noun* + -O- + -PHILE.]
A person who collects or is interested in gramophone records or compact discs.

discord /ˈdɪskɔːd/ *noun*. ME.
[ORIGIN Old French *descord*, *dis-* (mod. *discord(e)*), formed as DISCORD *verb*.]
1 Disagreement between persons; dissension, strife. ME.

SHAKES. *1 Hen. VI* An age of discord and continual strife.

apple of discord.

2 Lack of agreement between things; difference, incongruity. LME.

R. MACAULAY This makes a discord in the mind, the happiness and the guilt . . pulling in opposite directions.

3 MUSIC. Lack of harmony between notes sounded together, dissonance; a chord, interval, or note producing this, *spec*. any interval except the unison, octave, perfect fifth and fourth, major and minor third and sixth, and their octave. Cf. CONCORD *noun*[1] 2b. LME.
4 A clashing of sounds, a confused noise; a harsh or unpleasing sound. L16.
■ **diˈscordful** *adjective* (*rare*) full of discord, quarrelsome L16. **discordous** *adjective* (long *rare*) discordant L16.

discord /dɪˈskɔːd/ *verb intrans*. ME.
[ORIGIN Old French *descorder*, (also mod.) *dis-*, from Latin *discordare* be at variance, from *discors*, *discord-* discordant, formed as DIS- 2 + *cor*, *cord-* heart.]
1 Be in disagreement, quarrel, (*with*); dissent (*from*). ME.

CARLYLE We discorded commonly on two points.

2 Of sounds: be discordant, clash. Now *rare*. ME.
3 Be different (*from*), be inconsistent (*with*). LME.

R. FABYAN Thyse two nacions discorde in maners, but nat in clothing and in fayth. S. HIERON Not because it accordeth or discordeth with the original.

discordance /dɪˈskɔːd(ə)ns/ *noun*. ME.
[ORIGIN Old French *descordance*, (also mod.) *dis-*, from medieval Latin *discordantia*, from Latin *discordare*: see DISCORD *verb*, -ANCE.]
1 (A) lack of agreement or conformity. ME.
2 (A) discord of sounds. LME.
■ Also **discordancy** *noun* E17.

D

discordant /dɪˈskɔːd(ə)nt/ *adjective & noun*. LME.
[ORIGIN Old French *descordant*, (also mod.) *dis-* pres. pple of *discorder*: see DISCORD *verb*, -ANT[1].]
▸ **A** *adjective*. **1** Not in accord; at variance; disagreeing, differing; incongruous. (Foll. by *from*, *with*, †*to*.) LME.

GLADSTONE Testimony . . in no case discordant with that of the Iliad.

2 *spec*. Of a sound or musical instrument: inharmonious, dissonant; jarring. LME.

J. C. POWYS A series of shrill discordant screams.

3 Living in discord, quarrelsome. M16.

WELLINGTON He united that discordant and turbulent race.

4 GEOLOGY. Having a direction that cuts across that of adjacent or underlying strata. E20.
▸ †**B** *noun*. In *pl*. Discordant things, attributes, or propositions. LME–M16.
■ **discordantly** *adverb* LME.

discothèque /ˈdɪskətɛk/ *noun*. Also **-theque**. M20.
[ORIGIN French, orig. = record-library, after *bibliothèque*: cf. DISC *noun* 3b.]
= DISCO *noun* 1.

discounsel /dɪsˈkaʊns(ə)l/ *verb trans*. Long *rare*. Infl. **-ll-**, ***-l-**. L15.
[ORIGIN Old French *desconseillier* (mod. *déconseiller*), formed as DIS- 2, COUNSEL *verb*.]
†**1** Dissuade (*from* a course of action). L15–E17.
2 Advise against (an action or undertaking). L16.

discount /ˈdɪskaʊnt/ *noun*. E17.
[ORIGIN French †*descompte* (earlier *desconte*, now *décompte*), from *descompter*: see DISCOUNT *verb*.]
†**1** *gen*. A reduction in the amount or in the gross value of something. E17–L18.
2 *spec*. A deduction (usu. a certain percentage) made from an amount due or a price in return for prompt or early payment, or offered to special customers; any deduction made from a nominal value or price. L17.
3 **a** The percentage (representing the interest on the payment) deducted from the face value of a bill of exchange or promissory note when it changes hands before the due date. L17. ▸**b** STOCK EXCHANGE. The amount by which the price of a stock falls short of its issue price or the value of the assets it represents; *gen*. the amount by which an actual price falls short of a nominal one. E18.
4 The action or an act of discounting a bill, note, etc. M19.
– PHRASES: **at a discount** at less than the nominal value or price; *fig*. in low esteem: opp. ***at a premium***. ***trade discount***: see TRADE *noun*.
– ATTRIB. & COMB.: In the sense 'regularly offering goods at less than the standard price', as ***discount shop***, ***discount store***, etc. Special combs., as **discount-broker** a person who procures the discounting of bills of exchange, usu. by acting as intermediary; a dealer in bills; **discount house** (*a*) in Britain, a firm specializing in buying and selling bills of exchange; (*b*) (chiefly *US*) a discount shop (see above).

discount /dɪsˈkaʊnt, ˈdɪskaʊnt/ *verb trans*. E17.
[ORIGIN French †*descompter* (mod. *décompter*), in commercial senses prob. from Italian (*di*)*scontare*, both from medieval Latin *discomputare*, from Latin DIS- 2 + *computare* COMPUTE *verb*.]
▸ **I** †**1** Deduct or regard as deducted, esp. from a sum due. E17–E19.
2 Buy or sell (a bill of exchange) at a discount (DISCOUNT *noun* 3). L17.
3 Reduce (a price); reduce in price; *esp*. sell (goods) at a discount. M20.
▸ **II** *fig*. **4** Leave out of account as unimportant or irrelevant; allow for falsehood or exaggeration in (statements). E18.

C. J. WILLS One learns to mentally discount the statements made by the natives. G. GREENE He gave me . . good advice which I was unwise enough to discount. W. GOLDING That was the least of the dangers . . and one almost to be discounted.

5 Reduce the effect of (a possible future event or sensation) by taking it into account beforehand. Also, part with (a future good) for some present consideration. M19.

G. BRIMLEY Discounting immortality for pottage.

■ **diˈscountable** *adjective* that may be discounted; (of a period) within which a bill may be discounted: E19. **diˈscounter** *noun* (*a*) a person who discounts a bill; (*b*) a person engaged in discount trading: M18.

D

discountenance /dɪˈskaʊntɪnəns/ *noun. arch.* L16.
[ORIGIN Partly from Old French *descontenance*; partly from DIS- 2 + COUNTENANCE *noun*, after DISCOUNTENANCE *verb*.]
The fact or an act of discountenancing; disfavour or disapprobation shown.

SHELLEY The discountenance which Government will show to such an association.

discountenance /dɪsˈkaʊnt(ə)nəns, -tɪn-/ *verb trans.* L16.
[ORIGIN from DIS- 2 + COUNTENANCE *noun*, partly after French †*descontenancer*.]
1 Put out of countenance, abash, embarrass. Chiefly as ***discountenanced*** *ppl adjective.* L16.
2 Discourage with cold looks, express disfavour of, (esp. an activity, practice, etc.); refuse to sanction or allow. L16.

G. ORWELL 'Mrs.' was a word somewhat discountenanced by the Party.

■ **discountenancer** *noun* E17.

discouple /dɪsˈkʌp(ə)l/ *verb trans.* Now *rare.* L15.
[ORIGIN Old French *descupler* (mod. *découpler*), formed as DIS- 2, COUPLE *verb*.]
End the pairing of, uncouple.

discourage /dɪsˈkʌrɪdʒ/ *verb trans.* LME.
[ORIGIN Old French *descouragier* (mod. *décourager*), formed as DIS- 2, COURAGE.]
1 Deprive of courage, confidence, hope, or the will to proceed; dishearten, deject. LME.

J. CONRAD This discouraged Schomberg, who had looked up hopefully. A. J. CRONIN It must be dreadfully discouraging, to meet always with abuse.

2 Dissuade or deter *from* (†*for*, †*to do*). LME.
3 Inhibit or seek to prevent (an action etc.) by expressing disapproval. M17.

J. YEATS Laws were made to discourage usury.

■ **discourager** *noun* M17. **discouragingly** *adverb* in a discouraging manner L17.

discouragement /dɪsˈkʌrɪdʒm(ə)nt/ *noun.* M16.
[ORIGIN Old French *descouragement* (mod. *dé-*), formed as DISCOURAGE: see -MENT.]
1 The state of being discouraged; lack of inclination to act or make an attempt. M16.
2 The action or fact of discouraging. E17.
3 A discouraging thing, event, or influence. E17.

E. WAUGH Too hasty publication would be a discouragement to you now.

discourse /ˈdɪskɔːs/ *noun.* LME.
[ORIGIN Latin *discursus* running to and fro, (in late Latin) intercourse, (in medieval Latin) argument, from *discurs-* pa. ppl stem of *discurrere*, formed as DIS- 1 + *currere* run; form assim. to COURSE *noun*[1].]
1 The process or faculty of reasoning. Also ***discourse of reason***. Now *rare* or *obsolete*. LME.

W. RALEIGH The Dog . . we see is plentifully furnished with inward discourse.

†**2** Onward course (in space or time). M16–E17.
3 a (An) exchange of words; (a) conversation, (a) talk. Now *literary* or *arch.* M16. ▸†**b** Conversational power. L16–M17. ▸†**c** Familiar intercourse; familiarity. *rare* (Shakes.). Only in E17.

a DEFOE I have had a long discourse with my father. C. C. TRENCH A blue-stocking who engaged in learned discourse with . . Leibnitz. **b** SHAKES. *Com. Err.* I know a wench of excellent discourse, Pretty and witty. **c** SHAKES. *Haml.* If you be honest and fair, your honesty should admit no discourse to your beauty.

†**4** An account, a narrative. L16–M17.
5 A formal discussion of a topic in speech or writing; a treatise, homily, etc. L16.
6 LINGUISTICS. A connected series of utterances, forming a unit for analysis etc. M20.
– PHRASES: ***universe of discourse***: see UNIVERSE 4.

discourse /dɪsˈkɔːs/ *verb.* M16.
[ORIGIN from the noun, partly after French *discourir*.]
▸ **I 1** *verb intrans.* Hold discourse; converse, confer. M16.

L. M. MONTGOMERY You needn't stop to discourse with sympathetic listeners.

2 *verb intrans.* Speak or write at length on a topic. M16.

A. POWELL Mr. Templar . . discoursed . . of redemption dates. A. MASON He discoursed with erudition . . on whatever subject they cared to raise.

3 *verb trans.* Go through in speech or writing, tell, relate; confer about, discuss. *arch.* M16. ▸†**b** Utter, say; speak or write formally. E17–M18. ▸**c** Give out (music). *arch.* E17.

R. WHITLOCK Alcibiades cut of his Dogs Taile . . that so the talkative people might lesse discourse his other Actions. **b** JAS. HARRIS The Joy . . in recollecting what we have discoursed on these Subjects.

4 *verb trans.* Address words to; converse with; harangue. Now *arch.* & *dial.* L16.
5 *verb trans.* While *away* (time) in conversation. E17.
▸ †**II 6** *verb trans.* Turn over in the mind. M16–M17.
7 *verb intrans.* Pass from premisses to conclusions; reason. L16–L17.

■ **discourser** *noun* M16.

†**discoursive** *adjective.* L16.
[ORIGIN from DISCOURSE *verb* + -IVE: cf. DISCURSIVE.]
1 Having the faculty of reason. L16–L17.
2 Proceeding by reason or argument. L16–M18.
3 Passing from one thing to another; discursive. L16–E18.
4 Fond of conversation, talkative; of the nature of dialogue, conversational. L16–M17.

discourteous /dɪsˈkəːtjəs/ *adjective.* L16.
[ORIGIN from DIS- 2 + COURTEOUS.]
Lacking in courtesy; uncivil, rude.
■ **discourteously** *adverb* L16. **discourteousness** *noun (rare)* E18.

discourtesy /dɪsˈkəːtəsi/ *noun.* M16.
[ORIGIN from DIS- 2 + COURTESY *noun*.]
Impoliteness, lack of courtesy; an instance of this, a discourteous act.

†**discous** *adjective.* Only in 18.
[ORIGIN from mod. Latin *discosus*, from Latin DISCUS: see -OUS.]
Having a disc; discoid.

discover /dɪˈskʌvə/ *verb.* ME.
[ORIGIN Old French *descovrir* (mod. *découvrir*) from late Latin *discooperire*, from Latin DIS- 2 + *cooperire* COVER *verb*[2].]
▸ **I 1** *verb trans.* Make known, divulge, disclose, (a secret etc.). *arch.* ME. ▸†**b** *verb intrans.* Reveal one's secrets, confess. LME–L17.

SHAKES. *Much Ado* The Prince discovered to Claudio that he loved my niece. J. DAVIES They contain some secrets which Time will discover.

2 *verb trans.* Disclose the identity of (a person); betray. *arch.* ME.

C. KINGSLEY He was on the point of discovering himself to them.

3 *verb trans.* Expose to view, allow to be seen. *arch.* in *gen.* sense. LME. ▸**b** CHESS. Give (check) by removing a piece which stands between the checking piece and the king. L15. ▸**c** THEATRICAL. Present (a character) in a given position on the stage when the curtain rises. Usu. in *pass.* L18.

POPE We stand discover'd by the rising fires. H. ALLEN A bowl of soup, . . white rolls, and a bottle of wine discovered themselves. **c** E. O'NEILL At the rise of the curtain Ruth is discovered sitting by the stove.

4 *verb trans.* Exhibit, display, (a quality, feeling, etc.), esp. in action. *arch.* LME.

POPE A lofty gentleman Whose . . gait discovered when he had published a new book. H. BELLOC The greatness of the English soul is best discovered in that strong rebuke of excesses.

†**5** *verb trans.* & *intrans.* Orig. MILITARY, reconnoitre. Later *gen.*, explore (territory). LME–M19.

W. H. PRESCOTT He was empowered to discover and occupy the country for the distance of two hundred leagues.

6 *verb trans.* Become aware of for the first time (a thing or person previously unknown or overlooked); find. Freq., be the first to observe (a new country, a scientific phenomenon, etc.). M16. ▸**b** Catch sight of, espy. *arch.* L16. ▸**c** *verb trans.* Perceive for the first time the attractions or merits of; *esp.* be the first to recognize the potential of (a film star etc.). E20.

H. BLAIR Harvey discovered the circulation of the blood. W. S. MAUGHAM Though the police had looked with care, they had discovered no fingerprints. R. LYND We shall, perhaps, discover that freedom is better when we cease to possess it. **b** F. BROOKE From the top of the hill you discover Aden. **c** R. CHURCH I spent the time reading an author whom I had newly discovered—Charles Dickens.

†**7** *verb intrans.* Have or obtain a view; look, see. L16–E18.
†**8** *verb trans.* & *intrans.* Discern; distinguish (*between*, *from*). E17–L18.
▸ †**II 9** *verb trans.* Remove the covering from; *esp.* uncover (the head), unroof (a building). LME–M19.
10 Take off (a covering). M16–M19.

AV *Jer.* 13:22 For the greatnesse of thine iniquitie are thy skirts discouered.

■ **discovera'bility** *noun* discoverable quality M19. **discoverable** *adjective* able to be discovered L16. **discoverably** *adverb* M17. **discoverer** *noun* †(*a*) a person who discloses secrets, an informer; †(*b*) a military scout or spy; (*c*) a person who finds out or discovers something previously unknown: ME.

discovert /dɪsˈkʌvət/ *adjective* & *noun.* LME.
[ORIGIN Old French *descovert* (mod. *découvert*) pa. pple of *descovrir*: see DISCOVER.]
▸ **A** *adjective.* †**1** Uncovered, exposed, unprotected. LME–E16.
2 LAW. Of a woman: without a husband, not covert (COVERT *adjective* 5). M18.
▸ †**B** *noun.* An exposed state. Chiefly in ***at discovert***, off one's guard. LME–L16.
■ **discoverture** *noun* †(*a*) *rare* an indication, a manifestation; (*b*) LAW the state of being discovert: L16.

discovery /dɪˈskʌv(ə)ri/ *noun.* M16.
[ORIGIN from DISCOVER + -Y[3], after *recover, recovery*.]
1 The action or an act of revealing something secret or not generally known; disclosure. Now *rare* exc. LAW, (a) compulsory disclosure by a party to an action of relevant facts or documents. M16. ▸†**b** (A) display, (a) manifestation, (of a feeling or quality). L16–M18.

W. BLACKSTONE The bankrupt . . is bound upon pain of death to make a full discovery of all his estate. **b** S. JOHNSON His companions . . could make no discovery of their ignorance or surprise.

2 The action or an act of finding or becoming aware of for the first time; *esp.* the first bringing to light of a scientific phenomenon etc. Also, detection of a person. M16.

W. S. LANDOR Shew me . . a discoverer who has not suffered for his discovery . . whether a Columbus or a Galileo. C. BRONTË Anxious . . to avoid discovery, I had . . resolved to assume an alias. D. H. LAWRENCE She had made a strange discovery.

3 (An) exploration, (a) reconnaissance. Now *rare* or *obsolete*. E17.

DEFOE I had a great desire to make a more perfect discovery of the island.

4 Something discovered or brought to light. E17. ▸**b** A person whose talents are recognized and made known for the first time. M20.

C. DARWIN The principle is a modern discovery.

†**5** Information or evidence that bring something to light. M17–E18.
6 (**D-**.) A dessert apple of a variety with crisp flesh and bright red skin. L20.
– COMB.: **discovery method** a method of education in which pupils are encouraged to acquire knowledge by their own investigations rather than by listening and reading; **discovery well** the first successful oil well in a new field.

discreate /dɪskrɪˈeɪt/ *verb trans.* L16.
[ORIGIN from DIS- 2 + CREATE *verb*.]
Reduce (something created) to nothing or chaos.
■ **discre'ation** *noun* E17.

discredit /dɪsˈkrɛdɪt/ *noun.* M16.
[ORIGIN from DIS- 2 + CREDIT *noun*, after Italian (*di*)*scredito*, French *discrédit*.]
1 Loss or lack of credit; impaired reputation; disrepute, disgrace; an instance of this. M16.

B. JOWETT Such conduct brings discredit on the name of Athens.

2 Loss or lack of belief or confidence; disbelief, distrust. M17.

GEO. ELIOT There were obvious facts that at once threw discredit on the printed document.

3 Loss or lack of commercial credit. M18.

discredit /dɪsˈkrɛdɪt/ *verb trans.* M16.
[ORIGIN from DIS- 2 + CREDIT *verb*, after Italian (*di*)*screditare*, French *discréditer*.]
1 Refuse to credit, disbelieve. M16.
2 Take away the credibility of; destroy confidence in; cause to be disbelieved. M16.

R. LYND This explanation . . has been discredited in recent years.

3 Injure the reputation of; bring into disrepute. L16.

discreditable /dɪsˈkrɛdɪtəb(ə)l/ *adjective.* M17.
[ORIGIN from DIS- 2 + CREDITABLE.]
Bringing discredit to; shameful, disgraceful.
■ **discredita'bility** *noun* L19. **discreditably** *adverb* M19.

discreet /dɪˈskriːt/ *adjective.* ME.
[ORIGIN Old French & mod. French *discret*, *-ète* from Latin *discretus* pa. pple of *discernere* DISCERN, with late Latin & Proto-Romance sense from its deriv. *discretio(n-)* DISCRETION. Cf. DISCRETE *adjective*.]
1 Showing discernment or judgement in speech or action; judicious, prudent; intentionally unobtrusive. ME.

T. HARDY You should be more discreet in your bearing towards this soldier. F. FORSYTH Offering to the investor a highly discreet and even secretive service in banking.

2 Civil, polite, courteous. Chiefly *Scot.* ME.
■ **discreetly** *adverb* ME. **discreetness** *noun* the quality of being discreet, discretion LME.

discrepance /dɪsˈkrɛp(ə)ns/ *noun.* LME.
[ORIGIN Old French, formed as DISCREPANT: see -ANCE.]
1 = DISCREPANCY. Now *rare*. LME.
†**2** Distinction, difference. E16–E17.

discrepancy /dɪsˈkrɛp(ə)nsi/ *noun.* E17.
[ORIGIN Latin *discrepantia*, formed as DISCREPANT: see -ANCY.]
The quality of being discrepant; lack of correspondence, disagreement; an instance of this; an inconsistency.

E. A. FREEMAN There is little or no discrepancy as to the facts. R. TRAVERS He remarked on the numerous discrepancies in Butler's stories. E. FROMM The discrepancy between behaviour and character.

discrepant /dɪsˈkrɛp(ə)nt/ *adjective.* LME.
[ORIGIN Latin *discrepant-* pres. ppl stem of *discrepare* be discordant, formed as DIS- 1 + *crepare* to creak: see -ANT[1].]
1 Exhibiting difference, dissimilarity, or lack of agreement; discordant, inconsistent. (Foll. by *from*, †*to*.) LME.

A. STORR Basic social assumptions may be so widely discrepant that communication becomes impossible.

†2 Apart or separate in space. *rare*. L16–E19.

discrepate /dɪsˈkrɛpeɪt/ *verb*. *rare*. L16.
[ORIGIN Latin *discrepat-* pa. ppl stem of *discrepare*: see DISCREPANT, -ATE[3].]
†1 *verb intrans.* Differ (*from*), be discrepant. L16–M17.
2 *verb trans.* & *intrans.* Distinguish (one *from* another, *between*). M19.
■ **discreˈpation** *noun* †(*a*) difference; (*b*) discrimination: LME.

discrete /dɪˈskriːt/ *adjective* & *noun*. LME.
[ORIGIN Latin *discretus*: see DISCREET.]
▸ **A** *adjective*. **1** Separate, detached from others; individually distinct; not continuous or coalescent. LME.

W. J. ONG If we wish to take each poem individually as a discrete object existing in its own right. V. GLENDINNING The Anglo-Irish do not even constitute a discrete nationality.

2 Consisting of or pertaining to distinct or individual parts; (of a magnitude or quantity) not continuously variable, taking only certain values. L16.

H. HALLAM Dealing with continuous or geometrical, not merely with discrete or arithmetical quantity. H. M. ROSENBERG The energy of the particle can only have certain special discrete values.

†**3** GRAMMAR & LOGIC. Of a conjunction: adversative. Of a proposition: disjunctive. E–M17.
4 Not concrete or material, abstract. M19.
▸ **B** *noun*. A separate part or item. L19.
■ **discretely** *adverb* E18. **discreteness** *noun* M19.

†**discrete** *verb trans.* M17–M19.
[ORIGIN Latin *discret-*: see DISCRETION.]
Divide into discrete parts; separate completely.

discretion /dɪˈskrɛʃ(ə)n/ *noun*. ME.
[ORIGIN Old French & mod. French *discrétion* from Latin *discretio(n-)* separation, (in late Latin & Proto-Romance) discernment, from *discret-* pa. ppl stem of *discernere* DISCERN: see -ION.]
†**1** The faculty of discerning. ME–M17.

HOBBES The Discretion of times, places, and persons necessary to a good Fancy.

2 a Ability to discern what is right, fitting, or advisable, esp. as regards one's own conduct; the quality of being discreet; prudence, sound judgement. ME. ▸**b** Propriety of behaviour; civility, courtesy. *Scot.* L18.

a CONAN DOYLE Dr. Watson is the very soul of discretion. A. STORR Professional discretion means that the therapist is virtually unable to discuss his work with his family.

3 The action of discerning or judging; judgement; decision, discrimination. *obsolete* exc. in phrs. and as passing into sense 4. LME.

C. WHITEHEAD She put it to Myte's discretion whether he would continue to harbour a young knave.

4 Freedom to decide or act as one thinks fit, absolutely or within limits; having one's own judgement as sole arbiter. LME. ▸**b** LAW. A court's degree of freedom to decide a sentence, costs, procedures, etc. LME.

S. RAVEN It is at our discretion to make exceptions to the general rule.

†**5** With possess. adjective (as ***your discretion*** etc.): a title of respect to a bishop (or nobleman). LME–E16.
6 The action or result of separating or distinguishing; separation, disjunction, distinction. LME.
– PHRASES: **age of discretion** the age at which one is considered fit to manage one's affairs or take responsibility for one's actions. **at the discretion of** (to be settled or disposed of) according to the judgement or choice of. **use one's discretion** exercise one's judgement (rather than follow a prescribed rule etc.). **years of discretion** = ***age of discretion*** above.
■ **discretional** *adjective* discretionary M17. **discretionally** *adverb* M17. **discretionarily** *adverb* at one's discretion L17. **discretionary** *adjective* (*a*) pertaining to discretion, left to discretion; ***discretionary income***, income remaining after deduction of taxes, other mandatory charges, and expenditure on necessary items (cf. ***disposable income*** s.v. DISPOSABLE *adjective* 2); †(*b*) discreet: L17.

discretive /dɪˈskriːtɪv/ *noun* & *adjective*. L15.
[ORIGIN Late Latin *discretivus* serving to distinguish, from *discret-*: see DISCRETION, -IVE. Cf. Old French *discretif*, *-ive*.]
▸ †**A** *noun*. Something discretive; *spec.* a disjunctive conjunction or proposition. L15–E18.
▸ **B** *adjective*. **1** = DISJUNCTIVE *adjective*. L16.
†**2** Serving to distinguish or discriminate. E17–E19.
■ **discretively** *adverb* M17. **discretiveness** *noun* M19.

discretization /dɪˌskriːtʌɪˈzeɪʃ(ə)n/ *noun*. Also **-isation**. M20.
[ORIGIN from DISCRETE *adjective* + -IZATION.]
The process of making or the state of being discrete; *spec.* (MATH.), (a) representation or approximation by means of a discrete quantity.
■ **diˈscretize** *verb trans.* M20.

discriminable /dɪˈskrɪmɪnəb(ə)l/ *adjective*. M18.
[ORIGIN from DISCRIMINATE *verb* + -ABLE, after *separate* verb, *separable*.]
Able to be discriminated; distinguishable.
■ **discriminaˈbility** *noun* E20. **discriminably** *adverb* M20.

discriminal /dɪˈskrɪmɪn(ə)l/ *adjective*. *rare*. L17.
[ORIGIN Late Latin *discriminalis* serving to divide or separate, from Latin *discrimen*, *-min-*: see DISCRIMINATE *verb*, -AL[1].]
PALMISTRY. Designating the line on the palm between the hand and the arm.

discriminant /dɪˈskrɪmɪnənt/ *adjective* & *noun*. M19.
[ORIGIN Latin *discriminant-* pres. ppl stem of *discriminare* DISCRIMINATE *verb*: see -ANT[1].]
▸ **A** *adjective*. **1** Discriminating; showing discrimination or discernment. M19.
2 STATISTICS. Designating a function of several variates that is used to give the best classification of items for which values of the variates are available. M20.
▸ **B** *noun*. **1** MATH. A function derived from another function and providing information about its behaviour. M19.
2 *gen.* That which enables discrimination; a distinguishing feature, *spec.* a discriminant function. E20.

discriminate /dɪˈskrɪmɪnət/ *adjective*. E17.
[ORIGIN Latin *discriminatus* pa. pple, formed as DISCRIMINATE *verb*: see -ATE[2]. Cf. earlier INDISCRIMINATE.]
1 Distinct, distinguished. *arch.* E17.
2 Marked by discrimination or discernment; making careful or exact distinctions. E19.

T. R. MALTHUS Much may be done by discriminate charity.

■ **discriminately** *adverb* L18. **discriminateness** *noun* E18.

discriminate /dɪˈskrɪmɪneɪt/ *verb*. E17.
[ORIGIN Latin *discriminat-* pa. ppl stem of *discriminare*, from *discrimen*, *-min-* division, distinction, from *discernere* DISCERN: see -ATE[3].]
1 *verb trans.* Make or constitute a difference in or between; distinguish, differentiate. E17.

G. GROTE Capacities which discriminate one individual from another.

2 *verb trans.* Distinguish with the mind; perceive the difference in or between. M17.

I. BARROW We take upon us . . to discriminate the goats from the sheep. *Nature* Hearing in insects may discriminate the frequency, the intensity and the direction of the sound.

3 *verb intrans.* Make or recognize a distinction, esp. a fine one; provide or serve as a distinction; exercise discernment. L18.

H. T. BUCKLE It is by reason, and not by faith, that we must discriminate in religious matters. *Scientific American* A simple energy measurement serves to discriminate between the two kinds of event.

4 *verb intrans.* Make a distinction in the treatment of different categories of people or things, esp. unjustly or prejudicially *against* people on grounds of race, colour, sex, social status, age, etc. L19.

M. TWAIN To be discriminated against on account of my nationality. R. NIEBUHR Educational suffrage tests . . would discriminate in favour of the educated Negro against the servile, old-time Negro. L. P. HARTLEY We asked everyone we could, . . we didn't discriminate.

■ **discriminating** *ppl adjective* (*a*) constituting a distinction, affording ground for distinction; (*b*) perceiving or making distinctions with sensitivity, discerning: M17. **discriminatingly** *adverb* M19. **discriminatory** *adjective* discriminative; *esp.* practising or evincing racial, sexual, or similar discrimination: E19.

discrimination /dɪˌskrɪmɪˈneɪʃ(ə)n/ *noun*. M17.
[ORIGIN Late Latin *discriminatio(n-)*, formed as DISCRIMINATE *verb*: see -ATION.]
1 The action or an act of discriminating or distinguishing; the fact or condition of being discriminated or distinguished; a distinction made. M17. ▸**b** *spec.* The practice or an instance of discriminating against people on grounds of race, colour, sex, social status, age, etc.; an unjust or prejudicial distinction. L19. ▸**c** PSYCHOLOGY. The perception of a difference between two stimuli, esp. as evidenced by a different reaction to each. L19.

G. STANHOPE A perfect Discrimination shall then be made between the Good and Bad. I. MURDOCH He loves trouble, his own or other people's without discrimination. **b** A. G. GARDINER No people which tolerates titles, and so deliberately sets up social discriminations in its midst. B. SCHWARTZ A profound change . . in the attitude of that tribunal [the US Supreme Court] toward racial discrimination. M. L. KING The personal torment of discrimination cannot be measured. *Times* Employers who have cheated women of equal pay by job-grading schemes . . may be taken to court for sex discrimination. G. CLARE Officially there was no discrimination against Jews.

b *positive discrimination*: see POSITIVE *adjective*. ***reverse discrimination***: see REVERSE *adjective*.
2 Something which serves to distinguish; a difference, a distinguishing mark. Now *rare* or *obsolete*. M17.

S. JOHNSON Where we see . . the whole at once, we readily note the discriminations.

†**3** A recrimination. *rare*. M–L17.
4 The faculty of discriminating; the ability to observe accurately and make fine distinctions; perceptiveness, acuity, good judgement or taste. E19.

discriminative /dɪˈskrɪmɪnətɪv/ *adjective*. M17.
[ORIGIN from DISCRIMINATE *verb* + -IVE.]
1 Having the quality or character of observing or making distinctions with accuracy; showing discrimination, discerning. M17.

SOUTHEY Bombs and rockets are not discriminative.

2 Serving to discriminate or distinguish; distinctive, distinguishing. L17.

S. JOHNSON The discriminative excellence of Homer is elevation and comprehension of thought.

■ **discriminatively** *adverb* M17. **discriminativeness** *noun* M19.

discriminator /dɪˈskrɪmɪneɪtə/ *noun*. M19.
[ORIGIN formed as DISCRIMINATIVE + -OR.]
1 A person who discriminates. M19.
2 An electric circuit whose output depends on how some property of the input departs from a fixed value; *spec.* one for converting a frequency-modulated signal to an amplitude-modulated one. M20.
3 A quality or feature that enables distinctions to be made. M20.

discrown /dɪsˈkraʊn/ *verb trans.* L16.
[ORIGIN from DIS- 2 + CROWN *noun*, *verb*[1].]
Deprive of a crown or royal status; *fig.* deprive of supremacy, dignity, or adornment.

†**discruciate** *verb trans.* E17–L18.
[ORIGIN Latin *discruciat-* pa. ppl stem of *discruciare*, formed as DIS- 3 + *cruciare* to torment: see EXCRUCIATE *verb*, -ATE[3].]
Torture, excruciate, (chiefly *fig.*).

†**disculp** *verb trans.* *rare*. E17–M18.
[ORIGIN medieval Latin *disculpare*: see DISCULPATE.]
= DISCULPATE.

disculpate /dɪsˈkʌlpeɪt/ *verb trans.* L17.
[ORIGIN medieval Latin *disculpat-* pa. ppl stem of *disculpare*, from Latin DIS- 1 + *culpare* to blame, from *culpa* fault, blame: see -ATE[3]. Cf. EXCULPATE.]
Clear of blame or accusation; exculpate.
■ **disculˈpation** *noun* M18.

†**discumbent** *noun* & *adjective*. M16.
[ORIGIN Latin *discumbent-* pres. ppl stem of *discumbere* lie down, formed as DIS- 3 + *-cumbere*: see CUMBENT.]
▸ **A** *noun*. **1** A person reclining at table, a guest at a feast. M16–E17.
2 A person confined to bed. Only in M18.
▸ **B** *adjective*. Reclining. E–M18.
■ †**discumbency** *noun* reclining posture at meals M17–M18.

discumber /dɪsˈkʌmbə/ *verb trans.* E18.
[ORIGIN from DIS- 2 + CUMBER *verb*: cf. Old French *descombrer* (mod. *décombrer*).]
Relieve of a burden, disencumber.

discursion /dɪsˈkəːʃ(ə)n/ *noun*. M16.
[ORIGIN Old French, or late Latin *discursio(n-)*, from Latin *discurs-*: see DISCOURSE *noun*, -ION.]
†**1** The action of running or moving to and fro. *rare*. M16–L17.
2 Reasoning. *rare*. E17.
3 The action of moving away from the subject under discussion; (a) digression. M19.

discursive /dɪsˈkəːsɪv/ *adjective*. L16.
[ORIGIN medieval Latin *discursivus*, from *discurs-*: see DISCOURSE *noun*, -IVE.]
1 Passing rapidly or indiscriminately from subject to subject; rambling, digressive; extending over or dealing with a wide range of topics. L16.

H. G. WELLS My reading has been rather discursive.

2 Proceeding by argument or reasoning; ratiocinative; not intuitive. L16.

F. FERGUSSON The needs of the discursive intellect.

3 Running hither and thither. E17.
■ **discursively** *adverb* L17. **discursiveness** *noun* L17. **discurˈsivity** *noun* M20.

discursory /dɪsˈkəːs(ə)ri/ *adjective*. *rare*. L16.
[ORIGIN medieval Latin *discursorius*, from *discurs-*: see DISCOURSE *noun*, -ORY[2].]
†**1** Of the nature of discourse or reasoning. L16–E17.
2 Discursive, digressive. L19.

discus /ˈdɪskəs/ *noun*. M17.
[ORIGIN Latin from Greek *diskos*.]
1 A heavy thick-centred disc or plate thrown in ancient and modern athletic sports; the sporting event in which it is thrown. M17.
†**2** Any disc or disc-shaped body. L17–E18.

discuss /dɪˈskʌs/ *verb* & *noun*. LME.
[ORIGIN Latin *discuss-* pa. ppl stem of *discutere* dash to pieces, disperse, (in Proto-Romance) investigate, formed as DIS- 1 + *quatere* shake.]
▸ **A** *verb trans.* †**1 a** Drive away, dispel, disperse, (*lit.* & *fig.*); *spec.* (MEDICINE) disperse (a swelling, obstruction, etc.). LME–E19. ▸**b** Shake off; set free. M–L16.
†**2** Examine or investigate (a matter); try judicially. LME–E17.
†**3** Give judgement on (a matter). LME–L18.
†**4** Make known, declare. LME–M17.

SHAKES. *Hen. V* Art thou a gentleman? What is thy name? Discuss.

5 Investigate or examine by argument; debate; talk about (a topic) to, with, or *with* another person. LME.

R. L. STEVENSON I could see the pair discussing what they ought to do. H. BELLOC In a further paper I shall discuss the much-disputed point of authorship.

6 *LAW* (chiefly *Scot.*). Exhaust legal proceedings against (a debtor), esp. against the person primarily liable before proceeding against a surety. L16.
7 Consume (food etc.), esp. with leisurely enjoyment. Chiefly *joc.* E19.
▸ †**B** *noun.* = DISCUSSION 1, 2. M16–M17.
■ **discussant** *noun* a person who takes part in a discussion, esp. a prearranged one E20. **discusser** *noun* L16. **discussible** *adjective* M17.

discussion /dɪˈskʌʃ(ə)n/ *noun.* ME.
[ORIGIN Old French & mod. French from Latin *discussio(n-)*, formed as DISCUSS: see -ION.]
†**1** Judicial examination or decision. ME–E16.
2 Examination (*of* a point) by argument etc.; debate; an exchange of views; a conversation. M16.

H. J. LASKI A discussion group to thrash out the problems of governmental re-organisation. P. TILLICH One of the earliest philosophical discussions of courage, in Plato's dialogue Laches.

†**3** *MEDICINE.* The dissipation or dispersal of swellings, a tumour, etc. E17–M18.
4 *LAW* (chiefly *Scot.*). The exhaustion of legal proceedings against a debtor (see DISCUSS *verb* 6). L17.
5 The consumption *of* food etc., esp. with leisurely enjoyment. Chiefly *joc.* M19.
■ **discussional** *adjective* of the nature or pertaining to discussion M19. **discussionist** *noun* a debater M19.

discussive /dɪˈskʌsɪv/ *adjective & noun.* L16.
[ORIGIN medieval Latin *discussivus*, formed as DISCUSS: see -IVE.]
▸ **A** *adjective.* †**1** Having the property of dissipating swellings etc. L16–E18.
†**2** Able to settle a point in question; decisive. E–M17.
3 Of or pertaining to discussion or debate. *arch.* M17.
▸ †**B** *noun.* A preparation having the property of dissipating swellings etc. Only in 17.
■ **discussively** *adverb* (*rare*) E17.

discutient /dɪˈskjuːʃ(ə)nt/ *adjective & noun.* Now *rare* or *obsolete.* E17.
[ORIGIN Latin *discutient-* pres. ppl stem of *discutere*: see DISCUSS *verb*, -ENT.]
(A preparation) having the property of dissipating swellings etc.

disdain /dɪsˈdeɪn, -z-/ *noun.* ME.
[ORIGIN Anglo-Norman *dedeigne*, Old French *desdeign* (mod. *dédain*), formed as DISDAIN *verb*.]
1 a The feeling that is entertained towards something unworthy of notice or beneath one's dignity; scorn, contempt. ME. ▸**b** A feeling of this kind. *rare.* M17.

A. STORR Some schizoid patients . . may proclaim their disdain for convention by eccentricity in dress.

†**2** Anger or annoyance arising from offended dignity. ME–L17.
†**3** Loathsomeness; aversion. L16–M17.

disdain /dɪsˈdeɪn, -z-/ *verb.* LME.
[ORIGIN Old French *desdeignier* from Proto-Romance alt. of late Latin *dedignare*, classical Latin *dedignari*, from *de-* DE- 1 + *dignare*, *-ari* DEIGN.]
1 *verb trans.* Consider to be unworthy of oneself or of one's notice; regard with disdain; scorn (*to do, doing*). LME.

J. BARNES He wanted all writers to live obscurely in the provinces, . . disdain reputation.

†**2** *verb trans.* Be angry or offended at. LME–L17.
†**3** *verb intrans.* Be moved with indignation; be indignant (*at, that*); take offence. LME–L18.

W. TAYLOR Disdaining that the enemies of Christ should abound in wealth.

†**4** *verb trans.* Move to indignation or scorn; offend, displease. LME–E19.
■ **disdainable** *adjective* (*rare*) worthy of disdain E17. **disdainer** *noun* L16.

disdainful /dɪsˈdeɪnfʊl, -f(ə)l/ *adjective.* M16.
[ORIGIN from DISDAIN *noun* + -FUL.]
1 Full of or showing disdain; scornful, contemptuous. (Foll. by *of*, *to do.*) M16.
†**2** Hateful. M–L16.
■ **disdainfully** *adverb* M16. **disdainfulness** *noun* M16.

disdar /ˈdiːzdɑː/ *noun.* M18.
[ORIGIN Turkish *dizdar* from Persian *dizdār*, from *diz* castle + *-dār* holding, holder.]
hist. The warden of a castle or fort in Turkey, Persia, etc.

†**disdiapason** *noun.* E17–L18.
[ORIGIN Latin from Greek *dis dia pasōn*, from *dis* twice: see DIAPASON.]
MUSIC. The interval of a double octave; a fifteenth.

disease /dɪˈziːz/ *noun.* In sense 1 also (now usu.) **dis-ease** /dɪsˈiːz/. ME.
[ORIGIN Anglo-Norman *desease*, *dis-*, Old French *desaise*, from *des-* DIS- 2 + *aise* EASE *noun*. In sense 1 re-formed in E20 from DIS- 2 + EASE *noun*.]
1 Absence of ease; inconvenience; trouble. ME. ▸†**b** A cause of discomfort; an annoyance. LME–E18.
2 (A) disorder of structure or function in an animal or plant of such a degree as to produce or threaten to produce detectable illness or disorder; a definable variety of such a disorder, usu. with specific signs or symptoms or affecting a specific location; (an) illness, (a) sickness. LME.

GIBBON The legions of Augustus melted away in disease and lassitude. *Scientific American* Trichinosis . . is obviously a common infection but a rare disease.

Alzheimer's disease, ***coeliac disease***, ***deficiency disease***, ***Dutch elm disease***, ***foot-and-mouth disease***, ***industrial disease***, ***Parkinson's disease***, ***slimmers' disease***, etc.
3 *fig.* A bad quality, habit, or disposition regarded as affecting or having a hold on a person etc. E16.

T. FULLER Bad Latin was a catching disease in that age. S. BRETT The artistic temperament is a disease which afflicts amateurs.

British disease, ***English disease***, etc.
■ **diseaseful** *adjective* (now *rare*) †(*a*) troublesome; (*b*) full of or affected with disease; †(*c*) unwholesome: LME.

disease /dɪˈziːz/ *verb trans.* ME.
[ORIGIN Anglo-Norman var. of Old French *desaaisier*, from *desaise* noun (see DISEASE *noun*) after *aaisier*, *aiser* EASE *verb*.]
†**1** Deprive of ease, disturb; put to inconvenience; annoy. ME–L17.

J. KNOX He wold not disease hymself to heare a sermon.

2 Cause illness in; affect with disease. (Earlier in DISEASED 1.) L15.

fig.: E. HICKERINGILL Evil Ministers Disease the Common-wealth.

diseased /dɪˈziːzd/ *ppl adjective.* LME.
[ORIGIN from DISEASE *verb* + -ED[1].]
1 Affected with disease. LME.
2 Characterized by or symptomatic of disease. L16.
■ **diseasedly** /-zɪdli/ *adverb* L17. **diseasedness** /-zɪdnɪs/ *noun* E17.

disedify /dɪsˈɛdɪfʌɪ/ *verb trans.* E16.
[ORIGIN from DIS- 2 + EDIFY.]
Shock or weaken spiritually or morally.
■ **disedifiˈcation** *noun* M17.

disembark /dɪsɪmˈbɑːk/ *verb trans. & intrans.* L16.
[ORIGIN French *désembarquer*, Spanish *desembarcar*, or Italian *disimbarcare*, from Proto-Romance, formed as DIS- 2, French *embarquer*, EMBARK *verb*[1].]
Put or go ashore from a ship; remove from or leave an aircraft, train, etc.
■ ˌ**disembarˈkation** *noun* L18.

disembarrass /dɪsɪmˈbarəs/ *verb trans.* E18.
[ORIGIN from DIS- 2 + EMBARRASS *verb*, prob. after French †*désembarrasser* (now *débarrasser*).]
1 Free *from* an embarrassment, encumbrance, or complication; rid or relieve (oneself) *of.* E18.
2 Disentangle (one thing *from* another). M18.
■ **disembarrassment** *noun* E19.

disembody /dɪsɪmˈbɒdi/ *verb trans.* E18.
[ORIGIN from DIS- 2 + EMBODY.]
1 Separate (the soul) from the body; free (anything) from that in which it is embodied. Freq. as ***disembodied*** *ppl adjective.* E18.

J. A. SYMONDS Disembodying the sentiments which were incarnated in simple images.

2 Disband (a military corps etc.). *arch.* M18.
■ **disembodiment** *noun* M19.

disembogue /dɪsɪmˈbəʊg/ *verb & noun.* L16.
[ORIGIN Spanish *desembocar*, from *des-* DIS- 2 + *embocar* run into a creek or strait, from *en-* IN-[1] + *boca* mouth.]
▸ **A** *verb.* †**1** *verb intrans.* Of a sailor or vessel: come out of the mouth of a river, strait, etc., into the open sea. L16–E19.
2 *verb intrans. & trans.* Of a river, lake, etc.: flow or empty *into*; discharge into the sea etc. L16.

POPE The deep roar of disemboguing Nile. SOUTHEY Where wild Parana disembogues A sea-like stream.

3 *verb intrans. & trans.* Pour out; emerge or discharge in quantity. E17.

CARLYLE Paris disembogues itself . . to witness, with grim looks, the *Séance Royale.*

▸ †**B** *noun.* The mouth of a river. Only in 17.
■ **disemboguement** *noun* the action or place of disemboguing L17.

disembowel /dɪsɪmˈbaʊəl/ *verb trans.* Infl. **-ll-**, ***-l-**. E17.
[ORIGIN from DIS- 3 + EMBOWEL: cf. DISBOWEL.]
Remove the bowels or entrails of, eviscerate; rip up so as to cause the bowels to protrude.

fig.: Y. MENUHIN A cottage upright, disembowelled, its inner workings exposed on the floor.

■ **disembowelment** *noun* L19.

disembroil /dɪsɪmˈbrɔɪl/ *verb trans.* E17.
[ORIGIN from DIS- 2 + EMBROIL *verb*[1]. Cf. Spanish *desembrollar*.]
Extricate from confusion or entanglement.

disemburden /dɪsɪmˈbəːd(ə)n/ *verb trans. & intrans.* Also (*arch.*) **-burthen** /-ˈbəːð(ə)n/. E19.
[ORIGIN from DIS- 2 + EM-[1] + BURDEN *verb*.]
= DISBURDEN.

disenact /dɪsɪnˈakt/ *verb trans. rare.* M16.
[ORIGIN from DIS- 2 + ENACT *verb*.]
Repeal.
■ **diseˈnactment** *noun* (a) repeal M19.

disenamour /dɪsɪnˈamə/ *verb trans.* Also ***-or**. L16.
[ORIGIN from DIS- 2 + ENAMOUR.]
Free from being enamoured.

Nature He later became very much disenamoured with Marxism.

disenchant /dɪsɪnˈtʃɑːnt, dɪsɛn-/ *verb trans.* L16.
[ORIGIN Old French & mod. French *désenchanter*, formed as DIS- 2, ENCHANT *verb*.]
Free from enchantment or illusion.

DRYDEN A noble stroke or two Ends all the charms, And disenchants the grove. Q. BELL Virginia, who had been delighted by her first sight of the Italians, was becoming disenchanted.

■ **disenchanter** *noun* a person who removes enchantment M17. **disenchantment** *noun* the action of disenchanting; a disenchanted state: E17.

disencourage /dɪsɪnˈkʌrɪdʒ, dɪsɛn-/ *verb trans.* Now *rare* or *obsolete.* M17.
[ORIGIN from DIS- 2 + ENCOURAGE.]
Deprive of encouragement, discourage.
■ †**disencouragement** *noun* L16–E18.

disencumber /dɪsɪnˈkʌmbə, dɪsɛn-/ *verb trans.* L16.
[ORIGIN from DIS- 2 + ENCUMBER *verb*, prob. after Old French & mod. French *désencombrer*. Cf. DISCUMBER.]
Relieve of or free from encumbrance.
■ **disencumbrance** *noun* (now *rare*) deliverance or freedom from encumbrance E18.

disendow /dɪsɪnˈdaʊ, dɪsɛn-/ *verb trans.* M19.
[ORIGIN from DIS- 2 + ENDOW.]
Deprive or strip (esp. a Church) of endowments.
■ **disendower** *noun* M19. **disendowment** *noun* M19.

disenfranchise /dɪsɪnˈfrantʃʌɪz/ *verb trans.* E17.
[ORIGIN from DIS- 2, 3 + ENFRANCHISE.]
†**1** Set free, enfranchise. *rare.* E–M17.
2 Deprive of civil privileges or of voting rights; disfranchise. M17.
■ **disenfranchisement** /-ɪz-/ *noun* E18.

disengage /dɪsɪnˈgeɪdʒ/ *verb & noun.* E17.
[ORIGIN from DIS- 2 + ENGAGE *verb*, prob. after French *désengager*.]
▸ **A** *verb.* **1** *verb trans.* Free from engagement, promise, obligation, etc. *obsolete* exc. in DISENGAGED. E17.
2 *verb trans.* Loosen or free from something adhering, entangling, or interlocking; loosen (a bond). E17.

E. LANGLEY Gently we disengaged ourselves from the company and strolled off. R. COBB The priest eventually disengaged his hand from my friend's avid embrace.

3 *verb intrans.* Detach oneself; get loose. M17.
4 *verb intrans. FENCING.* Pass the point of one's sword over or under the opponent's blade to change the line of attack. L17.
▸ **B** *noun.* A fencer's movement to disengage. L18.

disengaged /dɪsɪnˈgeɪdʒd, dɪsɛn-/ *ppl adjective.* E17.
[ORIGIN from DISENGAGE + -ED[1].]
Free of engagement or obligation; not engaged; detached; *esp.* at leisure to attend to any visitor, business, etc.
■ **disengagedness** *noun* L17.

disengagement /dɪsɪnˈgeɪdʒm(ə)nt/ *noun.* M17.
[ORIGIN formed as DISENGAGED + -MENT, after ENGAGEMENT or French *désengagement*.]
1 Absence of engagement or involvement; the action of disengaging or of freeing from involvement. (Foll. by *from.*) M17. ▸**b** Liberation *of* gas, heat, etc. L18.

W. J. M. RANKINE Effecting . . disengagement by wheels in rolling contact. R. GARNETT That disengagement from all traditional and conventional influences . . which characterises younger men.

2 Freedom from (mental) occupation; detachment; ease of manner or behaviour. E18.
3 The breaking of an engagement to be married. L18.
4 *FENCING.* = DISENGAGE *noun.* L18.
5 A withdrawal of military forces; a renunciation of military or political influence in a specified area. M20.

disentail /dɪsɪnˈteɪl/ *verb & noun.* M17.
[ORIGIN from DIS- 2 + ENTAIL *verb*[2].]
▸ **A** *verb trans.* †**1** Divest, deprive, *of.* Only in M17.
2 *LAW.* Free from entail; break the entail of (an estate). M19.
▸ **B** *noun.* The act of breaking an entail. M19.
■ **disentailment** *noun* = DISENTAIL *noun* M19.

disentangle /dɪsɪnˈtaŋɡ(ə)l/ *verb*. L16.
[ORIGIN from DIS- 2 + ENTANGLE.]
▸ **I** *verb trans*. **1** Free (something) from that in or with which it is entangled; extricate; free *from* complications, difficulties, etc. L16.
G. BERKELEY To disentangle our minds from . . prejudices. E. BOWEN To disentangle her parasol from a long spray of creeper.
2 Bring out of a tangled state; unravel, untwist. M17.
E. K. KANE Patience to disentangle the knots of my harness.
▸ **II** *verb intrans*. **3** Be or become disentangled. E17.
■ **disentanglement** *noun* M18.

disenthral /dɪsɪnˈθrɔːl/ *verb trans*. Also *-**ll**. Infl. -**ll**-. M17.
[ORIGIN from DIS- 2 + ENTHRAL.]
Free from enthralment.
■ **disenthralment** *noun* E19.

disenthrone /dɪsɪnˈθrəʊn/ *verb trans*. E17.
[ORIGIN from DIS- 2 + ENTHRONE.]
= DETHRONE.
■ **disenthronement** *noun* L19.

disentitle /dɪsɪnˈtʌɪt(ə)l/ *verb trans*. M17.
[ORIGIN from DIS- 2 + ENTITLE *verb*.]
Deprive of a rightful claim (*to*).

disentomb /dɪsɪnˈtuːm/ *verb trans*. E17.
[ORIGIN from DIS- 2 + ENTOMB.]
Remove from a tomb; disinter, unearth, (*lit. & fig.*).
■ **disentombment** *noun* M19.

disentrail /dɪsˈɛntreɪl/ *verb trans*. Long *rare*. LME.
[ORIGIN from DIS- 2 + ENTRAIL *noun*[1].]
Remove the entrails of, disembowel; draw forth from the entrails.

disenvelop /dɪsɪnˈvɛləp, dɪsɛn-/ *verb trans*. Also (now *rare*) -**ope**. M17.
[ORIGIN from DIS- 2 + ENVELOP or ENVELOPE.]
Free from a wrapping or covering; *fig*. unfold, develop, (a meaning etc.).

disepalous /dʌɪˈsɛp(ə)ləs/ *adjective*. M19.
[ORIGIN from DI-[2] + SEPAL + -OUS.]
BOTANY. Having or consisting of two sepals.

disequilibrate /dɪsɪˈkwɪlɪbreɪt, ˌdɪsiːkwɪˈlʌɪbreɪt/ *verb trans*. L19.
[ORIGIN from DIS- 2 + EQUILIBRATE.]
Destroy the equilibrium of, throw out of balance.

disequilibrium /ˌdɪsiːkwɪˈlɪbrɪəm, dɪsɛ-/ *noun*. Pl. -**bria** /-brɪə/, -**briums**. M19.
[ORIGIN from DIS- 2 + EQUILIBRIUM.]
Lack or loss of equilibrium, instability; an imbalance.
J. M. KEYNES A most rapid and powerful corrective of real disequilibria in the balance of international payments.

†**disert** *adjective*. LME–L17.
[ORIGIN Latin *dis(s)ertus* pa. pple of *disserere* discuss, discourse, formed as DIS- 1, 1b + *serere* interweave, connect, compose.]
Fluent; well-spoken, eloquent.
■ †**disertly** *adverb* clearly, eloquently, in plain terms LME–L18.

disestablish /dɪsɪˈstablɪʃ/ *verb trans*. L16.
[ORIGIN from DIS- 2 + ESTABLISH.]
Terminate the establishment of, depose from an official position; *spec*. deprive (a Church) of a special state connection and support, remove from a position as the national or state Church.
■ **disestablisher** *noun* M19. **disesˈtablishment** *noun* the action or process of disestablishing, esp. a Church E19. **disestabˌlishmenˈtarian** *noun* an advocate of disestablishment L19. **disesˌtablishmenˈtarianism** *noun* (usu. as a factitious long word) L19.

disesteem /dɪsɪˈstiːm/ *noun*. E17.
[ORIGIN from DIS- 2 + ESTEEM *noun*. Cf. French †*désestime*, DISESTEEM *verb*.]
The action of disesteeming; the fact of being disesteemed; low estimation or regard.

disesteem /dɪsɪˈstiːm/ *verb trans*. & †*intrans*. with *of*. L16.
[ORIGIN from DIS- 2 + ESTEEM *verb*, perh. after French †*désestimer*.]
Have a poor opinion of, regard lightly; despise.
P. GOODMAN A commercially debauched popular culture makes learning disesteemed.
■ **diseˈsteemer** *noun* E17.

disestimation /ˌdɪsɛstɪˈmeɪʃ(ə)n/ *noun*. Long *rare*. L16.
[ORIGIN from DIS- 2 + ESTIMATION *noun*, after DISESTEEM *verb*.]
= DISESTEEM *noun*.

diseuse /diːˈzəːz, *foreign* dizøːz/ *noun*. Pl. pronounced same. L19.
[ORIGIN French = talker, fem. of *diseur*, from *dire* say.]
A female artiste who specializes in monologue.

disfame /dɪsˈfeɪm/ *noun*. *arch. rare*. LME.
[ORIGIN Orig. from Old French *desfame*, *dis-*, from *desfamer* DEFAME *verb*; later from DIS- 2 + FAME *noun*.]
Disrepute; defamation.

disfashion /dɪsˈfaʃ(ə)n/ *verb trans*. M16.
[ORIGIN from DIS- 2 + FASHION *verb*.]
Spoil the fashion or shape of, disfigure.

disfavour /dɪsˈfeɪvə/ *noun*. Also *-**or**. M16.
[ORIGIN from DIS- 2 + FAVOUR *noun*, prob. after French †*desfaveur*.]
1 Unfavourable regard, dislike, disapproval. M16.
J. GALSWORTHY He noticed with sour disfavour that June had left her wine-glass full of wine.
†**2** An act or expression of dislike or ill will. M16–M17.
3 The condition of being disliked or disapproved of. L16.
CARLYLE The poor young Prince . . had fallen into open disfavour.

disfavour /dɪsˈfeɪvə/ *verb trans*. Also *-**or**. M16.
[ORIGIN from DIS- 2 + FAVOUR *verb*.]
†**1** Spoil the looks or appearance of; disfigure. M16–E17.
2 Regard or treat with disfavour. L16.
†**3** Dislike. L16–M18.

disfavourable /dɪsˈfeɪv(ə)rəb(ə)l/ *adjective*. Long *rare*. Also *-**or**-. M16.
[ORIGIN from DIS- 2 + FAVOURABLE.]
Unfavourable.
■ **disfavourably** *adverb* M17.

disfeature /dɪsˈfiːtʃə/ *verb trans*. M17.
[ORIGIN from DIS- 2 + FEATURE *noun*. Cf. DEFEATURE *verb*.]
Disfigure, deface.

disfellowship /dɪsˈfɛlə(ʊ)ʃɪp/ *noun & verb*. E17.
[ORIGIN from DIS- 2 + FELLOWSHIP *noun*.]
▸ **A** *noun*. Lack of or exclusion from fellowship. E17.
▸ **B** *verb trans*. Infl. -**pp**-, *-**p**-. Exclude from (esp. religious) fellowship; excommunicate. Chiefly *US*. M19.

disfiguration /dɪsˌfɪɡjʊˈreɪʃ(ə)n, -ˌfɪɡə-/ *noun*. M17.
[ORIGIN from DISFIGURE *verb* + -ATION. Cf. Old French *desfiguration*.]
= DISFIGUREMENT.

disfigure /dɪsˈfɪɡə/ *verb trans*. LME.
[ORIGIN Old French *desfigurer* (mod. *dé-*) from Proto-Romance, from Latin DIS- 2 + *figura* FIGURE *noun*.]
1 Spoil the appearance or beauty of; deform, deface. LME.
LD MACAULAY Their diction was disfigured by foreign idioms. D. M. THOMAS Rather an ugly baby, disfigured by a hare lip.
†**2** Alter the figure or appearance of, disguise. LME–E18.
†**3** Carve (a peacock) at table. L15–E18.
■ **disfigurer** *noun* L18. **disfiguringly** *adverb* in a disfiguring manner; so as to disfigure: E20.

disfigurement /dɪsˈfɪɡəm(ə)nt/ *noun*. M17.
[ORIGIN from DISFIGURE + -MENT.]
1 The action of disfiguring; the fact of being disfigured. M17.
2 Something that disfigures; a deformity, a blemish. M17.

disflower /dɪsˈflaʊə/ *verb trans*. E17.
[ORIGIN from DIS- 2 + FLOWER *noun*.]
1 Deprive or strip of flowers; *fig*. rob of its beauty or excellence, spoil. E17.
†**2** Make to be no longer a flower. Only in E17.

disforest /dɪsˈfɒrɪst/ *verb trans*. E16.
[ORIGIN Anglo-Latin (cf. *disforestatio(n-)*), formed as DIS- 2 + FOREST *noun*. Cf. DE-AFFOREST, DEFOREST, DISAFFOREST.]
1 *hist*. = DISAFFOREST *verb* 1. E16.
2 Clear (land etc.) of forests or trees. M17.
■ ˌ**disforeˈstation** *noun* E17.

disform /dɪsˈfɔːm/ *verb*. LME.
[ORIGIN from DIS- 2 + FORM *verb*[1]. Cf. DEFORM *verb*.]
1 *verb trans*. Deform, disfigure, deface. *obsolete* exc. *dial*. LME.
2 *verb intrans*. Change form, lose form or arrangement. *rare*. M19.

disfranchise /dɪsˈfran(t)ʃʌɪz/ *verb trans*. LME.
[ORIGIN from DIS- 2 + FRANCHISE *verb*.]
1 Deprive of the rights and privileges of a free inhabitant of a borough, city, country, etc.; deprive of a right or privilege formerly held. LME.
2 *spec*. Deprive (a place) of the right of returning an elected representative, or (a person) of the right of voting in an election. E18.
■ **disfranchisement** /-ɪz-/ *noun* E17. **disfranchiser** *noun* M19.

disfunction *noun*, **disfunctional** *adjective* see DYSFUNCTION, DYSFUNCTIONAL.

disfurnish /dɪsˈfəːnɪʃ/ *verb trans*. M16.
[ORIGIN Old French *desfournir*, formed as DIS- 2, FURNISH *verb*.]
Deprive of or *of* appurtenances or belongings; make destitute *of*.
■ **disfurnishment** *noun* E17.

disgarnish /dɪsˈɡɑːnɪʃ/ *verb trans*. LME.
[ORIGIN Old French *desgarnir* (mod. *dé-*), formed as DIS- 2 + *garnir*: see GARNISH *verb*.]
Deprive of something that garnishes; despoil.

disgavel /dɪsˈɡav(ə)l/ *verb trans*. Infl. -**ll**-. L17.
[ORIGIN from DIS- 2 + GAVEL(KIND).]
hist. Relieve or exempt from the tenure of gavelkind.

disglorify /dɪsˈɡlɔːrɪfʌɪ/ *verb trans*. *rare*. L16.
[ORIGIN from DIS- 2 + GLORIFY.]
Deprive of glory; treat with dishonour. Usu. in *pass*.

disgorge /dɪsˈɡɔːdʒ/ *verb*. L15.
[ORIGIN Old French *desgorger* (mod. *dé-*), formed as DIS- 2, GORGE *noun*[1].]
1 *verb trans*. & *intrans*. Eject (matter) from or as from the throat; yield up, cease to hold on to, (esp. what has been wrongly appropriated). L15.
J. BUCHAN He . . was entitled to his share in the profits . . and he was determined to make Haraldsen disgorge. S. MIDDLETON A bus . . disgorged its complement of old-age pensioners.
2 *verb trans*. Discharge the contents of, empty. L16.
J. HEYWOOD Their stomacks some disgorg'd. ADDISON The four Rivers which disgorge themselves into the Sea of Fire.
■ **disgorgement** *noun* the action of disgorging L15. **disgorger** *noun* a thing which disgorges; *spec*. a device for extracting a hook from a fish's throat: M19.

disgown /dɪsˈɡaʊn/ *verb*. *arch*. M18.
[ORIGIN from DIS- 2 + GOWN *noun*.]
1 *verb intrans*. Take off one's gown. M18.
2 *verb trans*. Deprive of a gown; unfrock. L19.

disgrace /dɪsˈɡreɪs/ *noun*. L16.
[ORIGIN French *disgrâce* from Italian *disgrazia*, from *dis-* DIS- 2 + *grazia* from Latin *gratia* GRACE *noun*.]
1 Loss of high favour or respect, downfall from a position of honour; the state of being no longer held in honour. Formerly also, the disfavour shown to a person in such a state. L16.
LD MACAULAY The King . . had determined that the disgrace of the Hydes should be complete.
2 Loss of general or public respect; ignominy, shame. L16.
J. A. FROUDE The disgrace which the queen's conduct had brought upon her family. E. NESBIT Resistance was useless. There is no disgrace in yielding. E. TEMPLETON She was in disgrace at school.
†**3** A disfavour; a dishonour; an affront. L16–M18.
BACON The interchange continually of favours and disgraces.
†**4** (A) misfortune. L16–M18.
†**5** The expression of dishonour and reprobation; opprobrium, reproach; an expression or term of reprobation. L16–L17.
HOBBES Then Hector him with terms of great disgrace Reproved.
6 A thing or person involving dishonour; a cause of shame or reproach. L16.
G. STEIN He would be sure to turn out no good and be a disgrace to a German family.
7 Lack of grace. *rare*. L16.

disgrace /dɪsˈɡreɪs/ *verb trans*. M16.
[ORIGIN French *disgracier* from Italian *disgraziare*, from *disgrazia*: see DISGRACE *noun*.]
†**1** Spoil the (esp. outward) grace of; disfigure M16–L18.
W. COWPER Withered stumps disgrace the sylvan scene.
†**2** Put out of countenance; discomfit, dismay. M16–E17.
3 Dismiss from favour; degrade from a position of honour, rank, etc. M16.
LD MACAULAY Queensberry was disgraced for refusing to betray the interests of the Protestant religion.
†**4** Bring intentionally into disfavour or disgrace (*with* another); put to shame. M16–E18.
SHAKES. *Much Ado* As I wooed for thee to obtain her, I will join with thee to disgrace her.
5 Bring shame or discredit on; be a disgrace to. M16.
R. GRAVES I made the plea without stammering or forgetting my words or otherwise disgracing myself.
†**6** Speak of so as to dishonour; revile; speak slightingly of. M16–E19.
■ **disgracer** *noun* L16.

disgraceful /dɪsˈɡreɪsfʊl, -f(ə)l/ *adjective*. L16.
[ORIGIN from DISGRACE *noun* + -FUL.]
†**1** Lacking in grace; unbecoming, unpleasing. L16–E18.
2 Full of or involving disgrace; shameful, dishonourable. L16.
L. M. MONTGOMERY Mr. Phillips said my spelling was disgraceful.
3 Inflicting disgrace, degrading. Formerly also, opprobrious. E17.
J. REYNOLDS These . . disgraceful epithets with which the poor imitators are so often loaded. HARTLEY COLERIDGE It does not appear that Sir Samuel . . ever submitted to this disgraceful punishment.
■ **disgracefully** *adverb* E17. **disgracefulness** *noun* L16.

disgracious /dɪsˈɡreɪʃəs/ *adjective*. L16.
[ORIGIN French *disgracieux*, formed as DIS- 2, GRACIOUS.]
1 Ungracious, unfavourable, unkind. Now *rare* or *obsolete*. L16.
†**2** Out of favour; disliked. L16–E17.
3 Graceless, inelegant; unbecoming. L19.

D

disgrade /dɪsˈɡreɪd/ *verb trans.* LME.
[ORIGIN Old French *desgrader* var. of *degrader* DEGRADE *verb*.]
= DEGRADE *verb* 1.
■ **disgraˈdation** *noun* = DEGRADATION *noun*[1] 1 E18.

disgregate /ˈdɪsɡrɪɡeɪt/ *verb trans.* Now *rare*. LME.
[ORIGIN Late Latin *disgregat-* pa. ppl stem of *disgregare*, from Latin DIS- 1 + *gregare* collect into a flock, back-form. from *congregare* CONGREGATE *verb*: see -ATE[3].]
†**1** Dissipate, dispel. Only in LME.
†**2** Separate, sever, *from*. Only in L16.
3 Separate into individual parts, disintegrate. E17.
■ **disgreˈgation** *noun* disintegration, dispersal E17.

†**disgross** *verb trans.* M16–E19.
[ORIGIN Old French *desgrosser*, *-grossir* (mod. *dégrosser*, *-grossir*), formed as DIS- 2, GROSS *adjective*.]
Make finer; *spec.* reduce the thickness of (metal bars) in wire-making.

disgruntle /dɪsˈɡrʌnt(ə)l/ *verb trans.* M17.
[ORIGIN from DIS- 3 + GRUNTLE *verb*[1].]
Make discontented; put into a sulky humour. Chiefly as ***disgruntled*** *ppl adjective*.
■ **disgruntlement** *noun* moody discontent L19.

disguisal /dɪsˈɡʌɪz(ə)l/ *noun*. *rare*. M17.
[ORIGIN from DISGUISE *verb* + -AL[1].]
The action or an act of disguising.

disguise /dɪsˈɡʌɪz/ *noun*. ME.
[ORIGIN from the verb.]
†**1** Alteration of a customary style of dress; a new or strange fashion. ME–L16.
2 Alteration of dress, appearance, etc., to conceal identity; the state of being disguised in order to deceive. LME.

B. HARRIS In this extremity he left that City in disguise.

BLESSING ***in disguise***.
3 A garment, style, manner, etc., assumed for concealment or deception; a means of concealment or deception; a false appearance. L16.

W. BELSHAM This high-sounding language is merely the disguise of ignorance. G. MEREDITH Perfect candour can do more for us than a dark disguise. L. DEIGHTON The 'bookcase'.. proved to be an artful disguise for the doors of a cocktail cabinet.

4 The act or practice of disguising; concealment of reality under a false appearance. E17.

T. MEDWIN Friend.. to whom I communicate without disguise the inmost secrets of my breast.

†**5** A masque. E–M17.
6 Intoxication. Now *rare* or *obsolete*. E17.
■ **disguiseless** *adjective* M19.

disguise /dɪsˈɡʌɪz/ *verb trans.* ME.
[ORIGIN Old French *desguis(i)er* (mod. *déguiser*), formed as DIS- 2, GUISE *noun*.]
▸**I** †**1** Alter the usual style or fashion of dress of (a person); deck out. ME–L16.
†**2** Make different in appearance (*from* others, the proper or natural form, etc.); transform; disfigure. ME–L17. ▸**b** Alter or assume (clothing, a name) to conceal a person's identity. Only as ***disguised*** *ppl adjective*. LME–M17.

DRYDEN Faces.. disguised in death.

3 Change the dress or personal appearance of (a person) to conceal his or her identity; conceal the identity of by dressing *as* a particular (type of) person, *in* a particular garb, or *with* a particular feature. ME.

AV *1 Kings* 20:38 The prophet.. disguised himselfe with ashes vpon his face. G. B. SHAW The fugitive.., disguised in an old coat. H. ADAMS She disguised herself as a squire.

4 Deliberately alter the appearance of (a thing) so as to mislead or deceive; exhibit in a false light; misrepresent. LME.

T. GALE Plato's custome to desguise the Traditions he received from the Jews.

5 Conceal the nature or existence of (anything) by a counterfeit show or appearance. L16.

E. ROOSEVELT The low, gentle voice disguised a determination that could be as hard as steel. G. VIDAL Cave did not bother to disguise his boredom.

6 Hide (a material object), cover up. L16.

F. HERBERT Here in his quarters.. the ship's harsh metal was disguised with draperies.

7 Conceal the identity of under a different name or title. M17.
▸**II 8** Intoxicate, make drunk or tipsy. Chiefly as ***disguised*** *ppl adjective*. *arch. slang*. M16.
■ **disguisedly** /-zɪdli/ *adverb* in a disguised manner, in disguise L16. **disguisedness** /-zɪdnɪs/ *noun* the state of being disguised E17. **disguiser** *noun* †(*a*) *rare* a person who makes or wears newfangled or elaborate garments; †(*b*) a guiser, a mummer; (*c*) a person who or thing which disguises: LME. **disguising** *noun* (*a*) the action of the verb; (*b*) (*obsolete* exc. *hist.*) a masquerade, a performance by mummers etc.: LME.

disguisement /dɪsˈɡʌɪzm(ə)nt/ *noun*. L16.
[ORIGIN from DISGUISE *verb* + -MENT. Cf. Old French *desguisement* (mod. *déguisement*).]
1 The fact of disguising or of being disguised. L16.
2 Something which disguises or is used for disguise. L16.
3 In *pl.* Additions or accessories that alter the appearance; adornments. L16.

disgust /dɪsˈɡʌst/ *noun*. L16.
[ORIGIN French *desgoust* (now *dégoût*), from *desgouster* (mod. *dégoûter*), or from Italian *disgusto*, from *disgustare*: see DISGUST *verb*.]
1 (An instance of) repugnance or strong aversion; profound instinctive dissatisfaction; strong indignation. L16.

S. AUSTIN He soon retreated in disgust across the Alps. R. L. STEVENSON So many dead bodies lying all around, that I took a disgust of the place.. almost as strong as fear. A. S. NEILL They cannot overcome a sense of sin and shame and disgust.

2 Strong distaste for (some item of) food, drink, medicine, etc.; nausea. E17.
†**3** An outbreak of mutual ill feeling; a difference, a quarrel. E17–M18.
4 Something that causes strong dislike or repugnance; an annoyance, a vexation. Now *rare* or *obsolete*. M17.

disgust /dɪsˈɡʌst/ *verb*. E17.
[ORIGIN French *desgouster* or Italian *disgustare*, ult. formed as DIS- 2 + Latin *gustus* taste.]
†**1** *verb trans.* Have a strong distaste for or repugnance to; loathe. E17–L19.
2 *verb trans. & intrans.* Offend the senses or sensibilities (of); cause disgust (in). E17.

M. O. W. OLIPHANT He was disgusted with Phoebe for bringing the message. I. MURDOCH Drunkenness disgusts me.

3 *verb trans.* Arouse such disgust in (a person) as deters him or her from a proposed purpose. Foll. by *from*, *of*, *against*. E18.

J. O. JUSTAMOND The Monarch was ever soon disgusted of gratifications that were merely sensual.

■ **disgustedly** *adverb* in or with disgust M19. **disgusting** *ppl adjective* that disgusts, distasteful, sickening, repulsive M18. **disgustingly** *adverb* in a disgusting manner, so as to cause disgust; *colloq.* annoyingly: M18. **disgustingness** *noun* M19.

disgustful /dɪsˈɡʌstfʊl, -f(ə)l/ *adjective*. E17.
[ORIGIN from DISGUST *noun* + -FUL.]
1 Causing disgust; sickening; offensive; repulsive; shocking. E17.
2 Causing dislike; distasteful, displeasing. *arch.* E17.
3 Associated with or characterized by disgust. M19.

ALDOUS HUXLEY Studying Mr. Boldero with a close and disgustful attention.

■ **disgustfully** *adverb* M18. **disgustfulness** *noun* M19.

dish /dɪʃ/ *noun*.
[ORIGIN Old English *disċ* corresp. to Old Saxon *disk* (Dutch *disch*) table, Old High German *tisc* plate (German *Tisch* table), Old Norse *diskr*, all from Latin DISCUS discus, (Vulgate) dish, disc (of a sundial). Cf. DESK.]
1 A broad shallow flat-bottomed vessel for holding food to be cooked or served, now esp. one with a shape other than circular and having some depth; a glass vessel with a stem or base for holding an individual portion of food; in *pl.* also, table vessels collectively after use. OE.

J. STEINBECK Supper was over and the dishes dipped and wiped. D. WELCH The Boys moved about, serving.. vegetables from silver dishes. *Leicester Chronicle* A shallow ovenproof dish.

butter dish, ***chafing dish***, ***fruit dish***, etc. †**cast in a person's dish**, †**lay in a person's dish**, †**throw in a person's dish** reproach a person with.
2 A hollow vessel used for drinking or as a beggar's receptacle for alms; a cup. *arch.* LME.
clap dish: see CLAP *verb*[1].
3 a The food served in a dish; a particular form of prepared food. LME. ▸**b** An attractive person, esp. a woman. *slang*. E20. ▸**c *one's dish***, something exactly suited to one's taste. *slang*. E20.

a E. DAVID Interesting potato dishes invented by French cooks.

a dish of the day a dish specially featured on a day's menu. ***made dish***: see MADE *ppl adjective*. ***side dish***: see SIDE *noun*. **standing dish** a dish that appears daily or at every meal.
4 A dish or (*arch.*) cup with its contents; as much as a dish will hold. LME. ▸**b** *MINING*. A gallon of tin ore ready for the smelter; a measuring box for lead ore, by statute fixed to contain 15 pints. Also, the proportion of tin or lead ore paid as royalty to the owner of the mine. M16.

BYRON He sate him pensive o'er a dish of tea. V. WOOLF I must now pick a dish of raspberries for dinner.

5 Any shallow concave vessel or receptacle. M17.
evaporating dish.
6 A depression or concavity shaped like a dish, esp. in the side of a spoked wheel; the degree of such concavity; the condition of a wheel with such concavity. E19.
7 A microwave reflector or aerial with a shallow concave surface. Also ***dish aerial***, (US) ***dish antenna***. M20.
satellite dish: see SATELLITE *noun*.
– COMB.: ***dish aerial***, ***dish antenna***: see sense 7 above. **dishcloth** a cloth used for washing dishes (***dishcloth gourd***, any gourd of the genus *Luffa*, the fruit of which yields loofahs); **dish-clout** *arch.* & *dial.* = ***dishcloth*** above; **dish-cover** a cover put over a dish to keep food warm; **dish-faced** *adjective* having a concave face; *spec.* (of a dog) having the face concave from the indentation below the forehead to the nose; ***dish mop***: see MOP *noun*[3] 1; **dishpan** *N. Amer.*: in which dishes are washed up (***dishpan hands***: roughened by much washing up or use of detergents); **dishrag** = ***dishcloth*** above; **dishtowel** *Scot.* & *N. Amer.* a tea towel; **dishwasher** (*a*) a servant who washes dishes; a machine that does this automatically; (*b*) = WASHER *noun*[1] 1a; (*c*) *Austral.* the restless flycatcher, *Myiagra inquieta*, which has a repetitive call; **dishwater** the dirty water in which dishes have been washed; **dishwatery** *adjective* resembling dishwater.
■ **dishful** *noun* the contents of a dish, the quantity held by a dish ME.

dish /dɪʃ/ *verb*. LME.
[ORIGIN from the noun.]
1 *verb trans. & intrans.* Put (food) into a dish ready for the table. Freq. foll. by *out*, *up*. LME.

E. ACTON They [turnips] may be dished in the centre of.. mutton cutlets.

2 *verb trans.* **a** Present attractively for acceptance. Usu. foll. by *up*, †*out*. E17. ▸**b** Give *out* carelessly or indiscriminately. *slang*. M20.

a O. WELLES Gossip columnists who must daily dish up a ration of rumours, jokes, slanders.

b dish it out *N. Amer. colloq.* deal out punishment; fight hard.
3 a *verb intrans.* Be or become dish-shaped or concave. M17. ▸**b** *verb trans.* Make concave; *spec.* incline the spokes of (a wheel) towards the centre. Chiefly as ***dished*** *pa. pple*. M18.
4 *verb trans.* Defeat or swindle completely; ruin, spoil the chances of. *slang*. L17.

Listener Politicians love to dream of allying themselves with erstwhile enemies to dish their friends.

5 *verb intrans.* Of a horse: move its forefeet with a semicircular or scooping motion. M19.
■ **dishing** *verbal noun* (*a*) the action of the verb; (*b*) oblique positioning of the spokes of a wheel: L17.

dishabille *noun* var. of DÉSHABILLÉ.

†**dishabit** *verb trans.* *rare* (Shakes.). Only in L16.
[ORIGIN from DIS- 2 + HABIT *verb*.]
Remove from its resting place; dislodge.

dishallow /dɪsˈhaləʊ/ *verb trans.* M16.
[ORIGIN from DIS- 2 + HALLOW *verb*[1].]
Destroy the sanctity of.

disharmonic /dɪshɑːˈmɒnɪk/ *adjective*. L19.
[ORIGIN from DIS- 2 + HARMONIC.]
Not harmonic; anharmonic; disharmonious.

disharmonious /dɪshɑːˈməʊnɪəs/ *adjective*. M17.
[ORIGIN from DIS- 2 + HARMONIOUS.]
1 Not in harmony or agreement. M17.
2 Of sounds: discordant. L17.
■ **disharmoniously** *adverb* M17.

disharmonize /dɪsˈhɑːmənʌɪz/ *verb trans. & intrans.* Also **-ise**. E19.
[ORIGIN from DIS- 2 + HARMONIZE after DISHARMONY.]
Put or be out of harmony.

disharmony /dɪsˈhɑːməni/ *noun*. E17.
[ORIGIN from DIS- 2 + HARMONY, prob. after *discord*.]
1 Lack of harmony or agreement, discord; dissonance. E17.

CARLYLE Disharmony of mind and tongue.

2 Something discordant. M19.

Church Times This.. organist was really frightful in playing false notes and disharmonies.

dishdasha /ˈdɪʃdaʃə/ *noun*. Also **dishdash** /ˈdɪʃdaʃ/. L19.
[ORIGIN Arabic *dišdāša*.]
A long robe with long sleeves, traditional dress for men in the Arabian Peninsula and part of the Arab Mashriq countries.

†**disheart** *verb trans.* L16–E17.
[ORIGIN from DIS- 2 + HEART *noun*.]
= DISHEARTEN.

dishearten /dɪsˈhɑːt(ə)n/ *verb trans.* L16.
[ORIGIN from DIS- 2 + HEARTEN, or from DISHEART + -EN[5], after *hearten*.]
Cause to lose heart; make despondent.

G. ORWELL He had become much disheartened after losing money in a lawsuit.

■ **disheartenedness** *noun* dispirited condition L17. **dishearteningly** *adverb* in a way that disheartens M18. **disheartenment** *noun* the act of disheartening; a state of being disheartened, dejection: M19.

dishelm /dɪsˈhɛlm/ *verb*[1]. L15.
[ORIGIN from DIS- 2 + HELM *noun*[1], after Old French *desheaulmer*.]
†**1** *verb intrans.* Take off one's helmet. Only in L15.
2 *verb trans.* Strip of a helmet. E16.

dishelm /dɪsˈhɛlm/ *verb*[2] *trans.* M19.
[ORIGIN from DIS- 2 + HELM *noun*[2].]
Deprive of the helm or rudder.

disher /ˈdɪʃə/ *noun*. ME.
[ORIGIN from DISH *noun*, *verb* + -ER[1].]
1 A person who makes or sells dishes. Now *rare* or *obsolete*. ME.

2 A person who serves food. L16.

disherison /dɪsˈhɛrɪz(ə)n/ *noun*. Also (earlier) †**disheriteson**. ME.
[ORIGIN Old French *des(h)ereteisun*, *-eison*, from *des(h)eriter*: see DISHERIT, -ISON.]
The act of disinheriting; disinheritance.

†**disherit** *verb trans*. ME–L18.
[ORIGIN Old French *des(h)eriter* (mod. *déshériter*) from Proto-Romance, from Latin DIS- 2 + *hereditare* inherit. Superseded by DISINHERIT.]
Dispossess of or bar from an inheritance or (*fig*.) other possession or advantage; disinherit. (Foll. by *of*, (rare) *from*.)
■ †**disheritment** *noun* (*rare*) LME–L19.

†**disheriteson** *noun* see DISHERISON.

†**dishevel** *adjective* see DISHEVELY.

dishevel /dɪˈʃɛv(ə)l/ *verb trans*. Infl. **-ll-**, ***-l-**. L16.
[ORIGIN Prob. chiefly back-form. from DISHEVELLED: cf. French †*descheveler* (now *décheveler*).]
Loosen and throw about in disorder (hair etc.), make dishevelled.
■ **dishevelment** *noun* dishevelled or untidy state M19.

†**dishevelee** *adjective* see DISHEVELY.

dishevelled /dɪˈʃɛv(ə)ld/ *adjective*. Also ***-eled**. LME.
[ORIGIN from DISHEVELY + -ED[1].]
†1 Bare-headed; having one's hair hanging loose. LME–M17.
2 Of the hair: unconfined, hanging loose; (now usu.) disordered, unkempt. L16.
3 Having one's clothes etc. in disarray. E17.

CONAN DOYLE Ian Murdoch staggered into the room, pallid, dishevelled, his clothes in wild disorder.

4 *gen*. Untidy, disorderly. M17.

JAN MORRIS His house . . was . . stacked with books, and . . gloriously dishevelled.

†**dishevely** *adjective*. Also **-elee**, **-el**. LME–L15.
[ORIGIN Old French *deschevelé* pa. pple of *descheveler*, from *des-* DIS- 2 + *chevel* hair.]
= DISHEVELLED 1.

dishonest /dɪsˈɒnɪst/ *adjective*. LME.
[ORIGIN Old French *deshoneste* (mod. *déshonnête*) from Proto-Romance alt. of Latin *dehonestus*, from *honestus* HONEST *adjective*: see DE-, DIS-.]
†1 Bringing dishonour; shameful, discreditable. LME–M18.

MILTON That dishonest victory At Chaeronéa, fatal to liberty.

†2 Licentious, immoral. LME–M18.
3 **a** Of conduct, a statement, etc.: not straightforward or honourable; (now chiefly) fraudulent, of the nature of or involving theft, lying, or cheating. E17. ▸**b** Of a person: lacking in probity or integrity, untrustworthy; (now chiefly) apt to steal, cheat, lie, or act fraudulently. M18.

a LD MACAULAY A most dishonest and inaccurate French translation. J. LE CARRÉ It didn't appeal to Liz much, the secrecy, it seemed dishonest. **b** *Economist* 'Shrinkage' due to dishonest staff and shoplifters cost them £650m last year.

†4 Ugly, unsightly. M17–E18.
■ **dishonestly** *adverb* LME.

dishonest /dɪsˈɒnɪst/ *verb trans*. Long *rare*. LME.
[ORIGIN Old French *deshonester* from Proto-Romance alt. of Latin *dehonestare*, from *honestare* honour, adorn: see DE-, DIS-.]
†1 Bring shame on. LME–M17.
†2 Defame, calumniate. M16–E17.
3 Violate the chastity of; cause (a woman) to be sexually unfaithful. L16.
†4 Make ugly, deform. L16–M17.

dishonesty /dɪsˈɒnɪsti/ *noun*. LME.
[ORIGIN Old French *desho(n)nesté* from Proto-Romance, from (after Latin *honestas*, *-tat-* HONESTY) Latin *dehonestus*: see DISHONEST *adjective*.]
†1 Dishonour, shame; a dishonourable act. LME–L16.
†2 Sexual misconduct, unchastity; a lewd act. LME–M17.
†3 Foul or unsightly appearance; ugliness. LME–M16.
4 Lack of integrity or straightforwardness; *spec*. willingness to steal, cheat, lie, or act fraudulently. Also, a dishonest or fraudulent act. L16.

R. L. STEVENSON They could see no dishonesty where a man who is paid for an hour's work gives half an hour's . . idling in its place.

dishonor *noun*, *verb*, **dishonorable** *adjective* see DISHONOUR *noun* etc.

dishonour /dɪsˈɒnə/ *noun*. Also ***-honor**. ME.
[ORIGIN Old French *deshonor* (mod. *déshonneur*) from Proto-Romance, from Latin DIS- 2 + *honor* HONOUR *noun*.]
1 The reverse of honour or respect; a state of shame or ignominy. Also, a piece of ignominious treatment, an indignity. ME.

SHAKES. *Hen. VIII* So good a lady that no tongue could ever Pronounce dishonour of her.

do a dishonour to, **do dishonour to** treat with indignity, insult. **to the dishonour of** so as to bring into discredit.

2 A source or occasion of dishonour; a disgrace. M16.

R. EDEN They toke it for a dishonour, to . . forsake theyr Captayne.

3 Failure to honour a cheque or other financial obligation. M19.

dishonour /dɪsˈɒnə/ *verb trans*. Also ***-honor**. ME.
[ORIGIN Old French & mod. French *déshonorer* from medieval Latin *dishonorare*, from Latin DIS- 2 + *honorare* HONOUR *verb*.]
1 Treat with dishonour or indignity; behave irreverently towards. ME.
2 Bring dishonour or shame on by one's actions; disgrace. ME.

W. K. KELLY America . . dishonours herself by tolerating slavery.

3 Violate the chastity of, cause (a woman) to be sexually unfaithful. *arch*. LME.

M. AYRTON Theseus . . deserted Ariadne, dishonoured the queen of the Amazons.

4 (Of a bank) decline to accept or pay (a cheque etc.); default on (one's debts). E19.

Business Week 90% of the institutions surveyed showed no increase in losses as a result of dishonored checks.

■ **dishonourer** *noun* L17.

dishonourable /dɪsˈɒn(ə)rəb(ə)l/ *adjective*. Also ***-honor-**. LME.
[ORIGIN Orig. from DISHONOUR *verb* + -ABLE; in part from DIS- 2 + HONOURABLE.]
1 Entailing dishonour, ignominious. Of an action: base, discreditable. LME.

SHAKES. *Jul. Caes.* We petty men . . peep about To find ourselves dishonourable graves. G. B. SHAW It would have been dishonorable to betray her.

dishonourable discharge *US* discharge from the armed forces for dishonourable actions, such as theft or desertion, usu. by sentence of court martial.

†2 Of a person: held in low esteem. *rare*. E17–M18.
3 Of a person: having no sense of honour; unprincipled. L17.
■ **dishonourableness** *noun* E18. **dishonourably** *adverb* L16.

dishouse /dɪsˈhaʊs/ *verb trans*. L16.
[ORIGIN from DIS- 2 + HOUSE *noun*[1], *verb*[1].]
1 Oust from or deprive of a house. L16.
2 Clear (land) of houses. M17.

dishy /ˈdɪʃi/ *adjective*. *slang*. M20.
[ORIGIN from DISH *noun* + -Y[1].]
Very good-looking or attractive.

J. GARDNER Mm, is *that* him? . . He's dishy. B. W. ALDISS Singapore is the dishiest workshop ever invented.

disillusion /dɪsɪˈluːʒ(ə)n, -ˈljuː-/ *noun*. L16.
[ORIGIN from DIS- 3 (sense 1) & 2 (sense 2) + ILLUSION.]
†1 Illusion, delusion. L16–E17.
2 Disillusionment, disenchantment; an instance of this. M19.

H. ACTON The general climate was one of war weariness and disillusion after the elation of victory.

■ **disillusionary** *adjective* pertaining to or of the nature of disillusion L19.

disillusion /dɪsɪˈluːʒ(ə)n, -ˈljuː-/ *verb trans*. M19.
[ORIGIN from the noun.]
Deprive of belief in an illusion or ideal; disenchant, undeceive.

C. S. FORESTER Randall could not believe in victory: he had been disillusioned too often.

■ **disillusioner**, **disillusionist** *nouns* L19. **disillusionment** *noun* the action or an act of disillusioning; the state of being disillusioned; (a) disenchantment: M19.

disillusionize /dɪsɪˈluːʒ(ə)nʌɪz, -ˈljuː-/ *verb trans*. Also **-ise**. M19.
[ORIGIN from DISILLUSION *noun* + -IZE.]
= DISILLUSION *verb*.
■ **disillusionizer** *noun* L19.

disillusive /dɪsɪˈluːsɪv, -ˈljuː-/ *adjective*. L19.
[ORIGIN from DIS- 2 after *illusive*.]
Tending to disillusion.

disincentive /dɪsɪnˈsɛntɪv/ *noun & adjective*. M20.
[ORIGIN from DIS- 2 + INCENTIVE *noun*.]
(Constituting) a source of discouragement, esp. in an economic or commercial matter.
■ **disincentivize** *verb trans*. discourage, demotivate L20.

disincline /dɪsɪnˈklʌɪn/ *verb trans*. M17.
[ORIGIN from DIS- 2 + INCLINE *verb*.]
Make unwilling or averse. (Foll. by *for*, *to*, *from*, *to do*.)

D. CECIL A . . changeable temperament . . disinclined him to stick to any course of life for long.

■ **disincliˈnation** *noun* M17. **disinclined** *adjective* unwilling, averse M17.

disincommodate /dɪsɪnˈkɒmədeɪt/ *verb trans*. *rare*. M17.
[ORIGIN Blend of DISCOMMODATE and INCOMMODATE.]
Inconvenience, incommode.

disinfect /dɪsɪnˈfɛkt/ *verb trans*. L16.
[ORIGIN French *désinfecter*, from *dés-* DIS- 2 + *infecter* INFECT *verb*.]
†1 Rid (a person or place) of an infection. *rare*. L16–E18.
2 Cleanse (a room, clothes, etc.) from infection by destroying infecting micro-organisms, esp. by chemical means. M17.

N. MAILER The pills they kept to disinfect their drinking water. *Time* Phenols . . are employed by many plants and primitive animals to heal and disinfect wounds.

■ **disinfecter** *noun* M19. **disinfection** *noun* E19. **disinfector** *noun* M19.

D

disinfectant /dɪsɪnˈfɛkt(ə)nt/ *noun & adjective*. M19.
[ORIGIN French *désinfectant* pres. pple of *désinfecter*: see DISINFECT, -ANT[1].]
▸**A** *noun*. An agent (usu. chemical) used for disinfection. M19.
▸**B** *adjective*. Having the property of disinfecting. L19.

disinflation /dɪsɪnˈfleɪʃ(ə)n/ *noun*. L19.
[ORIGIN from DIS- 2 + INFLATION.]
1 = DEFLATION 3. L19.
2 *ECONOMICS*. The reversal of monetary inflation; the return to a state of equilibrium from an inflationary state. M20.
■ **disinflationary** *adjective* M20.

disinformation /ˌdɪsɪnfəˈmeɪʃ(ə)n/ *noun*. M20.
[ORIGIN from DIS- 2 + INFORMATION after Russian *dezinformatsiya*.]
(The dissemination of) deliberately false information, esp. as supplied by one government to another or to the public.
■ **disinˈform** *verb trans*. L20.

disingenuity /ˌdɪsɪndʒɪˈnjuːɪti/ *noun*. M17.
[ORIGIN from DISINGENUOUS after INGENUITY.]
1 Disingenuousness. M17.
2 A piece of unfair treatment or underhand dealing. L17.

disingenuous /dɪsɪnˈdʒɛnjʊəs/ *adjective*. M17.
[ORIGIN from DIS- 2 + INGENUOUS.]
Insincere, lacking in frankness or honesty; fraudulent.

W. GOLDING I should be disingenuous if I pretended not to be flattered.

■ **disingenuously** *adverb* M17. **disingenuousness** *noun* L17.

disinherison /dɪsɪnˈhɛrɪz(ə)n/ *noun*. M16.
[ORIGIN Alt. of DISHERISON after DISINHERIT.]
(An instance of) disinheritance.

disinherit /dɪsɪnˈhɛrɪt/ *verb trans*. LME.
[ORIGIN from DIS- 2 + INHERIT, superseding DISHERIT.]
Dispossess of or bar from an inheritance.

fig.: E. B. BROWNING Earth, methinks, Will disinherit thy philosophy.

■ **disinheritance** *noun* dispossession from an inheritance M16.

disintegrable /dɪsˈɪntɪɡrəb(ə)l/ *adjective*. L18.
[ORIGIN from DISINTEGRATE + -ABLE.]
Able to be disintegrated.

disintegrant /dɪsˈɪntɪɡr(ə)nt/ *adjective & noun*. M19.
[ORIGIN from DISINTEGRATE + -ANT[1].]
▸**A** *adjective*. Disintegrating; becoming disintegrated. M19.
▸**B** *noun*. An agent that causes disintegration. L19.

disintegrate /dɪsˈɪntɪɡreɪt/ *verb*. L18.
[ORIGIN from DIS- 2 + INTEGRATE *verb*.]
▸**I** *verb trans*. **1** Separate into its component parts or particles; reduce to fragments, break up, destroy the cohesion or integrity of. L18. ▸**b** *PHYSICS*. Produce the disintegration of (an atomic nucleus etc.). E20.

R. KIRWAN Marlites . . are not disintegrated by exposure to the atmosphere. G. MEREDITH We cannot modify our class distinctions without risk of disintegrating the social structure.

2 Separate or break off as particles *from* the whole mass. L19.
▸**II** *verb intrans*. **3** Undergo disintegration. M19.

R. P. WARREN The old stonework disintegrating into a heap of rubble.

■ **disintegrative** *adjective* tending to cause disintegration M19. **disintegratively** *adverb* L19. **disintegrator** *noun* M19.

disintegration /dɪsˌɪntɪˈɡreɪʃ(ə)n/ *noun*. L18.
[ORIGIN from DISINTEGRATE + -ATION.]
1 The action or process of disintegrating; the condition of being disintegrated. L18.

A. C. RAMSAY The constant atmospheric disintegration of cliffs. R. SCRUTON The disintegration of authority means the collapse of justice.

2 *PHYSICS*. The process in which an atomic nucleus changes into another nuclide by emitting one or more particles or splitting into smaller nuclei; the decay of a subatomic particle. E20.

Nature The disintegration-rate . . correctly specifies the strength of a radioactive source.

■ **disintegrationist** *noun* an advocate of disintegration L19.

disinter /dɪsɪnˈtəː/ *verb trans*. E17.
[ORIGIN French *désenterrer*, from *dés-* DIS- 2 + *enterrer* INTER *verb*.]
1 Remove (a buried object) from the ground; exhume. E17.

SIR T. BROWNE To disenterre the bodies of the deceased.

2 Take out as if from a tomb; bring out of concealment. E18.

G. GREENE How can I disinter the human character from the heavy scene?

†**disinteress** *verb*. E17–M17.
[ORIGIN French *désintéresser*, from *dés* DIS- 2 + *intéresser* INTERESS *verb*.]
= DISINTEREST *verb*.

†**disinteressed** *adjective*. E17.
[ORIGIN from DISINTERESS + -ED[1] or from DIS- 2 + *interessed* pa. ppl adjective of INTERESS *verb*.]
1 = DISINTERESTED 1. Only in 17.
2 = DISINTERESTED 2. E17–E18.

D

†**disinteressment** *noun*. M17–E18.
[ORIGIN French *désintéressement*, formed as DISINTERESSED + -MENT.]
Impartiality, disinterestedness.

disinterest /dɪsˈɪnt(ə)rɪst/ *noun*. M17.
[ORIGIN from DIS- 2 + INTEREST *noun*.]
1 Impartiality, disinterestedness. M17.
2 That which is contrary to interest or advantage; disadvantage, prejudice, injury. M17.

J. NORRIS Whatever . . tends to the Disinterest of the Public, is Evil.

3 Absence of interest (*in*), unconcern. L19.

disinterest /dɪsˈɪnt(ə)rɛst/ *verb trans*. Now *rare* exc. as next. E17.
[ORIGIN from DIS- 2 + INTEREST *verb*. Cf. DISINTERESS.]
Rid of interest or concern; detach from an interest or party. (Foll. by *in*, *of*, *from*.)

disinterested /dɪsˈɪnt(ə)rɪstɪd/ *adjective*. E17.
[ORIGIN from DISINTEREST *verb* + -ED[1], or from DIS- 2 + INTERESTED.]
1 Not interested, unconcerned, uninterested. E17.

P. ACKROYD He asked me with all the curiosity of a thoroughly disinterested person.

2 Not influenced by one's own advantage; impartial, free from personal interest. M17.

M. BEERBOHM May I assume that your love for me has been entirely disinterested?

— NOTE: Although it is the first recorded meaning and is commonly used, sense 1 is often regarded as incorrect.
■ **disinterestedly** *adverb* E18. **disinterestedness** *noun* L17.

disinteresting /dɪsˈɪnt(ə)rɪstɪŋ/ *adjective*. M18.
[ORIGIN from DIS- 2 + INTERESTING.]
Uninteresting, arousing no interest.

disintermediation /ˌdɪsɪntəmiːdɪˈeɪʃ(ə)n/ *noun*. M20.
[ORIGIN from DIS- 2 + INTERMEDIATION.]
ECONOMICS. Investment or borrowing of moneys without the mediation of a bank or other controlled institution; disinvestment from banks etc. in favour of direct investment in the securities market.
■ **disintermediate** *verb intrans. & trans*. L20.

disinterment /dɪsɪnˈtəːm(ə)nt/ *noun*. L18.
[ORIGIN from DISINTER + -MENT.]
1 Exhumation. L18.
2 Something disinterred. E19.

disintoxicate /dɪsɪnˈtɒksɪkeɪt/ *verb trans*. L17.
[ORIGIN from DIS- 2 + INTOXICATE *verb*.]
Free from intoxication or (*fig*.) enchantment.
■ **ˌdisintoxiˈcation** *noun* E20.

disintricate /dɪsˈɪntrɪkeɪt/ *verb trans*. Now *rare*. L16.
[ORIGIN from DIS- 2 + INTRICATE *verb*.]
Free from intricacy; disentangle, extricate.

disinvest /dɪsɪnˈvɛst/ *verb*. M17.
[ORIGIN from DIS- 2 + INVEST.]
1 *verb trans*. Deprive *of* that with which one is invested; divest. M17.
2 *verb intrans*. Remove financial investment. L20.

disinvestment /dɪsɪnˈvɛs(t)m(ə)nt/ *noun*. M20.
[ORIGIN from DIS- 2 + INVESTMENT.]
ECONOMICS. Withdrawal or realization of investments or assets; the process of disinvesting.

disinvitation /ˌdɪsɪnvɪˈteɪʃ(ə)n/ *noun*. *rare*. L17.
[ORIGIN from DIS- 2 + INVITATION.]
The withdrawal or cancellation of an invitation.

disinvite /dɪsɪnˈvʌɪt/ *verb trans*. L16.
[ORIGIN from DIS- 2 + INVITE *verb*.]
Withdraw or cancel an invitation to.

P. WYLIE Not being disinvited I tagged along.

— NOTE: Obsolete after L17; recorded again L19.

disinvoltura /disinvɔlˈtuːra/ *noun*. M19.
[ORIGIN Italian, from *disinvolto* unembarrassed, from *disinvolgere* unwind.]
Self-assurance; lack of constraint.

F. A. KEMBLE A woman, who moves with more complete *disinvoltura* in her men's clothes than most men do.

disjaskit /dɪsˈdʒɑːskɪt/ *adjective*. *Scot*. Also **-ket**, **-ked**. E19.
[ORIGIN Perh. alt. of *dejected*.]
Dilapidated; dejected; exhausted.

disject /dɪsˈdʒɛkt/ *verb trans*. L16.
[ORIGIN Latin *disject-* pa. ppl stem of *disicere*, formed as DIS- 1 + *jacere* to throw.]
Scatter, disperse; break up, dismember.
■ **disjection** *noun* M18.

disjecta membra /dɪsˌjɛktə ˈmɛmbrə/ *noun phr. pl*. E18.
[ORIGIN Alt. of Latin *disjecti membra poetae* limbs of a dismembered poet (Horace).]
Scattered remains. Cf. MEMBRA DISJECTA.

R. G. COLLINGWOOD A world full of shattered ideas, *disjecta membra* of old systems of life and thought.

disjoin /dɪsˈdʒɔɪn/ *verb*. LME.
[ORIGIN Old French *desjoign-* pres. stem of *desjoindre* (mod. *dé-*) from Latin *disjungere*, formed as DIS- 2 + *jungere* JOIN *verb*.]
1 *verb trans*. Put or keep apart; separate, sever. LME.
2 *verb trans*. Dissolve, break up; unfasten; separate into parts. Now *rare* or *obsolete*. L16.
3 *verb intrans*. Separate oneself (*from*); part, become separate. L16.

disjoint /dɪsˈdʒɔɪnt/ *adjective & adverb*. LME.
[ORIGIN Old French *desjoint* pa. pple of *desjoindre*: see DISJOIN.]
▸ **A** *adjective*. †**1** Disjointed, out of joint, disconnected. LME–E18.
2 Separate, separated; *spec*. (LOGIC, of two or more sets) having no elements in common. L16.
▸ †**B** *adverb*. Apart, asunder. Only in LME.
■ **disjointly** *adverb* (**a**) separately, apart; (**b**) *rare* disjointedly, disconnectedly: E17.

disjoint /dɪsˈdʒɔɪnt/ *verb*. LME.
[ORIGIN Orig. from DISJOINT *adjective & adverb*, later partly from DIS- 2 + JOINT *noun*.]
1 *verb trans*. Destroy the connection and arrangement of; dislocate, disturb. LME.

fig.: GIBBON A lyric writer of taste . . disjointing the order of his ideas.

2 *verb trans*. = DISJOIN 1. L16.

T. JEFFERSON Great Britain, disjointed from her colonies.

3 *verb trans*. Take to pieces. L16.

R. LOVELACE Like watches by unskilfull men Disjoynted, and set ill againe.

4 *verb intrans*. Be disjointed; suffer dislocation, come apart. E17.

SHAKES. *Macb*. Let the frame of things disjoint.

■ **disjointure** *noun* the fact of being disjointed; disconnection, separation: M18.

disjointed /dɪsˈdʒɔɪntɪd/ *ppl adjective*. L16.
[ORIGIN from DISJOINT *verb* + -ED[1].]
1 Of speech, writing, etc.: not properly connected; incoherent, rambling. L16.

J. GALSWORTHY In the fourth carriage a disjointed conversation was carried on.

2 Separated joint from joint, disconnected; consisting of separated or poorly connected parts. E17.

C. THIRLWALL The huge frame of the Persian empire was disjointed and unwieldy.

■ **disjointedly** *adverb* L19. **disjointedness** *noun* M17.

disjunct /ˈdɪsdʒʌŋkt/ *adjective & noun*. LME.
[ORIGIN Latin *disjunctus* pa. pple of *disjungere*: see DISJOIN.]
▸ **A** *adjective*. **1** Disjoined, separate, distinct. Now *rare* exc. *techn*. LME.

Scientific American Two disjunct areas in Malaya support a single species of tree.

2 LOGIC. †**a** = DISJUNCTIVE *adjective* 2. L16–M17. ▸**b** Designating each term of a disjunctive proposition. M19.
3 MUSIC. Designating motion by leaps of more than one degree of a scale (i.e. by intervals of more than a second); proceeding by or involving such leaps. Opp. CONJUNCT *adjective* 4. L17.
▸ **B** *noun*. LOGIC. Each of the terms of a disjunctive proposition. E20.
■ †**disjunctly** *adverb* M17–E18.

disjunction /dɪsˈdʒʌŋkʃ(ə)n/ *noun*. LME.
[ORIGIN Old French *disjunction* (mod. *-jonction*) or its source Latin *disjunctio(n-)*, from *disjunct-* pa. ppl stem of *disjungere*: see DISJOIN, -ION.]
1 The action of disjoining; the condition of being disjoined; separation. LME.

R. D. LAING The disjunction between his concept of her and her experience of herself.

2 LOGIC. (A statement expressing) the relation between statements of which the truth of one and only one is asserted (exclusive 'or'). Also = ALTERNATION 4 (inclusive 'or'). L16.

disjunctive /dɪsˈdʒʌŋktɪv/ *noun & adjective*. LME.
[ORIGIN Latin *disjunctivus*, from *disjunct-*: see DISJUNCTION, -IVE.]
▸ **A** *adjective*. **1** GRAMMAR. Of a conjunction: expressing an alternative, or implying an adversative relation between the clauses it connects (opp. ***copulative***). LME.
2 LOGIC. Asserting the truth of one or other of two or more statements; involving a premiss of this kind; of the nature of a disjunction. L16.
3 Having the property of disjoining; characterized by separation. L16.

G. STEINER The syntax and structure of the Indo-Germanic languages are strongly disjunctive.

▸ **B** *noun*. **1** GRAMMAR. A disjunctive conjunction. M16.
2 LOGIC. A disjunctive proposition or statement. M16.
■ **disjunctively** *adverb* in a disjunctive manner; alternatively, not jointly; adversatively L16.

disjuncture /dɪsˈdʒʌŋktʃə/ *noun*. LME.
[ORIGIN medieval Latin *disjunctura*, from *disjunct-*: see DISJUNCTION, -URE. Cf. Old French *desjointure*.]
Separation, disconnection; a breach, a hiatus; a disjointed state.

T. GOODWIN Disjunctures, or brokenness of bones. *Scientific American* Allegations . . of a disjuncture between academic medicine and the effective delivery of medical care.

disjune /dɪsˈdʒuːn/ *noun*. Chiefly *Scot*. *arch*. L15.
[ORIGIN Old French *desjeün* (mod. dial. *déjun*), from *desjeüner* (mod. *déjeuner*) to break fast, breakfast (noun), from *des-* DIS- 2 + *jeün* fasting from Latin *jejunus*.]
Breakfast.

disk *noun*, *verb*, **diskectomy** *noun* see DISC *noun*, *verb*, DISCECTOMY.

diskette /dɪˈskɛt/ *noun*. Also **discette**. L20.
[ORIGIN from DISK *noun* + -ETTE.]
COMPUTING. A small flexible plastic disk with a magnetic coating used as an inexpensive data-storage device of moderate capacity; a floppy disk; such a disk together with its protective envelope.

†**disleal** *adjective*. *rare* (Spenser). Only in L16.
[ORIGIN Italian *disleale*.]
Disloyal.

dislikable *adjective* var. of DISLIKEABLE.

dislike /dɪsˈlʌɪk; *contrasted with* like ˈdɪslʌɪk/ *noun*. L16.
[ORIGIN from the verb.]
†**1** Displeasure, disapproval, (as directed at some object). L16–M18.

W. PENN A letter from the government, in dislike of such proceedings.

2 The feeling that something is distasteful, unpleasant, unattractive, or objectionable. L16. ▸**b** A particular aversion, something disliked. E17.

P. G. WODEHOUSE His dislike amounted to positive loathing. A. LURIE The look of cool dislike on Steve's face. **b** G. L. HARDING Likes and dislikes in the way of scenery are so very personal. W. GASS Pa took a dislike to Hans and said I shouldn't go with Hans so much.

†**3** Disagreement, discord. L16–M17.
■ †**dislikeful** *adjective* (**a**) unpleasant; (**b**) characterized by dislike: only in L16.

†**dislike** *adjective*. L16–M17.
[ORIGIN from DIS- 2 + LIKE *adjective*.]
Unlike, dissimilar.
■ †**dislikeness** *noun*: only in 17.

dislike /dɪsˈlʌɪk/ *verb*. M16.
[ORIGIN from DIS- 2 + LIKE *verb*[1]: superseded MISLIKE.]
†**1** *verb intrans*. Be displeased, offended, or dissatisfied (*with*); disapprove (*of*). M16–L17.
†**2** *verb trans*. Displease, annoy, offend. Only in 3rd person. L16–E19.

SHAKES. *Oth*. I'll do't; but it dislikes me.

3 *verb trans*. Not like; have a distaste for, have an aversion or objection to. L16.

J. CONRAD A crowd, which disliked to be disturbed by sounds of distress. E. F. BENSON No young man dislikes being treated intimately by a woman. C. P. SNOW I disliked the sound of the job—I felt it was nothing like good enough.

4 *verb trans*. Show or express aversion to. *obsolete* exc. in ***disliking*** *ppl adjective*. E17.
■ **disliker** *noun* L16.

dislikeable /dɪsˈlʌɪkəb(ə)l/ *adjective*. Also **-likable**. M19.
[ORIGIN from DISLIKE *verb* + -ABLE.]
Able to be disliked; producing dislike, easy to dislike.

†**disliken** *verb trans*. *rare* (Shakes.). Only in E17.
[ORIGIN from DISLIKE *adjective* + -EN[5].]
Make unlike, disguise.

dislimn /dɪsˈlɪm/ *verb*. E17.
[ORIGIN from DIS- 2 + LIMN.]
1 *verb trans*. Obliterate the outlines of; efface, blot out. E17.
2 *verb intrans*. Become effaced; vanish. M19.

dislocate /ˈdɪslə(ʊ)kət/ *ppl adjective*. Now *rare* or *obsolete*. LME.
[ORIGIN medieval Latin *dislocatus* pa. pple of *dislocare*: see DISLOCATION, -ATE².]
Dislocated.

dislocate /ˈdɪslə(ʊ)keɪt/ *verb trans*. L16.
[ORIGIN Prob. back-form. from DISLOCATION, but perh. from DISLOCATE *adjective*: see -ATE³.]
1 Destroy or disturb the normal connection of (a joint or limb); displace (a bone) from its proper position. L16.
2 *gen*. Put out of a proper (or former) place; displace, shift. Now *rare*. E17.

G. MEREDITH No sooner was he comfortably established than she wished to dislocate him.

3 Put out of proper position or orientation in relation to adjoining parts. M17.

R. L. STEVENSON Something, flood or earthquake, had dislocated the whole structure at one joint, so that it hung two ways.

4 Put (affairs, the working of something) out of order or out of the normal course; upset, disrupt. M17.

M. L. KING To dislocate the functioning of a city without destroying it.

■ **dislocative** *adjective* (*rare*) serving to dislocate, causing dislocation. E19. **disloˈcatory** *adjective* causing dislocation. L19.

dislocation /dɪslə(ʊ)ˈkeɪʃ(ə)n/ *noun*. LME.
[ORIGIN Old French, or medieval Latin *dislocatio(n-)*, from *dislocat-* pa. ppl stem of *dislocare*, from Latin DIS- 1 + *locare* place: see -ATION.]
1 Displacement of a bone from its natural position in a joint; luxation. LME.
2 *gen*. Displacement; removal from a proper (or former) position. E17. ▸**b** GEOLOGY. The fracture of strata with upheaval or subsidence; a result of this, a fault. L17. ▸**c** CRYSTALLOGRAPHY. A displacement of the lattice structure of a crystal. M20.

New Republic The prevailing mood of Kafkaesque dislocation.

3 Disarrangement of parts; a disordered state. M17.

E. B. PUSEY The utter dislocation of society. V. WOOLF Something's wrong, he thought; there's a gap, a dislocation, between the word and the reality. *Adweek (US)* Recessions create dislocations in the labor force—furloughs, layoffs, all manner of unpleasantness.

4 MILITARY. The distribution of troops to a number of garrisons or stations. E19.

dislodge /dɪsˈlɒdʒ/ *verb*. LME.
[ORIGIN Old French *dislog(i)er*, from *des-* DIS- 2 + *logier*, (also mod.) *loger* LODGE *verb*.]
1 *verb trans*. Remove or turn out of a settled or established position; displace. LME. ▸**b** MILITARY. Drive (an enemy) from a lodgement or other established position. LME. ▸†**c** MILITARY. Shift the position of (a force, one's quarters). L15–L17. ▸**d** HUNTING. Drive (an animal) out of its lair. E17.

M. SHADBOLT It was as if a falling pebble had dislodged stones, and stones boulders.

†**2** *verb intrans*. MILITARY. Leave a place of encampment. L15–M18.
3 *verb intrans*. Leave the place where one lives or is staying; (of a thing) leave the place where it has been settled. Now *rare*. E16.

H. COGAN Proclaimed, that all persons . . should upon pain of death dislodge speedily out of the Island.

dislodgement /dɪsˈlɒdʒm(ə)nt/ *noun*. Also **-dgm-**. E18.
[ORIGIN from DISLODGE + -MENT.]
The action or an act of dislodging; displacement.

†**disloign** *verb trans*. *rare* (Spenser). Only in L16.
[ORIGIN Old French *desloignier*, from *des-* DIS- 1 + *loin* far.]
Remove to a distance.

dislove /dɪsˈlʌv/ *noun*. *rare*. M16.
[ORIGIN from DIS- 2 + LOVE *noun*.]
Disappearance of love; unfriendliness; hatred.

dislove /dɪsˈlʌv/ *verb trans*. Now *rare*. M16.
[ORIGIN from DIS- 2 + LOVE *verb*.]
Not love; hate; cease loving.

disloyal /dɪsˈlɔɪ(ə)l/ *adjective* & *noun*. L15.
[ORIGIN Old French *desloial* (mod. *déloyal*), from *des-* DIS- 2 + *loial* LOYAL.]
▸ **A** *adjective*. **1** Unfaithful to personal ties of duty or affection, as friendship, marriage, etc. L15.

SHAKES. *Rich. II* Thou dost suspect That I have been disloyal to thy bed. E. B. BROWNING Without a thought disloyal.

2 Untrue to a political allegiance, lacking loyalty to a government or other constituted authority. L16.
▸ **B** *noun*. A disloyal person; a traitor; a rebel. Now *rare*. E17.
■ **disloyalist** *noun* M19. **disloyally** *adverb* LME.

disloyalty /dɪsˈlɔɪ(ə)lti/ *noun*. LME.
[ORIGIN from DISLOYAL + -TY¹, or from DIS- 2 + LOYALTY: cf. Old French *desloyau(l)té* (mod. *déloyauté*).]
The quality of being disloyal; lack of loyalty; violation of allegiance or duty to one's country etc.

dismail /dɪsˈmeɪl/ *verb trans*. *arch*. LME.
[ORIGIN Old French *desmailler*, from *des-* DIS- 2 + *maille* MAIL *noun*².]
Divest of mail; break the mail off.

dismal /ˈdɪzm(ə)l/ *noun*. ME.
[ORIGIN Anglo-Norman *dis mal* from medieval Latin *dies mali* evil days; in branch II from the adjective.]
▸ **I** †**1** The 24 evil or unlucky days (two in each month) in the medieval calendar; *gen*. evil days; the time of old age. Only in ME.
▸ **II** †**2** The Devil. L15–L16.
†**3 a** A funeral mute. Only in E18. ▸**b** In *pl*. Mourning garments. M–L18.
4 One of the dreary tracts of swampy land on the eastern seaboard of the US. E18.
5 *the dismals*, low spirits, the 'dumps'. M18. ▸**b** In *pl*. Depressing circumstances, miseries. E19.

dismal /ˈdɪzm(ə)l/ *adjective*. LME.
[ORIGIN from DISMAL *noun* I.]
1 Designating each of the 24 evil or unlucky days of the medieval calendar. *obsolete* exc. *hist*. LME.

SPENSER An ugly feend, more fowle than dismall day.

†**2** *gen*. Boding or bringing misfortune and disaster; malign. L16–M17.
3 Of the nature of misfortune or disaster; calamitous. Now *rare*. L16.
4 Orig., causing dismay, dreadful. Now, causing gloom, depressing; sombre, dreary, cheerless. L16.

W. IRVING The sight of this wreck . . gave rise to many dismal anecdotes. E. F. BENSON Minorca . . had been a dismal failure. H. KELLER The weather has been awfully dismal. D. H. LAWRENCE The sea was grey and shaggy and dismal.

dismal Desmond a toy dog with drooping ears; *colloq*. a gloomy person. **dismal Jimmy** *colloq*. a gloomy person. **dismal science** *joc*. & *colloq*. economics.
5 Exhibiting or expressing gloom. E18.

G. BURNET Wrote dismal letters to the Court. W. IRVING The warriors returned, in dismal procession.

6 Feeble; inept. *colloq*. M20.

Economist Galsworthy's dismal efforts at working-class descriptions.

■ **disˈmality** *noun* dismal quality or state; an instance of this: E18. **dismalize** *verb trans*. make (more) dismal M18. **dismally** *adverb* L16. **dismalness** *noun* E17.

disman /dɪsˈman/ *verb trans*. Infl. **-nn-**. E17.
[ORIGIN from DIS- 2 + MAN *noun*.]
†**1** Deprive of personal existence or manhood. E–M17.
2 Deprive (a country etc.) of men. M19.

dismantle /dɪsˈmant(ə)l/ *verb trans*. L16.
[ORIGIN Old French *desmanteler* (mod. *démanteler* in military sense), from *des-* DIS- 2 + *manteler* fortify.]
1 Destroy the defensive capability of (a fortification etc.); raze; pull down, take to pieces, disassemble. L16.

H. COGAN Causing all the walls of it to be dismantelled, he razed the place quite to the ground. A. BROOKNER Watching tents being put up and dismantled. *Observer* When Great Britain dismantled the British Empire it gave the land back to the original owners.

2 Strip (something) of necessary equipment, covering, furniture, or apparatus; *esp*. strip (a fortress) of its defences, strip (a vessel) of its rigging. (Foll. by *of* the equipment, covering, etc.) E17.

JAMES SULLIVAN When Greece was dismantled by the Romans.

†**3** Divest of a mantle or cloak; uncloak (*lit*. & *fig*.). Only in 17.
†**4** Strip off or remove (a covering). E–M17.
■ **dismantlement** *noun* L19. **dismantler** *noun* M18.

dismark /dɪsˈmɑːk/ *verb trans*. *rare*. E17.
[ORIGIN French †*desmarquer* (now *dé-*) remove a mark from.]
Remove a (distinguishing) mark from.

dismarry /dɪsˈmari/ *verb trans*. *rare*. E16.
[ORIGIN Old French *desmarier* (mod. *dé-*), from *des-* DIS- 2 + *marier* MARRY *verb*.]
Annul the marriage of; divorce.

†**dismask** *verb trans*. L16–M17.
[ORIGIN French †*desmasquer* (now *dé-*), from *des-* DIS- 2 + *masquer* MASK *verb*².]
Divest of a mask or covering; unmask.

dismay /dɪsˈmeɪ/ *noun*. ME.
[ORIGIN from the verb.]
1 Loss of moral courage or resolution in the face of difficulty or danger; faintness of heart from terror or inability to cope with a situation; consternation, discouragement; keenly felt disappointment. ME.

G. B. SHAW My amusement at this soon changed to dismay. TOLKIEN 'Your news is all of woe!' cried Éomer in dismay.

†**2** Dismaying influence or operation. *rare* (Spenser). Only in L16.
■ **dismayful** *adjective* appalling L16. **dismayfully** *adverb* in dismay L16.

dismay /dɪsˈmeɪ/ *verb*. ME.
[ORIGIN from assumed Old French verb from Proto-Romance, from Latin DIS- 2 + Germanic base of MAY *verb*¹.]
1 *verb trans*. Fill with dismay; reduce to despair. Formerly also (*rare*), defeat or rout by sudden onslaught. ME.

J. G. FARRELL She hugged him tightly with tears in her eyes, dismayed at how much he had changed.

†**2** *verb intrans*. Become utterly discouraged or faint-hearted. LME–L16.
■ **dismayedness** *noun* dismayed condition L16. **dismayer** *noun* L16. **dismayingly** *adverb* so as to cause dismay (*rare* before E20) M18.

†**disme** *noun* var. of DIME.

dismember /dɪsˈmɛmbə/ *verb trans*. ME.
[ORIGIN Old French *desmembrer* (mod. *dé-*) from Proto-Romance (cf. medieval Latin *dismembrare*) from Latin DIS- 2 + *membrum* MEMBER *noun*. In sense 4 directly from DIS- 2 + MEMBER *noun* 2. Cf. DEMEMBER.]
1 Cut off the limbs of; tear or divide limb from limb. ME. ▸**b** Carve (a heron or certain other birds). *obsolete* exc. *hist*. LME. ▸**c** Sever (a limb) from or *from* the body; *fig*. separate (a part) from or *from* the main body. Now *rare*. L16.

P. D. JAMES Men wishing to be acquitted of murder should avoid dismembering their victims.

2 *fig*. Break up into smaller units, esp. so as to mutilate; *spec*. partition (an empire or other territory). ME.

J. R. GREEN Mercia had been dismembered to provide another earldom for his son.

3 Deprive of membership. M17.
■ **dismembered** *ppl adjective* that has been dismembered; *spec*. (HERALDRY) having the limbs narrowly separated from the body: M16. **dismemberer** *noun* L16.

dismemberment /dɪsˈmɛmbəm(ə)nt/ *noun*. M17.
[ORIGIN from DISMEMBER + -MENT.]
▸ **I 1** Expulsion from membership. *rare*. M17.
▸ **II 2** The action or an act of dismembering; a dismembered condition. M18.
3 A detached part formed by separation from the main body. M19.

†**dismembration** *noun*. M17–E19.
[ORIGIN medieval Latin *dismembratio(n-)*, from *dismembrare*, from Latin DIS- 2 + *membrum* MEMBER *noun*: see -ATION.]
= DEMEMBRATION.

dismiss /dɪsˈmɪs/ *noun*. Long *rare*. L16.
[ORIGIN from the verb.]
An act of dismissing; a dismissal.

dismiss /dɪsˈmɪs/ *verb*. Pa. t. & pple **dismissed**, †**dismist**. LME.
[ORIGIN medieval Latin *dismiss-* var. of Latin *dimiss-* pa. ppl stem of *dimittere*, from *di-* DI-¹ + *mittere* send: see DIS- 1. Cf. DIMISS, DIMIT *verb*¹.]
▸ **I** *verb trans*. **1** Free from custody or confinement. LME.

transf.: J. SYLVESTER Blushing Aurora had yet scarce dismist Mount Libanus from the Nights gloomy Mist.

†**2** Release from a legal liability; exclude from a legal advantage. (Foll. by *of*.) LME–M17.
3 Remove, esp. with dishonour, from a post or employment; discharge, expel. (Foll. by *from*, †*of*, or double obj.) LME. ▸**b** Pay off (a hired vehicle etc.). E17. ▸**c** CRICKET. Put (a batsman or side) out, esp. *for* a given score. L19.

J. R. GREEN The King dismissed those of his ministers who still opposed a Spanish policy. *Listener* He was dismissed the service and sent back to England.

†**4** Deprive or disappoint of an advantage. Foll. by *of*, *from*. L15–M17.
5 Permit or direct (a person) to go from one's presence; send away. M16. ▸**b** Let go, send away, (a thing); give egress to. E17.

G. VIDAL My father dismissed me with an awkward pat. **b** J. HAWKESWORTH As a slinger whirls a stone that he would dismiss with all his strength.

6 Send away in various directions, disperse, (an assembly etc.); disband (an army etc.). L16.
7 Banish from the mind (a thought, feeling, etc.); treat as unworthy of consideration. L16. ▸†**b** Allow to be forgotten; overlook (an offence, a promise made). E17–L18.

A. BLEASDALE He inspects the cigarette end and dismisses, reluctantly, the chances of smoking it. *Times* We trust that this unfounded . . allegation will be dismissed. L. HUDSON Lacan . . would certainly dismiss the present text as part of a cowardly Anglo-Saxon plot.

8 Send out of court; deny further hearing to (a legal action or claim). E17.
9 Reject (a person) as unsuitable; *spec*. put away, divorce, (a wife). E17.
10 Lay aside, get rid of. Now chiefly with abstract obj. L17.

HOBBES [Gods] can their form dismiss, And when they will, put on a new disguise.

11 Pass from the consideration of, bring (a subject) to an end; treat summarily. L17.

ADDISON I shall dismiss this Paper with a Story out of Josephus.

▸ **II** *verb intrans*. **12** Of a body of people: disperse from ordered assembly; (MILITARY, in *imper*.) used as a word of command at the end of drilling. E19.

A. S. NEILL The class refused to dismiss, they crowded round Dorothy.

■ **dismissable** *adjective* = DISMISSIBLE E19. **dismissible** *adjective* liable to be dismissed from office M19.

D

dismissal /dɪsˈmɪs(ə)l/ *noun*. E19.
[ORIGIN from DISMISS *verb* + -AL¹, repl. DISMISSION.]
The action or an act of dismissing.

Z. GREY Sampson had told me to clear out, and although I did not take that as a dismissal I considered I would be wise to leave the ranch at once. K. AMIS His dismissal of the captain of the Eleven off the first ball of the innings.

dismission /dɪsˈmɪʃ(ə)n/ *noun*. Now *rare*. M16.
[ORIGIN from DISMISS *verb* + -ION, after French †*desmission* (now *démission*): see DEMISSION *noun*¹.]
1 Removal from office or employment; discharge. Also, a notice of discharge. M16.
2 Release from confinement; liberation. E17.
3 The action of sending a person away; permission to go. Formerly freq., an official send-off. E17. ▸**b** The action of sending assembled persons away in various directions; dispersal; disbandment. M17.
4 Rejection, discarding; *spec.* repudiation of a wife. E17.
5 The action of dispelling or banishing from the mind. M18.

dismissive /dɪsˈmɪsɪv/ *adjective*. M17.
[ORIGIN from DISMISS *verb* + -IVE.]
Of the nature of or characterized by dismissal; tending to dismiss; suggesting unworthiness of any (further) consideration; disdainful.

Encounter Their dicta Relegated to dismissive footnotes.

■ **dismissively** *adverb* E20. **dismissiveness** *noun* L20.

dismissory /dɪsˈmɪs(ə)ri/ *adjective & noun*. Long *rare*. M17.
[ORIGIN Alt. of DIMISSORY after DISMISS *verb*.]
▸ **A** *adjective*. = DIMISSORY *adjective*. M17.
▸ †**B** *noun*. In *pl*. Letters dimissory. Only in E18.

dismoded /dɪsˈməʊdɪd/ *adjective*. L19.
[ORIGIN Alt. of DEMODED (cf. DÉMODÉ): see DIS- 2.]
Unfashionable.

dismount /dɪsˈmaʊnt/ *noun*. M17.
[ORIGIN from the verb.]
An act or method of dismounting (from a horse etc.).

dismount /dɪsˈmaʊnt/ *verb*. M16.
[ORIGIN from DIS- 2 + MOUNT *verb*, prob. after Old French *desmonter*, medieval Latin *dismontare*: cf. DEMOUNT *verb*.]
▸ **I** *verb trans*. **1** Take down (a thing) from that on which it is mounted; *esp.* remove (a gun) from its carriage. M16.
2 †**a** Come down from (a height). L16–M19. ▸**b** Get off (a horse). E17.
3 Throw (a person) down from a horse; unseat. Also, deprive (a cavalry unit) of mounts. L16.
†**4** Lower from a high position; *fig.* reduce in rank or esteem. L16–M18.

G. HERBERT His eyes dismount the highest Starre. W. PENN Drunkenness . . spoils Health, dismounts the Mind.

5 Remove (a gem etc.) from its setting or mount; take (a mechanism) from its framework, take apart. E17.
▸ **II** *verb intrans*. **6** Come down from or *from* a height. *arch*. L16.

T. HARDY Somerset dismounted from the stile.

7 Get off a horse etc. or a bicycle or motorcycle; alight from a vehicle. (Foll. by *from*.) L16.

GIBBON He . . dismounted to present the pilgrim with his camel. I. MURDOCH Mor dismounted at the drive, as the coarse gravel was not pleasant for cycling on. J. LE CARRÉ The bus . . was held up in a traffic jam near a tube station; he dismounted and caught a tube.

■ **dismountable** *adjective* able to be dismounted; (of a gun or cannon) that can be removed from its carriage for transport: E18.

dismutation /dɪsmjuːˈteɪʃ(ə)n/ *noun*. E20.
[ORIGIN from DIS- 3 + MUTATION.]
CHEMISTRY. Disproportionation, esp. involving both oxidation and reduction of a (usu. biological) compound.
■ **disˈmutase** *noun* an enzyme which catalyses a dismutation, esp. of superoxide ions into oxygen M20. **disˈmute** *verb intrans. & trans*. (cause to) undergo dismutation M20.

disna *verb* see DO *verb*.

disnaturalize /dɪsˈnatʃ(ə)r(ə)lʌɪz/ *verb trans*. Also **-ise**. E18.
[ORIGIN from DIS- 2 + NATURALIZE.]
= DENATURALIZE *verb*.

disnature /dɪsˈneɪtʃə/ *verb trans*. LME.
[ORIGIN Old French *desnaturer* (mod. *dé-*), from *des-* DIS- 2 + *naturer* to form, shape from medieval Latin *naturare*, from *natura* NATURE *noun*.]
Deprive of natural quality, character, appearance, etc.

Disneyesque /dɪznɪˈɛsk/ *adjective*. M20.
[ORIGIN from Walt(er Elias) *Disney* (1901–66), US cartoonist + -ESQUE. Cf. WALT DISNEY.]
Having the characteristics or in the style of the animated cartoons of Walt Disney or the company he founded.
■ ˌ**Disneyfiˈcation** *noun* the action or process of making Disneyesque; Disneyesque state: M20. ˈ**Disneyfy** *verb trans*. make Disneyesque L20. ˈ**Disneyland** *noun* [a large amusement park near Los Angeles] a fantastic or fanciful place, a never-never land M20.

disobedience /dɪsəˈbiːdɪəns/ *noun*. LME.
[ORIGIN Old French *desobedience* from Proto-Romance alt. of ecclesiastical Latin *inoboedientia*, from Latin *oboedientia* OBEDIENCE: see DIS- 2.]
The fact or condition of being disobedient; neglect or refusal to obey; an instance of this.
civil disobedience: see CIVIL *adjective*.
■ †**disobediency** *noun* L16–E18.

disobedient /dɪsəˈbiːdɪənt/ *adjective*. LME.
[ORIGIN Old French *desobedient* from Proto-Romance alt. of ecclesiastical Latin *inoboedient-*, from Latin *oboedient-* OBEDIENT: see DIS- 2.]
1 Refusing or failing to obey; neglectful or not observant of what is laid down as a command or duty; refractory, rebellious; insubordinate. LME.

SIR W. SCOTT These are not loving subjects, but disobedient rebels.

2 *transf*. Not yielding to treatment. L16.

E. DARWIN Medicines . . rendering . . parts of the system disobedient to stimuli.

■ **disobediently** *adverb* M16.

disobey /dɪsəˈbeɪ/ *verb*. LME.
[ORIGIN Old French & mod. French *désobéir* from Proto-Romance alt. of ecclesiastical Latin *inoboedire*, from Latin *oboedire* OBEY: see DIS- 2.]
1 *verb intrans*. Be disobedient; show disobedience (†*to* an authority). LME.
2 *verb trans*. Act in violation of the orders of (a person, a law, etc.); refuse or neglect to obey. LME.
■ **disobeyer** *noun* (*a*) *gen*. a person who disobeys; †(*b*) *spec*. a recusant, a rebel: LME.

†**disobligation** *noun*. E17.
[ORIGIN from DIS- 2 + OBLIGATION after DISOBLIGE.]
1 Freedom from obligation. E17–L18.
2 A disobliging act; an affront, a slight. M17–L18.

C. CIBBER Mrs. Oldfield receiv'd it rather as a favour than a disobligation.

3 The feeling of being disobliged; a grudge. M17–M18.

STEELE I . . shall never give a Vote out of Peevishness or personal Disobligation.

disoblige /dɪsəˈblʌɪdʒ/ *verb trans*. L16.
[ORIGIN Old French & mod. French *désobliger* from Proto-Romance, from DIS- 2 + Latin *obligare* OBLIGE.]
†**1** Release, set free, esp. from obligation or duty. L16–L17. ▸**b** Detach from an allegiance. M–L17.
2 Refuse to consider the wishes or convenience of; offend, affront. M17.
3 Incommode, trouble. *obsolete* exc. *dial*. M17.

S. JUDD I . . hope my presence, Madam, will not disoblige you.

■ **disobligement** *noun* (long *rare*) †(*a*) = DISOBLIGATION 1, 2; (*b*) = DISOBLIGATION 3: M17. **disobliging** *ppl adjective* (*a*) not disposed to consider another's wishes, unaccommodating; †(*b*) inconvenient: M17. **disobligingly** *adverb* M17. **disobligingness** *noun* M17.

disomic /dʌɪˈsəʊmɪk/ *adjective & noun*. E20.
[ORIGIN from DI-² + -SOME³ + -IC.]
BIOLOGY. ▸**A** *adjective*. Of, pertaining to, or having a chromosome represented twice in a chromosomal complement. E20.
▸ **B** *noun*. A disomic individual etc. M20.
■ ˈ**disome** *noun* a pair of homologous chromosomes E20.

†**disopinion** *noun*. L16.
[ORIGIN from DIS- 2 + OPINION *noun*.]
1 A difference of opinion; dissent. *rare*. L16–M17.
2 An adverse or low opinion (*of*); disesteem. E17–E18.

disorb /dɪsˈɔːb/ *verb trans*. E17.
[ORIGIN from DIS- 2 + ORB *noun*¹.]
1 Remove (a star etc.) from its sphere. E17.
2 Deprive of an orb as a symbol of sovereignty. M19.

†**disordain** *verb trans*. ME.
[ORIGIN Old French *desordener* (mod. *désordonner*) from Proto-Romance, from Latin DIS- 2 + *ordinare* ORDAIN.]
1 = DISORDER *verb* 5. Only in ME.
2 = DISORDER *verb* 1. Only in LME.

disorder /dɪsˈɔːdə/ *noun*. M16.
[ORIGIN from the verb, after French *désordre*.]
1 Lack of order or regular arrangement; disarray, a confused state. M16.

E. FERBER Books leaning . . against each other or fallen flat in zigzag disorder. H. M. ROSENBERG The presence of all types of defect increases the disorder of the crystal.

2 (A) disturbance, (a) commotion; *esp.* (a) breach of public order. M16.

A. J. P. TAYLOR There were fresh disorders [in India] . . . Gandhi, Nehru, and many other Congress leaders were again imprisoned. *Didcot Herald* Police report an increase in public disorder and violence due to drunkenness.

3 A breach of discipline or orderly conduct, an irregularity. Formerly *spec.*, an irregularity of conduct, a misdemeanour. L16.

G. BURNET The king had another mistress . . she fell into many scandalous disorders.

†**4** Agitation of mind, discomposure. L16–M19.
5 A disturbance of the normal state of the body or mind. L17.

J. K. JEROME We caught colds, and whooping cough, and all kinds of disorders. A. CLARE The prevalence of particular psychiatric disorders.

disorder /dɪsˈɔːdə/ *verb*. L15.
[ORIGIN App. an assim. to ORDER *verb* of earlier DISORDAIN. In sense 6 from DIS- 2 + ORDER *verb*.]
▸ **I** *verb trans*. **1** Upset the order or arrangement of; throw into confusion. L15.

E. BLUNDEN Even getting out of the narrow steep trenches with heavy equipment . . threatened to disorder the assault.

2 Upset the health or function of (the body etc.). M16.

G. BERKELEY The east wind . . never fails to disorder my head.

†**3** Disturb the mind or feelings of; discompose, agitate. Also, confuse (the features) with signs of mental agitation. L16–E19.

DEFOE I looked very earnestly at her; so that it a little disordered her.

†**4** *refl*. Violate moral order or rule; behave in a riotous or unrestrained manner. L16–M17.
†**5** Remove from holy orders, defrock. L16–L17.
6 Rescind an order for; countermand. M17.
▸ †**II** *verb intrans*. **7** Become disordered, fall into disarray. E16–M17.
■ **disordered** *ppl adjective* (*a*) that has been disordered; in a state of disorder; †(*b*) irregular, contrary to rule or law; †(*c*) riotous, disorderly: L15.

disorderly /dɪsˈɔːdəli/ *adjective & noun*. L16.
[ORIGIN from DISORDER *noun* + -LY¹.]
▸ **A** *adjective*. **1** Opposed to or violating public order or morality or constitutional authority; *esp.* unruly, turbulent, riotous. L16.

G. B. SHAW A gay, disorderly, anarchic spoilt child.

disorderly conduct *LAW* unruly or offensive behaviour constituting a minor offence. **disorderly house** *LAW* a building in which disorderly conduct takes place, *spec.* a brothel. ***drunk and disorderly***: see DRUNK *adjective* 1. ***idle and disorderly person***: see IDLE *adjective*.

2 Marked by lack of order or regularity; confused, irregular, untidy. M17.

G. BERKELEY A disorderly and confused chaos. D. H. LAWRENCE The long white locks fell unbraided and disorderly on either side of the . . face.

▸ **B** *noun*. A disorderly person. E19.
■ **disorderliness** *noun* L16.

disorderly /dɪsˈɔːdəli/ *adverb*. M16.
[ORIGIN formed as DISORDERLY *adjective & noun* + -LY².]
1 Not in accordance with order or rule; in an unruly or riotous manner. M16.
2 Without order or regular arrangement; confusedly, irregularly. M16.

disordinate /dɪsˈɔːdɪnət/ *adjective*. Long *rare*. LME.
[ORIGIN medieval Latin *disordinatus* inordinate, for classical Latin *inordinatus*, from *ordinatus* ORDINATE *adjective*: see DIS- 2.]
Transgressing the bounds of what is fitting or reasonable; unrestrained, inordinate.
■ **disordinately** *adverb* L15.

disordination /ˌdɪsɔːdɪˈneɪʃ(ə)n/ *noun*. Long *rare*. E17.
[ORIGIN medieval Latin *disordinatio(n-)* disarrangement, from *disordinat-* pa. ppl stem of *disordinare*, from Latin DIS- 2 + *ordinare* ORDAIN: see -ATION.]
The action of disarranging or putting out of order; disordered or uncoordinated condition.

disorganize /dɪsˈɔːɡənʌɪz/ *verb trans*. Also **-ise**. L18.
[ORIGIN French *désorganiser* from *des-* DIS- 2 + *organiser* ORGANIZE. This and related words date in English from the French Revolution.]
Destroy the organization, systematic arrangement, or orderly connection of; throw into confusion. Chiefly as ***disorganized*** *ppl adjective*.

J. RUSKIN A vast and disorganized mob, scrambling each for what he can get.

■ **disorganiˈzation** *noun* L18. **disorganizer** *noun* L18.

disorient /dɪsˈɔːrɪɛnt/ *verb trans*. M17.
[ORIGIN French *désorienter*, from *des-* DIS- 2 + *orienter* ORIENT *verb*.]
Cause (a person) to lose his or her sense of direction; make confused as to what is true or correct.

disorientate /dɪsˈɔːrɪənteɪt/ *verb trans*. E18.
[ORIGIN from DIS- 2 + ORIENTATE.]
1 Turn from the east, give an alignment other than eastern; change or vary the alignment of. E18.

R. F. CHAPMAN The membrane is usually . . made up . . of disoriented fibres in an amorphous matrix.

2 = DISORIENT. E18.
■ **disˌorienˈtation** *noun* (*a*) deviation from an eastern alignment; (*b*) the condition of having lost one's bearings; a confused mental state (sometimes caused by disease) in which a person's sense of time, place, or personal identity is disturbed: M19.

disour /ˈdɪzʊə, dɪˈzʊə/ *noun*. *obsolete* exc. *hist*. ME.
[ORIGIN Old French (mod. *diseur*), from *dire* say: see -OUR. Cf. DISEUSE.]
A professional storyteller, a minstrel; a jester.

disown /dɪsˈəʊn/ *verb trans.* E17.
[ORIGIN from DIS- 2 + OWN verb.]
†1 Cease to own; renounce possession of. Only in E17.
2 Refuse to acknowledge as one's own; disclaim, repudiate. M17. ▸b Refuse to acknowledge the authority of. L17.
R. G. COLLINGWOOD Bad art arises when instead of expressing these emotions we disown them. L. DURRELL Her family had disowned her and turned her out.
†3 Refuse to acknowledge or admit (something asserted); deny. M17–E18.
4 In the Society of Friends: expel, repudiate from membership. E18.
■ **disowner** *noun* L19. **disownment** *noun* the action or an act of disowning; *spec.* expulsion from the Society of Friends: E19.

†**dispaint** *verb trans. rare* (Spenser). Only in L16.
[ORIGIN from DIS- 1 + PAINT verb.]
Paint with various colours.

†**dispair** *verb trans.* L16–M18.
[ORIGIN from DIS- 2 + PAIR noun[1].]
End the pairing of, separate (things forming a pair).

†**disparage** *noun.* ME.
[ORIGIN Old French *desparage* unsuitable marriage, from *des-* DIS- 2 + *parage* equality of rank from Proto-Romance, from Latin *par* equal: see -AGE.]
1 Inequality of rank in marriage; an unequal match; disgrace resulting from this. ME–L16.
SPENSER Her friends . . Dissuaded her from such a disparage.
2 Disparagement, dishonour. LME–E17.

disparage /dɪˈsparɪdʒ/ *verb trans.* LME.
[ORIGIN Old French *desparagier*, formed as DISPARAGE noun.]
†1 Marry (oneself or another) to someone of unequal rank; degrade by such a match. LME–L18.
2 Bring discredit or reproach upon; dishonour; lower in esteem. LME.
†3 Degrade, lower in position or dignity; cast down in spirit. LME–E18.
POPE I am disparaged and disheartened by your commendations. ADDISON I'll not disparage myself to be a Servant in a House that is haunted.
4 Speak of or treat slightingly or critically; vilify; undervalue, depreciate. E16.
W. PLOMER Too loyal and fond a parent to say anything disparaging about him. P. MEDAWAR To express dissatisfaction with psychoanalysis is not to disparage psychological medicine as a whole.
■ **disparager** *noun* a person who disparages, a detractor E17. **disparagingly** *adverb* in a disparaging manner E18.

disparagement /dɪˈsparɪdʒm(ə)nt/ *noun.* L15.
[ORIGIN Old French, formed as DISPARAGE noun: see -MENT.]
1 Lowering of value, honour, or estimation; dishonour, disgrace, indignity, discredit; something that causes this. L15.
MILTON The learnedest of England thought it no disparagement to sit at his feet.
2 Marriage to a person of inferior rank; disgrace or dishonour incurred by this. *obsolete* exc. *hist.* E16.
3 The action or an act of referring to or treating in a slighting or depreciatory way; depreciation, detraction; undervaluing. L16.

disparate /ˈdɪsp(ə)rət/ *adjective & noun.* LME.
[ORIGIN Latin *disparatus* pa. pple of *disparare* separate, formed as DIS- 1 + *parare* prepare. In use often assoc. with Latin *dispar* unequal (cf. DISPARITY).]
▸ **A** *adjective.* 1 Essentially different or diverse in kind, unlike; incommensurable, without comparison or relation; composed of elements of this kind. LME.
E. JONES I can perceive a connexion between these apparently disparate topics. M. EDWARDES These problems faced a disparate group of people.
2 Unequal. M18.
F. W. FARRAR His authority was in no way disparate with theirs.
▸ **B** *noun.* A disparate thing or person; *esp.* in *pl.*, things so unlike that there is no basis for their comparison. L16.
■ **disparately** *adverb* L19. **disparateness** *noun* M17.

disparition /dɪspəˈrɪʃ(ə)n/ *noun.* Now *literary.* L16.
[ORIGIN French, from *disparaître* disappear, after *apparition*.]
(A) disappearance.

disparity /dɪˈsparɪti/ *noun.* M16.
[ORIGIN French *disparité* from late Latin *disparitas*, from *paritas* PARITY noun[1]: see DIS- 2.]
1 The quality of being unlike or different; dissimilarity, difference, incongruity; an instance of this. M16.
H. L. MENCKEN The disparity between the glorious . . passing imagined by the young soldier and the messy finish that is normally in store.
2 Inequality (of age, rank, strength, etc.); an instance of this. L16.
W. S. CHURCHILL He watched vigilantly for the chance of a battle, even at a disparity in odds.

dispark /dɪsˈpɑːk/ *verb trans.* M16.
[ORIGIN from DIS- 2 + PARK noun. Cf. French †*desparquer* (now *dé-*).]
Deprive of the status of a park; convert (parkland) to other uses.

dispart /dɪsˈpɑːt/ *noun.* L16.
[ORIGIN Uncertain: perh. from DISPART verb[1].]
1 The difference between the semidiameter of a gun at the base ring and at the swell of the muzzle. L16.
2 A sight mark placed on the muzzle of a gun, to make the line of sight parallel to the bore. Also ***dispart-sight***. L16.

dispart /dɪsˈpɑːt/ *verb*[1]. *arch.* L16.
[ORIGIN Italian (*di*)*spartire* divide, part, or Latin *dispartire* distribute, divide, formed as DIS- 1 + *partire* PART verb.]
1 *verb trans. & intrans.* Part asunder, split in two. L16.
J. WESLEY The Sea . . fled, Disparted by the wondrous Rod.
2 *verb trans.* Divide into parts or shares; distribute. E17.
F. ROBERTS The Old Testament . . is disparted by the Holy Ghost himself into two general heads.
3 *verb trans.* Separate, sever; dissolve (a union). M17.
■ **dispartment** *noun* (*rare*) a separation, a split L17.

dispart /dɪsˈpɑːt/ *verb*[2] *trans.* L16.
[ORIGIN from DISPART noun.]
1 Ascertain the dispart of (a gun); make allowance for the dispart in aiming (a gun). L16.
2 Provide (a gun) with a dispart-sight. M17.

dispassion /dɪsˈpaʃ(ə)n/ *verb & noun.* E17.
[ORIGIN from DIS- 2 + PASSION noun.]
▸ †**A** *verb trans.* Free from passion. Chiefly as ***dispassioned*** *ppl adjective.* E17–M18.
▸ **B** *noun.* Freedom from passion; calmness. Formerly also, apathy. L17.

dispassionate /dɪsˈpaʃ(ə)nət/ *adjective.* L16.
[ORIGIN from DIS- 2 + PASSIONATE adjective.]
Free from the influence or effect of strong emotion; calm; impartial.
J. R. GREEN A dispassionate fairness towards older faiths. E. BOWEN Matchett's voice was flat and dispassionate.
■ **dispassionately** *adverb* M17. **dispassionateness** *noun* M19.

dispatch /dɪˈspatʃ/ *noun.* Also **des-**. M16.
[ORIGIN from DISPATCH verb, or Italian *dispaccio*, Spanish *despacho*.]
▸ **I** An act or quality.
†1 Dismissal of a person after settlement of business; *spec.* official dismissal given to an ambassador on completion of his errand. M16–L17.
2 Killing; death by violence. L16.
happy dispatch *joc.* hara-kiri. ***hatches, matches, and dispatches***: see HATCH noun[2].
3 Settlement of business, accomplishment of a task; (prompt or speedy) performance. L16. ▸†**b** Conduct, management. *rare* (Shakes.). Only in E17.
H. MARTINEAU Three members of the Committee sit daily for the dispatch of common business. A. WILSON Sonia's voice was as cool . . as the quick despatch with which she wound the bandage round the little boy's arm. **b** SHAKES. *Macb.* You shall put This night's great business into my dispatch.
4 Prompt settlement or accomplishment; promptitude; speed, efficiency, rapidity of progress. L16.
CARLYLE All turns on dispatch; loiter a little, and Friedrich himself will be here again! R. BRADBURY She worked with energy and dispatch.
5 The sending of a messenger, letter, etc. to a destination or for a purpose. E17.
S. PEPYS To Woolwich to give order for the dispatch of a ship.
†6 The act of getting rid or disposing of something, esp. hastily. E–M17.
▸ **II** A thing.
7 A written message given or requiring fast delivery, *esp.* an official one on state or military matters; a piece sent in by a reporter. M16.
mentioned in dispatches distinguished by having one's actions commended in an official military dispatch.
8 An agency for the quick transmission of goods etc.; a conveyance by which goods or mail are dispatched. L17.
pneumatic dispatch: see PNEUMATIC adjective.
9 A false die with some faces bearing the wrong number of spots. *arch. slang.* E19.
– COMB.: **dispatch boat** a fast vessel for carrying dispatches; **dispatch box**, **dispatch case** a container for carrying official (esp. state) and other documents; an attaché case; **dispatch rider** a rider, esp. a motorcyclist or horseman, who carries (esp. military) dispatches.
■ **dispatchful** *adjective* †(**a**) having the quality of doing away with expeditiously; (**b**) *arch.* characterized by dispatch, expeditious, hasty: E17.

dispatch /dɪˈspatʃ/ *verb.* Also **des-**. E16.
[ORIGIN Italian *dispacciare* or Spanish *despachar* expedite, formed as DIS- 2 + base (of unknown origin) of Italian *impacciare* hinder, stop, Spanish, Portuguese *empachar* impede, embarrass.]
▸ **I** *verb trans.* 1 Send off to a particular destination or recipient or for a particular purpose. E16.
R. DAVENPORT Embassadors were dispatch'd to Bergamo. H. MACMILLAN I despatched a message to the new Prime Minister. A. TOFFLER The maintenance supervisor would dispatch a crew to repair the damage.
†2 Send away from one's presence or employment; dismiss, discharge. M16–M17.
3 Dismiss (a person) after settling his or her business; deal with and send away. Now *rare.* M16.
4 Get rid or dispose of (a person) by putting to death; execute, kill. Formerly also, get rid of or banish (anything), dispel. M16. ▸†**b** End (a person's life). L16–M17.
HENRY MILLER Like mopping up a battlefield: all those who are hopelessly disabled . . you dispatch with one swift blow.
dispatch out of life, **dispatch out of the world**, etc. (now *rare* or *obsolete*) kill.
5 Get (a task or piece of business) promptly done; accomplish, finish off, conclude. M16. ▸**b** Eat (food, a meal) quickly; consume, devour. *colloq.* E18.
J. PRIESTLEY Dominic easily dispatched this task in six days.
†6 Rid (esp. a person) of an encumbrance or hindrance; deliver, relieve; deprive. Foll. by *of*, *from*. M16–M17.
▸ **II** *verb intrans.* †7 Start promptly for a destination, hurry away. L16–E18.
8 Make haste (*to do*), be quick. *arch.* L16.
†9 Conclude or settle one's business; get through, have done (*with*). E–M17.
■ **dispatcher** *noun* (**a**) a person who or thing which dispatches, *esp.* a person who gives orders for the departure of goods or vehicles; (**b**) *arch. slang* = DISPATCH noun 9: M16.

†**dispeed** *verb trans.* E17–E19.
[ORIGIN App. from Italian †*dispedire*, from *dis-* DIS- 1 + *spedire* dispatch from Latin *expedire* (see EXPEDITE verb); infl. in spelling by SPEED verb.]
Dispatch, send off; *refl.* go away quickly.

dispel /dɪˈspɛl/ *verb.* Infl. **-ll-**. LME.
[ORIGIN Latin *dispellere*, formed as DIS- 1 + *pellere* to drive.]
1 *verb trans.* Drive away, banish, dissipate, (now, something abstract or vaporous). LME.
M. MITCHELL The fresh air could do little toward dispelling the sickening odours. *New York Law Journal* The court first dispelled any shareholder's liability under the restrictive covenant. J. CHEEVER Any sense of obligation . . was dispelled by their knowing that they were useful to their hostess. N. SAHGAL Cupboard doors were open to dispel monsoon damp.
2 *verb intrans.* Be dispelled. M17.
■ **dispeller** *noun* E18.

dispend /dɪˈspɛnd/ *verb trans.* Pa. t. & pple **dispended**, **dispent** /dɪˈspɛnt/. ME.
[ORIGIN Old French *despendre* expend from Latin *dispendere* weigh out, pay out, formed as DIS- 1 + *pendere* weigh.]
1 Pay out (money), expend (resources etc.). Now *rare* or *obsolete*. ME.
†2 Employ, consume, or occupy (time). ME–L16.
†3 Waste, squander. ME–L15.
†4 Distribute, dispense, esp. in charity to the poor. ME–M17.
†5 Bring to an end; exhaust, use up. Usu. in *pass.* LME–E16.

dispendious /dɪˈspɛndɪəs/ *adjective.* M16.
[ORIGIN from Latin *dispendiosus* hurtful, formed as DISPENDIUM: see -OUS. In sense 2 through French *dispendieux* expensive.]
†1 Harmful. Only in M16.
2 Expensive; extravagant. E18.

†**dispendium** *noun.* Pl. **-iums**, **-ia**. M17–E18.
[ORIGIN Latin, from *dispendere*: see DISPEND.]
Loss, waste; expenditure, expense.

dispensable /dɪˈspɛnsəb(ə)l/ *adjective.* In senses 1 & 2 also **-ible**. E16.
[ORIGIN medieval Latin *dispensabilis*, from Latin *dispensare* DISPENSE verb: see -ABLE, -IBLE.]
1 ECCLESIASTICAL. Subject to dispensation; *spec.* (of action normally prohibited) able to be permitted or condoned in special circumstances; (of a law, vow, etc.) able to be relaxed in special cases. E16.
2 Allowable, excusable. Now *rare* or *obsolete*. L16.
3 Able to be dispensed with or done without; not necessary, inessential; unimportant. M17.
■ **dispensaˈbility**, **dispensableness** *nouns* the quality of being dispensable M17.

dispensary /dɪˈspɛns(ə)ri/ *noun.* L17.
[ORIGIN medieval Latin *dispensarium* use as noun of neut. of *dispensarius*, from Latin *dispensare*: see DISPENSE verb, -ARY[1].]
1 A place, esp. a room in a doctor's surgery or a chemist's shop, in which medicines are dispensed; a public or charitable institution for dispensing medicines or giving medical advice. L17.
†2 A collection of different drugs. E–M18.

dispensate /dɪˈspɛnseɪt/ *verb trans. rare.* E18.
[ORIGIN Latin *dispensat-* pa. ppl stem of *dispensare*: see DISPENSE verb, -ATE[3].]
Dispense; distribute.

dispensation /dɪspɛnˈseɪʃ(ə)n/ *noun.* LME.
[ORIGIN Old French & mod. French from Latin *dispensatio(n-)* (in branch II as translation of Greek *oikonomia* in New Testament and patristic writers), formed as DISPENSATE: see -ATION.]
▸ **I** Dealing out, distribution.

D

1 The action or an act of dispensing or dealing out; distribution; disbursement; economical use or disposal. LME.

I. D'ISRAELI Elizabeth, a queen well known for her penurious dispensations. J. TULLOCH Changes in the dispensation of the Lord's Supper.

2 The process of dispensing a medicine or prescription. M17.

▸ **II** (A mode of) ordering, management.

3 The orderly administration of affairs committed to one's charge; stewardship. *arch.* LME.

4 The ordering of events by divine Providence. Formerly also *gen.*, ordering, management; (an) arrangement. LME. ▸**b** An arrangement made by providence or nature; a special dealing of providence with a community, family, or person; a judgement, (esp.) a blessing. M17.

b R. HOOKE So infinitely wise and provident do we find all the Dispensations in Nature. SIR W. SCOTT A humbling dispensation on the house of Peveril.

5 A religious system regarded as divinely ordained for a particular nation or period (freq. with specifying word); the age characterized by such a system; any established system under which one lives or works. M17.

W. BRUCE The Israelitish dispensation was abolished by the First Coming of Christ. J. BRAINE The last evening under the old dispensation I remember as one remembers the party on the eve of the mutiny.

▸ **III** Dispensing with a requirement.

6 *ECCLESIASTICAL.* (The granting of) a licence permitting in special circumstances the exemption of a person from a penalty or obligation of canon law. LME.

C. MCCULLOUGH Once your final vows are taken and you are ordained, . . there can be no going back, no dispensation. *transf.*: DRYDEN 'Tis a crime past dispensation.

7 The action of dispensing *with* something or doing without. L16.

8 The relaxation or suspension of a statute in a particular case. E17.

9 An exemption, a release from an obligation or requirement; a concession. E17.

S. JOHNSON Our intimacy was regarded by me as a dispensation from ceremonial visits. W. STYRON Moore gave us five days of absence—a fairly common dispensation during August.

■ **dispen'sational** *adjective* L19. **dispensationalism** *noun* (*CHRISTIAN THEOLOGY*) belief in a system of historical progression as revealed in the Bible, consisting of a series of (*spec.* seven) stages in God's self-revelation and plan of salvation E20. **dispensationalist** *noun* (*CHRISTIAN THEOLOGY*) an adherent of dispensationalism M20.

dispensative /dɪˈspɛnsətɪv/ *adjective*. Long *rare*. E16.
[ORIGIN Late Latin *dispensativus*, from Latin *dispensat-*: see DISPENSATE, -IVE. Cf. Old French & mod. French *dispensatif*, *-ive*.]
†**1** = DISPENSATORY *adjective* 1. E16–M17.
2 = DISPENSATORY *adjective* 2. E17.
■ **dispensatively** *adverb* L16.

dispensator /ˈdɪspɛnseɪtə/ *noun*. Now *rare*. LME.
[ORIGIN Anglo-Norman *dispensatour*, Old French *dispensateur* from Latin *dispensator*, from *dispensat-*: see DISPENSATE, -OR 2.]
A person who dispenses. Formerly, a steward.

dispensatory /dɪˈspɛnsət(ə)ri/ *noun*. M16.
[ORIGIN medieval Latin *dispensatorium* storeroom, pantry, pharmacopoeia, use as noun of neut. of late Latin *dispensatorius*: see DISPENSATORY *adjective*.]
1 A book containing a list of medicines with directions for their use and sometimes their composition and preparation; a pharmacopoeia. M16.
2 A dispensary; *gen.* a place where something is dispensed or given out. Now *rare* or *obsolete*. L16.
†**3** = DISPENSARY 2. M17–M18.

dispensatory /dɪˈspɛnsət(ə)ri/ *adjective*. M17.
[ORIGIN Late Latin *dispensatorius*, from Latin *dispensator* DISPENSATOR: see -ORY[1]. In sense 2 from medieval Latin eccl. use.]
†**1** (Of power) exercised by virtue of office; of or pertaining to an administrator or administration. M–L17.
2 That gives dispensations; able to dispense with laws or rules. M17.
■ **dispensatorily** *adverb* by dispensation M17.

dispensatrix /dɪspɛnˈseɪtrɪks/ *noun*. Pl. **-trices** /-trɪsiːz/. M19.
[ORIGIN Latin, fem. of DISPENSATOR: see -TRIX.]
A female dispenser.

dispense /dɪˈspɛns/ *noun*. ME.
[ORIGIN Old French *despense* from medieval Latin *dispensa* use as noun of fem. sing. of pa. pple of *dispendere*: see DISPEND. In senses 3 and 6 prob. from the verb.]
†**1** The act of spending; expenditure; in *pl.*, expenses, costs. ME–E18.
†**2** Means of meeting expenditure, money to spend; in *pl.*, supplies. LME–M17.
†**3** *ECCLESIASTICAL.* = DISPENSATION 6. L15–L18.
†**4** The act of dispensing or bestowing liberally. *rare* (Spenser). Only in L16.
†**5** A pantry, a buttery. Only in E17.
6 In full *dispense bar*. A bar in a club or hotel for the use of the staff. M20.

dispense /dɪˈspɛns/ *verb*. LME.
[ORIGIN Old French *despenser* from Latin *dispensare* weigh out, disburse, frequentative of *dispendere*: see DISPEND.]
▸ **I** *verb trans.* from classical Latin.
1 Distribute, deal out; give out as a share from a general stock. LME. ▸†**b** Spend, employ, (time or talents). E–M17.

S. BRETT The hostess . . dispensed cold tea. I. MCEWAN Patricians dispensing to their son or nephew . . the fruits of their sagacity and wealth.

2 Administer (a sacrament, justice, authority). LME.

J. A. MICHENER He dispensed an impartial justice which protected men in their ownership of . . property.

3 Make up (medicine) according to a prescription, give out (a prescribed medicine); carry out (a prescription). M16.

fig.: W. H. AUDEN Panic, shock, are dispensed in measured doses / by fool-proof engines.

▸ **II** *verb intrans. & trans.* from medieval Latin in eccl. use.
4 *verb intrans.* Use a power of granting dispensations; grant a dispensation (*in* a special case). LME.

C. O'CONOR The Pope could not dispense in the allegiance due by Catholics to their Sovereigns.

†**5** *verb trans.* Relax the law in reference to (some thing or person); permit (a person or act) by dispensation; condone. LME–M17.
†**6** *verb trans.* Do without, forgo. LME–M17.
7 *verb trans.* Grant (a person) a dispensation (*from* an obligation or promise). Formerly also, dissolve the obligation of (a vow) by ecclesiastical authority. M16.

J. G. COZZENS He was even dispensed from Lenten abstinence so he could dine with the worldly.

†**8** *verb intrans.* Make amends or compensation *for*. *rare* (Spenser). Only in L16.
▸ **III** *verb intrans.* Foll. by *with* (from sense 4).
†**9** Arrange to grant (a person) dispensation from a law, penalty, or duty; exempt or excuse (oneself) *from* doing something. LME–L18. ▸†**b** Compound with to gain exemption for an offence or a penalty. M16–M17.

H. LATIMER God had dispensed wyth theym to have manye wyues. **b** SHAKES. *2 Hen. VI* Canst thou dispense with heaven for such an oath?

10 Arrange to relax or remit the penalty or obligation of (a law or rule), esp. in a special case; give special exemption or relief from. LME.

R. BOLT The Pope dispensed with the Christian law forbidding a man to marry his brother's widow.

11 Relax the obligation of (a vow or promise); dissolve the binding force of (an oath), esp. in special circumstances. M16.
†**12** Disregard (a duty); fail to heed (one's religious faith). M16–M18.
†**13** Deal with (a breach of law) so as to condone it; permit or condone (something illegal or irregular) by dispensation. M16–E18.

ADDISON His religion dispenses with the violation of the most sacred engagements.

†**14** Deal with tolerantly; cope with; put up with. L16–L18.
15 Do away with (a requirement or necessity); make unnecessary or superfluous. L16.

F. HALL Familiar facts dispense with all need to draw on the imagination.

16 Excuse or put up with the absence of (a thing or person); forgo, do without. E17.

DICKENS Let us dispense with compliments. P. G. WODEHOUSE Suppose we dispense with coffee and go round and see him.

dispenser /dɪˈspɛnsə/ *noun*. LME.
[ORIGIN Partly from Old French *despenseor*, *-eur* from Latin *dispensator* DISPENSATOR; partly from Anglo-Norman *despens(i)er*, Old French *despensier*, *dis-* = medieval Latin *dispensarius*, from medieval Latin *dispensa* DISPENSE *noun*: see -ER[2].]
1 **a** A steward of a household. *arch.* LME. ▸**b** An administrator of the law, authority, etc. M17.
2 A person who dispenses or deals out; a spender. LME.
3 A person who dispenses medicines. M19.
4 A container designed to release a predetermined amount; (more fully *cash dispenser*) a machine from which an authorized person can withdraw cash and have a bank account automatically debited. M20.

dispensible *adjective* see DISPENSABLE.

dispensive /dɪˈspɛnsɪv/ *adjective*. Now *rare* or *obsolete*. L16.
[ORIGIN Latin *dispens-* pa. ppl stem of *dispendere*: see DISPEND *verb*, -IVE. Assoc. with DISPENSE *verb*.]
†**1** Subject to dispensation. Only in L16.
†**2** Characterized by or given to spending or disbursing. M–L17.
3 = DISPENSATORY *adjective* 2. E19.

dispeople /dɪsˈpiːp(ə)l/ *verb trans.* LME.
[ORIGIN Old French *despeupler* (mod. *dé-*) from Proto-Romance, from Latin DIS- 2 + *populus* PEOPLE *noun*. Cf. DEPEOPLE.]
1 Empty of people; depopulate. LME.
†**2** Exterminate (people). Also, make no longer a distinct people. L16–L17.
3 Remove all living creatures from. M17.
■ **dispeopler** *noun* E17.

dispermous /dʌɪˈspəːməs/ *adjective*. M18.
[ORIGIN from DI-[2] + Greek *sperma* seed + -OUS.]
BOTANY. Having two seeds.

dispermy /ˈdʌɪspəːmi/ *noun*. L19.
[ORIGIN formed as DISPERMOUS + -Y[3].]
BIOLOGY. The entrance of two sperms into a single egg.
■ **di'spermic** *adjective* E20.

dispersal /dɪˈspəːs(ə)l/ *noun*. E16.
[ORIGIN from DISPERSE *verb* + -AL[1].]
1 The action of dispersing; the condition or state of being dispersed; = DISPERSION 1. E16.
2 In full *dispersal area*, *dispersal point*. Any of several separated areas on an airfield where aircraft are parked to minimize their combined vulnerability to attack. M20.

disperse /dɪˈspəːs/ *adjective*. LME.
[ORIGIN In sense 1 from Old French *dispers*, in sense 2 from German *dispers*, both from Latin *dispersus* pa. pple of *dispergere*: see DISPERSE *verb*.]
†**1** Dispersed. LME–E16.
2 *CHEMISTRY.* Of a phase: dispersed in another. Of a system: consisting of one phase dispersed in another, continuous, phase. E20.

disperse /dɪˈspəːs/ *verb*. LME.
[ORIGIN Latin *dispers-* pa. ppl stem of *dispergere* scatter, formed as DIS- 1 + *spargere* strew.]
1 *verb trans.* Drive, throw, or send in different directions; scatter, rout. LME.

WORDSWORTH Her feet disperse the powdery snow. P. L. FERMOR The heralds were dispersed, the regiments disbanded . . long ago.

2 *verb trans.* Distribute from a main source or centre; put (books, currency, or commodities) in circulation; spread around, disseminate. LME.

C. BURNEY A practice . . thence dispersed into all parts of the Christian world.

3 *verb trans.* Place or station at widely separated points. Freq. in *pass.* E16.

N. MAILER The regiment was dispersed over an area twenty miles wide and more than ten miles deep.

†**4** *verb trans.* Separate into parts; divide. M16–E17.
†**5** *verb trans.* Make known; publish. M16–E17.
6 *verb trans.* Cause (esp. something unpleasant) to disappear; dispel, dissipate. M16.

G. W. KNIGHT A clear daylight now disperses the imaginative dark that has eclipsed Scotland.

7 *verb intrans.* Become dispelled or dissipated. L16.

R. L. STEVENSON The dust . . dispersed like the smoke of battle.

8 *verb intrans.* (Of people) separate and go different ways; (of a crowd or gathering) break up. M17.

E. HUXLEY Not only have Jews dispersed first from the Leylands, then to Chapeltown and now to other parts of the city.

9 *verb trans. PHYSICS.* Separate (light) into its constituent wavelengths. M17.
10 *verb trans. SCIENCE.* Distribute (a substance) as small particles throughout another, continuous, one, e.g. in a solution. E20.
■ **dispersa'bility** *noun* M20. **dispersable** *adjective* E19. **dispersant** *noun* an agent which causes or maintains a state of dispersion in a surrounding medium; a dispersing agent: M20. **dispersedly** *adverb* in a dispersed or scattered manner M16. **dispersedness** *noun* the condition or state of being dispersed or scattered L16. **disperser** *noun* L16. **dispersi'bility** *noun* M20. **dispersible** *adjective* M20.

dispersion /dɪˈspəːʃ(ə)n/ *noun*. LME.
[ORIGIN Late Latin *dispersio(n-)* scattering, formed as DISPERSE *verb*: see -ION.]
1 The action of dispersing or scattering abroad; diffusion, dissemination; the condition or state of being dispersed. LME. ▸**b** (Also **D-**.) = DIASPORA. LME.

b H. A. L. FISHER The Dutch settlers in Cape Colony were not imperialists, still less were the Dutch dispersion in the interior.

2 *PHYSICS.* The phenomenon by which light of different wavelengths is spread out by a prism etc. into a spectrum; a variation of speed of propagation of light, sound, etc., with wavelength; the degree of this. E18.
3 *MEDICINE.* The removal of inflammation, suppuration, etc., from a part. Now *rare* or *obsolete*. M18.
4 *STATISTICS.* The degree to which a set of observed values are spread over a range. L19.
5 *CHEMISTRY.* A mixture of one substance dispersed throughout another, continuous, one; an emulsion, aerosol, etc.; the state of being so dispersed. E20.
– COMB.: **dispersion hardening** hardening of an alloy by heating at high temperatures followed by rapid cooling, causing the dispersion of one constituent.

dispersive /dɪˈspəːsɪv/ *adjective*. E17.
[ORIGIN from DISPERSE *verb* + -IVE. Cf. Old French & mod. French *dispersif*, *-ive*.]
Having the character or quality of dispersing, serving or tending to disperse something; PHYSICS causing dispersion (of light etc.).
■ **dispersiveness** *noun* M19. **disperˈsivity** *noun* the degree to which the refractive index of a substance varies with wavelength E20.

dispersoid /dɪˈspəːsɔɪd/ *noun*. E20.
[ORIGIN from DISPERSE *adjective* + -OID.]
CHEMISTRY. A disperse system.

dispersonalize /dɪsˈpəːs(ə)n(ə)lʌɪz/ *verb trans*. Also **-ise**. L19.
[ORIGIN from DIS- 2 + PERSONALIZE.]
= DISPERSONATE 2.

dispersonate /dɪsˈpəːsəneɪt/ *verb trans*. E17.
[ORIGIN from DIS- 2 + Latin *persona* mask + -ATE[3].]
†**1** Strip of an assumed character, unmask. Only in E17.
2 Destroy or remove the personality of. Chiefly *refl*. E18.

dispersonify /dɪspəˈsɒnɪfʌɪ/ *verb trans*. M19.
[ORIGIN from DIS- 2 + PERSONIFY.]
Represent or regard as impersonal.
■ ˌ**dispersonifiˈcation** *noun* L19.

disphenoid /dʌɪˈsfiːnɔɪd/ *noun*. L19.
[ORIGIN from DI-[2] + SPHENOID.]
CRYSTALLOGRAPHY. A solid formed by eight similar scalene triangles, a tetragonal scalenohedron. Also, a crystal form like a double wedge formed by two pairs of scalene or isosceles triangles and having two planes of symmetry.

dispiece /dɪsˈpiːs/ *verb trans*. Now *rare*. L15.
[ORIGIN Old French *despiecer* (mod. *dépiécer*), from *des-* DIS- 1 + PIECE *noun*.]
Divide into pieces.

dispirit /dɪˈspɪrɪt/ *verb trans*. M17.
[ORIGIN from DIS- 2 + SPIRIT *noun*.]
†**1** Deprive of essential quality or force; deprive of vigour, weaken; deprive (liquor) of its spirit. M17–M18.
2 Lower the morale of, make despondent; dishearten. M17.

C. P. SNOW He was dispirited because his triumph . . had not been as intoxicating as he had imagined. T. GUNN I was trying to write novels and poetry, but the results were . . dispiriting.

■ **dispiritedly** *adverb* in a dispirited way M19. **dispiritedness** *noun* a dispirited state M17. **dispiritingly** *adverb* in a dispiriting manner L19. **dispiritment** *noun* dispiritedness, (a) disheartenment E19.

dispiteous /dɪsˈpɪtɪəs/ *adjective*. LME.
[ORIGIN Orig. var. of DESPITEOUS; later from DIS- 2 + PITEOUS.]
1 = DESPITEOUS 1. Now *arch*. *rare*. LME.
2 Orig., spiteful, malevolent, cruel. Later, pitiless, merciless. E16.
■ **dispiteously** *adverb* LME. **dispiteousness** *noun* M19.

displace /dɪsˈpleɪs/ *verb trans*. M16.
[ORIGIN Partly from DIS- 2 + PLACE *noun*[1]; partly after French †*desplacer* (now *dé-*), from *des-* DIS- 1, 2 + PLACE *noun*[1], *placer* to place. Cf. DEPLACE.]
1 Move from its proper or usual place. M16. ▸†**b** *fig*. Remove, banish. L16–L17.
displaced person: removed from his or her home country by military events or political pressure.
2 Remove from office. M16.
3 Replace with something else; take the place of, supplant. L18.

A. CHRISTIE She displaced Midge from the sofa, settled Gerda there. J. BARZUN The notion of helping a child has . . displaced that of teaching him.

■ **displaceaˈbility** *noun* L19. **displaceable** *adjective* L17. **displacer** *noun* L16.

displacement /dɪsˈpleɪsm(ə)nt/ *noun*. E17.
[ORIGIN from DISPLACE + -MENT; in sense 1 perh. from French †*desplacement*.]
1 Removal from office. *rare*. E17.
2 The moving of something from its place or position; the extent of such a movement; the difference or relation between an initial position of a body and a subsequent position. E19.

S. HAUGHTON A vertical displacement of the strata.

3 The removal of something by something else which takes its place; *spec*. the fact of a submerged or partly submerged body occupying a volume which would otherwise be occupied by the fluid; the amount or weight of fluid that would fill this volume in the case of a floating ship etc. E19. ▸**b** MECHANICS. The volume swept by a reciprocating system, as in a pump or engine. L19.

W. H. G. KINGSTON Her total length is 320 feet . . with a displacement of 11,407 tons.

VIRTUAL *displacement*.
4 ELECTRICITY. More fully ***electric displacement***. Orig., the polarized state of a dielectric in an electric field. Now, (a vector representing) the component of an electric field due to free separated charges, regardless of any polarization effects; the flux density of such a field. L19.
5 PSYCHOANALYSIS. The unconscious transfer of an emotion from its original object to something else; the unconscious substitution of an inoffensive concept or activity for one that is disturbing or unacceptable; an instance of such a transfer. E20.

H. SEGAL She considers an interest in the world to be a displacement from the basic interest in one's own and the parents' bodies.

– COMB.: **displacement activity** (an) animal or human activity that seems irrelevant to the situation in which it occurs; **displacement current** a notional electric current associated with a changing electric field not produced by an actual current, and proportional to the rate of change of displacement with time; **displacement pump** any pump in which liquid is moved out of the pump chamber by a moving surface or by the introduction of compressed air or gas; ***displacement ton***: see TON *noun*[1] 2; ***displacement tonnage***: see TONNAGE *noun*.

displacency /dɪsˈpleɪs(ə)nsi/ *noun*. Now *rare* or *obsolete*. M17.
[ORIGIN medieval Latin *displacentia* for Latin *displicentia* DISPLICENCY, or alt. of DISPLICENCY.]
= DISPLICENCY.

displant /dɪsˈplɑːnt/ *verb trans*. L15.
[ORIGIN French †*desplanter* (now *déplanter*) from Proto-Romance, from Latin DIS- 1 + *plantare* plant.]
1 Uproot (a plant). L15.
†**2** Remove from a town or country of settlement; undo the settlement of (a town, colony, etc.). L16–M17.
†**3** *fig*. Eradicate; supplant. E–M17.

display /dɪˈspleɪ/ *noun*. L16.
[ORIGIN from the verb.]
†**1** Presentation in writing; a description. L16–E18.
2 Something intended for people to look at; an exhibition, a show. M17. ▸**b** A visual presentation of data or signals on the screen of a cathode-ray tube etc.; a device or system used for this. Also more fully ***visual display***. M20.

M. MOORCOCK The better shops were filled with light and wonderful displays.

b ***visual display unit***: see VISUAL *adjective*. ***video display terminal***, ***video display unit***: see VIDEO *adjective* & *noun*.
3 The action or an act of displaying or exhibiting to view; (a) manifestation; exhibition, show. L17. ▸**b** The presentation of printed matter in such a way as to make it visually prominent. E19. ▸**c** A specialized pattern of behaviour used by a bird as visual communication. E20.

Economist Mrs Marcos's famous collection of shoes now on display in Manila. A. CHRISTIE This display of Edward's unerring and fastidious taste. **b** attrib.: *New Zealand Listener* The display size of the type used makes the distinctive form of the 'long s' self-evident. **c** A. MANNING Some birds have evolved elaborate mutual courtship displays.

4 Showiness, ostentation. E19.

BYRON As erring man should die, Without display, without parade.

– COMB.: **display cabinet**, **display case**: for displaying items for observation or inspection; **display type**: used for displaying printed matter.

display /dɪˈspleɪ/ *verb*. ME.
[ORIGIN Old French *despleier* (mod. *déployer* DEPLOY *verb*) from Latin *displicare* scatter, disperse, (in medieval Latin) unfold, formed as DIS- 1, 2 + *plicare* fold.]
▸ **I** *verb trans*. **1** Unfurl, unfold to view. *obsolete* exc. with implication of sense 3. ME.

POPE See . . her sable flag display'd.

2 Lay or place with the limbs extended; to extend (a limb, wing, etc.); *spec*. in HERALDRY, extend the wings of (a bird of prey) (chiefly as ***displayed ppl adjective***). ME. ▸†**b** Carve (a crane) for the table. L15–E19.

SPENSER Thou . . Thy careles limbs in loose sleep dost display.

3 Expose to view, make visible; show, exhibit. ME. ▸**b** TYPOGRAPHY. Make (matter) more prominent by using larger type, open layout, etc. L19.

J. BERGER A dress displayed in a shop window.

†**4** Describe in words, unfold in narrative; expound, explain. LME–E19.
5 Show (a quality) to be possessed by the subject; reveal; allow to be perceived, give evidence of, make manifest. L15.

G. SAINTSBURY They often display much more real critical power than later writers. S. NAIPAUL To bring the subject up was to display bad manners.

†**6** Get sight of. L16–E17.

SPENSER They . . did at last display That wanton Lady, with her lover.

†**7** Give voice to, utter. L16–M17.
8 Exhibit ostentatiously; make a show of. E17.

J. CONRAD The . . forecastle . . where he could display his talents.

▸ **II** *verb intrans*. †**9** Show off, behave ostentatiously. *rare* (Shakes.). Only in E17.
10 Of a bird: engage in or use display as visual communication. E20.

D. A. BANNERMAN A male gold-crest displaying to the lady of his choice.

■ **displayable** *adjective* (*rare*) M19. **displayer** *noun* E17.

†**disple** *verb trans*. L15–M17.
[ORIGIN App. from DISCIPLINE *noun* or *verb*.]
Subject to discipline, penance, or punishment, esp. as a religious practice.

SPENSER Bitter Penaunce, with an yron whip, Was wont him once to disple every day.

displeasance /dɪsˈplɛz(ə)ns/ *noun*. Long *arch*. *rare*. ME.
[ORIGIN Old French *desplaisance* (mod. *déplaisance*), formed as DISPLEASANT: see -ANCE.]
Displeasure. Formerly also, a grievance.

displeasant /dɪsˈplɛz(ə)nt/ *adjective*. Long *arch*. *rare*. LME.
[ORIGIN Old French *desplaisant* pres. pple of *desplaisir*: see DISPLEASE, -ANT[1].]
1 Unpleasant; displeasing. LME.
†**2** Displeased. L15–E18.
■ †**displeasantly** *adverb* M16–E18.

displease /dɪsˈpliːz/ *verb*. LME.
[ORIGIN Old French *desplais-* pres. stem of *desplaisir*, *desplaire* (mod. *déplaire*), from *des-* DIS- 2 + *plaisir* PLEASE *verb*.]
1 *verb intrans*. Cause dislike, be disagreeable, be offensive. LME.
2 *verb trans*. Be disagreeable to; offend, annoy; make indignant or angry. LME.
3 *verb trans*. In *pass*. Be dissatisfied or indignant. (Foll. by *with*, *at*, *to do*, *that*; †*of*, †*against*.) LME.
■ **displeasedly** *adverb* in a displeased manner, with displeasure E17. †**displeasedness** *noun* displeased state, discontent M16–E18. **displeasingly** *adverb* disagreeably, offensively M18. **displeasingness** *noun* the property of causing displeasure M17.

displeasure /dɪsˈplɛʒə/ *noun* & *verb*. LME.
[ORIGIN Old French *desplaisir* use as noun of inf.: see DISPLEASE. Later assim. to PLEASURE *noun*.]
▸ **A** *noun*. **1** The fact or condition of being displeased; dissatisfaction, disapproval; indignation, anger. LME.

J. P. DONLEAVY The most despicable letter I have ever had the displeasure to receive.

2 Something causing offence or trouble; injury, harm; an offence, a wrong. *arch*. LME.
†**3** Discomfort, unhappiness; sorrow, trouble; an instance of this, a pain. L15–L19.
†**4** A state of unfriendly relations; a disagreement. M–L16.
– PHRASES: †**take a displeasure**, **take displeasure** take offence, be displeased.
▸ **B** *verb trans*. = DISPLEASE 2. *arch*. M16.
■ **displeasurable** *adjective* (*rare*) L19. **displeasurably** *adverb* (*rare*) M17.

displenish /dɪsˈplɛnɪʃ/ *verb trans*. *Scot*. M17.
[ORIGIN from DIS- 2 + PLENISH *verb*.]
Deprive of furniture or supplies; divest of stock.

displicency /ˈdɪsplɪs(ə)nsi/ *noun*. M17.
[ORIGIN Latin *displicentia*, from *displicere* displease, formed as DIS- 2 + *placere* PLEASE *verb*: see -ENCY.]
The fact or condition of being displeased or dissatisfied.
■ †**displicence** *noun* E17–M18.

displode /dɪˈspləʊd/ *verb*. *arch*. M17.
[ORIGIN Latin *displodere* burst asunder, formed as DIS- 1 + *plaudere* clap.]
†**1** *verb trans*. Discharge with an explosion. M17–E18.
2 *verb intrans*. Explode. M18.
■ †**displosion** *noun* M17–L18.

dispondee /dʌɪˈspɒndiː/ *noun*. L16.
[ORIGIN Late Latin *dispondeus* from Greek *dispondeios*, formed as DI-[2] + *spondeios* SPONDEE.]
PROSODY. A double spondee.
■ **disponˈdaic** *adjective* L19.

dispone /dɪˈspəʊn/ *verb*. Chiefly *Scot*. LME.
[ORIGIN Latin *disponere* arrange, dispose, formed as DIS- 1 + *ponere* to place. Cf. DISPOSE *verb*.]
†**1** *verb trans*. Arrange, dispose. LME–E17.
†**2** *verb trans*. Dispose *to*, *for*; incline. LME–E17.
†**3** *verb trans*. Dispose of; give away. LME–M17.
4 *verb trans*. SCOTS LAW. Make over, convey, assign, grant. LME.
†**5** *verb intrans*. Foll. by *of*, (*up*)*on*: deal with, dispose of. LME–E19.
†**6** *verb intrans*. Order matters, make arrangements. LME–E18.
■ **dispoˈnee** *noun* (SCOTS LAW) a person to whom property is conveyed M18. **disponer**, **-or** *noun* †(**a**) a person who disposes or arranges; (**b**) LAW a person who conveys property to another, a settlor: L15.

disponent /dɪˈspəʊnənt/ *adjective*. E17.
[ORIGIN Latin *disponent-* pres. ppl stem of *disponere*: see DISPONE, -ENT.]
Disposing; inclining in a particular direction, or towards a particular end.

disponge *verb* see DISPUNGE.

disponible /dɪˈspəʊnɪb(ə)l, *foreign* dispɔnibl/ *adjective*. L19.
[ORIGIN from (the same root as) DISPONE + -IBLE, or from French *disponible*.]
Able to be assigned; at a person's disposal; amenable.
– NOTE: Freq. treated as French.
■ **disponiˈbility** *noun* M19.

D

D

disport /dɪˈspɔːt/ *noun. arch.* ME.
[ORIGIN Anglo-Norman *desport*, formed as DISPORT *verb*. Cf. DEPORT *noun*.]
1 Diversion; relaxation; amusement. ME.
2 A pastime; a game; a sport. LME.
†**3** Merriment, fun. LME–E19.

disport /dɪˈspɔːt/ *verb*. LME.
[ORIGIN Anglo-Norman, Old French *desporter* (French *déporter* DEPORT *verb*[2]), from *des-* DIS- 1 + *porter* carry, PORT *verb*[1].]
†**1** *verb trans.* Divert (from sadness etc.); amuse, entertain. LME–L17.

T. HERBERT All the way we sail'd . . we were disported by Whales.

2 *verb intrans. & refl.* Amuse or divert oneself; occupy oneself pleasurably. Now *esp.* play unrestrainedly, frolic, make a show of oneself. LME.

P. P. READ Eager to disport herself in her new clothes. H. L. MENCKEN Savage tribes who permit their children to disport freely.

■ **disportment** *noun* (an) amusement, (an) entertainment M17.

disposable /dɪˈspəʊzəb(ə)l/ *adjective & noun*. M17.
[ORIGIN from DISPOSE *verb* + -ABLE.]
▸ **A** *adjective*. **1** Able to be disposed or inclined; inclinable (*to* something). *rare*. M17.
2 Able to be disposed of or dealt with; able to be used, available; at a person's disposal. M17.

D. MASSON They were more disposable as literary ware.

disposable income income remaining after deduction of taxes and other mandatory charges, available to be spent or saved as one wishes (cf. ***discretionary income*** s.v. DISCRETION).

3 Designed to be thrown away after being used once, not to be laundered or refilled. M20.

Sunday Times Bed pans and bottles . . made of papier mâché, to be disposable.

▸ **B** *noun*. An article designed to be thrown away after being used once. M20.

P. LEACH Your basic choice is between washable nappies and disposables.

■ **disposaˈbility** *noun* M19.

disposal /dɪˈspəʊz(ə)l/ *noun*. M17.
[ORIGIN from DISPOSE *verb* + -AL[1].]
1 Power or right to dispose of or deal with as one pleases. Usu. in ***at one's disposal*** below. M17.

W. BLACKSTONE The lords, who had the disposal of these female heiresses in marriage.

at one's disposal available for one's use, subject to one's orders or decisions.

†**2** = DISPOSITION 3. M17–E18.

MILTON Tax not divine disposal.

3 The action of disposing of or getting rid of: the action of settling or dealing with. M17.

E. A. PARKES The disposal of the dead is always a question of difficulty. *Howard Journal* Children's hearings . . are concerned only with the disposal of the child.

garbage disposal unit: see GARBAGE *noun*. ***waste-disposal unit***: see WASTE *noun*.

4 The action of bestowing, giving, or making over; bestowal, assignment; sale. M17.

E. FROMM Via the legal power of the last will the disposal of our property is determined.

5 Arrangement, disposition. E19.
6 A waste-disposal unit. *N. Amer.* M20.

dispose /dɪˈspəʊz/ *noun*. Now *rare* or *obsolete*. L16.
[ORIGIN from the verb.]
†**1** = DISPOSAL *noun* 1. L16–M18.
†**2** = DISPOSAL *noun* 4. L16–L17.
†**3** = DISPOSAL *noun* 2, DISPOSITION 3. Only in 17.
†**4** = DISPOSITION 7. Only in E17.
5 A person's manner; an air. *rare*. E17.

SHAKES. *Oth.* He hath a person and a smooth dispose To be suspected.

dispose /dɪˈspəʊz/ *verb*. LME.
[ORIGIN Old French & mod. French *disposer* based on Latin *disponere* (see DISPONE) but re-formed after Latin pa. pple *dispositus* and Old French & mod. French *poser*: see POSE *verb*[1].]
▸ **I** *verb trans.* **1** Place suitably, at intervals, or in order; adjust; arrange in a particular way. LME. ▸**b** Put away or in its proper place. Now *rare*. LME.

C. HAMPTON The Indians . . dispose themselves on either side of the stage.

†**2** = sense 10 below. LME–L17.
†**3** Bestow, make over; deal out, dispense, distribute. LME–E19.
†**4** Formally assign or hand over. LME–M16.
5 Make fit or ready; prepare (*to do*; *for* something). *arch.* LME.

W. TAYLOR Those missionaries who are disposing themselves to visit the Syrian churches.

6 Bring into a mood or frame of mind favourable for something; incline *to* something; make willing *to do*; give (something) a tendency *to*. LME.

D. CECIL Prejudices . . disposed them to be cheerfully opposed to anything . . far-fetched or newfangled. M. SINCLAIR Knitting disposed her to long silences.

▸ **II** *verb intrans.* **7** Make arrangements; determine the course of events. LME.

Proverb: Man proposes, God disposes.

†**8** Settle matters, make terms. *rare* (Shakes.). Only in E17.
†**9** Foll. by (*up*)*on*: = senses 11, 12 below. *Scot.* M17–L18.
▸ **III** *verb intrans.* Foll. by *of*.
†**10** Make a disposition of; control, regulate, govern. M16–E19.
11 Get rid of; deal conclusively with, settle; *colloq.* kill. E17. ▸**b** Show (a claim, argument, or opponent) to be incorrect. L19. ▸**c** Consume (food or drink). *colloq.* L19.

A. J. CRONIN Searching for . . a remark which might tactfully dispose of the past and . . open out the future. J. FRAME A notice . . requesting that lunch wrappers be disposed of in the receptacle provided. G. GREENE It was always his first question and he was glad when he had disposed of it.

12 Transfer into the hands of another by sale or bequest. L17.

C. BLACKWOOD I would . . like you to be there when all my possessions are disposed of.

■ **disposer** *noun* E16.

disposed /dɪˈspəʊzd/ *ppl adjective*. LME.
[ORIGIN from DISPOSE *verb* + -ED[1].]
1 Arranged, appointed, prepared; suitably placed or situated. LME.

E. BOWEN She sat well back . . with knees jutting forward, disposed in this attitude almost in spite of herself.

†**2** In a (specified) condition of body or health. Also, in good health, not indisposed. LME–L17.
3 Having a (specified) disposition or turn of mind; in a (specified) mood. Formerly also, well-disposed, having a favourable disposition. LME.

ISAIAH BERLIN Humanitarian prophets . . generously disposed towards all mankind.

ill-disposed: see ILL *adverb*. ***well-disposed***: see WELL *adverb*.

4 Inclined, in the mood, prepared, (*to do*, *to*, *for*). LME. ▸†**b** Inclined to merriment; in a cheerful mood. L16–E17.

I. D'ISRAELI The French Cabinet was strongly disposed for a Spanish war. A. MOOREHEAD Nobody was disposed to listen to him.

5 Having a physical inclination or tendency (*to do*, *to*); subject, liable. LME.

J. GALSWORTHY Hereditarily disposed to myopia.

■ **disposedly** /-zɪdli/ *adverb* with a (good or dignified) bearing E17. **disposedness** /-zɪdnɪs/ *noun* L16.

disposition /dɪspəˈzɪʃ(ə)n/ *noun*. LME.
[ORIGIN Old French & mod. French from Latin *dispositio(n-)*, from *disposit-* pa. ppl stem of *disponere* DISPONE: see -ITION. Later assoc. with DISPOSE *verb*.]
1 The action of getting rid of or making over; bestowal by deed or will; = DISPOSAL 3, 4. LME.

STEELE The wanton disposition of the favours of the powerful.

2 Power of disposing, control; = DISPOSAL 1. LME.

GIBBON The choice of action or of repose is no longer in our disposition.

3 The action of ordering or regulating by (esp. divine) right or power; dispensation, direction, control. *arch.* LME.

DEFOE This seemed to me to be a disposition of Providence.

4 Arrangement of affairs, esp. for a particular purpose; condition of affairs; in *pl.*, preparations, plans. LME. ▸**b** MILITARY. The stationing of troops ready for attack or defence; their distribution and allocation; in *pl.*, military measures or preparations. E17.

H. WILSON I . . would make dispositions for the work of the day.

†**5** ASTROLOGY. The situation of a planet in a horoscope, as supposedly affecting events; *spec.* the state of being in the house of another planet. LME–M17.
6 Temperament or character, esp. as displayed in dealings with others; turn of mind. LME.

V. CRONIN Uncle Georg had a cheerful disposition and Sophie found it fun to be with him. J. P. STERN A disposition of mind aiming at the subjugation of any object outside myself.

7 The state or quality of being disposed (*to*, *to do*); inclination (*for*); the condition of being (favourably or unfavourably) disposed *towards*. LME. ▸†**b** A frame of mind; a mood. E–M18.

JOHN BROOKE He did not want a wife with a disposition to meddle in politics.

8 A tendency of anything physical (*to*, *to do*). LME. ▸†**b** An aptitude, a skill. *rare*. E17–M18.

W. HAMILTON The different dispositions of wool, silk, etc. to unite with the colouring particles.

†**9** Physical constitution of anything; physical condition of the body, state of health. LME–E19.
10 The fact of being set in order; spatial arrangement; relative position, esp. of constituent parts. L15.

A. GEIKIE Looking at the disposition of the Highland glens and straths.

■ **dispositional** *adjective* M19. **dispositionally** *adverb* E20. **dispositioned** *adjective* having a (specified) disposition or turn of mind M17.

dispositive /dɪsˈpɒzətɪv/ *adjective*. LME.
[ORIGIN Old French & mod. French *dispositif*, *-ive* or medieval Latin *dispositivus*, from Latin *disposit-*: see DISPOSITION, -IVE.]
1 That has the quality of disposing or inclining; contributory, conducive. LME.
2 Having the quality or function of directing or controlling; relating to control; chiefly *Scot.* & US LAW, dealing with disposition by deed or will; effecting disposition of an issue etc. E17.
†**3** Of or pertaining to a person's natural disposition or inclination. M–L17.
■ **dispositively** *adverb* (long *rare*) LME.

dispositor /dɪˈspɒzɪtə/ *noun*. L16.
[ORIGIN Latin = disposer, (in medieval Latin) dispositor, from *disposit-*: see DISPOSITION, -OR.]
ASTROLOGY. The planet in whose house a given planet is situated.

dispository /dɪˈspɒzɪt(ə)ri/ *adjective*. *rare*. E17.
[ORIGIN from Latin *disposit-* (see DISPOSITION) + -ORY[2].]
†**1** = DISPOSITIVE 1. E–M17.
2 = DISPOSITIVE 2. M20.

dispossess /dɪspəˈzɛs/ *verb & noun*. L15.
[ORIGIN Old French *despossesser*, formed as DIS- 2, POSSESS *verb*.]
▸ **A** *verb trans.* **1** Put out of possession; strip of possessions; oust, dislodge; deprive *of*. L15. ▸†**b** Expel or banish *from*; drive *out of*. E17–L18. ▸†**c** Foll. by double obj.: deprive (a person) of (a possession). *rare* (Shakes.). Only in E17.

J. F. W. HERSCHEL Two kinds of prejudices, which . . differ exceedingly in the difficulty of dispossessing them. A. BROOKNER A veteran, dispossessed of all his belongings, returning from the wars. c SHAKES. *Timon* I will choose Mine heir from forth the beggars of the world, and dispossess her all.

2 Free (a possessed person) *of* an evil spirit by exorcism. Formerly also, exorcize (an evil spirit). L16.
▸ **B** *noun*. Eviction of a tenant or squatter. *US*. L19.
attrib.: ***dispossess proceedings***, ***dispossess warrant***, etc.
■ **dispossessed** *ppl adjective & noun* (**a**) *ppl adjective* that has been dispossessed or deprived, esp. of a home; (**b**) *noun pl. the* people who are dispossessed: L16. **dispossession** *noun* the action or an act of dispossessing; deprivation of or ejection from a possession, *spec.* exorcism; the fact of being dispossessed: L16. **dispossessor** *noun* a person who dispossesses L16.

dispost /dɪsˈpəʊst/ *verb trans.* Now *rare* or *obsolete*. L16.
[ORIGIN from DIS- 2 + POST *noun*[4]: cf. French †*desposter* dispossess, *déposter* dismiss from service.]
Deprive of a post, dismiss from service.

disposure /dɪˈspəʊʒə/ *noun*. M16.
[ORIGIN from DISPOSE *verb* + -URE.]
†**1** = DISPOSITION 3. M16–L17.
2 Arrangement, order. Now *rare*. E17.
†**3** = DISPOSAL *noun* 1. Only in 17.
4 = DISPOSAL *noun* 3, 4. *arch.* M17.

dispraise /dɪsˈpreɪz/ *noun*. LME.
[ORIGIN from DIS- 2 + PRAISE *noun* or from the verb.]
†**1** Contempt. *rare*. Only in LME.
2 The action or fact of dispraising; disparagement; blame, censure. E16.

C. M. YONGE Charles VI would not hear a word in his dispraise.

3 An instance or act of dispraising; a cause of blame, discredit, or disgrace. M16.

dispraise /dɪsˈpreɪz/ *verb*. ME.
[ORIGIN Old French *despreisier* from Proto-Romance from Latin *depretiare* DEPRECIATE. Cf. DISPRIZE *verb*.]
1 a *verb trans.* Express disapproval of; find fault with; blame, censure. ME. ▸**b** *verb intrans.* Express disapproval or blame. L15.
†**2** *verb trans.* Despise, belittle. LME–E16.
■ **dispraiser** *noun* LME. **dispraisingly** *adverb* disparagingly E17.

dispread /dɪˈsprɛd/ *verb trans.* & (*rare*) *intrans. arch.* Also **disspread**. Pa. t. & pple **-spread**. L16.
[ORIGIN from DIS- 1 + SPREAD *verb*.]
Spread out or through; extend, expand, open out.

J. THOMSON Tyrant heat, dispreading through the sky. H. WILLIAMSON He saw, in hut after hut, figures dispread and inert on wet floors.

disprize /dɪsˈprʌɪz/ *noun*. Long *rare*. M16.
[ORIGIN from the verb, or from Old French *despris*, formed as DISPRIZE *verb*.]
Disparagement, contempt; belittlement.

disprize /dɪsˈprʌɪz/ *verb trans.* LME.
[ORIGIN Old French *desprisier* var. of *despreisier* DISPRAISE *verb*.]
Despise; disparage, decry, belittle.

disprofit /dɪsˈprɒfɪt/ *noun. arch.* **L15.**
[ORIGIN from DIS- 2 + PROFIT *noun*.]
1 Detriment, disadvantage. **L15.**
†**2** A disadvantage. **M16–L17.**

disprofit /dɪsˈprɒfɪt/ *verb trans. arch.* **L15.**
[ORIGIN from DIS- 2 + PROFIT *verb*.]
Bring disadvantage to; inconvenience.

disproof /dɪsˈpruːf/ *noun.* **LME.**
[ORIGIN from DIS- 2 + PROOF *noun*.]
The action or an act of disproving an assertion, claim, etc.; refutation; a disproving fact or piece of evidence.

disproportion /dɪsprəˈpɔːʃ(ə)n/ *noun.* **M16.**
[ORIGIN from DIS- 2 + PROPORTION *noun*, after French *disproportion*.]
1 Lack of proportion; the condition of being out of proportion. **M16.**

S. KITZINGER The baby cannot pass through the bones of the pelvis; this is called *disproportion*.

2 An instance of this; something out of proportion. **L16.**

B. JOWETT A leg too long, or some other disproportion. R. NIEBUHR Inequalities of privilege are due chiefly to disproportion of power.

disproportion /dɪsprəˈpɔːʃ(ə)n/ *verb trans.* **L16.**
[ORIGIN from the noun, after French *disproportionner*.]
Make or shape out of proportion; make disproportionate *to*.

SHAKES. *3 Hen. VI* To shape my legs of an unequal size; To disproportion me in every part. LYTTON Statutes that disproportion punishment to crime.

■ **disproportionable** *adjective* out of due proportion, disproportionate **L16.** **disproportionableness** *noun* **M17.** **disproportionably** *adverb* **E17.** **disproportioned** *ppl adjective* (*a*) disproportionate; †(*b*) *rare* (Shakes.), inconsistent: **L16.**

disproportional /dɪsprəˈpɔːʃ(ə)n(ə)l/ *adjective.* Long *rare.* **E17.**
[ORIGIN from DISPROPORTION *noun* + -AL[1].]
= DISPROPORTIONATE *adjective*.
■ **disproportionally** *adverb* **M18.**

disproportionality /ˌdɪsprəpɔːʃəˈnalɪti/ *noun.* **M17.**
[ORIGIN from DISPROPORTIONAL + -ITY.]
The quality of being disproportionate.

disproportionate /dɪsprəˈpɔːʃ(ə)nət/ *adjective.* **M16.**
[ORIGIN from DIS- 2 + PROPORTIONATE *adjective*, after French *disproportionné*.]
Lacking proportion, poorly proportioned; out of proportion (*to*); relatively too large or too small.

C. S. LEWIS His tiny, child-like snore, so disproportionate to his bulk. D. MURPHY The socially crippling effects of unmarried motherhood constituted an altogether disproportionate punishment for a momentary loss of control.

■ **disproportionately** *adverb* **L17.** **disproportionateness** *noun* **M17.**

disproportionate /dɪsprəˈpɔːʃ(ə)neɪt/ *verb intrans.* **M20.**
[ORIGIN Back-form. from DISPROPORTIONATION.]
CHEMISTRY. Undergo disproportionation.

disproportionation /ˌdɪsprəpɔːʃəˈneɪʃ(ə)n/ *noun.* **E20.**
[ORIGIN from DISPROPORTION *noun* or *verb* + -ATION.]
CHEMISTRY. A transfer of atoms or valency electrons between identical atoms or ions so as to give dissimilar products; decomposition in which a compound is both oxidized and reduced.

disprove /dɪsˈpruːv/ *verb trans.* Pa. pple **-proved**, (*arch.*) **-proven** /-ˈprəʊv(ə)n, -ˈpruːv(ə)n/. **LME.**
[ORIGIN Old French *desprover*, formed as DIS- 2, PROVE *verb*.]
1 Prove (an assertion, claim, etc.) to be false or erroneous; show the fallacy or non-validity of. **LME.**
2 Disapprove of. *obsolete* exc. *dial.* **LME.**
3 Prove the falsity or error of the statement(s) of (a person). Now *rare* or *obsolete*. **L16.**
■ **disprovable** *adjective* †(*a*) reprehensible; (*b*) able to be disproved, refutable: **M16.** **disproval** *noun* (*rare*) an act of disproving, a disproof **E17.** **disprovement** *noun* (*rare*) the action or fact of disproving, (a) disproof **L16.**

disprovide /dɪsprəˈvʌɪd/ *verb trans. arch.* **E16.**
[ORIGIN from DIS- 2 + PROVIDE.]
Fail to provide for; leave unprovided.

dispunct /dɪsˈpʌŋkt/ *verb trans. rare.* **L16.**
[ORIGIN Latin *dispunct-* pa. ppl stem of *dispungere* prick here and there, formed as DIS- 1 + *pungere* to prick.]
Mark (as) with a pen for omission or distinction; erase; distinguish, make prominent.

dispunge /dɪˈspʌndʒ/ *verb trans. arch.* In sense 1 also **dispong**e. **E17.**
[ORIGIN Partly from SPONGE *verb*, partly from EXPUNGE *verb* by substitution: see DIS- 1.]
1 Discharge or release as from a squeezed sponge. **E17.**
†**2** Delete, expunge. **E–M17.**

dispunishable /dɪsˈpʌnɪʃəb(ə)l/ *adjective.* **L16.**
[ORIGIN from DIS- 2 + PUNISHABLE. Cf. Anglo-Norman *dispunishable*.]
LAW. Free from liability to punishment or penalty; not punishable.

†**dispurse** *verb trans.* **L16–E18.**
[ORIGIN Alt.]
= DISBURSE *verb*.

†**dispurvey** *verb trans.* **LME–E17.**
[ORIGIN Old French *desporveeir*, formed as DIS- 2 + *porveeir*: see PURVEY *verb*.]
Rob or strip of provisions; make destitute. Usu. in *pass.*
■ †**dispurveyance** *noun* (*rare*) lack of provisions, destitution **L15–L16.**

disputable /dɪˈspjuːtəb(ə)l, ˈdɪspjʊtəb(ə)l/ *adjective.* **L15.**
[ORIGIN French, or Latin *disputabilis*, formed as DISPUTE *verb*: see -ABLE.]
1 Liable to be disputed; open to question; contentious. **L15.**

Church Times His highly disputable approach to the New Testament.

†**2** Disputatious. *rare* (Shakes.). Only in **L16.**
■ **diˈsputableness** *noun* **M17.** **disputably** *adverb* **M19.**

†**disputacity** *noun.* **M17–E18.**
[ORIGIN Irreg. from DISPUTATIOUS *adjective*: see -ACITY.]
Disputatiousness.

disputant /dɪˈspjuːt(ə)nt, ˈdɪspjʊt(ə)nt/ *noun & adjective.* **L16.**
[ORIGIN Latin *disputant-* pres. ppl stem of *disputare*: see DISPUTE *verb*, -ANT[1].]
▸ **A** *noun.* A person who disputes or argues; *esp.* one who engages in public debate or disputation. **L16.**
▸ **B** *adjective.* That disputes; engaged in debate or controversy. **L17.**

disputation /dɪspjuːˈteɪʃ(ə)n, -pjʊ-/ *noun.* **LME.**
[ORIGIN French from Latin *disputatio(n-)*, from *disputat-* pa. ppl stem of *disputare*: see DISPUTE *verb*, -ATION.]
1 The action of disputing or debating; argument, controversy; debate, discussion. Also, an instance of this. **LME.** ▸**b** *spec.* An exercise in which parties formally propose, attack, and defend a set question or thesis. **M16.**
†**2** Written discussion or treatment of a subject; a dissertation. **M16–E17.**
†**3** Doubtful or disputable condition; doubt. **M16–L17.**
†**4** Interchange of ideas; discourse, conversation. *rare* (Shakes.). Only in **L16.**

disputatious /dɪspjuːˈteɪʃəs, -pjʊ-/ *adjective.* **M17.**
[ORIGIN from DISPUTATION: see -OUS.]
Characterized by or given to disputation; prone to argue; fond of argument.

SIR W. SCOTT The wine rendered me loquacious, disputatious, and quarrelsome.

■ **disputatiously** *adverb* **M19.** **disputatiousness** *noun* **L17.**

disputative /dɪˈspjuːtətɪv/ *adjective.* **L16.**
[ORIGIN Late Latin *disputativus*, from Latin *disputat-*: see DISPUTATION, -ATIVE.]
1 Disputatious. **L16.**
†**2** That is the subject of disputation or dispute; controversial. **L16–E18.**
3 Of or pertaining to disputation. **M17.**
■ **disputatively** *adverb* **L16.** **disputativeness** *noun* **M19.**

disputator /ˈdɪspjʊteɪtə/ *noun. rare.* **L16.**
[ORIGIN Latin, from *disputat-*: see DISPUTATION, -ATOR.]
A disputant.

dispute /dɪˈspjuːt, ˈdɪspjuːt/ *noun.* **L16.**
[ORIGIN from the verb.]
†**1 a** A logical argument. *rare.* Only in **L16.** ▸**b** An oral or written discussion of a subject in which arguments for and against are put forward and examined. **E17–M19.**

b T. STANLEY He was the first that committed the disputes of Socrates his Master to writing.

2 An instance of disputing or arguing against something or someone, an argument, a controversy; *esp.* a heated contention, a disagreement in which opposing views are strongly held. **E17.**

Financial Times El Al, Israel's national airline, . . has been grounded for more than a month because of a labour dispute.

3 The act of disputing or arguing against something or someone; controversy, debate. **M17.**

J. WESLEY That once was in the Heat of Dispute. H. CECIL There was no dispute that this was the law, but Martin raised various defences.

beyond dispute, **past dispute**, **without dispute** certainly, indisputably, without question; ***be beyond dispute*** etc., be indisputable (*that*). **in dispute** being argued about.
†**4** Strife, contest; a fight, a struggle. **M17–M18.**

dispute /dɪˈspjuːt/ *verb.* **ME.**
[ORIGIN Old French *desputer*, (also mod.) *disputer* from Latin *disputare* estimate, (in late Latin) dispute, formed as DIS- 1 + *putare* reckon.]
▸ **I** *verb intrans.* **1** Contend with opposing arguments or assertions; argue; debate hotly, quarrel, have an altercation. (Foll. by *about*, *on*, *over*, †*against*, †*of*, a subject; *against*, *with*, an opponent.) **ME.**

R. W. EMERSON He disputed like a devil on these two points. QUILLER-COUCH Four children . . are disputing over a box of wooden soldiers. J. BUCHAN Always very ready to dispute about philosophy.

†**2** Contend physically, esp. by force of arms; struggle. **M17–E19.**
▸ **II** *verb trans.* **3** Discuss, debate, or argue (a question or point), esp. heatedly. Foll. by direct obj. or subord. clause **ME.**

J. RAY I will not dispute what Gravity is. H. MARTINEAU Disputing whether luxury be a virtue or a crime. B. WEBB One of the most hotly disputed questions within the Labour Party.

4 Maintain or defend (an assertion, claim, etc.) by argument or disputation; contend (that something is so). Now *rare* or *obsolete*. **LME.**

SWIFT And these, she offer'd to dispute, Alone distinguish'd man from brute.

5 Question the correctness or validity of (a statement or an alleged fact); argue with (a person). **E16.**

E. WAUGH They were disputing the bill. HARPER LEE A Cunningham disputed a Coningham over land titles and took to the law.

6 Contest, strive against, or resist (an action). **E17.**
7 Move or influence by disputation, argue or persuade (a person) *into* or *out of*. Now *rare* or *obsolete*. **M17.**
8 Contend or compete for the possession of; strive to gain against opposition. **L17.**

F. HOYLE They and their men disputed the possession of caves with bears and mountain lions.

■ **disputer** *noun* a person who disputes or is given to disputation **LME.**

disqualification /dɪsˌkwɒlɪfɪˈkeɪʃ(ə)n/ *noun.* **E18.**
[ORIGIN from DISQUALIFY *verb*: see -FICATION.]
1 Something which disqualifies; a ground or cause of incapacity. **E18.**

DICKENS I hope you don't think good looks a disqualification for the business.

2 The action of disqualifying; the fact or condition of being disqualified. **L18.**

Times A driver . . appealed successfully, against the disqualification order.

disqualify /dɪsˈkwɒlɪfʌɪ/ *verb trans.* **E18.**
[ORIGIN from DIS- 2 + QUALIFY.]
1 Deprive of the qualities required (*for* a situation, purpose, etc.); make unfit or unsuited; prevent by lack of qualification *from* doing. **E18.**

L. STEPHEN Strong passions and keen sensibilities may easily disqualify a man for domestic tranquillity.

2 Incapacitate legally, pronounce unqualified; debar from a competition because of an infringement of the rules; prohibit from driving. **E18.**

D. HUME It is usual for the Speaker to disqualify himself for the office. *Times* He also pleaded guilty to driving a bus while disqualified.

disquantity /dɪsˈkwɒntɪti/ *verb trans. rare.* **E17.**
[ORIGIN from DIS- 2 + QUANTITY *noun*.]
Make smaller, reduce; deprive of metrical quantity.

disquiet /dɪsˈkwʌɪət/ *noun.* **M16.**
[ORIGIN from DISQUIET *adjective*, *verb*.]
1 Absence of calmness or peace; disturbance; uneasiness, anxiety; unrest. **M16.**

S. AUSTIN The States of the Church and Naples were still in a state of universal disquiet and ferment. DAY LEWIS My father's moodiness was . . not a source of much disquiet or grievance.

†**2** A disturbance; a disquieting feeling or circumstance. **L16–M18.**

disquiet /dɪsˈkwʌɪət/ *adjective.* Now *rare.* **L16.**
[ORIGIN from DIS- 2 + QUIET *adjective*.]
Restless, uneasy; disturbed.

T. UNDERDOWN A sea, which . . was very disquiet. THACKERAY His mind was disquiet.

■ **disquietly** *adverb* †(*a*) disquietingly; (*b*) in a disquiet or uneasy manner: **E17.** **disquietness** *noun* **M16.**

disquiet /dɪsˈkwʌɪət/ *verb trans.* **E16.**
[ORIGIN from DIS- 2 + QUIET *verb*.]
Deprive of quietness, peace, or rest; trouble, alarm, worry; make uneasy or restless.

R. D. LAING This . . was profoundly disquieting. It baffled me. It *scared* me. H. KISSINGER What worried Paris could also disquiet Moscow and Damascus.

■ **disquietedly** *adverb* in a disquieted manner **M19.** **disquietedness** *noun* the state of being disquiet **L17.** **disquieter** *noun* **M16.** **disquietingly** *adverb* in a disquieting manner, disturbingly, worryingly **E20.**

disquieten /dɪsˈkwʌɪət(ə)n/ *verb trans.* **E20.**
[ORIGIN from DIS- 2 + QUIETEN *verb*.]
= DISQUIET *verb*.

†**disquietment** *noun.* **E17–L18.**
[ORIGIN from DISQUIET *verb* + -MENT.]
Disquiet; the action of disquieting; a disquieting circumstance.

D

disquietude /dɪsˈkwʌɪətjuːd/ *noun*. E18.
[ORIGIN from DISQUIET *adjective* + -TUDE, after *quietude*.]
1 Disquieted condition or state; disquiet. E18.
2 A feeling, occasion, or cause of disquiet; a disquieting circumstance. E18.

disquisition /dɪskwɪˈzɪʃ(ə)n/ *noun*. L15.
[ORIGIN Old French & mod. French from Latin *disquisitio(n-)*, from *disquisit-* pa. ppl stem of *disquirere*, formed as DIS- 1 + *quaerere* seek: see -ITION.]
†**1** A subject or topic for investigation. L15–M17.
2 Diligent or systematic search; investigation, examination. L16.
3 A treatise or discourse in which a subject is investigated and discussed; a long or elaborate treatise or discourse. M17.

J. COLVILLE The P.M.'s lengthy disquisitions in Cabinet on papers which he has not read.

■ **disquisitional** *adjective* of the nature of a disquisition E19. **disquisitionist** *noun* a person who writes or gives a disquisition M19.

disquisitive /dɪˈskwɪzɪtɪv/ *adjective*. M17.
[ORIGIN from Latin *disquisit-*: see DISQUISITION, -IVE.]
Characterized by or given to research or investigation; inquiring.

disquisitor /dɪˈskwɪzɪtə/ *noun*. M18.
[ORIGIN medieval Latin, formed as DISQUISITIVE: see -OR.]
A person who makes disquisition, an inquirer; a person who writes or gives a disquisition.

Disraelian /dɪzˈreɪlɪən/ *adjective*. L19.
[ORIGIN from *Disraeli* (see below) + -AN.]
Pertaining to, characteristic of, or resembling the Conservative statesman and writer Benjamin Disraeli (1804–81).

Daily Telegraph Seeking to give the Disraelian One Nation ideal more concrete expression.

†**disrange** *verb*. LME.
[ORIGIN Old French *desrangier*, *-rengier*, from *des-* DIS- 2 + *ranc*, *renc* (mod. *rang*) RANK *noun*. Cf. RANGE *verb*¹.]
1 *verb intrans.* & *refl.* Start out; fall out of rank. LME–E17.
2 *verb trans.* Throw out of order; disarrange. Only in L18.

disrank /dɪsˈraŋk/ *verb trans.* L16.
[ORIGIN from DIS- 2 + RANK *noun*.]
†**1** Throw out of rank or into disorder; confuse. L16–M17.
2 Deprive of rank, reduce to a lower rank; degrade. L16.

disrate /dɪsˈreɪt/ *verb trans.* E19.
[ORIGIN from DIS- 2 + RATE *noun*¹.]
Chiefly NAUTICAL. Reduce to a lower rating or rank, demote; remove from a rank or class.

disregard /dɪsrɪˈɡɑːd/ *noun*. M17.
[ORIGIN from DIS- 2 + REGARD *noun*.]
1 Lack of regard or respect; neglect. Now *esp.* the action of ignoring or treating as of no importance. (Foll. by *of*, *for*, †*to*.) M17.

D. NEAL The Bishops fell under a general disregard. J. ROSENBERG A complete disregard for social convention.

2 Part of a person's income not to be considered in the assessment of a state benefit. M20.

disregard /dɪsrɪˈɡɑːd/ *verb trans.* M17.
[ORIGIN from DIS- 2 + REGARD *verb*.]
Pay no regard to; *esp.* ignore, treat as of no importance. Formerly, neglect unduly, slight.
■ **disregardable** *adjective* M17. **disregardant** *adjective* disregarding, neglectful E19. **disregarder** *noun* M17.

disregardful /dɪsrɪˈɡɑːdfʊl, -f(ə)l/ *adjective*. M17.
[ORIGIN from DIS- 2 + REGARDFUL.]
Neglectful, careless.
■ **disregardfully** *adverb* M17. **disregardfulness** *noun* (*rare*) M18.

disrelish /dɪsˈrɛlɪʃ/ *noun*. E17.
[ORIGIN from the verb or from DIS- 2 + RELISH *noun*.]
Distaste, aversion. (Foll. by *for*, †*of*.)

disrelish /dɪsˈrɛlɪʃ/ *verb*. M16.
[ORIGIN from DIS- 2 + RELISH *verb* or *noun*.]
†**1** *verb trans.* Destroy the relish or flavour of; make distasteful. M16–M18.
2 *verb trans.* Have a distaste for; dislike. E17.

R. L. STEVENSON He so much disrelished some expressions of mine that . . he showed me to the door.

3 *verb intrans.* Be distasteful. M17.
†**4** *verb trans.* Be distasteful to; disgust. M17–E18.

disremember /dɪsrɪˈmɛmbə/ *verb trans.* & *intrans.* Chiefly *dial.* M17.
[ORIGIN from DIS- 2 + REMEMBER.]
Fail to remember; forget.

disrepair /dɪsrɪˈpɛː/ *noun*. L18.
[ORIGIN from DIS- 2 + REPAIR *noun*².]
The state of being out of repair, or in bad condition for lack of repairs.

E. WAUGH Carpet, curtains and upholstery were inspected for signs of disrepair. J. A. MICHENER A building fallen into sad disrepair.

disreputable /dɪsˈrɛpjʊtəb(ə)l/ *adjective* & *noun*. L18.
[ORIGIN from DIS- 2 + REPUTABLE, after *disrepute*.]
▸ **A** *adjective*. **1** Such as to bring something into disrepute; discreditable. L18.
2 Having a bad reputation; not respectable in character or appearance. E19.
▸ **B** *noun*. A disreputable person. M19.
■ **disreputaˈbility** *noun* M19. **disreputableness** *noun* E18. **disreputably** *adverb* L18.

disreputation /ˌdɪsrɛpjʊˈteɪʃ(ə)n/ *noun*. *arch.* E17.
[ORIGIN from DIS- 2 + REPUTATION.]
1 Loss of reputation; the action of bringing into disrepute; dishonour. E17. ▸†**b** A discrediting circumstance. E17–M18.
2 Lack of reputation, bad reputation; the condition of being in disrepute. M17.

disrepute /dɪsrɪˈpjuːt/ *noun*. M17.
[ORIGIN from DIS- 2 + REPUTE *noun*.]
Loss or absence of reputation; bad repute, dishonour, discredit.

H. T. BUCKLE It brings the administration of justice into disrepute.

disrespect /dɪsrɪˈspɛkt/ *noun*. E17.
[ORIGIN from DIS- 2 + RESPECT *noun*; or perh. from the verb.]
1 Lack of respect or courtesy; discourtesy. E17.

I. MURDOCH Finn has very little inner life. I mean no disrespect to him in saying this.

†**2** An act that shows disrespect. E17–E18.

disrespect /dɪsrɪˈspɛkt/ *verb trans.* E17.
[ORIGIN from DIS- 2 + RESPECT *verb*.]
Have or show no respect or reverence for; treat with disrespect.
■ **disrespecter** *noun* (*rare*) M17.

disrespectable /dɪsrɪˈspɛktəb(ə)l/ *adjective*. E19.
[ORIGIN from DIS- 2 + RESPECTABLE.]
Not worthy of respect, not respectable.
■ ˌ**disrespectaˈbility** *noun* M19.

disrespectful /dɪsrɪˈspɛktfʊl, -f(ə)l/ *adjective*. L17.
[ORIGIN from DIS- 2 + RESPECTFUL, after *disrespect*.]
Showing disrespect.
■ **disrespectfully** *adverb* L17. **disrespectfulness** *noun* L17.

†**disrespective** *adjective*. E17–M18.
[ORIGIN from DIS- 2 + RESPECTIVE *adjective*, after *disrespect*.]
Disrespectful.

disrobe /dɪsˈrəʊb/ *verb*. LME.
[ORIGIN from DIS- 2 + ROBE *verb* or *noun*¹, perh. after Old French *desrober*.]
1 *verb trans.* Divest of a garment; remove clothing or covering or some possession or quality from. (Foll. by *of*.) LME.
2 *verb intrans.* Undress; take off clerical robes. E18.
■ **disrobement** *noun* M18. **disrober** *noun* M17.

disroot /dɪsˈruːt/ *verb trans.* E17.
[ORIGIN from DIS- 2 + ROOT *verb*¹.]
1 Dislodge (something) from the place where it is fixed. E17.
2 Uproot (a plant). E19.

disrump /dɪsˈrʌmp/ *verb trans.* & *intrans.* L16.
[ORIGIN Latin *disrumpere*, formed as DIS- 1 + *rumpere* break.]
Break up; = DISRUPT.

disrupt /dɪsˈrʌpt/ *verb*. Pa. pple & ppl adjective **disrupted**, (earlier, now *poet.*) **disrupt**. LME.
[ORIGIN Latin *disrupt-* pa. ppl stem of *disrumpere*: see DISRUMP.]
1 *verb trans.* Break apart, burst, shatter; separate forcibly; *esp.* interrupt the normal continuity of (an activity etc.); throw into disorder. LME.

G. MEREDITH Leaving them . . disrupt, as by earthquake. E. FIGES The household routine had been totally disrupted. *Times* War veterans disrupt Senate hearings.

2 *verb intrans.* Burst open; be disrupted. *rare*. M17.
– NOTE: In sense 1 rare before 18 & only as pa. pple before 19.
■ **disrupter**, **disruptor** *nouns* L19.

disruption /dɪsˈrʌpʃ(ə)n/ *noun*. LME.
[ORIGIN Latin *disruptio(n-)*, formed as DISRUPT: see -ION.]
1 Disrupted condition, disorder; a disrupted part; a rent, a tear. LME.

Times Further disruption will be caused by a half-day strike tomorrow morning.

2 The action or an act of disrupting something. M17.

T. BURNET Great earthquakes and disruptions.

the Disruption the great split (of 1843) in the Established Church of Scotland, from which arose the Free Church of Scotland.
■ **disruptionist** *noun* a person who favours disruption. L19.

disruptive /dɪsˈrʌptɪv/ *adjective*. M19.
[ORIGIN from DISRUPT *verb* + -IVE.]
Causing or tending to cause disruption or disorder.

A. WEST A student they had come to look on as a disruptive nuisance. *Guardian* A commitment by returning miners to ensure the survival of their own pits will preclude disruptive action.

■ **disruptively** *adverb* L19. **disruptiveness** *noun* L19.

disrupture /dɪsˈrʌptʃə/ *noun* & *verb*. L18.
[ORIGIN from DISRUPT *verb* after *rupture*.]
▸ **A** *noun*. The action of disrupting; (a) disruption. L18.
▸ **B** *verb trans.* Break apart or off; divide by a rupture. E19.

diss /dɪs/ *noun*¹. M19.
[ORIGIN Algerian Arab. *dīs*.]
In Algeria, a Mediterranean grass, *Ampelodesmos mauritanica*, used for making cordage etc.

diss *adjective* & *verb*¹ var. of DIS *adjective* & *verb*¹.

diss *verb*² & *noun*² var. of DIS *verb*³ & *noun*².

dissatisfaction /ˌdɪ(s)satɪsˈfakʃ(ə)n, dɪˌsat-/ *noun*. M17.
[ORIGIN from DIS- 2 + SATISFACTION.]
1 The fact or condition of being dissatisfied. M17.
2 In *pl.* Feelings or expressions of discontent. M17.

dissatisfactory /ˌdɪ(s)satɪsˈfakt(ə)ri/ *adjective*. E17.
[ORIGIN from DIS- 2 + SATISFACTORY.]
Not satisfactory; causing dissatisfaction.

dissatisfied /dɪ(s)ˈsatɪsfʌɪd/ *ppl adjective*. M17.
[ORIGIN from DISSATISFY + -ED¹.]
1 Not satisfied; displeased; left with a feeling of dissatisfaction by the deficiency or inadequacy of something. M17.
2 Showing or expressing dissatisfaction. E19.
■ **dissatisfiedly** *adverb* E19. **dissatisfiedness** *noun* E18.

dissatisfy /dɪ(s)ˈsatɪsfʌɪ/ *verb trans.* M17.
[ORIGIN from DIS- 2 + SATISFY.]
Deprive of satisfaction; fail to satisfy, displease; disquiet.

dissava /dɪˈsɑːvə/ *noun*. L17.
[ORIGIN Sinhalese *disāva*.]
hist. A governor of an administrative district in Ceylon (Sri Lanka).

dissect /dɪˈsɛkt/ *verb*. L16.
[ORIGIN Latin *dissect-* pa. ppl stem of *dissecare*, formed as DIS- 1 + *secare* to cut.]
1 *verb trans.* Cut in pieces. L16.
dissecting aneurysm an annular blood-filled cavity in the wall of an artery where it has split.
2 *verb trans.* *spec.* Methodically cut up (an animal, plant, etc.) in order to show or examine the internal parts. L16. ▸**b** Take *out* an organ etc. without disturbing adjoining tissue. M19.
dissecting knife, *dissecting room*, etc.
3 *verb trans.* Examine minutely, part by part; analyse, criticize in detail. M17.
4 *verb intrans.* Perform dissection. L17.

WORDSWORTH Our meddling intellect Misshapes the beauteous forms of things:—We murder to dissect.

■ **dissectible** *adjective* (*rare*) E19. **dissective** *adjective* having the quality of dissecting; serving to dissect: M19.

dissected /dɪˈsɛktɪd/ *ppl adjective*. L16.
[ORIGIN from DISSECT + -ED¹.]
1 Divided into pieces; cut up for anatomical study. L16.
dissected map, **dissected picture**: that can be reassembled as an exercise or puzzle.
2 Having a divided form or structure; BOTANY (of a leaf) divided into many deep lobes. M17. ▸**b** PHYSICAL GEOGRAPHY. Formed by the dissection of a once flat plateau or plain. E20.

dissection /dɪˈsɛkʃ(ə)n/ *noun*. L16.
[ORIGIN from DISSECT + -ION; perh. partly from French *dissection*, medieval Latin *dissectio(n-)*, formed as DISSECT.]
1 The action or process of dissecting. L16. ▸**b** PHYSICAL GEOGRAPHY. The breaking up by erosion of a flat surface such as a plateau or plain into hills, or flat uplands, and valleys. E20.
2 Something which is the result or product of dissecting. L16.
3 Detailed analysis, minute examination. Formerly *spec.*, chemical analysis. E17.

dissector /dɪˈsɛktə/ *noun*. L16.
[ORIGIN mod. Latin, from Latin *dissect-*: see DISSECT, -OR.]
1 A person who dissects, esp. anatomically. L16.
2 A dissecting instrument. M19.

disseise /dɪsˈsiːz/ *verb trans.* Also **-ze**. ME.
[ORIGIN Anglo-Norman *disseisir*, Old French *dessaisir* dispossess, formed as DIS- 2, SEIZE *verb*.]
1 LAW (now *hist.*). Put out of actual seisin or possession; dispossess (a person) of estates etc., usually wrongfully or by force; oust. (Foll. by *of*, †*from*.) ME.
2 *gen.* Deprive, rob, rid, *of*. ME.
■ **disseiˈsee** *noun* a person who is disseised of an estate E16. **disseisor** *noun* a person who disseises LME. **disseisoress** *noun* a female disseisor L16. †**disseisure** *noun* = DISSEISIN 1 L16–E18.

disseisin /dɪsˈsiːzɪn/ *noun*. Also **-zin**. LME.
[ORIGIN Anglo-Norman *disseisine*, Old French *dessaisine*, formed as DIS- 2, SEISIN.]
1 LAW (now *hist.*). The act or fact of disseising; privation of seisin; *esp.* the wrongful appropriation of the lands or (formerly) the goods of another. LME.
novel disseisin, **new disseisin**, **fresh disseisin** disseisin of recent date.
2 *gen.* Dispossession. *arch.* L16.

M. BEERBOHM Why should the disseizin of his soul have seemed shameful to him?.. He was in love.

disseize *verb*, **disseizin** *noun* vars. of DISSEISE, DISSEISIN.

disselboom /ˈdɪs(ə)lbʊəm/ *noun. S. Afr.* E19.
[ORIGIN Dutch, from *dissel* shaft + *boom* beam, boom.]
The pole of a wagon.

dissemblable /dɪˈsɛmbləb(ə)l/ *adjective & noun.* LME.
[ORIGIN Old French *dessemblable*, from *dessembler*: see DISSEMBLANCE, -ABLE.]
▸ **A** *adjective.* Dissimilar; various. Now *rare* or *obsolete.* LME.
▸ **B** *noun.* In *pl.* Dissimilar things. *rare.* E20.

dissemblance /dɪˈsɛmbl(ə)ns/ *noun.* LME.
[ORIGIN In sense 1 from Old French *dessemblance* (mod. *dissemblance*), from *dessembler* be unlike, from *des-* DIS- 2 + *sembler* resemble, seem: see -ANCE. In sense 2 alt. of DISSIMULANCE after *dissemble.*]
1 Dissimilarity, (a) lack of resemblance. LME.
2 The action of dissembling, dissimulation. E17.

dissemble /dɪˈsɛmb(ə)l/ *verb*[1]. LME.
[ORIGIN Alt. of DISSIMULE, assoc. with SEMBLANCE.]
1 *verb trans. & intrans.* Conceal (one's character, a feeling, an intention, etc.) by feigning a different one. LME.

A. T. ELLIS None of them knew how unhappy she was, so she would have either to dissemble or explain. M. DRABBLE She had .. dissembled what gifts she had once had.

2 *verb trans.* Assume a false appearance of; feign, simulate; pretend (*that*, *to do*). Now only as ***dissembled*** *ppl adjective.* LME.
3 *verb trans.* Conceal the identity of, disguise. *arch.* L15.
4 *verb trans.* Pretend not to notice, turn a blind eye to; ignore (the fact *that*). E16.
■ **dissembler** *noun* a person who dissembles; a deceiver, a hypocrite: E16. **dissemblingly** *adverb* in a way that disguises one's real character or purpose M16.

dissemble /dɪˈsɛmb(ə)l/ *verb*[2]. LME.
[ORIGIN Old French *dessembler*, from *des-* DIS- 2 + *a-sembler* ASSEMBLE.]
†**1** *verb intrans.* = DISASSEMBLE 1. *rare.* LME.
2 *verb trans.* = DISASSEMBLE 2. L20.

†**dissembly** *noun.* L16–L17.
[ORIGIN Alt.]
(An) assembly.

SHAKES. *Much Ado* Is our whole dissembly appear'd?

disseminate /dɪˈsɛmɪneɪt/ *verb trans.* Pa. pple & ppl adjective **-ated**, (earlier) **-ate** /-ət/. LME.
[ORIGIN Latin *disseminat-* pa. ppl stem of *disseminare*, formed as DIS- 1 + *semen*, *semin-* seed: see -ATE[3].]
Scatter in different directions, as in sowing seed; spread, disperse; diffuse, promulgate, (opinions, knowledge, etc.); *spec.* (MEDICINE, chiefly as ***disseminated*** *ppl adjective*) spread throughout an organ or the body.

C. G. SELIGMAN The mass of the Fulani population .. is disseminated among diverse Negro populations. Q. BELL She collected and disseminated bad news.

disseminated sclerosis multiple sclerosis.
— NOTE: In isolated use before 17.
■ **disseminator** *noun* E17.

dissemination /dɪˌsɛmɪˈneɪʃ(ə)n/ *noun.* E17.
[ORIGIN Latin *disseminatio(n-)*, formed as DISSEMINATE: see -ATION.]
The action of disseminating; the fact or condition of being disseminated; dispersion, diffusion; promulgation.

disseminule /dɪˈsɛmɪnjuːl/ *noun.* E20.
[ORIGIN Irreg. from DISSEMINATION + -ULE.]
BOTANY. Any part of a plant that serves to propagate it, e.g. a seed or a fruit.

dissension /dɪˈsɛnʃ(ə)n/ *noun.* Also (now *rare*) **-ntion.** ME.
[ORIGIN Old French & mod. French from Latin *dissensio(n-)*, from *dissens-* pa. ppl stem of *dissentire*: see DISSENT *verb*, -ION.]
1 (A) disagreement of opinion, esp. such as leads to contention or strife. ME.

M. MITCHELL There were dissensions within the Confederate cabinet, disagreements between President Davis and his generals.

†**2** MEDICINE. (A) disturbance of the body producing illness. L16–E18.
†**3** Disagreement in matters of religion; = DISSENT *noun* 3. E18–E19.

†**dissensious** *adjective* var. of DISSENTIOUS.

dissensus /dɪˈsɛnsəs/ *noun.* M20.
[ORIGIN from DIS- 2 + CONSENSUS, or Latin *dissensus* disagreement, from *dissens-* pa. ppl stem of *dissentire*: see DISSENT *noun.*]
Widespread dissent; the reverse of consensus.

Encounter Differing viewpoints .. erupting into dissensus and minority positions.

dissent /dɪˈsɛnt/ *noun.* LME.
[ORIGIN from the verb.]
1 Opposition to a proposal or resolution; an instance of this. LME.

H. WILSON It was traditional for any minister who disagreed deeply with the decision to ask for his dissent to be recorded.

2 (A) difference of opinion, (a) disagreement. Formerly also, a quarrel. L16.

T. SPENCER I finde no dissent betweene any parties touching this precept.

3 *spec.* Difference of opinion on questions of religious doctrine or practice. L16. ▸**b** The state of being separated from a prevailing or established Church, esp. the Church of England; *spec.* Protestant Nonconformism. Also, the Nonconformist community. L18.

b LD MACAULAY The Church of Rome unites in herself all the strength of establishment and all the strength of dissent.

†**4** Difference in meaning, character, etc. E–M17.

dissent /dɪˈsɛnt/ *verb intrans.* LME.
[ORIGIN Latin *dissentire* differ in sentiment, formed as DIS- 1 + *sentire* feel. Cf. French *dissentir* (15).]
1 Withhold assent or consent from a proposal etc.; express opposition. (Foll. by *from*, (now *rare*) *to*.) LME.

B. CASTLE When he talked about freedom to dissent he hadn't meant that we should .. organize an anti-Government campaign.

2 Think differently; have a different opinion, disagree. (Foll. by *from*, *in* a subject; *from*, †*with* a person.) M16.

G. GROTE If the public dissent from our views, we say that they ought to concur with us.

3 *spec.* Differ in religious doctrine or practice, esp. from a prevailing or established Church. M16.
†**4** Be at loggerheads; quarrel. M16–M18.
†**5** Differ in meaning, nature, form, etc., (*from*). M16–M17.
■ **dissenting** *ppl adjective* (**a**) that dissents, esp. from the majority view; (**b**) differing in opinion on religious matters; *spec.* (**D-**) Nonconformist: M16. **dissentingly** *adverb* in a manner expressive of dissent E17. **dissentment** *noun* (*rare*) dissent L17.

dissentaneous /dɪs(ə)nˈteɪnɪəs/ *adjective. arch.* E17.
[ORIGIN Latin *dissentaneus* (from *dissentire* DISSENT *verb*) + -OUS.]
Not harmonizing, contradictory, discordant. (Foll. by *to*, *with*.)

dissenter /dɪˈsɛntə/ *noun.* M17.
[ORIGIN from DISSENT *verb* + -ER[1].]
1 A person who disagrees with an opinion, resolution, or proposal; a dissentient. M17.
2 A person who dissents in matters of religious belief or practice; *esp.* one who dissociates himself or herself from or *from* a prevailing or established Church. M17. ▸**b** *spec.* (Now usu. **D-**.) In England, a member of a Protestant Church or sect other than the Church of England; *hist.* (in Britain and Ireland) a member of any Church or sect, Protestant or Catholic, not established in the area concerned. Now somewhat *derog.* L17.
■ **dissenterism**, **D-** *noun* the principles and practice of Dissenters E19.

dissentient /dɪˈsɛnʃɪənt, -ʃ(ə)nt/ *noun & adjective.* E17.
[ORIGIN Latin *dissentient-* pres. ppl stem of *dissentire*: see DISSENT *verb*, -ENT.]
(A person) dissenting or expressing dissent, esp. from the majority or official view.

JO GRIMOND If dissentients could be persuaded to abstain instead of actually voting in a different lobby. A. BURGESS There will be no dissentient voices raised to this proposal.

■ **dissentience** *noun* (*rare*) M19.

dissention *noun* see DISSENSION.

dissentious /dɪˈsɛnʃəs/ *adjective.* Now *rare.* Also †**-nsious.** M16.
[ORIGIN from DISSENSION: see -IOUS. Cf. French †*dissentieux*, *-cieux.*]
Of, pertaining to, or marked by dissension; given to dissension, quarrelsome. Formerly also, inclined to dissent in matters of religion.

dissepiment /dɪˈsɛpɪm(ə)nt/ *noun.* E18.
[ORIGIN Latin *dissaepimentum*, from *dissaepire* make separate, formed as DIS- 1 + *saepire* divide off by a hedge, from *saepes* hedge: see -MENT.]
ZOOLOGY & BOTANY. A partition in some part or organ; a septum; *esp.* (**a**) a wall separating the cells of a syncarpous ovary or fruit; (**b**) one of the horizontal plates connecting the vertical septa in corals.
■ **dissepiˈmental** *adjective* M19.

dissert /dɪˈsəːt/ *verb.* E17.
[ORIGIN Latin *dissert-* pa. ppl stem of *disserere* treat of, discourse, formed as DIS- 1 + *serere* connect, join words in composition.]
†**1** *verb trans.* Discuss, examine. E17–E18.
2 *verb intrans.* Discourse, expatiate, (*on* a subject). Now *rare.* M17.

dissertate /ˈdɪsəteɪt/ *verb intrans.* Now *rare.* M18.
[ORIGIN Latin *dissertat-*: see DISSERTATION, -ATE[3].]
= DISSERT 2.

Times I am no scholar to dissertate on the innumerable versions of the *Pervigilium Veneris.*

dissertation /dɪsəˈteɪʃ(ə)n/ *noun.* E17.
[ORIGIN Latin *dissertatio(n-)*, from *dissertat-* pa. ppl stem of *dissertare* argue, debate, frequentative of *disserere*: see -ATION.]
†**1** Discussion, debate. E17–E18.
2 A spoken or written discourse on a subject, in which it is treated at length. M17. ▸**b** An extended scholarly essay submitted for a degree or other academic qualification. L19.
■ **dissertational** *adjective* pertaining to or of the nature of a dissertation or long discourse M19.

dissertative /ˈdɪsəteɪtɪv/ *adjective.* E19.
[ORIGIN from Latin *dissertat-*: see DISSERTATION, -IVE.]
Marked by or given to dissertations.

dissertator /ˈdɪsəteɪtə/ *noun.* L17.
[ORIGIN Late Latin = disputant, formed as DISSERTATIVE: see -OR.]
A person who gives a dissertation.

D

disserve /dɪ(s)ˈsəːv/ *verb trans. & intrans.* E17.
[ORIGIN from DIS- 2 + SERVE *verb*[1], prob. after Old French & mod. French *desservir.*]
Do a disservice (to), esp. when trying to help; serve badly or imperfectly.

M. SCHORER We can speak of good and bad technique, .. of technique which serves the novel's purpose, or disserves.

disservice /dɪ(s)ˈsəːvɪs/ *noun.* L16.
[ORIGIN from DIS- 2 + SERVICE *noun*[1]. Cf. French *desservice.*]
Detriment, injury; an unhelpful or harmful act.

P. GOODMAN You do a disservice to the .. poor by giving them money, because they will get into trouble.

■ **disserviceable** *adjective* tending to disserve; unhelpful, detrimental: M17.

†**dissettle** *verb trans.* M17–M18.
[ORIGIN from DIS- 2 + SETTLE *verb.*]
Make unsettled, disturb.

dissettlement /dɪ(s)ˈsɛt(ə)lm(ə)nt/ *noun.* M17.
[ORIGIN from DIS- 2 + SETTLEMENT.]
†**1** The action of unsettling; unsettled or disturbed condition. Only in M17.
2 Expulsion from a settled place of residence. *rare.* L19.

dissever /dɪ(s)ˈsɛvə/ *verb.* ME.
[ORIGIN Anglo-Norman *des(c)everer*, Old French *des(s)evrer* (mod., techn. *desseuvrer*) from late Latin *disseparare*, formed as DIS- 1 + Latin *separare* SEPARATE *verb.*]
1 *verb trans.* Separate, sunder, (a person or thing *from* another, two or more people or things from each other). ME.

F. TUOHY Some people, whose anxieties have almost dissevered them from the corporeal world.

2 *verb trans.* Divide into parts, cut up. LME.
†**3** *verb trans.* Break up, disperse, (a company or combination). LME–E17.
4 *verb intrans.* Become parted, break up. LME.

L. MACNEICE Drifting cloud and gauzy mist Brighten and dissever.

■ **disseverance** *noun* the action or an act of dissevering LME. **disseveˈration** *noun* = DISSEVERANCE L17. **disseverment** *noun* = DISSEVERANCE E17.

dissidence /ˈdɪsɪd(ə)ns/ *noun.* M17.
[ORIGIN French, or Latin *dissidentia*, from *dissident-*: see DISSIDENT, -ENCE.]
The state or fact of being dissident; disagreement in opinion, dissent; difference in character.

dissident /ˈdɪsɪd(ə)nt/ *adjective & noun.* M16.
[ORIGIN French, or Latin *dissident-* pres. ppl stem of *dissidere* sit apart, disagree, formed as DIS- 1 + *sedere* sit: see -ENT.]
▸ **A** *adjective.* **1** Differing in opinion, character, etc.; disagreeing. (Foll. by *from*.) M16.

J. R. LOWELL Men .. dissident .. in other respects, were agreed in resenting these impediments.

2 Dissenting in matters of religion. M19.
3 Voicing political dissent, usu. in a totalitarian (esp. Communist) state. M20.
▸ **B** *noun.* **1** *hist.* In Poland: a non-Catholic (esp. Orthodox) Christian. M18.
2 A person who disagrees, a dissentient. L18.
3 *spec.* A person who dissents from a prevailing or established form of religion; a dissenter. L18.
4 A person who openly opposes the policies of a totalitarian (esp. Communist) regime. M20.

dissilient /dɪˈsɪlɪənt/ *adjective. rare.* M17.
[ORIGIN Latin *dissilient-* pres. ppl stem of *dissilire* spring apart, formed as DIS- 1 + *salire* leap: see -ENT.]
Springing or tending to spring apart.

dissimilar /dɪˈsɪmɪlə/ *adjective & noun.* L16.
[ORIGIN from DIS- 2 + SIMILAR, after Latin *dissimilis*, French *dissimilaire.*]
▸ **A** *adjective.* Not similar; different in appearance, properties, or nature; unlike. (Foll. by *to*; also *from*, †*with*.) L16.

C. DARWIN We see countries closely corresponding in all their physical conditions, but with their inhabitants utterly dissimilar.

▸ **B** *noun.* A dissimilar thing. Usu. in *pl.* M17.
■ **dissimiˈlarity** *noun* (an instance of) dissimilar character; (a) difference: E18. **dissimilarly** *adverb* M18.

dissimilate /dɪˈsɪmɪleɪt/ *verb trans. & intrans.* M19.
[ORIGIN from DIS- 2 + Latin *similis* similar, after ASSIMILATE *verb*.]
Make or become different; *esp.* (LINGUISTICS) subject to or undergo dissimilation.
■ **dissimilatory** *adjective* (PHILOLOGY) pertaining to or produced by dissimilation E20.

dissimilation /ˌdɪsɪmɪˈleɪʃ(ə)n/ *noun.* M19.
[ORIGIN from DISSIMILATE after ASSIMILATION.]
1 The action of making dissimilar; the process of becoming dissimilar. M19.
2 *spec.* (LINGUISTICS) The differentiation of two identical sounds occurring near each other in a word by the change of one of them, as ***purple*** from Old English *purpuran*. L19.
3 BIOLOGY. Destructive metabolism, catabolism. L19.

D

dissimile /dɪˈsɪmɪli/ *noun.* L17.
[ORIGIN Latin, neut. of *dissimilis* (see DISSIMILITUDE) after SIMILE.]
RHETORIC. A comparison or illustration by contrast.

dissimilitude /dɪsɪˈmɪlɪtjuːd/ *noun.* LME.
[ORIGIN Latin *dissimilitudo*, from *dissimilis* unlike, formed as DIS- 2 + *similis* alike: see -TUDE.]
1 Dissimilarity, diversity; an instance of this. LME.
†**2** RHETORIC. = DISSIMILE. L16–M18.

†**dissimulance** *noun.* LME–E18.
[ORIGIN Latin *dissimulantia*, from *dissimulare*: see DISSIMULATE, -ANCE.]
= DISSIMULATION 1.

dissimulate /dɪˈsɪmjʊleɪt/ *verb.* LME.
[ORIGIN Latin *dissimulat-* pa. ppl stem of *dissimulare*, formed as DIS- 2, SIMULATE *verb*.]
1 *verb trans. & intrans.* = DISSEMBLE *verb*[1] 1. LME.
> ST G. J. MIVART The long dissimulated Atheism of Mill is now avowed. V. GLENDINNING Most people conceal a good deal of what they feel; Edith did not dissimulate.

†**2** *verb trans.* Combine with, neutralize, (an electric charge, electricity). M–L19.
– NOTE: Rare before L18.

dissimulation /dɪˌsɪmjʊˈleɪʃ(ə)n/ *noun.* LME.
[ORIGIN Old French & mod. French from Latin *dissimulatio(n-)*, formed as DISSIMULATE: see -ATION.]
1 The action of dissembling; concealment of one's true nature, feelings, etc.; pretence, hypocrisy. Formerly also, an instance of this. LME. ▸†**b** Disguised form. *rare* (Milton). Only in L17.
> STEELE Simulation is a Pretence of what is not, and Dissimulation a Concealment of what is. A. G. GARDINER I may . . only be truthful because I haven't courage enough for dissimulation. **b** MILTON Satan, bowing low His gray dissimulation, disappeared.

†**2** A flock *of* (small) birds. L15–L17.

dissimulator /dɪˈsɪmjʊleɪtə/ *noun.* E16.
[ORIGIN Latin, formed as DISSIMULATE: see -OR.]
A person who dissimulates; a dissembler.

†**dissimule** *verb trans. & intrans.* LME–M17.
[ORIGIN Old French & mod. French *dissimuler* from Latin *dissimulare*: see DISSIMULATE.]
= DISSEMBLE *verb*[1].
– NOTE: DISSEMBLE *verb*[1] developed from this word.

†**dissipable** *adjective.* E17–E18.
[ORIGIN Latin *dissipabilis*, from *dissipare*: see DISSIPATE, -ABLE.]
Able to be dissipated.

dissipate /ˈdɪsɪpeɪt/ *verb.* Pa. pple & ppl adjective **-ated**, †**-ate**. LME.
[ORIGIN Latin *dissipat-* pa. ppl stem of *dissipare*, formed as DIS- 1 + *supare* throw: see -ATE[3].]
▸ **I** *verb trans.* **1** Drive or cause to go in different directions; disperse (what has been concentrated). Formerly, spread out (troops). *arch.* LME. ▸†**b** Disperse in flight; rout. E17–L18.
> C. LAMB To pick up her wandering fruit, which some unlucky dray has just dissipated. C. SAGAN The outer layers of red giants are slowly dissipated into interstellar space.

2 Cause (an abstract thing) to disappear; *esp.* dispel (a feeling etc.) from the mind. LME.
> I. D'ISRAELI Cool shades and exquisite viands in a moment dissipated heat and hunger.

3 Reduce to dust, smoke, or impalpable form; destroy completely (material or abstract things). L15.
> T. R. MALTHUS Violent hurricanes, by which whole harvests are dissipated.

4 Cause to disappear into the atmosphere; disperse (vapour, a cloud, etc.); (of an electrical device etc.) lose (heat), convert (energy) into heat that is lost. M16.
> C. MCCULLOUGH The room . . reeked so of roses that open windows could not dissipate their heavy perfume.

5 Consume wastefully, squander, (money, resources, etc.). L17.
6 Divide (attention, mental activity, etc.) between a variety of objects. L17.
> K. M. E. MURRAY He should . . do one big thing well, rather than dissipate his energies on a number of minor works.

▸ **II** *verb intrans.* **7** Become dispersed; melt away, disappear; be reduced to dust or impalpable fragments. E17.
> F. KING A plume of smoke . . which uncurls and then slowly dissipates. A. T. ELLIS Claudia's anxiety dissipated.

8 Indulge in frivolous or dissolute pleasures; practise dissipation. M19.
> T. HOOK I was rather out of spirits, so I dissipated in a glass of negus.

■ **dissipated** *adjective* (*a*) that has been dissipated; (*b*) given to or marked by dissipation, dissolute: E17. **dissipater** *noun* L18. **dissipator** *noun* M16. **dissipative** *adjective* tending to dissipate; characterized by dissipation, esp. of energy as waste heat: L17. **dissipaˈtivity** *noun* L19.

dissipation /dɪsɪˈpeɪʃ(ə)n/ *noun.* LME.
[ORIGIN Old French & mod. French, or Latin *dissipatio(n-)*, formed as DISSIPATE: see -ATION.]
1 Reduction to an impalpable form; complete disintegration, dissolution. LME.
2 The action or an act of dispersing; dispersal; *spec.* (OPTICS) the spreading out of a beam of light. Also, dispersed condition. Now *rare* or *obsolete*. M16.
3 The continuous loss of energy or (formerly) substance, esp. from an electrical device, by its conversion into heat. E17.
4 Wasteful consumption of money, resources, etc.; squandering. M17.
5 (A source of) distraction of the mind from serious matters; (a) diversion, (an) amusement, now esp. of a frivolous or dissolute nature. M18.
> S. JOHNSON Change of place . . inevitably produces dissipation of mind. M. HOLROYD After the dissipations of London, both painters tried hard to discipline themselves.

6 Immoderate indulgence in physical pleasures; intemperate or dissolute living. L18.
> DICKENS Tupman was not in a condition to rise, after the unwonted dissipation of the previous night.

■ **dissipationless** *adjective* L20.

dissociable /*in sense* 1 dɪˈsəʊʃəb(ə)l, *in sense* 2 dɪˈsəʊʃɪəb(ə)l, -sɪ-/ *adjective.* E17.
[ORIGIN In sense 1, from DIS- 2 + SOCIABLE *adjective*. In sense 2, from French from Latin *dissociabilis*, from *dissociare*: see DISSOCIATE *verb*, -ABLE.]
1 Not sociable, uncompanionable; not well associated, ill-assorted. E17.
2 Able to be dissociated; separable. M19.
■ **dissociaˈbility** *noun* †(*a*) *rare* unsociableness; (*b*) dissociable character: M18. **dissociableness** *noun* unsociableness M19.

dissocial /dɪˈsəʊʃ(ə)l/ *adjective.* M18.
[ORIGIN from DIS- 2 + SOCIAL *adjective*.]
Disinclined or unsuitable for society; unsocial.
■ **dissociˈality** *noun* E19. **dissocialize** *verb trans.* make dissocial E19.

dissociate /dɪˈsəʊʃɪeɪt, -sɪ-/ *verb.* Pa. pple & ppl adjective **-ated**, (*rare*) **-ate** /-ət/. M16.
[ORIGIN Latin *dissociat-* pa. ppl stem of *dissociare*, formed as DIS- 1 + *sociare* join together, from *socius* companion: see -ATE[3].]
▸ **I** *verb trans.* **1** Cut off or free from association with something else; separate in fact or thought; disassociate. (Foll. by *from*.) M16.
> A. TUCKER Our very . . desires, which first bring us together, have a tendency likewise to dissociate us. V. BRITTAIN The whole subject of child-birth was completely dissociated in my mind from that of sex.

dissociate oneself from declare oneself unconnected with.
2 SCIENCE. Cause the dissociation of (a compound etc.). M19.
> S. WEINBERG The universe was so hot and dense that atoms were dissociated into their nuclei and electrons.

3 PSYCHIATRY. Cause (the personality, ideas, etc.) to undergo dissociation (DISSOCIATION *noun* 4). Chiefly as ***dissociated ppl adjective***. L19.
dissociated personality a pathological state of mind in which two or more distinct personalities coexist in the same person.
▸ **II** *verb intrans.* **4** Become dissociated; *spec.* (SCIENCE) undergo dissociation. M19.
■ **dissociative** *adjective* tending to dissociate; causing dissociation; ***dissociative hysteria***: see HYSTERIA 1: L19.

dissociation /dɪˌsəʊʃɪˈeɪʃ(ə)n, -sɪ-/ *noun.* E17.
[ORIGIN French, or Latin *dissociatio(n-)*, formed as DISSOCIATE: see -ATION.]
1 The action of dissociating; the condition of being dissociated; disassociation. E17.
2 *spec.* in SCIENCE. The usu. reversible breaking up of a compound into simpler substances, esp. by the action of heat on a gas or a solvent on a solute; the analogous breaking up of a molecule; the ionization of an atom. M19.
3 PSYCHOLOGY. The process or result of breaking up an association of ideas. L19.
4 PSYCHIATRY. A process, or the resulting condition, in which certain concepts or mental processes are separated from the conscious personality; *spec.* the state of a person suffering from dissociated personality. L19.
– COMB.: **dissociation constant** the product of the concentrations of dissolved ions in a solution, at equilibrium, divided by the concentration of the undissociated molecule.

dissogeny /dɪˈsɒdʒəni/ *noun.* M20.
[ORIGIN Alt. of DISSOGONY: see -GENY.]
ZOOLOGY. The condition, found esp. among certain ctenophores, in which an individual has two periods of sexual maturity, one in the larval and one in the adult stage.

dissogony /dɪˈsɒgəni/ *noun.* L19.
[ORIGIN from Greek *dissos* twofold + -GONY.]
ZOOLOGY. = DISSOGENY.

dissoluble /dɪˈsɒljʊb(ə)l/ *adjective.* M16.
[ORIGIN Old French, or Latin *dissolubilis*, from *dissolvere*, formed as DIS- 1, SOLVE: see -UBLE. Cf. earlier INDISSOLUBLE.]
1 Able to be broken down into elements or atoms; decomposable. M16.
2 Of a physical connection or (*fig.*) a bond or tie: able to be undone or broken. E17.
3 Able to be dissolved in a liquid; soluble. Now *rare*. M17.
■ **dissoluˈbility** *noun* E17.

dissolute /ˈdɪsəluːt/ *adjective & noun.* LME.
[ORIGIN Latin *dissolutus* loose, disconnected, pa. pple of *dissolvere* DISSOLVE *verb*.]
▸ **A** *adjective.* †**1** Having the connection dissolved; disconnected, disunited. LME–M17.
†**2** Relaxed, enfeebled; lacking firmness of texture or of temperament. LME–E19.
†**3** Having one's energies or attention relaxed; careless, negligent. LME–M18.
4 †**a** Unrestrained in behaviour; unruly, unbridled; lavish, wasteful. LME–E18. ▸**b** Undisciplined in style. Now *rare*. M16.
5 Lax in sexual matters, loose-living; abandoned, profligate. LME.
> J. BUTLER Untimely deaths occasioned by a dissolute course of life. L. HUDSON A grossly dissolute and unprincipled young man.

▸ **B** *noun.* A dissolute person. *rare*. E17.
■ **dissolutely** *adverb* LME. **dissoluteness** *noun* M16.

†**dissolute** *verb trans. rare.* E17–M18.
[ORIGIN from the adjective.]
Dissolve, break up, loosen. Chiefly as ***dissoluted ppl adjective***.

dissolution /dɪsəˈluːʃ(ə)n/ *noun.* LME.
[ORIGIN Old French & mod. French, or Latin *dissolutio(n-)*, from *dissolut-* pa. ppl stem of *dissolvere* DISSOLVE *verb*: see -ION.]
1 Reduction of a body or mass to its constituent elements; disintegration, decomposition. LME.
†**2** Harmful relaxation or softening; enfeeblement. LME–L17.
3 Unrestrained or dissolute conduct; laxity of morals. Formerly also, (an) extravagance; a dissolute practice. LME.
> JER. TAYLOR His youthful aptnesses to dissolution.

4 The undoing or severance of something that fastens or joins; *esp.* the dissolving of a partnership, union, etc. LME.
5 The action of bringing to an end; the state of being ended; destruction or ruin of an organized system etc. LME.
6 Extinction of life in a person; decease. E16.
> L. STRACHEY Minute descriptions of her mother's last hours, her dissolution, her corpse.

7 The dismissal or dispersal of an assembly, esp. of Parliament for new elections; termination of the existence of a constituted body or association. M16.
> H. P. BROUGHAM The dissolution of the monasteries in Henry VIII's reign. W. S. CHURCHILL The normal period between a Dissolution and the poll is seventeen days.

8 The process of dissolving or the state of being dissolved in liquid. Formerly, a solution. M16.
9 The melting of a substance at ambient temperature or (formerly) with the application of heat. L16.

dissolutive /dɪˈsɒljʊtɪv, ˈdɪsəluːtɪv, ˈdɪsəljuːtɪv/ *adjective.* Now *rare*. LME.
[ORIGIN medieval Latin *dissolutivus*, from *dissolut-*: see DISSOLUTION, -IVE.]
†**1** Having the property of causing to dissolve. LME–L17.
2 Pertaining to disintegration or dissolution. L19.

dissolvable /dɪˈzɒlvəb(ə)l/ *adjective.* M16.
[ORIGIN from DISSOLVE *verb* + -ABLE; repl. (in part) DISSOLUBLE.]
1 Able to be broken down into its constituent elements; decomposable. M16.
2 Able to be dissolved or (formerly) melted. M17.
3 Of a partnership, ordinance, etc.: able to be broken or annulled. L17.

dissolve /dɪˈzɒlv/ *noun.* E20.
[ORIGIN from the verb.]
CINEMATOGRAPHY, TELEVISION. A transition between scenes in which one gradually disappears from view at the same time as the following scene gradually appears. Also called ***mix***.
match dissolve: see MATCH *adjective*.

dissolve /dɪˈzɒlv/ *verb.* LME.
[ORIGIN Latin *dissolvere*, formed as DIS- 1 + *solvere* loosen, SOLVE.]
▸ **I** *verb trans.* **1** Break down (an object or substance) into its component parts; destroy the cohesion of, cause to

disintegrate. Now *rare* or *obsolete* exc. as assoc. with other senses. LME.

> J. PRIESTLEY Animal substances dissolved by putrefaction . . emit phlogiston.

2 Melt, esp. by the application of heat. Now *rare* or *obsolete*. LME.
3 Cause (a solid or gas) to be incorporated into a liquid so as to be indistinguishable from it; make a solution of. LME.

> T. H. HUXLEY All natural water . . contains such dissolved salts. E. O'NEILL Is it a powder you dissolve in wine?

dissolve away, **dissolve off**, **dissolve out** remove or extract by dissolving.
†**4** Make weak or languid; relax, enfeeble. LME–M16.
5 Loosen from what holds fast; unfasten, release. *arch.* LME.
†**6** Release from life. Usu. in *pass.*, die. LME–M18.
7 Cause to disappear gradually from sight or from existence; *CINEMATOGRAPHY, TELEVISION* cause (a scene) to fade as the following scene gradually appears. LME.

> J. TYNDALL That promise is a dream dissolved by the experience of eighteen centuries. G. GREENE The photographer had tried to dissolve in mist the rocky outline of the jaw.

†**8** *MEDICINE*. Disperse (morbid humours); reduce (a swelling); remove or assuage (a pain or ailment). LME–E18.
9 Dismiss, disperse, (an assembly); terminate the existence of (a constituted body or association, esp. Parliament). LME.

> J. REED The Second . . Congress of Soviets was dissolved, so that the members might hurry to their homes.

10 a Undo (a knot, a bond); *fig.* bring to an end (a partnership, union, marriage, etc.). LME. ▸†**b** Part, divide, (persons united to each other). L16–E17.

> **b** SHAKES. *Merry W.* She and I, long since contracted, are now so sure that nothing can dissolve us.

11 a Destroy the binding force or influence of; *spec.* (*LAW*) annul, abrogate, (an injunction). LME. ▸†**b** Reject the authority of. LME–M17. ▸†**c** Dispose of (an assertion etc.) as false or erroneous; refute. E16–M19.

> **a** S. HAZZARD Caro lifted her hands and dissolved the spell.

12 Solve, clear up, (a problem, doubt, etc.). *arch.* LME.
13 *fig.* Overwhelm emotionally; cause to melt (*into* tears etc.); immerse *in* pleasure or absorbing activity. E16.

> MILTON Anthems clear, As may . . Dissolve me into ecstasies. I. D'ISRAELI Henry Rantzall . . whose days were dissolved in the pleasures of reading.

▸ **II** *verb intrans.* **14** Lose solidity or cohesion; disintegrate; vanish or fade away gradually. Now usu. taken as *fig.* from sense 18. LME.

> J. L. WATEN I watched them get smaller in the distance and dissolve into the darkness. I. MURDOCH The painful concentration of her face increased and then dissolved as she . . began suddenly to weep.

15 Melt. Now *rare*. LME. ▸**b** *fig.* Give way to unrestrained expression of feeling; melt (*into* tears etc.); faint, swoon. E17.

> A. WINCHELL The dissolving ice of the glacier. **b** B. PYM The young men dissolved into helpless laughter.

16 Of an assembly or collective body: disperse, break up, disband. M16.

> F. O'BRIEN Groups would form . . and dissolve again quickly.

17 Lose its binding force or influence. E17.
18 Of a solid or gas: become incorporated in a liquid to form a solution. M17.

> B. NILSON Stir until the sugar dissolves.

19 *CINEMATOGRAPHY, TELEVISION*. Pass *to* or *into* a new scene by means of a dissolve. E20.
■ **dissolver** *noun* a person who or thing which dissolves; *spec.* an apparatus for dissolving film or television shots: LME. **dissolvingly** *adverb* in a dissolving manner E19.

dissolvent /dɪˈzɒlv(ə)nt/ *adjective & noun*. M17.
[ORIGIN Latin *dissolvent-* pres. ppl stem of *dissolvere*: see DISSOLVE *verb*, -ENT.]
▸ **A** *adjective*. Having the property of causing something to dissolve or of becoming dissolved. M17.
▸ **B** *noun*. An agent which dissolves something; a solvent. M17.

> J. RAY Fire—the only Catholic Dissolvent. F. MAHONY Wine is the great dissolvent of mistrust.

dissolvible /dɪˈzɒlvɪb(ə)l/ *adjective*. Now *rare* or *obsolete*. L17.
[ORIGIN from DISSOLVE *verb* + -IBLE, or alt. of DISSOLVABLE.]
= DISSOLVABLE.

dissonance /ˈdɪs(ə)nəns/ *noun*. LME.
[ORIGIN Old French & mod. French, or late Latin *dissonantia*, formed as DISSONANT: see -ANCE.]
1 Lack of agreement between things; discordance, discrepancy. LME.
COGNITIVE **dissonance**.
2 (An) unpleasant or jarring combination of sounds. L16.
3 *MUSIC*. (The quality of) a combination of notes producing beats or sounding as if it needs resolution; a note whose presence causes this. M17.
■ **dissonancy** *noun* (now *rare*) = DISSONANCE L16.

dissonant /ˈdɪs(ə)nənt/ *adjective & noun*. LME.
[ORIGIN Old French & mod. French, or Latin *dissonant-* pres. ppl stem of *dissonare* disagree in sound, formed as DIS- 1 + *sonare* SOUND *verb*[1]: see -ANT[1].]
▸ **A** *adjective*. **1** Not in agreement or accord in any respect; at variance, conflicting. (Foll. by *from*, *to*, (rare) *with*.) LME.

> BURKE The interests . . before that time jarring and dissonant, were . . adjusted.

2 Discordant in sound, jarring, inharmonious; *MUSIC* forming or of the nature of a dissonance. L16.

> J. BRYANT If the name was dissonant, and disagreeable to their ear, it was rejected as barbarous.

▸ **B** *noun*. A dissonant element; a harsh speech sound. M16.
■ **dissoˈnantal** *adjective* employing or characterized by dissonance M20. **dissonantly** *adverb* L18.

†**dissonate** *adjective*. M16–L18.
[ORIGIN Latin *dissonatus* pa. pple, formed as DISSONATE *verb*: see -ATE[2].]
= DISSONANT 1.

dissonate /ˈdɪs(ə)neɪt/ *verb*. *rare*. L19.
[ORIGIN Latin *dissonat-* pa. ppl stem of *dissonare*: see DISSONANT, -ATE[3].]
1 *verb intrans.* Of sounds: be dissonant. Chiefly as ***dissonating ppl adjective***. L19.
2 *verb trans.* Make dissonant. M20.

disspread *verb* var. of DISPREAD.

dissuade /dɪˈsweɪd/ *verb*. L15.
[ORIGIN Latin *dissuadere*, formed as DIS- 2 + *suadere* advise, persuade. Cf. French *dissuader*.]
1 *verb trans. & intrans.* Advise or urge (a person) against. (Foll. by *from* (an action etc., *doing*).) Now *rare*. L15.

> V. WOOLF The more she dissuaded, the more he was determined to go.

2 *verb trans.* Give advice against, discourage, (an action etc.). Now *rare*. E16.

> J. STEPHEN His . . friends anxiously dissuaded a journey so full of peril.

3 *verb trans.* Deflect (a person) by persuasion or influence (*from* (an action etc., *doing*)). L16.

> A. HOPKINS A crowd of anxious nannies trying to dissuade a capricious child from going too far.

■ **dissuader** *noun* a person who or thing which dissuades M16.

dissuasion /dɪˈsweɪʒ(ə)n/ *noun*. LME.
[ORIGIN Old French & mod. French, or Latin *dissuasio(n-)*, from *dissuas-* pa. ppl stem of *dissuadere*: see DISSUADE, -ION.]
The action or an act of dissuading; (an) exhortation against something.

dissuasive /dɪˈsweɪsɪv/ *adjective & noun*. E16.
[ORIGIN from Latin *dissuas-*: see DISSUASION, -IVE.]
▸ **A** *adjective*. Tending to dissuade. E16.
▸ **B** *noun*. A dissuasive speech or argument. E17.
■ **dissuasively** *adverb* M19. **dissuasiveness** *noun* E18.

†**dissuetude** *noun*. *rare*. LME.
[ORIGIN Late Latin *dissuetudo*, from *dissuet-* pa. ppl stem of *dissuescere* = classical Latin *desuescere*: see DESUETUDE.]
1 = DESUETUDE 1. LME–M18.
2 = DESUETUDE 2. Only in L16.

dissyllabic *adjective & noun*, **dissyllabize** *verb*, **dissyllable** *noun & adjective*, etc.: see DISYLLABIC etc.

dissymmetry /dɪˈsɪmɪtri/ *noun*. M19.
[ORIGIN from DIS- 2 + SYMMETRY.]
1 Lack of symmetry, asymmetry. M19.
2 Symmetry between two things related to each other in the way that an object is related to its image in a mirror. L19.
■ **dissyˈmmetric** *adjective* = DISSYMMETRICAL L19. **dissyˈmmetrical** *adjective* exhibiting dissymmetry; enantiomorphic: M19. **dissyˈmmetrically** *adverb* L19.

distad /ˈdɪstad/ *adverb*. E19.
[ORIGIN formed as DISTAL + -AD[3].]
ANATOMY. In the direction of the distal part of a limb etc.

distaff /ˈdɪstɑːf/ *noun & adjective*.
[ORIGIN Old English *distæf*, app. from the base of Middle Low German *dise*, *disene* distaff, bunch of flax (Low German *diesse*) rel. to DIZEN + STAFF *noun*[1].]
▸ **A** *noun*. Pl. **-staffs**, †**-staves**.
1 A cleft stick for holding wool or flax wound round for spinning by hand; the corresponding part of a spinning wheel. (Used as a symbol of women and women's work.) OE.

> SIR W. SCOTT Serving wenches . . sate plying their distaffs.

2 A female heir; *the* female line; *the* female sex. L15.

> B. HARRIS The Kingdom . . for want of an heir male . . falls to the Distaff.

– PHRASES: ***have tow on one's distaff***: see TOW *noun*[1] 1. ***Jupiter's distaff***. **St Distaff's Day** *arch.* 7 January, the day after Twelfth Day, on which women resumed their housework.

▸ **B** *attrib.* or as *adjective*. Female; of or pertaining to women. L16.

> S. T. WARNER A great-great uncle . . on the distaff side. *Rolling Stone* All her distaff classmates mooning nightly by their phones for a call.

distain /dɪˈsteɪn/ *verb trans. arch.* LME.
[ORIGIN Old French *desteign-* pres. stem of *desteindre* (mod. *déteindre*), from Proto-Romance, formed as DIS- 1, TINGE *verb*.]
1 Imbue or stain with a colour different from the natural one; discolour, stain, tinge. LME.

> C. MARLOWE The tears that so distain my cheeks.

2 Defile; bring a blot or stain on; sully, dishonour. LME.

> R. BURNS May coward shame distain his name, The wretch that dare not die!

†**3** Deprive of colour, brightness, or splendour, esp. by comparison; outshine. LME–M17.

distal /ˈdɪst(ə)l/ *adjective*. E19.
[ORIGIN Irreg. from DIST(ANT + -AL[1], after *dorsal* etc.]
SCIENCE. Situated away from the centre of the body or the point of attachment; further, more distant; *spec.* in *GEOLOGY*, designating or characteristic of an area far from but influenced by an area of activity, as a sedimentation zone, a volcanic vent, etc.
■ **distally** *adverb* L19.

Distalgesic /dɪst(ə)lˈdʒiːzɪk/ *noun*. Also **d-**. M20.
[ORIGIN from *Distillers'* Co. Ltd + ANALGESIC.]
(Proprietary name for) a brand of painkiller containing paracetamol and propoxyphene in tablet form.

distance /ˈdɪst(ə)ns/ *noun*. ME.
[ORIGIN Old French *destance*, (also mod.) *distance* or Latin *distantia*, from *distant-*: see DISTANT *adjective*, -ANCE.]
▸ **I** [Old French *destance*.]
†**1** The condition of being at variance; discord, dissension; dispute, debate. ME–M18.
†**2** A disagreement, a quarrel; an estrangement. ME–M17.
▸ †**II** [Latin *distantia*.]
3 Difference of quality or nature; diversity. LME–M16.
▸ **III** [Latin *distantia*, Old French & mod. French *distance*.]
4 The fact or condition of being apart or far off in space; remoteness. LME.

> SHELLEY Afar the Contadino's song is heard . . made sweet by distance. C. H. SISSON A bench some distance from the bed.

5 The extent of space lying between two points; the space to be passed over before reaching an object; an intervening space. LME. ▸**b** *FENCING*. A definite interval of space to be kept between two combatants. L16. ▸**c** *MILITARY*. The space between adjacent individuals when standing in rank; the space between the ranks. M17. ▸**d** *HORSE-RACING*. A distance of 240 yards (220 metres) or thereabouts; orig. (now *US*), the distance from the winning post which a horse must have reached when the winner finishes in order to qualify for a subsequent heat. L17. ▸**e** The range within which a boxer can strike his opponent. E19.

> W. S. MAUGHAM Excursions to places of interest within convenient distance. A. PATON He . . began to walk across the bare fields, measuring the distance with his strides.

6 The length of time between two events; an interval, an intervening period. Now only in ***distance of time***. LME. ▸**b** The scheduled length of a boxing match. Esp. in ***go the distance*** below. M20.

> S. FOOTE Take . . three times a day, at two hours distance. LD MACAULAY An apprehension not to be mentioned, even at this distance of time, without shame and indignation.

7 *MUSIC*. An interval. M16–L18.
8 (The part of a picture representing) the distant part of a landscape; the more remote part of what the eye can see; a point or region a long way away. M16.

> J. WILLOCK I was unable to walk to any distance. C. DARWIN The rocks . . appear from a distance of a brilliantly white colour. DAY LEWIS A bicycle-bell rings in the distance.

9 Remoteness in personal relations; lack or avoidance of intimacy or familiarity; aloofness, reserve. Formerly also, deference. L16.

> SHAKES. *Oth.* He shall in strangeness stand no further off Than in a politic distance. E. REVELEY A certain distance had to be maintained and he kept his own voice deliberately cool.

10 *fig.* Remoteness or lack of closeness in likeness, relationship, allusion, degree, etc. M17.
– PHRASES: **at a distance**, (*arch.*) **at distance** far off, not very near (***action at a distance***: see ACTION *noun* 1). **go the distance** *BOXING* complete the scheduled duration of a fight. **keep one's distance** remain a certain way away (*from*); avoid closeness; *fig.* avoid undue familiarity. **know one's distance** *arch.* recognize what degree of familiarity is appropriate. LONG-DISTANCE. ***lunar distance***: see LUNAR *adjective*. ***middle distance***: see MIDDLE *adjective*. ***polar distance***: see POLAR *adjective*. ***social distance***: see SOCIAL *adjective*. ***within a measurable distance of***: see MEASURABLE 1. **within hailing distance**, **within walking distance** near enough to reach easily by the specified means (cf. ***striking distance*** s.v. STRIKING *noun*).
– COMB.: **distance learning**: in which lessons are given by post, radio, etc., rather than in person; **distance post** *HORSE-RACING*:

marking a distance (sense 5d) before the winning post; **distance runner**: who competes in long- or middle-distance races.

distance /ˈdɪst(ə)ns/ *verb trans.* L16.
[ORIGIN from the noun.]
1 Place far off or not very near; separate by a space; dissociate (*from*). L16.
> T. FULLER The friendly Sea conveniently distanced from London. L. P. HARTLEY She had . . interests outside his range, interests which . . distanced her from him.

2 Leave far behind in a race etc.; outstrip (*lit.* & *fig.*). M17. ▸**b** HORSE-RACING. Beat by a distance (see DISTANCE *noun* 5d). L17. ▸**c** Keep far off from. Now *rare* or *obsolete*. E18.
3 Make to seem far off. L17.

distancy /ˈdɪst(ə)nsi/ *noun*. *rare*. E17.
[ORIGIN Latin *distantia* DISTANCE *noun*: see -ANCY.]
†**1** Disagreement, difference. Only in E17.
†**2** The condition of being far off in space. Only in M17.
3 Avoidance of familiarity or intimacy; aloofness; reserve. M19.

distant /ˈdɪst(ə)nt/ *adjective*. LME.
[ORIGIN Old French & mod. French, or Latin *distant-* pres. ppl stem of *distare* stand apart, formed as DIS- 1 + *stare* stand.]
1 Separate or apart in space by a specified interval. (Foll. by *from*.) LME.
> AV *Exod.* 36:22 One board had two tenons, equally distant one from another. E. WAUGH Quarter of a mile distant lay the low sea-front.

2 Separated by an unspecified but considerable space; far apart, not close together. LME.
3 Remote or not close in likeness, allusion, degree, etc.; *spec.* remotely related in kinship. M16. ▸†**b** Different in character or quality; various. M17–E18.
> ADDISON I could still discover a distant Resemblance of my old friend.

4 Standing, lying, or occurring far off; not close at hand, remote. L16. ▸**b** Of the eyes or an expression: focused on a distant point; giving an appearance of inattention to immediate surroundings. L19.
> T. HARDY As they approached . . distant shouts and rattles reached their ears. R. CAMPBELL The distant outline of peaks and bluffs far inland.

5 Far apart or remote in time. E17.
> J. WAIN Revenge was three years distant.

6 Reserved in personal relations; aloof; avoiding intimacy or familiarity. E18.
> A. N. WILSON Towards Sam, formerly his favourite, Fred was now distant, moody, cold.

– SPECIAL COLLOCATIONS: **distant early warning** *adjectival phr.* designating a radar system in N. America for giving early warning of a missile attack. **distant signal** a railway signal in advance of the home signal to give warning of the latter's setting.
■ **distantly** *adverb* LME. **distantness** *noun* (*rare*) M18.

†**distantial** *adjective*. M17–E18.
[ORIGIN formed as DISTANTIATE + -AL^1.]
Distant; diverse.

distantiate /dɪˈstanʃɪeɪt/ *verb trans.* E17.
[ORIGIN from Latin *distantia* DISTANCE *noun* + -ATE^3.]
†**1** Find the distance of. Only in E17.
2 Put or keep at a distance. M20.
■ **distantiˈation** *noun* the action of distantiating M20.

distaste /dɪsˈteɪst/ *noun*. L16.
[ORIGIN from DIS- 2 + TASTE *noun*^{1}, after Old French *desgoust* (mod. *dégoût*), Italian *disgusto* DISGUST *noun*.]
1 (A) dislike; (a) mild aversion; (a) preference for the absence or avoidance of something; repugnance. L16. ▸**b** *spec.* Dislike of food or drink; nausea; a bad taste in the mouth. Now *rare* or *obsolete*. L16.
> J. C. POWYS He experienced . . a vague, humorous distaste for his plump, unathletic body. J. L. WATEN Mother . . looked with distaste on the extravagant clothes of the dancers.

†**2** Unpleasantness; annoyance, discomfort. E17–E18.
†**3** Offence given or taken. E17–M18.
†**4** Mutual aversion, estrangement; a disagreement, a quarrel. Only in 17.

distaste /dɪsˈteɪst/ *verb*. Now *rare*. L16.
[ORIGIN from DIS- 2 + TASTE *verb*, after Old French *desgouster* (mod. *dégoûter*), Italian *(di)sgustare* DISGUST *verb*.]
1 *verb trans.* Have or conceive distaste for; regard with aversion; dislike mentally. L16. ▸†**b** *spec.* Dislike the taste of. L16–M17.
> R. L. STEVENSON A man . . whom I distasted at the first look, as we distaste a ferret or an earwig.

2 **a** *verb trans.* Excite the dislike or aversion of; displease, offend. Freq. in *pass.* (foll. by *with*, *at*). L16. ▸†**b** *verb intrans.* Cause displeasure or offence; be distasteful. E–M17.
> ADDISON I have . . been very much distasted at this way of writing.

†**3** *verb trans.* & *intrans.* Produce a nasty taste in the mouth (of); nauseate. Only in 17.
> SHAKES. *Oth.* Poisons Which at the first are scarce found to distaste.

†**4** *verb trans.* Spoil the taste or savour of. E–M17.

distasteful /dɪsˈteɪstfʊl, -f(ə)l/ *adjective*. E17.
[ORIGIN from DISTASTE *noun* + -FUL.]
1 Disagreeable (formerly esp. to the taste); causing dislike or disgust; unpleasant, offensive. E17.
> DRYDEN Why shou'd you pluck the green distasteful fruit. J. AMBROSE His work must not be made distasteful to him through too much drudgery.

†**2** Full of or exhibiting dislike or aversion; malevolent. E–M17.
> SHAKES. *Timon* After distasteful looks . . They froze me into silence.

■ **distastefully** *adverb* (*a*) in a manner causing distaste, unpleasantly; (*b*) (long *rare*) with dislike or aversion: E17. **distastefulness** *noun* (*a*) the quality of causing distaste, offensiveness; †(*b*) dislike, repugnance: E17.

distemper /dɪˈstɛmpə/ *noun*^{1}. M16.
[ORIGIN Partly from DISTEMPER *verb*^{1}, partly from DIS- 2 + TEMPER *noun*.]
1 Ill humour, bad temper; uneasiness; disaffection; *hist.* disturbance of the bodily humours. M16.
> W. TAYLOR Let us talk of these things . . without distemper and without eloquence.

2 Disturbed condition of the body or mind; ill health, illness; a mental or physical disorder, a disease, an ailment. L16. ▸†**b** Intoxication. L16–M17. ▸**c** (A) disturbed or disordered condition, esp. of society or (formerly) the weather. *arch.* E17. ▸**d** An often fatal virus disease of dogs characterized by catarrh, cough, and weakness; any of various other animal diseases. M18.
> BROWNING Eccentricity Nowise amounting to distemper. R. C. HUTCHINSON It was . . the slight distemper from pregnancy which made me speak so brusquely. N. MITFORD Having suffered, or enjoyed, most of the distempers in the medical dictionary.

†**3** A disproportionate mixture of parts; the state of having elements mixed in the wrong proportions. E–M17.

distemper /dɪˈstɛmpə/ *noun*^{2}. M17.
[ORIGIN from DISTEMPER *verb*^{2}, after French †*destrempe* (now *détrempe*).]
1 A method of painting in which powder colours are mixed with some glutinous substance dissolved in water, used esp. for scene-painting and interior walls. M17.
2 A liquid prepared for and used in this process; *spec.* whiting mixed with size and water, formerly used for ceilings etc. M19.

distemper /dɪˈstɛmpə/ *verb*^{1} *trans.* *arch.* ME.
[ORIGIN Late Latin *distemperare* soak, mix, affect by disproportionate mixture, formed as DIS- 2, TEMPER *verb*^{1}.]
†**1** Temper incorrectly by mixing elements in the wrong proportions; disturb the due proportion of. Only in ME.
2 Disturb the temper or feelings of; make ill-humoured or ill at ease; trouble, vex, upset. Now *rare* or *obsolete*. LME.
> JOSEPH HALL Vainely distempering himselfe about idle and frivolous questions.

3 Disorder the health of; make diseased or insane; affect with an illness. LME. ▸†**b** Intoxicate, make drunk. L15–L17.
> *fig.*: *Listener* The ITV companies are as distempered as parrots about the cash they have to shell out for Channel 4.

4 Disorder or spoil the condition of. Formerly, disturb the weather, air, etc., (usu. in *pass.*) of. LME.
> MILTON Sin, that first Distemper'd all things.

distemper /dɪˈstɛmpə/ *verb*^{2} *trans.* LME.
[ORIGIN Old French *destremper* or late Latin *distemperare* soak, macerate, formed as DIS- 1, 3, TEMPER *verb*^{1}.]
1 Treat with water etc. or other liquid; mix with a liquid to dissolve wholly or partly; dilute; steep. LME–M17.
> E. TOPSELL Give the Horse . . the quantity of a Hasel-nut distempered in a quart of Wine.

2 *fig.* Lessen the strength of by dilution; allay. *arch.* L16.
> N. HAWTHORNE The May sunshine was . . distempered with a very bitter east-wind.

3 Paint or colour in distemper. L19.
■ **distemperer** *noun* a person who paints in distemper L19.

distemperate /dɪˈstɛmp(ə)rət/ *adjective*. Now *rare* or *obsolete*. LME.
[ORIGIN Late Latin *distemperatus*, formed as DIS- 2, TEMPERATE *adjective*.]
†**1** Of the air, weather, etc.: not temperate; disturbed; inclement. LME–M17.
†**2** (Of the bodily humours) not properly tempered, disordered by excess or deficiency of some constituent; diseased; in bad health or poor condition. M16–M17.
3 Immoderate, excessive; intemperate. M16.

distemperature /dɪˈstɛmp(ə)rətʃə/ *noun*. M16.
[ORIGIN from DIS- 2 + TEMPERATURE.]
1 Disturbance of the weather; unhealthiness of the air; inclemency. *arch.* M16.
> T. HERBERT This distemperature by storms of Wind and Rain turns Summer into Winter.

2 = DISTEMPER *noun*^{1} 1, 2. *arch.* M16.
> LYTTON The distemperature of an over-laboured brain. SIR W. SCOTT Durward . . found the latter in a state of choleric distemperature.

3 (A) disturbed or disordered condition of society, the world, etc. Now *rare* or *obsolete*. L16.
4 Immoderation, excess; intemperance. *arch.* L16.

distempered /dɪˈstɛmpəd/ *ppl adjective*^{1}. LME.
[ORIGIN from DISTEMPER *verb*^{1} + -ED^1, perh. immed. after Old French *destempré* immoderate, deranged, or late Latin *distemperatus* DISTEMPERATE.]
1 Diseased; affected by a mental or physical disorder; now *esp.* (of feelings, ideas, etc.), disordered, disturbed. LME.
> SHAKES. *Sonn.* I, sick withal . . thither hied, a sad distemper'd guest, But found no cure. SWIFT His books, which his distempered imagination represented to him as alive.

†**2** = DISTEMPERATE 1. L15–E17.
†**3** (Of the bodily humours) = DISTEMPERATE 2; disturbed in temper or feelings; ill-humoured, troubled, vexed. L16–M18.
†**4** = DISTEMPERATE 3. L16–M17.
> W. LAUD He must answer for his own distempered language.

5 Disordered, spoiled, out of joint. E17.
> E. REYNOLDS The . . difficulties under which this distempered Kingdom is now groaning.

■ **distemperedly** *adverb* M17. **distemperedness** *noun* M17.

distempered /dɪˈstɛmpəd/ *ppl adjective*^{2}. E17.
[ORIGIN from DISTEMPER *verb*^{2} + -ED^1.]
†**1** Diluted; weakened by dilution. E17–M18.
2 Painted in or with distemper. L18.

distend /dɪˈstɛnd/ *verb trans.* & *intrans.* LME.
[ORIGIN Latin *distendere*, formed as DIS- 1 + *tendere* stretch. Cf. DISTENT.]
†**1** Stretch out, extend; spread out at full length or breadth; overstretch, overextend. LME–M19.
> DRYDEN On engines they distend their tortur'd joints.

2 Swell out or enlarge by pressure from within; expand or dilate by stretching. LME.
> W. IRVING I could see his . . nostrils distend with indignation. P. ACKROYD The meal . . distended my stomach.

■ **distendedly** *adverb* in a distended manner M18. †**distendible** *adjective* = DISTENSIBLE L17–M18.

distensible /dɪˈstɛnsɪb(ə)l/ *adjective*. E19.
[ORIGIN formed as DISTENSILE + -IBLE.]
Able to be distended.
■ **distensiˈbility** *noun* M18.

distensile /dɪˈstɛnsʌɪl/ *adjective*. M18.
[ORIGIN from Latin *distens-* (see DISTENSION) + -ILE.]
Distensible; capable of distending or causing distension.

distension /dɪˈstɛnʃ(ə)n/ *noun*. Also **-tention**. LME.
[ORIGIN Latin *distensio(n-)*, later var. of *distentio(n-)*, from *distent-*, *distens-* pa. ppl stem of *distendere* DISTEND: see -ION.]
1 The action of extending or straightening something; extension; straining. Now *rare* or *obsolete*. LME.
2 The action of distending; the condition of being distended; swelling beyond the normal or usual size. E17.

distent /dɪˈstɛnt/ *pa. pple* & *ppl adjective*. L16.
[ORIGIN Latin *distentus* pa. pple of *distendere* DISTEND.]
†**1** Extended. L16–L18.
2 Distended, swollen. E17.

distention *noun* var. of DISTENSION.

disthrone /dɪsˈθrəʊn/ *verb trans.* L16.
[ORIGIN from DIS- 2 + THRONE *noun*.]
Remove from a throne; dethrone (*lit.* & *fig.*).
■ **disthronement** *noun* dethronement L19.

distich /ˈdɪstɪk/ *noun*. Orig. in Latin form †**distichon**. E16.
[ORIGIN Latin *distichon* from Greek *distikhon*, use as noun (sc. *metron* metre) of neut. of *distikhos* of two rows or verses, formed as DI-^{2} + *stikhos* row, line of verse.]
PROSODY. A pair of verse lines, a couplet.
■ **distichal** *adjective* L18.

distichous /ˈdɪstɪkəs/ *adjective*. M18.
[ORIGIN from Latin *distichus* (from Greek *distikhos*: see DISTICH) + -OUS.]
(Having parts) arranged in two opposite rows; BOTANY arranged alternately in two vertical rows. Formerly also, dichotomous.
■ **distichously** *adverb* M19.

distil /dɪˈstɪl/ *verb* & *noun*. Also *-**ll**. LME.
[ORIGIN (Partly through Old French & mod. French *distiller*) from Latin *distillare* alt. of *destillare*, from *de-* DE- 1 + *stillare*, from *stilla* a drop.]
▸ **A** *verb*. Infl. **-ll-**.
1 *verb intrans.* Trickle down or fall in minute drops; issue in drops or as a fine moisture; ooze out. LME. ▸**b** *fig.* Come

or be manifested gently or gradually. E17. ▸**c** Drip or be wet *with*. E18.

POPE Soft showers distill'd, and suns grew warm in vain. **b** R. GRANT Thy bountiful care . . sweetly distils in the dew and the rain.

2 *verb trans.* Let fall or exude in minute drops, or in a vapour that condenses into drops. LME.

MILTON His dewie locks distill'd Ambrosia.

3 *verb trans.* Give out or impart (a quality, principle, etc.) in minute quantities, infuse. Formerly also, instil. (Foll. by *into*.) LME.

I. WALTON There was distilled into the minds of the common people . . venomous and turbulent principles.

4 *verb trans.* Subject to the process of distillation; convert (*into*), or drive (a volatile constituent) *off* or *out*, by this means. LME.

R. KIRWAN Brisson dissolved 2 oz. of the purest common salt in 16 oz. of distilled water. J. BELKNAP Molasses to be distilled into rum.

5 *verb trans.* Obtain, extract, produce, or make by distillation (*lit. & fig.*); *esp.* make (whisky etc.) by distilling raw materials. LME.

E. TEMPLETON Wondering how far her mother distilled her knowledge from actual experience. P. L. FERMOR A liqueur distilled from Tokay grapes.

6 *verb trans.* Extract the essence of (a plant etc. by distillation, a doctrine etc.); concentrate, purify. LME.

L. EDEL He distilled from the elaborate theorizing of the French poets the essence of symbolist doctrine.

7 *verb intrans.* Undergo distillation; vaporize and then condense; pass *over* as a vapour. LME.

H. DAVY The acid . . distills unaltered at 248° Fahrenheit.

†**8** *verb trans.* Melt, dissolve, (*lit. & fig.*). L15–E18.
9 *verb intrans.* Perform distillation. E17.
▸ †**B** *noun.* A vessel used in distillation; a still. E18–E19.
■ **distillable** *adjective* E17.

distillate /ˈdɪstɪleɪt/ *noun.* M19.
[ORIGIN from Latin *distillatus* pa. pple of *distillare*: see DISTIL, -ATE[2].]
A liquid formed by condensation of distilled vapour.

distillation /dɪstɪˈleɪʃ(ə)n/ *noun.* LME.
[ORIGIN Latin *destillatio(n-)* catarrh, (in late Latin) a dripping down, from *destillat-* pa. ppl stem of *destillare*: see DISTIL, -ATION.]
1 The action of trickling or falling down drop by drop. LME.
2 The action or process of vaporizing (some constituent of) a substance by heat, condensing it by cold in a special vessel, and re-collecting the liquid, esp. to free it of dissolved impurities or to separate it from a liquid with a different boiling point; the extraction of a volatile constituent by this means; the separation of volatile from non-volatile constituents by heating in a closed vessel. LME.
destructive distillation, **dry distillation** decomposition of a solid by heating it in a closed vessel and collecting the volatile constituents given off. FRACTIONAL *distillation*.
3 A product of distilling; something which distils or forms by distilling; a distillate; *fig.* the essence; an extract, an abstract. LME.
†**4** MEDICINE. Catarrh. M16–M18.

†**distillatory** *noun.* L15–M18.
[ORIGIN medieval Latin *distillatorium*, from Latin *distillat-*: see DISTILLATORY *adjective*, -ORY[1].]
An apparatus for distillation.

distillatory /dɪˈstɪlət(ə)ri/ *adjective.* L16.
[ORIGIN medieval Latin *distillatorius*, from Latin *distillat-* alt. of *destillat-*: see DISTILLATION, -ORY[2].]
Pertaining to or used in distillation.

distiller /dɪˈstɪlə/ *noun.* L16.
[ORIGIN from DISTIL *verb* + -ER[1].]
1 A person or thing which distils something; *spec.* a person who manufactures alcoholic liquor by distillation. L16.
2 An apparatus for distilling salt water at sea. L19.

distillery /dɪˈstɪləri/ *noun.* L17.
[ORIGIN from DISTILLER: see -ERY.]
†**1** The action of distilling, distillation. L17–E19.
2 A place for distilling something; *spec.* an establishment for distilling alcoholic liquor. M18.

distilment /dɪˈstɪlm(ə)nt/ *noun.* Also *-**ll**-. E17.
[ORIGIN from DISTIL *verb* + -MENT.]
A distilled essence (*lit. & fig.*); something produced by distillation.

distinct /dɪˈstɪŋkt/ *adjective & noun.* LME.
[ORIGIN Latin *distinctus* pa. pple of *distinguere* DISTINGUISH. Cf. Old French & mod. French *distinct* (14).]
▸ **A** *adjective* (orig. †*pa. pple*).
1 Distinguished, differentiated. Now *spec.* distinguished as not being the same; separate, individual. (Foll. by *from*.) LME. ▸**b** Separate from the rest; retaining its own identity. L16.

MILTON No place Is yet distinct by name. G. M. TREVELYAN To write the social as distinct from the political history of a nation. G. GORDON Human beings have approximately 200 distinct bones. **b** E. HUXLEY The segments of an orange, each distinct and yet wrapped in one skin. A. J. P. TAYLOR He assumed . . that he could keep his private life entirely distinct from his public image.

2 Readily distinguishable by the senses, esp. the sight or hearing, or by the mind; clear, plain, clearly perceptible; well-defined, unambiguous. LME. ▸**b** That is recognizably or perceptibly such; definite, unmistakable; pronounced, positive. E19.

S. JOHNSON When common words . . were less distinct in their signification. T. HARDY A face was bending over her, veiled, but still distinct. E. BOWEN Lots here could only be purchased on the distinct condition that houses of a fixed value were to be put up. **b** G. B. SHAW There is a distinct attempt to increase the feminine interest all through. E. F. BENSON She saw his eyes fixed on her in distinct disapproval. J. LE CARRÉ He had the distinct feeling that something was wrong.

3 Separated from others by distinguishing characters; recognizably different in nature or qualities (*from*). Also *emphatic*, having well-marked differences. E16.

LD MACAULAY The firelock of the Highlander was quite distinct from the weapon which he used in close fight. C. DARWIN No two marine faunas are more distinct, with hardly a fish, shell, or crab in common.

4 *pred.* Distinctively marked or adorned *with*. *arch.* L16.

TENNYSON The deep sphere overhead, Distinct with vivid stars.

5 Of sensory or mental perception: receiving or able to receive clear impressions. Formerly also, able to distinguish clearly; discriminating. E17.

R. W. EMERSON The droll disguises [of dreams] . . enhancing a real element, and forcing it on our distinct notice.

▸ †**B** *noun.* A separate person or thing. *rare* (Shakes.). Only in E17.
■ **distinctly** *adverb* †(*a*) separately, individually; (*b*) clearly, without obscurity; (*c*) (chiefly with adjectives or adjectival phrs.) decidedly, markedly: LME. **distinctness** *noun* distinct nature or quality L16.

distinction /dɪˈstɪŋkʃ(ə)n/ *noun.* ME.
[ORIGIN Old French & mod. French from Latin *distinctio(n-)*, from *distinct-* pa. ppl stem of *distinguere*: see DISTINGUISH, -ION.]
1 Each of the parts into which a whole is divided; a subdivision; a category. *obsolete* exc. *hist.* ME. ▸†**b** Rank, social class. E–M18.
2 The action of distinguishing or discriminating; the noting or making of a difference between things; the result of such action, a difference so made or appreciated. ME.

E. A. FREEMAN A distinction is drawn between the rule of William himself and the rule of his oppressive lieutenants. C. GEIKIE Jesus . . teaches universal love without distinction of race, merit, or rank.

a distinction without a difference an artificially created distinction, where no real difference exists.
†**3** The action of dividing; the fact of being divided; division, partition. LME–E18. ▸**b** Punctuation of a sentence; a punctuation mark. M16–M17.

DRYDEN The distinction of tragedy into acts.

4 The condition of being different or distinct; an instance of this, a difference. LME.

R. MACAULAY He has a keen . . insight into the distinction between essentials and non-essentials. A. MOOREHEAD The social distinctions remained: Burke and Wills were officers . . , Gray and King were men.

5 Something that differentiates; a distinguishing feature or property. LME.

J. BUTLER It may be spoken of as . . the distinction of the present [age] to profess a contracted spirit.

†**6** The ability to perceive differences; discernment, discrimination. LME–M18.
7 The quality of being clearly perceptible; clarity of perception. Formerly also, the process of making clear to the senses. Now *rare*. LME.

STEELE All the several Voices lost their Distinction, and rose up in a confused Humming. V. WOOLF I see you with extreme distinction.

8 (An instance of) excellence that sets a person or thing apart from others; (a) distinctive merit or good quality. Also, pre-eminent rank or position. L17. ▸**b** In certain examinations: an outstandingly good mark or grade. M20.

BURKE The chase of honours and distinction. L. STRACHEY He had served with distinction in the war against Napoleon. W. S. MAUGHAM Thick waving hair only sufficiently greying to add to the distinction of his appearance. A. J. P. TAYLOR New plays of distinction.

9 The showing of special honour or preferential regard. Also, an instance of this; a mark of honour. E18.

JAS. HARRIS For grammatical knowledge, we ought to mention with distinction the learned prelate, Dr. Lowth. W. S. CHURCHILL The new distinctions which have been created by His Majesty for service in the war.

distinctive /dɪˈstɪŋktɪv/ *adjective & noun.* LME.
[ORIGIN Late Latin *distinctivus*, from Latin *distinct-*: see DISTINCTION, -IVE.]
▸ **A** *adjective.* **1** Serving to differentiate or distinguish; peculiar to one person or thing as distinct from others, characteristic; having well-marked properties; easily recognized. LME.

I. D'ISRAELI Papist and Protestant now became distinctive names. C. N. ROBINSON A military organization, wearing a distinctive dress. C. G. SELIGMAN Their products are sufficiently well characterized to be distinctive. W. BOYD He saw the distinctive baldheaded . . figure of his father-in-law.

distinctive feature PHONOLOGY a minimal feature (e.g. voice, labiality) distinguishing one phoneme from another.
2 Having the faculty of perceiving differences; discriminating. *rare*. M17.
3 Having a separate or distinct character or status. *rare*. M19.

S. SMILES The refugees . . ceased to exist as a distinctive people.

4 HEBREW GRAMMAR. Of an accent: used in place of a stop to separate clauses. L19.
▸ **B** *noun.* **1** A distinguishing mark; a characteristic. E19.

M. B. KEATINGE The red umbrella, the distinctive of royalty here.

2 HEBREW GRAMMAR. A distinctive accent. L19.
■ **distinctively** *adverb* (*a*) with distinction of treatment; separately, individually; (*b*) characteristically: E17. **distinctiveness** *noun* †(*a*) power of distinguishing; (*b*) distinctive character, force, tendency, etc.: M17.

distingué /dɪˈstaŋgeɪ, *foreign* distɛ̃ge/ *adjective.* Fem. **-ée**. E19.
[ORIGIN French.]
Having an air of distinction; having a distinguished appearance or manner.

distinguish /dɪˈstɪŋgwɪʃ/ *verb.* L16.
[ORIGIN Irreg. from French *distinguer* or Latin *distinguere* + -ISH[2]: cf. EXTINGUISH.]
▸ **I** *verb trans.* †**1** Divide, separate; punctuate (writing). L16–E18.
2 Mentally divide *into* different kinds; classify. L16.
3 Serve to make different (*from*); constitute a difference between, differentiate. L16. ▸**b** Be a distinctive feature of; characterize. E17.

B. RUSSELL Self-consciousness is one of the things that distinguish men from animals. **b** LD MACAULAY He . . was distinguished by many both of the good and of the bad qualities which belong to aristocrats.

4 Recognize or treat as different (*from*), differentiate. L16. ▸**b** Separate as a distinct item. M19.

ISAIAH BERLIN Those quasi-aesthetic . . judgments which distinguish essential from inessential. W. GOLDING It was easy to distinguish him from the scattering of other figures by the strangeness of his dress. **b** J. E. T. ROGERS Items which used to be distinguished are lumped in one general sum.

5 Make a distinction in respect of; *esp.* draw distinctions between the meanings of (a word or statement). Also, put *away* or *out of*, or bring *into*, by making fine distinctions. Now *rare*. L16.

MILTON That Proverbial Sentence . . which also the Peripatetics do rather distinguish than deny.

6 Perceive distinctly by sight, hearing, or other sense; discern, pick out, esp. with difficulty. L16.

B. PYM Voices were heard . . and a few broken sentences could be distinguished.

7 Treat with special honour or attention. *arch.* E17.
8 Make noteworthy or outstanding in some respect. Now usu. *refl.* or *pass.* E17.

C. LAMB A peculiar sort of sweet pudding . . distinguished the days of his coming. J. RUSSELL Robert Haig distinguished himself in the battle by taking Lord Evers a prisoner.

▸ **II** *verb intrans.* **9** Perceive or mark the difference between things; discriminate, make a mental distinction, *between*. L16.

R. MACAULAY If he had known enough about Anglicanism to distinguish between one kind and another. C. HAMPTON We . . laid them on the ground, the corpses to one side and the living to another, although it was by no means easy to distinguish.

†**distinguish of**, †**distinguish upon** make distinctions between or in respect of.
■ **distinguisher** *noun* L16. **distinguishingly** *adverb* by way of distinction; markedly, pre-eminently: M17. **distinguishment** *noun* (now *rare* or *obsolete*) the action of distinguishing; the fact of being distinguished; (a) distinction: L16.

distinguishable /dɪˈstɪŋgwɪʃəb(ə)l/ *adjective.* L16.
[ORIGIN from DISTINGUISH + -ABLE.]
1 Able to be differentiated; recognizable as different. L16.
2 Discernible by the senses or the mind. E17.
3 Divisible into different kinds. M17.
†**4** Worthy of distinction; eminent, remarkable. E18–E19.

D

■ **distinguisha'bility** *noun* ability to be differentiated or distinguished **E20**. **distinguishableness** *noun* = DISTINGUISHABILITY **M18**. **distinguishably** *adverb* **E18**.

distinguished /dɪˈstɪŋɡwɪʃt/ *adjective*. **E17**.
[ORIGIN from DISTINGUISH + -ED¹.]
†**1** Separate, individually distinct. **E17–E19**.
†**2** Clearly perceptible; distinct, pronounced. Only in **18**.
3 Marked by outstanding excellence or eminence; remarkable (*for*). Now also of people: illustrious, of high social or professional standing. **E18**.

J. MILL The making of a new Nabob, the most distinguished of all occasions for presents. J. GALSWORTHY He cherished . . the secret theory that there was something distinguished somewhere in his ancestry. G. VIDAL Sooner or later, just about every distinguished man of state is exiled.

Distinguished Conduct Medal: awarded to warrant and non-commissioned officers and men in the British army and the Royal Air Force for distinguished conduct in action. **Distinguished Flying Cross**: awarded to commissioned and warrant officers in the Royal Air Force for distinguished conduct while flying in action. **Distinguished Flying Medal**: awarded to non-commissioned officers and men in the Royal Air Force for distinguished conduct while flying (other than in action). **Distinguished Service Medal**: the equivalent in the Royal Navy to the Distinguished Conduct Medal. **Distinguished Service Order**: a decoration awarded to British military, naval, and air force commissioned officers for distinguished conduct in action.

4 Having an air of distinction; stylish, distingué. **M18**.

S. GIBBONS She looked distinguished, elegant, and interesting.

5 Special, distinctive. Now *rare*. **M18**.
■ **distinguishedly** *adverb* **L17**.

distinguo /dɪˈstɪŋɡwəʊ/ *noun*. Pl. **-os**. **L19**.
[ORIGIN Latin = I distinguish.]
A distinction in thought or reasoning.

distomiasis /dɪstə(ʊ)ˈmʌɪəsɪs/ *noun*. Pl. **-ases** /-əsiːz/. **L19**.
[ORIGIN mod. Latin from French *distomiase*, from *Distoma*, a former genus of two-suckered trematode worms, the members of which are now referred to *Fasciola*, *Fasciolopsis*, etc.: see -IASIS.]
MEDICINE & VETERINARY MEDICINE. Infestation of the alimentary tract by flukes or parasitic trematode worms; *spec.* liver rot.
■ Also **distomatosis** /ˌdɪstə(ʊ)məˈtəʊsɪs, -stɒm-/ *noun*, pl. **-toses** /-ˈtəʊsiːz/, **L19**.

†**distort** *adjective*. **L16–M17**.
[ORIGIN Latin *distortus* pa. pple, formed as DISTORT *verb*.]
Distorted, awry.

SPENSER Her face was ugly, and her mouth distort.

distort /dɪˈstɔːt/ *verb*. **L15**.
[ORIGIN Latin *distort-* pa. ppl stem of *distorquere*, formed as DIS- 1 + *torquere* to twist.]
†**1** *verb trans.* Twist or wrench to one side. **L15–E18**.
2 *verb trans. fig.* Give an erroneous turn to, bias, (a person's thoughts, judgements, etc.); present a false account or interpretation of; alter so as to appear other than as it is; misrepresent. **L16**. ▸**b** *ELECTRICITY*. Charge the form of (a signal) during transmission or amplification, thus causing misrepresentation. **L19**.

I. D'ISRAELI To establish a pre-conceived theory . . the historian sometimes distorted facts. H. SPENCER Passion distorts judgment. G. GREENE His mother had deliberately distorted his age.

3 *verb trans. & intrans.* Alter to an unnatural shape by twisting; make or become misshapen; contort (the features). **M17**.

S. JOHNSON Any . . posture, long continued, will distort . . the limbs. J. GALSWORTHY Her face was distorted with anger. G. GREENE Those distorting mirrors at fairs. *Which?* On the hill, the jack mounting points distorted slightly.

■ **distortedly** *adverb* in a distorted manner **L17**. **distortedness** *noun* the quality or state of being distorted **L17**. **distortive** *adjective* tending to distort; constituting distortion: **E19**.

distortion /dɪˈstɔːʃ(ə)n/ *noun*. **L16**.
[ORIGIN Latin *distortio(n-)*, formed as DISTORT *verb*: see -ION.]
1 The action or an act of distorting or twisting out of shape (permanently or temporarily); (a) distorted condition; *spec.* a condition of the body or a limb in which it is twisted out of its natural shape. **L16**. ▸**b** (An) alteration of the shape of an image by a lens or mirror. **M18**. ▸**c** *ELECTRICITY*. Unwanted alteration of a waveform, esp. in an electronic device or in its passage through a medium, with consequent impairment of quality. **L19**.

T. MEDWIN That . . distortion generally known by the appellation of club-foot. C. BRONTË A . . marked expression of disgust, horror, hatred warped his countenance almost to distortion. **b** J. THURBER All the mirrors in the house were made of wavy glass and reflected images in fantastic distortions.

2 *fig.* The action of perverting words, facts, etc., from their natural interpretation or intent; misconstruction, misrepresentation. **M17**.

J. WESLEY What a frightful Distortion of my Words is this? L. STEPHEN He will be amused at the distortion of history.

3 A distorted form or image. **E19**.

A. BARRY Some remains of the objectionable distortion at the entrance from S. Stephen's Hall.

4 *PSYCHOANALYSIS*. The process of converting repressed elements to an acceptable form before they are presented to the conscious or dreaming mind. **E20**.
■ **distortional** *adjective* of or pertaining to distortion **L19**. **distortionist** *noun* a person who practises distortion, e.g. in drawing caricatures **M19**. **distortionless** *adjective* (*ELECTRICITY*) not producing or accompanied by any distortion **L19**.

distract /dɪˈstrakt/ *ppl adjective*. Long *arch.* **ME**.
[ORIGIN Latin *distractus* pa. pple of *distrahere*, formed as DIS- 1 + *trahere* draw, drag. Cf. DISTRACTED, DISTRAUGHT *adjective*.]
1 = DISTRACTED 5, 3. **ME**.
†**2** = DISTRACTED 1. **LME–L16**.
†**3** Drawn away, diverted; having the attention diverted. **LME–M16**.
4 = DISTRACTED 2. **L15**.

distract /dɪˈstrakt/ *verb trans.* Pa. pple **-ed**, †**distract**, (*arch.*) **distraught** /dɪˈstrɔːt/. **LME**.
[ORIGIN Latin *distract-* pa. ppl stem of *distrahere*: see DISTRACT *adjective* For origin of arch. pa. pple see DISTRAUGHT *adjective*.]
†**1** Draw in different directions; draw away or apart; separate, divide, (*lit.* & *fig.*). **LME–M17**. ▸**b** Disperse. **E–M17**.

HOBBES Being distracted in opinions.

2 Divide, break up, esp. so as to produce disorder or disintegration. Formerly also *fig.*, undo, spoil. Long *rare* or *obsolete*. **LME**.

J. FRYER The Power was distracted among the Captains of the Conqueror.

3 Orig., turn away from a purpose, destination, or position. Now, divert (the attention, a person) from or *from* something, esp. an intention or preoccupation; stop (a person) from attending fully to something. **LME**.

SIR T. BROWNE The needle . . being distracted, driveth that way where the . . powerfuller part of the earth is placed. J. HERSEY The motherless . . children were inconsolable. Father Cieslik worked hard to distract them. A. KOESTLER He wanted to avoid . . anything which might distract him from his task. G. GREENE Next day a number of things distracted me from the fate of Jones. R. HAYMAN He was easily distracted by noises through the wall.

4 Throw into a state of mind in which one does not know how to act; greatly perplex, bewilder; trouble, agitate. Usu. in *pass.* **LME**.

SOUTHEY Have fanatic dreams distraught his sense?

†**5** Derange; make mad. Usu. in *pass.* **LME–L18**.
6 Confuse by divergent aims or interests; cause dissension or disorder in; divide the inclination etc. *between* different objects. **L16**.

LD MACAULAY He was distracted between the fear of losing his ears and the fear of injuring his patron.

■ **distracta'bility** *noun* = DISTRACTIBILITY **M20**. †**distractful** *adjective* full of or fraught with distraction **M17–M18**. **distractible** *adjective* able to be distracted **M18**. **distracti'bility** *noun* the condition of being distractible; inability to maintain prolonged attention: **E20**. **distractingly** *adverb* in a manner that distracts; bewilderingly, maddeningly: **M19**. **distractive** *adjective* of distracting quality or tendency **E17**. **distractively** *adverb* **M19**. **distractor** *noun* (*US*) an incorrect option in a multiple-choice question **M20**.

distracted /dɪˈstraktɪd/ *ppl adjective*. **L16**.
[ORIGIN from DISTRACT *verb* + -ED¹. Cf. DISTRACT *adjective*, DISTRAUGHT *adjective*.]
1 Drawn apart; torn asunder; separated, divided. Long *rare*. **L16**.

T. FULLER By putting together distracted syllables.

2 Deranged; out of one's mind; crazed, insane. *arch.* **L16**.
3 Mentally drawn in different directions; confused by divergent aims or interests; affected by disorder or dissension. **L16**.
4 So confused or troubled that one hardly knows how to act; unable to settle because of worry, distress, etc.; troubled, disturbed. **E17**.

DRYDEN Where shall a Maid's distracted Heart find Rest? G. VIDAL I had never seen him so distracted.

†**5** In a condition of disorder or disintegration; driven hither and thither; in irregular motion, agitated. **M17–M19**.

T. HOOD The vapours fly Over the dark distracted sky.

■ **distractedly** *adverb* **L16**. **distractedness** *noun* (long *rare*) **E17**.

†**distractile** *adjective*. **E18–M19**.
[ORIGIN formed as DISTRACT *verb* + -ILE.]
Able to be stretched, extensible.

distraction /dɪˈstrakʃ(ə)n/ *noun*. **LME**.
[ORIGIN Old French & mod. French, or Latin *distractio(n-)*, formed as DISTRACT *verb*: see -ION.]
1 The action of drawing or forcing apart; forcible disruption, severance; division, separation; removal, dispersal. Now *rare* or *obsolete*. **LME**. ▸†**b** A severed or divided form, drawn apart from others. *rare* (Shakes.). Only in **E17**.

W. HAMILTON The parts which, by the distraction of the whole, come into view.

2 Diversion of the mind, attention, etc., from a particular object or course; the fact of having one's attention or concentration disturbed by something; amusement, relaxation. **LME**. ▸**b** An instance or occasion of this; something that distracts or diverts the mind or attention; distracting sounds, events, etc. **E17**.

AV *1 Cor.* 7:35 That you may attend vpon the Lord without distraction. **b** F. W. ROBERTSON The cares of this world—its petty trifling distractions. H. ACTON It was a distraction and a relief to write letters. J. MASTERS There was work to do, and continual distraction outside.

3 The fact or condition of being physically or mentally drawn in different directions by conflicting forces or emotions. **L16**. ▸**b** Disorder or confusion of affairs, resulting from internal conflict or dissension; the condition of a community torn by conflict or dissension. **M17**.

b STEELE My little affairs are in such distraction till I can come to an hearing in Chancery.

†**4** Mental derangement; insanity. **L16–L18**.

C. MATHER A distempered melancholy at last issued in an incurable distraction.

5 Extreme perturbation of mind or feelings; frenzy. **E17**.
to distraction almost to a state of madness, distractedly.
– COMB.: **distraction-behaviour**, **distraction-flight**, etc.: exhibited by a bird attempting to divert the attention of a possible predator.

distrain /dɪˈstreɪn/ *verb*. **ME**.
[ORIGIN Old French *destreign-* pres. stem of *destreindre* from Latin *distringere* draw asunder, formed as DI-¹ + *stringere* draw tight.]
▸**I** *LAW*. **1** *verb trans.* Constrain or force (a person), by seizure of a chattel, to meet an obligation; punish in this way for failure to meet an obligation; levy a distress on (a person) so that payment of money owed to one may be obtained. (Foll. by *to do*.) Now *rare* or *obsolete*. **ME**.

N. BACON All such as ought to be Knights and are not, shall be distrained to undertake the weapons of Knighthood. A. TUCKER When Squire Peremptory distrained his tenant for rent.

2 *verb intrans.* Impose a distress (*for* goods, *on* or *upon* a person or thing). **ME**.

MILTON Any seven or more of them . . may distrain and imprison. A. J. AYER When the authorities distrained on his effects, his friends raised the money . . for the first of his books to be put up for auction.

3 *verb trans.* Seize (a chattel) by way of distress; levy a distress on. **LME**.
▸†**II** *gen.* **4** *verb trans.* Press or grasp tightly; squeeze; confine, restrain. **LME–E16**.
5 *verb trans.* Of a circumstance or event: have in its hold; distress, oppress, afflict. **LME–E17**.
6 *verb trans.* Control by force, restrain, subdue. **LME–M16**.
7 *verb trans.* Force or compel (a person) *to do*. Only in **LME**.
8 *verb trans.* Strain out; extract by pressing or straining. **LME–M17**.
9 *verb trans.* Pull or tear off; tear apart. **LME–L16**.
10 *verb trans.* Seize, confiscate, annex. Also (*rare*), deprive (a person) *of*. **M16–E18**.
■ **distrainable** *adjective* liable to distraint; able to be distrained for: **L16**. **distrai'nee** *noun* a person who is distrained **L19**. **distrainer** *noun* = DISTRAINOR **E17**. **distrainment** *noun* the action or fact of distraining, distraint **LME**. **distrainor** *noun* a person who distrains **M16**.

distraint /dɪˈstreɪnt/ *noun*. **M18**.
[ORIGIN from DISTRAIN after *constraint*.]
LAW. = DISTRESS *noun* 3.

distrait /dɪˈstreɪ, ˈdɪstreɪ, *foreign* distrɛ/ *adjective*. Fem. **-aite** /-eɪt, *foreign* -ɛt/. **LME**.
[ORIGIN French from Old French *destrait* pa. pple of *destraire* from Latin *distrahere* DISTRACT *verb*.]
†**1** Distracted in mind; excessively perplexed or troubled. Only in **LME**.
†**2** Divided, separated. **LME–L16**.
3 Absent-minded, not paying attention; distraught. **M18**.

W. A. PERCY In a distrait moment she would sew crimson neat to shrimp pink.

– NOTE: Borrowed again from French in **18** after having become obsolete in **16**.

distraught /dɪˈstrɔːt/ *adjective*. **LME**.
[ORIGIN Alt. of DISTRACT *ppl adjective* by assim. to †*straught* pa. pple: see STRETCH *verb*. Cf. also DISTRACTED.]
1 = DISTRACTED 4. Formerly also, mentally drawn or driven in diverse directions or by conflicting emotions (cf. DISTRACTED 3). **LME**.

SPENSER I in minde remained . . Distraught twixt feare and pitie. E. WAUGH There came two distraught orphans to ask what arrangements their parents had made. R. ADAMS One of the boys . . began jabbering in a voice distraught with fear.

2 = DISTRACTED 2. **LME**.
†**3** Pulled apart or in different directions. **L16–M17**.

SPENSER His greedy throte . . in two distraught.

■ **distraughtly** *adverb* **E20**. **distraughtness** *noun* (*rare*) **L16**.

distraught *verb pa. pple*: see DISTRACT *verb*.

†**distream** *verb intrans. poet. rare.* **M17–M18.**
[ORIGIN Irreg. from DIS- 1 + STREAM *verb*.]
Flow away in a stream, stream down or away.

distress /dɪˈstrɛs/ *noun.* **ME.**
[ORIGIN Old French *destres(c)e*, *-esse* (mod. *détresse*) from Proto-Gallo-Romance, from Latin *district-* pa. ppl stem of *distringere*: see DISTRAIN.]
▸ **I** *gen.* **1** Severe pressure of trouble, pain, sickness, or sorrow; anguish, affliction; hardship, privation, lack of money or necessities. Also, an instance of this, a misfortune, a calamity; in *pl.*, difficult circumstances. **ME.** ▸**b** The state of a ship or aircraft when it needs help from threatened damage or danger. **M17.** ▸**c** A state of physical exhaustion or collapse; breathlessness; *MEDICINE* the state of an organ etc. that is not functioning normally or adequately. **E19.**

> JOSEPH HALL Being in great distress of Conscience. J. H. NEWMAN This event . . filled him with the utmost distress and despondency. DICKENS There is great distress here among the poor. L. STRACHEY The meagre grant . . had by no means put an end to his financial distresses. **b** LONGFELLOW Some ship in distress, that cannot live In such an angry sea.

c *FETAL* **distress.**
2 The action or fact of straining or pressing tightly; pressure, stress; pressure applied to produce or (occas.) prevent action (*lit. & fig.*). *obsolete* exc. *dial.* **ME.** ▸†**b** The overpowering pressure *of* an adverse force, weather, etc. **L15–L18.**

> **b** J. SMEATON Driven westward, by distress of weather.

▸ **II** *LAW.* **3** The action of distraining; the lawful seizure of another's chattel in order to make him or her meet an obligation or to obtain payment of money owed from the proceeds of their sale. **ME.**
4 A chattel seized in such an action. **LME.**
– COMB.: **distress gun**: used to fire a distress rocket; **distress rocket**: fired as a distress signal; **distress signal**: from a ship or aircraft in distress; **distress warrant**: *LAW* authorizing a distress.

distress /dɪˈstrɛs/ *verb trans.* **LME.**
[ORIGIN Anglo-Norman *destresser*, Old French *destrecier*, formed as DISTRESS *noun*.]
1 Subject to severe strain or pressure; exhaust, esp. by extreme physical exertion; afflict. **LME.**

> GOLDSMITH The . . servants of the crown . . distressed their private fortunes to gratify their sovereign. QUILLER-COUCH Their horses began to be distressed in the heavy sand.

†**2** Crush in battle, overwhelm, coerce; harass in war. **LME–L18.**
3 Constrain by force or the infliction of pain etc. (*to do*, *into*, *out of*). Now *rare*. **LME.**

> A. HAMILTON Men who can neither be distressed nor won into a sacrifice of duty.

4 Cause trouble, pain, anguish, or hardship to; vex, make unhappy. Now chiefly *refl.* or *pass.* **LME.**

> OED Do not distress yourself about the child, he is safe. J. C. POWYS Henry's crying . . rose to a pitch that was distressing to hear.

5 Steal (belongings); plunder (a person). Long *rare* or *obsolete*. **LME.**
6 *LAW.* Levy a distress on; distrain on. **LME.**
7 Damage (a piece of furniture, fabric, etc.) deliberately to simulate the effects of age and wear. **M20.**
■ **distressingly** *adverb* in a distressing manner, painfully **L18.**

distressed /dɪˈstrɛst/ *ppl adjective.* **L16.**
[ORIGIN from DISTRESS *verb* + -ED[1].]
1 Exhibiting or pertaining to distress; afflicted with pain or trouble; *spec.* living in impoverished circumstances. **L16.** ▸**b** Of property: offered for sale cheaply due to mortgage foreclosure or because it is part of an insolvent estate. Chiefly *US.* **E20.**

> J. TRUSLER Their poverty and distressed situation.

distressed area a region of high unemployment.
2 Of furniture, fabric, etc.: having simulated marks or other features of age and wear. **M20.**

> *Times* Distressed leathers give new interest to the uppers.

■ **distressedly** *adverb* **L19.** **distressedness** *noun* **L16.**

distressful /dɪˈstrɛsfʊl, -f(ə)l/ *adjective. literary.* **L16.**
[ORIGIN from DISTRESS *noun* + -FUL.]
1 Fraught with, causing, or involving distress; distressing, painful. **L16.** ▸†**b** Gained by severe exertion. *rare* (Shakes.). Only in **L16.**
2 = DISTRESSED 1. **E17.**
■ **distressfully** *adverb* **L16.** **distressfulness** *noun* **L19.**

distributary /dɪˈstrɪbjʊt(ə)ri/ *adjective & noun.* **M16.**
[ORIGIN formed as DISTRIBUTE + -ARY[1].]
▸ **A** *adjective.* †**1** Distinct, several. Only in **M16.**
2 That distributes; *spec.* designating a distributary of a canal, river, etc. **M19.**
▸ **B** *noun.* Something that distributes; *spec.* a branch of a river etc. which does not return to its parent branch after leaving it (as in a delta). **L19.**

distribute /dɪˈstrɪbjuːt, ˈdɪstrɪbjuːt/ *verb trans.* Pa. pple **-uted**, (long *rare*, *obsolete* exc. *Scot.*) **-ute**. **LME.**
[ORIGIN Latin *distribut-* pa. ppl stem of *distribuere*, formed as DIS- 1 + *tribuere* grant, assign.]
1 Deal out in portions or shares among a number of recipients; give a share of to each of a number of people. **LME.** ▸†**b** Deal out, administer, (justice etc.). **E17–M18.**

> T. HOOD Pray distribute my kindest regards amongst all friends. I. WALLACE She distributed memorandum pads, pencils, ashtrays.

2 Spread or disperse throughout a region; put at different points over an area; spread generally, scatter. **LME.**

> A. R. WALLACE Mammalia may be said to be universally distributed over the globe. *Times* The paper is not yet distributed in Scotland. *Which Computer?* A distributed intelligence network of POS VDU's.

3 Divide (a whole or collective body) into parts with distinct characters and functions. **L15.**

> GIBBON That great peninsula . . was distributed by Augustus into three provinces.

4 Divide mentally into classes, classify. Formerly also (*MATH.*), divide. **L16.**
5 *PRINTING* (chiefly *hist.*). Separate (type that has been set up) and return each character to its proper place in the case. **E17.**
6 *LOGIC.* Use (a term) in its full extension so that it refers to every individual of the class it designates. **E19.**
■ **distributable** *adjective* **M17.** **distribuˈtee** *noun* (*US LAW*) a person to whom a share falls in the distribution of the estate of a deceased person **L19.** **distributism** *noun* the theory or practice of an equal division of property; agrarianism: **E20.** **distributist** *adjective & noun* (**a**) *adjective* of or pertaining to distributism; (**b**) *noun* an advocate of distributism: **E20.**

distribution /dɪstrɪˈbjuːʃ(ə)n/ *noun.* **LME.**
[ORIGIN Old French & mod. French, or Latin *distributio(n-)*, formed as DISTRIBUTE: see -ION.]
1 The action of dealing out in portions or shares among a number of recipients; apportionment, allotment; *ECONOMICS* the dispersal of commodities among consumers effected by commerce. **LME.** ▸**b** *ECONOMICS.* The way in which individuals or classes share in the aggregate products of a community. **L17.**

> J. BUTLER All shall be set right at the final distribution of things. *Truck & Driver* The distribution of horticultural produce throughout the entire south and west of England. **b** J. S. MILL Diversities in the distribution of wealth.

2 The action of spreading or dispersing throughout a region; the state or manner of being located in different places all over a region. **LME.** ▸**b** *STATISTICS.* The way in which a particular characteristic is spread over the members of a class. **M19.** ▸**c** *LINGUISTICS.* The range of positions or contexts in which a linguistic element can occur. **M20.**

> B. LOVELL The distribution of the stars in the Milky Way. *Times* Weaknesses in distribution were blamed for the newspaper's non-arrival in areas of England and Wales.

b *FREQUENCY* **distribution**. **c** *complementary* **distribution**: see COMPLEMENTARY 2.
3 The division of a whole or collective body into parts, esp. with distinctive characters or functions; division and arrangement; classification. **M16.**

> R. W. EMERSON The distribution of land into parishes.

4 *ARCHITECTURE.* The arrangement of the various parts of a building, esp. of the interior divisions or rooms. **E18.**
5 *PRINTING* (chiefly *hist.*). The action or process of distributing type. **E18.**
6 *LOGIC.* The use of a term in its full extension to refer to every individual of the class it designates. **E19.**
– COMB.: **distribution board** a panel carrying the fuses etc. of a number of subsidiary electric circuits; **distribution function** *STATISTICS* a function whose value is either the frequency with which a variable has a value less than or equal to the argument of the function, or the probability that it has such a value; **distribution map**: showing the distribution of rainfall, population, crops, etc.
■ **distributional** *adjective* of or pertaining to distribution **M19.** **distributionally** *adverb* **M20.**

distributive /dɪˈstrɪbjʊtɪv/ *adjective & noun.* **LME.**
[ORIGIN Old French & mod. French *distributif*, *-ive* or late Latin *distributivus*, formed as DISTRIBUTE: see -IVE.]
▸ **A** *adjective.* **1** Having the property of distributing; characterized by dealing out in portions or by spreading; given to or engaged in distribution. **LME.**
distributive fault *GEOLOGY*: affecting several parallel planes each close to its neighbour.
2 Expressing distribution; *GRAMMAR & LOGIC* referring to each individual of a class, not to the class collectively. **LME.**
distributive adjective, **distributive pronoun**: denoting one or more individuals of a class, not the class collectively, e.g. ***each***, ***either***, ***every***.
3 Of, concerned with, or produced by distribution; *spec.* pertaining to or designating a political system etc. under which property is owned by the largest possible number of people. **M16.**
distributive justice justice consisting in the distribution of something in shares proportionate to each recipient's deserts; *esp.* justice concerned with the distribution of rights, duties, etc., among individuals and groups in society.
4 *MATH.* Governed by or stating the condition that when an operation is performed on two or more quantities already combined by a second operation, the result is the same as when it is performed on each quantity individually and the products then combined, e.g. that $a \times (b + c) = (a \times b) + (a \times c)$. **M19.**

> B. RUSSELL The associative, commutative, and distributive laws. A. G. HOWSON The binary operation $\cup$ is distributive over $\cap$.

▸ **B** *noun. GRAMMAR.* A distributive word. **M16.**
■ **distributively** *adverb* **L16.** **distributiveness** *noun* **M17.** **distribuˈtivity** *noun* (esp. *MATH.*) **M20.**

distributor /dɪˈstrɪbjʊtə/ *noun.* **LME.**
[ORIGIN from DISTRIBUTE + -OR.]
1 A person who distributes something; *spec.* an agent who markets goods, esp. a wholesaler. **LME.**
2 A thing that distributes a substance, power, etc. **M19.** ▸**b** A device in an internal-combustion engine for passing the current to each sparking plug in turn. **E20.**
■ **distributorship** *noun* the position of being a distributor, esp. of goods **E19.**

distributress /dɪˈstrɪbjʊtrɪs/ *noun.* **M17.**
[ORIGIN from DISTRIBUTOR + -ESS[1].]
A female distributor.

district /ˈdɪstrɪkt/ *noun & verb.* **E17.**
[ORIGIN French from medieval Latin *districtus* (territory of) jurisdiction, from Latin *district-* pa. ppl stem of *distringere*: see DISTRAIN. Cf. STRICT.]
▸ **A** *noun.* †**1** The territory under the jurisdiction of a feudal lord. Only in **17.**
2 An area of country marked off for a special administrative or electoral purpose, or forming the responsibility of a particular officer or administrative body. **M17.** ▸**b** *hist.* A division of an Indian province or presidency under British rule, formerly the major unit of civil administration. **L18.** ▸**c** A subdivision of a county or (since 1974) of a Scottish region. Orig. *US.* **E19.** ▸**d** A division of an Anglican parish with its own church or chapel and member of the clergy. **E19.** ▸**e** In Methodist Churches, a territorial division comprising a number of circuits. **M19.** ▸**f** An area assigned as the sphere of operation of a person or organization, esp. a midwife or a maternity hospital. **M19.**
London postal district, ***Metropolitan district***, ***police district***, etc. ***c FEDERAL district***. ***RURAL district***. ***URBAN district***.
3 An area with a recognizable identity or common characteristics; a locality, a region. **E18.**

> OED A manufacturing district; a purely agricultural district. E. BLISHEN The miserable greyness of the district. DAY LEWIS He was much sought after in the district as a 'healer'.

Lake District: see LAKE *noun*[2]. ***red-light district***: see RED *adjective*.
– COMB.: **district attorney** *US* a public official who acts as prosecutor for the state in a particular district; **district auditor** a civil servant responsible for auditing the accounts of local authorities; **district court** (**a**) *US* a Federal court of first instance; (**b**) *NZ* a court where all but the most serious civil and criminal cases are heard; **district heating**: of a district or group of buildings from a single central source of heat; **district nurse** a nurse who visits and treats patients in their homes, operating in an assigned area; **district visitor** a person appointed to work in a particular section of a parish under the direction of the parish clergy.
▸ **B** *verb trans.* Divide into districts. Chiefly *US.* **L18.**

†**district** *adjective.* **M16–E18.**
[ORIGIN Latin *districtus* strict, severe, pa. pple of *distringere*: see DISTRICT *noun & verb*.]
Strict, severe, exact.

distringas /dɪˈstrɪŋgas/ *noun.* **LME.**
[ORIGIN Latin = you shall distrain (the opening word(s) of the writ), subjunct. of *distringere* (in medieval Latin) DISTRAIN *verb*.]
LAW (chiefly *hist.*). A writ directing the sheriff to distrain upon a person or body.

†**distrouble** *verb trans.* **ME–E19.**
[ORIGIN Old French *destro(u)bler*, formed as DIS- 3, TROUBLE *verb*.]
Disturb, trouble greatly.

distrust /dɪsˈtrʌst/ *noun.* **M16.**
[ORIGIN from DIS- 2 + TRUST *noun*: cf. DISTRUST *verb*.]
1 Lack of trust or confidence; doubt, suspicion; an instance of this. **M16.**
†**2** The fact of being distrusted; loss of credit. *rare* (Milton). Only in **M17.**
†**3** Breach of trust. *rare* (Milton). Only in **M17.**
■ †**distrustless** *adjective* without distrust; confident, unsuspecting: **E17–M18.**

distrust /dɪsˈtrʌst/ *verb.* **LME.**
[ORIGIN from DIS- 2 + TRUST *verb* after French *défier* (cf. DEFY *verb*) or Latin *diffidere*.]
†**1** *verb intrans.* **a** Foll. by *of*: have a doubt or dread of, suspect. *rare.* Only in **LME.** ▸**b** Foll. by *of*, *in*, *to*: be without confidence in. **L16–L17.**
2 *verb trans.* Put no trust in, have no confidence in; have doubts about the reality, validity, or genuineness of. **M16.**

A. G. GARDINER Johnson.. loved liberty in its social meanings, but distrusted it as a political ideal. L. DURRELL My feeling of unreality had grown to such a pitch that at times I distrusted my own memory. T. CAPOTE Neighbours and old friends had suddenly to endure the unique experience of distrusting each other.

†**3** *verb trans.* Suspect *that* or (a person) *to be*. E17–E18.
■ **distruster** *noun* M17.

distrustful /dɪsˈtrʌs(t)fʊl, -f(ə)l/ *adjective*. L16.
[ORIGIN from DISTRUST *noun* + -FUL.]
1 Full of or marked by distrust; doubtful, suspicious; lacking confidence; diffident. (Foll. by *of*.) L16.

E. K. KANE I became.. distrustful as to the chance of our ever living to gain the open water.

2 Causing or giving rise to distrust. E17.

DICKENS Places that had shown ugly and distrustful all night long, now wore a smile.

■ **distrustfully** *adverb* E17. **distrustfulness** *noun* L16.

†**disturb** *noun*. L16–M17.
[ORIGIN from the verb.]
An act of disturbing; (a) disturbance.

MILTON Instant without disturb they took Allarm.

disturb /dɪˈstəːb/ *verb trans*. ME.
[ORIGIN Old French *desto(u)rber* from Latin *disturbare*, formed as DIS-3 + *turbare* disturb, from *turba* tumult, crowd. Cf. STURB.]
1 Agitate and destroy (quiet, peace, etc.); break up the tranquillity or calmness of; distract the attention of, intrude upon. ME. ▸**b** Physically agitate; move from a settled condition or position. L16. ▸**c** *refl.* Get up to greet or accommodate another person. Usu. in neg. contexts. L19.

A. HALEY He'd have to arrest him for disturbing the peace. G. VIDAL The slightest sound in the night disturbs me. D. M. THOMAS It was a strict rule not to disturb adults when they were resting. **b** H. BUTTES Mulberries.. disturbe the stomacke. T. HARDY A plough has never disturbed the turf. **c** T. L. PEACOCK The stranger was rising up, when Mr. Crotchet begged him not to disturb himself.

2 Worry, cause anxiety to. ME.

P. H. GIBBS Halliwell had a strained look, as though this signal .. had disturbed or distressed him. E. O'NEILL As though he were throwing off some disturbing thought.

3 Interfere with the settled course or operation of; put out of its course; frustrate, interrupt. ME.

B. JOWETT An error in the original number disturbs the whole calculation. G. B. SHAW It should.. be made an offence to disturb a performance which the Committee has not condemned.

4 †**a** Deprive *of*; turn or draw away *from* by disturbance. ME–M17. ▸**b** LAW. Deprive of the peaceful enjoyment or possession *of*. M16.
■ **disturbed** *ppl adjective* that has been disturbed; PSYCHIATRY emotionally or mentally unstable or abnormal: L16. **disturbedly** /-bɪdli/ *adverb* M18. **disturbingly** *adverb* to a disturbing degree L19.

disturbance /dɪˈstəːb(ə)ns/ *noun*. ME.
[ORIGIN Old French *desto(u)rbance*, formed as DISTURB *verb*: see -ANCE.]
1 The interruption and breaking up of a settled condition or of proper functioning; agitation (physical or social); an instance of this, *spec.* a breach of the public peace. ME.

E. JONES Complicated disturbances of sight and speech.

2 Interference with the continuance of any action or process. ME.

ADDISON That he may let the ship sail on without disturbance.

3 Mental discomposure or excitement. LME.
4 LAW. Interference with rights or property. L16.

disturbancy /dɪˈstəːb(ə)nsi/ *noun*. *rare*. L16.
[ORIGIN from DISTURBANCE or DISTURBANT + -ANCY.]
Disturbance.

disturbant /dɪˈstəːb(ə)nt/ *adjective & noun*. E17.
[ORIGIN Latin *disturbant-* pres. ppl stem of *disturbare*: see DISTURB *verb*, -ANT[1].]
▸ **A** *adjective*. That disturbs; disquieting. E17.
▸ **B** *noun*. A disturber. M19.

disturbative /dɪˈstəːbətɪv/ *adjective*. *rare*. L17.
[ORIGIN from Latin *disturbat-* pa. ppl stem of *disturbare* DISTURB *verb*: see -IVE.]
Of disturbing tendency or character.

disturber /dɪˈstəːbə/ *noun*. In sense 2 also **-or**. ME.
[ORIGIN Anglo-Norman *destourbour* (Old French *destorbëor*), formed as DISTURB *verb*: see -ER[2].]
1 A person who or thing which disturbs peace or quiet or causes disturbance. ME.
2 LAW (chiefly *hist.*). A person who hinders another in the lawful enjoyment of a right. L15.

distyle /ˈdʌɪstʌɪl/ *noun & adjective*. M19.
[ORIGIN from DI-[2] + Greek *stulos* column.]
ARCHITECTURE. (A structure) having or consisting of two columns.

disubstituted /dʌɪˈsʌbstɪtjuːtɪd/ *adjective*. E20.
[ORIGIN from DI-[2] + *substituted* pa. pple of SUBSTITUTE *verb*: see -ED[1].]
CHEMISTRY. Having two substituents in the molecule.

disulfide *noun* see DISULPHIDE.

disulfiram /dʌɪˈsʌlfɪram/ *noun*. M20.
[ORIGIN from DISUBSTITUTED + THIURAM.]
A white powder used esp. in the treatment of alcoholics to make the drinking of alcohol produce unpleasant after-effects; tetraethylthiuram disulphide, $(C_2H_5)_2NCSSCN(C_2H_5)_2$.
– NOTE: A proprietary name for this substance is ANTABUSE.

disulphide /dʌɪˈsʌlfʌɪd/ *noun*. Also (*US & CHEMISTRY*) **-fide**. M19.
[ORIGIN from DI-[2] + SULPHIDE *noun*.]
A compound in which two sulphur atoms are joined to another atom or group; an organic compound in which the group —S—S— is joined to different atoms. Formerly also, a compound in which a sulphur atom is joined to two other atoms.
– COMB.: **disulphide bond**: joining two sulphur atoms.

disunion /dɪsˈjuːnɪən/ *noun*. L15.
[ORIGIN from DIS- 2 + UNION *noun*[2].]
1 Breaking of union; separation, severance. L15.
2 Lack of union or unity; separated condition; dissension, disharmony. L16.
■ **disunionism** *noun* the doctrine of disunionists L19. **disunionist** *noun* a person who favours or works for the dissolution of a political union, *spec.* that of the US (before or during the Civil War) or that of Britain and Ireland M19.

disunite /dɪsjuːˈnʌɪt/ *verb*. M16.
[ORIGIN from DIS- 2 + UNITE *verb*.]
1 *verb trans.* Undo the union of; *esp.* cause dissension among, set at variance, alienate. (Foll. by *from*.) M16.

Time Chirac fears that the left, even disunited, could still win.

2 *verb intrans.* Separate; part; fall apart. M17.

disunity /dɪsˈjuːnɪti/ *noun*. M17.
[ORIGIN from DIS- 2 + UNITY *noun*[1].]
Lack of unity; a state of separation; dissension, discord.

†**disusage** *noun*. LME–E18.
[ORIGIN from DISUSE *verb* after *usage*. Cf. French †*désusage*.]
= DISUSE *noun* 2.

disusance /dɪsˈjuːz(ə)ns/ *noun*. *rare*. LME.
[ORIGIN formed as DISUSAGE after *usance*.]
= DISUSE *noun* 2.

disuse /dɪsˈjuːs/ *noun*. LME.
[ORIGIN from DIS- 2 + USE *noun*.]
†**1** The state of being or becoming unaccustomed (*to* something). LME–L18.
2 Discontinuance or prolonged suspension of use, practice, or exercise. M16.

S. T. WARNER The field-path to it is vanishing from disuse.

3 The state of being no longer in use. L17.

P. H. JOHNSON The wireless, with its earphones, fell into disuse since nobody cared to listen to it.

disuse /dɪsˈjuːz/ *verb trans*. LME.
[ORIGIN Old French *desuser*, from *des-* DIS- 2 + *user* USE *verb*.]
1 Make (a person) unaccustomed to something; cause to lose a habit. Usu. in *pass. obsolete* exc. *dial.* LME.
†**2** Misuse, use wrongly. Only in LME.
3 Cease to use. Chiefly as ***disused*** *ppl adjective*. L15.

CONAN DOYLE This house is older than the water-pipes. There must be a disused well somewhere.

disvalue /dɪsˈvaljuː/ *noun*. E17.
[ORIGIN from DIS- 2 + VALUE *noun*.]
†**1** Depreciation, disparagement. Only in 17.
2 Negative value or worth; a quality by virtue of which the absence of something is valued more than its presence. E20.

disvalue /dɪsˈvaljuː/ *verb trans*. E17.
[ORIGIN from DIS- 2 + VALUE *verb*.]
Place too little value on, undervalue. Formerly, devalue (*lit.* & *fig.*), disparage.
■ **disvaluable** *adjective* having negative value; bad: M20. **disvaluˈation** *noun* the action or an act of disvaluing E17.

†**disvelop** *verb trans*. L16–M18.
[ORIGIN Old French *desveloper* (mod. *développer*): see DEVELOP.]
Unfold, unfurl; display heraldically.

†**disventure** *noun*. E17–M18.
[ORIGIN Spanish *desventura*, from *des-* DIS- 2 + *ventura* VENTURE *noun*.]
A foolish or ill-starred venture.

disvisage /dɪsˈvɪzɪdʒ/ *verb trans*. *rare*. E17.
[ORIGIN Old French *desvisager* (mod. *dévisager*), from *des-* DIS- 2 + *visage* VISAGE *noun*.]
Disfigure.

disyllabic /dʌɪsɪˈlabɪk, dɪ-/ *adjective & noun*. Also **dissyll-**. M17.
[ORIGIN French *dissyllabique*, from Latin *disyllabus*: see DISYLLABLE, -IC.]
▸ **A** *adjective*. Having two syllables. M17.
▸ **B** *noun*. A disyllabic word. M20.

■ **disyllabically** *adverb* L19.

disyllabize /dʌɪˈsɪləbʌɪz, dɪ-/ *verb trans*. Also **dissyll-**, **-ise**. L19.
[ORIGIN from Latin *disyllabus* (see DISYLLABLE) + -IZE.]
Make disyllabic.

disyllable /dʌɪˈsɪləb(ə)l, dɪ-, ˈdʌɪsɪl-/ *noun & adjective*. Also **dissyll-**. L16.
[ORIGIN Alt. (after SYLLABLE *noun*) French *disyllabe*, from Latin *disyllabus* adjective from Greek *disullabos* of two syllables, formed as DI-[2] + *sullabē* SYLLABLE *noun*.]
▸ **A** *noun*. A disyllabic word or metrical foot. L16.
▸ **B** *adjective*. = DISYLLABIC *adjective*. M18.

dit /dɪt/ *noun*[1]. *arch.* L16.
[ORIGIN App. alt. of obsolete form of DITE *noun*[1] with substitution of short vowel.]
A poetical composition; a ditty.

dit /dɪt/ *noun*[2]. M20.
[ORIGIN Imit.]
In Morse telegraphy: a dot, *esp.* one spoken at the end of a character group.

dit *noun*[3] see DITE *noun*[2].

dit /dɪt/ *verb trans*. Now *Scot. & dial.* Infl. **-tt-**.
[ORIGIN Old English *dyttan*, prob. rel. to DOT *noun*[1].]
1 Stop up, shut, (an opening); fill *up* (a hole or gap). OE.
2 Obstruct the course or way of. ME.

dita /ˈdiːtə/ *noun*. L19.
[ORIGIN Tagalog *ditâ*.]
A tall evergreen tree of the Old World tropics, *Alstonia scholaris* (family Apocynaceae); (more fully ***dita bark***) the bark of this, which yields an antimalarial substance.

dital /ˈdʌɪt(ə)l/ *noun*. E19.
[ORIGIN from Italian *dito* finger, after *pedal*.]
A thumb key by which the pitch of a guitar or lute string can be raised a semitone.

ditch /dɪtʃ/ *noun*.
[ORIGIN Old English *dīc*, corresp. to Old Frisian, Old Saxon *dīk* ditch, dyke (Dutch *dijk*), Middle High German *tīch* (German *Teich* pond, pool), Old Norse *díki* ditch, DYKE *noun*[1].]
1 A long narrow hollow dug in the ground; a trench, a fosse. OE. ▸**b** *spec.* Such a hollow dug out to hold or conduct water; *rhet.* any watercourse or channel. ME. ▸**c** The trench or piece of ground immediately surrounding a bowling green. M19. ▸**d** The sea; *spec.* the English Channel; the North Sea. *slang*. E20.
†**2** Any hollow dug in the ground; a pit, cave, etc. Only in ME.
3 An embankment; a bank or mound of earth. Now *dial.* L15.
– COMB.: **ditchwater**: stagnant in a ditch (freq. in ***(as) dull as ditchwater***); **last ditch** a place of final desperate defence (***die in the last ditch***: see DIE *verb*[1], ***last-ditch***: see LAST *adjective*).
■ **ditchless** *adjective* L19.

ditch /dɪtʃ/ *verb*. LME.
[ORIGIN from the noun.]
1 *verb intrans.* Make a ditch or ditches. LME.
2 *verb trans.* Surround with a ditch; make a ditch for. Also foll. by *around* etc. LME.
3 *verb trans.* Dig ditches or furrows in for the purpose of drainage etc.; provide with ditches. LME.
4 *verb trans.* Clean out or repair (a ditch). L16.
5 *verb trans.* Throw into a ditch; drive (a vehicle) into a ditch; *US* derail (a train). E19.
6 *verb trans.* Put (a person) off a train. Usu. in *pass. US slang*. L19.
7 *verb trans.* Abandon, discard; leave in the lurch. *colloq.* E20.

A. BURGESS He ditches her after a night of love. M. AMIS I ditched the car and walked the last mile. *Dumfries Courier* Even some projects described as 'important'.. may be ditched as the Council draw up their priority lists.

8 *verb trans. & intrans.* Bring (an aircraft) down into the sea in an emergency. *slang*. M20.

ditcher /ˈdɪtʃə/ *noun*. LME.
[ORIGIN from DITCH *noun*, *verb* + -ER[1].]
1 A person who makes and repairs ditches. LME.
2 A machine for making ditches. M19.
3 BOWLS. A bowl which runs or is driven off the green. L19.
4 [With ref. to the Mahratta Ditch, a local fortification.] A resident of Kolkata (Calcutta). *slang*. L19.

ditchy /ˈdɪtʃi/ *adjective*. L18.
[ORIGIN from DITCH *noun* + -Y[1].]
Resembling a ditch; having many ditches or deep furrows.

†**dite** *noun*[1]. ME.
[ORIGIN Old French & mod. French *dit* saying, maxim (from Latin DICTUM), use as noun of pa. pple of *dire* say, from Latin *dicere*. Cf. DIT *noun*[1].]
1 Something composed and written down; a composition, a letter, a written message. ME–L16.
2 A composition in poetic form, or intended to be set to music; a song, a ditty. ME–M16.
3 Manner or mode of composition; form of speech; diction, language. *Scot.* LME–M16.

dite /dʌɪt/ *noun*². Also **dit** /dɪt/. E20.
[ORIGIN Unknown. Cf. DOIT *noun*.]
A very little, a jot. Only in ***not care a dite***, i.e. at all.

†**dite** *verb trans.* ME.
[ORIGIN Old French *dit(i)er* from Latin *dictare* frequentative of *dicere* say. Partly aphet. from INDICT *verb*¹.]
1 Compose, put in words; indite. ME–M19.
2 Dictate (what is to be written or done). LME–M19.
3 Summon, indict. LME–L18.

ditement /ˈdʌɪtm(ə)nt/ *noun. obsolete* exc. *dial.* ME.
[ORIGIN from DITE *verb* + -MENT.]
1 A summons, an indictment. ME.
†**2** A written or spoken composition. *Scot.* M16–E17.

diterpene /dʌɪˈtəːpiːn/ *noun.* E20.
[ORIGIN from DI-² + TERPENE.]
CHEMISTRY. Any terpene with the formula $C_{20}H_{32}$; a diterpenoid.
■ **diterpenoid** *noun & adjective* (of or pertaining to) any simple derivative of a $C_{20}H_{32}$ diterpene M20.

ditetragonal /dʌɪtɛˈtragən(ə)l/ *adjective.* L19.
[ORIGIN from DI-² + TETRAGONAL.]
CRYSTALLOGRAPHY. (Of a prism or pyramid of the tetragonal system) such that a horizontal cross-section has eight angles, alternate ones being equal; of or pertaining to such a crystal form.

ditheism /ˈdʌɪθiːɪz(ə)m/ *noun.* L17.
[ORIGIN from DI-² + THEISM *noun*¹.]
Belief in two supreme gods; religious dualism; *esp.* (***a***) the belief in two independent antagonistic principles of good and evil; (***b***) a form of belief which implies that Christ is not of one substance with God the Father.
■ **ditheist** *noun* a person who holds the doctrine of ditheism L17. **dithe'istic** *adjective* L17. **dithe'istical** *adjective* M18.

dithematic /dʌɪθɪˈmatɪk/ *adjective & noun.* L19.
[ORIGIN from DI-² + THEMATIC.]
PHILOLOGY. (A word) containing two significant thematic elements or stems.

dither /ˈdɪðə/ *noun. colloq.* or *dial.* E19.
[ORIGIN from the verb.]
1 A state of tremulous excitement or apprehension (chiefly in ***all of a dither***); vacillation; a state of confusion. E19.
2 The action of trembling or quivering; vibration, esp. (ENGINEERING) when caused deliberately for some purpose. L19.

dither /ˈdɪðə/ *verb.* M17.
[ORIGIN Var. of DIDDER.]
1 *verb intrans.* Tremble, quiver, thrill. *dial.* M17.
J. CLARE How have I joy'd, with dithering hands, to find Each fading flower.
2 *verb intrans.* Act hesitantly, vacillate, be undecided. *colloq.* E20.
G. GREENE He stood and dithered awkwardly while I got my drinks. E. LONGFORD For several years Kitty dithered between encouraging and checking their secret romance. G. SWIFT If we don't decide now we might dither for ever.
3 *verb trans.* Confuse, make nervous or (*Austral.*) drunk. Chiefly as ***dithered*** *ppl adjective.* E20.
■ **ditherer** *noun* M20.

dithery /ˈdɪð(ə)ri/ *adjective. colloq.* L19.
[ORIGIN from DITHER *verb* + -Y¹.]
Dithering, trembling.

dithio- /dʌɪˈθʌɪəʊ/ *combining form.*
[ORIGIN from DI-² + THIO-.]
Containing two sulphur atoms in the molecule, esp. in place of two oxygen atoms or joined together, as ***dithio-acid***.

dithionic /dʌɪθʌɪˈɒnɪk/ *adjective.* M19.
[ORIGIN from DI-² + Greek *theion* sulphur + -IC.]
CHEMISTRY. ***dithionic acid***, a strong dibasic acid, $H_2S_2O_6$, known only in solution and as crystalline salts.
■ **dithionate** *noun* a salt of dithionic acid M19.

dithionous /dʌɪˈθʌɪənəs/ *adjective.* M20.
[ORIGIN formed as DITHIONIC + -IC.]
CHEMISTRY. = HYDROSULPHUROUS.
■ **dithionite** *noun* = HYDROSULPHITE M20.

dithizone /dʌɪˈθʌɪzəʊn/ *noun.* E20.
[ORIGIN German *Dithizon*, formed as DI-², THIO-, AZO-, -ONE, elems. of the systematic name (see below).]
CHEMISTRY. A reagent used for the estimation and separation of lead and other metals; diphenylthiocarbazone, $C_{13}H_{12}N_4S$.

dithying /ˈdɪðɪɪŋ/ *adjective. poet.* E20.
[ORIGIN Alt. of *dithering* ppl adjective of DITHER *verb*.]
Quivering, trembling.

dithyramb /ˈdɪθɪram(b)/ *noun.* Also in Latin form **dithyrambus** /dɪθɪˈrambəs/, pl. **-bi** /-bʌɪ/. E17.
[ORIGIN Latin *dithyrambus* from Greek *dithurambos*.]
1 An ancient Greek choric hymn, vehement and wild in character; a Bacchanalian song. E17.
2 A passionate or inflated poem, speech, or writing. M17.
■ **dithy'rambist** *noun* a composer or declaimer of dithyrambs L19.

dithyrambic /dɪθɪˈrambɪk/ *adjective & noun.* E17.
[ORIGIN Latin *dithyrambicus* from Greek *dithurambikos*, from *dithurambos*: see DITHYRAMB, -IC.]
▸ **A** *adjective.* **1** Pertaining to or of the nature of a dithyramb; composing dithyrambs. E17.
2 Resembling a dithyramb in style; wild, vehement, boisterous. E17.
E. JONES A dithyrambic letter to the woman he felt so much nearer winning.
▸ **B** *noun.* A dithyramb; a dithyrambic verse etc.; a writer of a dithyramb. M17.
■ **dithyrambically** *adverb* L19.

ditone /ˈdʌɪtəʊn/ *noun.* E17.
[ORIGIN Late Latin *ditonum* from Greek *ditonon* ancient major third, neut. of *ditonos*, formed as DI-² + *tonos* TONE *noun*. Cf. TRIHEMITONE.]
MUSIC. An interval containing two whole tones; *esp.* the Pythagorean major third.

ditransitive /dʌɪˈtransɪtɪv, -ˈtrɑː-, -nz-/ *adjective.* M20.
[ORIGIN from DI-² + TRANSITIVE.]
LINGUISTICS. Of a verb: able to take an indirect object as well as a direct object.

ditriglyph /dʌɪˈtrʌɪglɪf/ *noun.* E18.
[ORIGIN French *ditriglyphe*, formed as DI-² + *triglyphe* TRIGLYPH.]
ARCHITECTURE. **1** The space between two triglyphs. *rare.* E18.
2 A spacing between columns of the Doric order which allows the use of two triglyphs in the frieze, between those over the columns; a horizontal distance in Doric architecture regarded as containing two triglyphs. L18.
■ **ditri'glyphic** *adjective* M19.

ditrigonal /dʌɪˈtrɪgən(ə)l/ *adjective.* L19.
[ORIGIN from DI-² + TRIGONAL.]
CRYSTALLOGRAPHY. (Of a prism or pyramid of the hexagonal system) such that a horizontal cross-section has six angles, alternate ones being equal; of or pertaining to such a crystal form.
■ **ditrigonally** *adverb* L19.

ditrochee /dʌɪˈtrəʊkiː/ *noun.* Also in Latin form **ditrochaeus** /dʌɪtrə(ʊ)ˈkiːəs/, pl. **-aei** /-iːʌɪ/. E18.
[ORIGIN Late Latin *ditrochaeus* from Greek *ditrokhaios*, formed as DI-² + *trokhaios* TROCHEE.]
PROSODY. A foot consisting of two trochees; a double trochee.
■ **ditro'chean** *adjective* containing two trochees M19.

ditsy *adjective* var. of DITZY.

dittander /dɪˈtandə/ *noun.* ME.
[ORIGIN formed as DITTANY, with ending perh. after Old French & mod. French *coriandre* CORIANDER.]
1 Pepperwort, *Lepidium latifolium.* ME.
†**2** = DITTANY 1. E–M17.

dittany /ˈdɪtəni/ *noun.* LME.
[ORIGIN Old French *dita(i)n* (from medieval Latin *dictamus*) & medieval Latin *ditaneum* (from late Latin *dictamnium*) from Latin *dictamnus*, *-um* from Greek *diktamnon*, perh. from *Diktē* mountain in Crete where it grows.]
1 A dwarf shrub, *Origanum dictamnus*, of the mint family with pink flowers and white woolly leaves, native to Crete and Greece and cultivated for window boxes etc.; formerly supposed to have the power to expel weapons. LME.
fig.: T. BRUGIS But this newes . . was a forcible dittany to drive this arrow out of the wound.
2 Orig., any of various plants resembling dittany, *spec.* = DITTANDER 1. Now (*US*), any plant of the genus *Cunila* of the mint family, sometimes grown as culinary herbs; spec. *C. origanoides.* M16.
3 The plant *Dictamnus albus*, fraxinella. E17.

dittay /ˈdɪteɪ, ˈdɪti/ *noun.* LME.
[ORIGIN Old French *dit(t)é*: see DITTY.]
SCOTS LAW (now *hist.*). The ground of indictment against a person for a criminal offence; such an indictment.

ditto /ˈdɪtəʊ/ *adjective, adverb, noun, & verb.* E17.
[ORIGIN Italian dial. (Tuscan) var. of *detto* said from Latin *dictus* pa. pple of *dicere* say.]
▸ **A** *adjective, adverb, & noun* (pl. **-os**).
†**1** In or of the month already named; the aforesaid month. Only in 17.
2 In the same way, similar(ly); the same; (the) aforesaid; (the same as, another of) what was mentioned above or previously. *colloq.* exc. in lists etc. (where usu. repr. by dots or commas under the matter repeated). L17. ▸**b** *noun.* A symbol representing the word 'ditto'. Also ***ditto mark***. L19.
S. THEMERSON Four Long Petticoats . . . Three Cambric ditto. R. ADAMS A great iron frying-pan and six ditto spoons. P. ACKROYD He blows up easy and down again ditto. A. BLOND Clauses requiring the author to return an advance are rarely invoked, ditto penalties for late delivery.
say ditto to to express agreement with what has been said by (another).
3 *noun.* Cloth of the same material. Chiefly in ***suit of dittos***, a suit of clothes of the same material and colour throughout. *arch.* M18.
4 *noun.* Something identical or similar; an exact resemblance; a repetition. L18.
L. OLIPHANT The upper fragment . . the ditto of which is to be found at Irbid.
5 (Also **D-**.) (Proprietary name for) a duplicator, a small offset press for copying. E20.
▸ **B** *verb.* Pa. t. & pple **dittoed** /ˈdɪtəʊd/.
1 *verb trans.* Produce (mechanically or otherwise) a duplicate of; match, equal. M19.
T. C. HALIBURTON Where will you ditto our fall? It whips English weather by a long chalk. *Canadian Journal of Linguistics* Papers which are privately circulated in dittoed form.
2 *verb intrans.* Say or do the same as another person; agree, echo. L19.

D

dittography /dɪˈtɒgrəfi/ *noun.* L19.
[ORIGIN from Greek *dittos* double + -GRAPHY.]
PALAEOGRAPHY. Unintentional repetition of a letter, word, etc., by a copyist; an instance of this.
■ **'dittogram** *noun* a dittograph L19. **'dittograph** *noun & verb* (***a***) *noun* a letter, word, etc., unintentionally repeated by a copyist; (***b***) *verb trans.* repeat by dittography: L19. **ditto'graphic** *adjective* L19.

dittology /dɪˈtɒlədʒi/ *noun.* L17.
[ORIGIN Greek *dittologia* repetition of words, formed as DITTOGRAPHY: see -LOGY.]
A twofold reading or interpretation.

ditty /ˈdɪti/ *noun & verb.* ME.
[ORIGIN Old French *dité* composition, treaty from Latin *dictatum* use as noun of neut. pa. pple of *dictare* DICTATE *verb*: see -Y⁵. Cf. DICTATE *noun*, DITE *noun*¹.]
▸ **A** *noun.* **1** Orig., a song, a lay. Now, a short simple song; a bird's song. ME.
2 Any composition in verse. LME.
†**3** The words or leading theme of a song; a subject, a theme. M16–L17.
▸ †**B** *verb.* **1** *verb trans.* Sing as a ditty; sing about (something); fit words to (music). L16–L18.
2 *verb intrans.* Sing a ditty. Only in M17.

ditty bag /ˈdɪtɪ bag/ *noun.* M19.
[ORIGIN from unkn. 1st elem. + BAG *noun*.]
A small bag used by sailors etc. to hold odds and ends.

ditty box /ˈdɪtɪ bɒks/ *noun.* L19.
[ORIGIN formed as DITTY BAG + BOX *noun*².]
A box used in the same way as a ditty bag.

ditzy /ˈdɪtsi/ *adjective.* Also **ditsy**. *N. Amer. slang.* L20.
[ORIGIN Unknown.]
(Of a woman) silly, scatterbrained; conceited, snobbish; (of a thing) intricate.
M. SAWYER I knew that it wasn't all designer labels and ditsy housewives.
■ **ditz** *noun* [back-form.] a scatterbrained person L20.

diuresis /dʌɪjʊ(ə)ˈriːsɪs/ *noun.* L17.
[ORIGIN mod. Latin, formed as DI-³ + Greek *ourēsis* urination.]
Increased excretion of urine, esp. of a temporary nature. Formerly, urination.

diuretic /dʌɪjʊ(ə)ˈrɛtɪk/ *adjective & noun.* LME.
[ORIGIN Old French & mod. French *diurétique* or late Latin *diureticus* from Greek *diourētikos*, from *diourein* urinate, formed as DI-³ + *ouron* urine: see -IC.]
▸ **A** *adjective.* **1** Causing diuresis. LME.
†**2** Of a person: urinating excessively. M18–E19.
▸ **B** *noun.* A diuretic agent. LME.
■ †**diuretical** *adjective & noun* = DIURETIC: only in 17. **diuretically** *adverb* M17.

diurnal /dʌɪˈəːn(ə)l/ *adjective & noun.* LME.
[ORIGIN Late Latin *diurnalis*, from Latin *diurnus* daily, from *dies* day: see -AL¹. Cf. JOURNAL *noun & adjective*.]
▸ **A** *adjective.* **1** Chiefly ASTRONOMY. Performed in or occupying one day. LME.
D. ADAMS The Earth moved slowly in its diurnal course.
diurnal arc: see ARC *noun* 1. ***diurnal circle***: see CIRCLE *noun*.
2 Belonging to each day; occurring or (*arch.*) published every day; daily; SCIENCE varying with a period of one day. L16.
T. HARDY The diurnal setting of the sun. J. C. POWYS His diurnal relaxation was his mid-day dinner at the Pilgrims'.
3 Of the day rather than the night (opp. ***nocturnal***); *spec.* (of an animal etc.) active only during the day. L19.
▸ **B** *noun.* **1** ECCLESIASTICAL. A book containing the daytime canonical hours. Formerly also, any book of devotion. M16.
2 A daybook, a diary. *arch.* E17.
3 A newspaper published daily; *loosely* any newspaper or periodical. *obsolete* exc. *hist.* M17.
■ **diurnalist** *noun* (now *rare* or *obsolete*) a writer of a journal; a journalist: M17. **diurnally** *adverb* E16.

diurnation /dʌɪəːˈneɪʃ(ə)n/ *noun.* M19.
[ORIGIN from Latin *diurnus* DIURNAL + -ATION, after *hibernation*.]
The habit in some animals of sleeping or remaining quiescent during the day.

diuturnal /dʌɪjʊˈtəːn(ə)l/ *adjective.* Now *rare.* L16.
[ORIGIN medieval Latin *diuturnalis*, from Latin *diuturnus* of long duration, from *diu* long, for a long time: see -AL¹.]
Of long duration, lasting.
■ Also †**diuturn** *adjective* LME–M17.

D

diuturnity /dʌɪjʊˈtəːnɪti/ *noun*. Now *rare*. LME.
[ORIGIN Latin *diuturnitas*, from *diuturnus*: see DIUTURNAL, -ITY.]
Long duration or continuance.

div /diːv/ *noun*[1]. L18.
[ORIGIN Persian *dīv* from Old Persian *daiva* (Avestan *daēva*) = Sanskrit DEVA.]
In Iranian (esp. Zoroastrian) mythology: a demonic power.

div /dɪv/ *noun*[2]. L19.
[ORIGIN Abbreviation.]
MATH. Divergence (DIVERGENCE 3) (of).

div /dɪv/ *noun*[3]. *slang*. L20.
[ORIGIN Abbreviation.]
A fool, an idiot; = DIVVY *noun*[2].

K. SAMPSON What a pompous, muscle-bound div he is!

Div. *abbreviation*.
Division.

diva /ˈdiːvə/ *noun*. L19.
[ORIGIN Italian from Latin = goddess.]
A distinguished female (esp. operatic) singer; a prima donna.

divagate /ˈdʌɪvəgeɪt/ *verb intrans. literary*. L16.
[ORIGIN Latin *divagat-* pa. ppl stem of *divagari* wander about, formed as DI-[1] + *vagari* wander: see -ATE[3].]
Wander about; stray from one place or subject to another; digress.
■ **divaˈgation** *noun* the action of divagating; (a) deviation, (a) digression: M16.

divalent /dʌɪˈveɪl(ə)nt/ *adjective*. M19.
[ORIGIN from DI-[2] + -VALENT.]
CHEMISTRY & IMMUNOLOGY. Having a valency of two.
■ **divalence** *noun* E20. **divalency** *noun* L19.

Divali *noun* var. of DIWALI.

divan /dɪˈvan, dʌɪˈvan, ˈdʌɪvan/ *noun*. L16.
[ORIGIN French, or Italian *divano*, from Turkish *dīvān* from Persian *dīvān* brochure, anthology, register, court, bench. Cf. DEWAN, DOUANE.]
1 An Eastern council of state; *spec.* (*hist.*) the privy council of the Ottoman Empire, presided over by the Sultan or the grand vizier. L16. ▸**b** Any council. *arch.* E17.
2 The hall where the Ottoman divan was held; a court of justice or council chamber. L16.
3 In Eastern countries, a room entirely open at one side towards a court, garden, river, etc. L17.
4 (Now the usual sense.) A couch or bed without a headboard or footboard. Orig., a low bench or a raised part of a floor forming a long seat against the wall of a room. E18.
5 (A smoking room attached to) a cigar shop. *arch.* E19.
6 An anthology of poems in Persian or another language such as Arabic; *spec.* a series of poems by one author, with rhymes usually running through the alphabet. E19.

divaricate /dʌɪˈvarɪkət, dɪ-/ *adjective*. L18.
[ORIGIN Latin *divaricatus*, formed as DIVARICATE *verb*, -ATE[2].]
Chiefly *BOTANY & ZOOLOGY*. Widely divergent; *esp.* (of a branch) having the stem almost at a right angle.
■ **divaricately** *adverb* M19.

divaricate /dʌɪˈvarɪkeɪt, dɪ-/ *verb*. E17.
[ORIGIN Latin *divaricat-* pa. ppl stem of *divaricare*, formed as DI-[1] + *varicare* stretch (the legs) apart, from *varicus* straddling: see -ATE[3].]
1 *verb intrans.* Stretch or spread apart; branch off, diverge; ramify. E17. ▸**b** *BOTANY & ZOOLOGY*. Diverge widely from a stem or main body. Chiefly as ***divaricated***, ***divaricating*** *ppl adjectives*. M17.

G. P. R. JAMES Where these two [roads] divaricated, the horseman stopped.

2 *verb trans.* Stretch or open wide apart. L17.

MARVELL I took my compasses, and divaricating them . . I drew the circular line.

3 *verb trans.* Cause to spread or branch out in different directions. Now *rare* or *obsolete*. L17.
■ **divaricatingly** *adverb* in a divaricating manner L19. **divaricator** *noun* something which divaricates; *esp.* (*SURGERY*) a hinged instrument for holding portions of tissue apart; (*ZOOLOGY*, more fully ***divaricator muscle***) a muscle that separates parts, e.g. opens a brachiopod shell: L19.

divarication /dʌɪˌvarɪˈkeɪʃ(ə)n, dɪ-/ *noun*. L16.
[ORIGIN medieval Latin *divaricatio(n-)*, formed as DIVARICATE *verb*: see -ATION.]
1 The action of divaricating, divergence; straddling of the legs; the state of spreading out or ramifying. L16.
2 A place where something branches off; something which branches off, a ramification. M17.
3 Divergence of opinion; disagreement. M17.

dive /dʌɪv/ *noun*. E18.
[ORIGIN from the verb.]
1 An act of diving; a swift descent (esp. head first) into or through water etc.; *spec.* one performed by projecting oneself upwards and inverting the body or somersaulting to keep the head first, esp. as a sport. E18.
nosedive: see NOSE *noun*. ***swallow dive***: see SWALLOW *noun*[1].
2 A sudden darting movement, esp. so as to disappear. L19.

OED He made a dive into the nearest shop.

3 A drinking den; a disreputable establishment. *colloq.* L19.
4 In football, boxing, etc. a feigned fall intended to deceive an opponent or referee. Freq. in ***take a dive***. M20.
– COMB.: **divemaster** a person who is in charge of an underwater diving expedition.

dive /dʌɪv/ *verb*. Pa. t. **dived**, (*N. Amer. & dial.*) **dove** /dəʊv/.
[ORIGIN Old English strong intrans. verb *dūfan* (pa. t. *dēaf*, pl. *dufon*), obsolete before 14, & weak trans. verb *dȳfan*, *dȳfde*, both from Germanic, cogn. with DEEP *adjective*, DIP *verb*. (Pa. t. *dove* app. after *drive*, *drove*, etc.)]
▸ **I** *verb intrans.* **1** Descend or plunge, esp. head first, into or through water etc.; execute a dive. OE. ▸**b** Of a submarine: descend so as to be entirely under water. L19. ▸**c** Of an aircraft: plunge steeply downwards at increasing or high speed. E20. ▸**d** In football, boxing, etc.: feign a fall to deceive an opponent or referee. M20.

P. H. JOHNSON He climbed onto a groin, stretched his arms and dived cleanly into the sparkling sea.

2 Of a thing: sink deeply into water etc.; penetrate into a body. Long *rare*. ME.

SHAKES. *John* To dive like buckets in concealed wells. J. DICKEY I . . saw him kill a quail . . , the arrow diving into the black feathers. *transf.*: POPE The fierce soul to darkness dived and hell.

3 Penetrate or search mentally *into* a matter. L16.
4 Put one's hand *into* water, a receptacle, etc., esp. in order to take something out; *arch. slang* pick pockets. L17.
5 Go suddenly or eagerly, esp. into or towards a place or thing. Foll. by preposition. M18.

QUILLER-COUCH A straight pathway dived between hazel-bushes and appeared again twenty feet above. G. B. SHAW A man of sense would have dived into the nearest cellar.

▸ **II** *verb trans.* **6** Dip, submerge, or plunge (a person or thing) *in* or *into* water etc. *arch.* OE.
7 Thrust (the hand or something held) *into*. L16.

E. WAUGH Corker began . . to dive his hand into his bosom and scratch his chest.

8 Penetrate or traverse by diving; dive into or through. Now *rare*. E17.

R. W. EMERSON He dives the hollow, climbs the steep.

– COMB.: **dive-bomb** *verb trans.* (of an aircraft) attack by releasing a bomb while diving towards the target; *slang* (of a bird) swoop down on and away again; release droppings over; **dive-bomber** an aircraft designed for dive-bombing.

dive-dap /ˈdʌɪvdap/ *noun*. Now *dial.* Also **-dop** /-dɒp/.
[ORIGIN Old English *dūfedoppa*, formed as DIVE *verb* + *doppa* agent noun from ablaut stem *dēop-*, *dup-* (*dop-*) dip. Cf. DABCHICK, DIDAPPER, DIVE-DAPPER.]
= DIDAPPER.

dive-dapper /ˈdʌɪvdapə/ *noun*. Now *dial.* M16.
[ORIGIN from DIVE-DAP: assim. to agent nouns. in -ER[1].]
= DIDAPPER.

dive-dop *noun* var. of DIVE-DAP.

†**divell** *verb trans.* E17–E19.
[ORIGIN Latin *divellere* tear apart, formed as DI-[1] + *vellere* tear.]
Tear or pull apart.

divellent /dɪˈvɛl(ə)nt, dʌɪ-/ *adjective*. Now *rare*. L18.
[ORIGIN Latin *divellent-* pres. ppl stem of *divellere*: see DIVELL, -ENT.]
Tending to cause separation or decomposition.

divellicate /dʌɪˈvɛlɪkeɪt/ *verb trans.* Now *rare*. M17.
[ORIGIN from DI-[1] + Latin *vellicat-* pa. ppl stem of *vellicare* pluck, pinch, from *vellere* tear: see -ATE[3].]
Tear apart, pull to pieces, (*lit. & fig.*).

diver /ˈdʌɪvə/ *noun*. L15.
[ORIGIN from DIVE *verb* + -ER[1].]
1 Any of various diving birds, *esp.* one of the family Gaviidae, comprising large waterbirds with straight sharply pointed bills. Cf. LOON *noun*[2] 1. L15.
great northern diver a large diver, *Gavia immer*, which breeds chiefly in forest lakes in N. America and visits the westernmost parts of Europe in winter. ***red-throated diver***: see RED *adjective*.
2 A person who dives, esp. as an occupation or a sport; an animal good at diving. E16.
pearl diver, ***scuba-diver***, etc.
3 A pickpocket. *arch. slang.* L16.
4 A thing made to plunge under water. L18.
Cartesian diver: see CARTESIAN *adjective*.
■ **diverless** *adjective* L20.

diverge /dʌɪˈvəːdʒ, dɪ-/ *verb*. M17.
[ORIGIN medieval Latin *divergere*, formed as DI-[1] + Latin *vergere* bend, turn, incline.]
1 *verb intrans.* Proceed in different directions from a point; take different courses, turn aside *from* a track or course, (*lit. & fig.*); differ. M17.

E. M. FORSTER A footpath diverged from the highroad. E. JONES As they grew up their interests diverged. M. M. KAYE Her unusual looks . . diverged too widely from the Indian ideal.

2 *verb trans.* Cause to diverge; deflect. M18.
diverging lens: causing light rays to diverge.
3 *verb intrans. MATH.* Of an infinite series: not converge (CONVERGE 2). L18.
■ **divergement** *noun* divergence M18. **diverger** *noun* a person whose thought is divergent (DIVERGENT 2) M20. **divergingly** *adverb* in a diverging manner, with divergence: L18.

divergence /dʌɪˈvəːdʒ(ə)ns, dɪ-/ *noun*. M17.
[ORIGIN from DIVERGE + -ENCE, perh. after French *divergence*.]
1 The action, fact, or property of diverging; movement in different directions from the same point so that the intervening distance continually increases; departure from a path or course (*lit. & fig.*). M17.

GLADSTONE The natural divergence of the two traditions. D. LINDSAY By making a long divergence they eventually got round to the other side.

2 A difference or conflict between opinions, interests, wishes, etc. L19.

L. STEPHEN There was the widest divergence of opinion as to our probable fate. W. S. CHURCHILL A divergence grew between the King and Marlborough.

3 *MATH.* The scalar product of the operator ∇ (see DEL) and any given vector. L19.
4 *METEOROLOGY & OCEANOGRAPHY*. A place where airflows or ocean currents diverge, characteristically marked by downwelling (of air) or upwelling (of water). M20.
■ **divergenceless** *adjective* (*MATH.*) having a divergence of zero M20. **divergency** *noun* divergent quality or state; (amount or degree of) divergence: E18.

divergent /dʌɪˈvəːdʒ(ə)nt, dɪ-/ *adjective*. L17.
[ORIGIN formed as DIVERGENCE + -ENT, perh. after French *divergent*.]
1 Diverging; of or pertaining to divergence; *MATH.* (of an infinite series) not convergent. L17.

C. DARWIN The Siamese have small noses, with divergent nostrils. H. MACMILLAN There seemed little likelihood of reconciling the divergent interests.

2 *PSYCHOLOGY*. Of thought: tending to produce a variety of unusual answers or responses; not habitually given to deductive reasoning. Cf. CONVERGENT 3. M20.
■ **divergently** *adverb* E19.

divers /ˈdʌɪvəz/ *adjective, pronoun, & adverb. arch.* ME.
[ORIGIN Old French & mod. French (fem. *diverse*) from Latin *diversus* pa. pple of *divertere* DIVERT. See also DIVERSE *adjective, pronoun, & adverb*.]
▸ **A** *adjective*. †**1** = DIVERSE *adjective* 1. ME–E18.
†**2** Differing from what is right, good, or profitable; perverse, cruel; adverse, unfavourable. ME–E17.
3 Various, sundry, several; more than one; some number of. ME.

G. SAINTSBURY Divers interpretations may be put on that story. R. H. MORRIESON Through divers landing windows, we saw *her*.

▸ **B** *pronoun*. Several, some number, (*of*). (Earlier as DIVERSE *pronoun*.) E16.

HOBBES He subdued divers of the islands.

▸ †**C** *adverb*. Diversely. L16–E18.
■ **diversly** *adverb* ME.

diverse /dʌɪˈvəːs, ˈdʌɪvəːs/ *adjective, pronoun, & adverb*. ME.
[ORIGIN Var. of DIVERS, later infl. by *adverse*, *perverse*, etc.]
▸ **A** *adjective*. **1** Different in character or quality; not of the same kind; unlike in nature or qualities. (Foll. by *from*, †*to*.) ME.

H. ARENDT They were a mixture of diverse elements: men as far apart as Zola and Péguy.

†**2** = DIVERS *adjective* 3. ME–E18.
†**3** = DIVERS *adjective* 2. LME–L15.
4 Differing from itself in different circumstances, at different times, or in different parts; varied; changeful. M16.

B. JOWETT The diverse and multiform nature of pleasure.

†**5** Distracting. *rare* (Spenser). Only in L16.
▸ †**B** *pronoun*. = DIVERS *pronoun*. LME–E18.
▸ †**C** *adverb*. Diversely. LME–E18.
■ **diversely** *adverb* ME. **diverseness** *noun* (now *rare*) the quality or state of being diverse; diversity: LME.

†**diverse** *verb*. ME.
[ORIGIN Old French *diverser* from medieval Latin *diversare* frequentative of Latin *divertere* DIVERT.]
1 *verb trans.* Make diverse or different; vary, change. ME–M17.
2 *verb intrans.* Be or grow diverse or different; vary; differ. Only in ME.
3 *verb trans. & intrans.* Turn aside. *rare*. LME–L16.

SPENSER The Redcrosse Knight diverst, but forth rode Britomart.

diversification /dʌɪˌvəːsɪfɪˈkeɪʃ(ə)n, dɪ-/ *noun*. E17.
[ORIGIN medieval Latin *diversificatio(n-)*, from *diversificat-* pa. ppl stem of *diversificare*: see DIVERSIFY, -ATION.]
1 The action of diversifying; the process of becoming diversified; the fact of being diversified. E17.
2 A diversified condition, form, or structure. Now *rare*. L17.

diversiform /dʌɪˈvəːsɪfɔːm, dɪ-/ *adjective*. E18.
[ORIGIN from late Latin *diversi-* combining form of *diversus* DIVERS + -FORM.]
Of various forms; differing in form.

diversify /dʌɪˈvəːsɪfʌɪ, dɪ-/ *verb*. **LME**.
[**ORIGIN** Old French *diversifier* from medieval Latin *diversificare* make unlike, from *diversus* **DIVERS**: see **-FY**.]
1 *verb intrans*. †**a** Exhibit or produce diversity; vary. **LME–E19**. ▸**b** Of a company etc.: enlarge or vary its range of products, field of operation, etc., esp. to reduce its dependence on a particular market etc.; engage in diversification *into*. **M20**.

b *Daily Telegraph* His gallery has ambitious ideas for diversifying into publishing.

2 *verb trans*. Make diverse, different, or varied; give variety or diversity to; vary, modify, variegate. **L15**. ▸†**b** Differentiate, make different, *from*. **L16–E18**.

POPE Swift trouts, diversify'd with crimson stains. **JAS. ROBERTSON** That charming lake and . . the diversified scenery around its wooded banks. **L. STRACHEY** Sometimes the solemnity of the evening was diversified by a concert.

■ **diversifier** *noun* (*rare*) **L19**.

diversion /dʌɪˈvəːʃ(ə)n, dɪ-/ *noun*. **LME**.
[**ORIGIN** Late Latin *diversio(n-)* turning away, from Latin *divers-* pa. ppl stem of *divertere* **DIVERT**: see **-ION**.]
1 The action or an act of diverting or turning aside from an expected or usual course, purpose, etc. **LME**.

DONNE A diversion . . from this rectitude, this uprightness. **E. BOWEN** The diversion of traffic out of blocked main thoroughfares into by-ways. **H. KISSINGER** The ABM . . was attacked as a wasteful diversion of resources from domestic priorities.

2 Something that diverts the mind from preoccupation or boredom; a pleasant mental distraction; an amusement, an entertainment, a pastime. **E17**.

W. TREVOR A seaside resort of limited diversions.

3 The turning away of the attention, thoughts, etc., esp. in a pleasurable way; distraction, recreation, amusement. **M17**.

J. AUSTEN All were finding . . diversion in the playful conceits they suggested.

4 Something intended to distract someone else's attention, *spec*. (**MILITARY**) a manoeuvre with this purpose. **M17**.

WELLINGTON To make the most powerful diversion which may be practicable on the coasts of the Red Sea. *New York Times* One frantic author, worried about a scene to be played on stage, knocked over an ashtray to create a diversion.

†**5** Something that diverts a person from a regular occupation. **M–L17**.
6 An alternative route; *spec*. one to be taken when a road is temporarily closed. **M20**.
■ **diversionary** *adjective* tending to a diversion, of the nature of a diversion **M19**. **diversionism** *noun* the activity of a diversionist **M20**. **diversionist** *noun* & *adjective* (**a**) *noun* (esp. in Communist usage) a saboteur, a conspirator against the state; (**b**) *adjective* of the nature of diversionism: **M20**.

diversity /dʌɪˈvəːsɪti, dɪ-/ *noun* & *adjective*. **ME**.
[**ORIGIN** Old French & mod. French *diversité* from Latin *diversitas*, from *diversus* **DIVERS**: see **-ITY**.]
▸ **A** *noun*. **1** The condition or quality of being diverse, different, or varied; variety, unlikeness. **ME**.

C. SAGAN Despite the apparent diversity of terrestrial life forms, they are identical in the deepest sense.

2 An instance of this; a distinction; a different kind, a variety (of a thing etc.). **ME**.

J. S. MILL People have diversities of taste.

†**3** Various kinds, variety (of things etc.). **LME–E17**.

SHAKES. *Temp*. Roaring, shrieking, . . And moe diversity of sounds, all horrible.

†**4** Contrariety to what is agreeable, good, or right; perversity, evil, mischief. **LME–E16**.
▸ **B** *attrib*. or as *adjective*. Designating radio reception in which a signal is received on several channels and the one least affected by fading etc. is automatically used. **M20**.

diversive /dʌɪˈvəːsɪv, dɪ-/ *adjective*. Long *rare*. **LME**.
[**ORIGIN** from Latin *divers-*: see **DIVERSION**, **-IVE**.]
Tending to divert or cause diversion; divertive.

divert /dʌɪˈvəːt, dɪ-/ *verb*. **LME**.
[**ORIGIN** French *divertir* from Latin *divertere*, formed as **DI-**[1] + *vertere* to turn.]
1 *verb trans*. Turn aside from a direction or course; cause (esp. traffic) to take a different route; alter (a course); turn *from* one destination or object *to* another. **LME**.

T. ARNOLD Some of the reinforcements . . were afterwards diverted to other services. **E. FIGES** I had to get planning permission to divert the stream.

2 *verb trans*. Turn (a purpose, feeling, etc.) elsewhere; interrupt the progress of (an action); avert, ward off. **LME**.

MILTON Which Omen . . God hath not diverted. **E. M. FORSTER** An opportunity of diverting the conversation while she recovered her composure.

3 *verb intrans*. Turn aside from a route, purpose, etc.; deviate, digress, (*lit*. & *fig*.). Now *arch*. & *formal*. **LME**.

W. MUNK He . . was bred to physic, but he diverted to the diplomatic life.

†**4** *verb intrans*. & *refl*. Separate *from*; part. **M16–E18**.
†**5** *verb trans*. Turn awry or out of true. *rare* (Shakes.). Only in **E17**.
6 *verb trans*. Draw (a person etc.) away *from* a particular course, design, etc.; draw (the attention etc.) away *from* one thing *to* another; distract. **E17**.

O. MANNING She diverted him by taking a small parcel from her handbag.

7 *verb trans*. Draw away from tedious or serious occupations; entertain, amuse. **M17**.

P. WARNER The higher ranks would divert themselves with hunting, drinking.

8 *verb trans*. Cause (time) to pass pleasantly; while away. Now *rare*. **E18**.
■ **diverter** *noun* **E17**. **diverti'bility** *noun* (*rare*) ability to be diverted **L19**. **divertible** *adjective* (*rare*) able to be diverted **L19**. **diverting** *ppl adjective* that diverts; *esp*. amusing, entertaining: **M17**. **divertingly** *adverb* **E18**. **divertingness** *noun* **L17**. **divertive** *adjective* (now *rare*) tending to divert; amusing, entertaining: **L16**. **divertor** *noun* a device or apparatus that diverts electricity, impurities, etc. **L19**.

†**diverticle** *noun*. **LME**.
[**ORIGIN** formed as **DIVERTICULUM**.]
1 A byway, a side road; a turning out of the main or direct way (*lit*. & *fig*.). **LME–L18**.
2 = **DIVERTICULUM** 2. Only in **M19**.

diverticulum /dʌɪvəˈtɪkjʊləm/ *noun*. Pl. **-la** /-lə/. **M17**.
[**ORIGIN** medieval Latin = byway, var. of Latin *deverticulum*, from *devertere* turn down or aside, from *de* **DE-** 1 + *vertere* to turn: see **-CULE**.]
†**1** A byway; a way out, a means of exit. **M17–E18**.
2 **MEDICINE**. A blind tube or sac forming a side-branch of a cavity or passage, *esp*. an abnormal one in the colon etc. **E19**.
Meckel's diverticulum: see **MECKEL** 1. ***Zenker diverticulum***, ***Zenker pulsion diverticulum***, ***Zenker's diverticulum***, ***Zenker's pulsion diverticulum***: see **ZENKER** *noun*[1].
■ **diverticular** *adjective* pertaining to, affecting, or of the nature of a diverticulum **M19**. **diverticulate** *adjective* having a diverticulum **L19**. ˌ**diverticuˈlectomy** *noun* (an instance of) surgical removal of an abnormal diverticulum **E20**. ˌ**diverticuˈlitis** *noun* (**MEDICINE**) inflammation of an abnormal diverticulum, esp. in the intestine **E20**. ˌ**diverticuˈlosis** *noun* (**MEDICINE**) the presence of abnormal diverticula, esp. in the intestine **E20**.

divertimento /dɪˌvəːtɪˈmɛntəʊ, -ˌvɛːt-/ *noun*. Pl. **-ti** /-ti/, **-tos**. **M18**.
[**ORIGIN** Italian = diversion.]
1 A diversion, an amusement. Long *rare*. **M18**.
2 **MUSIC**. A composition primarily for entertainment, *esp*. a suite for a small group of instruments or a single instrument; a light orchestral piece. **E19**.

divertisement /dɪˈvəːtɪzm(ə)nt/ *noun*. **M17**.
[**ORIGIN** French **DIVERTISSEMENT**.]
1 (An) entertainment, (an) amusement; = **DIVERSION** 2, 3. **M17**.
2 = **DIVERTISSEMENT** 1. *arch*. **M17**.

divertissement /diːvɛːˈtiːsmɒ̃; *foreign* divɛrtismɑ̃ (*pl. same*)/ *noun*. **E18**.
[**ORIGIN** French, from *divertiss-* stem of *divertir* **DIVERT**: see **-MENT**.]
1 **a** A short ballet or other entertainment between acts or longer pieces. **E18**. ▸**b** = **DIVERTIMENTO** 2. **L19**.
2 An entertainment; = **DIVERSION** 2. **E19**.

Dives /ˈdʌɪviːz/ *noun*. In sense 2 **d-**. **LME**.
[**ORIGIN** Late Latin (Vulgate *Luke* 16) = rich man, use as noun of Latin *dives* rich.]
1 (The type of) a rich man. **LME**.
2 *hist*. ***Dives costs***, legal costs on the ordinary rather than the reduced scale formerly allowed in certain cases. **M19**.

divest /dʌɪˈvɛst, dɪ-/ *verb*. **E17**.
[**ORIGIN** Alt. of **DEVEST** on Latin models in *di-*. Cf. medieval Latin *disvestire*, *di-*, *de-*.]
1 *verb trans*. Strip *of* a possession, right, or attribute; dispossess, deprive, *of*; free, rid, (esp. oneself) *of*. **E17**.

J. GALSWORTHY She could never divest herself of the feeling that the world was the most ungrateful place. **B. RUSSELL** As soon as we are able to divest our thoughts of irrelevant particularity.

2 *verb trans*. **a** Take off (a garment etc.); lay aside, abandon. Now *rare*. **E17**. ▸**b** Strip *of* a garment, covering, etc.; strip, undress. **E19**.

a **BROWNING** I will divest all fear. **b** **N. PODHORETZ** The . . young gentleman was forthwith divested of his . . red satin jacket.

3 *verb trans*. **LAW**. Take away (property etc. vested in someone); alienate. **L18**.
4 *verb trans*. & *intrans*. Sell off (a subsidiary company); get rid of, cease to hold, (an investment). **M20**.
■ **divestment** *noun* the action or an act of divesting; the state of being divested: **M18**. **divesture** *noun* & *verb* (**a**) *noun* = **DIVESTITURE** 2; (**b**) *verb trans*. undress: **M17**.

divestitive /dʌɪˈvɛstɪtɪv, dɪ-/ *adjective*. **E19**.
[**ORIGIN** formed as **DIVESTITURE** + **-IVE**.]
Having the property of divesting.

divestiture /dʌɪˈvɛstɪtʃə, dɪ-/ *noun*. **E17**.
[**ORIGIN** from medieval Latin *divestit-* pa. ppl stem of *divestire*: **DIVEST**: see **-URE**. Cf. medieval Latin *disvestitura*.]
1 Deprivation of a possession or right; dispossession; alienation. **E17**.
2 The action of stripping off clothing or getting rid of something. **E19**.
3 The process of breaking up a large company by selling off or forcing the sale of subsidiaries; withdrawal of investment. *US*. **M20**.

divi *noun* & *verb* var. of **DIVVY** *noun*[1] & *verb*.

dividant *adjective* see **DIVIDENT**.

D

divide /dɪˈvʌɪd/ *noun*. **M17**.
[**ORIGIN** from the verb.]
1 The act of dividing, esp. among a number of people. Formerly also, separation. **M17**.
2 A ridge or line of high ground forming the division between two valleys or river systems; a watershed; a dividing line, a boundary, (*lit*. & *fig*.). **E19**.
the Great Divide: *spec*. between life and death.

divide /dɪˈvʌɪd/ *verb*. **ME**.
[**ORIGIN** Latin *dividere* force apart, separate, remove. Cf. **DEVISE** *verb*.]
▸ **I** *verb trans*. **1** Separate into or *into* parts or smaller groups; split up; break or cut apart. **ME**. ▸**b** Penetrate by motion through; pass through or across. *arch*. **L16**.

I. MURDOCH Julius contented himself with dividing it into four pieces. **H. NICOLSON** I start dividing the primroses.

divide the hoof *arch*. (of an animal) have cloven hoofs.
2 Separate into branches, cause to fork. Usu. in ***pass***. **LME**.
3 Mark out into parts, in fact or thought; cause to consist of parts or distinct areas. Freq. in ***pass***. (Foll. by *into*.) **LME**.

L. DEIGHTON The wire roof divided the . . sky into a hundred rectangles. **G. GREENE** The house was divided into flats. **J. HAWKES** Walls dividing the rich pastures of the valley.

4 Separate into categories; classify. Formerly also, make distinctions with regard to. Usu. foll. by *into*. **LME**.

R. W. HAMILTON We commonly divide the people into agricultural and manufacturing.

5 Separate *from* another person or thing, or an adjacent part; cut off, isolate; be a boundary between; part, sunder. **LME**.

POPE What thin partitions Sense from Thought divide. **G. GREENE** The breadth of Lake Mälaren divided him from the workmen's quarters on the other bank.

6 Separate (people) in opinion, feeling, or interest; cause to disagree; set at variance. **LME**.

H. MACMILLAN Two great sources of dispute divided the successor states to the old Indian Empire.

7 Distribute or share out *between* or *among* two or more parties, objects of thought, etc., deal out (†*to*). Now also ***divide up***. **LME**. ▸**b** Take or have a portion of (something) along with another or others; share (*with*). **E16**.

K. VONNEGUT The government ought to divide up the wealth of the country equally. **T. CAPOTE** They divided between them the household chores, taking turns at the stove and the sink. **b** **DRYDEN** Let old Timotheus yield the prize, Or both divide the crown.

8 **MATH**. **a** Find how many times (one quantity) contains another. Foll. by *by* the latter quantity. **LME**. ▸**b** Of a quantity: be contained in (another quantity) without a remainder. **E18**.
†**9** **MUSIC**. Perform with divisions. Only in **L16**.
10 Cause (a legislative assembly etc.) to divide (see sense 14 below). **E17**.
▸ **II** *verb intrans*. **11** Become divided, undergo division; become separated into parts, or from something else or each other; admit of division; branch, ramify. **LME**. ▸**b** Of a Cambridge University term: reach its midpoint. **L18**.

SHAKES. *Lear* Love cools, friendship falls off, brothers divide. **O. MANNING** The street divided into smaller streets. *Nature* The scholarly reading population divides naturally into two types.

12 Make a separation or distinction; distinguish (*between*). Now chiefly in ***divide and rule*** below. **LME**.
divide and rule [translating Latin *divide et impera*] maintain supremacy over subjects or prospective antagonists by preventing them from making common cause.
13 **MATH**. Perform division. **E16**.
14 Of a legislative assembly etc.: separate into two groups according to which way a vote is cast, so that those for and those against may be counted. **M16**.
†**15** **MUSIC**. Perform or execute divisions. Only in **E17**.
†**16** Have a share. *rare* (Shakes.). Only in **E17**.
■ **dividable** *adjective* (**a**) able to be divided, divisible; †(**b**) *rare* having the function of dividing: **L16**.

divided /dɪˈvʌɪdɪd/ *ppl adjective*. **M16**.
[**ORIGIN** from **DIVIDE** *verb* + **-ED**[1].]
That has been divided; separated into parts; (of a verdict) not unanimous; discordant, at variance.

D. HALBERSTAM Not everyone loved her, people in that community were fiercely divided over her. **E. BOWEN** Emmeline gave them the best she could of her now divided attention.

divided against itself consisting of opposing factions. **divided highway** *N. Amer.* a dual carriageway. **divided skirt**: hanging like an ordinary skirt but with separate legs, as in trousers.
■ **dividedly** *adverb* E17. **dividedness** *noun* M17.

dividend /ˈdɪvɪdɛnd/ *noun.* L15.
[ORIGIN Anglo-Norman *dividende* from Latin *dividendum* use as noun of neut. gerundive of *dividere* DIVIDE *verb*: see -END.]
1 A portion or share of anything divided, *esp.* the share that falls to each party. *obsolete* exc. as *fig.* use of sense b. L15. ▸**b** A sum received periodically by a shareholder or creditor (cf. sense 4 below). L17.

S. JOHNSON A very liberal dividend of praise. **b** *fig.*: M. M. KAYE Those two hard years in the mountains . . had paid dividends at last, for they had toughened him.

b *cum dividend*: see CUM 2. *ex dividend*: see EX *preposition*.
2 MATH. A quantity which is to be divided by another (the divisor). M16.
†**3** The action or an act of dividing or sharing; (a) distribution. M16–E18.
4 A sum of money to be divided among a number of people, e.g. the creditors of an insolvent estate; *esp.* the payment made periodically by a company to its shareholders, usu. expressed as an amount per share; a similar payment made to members or customers of a cooperative in proportion to the amount spent; a payment made to a winner in a football pool. E17.
– COMB.: **dividend-stripping** the practice of buying securities ex dividend and selling them cum dividend before the next dividend is due in order to avoid the tax payable on dividends; **dividend warrant** the document by which a shareholder receives a dividend.
■ **dividendless** *adjective* L19.

†**divident** *noun & adjective.* In sense B.1 also **-ant**. LME.
[ORIGIN Latin *divident-* pres. ppl stem of *dividere* DIVIDE *verb*: see -ENT.]
▸ **A** *noun.* A person who or thing which divides or separates; something that forms the boundary between two regions etc., MATH. a divisor. LME–M17.
▸ **B** *adjective.* **1** Divided, separate. *rare* (Shakes.). Only in E17.
2 Distributive. Only in M17.

divider /dɪˈvʌɪdə/ *noun.* E16.
[ORIGIN from DIVIDE *verb* + -ER¹.]
1 A person who distributes or shares something. E16.
2 A person who or thing which divides a whole into parts or portions. M16. ▸**b** A partition or screen; *spec.* (in full ***room divider***) a screen, piece of furniture, etc., to divide a room into different areas. M20.
†**3** A person who makes philosophical distinctions. L16–E17.
4 A cause of dissension or discord. M17.
5 In *pl.* Measuring compasses worked by means of a screw fastened to one leg and passing through the other, esp. for setting to small intervals; a simple pair of compasses with steel points. E18.

divi-divi /ˈdɪvɪˌdɪvi/ *noun.* M19.
[ORIGIN Amer. Spanish from Carib.]
A flowering tree, *Caesalpinia coriaria*, of tropical America (also ***divi-divi tree***); its curled pods, used in tanning.

dividual /dɪˈvɪdjʊəl/ *adjective & noun. arch.* L16.
[ORIGIN from Latin *dividuus* (formed as DIVIDE *verb*) + -AL¹.]
▸ **A** *adjective.* **1** That is or may be divided or separated from something else; separate, distinct. L16.
2 Divided or divisible into parts; fragmentary. E17.
3 Divided between a number; shared, held in common. M17.
▸ †**B** *noun.* **1** Something (able to be) divided. Only in M17.
2 MATH. In division, each of the several parts of the dividend, yielding successively one figure or term of the quotient. E18–E19.
■ **dividually** *adverb* separately M17.

dividuality /dɪˌvɪdjʊˈalɪti/ *noun. rare.* E19.
[ORIGIN Back-form. from INDIVIDUALITY.]
The state of not being individual; lack of individuality.

dividuity /dɪvɪˈdjuːɪti/ *noun. rare.* M17.
[ORIGIN Latin *dividuitatem*, formed as DIVIDUAL: see -ITY.]
Divisible or divided quality or state.

dividuous /dɪˈvɪdjʊəs/ *adjective. rare.* M18.
[ORIGIN formed as DIVIDUAL + -OUS.]
1 = DIVIDUAL *adjective* 2. M18.
2 = DIVIDUAL *adjective* 1. E19.

divination /dɪvɪˈneɪʃ(ə)n/ *noun.* LME.
[ORIGIN Old French, or Latin *divinatio(n-)*, from *divinat-* pa. ppl stem of *divinare*: see DIVINE *verb*, -ATION.]
1 The action or practice of divining; an act of divining; insight into or discovery of the unknown or the future by supernatural or magical means; (an) augury, (a) prophecy. LME.

L. DURRELL The Grand Tarot for amateur divination. C. G. SELIGMAN Divination is performed by inspection of the stomach of a slaughtered cow, and interpretation of the flight of birds.

2 Guessing by happy instinct or unusual insight; successful conjecture; an inspired insight, a skilful forecast, a good guess. LME.

R. HUGHES She had not Rachel's clear divination: she never knew when she might offend. A. NIN At times I have intuitions, swift divinations.

divinator /ˈdɪvɪneɪtə/ *noun.* L15.
[ORIGIN Latin, from *divinat-*: see DIVINATION, -OR.]
A person who practises divination; a diviner, a soothsayer.
■ **diˈvinatory** *adjective* pertaining to a diviner or to divination, prophetic; conjectural: M16.

divine /dɪˈvʌɪn/ *noun¹ & adjective.* ME.
[ORIGIN Old French *devin*, fem. *-ine*, later (by assim. to Latin) *divin*, from Latin *divinus*, from *divus* godlike, god, rel. to *deus* god.]
▸ **A** *noun.* †**1** Theology, divinity. Only in ME.
†**2** Divination. Only in ME.
3 Divine nature, divinity. Now only as ***the divine***. *rare.* LME.
†**4** Divine service. L15–E17.
▸ **B** *adjective.* **1** Of or pertaining to God or a god. LME.

R. W. EMERSON Accept the place divine providence has found for you.

2 Given by or proceeding from God; sanctioned or inspired by God. LME.

J. WATERWORTH Did this unrivalled Biblist acknowledge any writings as divine, which the Jews did not receive as canonical?

divine right (of kings) *hist.* (the right deriving from) the doctrine that monarchs have authority from God alone, independently of their subjects' will.
3 Addressed or devoted to God; religious, sacred. LME.

I. WATTS Divine songs, attempted in easy language, for the use of children.

divine office: see OFFICE *noun* 4. **divine service** the public worship of God.
4 Partaking of the nature of God or a god; godlike; heavenly. LME. ▸†**b** Immortal, beatified. L16–M17.

R. A. KNOX They were not to think of Christ after a human fashion. His nature was Divine. R. G. COLLINGWOOD Some divine or at least spiritual being.

5 Superhumanly gifted, or beautiful; of surpassing excellence; *colloq.* excellent, delightful; as good as one could wish for. LME.

WORDSWORTH That mighty orb of song, The divine Milton. J. GRENFELL Isn't he divine? He is the best White Russian butler in the whole of New York.

divine proportion: that of the golden section.
6 Connected or dealing with divinity or sacred things; sacred. *arch.* LME.
†**7** Foreboding, prophetic. E–M17.

MILTON Yet oft his heart, divine of somthing ill, Misgave him.

■ **divineness** *noun* (now *rare*) LME.

divine /dɪˈvʌɪn/ *noun².* ME.
[ORIGIN Old French *devin* soothsayer, (later) *divin* theologian, from Latin *divinus* soothsayer, (in medieval Latin) theologian, use as noun of *divinus* adjective: see DIVINE *noun¹ & adjective*.]
†**1** A soothsayer; a prophet, a seer. ME–L16.
2 A person, usu. a cleric, skilled in divinity; a theologian. Formerly, any clergyman. LME.
†**3** A writer on the theology of a religious system other than Christianity; a priest or religious teacher of a religion other than Christianity. LME–E17.

divine /dɪˈvʌɪn/ *verb.* LME.
[ORIGIN Old French & mod. French *deviner*, formed as DIVINE *noun²* after Latin *divinare* foretell, predict.]
▸ **I** *verb trans.* †**1** Make out or interpret by supernatural or magical insight; disclose, make known. LME–E17.
2 Make out by sagacity, intuition, or fortunate conjecture; conjecture successfully; guess. LME.

L. STRACHEY He alone among public men had divined her feelings at Albert's death. R. H. MOTTRAM He has written to us, you will never divine from whence! Q. BELL Each divined that the other could become a formidable rival.

3 Have supernatural or magic insight into (things to come); have a presentiment of; predict or prophesy by some special intuition. LME.

S. BUTLER None . . could divine To which side Conquest would incline.

†**4** Conceive of, devise, or contrive by special inspiration or extraordinary sagacity. LME–L16.
†**5** Of a thing: foreshadow, prognosticate, portend; point out. L16–M19.

SWIFT A certain magick rod . . divines Whene'er the soil has golden mines. R. W. EMERSON All things wait for and divine him.

†**6** Make divine; canonize; divinize. L16–E17.
▸ **II** *verb intrans.* **7** Practise divination; obtain insight into or discovery of the unknown or the future by supernatural or magical means. LME.
divining rod = ***dowsing rod*** s.v. DOWSE *verb¹*.
8 Foretell the future by divine or superhuman power; prophesy. *arch.* LME.
9 Make an inference by sagacity, intuition, or fortunate conjecture; conjecture, guess. LME. ▸†**b** Foll. by *of*, *on*, *upon*: make conjectures about, augur from. LME–E18.

SHAKES. *Oth.* Something from Cyprus, as I may divine.

divinely /dɪˈvʌɪnli/ *adverb.* LME.
[ORIGIN from DIVINE *adjective* + -LY².]
1 With a superhuman excellence or perfection; *colloq.* excellently, delightfully, as well as one could wish. LME.

W. IRVING An elegant young man . . who danced a minuet divinely.

2 (As) by the agency or power of God or a god. L16.

G. W. KNIGHT They might be divinely inspired.

†**3** In a holy or pious manner. L16–L17.

diviner /dɪˈvʌɪnə/ *noun.* ME.
[ORIGIN Anglo-Norman *devinour*, *di-* = Old French *devineor* etc. (corresp. to Latin *divinator*), from *deviner*: see DIVINE *verb*, -ER². In sense 2, after Old French *divin* DIVINE *noun²*.]
1 A person who practises divination; *spec.* a dowser. ME. ▸**b** A successful conjecturer, a good guesser. L17.
†**2** A divine, a theologian; a wise man. LME–M16.
■ **divineˈress** *noun* (*arch.*) a female diviner LME.

diving /ˈdʌɪvɪŋ/ *verbal noun.* LME.
[ORIGIN from DIVE *verb* + -ING¹.]
The action of DIVE *verb*.
– COMB.: **diving bell** (*a*) a vessel open at the bottom and with a supply of air in which a person can be let down into deep water; (*b*) the air-filled web in which the water spider lives under water; **diving board** an elevated board, projecting over water, for diving from; **diving suit** a watertight suit, usu. with a helmet and air supply, for wearing when working under water.

diving /ˈdʌɪvɪŋ/ *ppl adjective.* L16.
[ORIGIN from DIVE *verb* + -ING².]
That dives.
diving beetle any of various predatory water beetles of the family Dytiscidae, which are enabled to dive by the air stored under their elytra. **diving duck** a duck that habitually dives under water for food; *spec.* any of a tribe of mostly freshwater ducks exemplified by the pochard, scaup, tufted duck, etc. **diving petrel** a petrel of the family Pelecanoididae.

divinify /dɪˈvɪnɪfʌɪ/ *verb trans.* M17.
[ORIGIN from Latin *divinus* DIVINE *adjective* + -FY, after *deify*.]
Make or regard as divine. Usu. in *pass.*

divinise *verb* var. of DIVINIZE.

divinitize /dɪˈvɪnɪtʌɪz/ *verb trans. rare.* Also **-ise**. M17.
[ORIGIN Irreg. from DIVINITY + -IZE.]
= DIVINIZE.

divinity /dɪˈvɪnɪti/ *noun.* ME.
[ORIGIN Old French & mod. French *divinité* from Latin *divinitat-* (in Vulgate translating Greek *theiotēs* and *theotēs*), from *divinus* DIVINE *adjective*: see -ITY.]
1 The organized body of knowledge dealing with the nature, attributes, and governance of God or *transf.* gods; theology. ME.

H. H. MILMAN He . . was versed in all the divinity of the Greeks. D. ATTENBOROUGH Darwin was far from being an atheist—he had . . taken a degree in divinity.

2 The character or quality of being God or sharing the nature of God; godhood; divine nature; deity, godhead. LME.

DAY LEWIS I grew up with certain assumptions . . : the divinity of Christ, the assurance of eternal life.

3 A divine or celestial being; a god, a goddess; *the* Deity. LME.

fig.: THACKERAY Composing a most flaming and conceited copy of verses to his divinity.

†**4** = DIVINATION 1. *rare.* LME–E17.
5 Quality, virtue, or power characteristic of or appropriate to God. E16.

SHAKES. *Merry W.* There is divinity in odd numbers, either in nativity, chance, or death.

6 More fully ***divinity fudge***. A kind of fudge made with beaten white of egg and nuts. *N. Amer.* E20.
– COMB.: **divinity calf** a dark brown calf leather with blind tooling, traditionally used for binding theological works; ***divinity fudge***: see sense 6 above.
■ **divinityship** *noun* (*a*) the status or personality of a divinity, godship; (*b*) *rare* skill in or knowledge of divinity: L16.

divinize /ˈdɪvɪnʌɪz/ *verb trans.* Also **-ise**. M17.
[ORIGIN French *diviniser*, from *divin* DIVINE *adjective*: see -IZE.]
Make divine; deify.
■ **diviniˈzation** *noun* M19.

divisa /dɪˈvisa/ *noun.* M20.
[ORIGIN Spanish = device, emblem, ult. from Latin *divis-*: see DEVICE, DIVISION.]
BULLFIGHTING. A bunch of coloured ribbons worn by a bull and denoting its breeder.

divisi /dɪˈviːsi/ *adverb, adjective, & noun.* M18.
[ORIGIN Italian = divided, pl. pa. ppl adjective of *dividere* divide.]
MUSIC. ▸**A** *adverb & adjective.* A direction: with a section of players divided into two or more groups each playing a different part. M18.
▸ **B** *noun.* (The use of) *divisi* playing or scoring. M20.

divisible /dɪˈvɪzɪb(ə)l/ *adjective.* LME.
[ORIGIN Old French & mod. French, or late Latin *divisibilis*, from Latin *divis-*: see DIVISION, -IBLE.]
1 Able to be divided (actually or in thought); distributable; distinguishable. LME.

J. PRIESTLEY Every particle of matter is infinitely divisible. T. DREISER Giving her the half of his property, stocks, ready money, and anything else that might be divisible.

2 *MATH.* Of a quantity: able to be divided without remainder *by* another quantity. Formerly, that is to be divided, forming the dividend. **L16.**

■ **divisiˈbility** *noun* **M17.** **divisibleness** *noun* (*rare*) divisibility **M17.** **divisibly** *adverb* **M16.**

division /dɪˈvɪʒ(ə)n/ *noun.* **LME.**

[ORIGIN Old French *devisiun*, *di-* (mod. *division*) from Latin *divisio(n-)*, from *divis-* pa. ppl stem of *dividere* DIVIDE *verb*: see -ION.]

▸ **I** An action or condition.

1 The action of dividing or state of being divided into parts or branches; separation, partition; severance; an instance of this. **LME.** ▸**b** (Also **D-**.) The separation of the members of a legislative body etc. into two groups in voting. **M16.** ▸**c** The splitting of the roots of a perennial plant into parts to be replanted separately, as a means of propagation. **E19.**

C. CAUDWELL The very division of industrial capitalism from agricultural capitalism has . . separated the country from the town. R. HOGGART There is a rough division of material into three themes. M. L. KING The . . division of India and Pakistan shattered his heart's desire for a united nation.

2 The action of distributing among a number; distribution, sharing; an instance of this. **LME.**

division of labour the assigning of different parts of a job or manufacturing process etc. to different people.

†**3** The action or an act of distinguishing, or of perceiving or making a difference; (a) distinction. **LME–E17.**

4 The fact of being divided in opinion, sentiment, or interest; dissension, discord; an instance of this, a disagreement. **LME.**

A. F. DOUGLAS-HOME Not to allow any division in the Cabinet which could be represented as a split on . . policy.

5 *MATH.* The action or process of dividing one quantity by another; a method of doing this. **LME.**

long division a method of division in which intermediate stages of the calculation are written down as it is made (used with divisors greater than 12). **short division** a method of division in which the quotient is written down directly (used with divisors up to 12).

6 *LOGIC.* The action of dividing a wider class into two or more kinds or classes; enumeration of the parts of a whole or of the meanings of a term. **M16.**

7 *MUSIC.* The execution of a rapid melodic passage, esp. by dividing each of a succession of long notes into several short ones; a florid phrase or melody; *spec.* a variation (usu. improvised) on an accompanying melody. Now *hist.* **L16.** ▸†**b** *fig.* Variation. *rare* (Shakes.). Only in **E17.**

b SHAKES. *Macb.* The king-becoming graces, . . I have no relish of them; but abound In the division of each several crime, Acting it many ways.

†**8** Disposition, arrangement. *rare* (Shakes.). Only in **E17.**

▸ **II** A cause or result of dividing.

9 Something that divides or marks separation; a dividing line or mark; a boundary; a partition. **LME.** ▸**b** At Cambridge University, the date that divides the term into two halves. **E19.**

E. RUTHERFORD The maximum excursion of the needle . . being not more than three scale divisions.

10 Each of the parts into which something is or may be divided; a portion, a section. **LME.** ▸**b** Any of several major parts into which an organization, esp. an army, is divided; *spec.* a group of Army brigades or regiments; a portion of a ship's company assigned to a particular service (in *pl.*, the parade of a ship's company according to its divisions); a group of (esp. soccer) teams within a league between which fixtures are arranged. **L16.** ▸**c** A portion of a country, county, etc., marked off for some political, administrative, judicial, etc., purpose; *spec.* a part of a county or borough returning a Member of Parliament. **M17.** ▸**d** *BIOLOGY.* A section of a taxonomic grouping; *BOTANY* a basic taxonomic grouping ranking above class and below kingdom, equivalent to a phylum; *ZOOLOGY* a subsidiary category between major levels of classification. **M19.** ▸**e** *hist.* Either of the two or three categories of imprisonment without hard labour or penal servitude to which an offender could be sentenced. **M19.**

F. SMYTH Over the years, more divisions of blood type . . have been discovered. *Practical Gardening* Divide and transplant border perennials, . . only replanting the strongest, healthiest divisions. **e** ALDOUS HUXLEY The appeal . . won't . . do any good except perhaps to change his six months from second to first division.

b *Family Division*: see FAMILY.

– COMB.: **division bell**: rung to announce an imminent parliamentary division; *division lobby*: see LOBBY *noun* 3a; **division sign** the sign ÷, placed between two quantities to denote that the one preceding the sign is to be divided by the one following it.

■ **divisionary** *adjective* (*rare*) divisional **M17.**

divisional /dɪˈvɪʒ(ə)n(ə)l/ *adjective.* **M17.**

[ORIGIN from DIVISION + -AL¹.]

1 Of the nature of division; pertaining to or characterized by division. **M17.**

2 Of or pertaining to a division. **M19.**

Divisional Court: consisting of two or three judges from a Division of the High Court.

■ **divisionaliˈzation** *noun* (the introduction of) a divisional organization or structure **M20.** **divisionalize** *verb trans.* organize (esp. a company) on a divisional basis **L20.** **divisionally** *adverb* **L18.**

divisionism /dɪˈvɪʒ(ə)nɪz(ə)m/ *noun.* **E20.**

[ORIGIN formed as DIVISIONAL + -ISM.]

ART. The practice of painting with pure colours, using the juxtaposition of contrasting unmixed colours in place of mixed colours.

■ **divisionist** *adjective & noun* (**a**) *adjective* of or pertaining to divisionism; (**b**) *noun* a practitioner or adherent of divisionism: **E20.**

divisive /dɪˈvʌɪsɪv/ *noun & adjective.* **M16.**

[ORIGIN Late Latin *divisivus*, from Latin *divis-*: see DIVISION, -IVE.]

▸ †**A** *noun.* Something which divides or separates. *rare.* Only in **M16.**

▸ **B** *adjective.* **1** Having the quality or function of dividing; causing or expressing division or distribution; making or perceiving distinctions, analytical. **L16.**

CARLYLE As the one spirit was intuitive, all-embracing . . so the other was scholastic, divisive.

2 Producing or tending to division of opinion, discord, or disunion. **M17.**

A. WEST The class of explosively divisive happenings that cause men and women to think *Enough!* and walk out on their lovers.

■ **divisively** *adverb* **L15.** **divisiveness** *noun* **M19.**

divisor /dɪˈvʌɪzə/ *noun.* **LME.**

[ORIGIN French *diviseur* or Latin *divisor*, from *divis-*: see DIVISION, -OR.]

MATH. **1** A quantity by which another (the ***dividend***) is to be divided. **LME.**

2 A quantity that divides another exactly without a remainder; a factor. **M16.**

divisory /dɪˈvʌɪz(ə)ri/ *adjective.* **E17.**

[ORIGIN medieval Latin *divisorius*, from Latin *divis-*: see DIVISION, -ORY².]

Pertaining to division or distribution among a number.

divorce /dɪˈvɔːs/ *noun.* **LME.**

[ORIGIN Old French & mod. French from Latin *divortium* separation, divorce, from *divortere*, *divertere* DIVERT.]

1 Legal dissolution of marriage by a court or other competent body, or according to recognized forms; a decree dissolving a marriage. **LME.**

G. GORER The people who would end the marriage legally, by divorce or separation.

attrib.: *divorce case*, *divorce court*, *divorce law*, etc.

2 Severance, complete separation, esp. of what ought to be or have been united. **LME.**

B. RUSSELL Slavery began the divorce between the purpose of the work and the purposes of the worker.

†**3** Something which causes divorce or separation. *rare* (Shakes.). **L16–E17.**

■ **divorceless** *adjective* not practising or liable to divorce **L16.**

divorce /dɪˈvɔːs/ *verb.* **LME.**

[ORIGIN Old French & mod. French *divorcer* from late Latin *divortiare*, from *divortium*: see DIVORCE *noun*.]

1 *verb trans.* Legally dissolve the marriage of (a husband and wife); separate (a spouse) by divorce *from*. Freq. in *pass.* **LME.**

SHAKES. *3 Hen. VI* I here divorce myself Both from thy table, Henry, and thy bed.

2 *verb trans.* Obtain a divorce from (a husband or wife). **LME.**

O. MANNING Quintin is married already and his wife won't divorce him.

3 *verb trans. fig.* Separate, sever, detach, (*from*). **LME.**

R. NIEBUHR If a socialist commonwealth should succeed in divorcing privilege from power.

4 *verb trans.* Dissolve (a marriage or union). *arch.* **L16.**

5 *verb trans. fig.* Put away, remove, dispel; repudiate. *arch.* **L16.**

SHAKES. *Rich. II* The man That would divorce this terror from my heart.

6 *verb intrans.* Legally dissolve one's marriage, obtain a divorce. **M17.**

J. CHEEVER She had left me twice before—the second time, we divorced and then remarried.

■ **divorceable** *adjective* **M17.** **divorcement** *noun* the action of divorcing; the fact of being divorced; (a) complete separation: **E16.** **divorcer** *noun* **E17.**

divorcé *noun* see DIVORCEE.

divorcee /dɪvɔːˈsiː/ *noun.* Also (earlier) ***divorcé***, (fem.) ***-ée***, /dɪˈvɔːseɪ/ (*pl. same*), dɪvɔːˈseɪ/. **E19.**

[ORIGIN Partly from French *divorcé(e)* use as noun of pa. ppl adjective of *divorcer* DIVORCE *verb*, partly from DIVORCE *verb* + -EE¹ after the French.]

A divorced person.

divot /ˈdɪvət/ *noun & verb.* **E16.**

[ORIGIN Unknown.]

▸ **A** *noun.* **1** A slice of earth with the grass growing on it, a sod, esp. as formerly used for roofing cottages etc.; such sods collectively. *Scot. & N. English.* **E16.**

fail and divot: see FAIL *noun*¹.

2 *GOLF.* A piece of turf cut out by the club head when a stroke is made. **L19.**

▸ **B** *verb. Scot.*

1 *verb trans.* Roof (a building) with divots. **L17.**

2 *verb intrans.* Cut divots. **L18.**

divulgate /dʌɪˈvʌlgeɪt, dɪ-/ *verb trans.* Now *rare.* Pa. pple & ppl adjective †**-ate** (earlier), **-ated.** **LME.**

[ORIGIN Latin *divulgat-* pa. ppl stem of *divulgare*: see DIVULGE, -ATE³.]

Make commonly known.

■ **divulˈgation** *noun* †(**a**) publication; (**b**) (a) disclosure: **M16.**

divulge /dʌɪˈvʌldʒ, dɪ-/ *verb.* **LME.**

[ORIGIN Latin *divulgare*, formed as DIS- 1 + *vulgare* publish, propagate, from *vulgus* common people.]

†**1** *verb trans.* Make publicly known; publish (a statement, book, etc.). **LME–L18.** ▸†**b** Make a public announcement about (a person). **L16–L17.**

b SHAKES. *Merry W.* I will . . divulge Page himself for a secure and wilful Actæon.

2 *verb trans.* Declare or tell openly (something private or secret); disclose, reveal. **E17.**

M. LAVIN Plans which . . he would shortly have to divulge to the family. G. SWIFT Freddie . . was a great blabber-mouth and divulged everything.

3 *verb intrans.* Become publicly known. *rare.* **E17.**

†**4** *verb trans.* Make common, impart generally. *rare* (Milton). Only in **M17.**

■ **divulgement** *noun* †(**a**) *rare* something that is divulged; (**b**) divulgence: **M17.** **divulgence** *noun* the action of divulging, disclosure **M19.** **divulger** *noun* **E17.**

divulsion /dʌɪˈvʌlʃ(ə)n, dɪ-/ *noun.* Now *rare.* **E17.**

[ORIGIN French, or Latin *divulsio(n-)*, from *divuls-*: see DIVULSIVE, -ION.]

The action of tearing or pulling apart; (a) violent separation.

divulsive /dʌɪˈvʌlsɪv, dɪ-/ *adjective.* Now *rare.* **E17.**

[ORIGIN from Latin *divuls-* pa. ppl stem of *divellere* (see DIVELL) + -IVE.]

Tending to tear apart.

Divvers /ˈdɪvəz/ *noun. Oxford Univ. slang.* Now *hist.* **L19.**

[ORIGIN from DIVINITY: see -ER⁶.]

Divinity moderations (the first public examination in divinity).

divvy /ˈdɪvi/ *noun*¹ *& verb. colloq.* Also **divi.** **L19.**

[ORIGIN Abbreviation of DIVIDEND.]

▸ **A** *noun.* A dividend; a share, a portion. **L19.**

▸ **B** *verb trans. & intrans.* Divide (*up*), share. **L19.**

divvy /ˈdɪvi/ *adjective*¹. *slang.* Now *rare.* **E20.**

[ORIGIN from DIVINE *adjective* + -Y¹. Cf. DEEVY.]

Delightful, 'divine', 'heavenly'.

divvy /ˈdɪvi/ *adjective*² *& noun*². *dial. & slang.* **L20.**

[ORIGIN Unknown.]

▸ **A** *adjective.* Foolish, idiotic. **L20.**

▸ **B** *noun.* A fool, an idiot. **L20.**

Diwali /dɪˈwɑːliː/ *noun.* Also **Dewali**, **Divali.** **L17.**

[ORIGIN Hindi *diwālī* from Sanskrit *dīpāvalī*, *dīpālī* row of lights, from *dīpa* light, lamp.]

A Hindu festival with lights, held over three nights in the period October to November.

diwan(i) *nouns* vars. of DEWAN(I).

dix /diːs/ *noun.* **L19.**

[ORIGIN French = ten, from Latin *decem*.]

The lowest trump in bezique and related card games, entitling a player to a score of ten points.

dix-huitième /dizɥitjɛm/ *adjective & noun.* **E20.**

[ORIGIN French = eighteenth.]

(Of or pertaining to) the eighteenth century in France.

Dixie /ˈdɪksi/ *noun*¹. *US.* **M19.**

[ORIGIN Unknown.]

The southern states of the US, the South.

– COMB.: **Dixieland** (**a**) Dixie; (**b**) a kind of jazz characterized by a rhythm strongly accenting the second and fourth beats and by collective improvisation.

■ **Dixiecrat** *noun* (*colloq.*) any of the southern Democrats who seceded from the party in 1948 in opposition to its policy of extending civil rights; any dissident or right-wing Democrat: **M20.**

dixie /ˈdɪksi/ *noun*². **E20.**

[ORIGIN Hindi *degcī* cooking pot from Persian *degča* dim. of *deg* iron pot.]

A large iron kettle or pot in which stew, tea, etc., is made or carried by soldiers etc.

dixit /ˈdɪksɪt/ *noun.* **L16.**

[ORIGIN Latin = he has said: see IPSE DIXIT.]

An utterance or statement (quoted as) already made.

DIY *abbreviation.*

Do-it-yourself.

D

D

diz /dɪz/ *verb & noun*. Now *rare*. Also **dizz**. **M17**.
[ORIGIN Back-form. from DIZZY *adjective* after *craze*, *crazy*, etc.]
▸ **A** *verb trans.* Infl. **-zz-**. Make dizzy or giddy. **M17**.
▸ **B** *noun*. The action of making dizzy or giddy. *rare*. **E19**.

dizen /ˈdʌɪz(ə)n, ˈdɪ-/ *verb trans.* Now *arch. & poet.* **M16**.
[ORIGIN from base repr. by the 1st syll. of DISTAFF and in Middle Dutch *disen* (perh. the immediate source): see -EN[5].]
†**1** Dress (a distaff) with flax etc. for spinning. **M–L16**.
2 Dress, esp. with finery; deck *out*, bedizen. Also foll. by *up*. **E17**.

dizygotic /dʌɪzʌɪˈɡɒtɪk/ *adjective*. **M20**.
[ORIGIN from DI-[2] + ZYGOTE + -IC.]
Of twins: derived from two separate ova, and so not identical.

dizygous /dʌɪˈzʌɪɡəs/ *adjective*. **M20**.
[ORIGIN from DI-[2] + Greek *zugon* yoke + -OUS.]
= DIZYGOTIC.

dizz *verb & noun* var. of DIZ.

dizzard /ˈdɪzɑːd/ *noun*. Now *rare* or *obsolete*. Also **disard**. **E16**.
[ORIGIN Uncertain: perh. modified from DISOUR; in sense 2 app. assoc. with DIZZY *adjective*.]
†**1** = DISOUR. **E16–E17**.
2 A fool, a blockhead. **M16**.

dizzy /ˈdɪzi/ *adjective*.
[ORIGIN Old English *dysiġ* = Old Frisian *dusig*, Middle Dutch *dosech*, *dösech*, Low German *dusig*, *dösig* giddy, Old High German *tusic* foolish, weak, from West Germanic: see -Y[1].]
1 Foolish, stupid. Long *obsolete* exc. *dial.* **OE**.
2 Having a sensation of whirling in the head with one's sense of balance disordered and a consequent tendency to fall; giddy. **ME**.
3 Mentally or morally unsteady or in a whirl; lacking mental or moral stability; *colloq.* scatterbrained. **E16**.

B. JOWETT My head is dizzy with thinking of the argument. D. HAMMETT A dizzy blonde that likes men and fun and hasn't got much sense.

4 Accompanied by or producing dizziness; making dizzy; *spec.* (of a mountain, tower, etc.) very high. **E17**.
5 Arising from or caused by giddiness; reeling, tottering. **E18**.

GEO. ELIOT Thought gave way to a dizzy horror, as if the earth were slipping away from under him.

6 Whirling rapidly (*lit. & fig.*). **L18**.
7 Startling, astonishing. *slang*. **L19**.
■ **dizzily** *adverb* **ME**. **dizziness** *noun* **OE**.

dizzy /ˈdɪzi/ *verb*.
[ORIGIN Old English *dysigan* = Old Frisian *dusia*; branch II re-formed from the adjective.]
▸ †**I** *verb intrans.* **1** Act foolishly or stupidly. **OE–ME**.
▸ **II** *verb trans.* **2** Make dizzy. **E16**.
3 Bewilder, confuse mentally. **E17**.

J. BARZUN World trade was increasing at a dizzying rate.

■ **dizzyingly** *adverb* in a dizzying manner, amazingly, bewilderingly **E20**.

Dizzyite /ˈdɪzɪʌɪt/ *noun*. **L19**.
[ORIGIN from *Dizzy*, nickname of Benjamin Disraeli (see below) + -ITE[1].]
A follower or admirer of the Conservative statesman and writer Benjamin Disraeli (1804–81).

DJ *abbreviation & verb*.
▸ **A** *abbreviation*. **1** Dinner jacket.
2 Disc jockey.
▸ **B** *verb intrans.* Pa. t. & pple **DJ'd**. Perform as a disc jockey, esp. in a club.

djellaba /ˈdʒɛləbə/ *noun*. Also **djellabah**, **jellaba**, **jelab** /ˈdʒɛləb/. **E19**.
[ORIGIN Moroccan Arab. *jellāb(a)*, *jellābiyya*: cf. GALABIYA.]
A loose hooded long-sleeved cloak of a kind worn orig. by Arab men in N. Africa.

djembe /ˈdʒɛmbə/ *noun*. **L20**.
[ORIGIN French *djembé*, from Mande *jembe*.]
A kind of goblet-shaped hand drum originating in West Africa.

djibba(h) *noun* var. of JIBBA.

djinn *noun* var. of JINN.

dkl *abbreviation*. *US*.
Dekaliter(s).

dkm *abbreviation*. *US*.
Dekameter(s).

DL *abbreviation*[1].
1 Deputy Lieutenant.
2 *N. Amer.* SPORT. Disabled list.

dl *abbreviation*[2].
Decilitre(s).

D.Litt. *abbreviation*.
Latin *Doctor Litterarum* Doctor of Letters.

dlr *abbreviation*.
Dollar.

DM *abbreviation*[1]. *hist.*
Deutschmark.

dm *abbreviation*[2].
Decimetre(s).

D-mark *abbreviation*.
Deutschmark.

DMD *abbreviation*.
Duchenne muscular dystrophy.

d.m.u. *abbreviation*.
Diesel multiple unit (railway vehicle).

D.Mus. *abbreviation*.
Doctor of Music.

DMZ *abbreviation*.
Demilitarized zone.

DNA /diːɛnˈeɪ/ *noun*. **M20**.
[ORIGIN Abbreviation of DEOXYRIBONUCLEIC *acid*.]
A nucleic acid in which the sugar component is deoxyribose; a self-replicating material present in nearly all living organisms, esp. in chromosomes, as the carrier of genetic information and the determiner of protein synthesis, and consisting of a very long double-stranded helical chain of sugars joined by phosphate bonds and cross-linked by pairs of organic bases. Cf. RNA.
– COMB.: **DNA polymerase** any of several enzymes which synthesize DNA and are responsible for its repair and replication; **DNA virus** a virus in which the genetic information is stored in the form of DNA.
■ **DNase** /diːɛnˈeɪz/ *noun* an enzyme which breaks DNA up into smaller molecules, a deoxyribonuclease **M20**.

DNB *abbreviation*.
Dictionary of National Biography.

DNR *abbreviation*.
1 Department of Natural Resources. *US*.
2 MEDICINE (orig. & chiefly *US*). Do not resuscitate.

DNS *abbreviation*.
COMPUTING. Domain name server (or system).

do /duː/ *noun*[1]. Pl. **dos**, **do's**. **L16**.
[ORIGIN from DO *verb*.]
1 a The action of doing; that which is done; business, concern; in *pl.*, affairs. Now *rare* or *obsolete*. **L16**. ▸**b** Something done in a set or elaborate manner; an entertainment; a party, a social function; a military engagement. *colloq.* **E19**. ▸**c** *sing.* & (usu.) in *pl.* Behaviour towards someone, treatment. Chiefly in ***fair dos***, equitable treatment, fair shares. *colloq.* **M19**.

a O. CROMWELL It's probable the Kirk has done their doo. **b** B. BAINBRIDGE Met him at a masonic do last year.

b *poor do*: see POOR *adjective*.
2 Commotion, trouble; a fuss, an ado. *obsolete* exc. *dial.* **L16**.
3 A swindle; an imposture; a hoax. *slang*. **E19**.
4 A success. Only in ***make a do of***. *Austral. & NZ colloq.* **E20**.
5 An instruction; an injunction to do something. Usu. in *pl.* in ***dos and don'ts***. **E20**.
6 = ***hairdo*** s.v. HAIR *noun*. *colloq.* **E20**.
7 Excrement. *nursery & slang*. **L20**.
– COMB.: **do-rag** *US black slang* a scarf or cloth worn to protect one's hairstyle.

do *noun*[2] var. of DOH.

do /duː, *unstressed* dʊ/ *verb*. Pres. indic.: 1, 2, *pl.*, & (*dial.*) 3 **do**; 3 **does** /dʌz, d(ə)z/; 2 (*arch.*) **doest** /ˈduːɪst/ (now confined to the principal verb), **dost** /dʌst, dəst/ (now usu. aux.); 3 (*arch. & poet.*) **doth** /dʌθ, dəθ/ or **doeth** /ˈduːɪθ/. Past indic.: **did** /dɪd/; also (*non-standard*) **done** /dʌn/, 2 (*arch.*) **didst** /dɪdst/. Pres. subjunct.: **do**. Past subjunct.: **did**. Imper. **do**. Pres. pple **doing** /ˈduːɪŋ/. Pa. pple **done**. Informal abbreviated forms: **didn't** /ˈdɪd(ə)nt/ = ***did not***; **doesn't** /ˈdʌz(ə)nt/ = ***does not***; **don't** /dəʊnt/ = ***do not***, (*non-standard*) ***does not***; **'s** /s/ = ***does*** (interrog.). Scottish forms: **dae** /deɪ/ = ***do***; **dinna** /ˈdɪnə/ = ***do not***, **disna** /ˈdɪznə/ = ***does not***. See also DUNNO.
[ORIGIN Old English *dōn* corresp. to Old Frisian *duā*, Old Saxon *dōn* (Dutch *doen*), Old High German *tuon* (German *tun*), from West Germanic from Indo-European stem repr. also by Sanskrit *dadhāmi* put, lay, Greek *tithēmi* I place, Latin *facere* make, do. Cf. DEED *noun*, DOOM *noun*[1].]
▸ **I** *verb trans.* as full verb.
1 a Put, place, (*lit. & fig.*). *obsolete* exc. *dial.*, with prepositions (see ***do off*** etc. below), & in ***do to*** DEATH. **OE**. ▸†**b** *refl.* Put or set oneself; proceed, go. Only in **ME**. ▸†**c** Use, disburse, (money) for a particular purpose. **LME–E16**.

a J. FOXE If I would not tell where I had done him. WILLIAM STEWART He did him in his will.

2 Confer on, impart to, (a person etc.); cause (a person etc.) to receive (something abstract, usu. good). Also foll. by *to* the recipient. **OE**.

LD BERNERS The which dyd them great trouble. F. MARRYAT I did a gipsy a good turn once. S. WALPOLE A day's sport which would have done credit to these modern days. M. KEANE A brisk walk would do you good. W. GOLDING To call them 'assistants' does their memory scant justice.

3 Perform, effect, engage in, be the agent of, (an action, good, work, etc.); carry out (a function, duty, etc.); carry out, obey, (a command, wish, etc.); follow (advice, a bidding); perform duly (a ritual, esp. penance); *arch.* commit (a crime). **OE**. ▸**b** In an interrog. or indef. clause introduced by *what*: follow as an occupation, work at for a living. **E20**.

AV *Matt.* 6:10 Thy will be done. DEFOE We knew not what to do with this poor girl. R. H. MOTTRAM Powerful, docile servants of a younger age, that could do the work of ten men. V. WOOLF As the whole thing is a bad joke, let us, at any rate, do our part. IRVING BERLIN Anything you can do, I can do better. E. WAUGH A smartly dressed young man was doing a brisk trade in bogus tickets. C. P. SNOW It doesn't do any harm to touch wood. **b** J. BETJEMAN You ask me what it is I do . . . I'm partly a liaison man and partly P.R.O.

4 a As pa. pple (*done*), esp. in perf. tenses. Accomplished, finished, brought to a conclusion; (of a wager etc.) accepted, agreed, (freq. *absol.* as *interjection*). **ME**. ▸**b** Exhaust; ruin, be the downfall of, (a person); *slang* beat up, kill, defeat. **LME**. ▸**c** In *pass.* Have nothing more to say or to do; have finished; (foll. by *with*) give up concern or lose interest in. **M18**.

a SWIFT When dinner is done. DICKENS 'Dine with me to-morrow.' . . 'Done!' RIDER HAGGARD By the time that the horses had done their forage. D. L. SAYERS Mr. Bunter congratulated himself on a number of things attempted and done. S. BECKETT Have you not done tormenting me? **c** F. MARRYAT One little bit more, and then I am done. E. REVELEY Heidi was soon done with literature.

5 Exert or use (one's best, one's diligence, etc.) in effecting something. **ME**.

DEFOE They bade the Swedes do their worst. P. H. JOHNSON I do my best for her.

†**6** Deliver (a message). **E16–E18**.
7 Deal with, do things to, perform actions on, (the nature of the action being usu. inferable from the obj. or subj.); *esp.* arrange (hair, flowers); decorate or clean (a room); cook (food), esp. to the right degree (usu. in *pass.*); wash (crockery); tend (a garden); attend to (a person), subject (a person) to immunization, a test, etc.; neuter or spay (an animal). **E16**.

M. DRABBLE The spaghetti was not quite done. J. WINTERSON She played *Lead Kindly Light*. Her doing the keys, and me doing the pedals.

8 Produce, bring into existence by one's action. **L16**. ▸**b** Of a public house, hotel, etc.: provide (meals, accommodation). **L20**.

C. HOLLYBAND We have done five or six copies in the same paper. E. NESBIT It's the pipe we did bubbles with in the summer. **b** W. J. BURLEY The Marina doesn't do meals other than breakfast.

9 Act (a play); play the part of. **L16**.

E. BOWEN Colonel Duperrier asked her to pour out tea and do hostess. *Times* Institutions under threat of closure . . are saying 'They're doing a Beeching on us.'

10 Work at, study; take (a course of instruction); (of an artist, reviewer, etc.) take as one's subject; translate (*into*). **M17**.

R. BUCHANAN There Amos often sat and did his accounts. O. W. HOLMES Life is painting a picture, not doing a sum. I. MURDOCH She'll . . do a secretarial course next year. G. SWIFT Children, do you remember when we did the French Revolution?

11 Hoax, cheat, swindle. *slang*. **M17**.
12 Traverse (a distance); attain, travel at, (a speed). **L18**.

T. MOORE Did the four miles in less than twenty minutes. G. B. SHAW The old cars only do twelve miles to the gallon. J. MASTERS Patrick passed us on his Norton, doing about seventy.

13 Break into, steal from, (a place). *slang*. **L18**.
14 Arrest; charge with an offence; convict. *slang*. **L18**.

S. TOWNSEND If he's not careful he will get done by the police for obscene language.

15 Visit, see the sights of, (a place); attend (an entertainment). *colloq.* **E19**.
16 Spend (a time) as a prisoner, serve. *slang*. **M19**.
17 Be sufficient for, satisfy, (a person). Cf. sense 27 below. *colloq.* **M19**.

M. GEE Will fish and chips do you?

18 Orig., drink (an alcoholic liquor). Now, take or smoke (a drug) otherwise than therapeutically. *slang*. **M19**.
19 Provide food or lodgings for; treat or entertain *well*. *colloq.* **L19**.

J. K. JEROME He said they would do him for the whole week at two pounds five.

20 Look after and manage (a horse); *dial. & NZ* look after, provide food for, (sheep). **L19**.
21 Have sexual intercourse with. *coarse slang*. **L19**.
22 Spend all of. Also foll. by *in*. *Austral. & NZ slang*. **L19**.
▸ **II** *verb intrans.* as full verb.
23 Act or behave in a specified way; perform some activity. **OE**. ▸**b** Perform deeds; be active. **LME**.

J. SELDEN Preachers say, Do as I say, not as I do. A. RADCLIFFE He had done imprudently to elect her for the companion of his whole life. N. MITFORD When in Rome . . we do as the Romans do. **b** LONGFELLOW Let us . . be up and doing. G. K. CHESTERTON At Trafalgar . . We did and died like lions. *Times* Younger people, with no money and no showrooms but ready to do for themselves.

24 Proceed in an emergency or difficulty; manage, get by. ME.

SHAKES. *Rich. II* How shall we do for money for these wars? R. MACAULAY They could just do on it . . with what she herself earned.

25 Fare, get on, make progress, *spec.* as regards health. Foll. by adverb, esp. *well*. ME.

SHAKES. *2 Hen. IV* May I ask how my lady his wife doth? E. B. BROWNING She was ill only three hours and is doing excellently now. M. DRABBLE Mrs Maugham had done well at school. J. GRENFELL Say how-do-you-do to Mr Hindhorst. C. CAUSLEY Telling him How the lobelias are doing.

26 In perf. tenses (***have done*** etc.). Make an end, conclude; cease to have dealings *with*. ME.

CARLYLE There is endless merit in a man's knowing when to have done. W. GOLDING Let us have done with her for a moment.

27 Serve a purpose, suffice; be adequate; be suitable, acceptable, or appropriate. Cf. sense 17 above. L16.

CHESTERFIELD Adieu, my dear! I find you will do. E. A. FREEMAN It would hardly have done to send him. I. MURDOCH Would the same time on Sunday morning do for Miles? P. CAMPBELL I had one fairly good dark suit . . that would do for the evenings.

▸ **III** As aux. verb (see also sense 35 below).

28 Causative uses. ▸†**a** Cause *that* a person or thing should do something; produce the effect *that*. OE–LME. ▸**b** With obj. & inf.: cause (a person etc.) to or *to* (do something, esp. know, or be done). Now *arch. rare*. OE. ▸†**c** With inf. only: cause to or *to* (do or be done). ME–M16.

b SPENSER Sometimes, to do him laugh, she would assay To laugh. SIR W. SCOTT We . . do thee, Sir Patrick Charteris . . to know, that [etc.].

29 As a substitute for a verb just used. ▸**a** *verb intrans.* Repl. a verb & its obj. (if any) in affirmatives, and in imperatives conveying assent to a request or suggestion. OE. ▸**b** *verb intrans. & trans.* (with *it*). Repl. a verb, with *as*, *it*, *so*, or *which* referring to the earlier verb or clause. OE. ▸**c** *verb trans. & intrans.* Repl. a verb and taking its construction(s). ME. ▸**d** *verb intrans.* Repl. a verb in an emphatic repetition. L16. ▸**e** *verb intrans.* Ellipt. for periphrastic aux. (sense 30 below). E17.

a JOHN COLLINS We pay double the price we formerly did. G. B. SHAW *Lady Farwaters*. May I try to explain? *The Clergyman*. Please do. D. ABSE I feel much better now than I did a month ago. **b** W. CRUISE Whoever wanted to surrender must . . do it in person. S. T. WARNER He told them to go away, he even begged them to do so. A. T. ELLIS The churches are closing, as the cinemas did. **c** GOLDSMITH I . . chose my wife, as she did her wedding-gown. **d** P. BEER He rang me up In a dream, My brother did. D. L. SAYERS 'Ev another crumpet, do, Mr. Bunter. **e** J. CONRAD Everybody supposed Haldin was in the provinces . . . Didn't you? E. BOWEN 'I cleared out.' 'So you did.'

30 As periphrastic aux. in past and pres. tenses. ▸**a** In simple affirmative sentences. Now *arch. & dial.* exc. LAW. OE. ▸**b** In affirmative sentences with inverted word order. OE. ▸**c** In questions and negations; now usual exc. with *dare*, *ought*; not used with *be*, *can*, *may*, or *must*, nor with *have* as aux. (nor, formerly, with *have* as verb trans.). LME. ▸**d** In affirmative sentences, used to give emphasis, esp. in contrast with what precedes or follows. L16.

a *Book of Common Prayer* O Lord, who . . didst fast fourty days and fourty nights. **b** J. CONRAD More than any other event does 'stranding' bring to the sailor a sense of . . failure. **c** H. HUNTER Do we not see there . . talents distracted? J. FISKE The popular histories do not have much to say about these eighteen days. ANTHONY SMITH Do you like water-melon? **d** T. HARDY At last a packet did indeed arrive at the village. S. SPENDER The Dents du Midi do look incredibly like teeth. R. P. JHABVALA For all she was so thin and white, she did look tough.

31 As periphrastic aux. in imperatives. ▸**a** Adding emphasis or urgency to an exhortation or command. OE. ▸**b** Used with *not* (colloq. jointly contr. to *don't*) as the now normal form of the neg. imper. L16.

a T. HARDY Do you hop up here. M. KEANE Oh Mother, do let them come. **b** J. CONRAD And don't you forget it. DYLAN THOMAS Do not go gentle into that good night.

32 In progressive active tense (***be doing***): ▸**a** Happen, go on; (of an activity or, formerly, an object) be doing done. Cf. ***nothing doing*** below. ME. ▸**b** In an interrog. or indef. clause introduced by *what*: have as an explanation or reason for being (in a place). M18.

S. PEPYS My closett is doing by upholsters. M. W. MONTAGU What is doing among my acquaintance at London. L. MANN He had invited her so that he might ascertain whether there was anything doing. **b** J. JOHNSTON What's that fellow doing here? I. MURDOCH She lay awake wondering what that . . hairy body was doing in her bed.

▸ **IV** *spec.* uses of parts of the verb (see also senses 4, 26, 32 above).

33 ***to do*** inf., after *be* (in 3rd person) or a noun: proper or necessary to be done; (formerly also) the thing to be done. Cf. TO-DO. ME.

P. A. MOTTEUX There was the Devil and all to do.

†**34** ***do*** imper.: go on! (as a word of encouragement or incitement). LME–E17.

35 ***done*** pa. pple: used as a perfective aux., and as adverb in senses 'already', 'completely'. *US dial.* E19.

J. H. BEADLE People have done forgot they had any Injun blood in 'em. E. T. WALLACE I don't know what you need with another boy. You done got four. F. O'CONNOR He done gone off with a woman.

36 ***don't***: used in 3rd person neg. imperatives after *let's*, in place of simple *not*. *US slang*. M20.

New Yorker Let's don't go yet.

– PHRASES: ***can do***: see CAN *verb*[1]. **do a —** *colloq.* behave like, do an impersonation of, (a specified person). ***do a guy***: see GUY *noun*[2]. ***do a hand's turn***: see HAND *noun*. ***do a line with***: see LINE *noun*[2]. ***do a number on***: see NUMBER *noun*. ***do any good***: see GOOD *noun*. ***do a person in the eye***: see EYE *noun*. **do a person proud**, **do oneself proud** *colloq.* give a person, oneself, reason for being proud, treat with honour or great generosity. ***do a person wrong***: see WRONG *noun*[2]. ***do a ton***: see TON *noun*[1]. ***do battle***: see BATTLE *noun*. ***do brown***: see BROWN *adjective* 3. ***do dirt to***: see DIRT *noun*. ***do good***: see GOOD *noun*. ***do homage***: see HOMAGE *verb* 1. **do it** (***a***) *colloq.* have sexual intercourse; (***b***) *slang* urinate; defecate; (***c***) succeed in a task etc. ***done to a turn***: see TURN *noun*. **don't — me** *colloq.* do not use the word — or mention the name of — to me. ***do one's bit***: see BIT *noun*[2]. ***do one's block***: see BLOCK *noun* 6b. **do oneself well** *colloq.* make liberal provision for one's creature comforts (cf. sense 17 above). **do one's head**, **do one's nut** *slang* become very worried or angry. ***do one's own thing***: see THING *noun*[1]. ***do one's scone***: see SCONE 3. ***do one's stuff***: see STUFF *noun*. ***do one's thing***: see THING *noun*[1]. ***do one's utmost***: see UTMOST *noun* 2b. **do or die** perform deeds in the face of great danger. ***do right by***: see RIGHT *noun*[1]. **do something for**, **do something to** *colloq.* enhance the appearance or quality of. **do the —** *colloq.* do what is (proper etc.), be (amiable etc.); (***do the dirty***: see DIRTY *noun*). ***do the other thing***: see OTHER *adjective*. ***do the ton***: see TON *noun*[1]. ***do the trick***: see TRICK *noun*. ***do things to***: see THING *noun*[1]. ***do to*** DEATH. ***do violence to***: see VIOLENCE. **do well for oneself** prosper. **do well out of** profit by, benefit from. ***do wonders***: see WONDER *noun*. ***do wrong to***: see WRONG *noun*[2]. ***do your worst***: see WORST *adjective, adverb, & noun*. ***get done with***: see GET *verb*. **have done it** *colloq.* have made a mess of something, incur disaster (see also ***do it*** above); ***that's done it***, (***a***) (expr. dismay or exasperation) the limit of tolerance has been reached, that is the last straw; (***b***) (expr. delight) that achieves the desired end, that has brought success. **have to do** (***a***) *arch. & dial.* have business or concern (freq. *interrog.*); (***b***) be connected *with*, have business *with*, (freq. in ***have nothing to do***, ***not have anything to do***). ***how do*** (***you do***)?: see HOW *adverb*. ***I never did!*** **it isn't done**, (less usu.) **it is not done** *colloq.* it contravenes custom, opinion, or propriety. ***make do***: see MAKE *verb*. ***no can do***: see CAN *verb*[1]. **nothing doing** nothing is happening, there is no business; *colloq.* there is no chance of success; I will not comply or accept. **not know what to do with oneself** be embarrassed, be bored. **no you don't** *colloq.* I will prevent you (from doing what you were about to do or have just begun). ***over and done with***: see OVER *adverb*. ***tell a person what to do with —***: see TELL *verb*. **that will do** (***a***) that is sufficient; (***b***) (as exclam.) stop that! **what did you do with it?**, **what shall I do with it?** etc., where did you, shall I, etc., put it? ***when all is said and done***: see SAY *verb*[1].

– WITH ADVERBS IN SPECIALIZED SENSES: **do away** †(***a***) *verb phr. trans.* dismiss, remove; (***b***) *verb phr. trans.*, & (now usu.) *intrans.* with *with* put an end to, abolish. **do down** †(***a***) put down (*lit. & fig.*); (***b***) *colloq.* overcome; cheat, swindle. **do in** *slang* damage greatly, ruin; murder; (see also sense 21 above, DONE *ppl adjective* 3). **do off** *arch.* take off, remove. **do on** *arch.* put on, don. **do out** †(***a***) put out (*of*), remove, extinguish; (***b***) clean, redecorate, refurbish, (a room); (***c***) ***do a person out of***, deprive of, esp. fraudulently or unfairly. **do over** (***a***) overlay, cover, *with*; (***b***) *slang* = sense 11 above; (***c***) *colloq.* wear out, tire out, (usu. in *pass.*); (***d***) *Austral. & NZ slang* handle (a person) roughly; (***e***) *slang* = sense 21 above; (***f***) = ***do out*** (b) above; (***g***) *N. Amer.* do again. **do up** †(***a***) put up, raise, open; (***b***) repair, renovate; (***c***) wrap up (a parcel), make into a parcel; (***d***) dress up, adorn; (***e***) *slang* ruin; get the better of; beat up; (see also DONE *ppl adjective* 3).

– WITH PREPOSITIONS IN SPECIALIZED SENSES: **do by** act towards or deal with (a person) in a specified way. **do for** (***a***) (now *colloq.*) act for, manage; provide for, attend to; *esp.* act as housekeeper for; (***b***) *colloq.* ruin, seriously damage or injure, destroy, kill; (see also sense 27 above). **do to**, (*arch.*) **do unto** = ***do by*** above; (see also sense 2 above). **do with** (***a***) deal with, have to do with; (***b***) put up with, tolerate, accept; manage with, find sufficient; ***could do with*** (*colloq.*), would find useful or should like to have; (see also senses 4,26 and in Phrases above). **do without** manage without (something specified or (*absol.*) understood contextually); complete a task without.

do. *abbreviation*.
Ditto.

DOA *abbreviation*.
Dead on arrival (at hospital etc.).

doab /ˈdəʊab/ *noun*. Also **duab** /ˈduːab/. E19.
[ORIGIN Urdu from Persian *dō-āb*, from *dō* two + *āb* water.]
A tongue or tract of land between two confluent rivers, esp. in the Punjab.

doable /ˈduːəb(ə)l/ *adjective*. LME.
[ORIGIN from DO *verb* + -ABLE.]
Able to be done; practicable.

do-all /ˈduːɔːl/ *noun*. Now *rare*. M17.
[ORIGIN from DO *verb* + ALL.]
A factotum.

doat *verb* var. of DOTE *verb*[1].

doater *noun* var. of DOTER.

doatish *adjective* var. of DOTISH.

doaty *noun* var. of DOTEY.

doaty *adjective* var. of DOTY *adjective*.

dob /dɒb/ *verb*. Infl. **-bb-**. E19.
[ORIGIN Var. of DAB *verb*.]
1 *verb trans.* Put down with an abrupt movement. *dial.* E19.
2 *verb trans. & intrans.* Throw (a stone etc.) at a target. *dial.* M19.
3 *verb trans.* (foll. by *in*) & *intrans.* (foll. by *on*): betray, inform against. *slang* (chiefly *Austral. & NZ*). M20.
4 *verb trans.* Foll. by *in*: contribute (money) to a common cause. *Austral. & NZ slang*. M20.

D

dobber /ˈdɒbə/ *noun*[1]. *US local*. E19.
[ORIGIN Dutch.]
The float of a fishing line.

dobber /ˈdɒbə/ *noun*[2]. M19.
[ORIGIN Prob. from DOB *verb* + -ER[1].]
1 A lump; something unusually large. *dial.* M19.
2 A large marble. Chiefly *dial.* L19.

dobbie *noun* var. of DOBBY.

dobbin /ˈdɒbɪn/ *noun*. L16.
[ORIGIN Personal name *Dobbin* (dim. of *Dob*), altered forms of *Robin*, *Rob*. Sense 2 is perh. a distinct word.]
1 (A pet name for) a draught horse or farm horse. Sometimes *derog.*, an old horse. L16.
2 A small drinking vessel; *esp.* a short thick glass tumbler. L18.

dobby /ˈdɒbi/ *noun*. Also **dobbie**. L17.
[ORIGIN Perh. a playful application of personal name *Dobbie*, from *Dob* (see DOBBIN) + -Y[6].]
1 A stupid fellow, a simpleton. *dial.* L17.
2 A spirit or apparition attached to a particular house or locality; *esp.* a household brownie. *dial.* L18.
3 In full ***dobby-horse***. A wooden figure of a horse, used in folk plays or fairgrounds. Cf. HOBBY HORSE *noun*. M19.
4 A mechanism attached to a loom for weaving small devices similar to but simpler than those produced by a Jacquard loom. L19.
– COMB.: **dobby-weave** a patterned weave consisting of small geometric devices repeated frequently.

dobchick *noun* see DABCHICK.

dobe /ˈdəʊbi/ *noun*. *US colloq.* Also **'dobe**, **dobie**, **doby**. M19.
[ORIGIN Aphet.]
= ADOBE.

Dobermann /ˈdəʊbəmən/ *noun*. Also **-man**. E20.
[ORIGIN Ludwig *Dobermann*, 19th-cent. German dog-breeder.]
In full ***Dobermann pinscher***. (An animal of) a medium-sized breed of dog with a smooth coat, freq. used as a guard dog.

dobey /ˈdəʊbi/ *verb trans. nautical slang*. Also **dhob-**. E20.
[ORIGIN from DHOBI.]
Wash (clothes). Chiefly as ***dobeying*** *verbal noun*.

dobie *noun* var. of DOBE.

dobla /ˈdəʊblə/ *noun*. *obsolete* exc. *hist.* L16.
[ORIGIN Spanish. Cf. *doble* double.]
An obsolete Spanish gold coin.

Dobos Torte /ˈdɒbɒʃ ˌtɔːtə/ *noun phr.* Also **Dobos Torta**. Pl. **Dobos Torten** /ˈtɔːt(ə)n/. E20.
[ORIGIN German *Dobostorte*, from J. C. *Dobós* (1847–1924), Hungarian pastry cook + *Torte* tart, pastry, cake (cf. TORTE). Cf. Hungarian *dobostorta*.]
A rich cake made of alternate layers of sponge and chocolate or mocha cream, with a crisp caramel topping.

dobra /ˈdɒbrə/ *noun*. L20.
[ORIGIN Portuguese *dôbra* doubloon.]
The basic monetary unit of São Tomé and Principe, equal to 100 centavos.

dobro /ˈdɒbrəʊ/ *noun*. Orig. *US*. Also **D-**. Pl. **-os**. M20.
[ORIGIN from the *Do(pěra) Bro(thers*, its Czech-American inventors.]
(US proprietary name for) a type of acoustic guitar with steel resonating discs inside the body under the bridge, popular for playing country and western music.

dobson /ˈdɒbs(ə)n/ *noun*. *US*. L19.
[ORIGIN Unknown.]
A larva of a dobsonfly, esp. *Corydalus cornutus*, used as fish bait.
– COMB.: **dobsonfly** a large neuropterous insect (family Corydalidae) of continents other than Europe, the larva of which is predatory and aquatic.

Dobsonian /dɒbˈsəʊnɪən/ *adjective & noun*. L20.
[ORIGIN from John *Dobson*, 20th-cent. US amateur astronomer: see -IAN.]
ASTRONOMY. ▸**A** *adjective*. Designating or pertaining to a large aperture, short focal length, low-cost Newtonian reflecting telescope, or the simple altazimuth mount used for it. L20.

▸ **B** *noun.* A Dobsonian telescope. **L20.**

Dobson unit /ˈdɒbs(ə)n ˌjuːnɪt/ *noun phr.* **L20.**
[ORIGIN G. M. B. *Dobson* (1889–1976), Brit. meteorologist and pioneer of atmospheric ozone measurement.]
A unit of measurement for the total amount of ozone in the atmosphere above a point on the earth's surface, one Dobson unit being equivalent to a layer of pure ozone 0.01 mm thick at standard temperature and pressure.

doby *noun* var. of DOBE.

doc /dɒk/ *noun*[1]. *colloq.* **M19.**
[ORIGIN Abbreviation of DOCTOR *noun*.]
A person who is a doctor or has the title 'Doctor', *esp.* a medical practitioner.

doc /dɒk/ *noun*[2]. *slang.* **L20.**
[ORIGIN Abbreviation.]
A documentary.

Doccia /ˈdɒtʃɪə/ *noun.* **M19.**
[ORIGIN See below.]
In full ***Doccia porcelain***, ***Doccia china***, etc. A type of porcelain made at Doccia, an Italian town near Florence.

docent /ˈdəʊs(ə)nt, *foreign* doˈtsɛnt/ *noun.* **L19.**
[ORIGIN German *Docent*, *Dozent*, from Latin *docent-*: see DOCENT *adjective*, and cf. PRIVATDOZENT.]
1 Orig. = PRIVATDOZENT. Now, in certain US universities and colleges, a member of the teaching staff below professorial rank. **L19.**
2 A (usu. voluntary) guide in a museum, art gallery, or zoo. Chiefly *US*. **E20.**

docent /ˈdəʊs(ə)nt/ *adjective.* **M17.**
[ORIGIN Latin *docent-* pres. ppl stem of *docere* teach: see -ENT.]
That teaches or instructs.

Docete /ˈdəʊsiːt/ *noun.* Pl. **Docetes**, also in Latin form **Docetae** /dəʊˈsiːtiː/. **L18.**
[ORIGIN medieval Latin *Docetae* from patristic Greek *Dokētai*, from Greek *dokein* seem, appear.]
ECCLESIASTICAL HISTORY. A Docetist. Usu. in *pl.*

Docetism /dəʊˈsiːtɪz(ə)m/ *noun.* Also **Doket-** /dəʊˈkiːt-/. **M19.**
[ORIGIN from DOCETE + -ISM.]
CHRISTIAN CHURCH. The belief or doctrine, held as a heresy by some early Christians, that Christ's body was either a phantasm or of real but celestial substance, and his sufferings only apparent.
■ **docetic**, **D-** *adjective* of or pertaining to Docetism or Docetists **M19.** **docetically** *adverb* **L19.** **Docetist** *noun* a follower of docetic teaching **L19.**

doch an doris *noun phr.* var. of DEOCH AN DORIS.

dochmius /ˈdɒkmɪəs/ *noun.* Pl. **-mii** /-mɪʌɪ/. **E19.**
[ORIGIN Latin from Greek *dokhmios* lit. 'slanted, oblique'.]
CLASSICAL PROSODY. A metrical foot having the basic form of an iambus followed by a cretic.
■ **dochmiac** *adjective* & *noun* (**a**) *adjective* of the nature of a dochmius; composed of dochmii; (**b**) *noun* a dochmiac foot or verse: **L18.**

docible /ˈdɒsɪb(ə)l/ *adjective. obsolete* exc. *dial.* **LME.**
[ORIGIN French, or late Latin *docibilis*, from *docere* teach: see -IBLE.]
1 Capable of learning, teachable; docile, tractable. **LME.**
2 Able to be imparted by teaching. Now *rare.* **M17.**
■ **dociˈbility** *noun* **E17.**

docile /ˈdəʊsʌɪl/ *adjective.* **L15.**
[ORIGIN Latin *docilis*, from *docere* teach. Cf. French *docile* (16).]
1 Apt or willing to learn; teachable. Now *rare.* **L15.**
> S. AUSTIN His docile and intelligent pupil.

2 Submissive to training or direction, not assertive; easily managed, tractable. **L18.**
> A. LEWIS The milk-white oxen waited Docile at the yoke. D. MURPHY I sat beside my mother like the most docile of Victorian daughters.

3 Of a thing: submitting readily to treatment. **L18.**
■ **docilely** *adverb* **M19.**

docility /də(ʊ)ˈsɪlɪti/ *noun.* **M16.**
[ORIGIN Latin *docilitas*, formed as DOCILE: see -ITY. Cf. French *docilité* (15).]
The quality of being docile. Now *esp.* amenability to training or direction, lack of assertiveness, tractability.

docimastic /dɒsɪˈmastɪk/ *adjective.* **M18.**
[ORIGIN Greek *dokimastikos*, from *dokimazein* test, scrutinize: see -IC.]
Of or pertaining to the assay of metals.

docimasy /ˈdɒsɪməsi/ *noun.* Now *rare.* **E19.**
[ORIGIN Greek *dokimasia*, from *dokimazein*: see DOCIMASTIC, -Y[3].]
Subjection of something to experimental tests; *esp.* the assaying of metallic ores.

docity /ˈdɒsɪti/ *noun. colloq.* & *dial.* **L17.**
[ORIGIN App. alt. of DOCILITY.]
Quickness of comprehension; gumption.

dock /dɒk/ *noun*[1].
[ORIGIN Old English *docce*, corresp. to Middle Dutch *docke-blaederen* (whence German *Dockenblätter*), Old Danish *ådokke* (= Old English *ēadocce*).]
Any of several coarse weeds of the genus *Rumex*, of the knotgrass family, with sheathing stipules, whorls of inconspicuous usu. greenish flowers, and large leaves popularly used to relieve nettle stings; esp. *R. obtusifolius* and *R. crispus*. Also, any of various unrelated coarse plants of similar habit, *esp.* burdock.
in dock, out nettle: a charm uttered in applying dock leaves to nettle stings; formerly also, a proverbial expression for changeableness and inconstancy. ***patience-dock***: see PATIENCE *noun*. ***sour dock***: see SOUR *adjective*.

dock /dɒk/ *noun*[2]. **LME.**
[ORIGIN Perh. identical with 2nd elem. of Old English *fingerdoccan* finger muscles, and corresp. to Frisian *dok* bunch, ball (of twine etc.), Middle & mod. Low German *dokke* bundle of straw, Old High German *tocka* (southern German *Docke*) doll. In sense 6 from DOCK *verb*[1].]
1 The solid fleshy or bony part of an animal's tail. **LME.**
2 A person's buttocks. Long *obsolete* exc. *Scot.* and in ***strong-docked*** s.v. STRONG *adjective*. **E16.**
†**3** The skirts of a garment. **E–M16.**
4 The stump left after a tail is docked; *gen.* (now *dial.*), a cut end of anything, a stump. **L16.**
5 Part of a crupper in the form of a ring through which a horse's tail is inserted; a crupper; a covering for a horse's tail. **E17.**
6 The action or an act of docking or cutting short. Now only *spec.* (*Scot.*), a haircut. **M17.**

dock /dɒk/ *noun*[3]. **LME.**
[ORIGIN Middle Low German, Middle Dutch *docke* (mod. *dok*), of unknown origin.]
1 An artificial basin, usu. with floodgates to control the water level, in which ships can be repaired, built, or loaded and unloaded. **LME.** ▸**b** A wharf or pier. Orig. *US*. **E19.** ▸**c** The body of water between adjacent wharves. **E19.**
†**2** The bed (in the sand or mud) in which a vessel lies dry at low water; the hollow made by a vessel lying in the sand. **L15–M17.**
†**3** A creek in which ships may lie on the mud or ride at anchor, according to the tide. **M–L16.**
†**4** A trench or canal to admit a boat. **M17–E18.**
5 *sing.* & (usu.) in *pl.* A range of docks (sense 1 above) together with the adjoining wharves, warehouses, and offices (***commercial docks***); a dockyard (***naval docks***). **E18.**
6 An enclosure in a platform into which a single railway line runs and terminates. **L19.**
7 THEATRICAL. More fully ***scene dock***. A storage space for scenes at the side or back of a stage. **L19.**
8 A raised platform from which lorries or railway trucks are loaded and unloaded. *N. Amer.* **E20.**
– PHRASES: ***dry dock***: see DRY *adjective*. **floating dock** a floating structure serving as a dry dock. **graving dock** a dry dock. **in dock** *colloq.* in or into hospital; in or into a garage for repair etc. ***wet dock***: see WET *adjective*.
– COMB.: **dock glass** a large wine glass of a type orig. used by excisemen for wine tasting; **dockland**, **D-** the area about a city's docks, esp. those of London; **dockside** *noun* & *adjective* (situated in) the area immediately adjacent to a dock; **docksman** a man employed at a dock; *spec.* one who opens and shuts dock gates; **dock warrant** a certificate given to the owner of goods warehoused at a dock.

dock /dɒk/ *noun*[4]. **L16.**
[ORIGIN Prob. orig. a cant word and identical with Flemish *dok* fowl pen, rabbit hutch.]
The enclosure in a courtroom in which the prisoner is placed during a criminal trial. Orig., one filled with prisoners whose trial was scheduled for the day (see ***bail-dock*** s.v. BAIL *noun*[2]).
in the dock *fig.* under scrutiny or interrogation for some suspected misdeed.
– COMB.: **dock brief** a brief handed in court directly to a barrister selected from those present by a prisoner in the dock (instead of through the agency of a solicitor).
– NOTE: Hardly known before **E19** exc. in *bail-dock*.

dock /dɒk/ *verb*[1] *trans.* **LME.**
[ORIGIN from DOCK *noun*[2].]
1 Cut short (a tail, hair, etc.); cut short the tail of (an animal). Formerly also, cut short the hair of (a person). **LME.**
2 Abridge or reduce by taking away a part; curtail; deprive *of*; *esp.* (*colloq.*) make a deduction from the pay of (a person) or from (pay) as a fine, subscription, etc. Also, deduct (something) *from* pay. **LME.**
> E. A. BARTLETT Her creditors have been docked of three-fourths of their due. A. J. CRONIN He's afraid to ask the Council for anything in case they dock his wretched salary to pay for it. A. S. NEILL He is docked of all his pocket money until the debt is paid. *Accountant* The . . company suddenly finds its contribution to group profits has been docked.

3 Put an end to (an entail) by breaking the line of succession to the estate. **E17.**
– COMB.: **dock-tailed** *adjective* with a tail cut short.

dock /dɒk/ *verb*[2]. **E16.**
[ORIGIN from DOCK *noun*[3].]
†**1** *verb trans.* Put (a vessel) into anchorage in a roadstead etc. **E16–E17.**
†**2** *verb trans.* Bring or put (a vessel) ashore to rest in the mud, or in a trench or creek. **L16–M18.**
> SHAKES. *Merch. V.* I should . . see my wealthy Andrew dock'd in sand.

3 a *verb trans.* Bring or put (a vessel) into dock. **E17.** ▸**b** *verb intrans.* Of a vessel or those aboard: come into dock; enter port. **L19.**
> **a** S. PEPYS We . . saw the manner and trouble of docking such a ship. **b** C. PRIEST The ship was always expected, whether we docked at noon or midnight.

4 *verb trans.* Provide (a port etc.) with docks. **M18.**
5 a *verb trans.* Join (a spacecraft) to another in space. **M20.** ▸**b** *verb intrans.* Join spacecraft in space; be joined to another spacecraft in space. **M20.**
> *New Scientist* Soviet designers are now providing their manned spacecraft with a docking tunnel.

dockage /ˈdɒkɪdʒ/ *noun*[1]. **M17.**
[ORIGIN from DOCK *noun*[3] + -AGE.]
(The charges for) docking facilities; docks collectively; the berthing of a vessel in a dock.

dockage /ˈdɒkɪdʒ/ *noun*[2]. **L19.**
[ORIGIN from DOCK *verb*[1] + -AGE.]
The action of docking an amount; deduction.

docken /ˈdɒk(ə)n/ *noun. Scot.* & *N. English.* **LME.**
[ORIGIN App. from Old English *doccan* pl. & infl. sing. of *docce* DOCK *noun*[1].]
= DOCK *noun*[1].

docker /ˈdɒkə/ *noun*[1]. **M18.**
[ORIGIN from DOCK *noun*[3] + -ER[1].]
1 A person who lives in or near a dock; (**D-**) *spec.* a native or inhabitant of Devonport, formerly called Plymouth Dock. **M18.**
2 A labourer in a dock. **L19.**

docker /ˈdɒkə/ *noun*[2]. **E19.**
[ORIGIN from DOCK *verb*[1] + -ER[1].]
A person who docks tails.

docker /ˈdɒkə/ *noun*[3]. *colloq.* (now *hist.*). **L19.**
[ORIGIN from DOCK *noun*[4] + -ER[1].]
A dock brief.

docket /ˈdɒkɪt/ *noun.* Also †**docquet(t)**, †**dogget(t)**. **L15.**
[ORIGIN Uncertain: perh. from DOCK *verb*[1] + -ET[1].]
1 An abridged account, a summary; an abstract. *obsolete* exc. *hist.* **L15.** ▸**b** An abstract of the contents of proposed letters patent, written on the monarch's bill which authorized their preparation and copied into a register. **M16.** ▸**c** LAW. An abridged account of judicial proceedings, esp. of a case in Chancery; a register of judicial decisions or cases. **M17.**
c †**strike a docket** enter a bond with the Lord Chancellor to show that a debtor is a bankrupt.
2 A list of law cases due to be heard or tried; *transf.* a list of matters for discussion or things to be done; an agenda. Freq. in ***on the docket***. *US*. **E18.**
> B. TARKINGTON The court had cleared up the docket by sitting to unseemly hours of the night.

3 A document or inscription giving particulars, esp. of something attached; *spec.* a label attached to goods to indicate their destination, nature, value, etc.; a customs warrant certifying that duty has been paid on goods entering; a warrant or voucher entitling the holder to obtain or receive something. Cf. DUCAT 3. **E18.**
> T. HOOD Tourists . . Provided with passport, that requisite docket. JOYCE The box of pawn-tickets . . had just been rifled and he took up idly . . the blue and white dockets.

4 A workman's record of jobs done during the day or week. **M20.**
5 A set of papers on a given topic; a file. **M20.**

docket /ˈdɒkɪt/ *verb trans.* Also †**docquet(t)**, †**dogget(t)**. **E17.**
[ORIGIN from the noun.]
†**1** Inscribe (letters patent etc.) with a docket. **E17–M19.**
2 LAW. Enter a summary of (a judgement etc.) in a register. **L17.**
3 Annotate (a letter or document) with a brief note of its contents etc. **M18.**
4 LAW. Enter (a case or suit) on the list of those due to be heard. *US*. **E19.**
5 *fig.* Assign to a category; classify. **M19.**
> D. WELCH He only looked at things in the room that he could date and docket. Other things were quite missed.

dockominium /dɒkəˈmɪnɪəm/ *noun. US.* **L20.**
[ORIGIN from DOCK *noun*[3] + CONDOMINIUM.]
A privately owned landing stage at a marina etc.; a waterfront condominium with a private landing stage.

dockyard /ˈdɒkjɑːd/ *noun.* **E18.**
[ORIGIN from DOCK *noun*[3] + YARD *noun*[1].]
An area with docks and workshops for the building, outfit, and repair of ships; *esp.* a Government establishment of this kind for the use of the Royal Navy.
– COMB.: **dockyard man**, (*colloq.*) **dockyard matey** a male employee in a Government dockyard.

Doc Martens *noun phr.* see DOCTOR MARTENS.

†docquet(t) *noun, verb* vars. of DOCKET *noun, verb*.

doct /dɒkt/ *adjective. rare.* E18.
[ORIGIN Latin *doctus* pa. pple of *docere* teach.]
Learned.

doctor /ˈdɒktə/ *noun.* ME.
[ORIGIN Old French *doctour* from Latin *doctor* teacher, from *doct-* pa. ppl stem of *docere* teach: see -OR.]
1 A person skilled in, and therefore entitled to teach or speak authoritatively on, any branch of knowledge; an eminently learned person. *arch.* ME.

POPE Who shall decide, when Doctors disagree?

2 CHRISTIAN CHURCH. **a** Any of certain theologians (orig. four each in the Western and the Eastern Church) whose canonization as saints is due esp. to their outstanding learning and influence. ME. ▸**b** A leading medieval schoolman. E17.
b *the Angelic Doctor*: see ANGELIC *adjective*[1] 2. *the Seraphic Doctor*: see SERAPHIC *adjective*.
3 A person who gives instruction in some branch of knowledge, or inculcates opinions or principles; a teacher. (Foll. by *of*.) Now *rare.* LME. ▸†**b** An assistant schoolmaster. *Scot.* M17–L18.

BURKE These new Doctors of the Rights of men.

4 A holder of the highest degree awarded in a university faculty or (now) by some other competent body. Now usu. used as a title preceding a name (freq. abbreviated to *Dr*); formerly also used as a form of address. LME.
Doctor of Civil Law, *Doctor of Divinity*, *Doctor of Philosophy*, etc.
5 A person who is learned in theology or law. *arch.* LME.
6 Orig., an authority on medicine or surgery; a doctor of medicine. Now, any medical practitioner, *esp.* one who is qualified or registered and (in Britain and Ireland) is not a surgeon; *spec.* a general practitioner; (chiefly as an official designation) a dentist; *N. Amer.* also (only as a title preceding a name), an ophthalmic optician, a veterinarian. Also used as a title preceding a name (freq. abbreviated to *Dr*) and used as a form of address. LME. ▸**b** *fig.* A thing that improves health or promotes well-being; *spec.* (**a**) *colloq.* a reviving drink; (**b**) *colloq.* in the W. Indies, southern Africa, and western Australia, a cool sea breeze which usually blows for part of the day in summer. M17. ▸**c** A person who mends or repairs things of a certain kind. L19.

G. GREENE Doctor Castle's study . . had been left unchanged after the doctor's death.

go for the doctor *Austral. & NZ slang* make every effort; bet heavily. **what the doctor ordered**, **just what the doctor ordered** *colloq.* something beneficial or desirable, esp. in a given situation. **you're the doctor** *colloq.* the decision is up to you. **c** *play-doctor*, *saw doctor*, *tree doctor*, etc.
7 A false or loaded die. *arch. slang.* L17.
8 = *surgeonfish* s.v. SURGEON *noun.* M18.
9 A blade for removing surplus ink, fibres, etc., in printing and paper-making machines. Also *doctor blade*. L18.
10 An added ingredient used to adulterate food or drink. L18.
11 A cook on board ship or (*US, Austral., & NZ*) in a camp. *slang.* E19.
12 ANGLING. A kind of hackled dry fly. M19.
silver doctor: see SILVER *noun & adjective*.
– COMB.: **doctor bird** *W. Indian* a hummingbird; **doctor blade** = sense 9 above; **doctor-fish** (**a**) = sense 8 above; (**b**) the tench; **Doctors' Commons** *hist.* (the site of) a London building occupied by the former College of Doctors of Laws, in which legal business relating to wills, marriage licences, divorce proceedings, etc., was transacted; *doctor's mandate*: see MANDATE *noun*; *doctor's orders*: see ORDER *noun*; **doctor's stuff**, **doctor-stuff** *derog. colloq.* medicine.
■ **doctorhood** *noun* the status or rank of a doctor L19. **doctorism** *noun* (**a**) the principles or practices of doctors; (**b**) a saying characteristic of doctors: M17. **doctorize** *verb trans.* (*rare*) = DOCTOR *verb* 1 E17. **doctorly** *adjective* like, characteristic of, or befitting a doctor L16.

doctor /ˈdɒktə/ *verb. colloq.* M16.
[ORIGIN Partly from DOCTOR *noun*, partly (in sense 2) from medieval Latin *doctorare* (see DOCTORATE *verb*).]
1 *verb intrans.* Cite learned persons. Only as *doctoring verbal noun. rare.* Only in M16.
2 *verb trans.* Confer the degree or title of doctor on; make a doctor; address as 'doctor'. L16.

J. R. LOWELL I have been over to Oxford to be doctored.

3 *verb trans.* Treat, as a doctor; give medical treatment to. E18. ▸**b** Repair, patch up, set to rights, (machinery etc.); take steps to improve or make acceptable. E19. ▸**c** Castrate or spay (an animal). E20.

S. BELLOW I doctored myself with tranquillizers. **b** A. BLOND A writer, gaining his main income . . from doctoring film scripts.

4 *verb trans.* Alter or disguise the appearance, flavour, or character of; falsify, tamper with, adulterate; 'cook'. L18.

P. V. PRICE As wine got old in cask . . it would be doctored . . with honey . . or fruit juices that might make it palatable. M. RICHLER He wasn't awfully good at school, and so . . he would doctor his report card.

5 *verb intrans.* Practise as a physician. Chiefly as *doctoring verbal noun.* M19.

A. D. T. WHITNEY Preaching ran in the King family, as politics or doctoring . . run in some others.

6 *verb intrans.* Receive treatment by a doctor. L19.
■ **doctorer** *noun* L19.

doctoral /ˈdɒkt(ə)r(ə)l/ *adjective.* L16.
[ORIGIN from DOCTOR *noun* + -AL[1].]
Of or pertaining to an eminently learned person or a teacher. Now *spec.* of or pertaining to (the holder of) a doctorate.
■ **doctorally** *adverb* L16.

doctorand /ˈdɒktərand/ *noun.* Also in Latin form **doctorandus** /dɒktəˈrandəs/, pl. **-di** /-dʌɪ/. E20.
[ORIGIN German from medieval Latin *doctorandus*.]
A candidate for a doctor's degree.

doctorate /ˈdɒkt(ə)rət/ *noun.* M17.
[ORIGIN Partly formed as DOCTORATE *verb*; partly from medieval Latin *doctoratus* = sense 2 below, from Latin DOCTOR *noun*: see -ATE[1].]
1 A person who has a doctor's degree. *rare.* M17.
2 The highest degree awarded in a university faculty or (now) by some other competent body; a doctor's degree. L17.

doctorate /ˈdɒktəreɪt/ *verb trans.* Now *rare.* Pa. pple **-ated**, (earlier) †**-ate**. L16.
[ORIGIN medieval Latin *doctorat-* pa. ppl stem of *doctorare*, from Latin DOCTOR *noun*: see -ATE[3].]
= DOCTOR *verb* 2.

doctoress *noun* var. of DOCTRESS.

doctorial /dɒkˈtɔːrɪəl/ *adjective.* E18.
[ORIGIN from DOCTOR *noun* + -IAL.]
= DOCTORAL.
■ **doctorially** *adverb* M19.

Doctor Martens /dɒktə ˈmɑːtɪnz/ *noun phr.* Also **Doctor Marten's**, **Doc M-**, **Dr M-**. L20.
[ORIGIN Klaus *Maertens*, German inventor of the sole.]
(Proprietary name for) a type of heavy (esp. laced) boot or shoe with a cushioned sole.

doctorship /ˈdɒktəʃɪp/ *noun.* L16.
[ORIGIN from DOCTOR *noun* + -SHIP.]
1 = DOCTORATE *noun* 2. L16.
2 The position, character, or function of a teacher or learned person; teaching; learning, scholarship. L16.
3 The personality or dignity of a doctor. Chiefly *joc.* or *iron.* as a title. E17.
4 The function or practice of a medical doctor; medical skill or attendance. M17.

doctress /ˈdɒktrɪs/ *noun.* Also **doctoress** /ˈdɒkt(ə)rɪs, -ɛs/. M16.
[ORIGIN from DOCTOR *noun* + -ESS[1], after French †*doctoresse*.]
1 A female teacher; a learned woman; a female holder of a doctor's degree. Now *rare* or *obsolete.* M16.
2 A female medical doctor, a lady doctor. L16.
3 A doctor's wife or daughter. *joc.* M18.

†doctrices *noun pl.* see DOCTRIX.

doctrinaire /dɒktrɪˈnɛː/ *noun & adjective.* E19.
[ORIGIN French, from DOCTRINE + *-aire* -ARY[1].]
▸ **A** *noun.* **1** In early 19th-cent. France, a member of a political movement which supported constitutional government and the reconciliation of the principles of authority and liberty. E19.
2 A person who tries to apply principle without allowance for circumstance; a pedantic theorist. M19.
▸ **B** *adjective.* Pertaining to or of the character of a doctrinaire; seeking to apply a doctrine in all circumstances; theoretical and unpractical. M19.
■ **doctrinairism** *noun* M19.

doctrinal /dɒkˈtrʌɪn(ə)l, ˈdɒktrɪn-/ *noun.* LME.
[ORIGIN Old French, from medieval Latin *doctrinale* use as noun of neut. of late Latin *doctrinalis*: see DOCTRINAL *adjective*.]
†**1** A textbook; a book of instruction on any subject. Orig. the title of a particular textbook on grammar. LME–M17.
2 In *pl.* Matters or points of doctrine or instruction. E17.

doctrinal /dɒkˈtrʌɪn(ə)l, ˈdɒktrɪn-/ *adjective.* LME.
[ORIGIN Late Latin *doctrinalis*, from *doctrina* DOCTRINE: see -AL[1].]
1 Of or pertaining to doctrine; dealing with or concerned with inculcating doctrine or doctrines. LME.

D. NEAL Doctrinal Puritans. J. A. FROUDE Doctrinal conservatism.

†**2** Serving to teach or instruct; instructive, didactic. L16–M17.
■ **doctrinalism** *noun* the laying of stress on, or rigid adherence to, doctrinal matters L19. **doctrinalist** *noun* M19. **doctrinally** *adverb* in a doctrinal way; as doctrine; as regards doctrine: LME.

doctrinarian /dɒktrɪˈnɛːrɪən/ *noun & adjective.* M18.
[ORIGIN from medieval Latin *doctrinare* (see DOCTRINATE) + -ARIAN.]
▸ **A** *noun.* †**1** A member of the Brothers of Christian Doctrine, or Christian Brothers, a lay teaching order instituted at Rheims in 1680. M–L18.
2 = DOCTRINAIRE *noun* 2. M19.
▸ **B** *adjective.* = DOCTRINAIRE *adjective.* L19.
■ **doctrinarianism** *noun* L19.

doctrinary /ˈdɒktrɪn(ə)ri/ *adjective.* M19.
[ORIGIN French DOCTRINAIRE: see -ARY[1].]
= DOCTRINAIRE *adjective.*
■ **doctriˈnarity** *noun* doctrinaire quality M19.

doctrinate /ˈdɒktrɪneɪt/ *verb. arch.* M17.
[ORIGIN medieval Latin *doctrinat-* pa. ppl stem of *doctrinare* teach, from *doctrina* DOCTRINE: see -ATE[3].]
†**1** *verb trans.* Teach, instruct. Only in M17.
2 *verb intrans.* Give instruction *on* a subject. *rare.* M19.

doctrine /ˈdɒktrɪn/ *noun.* LME.
[ORIGIN Old French & mod. French from Latin *doctrina* teaching, learning, from DOCTOR *noun*: see -INE[4].]
†**1** The action of teaching or instructing; a lesson; a precept. LME–E18. ▸†**b** Preaching. M16–E17.

AV *Mark* 4:2 And he . . said vnto them in his doctrine, Hearken.

2 That which is taught; instruction; a body of teaching, *esp.* that concerning a particular subject or set of beliefs; a dogma, a tenet; a political or ethical principle. LME.

BURKE The doctrine of the equality of all men. C. HILL The Laudians rejected the Calvinist doctrine of predestination.

MONROE DOCTRINE.
3 A body of principles or tenets, a system of beliefs; a theory; a branch of knowledge. Now *rare* or *obsolete.* LME.

EARL OF CHATHAM A . . notion of . . the solar system: together with the doctrine of comets.

†**4** Learning, knowledge. LME–E17.
†**5** Discipline. *rare.* L15–M16.
■ **doctrinism** *noun* adherence to or propounding of doctrine L19. **doctrinist** *noun* M19.

†doctrix *noun.* Pl. **-trixes**, **-trices**. E17–M18.
[ORIGIN Latin, fem. of DOCTOR *noun*.]
A female doctor.

docudrama /ˈdɒkjʊdrɑːmə/ *noun.* M20.
[ORIGIN from DOCUMENTARY + DRAMA.]
= *DRAMA-documentary*.

document /ˈdɒkjʊm(ə)nt/ *noun.* LME.
[ORIGIN Old French & mod. French from Latin *documentum* lesson, proof, instance, (in medieval Latin) written instruction, official paper, from *docere* teach: see -MENT.]
†**1** Teaching; (a piece of) instruction, a lesson; (a) warning. LME–E19.
†**2** Evidence, proof. Usu. foll. by *of*, *that*. LME–M19.
3 Something written, inscribed, engraved, etc., which provides evidence or information or serves as a record; *esp.* an official paper. LME.

A. E. STEVENSON Our great documents, from the Declaration of Independence to the Atlantic Charter. S. NAIPAUL His testament, a rambling document some forty pages long.

social document: see SOCIAL *adjective*.
– COMB.: **document case** a lightweight usu. flexible case for carrying papers.

document /ˈdɒkjʊmɛnt/ *verb trans.* M17.
[ORIGIN from DOCUMENT *noun*.]
†**1** Teach, instruct. M17–M18. ▸**b** Instruct or admonish authoritatively; rebuke. L17–E19.

BUNYAN That they might be documented in all good and wholesome things. **b** DRYDEN I am finely documented by my own daughter!

2 Prove or support by documentary evidence; record in documents. Freq. in *pass.* E18.

A. POWELL Like many Welsh families my father's had been documented from an early period.

3 Provide with documents, esp. legally required papers. Usu. in *pass.* E19.

J. ARNOULD By sailing his ship imperfectly or improperly documented, he forfeits his rights to protection under the policy.

4 Provide (a person) with evidence or information, keep informed. E19.
■ **docuˈmentable** *adjective* L16. **docuˈmentably** *adverb* L20.

documental /dɒkjʊˈmɛnt(ə)l/ *adjective.* L16.
[ORIGIN from DOCUMENT *noun* + -AL[1].]
†**1** Instructive; didactic. L16–E17.
2 Of or pertaining to documents; documentary. E19.
■ **docuˈmentalist** *noun* a person engaged in documentation M20.

documentary /dɒkjʊˈmɛnt(ə)ri/ *adjective & noun.* E19.
[ORIGIN formed as DOCUMENTAL + -ARY[1].]
▸ **A** *adjective.* **1** Of, pertaining to, or consisting of a document or documents. E19.

LD MACAULAY They were in possession of documentary evidence which would confound the guilty.

2 Affording evidence, evidential. *rare.* M19.
3 Relating to teaching or instruction. *rare.* L19.
4 Factual, realistic; *esp.* (of a film etc.) based on real events, places, or circumstances and usu. intended primarily to record or inform. E20.

Punch Most documentary films seem to hinge upon the exposition of some staple industry.

▸ **B** *noun.* A documentary film or programme. M20.

D. ADAMS One of our film producers is already making a fascinating documentary about the indigenous cavemen.

■ **ˌdocumenˈtarian** *noun* (**a**) a photographer of real events or places as a (historical) record; (**b**) = DOCUMENTARIST; (**c**) a historian who uses documentary evidence: M20. **documentarily** *adverb*

D

M19. **documentarist** *noun* a person who makes documentaries M20.

documentation /ˌdɒkjʊmɛnˈteɪʃ(ə)n/ *noun*. M18.
[ORIGIN from DOCUMENT *verb* + -ATION.]
†**1** Instruction, admonition. M18–M19.
2 The provision of documents. L19.
3 Preparation or use of documentary evidence or authorities. L19.
4 The process or speciality of accumulating and classifying documents and making them available to others. E20.
5 Documents collectively; the documents accompanying or belonging to something. E20.

Which Micro? The BBC Micro has . . excellent documentation.

documentative /dɒkjʊˈmɛntətɪv/ *adjective*. L20.
[ORIGIN formed as DOCUMENTATION + -IVE.]
Of the nature of a documentary; employing or providing documentation.

documentize /ˈdɒkjʊm(ə)ntʌɪz/ *verb trans*. Now *dial*. Also **-ise**. L16.
[ORIGIN from DOCUMENT *noun* + -IZE.]
1 Preach, moralize. Formerly, teach, instruct. L16.
†**2** Provide with evidence. Only in M18.

docusoap /ˈdɒkjʊsəʊp/ *noun*. L20.
[ORIGIN from DOCU(MENTARY + SOAP *noun*[1].]
A television documentary series following people in a particular occupation or location over a period of time.

docutainment /dɒkjʊˈteɪnm(ə)nt/ *noun*. *N. Amer*. L20.
[ORIGIN from DOCU(MENTARY + ENTER)TAINMENT.]
(A) documentary film or programme designed as entertainment.

DOD *abbreviation*. *US*.
Department of Defense.

dod /dɒd/ *noun*[1]. *Scot. & N. English*. ME.
[ORIGIN Rel. to DOD *verb*[1].]
A rounded summit or eminence, *esp.* one that is a lower summit or shoulder of a hill.

dod /dɒd/ *noun*[2]. M17.
[ORIGIN Cogn. with Dutch *dodde* in same sense.]
The greater reed mace, *Typha latifolia*.

dod /dɒd/ *noun*[3] *& interjection*. Chiefly *dial*. L17.
[ORIGIN Alt. Cf. DAD *noun*[2].]
God: used in oaths and exclamations, and (*US*) as an intensive with verbs and pa. pples.

C. E. CRADDOCK Dod-rot that critter.

– COMB.: **dod-rotted** *adjective* (*US*) damned, dratted.

dod /dɒd/ *noun*[4]. *Scot*. L18.
[ORIGIN Gaelic = peevishness.]
A fit of ill humour; usu. in *pl.*, sulks, esp. in ***take the dods***.

dod /dɒd/ *verb*[1] *trans*. *obsolete* exc. *dial*. Infl. **-dd-**. ME.
[ORIGIN Rel. to DOD *noun*[1]: ult. origin unknown. Cf. DODDY *noun*[2].]
Make the top of (something) blunt, rounded, or bare; shave the head of; lop (a tree); dehorn (an animal).

dod /dɒd/ *verb*[2] *trans*. *obsolete* exc. *dial*. Infl. **-dd-**. M17.
[ORIGIN Imit.: cf. DAD *verb*.]
Beat, knock.

†**doddard** *noun*. *rare*. L17–L18.
[ORIGIN App. from DOD *verb*[1] + -ARD: cf. *pollard*, DODDERED *adjective*[1].]
= DOTARD *noun*[2].

dodder /ˈdɒdə/ *noun*. ME.
[ORIGIN Corresp. to Middle Low German *dod(d)er*, Middle High German *toter* (German *Dotter*).]
1 Any plant of the genus *Cuscuta*, related to the bindweeds, comprising leafless threadlike twining plants with parasitic suckers. ME.
2 Any of various choking or climbing weeds. *dial*. L19.

dodder /ˈdɒdə/ *verb intrans*. E17.
[ORIGIN Alt. of or parallel to DADDER.]
1 Tremble or shake owing to frailty or illness. E17.
2 Walk unsteadily or falteringly, totter; be feeble. E19.
■ **dodderer** *noun* an infirm, feeble, or inept person E20. **doddering** *ppl adjective* that dodders; feeble in body or mind; inept, footling: M18. **dodderingness** *noun* E20. **doddery** *adjective* apt to tremble or totter, esp. from age or infirmity; faltering, shaky: M19.

doddered /ˈdɒdəd/ *adjective*[1]. L17.
[ORIGIN App. orig. from DOD *verb*[1] (cf. DODDARD, DODDLE *noun*[1], DOTTER *verb*); later also assoc. with DODDER *noun*.]
Of a tree, esp. an oak: having lost the top or branches, esp. through age and decay.

doddered /ˈdɒdəd/ *adjective*[2]. Chiefly *dial*. M19.
[ORIGIN from DODDER *verb* + -ED[1].]
Infirm, doddery; doddering; dilapidated.

dodderel /ˈdɒd(ə)r(ə)l/ *noun*. *dial*. E18.
[ORIGIN from DOD *verb*[1]: cf. DODDERED *adjective*[1], DOTTEREL.]
A doddered tree; a pollard.

doddie *noun* var. of DODDY *noun*[1], *noun*[2].

doddle /ˈdɒd(ə)l/ *noun*[1] *& adjective*. *obsolete* exc. *dial*. E17.
[ORIGIN from DOD *verb*[1]: cf. DODDARD.]
(Designating) a pollard.

doddle /ˈdɒd(ə)l/ *noun*[2]. *colloq*. M20.
[ORIGIN Uncertain: perh. from DODDLE *verb*.]
An easy task; something requiring little effort or skill; a walkover.

J. KELMAN It is never a doddle to beg from acquaintances.

doddle /ˈdɒd(ə)l/ *verb intrans*. L16.
[ORIGIN from obscure 1st elem. + -LE[3]. Cf. DADDLE *verb*, DAWDLE *verb*, DODDER *verb*, TODDLE *verb*.]
Walk with short, faltering, or unsteady steps; toddle; totter; dawdle.

doddy /ˈdɒdi/ *noun*[1]. Now *Scot*. Also **-ie**. L16.
[ORIGIN Abbreviation.]
= DODDYPOLL.

doddy /ˈdɒdi/ *noun*[2]. *Scot*. Also **-ie**. L18.
[ORIGIN from DOD *verb*[1] + -Y[6], -IE.]
A hornless cow or bull.

doddypoll /ˈdɒdɪpəʊl/ *noun*. *arch*. Also (earlier) †**dot(t)y-**. LME.
[ORIGIN App. from DOTE *verb*[1], later referred to DOD *verb*[1] + POLL *noun*[1]: cf. *roundhead*.]
A stupid person; a dolt, a blockhead.

dodeca- /ˈdəʊdɛkə/ *combining form* of Greek *dōdeka* twelve. Before a vowel **dodec-**.
■ **do'decamer** *noun* (CHEMISTRY) a compound whose molecule is composed of twelve molecules of monomer M20. **dodeca'meric** *adjective* (CHEMISTRY) of the nature of a decamer, consisting of a dodecamer or dodecamers M20. **dodecandrous** /dəʊdɪˈkandrəs/ *adjective* (BOTANY) having twelve stamens E19. **dodeca'phonic** *adjective* (MUSIC) pertaining to, using, or designating the twelve-note system M20. **dodecaphonist** /dəʊˈdɛkəf(ə)nɪst, dəʊdɪˈkaf(ə)nɪst/ *noun* (MUSIC) a composer of dodecaphonic music M20. **dodecaphony** /dəʊˈdɛkəf(ə)ni, dəʊdɪˈkaf(ə)ni/ *noun* (MUSIC) the twelve-note system M20. **dodecarchy** *noun* (government by) a ruling body of twelve M17. **dodecastyle** *noun* a portico or colonnade of twelve columns E19. **dodecasy'llabic** *adjective* (PROSODY) composed of dodecasyllables L19. **dodeca'syllable** *noun* (PROSODY) a word or line of twelve syllables M18.

dodecad /ˈdəʊdɪkad, dəʊˈdɛkad/ *noun*. Also **-ade** /-eɪd/. L17.
[ORIGIN from Greek *dōdeka* twelve, after *decade*.]
A group or set of twelve items.
■ Also †**dodecady** *noun*: only in E17.

dodecagon /dəʊˈdɛkəg(ə)n/ *noun*. M17.
[ORIGIN Greek *dōdekagōnon*, from *dōdeka* twelve + *-gōnos* -GON.]
GEOMETRY. A plane figure with twelve straight sides and twelve angles.

dodecahedrane /dəʊdɛkəˈhiːdreɪn/ *noun*. M20.
[ORIGIN from DODECAHEDRON + -ANE.]
CHEMISTRY. A crystalline hydrocarbon, $(CH)_{20}$, in which the carbon atoms of each molecule lie at the vertices of a regular dodecahedron.

dodecahedron /ˌdəʊdɛkəˈhiːdr(ə)n, -ˈhɛd-/ *noun*. Pl. **-dra** /-drə/, **-drons**. L16.
[ORIGIN Greek *dōdekaedron* neut. of *dōdekaedros*, from *dōdeka* twelve + *hedra* seat, face.]
GEOMETRY & CRYSTALLOGRAPHY. A solid figure or object with twelve plane faces; *esp.* (more fully ***regular dodecahedron***) one with twelve equal regular pentagonal faces.
■ **dodecahedral** *adjective* having the form of a dodecahedron; having twelve faces: L18. **dodecahedric** *adjective* = DODECAHEDRAL L19.

dodecane /ˈdəʊdɪkeɪn/ *noun*. L19.
[ORIGIN from DODECA- + -ANE.]
CHEMISTRY. Any of a series of saturated hydrocarbons (alkanes) with the formula $C_{12}H_{26}$; *spec.* (also *n-dodecane*) the unbranched isomer, $CH_3(CH_2)_{10}CH_3$.
■ **dodeca'noic** *adjective* = LAURIC M20.

†**dodecatemory** *noun*. E17–E18.
[ORIGIN Greek *dōdekatēmorion*, from *dōdekaton*, fem. *-tē*, twelfth + *morion* a part.]
A twelfth part; *esp.* (ASTROLOGY) each of the twelve houses of the zodiac; a twelfth part of a sign, 2½ degrees.

dodecyl /ˈdəʊdɪsʌɪl, -sɪl, dəʊˈdiːs-/ *noun*. L19.
[ORIGIN from DODECANE + -YL.]
CHEMISTRY. A radical $C_{12}H_{25}$·, derived from a dodecane. Usu. in *comb.*

dodgast /ˈdɒdgɑːst/ *verb trans*. *US dial*. L19.
[ORIGIN from DOD *noun*[3] + *gast*, prob. from BLAST *verb*.]
Confound, curse: used in oaths and exclamations. Chiefly as ***dodgasted*** *ppl adjective*.

dodge /dɒdʒ/ *noun*. L16.
[ORIGIN from the verb.]
1 An act of dodging; a quick sideways movement. Formerly, *the* slip. L16.

L. PARR He was forced to avoid him by giving a sudden dodge to one side.

2 A trick; an artifice, esp. as a means of eluding or cheating someone. E17.

DICKENS 'It was all false, of course?' 'All, sir . . , reg'lar do, sir; artful dodge'. V. WOOLF His little dodges deceived nobody.

on the dodge engaged in crooked or dishonest proceedings.
3 A clever or adroit expedient or stratagem; *colloq.* something showing ingenuity or shrewdness. M19.

F. C. BURNAND This is a queer sort of dodge for lighting the streets. H. A. VACHELL He had other dodges to capture trade.

– COMB.: **dodgeball** *N. Amer.* a game in which players, in teams, form a circle and try to hit opponents with a large ball.

dodge /dɒdʒ/ *verb*. M16.
[ORIGIN Unknown.]
†**1** *verb intrans.* Go this way and that in one's speech or behaviour; negotiate, haggle; dither. M16–M18.
2 *verb intrans.* Play fast and loose (esp. *with* a person); prevaricate. L16.
3 *verb trans.* Play fast and loose with; frustrate or impede by shifts and pretexts; trifle with. L16.
4 †**a** *verb intrans.* Use changes of position *with* a person to evade or catch him or her. M17–E18. ▸**b** *verb intrans.* Move to and fro, change position, esp. quickly; move quickly to evade a pursuer, blow, etc., or to gain an advantage. (Foll. by various prepositions, adverbs, and adverbial phrs.) L17. ▸**c** *verb trans.* Move up and down or to and fro (*lit. & fig.*); move suddenly, jerk; question or address at random rather than sequentially. E19.

a W. HUBBARD He began to dodge with his pursuers. **b** A. SILLITOE He dodged between tall green buses. J. B. PRIESTLEY It was . . easier too to dodge out of sight if we caught a glimpse of people who might be looking for us. J. OSBORNE I used to have to dodge downstairs for the post. **c** R. MARSH He made a snatch at it . . . Sydney dodged it out of his reach.

5 *verb trans.* Evade (a pursuer) by sudden changes of direction or (a blow) by sudden movement; evade, escape, esp. by cleverness or trickery. L17.

J. GALSWORTHY Haven't you attorneys invented a way yet of dodging this damned income tax? D. ABSE We crossed the road, dodging the traffic. D. ADAMS You can't dodge your responsibilities by saying they don't exist!

6 *verb intrans.* Of a bell in change-ringing: move one place contrary to the normal sequence, and then back again in the following round. L17.
7 *verb trans.* Follow stealthily and with subterfuges to avoid discovery; dog (a person's steps). Now *rare* or *obsolete*. E18.
8 *verb intrans.* (also foll. by *on*) & *trans.* Jog. *Scot. & N. English*. E18.
– PHRASES: **dodge Pompey** (*a*) *nautical slang* shirk work; (*b*) *Austral. slang* steal grass. ***dodge the column***: see COLUMN *noun* 4.

dodgem /ˈdɒdʒ(ə)m/ *noun*. E20.
[ORIGIN from DODGE *verb* + 'EM.]
A small electrically powered car at a funfair, driven in an enclosure with the aim of bumping other cars and avoiding bumps from them. Also ***dodgem car***.
– NOTE: Proprietary name (as *Dodg'em*) in the US.

dodger /ˈdɒdʒə/ *noun*. M16.
[ORIGIN from DODGE *verb* + -ER[1].]
1 A person who dodges; *esp.* an artful or elusive person. M16.
2 a A maize-flour cake. *US*. M19. ▸**b** A sandwich; bread; food. *Austral. & military slang*. L19.
3 A small handbill or circular. *US*. L19.
4 A screen on a ship's bridge etc. giving protection from spray. L19.

dodger /ˈdɒdʒə/ *adjective*. *Austral. slang*. M20.
[ORIGIN Unknown.]
Good, excellent.

dodgery /ˈdɒdʒəri/ *noun*. M17.
[ORIGIN from DODGE *noun* or *verb* + -ERY.]
The employment of dodges; trickery.

dodging /ˈdɒdʒɪŋ/ *verbal noun*. L16.
[ORIGIN from DODGE *verb* + -ING[1].]
The action of DODGE *verb*; an instance of this; PHOTOGRAPHY the deliberate modification of the intensity of a particular part of a photograph during processing or enlarging.

dodgy /ˈdɒdʒi/ *adjective*. M19.
[ORIGIN from DODGE *verb* + -Y[1].]
1 Full of trickery; cunning, artful. M19.
2 Difficult, awkward, unreliable; tricky, risky. *colloq*. L19.

H. PINTER It'd be a bit dodgy driving tonight.

■ **dodgily** *adverb* L19. **dodginess** *noun* L19.

dodkin /ˈdɒdkɪn/ *noun*. *obsolete* exc. *hist*. Also **dot-**, †**doit-**. LME.
[ORIGIN Middle Dutch *doytkin* dim. of *duit*, *deuyt* DOIT *noun*: see -KIN.]
A doit; any coin of very low value.

dodman /ˈdɒdmən/ *noun*. Now *dial*. M16.
[ORIGIN Unknown: cf. HODMANDOD.]
A snail.

dodo /ˈdəʊdəʊ/ *noun*. Pl. **-o(e)s**. E17.
[ORIGIN Portuguese *doudo* simpleton, fool.]
1 A large flightless bird, *Raphus cucullatus*, with stumpy wings, which inhabited Mauritius until it became extinct in the 17th cent. E17.
dead as a dodo, ***dead as the dodo***: see DEAD *adjective*. ***solitary dodo***: see SOLITARY *adjective*.
2 An old-fashioned, stupid, or inactive person or institution. *colloq*. L19.

Dodonean /dəʊdəˈniːən/ *adjective*. Also **-ian**. M16.
[ORIGIN from Latin *Dodonaeus* from Greek *Dōdōnaios*, from *Dōdōnē* Dodona: see -EAN, -IAN.]
Of or pertaining to Dodona in ancient Epirus, where there was an oracle of Zeus in an oak grove.

DoE *abbreviation*. *hist.*
Department of the Environment.

doe /dəʊ/ *noun*.
[ORIGIN Old English *dā*: ult. origin unknown.]
▸ **A** *noun*. **1** The female of a deer, *spec.* the fallow deer and roe deer. OE.
2 A female hare, rabbit, ferret, or rat. E17.
3 A (large) female kangaroo. *Austral.* M19.
– COMB.: **doe-eyed** *adjective* (esp. of a woman) having large gentle dark eyes; **doeskin** (*a*) (leather of) the skin of a doe; (*b*) a smooth closely cut woollen or twilled cloth.
▸ **B** *attrib.* or as *adjective*. (Of an animal) female; of or from a doe. LME.
– NOTE: The corresponding male animal is usu. called **buck**.

doegling /ˈdəːɡlɪŋ/ *noun*. Also **dog-**. M19.
[ORIGIN Faroese.]
A bottlenose whale, *Hyperoodon ampullatus*, of the N. Atlantic.

doek /dʊk/ *noun*. *S. Afr.* L18.
[ORIGIN Afrikaans = cloth: cf. DUCK *noun*[3].]
A cloth, *esp.* a headscarf.

doer /ˈduːə/ *noun*. ME.
[ORIGIN from DO *verb* + -ER[1].]
1 A person who does something; a person who acts rather than merely talking or thinking. ME.
2 A person who acts on behalf of another; an agent; a lawyer. Now *Scot.* LME.
3 A cheat. *slang*. M19.
4 An animal or plant that thrives (in a specified way). M19.
F. D. DAVISON Piebald was a good doer; . . that pony's head would go down to the food through it all.
5 A person of character; an eccentric person. *Austral. & NZ.* E20.
good doer a warm-hearted person. **hard doer** a tough character; an eccentric person, a character.

does, **doest**, **doeth** *verbs* see DO *verb*.

doff /dɒf/ *verb*. See also DAFF *verb*[2]. LME.
[ORIGIN Contr. of *do off*: see DO *verb*.]
1 a *verb trans.* Put or take off (a garment etc.); take off or raise (a hat), esp. in respect or greeting; *fig.* throw off, get rid of, (a mood etc.). Now *arch.* or *literary*. LME. ▸**b** *verb intrans.* Raise one's hat (*to* a person). *arch. rare.* L17.
K. TYNAN The royal courtesan doffs her baser attributes.
†**2** *verb trans.* Put (a person) *off* (with an excuse etc.). L16–M17.
3 *verb trans.* **a** Automatically remove (cotton etc.) from the carding cylinder during its progress through a carding machine. E19. ▸**b** Remove (empty bobbins or spindles) from a textile machine. M19.
■ **doffer** *noun* a person who or thing which doffs, esp. in textile manufacture E19.

dog /dɒɡ/ *noun & adjective*.
[ORIGIN Late Old English *docga* (once), of unknown origin.]
▸ **A** *noun*. **1** A carnivorous mammal, *Canis familiaris*, long domesticated for hunting or guarding, as a pet, etc., and existing in many diverse breeds. LOE. ▸**b** *spec.* A dog used for hunting; a hound. ME. ▸**c** A watchdog; *school slang* a child who keeps watch. LME. ▸**d** Any of various wild animals related to the dog or thought to resemble it; *spec.* (*a*) *US colloq.* a prairie dog; (*b*) *Austral.* a dingo. Usu. with specifying word or in *comb.* L18. ▸**e** In full **tinned dog**. Canned meat. *Austral. & NZ slang.* L19. ▸**f** In *pl. The* greyhound races. *colloq.* E20.
bulldog, **German shepherd dog**, **guide dog**, **gun dog**, **lapdog**, **longdog**, **sheepdog**, **watchdog**, etc. **d** **hyena dog**, **native dog**, **prairie dog**, etc.
2 As a term of abuse: a worthless or contemptible person; a wretch, a cur. ME. ▸**b** A person who betrays his or her associates; an informer. Chiefly in **turn dog** (**on**). *US, Austral., & NZ slang.* M19. ▸**c** An unattractive or unpleasant woman or girl. *slang*. M20.
SIR W. SCOTT Dog of an unbeliever . . darest thou press upon a Christian? **b** R. BOLDREWOOD Are you going to turn dog, now that you know the way in?
3 A male dog. Also, a male fox or wolf. LME.
4 Any of various mechanical devices, usu. with a tooth or claw, for gripping or holding; *esp.*: (*a*) a clamp for supporting something (e.g. part of a building) or holding something in place; (*b*) (in a firearm) = **doghead** below; (*c*) a grappling iron for gripping a log or other heavy object which has to be hoisted or held in position; (*d*) a projection or tooth acting as a detent; a catch which engages the teeth of a ratchet wheel. LME.
5 (Usu. **D-**.) *The* star Sirius (see **Dog Star** below); (more fully **Great Dog**) *the* constellation Canis Major, containing Sirius; (more fully **Lesser Dog**, **Little Dog**) *the* constellation Canis Minor. M16.
†**6** A kind of gun or cannon. M16–M17.
7 An andiron; an analogous support for a dog grate. Also **firedog**, **dog iron**. L16.
†**8** An adept *at* something. Also **old dog**. L16–E18.
9 A lively or rakish young man; (usu. with prec. adjective, in playful reproof or commiseration) a fellow, a chap. E17.
T. C. WOLFE That dull dog, Cicero. S. SASSOON He posed as a gay dog, chaffing the nurses.
10 Any of various atmospheric phenomena. Usu. as 2nd elem. of comb. (Earliest in **sun dog** s.v. SUN *noun*[1].) M17. WATER DOG.
11 *ellipt.* A dogfish. L17.
12 Any of several sorts of coin; *esp.* a copper coin formerly used in the W. Indies. Earliest in **black dog** s.v. BLACK *adjective*. E18.
13 Display, stylishness; pretentious airs, affected dignity. Esp. in **put on dog**, **put on the dog**. *colloq.* (chiefly *N. Amer.*). L19.
W. STEVENS Sweeney is completely without side or dog.
14 A sausage. Usu. in *pl. slang*. L19. ▸**b** A hot dog. M20.
15 In *pl.* [Abbreviation of *dog's meat*.] Feet. *rhyming slang*. E20.
16 Something that is or turns out worthless; a failure, a dud. *slang* (chiefly *N. Amer.*). M20.
New Yorker The enormous Cadillac . . turned out to be a dog and had to be junked.
17 A horse that is slow or difficult to handle. *slang*. M20.
– PHRASES: **bottom dog**: see BOTTOM *adjective*. **Danish dog**: see DANISH *adjective*. **die like a dog**, **die a dog's death** die shamefully. **dirty dog**: see DIRTY *adjective*. **dog and bone** *rhyming slang* a telephone. **dog-and-pony show** *N. Amer. colloq.* an elaborate formal occasion or display designed to attract people's attention, *esp.* a business briefing or sales presentation. **dog in the manger** a person who selfishly refuses to let others enjoy benefits for which he or she personally has no use. **dog on (it)**: see DOGGONE. **dogs of war** *fig.* the havoc accompanying war. **Great Dog**: see sense 5 above. **hair of the dog (that bit one)**: see HAIR *noun*. **help a lame dog over a stile** come to the aid of a person in need. **keep a dog and bark oneself** do the work for which one employs others (usu. in neg. & interrog. contexts). **lazy dog**: see LAZY *adjective*. **Lesser Dog**: see sense 5 above. **let sleeping dogs lie** refrain from intervening in a situation which is safest left alone. **like a dog with two tails** in a state of great delight. **Little Dog**: see sense 5 above. **Negro dog**: see NEGRO. **not a dog's chance** no chance whatever. **rain cats and dogs**: see CAT *noun*[1]. **running dog**: see RUNNING *ppl adjective*. **see a man about a dog**: see SEE *verb*. **short dog**: see SHORT *adjective*. SPOTTED **dog**. **the dog's bollocks** *coarse slang* a person or thing that is the best of its kind. **tinned dog**: see sense 1e above. **top dog**: see TOP *adjective*. **to the dogs** to ruin or destruction; **go to the dogs**, deteriorate shockingly; **send to the dogs**, **throw to the dogs**, discard as worthless. **try it on the dog**: see TRY *verb*. **turn dog**: see sense 2b above. **upper dog**: see UPPER *adjective*. **yellow dog**: see YELLOW *adjective*.
▸ **B** *attrib.* or as *adjective*. **1** Of or pertaining to dogs; canine. M16.
2 Of certain animals, esp. ones related to the dog: male. M16.
dog fox, **dog hyena**, **dog otter**, etc.
3 Of a language etc.: debased, corrupt, mongrel. E17.
dog Latin etc.
– COMB.: With certain adjectives in sense 'as — as a dog, thoroughly, extremely', as **dog-poor**, **dog-sick**, etc. Special combs., as †**dog-ape** a cynocephalus; **dogbane**, **dog's-bane** any of various plants reputedly poisonous to dogs; *esp.* any of various members of the genus *Apocynum* (family Apocynaceae); **dog biscuit** a hard dry savoury biscuit fed to dogs; *military slang* an army mattress; **dogbox** (*a*) a box or compartment for a dog or dogs to lie in; **in the dogbox** (*NZ slang*), in disfavour; (*b*) *Austral. & NZ slang* a compartment in a railway carriage without a corridor; a railway goods wagon; **dog-bramble** any of several thorny shrubs, *esp.* a N. American wild gooseberry, *Ribes cynosbati*; **dogcart** (*a*) a small cart drawn by dogs; (*b*) a two-wheeled open carriage with two cross-seats back to back, the rear one orig. made to shut up so as to form a box for sportsmen's dogs; **dog-cheap** *adjective & adverb* (*arch.*) costing very little; dirt cheap; **dog clutch** a (mechanical) clutch with the teeth of one part engaging in slots in the other; **dog cockle** any of numerous burrowing bivalve molluscs of the family Glycimeridae, having highly convex, almost spherical, shells; **dog collar** a collar for a dog's neck; *fig.* a close-fitting collar; *spec.* a clerical collar; also, a jewelled band worn by women, a choker; **dog daisy** the ox-eye daisy, *Leucanthemum vulgare*; *N. English* the common daisy, *Bellis perennis*; **dog days** the days about the time of the heliacal (or cosmical) rising of the Dog Star, traditionally regarded as the hottest and unhealthiest time of the year; *fig.* a period in which malignant influences prevail; **dog-eat-dog** *adjective* marked by mutually destructive competition; **dog-end** *slang* a cigarette end; **dogface** *US slang* a US soldier, esp. an infantryman; **dog-faced** *adjective* having a face like a dog; *spec.* designating baboons of the genus *Papio*, from their prognathous jaws; **dog fennel** the weed stinking camomile, *Anthemis cotula*; **dog-fall** WRESTLING: in which both wrestlers touch the ground together; **dog fence** *Austral.*: designed to exclude dingoes from a range; **dogfight** *noun & verb* (*a*) *noun* a fight between dogs; *fig.* a violent and confused fight; a fight between aircraft at close quarters; (*b*) *verb intrans.* take part in a dogfight; **dogfish** (*a*) any of various small sharks of the families Squalidae, Scyliorhinidae, and Triakidae; *esp.* the nurse hound or large spotted dogfish (*Scyliorhinus stellaris*), the lesser spotted dogfish (*S. canicula*), and the spur-dog or spiny or piked dogfish (*Squalus acanthias*); †(*b*) *fig.* a person held in contempt; **dog fly** [translating Greek *kunamuia*] any of various flies troublesome to dogs; now *esp.* (*US*) = **stable fly** s.v. STABLE *noun*[1]; **dog grass** (*a*) couch grass, *Leymus repens*; (*b*) *dial.* = **dogstail** below; **dog grate** a detached grate for a fireplace; **dog handler** a person, esp. a police officer, in charge of a dog or dogs; **doghead** the hammer of a gunlock; **dog-headed** *adjective* having a dog's head or a head like a dog's; **dog-hole** a hole fit for a dog; *derog.* a mean or cramped dwelling; **dog hook** an iron bar with a bent prong for securing or hoisting a log etc.; **doghouse** (*a*) (now *N. Amer.*) a kennel; (*b*) **in the doghouse** (*fig., colloq.*), in disgrace; (*c*) *colloq.* any small structure likened to a kennel, *esp.* a hut, a shelter; (*d*) *slang* a double bass; **dog-hutch** = **dog-hole** above; **dog-in-the-manger** *adjective* characteristic of a dog in the manger (see Phrases above); **dog iron**: see DOG *noun* 7; **dog-leech** (*a*) *arch.* a veterinary surgeon who treats dogs; †(*b*) an ignorant medical practitioner; **dogleg** GOLF a fairway which turns to left or right; **dogleg**, **dog-legged** *adjectives* bent like a dog's hind leg; **dog-leg fence**, **dog-legged fence** (*Austral. & NZ*), a fence made of logs or trees laid horizontally on crossing supports; **dog-leg stair**, **dog-legged stair**, a staircase without a well; **dog-lichen** a large prostrate leaflike lichen, *Peltigera canina*, with apothecia produced on upward-pointing narrow lobes; **dogman** *Austral.* a man who gives directional signals to a crane-operator on a building site, often riding on the goods lifted by the crane; **dog meat** prepared horseflesh or offal sold as food for dogs; **dog nail** a nail with a solid and slightly countersunk head; a large nail with a head projecting sideways; **dognap** a short sleep, a catnap; **dog-paddle** *noun & verb* (*colloq.*) (*a*) *noun* an elementary form of swimming stroke; (*b*) *verb intrans.* swim using this stroke; **dog race** a race between greyhounds; in *pl.* also, a meeting for such races; **dog-robber** *slang* (*a*) in *pl.*, civilian clothes worn by a naval officer on shore leave; (*b*) an army or navy officer's orderly; **dogrose** any of various related wild roses with faintly scented, usu. pale pink flowers, esp. *Rosa canina*; **dog's age** *slang* a very long time; **dog's-bane**: see **dogbane** above; **dog's breakfast** *slang* a mess; **dog's cabbage** a fleshy plant, *Theligonum cynocrambe*, grown as a pot-herb in Mediterranean regions; **dog's dinner** *slang* (*a*) **like a dog's dinner**, (dressed etc.) ostentatiously or overelaborately; (*b*) = **dog's breakfast** above; **dogshore** a temporary wooden support for a ship just before launching; **dogskin** (leather from or imitating) a dog's skin; †**dog's leather**: made from the skin of dogs; **dog-sleep** a light, fitful, or (formerly) feigned sleep; **dog's letter** [translating Latin *litera canina*] the letter R (from its resemblance in sound to the snarl of a dog); **dog's life** a life of constant harassment or drudgery; a miserable life; **dog's meat** (*a*) = **dog meat** above; *fig.* carrion; (*b*) *rhyming slang* feet (cf. sense 15 above); **dog's mercury**: see MERCURY *noun*; **dog's nose** a mixture of beer and gin or rum; **dog's onion**: see ONION *noun* 1b; **dogstail** a grass of the genus *Cynosurus*, with flowers in spikelike panicles, *esp.* (more fully **crested dogstail**) a common pasture grass, *C. cristatus*; **Dog Star** (*a*) the star Sirius, in the constellation of the Great Dog, the brightest of the fixed stars; (*b*) (in full **Lesser Dog star**) Procyon, a star of the first magnitude in the Little Dog; **dogstone** (*a*) a stone used for a millstone; (*b*) in *pl.* (now *rare* or *obsolete*) [translating medieval Latin *testiculus canis*], any of various British orchids; **dog's tongue** = **hound's tongue** s.v. HOUND *noun*[1]; **dog stove** = **dog grate** above; **dog's trick**: see **dog-trick** below; **dog tag** (*a*) a tag attached to a dog's collar, giving the owner's address, the dog's name, etc.; (*b*) *N. Amer. slang* a soldier's metal identity tag; **dog tent** a small tent shaped like a kennel; **dog tick** a tick which infests dogs; **dog-tired** *adjective* as tired as a dog after a long chase; utterly exhausted; **dog-town** *US* an area occupied by a colony of prairie dogs; **dog trials** *Austral. & NZ* sheepdog trials; **dog-trick** (now *rare* or *obsolete*), **dog's trick** a mean low-down trick; **dogtrot** an easy trot like that of a dog; **dog tucker** *Austral. & NZ* mutton used as food for working dogs; **dog vane** NAUTICAL a small improvised vane placed on a gunwale or shroud to show the direction of the wind; **dog violet** any of various related scentless violets, esp. *Viola riviniana*, common in woods and hedges; **dogwatch** (*a*) NAUTICAL either of the two shorter (two-hour) watches (4–6, 6–8 p.m.); (*b*) *US slang* a night shift, esp. in a newspaper office; **dog-weary** *adjective* = **dog-tired** above; **dog whelk** (*a*) any of various carnivorous marine gastropods of the family Nassariidae; (*b*) = **dog winkle** below; **dog-whipper** *hist.* an official formerly employed to whip dogs out of a church; a sexton, a beadle; **dog winkle** a carnivorous marine gastropod, *Nucella* (*Thais*) *lapillus*.
– NOTE: Perh. orig. applied to a particular breed, a mastiff or other powerful dog; adopted in this sense into Continental langs., at first usu. with the attribute 'English'. In Germanic langs. the generic name was *hund*: see HOUND *noun*.
■ **doglike** *adjective* (*a*) resembling (that of) a dog; (*b*) *fig.* excessively submissive or devoted: E16.

dog /dɒɡ/ *verb*. Infl. **-gg-**. E16.
[ORIGIN from the noun. In sense 8 back-form. from DOGGER *noun*[3].]
1 *verb trans.* Follow on the heels of; pursue closely (a person, a person's footsteps, etc.); *fig.* beset continually. E16.
S. NAIPAUL I went out into the lobby, dogged at a discreet distance by my spy. H. MOORE Insults and misunderstanding . . dogged him all his life.
2 *verb intrans.* Follow in close pursuit. E16.
3 *verb trans.* Drive or chase (esp. *out*) with a dog or dogs. L16.
4 *verb trans.* Fasten or secure by means of a (mechanical) dog. L16.
5 *verb trans.* In imprecations: damn. Chiefly in **be dogged if**. *US slang*. M19.
6 *verb intrans.* Go grouse-shooting using dogs to rouse the birds. Chiefly as **dogging** *verbal noun*. L19.
7 *verb intrans.* Betray someone; turn dog *on* (DOG *noun* 2b). *Austral. slang*. L19.
8 *verb intrans.* Hunt dingoes. Chiefly as **dogging** *verbal noun*. Cf. DOGGER *noun*[3]. *Austral.* E20.
9 *verb trans.* (esp. with *it*). Not try hard (at) or make an effort (over). *US slang*. E20.

dogan /ˈdəʊɡən/ *noun*. *Canad. slang*. M19.
[ORIGIN Uncertain: perh. from *Dogan*, an Irish surname.]
An Irish Roman Catholic.

dogana /də(ʊ)ˈɡɑːnə/ *noun*. M17.
[ORIGIN Italian: see DOUANE.]
In Italy (and Spain): a custom house; the customs.

D

D

dogaressa /dəʊgəˈrɛsə/ *noun*. E19.
[ORIGIN Italian, irreg. fem. of DOGE.]
hist. The wife of a doge.

dogate /ˈdəʊgeɪt/ *noun*. Also **dogeate** /-dʒ-/. E18.
[ORIGIN French *dogat* from Italian *dogato*, from DOGE: see -ATE[1].]
The position or status of a doge.

dogberry /ˈdɒgb(ə)ri, -bɛri/ *noun*[1]. Also †**dog's berry**. E16.
[ORIGIN from DOG *noun* + BERRY *noun*[1].]
The fruit of the wild cornel or dogwood, *Cornus sanguinea*; (in full ***dogberry tree***) the shrub itself. Also, (the fruit of) any of various other shrubs or small trees with fruit of poor eating quality, as the N. American mountain ash, *Sorbus americana*.

Dogberry /ˈdɒgbɛri, -b(ə)ri/ *noun*[2]. M19.
[ORIGIN A foolish constable in Shakespeare's *Much Ado*.]
An ignorant self-important petty official.

dogbolt /ˈdɒgbəʊlt/ *noun*. LME.
[ORIGIN Prob. from DOG *noun* + BOLT *noun*[1], but only readily so explained in sense 3.]
†**1** A butt for ridicule; a fool; a contemptible wretch. LME–E19.
†**2** A kind of bolt or blunt-headed arrow. L16–E17.
3 Any of various kinds of mechanical fastener. E19.

dogdom /ˈdɒgdəm/ *noun*. *joc.* M19.
[ORIGIN from DOG *noun* + -DOM.]
The world of dogs or dog-fanciers; dogs collectively.

doge /dəʊdʒ/ *noun*. M16.
[ORIGIN French (monosyllabic) from Italian (disyllabic) from Venetian Italian *doze* ult. from Latin DUX, *duc-* leader.]
hist. The chief magistrate in the former republics of Venice and Genoa.
■ **dogeship** *noun* the status, position, or personality of a doge L17.

dog-ear /ˈdɒgɪə/ *verb & noun*. Also (earlier) **dog's-** /ˈdɒgz-/. M17.
[ORIGIN from DOG *noun* (+ -'S[1]) + EAR *noun*[1].]
▸ **A** *verb trans.* Disfigure (a book etc.) by turning down the corners of the pages; make worn or grubby by repeated or careless use. Chiefly as ***dog-eared*** *ppl adjective*. M17.
▸ **B** *noun*. **I** Now usu. **dog-**.
1 The corner of the page of a book turned over or creased by repeated or careless use, or to keep a place. M18.
▸ **II dog's-** only.
2 NAUTICAL. A loop formed by a leech rope when a sail is reefed. M19.
3 NAUTICAL. A corner of a shark's-mouth in an awning. L19.

dogeate *noun* var. of DOGATE.

dogged /ˈdɒgɪd/ *adjective & adverb*. ME.
[ORIGIN from DOG *noun* + -ED[2]. Cf. CRABBED.]
▸ **A** *adjective*. †**1** Having the bad qualities of a dog; vicious, mean, spiteful; (of a thing) difficult to deal with, intractable. ME–L17.
2 a Bad-tempered, surly, morose. Now always with mixture of sense 2b: displaying sullen obstinacy. LME. ▸**b** Having the tenacity or persistence of a dog; stubborn, unyielding. L18.

> **a** S. PEPYS My wife in a dogged humour for my not dining at home. G. GISSING He had not spoken angrily but in a curiously dogged tone, with awkward emphasis. **b** C. STEAD I won't have this cussed obstinacy. I'll break that miserable dogged spirit of yours. D. ACHESON The dogged, unbeatable courage of the British. *Proverb*: It's dogged as does it.

3 *gen.* Having some other characteristic or habit of a dog; of or pertaining to a dog or dogs. Now *rare* or *obsolete*. LME.

> SHAKES. *John* Now for the bare-pick'd bone of majesty Doth dogged war bristle his angry crest.

▸ **B** *adverb*. †**1** Viciously, spitefully. Only in LME.
2 Excessively, thoroughly. *colloq. & dial.* E19.
■ **doggedly** *adverb* LME. **doggedness** *noun* M16.

dogger /ˈdɒgə/ *noun*[1]. ME.
[ORIGIN Middle Dutch = trawler, fishing boat.]
hist. A kind of two-masted fishing boat with bluff bows formerly used in the North Sea. Also ***dogger boat***.

dogger /ˈdɒgə/ *noun*[2]. L17.
[ORIGIN Perh. a deriv. of DOG *noun*.]
1 a A kind of ironstone found in globular concretions; a concretion of this. *dial.* L17. ▸**b** GEOLOGY. A large roughly spherical mass of sandstone. L19.
2 GEOLOGY. (**D-**.) The lowest division of the Middle Jurassic in Yorkshire, composed of marine sandstones and oolites; the Middle Jurassic system and period in Europe. E19.

dogger /ˈdɒgə/ *noun*[3]. *Austral.* L19.
[ORIGIN from DOG *noun* + -ER[1].]
A person who hunts dingoes. Cf. DOG *verb* 8.

doggerel /ˈdɒg(ə)r(ə)l/ *adjective & noun*. Also **doggrel** /ˈdɒgr(ə)l/. LME.
[ORIGIN App. from DOG *noun & adjective* (with contempt. force as in *dog Latin*): see -REL.]
▸ **A** *adjective*. Of verse: burlesque and composed in irregular rhythm; trivial, paltry; undignified. LME.

> BARONESS ORCZY His doggerel verse, 'We seek him here, we seek him there,' etc.

▸ **B** *noun*. Burlesque verse in irregular rhythm; (a specimen of) trivial or pedestrian verse. M17.
■ **doggerelize** *verb trans.* turn into doggerel E19. **doggerelizer** *noun* a writer of doggerel E19.

doggery /ˈdɒg(ə)ri/ *noun*. E17.
[ORIGIN from DOG *noun* + -ERY.]
1 Foul or abusive language. *rare*. E17.
2 Contemptible or dishonest behaviour. M19.
3 Dogs collectively; *fig.* [translating French *canaille*] a rabble. M19.
4 A cheap or disreputable saloon. *US slang*. M19.

doggess /ˈdɒgɪs/ *noun*. *joc.* M18.
[ORIGIN from DOG *noun* + -ESS[1].]
A female dog, a bitch.

†**dogget(t)** *nouns, verbs* vars. of DOCKET *noun, verb*.

doggie *noun* var. of DOGGY *noun*.

doggish /ˈdɒgɪʃ/ *adjective*. LME.
[ORIGIN from DOG *noun* + -ISH[1].]
1 Pertaining to or resembling (that of) a dog. LME.
2 *spec.* Having the bad qualities of a dog; malicious; surly, bad-tempered; snappish; spiteful. Now *rare*. LME.
■ **doggishly** *adverb* L16. **doggishness** *noun* L16.

doggo /ˈdɒgəʊ/ *adverb*. *slang*. L19.
[ORIGIN App. from DOG *noun* + -O.]
Without moving or making a sound; without doing anything that would draw attention to one's presence. Chiefly in ***lie doggo***.

doggone /ˈdɒgɒn/ *verb, adjective, adverb, & noun*. *colloq.* (chiefly *N. Amer.*). Also **dog-gone**, **dog-on**, & (esp. as verb) **dog gone**. E19.
[ORIGIN Prob. alt. of *God damn*.]
▸ **A** *verb trans.* (esp. with *it*). Damn, confound. E19.

> R. H. MORRIESON Doggone it, . . she *was* pretty.

▸ **B** *adjective*. Damned, confounded; (esp. with *I'm*) astonished, blowed. M19.

> S. LEWIS By golly, here they go and use up all the towels, every doggone one of 'em.

▸ **C** *adverb*. Confoundedly, damnably. L19.

> R. D. SAUNDERS You was so dog-gone proud of the blue coat.

▸ **D** *noun*. A damn. M20.

> E. CALDWELL That will be my ship coming in, and I don't give a dog-gone for the name you call it.

dog-goned /ˈdɒgɒnd/ *adjective*. *colloq.* (chiefly *N. Amer.*). M19.
[ORIGIN Prob. alt. of ***God-damned***.]
= DOGGONE *adjective*.

> C. E. MULFORD Well, I'll be dog-goned if here ain't Hopalong!

doggrel *adjective & noun* var. of DOGGEREL.

doggy /ˈdɒgi/ *noun*. Also **-ie**. L17.
[ORIGIN from DOG *noun* + -Y[6], -IE.]
1 A little dog; (a pet name for) a dog. L17.
2 MINING. = DEPUTY *noun* 2c. Orig., a subordinate to a butty (BUTTY *noun*[1] 2). *dial.* M19.
3 An officer's servant or assistant. Cf. ***dog-robber*** (b) s.v. DOG *noun*. *slang*. E20.
– COMB.: **doggy bag** a bag in which a diner may take away leftovers, *esp.* one provided by a restaurant; **doggy style** *colloq.* a position for sexual intercourse in which the woman, usu. on all fours, is penetrated from behind by the man.

doggy /ˈdɒgi/ *adjective*. LME.
[ORIGIN from DOG *noun* + -Y[1]. Cf. HORSY.]
†**1** = DOGGISH 2. LME–L16.
2 = DOGGISH 1. M19.

> A. BURGESS They looked up at me with eyes that would soon grow doggy and pleading.

3 Of a person: devoted to or concerned with dogs. M19.
4 Stylish, smart, dashing. Cf. DOG *noun* 13. *slang*. L19.

dogie /ˈdəʊgi/ *noun*. *N. Amer.* Also **dogy**. L19.
[ORIGIN Unknown.]
A neglected or undernourished calf on a range, *esp.* one without a mother.

dogless /ˈdɒglɪs/ *adjective*. M19.
[ORIGIN from DOG *noun* + -LESS.]
Having no dog.

dogling *noun* var. of DOEGLING.

dogma /ˈdɒgmə/ *noun*. Pl. **-mas**, **-mata** /-mətə/. M16.
[ORIGIN Late Latin from Greek *dogma*, *dogmat-* opinion, decree, from *dokein* seem good, think.]
1 An opinion, a belief; *spec.* a tenet or doctrine authoritatively laid down, esp. by a Church or sect; an arrogant declaration of opinion. M16.

> R. NIEBUHR The idea of the class struggle is a dogma which creates . . the conflict experience of the worker. R. LOWELL The year when Pius XII defined the dogma of Mary's bodily assumption.

2 Doctrines or opinions, esp. on religious matters, laid down authoritatively or assertively. L18.

> J. MORLEY It places character on the pedestal where Puritanism places dogma. G. BROWN What he didn't have was dogma—he accepted that there could be more than one way of accomplishing a purpose.

dogmatic /dɒgˈmatɪk/ *noun & adjective*. E17.
[ORIGIN Latin *dogmaticus* from Greek *dogmatikos*, from DOGMA: see -ATIC.]
▸ **A** *noun*. **1** = DOGMATIST *noun* 1. *obsolete* exc. *hist.* E17.
2 *sing.* & (now usu.) in *pl.* (treated as *sing.*). A system of dogma; *spec.* dogmatic theology. M19.
▸ **B** *adjective*. **1** Of philosophy or medicine: based on a priori assumptions rather than empirical evidence. L17.
2 Concerned with propounding opinions; *esp.* (of a person, writing, etc.) asserting doctrines or views in an opinionated or arbitrary manner. L17.

> G. MURRAY He lays down . . lots of rules, . . some of them hopelessly dogmatic and inhuman. J. K. GALBRAITH When people are least sure, they are often most dogmatic.

3 Of, pertaining to, or of the nature of a (religious) dogma or dogmas; doctrinal. L17.

> J. S. MILL A . . Christian in all but the dogmatic sense of the word.

dogmatic THEOLOGY.
■ **dogmatician** /-ˈtɪʃ(ə)n/ *noun* an expert in or student of dogmatics M19.

dogmatical /dɒgˈmatɪk(ə)l/ *adjective & noun*. E17.
[ORIGIN formed as DOGMATIC + -AL[1].]
▸ **A** *adjective*. = DOGMATIC *adjective*. E17.
▸ †**B** *noun*. In *pl.* Dogmatics. E17–E18.
■ **dogmaticalness** *noun* L17.

dogmatically /dɒgˈmatɪk(ə)li/ *adverb*. M17.
[ORIGIN from DOGMATIC *adjective* or DOGMATICAL *adjective*: see -ICALLY.]
In a dogmatic manner.

dogmatise *verb* var. of DOGMATIZE.

dogmatism /ˈdɒgmətɪz(ə)m/ *noun*. E17.
[ORIGIN French *dogmatisme* or late Latin *dogmatismus*, from Latin DOGMA: see -ISM.]
1 Positive assertion of dogmas or opinions; dogmatic character. Formerly also, the propounding of new doctrines. E17. ▸**b** A dogmatic tenet or system. *rare*. E19.
2 A system of philosophy with principles based on reasoning alone, not experience. L18.

dogmatist /ˈdɒgmətɪst/ *noun*. E16.
[ORIGIN French *dogmatiste* or late Latin *dogmatistes* from Greek, from *dogmatizein*: see DOGMATIZE, -IST.]
1 A philosopher or physician of a dogmatic school (see DOGMATIC *adjective* 1). E16.
†**2** A person who propounds new doctrines. L16–L18.
3 A person who dogmatizes; *esp.* one who asserts his or her opinions forcefully or in a doctrinaire manner. M17.

dogmatize /ˈdɒgmətʌɪz/ *verb*. Also **-ise**. E17.
[ORIGIN Old French & mod. French *dogmatiser* or late Latin *dogmatizare* from Greek *dogmatizein* lay down as one's opinion, from DOGMA: see -IZE.]
1 *verb intrans.* Speak or write authoritatively or imperiously without giving arguments or evidence in support of one's assertions. E17.

> A. S. NEILL I should not dare dogmatize about girls who never go to lessons.

2 *verb trans.* Formulate into a dogma; assert dogmatically. E17.

> *Daily Telegraph* I find the views expressed . . dogmatised to the point of polemic absurdity.

†**3** *verb intrans.* Teach new doctrines. Only in 17.
■ **dogmatiˈzation** *noun* (*rare*) L19. **dogmatizer** *noun* E17.

dognapping /ˈdɒgnapɪŋ/ *noun*. *colloq.* M20.
[ORIGIN from DOG *noun* after *kidnapping*.]
The stealing of dogs in order to get a ransom or reward from the owners, or to sell them.
■ **dognapper** *noun* M20.

do-good /ˈduːgʊd/ *noun & adjective*. M17.
[ORIGIN from *do good*: see GOOD *noun*.]
▸ **A** *noun*. **1** A person who or thing which does good or is of use. *obsolete* exc. as in sense 2. M17.
2 *spec.* = DO-GOODER. E20.
▸ **B** *adjective*. Designating or typical of a 'do-good'. M20.

do-gooder /duːˈgʊdə/ *noun*. *colloq.* E20.
[ORIGIN formed as DO-GOOD + -ER[1].]
A person who actively tries to help other people, *esp.* one regarded as unrealistic or officious.
■ **do-goodery** *noun* the activities or attitudes of do-gooders M20. **do-gooding** *adjective & noun* (*a*) *adjective* behaving as a do-gooder; (*b*) *noun* the activities of a do-gooder: M20. **do-goodism** *noun* = DO-GOODERY M20.

Dogra /ˈdəʊgrə/ *noun & adjective*. Also (see senses A.2, B. below) **-ri** /-ri/. M19.
[ORIGIN Dogri *dogrā*.]
▸ **A** *noun*. **1** Pl. **-s**, same. A member of a mainly Hindu people predominating in the Jammu district of the Indian state of Jammu and Kashmir. M19.
2 Usu. **-ri**. The Indo-Aryan language of this people. M20.

▸ **B** *adjective*. Of or pertaining to the Dogras or (usu. **-ri**) their language. **L19**.

Dogrib /ˈdɒɡrɪb/ *noun & adjective*. **L19**.
[ORIGIN from DOG *noun* + RIB *noun*, as translation of Dogrib *Thlingchadinne* dog's flank (from their legend that they are descended from a dog).]
▸ **A** *noun*. **1** A member of an Athabaskan people of NW Canada. **L19**.
2 The language of this people, belonging to the Na-Dene family. **E20**.
▸ **B** *adjective*. Of or pertaining to the Dogribs. **M20**.

dogsbody /ˈdɒɡzbɒdi/ *noun*. Also **dog's body**, **dog's-body**. **E19**.
[ORIGIN from DOG *noun* + -'S[1] + BODY *noun*.]
1 Peas boiled in a cloth. Also, sea biscuits soaked to a pulp with water and sugar. *nautical slang*. **E19**.
2 A person given a variety of menial tasks; *nautical slang* a junior officer. **E20**.

dog's-ear *verb & noun* see DOG-EAR.

dog's tooth /ˈdɒɡz tuːθ/ *noun phr*. **L16**.
[ORIGIN from DOG *noun* + -'S[1] + TOOTH *noun*.]
1 Now more fully ***dog's tooth violet***. Any of various spring-flowering plants of the genus *Erythronium* of the lily family, so called from the toothed perianth segments; esp. *E. dens-canis*, with mottled leaves and purplish flowers. **L16**.
2 More fully ***dog's tooth grass***. A creeping grass, *Cynodon dactylon*, common in warmer parts of the world and used for lawns and fodder. **E17**.
3 (A fabric in) a broken check pattern; = ***houndstooth*** s.v. HOUND *noun*[1]. **M20**.

dog-tooth /ˈdɒɡtuːθ/ *noun & verb*. **LME**.
[ORIGIN from DOG *noun* + TOOTH *noun*.]
▸ **A** *noun*. Pl. **-teeth**.
1 An eye tooth. **LME**.
2 A stone ornament with four leaves radiating from a raised central point, much used in Norman and Early English architecture. Also ***dog-tooth moulding***. **M19**.
3 = DOG'S TOOTH 3. **M20**.
– COMB.: **dog-tooth spar** a form of calcite with pointed scalenohedral crystals; **dog-tooth violet** = DOG'S TOOTH 1.
▸ **B** *verb trans*. Decorate with dog-tooth moulding. **M19**.

dogwood /ˈdɒɡwʊd/ *noun*. **L16**.
[ORIGIN from DOG *noun* + WOOD *noun*[1]. Cf. DOGBERRY *noun*[1].]
1 Any of various shrubs and small trees of the genus *Cornus* (family Cornaceae); their hard horny wood; *esp.* (***a***) the wild cornel, *C. sanguinea*, a shrub with dark red twigs and clusters of small white flowers; (***b***) *N. Amer.* (also ***flowering dogwood***) the flowering cornel, *C. florida*, a deciduous tree in which the flowers are surrounded by large petal-like bracts. **L16**.
2 (The wood of) any of various shrubs and trees suggesting the wild cornel in appearance or by the hardness of their wood; *esp.* (*W. Indian*) the leguminous tree *Piscidia piscipula*; *Austral.* the leguminous shrub *Jacksonia scoparia*. **L17**.

dogy *noun* var. of DOGIE.

DoH *abbreviation*.
Department of Health.

doh /dəʊ/ *noun*. Also **do**. **M18**.
[ORIGIN Italian *do* arbitrary syllable repl. UT.]
MUSIC. In solmization: the keynote of a major diatonic scale (also ***movable doh***); the note C (also ***fixed doh***).

doh /dəʊ/ *interjection*. **M20**.
[ORIGIN Natural exclam. Cf. OH *interjection*.]
Expr. frustration at the realization that things have turned out badly or not as planned, or that the speaker or someone else has just said or done something foolish.

N. HORNBY 'Doh,' said Marcus scornfully. 'Why would I want to go there?'

DOHC *abbreviation*.
Double overhead camshaft.

dohickey *noun* var. of DOOHICKEY.

dohyo /ˈdəʊjəʊ/ *noun*. Pl. **-os**. **E20**.
[ORIGIN Japanese, abbreviation of *dohyōba* wrestling arena, from *do* land, soil + *hyo* sack + *ba* arena.]
The ring within which sumo wrestling takes place.

DOI *abbreviation*.
COMPUTING. Digital object identifier.

doigté /dwate/ *noun*. **L19**.
[ORIGIN French, from *doigt* finger from Latin *digitus* DIGIT.]
FENCING. The use of the fingers and thumb in manipulating the sword.

doiled /dɔɪld/ *adjective*. *Scot.* Also **doilt**, **doylt**, /dɔɪlt/. **E16**.
[ORIGIN Unknown.]
Stupid, foolish; confused, affected in mind; wearied.

doily /ˈdɔɪli/ *adjective & noun*. Also **doyl(e)y**. **L17**.
[ORIGIN *Doiley* or *Doyley*, 17th-cent. London draper.]
▸ †**A** *adjective*. Designating a woollen material used esp. for summer wear; made of this material. **L17–E18**.
doily napkin = sense B.1 below.
▸ **B** *noun*. **1** [Ellipt. for *doily napkin* above.] A small ornamental napkin used at dessert. *arch.* **L18**.
2 A small light ornamental mat of paper or cloth, used on a plate beneath sandwiches, cakes, etc. **M19**.

doing /ˈduːɪŋ/ *noun*. **ME**.
[ORIGIN from DO *verb* + -ING[1].]
1 The action of DO *verb*; action, conduct; performance, execution, (*of* something). Freq. with possess., attributing responsibility to a specified agent. **ME**. ▸**b** Sexual intercourse. **E17**. ▸**c** Effort put into accomplishing something. *colloq.* **M20**.

SHAKES. *Tr. & Cr.* Things won are done; joy's soul lies in the doing. *Book of Common Prayer* This is the Lords doing: and it is marvellous in our eyes. R. LAWLER I'm not blamin' him. This is Barney's doin', he cooked this up. **c** L. NKOSI Took a bit of doing, but . . we pulled it off.

2 A deed, an action; an activity. Usu. (now always, exc. *Scot.*) in *pl.* **LME**. ▸**b** A scolding; a thrashing; a defeating. *colloq. & dial.* **E19**.

BARONESS ORCZY Feelings . . ran very high . . against the French and their doings. J. GALSWORTHY It was a habit with him to tell her the doings of his day.

3 In *pl.* Ingredients for a dish; a prepared or fancy dish; food, victuals; drink. *US dial. & Austral. slang*. **M19**.
4 In *pl.* Trimmings, ornaments, etc., for a dress. *US colloq.* **M19**.
5 In *pl.* (treated as *sing.* or *pl.*). A thing needed; requisites; something referred to without being named. *slang*. **E20**.

J. FOWLES There were all the doings to make tea with. P. LIVELY If either of you need the doings it's first right at the end of the passage.

6 In *pl.* Excrement. *slang*. **M20**.

doing /ˈduːɪŋ/ *ppl adjective*. **L16**.
[ORIGIN from DO *verb* + -ING[2].]
That does, acts, or performs; *spec.* busy; energetic.
up and doing: see UP *adverb*[2] & *adjective*[2].

doit /dɔɪt/ *noun*. Now *arch.* or *hist.* **L16**.
[ORIGIN Middle Low German *doyt* = Middle Dutch *duit*, *deuyt*. Cf. DODKIN.]
1 A small Dutch coin formerly in use, the eighth part of a stiver; any very small coin or sum. **L16**.
2 *fig.* A very small part *of* anything; a bit, a jot. Esp. in ***not care a doit***. **M17**.

doit /dɔɪt/ *verb*. *Scot. & N. English*. **M16**.
[ORIGIN Uncertain: perh. alt. of DOTE *verb*[1]. Cf. DOITED.]
1 *verb intrans.* Behave stupidly; be confused or enfeebled, esp. through old age or drink. **M16**.
2 *verb trans.* Make confused, befuddle; puzzle. Cf. earlier DOITED. **M18**.
3 *verb intrans.* Walk unsteadily. **L18**.

doited /ˈdɔɪtɪd/ *adjective*. *Scot. & N. English*. **LME**.
[ORIGIN Uncertain: perh. alt. of *doted* pa. pple of DOTE *verb*[1].]
Having the faculties impaired, esp. by age.

doitkin *noun* see DODKIN.

do-it-yourself /ˌduːɪtjəˈsɛlf, -tʃə-/ *noun & adjective*. **M20**.
[ORIGIN from *do it yourself* (DO *verb* 3).]
▸ **A** *noun*. The action or practice of doing practical work, esp. one's household repairs and maintenance, oneself, rather than paying to have it done. **M20**.
▸ **B** *adjective*. Pertaining to do-it-yourself; suitable or intended for use by a do-it-yourselfer or amateur; interested in do-it-yourself. **M20**.
■ **do-it-yourselfer** *noun* a person who practises do-it-yourself **M20**.

dojo /ˈdəʊdʒəʊ/ *noun*. Pl. **-os**. **M20**.
[ORIGIN Japanese, from *dō* way, pursuit + *-jō* a place.]
A room or hall in which judo or other martial arts are practised; an area of padded mats for the same purpose.

doke /dəʊk/ *noun*. Now *dial.* **E17**.
[ORIGIN Uncertain: cf. East Frisian *dōlke* small hollow, dimple. See also DOLK.]
A hollow; a dent; a dimple.

Doketism *noun* var. of DOCETISM.

dol /dəʊl/ *noun*. **M20**.
[ORIGIN Latin *dolor* pain.]
A unit of intensity of pain.

dol. *abbreviation*.
Dollar(s).

dolabriform /də(ʊ)ˈlabrɪfɔːm/ *adjective*. **M18**.
[ORIGIN from Latin *dolabra* pickaxe + -I- + -FORM.]
BOTANY & ENTOMOLOGY. Axe-shaped.

Dolby /ˈdɒlbi, ˈdəʊl-/ *noun*. **M20**.
[ORIGIN R. M. *Dolby* (b. 1933), US engineer.]
(Proprietary name for) a kind of electronic noise-reduction system used esp. to reduce tape hiss.
■ **Dolbyed** *adjective* (UK proprietary) provided with a Dolby **L20**. **Dolbyized** *adjective* (US proprietary) = DOLBYED **L20**.

dolcan /ˈdɒlkən/ *noun*. **M19**.
[ORIGIN from Italian *dolce* sweet: cf. Italian *dolciano*.]
A kind of soft-toned organ stop, wider at the top than at the bottom.

dolce far niente /ˌdoltʃe far niˈɛnte/ *noun phr.* **E19**.
[ORIGIN Italian = sweet doing nothing.]
Delightful idleness. Cf. FAR NIENTE.

Dolcelatte /dɒltʃɛˈlɑːteɪ/ *noun*. **M20**.
[ORIGIN Italian, lit. 'sweet milk'.]
(Proprietary name for) a kind of soft, creamy blue-veined Italian cheese, similar to Gorgonzola but milder.

dolce vita /doltʃe ˈviːta, dəʊltʃeɪ ˈviːtə/ *noun phr.* **M20**.
[ORIGIN Italian = sweet life.]
A life of luxury, pleasure, and self-indulgence. Freq. preceded by *the* or *la* /la/.

D

doldrum /ˈdɒldrəm/ *noun*. **L18**.
[ORIGIN Perh. from DULL *adjective* after *tantrum*.]
▸ **I** *sing.* †**1** A dull, sluggish, or stupid person. **L18–E19**.
▸ **II** In *pl.* (usu. with *the*).
2 A condition of dullness or drowsiness; low spirits, despondency. **E19**.
3 The condition of a ship which makes no headway. **E19**.
4 A region of calms, sudden storms, and light unpredictable winds near the Equator. **M19**.
5 *fig.* A state or period of little activity or progress in affairs. **L19**.

J. BARZUN Fiction languishes and the theater is in the doldrums.

dole /dəʊl/ *noun*[1]. Also (*Scot. & N. English*) **dale** /deɪl/.
[ORIGIN Old English *dāl* from Germanic base also of DEAL *noun*[1].]
†**1** The state of being divided; division. **OE–ME**.
2 †**a** A part or division of a whole. **OE–L16**. ▸**b** A portion of an area of land, esp. a common field. Chiefly *Scot. & N. English*. *obsolete* exc. *hist.* **ME**. ▸**c** A portion for sale; *Scot.* a former measure in which coal was sold. **E18**. ▸**d** MINING. A portion of ore. **E19**.
3 One's share, one's portion. *arch.* **ME**.
4 Fate, destiny; lot in life. Chiefly in ***happy man be his dole*** (proverbial). *arch.* **ME**.
†**5** Dealing, intercourse. **ME–M16**.
6 Dealing out, distribution, esp. of charitable gifts. **ME**.
7 That which is doled out, *esp.* a gift of food or money made in charity. **LME**. ▸†**b** A reward given to hounds. **L16–L17**. ▸**c** State relief paid to the unemployed. Usu. ***the dole***. *colloq.* **E20**.

c R. HOGGART A man out of work and drawing the dole.

c on the dole in receipt of unemployment benefit.

8 = DEAL *noun*[1] 3. *Scot.* **E18**.
– COMB.: **dole bludger** *Austral. & NZ* a person who draws unemployment benefit in preference to getting or seeking work; **dole queue** a queue of people waiting to collect unemployment benefit (*lit. & fig.*).

dole /dəʊl/ *noun*[2]. *arch. & dial.* Also **dool**, **dule**, /duːl/. **ME**.
[ORIGIN Old French *dol*, *doel*, *duel* (mod. *deuil*) mourning from popular Latin *dolus*, from Latin *dolere* grieve.]
1 Grief, sorrow; distress of mind. **ME**.
2 Mourning, lamentation. Chiefly in ***make dole***. **ME**.
3 A cause of grief; a grievous or piteous thing; a sorrow. **ME**.
†**4** Clothes etc. worn as a sign of mourning. **E16–M18**.
5 A funeral. *obsolete* exc. *dial.* **M16**.

dole /dəʊl/ *noun*[3]. **LME**.
[ORIGIN Latin *dolus* deceit from Greek *dolos*.]
†**1** Guile, deceit, fraud. **LME–M19**.
2 SCOTS LAW (now *hist.*). The wrongful intention necessary to make an act a crime. **M17**.

dole *noun*[4] var. of DOOL *noun*[1].

dole /dəʊl/ *verb*[1]. **ME**.
[ORIGIN Old French *doleir*, *doloir* (mod. (*se*) *douloir*) from Latin *dolere* grieve.]
†**1** *verb intrans.* Sorrow, lament. **ME–L18**.
2 *verb trans.* Mourn, bewail. *obsolete* exc. *Scot. dial.* **M16**.
3 *verb intrans.* Of a bird: coo. **M19**.

dole /dəʊl/ *verb*[2] *trans.* **LME**.
[ORIGIN from DOLE *noun*[1].]
1 Give as a dole; distribute as charity. **LME**.
†**2** Spread *about*, *around*; distribute. **E–M18**.
3 Give *out* in small quantities; deal *out* sparingly. **M18**.

A. MOOREHEAD At each meal he carefully doled out the food.

■ **doler** *noun* a person who doles something (usu. foll. by *out*) **L16**.

doleful /ˈdəʊlfʊl, -f(ə)l/ *adjective & noun*. **ME**.
[ORIGIN from DOLE *noun*[2] + -FUL.]
▸ **A** *adjective*. **1** Fraught with or causing sorrow, distressing; gloomy, dismal. **ME**.

MILTON Regions of sorrow, doleful shades.

2 Of a person etc.: full of pain, grief, or suffering; sorrowful; melancholy, discontented. **ME**.
3 Expressive of grief, suffering, or sad regret. **ME**.

DAY LEWIS Her pure, rather doleful voice.

▸ **B** *noun*. †**1** In *pl.* Mourning clothes. *rare*. Only in **M18**.
2 In *pl.* A doleful state, *the* dumps. *colloq.* **L18**.
■ **dolefully** *adverb* **ME**. **dolefulness** *noun* **LME**.

dolent /ˈdəʊl(ə)nt/ *adjective*. *arch.* **LME**.
[ORIGIN Old French & mod. French from Proto-Gallo-Romance, from Latin *dolent-* pres. ppl stem of *dolere* grieve: see -ENT.]
1 = DOLEFUL *adjective* 2. **LME**.

2 = DOLEFUL *adjective* 3. L15.
†**3** = DOLEFUL *adjective* 1. L15–L16.

dolerite /ˈdɒlərʌɪt/ *noun*. M19.
[ORIGIN French *dolérite*, from Greek *doleros* deceptive (because it was difficult to distinguish from diorite): see -ITE[1].]
An igneous rock chemically the same as basalt and gabbro but medium-grained with a usu. ophitic texture.
■ **doleˈritic** *adjective* M19.

dolesome /ˈdəʊls(ə)m/ *adjective*. Now *rare*. M16.
[ORIGIN from DOLE *noun*[2] + -SOME[1].]
= DOLEFUL *adjective* 1, 3.
■ **dolesomely** *adverb* L16. **dolesomeness** *noun* E17.

doless /ˈduːlɪs/ *adjective*. *dial.* & *colloq.* (chiefly *Scot.* & *US*). Also **do-less**. M18.
[ORIGIN from DO *verb* + -LESS.]
Lazy, good-for-nothing; lacking energy.
M. MEAD Too lazy, too do-less, to make an effort.

dolia *noun* pl. of DOLIUM.

doli capax /dɒlɪ ˈkapaks/ *adjectival phr.* L17.
[ORIGIN from Latin *doli* genit. sing. of *dolus* (see DOLE *noun*[3], DOLUS) + *capax* capable.]
LAW. Capable of having the intention to commit a crime or tort, esp. through being of sufficient age. Cf. DOLI INCAPAX.

dolicho- /ˈdɒlɪkəʊ/ *combining form* of Greek *dolikhos* narrow: see -O-. Cf. BRACHY-, PLATY-.
■ **dolichoˈpellic** *adjective* [Greek *pella* bowl] having or designating a pelvis whose anteroposterior diameter is nearly as great as its transverse diameter L19.

dolichocephalic /ˌdɒlɪkəʊsɪˈfalɪk, -kɛˈfalɪk/ *adjective*. Also †**-keph-**. M19.
[ORIGIN from DOLICHO- + -CEPHALIC.]
Long-headed; *spec.* having a cranial index of less than 75.
■ ˈ**dolichocephal** *adjective* & *noun* (pl. **-s**) [back-form. from mod. Latin pl.] †(**a**) *adjective* dolichocephalic; (**b**) *noun* a dolichocephalic person: L19. **dolichoˈcephali** *noun pl.* (now *rare* or *obsolete*) [mod. Latin] dolichocephals M19. **dolichoˈcephalism** *noun* dolichocephalic condition M19. **dolichoˈcephalous** *adjective* dolichocephalic M19. **dolichoˈcephaly** *noun* dolichocephalism M19.

dolichos /ˈdɒlɪkɒs/ *noun*. Pl. **-es**, same. L18.
[ORIGIN mod. Latin from Greek = long, with allus. to the length of the pods.]
Any of several tropical leguminous plants of the genus *Dolichos*, grown for food or fodder.

doli incapax /ˌdɒlɪ ɪnˈkapaks/ *adjectival phr.* L17.
[ORIGIN formed as DOLI CAPAX: see IN-[2].]
LAW. Not capable of forming the intent to commit a crime or tort, esp. through being too young. Cf. DOLI CAPAX.

†**doliman** *noun* see DOLMAN.

doline /dɒˈliːnə, -ˈliːn/ *noun*. Also **-ina** /-iːnə/. L19.
[ORIGIN German from Slovene *dolina* valley.]
A typically funnel-shaped basin in a karstic region.

do-little /ˈduːlɪt(ə)l/ *noun* & *adjective*. L16.
[ORIGIN from DO *verb* + LITTLE *noun*.]
▸ **A** *noun*. A person who does little; a lazy person. L16.
▸ **B** *adjective*. Lazy. L17.

dolium /ˈdəʊlɪəm/ *noun*. Pl. **-ia** /-ɪə/. L15.
[ORIGIN Latin *dolium*.]
ROMAN ANTIQUITIES. A large earthenware vessel for storing grain, wine, etc.

dolk /dɒlk/ *noun*. *obsolete* exc. *dial.* ME.
[ORIGIN Uncertain: for sense 1 cf. Old Frisian *dolch*, Old High German *tolg* wound; for sense 3 cf. DOKE.]
†**1** A wound; a scar. Only in ME.
2 = DOKE. E19.
3 A dab, a light blow. M19.

doll /dɒl/ *noun*[1]. M16.
[ORIGIN Pet form of female forename *Dorothy*, with *l* for *r* as in *Hal*, *Sal*, *Moll*, for *Harry*, *Sarah*, *Mary*.]
†**1** A female favourite, a mistress. M16–E17.
2 A small model of a human figure, usu. a child or woman, for use as a toy. L17. ▸**b** A ventriloquist's or puppeteer's dummy. L19. ▸**c** A hit or score in the game of Aunt Sally. L20.
C. MCCULLOUGH The doll had jointed arms and legs which could be moved anywhere.
Dutch doll, ***peg doll***, ***rag doll***, ***Russian doll***, ***walking doll***, etc.
3 A woman who is pretty but unintelligent or frivolous. L18. ▸**b** Any woman or girl, *esp.* an attractive one; occas., a pleasant or attractive man. *slang.* M19.
b R. LARDNER Betsy is some doll when she is all fixed up.
– COMB.: **doll-baby** *US* = sense 2 above; **doll hospital** *US* = ***doll's hospital*** below; **dollhouse** *N. Amer.* = ***doll's house*** below; **doll's hospital** an establishment that repairs dolls and sells materials for making them; **doll's house** a miniature toy house for dolls; a very small house.
■ **dolldom** *noun* the world of dolls M19. **dollhood** *noun* the state or condition of a doll, or of being like a doll L19. **dollship** *noun* (with possess. adjective, as ***her dollship*** etc.) a mock title of respect given to a doll M18.

doll /dɒl/ *noun*[2]. M20.
[ORIGIN Perh. var. of DOOL *noun*[1].]
HORSE-RACING. A hurdle used as a barrier.

†**doll** *verb*[1] *trans.* LME.
[ORIGIN Unknown.]
1 Warm moderately; mull. LME–M17.
2 Make (drink) stale or vapid. LME–M19.

doll /dɒl/ *verb*[2] *trans.* & *intrans. colloq.* E20.
[ORIGIN from DOLL *noun*[1].]
Foll. by *up*: dress up finely or elaborately; make (esp. oneself) smart.
H. L. WILSON Jeff said he'd also doll up in his dress suit and get shaved. F. ASTAIRE The Globe Theatre was all dolled up with fresh paint. J. KEROUAC Old Mr. Burke dolled himself up for a date.

dollar /ˈdɒlə/ *noun*. M16.
[ORIGIN Early Flemish, Low German *daler* (Dutch *daalder*) from German *Taler* (formerly also *thaler*), abbreviation of *Joachimst(h)aler* coin from the silver mine of *Joachimst(h)al*, i.e. Joachim's valley, now Jáchymov in the Czech Republic. Cf. THALER.]
1 *hist.* A German thaler; any of various northern European coins bearing an equivalent name. M16.
2 *hist.* A Spanish or Spanish-American peso or piece of eight (also largely used in the British N. American colonies at the time of the War of Independence). L16.
3 The basic monetary unit of the United States, equal to 100 cents; a basic monetary unit in Canada, Australia, New Zealand, and numerous other countries; a note or coin of the value of one dollar. L18.
4 A five-shilling piece, a crown. *slang. obsolete* exc. *hist.* E19.
– PHRASES: ***a million dollars***: see MILLION *adjective*. **be dollars to doughnuts**, **be dollars to buttons**, etc., *US* be a certainty (*that*). ***bottom dollar***: see BOTTOM *adjective*. ***like a million dollars***: see MILLION *adjective*. ***top dollar***: see TOP *adjective*.
– COMB.: **dollar area** those countries which have a currency linked to the US dollar; **dollarbird** the broad-billed roller, *Eurystomus orientalis*, a brown and blue-green bird of parts of Asia and Australia that has a round white patch on each wing; **dollar day** *N. Amer.*: when a shop makes special price reductions, usu. including some to a dollar; **dollar diplomacy**: which seeks to advance a country's financial and commercial interests abroad and hence its international influence; **dollar gap** the excess of a country's import trade with the dollar area over the corresponding export trade; **dollar mark**, **dollar sign** the symbol $, placed before a number to denote that many dollars; **dollar spot** a discoloured area caused by disease, esp. on a lawn; a fungal disease that affects lawns in this way.
■ **Dollardom** *noun* (now *rare*) (the inhabitants of) a place where the people's main aim is seen as amassing dollars; rich Americans collectively: M19. **dollariˈzation** *noun* the action or process of aligning a currency with the US dollar L20.

dollop /ˈdɒləp/ *noun* & *verb*. L16.
[ORIGIN Perh. of Scandinavian origin (cf. Norwegian dial. *dolp* lump).]
▸ **A** *noun*. **1** A clump of grass, weeds, etc., in a field. *obsolete* exc. *dial.* L16.
2 A shapeless, usu. large, lump or portion. *colloq.* E19.
L. CHAMBERLAIN Serve with a dollop of sour cream.
3 A slovenly woman; a trollop. *dial.* E19.
▸ **B** *verb trans.* **1** Tumble about. *dial.* E19.
2 Serve *out* or put *on* in substantial quantities. *colloq.* M19.

dolly /ˈdɒli/ *noun*[1]. E17.
[ORIGIN from DOLL *noun*[1] + -Y[6].]
†**1** **a** = DOLL *noun*[1] 1. *slang.* E17–M19. ▸**b** An untidy or lazy woman. *dial.* E19.
2 **a** A child's doll. See also ***corn dolly*** s.v. CORN *noun*[1]. L18. ▸**b** An attractive girl or young woman. *colloq.* E20.
b *Daily Mirror* Always falling wildly in and out of love with dishy dollies.
3 A short wooden pole with projecting pieces at one end and a handle at the other, used for stirring clothes in a washtub. Formerly also, a washtub; a machine for washing clothes. L18.
4 Something placed between a ram and a pile; a punch, *esp.* one for shaping the head of a rivet. M19.
5 A simple device for crushing auriferous quartz by repeated blows. *Austral.*, *S. Afr.*, & *NZ.* M19.
6 A small platform on wheels used as a conveyance; *spec.* one used as a mobile base for a film or television camera. E20.
7 In ball games, a ball that is easily caught or hit; CRICKET a donkey drop. *colloq.* E20.
8 The pivoted lever of a tumbler switch. M20.
9 A weighted barbless hook with a lure, used in fishing for snoek. *S. Afr.* M20.
– COMB.: **dolly-bag** = DOROTHY BAG; **dolly bird** *colloq.* an attractive but unintelligent young woman; **dolly mixture** a mixture of tiny sweets of various shapes and colours; a sweet from such a mixture; **dolly mop** *slang* (**a**) an unkempt or untidy woman; (**b**) a prostitute; **dolly peg** = sense 3 above; **dolly pot** *Austral.* & *NZ* in a dolly, the vessel in which quartz is crushed; **dolly-tub** (**a**) a washtub; (**b**) MINING a vessel in which ore is washed.

dolly /ˈdɒli/ *noun*[2]. M19.
[ORIGIN Hindi *ḍālī*.]
In the Indian subcontinent, an offering of fruit or flowers etc., presented usu. on a tray.

dolly /ˈdɒli/ *adjective*[1]. M19.
[ORIGIN from DOLL *noun*[1] + -Y[1].]
1 Resembling (that of) a doll. M19.
2 Stupid, foolish. L19.
JOYCE Grinning all over his big Dolly face.
3 Designating a very easy catch, shot, etc., in a ball game, esp. cricket. *colloq.* L19.
4 Of a person: attractive, stylish. Cf. ***dolly bird*** s.v. DOLLY *noun*[1]. *colloq.* M20.

†**dolly** *adjective*[2] var. of DOWIE.

dolly /ˈdɒli/ *verb*. M19.
[ORIGIN from DOLLY *noun*[1].]
1 *verb trans.* & *intrans.* Beat or crush (esp. quartz) using a dolly; extract (gold) in this way. M19.
2 *verb trans.* Wash or stir (clothes) in a dolly-tub. M19.
3 **a** *verb intrans.* Of a camera or its operator: travel on a dolly, esp. *in* towards the subject or *out* away from it. M20. ▸**b** *verb trans.* Move (esp. a camera) on a dolly. M20.
a M. AYRTON The camera dollies about all over the acres of smooth marble. *fig.*: G. MACBETH Someone dollied in to kill. **b** R. B. PARKER He was getting awkward to handle . . . They dollied him out.
4 *verb trans.* Doll or smarten *up*. *colloq.* M20.

Dolly Varden /dɒlɪ ˈvɑːd(ə)n/ *noun* & *adjective*. L19.
[ORIGIN A character in Dickens's *Barnaby Rudge*.]
1 (Designating) a print dress with a large flower pattern, worn with the skirt gathered up in loops. L19.
2 (Designating) a large hat, formerly worn by women, trimmed with flowers and with one side bent downwards. L19.
3 (Designating) a brightly spotted char, *Salvelinus malma*, that is a sporting fish of western N. America. L19.

dolman /ˈdɒlmən/ *noun*. In sense 1 also (earlier) †**doliman**. L16.
[ORIGIN In sense 1 from French *doliman*; in sense 2 from French *dolman* from German from Hungarian *dolmány*; both ult. from Turkish *dolama(n)*.]
1 A long Turkish robe open in front and with narrow sleeves. L16.
2 A hussar's jacket worn with the sleeves hanging loose. L19.
3 A woman's mantle with dolman sleeves. L19.
4 In full ***dolman sleeve***. A loose sleeve made in one piece with the body of a coat etc. M20.

dolmas /ˈdɒlməs/ *noun*. Pl. **dolmades** /dɒlˈmɑːðɛz/. Also **dolma**, pl. **-s**. L17.
[ORIGIN mod. Greek *ntolmas* from Turkish *dolma*, from *dolmak* fill, be filled.]
In the cookery of Greece, Turkey, and other East European countries: a dish of seasoned chopped meat and rice enclosed in a vine leaf, cabbage, pepper, etc.

dolmen /ˈdɒlmɛn/ *noun*. M19.
[ORIGIN French, perh. from Cornish *tolmen* hole stone.]
A megalithic structure found esp. in Britain and France, consisting of a large flat stone supported on stone slabs set vertically in the ground forming a burial chamber, probably orig. covered by an earth mound.
■ **dolˈmenic** *adjective* L19.

dolmus /ˈdɒlmʊʃ/ *noun*. Pl. same. M20.
[ORIGIN Turkish *dolmuş* filled, (as noun) dolmus.]
In Turkey, a shared taxi.

dolomite /ˈdɒləmʌɪt/ *noun*. L18.
[ORIGIN French *dolomi(t)e*, from D. *Dolomieu* (1750–1801), French geologist: see -ITE[1].]
A rock-forming mineral that is a hexagonal carbonate of calcium, magnesium, and usu. iron etc. and occurs as translucent crystals of various colours; a sedimentary rock composed chiefly of this mineral, alone or with calcite.
■ **dolomitic** /dɒləˈmɪtɪk/ *adjective* of the nature of or containing dolomite E19. **dolomitization** /ˌdɒləmɪtʌɪˈzeɪʃ(ə)n/ *noun* conversion into dolomite M19. **dolomitize** /ˈdɒləmɪtʌɪz/ *verb trans.* convert into dolomite (chiefly as ***dolomitized*** *ppl adjective*) L19.

Dolophine /ˈdɒləfiːn/ *noun*. *US*. M20.
[ORIGIN from *dolo-* of unknown origin + MOR)PHINE.]
Methadone.
– NOTE: Proprietary name in the US.

dolor *noun* see DOLOUR.

dolorific /dɒləˈrɪfɪk/ *adjective*. Now *rare*. M17.
[ORIGIN medieval Latin *dolorificus*, from Latin *dolor*: see DOLOUR, -FIC.]
Causing pain.

dolorifuge /ˈdɒlərɪfjuː(d)ʒ/ *noun*. L19.
[ORIGIN from Latin *dolor* (see DOLOUR) + -FUGE.]
Something that drives away pain.

dolorimeter /dɒləˈrɪmɪtə/ *noun*. M20.
[ORIGIN from Latin *dolor* (see DOLOUR) + -IMETER.]
An instrument for measuring (sensitivity to) pain.

doloroso /dɒləˈrəʊzəʊ/ *adjective*, *adverb*, & *noun*. E19.
[ORIGIN Italian = dolorous.]
MUSIC. (In) a plaintive or pathetic style.

dolorous /ˈdɒl(ə)rəs/ *adjective*. Now chiefly *literary*. LME.
[ORIGIN Old French *doleros* (mod. *douloureux*) from late Latin *dolorosus*, from Latin *dolor*: see DOLOUR, -OUS.]
1 Causing or accompanied by physical pain; painful. LME.
W. ROBERTS The dolorous sensations . . which constantly torment diabetic patients.
2 Causing or giving rise to grief or sorrow; distressing; dismal. LME.
W. BLACK We had a dolorous day of rain.
3 Full of sorrow; expressing sorrow. LME.
MILTON A dolorous groan.
■ **dolorously** *adverb* LME. **dolorousness** *noun* M16.

dolos /ˈdɒlɒs/ *noun*. *S. Afr.* Pl. **dolosse** /ˈdɒlɒsə/, (in sense 2) **dolossies** /ˈdɒlɒsɪz/. L19.
[ORIGIN Afrikaans, of unknown origin.]
1 An animal bone, esp. a knuckle bone, used for divination. Usu. in *pl.* L19.
2 In *pl.* Children's playthings; a game played with dolosse. E20.
3 Each of a series of interlocking concrete blocks used to guard against erosion by the sea. L20.

dolose /dəʊˈləʊs/ *adjective*. Now *rare*. M17.
[ORIGIN Latin *dolosus*, from *dolus*: see DOLE *noun*[3], -OSE[1].]
LAW. Characterized by criminal intention; deceitful. Cf. DOLOUS.

dolosse, **dolossies** *nouns* pls. of DOLOS.

dolostone /ˈdɒləstəʊn/ *noun*. M20.
[ORIGIN from DOLOMITE + STONE *noun*.]
GEOLOGY. (A) rock consisting of dolomite.

dolour /ˈdɒlə/ *noun*. Now *literary*. Also *-or. ME.
[ORIGIN Old French *dolo(u)r* (mod. *douleur*) from Latin *dolor* pain, grief: see -OUR, -OR.]
†**1** Physical suffering, pain; a pain, a painful affliction. ME–E18.
2 Mental pain or suffering; sorrow, distress; in *pl.* (now *rare*), griefs, sorrows. ME.
V. NABOKOV I spend my doleful days in dumps and dolours. T. ROETHKE I'm full of dolor and gloom about . . human existence.
†**3** The outward expression of grief; lamentation, mourning. ME–M17.
†**4** Indignation. E–M17.

dolous /ˈdəʊləs/ *adjective*. Now *rare*. E20.
[ORIGIN from Latin *dolus* (see DOLE *noun*[3]) + -OUS.]
LAW (chiefly *Scot.*) = DOLOSE.

dolphin /ˈdɒlfɪn/ *noun*. LME.
[ORIGIN Old French *daulphin* from Provençal *dalfin* from medieval Latin *dalphinus* for Latin *delphinus* from Greek *delphin* (earlier *delphis*). Cf. DAUPHIN, (earlier) DELPHIN.]
► **I 1** A toothed whale of the family Delphinidae, similar to a porpoise but longer and with a beaklike snout; *spec.* (more fully ***common dolphin***), *Delphinus delphis*; (in full ***river dolphin***) a similar toothed whale of the family Platanistidae, found only in some tropical rivers of S. America and southern Asia and without the social behaviour of true dolphins. In early use also, a fabulous fish of the R. Nile. LME. ▸**b** = DORADO 1. Cf. ***dolphinfish*** below. E17.
2 A figure of a dolphin in heraldry, sculpture, etc., usu. represented with a curved body and formerly symbolizing love, diligence, or swiftness. LME.
3 (Usu. **D-**.) *The* constellation Delphinus. LME.
4 a *hist.* Either of two handles cast solid with a cannon, nearly over the trunnions. E18. ▸**b** *NAUTICAL*. A strap of plaited rope, fastened round the mast of a square-rigged ship (***dolphin of the mast***) or hung below the gunwale as a fender. M18. ▸**c** *GREEK ANTIQUITIES*. A heavy weight suspended from a ship's mast, to be dropped into an enemy ship at close quarters. L18. ▸**d** *NAUTICAL*. A pile or group of piles in the seabed used as a mooring for ships, to mark a channel, or to protect the pier of a bridge; a mooring post or buoy. M19.
5 A black aphid, *Aphis fabae*, that attacks beans. L18.
► †**II 6** = DAUPHIN *noun* 1. LME–E18.
– COMB.: **dolphinfish** either of the two tropical marine fishes forming the family Coryphaenidae, marked by a long dorsal fin and a deeply forked tail (cf. DORADO 1); **dolphin-striker** *NAUTICAL* a short gaff spar fixed vertically under the bowsprit.
■ †**dolphinate** *noun* = DAUPHINATE: only in M17. **dolphined** *adjective* (*literary*) having, associated with, or containing dolphins E20. †**dolphiness** *noun* = DAUPHINESS M16–E17.

dolphinarium /dɒlfɪˈnɛːrɪəm/ *noun*. Pl. **-ia** /-ɪə/, **-iums**. M20.
[ORIGIN from DOLPHIN + AQU)ARIUM, after *oceanarium*.]
A large aquarium in which dolphins are kept and trained, usu. for public entertainment.

dolt /dəʊlt/ *noun* & *verb*. M16.
[ORIGIN Perh. ult. var. of *dulled* pa. pple & ppl adjective of DULL *verb*.]
► **A** *noun*. A dull stupid person, a fool, a blockhead. M16.
► †**B** *verb trans.* Make foolish; call a dolt; make a fool of. M16–L19.
■ **doltish** *adjective* somewhat dull and stupid, rather foolish M16. **doltishly** *adverb* L16. **doltishness** *noun* M16.

dolus /ˈdɒləs/ *noun*. E17.
[ORIGIN Latin: see DOLE *noun*[3].]
LAW. Deceit; intentional damage.
dolus bonus /ˈbɒnəs/ [= good] deceit not intended to cause damage. **dolus malus** /ˈmaləs/ [= bad] deceit with malicious intention to harm.

Dom /dɒm/ *noun*[1]. L17.
[ORIGIN In sense 1 abbreviation of Latin *dominus* lord, master; in sense 2 Portuguese *dom* from Latin *dominus*. Cf. DAN *noun*[1], DON *noun*[1], DAME.]
1 Master: used as a title preceding the names of some Roman Catholic ecclesiastical and monastic dignitaries, esp. of Benedictine and Carthusian monks. L17.
2 In Portugal and Brazil, used as a title of respect preceding male forenames, esp. of men of the royal family or the Church hierarchy. E18.

Dom /dəʊm/ *noun*[2] & *adjective*. E19.
[ORIGIN Hindi *Ḍom* from Sanskrit *Ḍom(b)a*.]
In the Indian subcontinent: (pertaining to or designating) a member of a very low caste.

dom /dəʊm/ *noun*[3]. M19.
[ORIGIN German from Latin *domus* house. Cf. DOME *noun*.]
A cathedral church in Germany, Austria, and other German-speaking areas. Cf. DOME *noun* 2.

-dom /dəm/ *suffix*.
[ORIGIN Old English *-dōm* = Old Saxon *-dōm* (Dutch *-dom*), Old High German *-tuom* (German *-tum*), use as suffix of Old English *dōm* DOOM *noun*[1], Old High German *tuom* position, condition, dignity.]
1 Forming nouns from nouns and adjectives with the senses 'rank, condition', 'domain', as in ***earldom***, ***freedom***, ***kingdom***.
2 Forming nouns from nouns as collect. pl. or with the sense 'the ways of —s' as in ***officialdom***.

domain /də(ʊ)ˈmeɪn/ *noun*. LME.
[ORIGIN French *domaine* alt. (by assoc. with Latin *dominus* lord, master) of Old French *demaine*, *demeine* DEMESNE.]
†**1** = DEMESNE *noun* 1. *rare*. LME–M17.
2 (A) heritable property; (an) estate or territory held in possession; lands, dominions. LME. ▸**b** An area under rule or influence; the area of activity of a person, institution, etc. M18. ▸**c** A public park or recreation ground; ***the Domain***, a park in Sydney popular for speech-making. *Austral.* & *NZ*. L19. ▸**d** *PHYSICS*. In a ferromagnetic material, a region in which all the atoms or ions are magnetically aligned in the same direction. E20.
W. S. CHURCHILL The Electoral Prince of Bavaria, heir to prodigious domains. A. J. TOYNBEE The traveller . . is entering the former domain of the Inca Empire. **b** P. NORMAN Nanny Belmayne's domain begins at the top of the first flight of stairs.
3 A sphere of thought or operation; the situations where a particular science, law, etc., is applicable. M18.
J. MACKINTOSH Contracting . . the domain of brutal force and of arbitrary will. G. B. SHAW An astronomer whose mental domain is the universe.
4 *MATH*. A set with two binary operations defined by postulates stronger than those for a ring but weaker than those for a field. L19.
5 *MATH*. The set of values that the independent variable of a function can take. E20.
6 *LOGIC*. The class of all terms bearing a given relation to a given term. E20.
B. RUSSELL If paternity be the relation, fathers form its domain.
7 *BIOCHEMISTRY*. A distinct region of a complex molecule or structure. M20.
8 *COMPUTING*. A subset of locations on the Internet or other network which share a common element of their IP address (indicating a geographical, commercial or other affiliation), or which are under the control of a particular organization or individual. L20.
– PHRASES: **eminent domain** *LAW* superiority of the sovereign power over all property in a state, with constitutional right of expropriation in the public interest. ***in the public domain***: see PUBLIC *adjective*.
– COMB.: **domain name** *COMPUTING* the part of a network address which identifies it as belonging to a particular domain; **Domain orator** *Austral.* a person who makes public speeches in the Domain.
■ **domainal** *adjective* M19.

domaine /dəˈmeɪn/ *noun*. M20.
[ORIGIN French: see DOMAIN.]
A vineyard. Usu. in ***domaine-bottled*** below.
– COMB.: **domaine-bottled** *adjective* (of a wine) bottled at the vineyard where the grapes of which it is made were grown.

domal /ˈdəʊm(ə)l/ *adjective* & *noun*. E18.
[ORIGIN In branch A.I from Latin *domus* house, (in medieval Latin) planetary house, in branch A.II from DOME *noun*: see -AL[1].]
► **A** *adjective* **I 1** Of or pertaining to a house or houses; domestic. E18.
2 *ASTROLOGY*. Of or pertaining to a house of the zodiac. E18.
► **II 3** Of, pertaining to, or shaped like a dome. E20.
4 *PHONETICS*. Of a speech sound: articulated with the tip of the tongue against the highest part (or dome) of the palate; cacuminal. E20.
► **B** *noun*. *PHONETICS*. A domal speech sound. E20.

domanial /də(ʊ)ˈmeɪnɪəl/ *adjective*. E19.
[ORIGIN French from medieval Latin *domanialis*, from *domanium* lordship, domain: see -IAL.]
Of or pertaining to (a) domain.

Domdaniel /dɒmˈdanɪəl/ *noun*. *literary*. E19.
[ORIGIN French, app. from Greek *dōma Daniēl* or Latin *domus Danielis* hall or house of Daniel.]
(The name of) a fabled underwater hall where a magician or sorcerer met with his disciples; *transf.* a den of iniquity, a hell.

dome /dəʊm/ *noun* & *verb*. E16.
[ORIGIN In sense A.1 directly from Latin *domus* house; in other senses from French *dôme* from Italian DUOMO (dial. *domo*) house, house of God, cathedral, cupola, from Latin *domus*.]
► **A** *noun*. **I** A house.
1 A house, a home; a stately building, a mansion. Now chiefly *literary*. E16.
SWIFT Sad charnel-house! a dismal dome, For which all mortals leave their home.
†**2** A cathedral church. Cf. DOM *noun*[3]. L17–M18.
► **II** A hemispherical surface.
3 A rounded vault forming (the chief part of) the roof of a building, and having an elliptical or polygonal base; a large cupola. M17. ▸**b** The revolving openable hemispherical roof of an astronomical observatory. M19. ▸**c** A stadium with a domed roof. Cf. ASTRODOME (b). *N. Amer.* M20.
M. GIROUARD A tower capped by a green copper dome.
4 The vaulted roof of a cavern or natural hollow; the concave vault of the sky; a natural canopy of trees etc. E18.
J. L. WATEN The high dome of light-blue sky.
5 A dome-shaped part of anything; a convex lid or cover. E18. ▸**b** The rounded summit of a natural object, as a mountain, hill, wave, etc. M19. ▸**c** In full ***dome fastener***. A press stud consisting of a rounded portion which clips into a socket, used esp. as a fastener for gloves. E20.
T. S. ELIOT The egg's well-rounded dome.
6 The head. *slang*. L19.
7 *GEOLOGY*. A dome-shaped landform or underground structure. E20.
N. CALDER Salt domes are favourite targets for oil prospectors.
– PHRASES: **Dome of Silence** (proprietary name for) a type of castor fitted to furniture.
– COMB.: ***dome fastener***: see sense 5c above; **dome-headed** *adjective* having a large rounded head; **dome-light**: with a dome-shaped cover or shade.
► **B** *verb trans.* **1** Cover (as) with a dome. L19.
2 *verb trans.* Make dome-shaped. L19.
MRS H. WARD The roof had been raised and domed.
3 *verb intrans.* Be or become dome-shaped. L19.
Scientific American A caldera whose floor has slowly domed upward in the millenniums since the eruption. *Nature* Towards the end of the Carboniferous period uplift . . and doming of the region took place.

domed /dəʊmd/ *adjective*. L18.
[ORIGIN from DOME + -ED[1], -ED[2].]
1 Dome-shaped, vaulted. L18.
2 Having a dome or domes. M19.

domelet /ˈdəʊmlɪt/ *noun*. L19.
[ORIGIN from DOME *noun* + -LET.]
A miniature dome.

doment /ˈduːm(ə)nt/ *noun*. *dial.* & *colloq.* E19.
[ORIGIN from DO *verb* + -MENT.]
A fuss, a performance; a to-do.

Domesday /ˈduːmzdeɪ/ *noun*. ME.
[ORIGIN Var. of DOOMSDAY.]
More fully ***Domesday Book***. A comprehensive record of the extent, value, ownership, and liabilities of lands in England, made in 1086 by order of William the Conqueror.
– NOTE: App. a popular name alluding to *doomsday* 'Day of Judgement', applied during 12 to the book as a final authority on matters about which it was referred to.

domestic /dəˈmɛstɪk/ *adjective* & *noun*. LME.
[ORIGIN Old French & mod. French *domestique* from Latin *domesticus*, from *domus* house, after *rusticus* RUSTIC *adjective* etc.]
► **A** *adjective*. **1** Of or pertaining to the home, house, or household; pertaining to one's home or family affairs. LME.
K. CLARK Ivory mirror cases and other domestic objects. A. THWAITE The two friends, the baby and the cat offered a picture of domestic bliss.
domestic bursar a person in charge of the administrative or financial affairs of a college or university. **domestic science** cookery and other household activities, as subjects to be taught. **domestic service** the position or occupation of a household servant.
2 Not wild; (of an animal) kept by or living with humans, tame; (of a plant) cultivated. L15.

D

T. HARDY A panting fox.. trotted past them tamely as a domestic cat.

domestic fowl a bird reared for meat, eggs, or feathers; in *pl.* poultry; *spec.* the widely domesticated form of the SE Asian jungle fowl, *Gallus gallus*, a cock, a hen, a chicken.

†3 Having the character or position of the inmate of a house, housed. Also, intimate, familiar, at home. (Foll. by *with*.) E16–M18.

CHESTERFIELD Domestic in the best company and the best families.

4 Of or pertaining to one's own country or nation; not foreign or international; indigenous; made in one's own country, not imported. M16.

W. S. CHURCHILL The domestic law of England was outraged by the arrogance.. of the French despot.

domestic trade: see TRADE *noun*. ***gross domestic product***: see GROSS *adjective*.

5 Attached to home; fond of home life or duties. M17.

J. H. NEWMAN It is praiseworthy and right to be domestic.

▸**B** *noun*. †1 A member of a household; someone living in the same house as another person; a member of the family (*lit. & fig.*). M16–M18.

2 A household servant. E17. ▸†**b** A domestic animal. *rare*. E–M18.

†3 An inhabitant of the same country; a native, a compatriot. Only in 17.

4 An article of home manufacture (usu. in *pl.*); *US* a plain cotton fabric. E17.

5 A kind of cigar. *US colloq.* (now *rare*). M19.

6 A violent quarrel between family members, esp. between husband and wife. *colloq.* (orig. *Police slang*). M20.

■ **domestical** *adjective & noun* (now *rare* or *obsolete*) (*a*) *adjective* domestic; (*b*) *noun* a domestic; a member of a household: LME. **domestically** *adverb* in a domestic way; as regards domestic matters or home life; familiarly: L16. **domesticism** /-sɪz(ə)m/ *noun* devotion to home life L18. **domesticize** /-sʌɪz/ *verb trans.* domesticate M17. †**domesticly** *adverb* M17–M18.

domesticable /dəˈmɛstɪkəb(ə)l/ *adjective*. E19.
[ORIGIN from DOMESTICATE *verb* + -ABLE.]
Able to be domesticated or tamed.

domesticate /dəˈmɛstɪkət/ *noun*. M20.
[ORIGIN from DOMESTICATE *verb*: see -ATE².]
A domesticated animal.

domesticate /dəˈmɛstɪkeɪt/ *verb*. M17.
[ORIGIN medieval Latin *domesticat-* pa. ppl stem of *domesticare*, from Latin *domesticus*: see DOMESTIC, -ATE³.]

1 *verb trans.* Settle as a member of a household; cause to feel at home; naturalize (esp. a plant or animal). M17.

GLADSTONE An element in the Greek nation originally foreign, but now domesticated.

2 *verb trans.* Accustom (an animal) to being kept by or to living with humans; bring under control, tame. M17.

C. G. SELIGMAN They possess no domesticated animals except the dog.

3 *verb trans.* Attach (a person) to home life and household matters; make domestic. M18.

G. GREENE The domesticated man with a devoted wife and six children to support. M. BRADBURY Henry has domesticated the space, and filled it with potted plants.

†4 *verb intrans.* Live on familiar terms or at home *with*; take up residence, settle down. M18–M19.

■ **domestiˈcation** *noun* the action of domesticating; the fact of being domesticated: L18. **domesticator** *noun* L19.

domesticity /dɒmɛˈstɪsɪti, dəʊm-/ *noun*. E18.
[ORIGIN from DOMESTIC + -ITY. Cf. French *domesticité*, late Latin *domesticitas*.]

1 The quality or state of being domestic; *esp.* (attachment to) home life. E18. ▸**b** The state in an animal of being domesticated. M19.

L. STEPHEN A masculine woman with no talent for domesticity.

2 In *pl.* Domestic affairs, arrangements, or concerns. E19.

domett /ˈdɒmɪt, dəˈmɛt/ *noun & adjective*. Also **domette** /dəˈmɛt/. E19.
[ORIGIN Perh. from a proper name.]
(Made of) a kind of plain cheap cloth with a cotton warp and a woollen weft (later cotton only).

domical /ˈdəʊmɪk(ə)l/ *adjective*. M19.
[ORIGIN from DOME *noun* + -ICAL.]
1 = DOMED 1. M19.
2 = DOMED 2. M19.
■ †**domic** *adjective* = DOMICAL: only in E19. **domically** *adverb* L19.

domicile /ˈdɒmɪsʌɪl, -sɪl/ *noun & verb*. Also **-cil** /-sɪl/. LME.
[ORIGIN Old French & mod. French from Latin *domicilium*, from *domus* house.]

▸**A** *noun*. 1 A place of residence or customary habitation; a home. LME.

2 LAW. The place of a person's permanent residence, which he or she leaves only temporarily. L17.

3 The fact of being resident; residence. M19.

4 The place at which a bill of exchange is made payable. L19.

▸**B** *verb*. 1 *verb trans.* Establish in a fixed residence; settle in a home. Usu. in *pass.* LME.

Photography A photographer and designer domiciled in France.

2 *verb trans.* Make (a bill of exchange) payable at a place specified by the acceptor. E19.

3 *verb intrans.* Have one's home, live. M19.

†**domiciliar** *adjective & noun*. *rare*. M17.
[ORIGIN medieval Latin *domiciliarius*: see DOMICILIARY, -AR¹.]

▸**A** *adjective*. Of or pertaining to one's domicile. Only in M17.

▸**B** *noun*. A canon of a minor order having no voice in a chapter. Only in M18.

domiciliary /dɒmɪˈsɪlɪəri/ *adjective*. L18.
[ORIGIN French *domiciliaire* from medieval Latin *domiciliarius*, from Latin *domicilium* DOMICILE: see -ARY¹.]
Of or pertaining to a person's home; occurring at home.

S. KITZINGER Her first domiciliary delivery.

domiciliary visit a visit by an official to a person's home, *esp.* one made by a doctor, midwife, etc., to see a patient.

domiciliate /dɒmɪˈsɪlɪeɪt/ *verb*. L18.
[ORIGIN from Latin *domicilium* DOMICILE + -ATE³, after French *domicilier*.]

1 *verb trans.* = DOMICILE *verb* 1. L18.

†2 *verb trans.* Accustom to a house or permanent dwelling place; domesticate (an animal). *rare*. L18–E19.

3 *verb intrans.* = DOMICILE *verb* 3. E19.

■ ˌ**domiciliˈation** *noun* L18.

†**domify** *verb trans.* LME–E18.
[ORIGIN French *domifier* from medieval Latin *domificare* build houses, from Latin *domus* house: see -FY.]
ASTROLOGY. Divide (the heavens) into twelve houses; locate (the planets) in their respective houses.
■ †**domification** *noun* E17–E18.

domina /ˈdɒmɪnə/ *noun*. Now *rare*. E18.
[ORIGIN Latin = mistress, lady.]
A lady of rank; the superior of a nunnery.

dominance /ˈdɒmɪnəns/ *noun*. E19.
[ORIGIN from DOMINANT: see -ANCE.]

1 The fact or position of being dominant; paramount influence, ascendancy, dominion, sway. E19.

D. ACHESON Two German bids for dominance in Europe. A. STORR Male therapists are often put off by dominance and assertiveness in women.

2 GENETICS. The phenomenon whereby, in an individual in whom two allelic forms of a gene are present, one is expressed to the exclusion of the other. E20.

3 ECOLOGY. The predominance of one or more species in a plant or animal community. E20.

■ **dominancy** *noun* dominant quality, position, or condition M19.

dominant /ˈdɒmɪnənt/ *adjective & noun*. LME.
[ORIGIN Old French & mod. French from Latin *dominant-* pres. ppl stem of *dominari* DOMINATE: see -ANT¹.]

▸**A** *adjective*. 1 Exercising chief authority or rule; ruling, prevailing; most influential. LME.

W. S. CHURCHILL His dominant theme was that conscience and the moral law must govern political decisions. J. F. LEHMANN My will remained dominant.. over my senses and emotions. C. P. SNOW How China could avoid becoming the dominant power on earth.

2 LAW. Designating (tenement of) land whose owner has an easement over someone else's land. E18.

3 MUSIC. Based on or pertaining to the dominant. M18.

Music Teacher Harmonizing a melody, employing inversions and the dominant seventh.

4 Occupying a commanding position; overtopping its surroundings; *spec.* (of a forest tree) having its crown free to light on all sides. M19.

J. TYNDALL A bay, sheltered by dominant hills.

5 GENETICS. Of a gene or allele: expressed even when inherited from only one parent. Of a hereditary trait: controlled by such a gene; appearing in an individual to the exclusion of its allelic counterpart, when alleles for both are present. Opp. ***recessive***. (Foll. by *to*, *over*.) E20.

6 ECOLOGY. Designating the predominant species in a plant or animal community. E20.

▸**B** *noun*. †1 = DOMINATION 3. Only in LME.

2 MUSIC. The fifth note of the diatonic scale of a key; the reciting note in a church mode, usu. a fifth or a third above the final. E19.

fig.: M. TRIPP If the keynote was tolerance, the dominant was fidelity.

3 GENETICS. A dominant gene or trait (see sense A.5 above). E20.

4 ECOLOGY. A predominant species of a plant or animal community. E20.

■ **dominantly** *adverb* so as to be dominant or to prevail; predominantly; GENETICS as a dominant trait: M19.

dominate /ˈdɒmɪneɪt/ *verb*. E17.
[ORIGIN Latin *dominat-* pa. ppl stem of *dominari* rule, govern, from *dominus* lord, master: see -ATE³.]

1 *verb trans.* Rule over, govern; control, master; have a commanding influence over; be the most influential or conspicuous thing in. E17.

T. H. HUXLEY The Germans dominate the intellectual world. W. BRONK Death dominates my mind. S. BRETT Bill and Carla's bedroom.. was dominated by an enormous circular bed.

2 *verb intrans.* Predominate, prevail; have a commanding influence (*over*); be the most influential or conspicuous person or thing present. E19.

ALDOUS HUXLEY She only wanted to dominate, to be the leader and make him do what she wanted. P. CAREY The distinctive odour of a mental hospital. Floor polish, methylated spirits and chlorine seemed to dominate.

3 *verb intrans.* Of something high or tall: occupy a commanding position (*over*). E19.

4 *verb trans.* Overlook (*lit. & fig.*). M19.

BOSW. SMITH This hill.. dominates the plain.

domination /dɒmɪˈneɪʃ(ə)n/ *noun*. LME.
[ORIGIN Old French & mod. French from Latin *dominatio(n-)*, formed as DOMINATE: see -ATION.]

1 The action of dominating; ascendancy, sway, control; the state of being dominated. LME.

G. VIDAL He was used to domination.. but it made him uneasy .. to feel that his own will was so easily bent by others. J. BERGER To liberate the Southern Slavs.. from the domination of the Hapsburgs.

†2 A territory under rule; a dominion. LME–M17.

3 In Christian theology, a member of the fourth order of the ninefold celestial hierarchy, ranking directly below the thrones and above the virtues (usu. in *pl.*). Also, a conventional representation of such a being. LME.

dominative /ˈdɒmɪnətɪv/ *adjective*. L16.
[ORIGIN Old French & mod. French *dominatif*, *-ive* or medieval Latin *dominativus*, formed as DOMINATE: see -ATIVE.]
Having the quality of ruling or dominating; of lordly authority.

dominator /ˈdɒmɪneɪtə/ *noun*. LME.
[ORIGIN Orig. from Old French & mod. French *dominateur*, later from, or assim. to, Latin *dominator*, formed as DOMINATIVE: see -OR.]

1 A person who or thing which dominates; a ruler, a lord. LME.

†2 *spec.* ASTROLOGY. A planet or sign that dominates a particular person or region. L16–M17.

dominatrix /dɒmɪˈneɪtrɪks/ *noun*. Pl. **-trices** /-trɪsiːz/. M16.
[ORIGIN Latin, fem. of *dominator*: see DOMINATOR, -TRIX.]
A female dominator or ruler.
– NOTE: Rare before L20.

domine /ˈdɒmɪni, ˈdʊə-/ *noun*. Also (esp. as a title) **D-**. M16.
[ORIGIN Latin, voc. of *dominus* lord, master. Cf. DOMINEE, DOMINIE.]

†1 Lord, master; sir: used in respectful address to a clergyman or a member of one of the professions. M16–L17.

2 = DOMINIE 1. Now *rare* or *obsolete*. E17.

3 A member of the clergy, a pastor; *esp.* a pastor of the Dutch Reformed Church. (Cf. DOMINEE, DOMINIE 2). *arch.* M17.

dominee /ˈdɒmɪni, ˈdʊə-/ *noun*. *S. Afr.* Also (esp. as a title) **D-**. M20.
[ORIGIN Afrikaans & Dutch from Latin DOMINE.]
A pastor of the Dutch Reformed Church.

domineer /dɒmɪˈnɪə/ *verb & noun*. L16.
[ORIGIN Dutch *domineren* from Old French & mod. French *dominer* from Latin *dominari* DOMINATE: see -EER.]

▸**A** *verb*. **I** *verb intrans.* 1 Rule arbitrarily or despotically; act imperiously; tyrannize; be overbearing. (Foll. by *over*.) L16. ▸†**b** Assume lordly airs, swagger. E17–M18.

ADAM SMITH The mercantile company which domineers in the East Indies. H. KELLER It pleased me to domineer over her, and she generally submitted to my tyranny.

†2 Revel; feast riotously. L16–L17.

SHAKES. *Tam. Shr.* Go to the feast, revel and domineer.

†3 Predominate, prevail. E17–E19.

4 Of something high or tall: tower (*over*, *above*); occupy a commanding position. M17.

▸**II** *verb trans.* 5 Govern imperiously, tyrannize over, dominate absolutely. M18.

6 Of something high or tall: tower over, command. E19.

▸**B** *noun*. A domineering manner or air; imperious swaggering. Now *rare*. E19.

■ **domineerer** *noun* (now *rare*) a person who domineers, a tyrant, a despot M17. **domineering** *adjective* (*a*) tyrannical; overbearing, offensively assertive or dictatorial; †(*b*) predominating, prevailing: L16. **domineeringly** *adverb* L17. **domineeringness** *noun* L19.

dominial /dəˈmɪnɪəl/ *adjective*. M18.
[ORIGIN from DOMINION + -AL¹.]
Of or pertaining to ownership.

dominical /dəˈmɪnɪk(ə)l/ *noun & adjective*. ME.
[ORIGIN Old French & mod. French, or late Latin *dominicalis*, from Latin *dominicus*, from *dominus* lord, master: see -ICAL.]
▸ **A** *noun*. CHRISTIAN CHURCH.
1 A book, garment, or other item intended for use on Sundays; *spec.* a veil formerly worn by women when receiving the Eucharist. Now *rare*. ME.
†**2** The Lord's day, Sunday. M16–L17.
†**3** = ***dominical letter*** (see sense B.2 below). L16–L17.
4 A person who observes the Christian Sunday but does not treat it strictly as representing the sabbath of the Israelites. M19.
▸ **B** *adjective*. **I** CHRISTIAN CHURCH. Also **D-**.
1 Of or pertaining to the Lord (Christ); Lord's. ME.
R. HARRIES The Church is not now regarded as a profession in which a career may be advanced. This is . . a return to more Dominical standards.
dominical day Sunday. **dominical year** the year of Our Lord (numbered from an assumed year of the birth of Jesus).
2 Of or pertaining to Sunday. LME.
dominical letter one of the seven letters A–G used to indicate the dates of Sundays in a particular year (sometimes printed in red, or distinctive type, in the calendar).
▸ †**II** Other uses.
3 Belonging or pertaining to a demesne or domain; domanial. M16–L18.

Dominican /dəˈmɪnɪk(ə)n/ *noun*[1] *& adjective*[1]. L16.
[ORIGIN medieval Latin *Dominicanus*, from *Dominicus* Latin name of St Dominic (Spanish *Domingo* de Guzmán): see below, -AN.]
A member of, designating or pertaining to, the Order of Friars Preachers (Black Friars), founded in 1215 by the Spanish priest St Dominic (*c* 1170–1221) as a mendicant order devoted to preaching and the study of theology.
■ †**Dominic** *noun & adjective* = DOMINICAN *noun*[1] *& adjective*[1] LME–L17. **Dominicaˈness** *noun* a Dominican nun M19.

Dominican /dɒmɪˈniːk(ə)n, dəˈmɪnɪk(ə)n/ *noun*[2] *& adjective*[2]. E19.
[ORIGIN from *Dominica* (see below), so called because discovered on a Sunday (Latin *dies dominica*) in 1493 + -AN.]
A native or inhabitant of, of or pertaining to, the island of Dominica in the Lesser Antilles.

Dominican /dəˈmɪnɪk(ə)n/ *noun*[3] *& adjective*[3]. M19.
[ORIGIN Spanish *Dominicana*, formed as DOMINICAN *adjective*[1] & *noun*[1] after *Santo Domingo* one of the earliest settlements and subsequently the capital of the Dominican Republic.]
A native or inhabitant of, designating or pertaining to, the Dominican Republic, which occupies the eastern half of the island of Hispaniola in the Greater Antilles.

Dominicker /ˈdɒmɪnɪkə/ *noun & adjective*. *US*. Also **d-**. E19.
[ORIGIN Alt. of *Dominica* (see DOMINICAN *noun*[2] *& adjective*[2]).]
(Designating) a hen of an American breed characterized by barred plumage and yellow legs.

dominie /*in sense 1* ˈdɒmɪni, *in senses 2 & 3* ˈdəʊmɪni, ˈdɒmɪni/ *noun*. L17.
[ORIGIN Alt. of DOMINE.]
1 A schoolmaster; a teacher. Now chiefly *Scot*. L17.
2 A pastor of the Dutch Reformed Church; *dial.* any minister. *US*. L17.
3 More fully ***dominie apple***. A variety of large apple. *US*. E19.

dominion /dəˈmɪnjən/ *noun*. ME.
[ORIGIN Old French from medieval Latin *dominio(n-)*, from *dominium* property, from *dominus* lord, master.]
1 A domain, a territory; *esp.* (*sing.* & in *pl.*) the land of a feudal lord; the territory of a particular ruler or government. ME. ▸**b** *hist.* (Also **D-**.) A country outside Great Britain or (in early use) England under the sovereignty of or owing allegiance to the Crown; *esp.* (the title of) any of the larger self-governing nations that belong or once belonged to the British Commonwealth. E17.
LD MACAULAY The wide dominion of the Franks was severed into a thousand pieces. **b** *attrib.*: A. F. DOUGLAS-HOME Her leaders could . . make a good case for Dominion status (i.e. complete independence within the Commonwealth) on the country's record and prospects.
b the Dominion *colloq.* (now *rare*) Canada. **the Old Dominion** *US colloq.* Virginia.
2 The power or right of governing; sovereign authority, lordship; dominance, influence, control. LME.
B. JOWETT For ages physicians have been under the dominion of prejudices. P. ACKROYD Neither tears nor hollow laughter hold dominion. J. C. OATES The dominion of men over beasts.
3 CHRISTIAN CHURCH. = DOMINATION 3. Usu. in *pl.* E17.
4 LAW. Ownership, property; right of possession. M17.
T. JEFFERSON Our Saxon ancestors held their lands . . in absolute dominion, unencumbered with any superior.
– COMB.: **Dominion day** *hist.* = ***Canada Day*** s.v. CANADA 1.

Dominique /ˈdɒmɪnɪk, dɒmɪˈniːk/ *noun & adjective*. *US*. Also **d-**. E20.
[ORIGIN French name for *Dominica* (see DOMINICAN *noun*[2] & *adjective*[2]).]
= DOMINICKER.

dominium /dəˈmɪnɪəm/ *noun*. M18.
[ORIGIN Latin: see DOMINION.]
LAW. Lordship, ownership, dominion. Chiefly as below.
dominium directum /dɪˈrɛktəm/ [= direct ownership] the rights reserved to a lord or superior. ***dominium utile*** /ˈjuːtɪli/ [= ownership of use] the rights (e.g. of possession or use) reserved to a tenant or vassal.

domino /ˈdɒmɪnəʊ/ *noun & interjection*. L17.
[ORIGIN French = hood worn by priests in winter (also in Spanish = a masquerade garment), prob. ult. from Latin *dominus* lord, master, but unexpl.]
▸ **A** *noun*. Pl. **-o(e)s**.
1 A garment worn to cover the head and shoulders; *spec.* a loose cloak with a mask for the upper part of the face, worn to conceal the identity at masquerades etc. L17.
fig.: DISRAELI As for Pantheism, it is Atheism in domino.
2 A person wearing a domino. M18.
3 Each of a set of small oblong pieces, usu. 28 in number and marked with 0 to 6 pips in each half, used in various matching and trick-taking games; in *pl.* (treated as *sing.*) & †*sing.*, the game played with such pieces, in which matching halves are placed in contact. L18. ▸**b** In *pl.* The teeth. *arch. slang*. E19. ▸**c** In *pl.* The keys of a piano. *arch. slang*. L19.
make the domino *colloq.* go out first in the game of dominoes; finish first.
4 [from the interjection] The end, the finish. Chiefly in ***be all domino***, be all up (*with*). *slang*. M19.
5 In full ***domino paper***. Paper printed with a design from a woodblock and coloured, used as wallpaper etc. M19.
– COMB.: **domino effect**: by which one event triggers a succession of other, often similar, events, like a falling domino at the beginning of a line of upended dominoes; ***domino paper***: see sense 5 above; **domino theory** the theory that a domino effect will occur, *spec.* (POLITICS) that when one country in SE Asia becomes Communist-controlled the same thing will happen to its neighbours.
▸ **B** *interjection*. Notifying that one has matched up all one's dominoes; *transf.* notifying or registering the end of something. M19.
■ **dominoed** *adjective* wearing a domino L19.

domitable /ˈdɒmɪtəb(ə)l/ *adjective*. *rare*. L17.
[ORIGIN from Latin *domitare* frequentative of *domare* to tame: see -ABLE. Cf. earlier INDOMITABLE.]
Tameable.

domite /ˈdəʊmʌɪt/ *noun*. E19.
[ORIGIN German *Domit*, from Puy de Dôme peak in the Massif Central, France: see -ITE[1].]
PETROGRAPHY. A trachyte containing biotite and oligoclase, *esp.* one containing tridymite.
■ **domitic** /dəˈmɪtɪk/ *adjective* L19.

†**domo** *noun* see DUOMO.

Dom Pedro /dɒm ˈpɛdrəʊ/ *noun phr. US*. Also **Don Pedro** /dɒn/. L19.
[ORIGIN Prob. from DOM *noun*[1], DON *noun*[1] + male forename *Pedro*.]
A card game like Sancho Pedro but in which the joker is used.

dompt /dɒm(p)t/ *verb trans. rare*. L15.
[ORIGIN French *dompter*: see DAUNT *verb*.]
Tame, subdue; daunt.

domus /ˈdəʊməs/ *noun*. M18.
[ORIGIN Latin = house.]
(The fellows of) an Oxford or Cambridge college with regard to its domestic affairs.

domy /ˈdəʊmi/ *adjective*. M19.
[ORIGIN from DOME + -Y[1].]
= DOMED.

don /dɒn/ *noun*[1]. E16.
[ORIGIN Spanish (in sense 1c Italian) from Latin *dominus* lord, master. Cf. DAME, DAN *noun*[1], DOM *noun*[1].]
1 a (**D-**.) Used as a title of respect preceding the forename of a Spanish man (orig. one of high rank) or (formerly, *joc.*) preceding the name or designation of any man. E16. ▸**b** A Spanish lord or gentleman. E17. ▸**c** A high-ranking or powerful member of the Mafia. *N. Amer. slang*. M20.
2 A distinguished or skilled man; a man who is outstanding in some way. *arch*. L16.
DRYDEN The great dons of wit.
3 At British universities, esp. Oxford and Cambridge: a head, fellow, or tutor of a college; a member of the teaching staff. M17.

don /dɒn/ *noun*[2]. Long *obsolete* exc. *dial*. L15.
[ORIGIN French from Latin *donum* gift.]
A donation, a gift.

don /dɒn/ *verb*. Infl. **-nn-**. LME.
[ORIGIN Contr. of *do on*: see DO *verb*.]
1 *verb trans.* Put on (a garment). LME.
D. BROWN He donned his hotel bathrobe and moved towards the door.
2 *verb refl.* & *intrans.* Dress oneself. Chiefly *N. English*. E19.
3 *verb trans.* Dress (a person) *in* a garment. Chiefly *N. English*. M19.
– NOTE: Became largely obsolete in 17; revived in 19.

dona /ˈdəʊnə/ *noun*. In sense 1 also ***doña*** /ˈdoɲa/; in sense 2 also **donah**, **doner**. E17.
[ORIGIN Portuguese *dona*, Spanish *doña*, from Latin *domina* fem. of *dominus*: see DON *noun*[1]. Cf. DONNA.]
1 (Used as a courtesy title preceding the name of) a Spanish or Portuguese lady. E17.
2 A woman; a girlfriend. *slang*. Now *rare*. M19.

Donald Duck /dɒn(ə)ld ˈdʌk/ *adjectival phr*. M20.
[ORIGIN See below.]
Designating or pertaining to the high-pitched nasal quality of the voice of the character Donald Duck in Walt Disney cartoon films.
Daily Telegraph The 'Donald Duck effect' results from divers having to breathe an oxy-helium mixture in depths greater than 600 ft.

D

donary /ˈdəʊn(ə)ri/ *noun*. L16.
[ORIGIN Latin *donarium*, from *donum* gift: see -ARY[1].]
A votive offering; a gift, a donation.

†**donatar** *noun* var. of DONATOR *noun*[2].

donatary *noun* var. of DONATORY.

donate /ˈdəʊneɪt/ *noun*. Also **-at** /-at/ E19.
[ORIGIN medieval Latin *donatus* pa. pple of *donare* give.]
A member or associate of any of certain religious orders.

donate /də(ʊ)ˈneɪt/ *verb*. L18.
[ORIGIN Back-form. from DONATION.]
1 *verb trans. & intrans.* Make a donation (of), esp. to a charity or institution. L18.
C. STEAD She loved to donate things made by herself to their festivals . . and sales of work.
2 *verb trans.* Present *with*. *rare*. M19.
3 *verb trans.* CHEMISTRY & PHYSICS. Of an atom etc.: lose (an electron) by partial transfer to a neighbouring atom, with formation of a bond. M20.

donatee /dəʊnəˈtiː/ *noun*. E18.
[ORIGIN from DONATE *verb* + -EE[1].]
A recipient of a donation.

†**Donatian** *noun*. E17–E19.
[ORIGIN from *Donatus* (see DONATIST) + -IAN.]
A Donatist.

donatio mortis causa /dəˌneɪʃɪəʊ ˌmɔːtɪs ˈkɔːzə/ *noun phr*. Pl. ***donationes mortis causa*** /dəneɪʃɪˌəʊniːz/. M17.
[ORIGIN Latin = gift by reason of death.]
LAW. A (revocable) gift of property made in expectation of the donor's death and taking effect thereafter.

donation /də(ʊ)ˈneɪʃ(ə)n/ *noun*. LME.
[ORIGIN Old French & mod. French from Latin *donatio(n-)*, from *donat-* pa. ppl stem of *donare* give, from *donum* gift: see -ATION.]
1 The action or an act of donating; *spec.* (LAW) the transfer of ownership as a free gift. LME.
J. HELLER The donation of all his organs and tissues for medical use. R. FULLER Far back it gave us life, although We now may look askance at the donation. *Chemistry in Britain* The donation of a lone pair of electrons from BCl into the empty 2p orbital of the trichloride.
2 The right of bestowing or conferring a benefice; gift. Now *rare*. M16.
W. PALEY Offices in the donation of the king.
3 A thing which is donated; a gift or contribution to a charity, fund, etc. L16.
B. T. WASHINGTON Small donations from persons of moderate means.

donationes mortis causa *noun phr.* pl. of DONATIO MORTIS CAUSA.

Donatism /ˈdəʊnətɪz(ə)m/ *noun*. L16.
[ORIGIN from DONATIST + -ISM.]
ECCLESIASTICAL HISTORY. The doctrine or principles of the Donatists.

Donatist /ˈdəʊnətɪst/ *noun & adjective*. ME.
[ORIGIN Late Latin *Donatista*, from *Donatus* 2nd Bishop of Carthage after Caecilian: see -IST.]
ECCLESIASTICAL HISTORY. ▸**A** *noun*. A member of a schismatic body of N. African Christians which originated when they declared invalid the consecration of Caecilian as Bishop of Carthage in 311. ME.
▸ **B** *adjective*. Of or pertaining to Donatism or the Donatists. E18.
– NOTE: Rare before L19.
■ **Donaˈtistic** *adjective* E19.

donative /ˈdəʊnətɪv/ *noun & adjective*. LME.
[ORIGIN Latin *donativum* largesse, from *donat-*: see DONATION, -IVE.]
▸ **A** *noun*. **1** A donation, a gift, a bounty, esp. given formally or officially. LME.
2 ECCLESIASTICAL HISTORY. A benefice which is not presentative but given directly. M16.
▸ **B** *adjective*. Of the nature of a donative; *esp.* (ECCLESIASTICAL HISTORY) (of a benefice) vesting or vested by donation (opp. PRESENTATIVE *adjective* 2). M16.

donator /də(ʊ)ˈneɪtə/ *noun*[1]. LME.
[ORIGIN Orig. from Old French & mod. French *donateur* or Latin *donator*, from *donat-*: see DONATION, -OR. In mod. use from DONATE *verb* + -OR.]

A person who makes a donation, a donor.

donator /ˈdə(ʊ)nətə/ *noun*². *Scot.* Also †**-ar**. **E16**.
[ORIGIN Old French *donatoire*, French *donataire*, or medieval Latin *donatorius*, *-arius*: see DONATORY, -OR, -AR².]
= DONATORY.

donatory /ˈdəʊnət(ə)ri/ *noun*. Also **-ary**. **E17**.
[ORIGIN medieval Latin *donatorius*, from *donat-*: see DONATION, -ORY¹; *donatary* by alt. (cf. medieval Latin *donatarius*, -ARY¹).]
A person who receives a donation, esp. (LAW) from the Crown in the event of a forfeiture, a failure of succession, etc.

donatrix /də(ʊ)ˈneɪtrɪks/ *noun*. Pl. **-trixes**, **-trices** /-trɪsiːz/. **M16**.
[ORIGIN Latin, fem. of *donator*: see DONATOR *noun*¹, -TRIX.]
A female donor.

Donau /ˈdɒnaʊ/ *adjective & noun*. **M20**.
[ORIGIN German = the river Danube.]
GEOLOGY. (Designating or pertaining to) a series of Lower Pleistocene glaciations in the Alps, preceding the Günz.

doncher /ˈdəʊntʃə/ *verb* (2 *sing. pres.*). *colloq.* Also **doncha**, **dontcha**, **dontcher**. **L19**.
[ORIGIN Repr. an informal pronunc.]
Don't you. Esp. in ***doncher know***.

done /dʌn/ *ppl adjective & noun*. **ME**.
[ORIGIN pa. pple of DO *verb*.]
▶ **A** *ppl adjective*. **1** *gen.* That has been done. Also foll. by adverb. Cf. esp. DO *verb* 4. **ME**.

J. CANNAN The Colonel Blimps from the done-up cottages. *New Yorker* A done deal.

hard done by: see HARD *adjective, adverb, & noun*.
2 Socially acceptable; customary. Usu. in neg. with *be*, & in ***the done thing***. *colloq.* **M19**.

T. HEALD Some people consider it 'not done' to wear one club tie in another club's premises.

3 Tired, exhausted; worn out. Usu. *pred.* foll. by *for*, *in*, *up*. *colloq.* **E20**.

A. MOOREHEAD We and our camels being just done up, and scarcely able to reach the depot. *What Video?* Throwing a done-for VCR into the bin?

done to the wide, **done to the world** *colloq.* absolutely worn out or defeated.
▶ **B** *noun*. A thing that is done. **M19**.
■ **doneness** *noun* (*colloq.*) the degree to which food is done or cooked; the state of being sufficiently cooked: **M20**.

done *verb* see DO *verb*.

donee /dəʊˈniː/ *noun*. **E16**.
[ORIGIN from DONOR: see -EE¹.]
1 A person to whom something is given or conveyed, esp. legally. **E16**.
2 A person who receives a blood transfusion. **E20**.

Donegal /dɒnɪˈɡɔːl, dʌn-, ˈdɒnɪɡɔːl, ˈdʌn-/ *noun*. **E20**.
[ORIGIN A county in NW Ireland.]
1 In full ***Donegal tweed***. A tweed characterized by bright flecks randomly distributed on a usu. light grey background, orig. woven in Co. Donegal. **E20**.
2 In full ***Donegal carpet***. A coarse knotted carpet of a kind orig. made in Co. Donegal. **E20**.

doner /ˈdʌnə/ *noun*¹. *dial.* **M19**.
[ORIGIN Prob. from DONE *ppl adjective* + -ER¹.]
A person or animal past hope or fated to die.

doner /ˈdɒnə, dəʊ-/ *noun*². **L20**.
[ORIGIN Abbreviation.]
= DONER KEBAB.

doner *noun*³ see DONA.

doner kebab /ˈdɒnə kɪˈbab, ˈdəʊ-, kə-, ˈbaːb/ *noun phr.* **M20**.
[ORIGIN Turkish *döner kebap*, from *döner* rotating + *kebap* KEBAB.]
A Turkish dish consisting of spiced lamb roasted on a vertical rotating spit and sliced thinly.

doney *noun* var. of DHONEY.

dong /dɒŋ/ *noun*¹. Pl. same. **E19**.
[ORIGIN Vietnamese.]
A monetary unit (now the basic unit) of Vietnam, now equal to 10 hào or 100 xu.

dong /dɒŋ/ *noun*². **L19**.
[ORIGIN Coined by Edward Lear.]
A fabulous creature represented as having a luminous nose.

dong /dɒŋ/ *noun*³. **L19**.
[ORIGIN from the verb.]
1 A deep resonant sound (as) of a large bell. **L19**.
2 A heavy blow, a punch. *Austral. & NZ colloq.* **M20**.

dong /dɒŋ/ *noun*⁴. *slang* (chiefly *N. Amer.*). **M20**.
[ORIGIN Uncertain: perh. from DONG *noun*³.]
The penis.

dong /dɒŋ/ *verb*. **L16**.
[ORIGIN Imit.]
1 *verb intrans.* (Of a large bell) sound resonantly; make a deep resonant sound like that of a large bell. **L16**.
2 *verb trans.* Hit, punch. *colloq.* (esp. *Austral. & NZ*). **L19**.

donga /ˈdɒŋɡə/ *noun*. **L19**.
[ORIGIN Nguni.]
1 A ravine or watercourse with steep sides. *S. Afr.* **L19**.
2 A broad shallow depression in the ground. *Austral. & NZ*. **E20**.
3 A makeshift shelter; a temporary dwelling. *Austral.* **E20**.

dongle /ˈdɒŋɡ(ə)l/ *noun*. **L20**.
[ORIGIN Arbitrary.]
COMPUTING. A software protection device which must be plugged into a computer to enable the protected software to be used on it.

Dongola /ˈdɒŋɡələ, dɒnˈɡəʊlə/ *noun*¹ *& adjective*. Also **d-**. **L19**.
[ORIGIN A district of Sudan.]
(Designating) a type of leather resembling kid, made from goat, sheep, or calf skin.

dongola /ˈdɒŋɡələ, dɒnˈɡəʊlə/ *noun*². Also **D-**. **L19**.
[ORIGIN Unknown: cf. DONGOLA *noun*¹ *& adjective*, *gondola*.]
A punt paddled by a team of people in a race. Chiefly in ***dongola race***, ***dongola racing***.

dong quai /dɒŋ ˈkweɪ, ˈkwʌɪ/ *noun phr.* **L20**.
[ORIGIN Chinese *dānggui*.]
Either of two aromatic herbs of the genus *Angelica* (family Umbelliferae, or Apiaceae), *A. sinensis* of China and *A. acutiloba* of Japan, the roots of which are used by herbalists to treat premenstrual syndrome and menopausal symptoms.

Donizettian /dɒnɪˈzɛtɪən, -ˈtsɛ-/ *adjective & noun*. **M19**.
[ORIGIN from *Donizetti* (see below) + -AN.]
▶ **A** *adjective*. Of, pertaining to, or characteristic of the Italian operatic composer Gaetano Donizetti (1797–1848) or his music. **M19**.
▶ **B** *noun*. An interpreter, student, or admirer of Donizetti or his music. **M20**.

donjon /ˈdɒndʒ(ə)n, ˈdʌn-/ *noun*. Also (now *rare*) **dungeon** /ˈdʌndʒ(ə)n/. See also DUNGEON *noun*. **ME**.
[ORIGIN See DUNGEON *noun*.]
1 The great tower or keep of a castle, in the innermost court or bailey. **ME**.
2 See DUNGEON *noun* 1.

Don Juan /dɒn ˈdʒʊən, ˈwaːn/ *noun*. **M19**.
[ORIGIN A legendary Spanish nobleman famous for his seductions. Cf. DON *noun*¹.]
A man with a reputation for seducing women; a libertine.
■ **Don Juanism** *noun* **L19**.

donk /dɒŋk/ *noun*. *colloq.* **E20**.
[ORIGIN Abbreviation of DONKEY.]
1 = DONKEY 1, 2. **E20**.

A. RANSOME Roger's being a donk and starting some silly game.

2 A donkey engine. **M20**.

donkey /ˈdɒŋki/ *noun*. **L18**.
[ORIGIN Unknown: in early use pronounced to rhyme with *monkey*, whence the proposed derivations from DUN *noun*¹ and the male personal name *Duncan* (cf. DICKY *noun*, NEDDY).]
1 A domesticated hoofed mammal of the horse family, *Equus asinus*, with long ears and a braying call, used as a beast of burden; an ass. **L18**.
2 A stupid or silly person. **M19**.
3 **a** In full ***donkey engine***. A small or auxiliary engine, esp. on a ship. **M19**. ▸**b** In full ***donkey pump***. A small or auxiliary pump. **M19**.
4 A simple card game often played with special cards. **E20**.
5 A low stool used by an artist at an easel. **M20**.
– PHRASES: **(a penny more and) up goes the donkey** *colloq.*: used with allusion to the cry of a travelling showman inviting contributions to complete a sum of money. **talk the hind leg(s) off a donkey** *colloq.* talk at very great length; talk persuasively.
– COMB.: **donkey deep** *NZ slang* much involved; **donkey derby** a race in which competitors are mounted on donkeys; a meeting for such races; **donkey drop** *colloq.* in cricket etc., a slow ball bowled or hit so that it travels in a high curve; ***donkey engine***: see sense 3a above. **donkey jacket** a thick weatherproof jacket worn esp. by workmen; **donkey-lick** *verb trans.* (*Austral. & NZ slang*) defeat easily or thoroughly; **donkeyman** a man in charge of a donkey engine; a man with responsibilities in a ship's engine room; ***donkey pump***: see sense 3b above. **donkey's breakfast** *slang* a straw mattress; **donkey-stone** *noun & verb* = *hearthstone* s.v. HEARTH; **donkey stool** = sense 5 above; **donkey's years** *colloq.* a very long time; **donkey vote** *Austral. & NZ colloq.*: in which a voter or voters allocate their preferences simply by going down the list of candidates on the voting paper; **donkey work** the hard or unattractive part of an undertaking.
■ **donkeydom** *noun* folly, stupidity **M19**. **donkeyish** *adjective* asinine, rather stupid or silly **M19**.

donna /ˈdɔnna, ˈdɒnə/ *noun*. **E17**.
[ORIGIN Italian from Latin *domina*: see DONA.]
(Used as a courtesy title preceding the name of) an Italian, or a Spanish or Portuguese, lady. See also PRIMA DONNA, SECONDA DONNA.

Donnan equilibrium /ˌdɒnən iːkwɪˈlɪbrɪəm, ɛkwɪ-/ *noun phr.* **E20**.
[ORIGIN F. G. *Donnan* (1870–1956), Brit. physical chemist.]
PHYSICAL CHEMISTRY. The equilibrium that exists between two ionic solutions when one or more of the ionic species cannot pass from one solution to the other, producing a difference in osmotic pressure and electrical potential between the solutions.

donnard *verb pa. pple*: see DONNER.

donnée /dɔne, ˈdɒneɪ/ *noun*. Also **donné**. **L19**.
[ORIGIN French, fem. pa. ppl adjective of *donner* give.]
1 A subject, theme, or motif of a literary work. **L19**.

J. CAREY Those vague economic données that we come to expect in a Dickens novel.

2 A datum, a given fact; a basic assumption. **L19**.

J. P. STERN Leaving . . the question of how such a reverence is possible, we may accept it as a metaphysical donnée.

donner /ˈdɒnə/ *verb trans.* *Scot. & N. English*. Pa. pple **donnered**, **donnard**. **E18**.
[ORIGIN Unknown.]
Daze, stun, stupefy. Chiefly as ***donnered*** *ppl adjective*.

donnish /ˈdɒnɪʃ/ *adjective*. **E19**.
[ORIGIN from DON *noun*¹ + -ISH¹.]
Resembling or characteristic of a college don; having a pedantic stiffness or gravity of manner.
■ **donnishly** *adverb* **E20**. **donnishness** *noun* **M19**.

donnot *noun* var. of DO-NOUGHT.

donnybrook /ˈdɒnɪbrʊk/ *noun*. **M19**.
[ORIGIN *Donnybrook*, a suburb of Dublin, Ireland, once famous for its annual fair.]
A scene of uproar and disorder; an uproarious meeting; a heated argument.

donor /ˈdəʊnə, -nɔː/ *noun*. **LME**.
[ORIGIN Anglo-Norman *don(o)ur*, Anglo-Norman & Old French *doneur*, from Latin *donator*: see DONATOR *noun*¹, -OR.]
1 A person who gives or (LAW) conveys something. **LME**.
2 A person or animal, or a corpse, that is used as a source of tissue for transplantation; a blood donor; a man who contributes semen for artificial insemination. **E20**.
universal donor: see UNIVERSAL *adjective*.
3 **a** CHEMISTRY. An atom, molecule, etc., that loses part of itself in combining with another; *esp.* an atom that gives up two valency electrons in forming a coordinate bond. **E20**. ▸**b** PHYSICS. An impurity atom in a semiconductor which has more valency electrons than the majority of atoms and effectively contributes a conducting electron to the material. **M20**.
– COMB.: **donor card** a card which a person carries to authorize the use of his or her body for transplant surgery after death; **donor country**: which gives economic aid to another country; **donor fatigue** a lessening of public willingness to respond generously to charitable appeals, resulting from the frequency of such appeals.
■ **donorship** *noun* **M20**.

do-nothing /ˈduːnʌθɪŋ/ *noun & adjective*. **L16**.
[ORIGIN from DO *verb* + NOTHING.]
▶ **A** *noun*. A person who does nothing; an idler. **L16**.
▶ **B** *adjective*. That does nothing; characterized by doing nothing; indolent, idle. **M19**.
■ **doˈnothingism** *noun* **M19**. **doˈnothingness** *noun* **E19**.

do-nought /ˈduːnɔːt/ *noun*. Now chiefly *dial.* Also **donnot** /ˈdɒnət/ **L16**.
[ORIGIN App. from *do nought*.]
A do-nothing; a good-for-nothing.

Donovan body /ˈdɒnəvən bɒdi/ *noun phr.* **E20**.
[ORIGIN C. *Donovan* (1863–1951), Irish physician.]
MEDICINE. The intracellular body characteristic of the lesions of donovanosis, identified as due to an anaerobic rod-shaped bacterium, *Calymmatobacterium granulomatosis*.
■ **donovaˈnosis** *noun*, pl. **-noses** /-ˈnəʊsiːz/, a chronic granulomatous skin disease of the inguinal and genital regions, endemic in southern India and the Caribbean and thought to be caused by the bacteria that form Donovan bodies; also called ***granuloma inguinale***: **M20**.

Don Pedro *noun phr.* var. of DOM PEDRO.

Don Quixote *noun* see QUIXOTE.

donship /ˈdɒnʃɪp/ *noun*. **E17**.
[ORIGIN from DON *noun*¹ + -SHIP.]
1 With possess. adjective (as ***his donship*** etc.): a title of respect given to a don (DON *noun*¹ 1). **E17**.
2 The status of being a don; possession of the title 'don'. **L18**.

donsie /ˈdɒnsi/ *adjective*. *Scot.* Also **-sy**. See also DAUNCY. **E18**.
[ORIGIN from Gaelic *donas* bad luck (from *dona* bad) + -IE. Cf. SONSY.]
1 Unlucky. **E18**.
2 Dejected, glum. **E18**.
3 Neat, tidy, esp. affectedly so. *Scot. & N. English*. Now *rare* or *obsolete*. **E18**.
4 Sickly; delicate, feeble. **L18**.
5 Badly behaved; bad-tempered. Now *rare* or *obsolete*. **L18**.
6 Stupid. **E19**.

don't /dəʊnt/ *noun*. **L19**.
[ORIGIN from *don't*: see DO *verb*.]
A prohibition; an injunction not to do something. Usu. in *pl.* in ***dos and don'ts***.

don't *verb* see DO *verb*.

don't-care /ˈdəʊntkɛː/ *adjective & noun.* L19.
[ORIGIN from *don't* (see DO verb) + CARE verb.]
▸ **A** *adjective.* Careless, indifferent; reckless. L19.
▸ **B** *noun.* A careless or indifferent person. E20.
■ **don't-ˈcarish** *adjective* M19. **don't-ˈcarishness** *noun* M19.

dontcha, **dontcher** *verbs* vars. of DONCHER.

don't-know /dəʊntˈnəʊ/ *noun.* L19.
[ORIGIN from *don't* (see DO verb) + KNOW verb.]
A person who does not know or disclaims knowledge; *esp.* one who is undecided when replying to an opinion poll or questionnaire.

donut *noun* see DOUGHNUT.

donzel /ˈdɒnz(ə)l/ *noun.* Now *arch.* or *hist.* L16.
[ORIGIN Italian *donzello* from Proto-Romance dim. of Latin *dominus* lord, master: see -EL[2]. Cf. DON noun[1], DAMSEL.]
A young gentleman not yet knighted; a squire, a page.

donzella /donˈdzella, dɒntˈsɛlə/ *noun.* Pl. ***-lle*** /-lle/, ***-llas*** /-ləz/. M19.
[ORIGIN Italian, fem. of *donzello*: see DONZEL.]
A young Italian or Provençal woman.

doo *noun* see DOVE noun.

doob /duːb/ *noun.* E19.
[ORIGIN Hindi *dūb* = Sanskrit *dūrvā*.]
In the Indian subcontinent, = DOG'S TOOTH 2.

doobie /ˈduːbi/ *noun. US slang.* M20.
[ORIGIN Unknown.]
A cannabis cigarette; cannabis.

doobry /ˈduːbri/ *noun. colloq.* L20.
[ORIGIN Origin unknown. Cf. DOODAD, DOOFER, DOOHICKEY.]
A thing that one cannot name precisely, a 'thingummy'.

New Statesman I've got to go down to Sainsbury's to get the doobry for the loo.

doocot /ˈduːkət/ *noun.* Orig. & chiefly *Scot.* LME.
[ORIGIN from DOO + COT noun[1].]
A dovecote; *Scot.* a type of large stone dovecote characteristic of the Scottish Lowlands.

doodad /ˈduːdad/ *noun. colloq.* (chiefly *N. Amer.*). E20.
[ORIGIN Unknown.]
Something not readily nameable, a 'thingummy'; *esp.* a fancy ornament of an unnecessary kind.

R. DAVIES Full of marquetry woodwork . . and filigree doodads around the ceiling.

doodah /ˈduːdɑː/ *noun. slang.* E20.
[ORIGIN The refrain *doo-da(h)* of the plantation song 'Camptown Races'.]
1 ***all of a doodah***, in a state of excitement; in a flap. E20.
2 = DOODAD. E20.

doodle /ˈduːd(ə)l/ *noun.* E17.
[ORIGIN Low German *dudel-* in *dudeltopf*, *-ldopp* simple fellow.]
1 A foolish person; a dolt, a ninny. *colloq.* E17.
2 = DOODLEBUG 1. *US colloq.* L19.
3 An idle scrawl or figure drawn absent-mindedly or to while away the time. M20.

doodle /ˈduːd(ə)l/ *verb*[1]. E19.
[ORIGIN from DOODLE noun.]
1 *verb trans.* Make a fool of; cheat. *dial.* E19.
2 *verb intrans. & trans.* Scrawl or draw absent-mindedly. M20.
■ **doodler** *noun* a person who draws doodles M20.

doodle /ˈduːd(ə)l/ *verb*[2] *trans.* Chiefly *Scot.* E19.
[ORIGIN German *dudeln*: cf. *Dudelsack* bagpipe.]
Play (a bagpipe).
– COMB.: **doodle-sack** a bagpipe.

doodlebug /ˈduːd(ə)lbʌg/ *noun.* M19.
[ORIGIN from DOODLE noun + BUG noun[2].]
1 The larva of the ant lion; any of various similar insects. *US.* M19.
2 A divining rod for finding oil etc.; any device used for the same purpose. *US colloq.* E20.
3 A prospector for oil etc. *US colloq.* M20.
4 Any of various kinds of small vehicle. *US colloq.* M20.
5 A flying bomb of the Second World War. *colloq.* M20.
■ **doodlebugger** *noun* (*US*) = sense 3 above M20.

doodle-doo /duːd(ə)lˈduː/ *noun.* L18.
[ORIGIN Abbreviation of COCK-A-DOODLE-DOO.]
A child's word for a cockerel.

doodly-squat /duːdlɪˈskwɒt/ *noun. N. Amer. slang.* M20.
[ORIGIN Perh. from fanciful extension of DOODLE verb + SQUAT verb.]
Nothing at all; (following a neg.) anything. Abbreviated to SQUAT noun[2].

doo-doo /ˈduːduː/ *noun. colloq.* M20.
[ORIGIN Perh. child's var. of POOH-POOH.]
Excrement, faeces.

fig.: K. LETTE I was in deep doo-doo. Circumstances had boxed me in like the sides of a coffin.

doofer /ˈduːfə/ *noun. colloq.* Also **-fah**; **-vah**, **-ver**, /-və/. M20.
[ORIGIN Prob. alt. of *do for* in phrs. like *that will do for now*.]
An unspecified object or device, a 'thingummy'.

doofus /ˈduːfʌs/ *noun. N. Amer. colloq.* Also **dufus**. M20.
[ORIGIN Perh. alt. of GOOFUS noun[1], or from Scots *doof* dolt.]
A stupid person, an idiot.

doohickey /ˈduːhɪki/ *noun. colloq.* (chiefly *N. Amer.*). Also **dohickey**, **doohicky**. E20.
[ORIGIN from DOO(DAD + HICKEY.]
An unspecified or unnameable object or device, *esp.* a mechanical one.

doojigger /ˈduːdʒɪgə/ *noun. US colloq.* M20.
[ORIGIN from DOO(DAD + JIGGER noun[1].]
A small object, a gadget, a 'thingummy'.

dool /duːl/ *noun*[1]. Also **dole** /dəʊl/. LME.
[ORIGIN Corresp. to Old Frisian *dōl* (Dutch *doel*) aim, mark.]
1 A boundary or landmark in the form of a post, stone, or unploughed strip. LME.
2 The goal in a game. *Scot.* M16.
hail the dool score a goal.

dool *noun*[2] var. of DOLE *noun*[2].

doolally /duːˈlali/ *adjective. slang* (orig. MILITARY). E20.
[ORIGIN *Deolali*, a town in India.]
Orig. (now less usual) ***doolally tap*** [Urdu from Persian *tap* fever]. Temporarily insane; deranged; crazy, foolish.

R. HILL Mrs Hardcastle . . has gone a bit doolally with grief.

Doolan /ˈduːlən/ *noun. NZ slang.* Also **d-**. M20.
[ORIGIN Prob. the Irish surname.]
A Roman Catholic, *spec.* an Irish one.

doolie /ˈduːli/ *noun.* Also **-ly**. E17.
[ORIGIN Hindi *ḍolī* dim. of *ḍolā* cradle, swing, litter, from Sanskrit *dolā*, *ḍolā* to swing.]
A simple litter, formerly used in the Indian subcontinent for transporting the wounded.

doom /duːm/ *noun*[1].
[ORIGIN Old English *dōm* = Old Frisian, Old Saxon *dōm*, Old High German *tuom*, Old Norse *dómr*, Gothic *dōms*, from Germanic, from a base meaning 'to place', 'to set', repr. also by DO verb. For the sense-development cf. Greek *themis* law (*the-* to place), Latin *statutum* STATUTE noun.]
1 A statute, a law; *gen.* an ordinance, a decree. *obsolete* exc. *hist.* OE.

J. LINGARD He revised the whole code of Anglo-Saxon law, and compiled a new book of dooms.

2 A judicial decision, *esp.* one formally pronounced; *spec.* a sentence of punishment. OE.

S. BECKETT To record the doom, don the black cap.

3 The process of judging, as in a court of law; a trial. *arch.* OE.

C. KINGSLEY The Judge is set, the doom begun!

†**4** Justice, equity. Chiefly in versions of Scripture or in scriptural allusions. OE–L16.
†**5** Right to judge; *gen.* power, authority. OE–LME.
6 The Last Judgement; a pictorial representation of this. Now chiefly in ***crack of doom***. *arch.* ME.

MILTON The wakefull trump of doom. J. T. MICKLETHWAITE The . . hobgoblins of mediaeval dooms.

Day of Doom (*a*) the Day of Judgement; †(*b*) *transf.* the last day of one's life.
†**7** Personal opinion or judgement. ME–E17.
†**8** Faculty of judging; discernment. LME–L17.

DRYDEN With . . unerring Doom, He sees what is, and was, and is to come.

9 Irrevocable lot, fate, destiny, (esp. evil). LME.

D. H. LAWRENCE She knew her life would be unhappy . . . Yet it was her doom She had to come back to him. T. H. WHITE It will be your glorious doom . . to enjoy the nobility of your proper title.

10 The fated ending to a person's life, career, or course of action; impending ruin or disaster. L16.

J. R. GREEN The minister's doom was sealed. V. GLENDINNING The atmosphere of impending doom . . lay heavily on them all.

– COMB.: **doombook** *hist.* a code of Germanic or Anglo-Saxon laws, *spec.* that ascribed to Alfred the Great; **doom-laden** *adjective* portending, suggesting, or predicting doom; **doom-ring** ARCHAEOLOGY a ring of stones forming the boundary of the old Norse courts of judgement; **doomsayer** = DOOMSTER 3; **doom-tree** *hist.*: on which condemned persons were hanged; **doomwatch** a watch for signs of impending disaster, esp. of environmental destruction; **doomwatcher** a person who takes part in a doomwatch or who predicts environmental disaster.
■ **doomful** *adjective* (*arch.*) fraught with impending disaster; fateful: L16. **doomfully** *adverb* M20.

doom *noun*[2] var. of DOUM.

doom /duːm/ *verb.* LME.
[ORIGIN from DOOM noun[1].]
▸ **I** *verb trans.* **1** Pass judgement on. *obsolete* exc. as in sense 2. LME.

P. FLETCHER There the equall Judge . . dooms each voice aright.

2 Give judgement against; sentence, condemn, (*to* a punishment). L16.

MILTON He dooms it as contrary to Truth. LD MACAULAY An act was passed which doomed him to perpetual exile.

3 Pronounce or fix as a sentence or fate; decree. *arch.* L16.

SHAKES. *Tit. A.* The Emperor in his rage will doom her death.

4 Destine inexorably *to* a (usu. unwelcome) fate or *to do*. Also *absol.*, consign to certain misfortune or destruction. Chiefly as ***doomed*** *ppl adjective.* E17.

G. F. KENNAN They thought Kornilov's venture doomed to failure. F. WELDON I . . cannot afford to throw anything away, and am doomed to wear it for ever.

▸ **II** *verb intrans.* **5** Give judgement; decide. Now *rare* or *obsolete.* L16.

doomer /ˈduːmə/ *noun. arch.* OE.
[ORIGIN from DOOM noun[1] + -ER[1]; later from DOOM verb.]
A person who tries a case or pronounces a sentence, *esp.* a judge.

dooms /duːmz/ *adverb. Scot. & N. English.* E19.
[ORIGIN Uncertain: perh. alt. of †*doon(s)* in same sense, from *doon* var. of DOWN adverb.]
Extremely, very; (with imprecatory force) deucedly.

doomsday /ˈduːmzdeɪ/ *noun.* In sense 2 **D-**. See also DOMESDAY. OE.
[ORIGIN from genit. of DOOM noun[1] + DAY noun.]
1 The day when God is expected to judge the world, the Day of Judgement; any day of decisive judgement or final dissolution. OE.
till doomsday to the end of the world; for ever.
2 = DOMESDAY. L16.
– COMB.: **doomsday machine**, **doomsday bomb** a hypothetical bomb capable of annihilating the world.

doomsman /ˈduːmzmən/ *noun. arch.* Pl. **-men**. ME.
[ORIGIN from DOOM noun[1] + -'S[1] + MAN noun.]
= DOOMSTER 1, DEEMSTER 1.

doomster /ˈduːmstə/ *noun.* LME.
[ORIGIN Var. of DEEMSTER after DOOM noun[1], verb.]
1 = DEEMSTER 1. *arch.* LME.
2 *Scot.* = DEMPSTER 2. *obsolete* exc. *hist.* E17.
3 A person who predicts disaster, esp. of a political or economic nature; a doomsayer. L20.

doomy /ˈduːmi/ *adjective.* M20.
[ORIGIN from DOOM noun[1] + -Y[1].]
Portending, suggesting, or predicting doom; ominous; gloomy, weird.

New Society Anyone who is less than doomy about Britain's population 'problem'. CLIVE JAMES 'Come with us', boomed a doomy tape, 'into the Mesozoic age.'

■ **doomily** *adverb* L20. **doominess** *noun* L20.

Doona /ˈduːnə/ *noun. Austral.* Also **d-**. L20.
[ORIGIN Perh. from Swedish *dun* down.]
(Proprietary name for) a quilted eiderdown or duvet.

doonga /ˈduːŋgə/ *noun.* Also **dunga**. E20.
[ORIGIN Hindi *ḍõgā*.]
In the Indian subcontinent, a flat-bottomed dugout with a square sail.

door /dɔː/ *noun.*
[ORIGIN Old English *duru* (fem. *u*-stem) = Old Frisian *dure*, Old Saxon *duru* & Old English *dor* (neut. *a*- stem) = Old Saxon *dor*, Old & mod. High German *tor* gate, Gothic *daur* both from Germanic, from Indo-European base repr. also by Latin *foris*, Greek *thura*, Sanskrit *dur*, *dvār*.]
▸ **I 1** A hinged or sliding barrier of wood, metal, etc., serving to open or close the entrance to a building, room, cupboard, vehicle, or other enclosure. OE. ▸**b** Indicating the room, house, etc., in a row or series, to which the door belongs. M17.

SIR W. SCOTT She stood before her lover's door and knocked for admittance. **b** J. MASTERS His office . . was three doors from the Collector's.

back door, ***French door***, ***front door***, ***patio door***, ***side door***, etc. ***double door***, ***folding door***, ***glass door***, ***sliding door***, etc.
2 An opening that can be closed by a door, a doorway. LME.
3 Something resembling a door in its movement or function; a lid, a valve, a cover; an opening. LME.
4 Either of the two boards or metal plates attached to the ends of a trawl net. E20.
▸ **II** *fig.* **5** A means of access, admission, or exit; a means to a specified end; a suitable occasion, an opportunity. Chiefly in phrs. below. OE.

A. W. KINGLAKE Which left open a door to future negotiation. H. KELLER I did not dream that that interview would be the door through which I should pass . . from isolation to friendship. M. L. KING A democratic educational system requires multiple doors.

– PHRASES: ***at DEATH's door***. **be at a person's door** = ***lie at a person's door*** below. ***behind CLOSED doors***. **close the door on**, **close the door to** make impossible, preclude. ***DARKEN a person's door(s)***. ***folding door(s)***: see FOLDING *ppl adjective.* ***foot in the door***: see FOOT noun. ***in doors***: see INDOORS adverb. †**is the wind in that door?** is the wind in that quarter? is that how matters are going? ***keep the wolf from the door***: see WOLF noun. **lay something at a person's door** impute something reprehensible etc. to a person. ***LEDGED door***. **lie at a person's door** be the fault or responsibility of a person. ***nail to the barn door***: see NAIL verb. ***next door***: see NEXT adjective. **open a door for**, **open a door to** provide an opportunity for, make possible. ***open door***: see OPEN adjective. **out of doors** (*a*) outside the house, in or into the open air; †(*b*) *fig.* out of place, irrelevant: see OUT-OF-DOORS. **show**

a person the door dismiss a person unceremoniously from one's presence. **shut the door on**, **shut the door to** = *close the door on* above. ***shut the stable door when the horse has bolted***: see STABLE *noun*[1]. ***toe in the door***: see TOE *noun*. ***Venetian door***: see VENETIAN *adjective*. **within door(s)** *arch.* in or into a building, indoors. WITHOUT DOOR, WITHOUT DOORS.

– COMB.: **doorbell** a bell inside a building that can be rung from outside to indicate that someone is at the door; **doorcase** = *door frame* below; **door cheek** (now *N. English*) = *doorpost* below; **door frame** the frame inside a doorway, in which the door is hung; **door head** the horizontal upper part of a door frame; **doorkeeper** a person who guards a door; a janitor; **doorknob**: for turning to release the catch of a door; ***door knocker***: see KNOCKER 2; **doorman** an attendant at the entrance to a shop, office, or place of entertainment; a doorkeeper; **doormat** a mat for wiping mud etc. from the shoes on entering a building; *fig.* a passive subservient person; **doornail** a large-headed nail with which doors were formerly studded for strength or ornament; now esp. in ***dead as a doornail*** (see DEAD *adjective*); **door plate** a plate on or by a front door of a building, bearing the name of the occupant(s) or the nature of the business conducted there; **doorpost** either of the two uprights in a door frame; a jamb; **door prize** *N. Amer.* a prize which each person present at an event has the chance to win, usually by means of a raffle or draw; **door sill** = SILL *noun*[1] 3a; **doorsman** *arch.* = *doorman* above; **door stead** (now *dial.*) = *doorway* below; **door stone** a flagstone situated in front of a door; **doorstop** a device fixed to the ground or the wall to prevent a door from opening too widely or from striking the wall; a weight or wedge that can be used to keep a door open; **door-to-door** *adjective* (of selling, canvassing, etc.) carried on systematically from house to house; **doorward** *arch.* a doorkeeper, a janitor; SCOTTISH HISTORY a warder of the royal palace; **doorway** the opening filled by a door; **dooryard** *N. Amer.* a yard or garden in front of the door of a house.

■ **doored** *adjective* having a door or doors LME. **doorless** *adjective* ME.

doorstep /ˈdɔːstɛp/ *noun, adjective, & verb.* E19.
[ORIGIN from DOOR + STEP *noun*[1].]

▸ **A** *noun.* **1** A step outside a (usu. outer) door, by which the threshold is raised above the level of the ground. E19. **on one's doorstep**, **on the doorstep** *fig.* very close to one.

2 A thick slice of bread. *slang.* L19.

▸ **B** *attrib.* or as *adjective.* Door-to-door; brought or made to people in their own homes. E20.

Modern Law Review He had foolishly signed a three-year magazine subscription contract with a doorstep salesman. *Times Lit. Suppl.* Doorstep jobs like delivering milk and selling insurance. *Times* Doorstep deliveries are losing ground to shop sales.

▸ **C** *verb.* Infl. **-pp-**.

1 *verb intrans.* Go from door to door selling, canvassing, etc. Earliest as ***doorstepping*** *verbal noun.* E20.

2 *verb trans.* Leave (a child) in the care of someone else. M20.

3 *verb trans. & intrans.* Call on or wait on the doorstep for (a person) without invitation or arrangement. L20.

Guardian The 'frightful men' from that newspaper who doorstepped her.

■ **doorstepper** *noun* a person who doorsteps L20.

doosra /ˈduːzrɑː/ *noun.* L20.
[ORIGIN Urdu *doosra* other one, second, from *doh* two.]
CRICKET. A ball which breaks from the leg (to a right-handed batsman), though bowled with an apparent off-break action, in order to deceive the batsman.

doovah, **doover** *nouns* vars. of DOOFER.

doo-wop /ˈduːwɒp/ *noun.* Also **doowhop**, **doowop**, & other vars. M20.
[ORIGIN App. imit.]
A style of pop music marked by the use of nonsense phrases as the main line or as harmony, which originated in the US in the 1950s.

doozer /ˈduːzə/ *noun. slang* (chiefly *N. Amer.*). M20.
[ORIGIN Uncertain: see DOOZY, -ER[1].]
= DOOZY *noun.*

doozy /ˈduːzi/ *adjective & noun. slang* (chiefly *N. Amer. & Austral.*). Also **-ie**. E20.
[ORIGIN Uncertain: perh. rel. to DOUSE *verb*[1].]

▸ **A** *adjective.* Excellent, stunning. E20.

▸ **B** *noun.* A thing of surpassing size or excellence; a stunner. E20.

dop /dɒp/ *noun*[1]. *obsolete* exc. *dial.* L16.
[ORIGIN from DOP *verb.*]
A quick bob or curtsy.

dop /dɒp/ *noun*[2]. E18.
[ORIGIN Dutch & Afrikaans = shell, husk. In senses 3 & 4 perh. a different word.]

†**1** The pupa case of an insect. *rare.* Only in E18.

2 A small copper cup into which a diamond is cemented while it is being cut or polished. M18.

3 In full ***dop brandy***. Brandy, esp. of a cheap or inferior kind. *S. Afr.* L19.

4 A tot of liquor, esp. of wine as given to farm labourers. *S. Afr.* M20.

dop /dɒp/ *verb. obsolete* exc. *dial.* Infl. **-pp-**. LME.
[ORIGIN from base of Old English *doppettan* immerse, baptize, from Germanic var. of base of DIP *verb*, DEEP *adjective*. Cf. also DAP *verb.*]

†**1** *verb intrans.* Plunge or sink suddenly into water etc.; dive, plop. LME–L17.

2 *verb intrans.* Make a quick bob or curtsy. M16.

†**3** *verb trans.* Dip or immerse quickly, as in baptism. M16–M17.

dopa /ˈdəʊpə/ *noun.* E20.
[ORIGIN German, from initial letters of DI-[2] + OXY- + PHENYL + ALANINE.]
An amino acid formed from tyrosine in the nerves and adrenal medulla as a precursor of dopamine, and given (as L-dopa) in the treatment of Parkinsonism; dihydroxyphenylalanine, $C_9H_{11}NO_4$.
L-**dopa** the laevorotary form of dopa, levodopa.

dopamine /ˈdəʊpəmiːn/ *noun.* M20.
[ORIGIN from DOPA + AMINE.]
BIOCHEMISTRY. An amine that occurs esp. in nervous and peripheral tissue as a neurotransmitter and a precursor of noradrenaline, adrenalin, and melanin; 3,4-dihydroxyphenylethylamine, $C_8H_{11}NO_2$.

■ **dopamiˈnergic** *adjective* releasing or involving dopamine as a neurotransmitter M20.

dopant /ˈdəʊp(ə)nt/ *noun.* M20.
[ORIGIN from DOPE *verb* + -ANT[1].]
A substance used to dope a semiconductor.

dopchick *noun* see DABCHICK.

dope /dəʊp/ *noun.* E19.
[ORIGIN Dutch *doop* sauce, from *doopen* dip, mix, adulterate. In branch II prob. orig. a distinct word.]

▸ **I** Senses orig. *US.*

1 A thick liquid, *esp.* one used as a lubricant. Also, a thick gravy. *US.* E19.

2 An absorbent material used to hold a lubricant or a high explosive. L19.

3 Orig., opium, *esp.* the thick treacly preparation used in opium-smoking. Now *gen.*, any narcotic or stupefying drug. Also, alcoholic drink. *slang.* L19.

4 A preparation, mixture, or medicinal drug not more precisely defined; 'stuff'. *slang.* L19. ▸**b** A drug etc. administered to a racehorse or greyhound to interfere with its performance, or to an athlete as a stimulus. L19. ▸**c** A varnish applied to the cloth surface of aeroplane parts to keep them taut and airtight. E20. ▸**d** A substance added to a fuel to increase its efficiency. M20.

A. D. GILLESPIE The hay fever is better now, more because the season is passing than by reason of the doctor's 'dopes'.

5 (A drink of) a carbonated beverage. *US slang.* E20.

6 Information, esp. on a particular topic or of a kind not generally divulged; essential facts or details. Also, statements designed to gloss over the truth; misleading talk. *slang.* E20.

Chicago Daily News What does the average layman think, upon getting all this reassuring dope? M. LEITCH If you want the inside story, names, dates, places, all the dope on . . the Brotherhood, I can supply it.

▸ **II 7** A foolish or silly person. *colloq.* (orig. *dial.*). M19.

T. ROETHKE He's a dope in some ways, but very honest.

8 A person under the influence of drugs or drink; a drug addict. *US slang.* E20.

– COMB.: **dope-fiend** *slang* a drug addict; **dope-ring** *slang* a group of people engaged in buying, selling, and using illicit drugs; **dope-runner** *slang* a person who smuggles or traffics in illicit drugs; **dope-sheet** *N. Amer. slang* a sheet of paper giving information or instructions; *spec.* one containing details of the horses entered for a race, with their past form.

dope /dəʊp/ *verb.* Orig. *US.* M19.
[ORIGIN from the noun.]

1 *verb trans.* Smear, daub; *spec.* apply dope to (the outer fabric of an aeroplane etc). M19.

2 *verb trans.* Treat with an adulterant; doctor. L19. ▸**b** Add an impurity to (a semiconductor) to produce a desired electrical characteristic. M20.

3 *verb trans.* Administer stimulating or stupefying drugs to (a horse, a person). L19.

4 *verb intrans.* Indulge in drug-taking. E20.

5 *verb trans.* Foll. by *out*: work out; infer or find out by surmising; reckon (*that*). *US.* E20.

R. H. DAVIS We would study the morning papers and . . from them try to dope out the winners. B. SCHULBERG I'm going to sell it to Hollywood. I even got the title all doped out. *Village Voice* She started reading the media . . to dope out the treatment of women.

■ **doper** *noun* a person who administers or (now chiefly) habitually takes drugs E20. **dopester** *noun* (*slang*) (**a**) a person who collects information on, and forecasts the results of, sporting events, elections, etc.; (**b**) a drug addict: E20.

dopey /ˈdəʊpi/ *adjective. slang* (orig. *US*). Also **dopy**. L19.
[ORIGIN from DOPE *noun* + -Y[1].]

1 Sluggish or stupefied (as) with a drug. L19.

G. ORWELL I was dopey from morphia but still in great pain.

2 Foolish, silly. L19.

R. JAFFE She decided that she would never talk about her dopey ambitions again.

■ **dopily** *adjective* M20. **dopiness** *noun* dopey quality; *spec.* (*NZ*) a deficiency disease in sheep: M20.

dopiaza /ˈdəʊpɪɑːʒə/ *noun.* L20.
[ORIGIN Urdu *dupiyāza*, from *du* two + *piyāz* onion (see below).]
An Indian dish of meat cooked with onions (which are divided into two portions, one cooked with the meat and one fried separately and added at the end).

doppelgänger /ˈdɒpəlgɛŋər; ˈdɒp(ə)lgɛŋə, -gaŋə/ *noun.* Also **-ganger**. M19.
[ORIGIN German, lit. 'double-goer'. Cf. DOUBLE-GANGER.]
A supposed spectral likeness or double of a living person.

Dopper /ˈdɒpə/ *noun. S. Afr.* Also **d-**. M19.
[ORIGIN Afrikaans, of unknown origin.]
A member of a strictly Calvinistic sect of the Dutch Reformed Church, proverbial for ultra-conservatism in ideas, manners, and dress.

doppie /ˈdɒpi/ *noun. S. Afr.* L19.
[ORIGIN Afrikaans, dim. of *dop* (DOP *noun*[2]).]

1 An empty cartridge case, a percussion cap. *colloq.* L19.

2 A grapeskin. M20.

doppione /dɒpˈpjone, dɒpɪˈəʊni/ *noun.* Pl. **-ni** /-ni/. M20.
[ORIGIN Italian, from *doppio* double.]
EARLY MUSIC. A double-bore woodwind instrument of the Italian Renaissance.

Doppler /ˈdɒplə/ *noun.* Also **d-**. L19.
[ORIGIN C. J. *Doppler* (1803–53), Austrian mathematician and physicist.]
Used *attrib.* and (formerly) in *possess.* with ref. to the effect explained by him (see below).
Doppler broadening: of spectral lines as a result of the different velocities of the emitting atoms giving rise to different Doppler shifts. **Doppler effect** the observed increase (or decrease) in the pitch or frequency of sound, light, and other waves when the source and observer are getting closer (or further away). **Doppler radar**: using the Doppler effect to ascertain the radial velocity of a detected object. **Doppler shift** the change in frequency caused by the Doppler effect. **Doppler width**: of spectral lines, due to Doppler broadening.

dopy *adjective* var. of DOPEY.

dor /dɔː/ *noun*[1]. Also **dorr**.
[ORIGIN Prob. imit. Cf. Middle Low German *dorte* drone.]

†**1** Any of various kinds of bee or buzzing fly. Also ***dor-bee***, ***dor-fly***, etc. OE–L17.

2 More fully ***dor beetle***. Any of various coleopterous insects that make a buzzing sound, *esp.* a dung beetle of the genus *Geotrupes*. LME.

– COMB.: ***dor-bee***: see sense 1 above; ***dor beetle***: see sense 2 above; **dor-bug** *US* any insect that makes a buzzing sound; ***dor-fly***: see sense 1 above; **dor-hawk** the nightjar.

†**dor** *noun*[2]. M16–M19.
[ORIGIN Rel. to DOR *verb*: perh. from Old Norse *dár* scoff, in phr. *draga dár at* make game of.]
Mockery. Chiefly in ***give someone the dor***, ***receive the dor***, etc.

dor /dɔː/ *verb trans.* Long *obsolete* exc. *dial.* L16.
[ORIGIN Rel. to DOR *noun*[2]: perh. from Old Norse *dára* mock, make sport of.]
Mock, make game of; confound, stupefy.
dor the dotterel cajole or hoax a simpleton.

DORA /ˈdɔːrə/ *abbreviation.*
hist. Defence of the Realm Act, an act providing the British Government with wide powers during the First World War.

dorado /dəˈrɑːdəʊ/ *noun.* Pl. **-os**. E17.
[ORIGIN Spanish = gilded, from late Latin *deauratus* pa. pple of *deaurare* gild over: see DORY *noun*[1].]

1 A dolphinfish, *Coryphaena hippurus*, noted for its splendid blue-green and silver colours and fast speed and caught as a sporting and food fish; = DOLPHIN 1b. E17.

2 (Usu. **D-**.) (The name of) a small constellation of the southern hemisphere, between Pictor and Reticulum; the Swordfish. L17.

3 A carplike game fish, *Salminus maxillosus*, of the characin family, found in S. American rivers and of a golden colour. L19.

dorcas /ˈdɔːkəs/ *noun*[1]. E19.
[ORIGIN mod. Latin, from *Gazella dorcas* (see below), from Greek *dorkas* deer, gazelle.]
More fully ***dorcas gazelle***. A small gazelle, *Gazella dorcas*, found in N. Africa and western Asia.

Dorcas /ˈdɔːkəs/ *noun*[2]. M19.
[ORIGIN A woman in *Acts* 9:36.]
(A meeting of) a society of women in a church, whose aim is to make and provide clothing for the poor. Also ***Dorcas meeting***, ***Dorcas society***.

– COMB.: **Dorcas basket**: of needlework for charitable purposes.

doré /*noun* ˈdɔːreɪ, -riː; *adjective* ˈdɔːreɪ, ˈdɒr-/ *noun & adjective.* L18.
[ORIGIN French, pa. pple of *dorer* gild from late Latin *deaurare*: see DORY *noun*[1].]

▸ **A** *noun.* The walleye, *Stizostedion vitreum. Canad.* L18.

▸ **B** *adjective.* METALLURGY. Containing gold. L19.

doria /ˈdɔːrɪə/ *noun.* Also **dorea**. L17.
[ORIGIN Hindi *ḍoriyā* striped cloth.]
A kind of striped Indian muslin, sometimes flowered between the stripes.

Dorian /ˈdɔːrɪən/ *noun & adjective*. M16.
[ORIGIN from Latin *Dorius* (from Greek *Dōrios* of Doris) + -IAN.]
▸ **A** *noun. hist.* A native or inhabitant of Doris (Doria), a division of ancient Greece. M16.
▸ **B** *adjective.* Of or pertaining to Doris (Doria). L16.
Dorian mode MUSIC (*a*) an ancient Greek mode, reputedly simple and solemn in character; (*b*) a church mode with D as the final and A as the dominant.

Doric /ˈdɒrɪk/ *adjective & noun*. In ARCHITECTURE orig. †**-ica**. M16.
[ORIGIN Latin *Doricus* from Greek *Dōrikos*, from *Dōrios*: see DORIAN, -IC.]
▸ **A** *adjective.* **1** Of or pertaining to Doris or the Dorians. M16. ▸**b** Of a dialect: broad; rustic. E17.
2 ARCHITECTURE. Designating the simplest and sturdiest of the three Greek orders, and its Roman adaptation, characterized by a capital consisting of a thick square abacus resting on an echinus and (in the case of Greek Doric) no base to the column. M16.
▸ **B** *noun.* **1** ARCHITECTURE. The Doric order. E17.
2 A broad or rustic dialect; *spec.* (*a*) the Doric dialect of ancient Greek; (*b*) a Scottish or northern form of English. M17.

C. GIBBON The good doctor dropped into the broadest Doric.

3 TYPOGRAPHY. (The name of) a kind of sans serif type. M19.

Dorise *verb* var. of DORIZE.

Dorism /ˈdɔːrɪz(ə)m/ *noun*. L17.
[ORIGIN Greek *Dōrismos* speaking Doric, from *Dōrizein*: see DORIZE, -ISM.]
1 A Doric form of expression. L17.
2 Culture of a Dorian character. L19.

Dorize /ˈdɔːrʌɪz/ *verb*. Now *rare*. Also **-ise**. L17.
[ORIGIN Greek *Dōrizein*: see -IZE.]
1 *verb intrans.* Behave like the Dorians; speak or write in Doric. L17.
2 *verb trans.* Make Dorian. M19.

dorje /ˈdɔːdʒeɪ/ *noun*. M19.
[ORIGIN Tibetan.]
A representation of a thunderbolt in the form of a short double trident or sceptre, held by lamas during prayers.

dork /dɔːk/ *noun. slang.* M20.
[ORIGIN Perh. var. of DIRK *noun*, infl. by DICK *noun*[1] 2.]
1 The penis. *N. Amer.* M20.
2 A stupid or contemptible person. L20.
■ **dorkiness** *noun* L20. **dorky** *adjective* L20.

Dorking /ˈdɔːkɪŋ/ *adjective & noun*. L18.
[ORIGIN A town in Surrey, England.]
▸ **A** *adjective.* (Designating a bird) of a breed of large white fowl with five toes. L18.
▸ **B** *noun.* (A fowl of) this breed. L18.

dorlach /ˈdɔːləx/ *noun. Scot.* L16.
[ORIGIN Gaelic. Cf. DOURLACH.]
†**1** A quiver. L16–E19.
2 A bundle formerly carried on the person by Highland troops; a kitbag; a portmanteau. M17.

dorm /dɔːm/ *noun. colloq.* E20.
[ORIGIN Abbreviation.]
= DORMITORY *noun* 1.

dormancy /ˈdɔːm(ə)nsi/ *noun*. L18.
[ORIGIN from DORMANT: see -ANCY.]
Dormant condition, esp. of a plant or seed.

dormant /ˈdɔːm(ə)nt/ *adjective & noun*. LME.
[ORIGIN Old French & mod. French, pres. pple of *dormir* from Latin *dormire* to sleep: see -ANT[1].]
▸ **A** *adjective.* **1** Fixed in position. Chiefly in ***dormant table***, ***dormant tree***. LME.
dormant tree a fixed horizontal beam; a sleeper.
2 In a state of rest; not in operation; in abeyance; latent. LME. ▸**b** Of an animal: with animation suspended. Of a plant or seed: with development suspended. L18.

T. H. HUXLEY Many volcanoes .. are merely dormant. *Times* The main clearing banks will not disclose how much is lying in dormant accounts. A. BROOKNER That fear that lies dormant even in the strongest heart.

dormant partner = ***sleeping partner*** s.v. SLEEPING *ppl adjective*. ***warrant dormant***: see WARRANT *noun*[1] 8.
3 HERALDRY. Of an animal: lying with its head resting on its paws and its eyes closed. Usu. *postpositive*. E16.
4 Sleeping; lying as in sleep; intellectually inactive. E17.
5 ***dormant window***, a dormer window. M17.
▸ **B** *noun.* †**1** = ***dormant tree*** above. LME–M17.
2 = ***dormant window*** above. E18.

dormer /ˈdɔːmə/ *noun*. L16.
[ORIGIN Old French *dormëor*, from *dormir* (see DORMANT) + *-ëor* -ER[2].]
1 A vertical window that projects from a sloping roof. Formerly, the window of a dormitory or bedroom. Also ***dormer window***. L16.
2 A room for sleeping in; a dormitory. *obsolete* exc. *hist.* E17.
†**3** = ***dormant tree*** s.v. DORMANT *adjective* 1. E17–M19.
– COMB.: **dormer bungalow**: having an upper storey with a dormer window in the roof space; **dormer room**: in the roof space of a house etc., lit by a dormer window.
■ **dormered** *adjective* M19.

dormeuse /dɔrmøːz (*pl. same*), dɔːˈməːz/ *noun*. M18.
[ORIGIN French, fem. of *dormeur* lit. 'sleeper', from *dormir*: see DORMANT.]
†**1** A cap or hood worn in bed. Only in M18.
2 A travelling carriage adapted for sleeping in. *obsolete* exc. *hist.* E19.
3 A kind of couch or settee. M19.

dormice *noun* pl. of DORMOUSE.

dormie *adverb & pred. adjective* var. of DORMY.

dormient /ˈdɔːmɪənt/ *adjective*. Now *rare*. M17.
[ORIGIN Latin *dormient-* pres. ppl stem of *dormire* to sleep: see -ENT.]
Sleeping; dormant, latent.

dormition /dɔːˈmɪʃ(ə)n/ *noun*. L15.
[ORIGIN French from Latin *dormitio(n-)*, from *dormit-* pa. ppl stem of *dormire* to sleep: see -ION.]
The act of sleeping; falling asleep; *fig.* death (of a holy person). Also (**D-**) in the Orthodox Church, (a feast commemorating) the passing of the Virgin Mary from earthly life.

dormitive /ˈdɔːmɪtɪv/ *adjective & noun*. L16.
[ORIGIN French *dormitif*, *-ive*, from Latin *dormit-*: see DORMITION, -IVE.]
▸ **A** *adjective.* Causing sleep, soporific. L16.
▸ **B** *noun.* A soporific medicine. Now *rare*. E17.

dormitory /ˈdɔːmɪt(ə)ri/ *noun*. LME.
[ORIGIN Latin *dormitorium* use as noun of neut. of *dormitorius*, from *dormit-*: see DORMITION, -ORY[1].]
1 A room for sleeping in; *spec.* a room or building in a school, monastery, or other institution containing beds, and sometimes divided into separate chambers. LME. ▸**b** A university or college hall of residence or hostel. *US.* M19. ▸**c** A town, village, or suburb where people live whose work is elsewhere in a neighbouring city or city centre. Also ***dormitory town*** etc. E20.
2 *fig.* A resting place. M17.
†**3** A cemetery; a grave, a vault. M17–L19.

†**dormitory** *adjective*. E17–M19.
[ORIGIN Latin *dormitorius*: see DORMITORY *noun*.]
Causing sleep.

Dormobile /ˈdɔːmə(ʊ)biːl/ *noun*. Also **d-**. M20.
[ORIGIN from DOR(MITORY *noun* + AUTO)MOBILE *noun* or MOBILE *adjective*.]
(Proprietary name for) a kind of van whose rear compartment has windows and can be used for sleeping and eating in.

dormouse /ˈdɔːmaʊs/ *noun & adjective*. LME.
[ORIGIN Origin unkn.; from 16 assoc. with French *dormir*, Latin *dormire*: see DORMANT.]
▸ **A** *noun.* Pl. **-mice** /-mʌɪs/.
1 Any rodent of the family Gliridae, comprising small, nocturnal, mostly arboreal animals of Europe, Asia, and N. Africa with soft fur and a sometimes bushy tail; *esp.* the British species, *Muscardinus avellanarius*, noted for its long period of hibernation. Also (usu. with specifying word), either of two similar rodents, *Platacanthomys lasiurus* of India and *Typhlomys cinereus* of China. LME.
edible dormouse: see EDIBLE *adjective*. ***fat dormouse***: see FAT *adjective*.
2 A sleepy or dozing person. M16.
▸ **B** *attrib.* or as *adjective*. Resembling (that of) a dormouse; sleepy, dozy. E17.

SHAKES. *Twel. N.* To awake your dormouse valour. *Listener* When some dormouse economist wakes up the whole monetary system will vanish like Alice's pack of cards.

dormy /ˈdɔːmi/ *adverb & pred. adjective*. Also **dormie**. M19.
[ORIGIN Unknown.]
Of a golfer: as many holes ahead of an opponent as there are holes to play.
attrib.: ***dormy one***, ***dormy two***, etc.

dornick /ˈdɔːnɪk/ *noun*[1]. Now *rare* or *obsolete*. Also (*Scot.*) **-ock**. LME.
[ORIGIN *Doornik*, Flemish name for Tournai.]
Any of various fabrics orig. manufactured at Doornik (Tournai) in SW Belgium; *esp.* (*a*) a silk or wool fabric formerly used for hangings, carpets, vestments, etc.; (*b*) a linen fabric used in Scotland for tablecloths, napkins, etc. Also, a cloth or covering made of such a fabric.

dornick /ˈdɔːnɪk/ *noun*[2]. *US dial.* Also **dar-** /ˈdɑː-/. M19.
[ORIGIN Cf. Irish *dornóg* handful, small stone.]
A stone, a pebble; a small boulder.

dornock *noun* see DORNICK *noun*[1].

doronicum /dəˈrɒnɪkəm/ *noun*. M16.
[ORIGIN mod. Latin from mod. Greek *dōronikon* from Persian *darūnak*.]
Any of various yellow-rayed plants of the genus *Doronicum*, of the composite family, esp. the early-flowering kinds grown in gardens.

Dorothy bag /ˈdɒrəθi bag/ *noun phr.* E20.
[ORIGIN from female forename *Dorothy*.]
A bag gathered at the top by a drawstring; *esp.* a woman's handbag of this form slung by loops from the wrist.

dorp /dɔːp/ *noun*. Now *S. Afr.* L15.
[ORIGIN Dutch: see THORP.]
A village, a small town, esp. in the Netherlands or (now) South Africa.

dorr *noun* var. of DOR *noun*[1].

dorsa *noun* pl. of DORSUM.

dorsad /ˈdɔːsad/ *adverb*. E19.
[ORIGIN from Latin *dorsum* back + -AD[3].]
ANATOMY & ZOOLOGY. Towards the dorsal side.

D

dorsal /ˈdɔːs(ə)l/ *adjective & noun*. LME.
[ORIGIN Old French & mod. French, or late Latin *dorsalis* from Latin *dorsualis*, formed as DORSUM: see -AL[1]. Cf. DOSSAL.]
▸ **A** *adjective.* †**1** Of a knife: having one cutting edge. LME–M16.
2 Of or pertaining to the back of a person or animal; situated on or near the back; shaped like the back, in the form of a ridge. LME.

T. PENNANT The dorsal and anal fins. QUILLER-COUCH A dorsal ridge of slate-coloured rock. S. KITZINGER Midwives sometimes prefer to have women in a dorsal or modified lithotomy position for examination.

3 ANATOMY, ZOOLOGY, etc. Pertaining to, situated on, or designating the part of any organ or structure that faces to the rear or the upper side, or is the upper, outer, or convex part; BOTANY relating to or designating the abaxial or inner surface of a carpel etc. or the surface of a thallus furthest from the substrate (i.e. the upper side). E19. ▸**b** PHONETICS. Of a speech sound: made with the back of the tongue. E20.

S. H. VINES The dorsal surface of ordinary leaves. R. F. CHAPMAN Immature insects nearly always have a line along the dorsal midline of the head.

▸ **B** *noun.* **1** A dorsal fin; a dorsal (thoracic) vertebra. M19.
2 ECCLESIASTICAL. = DOSSAL 2. L19.
3 PHONETICS. A dorsal sound. M20.
■ **dorˈsality** *noun* (PHONETICS) dorsal quality M20. **dorsalmost** *adjective* nearest to the back L19. **dorsally** *adverb* in a dorsal position or direction; on or towards the back: M19.

dorse /dɔːs/ *noun*[1]. E16.
[ORIGIN Latin DORSUM back, (in medieval Latin also) back of document (cf. ENDORSE *verb*).]
†**1** = DOSSAL. Only in E16.
2 The reverse side of a parchment or document; the cover of a book. M17.

dorse /dɔːs/ *noun*[2]. E17.
[ORIGIN Low German *dorsch* = Old Norse *torskr* codfish.]
A young cod.

dorsel *noun* var. of DOSSEL *noun*[1].

dorser *noun* var. of DOSSER *noun*[1].

Dorset /ˈdɔːsɪt/ *adjective & noun*. M18.
[ORIGIN See sense 1 below.]
1 *gen.* Used *attrib.* to designate things, esp. produce, from or characteristic of Dorset, a county in SW England. M18.
2 (Designating) either of two breeds of short-woolled sheep bred for meat: (*a*) (more fully ***Dorset Down***) a Down sheep with brown face and legs; (*b*) (more fully ***Dorset Horn***, ***Dorset Horned***) a sheep with a white face, and horns on the ewe and the ram; a sheep of either breed. E19.
3 (Designating) an extinct breed of pig; a pig of this breed, red with black markings. Also ***Dorset Gold Tip***. E20.
4 ***Dorset cheese***, blue vinny cheese. E20.

dorsi- /ˈdɔːsi/ *combining form*.
[ORIGIN formed as DORSUM + -I-.]
Of, to, or on the back. Also = DORSO-.
■ **dorˈsiferous** *adjective* (of a fern etc.) bearing seeds on the underside of a frond or leaf E18. **dorsifixed** *adjective* (BOTANY, of an anther) attached along its dorsal edge to the filament L19. **dorsiflex** *verb trans. & intrans.* bend (esp. the hand or foot) dorsally or towards its upper surface E20. **dorsiˈflexion** *noun* (*a*) *rare* a bow, a bending of the back; (*b*) the action of dorsiflexing: E19. **dorsiflexor** *noun* a muscle that dorsiflexes the hand or foot M20. **dorsiˈventral** *adjective* (*a*) BOTANY (of a leaf etc.) having unlike dorsal and ventral surfaces; (*b*) = DORSOVENTRAL: L19.

dorso- /ˈdɔːsəʊ/ *combining form*.
[ORIGIN formed as DORSUM + -O-.]
The back and (what is denoted by the 2nd elem.).
■ **dorsoˈlateral** *adjective* of, pertaining to, or involving the dorsal and lateral surfaces M19. **dorsoˈventral** *adjective* extending along or designating an axis joining the dorsal and ventral surfaces; of, pertaining to, or involving these surfaces: L19. **dorsoˈventrally** *adverb* in a dorsoventral direction L19.

dorsum /ˈdɔːsəm/ *noun*. Pl. **-sa** /-sə/. L18.
[ORIGIN Latin = back.]
1 A ridge, a long hill. L18.
2 ZOOLOGY & ANATOMY. The dorsal surface of a part, e.g. the hand or tongue. M19.

dort /dɔːt/ *noun*. *Scot.* M17.
[ORIGIN Rel. to DORT *verb*, DORTY: ult. origin unknown.]
sing. & (usu.) in *pl.* Sulkiness, ill humour, sulks. Chiefly in ***the dorts***.
Meg Dorts a peevish woman.

dort /dɔːt/ *verb intrans. Scot.* **E17.**
[ORIGIN Rel. to DORT *noun*, DORTY: ult. origin unknown.]
Sulk.

dorter /ˈdɔːtə/ *noun.* Also **-tour** /-tʊə/, **-toir** /-twɑː/. **ME.**
[ORIGIN Old French *dortour* (mod. *dortoir*) from Latin *dormitorium* DORMITORY *noun*.]
Chiefly *hist.* A bedroom, a dormitory, esp. in a monastery.

dorty /ˈdɔːti/ *adjective. Scot.* **E16.**
[ORIGIN Rel. to DORT *noun, verb*: ult. origin unknown.]
1 Sulky, bad-tempered; haughty. **E16.**
2 Fastidious. **L18.**
3 Sluggish. **E19.**
4 Delicate, feeble; (of an animal or plant) difficult to rear. **E20.**
5 Of the weather: dry. Of rain: holding off. **E20.**

dory /ˈdɔːri/ *noun*[1]. **ME.**
[ORIGIN French *dorée* use as noun of fem. pa. pple of *dorer* gild from late Latin *deaurare*, from Latin *de-* DE- 1 + *aurare* gild, from *aurum* gold.]
Any of several marine fishes constituting the family Zeidae, characterized by thin deep bodies; *esp.* = JOHN DORY.

dory /ˈdɔːri/ *noun*[2]. *N. Amer. & W. Indian.* Also **dorey**. **E18.**
[ORIGIN Uncertain: perh. from Miskito *dóri* dugout.]
A skiff, *esp.* a flat-bottomed one.

doryphore /ˈdɒrɪfɔː/ *noun.* **M20.**
[ORIGIN French = Colorado beetle, from Greek *doruphoros* spear carrier; coined by Sir Harold Nicolson.]
A self-righteously pedantic critic.

DoS *abbreviation.*
COMPUTING. Denial of service.

dosa /ˈdəʊsə/ *noun.* Pl. **-as**, **-ai** /-ʌɪ/. **M20.**
[ORIGIN Sanskrit *doṣā* from Tamil *tōcai*.]
In southern Indian cooking: a thin pancake made from rice flour and dal, typically served with a spiced vegetable filling.

dos-à-dos /dozado, dəʊzəˈdəʊ/ *adverb, noun, & adjective.* **M19.**
[ORIGIN French, from *dos* back: see DOSSIER. Cf. DO-SI-DO.]
▸ **A** *adverb.* Back to back. **M19.**
▸ **B** *noun.* Pl. same. A seat, carriage, etc., so constructed that the occupants sit back to back. *arch.* **M19.**
▸ **C** *adjective.* Designating binding or books in which two volumes are bound together facing in opposite directions and sharing a central board. **M20.**

dosage /ˈdəʊsɪdʒ/ *noun.* **M19.**
[ORIGIN from DOSE *verb, noun* + -AGE. Cf. French *dosage*.]
1 The operation of dosing; the addition or giving of a dose or doses. **M19.**

Nature Feeding tryptophan after dosage with monoamine oxidase inhibitors leads to an exacerbation of psychotic symptoms.

2 The size or frequency of a dose or doses. **L19.**

O. SACKS In the first week of medication . . the dosage was being slowly increased. J. R. S. FINCHAM The roentgen unit, in terms of which X-ray dosage is expressed.

3 A dose; *spec.* a small amount of sugar added to some wines before the final corking, to make them sweet. **L19.**

P. MATTHIESSEN The doctor thinks he has dysentery. . . and has pressed preventive dosages on all the rest of us. *Which?* The bottle is topped up with more of the same wine, plus the 'dosage'.

dose /dəʊs/ *noun.* **LME.**
[ORIGIN French from late Latin *dosis* from Greek = giving, gift, portion of medicine (Galen), from *didonai* give.]
1 A definite quantity of a medicine or drug (prescribed to be) given or taken at any one time. **LME.** ▸**b** An amount of ionizing radiation to which a person etc. is exposed. **E20.**

I. MURDOCH With a large dose of sleeping pills and alcohol in his body. R. MACAULAY I went and saw the camel, and gave it a dose of its sedative. M. MOORCOCK I was using cocaine in stronger and stronger doses.

a dose of one's own medicine: see MEDICINE *noun*[1]. **a dose of salts** a dose of laxative salts (***like a dose of salts***, very rapidly).
2 A definite quantity of something regarded as analogous in some respect to medicine. **E17.**

C. MERIVALE To repeat and daily increase the dose of flattery. L. BLUE Occasional doses of solitude increase my pleasure.

3 An unpleasant experience; a bout *of* an illness. **M19.**

Washington Post A badly sprained wrist and a heavy dose of the flu have kept him out of uniform.

4 (An infection with) venereal disease. *slang.* **E20.**
– COMB.: **dosemeter** = DOSIMETER; **dose-response curve** MEDICINE the relationship between the size of a dose and the extent of the response to it.

dose /dəʊs/ *verb trans.* **M17.**
[ORIGIN from DOSE *noun*: cf. French *doser*.]
1 Give doses of medicine to; add a dose to. **M17.**

V. S. REID Mother boils castor oil to dose him. R. TRAVERS Trying to poison his wife with dosed lemon syrup.

2 Divide into, or administer in, doses. **E18.**
3 Infect with venereal disease. *slang.* **M20.**
■ **doser** *noun* a person who gives a dose; *derog.* a physician: **L19.**

dosh /dɒʃ/ *noun. slang.* **M20.**
[ORIGIN Unknown.]
Money.

I. BANKS Ashley . . bought me drink . . even though she probably had less dosh than I did.

dosha /ˈdɒʃə, ˈdəʊʃə/ *noun.* **L20.**
[ORIGIN Sanskrit *doṣa*, lit. 'fault, disease' (esp. of the three humours of the body).]
In Ayurvedic medicine: each of three energies believed to circulate in the body and govern physiological activity.

do-si-do /dəʊzɪˈdəʊ, -sɪ-/ *noun & verb.* Also **-se-**. **E20.**
[ORIGIN Alt. of DOS-À-DOS.]
▸ **A** *noun.* Pl. **-os**. A figure in square dancing in which a facing couple pass round each other back to back, without turning, to finish in the same position they started from. **E20.**
▸ **B** *verb intrans.* Pres. pple & verbal noun **-do-ing**. Perform a do-si-do. **E20.**

dosimeter /dəʊˈsɪmɪtə/ *noun.* Also †**doso-**. **L19.**
[ORIGIN from DOSE *noun* + -IMETER, -OMETER.]
A device for measuring doses, esp. of ionizing radiation. Also called ***dosemeter***.
■ **dosiˈmetric** *adjective* **L19.** **dosimetry** *noun* **L19.**

doss /dɒs/ *noun. slang.* **L18.**
[ORIGIN Unknown. Cf. DOSS *verb*[2].]
1 A place for sleeping in; a bed; *esp.* a bed in a common lodging house. Also ***doss-down***. **L18.**
2 Sleep. **M19.**
3 An easy task giving the opportunity for idling, a soft option. **L20.**
– COMB.: **dosshouse** a common lodging house.

doss /dɒs/ *verb*[1]. **L16.**
[ORIGIN Perh. rel. to Middle Dutch *dossen*: see DOUSE *verb*[1].]
1 *verb trans.* & †*intrans.* Butt, toss, or gore (a person) with the horns. Now *dial.* **L16.**
2 *verb trans.* Toss (the horns). Now *dial.* **L16.**
3 *verb trans.* Throw or toss (something or oneself) *down* with force. *Scot.* **M18.**

doss /dɒs/ *verb*[2] *intrans. slang.* **L18.**
[ORIGIN Rel. to DOSS *noun*.]
1 Sleep or bed *down*, esp. at a common lodging house or in improvised accommodation. **L18.**

P. L. FERMOR Humble travellers in Holland could doss down in police stations.

2 Idle or waste time; fool *about*, mess *around*. **M20.**

dossal /ˈdɒs(ə)l/ *noun.* Also **-el**. **M17.**
[ORIGIN medieval Latin *dossale* neut. of *dossalis* for late Latin *dorsalis* DORSAL. Cf. Old French *dossal, -el*; DOSSER *noun*[1].]
1 An ornamental cloth forming a cover for the back of a seat. *arch.* **M17.**
2 ECCLESIASTICAL. An ornamental cloth hung at the back of an altar or at the sides of the chancel. **M19.**

dossel /ˈdɒs(ə)l/ *noun*[1]. *obsolete* exc. *dial.* Also **dorsel** /ˈdɔːs(ə)l/. **M18.**
[ORIGIN App. var. of DOSSER *noun*[1], with substitution of *-el* for -ER[2].]
A pannier or other basket borne by an animal. Cf. DOSSER *noun*[1] 2.

dossel *noun*[2] var. of DOSSAL.

dosser /ˈdɒsə/ *noun*[1]. *obsolete* exc. *hist.* Also **dorser** /ˈdɔːsə/. **ME.**
[ORIGIN Old French DOSSIER: cf. medieval Latin *dorsarium, dossarium*, from Latin DORSUM, popular Latin *dossum*, & see -ER[2].]
1 An ornamental cloth used to cover the back of a seat, esp. a throne or chair of state, or as a wall hanging. Cf. DOSSAL. Long *rare*. **ME.**
2 A basket carried on the back; a pannier borne by an animal. Cf. DOSSEL *noun*[1]. **LME.**

dosser /ˈdɒsə/ *noun*[2]. *slang.* **M19.**
[ORIGIN from DOSS *verb*[2] + -ER[1].]
A person who 'dosses'; a vagrant.

dosseret /ˈdɒsərɛt/ *noun.* **M19.**
[ORIGIN French, dim. of DOSSIER: see -ET[1].]
ARCHITECTURE. An additional block of stone placed above an abacus in the columns of many Byzantine and some Romanesque arcades.

dossier /ˈdɒsɪə, -ɪeɪ, -jeɪ/ *noun.* **L19.**
[ORIGIN French = bundle of papers in a wrapper having a label on the back, (in Old French = DOSSER *noun*[1]), from *dos* back (from popular Latin *dossum* for Latin DORSUM) + *-ier* -ARY[1].]
A collection of papers or information about a particular person or matter.

K. VONNEGUT Fred's dossier in the law firm's confidential files.

dossil /ˈdɒsɪl/ *noun.* Now *rare*. **ME.**
[ORIGIN Old French *do(i)sil* from Proto-Gallo-Romance (medieval Latin) *duciculus*, from Latin *ducere* lead, conduct.]
†**1** A plug for a barrel; a spigot. Cf. DOTTLE *noun*[2] 1. **ME–L15.**
2 A wad of lint or rag for stopping a wound etc. **L16.**

dost *verb* see DO *verb*.

Dostoevskian /dɒstɔɪˈɛfskɪən/ *adjective.* Also **Dostoiev-**, **Dostoyev-**. **E20.**
[ORIGIN from *Dostoevsky* (see below) + -AN.]
Pertaining to or characteristic of the Russian novelist Fedor Mikhailovich Dostoevsky (1821–81), or his works.

DOT *abbreviation*[1].
MEDICINE. Directly Observed Therapy, a system whereby a course of medication is taken under close supervision in order to ensure that the patient complies with the doctor's instructions.

DoT *abbreviation*[2].
1 In Canada and formerly the UK: Department of Transport.
2 In the US: Department of Transportation.

dot /dɒt/ *noun*[1].
[ORIGIN Old English *dott* (once); sense 2 may be from Dutch *dot* knot.]
†**1** The head of a boil. Only in OE.
†**2** A small lump, a clot. **L16–M19.**
3 A minute spot, speck, or mark; *esp.* a minute roundish mark written or printed. **M17.**

S. WYNTER Her white frock with the red dots.

4 *spec.* ▸**a** A point used in punctuation, as or as part of a punctuation mark, or to form part of or modify a letter or character. **M18.** ▸**b** MUSIC. A point placed after a note or rest to lengthen it by half as much again, or over a note to indicate that it is to be performed staccato. **E19.** ▸**c** The shorter of the two signals (the other being the dash) which in various combinations make up the letters of the Morse alphabet. **M19.** ▸**d** In *pl.* (The notes of) written or printed music. *colloq.* **E20.** ▸**e** A picture element in colour television; an area of phosphor on the inside of a television tube corresponding to this. **E20.**
5 A little child; a small creature. *colloq.* **M19.**

S. WATERS What a dot of a girl, to be so naughty!

– PHRASES: ***double dot***: see DOUBLE *adjective & adverb*. **off one's dot** *slang & dial.* out of one's senses (cf. DOTTY *adjective*[2] 2). **on the dot** punctually, at the precise moment. ***the year dot***: see YEAR *noun*[1]. **to a dot** exactly, precisely.
– COMB.: **dot-com** (also **dot.com**) [from the suffix *.com* in an Internet address, indicating a commercial site] a company which conducts its business on the Internet; **dot-commer** (also **dot.-commer**) an employee or owner of a company which conducts its business on the Internet; **dot map** a statistical map using dots as indicators of numbers or frequency; **dot matrix** a regular array of positions which are filled selectively to create a character (on a screen or on paper); also (in full ***dot matrix printer***) = ***matrix printer*** s.v. MATRIX *noun*; **dot-org** (also **dot.org**) [from the suffix *.org* in an Internet address, indicating a non-commercial site] a non-profit-making organization which conducts its business on the Internet; **dot plant** a garden plant that is planted singly to stand out against the surrounding plants; **dot stitch**: used in making dots in embroidery; **dot product** MATH. = ***scalar product*** s.v. SCALAR *adjective* 2.

dot /dɒt/ *noun*[2]. Pl. pronounced same. **M19.**
[ORIGIN Old French & mod. French from Latin *dos, dot-*: see DOWER.]
A dowry only the income from which is at the husband's disposal. Cf. DOTE *noun*[2].

dot /dɒt/ *verb trans.* Infl. **-tt-**. **M18.**
[ORIGIN from DOT *noun*[1].]
1 Mark with a dot or dots; fill *in* with dots. **M18.** ▸**b** Add the dot to (a letter *i* or *j*). Chiefly in ***dot the i's (and cross the t's)*** below. **M19.**

b H. JAMES It dots every i, it places every comma.

2 Jot *down*; write (*down*) compendiously. **L18.**
3 Occur singly throughout (an area etc.) or over (a surface). Usu. as DOTTED *adjective* 2. **L18.**

T. C. WOLFE Small houses dotted the land.

4 Disperse or scatter (*about*) like dots. Usu. as DOTTED *adjective* 3. **E19.**

Cookery Year Cut . . fat into small flakes and dot them evenly over two-thirds of the pastry.

5 Hit, strike. Esp. in ***dot a person one***. *slang.* **L19.**
– PHRASES & COMB.: **dot and carry (one)** = ***dot and go one*** below. **dot-and-carry(-one)** *noun & adjective* (*a*) *noun* (a teacher of) elementary arithmetic; (*b*) *adjective* = ***dot-and-go-one*** *adjective* below. **dot and go one** like a lame person, limpingly. **dot-and-go-one** *noun & adjective* (*a*) *noun* (the limp of) a person who is lame in one leg or has an artificial leg; (*b*) *adjective* limping, halting in gait. **dot the i's (and cross the t's)** *fig.* particularize minutely, complete in detail.
■ **dottable** *adjective* **M19.**

dotage /ˈdəʊtɪdʒ/ *noun.* **LME.**
[ORIGIN from DOTE *noun*[1] or *verb*[1] + -AGE. Cf. French *radotage*, from *radoter* talk idly or nonsensically.]
1 a The state of having the intellect impaired, esp. through old age; senility; imbecility; stupidity, folly; *one's second childhood*. **LME.** ▸**b** A stupid or foolish thought, word, or action. **E16.**

a LD MACAULAY Now fast sinking into dotage. E. GLASGOW Wait until I'm a hundred . . . Don't hurry me into my dotage.

2 a The action of doting on someone; foolish or excessive love or affection. **LME.** ▸**b** An object doted upon. **M17.**

dotaku /ˈdəʊtakuː/ *noun pl.* Also **dō-**. E20.
[ORIGIN Japanese, from *dō* bronze + *taku* bell-like musical instrument.]
Prehistoric Japanese bronze objects, shaped like bells and usu. decorated with geometric designs or scenes from life.

dotal /ˈdəʊt(ə)l/ *noun & adjective.* LME.
[ORIGIN Latin *dotalis*, from *dos* DOT *noun*²: see -AL¹. Perh. through Old French or (as adjective) French *dotal*, formed as DOT *noun*².]
▸ †**A** *noun.* A dowry. Only in LME.
▸ **B** *adjective.* Pertaining to or designating a dowry or dower. E16.

†**dotant** *noun. rare* (Shakes.). Only in E17.
[ORIGIN from DOTE *verb*¹ + -ANT¹. Cf. French *radotant*.]
= DOTARD *noun*¹.

dotard /ˈdəʊtəd/ *noun*¹ & *adjective*¹. LME.
[ORIGIN from DOTE *verb*¹ + -ARD. Cf. DOTTERED.]
▸ **A** *noun.* A person in his or her dotage; a stupid or foolish person. LME.
▸ **B** *adjective.* Senile; in one's second childhood; stupid, foolish. LME.

dotard /ˈdəʊtəd/ *noun*² & *adjective*². Also †**-tt-**. L16.
[ORIGIN Unknown. Cf. DODDARD, DOTTERED; also DOTE *noun*³, *verb*².]
(Designating) a tree that has lost its branches, esp. through age or decay.

dotate /dəʊˈteɪt/ *verb trans.* Now *rare.* Pa. pple **-ated**, †**-ate**. M16.
[ORIGIN Latin *dotat-* pa. ppl stem of *dotare*: see DOTATION, -ATE³.]
Endow.

dotation /dəʊˈteɪʃ(ə)n/ *noun.* LME.
[ORIGIN Old French & mod. French, or medieval Latin *dotatio(n-)*, from *dotare* endow, from *dos*, *dot-* DOT *noun*²: see -ATION.]
The action of endowing; (an) endowment.

dotchin /ˈdɒtʃɪn/ *noun.* L17.
[ORIGIN Chinese *dù ching*, from *dù* measure + *ching* steelyard.]
A small hand-steelyard used in southern China.

†**dote** *noun*¹. ME–M19.
[ORIGIN App. based on Middle Dutch *dote* folly.]
A foolish or weak-minded person; a dotard.

dote /dəʊt/ *noun*². *arch.* E16.
[ORIGIN French, obsolete var. of DOT *noun*².]
1 = DOT *noun*². E16.
†**2** A natural gift or endowment. Usu. in *pl.* M16–M17.

dote /dəʊt/ *noun*³. L19.
[ORIGIN Unknown. Cf. DOTE *verb*², DOTARD *noun*² & *adjective*².]
Decay in wood.

dote /dəʊt/ *verb*¹. Also **doat**. ME.
[ORIGIN Corresp. to Middle Dutch *doten* be silly (whence Old French *redoter*, mod. *radoter*). Cf. DOIT *verb*.]
▸ **I** *verb intrans.* **1** Be silly or deranged; act or talk foolishly or stupidly. ME.

COLERIDGE Others . . dote with a mad idolatry.

2 Have the intellect impaired through old age. ME.

G. CRABBE We grow unfitted for that world and dote.

3 Be infatuated; have or show excessive affection. (Foll. by *on*, *upon*, †*of*.) L15.

J. A. MICHENER He doted upon her and was enraptured when she presented him with two strong sons. J. BARNES Perhaps those who forgive and dote are more irritating than they ever suspect.

▸ **II** *verb trans.* †**4** Drive mad; make foolish; infatuate. L15–E17.
†**5** Have excessive affection for, dote on. L15–L17.
†**6** Say or think foolishly. M16–E17.
■ **dotingly** *adverb* in a doting manner or degree; infatuatedly; fondly: M16.

dote /dəʊt/ *verb*² *intrans. obsolete* exc. *dial.* & *US.* LME.
[ORIGIN Unknown. Cf. DOTE *noun*³, DOTARD *noun*² & *adjective*².]
Of a tree, timber, a seed, etc.: decay. Chiefly as ***doted***, ***doting*** *ppl adjectives.*

doter /ˈdəʊtə/ *noun.* Also **doater**. M16.
[ORIGIN from DOTE *verb*¹ + -ER¹.]
1 A person who is foolishly affectionate; a person who dotes. M16.
2 = DOTARD *noun*¹. E17.

dotey /ˈdəʊti/ *noun.* Chiefly *Irish.* Also **do(a)ty**. M17.
[ORIGIN Rel. to DOTE *verb*¹.]
A person, esp. a child, of whom one is fond. Usu. as a form of address.

doth *verb* see DO *verb*.

dotish /ˈdəʊtɪʃ/ *adjective. arch.* Also **doat-**. E16.
[ORIGIN from DOTE *noun*¹ + -ISH¹.]
Silly, stupid, childish.
■ **dotishness** *noun* L16.

dotkin *noun* var. of DODKIN.

†**dottard** *noun & adjective* var. of DOTARD *noun*² & *adjective*².

dotted /ˈdɒtɪd/ *adjective.* L18.
[ORIGIN from DOT *noun*¹, *verb*: see -ED², -ED¹.]
1 Formed of dots. L18. ▸**b** Of (an) engraving: executed by dots instead of lines; stippled. E19.
2 Irregularly marked with or occupied by dots or things occurring singly. L18. ▸**b** *spec.* Designating moths marked thus. M19.

W. GOLDING The beach . . was dotted with groups of boys. W. TREVOR He pulls the dotted handkerchief from his pocket.

3 Scattered (*about* etc.) like dots; occurring or situated singly here and there. E19.

P. SCOTT There were chairs dotted here and there on the lawn. M. SINCLAIR A tiny Dutch landscape . . . Trees dotted about.

4 Of a musical note, a symbol, etc.: having an added dot. M19.

F. A. G. OUSELEY One dotted semibreve in the canto fermo.

– SPECIAL COLLOCATIONS: **dotted line** a line of dots or small dashes, *esp.* one on a document to indicate the space left for a signature and therefore acceptance of its terms; (***dotted-line responsibility***, indirect responsibility to another in an organizational structure; ***sign on the dotted line***, agree fully or formally). **dotted rhythm** MUSIC: in which long notes alternate with short notes.

dottel *noun* var. of DOTTLE *noun*².

dotter /ˈdɒtə/ *noun.* M19.
[ORIGIN from DOT *verb* + -ER¹.]
A person who or thing which marks something with dots; an instrument for making dots.

dotter /ˈdɒtə/ *verb intrans.* Now *Scot.* LME.
[ORIGIN Rel. to DODDER *verb*, TOTTER *verb*.]
Move unsteadily; totter; fall.

dottered /ˈdɒtəd/ *adjective.* Now *Scot.* L16.
[ORIGIN Perh. alt. of DOTARD *adjective*¹ or *adjective*².]
Worn out or enfeebled with age.

dotterel /ˈdɒt(ə)r(ə)l/ *noun & adjective.* Also **dottrel** /ˈdɒtr(ə)l/. LME.
[ORIGIN from DOTE *verb*¹ + -REL.]
▸ **A** *noun.* **1** A small, exceptionally tame plover, *Eudromias morinellus*, found on open ground in northern Europe and northern Asia and migrating to the Mediterranean. Also (usu. with specifying word), any of several other plovers of Australia, New Zealand, and S. America of the genera *Eudromias*, *Charadrius*, and *Peltohyas*. LME.
2 A silly or deranged person; a dotard. Now *dial.* LME.
3 A doddered tree; a pollard. Now *dial.* E17.
▸ **B** *attrib.* or as *adjective.* **1** ***dotterel tree*** = sense A.3 above. Now *dial.* M16.
2 Foolish, doting. Now *rare* or *obsolete.* L16.

dottle /ˈdɒt(ə)l/ *noun*¹ & *adjective.* LME.
[ORIGIN from DOTE *verb*¹ or *noun*¹ + -LE¹.]
▸ **A** *noun.* A fool, a silly person; a dotard. Now *Scot.* LME.
▸ **B** *adjective.* In a state of dotage; deranged; silly. *Scot.* E19.
■ Also **dottled** *adjective* (*Scot.*) E19.

dottle /ˈdɒt(ə)l/ *noun*². Also **dottel**. LME.
[ORIGIN from DOT *noun*¹ + -LE¹.]
†**1** A plug for a barrel or other vessel. Cf. DOSSIL *noun* 1. LME–M18.
2 (A plug of) tobacco left at the bottom of a pipe after smoking. E19.

dottrel *noun & adjective* var. of DOTTEREL.

dottrified /ˈdɒtrɪfʌɪd/ *adjective.* Chiefly *Scot.* & *dial.* E19.
[ORIGIN from DOTE *verb*¹ + -ERY + -FY + -ED¹.]
Having the intellect impaired; stupefied, dazed.

dotty /ˈdɒti/ *adjective*¹. E19.
[ORIGIN from DOT *noun*¹ + -Y¹.]
Consisting of or characterized by dots; resembling a dot.

dotty /ˈdɒti/ *adjective*². L19.
[ORIGIN Perh. from DOTE *noun*¹ (cf. earlier DOTTYPOLL) or rel. to DOTTER *verb*.]
1 Having an unsteady or feeble gait. Now *rare.* L19.

D. ABSE Dotty, shifty points of glitterings.

2 Insane; harmlessly eccentric; silly; absurd, crazy; absurdly enthusiastic *about*. *colloq.* L19.

H. L. WILSON Mr. Jackson had chosen the part of Oswald, a youth who goes quite dotty. *Daily Telegraph* It was 'dotty' for the nation to spend £2 million trying to save a picture. B. BAINBRIDGE All foreigners are dotty about their mothers.

■ **dottily** *adverb* in an eccentric or absurd manner, to an eccentric or absurd degree M20. **dottiness** *noun* dotty quality, *esp.* insanity, eccentricity L19.

†**dottypoll** *noun* see DODDYPOLL.

doty *noun* var. of DOTEY.

doty /ˈdəʊti/ *adjective.* Also **doaty**. M19.
[ORIGIN Rel. to DOTE *noun*³, DOTARD *noun*² & *adjective*².]
Of wood: decayed, rotten.
■ **dotiness** *noun* L19.

†**dotypoll** *noun* see DODDYPOLL.

Douai *noun* var. of DOUAY.

douane /duːˈɑːn/ *noun.* M17.
[ORIGIN French from Italian *do(g)ana* from Arabic *dīwān* office from Old Persian *dīwān* DIVAN. Cf. DEWAN.]
A custom house in France or other Mediterranean country.
■ **douanier** /duːˈɑːnɪeɪ/ *noun* a customs officer, *esp.* one at a douane M18.

douar /ˈduːɑː, dwɑː/ *noun.* Also **dowar**, **duar**. E18.
[ORIGIN Colloq. Arabic form of Arabic *dawwār* circling, after French *douar*.]
In Arab countries, an encampment of tents, a village.

Douay /ˈdaʊeɪ, ˈduːeɪ/ *noun.* Also **Douai**. M19.
[ORIGIN A town (now *Douai*) in France (see below).]
In full ***Douay version***, ***Douay Bible***. An English translation of the Vulgate formerly used in the Roman Catholic Church, begun at Douai and completed there in 1609.

double /ˈdʌb(ə)l/ *noun.* ME.
[ORIGIN Partly (in branch I) from DOUBLE *adjective & adverb*, partly (in branch II) from DOUBLE *verb*.]
▸ **I 1** A double quantity; twice as much or as many. ME.

B. JOWETT Ten, which is the double of five.

2 *hist.* Any of various coins formerly current in France or Guernsey. ME.
†**3 a** A duplicate or copy of a document. LME–M18. ▸†**b** In *pl.* Twins. Only in L15. ▸**c** An exact counterpart; a person who is very like another; a wraith. L18.

c P. V. WHITE Her reflection is a double that she has grown to hate.

4 A double person or thing identified contextually, as a double victory, a double century, a double event, etc. L16. ▸**b** ROMAN CATHOLIC CHURCH (now *hist.*). [Ellipt. for *double feast*.] Any of the higher ranking feasts. L17. ▸**c** MILITARY. A double pace. Chiefly in ***at the double*** below. M19. ▸**d** A double measure of spirits. E20. ▸**e** A double room. *colloq.* M20.

b C. MACKENZIE We are going . . to keep the feast as the Feast of the Immaculate Conception, a double of the first class with octave.

c at the double in double time; *transf.* as fast as possible.
5 BELL-RINGING. A change in which two pairs of bells change places. L17.
6 PRINTING. An accidental duplication of a word or passage. Cf. DOUBLET 4b. E18.
7 MUSIC. A variation (usu. the theme with ornamentation) in 17th- and 18th-cent. music. E19.
8 An actor who takes two parts in the same performance. Also, an understudy. E19.
9 In *pl.* A game of tennis, badminton, etc., between two pairs of players rather than one. L19.
MIXED ***doubles***.
10 A bet on two horses in different races in which winnings from the first are placed on the later one. L19.
twin double: see TWIN *adjective & noun*.
11 CARDS (esp. BRIDGE). A call that doubles the value of the points to be won or lost on an opponent's bid. E20.
12 (A throw on) the narrow ring enclosed by the two outer circles of a dartboard, scoring double. M20.
▸ **II 13** A sharp turn made in running by a hunted animal; a sharp alteration in the course of a river; *fig.* an evasive turn or shift in action, argument, etc. L16.
14 A fold; a folded piece of material. Now *rare* or *obsolete.* L16.

double /ˈdʌb(ə)l/ *adjective & adverb.* ME.
[ORIGIN Old French *doble*, *duble* (mod. *double*) from Latin *duplus* DUPLE.]
▸ **A** *adjective.* **1** Consisting of two members, things, layers, sets, etc.; twofold, forming a pair; occurring twice, repeated. ME. ▸**b** Folded, doubled; bent, stooping forward, doubled up. LME. ▸**c** Having some essential part or feature present twice; (of a flower) having more than the usual number of petals, often owing to the conversion of stamens and sometimes carpels into petals; (of a domino) having the same number of pips in each half. LME.

SHAKES. *Mids. N. D.* Like to a double cherry . . , Two lovely berries moulded on one stem. STEELE Is Dimpple spelt with a single or double P? DICKENS Nickleby gave a double knock. L. DURRELL The double burden of her own poor circumstances and illness. **b** W. OWEN Bent double, like old beggars under sacks.

2 Having a twofold relation or application; dual; ambiguous. ME.

T. HERBERT The word μηλον admitting a double construction, sheep and apple. F. MARRYAT He . . is a double traitor.

3 Twice as much or as many; of twice the, or twice *the*, measure, amount, or capacity. (Formerly foll. by *of*, *over*, *to*.) ME.

A. DE MORGAN The average error of the first . . is double of that of the second. LD MACAULAY His army . . might easily have been increased to double the number.

4 Characterized by duplicity; false, deceitful. ME.

G. BURNET He was . . either very double or very inconstant.

5 Of two or more times the usual size, value, strength, etc. LME. ▸**b** MUSIC. Lower in pitch by an octave. L17.

D

V. Scannell Ten new pennies For a pint and a double gin.

▸ **B** *adverb*. †**1** After a numeral: times, -fold. ME–L17.

2 To twice the amount or extent; in two ways or respects; doubly. LME. ▸**b** In a pair or couple; two together; two at once. L16.

Keats Bright eyes were double bright. **b** R. B. Sheridan Content to ride double, behind the butler.

3 With duplicity, deceitfully. *rare*. L16.

– PHRASES: **double or quits** *colloq.* the next game, throw, etc., will decide whether the stake is to be doubled or cancelled. **see double** (seem to) perceive two images of one object.

D

– SPECIAL COLLOCATIONS & COMB.: ***double acrostic***: see ACROSTIC *noun* 1. **double-acting** *adjective* acting in two ways or directions; *spec.* (of an engine) in which pistons are pushed from both sides alternately. **double agent** a person who purports to spy for one country or organization while actually working for a hostile or rival one. **double album** two long-playing records or two cassettes packaged together and sold as a set. **double axe** an axe with two blades. **double-bank** *verb* (*a*) *verb trans.* provide or work with two sets of rowers, horses, etc., side by side; (*b*) *verb intrans. & trans.* (*Austral. & NZ*) ride two on (a horse or bicycle); carry (a second person) thus; cf. DOUBLE *verb* 17; (*c*) *verb trans. & intrans.* = ***double-park*** below. **double-banked** *adjective & adverb* designating, having, or with two (sets of) things side by side. **double bar** *MUSIC* a pair of closely spaced bar lines marking the end of a work or of a section of one. **double-bar** an Australian waxbill, *Poephila bichenovii*. **double-barrel** *adjective & noun* (*a*) *adjective* double-barrelled; (*b*) *noun* a double-barrelled gun; (a person with) a double-barrelled name. **double-barrelled** *adjective* (*a*) (of a gun) having two barrels; (*b*) serving a double purpose, twofold; (*c*) (of a surname) having two (usu. hyphenated) elements. ***double bassoon***: see BASSOON 1. **double bed** a bed for two people. **double bill** a cinema or theatre show with two principal items. **double bind** (*a*) *PSYCHOLOGY* a situation in which contradictory attitudes are expressed towards a child or other person, or contradictory demands are made of him or her, so that he or she cannot avoid being at fault; (*b*) *gen.* a situation in which either of two possible courses will be wrong; a dilemma. **double-bitted** *adjective*[1] having two bits. **double-bitted** *adjective*[2] (*NAUTICAL*) (of a cable) wound twice round the bitts or round two pairs of bitts. ***double blank***: see BLANK *noun* 11. **double-blind** *adjective & noun* (designating) a test etc. in which neither tester nor subject has knowledge of identities or other factors that might lead to bias. **double bluff** a bluff in which a person deliberately emphasizes one course of action etc. to suggest that a contradictory course will be taken, and then takes the first course. **double bogey** *GOLF* a score of two strokes over par. **double-bogey** *verb trans. & intrans.* (*GOLF*) complete (a hole) in two strokes over par. **double boiler** a saucepan with a detachable upper compartment heated by boiling water in the lower. **double bond** *CHEMISTRY* two covalent bonds between the same two atoms. **double-book** *verb trans. & intrans.* accept two mutually exclusive bookings for (the same room, seat, etc.); book (a person) into a room, seat, etc., also assigned to another. **double-breasted** *adjective* (of a jacket etc.) having a substantial overlap of material at the front, freq. fastened with two rows of buttons. **double bridle** a bridle comprising both curb and snaffle bits, each with its own set of reins. **double century** a score of 200, esp. in cricket; (a cycle ride of) 200 miles. **double-check** *verb trans.* verify twice or in two ways. **double chin** a chin with a fold of flesh under it. **double-chinned** *adjective* having a double chin. **double-click** *verb intrans. & trans.* press a mouse button twice in quick succession to select a file, program, or function: select (a file etc.) in this way. **double-clutch** *verb intrans.* (*US*) = ***double-declutch*** below. ***double coconut***: see COCONUT 4. ***double CONCERTO***. **double cream** thick cream containing a high proportion of fat. **double-crop** *verb trans.* cultivate (land) under a system of double cropping. **double cropping** the cultivation of two crops from the same land in a single season. **double cube** *ARCHITECTURE* a room of which the breadth is equal to the height and the length is double it. ***double dagger***: see DAGGER *noun*[1]. **double date** *colloq.* a social engagement involving two couples. **double-date** *verb intrans.* (*colloq.*) go on a double date. **double-dealer** a cheat, a deceiver. **double-dealing** deceit, treachery. **double-dealing** *adjective* deceitful, treacherous. **double-deck**, **double-decked** *adjectives* having two decks or layers. **double-decker** *noun & adjective* (designating) something with two decks or layers; *spec.* (designating) a bus, ship, etc., with an upper and a lower deck for passengers. **double-declutch** *verb intrans.* release and re-engage the clutch twice when changing gear in a motor vehicle. **double decomposition** *CHEMISTRY* the simultaneous decomposition of two compounds in a reaction with the formation of two new ones. **double-dig** *verb trans.* dig two spits deep, as in double digging. **double digging** digging in which one spit of soil is taken off and the underlying second spit broken up before being covered again. **double-digit** *adjective* = ***double-figure*** below. **double digits** = ***double figures*** below. **double-dink** *verb intrans. & trans.* (*Austral. & NZ slang*) carry (a person) as a second rider on a bicycle or horse. **double dip** *N. Amer.* an ice-cream cone with two scoops of ice cream. **double-dipper** *N. Amer., Austral., & NZ* a person who practises double-dipping. **double-dipping** *N. Amer., Austral., & NZ* the practice of commuting an occupational pension to a lump sum and then drawing a state pension that would not otherwise be due, or of receiving an income from two jobs, esp. a pension from a former job and a salary from a current one. **double door(s)** (*a*) a pair of doors side by side in one opening, meeting in the middle; (*b*) two doors situated one close behind the other. **double dot** *MUSIC* two dots placed side by side after a note to lengthen it by three-quarters of its value. **double-dot** *verb trans. & intrans.* (*MUSIC*) mark with or employ double dots (chiefly as ***double-dotted*** *ppl adjective*, ***double-dotting*** *verbal noun*). **double dummy** whist or bridge with two hands exposed, allowing every card to be located by the players. ***double Dutch***: see DUTCH *noun*[1]. **double-dye** *verb trans.* dye twice; *fig.* imbue or stain deeply with guilt; (chiefly as ***double-dyed*** *ppl adjective*). **double eagle** (*a*) a figure of an eagle with two heads; (*b*) *GOLF* = ALBATROSS 3; (*c*) a former US coin worth twenty dollars. **double-edged** *adjective* having two cutting edges; *fig.* acting both ways; damaging to the user as well as an opponent. **double-ender** something with both ends alike. **double-entry** a method of bookkeeping in which each transaction is entered twice, once to the credit of one account and once to the debit of another. **double event** the winning of two events at the same meeting or in the same season; a dual success or occurrence. **double exposure** *PHOTOGRAPHY* the action or result of exposing the same frame, plate, etc., on two occasions, either accidentally or deliberately. **double fault** *TENNIS* two consecutive faults in serving, together resulting in the loss of a point. **double-fault** *verb intrans.* commit a double fault. **double feast** *ROMAN CATHOLIC CHURCH* = DOUBLE *noun* 4b. **double feature** a cinema programme with two full-length films. **double fertilization** *BOTANY* the mode of fertilization in angiosperms, in which one sperm nucleus fuses with an egg nucleus to produce the embryo and the other fuses with the two polar nuclei to produce the endosperm. **double-figure** *adjective* equal in quantity, rate, etc., to a number, esp. a percentage, between 10 and 99 inclusive. **double figures** (a quantity, score, etc., equal to) a number between 10 and 99 inclusive. **double first** (a person gaining) first-class honours in two subjects or examinations at university. **double flat** *MUSIC* a sign (♭♭) placed before a note to indicate that it is to be lowered two semitones; a note so marked or lowered. **double fleece** *Austral. & NZ* a fleece from a sheep that has missed a shearing. **double-fronted** *adjective* having two fronts or faces; (of a house) having the principal windows on either side of the front door. ***double FUGUE***. **double glazing** (the provision of) two sheets of glass fixed one behind the other in a window to reduce heat loss, noise, etc. **double Gloucester (cheese)** [made at Berkeley, Gloucestershire] a firm cheese similar to Cheddar but milder. **double-handed** *adjective* (*a*) made to be lifted or held with two hands, two-handled; (*b*) capable of a double use, application, or action (*lit. & fig.*). **double harness** harness for two horses etc.; *fig.* matrimony, close partnership. ***double harp***: see HARP *noun*. **double-head** *verb* (*a*) *verb intrans.* (of a train) be pulled by two locomotives; (*b*) *verb trans.* (of two locomotives) jointly pull (a train) (usu. in *pass.*). **double-headed** *adjective* having a double head or two heads; double-ended; (of a train) pulled by two locomotives. **double-header** (*a*) *US* (*rare*) a kind of firework; (*b*) a train pulled by two locomotives; (*c*) *N. Amer.* two games or matches in succession between the same opponents. **double-hearted** *adjective* (*arch.*) deceitful, dissembling. **double-heartedness** *noun* (*arch.*) double-hearted nature. **double helix** a pair of helices intertwined about a common axis, esp. in the structure of the DNA molecule. **double-hung** *adjective* (of a window) consisting of two sliding vertical sashes. **double hyphen** a mark consisting of one hyphen above another, sometimes used at the end of a line to show that a hyphen would be there even if it were not a line end. **double image** (*a*) duplicate images of an object seen simultaneously, as when the eyes fail to focus; (*b*) *ART* an image, representation, etc., which allows two irreconcilable interpretations simultaneously. **double indemnity** *US* the provision for payment of double the face amount of an insurance policy when death occurs as a result of an accident. **double jeopardy** (the immunity which prevents) the prosecution of a person twice for the same offence. **double-jointed** *adjective* having joints that allow an unusual bending and flexibility of fingers, limbs, etc. **double-jointedness** double-jointed condition. **double knitting** (*a*) knitting that is tubular, for ties, belts, etc.; (*b*) knitting with yarn of double thickness; (more fully ***double knitting wool***, ***double knitting yarn***) yarn for knitting that is double the usual thickness. **double life** a life in which two different characters (and careers) are sustained simultaneously, of which usu. one is virtuous and one not. **double-lock** *verb trans.* lock by a double turn of the key. **double meaning** (possession of) two meanings; (use of) an ambiguous expression; *spec.* = DOUBLE ENTENDRE. **double-meaning** *adjective* having or employing a double meaning. **double-minded** *adjective* (*a*) in two minds, uncertain, wavering; †(*b*) having two meanings. **double-mindedness** double-minded quality or state. **double negative** *GRAMMAR* a construction containing two negative elements (esp. where one is redundant, now considered ungrammatical in standard English); *loosely*, either of the two negatives in such a construction. ***double nelson***: see NELSON *noun*[2]. ***double obelisk***: see OBELISK *noun* 2. ***double OXER***. **double paddle** a paddle with a blade at each end. **double-park** *verb trans. & intrans.* park (a vehicle) alongside another vehicle already parked at the roadside etc. **double play** *BASEBALL* a play in which two runners are put out. ***double PNEUMONIA***. **double precision** *COMPUTING* the use of twice the usual number of bits or words to represent a number. **double-precision** *adjective* (*COMPUTING*) having double precision. **double-queued** *adjective* (*HERALDRY*) (of an animal) having two tails. **double-quick** *adjective, adverb, noun, & verb* (*a*) *adjective* (*MILITARY*) designating the fastest marching time next to the run; (*b*) *adverb* in double-quick time; very quickly, smartly; (*c*) *noun* double-quick time; (*d*) *verb intrans.* (*MILITARY*) march in double-quick time. **double reed** a wind instrument reed with two slightly separated blades, as in the oboe and bassoon. **double-reef** *verb trans.* (*NAUTICAL*) reduce the spread of (a sail) by two reefs. **double refraction** the refraction of unpolarized light into two rays or beams going in different directions, producing a double image of an object; the property of causing this, exhibited by some crystals. **double rhyme** rhyme involving two syllables in each rhyming line. **double room** a bedroom for two people. **double salt** *CHEMISTRY* a salt which when crystalline is composed of two simple salts (which it usu. yields in solution) and has different properties from either. **double saucepan** = ***double boiler*** above. **double sharp** *MUSIC* a sign (𝄪) placed before a note to indicate that it is to be raised two semitones; a note so marked or raised. **double shuffle** a dance in which each foot in turn makes two shuffles. **double-shuffle** *verb intrans.* dance a double shuffle. **double-shot** *verb trans.* load (a gun) with a double quantity of shot. **double-space** *verb trans.* lay out (a text) with double spacing. **double spacing** spacing in which a line is left empty between successive lines of a (esp. typewritten) text. **doublespeak** language or talk that is (usu. deliberately) ambiguous or obscure. **double standard** (*a*) bimetallism; (*b*) (the application of) a standard, principle, etc., applied more strictly to some people or situations than others. **double star** a pair of stars that appear as one until viewed in a telescope, *esp.* a binary star. **double steal** *BASEBALL* a play in which two base-runners each steal a base. **double-stopping** *MUSIC* the sounding of two strings at once on an instrument to give an interval. **Double Summer Time** daylight saving in which clocks are two hours ahead of standard winter time. **double take** a delayed and usu. contradictory reaction to an occurrence or situation immediately after one's first reaction. **doubletalk** = ***doublespeak*** above. ***double team***: see TEAM *noun* 5a. **double-team** *verb* (*US*) (*a*) *verb intrans.* combine two teams into one; (*b*) *verb intrans.* bring double pressure to bear *on* a person; (*c*) *verb trans.* block (an opposing player) with two players. ***double tertian***: see TERTIAN *noun* 1. **doublethink** the mental capacity to accept as equally valid two entirely contradictory opinions or beliefs; the practice of doing this. **double tides** *adverbial phr.* twice as long or as hard, as hard or as much as possible (chiefly in ***work double tides***). **double time** (*a*) *MILITARY* a marching pace in which approximately twice as many steps per minute are made as in slow time; (*b*) *MUSIC* a rhythm made twice as fast as an earlier rhythm; (*c*) a rate of pay equal to twice the standard rate (given for working extra on holidays etc.). **double-time** *verb intrans.* march or play in double time. **double-tongued** *adjective* saying contradictory or inconsistent things; deceitful or insincere in speech. **double tonguing** *MUSIC* tonguing in which two alternating movements of the tongue are made (usu. as in sounding *t* and *k*), to facilitate rapid playing of a wind instrument. **double top** *DARTS* (a throw into) the double-scoring segment of the top (20) space of a dartboard, worth 40 points. **doubletree** [after ***singletree*** s.v. SINGLE *adjective & adverb*] a crossbar of a wagon with a swingletree at each end, enabling two horses to draw. **double vision** the simultaneous perception of two images of one object. **double wedding** a wedding of two couples at the same time. DOUBLE ***whammy***. **double-wide** *noun & adjective* (*US*) (designating) a semi-permanent mobile home consisting of two separate units connected on site. ***double yellow***: see YELLOW *noun*. ***double yellow line***: see YELLOW *adjective*.

■ **doublefold** *adjective & adverb* twofold ME. **doubleness** *noun* the quality or state of being double; duplicity, deceitfulness: LME.

double /ˈdʌb(ə)l/ *verb*. ME.

[ORIGIN Old French *dobler*, *dubler* (mod. *doubler*) from late Latin *duplare*, from Latin *duplus* DUPLE.]

1 *verb trans.* Make double; increase twofold; put two in the place of one; multiply by two; *arch.* amount to twice as much as. ME. ▸**b** *MUSIC*. Add the same note in a higher or lower octave to. M18. ▸**c** *CHESS*. Place a pawn or rook on the same file behind (another piece of the same kind and colour); place (two pawns or two rooks) thus. M18.

Shakes. *Lear* Thy fifty yet doth double five and twenty. B. Jowett Ignorance doubled by conceit of knowledge. O. Henry If I doubled the number of trips I would see her twice as often. G. Greene He doubled the tip.

2 *verb intrans.* Become twice as much or as many as before; increase twofold. ME.

C. Pebody The circulation doubled. A. Alvarez Whenever he relaxed everything doubled: two brandy glasses, . . two professors.

†**3** *verb trans.* Repeat, reiterate; *Scot.* make a copy or duplicate of. LME–E19. ▸**b** Speak with repetition of sounds; stammer. *rare*. LME–E17.

4 *verb trans.* (Now chiefly *HERALDRY*) add a second layer of material to, line, (a garment); cover (a ship) with an additional layer of planking. LME.

5 a *verb trans.* Fold (a cloth, paper, etc.) so as to bring the two parts into contact, parallel; bend (the body), esp. into a stooping or curled-up posture (also foll. by *up*); clench or close (the hand). LME. ▸**b** *verb intrans.* Become folded together or bent over; (of a person or limbs) bend double, stoop, curl up, (also foll. by *up*). M17. ▸**c** *verb trans.* Lay together and compress into one (two or more textile filaments or slivers). Freq. as ***doubling*** *verbal noun*. M19.

a Dryden The page is doubled down. Yeats He is all doubled up with age. R. Carver She doubled her legs under her. J. G. Cozzens A slow involuntary spasm doubled her. **b** OED The leaf has been folded, and tends to double over.

6 a *verb trans.* Sail round or to the other side of (a cape or headland). M16. ▸**b** *verb intrans.* Foll. by *upon*: enclose (an enemy fleet) from two sides. M18.

7 *verb intrans.* Make evasive turns or shifts; use duplicity, act deceitfully. Now *rare* or *obsolete*. M16.

8 a *verb intrans.* Turn suddenly and sharply in running, like a hunted animal; turn (*back*) in one's course; pursue a winding or tortuous course. L16. ▸**b** *verb trans.* Avoid or escape by so doubling; give the slip to. E19.

a Dryden See how he doubles, like a hunted hare. P. Warner They were completely fooled when he doubled on his tracks.

9 a *verb trans. MILITARY*. Make double the length of (a rank or file) by bringing up another rank or file; bring up (a rank or file) in this way. L16. ▸**b** *verb intrans. MILITARY*. Of a rank or file: march into position behind another so as to make it double. M17.

10 *verb intrans. & trans.* (Cause to) share a room or quarters with or *with* another, esp. where the accommodation is intended for one only. Usu. foll. by *up*. L18.

11 a *verb trans. THEATRICAL*. Perform (a part) in place of another player; stand in for (a player); combine the performance of (two parts) in a play etc. E19. ▸**b** *verb intrans.* Perform two parts or an additional part in a play etc.; perform or function in an additional capacity *as*. E20.

b C. P. Snow The governor of Kate's hospital also doubled as a trustee of the Opera. B. Moore The tobacconist's shop . . , which doubled as the post office.

12 *verb intrans.* March in double time; go at the double. L19.

13 *verb intrans. & trans.* BILLIARDS & SNOOKER etc. Of a ball: rebound from a cushion; *spec.* (of an object ball) rebound from one cushion and enter a pocket. Of a player: cause (a ball) to do this. L19.
14 *verb trans. & intrans.* BRIDGE. Counter (a bid) by declaring a double. L19.
15 *verb trans. & intrans.* MUSIC. Play on or *on* a second instrument in addition to a main one. E20.

L. FEATHER A clarinetist would double on tenor sax. *Gramophone* An arrangement for flute (doubling piccolo), two violas.. and piano.

16 *verb intrans.* Foll. by *up*: increase a stake in betting twofold. E20.
17 *verb trans.* Carry (a person) as a second rider on a bicycle. Cf. ***double-bank*** s.v. DOUBLE *adjective & adverb.* *Austral. & NZ.* M20.

doublé /duble/ *adjective.* M19.
[ORIGIN French, pa. pple of *doubler* line, DOUBLE *verb.*]
Covered or lined *with*; (of a book) having a doublure; plated *with* precious metal.

double bass /dʌb(ə)l 'beɪs/ *noun.* M18.
[ORIGIN from DOUBLE *adjective* + BASS *noun*[2], after Italian *contrabasso*: see CONTRABASS.]
The largest and deepest-toned instrument of the violin family, played with one end resting on the floor.

double-cross /dʌb(ə)l'krɒs/ *noun & verb.* Also **doublecross**. E19.
[ORIGIN from DOUBLE *adjective* + CROSS *noun.*]
▸ **A** *noun.* **1** In gaming, the cheating of two parties by trying to win a game or match after promising to lose it; *gen.* betrayal of a collaborator or partner in a dishonest or secret transaction. E19.
2 A plant variety that is a cross between two hybrids that are themselves crosses between separate inbred lines. E20.
3 An embroidery stitch consisting of one cross stitch superimposed on another. M20.
▸ **B** *verb trans.* Betray in a double-cross; cheat. E20.
■ **double-crosser** *noun* E20.

double entendre /ˌduːb(ə)l ɒ̃ː'tɒ̃ːdr(ə), *foreign* dubl ɑ̃tɑ̃ːdr/ *noun phr.* Pl. **double entendres** (pronounced same). L17.
[ORIGIN Obsolete French (now *double entente*) = double understanding.]
A double meaning; an ambiguous expression; a phrase with two meanings, one usually indecent. Also, the use of such a meaning or phrase.

double entente /dubl ɑ̃tɑ̃ːt/ *noun phr.* Pl. ***-s -s*** (pronounced same). L19.
[ORIGIN French: see DOUBLE ENTENDRE.]
= DOUBLE ENTENDRE.

double-face /'dʌb(ə)lfeɪs/ *noun & adjective.* E19.
[ORIGIN from DOUBLE *adjective* + FACE *noun*, or back-form. from DOUBLE-FACED.]
▸ **A** *noun.* **1** Duplicity. *rare.* E19.
2 A double-faced person. L19.
3 Double-faced fabric. M20.
▸ **B** *adjective.* = DOUBLE-FACED 2b. L19.

double-faced /dʌb(ə)l'feɪst/ *adjective.* M16.
[ORIGIN from DOUBLE *adjective* + FACE *noun* + -ED[2].]
1 Of a person: insincere, two-faced. M16.
2 Having two faces, sides, or aspects (*lit. & fig.*). L16. ▸**b** Of a fabric: finished on both sides. L19.

O. JESPERSEN Some phrases are.. double-faced. J. GALSWORTHY The double-faced stove in the centre.

■ **double-facedness** *noun* M19.

double-ganger /'dʌb(ə)lgaŋə/ *noun.* M19.
[ORIGIN Partial translation.]
= DOPPELGÄNGER.

double-gee /'dʌb(ə)ldʒiː/ *noun. Austral.* L19.
[ORIGIN Alt., after DOUBLE *adjective & adverb.*]
= DUBBELTJIE 2.

doubler /'dʌblə/ *noun*[1]. *obsolete* exc. *dial.* LME.
[ORIGIN Anglo-Norman *dobler*, *dubler* = Old French *do(u)blier* from medieval Latin *duplarium*, from Latin *duplus* DUPLE + *-arium* -ARY[1].]
A large plate or dish.

doubler /'dʌblə/ *noun*[2]. M16.
[ORIGIN from DOUBLE *verb* + -ER[1].]
A person who or thing which doubles something; *spec.* a device for doubling the voltage or frequency of a signal.

doubles ententes *noun phr.* pl. of DOUBLE ENTENTE.

doublet /'dʌblɪt/ *noun.* ME.
[ORIGIN Old French, from *double*: see DOUBLE *adjective*, -ET[1].]
1 *hist.* A close-fitting garment for the upper body formerly worn by men, with or without sleeves and a short skirt. ME.
doublet and hose (the type of) masculine attire; *arch.* light or informal attire (without a cloak or gown).
2 In *pl.* The same number on two dice thrown at once. LME. ▸†**b** A form of backgammon. Only in 17.
3 A counterfeit or simulated jewel composed of two pieces of crystal or glass cemented together with a layer of colour between them, or of a thin slice of a gem cemented on a piece of glass or inferior stone. LME.
4 Either of two things precisely alike or in some way identical; either of a pair; *esp.* either of two words in a language that have the same ultimate derivation. M16. ▸**b** PRINTING. = DOUBLE *noun* 6. M19. ▸**c** A story, episode, or saying occurring in two different biblical contexts and so regarded as derived from distinct sources. L19.

Verbatim The members of a doublet may have moved apart very little in meaning (as *frail*: *fragile*).

5 A pair, a couple; *spec.* a lens composed of two simple lenses; a magnifying glass consisting of this. E19. ▸**b** PHYSICS. A pair of related lines occurring close together in a spectrum; a pair of related atomic states or energy levels with slightly different energies. L19. ▸**c** A pair of words of equal length that have to be changed into each other in a word-ladder; in *pl.*, the pastime of doing this. L19.

b H. M. ROSENBERG The state is split by the crystalline electric field into two degenerate doublets.

doubleton /'dʌb(ə)lt(ə)n/ *noun.* E20.
[ORIGIN from DOUBLE *adjective* after SINGLETON.]
CARDS. A suit of which a hand contains only two cards; a pair of cards of such a suit; each card of such a pair.

doubling /'dʌblɪŋ/ *verbal noun.* LME.
[ORIGIN from DOUBLE *verb* + -ING[1].]
1 The action of DOUBLE *verb.* Also foll. by *up.* LME.

R. W. EMERSON The rapid doubling of the population. A. GARVE Intourist had given some of our booked rooms to a delegation from Mongolia, which meant a lot of doubling up. *Melody Maker* A violinist anxious to learn a 'doubling instrument'.

2 HERALDRY. The lining of a garment. L16.
3 A sudden change of direction; *fig.* an evasion, a deceitful action. E17.
4 The state of being folded; a fold. M17.

doubloon /dʌ'bluːn/ *noun.* E17.
[ORIGIN French *doublon* or its source Spanish *doblón*, from *doble* DOUBLE *adjective*: see -OON.]
1 *hist.* A Spanish gold coin, a pistole of double value. E17.
2 In *pl.* Money. *slang.* E20.

doublure /də'bluə, duː-; *foreign* dublyːr (*pl. same*)/ *noun.* L19.
[ORIGIN French = lining, from *doubler* to line: see -URE.]
An ornamental lining, usu. of leather, on the inside of a book cover.

doubly /'dʌbli/ *adverb.* LME.
[ORIGIN from DOUBLE *adjective* + -LY[2].]
1 In a double or twofold manner; in two ways; to a double degree, twice as much. LME.

SHAKES. *Rich. II* Thy blows, doubly redoubled. T. HARDY The duty of breaking the news was made doubly painful.

doubly incontinent unable to control urination and defecation.
†**2** Deceitfully. LME–M18.

doubt /daʊt/ *noun.* ME.
[ORIGIN Old French *dote*, *dute* (mod. *doute*), from *douter*: see DOUBT *verb.*]
1 a Uncertainty as to the truth or reality of something or as to the wisdom of a course of action; occasion or room for uncertainty. ME. ▸**b** A feeling of uncertainty; an inclination to disbelieve or hesitate; a reason to disbelieve or hesitate, a reservation. Usu. in *pl.* LME.

a G. B. SHAW There can be no doubt of that: everybody knows it. J. CONRAD He had little doubt.. of his power to get hold of the girl. M. EDWARDES The Committee.. casts doubt on the value of the Ryder report. **b** C. DARWIN One great authority.. entertains grave doubts on this subject. *Daily Telegraph* 3 per cent. of church-goers have doubts. D. LODGE I had my doubts but dutifully plied him with questions. JAN MORRIS He had doubts about the saint.

†**2 a** Apprehension, fear. ME–M17. ▸**b** A cause for fear; a risk, a danger. ME–L16.

LD BERNERS They dare not, for dought of Kyng Charlemayne.

†**3** A matter surrounded in uncertainty; a doubtful point. LME–L17.

AV *Dan.* 5:16 I haue heard of thee, that thou canst make interpretations, and dissolue doubts.

– PHRASES: ***benefit of the doubt***: see BENEFIT *noun*. **beyond a doubt**, **beyond all doubt**, **beyond doubt**, **beyond the shadow of a doubt** = ***without a doubt*** below. **make doubt** be uncertain, doubt, (*that*, *whether*). **in doubt** (*a*) in a state of mental uncertainty or indecision; (*b*) not certainly known or decided. **no doubt** in all likelihood, doubtless; orig. in stronger sense = ***without a doubt*** below. †**out of doubt** = ***without a doubt*** below. **without a doubt**, **without doubt** certainly, unquestionably.

doubt /daʊt/ *verb.* ME.
[ORIGIN Old French *doter*, *duter* (mod. *douter*) from Latin *dubitare* waver, hesitate, from *dubius* DUBIOUS. The Latinized spelling appeared in 15, following French †*doubter*.]
▸ **I** Be uncertain.
1 *verb intrans.* Be undecided in opinion or belief; be in doubt. (Foll. by *of.*) ME.

AV *Matt.* 14:31 O thou of little faith, wherefore didst thou doubt?

2 *verb trans.* Hesitate to believe or trust; feel uncertain of, call in question, have reservations about. ME.

DRYDEN He.. The beauty doubted, but believ'd the wife. A. RADCLIFFE My lord, you have never yet doubted my word. R. W. EMERSON They doubt a man's sound judgment if he does not eat with appetite.

3 *verb trans.* With clauses: feel uncertain *whether*, *if*; hesitate to believe, think it unlikely, that or *that* (chiefly *US* exc. as follows). After neg. or interrog. main clause foll. by *that*, *but that*, *but*. ME.

W. SELWYN It never was doubted, but that one partner might bind the rest. D. MAHON Death is near,.. I doubt if I shall survive another.. winter. W. GOLDING I doubt he'll bother to come.

†**4** *verb trans.* Hesitate, scruple, *to do*. ME–M18.
5 Of a thing: cause to doubt; make undecided. M19.

J. G. WHITTIER This.. somewhat doubted him at first, as the book was not canonical.

▸ **II** Fear, be in fear.
6 *verb trans.* †**a** Dread, be afraid of. ME–E18. ▸**b** Fear, be afraid, *that* or *lest*; fear that. *arch.* exc. *Scot. & dial.* LME.

a J. KELLY Do well and doubt no man.

7 *verb refl.* [= Old French *se douter*.] Be afraid (that). Now *rare* or *obsolete*. ME.

SIR W. SCOTT I doubt me his wits have gone a bell-wavering by the road.

†**8** *verb intrans.* Be in fear; be afraid (*of*). ME–L16.
9 *verb trans.* In weakened sense (app. infl. by branch I): anticipate (with fear) the possibility of; expect (esp. something unwelcome), suspect. Freq. foll. by *that*. *arch.* exc. *Scot. & dial.* E16.

W. H. PRESCOTT They doubted some sinister motive.. in the conduct of the French king. A. TROLLOPE I doubt that Thackeray did not write the Latin epitaph. D. L. SAYERS 'Hech, my lord,' said he, cheerfully. 'I dooted ye'd be here before verra long.' L. G. GIBBON Man, it's a fair tough case, I doubt I'll need your help.

■ **doubtable** *adjective* (*a*) uncertain, open to doubt; †(*b*) redoubtable: LME. **doubter** *noun* E17.

doubtful /'daʊtfʊl, -f(ə)l/ *adjective & noun.* LME.
[ORIGIN from DOUBT *noun* + -FUL.]
▸ **A** *adjective.* **1** Causing or subject to doubt; uncertain, questionable, ambiguous; that is only questionably, or is not unequivocally, such. LME. ▸**b** Unpredictable in result. LME. ▸**c** Of dubious character; not to be counted on in some capacity. M19.

ADDISON A doubtful Passage in a Latin Poet. C. DARWIN The question whether certain doubtful forms should be ranked as species or varieties. SCOTT FITZGERALD It was doubtful if he knew who Andrew Jackson was. E. F. SCHUMACHER A change which is not an unquestionable improvement is a doubtful blessing. **b** SOUTHEY The fight Hung doubtful. **c** R. MACAULAY She and that boy mix with some pretty doubtful company. T. E. LAWRENCE Don't put yourself about expecting me, for I'm a doubtful starter.

2 Feeling doubt or uncertainty; divided or unsettled in opinion. LME.

J. A. FROUDE He was doubtful of the prospects of the rebellion. B. JOWETT He was doubtful.. whether the ideal.. state could be realized.

†**3** To be feared; dreadful, terrible. LME–M16.
4 Such as gives cause for apprehension. *arch.* LME.

GIBBON The consul.. reported the doubtful and dangerous situation of the empire.

†**5** Full of fear; apprehensive (*that*). M16–L18.
▸ **B** *noun.* A doubtful person or thing; *esp.* a person who has not made up his or her mind on an issue. L16.
■ **doubtfully** *adverb* L15. **doubtfulness** *noun* LME.

doubting /'daʊtɪŋ/ *ppl adjective.* LME.
[ORIGIN from DOUBT *verb* + -ING[2].]
That doubts; sceptical. Formerly also, fearful.
doubting Thomas: see THOMAS *noun*[1] 1.
■ **doubtingly** *adverb* in a hesitant or doubting manner E16. **doubtingness** *noun* (*rare*) L18.

doubtless /'daʊtlɪs/ *adverb & adjective.* LME.
[ORIGIN from DOUBT *noun* + -LESS.]
▸ **A** *adverb.* **1** Without doubt; certainly, unquestionably. Now chiefly expressing concession of a statement. LME.

AV *Ps.* 126:6 He that goeth forth and weeping, bearing precious seed, shall doubtless come again with rejoicing.

2 In all likelihood; probably; no doubt. M17.

W. S. MAUGHAM He would marry again... Next time doubtless he would choose a different sort of woman.

▸ **B** *adjective.* Free from doubt; certain, indubitable. Formerly also, free from apprehension. LME.

SHAKES. *John* Pretty child, sleep doubtless and secure.

■ **doubtlessly** *adverb* = DOUBTLESS *adverb* LME. **doubtlessness** *noun* L19.

douc /duːk/ *noun.* L18.
[ORIGIN French from Vietnamese *douc*, *dok*.]
A langur, *Pygathrix nemaeus*, found in the forests of Vietnam. Also ***douc langur***.

D

douçaine /duːˈseɪn/ *noun*. **M20.**
[**ORIGIN** French, from *douce*: see **DOUCE**.]
EARLY MUSIC. A soft-toned reed instrument. Cf. **DOUCET** *noun* 2.

douce /duːs/ *adjective*. **ME.**
[**ORIGIN** Old French *dous* (mod. *doux*), fem. *douce* from Latin *dulcis* sweet. Cf. **DULCE** *adjective*.]
1 Pleasant, sweet. (Formerly a stock epithet of France.) Now *Scot. & N. English*. **ME.**
2 Quiet, sober, sedate. *Scot. & N. English*. **E18.**
A. M. SMITH The world of douce Edinburgh.
■ **doucely** *adverb* **E17**. **douceness** *noun* **E17**.

doucepere *noun* var. of **DOUZEPER**.

doucet /ˈduːsɪt/ *noun*. Also **dowset** /ˈdaʊsɪt/. **LME.**
[**ORIGIN** Old French, use as noun of *doucet*, *doucette* dim. of *doux*, **DOUCE**. Cf. **DULCET** *noun*, *adjective*.]
1 *COOKERY*. A sweet or sweetened dish. *obsolete* exc. *dial.* (in comb. ***doucet-pie***). **LME.**
†**2** A wind instrument resembling a flute. Cf. **DOUÇAINE**. Only in **LME**.
3 *HUNTING*. In *pl.* The testicles of a deer. **M16.**

†**doucet** *adjective* see **DULCET** *adjective*.

douceur /dusœːr, duːˈsəː/ *noun*. **LME.**
[**ORIGIN** French from Proto-Romance var. of Latin *dulcor* sweetness.]
1 Orig., sweetness of manner, amiability, (of a person). Now, agreeableness, charm (chiefly in ***douceur de vivre*** etc. below). **LME.**
F. BURNEY He . . answered with all his accustomed douceur and politeness. I. MURDOCH A curious relationship grew up between Michael and Dora, something . . which had for Michael a certain ease and *douceur*.
douceur de vie, ***douceur de la vie*** /də (la) vi/, ***douceur de vivre*** /də viːvr/ [French *vie* life, *vivre* live] the pleasure or amenities of life.
†**2** A complimentary speech or turn of phrase. **L17–E19.**
3 A conciliatory present; a gratuity, a bribe. **M18.**
N. GULBENKIAN When I have a bet, a winning one, . . all my servants get a little *douceur*.
4 A tax benefit available to a person who sells a work of art by private treaty to a public collection rather than on the open market. **L20.**

douche /duːʃ/ *noun & verb*. **M18.**
[**ORIGIN** French from Italian *doccia* conduit pipe, from *docciare* pour by drops from Proto-Romance, from Latin *ductus* **DUCT** *noun*.]
▸ **A** *noun*. (The application of) a jet of (esp. cold) liquid or air to a part of the body, as a form of bathing or for medicinal purposes; *spec.* the flushing of the vagina, as a contraceptive measure. Also, a syringe or similar device for producing such a jet. **M18.**
fig.: P. BROOK From the fanatical chastity of Isabella and the mystery of the Duke we are plunged back to Pompey and Barnadine for douches of normality.
– **COMB.**: **douche bag** a small syringe for douching the vagina, esp. as a contraceptive measure.
▸ **B** *verb*. **1** *verb trans.* Administer a douche to. **M19.**
2 *verb intrans.* Take a douche; *spec.* take a vaginal douche, esp. as a contraceptive measure. **M19.**

doucin /ˈduːsɪn, *foreign* dusɛ̃/ *noun*. **L16.**
[**ORIGIN** French, formed as **DOUCE**.]
A sweet variety of wild apple, used as a stock.

dough /dəʊ/ *noun*.
[**ORIGIN** Old English *dāg* = Middle Low German *dēch* (Dutch *deeg*), Old High German *teic* (German *Teig*), Old Norse *deig*, Gothic *daigs*, from Germanic, from Indo-European base meaning 'smear, knead'. Cf. **DUFF** *noun*².]
1 A mass of flour that has been moistened and kneaded for making into bread, pastry, cakes, etc. **OE.**
one's cake is dough one's project has failed.
2 Any soft pasty mass. **M16.**
3 Money. *slang* (chiefly *N. Amer.*). **M19.**
M. PUZO Twenty million bucks is a lot of dough.
– **COMB.**: **dough-baked** *adjective* imperfectly baked, so as to remain doughy; *fig.* deficient in reason or sense; **doughboy** (*a*) a boiled flour dumpling; (*b*) *US colloq.* an infantryman; **dough-face** (*a*) a mask made of dough; (*b*) *US HISTORY* a northern congressman who supported the South, esp. on the question of slavery; **dough trough** a trough or vessel in which dough is placed to rise.

dough /dəʊ/ *verb*. *rare*. **M17.**
[**ORIGIN** from the noun.]
†**1** *verb intrans.* Work with dough; be a baker. Only in **M17**.
2 *verb trans.* Make into dough; mix *in* with dough. **L19.**

doughnut /ˈdəʊnʌt/ *noun*. Also (*N. Amer.*) **donut**. **L18.**
[**ORIGIN** from **DOUGH** *noun* + **NUT** *noun*.]
1 A small spongy cake of sweetened and fried dough, freq. ring-shaped, or spherical with a jam or cream filling. **L18.**
be dollars to doughnuts: see **DOLLAR**.
2 Any of various circular objects with a hole in the middle, *esp.* a car or aircraft tyre. *colloq.* **E20.** ▸**b** A toroidal vacuum chamber in some particle accelerators. **M20.**

dought /daʊt/ *noun*. Now *Scot. rare*. **ME.**
[**ORIGIN** Orig. perh. repr. Old English *dugup* worth, virtue, manhood, from *dugan*: see **DOW** *verb*¹. Later, back-form. from **DOUGHTY**.]
Power, strength, ability.

doughty /ˈdaʊti/ *adjective*. Now *arch.* or *joc.*
[**ORIGIN** Late Old English *dohtig*, earlier *dyhtig* = Middle Low German, Middle Dutch *duchtich* (Dutch *duchtig*), Middle High German *tühtic* (German *tüchtig*), from Germanic: see **DOW** *verb*¹.]
Fearless and resolute; stout-hearted. **OE.**
SIR W. SCOTT After this doughty resolution, I went doggedly to work. R. COBB A . . doughty fighter against bureaucracy.
■ **doughtily** *adverb* **ME**. **doughtiness** *noun* **ME**.

doughy /ˈdəʊi/ *adjective*. **E17.**
[**ORIGIN** from **DOUGH** *noun* + **-Y**¹.]
Resembling dough in appearance or consistency; (of bread etc.) imperfectly baked.
J. M. GOOD A pallid doughy countenance. *fig.*: SHAKES. *All's Well* All the unbak'd and doughy youth of a nation.
■ **doughiness** *noun* **E17**.

Douglas /ˈdʌɡləs/ *noun*¹. **M19.**
[**ORIGIN** David *Douglas* (1798–1834), Scot. botanical explorer.]
1 ***Douglas fir***, ***Douglas spruce***, ***Douglas pine***, a very tall coniferous timber tree, *Pseudotsuga menziesii*, native to western N. America. **M19.**
2 ***Douglas squirrel***, a chickaree, *Tamiasciurus douglasi*. *N. Amer.* **L19.**

Douglas /ˈdʌɡləs/ *noun*². **M19.**
[**ORIGIN** James *Douglas* (1675–1742), Scot. physician.]
ANATOMY. Used in *possess.* or after *of* to designate anatomical structures described by or named after Douglas.
Douglas's pouch = ***RECTO-UTERINE pouch***.

Douglas /ˈdʌɡləs/ *noun*³. *Austral. slang*. **E20.**
[**ORIGIN** The *Douglas* Axe Manufacturing Co., orig. of East *Douglas*, Massachusetts, US.]
(A name for) an axe.
swing Douglas: see **SWING** *verb*.

Douglasite /ˈdʌɡləsʌɪt/ *noun & adjective*. *hist.* **M20.**
[**ORIGIN** from *Douglas* (see below) + **-ITE**¹.]
▸ **A** *noun*. A supporter of the economic theories of social credit of Major C. H. Douglas (1879–1952). **M20.**
▸ **B** *adjective*. Pertaining to or characteristic of Douglasites. **M20.**

Doukhobor *noun* var. of **DUKHOBOR**.

doula /ˈduːlə/ *noun*. **M20.**
[**ORIGIN** mod. Greek, from ancient Greek *doulē* bondswoman, fem. of *doulos* born bondsman, slave.]
A person, typically an experienced mother, who provides emotional support, practical help, and advice to a woman during pregnancy and childbirth and for the first few weeks after birth.

doulocracy *noun* var. of **DULOCRACY**.

Doulton /ˈdəʊlt(ə)n/ *adjective & noun*. **L19.**
[**ORIGIN** John *Doulton* (1793–1873), English potter.]
(Proprietary name designating) pottery or porcelain made at the factories of John Doulton or his successors.

doum /duːm/ *noun*. Also **doom**. **E18.**
[**ORIGIN** Arabic *dawm*, *dūm*.]
More fully ***doum palm***. An Egyptian palm, *Hyphaene thebaica*, usu. with a dichotomously branched trunk, bearing an edible fruit the size of an apple.

doup /duːp/ *noun*. *Scot.* **E16.**
[**ORIGIN** Cf. Old Norse *daup*.]
1 A hollow bottom; *esp.* the bottom of an eggshell. *obsolete* exc. *dial.* **E16.**
2 The buttocks. **M17.**
3 The end or last part of anything, as a candle. **E18.**

douppion *noun* var. of **DUPION**.

dour /ˈdʊə/ *adjective*. Orig. *Scot.* **LME.**
[**ORIGIN** Prob. from Gaelic *dúr* dull, stupid, obstinate = Middle Irish & mod. Irish *dúr*, perh. from Latin *durus* hard.]
1 Severe, stern, relentless; fierce, bold. *Scot. & N. English*. **LME.**
J. DALRYMPLE He led a dour and hard lyfe. LYTTON Tostig is a man . . dour and haughty. F. ORMSBY Never again would dour fields lie Quite so forbidding, stones be so bare.
2 Obstinate, stubborn. *Scot. & N. English*. **LME.**
J. BUCHAN I know the ways of those London journalists, and they're a dour crop to shift.
3 Gloomily taciturn; sullen. **L15.**
P. THEROUX These Indians are habitually dour—their faces wrinkled into frowns. J. STEINBECK She had a dour Presbyterian mind.
■ **dourly** *adverb* **L15**. **dourness** *noun* **LME**.

dourine /ˈdʊəriːn/ *noun*. **L19.**
[**ORIGIN** French.]
A chronic, usu. fatal, venereal disease of horses caused by a trypanosome.

†**dourlach** *noun*. *Scot.* Only in **19**.
[**ORIGIN** App. var. of **DORLACH**.]
A short sword; a dagger.

douro *noun* var. of **DURO**.

douroucouli /dʊərʊˈkuːli/ *noun*. Also **-coli** /-ˈkɒli/. **M19.**
[**ORIGIN** Prob. a S. Amer. Indian name.]
= ***night monkey*** s.v. **NIGHT** *noun*.

dourra *noun* var. of **DURRA**.

douse /daʊs/ *noun*. **M16.**
[**ORIGIN** from **DOUSE** *verb*¹. Cf. **DOUST**.]
A dull heavy blow.

douse /daʊs/ *verb*¹ *trans.* Also **dowse**. **M16.**
[**ORIGIN** Perh. rel. to similar and partly synon. Middle Dutch, Low German *dossen*, Dutch *doesen*, German dial. *dusen* beat, strike. Cf. **DOSS** *verb*¹.]
1 Strike, knock, punch. Now *dial.* **M16.**
2 *NAUTICAL*. Lower (a sail etc.) or slacken (a rope) suddenly or in haste; close (a porthole). **E17.**
E. JONG 'Dowse your Topsail and salute her!' I cried.
3 Throw *down* with force; *fig.* put down or pay out (money). Chiefly *dial.* **L18.**
4 Take off (clothes, esp. a hat). **L18.**
■ **douser** *noun*¹ a heavy blow **L18**.

douse /daʊs/ *verb*². **E17.**
[**ORIGIN** Prob. imit. (cf. *souse*), but perh. identical with **DOUSE** *verb*¹.]
1 *verb trans.* Plunge vigorously into water or other liquid; immerse (*in*). **E17.**
fig.: L. MACNEICE When we were children Spring was easy, Dousing our heads in suds of hawthorn.
2 *verb trans.* Wet thoroughly with a liquid, drench. (Usu. foll. by *with*, *in*.) **E17.**
B. CHATWIN He had doused himself once a week in the wash-house. T. KENEALLY The pyre . . was doused in fuel and lit.
3 *verb intrans.* Plunge or be plunged into water. **E17.**
4 Put out, extinguish, (a light, fire, etc.). Also *fig.*, suppress (a feeling), put an end to (an activity). **L18.**
T. E. LAWRENCE I see the Corporal's cigarette doused. L. GARFIELD With the moon now doused in a creeping sea of cloud. T. CAPOTE Dick doused the flashlight. E. BIRNEY His spirits, never easy to douse, were sustained by his . . winnings at black jack.
■ **douser** *noun*² (*a*) someone who drenches another person; (*b*) a screen in a projector which cuts off the light before it reaches the film: **L19**.

†**doust** *noun*. **E17–E18.**
[**ORIGIN** Perh. alt. of **DOUSE** *noun*.]
A firm blow; a punch.

dout /daʊt/ *verb & noun*. Also (now only as noun) **dowt**. **E16.**
[**ORIGIN** Contr. of *do out*: see **DO** *verb*.]
▸ **A** *verb trans.* Extinguish, put out, (a fire or light). *obsolete* exc. *dial.* **E16.**
▸ **B** *noun*. **1** A thing which extinguishes something. *obsolete* exc. *dial.* **L16.**
2 A cigarette end. *Scot. colloq.* **M20.**
■ **douter** *noun* (*obsolete* exc. *dial.*) a person who or thing which extinguishes something **E17**.

douzaine /duːˈzeɪn/ *noun*. **L18.**
[**ORIGIN** French = **DOZEN** *noun*.]
In Guernsey and Alderney, a body of twelve people elected to represent a parish.
■ **douzainier**, **-zenier** /duːzəˈnɪə/ *noun* a member of a douzaine **L17**.

douzeper /ˈduːzəpɛː/ *noun*. *arch.* Also **doucepere** /ˈduːs-/. **ME.**
[**ORIGIN** Orig. in pl. form *douzepers* from Old French *douze pers* (mod. *douze pairs*) twelve peers.]
Each of the twelve paladins of Charlemagne, the bravest of his knights; any of the twelve chief peers of France, temporal and spiritual, regarded as their symbolic heirs; *fig.* any illustrious person. Usu. in *pl.*

dove /dʌv/ *noun*. Also (*Scot.*) **doo** /duː/. **ME.**
[**ORIGIN** Old Norse *dúfa* = Old Frisian *dūve*, Old Saxon *duba* (Dutch *duif*), Old High German *tūba* (German *Taube*), Gothic *dūbo*, from Germanic base taken to be imit. of the bird's cry.]
1 Any bird of the family Columbidae; a pigeon; *esp.* a turtle dove or similar small pigeon. Formerly (now *dial.*), any of the native British pigeons. (In Christian symbolism typifying gentleness and harmlessness.) **ME.** ▸**b** ***Greenland dove***, the black guillemot. Cf. **DOVEKIE**. *dial.* **L17.**
collared dove, ***ringdove***, ***rock dove***, ***stock dove***, ***turtle dove***, etc.
2 A person, esp. a woman, for whom one feels tender affection. Chiefly in ***my dove***. **LME.**
TENNYSON She is coming, my dove, my dear.
3 An image of a dove as a symbol of innocence, harmlessness, or peace. Also (*CHRISTIAN CHURCH*), a vessel formerly used to enclose the pyx. **E16.**
4 a In full ***dove-colour***. A warm grey with a tone of pink or purple. **L16.** ▸**b** A dove-coloured marble. **E19.**
5 A gentle or innocent person. Formerly, a simpleton. **L16.**
soiled dove: see **SOILED** *adjective*¹.
6 *CHRISTIAN CHURCH*. [Cf. *Luke* 3:22 etc.] The Holy Spirit, esp. in his outward manifestation. **E18.**
7 (Usu. **D-**.) *The* constellation Columba. Also ***Noah's Dove***, ***the Dove of Noah***. **L18.**
8 *POLITICS*. A person who believes in a policy of negotiation and conciliation rather than warfare or confrontation. Opp. ***hawk***. **M20.**
S. BRILL Gibbons . . had gone to North Vietnam . . with some fellow doves in search of peace feelers.

– **COMB.**: ***dove-colour***: see sense 4a above; **dove-eyed** *adjective* having mild or gentle eyes like a dove's; **dove-flower** an orchid, *Peristeria elata*, native to Central America and northern S. America; **dove-hawk** *dial.* the hen harrier; **dovehouse** a dovecote; **dove-marble** = sense 4b above; **dove orchid** = ***dove-flower*** above; **dove's-foot (cranesbill)** a cranesbill, *Geranium molle*, with small pink flowers and round, softly hairy, deeply divided leaves; **dove tree** a deciduous tree, *Davidia involucrata*, native to China, with heads of small petalless flowers subtended by huge white bracts.

■ **dovelet** *noun* a young or small dove **E19**. **dovelike** *adjective* resembling (that of) a dove; *esp.* gentle, peace-loving: **L16**. **doveling** *noun* = DOVELET; also, (a term of endearment for) a small child: **E17**.

dove /dəʊv/ *verb*[1] *intrans. Scot. & N. English.* **L18**.
[ORIGIN Rel. to Old English *dofung* dotage; Old Norse *dofna*, Gothic *daubnan* become heavy, flat, or dead. Cf. earlier DOVER.]
1 Doze, become drowsy. **L18**.
2 Be stupid. *Scot.* **E19**.

dove *verb*[2] *pa. t.*: see DIVE *verb*.

dovecote /ˈdʌvkəʊt/ *noun*. Also **-cot** /-kɒt/. See also DOOCOT. **LME**.
[ORIGIN from DOVE *noun* + COTE *noun*[1].]
A structure housing doves or pigeons, usu. placed at a height above the ground and with entrances for the birds to fly in by.
flutter the dovecotes, **cause a flutter among the dovecotes** startle or perturb a sedate or conventionally minded community.

dovekie /ˈdʌvki/ *noun*. **E19**.
[ORIGIN Scot. dim. of DOVE *noun*.]
Orig., the black guillemot, *Cepphus grylle* (cf. DOVE *noun* 1b). Now usu. the little auk, *Alle alle* (its usual name in N. Amer.).

dover /ˈdəʊvə/ *verb & noun*. *Scot. & N. English.* **E16**.
[ORIGIN App. from (the same root as) DOVE *verb*[1]: see -ER[5].]
▸ **A** *verb*. **1** *verb intrans. & trans.* (Cause to) doze or be unconscious. **E16**.
2 *verb intrans.* Wander aimlessly or confusedly; walk unsteadily. *Scot.* **E19**.
▸ **B** *noun*. A light or fitful sleep; a doze. **E19**.

Dover's powder /ˈdəʊvəz paʊdə/ *noun phr.* **E19**.
[ORIGIN Thomas *Dover* (1660–1742), English physician.]
PHARMACOLOGY. A mixture of opium and ipecacuanha, formerly much used as an anodyne and diaphoretic.

dovetail /ˈdʌvteɪl/ *noun & verb*. **M16**.
[ORIGIN from DOVE *noun* + TAIL *noun*[1].]
▸ **A** *noun*. **1** A joint formed by one or more tenons in the shape of a dove's tail, i.e. a reversed wedge, fitting into mortises of corresponding shape. **M16**.
2 A tenon or mortise of such a joint. **L17**.
3 *HERALDRY.* A dovetailed line of partition. **L17**.
– **COMB.**: **dovetail joint** = sense 1 above; **dovetail moulding** *ARCHITECTURE*: composed of alternating triangles and reversed triangles.
▸ **B** *verb*. **1** *verb trans.* Fit together or join with a dovetail. **M16**.
2 *verb trans. & intrans.* (*fig.*) Fit together or become adjusted perfectly, so as to form a compact or harmonious whole. (Foll. by *with*, *into*.) **E19**.

A. GEIKIE The readiness with which Forbes had begun to dovetail zoology and geology. C. S. LEWIS Every problem of conduct was dovetailed into a complex and rigid moral theology. P. L. FERMOR Meals within meals dovetailing so closely . . that there is hardly an interprandial moment.

■ **dovetailed** *adjective* (**a**) joined by means of a dovetail; (**b**) (having an end) shaped like a dove's tail or inverted triangle; (**c**) *HERALDRY* (of a line of partition) forming a row of inverted triangles with open apices, as in a dovetail joint: **M17**. **dovetailer** *noun* a machine for making dovetails; a person who dovetails: **E19**.

dovey /ˈdʌvi/ *noun*. Also **dovie**. **M18**.
[ORIGIN Dim. or pet form of DOVE *noun*: see -Y[6], -IE.]
Used as a term of endearment: little dove. Cf. LOVEY, LOVEY-DOVEY.

dovish /ˈdʌvɪʃ/ *adjective*. **M16**.
[ORIGIN from DOVE *noun* + -ISH[1].]
†**1** Of simplicity etc.: like that of a dove. Only in **M16**.
2 Chiefly *POLITICS*. Inclined to advocate negotiation and conciliation (cf. DOVE *noun* 8); conciliatory. Opp. ***hawkish***. **M20**.
■ **dovishness** *noun* **M20**.

dow /daʊ/ *noun*[1]. *slang.* **E19**.
[ORIGIN Abbreviation.]
A dowager.

Dow /daʊ/ *noun*[2]. **M20**.
[ORIGIN Abbreviation.]
The Dow-Jones average.

dow *noun*[3] var. of DHOW.

dow /daʊ/ *verb*[1] *intrans.* Now *Scot. & N. English.*
[ORIGIN Old English *dugan* corresp. to Old Saxon *dugan*, Old High German *tugan* (German *taugen*), Old Norse *duga*: a Germanic preterite-present verb rel. to DOUGHTY.]
†**1** Be good, strong, vigorous, virtuous, valiant, or manly. Only in **OE**.
†**2** Be of use or profit to a person, avail. Usu. *impers.* in (***it***) *dows* etc. **OE–L16**.
†**3** Be valid or of value; be worth or good for something. **ME–L18**.
†**4** Be good, fitting, or proper for someone; become, befit, behove. Usu. *impers.* in ***it dows*** etc. Only in **ME**.
5 Have the strength or ability, be able (to do something). Usu. in neg. contexts. Now *rare* exc. *poet.* **ME**.
6 Do well, thrive, prosper. **ME**.

†**dow** *verb*[2] see DUE *verb*.

dowable /ˈdaʊəb(ə)l/ *adjective*. Now *rare*. **LME**.
[ORIGIN Anglo-Norman, from Old French & mod. French *douer* endow: see DOWAGER, -ABLE.]
LAW. Entitled to dower; able to be endowed.

dowager /ˈdaʊədʒə/ *noun*. **M16**.
[ORIGIN Old French *douag(i)ere*, from *douage* dower, from *douer* portion out, endow, from Latin *dotare*: see DOWER, -ER[2].]
1 A widow holding title or rank, or property, derived from her late husband. Freq. appositive, as ***queen dowager***, ***princess dowager***, ***countess dowager*** or ***dowager countess***, etc. **M16**.

D. HUME He espoused Eleanor, dowager of William Earl of Pembroke. E. A. FREEMAN A marriage with their dowager aunt. J. GRENFELL The Dowager Duchess cuts the cake.

2 A dignified elderly lady. *colloq.* **E19**.
dowager's hump forward curvature of the spine resulting in a stoop, caused by collapse of the front edges of the thoracic vertebrae and associated typically with women with osteoporosis.
■ **dowagerly** *adjective* (*rare*) **M19**.

dowar *noun* var. of DOUAR.

dowd /daʊd/ *noun*[1]. **ME**.
[ORIGIN Unknown. In mod. use partly back-form. from DOWDY *adjective*.]
A person, usu. a woman, of dull unfashionable appearance; a dowdy woman.

dowd /daʊd/ *noun*[2]. *obsolete* exc. *dial.* **M18**.
[ORIGIN Unknown: cf. DOWDY *noun*[2].]
A woman's cap or nightcap.

dowdy /ˈdaʊdi/ *noun*[1] & *adjective*. **L16**.
[ORIGIN from DOWD *noun*[1] + -Y[6].]
▸ **A** *noun*. A woman who is shabbily, unfashionably, or unattractively dressed. **L16**.
▸ **B** *adjective*. (Of a person, esp. a woman) shabbily, badly, or unattractively dressed; (of a garment) lacking smartness and freshness, shabby, unattractively dull. **L17**.

R. WEST I can't stand by and see my sister turning into a dowdy, middle-aged frump.

■ **dowdily** *adverb* **L19**. **dowdiness** *noun* **M19**. **dowdyish** *adjective* **E19**. **dowdyism** *noun* dowdy character or quality **M19**.

dowdy /ˈdaʊdi/ *noun*[2]. *obsolete* exc. *dial.* **L18**.
[ORIGIN Unknown: cf. DOWD *noun*[2].]
= DOWD *noun*[2].

dowel /ˈdaʊəl/ *noun & verb*. **ME**.
[ORIGIN Perh. from Middle Low German *dovel*, corresp. to Old High German *tubili* (Middle High German *tübel*: German *Döbel* after Low German) from Germanic from Indo-European, whence Greek *tuphos* wedge.]
▸ **A** *noun*. A short round rod that projects from one (usu. wooden) surface and fits into a matching hole in another, so as to hold the two together without showing; a headless wooden pin used similarly. Also ***dowel pin***. **ME**.
▸ **B** *verb trans.* Infl. **-ll-**, ***-l-**. Fasten with a dowel or dowels. **L17**.
■ **dowelled** *adjective* **E19**. **dowelling** *noun* (**a**) the action of the verb; (**b**) wood in cylindrical form suitable for cutting into dowels: **L19**.

do-well /ˈduːwɛl/ *noun*. **LME**.
[ORIGIN from DO *verb* + WELL *adverb*.]
1 The action of doing well. Freq. personified. *obsolete* exc. *dial.* **LME**.
2 A prosperous person. *rare*. **M19**.

dower /ˈdaʊə/ *noun & verb*. **LME**.
[ORIGIN Old French *douaire* from medieval Latin *dotarium*, from Latin *dotare* endow, from *dos*, *dot-* dowry, DOT *noun*[2], rel. to *dare* give: see -ARY[1].]
▸ **A** *noun*. **1** *LAW* (now *hist.*). The share of a dead man's estate that was formerly allowed to his widow for life. **LME**.
2 = DOWRY 2. Now *arch. & poet.* **LME**.
3 An endowment or gift of nature; a talent. **LME**.
– **COMB.**: **dower chest** (**a**) a wedding chest; (**b**) *US* a hope chest; **dower house** a smaller house on the estate of a large one, forming part of a widow's dower and intended as her place of residence; **dower land**: forming part of a widow's dower.
▸ **B** *verb trans.* **1** Give a dowry to; endow *with* a dowry. **L15**.

E. BOWEN The daughters should be well dowered with Bland money.

2 Endow *with* an attribute, talent, or gift. **L18**.

E. M. FORSTER A man dowered with coarse kindliness, and rustic strength.

■ †**doweress** *noun* a widow holding a dower; a dowager: **E16–E19**. **dowerless** *adjective* **E17**.

dowf /daʊf/ *noun, adjective, & verb*. *Scot.* (now *dial.*) & *N. English.* **LME**.
[ORIGIN Uncertain: perh. from Old Norse *daufr* deaf.]
▸ **A** *noun*. **1** A spiritless, stupid, or gloomy person. **LME**.
2 A dull blow. **E18**.
▸ **B** *adjective*. **1** Of a person, a sound, or (formerly) the weather: dull. Of a person: lacking spirit or energy; gloomy. **E16**.
†**2** Of an excuse: unconvincing, feeble. **L18–M19**.
3 Of wood or vegetation: decayed. Of ground: unfertile. **E19**.
▸ **C** *verb*. **1** *verb intrans. & trans.* Be or make dull or sluggish. **E19**.
2 *verb trans.* Hit with something soft; thump. **E19**.
3 *verb trans.* Bounce (a ball). Now *rare*. **E19**.
■ **dowfness** *noun* lack of spirit **E16**.

D

dowfart /ˈdaʊfət/ *noun & adjective*. *Scot. arch.* **E18**.
[ORIGIN from DOWF + *-art* -ARD. Cf. DUFFER *noun*[2].]
▸ **A** *noun*. A dull or stupid person. **E18**.
▸ **B** *adjective*. Dull, stupid. **L18**.

dowie /ˈdaʊi/ *adjective*. *Scot. & N. English.* Also †**dolly**. **E16**.
[ORIGIN Uncertain: perh. ult. from DULL *adjective* + -Y[1].]
Dull and lonely; dreary; dismal.

dowitcher /ˈdaʊɪtʃə/ *noun*. **M19**.
[ORIGIN Iroquoian: cf. Mohawk *tawistawis* snipe.]
Either of two wading birds of the genus *Limnodromus* (family Scolopacidae), related to the sandpiper and breeding in Arctic and subarctic regions, *L. griseus* or *L. scolopaceus*, the short- and long-billed dowitchers of N. America.

Dow-Jones /daʊˈdʒəʊnz/ *noun*. Also **Dow Jones**. **E20**.
[ORIGIN from *Dow Jones & Co.*, Inc., US financial news agency, from C. H. *Dow* (1851–1902) & E. D. *Jones* (*c* 1855–1920).]
In full ***Dow-Jones average***, ***Dow-Jones industrial average***. An index of the average level of share prices on the New York Stock Exchange at any time, based on the daily price of a selection of representative stocks. Cf. Dow *noun*[2].

dowl /daʊl/ *noun*. Now *dial.* **LME**.
[ORIGIN Perh. rel. to DOWN *noun*[2].]
A barb of a feather; down, fluff.

dowlas /ˈdaʊləs/ *noun & adjective*. **ME**.
[ORIGIN *Daoulas*, a village in Brittany.]
▸ **A** *noun*. Orig., a coarse kind of linen. Now, a strong calico made in imitation of it. **ME**.
▸ **B** *attrib.* or as *adjective*. Made of dowlas. **M16**.

dowless /ˈdaʊlɪs/ *adjective*. *Scot.* **L18**.
[ORIGIN from DOW *verb*[1] + -LESS.]
Without strength or energy; feeble; infirm.

dowly /ˈdaʊli/ *adjective*. *N. English.* **LME**.
[ORIGIN Uncertain: perh. rel. to DOWIE.]
Doleful, miserable, gloomy, lonely.

down /daʊn/ *noun*[1].
[ORIGIN Old English *dūn* = Old Frisian *dūne*, Old Saxon *dūna* (Dutch *duin*, cf. DUNE), perh. ult. from a Celtic word whence also Old Irish & mod. Irish *dún*, Welsh †*din*, fort, cogn. with Old English *tūn* TOWN *noun*.]
1 A hill. *obsolete* exc. as passing into sense 2. **OE**.
2 An open tract of high ground; *spec.* in *pl.*, (*the*) treeless undulating chalk uplands of S. and SE England and elsewhere, traditionally a major source of pasturage. **ME**.

R. KIPLING Little, lost, Down churches praise The Lord who made the hills.

dale and down (now *arch. & poet.*) lowland and upland. **North Downs** *the* hills forming a ridge across Kent and Surrey. **South Downs** *the* hills forming a ridge across Sussex and Hampshire. **The Downs** (**a**) see sense 2 above; (**b**) part of the sea (opposite the North Downs) off east Kent.

3 A sandhill, a dune. Now *rare*. **E16**.
4 (**D-**.) (A sheep of) any of several short-woolled hornless breeds originally raised on the English downs, or bred from such a breed. (Earliest in SOUTHDOWN.) **L18**.
Dorset Down, ***Hampshire Down***, ***Oxford Down***, etc.
– **COMB.**: **downland** land forming downs.
■ **downlike** *adjective* resembling downland or a down **L17**.

down /daʊn/ *noun*[2]. **ME**.
[ORIGIN Old Norse *dúnn*, whence Low German *dune*, German *Daune*.]
1 Soft loose fluffy feathers, as on young birds (used in cushions, quilts, etc.). **ME**.

L. MACNEICE Baby pigeons covered with yellow down.

2 Fine short soft hairs on some plants, fruits, and seeds. **LME**.
thistledown: see THISTLE.
3 (A mass of) short soft hair on the skin, *spec.* that which appears on a boy's face at puberty. **L16**.

DRYDEN The callow down began To shade my chin, and call me first a man. D. LESSING A tiny down on his bare forearm gleamed gold. D. JACOBSON There was no down on . . her cheeks or upper lip.

4 Any material of a soft fluffy nature. **E17**.

A. REID Nitre . . effloresces . . on their surface, in the form of a crystalline down.

■ **downless** *adjective* **L16**.

D

down /daʊn/ *noun*[3] *& interjection*. L16.
[ORIGIN from DOWN *adverb* or ellipt. for 'downward motion'.]
1 a *noun & interjection*. Used as a meaningless word in the refrains of popular songs. Also ***derry down***. Cf. DERRY 1. L16. ▸†**b** The burden or refrain of a song. E–M17.
2 A descent (*lit. & fig.*); a reverse of fortune. Chiefly in ***ups and downs*** (see UP *noun*). E18. ▸**b** An act of throwing or putting something down; *spec.* in American and Canadian football, (***a***) a play to advance the ball; (***b***) each of a fixed number of attempts to advance the ball 10 yards. M19. ▸**c** A feeling or period of depression or low spirits or lack of vigour. *colloq.* M20.

Times The index spent most of the morning on the down.

†**3** A suspicion; a suggestion of illegality. *slang*. E–M19.
4 A tendency to view with suspicion and disapproval; a prejudice, a grudge, a resentment. Chiefly in ***have a down on***. *colloq.* M19.

Abingdon Herald One of the men . . had a particular down on drugs because a member of his family had got into serious trouble with them. M. BINCHY You've always had a down on her.

5 *DOMINOES*. The play of the first piece. L19.
6 The position or action of a dog lying down in response to a command. M20.

down /daʊn/ *verb*[1] *trans. rare*. E17.
[ORIGIN from DOWN *noun*[2].]
Cover or line with down, make downy.

down /daʊn/ *verb*[2]. L17.
[ORIGIN from DOWN *adverb*.]
▸ **I** *verb intrans.* Now *rare*.
1 Foll. by *with*: put or throw down; have done with. L17.
2 Come or go down, descend. E19.
3 Foll. by *on, upon*: come down on, attack (*lit. & fig.*). M19.
▸ **II** *verb trans.* †**4** with *it*. Move downwards, descend. Only in M18.
5 Bring, put, throw, or knock down; get the better of. L18.

S. JOHNSON He talked of one whom he did not know, but I *downed* him with the King of Prussia. R. S. SURTEES His horse . . had downed him three times. *Sun (Baltimore)* The American fighters reported downing 110 of the Nazi interceptors. *Globe & Mail (Toronto)* London Lords downed Kitchener Oaks 31–14 yesterday. *New Yorker* Downed trees with their roots . . sticking high in the air.

down tools stop work, esp. as a form of industrial action.
6 Drink, esp. all of. *colloq.* E20.

W. SOYINKA A waiter refills his glass; he downs it.

down /daʊn/ *adverb & adjective*. Superl. DOWNMOST. OE.
[ORIGIN Aphet. from ADOWN.]
▸ **A** *adverb &* (after *be* or other copula) *pred. adjective*.
▸ **I** Denoting motion or direction in space.
1 In a descending direction; from above, to the ground, to a lower place. OE.

O. MANNING The bamboo blinds were pulled down. C. P. SNOW She looked down at her plate. M. ROBERTS I go up and down like a seesaw.

2 To a place regarded as lower in position; e.g. in the direction of a current; with the wind; from the capital to the country; away from university; from the House of Lords to the House of Commons. ME.

GOLDSMITH We caught him up accidentally in our journey down. N. MARSH Twenty years ago this month I came down from Cambridge.

▸ **II** Denoting position in space.
3 In a low or lowered situation or position; on the ground or floor. ME.

M. EDGEWORTH The new carpet is down in the two drawing rooms.

4 At a place or in a situation regarded as lower in position; e.g. at a distance from the capital, not at one's university. M19. ▸**b** = DOWNSTAGE *adverb*. L19.

F. MARRYAT A gentleman who lived down in Hampshire. R. DAVIES A smile that would have melted . . a lad down from Cambridge.

▸ **III** Of posture, position, attitude, etc.
5 In or into a fallen, sitting, or overturned posture or position. ME.

D. H. LAWRENCE The minister flushed with confusion and sat down again. E. M. FORSTER All the flats . . might be pulled down, and new buildings . . arise.

6 So as to bring down, reach, or overtake by the action of the verb. M17.
pull down, ride down, run down, throw down, etc.
7 Prostrate from illness, esp. *with* (formerly *in*) a specified ailment; ill. E18.

WOODES ROGERS We have now about 50 men down. DAY LEWIS Struck down by some obscure glandular disease.

▸ **IV** Particular varieties of direction or position.
8 Of the sun, moon, etc.: below the horizon, set. ME.

L. BINYON At the going down of the sun and in the morning.

9 In ref. to (the payment of) a sum of money: (laid) on the table or counter; (paid) on the spot or on the instant. LME.

P. PORTER A suit . . easily got for two pounds down.

10 Downstairs; to the ground floor, basement, etc., from an upper floor or room, *esp.* from one's bedroom or to the dining room; on a lower floor after getting up and leaving an upstairs bedroom. L16.

D. H. LAWRENCE Presently he came down dressed. D. HALLIDAY Anne-Marie had got breakfast, but no one was down.

11 Down the throat, into the stomach. L16.

M. B. KEATINGE Which homely fare they wash down with a spoonful of light wine.

12 On paper or other surface used for writing; in writing, in print; in a programme or schedule. L16.

T. HARDY When he had jotted down something he went to the telescope again. *Guardian* Angus Wilson . . was down to chair Saturday's session.

13 Below the surface or to the bottom of the water; into the depths of the sea. Usu. with *go*. E17.

W. COWPER When Kempenfelt went down With twice four hundred men.

14 (Filling or to fill spaces) along a vertical line of a crossword puzzle. Usu. following the number of the word or clue (passing into *adjective*). E20.

R. RENDELL How many letters in fifteen down.

▸ **V** Of order, time, condition, quality, or value.
15 In or into a position regarded as lower or inferior, a state of subjection, discomfiture, etc. ME. ▸**b** So as to make silent, submissive, etc., by the action of the verb. L16. ▸**c** Behind one's opponent or opponents in a game or competition by a stated number of points. L19.

H. REED If the spirit of a nation goes down, its poetry will go down with it. **b** A. BIRRELL He was immediately frowned down by Mrs. Snagsby. **c** H. H. HILTON At the fourteenth hole he was one down.

b ***howl down, shout down***, etc.
16 From an earlier to a later time. LME.

G. BERKELEY Throughout all ages down to our own. O. HENRY They hand it down from one generation to another.

17 To or at a value, price, or rate that is lower than or no higher than previously. L16.

W. LONGMAN Employers . . combined to keep down wages. J. STEINBECK Wages went down and prices went up. P. LARKIN His temperature was down this morning nearly a whole point.

18 From a roused, excited, distressed, or violent state; in or into a state of calm or quiescence. L16.

COLERIDGE Down dropt the breeze. W. S. MAUGHAM Women felt a little irritable at times, but . . they'd calm down after a bit.

19 In or into a state of depression or low spirits or lack of vigour. *colloq.* E17.

H. D. THOREAU The Captain is rather down about it, but I tell him to cheer up. L. K. JOHNSON Don't let problems get you down. *Sunday Times* She was looking a little down because she had had . . gastro-enteritis.

20 To a smaller size or bulk, finer particles, or a thinner consistency. M17.

M. B. KEATINGE Ground down into dust.

boil down, melt down, thin down, water down, etc.
21 In or into a state weaker, milder, or less pronounced in quality. E19.

A. GILBERT 'Can't you keep that radio down?' the landlady would implore.

soften down, tone down, etc.
22 Aware, alert; wise *to*. *arch. slang*. E19.
23 Chiefly *COMPUTING*. Out of action; in or into a state of being unavailable for use. M20.

Times The computer's down again.

▸ **VI 24** With ellipsis of verb of action (esp. *sit, lie*), *imper.*, & after aux. verbs. LME.

SHAKES. *Coriol.* Down, ladies, let us shame him with our knees. SHELLEY Long live Iona! down with Swellfoot! F. MARRYAT Down, Smoker, good dog! W. H. SMYTH Down oars! . . Down with the helm. R. BRIDGES That house . . That blocks the way must down.

– PHRASES: **be down on** (***a***) *arch. slang* understand, be wise to; (***b***) assail, fall upon; (***c***) disapprove of. **cash down** money paid at once, (as though) laid on a counter. ***do down***: see DO *verb*. **down along** *dial. & colloq.* in or to the West Country of England. **down-and-dirty** *colloq.* (***a***) unprincipled, devious, viciously competitive; (***b***) earthy, raunchy; rough, sleazy, gritty. **down and out** [with allus. to a boxer who is knocked out] beaten in the struggle of life, completely without resources or means of livelihood. ***down at heel***: see HEEL *noun*[1]. **down east, Down East** *N. Amer.* (in or into) the north-eastern coastal part of the US (esp. Maine) or the Maritime Provinces of Canada. ***down in the dumps***: see DUMP *noun*[1] 2. **down in the mouth** *colloq.* dejected, miserable. ***down on one's luck***: see LUCK *noun*. **down south** (in or into) the southern part of a country. **down to** (***a***) as far as (the lowest, smallest, least, or last item or member); (***b***) attributable to; (***c***) the responsibility of, up to. ***down to earth***: see EARTH *noun*[1]. ***down to the ground***: see GROUND *noun*. **down under, Down Under** *colloq.* (in or to) the antipodes, Australia or New Zealand. ***eyes down***: see EYE *noun*. ***hands down***: see HAND *noun*. ***hull down***: see HULL *noun*[2]. ***let one's hair down***: see HAIR *noun*. ***thumbs down***: see THUMB *noun*. ***two-up and two-down, two-up two-down***: see TWO *noun* 4. ***with one's PANTS down, with one's TROUSERS down***.
▸ **B** *attrib. adjective*. **1** Directed downwards; descending. M16. ▸**b** Of a train or coach: travelling away from the capital or principal terminus. Of a line or platform: used by such a train. M19.
†**2** Downright, positive. Only in E17.
3 That is in low spirits or poor health; lacking vigour. Now *rare* or *obsolete* exc. as *pred. adjective* (see DOWN *adverb* 19 above). M17. ▸**b** Causing or characterized by depression or low spirits or lack of vigour. *slang*. M20.

b T. LEARY Alcohol is a 'down' experience. It narrows consciousness and makes you rather sloppy. S. TUROW A down week with a couple of lighter spots.

4 Of a crossword clue or answer: that fills or is intended to fill the spaces along a vertical line of the puzzle. Cf. sense A.14 above. E20.
5 *PARTICLE PHYSICS*. Designating a *d* quark. Cf. UP *adjective*[1] 6. L20.
– SPECIAL COLLOCATIONS: **down lead** a wire connecting an elevated aerial to a receiver or transmitter. **down payment** an initial payment made at the time that something is bought on credit. **down timber** *N. Amer.* (timber from) fallen trees brought down by wind, storm, or other natural agency. See also DOWN-.
– NOTE: In *PARTICLE PHYSICS*, the symbols *d* and *u* (M20) appeared in print earlier than the descriptions *down* and *up* (cf. sense B.5 above).

down /daʊn/ *preposition*. LME.
[ORIGIN from DOWN *adverb*. Cf. ADOWN *preposition*.]
1 In a descending direction along, through, or into; from the top to the bottom of; from a higher to a lower part of. LME. ▸**b** At or in a lower part of. M18.

E. BOWEN For two-and-a-half hours, up hill, down dale, they had been rushing through cold scenery. M. AMIS I came down the steps. **b** M. B. KEATINGE In the timbered parts of France, down the Loire.

2 To or at a place regarded as lower than or as a lower part of; along the course or extent of. LME.

N. COX Some Hares will go up one side of the Hedge, and come down the other. V. WOOLF Endless avenues down which . . he might wander. A. PRICE Paris is only about seventy miles down the road. M. BRADBURY The Kirks . . believe in dividing all tasks equally down the middle, half for you, half for me.

3 (Down) to; (down) at. *colloq.* L19.

A. BUZO Been down the pub for lunch? W. FAULKNER When you are relieved, go down your dugout and stay there. R. RENDELL We've got more . . than they've got down the library.

– PHRASES: **down cellar** *N. Amer.* in or into the cellar. **down home** *N. Amer.* at or to one's home; see also DOWN-HOME. ***down one's street***: see STREET *noun*. **down the course** (of a horse) trailing some way behind the leaders in a race; **down the drain, down the pan** *colloq.* lost, wasted. **down the road** *N. Amer. colloq.* in the future, later on. **down the track** *Austral. & NZ slang* in the future, later on. **down the tube(s)** *colloq.* lost; wasted. **down town** into a town from a higher or outlying part (see also DOWNTOWN). ***right down one's street***: see STREET *noun*.

down- /daʊn/ *prefix*.
[ORIGIN Repr. DOWN *adverb, preposition*.]
Prefixed to nouns, adjectives, and verbs in various relations and in various senses, esp. indicating (***a***) position below, at a lower level (of), or further from the interior or source (of), as ***downhole, downrange, downside***; (***b***) motion or direction down, downwards, to a lower level (of), or further away from the interior or source (of), as ***downcurved, downpipe, downrate***.
■ **downbow** *noun* (*MUSIC*) a stroke in which a bow is drawn across a string from the heel to the tip L19. **downburst** *noun* a strong downward current of air from a cumulonimbus cloud, usu. associated with intense rain or a thunderstorm L20. **down-calving** *adjective* (of a cow or heifer) near the time of calving L19. **down-ˈchannel** *adverb & adjective* (moving, leading, etc.) towards the lower end of a channel M19. **downcoast** *adjective & adverb* (situated, extending, etc.) further down the coast L19. **downcourt** *adjective & adverb SPORT* to or into the opposite end of the court, esp. in basketball M20. **downcurrent** *noun* a descending current of air or water M19. **downcurved** *adjective* curved downwards M20. **down-dip** *adjective & adverb* (situated or occurring) in a direction downwards along the dip E20. **downdraught** *noun* (***a***) *Scot.* a ne'er-do-well, a profligate; a depressing influence; (***b***) a descending current of air, esp. down a chimney into a room: M19. **down-ˈeaster** *noun* (*N. Amer.*) a person who lives or was born Down East E19. **downface** *verb trans.* contradict, controvert; browbeat; outwit: E20. **downfault** *verb trans.* (*GEOLOGY*) move downwards in faulting M20. **downfold** *noun* (*GEOLOGY*) a syncline E20. **downforce** *noun* a force produced by a combination of air resistance and gravity which acts on a moving vehicle with the effect of pressing it down towards the ground and giving it increased stability L20. **downglide** *noun* (*PHONETICS*) a glide from a relatively high tone to a lower one M20. †**down-gyved** *adjective* (*rare*, Shakes.) hanging down like fetters: only in E17. **downhaul** *noun* (*NAUTICAL*) a rope by which a sail, spar, or flag is hauled down; a rope that stops the end of a spinnaker boom from lifting: M17. **down-ˈhome** *adjective* (chiefly *N. Amer.*) pertaining to, or reminiscent of, one's home; unaffected, unpretentious: E20. **downlight, downlighter** *nouns* a light placed or designed to throw illumination downwards M20. **downlink** *noun* a telecommunications link for signals coming from a spacecraft to earth L20. †**downlooked** *adjective* having downward or downcast looks, guilty-looking; demure: M17–E19. **downlooking** *adjective* that looks down L18. **downpipe** *noun* a pipe leading downwards, *esp.* one to carry rainwater from a roof to a drain M19. **downplay** *verb*

trans. play down, make little of M20. **downrange** *adverb & adjective* (situated or occurring) at a point along the course of a missile, spacecraft, etc., or beyond the (intended) landing place M20. **downset** *noun* †(***a***) *rare* a going down or setting (as) of the sun; (***b***) *Scot.* an establishment, a settlement; (***c***) *rare* a rebuke: E17. **downspout** *noun* (chiefly *US*) a downpipe from a roof L19. **down'stage** *adverb, adjective,* & (after prepositions) *noun* (at or towards, of or pertaining to) the front of a theatre stage L19. **downstart** *noun* [after *upstart*] a person who has descended to, or falsely claims to originate from, a humble social position L19. **down-street** *adverb* (*colloq. & dial.*) down the street; in, into, or towards the lower part of a town: E19. **downstroke** *noun* a downward stroke, esp. of a pen etc. on paper M19. **downsun** *adverb & adjective* in a direction away from the sun M20. **down-the-line** *adjective & noun* (***a***) *adjective* thorough, out and out; (***b***) *adjective & noun* (designating) trapshooting in which shooters stand at fixed firing positions along a straight line, and move to the next position on the line after a certain number of shots: M20. **down time** *noun* (***a***) time, or an occasion, when a machine, computer, or vehicle is out of action or not available for use; (***b***) (an opportunity for) time off; a rest: M20. **down-to-date** *adjective* up-to-date L19. **downtoner** *noun* (LINGUISTICS) an adjective or adverb which reduces the force of what it qualifies, or constitutes a weak or partial denial of it M20. **downtrend** *noun* a downward tendency, esp. in economic conditions E20. **downturn** *noun* a downward turn, esp. in economic conditions E20. **downwarp** *noun & verb* (GEOLOGY) (***a***) *noun* a gentle extensive depression of the earth's surface; (***b***) *verb trans. & intrans.* (cause to) undergo downwarping: E20. **downwarping** *noun* (GEOLOGY) the local sinking of the earth's surface to form a downwarp E20. **downwash** *noun* (AERONAUTICS) the downward deflection of an airstream by a wing etc. E20. **down'weigh** *verb trans.* weigh down, depress, (*lit. & fig.*); outweigh: E17. **downzone** *verb trans.* (*US*) assign (land, property) to a lower, more restrictive zoning grade M20.

down-and-out /'daʊnən(d)aʊt/ *noun. colloq.* E20.
[ORIGIN from ***down and out*** s.v. DOWN *adverb.*]
A person completely without resources or means of livelihood; a vagrant, a tramp.

> HUGH WALPOLE A down-and-out with holes in his boots. R. HARRIES Someone mentally holding her nose whilst coldly dishing out soup to a down-and-out.

▪ Also **down-and-outer** *noun* E20.

downbear /daʊn'bɛː/ *verb trans.* Now *rare.* Infl. as BEAR *verb*¹; pa. t. usu. **-bore** /-'bɔː/, pa. pple usu. **-borne** /-'bɔːn/. ME.
[ORIGIN from DOWN- + BEAR *verb*¹.]
Bear or press down, cause to sink, (*lit. & fig.*).

downbeat /'daʊnbiːt/ *noun & adjective.* L19.
[ORIGIN from DOWN- + BEAT *noun*¹.]
▸ **A** *noun.* A downward beat; MUSIC the first or most heavily accented beat of a measure (indicated by a conductor's downward beat). L19.
▸ **B** *adjective.* Pessimistic, gloomy; relaxed, unemphatic. M20.

downcast /'daʊnkɑːst/ *noun.* ME.
[ORIGIN from DOWN- + CAST *noun*¹.]
1 The action of casting down (*lit. & fig.*); destruction, ruin; the downward direction of a look; GEOLOGY = DOWNTHROW *noun* 2. ME.
2 The introduction of fresh air down a shaft into a mine; a shaft by which this is done (also ***downcast shaft***). M19.

downcast /'daʊnkɑːst/ *adjective.* E17.
[ORIGIN Partly from DOWN- + CAST *ppl adjective*, partly as pa. pple of DOWNCAST *verb.*]
1 Cast down, destroyed. Chiefly *fig.*, dispirited, depressed. E17.

> S. T. WARNER He'll get over it . . ; but just now he's dreadfully downcast. D. LODGE She was a bit downcast by this chilly reception.

2 Of a look, the eyes, etc.: directed downwards, lowered. E17.

> L. P. HARTLEY Her downcast eyes were bent in an ecstasy of maternal devotion on the doll.

downcast /daʊn'kɑːst/ *verb trans.* Now only *poet.* Pa. t. & pple **downcast**. ME.
[ORIGIN from DOWN- + CAST *verb.*]
Cast down (*lit. & fig.*); destroy, ruin; make dispirited, depress.

downcome /'daʊnkʌm/ *noun.* LME.
[ORIGIN from DOWN- + COME *verb*; cf. *income.*]
(A) downcoming; a downward swoop by a hawk or falcon.

downcomer /'daʊnkʌmə/ *noun.* M19.
[ORIGIN from DOWN- + COMER.]
A pipe for conveying gas, steam, etc., down from the top of a furnace or boiler; a downpipe.

downcoming /'daʊnkʌmɪŋ/ *ppl adjective.* M19.
[ORIGIN from DOWN- + COMING *adjective.*]
That comes down or onwards.

down-coming /'daʊnkʌmɪŋ/ *noun.* ME.
[ORIGIN from DOWN- + COMING *noun.*]
The action or an act of coming down (*lit. & fig.*); (a) descent; (a) downfall.

downconverter /'daʊnkənvəːtə/ *noun.* M20.
[ORIGIN from DOWN- + CONVERTER.]
ELECTRONICS. A device that downconverts a signal.
▪ **downconversion** *noun* conversion (of a signal) to a lower frequency, esp. in television reception M20. **downconvert** *verb trans.* subject to downconversion M20.

downcountry /'daʊnkʌntri, *as adjective & adverb also* daʊn'kʌntri/ *noun, adjective, & adverb.* E19.
[ORIGIN from DOWN- + COUNTRY.]
▸ **A** *noun.* In N. America, Australia, New Zealand, and other countries: *the* flat or low-lying part of the country as opp. to the hilly regions; *the* more densely settled regions. E19.
▸ **B** *adjective.* Situated in or pertaining to the downcountry; (of a person) from the downcountry. L19.
▸ **C** *adverb.* In, into, or towards the downcountry. L19.

downed /daʊnd/ *adjective.* E20.
[ORIGIN from DOWN *verb*¹, *noun*²: see -ED¹, -ED².]
Covered or lined with down.

downer /'daʊnə/ *noun*¹. *colloq.* E20.
[ORIGIN from DOWN *noun*³ + -ER⁶.]
= DOWN *noun*³ 4.

downer /'daʊnə/ *noun*². *slang.* M20.
[ORIGIN from DOWN *verb*² or *adverb* + -ER¹.]
1 A drug, esp. a barbiturate pill, with a depressant or tranquillizing effect. M20.
2 A depressing person or event; a failure. L20.

downfall /'daʊnfɔːl/ *noun.* ME.
[ORIGIN from DOWN- + FALL *noun*¹.]
1 (The cause of) a fall from prosperity, high estate, etc.; a person's ruin. ME.

> W. IRVING The downfall of his great expectations. R. P. GRAVES The . . intellectual arrogance which led to his downfall in Greats.

2 The action of falling down; sudden descent. Now *rare.* LME. ▸**b** A great fall of water; a downpour. E17.

> TENNYSON 'Tween the spring and downfall of the light.

3 A steep descent, a precipice; an abyss, a gulf, a pit. *obsolete* exc. *Scot.* M16.

downfall /'daʊnfɔːl/ *verb intrans.* Now chiefly *literary.* Pa. t. **-fell** /-fɛl/; pa. pple **-fallen** /-fɔːl(ə)n/. ME.
[ORIGIN from DOWN *adverb* + FALL *verb.*]
Fall down; have a downfall. Chiefly as ***downfallen*** *ppl adjective*, ***downfalling*** *verbal noun & ppl adjective.*

downfield /*as adverb* daʊn'fiːld, *as adjective* 'daʊnfiːld/ *adverb & adjective.* E20.
[ORIGIN from DOWN- + FIELD *noun.*]
▸ **A** *adverb.* **1** SPORT. = UPFIELD *adverb* 1. E20.
2 CHEMISTRY & PHYSICS. In a direction corresponding to a smaller field strength. M20.
▸ **B** *adjective.* **1** SPORT. = UPFIELD *adjective.* M20.
2 CHEMISTRY & PHYSICS. Situated of occurring in the direction of smaller field strengths. M20.

downgrade /'daʊngreɪd/ *noun.* Orig. *US.* M19.
[ORIGIN from DOWN- + GRADE *noun.*]
A downward gradient, esp. on a railway or road; a downward course (*lit. & fig.*).

> M. RENAULT A steep downgrade for which he had put the car in second. *Sun (Baltimore)* Profits are on the downgrade.

downgrade /'daʊngreɪd, daʊn'greɪd/ *verb trans.* M20.
[ORIGIN from the noun.]
Lower in rank, grade, status, or estimation; demote; belittle.

> A. LURIE Kenneth's odd lack of sympathy with people's love affairs . . , his tendency to rather downgrade that side of things. *Times* Brokers Laing & Cruickshank . . has now downgraded its estimate for the year from £18m to £15m.

downhearted /daʊn'hɑːtɪd/ *adjective.* M17.
[ORIGIN from DOWN *adjective* + HEART *noun* + -ED².]
In low spirits, discouraged, dejected.
▪ **downheartedly** *adverb* M17. **downheartedness** *noun* E19.

downhill /*as noun & attrib. adjective* 'daʊnhɪl; *as adverb & pred. adjective* daʊn'hɪl/ *noun, adverb, & adjective.* M16.
[ORIGIN from DOWN- + HILL *noun.*]
▸ **A** *noun.* **1** The downward slope of a hill; a decline, a descent, (*lit. & fig.*). M16.
downhill of life the later half of life.
†**2** In *pl.* False dice which give low numbers. *slang.* L17–E19.
3 SKIING. A downhill race. M20.
▸ **B** *adverb & adjective.* **1** *adverb* & (after *be* or other copula) *pred. adjective.* Down a slope, esp. of a hill; in a descending direction; on a decline, downwards, (*lit. & fig.*); in a worsening situation; in a situation free of difficulty or impediments. E17.

> E. BOWEN The road coming downhill from the north-west turned south. R. ADAMS A stone rolled downhill. *Gay News* From this point it is downhill all the way: a host of deprivations and disasters. *Guardian* It was downhill from then on, though it actually took a year to secure the country completely.

go downhill *fig.* deteriorate.

2 *attrib. adjective.* Sloping or descending downwards; declining (*lit. & fig.*); occurring down a slope, esp. of a hill. E18.

> J. A. FROUDE The monks had travelled swiftly on the downhill road of human corruption. *Globe & Mail (Toronto)* The dangerous downhill pistes of Europe.

▪ **down'hiller** *noun* a skier who takes part in downhill races M20.

downhole /*as adjective* 'daʊnhəʊl, *as adverb* daʊn'həʊl/ *adjective & adverb.* M20.
[ORIGIN from DOWN- + HOLE *noun*¹.]
Chiefly OIL INDUSTRY. ▸**A** *adjective.* Used, occurring, or performed down or in a well or hole drilled in the earth's surface. M20.
▸ **B** *adverb.* Down or in a drilled hole or well. M20.

D

Downing Street /'daʊnɪŋ striːt/ *noun phr.* L18.
[ORIGIN A street in London containing the official residence of the Prime Minister and the Foreign and Commonwealth Office, from Sir George *Downing* (c 1624–84), English diplomat and owner of the site.]
The British Government; the Prime Minister; (formerly) the Foreign and Commonwealth Office.

downish /'daʊnɪʃ/ *adjective.* L17.
[ORIGIN from DOWN *adjective* + -ISH¹.]
Somewhat downcast.

down-lie /daʊn'lʌɪ/ *verb intrans.* Now *rare* exc. *N. English.* Pa. t. **-lay** /-'leɪ/, pa. pple **-lain** /-'leɪn/, pres. pple **-lying** /-'lʌɪɪŋ/. E16.
[ORIGIN from DOWN- + LIE *verb*¹.]
Lie down, go to bed. Also, be in labour, give birth. Chiefly as ***down-lying*** *verbal noun & ppl adjective.*

download *verb & noun.* L20.
[ORIGIN from DOWN- + LOAD *verb.*]
▸ **A** *verb trans.* Copy (data) from one computer system to another or to a disk. L20.

> *Popular Science* Customers can download music directly to their portable MP3 players.

▸ **B** *noun.* The action or process of copying data in such a way; a computer file transferred in such a way. L20.

> T. CLANCY With the download complete, she made sure she'd backed it up.

▪ **downloadable** *adjective.* L20.

down-low /'daʊnləʊ/ *noun. US black slang.* L20.
[ORIGIN from DOWN *adjective* + LOW *adjective.*]
on the down-low, on the quiet, in secret; *spec.* (of a man) engaging in secretive homosexual activity.

downmarket /*as adjective* 'daʊnmɑːkɪt, *as adverb* daʊn'mɑːkɪt/ *adjective & adverb.* L20.
[ORIGIN from DOWN- + MARKET *noun.*]
▸ **A** *adjective.* Of or relating to the cheaper end of the market; cheap, with popular appeal. L20.
▸ **B** *adverb.* Towards the cheaper end of the market. L20.

downmost /'daʊnməʊst/ *adverb & adjective.* L18.
[ORIGIN from DOWN *adverb & adjective* + -MOST.]
Furthest down.

downpour /'daʊnpɔː/ *noun.* E19.
[ORIGIN from (the same root as) DOWNPOUR *verb.*]
A pouring down; *esp.* a heavy fall of rain.

downpour /daʊn'pɔː/ *verb intrans. & trans.* L18.
[ORIGIN from DOWN- + POUR *verb.*]
Pour downwards.

> J. CARROLL Colman let his hand wind through her downpouring hair.

downrate /daʊn'reɪt/ *verb trans.* M20.
[ORIGIN from DOWN- + RATE *verb*¹.]
Reduce the rating of, downgrade; decrease the size, value, or performance of.

downright /'daʊnrʌɪt; *also* (*as following adverb*) daʊn'rʌɪt/ *adverb, adjective, & noun.* ME.
[ORIGIN Aphet. from ADOWNRIGHT.]
▸ **A** *adverb.* †**1** Straight down; vertically downwards. ME–M18.

> POPE He . . Shot to the black abyss, and plung'd downright.

2 Thoroughly, absolutely, positively. Usu. foll. by adjective or ppl adjective. ME.

> R. FALCONER Killed four downright. D. PIPER When one compromises in art, the results are often artistically mediocre if not downright bad.

†**3** In a direct or straightforward manner; plainly, definitely. Only in 17.

> SHAKES. *A.Y.L.* You have heard him swear downright he was.

†**4** At once, immediately. M17–E18.
▸ **B** *adjective.* **1** Directed straight downwards; vertical; directly descending. M16.

> BUNYAN He gave him again a down-right blow, and brought him upon his knees.

2 That is thoroughly or entirely the thing specified; out-and-out, positive; nothing less than. M16.

B. Jowett He is a downright atheist. B. Bettelheim The number of inadequacies and downright errors in the translations is enormous.

3 Plain, definite, straightforward; not circuitous; (of a person's speech or behaviour) so direct as to be blunt. **E17.**

R. G. Collingwood Hobbes accepted the same position and stated it, with his usual trenchancy, in a more downright form. H. E. Bates A true downright Evensford character who . . did not care a damn for her or anyone else.

▸ **C** *noun.* †**1** A vertical line, a perpendicular. Only in **L17.**

D

2 In *pl.* A grade of wool next above seconds in some classifications. **L18.**

■ **downrightly** *adverb* **M17.** **downrightness** *noun* **E17.**

downriver /*as adverb* daʊnˈrɪvə, *as adjective* ˈdaʊnrɪvə/ *adverb & adjective.* **M19.**

[**ORIGIN** from **DOWN-** + **RIVER** *noun*[1].]

▸ **A** *adverb.* Away from the source of a river. **M19.**

▸ **B** *adjective.* Situated or occurring further down a river; leading or directed away from the source of a river. **L19.**

downrush /ˈdaʊnrʌʃ/ *noun.* **M19.**

[**ORIGIN** from **DOWN-** + **RUSH** *noun*[2].]

A downward rush; a rapid descent.

Down's /daʊnz/ *noun. colloq.* exc. *attrib.* **L20.**

[**ORIGIN** Abbreviation.]

= **DOWN'S SYNDROME.**

downscale /ˈdaʊnskeɪl/ *adjective & verb. US.* **M20.**

[**ORIGIN** from **DOWN-** + **SCALE** *noun*[4], *verb*[2].]

▸ **A** *adjective.* At the lower end of the social scale; of low quality; downmarket. **M20.**

▸ **B** *verb trans.* Reduce the scale of, scale down. **M20.**

downshift *noun & verb.* **M19.**

[**ORIGIN** from **DOWN-** + **SHIFT** *noun.*]

▸ **A** *noun.* **1** A movement downwards; a downward change or tendency. **M19.**

2 A change to a lower gear in a motor vehicle or bicycle. **M20.**

3 An instance of changing a financially rewarding but stressful career or lifestyle for a less pressured but more fulfilling one. **L20.**

▸ **B** *verb intrans.* **1** Change to a lower gear in a motor vehicle or bicycle. **M20.** ▸**b** Slow down; slacken off. **M20.**

2 Change a financially rewarding but stressful career or lifestyle for a less pressured and less highly paid but more fulfilling one. **L20.**

downside /ˈdaʊnsʌɪd/ *noun, adverb, & adjective.* **L17.**

[**ORIGIN** from **DOWN-** + **SIDE** *noun.*]

▸ **A** *noun.* **1** The underside. Only in ***downside up.*** **L17.**

2 A risk of falling in value; a downward trend or movement; a negative aspect of something; a drawback. **M20.**

Times There is little downside in the shares. *Daily Express* The political downside . . exceeds anything positive that could come out of it.

on the downside falling in value.

▸ **B** *adverb.* Upside down, downwards. **M19.**

▸ **C** *adjective.* (At risk of) falling in value; negative in aspect; constituting a drawback. **M20.**

National Observer (US) What is the upside potential contrasted with the downside risk?

downsize /ˈdaʊnsʌɪz/ *verb trans.* Orig. *US.* **L20.**

[**ORIGIN** from **DOWN-** + **SIZE** *verb*[1].]

Make (something) smaller; *spec.* (***a***) design or build (a car) of smaller overall dimensions, esp. without reducing interior capacity; (***b***) **COMMERCE** make (a company or organization) smaller by shedding staff.

R. Gervais & S. Merchant Jennifer is talking of either downsizing Swindon branch or this branch.

downslope /ˈdaʊnsləʊp/ *noun, adverb, & adjective.* **E20.**

[**ORIGIN** from **DOWN-** + **SLOPE** *noun*[1].]

▸ **A** *noun.* A downward slope. **E20.**

▸ **B** *adverb.* At or towards a lower point on a slope. **E20.**

▸ **C** *adjective.* Caused by, occurring, or acting on a downward slope; descending. **M20.**

Downsman /ˈdaʊnzmən/ *noun.* Pl. **-men.** **E20.**

[**ORIGIN** from **DOWN** *noun*[1] + **-S**[1] + **MAN** *noun.*]

A man who lives on or is a native of the Sussex Downs.

Down's syndrome /ˈdaʊnz sɪndrəʊm/ *noun phr.* Also **Down syndrome** /ˈdaʊn sɪndrəʊm/. **M20.**

[**ORIGIN** J. H. L. *Down*, English physician (1828–96).]

A congenital condition (usu. due to an extra chromosome) causing intellectual impairment and physical abnormalities including short stature and a broad facial profile.

– **NOTE:** The term is now used in preference to the older *mongolism*, which is considered offensive.

downstairs /ˈdaʊnstɛːz/ *adjective.* Also **-stair** /-stɛː/. **E19.**

[**ORIGIN** from **DOWNSTAIRS** *adverb & noun.*]

Situated or occurring downstairs or below stairs.

M. R. Mitford Her down-stair life was less happy. W. Faulkner He looked through a downstairs window.

downstairs /daʊnˈstɛːz; *as noun also* ˈdaʊnstɛːz/ *adverb & noun.* **L16.**

[**ORIGIN** from **DOWN** *preposition* + **STAIR** + **-S**[1].]

▸ **A** *adverb.* Down the stairs; to, on, or of the ground floor or lower floors of a house etc. **L16.**

E. Waugh All I possess . . is downstairs in your hall. E. J. Howard To stay downstairs after the others had all gone up to bed.

▸ **B** *noun.* The ground floor or lower floors of a house etc. **M19.**

New Yorker When the children grew up they would often be given the downstairs to live in.

downstate /ˈdaʊnsteɪt/ *noun, adverb, & adjective. US.* **E20.**

[**ORIGIN** from **DOWN-** + **STATE** *noun.*]

▸ **A** *noun.* The region of a state remote from large cities, a rural area. **E20.**

▸ **B** *adverb.* In or to the part of a state remote from large cities, esp. the southern part. **M20.**

▸ **C** *adjective.* Of, pertaining to, or characteristic of an area downstate; situated downstate. **M20.**

■ **downstater** *noun* a person from downstate **E20.**

downstream /*as adverb* daʊnˈstriːm; *as adjective* ˈdaʊnstriːm/ *adverb & adjective.* **L18.**

[**ORIGIN** from **DOWN-** + **STREAM** *noun.*]

▸ **A** *adverb.* **1** In the direction in which a stream or river flows. **L18.**

2 **BIOLOGY.** Towards the part of a sequence of genetic material where transcription takes place later than at a given point. Opp. **UPSTREAM** *adverb* 3. **L20.**

▸ **B** *adjective.* **1** Situated or occurring downstream. **M19.**

2 **OIL INDUSTRY.** Pertaining to, involved in, or designating activities other than exploration and extraction. **M20.**

down-swept /ˈdaʊnswɛpt/ *adjective.* **E20.**

[**ORIGIN** from **DOWN-** + **SWEPT** *ppl adjective.*]

Having a downward sweep, curved downwards.

downswing /ˈdaʊnswɪŋ/ *noun.* **L19.**

[**ORIGIN** from **DOWN-** + **SWING** *noun*[1].]

1 **GOLF.** The descending movement of the club when a player is about to hit the ball. **L19.**

2 (A period marked by) a downward trend, esp. in economic conditions. **M20.**

Down syndrome *noun phr.* var. of **DOWN'S SYNDROME.**

downtempo /daʊnˈtɛmpəʊ/ *adjective & adverb.* **M20.**

[**ORIGIN** from **DOWN-** + **TEMPO** *noun*[1].]

MUSIC. At or having a slow tempo.

downthrew *verb pa. t.*: see **DOWNTHROW** *verb.*

downthrow /ˈdaʊnθrəʊ/ *noun.* **E17.**

[**ORIGIN** from **DOWN-** + **THROW** *noun*[2].]

1 A throwing or being thrown down; an overthrow, a downfall. *rare.* **E17.**

2 **GEOLOGY.** The downward movement of strata on one side of a fault; the extent of this. **M19.**

downthrow /daʊnˈθrəʊ/ *verb.* Infl. as **THROW** *verb*; pa. t. usu. **-threw** /-ˈθruː/, pa. pple usu. **-thrown** /-ˈθrəʊn/. **L16.**

[**ORIGIN** from **DOWN-** + **THROW** *verb.*]

1 *verb trans.* Throw down, overthrow; **GEOLOGY** cause to sink in relation to adjacent rocks. **L16.**

2 *verb intrans.* **GEOLOGY.** Give rise to a downthrow; sink. **L20.**

downtown /*as adverb* daʊnˈtaʊn; *as adjective or noun* ˈdaʊntaʊn/ *adverb, adjective, & noun.* Chiefly *N. Amer.* **E19.**

[**ORIGIN** from **DOWN-** + **TOWN** *noun.*]

▸ **A** *adverb.* In or into the lower or more central part or the business part of a town or city. **E19.**

R. Jaffe Let's go downtown to the doughnut shop.

▸ **B** *adjective.* Situated or occurring downtown; pertaining to or characteristic of such an area. **M19.**

B. Ulanov Squalid little towns in downtown New York.

▸ **C** *noun.* The downtown part of a town or city; a downtown area. **M19.**

Globe & Mail (Toronto) A . . property just 18 minutes to downtown. *Billings (Montana) Gazette* Designers . . have long warned the downtowns were doomed.

■ **down'towner** *noun* an inhabitant or frequenter of a downtown area **M19.**

downtrodden /ˈdaʊntrɒd(ə)n/ *adjective & pa. pple.* **M16.**

[**ORIGIN** from **DOWN-** + **TRODDEN.**]

1 Trampled down; beaten down (as) by treading. **M16.**

Longfellow The flowers, downtrodden by the wind.

2 Crushed by oppression or tyranny; oppressed, kept under. **L16.**

J. Martineau The downtrodden serfs of Franconia. R. P. Graves Although quiet and studious, Alfred was not downtrodden by any of the boys for long.

■ Also **'downtrod** *adjective & pa. pple* **M16.**

downward /ˈdaʊnwəd/ *adverb, adjective, & preposition.* **ME.**

[**ORIGIN** Aphet. from **ADOWNWARD.**]

▸ **A** *adverb.* **1** = **DOWNWARDS** 1. **ME.**

2 = **DOWNWARDS** 2. **ME.**

3 = **DOWNWARDS** 3. **E17.**

▸ **B** *adjective.* **1** Lying or situated below; lower. *rare.* **ME.**

Dryden Aurora . . lights the downward Heav'n.

2 Directed, moving, extending, pointing, leading, etc., towards what is lower; inclined downward. **M16.**

E. A. Freeman Steps in a downward scale. T. H. Huxley The downward current of the river. *National Observer (US)* With our new downward mobility, the quasi marriage is apt to be a . . college-bred phenomenon.

▸ †**C** *preposition.* = **DOWN** *preposition* 1. *rare.* Only in **LME.**

■ **downwardly** *adverb* (***downwardly***: see **MOBILE** *adjective* 4) **M19.** **downwardness** *noun* **M19.**

downwards /ˈdaʊnwədz/ *adverb.* **LME.**

[**ORIGIN** from **DOWNWARD**: see **-WARDS.**]

1 Towards a lower place or position; towards what is below; with a descending motion or tendency. **LME.**

R. Lehmann Small, thick writing, . . running downwards on the page. V. Woolf She ferreted in her bag; then held it up mouth downwards. M. Sinclair From his nose and cheek-bones downwards his beard hung straight.

2 Towards something which is lower in order, inferior, or less important. **M17.**

Television Teletext improvements have to be downwards compatible so that older decoders will receive something recognisable.

3 Onward from an earlier to a later time. **L19.**

L. O. Pike From the time of Glanville downwards.

downwell /*as adjective* ˈdaʊnwɛl, *as adverb* daʊnˈwɛl/ *adjective & adverb.* **M20.**

[**ORIGIN** from **DOWN-** + **WELL** *noun*[1].]

OIL INDUSTRY. ▸**A** *adjective.* = **DOWNHOLE** *adjective.* **M20.**

▸ **B** *adverb.* = **DOWNHOLE** *adverb.* **L20.**

downwell /daʊnˈwɛl/ *verb intrans.* **M20.**

[**ORIGIN** from **DOWN-** after *upwell.*]

Of seawater etc.: sink in a downward current.

■ **downwelling** *noun* downward movement of fluid in the sea or the atmosphere; a downward current: **M20.**

downwind /daʊnˈwɪnd/ *adverb & adjective.* Also as two words. **E19.**

[**ORIGIN** from **DOWN-** + **WIND** *noun*[1].]

▸ **A** *adverb.* In the direction of the wind. **E19.**

▸ **B** *adjective.* Occurring or situated downwind. **L19.**

■ **downwinder** *noun* (chiefly *US*) a person living downwind of a nuclear test site or nuclear reactor, and (liable to be) affected by fallout or radiation leaks **L20.**

downy /ˈdaʊni/ *noun. slang.* **E19.**

[**ORIGIN** from **DOWNY** *adjective*[1].]

†**1** A shrewd, sharp, or knowing person. Only in **E19.**

2 A bed. **M19.**

do the downy lie in bed.

downy /ˈdaʊni/ *adjective*[1]. **M16.**

[**ORIGIN** from **DOWN** *noun*[2] + **-Y**[1]. In sense 5 also infl. by **DOWN** *adverb* 22.]

1 Covered with down, esp. as a distinguishing epithet of plants and animals or as connoting youth, immaturity, or innocence. **M16.**

H. Keller Large, downy peaches. R. Kipling It brought not the faintest flush to Stalky's downy cheek.

downy birch: see **BIRCH** *noun.* **downy woodpecker** a small black and white woodpecker, *Picoides pubescens*, of N. America.

2 Of the nature of or like down; feathery; fluffy. **L16.**

R. H. Dana Thick downy feathers, taken from the breasts of various birds. Sherwood Anderson His eyebrows, and the downy beard . . were pale.

downy mildew mildew marked by a whitish down composed of fungal sporangiophores or conidiophores and penetrating more deeply into the plant than powdery mildew; a lower fungus of the family Peronosporaceae which causes this.

3 Made of or containing down. **L16.**

Pope Belinda still her downy pillow prest.

4 Soft and yielding as down. **E17.**

E. Young Time steals on with downy Feet.

5 Shrewd, sharp, knowing. *slang.* **E19.**

M. E. Braddon You're the downiest bird—I beg your pardon, the cleverest woman I ever met with.

■ **downily** *adverb* (*rare*) **M19.** **downiness** *noun* **L17.**

downy /ˈdaʊni/ *adjective*[2]. **L17.**

[**ORIGIN** from **DOWN** *noun*[1] + **-Y**[1].]

Of the nature of a down or downland; characterized by downs.

J. L. Motley A rolling, downy country.

dowry /ˈdaʊ(ə)ri/ *noun.* **ME.**

[**ORIGIN** Anglo-Norman *dowarie* = Old French & mod. French *douaire* **DOWER.**]

†**1** = **DOWER** *noun* 1. **ME–M19.**

2 Property or money brought by a bride to her husband; the portion given with the bride. **LME.**

3 A present made by a man to the father of his prospective bride as a condition of her being allowed to marry. Formerly, a present given by one spouse to the other. **LME.**

4 = **DOWER** *noun* 3. **LME.**

†5 The property or endowment of a church. LME–L15.
■ **dowryless** *adjective* E20.

Dowsabel /ˈdaʊsəbɛl/ *noun*. Long *arch*. L16.
[ORIGIN Alt. (through French) of female forename *Dulcibella*.]
A sweetheart, a pet. Freq. as a form of address.

dowse /daʊz/ *verb*[1] *intrans*. L17.
[ORIGIN Unknown.]
Search for hidden water, mineral deposits, etc., by passing a forked stick or rod over the surface of the ground under which it is hoped to find them, so that it might dip suddenly when brought over the right spot.
– COMB.: **dowsing rod** a forked stick or rod which is held in the hands and passed over the surface of the ground in dowsing; also called *divining rod*.
■ **dowser** *noun* a person who dowses, or has the gift of dowsing M19.

dowse *verb*[2] var. of DOUSE *verb*[1].

dowset *noun* var. of DOUCET *noun*.

dowt *verb & noun* see DOUT.

doxographer /dɒkˈsɒɡrəfə/ *noun*. L19.
[ORIGIN from Greek *doxa* opinion + -O- + -GRAPHER.]
A writer who collected and recorded the opinions of the ancient Greek philosophers.
■ **doxoˈgraphic** *adjective* of or pertaining to (the work of) a doxographer or the doxographers M20. **doxoˈgraphical** *adjective* = DOXOGRAPHIC L19. **doxography** *noun* the branch of knowledge that deals with doxographic writings; a collection of doxographic writings: M20.

doxology /dɒkˈsɒlədʒi/ *noun*. Also **D-**. M17.
[ORIGIN medieval Latin *doxologia* from Greek, from *doxa* expectation, opinion, repute, glory, from *dokein*: see DOCETIC, -OLOGY.]
CHRISTIAN CHURCH. †**1** The utterance of praise to God, thanksgiving. Only in M17.
2 A liturgical formula of praise to God. M17.

Daily Telegraph The doxology which has been commonly added to the Lord's Prayer since the second century.

Greater Doxology the *Gloria in excelsis*. **Lesser Doxology** the *Gloria Patri*.
■ **doxoˈlogical** *adjective* pertaining to or of the nature of a doxology M17. **doxoˈlogically** *adverb* L19. **doxologize** *verb* (*a*) *verb intrans*. say a doxology; (*b*) *verb trans*. address a doxology to: E18.

doxorubicin /dɒksəʊˈruːbɪsɪn/ *noun*. L20.
[ORIGIN from D(E)OX(Y- + -O- + Latin *rubus* red + -I- + -MY)CIN.]
An antibiotic produced by a streptomycete and used to treat leukaemia and various tumours, including cancer.

doxy /ˈdɒksi/ *noun*[1]. *arch*. or *joc*. (orig. *slang*). M16.
[ORIGIN Unknown.]
Orig., a beggar's female companion. Now, a mistress or girlfriend; a prostitute or promiscuous woman.

doxy /ˈdɒksi/ *noun*[2]. *arch*. *joc*. M18.
[ORIGIN from *orthodoxy*, *heterodoxy*, etc.]
Opinion, esp. on theological matters.

doxycycline /dɒksɪˈsʌɪkliːn/ *noun*. M20.
[ORIGIN from D(E)OXY- + TETRA)CYCLINE.]
A broad-spectrum antibiotic of the tetracycline group which has a long half-life in the body.

doyen /ˈdɔɪən, ˈdwɑːjã/ *noun*. LME.
[ORIGIN French: see DEAN *noun*[1].]
†**1** A leader or commander of ten. *rare*. Only in LME.
2 The most senior or most prominent of a particular category or body of people. L17.

C. R. ATTLEE Smuts was the doyen and the only one of us who had taken part in the conduct of the First World War. J. GROSS Saintsbury had become generally accepted as the doyen of academic critics, the nearest thing to a Critic Laureate.

Doyenne /dwɑːˈjɛn/ *noun*[1]. Also **Doyenné** /dwɑːˈjɛneɪ/. M18.
[ORIGIN French (*poire de*) *doyenné* deanery (pear), formed as DOYEN.]
Any of several varieties of dessert pear.
Doyenne du Comice /duː kɒˈmiːs/ [French: see COMICE] a large yellow late-fruiting variety of dessert pear that is a favourite for cultivation.

doyenne /ˈdɔɪɛn, dɔɪˈɛn, dwɑːˈjɛn/ *noun*[2]. M19.
[ORIGIN French, fem. of DOYEN.]
A female doyen.

doyley *noun* var. of DOILY.

doylt *adjective* var. of DOILED.

doyly *noun* var. of DOILY.

doz. /dʌz/ *noun*. L19.
[ORIGIN Abbreviation.]
= DOZEN *noun*.

doze /dəʊz/ *verb*[1] & *noun*. M17.
[ORIGIN Unknown: perh. earlier in dialect use. Cf. Danish *døse* make drowsy.]
▸ **A** *verb*. **1** *verb trans*. Stupefy, muddle; make drowsy or dull; bewilder, perplex. *obsolete* exc. *Scot*. *dial*. M17.

DEFOE The tobacco had . . dozed my head.

2 *verb intrans*. Sleep drowsily, be half asleep; fall into a light sleep. L17.

R. B. SHERIDAN I have been dozing over a stupid book. M. SHADBOLT He dozed uneasily, in fits and starts.

doze off fall lightly asleep.
3 *verb trans*. Foll. by *away*, *out*: pass or spend (time) in dozing. L17.
▸ **B** *noun*. A spell of dozing; a short light sleep. M18.
■ **dozed** *ppl adjective* (*a*) stupefied, drowsy; (*b*) (of timber) decayed inside: M17. **dozedness** *noun* (now *rare*) drowsiness, sleepiness M17.

doze /dəʊz/ *verb*[2] *trans*. *colloq*. M20.
[ORIGIN Back-form. from DOZER *noun*[2].]
Clear, level, or move, with a bulldozer; use a bulldozer on.

dozen /ˈdʌz(ə)n/ *noun & adjective* (in mod. usage functioning like a *determiner*). ME.
[ORIGIN Old French *dozeine*, *-aine* (mod. *douzaine*) from Proto-Romance, ult. from Latin *duodecim* twelve.]
▸ **A** *noun*. Pl. same (after a numeral or quantifier), **-s**.
1 A group or set of twelve or *colloq*. approximately twelve (*of* a particular class). ME. ▸**b** In *pl*. As many as might number a few dozen; a lot *of*. *colloq*. M18. ▸**c** A dozen lashes of the whip. M19. ▸**d** *the dozens*, an exchange of insults, usu. about the other person's mother or family, engaged in as a game or ritual among black Americans. Freq. in *play the dozens*. E20.

D. L. SAYERS And another dozen of Bass while it settles. G. B. SHAW She wants him to buy her another dozen. W. FAULKNER A face, then three, then a dozen, turned to look at him. **b** D. H. LAWRENCE Dozens of men were lounging round the cart.

a dime a dozen: see DIME 2. *baker's dozen*: see BAKER. **by the dozen** in large quantities. **daily dozen** *colloq*. physical exercises done daily on rising. **devil's dozen** thirteen. *half a dozen*: see HALF *adjective*. *half-dozen*: see HALF-. **long dozen** thirteen. *rump and dozen*: see RUMP *noun*. *talk nineteen to the dozen*: see TALK *verb*.
†**2** A kind of kersey. Usu. in *pl*. LME–E18.
†**3** The town council of a borough. *Scot*. LME–L16.
▸ **B** *adjective*. After an article, numeral, or quantifier: twelve. LME.

M. AYRTON There are a dozen small bronzes.

■ **dozenth** *adjective* twelfth E18.

dozen /ˈdəʊz(ə)n/ *verb intrans*. *Scot*. & *N. English*. E18.
[ORIGIN Back-form. from DOZENED.]
Become torpid, numb, or stiff with cold.

dozened /ˈdəʊz(ə)nd/ *adjective*. *Scot*. & *N. English*. LME.
[ORIGIN Unknown.]
1 Stupefied, dazed. LME.
2 Torpid; numb; stiff with cold. L16.

dozener /ˈdʌz(ə)nə/ *noun*. M16.
[ORIGIN Prob. from Anglo-Norman *doseyner* from *dizeiner*, Old French *disenier* (mod. *dizenier*) leader of ten (cf. DECENER), from Old French & mod. French DIX + *-ain* from Latin *-eni*: see -ER[2].]
hist. The constable or other officer of a borough in some localities.

dozer /ˈdəʊzə/ *noun*[1]. E18.
[ORIGIN from DOZE *verb*[1] + -ER[1].]
A person who dozes.

dozer /ˈdəʊzə/ *noun*[2]. *colloq*. M20.
[ORIGIN Abbreviation.]
= BULLDOZER.

dozy /ˈdəʊzi/ *adjective & noun*. L17.
[ORIGIN from DOZE *verb*[1] + -Y[1].]
▸ **A** *adjective*. **1** Sleepy, drowsy; *colloq*. slow on the uptake, stupid, lazy. L17.
2 Of timber or fruit: in a state of incipient decay. L19.
▸ **B** *noun*. A dozy person. *colloq*. M19.
■ **dozily** *adverb* M19. **doziness** *noun* L17.

dozzle /ˈdɒz(ə)l/ *noun*. M20.
[ORIGIN Unknown.]
A hollow heat-resistant brick fitted to the top of an ingot mould to provide a reservoir of molten metal, which flows downward to fill cavities in the ingot.
■ Also **dozzler** *noun* E20.

dozzle /ˈdɒz(ə)l/ *verb trans*. Long *obsolete* exc. *dial*. M17.
[ORIGIN Frequentative of DOZE *verb*[1]: see -LE[3].]
Make stupid; stupefy.

DP *abbreviation*.
1 Data processing.
2 Displaced person.

D.Phil. *abbreviation*.
Doctor of Philosophy.

dpi *abbreviation*.
COMPUTING. Dots per inch, a measure of the resolution of printers, scanners, etc.

DPP *abbreviation*.
Director of Public Prosecutions.

DPT *abbreviation*.
Diphtheria, pertussis, and tetanus, a combined vaccine given to young children.

Dr *abbreviation*.
Doctor.

Dr. *abbreviation*[1].
Drive (in addresses).

dr. *abbreviation*[2].
1 Drachm(s).
2 Drachma(s).
3 Dram(s).

drab /drab/ *noun*[1]. *arch*. E16.
[ORIGIN Perh. from Dutch or Low German; cf. Dutch *drab* dregs, Low German *drabbe* thick dirty liquid, *drabbig* muddy. Cf. DRABBLE.]
1 An unkempt or untidy woman. E16.

BETTY SMITH He was so handsome that Francie felt like a dark drab alongside of him.

2 A prostitute. M16.
■ **drabbish** *adjective*[1] M16. **drabby** *adjective*[1] E17.

D

drab /drab/ *noun*[2] & *adjective*. M16.
[ORIGIN Prob. alt. of Old French *drap* cloth: see DRAPE *verb*. Cf. DRAP-DE-BERRY.]
▸ **A** *noun*. **I 1** Any of various undyed cloths of a dull neutral colour. M16.
▸ **II** [absol. use of the adjective]
2 A dull light brown colour; cloth or clothing, *esp*. (in *pl*.) breeches, of this colour. E19.

M. R. MITFORD Woe to white gowns! Woe to black! Drab was your only wear.

3 Any of various dull-coloured moths. E19.
4 In *pl*. The long wing feathers of a female ostrich near the junction with the body. *S. Afr*. L19.
5 A dull or lifeless character or appearance; monotony. E20.

Westminster Gazette The one sustained note of colour in the dreary drab of Irish life.

▸ **B** *adjective*. Compar. & superl. **-bb-**.
1 Of a dull light brown colour. L18.

G. DOWNES The cottages . . were of a deep drab hue.

2 Dull, monotonous; lacking brightness or colour. L19.

J. BUCHAN Sansculottes who sought to . . reduce the great to a drab level of mediocrity. A. EDEN In the cold and rain of mid-winter the prospect was drab and dour.

■ **drabbiness** *noun* the state or quality of being drabby L19. **drabbish** *adjective*[2] somewhat drab in colour or appearance M19. **drabby** *adjective*[2] rather drab, drabbish M19. **drably** *adverb* L19. **drabness** *noun* L19.

drab /drab/ *noun*[3]. Long *rare*. M18.
[ORIGIN Unknown.]
A wooden case with a sloping bottom in which the remaining liquid was separated from salt after boiling.

drab /drab/ *noun*[4]. E19.
[ORIGIN Perh. redupl. of DRIB *noun*.]
A small or petty amount. Chiefly in *dribs and drabs* (see DRIB *noun*).

drab /drab/ *verb intrans*. *arch*. Infl. **-bb-**. L16.
[ORIGIN from DRAB *noun*[1].]
Associate with prostitutes, whore.

draba /ˈdreɪbə/ *noun*. Also **D-**. E17.
[ORIGIN mod. Latin from Greek *drabē* kind of cress.]
Any cruciferous plant of the genus *Draba*, comprising spring-flowering alpines.

drabant /drəˈbant/ *noun*. *obsolete* exc. *hist*. E18.
[ORIGIN Swedish (= German *Trabant*, Italian *trabante*, French *traban*, *draban*, Czech & Polish *drabant*, Hungarian *darabont*, Romanian *dorobant*) ult. from Turkish *derban* from Persian *darbān* porter, guard. Cf. TRABANT.]
A halberdier; a member of the Swedish monarch's bodyguard.

drabbet /ˈdrabɪt, drəˈbɛt/ *noun*. E19.
[ORIGIN from DRAB *noun*[2] + -ET[1].]
A coarse drab linen formerly used for workmen's clothes.

drabble /ˈdrab(ə)l/ *verb intrans*. & *trans*. LME.
[ORIGIN Low German *drabbelen* walk or paddle in water or mire: cf. DRAB *noun*[1], -LE[3].]
Become or make dirty and wet by contact with water or mud.

R. KIPLING The sad valleys all drabbled with rain.

drabbler /ˈdrablə/ *noun*. Also **drabler**. L16.
[ORIGIN from DRABBLE *verb*: see -ER[1].]
NAUTICAL. An additional length of canvas laced to the foot of a bonnet to give a greater area of sail.

†**drab-de-Berry** *noun* var. of DRAP-DE-BERRY.

drabi /ˈdrabi/ *noun*. E20.
[ORIGIN Alt. of DRIVER.]
In the Indian subcontinent: a muleteer.

drabler *noun* var. of DRABBLER.

drac *noun* var. of DRACH.

dracaena /drəˈsiːnə/ *noun*. E19.
[ORIGIN mod. Latin from Greek *drakaina* fem. of *drakōn* DRAGON.]
Any of two genera of numerous shrubs and trees of the agave family that belong to the genera *Dracaena* and *Cordyline* and are grown for their ornamental foliage.

D

drach /drak/ *noun. colloq.* Also **drac(k)**. M20.
[ORIGIN Abbreviation.]
= DRACHMA 4.

drachm /dram/ *noun. arch.* LME.
[ORIGIN Old French *dragme* or late Latin *dragma* var. of Latin DRACHMA. Cf. DRAM *noun*[1].]
1 = DRACHMA 2. Now *rare* or *obsolete*. LME. ▸**b** = DIRHAM. Now *rare* or *obsolete*. M16.
2 A unit of weight orig. equal to the weight of a drachma; an apothecaries' weight of ⅛ ounce (60 grains); an avoirdupois weight of 1/16 ounce (approx. 27.344 grains). Also = ***fluid drachm*** s.v. FLUID *adjective*. LME.
3 *fig.* A small quantity. LME.

T. HARDY 'Now do you see the truth?' she whispered . . without a drachm of feeling.

drachma /ˈdrakmə/ *noun*. Pl. **-mas**, **-mae** /-miː/. E16.
[ORIGIN Latin from Greek *drakhmē* an Attic weight and coin. Cf. DRACHM, DRAM *noun*[1].]
1 = DRACHM 2. Now *rare* or *obsolete*. E16.
2 *hist.* The principal silver coin of ancient Greece. L16.
3 *hist.* The ancient Jewish quarter-shekel. L16.
4 The basic monetary unit of modern Greece until the introduction of the euro in 2002, equal to 100 lepta. L19.

drack *noun* var. of DRACH.

drack /drak/ *adjective. Austral. slang.* M20.
[ORIGIN Perh. from (the same root as) DRACULA, but cf. DRECK.]
Unattractive, uninteresting, inferior.

drackly /ˈdrakli/ *adverb. dial.* L19.
[ORIGIN Alt. of DIRECTLY.]
drackly minute, at once; *the* or *this* very minute (*that*).

Draco /ˈdreɪkəʊ/ *noun*. M17.
[ORIGIN Latin: see DRAGON.]
(The name of) a constellation of the northern hemisphere between Ursa Minor and Hercules.

dracocephalum /drakəˈsɛf(ə)ləm/ *noun*. M19.
[ORIGIN mod. Latin, from Greek *drakōn* DRAGON + *kephalē* head.]
Any plant of the genus *Dracocephalum* of the mint family, comprising annual and perennial plants with spikes or racemes of flowers.

dracone /ˈdrakəʊn/ *noun*. M20.
[ORIGIN Greek *drakōn* DRAGON.]
A large flexible sausage-shaped container for liquids, to be towed on the surface of the sea.

draconian /drəˈkəʊnɪən, dreɪ-/ *adjective*. Also **D-**. L19.
[ORIGIN from Greek *Drakōn* Draco (see below) + -IAN.]
Of, pertaining to, or characteristic of the supposed Athenian legislator Draco (fl. *c* 620 BC) or the severe penal code attributed to him; harsh, cruel; severe, strict.

S. RUSHDIE The threat . . could never be eliminated unless he . . were empowered to take draconian punitive measures. R. C. A. WHITE Failure to respond has draconian consequences.

draconic /drəˈkɒnɪk, dreɪ-/ *adjective*. L17.
[ORIGIN Partly from Greek *drakōn* DRAGON, partly formed as DRACONIAN: see -IC.]
1 Of, pertaining to, or of the nature of, a dragon. L17.
2 (Also **D-**.) = DRACONIAN. E18.
3 ASTRONOMY. [Cf. DRAGON *noun* 7.] ***draconic month***, ***draconic period***, the period of 27.2122 days between successive passages of the moon through the ascending or the descending node. L19.
■ **draconically** *adverb* in a draconian manner, rigorously, severely M17.

Draconid /ˈdreɪkənɪd/ *noun & adjective*. E20.
[ORIGIN from Latin DRACO (see also DRAGON) + -ID[3].]
ASTRONOMY. (Designating) any of a shower of meteors seeming to radiate from the constellation Draco in October in some years, associated with Comet Giacobini–Zinner. Also called *Giacobinid*.

draconites /drakəˈnʌɪtiːz/ *noun*. L15.
[ORIGIN Latin *draconitis*, formed as DRACONID.]
A fabled precious stone supposed to have been formed in the brain of a dragon.

dracontiasis /drakɒnˈtʌɪəsɪs/ *noun*. Pl. **-ases** /-əsiːz/. L19.
[ORIGIN from Greek *drakontion* Guinea worm + -IASIS.]
MEDICINE. The condition of having a Guinea worm or its larvae inside the body.

dracontine /drəˈkɒntʌɪn/ *adjective. rare.* E19.
[ORIGIN formed as DRACONTIASIS + -INE[1].]
= DRACONIC 1.

Dracula /ˈdrakjʊlə/ *noun*. M20.
[ORIGIN Count *Dracula*, a Transylvanian vampire king depicted in Bram Stoker's novel *Dracula* of 1897.]
A person of grotesque, terrifying, and savage character.

dracunculus /drəˈkʌŋkjʊləs/ *noun*. Pl. **-li** /-lʌɪ, -liː/. E17.
[ORIGIN Latin, formed as DRACONID + *-culus* -CULE.]
1 = DRAGON 10. *rare*. E17.
2 The Guinea worm. E18.
3 = DRAGONET 2. M18.
■ **dracunculiasis** /-ˈlʌɪəsɪs/ *noun*, pl. **-ases** /-əsiːz/, = DRACONTIASIS M20. **dracuncuˈlosis** *noun*, pl. **-loses** /-ˈləʊsiːz/, = DRACONTIASIS M20.

draegerman /ˈdreɪɡəmən/ *noun. N. Amer.* Pl. **-men**. E20.
[ORIGIN from A. B. *Dräger* (1870–1928), German inventor of a type of breathing apparatus, + MAN *noun*.]
A member of a crew trained for underground rescue work.

draff /draf/ *noun*. ME.
[ORIGIN Perh. repr. an Old English word = Middle Low German, Middle Dutch *draf*, Old High German pl. *trebir* (German *Treber*, *Träber* husks, grains), also rel. to Old Norse *draf* draff, husks, Norwegian *drav* mash. Perh. rel. to DRIVEL *verb*.]
Dregs, lees; refuse; *esp.* the grains of malt left after brewing or distilling.

fig.: MILTON The brood of Belial, the draffe of men.

– COMB.: **draffsack** (now *dial.*) a sack of draff; *fig.* a big paunch; a lazy glutton.
■ **draffy** *adjective* full of dregs or draff; worthless: E17.

draft /drɑːft/ *noun & adjective*. M16.
[ORIGIN Repr. mod. pronunc. of DRAUGHT *noun*.]
▸ **A** *noun*. **I 1** *gen.* = DRAUGHT *noun*. Now chiefly *N. Amer.* M16.
▸ **II** *spec.* **2** A plan, a drawing, *esp.* one showing work to be executed. Formerly also, a chart. (Earlier as DRAUGHT *noun* 26 and in DRAFTSMAN 1.) L17.
3 A preliminary version or rough form of something to be written or printed, esp. an official document. (Earlier as DRAUGHT *noun* 25.) M18.

R. WEST An ordinary swan or goose quill for the rough draft, and for his fair copy the crow quill. B. CASTLE The original draft of the industrial policy White Paper had been pretty unsatisfactory.

4 The turn of a balance as the lighter side becomes the heavier; a deduction from gross weight allowed for this. (Earlier as DRAUGHT *noun* 12.) Now *rare*. M18.
5 The drawing off or selection of a detachment (esp. of livestock or troops) from a larger group for a special duty or purpose; *US* selective conscription. Also, a group or individual selected in this way; a contingent, a reinforcement. (Earlier as DRAUGHT *noun* 16.) L18. ▸**b** In full ***draft ewe***. A ewe selected from a flock. M19.

WELLINGTON If the bullocks are not occasionally recruited by drafts of fresh calves. J. T. ADAMS There was no draft, there were only . . volunteers. *attrib.*: *Listener* Students . . were protesting against the war by turning in their draft cards.

6 The drawing of money by a written order; a bill or cheque drawn, esp. by one branch of a bank on another. (Earlier as DRAUGHT *noun* 15.) L18. ▸**b** *fig.* A demand or claim made *on* a person's friendship, confidence, etc. M19.

G. J. GOSCHEN Teas shipped from China . . are generally paid for by a draft . . on a London merchant.

7 A groove near the edge of a stone to serve as a guide for a stonecutter. (Earlier as DRAUGHT *noun* 28.) L19.
▸ **B** *attrib.* or as *adjective*. **1** = DRAUGHT *adjective* 1, 2. Now chiefly *US*. E17.
2 Prepared as a draft. L19.

draft /drɑːft/ *verb trans.* E18.
[ORIGIN Partly from the noun, partly repr. pronunc. of DRAUGHT *verb*.]
1 Remove or select (esp. livestock or troops) from a larger body for a special purpose; *US* conscript (*lit.* & *fig.*); persuade or force (a reluctant person) to stand for office. E18.

E. J. HOWARD I volunteered for the army and got drafted into the Royal Corps of Signals. G. BOYCOTT A practice match . . with local builders drafted in as reinforcements. N. PODHORETZ With conscription still in effect . . I was certain to be drafted.

2 Make a draft of (something to be written etc.); draw up in a preliminary form. (Earlier as DRAUGHT *verb* 1.) E19.

P. THEROUX A Patagonian lawyer who had helped to draft the legal aspects of the treaty.

3 Cut a draft on (a stone). Chiefly as ***drafted*** pa. pple. (Earlier as DRAUGHT *verb* 3.) L19.
■ **drafˈtee** *noun* (*US*) a conscript M19. **drafter** *noun* (*a*) a person employed in drafting livestock; (*b*) a person who prepares preliminary drafts; a draftsman; (*c*) a draught horse; a horse used in drafting livestock: E19.

draftsman /ˈdrɑːf(t)smən/ *noun*. Pl. **-men**. M17.
[ORIGIN from DRAFT *noun* + -'S[1] + MAN *noun*. Cf. DRAUGHTSMAN.]
1 = DRAUGHTSMAN 1. Now chiefly *N. Amer.* M17.
2 A person who drafts or draws up a document, esp. a legal clause or a parliamentary bill. M18.
■ **draftsmanship** *noun* the function, quality, or art of a draftsman; skill in drafting documents etc.; (cf. DRAUGHTSMANSHIP): L19.

†**drafty** *adjective*[1]. L16–E19.
[ORIGIN Unknown.]
Rubbishy, filthy, (*lit.* & *fig.*).

drafty *adjective*[2] see DRAUGHTY *adjective*.

drag /drag/ *noun*. ME.
[ORIGIN Partly from the verb, partly from Middle Low German *dragge* grapnel. See also DRUG *noun*[2].]
1 AGRICULTURE. **a** A heavy harrow used for breaking up the surface of land. ME. ▸**b** Any of several implements with prongs or claws. L18.
2 A dragnet; an apparatus for dragging a river etc. or for dredging. ME.
3 †**a** A raft. LME–E17. ▸**b** A sledge. L16. ▸**c** Any wheeled vehicle. Now *spec.* (*a*) *hist.* a private horse-drawn coach like a stagecoach; (*b*) *slang* a car. M18. ▸**d** More fully ***drag race***. A motor race run over a straight ¼ mile as a test of acceleration, usu. between two cars at a time. M20.
4 A hook with which something is dragged. *obsolete* exc. *dial.* L15.
5 Something that impedes movement; *spec.* an iron shoe that can be applied to a wheel as a brake. E18. ▸**b** The force resisting the motion of a body through a liquid or gas. E20.

fig.: I. ZANGWILL She was a drag on his career.

6 HUNTING. **a** The scent left by a fox or other hunted animal; a strong-smelling lure for hounds in place of this. M18. ▸**b** A hunt following an artificial drag; a club that organizes such hunts. Also ***drag hunt***. E19.

LD RAVENSWORTH His bloodhounds sniff the drag Of . . antlered stag.

7 †**a** The robbery of a vehicle. *slang*. L18–E19. ▸**b** A prison sentence of three months. *slang*. M19.
8 The action or fact of dragging; forcible motion or progress against resistance. E19.

H. ALLEN The ship . . began to drift down the river, . . gathering way as the drag of the ebb became heavier.

9 A boring or dreary person or event. E19.

J. DIDION Doris Jeanne thought California was strictly a drag.

10 The slow-moving part of a herd on a cattle drive. M19.
11 A street, *esp.* (also ***main drag***) the principal street of a town. *slang*. M19.
12 Women's clothes as worn by a man; (less commonly) men's clothes as worn by a woman; a party at which such clothes are worn; *gen.* clothes. Freq. in ***in drag***. L19.

Listener Laurence Olivier, doing his Othello voice and attired . . in Arab drag. A. BEATTIE He . . acted in a porn film about the war, in drag.

13 A relationship where a person has influence over someone; influence. *US slang*. L19.

G. ADE He knows I've got a drag in the precinct. J. T. FARRELL He grew up with guys who got plenty of drag in this town.

14 An inhalation of smoke from a cigarette etc.; a spell of smoking a cigarette etc. *slang*. E20.

D. LODGE Another joint was circulating, and this time Philip took a drag or two.

15 MUSIC. A drum stroke consisting of two or more grace notes preceding a beat. E20.
16 (Music for) a kind of slow dance. *US*. E20.
– COMB.: **drag act** an act by a drag artist or drag artists; **drag anchor** = *SEA anchor*; **drag artist** a performer in a variety show etc. who appears in drag; **drag chain** (*a*) a chain used to retard the motion of a vehicle; *fig.* a check, a hindrance; (*b*) a strong chain for coupling railway vehicles; **drag hook** (*a*) a hook used for dragging; (*b*) a hook on the end of a drag chain; **drag hound** a hound used for drag hunting; ***drag hunt***: see sense 6b above; **drag hunting** the sport of following with hounds the trail supplied by an artificial drag; **dragline** a rope by which a bucket or grab is drawn towards an excavator; (also ***dragline excavator***) an excavator with this; **drag queen** *slang* a male homosexual transvestite; ***drag race***: see sense 3d above; **drag racing** the holding of or participation in drag races; **drag rope** a rope used for haulage; **drag saw**: with which the effective stroke is given by the pull rather than by the thrust; **drag staff** *hist.* a trailing pole hinged to the rear of a coach etc. to check backward movement when stopped on a steep slope; **drag strut** AERONAUTICS a strut used to strengthen a wing against forces arising from drag.

drag /drag/ *verb*. Infl. **-gg-**. LME.
[ORIGIN Old Norse *draga* or obscurely developed from Old English *dragan*: see DRAW *verb*.]
▸ **I 1** *verb trans.* Draw or pull along with force, difficulty, or friction; allow (the feet, a tail, etc.) to trail along the ground. LME. ▸**b** Of a ship: trail (an anchor) along the seabed after it has come adrift. L17. ▸**c** Foll. by adverb or preposition: take or escort (a person) to or away from a place or event despite his or her reluctance. *colloq.* L18. ▸**d** COMPUTING. Move (a window, icon, or other image) across a computer screen using a tool such as a mouse. L20.

T. WILLIAMS She has dragged her wardrobe trunk into the centre of the bedroom. *fig.*: J. T. STORY All this is going to be dragged through a coroner's court. **c** J. BENTHAM I have to regret being the cause . . of dragging you out thus early. J. CANNAN I was dragged to an Old Tyme Dance in the Town Hall.

drag ass: see ASS *noun*[2]. **drag one's feet**, **drag one's heels** *fig.* be deliberately slow or reluctant in accomplishing or proceeding with something. **drag the chain** *Austral. & NZ slang* work slowly or lazily, lag behind others. **drag through the mud** publish unpleasant information or allegations about. **d drag-and-drop** COMPUTING (*a*) *adjective* designating or permitting a method of moving or copying images, text, etc., from one part of the display screen to another using a mouse or similar device; (*b*) *verb trans.* move or copy using such a method.
2 *verb intrans.* Hang back with a retarding tendency; lag behind, esp. in singing or playing. E16.

OED The quartet was not sung in time, the tenor dragged.

3 *verb intrans.* Trail or hang under its own weight while being moved; (of a door) catch on the ground. **M17.**

W. GOLDING He . . limped forward, left foot dragging a little.

4 *verb trans.* Protract, prolong, or continue tediously. Now usu. foll. by *out*. **L17.**

5 *verb intrans.* Advance or progress slowly and painfully; be tediously prolonged; become tedious by protraction. Freq. foll. by *on*. **M18.**

G. GISSING Winter dragged to its end. ANNE STEVENSON Schoolgirls dragging in crocodile/through the damp lanes.

6 *verb intrans.* Suck *on* or *at* a cigarette etc. to draw in the smoke. *colloq.* **E20.**

▸ **II 7** *verb trans.* Catch by means of a dragnet or dredging. **LME.**

8 *verb trans. & intrans.* Draw a dragnet, grapnel, etc., along the bed of (a river etc.) to clear it or free objects; search in this way for a body. **M16.**

J. FOWLES The police were going to drag the ponds.

9 *verb trans.* Break up the surface of (land) with a drag or heavy harrow. **E18.**

10 *verb trans.* Put a drag on (a wheel or vehicle); impede in this way. **E19.**

11 *verb trans.* Rob (a vehicle). *slang.* **E19.**

12 *verb intrans.* Race a motor vehicle, take part in a drag race. *N. Amer.* **M20.**

– WITH ADVERBS IN SPECIALIZED SENSES: **drag in** introduce (a topic) in a forced manner or needlessly. **drag up** *colloq.* (*a*) rear (a child) roughly and without proper training (freq. in *pass.*); (*b*) deliberately mention (a subject or event, usu. unpleasant, that is generally forgotten or ignored).

■ **dragger** *noun* (*a*) a person who or thing which drags; (*b*) *N. Amer.* a fishing boat which uses a dragnet: **L15.** **draggingly** *adverb* slowly and with difficulty **L19.**

†dragant *noun*. Also **dragagant**. **ME–E18.**

[ORIGIN Old French from Latin *tragacantha*: see TRAGACANTH. Cf. ADRAGANT.]

Tragacanth.

dragée /ˈdrɑːʒeɪ; *foreign* draʒe (*pl. same*)/ *noun*. **L17.**

[ORIGIN French: see DREDGE *noun*[1].]

A sweet consisting of a centre covered with some coating, *esp.* a sugared almond etc. or a chocolate; a small silver-coated sugar ball for use in cake decoration; a sweet used as a vehicle for a medicine or drug. Formerly also, a mixture of spices etc. Cf. DREDGE *noun*[1] 1.

drageoir /draʒwaːr/ *noun*. Pl. pronounced same. **M19.**

[ORIGIN French, formed as DRAGÉE.]

A box for holding sweets.

draggle /ˈdrag(ə)l/ *verb*. **E16.**

[ORIGIN Dim. & frequentative of DRAG *verb*: see -LE[3].]

1 *verb trans.* Make dirty, untidy, and usu. wet, esp. by trailing through something. **E16.**

CARLYLE The wet day draggles the tricolor. T. HARDY Lifting her skirts to avoid draggling them in the white dust. S. LEACOCK All draggled with the mud and rain he stood. R. MACAULAY Her draggled hair drooping like dark seaweed round her face.

2 *verb intrans.* Trail on the ground; hang trailing or untidily. **L16.**

3 *verb intrans.* Come on or follow slowly; lag; straggle in the rear. **L16.**

draggle-tail /ˈdrag(ə)lteɪl/ *noun & adjective*. **L16.**

[ORIGIN from DRAGGLE + TAIL *noun*[1].]

▸ **A** *noun*. **1** A bedraggled person or animal; *esp.* (*arch.*) a woman with draggled or untidily trailing skirts. **L16.**

SWIFT What a draggletail she will be before she gets to Dublin.

2 In *pl.* Skirts that trail on the ground. *arch.* **M19.**

▸ **B** *attrib.* or as *adjective*. Draggle-tailed; draggled. **E17.**

A. CARTER In the long, rank, soaking grass among draggletail dog-daisies.

■ **draggle-tailed** *adjective* **M17.** **draggle-tailedness** *noun* **L19.**

draggly /ˈdragli/ *adjective*. **M19.**

[ORIGIN from DRAGGLE *verb* + -Y[1].]

Inclined to draggle.

draggy /ˈdragi/ *adjective*. **L19.**

[ORIGIN from DRAG *verb* + -Y[1].]

1 Inclined to drag or cause dragging; heavy; slow; lacking liveliness. **L19.**

2 Tedious; boring. *colloq.* **E20.**

■ **dragginess** *noun* **L19.**

dragnet /ˈdragnɛt/ *noun*. **M16.**

[ORIGIN from DRAG *noun* + NET *noun*[1]. Cf. Old English *drægnet*, Swedish *draggnot*; also DRAY *noun*[1].]

A net drawn through a river or across ground to trap fish or game; *fig.* a means of systematically discovering criminals or criminal activity.

dragoman /ˈdragə(ʊ)mən/ *noun*. Pl. **-mans**, **-men**. **LME.**

[ORIGIN Obsolete French (now *drogman*) from Italian *dragomanno* from medieval Greek *dragoumanos* from Arabic *tarjumān* (formerly with -g-), from *tarjama* interpret: rel. to Aramaic *targēm* interpret, Akkadian *targumannu* interpreter. Cf. TARGUM, TRUCHMAN.]

An interpreter, a guide; *esp.* a person employed as a guide or courier in countries where Arabic, Turkish, or Persian is spoken.

dragon /ˈdrag(ə)n/ *noun & adjective*. **ME.**

[ORIGIN Old French & mod. French from Latin *draco*, *dracon-* from Greek *drakōn* serpent.]

▸ **A** *noun*. **†1** A huge serpent or snake. **ME–E18.**

2 A mythical monster like a huge reptile, combining ophidian and crocodilian structure, usu. with wings and claws and often breathing fire. **ME.** ▸**b** A creature or person represented in a role like that of some dragon of legend, e.g. as a watchful guardian of treasure. **L16.**

SHAKES. *John* Saint George, that swing'd the dragon. SIR W. SCOTT They . . faced the dragon's breath of fire.

3 A representation or figure of a dragon. Formerly, an ensign or standard depicting a dragon. **ME.** ▸**b** (Usu. **D-**.) *The* constellation Draco. **M16.** ▸**c** In full ***dragon china***. A kind of porcelain decorated with designs of dragons. **L18.** ▸**d** Any of twelve tiles so designated which make up one of the suits in mah-jong. **E20.**

4 In biblical translations: (*a*) a large sea creature; †(*b*) a jackal. **ME.**

AV *Ps.* 74:13 Thou brakest the heads of the dragons in the waters.

5 More fully ***the Dragon***, ***the old Dragon***. Satan. *arch.* **ME.**

6 a A devilish or wicked person. **LME.** ▸**b** A fierce person; *esp.* an aggressively watchful or protective woman, a duenna. **M18.**

b R. CHURCH The headmistress, a formidable dragon . . , terror of the slum mothers.

†7 ASTRONOMY. The part of the moon's apparent path which lies south of the ecliptic. **LME–E16.**

†8 A shooting star with a luminous tail. **LME–L18.**

9 Death. *arch.* **E16.**

10 More fully ***dragon arum***. A Mediterranean arum, *Dracunculus vulgaris*, having a large spathe that is dark purple on the inside and a dark purple spadix. Also ***green dragon***. Cf. DRAGONS. **M16.**

†11 = DRAGOON *noun* 1, 2. **E17–M19.**

12 = DRAGONET 2. Formerly, any of various other fishes, *esp.* an anglerfish (*Lophius*). **E17.**

†13 A small cataract in a horse's eye. **E17–E18.**

14 = ***flying lizard*** s.v. FLYING *ppl adjective*. **E19.**

15 = DRAGOON *noun* 4. **M19.**

– PHRASES: **chase the dragon** *slang* take heroin etc. by heating it in tinfoil and inhaling the fumes through a tube or roll of paper. ***flying dragon***: see FLYING *ppl adjective*. ***Komodo dragon***. ***Rouge Dragon***: see ROUGE *adjective*. ***SEA dragon***.

▸ **B** *attrib.* or as *adjective*. Of a dragon; like (that of) a dragon. **E17.**

– COMB. & SPECIAL COLLOCATIONS: ***dragon arum***: see sense A.10 above; **dragon boat** (*a*) a beaked galley, or ship of war of the Vikings; (*b*) a boat of a traditional Chinese design, orig. made of teak and typically decorated to resemble a dragon, propelled with paddles by a large crew and used for racing at an annual Spring festival; ***dragon china***: see sense A.3c above; **dragonfish** †(*a*) = DRAGONET 2; (*b*) any of various long slender marine fishes of the order Stomiiformes; (*c*) a fish of Antarctic seas of the family Bathydraconidae; (*d*) = ***SEA-moth***; **dragonfly** any insect of the suborder Anisoptera (order Odonata), comprising predatory insects with a long slender body, a large head, and two unequal pairs of large transparent wings that are spread while resting; any other odonate insect; **dragon root** either of two stemless tuberous hardy plants of the lily family, *Arisaema dracontium* and *A. triphyllum*, native to N. America; **dragon's blood** any of various red plant resins; *esp.* that which exudes from the fruit of some palms of the genus *Daemonorops*, used as a colouring for varnishes; **dragon's head** (*a*) ASTROLOGY [cf. sense 7 above] the ascending node of the moon's orbit; (*b*) *arch.* the heraldic tincture tenné when blazoning is by the heavenly bodies; (*c*) BOTANY = DRACOCEPHALUM; **dragon ship** *hist.* a Viking longship, esp. one ornamented with a beaked prow; **dragon's tail** (*a*) ASTROLOGY [cf. sense 7 above] the descending node of the moon's orbit; (*b*) *arch.* the heraldic tincture sanguine when blazoning is by the heavenly bodies; ***dragon's mouth*** = ARETHUSA. **dragon's teeth** (*a*) (something likened to) the teeth of the dragon killed by Cadmus in Greek legend, which when he sowed them turned into armed men; (*b*) *colloq.* upward-pointing obstacles laid in the ground to stop tanks etc. passing or to slow traffic down; **dragon tree** a tall tree, *Dracaena draco* (cf. DRACAENA), of the Canary Islands that has orange berries and panicles of greenish flowers and whose stem is a source of dragon's blood; **Dragon variation** CHESS a form of the Sicilian defence involving a fianchetto of the Black king's bishop. **dragonwort** †(*a*) = sense 10 above; (*b*) the plant bistort or snakeweed, *Polygonum bistorta*.

■ **dragoˈness** *noun* a female dragon; a woman who is a dragon: **M17.** **dragonish** *adjective* (*a*) of the nature or character of a dragon; fierce, severe; (*b*) somewhat like a dragon in shape: **M16.** **dragonism** *noun* (*rare*) †(*a*) dragonish nature; devilry; (*b*) jealous and watchful guardianship: **L16.** **dragonize** *verb* (*a*) *verb trans.* turn into a dragon; (*b*) *verb trans. & intrans.* guard or watch (over) like a dragon: **M19.**

dragonet /ˈdragənɪt/ *noun*. **ME.**

[ORIGIN Old French & mod. French, dim. of DRAGON: see -ET[1].]

1 A young or small dragon. **ME.**

2 Any of various perciform marine fishes of the family Callionymidae, which tend to lie partly buried in the seabed and in the case of males are brilliantly coloured, esp. *Callionymus lyra* of the NE Atlantic. **M18.**

dragonnade /dragəˈneɪd/ *noun & verb*. Orig. **†dragoonade**. **E18.**

[ORIGIN French, formed as DRAGOON *noun*: see -ADE.]

▸ **A** *noun sing.* & (usu.) in *pl.* A persecution conducted by Louis XIV against French Protestants in the 1680s, in which dragoons were quartered on them; any persecution conducted with the aid of troops. **E18.**

▸ **B** *verb trans.* Subject to dragonnades. **L19.**

†dragons *noun*. **LME–M18.**

[ORIGIN Old French *dragance* var. of *dragonce* from late Latin *dracontia* from Greek *drakontion*, from *drakōn* DRAGON.]

= DRAGON *noun* 10.

dragoon /drəˈguːn/ *noun*. **E17.**

[ORIGIN French DRAGON: see -OON.]

†1 A kind of carbine or musket. **E–M17.**

2 Orig., a mounted infantryman. Now, a member of any of several cavalry regiments in the British army. **E17.**

3 A rough fierce man. **E18.**

4 A pigeon that is a cross between a horseman and a tumbler. **E18.**

dragoon /drəˈguːn/ *verb trans.* **L17.**

[ORIGIN from the noun after French *dragonner*.]

1 Set dragoons upon; force or drive with the aid of dragoons; persecute, oppress. **L17.**

D. NEAL His brother of France . . was dragooning his Protestant subjects out of his kingdom. J. COLVILLE He . . dragooned the Chiefs of Staff and Ismay in the War Room.

2 Force *into* a course of action etc. by rigorous or harassing measures. **L17.**

E. BOWEN Dragooning the lower classes into healthy activities.

†dragoonade *noun* see DRAGONNADE.

†dragooner *noun*. **M17.**

[ORIGIN In senses 1 perh. from German *Dragoner* formed as DRAGOON *noun*. In sense 2 from DRAGOON *verb* + -ER[1].]

1 = DRAGOON *noun* 2. **M17–E18.**

2 A person who dragoons or takes part in dragonnades; a rigid persecutor. **L17–E19.**

dragsman /ˈdragzmən/ *noun*. Pl. **-men**. **E19.**

[ORIGIN from DRAG *noun* + -'S[1] + MAN *noun*.]

1 The driver of a drag (see DRAG *noun* 3c). **E19.**

2 A person who steals from vehicles. *slang.* **E19.**

dragster /ˈdragstə/ *noun*. **M20.**

[ORIGIN from DRAG *noun* + -STER.]

A car built or modified for use in drag races.

drail /dreɪl/ *verb & noun*. **L16.**

[ORIGIN App. alt. of TRAIL *verb*.]

▸ **A** *verb*. **1** *verb trans. & intrans.* (Cause to) trail, draggle. *obsolete* exc. *dial.* **L16.**

2 *verb intrans.* Fish with a drail. *N. Amer.* **M17.**

▸ **B** *noun*. **1** A ring etc. to which a tie may be secured; *spec.* (*hist.*) a metal ring on a horse-drawn plough to which a trace was attached. **L16.**

2 A fish hook weighted to enable it to be dragged through water at a depth; a line with such a hook. *N. Amer.* **M17.**

drain /dreɪn/ *noun*. **ME.**

[ORIGIN from the verb.]

1 A channel or pipe along which liquid drains away; *esp.* (*a*) a pipe for leading away rainwater etc.; (*b*) an open channel made to drain an area of land; an artificial river. **ME.** ▸**b** MEDICINE. A tube or wick for draining a wound or abscess. **M19.** ▸**c** ELECTRONICS. (The material forming) the part of a field-effect transistor to which the current carriers flow after passing the gate. Opp. SOURCE *noun* 5c. **M20.**

L. LEE We found the drain blocked already and the yard full of water.

down the drain: see DOWN *preposition*. ***French drain***: see FRENCH *adjective*. **laugh like a drain** *colloq.* laugh loudly, guffaw.

2 The action or an act of draining; drainage. Now only *fig.*, a continual loss, demand, or expenditure. **E18.**

A. WILSON At fifty-seven he could not afford . . such exacting drains upon his creative energies. M. FONTEYN The drain of top dancers and choreographers leaving the country.

brain drain: see BRAIN *noun*.

3 A small (remaining) quantity of liquid; in *pl.*, dregs; *slang* a drink. **E19.**

– COMB.: **drainboard** *N. Amer.* = ***draining board*** s.v. DRAIN *verb*; **draincock**: for draining the water out of a boiler etc; **drainpipe** a pipe for carrying off surplus water or liquid refuse from a building; *attrib.* (of trousers etc.) very narrow; in *pl.*, narrow tight-fitting trousers.

drain /dreɪn/ *verb*.

[ORIGIN Old English *drēahnian*, *drēhnian*, prob. from Germanic base repr. also by DRY *adjective*.]

†1 *verb trans.* Strain (liquid) through any porous medium. **OE–M17.**

2 *verb trans.* Drink (liquid, a drink) to the last drops. **LME.**

W. BOYD The little boys were noisily draining soft drinks.

drain the lees, ***drain to the lees***: see LEES.

3 *verb trans.* Empty by drinking, drink dry. **LME.**

DICKENS They had drained the cup of life to the dregs. E. CRISPIN Widger picked up his glass, drained it at a gulp, and put it down.

D

4 *verb trans.* Cause (a liquid) to come out of or leave something gradually or in small quantities, esp. by means of a pipe, channel, etc.; carry *off* or *away* thus; *fig.* cause gradually to disappear or go to waste. **M16.**

> M. FRAYN Held upside down to drain the water out of its works.

†**5** Let fall in drops. *rare* (Shakes.). Only in **L16.**
6 *verb trans.* Cause water etc. to flow from or out of; make (a marsh etc.) dry by providing an outflow for water; (of a river) receive water from (a specified area); remove purulent matter from (an abscess). **L16.** ▸**b** Deprive of strength, resources, vitality, etc.; exhaust emotionally. **M17.**

> *fig.*: E. BOWEN Lounge and drawing-room had been drained of their usual occupants. **b** *Daily Telegraph* We are thoroughly exasperated and drained by the whole thing.

7 *verb intrans.* Of liquid: flow away or out. Usu. foll. by *away*, *off*. **L16.**

> *fig.*: P. BARKER A rush of colour to her face . . drained away as quickly as it came, leaving her even whiter. SLOAN WILSON Suddenly the tension drained out of him, and he felt relaxed.

8 *verb intrans.* Become dry or drier as a result of water draining away. **L17.**

> *Practical Photography* Pick up the print with tongs, allow it to drain and then transfer to the stop bath.

– COMB.: **draining board** a sloping, usu. grooved, board on which washed dishes etc. are put to drain into an adjacent sink.
■ **drainable** *adjective* **E17.**

drainage /ˈdreɪnɪdʒ/ *noun.* **M17.**
[ORIGIN from DRAIN *verb* + -AGE.]
1 The action of draining something; the manner in which something is drained. **M17.**

> *fig.*: W. IRVING This constant drainage of the purse.

2 Water etc. carried away by a drain. **M19.**
3 A system of drains; a means of draining. **L19.**
4 An area drained; a river valley, a drainage basin. Chiefly *US*. **L19.**
– COMB.: **drainage basin** = BASIN 6(a); **drainage tube** MEDICINE a tube, usu. with lateral perforations, for draining a wound etc.

drainer /ˈdreɪnə/ *noun.* **L16.**
[ORIGIN from DRAIN *verb* + -ER¹.]
1 A thing that acts as a means of draining something; *esp.* a container in which wet things are put to drain. **L16.** ▸**b** = ***draining board*** s.v. DRAIN *verb*. **M20.**
2 A person who drains, *esp.* one who makes field drains. **E17.**

drainless /ˈdreɪnlɪs/ *adjective.* **E19.**
[ORIGIN from DRAIN *noun* + -LESS.]
1 Inexhaustible. *poet.* **E19.**
2 Not provided with drains. **E20.**

drake /dreɪk/ *noun*¹.
[ORIGIN Old English *draca* = Old Frisian, Middle Low German, Middle Dutch *drake* (Dutch *draak*), Old High German *trahho* (German *Drache*), from West Germanic from Latin *draco* DRAGON.]
1 A dragon (cf. FIREDRAKE 1); an ensign or standard depicting a dragon. *arch.* **OE.**
†**2** A fiery meteor. (Surviving longer in FIREDRAKE 2.) **ME–E17.**
3 [from Low German.] A kind of small cannon. *obsolete* exc. *hist.* **E17.**
4 ANGLING. (An artificial fly imitating) a mayfly, esp. (***green drake***) a subimago or (***grey drake***) a gravid female of *Ephemera*. Also ***drake-fly***. **M17.**

drake /dreɪk/ *noun*² & *adjective.* **ME.**
[ORIGIN Corresp. to Low German *drake*, *drache* from West Germanic base repr. also by 2nd elem. of Old High German *antrahho*, *antrehho* (German *Enterich*).]
▸ **A** *noun.* A male duck. **ME.**
drake's tail an unruly tuft or curl of hair at the back of the head. ***ducks and drakes***, ***duck and drake***: see DUCK *noun*¹.
▸ **B** *attrib.* or as *adjective.* Designating a duck that is male. **L19.**

Drake /dreɪk/ *noun*³. **L20.**
[ORIGIN Frank D. *Drake* (b. 1930), US astrophysicist.]
ASTRONOMY. ***Drake equation***, ***Drake's equation***, a speculative equation which gives an estimate of the likelihood of discovering intelligent extraterrestrial life in the galaxy, expressed as the product of a series of factors such as the number of stars, the fraction of stars with planets, the fraction of planets on which life evolves, the average lifetime of a civilization, etc.

Dralon /ˈdreɪlɒn/ *noun.* Also **d-**. **M20.**
[ORIGIN After NYLON.]
(Proprietary name for) an acrylic textile fibre; fabric made from this.

> S. TOWNSEND This . . reduced me to silent sobs into the Dralon cushions.

DRAM /ˈdiːram/ *abbreviation.*
COMPUTING. Dynamic random access memory.

dram /dram/ *noun*¹ & *verb.* **LME.**
[ORIGIN Old French *drame* or medieval Latin *drama*, vars. of Old French *dragme*, late Latin *dragma*: see DRACHM.]
▸ **A** *noun.* †**1** = DRACHMA 2. **LME–M16.**
2 = DRACHM 2. Now chiefly *US*. **LME.**
fluid dram: see FLUID *adjective*.
3 *fig.* = DRACHM 3. **M16.**
4 A small drink of spirits etc. **E18.**

> A. S. NEILL He always brought a flask of whisky and gave each one a dram.

– COMB.: **dram-drinker** a tippler; **dram-shop** *US* (*arch.*) an establishment where spirits are sold, a bar-room.
▸ **B** *verb trans.* & *intrans.* Infl. **-mm-**. (Cause to) drink drams, tipple. Now *rare* or *obsolete*. **E18.**

dram /dram/ *noun*² & *adjective.* **M17.**
[ORIGIN Abbreviation of *Drammen* (see below).]
(Designating) timber from the town of Drammen in Norway.

dram /drɑːm/ *noun*³. **L20.**
[ORIGIN Armenian, lit. 'coin, money' from Greek *drakhmē* DRACHMA.]
The basic monetary unit of Armenia, equal to 100 luma.

drama /ˈdrɑːmə/ *noun.* Orig. †**drame**. **E16.**
[ORIGIN (French *drame* from) late Latin *drama* from Greek *drama(t-)*, from *dran* do, act, perform.]
1 A play for acting on stage, radio, etc., esp. one with high emotional content. **E16.**
lyric drama: see LYRIC *adjective* 1. ***music drama***: see MUSIC *noun*.
2 The dramatic art; the composition and presentation of plays. Formerly usu. ***the drama***. **E17.**

> L. C. KNIGHTS Restoration drama—tragedy as well as comedy— . . is insufferably dull.

3 A situation in which there is conflict; *esp.* a dramatic series of events leading up to a particular outcome. **E18.**

> R. V. JONES After the drama of Dunkirk the next few days were surprisingly quiet.

4 Dramatic quality; interest, excitement. **M20.**

> L. MACNEICE The hills to-day were monotonous, lacking in drama.

– COMB.: **drama-documentary** a film (esp. for television) dramatizing or based on real events; **drama queen** *colloq.* a person who responds to situations in a melodramatic manner.

Dramamine /ˈdraməmiːn/ *noun.* Also **d-**. **M20.**
[ORIGIN from *dram-*, of unknown origin + AMINE.]
PHARMACOLOGY. (Proprietary name for) an antihistamine used to counter nausea, esp. travel sickness.

dramatic /drəˈmatɪk/ *adjective* & *noun.* **L16.**
[ORIGIN Late Latin *dramaticus* from Greek *dramatikos*, from *dramat-* DRAMA: see -IC.]
▸ **A** *adjective.* **1** Of or pertaining to drama; dealing with or employing the forms of drama. **L16.**

> M. SPARK Jenny was already showing her dramatic talent.

dramatic irony see IRONY 4.
2 Characteristic of drama or a play-actor, theatrical; fit for representation in a drama, striking, impressive; sudden. **E18.**

> M. PEAKE He took a dramatic step towards Lady Cora. I. D. SMITH There are going to be no dramatic changes in Rhodesia. O. MANNING A dramatic range of high ridges could be seen on the horizon.

▸ **B** *noun.* †**1** A dramatic poet; a dramatist. **M17–M18.**
2 In *pl.* Dramatic compositions or presentations (now chiefly in ***amateur dramatics***); dramatic behaviour. **L17.**

> A. BROOKNER Monica's face dropped . . . No dramatics, please, thought Edith.

■ **dramatical** *adjective* (now *rare*) = DRAMATIC *adjective* 1 **M17.** **dramatically** *adverb* in a dramatic manner; with dramatic or theatrical effect: **M17.** **dramaticism** /-sɪz(ə)m/ *noun* dramatic quality **M19.** **dramaticule** *noun* (*rare*) a minor or insignificant drama **E19.**

dramatise *verb* var. of DRAMATIZE.

dramatism /ˈdramətɪz(ə)m/ *noun.* **M19.**
[ORIGIN from Greek *dramat-* DRAMA + -ISM.]
1 Dramatization. *rare.* **M19.**
2 Dramatic quality. *rare.* **L19.**
3 A theory of social action that analyses behaviour in terms of dramatic forms and convention. **L20.**

dramatis personae /ˌdramətɪs pəːˈsəʊnʌɪ, -niː/ *noun pl.* (freq. treated as *sing.*). **M18.**
[ORIGIN Latin *dramatis personae* persons of the drama.]
The (list of) characters in a play; *fig.* the participants in an event etc.

dramatist /ˈdramətɪst/ *noun.* **L17.**
[ORIGIN from Greek *dramat-* DRAMA + -IST.]
A person who writes dramas or (formerly) dramatic poetry; a playwright.

dramatistic /draməˈtɪstɪk/ *adjective.* **M20.**
[ORIGIN formed as DRAMATIST + -IC.]
SOCIOLOGY. Of or pertaining to dramatism.
■ **dramatistically** *adverb* **M20.**

dramatize /ˈdramətʌɪz/ *verb.* Also **-ise**. **L18.**
[ORIGIN from Greek *dramat-* DRAMA + -IZE.]
1 *verb trans.* Put into dramatic form; adapt (a novel etc.) as a play. **L18.** ▸**b** *verb intrans.* Write plays. **E19.**

> SIR W. SCOTT They are busy dramatizing the Lady of the Lake here.

2 a *verb trans.* Describe or represent dramatically; make dramatic. **E19.** ▸**b** *verb intrans.* & *refl.* Behave dramatically or theatrically. **L19.**

> **a** A. WESKER She manages to dramatize the smallest piece of gossip into something significant. **b** G. VIDAL Enid's dramatizing herself, that's all.

3 *verb intrans.* Be adaptable as a play. **E19.**
■ **dramatiˈzation** *noun* the action of dramatizing; a dramatized version: **L18.**

dramaturge /ˈdramətəːdʒ/ *noun.* Also **-g**; ***Dramaturg*** /draməˈtʊrk/, pl. ***-gen*** /-gən/. **M19.**
[ORIGIN French *dramaturge*, German *Dramaturg*, from Greek *dramatourgos*, from *dramat-* DRAMA + *-ergos* worker.]
A dramatist; *spec.* a reader and literary editor etc. to a permanent theatrical company.

dramaturgy /ˈdramətəːdʒi/ *noun.* **E19.**
[ORIGIN Greek *dramatourgia* composition of dramas (from *dramatourgos* DRAMATURGE: see -Y³), prob. after German *Dramaturgie*.]
1 Dramatic composition; the dramatic art. **E19.**
2 Dramatic or theatrical acting. Now *rare*. **M19.**
3 SOCIOLOGY. A theory which interprets individual behaviour as the dramatic projection of a chosen self. **M20.**
■ **dramaˈturgic**, **dramaˈturgical** *adjectives* **M19.** **dramaˈturgically** *adverb* **M20.** **dramaturgist** *noun* a dramatist **E19.**

Drambuie /dramˈbuːi, -ˈbjuːi/ *noun.* Also **d-**. **L19.**
[ORIGIN from Gaelic *dram buidheach* satisfying drink.]
(Proprietary name for) a Scotch whisky liqueur; a drink of this.

†**drame** *noun* see DRAMA.

dramedy /ˈdrɑːmədi/ *noun.* **E20.**
[ORIGIN Blend of DRAMA and COMEDY.]
An artwork, now esp. a television programme or film, in which the comic elements derive mainly from character and plot development.

drammock /ˈdramək/ *noun.* *Scot.* *arch.* **M17.**
[ORIGIN Gaelic *dramag*.]
Oatmeal mixed with cold water.

Drang /draŋ/ *noun*¹. **M19.**
[ORIGIN German.]
Strong tendency, pressure; urge, strong desire. Chiefly in phrs.
Drang nach Osten /nax ˈɔstən/ [lit. 'drive towards the east'] *hist.* a German imperialistic policy of eastward expansion. STURM UND DRANG.

drang *noun*² var. of DRONG.

drank *verb pa. t.* & *pple*: see DRINK *verb*.

drant /drant/ *noun* & *verb.* *Scot.* & *dial.* Also **draunt** /drɔːnt/. **E18.**
[ORIGIN App. onomatopoeic after DRAWL or DRONE *noun*, *verb* and RANT.]
▸ **A** *noun.* A drone; a drawl. **E18.**
▸ **B** *verb intrans.* Speak with a drawl. **E18.**

drap *noun* see DROP *noun*.

drápa /ˈdrɑːpə, ˈdraʊpə/ *noun.* Pl. ***-pur*** /-pʊə/. **M19.**
[ORIGIN Old Norse, prob. from *drepa* to strike.]
An old Icelandic heroic and laudatory poem.

†**drap-de-Berry** *noun.* Also **drab-**, **-du-**; **D-**. **E17–E19.**
[ORIGIN French = cloth of Berry.]
A type of woollen cloth from Berry in France.

drape /dreɪp/ *noun.* **M17.**
[ORIGIN Partly from French *drap* (see DRAPE *verb*), partly from DRAPE *verb*.]
1 Cloth; (a piece of) drapery. **M17.**
2 A curtain. Usu. in *pl.* *N. Amer.* **E20.**
3 *sing.* & (usu.) in *pl.* A man's suit, *esp.* one comprising a long jacket and narrow trousers. *slang.* **M20.**
4 The way a garment or fabric hangs. **M20.**
5 SURGERY. A sterilized covering for use in an operation. **M20.**
– COMB.: **drape jacket** *slang* the jacket of a drape suit; **drape suit** *slang* = sense 3 above.

drape /dreɪp/ *verb.* **LME.**
[ORIGIN In sense 1 from Old French & mod. French *draper*, from *drap* cloth from late Latin *drappus*, perh. of Celtic origin: cf. DRAB *noun*². In other senses back-form. from DRAPERY suggested by mod. French *draper*.]
†**1** *verb trans.* & *intrans.* Weave; make by weaving. **LME–L17.**
2 *verb trans.* Cover, hang, or adorn (as) with cloth or drapery; cover with a sterilized drape. **M19.**

> D. LODGE Another girl whose blonde head is becomingly draped with a black lace mantilla. G. SWIFT The body on the stretcher . . was entirely draped by the red blanket.

3 *verb trans.* Arrange or place (clothing etc.) *around* something, esp. in graceful folds. Also foll. by *about*, *over*. **M19.**

> I. MCEWAN Mary appeared . . , a cardigan draped around her shoulders. *fig.*: J. T. FARRELL Clouds . . draping shadows over the park.

4 *verb intrans.* Of fabric or a garment: admit of being (readily) draped. **M20.**
5 *verb refl.* Place (oneself) on or against something for support, esp. in drunken unsteadiness. *colloq.* **M20.**

■ **drapea'bility**, **drapa'bility** *noun* drapeable quality L20. **drapeable**, **drapable** *adjective* (of fabric etc.) that hangs easily, without stiffness M20. **draping** *ppl adjective* hanging in graceful folds or sheets L19.

draper /ˈdreɪpə/ *noun*. LME.
[ORIGIN Anglo-Norman, & Old French & mod. French *drapier*, from *drap* cloth: see DRAPE *verb*, -ER².]
Orig., a maker of (woollen) cloth. Now, a dealer in cloth.

drapery /ˈdreɪp(ə)ri/ *noun & verb*. ME.
[ORIGIN Old French & mod. French *draperie*, from *drap* cloth (see DRAPE *verb*), *drapier* DRAPER: see -ERY.]
► **A** *noun*. **1** Cloth, fabrics. ME.
†**2** The place where a draper works. LME–E17.
3 The trade of a draper. L15.
4 The artistic arranging of clothing in painting and sculpture. E17.
5 Cloth with which something is draped; hangings; clothing, *esp.* clothing that hangs; in *pl.*, curtains. L17.

W. HOLTBY The flying drapery of her lilac tunic. O. MANNING The monstrous catafalque appeared, black and blackly ornamented with fringed draperies. *fig.*: W. HOWITT Nature is stripped of all her summer drapery.

– COMB.: **drapery artist**, **drapery drudge** an artist employed to paint in the drapery of another's painting(s).
► **B** *verb trans.* Cover with drapery; drape. E19.

†**drapet** *noun*. *rare*. L16–L18.
[ORIGIN Italian *drappetto* dim. of *drappo* cloth from late Latin *drappus*.]
A cloth, a covering.

drappie /ˈdrapi/ *noun*. *Scot.* Also **-ppy**. L18.
[ORIGIN from DRAP *noun* + -IE, -Y⁶.]
A little drop, *spec.* of spirits.

drápur *noun* pl. of DRÁPA.

drastic /ˈdrastɪk, ˈdrɑː-/ *adjective & noun*. L17.
[ORIGIN Greek *drastikos* active, effective, from *dran* do: see -IC.]
► **A** *adjective*. **1** Of a medicine: acting strongly or violently. L17.
2 *gen.* Vigorous and decisive; having violent effects; severe. E19.

W. S. CHURCHILL Drastic measures were necessary. A. BRINK If you don't put an end to it soon something drastic will happen.

► **B** *noun*. A drastic medicine; *esp.* a strong laxative. L18.
■ **drastically** *adverb* M19.

drat /drat/ *verb trans. & intrans.* Infl. **-tt-**. E19.
[ORIGIN Aphet. from *od-rat*, from OD *noun*¹ + RAT *verb*².]
Damn, confound: used in exclamations of angry annoyance.

A. TROLLOPE Drat their impudence. J. HARTLEY It's that dratted dog after th' cat. *People* 'Oh drat it!' said Mrs. Fairbanks. BEVERLEY CLEARY 'Drat!' said Mitchell, kicking the fence and wishing he knew what to do.

dratch /dratʃ/ *verb intrans.* Now *Scot. & dial.* Also **dretch** /drɛtʃ/. ME.
[ORIGIN Unknown.]
Delay, linger; dawdle.

dratchell /ˈdratʃ(ə)l/ *noun*. *Scot. & dial.* Also **drotchell** /ˈdrɒtʃ(ə)l/. M18.
[ORIGIN Uncertain: perh. rel. to DRATCH.]
A slovenly, untidy, or disreputable woman.

draught /drɑːft/ *noun & adjective*. See also DRAFT *noun*. ME.
[ORIGIN Old Norse *dráttr* = Middle Dutch *dragt*, Old High German *traht* (German *Tracht*), from Germanic base of DRAW *verb*.]
► **A** *noun*. **I** Senses in which the dominant idea is of an action.
1 The action or an act of pulling something along, esp. a vehicle or farm implement; traction. ME. ►**b** *fig.* Attraction; tendency, inclination; impulse. (Foll. by *to*, *towards*.) *arch.* ME.

Daily Telegraph Horses . . were far too valuable to use for draught.

2 The action or an act of drawing a net for fish etc. ME. ►**b** A site where a net is customarily drawn. LME.
3 A single act of drinking or of inhaling tobacco smoke etc.; (long *obsolete* exc. *Scot.*) breathing; an amount drunk or inhaled at one go. ME. ►**b** *fig.* The taking in by the senses or the mind of something that affects one deeply; something experienced deeply. LME. ►**c** A dose of medicine; a potion. M17.

A. WILSON She stood by the open window, drawing in great draughts of . . air. A. UTTLEY He drained the cup at a draught. **b** S. JOHNSON Make the draught of life sweet or bitter.

c black draught *hist.* a purgative medicine (*lit.* & *fig.*).
†**4** The action of drawing a bow; a bowshot. ME–E17.
5 A stroke with a weapon. Long *obsolete* exc. *dial.* ME.
†**6** The action of drawing a brush, pencil, etc., across a surface; a mark so made. ME–M17. ►**b** Drawing (as an art). M16–M18.
†**7** A course followed, a way; *fig.* a way of behaving. Only in ME.
8 †**a** A move in chess etc. LME–M17. ►**b** In *pl.* (usu. treated as *sing.*). A game in which two players each start with 12 (or occas. 20) pieces of equal value on opposite sides of a chequered board, the pieces being moved diagonally with the aim of capturing those of the opponent. LME. ►**c** Each of the pieces used in the game of draughts. L19.
b Polish draughts: see POLISH *adjective*.
9 The action of drawing a saw through a block of wood or stone; a measure of timber etc. so cut. LME.
10 The action of drawing out to a greater length, stretching; something drawn out or spun, a thread. LME.
11 The action of drawing liquor from a cask etc.; the condition of being (ready to be) so drawn. LME.
on draught (of beer etc.) ready to be drawn from a cask, not bottled or canned etc.
12 = DRAFT *noun* 4. Now *rare* or *obsolete*. L15.
†**13** (An) extraction, (a) derivation; an act of drawing a lot. Long *rare* or *obsolete*. L15.
14 The depth of water needed to float a ship. E17.
15 The drawing of money by a written order (cf. DRAFT *noun* 6). Formerly also, the order itself. M17.
16 (The selection of) a detachment drawn from a larger group (see DRAFT *noun* 5). E18.
► **II** Senses in which the dominant idea is that of something drawn.
17 An amount or thing that is pulled or carried, esp. as a measure; a load. Now *rare* exc. *techn.* ME.
18 The quantity of fish taken in one drawing of the net; a catch. LME. ►**b** A unit of weight of eels, equal to 20 lb (approx. 9.1 kg). M19.

TINDALE *Luke* 5:9 He was vtterly astonyed . . at the draught of fisshe.

†**19** More fully ***draught-bridge***. A drawbridge. LME–M16.
20 The entrails of an animal removed prior to cooking. Now *obsolete* or *dial.* LME.
†**21** A passage of writing; an extract. LME–E17.
22 A thing drawn up or devised; a scheme, a plan, a design; a plot. Now *rare* or *obsolete*. LME.
23 A thing which is drawn on paper etc.; a drawing, a sketch. Now *rare* or *obsolete* in *gen.* sense. LME. ►**b** Representation in sculpture; a sculptured figure. M–L17.

S. JOHNSON He . . embellished [his pages] with elegant draughts and illuminations.

24 A sketch in words; a brief account; an outline, an abstract. Now *rare*. E16.

J. LOCKE Thus I have, in a short draught, given a view of our original Ideas.

25 = DRAFT *noun* 3. Also, an artist's initial or preparatory sketch etc. E16.
26 = DRAFT *noun* 2. L16.
27 WEAVING. The succession in which the threads of the warp are inserted into the heddles of the loom to produce the required pattern. E19.
28 = DRAFT *noun* 7. M19.
► **III** A thing that draws or is used in drawing; a current.
29 **a** A thing used in pulling; *esp.* a harness for horses to draw with. LME. ►**b** A team of horses etc. used for draught together with the vehicle drawn. Now *dial.* E16.
30 A flow, esp. of liquid. LME. ►**b** The course of a stream; a narrow valley. M17.

P. LEACH Sometimes the draught reflex makes the second breast leak milk while the baby sucks from the first.

31 More fully ***draught-house***. A privy, a lavatory. Now *rare* or *obsolete*. LME.
†**32** A cesspool, a sewer; a drainage channel. E16–E18.
33 A current of air in a room, chimney, or other confined space. L18.

DICKENS A sore throat, from sitting in constant draughts.

feel the draught: see FEEL *verb*.
► **B** *attrib.* or as *adjective*. **1** Of an animal: used for pulling a cart, plough, etc.; of a breed suitable for this. LME.
2 Of beer etc.: on draught (see sense 11 above). M19.
3 = DRAFT *adjective* 2. L19.
– COMB. & SPECIAL COLLOCATIONS: **draughtboard** a chequered board (identical to a chessboard) used for the game of draughts; ***draught-bridge***: see sense 19 above; **draught ewe** = DRAFT *noun* 5b; **draught excluder** a device or material for excluding draughts, esp. from doors or windows; †**draught-hound**: used for tracking by scent; **draught horse** a strong horse used for or of a breed suitable for draught; ***draught-house***: see sense 31 above; **draught-net** a net that is drawn for fish; **draughtproof** *adjective & verb* (**a**) *adjective* proof against draughts; (**b**) *verb trans.* make draughtproof (usu. in *pass.*); **draught-screen**: for shelter against draughts; **draught-tree** (now *rare* or *obsolete*) the pole of a wagon etc. to which the drawing gear is attached.

draught /drɑːft/ *verb trans.* M17.
[ORIGIN from the noun Cf. DRAFT *verb*.]
1 = DRAFT *verb* 2. M17.
2 = DRAFT *verb* 1. E18.
3 = DRAFT *verb* 3. M19.

draughtman /ˈdrɑːftmən/ *noun*. *rare*. Pl. **-men**. E18.
[ORIGIN from DRAUGHT *noun* + MAN *noun*.]
†**1** ***morning's draughtman***, a man who indulges in a morning draught of liquor; a tippler. Only in E18.
2 A draughtsman; *spec.* = DRAUGHTSMAN 3. M19.
■ **draughtmanship** *noun* = DRAUGHTSMANSHIP L19.

draughtsman /ˈdrɑːf(t)smən/ *noun*. Pl. **-men**. E18.
[ORIGIN from DRAUGHT *noun* + -'S¹ + MAN *noun*. Cf. earlier DRAFTSMAN.]
1 A person whose profession is to make drawings, plans, or sketches; a person skilled in drawing or designing. E18.

J. W. BURGON Though he was no draughtsman, he was the author of a large portfolio of portraits.

2 = DRAFTSMAN 2. E19.
3 = DRAUGHT *noun* 8c. Cf. DRAUGHTMAN 2. L19.
■ **draughtsmanship** *noun* the function, quality, or art of a draughtsman; skill in draughting or drawing; (cf. DRAFTSMANSHIP): M19.

D

draughtsperson /ˈdrɑːf(t)spəːs(ə)n/ *noun*. L20.
[ORIGIN formed as DRAUGHTSMAN + PERSON *noun*.]
= DRAUGHTSMAN 1.

draughtswoman /ˈdrɑːf(t)swʊmən/ *noun*. Pl. **-women** /-wɪmɪn/. M19.
[ORIGIN formed as DRAUGHTSMAN + WOMAN *noun*.]
A female draughtsman.

draughty /ˈdrɑːfti/ *adjective*. Also *__drafty__. E19.
[ORIGIN from DRAUGHT *noun* + -Y¹.]
1 Artful, crafty. *Scot.* E19.
2 Letting in draughts, subject to draughts. M19.
■ **draughtiness** *noun* L19.

draunt *noun & verb* var. of DRANT.

drave /dreɪv/ *noun*. *Scot. & N. English*. L16.
[ORIGIN formed as DROVE *noun*.]
A communal fishing expedition in which each participant supplies a net and takes a share of the profit; a haul of fish; a shoal.

drave *verb pa. t.*: see DRIVE *verb*.

Dravidian /drəˈvɪdɪən/ *adjective & noun*. M19.
[ORIGIN from Sanskrit *drāviḍa* pertaining to the Tamils from *Dravida* Tamil: see -IAN.]
1 (Of, pertaining to, or designating) any of a group of languages spoken chiefly in southern India and Sri Lanka, including Tamil, Telugu, and Brahui. M19.
2 (Of, pertaining to, or designating) a member of a dark-skinned people of southern India and Sri Lanka that mostly speak a Dravidian language, including Tamils and Kanarese. M19.

Dravidic /drəˈvɪdɪk/ *adjective*. M19.
[ORIGIN formed as DRAVIDIAN: see -IC.]
Dravidian.

draw /drɔː/ *noun*. LME.
[ORIGIN from the verb.]
1 The action or an act of drawing. LME. ►**b** *The* action of drawing a revolver from its holster in order to shoot. M19. ►**c** A suck at a pipe, cigarette, etc.; a smoke. Chiefly *dial. & N. Amer.* L19.

Abingdon Herald The first draw of the day was in Flamborough, where a fox was killed.

2 **a** A drawer of a cabinet. *US*. L17. ►**b** (The movable part of) a drawbridge. *US*. L18.
3 An event in which lots are drawn, a raffle; an order of contestants etc. decided in this way; a lot drawn. M18.
luck of the draw: see LUCK *noun*.
4 Attractive power or effect; a person or thing drawing or able to draw custom, attention, etc. *colloq.* E19.

A. WILSON His name would still be a great draw for bourgeois audiences.

5 Something or someone used to elicit a person's knowledge or intentions; a person from whom such information may be extracted. *arch. slang*. E19.
6 Orig. †***draw game***, †***draw race***, etc. A game etc. which has ended without an outright winner; a drawn game. E19.
hold to a draw: see HOLD *verb*.
7 An amount drawn or drawn out etc. E19.
8 CRICKET. A stroke to the leg side (no longer used) in which the batsman deflected the ball so that it passed between the wicket and his legs; a player positioned to field balls so hit. M19.
9 **a** More fully ***draw poker***. The standard form of the game of poker. M19. ►**b** The deal in poker after discarding. L19.
10 A shallow valley. *US*. L19.
11 A cavity inside cast metal resulting from shrinkage during solidification. E20.
12 Cannabis, esp. when smoked or prepared for smoking. *slang*. L20.

draw /drɔː/ *verb*. Pa. t. **drew** /druː/; pa. pple **drawn** /drɔːn/.
[ORIGIN Old English *dragan* = Old Norse *draga*, Old Frisian *draga*, Old Saxon *dragan* (Dutch *dragen*), Old High German *tragan* (German *tragen*), Gothic (*ga*)*dragan*.]
► **I** Cause to move, pull.
1 **a** *verb trans.* Cause (something) to move towards, or past a part of, oneself by the application of force; pull. OE.

▸**b** *verb trans. & intrans.* Pull (something, esp. a vehicle or its load) so as to make it follow along behind; *hist.* drag (a criminal) on a hurdle etc. to the place of execution. Formerly also *fig.*, agree (*with*); be in a like situation *with*. ME. ▸**c** *verb intrans.* Be drawn; admit of being drawn. M17.

a ADDISON He drew a Paper of Verses out of his Pocket. F. BURNEY I.. drew my hat over my face. G. GREENE Josef.. drew the string on which the revolver dangled a couple of inches higher. I. MCEWAN He took her wrist and drew her into the street. *refl.*: W. C. RUSSELL Wilfrid.. drew himself erect. **b** SHAKES. *Oth.* Think every bearded fellow that's but yok'd May draw with you. D. BAGLEY There were carts pushed by hand or drawn by donkey.

†**2** *verb trans.* Tear apart; pull *in pieces*, *asunder*. ME–E18.

3 a *verb trans. & intrans.* Pull back the string of (a bow) ready to shoot; pull back (the arrow) on the string; hoist (a sail); pull up (a drawbridge); pull out (a bolt, an organ stop); haul in (a net). ME. ▸**b** *verb trans.* Pull (a veil etc.) over something so as to conceal it; pull (a curtain, blinds) open or shut. LME.

a AV *1 Kings* 22:34 A certain man drew a bow at a venture. W. LONGMAN He then drew the bolt, the door was opened. T. H. WHITE Boys.. are inclined to catch hold of the nock of the arrow when they draw.

4 *verb trans.* Cause to come, move, or go (from or to some place, position, or condition); lead, bring, take, convey, put. *obsolete* exc. as assoc. with other senses. ME.

T. HERBERT Hee.. drawes his forces against Rantas. W. IRVING He hastened to draw him from the seductions of the garden.

†**5** *verb trans.* Render into another style of writing; translate. ME–M16.

†**6** *verb trans. fig.* Adduce, appeal to for confirmation; assign, attribute; turn aside to a purpose, pervert. ME–E18.

7 *verb trans. & intrans.* Contract, shrink; pull or become out of shape or place. Usu. as DRAWN *adjective*. LME.

†**8** *verb trans.* Construct (a ditch, canal, wall) from one point to another. LME–L18.

†**9** *verb trans.* Pass (food) through or *through* a strainer; bring to the required consistency thus. LME–L18.

†**10** Operate on (a number) with one of the processes of arithmetic: add *to*, *together*; multiply *into*; subtract *out of*. LME–E19.

11 *verb trans.* NAUTICAL. Of a ship: require (a specified depth of water) for floating. M16.

J. CONRAD She drew too much water to cross the bar.

†**12** *verb trans.* Bring (the edges of a tear etc.) together by sewing; mend (a rent). L16–E17.

13 *verb trans.* In various games, direct or divert (a ball) in some way; *spec.* in CRICKET (now *rare*), divert (the ball) to the leg side of the wicket with the bat; GOLF drive (the ball) purposely to the left of a right-handed player or vice versa; BOWLS cause (the bowl) to travel in a curve to the desired point. M19.

▸ **II** Come; go.

14 *verb intrans.* Come *together*; move or make one's way *towards*; also with adverbs in specialized senses (see below). Formerly without adverb or adverbial phr.: move, come, go. OE.

†**15** *verb refl.* Go *towards* or *to*; withdraw *from*. ME–E17.

W. RALEIGH As their people increased, they drew themselves more westerly towards the Red sea.

†**16** *verb intrans.* Tend, approach, *to* or *towards* some condition, state, etc. ME–E17.

R. KNOLLES Of a darke colour, somewhat drawing toward a violet.

17 *verb intrans.* Move in time *to* or *towards* an event, a particular time, etc. ME.

B. JOWETT The days of Socrates are drawing to a close.

18 *verb intrans.* HUNTING. Of a hound etc.: track game by its scent; move slowly towards the game after pointing. (Foll. by *after*, *on*, *upon*.) L16.

19 *verb intrans.* Gradually get further *away from* or gain *on* an antagonist or competitor in a race etc. E19.

▸ **III** Take in; attract.

20 a *verb trans.* Take (a breath); take (air etc.) into the lungs. See also ***draw breath*** s.v. BREATH. ME. ▸**b** *verb intrans.* Of a chimney, pipe, etc.: promote or allow a current of air through it. Of a smoker: suck *at* a pipe etc. M18.

b F. MARRYAT The fire does not draw well. R. CHANDLER I finished filling the pipe, put a match to it, got it drawing.

21 *verb trans.* Attract by physical force, as a magnet; tend to become covered or affected with (rust etc.). ME.

E. KIRKE The rod draws the electricity from the air. *fig.*: J. TILLOTSON The blessings it will draw down upon us.

22 a *verb trans.* Attract (a person) by affecting his or her inclination, sympathies, etc.; cause (the mind, eyes, etc.) to become directed *to*, *from*, etc., or attracted; lead (a person) into, from, etc. (a course of action, condition, etc.). ME. ▸**b** *verb intrans.* Exercise allurement or attraction; prove an attraction; attract crowds. L16.

a ADDISON To draw the Eyes of the World upon her. THOMAS HUGHES It is wonderful.. how you feel drawn to a man who feeds you well. L. J. JENNINGS A great bereavement.. drew his mind from public affairs. G. GREENE I feel an enormous desire to draw attention to myself. S. BELLOW He did not want to be drawn into a quarrel. **b** J. R. LOWELL Mr. Emerson always draws.

23 *verb intrans. & †trans.* Gather together, collect, assemble. ME.

A. RADCLIFFE Our desolate party drew round it.

24 *verb trans.* Cause (an enemy etc.) to fall *on* or *upon* a person; bring (disaster etc.) *on* or *upon*; bring about as a result, bring on. ME.

T. MARTIN Rage drew on Thyestes the vengeance of heaven.

25 *verb trans.* Induce (a person) *to do*. M16.

M. LASKI One of the things that had drawn him to ask her to dance.

▸ **IV** Take out; deprive.

26 a *verb trans.* Remove or extract (an object) from what it is fixed or embedded in; *esp.* take (a playing card or suit) from a pack. (Foll. by *from*.) ME. ▸**b** *verb trans. & intrans.* Take (a weapon) from a sheath or holster in readiness for immediate use. ME.

T. HARDY He drew the corks of the mineral waters. H. ROTH He would draw several of her teeth. E. BOWEN He kept drawing long black horsehairs from the seat of his chair. **b** R. JARRELL He drew a big revolver and he shot me.

27 a *verb trans. & intrans.* Pull or take (one thing) from a number in order to decide something by chance; obtain or win (something) in this way. ME. ▸**b** *verb trans.* Set apart (sheep) from a flock; separate (seeds) from the husks. L15.

a STEELE Neither of them had drawn the Thousand Pound. W. MORRIS We.. shared the spoil by drawing short and long. TOLKIEN They now drew lots for the watches.

28 a *verb trans. & †intrans.* Raise (water) from a well etc. by hauling or pumping; obtain (beer etc.) from a cask or (water) from a tap; run (a bath); cause (blood) to flow from an incision etc. ME. ▸**b** *verb trans.* Extract (liquor, juice, etc.) by suction, pressure, infusion, or distillation. M16. ▸**c** *verb intrans.* Of tea: infuse. E19.

a H. ROBBINS He.. walked over to the sink, and drew a glass of water. **c** F. TUOHY The two women.. waited for the Indian tea to draw.

29 a *verb trans.* Take or obtain *from* a source; derive; deduce, infer, (a conclusion). ME. ▸**b** *verb trans.* Take, receive, or obtain (money) from a source of supply. L16. ▸**c** *verb intrans.* Obtain information, resources, etc., *from*. E19.

a A. FLEMING The stocke from whence he draweth his descent. *Daily Telegraph* Gilt-edged investors were looking a bit happier... drawing comfort from the improving pound. **b** B. PYM Letty had been retired for a week and had drawn the first payment of her pension.

30 *verb trans.* Cause to come out or appear; elicit, evoke; *spec.* cause (a particular playing card) to be played by another player. ME.

31 *verb trans.* Extract something from; empty, drain, exhaust, deplete; *spec.* disembowel (a fowl etc., *hist.* a criminal after hanging). ME. ▸**b** Remove coals from (a fire, furnace, etc.). E19.

32 *verb trans.* Drag or pull a net through or along (a river etc.) for fish; search (a wood etc.) for game. LME.

A. EDEN Hounds were drawing the home coverts.

33 *verb trans. & intrans.* **a** Cause a flow of (blood, matter, etc.) to a particular part of the body; promote suppuration. LME. ▸**b** Drain off or away, esp. by means of a channel. E17.

R. D. BLACKMORE His poultice began to draw.

†**34** *verb trans.* Withdraw (stakes, a racehorse, etc.). L16–M19.

35 *verb trans.* Force (a badger or fox) from its hole. M19.

36 *verb trans.* Elicit information or conversation from (a person). *colloq.* M19.

J. SIMMS I tried to involve him in a political discussion,.. but he refused to be drawn.

37 *verb trans.* Rouse (a person) to action, speech, or anger; irritate, exasperate. *colloq.* M19.

38 *verb trans. & intrans.* Finish (a game etc.) with no one a winner or scores equal. (Earlier as DRAWN *ppl adjective* 2.) M19.

▸ **V** Extend.

39 *verb trans.* Pull out to a greater length; extend, lengthen; prolong, protract. Usu. foll. by *out*. ME. ▸**b** Make (wire) by drawing metal through successively smaller holes; elongate and attenuate (a sliver of cotton etc.) by passage through pairs of rollers revolving at successively greater speeds. E16.

T. ELLWOOD I Prayed often, and drew out my Prayers to a great length. P. THEROUX A man melting tubes of glass and drawing them thin.

†**40** *verb trans. & intrans.* Amount to or *to*. LME–M16.

41 *verb intrans.* NAUTICAL. Of a sail: swell out tightly with the wind. E17.

▸ **VI** Make, depict.

42 a *verb trans.* Trace (a line or figure), make (a picture), by drawing a pen, pencil, etc., across a surface; cut (a furrow) with a ploughshare. ME. ▸**b** *verb intrans.* Draw pictures, practise the art of drawing. M16. ▸**c** *verb trans.* Represent by a drawing, depict; *fig.* represent in words, describe. L16.

a J. RHYS She took a sharp stick and drew lines and circles on the earth under the tree.

43 = ***draw up*** (b) below. Formerly also, write (a story), compose (a song). ME.

L. STEPHEN Langton had employed Chambers.. to draw his will.

†**44** *verb trans.* Devise, contrive; set in order, arrange. M16–M17.

F. HAWKINS The matter of any Book or Science, drawn into Indexes or Tables.

45 *verb trans.* Shape or carve (stone, wood, etc.) by shaving thin slices off it. M17.

46 *verb trans.* Write out (a cheque etc.) in due form to authorize payment. (Foll. by *on*, *upon* the person etc. that has to pay.) M17.

47 *verb intrans.* Draw a cheque etc. *on* or *upon* a person etc.; call *on* or *upon* a person for or *for* funds, or any source for or *for* something. L17.

P. ACKROYD There were few intellectual models upon which to draw. V. GLENDINNING Edith was drawing deeply on her childhood memories for this poetry.

48 *verb trans.* Make, formulate, (a comparison, contrast, distinction, etc.). L18.

– PHRASES: ***draw a bead on***: see BEAD *noun* 4c. **draw a blank** fail in a search; elicit no response. ***draw a veil*** (***over***): see VEIL *noun* 5. **draw bit**, **draw bridle**, **draw rein** check one's horse or (*fig.*) oneself. ***draw breath***: see BREATH. ***draw bridle***: see ***draw bit*** above. ***draw in one's horns***: see HORN *noun*. **draw it mild** *fig.* [from drawing beer] be moderate, not exaggerate. **draw level** (**with**) come from behind to a position alongside in a race etc. ***draw one's steel***: see STEEL *noun*[1]. ***draw pig on pork***, ***draw pig on bacon***: see PIG *noun*[1]. **draw one's sword against** take up arms against, attack (*lit. & fig.*). ***draw rein***: see ***draw bit*** above. ***draw steel***: see STEEL *noun*[1]. ***draw straws***: see STRAW *noun*. ***draw stumps***: see STUMP *noun*[1]. ***draw the badger***: see BADGER *noun*[2] 1. **draw the cloth** *arch.* remove the tablecloth after a meal, clear away. ***draw the line at***: see LINE *noun*[2]. ***draw the longbow***: see LONG *adjective*[1]. ***draw the short straw***: see STRAW *noun*. ***draw the stumps***: see STUMP *noun*[1].

– WITH ADVERBS IN SPECIALIZED SENSES: **draw back** move backwards from one's position, *fig.* withdraw from an undertaking. **draw down** (*a*) make (metal, plastic) thinner by hammering, stretching, etc.; (*b*) make a drawing of (a loan), borrow. **draw forth** evoke. **draw in** (*a*) entice (*to do*); deceive, take in; persuade to take part; make to include in a conversation; (*b*) draw tight, cause to shrink; (*c*) (of a day) approach its end, (of night) approach, (of successive evenings) become shorter; (*d*) (of a train etc.) enter a station; (of a vehicle) move towards the side of the road; (*e*) = sense 20a above. **draw near** (**to**) approach (*lit. & fig.*). **draw off** (*a*) withdraw (troops); move off; (*b*) drain away by a tap etc., esp. without disturbing the bottom or sediment of the liquid. **draw on** (*a*) come near; (*b*) bring on, involve as a consequence; (*c*) entice, allure; (*d*) pull on (a garment etc.). **draw out** (*a*) = ***draw up*** (b) below; (*b*) elicit, evoke; (*c*) lead out, detach, or array (troops); (of troops) move out of camp etc.; (*d*) induce to talk; (*e*) (of successive days) grow longer; (*f*) (of a train etc.) leave a station; (of a vehicle) move away from the side of the road. **draw up** (*a*) bring (esp. troops) or come into regular order; (*b*) compose (a document), esp. in a formally correct way; write out in due form; (*c*) come up *with*, come close *to*; gain on or overtake an antagonist in a race; (*d*) bring or come to a halt, pull up; (*e*) make *oneself* stiffly erect; (*f*) take up *with* (a person).

draw- /drɔː/ *combining form.*

[ORIGIN Repr. DRAW *noun*, *verb*.]

In combs. in various relations and with various senses, as 'that is drawn', 'that draws', 'involving drawing'.

■ **drawbench** *noun* a machine with a bed along which wire etc. can be reduced in cross-section by being drawn through a restricting aperture M19. **draw boy** *noun* (*hist.*) the boy who pulled the strings of a draw loom; the device by which this was later effected: M18. **drawcard** *noun* something that attracts attention or custom M20. **draw-gate** *noun* a sluice gate L18. **draw-glove(s)** *noun* (*hist.*) a parlour game which consisted in a race at drawing off gloves when certain words were spoken M17. **draw hoe** *noun* a hoe used with a pulling action E19. **draw-in** *noun* (*a*) *rare* something that draws things in; (*b*) a lay-by: M19. **draw-kiln** *noun* a limekiln from which the burned lime is drawn out at the bottom E19. **drawknife** *noun* (*a*) a blade with a handle at each end at right angles to it, drawn towards the user to remove wood from a surface; (*b*) = ***drawing-knife*** (a) s.v. DRAWING *verbal noun*: E18. **draw-leaf** *noun* an extending leaf of a draw-table M20. **draw loom** *noun* (*hist.*) a loom used for figure weaving, in which the warp threads passed through loops in strings which were pulled in a particular order to produce a pattern M19. **draw-net** *noun* a dragnet E17. **draw-off** *adjective* designating a tap by which liquid may be drawn from a vessel E20. **drawplate** *noun* a plate with a number of graduated apertures through which wire or metal strip can be drawn to make it thinner M19. ***draw poker***: see DRAW *noun* 9a. **draw-shave** *noun* a drawknife for shaving spokes etc. E19. **draw sheet** *noun* a sheet so placed that it can be taken from under a patient without remaking the whole bed L19. **drawstop** *noun* an organ stop which is pulled out to admit air to a rank of pipes L19. **drawstring** *noun* a string, cord, etc., that can be pulled to tighten the mouth of a bag, the waist of a garment, etc. M19. **draw-table** *noun* a table with parts that can be pulled out to make it larger E20. **draw-well** *noun* a deep well from which water is drawn by a bucket suspended on a rope LME. **draw-works** *noun pl.* the machinery in an oil derrick for raising and lowering the drill pipe and providing the power for turning it E20.

drawable /'drɔː(r)əb(ə)l/ *adjective*. LME.
[ORIGIN from DRAW *verb* + -ABLE.]
Able to be drawn.

drawback /'drɔːbak/ *noun & adjective*. E17.
[ORIGIN from *draw back* s.v. DRAW *verb*.]
▸ **A** *noun*. †**1** A person who draws back or hesitates. Only in E17.
2 A refund of excise or import duty when the imported item is subsequently exported or used in producing an export. Formerly, the action of getting such a refund. L17. ▸**b** A deduction, a diminution. Foll. by *from*. M18.
3 Something that hinders progress or impairs satisfaction; a hindrance, a disadvantage. E18.

P. WARNER The greatest drawback to armour was its suffocating effect. D. M. THOMAS Except for the major drawback of being apart from her husband, she was busy and contented.

4 In iron-founding, a removable part of a mould. M19.
5 The inhalation of smoke from a cigarette etc. *Austral.* M20.
▸ **B** *attrib.* or as *adjective*. (Having a part) that can be drawn back. E18.

drawbar /'drɔːbɑː/ *noun*. M16.
[ORIGIN from DRAW- + BAR *noun*¹.]
1 A bar that can be removed, esp. in a fence to allow passage. M16.
2 A bar on a vehicle to which something can be attached to pull it or be pulled. M19.
3 A submerged fireclay block used in glass-making to stabilize the position of sheet glass during drawing. M20.
4 Any of a number of bars that may be pulled out to control harmonics on an electric organ. M20.

drawbridge /'drɔːbrɪdʒ/ *noun*. ME.
[ORIGIN from DRAW- + BRIDGE *noun*¹.]
1 A bridge or section of a bridge hinged at one end for drawing up and lowering to prevent or permit passage across it or to open or close a channel spanned by it. ME.
2 A movable bridge or gangway on a ship etc. M19.

Drawcansir /'drɔːkansə, drɔː'kansə/ *noun*. L17.
[ORIGIN A blustering braggart in Villiers's 'The Rehearsal' (1672), who in the last scene enters a battle and kills all the combatants, from burlesque alt. of *Almanzor* in Dryden's 'Conquest of Granada' (1670–2), perh. intended to suggest *draw a can* (of liquor).]
A person formidable to both friend and enemy; a fierce swashbuckler.

drawdown /'drɔːdaʊn/ *noun*. L18.
[ORIGIN from *draw down* s.v. DRAW *verb*.]
†**1** Something that is drawn down. *rare*. Only in L18.
2 (A) lowering of the water level in a lake etc.; a withdrawal of water or oil from a reservoir etc. M20.
3 An act of raising money through loans; borrowing. L20.

drawee /drɔː(r)'iː/ *noun*. M18.
[ORIGIN from DRAW *verb* + -EE¹.]
The person, bank, etc., on whom a bill of exchange is drawn.

drawer /*in branch I* 'drɔː(r)ə; *in branches II, III* drɔː/ *noun*. ME.
[ORIGIN from DRAW *verb* + -ER¹, in branch II after Old French & mod. French *tiroir*, from *tirer* draw.]
▸ **I 1** A person who or thing which draws. ME. ▸**b** A tapster. *arch.* M16. ▸**c** A person who makes a drawing; a draughtsman. L16. ▸**d** A person who draws a bill of exchange. L17. ▸**e** A legal draftsman. L18.
2 An instrument, tool, etc., for drawing out or extracting. Long *rare*. M16.
▸ **II 3** In *pl.* Knickers, underpants, briefs. Formerly also, any garment worn next to the body below the waist; stockings. M16.

D. L. SAYERS The Dean . . thinks a brassière and a pair of drawers rather unsuitable for sun-bathing in the quad.

droopy drawers.
▸ **III 4** A box-shaped receptacle made to slide horizontally in and out of a frame or a table for access. L16.

R. RENDELL The drawers in the two bedside tables were pulled out.

bottom drawer: see BOTTOM *adjective*. *top drawer*: see TOP *adjective*.
5 In *pl.* = *chest of drawers* s.v. CHEST *noun*. L17.

drawing /'drɔː(r)ɪŋ/ *noun*. ME.
[ORIGIN from DRAW *verb* + -ING¹. In branch II abbreviation of WITHDRAWING.]
▸ **I 1** *gen.* The action of DRAW *verb*; an instance of this, *esp.* a raffle. ME.

JER. TAYLOR Little drawings aside of the curtains of peace. B. WEBB There has been a rapid drawing together . . of Liberals and Conservatives against Labour.

deep drawing: see DEEP *adverb*.
2 *spec.* The action of drawing a line on paper etc.; the art of representing or figuring by means of lines, esp. in monochrome; representation in which delineation of form is primary. LME.

J. REYNOLDS Painting comprises both drawing and colouring.

out of drawing incorrectly drawn, esp. as regards perspective. *technical drawing*: see TECHNICAL *adjective*.
3 A picture, diagram, or representation of something drawn in monochrome or in which delineation of form is primary. L17. ▸**b** The arrangement of the lines in a drawing which determine form. M18.

W. S. MAUGHAM On the walls were drawings by the great French masters.

detail drawing, *exploded drawing*, *working drawing*, etc.
4 Something which is drawn out or obtained by drawing; in *pl.*, money drawn out of a business or account. M19. **drawing of tea** an amount of tea leaves taken to make a pot of tea.
▸ **II 5** = WITHDRAWING. Only in *drawing-chamber* below, DRAWING ROOM. LME.
– COMB.: **drawing account** an account from which money can be drawn, esp. against credited future earnings or an allowance of expenses; **drawing block** a pad of drawing paper; **drawing board**: on which paper may be spread for drawing plans etc. on; *back to the drawing board* (*colloq.*), back to begin afresh (after the failure of an enterprise); **drawing book** a book for drawing in or containing designs to be copied; †**drawing-chamber** a private room; a drawing room; **drawing knife** (*a*) a farrier's knife for trimming hoofs; (*b*) = *drawknife* (a) s.v. DRAW-; **drawing master** a teacher of drawing; **drawing paper** stout paper for drawing on; **drawing pin**: with a round flat head for fastening paper to a drawing board or other surface; **drawing string** = *draw string* s.v. DRAW-.

drawing /'drɔː(r)ɪŋ/ *ppl adjective*. LME.
[ORIGIN from DRAW *verb* + -ING².]
That draws, esp. a vehicle, matter from a wound, or an audience.
drawing card = DRAWCARD.

drawing room /'drɔː(r)ɪŋrʊm, -ruːm/ *noun & adjective phr.* M17.
[ORIGIN Abbreviation of *WITHDRAWING-room*.]
▸ **A** *noun*. **1** Orig., a private room attached to a more public one. Now, a room where guests can be formally received and to which they can retire after dinner; a sitting room. M17. ▸**b** The company assembled in a drawing room. M19. ▸**c** A private compartment in a train. *US*. M19.
2 *hist.* A levee; a formal reception, esp. at court. E18.
▸ **B** *attrib.* or as *adjective*. Suitable for or characteristic of a drawing room; *esp.* (of a story, song, play, etc.) distinguished by an observance of social proprieties; polite, restrained. M19.
■ **drawing-roomy** *adjective* E20.

drawish /'drɔː(r)ɪʃ/ *adjective*. E20.
[ORIGIN from DRAW *noun* + -ISH¹.]
Of a game of chess: likely to lead to a draw.

drawk /drɔːk/ *noun*. Now *dial.* ME.
[ORIGIN medieval Latin *drauca*.]
Any of several weeds that grow in corn, *esp.* brome, darnel, or wild oats.

drawl /drɔːl/ *verb & noun*. L16.
[ORIGIN Prob. orig. slang from East Frisian, Low German, Dutch *dralen* delay, linger. Cf. DRAIL.]
▸ **A** *verb*. **1** *verb intrans. & trans.* (usu. foll. by *out*). Speak or utter with indolence or deliberate slowness; speak or utter with vowels more prolonged than is usual. L16.
2 *verb intrans.* Move slowly and loiteringly, crawl; trail. Now *rare*. L16.

W. OWEN The blind-cord drawls across the window sill.

3 *verb trans.* Pull slowly or with effort, drag; drag *on* or *out* in time; cause to pass slowly *away*. L16.
▸ **B** *noun*. The action of drawling; a slow indolent utterance; speech or an accent with vowels more prolonged than is usual. M18.

R. LEHMANN 'No, I can't imagine,' said Madeleine in a thoughtful drawl.

■ **drawler** *noun* M19. **drawlingly** *adverb* in a drawling manner M18.

drawlatch /'drɔːlatʃ/ *noun & verb*. ME.
[ORIGIN from DRAW *verb* + LATCH *noun*¹.]
▸ **A** *noun*. **1** A sneak thief. *obsolete* exc. *dial.* ME.
2 A lazy or worthless person. *derog. arch.* M16.
▸ **B** *verb intrans.* Act in a sneaky way; dawdle, waste time. *obsolete* exc. *dial.* L16.

drawly /'drɔːli/ *adjective*. E19.
[ORIGIN from DRAWL *noun* + -Y¹.]
Of the nature of a drawl; characterized by drawling.

drawn /drɔːn/ *adjective*. ME.
[ORIGIN pa. pple of DRAW *verb*.]
1 That has been drawn; *spec.* (of a gun etc.) taken out ready for immediate use; (of a line, picture, etc.) formed on paper etc.; (of wire, glass, etc.) made by drawing. ME.

A. K. GREEN A long drawn-out tale.

deep-drawn: see DEEP *adverb*.
2 Of a battle, game, etc.: ended without an outright winner; resulting in a draw. Of a position in chess: resulting in a draw if both players make the best moves. E17.
3 Of fabric, a garment, etc.: gathered. M19.
4 Of a face, expression, etc.: distorted or lined by pain, anxiety, or fear. L19.
5 Of a shoot or plant: thin and elongated, spindly. L19.
– SPECIAL COLLOCATIONS: **drawn butter** melted butter. **drawn-thread work**, **drawn work** ornamental work on a fabric done by drawing out threads, usu. with additional needlework.

dray /dreɪ/ *noun*¹ *& verb*. LME.
[ORIGIN Corresp. formally to Old English *dræge* (also *drægnet*) dragnet, from base of *dragan* DRAW *verb* & Anglo-Latin *dreia*. Cf. Middle Low German *drage* bier, litter (German *Trage* hand-barrow, litter).]
▸ **A** *noun*. **1** A cart without wheels, a sledge. Now *dial.* & *US*. LME.
2 A low cart without sides used esp. by brewers for carrying heavy loads. (Earliest in *drayman*.) L16.
3 A two-wheeled cart. *Austral.* & *NZ*. E19.
– COMB.: **dray cart** = senses 1, 2 above; **dray horse** a large strong horse used for pulling a dray; **drayman** the driver of a dray, *esp.* a brewer's driver; **dray-road**, **dray-track** (chiefly *Austral.* & *NZ*) a road or track used chiefly by drays, a narrow track.
▸ **B** *verb trans.* Convey by dray; bring *up* or *in* by dray. M19.
■ **drayage** *noun* (*a*) conveyance by dray; (*b*) the charge for this: L18.

dray *noun*² var. of DREY.

dread /drɛd/ *noun*. ME.
[ORIGIN from DREAD *verb*.]
1 Extreme fear or apprehension; great awe. ME.

C. CONNOLLY The dread of loneliness being keener than the fear of bondage, we get married. J. COE The sight of these men filled me with dread.

†**2** Doubt; risk of something being otherwise. ME–M16.
3 An object or cause of dread. ME.

MILTON Shouting to behold Their once great dread, captive and blind before them.

4 A sudden take-off and flight by a colony of gulls or other birds. M20.
5 A Rastafarian; a person who wears dreadlocks; in *pl.*, dreadlocks. L20.
– COMB.: **dreadlocks** a Rastafarian hairstyle in which the hair is twisted while wet into tight braids or ringlets hanging down on all sides.

†**dread** *adjective*¹. Only in ME.
[ORIGIN Aphet. from ADRAD with assim. to DREAD *noun*.]
Afraid, terrified.
– NOTE: Survives in derivs. DREADLY, DREADNESS.

dread /drɛd/ *adjective*². LME.
[ORIGIN pa. pple of DREAD *verb*.]
1 Feared greatly; dreadful, awful. LME.

F. W. FABER A bondage dreader far than death. R. ELLISON The dread possibility . . of being expelled.

2 Held in awe, revered. *arch.* LME.

SHAKES. *2 Hen. VI* A messenger from Henry, our dread liege.

dread /drɛd/ *verb*. Earlier †**a-**. Pa. t. & pple **dreaded**, †**dred**. See also YDRED.
[ORIGIN Old English *adrǣdan* late form of *ondrǣdan* = Old Saxon *antdrāden*, Old High German *intrātan*, from *ond-*, *and-* (as in ANSWER *noun*) + a West Germanic base of unknown origin. Aphet. in Middle English after which *adread* is not recorded.]
1 *verb trans.* Fear greatly; regard with awe. OE.
2 *verb trans.* Have a shrinking apprehension of; look forward to with anxiety or fear; be afraid *that*, *to do*. OE. ▸†**b** Fear for. *rare*. M–L16.

T. MOORE I sometimes dread that all is not right at home. J. BUCHAN The thing I hoped for and had dreaded to miss. P. ROSE Mrs Ruskin hated Scotland and . . dreaded going there.

†**3** *verb intrans.* Be greatly afraid. OE–M19.

AV *1 Chron.* 22:13 Dread not, nor be dismayed.

4 *verb refl.* Fear, be afraid. Now only foll. by subord. clause. Long *arch.* OE.
5 *verb trans.* Cause to fear; terrify. Long *obsolete* exc. *Scot. arch.* ME.
■ **dreaded** *ppl adjective* regarded with dread; *joc.* & *colloq.* regarded with mock fear or light-hearted contempt: M16. **dreader** *noun* (now *rare*) M16. **dreadingly** *adverb* (*rare*) with dread L16.

dreadful /'drɛdfʊl, -f(ə)l/ *adjective, adverb, & noun*. ME.
[ORIGIN from DREAD *noun* + -FUL.]
▸ **A** *adjective*. †**1** Full of dread; terrified; awed. ME–M17.
2 Inspiring dread or awe; formidable; terrible. ME.

H. JAMES He was haunted . . with dreadful visions of what might have befallen her.

3 Exceedingly bad, long, or boring; troublesome, disagreeable, horrid. *colloq.* E18.

G. VIDAL The acoustics of the Odeon are dreadful.

▸ **B** *adverb*. Dreadfully. Now *non-standard*. L17.
▸ **C** *noun*. A story in a crudely sensational style; a cheap book or magazine of such stories. L19.

D

penny dreadful: see PENNY *adjective*.
■ **dreadfully** *adverb* †(*a*) with fear or awe; (*b*) terribly, fearfully; *colloq.* exceedingly: ME. **dreadfulness** *noun* †(*a*) the state of having fear or dread; (*b*) the quality of being dreadful or fearsome: LME.

dreadless /ˈdrɛdlɪs/ *adjective & adverb*. Now *rare*. LME.
[ORIGIN from DREAD *noun* + -LESS.]
▸ **A** *adjective*. Without dread; fearless; without danger, secure. LME.
▸ †**B** *adverb*. Without doubt or fear of mistake. LME–M16.
■ **dreadlessly** *adverb* E17. **dreadlessness** *noun* L16.

dreadly /ˈdrɛdli/ *adverb*. *arch.* ME.
[ORIGIN from DREAD *adjective*[1] + -LY[2].]
1 In a manner that inspires dread. ME.
2 With dread or awe. *rare*. L17.

dreadness /ˈdrɛdnɪs/ *noun*. Long *arch. rare*. ME.
[ORIGIN from DREAD *adjective*[1] + -NESS.]
Dreadfulness.

dreadnought /ˈdrɛdnɔːt/ *noun & adjective*. Also **-naught**, (in sense 3) **D-**. E19.
[ORIGIN from DREAD *verb* + NOUGHT *noun*. In sense A.3 from the name of a particular Brit. battleship.]
▸ **A** *noun*. **1** A heavy overcoat; a type of thick woollen cloth used for such overcoats. Cf. FEARNOUGHT. *arch.* E19.
2 A fearless person. E19.
3 *hist.* Any of a class of battleships (orig. superior to all their predecessors) whose main armament was entirely big guns of the same calibre. E20.
▸ **B** *adjective*. Fearless. *rare*. M19.

dream /driːm/ *noun*[1]. Long *obsolete* exc. perh. in DREAM-HOLE.
[ORIGIN Old English *drēam* corresp. to Old Saxon *drōm* joy, music (also dream).]
†**1** Joy, gladness, mirth. OE–ME.
2 Music, melody; sound, noise. OE.

dream /driːm/ *noun*[2] *& adjective*. ME.
[ORIGIN Corresp. in sense to Old Frisian *drām*, Old Saxon *drōm* (Dutch *droom*), Old High German *troum* (German *Traum*), Old Norse *draumr*. Perh. rel. to DREAM *noun*[1].]
▸ **A** *noun*. **1** A series of thoughts, images, sensations, or emotions occurring in the mind during sleep. ME.

S. JOHNSON Striving, as is usual in dreams, without ability to move.

2 A vision of the imagination indulged in when awake, *esp.* one prompted by desire, hope, or ambition; a flight of fancy; a state of mind in which awareness of immediate reality is temporarily shut out, a reverie. LME.

W. DAMPIER These may seem to the Reader but Golden Dreams. G. GREENE He stood in a dream, fingering his long grey moustache.

3 Something seen in a dream; a vision. M17.

MILTON Suddenly stood at my Head a dream.

4 An exceptionally enjoyable or attractive person or thing. L19.

K. TENNANT I picked up a dress in Innes thats a dream.

5 An enduring hope or aspiration; an ideal. E20.

L. M. MONTGOMERY It's always been one of my dreams to live near a brook. M. MITCHELL He was still a young girl's dream of the Perfect Knight.

– PHRASES: ***American dream***: see AMERICAN *adjective*. **in your dreams** *colloq.* (as a sarcastic or resigned comment on an unlikely situation): you are deluding yourself, that cannot happen. **like a dream** *colloq.* easily, effortlessly. ***loves' young dream***: see LOVE *noun*. OPIUM **dream**. ***sweet dreams***: see SWEET *adjective & adverb*. **waking dream** an involuntary dream occurring when awake. ***wet dream***: see WET *adjective*.
▸ **B** *attrib.* or as *adjective*. Such as one dreams of or longs for; ideal; perfect. Cf. DREAMY 4. L19.

P. G. WODEHOUSE I wasn't everybody's dream girl. D. EDEN She planned her dream home.

– COMB. & SPECIAL COLLOCATIONS: **dreamboat** *colloq.* a very attractive thing or person (esp. of the opposite sex); **dream-book**: containing interpretations of dreams; **dreamcatcher** a N. American Indian charm, consisting of a wooden or leather hoop with a webbed centre made of strands of thread, which is decorated with feathers, stones, beads, etc. and hung above the bed to catch dreams (usu. described as entrapping bad dreams, but sometimes said to preserve good dreams); **dreamland** an ideal or imaginary land; **dreamscape** a scene dreamed; a dream-like picture, a dreamworld; a (literary) description of a dream; **dream ticket** (the conjunction of) an ideal pair of candidates standing together for political office; **Dreamtime** (in the mythology of some Australian Aborigines) a collection of events long before living memory when the first ancestors were created; the era when these events occurred; = ALCHERINGA; **dream vision** (a poem in) a form freq. used by medieval poets, in which the poet recounts an alleged dream often open to allegorical interpretation; **dreamworld** a state of mind distanced from reality.
■ **dreamery** *noun* (*a*) a place conducive to dreaming; (*b*) dreaminess; the material of dreams: E19. **dreamful** *adjective* full of dreams; dreamy: M16. **dreamfully** *adverb* L19. **dreamfulness** *noun* E20. **dreamish** *adjective* (*rare*) rather dreamy L16. **dreamless** *adjective* E17. **dreamlessly** *adverb* L19. **dreamlessness** *noun* E20. **dreamlike** *adjective* appearing unreal, vague, or shadowy, as in a dream E19.

dream /driːm/ *verb*. Pa. t. **dreamed** /drɛmt, driːmd/, **dreamt** /drɛmt/. ME.
[ORIGIN from (the same root as) DREAM *noun*[2].]
1 *verb intrans.* Experience dreams during sleep (*of*, *about*, †*on*). ME.
2 *verb trans.* See, hear, or feel in a dream; experience or imagine (a dream, vision, etc.) in sleep. Foll. by simple obj., *that*. ME.

HOBBES He dreamed that God spake to him. TENNYSON Last night . . I dream'd a vision of the dead.

3 *verb trans.* Imagine as in a dream; picture to oneself; believe possible (*that*). Usu. in neg. contexts. LME.

J. BUCHAN He did not dream that it would be his fate to fall . . under the walls of Arras. T. GUNN Dreaming the flower I have never seen.

4 *verb intrans.* Think *of* as at all possible or appropriate; have any conception *of*. Usu. in neg. contexts. M16.

SHAKES. *Haml.* There are more things in heaven and earth, Horatio, Than are dreamt of in your philosophy. K. AMIS I wouldn't dream of doing anything behind his back.

5 *verb intrans.* Fall into reverie; indulge in daydreams. (Foll. by *of*.) Cf. DAYDREAM *verb*. M16.

R. LEHMANN Dinah . . had dreamed always of living in the country. P. KAVANAGH He walked slowly, dreaming, along the narrow path.

6 *verb intrans.* †**a** Act dreamily, procrastinate. Only in M16. ▸**b** Hover or hang dreamily or lightly. M19.

b N. HAWTHORNE Mist . . dreamed along the hills.

7 *verb trans.* Bring (esp. oneself) in a dream to a specified state or place. E18.

R. H. FROUDE I may dream myself among lakes and mountains.

– WITH ADVERBS IN SPECIALIZED SENSES: **dream away** spend or lose (time etc.) dreamily or unpractically. **dream on!** *colloq.* used as an ironic comment on the unlikely or impractical nature of a plan or aspiration. **dream up** think up, devise, invent.
■ **dreamer** *noun* a person who dreams; a visionary; *esp.* an idle or unpractical person: ME. **dreaming** *noun* (*a*) the action of DREAM *verb*; (*b*) (**D-**) (in the mythology of some Australian Aborigines) Dreamtime or alcheringa, esp. as manifested in the natural world and celebrated in ritual: ME. **dreamingly** *adverb* in a dreaming or dreamlike manner M16.

dream-hole /ˈdriːmhəʊl/ *noun*. Now *rare*. M16.
[ORIGIN Perh. from DREAM *noun*[1] (as referring to holes by which the sound of bells escaped) + HOLE *noun*[1].]
An opening in an outside wall of a church tower, barn, etc.

dreamy /ˈdriːmi/ *adjective*. M16.
[ORIGIN from DREAM *noun*[2] + -Y[1].]
1 Full of dreams; characterized by dreaming; causing dreams. M16.

TENNYSON Within the dreamy house, The doors upon their hinges creak'd. E. K. KANE A dreamy but intense slumber.

2 Given or pertaining to reverie; fanciful; unpractical. E19.

G. STEIN She was always sort of dreamy and not there.

3 Such as might occur in a dream, dreamlike; vague, indistinct; misty, cloudy. M19.

B. JOWETT He has a dreamy recollection of hearing [it]. D. H. LAWRENCE He lay there . . , his face all dreamy and boyish, very unusual.

4 Perfect, ideal; delightful. Cf. DREAM *adjective*. *colloq.* L19.

N. BLAKE The water's absolutely dreamy And I bet you're a super swimmer.

■ **dreamily** *adverb* M19. **dreaminess** *noun* L18.

drear /drɪə/ *noun*. M16.
[ORIGIN Back-form. from DREARY.]
†**1** Dreariness, sadness, gloom. M16–M19.
2 A dreary person. *colloq.* M20.

drear /drɪə/ *adjective*. Chiefly *poet.* E17.
[ORIGIN Abbreviation.]
= DREARY *adjective* 3.

dreary /ˈdrɪəri/ *adjective & noun*.
[ORIGIN Old English *drēorig*, from *drēor* gore from Germanic, from base of Old English *drēosan* drop, fall, Old Saxon *driosan*, Gothic *driusan*, and Old Saxon *drōr*, Old High German *trōr*, Old Norse *dreyri* gore, blood, Middle High German *trürec* (German *traurig* sorrowful): see -Y[1].]
▸ **A** *adjective*. †**1** Gory, bloody; cruel; dreadful. OE–E17.
2 Of a person etc: sad, melancholy. Now *rare* or *obsolete*. OE.
3 Dismal, gloomy; dull, tediously uninteresting. M17.

OED A dreary speech by a dreary orator. D. M. THOMAS The dreary yard with its rubbish heaps, and the backs of more slums.

▸ **B** *noun*. A dreary person. *colloq.* E20.
■ **drearihead** *noun* (*arch.*) [-HEAD[1]] (*a*) sadness; (*b*) gloominess, dreariness: ME. **drearihood** *noun* (*arch.*) = DREARIHEAD M17. **drearily** *adverb* OE. **feariment** *noun* (*arch.*) (the expression of) dreary condition L16. **dreariness** *noun* †(*a*) sadness, sorrowfulness; (*b*) dismal or gloomy character, tedious dullness: OE. **drearisome** *adjective* (chiefly *dial.*) [-SOME[1]] dreary, desolate M17.

dreck /drɛk/ *noun*. *slang*. Also **drek**. E20.
[ORIGIN from Yiddish *drek* (German *Dreck*) filth, dregs, dung from Middle High German *drec* from Germanic base repr. also by Old English *þreax* rubbish, rottenness, Old Norse *þrekkr*, Old Frisian *threkk*, prob. connected with Greek *skatos* dung, *sterganos* privy, lavatory, Latin *stercus* excrement.]
Rubbish, trash.

†**dred** *verb pa. t. & pple*: see DREAD *verb*.

dredge /drɛdʒ/ *noun*[1]. ME.
[ORIGIN Old French *dragie*, (also mod.) DRAGÉE, in medieval Latin *drageia*, *dragetum*, *-ata* perh. from Latin *tragemata* spices from Greek.]
†**1** A comfit, a sweet consisting of a coated seed or grain of spice, a dragée. Also, a mixture of spices etc. ME–E17.
2 A mixture of grains, esp. oats and barley, sown together. Also ***dredge corn***. ME.

dredge /drɛdʒ/ *noun*[2]. L15.
[ORIGIN Perh. from Middle Dutch *dregghe* grappling hook, but the final consonant of the English word suggests a native origin. Perh. rel. to DRAG *noun*. Earliest in *dredge-boat*.]
An apparatus for collecting and bringing up objects or material from the bed of a river etc. by dragging or scooping; a dragnet; a boat or machine for dredging.
– COMB.: **dredge-boat** a boat used for dredging.

dredge /drɛdʒ/ *verb*[1]. E16.
[ORIGIN from DREDGE *noun*[2].]
1 *verb trans.* Bring *up* or collect, clear *out* or *away*, using a dredge. E16.

fig.: C. S. FORESTER Randall raked back in his memory, trying to dredge up the schoolboy geography he had once learned.

2 *verb intrans.* Use a dredge. L17.
3 *verb trans.* Clean out the bed of (a river etc.) using a dredge; search in this way. M19.

V. WOOLF The pool had been dredged and a thigh bone recovered.

dredge /drɛdʒ/ *verb*[2] *trans.* Also †**drudge**. L16.
[ORIGIN from DREDGE *noun*[1].]
1 Sprinkle with a powdered substance, esp. flour, sugar, or (orig.) a mixture of spices. L16.

fig.: D. W. JERROLD His . . hair was dredged with grey.

2 Sprinkle (a powdered substance) *over*. M17.
– COMB.: **dredging box** = DREDGER *noun*[2].

dredger /ˈdrɛdʒə/ *noun*[1]. E16.
[ORIGIN from DREDGE *verb*[1] + -ER[1].]
1 A person who uses a dredge-boat or dredging apparatus, esp. for collecting oysters. E16.
2 A boat or machine used for dredging. E17.

dredger /ˈdrɛdʒə/ *noun*[2]. Also †**drudger**. M17.
[ORIGIN from DREDGE *verb*[2] + -ER[1].]
A container with a perforated lid for sprinkling a powdered substance, esp. sugar or flour.

dree /driː/ *noun*. *arch.* LME.
[ORIGIN from the verb.]
Suffering, grief, trouble.
– NOTE: In isolated use before L19.

dree *adjective & adverb* see DREICH.

dree /driː/ *verb*. Long *Scot. & N. English* exc. *arch.* Also **drie**. Pa. t. & pple **dreed**.
[ORIGIN Old English *drēogan* from Germanic base repr. also by Gothic *driugan* do military service, Old Norse *drýgja* perpetrate, practise.]
1 *verb trans.* †**a** Perform (service); do (a person's will); commit (sin). OE–ME. ▸**b** Do, perform, (penance). ME.
2 *verb trans.* Endure, undergo, (something burdensome, painful, etc.). OE.

E. GASKELL To dree all the cruel slander they'll put upon him.

dree one's weird submit to one's fate.
3 *verb intrans.* Endure, continue, last. ME.
4 *verb trans.* Pass, spend, (time, one's life). Also foll. by *forth*, *out*. ME.
– NOTE: As an archaism, following use by Sir Walter Scott.

dreep /driːp/ *verb & noun*. Now chiefly *dial.*
[ORIGIN Old English *drēopan* = Old Saxon *driopan*, Old High German *triofan*, Old Norse *drjúpa*, from Germanic base of DROP *verb*: cf. DRIP *noun*, *verb*. In Scot. a dial. var. of DRIP *verb*.]
▸ **A** *verb intrans.* **1** Fall in drops; drip. OE.
2 Droop; *fig.* lose courage; walk very slowly; act lethargically. LME.

L. A. G. STRONG A shuffling, dreeping old crone.

▸ **B** *noun*. **1** A wet, dripping, condition. M19.
2 An ineffective, spiritless, or mournful person; a 'drip'. E20.
■ **dreepy** *adjective* droopy, spiritless L19.

dreg /drɛg/ *noun & verb*. ME.
[ORIGIN Prob. of Scandinavian origin: cf. Old Norse pl. *dreggjar*, Middle Swedish *drägg*, Swedish pl. *drägg*.]
▸ **A** *noun sing.* & (usu.) in *pl.*
1 The sediment of a liquor; grounds, lees. ME.

DICKENS He flings the dregs of his wine at Edwin.

†**2** Excrement; rubbish; corrupt matter. ME–M17.
3 The most worthless part or parts; the refuse. M16.

W. STYRON *You* must be part of the bottomless dregs of this loathsome city.

4 The last remains or traces; *sing.* a small remnant, a small quantity or drop. **L16.**

E. BOWEN At first, in those dregs of daylight, he saw nobody there.

▸ †**B** *verb trans.* Infl. **-gg-**. Make dreggy. *rare.* **E17–E19.**

▪ **dreggish** *adjective* (now *rare*) of the nature of dregs or refuse; affected by dregs; *fig.* base, vile: **M16. dreggy** *adjective* containing dregs; of the nature of dregs; turbid, polluted; impure: **LME.**

dreich /driːx/ *adjective & adverb.* Long *obsolete* exc. *Scot. & N. English.* Also **driech, driegh, dree** /driː/. **ME.**
[ORIGIN formed as DREE *verb*, corresp. to Old Norse *drjúgr* enduring, lasting.]
▸ **A** *adjective.* †**1** Patient, long-suffering. Only in **ME.**
†**2** Heavy, mighty, great; fierce. Only in **LME.**
3 Long; tedious, persistent; slow, tardy; dreary, miserable, gloomy, bleak. **LME.**

R. L. STEVENSON My life is a bit driegh . . . I see little company. D. H. LAWRENCE A grey, dree afternoon.

▸ **B** *adverb.* = DREICHLY. **ME.**

▪ **dreichly** *adverb* †(*a*) heavily, mightily, vehemently; in a dreich manner; (*b*) slowly, persistently: **LME.**

dreidel /ˈdreɪd(ə)l/ *noun.* Chiefly *N. Amer.* Also **dreidl**. **M20.**
[ORIGIN Yiddish *dreydl*, from Middle High German *dræ(je)n* (German *drehen*) turn.]
A four-sided spinning top with a Hebrew letter on each side; a game of put-and-take played with this, esp. at Hanukkah.

dreigh *adjective & adverb* var. of DREICH.

dreikanter /ˈdrʌɪkɑːntə, -kan-/ *noun.* Pl. same, **-s**. **E20.**
[ORIGIN German, lit. 'three-edged thing', from *drei* three + *Kante* edge: see CANT *noun*[1], -ER[1].]
An angular faceted pebble whose surface has been cut by wind-blown sand, *esp.* one with three facets.

drek *noun* var. of DRECK.

drench /drɛn(t)ʃ/ *noun.*
[ORIGIN Old English *drenċ* from Germanic, from var. of base of DRINK *verb*; corresp. to Old Saxon *dranc*, Old High German *tranc(h)* (German *Trank*), Old Norse *drekka*, Gothic *dragk*.]
†**1** *gen.* A drink, a draught. **OE–ME.**
2 A medicinal or poisonous draught; a potion. *arch.* **OE.**
3 A drink or dose of medicine given to an animal. **M16.**
4 The act of drenching or soaking; a soaking, a downpour. **E19.**

F. NORRIS The horse, restive under the drench of the rain, moved uneasily. *fig.*: A. THWAITE Sun's incessant drench.

drench /drɛn(t)ʃ/ *verb.*
[ORIGIN Old English *drenċan* = Old Frisian *drenza*, Old Saxon *drenkian* (Dutch *drenken*), Old High German *trenchen* (German *tränken*), Old Norse *drekkja*, Gothic *dragkjan*, from Germanic.]
1 *verb trans.* Force (an animal) to take a draught of medicine; *arch.* force (a person) to drink. **OE.**
drenching gun a device for giving a medicinal drench to an animal.
†**2** *verb trans. & intrans.* Drown; (cause to) sink in water. **ME–M17.**
3 *verb trans.* **a** Wet thoroughly (as) by immersion; soak, steep. **ME.** ▸**b** Wet thoroughly with falling or thrown liquid. **M16.**

a A. DAVIS Sweat drenched my clothes before I had hardly gotten started. A. T. ELLIS I fell in that bloody stream and I'm drenched. **b** R. L. STEVENSON A drenching rain.

4 *verb trans. fig.* Overwhelm; saturate as in a liquid, cover thoroughly all over. Formerly also, plunge *in* or *into* despair, sin, etc. **ME.**

W. GOLDING Half the plain and the mountains . . were drenched in milky light. A. COOKE His unique popularity in being drenched by a continuous blizzard of invitations.

▪ **drencher** *noun* a person who or thing which drenches; *esp.* a drenching shower; a drenching gun: **ME.**

dreng /drɛŋ/ *noun.* **OE.**
[ORIGIN Old Norse *drengr* young man, lad, fellow (Swedish *dräng* man, servant, Danish *dreng* boy, apprentice).]
ENGLISH HISTORY. A free tenant, esp. in ancient Northumbria, holding by a tenure partly military, partly servile.
▪ **drengage** *noun* the tenure or service of a dreng **L17.**

Dresden /ˈdrɛzd(ə)n/ *adjective & noun.* **M18.**
[ORIGIN See below.]
▸ **A** *adjective.* **1** Designating (a piece of) china made at Meissen, near Dresden, Germany, with elaborate decoration and delicate colouring. **M18.**
2 Having a delicate or frail prettiness. **E20.**
▸ **B** *noun.* Dresden china. **M18.**
▪ **Dresdener** *noun* a person who lives in or comes from Dresden **L19.**

dress /drɛs/ *noun.* **M16.**
[ORIGIN from the verb.]
1 The action or an act of dressing. Now *rare* or *obsolete.* **M16.**
2 Clothing, *esp.* outer clothing; clothing belonging to a particular occupation, country, or (esp. formal or ceremonial) occasion. **M16.**

DICKENS Your black silk frock will be quite dress enough. J. CONRAD The dress I wore was . . that of a sailor come ashore from some coaster. A. LURIE Fashion, as opposed to mere dress, is . . sprinkled with foreign terms.

battledress, *evening dress*, *fancy dress*, *full dress*, *morning dress*, etc.

3 *transf.* External covering, *esp.* the plumage of a bird; outward form. **E17.**

H. J. LASKI The *Letter Concerning Toleration* was published in its Latin dress, and four years afterwards an English translation appeared.

4 Orig., a suit of clothes, an outfit, an article of clothing. Now, a woman's or girl's garment consisting of a skirt and a bodice; (with qualifying noun) a garment for a specified occasion or part of the body. **M17.**

DAY LEWIS She wears a long dress with a dark band above the hem.

cocktail dress, *headdress*, *nightdress*, etc.

†**5** A dressing for a wound. **L17–L18.**
6 A finish put on something to set off its appearance. **L19.**
– ATTRIB. & COMB.: In the sense 'constituting or worn (as part of) full dress', as **dress shirt**, **dress shoes**, **dress sword**, **dress uniform**, etc. Special combs., as **dress agency** an agency, shop, etc., that buys used clothes privately and resells them; **dress-carriage**: reserved for state or semi-state occasions; **dress circle** the lowest and most expensive gallery of seats in a theatre etc., in which evening dress was at one time required; **dress coat** a man's swallow-tailed coat used for formal dress; **dress code** a set of rules or guidelines specifying the approved manner of dress at a school, place of work, social occasion, etc. **dress-conscious** *adjective* aware of what is fashionable in dress, particular about clothes; **dress house** (now *rare*) a brothel; **dress-improver** *hist.* = BUSTLE *noun*[2]; **dress length** a piece of material sufficient to make a dress; **dressmake** *verb intrans.* make dresses, do dressmaking; **dressmaker** a person, usu. a woman, who makes dresses (***dressmaker's dummy***: see DUMMY *noun* 5b); **dressmaking** the action or occupation of making dresses; **dress parade** (*a*) a display of clothes by mannequins; (*b*) a military parade in full dress uniforms; **dress preserver** = *dress shield* below; **dress rehearsal** a rehearsal in full costume, *esp.* a final such rehearsal; *transf.* a (final) practice session; **dress sense** a feel for the appropriateness of certain garments to a certain person (esp. oneself) or occasion; **dress shield** a piece of waterproof or other material fastened under the armpit of a dress to protect it from perspiration; **dress shirt** a shirt for wearing with evening dress; **dress weight** (*a*) a small weight placed in the hem of a dress etc.; (*b*) cloth of a suitable weight for making into dresses.

dress /drɛs/ *verb.* Pa. t. & pple **dressed** /drɛst/, (*arch. & poet.*) **drest** /drɛst/. **ME.**
[ORIGIN Old French & mod. French *dresser* from Proto-Romance, from Latin *directus* DIRECT *adjective*.]
▸ **I** Make straight; order; make ready.
†**1** *verb trans.* Put to rights, set in order, put straight. **ME–L17.** ▸**b** Place or set in position. **LME–E16.**
†**2** **a** *verb trans.* Erect, set *up*, make straight. **LME–L16.** ▸**b** *verb refl. & intrans.* Raise oneself, rise. **LME–L15.**
3 *verb trans.* †**a** *gen.* Make ready, prepare; arrange, draw up. **LME–M18.** ▸**b** Treat or prepare (something) in a way proper to its character or purpose; smooth (stone, a line of cast type); prepare and finish (a skin, leather, fabric, etc.); prepare (ore) for further processing by removing waste. **L15.** ▸**c** Cleanse (corn) from chaff etc. **M17.** ▸**d** Remove (something) in the process of preparing, purifying, or cleansing. **E18.** ▸**e** ANGLING. Prepare (a fly) for use on a fish hook. **M19.**

b R. GRAVES The dressed stones of the rampart.

4 *verb trans.* Prepare (esp. an animal carcass) for use as food. **LME.** ▸**b** Add a sauce or other mixture to (food, esp. a salad). **L18.**

B. MACDONALD I could dress chickens . . in about two minutes without once tearing the skin. **b** J. AUSTEN These two girls had been . . dressing a sallad and cucumber.

†**5** *verb refl. & intrans.* Prepare (oneself). (Foll. by *for*, *to do*.) **LME–L16.**
6 **a** *verb trans.* Attire in suitable or fine clothing; array; adorn with apparel. Now often simply, put clothes on, clothe. **LME.** ▸**b** *verb refl. & intrans.* Put on one's clothes; wear clothes in a specified way; *spec.* put on clothes appropriate to a formal or ceremonial occasion. **M17.** ▸**c** *verb intrans.* Of a male: have the genitals habitually on one or other side of the fork of the trousers. **M20.**

a M. R. MITFORD Good Mr. Norris . . dressed his little daughter's doll. J. STEINBECK He himself was dressed in new white clothes. **b** S. JOHNSON He was come back to dress himself for a ball. F. A. KEMBLE It is close upon time to dress for dinner. J. RHYS Get up and dress yourself, and come downstairs. N. SHUTE She dressed in the red shirt and slacks that she had worn when she had met Dwight first. H. ROTH Even when you go to the market, you dress like a lady.

a dressed to kill dressed to create a striking impression, often in very smart or sophisticated clothes. ***dressed up to the nines***: see NINE *noun* 2. ***mutton dressed as lamb***: see MUTTON.

7 *verb trans.* Equip; adorn, deck; *spec.* adorn (a ship) with flags etc.; display goods in (a shop window) in an artistic or attractive way. **LME.** ▸**b** Equip (a play etc.) with appropriate costumes. **M18.** ▸**c** Fill (a theatre etc.) by means of complimentary tickets. **L19.**

T. GAGE The Chamber was richly dressed and hung with many pictures, and with hangings. J. CLAVELL A high matted roof dressed with white silk.

8 *verb trans.* Treat (a person) with deserved firmness or severity; thrash; scold. Now usu. foll. by *down*. **LME.**
†**9** *verb trans.* Train or break in (a horse etc.). **LME–L18.**
10 *verb trans.* Treat (a wound, a wounded person) with remedies; apply a dressing to. **L15.**

R. L. STEVENSON He had recently been wounded, and still more recently dressed. S. SASSOON The little doctor . . would soon be dressing the wounds of moaning men.

11 Cultivate, tend, (a field, garden, plant, etc.); treat with manure, compost, or other fertilizer or food. **E16.**
12 Comb, brush, or arrange (the hair). **E16.** ▸**b** Groom (a horse etc.). **M16.**
13 MILITARY. **a** *verb trans.* Draw up (troops, a body of men, etc.) in proper alignment; correct the alignment of. **M18.** ▸**b** *verb intrans.* Come into the correct place in line etc. **L18.**

a A. W. KINGLAKE The battalion dressed its ranks with precision.

14 *verb trans.* Make (an artificial fly) for use in fishing. **E19.**
15 *verb intrans.* Of food: turn out (well etc.) when dressed. Of stone etc.: be (easily etc.) dressed. **E19.**
▸ †**II** Direct.
16 *verb trans.* Straighten the course of (*lit. & fig.*); direct, guide; turn or send in a given direction. **ME–L16.**
17 *verb refl. & intrans.* Go, set off, proceed. **LME–L16.**
18 *verb trans.* Address (words) *to*. **LME–M17.**
– WITH ADVERBS IN SPECIALIZED SENSES: **dress down** dress informally or less formally than would be expected; ***dress-down day***, ***dress-down Friday***: on which employees are encouraged to dress informally. **dress out** attire conspicuously. **dress up** dress elaborately or in masquerade; put on or wear one's best clothes or clothes for a formal occasion; *fig.* disguise by embellishment; (esp. of a child) dress oneself in a costume or in special clothes as an entertainment.
– COMB.: **dress-up** *noun & adjective* (*a*) *noun* the action of dressing up, esp. in one's best clothes; an occasion or gathering which requires formal dress; (*b*) *adjective* requiring or designating formal dress.

dressage /ˈdrɛsɑːʒ, -ɑːdʒ/ *noun.* **M20.**
[ORIGIN French, lit. 'training', from *dresser* to train, drill.]
The training of a horse in obedience and deportment; the execution by a horse of precise movements in response to its rider.

dresser /ˈdrɛsə/ *noun*[1]. **ME.**
[ORIGIN from DRESS *verb* + -ER[1].]
1 A person who prepares, treats, finishes, or otherwise dresses some material or piece of equipment. **ME.**
2 A person who dresses another. **E17.** ▸**b** *spec.* A person whose job is to look after theatrical costumes and help actors to dress. **M19.**
3 A tool or machine used in the operation of dressing. **E17.**
4 A person who dresses elegantly or in a specified way. **L17.**

LYTTON The most perfect dresser that even France could exhibit.

5 A surgeon's assistant who helps in hospital operations. **M18.**
6 MILITARY. A person from whom a parading body of troops takes its alignment. **L18.**

dresser /ˈdrɛsə/ *noun*[2]. **LME.**
[ORIGIN Old French *dresseur*, *dreçor* (mod. *dressoir*), from *dresser* prepare: see -ER[2].]
1 *hist.* A sideboard or table in a kitchen on which food could be prepared; a table in a dining room or hall from which dishes were served or on which plate was displayed. **LME.**
2 A kind of sideboard surmounted by shelves for storing and displaying dishes, plates, kitchen utensils, etc. **M16.**
Welsh dresser: see WELSH *adjective*.
3 A dressing table; a bureau. *N. Amer.* **L19.**

dressing /ˈdrɛsɪŋ/ *noun.* **LME.**
[ORIGIN from DRESS *verb* + -ING[1].]
1 *gen.* The action of DRESS *verb*; an instance of this. **LME.**

J. K. JEROME As a girl, she never understood dressing.

window dressing: see WINDOW *noun*.

2 *spec.* ▸**a** The action of preparing or finishing various materials. **LME.** ▸**b** A beating, a thrashing; a scolding, an upbraiding. Now usu. ***dressing-down***. **M18.** ▸**c** MILITARY. The proper alignment of troops. **L18.** ▸**d** ***dressing up***, the action or practice of dressing in masquerade or in special clothes as an entertainment, or of dressing in one's best clothes or clothes for a formal occasion. **M19.**

d *attrib.*: A. WILSON Strange old hats and frocks in the dressing-up box in the nursery.

a mineral dressing, ***ore dressing***, etc.

3 (A) sauce or other mixture added to food, esp. a salad; a seasoning; stuffing. **E16.**
French dressing, ***salad dressing***, ***thousand island dressing***, ***vinaigrette dressing***, etc.
4 *sing.* & (usu.) in *pl.* (Decorative) clothing. Now *rare*. **E17.**
5 A piece of material placed directly on to a wound or diseased area. **E18.**

6 Manure, compost, or other fertilizer spread over or ploughed into land to improve it. M18.

Practical Gardening A dressing of bonemeal during the late autumn is usually productive.

7 A glaze, stiffening, or other preparation used in the finishing of fabrics. E19.

– COMB.: **dressing box** (now *rare*) a dressing case; **dressing case**: used for holding toilet articles; **dressing chest** a piece of bedroom furniture with a flat top and storage facilities, for use while dressing (***duchesse dressing chest***: see DUCHESSE 2); **dressing comb**: used for dressing the hair; **dressing forceps**: used in applying and removing surgical dressings; **dressing gown** a loose robe worn while one is not fully dressed, while resting, etc.; *hist.* any loose informal gown; **dressing room** a place for dressing or for changing one's clothes, esp. in a theatre, a sports centre, or attached to a bedroom; **dressing station** a place for giving emergency treatment to the wounded; **dressing table** a piece of bedroom furniture with a flat top, an upright mirror, and usu. drawers underneath for use while dressing, arranging one's hair, applying make-up, etc. (***duchesse dressing table***: see DUCHESSE 2).

dressy /ˈdrɛsi/ *adjective*. M18.
[ORIGIN from DRESS *noun* + -Y[1].]
1 Attentive to dress; given to elaborate or noticeably smart dressing. M18. ▸**b** *fig.* Excessively elaborate. M19.

DAY LEWIS He was a dressy man, keeping his trousers in a press and trees in his shoes.

2 Of a garment or accessory: suitable for a formal occasion, stylish. Of an occasion or function: requiring formal dress or one's best clothes. L18.

M. GEE Why do you always wear those earrings? They're much too dressy.

■ **dressiness** *noun* E19.

dretch *verb* var. of DRATCH.

drew /druː/ *noun*. *obsolete* exc. *dial.* LME.
[ORIGIN Unknown.]
A drop, a very small amount of liquid.

drew *verb pa. t.*: see DRAW *verb*.

drey /dreɪ/ *noun*. Also **dray**. E17.
[ORIGIN Unknown.]
A squirrel's nest.

Dreyfusard /ˈdreɪfʊsɑː, -ɑːd/ *noun*. L19.
[ORIGIN French, from *Dreyfus* (see below) + -ARD.]
A defender or supporter of Alfred Dreyfus (1859–1935), a Jewish Frenchman convicted of treason in 1894 and declared innocent in 1906.

drib /drɪb/ *noun*. Chiefly *Scot.* & *dial.* exc. in phr. below. E18.
[ORIGIN from the verb or DRIBBLE *noun*, DRIBLET.]
An insignificant quantity; a driblet.
dribs and drabs *colloq.* [DRAB *noun*[4]] small and intermittent sums or amounts.

drib /drɪb/ *verb*. Infl. **-bb-**. E16.
[ORIGIN Alt. of DRIP *verb*.]
†**1** *verb intrans.* Fall in drops; *fig.* go on little by little. Only in E16.
2 *verb trans.* Let fall in drops; *fig.* utter as in driblets. Now *rare*. M16.
†**3** *verb trans.* Shoot (an arrow) so that it falls short or wide of the mark. Cf. DRIBBLE *verb* 1. M–L16.

dribble /ˈdrɪb(ə)l/ *noun*. L17.
[ORIGIN from the verb.]
1 A small barely continuous stream, a trickle; a small amount of liquid; a small stream of saliva. L17.
2 A field drain of broken stones, between which the water trickles. *local.* M19.
3 In football etc., an act of dribbling. L19.
■ **dribbly** *adjective* given to or marked by dribbling E20.

dribble /ˈdrɪb(ə)l/ *verb*. M16.
[ORIGIN Frequentative of DRIB *verb*: see -LE[3]. In sense 4 perh. infl. by DRIVEL *verb*. With sense 5 (perh. a different word) cf. Dutch *dribbelen* toddle, trip.]
†**1** *verb trans.* & *intrans.* Shoot (an arrow), be shot, short or wide of the mark. Cf. DRIB *verb* 3. M16–E17.
2 *verb trans.* Allow to flow in a trickle or in slow drops; give out in driblets. (Foll. by *out*, *away*, *forth*.) L16.

W. S. CHURCHILL It is a perilous policy to dribble out reinforcements and to fritter away armies.

3 *verb intrans.* Flow or run out in a trickle or in slow drops. E17.

S. RAVEN The scraps of paper dribbled through his fingers like confetti. *fig.*: C. P. SNOW Margaret . . did not let the chit-chat dribble on.

4 *verb intrans.* Let saliva trickle from the mouth. L17.

E. M. BRENT-DYER Mamma says . . Geoff must be starting to teethe because he dribbles so much.

5 *verb trans.* & *intrans.* In football, hockey, basketball, and other games: keep (the ball or puck) moving in front of one by a succession of pushes or taps. M19.

J. LEHANE The player dribbles with his right hand, . . using proper fingertip control to keep the ball below knee level. M. ROBERTS Her eyes on the ball which she dribbled expertly.

■ **dribbler** *noun* a person who dribbles, esp. at football etc. M19. **dribbling** *verbal noun* (*a*) *rare* a quantity given out in driblets; (*b*) the action of the verb: L16. **dribbling** *ppl adjective* that dribbles; *fig.* insignificant, made up of petty items: L16.

dribblet *noun* var. of DRIBLET.

driblet /ˈdrɪblɪt/ *noun*. Also **-bb-**. L16.
[ORIGIN from DRIB *verb* + -LET.]
1 A small sum of money. Formerly *spec.*, a small debt. L16.
2 A small or insignificant quantity or part. L17.

V. SACKVILLE-WEST These bits of information were imparted . . in driblets and with caution.

3 A thin stream or small quantity of liquid. M19.

R. K. NARAYAN The river trickling away in minute driblets.

– COMB.: **driblet cone**: produced by successive ejections of small amounts of lava.

†**dricksie** *adjective* see DRUXY.

driddle /ˈdrɪd(ə)l/ *verb* & *noun*. *Scot.* E17.
[ORIGIN Imit., infl. by *dribble*, *diddle* & perh. Norwegian dial. *dritla* walk slowly trailing something.]
▸ **A** *verb*. **1** *verb intrans.* Walk slowly or uncertainly; work in a dilatory way; waste one's time. E17.
2 *verb intrans.* & *trans.* Spill, dribble, trickle. E19.
3 *verb intrans.* Play the fiddle. M19.
▸ **B** *noun*. **1** A dawdler; an idler; an awkward person. E19.
2 = DRIBLET 3. M19.

drie *verb* var. of DREE *verb*.

driech *adjective* & *adverb* var. of DREICH.

dried /drʌɪd/ *ppl adjective*. ME.
[ORIGIN from DRY *verb* + -ED[1].]
1 Deprived of moisture, desiccated. Also ***dried-off***, ***dried-out***, ***dried-up***. ME.
cut and dried: see CUT *ppl adjective* 1.
2 *spec.* Of food: preserved by the removal of its natural moisture. LME.

dried *verb pa. t.* & *pple* of DRY *verb*.

driedoring /ˈdrɪdʊərɪŋ/ *noun*. *S. Afr.* Also **-doorn** /-dʊər(ə)n/. E19.
[ORIGIN Afrikaans, from Dutch *drie* THREE + *doorn* THORN *noun*.]
Any of several thorny flowering shrubs and small trees of the dry plains of southern and tropical Africa, esp. *Rhigozum trichotomum*.

driegh *adjective* & *adverb* var. of DREICH.

drier /ˈdrʌɪə/ *noun*. Also **dryer**. ME.
[ORIGIN from DRY *verb* + -ER[1].]
1 A person engaged in drying. ME.
2 A natural agency that removes moisture. E16.
3 A substance mixed with oil paint, oil, ink, etc., to make it dry more quickly. M19.
4 A machine or appliance for drying laundry, hair, etc. L19.
hairdryer, ***spin drier***, ***tumble drier***, etc.
5 A substance that dries (quickly or slowly). L19.
– COMB.: **drier-up** a person who does the drying when dishes etc. are washed.

drieth *noun* var. of DRYTH.

drift /drɪft/ *noun*. ME.
[ORIGIN Orig. from Old Norse *drift* snowdrift; later from Middle Dutch *drift* drove, course, current = Old Frisian (*ur*)*drift* expulsion, Middle High German, German *Trift* passage for or of cattle, pasturage, drove, from Germanic base of DRIVE *verb*.]
▸ **I** Something driven.
1 An accumulation of snow, sand, etc., driven together by the wind. ME.

T. HERBERT The sands by the fury of Tempests lie in great drifts. M. ARNOLD The field Strewn with . . yellow drifts Of wither'd leaves.

snowdrift: see SNOW *noun*[1].
2 A driving mass of rain, dust, etc. LME.

TENNYSON Thro' scudding drifts the rainy Hyades Vext the dim sea.

3 A body of animals (rarely, persons) driven or moving along together. Formerly also, a flock of birds. Now *dial.* LME.

J. M. SYNGE You'll lose my drift of heifers and my blue bull.

4 A tool for driving or ramming in piles etc. Also = ***drift pin*** below. M16.
5 A floating log or mass of wood driven by the current. E17.
6 GEOLOGY. Material originally deposited by a current of ice, water, or air; *spec.* Pleistocene glacial and fluvioglacial deposits left when the ice sheet retreated. M19.
7 A set of fishing nets. Also = ***drift net*** below. M19.
8 A large irregular mass of flowering plants, *esp.* ones planted in a garden. E20.

W. BRONK Great drifts of purple flowers hold / the roadside.

9 ASTRONOMY. Either of two groups of stars that appear to have some motion towards one or other vertex in the sky. E20.
▸ **II** The action of driving.
10 The action of driving or impelling; *esp.* (*hist.*) the driving of all the cattle within a forest to a particular place on a fixed day, with a view to establishing ownership, levying fines, etc. LME.

R. SOUTH A man being under the drift of any passion, will still follow the impulse of it.

11 The fact or state of being driven (as) by a current; any slow steady movement in some direction. LME. ▸**b** MOTOR RACING. A controlled skid, used in taking bends. M20. ▸**c** *fig.* The practice of waiting on events; inaction. Chiefly in ***policy of drift***. M20.

M. WEBB The night was full of the smell of . . moss, with a drift of primrose scent now and again. *Listener* The drift [of the population] away from the big cities continues. **c** W. S. CHURCHILL Resolved to be irresolute, adamant for drift.

CONTINENTAL ***drift***. ***urban drift***: see URBAN *adjective*.
12 The aim or purpose of an activity. Now chiefly, the tenor or purport of speech or writing. LME.

W. COWPER My sole drift is to be useful. A. BURGESS I do not quite understand the drift of your statement. D. LODGE Philip was able to follow his drift pretty well.

†**13** A scheme, a plot. E16–L17.
14 The natural course or tendency *of* events, actions, etc.; a trend. M16.

H. J. LASKI The drift of opinion in . . Europe was towards benevolent despotism.

wage drift: see WAGE *noun*.
†**15** Delay, procrastination. *Scot.* M16–M17.
16 (The amount of) deviation from a course (e.g. of an aircraft, projectile, migrating bird), esp. as a result of a current. L17.
17 A slow variation in the characteristics or operation of an electric circuit or device. L19.
†**18** AERONAUTICS. Drag, air resistance. L19–E20.
19 LINGUISTICS. Gradual modification of a language, as brought about by internal changes rather than external influences. E20.
▸ **III** A course along which something is driven.
20 A horizontal passage in a mine, *esp.* one following a mineral vein; an inclined tunnel dug from the surface to a seam of coal etc. Also ***driftway***. E17.
21 More fully ***driftway***. A lane along which animals are driven. *local.* E17.
22 A ford. *S. Afr.* L18.
23 Each of the rows in which underwood is laid when felled. E19.
– COMB.: **drift anchor** = ***SEA anchor***; **drift bottle**: thrown into the sea to determine currents; **drift ice** detached pieces of ice drifting with the wind or ocean currents; **drift indicator** an instrument for showing the drift of an aircraft; **drift mine**: to which access is gained by a drift; **drift mining**: by means of drifts (rather than shafts or open working); **drift net** a large net for herrings etc., kept upright by weights at the bottom and floats at the top and allowed to drift with the tide; **drift pin** a steel pin driven into a hole in a piece of metal to enlarge or shape it; **drift sight** = ***drift indicator*** above; ***driftway***: see senses 20, 21 above; **driftweed** (*a*) seaweed driven ashore by the waves; (*b*) either of two kinds of seaweed, gulfweed, *Sargassum bacciferum*, and tangle, *Laminaria digitata*; **driftwood** wood floating about on, or cast ashore by, the water.

drift /drɪft/ *verb*. M16.
[ORIGIN from the noun.]
†**1** *verb trans.* Subject (a person, a legal action, etc.) to delays. *Scot.* M16–M17.
2 *verb trans.* Of a current of water or air: drive or carry along. E17. ▸**b** Allow (a fishing net) to be borne by the current. M19.

J. CONRAD The light winds and strong currents . . had drifted the boat about.

3 *verb trans.* & *intrans.* Blow or be blown into heaps. M18. ▸**b** Cover or become covered with snowdrifts. M19.

J. STEINBECK The wind . . drifted the sand of the country like snow. E. SHANKS The withered leaves that drift in Russell Square. **b** R. W. EMERSON Struggling through the drifted roads.

4 *verb intrans.* Be driven along (occas., off course) by a current of water or air; move with the stream or wind; gradually deviate from a position or course. M18. ▸**b** *transf.* & *fig.* Move passively or aimlessly; be brought involuntarily or imperceptibly *into* a condition, a way of life, etc. E19.

J. BARTH The boat wouldn't be moored, but would drift up and down the river on the tide. S. KING A little snow began to drift down from the sky. *Nature* The satellite tends to drift slowly in longitude. **b** A. MACLEAN His eyes closed and I thought he was drifting off into sleep. A. HAILEY It was uncharacteristic . . for him merely to 'go along' and let things drift.

5 *verb intrans.* Come, go, or move in a casual or aimless manner. Also, depart. *colloq.* M19.

M. TWAIN Some . . will have to drift around to two or three hotels . . before they find accommodations. V. WOOLF He had left Cambridge after two terms . . and then travelled and drifted. E. BOWEN The children . . drifted amiably into the informal classrooms.

drift apart (of partners in a marriage or other relationship) suffer a gradual loss of affection or contact.
6 *verb trans.* MECHANICS. Enlarge (a hole) with a drift pin. M19.

7 *verb trans. & intrans.* MINING. Excavate a drift (in), tunnel (through). **M19.**
8 *verb trans.* Drive (animals) slowly, allowing them to feed as they go. *US.* **L19.**
■ **driftage** *noun* the process or extent of drifting; drifted material: **M18.** **drifting** *verbal noun* (*a*) the action of the verb; (*b*) in *pl.*, that which is drifted: **E17.** **driftingly** *adverb* †(*a*) dilatorily; (*b*) in a drifting way: **L16.**

drifter /ˈdrɪftə/ *noun.* **M19.**
[ORIGIN from DRIFT *verb* + -ER[1].]
1 MINING. **a** A person who excavates drifts. **M19.** ▸**b** A percussion drill driven by compressed air used in drifting. **E20.**
2 A boat or person engaged in fishing with a drift net; a fishing vessel etc. used by the Royal Navy, esp. in wartime, for patrolling, conveying stores, etc. **L19.**
3 = *drift bottle* s.v. DRIFT *noun.* **L19.**
4 A person leading an aimless or vagrant way of life. **L19.**
5 A wind causing snow to drift. **E20.**

driftless /ˈdrɪftlɪs/ *adjective.* **E19.**
[ORIGIN from DRIFT *noun* + -LESS.]
1 Aimless, without a purpose. **E19.**
2 GEOLOGY. Free from drift. **L19.**

drifty /ˈdrɪfti/ *adjective.* **L16.**
[ORIGIN from DRIFT *noun* + -Y[1].]
†**1** Full of secret aims; wily. Only in **L16.**
2 Containing much driving snow or many snowdrifts. **M18.**
3 Of a garment: flowing. **L19.**

drill /drɪl/ *noun*[1]. Now *rare* or *obsolete.* **LME.**
[ORIGIN Rel. to DRILL *verb*[2]. Sense 1 is perh. a different word.]
†**1** A small amount of liquid imbibed. Only in **LME.**
2 A small stream; a rill. **E17.**

drill /drɪl/ *noun*[2]. **E17.**
[ORIGIN from DRILL *verb*[3]. In sense 1 prob. from Dutch *dril*, *drille*.]
1 A tool or machine for making holes in bulk material, or sinking wells, by using a rotating cutting tip or a reciprocating hammer or chisel; *spec.* a dentist's rotary tool for cutting away part of a tooth etc. **E17.** ▸**b** A univalve mollusc, *Urosalpinx cinerea*, which bores into the shells of young oysters. Also *oyster drill*. **L19.**
Archimedean drill, *diamond drill*, *hammer drill*, *percussion drill*, etc.
2 (Repeated) training or instruction in military exercises; a form or instance of this. **M17.** ▸**b** *transf.* Intensive instruction or training in a subject. **E19.**

T. HEGGEN Loading drill on the five-inch gun. S. HILL The days were taken up with a succession of drills and parades and inspections.

b *Swedish drill.*
3 A person who drills soldiers. **E19.**
4 *The* correct or recognized procedure. *colloq.* **M20.**

D. O'GRADY Angle parking was the drill, front to kerb.

– COMB.: **drill-book** a manual of instruction in military drill; **drillmaster** a person who instructs or leads others in military drills and marching; **drill pipe** OIL INDUSTRY piping which carries and rotates the bit during drilling and conveys the circulating mud; **drill press** a machine tool for drilling holes, set on a fixed stand; **drill sergeant** a non-commissioned officer who trains soldiers in military exercises; **drill ship**: used to support a drilling rig; **drill stem** OIL INDUSTRY in percussion drilling, a heavy metal rod added above the bit to give weight; in rotary drilling, = KELLY *noun* 4; also, the whole drill string; *drill-stem test*, a test of potential made by sampling from a partly drilled well; *drill string*: see STRING *noun* 22b.

drill /drɪl/ *noun*[3]. **M17.**
[ORIGIN Prob. of African origin: cf. MANDRILL.]
A W. African baboon, *Mandrillus leucophaeus*, allied to the mandrill.

drill /drɪl/ *noun*[4]. **E18.**
[ORIGIN Perh. a use of DRILL *noun*[1].]
1 A small furrow in which seed is sown; a ridge with such a furrow on its top; a row of seeds so sown. **E18.**

C. S. LEWIS Just ordinary drills of cabbages.

2 A machine which makes drills, sows seed in them, and covers the seed sown. **M18.**

drill /drɪl/ *noun*[5] *& adjective.* **E18.**
[ORIGIN Abbreviation of DRILLING *noun.*]
(Made of) a tough twilled cotton or linen fabric.

W. HOLTBY Farmers' wives in white drill overalls.

†**drill** *verb*[1]. **ME.**
[ORIGIN Unknown.]
1 *verb trans. & intrans.* Make postponement or delay (of). Only in **ME.**
2 *verb trans.* Foll. by *away*, *on*, *out*: protract; fritter (time) away, fill (time) aimlessly. **M17–M18.**

J. USSHER Purposely drilling out the time, hoping to encline the Senate to favour his designe.

3 *verb trans.* Lead (a person) *on*; entice (a person) *in*, *into*, or *out of* something. Also foll. by *along*. **M17–M18.**

R. HEAD [He] was pickt up by a pack of Rogues in the streets and drilled into a Tavern. T. GRAY He drilled him on with various pretences.

†**drill** *verb*[2] *intrans.* **E17–L18.**
[ORIGIN App. var. of TRILL *verb*[1]: rel. to DRILL *noun*[1].]
Flow in a small stream or in drops; trickle.

drill /drɪl/ *verb*[3]. **E17.**
[ORIGIN Middle Dutch *drillen* bore, turn in a circle, brandish = Middle Low German *drillen* roll, turn, whence Middle & mod. High German *drillen* turn, round off, bore, drill soldiers.]
▸ **I** Make a hole (in).
1 *verb trans.* Make a hole or passage in (something), esp. with a drill. **E17.** ▸**b** Produce (a hole) or sink (an oil well) by or as by drilling. **M17.** ▸†**c** Turn round and round; churn (butter). **L17–M19.**

R. JEFFERIES Rabbit-holes drill the bank everywhere. **b** J. HIGGINS The bullet drilled a neat hole through the windscreen.

2 *verb intrans.* Drill a hole or well. **L17.**

N. CALDER Equipped for drilling into the bed of the deep ocean. *Economist* Five rigs are now drilling.

drilling mud: see MUD *noun*[1]. **drilling rig** a structure above an oil well etc. containing the machinery needed to drill it. *drilling string*: see STRING *noun* 22b.
3 *verb trans.* Shoot (a person). *colloq.* **E19.**
4 *verb intrans.* Foll. by *down*: access data which is in a lower level of a hierarchically structured database. **L20.**
▸ **II** Military & derived senses.
5 *verb trans. & intrans.* Train or be trained in military exercises and the use of arms. **E17.**

E. LINKLATER The whole army would be paraded and drilled in a variety of movements. C. MILNE We drilled on the Square, marching and counter-marching.

6 *verb trans. & intrans.* Instruct or be instructed (*in* a subject) by repeated exercises. Also, regulate (affairs) exactly. **E17.**

E. K. KANE We had drilled with knapsacks and sledge till we were almost martinets in our evolutions on the ice. H. KELLER I had been well drilled in English by Miss Sullivan. N. PODHORETZ I needed repeated drilling before the lesson of those negotiations could . . sink in.

7 *verb trans.* Inculcate (knowledge etc.) *into* a person by strict methods. **M19.**

A. KOESTLER The necessity to drill every sentence into the masses by . . endless repetition.

■ **drillable** *adjective* **L19.** **driller** *noun*[1] (*a*) a person who teaches or practises military drill; (*b*) a person who or a machine which drills holes or wells: **M17.**

drill /drɪl/ *verb*[4] *trans.* **M18.**
[ORIGIN from DRILL *noun*[4].]
1 Sow (seed) in drills, rather than broadcast; raise (a crop) in drills. **M18.**
direct drilling: see DIRECT *adjective.*
2 Sow or plant (ground) in drills. **L18.**
■ **driller** *noun*[2] **L18.**

drilling /ˈdrɪlɪŋ/ *noun.* **M17.**
[ORIGIN Alt. of German *Drillich*, earlier †*drilich* from Latin *trilix*, *trilic-* triple-twilled, from *tri-* three + *licium* thread.]
= DRILL *noun*[5].

drily /ˈdrʌɪli/ *adverb.* Also **dryly**. **LME.**
[ORIGIN from DRY *adjective* + -LY[2].]
In a dry manner, with dryness, (chiefly *fig.*).

GOLDSMITH The poet either drily didactive . . or triflingly volatile. T. HARDY He said drily that he could manage to do that, not without some contempt for the state of her knowledge. A. KOESTLER He finished a shade more drily, without warmth in his voice. J. M. COETZEE Before he could chew his stomach began to retch drily.

Drinamyl /ˈdrɪnəmɪl/ *noun.* Also **d-**. **M20.**
[ORIGIN from D(EXT)R(O- + AMPHETAM)IN(E + AMYL.]
PHARMACOLOGY. (Proprietary name for) a stimulant drug prepared from dexamphetamine and amylobarbitone.

dring *noun*, *verb* vars. of THRING *noun*[1], *verb.*

drink /drɪŋk/ *noun.* **OE.**
[ORIGIN from the verb.]
1 Liquid swallowed or suitable for swallowing, esp. to quench thirst or as refreshment or nourishment. **OE.** ▸**b** *transf.* Liquid absorbed or taken in by anything. **E17.**

AV *Matt.* 25:42 I was thirstie, and ye gaue me no drinke. LD MACAULAY The crews had better food and drink than they had ever had before. **b** EVELYN If they [plants] shrivel and fold up, give them Drink.

2 A particular kind of liquid for drinking; a beverage. **OE.**

D. LODGE A small kiosk that sold tea, fizzy drinks, . . bread.

3 *spec.* Intoxicating drink, alcohol; (excessive or habitual) indulgence in this. **OE.**

J. B. GOUGH Who ever saw me the worse for drink? CONAN DOYLE A rough, uncouth man, with . . a perpetual smell of drink. R. TRAVERS Drink was the reason of his downfall.

4 A glass or portion of (*spec.* alcoholic) liquid for drinking. Also, a quantity of liquid swallowed at one draught. **OE.** ▸**b** A medicinal potion. **ME.**

G. B. SHAW He goes to the sideboard for a drink of lemonade. J. WAIN He took a long drink of gin . . and put down his empty glass. B. GELDOF Daphne and I were engaged in a bout of spontaneous nobbing . . . We went for a drink afterwards.

5 *the drink*, the sea; some large body of water. *colloq.* **M19.**

– PHRASES: *be meat and drink to*: see MEAT *noun.* **in drink** inebriated, drunk. *long drink*: see LONG *adjective*[1]. *mix one's drinks*: see MIX *verb.* **on the drink** *colloq.* indulging in alcohol (to excess). *short drink*: see SHORT *adjective.* *soft drink*: see SOFT *adjective.* *strong drink*: see STRONG *adjective.* *tall drink*: see TALL *adjective.* **the Big Drink** (*a*) the Mississippi; (*b*) the Atlantic.
– ATTRIB. & COMB.: Esp. (freq. in *pl.*) with ref. to alcoholic drinks, as *drinks party*, *drinks table*, *drinks tray*, etc. Special combs., as **drink-money** [cf. French *pourboire*] a gratuity to be spent on drinks; **drink-offering** a libation of wine or other liquid to a god. **drink-taken** *adjective* [misunderstanding of Anglo-Ir. *have drink taken* = have taken drink] suffering from the effects of alcohol.
■ **drinkless** *adjective* **ME.**

D

drink /drɪŋk/ *verb.* Pa. t. **drank** /draŋk/, (now *non-standard*) **drunk** /drʌŋk/. Pa. pple **drunk**, (now *non-standard*) **drank**, (*arch.*) **drunken** /ˈdrʌŋkən/. See also DRUNK, DRUNKEN *adjectives.*
[ORIGIN Old English *drincan* = Old Frisian *drinka*, Old Saxon *drinkan* (Dutch *drinken*), Old High German *trinkan* (German *trinken*), Old Norse *drekka*, Gothic *drigkan*, from Germanic.]
1 *verb trans.* Swallow and take (liquid), or the liquid in (a vessel), into the stomach, esp. to quench thirst or as refreshment or nourishment; swallow (something solid) in a liquid. **OE.**

H. ROTH He drank the water in breathless . . gulps. B. PYM She drank two glasses of gin.

2 *verb intrans.* Swallow a liquid, take a drink. (Foll. by *from*, *out of*, †*in* a vessel, *of* the liquid or source.) **OE.**

J. STEINBECK Kino drank long and thirstily at the pool.

3 *verb intrans. spec.* Take or be in the habit of taking alcoholic drink, esp. to excess. **ME.**

OED Poor woman! her husband drinks. S. KING Sometimes when he drank he turned mean.

4 a *verb intrans.* Foll. by *to*: drink in honour of, toast; take a ceremonial drink from one's glass to express one's hopes for (a person's health, the success of an enterprise, etc.) or the health, success, etc., of (a person etc.). Formerly, offer a drink to (a person) after first taking a sip from it. **ME.** ▸**b** *verb trans.* Toast, drink to, (a person's health or (*arch.*) a person); wish (health, success, etc.) to or *to* a person etc. by drinking. Also, respond to or mark (a toast) by drinking. **LME.**

a SHAKES. *2 Hen. VI* Here, neighbour Horner, I drink to you in a cup of sack. R. V. JONES We still drink at the annual dinner to the memory of the Old Boys who fell. **b** BURKE We drank the man we were so much obliged to. JOHN MAYNE 'The King' and other loyal toasts . . Were drank aloud. E. WAUGH Miss Runcible's health was widely drunk in the refreshment tent. T. S. ELIOT I'll have a glass of sherry, To drink success to the flat.

†**5** *verb trans. & intrans. fig.* Suffer, have painful experience (of). **ME–L17.**

AV *Job* 21:20 His eyes shall see his destruction, and he shall drinke of the wrath of the Almightie.

6 *verb trans. fig.* Take eagerly into the mind or consciousness, esp. through the senses; look at or listen to with delight or agreement. Usu. foll. by *in*. **ME.**

SHAKES. *Rom. & Jul.* My ears have not yet drunk a hundred words Of thy tongue's uttering. J. BUCHAN We halted on the top of the Lammer Law to drink in the view.

7 *verb trans. transf.* Of a porous substance, a plant, etc.: absorb (moisture). Freq. foll. by *in*, *up*. **LME.**
8 *verb intrans.* Of wine etc.: have a specified flavour or character when drunk. **LME.**

C. RAY A vintage which was (as the wine merchants say) 'drinking very nicely now'.

9 *verb trans.* Spend or waste (money) on liquor. Also foll. by *away*, *up*. **LME.**
10 *verb trans.* with compl. Reduce to a specified state by drinking. **L16.**

P. HAWKER We having nearly drunk the landlord out of . . his . . wine. J. CONRAD Her skipper drank himself to death.

†**11** *verb trans.* Inhale (tobacco smoke); smoke (tobacco etc.). **L16–L18.**
– PHRASES & COMB.: **drink and drive** drive a motor vehicle soon after drinking alcohol or with too much alcohol in one's blood. **drink-and-drive** *adjective* = *drink-drive adjective* below. **drink deep** take a copious draught or draughts. **drink-drive** *adjective* pertaining to (the laws relating to) drink-driving. **drink-driving** driving a motor vehicle with the proportion of alcohol in one's blood greater than the legal limit. **drink hail** *imper.* (*hist.*) drink health, drink good luck (the customary reply to a pledge in drinking in early English times: cf. WASSAIL). **be drinking in the last chance saloon** *colloq.* have one final chance to put right a difficult situation. *drink like a fish*: see FISH *noun*[1]. *drink one's fill*: see FILL *noun*[1] 1. *drink the three outs*: see OUT *noun* 2. *drink the waters*: see WATER *noun* 5. *drink with the flies*: see FLY *noun*[1]. **drink under the table** surpass (a drinking companion) in ability to stay sober.
– WITH ADVERBS IN SPECIALIZED SENSES: **drink down** (*a*) swallow straight off; (*b*) extinguish the thought of (something) by taking an alcoholic drink; (*c*) = *drink under the table* above. **drink in** welcome in (an occasion) with festive drinking; see also senses 6, 7 above. **drink off**, (now *dial.*) **drink out** consume the whole of (a drink) at one go. **drink up** drink the whole of; drink what remains (of); see also senses 7, 9 above.

D

drinkable /ˈdrɪŋkəb(ə)l/ *adjective & noun*. LME.
[ORIGIN from DRINK *verb* + -ABLE.]
▸ **A** *adjective*. Able to be drunk, suitable for drinking. LME.
▸ **B** *noun*. A drinkable substance, an item of drink. Usu. in *pl*. E18.
■ **drinkaˈbility** *noun* M19. **drinkably** *adverb* sufficiently to be drinkable, so as to be drinkable M17.

drinker /ˈdrɪŋkə/ *noun*. OE.
[ORIGIN from DRINK *verb* + -ER¹.]
1 A person who drinks; *spec*. one who takes alcoholic drinks, esp. to excess. OE.

OED His father was a hard drinker. A. PRICE The pub's early evening drinkers.

social drinker: see SOCIAL *adjective*.
2 (In full ***drinker caterpillar***) the caterpillar of a large brownish European moth, *Euthrix* (*Philudoria*) *potatoria*, which shows a predilection for taking up water; (in full ***drinker moth***) the moth itself. L17.
3 A vessel or device from which an animal can drink. M20.

drinkery /ˈdrɪŋk(ə)ri/ *noun*. M19.
[ORIGIN from DRINK *noun* + -ERY.]
A place where alcoholic drink is supplied.

drinkie /ˈdrɪŋki/ *noun*. *nursery & joc*. Also **drinky**. M20.
[ORIGIN Dim. of DRINK *noun*: see -IE, -Y⁶.]
sing. & in *pl*. A drink.

ALAN BENNETT Come along now let's give you a drinkie. N. BAWDEN Nearly feeding time, isn't it? Anyone ready for drinkies?

drinking /ˈdrɪŋkɪŋ/ *verbal noun*. ME.
[ORIGIN from DRINK *verb* + -ING¹.]
1 The action of DRINK *verb*; *spec*. the taking of alcoholic drink, esp. to excess. ME.
social drinking: see SOCIAL *adjective*.
2 An occasion of convivial drinking. Now *rare* or *obsolete*. LME.
– COMB.: **drinking bout** a spell of hard drinking; **drinking fountain** a device that can be made to produce a little jet of water for drinking from; **drinking horn** *hist*. a drinking vessel carved from an animal's horn; **drinking problem** *euphem*. an addiction to alcohol, a habit of drinking too much; **drinking song** a hearty song about (and usu. sung at the time of) convivial drinking; **drinking up** the finishing of a drink (***drinking-up time***, a short period legally allowed for the consumption of drinks bought before closing time in a public house); **drinking water** water reserved, or pure enough, for drinking.

drinky *noun* var. of DRINKIE.

drinky /ˈdrɪŋki/ *adjective*. *colloq. & dial*. M19.
[ORIGIN from DRINK *noun* + -Y¹.]
(Somewhat) drunk.

drip /drɪp/ *noun*. LME.
[ORIGIN from the verb.]
1 †**a** A falling drop. LME–M16. ▸**b** *sing*. & in *pl*. Liquid which drips or falls in drops. E18.

b V. L. CAMERON An awning . . to keep the drips off.

2 a A projection on a cornice, sill, etc., designed to deflect rainwater from the wall below. M17. ▸**b** Each of a series of steps on a gently sloping roof. E18.
3 The act or fact of dripping; the sound made by falling drops. L17. ▸**b** MEDICINE. The continuous slow introduction of fluid into the body, usu. intravenously; fluid so introduced; an apparatus used for this purpose, having a chamber through which the fluid can be seen to drip. M20.

BYRON On the ear Drops the light drip of the suspended oar.

4 The angle made by a stratum with the horizontal; dip; (cf. DRIP *verb* 4). Now *rare* or *obsolete*. M19.
5 A receptacle for waste or overflow. L19.
6 *fig*. **a** Nonsense, flattery; sentimental drivel. *slang*. E20. ▸**b** A stupid, feeble, or dull person. *slang*. M20. ▸**c** A grumble, a complaint. *slang*. M20.
– PHRASES: **in a drip** in a dripping condition; saturated.
– COMB.: **drip coffee** *N. Amer*.: made by allowing boiling water to percolate through ground coffee; **drip culture** hydroponic growth of plants using a drip-feed; **drip-drip** (the sound of) continuous dripping; **drip-feed** a method of feeding, lubrication, etc., in which liquid is supplied drop by drop; **drip joint** an overlapping joint in metal roofing designed to keep out rainwater; **drip mat** a small mat placed under a glass etc. to catch drips; **drip painting** a method of painting by which the colour is dripped on to the surface, not applied directly; a painting so produced; **drip pan**: to catch drops of liquid; **dripstone** (*a*) a moulding or cornice over a door, window, etc., to deflect the rain; (*b*) a porous stone used as a filter; (*c*) a stone structure produced by dripping water; a stalactite, a stalagmite; **drip tray** = ***drip pan*** above.

drip /drɪp/ *verb*. Infl. **-pp-**.
[ORIGIN Old English *dryppan*, *drȳpan*, from Germanic base also of DROP *noun*, Middle Danish *drippe* verb (Danish *dryppe*). Cf. DREEP.]
1 *verb trans*. Let (a liquid) fall in drops; let (drops) fall. OE.

G. GREENE He dripped the heavy black oil into the well of each machine. J. STEINBECK His head still dripped water from the scrubbing and dousing.

2 *verb intrans*. Be so wet (*with* liquid) as to shed drops. OE.

H. MARTINEAU Girls wrung out their dripping hair. D. DUNN Underwear Drips from sagging clothes lines. *fig*.: A. PRICE Great-great-grandmother, dripping with jewels.

dripping wet very wet.
3 *verb intrans*. Fall in drops. OE.

J. TYNDALL The rain . . came through the roof, and dripped from the ceiling.

†**4** *verb intrans*. Slope, slant, dip. Cf. DRIP *noun* 4. E–M18.
5 *verb intrans*. Complain, grumble. *slang*. M20.

drip-drop /ˈdrɪpdrɒp/ *noun & verb*. M19.
[ORIGIN from DRIP *noun*, *verb* + DROP *noun*, *verb*.]
▸ **A** *noun*. Continuous dripping with alternation of sound. M19.
▸ **B** *verb intrans*. Infl. **-pp-**. Pass very slowly, like dripping water. L19.

drip-dry /*as verb* drɪpˈdrʌɪ; *as adjective & noun* ˈdrɪpdrʌɪ/ *verb*, *adjective*, *& noun*. M20.
[ORIGIN from DRIP *verb* + DRY *adjective*.]
▸ **A** *verb*. **1** *verb intrans*. Of a garment or fabric: dry without creases when hung up to drip after being washed. M20.
2 *verb trans*. *& intrans*. Dry (a garment etc.) by hanging up to drip. M20.
▸ **B** *adjective & noun*. (A garment or fabric) that will drip-dry. M20.

dripping /ˈdrɪpɪŋ/ *verbal noun*. LME.
[ORIGIN from DRIP *verb* + -ING¹.]
1 The fall of liquid in drops; *sing*. & (usu.) in *pl*., liquid so falling. LME.
2 *spec*. Fat melted from roasting meat and eaten cold or used in cooking. LME.
– COMB.: **dripping crust** a pastry crust made with dripping; **dripping pan**: used to catch the dripping from roasting meat; **dripping toast**: spread with dripping.

dripple /ˈdrɪp(ə)l/ *verb intrans*. E19.
[ORIGIN Blend of DRIP *verb* and DRIBBLE *verb*.]
1 Trickle; flow in a small stream. E19.
2 Drip with moisture. E19.

drippy /ˈdrɪpi/ *adjective*. E19.
[ORIGIN from DRIP + -Y¹.]
1 Characterized by dripping; wet, rainy. E19.
2 Drivelling, sloppily sentimental; (of a person) feeble or dull. M20.

R. TREMAIN I thought the idea of a Medieval Romance sounded drippy.

drisheen /drɪˈʃiːn/ *noun*. E20.
[ORIGIN Irish *drisín* intestine.]
A sausage made from sheep's blood, oatmeal, milk, and seasoning.

drive /drʌɪv/ *noun*. L17.
[ORIGIN from the verb.]
1 The action or an act of driving, esp. game or livestock; *US* a round-up of cattle. L17. ▸**b** *spec*. A journey or ride in a vehicle under one's direction. L18. ▸**c** A forceful stroke made by driving the ball in various games; *colloq*. a hard punch. M19.

S. W. BAKER After the tiger has killed a buffalo, there is much art required in the conduct of the drive. J. M. HUNTER Cowboys returning home after the drives. C. MAIR When it is mainly saw-logs that are cut, the fully improved streams make the drive easy. **b** R. LOWELL I was . . taken on Sunday afternoon drives through the suburbs. **c** M. FRAYN He selected a club from the golf bag . . and began practising drives from a tee. B. C. PELTON The forehand drive [in badminton] . . is flat, hard, and hit from a sidearm position.

2 A road for vehicles; (in proper names) a road represented as pleasant to drive along or with fine views; *esp*. a private road leading to a house. E19. ▸**b** A broad track in a wood. L19.

S. MIDDLETON He parked in the street, though he knew there would be room on the drive. J. MCCLURE 'Did Zondi give you Sally's address . . ?' 'It's 39 Woodland Drive, Parktown.'

3 A quantity of timber (to be) floated downstream. *N. Amer*. M19.
4 Pressure exerted on or by a person. M19.

W. ARTHUR The constant drive of work has . . driven a postponable duty out of the way.

5 MINING. = DRIFT *noun* 20. M19.
6 An organized effort to gain a particular end; an intensive campaign. L19. ▸**b** MILITARY. A forceful advance or attack. E20.

Times Weekly The export drive of the motor industry. *QuarterBack* The 80-yard, 13-play drive . . has its place in pro football lore.

ECONOMY *drive*.
7 An occasion at which several sets of people play whist or another game. E20.
beetle drive, ***domino drive***, ***whist drive***, etc.
8 PSYCHOLOGY & ZOOLOGY. An inner urge to satisfy some basic need or motivation; persistent behaviour directed towards a goal. E20.

R. FINE The individual finds it difficult to recognize his unconscious emotional drives. N. TINBERGEN When an animal's fighting drive is aroused.

9 Determination to achieve one's purpose; energy, initiative, persistence. E20.

M. MCCARTHY I have the drive but lack the talent. LD BRAIN With characteristic drive and organizing ability Cairns built up the neurosurgical department.

10 a A mechanism for transmitting (esp. rotary) motion to the wheels of a vehicle, a turntable, etc. E20. ▸**b** The position of the driving controls of a motor vehicle, specified as on the left- or the right-hand side. M20. ▸**c** In a motor vehicle with automatic transmission: the position of the selector lever in which the gears are automatically changed as required. M20. ▸**d** COMPUTING. = ***disc drive*** s.v. DISC *noun*. M20.

a N. SHUTE A big four-wheel-drive truck. **b** P. P. READ A white Jaguar . . with French registration plates and a left-hand drive. **c** *Times* The coroner said the selector lever must have been in 'drive'.

a belt drive, ***chain drive***, etc.
11 ELECTRICITY. The signal supplied as the input to a transistor, amplifier, etc. M20.
12 A thrill, a feeling of exhilaration, *esp*. one induced by drugs. *US slang*. M20.
– PHRASES ETC.: ***direct-drive***: see DIRECT *adjective*. ***final drive***: see FINAL *adjective*. **full drive** (now *rare* or *obsolete*) at full speed, with maximum impetus.

drive /drʌɪv/ *verb*. Pa. t. **drove** /drəʊv/, (*arch*.) **drave** /dreɪv/; pa. pple **driven** /ˈdrɪv(ə)n/.
[ORIGIN Old English *drīfan* = Old Frisian *drīva*, Old Saxon *drīban* (Dutch *drijven*), Old High German *trīban* (German *treiben*), Old Norse *drífa*, Gothic *dreiban*, from Germanic.]
▸ **I** Force (a living being, a vehicle, etc.) to move on.
1 *verb trans*. Urge (animals, people) in some (usu. specified) direction by blows, shouts, etc. OE.

J. BUCHAN I helped to drive sheep to the local market.

2 a *verb trans*. *& intrans*. Cause (animals, an enemy) to flee before one, esp. into an area where they can be captured or killed; cause (bees) to enter a new hive; *hist*. impound a tenant's cattle in lieu of unpaid rent. ME. ▸**b** *verb trans*. Search (an area) for game, cattle, etc.; clear (an area) of animals etc. LME.

a SIR W. SCOTT Drive the fleet deer the forest through. J. FORBES To encircle the herd, and to await his signal to commence driving. J. INGLIS The Indian jackal . . can fight in an ugly way when driven into a corner. G. L. HARDING The Muslims were driven back and their three great leaders . . were killed.

3 *verb trans*. Compel to leave or go (*out*; *to*, *from*, *out of* a place). ME.

G. B. SHAW I am sent . . to drive the English away from Orleans and from France. J. STEINBECK The sun . . drove the fog headlong from the sky.

4 *verb trans*. Impel (a person etc.) powerfully and irresistibly; bring forcibly into or out of some state, or into the state of being (mad etc.). (Foll. by *to do*; *to*, *into* an action; *into*, *out of*, etc., a state.) ME. ▸**b** Urge on; force to work, *esp*. overwork. M17.

O. HENRY Driven by hunger, he had committed an onslaught upon a bottle of . . infant's food. QUILLER-COUCH His isolation . . drove him to return the men's friendship. W. S. CHURCHILL His foreign policy had driven the Scots into alliance with France. P. TILLICH His anxiety does not drive him to the construction of imaginary worlds. R. TRAVERS The death of his wife had driven Weller into a deep melancholia. G. PALEY This place drives me nuts. **b** A. WILSON Young people need leading, not driving.

†**5** *verb intrans*. Ride hard on horseback. ME–L15.
6 a *verb trans*. Orig., control and guide (a draught animal or the vehicle drawn). Now usu., operate and control the course of (a motor vehicle, locomotive, etc.). LME. ▸**b** *verb intrans*. (Be competent to) drive a vehicle; drive a draught animal; travel in a vehicle under one's control or direction; (of a vehicle) travel under a driver's control. L16. ▸**c** *verb trans*. Convey or carry in a vehicle. M17.

P. GOODMAN Kids of other periods drove the horses at an early age; in rural places they drive cars at fourteen. **b** *Sunday Express* We drove back to her home. M. DRABBLE She drives quite well. *Times* The security van was . . driving north in the inside lane. **c** M. AMIS I offered to drive her home in my powerful green car.

7 *verb trans*. *fig*. Direct (guilt, blame, etc.) *on* or *upon* a person. Now *rare* or *obsolete*. LME.
▸ **II** Impel (matter) by physical force.
8 *verb trans*. Cause (an object) to move by applying force to it; propel, carry or send along; *N. Amer. & NZ* guide the course of (timber floating downstream). OE. ▸**b** Supply motive power for (machinery etc.), electrical power to (a device), or chemical power for (a reaction or phenomenon). L16.

C. M. YONGE Alice and I used to drive hoops. J. CONRAD A ship may be 'driven ashore' by stress of weather. **b** N. NICHOLSON Every wagon of cold coal Is fire to drive a turbine wheel. *Which?* You will normally need a more powerful amplifier to drive a less efficient speaker. *Scientific American* The bioluminescence of fireflies . . is driven by a sequence of chemical reactions.

9 a *verb trans.* Impel forcibly; throw, hit; hit (a ball) hard; CRICKET hit (the ball) with the bat swung freely downwards; hit a ball delivered by (a bowler) in this way; TENNIS & BADMINTON etc., hit (the ball, the shuttlecock) with a freely swung racket; GOLF hit (the ball) with a powerful stroke, esp. from a tee using a driver. OE. ▸**b** *verb intrans.* Drive a ball (in golf etc.); make a driving shot; (of a cricket bat) be suited to doing this. E19.

b M. McCormack He missed from four feet after driving into the rough.

10 a *verb trans.* Force by a blow or thrust (*into, through*, etc.); *spec.* force (a nail, stake, etc.) into or *into* a solid body by repeated blows. ME. ▸**b** *verb intrans.* Of a nail etc.: go when driven. E18.

a A. Ransome She . . grabbed one of the big spades and drove it as hard as she could into the ground. J. Steinbeck His father set another nail and drove it in. A. Gray He . . drove his fist hard into her stomach.

11 *verb intrans. & trans.* Aim (a blow or missile), strike, (*at*). Also ***let drive***. LME.

Swift [He] let drive at us with a large folio. E. O'Neill He lets drive a terrific swing, his fist landing full on the . . face.

12 *verb trans. & intrans.* Cause (a tunnel, cavity, etc.) to penetrate solid material; *spec.* bore (a tunnel) horizontally or nearly so. L15.

13 *verb trans.* Spread, or (formerly) beat, out thinly. Now only of colour painting. L15.

14 *verb trans.* Separate (feathers or down) by a current of air so that the lightest are driven off and may be collected. (Earlier as DRIVEN *ppl adjective* 2.) L17.

▸**III** Maintain (a course).

15 *verb trans.* Carry on vigorously, engage in, practise, (a custom, trade, etc.); carry through, perform; bring to a conclusion, conclude, (a transaction). Also foll. by *on, through*. *arch.* exc. in ***drive a hard bargain*** below. OE.

Swift We drove on the war at a prodigious disadvantage. Ld Auckland The Portuguese princess spoke French sufficient to drive a conversation.

16 *verb intrans.* Advance quickly; come with violence; rush, hasten; work hard (*at*). OE. ▸**b** Play music energetically or with a strong rhythm. *colloq.* M20.

W. Clubbe In swarms again they seek the Hive As fast as ever they can drive. T. Gray I have been driving away at the 'Flora', of late, very hard. **b** J. Lennon I was rhythm guitarist . . . I can make a band drive.

17 a *verb trans.* Move along, esp. with force, under the action of wind, a current, etc.; float along, drift. ME. ▸**b** *verb intrans. fig.* Proceed in a course; tend. LME.

a Longfellow A mist was driving down the British Channel. C. Francis Often ships would drive straight up on to the rocks.

▸**IV** Other uses.

18 *verb trans. & intrans.* Protract, prolong, (time or occupation); put off, defer. Also foll. by *off, out, on*. ME.

†**19** *verb trans.* Live out, endure, (one's days, fate); experience (hardship, grief, etc.). Only in ME.

†**20 a** *verb trans. & intrans.* While *away*, pass, spend, (time). (Foll. by *off, over*, etc.) ME–E19. ▸**b** *verb intrans.* Of time: pass away. LME–L18.

†**21** *verb trans.* **a** Conclude, infer, deduce. (Foll. by *out*.) LME–L17. ▸**b** Derive *from* a source. M–L16.

22 *verb trans.* Fish with a drift net. L17.

– PHRASES: †**drive a buck (of clothes)** carry out buck-washing. ***drive a coach and horses through***, ***drive a coach and six through***: see COACH *noun* 1. **drive a hard bargain** be severe or uncompromising in making a bargain, settlement, etc. **drive a quill**, **drive a pen** write; work in an office. **drive the centre**, **drive the cross**, **drive the nail** US make a perfect shot, hit the centre of a target. **drive the green** GOLF hit the ball from a tee on to the green. ***drive to the wall***, ***drive up the wall***: see WALL *noun*[1].

– WITH ADVERBS & PREPOSITIONS IN SPECIALIZED SENSES: **drive at** have as one's meaning or purpose (now usu. in rel. or interrog. clause with *what*). **drive off** (*a*) cause (liquid) to leave a solution as vapour, by heating; (*b*) leave in a vehicle; (*c*) GOLF drive a ball from the tee. **drive out** (*a*) oust, take the place of, (a person); (*b*) TYPOGRAPHY respace (type) to cover a larger area, move (type) forward to accommodate an insertion etc.; (*c*) see also senses 3, 22a above. **drive over** = *drive out* (b) above.

– COMB.: **drive belt**: that transmits torque; **drive-by** *adjective & noun* (designating) an action, esp. a shooting or murder, carried out from a passing vehicle; **drive-by-wire** *adjective & noun* (designating) a semi-automatic and typically computer-regulated system for controlling the engine, handling, suspension, etc. of a motor vehicle; **drive-in** *adjective & noun* (designating) a cinema, bank, restaurant, etc., that can be visited without getting out of one's car; **drive-on** *adjective* (of a ship) on to which a motor vehicle may be driven from land; **driveshaft**: that transmits torque; **drive system** *Austral. & NZ* a method of felling trees in hilly country by making one at the top of a hill topple on to others partly cut through; **drive-through** *noun & adjective* (chiefly *N. Amer.*) (*a*) *noun* a restaurant, shop, etc., with a window to which customers drive to be served; (*b*) *adjective* designating the window of a drive-through; (of a place) suitable for driving through; **drivetrain** the system in a motor vehicle which connects the transmission to the drive axles; **drive-yourself** *adjective & noun* (designating) a motor vehicle hired out and driven by the hirer.

■ **drivaˈbility** *noun* the capacity of a motor vehicle for being driven, esp. easily or economically L20. **drivable** *adjective* able to be driven, suitable for driving M19.

†**drivel** *noun*[1]. ME–L16.

[ORIGIN App. from Low German: cf. Middle Dutch *drevel* scullion, turnspit from *drivan* to drive.]

1 A driving tool or implement; a carpenter's punch. ME–L16.

2 A servant doing menial work; a drudge. ME–L16.

3 A fool, an imbecile. L15–L16.

4 A dirty slovenly person. M–L16.

drivel /ˈdrɪv(ə)l/ *noun*[2]. ME.

[ORIGIN from the verb.]

1 Spittle trickling from the mouth, slaver. Now *rare*. ME.

2 Silly nonsense, twaddle. M19.

drivel /ˈdrɪv(ə)l/ *verb*. Infl. **-ll-**, *-**l**-.

[ORIGIN Old English *dreflian* (in pres. pple glossing medieval Latin *reumaticus* rheumy), perh. rel. to DRAFF: cf. -LE[3].]

1 a *verb intrans.* Let saliva or mucus trickle from the mouth or nose; dribble, slobber. OE. ▸†**b** *verb trans.* Let (saliva etc.) trickle from the mouth or nose; allow to flow *out* through a crack. L16–E18. ▸†**c** *verb intrans.* (Of saliva etc.) escape from the mouth or nose; trickle. E17–L18.

2 a *verb intrans.* Talk in a childish or idiotic way. LME. ▸**b** *verb trans.* Say in a childish or idiotic way. Now *rare*. M18.

3 *verb trans.* Fritter *away* or drag *out* in a childish or idiotic way. M18.

■ **driveller** *noun* M16. **drivelling** *ppl adjective* (*a*) childish, idiotic; (*b*) slavering, dribbling: LME. **drivellingly** *adverb* M18.

driven /ˈdrɪv(ə)n/ *ppl adjective*. L15.

[ORIGIN pa. pple of DRIVE *verb*.]

1 Of snow: piled into drifts or made smooth by the wind. Chiefly in ***white as driven snow***, ***pure as the driven snow***, etc. L15.

2 Of feathers or down: selected by driving so as to get only the lightest. (Cf. DRIVE *verb* 14.) E17.

Shakes. *Oth.* My thrice-driven bed of down.

3 Urged onward, impelled; forced; powered; (of a person) showing intensity or compulsion in his or her behaviour; having as the chief reason or determinant the thing specified. Freq. as 2nd elem. of comb. M17.

B. Friedan One, after five years of therapy, was no longer a driven woman.

consumer-driven, ***market-driven***, ***receipt-driven***, etc. **driven well** US a tube well.

driven *verb pa. pple*: see DRIVE *verb*.

driver /ˈdrʌɪvə/ *noun*. LME.

[ORIGIN from DRIVE *verb* + -ER[1].]

1 A person who drives a vehicle, cattle, etc. LME. ▸**b** The overseer of a gang of slaves; *slang* a hard or exacting supervisor or manager. M18. ▸**c** CRICKET. A batsman skilled at driving. E20.

bus-driver, ***cab-driver***, ***engine driver***, ***taxi-driver***, etc. **in the driver's seat** in control.

2 A boat used in fishing with a drift net. M17.

3 A tool or instrument for driving, as a punch or tamping iron. L17. ▸**b** GOLF. A wooden-headed club (now always straight-faced) for driving off. M19.

4 NAUTICAL. Orig., an additional sail set square on the mizzenmast to take advantage of a following wind. Now, a spanker, *esp.* a small one. M18.

5 Part of a machine or electrical device which transmits or provides power to another part. M19.

6 In full ***driver ant***. Any of various blind tropical ants of the subfamily Dorylinae, esp. of the genera *Eciton* (in America) and *Anomma* (in Africa), which migrate in large columns that prey mainly on insects and spiders. Also called ***army ant***, ***visiting ant***. M19.

7 A horse trained to be driven in harness. *US*. L19.

8 A leather strap on sheep-shearers' hand shears to prevent the hand from slipping on to the blades. *Austral. & NZ*. E20.

■ **driverless** *adjective* L19.

driveway /ˈdrʌɪvweɪ/ *noun*. Chiefly *N. Amer.* M19.

[ORIGIN from DRIVE *verb* + WAY *noun*.]

1 A passageway by which hay, grain, etc., can be taken into a barn. M19.

2 A course along which game is driven in hunting. L19.

3 A road along which animals or vehicles are driven; *spec.* a private road leading to a house, a drive. L19.

4 A scenic highway. *Canad.* E20.

driving /ˈdrʌɪvɪŋ/ *verbal noun*. LME.

[ORIGIN from DRIVE *verb* + -ING[1].]

The action of DRIVE *verb*.

– ATTRIB. & COMB.: Esp. in the senses 'relating to driving a horse or a vehicle', as ***driving gloves***, ***driving school***, ***driving whip***, 'relating to or used for the transmission of power', as ***driving axle***, ***driving gear***. Special combs., as **driving band** (*a*) = *driving belt* below; (*b*) a band of soft metal on a projectile with which the rifling of a gun barrel engages to impart rotary motion; **driving belt** a broad flat strap passing round two wheels or shafts to transmit motion from one to the other; **driving box** the seat on which the driver of a horse-drawn carriage sits; **driving iron** GOLF = DRIVER 3b; formerly, any of various iron clubs; **driving licence** an official document authorizing a person to drive a motor vehicle; **driving range** GOLF an area equipped for practising driving; **driving seat** the seat on which the driver of a vehicle sits; ***in the driving seat***, in control; **driving test** a test of a person's competence to drive which has to be passed before he or she is allowed to drive without individual restriction; **driving wheel** each of the wheels by which the power of a motor vehicle, locomotive, etc., is conveyed to the road or track.

driving /ˈdrʌɪvɪŋ/ *ppl adjective*. ME.

[ORIGIN from DRIVE *verb* + -ING[2].]

1 Setting in motion; impelling, actuating. ME.

driving force, **driving power** the force or power by which a machine or vehicle is driven; *fig.* a source of energy, a person who or thing which strongly motivates.

2 Moving along rapidly, esp. before the wind. E17.

Dryden Perpetual Sleet, and driving Snow.

3 Energetic, dynamic, forceful. Chiefly *US*. M19.

D. Norden A driving up-tempo version of 'I met her on the Beach.'

drizzle /ˈdrɪz(ə)l/ *noun & verb*. M16.

[ORIGIN Prob. from Old English *drēosan* to fall = Old Saxon *driusan*, Gothic *driusan*: see DREARY, -LE[1].]

▸**A** *noun*. **1** Rain that falls in fine spraylike droplets; an example of this. M16.

P. Theroux The rain was not a brisk purifying downpour, but a dark tedious drizzle.

2 A tiny trickle. E18.

Listener They have also produced a drizzle of mediocre sit-coms.

▸**B** *verb*. **1** *verb intrans.* Rain or fall in fine spraylike drops. Usu. *impers.* in ***it drizzles***, ***it is drizzling***, etc. M16.

R. Macaulay Rain had begun to drizzle. J. Buchan The following morning it still drizzled. *transf.*: *Nature* Magnetospheric electrons constantly drizzle down into the stratosphere.

2 *verb trans.* Shed in fine drops; sprinkle (a liquid), let fall in a thin trickle. M16.

Shakes. *Jul. Caes.* Fierce fiery warriors fight upon the clouds . . Which drizzled blood upon the Capitol. C. McCullough Meggie beat green food coloring into a bowl of runny icing and began to drizzle it over already baked fir trees.

3 *verb trans. & intrans.* Sprinkle or wet (esp. food) with liquid in fine drops or a thin trickle. E19.

Freetime Fill it with . . ice cream, drizzle with hot chocolate.

4 *verb intrans.* Pick the gold thread out of discarded tassels, embroideries, etc., into which it was woven. L19.

■ **drizzling** *ppl adjective* that drizzles; drizzly: M16. **drizzly** *adjective* of the nature of drizzle; marked by drizzling rain: L17.

Dr Martens *noun phr.* var. of DOCTOR MARTENS.

drog /drəʊɡ/ *verb trans.* Also **drogue**. L17.

[ORIGIN Uncertain: perh. back-form. from or formed as DROGHER.]

Carry in a drogher.

drogher /ˈdrəʊɡə/ *noun*. Also **drog(g)er**, **droguer**. M17.

[ORIGIN French †*drogueur* a ship that fished and dried herring and mackerel from Dutch *droger* drier, from *droogen* to dry.]

A W. Indian coasting vessel; any slow coasting vessel.

drogue /drəʊɡ/ *noun*. E18.

[ORIGIN Unknown.]

1 A board, tub, etc., attached to the end of a harpoon line to check a whale's progress. E18.

2 A canvas cone open at both ends or other device towed behind a sailing vessel to slow it down. L19.

3 A fabric cone or cylinder open at both ends and towed behind an aircraft to serve as a brake or target; a similar device used as a windsock or an auxiliary parachute. E20.

attrib.: ***drogue parachute***.

4 A funnel-shaped device at the end of the supply line from a tanker aircraft, which receives the probe from an aircraft to be refuelled in flight. M20.

drogue *verb* var. of DROG.

droguer *noun* var. of DROGHER.

droid /drɔɪd/ *noun*. L20.

[ORIGIN Abbreviation of ANDROID.]

1 A robot or automaton, esp. a humanoid one; an android.

2 COMPUTING. A program which automatically collects information from remote systems.

droit /drɔɪt, *foreign* drwa/ *noun*[1]. LME.

[ORIGIN Old French & mod. French from Proto-Romance use as noun of var. of Latin *directum* neut. of *directus* DIRECT *adjective*.]

1 A right; a legal claim; something to which one has a legal claim; a due. LME.

droit of Admiralty a right by which proceeds arising from wrecks, the seizure of enemy ships, etc., could be claimed by the Court of Admiralty and are now paid into the Exchequer. **droit de suite** LAW the right of an artist or his or her heirs to receive a fee when one of his or her works is resold. **droit du seigneur**, **droit de seigneur**, **droits du seigneur**, **droits de seigneur** /drwɑː duː sɛnˈjəː; *foreign* drwa dy sɛɲœːr; də/ an alleged custom by which a medieval feudal lord might have sexual intercourse with a vassal's bride on the wedding night.

†**2** Law, right, justice; a law. L15–M16.

†**droit** *noun*[2]. M16–M19.

[ORIGIN Unknown.]

A very small unit of weight, equal to 1/480 grain (about 0.135 mg).

D

droitural /ˈdrɔɪtjər(ə)l/ *adjective*. M18.
[ORIGIN from French *droiture* straightness, rightness (from medieval Latin *drectura* from Latin *directura*, from *direct-* pa. ppl stem of *dirigere* DIRECT *verb*: see -URE) + -AL¹.]
LAW (now *hist.*). Relating to a right to property, as distinguished from possession.

droke /drəʊk/ *noun*. *dial. & Canad.* L18.
[ORIGIN Unknown.]
1 A groove, a furrow; a ditch; a narrow usu. steep passageway; a valley. L18.
2 A clump or belt of trees. E19.

droll /drəʊl/ *noun*. *arch.* M17.
[ORIGIN French *drôle*, perh. from Middle Dutch *drolle* (mod. *drol*) imp, goblin.]
1 A humorist, a jester; a buffoon. M17.
†**2** A comedy, a farce; an enacted piece of buffoonery; a puppet show. M17–E19.
†**3** The action of jesting; burlesque writing or style. L17–M19.

droll /drəʊl/ *adjective*. E17.
[ORIGIN French *drôle*, earlier *drolle*, formed as DROLL *noun*.]
Amusing, now esp. in a dry or whimsical way; queer, odd, surprising.

SIR W. SCOTT A droll sort of house . . a pretty, somewhat fantastical residence. P. G. WODEHOUSE His sudden grab at the hair of any adult . . within reach was very droll. E. WAUGH A pretty, droll girl. C. SANDBURG He enjoyed droll stories.

■ **drollish** *adjective* L17. **drollness** *noun* E19. **drolly** /ˈdrəʊl-li/ *adverb* M17.

droll /drəʊl/ *verb*. *arch.* M17.
[ORIGIN French †*drôler* play the wag, formed as DROLL *noun*.]
1 *verb intrans.* Make fun; jest, joke; lark about. (Foll. by *with*, *at*, *on*, *upon*.) M17.
2 *verb trans.* Send *away* or *off* by laughter or mockery; bring *forth* like a jester or buffoon. Formerly also, laugh (a person) *out of* or *into* something. M17.

drollery /ˈdrəʊləri/ *noun*. L16.
[ORIGIN French *drôlerie*, formed as DROLL *noun*; see -ERY.]
†**1** A comic picture; a caricature. L16–L19.
†**2** = DROLL *noun* 2. E17–M19.
3 A joke; a funny story. M17.

H. CARPENTER The rather feeble drolleries of the early limerick books.

4 Joking, buffoonery. M17.

G. MAXWELL There seems no end to its fun, its energy, its drollery.

5 The quality of being droll; droll humour. M18.

C. S. LEWIS Drollery, whimsicality, the kind of humour that borders on the fantastic, was my line.

dromaeosaur /ˈdrəʊmɪə(ʊ)sɔː/ *noun*. L20.
[ORIGIN from mod. Latin *Dromaeosaurus* (genus name), from Greek *dromaios* swift-running + *sauros* lizard.]
Any of various carnivorous bipedal dinosaurs of the family Dromaeosauridae, whose members (including deinonychus and the velociraptors) had a large curved slashing claw on each hind foot.
■ Also **dromaeoˈsaurid** *noun* L20.

drome /drəʊm/ *noun*. *colloq.* Also **'drome**. E20.
[ORIGIN Abbreviation.]
1 = AERODROME 1. E20.
2 = AERODROME 2. E20.

-drome /drəʊm/ *suffix*.
[ORIGIN Repr. Greek *dromos* course, running, avenue, rel. to *dramein* run.]
Forming nouns denoting (*a*) a place for running, a course, etc., as in AERODROME 2, HIPPODROME; (*b*) a thing that runs, as in AERODROME 1, PALINDROME. Cf. also SYNDROME.

dromedary /ˈdrɒmɪd(ə)ri, ˈdrʌm-/ *noun*. ME.
[ORIGIN Old French *dromedaire* (mod. *dromadaire*) or late Latin *dromedarius* adjective (sc. *camelus*), from Latin *dromas*, *dromad-* dromedary (from Greek = runner) + *-arius* -ARY¹.]
1 A camel of a swift and light breed (usu. the Arabian or one-humped camel) specially reared and trained for riding. ME.
†**2** = DROMOND. L15–M16.
3 A stupid bungling person. Now *dial.* M16.

dromic /ˈdrɒmɪk/ *adjective*. M19.
[ORIGIN Greek *dromikos*, from *dromos*: see -DROME, -IC.]
Suitable for racing; pertaining to or of the form of a racecourse; *spec.* designating the basilican type of Orthodox church.
■ Also **dromical** *adjective* M17.

dromoi *noun* pl. of DROMOS.

dromomania /drɒməˈmeɪnɪə/ *noun*. E20.
[ORIGIN from Greek *dromos* (see -DROME, -O-) + -MANIA.]
A mania for roaming or running.
■ **dromomaniac** *noun* a person who has such a mania; (*joc.* or *slang*) an athlete: M20.

dromond /ˈdrɒmənd, ˈdrʌm-/ *noun*. ME.
[ORIGIN Anglo-Norman *dromond*, Old French *dromon(t)*, from late Latin *dromo*, *dromon-*, from late Greek *dromōn*, from Greek *dromos*: see -DROME.]
hist. A very large medieval ship formerly used in war and trade.

dromos /ˈdrɒmɒs/ *noun*. Pl. **-moi** /-mɔɪ/. M19.
[ORIGIN Greek: see -DROME.]
GREEK ANTIQUITIES. An avenue or entrance passage to an ancient temple, tomb, etc., often between rows of columns or statues.

drone /drəʊn/ *noun*.
[ORIGIN Old English *drān*, *drǣn*, corresp. to Old Saxon *drān*, *dreno*, Middle Low German *drāne*, *drōne* (Low German *drōne*), Old High German *treno* (Middle High German *tren(e)*, German dial. *Dräne*), prob. from West Germanic word meaning 'to boom'. In branch II partly from the verb.]
▸ **I 1** A male bee in a colony of bees, which does no work but can fertilize the queen. OE.
2 An indolent person; an idler. E16.
3 A pilotless aircraft or missile directed by remote control. M20.
▸ **II 4** A continuous steady deep humming or buzzing sound; *spec.* a continuous low note produced by a musical instrument. E16.

P. H. GIBBS The drone of German aeroplanes. A. BURGESS The power-house drone of the refrigerator.

5 A bagpipe or other musical instrument that produces a continuous low tone. E16.
6 a A bass pipe of a bagpipe, which emits only one continuous tone. L16. ▸**b** On a stringed instrument, a string used to produce a continuous droning sound. L18.
7 A monotonous tone of speech. L18.
8 A monotonous speaker. L18.
– COMB.: *drone-bee* = sense 1 above; *drone-beetle*: see DOR *noun*¹ 2; **drone fly** a flower-fly, *Eristalis tenax*, similar to the honeybee in appearance and behaviour.
■ **dronage** *noun* the condition of a drone or male bee M19.

drone /drəʊn/ *verb*. E16.
[ORIGIN from the noun.]
▸ **I 1** *verb intrans.* Act in a sluggish or indolent manner. E16.
2 *verb trans.* Pass *away*, drag *out*, (life, time) sluggishly and indolently. M18.
▸ **II 3** *verb intrans.* Emit a drone; hum on one note; talk monotonously; fly or travel with a droning sound. E16.

DAY LEWIS On and on droned the voices. G. GREENE A mosquito droned to the attack.

†**4** *verb trans.* Play (a bagpipe); smoke (a pipe). M16–E17.
5 *verb trans.* Utter, give *out*, in a drone. E17.

THACKERAY Penitents . . droning their dirges.

■ **droner** *noun* M16. **droningly** *adverb* in a droning way, boringly L19.

drong /drɒŋ/ *noun*. *dial.* Also **drang** /draŋ/. L18.
[ORIGIN from ablaut var. of base of DRING *verb*, THRING *verb*.]
A narrow lane or passage.

drongo /ˈdrɒŋgəʊ/ *noun*. Pl. **-o(e)s**. M19.
[ORIGIN Madagascan name.]
1 Any of several black birds with long forked tails that belong to the passerine family Dicruridae and occur in Africa, southern Asia, and Australia. M19.
2 A stupid, foolish, or incompetent person. *Austral. & NZ slang*. M20.

J. CLEARY You're just a bloody drongo who doesn't know any better.

dronish /ˈdrəʊnɪʃ/ *adjective*. L16.
[ORIGIN from DRONE *noun* + -ISH¹.]
Of the nature of a drone or male bee; living on another's labour; indolent, sluggish.

drony /ˈdrəʊni/ *adjective*. L18.
[ORIGIN from DRONE *noun* + -Y¹.]
1 Resembling a drone or male bee; sluggish. L18.
2 Characterized by a monotonous tone, boring to listen to. E19.

droob /druːb/ *noun*. *Austral. slang*. M20.
[ORIGIN Uncertain: perh. alt. of DROOP *noun*.]
An unprepossessing or contemptible person, esp. a man.
■ **drooby** *adjective* L20.

droog /druːg/ *noun*. *slang*. M20.
[ORIGIN Alt. of Russian *drug* friend: coined by Anthony Burgess in *A Clockwork Orange* (1962).]
A member of a gang; a young thug.

drook *verb* var. of DROUK.

drool /druːl/ *noun*. E19.
[ORIGIN Cf. DROOL *verb*².]
1 A slow or slothful person. *Scot.* E19.
2 Spittle; = DRIVEL *noun*² 1. *US colloq.* M19.
3 = DRIVEL *noun*² 2. *colloq.* E20.

drool /druːl/ *verb*¹ *intrans. & trans. obsolete* exc. *Scot.* (now *rare*). M17.
[ORIGIN Unknown.]
Make a mournful sound; utter mournfully.

drool /druːl/ *verb*². E19.
[ORIGIN Contr. of DRIVEL *verb*.]
1 *verb intrans. & (rare) trans.* Dribble; salivate in anticipation. E19.

A. HAMILTON There may be drooling of saliva. T. HARDY The glebe cow drooled. K. TENNANT Cooking . . of such a quality that the boarders were . . drooling impatiently long before the bell went.

2 *verb intrans.* Talk foolishly or nonsensically; ramble (*on*). L19.

J. CAREY He had tried nursing his wife, and soon got sick of her drooling inanities.

3 *verb intrans.* Express or feel inordinate sentimentality or enthusiasm. (Foll. by *over*.) M20.

W. STYRON Those stacks of records of yours make me drool. A. COOKE When Brando came out with one sweat shirt, the town drooled over him.

■ **drooler** *noun* L19.

droop /druːp/ *noun*. M17.
[ORIGIN formed as DROOP *adjective*.]
1 The act or fact of drooping; a drooping attitude; a loss of energy or spirit. M17.

A. TYLER A slump in his posture, a little droop to his shoulders. *Hi-Fi News* Some power supply droop.

2 A fool; an ineffectual languid person. M20.
– COMB.: **droop-snoot**, **droop-snooter** *colloq.* (an aircraft with) a nose that can be lowered to increase visibility.

droop /druːp/ *adjective*. E16.
[ORIGIN from the verb.]
Drooping. Chiefly in parasynthetic combs., as *droop-wristed*.

droop /druːp/ *verb*. ME.
[ORIGIN Old Norse *drúpa* hover, hang the head for sorrow, from Germanic base also of DROP *noun*.]
1 *verb intrans.* Hang or sink down, as from weariness; bend or slope downwards; (of the eyes) look downwards; (of the eyelids) fall. ME.

V. WOOLF Two cracked vases, from which red flowers drooped.

2 *verb intrans.* **a** Flag in spirit or courage, lose heart. ME. ▸**b** Lose energy, flag, languish; become less in size, quantity, value, or importance. LME.

b *Daily Telegraph* The exchange rate has begun to droop.

3 *verb intrans.* Sink; decline, draw to a close. Now only *poet.* (of the sun, day, etc.). LME.
†**4** *verb intrans.* Sink or crouch out of sight; lie hidden. LME–L15.
5 *verb trans.* Allow to hang or sink down; bend downwards; cast down (the eyes or face). L16.

T. C. WOLFE The honeysuckle drooped its heavy mass upon the fence.

■ **drooper** *noun* L16. **droopingly** *adverb* in a drooping or dejected manner LME. **droopingness** *noun* a drooping state or condition M17.

droopy /ˈdruːpi/ *adjective*. ME.
[ORIGIN from DROOP *verb* or Old Norse *drúpr* drooping spirits: see -Y¹.]
Dejected, gloomy; drooping.
droopy drawers *slang* an untidy, sloppy, or depressing person.
■ **droopiness** *noun* E19.

drop /drɒp/ *noun*. Also (*Scot.*) **drap** /drap/.
[ORIGIN Old English *dropa* corresp. to Old Saxon *dropo*, Old Norse *dropi*, with var. corresp. to Old High German *tropfo* (German *Tropfen*), from Germanic, from weak grade of base also of DROOP *verb*: cf. DRIP *noun*. In branch II from the verb.]
▸ **I 1** A small round pear-shaped or hemispherical mass of liquid that hangs or falls separately or adheres to a surface; a liquid globule; (*ellipt.* or contextually) a teardrop, a drop of blood, etc. OE. ▸**b** In dispensing medicine: the smallest separable quantity of a liquid; *sing.* & (usu.) in *pl.*, a medicinal solution applied in drops. LME.

DRYDEN On his . . Ears . . Sweat in clammy Drops appears. DEFOE They would be faithful to him to the last drop. J. C. POWYS A faint trickle of water . . fell down drop by drop into the ditch. R. HUGHES The moisture from the mist collected on my hair, and two drops rolled over . . my cheek.

dewdrop, *raindrop*, *teardrop*, etc. *drop serene*: see SERENE *adjective*. *hanging drop*: see HANGING *adjective*. **b** *ear-drops*, *eye-drops*, etc.

†**2** A disease (supposedly) characterized by drops; *esp.* gout. OE–M16.
3 Any minute quantity of liquid; *fig.* a particle or minute amount of something abstract. ME. ▸**b** *spec.* A small portion or quantity of alcoholic drink. *colloq.* L17.

S. O'CASEY I just come in for a drop o' milk for a cup o' tea. D. CUSACK To add one more drop of bitterness to the sorrow she is already experiencing. **b** E. O'NEILL He never touched a drop till he was forty.

a drop in the bucket, **a drop in the ocean** a negligibly small amount in proportion to the whole or to what is needed. **b have a drop in one's eye** show slight signs of intoxication. **have had a drop too much** *colloq.* be drunk.

4 A spot of colour on a surface; *fig.* a stain, a spot. Now *rare* or *obsolete*. LME.
rosy drop: see ROSY *adjective*.
5 Something resembling a drop of liquid in size, shape, or pendulous quality; *spec.* a (pendent) ornament or bead

of glass, metal, etc., as in an earring or chandelier. **E16.** ▸**b** A piece of small shot. *Scot.* **E17.** ▸**c** A small chiefly round sweet, lozenge, or other confection. **L17.** ▸**d** *ARCHITECTURE.* = GUTTA *noun*[1] 2. **L17.**
ear-drops: see EAR *noun*[1]. **Prince Rupert's drop, Rupert's drop** a tadpole-shaped bubble of glass which bursts explosively when the tail is broken in any part. **c** *acid drop*, *chocolate drop*, *cough drop*, *pear drop*, etc.
†**6** In full ***drop weight***. An old Scottish weight equal to 1/16 ounce. **M16–E19.**
▸ **II 7** The action or an act of falling or letting fall abruptly or in drops; (a) dropping. Formerly, a drip, a shower. **LME.** ▸**b** *fig.* A decrease in something that can be measured or quantified. **M19.** ▸**c** *SPORT.* = DROP KICK, DROP STROKE. **M19.** ▸**d** An act of dropping men, supplies, etc., by parachute; the landing of an aircraft. **M20.**

> BROWNING The drop of the woodland fruit's begun. H. JAMES His expectation had had a drop. **b** J. C. OATES Despite the drop in temperature she left her French doors open. *New York Times* You get a significant drop in voting if you have a light mist on election day.

at the drop of a hat *colloq.* promptly, without hesitation.
8 Something that drops; *dial.* a windfall. **E18.** ▸**b** *THEATRICAL.* A painted curtain or piece of scenery lowered on to the stage. **M19.** ▸**c** (The number of) the young produced at a birth. **L19.**
b *act-drop*: see ACT *noun*. *backdrop*: see BACK-.
9 A small platform or trapdoor which is withdrawn from under the feet of a person being hanged; *the* gallows. **L18.**
10 The depth to which something sinks, falls, or is below the general level. **L18.**
11 A descent of sufficient size and steepness for a person to be able to fall down it; the distance of the bottom below the top. **E19.**

> M. LOWRY Trees . . grew down into the gulch, their foliage partly obscuring the terrific drop. G. ORWELL A sheer drop of ten or twenty metres, with boulders at the bottom.

12 *The* advantage over someone; *spec.* the fact of having someone covered with a firearm. Chiefly in ***get the drop (on)***, ***have the drop (on)***. *colloq.* **M19.**
13 A letterbox. *US.* **L19.**
14 A receiver of stolen goods; a fence. *criminals' slang.* **E20.**
15 A hiding place for stolen or illicit goods; in espionage, a place where items may be collected by a confederate. **M20.**

> *New Yorker* One of the nearby stores is a heroin drop.

16 A delivery of goods from a lorry. **M20.**
17 *CARDS.* A situation in which a card is dropped (DROP *verb* 29). **M20.**
18 Money given as alms or a bribe; the action of so giving money. *slang.* **M20.**
■ **dropless** *adjective* **LME.** **droplike** *adjective* resembling (that of) a drop of liquid **L19.** **dropwise** *adverb* in drops **L17.**

drop /drɒp/ *verb.* Infl. **-pp-**. Pa. t. & pple **dropped**, (*arch.*) **dropt**.
[ORIGIN Old English *drop(p)ian*, formed as the noun.]
▸ **I** *verb intrans.* **1** Of a liquid: fall in drops; drip. **OE.**

> OED Sweat dropped from his brow.

2 Give off moisture in drops; drip (*with*). **ME.**

> LD MACAULAY The rabble of Comus . . dropping with wine.

3 Allow or cause drops to fall; weep. **LME.**
4 Descend freely under the action of gravity; reach the ground after doing this. **LME.** ▸**b** Of ground etc.: incline or fall steeply to a lower level. Of a sail: have a specified vertical depth. **M18.**

> W. COWPER His apples might hang till they dropt from the tree. E. HEMINGWAY It was snowing and the flakes were dropping diagonally through the pines. R. MACAULAY Barbary swung herself through the window, dropped lightly on her feet. **b** R. L. STEVENSON Mountain forests, dropping thousands of feet toward the far sea-level.

5 Of a person or animal: sink to the ground, allow oneself to fall, esp. because exhausted, wounded, or dead. **LME.** ▸**b** Die. **M17.** ▸**c** Of a dog: crouch down abruptly at the sight of game. **M19.**

> C. P. SNOW They would be working till they dropped. I. WALLACE Edna Foster dropped into her . . chair with a sigh of relief.

6 Call *in* or *by* as a casual or unexpected visitor; come or go *back*, *over*, *into*, etc., in a casual or undesigned way; come *across* or *upon* a person or thing. **M17.**

> CONAN DOYLE We could drop in on each other in the evenings without an invitation. L. HUGHES Drop by Sunday and lemme know for sure. J. GARDNER I'll drop back later to see how you're doing. SLOAN WILSON If you would care to drop into my office . . we can work something out.

7 Pass easily or imperceptibly *into* a condition; fall *asleep*. **M17.**

> A. B. EDWARDS We soon dropped back into the old life of sight-seeing and shopping.

8 Drop anchor. **M17.**
9 Come to an end through not being kept up; lapse. **L17.**

> J. GALSWORTHY George yawning, the conversation dropped.

10 Fall in amount, degree, or pitch. Of the face: become downcast. **E18.**

> H. JAMES The storm of the night . . had dropped. SCOTT FITZGERALD Her voice, dropping an octave lower, filled the room with . . scorn. M. EDWARDES The British market for trucks had dropped alarmingly. *Financial Times* MTD (Mangula) dropped 16 to 54p.

11 Be carried gently downstream by the wind or current. Usu. foll. by *down*. **L18.**
12 Fall *behind*, *to the rear*, etc., through allowing others to pass one. **E19.**
13 Spend or lose money; give a tip. *slang.* **L19.**
14 Of a playing card: be dropped (see sense 29 below). **M20.**
▸ **II** *verb trans.* **15** Let (a liquid) fall in drops; shed (tears). **ME.**
16 Allow (something) to fall by relaxing one's hold or ceasing to give support; allow or cause to drop; *spec.* allow (esp. troops, supplies) to fall by parachute. In early use also *fig.*, perpetrate (a trick etc.). **ME.** ▸**b** Bring to the ground by a blow or shot. **E18.**

> *Times* The first atomic bomb had been dropped . . on Hiroshima. J. ORTON He takes it off, kicks away his shoes and drops his trousers. ROBERT ANDERSON Laura stoops and picks up the raincoat which Tom has dropped. **b** J. W. SCHULTZ He fired his Henry rifle . . dropping two of the enemy.

17 Sprinkle with drops; *transf.* dot with spots of colour. *arch.* **LME.**

> S. ROGERS Fish . . dropt with crimson and gold.

18 Utter or mention casually or as if unconsciously; let fall (a hint etc.). **E17.**

> J. BETJEMAN His womenfolk . . smooth their . . twinsets And drop the names of earls.

name-drop: see NAME *noun*.
19 Abandon, cease to continue or pursue, (an activity, practice, study, etc.); give up association with (a person). **E17.** ▸**b** Discard from a team; *gen.* (chiefly *US*) dismiss from employment. *colloq.* **M19.** ▸**c** Lose (a game etc.) unexpectedly. Chiefly *US.* **M20.**

> R. TRAVERS When the jury failed to agree the prosecution was dropped. J. CHEEVER I've never liked her parties, and I'm glad she's dropped us. W. MARCH When you get this letter, drop everything . . and come back to me. M. ROBERTS Helen is glad to drop the subject. **b** G. BOYCOTT He was dropped by England after a couple of Test matches.

20 Give birth to; lay (an egg). **M17.**
21 Lose, give, or part with (money). *slang.* **L17.**
22 Bend the knees and lower the body to make (a curtsy). **L17.**
23 Send (a note etc.) in a casual manner. **M18.**

> T. SHARPE I was about to drop you a line asking if I could see you.

24 Set down (a passenger) from a vehicle or ship, esp. on the way to another destination; leave (a packet) at a house etc. **L18.**

> A. BURGESS Drop me outside the town. I can pick up a trishaw. N. MAILER The newspapers were already being dropped at the early morning stands.

25 Omit (a letter or syllable) in reading or pronunciation. **M19.**
26 Lower (the eyes), esp. from modesty or shame. **M19.**
27 Lower the level or position of; *transf.* reduce the pitch or loudness of (the voice). **M19.**

> E. WAUGH Anthony dropped his voice to a . . whisper.

28 *RUGBY.* Score (a goal) by a drop kick. **L19.**
29 Play (a lower card) in the same trick as a higher one, esp. because of the need to follow suit. **M20.**
30 Put into circulation (counterfeit money, forged cheques). *slang.* **M20.**
31 Take (a drug) orally. *slang.* **M20.**
32 Sing or perform (rap music); release (a musical recording); select and play (a record). *slang.* **L20.**
– PHRASES: ***drop a brick***: see BRICK *noun*. ***drop anchor***: see ANCHOR *noun*[1]. **drop astern** outdistance (a boat), leave in the rear. ***drop a CLANGER***. ***drop a stitch***: see STITCH *noun*[1]. **drop dead!** *slang* an exclam. expressing intense scorn of the person addressed. **drop-eared** *adjective* (of a dog) having ears that hang down; opp. PRICK-EARED 1. **drop it!** stop that! have done! stop talking or arguing about that! ***drop one's aitches***: see AITCH. ***drop one's bundle***: see BUNDLE *noun*. **drop short** fall short (*of*). **fit to drop**, **ready to drop** worn out, exhausted. ***let drop***: see LET *verb*[1]. ***the bottom drops out of***: see BOTTOM *noun*. ***the penny drops***: see PENNY *noun*.
– WITH ADVERBS & PREPOSITIONS IN SPECIALIZED SENSES: **drop away** fall away or be lost gradually. **drop down to** = *drop to* below. **drop in** come in one by one or at intervals; (see also sense 6 above). **drop into** *colloq.* attack fiercely. **drop off** (*a*) *verb phr. intrans.* gradually withdraw or cease to come, diminish; (*b*) *verb phr. intrans.* die; fall asleep; (*c*) *verb phr. trans.* = sense 24 above. **drop on** come down heavily on; reprimand, punish; (usu. in *pass.*). **drop on to** = *drop to* below. **drop out** (*a*) cease to appear or participate in an activity; *spec.* abandon one's studies from deliberate choice; withdraw from conventional society; (*b*) remove dots from (an area of a halftone picture or plate). **drop to** *slang* (chiefly *US & Austral.*) become aware of, recognize, realize.

drop- /drɒp/ *combining form.*
[ORIGIN Repr. DROP *verb*, *noun*.]
Prefixed to words, esp. nouns, in various senses, as 'that drops', 'involving a drop', 'shaped like a drop'.
■ **drop-black** *noun* bone-black ground into water, formed into drops, and dried **L19.** **drop curtain** *noun* (*THEATRICAL*) = *act-drop* s.v. ACT *noun* **M19.** **drop-dead** *adjective* (*slang*) (*a*) designating the latest date or time by which something can be done; (*b*) that surprises one, *esp.* outstandingly attractive, stunning: **M20.** **drop-down** *adjective* (*a*) that drops down or unfolds when required; (*b*) *COMPUTING* (of a menu) appearing below a menu title when selected and remaining until used or dismissed: **M20.** **drop-fly** *noun* = DROPPER *noun* 3 **L19.** **drop-forge** *verb trans.* make by drop-forging **L19.** **drop-ˈforging** *noun* forging in which a drop hammer falls repeatedly on to heated metal, forcing it into a die; a forging made in this way: **L19.** **drop hammer** *noun* a heavy weight raised mechanically and allowed to drop, as used in drop-forging and pile-driving; a drop-forging machine: **M19.** **drop-handle** *noun* a handle that hangs down when not held **L19.** **drop-ˈhandlebar(s)** *noun* a bicycle handlebar, bicycle handlebars, in which the handles are bent below the rest of the bar **M20.** **drophead** *adjective & noun* (*a*) (designating) a sewing machine, typewriter, etc., that can be lowered into a table etc. so as to leave a flat top; (*b*) (having) a car roof that can be folded down or removed; (*c*) (designating) a chapter-heading lower down the page than the first line of ordinary pages: **L19.** **drop initial** *noun phr.* (*TYPOGRAPHY*) = *drop-letter* (b) below **M20.** **drop-keel** (*a*) a centreboard; (*b*) a projecting keel: **L19.** **drop kick** *noun & verb transitive* (*RUGBY*) (make) a kick by dropping the ball and kicking it as it drops or after it bounces: **M19.** **drop-leaf** *noun & adjective* (having) a hinged flap on a table or desk which can be raised to increase the surface area: **L19.** **drop-letter** *noun* (*a*) *N. Amer.* a letter posted at a post office for local delivery or collection from that office; (*b*) *TYPOGRAPHY* a large letter at the beginning of a section of text, occupying more than the depth of one line: **M19.** **drop-light** *noun* (*a*) *US* a portable gas lamp attached to the gas pipe by a flexible tube; (*b*) an electric light suspended from the ceiling: **L19.** **drop-line** *noun* a weighted fishing line for fishing near the bottom of a river etc. **M19.** **drop-press** *noun*: in which metal is formed using a drop hammer **M19.** **drop-ripe** *adjective* (of fruit) ripe enough to drop: **E18.** **drop scene** *noun* a drop curtain; the final scene of a drama, a denouement: **E19.** **drop scone** *noun* a small pancake formed by dropping spoonfuls of batter on a hot surface; a griddle cake: **L19.** **dropseed** *noun* a grass that readily drops its seed, esp. *Muhlenbergia diffusa* **M19.** **drop shot** *noun* (*a*) small gunshot; (*b*) = *drop stroke* below: **L17.** **drop shoulder** *noun* a style of shoulder on a garment cut so that the seam is positioned on the upper arm rather than the shoulder **E20.** **drop-ship** *verb trans.* provide (goods) by direct delivery from the manufacturer to the retailer or customer **M20.** **dropside** *noun & adjective* (having) a side of a cot or lorry that drops down **E20.** **dropstone** *noun* †(*a*) a stalactite, a stalagmite; (*b*) *GEOLOGY* a stone embedded in a sedimentary deposit and believed to have got there after being released from a melting glacier: **L17.** **drop stroke** *noun* a soft stroke or shot in tennis, squash, etc., causing the ball to drop abruptly after crossing the net or hitting the wall **L19.** **drop tank** *noun* an aircraft fuel tank that can be dropped when empty **M20.** **drop test** *noun phr.* a test of the strength of an object, in which it is dropped from a height under controlled conditions, or a set weight is dropped on it from a given height **L19.** **drop-testing** *verbal noun* the performance of a drop test **E20.** **drop waist** *noun* a style of waistline on a dress cut so that the seam is positioned at the hips rather than the waist **E20.**

drop-in /ˈdrɒpɪn/ *noun & adjective.* **E19.**
[ORIGIN from *drop in*: see DROP *verb* 6.]
▸ **A** *noun.* **1** An unexpected or informal visitor or visit. *colloq.* **E19.**
2 A place or function at which one can turn up informally, without prior appointment or referral. *colloq.* (chiefly *N. Amer.*). **M20.**
▸ **B** *adjective.* **1** Designed to drop into position. **E20.**
2 Of a place or function: at which one may turn up informally, without prior appointment or referral. **M20.**

droplet /ˈdrɒplɪt/ *noun.* **E17.**
[ORIGIN from DROP *noun* + -LET.]
A minute drop.
– COMB.: **droplet infection**: conveyed by droplets of mucus sprayed into the air when a person coughs etc.

†**dropling** *noun.* **E17–L18.**
[ORIGIN from DROP *noun* + -LING[1].]
A little drop.

drop-off /ˈdrɒpɒf/ *adjective & noun.* **E20.**
[ORIGIN from ***drop off*** s.v. DROP *verb*.]
▸ **A** *adjective.* Of or pertaining to dropping off; (of a place) where things or people can be dropped off or set down. **E20.**
▸ **B** *noun.* **1** An act or instance of dropping off; *spec.* a diminution, a decrease; a slowing down. **E20.**

> *National Observer (US)* There is a small extra charge . . for drop offs and pickups in Lincoln. *Nature* A reflectance spectrum showing a steep dropoff in the UV.

2 A declivity; a steep drop; a cliff. *N. Amer.* **M20.**

drop-out /ˈdrɒpaʊt/ *noun.* **L19.**
[ORIGIN from ***drop out*** s.v. DROP *verb*.]
1 *RUGBY.* A drop kick made from within the defending team's 22-metre (formerly 25-yard) line in order to restart play after the ball has gone dead. **L19.**
2 On a bicycle, a small U-shaped end to a fork or stay, made to receive the axle. **E20.**
3 A person who drops out of a course of activity or study, or who abandons conventional society in favour of an alternative lifestyle. *colloq.* **M20.**

D

L. BANGS A semiliterate grass-smoking dropout.

4 On a halftone picture or plate, a highlight area from which the tiny dots produced by the screen have been removed; a halftone with such an area. Also ***drop-out halftone***. M20.

5 A flaw or loss of coating on magnetic tape or disc; a momentary loss of recorded signal due to this; an error in data caused by the failure to read a bit or sequence of bits. M20.

What Video? A high grade chrome tape . . with improved signal-to-noise ratio and less dropout.

D

droppable /ˈdrɒpəb(ə)l/ *adjective*. E20.
[ORIGIN from DROP *verb* + -ABLE.]
Able to be dropped or (esp.) discarded.

dropped /drɒpt/ *ppl adjective*. Also (*arch.*) **dropt**. L15.
[ORIGIN from DROP *verb* + -ED¹.]
†**1** Marked with specks or spots. L15–E17.
2 That has been dropped; lowered; having a lower position than usual. L16.
dropped handlebar(s) = ***drop-handlebar(s)*** s.v. DROP-. **dropped kerb** a small ramp built into the kerb of a pavement to aid people using pushchairs or wheelchairs. **dropped scone** = ***drop scone*** s.v. DROP-.
3 Of an egg: poached. *Scot. & US*. E19.
4 RUGBY. Of a goal: scored from a drop kick. L19.

dropper /ˈdrɒpə/ *noun*. M17.
[ORIGIN from DROP *verb* + -ER¹.]
1 A person who drops or lets something fall in drops. Formerly (*slang*), a distiller. M17. ▸**b** A person who passes forged cheques, counterfeit money, etc. *slang*. M20. ▸**c** A person who delivers goods (formerly esp. illicit liquor) to a retailer. *Austral. & NZ colloq*. M20.
2 ***dropper-in***, a casual caller. E19.
3 In fly-fishing, an artificial fly attached to a leader above the tail fly. Also ***dropper-fly***. M19.
4 MINING. A vein branching off a main lode. M19.
5 A short glass tube with a rubber bulb at one end and a narrow opening at the other end, for administering a liquid in drops. L19.
6 HORTICULTURE. A shoot growing downwards from the base of a bulb and itself developing a bulb at the apex. L19.
7 A vertical part of a fence etc.; *esp*. a light vertical lath used between the main uprights to keep the wires spaced. Chiefly *Austral., NZ, & S. Afr*. L19.

dropping /ˈdrɒpɪŋ/ *verbal noun*. OE.
[ORIGIN from DROP *verb* + -ING¹.]
1 The action of DROP *verb*; an instance of this. OE.
2 That which falls or is shed in drops, as rain or melted wax. Usu. in *pl*. LME.

T. TROLLOPE Collecting the droppings from the great wax candles.

3 *spec*. The excrement of animals, birds, etc.; a lump of this. Usu. in *pl*. L15.
†**4** *sing*. & in *pl*. The eaves from which water drops. L16–E18.
5 In *pl*. Waste material cast off from a machine in certain processes of textile manufacture. E20.
– COMB.: **dropping bottle**: used to supply fluid in small quantities; **dropping field**, **dropping point** a place prepared for the dropping of troops, supplies, bombs, etc., from an aircraft; **dropping well**: formed by the dropping of water from above; **dropping zone** = ***dropping field*** above.

dropping /ˈdrɒpɪŋ/ *ppl adjective*. LME.
[ORIGIN from DROP *verb* + -ING².]
1 Falling in drops; having moisture falling off in drops, dripping; rainy. LME.
2 *gen*. Falling; decreasing. E18.
3 Of gunfire or a shot: desultory, not continuous. E18.
■ **droppingly** *adverb* drop by drop; *fig*. one by one: LME.

droppy /ˈdrɒpi/ *adjective*. Now *dial*. M17.
[ORIGIN from DROP *noun* + -Y¹.]
Dripping, rainy.

dropsical /ˈdrɒpsɪk(ə)l/ *adjective*. L17.
[ORIGIN from DROPSY + -ICAL, after *hydropical*.]
1 Of, pertaining to, or resembling dropsy. L17.
2 Affected with or subject to dropsy. L17.
3 Enlarged, swollen; saturated with water. E18.

L. WHISTLER The swollen populations, wretched in the dropsical cities.

■ **dropsically** *adverb* L18.

dropsied /ˈdrɒpsɪd/ *adjective*. E17.
[ORIGIN from DROPSY + -ED².]
Swollen (as) with water; turgid; watery.

dropsy /ˈdrɒpsi/ *noun & adjective*. ME.
[ORIGIN Aphet. from HYDROPSY.]
▸**A** *noun*. **1** A condition marked by an excess of watery fluid in the tissues or cavities of the body. ME.
†**2** An insatiable thirst or craving. M16–E18.
3 Money, esp. paid as a tip or bribe. *slang*. M20.
▸†**B** *adjective*. = DROPSICAL 2, 3. L15–L17.

dropt *verb pa. t. & pple*: see DROP *verb*.

dropwort /ˈdrɒpwəːt/ *noun*. LME.
[ORIGIN from DROP *noun* + WORT *noun*¹, on account of the tuberous root-fibres.]
1 A plant of calcareous grassland, *Filipendula vulgaris*, allied to meadowsweet. LME.
2 Now only more fully ***water dropwort***. Any of several aquatic or marsh-loving umbellifers of the genus *Oenanthe*. L16.
hemlock water dropwort: see HEMLOCK *noun*.

drosera /ˈdrɒs(ə)rə/ *noun*. E19.
[ORIGIN mod. Latin from Greek *droseros* dewy.]
Any plant of the genus *Drosera*, sundew; a powder prepared from this, formerly used against respiratory ailments.

droshky /ˈdrɒʃki/ *noun*. Also **-sky** /-ski/. E19.
[ORIGIN Russian *drozhki* pl., dim. of *drogi* wagon, hearse, pl. of *droga* centre pole of a carriage.]
A low open horse-drawn carriage used esp. in Russia; any horse-drawn passenger vehicle.

drosometer /drɒˈsɒmɪtə/ *noun*. E19.
[ORIGIN from Greek *drosos* dew + -OMETER.]
An instrument for measuring the amount of dew deposited.

drosophila /drɒˈsɒfɪlə/ *noun*. E19.
[ORIGIN mod. Latin, from Greek *drosos* dew + *philos* loving.]
A fruit fly of the genus *Drosophila*, much used as an experimental subject in genetics.
■ **drosophilist** *noun* a person who studies or uses drosophilas M20.

drosophyllum /drɒˈsɒfɪləm/ *noun*. L19.
[ORIGIN mod. Latin, from Greek *drosos* dew + *phullon* leaf.]
A subshrub, *Drosophyllum lusitanicum*, of the sundew family, native to SW Europe and NW Africa and with leaves that secrete drops of glutinous fluid by which insects are captured.

dross /drɒs/ *noun & verb*.
[ORIGIN Old English *drōs* = Middle Dutch *droes(e)* dregs. Cf. Middle Low German *drōsem*, Middle Dutch *droesen(e)* (Dutch *droesem*), Old High German *truosana* (German *Drusen*) dregs, lees, corresp. to Old English genit. pl. *drōsna*.]
▸**A** *noun*. **1** Impurities separated from metal by melting; the scum which forms on the surface of molten metal. OE.
2 Foreign matter mixed with anything; dregs of wine, chaff of corn, etc. LME. ▸**b** MINING. Iron pyrites in coal; waste from the sorting of coal. E19.
3 *gen*. Refuse, rubbish, worthless matter, esp. as contrasted with or separated from something of value. LME.

J. LONDON His face was transfigured, purged of all earthly dross, and pure and holy. L. DEIGHTON He asked me what I thought about the crowd she was running around with. I told him they were absolute dross.

▸**B** *verb trans*. †**1** Make impure; corrupt. Only in M17.
†**2** Sift *out* as dross. Only in M17.
3 Free from dross. L19.
4 Convert (an impurity in metal) into dross that can be removed. L19.
■ **drossiness** *noun* the quality or condition of being drossy M17. **drossy** *adjective* characterized by or containing dross, impure LME.

drostdy /ˈdrɒsti, drɒs(t)ˈdeɪ/ *noun*. *S. Afr*. Pl. **-dies**. L18.
[ORIGIN Afrikaans from Dutch *drost* bailiff.]
1 *hist*. The district under a landdrost. L18.
2 A building that was formerly the official residence of a landdrost. L18.

drotchell *noun* var. of DRATCHELL.

dróttkvætt /ˈdrəʊtkvʌɪt/ *noun*. Also ***dróttkvæði*** /ˈdrəʊtkvʌɪði/. L18.
[ORIGIN Old Norse = court poem.]
A complex verse form used by the skaldic poets of early Scandinavia.

drought /draʊt/ *noun*. Also (now *Scot., Irish, US, dial., & poet.*) **drouth** /draʊθ, *Scot*. druːθ/.
[ORIGIN Late Old English *drūgaþ*, from Germanic base of DRY *adjective*. Cf. Middle & mod. Low German *drogede*, Middle Dutch & mod. Dutch *droogte*, from *droog* dry. For *drouth* cf. *highth* HEIGHT *noun* and see -TH¹.]
1 Dryness, aridity, lack of moisture. *arch. & poet*. LOE.

TENNYSON The burning drouth Of that long desert to the south.

†**2** Dry country; a desert. *rare*. LOE–L17.
3 A prolonged period of abnormally low rainfall, leading to a shortage of water. ME.

W. STYRON What began as a simple dry spell developed into a searing drought. *Times* In times of drought, many Africans do not survive.

4 Thirst. *arch., poet., & dial*. LME.
5 *fig*. Absence or shortage of anything necessary or desirable; a prolonged deficiency. E17.

T. MIDDLETON A drouth of virtue, And dearth of all repentence.

■ **droughted** *adjective* affected by drought M20.

droughty /ˈdraʊti/ *adjective*. Also (now *Scot., Irish, US, dial., & poet.*) **drouthy** /ˈdraʊθi, *Scot*. ˈdruːθi/. L15.
[ORIGIN from DROUGHT + -Y¹.]
1 Dry, arid; lacking rain. L15.
2 Thirsty; fond of (alcoholic) drink. E17.
■ **droughtily** *adverb* without drink M20. **droughtiness** *noun* E18.

drouk /druːk/ *verb trans*. *Scot. & N. English*. Also **drook**. E16.
[ORIGIN Unknown. Cf. Old Norse *drukna* be drowned, *drukkit* drunk.]
Drench, as with heavy rain.

drouth *noun*, **drouthy** *adjective* see DROUGHT, DROUGHTY.

drove /drəʊv/ *noun*.
[ORIGIN Old English *drāf*, from ablaut var. of base of DRIVE *verb*.]
†**1** The action of driving. Only in OE.
2 A number of cattle, horses, sheep, or goats being driven in a body or moving together; a herd, a flock. OE.

S. LEACOCK Droves of young lambs with their shepherds, proceeding to market.

3 *transf*. A (moving) crowd or group of other animals or of people; a horde, a shoal, a multitude; *sing*. & (esp.) in *pl*., a large number. OE.

S. MIDDLETON One needs no brains to pass, but candidates fail in droves.

4 A channel for drainage or irrigation. OE.
5 An unenclosed road or track, chiefly for cattle, esp. in the Fens. M17.
6 A broad chisel for use by stonemasons. E19.
– COMB.: **drove road** an ancient unmetalled road for cattle.

drove /drəʊv/ *verb*¹. M17.
[ORIGIN from DROVE *noun*, or (in sense 1) back-form. from DROVER.]
1 *verb intrans. & trans*. Drive (cattle etc.); be a drover. M17.
2 *verb trans*. Dress (stone) in parallel lines using a drove. E19.

drove *verb*² *pa. t.*: see DRIVE *verb*.

drover /ˈdrəʊvə/ *noun*. LME.
[ORIGIN from DROVE *noun* + -ER¹.]
1 A person who drives cattle or other livestock to market; a dealer in livestock. LME.
2 A boat used for fishing with a drift net. L16.

drow /draʊ, drəʊ/ *noun*¹. *Scot*. L16.
[ORIGIN Perh. from ablaut var. of base of DREE *verb*.]
A fit of illness, a fainting fit, a qualm.

drow /draʊ, drəʊ/ *noun*². *Scot*. E17.
[ORIGIN Unknown.]
A cold wet mist; a drizzling shower.

drowk /draʊk/ *verb intrans*. *obsolete* exc. *dial*. E16.
[ORIGIN Unknown.]
Droop.

drown /draʊn/ *verb*. Pa. t. & pple **drowned** /draʊnd/, (*arch. & dial.*) **drownded** /ˈdraʊndɪd/. ME.
[ORIGIN Rel. to Old Norse *drukkna* be drowned, from Germanic base of DRINK *verb*. Prob. already in Old English.]
1 *verb intrans*. Suffer death by suffocation in liquid. ME.

E. HEMINGWAY I thought . . I would drown because of my boots, but I thrashed and fought through the water.

2 *verb trans*. Kill by suffocation in liquid. Of a liquid: kill by suffocation. ME.

SHAKES. *3 Hen. VI* I'll drown more sailors than the mermaid slay. G. B. SHAW Someday you'll walk into the river and drown yourself.

like a drowned rat very wet and bedraggled.
†**3** *verb intrans. & trans*. (Cause to) sink; go or send to the bottom of the sea etc. ME–E17.
4 *verb trans*. Submerge, inundate, flood; drench; add a lot of or too much water to. ME. ▸**b** Foll. by *out*: drive out (people etc.), prevent (work), by flooding. L17.

C. BOYLE Once they drowned a whole village To make a reservoir. P. FITZGERALD The sea had drowned the woodlands in salt.

drowned valley: wholly or partly submerged by a change in sea level.
5 *verb trans*. Make inaudible, ineffective, or unidentifiable by being louder, stronger, etc.; overwhelm, swamp, dilute excessively. Also foll. by *out*. ME. ▸**b** Stupefy (oneself) with alcoholic drink; deaden (sorrow etc.) with drink. (Foll. by *in* drink.) LME.

Scientific American The orchestra's much stronger sounds would drown out the singer's. *Photography* An incredibly tedious press release . . drowns the disturbing message of this exhibition. **b** J. M. SYNGE And I swamped and drownded with the weight of drink. E. O'NEILL I might as well forget her . . and drown my sorrows.

†**6** *verb trans*. LAW. Nullify by merging in something greater. M17–E19.
■ **drowner** *noun* (*a*) a person or thing which drowns; (*b*) a manager of water meadows: M16. **drowningly** *adverb* so as to drown E19.

drowse /draʊz/ *noun*. L17.
[ORIGIN from the verb.]
The action or an act of drowsing; the state of being half asleep.

drowse /draʊz/ *verb*.
[ORIGIN Old English *drūsian* from Germanic base also of *drēosan* fall: see DREARY. Later back-form. from DROWSY.]
†1 *verb intrans.* Sink, droop; become slow. Only in OE.
2 *verb intrans.* Be drowsy or half asleep; doze (*off*). L16.
D. JACOBSON I would fall into a doze, wake . . , drowse again.
3 *verb intrans.* Be or become inactive, dull, or sluggish. *arch.* L16.
TENNYSON Let not your prudence . . drowse.
4 *verb trans.* Make drowsy; *arch.* make dull or lethargic. E17.
A. S. BYATT Marcus, drowsed by the fire, . . nodded and jerked awake.
5 *verb trans.* Pass *away* (time) drowsily or in drowsing. M19.
M. M. KAYE Men and animals . . drowsed away the slow hours until the sun was low.

drowsy /ˈdraʊzi/ *adjective*. L15.
[ORIGIN Prob. from stem of Old English *drūsian*: see DROWSE *verb*.]
1 Inclined to sleep; heavy with sleep, sleepy; half asleep. L15.
B. A. STAPLES I felt a little drowsy.
2 Caused or characterized by sleepiness or inactivity. E16.
E. TAYLOR The drowsy afternoon quiet was broken abruptly by a bell ringing.
3 Inducing sleepiness; soporific. L16.
4 Heavy, dull; sluggish, lethargic. *arch.* L16.
– COMB.: **drowsy-head** a sleepy or sluggish person.
■ **drowsihead** *noun* (*arch.*) drowsiness L16. **drowsily** *adverb* L15. **drowsiness** *noun* (**a**) sleepiness, the state of being drowsy; (**b**) *arch.* lethargy, sloth: M16.

Dr Strangelove /dɒktə ˈstreɪn(d)ʒlʌv/ *noun*. M20.
[ORIGIN A character in a film of that title (1963).]
A person who ruthlessly considers or plans nuclear warfare. Cf. STRANGELOVE.

drub /drʌb/ *noun & verb*. E17.
[ORIGIN Prob. ult. from Arabic *ḍaraba* beat, (pronounced *ḍreb* or similarly in NW Africa).]
▸ **A** *noun*. A blow, a thump. Formerly *spec.*, a bastinado. E17.
▸ **B** *verb*. Infl. **-bb-**.
1 *verb trans.* Beat with a stick; cudgel, flog, thump; beat in a fight or contest. Formerly *spec.*, bastinado. M17.
W. BESANT He drubbed and belaboured his servants every day. S. KINGSLEY We must drub the enemy and drub him soundly. *Toronto Star* It was no contest last night as the Islanders drubbed the Habs, 7–0.
2 *verb trans.* Drive (an idea etc.) *into* or *out of* a person, drive (a person) *into* or *out of* a habit etc., by drubbing. L17.
3 *verb trans.* Abuse or criticize roundly. E19.
4 *verb trans. & intrans.* Beat, beat *on*, (a drum etc.), hit repeatedly; stamp (one's foot). M19.
W. D. HOWELLS Teaching the young . . how to drub the piano. C. RAINE Thugs who drub The helpless air with clubs.
5 *verb intrans.* Give out a sound of being beaten. M19.
S. MIDDLETON The signal drubbed on unanswered.
■ **drubber** *noun* E18. **drubbing** *verbal noun* (**a**) the action of the verb; (**b**) a beating, a thrashing: M17.

†**drubly** *adjective*. OE–E16.
[ORIGIN Old English *drōflic*, prob. infl. by obsolete Middle English *trouble* adjective = disturbed, from Old French from base of TROUBLE *verb*. Cf. DRUMLY.]
Stirred up, turbid, (*lit. & fig.*).

drucken *adjective* see DRUNKEN *adjective*.

drudge /drʌdʒ/ *noun*¹. L15.
[ORIGIN from or rel. to DRUDGE *verb*.]
A person who does heavy, unpleasant, or servile work; a dogsbody, a hack.
ANTHONY WOOD He was the common drudge . . to make, correct, or review the Latine Sermons. M. DRABBLE All I am is a servant, . . a household drudge.

†**drudge** *noun*² var. of DREDGE *noun*².

drudge /drʌdʒ/ *verb*. ME.
[ORIGIN Perh. from stem of Old English *drēogan* DREE *verb* or var. of DRUG *verb*¹.]
1 *verb intrans.* Work hard at heavy, unpleasant, or servile tasks; toil. In early use, carry a heavy burden. ME.
E. BLISHEN My father had been out . . enjoying himself while she drudged at home. R. CHURCH Drudging sullenly at subjects I despised.
2 *verb trans.* Pass (time) *away* in drudgery; (foll. by *out*) perform as drudgery; (foll. by *down*) repress with drudgery. M17.
3 *verb trans.* Subject to drudgery. *rare*. E19.
– NOTE: Some or all apparent early examples may in fact belong to DRUG *verb*¹.
■ **drudgingly** *adverb* in a drudging manner L17.

drudger /ˈdrʌdʒə/ *noun*¹. M18.
[ORIGIN from DRUDGE *verb* + -ER¹.]
A person who drudges.

†**drudger** *noun*² var. of DREDGER *noun*².

drudgery /ˈdrʌdʒ(ə)ri/ *noun*. M16.
[ORIGIN from DRUDGE *noun*¹ + -ERY.]
The work of a drudge; heavy, unpleasant, or servile work; wearisome toil; a heavy, unpleasant, or servile task.

drug /drʌg/ *noun*¹. LME.
[ORIGIN Old French & mod. French *drogue*, of unknown origin.]
1 Any substance that affects the physical or mental functioning of a living organism; *esp.* one used for the treatment or prevention of an ailment or disease. Formerly also, any substance used in chemistry, dyeing, or any technical process. Orig. in *pl.* LME. ▸**b** A stimulant or narcotic taken otherwise than medicinally, *esp.* one that is addictive or subject to legal restriction. L19.
T. CORYAT Women . . annoint their haire with oyle, or some other drugs. J. H. BURN A healthy person ought to fall asleep without needing a drug. **b** M. AMIS The drugs I like are cocaine and mandrax. D. SHANNON That psychiatrist, after I'd listened to him half an hour I thought he was on drugs himself.
controlled drug: see CONTROL *verb* 2a. ***miracle drug***: see MIRACLE *noun*. ***orphan drug***: see ORPHAN *adjective*. **b *dangerous drug***: see DANGEROUS *adjective* 2.
2 A commodity no longer in demand and so unsaleable. Now usu. ***a drug on the market***, ***a drug in the market***. M17.
– COMB.: **drug abuse** the non-medicinal or excessive use of drugs; **drug addict** a person with an addiction to a drug; **drug addiction** addiction to a drug or drugs; **drug bust** a seizure of illegal drugs by the police or other law enforcement agency; **drug buster** *colloq.* a member of a drug squad; **drug dealer**, **drug peddler**, **drug pusher** a person who sells drugs illegally; **drug squad**, **drugs squad** a division of a police force appointed to investigate crimes involving illegal drugs; **drugstore** *N. Amer.* a chemist's shop also selling miscellaneous articles and often light refreshment (***drugstore cowboy***, a braggart, a loafer; a person who is not a cowboy but dresses like one); **drug traffic** illegal dealing in (addictive) drugs.
■ **drugless** *adjective* L19.

drug /drʌg/ *noun*². *obsolete* exc. *dial.* M17.
[ORIGIN from or rel. to DRUG *verb*¹.]
A low truck for carrying timber etc.

drug /drʌg/ *verb*¹ *intrans. & trans.* Long *obsolete* exc. *dial.* Infl. **-gg-**. L15.
[ORIGIN Perh. rel. to DRAG *verb*.]
Pull, drag.
– NOTE: See note s.v. DRUDGE *verb*.

drug /drʌg/ *verb*². Infl. **-gg-**. E17.
[ORIGIN from DRUG *noun*¹.]
1 *verb trans.* Mix or adulterate (food or drink) with a drug, esp. a narcotic or poison. E17.
SHAKES. *Macb.* I have drugg'd their possets.
2 *verb trans.* Administer a drug to (a person etc.), esp. in order to stupefy or poison; *fig.* stupefy; (now *arch.*) nauseate, cloy. M17.
W. COWPER Some baneful herb Which cast into our cup shall drug us all. V. BRITTAIN The . . music of the Mass drugged my senses with anodyne sweetness. T. KENEALLY Farmers . . kept drugging him from flasks of rum.
3 *verb intrans.* Take drugs; *esp.* habitually indulge in narcotics etc. L19.
H. C. BAILEY I don't drink and I don't drug.

drugger /ˈdrʌgə/ *noun*. L16.
[ORIGIN from DRUG *noun*¹, *verb*² + -ER¹.]
†1 = DRUGGIST. L16–M18.
2 A person who administers a drug. M19.
3 A user of (addictive or narcotic) drugs; a drug addict. *colloq.* M20.

druggery /ˈdrʌg(ə)ri/ *noun*. Now *rare*. E16.
[ORIGIN French *droguerie*, formed as DRUG *noun*¹: see -ERY.]
1 Drugs collectively; the subject of medicine. E16.
2 A place where drugs are kept. M19.

drugget /ˈdrʌgɪt/ *noun & adjective*. M16.
[ORIGIN French *droguet*, of unknown origin.]
▸ **A** *noun*. A coarse woven fabric used for floor and table coverings; such a covering. Formerly, (a garment made of) cloth made of wool (alone or with silk or linen) and used for clothing. M16.
▸ **B** *attrib.* or as *adjective*. Made of drugget. L16.

druggie *noun* var. of DRUGGY *noun*.

druggist /ˈdrʌgɪst/ *noun*. Now *N. Amer.* E17.
[ORIGIN French *droguiste*, formed as DRUG *noun*¹: see -IST.]
A dealer in medicinal drugs; *spec.* = CHEMIST 4.

druggister /ˈdrʌgɪstə/ *noun*. *obsolete* exc. *dial.* M17.
[ORIGIN from DRUGGIST + -ER¹.]
= DRUGGIST.

druggy /ˈdrʌgi/ *noun*. *slang*. Also **-gie**. M20.
[ORIGIN from DRUG *noun*¹ + -Y⁶, -IE.]
= DRUGGER 3.

druggy /ˈdrʌgi/ *adjective*. L16.
[ORIGIN from DRUG *noun*¹ + -Y¹.]
1 Of, pertaining to, or of the nature of a medicinal drug. L16.
H. JAMES The druggy aroma.
2 Of, pertaining to, or characteristic of narcotic etc. drugs or users of such drugs. *colloq.* M20.
Times I was enmeshed in a very druggy crowd at the time.

†**drugster** *noun*. E17–E18.
[ORIGIN from DRUG *noun*¹ + -STER.]
= DRUGGIST.

Druid /ˈdruːɪd/ *noun & adjective*. Also **d-**. M16.
[ORIGIN French *druide* or Latin *druidae*, *druides* pl. from Greek *druidai* from Gaulish *druides*.]
▸ **A** *noun*. **1** A member of an order of priests and teachers among the Celts of ancient Gaul, Britain, and Ireland, later reputed to be magicians and soothsayers. M16.
2 A philosophic bard or poet; a priest, a chaplain. M17.
3 A member of any of various groups that are held to be present-day representatives of ancient Druidism or to be derived from it; (a title of) any of certain officers of the Welsh Gorsedd. M19.
▸ **B** *adjective*. Of or pertaining to Druids. L17.
T. WARTON Here Poesy . . In Druid songs her solemn spirit breath'd.
Druid stone: of which the megalithic monument Stonehenge on Salisbury Plain in Wiltshire is made.
■ **Drui'dess** *noun* (now *rare*) a female Druid M18. **Dru'idic** *adjective* = DRUID *adjective* L18. **Dru'idical** *adjective* = DRUID *adjective* M18. **Druidism** *noun* the religious and philosophical system of Druids E18. **Druidry** *noun* (*rare*) = DRUIDISM M19.

drum /drʌm/ *noun*¹. LME.
[ORIGIN Prob. from Middle Dutch, Low German *tromme* of imit. origin. Cf. DRUMSLADE.]
▸ **I 1** An instrument of music or communication sounded by striking and made of a pliable membrane stretched taut over the open end of a hollow cylinder or hemisphere or over a thin hoop; a percussion instrument consisting of some form of hollow body but without a membrane. LME. ▸**b** The body of a banjo. L19.
LONGFELLOW Our hearts . . , like muffled drums, are beating Funeral marches to the grave. *Scientific American* Such percussion instruments as steel drums and hollow-log drums.
bass drum, ***kettledrum***, ***side drum***, ***snare drum***, ***tenor drum***, etc. **beat the drum(s)**, **beat the big drum(s)**, **thump the drum(s)**, **thump the big drum(s)** make loud or ostentatious advertisement or protest.
2 **a** MILITARY. A drummer. Formerly also, a man or a small party sent with a drum as a messenger to an enemy. E16. ▸**b** In *pl.* The percussion section or drum kit of a pop, rock, or jazz group. E20.
3 The sound of the instrument; a noise like that of a drum. M17. ▸**b** Any fish of the percoid family Sciaenidae, found mainly in shallow sea and able to make a drumming noise; a croaker. M17.
O. HENRY The soft drum of the ponies' hoofs.
b *red drum*: see RED *adjective*.
4 *hist.* Orig., an evening party or assembly. Later, a tea party, esp. when joined by more guests after the meal. M18.
5 ***the drum***, the facts; reliable or inside information. *Austral. & NZ slang*. E20.
▸ **II** Something likened to a drum in shape or function.
6 The tympanic membrane, the eardrum. Formerly also, the middle ear. E17.
7 A cylindrical appliance or part of a machine; *spec.* a cylinder round which a rope, belt, etc., passes. E18. ▸**b** (The contents of) the cartridge-holding part of a machine gun. L19. ▸**c** COMPUTING. More fully ***magnetic drum***. A data-storage device in the form of a rotatable cylinder with a magnetizable outer surface. M20.
brake drum: see BRAKE *noun*⁷.
8 ARCHITECTURE. The solid part of a Corinthian or Composite capital; one of the cylindrical blocks forming the shaft of a column; the vertical wall supporting a dome. E18.
9 A cylindrical container for packing dried fruit, holding oil, etc. L18. ▸**b** The bundle of a tramp, miner, etc., a swag. *Austral. & NZ slang*. M19. ▸**c** A tin in which tea etc. is made, a billycan. *slang*. M20.
10 ZOOLOGY. An organ which produces or amplifies the natural sound of certain animals. E19.
11 A cylinder hoisted (together with a cone) by coastguards etc. to give warning of a strong gale. M19.
– COMB.: **drum and bass** a type of dance music characterized by bare instrumentation consisting largely of electronic drums and bass, originating in Britain during the early 1990s; ***drum-and-trumpet history***: see HISTORY *noun*; **drumbeat** a beat on a drum; **drum brake**: in which brake shoes on the vehicle press against a brake drum on the wheel; **drumfire** heavy continuous rapid artillery fire; *fig.* a barrage of criticism etc.; **drumfish** *noun & verb* (**a**) *noun* = sense 3b above; (**b**) *verb intrans.* (*US*) fish for drumfish; **drum kit**: see KIT *noun*¹ 2d; **drum machine** an electronic device that imitates the sound of percussion instruments; **drum major** †(**a**) the chief drummer of a regimental band; (**b**) *arch.* an NCO in command of the drummers of a regimental band; (**c**) the leader of a marching band; **drum majorette** (orig. *US*) a female leader of a marching band; a girl who leads or takes part in a parade etc. twirling a baton; **drum pad** an electronic device with one or more flat pads which imitate the sounds of a drum kit when struck; **drum printer**: in which the paper is hammered against a drum with as many circular bands of types on it as there are printing positions on a line; **drum roll** a rapid succession of

D

D

notes sounded on a drum; **drum tower**: of cylindrical, usu. squat form, as at the angle of a castle wall.
■ **drummy** *adjective* like the sound of a drum; characterized by a drum: M19. †**drumster** *noun* (*rare*) a drummer L16–M19.

drum /drʌm/ *noun*². *Scot. & Irish*. E18.
[ORIGIN Gaelic & Irish *druim* back, ridge.]
A long narrow hill often separating two parallel valleys; a drumlin.

drum /drʌm/ *noun*³. *slang*. L18.
[ORIGIN Uncertain: perh. from Romany. Cf. Romanian *drum*, Greek *dromos* street.]
†**1** A street. L18–L19.
2 A house, a lodging; a room, a flat; a low dive, a brothel; *US* a saloon, a nightclub. M19.

drum /drʌm/ *verb*. Infl. **-mm-**. L16.
[ORIGIN from DRUM *noun*¹.]
▸ **I** *verb intrans*. **1** Beat or play (as) on a drum; make a continuous noise by rapidly repeated blows. L16.

> DRYDEN Heart.. take thy rest..; For thou shalt drum no more. E. BOWEN Rain.. still drummed through the leaves. J. STEINBECK Lennie drummed on the table with his fingers. T. C. WOLFE A woodpecker drummed on.. a.. chestnut-tree.

2 Sound like a drum; resound. E17.
3 Of a bird, insect, etc.: make a loud reverberating noise, as by the quivering of the wings. E19.

> J. E. TAYLOR Flies and gnats drum around you.

4 Solicit orders, canvass, (*for*). *US*. M19.
5 Foll. by *up*: make tea etc. in a billycan; prepare a rough-and-ready outdoor meal. *slang*. E20.
6 Steal from unoccupied premises. Cf. sense 12b below. *slang*. E20.
▸ **II** *verb trans*. **7** Summon (as) by the beat of a drum; *esp*. attempt to obtain (custom etc.) by canvassing or soliciting. (Foll. by *up*.) E17.

> E. BLISHEN The paralysis of conventional training during the war years had made it necessary to drum up new teachers in a hurry. CLIVE JAMES I finally drummed up the courage to take a look. *Times* It was difficult to drum business in the money markets yesterday.

8 Cashier with drums beaten to heighten disgrace; expel or dismiss with ignominy. (Foll. by *out*.) M18.

> T. AMORY They.. ought to be drummed out of society.

9 Drive (a person etc. *into* a state, or a lesson, idea, etc., *into* a person) by constant repetition. E19.

> H. BUSHNELL Small children are.. drummed into apathy by dogmatic catechisms. M. MEYER Continually drumming into him the importance of duty.

10 Beat (one's fingers etc.) repeatedly on a surface, as if drumming. (Foll. by *on*, *upon*.) M19.
11 Play (a tune) on or as on a drum. M19.
12 Hit repeatedly; *dial*. thrash, beat, (a person). L19. ▸**b** Knock at (a house) to check whether it is unoccupied before attempting a robbery; reconnoitre with a view to robbery. Cf. sense 6 above. *slang*. M20.
13 Inform, warn; give (a person) 'the drum' (DRUM *noun*¹ 5). *Austral. & NZ slang*. E20.

> S. L. ELLIOTT Someone musta drummed him Vic had extra razor blades.

drumble /ˈdrʌmb(ə)l/ *noun*. M16.
[ORIGIN from the verb.]
An inert or sluggish person, a drone.

drumble /drʌmb(ə)l/ *verb intrans*. Now *dial*. ME.
[ORIGIN Imit.]
1 Drone; mumble. ME.
2 Be sluggish; move sluggishly. L16.
– COMB.: **drumbledore** a bumblebee; a dor; *fig*. a heavy stupid person; **drumbledrone** a drone-bee; a bumblebee.

drumhead /ˈdrʌmhɛd/ *noun & adjective*. E17.
[ORIGIN from DRUM *noun*¹ + HEAD *noun*.]
▸ **A** *noun*. **1** The stretched skin or membrane of a drum. E17.
2 The eardrum. Cf. DRUM *noun*¹ 6. M17.
3 The top of a capstan or a mechanical drum. L17.
4 More fully ***drumhead cabbage***. A flat-topped variety of cabbage. L18.
▸ **B** *attrib*. or as *adjective*. Held or done during military operations or with men in battledress; resembling or characteristic of a summary court martial so held. M19.

> J. R. LOWELL There was more reason in the drumhead religious discipline.. than he may have thought. D. ACHESON Resistance groups hunting out and executing, after drumhead trials, collaborators. *Daily Telegraph* Servicemen.. have the freedom of the town and were planning.. a drumhead service in the market square.

drumlin /ˈdrʌmlɪn/ *noun*. M19.
[ORIGIN App. from DRUM *noun*² + *-lin* repr. -LING¹.]
A long low oval mound of compacted boulder clay rounded and smoothed by past glacial action.
■ **drumlinized** *adjective* formed into or covered with drumlins E20. **drumlinoid** *adjective & noun* (a hill, rock mass, etc.) resembling a drumlin in shape L19.

drumly /ˈdrʌmli/ *adjective*. Orig. *Scot*. Also **-lie**. E16.
[ORIGIN App. nasalized var. of DRUBLY.]
(Of the sky, a person's looks, etc.) gloomy, cloudy, troubled; (of water) turbid, not clear; *fig*. muddled, confused, obscure; giddy.

drummer /ˈdrʌmə/ *noun*. L16.
[ORIGIN from DRUM *verb* + -ER¹.]
1 A person who beats a drum. L16.
2 Any animal which makes a drumming noise or action. E18.
3 A person who solicits custom or orders; a commercial traveller; a salesman. *colloq*. E19.
4 A thief; a housebreaker. *slang*. M19.
5 A swagman, a tramp. *Austral. & NZ slang*. L19.
6 The slowest shearer in a shed. *Austral. & NZ slang*. L19.

drumming /ˈdrʌmɪŋ/ *verbal noun*. L16.
[ORIGIN from DRUM *verb* + -ING¹.]
The action of DRUM *verb*; an instance of this; a sound like a drum.

Drummond light /ˈdrʌmənd lʌɪt/ *noun phr*. M19.
[ORIGIN T. *Drummond* (1797–1840), Scot. engineer.]
A powerful lamp producing limelight.

†**drumslade** *noun*. E16.
[ORIGIN Alt. of Low German *trommelslag* drum beat, from *trommel* drum (formed as DRUM *noun*¹) + *slag* beat.]
1 A drum. E16–M17.
2 A drummer. E16–L18.

drumstick /ˈdrʌmstɪk/ *noun*. L16.
[ORIGIN from DRUM *noun*¹ + STICK *noun*¹.]
1 A stick for beating a drum. L16.
2 The lower joint of the leg of a cooked or dressed fowl. M18.
3 In full ***drumstick tree***. Either of two trees, *Cassia sieberana*, an African shower tree valued for its timber, and *Moringa oleifera*, the Indian horseradish tree. M19.
4 CYTOLOGY. An appendage of the nucleus of a polymorphonuclear leucocyte, characteristic of females. M20.
– COMB.: **drumstick primula** a primula, *Primula denticulata*, with a globular head of usu. purplish flowers on an erect stem; ***drumstick tree***: see sense 3 above.

drungar /ˈdrʌŋgə/ *noun*. E17.
[ORIGIN medieval Latin *drungarius*, from late Latin *drungus* body of soldiers: see -AR².]
hist. ***drungar of the fleet***, a Byzantine admiral.

drunk /drʌŋk/ *adjective & noun*. ME.
[ORIGIN pa. pple of DRINK *verb*, shortened from DRUNKEN *verb*. Cf. DRUNKEN *adjective*.]
▸ **A** *adjective* (now usu. *pred*.).
1 Affected by alcohol in the body to such an extent that one is without full or proper control of one's faculties or behaviour; inebriated; intoxicated; *fig*. overcome *with* emotion etc. ME.

> J. R. GREEN Napoleon was drunk with success. W. OWEN Many had lost their boots But limped on.. Drunk with fatigue. I. WALLACE She wondered why three drinks had not made her drunk.

appeal from Philip drunk to Philip sober suggest that an opinion etc. represents a passing mood only. ***blind drunk***: see BLIND *adverb*. ***dead drunk***: see DEAD *adverb*. **drunk and disorderly** (committing the offence of) creating a public disturbance under the influence of alcohol. **drunk as a fiddler**, **drunk as a lord**, & vars., very drunk.
†**2** = DRUNKEN *adjective* 3. LME–L17.
3 = DRUNKEN *adjective* 4. M19.
– COMB.: **drunk-driving** *N. Amer*. = ***drink-driving*** s.v. DRINK *verb*.
▸ **B** *noun*. **1** A drinking bout; a period or state of drunkenness. *slang*. L18.
2 A person who is drunk or is frequently drunk. M19.
– COMB.: **drunk tank** *N. Amer. slang* a large prison cell for the detention of drunks.
■ **drunkery** *noun* (*derog*.) a place to get drunk in; a public house, a bar: E19. **drunkish** *adjective* E18. **drun'kometer** *noun* (*US*) an instrument for determining the level of alcohol in the breath (cf. BREATHALYSER) M20.

drunk *verb pa. t. & pple*: see DRINK *verb*.

drunkard /ˈdrʌŋkəd/ *noun*. ME.
[ORIGIN Prob. from Middle Low German *drunkert*, from *drunken*; cf. Middle Dutch *dronker*, Dutch *dronkaard*, whence early mod. French *dronquart*: see -ARD.]
1 A person inordinately fond of drinking alcohol, esp. to excess; a person who is habitually drunk. ME.
2 The marsh marigold. L19.

drunken /ˈdrʌŋk(ə)n/ *adjective* (now usu. *attrib*.). Also (*Scot*.) **drucken** /ˈdrʌk(ə)n/. OE.
[ORIGIN pa. pple of DRINK *verb*: cf. DRUNK *adjective*. Scot. form from Old Norse.]
1 a = DRUNK *adjective* 1. OE. ▸**b** Habitually or frequently drunk. M16.

> **a** V. WOOLF He lurches back to his seat like a drunken sailor. *fig*.: E. K. KANE We were so drunken with cold that we strode on steadily. **b** E. E. NAPIER Drunken, lazy, good-for-nothing fellows.

2 Proceeding from or pertaining to drink or drunkenness. LME.

> S. JOHNSON Men who.. destroy in a drunken frolick the happiness of families. BURKE The delirium of a low, drunken alehouse.

3 Of a thing: drenched, saturated with moisture. Now *rare* or *obsolete*. LME.
4 Uneven, unsteady; reeling in motion or course. L18.
■ **drunkenly** *adverb* L16. **drunkenness** /-n-n-/ *noun* the state of being drunk (*lit. & fig*.); intoxication; the habit of drinking to excess: OE. †**drunkensome** *adjective* = DRUNKEN 1b ME–M19.

drunken *verb pa. pple*: see DRINK *verb*.

†**drunkness** *noun*. ME–E18.
[ORIGIN Syncopated from DRUNKENNESS.]
= DRUNKENNESS.

drupe /druːp/ *noun*. M18.
[ORIGIN Latin *drupa*, *druppa* overripe olive (in mod. Latin, drupe) from Greek *druppa* olive.]
A fleshy indehiscent fruit with an outer skin and a central stone enclosing the seed (e.g. a cherry, a plum).
■ **dru'paceous** *adjective* of the nature of a drupe; bearing drupes: E19. **drupelet** /ˈdruːplɪt/ *noun* a little drupe forming part of a compound fruit like a blackberry L19. **drupel** /ˈdruːp(ə)l/ *noun* [mod. Latin *drupella*] = DRUPELET M19.

druse /druːz/ *noun*¹. E19.
[ORIGIN French from German, = Middle Low German *drūse*, *drose*, Dutch *droes*.]
(A cavity in a rock lined with) a crust of small projecting crystals.
■ **drusy** *adjective* covered or lined with a druse; containing druses, of the nature of a druse: L18.

Druse *noun*² & *adjective* var. of DRUZE *noun & adjective*.

druther /ˈdrʌðə/ *adverb & noun*. *N. Amer*. L19.
[ORIGIN from a US dial. pronunc. of *would rather*. Cf. RUTHER, RATHER *noun*.]
▸ **A** *adverb*. Rather, by preference. L19.

> D. BAKER Would you druther I wouldn't go?

▸ **B** *noun*. In *pl*. Preference, choice; one's way in a matter. L19.

> *Globe & Mail (Toronto)* If Robert Stanfield had his druthers, he would announce his retirement about May.

druxy /ˈdrʌksi/ *adjective*. Also (earlier) †**dricksie**. L16.
[ORIGIN Unknown.]
Of timber: having decayed spots hidden by healthy wood.

Druze /druːz/ *noun & adjective*. Also **-se**. L18.
[ORIGIN (French from) Arabic *Durūz* pl. of *Durzī* var. of *Darazī*, from the name of Muḥammad ibn Ismā'īl ad-*Darazī* (d. 1019), one of the founders.]
▸ **A** *noun*. Pl. same, **-s**. A member of a small religious and political sect, orig. an offshoot of the Ismaili Shiite Muslims, that lives chiefly in Syria and Lebanon and believes in the divinity of the 6th Fatimid caliph of Egypt (d. 1020). L18.
▸ **B** *adjective*. Of, pertaining to, or designating the Druze. L18.
■ Also **Druzian** †*noun & adjective* L16.

druzhina /ˈdruʒiːnə/ *noun*. Pl. **-nas**, **-ny** /-ni/. L19.
[ORIGIN Russian, from *drug* friend + *-ina* group suffix.]
hist. **1** The retinue or bodyguards of a Russian prince. L19.
2 In the USSR: a military or police unit; *spec*. a detachment of volunteers assuming police powers. M20.
■ **druzhinnik** /ˈdruʒiːnɪk/ *noun* pl. **-i** /-i/, a member of a druzhina M20.

dry /drʌɪ/ *noun*. Pl. **dries**, **drys**. ME.
[ORIGIN from the adjective.]
1 Dryness, esp. of the atmosphere; drought. ME. ▸**b** *The* dry season. Chiefly *Austral. colloq*. L19.
2 *The* land (as opp. to the sea). ME.
3 A place for drying things. L19.
4 A person who opposes the sale and consumption of alcohol; a prohibitionist. *colloq*. L19.
5 A desert, a waterless area. *Austral*. E20.
6 A dry wine, cocktail, or other drink. M20.
7 The process or an act of drying. M20.
8 THEATRICAL. An act of forgetting one's lines on the stage. M20.
9 A British Conservative politician (esp. in the 1980s) in favour of strict monetarist policies. *colloq*. L20.

dry /drʌɪ/ *adjective & adverb*.
[ORIGIN Old English *drȳge* rel. to Middle & mod. Low German *dröge*, *dreuge*, Middle Dutch *drōghe* (Dutch *droog*), from Germanic.]
▸ **A** *adjective*. **I** As a physical quality.
1 Lacking or free from moisture. OE. ▸**b** *hist*. Designating a quality associated with dryness and regarded in medieval and later times as one of four qualities inherent in all things; having a preponderance of this quality. Cf. ***moist***, ***hot***, ***cold***. OE. ▸**c** Lacking or free from rain; having scanty or deficient rainfall. ME. ▸**d** Free of tears; not accompanied by weeping. LME.

> N. GORDIMER You had no dry clothes to replace wet ones. P. S. BUCK With this dry wind the wheat seed.. could not sprout. **c** H. QUICK The pedestrian made his way over earth paths in dry and through puddles of mud in wet weather.

2 Having lost its natural moisture; desiccated, parched. OE. ▸**b** Of a watercourse, pond, etc., or moisture on a surface: having disappeared by evaporation, draining, wiping, etc.; dried up. **LME.**

C. FREEMAN His mouth was dry. A. N. WILSON He nibbled his dry little bit of seed cake. **b** I. WATTS Let our songs abound, And ev'ry tear be dry. E. HEMINGWAY A .. bridge across what was usually a dry river-bed.

3 Not in, on, or under water; (of a boat, fish, etc.) beached, stranded. **ME.**
4 Of bread: served without butter or other spread. **ME.**
5 Of a person: wanting drink, thirsty. Of a thing or condition: causing thirst. **LME.** ▸**b** Not accompanied by or associated with (alcoholic) drink; *spec.* (of a person) favouring the prohibition of the liquor trade; (of a place) where alcoholic drink is banned. **L15.** ▸**c** Abstaining from alcohol, esp. after overindulging; having stopped taking an addictive drug. **M20.**

T. HARDY I am sometimes that dry in the dog days that I could drink a quarter-barrel. OED Better have a pint; it's dry work. **b** T. H. WHITE Bottles of wine were opened so that it should not be a dry meeting.

6 Not or no longer yielding water or other liquid; (of a cow etc.) not yielding milk. **LME.**

H. FAST The well is good, and it's never gone dry.

7 *MEDICINE.* Not accompanied by a discharge; (of a cough) without phlegm; (of a wound) not discharging blood or pus. **LME.** ▸†**b** Occurring without bloodshed. Of a blow: bruising rather than breaking the skin; *loosely* hard, severe. **M16–L18.**
8 Solid, not liquid; of or pertaining to solid substances or commodities. **L17.**

G. OGLE Neither the Wine nor dry Provisions were come.

9 Of a wall: made without using mortar. See also ***drywall*** below. **E18.**
10 Designating a process or apparatus in which no liquid is used. **L18.**

J. BOWYER Warm air heating, the only dry central heating system.

11 Of a young child: continent of urine. **M20.**
▸**II** *fig.* **12** Orig., lacking religious ardour. Now, unemotional, impassive; without sympathy or cordiality. **ME.** ▸†**b** Of a person: miserly; unresponsive, reserved. **M16–L17.**

A. F. DOUGLAS-HOME A dry, tight-lipped, meticulous character, with little or no sense of humour.

13 Giving no satisfaction or result; barren, unproductive. **ME.**
14 Expressed in or marked by a matter-of-fact tone with feigned unawareness of humour. **M16.**

R. C. HUTCHINSON He talked with dry appreciation of eccentrics he had travelled with.

15 Of rent, fees, etc.: paid in cash. Now *rare* or *obsolete*. **L16.**
16 Not enlarged upon; plain, bare, matter-of-fact. **E17.**

M. W. MONTAGU I would willingly return .. something more .. than dry thanks impertinently expressed.

17 Uninteresting, unattractive, dull. **E17.**

M. PATTISON Annals .. valuable to the antiquary, but dry and profitless to others.

18 *ART.* Characterized by stiff and formal outlines, construction, etc. **E18.**

T. E. HULME A poem which is all dry and hard, a properly classical poem.

19 Of wine etc.: having all or most of the sugar fermented into alcohol; not sweet (formerly, not tasting sweet or fruity). **E18.**

J. ASHBY-STERRY In Mrs. Williams' driest sherry He toasts the Lass of Bolney Ferry!

20 Of a sound: harsh, rasping. Of a sound, an acoustic, a room, etc.: lacking warmth or resonance. **E18.**

– PHRASES: **(as) *dry as a chip***: see CHIP *noun*. **(as) *dry as a whistle***: see WHISTLE *noun*. **(as) dry as dust** extremely dry; *spec.* extremely dull and uninteresting, arid, unrewarding (cf. DRYASDUST). ***extra dry***: see EXTRA *adverb*. ***high and dry***: see HIGH *adjective*. ***home and dry***: see HOME *adverb*. ***keep one's powder dry***: see POWDER *noun*[1]. ***milk dry***: see MILK *verb*. ***run dry***: see RUN *verb*. ***suck dry***: see SUCK *verb*.

– SPECIAL COLLOCATIONS & COMB.: **dry battery** a battery consisting of dry cells; a dry cell. **dry-blow** *verb* (*Austral. & NZ*) (**a**) *verb intrans.* perform dry-blowing; (**b**) *verb trans.* seek for gold in (a material or place) by dry-blowing; (**c**) *verb trans.* attempt to clean without using water. **dry-blower** *Austral. & NZ* (**a**) a person who performs dry-blowing; a gold-miner; (**b**) a sieve etc. used in dry-blowing. **dry-blowing** *Austral. & NZ* the separation of gold from the soil etc. in which it is found by means of an air current. ***dry-bob***: see BOB *noun*[5]. **dry-bulb** *adjective* designating (the temperature measured with) a thermometer with an ordinary exposed bulb, usu. used along with a wet-bulb one. ***dry canteen***: see CANTEEN 1. **dry cell** a voltaic cell in which the electrolyte is in the form of a paste or is otherwise prevented from spilling. **dry-clean** *verb* (**a**) *verb trans.* clean (a garment, textile, etc.) using an organic solvent, without water; (**b**) *verb intrans.* (of a garment etc.) have the property that it can be dry-cleaned. **dry-cleaner** an establishment that carries out dry-cleaning. **dry-cure** *verb trans.* preserve (meat etc.) by salting and drying, rather than pickling. **dry death** (**a**) death without bloodshed; (**b**) (*rare*, Shakes.) death other than by drowning. **dry diggings** gold diggings away from a river or stream. **dry dock** a narrow basin into which a vessel may be floated and the water then pumped out so that repairs can be carried out on the hull. **dry-dock** *verb trans.* place (a vessel) in dry dock for repairs. ***dry distillation***: see DISTILLATION 2. **dry farming** (chiefly *N. Amer.*) a method of farming in semi-arid areas without the aid of irrigation; dry-land farming. **dry fly** *ANGLING* an artificial fly which floats lightly on the water. **dry-fly** *verb intrans.* fish with a dry fly. **dry-foot** *adverb* without wetting the feet (†*draw dry-foot*, †*hunt dry-foot*, track game by the mere scent of the feet). **dry-fry** *verb trans.* fry in a pan without fat or oil. **dry fuck** *US coarse slang* an act of sexual intercourse that is simulated or unsatisfactory. ***dry GANGRENE***. **dry goods** (chiefly *N. Amer.*) drapery and haberdashery. **dry hole** a well drilled for oil or gas but yielding none. **dry ice** carbon dioxide in the form of a solid block, which sublimes at −78°C and is used as a refrigerant. **dry joint** a soldered joint with faulty electrical continuity. DRY LAND. **dry lease** an arrangement covering the hire of an aircraft which does not include provision of a flight crew. **dry light**: in which one sees things without prejudice, uninfluenced by personal predilection. ***dry Martini***: see MARTINI *noun*[2]. ***dry mass***: see MASS *noun*[1]. **dry matter** *NZ* feedstuff for farm animals. **dry measure** a measure of capacity for corn etc. **dry milk** *US* dried milk. **dry mounting**: in which paper impregnated with shellac, or a coating of shellac, is placed between the print etc. and the mount, the whole then being pressed between hot plates to produce bonding. DRY NURSE. **dry point** a needle for engraving without acid on bare copper plate; engraving by this means; (a print made from) an engraving so produced. ***dry prune***: see PRUNE *noun* 2. **dry-roast** *verb trans.* roast without fat or oil. **dry rot** a type of decay of wood in poorly ventilated or humid conditions, in which the cellulose is attacked and the wood readily reduced to a powder; the fungus *Serpula lacrymans*, which causes this; *fig.* unsuspected moral or social decay. **dry-rotten** *adjective* decayed with dry rot. **dry run** (**a**) *US* a stream bed which is filled only after rain; (**b**) *colloq.* a rehearsal, a try-out. **dry-salt** *verb trans.* = ***dry-cure*** above. **dry-salter** *hist.* a dealer in drugs, dyestuffs, gums, oils, tinned or pickled foodstuffs, etc. **dry saltery** a dry-salter's store; *sing.* & in *pl.*, the commodities sold at such a store. ***dry scall***: see SCALL *noun*. **dry season** a period of a month or more each year in tropical and subtropical regions when there is little or no rainfall. **dry shampoo** a cleaner for the hair, upholstery, etc., which does not need water. **dry shave** a shave without water, soap, or other lubricant. **dry shaver** an electric or other razor for use without water. **dry-shod** *adverb* without wetting one's shoes. **dry sink** *N. Amer.* an antique (usu. wooden) kitchen cabinet with an inset sink, now usu. used as a plant holder or for some other purpose. **dry-ski** *adjective* designating a school etc. for indoor training in skiing. **dry slope** a slope with an artificial surface on which to ski. **dry spell** a period of dry weather. ***dry steam***: see STEAM *noun*. **drystone** *adjective* designating a stone wall built without using mortar. **drysuit** a diving suit under which warm clothing can be worn. **dry valley**: in which the original river or stream has disappeared. **drywall** plasterboard (see also sense 9 above). ***dry wash***: see WASH *noun* 5c. ***dry way***: see WAY *noun*. **dry well** = ***dry hole*** above.

▸**B** *adverb.* In a dry way; without the use of liquid; without drawing blood. **L15.**

dry /drʌɪ/ *verb.* Pa. t. & pple **dried** /drʌɪd/. See also DRIED *ppl adjective*.
[ORIGIN Old English *drȳgan* verb trans., *drūgian* verb intrans., formed as DRY *adjective*.]
▸**I** *lit.* **1** *verb trans.* Remove the moisture from by wiping, evaporation, draining, etc. (freq. foll. by *off*, *out*, *up*); preserve (food etc.) by the removal of its natural moisture. **OE.** ▸**b** Stop the flow of milk of (a cow or other mammal). Also foll. by *off*, *up*. **M16.**

E. O'NEILL She dries her eyes and regains her composure. E. HEMINGWAY Make a fire in the kitchen and dry your things.

2 *verb intrans.* Lose moisture by wiping, evaporation, drainage, etc. Also foll. by *off*, *out*. **OE.** ▸**b** Of a well, spring, etc.: cease to give water. Usu. foll. by *up*. **ME.** ▸**c** Of a cow etc.: cease to give milk. **E19.**

G. B. SHAW His clothes are drying in the sun. J. BUCHAN Acres of spongy ground which .. dried up at the first frosts. **b** *fig.*: M. DE LA ROCHE The fount of his gratitude must dry up from the unceasing flow.

dry straight *fig.* come right eventually. ***hang out to dry***, ***hang one's bat out to dry***: see HANG *verb*.

3 *verb trans.* Remove (water, moisture) by evaporation, drainage, etc. (also foll. by *up*); wipe away (tears). **ME.**
4 *verb intrans.* Of water etc.: disappear by evaporation etc. Freq. foll. by *up*. **ME.**

SHAKES. *All's Well* Great floods have flown From simple sources, and great seas have dried. TENNYSON The sap dries up: the plant declines.

5 *verb intrans.* Dry crockery, cutlery, etc., after it has been washed. Also foll. by *up*. **M20.**
▸**II** *fig.* **6** *verb intrans.* Foll. by *up*: stop, cease; come to an end; *spec.* stop talking. *colloq.* **M19.**

SCOTT FITZGERALD 'Oh, dry up!' retorted Basil. *New York Times* As selling dried up, the glamours gained on new buying.

7 a *verb intrans.* Forget one's lines on stage. Also foll. by *up*. **L19.** ▸**b** *verb trans.* Foll. by *up*: cause (a performer) to forget lines. **E20.**

L. A. G. STRONG A colleague of mine once dried in the middle of a scene.

8 *verb intrans.* & *trans.* Foll. by *out*: (cause to) undergo treatment for drug or alcohol addiction. **M20.**

dryad /ˈdrʌɪəd, -ad/ *noun.* Also **D-**. Pl. **-ads**, **-ades** /-ədiːz/. **LME.**
[ORIGIN Old French & mod. French *dryade* from Latin *Dryades* pl. of *Dryas* from Greek *Druas*, *Druades*, from *drus* tree: see -AD[1].]
CLASSICAL MYTHOLOGY. A nymph supposed to inhabit trees, a wood nymph.

transf.: BYRON The palm, the loftiest dryad of the woods.

dryad's saddle a common bracket fungus, *Polyporus squamosus*, having a scaly yellowish-brown upper surface and edible when young.
■ **dry'adic** *adjective* **L19.**

D

dryas /ˈdrʌɪəs/ *noun.* **L18.**
[ORIGIN Latin: see DRYAD.]
1 Any of several creeping alpines of the genus *Dryas*, belonging to the rose family and having white or yellowish flowers. **L18.**
2 (**D-**.) *GEOLOGY.* A type of clay or a subarctic phase characterized by the growth of dryases. **E20.**

Dryasdust /ˈdrʌɪəzdʌst/ *noun.* **M19.**
[ORIGIN Dr *Dryasdust*, a fictitious character (from (**as**) **dry as dust** s.v. DRY *adjective*) to whom Sir Walter Scott dedicated novels.]
A laborious dull antiquarian or historian; a scholar occupied with uninteresting details.

Drydenian /drʌɪˈdiːnɪən/ *adjective.* **L17.**
[ORIGIN from *Dryden* (see below) + -IAN.]
Of, pertaining to, or resembling the English poet, dramatist, and critic John Dryden (1631–1700), his works, or his style.
■ Also **Drydenish** /ˈdrʌɪd(ə)nɪʃ/ *adjective* **L17.**

dryer *noun* var. of DRIER.

drying /ˈdrʌɪɪŋ/ *verbal noun.* **LME.**
[ORIGIN from DRY *verb* + -ING[1].]
The action of DRY *verb*. Also ***drying-off***, ***drying-out***, ***drying-up***.

H. OLDENBURG The too hasty drying thereof spoils it. I. SHAW Jean was spending more and more time in drying-out clinics.

– ATTRIB. & COMB.: in the sense 'used in or for drying something', as ***drying closet***, ***drying floor***, ***drying green***, ***drying rack***, etc. Special combs., as **drying day** a specified (good etc.) type of day for the drying of washing outdoors.

drying /ˈdrʌɪɪŋ/ *ppl adjective.* **LME.**
[ORIGIN from DRY *verb* + -ING[2].]
That dries; causing drying; in the process of drying. *spec.* that dries quickly.

W. B. CARPENTER A cold drying wind. W. FAULKNER His boots and puttees not caked with the drying mud of trenches.

drying oil: that thickens or hardens on exposure to air.

dryish /ˈdrʌɪɪʃ/ *adjective.* **E18.**
[ORIGIN from DRY *adjective* + -ISH[1].]
Somewhat dry.

dry land /*noun phr.* drʌɪ ˈland; *adjective* ˈdrʌɪland/ *noun phr.* & *adjective.* As adjective usu. **dry-land**. **ME.**
[ORIGIN from DRY *adjective* + LAND *noun*[1].]
▸**A** *noun phr.* **1** Land as opp. to the sea, a river, etc.; land that is dry, not swampy or under water. **ME.**
2 *sing.* & (usu.) in *pl.* An area, or land, where rainfall is low, esp. when farmed without irrigation. Chiefly *N. Amer.* **E20.**
▸**B** *attrib.* or as *adjective.* **1** Living or occurring on the land. **L17.**
2 Established or (able to be) grown or bred on dry lands; (of farming) practised on dry lands without irrigation. Chiefly *N. Amer.* **L19.**
■ **dry'lander** *noun* (*N. Amer.*) a person who has settled on or who farms dry lands **E20.**

dryly *adverb* var. of DRILY.

dryness /ˈdrʌɪnɪs/ *noun.* **LME.**
[ORIGIN from DRY *adjective* + -NESS.]
The state or condition of being dry (*lit.* & *fig.*); absence or deficiency of moisture; prohibition of alcohol; absence of emotion or cordiality; dullness, lack of interest.

dry nurse /ˈdrʌɪnəːs/ *noun* & *verb.* **M16.**
[ORIGIN from DRY *adjective* + NURSE *noun*[1].]
▸**A** *noun.* **1** A woman who looks after a baby but does not breastfeed it. Opp. ***wet nurse***. **M16.**
2 *fig.* A person who coaches another (esp. a superior) in his or her duties. *arch.* **E17.**
▸**B** *verb trans.* (With hyphen.) Look after (another person's baby); be a dry nurse to (*lit.* & *fig.*). **L16.**

Dryopithecus /drʌɪəʊˈpɪθɪkəs/ *noun.* **M19.**
[ORIGIN mod. Latin, from Greek *drus* tree + *pithēkos* ape.]
A member of the fossil genus *Dryopithecus* of partly tree-dwelling Old World anthropoid apes of Miocene times, ancestral to present-day African pongids.
■ **dryopithecine** /-siːn/ *adjective* & *noun* (**a**) *adjective* of, pertaining to, or designating the Dryopithecinae, a subfamily of the Pongidae including Dryopithecus and believed to be ancestral to humans; designating a five-cusped tooth pattern found in Dryopithecus and in the lower molars of humans and other hominoids; (**b**) *noun* a dryopithecine individual: **M20.**

dryster /ˈdrʌɪstə/ *noun.* Now *arch.* or *hist.* **ME.**
[ORIGIN from DRY *verb* + -STER.]
A person employed in drying something.

D

dryth /drʌɪθ/ *noun. obsolete* exc. *dial.* Also **drieth**. M16.
[ORIGIN from DRY *adjective* + -TH[1], after *warmth*.]
1 Dryness, dry condition. M16.
2 Thirst. M16.
3 Dry weather, drought. L16.

dry-up /ˈdrʌɪʌp/ *noun*. L19.
[ORIGIN from *dry up*: see DRY *verb*.]
An act or instance of drying up.

DS *abbreviation.*
1 Dal segno.
2 Disseminated sclerosis.

Ds *symbol.*
CHEMISTRY. Darmstadtium.

DSC *abbreviation.*
Distinguished Service Cross.

D.Sc. *abbreviation.*
Doctor of Science.

DSIR *abbreviation.*
Chiefly *hist.* Department of Scientific and Industrial Research.

DSL *abbreviation.*
Digital subscriber line, a technology for the high-speed transmission of digital information over standard telephone lines.

DSM *abbreviation.*
Distinguished Service Medal.

DSO *abbreviation.*
(Companion of the) Distinguished Service Order.

DSP *abbreviation.*
COMPUTING & AUDIO. Digital signal processing (or processor).

DSS *abbreviation. hist.*
Department of Social Security.

DST *abbreviation.*
Daylight saving time.

DT *abbreviation.*
Delirium tremens. See also **DTs**.

DTD *abbreviation.*
COMPUTING. Document type definition, a document that defines the tagging structure of an SGML or XML document.

DTI *abbreviation.*
Department of Trade and Industry.

DTP *abbreviation.*
Desktop publishing.

DTp *abbreviation. hist.*
Department of Transport.

DTs /diːˈtiːz/ *abbreviation.*
Delirium tremens.

DTV *abbreviation.*
Digital television.

DU *abbreviation.*
1 Depleted uranium.
2 Dobson unit.

duab *noun* var. of DOAB.

duad /ˈdjuːad/ *noun*. M17.
[ORIGIN Greek *duas*, *duad-* the number two (see -AD[1]), prob. infl. by Latin *duo*. Cf. DYAD.]
A combination of two; a couple, a pair.
■ **duˈadic** *adjective* of, pertaining to, or consisting of a duad or duads L19.

dual /ˈdjuːəl/ *noun & adjective*. LME.
[ORIGIN Latin *dualis*, from *duo* two: see -AL[1].]
▸ **A** *noun*. †**1** Either of the two middle incisor teeth in each jaw. LME–M16.
2 GRAMMAR. A form of nouns, verbs, etc., denoting two people or things (in addition to singular and plural); a word in this number. M17.
3 In a chess problem, an alternative second or later move by White that fulfils the stipulations in a manner not intended by the composer. L19.
▸ **B** *adjective*. **1** Of or pertaining to two; shared by two, joint; *spec.* (GRAMMAR) denoting two people or things. E17.
2 Composed or consisting of two parts; twofold, double. M17.

> F. O'BRIEN His laugh had a dual function, partly to applaud his jest, partly to cloak his anger. S. SONTAG Everyone . . holds dual citizenship in the kingdom of the well and in the kingdom of the sick.

– SPECIAL COLLOCATIONS & COMB.: **dual carriageway** a road with a dividing strip between traffic going in opposite directions. **dual control** (*a*) control exercised by two parties jointly; (*b*) in *pl.*, duplicated controls in an aircraft, motor vehicle, etc., for instructor and learner. **dual-control** *adjective* (of a vehicle or aircraft) controllable by both instructor and learner. **dual in-line** *adjective* (ELECTRONICS) denoting an integrated circuit package consisting of a rectangular sealed unit with two parallel rows of downward-pointing pins. **dual number** GRAMMAR = sense A.2 above. **dual personality** two distinct personalities in one individual. **dual-purpose** *adjective* serving two purposes; *spec.* (of a car) usable for passengers and goods. **dual-standard** *adjective* (of equipment etc.) capable of working to either of two specifications.
■ **dually** *adverb* in a dual manner; GRAMMAR in the dual number: M17.

dual /ˈdjuːəl/ *verb trans.* Infl. **-ll-**, *-**l-**. E20.
[ORIGIN from the adjective.]
1 CHESS. In *pass.*, admit of a dual (see DUAL *noun* 3). E20.
2 Convert into dual form; *spec.* make (a road) into a dual carriageway. M20.

dualise *verb* var. of DUALIZE.

dualism /ˈdjuːəlɪz(ə)m/ *noun*. L18.
[ORIGIN from DUAL *adjective* + -ISM, after French *dualisme*.]
1 A theory or system of thought which recognizes two independent principles (cf. MONISM, PLURALISM 2); *spec.* (*a*) the theory that mind and matter exist as separate entities; (*b*) the doctrine that there are two conflicting powers, good and evil, in the universe; (*c*) the doctrine that Christ had two natures, human and divine. L18.

> D. R. HOFSTADTER Dualism is the conceptual division of the world into categories.

2 The state of being dual; twofold division, duality. M19.

> R. W. EMERSON An inevitable dualism bisects nature, so that each thing is a half, and suggests another thing to make it whole. M. S. LIVINGSTON Wave-particle dualism in the properties of light.

3 GRAMMAR. The fact of expressing two in number. L19.

dualist /ˈdjuːəlɪst/ *noun*. M17.
[ORIGIN from DUAL *adjective* + -IST. In sense 1 after PLURALIST, in sense 2 after French *dualiste*.]
†**1** A holder of two benefices. Only in M17.
2 A person who holds any of the doctrines of dualism. E19.

dualistic /djuːəˈlɪstɪk/ *adjective*. L18.
[ORIGIN from DUALIST + -IC, after French *dualistique*.]
1 Of or pertaining to dualism; of the nature of dualism. L18.
2 Dual. M19.
■ **dualistically** *adverb* M19.

duality /djuːˈalɪti/ *noun*. LME.
[ORIGIN Late Latin *dualitas* dual nature, from Latin *dualis* DUAL *adjective*: see -ITY. In sense 2 app. after PLURALITY: cf. DUALIST.]
1 The state or condition of being dual or having two parts or natures; twofold condition, dualism. LME.
principle of duality: see PRINCIPLE *noun*.
†**2** The simultaneous holding of two benefices. E–M17.

dualize /ˈdjuːəlʌɪz/ *verb trans.* Also **-ise**. M19.
[ORIGIN from DUAL *adjective* + -IZE.]
Make or regard as dual.

duan /ˈduːən/ *noun*. M18.
[ORIGIN Gaelic & Irish.]
A (Gaelic or Irish) poem, song, or canto.

duar *noun* var. of DOUAR.

duarchy /ˈdjuːɑːki/ *noun*. L16.
[ORIGIN from Latin (or irreg. from Greek) *duo* two, after *monarchy* etc.]
Government by two joint rulers; a diarchy.

dub /dʌb/ *noun*[1]. *Scot. & N. English*. Also **dib** /dɪb/. LME.
[ORIGIN Unknown. Cf. Middle Low German, Low German, West Frisian *dobbe*.]
1 A muddy or stagnant pool, a puddle. LME.
2 A deep dark pool in a river or stream. M16.
– COMB.: **dub-skelper** a person who splashes through puddles; *fig.* an idle person, a vagrant.

dub /dʌb/ *noun*[2]. L16.
[ORIGIN Imit.: cf. DUB-A-DUB, RUB-A-DUB.]
1 The beat or the sound of a drum. L16.
2 A tap, a blow (resembling a drum beat). M17.

> N. HAWTHORNE Jotting down each dull footstep with a melancholy dub of his staff.

dub /dʌb/ *noun*[3]. *criminals' slang.* In sense 2 also **dubs**. L17.
[ORIGIN Rel. to DUB *verb*[3].]
1 A key, a picklock. L17.
2 A turnkey, a jailer. E19.

dub /dʌb/ *noun*[4]. *obsolete* exc. *hist.* L18.
[ORIGIN Telugu *dabbu*.]
A small copper coin formerly used in parts of India.

dub /dʌb/ *noun*[5]. *slang* (orig. *US*). L19.
[ORIGIN Perh. from DUB *verb*[1] 10.]
An inexperienced or unskilful person; a fool, a duffer.

dub /dʌb/ *noun*[6]. L20.
[ORIGIN from DUB *verb*[5].]
1 A remixed version of a piece of recorded (esp. black) music, usu. with the melodic line removed and special effects added. L20.
2 A kind of black performance poetry, orig. accompanied by dub music. L20.

dub /dʌb/ *verb*[1] *trans.* Infl. **-bb-**. LOE.
[ORIGIN Anglo-Norman *duber*, aphet. from *aduber*, Old French *adober* (mod. *adouber*) equip with armour, repair, mend: ult. origin unknown.]
▸ **I** Give (a title) to. With obj. & compl., or (now *rare*) simple obj.
1 Confer knighthood on by ceremonially touching on the shoulder with a sword; make (a person) a knight. LOE.

> C. KINGSLEY Thou wast dubbed knight in this church. O. NEUBECKER It was the custom to dub new knights before the beginning of the fighting.

2 Invest with a dignity or title; give a name, description, or nickname to. Now freq. *joc.* ME.

> POPE A Man of wealth is dubb'd a Man of worth. T. HARDY She was light and slight, of the type dubbed elegant. A. J. TOYNBEE The officiants are medicine men, though, to save appearances, they are dubbed 'sacristans'. M. EDWARDES The media dubbed it the 'tea break strike'.

▸ **II** Dress; trim.
†**3** Equip, clothe, adorn. ME–E18.
4 ANGLING. Make up (an artificial fly); dress (a hook) *with* a fly. LME.
†**5** Disguise (inferior goods); adulterate (wine). Only in LME.
6 Cut off the comb and wattles of (a cock). L16.
7 Smear or rub (now *spec.* hide, leather) with grease. Cf. DUBBING 4, DUBBIN. E17.
8 Trim or crop (trees, hedges, etc.). *obsolete* exc. *dial.* M17.
9 Trim or make smooth with an adze. E18.
10 Make blunt; beat flat. M18.
11 Dress (cloth); *spec.* beat with teazels in order to raise nap. *obsolete* exc. *dial.* E19.

dub /dʌb/ *verb*[2]. Infl. **-bb-**. L15.
[ORIGIN Imit. Cf. East Frisian *dubben* butt, beat, strike.]
1 *verb trans.* Thrust, poke, prod. Formerly also, strike, hit. L15. ▸**b** *verb intrans.* Make a thrust; poke *at*. M19.
2 *verb intrans. & trans.* Beat (a drum); (of a drum) beat, sound. Cf. DUB-A-DUB, RUB-A-DUB. L16.

dub /dʌb/ *verb*[3] *trans. slang.* Infl. **-bb-**. L17.
[ORIGIN Perh. from DUP *verb* = do up. Cf. DUB *noun*[3].]
†**1** Unlock, open (a door). L17–L18.
2 Shut or lock *up*. M18.

dub /dʌb/ *verb*[4] *intrans. slang.* Infl. **-bb-**. E19.
[ORIGIN Unknown.]
Foll. by *up*, *in*: give money, make a contribution, pay up, chip in.

dub /dʌb/ *verb*[5] *trans.* Infl. **-bb-**. E20.
[ORIGIN Abbreviation of DOUBLE *verb*.]
Add (sounds or music) to a film, recording, or broadcast; provide (a film etc.) with an alternative soundtrack, esp. in a different language; transfer or combine (recorded soundtracks). Freq. as ***dubbed*** *ppl adjective*, ***dubbing*** *verbal noun*.

> F. ASTAIRE The foot sounds had to be dubbed in, due to the difficulty of picking them up . . on the set during shooting. J. D. WATSON Dubbed voices uttered words of uncontrolled passion.

dub-a-dub /ˈdʌbədʌb, dʌbəˈdʌb/ *noun, adjective, adverb, & verb*. M16.
[ORIGIN Imit. Cf. DUB *noun*[2], RUB-A-DUB.]
▸ **A** *noun, adjective, & adverb*. (With, like) the sound made in beating a drum. M16.
▸ **B** *verb trans. & intrans.* Infl. **-bb-**. Beat (a drum); drum. L16.

dubash /duːˈbɑːʃ/ *noun*. L17.
[ORIGIN Hindi *dubhāṣī*, from *du-* two + Sanskrit *bhāṣā* language.]
In the Indian subcontinent: an interpreter, an intermediary, a mercantile broker.

dubba /ˈdʌbə/ *noun*. Also **dubber**. L17.
[ORIGIN Hindi *ḍabbā*, Urdu *dabbah*.]
In the Indian subcontinent: a leather bottle or skin bag, used chiefly for holding oil, ghee, etc.

dubbeltjie /ˈdœbəlki, -tʃi/ *noun*. *S. Afr.* L17.
[ORIGIN Sense 1 from Afrikaans from Dutch *dubbeltje* double stiver, two-penny piece. Sense 2 is prob. a different word. See also DOUBLE-GEE.]
1 A Dutch two-stiver coin or an English penny, both formerly current in South Africa; in *pl.*, money. *obsolete* exc. *hist.* L17.
2 Any of various trailing weeds with spiny burs, esp. *Tribulus terrestris* or *Emex australis*; one of these burs. L18.

dubber *noun* var. of DUBBA.

dubbin /ˈdʌbɪn/ *noun & verb*. E19.
[ORIGIN Alt. of DUBBING 4.]
▸ **A** *noun*. A preparation of grease for softening and waterproofing leather. E19.
▸ **B** *verb trans.* Apply dubbin or a similar substance to. L19.

dubbing /ˈdʌbɪŋ/ *noun*. ME.
[ORIGIN from DUB *verb*[1] + -ING[1].]
1 The action of DUB *verb*[1] I; the conferring of knighthood, the giving of a name or title. ME.
†**2** Attire, dress, array. Only in ME.
3 ANGLING. The preparation of an artificial fly; the materials used in this. L17.
4 = DUBBIN *noun*. Now *rare* or *obsolete*. L18.
5 Trimming with an adze etc.; smoothing, levelling. E19.

dubby /ˈdʌbi/ *adjective. colloq. & dial.* E19.
[ORIGIN from DUB *verb*[1] + -Y[1].]
Blunt; short, dumpy.

duberous /ˈdjuːb(ə)rəs/ *adjective. dial. & joc.* L18.
[ORIGIN Alt. of DUBIOUS.]
Dubious, doubtful, unsure.

dubiety /djuːˈbʌɪɪti/ *noun.* M18.
[ORIGIN Late Latin *dubietas*, from *dubium*: see DUBIOUS, -ITY.]
The state or quality of being dubious; uncertainty; an instance of this.

dubiosity /djuːbɪˈɒsɪti/ *noun.* M17.
[ORIGIN formed as DUBIOUS + -ITY.]
1 A doubtful matter, an uncertainty. M17.
2 Doubt, uncertainty. M19.

dubious /ˈdjuːbɪəs/ *adjective.* M16.
[ORIGIN from Latin *dubiosus*, from *dubium* doubt: see -OUS.]
1 Giving rise to doubt; of questionable value or truth; uncertain, vague. M16. ▸**b** Of uncertain outcome. M17. ▸**c** Of questionable character; suspect, untrustworthy. M19.

T. HEGGEN The islands began to grow dubious on the horizon. J. F. LEHMANN I had the dubious satisfaction of knowing that I had been 'put on their files'. **b** MILTON His utmost power . . oppos'd In dubious Battel on the Plains of Heav'n. **c** W. S. CHURCHILL He resorted to dubious methods of raising money. J. ROSENBERG The quack . . equipped with all the paraphernalia of his dubious profession.

2 Wavering in opinion, hesitant, inclined to doubt; expressing uncertainty. M17.

A. HELPS I followed them, dubious as to whether I should ultimately interfere. CONAN DOYLE The Inspector rubbed his chin and looked at me with dubious eyes.

■ **dubiously** *adverb* M17. **dubiousness** *noun* M17.

dubitable /ˈdjuːbɪtəb(ə)l/ *adjective.* E17.
[ORIGIN Latin *dubitabilis*, from *dubitare* to doubt: see -ABLE. Cf. earlier INDUBITABLE.]
Open to doubt or question, able to be doubted.
■ **dubitably** *adverb* M19.

dubitant /ˈdjuːbɪt(ə)nt/ *adjective.* E19.
[ORIGIN Latin *dubitant-* pres. ppl stem of *dubitare* to doubt: see -ANT[1].]
Doubting, having doubts, hesitant.

dubitate /ˈdjuːbɪteɪt/ *verb intrans.* E19.
[ORIGIN Latin *dubitat-* pa. ppl stem of *dubitare* to doubt: see -ATE[3].]
Doubt, hesitate, waver.

dubitation /djuːbɪˈteɪʃ(ə)n/ *noun.* LME.
[ORIGIN Old French & mod. French from Latin *dubitatio(n-)*, formed as DUBITATE: see -ATION.]
The action of doubting; (a) doubt.

dubitative /ˈdjuːbɪtətɪv/ *adjective.* E18.
[ORIGIN Old French & mod. French *dubitatif*, *-ive* or late Latin *dubitativus*, formed as DUBITATE: see -ATIVE.]
Inclined to doubt; expressing doubt or hesitation.
■ **dubitatively** *adverb* E17.

Dublin Bay prawn /ˌdʌblɪn beɪ ˈprɔːn/ *noun phr.* M20.
[ORIGIN *Dublin*: see DUBLINER.]
= NORWAY *lobster*. In *pl.*, scampi.
■ Also **Dublin prawn** *noun phr.* E20.

Dubliner /ˈdʌblɪnə/ *noun.* E20.
[ORIGIN from *Dublin* (see below) + -ER[1].]
A native or inhabitant of Dublin, capital city of the Republic of Ireland.

dubnium /ˈdʌbnɪəm/ *noun.* L20.
[ORIGIN from *Dubna* near Moscow in Russia, site of the Joint Nuclear Institute in which element 105 was created, + -IUM.]
A radioactive transuranic chemical element (atomic no. 105), produced artificially (symbol Db).
– NOTE: The name was orig. proposed for the element 104 (rutherfordium).

Dubonnet /duːˈbɒneɪ; *foreign* dybɔnɛ (*pl. same*)/ *noun.* E20.
[ORIGIN Name of a family of French wine merchants.]
Proprietary name for a sweet French flavoured wine drunk as an aperitif.

dubs *noun*[2] see DUB *noun*[3].

dubs /dʌbz/ *interjection & noun*[1]. *local.* E19.
[ORIGIN Abbreviation of *doubles*. Cf. DIBS *interjection & noun*[3].]
(A situation provoking) a cry used in games of marbles; a marble used in certain games.

ducal /ˈdjuːk(ə)l/ *adjective.* L15.
[ORIGIN French, from *duc* DUKE *noun*: see -AL[1].]
1 Of or pertaining to a duke or dukedom; characteristic of or like a duke. Also, of a doge. L15.
2 Of the rank of duke. L18.
■ **ducally** *adverb* in a ducal manner; as a duke: E19.

ducape /ˈdjuːkeɪp/ *noun.* M17.
[ORIGIN Unknown.]
A heavy silk dress fabric.

ducat /ˈdʌkət/ *noun.* Also (esp. in sense 3) **ducket(t)**. LME.
[ORIGIN Italian *ducato* or its source, medieval Latin *ducatus* DUCHY.]
1 Orig., a silver coin minted by Roger II of Sicily, as Duke of Apulia, in 1140. Later, any of various gold or silver coins formerly current in most European countries. LME.
2 A piece of money. In *pl.*, money, cash. *arch. colloq.* L18.
3 A ticket; *esp.* a railway or admission ticket. Cf. DOCKET *noun* 3. *slang.* L19.

ducatoon /dʌkəˈtuːn/ *noun.* E17.
[ORIGIN French *ducaton* from Italian *ducatone*, formed as DUCAT: see -OON.]
hist. A silver coin formerly current in some European countries.

duce /ˈduːtʃeɪ/ *noun.* Also **D-**. E20.
[ORIGIN Italian = leader.]
A leader; *spec.* ***il Duce*** /iːl/ [Italian = the], ***the Duce***, the title assumed by Benito Mussolini (1883–1945), creator and leader of the Fascist State in Italy.

duces *noun*[1] pl. of prec.

duces *noun*[2] *pl.* see DUX.

duces tecum /djuːsiːz ˈtiːkəm/ *noun phr.* E17.
[ORIGIN Latin (*sub poena*) *duces tecum* (under penalty) you shall bring with you.]
LAW (now *hist.*). A writ commanding a person to produce documentary evidence in court or at a deposition. Also ***subpoena duces tecum***.

Duchenne /duːˈʃɛn/ *noun.* L19.
[ORIGIN G. B. A. *Duchenne* (1806–75), French neurologist.]
MEDICINE. Used *attrib.* and in *possess.* to designate a severe form of muscular dystrophy described by Duchenne.

duchess /ˈdʌtʃɪs, -ɛs/ *noun.* Also (esp. in titles) **D-**. Also †**dutchess**. LME.
[ORIGIN Old French & mod. French *duchesse* from medieval Latin *ducissa*, from Latin *dux*, *duc-*: see DUKE *noun*, -ESS[1].]
▸**I 1** A lady of nobility; *spec.* (*a*) the wife or widow of a duke; (*b*) a woman holding a title equivalent to duke in her own right. LME.
grand duchess: see GRAND *adjective*[1].
2 A woman of imposing or showy appearance. *slang.* L17.
3 A girl or woman, *spec.* one's wife or mother; a costermonger's wife. Also used as a familiar form of address. Cf. DUTCH *noun*[2]. *slang.* E20.
▸**II 4** A roofing slate of a large size. Cf. COUNTESS 2, LADY *noun* 11. E19.
5 A size of writing paper. E20.
▸**III** Cf. DUCHESSE.
6 = DUCHESSE 1. E19.
– COMB.: **duchess potatoes** = *DUCHESSE* ***potatoes***; **duchess sleeve** = *DUCHESSE* ***sleeve***.

duchesse /duːˈʃɛs; ˈdʌtʃɪs, -ɛs; *foreign* dyʃɛs (*pl. same*)/ *noun.* Also **D-**. L18.
[ORIGIN French: see DUCHESS.]
1 A chaise longue consisting of two facing armchairs connected by a detachable footstool. L18.
2 More fully ***duchesse dressing chest***, ***duchesse dressing table***, ***duchesse table***. A dressing table with a pivoting mirror. M19.
3 More fully ***duchesse satin***, ***satin duchesse***. A soft heavy kind of satin. L19.
– COMB.: ***duchesse dressing chest***, ***duchesse dressing table***: see sense 2 above; **duchesse lace** a kind of Brussels pillow lace, worked with fine thread in large sprays; **duchesse potatoes** mashed potatoes mixed with egg, baked or fried in small cakes or used as garnish; ***duchesse satin***: see sense 3 above; **duchesse set** a set of fabric or lace mats for a dressing table; **duchesse sleeve** an ornately trimmed sleeve covering two-thirds of the arm; ***duchesse table***: see sense 2 above; **duchesse toilet cover** a fabric or lace mat for a dressing table.

duchy /ˈdʌtʃi/ *noun.* LME.
[ORIGIN Partly from Old French *duché* fem., later form of *duchée* from Proto-Romance, from Latin *dux*, *duc-*, partly from Old French & mod. French *duché* masc. from medieval Latin *ducatus* territory of a duke, from Latin *dux*, *duc-*: see DUKE *noun*, -Y[5].]
1 The territory ruled by a duke or duchess. LME.
grand duchy: see GRAND *adjective*[1].
2 *spec.* (**D-**.) Each of the royal dukedoms of Cornwall and Lancaster, having certain estates, revenues, and jurisdictions of their own. L15.

duck /dʌk/ *noun*[1]. Pl. **-s**, (in sense 1, also) same.
[ORIGIN Old English *duce* or *dūce*, from Germanic base of DUCK *verb*.]
1 Any of numerous swimming birds belonging to the family Anatidae, distinguished from the swans and geese (also Anatidae) esp. by their generally smaller size. Also *spec.*, any of the domesticated forms of the mallard or wild duck *Anas platyrhynchos.* OE. ▸**b** *spec.* The female of this fowl, (the male being the ***drake***). LME. ▸**c** The flesh of this fowl as food. L18.
dabbling duck, ***diving duck***, ***eider duck***, ***ferruginous duck***, ***harlequin duck***, ***long-tailed duck***, ***mandarin duck***, ***Muscovy duck***, ***ruddy duck***, ***shelduck***, ***swallow-tailed duck***, ***tree duck***, ***tufted duck***, ***velvet duck***, ***wood duck***, etc.
2 a As a term of familiarity or endearment: darling, dear; an attractive thing. Cf. DUCKS, DUCKY *noun. colloq.* L16. ▸**b** A fellow, a chap; an individual. *slang* (chiefly *US*). M19.

a C. H. SPURGEON Her child . . was so much her 'duck' that he grew up to be a goose. *Sun* Nutty Nottingham Council has banned workers calling each other 'love' or 'duck' under new anti-sexism laws. **b** M. TWAIN Are you the duck that runs the gospel-mill next door?

3 A British soldier of the Bombay Presidency. *colloq.* (now *hist.*). E19.
4 A children's game in which a small stone is placed on a larger and the players throw stones to try to dislodge it; the target stone used in this. E19.
5 *CRICKET.* Orig. ***duck egg***, ***duck's egg***. A score of nought by a batsman. M19.

F. RAPHAEL Julia clean-bowled him for a duck.

6 A savoury meatball, a faggot. L19.
– PHRASES: **a duck of a —** a dear, sweet, pretty, or desirable —. BOMBAY DUCK. ***break one's duck***: see BREAK *verb*. **dead duck** *slang* (orig. *US*) a useless person or thing, a failure, a bankrupt. **ducks and drakes**, **duck and drake** a pastime in which a flat stone is bounced across the surface of water; idle play (***make ducks and drakes of***, ***play ducks and drakes with***, trifle with, use recklessly, squander). **fine weather for ducks** wet, rainy weather. **lame duck** a disabled or powerless person or thing; *spec.* a person or company who cannot meet financial obligations. **like a duck in thunder**, **like a duck in a thunderstorm**, **like a dying duck in a thunderstorm** with upturned eyes, looking flabbergasted or distressed. **like water off a duck's back** producing no effect. ***Lord love a duck***: see LOVE *verb* 1. ***ruptured duck***: see RUPTURE *verb* 1. **sitting duck** a target that one cannot (or should not) miss. **take to something like a duck to water** take to something very readily.
– COMB.: **duck ant** a termite; **duck arse**, **duck's arse**, (*US*) **duck ass**, **duck's ass** a hairstyle with the back hair tapered like a duck's tail; abbreviation ***d.a.***; **duckbill** (*a*) = PLATYPUS; (*b*) ***duckbill wheat***, red wheat or rivet-wheat; (*c*) = ***duck's bill*** below; (*d*) = ***duck-billed dinosaur*** below; **duck-billed** having a bill like a duck; ***duck-billed dinosaur***, a hadrosaur; ***duck-billed*** PLATYPUS; **duckboard** a (slatted) board laid to facilitate movement over soft ground or fragile surfaces; **duck decoy** = DECOY *noun* 1; **duck-dive** *noun & verb* (make) a vertical dive down into the water; **duck egg**, **duck's egg** (*a*) the egg of a duck; (*b*) see sense 5 above; (*c*) a pale greenish-blue colour (freq. *attrib.*); **duck hawk** (*a*) *N. Amer.* the peregrine; (*b*) *dial.* the marsh harrier; **duckmeat**, **duck's meat** = ***duckweed*** below; **duck-mole** *Austral.* = PLATYPUS; **duck mussel** a freshwater bivalve mollusc, *Anodonta anatina*, smaller and darker than the related swan mussel; **duckpin** *US* a short squat bowling pin; ***duck's egg***: see ***duck egg*** above; **duck-shot**: of a size suitable for shooting wild ducks; **duck-shove** *verb intrans. & trans.* (*Austral. & NZ slang*) (*a*) engage in sharp practice, act unethically; (*b*) evade responsibility (for); ***duck's meat***: see ***duckmeat*** above; **duck soup** *slang* (orig. & chiefly *US*) an easy task, a pushover; ***duck's arse***, ***duck's ass***: see ***duck arse*** above; **duck's bill** (an object having the spatulate shape of) the bill of a duck (freq. *attrib.*); **duck's disease** *joc.* short legs; **duckstone** = sense 4 above; **ducktail** (*a*) *S. Afr.* a young hooligan; (*b*) = ***duck arse*** above; **duckwalk** (*a*) a duckboard track; (*b*) a waddle; a walk in a squatting position; **duckweed** any of various tiny aquatic plants belonging to the genus *Lemna* and related genera of the family Lemnaceae, which freq. carpet the surface of stagnant water and which consist of a flattened or gibbous frond bearing a minute flower in a lateral pocket; *collect.* a mass of such plants.

duck /dʌk/ *noun*[2]. M16.
[ORIGIN from DUCK *verb*.]
1 A rapid jerky lowering of the head or body; a rapid evasive movement. M16.
2 A quick plunge in water, a dip. M19.

duck /dʌk/ *noun*[3] *& adjective.* M17.
[ORIGIN Middle Dutch & mod. Dutch *doek* linen, linen cloth = Old Frisian, Old Saxon *dōk*, Old High German *tuoh* (German *Tuch*), of unknown origin.]
▸**A** *noun.* **1** A strong untwilled linen or cotton fabric used for outer clothing (esp. by sailors), small sails, etc. M17.
2 In *pl.* Trousers of this material. E19.
▸**B** *adjective.* Made of duck. M19.

duck /dʌk/ *noun*[4]. *colloq.* Also **DUKW**, **dukw**. M20.
[ORIGIN Alt. (after DUCK *noun*[1]) of *DUKW*, a combination of factory serial letters designating features of the vehicle.]
An amphibious lorry, a landing craft.

duck /dʌk/ *verb.* ME.
[ORIGIN Corresp. to Old Frisian *dūka*, Middle Low German, Middle Dutch *dūken* (Dutch *duiken*), Old High German *tūhhan* (German *tauchen*), from Germanic. Prob. already in Old English: cf. DUCK *noun*[1].]
▸**I** *verb intrans.* **1** Suddenly go under water and emerge; dip the head rapidly under water; plunge, dive; descend rapidly. ME.

W. GOLDING She . . stepped down into cooler water, ducked, then got out.

2 Bend or stoop quickly; bob, lower the head suddenly, esp. as an evasive measure; move quickly and unobtrusively. M16.

J. KOSINSKI Someone threw an apple-core; I ducked and it hit the principal. J. ARCHER Charles ducked into a nearby phone booth and rang Clive. *fig.*: BROWNING Law ducks to Gospel here.

duck and cover [with ref. to a civil-defence slogan used in the US *c* 1950] *US* take action to protect oneself from danger, esp. where such action is likely to prove completely inadequate.
3 Back *out*, withdraw, abscond. *colloq.* L19. ▸**b** *BRIDGE.* Play a low card to a trick rather than attempt to win with a high card. E20.

D. ABSE I had ducked out from a lecture. H. CARPENTER His third novel . . ducked out of contemporary social issues entirely.

▸**II** *verb trans.* **4** Submerge or dip (a person or thing) briefly (*in*, *into*, *under* water etc.). ME.

SIR W. SCOTT Duck her in the loch, and then we will see whether she is witch or not.

5 Lower (esp. the head) momentarily; jerk down. L16.

D

T. HEGGEN He ducked his head below the level of the rail and crouched there.

duck up NAUTICAL haul up (the foot of a sail etc.) to allow the steersman a view forward.

6 Get away from, avoid, dodge. *colloq.* L19. ▸**b** BRIDGE. Deliberately lose (a trick) or fail to beat (a card) by playing a low card. E20.

R. HYDE Soldiers who had ducked the church parades. G. SWIFT I'm not trying to duck your questions. I'll answer them.

■ **ducker** *noun* (*a*) a person who ducks or dives under water; (*b*) (*obsolete* exc. *dial.*) a diving bird: L15.

D

ducket(t) *noun* see DUCAT.

duckie *noun* var. of DUCKY *noun*.

ducking /ˈdʌkɪŋ/ *verbal noun*[1]. M16.
[ORIGIN from DUCK *verb* + -ING[1].]
The action of DUCK *verb*.
– COMB.: **ducking pond** *noun*[1] *hist.* a pond into which offenders were ducked; **ducking stool** *hist.* a chair at the end of a rising and falling pole, formerly used to duck scolds and other offenders in water.

ducking /ˈdʌkɪŋ/ *noun*[2]. L16.
[ORIGIN from DUCK *noun*[1] + -ING[1].]
The catching, hunting, or shooting of wild ducks.
– COMB.: **ducking pond** *noun*[2] a pond on which ducks may be hunted or shot.

ducking /ˈdʌkɪŋ/ *noun*[3]. E19.
[ORIGIN from DUCK *noun*[3] + -ING[3].]
= DUCK *noun*[3].

duckling /ˈdʌklɪŋ/ *noun*. LME.
[ORIGIN from DUCK *noun*[1] + -LING[1].]
A young duck.
ugly duckling: see UGLY *adjective*.

ducks /dʌks/ *noun*. *colloq.* M20.
[ORIGIN from DUCK *noun*[1] + -S[4].]
= DUCKY *noun*. Cf. DUCK *noun*[1] 2a.

ducky /ˈdʌki/ *noun*. *colloq.* Also **duckie**. M16.
[ORIGIN from DUCK *noun*[1] + -Y[6].]
†**1** A woman's breast. M16–M19.
2 As a term of familiarity or endearment: darling, dear. Cf. DUCK *noun*[1] 2a, DUCKS. E19.

ducky /ˈdʌki/ *adjective*. *colloq.* L19.
[ORIGIN from DUCK *noun*[1] + -Y[1].]
Sweet, pretty; fine, splendid.

duct /dʌkt/ *noun*. M17.
[ORIGIN Latin *ductus* leading, (in medieval Latin) aqueduct, from *duct-* pa. ppl stem of *ducere* to lead. Cf. DUCTUS.]
▸ **I** †**1** The action of leading; guidance. M–L17.
†**2** Course, direction. M17–E18.
3 A stroke drawn or traced as part of a letter; the manner of making such a stroke. M18.
▸ **II 4** ANATOMY & ZOOLOGY. A tube or passage in the body for conveying fluids (now usu. lymph or glandular secretions). Cf. earlier DUCTUS 2. L17. ▸**b** BOTANY. Any of the vessels of the vascular tissue of plants, containing air, water, etc. M19.
ejaculatory duct, ***Müllerian duct***, ***parotid duct***, ***vitelline duct***, ***Wolffian duct***, etc.
5 A channel or tube made for conveying liquid, gas, air, electric cable, etc.; *spec.* a trough in a printing machine which holds the ink and controls its flow to the rollers. E18.
– COMB.: **duct tape** *N. Amer.* strong cloth-backed waterproof adhesive tape; **ductwork** a system of ducts for conveying gases, liquids, etc.
■ **ductal** *adjective* M19. **ducting** *noun* a system of ducts; tubing, piping: M20.

duct /dʌkt/ *verb trans.* M20.
[ORIGIN from the noun.]
Convey through a duct; provide with a duct or ducts (chiefly as ***ducted*** *ppl adjective*).
ducted fan, **ducted propeller** (in a turbine) a multibladed fan, propeller, rotating inside a coaxial duct which prevents radial flow at the blade tips.

ductible /ˈdʌktɪb(ə)l/ *adjective*. Long *rare*. LME.
[ORIGIN Obsolete French, from Latin *duct-*: see DUCT *noun*, -IBLE.]
= DUCTILE.

ductile /ˈdʌktʌɪl/ *adjective*. ME.
[ORIGIN Old French, or Latin *ductilis*, formed as DUCT *noun*: see -ILE.]
1 Flexible, pliant, malleable. ME. ▸**b** *spec.* Of a material, esp. metal: able to be drawn out into wire, tough. E17. ▸**c** Of liquid: (able to be) conducted through channels. E18.

J. H. BURTON The Roman law . . has proved extremely ductile and accommodating. **b** J. S. FOSTER Ductile materials which allow them to yield rather than break.

2 (Of a person etc.) able to be led or drawn, docile; tractable, open to persuasion. E17.

MRS H. WARD The man . . was in truth childishly soft and ductile.

ductility /dʌkˈtɪlɪti/ *noun*. M17.
[ORIGIN from DUCTILE + -ITY.]
1 Ability of a material to be drawn out into wire, extended, or worked upon; malleability, pliableness. M17.
2 Tractableness, docility. M17.

ductless /ˈdʌktlɪs/ *adjective*. M19.
[ORIGIN from DUCT *noun* + -LESS.]
ANATOMY. Having no duct; *spec.* (of a gland) that secretes directly into the bloodstream, endocrine.

ductor /ˈdʌktə/ *noun*. *rare*. LME.
[ORIGIN Latin = leader, from *duct-*: see DUCT *noun*, -OR.]
†**1** A leader; an officer. LME–E17.
†**2** A line running in some direction. Only in M17.
3 A roller forming part of the ink duct of a printing machine from which other rollers derive ink. M19.

ductule /ˈdʌktjuːl/ *noun*. L19.
[ORIGIN Latin, dim. of *ductus*: see DUCT *noun*.]
ANATOMY. A minute duct.

†**ducture** *noun*. E17.
[ORIGIN from Latin *duct-* (see DUCT *noun*) + -URE, after *fracture* etc.]
1 A stroke drawn or traced. Only in E17.
2 Leading, guidance. E17–E18.
3 Extension or movement. Only in L17.
4 A channel. Only in L17.

ductus /ˈdʌktəs/ *noun*. M17.
[ORIGIN Latin: see DUCT *noun*.]
†**1** = DUCT *noun* 2. Only in M17.
2 ANATOMY. = DUCT *noun* 4. Now only in mod. Latin names of particular vessels. M17.
3 = DUCT *noun* 3. L19.

ductus litterarum /ˌdʌktəs lɪtəˈrɑːrəm/ *noun phr.* L19.
[ORIGIN mod. Latin, from Latin *ductus* (see DUCTUS) + *litterarum* genit. pl. of *littera* letter.]
The general shape and formation of letters and their combinations in manuscripts, the study of which may enable the restoration of true readings in a corrupt text.

dud /dʌd/ *noun & adjective*. *slang & dial.* ME.
[ORIGIN Unknown.]
▸ **A** *noun*. **1** An article of clothing. Now only in *pl.*, clothes; effects, things. ME. ▸**b** In *pl.* Rags, ragged clothes. E16.

S. L. ELLIOTT These are me clean duds for meetin' Rosebud at the station.

lag of duds: see LAG *noun*[1] 3.
2 A useless or ineffective person. E19.

J. GALSWORTHY It's when you don't understand that you feel such a dud. R. GRAVES An expert on shell-fish, otherwise a dud.

3 A counterfeit, useless, futile, or unsatisfactory thing; *esp.* (*a*) a bomb, firework, etc., that fails to go off; (*b*) a dishonoured cheque. L19.
▸ **B** *adjective*. Counterfeit; bad, useless, worn out, ineffective, unsatisfactory. E20.

H. ROSHER As luck would have it, the weather was dud. E. HEATH The dud engine would have to be changed.

■ **duddery** *noun* (*dial.*) a place where woollen cloth is sold or manufactured M16. **duddy** *adjective* (*Scot.*) ragged E18.

dude /duːd, djuːd/ *noun & verb*. *slang* (orig. *US*). L19.
[ORIGIN Prob. from German dial. = fool (cf. Low German *dudenkop* 'stupid head').]
▸ **A** *noun*. **1** A fastidious, aesthetic person; a dandy, a fop. *slang*. L19.
2 A holidaymaker in the western US, *esp.* one who holidays on a ranch; a tenderfoot. L19.
3 A fellow, a guy. E20.
– COMB.: **dude ranch** a ranch which provides entertainment for tourists etc.
▸ **B** *verb intrans. & refl.* Dress oneself (*up*) as or like a dude. L19.
■ **dudess**, **dudine** /duːˈdiːn, djuː-/ *nouns* a female dude L19. **dudish** *adjective* characteristic of a dude; foppish: L19.

dudeen /duːˈdiːn/ *noun*. *Irish*. Also **dudheen**. M19.
[ORIGIN Irish *dúidín* dim. of *dúd* pipe: see -EEN[2].]
A short clay tobacco pipe.

dudgeon /ˈdʌdʒ(ə)n/ *noun*[1]. LME.
[ORIGIN Uncertain: cf. Anglo-Norman *digeon* (14th cent.).]
1 A kind of wood used esp. for the handles of knives, daggers, etc. *obsolete* exc. *hist.* LME.
2 a In full ***dudgeon-dagger***. A dagger with a hilt made of dudgeon. Also, a butcher's steel for sharpening knives. *arch.* L16. ▸†**b** The hilt of a dagger, made of dudgeon. *rare* (Shakes.). Only in E17.

dudgeon /ˈdʌdʒ(ə)n/ *noun*[2]. L16.
[ORIGIN Unknown.]
Resentment; a feeling of anger or offence. Chiefly in ***in dudgeon***, ***in high dudgeon***, ***in great dudgeon***, in angry resentment, having taken offence.

SIR W. SCOTT They often parted in deep dudgeon. R. L. STEVENSON I was old and spiteful . . and retired to pour forth my dudgeon to Fanny. D. M. DAVIN He would construe some jest as an insult, and withdraw in a dudgeon.

dudheen *noun* var. of DUDEEN.

due /djuː/ *noun*. LME.
[ORIGIN French *du* (now *dû*) use as noun of pa. pple of *devoir* owe from Latin *debere*: see DUE *adjective & adverb*.]
†**1** Something which is due; a debt. LME–L17.
2 With possess. of the person owed: something which is due to a person legally or morally; one's rights, one's deserts; one's due share or quantity *of*. LME.

JOHN BROOKE The second monarch . . has received less than his due from historians. D. L. SAYERS He had . . missed the promotion he felt to be his due. J. OSBORNE Even from other young women . . she receives her due of respect and admiration.

give a person his or her due treat a person fairly or with justice. **give the devil his due** treat even a bad or undeserving character with justice.
3 a *sing.* & (usu.) in *pl.* An obligatory payment; a fee, a tribute, a toll; a legal charge; *spec.* the membership fee for a college, club, etc. LME. ▸**b** *gen.* In *pl.* With possess. of the person owing: something which is owed by a person; one's debts; *fig.* one's obligations, one's responsibilities. M18.

a P. SCOTT It was like belonging to a Union without having to pay the dues.

a pay one's dues *fig.* fulfil one's obligations; undergo hardships to succeed or gain experience.
†**4** Something which is due to be done; (a) duty. LME–L17.
†**5** Right, just title. L16–M17.
6 NAUTICAL. Something duly or thoroughly done. M19.
for a full due thoroughly, so that it will not need to be done again.

due /djuː/ *adjective & adverb*. ME.
[ORIGIN Old French *deü* (mod. *dû*, fem. *due*) from Proto-Romance var. of Latin *debitus* (cf. DEBIT *noun*) pa. pple of *debere* owe.]
▸ **A** *adjective*. **1** That is owing or payable as an obligation or debt. ME.

J. R. GREEN The amount of service due from the serf had become limited by custom.

fall due, **become due** become immediately payable.
2 That ought to be or to be done; fitting, proper, rightful, appropriate. ME.

H. GREEN Everything must proceed, and in due order. I. WATT His . . sense that due decorums must also be attended to.

due diligence LAW reasonable steps taken by a person in order to avoid committing an offence, especially in buying or selling something. **due process (of law)** fair treatment through the normal judicial system, especially as a citizen's entitlement. **in due course**, **in due time**, etc., after a suitable interval, at the proper time. ***with all due respect***: see RESPECT *noun*.
†**3** *pred.* Foll. by *to*: belonging to or incumbent upon by right or as a duty or necessity. LME–M17.
4 *pred.* That ought to be given, granted, or administered *to*. LME.

STEELE The first Place among our English Poets is due to Milton.

5 Merited, deserved. LME.

JOSEPH HALL The Lord . . shall execute due vengeance upon Satan. H. ADAMS Somewhat more than her due share of conventional moral reproof.

6 Adequate, sufficient. LME.

J. WESLEY A due Degree of Exercise.

7 ***due to***: ▸**a** *adjectival phr.* Attributable to, ascribable to. M17. ▸**b** *prepositional phr.* Because of, on account of, owing to. Often considered *erron.* L19.

a E. M. FORSTER Death . . was due to heart disease. B. BAINBRIDGE He liked touching people—it was due to him being a foreigner. **b** J. D. MACDONALD The beach dwindled due to erosion.

8 *pred.* Expected, intended, or under engagement to arrive or appear, or *to do* something, at a specified time or *absol.* now; scheduled or in line *for* something at a specified time or *absol.* now. M19.

F. M. FORD He advised me to buy Caledonian Deferred, since they were due to rise. L. MACNEICE My boat to Lochboisdale—due at 5.30. K. AMIS They were due back the day before yesterday. A. PRICE He was due for a CID transfer in a few months' time. F. WELDON Susan enquires when the baby is due.

– SPECIAL COLLOCATIONS: **due date**: on which something falls due, esp. the payment of a bill or the expected birth of a baby.
▸ **B** *adverb*. **1** = DULY. *arch.* L16.

SHAKES. *2 Hen. IV* Every third word a lie, duer paid to the hearer than the Turk's tribute.

2 Of a compass point, or a direction: exactly, directly. L16.

M. INNES There is a . . mission station about eighty miles due north. G. L. HARDING From Karak the road runs almost due south.

– NOTE: *Due to* as a prepositional phr. in the sense 'because of' is traditionally condemned as incorrect on the grounds that *due* is an adjective and should not be used as a preposition; *owing to* is often recommended as a better alternative. However, the prepositional use is now common in all types of literature and is regarded as part of standard English.
■ **dueful** *adjective* (*arch.*) due, appropriate L16. **dueness** *noun* LME.

†**due** *verb trans.* Also (earlier) **dow**. ME–L16.
[ORIGIN Old French & mod. French *douer*: see ENDOW. Later form after ENDUE.]
Endow.

duel /ˈdjuːəl/ *noun*. L15.
[ORIGIN Italian *duello* or Latin *duellum*, arch. form of *bellum* war, used in medieval Latin for judicial single combat.]
1 **a** A judicial single combat. *obsolete* exc. *hist.* L15. ▸**b** Chiefly *hist.* A private fight between two people, prearranged and fought with deadly weapons, usually in the presence of two seconds, in order to settle a quarrel. E17.
2 Any contest between two people, parties, animals, or forces. L16.
3 Duelling as a practice. *rare*. E17.

duel /ˈdjuːəl/ *verb*. Infl. **-ll-**, *__-l-__. M17.
[ORIGIN from the noun.]
1 *verb intrans.* Fight a duel or duels. M17.
duelling pistol a long-barrelled pistol of a type made in identical pairs and used for duelling.
†**2** *verb trans.* Encounter or overcome in a duel. M17–E18.
■ **dueller** *noun* a duellist E17.

duellist /ˈdjuːəlɪst/ *noun*. Also ***duelist**. L16.
[ORIGIN from DUEL *noun* + -IST, after French *duelliste* or Italian *duellista*.]
A person who fights a duel or duels.

duello /djuːˈɛləʊ/ *noun*. Pl. **-os**. L16.
[ORIGIN Italian = duel.]
1 Duelling, as a custom; the established code of duellists. L16.
2 A duel. Now *rare* or *obsolete*. E17.

duende /duːˈɛndeɪ, *foreign* ˈdwende/ *noun*. E20.
[ORIGIN Spanish.]
1 A ghost, an evil spirit. E20.
2 Inspiration, magic. M20.

duenna /djuːˈɛnə/ *noun*. M17.
[ORIGIN Spanish *dueña*, †*duenna* from Latin *domina* lady, mistress.]
1 An older woman acting as governess and companion to one or more girls, esp. within a Spanish family. M17.
2 A chaperone. E18.

duet /djuːˈɛt/ *noun & verb*. M18.
[ORIGIN German *Duett* or Italian *duetto*, from *duo* two: see DUO, -ET[1].]
▸ **A** *noun*. MUSIC. (A composition for) two voices or two performers. M18.

fig.: S. MIDDLETON The conversation became a duet between the Hollies and Terry.

▸ **B** *verb intrans.* Infl. **-tt-**. Perform a duet (*with*). E19.
■ **duettist** *noun* a person who takes part in a duet L19.

duettino /djuːɛˈtiːnəʊ/ *noun*. Pl. **-os**. M19.
[ORIGIN Italian, dim. of DUETTO.]
A short duet.

duetto /djuːˈɛtəʊ/ *noun*. Pl. **-os**. E18.
[ORIGIN Italian, dim. of *duo* duet: see DUO.]
= DUET *noun*.

duff /dʌf/ *noun*[1]. L18.
[ORIGIN Unknown: cf. DUFF *verb*[2], DUFFER *noun*[1].]
1 Something worthless; counterfeit money; smuggled goods; the passing or selling of such things. *slang*. L18.
2 Decaying vegetable matter covering forest ground. *Scot. & US*. E19.
3 Coal dust; dross. M19.

duff /dʌf/ *noun*[2]. M19.
[ORIGIN North. var. of DOUGH *noun*. Cf. *enough*.]
1 Dough, paste. *dial.* M19.
2 A boiled pudding; a dumpling. M19.

R. H. DANA Christmas . . . The only change was that we had a 'plum duff' for dinner.

duff /dʌf/ *noun*[3]. *colloq.* M19.
[ORIGIN Uncertain; prob. = DUFF *noun*[1].]
The buttocks.

R. CRITCHFIELD These are not people who sit on their duff, expecting a handout.

duff /dʌf/ *noun*[4]. *slang* (orig. *Austral.*). M20.
[ORIGIN Uncertain; perh. rel. to DUFF *noun*[1].]
up the duff, pregnant.

duff /dʌf/ *adjective*. *colloq.* L19.
[ORIGIN Perh. from DUFF *noun*[1], but cf. DUFFER *noun*[2].]
Worthless, false, bad, defective, dud.

J. LYMINGTON I went down to the pub because the play was so duff. *Which?* To find the duff bulb you'll have to test each bulb in turn.

duff /dʌf/ *verb*[1] *trans. & intrans.* E19.
[ORIGIN Back-form. from DUFFER *noun*[2].]
In golf, mishit (a shot or a ball); *gen.* make a mess of (something), bungle.

duff /dʌf/ *verb*[2]. *slang.* M19.
[ORIGIN Perh. back-form. from DUFFER *noun*[1].]
1 *verb trans.* Falsify (a thing); pass off (a worthless article) as valuable. M19.
2 *verb trans.* Alter the brands on (stolen cattle); rustle (cattle); graze (stock) illicitly on another's land. *Austral.* M19.
3 *verb trans.* Cheat (a person). M19.
4 *verb intrans.* With *up*: become foggy or hazy. L19.
5 *verb trans.* With *up*: beat up. M20.

C. GLAZEBROOK I was always getting duffed up at school.

■ **duffing** *adjective* (**a**) that duffs something; (**b**) counterfeit, worthless but passed off as valuable: M19.

duffadar *noun* var. of DAFADAR.

duffel *noun* var. of DUFFLE.

duffer /ˈdʌfə/ *noun*[1]. M18.
[ORIGIN Unknown: cf. DUFF *noun*[1].]
1 A person who sells worthless articles as valuable on false pretences. M18.
2 A pedlar, a hawker. L18.
3 A person who duffs cattle. *Austral.* M19.

duffer /ˈdʌfə/ *noun*[2] *& verb*. *colloq.* M19.
[ORIGIN Perh. alt. of DOWFART.]
▸ **A** *noun*. **1** A useless, incompetent, or stupid person. M19.

M. E. BRADDON I was always a duffer at dancing.

2 A useless or defective article; *esp.* a counterfeit coin. M19.
3 An unproductive mine or claim. *Austral. & NZ*. M19.
▸ **B** *verb intrans.* Of a mine: prove no good, give *out*. *Austral. & NZ*. L19.

duffle /ˈdʌf(ə)l/ *noun & adjective*. Also **duffel**. M17.
[ORIGIN from *Duffel*, a town in Belgium.]
▸ **A** *noun*. **1** A coarse woollen cloth with a thick nap. M17.
2 Sporting or camping equipment; food and clothing. Chiefly *US*. M19.
3 = ***duffle coat*** below. M20.
▸ **B** *attrib.* or as *adjective*. Made of duffle. L17.
– SPECIAL COLLOCATIONS & COMB.: **duffle bag** a cylindrical canvas bag closed by a drawstring. **duffle coat** a coat made of duffle; *spec.* a warm coat with a hood, fastened at the front with toggles.

dufrenite /duːˈfreɪnʌɪt, djuː-/ *noun*. M19.
[ORIGIN from Pierre *Dufrenoy* (1792–1857), French mineralogist + -ITE[1].]
MINERALOGY. A monoclinic hydrated basic phosphate of ferrous and ferric iron, usu. occurring as dark-green to brown botryoidal masses or crusts.

dufrenoysite /duːfrɪˈnɔɪzʌɪt, djuː-/ *noun*. M19.
[ORIGIN formed as DUFRENITE + -*s*- + -ITE[1].]
MINERALOGY. A monoclinic sulphide of lead and arsenic usu. occurring as grey prisms with a metallic lustre.

dufter /ˈdʌftə/ *noun*. L18.
[ORIGIN Urdu from Arabic, Persian *daftar* register from Greek *diphthera* hide. Cf. DEFTERDAR.]
In the Indian subcontinent: an official register or record; also, a business office.

dufus *noun* var. of DOOFUS.

dug /dʌg/ *noun*. M16.
[ORIGIN Unknown.]
The udder of a female mammal, *derog.* a woman's breast; a teat, a nipple.
■ **duggy** *adjective* (*rare*) having large dugs E17.

dug *verb pa. t. & pple*: see DIG *verb*.

dugite /ˈdjuːgʌɪt/ *noun*. L19.
[ORIGIN Nyungar *dukayj*.]
A highly venomous elapid snake, *Pseudonaja affinis*, of SW Australia, similar to the related brown snakes.

dugong /ˈduːgɒŋ, ˈdjuː-/ *noun*. Pl. **-s**, same. E19.
[ORIGIN Ult. from Malay *duyung*.]
A sirenian, *Dugong dugon*, inhabiting coastal waters of the Indian Ocean, the SW Pacific, and adjacent seas.

dugout /ˈdʌgaʊt/ *ppl adjective & noun*. E18.
[ORIGIN from *dug* pa. pple of DIG *verb* + OUT *adverb*. Cf. *dig out* s.v. DIG *verb*.]
▸ **A** *ppl adjective*. Hollowed out by digging; excavated; *esp.* (of a canoe) made from a hollowed out tree trunk. E18.
▸ **B** *noun*. **1** A dugout canoe. E19.
2 **a** A rough dwelling hollowed out in a bank or hillside and roofed with turf, canvas, etc. Chiefly *US*. M19. ▸**b** A hollowed-out roofed shelter used in trench warfare; an underground shelter for protection from air raids or nuclear attack. E20. ▸**c** A low shelter at the side of a baseball, football, etc., pitch, with seating for the team manager, trainer, players, etc. Orig. *US*. E20.
3 A person of outdated appearance or ideas; *spec.* a retired officer recalled to service. *slang*. M19.

duh /dʌ, də/ *interjection*. *colloq.* M20.
[ORIGIN Imit. Cf. DOH.]
Expr. inarticulacy or incomprehension; implying that someone has said something foolish or extremely obvious.

DUI *abbreviation*. *US*.
Driving under the influence (of drugs or alcohol).

duiker /ˈdʌɪkə, *foreign* dœɪkər/ *noun*. *S. Afr.* Also **duyker**. Pl. **-s**, same. L18.
[ORIGIN Dutch = diver from Middle Dutch *dûker*, from *dûken* dive, DUCK *verb*; sense 1 from the animal's habit of plunging through bushes when alarmed.]
1 Any of various small African antelopes of the genera *Cephalophus* and *Silvicapra*; spec. *S. grimmia*, widespread in southern African savannah and bush. L18.
2 A cormorant. M19.

du jour /dy ʒuːr, d(j)uː ˈʒʊə/ *adjectival phr.* Also (*erron.*) ***de jour***. L20.
[ORIGIN French, lit. 'of the day'. Cf. ***plat du jour*** s.v. PLAT *noun*[4].]
Used to describe something that is enjoying great but probably short-lived popularity or publicity.

Guardian The media eagerly hyped the issue *du jour*.

duka /ˈduːkə/ *noun*. E20.
[ORIGIN Kiswahili from Arabic *dukkān* shop, store, business.]
In Kenya, a shop, a store.

duk-duk /ˈdʌkdʌk/ *noun*. L19.
[ORIGIN Local name.]
(A member of) a secret society in New Britain (Papua New Guinea) which executes justice and practises sorcery.

duke /djuːk/ *noun*. Also (esp. in titles) **D-**. OE.
[ORIGIN Old French & mod. French *duc* from Latin DUX, *duc-* leader, rel. to *ducere* to lead.]
1 In some European countries: a sovereign prince, the ruler of a duchy. OE. ▸†**b** = DOGE. M16–E19.
2 †**a** A leader; a captain, a general; a chief, a ruler. ME–L16. ▸**b** ROMAN HISTORY. [Latin DUX.] A provincial military commander under the later emperors. M17.
3 In Britain and some other countries: a male holding the highest hereditary title of nobility (ranking next below a prince). LME.
4 More fully ***duke cherry***. A hybrid between the sweet cherry, *Prunus avium*, and sour cherry, *P. cerasus*; the fruit of such a tree. M17.
5 [from *Duke of Yorks* below.] A hand, a fist, a finger. Usu. in *pl.* *slang*. L19. ▸**b** The verdict in a boxing match (from the practice of raising the victor's arm). *slang*. M20.

J. MITFORD Always ready with dukes up to go to the offensive. **b** D. RUNYON Ledoux gets the duke by unanimous vote of the officials.

– PHRASES: ***dine with Duke Humphrey***: see DINE *verb* 1. ***duke cherry***: see sense 4 above. ***Duke of Argyll's tea plant***: see ***tea plant*** s.v. TEA *noun*. ***Duke of Argyll's tea tree***: see TEA TREE 3. **Duke of Burgundy (fritillary)** a small European butterfly, *Hamearis lucina* (family Riodinidae or Nemeobiidae), which resembles a fritillary and has dark brown wings with rows of orange markings. ***Duke of Exeter's*** DAUGHTER. **Duke of Yorks** *rhyming slang* 'forks', i.e. fingers, hands, fists. ***Iron Duke***: see IRON *noun & adjective*. ***grand duke***: see GRAND *adjective*[1]. **royal duke** a duke who is also a royal prince.
■ **dukeling** *noun* (**a**) a petty duke; (**b**) *arch.* a duke's child: E17. **dukely** *adjective* (*rare*) belonging to or befitting a duke L16. **dukeship** *noun* the office of a duke; (a humorous title for) a duke: M16.

duke /djuːk/ *verb*. LME.
[ORIGIN from the noun.]
1 *verb trans.* Confer dukedom on. LME.
2 *verb intrans. & trans.* (with *it*). Act as a duke. E17.
3 *verb trans. slang*. Shake hands with. M19.
4 *verb trans. & intrans.* Fight with the fists, box, punch. Also ***duke it out***. *US slang*. M20.

dukedom /ˈdjuːkdəm/ *noun*. LME.
[ORIGIN from DUKE *noun* + -DOM.]
1 The territory ruled by a duke; a duchy. LME.
2 The dignity or office of a duke. L15.

dukery /ˈdjuːkəri/ *noun*. M16.
[ORIGIN from DUKE *noun*: see -ERY, -RY.]
1 †**a** The dignity or office of a duke. M–L16. ▸**b** A duchy. *rare*. M19.
2 The residence or estate of a duke; *spec.* (***the Dukeries***) an area of N. Nottinghamshire containing several ducal estates. E19.

Dukhobor /ˈduːkəbɔː/ *noun*. Also **Doukh-**. L19.
[ORIGIN Russian, from *dukh* spirit + *borets* wrestler.]
A member of a Russian Christian sect similar to the Society of Friends, many members of which migrated to Canada in 1899 after persecution for refusing military service.

dukun /ˈduːkʌn/ *noun*. *SE Asian*. E20.
[ORIGIN Indonesian.]
A traditional healer believed to have spiritual and occult powers.

dukw *noun* var. of DUCK *noun*[4].

dulcamara /dʌlkəˈmɛːrə/ *noun*. L16.
[ORIGIN medieval Latin, from Latin *dulcis* sweet + *amara* bitter.]
(A medicinal extract from) woody nightshade or bittersweet, *Solanum dulcamara*.

dulce /ˈduːlseɪ/ *noun*. M17.
[ORIGIN Sense 1 from the adjective; sense 2 from Spanish.]
†**1** Sweetness, gentleness. M17–E18.
2 A sweet substance; a sweet wine. M19.

D

†dulce *adjective*. L15–E18.
[ORIGIN Latin *dulcis* or a refashioning of DOUCE after the Latin.]
Sweet (to the senses); agreeable; soothing.

dulce de leche /ˈdʌlˌseɪ də ˈlɛtʃeɪ/ *noun*. E20.
[ORIGIN Amer. Spanish, from *dulce* sweet + *de* of + *leche* milk.]
A sweet Argentinian spread or sauce made from caramelized milk.

dulcet /ˈdʌlsɪt/ *noun*. LME.
[ORIGIN from (the same root as) DULCET *adjective*. Cf. DOUCET *noun*.]
†**1** = DOUCET *noun* 2. Only in LME. ▸**b** A dulcet note or tone. Only in L16.
†**2** = DOUCET *noun* 3. L16–M17.
3 MUSIC. A soft organ stop of 4-ft length and pitch. L19.

dulcet /ˈdʌlsɪt/ *adjective*. Also †**doucet**. LME.
[ORIGIN Old French & mod. French *doucet* dim. of *doux*, fem. *douce*, refashioned after Latin *dulcis*: see -ET[1].]
1 Sweet to the taste or smell. *arch.* LME.
> LONGFELLOW Catawba wine Has a taste more divine, More dulcet, delicious, and dreamy.

2 Sweet to the eye, (now esp.) ear, or feelings; pleasing to hear; soothing, mild. LME.
> C. BAX The climate there is so dulcet that they are immune from all disease. K. CROSSLEY-HOLLAND Light-headed with desire, wholly taken in by her dulcet tones.

■ **dulcetly** *adverb* M19. **dulcetness** *noun* E16.

dulcian /ˈdʌlsɪən/ *noun*. M19.
[ORIGIN German *Dulzian*, or from DULCIANA. Cf. Old French *doulçaine* etc., a kind of flute.]
1 *hist.* An early one-piece bassoon. M19.
2 = BASSOON 2. Also = DULCIANA. M19.

dulciana /dʌlsɪˈɑːnə/ *noun*. L18.
[ORIGIN medieval Latin, from Latin *dulcis* sweet.]
MUSIC. A small-scaled, soft, open metal diapason usu. of 8-ft length and pitch.

dulcifluous /dʌlˈsɪflʊəs/ *adjective*. *rare*. E18.
[ORIGIN from Latin *dulcis* sweet + *-fluus* flowing + -OUS.]
Sweetly or softly flowing.

dulcify /ˈdʌlsɪfʌɪ/ *verb trans*. L16.
[ORIGIN Latin *dulcificare*, from *dulcis* sweet: see -FY.]
1 Make sweet to the taste, sweeten; *fig.* sweeten in temper, mollify. L16.
†**2** CHEMISTRY. Wash the soluble salts out of; neutralize the acidity of. E17–E19.
■ **dulcification** *noun* E17.

dulciloquent /dʌlˈsɪləkwənt/ *adjective*. M17.
[ORIGIN from Latin *dulcis* sweet + *loquens* pres. pple of *loqui* speak: see -ENT.]
Speaking sweetly.

dulcimer /ˈdʌlsɪmə/ *noun*. L15.
[ORIGIN Old French *doulcemer*, *-mele* corresp. to Spanish †*dulcemele*, Italian *dolcemelle*, presumably from Latin = sweet song.]
1 A musical instrument with metal strings of graduated length over a trapezoidal soundbox, struck with hammers. L15.
2 More fully ***Appalachian dulcimer***. An American folk instrument, a kind of zither. M20.

dulcin /ˈdʌlsɪn/ *noun*. Also **-ine**. M19.
[ORIGIN from Latin *dulcis* sweet + -IN[1].]
CHEMISTRY. †**1** = DULCITOL. M19–E20.
2 A synthetic compound, *p*-ethoxyphenylurea, $C_9H_{12}N_2O_2$, formerly used as a sweetening agent. L19.

dulcinea /dʌlsɪˈniːə, -ˈsɪnɪə/ *noun*. M17.
[ORIGIN *Dulcinea*, object of Don Quixote's devotion in the book by M. Cervantes.]
An idolized and idealized woman; a sweetheart.

dulcite /ˈdʌlsʌɪt/ *noun*. Now *rare* or *obsolete*. M19.
[ORIGIN from Latin *dulcis* sweet + -ITE[1].]
CHEMISTRY. = DULCITOL.

dulcitol /ˈdʌlsɪtɒl/ *noun*. L19.
[ORIGIN from DULCITE + -OL.]
CHEMISTRY. A hexahydric alcohol, $C_6H_{14}O_6$, which is a reduced counterpart of galactose and occurs in certain plants.

dulcitone /ˈdʌlsɪtəʊn/ *noun*. L19.
[ORIGIN from Latin *dulcis* sweet + TONE *noun*.]
MUSIC. A keyboard instrument with steel forks struck by hammers.

dulcitude /ˈdʌlsɪtjuːd/ *noun*. Now *rare*. E17.
[ORIGIN Latin *dulcitudo*, from *dulcis* sweet: see -TUDE.]
Sweetness.

dulcorous /ˈdʌlk(ə)rəs/ *adjective*. *rare*. L17.
[ORIGIN from Latin *dulcor* sweetness + -OUS.]
Sweet.

dule *noun* var. of DOLE *noun*[2].

dulia /djʊˈlʌɪə/ *noun*. LME.
[ORIGIN medieval Latin from Greek *douleia* servitude, from *doulos* slave.]
ROMAN CATHOLIC CHURCH. The veneration properly given to saints and angels. Cf. HYPERDULIA, LATRIA.

dull /dʌl/ *adjective*.
[ORIGIN Old English *dol* = Old Saxon (Dutch) *dol*, Old High German *tol* (German *toll*); superseded in Middle English by forms from cognate Middle Low German, Middle Dutch *dul*.]
1 Slow of understanding, not quick-witted; obtuse, stupid. In early use also occas., fatuous, foolish. OE.
> H. JAMES Her quick perception . . made him feel irretrievably dull.

2 Of an edge or weapon: blunt. ME.
> SHAKES. *Rich. III* The murd'rous knife was dull . . Till it was whetted on thy stone-hard heart.

3 Without keen sensation; insensible, inanimate, benumbed; *dial.* hard of hearing, deaf. LME. ▸**b** Of pain etc.: indistinctly felt, not acute. E18.
> TENNYSON You never would hear it; your ears are so dull. **b** OED A sharp pain, followed by a dull ache.

4 Slow-moving, sluggish; inactive; drowsy. LME. ▸**b** Of trade: slow, stagnant, not brisk. Of goods etc.: not easily saleable. E18.
> R. CHANDLER About four in the morning, when . . the crew were all dull with fatigue. A. SILLITOE Coal to bank up the dull fire.

5 Of a person, a mood, etc.: depressed, listless, not lively or cheerful. LME.
> DICKENS When other people were merry, Mrs. Varden was dull.

6 Uninteresting; uneventful: unexciting, tedious, boring. LME.
> A. S. NEILL There is always something happening . . there isn't a dull day in the whole year.

7 Of colour, sound, taste, etc.: not bright, vivid, or keen; dim, indistinct, insipid. LME. ▸**b** Of weather: overcast, cloudy; gloomy. L16.
> J. CONRAD The sun sank low, and from glowing white changed to a dull red. **b** J. TYNDALL Dawn was dull, but the sky cleared as the day advanced.

— COMB. & SPECIAL COLLOCATIONS: **dull emitter** a thermionic valve filament which operates at a relatively low temperature; a valve with such a filament; **dull-head** a stupid person, a blockhead; **dull-headed** *adjective* stupid, slow-witted; †**dull-pate** = ***dull-head*** above; **dull-witted** *adjective* = ***dull-headed*** above.
■ **dullify** *verb trans.* (*colloq.*, now *rare*) make dull M17. **dullish** *adjective* rather dull LME.

dull /dʌl/ *verb*. ME.
[ORIGIN from the adjective.]
1 *verb trans.* Make sluggish or inert; make stupid or unresponsive. ME.
> R. LEHMANN Dancing dulls the brain a bit.

2 *verb trans.* Make blunt. ME.
> B. CORNWALL Your sword is dulled With carnage.

dull the edge of *fig.* make less sensitive, interesting, or effective.
†**3** *verb trans.* Make listless, depressed, or gloomy. LME–E17.
4 *verb trans.* Make less sensitive; blunt the keenness of (senses, feelings, etc.). LME.
> TENNYSON Weeping dulls the inward pain. B. MALAMUD His hearing is dulled in the right ear since Berezhinsky hit him.

5 *verb trans.* Take away the brightness, clearness, or intensity of; make indistinct; tarnish. LME.
> M. SINCLAIR Smears of damp dulled the polished lid of the piano.

6 *verb intrans.* Become dull(er); become sluggish or stupid; become blunt; grow dim or tarnished. LME.
> G. P. SCROPE Lava . . at a white heat, gradually dulling to a faint red.

dullard /ˈdʌləd/ *noun & adjective*. ME.
[ORIGIN Prob. from Middle Dutch *dull-*, *dollaert*, from *dul* DULL *adjective*: see -ARD.]
▸ **A** *noun*. A dull or stupid person; a dolt, a dunce. ME.
▸ **B** *adjective*. Dull, stupid. L16.

dullness /ˈdʌlnɪs/ *noun*. Also **dulness**. LME.
[ORIGIN from DULL *adjective* + -NESS.]
The quality or state of being dull.

dullsville /ˈdʌlzvɪl/ *noun*. *N. Amer. slang*. Also **D-**. M20.
[ORIGIN from DULL *adjective* + *-s-* + -VILLE.]
A town, place, or situation of extreme dullness or boredom.

dully /ˈdʌli/ *adjective*. Long *rare*. L15.
[ORIGIN from DULL *adjective* + -Y[1].]
1 Gloomy, dreary, miserable. L15.
2 Faint, indistinct. M19.

dully /ˈdʌl-li/ *adverb*. LME.
[ORIGIN from DULL *adjective* + -LY[2].]
In a dull manner.

dulness *noun* var. of DULLNESS.

dulocracy /djuːˈlɒkrəsi/ *noun*. *rare*. Also **doul-** /duː-/. M17.
[ORIGIN Greek *doulokratia*, from *doulos* slave: see -CRACY.]
Government by slaves.

dulosis /djuːˈləʊsɪs/ *noun*. E20.
[ORIGIN Greek *doulōsis* slavery, from *douloun* enslave, from *doulos* slave.]
ENTOMOLOGY. The enslavement by certain kinds of ant of worker ants of other species.
■ **dulotic** /-ˈlɒtɪk/ *adjective* E20.

dulse /dʌls/ *noun*. Also (*Scot.*) **dilse** /dɪls/. E17.
[ORIGIN Irish, Gaelic *duileasg* = Welsh *delysg*, *dylusg*.]
An edible seaweed, *Rhodymenia palmata*, with dark red, palmately divided fronds.

dulsome /ˈdʌlsəm/ *adjective*. *obsolete* exc. *dial.* E17.
[ORIGIN from DULL *adjective* + -SOME[1].]
Dull, dreary, dismal.

duly /ˈdjuːli/ *adverb*. LME.
[ORIGIN from DUE *adjective* + -LY[2].]
In due manner, order, form, or season; correctly, properly, fitly; punctually; sufficiently.
> E. YOUNG The Man Is yet unborn, who duly weighs an Hour. J. BUCHAN The altar was being duly prepared for the victim. D. CECIL At . . the correct age for first love, he duly fell in love with her.

Duma /ˈduːmə, ˈdjuː-/ *noun*. L19.
[ORIGIN Russian.]
A Russian elective municipal council; *spec.* (***a***) the elective legislative council of state of 1905–17 (***b***) the lower house of the modern Russian parliament.

dumb /dʌm/ *adjective & noun*.
[ORIGIN Old English *dumb* = Old Frisian, Old Saxon *dumb* (Dutch *dom*) stupid, Old High German *tumb* stupid, deaf (German *dumm* stupid), Old Norse *dumbr*, Gothic *dumbs* mute. In sense 4 prob. reinforced by German *dumm*, Dutch *dom*.]
▸ **A** *adjective*. **1** Lacking the faculty of speech, either abnormally (in humans) or normally (in other animals and things). OE. ▸**b** Temporarily deprived of speech by surprise, shock, grief, or fear. Chiefly in ***strike dumb***. ME. ▸**c** Inarticulate; having no voice in government etc. M19.
(*as*) ***dumb as a beetle***, (*as*) ***dumb as a stone***, etc.
2 Not emitting or accompanied by sound; silent, mute; drowned out. OE. ▸**b** Of an action, an expression, etc.: performed or made without speech. M16.
> SHELLEY Its thunder made the cataracts dumb. TENNYSON The streets are dumb with snow. **b** DICKENS Pleasant answered with a short dumb nod. G. GREENE He was aware . . of her dumb approval.

3 Persistently silent; taciturn; reticent. ME.
> SHAKES. *Haml.* This spirit, dumb to us, will speak to him.

4 Stupid, ignorant, foolish. ME. ▸**b** Of a computer terminal: not having independent data-processing capability. Opp. INTELLIGENT *adjective*. L20.
> D. HAMMETT I'm not dumb enough to fall for that.

5 Meaningless, senseless. Now *rare*. M16.
> TINDALE The byshop of Rome . . with his domme traditions.

6 Lacking some expected quality, feature, or accessory. Usu. *attrib.* (as in some special collocations below). L16.
▸ **B** *absol.* as *noun*. A dumb person. Long chiefly *collect. pl.*, *the* dumb people as a class. OE.
— SPECIAL COLLOCATIONS & COMB.: ***deaf and dumb***: see DEAF *adjective & noun*. **dumb ague** *arch.* malarial fever without clearly defined episodic attacks. **dumb animal** an animal regarded pityingly or contemptuously as without speech. **dumb-ass** *adjective* (*N. Amer. colloq.*) stupid, brainless. **dumb barge**: without means of propulsion. **dumb blonde** a pretty but stupid blonde person (usu. female). **dumb cane** a W. Indian plant, *Dieffenbachia seguine*, of the arum family, with an acrid juice which swells the tongue and destroys the power of speech. **dumb chum** *joc.* = ***dumb friend*** below. **dumb cluck** *slang* a stupid person, a blockhead. ***dumb crambo***: see CRAMBO 2. **dumb friend** *joc.* a domestic animal. **dumbhead** *slang* a stupid person, a blockhead. **dumb iron** either of a pair of curved side-members of a motor-vehicle chassis, joining it to the front springs. **dumb nettle** = ***dead-nettle*** s.v. DEAD *adjective*. **dumb ox** *colloq.* a stupid, awkward, or taciturn person (***the dumb ox*** St Thomas Aquinas). **dumb peal** a muffled peal of bells. **dumb piano** a set of piano keys for exercising the fingers. **dumb play** = ***dumbshow*** (b) below. **dumb sheave** NAUTICAL a sheaveless block having a hole for a rope to be rove through. **dumbshow** (***a***) in early drama, a part of a play acted without words, exhibiting additional action or simply emblematical; (***b***) significant action without speech; an instance of this. **dumbstricken**, **dumbstruck** *adjectives* rendered temporarily speechless. **dumb waiter** a movable table, esp. with revolving shelves, for use in a dining room; a small lift for conveying food, tableware, etc.
— NOTE: Although the sense 'lacking the faculty of speech' is the original one, it has been overwhelmed by sense 4 to such an extent that it is likely to cause offence when used of people. Alternatives such as *speech-impaired* are preferred.
■ **dumbly** *adverb* M16. **dumbness** *noun* the quality or condition of being dumb, inability to speak (***deaf-dumbness***: see DEAF *adjective & noun*) LME.

dumb /dʌm/ *verb*. ME.
[ORIGIN from the adjective.]
†**1** *verb intrans.* Become dumb or silent. Only in ME.
2 *verb trans.* Make dumb or silent. E17.
3 *verb trans. & intrans.* ***dumb down***, simplify or reduce the intellectual content of (written or broadcast material etc.), esp. in order to appeal to a mass audience. *colloq.* (orig. *US*). M20.

P. BRONSON Having to translate his work into dumbed-down metaphors for the shiny-shoe set.

dumb-bell /ˈdʌmbɛl/ *noun*. Also **dumbell**. E18.
[ORIGIN from DUMB *adjective* + BELL *noun*[1].]
1 Formerly, an apparatus like that for ringing a church bell, used for exercise. Now, a short bar weighted at each end with a ball or disc, used usu. in pairs for exercising the muscles. E18.
2 An object shaped like a dumb-bell, with two rounded masses connected by a narrow bar. M19.
3 A stupid person, a blockhead. *slang*. E20.

dumb-dumb /ˈdʌmdʌm/ *noun*. *slang* (orig. *US*). Also **dum-dum**. L20.
[ORIGIN Redupl. of DUMB *adjective*.]
A stupid person, a blockhead.

dumbell *noun* var. of DUMB-BELL.

dumbfound /dʌmˈfaʊnd/ *verb trans.* Also **dumfound**. M17.
[ORIGIN App. from DUMB *adjective* + CONFOUND.]
Strike dumb; confound, nonplus. Chiefly as ***dumbfounded*** *ppl adjective*.

dumbfounder /dʌmˈfaʊndə/ *verb trans.* Also **dumfounder**. E18.
[ORIGIN from DUMBFOUND, assim. to FOUNDER *verb*.]
= DUMBFOUND. Chiefly as ***dumbfoundered*** *ppl adjective*.

dumble /ˈdʌmb(ə)l/ *noun*. *dial*. L16.
[ORIGIN App. formed as DUMMEL. Cf. DRUMBLE *noun*.]
A bumblebee. Also ***dumble-bee***.
– COMB.: **dumbledore** a loud buzzing insect, esp. a bumblebee.

dumbo /ˈdʌmbəʊ/ *noun*. *slang*. Pl. **-os**. M20.
[ORIGIN from DUMB *adjective* + -O, with pronunc. infl. by JUMBO.]
A stupid person, a blockhead.

D. GLAZER She didn't want Wayne to think she was a dumbo.

†**dumby** *noun* & *adjective* var. of DUMMY *noun* & *adjective*.

dum casta /dʌm ˈkastə/ *noun* & *adjectival phr.* L19.
[ORIGIN Abbreviation of Latin *dum sola et casta vixerit* as long as she shall live alone and chaste.]
LAW (now *hist.*). (Designating) a clause conferring on a woman a benefit which is to cease should she (re)marry or enter a new relationship.

dumdum /ˈdʌmdʌm/ *noun*. Also **dum-dum**. L19.
[ORIGIN *DumDum*, a town and arsenal near Kolkata (Calcutta), India, where the bullets were first produced.]
In full ***dumdum bullet***. A kind of soft-nosed bullet that expands on impact to inflict extensive injuries.

dum-dum *noun*[1] var. of DUM-DUM.

dum-dum *noun*[2] var. of DUMB-DUMB.

dumfound, **dumfounder** *verbs* vars. of DUMBFOUND, DUMBFOUNDER.

dumka /ˈdʊmkə/ *noun*. Pl. **-kas**, **-ky** /-ki/. L19.
[ORIGIN Czech & Polish from Ukrainian.]
An alternately melancholy and cheerful piece of Slavonic music.

dummel /ˈdʌm(ə)l/ *noun* & *adjective*. *dial*. L16.
[ORIGIN App. formed as DUMBLE. Cf. DRUMBLE *noun*.]
▸ **A** *noun*. A stupid person. L16.
▸ **B** *adjective*. Stupid; sluggish. L19.

dummerer /ˈdʌmərə/ *noun*. *slang*. *obsolete* exc. *hist.* M16.
[ORIGIN from DUMB *adjective*.]
A beggar pretending to lack the faculty of speech.

dummkopf /ˈdʊmkɒpf/ *noun*. *slang* (orig. *US*). Also †**domcop**. E19.
[ORIGIN German, from *dumm* (see DUMB *adjective*) + *Kopf* head. Var. from Dutch.]
A stupid person, a blockhead.

dummy /ˈdʌmi/ *noun* & *adjective*. Also †**dumby**. L16.
[ORIGIN from DUMB *adjective* + -Y[6].]
▸ **A** *noun*. **1** A person who cannot speak. *colloq*. L16. ▸**b** A beggar pretending to be both deaf and unable to speak. L19.
2 a WHIST. A hand dealt to an imaginary fourth player which is turned up and played by one of the other players as partner; (a game played with) this imaginary player. M18. ▸**b** BRIDGE. The partner of the declarer, whose cards are exposed after the first lead; this player's hand. L19.
3 A stupid person, a blockhead. L18.

New Yorker You've just been had, dummy.

4 A person taking no real part or present only for appearances, a figurehead; a person who is merely a tool of another; *Austral.* & *NZ hist.* a person who bought land on behalf of another who was not entitled to buy it. M19.

D. BAGLEY Our . . corporation might have caught a tiger by the tail—Favel is no one's dummy.

5 An object serving to replace the genuine or usual one; a substitute, an imitation; a counterfeit. M19. ▸**b** *spec.* A model of a human body to hang or display clothes on; a (usu. adjustable) model of a human torso to fit clothes on. Also ***dress-maker's dummy***, ***tailor's dummy***. M19. ▸**c** A set of sheets of paper made up to resemble a book etc.; a mock-up of a newspaper etc. M19. ▸**d** A model of a human body used as a target in shooting or bayonet practice or in safety tests for vehicles etc. L19. ▸**e** A teat of rubber, plastic, etc., given to a baby to suck as a comforter. E20. ▸**f** In football and other games, a feigned pass or kick intended to deceive an opponent. E20. ▸**g** A model of a person or animal made by a ventriloquist to appear to talk etc. Also ***ventriloquist's dummy***. M20. ▸**h** COMPUTING. An instruction or sequence of data that merely occupies space. M20.

R. V. JONES The warhead was a dummy made of concrete. P. PARISH Half the patients are given the true drug, half are given the dummy.

6 A barge, vehicle, etc., with no means of propulsion. M19.
– PHRASES: ***double dummy***: see DOUBLE *adjective* & *adverb*. ***dress-maker's dummy***: see sense 5b above. **in dummy** in dummy form. **sell a dummy (to)**, **sell the dummy (to)** in football and other games, deceive (an opponent) by a feigned pass or kick. ***tailor's dummy***: see sense 5b above. ***ventriloquist's dummy***: see sense 5g above.
▸ **B** *attrib.* or as *adjective*. That is a dummy, of the nature of a dummy; counterfeit, sham. M19.
– SPECIAL COLLOCATIONS & COMB.: **dummy run** a practice, a trial run, a rehearsal. **dummy teat**, **dummy tit** a baby's dummy (see sense A.5e above).

dummy /ˈdʌmi/ *verb*. L19.
[ORIGIN from the noun.]
1 *verb trans.* & *intrans.* *Austral.* & *NZ hist.* Acquire (land) by acting as a dummy (see DUMMY *noun* 4). L19.
2 *verb trans.* Make a dummy or imitation of. E20.
3 *verb intrans.* Foll. by *up*: refuse to talk, keep quiet. *US slang*. E20.
4 *verb trans.* & *intrans.* FOOTBALL etc. Sell a dummy (to); feign (a pass); make (one's way) by selling a dummy or dummies. M20.

dumortierite /djʊˈmɔːtjərʌɪt/ *noun*. L19.
[ORIGIN from V.-E. *Dumortier* (1802–76), French geologist + -ITE[1].]
MINERALOGY. An orthorhombic borosilicate of aluminium occurring as small violet or blue needles or fibrous masses, esp. in gneisses and schists.

dumosity /djuːˈmɒsɪti/ *noun*. *rare*. M17.
[ORIGIN from Latin *dumosus* bushy, from *dumus* thorn bush, bramble: see -ITY.]
Dense bushy growth; a mass of bushes or brambles.

dump /dʌmp/ *noun*[1]. E16.
[ORIGIN Prob. of Low German or Dutch origin and a fig. use of Middle Dutch *domp* exhalation, mist, rel. to DAMP *noun*.]
†**1** A reverie; *sing.* & in *pl.* perplexity, absence of mind. E16–L17.
2 A fit of depression. Now only in ***the dumps***, a state of depression, low spirits. *colloq*. E16.
down in the dumps, **in the dumps** depressed, low spirited.
†**3** A melancholy tune or song. M16–M19.

dump /dʌmp/ *noun*[2]. L18.
[ORIGIN App. identical with 1st elem. of DUMPLING.]
1 An object of a dumpy shape; a dumpy person. L18.

CARLYLE A . . vulgar little dump of an old man.

2 A small coin; a trivial sum; a jot; *spec.* (AUSTRAL. HISTORY) a circular piece removed from the centre of a (holey) dollar and issued as currency. E19.

G. K. CHESTERTON I do not care a dump whether they know the alphabet.

dump /dʌmp/ *noun*[3]. *dial*. L18.
[ORIGIN Perh. from Norse: cf. Norwegian *dump* pit, pool.]
A deep hole in the bed of a river or pond.

dump /dʌmp/ *noun*[4]. L18.
[ORIGIN from DUMP *verb*[1].]
1 A heap or pile of refuse or waste material; a place where refuse etc. is deposited; *esp.* (*US* & *S. Afr.*) a pile of earth, ore, etc., from mining operations, or the place where this is deposited. L18. ▸**b** (The site of) a store of provisions, ammunition, equipment, etc., deposited for later use. E20.

b J. HILTON Cans of petrol were fetched from a dump close by.

mine dump.
2 A dull abrupt thud; a bump. E19. ▸**b** *Surfing slang*. = DUMPER 2. M20.

B. M. CROKER Mrs. Brande . . was now let down with a dump.

3 An act or the practice of dumping. L19. ▸**b** An act of defecation. Chiefly *N. Amer.* M20. ▸**c** COMPUTING. The process or result of dumping data; a printout or listing of stored data, esp. of the complete contents of a computer's memory. M20.

b W. H. AUDEN To start the morning With a satisfactory Dump.

4 An unpleasant, shabby, or dreary place. *colloq*. L19.

G. PALEY You could have a decent place on a decent street instead of this dump.

– COMB.: **dump bin** a promotional box in a shop for displaying books or other items; **dump tank**: into which liquid can be rapidly discharged; **dump truck** etc. (chiefly *N. Amer.*) = DUMPER *truck* etc.; **dump valve**: allowing the rapid discharge of a liquid.

dump /dʌmp/ *verb*[1]. ME.
[ORIGIN Perh. from Old Norse; cf. Danish *dumpe*, Norwegian *dumpa* fall suddenly, fall plump. In mod. use partly imit: cf. THUMP *verb*.]
†**1** *verb intrans.* & *trans.* Fall or drop with sudden force; plunge. Only in ME.
2 *verb trans.* Strike heavily, thump. *Scot.* L16.
3 *verb trans.* Throw down in a lump; deposit unceremoniously; tip out (rubbish etc.); drop, esp. with a bump. Orig. *US*. L18. ▸**b** Put (goods) on the market in large quantities and at low prices; *spec.* send (goods unsaleable in the home market) to a foreign market for sale at a lower price. M19. ▸**c** Discard; abandon; get rid of. *colloq*. E20. ▸**d** *verb trans.* & *intrans.* Void (as) excrement, defecate. Chiefly *N. Amer.* E20. ▸**e** Of a wave: hurl (a swimmer or surfer) down with great force. *Surfing slang*. M20. ▸**f** COMPUTING. Copy (stored data) to a different location (esp. an external storage medium); list (stored data). M20.

J. B. PRIESTLEY Oakroyd's reply . . was to fetch his bag of tools and dump it down at the other's feet. A. TOFFLER Industrial waste dumped into a river can turn up . . thousands of miles away in the ocean. *fig.*: E. REVELEY He . . decided to dump the whole thing . . into the laps of his superiors. **b** P. CAREY There was a surfeit and . . talk of dumping grain on the world market. **c** D. STIVENS You've dumped plenty of fellows before.

d dumping syndrome MEDICINE a group of symptoms, including abdominal discomfort and distension and sometimes abnormally rapid bowel evacuation, occurring after meals in some patients who have undergone gastric surgery. **dump on** *colloq.* criticize severely, treat with scorn or contempt, defeat heavily.
4 *verb trans.* Compress (a wool bale) (as) by hydraulic pressure. *Austral.* & *NZ*. M19.

†**dump** *verb*[2] *intrans.* & *trans.* M16–M19.
[ORIGIN from DUMP *noun*[1].]
Fall or cast into depression, gloom, or abstraction.

dumper /ˈdʌmpə/ *noun*. L19.
[ORIGIN from DUMP *verb*[1] + -ER[1].]
1 A person who or thing which dumps; *esp.* (in full ***dumper truck***) a truck etc. with a body that tilts or opens at the back for unloading. L19.
2 A large wave which hurls a swimmer or surfer down with great force. *Surfing slang*. E20.

dumpish /ˈdʌmpɪʃ/ *adjective*. E16.
[ORIGIN from DUMP *noun*[1] + -ISH[1].]
†**1** Dull, slow-witted; abstracted. E16–L17.
2 Dejected, melancholy; down in the dumps. M16.
■ **dumpishly** *adverb* E17. **dumpishness** *noun* M16.

dumpling /ˈdʌmplɪŋ/ *noun*. E17.
[ORIGIN Uncertain: cf. DUMP *noun*[2], -LING[1].]
1 A (usu. globular) mass of dough boiled or baked either plain or enclosing fruit etc. E17.
Norfolk dumpling.
2 A small fat person or animal. E17.

DICKENS A nice little dumpling of a wife.

dumpoked /ˈdʌmpəʊkt/ *adjective*. L17.
[ORIGIN Urdu *dampukt*, from Persian *dam* breath, vapour + *puktah* cooked.]
INDIAN COOKERY. Of meat, esp. fowl: boned, steamed, and stuffed.
■ **dumpoke** *noun* a dish of dumpoked meat L17.

Dumpster /ˈdʌm(p)stə/ *noun*. *N. Amer.* Also **d-**. M20.
[ORIGIN from DUMP *verb*[1] + -STER.]
(US proprietary name for) a very large container for rubbish, a skip.

dumpty /ˈdʌm(p)ti/ *noun* & *adjective*. E19.
[ORIGIN Var. of DUMPY *adjective*[2] & *noun*. Cf. HUMPTY-DUMPTY.]
= DUMPY *adjective*[2] & *noun*.

dumpy /ˈdʌmpi/ *adjective*[1]. E17.
[ORIGIN from DUMP *noun*[1] + -Y[1].]
Dejected; melancholy; down in the dumps.

dumpy /ˈdʌmpi/ *adjective*[2] & *noun*. M18.
[ORIGIN from 1st elem. of DUMPLING (cf. DUMP *noun*[2]) + -Y[1].]
▸ **A** *adjective*. Short and stout; rounded. M18.
dumpy level a spirit level used in surveying, having a short telescope with a large aperture.
▸ **B** *noun*. A dumpy person, animal, or thing. E19.
■ **dumpily** *adverb* L19. **dumpiness** *noun* E19.

dun /dʌn/ *noun*[1]. LME.
[ORIGIN from DUN *adjective*.]
1 (A name for) a horse. Now *spec.* a dun horse. LME.
2 Dun colour; a dun hue. M16.

T. HARDY When beeches drip in browns and duns.

3 ANGLING. (An artificial fly imitating) any of various dusky-coloured flies, esp. mayflies in the subimago stage. L17.

dun /dʌn/ *noun*[2]. E17.
[ORIGIN Abbreviation of DUNKIRK privateer.]
1 A person who duns; an importunate creditor; a debt collector. E17.

R. GRAVES Creditors dog my steps, duns rap perpetually at my door.

2 A demand for money, esp. in payment of a debt. L17.

D

D

dun /dʌn/ *noun*³. L18.
[ORIGIN Irish *dún*, Gaelic *dùn* hill, hill fort, Welsh †*din*.]
A prehistoric hill fort or fortified eminence, esp. in Scotland or Ireland.

dun /duːn/ *noun*⁴. Also **dhoon** & other vars. E19.
[ORIGIN Hindi *dūn*.]
Any of the wide flat valleys in the Siwalik hills, lying parallel to the base of the Himalayas; *spec.* *the* valley of Dehra in Uttar Pradesh, India.

dun /dʌn/ *adjective*.
[ORIGIN Old English *dun(n)* = Old Saxon *dun* date-brown, nut-brown, prob. rel. to Old Saxon *dosan*, Old High German *tusin* (cf. DUSK *adjective*).]
1 Of a dull or dingy brown colour, dull greyish-brown; *spec.* (of a horse) of a sandy grey colour with black legs, mane, and tail, and usu. a dark dorsal stripe. OE.
SHAKES. *Sonn.* If snow be white, why then her breasts are dun.
2 Dark, dusky; murky; gloomy. *poet.* ME.
WILLIAM COLLINS Dun Night has veil'd the solemn view.
– SPECIAL COLLOCATIONS & COMB.: **dun-bar** a noctuid moth, *Cosmia trapezina*, with two grey-brown bands on the forewing. **dun-bird** the pochard. **dun-diver** a female or immature goosander or merganser.
■ **dunness** /-n-n-/ *noun* E17. **dunnish** *adjective* rather dun or dusky E16.

dun /dʌn/ *verb*¹ *trans.* Infl. **-nn-**. OE.
[ORIGIN from the adjective.]
Make dun or dingy; darken or dull the colour of.

dun /dʌn/ *verb*² *trans.* Infl. **-nn-**. M17.
[ORIGIN from DUN *noun*².]
Make repeated and persistent demands upon, esp. for money owed; pester, plague, assail constantly.
J. A. MICHENER The bank was dunning them to repay a small loan.

dunam /ˈdʊnəm/ *noun*. E20.
[ORIGIN mod. Hebrew *dūnām*, Arabic *dūnum* from Ottoman Turkish *dūnum*, Turkish *dönüm*, from *dönmek* go round.]
A variable measure of land used in the Ottoman Empire and its successor states, including Israel (where it is equal to about 900 sq. metres).

dunce /dʌns/ *noun & verb*. E16.
[ORIGIN from John *Duns* Scotus (*c* 1266–1308), scholastic theologian, whose followers were a predominating scholastic sect until discredited by humanists and reformers in the 16th cent.]
▸ **A** *noun*. †**1** An adherent of Duns Scotus, a Scotist; a hair-splitter, a sophist. Freq. *attrib.*, as ***dunce man***, ***dunce prelate***. E16–M17.
†**2** A copy of the works of Duns Scotus; a book embodying his teaching on theology or logic. M16–M17.
†**3** A dull book-learned pedant. L16–M18.
T. FULLER A dunce, void of learning but full of books.
4 A person who shows no capacity for learning; a dullard, a blockhead. L16.
R. W. DALE Some boys remain dunces though they are sent to the best schools.
dunce's cap a paper cone formerly put on the head of a dunce at school as a mark of disgrace.
▸ **B** *verb trans.* Puzzle; make a dunce of. Now *rare*. L16.
■ **duncedom** *noun* dunces collectively; a dunce's condition or character: E19. **duncehood** *noun* the condition or character of a dunce; stupidity: E19. **duncery** *noun* †(**a**) the practice or character of a Scotist; (**b**) the state, practice, or character of a dunce; stupidity: L16. **duncical** *adjective* †(**a**) of or pertaining to the Scotists; (**b**) of or pertaining to a dunce; stupid: M16. **duncify** *verb trans.* (*rare*) make a dunce of L16.

dunch /dʌn(t)ʃ/ *adjective*. Long *dial.* L16.
[ORIGIN Unknown: cf. DUNNY *adjective*².]
1 Deaf. L16.
2 Blind. L17.
3 Of bread etc.: heavy, doughy. M19.
4 Stupid; dull. M19.

dunch /dʌn(t)ʃ/ *verb & noun*. Chiefly *dial.* ME.
[ORIGIN Unknown.]
▸ **A** *verb trans.* Strike with a short rapid blow. Now *esp.* jog with the elbow. ME.
▸ **B** *noun*. A jog with the elbow; a sharp shock. LME.

duncish /ˈdʌnsɪʃ/ *adjective*. M19.
[ORIGIN from DUNCE + -ISH¹.]
Of the nature of or characteristic of a dunce; stupid.
■ **duncishly** *adverb* M19. **duncishness** *noun* E19.

Dundee /dʌnˈdiː, ˈdʌndiː/ *noun*. M19.
[ORIGIN A Scottish city on the Firth of Tay.]
1 ***Dundee rambler***, a variety of rambling rose. M19.
2 ***Dundee marmalade***, (proprietary name for) a kind of marmalade orig. made in Dundee. M19.
3 ***Dundee cake***, a kind of rich fruit cake usu. decorated with split almonds. L19.

dunder /ˈdʌndə/ *noun*¹. L18.
[ORIGIN from Spanish *redundar* overflow.]
The lees or dregs of cane juice, used in rum distillation.

dunder *noun*² & *verb* var. of DUNNER *noun*² & *verb*.

dunderhead /ˈdʌndəhɛd/ *noun*. E17.
[ORIGIN Perh. from DUNDER *noun*² + HEAD *noun*.]
A ponderously stupid person, a numbskull.
■ **dunderheaded** *adjective* stupid, thickheaded E19.

dunderpate /ˈdʌndəpeɪt/ *noun*. *arch.* L17.
[ORIGIN formed as DUNDERHEAD + PATE *noun*¹.]
= DUNDERHEAD.

Dundonian /dʌnˈdəʊnɪən/ *noun*. L19.
[ORIGIN from DUNDEE after *Aberdonian*.]
A native or inhabitant of the Scottish city of Dundee.

Dundreary /dʌnˈdrɪəri/ *noun*. *arch.* Pl. **-ries**, **-rys**. M19.
[ORIGIN Lord *Dundreary*, a character in T. Taylor's comedy *Our American Cousin* (1858).]
In *pl.*, or *sing.* in ***Dundreary weepers***, ***Dundreary whiskers***. Long side whiskers worn without a beard. Cf. PICCADILLY 1.

dunducketty /dʌnˈdʌkəti/ *adjective*. *colloq.* & *dial.* E19.
[ORIGIN App. from DUN *adjective* + DUCK *noun*¹.]
Of a dull, drab, muddy colour.

dune /djuːn/ *noun*. L18.
[ORIGIN Old French & mod. French from Middle Dutch *dūne* (Dutch *duin*) = Old English *dūn* DOWN *noun*¹.]
A mound or ridge of loose sand, or other sediment, formed by the wind, esp. on the sea coast.
– COMB.: ***dune buggy***: see BUGGY *noun*.

dung /dʌŋ/ *noun*.
[ORIGIN Old English *dung* = Old Frisian, Middle Dutch *dung(e)*, Old High German *tunga* manuring (German *Dung* manure): cf. Swedish *dynga* muck, dung, Danish *dynge* heap, Icelandic *dyngja* heap, dung: ult. origin unknown.]
1 Manure; the faeces of an animal or occas. a person. OE.
2 Something morally filthy or defiling; something vile. ME.
AV *Phil.* 3:8 I have suffered the losse of all things, and doe count them but doung, that I may win Christ.
3 A journeyman tailor who submits to terms of employment rejected by his fellows. *slang. obsolete* exc. *hist.* M18.
– COMB.: **dung beetle** any of various beetles which lay their eggs in dung or roll up balls of dung for their larvae to feed on; **dung cart**: for conveying manure; **dung fly** a dipteran insect of the family Scatophagidae, laying its eggs in fresh dung; *esp.* the yellow-brown *Scatophaga stercoraria*; **dung fork**: for spreading manure; **dungheap** a dunghill; **dung pot** (*dial.* exc. *hist.*) a horse-drawn tub etc. for carrying manure; **dungworm** an earthworm found in cow dung, *esp.* one used as bait.
■ **dungy** *adjective* resembling (that of) dung; foul; containing much dung: E17.

dung /dʌŋ/ *verb*¹.
[ORIGIN Old English *dyngian*, formed as DUNG *noun*. In Middle English assim. to, or formed anew from, the noun.]
1 *verb trans.* Manure with dung. OE.
2 *verb intrans.* Excrete dung. LME.
3 *verb trans.* Immerse (calico) in a preparation containing cow dung or equivalent chemicals, to remove superfluous mordant. *obsolete* exc. *hist.* M19.

dung *verb*² *pa. pple*: see DING *verb*¹.

dunga *noun* var. of DOONGA.

dungaree /dʌŋgəˈriː/ *noun*. L17.
[ORIGIN Hindi *duṅgrī*.]
A coarse Indian calico; in *pl.*, overalls or trousers of dungaree or a similar material, *esp.* trousers with a bib.

Dungeness /dʌndʒəˈnɛs/ *noun*. E20.
[ORIGIN *Dungeness*, a fishing village on the coast of Washington State.]
Dungeness crab, a large crab, *Cancer magister*, found off the west coast of N. America and popular as food.

dungeon /ˈdʌndʒ(ə)n/ *noun*. Also (*arch.*) **donjon** /ˈdɒndʒ(ə)n, ˈdʌn-/. See also DONJON. ME.
[ORIGIN Old French & mod. French *donjon* from Proto-Gallo-Romance = 'lord's tower' or 'mistress tower' (in medieval Latin *dangio(n-)*, *dunjo(n-)*, *donjo(n-)*), from Latin *dominus* master, lord.]
1 A strong subterranean cell for prisoners; a deep dark vault. ME.
A. CARTER Dungeons . . had been converted into cellars for his wines. *fig.*: G. R. PORTER Palissy . . confined within the dungeon of his own breast, those feelings of bitterness.
Dungeons & Dragons (proprietary name for) a fantasy role-playing game set in an imaginary world based loosely on medieval myth.
2 See DONJON 1.

dungeon /ˈdʌndʒ(ə)n/ *verb trans.* E17.
[ORIGIN from the noun.]
Put or keep in a dungeon; imprison.

dunghill /ˈdʌŋhɪl/ *noun & adjective*. ME.
[ORIGIN from DUNG *noun* + HILL *noun*.]
▸ **A** *noun*. **1** A heap of dung or refuse in a farmyard etc. ME.
2 *transf.* & *fig.* **a** A mass of filth; a disgusting place or situation. E16. ▸**b** A vile or base person. M16. ▸**c** [from *dunghill cock* below.] A coward. *arch.* M18.
– COMB.: **dunghill cock**, **dunghill fowl**, etc., (*arch.*) a common barnyard fowl as opp. to a gamecock.
▸ **B** *attrib.* or as *adjective*. Vile as a dunghill; base; cowardly. *arch.* LME.

dunite /ˈdʌnʌɪt/ *noun*. M19.
[ORIGIN from *Dun* Mountain, New Zealand (where first described) + -ITE¹.]
GEOLOGY. A coarse-grained igneous rock consisting essentially of olivine, with chromite xenoliths.

duniwassal /ˈduːnɪwas(ə)l/ *noun*. *Scot.* Now *arch.* or *hist.* M16.
[ORIGIN from Gaelic *duine* man + *uasal* noble, of gentle birth.]
A (Highland) gentleman of secondary rank.

dunk /dʌŋk/ *noun*. M20.
[ORIGIN from the verb.]
BASKETBALL. In full ***dunk shot***. A shot made by jumping and pushing the ball down through the basket from above.

dunk /dʌŋk/ *verb trans.* Orig. *US*. E20.
[ORIGIN Pennsylvanian German *dunke* to dip, from German *tunken* (Old High German *dunkōn*, Middle High German *tunken*, *dunken*). Cf. DUNKER.]
1 Dip (bread, a biscuit, etc.) in a drink or soup while eating; immerse (*lit.* & *fig.*). E20.
2 BASKETBALL. Shoot (the ball) down through the basket by jumping so that the hands are above the ring. M20.

Dunkard /ˈdʌŋkəd/ *noun*. *US*. M18.
[ORIGIN formed as DUNKER *noun*¹: see -ARD.]
= DUNKER *noun*¹.

Dunker /ˈdʌŋkə/ *noun*¹. Also **T-** /t-/. E18.
[ORIGIN Pennsylvanian German, formed as DUNK *verb*: see -ER¹.]
A member of a US religious sect, deriving orig. from German Baptists, who administer baptism by triple immersion.

dunker /ˈdʌŋkə/ *noun*². Orig. *US*. E20.
[ORIGIN from DUNK *verb* + -ER¹.]
A person who dunks bread, biscuit, etc.; a basketball player who dunks the ball.

Dunkirk /dʌnˈkəːk, dʌŋˈk-/ *noun*. L16.
[ORIGIN Seaport of France (French *Dunkerque*). Cf. DUN *noun*².]
1 A privateer (from Dunkirk). Long *obsolete* exc. *hist.* L16.
2 (The scene of) a withdrawal under fire such as or comparable with the evacuation of British forces in France from Dunkirk between 29 May and 3 June, 1940; a momentous crisis. M20.
– COMB.: **Dunkirk spirit** refusal to surrender or despair in a time of crisis.
■ **Dunkirker** *noun* (**a**) a native or inhabitant of Dunkirk; (**b**) (*obsolete* exc. *hist.*) = DUNKIRK 1: L16.

dunlin /ˈdʌnlɪn/ *noun*. Pl. **-s**, same. M16.
[ORIGIN Prob. formed as DUN *adjective* + -LING¹, from its greyish-brown upperparts (in winter).]
A sandpiper, *Calidris alpina*, occurring throughout the holarctic region.

Dunlop /ˈdʌnlɒp/ *noun*. E19.
[ORIGIN A parish near Ayr in SW Scotland.]
In full ***Dunlop cheese***. A full-cream hard cheese originally made in Dunlop.

dunnage /ˈdʌnɪdʒ/ *noun & verb*. Also (earlier) †**denn-**. ME.
[ORIGIN Unknown.]
Chiefly NAUTICAL.
▸ **A** *noun*. Mats, brushwood, gratings, etc., stowed among a cargo to prevent wetting or chafing; *colloq.* miscellaneous baggage, a sailor's belongings. ME.
– COMB.: **dunnage bag** a kitbag.
▸ **B** *verb trans.* Stow with dunnage. M19.

dunnakin *noun* var. of DUNNIKEN.

dunnamany /ˈdʌnəmɛni/ *verb intrans.* *colloq.* M19.
[ORIGIN Repr. informal pronunc.]
Chiefly as 1st person sing.: don't know how many.

dunnart /ˈdʌnɑːt/ *noun*. E20.
[ORIGIN Nyungar *dunard*.]
Any of various small insectivorous marsupials of the genus *Sminthopsis*, of Australia and New Guinea.

dunner /ˈdʌnə/ *noun*¹. L17.
[ORIGIN from DUN *verb*² + -ER¹.]
= DUN *noun*² 1.

dunner /ˈdʌnə/ *noun*² & *verb*. *Scot.* Also **dunder** /ˈdʌndə/. L18.
[ORIGIN Perh. imit., or frequentative rel. to DIN *noun*, *verb*. Perh. earlier in DUNDERHEAD.]
▸ **A** *noun*. A resounding noise; a jarring blow. L18.
▸ **B** *verb intrans.* Resound; fall or strike with a reverberating noise. E19.

dunniken /ˈdʌnɪkɪn/ *noun*. *dial.* & *slang*. Also **dunnakin** & other vars. L18.
[ORIGIN Uncertain: perh. formed as DUNNY *noun* + KEN *noun*².]
An earth closet; a lavatory, *esp.* an outside one.

dunno /ˈdʌnəʊ, dəˈnəʊ/ *verb trans.* & *intrans.* *colloq.* M19.
[ORIGIN Repr. an informal pronunc.]
Chiefly as 1st person sing.: do not know.
C. MORGAN Well, I dunno. P'raps I'm wrong.

dunnock /ˈdʌnək/ *noun*. L15.
[ORIGIN App. from DUN *adjective* + -OCK.]
A small brown woodland or garden bird, *Prunella modularis*, with dark grey head and breast. Also called ***hedge sparrow***.

dunny /ˈdʌni/ *noun*. In sense 1 also †**danna**. E19.
[ORIGIN Uncertain: perh. from DUNG *noun*. May be earlier in DUNNIKEN, of which sense 3 is an abbreviation.]
1 Dung, faeces. Usu. *attrib. slang*. E19.
2 An underground passage or cellar, esp. in a tenement. *Scot*. E20.
3 An earth closet; a lavatory, *esp*. an outdoor one. *slang* (chiefly *Austral. & NZ*). M20.

dunny /ˈdʌni/ *adjective*[1]. E16.
[ORIGIN from DUN *adjective* + -Y[1].]
Somewhat dun or greyish-brown; dunnish.

dunny /ˈdʌni/ *adjective*[2]. *dial*. E18.
[ORIGIN Unknown: cf. DUNCH *adjective*.]
Dull of hearing, deaf; dull-witted, stupid.

Dunstable /ˈdʌnstəb(ə)l/ *adjective & noun*. M16.
[ORIGIN A town in Bedfordshire, England.]
▸**A** *adjective*. **1** Connected with or made in Dunstable. M16. ▸**b** *spec*. Designating a kind of straw plait, or the method of plaiting it. *obsolete* exc. *hist*. L18.
Dunstable way *arch*. the road from London to Dunstable (part of the Roman Watling Street), regarded as the type of a direct route or straightforward course.
2 [from ***Dunstable way*** above.] Direct, straightforward, downright. *arch*. L16.
▸**B** *noun*. ***plain Dunstable***, ***downright Dunstable***, something direct or simple, *esp*. plain language, the simple facts. *arch*. L16.

> V. WOOLF The plain Dunstable of the matter is, I'm not in the mood.. to-night.

dunster /ˈdʌnstə/ *noun*. *obsolete* exc. *hist*. E17.
[ORIGIN *Dunster* (see below).]
A woollen cloth made in or near the town of Dunster in Somerset, England.

dunstone /ˈdʌnstəʊn/ *noun*. *local*. L18.
[ORIGIN from DUN *adjective* + STONE *noun*.]
Any of various kinds of stone of a dun or dull brown colour, *esp*. dolerite or magnesian limestone.

dunt /dʌnt/ *noun & verb*. *Scot. & dial*. LME.
[ORIGIN Perh. var. of DINT *noun*. Cf. DENT *noun*[1].]
▸**A** *noun*. **1** A firm dull-sounding blow. LME.
2 A beat or palpitation of the heart. M18.
3 A wound made by a firm blow. L19.
▸**B** *verb*. **1** *verb trans*. Hit or knock firmly with a dull sound; drive *out* by so knocking. L15.
2 *verb intrans*. Of the heart: beat violently. M16.

dunter /ˈdʌntə/ *noun*. *local*. L17.
[ORIGIN from DUNT + -ER[1].]
The eider.

duo /ˈdjuːəʊ/ *noun*. Pl. **-os**. L16.
[ORIGIN Italian (whence also French) from Latin = two.]
1 MUSIC. A duet. L16.
2 Two people; a couple; *esp*. a pair of entertainers. L19.

duo- /ˈdjuːəʊ/ *combining form*.
[ORIGIN from Latin *duo* two. Corresp. to Greek *duo*.]
Prefixed to other Latin roots to form composite numerals (***duodecimal***), and irreg. used with other words as equivalent to BI- or DI-[2] (***duopoly***, ***duotone***).

duodecad /djuːə(ʊ)ˈdɛkad/ *noun*. Also **-ade** /-eɪd/. E17.
[ORIGIN Late Latin *duodecas*, *-cad-* twelve: cf. DECADE.]
A group of twelve; a period of twelve years.

duodecennial /ˌdjuːə(ʊ)dɪˈsɛnɪəl/ *adjective*. M17.
[ORIGIN from Latin *duodecennium* period of twelve years, from *duodecim* twelve + *annus* year: see -AL[1].]
Of twelve years.

duodecimal /djuːə(ʊ)ˈdɛsɪm(ə)l/ *adjective & noun*. L17.
[ORIGIN from Latin *duodecimus* twelfth + -AL[1]: cf. DECIMAL.]
▸**A** *adjective*. Of twelfths or twelve; reckoning or reckoned by twelve. L17.
▸**B** *noun*. In *pl*. (treated as *sing*.). = CROSS-MULTIPLICATION. E18.
■ **duodecimally** *adverb* E19.

duodecimo /djuːəʊˈdɛsɪməʊ/ *noun & adjective*. M17.
[ORIGIN Latin (*in*) *duodecimo* in a twelfth (*sc*. of a sheet), formed as DUODECIMAL.]
▸**A** *noun*. Pl. **-os**. A size of book or paper in which each leaf is one-twelfth of a standard printing sheet. (Abbreviation ***12mo***.) M17.
▸**B** *attrib*. or as *adjective*. Of this size, in duodecimo; *fig*. diminutive. L18.

duoden- *combining form* see DUODENO-.

duodenal /djuːəˈdiːn(ə)l/ *adjective*. M19.
[ORIGIN from DUODENUM + -AL[1].]
Of or pertaining to the duodenum.

duodenary /djuːəˈdiːnəri/ *adjective*. M19.
[ORIGIN Latin *duodenarius* containing twelve, from *duodeni* distrib. of *duodecim* twelve: see -ARY[1].]
= DUODECIMAL *adjective*.

duodeno- /djuːəˈdiːnəʊ/ *combining form* of next: see -O-. Before a vowel also **duoden-**.
■ **duodeˈnectomy** *noun* (an instance of) surgical removal of all or part of the duodenum E20. **duodeˈnitis** *noun* inflammation of the duodenum M19. **duodeno-jeˈjunal** *adjective* of or pertaining to the duodenum and jejunum L19. **duodeˈnostomy** *noun* (an instance of) surgical opening of the duodenum, usu. for the purpose of introducing food L19.

duodenum /djuːəˈdiːnəm/ *noun*. LME.
[ORIGIN medieval Latin (so called from its length = twelve fingers' breadth), from Latin *duodeni*: see DUODENARY.]
ANATOMY. The first portion of the small intestine immediately beyond the stomach, leading to the jejunum.

duologue /ˈdjuːəlɒg/ *noun*. M18.
[ORIGIN from DUO- after *monologue*.]
A conversation between two people; a dramatic piece with two actors.

duomo /ˈdwəʊməʊ, *foreign* ˈdwomo/ *noun*. Also (earlier) †**domo**. Pl. **-mos** /-məʊz/, **-mi** /-mi/. M16.
[ORIGIN Italian: see DOME *noun*.]
An Italian cathedral.

duopoly /djʊˈɒpəli/ *noun*. E20.
[ORIGIN from DUO- after *monopoly*.]
A condition in which there are only two suppliers of a certain commodity, service, etc.; the domination of a particular market by two firms; control or domination by two people or groups; two suppliers, firms, etc., controlling a particular market.
■ **duopolist** *noun* a firm etc. operating in a duopoly M20. **duopoˈlistic** *adjective* M20.

duotone /ˈdjuːətəʊn/ *noun & adjective*. E20.
[ORIGIN from DUO- + TONE *noun*.]
▸**A** *noun*. (The process of making) a halftone illustration in two colours from the same original using different screen angles. E20.
▸**B** *attrib*. or as *adjective*. Made by this process; *gen*. of or in two tones or colours. E20.

dup /dʌp/ *verb trans*. *dial*. or *arch*. Infl. **-pp-**. M16.
[ORIGIN Contr. of *do up* s.v. DO *verb*.]
Open (a door, gate, etc.).

dupable /ˈdjuːpəb(ə)l/ *adjective*. Also **dupeable**. M19.
[ORIGIN from DUPE *verb*[1] + -ABLE.]
Able to be duped; gullible.
■ **dupaˈbility** *noun* M19.

dupatta /dʊˈpʌtə/ *noun*. E17.
[ORIGIN Hindi *dupaṭṭā*, from *do* two + *paṭṭā* (piece or strip of cloth) having two breadths.]
A length of material worn as a scarf or head covering, typically with a shalwar kameez, by women from the Indian subcontinent.

dupe /djuːp/ *noun*[1]. L17.
[ORIGIN French, joc. application of dial. *dupe* hoopoe, from the bird's supposedly stupid appearance.]
A person who allows himself or herself to be deluded; a victim of deception.

> SIR W. SCOTT The ready dupe of astrologers and soothsayers. R. P. WARREN He had been the dupe in the game which the senator was playing.

dupe /djuːp/ *noun*[2] *& adjective*. *colloq*. E20.
[ORIGIN Abbreviation of DUPLICATE *adjective & noun*.]
Chiefly CINEMATOGRAPHY. ▸**A** *noun*. A duplicate; *spec*. a duplicate negative made from a positive print. E20.
▸**B** *adjective*. Duplicate. M20.

dupe /djuːp/ *verb*[1] *trans*. M17.
[ORIGIN formed as DUPE *noun*[1], after French *duper*.]
Deceive, mislead, make a dupe of; cheat.
■ **duper** *noun* L18. **dupery** *noun* the action of duping, deception; the condition of a person who is duped: M18.

dupe /djuːp/ *verb*[2] *trans*. *colloq*. E20.
[ORIGIN from DUPE *noun*[2].]
CINEMATOGRAPHY. Make a dupe of (see DUPE *noun*[2]).

dupeable *adjective* var. of DUPABLE.

dupion /ˈdjuːpɪən/ *noun*. Also **douppion** /ˈduːp-/, **dupp-** /ˈdʌp-/. E19.
[ORIGIN French *doupion* = Italian *doppione*, from *doppio* double.]
1 A double cocoon made by two silkworms. E19.
2 (A rough irregular silk made from) the thread of double cocoons; an imitation of this made from other fibres. E20.

duplation /djuːˈpleɪʃ(ə)n/ *noun*. LME.
[ORIGIN Late Latin *duplatio(n-)*, from Latin *duplat-* pa. ppl stem of *duplare* to double: see -ATION.]
The process of doubling; multiplication by two.

duple /ˈdjuːp(ə)l/ *adjective & noun*. M16.
[ORIGIN Latin *duplus*, from *duo* two.]
▸**A** *adjective*. Double, twofold. Now *rare* exc. as below. M16.
duple proportion, **duple ratio**: that of 2 to 1. **duple rhythm**, **duple time** MUSIC: in which there are two beats in a bar.
▸†**B** *noun*. = DOUBLE *noun* 1. E17–L18.

duplet /ˈdjuːplɪt/ *noun*. M17.
[ORIGIN from DUPLE, after DOUBLET: see -ET[1].]
†**1** In *pl*. = DOUBLET 2. *rare*. Only in M17.
2 MUSIC. A group of two equal notes, *spec*. occurring in music with an odd number of beats in a bar. E20.

duplex /ˈdjuːplɛks/ *noun*. E20.
[ORIGIN from the adjective.]
1 A two-family house; an apartment occupying two storeys. *N. Amer*. E20.
2 BIOCHEMISTRY. A double-stranded polynucleotide molecule. M20.

duplex /ˈdjuːplɛks/ *adjective*. M16.
[ORIGIN Latin, from *duo* two + *plic-* base of *plicare* to fold.]
1 Having two parts, twofold, dual; combining two elements, esp. with similar functions. M16. ▸**b** METALLURGY. Designating or made by a steel-making process employing successive treatment in two furnaces or by two methods. E20. ▸**c** Designating paper or board made from two differently coloured layers of paper, or coloured differently on either side. E20. ▸**d** GENETICS. Of a polyploid individual: having the dominant allele of a particular gene represented twice (either homozygously or heterozygously). E20. ▸**e** BIOCHEMISTRY. Of a molecule or structure: having two polynucleotide strands linked side by side. M20.
duplex escapement in a clock or watch, an escapement in which the escape wheel has both spur and crown teeth.
2 TELECOMMUNICATIONS. Pertaining to or designating the transmission or reception of two signals simultaneously in opposite directions over one channel or with one aerial. Cf. DIPLEX. L19.
■ **duˈplexity** *noun* (*rare*) duplex quality E19.

duplex /ˈdjuːplɛks/ *verb*. L19.
[ORIGIN from the adjective.]
1 *verb trans*. TELECOMMUNICATIONS. Make (a cable, system, etc.) duplex (DUPLEX *adjective* 2). L19.
2 *verb intrans*. METALLURGY. Make steel by a duplex process. Chiefly as ***duplexing*** *verbal noun*. E20.
■ **duplexer** *noun* (TELECOMMUNICATIONS) a device enabling duplex transmission or reception of radio signals M20.

duplex querela /ˌdjuːplɛks kwɪˈriːlə, -ˈreɪlə/ *noun*. E18.
[ORIGIN Law Latin, lit. 'double complaint'.]
ECCLESIASTICAL LAW. The procedure in the Anglican Church by which a priest may challenge a bishop who refuses to institute him to a benefice to which he has been presented; a court's direction to a bishop to proceed with the institution.

duplicable /ˈdjuːplɪkəb(ə)l/ *adjective*. E20.
[ORIGIN from DUPLIC(ATE *verb* + -ABLE.]
Able to be duplicated.
■ **duplicaˈbility** *noun* E20.

duplicate /ˈdjuːplɪkət/ *adjective & noun*. LME.
[ORIGIN Latin *duplicatus* pa. pple, formed as DUPLICATE *verb*: see -ATE[2].]
▸**A** *adjective*. **1** Double, consisting of two corresponding parts, existing in two examples. LME.
2 Doubled, consisting of twice the number or quantity. M16.
3 Exactly like some other thing (with any number of copies or specimens). E19.

> R. W. EMERSON The duplicate copy of Florio, which the British Museum purchased.

4 GENETICS. Of genes: indistinguishable in effect. E20.
– SPECIAL COLLOCATIONS: **duplicate bridge**, **duplicate whist**: in which the same hands are played successively by different players. **duplicate proportion**, **duplicate ratio**: of the squares of two numbers. ***duplicate whist***: see ***duplicate bridge*** above.
▸**B** *noun*. **1** Each of two things exactly alike; *esp*. the one which is made from or after the other; a second copy, with equal legal force, of an original letter or document. M16. ▸**b** A pawnbroker's ticket. *arch*. M19.

> W. STUBBS The rolls of the treasurer and chancellor were duplicates. B. PLAIN He wanted to have a picture of you.. so I had a duplicate made of the one on my night table.

in duplicate in two exactly corresponding copies.
2 Either of two or more specimens of a thing exactly or virtually alike; a thing which is the exact counterpart of another, regarded as the original; an additional specimen of a stamp or other item in a collection. L17.

> C. LAMB As if a man should suddenly encounter his own duplicate.

3 = ***duplicate bridge***, ***duplicate whist*** above. L19.

duplicate /ˈdjuːplɪkeɪt/ *verb*. L15.
[ORIGIN Latin *duplicat-* pa. ppl stem of *duplicare*, to double, formed as DUPLE: see -ATE[3].]
1 *verb trans*. Make or be a double or exact copy of; repeat; provide in duplicate or multiple. L15.

> C. BEATON She never ordered one thing of a kind, but duplicated each item by the dozens. J. RABAN The formation.. more exactly duplicated the geological structure of Saudi Arabia's richest oil field. *Dirt Bike* Do not attempt to duplicate any stunts that are beyond your own capabilities.

duplicating machine a machine for making copies of documents, drawings, etc., from a stencil sheet.
2 *verb trans*. Double; multiply by two; redouble. L16.
3 *verb intrans*. ECCLESIASTICAL. Celebrate the Eucharist twice in one day. L18.
■ **duplicative** *adjective & noun* (**a**) *adjective* having the quality of doubling or producing double; (**b**) *noun* an addition that constitutes a duplicate: L19.

D

D

duplication /djuːplɪˈkeɪʃ(ə)n/ *noun*. LME.
[ORIGIN Old French & mod. French, or Latin *duplicatio(n-)*, formed as DUPLICATE *verb*: see -ATION.]
1 MATH. Multiplication by two. Now *rare* or *obsolete*. LME.
duplication of a cube MATH. the problem of finding the side of a cube having twice the volume of a given cube; the Delian problem.
2 *gen*. The action of doubling or duplicating; repetition of an action or thing; division into two by natural growth or spontaneous division. L16. ▸**b** GENETICS. The existence in a chromosome set of two copies of a particular segment; the duplicated segment itself; the process by which it arises. E20.
†**3** ANATOMY. A folding, a doubling; a fold. L16–M18.
4 LAW (now *hist.*). A pleading on the part of a defendant in reply to a replication. E17.
5 ECCLESIASTICAL. The celebration of the Eucharist twice in one day by the same priest. M19.
6 A duplicate copy; a counterpart. L19.

duplicato- /djuːplɪˈkeɪtəʊ/ *combining form*. M18.
[ORIGIN from Latin *duplicatus*: see DUPLICATE *adjective & noun*, -O-.]
BOTANY. Doubly.
■ **duplicato-ˈdentate** *adjective* doubly dentate M19.

duplicator /ˈdjuːplɪkeɪtə/ *noun*. L19.
[ORIGIN from DUPLICATE *verb* + -OR.]
A person who or thing which duplicates; *spec.* = ***duplicating machine*** s.v. DUPLICATE *verb* 1.

duplicature /ˈdjuːplɪkeɪtʃə, -kətjʊə/ *noun*. L17.
[ORIGIN French, formed as DUPLICATE *verb*: see -URE.]
Chiefly ANATOMY. A doubling; a fold.

duplicitous /djuːˈplɪsɪtəs, djʊ-/ *adjective*. L19.
[ORIGIN from DUPLICITY: see -OUS.]
Characterized by or displaying duplicity; *esp.* deceitful, two-faced.
■ **duplicitously** *adverb* M20. **duplicitousness** *noun* M20.

duplicity /djuːˈplɪsɪti, djʊ-/ *noun*. LME.
[ORIGIN Old French & mod. French *duplicité* or late Latin *duplicitas*, formed as DUPLEX *adjective*, *duplic-*: see -ITY.]
1 The quality of being deceitful in manner or conduct; the practice of being two-faced, of dishonestly acting in two opposing ways; deceitfulness; double-dealing. LME.
S. KAUFFMANN Now he lay there stroking her hair and thinking of his wife, hating his duplicity.
2 The state of being numerically or physically double; doubleness. *arch.* L16.
G. F. CHAMBERS The duplicity of Saturn's ring.
3 LAW. The coupling of two or more matters in one plea or charge. M19.

duply /djʊˈplʌɪ/ *verb & noun*. *Scot. obsolete* exc. *hist.* E16.
[ORIGIN medieval Latin *duplica*: cf. French *duplique*, and REPLY *noun* = French *réplique*.]
▸ **A** *verb intrans.* LAW. Make a duply. E16.
▸ **B** *noun* (usu. in *pl.*).
1 LAW. A rejoinder that was formerly given to a pursuer's reply; a second reply. L16.
2 In a debate, the rejoinder that comes fourth after the original assertion. M17.
SIR W. SCOTT Answers, replies, duplies, triplies, quadruplies, followed thick upon each other.

dupondius /djuːˈpɒndɪəs/. *noun*. Pl. **-ii** /-ɪʌɪ/. E17.
[ORIGIN Latin.]
ROMAN ANTIQUITIES. A bronze or brass coin of the value of two asses.

duppion *noun* var. of DUPION.

duppy /ˈdʌpi/ *noun*. *W. Indian*. L18.
[ORIGIN Uncertain: perh. W. African.]
A ghost or spirit, usu. a malevolent one but occas. a good-natured one.

Dupuytren /djʊˈpwiːtrɒ̃, -trən/ *noun*. L19.
[ORIGIN Baron Guillaume *Dupuytren* (1777–1835), French surgeon.]
MEDICINE. **1** ***Dupuytren's contraction***, ***Dupuytren's contracture***, fixed forward curvature of one or more fingers due to fixation of the finger tendons and their sheaths to the skin of the palm. L19.
2 ***Dupuytren's fracture***, a fracture of the fibula just above the malleolus. L19.

dura /ˈdjʊərə/ *noun*[1]. L19.
[ORIGIN Abbreviation.]
= DURA MATER.

dura *noun*[2] var. of DURRA.

durability /djʊərəˈbɪlɪti/ *noun*. LME.
[ORIGIN Old French & mod. French †*durabilité* from late Latin *durabilitas*, from *durabilis*: see DURABLE, -ITY.]
The quality of being durable.

durable /ˈdjʊərəb(ə)l/ *adjective & noun*. ME.
[ORIGIN Old French & mod. French from Latin *durabilis*, from *durare* see DURE *verb*, -ABLE.]
▸ **A** *adjective*. **1** Steadfast, unyielding; able to endure fatigue or discomfort. *obsolete* exc. *dial.* ME.
2 Capable of lasting; persistent; permanent, not transitory. LME.
E. POUND Prose of permanent or durable interest.
3 Able to withstand change, decay, or wear. LME. ▸**b** *spec.* Designating goods which remain useful over a period of time, as distinguished from those produced for immediate consumption. M20.
R. L. STEVENSON The sandy peninsula of San Francisco . . shaken . . by frequent earthquakes, seems in itself no very durable foundation.
▸ **B** *noun*. A durable manufactured article. Usu. in *pl.* M20.
consumer durable.
■ **durableness** *noun* (now *rare*) durability L16. **durably** *adverb* L15.

durain /ˈdjʊəreɪn/ *noun*. E20.
[ORIGIN from Latin *durus* hard, after FUSAIN.]
GEOLOGY. One of the lithotypes of coal, being a hard, compact material of dull grey-black appearance.

dural /ˈdjʊər(ə)l/ *adjective*. L19.
[ORIGIN from DURA *noun*[1] + -AL[1].]
Of or pertaining to the dura mater.

Duralumin /djʊˈraljʊmɪn/ *noun*. E20.
[ORIGIN Uncertain: perh. from *Düren*, a town in Germany, or from Latin *durus* hard; (see ALUMINIUM).]
(Proprietary name for) any of a series of aluminium alloys which contain copper and other elements and combine strength and hardness with lightness.

dura mater /djʊərə ˈmeɪtə/ *noun phr.* LME.
[ORIGIN medieval Latin *dura mater* 'hard mother', inexact translation of Arabic *al-'umm al-jāfiya* 'coarse mother' (*al'-umm* 'mother' indicating a relationship between parts). Cf. PIA MATER.]
ANATOMY. The dense, tough, fibrous lining of the cranial cavity and spinal canal, serving as the outermost envelope of the brain and spinal cord. Abbreviation DURA *noun*[1].

duramen /djʊˈreɪmɛn/ *noun*. M19.
[ORIGIN Latin = hardness, from *durare*: see DURE *verb*.]
BOTANY. The heartwood of a tree or other woody plant.

durance /ˈdjʊər(ə)ns/ *noun*. *arch.* LME.
[ORIGIN Old French, formed as DURE *verb*: see -ANCE.]
†**1** Continuance, duration. LME–L17. ▸**b** Lasting quality, durability. L16–M19.
2 Imprisonment or forced confinement. Now esp. in ***in durance vile***. Cf. DURESS 4. E16.
M. LOWRY I was thrown for a time, in Mexico, as a spy, into durance vile.
†**3** A hard-wearing woollen or worsted cloth, in appearance like buff leather. Cf. DURANT *noun*. L16–E18.
4 Endurance (of fatigue etc.). *arch.* L16.

durant /ˈdjʊər(ə)nt/ *adjective & noun*. LME.
[ORIGIN Old French & mod. French, pres. pple of *durer*: see DURE *verb*, -ANT[1].]
▸ †**A** *adjective*. Lasting, continuous; current. LME–M17.
▸ **B** *noun*. A hard-wearing woollen cloth; a variety of tammy. (Cf. DURANCE 3.) *obsolete* exc. *hist.* E18.

durante /ˈdjʊəranti/ *pres. pple & preposition*. LME.
[ORIGIN Latin, abl. sing. of *durans* enduring.]
During. *obsolete* exc. in Latin phrs.
durante beneplacito /bɛnɪˈplasɪtəʊ/ during pleasure. ***durante vita***, ***vita durante*** /ˈviːtə/ while life continues.

duration /djʊəˈreɪʃ(ə)n/ *noun*. LME.
[ORIGIN Old French from medieval Latin *duratio(n-)*, from Latin *durat-* pa. ppl stem of *durare*: see DURE *verb*, -ATION.]
1 The continuance or length of time; the time during which anything continues. LME. ▸†**b** Durability, permanence. M17–M18. ▸**c** PHONETICS. The length of a sound. L19.
R. L. STEVENSON We discussed the probable duration of the voyage. H. READ There was no permanency in his life, no sense of duration. H. KISSINGER A campaign of eight weeks' duration. **b** J. HANWAY The brick . . appears to be ill prepared for duration.
for the duration until the end of the (current) war; for a long or an unconscionably long time.
†**2** Hardening. E–M17.
■ **durational** *adjective* L19. **durationless** *adjective* having no duration E20.

durative /ˈdjʊərətɪv/ *adjective & noun*. L19.
[ORIGIN from DURATION + -IVE.]
▸ **A** *adjective*. Continuing; *spec.* in GRAMMAR, denoting continuing action. L19.
▸ **B** *noun*. GRAMMAR. A verb in the durative aspect. E20.
■ **duratively** *adverb* E20. **duraˈtivity** *noun* E20.

durbar /ˈdəːbɑː/ *noun*. E17.
[ORIGIN Urdu from Persian *darbār* court.]
1 A public levee held by an Indian ruler or by a British ruler in India. Also, the court of an Indian ruler. E17.
2 A hall or place of audience where durbars were held. E17.

durchkomponiert /ˈdʊrçkɔmponiːrt/ *adjective*. L19.
[ORIGIN German, from *durch* through + *komponiert* composed.]
MUSIC. (Of composition) having a formal design which does not rely on repeated sections; *esp.* (of song) having different music for each stanza; through-composed.

dure /djʊə/ *adjective*. *arch.* LME.
[ORIGIN Old French & mod. French *dur* from Latin *durus* hard.]
Hard (*lit.* & *fig.*).

dure /djʊə/ *verb*. ME.
[ORIGIN Old French & mod. French *durer* from Latin *durare* harden, endure, from *durus* hard.]
1 *verb intrans.* Last, continue in existence. *arch.* & *dial.* ME.
†**2** *verb intrans.* Hold out, persist, survive; continue in a certain state or condition. ME–L16.
†**3** *verb intrans.* Extend, stretch out into space. ME–E16.
†**4** *verb trans.* Sustain, undergo, endure. ME–L16.
5 *verb intrans.* Harden. Now *rare* or *obsolete*. LME.
■ †**dureful** *adjective* lasting, durable L16–E17.

Düreresque /djʊərəˈrɛsk/ *adjective*. M19.
[ORIGIN from *Dürer* (see below) + -ESQUE.]
In the style or manner of the German painter and engraver Albrecht Dürer (1471–1528).

duress /djʊ(ə)ˈrɛs, ˈdjʊərɛs/ *noun*. Also †**-esse**. ME.
[ORIGIN Old French *duresse* from Latin *duritia*, from *durus* hard: see -ESS[2].]
†**1** Harsh treatment; oppression, cruelty; harm, injury. ME–L17.
†**2** Hardness; roughness, violence; endurance, firmness. LME–M17.
3 Constraint, compulsion, esp. through imprisonment, threats, or violence; *spec.* in LAW, constraint illegally exercised to force a person to perform an act. LME.
J. L. AUSTIN Voidable for duress or undue influence. A. FRASER A laborious composition, no doubt written under duress.
4 Forced confinement, imprisonment. Cf. DURANCE 2. LME.
J. MCCARTHY Some of the missionaries had been four years in duresse.

du reste /dy rɛst/ *adverbial phr.* E19.
[ORIGIN French, lit. 'of the rest'.]
Besides, moreover.

Durex /ˈdjʊərɛks/ *noun*. Also **d-**. Pl. same. M20.
[ORIGIN Invented word.]
(Proprietary name for) a contraceptive sheath, a condom.

durgah *noun* var. of DARGAH.

Durham /ˈdʌrəm/ *noun*. L18.
[ORIGIN See below.]
Used *attrib.* to designate things originating in or associated with the city of Durham in NE England.
Durham mustard *hist.* ground mustard orig. produced in Durham in the 18th cent. **Durham quilt** a quilt made by sewing together a piece of fabric, an inner wad, and a lining, the stitches making decorative patterns. ***Durham shorthorn***: see ***shorthorn*** s.v. SHORT *adjective*.

durian /ˈdʊərɪən/ *noun*. L16.
[ORIGIN Malay, from *duri* thorn, prickle.]
A Malayan tree, *Durio zibethinus*, of the bombax family, widely grown in tropical Asia; the spinous fruit of this, the pulp of which is foul-smelling but palatable.

duricrust /ˈdjʊərɪkrʌst/ *noun*. E20.
[ORIGIN from Latin *durus* hard + -I- + CRUST *noun*.]
GEOLOGY. A hard crust formed at or near the ground surface in semi-arid climates by the deposition of minerals from groundwater which rises by capillary action and evaporates.

during /ˈdjʊərɪŋ/ *preposition & conjunction*. LME.
[ORIGIN pres. pple of DURE *verb* (see -ING[2]), after Old French *durant* & Latin abl. absol., as DURANTE *vita*, *vita durante*.]
▸ **A** *preposition*. Throughout the duration of; in the course of, in the time of. LME.
J. CONRAD Some time during the night the crew came on board. M. AMIS During the early months of the year, the air was like cold washing-up. A. N. WILSON Hilaire Belloc was born during a thunderstorm.
▸ †**B** *conjunction*. While (*that*); until (*that*). L16–L17.

†**durity** *noun*. LME–L19.
[ORIGIN Latin *duritas*, from *durus* hard: see -ITY.]
Hardness (*lit.* & *fig.*).

†**durk** *noun & verb* see DIRK.

Durkheimian /dəːkˈhʌɪmɪən/ *adjective & noun*. E20.
[ORIGIN from Émile *Durkheim* (see below) + -IAN.]
▸ **A** *adjective*. Of or characteristic of the French sociologist Émile Durkheim (1858–1917) or his sociological theories. E20.
▸ **B** *noun*. A follower or adherent of Durkheim. M20.

durmast /ˈdəːmɑːst/ *noun*. L18.
[ORIGIN Perh. orig. erron. for *dunmast*, from DUN *adjective* + MAST *noun*[2].]
More fully ***durmast oak***. A Eurasian oak, *Quercus petraea*, which bears sessile acorns and grows chiefly on acid soils.

durn /dəːn/ *noun*[1]. Now *dial.* ME.
[ORIGIN Uncertain: perh. from Norse. Cf. in same sense Old Swedish *dyrni*, Norwegian *dyrn*, Swedish dial. *dörne*, ult. from Germanic base of DOOR *noun*.]

1 A solid wood doorpost; *sing.* & (usu.) in *pl.*, the framework of a doorway. ME.
2 MINING. In *pl.* (treated as *sing.*). A frame of timbering. L18.

durn *noun*², *adjective, adverb, & verb*: see DARN *noun*² etc., DARN *verb*².

duro /ˈdʊərəʊ/ *noun*. Also **douro**. Pl. **-os**. L18.
[ORIGIN from Spanish *peso duro* hard or solid piastre.]
In Spanish America and (formerly) Spain: a peso or dollar coin (as opp. to a note).

Duroc /ˈdjʊərɒk/ *noun*. L19.
[ORIGIN A stallion owned by Isaac Frink, sheriff of Saratoga Co., N.Y., and said to have been bought on the same day (in 1823) as the pigs from which he developed the breed.]
Orig., (a pig of) a breed developed in New York State. Now (also ***Duroc-Jersey***), (a pig of) a breed derived by crossing the original breed with the Jersey Red. Also ***Duroc pig***.

duroy /djʊˈrɔɪ/ *noun*. *obsolete* exc. *hist.* E17.
[ORIGIN Unknown. Cf. CORDUROY *noun*.]
A kind of lightweight worsted material formerly made in western England, used for men's clothing.

durra /ˈdʊrə, ˈdʊərə/ *noun*. Also **dhurra**, **dourra**, **dura**, & other vars. L18.
[ORIGIN Arabic *ḏura*.]
A variety of grain sorghum, *Sorghum bicolor* var. *durra*, grown esp. in N. Africa and the Indian subcontinent.

durrie, **durry** *nouns* vars. of DHURRIE.

durst *verb pa. t.*: see DARE *verb*¹.

durum /ˈdjʊərəm/ *noun*. E20.
[ORIGIN Latin, neut. of *durus* hard.]
In full ***durum wheat***. A type of wheat grown in arid regions, *Triticum durum*, marked by hard seeds rich in gluten, which are used in the manufacture of pasta.

durwan /dəːˈwɑːn/ *noun*. L18.
[ORIGIN Urdu *darwān* from Persian.]
In the Indian subcontinent: a porter, a doorkeeper.

durzi /ˈdəːzi/ *noun*. E19.
[ORIGIN Urdu from Persian *darzī*.]
In the Indian subcontinent: a tailor.

†**dush** *verb & noun*. *Scot. & N. English*. ME.
[ORIGIN Perh. alt. of DASH *verb*¹: cf. CRUSH *verb*, CRASH *verb*.]
▸ **A** *verb*. **1** *verb intrans.* Rush; strike against something; fall heavily. ME–E19.
2 *verb trans.* Rush or throw down violently. LME–E19.
▸ **B** *noun*. A violent blow or impact; the sound of violent collision. LME–E20.

dusk /dʌsk/ *adjective & noun*.
[ORIGIN Old English *dox* rel. to Old Saxon *dosan*, Old High German *tusin* darkish (of colour), dull, from Germanic base repr. also by Latin *fuscus* dark, dusky. Metathesized in Middle English. Cf. DUN *adjective*.]
▸ **A** *adjective*. **1** Dark, shadowy; dusky. Now *poet.* OE.
†**2** Obscure, veiled from perception. ME–L16.
▸ **B** *noun*. **1** The darker stage of twilight; the time of this. E17.
R. L. STEVENSON The mail picked us up about dusk at the Royal George. J. WAIN The long golden evening gradually yielded first to twilight and then to a deep dusk, through which we could barely discern each other's faces.
2 Shade, shadow; gloom; duskiness. E18.
TENNYSON In the dusk of thee [Old Yew], the clock Beats out the little lives of men.
■ **dusken** *verb trans. & intrans.* (*rare*, now *poet.*) make or become dusky or obscure M16. **duskly** *adverb* (*poet.*) M19. **duskness** *noun* (now *poet.*) LME.

dusk /dʌsk/ *verb*. Now chiefly *poet.*
[ORIGIN Old English *doxian*, formed as DUSK *adjective & noun* Metathesized or re-formed in Middle English.]
1 *verb intrans.* Become dusk or dim; grow dark; be dusky. OE.
TENNYSON Little breezes dusk and shiver. G. GISSING When it began to dusk.. supper was prepared.
2 *verb trans.* Make dusky; darken, dim, obscure. LME.
fig.: LD BERNERS Vnderstandyng, which is dusked in errours.

duskish /ˈdʌskɪʃ/ *adjective*. M16.
[ORIGIN from DUSK *adjective & noun* + -ISH¹.]
Rather dusky; somewhat dark.
■ **duskishly** *adverb* L16. **duskishness** *noun* M16.

dusky /ˈdʌski/ *adjective*. M16.
[ORIGIN from DUSK *adjective & noun* + -Y¹.]
1 Somewhat black or dark in colour; darkish. M16. ▸**b** *euphem.* Of a person: black. Esp. *Austral.*, Aboriginal. E19.
R. T. PETERSON The immature Blue-faced Booby is dusky-brown with a white belly.
dusky cranesbill a European cranesbill, *Geranium phaeum*, with usu. dark purple flowers. ***dusky perch***: see PERCH *noun*¹. **dusky titi** a mainly grey-brown cebid monkey, *Callicebus moloch*, occurring in the forests of tropical America.
2 Shady or shadowy; deficient in light; dim, obscure. L16.
SHAKES. 1 *Hen. VI* Here dies the dusky torch of Mortimer, Chok'd with ambition of the meaner sort. H. JAMES Dusky with the shade of magnificent elms.
3 *fig.* Gloomy, melancholy. Now *rare* or *obsolete*. E17.
W. FALCONER Here no dusky frown prevails.
■ **duskily** *adverb* E17. **duskiness** *noun* E17.

Dussehra /ˈdʌʃərə, -ʃ-/ *noun*. Also **Dashera**, **Dassera**, & other vars. L18.
[ORIGIN Hindi *dasahrā* from Sanskrit *daśaharā*.]
The tenth (final) day of the Hindu autumn festival of Navaratri.

dust /dʌst/ *noun*.
[ORIGIN Old English *dūst* = Old Frisian *dūst*, Middle Dutch *donst*, *dūst* (Low German *dust*, Dutch *duist* meal-dust, bran), Old Norse *dust*. Cf. Old High German *tun(i)st* wind, breeze, Low German *dunst* vapour.]
1 Finely powdered earth or other matter lying on the ground or on surfaces, or carried about by the wind; any substance pulverized; fine particles of matter; an example of this. OE. ▸**b** This and other household refuse. Usu. in *comb.*, as ***dustbin***, ***dustman***, etc. E18. ▸**c** Pollen; spores. L18.
J. BRAINE There wasn't one chip, one scratch, one speck of dust anywhere. E. WELTY The peppering of red road dust on the old man's hat. U. LE GUIN Drought had.. dried the soil to a fine grey dust, that now rose up on every wind.
brick dust, ***coal dust***, ***gold dust***, ***sawdust***, ***stardust***, etc.
2 *fig.* **a** (The material of) the human frame. (Cf. *Genesis* 2:7, 3:19.) *arch.* OE. ▸**b** A dead person's remains. OE. ▸**c** As the type of that which is worthless or contemptible, or occupies the lowest position. ME.
a R. GRANT Frail children of dust. **b** SHAKES. *Haml.* May not imagination trace the noble dust of Alexander till 'a find it stopping a bung-hole? **c** C. N. ROBINSON The Navy that.. humbled to the dust the pride of France.
3 A particle of matter, a pinch of something. Now *rare*. L16.
SHAKES. *John* A grain, a dust, a gnat, a wandering hair.
4 A cloud of finely powdered earth or of other fine particles floating in the air; *fig.* confusion, turmoil, disturbance; *slang* a row, an uproar. L16.
T. BROWN Quarrel and raise a Dust about nothing. R. CARSON Drifting arsenic dusts.. spread over neighbouring farms.
5 Money; cash. *arch. slang*. E17.
6 An act of cleaning by wiping off dust. L20.
– PHRASES (chiefly *fig.*): ***bite the dust***: see BITE *verb*. ***bulldust***: see BULL *noun*¹ & *adjective*. ***cosmic dust***: see COSMIC 3. ***dry as dust***: see DRY *adjective*. **dust and ashes** something very disappointing or disillusioning. ***happy dust***: see HAPPY *adjective*. **in the dust** dead and buried. ***kiss the dust***: see KISS *verb*. **not see a person for dust** find a person hastily departed. **shake the dust off one's feet** depart indignantly or disdainfully (cf. *Matthew* 10:14). **throw dust in a person's eyes** mislead a person by misrepresentation or by diverting attention from a point. **wait until the dust settles** wait until a situation calms down.
– COMB.: **dust bath** a bird's rolling in or sprinkling itself with dust to clean its feathers; **dustbin** a container for household refuse; **dust bowl** an area of land made unproductive by wind erosion of soil, esp. following loss of vegetation through drought, inappropriate farming practices, etc.; **dust box** (*a*) *arch.* a box from which a fine powder is sprinkled on wet ink to dry it; (*b*) (chiefly *Austral.*) a dustbin; **dust bunny** *N. Amer. colloq.* a ball of dust and fluff; **Dustbuster** (chiefly *N. Amer.*) (proprietary name for) a hand-held battery-powered vacuum cleaner; **dust cap** a cap to protect something from dust; **dustcart** a vehicle for collecting household refuse; **dust cloth**: put over things as a protection from dust; **dustcoat**: worn as a protection against dust; **dust-colour** dull light brown; **dust cover** a removable cover to protect furniture etc. from dust; a dust jacket; ***dust devil***: see DEVIL *noun* 12; **dust disease** *colloq.* pneumoconiosis; **dustheap** a heap of household refuse; ***dust jacket***: see JACKET *noun* 3b; **dustman** (*a*) a man employed to remove refuse from dustbins; (*b*) a sandman; **dustpan** a hand-held receptacle into which dust can be brushed from the floor; **dust sheet** a cover to protect furniture etc. from dust; **dust shot** the smallest size of gunshot; **dust storm** a dry storm in which clouds of dust or sand are raised and carried along; **dust trap** something in or on or under which dust readily collects; **dust-up** *colloq.* a fight, a disturbance; **dust wrapper** a dust jacket.
■ **dustless** *adjective* E17.

dust /dʌst/ *verb*. ME.
[ORIGIN from the noun Cf. Old Norse *dusta*.]
†**1** *verb intrans.* Be dusty. Only in ME.
†**2** *verb trans. & intrans.* (Cause to) crumble into dust. LME–L17.
3 *verb trans.* Make dusty. M16.
J. A. FROUDE We go out.. and dust our feet along its thoroughfares.
4 *verb trans.* Free from dust; wipe, brush, or beat the dust from. M16. ▸**b** Brush, shake, or rub off as dust. L18.
A. PATON He dusted his feet on the frayed mat outside Kumalo's door. N. MONSARRAT The rooms were.. cleaned, dusted, polished, and set to rights. **b** S. LEWIS He dusted the cigar-ash off his vest.
dust a person's jacket *colloq.* thrash a person.
5 *verb trans.* Sprinkle with dust or powder; sprinkle powdered insecticide etc. on (a crop), esp. from the air. L16. ▸**b** Strew or sprinkle as dust or powder. L18. ▸**c** *verb refl.* & *intrans.* Of a bird: take a dust bath. L18.
W. CATHER Marie took out.. rolls, and began to dust them over with powdered sugar. **b** B. SPOCK It should be dusted on your hand first.. and then rubbed gently on his [the baby's] skin.
6 *verb trans.* Beat; strike. Now *colloq. & dial.* E17.
M. TWAIN So she.. dusted us both with the hickry.
7 *verb intrans.* Ride or go quickly; hurry. *slang* (chiefly *US*). M17.
– WITH ADVERBS IN SPECIALIZED SENSES: **dust down** wipe or brush the dust from. **dust off** (*a*) = ***dust down*** above; (*b*) *US slang* = sense 7 above; (*c*) *US slang* defeat, kill, get rid of.

dustak /ˈdʌstək/ *noun*. *obsolete* exc. *hist.* Also **-stu(c)k**. M18.
[ORIGIN Urdu *dastak* from Persian.]
In the Indian subcontinent: a pass, a permit.

duster /ˈdʌstə/ *noun*. L16.
[ORIGIN from DUST *noun* or *verb* + -ER¹.]
1 A cloth, brush, or other article for dusting surfaces. L16. ▸**b** A person who dusts. M19.
feather duster: see FEATHER *noun*. ***linen duster***: see LINEN *adjective* & *noun*.
2 A device for sifting or applying dust; a sieve. M17.
3 A dustcoat. Now usu. a woman's loose casual full-length coat. Also ***duster coat***. M19.
4 NAUTICAL. An ensign, a flag. *slang*. E20.
red duster: see RED *adjective*.

dusting /ˈdʌstɪŋ/ *verbal noun*. E17.
[ORIGIN from DUST *verb* + -ING¹.]
1 The action of DUST *verb*; *esp.* (*a*) the removal of dust from furniture etc. by wiping or brushing; (*b*) the action or result of sprinkling with dust or powder; a quantity of dust or powder sprinkled over something. E17.
DICKENS Mrs. Bardell resumed her dusting. L. BLUE Scatter liberally with sugar and a dusting of cinnamon. *fig.*: B. BAINBRIDGE He had a nice chest.. with only a dusting of freckles between his shoulders.
crop dusting: see CROP *noun*.
2 A thrashing; a fight. *colloq.* L18.
– COMB.: **dusting powder** a powder for dusting, *esp.* talcum powder.

dustoor, **dustoory** *nouns* vars. of DASTUR *noun*², DASTURI.

dustu(c)k *noun* var. of DUSTAK.

dusty /ˈdʌsti/ *adjective*. OE.
[ORIGIN from DUST *noun* + -Y¹.]
1 Full of, abounding with, or strewn with dust. OE.
2 Of the nature of or pertaining to dust; finely powdered like dust. LME.
3 Of colour: appearing as though sprinkled with dust, dull. E17.
4 *fig.* Mean, worthless; uninteresting, 'dry as dust'; vague, unsatisfactory. E17.
– SPECIAL COLLOCATIONS & PHRASES: **dusty answer** an unsatisfactory answer; a rebuff. **dusty miller** (*a*) any of several plants grown for their ornamental greyish or whitish foliage, *esp.* silver ragwort, *Senecio cineraria*, snow in summer, *Cerastium tomentosum*, and a N. American mugwort, *Artemisia stellerana*; (*b*) a kind of artificial fishing fly; (*c*) *US* any of various speckled noctuid moths. **not so dusty**, **none so dusty** *colloq.* not so bad, fairly good.
■ **dustily** *adverb* L16. **dustiness** *noun* L16.

Dusun /ˈduːs(ə)n/ *noun & adjective*. L18.
[ORIGIN Malay *dusun* orchard, village.]
▸ **A** *noun*. Pl. same, **-s**.
1 (**d-**.) In Malaysia: a village, a cultivated area. L18.
2 A member of a Dayak people inhabiting the Malaysian state of Sabah (N. Borneo); the Indonesian language of this people. M19.
▸ **B** *attrib.* or as *adjective*. Of or pertaining to the Dusun or their language. M19.

Dutch /dʌtʃ/ *noun*¹. LME.
[ORIGIN from the adjective.]
▸ **I 1** The West Germanic language of the area of north and central Europe now largely comprising Germany, Austria, Switzerland, and the Low Countries; any dialect of this language. Without specifying word (as *High*, *Low*). *obsolete* exc. *hist.* LME.
2 *spec.* The language of the Netherlands (spoken also in what is now N. Belgium: cf. ***Flemish***). E18. ▸**b** Afrikaans. *S. Afr.* M18.
3 The German language as spoken by American immigrants from Germany or by Americans of German descent. Now *spec.* Pennsylvania Dutch. *US*. M18.
▸ **II 4** *collect. pl.* Formerly *gen.*, the people of the area of north and central Europe in which German or Dutch is spoken. Now *spec.* (*a*) the people of the Netherlands; (*b*) *S. Afr.*, *derog.* the Afrikaans-speakers, the South Africans of Dutch descent; (*c*) *US* the American immigrants from Germany or the Americans of German descent, *esp.* the Pennsylvania Dutch. L16.
beat the Dutch *US* be or do something extraordinary or startling (chiefly in ***that beats the Dutch***).
▸ **III 5** Desertion, escape, suicide. Chiefly in ***do a Dutch***, ***do the Dutch***. *slang* (orig. *US*). E20.
6 ***in Dutch***, in disgrace, in trouble. *slang* (orig. *US*). E20.
– PHRASES: ***Cape Dutch***: see CAPE *noun*¹. **double Dutch** gibberish, completely incomprehensible language. **High Dutch** (*a*) *arch.* High German; (*b*) *S. Afr.* Netherlands Dutch as opp. to Afrikaans. **Low Dutch** (*a*) Low German (in the wider sense: see GERMAN *noun*¹ & *adjective*¹), (*b*) *arch.* Netherlands Dutch; (*c*) *rare*. Afrikaans;

D

D

(*d*) (in this dictionary) Dutch and Low German (Middle and Modern). *PENNSYLVANIA* ***Dutch***. ***South African Dutch***: see SOUTH.

Dutch /dʌtʃ/ *noun*[2]. *slang*. L19.
[ORIGIN Abbreviation.]
= DUCHESS *noun* 3.

Dutch /dʌtʃ/ *adjective & adverb*. ME.
[ORIGIN Middle Dutch *dutsch* Dutch, Netherlandish, German (Dutch *duitsch* German) = Old English *þēodisc* Gentile, Old Saxon *þiudisc*, from Germanic, formed as Old English *þeod* people, -ISH[1]. Cf. Old High German *diutisc* national, popular, vulgar. In spec. US uses translating German *deutsch*, *Deutsche*.]
▸ **A** *adjective*. **1** Of, pertaining to, or designating the Germanic people of the area of north and central Europe now largely comprising Germany, Austria, Switzerland, and the Low Countries, or of any part of this area; of, pertaining to, or designating the West Germanic language of this people or any of its dialects; Teutonic. Without specifying word (as *High*, *Low*). *obsolete* exc. *hist.* ME.
2 *spec.* Of, pertaining to, or designating the people of the Netherlands (Holland) or their language (spoken also in what is now N. Belgium: cf. ***Flemish***); native to or originating in the Netherlands; characteristic of or attributed (often casually, usu. derogatorily) to the people of the Netherlands. E17. ▸**b** Of, pertaining to, or designating South Africans of Dutch descent; Afrikaans-speaking; of Afrikaans. *S. Afr., derog.* M18.
3 Of, pertaining to, or designating American immigrants from Germany or Americans of German descent, or the German language as spoken by them. Now *spec.* Pennsylvania Dutch. *US*. M18.
– PHRASES: As for DUTCH *noun*[1].
– SPECIAL COLLOCATIONS: **Dutch act** *US slang* = DUTCH *noun*[1] 5 (chiefly in ***do a Dutch act***, ***do the Dutch act***). ***Dutch auction***: see AUCTION *noun* 1. **Dutch bargain**: concluded by drinking together. **Dutch barn** a roof, supported on poles, over hay etc. **Dutch cap** (*a*) a woman's lace cap with a triangular piece turned back on each side; (*b*) a contraceptive diaphragm. **Dutch cheese** a cheese from the Netherlands, characteristically spherical in shape. ***Dutch clover***: see CLOVER *noun*. ***Dutch courage***: see COURAGE *noun* 4. **Dutch defence** *CHESS* a defence replying to the queen's pawn opening with a two-square move of the king's bishop's pawn. **Dutch doll** a jointed wooden doll. **Dutch elm disease** a destructive disease of elms (first found in the Netherlands) caused by infestation with the fungus *Ceratocystis ulmi* and spread by bark beetles. **Dutch feast**: at which the host gets drunk before the guests. **Dutch hoe** a hoe used with a pushing action. **Dutch interior** a painting of the interior of a Dutch room or house, by or in the style of Pieter de Hooch (1629–83). **Dutch light** a cold frame in which the glass is a single large pane. **Dutch lunch**: at which each person pays for his or her own share. **Dutch metal** an alloy of copper and zinc imitating gold leaf. ***Dutch nightingale***: see NIGHTINGALE *noun*[1] 3. ***Dutch oven***: see OVEN *noun* 2. **Dutch pink** a yellow lake pigment. **Dutch reckoning** *slang* faulty reckoning. **Dutch roll** *AERONAUTICS* a short-period lateral oscillation of an aircraft. **Dutch rush** the rough horsetail, *Equisetum hyemale*. **Dutch tile** a kind of glazed white tile painted with traditional Dutch motifs in blue or brown. **Dutch treat** a party, or outing, meal, etc., at which each person pays for his or her own share of the expenses. **Dutch uncle** a well-disposed, authoritative person (***talk to like a Dutch uncle***, lecture with kindly severity). **Dutch wife** (*a*) a frame of cane etc. used for resting the limbs in bed; (*b*) an artificial sexual partner.
– COMB.: **Dutchland** †(*a*) [from German *Deutschland*] Germany; (*b*) *rare* the Netherlands.
▸ **B** *adverb*. In a Dutch fashion. Now chiefly in ***go Dutch***, pay for one's own share, share the expense, of food, drink, entertainment, etc. E17.
– NOTE: Although some early uses refer to the area which is now the Netherlands, the restriction of *Dutch* to this (to the exclusion of Germany etc.) took place during 17 with the country's independence and increasing contact with Britain.
■ †**Dutcher** *noun* (*rare*) one of the Dutch (see DUTCH *noun*[1] 4) L17–E19. **Dutchify** *verb trans.* make Dutch, give a Dutch character to L17. **Dutchy** *noun* (*slang, derog.*) a Dutchman, a German M19.

Dutch /dʌtʃ/ *verb trans. obsolete* exc. *hist.* M18.
[ORIGIN from the adjective.]
Clarify and harden (quills) in hot sand or flames.

†**dutchess** *noun* var. of DUCHESS.

dutchie /ˈdʌtʃi/ *noun*. *W. Indian*. M20.
[ORIGIN from *Dutch pot*.]
A large heavy cooking pot.

Dutchman /ˈdʌtʃmən/ *noun*. Pl. **-men**. LME.
[ORIGIN from DUTCH *adjective* + MAN *noun*.]
1 *gen.* A man who is a member of a Teutonic nation; a German. Long *obsolete* exc. as below. LME.
2 An adult male native or inhabitant of the Netherlands. L16.
3 A Dutch ship. M17.
4 An adult male American immigrant from Germany or American of German descent, *spec.* a Pennsylvania Dutchman (see PENNSYLVANIA); *slang* any adult male German. *US*. L18.
5 An adult male European or foreigner. *slang* (chiefly *US*). M19.
6 A piece of wood or stone used to repair a flaw or fault or to patch up bad workmanship. Chiefly *US*. M19.
– PHRASES: **Dutchman's breeches** (*a*) a plant of the fumitory family, *Dicentra cucullaria*, which is native to eastern N. America and bears white, spurred flowers (from the shape of which the name is derived) and finely divided leaves; (*b*) *slang* (orig. *NAUTICAL*) a small patch of blue sky. **Dutchman's pipe** a climbing vine of the birthwort family, *Aristolochia durior*, which is native to eastern N. America and bears hook-shaped tubular flowers. **Flying Dutchman** (the captain of) a spectral ship supposedly doomed to sail the seas forever. **or I'm a Dutchman**, **I'm a Dutchman if**: used to express one's disbelief or as a way of underlining an emphatic assertion.
■ **Dutchwoman** *noun*, pl. **-women**, †(*a*) a woman of a Teutonic nation, a German woman; (*b*) a woman of the Netherlands: L18.

duteous /ˈdjuːtɪəs/ *adjective*. L16.
[ORIGIN from DUTY + -OUS. Cf. BEAUTEOUS.]
Characterized by the performance of duty to a superior; dutiful; obedient, subservient.
■ **duteously** *adverb* E19. **duteousness** *noun* M17.

dutiable /ˈdjuːtɪəb(ə)l/ *adjective*. L18.
[ORIGIN from DUTY + -ABLE.]
Liable to customs or other duties.

dutied /ˈdjuːtɪd/ *adjective*. *US*. L18.
[ORIGIN from DUTY + -ED[2].]
Dutiable.

dutiful /ˈdjuːtɪfʊl, -f(ə)l/ *adjective*. M16.
[ORIGIN from DUTY *noun* + -FUL.]
Regular or willing in obedience or service; conscientious.
■ **dutifully** *adverb* M16. **dutifulness** *noun* L16.

dutiless /ˈdjuːtɪlɪs/ *adjective*. Long *arch. rare*. L16.
[ORIGIN from DUTY + -LESS.]
Not dutiful.

du tout /dy tu/ *adverbial phr.* E19.
[ORIGIN French, abbreviation of *pas du tout*.]
Not at all; by no means.

duty /ˈdjuːti/ *noun & adjective*. LME.
[ORIGIN Anglo-Norman *deweté*, *dueté*, from *du(e)* DUE *adjective*: see -TY[1].]
▸ **A** *noun*. **1** That which is owed; what one owes; one's due; a debt of money, goods, or service. Long *obsolete* exc. as below. LME.

> TINDALE *Matt.* 20:14 Take that which is thy duty. E. COKE If *A.* be accountable to *B.* and *B.* releaseth him all his duties.

2 A payment due and enforced by law or custom; now *esp.* the payment to the public revenue levied on the import, export, manufacture, or sale of goods, on the transfer of property, for licences etc., for legal recognition of documents, etc. Freq. in *pl.* LME. ▸†**b** Payment for the services of the Church. Usu. in *pl.* LME–M16. ▸**c** *SCOTS LAW*. A payment made by a vassal to a superior in recognition of feudal authority. M16.
customs duty, ***death duty***, ***excise duty***, ***probate duty***, ***stamp duty***, etc. ***countervailing duty***: see COUNTERVAIL *verb* 5. ***umboth duty***: see UMBOTH 2.
3 The behaviour due to a superior; homage; deference; an expression of respect. LME.

> N. ROWE What Duty, what Submission shall they not pay to that Authority? T. H. WHITE Hob made a duty to Merlyn, who returned it courteously.

4 The action or behaviour due by moral or legal obligation; an obligation; the binding force of what is morally right. LME.

> P. G. WODEHOUSE With your magnificent physique . . it is your duty to the future of the race to marry. A. S. NEILL Women . . compelled by a sense of duty to . . look after elderly parents. D. MURPHY It was a parental duty to try to persuade me to rethink. *personified*: WORDSWORTH Stern Daughter of the Voice of God! O Duty!

5 (An) action required by one's business, occupation, or function; the performance of or engagement in the activities required by one's business, occupation, or function. LME. ▸**b** *ECCLESIASTICAL*. Performance of the prescribed services or offices of the Church; *ROMAN CATHOLIC CHURCH* attendance at services and confession. E16.

> V. BRITTAIN He was transferred to the Somerset Light Infantry for temporary duty. E. LONGFORD His duties were to supervise the various harbour works, lifeboats and salvage.

do duty as, **do duty for** serve as or pass for (something else). **do one's duty** *euphem.* defecate, urinate. ***heavy-duty***: see HEAVY *adjective*. **off duty** not on duty, not engaged in one's duties; spent, engaged in, etc., when not on duty. **on duty** engaged in one's business or occupation or in performing one's function.
6 A measure of an engine's effectiveness expressed in units of work done per unit of fuel. E19.
– COMB.: **duty-bound** *adjective* obliged by duty; **duty cycle** the cycle of operation of a device acting intermittently; the time occupied by this, esp. as a fraction of available time; **duty-free** *adjective, adverb, & noun* (*a*) *adjective & adverb* exempt from payment of customs and excise duty, esp. as a small personal allowance on (re-)entering a country; (***duty-free shop***: at which duty-free goods are sold); (*b*) *noun* a duty-free article; **duty-paid** *adjective* (of goods) on which customs or excise duty has been paid.
▸ **B** *attrib.* or as *adjective*. **1** Of a visit, call, or other undertaking: done as a duty rather than as a pleasure. E19.

> C. ISHERWOOD A duty-party, given once a year, to all the relatives, friends and dependents of the family. A. CHRISTIE We had him to lunch with some other Duty people.

2 Of a person: having specific duties; being on duty. L19.

> P. LAURIE The Duty Officer, an elderly inspector.

duumvir /djuːˈʌmvə/ *noun*. Pl. **-virs**, in Latin form **-viri** /-vɪraɪ/. E17.
[ORIGIN Latin, sing. from *duum virum* genit. pl. of *duo viri* two men.]
In *ROMAN HISTORY*, of a pair of coequal magistrates or officials; *gen.* either of two people with joint authority, a coalition of two people.
■ **duumvirate** *noun* [Latin *duumviratus*] (*a*) the position or office of duumvirs; the joint authority of two people; (*b*) two people with joint authority, the members of a coalition of people: M17.

duvet /ˈdjuːveɪ, ˈduː-/ *noun*. M18.
[ORIGIN French = DOWN *noun*[2].]
A thick soft quilt used instead of other bedclothes. Also called ***continental quilt***.
– COMB.: **duvet day** *colloq.* an unscheduled extra day's leave from work, taken to alleviate stress or pressure and sanctioned by one's employer.

Duvetyn /ˈdjuːvɪtɪn, ˈdʌvtɪn/ *noun*. Also **d-**. E20.
[ORIGIN formed as DUVET.]
(Proprietary name for) a soft worsted and silk material.

dux /dʌks/ *noun*. Pl. **duces** /ˈdjuːsiːz/, **duxes**. M18.
[ORIGIN Latin = leader.]
1 *MUSIC*. The subject of a fugue or canon; the leading voice or instrument in a fugue or canon. Opp. COMES. M18.
2 The top pupil in a class or school. Chiefly *Scot.*, *NZ*, & *S. Afr.* L18.

duxelles /ˈdʌks(ə)lz, *foreign* dyksɛl/ *noun*. L19.
[ORIGIN Marquis *d'Uxelles*, 17th-cent. French nobleman.]
A seasoning or sauce of shallots, parsley, onions, and mushrooms.

duyker *noun* var. of DUIKER *noun*.

DV *abbreviation*.
Latin *Deo volente* God willing.

dvandva /ˈdvandvə/ *noun*. M19.
[ORIGIN Sanskrit *dvandva* from *dva* two.]
LINGUISTICS. More fully ***dvandva compound***. A compound word containing two elements as if joined by *and*, as ***whisky-soda***.

DVD *abbreviation*.
Digital versatile (or video) disc.

DVD-R *abbreviation*.
DVD recordable.

DVD-ROM *abbreviation*.
DVD (with) read-only memory.

DVD-RW *abbreviation*.
DVD rewritable.

DVLA *abbreviation*.
Driver and Vehicle Licensing Agency.

DVM *abbreviation*.
Doctor of Veterinary Medicine.

Dvořákian /(d)vɔːˈʒakɪən/ *adjective & noun*. L19.
[ORIGIN from *Dvořák* (see below) + -IAN.]
▸ **A** *adjective*. Of, pertaining to, or characteristic of the Czech composer Antonín Leopold Dvořák (1841–1904) or his music. L19.
▸ **B** *noun*. An interpreter, student, or admirer of Dvořák or his music. L20.

DVR *abbreviation*.
Digital video recorder.

DVT *abbreviation*.
Deep-vein thrombosis.

dwale /dweɪl/ *noun*. ME.
[ORIGIN Prob. of Scandinavian origin: cf. Danish *dvale* dead sleep, stupor, *dvaledrik* sleeping draught.]
†**1** A stupefying or soporific drink, *esp.* the juice or infusion of belladonna. ME–E17.
2 Belladonna, deadly nightshade. Formerly also, any of various other plants yielding similar narcotic preparations. LME.
3 *HERALDRY*. The tincture sable in the fanciful blazon of arms of peers. Long *obsolete* exc. *hist.* M16.

dwam /dwɑːm/ *noun & verb*. *Scot.*, *N. Irish*, & *N. English*. Also **dwalm**. E16.
[ORIGIN from Germanic base of DWELL *verb*. Cf. Old English *dwolma* confusion, chaos, Old High German *twalm*, Middle Dutch *dwelm* stupefaction, giddiness, Old Saxon *dwalm* delusion.]
▸ **A** *noun*. A fainting fit; dizziness, giddiness. E16.
▸ **B** *verb intrans.* Faint, swoon; fail in health. E16.

dwang /dwaŋ/ *noun*. Chiefly *Scot.* L15.
[ORIGIN Cf. Dutch *dwang* force, compulsion, constraint.]
A short piece of timber used for any of various purposes; *esp.* one inserted between joists or studs to prevent distortion. Also, a crowbar, a wrench.

dwarf /dwɔːf/ *noun & adjective*.
[ORIGIN Old English *dweorg*, *dweorh* = Old Frisian *dwirg*, Middle Dutch *dwerch* (Dutch *dwerg*), Old High German *twerg* (German *Zwerg*), Old Norse *dvergr*, from Germanic.]
▸ **A** *noun*. Pl. **dwarfs**, **dwarves** /dwɔːvz/.
1 An abnormally undersized person. Now regarded as *offensive*. OE. ▸**b** Any of a mythical race of diminutive beings, typically skilled in mining and metalworking and often possessing magical powers, figuring esp. in Scandinavian folklore. ME.

fig.: H. BELLOC Many troubles that seem giants at evening are but dwarfs at sunrise. **b** C. S. LEWIS The old bright-hooded, snowy-bearded dwarfs we had in those days before.. Walt Disney vulgarised the earthmen.

2 An animal or plant of much smaller size than the average of its kind or species. M17.
3 ASTRONOMY. A small dense star. Freq., a main-sequence star as opp. to a superdense star or to a giant or super-giant. E20.
brown dwarf: see BROWN *adjective*. ***red dwarf***: see RED *adjective*. ***white dwarf***: see WHITE *adjective*.
▸ **B** *adjective*. Of or pertaining to a dwarf, dwarfish; of unusually small stature or size, diminutive; puny, stunted (naturally or deliberately); *esp.* designating species or varieties of plants and animals which are much smaller than the average of their kind. L16.
dwarf wall a low wall; *spec.* one forming the base of a palisade or railing, or supporting the joists under a floor.
■ **dwarfism** *noun* the condition or character of being a dwarf; abnormally short stature: M19. **dwarfling** *noun* a small dwarf E17. **dwarfness** *noun* M17. **dwarfy** *adjective* of the nature of a dwarf, dwarfish E17.

dwarf /dwɔːf/ *verb*. E17.
[ORIGIN from the noun.]
1 *verb trans.* Stunt, restrict the growth of; stunt the development or extent of (*lit.* & *fig.*). E17.

R. W. EMERSON The incessant repetition of the same hand-work dwarfs the man, robs him of his strength, wit, and versatility. *Which?* Commercial growers.. often dwarf the plants with chemicals.

2 *verb trans.* Cause to look or seem small by contrast or by distance (*lit.* & *fig.*). M19.

B. WEBB Our close comradeship.. the ideal marriage—dwarfs all other human relationships. J. LE CARRÉ The wharf.. dwarfed by the decks of cargo ships.

3 *verb intrans.* Become dwarf or (relatively) undersized. M19.

TENNYSON By him [Mark Antony] great Pompey dwarfs.

dwarfish /ˈdwɔːfɪʃ/ *adjective*. M16.
[ORIGIN from DWARF *noun* & *adjective* + -ISH¹.]
Approaching the size of a dwarf; resembling (that of) a dwarf; of below average size or stature, diminutive, puny.
■ **dwarfishly** *adverb* M18. **dwarfishness** *noun* M17.

dwarves *noun pl.* see DWARF *noun*.

dweeb /dwiːb/ *noun*. *US slang*. L20.
[ORIGIN Unknown.]
A person who is boringly conventional, puny, or studious.

S. J. GOULD Any kid with a passionate interest in science was a.. dweeb.

■ **dweeby** *adjective* L20.

dwell /dwɛl/ *noun*. ME.
[ORIGIN from the verb. Cf. also Old Norse *dvǫl* stay, delay.]
†**1** Delay, stay, stoppage; continuance in a state or place. ME–M16.
2 A slight regular pause in the motion of (a part of) a machine, allowing time for its own or another part's operation. M19.

dwell /dwɛl/ *verb*. Pa. t. & pple **dwelt** /-t/, **dwelled**.
[ORIGIN Old English *dwellan* corresp. to Old Saxon *bi-dwellian* hinder, Middle Dutch *dwellen* stun, perplex, Old High German, Middle High German *twellen* delay, harass, Old Norse *dvelja* (*verb trans.*) delay, (*verb intrans.* & *refl.*) tarry, stay, from Germanic.]
†**1** *verb trans.* Mislead, delude; stun, stupefy. OE–ME.
†**2** *verb trans.* Hinder, delay. Only in OE.
†**3** *verb intrans.* Tarry, delay; discontinue an action. ME–L15.
†**4** *verb intrans.* Continue in existence, last, persist; remain. Only in ME.
5 *verb intrans.* Continue for a time in a place, state, or condition. ME. ▸**b** Of a horse: be slow in raising the feet, pause before taking a jump. M18. ▸**c** Of (part of) a machine: pause slightly during its working (cf. DWELL *noun* 2). M19.

SHAKES. *Merch. V.* I'll rather dwell in my necessity. *Horse & Hound* Here hounds dwelt round the buildings for a while.

6 *verb intrans.* Reside, live, have one's home. *literary*. ME. ▸†**b** *verb trans.* Inhabit. E16–L18. ▸†**c** *verb trans.* Cause to reside *in*. *rare* (Milton). Only in M17.

R. L. STEVENSON I see.. men dwell in contentment with noisy scullions. W. GASS Living in a city, among so many, dwelling in the heat and tumult of incessant movement.

7 *verb intrans.* Foll. by *on*, *upon*, †*in*: keep one's attention fixed on (an object); ponder, consider (a matter) at length; write or speak at length on (a subject). ME.

B. PYM She preferred not to dwell on how it might work, not to speculate. A. WILSON The speech dwelt mainly on defeat and the saving power of evil.

– COMB.: **dwell time** (chiefly *techn.*) time spent stationary or in the same area or state.
■ **dweller** *noun* LME.

dwelling /ˈdwɛlɪŋ/ *noun*. ME.
[ORIGIN from DWELL *verb* + -ING¹.]
1 The action of DWELL *verb*. ME.
2 A place of residence; a habitation, a house. LME.
– COMB.: **dwelling house**: used as a residence, not for business purposes; **dwelling place** a place of residence, an abode, a house.

dwelt *verb pa. t.* & *pple*: see DWELL *verb*.

DWEM *abbreviation*.
Dead white European male.

DWI *abbreviation*. *US*.
Driving while intoxicated.

dwile /dwʌɪl/ *noun*. *dial.* E19.
[ORIGIN Cf. Dutch *dweil* mop.]
A floorcloth, a mop, a flannel.
– COMB.: **dwile-flonking** [*flonking* prob. regional var. of *flinging*] an English pub game involving the throwing of beer-soaked cloths according to certain specified rules, which vary from region to region.

dwindle /ˈdwɪnd(ə)l/ *verb* & *noun*. L16.
[ORIGIN Frequentative of DWINE: see -LE³.]
▸ **A** *verb*. **1** *verb intrans.* Become reduced in size or quantity; shrink; waste away. L16. ▸**b** *fig.* Diminish in quality, value, or importance; decline, degenerate. L17.

J. B. PRIESTLEY The sun came struggling through again and the rain dwindled to a few glittering drops. R. C. HUTCHINSON The uproar had dwindled to silence. **b** G. MURRAY The great hope had dwindled to be very like despair.

2 *verb trans.* Cause to shrink, reduce gradually in size. *rare*. M17.
▸ **B** *noun*. The process of dwindling. Also, a dwindled object. *rare*. M18.

dwine /dwʌɪn/ *verb*. Now *arch.*, *Scot.*, & *dial.*
[ORIGIN Old English *dwīnan* = Middle & mod. Low German, Middle Dutch *dwīnen*, Old Norse *dvína*. Cf. DWINDLE.]
1 *verb intrans.* Waste or pine away; fade, wither. OE.
2 *verb trans.* Cause to pine or waste away. *rare*. L16.

DWM *abbreviation*.
1 Dead white male.
2 Divorced white male.

dwt *abbreviation*.
Pennyweight (*d* = Latin *denarius* penny).

d.w.t. *abbreviation*.
Dead weight tonnage.

Dy *symbol*.
CHEMISTRY. Dysprosium.

dy /dʌɪ/ *noun*. M20.
[ORIGIN Swedish = mire, ooze from Old Norse *dý*: perh. from Germanic base of DUNG *noun*.]
A sediment rich in allochthonous organic matter deposited in nutrient-poor lakes. Cf. GYTTJA.

dyad /ˈdʌɪad/ *noun*. L17.
[ORIGIN Late Latin *dyad-*, *dyas* from Greek *duad-*, *duas*, from *duo* two: see -AD¹. Cf. DUAD.]
▸ **A** *noun*. **1** The number two; a group of two, a pair; a twofold entity. L17. ▸**b** PROSODY. A group of two lines with different rhythms. L19. ▸**c** MATH. An operator which is a combination of two vectors. Now *rare*. L19.
†**2** CHEMISTRY. A divalent atom or radical. M–L19.
▸ **B** *attrib.* or as *adjective*. = DYADIC *adjective*. M19.

dyadic /dʌɪˈadɪk/ *adjective* & *noun*. Also **diadic**. E18.
[ORIGIN Greek *duadikos*, from *duad-*, *duas*: see DYAD, -IC.]
▸ **A** *adjective*. **1** Of, pertaining to, or of the nature of a dyad; double, twofold. E18.
2 PHILOSOPHY. Designating or pertaining to a relationship between exactly two entities, or a predicate expressing such a relationship. L19. ▸**b** MATH. & COMPUTING. Designating an expression, operator, etc., which requires or acts on two arguments. M20.
▸ **B** *noun*. MATH. A vector dyad or combination of dyads. Now *rare*. L19.

Dyak *noun* & *adjective* var. of DAYAK.

dyarchy *noun* var. of DIARCHY.

dybbuk /ˈdɪbʊk/ *noun*. Also **dibbuk**. Pl. **-im** /-ɪm/, **-s**. E20.
[ORIGIN Yiddish *dibek* from Hebrew *dibbūq*, from *dāḇaq* cling, cleave.]
In Jewish folklore, a malevolent wandering spirit that enters and possesses the body of a living person until exorcized.

dye /dʌɪ/ *noun*. Also †**die**.
[ORIGIN Old English *dēah*, *dēag* from Germanic. Obsolete after ME until re-formed from the verb in L16.]
1 Colour produced by or as by dyeing; shade, hue, tinge. Now chiefly *fig.* OE.

J. WILSON Wings and crests of rainbow dyes. C. STEAD Not a householder in Annapolis but considered Eastport a civic disgrace of deep dye.

2 A (natural or synthetic) substance used for dyeing; *esp.* a colouring matter used in solution. OE.

New Scientist Whereas dyes react with material at a molecular level, pigments are generally macromolecular.

adjective dye: see ADJECTIVE *adjective* 2. ***basic dye***: see BASIC *adjective* 2. ***direct dye***: see DIRECT *adjective*.
– COMB.: **dye-house** a building in which a dyer works; **dye laser** a tunable laser using the fluorescence of an organic dye; **dyeline** (a print made by) the diazo process; **dyestuff**, **dyeware** (a substance yielding) a dye; **dyewood**: yielding a dye.

dye /dʌɪ/ *verb*. Also †**die**. Pa. t. & pple **dyed**; pres. pple **dyeing**.
[ORIGIN Old English *dēagian* perh. of Germanic origin. Not recorded again until LME.]
1 *verb trans.* Colour, stain, tinge, suffuse; *esp.* impregnate with colouring matter, change the colour of by means of a (natural or synthetic) colouring material in solution. With compl.: make (a thing) a specified colour (thus), or *of*, *into*, *to* a colour. OE. ▸**b** *verb intrans.* or with compl. only: (have the ability to) impart colour to a thing. LME.

J. GALSWORTHY Swithin stared at her; a dusky orange dyed his cheeks. DYLAN THOMAS Mrs Beynon's new mauve jumper, it's her old grey jumper dyed. F. WELDON Colleen dyed her white.. shirt bright red. **b** J. LINDLEY Genista tinctoria.. Dyes yellow.

dyed-in-the-grain, **dyed-in-grain** (*a*) dyed in kermes; dyed in any fast colour; dyed in the fibre or thoroughly; (*b*) *fig.* = ***dyed-in-the-wool*** (b). **dyed-in-the-wool**, **dyed-in-wool** (*a*) *lit.* (now *rare*) dyed while the material is in a raw state, and hence more thoroughly and permanently; (*b*) *fig.* unchangeable, inveterate.
2 *verb intrans.* Take a colour (well or badly) in the process of dyeing. L19.

dyeable /ˈdʌɪəb(ə)l/ *adjective*. M20.
[ORIGIN from DYE *verb* + -ABLE.]
Able to be dyed.
■ **dyeaˈbility** *noun* M20.

dyer /ˈdʌɪə/ *noun*. LME.
[ORIGIN from DYE *verb* + -ER¹.]
A person whose occupation is the dyeing of cloth etc.
In *possess.* in names of plants yielding dyes: **dyer's broom** = ***dyer's greenweed*** below. ***dyer's greenweed***: see **greenweed** s.v. GREEN *adjective*. **dyer's rocket** the plant weld, *Reseda luteola*. **dyer's weed** (*a*) = ***dyer's greenweed*** above; (*b*) = ***dyer's rocket*** above.
■ **dyery** *noun* a place or building where dyeing is carried out M18.

dyester /ˈdʌɪstə/ *noun*. Now *Scot. arch.* LME.
[ORIGIN from DYE *verb* + -STER.]
= DYER.

dying /ˈdʌɪɪŋ/ *verbal noun*¹ & *adjective*¹. ME.
[ORIGIN from DIE *verb*¹ + -ING¹.]
▸ **A** *noun*. The action of DIE *verb*¹. ME.
▸ **B** *attrib.* or as *adjective*. Of or connected with death or dying; done, occurring, or (of words, a wish, etc.) expressed at the time of death. L16.
dying oath made at, or with the solemnity proper to, death. **to one's dying day**, **until one's dying day** for the rest of one's life.

dying /ˈdʌɪɪŋ/ *ppl adjective*² & *noun*². LME.
[ORIGIN from DIE *verb*¹ + -ING².]
▸ **A** *ppl adjective*. That dies; at the point of death; mortal; *fig.* that ends, ceases, fades. LME.
dying god: whose death is commemorated annually, typifying the seasonal death of vegetation.
▸ **B** *absol.* as *noun pl.* *The* people who are dying, as a class. L18.
■ **dyingly** *adverb* in a dying manner, in dying LME. **dyingness** *noun* dying or languishing quality E18.

dyke /dʌɪk/ *noun*¹. Also **dike**. ME.
[ORIGIN Old Norse *dík*, *díki* or (branch II) Middle Low German *dīk* dam, Middle Dutch *dijc* ditch, pool, mound, dam (Dutch *dijk* dam): see DITCH *noun*.]
▸ **I** Something dug out.
†**1** A long narrow excavation, a ditch (as a boundary marker, defensive measure, etc.). ME–L16.
†**2** Any hollow dug in the ground; a pit, cave, etc. ME–L15.
3 A hollow dug out to hold or conduct water; a drainage ditch; any watercourse or channel. LME.

POPE Thames, The King of dykes!

4 A lavatory. *slang*. E20.
▸ **II** Something built up.
5 †**a** The wall of a city; a fortification. ME–M16. ▸**b** A low wall of turf or stone serving as a division or enclosure. LME.

b R. SIBBALD The Ruins of a dry-stone dyke.

6 A bank formed by throwing up the earth from a ditch. L15.
7 A (raised) causeway. L15.
8 An embankment, long ridge, or dam against flooding, esp. as built in the Netherlands against the sea. M17.

J. A. MICHENER He might by building a dyke hold back the wadi and prevent it from washing away the fields.

9 *fig.* A barrier, an obstacle, a defence. L18.

BYRON He there builds up a formidable dyke Between his own and others' intellect.

10 **a** MINING. A fissure filled with rock; a fault. *dial.* L18. ▸**b** GEOLOGY. A sheet of rock filling a fissure; *esp.* a mass of igneous rock that has intruded upwards through strata, sometimes showing as a ridge at the surface. **E19.**

– **COMB.:** **dyke-reeve** [perh. alt. of DYKE-GRAVE] *hist.* an officer who had charge of the drains and sea banks in fenland counties.

dyke /dʌɪk/ *noun*². *slang. derog.* Also **dike**. **M20.**
[ORIGIN Unknown: cf. BULL-DYKE, earlier BULL-DYKER.]
A (masculine) lesbian; a masculine woman.
■ **dykey** *adjective* having the appearance or characteristics of a lesbian **M20.**

dyke /dʌɪk/ *verb*. Also **dike**. **ME.**
[ORIGIN from DYKE *noun*¹: cf. DITCH *verb*.]
1 *verb intrans.* Make a dyke, ditch, or excavation; dig. **ME.**
2 *verb trans.* Provide with a dyke or dykes, for defence or (later) as a protection against flooding or to improve drainage. **ME.**
3 *verb trans.* Clean out (a ditch or watercourse). Now *rare* or *obsolete*. **E16.**
■ **dyker** *noun* a person who constructs or works at dykes **OE.**

D

dyke-grave /ˈdʌɪkgreɪv/ *noun*. Also **dike-**. **M16.**
[ORIGIN Middle Dutch *dijcgrave*, from *dijc* (see DYKE *noun*¹) + *grave* (mod. *graaf*) GRAVE *noun*².]
hist. A dyke-reeve; an officer in the Netherlands with similar duties.

dyn *abbreviation*.
Dyne(s).

dynameter /dʌɪˈnamɪtə/ *noun*. **E19.**
[ORIGIN from Greek *dunamis*: see DYNAMIC, -METER.]
= DYNAMOMETER 2.

dynamic /dʌɪˈnamɪk/ *adjective & noun*. **E19.**
[ORIGIN French *dynamique* from Greek *dunamikos*, from *dunamis* force, power: see -IC.]
▸ **A** *adjective*. **1** Of or relating to force producing motion (opp. ***static***). **E19.** ▸**b** Of or pertaining to the science of dynamics. **M19.**

J. TYNDALL According to the dynamic view . . heat is regarded as a motion.

2 *PHILOSOPHY.* Of or relating to dynamism (DYNAMISM 1). **E19.**
3 Active, potent, energetic, forceful; characterized by action or change. **M19.**

M. MCCARTHY Kay and Harald were too busy and dynamic to let convention cramp their style. J. BARNES Adolescence is a dynamic period, the mind and body thrusting forward to new discoveries all the time.

4 *MEDICINE.* Affecting bodily function, as opp. to causing pathological organic change. **M19.**
5 *MUSIC, ELECTRONICS*, etc. Of or relating to the volume of sound produced by a voice, instrument, or sound recording equipment. **L19.**

Gramophone It sounds . . wider in dynamic range . . than most broadcasts of that period.

6 *GRAMMAR.* Of a verb: expressing an action, activity, event, or process. **L19.**
7 *COMPUTING.* Of a memory or store: orig., having a moving component; now usu., depending on an applied voltage to refresh it periodically. **M20.**

– **SPECIAL COLLOCATIONS:** **dynamic equilibrium** a state of balance between continuing processes. **dynamic friction**: between surfaces in relative motion. **dynamic metamorphism** *GEOLOGY*: produced by mechanical forces. **dynamic pressure**: due to the motion of a fluid. **dynamic pricing** the practice of pricing items at a level determined by a particular customer's perceived ability to pay. **dynamic range** the difference between the softest and loudest levels of recorded sound etc. ***dynamic viscosity***: see VISCOSITY 2.

▸ **B** *noun*. †**1** = DYNAMICS 1. Only in **L19.**
2 An energizing or a motive force. **L19.**

H. KISSINGER It could no longer conquer the world . . . The dynamic had gone. T. O'BRIEN Sarah . . understood the dynamic of our age. It was all escalation.

3 = DYNAMICS 3. **M20.**

dynamical /dʌɪˈnamɪk(ə)l/ *adjective*. **E19.**
[ORIGIN formed as DYNAMIC + -ICAL.]
1 = DYNAMIC *adjective* 1. **E19.**
2 *THEOLOGY.* Of or relating to inspiration as endowing with divine power rather than promoting mechanical action. **M19.**
3 *PHILOSOPHY.* = DYNAMIC *adjective* 2. **M19.**
4 *MEDICINE.* = DYNAMIC *adjective* 4. *rare*. **M19.**

dynamically /dʌɪˈnamɪk(ə)li/ *adverb*. **M19.**
[ORIGIN from DYNAMIC *adjective* or DYNAMICAL: see -ICALLY.]
In a dynamic or dynamical manner; as regards dynamics.

dynamicist /dʌɪˈnamɪsɪst/ *noun*. **M20.**
[ORIGIN from DYNAMICS + -IST.]
An expert in or student of the science of dynamics.

dynamics /dʌɪˈnamɪks/ *noun pl.* **L18.**
[ORIGIN formed as DYNAMIC: see -ICS.]
1 (Treated as *sing.*) The branch of mechanics that treats of motion in itself, and of the motion of bodies or matter under the influence of forces (including ***kinematics*** and ***kinetics***: opp. ***statics***). **L18.** ▸**b** That branch of any science in which forces or changes are considered. **M19.**

b J. S. MILL Social Dynamics is the theory of society considered in a state of progressive movement. C. LYELL Those . . conversant with dynamics of glacier motion.

2 The motive forces, physical or moral, in any sphere; the dynamic properties of a system. **M19.**

G. GORER This absence of overt aggression, calls for an explanation if the dynamics of English character are to be . . described. T. BARR Every scene should have some changes and dynamics in it.

3 *MUSIC, ELECTRONICS*, etc. The variation or amount of volume of sound in a musical performance, sound recording, etc. **L19.**

A. COPLAND Merely by changing the dynamics . . one can transform the emotional feeling of the very same . . notes.

dynamise *verb* var. of DYNAMIZE.

dynamism /ˈdʌɪnəmɪz(ə)m/ *noun*. **M19.**
[ORIGIN from Greek *dunamis* force, power + -ISM.]
1 *PHILOSOPHY.* Any system or theory which holds that the phenomena of matter or mind are due merely to the action of forces. **M19.**
2 Dynamic character, the operation of force; energizing action or power; energy, drive. **M19.**
■ **dynamist** *noun* (**a**) = DYNAMICIST; (**b**) an adherent of philosophical dynamism: **M19.** **dynaˈmistic** *adjective* **L19.**

dynamitard /dʌɪnəmɪˈtɑːd/ *noun*. Now *rare*. **L19.**
[ORIGIN from DYNAMITE after *communard*, prob. after rare obsolete French.]
= DYNAMITER (b).

dynamite /ˈdʌɪnəmʌɪt/ *noun, verb, & adjective*. **M19.**
[ORIGIN from Greek *dunamis* force, power + -ITE¹.]
▸ **A** *noun*. **1** A high explosive consisting of nitroglycerine absorbed in an inert material such as kieselguhr. **M19.**
2 *fig.* Something or someone potentially dangerous, disruptive, or devastating to an opponent etc. **E20.**

Guardian Withdrawal may be political dynamite. J. DIDION We've got a new Arabian at the ranch . . . Pereira blue mare, dynamite.

3 Heroin or a similar drug. *slang*. **E20.**
▸ **B** *verb trans.* Blow up, wreck, or charge with dynamite or a similar explosive. **L19.**
▸ **C** *adjective*. Powerful; explosive; extraordinarily good. *slang*. **M20.**
■ **dynamiter** *noun* (**a**) a person who employs dynamite or a similar explosive; (**b**) *spec.* a person who causes explosions as a means of attacking a government or political system: **L19.**

dynamize /ˈdʌɪnəmʌɪz/ *verb trans.* Also **-ise**. **M19.**
[ORIGIN from DYNAMIC + -IZE.]
Endow with power; make (more) dynamic. Orig. *spec.* in *HOMEOPATHY*, make (a medicine) more active by pulverizing or shaking.
■ **dynamiˈzation** *noun* **M19.**

dynamo /ˈdʌɪnəməʊ/ *noun*. Pl. **-os**. **L19.**
[ORIGIN Abbreviation of *dynamo-electric machine* (see DYNAMO-).]
1 A machine which converts mechanical energy into electric energy by electric induction, usu. by a rotating conductor in a magnetic field. **L19.**
2 *transf.* & *fig.* Something or someone very energetic or active; a source of power energizing a system; *esp.* the postulated system of circulating electric currents within the earth's core which is believed to generate the earth's magnetic field. **L19.**

D. OGILVY I have to rely on . . empirical techniques for spotting creative dynamos. E. J. KORMONDY The turnover of phosphorus may be . . sufficient to turn the ecosystem dynamo.

dynamo- /ˈdʌɪnəməʊ/ *combining form* of Greek *dunamis* force, power: see -O-.
■ **dynamo-eˈlectric** *adjective* of or pertaining to the conversion of mechanical to electric energy; ***dynamo-electric machine*** (now *hist.*) = DYNAMO 1: **L19.** **dynamoˈgenesis**, **dynaˈmogeny** *nouns* the generation of (increased) nervous or mental activity **L19.** **dynamometaˈmorphism** *noun* (*GEOLOGY*) = ***dynamic metamorphism*** s.v. DYNAMIC *adjective* **L19.**

dynamometer /dʌɪnəˈmɒmɪtə/ *noun*. **E19.**
[ORIGIN French *dynamomètre*, formed as DYNAMO- + -METER.]
1 An instrument for measuring the mechanical energy exerted by an animal, engine, etc., or by the action of a force. **E19.**
2 An instrument for measuring the magnifying power of a telescope. **M19.**

– **COMB.:** **dynamometer car** a railway vehicle containing equipment for measuring and recording the performance of a locomotive pulling the vehicle.
■ **dynamoˈmetric**, **dynamoˈmetrical** *adjectives* of or pertaining to the measurement of force or the use of a dynamometer **M19.** **dynamometry** *noun* **L19.**

dynamotor /ˈdʌɪnəməʊtə/ *noun*. **E20.**
[ORIGIN from Greek *dunamis* force, power + MOTOR *noun*.]
A form of rotary converter combining an electric motor and a generator.

dynast /ˈdɪnəst, ˈdʌɪnəst, -ast/ *noun*. **M17.**
[ORIGIN Latin *dynastes* from Greek *dunastēs*, from *dunasthai* be able, be powerful.]
A person in (esp. hereditary) power, a ruler; a member or founder of a dynasty.

dynastic /dɪˈnastɪk, dʌɪ-/ *noun & adjective*. **E17.**
[ORIGIN Greek *dunastikos*, from *dunastēs*: see DYNAST, -IC.]
▸ †**A** *noun*. = DYNAST. Only in **E17.**
▸ **B** *adjective*. Of, pertaining to, or connected with a dynasty or dynasties. **E19.**
■ **dynastical** *adjective* = DYNASTIC **M18.** **dynastically** *adverb* **M19.** **dynasticism** /-sɪz(ə)m/ *noun* the dynastic principle, the system of ruling dynasties **L19.**

dynasty /ˈdɪnəsti/ *noun*. **LME.**
[ORIGIN French *dynastie* or late Latin *dynastia* from Greek *dunasteia* power, domination, from *dunastēs*: see DYNAST, -Y³.]
†**1** Lordship, sovereignty, power; regime. **LME–M19.**
2 A succession of hereditary rulers; a line or family of monarchs. **LME.**
3 A succession of leaders in any sphere; a prominent family spanning a number of generations. **E19.**

dyne /dʌɪn/ *noun*. **L19.**
[ORIGIN French, from Greek *dunamis* force, power.]
PHYSICS. The unit of force in the centimetre-gram-second system, equal to 10^{-5} newton; the force that, acting on a mass of one gram, gives the mass an acceleration of one centimetre per second per second.

dynode /ˈdʌɪnəʊd/ *noun*. **M20.**
[ORIGIN formed as DYNE + -ODE².]
PHYSICS. An electrode which emits secondary electrons, used in electron multipliers etc.

Dyophysite /dʌɪˈɒfɪsʌɪt/ *noun*. **M19.**
[ORIGIN Late Greek *duophusitai*, from *duo* two + *phusis* nature.]
THEOLOGY. A person who holds the doctrine of the coexistence of two natures, divine and human, in Christ. Cf. MONOPHYSITE.

Dyothelite /dʌɪˈɒθɪlʌɪt/ *noun*. Also **-lete** /-liːt/. **M19.**
[ORIGIN from Greek *duo* two + *thelētēs* agent noun from *thelein* to will + -ITE¹, after MONOTHELITE.]
THEOLOGY. A person who holds the (orthodox) doctrine that Jesus had two wills, divine and human. Cf. MONOTHELITE.

dypsomania *noun* var. of DIPSOMANIA.

dys- /dɪs/ *prefix*.
[ORIGIN Greek *dus-*, cogn. with Sanskrit *dus-*, Old High German *zur-* (German *zer-*), Old Norse *tor-*, Old English TO-².]
Forming nouns and adjectives with the sense 'bad, difficult, unfavourable, abnormal, impaired' (opp. EU-). In *MEDICINE*, often with counterparts of related meaning in A-¹⁰.
■ **dyˈsarthria** *noun* difficult or unclear articulation of (otherwise normal) speech **L19.** **dyscalˈculia** *noun* severe difficulty in calculation, as a result of cerebral disorder **M20.** **dyschezia** /dɪsˈkiːzɪə/ *noun* [Greek *khezein* defecate] difficult or painful defecation **M19.** **dyskiˈnesia** *noun* an abnormality or impairment of voluntary movement **E18.** **dysˈlalia** *noun* a speech disorder, *esp.* one in which a person uses words or sounds peculiar to himself or herself **M19.** **dysˈphonia** *noun* difficulty in speaking due to a disorder of the throat, mouth, or vocal organs **E18.** **dysˈphotic** *adjective* (of ocean depths etc.) receiving insufficient light to bring about photosynthesis **E20.** **dysˈprosody** *noun* abnormality of speech inflection, stress, and rhythm, occurring in aphasia **M20.** **dysˈrhythmia** *noun* an abnormality of physiological rhythm, esp. in the electrical activity of the brain **E20.** **dysˈrhythmic** *adjective* of or pertaining to dysrhythmia **M20.** **dysteleoˈlogical** *adjective* of, pertaining to, or marked by dysteleology **M19.** **dysteleˈology** *noun* the denial of final causes or purpose in natural phenomena (opp. TELEOLOGY); biological study conforming to this viewpoint: **M19.** **dysˈthymia** *noun* [Greek *dusthumia*] *PSYCHIATRY* depression, despondency **M19.** **dysˈthymic** *adjective* (*PSYCHIATRY*) of, pertaining to, or suffering from dysthymia **M20.**

dysaesthesia /dɪsɪsˈθiːzɪə/ *noun*. Also ***dysesth-**. Pl. **-iae** /-iiː/. **E18.**
[ORIGIN mod. Latin from Greek *dusaisthēsia*, from *dus-* DYS- + *anaisthēsia* ANAESTHESIA.]
MEDICINE. An abnormal (unpleasant) sensation felt when touched, caused by disease or dysfunction of sensory tracts or peripheral nerves; the state of having sensations of this kind. Cf. PARAESTHESIA.

dyscrasia /dɪsˈkreɪsɪə, -zɪə/ *noun*. **LME.**
[ORIGIN Late Latin from Greek *duskrasia* bad temperament or mixture, from *dus-* DYS- + *krasis* CRASIS: see -IA¹. Cf. DYSCRASY.]
MEDICINE. Orig., an imbalance of humours, a distemper. Now, any abnormal or disordered state of the body or bodily part.
■ **dyscrasic** *adjective* of the nature of, pertaining to, or affected by dyscrasia **L19.**

dyscrasite /ˈdɪskrəsʌɪt/ *noun*. **M19.**
[ORIGIN from Greek *duskrasia*: see DYSCRASIA, -ITE¹.]
MINERALOGY. A native alloy of antimony and silver belonging to the orthorhombic system and usu. occurring as masses of pyramidal crystals.

†**dyscrasy** *noun*. **LME–M19.**
[ORIGIN Partly formed as DYSCRASIA, partly from Old French *dyscrasie*: see -Y³.]
= DYSCRASIA.

dysenteric /dɪsɛnˈtɛrɪk/ *noun & adjective*. **LME.**
[ORIGIN Latin *dysentericus* from Greek *dusenterikos*, from *dusenteria*: see DYSENTERY, -IC.]
▸ †**A** *noun*. Dysentery, or a disorder associated with it. Only in **LME.**
▸ **B** *adjective*. Of, pertaining to, or of the nature of dysentery; affected with or suffering from dysentery. **E18.**

■ †**dysenterical** *adjective*: only in 17.

dysentery /ˈdɪs(ə)nt(ə)ri/ *noun*. LME.
[ORIGIN Old French *dissenterie* or Latin *dysenteria* from Greek *dusenteria*, from *dusenteros* afflicted in the bowels, from *dus-* DYS- + *entera* bowels: see -Y³.]
Inflammation of the mucous membranes of the large intestine, with griping pains, diarrhoea, and evacuation of mucus and blood. Now *spec.* this condition as a result of bacterial or amoebic infection.

dysesthesia *noun* see DYSAESTHESIA.

dysfunction /dɪsˈfʌŋkʃ(ə)n/ *noun*. Also **dis-**. E20.
[ORIGIN from DYS- + FUNCTION *noun*.]
Orig. & chiefly MEDICINE. An abnormality or impairment of function.

A. KOESTLER I have never had any glandular disfunction. A. BURGESS The heating was in a state of dysfunction.

dysfunctional /dɪsˈfʌŋkʃ(ə)n(ə)l/ *adjective*. Also **dis-**. M20.
[ORIGIN from DYSFUNCTION + -AL¹.]
1 Of or relating to dysfunction; exhibiting dysfunction. M20.
2 SOCIOLOGY. Relating to or designating relationships, social interactions, etc., which are harmful for the emotional well-being of those who participate in them. M20.
■ **dysfunctioˈnality** *noun* M20. **dysfunctionally** *adverb* M20.

dysgenic /dɪsˈdʒɛnɪk/ *adjective*. E20.
[ORIGIN from DYS- + -GENIC.]
Exerting a detrimental effect on later generations; tending to racial degeneration. Opp. EUGENIC.
■ **dysgenically** *adverb* M20. **dysgenics** *noun* (the branch of knowledge that deals with) racial degeneration E20.

dysgraphia /dɪsˈgrafɪə/ *noun*. M20.
[ORIGIN from DYS- + Greek *graphia* writing.]
Difficulty in writing coherently, as a symptom of cerebral disease or damage. Cf. AGRAPHIA.
■ **dysgraphic** *adjective & noun* (*a*) *adjective* of, pertaining to, or affected with dysgraphia; (*b*) *noun* a person affected with dysgraphia: M20.

dyskaryosis /ˌdɪskarɪˈəʊsɪs/ *noun*. M20.
[ORIGIN from DYS- + KARYO- + -OSIS.]
Abnormality of the nucleus of a cell, *spec.* as an indication of malignant or pre-malignant change in a vaginal smear or other cytological preparation.

dyslexia /dɪsˈlɛksɪə/ *noun*. L19.
[ORIGIN from DYS- + Greek *lexis* speech (conf. with Latin *legere* read) + -IA¹.]
A developmental disorder marked by difficulty in reading, or in understanding written words, without general intelligence being affected. Cf. ALEXIA.
■ **dyslectic** *adjective & noun* = DYSLEXIC M20. **dyslexic** *adjective & noun* (*a*) *adjective* of, pertaining to, or affected with dyslexia; (*b*) *noun* a person affected with dyslexia: M20.

dyslogistic /dɪsləˈdʒɪstɪk/ *adjective*. E19.
[ORIGIN from DYS- + EULOGISTIC.]
Expressing disapproval, having a bad connotation, opprobrious.
■ **dyslogistically** *adverb* M19. ˈ**dyslogy** *noun* (*rare*) censure, disparagement M19.

dysmenorrhoea /ˌdɪsmɛnəˈriːə/ *noun*. Also ***-rrhea**. E19.
[ORIGIN from DYS- + MENORRHOEA.]
MEDICINE. Painful menstruation.
■ **dysmenorrhoeal** *adjective* = DYSMENORRHOEIC M19. **dysmenorrhoeic** *adjective* of, pertaining to, or affected with dysmenorrhoea L19.

dysmorphia /dɪsˈmɔːfɪə/ *noun*. L19.
[ORIGIN Greek, = misshapenness, ugliness.]
MEDICINE. Deformity or abnormality in the shape or size of a specified part of the body.
■ **dysmorphic** *adjective* M20.

dyspareunia /dɪspəˈruːnɪə/ *noun*. L19.
[ORIGIN from DYS- + Greek *pareunos* lying with, from *para* beside + *eunē* bed: see -IA¹.]
MEDICINE. Difficult or painful sexual intercourse.

dyspathy /ˈdɪspəθi/ *noun*. M16.
[ORIGIN French †*dispathie*, taken as the opposite of Greek *sumpatheia* SYMPATHY.]
†**1** MEDICINE. Non-susceptibility to a disease. Only in M16.
2 Antipathy, (a) dislike; (a) disagreement of feeling. Opp. ***sympathy***. E17.

dyspepsia /dɪsˈpɛpsɪə/ *noun*. E18.
[ORIGIN Latin from Greek *duspepsia*, from *duspeptos* difficult of digestion, from *dus-* DYS- + *peptos* cooked, digested: see -IA¹.]
Indigestion; abdominal pain or discomfort associated with taking food.
■ Also **dyspepsy** *noun* (now *rare*) M17.

dyspeptic /dɪsˈpɛptɪk/ *adjective & noun*. L17.
[ORIGIN from Greek *duspeptos*: see DYSPEPSIA, -IC.]
▸ **A** *adjective*. †**1** Indigestible; causing dyspepsia. *rare*. Only in L17.
2 Of or pertaining to dyspepsia; subject to or suffering from dyspepsia; despondent (as) through dyspepsia. E19.
▸ **B** *noun*. A person subject to or suffering from dyspepsia. E19.
■ **dyspeptical** *adjective* (*rare*) = DYSPEPTIC *adjective* 2 E19. **dyspeptically** *adverb* M19.

dysphagia /dɪsˈfeɪdʒɪə, -dʒə/ *noun*. L18.
[ORIGIN mod. Latin, from Greek *dus-* DYS- + -PHAGIA.]
MEDICINE. Difficulty in swallowing, as a symptom of disease.

dysphemia /dɪsˈfiːmɪə/ *noun*. L19.
[ORIGIN Greek *dusphēmia* evil language, from *dus-* DYS- + *phēmē* speaking: see -IA¹.]
MEDICINE. Stammering.

dysphemism /ˈdɪsfɪmɪz(ə)m/ *noun*. L19.
[ORIGIN from DYS- after *euphemism*.]
The substitution of a derogatory or unpleasant term for a pleasant or neutral one; a term so used. Opp. EUPHEMISM.
■ **dyspheˈmistic** *adjective* M20.

dysphoria /dɪsˈfɔːrɪə/ *noun*. M19.
[ORIGIN Greek *dusphoria* malaise, discomfort, from *dusphoros* hard to bear, from *dus-* DYS- + *pherein* to bear: see -IA¹.]
A state of unease or discomfort; *esp.* an unpleasant state of mind marked by malaise, depression, or anxiety. Opp. EUPHORIA.
■ **dysphoric** *adjective* M20.

dysplasia /dɪsˈpleɪzɪə/ *noun*. E20.
[ORIGIN from DYS- + -PLASIA.]
MEDICINE. Abnormal growth or development of body tissue.
■ **dysˈplastic** *adjective* of, pertaining to, or characterized by dysplasia E20.

dyspnoea /dɪspˈniːə/ *noun*. Also ***-pnea**. M17.
[ORIGIN Latin from Greek *duspnoia*, from *dus-* DYS- + *pnoē* breathing: see -A¹.]
MEDICINE. Difficulty in breathing or shortness of breath, as a symptom of disease.
■ **dyspnoeal** *adjective* = DYSPNOEIC L19. **dyspnoeic** *adjective* of, pertaining to, or affected with dyspnoea M19.

dyspraxia /dɪsˈpraksɪə/ *noun*. E20.
[ORIGIN from DYS- + Greek *praxis* action.]
MEDICINE. A developmental disorder of the brain in childhood causing difficulty in activities requiring coordination and movement.
■ **dyspraxic** *noun & adjective* M20.

dysprosium /dɪsˈprəʊzɪəm/ *noun*. L19.
[ORIGIN from Greek *dusprositos* difficult of access + -IUM.]
CHEMISTRY. A metallic chemical element, atomic no. 66, of the lanthanide series (symbol Dy).

dyss /dɪs/ *noun*. Also **dysse**. Pl. **dysser** /ˈdɪsə/. M20.
[ORIGIN Danish *dysse*.]
ARCHAEOLOGY. A megalithic chambered tomb of a kind found in Denmark.

dystocia /dɪsˈtəʊsɪə/ *noun*. Also **-ch-** /-k-/. E18.
[ORIGIN Greek *dustokia*.]
MEDICINE. Difficult or abnormally painful childbirth.
■ **dystocial** *adjective* E19.

dystonia /dɪsˈtəʊnɪə/ *noun*. E20.
[ORIGIN from DYS- + TONE *noun* + -IA¹.]
MEDICINE. A state of abnormal muscle tone; *esp.* a postural disorder marked by spasm of the trunk, neck, shoulders, or limbs and due to disease of the basal ganglia of the brain.
■ **dystonic** *adjective* E20.

dystopia /dɪsˈtəʊpɪə/ *noun*. L18.
[ORIGIN from DYS- + UTOPIA.]
An imaginary place or condition in which everything is as bad as possible. Opp. UTOPIA.
– NOTE: In isolated nonce uses before M20.
■ **dystopian** *adjective & noun* M19.

D

dystrophia /dɪsˈtrəʊfɪə/ *noun*. L19.
[ORIGIN from Greek *dus-* DYS- + *-trophia* nourishment.]
MEDICINE. Impaired nourishment of a bodily part; any unexplained abnormality of tissue. Cf. DYSTROPHY.
dystrophia myotonica /mʌɪəˈtɒnɪkə/ a form of dominantly inherited muscular dystrophy accompanied by myotonia.

dystrophic /dɪsˈtrɒfɪk, -ˈtrəʊf-/ *adjective*. L19.
[ORIGIN formed as DYSTROPHIA + -IC. In sense 2 from German *dystroph*.]
1 MEDICINE. Of, pertaining to, or affected with dystrophia or (muscular) dystrophy. L19.
2 Of a lake: having brown water due to the presence of much dissolved organic matter and little oxygen. M20.

dystrophin /dɪsˈtrəʊfɪn/ *noun*. L20.
[ORIGIN from DYSTROPH(Y + -IN¹.]
BIOCHEMISTRY. A protein that is present in normal skeletal muscle but absent from the muscle of individuals with Duchenne muscular dystrophy, this deficiency being thought to cause the disease.

dystrophy /ˈdɪstrəfi/ *noun*. L19.
[ORIGIN formed as DYSTROPHIA: see -TROPHY.]
MEDICINE. = DYSTROPHIA. Chiefly in ***muscular dystrophy***, any of a group of hereditary diseases marked by progressive wasting of certain muscles.

dysuria /dɪsˈjʊərɪə/ *noun*. LME.
[ORIGIN Late Latin *dysuria* from Greek *dusouria*, from *dus-* DYS- + *ouron* urine: see -IA¹. Cf. DYSURY.]
MEDICINE. Painful or difficult urination.
■ **dysuric** *adjective* of, pertaining to, or affected with dysuria M19.

†**dysury** *noun*. E16–M19.
[ORIGIN Partly formed as DYSURIA, partly from Old French *dissurie*: see -Y³.]
= DYSURIA.

dytiscid /dɪˈtɪskɪd, -sɪd/ *noun & adjective*. M19.
[ORIGIN formed as DYTISCUS: see -ID³.]
ENTOMOLOGY. ▸**A** *noun*. Pl. **-ids**, **-ides** /-ɪdiːz/. A member of the family Dytiscidae, which includes most water beetles (including *Dytiscus*). M19.
▸ **B** *adjective*. Of, pertaining to, or designating this family. L19.

dytiscus /dɪˈtɪskəs/ *noun*. M19.
[ORIGIN mod. Latin (see below), irreg. from Greek *dutikos* able to dive, from *duein* to dive.]
ENTOMOLOGY. A member of the genus *Dytiscus* of large carnivorous water beetles; *esp.* the great diving beetle, *D. marginalis*.

dyvour /ˈdʌɪvə/ *noun*. *Scot.* L15.
[ORIGIN Unknown.]
A bankrupt; a debtor; a beggar.

dzho *noun* var. of DZO.

dziggetai /ˈdzɪgətʌɪ, ˈdʒɪg-/ *noun*. L18.
[ORIGIN Mongolian *chikitei*, having ears, eared, from *chiki* ear.]
= KYANG.

dzo /zəʊ, zəʊ/ *noun*. Also **dzho**, **zho**, **zo**. Pl. **-os**, same. M19.
[ORIGIN Tibetan *mdso*.]
A hybrid between a yak and a domestic cow.

dzong *noun* var. of JONG *noun*².

Dzongkha /ˈdzɒŋkə/ *noun & adjective*. E20.
[ORIGIN Tibetan.]
(Of or pertaining to) the form of Tibetan used as the official language of Bhutan.

Ee

E, e /iː/.
The fifth letter of the modern English alphabet and of the ancient Roman one, repr. the Semitic ∃ (= *h*), but adopted by the Greeks (and from them by the Romans) as a vowel. The sound orig. represented by the letter probably varied from a mid-front to a low front vowel. For its principal mod. sounds see the Key to the Pronunciation. Pl. **ees**, **E's**, **Es**.
▸ **I 1** The letter and its sound.
2 The shape of the letter.
E-shaped *adjective* having a shape or a cross-section like the capital letter E.
▸ **II** Symbolical uses.
3 Used to denote serial order; applied e.g. to the fifth group or section, sheet of a book, etc.
4 *MUSIC*. (Cap. E.) The third note of the diatonic scale of C major. Also, the scale of a composition with E as its keynote.
5 *LOGIC*. (Cap. E.) A proposition which is universal and negative.
6 The fifth hypothetical person or example.
7 *MATH*. (Italic *e*.) The irrational number 2.71828 . . . , equal to the limit of $(1 + 1/n)^n$ as n tends to infinity; the sum $1 + 1/1! + 1/2! + 1/3! + \ldots$, where ! denotes a factorial.
8 (Usu. cap. E.) Designating the fifth highest class (of academic marks etc.).
9 *E-layer*, a stratum of the ionosphere between the lowest (D-) and highest (F-) layers, able to reflect long radio waves. Also called ***Heaviside layer***, ***Kennelly layer***, ***Kennelly–Heaviside layer***.
▸ **III 10** Abbrevs.: **E.** = east(ern); *slang* ecstasy (the drug); Egyptian; Engineering; European (as *e* or *E*, printed on packets to denote that the weight is one that complies with a relevant European Union directive); in ***E number***, (a code number preceded by the letter E, assigned to) an additive that accords with EU Food Additive directives; (as *prefix*) exa-. **E**, **e** (*PHYSICS*) = energy. **€** = euro(s).

e- /ɪ, ɛ/ *prefix*[1].
Repr. Latin *e-* var. of EX-[1] before consonants exc. *c*, *f*, *h*, *p*, *q*, *s*, *t*. Also used (in preference to *ex-*) to form adjectives (chiefly in -ATE[2]) with non-Latin sense 'not having, deprived of', as ***ecaudate***.

e- /iː/ *prefix*[2].
[ORIGIN from *e-* (in ELECTRONIC *adjective*), after EMAIL *noun*.]
Denoting the use of electronic data transfer in cyberspace for information exchange and financial transactions, esp. through the Internet.
■ **e-book** *noun* an electronic version of a printed book which can be read on a personal computer or specifically designed handheld device L20. **e-business**, **e-commerce** *nouns* commercial transactions conducted electronically on the Internet L20. **e-fit** *noun* an electronically created picture of the face of a person who is sought by the police L20. **e-ticket** *noun* (proprietary name in the US for) a reservation for an airline flight for which the details are recorded electronically rather than printed on a paper ticket L20. **e-zine** /ˈiːziːn/ *noun* a magazine published only in electronic form on a computer network L20.

ea /iːə/ *noun*. Long *obsolete* exc. *dial.* Also **eau** /əʊ/.
[ORIGIN Old English *ēa*. Var. as if from French *eau* water.]
A stream, a watercourse; a drainage canal, a sewer.

ea. *abbreviation*.
Each.

each /iːtʃ/ *adjective* (in mod. usage also classed as a *determiner*) & *pronoun*.
[ORIGIN Old English *ǣlć* = Old Frisian *ellik*, *elk*, *ek*, Middle Low German *ellik*, Middle Dutch *elic*, *ellic*, Middle & mod. Low German, Middle Dutch & mod. Dutch *elk*, Old High German *eogilīh* (German *jeglich*), from West Germanic phr. = ever alike, formed as AYE *adverb*[1] + ALIKE *adjective*.]
▸ **A** *adjective*. Used before a sing. noun to give the same sense in relation to individuals as does *both* or *all* before the pl. noun in relation to the category or aggregate of them (almost = EVERY, but with reference rather to the separate members). (Preceding the noun and adjectives, but before the def. article or possess. adjectives. Formerly also with *a(n)* interposed before the noun). OE.

E. YOUNG Each night we die, Each morn are born anew. J. CONRAD Each day of the ship's life. W. FAULKNER Creeping up toward the collar . . and across toward each armpit.

each and every — every single —. **each way** *BETTING* to win or to be placed.
▸ **B** *pronoun*. **1** Each one, each person: referring individually to things or people previously specified or implied, or following (after *of*). OE.

J. COULTER They each have long spades. S. T. WARNER He gave each of the islanders a ginger-bread nut. SCOTT FITZGERALD They were sitting at different ends of the room, each wearing a green eye-shade. J. BUCHAN Wood, sea and hill . . have never lost their spell for me. But the spell of each was different. T. S. ELIOT I have heard the mermaids singing, each to each. G. GREENE Long tables with an urn at the end of each. C. P. SNOW Each thought the other a master of his trade.

all and each (*arch.*), **each and all** all collectively and individually. **each other** (used as a compound reciprocal pronoun) one another (in accus., dat., or genit.), each . . . the other, each . . . another.
2 Distributed or in relation to each member of an aggregate. Freq. with ref. to price: apiece, for each one. OE.

DRYDEN Studious of Honey, each in his Degree. SHAFTESBURY We have each of us a daemon. OED I paid sixpence each for them. E. BAKER At every intersection old men held out eight arms each, pointing the ways to heaven.

each to each with exact correspondence of members or parts.

eager /ˈiːɡə/ *adjective*. ME.
[ORIGIN Anglo-Norman *egre*, Old French & mod. French *aigre* from Proto-Romance from Latin *acer*, *acr-*.]
1 Sharply perceived by the taste or other senses; pungent, acrid; sharp, biting; sour, tart; (of air etc.) cold. Now *rare* or *obsolete*. ME.

SHAKES. *Haml.* It is a nipping and an eager air.

2 Ardent, impetuous; fierce. *obsolete* exc. *dial.* ME.
3 Of a person, an action, etc.: full of or manifesting keen desire or appetite; impatiently longing. ME.

G. BERKELEY Those gentlemen who are called men of pleasure, from their eager pursuit of it. TOLKIEN An eager light was in their eyes. W. GOLDING He was poor, hard-working, eager to improve himself. H. CARPENTER The greedy populace, eager for gold and jewels.

eager beaver: see BEAVER *noun*[1].
†**4** Hungry; hungry-looking. L15–M18.
†**5** Of metal: brittle. L16–M18.
■ **eagerly** *adverb* ME. **eagerness** *noun* LME.

eagle /ˈiːɡ(ə)l/ *noun*. ME.
[ORIGIN Anglo-Norman *egle*, Old French & mod. French *aigle* from Latin *aquila*.]
1 Any of various large diurnal birds of prey belonging to the family Accipitridae, renowned for keen vision and powerful flight. ME.
bateleur eagle, ***fish eagle***, ***golden eagle***, ***harpy eagle***, ***sea eagle***, etc. ***bald eagle***: see BALD *adjective*. ***legal eagle***: see LEGAL *adjective*.
2 A representation or figure of an eagle, esp. as an ensign in the Roman or French imperial armies, or as an armorial bearing. ME. ▸**b** *spec.* A figure of the bald eagle as the emblem of the United States; ***the Eagle***, the US. L18.
double eagle: see DOUBLE *adjective & adverb*.
3 An object, esp. a lectern, made in the form of an eagle. LME.
4 (Usu. **E-**.) *The* constellation Aquila. LME.
5 A coin bearing the image of an eagle; *esp.* a US gold coin worth ten dollars. M18.
6 *GOLF*. A hole played in two strokes under par or bogey. E20.
– COMB.: **eagle eye** a keen eye; **eagle-eyed** *adjective* keen sight(ed); **eagle-hawk** *Austral.* the wedge-tailed eagle, *Aquila audax* (***whistling eagle-hawk***: see WHISTLING *adjective*); **eagle owl** any of several very large owls of the genus *Bubo*, with ear tufts, esp. *B. bubo* of Eurasia and N. Africa; **eagle ray** any of various large rays which constitute the family Myliobatidae, with long pointed pectoral fins; spec. *Myliobatis aquila*, of the Mediterranean and eastern Atlantic; **eagle-stone** = AETITES.
■ **eaglet** *noun* a young eagle L16.

eagle /ˈiːɡ(ə)l/ *verb*. M17.
[ORIGIN from the noun.]
1 *verb intrans. & trans.* (with *it*). Fly like an eagle. *rare*. M17.
2 *verb trans. GOLF*. Play (a hole) in two strokes under par or bogey. M20.

eagle-wood /ˈiːɡ(ə)lwʊd/ *noun*. E18.
[ORIGIN translating Portuguese *pao de aguila* wood of AGILA, confused with Latin *aquila* eagle. Cf. French *bois d'aigle*.]
Aloes wood.

eagre /ˈeɪɡə, ˈiː-/ *noun*. E17.
[ORIGIN Unknown.]
A tidal bore in a river; now *esp.* that in the River Trent.

ealdorman *noun* see ALDERMAN.

Eames chair /ˈiːmz tʃɛː/ *noun phr.* M20.
[ORIGIN from *Eames* (see below).]
(Proprietary name for) a chair designed by the US architect and designer Charles Eames (1907–78), or in the functional style popularized by him; *esp.* an office chair of moulded plastic and plywood.

ean /iːn/ *verb trans. & intrans.*
[ORIGIN Old English *ēanian* from Germanic.]
= YEAN.
■ **eanling** *noun* a young lamb L16.

-ean /ˈiːən, ɪən/ *suffix*.
[ORIGIN from Latin or Greek ending (see below) + -AN.]
Forming adjectives (often used as nouns) with the sense 'of, belonging to, characteristic of', chiefly anglicizations of Latin adjectives in *-aeus*, *-eus*, and Greek adjectives in *-aios*, *-eios*, as ***empyrean***, ***Epicurean***, ***Euclidean***, ***European***, ***Herculean***, ***Jacobean***, ***subterranean***, only rarely in English formations (as ***Caribbean***, ***Tyrolean***) exc. where the root itself provides *-e-* (-IAN being more usual), as ***Carlylean***. Often with parallel forms in -IAN.

E. & O. E. *abbreviation*.
Errors and omissions excepted.

ear /ɪə/ *noun*[1].
[ORIGIN Old English *ēare* = Old Frisian *āre*, Old Saxon, Old High German *ōra* (Dutch *oor*, German *Ohr*), Old Norse *eyra*, Gothic *ausō*, from Germanic, from Indo-European base also of Latin *auris*, Greek *ous*, *ōs*.]
▸ **I 1** The organ of hearing in humans and animals, considered with regard to its function or to its structure (in mammals divisible generally into the ***external ear***, ***middle ear***, and ***inner ear***: see below). OE. ▸**b** The imagined organ of hearing of the mind, the heart, or other quasi-personified object. LME.

H. C. JACKSON Rumours have come to my ears. W. N. HODGSON The summons in our ears was shrill. *fig.*: T. H. WHITE He listened to their difficulties with an impatient ear. **b** *Proverb*: Walls have ears (i.e. there may be listeners anywhere). J. H. BURTON The illustrious Eastern conqueror, whose name fills the ear of fame.

2 *spec.* The external ear. OE.

J. T. FARRELL Plunked in here all afternoon without even room to wriggle my ears.

3 Voluntary hearing, listening, attention. ME.

C. CHAPLIN Mother . . kept an alert ear on the way we talked, correcting our grammar.

4 *sing.* & in *pl.* The sense of hearing; auditory perception. ME.

CHESTERFIELD Most people have ears, but few have judgement.

5 The faculty of discriminating sounds; esp. the ability to recognize musical intervals (more fully ***ear for music***, ***musical ear***). E16.

P. H. NEWBY I understand Arabic. I've an ear for languages.

▸ **II** An object resembling the external ear in appearance, shape, position, or function.
†**6** An atrium of the heart. LME–L17.
7 The handle of a drinking vessel, bottle, etc. LME.
8 A projection on the side of a tool or a piece of machinery, serving as a support, handle, etc. L16.
9 *ZOOLOGY & BOTANY*. = AURICLE 3. L17.
10 In *pl.* A Citizens' Band radio; the aerial of such a radio. Chiefly in ***have one's ears on***. *US slang*. L20.
– PHRASES: **about one's ears** down upon oneself. **all ears** eagerly attentive. ***a word in a person's ear***: see WORD *noun*. BELIEVE **one's ear(s)**. ***bend someone's ear***: see BEND *verb*. ***cauliflower ear***: see CAULIFLOWER *noun*. **close one's ears** refuse to listen. CLOTH ***ears***. ***cock one's ears***, ***cock the ears***: see COCK *verb*[1] 6. **dry behind the ears** mature, experienced. ***ear for music***: see sense 5 above. **external ear** the pinna, with or without the meatus leading to the eardrum. ***fall on deaf ears***: see DEAF *adjective* 3. **fall on someone's ear(s)** be heard by someone. **gain the ear of** obtain the favourable attention of. ***get the right sow by the ear***, ***get the wrong sow by the ear***: see SOW *noun*[1]. **give ear** listen. ***go away with a flea in one's ear***: see FLEA *noun*. **go in at one ear and out at the other**, **go in one ear and out the other** be heard but leave no impression. **have a person's ear** have a person's favourable attention. ***have a wolf by the ears***: see WOLF *noun*. **have by the ears** keep or obtain a secure hold on. **have one's ear to the ground** be on the alert regarding rumours or trend of opinion. **have the ear of** have the favourable attention of. ***have the right sow by the ear***, ***have the wrong sow by the ear***: see SOW *noun*[1]. ***head over ears***: see ***over ears*** below. ***hold a wolf by the ears***: see WOLF *noun*. **inner ear**, **internal ear** the labyrinth of the temporal bone, containing the semicircular canals and the cochlea. **lead by the ears** keep in abject dependence. ***lend an ear***, ***lend one's ears***: see LEND *verb*. ***long ear***: see LONG *adjective*[1]. **middle ear** the eardrum and the space (containing the ossicles) between the eardrum and the inner ear. ***musical ear***: see sense 5 above. ***music to one's ears***: see MUSIC *noun*. **on one's ear** (***a***) roused, indignant; (***b***) drunk. ***one's ears burn***: see BURN *verb* 4. **open one's ears** listen. **outer ear** = ***external ear*** above. **out on one's ear** dismissed ignominiously. **over ears**, **over head and ears**, **head over ears** deeply immersed (*lit. & fig.*). ***pin a person's ears back***, ***pin one's ears back***: see PIN *verb*. ***play by ear***, ***play it by ear***: see PLAY *verb*. ***prick one's ears***, ***prick up one's ears***, ***prick the ears***, ***prick up the ears***: see PRICK *verb*. ***sea-ear***: see SEA. ***send away***

with a flea in his or her ear: see FLEA *noun*. **set by the ears** put at variance, cause to quarrel. *speak in a person's ear*: see SPEAK *verb*. *stop one's ears*: see STOP *verb*. *talk a person's ear off*: see TALK *verb*. *thick ear*: see THICK *adjective*. *third ear*: see THIRD *adjective & noun*. *tin ear*: see TIN *noun & adjective*. *turn a deaf ear (to)*: see DEAF *adjective* 3. **up to the ears** *colloq.* very deeply involved (*in*). **wet behind the ears** immature, inexperienced. *with a flea in one's ear*: see FLEA *noun*. *would give one's ears*: see GIVE *verb*.

– COMB.: **earache** pain in the (middle) ear; **earbash** *verb intrans. & trans. (slang)* talk inordinately (to); **earbasher** *slang* a chatterer, a bore; **ear-biter** *slang* a habitual borrower of money; **earbud** a very small headphone, worn inside the ear; **ear candling** the practice of inserting the tapered end of a special candle into the ear, with the supposed effect that earwax and other impurities are drawn out of the ear by a partial vacuum created by the candle flame; **ear candy** *colloq.* light popular music that is pleasant and entertaining but intellectually undemanding (cf. *eye candy* s.v. EYE *noun*); **ear-clip** an earring, esp. one that clips on; **ear covert** = AURICULAR *noun* 2; **ear defenders** (a pair of) plugs or earmuffs which protect the eardrums from loud or persistent noise; **ear-drops** (*a*) medicinal drops for the ear; (*b*) hanging earrings; **eardrum** the membrane of the middle ear, closing the inner end of the external auditory meatus and serving to transmit sound to the ossicles; also, the entire hollow part of the middle ear; †**ear finger** the little finger (as most easily inserted into the ear); **ear flap** (*a*) = *ear lobe* below; (*b*) a flap of material covering the ear; **earhole** the orifice of the ear; **ear-lap**, **ear lobe** the lower soft pendulous part of the external ear; **earlock** a lock of hair over or above the ear; **earmuff** a covering for the ear to protect it from cold, noise, etc.; **earphone** a device worn on the ear to aid hearing or to listen to radio, telephone, etc., communication; **ear-pick**, **ear-picker** an instrument for clearing the ear of wax etc.; **earpiece** (*a*) a part of a helmet covering the ear; (*b*) an apparatus designed to be applied to the ear, as part of a telephone, radio receiver, etc.; **ear-piercing** *adjective* shrill; **earplug** (*a*) an ornament worn in the lobe of the ear; (*b*) a wad of cotton wool, wax, etc., placed in the ear to keep out cold air, water, or excessive noise; **earring** an ornament, orig. always a ring, now often a drop, stud, etc., worn on the lobe of the ear; **earringed** *adjective* wearing earrings; **ear shell** (the shell of) an edible mollusc of the genus *Haliotis*, an abalone; **ear-splitting** *adjective* excessively loud; **ear trumpet** a conical tube (formerly) used by the partially deaf as an aid to hearing; **ear tuft** either of a pair of tufts of longer feathers on the top of the head of a bird, esp. of some owls; **earwax** a yellow waxy secretion which collects in the external ear; **earwitness**: whose testimony is based on his or her own hearing.

■ **earful** *noun (colloq.)* a large quantity of talk; a strong reprimand: E20. **earlike** *adjective* resembling an ear in shape E19.

ear /ɪə/ *noun*².
[ORIGIN Old English *ēar* = Old Frisian *ār*, Old Saxon *ahar* (Dutch *aar*), Old High German *ahir*, *ehir* (German *Ähre*), Old Norse *ax*, Gothic *ahs*, from Germanic base rel. to Latin *acus*, *acer-* husk, chaff. See also ICKER.]
A spike or head of corn; the part of a cereal plant which contains its flowers or seeds; *N. Amer.* a head of maize.

R. GRAVES The little corn that had been planted withered before it came to an ear.

in the ear at the stage when ears are borne.

ear /ɪə/ *verb*¹ *trans.* Now *arch. & dial.*
[ORIGIN Old English *erian* = Old Frisian *era*, Old Saxon *erian*, Old High German *erren*, Old Norse *erja*, Gothic *arjan*, from Indo-European base repr. also by Latin *arare*.]
Plough, till (the ground); turn *up* by ploughing.

fig.: SHAKES. *Ant. & Cl.* The Sea.. which they ear and wound With keels.

ear /ɪə/ *verb*² *intrans.* LME.
[ORIGIN from EAR *noun*².]
Of corn or maize: produce ears, come into ear.

ear *adverb, preposition, & conjunction* see ERE.

eared /ɪəd/ *adjective*¹. LME.
[ORIGIN from EAR *noun*¹ + -ED².]
Having ears or earlike appendages; (with specifying word) having ears of a specified kind.
eared seal any of various seals of the family Otariidae, comprising the fur seals and sea lions.

eared /ɪəd/ *adjective*². LME.
[ORIGIN from EAR *noun*² or *verb*²: see -ED², -ED¹.]
Of corn etc.: having ears, that has come into ear.

earing /ˈɪərɪŋ/ *noun*. Also **-rr-**. E17.
[ORIGIN from EAR *noun*¹ + -ING¹ or RING *noun*¹.]
NAUTICAL. Any of a number of small ropes used to fasten the upper corners of a square sail to its yard.

earl /əːl/ *noun*. Also (esp. in titles) **E-**.
[ORIGIN Old English *eorl* = Old Saxon, Old High German *erl*, Old Norse *jarl*, of unknown origin. Cf. JARL.]
1 In the Old English constitution: a man of noble rank, as distinguished from a churl (see CHURL *noun* 2); a hereditary nobleman ranking directly above a thane (THANE 3). OE. ▸†b A warrior, a (brave) man. *poet.* Only in OE.
2 *hist.* A Danish under-king, a jarl; (under Cnut and his successors), a governor of one of the great divisions of England, as Wessex, Mercia, etc. OE.
3 A British or Irish nobleman ranking below a marquess and above a viscount, corresponding to the European *count*. Cf. COUNTESS. OE. ▸†b = COUNT *noun*². OE–L18.

– COMB. & PHRASES: **Earl Grey** a superior type of tea flavoured with bergamot; **Earl Marshal** a high officer of state in Britain (now hereditary in the line of the Dukes of Norfolk), orig. deputizing for the Constable of England as judge of the court of chivalry, now presiding over the College of Arms and having ceremonial duties on various Royal occasions; *earl palatine*: see PALATINE *adjective*¹.

■ **earldom** *noun* (*a*) (*obsolete* exc. *hist.*) the territory governed by an earl; (*b*) the rank or dignity of an earl: OE. **earlship** *noun* (*a*) = EARLDOM (b); †(*b*) nobility, manliness: OE.

earless /ˈɪəlɪs/ *adjective*. E17.
[ORIGIN from EAR *noun*¹ + -LESS.]
1 Having no ears. E17.
2 Without a sense of hearing; without an ear for music; *poet.* where nothing is heard. E19.

WORDSWORTH In some deep dungeon's earless den.

earlet /ˈɪəlɪt/ *noun*. E17.
[ORIGIN from EAR *noun*¹ + -LET.]
†1 An earring. Only in E17.
2 Something resembling a small ear; (formerly) an atrium of the heart. M17. ▸b A tragus, esp. when largely developed as in some bats. M19.

early /ˈəːli/ *adjective & noun*. ME.
[ORIGIN from the adverb, after Old Norse *árligr*.]
▸ **A** *adjective*. **1** Designating, belonging to, or existing, occurring, etc., near to the beginning of a period of time, as the morning, the day, the evening, the year, a lifetime. ME.

W. COWPER Our most important are our earliest years. H. JAMES She had come up.. by an early train. DAY LEWIS My earliest memory is a smell of bacon. I. MURDOCH Women pick up these conventions at such an early age. U. BENTLEY In the early hours of the next morning.

2 Designating, belonging to, or relating to the initial stage of an epoch, of a person's development, of the history of a people, of the world, of a science, etc.; ancient. L17.

J. BONNYCASTLE Astronomy is a science of the earliest antiquity. LD MACAULAY Early fathers of the Church. P. G. WODEHOUSE The gruesome Early Victorianness of it all.

3 Near the beginning in serial order. E18.

OED The early chapters of the book. L. HELLMAN Mr. Goldwyn was in his early fifties when we first met.

4 Connected with the initial part of any division of time, continuous action, etc.; occurring before it is too late; arriving, occurring, etc., before the usual or expected time. In *compar.* & *superl.*, former, foremost, first (in time). M18. ▸b Of a future date or event: not remote, near at hand. M19.

B. GOOCH This consideration shou'd engage our earliest.. attention. LD MACAULAY Henry Wharton.. whose early death was soon after deplored by men of all parties. A. CHRISTIE The train couldn't have been ten minutes early. J. F. LEHMANN An elation I had not known since the early days at The Hogarth Press. I. MURDOCH Dark.. clumps of green betokened the early tulips. *Financial Times* It is still too early to predict how far they will get. **b** D. LIVINGSTONE There being no prospect of an early peace.

– PHRASES & SPECIAL COLLOCATIONS: **early closing** orig. (usu. *attrib.*), the reduction of the daily hours in certain trades; now, the closing of business premises at the end of the morning on a certain day of the week. **early days** early in time for something (to happen etc.). **early doors** *adverbial phr. (colloq.)* [app. orig. with ref. to admission to a music hall some time before the start of the performance] early on, esp. in a game or contest. **Early English** ARCHITECTURE the first stage of English Gothic (13th cent.), with pointed arches, lancet windows, and simple tracery. **early grave** an untimely or premature death. **early hours** the hours immediately after midnight. **early leaver** a pupil who leaves school without completing the session or the full course of study. **early music**: of the earliest times up to and including the Renaissance. **early night** a night when one goes to bed before the usual time. **early purple orchid**, **early purple orchis** a common spring-flowering woodland orchid, *Orchis mascula*, with purple flowers. **early retirement**: from one's occupation before the statutory age, esp. in return for a financial consideration. **early riser** a person who habitually gets up early from bed. *early spider orchid*: see *spider orchid* s.v. SPIDER *noun*. *early* STIRRER. **early warning**: esp. of missile attacks. **early wood** the less dense inner part of the annual ring of a tree. **keep early hours** rise and retire early. **take an early bath** *colloq.* (*a*) be sent off in a game; (*b*) fail early on in a race or contest. *the early bird*: see BIRD *noun*.

▸ **B** *ellipt.* as *noun*. **1** Early morning; an early occasion. Usu. in *superl.*: *at the earliest*, in the earliest possible eventuality. LME.

SHAKES. *Oth.* To-morrow with your earliest Let me have speech with you.

2 An early fruit or vegetable. Usu. in *pl.* M19.
3 In *pl.* Early years or days. E20.

■ †**earlily** *adverb* M17–E18. **earliness** *noun* L16. **earlyish** *adjective & adverb* somewhat early; early on: M19.

early /ˈəːli/ *adverb*. OE.
[ORIGIN from ERE + -LY², after Old Norse *árliga*.]
1 Near the beginning of a period of time, esp. of the morning, the day, the year, a lifetime. OE.

J. MORLEY Voltaire perceived very early in life that to be needy was to be dependent. S. LEACOCK We got out early, just after sunrise. K. AMIS One clear, bright morning early in April.

early and late at all hours, incessantly.
2 Far back in date, anciently. ME.

LD MACAULAY As early as the reign of Elizabeth.

3 At a time before something else; in good time; before the usual time, prematurely; in *compar.*, beforehand, previously. ME.

W. WOTTON This Abuse was early redrest. G. GREENE Winter had fallen early on the House of Stare. J. MITCHELL Her husband had died two years earlier.

early on at an early stage.
4 Near the beginning of a sequence. L19.

OED His name appears very early in the list.

earmark /ˈɪəmɑːk/ *noun & verb*. LME.
[ORIGIN from EAR *noun*¹ + MARK *noun*¹.]
▸ **A** *noun*. **1** A mark in the ear of a sheep or other animal, indicating ownership or identity. LME.
2 *transf. & fig.* A mark of ownership or identification. L16.
▸ **B** *verb trans.* **1** Mark (an animal) in the ear as a sign of ownership or identity; *gen.* mark as one's own by means of an identifying sign. L16.
2 Set aside (money etc.) for a particular purpose. L19.

E

earn /əːn/ *verb*¹ *trans.*
[ORIGIN Old English *earnian* = Middle Low German *arnen*, Old High German *arnēn*, *arnōn* reap, from West Germanic, from base rel. to Old English *esne* labourer, man, Old High German *esni*, Gothic *asneis* hired labourer.]
1 Receive or be entitled to (money, wages, etc.) in return for work done or services rendered; bring in as income; obtain or deserve in return for efforts or merit. OE. ▸b Of money etc. invested, an asset: gain as interest or profit. L19.

E. WAUGH Twenty pounds! Why, it takes me half a term to earn that. L. HELLMAN I earn a living as a carpenter. M. GORDON A child didn't have to earn its mother's love. *absol.*: C. HAMPTON If the public stop wanting me, I stop earning.

earn an honest penny: see HONEST *adjective*. **earned income**: from work or services; cf. UNEARNED 2; *earn one's keep*: see KEEP *noun*. **earn out** (of an author, book, recording artist, etc.) generate sufficient income through sales to equal the amount paid in an advance or royalty. *pay as you earn*: see PAY-. *save as you earn*: see SAVE *verb* 12.
2 Of a quality, an action, etc.: acquire for a person (a name, reputation, reproach, etc.), incur. L16.

E. WAUGH His comparative old age had earned him the sobriquet of 'uncle'.

3 BASEBALL. Score (a run) without any error by the fielding side. M19.
■ **earner** *noun* a person who or thing which earns; a profitable activity, *esp.* (*colloq.*) an easy means of making money: E17.

earn /əːn/ *verb*² *trans. & intrans. dial.* Also (*Scot. & N. English*) **yearn** /jəːn/.
[ORIGIN Old English *ġeirnan*, formed as Y- + metath. alt. of *rinnan* RUN *verb*. See also EARNING *noun*². Cf. RENNET *noun*¹.]
Coagulate, curdle.

†**earn** *verb*³ *intrans.* L16.
[ORIGIN App. var. of YEARN *verb*¹.]
1 Desire strongly, long. L16–M17.
2 Grieve. L16–E18.

earnest /ˈəːnɪst/ *noun*¹.
[ORIGIN Old English *eornust*, *-ost* = Middle Low German *ernest*, Old High German *ernust* (German *Ernst*), from base repr. also by Old Norse *ern* brisk, vigorous, Gothic *arniba* safely, of unknown origin.]
1 Seriousness, as opp. to jest. Now only in ***in earnest***, ***in real earnest***, etc., serious(ly), intense(ly), sincere(ly). OE.

J. WESLEY I am in great Earnest when I declare.. that I have a deep conviction. L. GARFIELD The snow.. began again in earnest.

†2 Ardour in battle; intense passion. Only in ME.

earnest /ˈəːnɪst/ *noun*². ME.
[ORIGIN Prob. ult. from Old French *erres* ARLES, assim. first to -NESS, then to EARNEST *noun*¹.]
(A sum of) money given in part-payment, esp. for the purpose of binding a bargain; *fig.* a foretaste, token, or pledge of one's intention or of what is to come.

R. MACAULAY Destruction, savagery; an earnest.. of the universal doom. J. RATHBONE What earnest can you give me that you will perform what you promised?

– COMB.: **earnest money**, **earnest penny** a small sum of money paid to secure a bargain.

earnest /ˈəːnɪst/ *adjective & adverb*.
[ORIGIN Old English *eornost(e)* = Old Frisian *ernst*, Middle Low German *ernest*, formed as EARNEST *noun*¹.]
▸ **A** *adjective*. **1** Serious in intention, not trifling; zealous, intense, ardent; resulting from or displaying sincere conviction. OE.

I. D'ISRAELI There was a good deal of earnest impetuosity in his temper. H. KELLER The thought of going to college took root in my heart and became an earnest desire. E. M. FORSTER The chapel was.. filled with an earnest congregation.

2 Weighty, important. *rare.* M16.

S. RICHARDSON Sir Charles had earnest business in town.

▸ †**B** *adverb*. In an earnest manner, earnestly. E17–L18.
■ **earnestly** *adverb* OE. **earnestness** *noun* M16.

earnful /ˈəːnfʊl, -f(ə)l/ *adjective*. *obsolete* exc. *dial.* E16.
[ORIGIN Alt. of YEARNFUL. Cf. EARN *verb*³.]
Full of longing desire; sorrowful.

E

earning /ˈəːnɪŋ/ *noun*[1]. **OE.**
[ORIGIN from EARN *verb*[1] + -ING[1].]
†**1** The fact of deserving, merit; one's desert. **OE–ME.**
†**2** In *pl.* Gain, profit. **ME–E18.**
3 In *pl.* The amount of money earned; income from work etc. **M18.**

> J. CHANG He supplemented his earnings from the bookshop with an evening job . . in a cinema.

immoral earnings: from prostitution. ***invisible earnings***: see INVISIBLE *adjective*.
4 The action of becoming entitled to payment in return for work carried out. **L19.**
– COMB.: **earnings-related** *adjective* (of a pension, benefit, etc.) proportionate to a person's earned income over a specified period.

earning /ˈəːnɪŋ/ *noun*[2]. *obsolete* exc. *Scot. & dial.* In sense 1 also (*Scot. & N. English*) **yearn-** /ˈjəːn-/. **ME.**
[ORIGIN from EARN *verb*[2] + -ING[1].]
1 A means of curdling milk; rennet. **ME.**
2 The curdling of milk for cheese. **L18.**

earring *nouns* see EAR *noun*[1], EARING.

earshot /ˈɪəʃɒt/ *noun*. **E17.**
[ORIGIN from EAR *noun*[1] + SHOT *noun*[1], after *bowshot* etc.]
The distance over which something may be heard; hearing. Chiefly in ***within earshot***, ***out of earshot***.

earth /əːθ/ *noun*[1].
[ORIGIN Old English *eorþe* = Old Frisian *erthe*, Old Saxon *erþa* (Dutch *aarde*), Old High German *erda* (German *Erde*), Old Norse *jǫ rð*, Gothic *airþa*, from Germanic.]
▸ **I** (The material of) the ground.
1 The ground considered as a surface, a solid stratum, or a place of burial. **OE.**
2 The soil as suitable for cultivation. **OE.**
3 The material which makes up the earth's surface; soil, mould, dust, clay. **OE.** ▸**b** This as one of the four elements of the ancients. **ME.** ▸†**c** Clay as a material for pottery. (Cf. EARTHEN *adjective* 1b, EARTHENWARE.) **ME–M17.**

> *attrib.*: J. STEINBECK He threw it down and beat it into the earth floor with his fist.

4 A particular substance having properties of stability, dryness, non-volatility, lack of taste or smell, etc., associated with the material of the ground; *spec.* in CHEMISTRY, a metallic oxide with these properties. Usu. with specifying word. **ME.**
5 (The material of) the human body. **ME.**

> SHELLEY The indignant spirit cast its mortal garment Among the slain—dead earth.

6 The lair of a burrowing animal, esp. a fox. **LME.**
7 The ground regarded as having zero electrical potential; electrical connection with the ground, whether intentional or otherwise; an electrical terminal to which such a connection should be made; a conductor kept at zero potential (by making direct or indirect contact with the ground). Freq. *attrib.* **M19.**
earth connection, *earth leakage*, *earth wire*, etc.
▸ **II** The world.
8 The land and the sea, as distinguished from the sky; (also **E-**) the planet on which humankind lives; the present abode of humankind as distinguished from heaven or hell as places of future existence. **OE.** ▸**b** The inhabitants of the world collectively. **LME.** ▸**c** A world resembling the earth; a (habitable) planet. **L17.**

> J. SCOTT Spreading . . even to the utmost ends of the earth. R. C. TRENCH Earth is not a shadow of heaven, but heaven . . a dream of earth. C. SAGAN Tiny intrepid unmanned spacecraft from the world called Earth. **b** AV *Gen.* 11:1 And the whole earth was of one language, and one speech.

9 The dry land as distinguished from the sea. **OE.**
10 A country, a territory. *arch.* **OE.**
11 ***the earth***, a great or excessive amount, esp. of money. *colloq.* **E20.**

> A. CHRISTIE Would it be terribly expensive? . . She'd heard they charged the earth.

– PHRASES ETC.: *ALKALINE* ***earth***. **back to earth** = *down to earth* below. ***brown earth***: see BROWN *adjective*. **down to earth** back to reality from fantasy. **down-to-earth** *adjective* plain-spoken, unpretentious; practical, realistic. ***fruits of the earth***: see FRUIT *noun* 1. ***fuller's earth***: see FULLER *noun*[1]. ***go the way of all the earth***: see GO *verb*. **go to earth** (of a hunted animal) hide itself in a burrow; *fig.* go into hiding. ***green earth***: see GREEN *adjective*. **lay in the earth** bury (a person). ***like nothing on earth***: see NOTHING *pronoun & noun*. ***mother earth***: see MOTHER *noun*[1]. ***move heaven and earth***: see HEAVEN *noun*. **on earth** existing anywhere; (*no person on earth*, *no place on earth*, etc., no person, place, etc., at all; as an intensive: ***who on earth . . . ?***, ***what on earth . . . ?***, ***where on earth . . . ?***). ***rare earth***: see RARE *adjective*[1]. ***red earth***: see RED *adjective*. **run to earth** chase (a fox etc.) to its lair; *fig.* find after long searching. ***scorched earth policy***: see SCORCH *verb*[1]. **spaceship earth** the world considered as a planet with finite resources common to all humankind. ***the ends of the earth***, ***the end of the earth***: see END *noun* 1. ***the salt of the earth***: see SALT *noun*[1]. ***white earth***: see WHITE *adjective*. ***yellow earth***: see YELLOW *adjective*.
– COMB.: **earth almond** = CHUFA; **earth ball** a fungus, *Scleroderma aurantium*, forming spherical fruiting bodies on the ground beneath esp. birch trees; **earth-born** *adjective* (*poet. & rhet.*) (**a**) born by emerging from the earth; (**b**) born on earth, of earthly or mortal race; (**c**) (of a thing) arising from or produced by the earth; **earth closet** a lavatory in which earth is used to cover excreta; **earth colour** a pigment obtained from the earth, as an ochre or umber; **earthfast** *adjective* fixed in the ground; **earth god**, **earth goddess**: of the earth, concerned with fertility and usu. the underworld; **earth house** an underground dwelling; *fig.* the grave; **earth hunger** a strong desire to own or control land; **earthlight** (**a**) = *earthshine* below; (**b**) a light of unknown origin seen apparently emerging from the ground; **earth-man** (**a**) a man whose interest lies in the material rather than the spiritual world; (**b**) (chiefly SCIENCE FICTION) a man living on or native to the planet Earth; **earth mother** a spirit or being symbolizing the earth; *fig.* a sensual and maternal woman; **earth mover** a vehicle or machine designed for earth moving; **earth moving** the excavation of large quantities of soil; **earthnut** (any of various plants bearing) an edible roundish tuber or other underground body; *spec.* (**a**) = *pignut* (a) s.v. PIG *noun*[1]; (**b**) = PEANUT *noun* 1; **earth pig** = AARDVARK; **earth pillar** GEOLOGY a free-standing column of earth, usu. one capped by a stone protecting the top from erosion; **earthquake** a (violent) movement or shaking of the earth's surface usu. due to geological forces or volcanic action; *fig.* a major social etc. disturbance; **earth-rise** the apparent rise of the earth over the moon's horizon as seen from the moon; **earth science(s)**: dealing with the various aspects of the physical constitution of the earth, as geology, geophysics, oceanography, meteorology, etc.; **earth-shaking**, **earth-shattering** *adjectives* (*fig.*) extremely important, momentous; having a devastating effect; **earthshine** the sun's light reflected from the earth, *esp.* that which illuminates the moon; **earth-soul** the supposed collective consciousness of the earth or humankind; **earthstar** any fungus of the genus *Geastrum*, the fruiting bodies of which grow on the ground and split into lobes which fold back giving a star-shaped structure; esp. *G. triplex*, found in woodland; **earth station** a transmitting station which retransmits signals received from satellites; an aerial for receiving such signals; ***earth tremor***: see TREMOR *noun* 3; **earth-wax** = OZOCERITE; **earth-woman** (chiefly SCIENCE FICTION) a woman living on or native to the planet Earth; **earthwork** an embankment, fortification, etc., made of earth; the process of excavation or building in earth; **earthworm** (**a**) an oligochaete worm which burrows in the soil and has a soft moist reddish body; (**b**) *fig.* an abject or contemptible person.
■ **earthlike** *adjective* (**a**) resembling (that of) the planet earth; (**b**) resembling earth or soil: **L19.**

earth /əːθ/ *noun*[2]. *obsolete* exc. *dial.*
[ORIGIN Old English (West Saxon) *ierþ* from Germanic, from Indo-European base also of EAR *verb*[1]: see -TH[1].]
The action or an act of ploughing.

earth /əːθ/ *verb*. **ME.**
[ORIGIN from EARTH *noun*[1].]
1 *verb trans.* Bury (a corpse). *obsolete* exc. *dial.* **ME.**
2 *verb trans.* Drive (a fox etc.) to its earth. **L16.**
3 *verb refl. & intrans.* Hide oneself underground; go into an earth. **E17.**
4 *verb trans.* Plunge or hide underground; cover with earth. *poet.* **M17.**
5 *verb trans.* Cover (the roots and stems of plants) with heaped-up earth. Usu. foll. by *up*. **M17.**
6 *verb trans.* Connect electrically with (an) earth. **L19.**

earth-board /ˈəːθbɔːd/ *noun*. **M17.**
[ORIGIN from EARTH *noun*[1] or *noun*[2] + BOARD *noun*.]
The mould board of a plough.

earthbound /ˈəːθbaʊnd/ *ppl adjective*[1]. **E17.**
[ORIGIN from EARTH *noun*[1] + *bound* pa. pple of BIND *verb*.]
Fixed on or in the earth's surface; restricted to the planet Earth or to worldly concerns.

> SHAKES. *Macb.* Who can impress the forest, bid the tree Unfix his earthbound root? DAY LEWIS Earth's first faint tug at the earthbound soul.

earthbound /ˈəːθbaʊnd/ *ppl adjective*[2]. **M20.**
[ORIGIN from EARTH *noun*[1] + BOUND *ppl adjective*[2].]
Moving towards the earth.

earthen /ˈəːθ(ə)n/ *adjective*. **ME.**
[ORIGIN from EARTH *noun*[1] + -EN[4].]
1 Made of earth. **ME.** ▸**b** Made of baked clay. **LME.**
2 Characteristic of the earth, esp. as opp. to heaven; materialistic, earthly. **L16.**

earthenware /ˈəːθ(ə)nwɛː/ *noun & adjective*. **M17.**
[ORIGIN from EARTHEN + WARE *noun*[2].]
▸ **A** *noun*. (Vessels or other objects made of) baked clay, esp. the opaque usu. porous kind baked at a relatively low temperature. **M17.**
▸ **B** *attrib.* or as *adjective*. Made of earthenware. **E19.**

earthiness /ˈəːθɪnɪs/ *noun*. **LME.**
[ORIGIN from EARTHY *adjective* + -NESS.]
1 The quality of resembling earth as a substance or (*hist.*) as one of the four elements. **LME.** ▸†**b** Earthy matter. **E16–L17.**
2 Earthliness, worldliness; the condition of being earthy or coarse. **L17.**

earthliness /ˈəːθlɪnɪs/ *noun*. **M16.**
[ORIGIN from EARTHLY *adjective* + -NESS.]
†**1** = EARTHINESS 1. **M16–M17.**
2 The quality or state of being earthly or terrestrial; worldliness, materialism. **L16.**

earthling /ˈəːθlɪŋ/ *noun*. **L16.**
[ORIGIN from EARTH *noun*[1] + -LING[1].]
1 An inhabitant of the earth. **L16.**
2 A worldly or materialistic person. **E17.**

earthly /ˈəːθli/ *adjective, adverb, & noun*. **OE.**
[ORIGIN from EARTH *noun*[1] + -LY[1].]
▸ **A** *adjective*. **1** Of or pertaining to the earth, terrestrial; worldly, material. Opp. ***celestial***, ***heavenly***, ***spiritual***. **OE.**

> I. MURDOCH This earthly joy was being . . transformed into a heavenly joy.

earthly paradise: see PARADISE *noun* 1.
2 Pertaining to or resembling earth as a substance; earthy. *arch.* **LME.** ▸†**b** Pale or lifeless as earth. *rare* (Shakes.). Only in **L16.**
†**3** Existing or living in or on the ground. **L16–M17.**
4 On earth, at all. Only in neg. & interrog. contexts. *colloq.* **M18.**

> ARNOLD BENNETT There's no earthly reason why you should not go back. G. GREENE What earthly difference does it make?

▸ **B** *adverb*. On earth, in any way, at all. *rare*. **LME.**

> SIR W. SCOTT I do not know earthly where to go or what to do.

▸ **C** *ellipt.* as *noun*. An earthly chance, use, hope, difference, etc.; any chance etc. whatever. Only in neg. contexts. *colloq.* **L19.**

> K. MANSFIELD He hadn't a ghost of a chance, he hadn't an earthly.

earthward /ˈəːθwəd/ *adverb & adjective*. **LME.**
[ORIGIN from EARTH *noun*[1] + -WARD.]
▸ **A** *adverb*. Orig. ***to the earthward***. Towards the earth. **LME.**
▸ **B** *adjective*. Moving or directed towards the earth. **M19.**
■ Also **earthwards** *adverb* **M19.**

earthy /ˈəːθi/ *adjective*. **LME.**
[ORIGIN from EARTH *noun*[1] + -Y[1].]
1 Resembling or suggestive of earth as a substance; having the physical qualities characteristic of earth; (of a mineral) lustreless, friable, and rough to the touch. **LME.** ▸**b** Made of earth; soiled with earth. **LME.**

> E. FIGES Strong earthy smells which come from out of doors. **b** G. DURRELL Andraia now emerged, scratched and earthy.

2 Pertaining to the earth, living or existing on earth; worldly, concerned with material rather than spiritual matters. *arch.* **LME.**

> SHAKES. *John* What earthy name to interrogatories Can task the free breath of a sacred king?

†**3** Pertaining to or having the qualities of earth as one of the four elements; heavy, gross, dull. **LME–L17.**
4 *fig.* (orig. from 3). Coarse, unrefined, crude; grossly material. **L16.**

> B. MACDONALD She was a very kind neighbour . . but she was earthy and to the point. L. VAN DER POST His language . . could be just as earthy as it was poetic. T. C. WOLFE It amused her . . to listen to Mary's obscene earthy conversation.

5 Pertaining to the ground or what is below the ground; subterranean. **M17.**

> DRYDEN Those earthy spirits black and envious are.

6 Of the nature of or pertaining to a substance of the kind called an earth. **E18.**
7 Electrically connected to earth; at zero electrical potential. **L19.**

earwig /ˈɪəwɪg/ *noun & verb*.
[ORIGIN Old English *ēarwicga*, from *ēare* EAR *noun*[1] + *wicga* earwig, prob. rel. to WIGGLE *verb*: the insect was formerly believed to crawl into the human ear.]
▸ **A** *noun*. **1** An insect of the order Dermaptera, esp. the common *Forficula auricularia*, characterized by an elongated, flattened body with large terminal forceps. **OE.** ▸**b** A small centipede. *US*. **L19.**
†**2** A whisperer; a flatterer; an insincere follower. **LME–L18.**
▸ **B** *verb trans.* Infl. **-gg-**. Pester with private importunities; influence by secret communications. *arch.* **M19.**

ease /iːz/ *noun*. **ME.**
[ORIGIN Anglo-Norman *ese*, Old French *eise*, (also mod.) *aise* †elbow room, †favourable occasion, convenience, from Proto-Romance alt. of Latin *adjacens* use as noun of pres. pple of *adjacere*: see ADJACENT.]
†**1** Opportunity, means or ability to do something. **ME–L15.**
2 Comfort, convenience; formerly also, advantage, enjoyment. **ME.** ▸†**b** A convenience, a luxury. **LME–M17.**

> HOBBES The ease, and benefit the Subjects may enjoy. T. JEFFERSON The portion which came . . to Mrs. Jefferson . . doubled the ease of our circumstances.

3 Absence of pain or discomfort; freedom from annoyance. **ME.** ▸**b** *spec.* Freedom from embarrassment or awkwardness in social behaviour. **M18.**

> S. JOHNSON Ease, a neutral state between pain & pleasure. **b** F. TUOHY A lack of ease, something ponderous and embarrassing in his manner.

4 Relief of pain, discomfort, or annoyance. Usu. foll. by *from*. **LME.** ▸**b** Alleviation of a constraint, burden, or obligation. Now *rare*. **LME.** ▸†**c** An act or means of relieving pain, discomfort, an obligation, etc. **LME–M18.**

> E. W. LANE Liberate him, said the King, and give us ease. CONAN DOYLE It was half a sleep and half a faint, but at least it was ease from pain.

5 Freedom from toil; leisure; idleness, sloth. LME. ▸**b** Indifference, unconcern. *rare*. E19.

> R. ELLIS Ease hath entomb'd princes of old renown. J. BUCHAN The position of a judge was the most honourable . . —ease without idleness, an absorbing intellectual pursuit. **b** J. BENTHAM It is a matter of ease to me not to know.

6 Absence of awkwardness or difficulty; dexterity. Chiefly in ***with ease***, easily. E17.

> L. C. KNIGHTS The sinewy ease of Dryden's satires. M. KEANE He jumped up and settled himself with neat ease in the saddle.

– PHRASES: **at ease**, **at one's ease** (*a*) comfortable, relaxed; without annoyance or embarrassment; †(*b*) well-to-do. ***chapel of ease***: see CHAPEL *noun*. ***ill at ease***: see ILL *adjective & adverb*. **put a person at his or her ease**, **set a person at his or her ease** avoid embarrassing a person by undue formality. **set at ease** reassure, relieve from anxiety. **stand at ease** MILITARY stand on parade in a relaxed attitude with the feet apart. **take one's ease** make oneself comfortable, relax. ***with ease***: see sense 6 above.

■ **easeless** *adjective* without ease; *esp.* without relief (from pain etc.): L16.

ease /iːz/ *verb*. ME.

[ORIGIN Orig. from Old French *aisier*, *aaisier*, from phr. *a aise* at ease; later directly from the noun.]

▸ **I** *verb trans.* **1** Make more comfortable, relieve from physical pain or discomfort. ME. ▸†**b** Refresh with rest or food; show hospitality to. ME–L17.

> E. M. FORSTER The driver . . had got out to ease the horses.

ease nature, **ease oneself** urinate or (*esp.*) defecate.

2 Relieve (a person who is oppressed, troubled, etc.) of a burden, pain, or anxiety; give relief to; help, assist. Also foll. by *of*, †*from*. ME. ▸**b** Rob, deprive *of*. *joc.* E17.

> T. URQUHART He . . gave unto each . . a horse to ease them on their way. G. BORROW A powerful priest . . has . . eased me of my sins.

3 Give mental relief to; comfort, relieve (the mind or heart). LME.

> CONAN DOYLE It would ease my mind if someone knew the truth before I died.

4 Relieve (pain, distress, etc.); lighten (a burden etc.). LME.

> P. H. GIBBS The food was hardly enough to ease the pangs of hunger.

5 Make easy or easier, facilitate. LME.

> A. G. GARDINER Otmar eased the passage up the slope by zigzagging.

6 Slacken, make less tight; cause to work more freely, esp. by altering or loosening. Freq. NAUTICAL, slacken (a rope, sail, etc.). E17. ▸**b** Reduce the engine speed of (a ship etc.). M19.

> G. S. NARES The earings are eased down. OED Tell the carpenter to ease the door a little. K. WARREN The first timetable was clearly much too tight, being eased by 14 minutes on 7 August.

ease the helm reduce the angle of the helm in a steamship to slow down the rate of swing.

7 Move gently or gradually *down*, *into*, *out of*, etc., L17. ▸**b** DRESSMAKING. Join by edges of unequal length, distributing the excess of one evenly along the join. Also foll. by *in*. M20.

> I. FLEMING He eased the cylinder out of his pocket. J. CHEEVER The conductor . . eased her down the steps.

ease in, **ease into** break in gently to (work etc.); manoeuvre into (a place, appointment, etc.). **ease out** manoeuvre out of a place, appointment, etc.

▸ **II** *verb intrans.* †**8** Take one's ease, rest. Only in LME.

9 Slacken, cease; become less burdensome; relax or cease one's efforts, *spec.* in rowing. Freq. with adverbs. L16. ▸**b** Of shares: become easier, fall a little in value. E20.

> M. TWAIN When . . approaching the shoalest part of the reef, the command is given to 'Ease all!' E. F. NORTON The slope began to ease off. K. ISHIGURO The rain had eased to a drizzle.

10 **a** Move oneself gently or effortlessly. Chiefly *N. Amer.* E20. ▸**b** Pass gently or easily, drift; seep. L20.

> **a** R. CARVER He eased in behind the steering wheel.

■ **easer** *noun* L16.

easeful /ˈiːzfʊl, -f(ə)l/ *adjective*. LME.

[ORIGIN from EASE *noun* or *verb* + -FUL.]

1 That gives ease, comfort, or relief; soothing. LME.

> S. RUSHDIE The disillusioning discovery that . . suffering, not easeful joy, was the human norm.

2 Unoccupied, at rest; indolent, slothful. E17.

> S. SONTAG My affections were never guided by the desire to lead an easeful life.

■ **easefully** *adverb* E17. **easefulness** *noun* M17.

easel /ˈiːz(ə)l/ *noun*. L16.

[ORIGIN Dutch *ezel* = German *Esel* ass. Cf. HORSE *noun* 8.]

A (usu. wooden) frame used to support a picture, a blackboard, etc.

– COMB.: **easel-picture**: painted at an easel or small enough to stand on one.

easement /ˈiːzm(ə)nt/ *noun*. LME.

[ORIGIN Old French *aisement*, from *aisier* EASE *verb*: see -MENT.]

1 Relief from pain, discomfort, or any burden; alleviation. LME. ▸†**b** *spec.* The relieving of the body by defecation or urination. LME–E18. ▸†**c** *spec.* Refreshment by food and rest; accommodation, hospitality. LME–E19.

> W. S. CHURCHILL An easement in the drastic petrol rationing system.

2 (An) advantage, convenience, comfort; formerly also, gratification, enjoyment. LME.

> R. V. JONES I had no easements such as a staff car.

3 A (supplementary) building, room, shed, etc., provided for the sake of convenience. *arch.* LME.

4 The right or privilege of using something not one's own; *spec.* in LAW, an entitlement to rights (e.g. right of way) over another's land. LME.

easily /ˈiːzɪli/ *adverb*. Formerly compared †**-lier**, †**-liest**. ME.

[ORIGIN from EASY *adjective* + -LY².]

1 Comfortably; in a relaxed fashion; without pain or anxiety; self-indulgently. ME.

> J. KOSINSKI Four men entered the room, talking and smiling easily.

2 With little labour or difficulty. ME.

> J. BUCHAN He would have beaten me easily if the course had been longer. E. BOWEN Anna could remember being a child more easily . . than she could remember being Portia's age.

3 Smoothly, freely. LME.

> M. KEANE She . . shut the drawer, then tried it again to see if it slid and ran easily.

4 Without hurry, gradually; calmly, quietly. *obsolete* exc. *dial.* LME.

†**5** ***but easily***, only indifferently, only poorly. LME–M16.

6 With little resistance or reluctance. M17.

> DAY LEWIS The small fatalists accept more easily than most philosophers the knowledge that what is is.

7 At least; without doubt; by a comfortable margin. *colloq.* M20.

> C. P. SNOW She was easily the most attractive woman there.

easiness /ˈiːzɪnɪs/ *noun*. LME.

[ORIGIN from EASY *adjective* + -NESS.]

1 Tranquillity, (spiritual) comfort. *rare*. LME.
2 The quality of not being difficult; facility. LME.
3 Gentleness, indulgence. LME.
4 The quality of being relaxed in manner, style, etc. M16.
5 Indifference; indolence. L16.
†**6** The quality of being easily influenced; lack of firmness. E17–L18.

eassel /ˈiːs(ə)l/ *adverb*. *Scot.* L18.

[ORIGIN Obscurely from EAST.]

Eastward, easterly.

east /iːst/ *adverb*, *adjective*, & *noun*.

[ORIGIN Old English *ēast-* = Old Frisian *āst*, Old Saxon, Old High German *ōst* (Dutch *oost*, German *ost*) repr. of Germanic base (with suffix in Old English *ēastan*, Old Saxon, Old High German *ōstana*, Old Norse *austan* from the east), from Indo-European, whence also Latin *aurora* dawn, Greek *auōs* dawn, *aurion* tomorrow (cf. Sanskrit *usas* morning, dawn); as simple adverb = Old Saxon, Old High German *ōstar*, Old Norse *austr* toward the east, from Germanic.]

▸ **A** *adverb*. †**1** From the east. OE–ME.

2 In the direction of that part of the horizon where the sun rises, in the direction of the earth's diurnal rotation about the polar axis; towards the cardinal point which is 90 degrees clockwise from the north point. OE. ▸**b** Foll. by *of*: further in this direction than. L18.

▸ **B** *adjective*. **1** (Also **E-**.) Designating (a person or the people of) the eastern part of a country, region, city, etc. OE.

East Africa, *East London*, *East Midlands*, *East Sussex*, etc.

2 Situated in or lying towards the east or eastern part of something; on the easterly side. ME. ▸**b** Facing east. M17. ▸**c** *spec.* Designating or situated in the end of a Christian church that contains the (high) altar, traditionally but not necessarily the geographical east. E18.

> G. GREENE The wind's east, and I'm damned if it hasn't begun to rain.

3 Of or pertaining to the east; (of a wind) coming from the east. LME.

▸ **C** *noun*. In senses 1, 2, 3 usu. with *the*.

1 (The direction of) that part of the horizon or the sky where the sun rises; *spec.* the cardinal point which is 90 degrees clockwise from the north point. ME.

> SHAKES. *Much Ado* The gentle day . . Dapples the drowsy east with spots of grey.

2 (Freq. **E-**.) The eastern part of the world relative to another part, or of a (specified) country, region, town, etc.; *spec.* (*a*) that part of the world which lies to the east of Europe, the culture and civilization of that part; (*b*) *hist.* = ***Eastern Empire*** s.v. EASTERN; (*c*) *hist.* the Communist states of eastern Europe. Also (*transf.*), the inhabitants of such a part of the world, such a region, country, etc. ME.

3 The east wind. Chiefly *poet.* M18.

4 (**E-**.) In bridge, (formerly) whist, or other four-handed partnership game: the player who occupies the position so designated, and who sits opposite 'West'. In mah-jong, = ***east wind*** (a) below. E20.

– SPECIAL COLLOCATIONS, PHRASES, & COMB.: **eastabout** *adverb* (NAUTICAL) by an easterly route; eastwards. **East African** (a native or inhabitant) of eastern Africa. **east and west** lengthwise along a line from east to west. ***East Anglian***. **eastbound** *adjective & noun* (*a*) *adjective* travelling or heading eastwards; (*b*) *noun* (chiefly *N. Amer.*) an eastbound train. **east-by-north**, **east-by-south** (in the direction of) the compass point 11¼ degrees or one point north, south, of the east point. **East Coaster** a native or inhabitant of the east coast of a country. **East Coast fever** a severe form of theileriasis affecting cattle esp. in Africa. †**East Country** the Baltic countries. **east end** the eastern part of something, esp. a church; *spec.* (***East End***) the eastern part of London, including the docks. **East Ender** a native or inhabitant of London's East End. ***East Germanic***. **East India** *hist.* the whole of SE Asia to the east of and including India; ***East India Company***, a company formed to trade with East India, esp. the English company incorporated in 1600 and dissolved in 1874; ***East India mahogany***, a leguminous tree, *Pterocarpus dalbergioides*. ***East Indiaman***. **East Indies** †(*a*) = ***East India*** above; (*b*) the region of the Malay archipelago. **east-north-east** (in the direction) midway between east and north-east. **East Side** *US* the eastern part of Manhattan. **East Sider** *US* a native or inhabitant of Manhattan's East Side. **east-south-east** (in the direction) midway between east and south-east. **east wind** (*a*) (usu. with cap. initials) one of the four players in mah-jong, the player who throws the highest score and draws the first four tiles at the outset of the game, preceding South Wind; (*b*) each of four tiles so designated, which with north, south, and west winds make up the suit of winds in mah-jong; (see also sense B.3 above). ***Far East***: see FAR *adjective*. ***Middle East***: see MIDDLE *adjective*. ***Near East***: see NEAR *adjective*. **to the east (of)** in an easterly direction (from).

■ **eastmost** *adjective* (chiefly *Scot.*) easternmost ME.

Easter /ˈiːstə/ *noun*.

[ORIGIN Old English *ēastre*, pl. *ēastron* (also *ēastro*, *-a*) = Old Frisian *āsteron*, Old High German *ōstarūn* (German *Ostern* pl.) app. from *Ēostre* Northumbrian var. of *Ēastre*, a goddess whose feast was celebrated at the vernal equinox, from Germanic, cogn. with Sanskrit *usrā* dawn. Cf. EAST.]

1 The most important of the Christian festivals, commemorating the resurrection of Christ and observed annually on the Sunday which follows the first full moon after the vernal equinox; *colloq.* Easter week or the weekend from Friday to Monday including Easter Sunday (see below). OE.

†**2** The Jewish passover. OE–E17.

– COMB.: **Easter bunny** (a representation of) a rabbit popularly said to bring gifts to children at Easter; **Easter Day** = ***Easter Sunday*** below; **Easter-dues** money payable at Easter to the incumbent of a parish by the parishioners; **Easter egg** (*a*) an egg given as a gift at Easter (orig. a painted hard-boiled hen's egg, now usu. one made of chocolate); (*b*) an unexpected or undocumented feature in a piece of computer software or on a DVD; **Easter lily** (chiefly *N. Amer.*) any of various spring-flowering lilies or similar plants; *spec.* a tall cultivated variety of *Lilium longiflorum*, a white-flowered lily native to Japan; **Easter Monday** the Monday after Easter Sunday; **Easter-offering(s)** orig. = ***Easter-dues*** above; now usu. the proceeds of the Easter Sunday collection; **Easter Parade** a parade or pageant held at Eastertime, esp. of people in new or striking clothes. **Easter sitting(s)** = ***Easter term*** (a) below; **Easter Sunday**: on which the festival of Easter is observed; **Easter term** (*a*) a term in the courts of law, formerly movable and occurring between Easter and Whitsuntide, but now fixed within a certain period; (*b*) in the older universities, a term formerly occurring between Easter and Whitsuntide and now included in the Trinity term; in some universities and schools, the term between Christmas and Easter; **Eastertide** the period from Easter Sunday until Pentecost (formerly until Ascension Day); **Eastertime** Easter Sunday and the following days up to Ascensiontide; **Easter week**: beginning with Easter Sunday.

easter /ˈiːstə/ *adjective*. *obsolete* exc. *Scot.* & *dial.* LME.

[ORIGIN Perh. repr. Old English compar. *ēasterra* (cf. Old Norse *austarr* more to the east), formed as EAST + -ER³.]

Lying towards or nearest the east; eastern.

Easterling /ˈiːstəlɪŋ/ *noun*. Also **e-**. LME.

[ORIGIN App. from EASTER *adjective* + -LING¹, prob. after Dutch *oosterling*.]

1 A native or inhabitant of eastern Germany or the Baltic coasts, *esp.* a citizen of the Hanse towns. *obsolete* exc. *hist.* LME.

2 *gen.* A native or inhabitant of an eastern country or district; a member of the Orthodox Church. *arch.* M16.

easterly /ˈiːstəli/ *adverb*, *adjective*, & *noun*. LME.

[ORIGIN Prob. from EASTER *adjective* + -LY², -LY¹.]

▸ **A** *adverb*. **1** In an eastward position or direction, towards the east. LME.

> R. GRAVES The full moon easterly rising, furious, Against a winter sky ragged with red.

2 Esp. of a wind: (nearly) from the east. L16.

▸ **B** *adjective*. **1** Situated towards or facing the east; directed towards the east. M16.

> E. DUNKIN The most easterly part of this constellation.

2 Esp. of a wind: coming (nearly) from the east. M16.

▸ **C** *noun*. An easterly wind. Usu. in *pl.* E20.

> R. FRAME Aldeburgh with its biting easterlies and . . flat leaden skies.

■ **easterliness** *noun* (*rare*) E20.

†**eastermost** *adjective*. **M16–M19**.
[**ORIGIN** from **EASTER** *adjective* + **-MOST**.]
= **EASTERNMOST**.

eastern /ˈiːst(ə)n/ *adjective & noun*.
[**ORIGIN** Old English *ēasterne* = Old Saxon, Old High German *ōstroni*, Old Norse *austrœnn*, from Germanic, from base of **EAST**.]
▸ **A** *adjective*. **1** Of, pertaining to, or characteristic of the east or its inhabitants, *esp*. of or pertaining to the part of the world east of Europe; living in or originating from the east. **OE**. ▸**b** *spec*. Situated or living in the (north-)east of the US, esp. New England; of, from, or relating to this region. **L18**.

> **SHAKES**. *Ant. & Cl*. Oh Eastern star! **J. CONRAD** Easy enough to dispose of a Malay woman, a slave after all, to his Eastern mind.

Eastern ABNAKI. **Eastern Church** the Orthodox Church. **Eastern Empire** the more easterly of the two parts into which the Roman Empire was divided in AD 395. ***Eastern HEMISPHERE***. **Eastern Standard time**, **Eastern time** the standard time used in the eastern parts of Canada and the US, or in eastern Australia. ***Far Eastern***: see **FAR** *adjective*. ***Middle Eastern***: see **MIDDLE** *adjective*. ***Near Eastern***: see **NEAR** *adjective*.
2 Of a wind: blowing from the east. *poet*. **OE**.
3 Situated in the east; directed, facing, or lying towards the east; having a position relatively east. **LME**.

> **ADDISON** The eastern end of the isle rises up in precipices. **J. TYNDALL** A pale light now overspread the eastern sky.

▸ **B** *noun*. **1** A native or inhabitant of the east. *rare*. **OE**.
2 A member of the Orthodox Church. **M19**.
■ **easterner** *noun* (**a**) a native or inhabitant of the eastern part of a country, esp. the eastern states of the US; (**b**) *hist*. an opponent of the concentration of forces on the Western Front in the First World War (cf. **WESTERNER** (b)): **M19**. **easternmost** *adjective* situated furthest to the east; most easterly: **L18**.

East Indian /iːst ˈɪndɪən/ *adjectival & noun phr*. **M16**.
[**ORIGIN** from ***East India*** s.v. **EAST** + **-AN**.]
▸ **A** *adjectival phr*. Chiefly *hist*. Of or pertaining to the region of the Malay archipelago or (formerly) the whole of SE Asia and India. **M16**.
East Indian walnut = **KOKKO** 1.
▸ **B** *noun phr*. **1** = **EURASIAN** *noun*. *obsolete* exc. *hist*. **E19**.
2 A resident of the West Indies descended from the indigenous peoples of the Indian subcontinent. **M20**.

easting /ˈiːstɪŋ/ *noun*. **E17**.
[**ORIGIN** from **EAST** + **-ING**[1].]
1 Chiefly **NAUTICAL**. Distance travelled or measured eastward. **E17**.
2 **CARTOGRAPHY**. Distance eastward from a point of origin (freq. from the south-west corner of a map); a figure representing this, expressed by convention as the first part of a grid reference (usu. in *pl*. or more fully ***easting coordinate***). Cf. **NORTHING** 2. **M18**.
3 Easterly tendency; a running or shifting eastward. **M19**.

Eastlake /ˈiːstleɪk/ *adjective & noun*. **L19**.
[**ORIGIN** See below.]
(Designating) furniture associated with the English designer Charles Locke Eastlake (1836–1906) and his book *Hints on Household Taste* (1878).

eastland /ˈiːstlənd/ *noun*. *obsolete* exc. *hist*. or *poet*. **OE**.
[**ORIGIN** from **EAST** + **LAND** *noun*[1].]
An eastern country or district; *spec*. (**E-**) the Baltic countries (= ***East Country*** s.v. **EAST**).

eastward /ˈiːstwəd/ *adverb, adjective, & noun*. **OE**.
[**ORIGIN** from **EAST** + **-WARD**.]
▸ **A** *adverb*. Towards the east (*of*); in an easterly direction. **OE**.

> **AV** *1 Kings* 17:3 Get thee hence, and turne thee Eastward.

▸ **B** *adjective*. Situated or directed towards the east; moving or facing towards the east. **LME**.
eastward position: of the celebrant standing in front of and facing the altar (and so facing east) in the Eucharist.
▸ **C** *noun*. The direction or area lying to the east or east *of* a place etc.; *US* the eastern side or part, esp. of the US. **M17**.
■ **eastwardly** *adverb & adjective* (**a**) *adverb* in or from an easterly direction; (**b**) *adjective* moving, lying, or facing towards the east; (of a wind) blowing (nearly) from the east: **M17**. **eastwards** *adverb* = **EASTWARD** *adverb* **E16**.

easy /ˈiːzi/ *adjective, adverb, & noun*. **ME**.
[**ORIGIN** Anglo-Norman *aisé*, Old French *aisié* (mod. *aisé*), pa. pple of *aisier* put at ease: see **EASE** *verb*, **-Y**[5].]
▸ **A** *adjective*. **1** Characterized by ease or rest; comfortable, quiet, tranquil. **ME**. ▸**b** Conducive to ease or comfort. **LME**.

> **DEFOE** My Condition began now to be . . much easier to my mind. **H. BELLOC** The River Sarthe . . runs . . through easy meadow-land.

make life easy (***for***): see **LIFE** *noun*. **b easy on the eye(s)**, **easy to look at** *colloq*. pleasant to look upon.
2 Presenting few difficulties; offering little resistance; (of an action, task, object, etc.) that can be accomplished with little effort. **ME**.

> **W. CATHER** It's awfully easy to rush into a profession you don't really like. **G. GREENE** We were an easy target in the light of the flames. **M. AMIS** People are easy to frighten.

(***as***) ***easy as ABC***, (***as***) ***easy as falling off a log***, (***as***) ***easy as kiss my hand***, (***as***) ***easy as pie***, (***as***) ***easy as winking***, etc. **easy of access** easily reached.
†**3** Of a person: lenient, gentle. **ME–E18**.

> **R. BENTLEY** Pisistratus . . a generous and easie Governour.

4 Of motion etc.: unhurried, gentle, slow, not hard-pressed. **LME**.

> **E. TOPSELL** They have a very slow and easie pace.

5 Free from anxiety or care. **LME**.

> **J. M. COETZEE** There is nothing special about you, you can rest easy about that. **M. ROBERTS** Smiling, easy, with not a care in the world.

6 Esp. of manner, movement, etc.: free from constraint or awkwardness, smooth. **LME**. ▸**b** Of literary composition etc.: showing no trace of effort, fluent. **E18**.

> **ROBERT ANDERSON** They are easy with each other, casual. **A. THWAITE** Ibsen was never an easy man.

free and easy: see **FREE** *adjective*.
7 Of a condition, penalty, etc.: moderate, not oppressive or burdensome. **LME**.

> **S. PEPYS** Secure it for me on the easiest terms you can.

at an easy rate: see **RATE** *noun*[1].
8 Moved without difficulty to action or belief; compliant, yielding; (esp. of a woman) promiscuous. **LME**.

> **LD MACAULAY** Juries were no longer so easy of belief. **S. BELLOW** Mimi, isn't that her name? She looks like an easy broad.

I'm easy *colloq*. I'm agreeable (to whatever is proposed), I don't mind. **of easy virtue** *arch*. or *joc*. (of a woman): promiscuous.
9 That is obtained with little effort or sacrifice. **LME**.

> **DRYDEN** The Swain . . Receives his easy Food from Nature's Hand.

†**10** Insignificant, of little importance; not very good. **LME–M17**.
11 Loosely fitting; not tight. **L16**.

> **SHAKES**. *All's Well* This woman's an easy glove, my lord; she goes off and on at pleasure.

12 = ***easy-going*** (a) below. **M17**.

> **DRYDEN** Easy Sloath. **W. SANSOM** We're easy folk in these parts, we leave doors unlocked.

13 Well off, comfortable. **E18**.

> **G. BERKELEY** Men easy in their fortunes, and unprovoked by hardships of any sort.

14 **STOCK EXCHANGE** etc. Not much in demand; not showing eager demand. **M19**.
▸ **B** *adverb*. (Now chiefly *colloq*.)
1 Without difficulty. **LME**.

> **BYRON** A wavering spirit may be easier wreck'd. **H. REED** You can do it quite easy.

come easy to present little difficulty to. **easy come easy go** what is easily acquired is soon lost or spent.
2 Not tightly; with freedom of movement. **E18**.

> **KEATS** The bolts full easy slide.

3 At a leisurely pace, without exertion; in a relaxed manner; comfortably, calmly. **L18**.

> **T. FORREST** Which kept the vessel's head to the sea, and made her lie easy.

easy does it go carefully, take your time. **easy on** do not be alarmed. **go easy** act or proceed cautiously (***go easy with***, ***go easy on***, use sparingly). **take it easy** proceed comfortably or carefully; do no more than one has to; relax. *In commands*: **easy!** (move) gently. **easy all!** stop (rowing). **stand easy!** *MILITARY*: with greater freedom or informality than 'at ease'.
– **SPECIAL COLLOCATIONS & COMB.**: **easy-care** *adjective* (of esp. man-made fabrics) serviceable, simple to wash, dry, etc. **easy chair** an upholstered chair, usu. with arms, designed for comfort. **easy circumstances** affluence. **easy game** *colloq*. someone or something overcome, outwitted, or persuaded without difficulty. **easy-going** (**a**) fond of comfort, indolent, not strict, taking things as they come; (**b**) (of a horse) having an easy gait. **easy listening** (recorded) popular music that is tuneful and undemanding. **easy meat** = ***easy game*** above. **easy money** money obtained without effort (and often illegally) or (*STOCK EXCHANGE* etc.) at low interest. **easy-paced** *adjective* (of a cricket pitch or golf course) allowing the ball to come at an easy pace off or along it. **easy-peasy** *slang*. [redupl.] very simple. **easy rider** *US slang* (**a**) a sexually satisfying lover; (**b**) a guitar. **Easy Street** *colloq*. comfortable circumstances, affluence. ***easy touch***: see **TOUCH** *noun*. ***easy virtue***: see sense 8 above.
▸ **C** *noun*. A rest, a breather. *colloq*. **L19**.

> **G. R. LOWNDES** We took a day's easy . . by the salmon pool.

easy /ˈiːzi/ *verb*. **M16**.
[**ORIGIN** from the adjective.]
†**1** *verb trans*. Facilitate; assist. Only in **M16**.
2 *verb trans. & intrans*. **ROWING**. (Cause to) cease rowing. **M19**.

eat /iːt/ *noun*. Now *colloq*.
[**ORIGIN** Old English *ǣt* = Old Frisian *ēt*, Old Saxon *āt*, Old High German *āz*; in mod. use from the verb.]
1 Food. Now only in *pl*., things to eat. **OE**.

> **J. P. DONLEAVY** On the table were eats the like of which . . have never been seen on this isle.

2 An act of eating, a meal. **OE**.

> **J. FRAME** Goodbye and thank you for the little eat.

eat /iːt/ *verb*. Pa. t. **ate** /eɪt, ɛt/, (*obsolete* exc. *Scot. & dial*.) **eat**. Pa. pple **eaten** /ˈiːt(ə)n/, †**eat**.
[**ORIGIN** Old English *etan* = Old Frisian *eta*, Old Saxon *etan* (Du *eten*), Old High German *ezzan* (German *essen*), Old Norse *eta*, Gothic *itan*, from Germanic, from Indo-European base of Latin *edere*, Greek *edein*.]
▸ **I** Consume for nutriment.
1 *verb trans*. Have as food; take into the mouth, masticate if necessary, and swallow (solid food; also fluid, e.g. soup, for which a spoon is used). **OE**. ▸†**b** *fig*. Submit to, accept meekly (an insult, an injury, etc.). **LME–E17**. ▸**c** *fig*. Receive (esp. a stage performance) with vigorous enjoyment; acclaim. (Foll. by *up*.) *colloq*. **E20**. ▸**d** Perform fellatio or cunnilingus on (a person). *US slang*. **E20**.

> **J. M. SYNGE** He eat the insides of a clock and died after. **D. ATTENBOROUGH** Some caterpillars have made themselves unpleasant to eat. **M. AMIS** They found out he was eating his diet *and* his normal food. **c N. MITFORD** London society . . simply ate Cedric up.

2 *verb intrans*. Consume food, take a meal; feed (†*on*, †*upon*); *arch*. eat some *of* a food. **OE**.

> **AV** *Exod*. 34:15 Lest . . thou eate of his sacrifice. **POPE** Yet on plain pudding deign'd at home to eat. **G. VIDAL** You lovely ones must have dinner with me this evening, otherwise I must eat alone.

3 *verb trans*. Leave (grain, grass, etc.) to animals to be eaten. Foll. by *with*. **E16**.

> *Perthshire Journal* The pasture . . he intended to eat with sheep.

4 *verb intrans*. Have a certain consistency or flavour when eaten. **L16**.

> **SHAKES**. *All's Well* Like one of our French wither'd pears: . . it eats drily.

5 *verb trans*. Provide with food. *US slang*. **M19**.

> **J. T. TROWBRIDGE** I might hide ye; but I can't eat ye.

▸ **II** Destroy by devouring.
6 *verb trans*. Devour, consume; feed destructively on (crops, vegetation, etc.). **OE**. ▸**b** Bother, vex; make anxious. *colloq*. (orig. *US*). **L19**.

> **AV** *Exod*. 10:12 Stretch out thine hand . . for the locusts, that they may . . eate euery herbe of the land. **OED** He went to Africa, and got eaten by a lion. *fig*.: **SHAKES**. *Rich. III* Or, earth, gape open wide and eat him quick. **A. S. NEILL** If you throw any nutshells on that floor Mrs. Findlay will eat you. **b A. MILLER** He thinks I've been spiting him all these years and it's eating him up.

7 *verb trans*. Gnaw, wear away by gnawing; destroy gradually or insidiously by corrosion, erosion, disease, etc. **ME**.

> **AV** *Acts* 12:23 Hee was eaten of wormes and gave up the ghost. **COLERIDGE** His limbs The silent frost had eat, scathing like fire. **J. HODGSON** The cliffs chalky and stratified, . . eaten into caves.

8 *verb intrans*. Make a way (*into*, *through*) by gnawing, corrosion, etc. **E17**.

> *fig*.: **E. BIRNEY** Night's dissolvent eats into the west / browning the stippled mauve.

9 *verb trans*. Make (a hole, a passage, one's way) by gnawing, corrosion, etc. **L17**.

> **DRYDEN** The slow creeping Evil eats his way . . and makes the Life his Prey. **T. H. HUXLEY** Little water-courses may be eaten out of solid rock by a running stream.

– **PHRASES, & WITH ADVERBS IN SPECIALIZED SENSES**: **eat away** destroy gradually (*lit. & fig*.). **eat crow** *N. Amer*. submit to humiliation. **eat Chinese**, **eat Indian**, etc., have a meal of Chinese, Indian, etc., food. **eat dinners** = ***eat one's terms*** below. ***eat dirt***: see **DIRT** *noun*. ***eat humble pie***: see **HUMBLE** *adjective*[1]. **eat its head off** (of an animal) cost more for food than it will sell for. ***eat like a horse***: see **HORSE** *noun*. **eat off** clear off (a crop) by feeding it to animals. ***eat one's cake and have it***: see **CAKE** *noun*. **eat one's heart** (**out**) brood or suffer with grief or longing. **eat one's terms** be studying for the Bar, and therefore having to dine a certain number of times in the Hall of an Inn of Court. **eat one's words** retract, usu. in a humiliated manner, something one has said. **eat oneself sick** eat until one vomits or feels ill. **eat out** (**a**) *verb phr. trans*. destroy parasitically or corrosively; (**b**) *verb phr. trans*. encroach upon (space; formerly also, time); (**c**) *verb phr. intrans*. take a meal elsewhere than at one's residence. **eat out of a person's hand** be entirely submissive or obedient to a person. **eat out of house and home** (usu. *hyperbol*.) ruin (a person) by eating all he or she has. ***eat the bread of***: see **BREAD** *noun*[1]. **eat the wind out of** *NAUTICAL* sail to windward of (another vessel). **eat up** (**a**) consume completely or wastefully; (**b**) consume all the resources of; (**c**) annex rapaciously; (**d**) assimilate the ideas of; (**e**) absorb; (**f**) wear out the life of (*with* remorse etc.); (**g**) traverse (a distance) rapidly; (**h**) finish eating; (see also sense 1c above). ***have one's cake and eat it*** etc.: see **CAKE** *noun*. **he won't eat you**, **it won't eat you**, etc., he etc. will not injure or harm you.
– **COMB.**: **eat-in** *adjective* (*N. Amer*.) designating a kitchen designed for eating in as well as cooking.
■ **eatery** *noun* (*colloq*., chiefly *N. Amer*.) a restaurant or cafe. **E20**.

eatable /ˈiːtəb(ə)l/ *adjective & noun*. **LME**.
[**ORIGIN** from **EAT** *verb* + **-ABLE**.]
▸ **A** *adjective*. Able to be eaten; edible; palatable. **LME**.
▸ **B** *noun*. An article of food. Usu. in *pl*. **L17**.

eatage /ˈiːtɪdʒ/ *noun. N. English.* **M17.**
[ORIGIN from EAT *verb* + -AGE.]
1 Grass available (only) for grazing, esp. the aftermath. **M17.**
2 The right of using for pasture. **M19.**

eaten *verb pa. pple*: see EAT *verb*.

eater /ˈiːtə/ *noun.* **OE.**
[ORIGIN from EAT *verb* + -ER[1].]
1 A person, animal, or thing that eats (*lit.* & *fig.*); a person who or animal which eats a specified food, or in a specified way. **OE.**

COVERDALE *Ezek.* 36:13 Thou art an eater vp of men, and a waister of thy people. J. L. WATEN Ginger was a slow eater.

ANTEATER. ***bee-eater***: see BEE *noun*[1]. **big eater** a person with a large appetite.

2 A fruit suitable for eating raw. **E20.**

P. LOVESEY She offered apples, but . . her eaters had gone soft.

eath /iːθ/ *adjective & adverb.* Now *Scot.* & *dial.* Also (*Scot.*) **eith**.
[ORIGIN Old English *ēaþe*, *ȳþe* adjective = Old Saxon *ōþi*, Old High German *ōdi*; Old English *ēaþe* adverb = Old Saxon *ōþo*, Old High German *ōdo*, Old Norse *auð-*; both from Germanic.]
▶ **A** *adjective.* Easy, presenting little difficulty. **OE.**
▶ **B** *adverb.* Easily. **OE.**
■ Also **eathly** *adverb* & †*adjective* **OE.**

eating /ˈiːtɪŋ/ *verbal noun.* **ME.**
[ORIGIN from EAT *verb* + -ING[1].]
The action or habit of taking food; in *pl.*, things or quantities eaten.
– COMB.: **eating apple** etc.: suitable for eating raw; **eating house** (*a*) a restaurant; †(*b*) a refectory; ***eating irons***: see IRON *noun* 16.

eau /əʊ; *foreign* o/ *noun*[1]. Pl. **eaux** (pronounced same). **M18.**
[ORIGIN French.]
The French for 'water', occurring in various phrases used in English.
■ **eau de Cologne** /əʊdəkəˈləʊn/ a lightly scented perfume made orig. at Cologne **E19.** **eau de Javelle**, **eau de Javel**, /əʊ də ʒaˈvɛl/ Javelle water **E19.** **eau de Luce** /əʊdəˈluːs/ (*obsolete* exc. *hist.*) a medicinal preparation of alcohol, oil of amber, oil of lavender, and ammonia **M18.** **eau de Nil** /əʊdəˈniːl, *foreign* odnil/ [lit. 'water of (the) Nile'] a pale greenish colour (supposedly resembling Nile water) **L19.** **eau de toilette** /əʊ də twɑːˈlɛt, *foreign* o də twalɛt/, pl. **eaux de toilette**, (a) toilet water **E20.** **eau de vie** /əʊdəˈviː, *foreign* odvi/, pl. **eaux de vie**, [lit. 'water of life'] (a) brandy **M18.** **eau sucreé** /əʊ ˈsuːkreɪ, *foreign* o sykre/ water with sugar in it **E19.** SALLE *d'eau*.

eau *noun*[2] see EA.

eaux *noun* pl. of EAU.

eave /iːv/ *noun sing.* **E17.**
[ORIGIN from EAVES, with -s taken as pl. suffix -S[1].]
= EAVES.
■ **eaved** *adjective* provided with eaves **M19.** **eaving** *noun* = next **L16.**

eaves /iːvz/ *noun pl.* (orig. †*sing.*).
[ORIGIN Old English *efes*, corresp. to Old Frisian *ose*, Middle Low German *ovese*, Flemish *oose*, Middle Dutch *ovese*, *ose*, Old High German *obasa*, *-isa*, Middle High German *ob(e)se* (German dial. *Obsen*) eaves, porch, Old Norse *ups*, Gothic *ubizwa* porch, from Germanic, prob. from base of OVER *adverb*. See also EAVE.]
1 The projecting edge of a roof or thatch, which overhangs the side of the building. **OE.** ▸**b** The edge or margin of a wood or forest. Long *arch. rare.* **OE.**

MILTON Ushered with a shower still . . With minute-drops from off the eaves. N. GORDIMER A rim of shady light where the mud walls did not meet the eaves. **b** TOLKIEN They had reached the eaves of Mirkwood.

2 *transf.* Something that projects or overhangs slightly. **ME.**

G. BORROW A leather hat . . with the side eaves turned up.

– COMB.: **eaves-board**, **eaves-catch** a horizontal board fixed under the eaves, making the lowest tile course(s) incline less steeply than the rest of the roof; **eavestrough** a rainwater gutter under the eaves.

eavesdrop /ˈiːvzdrɒp/ *noun.* **LME.**
[ORIGIN Prob. from Old Norse *upsardropi*, from *ups* EAVES + *dropi* DROP *noun*. Cf. Old English *yfæsdrypæ* 'eaves-drip', West Frisian *œsdrip*, *-drup*, Flemish *oosdrup* eaves.]
The dripping of water from the eaves of a house; the ground on which such water falls.

eavesdrop /ˈiːvzdrɒp/ *verb trans.* & *intrans.* Infl. **-pp-**. **E17.**
[ORIGIN Back-form. from EAVESDROPPER.]
Listen secretly to (a person, private conversation), orig. by standing beneath the eaves of a house. Formerly also, stand beneath the eaves of (a building) in order to overhear conversation within.

J. SHIRLEY It is not civil to eavesdrop him. C. ISHERWOOD George eavesdrops on their conversation. A. HAILEY Yvette started to eavesdrop by making tape recordings.

eavesdropper /ˈiːvzdrɒpə/ *noun.* **LME.**
[ORIGIN from EAVESDROP *noun* + -ER[1].]
A person who eavesdrops (formerly an indictable public nuisance).

ébauche /eboːʃ/ *noun.* Pl. pronounced same. **E18.**
[ORIGIN French.]
1 A sketch; a rough-hewn sculpture; a first draft. **E18.**
2 A partly finished watch movement. **E20.**

eBay /ˈiːbeɪ/ *verb trans.* & *intrans.* **L20.**
[ORIGIN The proprietary name of a popular Internet auction site.]
Buy and sell goods using eBay or a similar Internet auction site.

Word Never drink and eBay.

■ **eBayer** *noun* a person who buys and sells goods on an Internet auction site **L20.**

ebb /ɛb/ *noun & adjective.*
[ORIGIN Old English *ebba* = Middle & mod. Low German, Middle Dutch & mod. Dutch *ebbe* (Dutch *eb*), from West Germanic, from base of OF *preposition*, as if meaning 'a running off or away'.]
▶ **A** *noun.* **1** The outward movement of the tide; the return of tidewater towards the sea. Opp. ***flow***. **OE.**

S. BECKETT I didn't have to row, the ebb was carrying me out.

2 *gen.* A flowing away, a subsiding; *fig.* decline, decay; a change to a less favourable state. **LME.** ▸**b** A point or state of decline or depression; esp. in ***at a low ebb***. **L16.**

JOSEPH HALL This . . was the Ebbe of his greatnesse. A. C. SWINBURNE Her ebbs and flows of passion. **b** F. MUIR The scene where Eliza . . at her lowest ebb, had decided to run for it.

†**3** In *pl.* Shallows. **L16–E19.**
– COMB.: **ebb-tide** = sense 1 above.
▶ **B** *adjective.* **1** (Of water, a well, a furrow, etc.) shallow, not deep; having a short supply. *obsolete* exc. *dial.* **LME.**

R. LEIGHTON This Apostle . . drew from too full a spring to be ebb of matter.

2 Near the surface. *obsolete* exc. *dial.* **E17.**

R. PLOT Sometimes it lyes so ebb . . that they plow up the head of it.

ebb /ɛb/ *verb.*
[ORIGIN Old English *ebbian* (from EBB *noun*) = Middle & mod. Low German, Middle Dutch & mod. Dutch *ebben*.]
1 *verb intrans.* Of the sea, tidal water, etc.: flow back, recede. Freq. in ***ebb and flow***. Cf. FLOW *verb* 10. **OE.**

SHAKES. *L.L.L.* The sea will ebb and flow. R. HUGHES The water of the bay began to ebb away.

2 *verb intrans. gen.* Flow out or away; sink lower, subside; *fig.* decline, decay; fade or waste away. **ME.**

DEFOE As my money declined, their respect would ebb with it. H. JAMES The flood of summer light had begun to ebb. B. CHATWIN Her strength ebbed away on a diet of corned beef and packet potato.

3 *verb trans.* Prevent (fish etc.) from returning to sea with the ebb-tide. **L15.**

EBCDIC /ˈɛbsɪdɪk/ *abbreviation.*
Extended Binary Coded Decimal Interchange Code, a standard 8-bit character code used in computing and data transmission.

EBD *abbreviation.*
Emotional and behavioural difficulties (or disorder).

†**ebdomadary** *noun* see HEBDOMADARY *noun*.

ebene /ˈiːbiːn/ *noun.* **L20.**
[ORIGIN Yanomami.]
Any of various mixtures of plant materials including psychoactive substances, *esp.* the bark and resin of some trees of the genus *Viola* (family Myristicaceae) used by the Yanomami people of Venezuela as hallucinogenic snuff.

Ebenezer /ɛbɪˈniːzə/ *noun.* **L17.**
[ORIGIN Hebrew *'eḇen hā-'ezer* lit. 'stone of the help', name of the memorial stone set up by Samuel after the victory of Mizpeh (1 *Sam.* 7:12).]
1 ***raise one's Ebenezer***, ***set up one's Ebenezer***, express gratitude for divine help in reaching one's present circumstances. **L17.**
2 [App. by misunderstanding of 'raise'.] Temper, anger. *US slang.* **M19.**
3 A Nonconformist chapel. **M19.**

ébéniste /ebenist/ *noun.* Pl. pronounced same. **E20.**
[ORIGIN French, from *ébène* ebony + *-iste* -IST.]
An ebonist; *spec.* a French cabinetmaker who veneers furniture (orig. with ebony).

Ebionite /ˈiːbjənʌɪt/ *noun & adjective.* **LME.**
[ORIGIN medieval Latin *ebionita*, from Hebrew *'eḇyōn* poor: see -ITE[1].]
Of or pertaining to, a member of, a Christian sect of the 1st to 3rd cents. which held that Jesus was a mere man and that the Mosaic law was binding on Christians.
■ **Ebioˈnitic** *adjective* pertaining to the Ebionites or their beliefs **M19.** **Ebionitism** *noun* (tendency towards) the beliefs or practices of the Ebionites **L18.**

EBIT *abbreviation.*
FINANCE. Earnings before interest and tax.

EBITDA *abbreviation.*
FINANCE. Earnings before interest, taxes, depreciation, and amortization.

Eblaite /ˈɛbləʌɪt, ˈiːb-/ *noun & adjective.* **L20.**
[ORIGIN from *Ebla*, ancient name of the city of Tell Mardikh in northern Syria + -ITE[1].]
▶ **A** *noun.* **1** An inhabitant of ancient Ebla. **L20.**
2 A Semitic language known from tablets of *c* 2400 BC discovered at the site of Ebla. **L20.**
▶ **B** *adjective.* Of or pertaining to ancient Ebla, its inhabitants, or this language. **L20.**

Eblis /ˈɛbliːs/ *noun.* Also **I-** /ˈɪ-/. **L18.**
[ORIGIN Arabic *Iblīs* prob. contr. of Greek *diabolos* DEVIL *noun*.]
The Devil in Islam.

Ebo *noun & adjective* var. of IGBO.

E-boat /ˈiːbəʊt/ *noun.* Now *hist.* **M20.**
[ORIGIN from enemy + BOAT *noun*.]
A German torpedo boat during the Second World War.

Ebola /iːˈbəʊlə, əˈbəʊlə/ *noun.* **L20.**
[ORIGIN The name of a river and district in the Democratic Republic of Congo (Zaire), where the disease was first observed in 1976.]
Used ***attrib.*** with reference to a tropical African filovirus that causes a severe, infectious, generally fatal haemorrhagic disease in humans. Esp. in ***Ebola fever***, ***Ebola virus***.

E-bomb /ˈiːbɒm/ *noun.* **L20.**
[ORIGIN from electromagnetic + BOMB *noun*.]
A weapon that can produce electromagnetic waves sufficiently powerful to cause widespread damage to electronic equipment.

ebon /ˈɛb(ə)n/ *noun & adjective.* Now only *poet.* **LME.**
[ORIGIN Old French *eban* (mod. *ébène*) = medieval Latin *ebanus*, var. of Latin *ebenus* from Greek *ebenos* ebony tree.]
▶ **A** *noun.* **1** The wood ebony. Also ***ebon-wood***. **LME.**
†**2** An ebony tree. Also ***ebon tree***. **LME–E17.**
▶ **B** *adjective.* Made of ebony; black as ebony. **L16.**

fig.: SHAKES. *Ven. & Ad.* Death's ebon dart.

Ebonics /ɛˈbɒnɪks/ *noun.* Orig. and chiefly *US.* **L20.**
[ORIGIN Blend of EBONY *noun* + PHONICS.]
Black American English, esp. when considered as a distinct language or creole with linguistic features related to those of African languages, rather than as a nonstandard variety of English.

ebonite /ˈɛbənʌɪt/ *noun.* **M19.**
[ORIGIN from EBONY + -ITE[1].]
= VULCANITE 2.

ebony /ˈɛb(ə)ni/ *noun & adjective.* **LME.**
[ORIGIN from EBON, perh. after IVORY.]
▶ **A** *noun.* **1** The hard, heavy, black or very dark timber of any of various tropical trees, esp. of the genus *Diospyros* (family Ebenaceae), native to W. Africa, India, Sri Lanka, and SE Asia. Also ***ebony-wood***. **LME.**
2 A tree yielding this wood. Also ***ebony tree***. **M18.**
3 A very dark brown or black colour. **E19.** ▸**b** A black person. *US. arch.* **M19.**
▶ **B** *adjective.* Made of ebony; of the colour of ebony. **M17.**
■ **ebonist** *noun* a worker or dealer in ebony or other ornamental woods **E18.** **ebonize** *verb trans.* make (furniture etc.) look like ebony **M19.**

éboulement /ebulmɑ̃/ *noun.* Pl. pronounced same. **E19.**
[ORIGIN French, from *ébouler* crumble.]
A crumbling and falling of rock etc.; a landslide.

ebracteate /ɪˈbraktɪət, -eɪt/ *adjective.* **M19.**
[ORIGIN mod. Latin *ebracteatus*, from Latin *e-* E- + *bractea* BRACT: see -ATE[2].]
BOTANY. Having no bracts.

EBRD *abbreviation.*
European Bank for Reconstruction and Development.

ebriety /ɪˈbrʌɪəti/ *noun. literary.* **LME.**
[ORIGIN French *ébriété* or Latin *ebrietas*, from *ebrius* drunk: see -ITY.]
Drunkenness, the state or habit of intoxication; *fig.* excitement; formerly also, an instance of drunkenness.

ebriosity /iːbrɪˈɒsɪti/ *noun. rare.* **M17.**
[ORIGIN Latin *ebriositas*, from *ebriosus* habitually drunk: see -OSITY.]
(Habitual) intoxication; excitement.

ebrious /ˈiːbrɪəs/ *adjective.* Now *rare.* **M16.**
[ORIGIN from Latin *ebrius* + -OUS.]
Drunken; characteristic of intoxication.
■ Also **ebriose** *adjective* (*joc.*) **L19.**

†**ebullate** *verb intrans.* **E17–M18.**
[ORIGIN Late Latin *ebullare*, var. of *ebullire*: see EBULLIENT, -ATE[3].]
Boil.

ebulliate /ɪˈbʌlɪeɪt/ *verb intrans.* & *trans. rare.* **L16.**
[ORIGIN Irreg. from Latin *ebullire*: see EBULLIENT, -ATE[3].]
Boil.

ebullience /ɪˈbʌlj(ə)ns, -ˈbʊl-/ *noun.* **M18.**
[ORIGIN from EBULLIENT: see -ENCE.]
Ebullient quality; enthusiasm, exuberance; a boiling up as of liquid (chiefly *fig.*).
■ Also **ebulliency** *noun* **M17.**

ebullient /ɪˈbʌljənt, -ˈbʊl-/ *adjective.* **L16.**
[ORIGIN Latin *ebullient-* pres. ppl stem of *ebullire* boil up, from *e-* E- + *bullire* BOIL *verb*: see -ENT.]
1 Boiling; agitated as if boiling. **L16.**

G. P. SCROPE Lava in a liquid and ebullient state.

†**2** Of the bodily humours: hot, effervescent, agitated. **E17–M18.**

E. YOUNG They scarce can swallow their ebullient spleen.

3 (The usual sense.) Bubbling over with enthusiasm or excitement; exuberant. M17.

W. HOLTBY Leaping, slavering, wild, restless, beautiful, ebullient dog. S. NAIPAUL The atmosphere . . was as ebullient and as joyous as a Civil Rights rally in the early 1960s.

■ **ebulliently** *adverb* L19.

ebulliometer /ɪˌbʌlɪˈɒmɪtə, -ˌbʊl-/ *noun*. M20.
[ORIGIN French *ébulliomètre*, from Latin *ebullire*: see EBULLIENT, -OMETER.]
= EBULLIOSCOPE.

ebullioscope /ɪˈbʌlɪə(ʊ)skəʊp, -ˈbʊl-/ *noun*. M19.
[ORIGIN French *ébullioscope*, from Latin *ebullire*: see EBULLIENT, -O-, -SCOPE.]
An instrument for the precise measurement of boiling points.
■ **ebullioˈscopic** *adjective* of or pertaining to ebullioscopy or an ebullioscope E20. **ebullioscopy** /-ˈɒskəpi/ *noun* the precise measurement of boiling points, *spec.* (CHEMISTRY) as a means of determining the molecular weight of a compound from the rise in the boiling point of a liquid when the compound is dissolved in the liquid E20.

ebullism /ˈɛbʌlɪz(ə)m/ *noun*. M20.
[ORIGIN from Latin *ebullire*: see EBULLIENT, -ISM.]
The formation of bubbles in body fluids owing to reduced ambient pressure.

ebullition /ɛbəˈlɪʃ(ə)n, -bʊ-/ *noun*. LME.
[ORIGIN Late Latin *ebullitio(n-)*, from *ebullit-* pa. ppl stem of *ebullire*: see EBULLIENT, -ITION.]
†**1** MEDICINE. A state of agitation of the bodily humours, ascribed to heat. LME–M18.
2 *fig.* (now taken as from sense 3). Agitation, commotion; a sudden outburst of war, emotion, etc. M16.

S. JOHNSON Such faults may be said to be ebullitions of genius. W. S. CHURCHILL We expected a certain amount of local ebullition while matters readjusted themselves.

3 *lit.* Boiling; the bubbling and agitation of a heated liquid. L16. ▸**b** The action of overflowing or rushing out in a state of turbulence; rapid bubbling, effervescence. L16.

D. BREWSTER Fluids of easy ebullition. **b** C. LYELL A great ebullition of gas.

†**ebulum** *noun*. OE–M18.
[ORIGIN Latin.]
Danewort. In later use, elderberry wine.

eburnation /iːbəːˈneɪʃ(ə)n/ *noun*. M19.
[ORIGIN from Latin *eburnus* made of ivory, from *ebur*: see IVORY, -ATION.]
MEDICINE. The exposure of a hard dense surface on a bone due to the wearing down of cartilage, esp. in osteoarthritis.

eburnean /ɪˈbəːnɪən/ *adjective*. Also **-ian**. M17.
[ORIGIN from Latin *eburneus* made of ivory, from *ebur*: see IVORY, -AN, -IAN.]
Made of or resembling ivory.

EBV *abbreviation*.
Epstein–Barr virus.

EC *abbreviation*.
1 East Central.
2 European Commission.
3 European Community.
4 Executive Committee.

ecad /ˈiːkad/ *noun*. E20.
[ORIGIN from Greek *oikos* house + -AD[1].]
ECOLOGY. An organism modified by its environment.

écarté /eɪˈkɑːteɪ; *foreign* ekarte (*pl. same*)/ *noun*. E19.
[ORIGIN French, pa. pple of *écarter* discard, from *é-* (formed as ES-) + *carte* CARD *noun*[2].]
1 A card game for two people in which cards may be exchanged for others and those from the two to the six are excluded. E19.
2 BALLET. A pose with one arm and one leg extended, the body being at an oblique angle to the audience. E20.

ecaudate /ɪˈkɔːdeɪt/ *adjective*. M19.
[ORIGIN mod. Latin *ecaudatus*, from Latin E- + CAUDA: see -ATE[2].]
ZOOLOGY. Tailless, or having only a very short tail.

ecbatic /ɛkˈbatɪk/ *adjective*. M19.
[ORIGIN Greek *ekbatikos*, from *ekbasis* digression, from stem of *ekbainein* go out, digress: see -IC.]
GREEK GRAMMAR. Of a clause or conjunction: denoting a result or consequence as distinct from a purpose or intention.

ecbolic /ɛkˈbɒlɪk/ *noun & adjective*. M18.
[ORIGIN from Greek *ekbolē* expulsion + -IC.]
MEDICINE. (An agent) that induces expulsion of the fetus.

ecce /ˈɛki, ˈɛtʃeɪ, ˈɛksi/ *interjection*. LME.
[ORIGIN Latin.]
Lo!; behold.
Ecce Homo /ˈhəʊməʊ/ behold the Man (*John* 19:5); (as *noun phr.*) a portrayal of Jesus wearing the crown of thorns. **ecce signum** /ˈsɪgnəm/ behold the sign.
■ †**ecceity** *noun* [medieval Latin *ecceitas*: see -ITY] the quality of being present M16–E18.

eccentric /ɪkˈsɛntrɪk, ɛk-/ *noun & adjective*. Also (chiefly in sense B.3) **exc-**. LME.
[ORIGIN Late Latin *eccentricus* adjective, from Greek *ekkentros*, from *ek-* EX-[2] + *kentron*: see CENTRE *noun*, -IC.]
▸ **A** *noun*. **1** ASTRONOMY. *hist.* A circle or orbit not having the earth precisely in its centre. LME.
2 A disc or wheel mounted eccentrically on a revolving shaft so as to transmit a backward-and-forward motion (esp. to the slide valve of a steam engine) through a linkage consisting of a ring (or strap) and connecting rod. E19.
3 A person whose behaviour is habitually unusual or whimsical. M19.
▸ **B** *adjective*. **1** Of a circle: not concentric with another (foll. by *to*). Of two or more circles: not mutually concentric. M16.
2 Of orbital motion: not referrable to a fixed centre; not circular. Of a curve or orbit: deviating from a circular form. E17.
3 That has its axis, point of support, etc., not centrally placed. Of an axis etc.: not passing through the centre, not central. M17. ▸**b** (*attrib.* use of the *noun*.) Worked by or connected with an eccentric (sense A.2 above). E19.
eccentric projection: see PROJECTION 7.
4 Irregular, anomalous, capricious; (of a person) unconventional and slightly strange, habitually unusual, odd. M17.

V. S. PRITCHETT His eccentric interpretation of the Christian ethic. A. CARTER Eccentric boots that laced up to her knee but left her toes bare. *Independent on Sunday* An eccentric old gent is regarded as great fun and everyone wants to dine with him.

■ **eccentrical** *adjective* †(**a**) = ECCENTRIC *adjective* 1, 2; (**b**) = ECCENTRIC *adjective* 4: M16. **eccentrically** *adverb* L17.

eccentricity /ɛksɛnˈtrɪsɪti/ *noun*. In sense 1 also **exc-**. M16.
[ORIGIN from ECCENTRIC + -ITY.]
1 The quality of being abnormally centred or of not being concentric. M16. ▸**b** Deviation of a curve, orbit, etc., from circularity; the extent of such deviation (for an ellipse, equal to the distance between the foci divided by the length of the major axis). L17. ▸†**c** Distance from the centre. E–M19.
2 The quality or habit of deviating from what is usual or customary; oddity, whimsicality; an instance of eccentric behaviour, etc. L17.

E. WAUGH Mrs M's latest eccentricity is to put bricks in the lavatory cisterns to save water. H. ACTON She was able to laugh at his foibles with a secret admiration for the vigorous eccentricity of his character.

ecchondroma /ɛkɒnˈdrəʊmə/ *noun*. Pl. **-mas**, **-mata** /-mətə/. L19.
[ORIGIN mod. Latin, from Greek *ek* out + CHONDROMA.]
MEDICINE. A chondroma growing outwards from the surface of a bone or cartilage. Cf. ENCHONDROMA.

ecchymoma /ɛkɪˈməʊmə/ *noun*. Now *rare* or *obsolete*. Pl. **-mas**, **-mata** /-mətə/. M16.
[ORIGIN mod. Latin from Greek *ekkhumōma*, from *ekkhumonathai* extravasate blood: see -OMA.]
MEDICINE. A swelling caused by bleeding beneath the skin. Cf. ECCHYMOSIS.

ecchymosis /ɛkɪˈməʊsɪs/ *noun*. Pl. **-moses** /-ˈməʊsiːz/. M16.
[ORIGIN mod. Latin from Greek *ekkhumōsis*, from *ekkhumonathai*: see ECCHYMOMA, -OSIS.]
MEDICINE. An area of discoloration and occas. swelling due to bleeding beneath the skin, whether through injury (bruising) or other cause.
■ **ecchymosed** *adjective* [from French *ecchymosé*] affected with ecchymosis M19.

Eccles. *abbreviation*.
Ecclesiastes (in the Bible).

Eccles cake /ˈɛk(ə)lz keɪk/ *noun phr.* L19.
[ORIGIN *Eccles*, a town in Greater Manchester, England.]
A round cake of pastry filled with currants etc.

ecclesia /ɪˈkliːzjə/ *noun*. L16.
[ORIGIN ecclesiastical Latin from Greek *ekklēsia* assembly, (eccl.) church, from *ekklētos* pa. ppl adjective of *ekkalein*, from *ek-* EX-[2] + *kalein* call, summon.]
hist. A regularly convoked assembly; *esp.* the general assembly of Athenian citizens. Also, later, the Christian Church.

ecclesial /ɪˈkliːzj(ə)l/ *adjective*. M17.
[ORIGIN Old French *ecclésial*, formed as ECCLESIA + -AL[1].]
Ecclesiastical.
– NOTE: Rare before M20.

ecclesiarch /ɪkˈliːzɪɑːk/ *noun*. L18.
[ORIGIN from Greek *ekklēsia* church + -ARCH.]
A ruler of the Christian Church.

ecclesiast /ɪˈkliːzɪast/ *noun*. LME.
[ORIGIN ecclesiastical Latin *ecclesiastes* from Greek *ekklēsiastēs* member of an assembly, from *ekklēsia*: see ECCLESIA. In the Septuagint rendering Hebrew *qōheleṯ*.]
1 (**E-**.) *The* author of the biblical book Ecclesiastes: Solomon. LME.
2 A functionary or administrator of the Christian Church. LME.
3 *hist.* A member of the Athenian ecclesia. M19.

ecclesiastic /ɪˌkliːzɪˈastɪk/ *adjective & noun*. LME.
[ORIGIN French *ecclésiastique* or ecclesiastical Latin *ecclesiasticus* from Greek *ekklēsiastikos*, from *ekklēsiastēs*: see ECCLESIAST, -IC.]
▸ **A** *adjective*. **1** = ECCLESIASTICAL *adjective* 1. LME.
2 = ECCLESIASTICAL *adjective* 2. E17.
▸ **B** *noun*. †**1** In *pl.* = ECCLESIASTICAL *noun* 1. E17–M18.
2 A member of the clergy, a priest. M17.
■ **ecclesiasticism** /-sɪz(ə)m/ *noun* ecclesiastical spirit or principles; attention, esp. overattention, to details of ecclesiastical practice or administration: M19. **ecclesiasticize** /-sʌɪz/ *verb trans.* make ecclesiastical M19.

ecclesiastical /ɪˌkliːzɪˈastɪk(ə)l/ *adjective & noun*. LME.
[ORIGIN from ECCLESIASTIC + -AL[1].]
▸ **A** *adjective*. **1** Of or pertaining to the Christian Church. Opp. *civil* or *secular*. LME.
2 Of or pertaining to the Christian clergy; clerical. M16.
– SPECIAL COLLOCATIONS: **Ecclesiastical Commission**, **Ecclesiastical Commissioners** *hist.* (the members of) a body, subordinate to the Privy Council, which managed the estates and revenues of the Church of England from 1835 to 1948. **ecclesiastical courts**: for maintaining the discipline of the Church of England and administering ecclesiastical law. **ecclesiastical law**: derived from canon and civil law, administered in ecclesiastical courts. *ecclesiastical year*: see YEAR *noun*[1].
▸ **B** *noun*. **1** In *pl.* Matters concerning the Christian Church. M17.
2 = ECCLESIASTIC *noun* 2. *rare*. L19.
■ **ecclesiastically** *adverb* L16.

ecclesiastico- /ɪˌkliːzɪˈastɪkəʊ/ *combining form*. L17.
[ORIGIN formed as ECCLESIASTICAL + -O-.]
Used chiefly to form adjectives from adjectives with the sense 'ecclesiastical and—', 'ecclesiastically', as *ecclesiastico-conservative*, *ecclesiastico-military*.

ecclesiolatry /ɪˌkliːzɪˈɒlətri/ *noun*. M19.
[ORIGIN from ECCLESIA + -O- + -LATRY.]
Excessive reverence for the Christian Church or church traditions.

ecclesiology /ɪˌkliːzɪˈɒlədʒi/ *noun*. M19.
[ORIGIN formed as ECCLESIOLATRY + -OLOGY.]
1 The branch of knowledge that deals with the Christian Church or churches, esp. church building and decoration. M19.
2 Theology as applied to the nature and structure of the Christian Church. M20.
■ **eˌcclesioˈlogic** *adjective* L19. **eˌcclesioˈlogical** *adjective* M19. **eˌcclesioˈlogically** *adverb* L19. **ecclesiologist** *noun* M19.

Ecclus *abbreviation*.
Ecclesiasticus (Apocrypha).

†**eccoprotic** *adjective & noun*. M17–E19.
[ORIGIN Greek *ekkoprōtikos*, from *ekkoproun* evacuate (the bowels), from *ek-* EX-[2] + *kopros* dung: see -IC.]
(A drug) having a mildly laxative effect.

eccrine /ˈɛkrʌɪn, -krɪn/ *adjective*. M20.
[ORIGIN from Greek *ekkrinein* secrete, from *ek-* EX-[2] + *krinein* to separate: see -INE[1].]
PHYSIOLOGY. Designating or pertaining to multicellular glands which do not lose cytoplasm in their secretions, esp. the sweat glands on the hands and feet. Cf. APOCRINE.

ecdysiast /ɛkˈdɪzɪast/ *noun*. M20.
[ORIGIN formed as ECDYSIS after *enthusiast*.]
A striptease artist.
■ **ecdysiasm** *noun* the art or occupation of striptease M20.

ecdysis /ˈɛkdɪsɪs, ɛkˈdʌɪsɪs/ *noun*. Pl. **-dyses** /-dɪsiːz, -ˈdʌɪsiːz/. M19.
[ORIGIN Greek *ekdusis*, from *ekduein* put off, shed, from *ek-* EX-[2] + *duein* put.]
The action or process of shedding an outer skin or integument, as in insects, reptiles, etc.
■ **ecdysial** /-ˈdɪz-/ *adjective* E20. **ecdysone** *noun* (BIOCHEMISTRY) a steroid hormone that controls moulting in insects and other arthropods M20.

ECG *abbreviation*.
electrocardiogram.

ecgonine /ˈɛkgəʊniːn, -nɪn/ *noun*. M19.
[ORIGIN from Greek *ekgonos*, from *ek* out of + *gon-*, *gen-* to produce: see -INE[5].]
CHEMISTRY. An alkaloid, $C_9H_{15}NO_3$, obtained by the hydrolysis of cocaine.

†**eche** *verb* var. of EKE *verb*.

echelle /eɪˈʃɛl/ *noun*. *obsolete* exc. *hist.* L17.
[ORIGIN French *échelle*: see ECHELON *noun*.]
An arrangement of ribbons in the form of a ladder, decorating the front of the stomacher of a dress, etc.

echelon /ˈɛʃəlɒn, ˈeɪʃ-/ *noun*. Also †**-ll-**. L18.
[ORIGIN French *échelon*, from *échelle* ladder from Latin *scala*: see SCALE *noun*[4], -OON.]
1 An arrangement of troops or equipment in parallel lines such that the end of each line is stepped somewhat sideways from that in front; *gen.* a formation of people or things arranged, individually or in groups, in a similar stepwise fashion. Also *echelon arrangement*, *echelon formation*, etc. L18.
in echelon arranged in an echelon; cf. EN ÉCHELON.

2 Each of the divisions of an echelon formation. **E19.** ▸**b** Each of the subdivisions of the main supply service for troops in warfare. **E19.**
b *rear echelon*: see **REAR** *adjective*[1].
3 (A group of people occupying) a particular level in any organization. **M20.**

Times The higher echelons of the law and politics have become almost an Oxford preserve.

echelon /ˈɛʃəlɒn, ˈeɪʃ-/ *verb trans.* **M19.**
[**ORIGIN** from the noun or French *échelonner*.]
Arrange in an echelon formation. Freq. as ***echeloned*** *ppl adjective.*

†**echeneis** *noun. rare.* **L16–L18.**
[**ORIGIN** Greek *ekhenēis*, from *ekhein* to hold + *naus* (dat. *nēi*) ship, from its supposed power to hold back a ship.]
= **REMORA** 1.

echeveria /ɛtʃɪˈvɪərɪə/ *noun.* **M19.**
[**ORIGIN** mod. Latin *Echeveria* (see below), from Anastasio *Echeverria* or *Echeveri*, 19th-cent. Mexican botanical illustrator: see **-IA**[1].]
Any of various succulent plants of the genus *Echeveria* (family Crassulaceae) native to S. and Central America.

échevin /ˈeɪʃəvɛ̃/ *noun.* Pl. pronounced same. **L17.**
[**ORIGIN** French.]
In France, a municipal magistrate. In Belgium, a civic dignitary next in rank to the mayor.

echidna /ɪˈkɪdnə/ *noun.* **E19.**
[**ORIGIN** mod. Latin *Echidna* former genus name from Greek *ekhidna* viper.]
Either of two spiny insectivorous monotreme mammals, *Tachyglossus aculeatus* (more fully ***short-nosed echidna***), native to Australia and New Guinea, and *Zaglossus bruijni* (more fully ***long-nosed echidna***), native to New Guinea. Also called ***spiny anteater***.

echinacea /ˌɛkɪˈneɪsɪə/ *noun.* **M19.**
[**ORIGIN** mod. Latin (see below), from Greek *ekhinos* hedgehog.]
Any of various plants of the N. American genus *Echinacea* (family Compositae), members of which have flowers with a raised cone-like centre appearing to consist of soft spines; *esp.* the purple-flowered *E. purpurea*, used in herbal medicine for its antibiotic and wound-healing properties.

echinate /ˈɛkɪneɪt/ *adjective.* **L17.**
[**ORIGIN** Latin *echinatus*, from **ECHINUS**: see **-ATE**[2].]
BOTANY. Covered with rigid bristles or prickles.

echinate /ˈɛkɪneɪt/ *verb.* **M17.**
[**ORIGIN** formed as **ECHINATE** *adjective*: see **-ATE**[3].]
1 *verb trans. BOTANY.* As ***echinated*** *ppl adjective* = **ECHINATE** *adjective.* **M17.**
2 *verb trans. & intrans. ZOOLOGY.* Of a sponge spicule: project from (the fibrous skeleton) at an acute angle. **L19.**

echini *noun* pl. of **ECHINUS.**

echinite /ˈɛkɪnʌɪt/ *noun.* **M18.**
[**ORIGIN** from **ECHINUS** + **-ITE**[1].]
PALAEONTOLOGY. A fossil echinoderm.

echino- /ɪˈkʌɪnəʊ, ˈɛkɪnəʊ/ *combining form* of Greek *ekhinos* hedgehog, sea urchin: see **-O-**.
■ **echino'pluteus** *noun* (*ZOOLOGY*) the free-swimming larval form of a sea urchin **E20.**

echinococcus /ɪˌkʌɪnə(ʊ)ˈkɒkəs/ *noun.* Pl. **-cocci** /-ˈkɒk(s)ʌɪ, -ˈkɒk(s)iː/. **M19.**
[**ORIGIN** mod. Latin *Echinococcus* (see below), formed as **ECHINO-** + Greek *kokkos* seed, grain.]
A tapeworm (formerly *spec.*, an encysted larval form) of the genus *Echinococcus*, members of which occur as adults in the intestines of dogs, wolves, etc., and as larval hydatid cysts in sheep and other animals, and sometimes humans.
■ **echinococcosis** /-kəˈkəʊsɪs/ *noun* (*MEDICINE*) hydatid disease caused by echinococci **E20.**

echinoderm /ɪˈkʌɪnə(ʊ)dəːm, ˈɛkɪn-/ *noun.* **M19.**
[**ORIGIN** formed as **ECHINO-** + Greek *derma*, *-mat-* skin.]
ZOOLOGY. Any member of the phylum Echinodermata of coelomate, radially symmetric animals including the starfishes, brittlestars, sea urchins, sea cucumbers, and crinoids.
■ **echino'dermal**, **echino'dermatous** *adjectives* of, pertaining to, or characteristic of the echinoderms **M19.**

echinoid /ˈɛkɪnɔɪd/ *noun & adjective.* **M19.**
[**ORIGIN** from **ECHINUS** + **-OID.**]
ZOOLOGY. ▸**A** *noun.* An echinoderm of the class Echinoidea: a sea urchin. **M19.**
▸**B** *adjective.* Of, belonging to, or characteristic of the class Echinoidea or sea urchins. **M19.**

echinulate /ɪˈkɪnjʊlət/ *adjective.* **M19.**
[**ORIGIN** formed as **ECHINUS** + **-ULE** + **-ATE**[2], after **AURICULATE** etc.]
Having or covered with small prickles.

echinus /ɪˈkʌɪnəs/ *noun.* Pl. **-ni** /-nʌɪ/. **LME.**
[**ORIGIN** Latin from Greek *ekhinos* hedgehog, sea urchin. The origin of sense 2 (also in Latin & Greek) is unkn.]
1 A sea urchin. Now *spec.* a member of the genus *Echinus*, which includes the common edible sea urchin *E. esculentus*. **LME.**
2 *ARCHITECTURE.* An ovolo moulding next below the abacus of a capital. **M16.**

echites /ɪˈkʌɪtiːz/ *noun.* Pl. same. **LME.**
[**ORIGIN** Greek *ekhitēs*, from *ekhis* viper.]
†**1** = **AETITES. LME–M18.**
2 A climbing plant of the neotropical genus *Echites*, of the dogbane family. **M18.**

echium /ˈɛkɪəm/ *noun.* **L19.**
[**ORIGIN** mod. Latin (see below) from Greek *ekhion*, from *ekhis* viper, with allus. to the spotted stem.]
A plant or shrub of the Eurasian genus *Echium*, of the borage family, e.g. viper's bugloss, *E. vulgare*.

echiuroid /ˈɛkɪjʊ(ə)rɔɪd, ɛkɪˈjʊərɔɪd/ *noun & adjective.* **L19.**
[**ORIGIN** from mod. Latin *Echiuroidea* phylum name (see below), from *Echiurus* genus name, from Greek *ekhis* viper + *oura* tail: see **-OID.**]
ZOOLOGY. ▸**A** *noun.* Any member of the phylum Echiura (formerly Echiuroidea) of unsegmented marine worms, which have an anterior flattened unretractable proboscis; a spoonworm. **L19.**
▸**B** *adjective.* Of, belonging to, or characteristic of this phylum. **L19.**

echo /ˈɛkəʊ/ *noun.* Pl. **-oes**, (*rare*) **-os. ME.**
[**ORIGIN** Old French & mod. French *écho* or Latin *echo* from Greek *ēkhō* rel. to *ēkhē* sound.]
1 A repetition of a sound or sounds due to the reflection of the sound waves; the secondary sound(s) so produced. **ME.** ▸**b** The cause of such repetition of sound personified; in Greek mythology (**E-**), the name of an oread. **LME.** ▸**c** The reflection of a radio wave, ultrasonic signal, etc.; a reflected radio etc. signal. **E20.**

A. GRAY What seemed like echoes were the footsteps of someone behind. **b** SHAKES. *Rom. & Jul.* The cave where Echo lies. P. G. WODEHOUSE Don't repeat everything I say, as if you were an echo in the Swiss mountains. **c** R. V. JONES Detecting aircraft by echoes arising from reflected radio waves.

to the echo so strongly as to produce echoes.
2 A person who reflects or imitates the language or opinions of others; a person who assents merely to flatter. Freq. in titles of newspapers. **ME.**

M. L. KING How often the church has been an echo rather than a voice.

3 In verse, the repetition of the concluding syllables of a line to form the next line. **L16.**
4 A repetition or close imitation of an idea, a style, effect, etc.; a weakened reproduction. **E17.**

FRANCIS THOMPSON No man can admire . . that of which he has no echo in himself. R. G. COLLINGWOOD Thus . . the sound of his groans, produces in us an echo of his pain.

5 *MUSIC.* A section of an organ, or occas. a separate instrument, located away from the main instrument or enclosed, and used to produce softer and seemingly more distant sounds. Also ***echo organ***. **E18.**
6 *BRIDGE & WHIST.* A conventional play of a higher card in a suit followed by a lower, used to request a further lead of that suit by one's partner or to indicate the number of cards held in that suit. Also called ***peter***. **M19.**
– **COMB.**: **echocardiogram** a tracing or image obtained by echocardiography; **echocardiographer** a person who uses echocardiography; **echocardiography** examination of the heart by means of ultrasound; **echo chamber**: for producing reverberation of sounds; **echoencephalogram** a tracing or image obtained by echoencephalography; **echoencephalography** examination of the inside or contents of the skull by means of ultrasound; **echolocate** *verb trans.* locate by echolocation; **echolocation** location of objects by means of reflected sound (usu. ultrasound); **echometer** †(*a*) a device for measuring the duration of sounds; (*b*) an echo sounder; ***echo organ***: see sense 5 above; **echo sounder** an apparatus for echo-sounding; **echo-sounding** the action or process of ascertaining depths or other distances by means of the time taken to receive an echo from a distant object, e.g. the seabed; **echo verse**: using the technique of the echo (sense 3).
■ **echogram** *noun* a record made by an echo sounder **M20.** **echograph** *noun* a recording echo sounder **M20.** **echoless** *adjective* **E18.**

echo /ˈɛkəʊ/ *verb.* **M16.**
[**ORIGIN** from the noun.]
1 *verb intrans.* Of a sound: be repeated as an echo, reverberate. **M16.**

K. MANSFIELD His long swinging steps echoed over the bare floor.

2 *verb intrans.* Of a place: resound with an echo, give rise to echoes. **L16.**

W. STYRON The cavernous room echoed with a tomblike roar to my sudden sneeze.

3 *verb trans.* Repeat (a sound, voice, etc.) by reflection or as if by reflection; repeat the words of, imitate or resemble the style, effect, etc., of; flatter by servile assent. **L16.**

CONAN DOYLE Ugly rumours which . . agitated the University and were echoed in the learned societies. N. O. BROWN Murry, echoing . . D. H. Lawrence, adopts a stance of moral superiority.

†**4** *verb intrans.* Act as an echo *to*. **M17–M18.**
5 *verb intrans. BRIDGE & WHIST.* Play an echo. **L19.**
■ **echoer** *noun* **E19.** **echoingly** *adverb* with an echo **M19.**

echoey /ˈɛkəʊi/ *adjective.* Also **echoy. M19.**
[**ORIGIN** from **ECHO** *noun* + **-Y**[1].]
Of the nature of or like an echo; liable to resound with echoes.

echoic /ɛˈkəʊɪk/ *adjective.* **L19.**
[**ORIGIN** from **ECHO** *noun* + **-IC.**]
Onomatopoeic; imitative of a sound.

echoism /ˈɛkəʊɪz(ə)m/ *noun.* **L19.**
[**ORIGIN** from **ECHO** *noun* + **-ISM.**]
Onomatopoeia.

echolalia /ɛkəʊˈleɪlɪə/ *noun.* **L19.**
[**ORIGIN** mod. Latin, from Greek *ēkhō* echo + **-LALIA.**]
The meaningless repetition of words and phrases, esp. as a sign of schizophrenia; repetition of speech by a child learning to talk.
■ **echolalic** *adjective* **M20.**

echopraxia /ɛkəʊˈpraksɪə/ *noun.* **E20.**
[**ORIGIN** mod. Latin, from Greek *ēkhō* echo + *praxis* action: see **-IA**[1].]
The meaningless repetition or imitation of the movements of others, as a psychological disorder.
■ **echopractic** *adjective* **E20.**

echovirus /ˈɛkəʊvʌɪrəs/ *noun.* Also **ECHO virus. M20.**
[**ORIGIN** from enteric cytopathogenic human orphan + **VIRUS.**]
MEDICINE. Any of a group of enteroviruses which are often asymptomatic but may cause mild meningitis, respiratory symptoms like those of a cold, etc.

echoy *adjective* var. of **ECHOEY.**

echt /ɛçt/ *adjective & adverb.* **E20.**
[**ORIGIN** German.]
Authentic(ally), genuine(ly), typical(ly).

C. LAMBERT England has never produced an artist so 'echt-English' as Mussorgsky is 'echt-Russian'. N. FREELING Are you married? . . I see your ring, but is that camouflage or *echt*?

ECJ *abbreviation.*
European Court of Justice.

eclair /eɪˈklɛː, ɪ-/ *noun.* Also **éclair. M19.**
[**ORIGIN** French *éclair*, lit. 'lightning'.]
A small finger-shaped cake of choux pastry, filled with cream and iced, esp. with chocolate icing.

eclaircise /ɪˈklɛːsʌɪz/ *verb trans. rare* (chiefly *US*). **M18.**
[**ORIGIN** Back-form. from **ÉCLAIRCISSEMENT**, assim. to *-ise*, **-IZE.**]
Make clear, elucidate.

éclaircissement /eklɛrsismɑ̃/ *noun.* Pl. pronounced same. **M17.**
[**ORIGIN** French, from *éclairciss-* lengthened stem of *éclaircir* clear up formed as **EX-**[1], *clair* clear: see **CLEAR** *adjective*, **-MENT.**]
A clarification of what is obscure or misunderstood; an explanation.

eclampsia /ɪˈklam(p)sɪə/ *noun.* **M19.**
[**ORIGIN** mod. Latin from French *éclampsie* irreg. from Greek *eklampsis* sudden development, from *eklampein* shine out.]
MEDICINE. A dangerous disorder of late pregnancy characterized by high blood pressure, albuminuria, and fits. (See also **PRE-ECLAMPSIA.**)
■ **eclamptic** *adjective* **M19.**

éclat /ɛˈklɑː, ˈeɪklɑː, *foreign* ekla/ *noun & verb.* **L17.**
[**ORIGIN** French, from *éclater* burst out.]
▸**A** *noun.* **1** Radiance, dazzling effect (now only *fig.*); brilliant display. **L17.**

G. ETHEREGE The Eclat of so much beauty . . ought To have charm'd me sooner.

†**2** Ostentation, publicity; public exposure, scandal; a sensation. **L17–L19.**
3 Social distinction; celebrity, renown. **M18.**
4 Conspicuous success; universal acclamation. Chiefly in ***with éclat***, ***with great éclat***, etc. **M18.**
▸**B** *verb trans. & intrans.* Make or become known or notorious. *rare.* **M18.**

eclectic /ɪˈklɛktɪk/ *adjective & noun.* **L17.**
[**ORIGIN** Greek *eklektikos*, from *eklegein* to select, from *ek-* **EX-**[2] + *legein* choose.]
▸**A** *adjective.* **1** Designating, of, or belonging to a class of ancient philosophers who selected from various schools of thought such doctrines as pleased them. **L17.**
2 Made up of selections. *rare.* **E19.**
3 *gen.* That borrows freely or is derived from various sources or systems; broad rather than exclusive in matters of opinion, taste, etc. **M19.**

DISRAELI With . . an eclectic turn of mind, Mr. Vavasour saw something good in everybody. A. TATE The eclectic miscellany of easy speculations and solutions to which his more sensitive contemporaries succumbed.

▸**B** *noun.* A person who is eclectic in method or outlook; *hist.* an eclectic philosopher. **E19.**
■ **eclectical** *adjective* = **ECLECTIC** *adjective* **M19.** **eclectically** *adverb* **M19.** **eclecticism** /-sɪz(ə)m/ *noun* eclectic philosophy; an eclectic outlook or method: **L18.** **eclectism** *noun* = **ECLECTICISM M19.**

E

†eclegme *noun*. E17–E18.
[ORIGIN medieval Latin *eclegma* alt. of Latin *ecligma* from Greek *ekleigma*, from *ekleikhein* lick out.]
MEDICINE. A linctus or syrupy medicine which is licked off the spoon.

eclipse /ɪˈklɪps/ *noun*. ME.
[ORIGIN Old French & mod. French *e(s)clipse* (mod. *éclipse*) from Latin *eclipsis* from Greek *ekleipsis*, from *ekleipein* be eclipsed, leave its place, fail to appear, from *ek-* EX-² + *leipein* leave.]
1 The interception of the light of a celestial object by the intervention of another object between that object and the observer, or between that object and what illuminates it (as when a satellite enters the shadow of its primary). ME. ▸**b** A temporary or permanent deprivation of light. E16.

JAS. HARRIS Often had mankind seen the sun in eclipse. **b** MILTON Blind among enemies.. Irrecoverably dark, total eclipse.

annular eclipse: see ANNULAR 1. **eclipse of the moon**, **lunar eclipse**: caused by the interposition of the earth between the sun and moon, such that the moon is darkened. **eclipse of the sun**, **solar eclipse**: caused by the interposition of the moon between the sun and earth, covering all or part of the sun's disc as seen from the earth. ***lunar eclipse***: see ***eclipse of the moon*** above. ***solar eclipse***: see ***eclipse of the sun*** above. ***total eclipse***: see TOTAL *adjective*.

2 *fig.* Obscuration, obscurity; dimness; loss of brilliance or splendour. LME.

G. HUNTINGTON His interest in a subject could undergo an eclipse and disappear altogether. W. S. CHURCHILL Jackson, from whom so much had been hoped, appeared in physical eclipse.

3 *ORNITHOLOGY*. A plumage phase of a bird (esp. of a male duck) during a postnuptial moult when distinctive marking or coloration tends to become obscured. M19.

D. A. BANNERMAN The male [mallard] in eclipse resembles the female closely.

eclipse /ɪˈklɪps/ *verb*. ME.
[ORIGIN Old French & mod. French *éclipser*, formed as ECLIPSE *noun*.]
1 *verb trans*. Of a celestial object: intervene so as to cause the eclipse of (another object). Also *gen.*, intercept light so as to obscure. ME.

L. DEIGHTON The.. fog that eclipsed his forward vision.

2 *verb trans*. Cast a shadow on, obscure, deprive of lustre. LME. ▸†**b** Put out of sight; extinguish (life). L16–M17.

E. REVELEY It was all beginning to sound horribly plausible, and George felt his humour quickly eclipsed. **b** SHAKES. *1 Hen. VI* Born to eclipse thy life this afternoon.

3 *verb trans*. Make dim by comparison; surpass in brilliance etc., outshine. LME.

DISRAELI One must sing in a room or the nightingales would eclipse us. A. GRAY He had.. expected it to eclipse the work of everyone else.

†**4** *verb intrans*. Suffer an eclipse. LME–M18.

MILTON The night-hag.. comes.. to dance With Lapland witches while the.. moon Eclipses at their charms.

5 *verb trans*. Orig., elide or omit (a sound) in pronunciation. Now *spec.* (in Irish and Welsh) cause the eclipsis of (a sound). L16.
– PHRASES: **eclipsing binary**, **eclipsing variable** *ASTRONOMY* a binary star system whose brightness varies periodically as the dimmer component passes in its orbit in front of the brighter and vice versa.
■ **eclipsable** *adjective* able to undergo eclipsis M19. **eclipser** *noun* L16.

eclipsis /ɪˈklɪpsɪs/ *noun*. Pl. **eclipses** /ɪˈklɪpsiːz/. M16.
[ORIGIN Greek *ekleipsis*: see ECLIPSE *noun*. In sense 1 perh. confused with ELLIPSIS.]
†**1** (An) ellipsis; a mark indicating this. M16–E18.
2 In Irish and Welsh, a change in an initial consonantal sound under the (historical) influence of a preceding nasal. M19.

ecliptic /ɪˈklɪptɪk/ *noun & adjective*. LME.
[ORIGIN Latin *eclipticus* adjective from Greek *ekleiptikos*, from *ekleipein*: see ECLIPSE *noun*, -IC.]
▸ **A** *noun*. The great circle of the celestial sphere representing the sun's apparent path during a year (so called because eclipses of the sun or moon can occur only when the moon is close to this circle). LME.
▸ **B** *adjective*. Of or pertaining to an eclipse, eclipses, or the ecliptic. LME.
■ **ecliptical** *adjective* (*rare*) = ECLIPTIC *adjective* M16.

eclogite /ˈɛklɒdʒʌɪt/ *noun*. M19.
[ORIGIN French, from Greek *eklogē*, with allus. to its selective content: see ECLOGUE, -ITE¹.]
GEOLOGY. Any of a class of dense, granulose, metamorphic rocks consisting largely of garnet and a pyroxene together with other distinctive minerals.

eclogue /ˈɛklɒg/ *noun*. Also †**eg-**. LME.
[ORIGIN Latin *ecloga* from Greek *eklogē* selection, esp. of poems, from *eklegein*: see ECLECTIC.]
A short poem, *esp.* a pastoral dialogue such as those of Virgil.

eclosion /ɪˈkləʊʒ(ə)n/ *noun*. L19.
[ORIGIN French *éclosion*, from *éclore* to hatch, ult. formed as EX-¹ 1 + Latin *claudere* to close.]
Emergence from concealment; *esp.* the emergence of an insect from the pupa, or a larva from the egg.

ECM *abbreviation*.
Electronic countermeasures.

ECN *abbreviation*.
Electronic communications network.

eco- /ˈiːkəʊ, ˈɛkəʊ/ *combining form*.
[ORIGIN Extracted from ECOLOGY.]
Of or pertaining to ecology, ecological; environmental.
■ **ecocaˈtastrophe** *noun* (an occurrence of) major damage to the natural environment, esp. where caused by human activity M20. **ecoˈcentrism** *noun* the view or belief that environmental concerns should take precedence over the needs and rights of human beings L20. **ecoˈcidal** *adjective* designed or tending to damage the natural environment L20. **ecocide** *noun* (esp. wilful) destruction of the natural environment M20. **ecoclimate** *noun* the climate of a particular habitat M20. **eco-friendly** *adjective* (*colloq.*) avoiding harm to the natural environment L20. **ecogeoˈgraphic**, **eco-geoˈgraphical** *adjectives* pertaining to location and environment M20. **eco-label** *noun* a label identifying manufactured products that satisfy certain conditions of environmental significance L20. **ecophene** /-fiːn/ *noun* [PHEN(OTYP)E] any of the range of phenotypes produced by one genotype in reaction to extremes of habitat E20. **ecophysiˈology** *noun* the study of the interrelationship between the normal physical function of an organism and its environment M20. **eco-raider** *noun* (*US*) a person who makes violent attacks in order to protect the natural environment L20. **ecoregion** *noun* an area defined in terms of its natural features and environment M20. **ecosphere** *noun* (**a**) the region of space (around the sun or a star) within which conditions compatible with the existence of life (esp. on planets) may theoretically occur; (**b**) = BIOSPHERE: M20. **ecosystem** *noun* a system of organisms occupying a habitat, together with those aspects of the physical environment with which they interact M20. **ecotone** *noun* [Greek *tonos* tension] a region of transition between two ecological communities E20. **Ecoˈtopia** *noun* [after *Utopia*] an ecologically ideal region or form of society L20. **ecotype** *noun* a subspecies occupying a particular habitat E20. **eco-warrior** *noun* a person actively involved in protecting, or preventing damage to, the environment L20.

†**ecod** *interjection*. M18–M19.
[ORIGIN formed as AGAD.]
= EGAD.

ecofeminism /iːkəʊˈfɛmɪnɪz(ə)m, ɛkəʊ-/ *noun*. L20.
[ORIGIN from ECO- + FEMINISM.]
A theory and movement which combines ecological concerns with feminist ones, regarding both as resulting from male domination of society.
■ **ecofeminist** *noun & adjective* L20.

E. coli *abbreviation*.
Escherichia coli (see COLI).

ecological /iːkəˈlɒdʒɪk(ə)l, ɛk-/ *adjective*. Also †**oe-**. L19.
[ORIGIN from ECOLOGY + -ICAL.]
Of, belonging to, or concerned with ecology.
ecological footprint the amount of land required to sustain a person or society.
■ **ecologic** *adjective* = ECOLOGICAL L19. **ecologically** *adverb* E20.

ecology /ɪˈkɒlədʒi, ɛ-/ *noun*. Also †**oe-**. L19.
[ORIGIN from Greek *oikos* house: see -OLOGY.]
1 The branch of biology that deals with organisms' relations to one another and to the physical environment in which they live; (the study of) such relations as they pertain to a particular habitat or a particular species. Also *spec.*, = ***human ecology*** below. L19.

Nature The ecology of a glacial lake. *fig.*: *Church Times* The finely balanced ecology of public-service broadcasting.

human ecology the branch of knowledge that deals with the interaction of humans with their environment.
2 (Also **E-**.) The political movement that seeks to protect the environment, esp. from pollution. Usu. *attrib.* L20.
■ **ecologist** *noun* M20.

Econ. *abbreviation*.
Economics.

econobox /ɪˈkɒnəbɒks/ *noun*. *N. Amer. colloq., derog.* L20.
[ORIGIN from ECONO(MICAL + BOX *noun*².]
A car that is reliable and economical to run but is considered unremarkable or unfashionable in its styling.

econometric /ɪˌkɒnəˈmɛtrɪk/ *adjective*. M20.
[ORIGIN from ECONOMY + -METRIC.]
Of, pertaining to, or concerned with econometrics.
■ **econometrical** *adjective* = ECONOMETRIC L20. **econometrically** *adverb* L20. **econometrician** /-məˈtrɪʃ(ə)n/ *noun* a student of or specialist in econometrics M20. **econometrist** *noun* = ECONOMETRICIAN L20.

econometrics /ɪˌkɒnəˈmɛtrɪks/ *noun*. M20.
[ORIGIN formed as ECONOMETRIC: see -ICS.]
The branch of economics that deals with the application of mathematics, esp. statistics, to economic data.

economic /iːkəˈnɒmɪk, ɛk-/ *noun & adjective*. Also (earlier) †**oe-**. LME.
[ORIGIN Old French & mod. French *économique* or Latin *oeconomicus* from Greek *oikonomikos*, from *oikonomos*: see ECONOMY, -IC.]
▸ †**A** *noun sing*. (see also ECONOMICS). Household management, housekeeping; a person versed in this. LME–M17.
▸ **B** *adjective* †**1 a** Of or relating to household management. L16–L18. ▸**b** Relating to the management of private, domestic, etc., finances; *gen.* (passing into sense 4), relating to monetary considerations, financial. M19.

a W. COWPER That I in wisdom œconomic aught Pass other women. **b** J. BRAINE It hadn't the remotest connection with.. economic necessity, it was.. self-indulgence. *Which?* The main economic drawback of the diesel car—its price—remains.

2 = ECONOMICAL 4. Now *rare*. M18.

M. EDGEWORTH I never saw any one so economic of her smiles.

3 *THEOLOGY*. Pertaining to or marked by economy in doctrine or divine government. E19.
4 Of, pertaining to, or concerned with economics; relating to the wealth of a community or nation. M19. ▸**b** Maintained for profit, on a business footing; paying (at least) the expenses of its operation or use. M19. ▸**c** Of a subject: studied from a utilitarian or material standpoint. M19.

A. J. P. TAYLOR The British government had developed a conscious economic policy.. during the first World war.

c ***economic geology***, ***economic history***, etc.
– SPECIAL COLLOCATIONS: ***economic*** GEOGRAPHY. ***economic growth***: see GROWTH *noun* 1c. **economic man** a (hypothetical) man who manages his finances strictly according to his own material interests. **economic migrant** a person who moves from one country or area to another in order to improve his or her standard of living. **economic rent** (**a**) a rent that brings a fair return on capital and current expenditure; (**b**) *ECONOMICS* the amount by which what is paid to a particular economic factor, e.g. a worker, land, etc., exceeds the minimum payment necessary to keep that factor in its present use or employment. **economic warfare** the use by a state of measures (e.g. blockade) whose primary effect is to harm the economy of another state.

economical /iːkəˈnɒmɪk(ə)l, ɛk-/ *adjective*. Also (earlier) †**oe-**. L15.
[ORIGIN formed as ECONOMIC + -AL¹.]
†**1** = ECONOMIC *adjective* 1a. L15–M18.
2 *THEOLOGY*. = ECONOMIC *adjective* 3. L16.
3 = ECONOMIC *adjective* 1b, 4. L18.
4 (The usual sense.) Characterized by or tending to economy; careful of resources, not wasteful; sparing, thrifty. L18.

R. KIPLING She's economical (I call it mean) in her coal. T. S. ELIOT Then we can share a taxi, and be economical. *Minicomputer Forum* An economical way of providing online computer services.

economical with the truth discreditably reticent.
■ **economically** *adverb* (**a**) *THEOLOGY* according to divine economy; (**b**) with economy, not wastefully; (**c**) as regards economics: L17.

economics /iːkəˈnɒmɪks, ɛk-/ *noun pl*. (usu. treated as *sing.*). Also (earlier) †**oe-**. L16.
[ORIGIN from ECONOMIC + -S¹, orig. after Latin *oeconomica*, Greek *ta oikonomika*, a treatise by Aristotle.]
†**1 a** (A treatise on) household management. Cf. ECONOMIC *noun*. L16–L18. ▸**b** The management of private or domestic finances; pecuniary position, monetary matters. M19.

b CARLYLE The family economics getting yearly more propitious.

2 The branch of knowledge that deals with the production and distribution of wealth in theory and practice; the application of this discipline to a particular sphere; the condition of a state etc. as regards material prosperity; the financial considerations attaching to a particular activity, commodity, etc. L18.

M. PYKE One of the principles of economics unfortunately is, that in times of scarcity prices rise. J. S. FOSTER His choices must be made in terms of.. the economics of the end result.

economise *verb* var. of ECONOMIZE.

economism /ɪˈkɒnəmɪz(ə)m/ *noun*. E20.
[ORIGIN French *économisme*, formed as ECONOMY: see -ISM.]
Belief in the primacy of economic causes or factors.

economist /ɪˈkɒnəmɪst/ *noun*. Also (earlier) †**oe-**. L16.
[ORIGIN from Greek *oikonomos*: see ECONOMY, -IST.]
†**1** A person who manages a household. L16–M19.
2 A person who attends to the effective use of resources, esp. money; an advocate or practitioner of economy, a thrifty person. E18.
3 a [French *économiste*.] A member of an 18th-cent. French philosophical school which advocated adherence to a supposed natural order of social institutions. M18. ▸**b** A believer in or advocate of economism. M20.
4 An expert in or student of economics. E19.
– PHRASES: **political economist** an expert in or student of political economy.

economize /ɪˈkɒnəmʌɪz/ *verb*. Also **-ise**, (earlier) †**oe-**. M17.
[ORIGIN formed as ECONOMIST + -IZE.]
†**1** *verb intrans*. Manage a household. Only in M17.
†**2** *verb trans*. Manage, organize. Only in L17.
3 *verb intrans*. Practise economy; reduce expenses; make savings *in* or *on* a commodity etc. L18.

J. CARLYLE Light is one of the things I do not like to economise in. P. H. GIBBS Your father wants us to economize He's getting worried about the new taxes.

4 *verb trans.* Use sparingly; make a saving in. **E19.**

G. GREENE Stooped . . under a single globe, economising fuel.

5 *verb trans.* Make (productive) use of; turn to the best account. *arch.* **M19.**

ALLAN RAMSAY Who knows . . what motive powers may . . be economised.

■ **economiˈzation** *noun* **M19. economizer** *noun* (*a*) a person who economizes; (*b*) a device intended to effect a saving in the use of fuel etc.: **M19.**

economy /ɪˈkɒnəmi/ *noun & adjective.* Also (earlier) †**oe-. L15.**
[ORIGIN Old French & mod. French *économie* or Latin *oeconomia* from Greek *oikonomia*, from *oikonomos* manager of a household, steward, from *oikos* house: see -NOMY.]

▶ **A** *noun.* **I** Management.

1 The management or administration of the resources (freq. *spec.* financial resources) of a community or establishment; the art or science of managing material resources. **L15.**

T. PENNANT Rural æconomy is but at a low ebb here. E. F. BENSON It is better economy . . to pay three-halfpence for an egg you can eat than a penny for one you can't.

black economy: see BLACK *adjective*. ***political economy*** the branch of economics that deals with the economic problems of government; *arch.* = ECONOMICS 2.

2 †**a** Household management. **M16–L17.** ▸**b** The manner of ordering a household or domestic etc. finances. *arch.* **E18.**

b J. PRIESTLEY Impertinence . . to watch over the œconomy of private people.

3 The careful or sparing use of resources; frugality; the effecting of saving *in* a commodity etc. **L17.** ▸**b** An instance or a means of reducing expenditure or saving. **L18.** ▸**c** The cheapest class of some service or product, *esp.* of air travel. **M20.**

C. DARWIN The economy shown by nature in her resources. J. KOSINSKI Splitting each match in halves for economy. **b** J. O'HARA What a foolish economy it is to save money on an orchestra. H. MACMILLAN Among the Government economies . . was a further cut . . in staff to Government Departments.

economy of scale: resulting from the greater efficiency of large-scale processes. **b** ***false economy***: see FALSE *adjective*.

▶ **II** Constitution; economic system.

4 The constitution, organization, or structure of something; an ordered system. *arch.* (exc. as in sense 5 below). **L16.** ▸†**b** Physical arrangement or structure; layout. **L17–M18.**

D. HUME With regard to the œconomy of the mind . . all vice is indeed pernicious. H. DAVY Water is absolutely necessary to the economy of vegetation. **b** MILTON Such œconomy or disposition of the fable as may stand best with . . decorum.

5 The organization or ordered state of a community or nation as regards its (esp. material) resources and concerns; the (economic) condition of a state etc. **M17.**

A. J. P. TAYLOR It seems that statesmen can do nothing right when the economy is going wrong. J. W. KRUTCH A pastoral or even a hunting economy capable of supporting the very small remaining population.

mature economy: see MATURE *adjective*. MIXED ***economy***. PLANNED ***economy***. ***wage economy***: see WAGE *noun*.

▶ **III** THEOLOGY. **6** The method of divine government of (an aspect or part of) the world; a system of this suited to particular circumstances. **M17.**

F. MYERS Egyptian influence in the Mosaic Economy.

7 The presentation of doctrine or, by extension, 'truth', in such a way as to suit particular circumstances. Occas. in a bad sense (infl. by sense 3 etc.): discreditable reticence. **L18.**

transf.: OED I do not impute falsehood . . , but I think there has been considerable economy of truth.

▶ **B** *attrib.* or as *adjective.* (Of a product) offering the best value for money, inexpensive; of economy class; designed to be economical to use. **E19.**

– COMB. & SPECIAL COLLOCATIONS: **economy class** the cheapest class of air travel, hotel accommodation, etc.; ***economy-class syndrome***, deep-vein thrombosis said to be caused by periods of prolonged immobility on long-haul flights; **economy drive** a campaign to make savings by reducing expenses; **economy size** a size (usu. the largest in a range) in which goods are sold as offering the customer the best value for money. **economy-size, economy-sized** *adjectives* of an economy size.

– NOTE: Adjective rare before **20.**

écorché /ˈɛkɔːʃeɪ; *foreign* ekɔrʃe (*pl. same*)/ *noun.* **M19.**
[ORIGIN French, pa. pple of *écorcher* flay.]
ART. An anatomical subject treated so as to display the musculature.

écossaise /ɛkɒˈseɪz, *foreign* ekɔsɛːz/ *noun.* Pl. pronounced same. **M19.**
[ORIGIN French, fem. of *écossais* Scottish.]
(A dance to) a lively tune in duple time.

ecotage /ˈiːkətɑːʒ, ˈɛ-/ *noun.* **L20.**
[ORIGIN from ECO- after *sabotage*.]
Sabotage carried out for ecological reasons.
■ **ecoteur** /iːkəˈtəː, ɛ-/ *noun* [after *saboteur*] a person who carries out ecotage **L20.**

ecoterrorism /iːkəʊˈtɛrərɪz(ə)m, ɛkəʊ-/ *noun.* **L20.**
[ORIGIN from ECO- + TERRORISM.]
Violence carried out to further environmentalist ends. Also, the action of causing deliberate environmental damage in order to further political ends.
■ **ecoterrorist** *noun* **L20.**

ecotoxicology /ˌiːkəʊtɒksɪˈkɒlədʒi, ˌɛkəʊ-/ *noun.* **L20.**
[ORIGIN from ECO- + TOXICOLOGY.]
The branch of science concerned with the nature, effects, and interactions of substances that are harmful to the environment.
■ **ecotoxicoˈlogical** *adjective* **L20**; **ecotoxiˈcologist** *noun* **L20.**

ECOWAS *abbreviation.*
Economic Community of West African States.

ecphonesis /ɛkfəˈniːsɪs/ *noun.* Now *rare* or *obsolete*. Pl. **-neses** /-ˈniːsiːz/. **L16.**
[ORIGIN Greek *ekphōnēsis*, from *ekphōnein* cry out, from *ek-* EX-[2] + *phōnein* speak.]
RHETORIC. An exclamation.

†**ecphractic** *adjective.* **M17–L19.**
[ORIGIN Greek *ekphraktikos*, from *ekphrassein* remove obstructions: see -IC.]
MEDICINE. Laxative.

ecphrasis /ˈɛkfrəsɪs/ *noun.* Also **ek-**. Pl. **-ases** /-əsiːz/. **E18.**
[ORIGIN Greek *ekphrasis*, from *ekphrazein*, from *ek-* EX-[2] + *phrazein* speak.]
RHETORIC. A lucid, self-contained explanation or description.

écrevisse /ɛkrəvis/ *noun.* Pl. pronounced same. **M18.**
[ORIGIN French.]
A crayfish.

ecru /ˈeɪkruː, ɛˈkruː/ *adjective & noun.* **M19.**
[ORIGIN French *écru* raw, unbleached.]
(Of) the colour of unbleached linen; light fawn.

†**ecstacy** *noun & verb* var. of ECSTASY.

ecstasiate /ɛkˈsteɪzɪeɪt/ *verb trans. & intrans.* **E19.**
[ORIGIN from ECSTASY + -ATE[3].]
= ECSTASIZE.

ecstasis /ˈɛkstəsɪs/ *noun.* **L16.**
[ORIGIN mod. Latin from Greek *ekstasis*: see ECSTASY.]
Ecstasy.

ecstasize /ˈɛkstəsʌɪz/ *verb trans. & intrans.* Also **-ise. M19.**
[ORIGIN from ECSTASY + -IZE.]
Throw into an ecstasy; go into ecstasies.

ecstasy /ˈɛkstəsi/ *noun & verb.* Also †**ex(s)t-**, †**-acy. LME.**
[ORIGIN Old French *extasie* from late Latin *extasis* from Greek *ekstasis*, from *eksta-* stem of *existanai* put out of place, formed as EX-[2] + *histanai* to place: see -Y[3].]

▶ **A** *noun.* **1** The state of being distracted by some emotion; a frenzy, a stupor. *arch.* **LME.**

SHAKES. *Macb.* On the torture of the mind to lie In restless ecstasy. W. OWEN Gas! Gas! Quick, boys!—An ecstasy of fumbling, Fitting the clumsy helmets just in time.

an ecstasy of rage, ***ecstasies of despair***, etc.

2 An exalted state of feeling, now esp. of rapture; overwhelming happiness or joyful excitement. Freq. in *pl.* **E16.**

D. H. LAWRENCE His presence . . touched her with an ecstasy, a thrill of pure intoxication.

in ecstasies extremely delighted, filled with pleasure.

†**3** Orig., a swoon, a trance. Later (MEDICINE), a pathological state of absorption and unresponsiveness. **L16–L19.**

4 A state of trance or rapture such as is supposed to accompany religious, prophetic, or mystical inspiration; poetic frenzy. **M17.**

MILTON Certaine women in a kind of ecstasie foretold of calamities to come. T. GRAY He that rode sublime Upon the seraph wings of ecstacy.

5 (Freq. **E-**.) A hallucinogenic drug, = ***MDMA*** s.v. **M, M. L20.**

▶ **B** *verb trans.* Send into a state of ecstasy; enrapture. Now *rare*. **E17.**

ecstatic /ɪkˈstatɪk, ɛk-/ *adjective & noun.* Also †**ex(s)t-. L16.**
[ORIGIN French *extatique* from Greek *ekstatikos*, from *eksta-*: see ECSTASY, -IC.]

▶ **A** *adjective.* Of the nature of, characterized by, or producing ecstasy; enraptured, extremely delighted. **L16.**

POPE In trance extatic may thy pangs be drowned. M. LASKI Ecstatic with happiness Margaret fox-trotted in her father's arms. R. WEST An ecstatic sense of ease.

▶ **B** *noun.* **1** A person who is subject to spells of (esp. mystical etc.) ecstasy. **M17.**

2 In *pl.* Transports of ecstasy (usu. *iron.*). **E19.**

■ **ecstatical** *adjective* (*arch.*) = ECSTATIC *adjective* **E17. ecstatically** *adverb* **M17.**

ECT *abbreviation.*
Electroconvulsive therapy.

ectasia /ɛkˈteɪzɪə/ *noun.* **L19.**
[ORIGIN mod. Latin, formed as ECTASIS with irreg. substitution of -IA[1].]
MEDICINE. Dilatation of a blood vessel or vessels, esp. when congenital and extensive. Cf. ANEURYSM.

ectasis /ˈɛktəsɪs/ *noun. rare* (only in Dicts.) or *obsolete*. Pl. **-ases** /-əsiːz/. **M16.**
[ORIGIN Late Latin from Greek *ektasis*, from *ekteinein* stretch out, from *ek-* EX-[2] + *teinein* stretch.]
The extension of a short syllable. Also, = ECTASIA.

ectene /ˈɛktɪni/ *noun.* Also **ek-. M19.**
[ORIGIN ecclesiastical Greek, from *ektenēs* extended.]
GREEK ORTHODOX CHURCH. A litany recited by a deacon and choir.

Ecthesis /ˈɛkθɪsɪs/ *noun.* **E18.**
[ORIGIN Greek *ekthesis* exposition, formed as EX-[2] + THESIS.]
THEOLOGY. An edict of the Emperor Heraclius of 638 maintaining the Monothelite doctrine that Jesus had only one (divine) will.

ecthlipsis /ɛkˈθlɪpsɪs/ *noun.* Pl. **-pses** /-psiːz/. **L16.**
[ORIGIN mod. Latin from Greek *ekthlipsis*, from *ekthlibein* squeeze out.]
CLASSICAL PROSODY. The removal of a syllable ending in *m* before a vowel.

ecthyma /ɛkˈθʌɪmə/ *noun.* **M19.**
[ORIGIN mod. Latin from Greek *ekthuma*, from *ekthnein* break out as heat or bodily humours.]
MEDICINE. An ulcerative impetigo affecting also lower layers of the skin.

ecto- /ˈɛktəʊ/ *combining form.*
[ORIGIN Repr. Greek *ekto-* stem of *ektos* adverb: see -O-.]
Outside, external.
■ **ectocrine** /-krʌɪn, -krɪn/ *noun* (BIOLOGY) any metabolite that is released into an organism's environment and influences the vital processes of other organisms **M20. ectoloph** *noun* (ZOOLOGY) the outer ridge on the crown of a lophodont tooth **E20. ectoˈparasite** *noun* a parasite that inhabits the outer surface of the body (as skin, fur, feathers, etc.) of its host **M19. ectoˈpterygoid** *adjective & noun* (ZOOLOGY) (designating or pertaining to) a palatal bone of most reptiles and some amphibians, lateral to the pterygoid **L19. ectoˈthermic** *adjective* (ZOOLOGY) dependent on external sources of body heat (cf. POIKILOTHERMIC): **M20. ectotrophic** /-ˈtrəʊfɪk, -ˈtrɒfɪk/ *adjective* (BOTANY) (of a mycorrhiza) forming tissue on the surface of roots **L19.**

ectoblast /ˈɛktə(ʊ)blast/ *noun.* **M19.**
[ORIGIN from ECTO- + -BLAST.]
BIOLOGY. = EPIBLAST.
■ **ectoˈblastic** *adjective* **L19.**

ectoderm /ˈɛktə(ʊ)dəːm/ *noun.* **M19.**
[ORIGIN from ECTO- + Greek *derma* skin.]
BIOLOGY. The outer germ layer of the embryo in early development, giving rise to epidermis and neural tissue; cells or tissue derived from this; such cells as forming the outer layer of the body of a coelenterate etc.
■ **ectodermal** *adjective* of, pertaining to, or derived from the ectoderm **L19.**

ectogenesis /ɛktə(ʊ)ˈdʒɛnɪsɪs/ *noun.* **E20.**
[ORIGIN from ECTO- + -GENESIS.]
BIOLOGY. Reproduction occurring outside the body.
■ **ectogeˈnetic, ectogenic** *adjectives* **E20.**

ectomorph /ˈɛktə(ʊ)mɔːf/ *noun.* **M20.**
[ORIGIN from ECTO- + -MORPH.]
A person of lean build (with noticeable development of tissue derived from the embryonic ectoderm, as the skin and nervous system).
■ **ectoˈmorphic** *adjective* of, pertaining to, or characteristic of an ectomorph; of the nature of an ectomorph: **M20. ectomorphy** *noun* the state or property of being an ectomorph **M20.**

-ectomy /ˈɛktəmi/ *suffix.*
[ORIGIN from Greek *ektomē* excision, from *ek-* EX-[2] + *temnein* to cut: cf. -TOMY.]
Forming nouns denoting surgical operations in which some part is removed, as ***appendicectomy***, ***hysterectomy***, ***tonsillectomy***, etc.

ectopia /ɛkˈtəʊpɪə/ *noun.* **M19.**
[ORIGIN mod. Latin, from Greek *ektopos* out of place from *ek-* EX-[2] + *topos* place: see -IA[1].]
MEDICINE. The presence of an organ, cells, or tissue at an abnormal site.

ectopic /ɛkˈtɒpɪk/ *adjective.* **L19.**
[ORIGIN from ECTOPIA + -IC.]
MEDICINE. Occurring in an abnormal position or place; *esp.* (of pregnancy) characterized by development of the fetus elsewhere than in the uterus.
ectopic beat = EXTRASYSTOLE.
■ **ectopically** *adverb* **M20.**

ectoplasm /ˈɛktə(ʊ)plaz(ə)m/ *noun.* **L19.**
[ORIGIN from ECTO- + -PLASM.]
1 BIOLOGY. The outer, clear, non-granular part of the cytoplasm in some cells (e.g. amoeba). Now *rare*. **L19.**
2 A viscous substance supposed to exude from the body of a medium during a spiritualistic trance. **E20.**
■ **ectoˈplasmic** *adjective* of, pertaining to, of the nature of, or resembling ectoplasm **L19. ectoˈplasmically** *adverb* in the manner of ectoplasm **M20. ectoˈplastic** *adjective* = ECTOPLASMIC **E20.**

E

ectoproct /ˈɛktə(ʊ)prɒkt/ *noun & adjective.* E20.
[ORIGIN from mod. Latin *Ectoprocta* (see below), formed as ECTO- + Greek *prōktos* anus.]
ZOOLOGY. ▸**A** *noun.* A bryozoan of the coelomate phylum Ectoprocta, having the anus opening outside the lophophore. Cf. ENTOPROCT. E20.
▸**B** *adjective.* Of, belonging to, or characteristic of Ectoprocta. E20.
■ **ectoˈproctan** *adjective & noun* = ECTOPROCT M20. **ectoˈproctous** *adjective* = ECTOPROCT *adjective* L19.

ectrodactyly /ɛktrə(ʊ)ˈdaktɪli/ *noun.* L19.
[ORIGIN from Greek *ektrōma* or *ektrōsis* miscarriage, abortion (from *ek-* EX-² + *trō-* to damage) + *daktulos* finger: see -Y³.]
MEDICINE. Congenital absence of digits.
■ **ectrodacˈtylia** *noun* (*rare*) = ECTRODACTYLY M19. **ectrodactylism** *noun* = ECTRODACTYLY L19.

ectromelia /ɛktrə(ʊ)ˈmiːlɪə/ *noun.* E20.
[ORIGIN formed as ECTRODACTYLY + Greek *melos* limb + -IA¹.]
MEDICINE. **1** Congenital absence of a limb or limbs. E20.
2 A viral disease of mice which may cause the loss of limbs. M20.

ectropion /ɛkˈtrəʊpɪən/ *noun.* L17.
[ORIGIN mod. Latin *ectropium*, Greek *ektropion*, from Greek *ek-* EX-² + *trepein* to turn.]
MEDICINE. Eversion of the eyelid.

ectype /ˈɛktʌɪp/ *noun.* M17.
[ORIGIN Greek *ektupon* neut. of *ektupos* worked in relief, from *ek-* EX-² + *tupos* figure: see TYPE *noun.*]
A replica or copy of an original, a reproduction. Formerly also, an impression in wax etc.
■ **ectypal** *adjective* of, pertaining to, or of the nature of, an ectype M17.

ecu /ˈɛkjuː, ˈiː-, ˈeɪ-; -kuː/ *noun.* Pl. same, **-s.** L20.
[ORIGIN Abbreviation for *European Currency Unit.*]
= EURO *noun*³ 3.

écu /ˈɛkuː, *foreign* eky (*pl. same*)/ *noun.* L16.
[ORIGIN French from Latin *scutum* shield.]
A French gold or silver coin orig. bearing three fleurs-de-lis on a shield, differing in value at different periods (usu. three or five francs).

Ecuadorian /ɛkwəˈdɔːrɪən/ *adjective & noun.* Also **-rean.** M19.
[ORIGIN from *Ecuador* (see below) + -IAN.]
▸**A** *adjective.* Of, belonging to, or characteristic of Ecuador, an equatorial country in S. America. M19.
▸**B** *noun.* A native or inhabitant of Ecuador. M19.

ecuelle /ɛˈkwɛl/ *noun.* Also **é-.** M19.
[ORIGIN French *écuelle* ult. from Latin *scutella*.]
1 A two-handled soup bowl. M19.
2 The process or apparatus by which oils are extracted from the peel of citrus fruit. L19.

ecumaniac /iːkjʊˈmeɪnɪak, ɛk-/ *noun. colloq.* M20.
[ORIGIN from ECUMENICAL + -MANIAC.]
A zealous or overzealous supporter of ecumenism.

ecumenical /iːkjʊˈmɛnɪk(ə)l, ɛ-/ *adjective.* Also (earlier) **oe-** /iː-/. L16.
[ORIGIN from late Latin *oecumenicus* from Greek *oikoumenikos* of or belonging to *hē oikoumenē* the (inhabited) earth, the whole world: see -AL¹.]
1 Of or belonging to the whole Christian world or the universal Church. In recent use freq.: marked by ecumenism, seeking (worldwide) Christian unity that transcends doctrinal differences; of or representing Christians of several denominations; interdenominational. L16.
ecumenical council any of various representative councils of the church worldwide (since the 9th cent., of the Roman Catholic Church alone) whose decisions are considered authoritative. **Ecumenical Patriarch** (a title of) the Patriarch of Constantinople.
2 Universal, general, worldwide. E17.
– NOTE: The spelling with *e-* is not recorded before M19.
■ **ecumenic** *adjective* = ECUMENICAL L16. **ecumenicalism** *noun* ecumenicity; (esp.) ecumenism: L19. **ecumenicality** *noun* = ECUMENICITY M19. **ecumenically** *adverb* M18. **ecumeˈnicity** *noun* [ecclesiastical Latin *oecumenicitas*] ecumenical character; (Christian) universality; ecumenism: M19. **ecumenics** *noun* (**a**) the branch of knowledge that deals with the Christian Church as a unity; (**b**) ecumenism: M20.

ecumenism /ɪˈkjuːmənɪz(ə)m/ *noun.* M20.
[ORIGIN from ECUMENICAL + -ISM.]
Belief in or striving for the worldwide unity of Christians, transcending differences of doctrine.
■ **ecumenist** *noun* an adherent of ecumenism M20.

eczema /ˈɛksɪmə, ˈɛkzɪmə/ *noun.* M18.
[ORIGIN mod. Latin from Greek *ekzema*, *-mat-*, from *ekzein* boil over, (of disease) break out, from *ek-* EX-² + *zein* to boil.]
Non-infective superficial inflammation of the skin, usu. with itching and vesicular discharge. Cf. DERMATITIS.
■ **eczematous** /ɛkˈsɛ-, ɛkˈzɛ-/ *adjective* of or pertaining to eczema; characterized by eczema: M19.

ED *abbreviation.*
1 Erectile disfunction.
2 *US* Emergency department.

ed. /ɛd/ *abbreviation.*
1 Edited (by).
2 Edition.
3 Editor.
4 Educated (at).
5 Education.

-ed /d, ɪd, t, (*see below*)/ *suffix*¹. Also **-d**, **-'d**, (see below). See also -T³.
[ORIGIN Old English *-ed*, *-ad*, *-od* (*-ud*), *-d* repr. Germanic ppl suffix from Indo-European.]
Forming the pa. t. & pple of weak verbs; also ppl adjectives having the same form as such pa. pples, with senses (of verb trans.) 'that has been subject to the verbal action, that expresses subjection to the verbal action', (of verb intrans.) 'that has performed the verbal action, that habitually performs the verbal action in the stated manner.' In the 15–17 cents. often added without change of meaning to adapted forms of Latin pa. pples and ppl adjectives in -ATE². Cf. -EN⁶.
– NOTE: Mod. English usage is as follows: (i) Pronunciation /ɪd/ after /t/, /d/, and after other consonants in some ppl adjectives and derived adverbs in general use, more widely in arch. and poet. use. Orthographic representation *-ed*, in arch. and poet. use sometimes *-èd*. Examples: ***folded***, ***listed***, ***blessed*** (*ppl adjective*), ***learned*** (*ppl adjective*), ***advisedly***, ***markedly***, ***hornèd*** (arch. & poet.). (ii) Pronunciation /t/ after voiceless consonants other than /t/, except in some ppl adjectives etc. (see (i) above). Orthographic representation *-d* after *-e*, otherwise *-ed*; after a shortened vowel, in some irreg. forms, and in arch. and poet. use also *-t*. Cf. -T³. Examples: ***baked***, ***peeped***, ***pushed***, ***crept***, ***slept***, ***bought*** (irreg.), ***blest*** (arch. & poet.), ***wrapt*** (arch. & poet.). (iii) Pronunciation /d/ after voiced consonants other than /d/, except in some ppl adjectives etc. (see (i) above), and after vowels. Orthographic representation *-d* after *-e* and after *-l* in some irreg. forms, otherwise *-ed*, also *'d* after *-a* and more widely in arch. and poet. use. Examples: ***inclined***, ***refereed***, ***carried***, ***cried***, ***sold*** (irreg.), ***absorbed***, ***rigged***, ***seemed***, ***hallowed***, ***huzzaed*** or ***huzza'd***, ***climb'd*** (arch. & poet.).

-ed /d, ɪd, t (*as prec.*)/ *suffix*². Also **-d**, **'d**, (as prec.).
[ORIGIN Old English *-ede* = Old Saxon *-ōdi*, from Germanic.]
Forming adjectives from nouns with the senses 'possessing, provided with, characterized by', as ***bearded***, ***moneyed***, ***jaundiced***, 'having the character of', as ***bigoted***, ***dogged***. Used freely to form adjectives from collocation of adjective & noun, as ***quick-witted***, ***three-cornered***, ***good-humoured***.

edacious /ɪˈdeɪʃəs/ *adjective.* Now *literary* or *joc.* E19.
[ORIGIN from Latin *edac-*, *edax* (from *edere* eat) + -OUS: see -ACIOUS.]
Of or relating to eating; voracious; *fig.* greedy.

J. R. LOWELL The edacious tooth of Time.

■ **edacity** *noun* the quality of being edacious; capacity for eating: E17.

Edam /ˈiːdam/ *noun.* E19.
[ORIGIN A town near Amsterdam, in the Netherlands.]
In full ***Edam cheese***. A mild spherical pressed Dutch cheese, usu. yellow with a red rind.

edamame /ˌɛdəˈmɑːmeɪ/ *noun.* M20.
[ORIGIN Japanese, lit. 'beans on a branch'.]
A Japanese dish of salted green soybeans boiled in their pods, usu. served as a snack or appetizer.

edaphic /ɪˈdafɪk/ *adjective.* L19.
[ORIGIN from Greek *edaphos* floor + -IC.]
BIOLOGY. Of the soil; produced or influenced by the soil.
■ **edaphically** *adverb* M20.

EDD *abbreviation.*
English Dialect Dictionary.

Edda /ˈɛdə/ *noun.* L17.
[ORIGIN Either from the name of the great-grandmother in the Old Norse poem *Rígsþul* or from Old Norse *óðr* poetry.]
Either of two Icelandic books, (**a**) the ***Elder Edda*** or ***Poetic Edda***, a collection, made *c* 1200, of ancient Old Norse poems on mythical and traditional subjects; (**b**) the ***Younger Edda*** or ***Prose Edda***, a miscellaneous handbook to Old Norse poetry, written *c* 1230.
■ **Eddaic** /ɛˈdeɪɪk/ *adjective* of, pertaining to, or resembling the contents of, the Eddas L19. **Eddic** *adjective* = EDDAIC M19.

edder /ˈɛdə/ *verb & noun.* Now *dial.* Also **ether** /ˈɛðə/. E16.
[ORIGIN Doubtfully identified with Old English *eodor*, *eder* enclosure. Cf. YEDDER.]
▸**A** *verb trans.* Interlace or bind (a hedge etc.) at the top with osiers, withes, etc. E16.
▸**B** *noun.* Osiers etc. used for this purpose. L16.

eddish /ˈɛdɪʃ/ *noun.* Now *dial.* OE.
[ORIGIN Unknown. Sense 2 perh. a different word, but cf. Old English *edisċhenn* quail, perh. 'stubble-hen'.]
†**1** A park or enclosed pasture for cattle. Only in OE.
2 Grass, clover, etc., which grows again; an aftermath; stubble, a stubble field. LME.

eddo /ˈɛdəʊ/ *noun.* Chiefly *W. Indian.* Pl. **-oes.** L17.
[ORIGIN Of W. African origin: cf. Fante *edwó(w)* yam, *ndwo(w)* root.]
1 A tuber of (a variety of) taro; a similar edible tuber. Usu. in *pl.* L17.
2 A plant bearing such tubers. M18.

eddy /ˈɛdi/ *noun & verb.* LME.
[ORIGIN Prob. from base of Old English *ed-* again, back. Cf. Old Norse *iða* eddy.]
▸**A** *noun.* A circular or contrary motion in water, esp. at the side of the main current; a similar motion in air, fog, smoke, etc.; a small whirlpool or vortex. LME.

G. ORWELL Little eddies of wind were whirling dust and torn paper into spirals. *fig.*: P. ACKROYD Eddies of loud, barking laughter swept across the room.

– COMB.: **eddy current** a localized circulating current induced within the body of an electrical conductor by magnetic field variation; **eddy-wind**: that moves in an eddy.
▸**B** *verb trans. & intrans.* (Cause to) move in an eddy or eddies. M18.

L. LEE This fearful spice, eddying up from its box. R. GRAVES Not enough breeze to eddy a puff of smoke.

■ **eddyless** *adjective* E17.

edelweiss /ˈeɪd(ə)lvʌɪs/ *noun.* Pl. same. M19.
[ORIGIN German, from *edel* noble + *weiss* white.]
A plant of the composite family, *Leontopodium alpinum*, of the Alps and other European mountains, bearing small heads surrounded by conspicuous white woolly bracts spreading like a star.

edema *noun* see OEDEMA.

Eden /ˈiːd(ə)n/ *noun.* ME.
[ORIGIN Late Latin (Vulgate), Greek (Septuagint) *Ēdēn*, Hebrew *'ēḏen*, perh. from Akkadian *edinu* from Sumerian *eden* plain, steppe, assoc. with Hebrew *'ēḏen* delight.]
The abode of Adam and Eve in the biblical account of creation; a delightful abode, a paradise, a state of supreme happiness. Also ***garden of Eden***.

SHAKES. *Rich. II* This scept'red isle, . . This other Eden, demi-paradise.

■ **Edenic** /ɪˈdɛnɪk/ *adjective* of, pertaining to, or resembling Eden M19.

edenite /ˈiːd(ə)nʌɪt/ *noun.* M19.
[ORIGIN from *Edenville*, Orange County, New York + -ITE¹.]
MINERALOGY. A light-coloured variety of hornblende containing relatively little iron.

edentate /ɪˈdɛnteɪt/ *adjective & noun.* E19.
[ORIGIN Latin *edentatus* pa. pple of *edentare* render toothless, from *e-* E- + *dent-*, *dens* tooth: see -ATE².]
▸**A** *adjective.* Having few or no teeth; *spec.* (*ZOOLOGY*) of or pertaining to the mammalian order Edentata, members of which (anteaters, sloths, and armadillos) lack incisor and canine teeth. E19.
▸**B** *noun.* An edentate mammal. M19.

edentulous /ɪˈdɛntjʊləs/ *adjective.* E18.
[ORIGIN from Latin *edentulus*, from *e-* E- + *dent-*, *dens* tooth: see -ULOUS.]
Having no teeth, toothless.

edestin /ɪˈdɛstɪn/ *noun.* L19.
[ORIGIN from Greek *edestos* eatable + -IN¹.]
BIOCHEMISTRY. A globulin found in wheat, hempseed, etc.

edge /ɛdʒ/ *noun.*
[ORIGIN Old English *eċġ* = Old Frisian *egg*, Old Saxon *eggia* (Dutch *egge*), Old High German *ekka* (German *Ecke*), Old Norse *egg*, from Germanic, from Indo-European base meaning 'be sharp or pointed', as in Latin *acies* edge, Greek *akis* point.]
▸**I** Something that cuts.
1 The sharpened side of the blade of a cutting instrument or weapon. OE. ▸**b** A cutting weapon or tool. *poet.* OE. ▸**c** The sharpness given to a blade by whetting. LME.

A. DUGGAN He carried a curved scimitar, so that in his fencing he relied on the edge and neglected the point. **b** SHAKES. *Coriol.* Men and lads, Stain all your edges on me. **c** T. HARDY A sword that has no edge. *fig.*: A. N. WILSON What gives Belloc's fiction its cutting edge.

2 *fig.* Effectiveness; trenchant force; keenness. L16. ▸†**b** Ardour; in a weaker sense: inclination. L16–M19. ▸**c** An advantage, superiority. Chiefly in ***have the edge*** (foll. by *on*, *over*). *colloq.* E20. ▸**d** A state of intoxication. *US colloq.* E20.

K. GRAHAME The edge of their hunger was somewhat dulled. E. GLASGOW The March wind had a biting edge. S. HILL His voice had taken on an edge of sarcasm. M. HUNTER The tension in our household took on an unbearable edge. **c** *Listener* Labour's special relationship with the working classes . . was supposed to give it an edge over the tories. P. ROTH In the shoulders and chest I had the edge.

▸**II** Something sharp or narrow.
3 The crest of a narrow ridge; a perilous path on a ridge. LME.

fig.: POPE Each . . Greek . . Stands on the sharpest edge of death or life.

4 The narrow surface or side of a thin object; in *BOOKBINDING*, each of the three surfaces (***top edge***, ***bottom edge***, and ***fore-edge***) not protected by the binding. M17.

L. STERNE Laying the edge of her finger across her two lips.

5 A line along which two surfaces of a solid intersect. In *SKATING*, the inner or outer side of the blade of a skate. L18.
▸**III** A boundary, a margin.
6 The boundary line of a surface or region, a border; the region adjacent to this, a margin. LME. ▸**b** The edging of a garment, curtain, etc. E16.

E. HEMINGWAY Whitewashed stones that marked the edge of the road. G. GREENE A table at the edge of the dance floor.

7 The brink or verge of a bank or precipice; the area close to a steep drop. LME.

> R. POLLOK Toppling upon the perilous edge of Hell. DAY LEWIS Leaning so far over the edge of it [a pulpit] . . that he all but pitched head first into the congregation.

8 *fig.* The beginning *of* a portion of time, *of* a season; the limit *of* a quality or emotion; (*colloq.*) *the* limit of what is reasonable or decent. E17.

> S. JOHNSON I made a journey to Staffordshire on the edge of winter. E. BOWEN He would go over the edge, quite mad. J. BUCHAN I came to the edge of fear.

– PHRASES ETC.: †**back and edge** adjoining, close by. ***bottom edge***: see sense 4 above. **edge to edge** with edges adjacent. ***fore-edge***: see sense 4 above. **give an edge to** sharpen, make keener, stimulate. ***knife-edge***: see KNIFE *noun*. ***leading edge***: see LEADING *adjective*. ***not put too fine an edge on it***, ***not put too fine an edge upon it***: see FINE *adjective*. **on edge** nervously irritable, excited, keyed up. **on the edge of** on the point of (an action); almost involved in or affected by. ***on the ragged edge***: see RAGGED *adjective*. ***razor edge***, ***razor's edge***: see RAZOR. **set an edge on**, **set an edge upon** = *give an edge to* above. **set a person's teeth on edge** cause a person acute irritation or discomfort, as if from eating sour fruit. **take the edge off** blunt, weaken, dull (a person's appetite, argument, tone of voice, etc.). **the edge of the sword** *rhet.* the instrument of slaughter or conquest. **the rough edge of one's tongue**, **the sharp edge of one's tongue** abusiveness, reviling. ***top edge***: see sense 4 above. ***trailing edge***: see TRAILING *adjective*.

– COMB.: **edge city** a relatively large urban area situated on the outskirts of a city, usu. beside a major road; **edge connector** *ELECTRONICS* a connector with a row of contacts, fitted to the edge of a printed circuit board to facilitate connection to external circuits; **edge-on** with the edge foremost; **edge-rail** a railway rail which bears the wheels on its edge; **edge-runner** an apparatus for crushing stone, fibres, or other material; **edge tool** (*a*) any implement with a sharp cutting edge (now chiefly *fig.*); (*b*) a hand-worked or machine-operated cutting tool; **edge well**: located at or near the edge of an oilfield or gas field.

■ **edgeless** *adjective* L16.

edge /ɛdʒ/ *verb*. ME.
[ORIGIN from the noun: see also EGG *verb*[1].]

1 *verb trans.* Give an edge, impart sharpness, to (a weapon, tool, etc.). ME. ▸**b** *fig.* Give keenness or incisive force to (appetite, wit, endeavour, etc.). L16. ▸**c** Urge on, incite, encourage. Now only with *on*. Cf. EGG *verb*[1]. L16.

> POPE Thy sure divinity shall . . edge thy sword to reap the glorious field. **b** G. BRIMLEY The piercing cold of the night-wind edged with sea-salt.

2 *verb trans.* Set (the teeth) on edge. *obsolete* exc. *dial.* ME.

3 *verb trans.* Provide with or *with* an edging; form a border to. M16. ▸**b** Enclose, surround; go round the edge of. M17.

> J. STEINBECK The concrete highway was edged with a mat of tangled, broken, dry grass. O. MANNING The single rusted rail that edged the quay. **b** POPE A bay there lies, Edg'd round with cliffs. A. TYLER She edged puddles . . and hopped across flowing gutters.

4 *verb intrans.* Move edgeways; advance, esp. gradually and obliquely. Orig. chiefly *NAUTICAL*. E17. ▸**b** *verb trans.* Insinuate *into* a place; push by imperceptible degrees (*away*, *in*, *off*, *out*, etc.); make (one's way) thus. L17.

> F. MARRYAT The . . admiral edged away with his squadron. M. AMIS I stayed where I was while Rachel edged forward with the queue. **b** S. CENTLIVRE A Son of One and Twenty, who wants . . to edge himself into the Estate! W. IRVING Every one edging his chair a little nearer. S. O'FAOLÁIN I . . edged my bicycle through the creaking gate.

5 *verb trans.* *CRICKET*. Deflect (the ball) with the edge of the bat. E20.

> *Times* Fortunate . . to edge Wilson only just wide of . . gully.

6 Defeat by a small margin. *N. Amer.* M20.

> *Globe & Mail (Toronto)* The Jays edged the Royals 6–5.

■ **edged** *adjective* (*a*) having a cutting edge; (*b*) having an edge or border (of a specified kind): ME. **edger** *noun* (*a*) a person whose job is to make or otherwise work on the edge of an article; (*b*) a tool for making or trimming an edge: L16. **edging** *noun* (*a*) the action of the verb (***edging shears***: for trimming the edges of a lawn); (*b*) something forming an edge; a border, fringe, etc., sewn on the edge of a garment, curtain, etc.; a border surrounding a flower bed: LME.

edgeways /ˈɛdʒweɪz/ *adverb*. Also (*rare*) **-way** /-weɪ/. M16.
[ORIGIN from EDGE *noun* + -WAYS.]

With the edge foremost, uppermost, or towards the spectator.

get a word in edgeways: see WORD *noun*.

edgewise /ˈɛdʒwʌɪz/ *adverb*. E18.
[ORIGIN from EDGE *noun* + -WISE.]

1 = EDGEWAYS. E18.

2 Edge to edge. M19.

edgy /ˈɛdʒi/ *adjective*. L18.
[ORIGIN from EDGE *noun* + -Y[1].]

1 Having an edge or edges; sharp-edged. L18. ▸**b** Of a painting: having the contours too hard. E19.

2 *fig.* Having one's nerves on edge; irritable, testy. M19. ▸**b** Eager; alert, sharp. *Scot.* & *dial.* M19.

> I. RANKIN He'd been edgy during the conversation, as though expecting some awkward question.

3 Challenging received ideas or prevailing sensibilities; experimental or cutting edge. L20.

> *Glamour* Sling a wide belt over a dress for an edgy but girlie look.

■ **edgily** *adverb* M19. **edginess** *noun* E19.

edh *noun* var. of ETH.

EDI *abbreviation*.
Electronic data interchange, a standard for exchanging information between computer systems.

edible /ˈɛdɪb(ə)l/ *adjective*. L16.
[ORIGIN Late Latin *edibilis*, from *edere* eat: see -IBLE.]

▸ **A** *adjective*. Eatable, fit to be eaten. L16.

edible crab a large European crab, *Cancer pagurus*, caught for food. **edible dormouse** a nocturnal dormouse, *Glis glis*, of western Eurasia, resembling a squirrel, valued as food in some countries. **edible frog** a green frog, *Rana esculenta*, native to Continental Europe and introduced in Britain. **edible snail** a large European snail, *Helix pomatia*, valued as a delicacy.

▸ **B** *noun*. A thing that is edible, an article of food. Usu. in *pl.* M17.

■ **edi'bility** *noun* M19. **edibleness** *noun* L18.

edict /ˈiːdɪkt/ *noun*. ME.
[ORIGIN Latin *edictum* use as noun of neut. pa. pple of *edicere* proclaim, from *e-* E- + *dicere* say, tell.]

1 An order proclaimed by authority; an ordinance or proclamation having the force of law; *esp.* (*hist.*) any of those issued by the Roman praetors and emperors, or the French monarchs. ME.

> W. STYRON I got to read it and you got to sign it. That's the edict of the court. *fig.*: R. HOOKER The generall Edicts of nature.

Edict of Nantes an edict issued by Henry IV of France in 1598, granting toleration to the Protestants (revoked by Louis XIV in 1685).

2 *SCOTTISH HISTORY*. A proclamation made in some public place whereby all concerned were summoned to appear before the courts. E18.

edictal /ɪˈdɪkt(ə)l/ *adjective*. L17.
[ORIGIN Late Latin *edictalis*, formed as EDICT: see -AL[1].]

1 *SCOTTISH HISTORY*. Done by means of public proclamation (see EDICT 2). L17.

2 Of or pertaining to an edict or edicts; consisting of edicts. M19.

■ **edictally** *adverb* (chiefly *Scot.*) by means of an edict or edicts L17.

edicule *noun* var. of AEDICULE.

edification /ˌɛdɪfɪˈkeɪʃ(ə)n/ *noun*. LME.
[ORIGIN Latin *aedificatio(n-)*, from *aedificat-* pa. ppl stem of *aedificare* build: see EDIFY, -ATION.]

1 Building, construction. *arch.* LME. ▸†**b** A building. LME–M17.

2 The building up of the church, or the soul, in faith and holiness; the imparting of moral and spiritual stability and strength by suitable instruction and exhortation. LME.

> J. H. NEWMAN In providing for the religious necessities of posterity, they were directly serving their own edification.

3 Mental or moral improvement, enlightenment, or instruction. LME.

> B. JOWETT Kindly answer, for the edification of the company and myself. A. SCHLEE He had been distributing tracts for the edification of their fellow passengers.

edificatory /ˌɛdɪfɪˈkeɪt(ə)ri/ *adjective*. M17.
[ORIGIN Late Latin *aedificatorius*, from *aedificat-*: see EDIFICATION, -ORY[2].]

Intended or suitable for (esp. religious) edification.

edifice /ˈɛdɪfɪs/ *noun*. LME.
[ORIGIN Old French & mod. French *édifice* from Latin *aedificium*, from *aedis*, *aedes* (see EDIFY) + *-fic-* var. of *fac-* stem of *facere* make.]

1 A building, esp. a large and stately one; *fig.* a large and complex construction (freq. abstract). LME.

> H. JAMES He had been living . . in an edifice of red brick, with granite copings and an enormous fan-light over the door. R. M. PIRSIG One logical slip and an entire scientific edifice comes tumbling down.

†2 The process of building; architectural style. L16–M17.

■ **edificial** /ɛdɪˈfɪʃ(ə)l/ *adjective* [late Latin *aedificialis*] *rare* (*a*) of the nature of an edifice; (*b*) architectural: M17.

edify /ˈɛdɪfʌɪ/ *verb*. ME.
[ORIGIN Old French & mod. French *édifier* from Latin *aedificare*, from *aedis*, *aedes* dwelling, temple, (orig.) hearth + *-ficare*: see -FY.]

1 *verb trans.* & †*intrans.* Construct (a building), build. *arch.* ME. ▸†**b** *verb trans.* Provide with buildings. LME–L16.

> LONGFELLOW The names of all who had died in the convent since it was edified.

2 *verb trans. gen.* Construct, make, set up, establish; build up, strengthen. *arch.* ME. ▸†**b** *verb intrans.* Take form, grow; *fig.* prosper, achieve success. LME–M17.

> SIR T. BROWNE Edified out of the Rib of Adam. SWIFT To edify a name and reputation.

3 *verb trans.* **a** Build up (the church, the soul) in faith and holiness; benefit or strengthen spiritually. ME. ▸**b** Improve in a moral sense; inform, instruct. LME.

> **a** E. A. FREEMAN He was much edified by the king's prayers and almsdeeds. **b** J. BUCHAN He was a preacher at heart, as every young Scotsman is, since we have all a craving to edify our fellows.

†4 *verb intrans.* Profit spiritually or morally; gain instruction. E17–M19.

■ **edifier** *noun* LME. **edifying** *adjective* that edifies; that tends to moral or spiritual improvement; instructive: E16. **edifyingly** *adverb* M17.

Edipal *adjective* see OEDIPAL.

edit /ˈɛdɪt/ *noun*. M20.
[ORIGIN from the verb.]

An act or spell of editing a recording etc.; the action or process of editing; a feature or facility that allows for or performs editing.

E

edit /ˈɛdɪt/ *verb trans.* L18.
[ORIGIN Partly from French *éditer* publish, edit (based on *édition*: see EDITION); partly back-form. from EDITOR *noun*.]

†1 Publish (a literary work previously existing in manuscript). Only in L18.

2 Prepare an edition of (a work or works by an earlier author); bring into order for publication, after compilation by others or oneself; act as editor of (a newspaper etc.); reword for a purpose. L18. ▸**b** Prepare (a film, tape, etc.) by rearrangement, cutting, or collation of recorded material to form a unified sequence. E20.

> K. AMIS He gave a compressed, but otherwise only slightly edited, account of his past relations with Margaret.

edit out remove from the final version of a book, account, film, etc.

■ **editable** *adjective* M20.

edition /ɪˈdɪʃ(ə)n/ *noun*. LME.
[ORIGIN Old French & mod. French *édition* from Latin *editio(n-)*, from *edit-* pa. ppl stem of *edere* put forth, from *e-* E- + *dare* put.]

1 A form or version of a literary work at its first publication, and after each revision, enlargement, abridgement, or change of format; one copy in such a form; the entire number of similar copies of a book, newspaper, etc., issued at one time; the entire number of any product issued at one time. LME.

> R. TRAVERS Butler composed another notice . . taking it to the newspaper office in time to catch . . Saturday's edition. D. MURPHY He chanced to notice the ten-volume 1840 edition of Sismondi's *Histoire*.

facsimile edition, ***first edition***, ***limited edition***, ***paperback edition***, ***pocket edition***, ***revised edition***, ***special edition***, ***variorum edition***, etc.

†2 The action of putting forth; publication. M16–M17.

†3 The action of producing or bringing into existence; birth, creation (of orders of knighthood, etc.), extraction, origin. L16–L17.

4 Any of several forms or versions resembling another in which a thing or person appears at different times; the whole number of any product issued at one time. E17.

> DONNE All the vertuous Actions they expresse, Are but a new, and worse edition Of her some one thought. M. ALLINGHAM A larger-than-life edition of his stage self. H. MOORE Of a very small piece [of sculpture] one doesn't mind if the edition goes to ten.

■ **editionize** *verb trans.* produce (a newspaper) in several editions L20.

editio princeps /ɪˌdɪʃɪəʊ ˈprɪnsɛps/ *noun phr.* Pl. ***editiones principes*** /ɪdɪʃɪˌəʊniːz ˈprɪnsɪpiːz/. E19.
[ORIGIN mod. Latin, from Latin *editio* (see EDITION) + PRINCEPS.]

The first printed edition of a book.

editor /ˈɛdɪtə/ *noun* & *verb*. M17.
[ORIGIN Latin = producer, exhibitor, from *edit-*: see EDITION, -OR.]

▸ **A** *noun*. †1 The publisher of a book. Only in M17.

2 A person who edits material for publication, broadcasting, etc.; a person who prepares an edition of a literary work; a person who selects or commissions material for publication. E18.

3 A person who has charge of the running and contents of a newspaper, periodical, etc., or of a particular section of the publication; a person who is responsible for the style and content of a reference book. L18. ▸**b** The head of a department of a publishing house. E20.

city editor, ***financial editor***, ***sports editor***, etc.

4 A person who cuts and edits films or tapes. E20.

5 *COMPUTING*. A program enabling the user to alter programs or to alter or rearrange textual or other information held in a computer. M20.

– PHRASES & COMB.: ***copy editor***: see COPY *noun*[1]. **editor-in-chief** the chief editor of a publication, in a publishing house, etc. ***literary editor***: see LITERARY *adjective*.

▸ **B** *verb trans.* Edit. *rare*. M20.

■ **editorship** *noun* the duties, functions, and office of an editor L18. **editress** *noun* a female editor L18. **editrix** *noun* = EDITRESS *noun* E20.

editorial /ɛdɪˈtɔːrɪəl/ *adjective* & *noun*. M18.
[ORIGIN from EDITOR + -IAL.]

▸ **A** *adjective*. Of or pertaining to an editor or editing; written by or as by the editor, distinguished from news

and advertising matter; of or pertaining to an editorial. M18.
▸**B** *noun*. A newspaper article written by, or under the direct responsibility of, the editor. M19.
■ **editorialist** *noun* a person who writes editorials, or makes editorial comment E20. **editorialize** *verb* (*a*) *verb intrans.* write editorials; comment editorially; (*b*) *verb trans.* add editorial comment to: M19. **editorially** *adverb* in an editorial manner or capacity E19.

Edo /ˈɛdəʊ/ *noun & adjective*. Pl. of noun **-os**, same. L19.
[ORIGIN Edo name of Benin City.]
(Of, pertaining to, or designating) a people inhabiting the district of Benin in Nigeria; (of) the Kwa language of this people.

EDP *abbreviation*.
Electronic data processing.

EDT *abbreviation*. *US*.
Eastern Daylight Time.

EDTA *abbreviation*.
CHEMISTRY. Ethylenediamine tetra-acetic acid, a crystalline acid, $(CH_2COOH)_2NCH_2CH_2N(CH_2COOH)_2$, widely used as a chelating agent, esp. in the form of its salts.

educable /ˈɛdjʊkəb(ə)l, ˈɛdʒʊ-/ *adjective*. M19.
[ORIGIN formed as EDUCATABLE.]
Able to be educated.
■ **educaˈbility** *noun* E19.

educatable /ˈɛdjʊkeɪtəb(ə)l/ *adjective*. M19.
[ORIGIN from EDUCATE + -ABLE.]
= EDUCABLE.
■ **educataˈbility** *noun* L19.

educate /ˈɛdjʊkeɪt/ *verb trans.* Pa. pple **-ated**, (*obsolete* exc. *Scot.*) **-ate**. LME.
[ORIGIN Latin *educat-* pa. ppl stem of *educare* rel. to *educere* EDUCE: see -ATE³.]
1 Bring up (children) so as to form their habits, manners, intellectual aptitudes, etc.; *spec.* instruct, provide schooling for. LME. ▸†**b** Rear by attention to physical needs. Only in 17.

B. JOWETT The youth of a people should be educated in forms . . of virtue. O. MANNING He had been educated at an English public school.

2 Train so as to develop intellectual or moral powers generally, or in a particular mental or physical faculty; instruct, discipline. M19.

T. S. ELIOT The multiplication of critical books . . may supply opinion instead of educating taste. A. LOOS I ought . . to educate Piggie how to act with a girl like American gentlemen.

educated guess: based on experience.
■ **educator** *noun* [Latin] M16. **educatory** *adjective* that has an educating influence M19.

education /ɛdjʊˈkeɪʃ(ə)n/ *noun*. M16.
[ORIGIN Old French & mod. French *éducation* or Latin *educatio(n-)*, formed as EDUCATE: see -ATION.]
†**1** The process of nourishing or rearing. M16–M17.

R. LOVELL They delight in woods, and places of their first education.

2 The process of bringing up children in particular manners, habits, or ways of life. *obsolete* exc. with the notion of 3. M16. ▸**b** The training of animals. M16.

SHAKES. *Tam. Shr.* Christopher Sly, . . by education a cardmaker.

3 The systematic instruction, schooling, or training of children and young people, or, by extension, instruction obtained in adult life; the whole course of such instruction received by a person. Also, provision of this, as an aspect of public policy. E17.

S. GIBBONS The education bestowed on Flora Poste by her parents had been expensive, athletic and prolonged. H. KELLER The next important step in my education was learning to read. A. J. P. TAYLOR The committee recommended economies in education and public health.

primary education, ***secondary education***, ***tertiary education***. ***adult education***: see ADULT *adjective* 2. COLLEGE ***of education***. ELEMENTARY ***education***. ***further education***: see FURTHER *adjective* 2. ***higher education***: see HIGHER *adjective*. ***physical education***: see PHYSICAL *adjective*. ***public education***: see PUBLIC *adjective & noun*.
4 The development of mental or physical powers; moulding of (some aspect of) character. M19.

H. E. MANNING Education is the formation of the whole man—intellect . . character, mind, and soul. DAY LEWIS Monart did more than any other place for my sensuous education.

■ **educatioˈnese** *noun* (*derog.*) jargon-ridden language supposedly characteristic of educationalists and educational administrators M20. **educationist** *noun* = EDUCATIONALIST E19.

educational /ɛdjʊˈkeɪʃ(ə)n(ə)l/ *adjective*. M17.
[ORIGIN from EDUCATION + -AL¹.]
†**1** Due to or arising from education. M17–E19.
2 Of, pertaining to, or concerned with education. Also, educative. E19.
■ **educationalist** *noun* a student of the methods of education; an advocate of education: M19. **educationally** *adverb* with reference to education; ***educationally subnormal*** (*hist.*) having learning difficulties and unable to be taught in ordinary schools: M19.

educative /ˈɛdjʊkətɪv/ *adjective*. M19.
[ORIGIN formed as EDUCATE + -IVE.]
Of or pertaining to education; conducive to education, having the power of educating.

educe /ɪˈdjuːs/ *verb trans.* LME.
[ORIGIN Latin *educere*, from *e-* E- + *ducere* to lead.]
†**1** Lead or draw out; MEDICINE remove by drawing out. LME–M17.
2 Bring out or develop from latent or rudimentary existence; elicit; evoke. E17.

T. GALE Chaos was that ancient slime, out of which al things were educed.

3 Infer (a principle etc.) *from* a set of data. M19.

J. BARZUN In most subjects few attempts are made to educe principles from ever larger masses of facts.

■ **educible** *adjective* L17.

educrat /ˈɛdjʊkrat, ˈɛdʒʊ-/ *noun*. *N. Amer. derog.* M20.
[ORIGIN from EDU(CATION + -CRAT.]
An educational administrator or theorist.

educt /ˈiːdʌkt/ *noun*. L17.
[ORIGIN Latin *eductum* neut. pa. pple of *educere* EDUCE.]
†**1** That which is brought forth as young. Only in L17.
†**2** CHEMISTRY. A component of a substance, which is released by the substance's decomposition. L18–L19.
3 That which is educed; a result of inference or development. E19.

eduction /ɪˈdʌkʃ(ə)n/ *noun*. LME.
[ORIGIN Latin *eductio(n-)*, from *educt-* ppl stem of *educere*: see EDUCE, -ION.]
†**1** A leading or putting out; MEDICINE a removal by drawing out. LME–E18.
2 The action or result of educing. Also, an educt, an inference. M17.
†**3** The exhaust of steam from a cylinder in a steam engine. L18–M19.
■ **eductive** *adjective* [medieval Latin *eductivus*] tending to educe LME.

edulcorate /ɪˈdʌlkəreɪt/ *verb trans.* M17.
[ORIGIN medieval Latin *edulcorat-* pa. ppl stem of *edulcorare*, from *e-* E- + late Latin *dulcor* sweetness, from Latin *dulcis* sweet: see -ATE³.]
†**1** Sweeten, make sweet. M17–E18.
2 Purify or soften by removing acid properties. M17.
3 Free from soluble impurities by washing or filtration. M17.
■ **edulcoˈration** *noun* M18.

edutainment /ɛdjʊˈteɪnm(ə)nt/ *noun*. L20.
[ORIGIN from EDU(CATION + ENTER)TAINMENT.]
Computer games, or other forms of entertainment, having an educational aspect.

Edw. *abbreviation*.
Edward.

Edward /ˈɛdwəd/ *noun*. L16.
[ORIGIN Male forename.]
Any of various coins issued in the reign of any of the Kings of England or Great Britain called Edward.

Edwardian /ɛdˈwɔːdɪən/ *adjective & noun*. M19.
[ORIGIN from EDWARD + -IAN.]
▸**A** *adjective*. Belonging to or characteristic of the reign of any of the King Edwards of England or Great Britain; *spec.* of Edward VII or his reign (1901–10). M19.
▸**B** *noun*. **1** A past or present member of a school named after a King, or Saint, Edward. L19.
2 A person of the period of Edward VII. E20.
■ **Edwardiˈana** *noun pl.* [-ANA] publications or other items concerning or associated with a school named after King, or Saint, Edward or the reign of Edward VII E20. **Edwardianism** *noun* the collective characteristics, or a sentiment or expression, of the reign of Edward VII M20. **ˈEdwardine** *adjective* belonging to or characteristic of the reign of Edward VI or VII M19.

EE *abbreviation*.
Early English.

'ee *pers. pronoun* see YE *pronoun*.

-ee /iː/ *suffix*¹.
[ORIGIN from or after Anglo-Norman *-é* pa. ppl suffix from Latin *-atus* -ATE².]
1 Used orig. in legal terms (with corresp. agent nouns in *-or*) to form nouns from verbs (occas. Latin ppl stems), with the sense 'person affected directly or indirectly by the verbal action', as ***appellee***, ***legatee***, ***lessee***, ***vendee***. Now used more widely (without corresp. terms in *-or*) to form nouns. (*a*) from verbs, with the sense 'person subject to an action or involved in an action', as ***employee***, ***payee***, ***devotee***, ***escapee***, ***conferee***, ***standee***; (*b*) from nouns, with the sense 'person having to do with', as ***bargee***, ***patentee***; (*c*) from adjectives, with the sense 'person described as', as ***absentee***.
2 Used to Anglicize mod. French nouns in *-é* (from pples), as ***debauchee***, ***refugee***.

-ee /iː/ *suffix*².
[ORIGIN Unknown.]
Forming diminutives, as ***bootee***, ***coatee***, or with vague or fanciful sense, as ***goatee***, ***settee***.

EEA *abbreviation*.
European Economic Area.

EEC *abbreviation*.
European Economic Community.

EEG *abbreviation*.
Electroencephalogram.

eejit /ˈiːdʒɪt/ *noun*. *dial.* (chiefly *Scot. & Irish*). L19.
[ORIGIN Repr. a pronunc.]
= IDIOT *noun* 1.
■ **eejity** *adjective* idiotic M20.

eel /iːl/ *noun & verb*.
[ORIGIN Old English *ǣl* = Old Frisian *ēl*, Old Saxon, Old High German *āl* (Dutch *aal*, German *Aal*), Old Norse *áll*, from Germanic, of unknown origin.]
▸**A** *noun*. **1** Any of various snakelike fishes of the genus *Anguilla*, members of which spend most of their lives in fresh water but breed in warm deep oceans. Also (usu. with specifying word), any of numerous slender, elongated fishes belonging to the order Anguilliformes (which includes *Anguilla*) or (*loosely*) other orders. OE.
conger eel, ***moray eel***, ***sand eel***, ***snipe eel***, etc. ***electric eel***: see ELECTRIC *adjective*. **jellied eels** cooked eels set in jelly. ***silver eel***: see SILVER *noun & adjective*. SPINY ***eel***.
2 The eel as the proverbial type of something slippery or evasive; a slippery or evasive person or thing. E16.
3 A microscopic nematode worm, as found in fermented flour paste, vinegar, etc. *arch. colloq.* M17.
– COMB.: **eel-fare** the passage of young eels upriver; (in *pl.*) a brood of young eels (cf. ELVER); **eelgrass** (*a*) = ZOSTERA; (*b*) *US* = ***tape-grass*** s.v. TAPE *noun*; **eelpout** †(*a*) a burbot; (*b*) any small thick-lipped fish of the family Zoarcidae, *esp.* the viviparous blenny, *Zoarces viviparus*; **eelskin** (material similar to) the skin of an eel; **eel spear** a pronged instrument for transfixing eels; **eelworm** a nematode worm, *esp.* one parasitic on plants.
▸**B** *verb*. **1** *verb intrans.* Fish for eels. Chiefly as ***eeling*** *verbal noun*. L18.
2 *verb trans. & intrans.* Move like an eel. Also ***eel one's way***. E20.
■ **eelery** *noun* a place where eels are caught M19. **eel-like** *adjective* L17. **eely** *adjective* M17.

Eem /iːm/ *adjective & noun*. L19.
[ORIGIN A river in the Netherlands.]
GEOLOGY. (Designating or pertaining to) the last interglacial stage of the Pleistocene in northern Europe, preceding the Weichsel glaciation.
■ Also **ˈEemian** *adjective & noun* E20.

e'en *adverb* see EVEN *adverb*.

-een /iːn/ *suffix*¹.
[ORIGIN Repr. French *-ine*.]
Forming names of fabrics, usu. of an inferior or coarser quality than that denoted by the root word, as ***sateen***, ***velveteen***.

-een /iːn/ *suffix*².
[ORIGIN Repr. Irish *-in* dim. suffix.]
Used in adoptions of Irish diminutives, as ***colleen***, ***dudeen***, ***poteen***, ***spalpeen***, and in (orig. Irish) formations on English words, as ***buckeen***, ***squireen***.

e'er *adverb* see EVER.

-eer /ˈɪə/ *suffix*.
[ORIGIN Repr. French *-ier* from Latin *-arius*: cf. -IER, -ARY¹.]
1 Forming nouns from nouns, with the sense 'person concerned with', as ***auctioneer***, ***mountaineer***, occas. with derog. implication, as ***profiteer***, ***sonneteer***; occas. with ref. to things, as ***gazetteer***, ***muffineer***.
2 Forming verbs from these nouns, freq. as back-forms. from derivs. in *-eering*, with the sense 'be concerned with', as ***electioneer***, ***profiteer***.

eerie /ˈɪəri/ *adjective*. Orig. *Scot. & N. English*. ME.
[ORIGIN Prob. repr. Old English *earg* cowardly.]
1 Fearful, usu. superstitiously. Now *rare*. ME.

R. TANNAHILL The watch-dog's howling . . makes the nightly wanderer eerie.

2 Inspiring unease or fear; spine-tingling; strange, weird, gloomy. L18.

J. G. FARRELL There was something eerie about this vast shadowy cavern and the Major . . felt a shiver of apprehension. A. PRICE His eerie faculty for total recall of every fact.

– NOTE: Not in general use before 19.
■ **eerily** *adverb* M19. **eeriness** *noun* LME.

EETPU *abbreviation*.
Electrical, Electronic, Telecommunications, and Plumbing Union.

Eeyorish /ˈiːɔːrɪʃ/ *adjective*. *colloq.* Also **Eeyoreish**. L20.
[ORIGIN from *Eeyore*, a donkey in A. A. Milne's *Winnie-the-Pooh*, characterized by his gloomy outlook on life, + -ISH *suffix*¹.]
Pessimistic or gloomy.

Daily Telegraph The association points out, in its Eeyorish way, that we are not really getting something for nothing.

ef- /ɪf, *stressed* ɛf/ *prefix.*
Assim. form of Old French ES- and EX-[1] before *f.*

EFA *abbreviation.*
Essential fatty acid.

eff /ɛf/ *verb. slang.* M20.
[ORIGIN from name of letter F, F, euphem. abbreviation of FUCK *verb.*]
1 *verb trans. & intrans.* = FUCK *verb* (used as an expletive on its own account, as a milder alternative to ***fuck***, or as a euphemistic report of the use of the full word). M20.
2 *verb intrans.* Utter ***fuck*** or an equivalent word. Esp. in ***eff and blind***, use strong expletives, swear continuously. M20.
■ **effer** *noun* M20. **effing** *ppl adjective & adverb* = FUCKING M20.

effable /ˈɛfəb(ə)l/ *adjective.* E17.
[ORIGIN Obsolete French, or Latin *effabilis*, from *effari* to utter, from EF- + *fari* speak: see -ABLE. Cf. earlier INEFFABLE.]
That can or may be expressed or described in words. Now only in antithesis to ***ineffable***.

Observer Trying to take on the ineffable, philosophers are always running the risk of making the eminently effable (chairs, tables and so on) entirely mysterious.

efface /ɪˈfeɪs/ *verb trans.* L15.
[ORIGIN Old French & mod. French *effacer*, from *es-* (see ES-, EF-) + *face* FACE *noun.*]
†**1** Pardon or obtain absolution for (an offence). L15–M18.

J. WESLEY In tender Mercy Look on me, And all my Sins efface.

2 Rub out or obliterate (writing, marks, painted or sculptured figures, etc.) from a surface. E17. ▸**b** Erase (words or sentences) from a document. Now only *fig.* M18.

A. NIN Inscriptions on the walls, half effaced by time. **b** LD MACAULAY To efface the penal laws from the statute book.

3 *gen.* Cause to disappear entirely, remove all trace of; *fig.* wipe out or obliterate (a memory or mental impression). E17.

H. A. L. FISHER The strong provincial feelings of Burgundy and Aquitaine . . were not allowed altogether to efface the historic image of Rome. SLOAN WILSON Before daylight, they had effaced all signs of the struggle and dragged the bodies into the woods.

4 Outshine, eclipse, utterly surpass. E18. ▸**b** *refl.* Treat or regard oneself as insignificant; allow oneself to be overlooked or ignored. L19.

M. W. MONTAGU Her beauty effaced everything I have seen. **b** C. P. SNOW Orbell, who had been quiet all the evening, was effacing himself and listening.

5 Greatly distort (the cervix or umbilicus), usu. through the distension of an adjacent organ in the course of labour. E20.
■ **effaceable** *adjective* M19. **effacement** *noun* L18.

†**effatum** *noun.* Pl. **-ta**. Also anglicized as **effate**. M17–L18.
[ORIGIN Latin, use as noun of neut. pa. pple of *effari*: see EFFABLE.]
A saying, dictum, or maxim.

effect /ɪˈfɛkt/ *noun.* LME.
[ORIGIN Old French (mod. *effet*), or Latin *effectus*, from *effect-* pa. ppl stem of *efficere* accomplish, from EF- + *facere*, *fic-* make, do.]
1 Something accomplished, caused, or produced; a result, a consequence. LME. ▸**b** Results in general; the quality of producing a result, efficacy. LME. ▸**c** A particular phenomenon (chiefly in physical science), usu. named after its discoverer or describer. M19.

H. H. WILSON The beneficial effects of their interposition had given shelter and security to private trade. D. DAVIE Always the overt intention is to exalt poetry; and always the effect is to emasculate it. **b** MILTON This Tree . . is of Divine effect To open Eyes. J. PRIESTLEY A law was made . . but it had little effect.

c *Auger effect, Compton effect, Doppler effect, Faraday effect, Hall effect, night effect, Peltier effect, Raman effect, shot effect, surface effect, Wallace effect, Weissenberg effect, Zeeman effect*, etc.

†**2** A contemplated result, a purpose. LME–M17.
3 Accomplishment, fulfilment; *obsolete* exc. in ***bring to effect*** etc. below. LME.
†**4** An outward sign, an appearance; a phenomenon. LME–M17.
†**5** Reality, fact, as opp. to appearance. LME–L17.
6 Operative influence. LME.

A. KOESTLER Liquor did not seem to have a stimulating effect on him. DAY LEWIS The full effect of my mother's death . . did not show itself until my adolescence.

7 †**a** Something attained or acquired as the result of an action. *rare* (Shakes.). Only in E17. ▸**b** In *pl.* Property (excluding real property); goods, belongings. E18.

b S. SONTAG To burn the clothes and other effects of someone who died of TB.

8 The impression produced on a spectator or listener by a work of art or literature, a performance, etc. M18. ▸**b** A (pleasing or remarkable) combination of colour or form in a picture, landscape, etc. L19. ▸**c** Lighting, sound, etc., used to enhance a play, film, broadcast, etc.; the means of producing this. Freq. in *pl.* L19.

J. AGATE William Devlin . . has already played Clemenceau with magnificent effect. R. DAVIES People are always charmed by clever mechanisms that give an effect of life. **b** H. READ Certain effects which he obtained—the representation of mist, of foam, of swirling water—still baffle our analysis. **c** T. BARR When the filmed sequences are assembled . . sound effects and music are added. A. ROAD The technical tricks—the visual and electronic effects which are so much a part of *Doctor Who*.

– PHRASES: **bring to effect** accomplish, realize. **bring into effect**, **carry into effect** realize, make operative. ***cause and effect***: see CAUSE *noun*. **for effect** for the sake of making an impression on an audience. **give effect to** make operative, put into force. ***ill effect***: see ILL *adjective & adverb*. **in effect** (*a*) in fact, in reality; (*b*) virtually, for all practical purposes. **law of effect** (PSYCHOLOGY): that a response to a stimulus will be more probably learned if it proves to be accompanied or followed by an event satisfying to the organism. **leave no effects** leave nothing for one's heirs. **no effects** no or insufficient funds (written by a banker on a dishonoured cheque). **of no effect**, †**of none effect** having no result, unsuccessful. **personal effects** one's own movable property, personal belongings. **put into effect** accomplish, realize, make operative. ***spot effect***: see SPOT *noun & adjective*. **take effect** prove successful; become operative, come into force (*from* a certain date). **to the effect that** to that end, with that significance. **to this effect**, **to that effect** having this, that, result or implication. **with effect from** coming into operation at (a certain time).
■ **effectless** *noun* L16.

effect /ɪˈfɛkt/ *verb.* L16.
[ORIGIN from the noun.]
1 *verb trans. &* †*intrans.* Bring about (an event or result); accomplish (an intention or desire). L16. ▸†**b** Produce (a state or condition). L16–M17. ▸**c** Make, construct, build. Now *rare* or *obsolete*. L18.

G. M. TREVELYAN Corn Law Repeal . . effected no immediate economic or social revolution. R. C. A. WHITE A police officer may use reasonable force . . to effect the arrest.

†**2** *verb trans.* Give effect to (an intention); fulfil (a promise). L16–M17.
■ **effecter** *noun* a person who or thing which brings about an event, accomplishes a purpose, etc. E17. **effectible** *adjective* M17. **effector** *noun* (*a*) = EFFECTER; (*b*) (BIOLOGY, freq. *attrib.*) an organ or cell acting in response to a stimulus: E17.

effective /ɪˈfɛktɪv/ *adjective & noun.* LME.
[ORIGIN Latin *effectivus*, from *effect-*: see EFFECT *noun*, -IVE.]
▸ **A** *adjective.* †**1** Concerned with or having the function of accomplishing or executing. LME–E17.
2 Powerful in effect; effectual; efficient, efficacious. LME. ▸**b** Making a strong impression; striking, vivid. M19.

C. S. FORESTER He judged that . . silence would be more effective than speech. *Which Micro?* Four effective, if not brilliant, items of software. **b** J. CONRAD The white stairs, the deep crimson of the carpet, and the light blue of the dress made an effective combination of colour.

†**3** That is concerned in the production *of* an event or condition; having the power of acting on objects. L16–L17.
4 Fit for work or (esp. military) service. L17.
5 Having an effect or result. M18. ▸**b** Actually usable or brought to bear; equivalent in its effect. L18. ▸**c** GRAMMAR. = PERFECTIVE *adjective* 3. M20.

J. H. BURTON The honour of the first effective shot.

b effective temperature PHYSICS the temperature of an object calculated from the radiation emitted by the object, assuming it to behave as a black body.

6 Actual, in effect; (of an order etc.) operative, in force. L18.

J. C. RANSOM Classical and medieval philosophies and sciences which have passed from our effective knowledge.
C. V. WEDGWOOD The King would remain as the respected figurehead, but effective power . . would be exercised by the gentry, the lawyers, and the merchants.

▸ **B** *noun.* †**1** An efficient cause. Only in 17.
2 An effective serviceman or other person. Usu. in *pl.* E18.
3 GRAMMAR. = PERFECTIVE *noun* 2. M20.
■ **effectively** *adverb* LME. **effectiveness** *noun* the quality of being effective E17. **effecˈtivity** *noun* (the degree of) effectiveness M19.

effectual /ɪˈfɛktʃʊəl/ *adjective.* LME.
[ORIGIN medieval Latin *effectualis*, from Latin *effectus*: see EFFECT *noun*, -AL[1].]
1 Efficacious, producing the intended result, effective. LME. ▸**b** Of a legal document etc.: valid, binding. LME.
†**2** Of a prayer or plea: earnest, zealous, urgent. LME–E17.
†**3** Real, actual, in existence. LME–M17.
†**4** Pertinent, to the point; conclusive. L16–L17.
– SPECIAL COLLOCATIONS: **effectual calling** THEOLOGY the action of the Holy Spirit in instilling Christian faith. **effectual grace** THEOLOGY the special grace given to those elected to salvation.
■ **effectuˈality** *noun* effectual quality M17. **effectually** *adverb* LME. **effectualness** *noun* (now *rare*) M16.

effectuate /ɪˈfɛktʃʊeɪt/ *verb trans.* L16.
[ORIGIN medieval Latin *effectuat-* pa. ppl stem of *effectuare*, from *effectus*: see EFFECT *noun*, -ATE[3].]
Cause to happen, put into effect, accomplish.
■ **effectuˈation** *noun* E17.

effeir /ɪˈfɪə/ *noun & verb. Scot.* LME.
[ORIGIN Alt. of AFFAIR.]
▸ **A** *noun.* †**1** A concern, a cause, an important matter. LME–E17.
2 Appearance, array; show, pomp, ceremony. Long *obsolete* exc. (*hist.*) in ***effeir of war***. LME.
▸ **B** *verb intrans. obsolete* exc. SCOTS LAW.
1 Appertain, fall by right. Esp. in ***as effeirs***, in the proper way, as appropriate. LME.
2 Be appropriate, pertain, relate *to*. M16.

effeminacy /ɪˈfɛmɪnəsi/ *noun.* E17.
[ORIGIN from EFFEMINATE *adjective & noun* + -ACY.]
1 The presence of feminine characteristics in a man; unmanly weakness or delicacy. E17.
†**2** Addiction to womanizing. M–L17.

effeminate /ɪˈfɛmɪnət/ *adjective & noun.* LME.
[ORIGIN Latin *effeminatus* pa. pple of *effeminare* make feminine, from EF- + *femina* woman: see -ATE[2].]
▸ **A** *adjective.* **1** (Of a man) having characteristics regarded as feminine or unmanly; delicate, feeble, self-indulgent. LME. ▸**b** Characterized by or proceeding from unmanly weakness, softness, or delicacy. L16. ▸†**c** Gentle, tender, compassionate. Only in L16.

J. BRAINE Despite the manicure and the diamond ring he didn't look effeminate. **b** GIBBON Rome was . . humbled beneath the effeminate luxury of Oriental despotism. **c** SHAKES. *Rich. III* Your tenderness of heart And gentle, kind, effeminate remorse.

†**2** Excessively amorous; addicted to womanizing. L15–L16.
▸ **B** *noun.* An effeminate man. L16.
■ **effeminately** *adverb* E16. **effeminateness** *noun* L16.

effeminate /ɪˈfɛmɪneɪt/ *verb.* Now *rare* or *obsolete*. LME.
[ORIGIN Latin *effeminat-* pa. ppl stem of *effeminare*: see EFFEMINATE *adjective & noun*, -ATE[3].]
†**1** *verb intrans.* Become womanish or unmanly; grow weak. LME–E17.
2 *verb trans.* Make womanish or unmanly; enervate, enfeeble. M16.
†**3** *verb trans.* Make into or represent as a woman. L17–M18.

effeminize /ɪˈfɛmɪnʌɪz/ *verb trans.* Now *rare*. Also **-ise**. E17.
[ORIGIN from EFFEMINATE *adjective* + -IZE.]
Make effeminate.

effendi /ɛˈfɛndi/ *noun.* E17.
[ORIGIN Turkish *efendi* from mod. Greek *aphentē* voc. of *aphentēs* from Greek *authentēs* lord, master.]
A man of education or social standing in an eastern Mediterranean or Arab country. Freq. (usu. *hist.*) as a title of respect or courtesy in Turkey or (former) Turkish territory.

efferent /ˈɛf(ə)r(ə)nt/ *adjective.* M19.
[ORIGIN Latin *efferent-* pres. ppl stem of *efferre*, from EF- + *ferre* bring, carry: see -ENT.]
ANATOMY. Conducting outwards (of a nerve: away from the central nervous system; of a blood vessel: away from an organ). Opp. AFFERENT.

effervesce /ɛfəˈvɛs/ *verb intrans.* E18.
[ORIGIN Latin *effervescere*, from EF- + *fervescere* inceptive of *fervere* be hot, boil: see -ESCE.]
†**1** Break into violent chemical action. E–M18.
2 Give off bubbles of gas, *esp.* as a result of chemical action; bubble. L18. ▸**b** Of a gas: issue in bubbles. M19.
3 *fig.* Show great excitement or enthusiasm; become lively or vivacious. M19.

effervescence /ɛfəˈvɛs(ə)ns/ *noun.* E17.
[ORIGIN formed as EFFERVESCENT: see -ESCENCE.]
†**1** The action of boiling up. E17–E18.
2 The action of bubbling up as if boiling; the vigorous rise of bubbles of gas from a liquid, *esp.* as a result of chemical action. L17.
3 *fig.* Vigorous action, exuberance, vivacity. M18.
■ **effervescency** *noun* effervescent condition, effervescence L17.

effervescent /ɛfəˈvɛs(ə)nt/ *adjective.* L17.
[ORIGIN Latin *effervescent-* pres. ppl stem of *effervescere*: see EFFERVESCE, -ESCENT.]
†**1** Boiling, bubbling with heat. Only in L17.
2 Having the property of effervescing; bubbly, fizzy; *fig.* exuberant. M19.

effete /ɪˈfiːt/ *adjective.* E17.
[ORIGIN Latin *effetus* exhausted as by bearing young, from EF- + *fetus* breeding: see FETUS.]
†**1** No longer fertile; past producing offspring. E17–M19.

CARLYLE Nature . . was as if effete now; could not any longer produce Great Men.

†**2** Of a substance or object: that has lost its special virtue or quality, exhausted, worn out. M17–M19.

EVELYN That imprison'd and Effœte Air, within the Green-house.

3 No longer vigorous or capable of effective action; decadent, degenerate. L18. ▸**b** Weak, ineffectual; effeminate. E20.

R. FRY The worn-out rags of an effete classical tradition long ago emptied of all meaning. **b** A. BROOKNER Next to her, Frederick appears effete, decorative, luxurious.

■ **effeteness** *noun* M19.

†**efficace** *noun.* ME–E18.
[ORIGIN Old French from Latin *efficacia*: see EFFICACY.]
Efficacy, effect.

E

efficacious /ɛfɪˈkeɪʃəs/ *adjective*. E16.
[ORIGIN from Latin *efficac-*, *efficax*, from *efficere*: see EFFECT *noun*, -ACIOUS.]
That does or is certain to produce the intended effect; effective.

P. MEDAWAR At present there is no convincing evidence that psychoanalytic treatment as such is efficacious.

■ **efficaciously** *adverb* M17. **efficaciousness** *noun* M17.

efficacity /ɛfɪˈkasɪti/ *noun*. LME.
[ORIGIN Old French & mod. French *efficacité* from Latin *efficacitas*, from *efficax*: see EFFICACIOUS, -ACITY.]
= EFFICACY.

efficacy /ˈɛfɪkəsi/ *noun*. E16.
[ORIGIN Latin *efficacia*, from *efficax*: see EFFICACIOUS, -Y[3].]
1 Power or capacity to produce effects; (an) ability to bring about the intended result. E16.
†**2** An effect. M16–M17.

E

efficience /ɪˈfɪʃ(ə)ns/ *noun*. Now *rare* or *obsolete*. M17.
[ORIGIN formed as EFFICIENT: see -ENCE.]
Causative or productive activity. Also, efficacy.

efficiency /ɪˈfɪʃ(ə)nsi/ *noun*. L16.
[ORIGIN Latin *efficientia* formed as EFFICIENT: see -ENCY.]
1 The fact of being an efficient cause. Now *rare* or *obsolete*. L16. ▸†**b** The action of an efficient cause; production. M–L17.
2 The quality of being efficient; the ability to accomplish or fulfil what is intended; effectiveness, competence. M17.

R. WHATELY The penalty annexed to any law is an instance, not of its efficiency, but . . of its failure. F. TUOHY He conducted his course at the University with an efficiency which shone beside the amateurish efforts of his colleagues.

3 PHYSICS. †**a** The work done by a force in operating a machine; the total energy expended by a machine. E–M19. ▸**b** The ratio of useful work performed by a device or system to the total energy input. M19.
b *thermal efficiency*: see THERMAL *adjective*.
4 In full ***efficiency apartment***. A room or small flat with limited washing and cooking facilities. *N. Amer.* M20.
– COMB.: *efficiency apartment*: see sense 4 above; **efficiency audit** an examination of a business etc. to ascertain the efficiency of its procedures; **efficiency bar** a point on a salary scale which may not be passed until the employee's efficiency is proved; **efficiency engineer**, **efficiency expert**: who advises on the efficiency of an organization or production process.

efficient /ɪˈfɪʃ(ə)nt/ *adjective & noun*. LME.
[ORIGIN Latin *efficient-* pres. ppl stem of *efficere*: see EFFECT *noun*, -ENT.]
▸ **A** *adjective*. **1** Making, causing; that makes a thing what it is. Usu. with *cause*. Cf. DEFICIENT *adjective* 1. LME.
2 Effective, producing the desired result with the minimum wasted effort; (of a person) capable, competent; PHYSICS characterized by high (or specified) efficiency. L18.

H. B. STOWE He was an expert and efficient workman. G. GREENE The appeal to sentiment was heartlessly efficient; it had struck him in the place where he was most vulnerable and at the hour when he was most alone.

▸ †**B** *noun*. **1** That which makes a thing what it is; the cause of an effect. L16–E19.
2 A trained soldier, *esp.* one volunteering for service. M–L19.
■ **efficiently** *adverb* †(*a*) as by an efficient cause; (*b*) in an efficient manner, effectively: E17.

†**effierce** *verb trans. rare* (Spenser). Only in L16.
[ORIGIN from EF- + FIERCE.]
Make fierce, madden.

effigial /ɪˈfɪdʒɪəl/ *adjective*. *rare*. E18.
[ORIGIN from Latin *effigies* EFFIGY + -AL[1].]
Of the nature of an effigy.

effigiate /ɪˈfɪdʒɪeɪt/ *verb trans*. Now *rare*. E17.
[ORIGIN Late Latin *effigiat-* pa. ppl stem of *effigiare*, from *effigies*: see EFFIGY, -ATE[3].]
Present a likeness of, portray.
■ **effigiˈation** *noun* the action of representing; a likeness: M16.

effigy /ˈɛfɪdʒi/ *noun*. Also (*arch.*) **effigies** /ɪˈfɪdʒiiːz/ (pl. same). M16.
[ORIGIN Latin *effigies*, from *effig-* stem of *effingere*, from EF- + *fingere* fashion, shape.]
A representation of (usu.) a person in the form of a sculptured figure or a dummy. Also, a portrait on a coin.

C. V. WEDGWOOD The validity of the seal . . , which bore the name and effigy of King Charles. C. THUBRON Some Russians suspect this is not Lenin's body at all, but an effigy.

burn in effigy, **hang in effigy**, etc., subject an image of (a person) to a semblance of a punishment desired for the original (formerly also done in the case of a criminal who had fled from justice).
– COMB.: **effigy mound** a prehistoric earth mound in the shape of an animal.
– NOTE: The sing. *effigy* is not recorded before M17. Earlier examples are either pl. or in Latin forms.

efflation /ɪˈfleɪʃ(ə)n/ *noun*. Now *rare*. L16.
[ORIGIN Late Latin *efflatio(n-)*, from *efflat-* pa. ppl stem of *efflare*, from EF- + *flare* to blow: see -ATION.]
Blowing out, expulsion of breath; a breath, an emanation.

effleurage /ɛfləːˈrɑːʒ/ *noun & verb*. L19.
[ORIGIN French, from *effleurer* stroke lightly.]
▸ **A** *noun*. The technique or process of massaging with a circular stroking movement of the flat or heel of the hand. L19.
▸ **B** *verb intrans. & trans.* Perform this kind of massage (on). L19.

effloresce /ɛfləˈrɛs/ *verb intrans*. L18.
[ORIGIN Latin *efflorescere*, from EF- + *florescere* inceptive of *florere* to blossom, from *flor-*, *flos* flower: see -ESCE.]
1 Bloom, burst out into or as into flower. L18.
2 a CHEMISTRY. Of a crystalline substance: turn to fine powder through loss of water or exposure to air. L18. ▸**b** Of a salt: be carried in solution to the surface of the ground etc. and crystallize there. Of the ground, a wall, or other surface: become covered with particles of a salt. E19.
3 *fig.* Blossom out; become manifest. M19.

efflorescence /ɛfləˈrɛs(ə)ns/ *noun*. E17.
[ORIGIN from Latin *efflorescent-* pres. ppl stem of *efflorescere*, partly through French: see EFFLORESCE, -ENCE.]
1 The process, or period, of flowering. Chiefly *fig.* E17.

R. FRY The change in art is merely the efflorescence of certain long prepared . . effects.

†**2** Colour developed on the skin; MEDICINE a pathological redness or rash. M17–L19.
3 The process of efflorescing of a salt; a powdery deposit resulting from this. M17.
■ **efflorescent** *adjective* that effloresces; resembling or forming an efflorescence E19.

effluence /ˈɛflʊəns/ *noun*. LME.
[ORIGIN Old French & mod. French, or medieval Latin *effluentia*, formed as EFFLUENT: see -ENCE.]
1 A flowing out (esp. of light, electricity, etc., or *fig.*). LME.
2 That which flows out; an emanation. E17.

effluent /ˈɛflʊənt/ *adjective & noun*. LME.
[ORIGIN Latin *effluent-* pres. ppl stem of *effluere*: see EFFLUVIUM, -ENT.]
▸ **A** *adjective*. That flows forth or out. LME.
▸ **B** *noun*. A stream or liquid flowing out; *esp.* waste discharged from an industrial process, sewage tank, etc. M19.

effluvium /ɪˈfluːvɪəm/ *noun*. Pl. **-ia** /-ɪə/, †**-iums**. M17.
[ORIGIN Latin, from *effluere*, from EF- + *fluere* to flow: see -IUM.]
†**1** A flowing out. M17–E18.
2 Chiefly *hist.* An outflow or stream of imperceptible particles, esp. as supposedly transmitting electrical or magnetic influence etc. M17.

R. BOYLE The Effluvia of the Load-stone. W. COWPER Attracted by the effluvia of my genius.

3 An (esp. unpleasant) exhalation affecting the lungs or the sense of smell. M17.

ADDISON The miraculous Powers which the Effluviums of cheese have. C. DARWIN The whole air tainted with the effluvium.

– NOTE: Pl. *effluvia* sometimes treated as *sing.*

efflux /ˈɛflʌks/ *noun*. M16.
[ORIGIN medieval Latin *effluxus*, from *efflux-* pa. ppl stem of *effluere*: see EFFLUVIUM.]
1 A flowing out (of liquid, gas, etc., or *fig.*). M16.

J. M. KEYNES An influx of money into one country means an efflux from another.

2 The lapse of time; passing away, expiry. M17.

T. MANTON That efflux of time . . between Christ's ascension and his second coming.

3 That which flows out; an emanation. M17.

GLADSTONE The Established Church of Scotland . . was the efflux of the mind of the people.

effluxion /ɪˈflʌkʃ(ə)n/ *noun*. E17.
[ORIGIN Old French & mod. French, or late Latin *effluxio(n-)*, from *efflux-*: see EFFLUX, -ION.]
1 The passing of time; the expiry or completion of a period; LAW the expiration of a limited-time agreement or contract. E17.
2 The action or process of flowing out. M17.

efforce /ɪˈfɔːs/ *verb trans*. Long *rare* or *obsolete*. E16.
[ORIGIN French *efforcer*: see EFFORT.]
Force; compel; force open or out.

efform /ɪˈfɔːm/ *verb trans*. Now *rare*. L16.
[ORIGIN Late Latin *efformare* from Latin *formare*: see EF-, FORM *verb*[1].]
Shape, mould.

effort /ˈɛfət/ *noun*. L15.
[ORIGIN Old French & mod. French, earlier nom. *esforz*, from *esforcier* (now *efforcer*) from Proto-Romance, from Latin EF- + *fortis* strong.]
†**1** Power; (in *pl.*) properties. L15–L17.
2 Exertion or striving, physical or mental; a vigorous attempt (*at*, *to do*). L15. ▸**b** The result of any concentrated or special activity; *colloq.* an achievement, a product, anything made. M19.

A. KOESTLER With a considerable effort of will he rose . . and shuffled to the bathroom. J. RHYS I make no effort to save myself. M. KEANE Praising just a little, demanding always more effort, a higher standard of perfection. **b** A. D. SEDGWICK The Venus is an effort of Ruth's. J. D. WATSON Stepped back from the lab bench and surveyed the afternoon's effort.

3 PHYSICS. Force applied to a thing in motion along the direction of motion. M19.
■ **effortful** *adjective* exhibiting, full of, or requiring effort E20. **effortfully** *adverb* M20.

effortless /ˈɛfətlɪs/ *adjective*. E19.
[ORIGIN from EFFORT + -LESS.]
1 Making no effort; passive. *arch.* E19.
2 Not involving or requiring effort; easy. M19.
■ **effortlessly** *adverb* M19. **effortlessness** *noun* L19.

effraction /ɪˈfrakʃ(ə)n/ *noun*. *rare*. M19.
[ORIGIN French from medieval Latin *effractio(n-)*, from Latin *effract-* pa. ppl stem of *effringere*, from EF- + *frangere* break: see -ION.]
Breaking and entering, burglary.

†**effray** *verb trans*. Chiefly *Scot.* LME.
[ORIGIN French *effrayer*: see AFFRAY *verb*.]
1 Frighten; alarm. LME–E19. ▸**b** Scare off. L16–E17.
2 Be afraid of. L15–E16.

†**effronted** *adjective*. L16–L17.
[ORIGIN from French *effronté*: see EFFRONTERY, -ED[1].]
Shameless, barefaced, insolent.

effrontery /ɪˈfrʌnt(ə)ri/ *noun*. L17.
[ORIGIN French *effronterie*, from *effronté* from Proto-Romance, from late Latin *effrons* barefaced, from EF- + *front-*, *frons* forehead: see -ERY.]
Shameless audacity; insolence; cheek.

effulge /ɪˈfʌldʒ/ *verb*. *poet.* (now *rare*). E18.
[ORIGIN Latin *effulgere*: see EFFULGENT.]
1 *verb trans.* Flash out (light). E18.
2 *verb intrans.* Shine out brilliantly. M18.

effulgence /ɪˈfʌldʒ(ə)ns/ *noun*. M17.
[ORIGIN Late Latin *effulgentia*, formed as EFFULGENT: see -ENCE.]
Effulgent quality; splendid radiance.

MILTON On thee Impresst the effulgence of his Glorie abides.

effulgent /ɪˈfʌldʒ(ə)nt/ *adjective*. M18.
[ORIGIN Latin *effulgent-* pres. ppl stem of *effulgere* shine brightly, from EF- + *fulgere* shine: see -ENT.]
Shining out brilliantly; radiant; resplendent. Freq. *fig.*

effund /ɪˈfʌnd/ *verb trans*. Now *rare*. LME.
[ORIGIN Latin *effundere*, from EF- + *fundere* pour.]
Pour out (*lit.* & *fig.*).

†**effuse** *noun*. *rare*. L16–M17.
[ORIGIN from the verb.]
Effusion (of blood).

effuse /ɪˈfjuːs/ *adjective*. M16.
[ORIGIN Latin *effusus* pa. pple of *effundere* EFFUND.]
†**1** Poured out freely; overflowing; unrestrained. M16–M18.
2 CONCHOLOGY. Of a shell: having lips separated by a groove. *rare*. M19.
3 BOTANY. Of an inflorescence: spreading loosely. L19.

effuse /ɪˈfjuːz/ *verb trans*. LME.
[ORIGIN Latin *effus-* pa. ppl stem of *effundere* EFFUND.]
Pour forth or out (liquid, air, light, smell, or *fig.*); in *pass.*, be extravasated.

SHAKES. *1 Hen. VI* Maiden blood, thus rigorously effus'd Will cry for vengeance.

effusion /ɪˈfjuːʒ(ə)n/ *noun*. LME.
[ORIGIN Old French & mod. French, or Latin *effusio(n-)*, formed as EFFUSE *verb*: see -ION.]
1 A pouring forth (*lit.* & *fig.*); shedding; unrestrained utterance; effusiveness. LME. ▸**b** MEDICINE. Escape of fluid (as blood or pus) into a body cavity; accumulation of fluid in a body cavity. M18.

J. F. W. HERSCHEL The effusion of lava. F. W. FARRAR The fulfilment of Christ's promise in the effusion of His Spirit. P. CAREY He was hurt . . by Harry's lack of effusion in the greeting.

†**2** Dispersion; confused downfall. LME–E18.
3 Something poured out (*lit.* & *fig.*); *esp.* (usu. *derog.*) a literary composition or speech regarded as an outpouring of emotion etc. E17.

V. GLENDINNING Would-be poets who bothered her with their worthless effusions.

effusive /ɪˈfjuːsɪv/ *adjective*. M17.
[ORIGIN formed as EFFUSE *verb* + -IVE.]
1 Pouring out, overflowing. Chiefly *fig.* (of speech, emotion, etc.): exuberant, demonstrative. M17.

J. MCCARTHY Peel . . was not effusive; he did not pour out his emotions.

†**2** That proceeds from an outpouring. Only in 18.

POPE The floor Washed with th' effusive wave.

3 GEOLOGY. Of rock: poured out when molten and later solidified. Also, marked by outpouring of igneous rock. L19.

■ **effusively** *adverb* L19. **effusiveness** *noun* L19.

Efik /ˈɛfɪk/ *adjective & noun.* M19.
[ORIGIN Efik.]
▸ **A** *adjective.* Of, pertaining to, or designating a people of southern Nigeria closely related to the Ibibio, or their Niger-Congo language. M19.
▸ **B** *noun.* Pl. same. A member of the Efik people; the Efik language. M19.

EFL *abbreviation.*
English as a foreign language.

efreet *noun* var. of AFREET.

eft /ɛft/ *noun.* Also †**ewt**.
[ORIGIN Old English *efeta*, of unknown origin. Cf. NEWT.]
A newt. Formerly also, a lizard.

eft /ɛft/ *adverb.* Long *arch. & dial.*
[ORIGIN Old English *eft* = Old Frisian, Old Saxon *eft*, Middle Low German, Middle Dutch *echt*, Old Norse *ept*, *eft*, from Germanic base of AFTER *adverb*.]
A second time, again; moreover; afterwards.

EFTA /ˈɛftə/ *abbreviation.*
European Free Trade Association.

EFTPOS *abbreviation.*
Electronic funds transfer at point of sale.

eftsoons /ɛftˈsuːnz/ *adverb.* Also (earlier) **-soon**.
[ORIGIN Old English *eftsōna*, formed as EFT *adverb* + *sōna* SOON *adverb*: see -S³.]
†**1** A second time, again; moreover. OE–M17.
2 (Soon) afterwards. *arch. & joc.* ME.
†**3** Occasionally; repeatedly. LME–E18.

e.g. *abbreviation.*
Latin *Exempli gratia* for example.

EGA *abbreviation.*
COMPUTING. Enhanced graphics adapter.

egad /ɪˈgad/ *interjection. arch.* L17.
[ORIGIN formed as AGAD.]
Expr. amazement or emphasis.

egalitarian /ɪˌgalɪˈtɛːrɪən/ *adjective & noun.* L19.
[ORIGIN from French *égalitaire*, formed as ÉGALITÉ: see -ARIAN.]
▸ **A** *adjective.* That asserts the equality of all humankind; of, relating to, or holding the principle of equal treatment for all persons. L19.
▸ **B** *noun.* A person who holds egalitarian views. E20.
■ **egalitarianism** *noun* E20.

égalité /egalite/ *noun.* L18.
[ORIGIN French, from *égal* from Latin *aequalis* EQUAL *adjective*: see -ITY.]
= EQUALITY 2.

egality /ɪˈgalɪti/ *noun.* Long *rare.* LME.
[ORIGIN French *égalité*: see ÉGALITÉ, -ITY.]
= EQUALITY.

egall /ˈɛgal/ *adjective. obsolete* exc. *dial.* LME.
[ORIGIN Old French & mod. French *égal* from Latin *aequalis* EQUAL *adjective*.]
= EQUAL *adjective*.
■ **egally** *adverb* LME.

Egeria /ɪˈdʒɪərɪə/ *noun.* E17.
[ORIGIN A Roman goddess said to have instructed Numa Pompilius.]
A tutelary divinity; a patroness and adviser.

egest /ɪˈdʒɛst/ *verb trans.* L15.
[ORIGIN Latin *egest-* pa. ppl stem of *egerere*, from *e-* E- + *gerere* bear, carry.]
Excrete; expel from the body.

egesta /ɪˈdʒɛstə/ *noun pl.* E18.
[ORIGIN Latin, use as noun of neut. pl. of *egestus* pa. pple of *egerere*: see EGEST.]
Egested matter; excreta.

egestion /ɪˈdʒɛstʃ(ə)n/ *noun.* LME.
[ORIGIN Latin *egestio(n-)*, formed as EGEST: see -ION.]
1 The action of discharging or excreting from the body (opp. ***ingestion***). Formerly *spec.*, defecation. LME.
†**2** Egested matter; excreta. LME–L17.
■ **egestive** *adjective* of or pertaining to egestion L17.

egg /ɛg/ *noun.* ME.
[ORIGIN Old Norse: superseding cognate EY *noun*.]
1 A (more or less) spheroidal body produced by the female of birds and other animal species, containing the germ of a new individual enclosed in a shell or firm membrane. ME. ▸**b** *spec.* The egg of the domestic fowl (as an article of food). ME. ▸**c** Material from inside an egg, esp. as used in or as food. LME.

> **b** SHAKES. *1 Hen. IV* They are up already and call for eggs and butter.

c ***coddled egg***, ***devilled egg***, ***fried egg***, ***poached egg***, ***scrambled egg(s)***, etc.
2 Something resembling an egg in shape or appearance. L16. ▸**b** A bomb, a mine. *slang.* E20.
3 A person, usu. of a specified character. *colloq.* E17.

> C. MACKENZIE Oxford was divided into Bad Men and Good Eggs. *Punch* Cheerio, old egg.

4 More fully ***egg cell***. The female gamete or reproductive cell in animals or plants; an ovum. L19.
– PHRASES: ***ant eggs***, ***ants'-eggs***: see ANT *noun*. **as sure as eggs is eggs**, **as sure as eggs are eggs** *colloq.* undoubtedly. ***bad egg***: see BAD *adjective*. ***cock's egg***: see COCK *noun*¹. ***curate's egg***: see CURATE *noun*. ***duck egg***, ***duck's egg***: see DUCK *noun*¹. **egg and anchor**, **egg and dart**, **egg and tongue** ARCHITECTURE types of moulding with alternating egg-shaped and triangular figures. **egg-and-spoon race**: in which runners carry an egg in a spoon. **egg on one's face** *colloq.* a condition of looking foolish or being embarrassed or humiliated by the turn of events. **eggs and bacon** *dial.* any of several plants combining shades of yellow and orange or red in the corolla, *esp.* bird's-foot trefoil, *Lotus corniculatus*, and yellow toadflax, *Linaria vulgaris*. **have all one's eggs in one basket** risk everything on a single venture. ***lay an egg***: see LAY *verb*¹. ***nest egg***: see NEST *noun*. ***Orphic egg***: see ORPHIC *adjective* 1. ***philosophers' egg***: see PHILOSOPHER. ***Scotch egg***: see SCOTCH *adjective*. ***teach one's* GRANDMOTHER *to suck eggs***. **tread on eggs** walk warily, proceed cautiously.
– COMB.: **egg beater** (**a**) = ***egg whisk*** below; (**b**) *US slang* a helicopter; **egg-bound** *adjective* (of a hen) unable through weakness or disease to expel its eggs; **egg box**, **egg carton**: containing individual spaces for the safe carriage of eggs; **eggbutt snaffle**: with a pair of rings that are joined to the mouthpiece of the bit by a hinge (instead of rings that pass through a hole at each end of the mouthpiece); **egg case** a hollow usu. rigid protective structure secreted by various invertebrates, in which eggs develop; ***egg cell***: see sense 4 above; **egg-coddler** a device for lightly cooking an egg; ***egg cosy***: see COSY *noun* 1; **egg cream** *US* a drink composed of milk and soda water, with syrup for added flavour; **eggcup** a small cup-shaped receptacle for holding a boiled egg while it is eaten; **egg custard** a baked usu. sweetened mixture of eggs and milk; a portion of this, as a dessert; **egg dance** a dance blindfold among eggs; *fig.* an intricate or delicate activity; **egg-drop (soup)** a Chinese soup made by trailing beaten egg into a simmering meat broth; **egg-eater** a southern African snake of the genus *Dasypeltis* that eats eggs; **egg-flip** = ***egg-nog*** below; **egg flower soup** = ***egg-drop (soup)*** above; **egg-nog** a hot or cold alcoholic drink with added egg and usu. milk; **eggplant** (now chiefly *N. Amer.*) the aubergine plant (orig. the form bearing white fruit); its fruit, an aubergine; **egg-plum** a small egg-shaped yellow plum; **egg roll** a spring roll; **Egg Saturday** the Saturday before Shrove Tuesday; **egg sauce** a savoury milk-based sauce to which boiled egg has been added; **eggs Benedict** a dish consisting of poached eggs on a slice of ham on toast, with a covering of hollandaise sauce; **egg-shaped** *adjective* elongated and rounded with one end broader than the other; **egg slice** a kitchen utensil with a flat blade for lifting cooked eggs out of a pan; **egg-slicer** a kitchen utensil with parallel wires on a hinged frame for slicing hard-boiled eggs; **egg spoon** a spoon for eating boiled eggs, smaller than a teaspoon; **egg tempera** a medium for painting consisting of tempera colours mixed with egg yolk; **egg timer** a device for timing the cooking of eggs; *spec.* a sealed glass vessel with a narrow neck in the middle and containing some sand, the fall of which when the vessel is inverted occupies a known time; **egg tooth** a hard white protuberance on the beak or jaw of an embryonic bird or reptile which is used to crack the egg and is discarded after hatching; **egg whisk**: for beating eggs to a froth; **egg white** = WHITE *noun* 1; ***egg yolk***: see YOLK *noun*¹.
■ **eggery** *noun* (**a**) a collection of eggs; (**b**) an establishment for the production of eggs: M19. **eggler** *noun* (*dial.*) [perh. after *pedlar*] an egg-dealer L18. **eggless** *adjective* E20.

egg /ɛg/ *verb*¹ *trans.* ME.
[ORIGIN Old Norse *eggja* (Danish *egge*) = EDGE *verb*.]
Incite, urge; provoke, tempt. Now always foll. by *on* (*to do*, *to* an act).

> B. BAINBRIDGE I egged him on . . . It wasn't his fault.

egg /ɛg/ *verb*². L18.
[ORIGIN from the noun.]
1 *verb intrans.* Collect or go looking for birds' eggs. L18.
2 *verb trans.* Add egg to; cover with egg. M19.
3 *verb trans.* Pelt with eggs. M19.

eggar /ˈɛgə/ *noun.* Also **egger**. E18.
[ORIGIN Prob. from EGG *noun* + -ER¹.]
Any of several large brown lasiocampid moths, *esp.* (more fully ***oak eggar***) *Lasiocampa quercus*, which makes egg-shaped cocoons. Also more fully ***eggar moth***.

egger /ˈɛgə/ *noun*¹. M19.
[ORIGIN from EGG *verb*² or *noun* + -ER¹.]
A collector of birds' eggs.

egger *noun*² var. of EGGAR.

egghead /ˈɛghɛd/ *noun. colloq.* E20.
[ORIGIN from EGG *noun* + HEAD *noun*.]
A person regarded as intellectual or highbrow.
■ **eggheaded** *adjective* (**a**) having an egg-shaped head; (**b**) *colloq.* intellectual, highbrow: E20. **eggheadedness** *noun* M20.

eggshell /ˈɛgʃɛl/ *noun & adjective.* LME.
[ORIGIN from EGG *noun* + SHELL *noun*.]
▸ **A** *noun.* The thin shell or external covering of a bird's egg. LME.
walk on eggshells = ***tread on eggs*** s.v. EGG *noun*.
▸ **B** *adjective.* Having the delicacy of an eggshell; (of a paint or finish) having the slight sheen or the pale colour of a bird's egg. LME.

> DAY LEWIS A sky of egg-shell blue.

eggshell china: of extreme thinness and delicacy.
■ **eggshell-ful** *noun* as much as the shell of a hen's egg could hold LME.

eggy /ˈɛgi/ *adjective*¹. E18.
[ORIGIN from EGG *noun* + -Y¹.]
Containing an egg or eggs; rich in eggs. Also, stained with egg.

eggy /ˈɛgi/ *adjective*². *colloq. & dial.* M20.
[ORIGIN from EGG *verb*¹ + -Y¹.]
Annoyed, irritated.

†**eglantere** *noun* var. of EGLATERE.

eglantine /ˈɛgləntʌɪn/ *noun.* LME.
[ORIGIN French *églantine* from Old French *aiglent* from Proto-Romance, from (after Latin *spinulentus* thorny) Latin *acus* needle, *aculeus* prickle, sting: see -INE¹.]
Any of several hedge shrubs; *spec.* the sweet briar, *Rosa rubiginosa*. Also occas. (chiefly *dial.*), the dogrose *Rosa canina*; the honeysuckle *Lonicera periclymenum*.

E

†**eglatere** *noun.* Also (earlier) **eglantere**, **eglent-**. LME–M19.
[ORIGIN Anglo-Norman *eglanter*, Old French *aiglentier*, (also mod.) *églantier*, from *aiglent* (see EGLANTINE) + *-ier* -ER².]
Eglantine, sweet briar.

†**eglogue** *noun* var. of ECLOGUE.

églomisé /eglɔmize/ *adjective & noun.* Pl. of noun pronounced same. L19.
[ORIGIN French, from *Glomy*, 18th-cent. Parisian picture-framer.]
▸ **A** *adjective.* Of glass: decorated on the back with engraved gold or silver leaf or paint. Freq. in ***verre églomisé*** /vɛːr/ [= glass]. L19.
▸ **B** *noun.* (A panel of) *verre églomisé*. L19.

EGM *abbreviation.*
Extraordinary general meeting.

†**egma** *noun. rare* (Shakes.). Only in L16.
[ORIGIN Alt.]
An enigma.

ego /ˈiːgəʊ, ˈɛ-/ *noun.* Pl. **-os**. E19.
[ORIGIN Latin = I *pronoun*.]
1 METAPHYSICS. Oneself, the conscious thinking subject. Also *joc.* E19.
2 PSYCHOANALYSIS. That part of the mind which has a sense of individuality and is most conscious of self; *spec.* according to Freud, the part which mediates between the id and the superego and deals with external reality. L19.
3 Self-esteem, self-importance; a person's sense of this in himself or herself. L19.

> D. CARNEGIE Bores intoxicated with their own egos, drunk with a sense of their own importance.

– COMB.: **ego-ideal** (**a**) PSYCHOLOGY a part of the mind that is evolved from the ego by awareness of parental and social standards and tries to impose upon it concepts of ideal behaviour; the superego; (**b**) a person's ideal conception of himself or herself; **ego-identity** PSYCHOLOGY a person's sense of identity as gained from self-perception and others' perception of him or her; **ego-psychology** a form of psychoanalysis dealing mainly with the ego, esp. as regards its control of libidinal impulses and its understanding of the external environment; **egosurf** *verb intrans.* (*colloq.*) search the Internet for instances of one's own name or links to one's own website; **ego trip** *colloq.* an activity etc. devoted to increasing one's self-esteem; **ego-trip** *verb intrans.* (*colloq.*) indulge in an ego trip.
■ **egoless** *adjective* M20. **egolessness** *noun* L20.

egocentric /ɛgə(ʊ)ˈsɛntrɪk, iː-/ *adjective & noun.* E20.
[ORIGIN from EGO + -CENTRIC.]
▸ **A** *adjective.* Centred in the ego; self-centred, egotistical. E20.
▸ **B** *noun.* An egocentric person. M20.
■ **egocentrically** *adverb* M20. **ˌegocenˈtricity** *noun* E20. **egocentrism** *noun* E20.

egoism /ˈɛgəʊɪz(ə)m, ˈiː-/ *noun.* L18.
[ORIGIN French *égoïsme* from mod. Latin *egoismus*, from Latin EGO: see -ISM.]
1 Solipsism. *obsolete* exc. *hist.* L18.
2 **a** A selfish aim or act. L18. ▸**b** The ethical theory which regards self-interest as the foundation of morality (opp. TUISM); systematic selfishness. E19.

> **b** H. SPENCER The promptings of egoism are duly restrained by regard for others.

3 = EGOTISM 1. E19.
4 The habit of seeing matters chiefly as they concern oneself, self-centredness; self-opinionatedness. M19.

egoist /ˈɛgəʊɪst, ˈiː-/ *noun.* L18.
[ORIGIN French *égoïste*, formed as EGO: see -IST.]
1 A solipsist. *obsolete* exc. *hist.* L18.
2 A systematically selfish person; a self-centred or self-opinionated person. E19.
■ **egoˈistic** *adjective* M19. **egoˈistical** *adjective* M19. **egoˈistically** *adverb* L19.

egoity /ɪˈgəʊɪti/ *noun.* Now *rare.* M17.
[ORIGIN formed as EGO + -ITY.]
That which forms the essence of personal identity; selfhood.

E

egomania /ɛgə(ʊ)'meɪnɪə, iː-/ *noun*. E19.
[ORIGIN from EGO + -MANIA.]
Morbid egotism; obsessive self-love or self-centredness.
■ **egomaniac** *noun & adjective* (*a*) *noun* a person with egomania; (*b*) *adjective* = EGOMANIACAL: L19. ˌ**egomaˈniacal** *adjective* characteristic of or affected with egomania M20.

egotise *verb* var. of EGOTIZE.

egotism /'ɛgətɪz(ə)m, 'iː-/ *noun*. E18.
[ORIGIN formed as EGO + -ISM, with euphonic *t*.]
1 Too frequent use of first person pronouns; the practice of continually talking about oneself. E18.
2 Self-conceit; selfishness. L18.

egotist /'ɛgətɪst, 'iː-/ *noun*. E18.
[ORIGIN from EGOTISM + -IST.]
A person characterized by egotism.
■ **egoˈtistic** *adjective* M19. **egoˈtistical** *adjective* E19. **egoˈtistically** *adverb* E19.

egotize /'ɛgətʌɪz, 'iː-/ *verb intrans*. Also **-ise**. L18.
[ORIGIN from EGOT(ISM + -IZE.]
Talk or write in an egotistic way.

egregious /ɪ'griːdʒəs/ *adjective*. M16.
[ORIGIN from Latin *egregius* surpassing, illustrious, from *e-* E- + *greg-*, *grex* flock: see -IOUS.]
1 Remarkably good; outstanding, striking; distinguished, excellent. Now *rare*. M16.
2 Remarkable in a bad sense; gross, flagrant; shocking. L16.

N. PEVSNER Pages 122–3 are a masterpiece of egregious diddling. C. P. SNOW The most egregious man who had ever been awarded fifteen honorary degrees.

3 Prominent, protruding. *rare*. L16.
■ **egregiously** *adverb* M16. **egregiousness** *noun* E17.

egress /'iːgrɛs/ *noun*. M16.
[ORIGIN Latin *egressus*, from *egress-* pa. ppl stem of *egredi* go out, from *e-* E- + *gradi* proceed, step.]
1 The action of going out or coming out; the right or freedom to do this. M16.

R. RENDELL Lodged in the . . skull, egress stopped by the frontal bone, was a bullet.

2 ASTRONOMY. The end of an eclipse, occultation, or transit; emersion. M17.
3 A way out; an outlet (*lit. & fig.*). L17.

R. WEST A position from which there seemed no egress save by way of someone's pain.

egress /ɪ'grɛs/ *verb intrans*. L16.
[ORIGIN from the noun.]
Go out; issue forth.
■ **egressive** *adjective* (*a*) tending to egress; characterized by egression; (*b*) PHONETICS (of a speech sound) made with expulsion of air; (of an airflow) outward: L17.

egression /iː'grɛʃ(ə)n, ɪ-/ *noun*. LME.
[ORIGIN Latin *egressio(n-)*, from *egress-*: see EGRESS *noun*, -ION.]
1 = EGRESS *noun* 1. LME.
†**2** Emergence *from* a specified condition; a departure from the norm; an outburst. E16–M18.

egret /'iːgrɪt, 'ɛ-/ *noun*. LME.
[ORIGIN Anglo-Norman *egrette*, Old French & mod. French *aigrette* from Provençal *aigreta*, from stem of *aigron* corresp. to Old French HERON: see -ET[1].]
1 Any of several kinds of heron, mostly of the genus *Egretta*, white, and with long plumes in the breeding season. LME.
CATTLE *egret*. *great white egret*, *great egret*: see GREAT *adjective*. *snowy egret*: see SNOWY *adjective*.
†**2** = AIGRETTE. Only in M17.
3 The feathery pappus of the seed of the dandelion, thistle, etc. L18.

†**egriot** *noun* var. of AGRIOT.

egromancy /'ɛgrəmansi/ *noun*. *arch*. LME.
[ORIGIN Alt.]
Necromancy.

egurgitate /ɪ'gəːdʒɪteɪt/ *verb trans*. *rare*. M17.
[ORIGIN from REGURGITATE, with substitution of prefix: see E-.]
Vomit; *fig*. eject, utter.

egusi /ɛ'gʌsi/ *noun*. E20.
[ORIGIN Yoruba.]
Watermelon seeds, as an item of food.

Egyptian /ɪ'dʒɪpʃ(ə)n/ *adjective & noun*. ME.
[ORIGIN from *Egypt* (see below) + -IAN.]
▸ **A** *adjective*. **1** Of, pertaining to, or native to Egypt, a country in NE Africa. Also, of or pertaining to the language Egyptian (see below). ME.
2 Gypsy. *joc. rare*. M18.
3 Designating a style of lettering with no serifs and minimal variation of thickness in the strokes. Also, designating a typeface with large block serifs. E19.
– SPECIAL COLLOCATIONS: **Egyptian bean** = LABLAB. **Egyptian black** stoneware made by Wedgwood and his successors from clay stained black by added iron oxide or manganese oxide. **Egyptian days** (*obsolete* exc. *hist.*) the 24 evil or unlucky days of the medieval calendar. **Egyptian goose** an African sheldgoose, *Alopochen aegyptiacus*, that has been introduced into Britain. **Egyptian lily** the arum lily, *Zantedeschia aethiopica*. **Egyptian lotus** either of two water lilies, the blue-flowered *Nymphaea caerulea* and the white-flowered *N. lotus*, regarded as sacred in ancient Egypt. **Egyptian onion** a form of tree onion. **Egyptian plover** = *crocodile bird* s.v. CROCODILE *noun*. **Egyptian vulture** a black and white vulture, *Neophron percnopterus*. **Egyptian wheel** = NORIA.
▸ **B** *noun*. **1** A native or inhabitant of Egypt. ME.
2 A Gypsy. *arch*. E16.
3 The Hamito-Semitic language used in Egypt until the 3rd cent. AD. M16.
4 Egyptian lettering or type. M19.
5 An Egyptian cigarette. L19.
■ **Egyptianism** *noun* Egyptian characteristics, inclination to Egyptian ways E19. **Egyptianiˈzation** *noun* the action of Egyptianizing something M20. **Egyptianize** *verb* †(*a*) *verb intrans*. behave like an Egyptian; (*b*) *verb trans*. make like Egypt or an Egyptian; *spec*. (*hist.*, of the Egyptian Government) transfer into Egyptian hands (property or interests in the hands of non-Egyptians): M17.

Egypticity /iːdʒɪp'tɪsɪti/ *noun*. L19.
[ORIGIN from *Egypt* (see EGYPTIAN) + -ICITY.]
The character or quality of being Egyptian.

Egyptizing /'iːdʒɪptʌɪzɪŋ/ *ppl adjective*. Also **-ising**. M19.
[ORIGIN from *Egypt* (see EGYPTIAN) + -IZE + -ING[2].]
Becoming Egyptian in character.

Egypto- /ɪ'dʒɪptəʊ/ *combining form*. M19.
[ORIGIN from Greek *Aiguptos* Egypt: see -O-.]
Used in senses 'Egyptian and —', as ***Egypto-Arabic*** etc.; 'Egypt', as ***Egyptomania*** etc.

Egyptology /iːdʒɪp'tɒlədʒi/ *noun*. M19.
[ORIGIN from *Egypt* (see EGYPTIAN) + -OLOGY.]
The branch of archaeology that deals with Egyptian antiquities.
■ **Eˌgyptoˈlogical** *adjective* M19. **Egyptologist** *noun* M19.

eh /eɪ/ *interjection*. M16.
[ORIGIN Natural exclam. Cf. EIGH, earlier AY *interjection*[2].]
†**1** Expr. sorrow. Only in M16.
2 *interrog*. Inviting assent or conveying emphasis. *colloq*. L18.

J. M. SYNGE You want someone to look after you eh?

3 *interrog*. Expr. a request for the repetition or clarification of something just said. *colloq*. M19.

T. BACON Eh? What's that, Sackville?

eicos- /'ʌɪkɒs/ *combining form*. Also **eicosa-** /'ʌɪkɒsə/, **eicosi-** /'ʌɪkɒsi/.
[ORIGIN formed as ICOS-.]
Orig. = ICOS-. Now *spec*. in CHEMISTRY, forming names of compounds or radicals containing twenty atoms of an element, usu. carbon.
■ **eicosapentaeˈnoic eicosapenteˈnoic** *adjective*: ***eicosapentaenoic acid***, ***eicosapentenoic acid***, a polyunsaturated fatty acid, $C_{19}H_{29}COOH$, which is present in fish oils and is a metabolic precursor of prostaglandins in humans M20. **eicoseˈnoic** *adjective*: ***eicosenoic acid***, an unsaturated fatty acid, $C_{19}H_{37}COOH$, which is present in fish oils and the wax of some plant seeds M20.

†**eicosahedron** *noun* var. of ICOSAHEDRON.

eicosane /'ʌɪkɒseɪn/ *noun*. Also **icos-**. L19.
[ORIGIN from EICOS- + -ANE.]
CHEMISTRY. Any saturated hydrocarbon having the formula $C_{20}H_{42}$, of which there are many isomers; *spec*. the normal straight-chain isomer.
■ **eicosaˈnoic** *adjective* = ARACHIDIC E20. **eiˈcosanoid** *noun* any of a group of biologically active compounds with the same carbon skeleton as eicosane, *esp*. one of those occurring as metabolites of certain fatty acids L20.

Eid /iːd/ *noun*. Also **Id**. L17.
A Muslim feast day:
Eid ul-Adha /ʊlə'dɑː/, **Eid ul-Azha** /ʊlə'zɑː/, the feast marking the culmination of the annual pilgrimage to Mecca (also called ***Greater Bairam***). **Eid ul-Fitr** /ʊl'fɪtrə/, **Eid al-Fitr** /al-/, the feast marking the end of the Ramadan fast (also called ***Lesser Bairam***).

eident /'ʌɪd(ə)nt/ *adjective*. *Scot*. Also **-ant**, **id-**. ME.
[ORIGIN Old Norse *iðinn* with assim. to pres. pples in *-and*.]
1 Industrious, diligent; conscientious, attentive. ME.
2 Continual, persistent. ME.
■ **eidently** *adverb* ME.

eider /'ʌɪdə/ *noun*. L17.
[ORIGIN Icelandic *æður* genit. *æðar* in *æðarfugl* eider duck from Old Norse *æðr*. See also EIDERDOWN.]
1 Any large northern sea duck of the genera *Somateria* and *Polysticta*; spec. *S. mollissima*, the male of which is largely black and white and the female dull brown, and which is the source of eider down. Also ***eider duck***. L17.
king eider an Arctic eider, *Somateria spectabilis*, distinguished by the orange bill and frontal shield of the male.
2 = EIDERDOWN 1. M18.

eiderdown /'ʌɪdədaʊn/ *noun*. Also **eider-down** (the usual form in sense 1). M18.
[ORIGIN Icelandic *æðardúnn*, formed as EIDER, DOWN *noun*[2].]
1 The soft feathers from the breast of the eider *Somateria mollissima*, with which it lines its nest. M18.
2 A quilt filled with this or with another soft material. L19.
3 A thick soft heavily napped fabric. L19.

eidetic /ʌɪ'dɛtɪk/ *adjective & noun*. E20.
[ORIGIN from Greek *eidētikos*, from *eidos* form: see -ETIC.]
PSYCHOLOGY. ▸ **A** *adjective*. Of, pertaining to, or designating a recollected mental image having unusual vividness and detail, as if actually visible; (of a person) capable of perceiving such images. E20.
▸ **B** *noun*. A person able to perceive eidetic images. E20.
■ **eidetically** *adverb* E20. **eidetiker** /ʌɪ'dɛtɪkə/ *noun* [German] a person with the faculty of seeing eidetic images L20.

eidolon /ʌɪ'dəʊlɒn/ *noun*. Pl. **-la** /-lə/, **-lons**. M17.
[ORIGIN Greek *eidōlon*: see IDOL.]
†**1** An emanation considered by atomic philosophers to constitute the visible image of an object. *rare*. Only in M17.
2 A spectre, a phantom. Also, an idealized image. E19.

E. A. POE An Eidolon named Night On a black throne. M. RENAULT She was the perennial *eidolon*, the clean pampered harlot.

Eidophusikon /ʌɪdə(ʊ)'fjuːzɪkɒn/ *noun*. *obsolete* exc. *hist*. Also **-con**. L18.
[ORIGIN from Greek *eidos* form + *phusikon* neut. of *phusikos* natural, from *phusis* nature.]
A kind of lantern depicting natural scenes and phenomena.

†**eidouranion** *noun*. L18–E19.
[ORIGIN formed as EIDOPHUSIKON + *ouranos* heaven.]
A mechanical device that represented the motions of celestial objects.

eigen- /'ʌɪgən/ *combining form*.
[ORIGIN German *eigen* OWN *adjective*.]
Used in MATH. & PHYSICS with general sense 'characteristic, proper', orig. in compounds adopted from German with translating of the second elem. only.
■ **eigenfrequency** *noun* any of the resonant frequencies of a system M20. **eigenfunction** *noun* each of a set of independent functions which are the solutions to a given differential equation E20. **eigenstate** *noun* a quantum-mechanical state corresponding to an eigenvalue of a wave equation M20. **eigentone** *noun* a frequency at which acoustic resonance occurs in a given enclosed space M20. **eigenvalue** *noun* (*a*) each of a set of values of a parameter for which a differential equation has a non-zero solution (an eigenfunction) under given conditions; (*b*) any of the numbers such that a given matrix minus that number times the identity matrix has zero determinant: E20. **eigenvector** *noun* a vector which when operated on by a given operator gives a scalar multiple of that vector M20.

eigh /eɪ/ *interjection*. *dial*. M18.
[ORIGIN Natural exclam.: cf. EH.]
Expr. surprise or affirmation.

eight /eɪt/ *adjective & noun* (*cardinal numeral*).
[ORIGIN Old English *ehta* (*eahta*, *ahta*) = Old Frisian *achta*, *acht(e)*, Old Saxon, Old High German *ahto* (Dutch, German *acht*), Old Norse *átta*, Gothic *ahtau*, from Germanic from Indo-European, whence also Latin *octo*, Greek *oktō*, Sanskrit *aṣṭā*.]
▸ **A** *adjective*. One more than seven (a cardinal numeral represented by 8 in arabic numerals, viii, VIII in roman). OE.

E. O'NEILL A small, square compartment about eight feet high. A. J. P. TAYLOR Trade union membership reached a peak of over eight million. W. BOYD One of eight hotels in Nairobi. *Financial Times* The amendment . . gives shareholders a majority (eight-fifteenths) of the seats.

an eight days, **eight days** *arch*. a week.
▸ **B** *noun*. **1** Eight persons or things identified contextually, as parts or divisions, years of age, points, runs, etc., in a game, chances (in giving odds), minutes, inches, shillings (now *hist.*), pence, etc. OE.

TENNYSON Eight that were left to make a purer world. DAY LEWIS I had had diphtheria at the age of eight or nine.

piece of eight [*sc.* reals], **real of eight** *hist*. a Spanish dollar.
2 One more than seven as an abstract number; the symbol(s) or figure(s) representing this (8 in arabic numerals, viii, VIII in roman); (more fully ***figure of eight***) a figure shaped like 8, esp. in ice skating. OE.
lazy eight: see LAZY *adjective*.
3 The time of day eight hours after midnight or midday (on a clock, watch, etc., indicated by the numeral eight displayed or pointed to). Also ***eight o'clock***. LME.

R. MAUGHAM I'm at work from eight in the morning.

4 The eighth of a set or series with numbered members, the one designated eight, (usu. ***number eight***, or with specification, as ***book eight***, ***chapter eight***, etc.); a size etc. denoted by eight, a shoe, glove, garment, etc., of such a size, (also ***size eight***). E16.

A. AYCKBOURN My slippers are eights.

factor eight: see FACTOR *noun* 7c. **one over the eight** *slang* (*a*) *noun* one alcoholic drink too many; (*b*) *adjective* slightly drunk.
5 A set of eight; a thing having a set of eight as an essential or distinguishing feature; *spec*. (*a*) a playing card marked with eight pips or spots; (*b*) a crew of eight in a rowing boat; in *pl.*, boat races (esp. at Oxford) between such crews; (*c*) an eight-oared boat; (*d*) in *pl.*, eight leaves to the sheet in a printed book, octavo; (*e*) a line or verse with eight syllables; (*f*) an engine or motor vehicle with eight cylinders. L16.
middle eight: see MIDDLE *adjective*. ***V-eight***: see V, V 2.

6 Each of a set of eight; *spec.* a large plant pot of which eight are formed from one cast of clay. E19.
– COMB.: Forming compound cardinal numerals with multiples of ten from twenty to ninety, as ***thirty-eight***, (arch.) ***eight-and-thirty***, etc., and (arch.) their corresponding ordinals, as ***eight-and-thirtieth*** etc., and with multiples of a hundred, as **208** (read ***two hundred and eight***, US also ***two hundred eight***), **5008** (read ***five thousand and eight***, US also ***five thousand eight***), etc. With nouns + -ER[1] forming nouns with the sense 'something (identified contextually) being of or having eight —s', as ***eight-seater***, ***eight-wheeler***, etc. Special combs., as **eight ball** *N. Amer.* (the black ball, numbered eight, in) a variety of the game of pool; ***behind the eight ball***, at a disadvantage, baffled; **eight-day clock** a clock that goes for eight days without being wound up; **eightpence** eight pence, esp. of the old British currency before decimalization; **eightpenny** *adjective* worth or costing eightpence; **eight-pounder** a gun throwing a shot that weighs eight pounds; **eight-square** *adjective & adverb* [after *four-square*] in the form of a regular octagon, with eight equal sides.
■ **eightfold** *adjective & adverb* (***a***) *adjective* eight times as great or as numerous; having eight parts, divisions, elements, or units; (***eightfold path***, the Buddhist path to nirvana, comprising eight aspects in which an aspirant must become practised; ***eightfold way*** (Physics), the grouping of hadrons into supermultiplets by means of SU(3)); (***b***) *adverb* to eight times the number or quantity: OE.

eighteen /eɪˈtiːn, ˈeɪtiːn/ *adjective & noun (cardinal numeral)*.
[ORIGIN Old English *e(a)htatēne* = Old Frisian *achtatīne*, Old Saxon *ahtotian* (Dutch *achttien*), Old High German *ahtozehan* (German *achtzehn*), Old Norse *átján*, from Germanic base of EIGHT, -TEEN.]
▸ **A** *adjective*. One more than seventeen (a cardinal numeral represented by 18 in arabic numerals, xviii, XVIII in roman). OE.

SIR W. SCOTT About eighteen years since.

▸ **B** *noun*. **1** Eighteen persons or things identified contextually, as years of age, chances (in giving odds), minutes, shillings (now *hist.*), pence, etc. OE.

D. H. LAWRENCE Our boys must stay at school till they are eighteen. A. J. P. TAYLOR Though 140 Labour M.P.s elected in 1929 belonged to the I.L.P., only eighteen pledged themselves to support its policy.

2 One more than seventeen as an abstract number; the symbols or figures representing this (18 in arabic numerals, xviii, XVIII in roman). LME.
3 The eighteenth of a set or series with numbered members, the one designated eighteen, (usu. ***number eighteen***, or with specification, as ***book eighteen***, ***chapter eighteen***, etc.); a size etc. denoted by eighteen, a garment etc. of such a size, (also ***size eighteen***). E16.
4 A set of eighteen; a thing having a set of eighteen as an essential or distinguishing feature; *spec.* (***a***) in *pl.*, eighteen leaves to the sheet in a printed book, octodecimo; (***b***) a team of eighteen in Australian Rules football. L17.
– COMB.: Forming compound numerals with multiples of a hundred, as **518** (read ***five hundred and eighteen***, US also ***five hundred eighteen***), **5018** (read ***five thousand and eighteen***, US also ***five thousand eighteen***), etc. In dates used for one thousand eight hundred, as **1812** (read ***eighteen twelve***), ***eighteen-nineties***, etc. With nouns + -ER[1] forming nouns with the sense 'something (identified contextually) being of or having eighteen —s', as ***eighteen-tonner***, ***eighteen-wheeler***, etc. Special combs., as **eighteen-pounder** a gun throwing a shot that weighs eighteen pounds.
■ **eighteenmo** *noun*, pl. **-os**, octodecimo E19.

eighteenth /eɪˈtiːnθ, ˈeɪtiːnθ/ *adjective & noun (ordinal numeral)*.
[ORIGIN Old English *e(a)htotēoþa*, repl. in Middle English by forms from EIGHTEEN + -TH[2]. Cf. Old Frisian *ahtatinda*, *ahtendesta*, *achtiensta*, Old Norse *átjándi*.]
▸ **A** *adjective*. Next in order after the seventeenth, that is number eighteen in a series, (represented by 18th). OE.

ALDOUS HUXLEY In the eighteenth century, when logic and science were the fashion. W. FAULKNER His eighteenth birthday and legal age for joining up.

▸ **B** *noun*. **1** The eighteenth person or thing of a category, series, etc., identified contextually, as day of the month, (following a proper name) person, esp. monarch or pope, of the specified name, etc. OE.

LONGFELLOW On the eighteenth of April, in Seventy-five.

2 *MUSIC*. An interval embracing eighteen notes on the diatonic scale; a note an eighteenth above another given note; a chord of two notes an eighteenth apart. L19.
– COMB.: Forming compound ordinal numerals with multiples of a hundred, as ***three-hundred-and-eighteenth*** (**318th**), ***five-thousand-and-eighteenth*** (**5018th**), etc.
■ **eighteenthly** *adverb* in the eighteenth place L17.

eighth /eɪtθ/ *adjective & noun (ordinal numeral)*.
[ORIGIN Old English *e(a)htoþa* = Old Frisian *achte*, Old High German *ahtodo* (German *achte*), from Germanic, from base of EIGHT, -TH[2].]
▸ **A** *adjective*. Next in order after the seventh, that is number eight in a series, (represented by 8th). OE.

S. KUNITZ Doomsday is the eighth day of the week.

eighth note *MUSIC* (*N. Amer.*) a quaver. **eighth part** *arch.* = sense B.3 below. ***eighth wonder of the world***: see WONDER *noun*.
▸ **B** *noun*. **1** The eighth person or thing of a category, series, etc., identified contextually, as day of the month, (following a proper name) person, esp. monarch or pope, of the specified name, etc. OE.

JOYCE An animated altercation . . as to whether the eighth or the ninth of March was the correct date of the birth of Ireland's patron saint. R. BOLT Our Sovereign Lord, Harry, . . The Eighth of that name.

†**2** *MUSIC*. An octave; a note an octave above another given note. LME–E18.
3 Each of eight equal parts into which something is or may be divided, a fraction which when multiplied by eight gives one, (= ***eighth part*** above). M16.

Economist Five-eighths of our income is going to be spent for us by the state.

– COMB.: Forming compound ordinal numerals with multiples of ten, as ***forty-eighth*** (***48th***), ***five-thousand-and-eighth*** (***5008th***), etc.
■ **eighthly** *adverb* in the eighth place L16.

eightieth /ˈeɪtɪɪθ/ *adjective & noun (ordinal numeral)*. LME.
[ORIGIN from EIGHTY + -TH[2].]
1 *adjective & noun* (The person or thing) next in order after the seventy-ninth, that is number eighty in a series, (represented by 80th). LME.
2 *noun*. Each of eighty equal parts into which something is or may be divided, a fraction which when multiplied by eighty gives one. M19.
– COMB.: Forming compound numerals with multiples of a hundred, as ***two-hundred-and-eightieth*** (**280th**), ***five-thousand-and-eightieth*** (**5080th**), etc., and (arch.) with numerals below ten, as ***five-and-eightieth*** etc.

eightsome /ˈeɪts(ə)m/ *pronoun, noun, & adjective*. ME.
[ORIGIN from EIGHT + -SOME[2].]
▸ **A** *pronoun & noun*. **1** Formerly, eight in all. Now, a group of eight. Chiefly *Scot.* ME.
†**2** One of eight. LME–M16.
3 *ellipt.* An eightsome reel. E20.
▸ **B** *attrib.* or as *adjective*. For eight; *esp.* (of a dance) performed by eight people together. M16.

eighty /ˈeɪti/ *adjective & noun (cardinal numeral)*.
[ORIGIN Old English *hunde(a)htatig*, from *hund* of uncertain origin + *e(a)hta* EIGHT + *-tig* -TY[2]. 1st elem. lost early in Middle English (cf. SEVENTY).]
▸ **A** *adjective*. Eight times ten (a cardinal numeral represented by 80 in arabic numerals, lxxx, LXXX in roman). OE.
▸ **B** *noun*. **1** Eighty persons or things identified contextually, as years of age, points, runs, etc., in a game, chances (in giving odds), etc. OE.

SCOTT FITZGERALD A . . bungalow at eighty a month. W. FAULKNER He would live to be eighty.

2 Eight times ten as an abstract number; the symbols or figures representing this (80 in arabic numerals, lxxx, LXXX in roman). LME.
3 The eightieth of a set or series with numbered members, the one designated eighty, (usu. ***number eighty***, or with specification, as ***chapter eighty***, ***verse eighty***, etc.); a size etc. denoted by eighty (also ***size eighty***). E16.
4 Any of a set of eighty; *spec.* a small plant pot of which eighty are formed from one cast of clay. E19.
5 In *pl.* The numbers from 80 to 89 inclusive, esp. denoting years of a century or units of a scale of temperature; *one's* years of life between the ages of 80 and 89. L19.

E. O'NEILL The rural taste for grandeur in the eighties.

– COMB.: Forming compound numerals (cardinal or ordinal) with numerals below ten, as ***eighty-nine***, (arch.) ***nine-and-eighty***, (**89**), ***eighty-first*** (**81st**), etc., and (cardinals) with multiples of a hundred, as **380** (read ***three hundred and eighty***, US also ***three hundred eighty***), **5080** (***five thousand and eighty***, US also ***five thousand eighty***), etc. Special combs., as **eighty-six** *noun & verb* (*US slang*) (***a***) *noun* an item on a menu that is not available; a customer who is not to be served; (***b***) *verb trans.* bar or eject (a person) from a place; reject, abandon.

eigne /eɪn/ *noun & adjective*. Formerly also †**ayne**. LME.
[ORIGIN Old French *ainz né* (mod. *aîné*) earlier born.]
▸ †**A** *noun*. In *pl.* Elders. Only in LME.
▸ **B** *adjective*. *LAW* (now *hist.*). Firstborn, eldest. Usu. *postpositive*. L15.

eik *noun, verb* see EKE *noun, verb*.

eikonal /ˈʌɪkən(ə)l, ʌɪˈkəʊn(ə)l/ *noun & adjective*. E20.
[ORIGIN from Greek *eikōn* image + -AL[1].]
PHYSICS. ▸ **A** *noun*. The optical path length of a ray between specified points. Also, the time taken for a wavefront to reach a specified point. E20.
▸ **B** *adjective*. **1** Designating an expression that gives the eikonal in terms of the wave velocity. M20.
2 Designating a method of approximately representing the behaviour of particles by means of eikonals. M20.

eild /iːld/ *adjective*. *Scot.* E18.
[ORIGIN Prob. var. of YELD *adjective*.]
Of a cow or other animal: not yielding milk; barren.

-ein /iːn, ɪn/ *suffix*.
Var. of -IN[1], used in names of some chemical compounds, as ***fluorescein***, ***phenolphthalein***.

-eine /iːɪn, iːn/ *suffix*.
Var. of -INE[5], used in names of some chemical compounds, as ***cysteine***.

Einfühlung /ˈaɪnfyːlʊŋ, ˈʌɪnfuːləŋ/ *noun*. E20.
[ORIGIN German, from *ein-* into + *Fühlung* feeling, from *fühlen* FEEL *verb*.]
Empathy.

einkorn /ˈʌɪnkɔːn/ *noun*. E20.
[ORIGIN German, from *ein* one + *Korn* CORN *noun*[1], seed.]
An inferior kind of diploid wheat, *Triticum monococcum*, with one-grained spikelets that was eaten in prehistoric times but is now grown only as fodder, in parts of Europe.

Einstein /ˈʌɪnstʌɪn/ *noun*. E20.
[ORIGIN See EINSTEINIAN.]
1 ***Einstein effect***, ***Einstein shift***, the lengthening of the wavelength of radiation as a result of its passage through a strong gravitational field. E20.
2 (**e-**.) A unit of quantity of light, equal to Avogadro's number of photons. M20.
– COMB.: **Einstein–Bose statistics** = BOSE–EINSTEIN STATISTICS.

Einsteinian /ʌɪnˈstʌɪnɪən/ *adjective*. E20.
[ORIGIN from *Einstein* (see below) + -IAN.]
Of, pertaining to, or characteristic of the German-born US physicist Albert Einstein (1879–1955) or his theories.

einsteinium /ʌɪnˈstʌɪnɪəm/ *noun*. M20.
[ORIGIN formed as EINSTEINIAN + -IUM.]
A radioactive metallic chemical element of the actinide series, atomic no. 99, which is produced artificially (symbol Es).

eirenic, **eirenical** *adjectives* vars. of IRENIC, IRENICAL.

eirenicon /ʌɪˈriːnɪkɒn/ *noun*. Also (earlier) **iren-**. E17.
[ORIGIN Greek *eirēnikon* neut. sing. of *eirēnikos* IRENIC.]
A conciliatory proposal, an attempt to make peace, esp. in a Church or between Churches.

eisegesis /ʌɪsɪˈdʒiːsɪs/ *noun*. L19.
[ORIGIN Greek *eisēgēsis* a bringing in, from *eisēgeisthai* introduce, from *eis* in + *ēgeisthai* to guide.]
The interpretation of a (scriptural) text in a way that is biased by one's own ideas.
■ **eisegetical** *adjective* L19.

†**eisel** *noun*. ME–M17.
[ORIGIN Old French *aisil* from Latin *acetum*, with unexpl. ending.]
Vinegar.

Eisenhower jacket /ˈʌɪz(ə)nhaʊə ˌdʒakɪt/ *noun phr.* M20.
[ORIGIN Dwight D. *Eisenhower* (1890–1969), US soldier and President.]
A US military uniform jacket; a short jacket resembling this.

eisteddfod /ʌɪˈstɛðvɒd, ʌɪˈstɛdvəd/ *noun*. Pl. **-fods**, **-fodau** /-vɒdʌɪ/. E19.
[ORIGIN Welsh = session, from *eistedd* sit.]
A congress of Welsh bards; a national or local gathering (in Wales, or in other places with a strong Welsh influence) for competitions of literature, music, folk dance, etc.; *spec.* (**E-**, in full ***Royal National Eisteddfod***) an annual national gathering of this kind.
■ **Eisteddfodic** /ʌɪstɛðˈvɒdɪk/ *adjective* L19.

Eiswein /ˈaɪsvaɪn/ *noun*. M20.
[ORIGIN German, from *Eis* ICE *noun* + *Wein* WINE *noun*.]
Wine made from ripe grapes picked while covered with frost.

eis wool /ˈʌɪs wʊl/ *noun phr.* L19.
[ORIGIN from German *Eis* ICE *noun* + WOOL *noun*.]
A fine glossy type of wool used for scarfs, shawls, etc. Also called ***ice-wool***.

eith *adjective & adverb* see EATH.

either /ˈʌɪðə, ˈiː-/ *adjective* (in mod. usage also classed as a *determiner*), *pronoun*, *adverb*, *& conjunction*.
[ORIGIN Old English *ǣġþer* contr. form of *ǣġ(e)hwæþer* = Old Frisian *ēider*, Middle Low German, Middle Dutch *ed(d)er* (as adverb), Old High German *eogihwedar* (Middle High German *iegeweder*), from Germanic phr. from bases of AYE *adverb*[1], WHETHER *adjective*, etc.]
▸ **A** *adjective*. **1** Each — of two. Occas., each — of more than two. OE. ▸†**b** Both. Also ***either both***. M16–E17.

E. WAUGH Dame Mildred and Miss Tin sat on either side of the Emperor. S. BELLOW He had a cup of coffee in either hand. B. BAINBRIDGE He had lived in Dublin and Paris and London and had been equally at home in either capital.

2 One or other — of two. Occas., any one — of more than two. ME.

J. S. LE FANU Her watch . . being seldom more than twenty minutes wrong, either way. J. STEINBECK In either case it was none of their business.

▸ **B** *pronoun*. **1** Each of two. (Foll. by *of*: with sing. & †pl. concord.) OE. ▸**b** Each of more than two. (Foll. by *of*.) L16.

SPENSER So parted they, as eithers way them led. G. GREENE If an English election is less complex than an American, a Haitian is simpler than either. **b** W. D. HOWELLS Just above the feet, at either of the three corners.

2 One or other of two. (Foll. by *of*: with sing. & (*colloq.*) pl. concord.) M16. ▸**b** Any one of more than two. (Foll. by *of*.) E17.

E

J. RUSKIN I don't mean that either of the writers I name are absolutely thus narrow in their own views. H. JAMES It was impossible to make out from the countenance of either whether a sound had passed between them. SCOTT FITZGERALD Either of them had only to mention the word 'mortifying' to send them both into riotous gasps. **b** T. HARDY 'Did you walk in through Giant's Ear, or Goblin's Cellar, or Grim Billy?' 'We did not enter by either of these.'

▸ **C** *adverb & conjunction*. †**1** Both — *and*. OE–ME.
2 Followed by coordinate *or*, †*other*, †*either*, (in neg. contexts, *colloq.*) *nor*: as one supposition or equally possible alternative; as one of mutually exclusive possibilities. LME.

B. JOWETT A narration of events, either past, present, or to come. J. MITCHELL The signatories hoped that the Ngulu would not suffer, either directly or indirectly, by the withdrawal of British rule. J. BERGER She . . either had to lean back . . . or else stare at his watch-chain. *New York Times* Personally I don't think either Moscow or Washington are going to play any major role. N. ALGREN Without either taking the hand nor lowering his left.

E

†**3** Or. LME–E17.
4 Following *or*: as an alternative; in addition. *arch.* LME.
5 In neg. & interrog. contexts: any more than the other; likewise; moreover. In hypothetical & conditional contexts: for that matter. E19.

J. CONRAD She was a good ship . . and not old either. E. WAUGH He can't bear it and he's not much use at it either. M. AMIS You don't agree? I don't agree either.

– COMB.: **either/or** *noun & adjective* (involving) an unavoidable choice between alternatives.

eiusdem generis *adverbial & adjectival phr.* var. of EJUSDEM GENERIS.

ejaculate /ɪˈdʒakjʊlət/ *noun*. E20.
[ORIGIN from the verb: see -ATE².]
Ejaculated semen; a quantity of semen ejaculated at one time.

ejaculate /ɪˈdʒakjʊleɪt/ *verb*. L16.
[ORIGIN Latin *ejaculat-* pa. ppl stem of *ejaculari*, from *e-* E- + *jaculari* to dart, from *jaculum* dart, javelin, from *jacere* to throw: see -ATE³.]
1 a *verb trans.* Forcefully eject (semen) on achieving orgasm; suddenly eject (any matter) from the human, animal, or plant body. L16. ▸**b** *verb intrans.* Ejaculate semen on achieving orgasm. L19.
†**2** *verb trans.* **a** Throw or shoot out suddenly and quickly. E17–M18. ▸**b** Give off, emit. M17–M19.
3 *verb trans.* Say suddenly or quickly, esp. with feeling. M17.

J. G. FARRELL 'Pure reason!' ejaculated the Magistrate.

■ **ejaculative** /-lətɪv/ *adjective* of the nature of an ejaculation; pertaining to ejaculation: M17. **ejaculator** *noun* a muscle that brings about ejaculation of semen; a person who ejaculates: E18.

ejaculation /ɪˌdʒakjʊˈleɪʃ(ə)n/ *noun*. E17.
[ORIGIN French *éjaculation*, from *éjaculer* from Latin *ejaculari*: see EJACULATE *verb*, -ATION.]
1 The action or an act of ejaculating matter from the body etc.; *spec.* the discharge of semen during orgasm. E17.

J. L. HARPER Where a seed is dispersed by ejaculation from a capsule.

premature ejaculation ejaculation of semen during sexual intercourse before penetration or immediately after it.
†**2** The action or an act of throwing, throwing up, or shooting out; emission of radiation. E17–E19.
3 Something that is ejaculated; *esp.* a short prayer hastily made; a sudden expression of emotion. E17.

CONAN DOYLE Cunning questions and ejaculations of wonder.

4 The action of saying something suddenly and with feeling. M17.

ejaculatio praecox /ɪdʒakjʊˌleɪʃɪəʊ ˈpriːkɒks/ *noun phr.* L19.
[ORIGIN mod. Latin, from Latin *ejaculat-* (see EJACULATE *verb*) + *praecox* premature: see PRECOCIOUS.]
Premature ejaculation.

ejaculatory /ɪˈdʒakjʊlət(ə)ri/ *adjective*. M17.
[ORIGIN from EJACULATE *verb* + -ORY².]
1 Of the nature of or resembling a spoken ejaculation. M17.
2 Involved with ejaculation, esp. of semen. M17.
ejaculatory duct: carrying semen to the urethra from where the vas deferens joins the excretory duct of the seminal vesicle.

eject /ˈiːdʒɛkt/ *noun*. L19.
[ORIGIN Latin *ejectum* neut. pa. pple of *e(j)icere* (see EJECT *verb*), after *subject*, *object*.]
A mental state or a sensation that cannot be an object of one's own consciousness but is inferred to exist.

eject /ɪˈdʒɛkt/ *verb*. LME.
[ORIGIN Latin *eject-* pa. ppl stem of *e(j)icere*, from *e-* E- + *jacere* to throw.]
1 *verb trans.* Throw out (material, an object) from within; cause to be thrown out; discharge forcefully or violently. LME.

C. LYELL If stones are thrown into the Crater they are instantly ejected. J. WYNDHAM I ejected the two spent cartridge cases, and reloaded.

2 *verb trans.* Drive out from or *from* a place by force or with indignity. LME.

M. MEYER The little kingdoms . . had risen against and ejected their tyrants. D. M. DAVIN I had to eject from the pub a drunk and troublesome Canadian soldier.

3 *verb trans.* Expel (a person) from or *from* a position or office; dispossess (an occupier) by legal means. LME.
4 *verb trans. fig.* Emit, give out. L16.
5 *verb intrans.* Leave an aircraft or spacecraft as an emergency procedure; bale out. M20.
– COMB.: **eject button**: that is pressed in order to eject a cassette or disc from a machine.

ejecta /ɪˈdʒɛktə/ *noun pl.* (treated as *pl.* or *sing.*). L19.
[ORIGIN Latin, neut. pl. of pa. pple of *e(j)icere* EJECT *verb*.]
1 Matter that is thrown out of a volcano or a star. L19.
2 Material discharged from the body, *esp.* vomit. L19.

ejectamenta /ɪˌdʒɛktəˈmɛntə/ *noun pl.* M19.
[ORIGIN Latin, pl. of *ejectamentum*, from *ejectare* frequentative of *e(j)icere* EJECT *verb*: see -MENT.]
= EJECTA 1.

ejection /ɪˈdʒɛkʃ(ə)n/ *noun*. LME.
[ORIGIN Old French & mod. French *éjection* or Latin *ejectio(n-)*, formed as EJECT *verb*: see -ION.]
1 The action or an act of ejecting something or someone. LME. ▸**b** An emergency procedure in which a pilot is catapulted out of and away from an aircraft. M20.
2 Something that has been ejected. M17.
– COMB.: **ejection seat** an aircraft pilot's seat that can be caused to eject its occupant.

ejective /ɪˈdʒɛktɪv/ *adjective & noun*. M17.
[ORIGIN from EJECT *verb* + -IVE.]
▸ **A** *adjective*. **1** Having the function or power of ejecting. M17.
2 PHONETICS. Of a consonant: not pulmonic, but articulated by closing the glottis, so as to produce a compression of air which is then forcefully released. M20.
▸ **B** *noun*. PHONETICS. An ejective consonant. M20.

ejectment /ɪˈdʒɛktm(ə)nt/ *noun*. Chiefly *hist.* E16.
[ORIGIN Law French *ejectement*, from French *éjecter* formed as EJECT *verb*: see -MENT.]
1 (An) ejection of a person from a place or office, *spec.* (LAW) of a tenant or occupier from property. E16.
2 LAW (now *hist.*). An action in which a person ejected from property seeks to recover possession and damages. L17.

ejector /ɪˈdʒɛktə/ *noun*. M17.
[ORIGIN from EJECT *verb* + -OR.]
1 A person who ejects someone, *spec.* (LAW) a tenant or occupier from property. M17.
2 An appliance or part that serves to eject something, e.g. a cartridge from a gun. L19.
– COMB.: **ejector seat** = EJECTION *seat*.

ejido /eˈxiðo, eɪˈhiːdəʊ/ *noun*. Pl. **-os** /-ɔs, -əʊz/. L19.
[ORIGIN Mexican Spanish from Spanish = common land (on the road leading out of a village) from Latin EXITUS.]
In Mexico: a cooperative farm; a piece of land farmed communally.
■ **ejidal** *adjective* /exiˈðal, eɪˈhiːd(ə)l/ M20.

†**ejulation** *noun*. E17–E18.
[ORIGIN Latin *ejulatio(n-)*, from *ejulat-* pa. ppl stem of *ejulare* wail: see -ATION.]
(A) lamentation.

ejusdem generis /eɪˌ(j)ʊsdɛm ˈdʒɛnərɪs/ *adverbial & adjectival phr.* Also ***eius-***. M17.
[ORIGIN Latin.]
LAW. ▸ **A** *adverbial phr.* As of the same kind. (Foll. by *with*.) M17.

Daily Telegraph 'Other records' . . had to be construed *eiusdem generis* with 'ledgers, day books, cash books and account books'.

▸ **B** *adjectival phr.* Designating the rule of interpretation that general words following an enumeration of particulars are to be understood as limited to the same general category as is jointly implied by the particulars. L19.

eka- /ˈeɪkə/ *combining form*. L19.
[ORIGIN Sanskrit = one.]
Prefixed to the name of an element to denote the element expected or postulated to occupy the next lower position in the same group or subgroup of the periodic table, as ***eka-bismuth***.

ek dum /eɪk ˈdʌm/ *adverbial phr.* Also ***ek dam***. L19.
[ORIGIN Hindi, Urdu, from *ek* one + Urdu *dam* breath.]
At once, immediately.

eke /iːk/ *noun*. Now chiefly *Scot.* Also (the usual *Scot.* form) **eik** /ɪk, eɪk/.
[ORIGIN Old English *ēaca* = Old Frisian *āka*, Old Norse *auki*, from base also of EKE *verb*.]
▸ **I** *gen.* **1** An addition, an increase; an extension. OE.
▸ **II** *spec.* **2** A tag at the end of a bell rope. Now *rare* or *obsolete*. E16.
3 LAW. An appendix or supplement to a document; a codicil; *esp.* one added to include property not covered by the original document. M16.
4 A ring on which a beehive is stood to increase the capacity. Now *dial.* E18.
5 A patch or gusset on a garment. L18.
6 An additional drink, an extra tot. Now *dial.* M19.

eke /iːk/ *verb*. Also †**eche**; (the usual *Scot.* form) **eik** /ɪk, eɪk/.
[ORIGIN Old English *ēacan*, *-ian* (verb intrans.), *ēcan* (verb trans.), = Old Frisian *āka*, Old Saxon *ōkian*, Old Norse *auka*, Gothic *aukan* rel. to Latin *augere* increase, Greek *aukhein*. Partly from the noun.]
1 *verb trans.* & †*intrans.* Increase, lengthen. Now chiefly *Scot.* OE. ▸**b** *verb trans.* Add to by way of repair, patch. *Scot.* E18.
2 *verb trans.* Add (*to*). Now *Scot.* OE.
3 *verb trans.* Foll. by *out*: cause to last longer by economical use or by expedients; make up for deficiencies in, supplement, (*with*). L16.

J. K. JEROME His German was easy to understand and he knew a little English with which to eke it out. G. GREENE Spending a little love at a time, eking it out here and there, on this man and that. A. BLOND Bookshops . . eke out their turnover with stationery.

4 *verb trans.* Contrive to make (a living) or to support (an existence) by makeshifts. Usu. foll. by *out*. E19.

Discovery The settlers eked out a bare existence from such poor land.

eke /iːk/ *adverb*. *arch.*
[ORIGIN Old English *ē(a)c* = Old Frisian *āk*, Old Saxon *ōk* (Dutch *ook*), Old High German *ouh* (German *auch*), Old Norse, Gothic *auk*, perh. from Indo-European (cf. Greek *au ge* again) or rel. to EKE *verb*.]
Also; in addition.

eke-name /ˈiːkneɪm/ *noun*. Now *rare*. ME.
[ORIGIN from EKE *noun* + NAME *noun*: cf. Old Norse *aukanafn*. See NICKNAME.]
An additional name; a nickname.

EKG *abbreviation*. *N. Amer.*
[ORIGIN German *Elektrokardiogramm*.]
Electrocardiogram.

eking /ˈiːkɪŋ/ *noun*. LME.
[ORIGIN from EKE *verb* + -ING¹.]
1 The action of increasing or adding something. Now chiefly *Scot.* LME.
2 An increase. Now *rare*. LME.
†**3** A protuberance, a projection. Only in LME.
4 NAUTICAL. A piece of wood inserted to make good a deficiency. Also, the carving under the lower part of a quarter-piece. E19.

ekistics /ɪˈkɪstɪks/ *noun*. M20.
[ORIGIN from Greek *oikistikos* relating to settlement, from *oikizein* settle (a colony), from *oikos* house: see -ICS.]
The branch of knowledge that deals with human settlements and the way they develop and adapt.
■ **ekistic** *adjective* M20. **ekiˈstician** *noun* an expert in or student of ekistics M20.

ekka /ˈɛkə/ *noun*¹. E19.
[ORIGIN Hindi *ikkā* lit. 'single', from Sanskrit *eka* one.]
In the Indian subcontinent: a small one-horse vehicle.

Ekka /ˈɛkə/ *noun*². *Austral. colloq.* M20.
[ORIGIN Alt. of *exhibition*.]
The Queensland Royal Show ('Brisbane Exhibition'), held each August.

ekker /ˈɛkə/ *noun*. *school & Univ. slang*. L19.
[ORIGIN from initial sounds of EXERCISE *noun* + -ER⁶.]
(Physical) exercise.

ekphrasis *noun* var. of ECPHRASIS.

ektene *noun* var. of ECTENE.

el /ɛl/ *noun*. *US colloq.* E20.
[ORIGIN Abbreviation of *elevated*.]
An elevated railway.

-el /əl, (ə)l/ *suffix*¹ (not productive).
Var. of -LE¹ retained after *ch*, soft *g*, *n*, *r*, *s*, *sh*, *th*, and *v*, as in ***kernel***, ***swivel***, ***teasel***.

-el /ɛl, (ə)l/ *suffix*² (not productive).
[ORIGIN Old French & mod. French: cf. -LE².]
Occurring in nouns and (occas.) adjectives.
1 Repr. Old French *-el* masc. (mod. *-eau*), *-elle* fem., from Latin *-ellus*, *-ella*, *-ellum* dim. suffix, as in ***bowel***, ***chapel***, ***novel***, ***tunnel***.
2 Repr. Old French *-el* from Latin *-ali-* (see -AL¹) adjectival suffix, as in ***vowel***.

Ela /ˈiːlɑː/ *noun*. *obsolete* exc. *hist.* Also **E la**. LME.
[ORIGIN from E as a pitch letter + *la*: see ELAMI.]
MEDIEVAL MUSIC. The note E in the 7th hexachord of Guido d'Arezzo (*c* 990–1050), where it was sung to the syllable *la*, the highest note in Guido's scale; *fig.* as a type of something high or extravagant. Cf. ALAMIRE, ARE *noun*¹, BEFA, CEFAUT, ELAMI, etc.

elaborate /ɪˈlab(ə)rət/ *adjective*. L16.
[ORIGIN Latin *elaboratus* pa. pple of *elaborare*: see ELABORATE *verb*, -ATE².]
†**1** Produced by labour. L16–E19.

S. JOHNSON He has no elegances either lucky or elaborate.

2 Worked out or accomplished in great detail; full of detail, intricate, complicated; minutely careful, painstaking. E17.

J. MORLEY He read Shakespeare, and made an elaborate study of his method. S. LEWIS The rites of preparing for bed were elaborate. R. P. GRAVES Adams had fitted Perry Hall with elaborate precautions against burglary. G. VIDAL A kind of skirt . . tied at the waist with an elaborate belt.

■ **elaborately** *adverb* L16. **elaborateness** *noun* M17.

elaborate /ɪˈlabəreɪt/ *verb*. Pa. pple **-ated**, (earlier) †**-ate**. L16.
[ORIGIN Latin *elaborat-* pa. ppl stem of *elaborare*, from *e-* E- + *labor* LABOUR *noun*: see -ATE[3].]
1 *verb trans.* Produce by effort or labour; make from raw material or simpler constituents; work out in more detail, develop. L16.

R. BOYLE Honey . . is elaborated by the Bee. W. STYRON He was going to continue, to elaborate and embellish this idea. A. LURIE I began jabbering, elaborating excuses. E. H. GOMBRICH He went out . . to make sketches from nature, and then elaborated them in his studio.

2 *verb intrans.* Become elaborate. L19.
3 *verb intrans.* Explain something in detail. (Foll. by *on*.) M20.

N. CHOMSKY This is . . a familiar observation, and I need not elaborate on it.

■ **elaborative** *adjective* M19. **elaborator** *noun* L19.

elaboration /ɪˌlabəˈreɪʃ(ə)n/ *noun*. LME.
[ORIGIN Latin *elaboratio(n-)*, formed as ELABORATE *verb*: see -ATION.]
1 The production of chemical substances by natural agencies, esp. in the body. Now *rare*. LME.
2 *gen.* The action or process of elaborating. E17.

A. PRICE 'You know Master Charlie well, do you?' . . Audley waited for elaboration, but none came.

3 Something produced by or consisting in this. M18.

J. BUCHAN His taste was fastidious, his courtesy of an old-fashioned elaboration.

4 The state of being elaborated; elaborateness. E19.

M. O. W. OLIPHANT Copies exist in various stages of elaboration.

elaboratory /ɪˈlab(ə)rət(ə)ri/ *noun*. M17.
[ORIGIN from ELABORATE *verb* + -ORY[1], after *laboratory*.]
1 A laboratory. *obsolete* exc. *hist.* M17.
2 An organ or part where a natural product is formed. Now *rare* or *obsolete*. M17.

elaeolite /ɪˈliːəlʌɪt/ *noun*. Also **eleo-**. E19.
[ORIGIN from Greek *elaion* oil + -LITE.]
GEOLOGY. Nepheline, *esp.* a coarse-grained translucent variety with a greasy lustre.

elaidic /ɛləˈɪdɪk/ *adjective*. M19.
[ORIGIN from Greek *elaion* oil + -ID(E + -IC.]
CHEMISTRY. ***elaidic acid***, a solid acid isomeric with oleic acid, of which it is the *trans* analogue.

elain /ɪˈleɪɪn/ *noun*. Now *rare* or *obsolete*. E19.
[ORIGIN formed as ELAIDIC + -IN[1].]
CHEMISTRY. = OLEIN.

Elami /iːlɑːˈmiː/ *noun*. *obsolete* exc. *hist.* Also **E la mi**. LME.
[ORIGIN from *E* as a pitch letter + *la*, *mi*, designating tones in the solmization of Guido d'Arezzo (*c* 990–1050).]
MEDIEVAL MUSIC. The note E in Guido d'Arezzo's 1st, 2nd, 4th, and 5th hexachords, where it was sung to the syllable *la* or *mi*. Cf. ALAMIRE, ARE *noun*[1], BEFA, CEFAUT, ELA, etc.

Elamite /ˈiːləmʌɪt/ *noun & adjective*. *hist.* LME.
[ORIGIN from *Elam* (see below) + -ITE[1].]
▸**A** *noun*. A native or inhabitant of Elam, an ancient country in the south-west of present-day Iran; the language of this country (also called ***Susian***). LME.
▸**B** *adjective*. Of, pertaining to, or designating the Elamites, their language, or their country. L19.

elan /eɪˈlɒ̃, eɪˈlan, *foreign* elɑ̃/ *noun*. Also **élan**. M19.
[ORIGIN French *élan*, formed as ELANCE.]
Vivacity; energy arising from enthusiasm.
élan vital /vitalˌ viːˈtɑːl/ an intuitively perceived life force in Bergson's philosophy; any mysterious life force, *esp.* one supposed to have caused the variations from which new species have emerged.

elance /ɪˈlɑːns/ *verb trans.* *arch.* E18.
[ORIGIN French *élancer*, from *é-* (formed as ES-) + *lancer* LANCE *verb*.]
Cast or throw (a lance, dart, etc.); launch.

eland /ˈiːlənd/ *noun*. L18.
[ORIGIN Afrikaans from Dutch = elk from German †*Elend* (now *Elen*) from Lithuanian *élnis*.]
Either of two large African antelopes of the genus *Taurotragus*, with spiral horns, *T. oryx* (more fully ***common eland***) and *T. derbianus* (more fully ***giant eland***).

elanguescence /iːlaŋˈgwɛs(ə)ns/ *noun*. M19.
[ORIGIN from Latin *elanguescent-* pres. ppl stem of *elanguescere* lose strength, from *e-* E- + *languescere* become weak, from *languere* be weak, LANGUISH: see -ESCENCE.]
The process of gradually fading away into non-existence.

elapid /ˈɛləpɪd/ *noun & adjective*. L19.
[ORIGIN mod. Latin *Elapidae* (see below), from *Elaps* genus name, from Greek *elaps* alt. of *ellops*: see -ID[3].]
(A snake) of the family Elapidae, the members of which are highly poisonous and include the cobras and usu. the sea snakes.

elapse /ɪˈlaps/ *noun*. L17.
[ORIGIN from the verb.]
1 A flowing out or away; chiefly *fig.*, an emanation, an effluence. Now *rare* or *obsolete*. L17.
2 A passage of time. L18.

elapse /ɪˈlaps/ *verb*. L16.
[ORIGIN Latin *elaps-* pa. ppl stem of *elabi* slip away, from *e-* E- + *labi*: see LAPSE *noun*.]
†**1** *verb intrans.* Slip away (from a place, from memory), leave unobtrusively; lapse *into* a condition. L16–M18.
2 *verb intrans.* Of time or a period of time: pass by, pass. M17.

C. CHAPLIN Six weeks had elapsed and still Sydney had not returned.

†**3** *verb trans.* Allow (time) to pass, pass (time). M17–E18.
■ †**elapsion** *noun* (*rare*) the action of elapsing; also, subsidence: M17–L18.

elasipod /ɪˈlasɪpɒd/ *noun & adjective*. L19.
[ORIGIN mod. Latin *Elasipoda* (see below), from Greek *elasmos* beaten metal + -I- + Greek *pod-*, *pous* foot.]
ZOOLOGY. (Of or designating) a holothurian of the order Elasipoda, found mainly in deep water and with shield-shaped buccal tentacles and no respiratory tree.

elasmobranch /ɪˈlazməbraŋk/ *noun & adjective*. L19.
[ORIGIN mod. Latin *Elasmobranchii* pl., from Greek *elasmos* beaten metal + *bragkhia* gills.]
(Designating) any fish of the larger of the two groups of cartilaginous fishes, comprising sharks, rays, and skates.

elasmosaur /ɪˈlazməsɔː/ *noun*. Also in mod. Latin form **elasmosaurus** /ɪˌlazməˈsɔːrəs/, pl. **-ruses**, **-ri** /-rʌɪ/. L19.
[ORIGIN mod. Latin (see below), from Greek *elasmos* beaten metal + -SAUR.]
A plesiosaur of the genus *Elasmosaurus* with a long neck shaped like that of a swan.

elasmotherium /ɪˌlazməˈθɪərɪəm/ *noun*. Also anglicized as **elasmothere** /ɪˈlazməθɪə/. L19.
[ORIGIN mod. Latin (see below), from Greek *elasmos* beaten metal + *thērion* wild animal.]
PALAEONTOLOGY. A large extinct animal of the genus *Elasmotherium*, resembling a rhinoceros.

elastance /ɪˈlast(ə)ns/ *noun*. L19.
[ORIGIN from ELASTIC + -ANCE.]
1 ELECTRICITY. The reciprocal of capacitance. L19.
2 PHYSIOLOGY. The reciprocal of compliance. M20.

elastane /ɪˈlasteɪn/ *noun*. L20.
[ORIGIN from ELAST(IC + -ANE.]
A highly elastic polyurethane material, composed of any of various man-made elastomeric fibres, used esp. to make hosiery, underwear, and other close-fitting garments.
– NOTE: Proprietary names for such materials are LYCRA, SPANDEX.

elastase /ɪˈlasteɪz/ *noun*. M20.
[ORIGIN from ELASTIN + -ASE.]
A pancreatic enzyme which digests elastin.

elastic /ɪˈlastɪk/ *adjective & noun*. M17.
[ORIGIN mod. Latin *elasticus* from Greek *elastikos*, from *ela-* stem of *elaunein* to drive.]
▸**A** *adjective*. †**1** (Of a gas) having the property of expanding spontaneously to fill whatever space is available; pertaining to or causing this expansion. M17–M18.
2 That spontaneously resumes its normal bulk or shape after contraction, expansion, or distortion by an external force; of or pertaining to this property or phenomenon. L17. ▸**b** *fig.* Of a person or feeling: not permanently or easily depressed; buoyant. L18. ▸**c** PHYSICS. Of a collision, or scattering of subatomic particles: not involving any loss of kinetic energy. M19.

Focus This narrow cable is elastic but hard-wearing.
b LD MACAULAY Those elastic spirits . . had borne up against defeat.

3 Able to be stretched without permanent alteration of size or shape; made of or containing material of this kind. L18. ▸**b** *fig.* Flexible, springy; accommodating; loose. M19. ▸**c** ECONOMICS. Of demand or supply: sensitive to changes in price or income. L19.

b CONAN DOYLE Even the rigid British law becomes human and elastic. E. BLISHEN Many of the contributors had an elastic sense of time.

▸**B** *noun*. Elastic cord or fabric, usu. woven with strips of rubber. M19.
– SPECIAL COLLOCATIONS & COMB.: ***elastic band***: see BAND *noun*[2] 2. **elastic cartilage** a yellowish kind of cartilage containing elastic fibres, present in the ear and larynx. **elastic deformation** in a metal or other elastic material, distortion under stress that is followed by a full recovery of the original size and shape (cf. ***plastic deformation*** s.v. PLASTIC *adjective* 4b). **elastic fibre** ANATOMY a yellowish fibre composed chiefly of elastin and occurring in networks or sheets in elastic tissue, to which it imparts elasticity. **elastic limit** the extent to which a body may be stretched without permanent alteration of size or shape. ***elastic modulus***. **elastic-side** *Austral.* a boot without laces and with an elastic gusset at each side (usu. in *pl.*). ***elastic stocking***: see STOCKING *noun*[1] 2. **elastic tissue** ANATOMY connective tissue of the kind that occurs in the dermis and the walls of arteries, composed chiefly of elastic fibres.
■ **elastically** *adverb* M19. **elasticated** *adjective* (of a cloth or garment) made elastic by incorporating elastic thread or fabric E20. **elastician** /iːlaˈstɪʃ(ə)n, ɛ-/ *noun* an expert in or student of elasticity, as a physical phenomenon or property L19. **elasticized** *adjective* = ELASTICATED E20.

elasticity /ɛlaˈstɪsɪti, iː-, ɪ-/ *noun*. M17.
[ORIGIN from ELASTIC + -ITY.]
1 The state or quality of being elastic (*lit.* & *fig.*). M17.
MODULUS of elasticity.
2 ECONOMICS. Sensitivity of demand or supply to changes in price or income; *spec.* the ratio of the proportionate change in the former to the proportionate change in the latter. L19.

elastin /ɪˈlastɪn/ *noun*. L19.
[ORIGIN from ELASTIC + -IN[1].]
BIOCHEMISTRY. An elastic fibrous protein that is the chief constituent of elastic fibres and elastic tissue.

E

elastohydrodynamic /ɪˌlastəʊhʌɪdrə(ʊ)dʌɪˈnamɪk/ *adjective*. M20.
[ORIGIN from ELASTIC + -O- + HYDRODYNAMIC.]
Pertaining to or involving the elastic properties of a liquid or situations where these become significant.

elastomer /ɪˈlastəmə/ *noun*. M20.
[ORIGIN from ELASTIC + -O- + -MER.]
A polymer possessing the elastic properties of rubber.
■ **elastoˈmeric** *adjective* M20.

Elastoplast /ɪˈlastəplɑːst/ *noun*. E20.
[ORIGIN from ELASTIC + -O- + PLASTER *noun*.]
(Proprietary name for) a sticking plaster.

†**elatcha** *noun*. E17–E19.
[ORIGIN Turkish *alaca* particoloured.]
A patterned silk fabric from Turkestan.

elate /ɪˈleɪt/ *adjective*. Now *rare*. LME.
[ORIGIN Old French *elat* proud, and (later) its source Latin *elatus* pa. pple of *efferre*: see ELATE *verb*, -ATE[2].]
Exalted, lofty, proud; in high spirits, exultant.

elate /ɪˈleɪt/ *verb trans.* L16.
[ORIGIN Latin *elat-* pa. ppl stem of *efferre*, from EF- + *ferre* BEAR *verb*[1]: see -ATE[3].]
†**1** Raise, elevate. L16–L18.
2 Lift the spirits of, fill with elation; inspire with pride. Chiefly as ***elated*** *ppl adjective*. E17.

R. L. STEVENSON I was greatly elated with my new command.

■ **elatedly** *adverb* M17. **elatedness** *noun* M18. **elatement** *noun* = ELATION M18.

elater /ˈɛlətə/ *noun*. M17.
[ORIGIN Greek *elatēr* driver, from *ela-* stem of *elaunein* to drive.]
†**1** The elastic property of gases; elasticity, spring; tone. M17–M18.
2 A click beetle. E19.
3 BOTANY. An elongated appendage in the spore case of a liverwort, or attached to the spore of a horsetail, which uncoils as it dries and aids in the dispersal of spores. M19.

elaterite /ɪˈlatərʌɪt/ *noun*. E19.
[ORIGIN formed as ELATER + -ITE[1].]
An asphaltic pyrobitumen that is soft and elastic when freshly cut and becomes hard and brittle in air.

elaterium /ɛləˈtɪərɪəm/ *noun*. M16.
[ORIGIN Latin from Greek *elatērion*, from *ela-*: see ELATER, -IUM.]
A precipitate from the juice of the squirting cucumber (*Ecballium elaterium*), formerly used as a drastic purgative and emetic.

elation /ɪˈleɪʃ(ə)n/ *noun*. LME.
[ORIGIN Old French *elacion*, and (later) its source Latin *elatio(n-)*, from *elat-*: see ELATE *verb*, -ATION.]
1 a Elevation of mind due to success; pride, vainglory. Now *rare*. LME. ▸**b** Elevation of spirits; a feeling of pleasurable self-satisfaction and self-assurance. M18.

b M. MEYER His moods varied from elation to the blackest depression. A. SILLITOE He walked back . . with a tremendous feeling of elation and freedom, hardly able to believe it belonged to him.

†**2** Lifting, elevation; carrying out. L15–L17.

elative /ɪˈleɪtɪv/ *adjective & noun*. L16.
[ORIGIN from ELATE *verb* + -IVE.]
▸**A** *adjective*. **1** That elates. *rare*. L16.
2 GRAMMAR. **a** Designating, being in, or pertaining to a case in some languages that expresses motion away from. M19. ▸**b** Having a superlative and intensive force. E20.
▸**B** *noun*. GRAMMAR. The elative case; a word, form, etc., in the elative case. E20.

elbow /ˈɛlbəʊ/ *noun*.
[ORIGIN Old English *el(n)boga* = Middle Dutch *elleboghe* (Du *elleboog*), Old High German *elinbogo* (German *Ellenbogen*), Old Norse *ǫlnbogi*, from Germanic, from bases of ELL *noun*[1] and BOW *noun*[1].]
1 The outer, bony part of the arm at the place where it bends; the part of a garment that covers this. Also, the elbow joint. OE. ▸**b** The analogous part in the shoulder or hock of a quadruped. E17. ▸**c** A (usu. temporary) loss of dexterity and accuracy in a tennis player's racket arm. Usu. preceded by *the*. L20.
2 Something resembling an elbow; *spec.* (**a**) a sharp bend in a road, river, etc.; (**b**) a projecting corner; (**c**) MECHANICS a piece of piping etc. bent through an angle. L16.

3 An arm of a chair, made to rest the elbow on. *obsolete* exc. in ***elbow chair*** below. E17.

– PHRASES: **at one's elbow** close at hand. ***bend one's elbow***: see BEND *verb*. ***crook one's elbow***: see CROOK *verb* 1. **give the elbow**, **give the big elbow** *colloq.* send away, dismiss, or reject (a person). ***lift one's elbow***: see LIFT *verb*. ***more power to your elbow*** etc.: see POWER *noun*. **out at elbows** worn out, threadbare; scruffy; poor. ***not know one's arse from one's elbow***: see ARSE *noun* 1. **rub elbows**: see RUB *verb*. †**rub the elbow** show oneself pleased. ***shake one's elbow***: see SHAKE *verb*. ***tennis elbow***: see TENNIS *noun*. **up to the elbows** *colloq.* busily engaged *in*.

– COMB.: **elbow chair** (*hist.* exc. *US*): with supports for the arms; **elbow grease** *joc.* vigorous rubbing; hard manual work or physical effort; **elbow joint**: between the humerus in the upper arm and the radius and ulna in the forearm; **elbow-length** *adjective* (of a sleeve or garment) reaching to the elbow; **elbow pad**: for protecting the elbow of a garment against wear or the elbow of a person against injury; **elbow room** *colloq.* (adequate) space to move or work in; **elbow sleeve**: reaching only to the elbow.

E

elbow /ˈɛlbəʊ/ *verb*. E17.
[ORIGIN from the noun.]
1 *verb trans.* Thrust with the elbow, nudge. E17. ▸b Move aside using the elbow. Chiefly *fig.* & foll. by preposition or adverb. E18.

R. COOVER Passengers protested at the shoving... A woman complained about getting elbowed. b J. CARY Yells.. like the shrieks of monkeys elbowed off their perch.

†2 *verb intrans.* Use the elbows in pushing. M17–L19.
3 *verb trans.* Make (one's way), esp. through a throng, by pushing with the arms. L18.
4 *verb intrans.* Make a detour; follow an indirect or erratic route. E19.
■ **elbowing** *noun* the action of thrusting with the elbow; a thrust with the elbow, a nudge: E19.

el cheapo /ɛl ˈtʃiːpəʊ/ *adjectival & noun phr.* *N. Amer. & Austral. slang*. L20.
[ORIGIN from CHEAP *adjective* after Spanish such as *El Dorado*, *El Greco*.]
▸ **A** *adjectival phr.* Cheap; of inferior quality. L20.
▸ **B** *noun phr.* Pl. **-os**. Something cheap or inferior. L20.

elchee /ˈɛltʃi/ *noun*. L16.
[ORIGIN Turkish *elçi*, from *el* (the representative of) an independent political unit.]
An ambassador, esp. in the Middle East.

eld /ɛld/ *noun*.
[ORIGIN Old English (Anglian) *eldu*, (West Saxon) *ieldu* = Old Frisian *elde*, Old Saxon *eldi*, Old High German *elti*, Old Norse *elli*, from Germanic: cf. OLD *noun*¹, *noun*².]
1 The age or time of life which a person has reached. *obsolete* exc. *dial.* OE.
†2 An age of the world, an era. OE–E16.
3 Old age. *arch. & poet.* OE. ▸†b Old people; old men; senate, aristocracy. OE–L16. ▸c An old person; an old man. *poet.* L18.

C. KINGSLEY His beard was white with eld.

†4 Conventional or legal age; a person's majority. ME–E16.
†5 Duration of existence; time as a wearing or destroying agency. LME–M18.
6 The old days, antiquity; people of former times. *arch. & poet.* LME.

SHAKES. *Merry W.* The superstitious idle-headed eld Receiv'd, and did deliver to our age, This tale of Herne the Hunter.

eld /ɛld/ *adjective*. *arch. & poet.* E17.
[ORIGIN from the noun: see OLD *adjective*.]
Old, aged.

eld /ɛld/ *verb intrans.* Long *obsolete* exc. *dial.*
[ORIGIN Old English (West Saxon) *ealdian*, from *eald* OLD *adjective*; cf. Old Frisian *aldia*, Old High German *altēn*, Gothic *us*)*alþan*.]
Grow old.

elder /ˈɛldə/ *noun*¹.
[ORIGIN Old English *ellærn*, corresp. to Middle Low German *ellern*, *elderne*, *elhorn*, *alhorn*, prob. orig. an adjective formation like Old & mod. High German *ahorn* maple, corresp. to Latin *acernus* of maple.]
1 A common British shrub or low-growing tree, *Sambucus nigra*, of the honeysuckle family, with cymes of creamy-white flowers, small black berries, and pinnate leaves; any of various other trees of the genus *Sambucus*. Also ***elder tree***. OE.
dwarf elder = ***danewort*** s.v. DANE *noun*.
2 Any of several unrelated plants resembling the elder in leaf or flower. L16.
box elder, ***ground elder***, ***marsh elder***, ***water elder***, etc.
– COMB.: **elderberry** the black fleshy fruit of the elder; ***elder tree***: see sense 1 above.

elder /ˈɛldə/ *adjective & noun*².
[ORIGIN Old English *eldra*, *-re* (*ieldra*, *-re*) = Old Frisian *alder*, *elder*, Old Saxon *aldira*, Old High German *altiro*, *eltiro* (German *älter*), Old Norse *ellri*, Gothic *alþiza*: see -ER³. Rel. to ELD *noun*, OLD *adjective*.]
▸ **A** *adjective*. 1 Earlier-born (of two related or indicated persons, esp. children or siblings). Freq. after possess. pronoun. OE.

I. MURDOCH He turned to her.. as to a mother or an elder sister. J. GROSS The elder Gosse was a naturalist.

2 *gen.* Older. Now only *attrib.*, without *than*. *arch.* OE.

SHAKES. *Merch. V.* How much more elder art thou than thy looks?

3 Ancient; of or pertaining to ancient or earlier times. LME.

SOUTHEY Huge as the giant race of elder times.

†4 Of or pertaining to the later period of a person's life. L16–M18.
†5 (Of an obligation, right, or title) of longer standing, prior; (of an official etc.) of longer service, senior. M17–M18.
– SPECIAL COLLOCATIONS & COMB.: **Elder Brother**, pl. **Elder Brethren**, each of thirteen senior members of Trinity House. **elder-brotherly** *adjective* pertaining to or appropriate to an elder brother. **eldercare** *N. Amer.* the care of infirm older people. **elder hand** the person in a card game for two who is first to be dealt to and therefore begins the play. **elder-sisterly** *adjective* pertaining to or appropriate to an elder sister. **elder statesman** (*a*) any of the Japanese statesmen who mainly directed the evolution of Japan in the late 19th cent.; (*b*) a person of ripe years and experience whose opinions are respected.
▸ **B** *noun*. 1 The elder person (of two), *esp.* the elder child or sibling. Usu. after *the* or possess. pronoun. OE.

E. B. BROWNING My cousin..; My elder by a few years. D. H. LAWRENCE They were pale mites, the elder about ten years old.

†2 A parent; an ancestor; a predecessor. Usu. in *pl.* OE–E17.
3 A person who is older than another who is indicated. Usu. in *pl.* after possess. pronoun. LME. ▸b An old person. L16.

W. BRONK Children.. are shocked by things their elders do unthinking.

4 Now chiefly *hist.* & ANTHROPOLOGY. A (usu. male) person having authority because of advanced age; a member of a governing body or class consisting of men chosen for their age and experience. LME.

P. GALLICO A sweet and gentle people presided over by a tall, stately elder. T. KENEALLY Tribal elders, who.. knew where the soul-stones of each man were hidden.

5 ECCLESIASTICAL. An official or minister in the early Church and in various Protestant, esp. Presbyterian, denominations; *US dial.* a minister of any denomination. LME. ▸b A member of the Society of Friends responsible for the organization and conduct of meetings for worship. E18.
lay elder: see LAY *adjective*. PRESIDING ***elder***. ***ruling elder***: see RULING *adjective*.
■ **elderhood** *noun* the position of an elder, seniority; a body of elders: L16.

elder /ˈɛldə/ *verb*. M19.
[ORIGIN from ELDER *adjective & noun*².]
†1 *verb trans.* with *it*. Play the elder. *rare*. Only in M19.
2 *verb intrans.* Become older; begin to show signs of age. *colloq. & poet.* L19.
3 *verb trans.* Make a request to or admonish (a person) in one's capacity as an elder in a meeting of the Society of Friends. E20.

elderly /ˈɛldəli/ *adjective & noun*. E17.
[ORIGIN from ELDER *adjective* + -LY¹.]
▸ **A** *adjective*. 1 Somewhat old; (of a person) past middle age; (of a thing) not new or recent, showing signs of age. E17.

LD MACAULAY The elderly inhabitants could still remember the time when the first brick house.. was built.

2 Of or pertaining to a person in later life. L17.
▸ **B** *absol.* as *noun pl.* The people who are elderly, as a class. Also *sing.* (*rare*), an elderly person. M19.

Observer The House of Lords is a model of how to care for the elderly.

■ **elderliness** *noun* L19.

eldern /ˈɛld(ə)n/ *adjective*. ME.
[ORIGIN from ELDER *adjective* + -EN⁴, added exceptionally to an adjective (cf. OLDEN *adjective*).]
1 Elderly. *obsolete* exc. *Scot.* ME.
2 = ELDER *adjective* 3. *arch.* ME.

eldership /ˈɛldəʃɪp/ *noun*. M16.
[ORIGIN from ELDER *adjective & noun*² + -SHIP.]
1 The position of being the elder; seniority of age. M16.
2 ECCLESIASTICAL. a A body of elders, elders collectively. M16. ▸b The office or position of church elder. L16.

eldest /ˈɛldɪst/ *adjective & noun*.
[ORIGIN Old English *eldest* (*ieldest*) = Old Frisian *eldest*, Old High German *altist* (German *ältest*), Old Norse *ellztr*, Gothic *altista*: see -EST¹. Rel. to ELDER *adjective*.]
▸ **A** *adjective*. 1 Firstborn, oldest surviving, (of a group of siblings or a family). OE.

R. GARNETT Carlyle was the eldest of nine children. D. H. LAWRENCE Mr. Leivers and Edgar, the eldest son, were in the kitchen.

†2 *gen.* Oldest, of the greatest age. OE–L19.
3 Earliest, first produced; most ancient. *arch.* OE.

DRYDEN Self-defence is Nature's Eldest Law.

– SPECIAL COLLOCATIONS: **eldest hand** the person in a card game for three or more who is first to be dealt to and therefore begins the play.
▸ **B** *noun*. The eldest person, esp. of children or siblings. OE.

G. B. SHAW I shouldnt know my two eldest if I met them. E. O'NEILL The eldest is about fourteen, the two others thirteen and twelve.

elding /ˈɛldɪŋ/ *noun*. *obsolete* exc. *dial.* ME.
[ORIGIN Old Norse, from *eldr* fire.]
Fuel.

Eldonian /ɛlˈdəʊnɪən/ *adjective*. L19.
[ORIGIN from *Eldon* (see below) + -IAN.]
Of, pertaining to, or characteristic of John Scott, Lord Eldon (1751–1838), regarded as typical of diehard toryism, or his political beliefs.
■ Also **Eldonine** /ˈɛldənʌɪn/ *adjective* M19.

El Dorado /ɛl dəˈrɑːdəʊ/ *noun*. Also **Eldorado**. Pl. **-os**. E19.
[ORIGIN Spanish, name of a non-existent country or city having much gold, once believed to exist on the Amazon, from *el* the + DORADO.]
A place of fabulous wealth or opportunity.

eldress /ˈɛldrɪs/ *noun*. M17.
[ORIGIN from ELDER *noun*² + -ESS¹.]
A female church elder.

eldritch /ˈɛl(d)rɪtʃ/ *adjective*. Orig. *Scot.* E16.
[ORIGIN Uncertain: perh. connected with ELF *noun*¹.]
Weird, ghostly, unnatural; hideous.

A. T. ELLIS Lydia gave a screech of eldritch mirth.

†**ele** *noun* see AISLE.

Eleatic /ɛlɪˈatɪk/ *adjective & noun*. L17.
[ORIGIN Latin *Eleaticus*, from *Elea*: see below and -ATIC.]
▸ **A** *adjective*. Of or pertaining to Elea, an ancient Greek city in SW Italy, or *spec.* the monistic school of philosophy that flourished there in the 6th and 5th cents. BC, propounded by Parmenides, Zeno, and others. L17.
▸ **B** *noun*. An Eleatic philosopher. M19.
■ **Eleaticism** /-sɪz(ə)m/ *noun* Eleatic philosophy or doctrines M19.

elecampane /ˌɛlɪkamˈpeɪn/ *noun*. LME.
[ORIGIN Ult. from medieval Latin *enula campana* (*enula* from Latin *inula* from Greek *helenion* elecampane; *campana* prob. 'of the fields', fem. adjective from Latin *campus*: see CAMP *noun*².]
1 A tall perennial yellow-rayed plant of the composite family, *Inula helenium*, with a bitter root formerly much used to treat pulmonary complaints. LME.
2 The candied root of this plant, formerly eaten as a sweet. E19.

elect /ɪˈlɛkt/ *adjective & noun*. LME.
[ORIGIN Latin *electus* pa. pple of *eligere*, from *e-* E- + *legere* choose.]
▸ **A** *adjective*. 1 Chosen for an office or position; *esp.* chosen but not yet installed. Usu. *postpositive*. LME.

C. WILMOT The Bride elect dissolved in tears. T. HEGGEN He went down to take among the crew his rightful place as hero-elect of a legend in the making.

2 *gen.* Picked out, chosen; select, choice. L15.
3 THEOLOGY. Chosen by God for salvation. E16.

R. HOOKER The elect Angels are without possibilitie of falling.

▸ **B** *noun*. †1 A choice. Only in LME.
†2 A person chosen for an office or position, esp. a bishopric. LME–E18.
3 THEOLOGY. †a A person chosen by God, esp. for salvation. LME–M17. ▸b ***the elect***, those chosen by God for salvation. M16.
4 *hist.* In the Royal College of Physicians, each of the eight officers who formerly granted licences and elected the President. E16.
5 A specially chosen group of people; an elite. E17.

elect /ɪˈlɛkt/ *verb*. LME.
[ORIGIN Latin *elect-* pa. ppl stem of *eligere*: see ELECT *adjective & noun*.]
†1 a *verb trans.* Pick out, select (a person or thing), usu. for a particular purpose. LME–E19. ▸b *verb trans. & intrans.* THEOLOGY. Of God: choose (a person) in preference to others for salvation or the receipt of some blessing. M16.
2 *verb trans.* Choose (a person) by vote for an office or position. Also foll. by *to* the office & with the title of the office as 2nd or only obj. LME.

H. COX Each Town Council elected a delegate. E. WAUGH I have been elected chairman of the Parish Council.

3 *verb trans. & intrans.* Choose (a thing, *to do* an action) in preference to an alternative. E16.

R. C. A. WHITE Anyone could elect to be tried by jury. Y. MENUHIN Except for electing the violin.. I scarcely disturbed the family pattern.

■ **electaˈbility** *noun* the property of being electable, eligibility for election L20. **electable** *adjective* able or qualified to be elected L19.

election /ɪˈlɛkʃ(ə)n/ *noun*. ME.
[ORIGIN Old French & mod. French *élection* from Latin *electio(n-)*, from *elect-*: see ELECT *verb*, -ION.]
1 The formal choosing of a person for an office or position, usu. by vote; the fact of being chosen. ME. ▸b *spec.* The choice of a person to fill a vacancy in a representative body by a vote among those represented; an occasion of such choice; the accompanying proceedings. M17.

S. AUSTIN The empire . . had waived the right . . to interfere in the election of the pope. J. GALSWORTHY He was not seeking election. H. FAST Her election to that very select body was no problem. **b** *Daily Telegraph* If Mrs Thatcher wins the next election, Labour will have lost four in a row.

b *election address*, *election manifesto*, etc. BY-ELECTION. **general election**: in which voting, usu. for a government, takes place in all the constituencies of a state.

2 The exercise of deliberate choice or preference, esp. in relation to conduct; *LAW* the right, opportunity, or duty of choosing between courses of action, the exercise of which will preclude the elector from subsequently seeking to rely on the others. LME. ▸†**b** Judicious selection, discrimination. M16–E17.

Daily Telegraph Thompson . . was committed to Southwark Crown Court for trial . . at his own election.

3 *THEOLOGY.* The choosing by God of some persons but not others for salvation, or for the receipt of some blessing. LME.

4 *ASTROLOGY.* The choosing of a propitious time for an undertaking; the time chosen. *obsolete* exc. *hist.* LME.

†**5** The selecting of a thing, esp. a medicinal herb, for a particular purpose. E17–E18.

– COMB.: **election bun**, **election cake** *US*: varieties of fancy bread; **election commissioner** any of a body of men appointed to inquire into corruption at an election or (*US*) to take charge of an election; **election petition**: calling for an inquiry into the validity of the election of a Member of Parliament.

▪ **electional** *adjective* (*ASTROLOGY*) M17.

electioneer /ɪˌlɛkʃəˈnɪə/ *verb & noun*. M18.
[ORIGIN from ELECTION + -EER.]
▸ **A** *verb intrans.* Be active or campaign in a (political) election. M18.
▸ **B** *noun.* A person who electioneers or has expertise in electioneering. M19.
▪ **electioneerer** *noun* E19.

elective /ɪˈlɛktɪv/ *adjective & noun*. LME.
[ORIGIN Old French & mod. French *électif*, *-ive*, from late Latin *electivus*, formed as ELECT *verb*: see -IVE.]
▸ **A** *adjective*. **1** Pertaining to or proceeding from choice; voluntary, optional. *obsolete* exc. as below. LME. ▸**b** (Of a course or subject at college or high school) taken at the choice of the student, optional; of, pertaining to, or containing such courses etc. Orig. *US*. M19. ▸**c** *MEDICINE.* Of an operation: at the option of the doctor or patient, not urgently necessary. M20.
2 Appointed by election; derived from or dependent on election. L15. ▸†**b** Subject to election at specified intervals. M17–M18.

E. A. FREEMAN The hereditary prince may be exchanged for an elective chief magistrate. *New York Times* You have to know when to get into politics in terms of elective office.

3 Having the power to elect. M17.
4 Pertaining to election; based on the principle of election. M17.

C. MERIVALE A preference of the elective to the hereditary principle in every department of government.

5 Orig. *CHEMISTRY.* Having a tendency to act on or be concerned with some things rather than others; preferential; sympathetic. M18.

J. TYNDALL Light . . which has been sifted . . by elective absorption. PERRY ANDERSON Traditional British culture has an elective affinity with certain types of expatriate.

▸ **B** *noun*. †**1** An elected representative. Only in E18.
2 An elective subject or course of study. Orig. *US*. M19.
▪ **electively** *adverb* LME. **electiveness** *noun* (*rare*) M19.

elector /ɪˈlɛktə/ *noun*. LME.
[ORIGIN (Old French & mod. French *électeur* from) Latin *elector*, formed as ELECT *verb*: see -OR.]
1 A person who has the right to vote in an election; *spec.* one who has the parliamentary vote; *US* a member of the Electoral College. LME.
2 *hist.* (Also **E-**.) Each of the Princes of Germany entitled to elect the Holy Roman Emperor. More fully ***prince-elector***. E16.

electoral /ɪˈlɛkt(ə)r(ə)l/ *adjective*. M17.
[ORIGIN from ELECTOR + -AL[1].]
1 Relating to or composed of electors. M17.
electoral college a body of electors to a particular office, *esp.* one chosen or appointed from a larger group; *spec.* (**a**) the princes who elected the Holy Roman Emperor; (**b**) *US* the group of electors from within each state chosen to elect the President and Vice-President.
2 *hist.* (Also **E-**.) Holding rank as, or belonging to, a German elector. L17.

HOR. WALPOLE George the first, while electoral prince, had married his cousin.

▪ **electorally** *adverb* with reference to electors or elections L18.

electorate /ɪˈlɛkt(ə)rət/ *noun*. E17.
[ORIGIN from ELECTOR + -ATE[1].]
1 *hist.* The rank or territory of a German elector. E17.
2 The area represented by an elected Member of Parliament in Australia or New Zealand. M19.
3 A body of electors; (the number of) all those entitled to vote in a country or constituency. L19.

†**electoress** *noun* var. of ELECTRESS.

electorial /ɪlɛkˈtɔːrɪəl/ *adjective*. L18.
[ORIGIN from ELECTOR + -IAL.]
= ELECTORAL.

electorship /ɪˈlɛktəʃɪp/ *noun*. L16.
[ORIGIN from ELECTOR + -SHIP.]
1 The state or condition of an elector or a member of an electoral college. L16.
2 *hist.* The position of being a German elector; the dominions of an elector. E17.

Electra /ɪˈlɛktrə/ *noun*. E20.
[ORIGIN In Greek tragedy, the daughter of Agamemnon and Clytemnestra who caused the death of the latter in revenge for the murder of the former.]
PSYCHOLOGY. ***Electra complex***, a daughter's subconscious sexual attraction to her father and hostility to her mother. Cf. OEDIPUS.

†**electral** *adjective*. L17–M18.
[ORIGIN from Latin *electrum* amber + -AL[1].]
Electrical.

electress /ɪˈlɛktrɪs/ *noun*. Also †**-oress**; **E-**. E17.
[ORIGIN from ELECTOR + -ESS[1].]
hist. The wife of a German elector.

electret /ɪˈlɛktrɪt/ *noun*. L19.
[ORIGIN from ELECTR(ICITY + MAGN)ET.]
PHYSICS. A permanently polarized piece of dielectric material, analogous to a permanent magnet.

electric /ɪˈlɛktrɪk/ *adjective & noun*. M17.
[ORIGIN mod. Latin *electricus*, from Latin *electrum* amber from Greek *ēlektron* (because rubbing amber produces electrostatic phenomena): see -IC.]
▸ **A** *adjective*. **1** Of a substance or object: capable of developing electricity when rubbed. M17.
2 Operating by means of electricity; caused or produced by electricity; (capable of) producing electricity; = ELECTRICAL *adjective* 2. L17.
electric battery, *electric cooker*, *electric generator*, etc.
3 *fig.* Suddenly exciting or thrilling, as if caused by electricity; stimulating; full of tension. E19.

Gramophone The electric urgency of the performance. Y. MENUHIN Bucharest was bustling, . . the air electric with life and enterprise. G. GREENE The strange electric beauty of Miss Elsa Lanchester as Frankenstein's second monster.

– SPECIAL COLLOCATIONS: **electric arc** = ARC *noun* 4. ***electric blanket***: see BLANKET *noun*. **electric blue** a steely or brilliant light blue. **electric chair**: in which a criminal is placed to be judicially electrocuted. **electric charge** the quantity whose presence or flow constitutes electricity and which is associated with certain subatomic particles; an amount of this on or in a body. **electric circuit** = CIRCUIT *noun* 9. **electric eel** an elongated S. American freshwater fish, *Electrophorus electricus*, which possesses electric organs and can give a severe electric shock. **electric eye** (**a**) a photoelectric cell that operates a relay when a beam of light illuminating it is interrupted; (**b**) a miniature cathode-ray tube used as a tuning indicator. **electric fence** a fence (often of a single strand of wire) maintained at a low voltage to give a mild shock to an animal touching it. **electric field** a field of force which is electrical in nature. **electric fire** a space heater, usu. a portable one for domestic use, in which the heat is produced by the passage of an electric current. **electric guitar**: in which the vibrations of the strings are not amplified by the body of the instrument but are converted by a pick-up into electrical signals and amplified by an independent amplifier and speaker. **electric organ** (**a**) a part of the body surface in certain fishes which develops an external electric field or voltage; (**b**) an organ operated electrically, *esp.* one in which the sound is produced by electro-acoustic or electromechanical means. **electric ray** any ray of the order Torpediniformes, as the Atlantic torpedo ray, *Torpedo nobiliana*, which possess electric organs and can give an electric shock. **electric shock** the effect on a person or animal of a sudden flow of electric current through the body, usu. causing stimulation of the nerves and contraction of muscles. **electric storm** a violent disturbance of the electric field in the atmosphere; a thunderstorm. ***electric telegraph***: see TELEGRAPH *noun* 1. ***electric torch***: see TORCH *noun* 1.
▸ **B** *noun*. **1** A substance that can be given an electrostatic charge by friction. *arch.* M17.
2 A thing operated by electricity rather than by other means; *esp.* an electric vehicle, an electric light. L19.

Sunday Express Petrol mowers . . need more attention than electrics.

3 An electric wire; an electric circuit; an electrical device. Usu. in *pl.* E20.

G. B. SHAW All the drains and telephones and electrics torn up.

4 In *pl.* Shares in electric or electrical engineering companies. M20.

electrical /ɪˈlɛktrɪk(ə)l/ *adjective & noun*. M17.
[ORIGIN from ELECTRIC + -AL[1].]
▸ **A** *adjective*. **1** = ELECTRIC *adjective* 1. M17–M18.
2 Of or pertaining to electricity; of the nature of electricity; = ELECTRIC *adjective* 2. M17.

M. SHELLEY He constructed a small electrical machine.

3 *fig.* = ELECTRIC *adjective* 3. L18.
4 Charged with electricity. E19.
– SPECIAL COLLOCATIONS: **electrical conductivity** a measure of the rate at which electricity can pass through a body, the reciprocal of resistivity. **electrical engineer** an expert in electrical engineering. **electrical engineering**: that deals with the utilization of electricity, esp. electric power. **electrical storm** = ***electric storm*** s.v. ELECTRIC *adjective*.
▸ **B** *noun*. **1** In *pl.* = ELECTRIC *noun* 4. L20.
2 In *pl.* Electrical products; *esp.* domestic electrical appliances. L20.

electrically /ɪˈlɛktrɪk(ə)li/ *adverb*. E19.
[ORIGIN from ELECTRIC *adjective* or ELECTRICAL *adjective*: see -ICALLY.]
1 By means of electricity; as regards electricity. E19.
2 *fig.* With suddenness, rapidity, or force suggestive of electricity. M19.

electrician /ɪlɛkˈtrɪʃ(ə)n, ɛl-/ *noun*. M18.
[ORIGIN from ELECTRIC + -IAN: see -ICIAN.]
A person who installs or repairs electrical equipment; an expert in or student of electricity.
electrician's tape = ***insulating tape*** s.v. INSULATE *verb*.

electricise *verb* var. of ELECTRICIZE.

electricity /ɪlɛkˈtrɪsɪti, ɛl-, iːl-/ *noun*. M17.
[ORIGIN from ELECTRIC + -ITY.]
1 A property of matter or a phenomenon which manifests itself when substances such as glass and amber are rubbed, when a metal wire is moved through a magnetic field, and in other circumstances, and which is now regarded as a form of energy occurring in two modes (positive and negative) as an intrinsic property of electrons and some other subatomic particles; a flow of this energy, an electric current, esp. as a source of power. M17. ▸**b** A supply of electric current laid on in a building or room. M20.

S. LEWIS Throughout, electricity took the place of candles and . . hearth-fires. **b** J. D. WATSON Their host . . kept his house free of gas and electricity. R. JEFFRIES Electricity cuts, roads blocked by snow.

electricity meter, *electricity pole*, etc. ***static electricity***: see STATIC *adjective*.
2 The branch of science that deals with electricity. M18.

electricize /ɪˈlɛktrɪsʌɪz/ *verb trans. rare*. Also **-ise**. L19.
[ORIGIN formed as ELECTRICITY + -IZE.]
= ELECTRIFY 1.

electride /ɪˈlɛktrʌɪd/ *noun*. L20.
[ORIGIN from ELECTRON *noun*[2] + -IDE.]
An ionic solid whose crystal lattice consists of cations and electrons, rather than cations and anions as in a salt.

electrification /ɪˌlɛktrɪfɪˈkeɪʃ(ə)n/ *noun*. M18.
[ORIGIN from ELECTRIFY: see -FICATION.]
1 The action or process, or an act, of electrifying. M18.

P. D. JAMES With the electrification of the north-east suburban line, Wrentham Green had increasingly become a commuter town.

2 The state of being electrified (*lit.* & *fig.*). L18.

electrify /ɪˈlɛktrɪfʌɪ/ *verb trans*. M18.
[ORIGIN from ELECTR(IC + -I- + -FY.]
1 Charge with electricity; pass an electric current through, *esp.* give (a person) an electric shock. M18.

P. CAREY The tenfoot high electrified fence.

2 *fig.* Cause sudden or dramatic excitement in. M18.

M. L. KING He electrified the public with his description of . . the spiritual emptiness of contemporary society. DAY LEWIS The effect . . was electrifying.

3 Convert to electric operation. E20.
▪ **electrifier** *noun* M19.

electrize /ɪˈlɛktrʌɪz/ *verb trans.* Now *rare* or *obsolete*. Also **-ise**. M18.
[ORIGIN from ELECTR(IC + -IZE.]
= ELECTRIFY 1.
▪ **electriˈzation** *noun* M18.

electro /ɪˈlɛktrəʊ/ *noun*. Pl. **-os**. M19.
[ORIGIN from ELECTRO-.]
1 An electroplated coating; electroplate. M19.
2 An electrotype. L19.
3 A style of dance music with a fast electronic beat backed by a synthesizer. L20.

electro- /ɪˈlɛktrəʊ/ *combining form* of ELECTRIC, ELECTRICITY: see -O-.
1 As a formative elem. of many scientific and techn. words.
2 Forming combs. denoting (styles of) pop music performed using electronic equipment, as ***electro-funk***, ***electro-pop***, etc. L20.
▪ **electro-aˈcoustic**, **electro-aˈcoustical** *adjectives* involving the direct conversion of electrical into acoustic energy or vice versa; (of music) performed or composed with the creative use of electronic equipment: M20. **electro-aˈcoustics** *noun* the branch of science that deals with electro-acoustic phenomena and devices E20. **electro-ˈacupuncture** *noun* acupuncture in which the needles used carry an electric current L20. **electro-aˈnalysis** *noun* chemical analysis by means of electrolytic techniques E20. **electro-anaˈlytical** *adjective* of or pertaining to electro-analysis E20. **electrobioˈlogical** *adjective* of or pertaining to electrobiology M19. **electrobiˈologist** *noun* an expert in electrobiology; a student or practitioner of electrobiology: M19. **electrobiˈology** *noun* (**a**) the branch of science that deals with the electrical phenomena of living organisms; (**b**) *hist.* a particular method of hypnotism: M19. **electroˈcardiogram** *noun* (*MEDICINE*) a chart or record

E

E

produced by an electrocardiograph E20. **electro'cardiograph** *noun* (MEDICINE) an instrument that records or displays the electrical activity of the heart by means of electrodes attached to the skin E20. **electrocardio'graphic** *adjective* (MEDICINE) involving or pertaining to electrocardiography E20. **electrocardio'graphically** *adverb* (MEDICINE) by means of electrocardiography E20. **electrocardi'ography** *noun* (MEDICINE) the practice or technique of using an electrocardiograph or electrocardiograms E20. **electro'cautery** *noun* cautery by means of an electrically heated instrument L19. **electro'chemical** *adjective* involving electricity as applied to or occurring in chemistry; of or pertaining to electrochemistry; ***electrochemical series***, a list of chemical elements in order of the electrical potentials generated by immersion in a standard solution: M19. **electro'chemically** *adverb* in accordance with the laws of electrochemistry M19. **electro'chemist** *noun* an expert or worker in, or a student of, electrochemistry M19. **electro'chemistry** *noun* the branch of science that deals with the relation between electrical and chemical phenomena and the interconversion of these forms of energy E19. **electro'chromic** *adjective* of or pertaining to electrochromism, esp. as used in the construction of displays M20. **electro'chromism** *noun* a reversible change in the colour of a dye, caused by an electric field M20. **electrocoagu'lation** *noun* the use of electrical means to destroy or harden tissue or to control bleeding E20. **electrocoat**, **electro-coating** *nouns* a process in which an object to be coated is made an electrode in a colloidal suspension of coating particles M20. **electro-con'vulsive** *adjective* designating a method of treating certain mental illnesses in which an electric current is passed through the brain so as to produce a convulsion (cf. *ECT* s.v. E, E 10); designating a shock given in this way: M20. **electro'corticogram** *noun* (MEDICINE) a chart or record of the electrical activity of the brain made using electrodes in contact with it M20. **electrocyte** *noun* a cell generating electricity in the electric organ of a fish L20. **electrode'posit** *verb trans.* deposit in the course of electrodeposition M19. **electrodepo'sition** *noun* the deposition of a substance, esp. a metal coating, at an electrode by means of electrolysis M19. **electro'dermal** *adjective* of or pertaining to measurement of the electrical conductivity of the skin, esp. as a guide to a person's emotion M20. **electrodi'alysis** *noun* dialysis in which the movement of ions is aided by an electric field applied across a membrane by electrodes on either side E20. **electroen'cephalogram** *noun* (MEDICINE) a chart or record that is produced by an electroencephalograph M20. **electro-en'cephalograph** *noun* (MEDICINE) an instrument that records or displays the electrical activity of the brain, using electrodes attached to the scalp M20. **electroencepha'lographer** *noun* (MEDICINE) a person who uses an electroencephalograph M20. **electroencephalo'graphic** *adjective* (MEDICINE) involving or pertaining to electroencephalography M20. **electroencephalo'graphically** *adverb* (MEDICINE) by means of electroencephalography M20. **electroencepha'lography** *noun* (MEDICINE) the practice or technique of using an electroencephalograph or electroencephalograms M20. **electrofish** *verb trans.* fish (a stretch of water) using electrocution or a weak electric field M20. **electro'focusing** *noun* = ***isoelectric focusing*** s.v. ISOELECTRIC *adjective* 2b M20. **electroform** *verb & noun* (**a**) *verb trans.* make by electrodeposition on to a mould; (**b**) *noun* an article made by electroforming: M20. **electro'fusion** *noun* fusion in cells or materials that is induced by means of an electric current L19. **electrogasdy'namic** *adjective* pertaining to or involving the transport of charged particles through an electric field by a current of gas, or the generation of electricity by this means M20. **electrogasdy'namics** *noun* the branch of technology dealing with electrogasdynamic phenomena and devices M20. **electro'genesis** *noun* the production of electricity, esp. by organic tissue L19. **electroglow** *noun* (ASTRONOMY) an emission of ultraviolet light from the upper atmospheres of Jupiter, Saturn, and Uranus on the side facing the sun L20. **electro-hy'draulic** *adjective* (**a**) pertaining to or designating a hydraulic system that is powered or controlled electrically; (**b**) involving or employing a high-voltage electrical discharge produced in a liquid: E20. **electro-hy'draulically** *adverb* by means of an electro-hydraulic system M20. **electro-hy'draulics** *noun* the branch of science that deals with electro-hydraulic phenomena M20. **electrojet** *noun* an intense electric current occurring in a narrow belt in the lower ionosphere near the magnetic equator and where there are strong auroral displays M20. **electroki'netic** *adjective* (**a**) of or pertaining to the flow of electricity; (**b**) of or pertaining to motion of particles in a fluid, or of a fluid over a surface, that is associated with a difference of electric potential: L19. **electroless** *adjective* of, pertaining to, or designating a method of plating by chemical and not electrical means M20. **elec'trologist** *noun* a person who practises electrology M20. **elec'trology** *noun* †(**a**) *rare* the branch of science that deals with electricity; (**b**) the removal of hair and skin blemishes electrically through the use of pointed electrodes: M19. **electrolumi'nescence** *noun* luminescence produced electrically, esp. in a phosphor by the application of a voltage L19. **electrolumi'nescent** *adjective* of, pertaining to, or exhibiting electroluminescence; (capable of) producing light by electroluminescence: E20. **electro'matic** *adjective* [after *automatic*] designating various kinds of electrical, often automatic, equipment E20. **electrome'chanical** *adjective* designating a mechanical device which is electrically operated; of, pertaining to, or involving such a device: L19. **electrome'chanically** *adverb* by electromechanical means M20. **electro'medical** *adjective* designating an electrical device used for medical purposes; of or pertaining to the use of such devices: L19. **electrometa'llurgic**, **electrometa'llurgical** *adjectives* of or pertaining to electrometallurgy M19. **electrome'tallurgy** *noun* metallurgy that involves the use of electricity, esp. in electrolytic methods of winning or purifying metals M19. **elec'trometer** *noun* any instrument for measuring small voltages while taking negligible current M18. **electro'metric** *adjective* = ELECTROMETRICAL L19. **electro'metrical** *adjective* of or pertaining to an electrometer; involving or employing the measurement of voltage: L18. **elec'trometry** *noun* the practice or technique of using an electrometer M19. **electromi'gration** *noun* the migration of particles in an electric field M20. **electro'myogram** *noun* (MEDICINE) a chart or record produced by an electromyograph E20. **electro'myograph** *noun* (MEDICINE) an instrument that records, displays, or converts into sound the electrical activity of muscle, using electrodes attached to the skin or inserted into the muscle M20. **electromyo'graphic** *adjective* (MEDICINE) involving or pertaining to electromyography E20. **electromyo'graphically** *adverb* (MEDICINE) by means of electromyography E20. **electromy'ography** *noun* (MEDICINE) the practice or technique of using an electromyograph or electromyograms E20. **electro'negative** *adjective* †(**a**) electrically negative; (**b**) CHEMISTRY going to the positive electrode in electrolysis; having a tendency to attract electrons: E19. **electro'negatively** *adverb* (CHEMISTRY) as an electronegative substance E20. **electronega'tivity** *noun* (CHEMISTRY) the degree to which an atom etc. attracts electrons; the state of being electronegative: E20. **electro'neutral** *adjective* (CHEMISTRY) electrically neutral M20. **electroneu'trality** *noun* (CHEMISTRY) the state of being electrically neutral M20. **electrony'stagmogram** *noun* (MEDICINE) a chart or record that is produced by an electronystagmograph L20. **electrony'stagmograph** *noun* (MEDICINE) an electro-oculograph that is used in electronystagmography M20. **electronystagmo'graphic** *adjective* (MEDICINE) of or pertaining to electronystagmography M20. **electronystagmo'graphically** *adverb* (MEDICINE) by means of electronystagmography L20. **electronystag'mography** *noun* the investigation of nystagmus by electro-oculographic means E20. **electro-'oculogram** *noun* (MEDICINE) (**a**) a chart or record produced by an electro-oculograph; (**b**) = ELECTRO-OCULOGRAPH: M20. **electro-'oculograph** *noun* (MEDICINE) an instrument that records the varying electric potentials of points near the eye as a guide to eye movement M20. **electro-oculo'graphic** *adjective* (MEDICINE) of or pertaining to electro-oculography M20. **electro-oculo'graphically** *adverb* (MEDICINE) by means of electro-oculography M20. **electro-ocu'lography** *noun* (MEDICINE) the use of an electro-oculograph or electro-oculograms M20. **electro-'optic** *adjective* pertaining to or involving the effect of an electric field on light; of or pertaining to electro-optics: L19. **electro-'optical** *adjective* = ELECTRO-OPTIC E20. **electro-'optically** *adverb* by means of an electro-optic device or effect E20. **electro-'optics** *noun* the branch of science that deals with the effect of electric fields on light and the optical properties of substances L19. **electro-os'mosis** *noun* osmosis under the influence of an electric field E20. **electro-os'motic** *adjective* of, pertaining to, or involving electro-osmosis E20. **electro-os'motically** *adverb* by means of or as regards electro-osmosis E20. **electropaint**, **electropainting** *nouns* the application of paint by electrocoating M20. **electrophile** *noun* (CHEMISTRY) an electrophilic substance or molecule E20. **electro'philic** *adjective* (CHEMISTRY) having or involving an affinity for electrons M20. **electrophoto'graphic** *adjective* of, pertaining to, or produced by electrophotography M20. **electropho'tography** *noun* any of various techniques in which fixed images are obtained by means of electricity; *esp.* one that makes use of the photoconductive properties of certain materials, as in xerography: L19. **electrophysio'logical** *adjective* of or pertaining to electrophysiology or its subject matter M20. **electrophysio'logically** *adverb* by means of or as regards electrophysiology M20. **electrophysi'ologist** *noun* an expert in or student of electrophysiology L19. **electrophysi'ology** *noun* the branch of physiology that deals with the electrical phenomena associated with nervous and other bodily activity; the electrical phenomena *of* a bodily process or organ: M19. **electroplaque** *noun* (ZOOLOGY) a flattened electrocyte L20. **electroplax** *noun* (ZOOLOGY) = ELECTROPLAQUE E20. **electroplexy** *noun* [APO)PLEXY] electroconvulsive therapy M20. **electropneu'matic** *adjective* involving both electric and pneumatic power or operation L19. **electro'polish** *verb trans.* polish (metal) by electrolysis M20. **electro'positive** *adjective* †(**a**) electrically positive; (**b**) CHEMISTRY going to the negative electrode in electrolysis; having valence electrons that are readily removed: E19. **electro'positively** *adverb* (CHEMISTRY) as an electropositive substance E20. **electroposi'tivity** *noun* the degree to which an atom etc. tends to form a positive ion; the state of being electropositive: M20. **electrore'ception** *noun* (ZOOLOGY) the detection of electric fields or currents by an animal L20. **e'lectrore,ceptor** *noun* (ZOOLOGY) a sensory receptor that responds to an electric field or current M20. **electrore'duction** *noun* chemical reduction by electrolytic means E20. **electro'retinogram** *noun* (MEDICINE) a chart or record of the electrical activity of the retina M20. **electro'retinograph** *noun* (MEDICINE) an instrument that records or displays the electrical activity of the retina L20. **electroretino'graphic** *adjective* (MEDICINE) involving or pertaining to electroretinography M20. **electroreti'nography** *noun* (MEDICINE) the practice or technique of using electroretinograms M20. **electroscope** *noun* an electrostatic instrument for detecting the presence and sign of electric charge, used also to ascertain the degree of ionization of the air E19. **electro'scopic** *adjective* of, pertaining to, or involving an electroscope M19. **electroshock** *noun* (MEDICINE) an electric shock; the therapeutic use of electric shocks: M19. **electro-'silver** *noun* articles electroplated with silver L19. **electro-slag** *adjective* designating a process for welding or refining metal in which an electric current is passed into the metal through a layer of slag lying on top of it M20. **electro'striction** *noun* the elastic deformation of a dielectric in an electric field when independent of the reversal of the field and proportional to the square of the field strength E20. **electro'strictive** *adjective* of, pertaining to, or employing electrostriction M20. **electro'surgery** *noun* surgery using (esp. high-frequency) electricity L19. **electro'surgical** *adjective* by means of or using electrosurgery E20. **electro'synthesis** *noun* chemical synthesis effected by electricity L19. **electro'technical** *adjective* of or pertaining to electrotechnics L19. **electrotech'nician** *noun* an expert in or student of electrotechnics E20. **electro'technics** *noun* electrical technology, electrical engineering L19. **electrothera'peutic**, **electrothera'peutical** *adjectives* of or pertaining to electrotherapy E20. **electrothera'peutics** *noun* = ELECTROTHERAPY M19. **electro'therapy** *noun* medical treatment by means of electricity, as in diathermy and electroconvulsive therapy L19. **electro'therapist** *noun* a person who employs electrotherapy E20. **electro'thermal**, **electro'thermic** *adjectives* using or involving the conversion of electricity into heat L19. **electro'tin** *verb trans.* coat with tin electrolytically L19. **electro'valence**, **electro'valency** *nouns* (CHEMISTRY) valency, or a bond, in which oppositely charged ions are bound together by the electrostatic attraction between them E20. **electro'valent** *adjective* (CHEMISTRY) of, pertaining to, or designating (an) electrovalency E20. **electrovi'scosity** *noun* the property of being electroviscous; the component of the viscosity of a substance that is due to the electroviscous effect: M20. **electro'viscous** *adjective* having a viscosity that depends on any electric field that is present; of or pertaining to electroviscosity: M20. **electro'weak** *adjective* (PHYSICS) pertaining to or designating the weak and electromagnetic interactions regarded as different low-energy manifestations of a single interaction L20.

electrocute /ɪˈlɛktrəkjuːt/ *verb trans.* L19.

[ORIGIN from ELECTRO- after *execute*.]

1 Put to death by a strong electric current as a means of capital punishment. L19.

2 Cause death of by electric shock. E20.

■ **electro'cution** *noun* execution by electricity; death caused by electricity: L19.

electrode /ɪˈlɛktrəʊd/ *noun*. M19.

[ORIGIN from ELECTRIC + Greek *hodos* way, after *anode*, *cathode*.]

A conductor by which electricity enters or leaves an object, substance, or region.

A. CLARE Two electrodes . . are applied to the anterior temporal areas of the scalp.

■ **electrodeless** *adjective* L19.

electrodynamic /ɪˌlɛktrə(ʊ)dʌɪˈnamɪk/ *adjective*. E19.

[ORIGIN from ELECTRO- + DYNAMIC.]

Of or pertaining to the interactions of electric currents with magnetic fields or with other electric currents; (of a device) employing the effects of such an interaction.

■ **electrodynamical** *adjective* = ELECTRODYNAMIC E20. **electrodynamics** *noun* the branch of physics that deals with electrodynamic phenomena E19.

electrogenic /ɪˌlɛktrə(ʊ)ˈdʒɛnɪk/ *adjective*. L19.

[ORIGIN from ELECTRO- + -GENIC.]

That produces electricity; *spec.* (PHYSIOLOGY) tending to produce a change in electric potential.

electrogenic pump: that transfers ions through a cell membrane and alters the potential across the membrane.

■ **e,lectroge'nicity** *noun* M20.

electrolier /ɪˌlɛktrəˈlɪə/ *noun*. L19.

[ORIGIN from ELECTRO- after *chandelier*.]

A chandelier in which the lights are electric.

electrolyse /ɪˈlɛktrəlʌɪz/ *verb trans.* Also *-**lyze**. M19.

[ORIGIN from ELECTROLYSIS after *analyse*.]

Subject to electrolysis; pass an electric current through (a liquid) so as to cause decomposition.

■ **electroly'sation** *noun* the process of electrolysing M19. **electrolyser** *noun* L20.

electrolysis /ɪˌlɛkˈtrɒlɪsɪs, ˌɛlɛkˈtrɒlɪsɪs/ *noun*. M19.

[ORIGIN from ELECTRO- + -LYSIS.]

1 Chemical decomposition produced by the passage of an electric current through a liquid; the process of passing a current through a liquid to produce a chemical reaction at the electrodes. M19.

2 MEDICINE. The destruction of tumours and calculi by passing an electric current through them. Now *rare*. M19.

3 The removal of body hair by passing an electric current through the root. E20.

electrolyte /ɪˈlɛktrəlʌɪt/ *noun*. M19.

[ORIGIN from ELECTRO- + Greek *lutos* released, from *luein* to release.]

A liquid which contains ions and can be decomposed by electrolysis; *spec.* one used as battery fluid. Also, a substance which gives rise to ions when dissolved, usu. in water, or fused; the ionized or ionizable constituents of a living cell, blood, or other tissue.

electrolytic /ɪˌlɛktrəˈlɪtɪk/ *adjective & noun*. M19.

[ORIGIN from ELECTROLYTE + -IC.]

▸ **A** *adjective*. Of, pertaining to, or produced by electrolysis; employing or involving electrolysis. M19.

▸ **B** *noun*. Copper that has been refined by electrolysis. E20.

■ **electrolytical** *adjective* = ELECTROLYTIC *adjective* M19. **electrolytically** *adverb* by means of electrolysis; as regards electrolysis: L19.

electrolyze *verb* see ELECTROLYSE.

electromagnet /ɪˌlɛktrə(ʊ)ˈmagnɪt/ *noun*. M19.

[ORIGIN from ELECTRO- + MAGNET.]

A piece of soft iron surrounded by a coil of wire so that it can be made temporarily magnetic by passing an electric current through the wire.

electromagnetic /ɪˌlɛktrə(ʊ)magˈnɛtɪk/ *adjective*. E19.

[ORIGIN from ELECTRO- + MAGNETIC.]

Of or pertaining to the interrelation of electric currents or fields and magnetic fields; having both electric and magnetic aspects or properties.

electromagnetic radiation: consisting of electromagnetic waves (e.g. light, radio waves, X-rays). **electromagnetic spectrum** the range of wavelengths or frequencies over which electromagnetic radiation extends. **electromagnetic units** a largely disused system of electrical units based on the force between two magnetic poles, assuming the permeability of the vacuum to be 1. **electromagnetic wave** a wave consisting of a travelling periodic fluctuation in both an electric and a magnetic field, these fields being at right angles to each other and to the direction of propagation of the wave.

■ **electromagnetically** *adverb* by means of electromagnetism L19. **e,lectro'magnetism** *noun* electromagnetic phenomena and properties; the branch of physics that deals with these: E19.

electromeric /ɪˌlɛktrə(ʊ)ˈmɛrɪk/ *adjective*. E20.
[ORIGIN from ELECTRO- after ISOMERIC.]
CHEMISTRY. Of, pertaining to, or designating a postulated displacement of electrons in a molecule during a reaction.

electromotive /ɪˌlɛktrəˈməʊtɪv/ *adjective*. E19.
[ORIGIN from ELECTRO- + MOTIVE *adjective*.]
Pertaining to the flow of an electric current. Chiefly in ***electromotive force*** below.
electromotive force a force or difference in potential that tends to give rise to an electric current; abbreviation ***emf***, ***EMF***.

electromotor /ɪˈlɛktrə(ʊ)məʊtə/ *noun*. E19.
[ORIGIN from ELECTRO- + MOTOR *noun*.]
Orig., a metal serving as an element of a voltaic cell. Now, an electric motor.

electron /ɪˈlɛktrɒn/ *noun*[1]. M19.
[ORIGIN Greek *ēlektron*.]
= ELECTRUM 1.

electron /ɪˈlɛktrɒn/ *noun*[2]. L19.
[ORIGIN from ELECTRIC + -ON.]
A stable subatomic particle which has a constant charge of negative electricity, is a constituent of all atoms, and is the primary carrier of electric current in solids. Cf. LEPTON *noun*[2].
Auger electron: see AUGER *noun*[2] 2. ***planetary electron***: see PLANETARY *adjective*. **positive electron** = POSITRON.
– COMB.: **electron diffraction** the diffraction of a beam of electrons by atoms and molecules (used to investigate crystal structure); **electron gun** a device in which electrons from a heated cathode are emitted as a narrow beam, e.g. in a cathode-ray tube; **electron lens** a device for focusing a beam of electrons by means of a magnetic or electric field; **electron micrograph** a magnified image obtained with an electron microscope; **electron microscope**: using a beam of electrons focused by electron lenses in order to achieve much greater magnification and resolution than is possible with light; **electron multiplier** a device for amplifying a current of electrons by utilizing secondary emission of electrons at a succession of anodes; **electron optics** the branch of physics that deals with the behaviour of electrons and electron beams in magnetic and electric fields; **electron pair** (*a*) *CHEMISTRY* two electrons of opposite spin occupying the same orbital in an atom or molecule; (*b*) *PHYSICS* an electron and a positron produced together by a high-energy reaction; ***electron shell***: see SHELL *noun* 23; **electron spin resonance** resonance in which the transition involved is that of electrons between states of different spin (used to investigate molecular structure etc.); **electron tube** an evacuated or gas-filled tube in which a current of electrons flows from one electrode to another; **electronvolt** a unit of energy equal to that gained or lost by an electron moving through a potential difference of 1 volt, equal to 1.602×10^{-19} joule (symbol eV).

electronic /ɪlɛkˈtrɒnɪk, ɛl-/ *adjective*. E20.
[ORIGIN from ELECTRON *noun*[2] + -IC.]
1 Of or pertaining to the electron or electrons. E20.

> C. P. SNOW The electronic structure of the specific atoms. P. W. ATKINS Electronic transitions, when electrons are shifted from one region of an atom or molecule to another.

2 Designating a device that operates according to the principles or methods of electronics, such as a transistor microchip, or electron tube; operating by means of or employing such devices; (of a musical instrument) generating sound by such devices rather than by mechanical vibration; (of music) using sounds generated or modified electronically and usu. recorded on tape. E20.

> *Times* The largest dollar order for electronic equipment . . yet received in this country.

3 Of or pertaining to electronics; (of a person) expert in electronics. M20.

> M. MCLUHAN The new electronic and organic age. *Physics Bulletin* The central part to be played by the electronics industry, and the electronic technician in particular.

4 Using the electronic transmission or storage of information, as by television or computer. L20.

> *Daily Telegraph* Evangelists who have made the Electronic Church of the airwaves a power in the . . life of the United States. *British Medical Journal* The launch of an electronic journal, Clinical Notes On-line.

– SPECIAL COLLOCATIONS: **electronic flash** a very brief but bright flash of light obtained by discharging a capacitor through a gas-discharge tube; a flashgun that produces such a flash. **electronic mail** the sending of non-spoken information between individuals over a telecommunication network to a location where it is stored for subsequent retrieval, usu. in a computer; information sent in this way. **electronic publishing** the issuing of texts as electronic files rather than on paper. ***electronic tag***: see TAG *noun*[1] 10g. ***electronic tagging***: see TAGGING *noun* 1(a). **electronic typewriter**: in which solid-state circuitry is used to provide facilities such as the storage of typed characters.
■ **electronically** *adverb* by electronic means; as regards an electron or electrons: E20.

electronica /ɪlɛkˈtrɒnɪkə/ *noun*. L20.
[ORIGIN from ELECTRONIC + -A[3].]
1 Electronic music, *spec.* a type deriving from techno and rave music and having an ambient or cerebral quality. L20.
2 Electronic devices or technology considered collectively. L20.

electronics /ɪlɛkˈtrɒnɪks, ɛl-/ *noun*. E20.
[ORIGIN formed as ELECTRONIC + -ICS.]
The branch of physics and technology that deals with the behaviour and flow of electrons, esp. in devices and circuits in which the flow is controlled and utilized.

electronographic /ɪˌlɛktrɒnəˈgrafɪk/ *adjective*. M20.
[ORIGIN from ELECTRON *noun*[2] + -O- + -GRAPHIC.]
1 Employing or designating a printing process in which ink is transferred without pressure by utilizing electrostatic attraction. M20.
2 Pertaining to or designating an image tube in which photoelectrons are accelerated and focused on a sensitive emulsion to form an image. M20.
■ **eˈlectronograph** *noun* an image obtained by electronography L20. **eˌlectroˈnography** *noun* (the use of) electronographic techniques M20.

electrophone /ɪˈlɛktrəfəʊn/ *noun*. M19.
[ORIGIN from ELECTRO- + -PHONE.]
1 *hist.* An instrument which produced sounds in response to an electric current, e.g. from an induction coil or telephone. M19.
2 Any musical instrument in which the sound is electronically generated or amplified. M20.

electrophonic /ɪˌlɛktrə(ʊ)ˈfɒnɪk/ *adjective*. M19.
[ORIGIN from ELECTROPHONE + -IC.]
1 Of, pertaining to, or designating an electrophone; (of music) electronic. M19.
2 Of, pertaining to, or designating a sensation of sound produced by the passage of an alternating current or electromagnetic waves through a person. M20.

electrophoresis /ɪˌlɛktrə(ʊ)fəˈriːsɪs/ *noun*. E20.
[ORIGIN from ELECTRO- + Greek *phorēsis* being carried.]
1 The migration of molecules or colloidal particles through a liquid or gel under the influence of an applied electric field; a technique employing this to separate, identify, or measure the components of protein mixtures etc. E20.
2 *MEDICINE*. = CATAPHORESIS 1. L20.
■ **electrophorese** /-ˈriːz/ *verb trans.* subject to electrophoresis L20. **electrophoretic** *adjective* E20. **electrophoretically** *adverb* M20.

electrophorus /ɪlɛkˈtrɒf(ə)rəs, ɛl-/ *noun*. Also anglicized as **electrophore** /ɪˈlɛktrəfɔː/. L18.
[ORIGIN from ELECTRO-: see -PHORE.]
A simple device for building up a static charge, consisting of a dielectric disc that is given a negative charge by friction, and a metal plate that is placed on the disc and then earthed, so that it acquires a positive charge when it is removed.

electroplate /ɪˈlɛktrə(ʊ)pleɪt, ɪˌlɛktrə(ʊ)ˈpleɪt/ *verb* & *noun*. M19.
[ORIGIN from ELECTRO- + PLATE *verb*, *noun*.]
▸ **A** *verb trans.* Give (a metal article) a coating of silver, chromium, or other metal by use as the cathode, with the coating metal as the anode, in an electrolytic bath. M19.
▸ **B** *noun*. **1** Electroplated articles. M19.
2 *BIOLOGY*. = ELECTROPLAQUE. M20.
■ **electroplater** *noun* M19.

electroporation /ɪˌlɛktrə(ʊ)pəˈreɪʃ(ə)n/ *noun*. L20.
[ORIGIN from ELECTRO- + PORE *noun*[1] + -ATION.]
BIOLOGY. The process of introducing DNA or chromosomes into cells using an electrical pulse to create temporary pores in the cell membranes.
■ **eˈlectroporate** *verb* L20.

electrostatic /ɪˌlɛktrə(ʊ)ˈstatɪk/ *adjective*. M19.
[ORIGIN from ELECTRO- + STATIC, after *hydrostatic*.]
Of or pertaining to stationary electric charges or electrostatics; employing or designating a steady electric field.

> H. M. ROSENBERG Electrons can be focussed into narrow beams by electrostatic or magnetic lenses.

electrostatic units a system of electrical units based on the force between two electric charges, assuming the permittivity of the vacuum to be 1.
■ **electrostatical** *adjective* = ELECTROSTATIC M19. **electrostatically** *adverb* L19.

electrostatics /ɪˌlɛktrə(ʊ)ˈstatɪks/ *noun*. E19.
[ORIGIN from ELECTRO- + STATICS.]
The branch of physics that deals with electrostatic phenomena and properties.

electrotonic /ɪˌlɛktrə(ʊ)ˈtɒnɪk/ *adjective*. M19.
[ORIGIN from ELECTRO- + TONIC *adjective*.]
1 Designating the state of an electric conductor in the vicinity of another conductor through which an electric current is flowing. Now *rare* or *obsolete*. M19.
2 *BIOLOGY*. Characterized by electrotonus; of, pertaining to, or designating the steady flow of electric charge in a cell or tissue in the absence of action potentials. M19.

electrotonus /ɪlɛkˈtrɒtənəs, ɛl-/ *noun*. M19.
[ORIGIN from ELECTRO- + TONE *noun*, TONUS.]
The altered state of a nerve due to the passage of a steady electric current through it.

electrotype /ɪˈlɛktrə(ʊ)tʌɪp/ *noun*, *adjective*, & *verb*. M19.
[ORIGIN from ELECTRO- + -TYPE.]
▸ **A** *noun*. A duplicate made by electroplating an object or a mould of it; a relief printing block made in this way. M19.
▸ **B** *adjective*. Pertaining to or designating an electrotype. M19.
▸ **C** *verb trans.* Make an electrotype of. M19.
■ **electrotyper** *noun* L19.

electrum /ɪˈlɛktrəm/ *noun*. LME.
[ORIGIN Latin from Greek *ēlektron*.]
1 A native mixture of gold with 20 per cent or more of silver; a pale yellow alloy with the same composition, used in jewellery. LME.
†**2** Amber. LME–L18.
3 An alloy of copper, nickel, and zinc. L19.

electuary /ɪˈlɛktjʊ(ə)ri/ *noun*. *arch.* LME.
[ORIGIN Late Latin *elect(u)arium*, prob. from Greek *ekleikton*, from *ekleikhein* lick up.]
1 A medicinal substance mixed with honey or syrup. LME.
†**2** = ELECTRUM 1, 2. M16–M17.

eledone /ɛlɪˈdəʊni/ *noun*. M19.
[ORIGIN mod. Latin (see below) from Greek *eledōnē* a kind of polypus.]
An eight-armed bottom-dwelling cephalopod of the genus *Eledone*, related to the octopus.

eleemosynary /ˌɛliːˈmɒsɪnəri, -ˈmɒz-/ *noun* & *adjective*. L16.
[ORIGIN medieval Latin *eleemosynarius*, (in sense A.1) *-synarium*, from ecclesiastical Latin *eleemosyna* alms from Greek *eleēmosunē* compassionateness, from *eleēmōn* compassionate, from *eleos* mercy: see -ARY[1]. Cf. ALMS.]
▸ †**A** *noun*. **1** = ALMONRY. L16–L17.
2 = ALMONER. *rare*. M17–E19.
3 A person who is dependent on alms. M–L17.
▸ **B** *adjective*. **1** Of, pertaining to, or of the nature of, alms or almsgiving; charitable. E17.

> C. BRONTË Eleemosynary relief never yet tranquillized the working classes.

2 Dependent on or supported by alms. M17.

> N. HAWTHORNE Threw forth . . food, for the flock of eleemosynary doves.

elegance /ˈɛlɪg(ə)ns/ *noun*. E16.
[ORIGIN French *élégance* from Latin *elegantia*, from *elegant-*: see ELEGANT, -ANCE.]
1 The state or quality of being elegant; refined luxury; tasteful correctness; ingenious simplicity. E16.
2 Something that is elegant; a refinement. L17.

elegancy /ˈɛlɪg(ə)nsi/ *noun*. M16.
[ORIGIN Latin *elegantia*: see ELEGANCE, -ANCY.]
1 = ELEGANCE 1. Now *rare*. M16.
2 = ELEGANCE 2. L16.

elegant /ˈɛlɪg(ə)nt/ *adjective*. L15.
[ORIGIN Old French & mod. French *élégant* or Latin *elegant-*, *elegans* rel. to *eligere* to select: see ELECT *verb*, -ANT[1].]
1 Of a person: that dresses tastefully. L15.
2 Characterized by grace of form, style, or movement; refined; graceful, free from awkwardness, coarseness, or clumsiness. E16.

> I. MURDOCH The long loose robes, too elegant to be called dressing-gowns, which she . . put on in the evenings. R. CONQUEST A statesmanlike speech in very elegant French.

elegant variation *iron.* the stylistic fault of deliberately avoiding repetition by using different words for the same thing.
3 Of a person: correct and delicate in taste. Now only in ***elegant scholar***. E17. ▸**b** Refined in manners and habits (formerly also in feeling). E18.
4 Characterized by refined luxury. L17.

> WILKIE COLLINS He felt languid pulses in elegant bedrooms.

5 Of interests, activities, etc.: appropriate to people of refinement and cultivated taste. E18.

> W. M. CRAIG A high state of the elegant arts . . is indicative of great advancement in civilization.

6 Ingeniously simple and effective. E18.

> W. MEID An elegant solution of this long-standing riddle.

7 Excellent, first-rate. *US*. M18.
■ **elegantly** *adverb* E16.

élégante /elegɑ̃ːt/ *noun*. Pl. pronounced same. L18.
[ORIGIN French, fem. of *élégant* ELEGANT.]
A fashionable woman.

elegiac /ɛlɪˈdʒʌɪək/ *adjective* & *noun*. L16.
[ORIGIN French *élégiaque* or late Latin *elegiacus* from Greek *elegeiakos*, from *elegeia*, *elegeion* ELEGY: see -AC.]
▸ **A** *adjective* **1 a** *PROSODY*. Used in or appropriate to elegies. L16. ▸**b** Of a poet: that writes in an elegiac metre, or in a mournful or pensive style. L16.

> **a** SIR W. SCOTT Hast thou no elegiac verse For Brunswick's venerable hearse?

a elegiac couplet, **elegiac distich**: composed of a dactylic hexameter followed by a dactylic pentameter. **elegiac stanza** a quatrain of iambic pentameters rhyming *abab*.
2 Pertaining to or of the nature of an elegy; mournful, melancholy. E17.

E

E

L. LEE Mother's lamentations reach elegiac proportions.

▸ **B** *noun*. In *pl*. Elegiac verses. L18.

■ **elegiacal** *adjective* (*arch.*) = ELEGIAC *adjective* LME. **elegiacally** *adverb* L20.

elegiast /ɪˈlɛdʒɪast/ *noun*. *rare*. M18.
[ORIGIN from ELEGY after *ecclesiast*.]
A writer of elegies.

elegit /ɪˈliːdʒɪt/ *noun*. E16.
[ORIGIN Latin, 3rd person sing. perf. of *eligere* choose, a word occurring in the writ.]
LAW (now *hist.*). A writ of execution by which a judgement creditor was put in possession of all or (earlier) half the goods and lands of a debtor, until the claim was satisfied; the right secured by such a writ.

elegy /ˈɛlɪdʒi/ *noun*. E16.
[ORIGIN French *élégie* or Latin *elegia* from Greek *elegeia*, from *elegos* mournful poem: see -Y³.]
1 A song of lamentation, esp. for the dead; a poem written in an elegiac metre. E16.
2 A poem, or poetry, written in elegiac metre, or for which this metre would have been used in classical times. L16.
■ **elegize** *verb intrans. & trans.* compose an elegy (on); write in a mournful style: E18.

eleme /ˈɛlɪmi/ *noun & adjective*. L19.
[ORIGIN Turkish = something selected.]
(Designating) a kind of dried fig from Turkey.

element /ˈɛlɪmənt/ *noun*. ME.
[ORIGIN Old French & mod. French *élément* from Latin *elementum* (esp. in pl.) principle, rudiment, letter of the alphabet, used as translation of Greek *stoikheion* step, component part.]
▸ **I** The four elements.
1 Earth, air, fire, or water (these being collectively regarded as the constituents of the material world by ancient and medieval philosophers). ME.
2 In *pl*. Atmospheric agencies, *esp.* wind and storm. Chiefly as ***the elements***. ME.
3 †**a** Any of the celestial spheres of ancient cosmology; a celestial object. ME–E17. ▸**b** The sky. *obsolete* exc. *dial.* L15.
4 One of the four elements that is the natural abode of a person etc.; *gen.* one's natural surroundings, one's appropriate or favourite sphere of operation. L16.

G. GISSING Clifford was never so much in his element as when conversing of art. *Truth* Early nineteenth century in character, he was . . out of his element in this neo-Georgian era.

5 A primordial principle, a source, an origin. *rare*. E17.
▸ **II** Component part.
6 Any of the relatively simple substances of which a complex substance or material body is compounded; in *pl.*, the raw material of anything. Orig. *spec.* as in branch I. LME. ▸**b** *spec.* in *SCIENCE*. Any of the substances (numbering more than 100) that cannot be chemically interconverted or broken down into simpler substances and are primary constitutents of matter. M17.

SHAKES. *Temp.* The elements Of whom your swords are temper'd. **b** *Practical Gardening* The principal elements obtained from the soil are nitrogen, potassium, phosphorus, calcium and magnesium.

b the elements of the elements that are present in (a compound), in the proportion in which they are present. ***trace element***: see TRACE *adjective*.
7 In *pl*. Orig., the letters of the alphabet. Now, the rudiments of learning; the first principles of a subject. LME. ▸**b** (Usu. **E-**.) In *pl*. (The name of) a class in a Roman Catholic school, college, or seminary, now only *spec.* the first and most junior class, immediately below Figures, in certain Jesuit schools. M19.

J. GLASSCO We learned the elements of cookery.

The Elements Euclid's fundamental treatise on geometry.
8 *CHRISTIAN CHURCH*. The bread or the wine used in the Eucharist. Usu. in *pl*. M16.
9 A constituent part of an abstract whole; a usu. small amount *of* some quality or characteristic present in something, a hint. L16. ▸**b** = PARAMETER 2. Usu. in *pl*. L18.

T. COLLINS Rory's character was made up of two fine elements, the poetic and the prosaic. *Annual Register* The Communist-led elements among the workers. B. WEBB A meeting ground for all elements in the Party. D. LODGE A certain immunity from assault, though an element of risk remained.

10 *MATH*. **a** An infinitesimal portion *of* length, mass, etc. E18. ▸**b** Each of the symbols or quantities that constitute a matrix or determinant. M19. ▸**c** Each of the entities of which a set is composed. M19.
11 Each of the facts or conditions which enter into a process, deliberation, etc.; a contributory factor. E19.

H. KISSINGER In that relationship the central element would have to be Anglo-French understanding and cooperation.

12 A component part of a structure or device; *spec.* the resistance wire that provides the heat in an electric fire, cooker, etc. M19. ▸**b** A definite small part of an animal or plant structure. M19.

SLR Camera The new lens . . has 10 elements in 9 groups.

b ***sieve element***, ***tracheary element***, etc.

element /ˈɛlɪmənt/ *verb trans*. LME.
[ORIGIN from the noun.]
Make or compound from elements. Now only *fig.*, compose, constitute.

elemental /ɛlɪˈmɛnt(ə)l/ *adjective & noun*. L15.
[ORIGIN medieval Latin *elementalis*, from Latin *elementum*: see ELEMENT *noun*, -AL¹.]
▸ **A** *adjective*. **1** Of or pertaining to any or all of the four elements. L15. ▸**b** Of or pertaining to the powers of nature; personifying a phenomenon or aspect of nature; *fig.* comparable to or suggestive of the great forces of nature. E19.

b GLADSTONE Amphitrite appears in the Odyssey only as an elemental power. E. BOWEN For all her . . tentative cosmetics she was suddenly elemental and heroic.

†**2** Pertaining to the sky; governed by celestial influences. E16–E17.
†**3** Composed of or produced by the four elements; material, not formal; inorganic, not vital. Of fire: physical, actual, not spiritual or figurative; in its hypothetical pure condition rather than the impure form known by experience. M16–M18.
4 Of the nature of an ultimate constituent; basic, primary; *SCIENCE* (of a chemical element) not combined with another element; of or pertaining to the elements. M16.

E. V. NEALE The primitive elemental operations of thought. J. BARZUN Intent upon a few elemental goals . . —food, shelter, love, survival. *Scientific American* Graphite, the commonest form of elemental carbon. *Times Lit. Suppl.* Three laboratories analysed the elemental composition of the torc.

5 = ELEMENTARY 3. Now *rare*. L16.
6 That is an essential or constituent part. M17.
▸ **B** *noun*. A supernatural entity or force regarded by occultists as capable of producing physical manifestations. L19.
■ **elementally** *adverb* M17.

elementalism /ɛlɪˈmɛnt(ə)lɪz(ə)m/ *noun*. M19.
[ORIGIN from ELEMENTAL + -ISM.]
1 The identification of divinities with the powers of nature. M19.
2 An elemental quality or state. E20.

Dance Theatre Journal The passionate, motivated elementalism of Modern Dance.

3 The semantic separation of things which are empirically or physically inseparable. M20.

elementary /ɛlɪˈmɛnt(ə)ri/ *adjective*. LME.
[ORIGIN Latin *elementarius*, from *elementum*: see ELEMENT *noun*, -ARY¹.]
†**1** = ELEMENTAL *adjective* 3. LME–L18.
2 = ELEMENTAL *adjective* 1. Now *rare*. M16.
3 Of the nature of elements or rudiments; introductory; fundamental; relating to the first principles of learning; simple, easy. M16.

J. S. MILL Elementary maxims of prudence. CONAN DOYLE 'Excellent!' I cried. 'Elementary,' said he.

4 = ELEMENTAL *adjective* 4. E17.
5 *MATH*. That is an element of length, mass, etc. L19.
– SPECIAL COLLOCATIONS: **elementary education** formal education at an elementary level in basic subjects. **elementary particle** *PHYSICS* a subatomic particle, *esp.* one not known to be decomposable into other particles. **elementary school** a school providing elementary education; *spec.* (*a*) *hist.* a school intended for children between the ages of 5 and 13; (*b*) *N. Amer.* a primary school. **elementary teacher** a teacher in an elementary school.
■ **elementarily** *adverb* L16. **elementariness** *noun* M17. **elementarity** *noun* the property of being elementary M17.

elemi /ˈɛləmi/ *noun*. M16.
[ORIGIN mod. Latin from Arabic *al-lāmī*.]
Any of various oleoresins obtained from tropical trees of the family Burseraceae and used in varnishes and ointments; *esp.* (more fully ***American elemi***) that from the gumbo-limbo tree, *Bursera simaruba*, and (more fully ***Manila elemi***) that from *Canarium luzanicum* of the Philippines. Also more fully ***gum elemi***.

†**elench** *noun*. LME.
[ORIGIN Latin ELENCHUS.]
LOGIC. **1** = ELENCHUS. LME–M17.
2 A sophistical argument, a fallacy. LME–L17.

elenchtic *adjective* var. of ELENCTIC.

elenchus /ɪˈlɛŋkəs/ *noun*. Pl. **-chi** /-kʌɪ/. M17.
[ORIGIN Latin from Greek *elegkhos* argument of refutation.]
LOGIC. A syllogism in refutation of a syllogistic conclusion; a logical refutation.
Socratic elenchus: see SOCRATIC *adjective*.

elenctic /ɪˈlɛŋktɪk/ *adjective*. Also **-ch-**. E19.
[ORIGIN Greek *elegktikos*, from *elegkhein* refute: see -IC.]
Pertaining to or designating reasoning which proves indirectly, esp. refutation by question and answer. Cf. DEICTIC.
■ †**elenctical** *adjective* L16–L17.

elenge /ˈɛlɪndʒ/ *adjective*. *obsolete* exc. *dial.*
[ORIGIN Old English *ǣlenge*, from stressed var. of A-¹ + *lenge* from var. of Germanic base of LONG *adjective*¹.]
1 Long, protracted; tedious. OE.
2 Solitary, remote; dreary, miserable; unhappy. ME.
†**3** Strange, unusual; foreign. LME–L18.

eleolite *noun* var. of ELAEOLITE.

Eleonora /ɛlɪəˈnɔːrə/ *noun*. M19.
[ORIGIN *Eleonora* of Arborea (c 1350–1404), a princess of Sardinia.]
Eleonora falcon, ***Eleonora's falcon***, a long-winged migratory falcon, *Falco eleonorae*, similar to but larger than the hobby, which occurs on islands and cliffs in the Mediterranean area.

elephant /ˈɛlɪf(ə)nt/ *noun*. Also (*arch.*) **oli-** /ˈɒlɪ-/. ME.
[ORIGIN Old French *olifant*, *elefant* (mod. *éléphant*) from Proto-Romance alt. of Latin *elephantus*, *elepha(n)s* from Greek *elephas*, *elephant-* ivory, elephant, prob. of alien origin; English *el-* by assim. to Latin.]
1 The largest living land mammal, with a prehensile trunk used for taking up food and water, a hairless body, and usu. a pair of long curved tusks, of which two species remain in existence. ME.
2 Ivory; a horn or trumpet of ivory. *arch.* ME.
†**3** = ELEPHANTA. E17–E18.
4 In full ***elephant paper***. A former large size of drawing paper, typically 28 × 23 inches (approx. 711 × 584 mm). E18.
5 A shade of grey. L19.
6 (The emblem of) the Republican Party. *US colloq.* L19.
7 A corrugated iron dugout or Nissen hut. Also ***elephant dugout***, ***elephant hut***. *military slang*. E20.
– PHRASES: **African elephant** the larger of the two species of elephant, *Loxodonta africana*, with large ears. **elephant in the room** (orig. *US*) a major problem or controversial issue which is obviously present but avoided as a subject for discussion. **Indian elephant** the smaller of the two species of elephant, *Elephas maximus*, with proportionately smaller ears. **Order of the Elephant** a Danish order of knighthood. ***pink elephant***: see PINK *adjective*². **see the elephant** *US* see the sights; see the world, get experience of life. ***white elephant***: see WHITE *adjective*.
– COMB.: **elephant bird** = AEPYORNIS; ***elephant dugout***: see sense 7 above; **elephant fish** (*a*) a large silvery chimaeroid fish, *Callorhinchus milii*, of Australia and New Zealand, with a long flexible snout bent sharply downwards at the tip; (*b*) = ***elephant-snout fish*** below; **elephant grass** any of various tall robust tropical grasses and grasslike plants, *esp.* the African *Pennisetum purpureum*; ***elephant hut***: see sense 7 above; **elephant joke** a child's nonsense riddle with an elephant as the subject; ***elephant paper***: see sense 4 above; **elephant seal** either of two very large seals of the genus *Mirounga*, of which the males have inflatable snouts; **elephant's ear** any of various ornamental plants, esp. species of begonia, with large heart-shaped leaves; **elephant's foot** either of two southern African yams, *Dioscorea elephantipes* and *D. sylvatica*, with large woody edible tubers projecting above the ground; **elephant shrew** any mammal of the African order Macroscelididae, comprising small insectivorous creatures with a long snout and small hind limbs; **elephant-snout fish** any of various mormyrids with an elongated snout that resembles an elephant's trunk; **elephant's teeth** ivory; **elephant trunk snake** the wart snake of Java, *Acrochordus javanicus*, which has flabby skin.

elephanta /ɛlɪˈfantə/ *noun*. Also **-ter** /-tə/. E18.
[ORIGIN Portuguese *elephante*, fem. *-ta* from Proto-Romance: see ELEPHANT.]
A violent storm at the end (or the beginning) of a monsoon.

elephantiasis /ˌɛlɪf(ə)nˈtʌɪəsɪs/ *noun*. Pl. **-ases** /-əsiːz/. M16.
[ORIGIN Latin from Greek, from *elephas*: see ELEPHANT, -IASIS.]
1 *MEDICINE*. A condition in which a part of the body, usu. a limb, is grossly enlarged, esp. when due to obstruction of the lymphatics by filarial worms. Formerly also, any of various diseases characterized by swelling or by alteration of the skin, *esp.* lepromatous leprosy. M16.
2 *fig.* A great or undue expansion or enlargement. M19.

elephantic /ɛlɪˈfantɪk/ *noun & adjective*. *rare*. L15.
[ORIGIN Late Latin *elephanticus*, from Latin *elephantus* ELEPHANT: see -IC.]
▸ †**A** *noun*. Leprosy. Only in L15.
▸ **B** *adjective*. Elephantine. L16.

elephantine /ɛlɪˈfantʌɪn/ *noun & adjective*. E16.
[ORIGIN Latin *elephantinus* from Greek *elephantinos*, from *elephant-*: see ELEPHANT, -INE¹.]
▸ †**A** *noun*. Ivory. Only in E16.
▸ **B** *adjective* **1 a** Resembling an elephant in size or strength; (of a task) requiring the strength of an elephant. E17. ▸**b** Resembling an elephant in manner; clumsy, unwieldy. M19.
2 Of or pertaining to an elephant or elephants. L17.
3 *ROMAN ANTIQUITIES*. Made of ivory. Only in ***elephantine book***. L17.

elephantoid /ɛlɪˈfantɔɪd/ *adjective*. M19.
[ORIGIN from ELEPHANT + -OID.]
= ELEPHANTINE *adjective* 1, 2.

elephantry /ˈɛlɪf(ə)ntri/ *noun*. M18.
[ORIGIN from ELEPHANT after *cavalry*.]
Troops mounted on elephants.

Elers ware /ˈɛləz wɛː/ *noun phr.* **M19.**
[ORIGIN David (1656–1742) and John Philip (1664–1738) *Elers*.]
Red stoneware made in Staffordshire in the 17th cent., *esp.* that made by the Elers brothers.

eleusine /ɛljʊˈsʌɪni/ *noun.* **E19.**
[ORIGIN mod. Latin, from Greek *Eleusin-*, *Eleusis*: see ELEUSINIAN.]
Any of several kinds of millet of the genus *Eleusine* with fingered spikes, much grown as cereals in dry areas of India, Africa, etc.

Eleusinian /ɛljʊˈsɪnɪən/ *adjective.* **M17.**
[ORIGIN from Latin *Eleusinius* adjective (from Greek *Eleusinios*) + -AN.]
Belonging to Eleusis, a village near Athens which in classical times was a town famous for its cult of the corn goddess Demeter.
Eleusinian mysteries the ritual celebrations that were held annually at Eleusis in honour of Demeter.

eleutherian /ɛljʊˈθɪərɪən/ *noun & adjective. rare.* **E17.**
[ORIGIN from Greek *eleutherios* (from *eleutheros* free) + -AN.]
▸ **A** *noun.* A deliverer. **E17.**
▸ **B** *adjective.* Designating Zeus as protector of political freedom. **E19.**

eleuthero- /ɪˈljuːθərəʊ/ *combining form* of Greek *eleutheros* free: see -O-.
▪ **eleutheroˈmania** *noun* a frantic desire for freedom **M19.** **eleutheroˈmaniac** *noun & adjective* (a person) possessed by eleutheromania **M19.**

elevate /ˈɛlɪveɪt/ *verb trans.* Pa. pple **-ated**, (earlier, now *poet.*) **-ate. LME.**
[ORIGIN Latin *elevat-* pa. ppl stem of *elevare*, from *e-* E- + *levare* lighten, raise: see -ATE³.]
▸ **I 1** Raise above the usual position or level, or above the level of surrounding objects. **LME.** ▸**b** Orig., hold up to view. Now only *spec.* (CHRISTIAN CHURCH), hold up (the host, the chalice) after speaking the words of institution over it in the Eucharist. **E17.**
D. LARDNER The rope by which the bucket is elevated. J. ROSENBERG Rembrandt . . introduced steps in the background to elevate the rear group.
†**2** Raise in the form of vapour; evaporate. **LME–E18.**
†**3** Erect, build. **LME–L18.**
4 Raise the spirits of; elate, exhilarate. Formerly also, inflate with pride. Now chiefly *joc.*, inebriate. **LME.**
C. RAYNER Fenton was elevated tonight by the splendour of the house, the elegance of the company.
5 Raise in status, rank, or importance; exalt; promote. **L15.**
CONAN DOYLE He could elevate my simple art . . into a prodigy. C. RYAN He had been elevated to the rank of Field Marshal too quickly.
6 Raise the pitch of (the voice). **E17.**
7 Turn or direct upwards (one's eyes, a glance, a gun); *fig.* lift up (one's hopes or thoughts). *arch.* **E17.**
8 Raise the moral, intellectual, or cultural level of. **E17.**
H. T. BUCKLE There is hardly any virtue which so elevates our character as moral courage. *absol.*: M. GRAY The kind of sorrow that purifies and elevates.
▸ †**II 9** Reduce in status or importance, depreciate. **M16–L18.**

elevated /ˈɛlɪveɪtɪd/ *adjective & noun.* **M16.**
[ORIGIN from ELEVATE + -ED¹.]
▸ **A** *adjective.* That has been elevated; raised (*lit.* & *fig.*); exalted, lofty; *joc.* inebriated. **M16.**
elevated railway, **elevated road**, etc.: running above ground level on columns etc.
▸ **B** *ellipt.* as *noun.* An elevated railway; a train running on this. *US.* **L19.**
▪ **elevatedly** *adverb* **L16.** **elevatedness** *noun* **M18.**

elevation /ɛlɪˈveɪʃ(ə)n/ *noun.* **LME.**
[ORIGIN Old French & mod. French *élévation* or Latin *elevatio(n-)*, formed as ELEVATE: see -ATION.]
1 The action or process, or an act, of elevating; the state or fact of being elevated. **LME.** ▸**b** CHRISTIAN CHURCH. The holding up of the host in the Eucharist. **L16.** ▸**c** BALLET. A dancer's leap; the ability to attain height and perform movements while in the air. Also, the action of tightening the muscles and achieving an erect posture. **M19.**
J. WOODWARD The disruption of the strata, the elevation of some, and depression of others. L. STRACHEY His sudden elevation to the throne. S. O'FAOLÁIN The glow of spiritual elevation died from his face.
2 A raised area, esp. of the ground; a swelling on the skin. **LME.**
C. SAGAN Measurements concerning the mountains and elevations of Mars.
3 a The angular height of a body or point in the sky, esp. the celestial pole. Formerly also, the pole's height at any one place, the latitude of a place. **LME.** ▸**b** The angle at which a gun or any line of direction is inclined to the horizontal. **L17.** ▸**c** Altitude above sea level; height above ground level. **M18.**
c J. TYNDALL What was snow at the higher elevations changed to rain lower down.
4 Loftiness; grandeur, dignity. **M17.**
J. MORLEY The classic form, its dignity, elevation, and severity.
5 A drawing or diagram made by projection on a vertical plane; a frontal or side view, esp. of a building. Cf. PLAN *noun* 3a. **M18.**
▪ **elevational** *adjective* (ARCHITECTURE) of or pertaining to an elevation **E20.**

elevator /ˈɛlɪveɪtə/ *noun.* **M17.**
[ORIGIN mod. Latin, formed as ELEVATE: see -OR. In mod. use directly from ELEVATE.]
1 ANATOMY. = LEVATOR 1. Now *rare.* **M17.**
2 A machine for raising corn or grain; a hoist in the form of an endless belt or chain with scoops or the like. **L18.** ▸**b** A building for the storage of grain and equipped with a grain elevator. *N. Amer.* **M19.**
3 SURGERY. An instrument for lifting depressed broken bone, esp. of the skull; an instrument for stripping periosteum from bone; a dental instrument for easing a tooth from a socket. **E19.**
4 A platform or compartment for raising and lowering people or things to different levels, a lift. *N. Amer.* **L19.**
5 Either of a pair of hinged flaps on the stabilizing wings or tailplane of an aircraft, used to vary the angle of pitch. **E20.**
6 (**E-.**) In *pl.* (Proprietary name for) shoes with a raised insole intended to make a person appear taller. Also (in *sing.* or *pl.*) ***elevator shoe***. *N. Amer.* **M20.**
– COMB.: **elevator music** (chiefly *N. Amer.*) bland recorded background music; **elevator pitch** [from the idea of having to impress a senior executive during a brief ride in an elevator] *colloq.* (chiefly *US*) a succinct and persuasive sales pitch.

elevatory /ɛlɪˈveɪt(ə)ri/ *noun & adjective.* **LME.**
[ORIGIN medieval Latin *elevatorium*, formed as ELEVATE: see -ORY²; as adjective directly from ELEVATE.]
▸ **A** *noun.* = ELEVATOR 3. Now *rare* or *obsolete.* **LME.**
▸ **B** *adjective.* Of or pertaining to elevation; that tends to elevate (*lit.* & *fig.*). **E19.**

élève /elɛːv/ *noun.* Pl. pronounced same. Also ***eleve*** /ɛˈlɛv/. **M18.**
[ORIGIN French *élève*, from *élever* raise, bring up, from *é-* (formed as ES-) + *lever* lift from Latin *levare*.]
A pupil, a scholar.

eleven /ɪˈlɛv(ə)n/ *adjective & noun (cardinal numeral).*
[ORIGIN Old English *endleofon*, *-lufon*, *ellefne* = Old Frisian *andlova*, *elleva*, *al-*, *elvene*, Old Saxon *elleban*, Old High German *einlif*, (Dutch, German *elf*), Old Norse *ellifu*, Gothic *ainlif*, from Germanic, from base of ONE *adjective* + base repr. also by TWELVE.]
▸ **A** *adjective.* One more than ten (a cardinal numeral represented by 11 in arabic numerals, xi, XI in roman). **OE.**
New York Times Eleven thousand Palestinian guerrillas . . left West Beirut. *Washington Post* Eleven-twelfths of both amounts would be taxable.
▸ **B** *noun.* **1** Eleven persons or things identified contextually, as years of age, points, runs, etc., in a game, chances (in giving odds), minutes, inches, shillings (now *hist.*), pence, etc. **OE.**
W. S. GILBERT He's a bit undersized, and you don't feel surprised / when he tells you he's only eleven. A. J. P. TAYLOR Eleven of the Liberals who voted against Lloyd George.
the Eleven the Apostles, without Judas.
2 One more than ten as an abstract number; the symbols or figures representing this (11 in arabic numerals, xi, XI in roman). **LME.**
3 The eleventh of a set or series with numbered members, the one designated eleven, (usu. ***number eleven***, or with specification, as ***book eleven***, ***chapter eleven***, etc.); a size etc. denoted by eleven, a shoe etc. of such a size, (also ***size eleven***). **LME.**
J. LE CARRÉ An eleven bus will take me to Hammersmith.
up to eleven [with ref. to a scene in the film *This is Spinal Tap* (1984), featuring a supposedly louder amplifier with control knobs having 11 rather than 10 as the top setting] *colloq.* up to maximum volume on an amplifier etc.
4 The time of day eleven hours after midnight or midday (on a clock, watch, etc., indicated by the numeral eleven displayed or pointed to). Also ***eleven o'clock***. **M16.**
G. B. SHAW It enables Parliament to do things at eleven at night that no sane person would do at eleven in the morning.
5 A set of eleven; a thing having a set of eleven as an essential or distinguishing feature; *spec.* a team of eleven at soccer, hockey, or cricket. **M18.**
S. RAVEN Give the first eleven a little practice.
– COMB.: Forming compound numerals with multiples of a hundred, as **611** (read ***six hundred and eleven***, US also ***six hundred eleven***), etc. In dates used for one thousand one hundred, as **1150** (read ***eleven fifty***), ***eleven-eighties***, etc. Special combs., as **elevenpence** eleven pence, esp. of the old British currency before decimalization; **elevenpenny** *adjective* worth or costing elevenpence; **eleven-plus** *noun & adjective* (designating) an examination formerly taken by schoolchildren to determine what kind of school they should go to for their secondary education (beginning in their twelfth year).
▪ **elevener** *noun* (*dial.*) a drink or light meal taken at about 11 a.m. **E19.** **elevenfold** *adjective & adverb* (**a**) *adjective* eleven times as great or as numerous; having eleven parts, divisions, elements, or units; (**b**) *adverb* to eleven times the number or quantity: **OE.**

elevenses /ɪˈlɛv(ə)nzɪz/ *noun pl. colloq.* Also (earlier, *dial.*) **elevens. L18.**
[ORIGIN from ELEVEN + -S¹ + *-es* var. of -S¹.]
Light refreshment taken at about 11 a.m.

eleventh /ɪˈlɛv(ə)nθ/ *adjective & noun (ordinal numeral).*
[ORIGIN Old English *endleofeþa*, formed as ELEVEN (superseding *endlyfta*, *ællefta* = Old Frisian *andlofta*, *ellefta*, Old Saxon *ellifto*, Old High German *einlifto*, (Dutch *elfde*, German *elfte*), Old Norse *ellifti*, from Germanic), repl. in Middle English by forms from ELEVEN + -TH².]
▸ **A** *adjective.* Next in order after the tenth, that is number eleven in a series, (represented by 11th). **OE.**
A. THWAITE The eleventh child of William Grosse. A. J. P. TAYLOR Cotton fell from third to eleventh place among British industries.
at the eleventh hour, **eleventh-hour** *adjective* at the latest possible moment. **eleventh commandment** *joc.* & *iron.* a rule to be observed as strictly as the Ten Commandments; *spec.* (**a**) one should avoid being found out; (**b**) *US* a Republican should not speak ill of another Republican. **eleventh part** *arch.* = sense B.2 below.
▸ **B** *noun.* **1** The eleventh person or thing of a category, series, etc., identified contextually, as day of the month, (following a proper name) person, esp. monarch or pope, of the specified name, etc. **OE.**
G. B. SHAW Even Louis the Eleventh had to tolerate his confessor, standing for the eternal against the temporal throne. W. FAULKNER 10:00 P.M. March eleventh.
2 Each of eleven equal parts into which something is or may be divided, a fraction which when multiplied by eleven gives one, (= ***eleventh part*** above). **M16.**
Washington Post One-eleventh of the eligible vehicle owners.
3 MUSIC. An interval embracing eleven consecutive notes in the diatonic scale, equivalent to an octave and a fourth; a note an eleventh above another note; a chord of two notes an eleventh apart, or based around the eleventh of a note. **L16.**
– COMB.: Forming compound ordinal numerals with multiples of a hundred, as ***two-hundred-and-eleventh*** (**211th**) etc.
▪ **eleventhly** *adverb* in the eleventh place **L16.**

E

elevon /ˈɛlɪvɒn/ *noun.* **M20.**
[ORIGIN from ELEV(ATOR + AILER)ON.]
A hinged flap on the trailing edge of a delta wing, taking the place of both aileron and elevator in a conventional aircraft.

ELF *abbreviation.*
Extremely low frequency.

elf /ɛlf/ *noun*¹. Pl. **elves** /ɛlvz/.
[ORIGIN Old English *elf* non-WS var. of earlier form of *ylf* = Middle Dutch *elf* from base also of Old English *ælf* = Old Saxon, Middle Low German *alf*, Middle High German *alp* (German *Alp* nightmare), Old Norse *álfr*.]
1 Esp. in Germanic mythology: a supernatural, usu. small being with magical powers for good or evil (sometimes distinguished from a fairy as being male, or, formerly, inferior or more malignant). **OE.**
2 A mischievous or spiteful creature. **M16.**
3 A dwarf. **M16.**
4 A child, *esp.* one that is wilful; a small animal. **L16.**
– COMB.: **elf-arrow** *arch.* a flint arrowhead (regarded as an elves' weapon); **elf-bolt** = ***elf-arrow*** above; **elf-dock** elecampane; **elflock** a tangled mass of hair; **elflocked** *adjective* having elflocks; **elf-shoot** *verb trans.* (*dial.*) shoot with an elf-arrow; **elf-shot** (**a**) a disease, esp. of livestock, attributed to the agency of elves; (**b**) *Scot.* = ***elf-arrow*** above.

elf /ɛlf/ *noun*². *S. Afr.* Also **elft. M18.**
[ORIGIN Afrikaans from Dutch *elft* shad.]
= ***bluefish*** (a) s.v. BLUE *adjective.*

†**elf** *verb trans. rare.* **E17–L18.**
[ORIGIN from ELF *noun*¹.]
Tangle or twist (hair) as an elf might.

elfin /ˈɛlfɪn/ *adjective & noun.* **L16.**
[ORIGIN from ELF *noun*¹, prob. suggested by Middle English *elvene* genit. pl., and infl. by *Elphin* a character of Arthurian romance.]
▸ **A** *adjective.* **1** Of, pertaining to, or produced by an elf or elves; of the nature of an elf. **L16.**
2 Of a person or their face: small and delicate, esp. with an attractively mischievous or strange charm. **L18.**
www.fictionpress.com She had long golden-brown hair, emerald eyes and delicate elfin features.
– SPECIAL COLLOCATIONS: **elfin-tree** a dwarf, crooked tree such as is found in alpine regions; **elfin-wood** a wood composed of elfin-trees.
▸ **B** *noun.* **1** An elf. **L16.**
2 The land or realm of the elves. *Scot.* **L16.**
3 A child. **M18.**

elfish /ˈɛlfɪʃ/ *adjective.* **M16.**
[ORIGIN from ELF *noun*¹ + -ISH¹.]
Elvish. Formerly also (of a thing), unmanageable.

G. GREENE A little Robin Goodfellow of a man, full of elfish tricks.

elft *noun* var. of ELF *noun*[2].

Elgarian /ɛl'ɡɑːrɪən, -'ɡɛː-/ *adjective & noun*. E20.
[ORIGIN from *Elgar* (see below) + -IAN.]
▶ **A** *adjective*. Of, pertaining to, or characteristic of the English composer Sir Edward Elgar (1857–1934) or his music, known for its noble pageantry and romantic fervour. E20.
▶ **B** *noun*. A devotee or interpreter of Elgar's music. L20.

elhi /ɛl'hʌɪ/ *adjective*. *N. Amer.* M20.
[ORIGIN from *el(ementary school* + *hi(gh school.*]
Of publishing or educational material: aimed at students of elementary to high school level. Also designating such a student.

E

Elian /'iːlɪən/ *adjective & noun*. E20.
[ORIGIN from *Elia* (see below) + -AN.]
▶ **A** *adjective*. Of or pertaining to the pseudonymous *Essays of Elia* (1823), or their author Charles Lamb (1775–1834). E20.
▶ **B** *noun*. An admirer or student of 'Elia'. E20.

†**elicit** *adjective*. E17–M18.
[ORIGIN Latin *elicitus* pa. pple of *elicere*: see ELICIT *verb*.]
PHILOSOPHY. Of an act: evolved immediately from an active power or quality.

elicit /ɪ'lɪsɪt/ *verb trans.* M17.
[ORIGIN Latin *elicit-* pa. ppl stem of *elicere* draw forth by trickery or magic, from *e-* E- + *lacere* deceive.]
1 Draw forth, bring out, from being only latent or potential. M17.

G. J. ADLER Having elicited sparks from two flints he lighted a large fire.

2 Bring out (truths etc.) from being only implied; draw out (information) from a person; evoke, stimulate, (a response, a reaction). (Foll. by *from*.) L17.

G. GREENE I was unable to elicit from any of the waiters . . the identity of the gentleman. A. BRINK Two more letters . . failed to elicit even an acknowledgement of receipt. L. HUDSON The smell of scent . . elicited a dream in which he was in a perfume shop. E. H. GOMBRICH As so often happens, the demand elicited a supply.

■ **eliciˈtation** *noun* M17. **elicitor** *noun* a person who or thing which elicits M19.

†**elicitate** *verb trans. rare.* M17–M19.
[ORIGIN Orig. formed as ELICIT *verb* + -ATE[3]; later perh. back-form. from ELICITATION.]
Elicit.

elide /ɪ'lʌɪd/ *verb trans.* M16.
[ORIGIN Latin *elidere* crush out, from *e-* E- + *laedere* to dash.]
†**1** **a** Annul, quash, do away with. Chiefly SCOTS LAW. M16–L19. ▸**b** Make of no account, weaken or destroy, (the force of evidence). L16–L17.
2 Omit (a sound, syllable, etc.) by elision. L18.

A. S. BYATT He had a mannered Oxford voice, elided words, and used the pronoun 'one' frequently.

3 Pass over in silence; suppress, strike out, or omit, often by running several items together. M19.

F. PALGRAVE Gibbon and Sismondi have elided these monarchs.

eligible /'ɛlɪdʒɪb(ə)l/ *adjective & noun*. LME.
[ORIGIN French *éligible* from late Latin *eligibilis*, from *eligere* choose: see -IBLE.]
▶ **A** *adjective*. **1** Fit or entitled to be chosen for a position, award, etc. LME.

G. GORER Never more than half the families eligible for membership were actually members at any one time.

†**2** Subject to appointment by election. M17–M18.
3 That is a matter of choice or preference. *rare.* M18.
4 Desirable, suitable, esp. as a partner in marriage. M18.

O. MANNING Edwina was unmarried and reputed to be the most eligible girl in Cairo.

▶ **B** *noun*. An eligible person or thing; *spec.* a desirable marriage partner. M19.
■ **eligiˈbility** *noun* M17. **eligibleness** *noun* eligibility L17. **eligibly** *adverb* E19.

eliminable /ɪ'lɪmɪnəb(ə)l/ *adjective*. M19.
[ORIGIN from ELIMINATE + -ABLE.]
Able to be eliminated.
■ **eliminaˈbility** *noun* the property or quality of being eliminable M20.

eliminant /ɪ'lɪmɪnənt/ *adjective & noun*. L19.
[ORIGIN Latin *eliminant-* pres. ppl stem of *eliminare*: see ELIMINATE, -ANT[1].]
▶ **A** *adjective*. Causing or promoting excretion, esp. of harmful substances. L19.
▶ **B** *noun*. **1** MATH. A function obtained by eliminating variables from a set of homogeneous polynomial equations. L19.
2 MEDICINE. An eliminant agent. L19.

eliminate /ɪ'lɪmɪneɪt/ *verb trans.* M16.
[ORIGIN Latin *eliminat-* pa. ppl stem of *eliminare* thrust out of doors, expel, from *e-* E- + *limin-*, *limen* threshold: see -ATE[3].]
1 Drive out, expel. Now *rare* or *obsolete*. M16. ▸†**b** Divulge (a secret); set at liberty. E17–M18.
2 Remove, get rid of, do away with; cause to exist no longer; *spec.* (**a**) exclude from further participation in a competition etc. by defeat; (**b**) murder. E18.

Times Lit. Suppl. The result of the late war has been to eliminate Germany from the map. T. BENN We aim to eliminate poverty. M. MCCARTHY Modern machinery and factory processes . . had eliminated all danger of bacteria.

3 **a** PHYSIOLOGY. Expel (waste matter etc.) from the body. L18. ▸**b** CHEMISTRY. Remove (a simpler substance) from a compound. L19.
4 MATH. Get rid of (a quantity in an equation) by combining equations. M19.
5 Ignore as irrelevant to an argument or idea. M19.
6 Extract, isolate, disentangle (a fact, principle, etc.) from a mass of details; elicit, deduce. *colloq.* M19.
■ **eliminative** *adjective* that eliminates or tends to eliminate M19. **eliminator** *noun* a person who or thing which eliminates L19. **eliminatory** *adjective* (*rare*) of or pertaining to elimination M19.

elimination /ɪˌlɪmɪ'neɪʃ(ə)n/ *noun*. E17.
[ORIGIN from ELIMINATE + -ATION.]
The action of eliminating or being eliminated.

Wavelength He came close to elimination in the third round. *Observer* Keeping well topped up with water . . may assist in the elimination of bodily toxins.

– COMB.: **elimination diet** a procedure used to identify foods which a person is intolerant of, in which all suspected foods are excluded from the diet and then reintroduced one at a time.

ELINT /ɪ'lɪnt/ *noun*. Also **Elint**. M20.
[ORIGIN from *el(ectronic int(elligence.*]
Covert intelligence-gathering by electronic means. Freq. *attrib.*

elinvar /'ɛlɪnvɑː/ *noun*. E20.
[ORIGIN French *élinvar*, from *élasticité invariable* invariable elasticity.]
An alloy, mainly of iron and nickel, whose modulus of elasticity is relatively independent of temperature changes.

eliotropus *noun* see HELIOTROPE.

eliquate /'ɛlɪkweɪt/ *verb*. LME.
[ORIGIN Latin *eliquat-* pa. ppl stem of *eliquare* (in late Latin) liquefy, dissolve, from *e-* E- + *liquare* melt, dissolve, liquefy: see -ATE[3].]
†**1** *verb trans.* Melt; liquefy; cause to dissolve or flow freely. LME–E18.
2 *verb trans. & intrans.* Separate by partial fusion. *rare.* M19.

eliquation /ɛlɪ'kweɪʃ(ə)n/ *noun*. E17.
[ORIGIN Late Latin *eliquatio(n-)*, formed as ELIQUATE: see -ATION.]
†**1** Liquefaction. E17–M18.
2 = LIQUATION 1. M18.

ELISA /ɪ'lʌɪzə/ *abbreviation*.
BIOCHEMISTRY. Enzyme-linked immunosorbent assay, an immunological assay technique making use of an enzyme bonded to a particular antibody or antigen.

elision /ɪ'lɪʒ(ə)n/ *noun*. L16.
[ORIGIN Late Latin *elisio(n-)*, from Latin *elis-* pa. ppl stem of *elidere*: see ELIDE, -ION.]
1 (An) omission of a sound, syllable, etc., running together the sounds on either side of it; (an) omission of a passage in a book etc. L16.

STEELE The . . Elisions, by which Consonants of most obdurate Sound are joined together.

2 A mechanical breaking or disruption. Now *rare* or *obsolete*. E17.
†**elision of the air**: formerly assigned as the cause of sound.

elisor /ɪ'lʌɪzə/ *noun*. LME.
[ORIGIN Old French *esliseor* (later *elisour*), from *e(s)lis-* stem of *eslire* choose, elect.]
†**1** = ELECTOR 1, 2. LME–E16.
2 LAW. Either of two people appointed in certain cases to select a jury. Now chiefly *US*. E17.

elite /eɪ'liːt, ɪ-/ *noun & adjective*. Also **élite**. L18.
[ORIGIN French *élite*, use as noun of fem. of obsolete pa. pple of *élire*, †*eslire* from Proto-Romance var. of Latin *eligere* ELECT *verb*.]
▶ **A** *noun*. **1** The choice part, the best, (of society, a group of people, etc.); a select group or class. L18.

K. M. E. MURRAY Oxford still catered . . for the social elite, who could afford to go to the University as a . . luxury. R. RENDELL She . . spoke of her family and its immediate circle as of an élite.

social elite: see SOCIAL *adjective*.
2 A size of type used on typewriters, having twelve characters to the inch. E20.
▶ **B** *attrib. adjective*. Of or belonging to an elite; exclusive. M19.

A. MACLEAN They were élite soldiers . . ruthless men . . ruthlessly trained.

■ **elitism** *noun* advocacy of or reliance on the leadership or dominance of a select group M20. **elitist** *adjective & noun* (a person) practising elitism M20.

elixate /ɪ'lɪkseɪt/ *verb trans.* LME.
[ORIGIN Latin *elixat-* pa. ppl stem of *elixare* boil thoroughly: see -ATE[3].]
1 Boil; obtain an extract of by boiling. Now *rare* or *obsolete*. LME.
2 Steep (in water); macerate. Now *rare*. M17.
■ **eliˈxation** *noun* (now *rare*) (**a**) the action of boiling; †(**b**) digestion: E17.

elixir /ɪ'lɪksə, -sɪə/ *noun*. LME.
[ORIGIN medieval Latin from Arabic *al-ʾiksīr*, from *al-* AL-[2] + Greek *xērion* desiccative powder for wounds, from *xēros* dry.]
1 ALCHEMY. A preparation by means of which it was hoped to change metals into gold; spec. *the* philosopher's stone. LME.
2 More fully ***elixir of life*** [medieval Latin *elixir vitae*]. A supposed drug or essence capable of prolonging life indefinitely. L15.
†**3** A strong extract or tincture. L15–E19.
4 The quintessence or kernel of a thing. E17.

W. CHILLINGWORTH The . . Elixir of all that can be said in defence of your church and doctrine.

5 A sovereign remedy; an aromatic solution used as a medicine or a flavouring (foll. by *of*). M17.

P. FLETCHER The best Elixar for souls drooping pain.

■ †**elixirate** *verb trans. & intrans.* distil, refine by distillation; purify: E17–M18.

†**elixiviate** *verb trans. rare.* L17–M18.
[ORIGIN from *e-* E- + LIXIVIATE.]
Clear from lixivium or lye; refine thoroughly.

Elizabethan /ɪˌlɪzə'biːθ(ə)n/ *adjective & noun*. E19.
[ORIGIN from *Elizabeth*, the name of two queens, the 1st of England and the 2nd of the UK + -AN.]
▶ **A** *adjective*. **1** Of, belonging to, or characteristic of the period of Elizabeth I (reigned 1558–1603), Queen of England. E19.

T. HOOD A large Elizabethan ruff.

2 Of or belonging to the period of Elizabeth II (reigned from 1952), Queen of the United Kingdom. M20.
▶ **B** *noun*. **1** A person, esp. a poet or dramatist, of the reign of Elizabeth I. Usu. in *pl.* E19.
2 A person of the reign of Elizabeth II. M20.
■ **Elizabethanism** *noun* (**a**) a work of literature of the period of Elizabeth I; (**b**) a manner or style characteristic or imitative of that of her reign: L19.

elk /ɛlk/ *noun*[1]. Pl. same, **-s**. L15.
[ORIGIN Prob. repr. Old English *elh*, *eolh* with k for h /x/ as in dial. *dwerk* (Old English *dweorh*) DWARF *noun*, *fark* (Old English *fǣrh*) FARROW *noun*, *selk* (Old English *seolh*) SEAL *noun*[1].]
1 The largest living deer, *Alces alces*, found in northern parts of Europe, Asia, and N. America, and having a growth of skin hanging from the neck and (in males) very large horns. In N. America also called ***moose***. L15.
†**2** = ELAND. *S. Afr.* Only in 18.
3 = WAPITI. Also more fully ***American elk***. *N. Amer.* L19.
4 In the Indian subcontinent, the sambar, *Cervus unicolor*. L19.
5 (**E-**.) A member of the Benevolent and Protective Order of Elks, a US social and charitable organization. Usu. in *pl.* L19.
– PHRASES & COMB.: ***American elk***: see sense 3 above. **elkhorn (coral)** a coral of the genus *Acropora* with sturdy antler-like branches. **elk hound** a large thick-coated hunting dog of Scandinavian origin. ***Irish elk***: see IRISH *adjective*.

elk /ɛlk/ *noun*[2]. *obsolete* exc. *dial.* M16.
[ORIGIN Unknown.]
A wild swan. Also, a wild goose.

ell /ɛl/ *noun*[1].
[ORIGIN Old English *eln* = Old Frisian *(i)elne*, Old Saxon *elina*, Middle Dutch *elne*, *elle* (Dutch *el*), Old High German *elina* (German *Elle*), Old Norse *ǫln* (*aln-*), Gothic *aleina*, orig. arm, forearm, cogn. with Latin ULNA, Greek *ōlenē* elbow. For loss of final *n* cf. MILL *noun*[1].]
1 *hist.* A measure of length, varying in different countries: in England equal to 45 inches; in Scotland equal to 37.2 inches; in the Low Countries equal to 27 inches. OE.
†**2** A measuring rod; = ELL-WAND 2. ME–M18.
†**3** = ULNA. Cf. ELL-WAND 1. E–M17.

ell /ɛl/ *noun*[2]. *dial.* & *US*. L18.
[ORIGIN Repr. pronunc. of *L*, *l* as the letter's name.]
The letter L, l; *spec.* an extension of a building etc. which is at right angles to the main part; a lean-to.

T. BERGER The dining ell off the living room.

-ella /'ɛlə/ *suffix*.
Repr. Italian or Latin dim. suffix, as ***mozzarella***, ***nassella***; *spec.* in BIOLOGY in names of genera of bacteria, as ***Legionella***, ***Salmonella***.

ellagic /ɛ'ladʒɪk/ *adjective*. E19.
[ORIGIN French *ellagique*, from anagram of *galle* gall nut (*gallique* GALLIC *adjective*[2] being already in use): see -IC.]
ellagic acid, a tetracyclic phenolic compound, $C_{14}H_6O_8$, found in oak bark and galls and in bezoars and used as a local haemostatic.
■ **ellagiˈtannin** *noun* (CHEMISTRY) any tannin that on hydrolysis gives ellagic acid and a sugar L19.

Ellingtonian /ɛlɪŋˈtəʊnɪən/ *adjective & noun*. M20.
[ORIGIN from *Ellington* (see below) + -IAN.]
▸ **A** *adjective*. Of, pertaining to, or characteristic of the distinctively brilliant and atmospheric music of Edward ('Duke') Ellington (1899–1974), US jazz musician. M20.
▸ **B** *noun*. A devotee or follower of Duke Ellington or his music. M20.

ellipse /ɪˈlɪps/ *noun*. L17.
[ORIGIN French from Latin *ellipsis*: see ELLIPSIS.]
1 One of the conic sections, a symmetrical closed curve traced by a point moving in a plane so that the sum of its distances from two other points is constant; the cross-section of a cone that is cut by a plane making a smaller angle with the base of the cone than the side of the cone makes. L17.

A. KOESTLER Comets were shown to move either in very elongated ellipses or in parabolas.

2 GRAMMAR. = ELLIPSIS 1. *rare*. M19.
■ **ellipsograph** *noun* an instrument for drawing ellipses L19.

ellipsis /ɪˈlɪpsɪs/ *noun*. Pl. **ellipses** /ɪˈlɪpsiːz/. M16.
[ORIGIN Latin from Greek *elleipsis* defect, ellipse, grammatical ellipsis from *elleipein* leave out, fall short, fail, from *en* in + *leipein* leave.]
1 GRAMMAR. (An) omission from a sentence of one or more words which would be needed to complete the sense or construction or which occur in the original; the omission of a sentence at the end of a paragraph; a set of dots etc. used to indicate such omission. Formerly, elision of a vowel. M16.
2 = ELLIPSE 1. Now *rare* or *obsolete*. L16.

ellipsoid /ɪˈlɪpsɔɪd/ *noun & adjective*. E18.
[ORIGIN from ELLIPSE + -OID.]
▸ **A** *noun*. A solid or surface of which at least one set of parallel cross-sections are ellipses and the rest circles. E18.
ellipsoid of revolution: obtained by rotating an ellipse about one of its axes.
▸ **B** *adjective*. = ELLIPSOIDAL. M19.
■ **ellipˈsoidal** *adjective* having the nature or shape of an ellipsoid M19. **ellipˈsoidally** *adverb* L19.

elliptic /ɪˈlɪptɪk/ *adjective*. E18.
[ORIGIN Greek *elleiptikos* defective, from *elleipein*: see ELLIPSIS, -IC.]
That has the form of an ellipse; pertaining to ellipses.
elliptic geometry a non-Euclidean geometry defined so that all straight lines converge.
■ **ellipticity** /ɛlɪpˈtɪsɪti/ *noun* elliptic form; degree of deviation from circularity (or sphericity), *spec.* the difference in length of the major and minor axes divided by that of the major (or minor) axis: M18.

elliptical /ɪˈlɪptɪk(ə)l/ *adjective & noun*. M17.
[ORIGIN from ELLIPTIC + -AL[1].]
▸ **A** *adjective*. **1** = ELLIPTIC M17.
2 GRAMMAR. Characterized by ellipsis; *spec.* (of sentences etc.) defective, lacking a word or words needed to complete the sense. L18.
▸ **B** *noun*. An elliptical galaxy. M20.
■ **elliptically** *adverb* in an elliptical manner; ***elliptically polarized***, (of light) having a rotating plane of polarization and an electric field vector whose amplitude varies along an elliptic curve: E19. **ellipticalness** *noun* (*rare*) L17.

†**ellops** *noun*. E17.
[ORIGIN Greek *el(l)ops*.]
1 A kind of fish mentioned by the ancients. E17–L19.
2 A kind of snake. *rare* (Milton). Only in M17.

-ellum /ˈɛləm/ *suffix*.
[ORIGIN Latin: see -LE[2].]
Forming dim. nouns, as ***capitellum***, ***flagellum***.

ell-wand /ˈɛlwɒnd/ *noun*. Chiefly *Scot. & N. English*. LME.
[ORIGIN from ELL *noun*[1] + WAND *noun*.]
†**1** = ULNA. Cf. ELL *noun*[1] 3. Only in LME.
2 An ell-measure: a yard-measure. L15.
3 The group of stars forming the belt in the constellation Orion. E16.

elm /ɛlm/ *noun*.
[ORIGIN Old English *elm* corresp. to Middle Low German, Old High German *elm(boum, elmo* (Middle High German *elme, ilme*, German dial. *Ilm*) and, with vowel variation, Old Norse *álmr* (Swedish, Norwegian *alm*), Latin *ulmus*.]
1 Any of various deciduous trees with serrate leaves, of the genus *Ulmus* and other genera of the family Ulmaceae; *esp.* (***a***) (more fully ***English elm***) the European *U. procera*, once common as a hedge tree in central and southern England; (***b***) (more fully ***American elm*** or ***white elm***) *U. americana*, a tree with pale bark of eastern N. America; (***c***) = WYCH ELM. Also more fully ***elm tree***. OE.
red elm, ***slippery elm***, ***Spanish elm***, ***water elm***, etc.
2 The wood of the elm. L16.
■ **elmen** *adjective* (now *arch. & dial.*) (***a***) made of elm; (***b***) of or pertaining to the elm; ***elmen tree***, an elm: LME. **elmy** *adjective* containing many elms, consisting of elms M18.

El Niño /ɛl ˈniːnjəʊ/ *noun phr*. Pl. **-os**. L19.
[ORIGIN Spanish *El Niño (de Navidad)* the (Christmas) child, with ref. to beginning in late December.]
Formerly, an annual warm southward current off northern Peru. Now, an irregularly occurring southward current in the equatorial Pacific Ocean, associated with weather changes and ecological damage; these associated phenomena.

elocution /ɛləˈkjuːʃ(ə)n/ *noun*. LME.
[ORIGIN Latin *elocutio(n-)*, from *elocut-* pa. ppl stem of *eloqui*: see ELOQUENT, -ION.]
†**1** Oratorical or literary expression; literary style as distinguished from matter; the art of appropriate and effective expression. LME–M19.

H. NEVILLE A Person of good Learning and Elocution.

†**2** Eloquence, oratory. L16–L18.

POPE When he speaks, what elocution flows!

3 The art of (public) speaking, esp. of pronunciation, delivery, gesture, and voice production. E17.

C. CIBBER True theatrical elocution.

4 Manner or style of speaking. E17.

BURKE You have a natural, fluent, and unforced elocution.

■ **elocute** *verb intrans.* (*joc.*) [back-form. after *execute* etc.] practise elocution; declaim in an elocutionary manner: L19. **elocutional** *adjective* = ELOCUTIONARY M20. **elocutionally** *adverb* M20. **elocutionary** *adjective* of or pertaining to elocution M19. **elocutionist** *noun* a person proficient in elocution M19. **elocutionize** *verb intrans.* (***a***) use florid or eloquent language; (***b***) speak or read in public: M19.

elocutory /ɛləˈkjuːt(ə)ri/ *adjective*. *rare*. E19.
[ORIGIN from Latin *elocut-*: see ELOCUTION, -ORY[2].]
= ELOCUTIONARY.

elodea /ɛləˈdiːə, ɪˈləʊdɪə/ *noun*. L19.
[ORIGIN mod. Latin, from Greek *helōdēs* marshy.]
Any of various aquatic plants of the N. and S. American genus *Elodea*, of the frogbit family, with whorled leaves and small white or lilac flowers arising from axillary spathes; esp. *E. canadensis* (Canadian waterweed), widely naturalized in Europe.

éloge /elɔːʒ/ *noun*. Pl. pronounced same. M16.
[ORIGIN French, from Latin *elogium* short saying or epitaph, altered from Greek *elegeia* ELEGY: app. confused with EULOGIUM, EULOGY.]
†**1** A commendation; an encomium. M16–E19.
2 A discourse in honour of a deceased person; *esp.* that pronounced on a member of the French Academy by his successor. E18.
– NOTE: Treated as alien in recent use, but formerly naturalized.

†**elogium** *noun*. L16–L18.
[ORIGIN Latin: see ÉLOGE.]
= ELOGY.

†**elogy** *noun*. L16.
[ORIGIN Anglicized from ELOGIUM: see -Y[4].]
1 A saying, an expression; an explanatory inscription. L16–M17.
2 A brief summary of a person's character, *esp.* a eulogy. E17–M18.
3 A biographical notice. Only in M17.
4 A funeral oration. Only in L17.

Elohim /ɛˈləʊhɪm, ɛləʊˈhiːm/ *noun*. L16.
[ORIGIN Hebrew *'ĕlōhīm*.]
In the Old Testament and Hebrew Scriptures: God. Cf. JEHOVAH, YAHWEH.
■ **Elohist** *noun* the author(s) of the Elohistic parts of the Pentateuch (cf. JEHOVIST 2) M19. **Eloˈhistic** *adjective* of, pertaining to, or designating the parts of the Pentateuch in which *Elohim* is used as the name of God M19.

eloign /ɪˈlɔɪn/ *verb trans*. Also †**eloin**. L15.
[ORIGIN Old French *esloignier* (mod. *éloigner*) from Proto-Romance, for late Latin *elongare*: see ELONGATE *verb*.]
1 †**a** Remove, set at a distance (*from*). L15–L17. ▸**b** *refl.* Retire to a distance, go away. Now *rare*. M16.
2 Remove out of legal jurisdiction. *arch*. M16.
3 Take or send away (property). M17.
■ †**eloignment** *noun* (***a***) removal; (***b***) distance, separation: L17–M18.

elongate /ˈiːlɒŋgeɪt/ *adjective*. E19.
[ORIGIN Late Latin *elongatus* pa. pple of *elongare*: see ELONGATE *verb*, -ATE[2].]
Chiefly BOTANY & ZOOLOGY. Having a slender form; long in relation to its width.

elongate /ˈiːlɒŋgeɪt/ *verb*. Pa. pple **-ated**, †**-ate**. LME.
[ORIGIN Late Latin *elongat-* pa. ppl stem of *elongare*, from Latin *e-* E- + *longe* far off, *longus* long: see -ATE[3].]
†**1** *verb trans.* Remove, set at a distance (*from*). LME–M16.
2 *verb trans.* Make longer (esp. relative to the width), draw out; prolong. L16.
3 *verb intrans.* Recede; *obsolete* exc. ASTRONOMY, (of a celestial object) move so as to increase its angular distance from the sun or a particular point on the celestial sphere. M17.
4 *verb intrans.* BOTANY. Grow, become longer; have a slender or tapering form. E19.

elongated /ˈiːlɒŋgeɪtɪd/ *adjective*. M18.
[ORIGIN from ELONGATE *verb* + -ED[1].]
1 That has been elongated; made longer. M18.
2 Long in relation to its width. M19.

elongation /iːlɒŋˈgeɪʃ(ə)n/ *noun*. LME.
[ORIGIN Late Latin *elongatio(n-)*, formed as ELONGATE *verb*: see -ATION.]
1 The action or process, or an act, of elongating. LME.

D. BREWSTER The figure will undergo most curious elongations and contractions.

2 ASTRONOMY. Orig., the angular distance of a celestial object from a particular point on the celestial sphere. Now, the difference in celestial longitude between a planet and the sun or between a moon and its planet. LME.
†**3** Removal to a distance; departure; remoteness. L15–L18.
4 The state of being elongated; an extension, a continuation. M18.
5 The amount of extension of something under stress, usu. expressed as a percentage of the original length. L19.
■ **elongational** *adjective* L20.

†**elonge** *noun* see ALLONGE.

elope /ɪˈləʊp/ *verb intrans*. L16.
[ORIGIN Anglo-Norman *aloper*, perh. from a Middle English word rel. to LEAP *verb*.]
1 Run away, abscond. Now *rare*. L16.

DICKENS The . . valet . . eloped with all the cash and moveables.

2 Orig. in LAW, run away from one's husband with a lover. Now, run away with a lover, or together, esp. to get married. E17.

M. DRABBLE They fell in love and eloped to Germany.

■ **elopement** *noun* L16. **eloper** *noun* M18.

eloquence /ˈɛləkwəns/ *noun*. LME.
[ORIGIN Old French & mod. French *éloquence* from Latin *eloquentia*, from *eloquent-*: see ELOQUENT, -ENCE.]
1 *sing.* & (*arch.*) in *pl.* The fluent, forcible, and apt use of language, so as to appeal to reason or emotion; the quality of being eloquent; eloquent language. LME.

LYTTON Her father's eloquence had descended to her. R. GRAVES The loud, persistent eloquence of an auctioneer in the slave-market. *fig.*: L. HUDSON His musical eloquence left wild beasts spellbound.

†**2** Speech in general. LME–M17.
3 The art of rhetoric. E17.

eloquent /ˈɛləkwənt/ *adjective*. LME.
[ORIGIN Old French & mod. French *éloquent* from Latin *eloquent-* pres. ppl stem of *eloqui* speak out, from *e-* E- + *loqui* speak: see -ENT.]
Possessing, exercising, or characterized by eloquence; expressive, persuasive. Also foll. by *of*.

A. FORBES His whole attitude eloquent of discouragement. L. DURRELL Pursewarden . . behind an armchair . . was making eloquent gestures at everyone.

■ **eloˈquential** *adjective* (*rare*) of or pertaining to eloquence LME. **eloquently** *adverb* LME.

elpee /ɛlˈpiː/ *noun*. L20.
[ORIGIN Repr. pronunc. of *LP* = *long-player*.]
A long-playing record.

Elsan /ˈɛlsan/ *noun*. M20.
[ORIGIN App. from *E. L.* Jackson, manufacturer + SAN(ITATION.]
(Proprietary name for) a transportable lavatory employing chemicals to render wastes inoffensive.

else /ɛls/ *adverb & noun*.
[ORIGIN Old English *elles* = Old Frisian *elles, -is*, Middle Dutch *els*, Old High German *elles, alles*, Old Swedish *äljes* (Swedish *eljest*), genit. sing. (corresp. to Gothic *aljis*) of Germanic word rel. to Latin *alius*, Greek *allos*.]
▸ **A** *adverb*. **1** In addition to, or in place of, the person or thing just mentioned or alluded to; besides; instead. Used after (formerly also before) an indef., rel., or interrog. pronoun and certain other words (as *nothing*, *everybody*, *someone*; *much*, *little*). OE. ▸**b** Used after an indef., rel., or interrog. adjective, with a noun interposed or (formerly) following. *arch*. OE. ▸**c** In (some, any, what, etc.) other manner, time, or place. Used after adverbs or adverbial phrs. correl. with the prons. mentioned in sense 1. ME.

V. WOOLF We have done little else and thought of little else all day. W. HOLTBY There's no one else who can run the company. D. CUSACK Someone else will take your classes for the day. R. OWEN Girls . . wearing bikinis . . and not much else. A. BROOKNER Edith, what else will you do? **b** G. CHAPMAN She kept his person from all else recourse. E. GELLNER Sure of his daily bread, and a good deal else besides. R. ADAMS The din obliterated every noise else. **c** R. POLLOK Sinks—where could he else?—to endless woe. G. GREENE Can't we have dinner somewhere else?

something else: see SOMETHING *pronoun & noun*.
2 †**a** In a different manner; in a different direction. OE–L16. ▸**b** At another time, at other times; on a previous occasion; already. Now *Scot*. LME.
3 In another case; otherwise; if not, (after a neg.) if so. Now usu. (exc. *colloq.* & *literary*) with prec. *or*. OE. ▸**b** If it is not believed; for confirmation. Now *rare* exc. *dial*. L16. ▸**c** Before an adjective: in other respects, otherwise. *rhet*. E19.

J. H. NEWMAN Else how should anyone be saved? I. MURDOCH I will succeed in art, or else in business. D. WELCH Don't squirm, else I'll cut you. **c** N. HAWTHORNE To wander with her through places else so desolate.

or else (***a***) or if not, or otherwise; (***b***) *colloq.* a warning or threat of the consequences should a previously expressed order, expectation, etc., not be carried out or realized.
– COMB.: **elsehow** *adverb* (now *dial.*) in some other way, in other ways; **elsewhen** *adverb* (now *rare*) at or in another time, at other times; **elsewhence** *adverb* (*arch.*) from some other place;

E

elsewhither *adverb* (*arch.*) (**a**) to some other place; †(**b**) to whatever place.
▸ †**B** *noun ellipt.* Something else; anything else. **OE–L16.**
SHAKES. *John* Bastards and else.
– NOTE: After *nobody, somebody, anybody, everybody* (also *someone* etc.), *what*, & *who*, the possess. is formed by inflecting *else*, e.g. *nobody else's*.

elsewhere /ɛlsˈwɛː, ˈɛlswɛː/ *adverb & noun.* **OE.**
[ORIGIN from ELSE + WHERE.]
▸ **A** *adverb.* **1** At or in some other place or other places. **OE.**
O. MANNING You'd be better off elsewhere. *Gramophone* Financial restrictions in Britain and elsewhere.
2 To some other place. **E16.**
GOLDSMITH If used ill in our dealings with one man we . . go elsewhere.
▸ **B** *noun.* Another place. **L20.**

elsewise /ˈɛlswʌɪz/ *adverb.* **M16.**
[ORIGIN from ELSE + -WISE.]
In some other manner; otherwise.

elsin /ˈɛlsɪn/ *noun.* Now *Scot. & N. English.* **ME.**
[ORIGIN App. from Middle Dutch *elsen(e* (Dutch *els*) from Germanic, from base also of AWL.]
An awl.

Elster /ˈɛlstə/ *adjective & noun.* **M20.**
[ORIGIN Tributary of the River Elbe in Germany.]
GEOLOGY. (Designating or pertaining to) a Pleistocene glaciation in northern Europe.
■ Also **Elsterian** /ɛlˈstɪərɪən/ *adjective & noun* **M20.**

ELT *abbreviation.*
English language teaching.

eluant *noun* var. of ELUENT.

eluate /ˈɛljuːət, -eɪt/ *noun.* **M20.**
[ORIGIN from Latin *eluere*: see ELUTE, -ATE³.]
CHEMISTRY. The solution obtained by eluting something.

elucidate /ɪˈluːsɪdeɪt, ɪˈljuː-/ *verb trans.* **M16.**
[ORIGIN Late Latin *elucidat-* pa. ppl stem of *elucidare*, from *e-* E- + *lucidus* LUCID: see -ATE³.]
Make lucid or clear. Now only *fig.*, throw light upon, explain, clarify.
LD MACAULAY His notes have the rare merit of really elucidating the text.
■ **elucidative** *adjective* = ELUCIDATORY **E19.** **elucidator** *noun* **M17.** **elucidatory** *adjective* that elucidates something **L18.**

elucidation /ɪˌluːsɪˈdeɪʃ(ə)n, ɪˌljuː-/ *noun.* **L16.**
[ORIGIN medieval Latin *elucidatio(n-)*, formed as ELUCIDATE: see -ATION.]
1 The action or process of elucidating something. **L16.**
2 Something that elucidates another thing; an explanation. **M17.**

elucubrate /ɪˈluːkjʊbreɪt, ɪˈljuː-/ *verb trans.* Now *rare.* **M16.**
[ORIGIN Latin *elucubrat-* pa. ppl stem of *elucubrare* compose by lamplight: see -ATE³.]
Compose by working at night; *gen.* study.

elucubration /ɪˌluːkjʊˈbreɪʃ(ə)n, ɪˈljuː-/ *noun.* Now *rare.* **M17.**
[ORIGIN Late Latin *elucubratio(n-)*, formed as ELUCUBRATE: see -ATION.]
1 The action or an act of studying or composing, esp. at night or with great application. **M17.**
2 The result of this; a literary composition. **M17.**

elude /ɪˈluːd, ɪˈljuːd/ *verb trans.* **M16.**
[ORIGIN Latin *eludere*, from *e-* E- + *ludere* to play.]
†**1** Delude; baffle; disappoint. **M16–E18.**
2 Evade the force of (an argument). **E17.**
3 Escape adroitly from, evade, (danger, difficulty, a person's grasp, etc.); slip away from (a pursuer); fail to be caught or grasped by (*lit. & fig.*). **M17.** ▸**b** Fail to be discovered or explained by. **L18.**
P. G. WODEHOUSE Quite a simple and obvious idea, but till now it had eluded her. J. THURBER Zigzagging across the North Atlantic, to elude the last submarines of the war. **b** R. L. STEVENSON He eluded the notice of the officials.
4 Evade compliance with or fulfilment of (a law, request, obligation, etc.). **M17.**
■ **eluder** *noun* **M17.**

eludible /ɪˈluːdɪb(ə)l, ɪˈljuː-/ *adjective. rare.* **E18.**
[ORIGIN from ELUDE *verb* + -IBLE. Earlier in INELUDIBLE.]
Able to be eluded, avoidable, escapable.

eluent /ˈɛljʊənt/ *noun.* Also **-ant.** **M20.**
[ORIGIN Latin *eluent-* pres. ppl stem of *eluere*: see ELUTE, -ENT, -ANT¹.]
CHEMISTRY. A solvent used to elute adsorbed material, esp. in chromatography.

Elul /ˈiːlʌl, ˈɛ-/ *noun.* **M16.**
[ORIGIN Hebrew *'ĕlūl*.]
In the Jewish calendar, the twelfth month of the civil and sixth of the religious year, usu. coinciding with parts of August and September.

elumbated /ɪˈlʌmbeɪtɪd/ *adjective.* Now *joc. rare.* **L18.**
[ORIGIN from Latin *elumbis* having a dislocated hip (from *e* out + *lumbus* loin) + -ATE³ + -ED¹.]
Weakened in the loins.

elusion /ɪˈluːʒ(ə)n, ɪˈljuː-/ *noun.* **M16.**
[ORIGIN Late Latin *elusio(n-)* deception, trickery, from Latin *elus-* pa. ppl stem of *eludere*: see ELUDE, -ION.]
†**1** The action of deluding someone; an illusion. **M16–L17.**
2 (An) escape; (an) evasion. Now *rare.* **E17.**

elusive /ɪˈluːsɪv, ɪˈljuː-/ *adjective.* **E18.**
[ORIGIN from Latin *elus-*: see ELUSION, -IVE.]
1 That fails or refuses to be caught by someone or something. Foll. by *of.* **E18.**
R. SAVAGE The grot, elusive of the noontide ray.
2 Of an argument or answer: evasive. **E18.**
3 Difficult to catch or grasp (*lit. & fig.*); eluding distinct perception or precise definition; difficult to find, remember, or attain. **M18.**
M. L. KING Since emancipation, Negroes had searched for the elusive path to freedom. E. F. BENSON Her ideal life . . hitherto had seemed distant and elusive. A. JOHN His deer . . were too elusive; no hit was scored.
■ **elusively** *adverb* **L19.** **elusiveness** *noun* **L19.**

elusory /ɪˈluːs(ə)ri, ɪˈljuː-/ *adjective.* **E17.**
[ORIGIN medieval Latin *elusorius*, from Latin *elus-*: see ELUSION, -ORY².]
Tending to elude; evasive.

elute /ɪˈluːt, ɪˈljuːt/ *verb.* **M18.**
[ORIGIN Latin *elut-* pa. ppl stem of *eluere* wash out, from *e-* E- + *luere* wash.]
†**1** *verb trans.* Wash out, cleanse. *rare.* Only in **M18.**
2 *verb trans.* Remove (adsorbed material) by washing the adsorbent with a solvent, esp. as a chromatographic technique. **M20.**
3 *verb intrans.* Of adsorbed material: be eluted. **L20.**

elution /ɪˈluːʃ(ə)n, ɪˈljuː-/ *noun.* **E17.**
[ORIGIN Late Latin *elutio(n-)*, formed as ELUTE: see -ION.]
1 Washing to remove impurity. Now *rare* or *obsolete.* **E17.**
2 The action or process of eluting; removal of adsorbed material. **E20.**

elutriate /ɪˈluːtrɪeɪt, ɪˈljuː-/ *verb trans.* **M18.**
[ORIGIN Latin *elutriat-* pa. ppl stem of *elutriare* wash out, from *e-* E- + *lutriare* wash.]
Decant; purify by straining; *techn.* separate (lighter and heavier particles) using a flow of liquid or gas.
■ **elutriˈation** *noun* **M17.** **elutriator** *noun* an apparatus used for elutriating something **E20.**

eluvial /ɪˈluːvɪəl, ɪˈljuː-/ *adjective.* **M19.**
[ORIGIN from *e-* E- after *alluvial*.]
1 Of, pertaining to, or of the nature of eluvium. **M19.**
2 Designating soil and soil horizons that have been subject to eluviation. **E20.**

eluviate /ɪˈluːvɪeɪt, ɪˈljuː-/ *verb trans.* **E20.**
[ORIGIN from Latin *eluvio* washing away (from *eluere*: see ELUTE) + -ATION.]
Subject (soil) to eluviation. Usu. as ***eluviated*** *ppl adjective.*
■ **eluviˈation** *noun* the movement of esp. colloidal material in suspension or solution through the soil **E20.**

eluvium /ɪˈluːvɪəm, ɪˈljuː-/ *noun.* **L19.**
[ORIGIN mod. Latin, from *e-* E- after *alluvium*.]
PHYSICAL GEOGRAPHY. Debris formed *in situ* by erosion or deposited by the wind.

elvan /ˈɛlv(ə)n/ *noun.* **E18.**
[ORIGIN Uncertain: perh. from Cornish from Welsh *elfen* element.]
In Cornwall: hard intrusive igneous rock.

elven /ˈɛlv(ə)n/ *noun & adjective.*
[ORIGIN Old English *ælfen, elfen*, repr. Germanic fem. of ELF *noun*¹.]
▸ †**A** *noun.* An elf; orig. *spec.* a female elf. **OE–ME.**
▸ **B** *attrib. adjective.* Of or pertaining to elves; that is an elf. Long *arch. rare.* **ME.**

elver /ˈɛlvə/ *noun.* **M17.**
[ORIGIN Alt. of dial. form of EEL *fare*.]
A young eel.

elves *noun* pl. of ELF *noun*¹.

elvish /ˈɛlvɪʃ/ *adjective.* **ME.**
[ORIGIN from ELF *noun*¹, *elv-* + -ISH¹.]
Of or pertaining to an elf or elves; of the nature of or resembling an elf; supernatural, weird; mischievous. Formerly also, spiteful, peevish; (of an illness) troublesome.

Elysian /ɪˈlɪzɪən/ *adjective.* **M16.**
[ORIGIN from ELYSIUM + -AN.]
Of, pertaining to, or resembling Elysium; paradisal, glorious.
Elysian fields = ELYSIUM 1.

Elysium /ɪˈlɪzɪəm/ *noun & adjective.* **L16.**
[ORIGIN Latin from Greek *Elusion* (sc. *pedion* plain).]
▸ **A** *noun.* **1** The home of the blessed after death, *spec.* in GREEK MYTHOLOGY. **L16.**
2 A place or state of perfect happiness. **L16.**
▸ †**B** *adjective.* = ELYSIAN. **E17–M18.**

elytro- /ˈɛlɪtrəʊ/ *combining form* (now *rare*) of Greek *elutron* sheath: see -O-.
Used chiefly in MEDICINE, with sense 'of the vagina'. Cf. COLPO-.

elytron /ˈɛlɪtrɒn/ *noun.* Pl. **-tra** /-trə/. **M18.**
[ORIGIN Greek *elutron* sheath.]
1 A sheath, a covering, *spec.* that of the spinal cord. Now *rare* or *obsolete.* **M18.**
2 Each of the horny forewings of a coleopterous insect, which form protective sheaths for the hindwings. Cf. TEGMEN. **L18.**
3 Any of a number of plates or scales on the parapodia of some polychaete worms. **M19.**
■ **elytral** *adjective* **L19.**

Elzevir /ˈɛlzɪvɪə/ *adjective & noun.* Also **-vier.** **E18.**
[ORIGIN Dutch *Elsevier*, mod. Latin *Elzevirius*: see below.]
1 (Designating) a book printed in Elzevir type (see sense 2 below) or by a member of the Elsevier family, who were printers in the Netherlands, 1583–1712, and famous for their editions of the classics. **E18.**
2 (Designating) type or a typeface adopted by the Elseviers or based on theirs. **E18.**
■ **Elzeˈvirian** *adjective & noun* (**a**) *adjective* of, pertaining to, or in the style of the Elseviers; (**b**) *noun* a collector of Elzevir editions: **E19.**

em /ɛm/ *noun.* **ME.**
[ORIGIN Repr. pronunc. of *M, m* as the letter's name; in sense 2 with ref. to this letter as having a width equal to the body. Cf. EN.]
1 The letter M, m. **ME.**
2 TYPOGRAPHY. A unit of horizontal measurement in typesetting, equal to the body of any size of metal type or the nominal type-size in photosetting, used for calculating the extent of a line or text; *loosely* a length of 12 points. **L18.**
– COMB.: **em dash** an em rule; **em quad, em quadrat** a square spacing unit; **em rule** a rule an em long, a dash (used to indicate pauses and parentheses in a text).

em- /ɪm, ɛm/ *prefix*¹.
[ORIGIN Repr. Old French & mod. French assim. form of EN-¹ before *b, p*, and (occas.) *m*.]
Used in words adopted from French and in English words modelled on these as a freely productive prefix, forming verbs, as ***embark, embed, embitter, embrighten, empower, empurple.*** Often with parallel forms in IM-¹.

em- /ɪm, ɛm/ *prefix*² (not productive).
Repr. Greek assim. form of EN-² before *b, m, p, ph.*

'em /əm/ *pronoun.* Now *colloq.* **ME.**
[ORIGIN Orig. alt. of HEM *pronoun.* Now regarded as abbreviation of THEM.]
Them.

†**emacerate** *verb trans.* **E16–E18.**
[ORIGIN Latin *emaceratus*, from *e-* E- + *maceratus* pa. pple of *macerare*: see MACERATE *verb*, -ATE³.]
Emaciate; impoverish (soil).

emaciate /ɪˈmeɪsɪeɪt, ɪˈmeɪʃ-/ *verb trans.* & (*rare*) *intrans.* Pa. pple **-ated**, (now *rare* or *obsolete*) **-ate** /-ət/. **E17.**
[ORIGIN Latin *emaciat-* pa. ppl stem of *emaciare*, from *e-* E- + *macies* leanness: see -ATE³.]
Make or become abnormally thin or wasted. Chiefly as ***emaciated*** *ppl adjective.*

emaciation /ɪˌmeɪsɪˈeɪʃ(ə)n, ɪˌmeɪʃ-/ *noun.* **M17.**
[ORIGIN Latin *emaciatio(n-)*, formed as EMACIATE: see -ATION.]
The action or process of emaciating someone; the state of being emaciated.

emacity /ɪˈmasɪti/ *noun. rare.* **M17.**
[ORIGIN Latin *emacitas*, from *emac-*, *emax* fond of buying, from *emere* buy: see -ACITY.]
Fondness for buying.

email /ˈiːmeɪl/ *noun & verb.* Also **e-mail.** **L20.**
[ORIGIN Abbreviation.]
▸ **A** *noun.* = ELECTRONIC ***mail.*** **L20.**
▸ **B** *verb trans. & intrans.* Send an email (to); send (a message) by email. **L20.**
■ **emailer** *noun* **L20.**

email ombrant /ɛmeɪl ˈɒmbrənt, *foreign* emaːj ɔ̃brɑ̃/ *noun phr.* Also **é-.** Pl. **email ombrants**, ***émaux ombrants*** /emo ɔ̃brɑ̃/. **L19.**
[ORIGIN French *émail ombrant*, from *émail* enamel + *ombrer* to shade: see -ANT¹.]
A form of decoration in which a coloured glaze is laid over intagliated earthenware or porcelain to give a monochrome picture.

emakimono /ɪˌmakɪˈmoːno, ɪmakɪˈməʊnəʊ/ *noun.* Pl. same. **M20.**
[ORIGIN Japanese, from *e* painting, picture + *makimono* MAKIMONO.]
A Japanese scroll containing pictures representing a narrative; a pictorial *makimono.*

emalangeni *noun* pl. of LILANGENI.

emanant /ˈɛmənənt/ *adjective. arch.* **E17.**
[ORIGIN Latin *emanant-* pres. ppl stem of *emanare*: see EMANATE, -ANT¹.]
That emanates from a source.

emanate /ˈɛməneɪt/ *verb.* **M18.**
[ORIGIN Latin *emanat-* pa. ppl stem of *emanare*, from *e-* E- + *manare* to flow.]
1 *verb intrans.* Come (as) from a source; issue, proceed, (*from*). **M18.**
E. B. TYLOR Sparks emanating from the flint and steel.

2 *verb trans.* Cause (esp. something abstract or intangible) to emanate. L18.

> W. FAULKNER Bookcases.. emanating an atmosphere of.. meditation.

■ **ˈemanatist** *noun & adjective* (THEOLOGY) (*a*) *noun* a person who believes in a theory of emanation; (*b*) *adjective* = EMANATIONIST: M19. **ˈemanative** *adjective* tending to emanate or to emit something; resembling or due to emanation; pertaining to a theory of emanation: M17. **ˈemanatory** *adjective* (*a*) resembling an emanation, derivative; (*b*) = EMANATIONIST: M17.

emanation /ɛməˈneɪʃ(ə)n/ *noun.* L16.
[ORIGIN Late Latin *emanatio(n-)*, formed as EMANATE: see -ATION.]
▸ **I 1** The process of coming from a source; THEOLOGY the generation of the Son, or the procession of the Holy Spirit, from the Father. L16.
2 The action of emitting or evolving something. M18.
▸ **II 3** A virtue, power, or other abstract quality (regarded as) emanating from something. L16. ▸**b** A necessary consequence. (Foll. by *of*, *from*.) E18.
4 A person who or thing which emanates from God. M17.
5 Something that emanates from a material object, *esp.* something intangible; *spec.* a flash or beam of light. M17. ▸**b** SCIENCE. A radioactive gas emitted by a solid as a product of its radioactive decay; *spec.* the element radon. E20.

> J. GALSWORTHY The savour, like nothing but the emanation of a refined cheese.

■ **emanational** *adjective* M19. **emanationism** *noun* the doctrine that the (spiritual) universe derives its existence from the essence of God and not from an act of creation out of nothing L19. **emanationist** *adjective* of or pertaining to a theory of emanation M20.

emancipate /ɪˈmansɪpeɪt/ *verb trans.* Pa. pple **-ated**, (now *poet.*) **-ate** /-ət/. E17.
[ORIGIN Latin *emancipat-* pa. ppl stem of *emancipare*, from *e-* E- + *mancipium* slave: see -ATE³. In sense 3 because emancipation in Roman Law was effected by a fictitious sale.]
▸ **I 1** Release from control or restraint, esp. a legal or political one. E17. ▸**b** ROMAN & CIVIL LAW. Set free (a child) from the power of the father or parents, orig. of the Roman *paterfamilias*. M17. ▸**c** AUSTRAL. HISTORY. Discharge (a convict) following a pardon, or after he or she has completed a sentence. L18.

> ADAM SMITH A parcel of emancipated slaves. *refl.*: A. STORR Growing up, a child gradually emancipates itself from dependence.

2 Cause to be less bound by social conventions, moral restraints, intellectual prejudices, etc. Freq. as **emancipated** *ppl adjective.* Cf. LIBERATE *verb* 4. M17.

> J. CONRAD Antonia.. offered him her hand (in her emancipated way).

▸ **†II 3** Enslave. *rare.* E17–M18.
■ **emancipative** *adjective* = EMANCIPATORY M19. **emancipator** *noun* L18. **emancipatory** /ɪˈmansɪpət(ə)ri, ɪˌmansɪˈpeɪt(ə)ri/ *adjective* that has the function or effect of emancipating M17.

emancipation /ɪˌmansɪˈpeɪʃ(ə)n/ *noun.* M17.
[ORIGIN Latin *emancipatio(n-)*, formed as EMANCIPATE: see -ATION.]
The action or process of emancipating.
Catholic Emancipation *hist.* the freeing of Roman Catholics from the civil disabilities imposed by English law until 1829.
■ **emancipationist** *noun* an advocate of the emancipation of any section of society, esp. (*hist.*) slaves E19.

emancipist /ɪˈmansɪpɪst/ *noun.* E19.
[ORIGIN from Latin *emancipare* (see EMANCIPATE) + -IST.]
AUSTRAL. HISTORY. An ex-convict who had been pardoned or had completed his or her sentence.

†emane *verb.* M17.
[ORIGIN Old French & mod. French *émaner* or Latin *emanare*: see EMANATE.]
1 *verb intrans.* = EMANATE 1. M17–E19.
2 *verb trans.* = EMANATE 2. *rare.* E18–E19.

emarginate /ɪˈmɑːdʒɪnət/ *adjective.* L18.
[ORIGIN Latin *emarginatus* pa. pple of *emarginare*: see EMARGINATE *verb*, -ATE².]
BOTANY & ZOOLOGY. Notched at the edge.

emarginate /ɪˈmɑːdʒɪneɪt/ *verb trans.* E17.
[ORIGIN Latin *emarginat-* pa. ppl stem of *emarginare* remove the edge of, from *e-* E- + *margin-*, *margo* edge: see -ATE³.]
†1 Remove dead or diseased material from the edge of (a wound or sore). E–M17.
2 BOTANY & ZOOLOGY. Make emarginate. Chiefly as **emarginated** *ppl adjective.* M18.
■ **emargiˈnation** *noun* L17.

emasculate /ɪˈmaskjʊlət/ *adjective.* E17.
[ORIGIN Latin *emasculatus* pa. pple of *emasculare*: see EMASCULATE *verb*, -ATE².]
Emasculated.

emasculate /ɪˈmaskjʊleɪt/ *verb trans.* E17.
[ORIGIN Latin *emasculat-* pa. ppl stem of *emasculare* castrate, from *e-* E- + *masculus* male: see -ATE³.]
1 Castrate; MEDICINE remove the penis of. E17.
2 Deprive of force and vigour; weaken, make effeminate; *esp.* take the force out of (literary work, legislation, etc.) by alterations. E17.
■ **emascuˈlation** *noun* E17. **emasculative** *adjective* that tends to emasculate L19. **emasculator** *noun* L19. **emasculatory** *adjective* = EMASCULATIVE L19.

émaux ombrants *noun phr.* see EMAIL OMBRANT.

embale /ɪmˈbeɪl/ *verb trans.* E18.
[ORIGIN from EM-¹ + BALE *noun*³.]
Wrap up in packages.

emball /ɪmˈbɔːl, ɛm-/ *verb trans.* L16.
[ORIGIN from EM-¹ + BALL *noun*¹.]
1 Encompass with a sphere. L16.
†2 Invest with an orb as the emblem of royalty. *rare* (Shakes.). Only in E17.

†emballage *noun. rare.* E18–E19.
[ORIGIN French, from *emballer* pack or wrap up, formed as EM-¹ + *balle* BALE *noun*³: see -AGE.]
1 Wrappings, packaging. Only in E18.
2 The action of wrapping or packing up. Only in E19.

embalm /ɪmˈbɑːm, ɛm-/ *verb trans.* Also **†im-**. ME.
[ORIGIN Old French & mod. French *embaumer*, formed as EM-¹ + *baume* BALM *noun*¹.]
1 Preserve (a corpse) from decay, orig. by applying spices, now usu. by arterial injection of a preservative. ME.
2 Endow with balmy fragrance. Formerly, anoint with aromatic spices or oil. LME.

> MILTON The buxom air, imbalm'd with odours. L. LEE I was daily embalmed with camphorated oils.

3 *fig.* Preserve from oblivion; keep in (usu. honoured) remembrance. E17.

> TENNYSON Embalm in dying songs a dead regret.

■ **embalmer** *noun* L16. **embalmment** *noun* (*a*) a preparation used in embalming; (*b*) the process of embalming: E17.

embank /ɪmˈbaŋk, ɛm-/ *verb trans.* Also **†im-**. L16.
[ORIGIN from EM-¹, IM-¹ + earlier synon. BANK *verb*¹.]
Enclose or confine (a river etc.) by banks, dykes, etc.
■ **embanker** *noun* a person who builds embankments M19.

embankment /ɪmˈbaŋkm(ə)nt, ɛm-/ *noun.* L18.
[ORIGIN from EMBANK + -MENT.]
1 A long bank or mound for confining a river etc. within fixed limits or for carrying a road, railway, or canal. L18.
2 The action or process of embanking. L19.
– COMB.: **embankment wall** *Austral.* a retaining wall.

embar /ɪmˈbɑː, ɛm-/ *verb trans.* Also **†im-**. Infl. **-rr-**. L15.
[ORIGIN Old French & mod. French *embarrer*, formed as EM-¹ + *barrer* BAR *verb*.]
†1 Break inward the bars of (a helmet). Only in L15.
†2 Exclude or debar (a person) from something. Also foll. by *to do.* E16–E17.
†3 Oppose a barrier to, obstruct; impede (trade) by an embargo; LAW prohibit or bar by legal enactment. M16–M17.
4 Enclose within bars; cage, imprison. Freq. *fig.* L16.

embarcadero /ɛmˌbɑːkəˈdɛːrəʊ/ *noun.* US. Pl. **-os**. M19.
[ORIGIN Spanish, from *embarcar* embark.]
A wharf, a quay.

embarcation *noun* var. of EMBARKATION.

†embarge *noun & verb.* Also **im-**. L16–M17.
[ORIGIN formed as EMBARGO.]
= EMBARGO *noun & verb.*
■ **†embargement** *noun* L16–E17.

embargo /ɛmˈbɑːgəʊ, ɪm-/ *noun & verb.* Also **†im-**. See also EMBARGE. E17.
[ORIGIN Spanish, from *embargar* arrest, impede, from Proto-Romance, from Latin *in-* IM-¹ + *barra* BAR *noun*¹.]
▸ **A** *noun.* Pl. **-oes**.
1 An order prohibiting ships from entering or leaving a country's ports, usu. issued in anticipation of war. E17.
2 An official, usu. temporary, prohibition of a particular commercial activity, or of trade in general, with another country. M17.

> DEFOE Trade was.. under a general Embargo.

3 *gen.* A prohibition, an impediment. L17.

> J. AUSTEN She wanted to talk, but there seemed an embargo on every subject. *Daily Telegraph* Blamed newspapers for having ignored his embargo—journalists usually receive copies.. a day or two beforehand.

▸ **B** *verb trans.* **1** Seize, confiscate; *spec.* seize, requisition, or impound (ships, goods, etc.) for the service of the state. M17.
2 Place (ships, trade, etc.) under an embargo. M18.

embark /ɪmˈbɑːk, ɛm-/ *verb*¹. Also **†im-**, **†-barque**. M16.
[ORIGIN French *embarquer*, formed as EM-¹ + *barque* BARK *noun*³.]
▸ **I 1** *verb trans.* Put or take on board a ship or aircraft. M16.

> E. J. HOWARD The destroyer.. had embarked all the men off the transports.

2 *verb intrans.* Go on board a ship or aircraft. (Foll. by *on* the ship etc., *for* the destination.) M16.

> V. CRONIN They embarked on a galley and two small pleasure ships. JANET MORGAN Archie's squadron.. was to move to Southampton to embark for France.

3 *verb intrans.* Set out *on* an activity or enterprise, make a start. Also foll. by *upon*, *in*. M17.

> J. HERRIOT Once you embark on a life of crime it gets easier all the time.

▸ **II 4** *verb trans.* Invest (money) in an undertaking; involve (a person) in an activity or enterprise. (Foll. by *in*, *on*.) L16.

> E. H. HUTTEN This failure may embark us on two different courses of action.

■ **embarkment** *noun* (now *rare*) = EMBARKATION 1 L16.

†embark *verb*² var. of IMBARK *verb*¹.

embarkation /ɛmbɑːˈkeɪʃ(ə)n/ *noun.* Also **-cation**, **†im-**. M17.
[ORIGIN from EMBARK *verb*¹ + -ATION. In sense 2 from French *embarcation* from Spanish *embarcación*.]
1 The action or process of embarking. M17.

> *attrib.*: R. KIPLING Every one was new to embarkation-duty.

†2 A ship, a boat. L17–L19.
†3 A body of troops on board ship. E–M18.
– COMB.: **embarkation leave**: taken by a member of the armed forces prior to being sent abroad.

†embarn *verb* var. of IMBARN.

†embarque *verb* var. of EMBARK *verb*¹.

embarras /ɑ̃bara/ *noun.* Pl. pronounced same. M17.
[ORIGIN French, formed as EMBARRASS.]
1 Embarrassment. Now only in phrs. below. M17.
embarras de choix, ***embarras de richesse(s)*** /də ʃwa, də riʃɛs/ [French = of choice, of riches] more choices, more resources, than one knows what to do with.
2 An accumulation of driftwood (partially) blocking a waterway. *N. Amer.* Now *rare* or *obsolete.* L18.

embarrass /ɪmˈbarəs, ɛm-/ *verb trans.* E17.
[ORIGIN French *embarrasser* from Spanish *embarazar* prob. from Portuguese *embaraçar*, from *baraço* halter.]
1 Hamper, impede, (a person, movement, or action). *arch.* E17.
2 Perplex, throw into doubt or difficulty. *arch.* L17.

> H. H. MILMAN Frederick.. embarrassed them with the choice among five prelates.

3 Make difficult, complicate, (a question, subject, etc.). *arch.* M18.
4 Cause (a person) to feel awkward, self-conscious, or ashamed. E19.

> F. TUOHY He embarrassed everyone by bursting into tears.

■ **embarrassingly** *adverb* in an embarrassing manner or degree L19.

embarrassed /ɪmˈbarəst, ɛm-/ *adjective.* L17.
[ORIGIN from EMBARRASS + -ED¹.]
1 Perplexed, confused; having or expressing a feeling of awkwardness or self-consciousness. L17.

> O. MANNING Arnold gave an embarrassed grunt and excused his emotions.

2 Of a route: obstructed. Now only *fig.* E18. ▸**b** Having difficulty in meeting financial obligations; short of money. L19.

> W. S. GILBERT Whose middle-class lives are embarrassed by wives who long to parade as 'My Lady'.

3 Of a sentence, narrative, etc.: involved, confused. Now *rare* or *obsolete.* M18.
■ **embarrassedly** *adverb* L19.

embarrassment /ɪmˈbarəsm(ə)nt, ɛm-/ *noun.* L17.
[ORIGIN from EMBARRASS + -MENT.]
1 An embarrassed state or condition; *esp.* a feeling of awkward confusion or self-consciousness. L17. ▸**b** A state of financial difficulty; shortage of money. M19.
2 A thing which embarrasses; in *pl.*, financial difficulties. E18.
– PHRASES: **embarrassment of riches** = EMBARRAS *de richesse(s)*.

†embarren *verb trans.* L15–E19.
[ORIGIN from EM-¹ + BARREN *adjective.*]
Make barren.

†embase *verb trans.* Also **im-**. M16.
[ORIGIN Alt. of ABASE, DEBASE, by substitution of EM-¹, IM-¹.]
1 Make lower (*lit.* & *fig.*); reduce in rank or dignity; humiliate; degrade. M16–M19.
2 Debase (coin); *fig.* impair, corrupt. M16–M18.
3 Devalue (coinage); reduce the price of (goods); *fig.* depreciate, discredit. L16–L17.
■ **†embasement** *noun* L16–E18.

embassade, **embassador**, **embassadress** *nouns* see AMBASSADE, AMBASSADOR, AMBASSADRESS.

embassage /ˈɛmbəsɪdʒ/ *noun.* Also (earlier) **am-** /am-/. L15.
[ORIGIN from Old French *ambasse* message, embassy + -AGE.]
1 = EMBASSY 1. *arch.* L15.
2 The business or message of an ambassador. E16.
3 A body of people sent as a deputation to a head of state; an ambassador and his or her retinue or staff. M16.

embassy /ˈɛmbəsi/ *noun.* Also (now *rare*) **am-** /am-/. L16.
[ORIGIN Old French *ambassé*, *-axée*, *-asée*, corresp. to Provençal *ambaissada*, Old Spanish *ambaxada*, Italian *ambasciata*, medieval Latin *ambasc(i)ata*, all from Proto-Romance: see AMBASSADOR, -Y⁵.]

E

E

1 The position or function of an ambassador. Also, the sending of ambassadors. L16.

SHAKES. *L.L.L.* Here comes in embassy The French king's daughter. SAKI Scuttering footsteps and hurried embassies for outside help.

†**2** = EMBASSAGE 2. L16–M18.

3 The official residence or offices of an ambassador. Also = EMBASSAGE 3. L16.

LYTTON A brilliant ball at the Palazzo of the Austrian embassy at Naples. R. GRAVES Send an embassy to the Great King.

embathe /ɪmˈbeɪð, ɛm-/ *verb trans. poet.* Also †**im-**. L15.
[ORIGIN from EM-[1], IM-[1] + BATHE *verb*.]
Bathe; immerse; wet.

embattle /ɪmˈbat(ə)l, ɛm-/ *verb*[1]. Also †**im-**. ME.
[ORIGIN Old French *embataillier*, formed as EM-[1], BATTLE *noun*.]
1 *verb trans.* Set in battle array; make ready or arm for battle. ME.
2 *verb refl.* & †*intrans.* Take up a battle position. LME.
3 *verb trans.* Fortify (a building, town, etc.). LME.
– NOTE: In sense 3 not always distinguishable from EMBATTLE *verb*[2].
■ **embattled** *ppl adjective*[1] (*a*) that has been embattled; armed; fortified; (*b*) that is under attack, threat, or pressure; subject to conflict or controversy: L15. **embattlement** *noun*[1] the state of being embattled L20.

embattle /ɪmˈbat(ə)l, ɛm-/ *verb*[2] *trans.* LME.
[ORIGIN from EM-[1] + Old French *bataillier*, formed as BATTLE *noun*: cf. BATTLEMENT.]
Provide with battlements. Cf. EMBATTLE *verb*[1].
■ **embattled** *ppl adjective*[2] (*a*) having battlements; (*b*) (esp. HERALDRY) having an edge shaped like battlements: LME. **embattlement** *noun*[2] = BATTLEMENT LME. **embattling** *noun* (HERALDRY) a battlement or crenellation M18.

embay /ɪmˈbeɪ, ɛm-/ *verb*[1] *trans.* L16.
[ORIGIN from EM-[1] + BAY *noun*[3].]
1 Enclose (as) in a bay, recess; shut in; surround. L16.

W. C. WILLIAMS Beds for the poor and sick embayed into the wall.

2 Put or force (a boat) into a bay. E17.

C. FRANCIS Ships were embayed between two headlands and tacked back and forth for days.

3 In *pass.* Be formed into bays. M19.

G. E. HUTCHINSON Embayed coast lines.

■ **embayment** *noun* a bay; a recess in a coastline forming a bay; a recess like a bay: E19.

†**embay** *verb*[2] *trans. poet.* L16–M18.
[ORIGIN from EM-[1] + BAY *verb*[3].]
Bathe; drench, steep.

embed /ɪmˈbɛd, ɛm-/ *verb & noun.* Also **im-** /ɪm-/. Infl. **-dd-**. L18.
[ORIGIN from EM-[1], IM-[1] + BED *noun*.]
▸ **A** *verb trans.* **1** Fix firmly in a surrounding mass of solid or semi-solid material. L18.

H. READ The colour and shape of every stone embedded in the footpath.

2 Of a surrounding mass: enclose firmly. M19.
3 Place or secure within something else, esp. within a larger or firmer entity; cause to be wholly contained within. M19. ▸**b** LINGUISTICS. Place (a clause etc.) within a larger unit of meaning, e.g. another clause, a sentence, etc. Freq. as ***embedded*** *ppl adjective.* M20. ▸**c** MATH. Incorporate (a structured set) into a larger structure while preserving the main features; *spec.* represent (a graph) *in* a given surface so that no two edges intersect. M20. ▸**d** Attach (a journalist) to a military unit during a conflict. L20.

J. R. LOWELL The winged seeds of his thought embed themselves in the memory. H. KISSINGER He embedded his main observations in easy banter. **c** *Personal Computer World* You can . . embed validation rules within the program that defines the screen layout.

▸ **B** *noun.* A journalist who is attached to a military unit during a conflict. L20.
■ **embeddable** *adjective* M20. **embeddedness** *noun* the state or property of being embedded E20. **embedment** *noun* (*a*) the action of embedding; (*b*) a thing which contains something else embedded in it: E19.

embellish /ɪmˈbɛlɪʃ, ɛm-/ *verb trans.* Also †**im-**. LME.
[ORIGIN Old French & mod. French *embelliss-* lengthened stem of *embellir*, formed as EM-[1] + *bel* beautiful: see -ISH[2].]
Orig., beautify. Now *spec.*, adorn, ornament, decorate; heighten (a narrative) with elaborate or fictitious additions.

S. HAZZARD Brushes and hand-mirrors . . , each embellished with a crest. R. COBB A very personal account . . often embellished by my own imagination.

■ **embellisher** *noun* L15.

embellishment /ɪmˈbɛlɪʃm(ə)nt, ɛm-/ *noun.* Also †**im-**. L16.
[ORIGIN from EMBELLISH + -MENT. Cf. Old French & mod. French *embellissement*.]
1 The action of embellishing. L16.
2 A thing which embellishes; an ornament, a decoration, an adornment; also, an exaggeration. M17.

ember /ˈɛmbə/ *noun*[1].
[ORIGIN Old English *ǣmyrġe*, *ǣmerġe* = Middle Low German *ēmere*, Old High German *eimuria* pyre (Middle High German *eimere*), Old Norse *eimyrje* (Danish *emmer*, Swedish *mörja*) embers, from Germanic base. For the intrusive *b* cf. *slumber*.]
1 A hot fragment left in a dying fire, or cast out of a fire. Usu. in *pl.* OE.
2 In *pl. fig.* The fading traces of a passing activity, state, etc. E16.

J. BENTHAM Success does not . . arise out of the embers of ill-success.

■ **embered** *adjective* strewn with or burnt to embers L16.

ember /ˈɛmbə/ *noun*[2]. *dial.* Also **emmer** /ˈɛmə/, **immer** /ˈɪmə/, & other vars. L17.
[ORIGIN Norwegian *immer*, *imbre*.]
The great northern diver, *Gavia immer*. Also more fully ***ember goose***.

Ember /ˈɛmbə/ *adjective & noun*[3]. Also **e-**.
[ORIGIN Old English *ymbren*: perh. alt. of *ymbryne* period, revolution of time, from *ymb* about, around + *ryne* course; perh. based partly on ecclesiastical Latin *quatuor tempora* (cf. German *Quatember*).]
CHRISTIAN CHURCH. ▸**A** *adjective.* Designating each of four periods, one in each season of the year, which were times of fasting but in Anglican Churches are now associated with ordinations. Chiefly in ***Ember day(s)*** below. OE.
Ember day a Wednesday, Friday, or Saturday immediately after (1) the first Sunday in Lent, (2) Pentecost, (3) Holy Cross Day (14 September), or (4) St Lucy's Day (13 December), which traditionally have been fast days. **Ember eve** *rare* (Shakes.) the vigil of an Ember day. **Embertide** one of the seasons or times of Ember days. **Ember week** a week in which Ember days occur.
▸ †**B** *noun.* An Ember day. OE–L16.

embetter /ɪmˈbɛtə, ɛm-/ *verb trans.* Now *rare.* Also †**im-**. M16.
[ORIGIN from EM-[1], IM-[1] + BETTER *adjective*.]
Make better.

embezzle /ɪmˈbɛz(ə)l, ɛm-/ *verb trans.* LME.
[ORIGIN Anglo-Norman *embesiler*, formed as EM-[1] + *besiler* in same sense (whence BEZZLE *verb*) = Old French *besillier* maltreat, ravage, destroy; of unknown origin.]
†**1** Make off with (provisions, money, etc.); steal. LME–M18. ▸**b** Steal or fraudulently destroy (a legal document); tamper with (any document). LME–L17.
†**2** Weaken, impair. M16–L17. ▸**b** Squander, dissipate. L16–L18.
3 Esp. of an employee or servant: misappropriate or steal (money, goods, etc.) belonging to or on their way to an employer or master, in violation of trust or duty. L16.

G. GREENE A sense of guilt . . as though he had embezzled the company's money.

■ **embezzlement** *noun* the action or an act of embezzling; misappropriation of entrusted money etc.: M16. **embezzler** *noun* M17.

embind /ɪmˈbʌɪnd, ɛm-/ *verb trans. rare.* Also †**im-**. Pa. t. & pple **-bound** /-ˈbaʊnd/. E17.
[ORIGIN from EM-[1], IM-[1] + BIND *verb*.]
Confine, hold fast.

embitter /ɪmˈbɪtə, ɛm-/ *verb trans.* Also †**im-**. L15.
[ORIGIN from EM-[1], IM-[1] + BITTER *adjective*.]
▸ **I 1** Make (a person or feeling) intensely hostile, bitter, or discontented; exacerbate (a quarrel). L15.

R. LINDNER A soured woman . . embittered for life by her illegitimacy.

2 Increase the bitterness or pain of. M17.

J. R. GREEN His failure was embittered by heavier disasters elsewhere.

3 Spoil the sweetness of, sour, (existence, pursuits, etc.). L17.
▸ **II 4** Make bitter to the taste. Now *rare.* E17.
■ **embitterer** *noun* M18. **embitterment** *noun* the action of embittering; the state of being embittered: M17.

emblaze /ɪmˈbleɪz, ɛm-/ *verb*[1] *trans.* Also **im-** /ɪm-/. L15.
[ORIGIN from EM-[1], IM-[1] + BLAZE *noun*[1].]
1 Light up, cause to glow. L15.
2 Fill with flames, set ablaze. E18.
■ **emblazer** *noun* L18.

emblaze /ɪmˈbleɪz, ɛm-/ *verb*[2] *trans.* Now *rare* or *obsolete.* E16.
[ORIGIN from EM-[1] + BLAZE *verb*[2].]
1 Adorn with heraldic devices; (infl. by EMBLAZE *verb*[1]) make resplendent. E16.
†**2** Describe in heraldic terms; represent heraldically; depict or paint in colour. L16–L18.
3 Inscribe or portray conspicuously. L16.
4 Make famous or notorious. L16.
– NOTE: Largely superseded by EMBLAZON *verb*.

†**emblazon** *noun.* M16–M17.
[ORIGIN App. from the verb.]
The heraldic depiction of armorial bearings.

emblazon /ɪmˈbleɪz(ə)n, ɛm-/ *verb trans.* L16.
[ORIGIN from EM-[1] + BLAZON *verb*.]
1 Inscribe or portray conspicuously, (as) on a heraldic shield; adorn with heraldic devices or conspicuously; depict or paint (armorial bearings) in colour; inscribe with words. L16.

J. MORLEY He emblazoned it on a banner. J. MARQUAND The lantern carriers . . bearings lights emblazoned with the master's name.

2 Celebrate, extol; make illustrious. L16.

J. BARZUN The . . word 'education', . . which we now find emblazoned in all the mansions of life.

■ **emblazoner** *noun* L16. **emblazonment** *noun* the action of emblazoning; a heraldic device or decoration: L18.

emblazonry /ɪmˈbleɪz(ə)nri, ɛm-/ *noun.* M17.
[ORIGIN from EMBLAZON *verb* + -RY.]
1 = BLAZONRY 1; symbolic ornamentation. M17.
2 = BLAZONRY 2; brilliant representation or embellishment (visual or verbal). E19.

emblem /ˈɛmbləm/ *noun.* E17.
[ORIGIN Latin *emblema* inlaid work, raised ornament from Greek *emblēma* insertion, from *emballein* throw in, insert, formed as EM-[2] + *ballein* throw.]
1 An object, or a picture of one, serving as a symbolic representation of a quality, action, type of person, etc. E17.

K. CLARK Those two emblems of lust and ferocity, the unicorn and the lion. D. STOREY A row of banners . . each bearing the emblem of a saint or an apostle.

2 A heraldic device or symbolic object used as the distinctive badge of a family, nation, organization, etc. E17.

TOLKIEN A small shield . . bore the running horse . . that was the emblem of the House of Eorl.

3 A symbol or token *of* something; a typical instance; a person who exemplifies a specified quality. E17.

P. ACKROYD Their first encounter . . had become an emblem of the way things were.

4 A drawing or picture expressing a moral fable or allegory; a fable or allegory which may be so expressed. E17.
†**5** An ornament of inlaid work. E17–L18.
– COMB.: **emblem book**: containing drawings accompanied by allegorical interpretations.
■ **emblemize** *verb trans.* = EMBLEMATIZE M17.

emblem /ˈɛmbləm/ *verb trans.* L16.
[ORIGIN from (the same root as) EMBLEM *noun*.]
Be the emblem of; express by means of an emblem, symbolize; provide with an emblem.

emblema /ɛmˈbliːmə/ *noun.* Pl. **-mata** /-mətə/. M19.
[ORIGIN Latin: see EMBLEM *noun*.]
CLASSICAL ART. A carved or mounted ornament in relief.

emblematic /ɛmbləˈmatɪk/ *adjective.* M17.
[ORIGIN from Greek *emblēmat-*, *-ma* (see EMBLEM *noun*) + -IC, after French *emblématique*: see -ATIC.]
Pertaining to, of the nature of, or serving as an emblem; symbolic, typical, (*of*).
■ **emblematical** *adjective* = EMBLEMATIC M17. **emblematically** *adverb* E17.

emblematise *verb* var. of EMBLEMATIZE.

emblematist /ɛmˈblɛmətɪst/ *noun.* M17.
[ORIGIN formed as EMBLEMATIC: see -IST.]
A person who invents or uses emblems; a composer of allegories.

emblematize /ɛmˈblɛmətʌɪz/ *verb trans.* Also **-ise**. E17.
[ORIGIN formed as EMBLEMATIST + -IZE.]
1 Serve as an emblem of; represent mystically, allusively, or allegorically. E17.
2 Of a person: represent using an emblem. M18.

emblements /ˈɛmblɪm(ə)nts/ *noun pl.* L15.
[ORIGIN Old French *emblaement*, from *emblaer*, *emblaier*, (also mod.) *emblaver* sow with corn, from *blé* corn.]
LAW. The profits of sown land; *spec.* annually produced plant crops, deemed personal property even when still attached to the soil, and even after unexpected loss of the land before the harvest.

emblic /ˈɛmblɪk/ *noun.* M16.
[ORIGIN medieval Latin *emblicus* from Arabic *amlaj* from Old Persian (Persian *ām(u)la*): cf. Sanskrit *āmalaka*.]
(The fruit of) a deciduous tree, *Phyllanthus emblica*, of the euphorbia family, native to tropical Asia.

†**embliss** *verb trans. rare.* LME–L18.
[ORIGIN from EM-[1] + BLISS *noun*.]
Make happy.

embloom /ɪmˈbluːm, ɛm-/ *verb trans.* Now *rare* or *obsolete.* E16.
[ORIGIN from EM-[1] + BLOOM *noun*[1].]
Give a bloom to.

emblossom /ɪmˈblɒsəm, ɛm-/ *verb trans.* Also **im-** /ɪm-/. M18.
[ORIGIN from EM-[1], IM-[1] + BLOSSOM *noun*.]
Load or cover with blossoms.

embodiment /ɪmˈbɒdɪm(ə)nt, ɛm-/ *noun.* Also (now *rare*) **im-** /ɪm-/. E19.
[ORIGIN from EMBODY + -MENT.]
1 A material or actual thing or person in which an abstract principle, concept, etc., is realized or concretely expressed; a person who is a typical expression *of* a quality, sentiment, etc. E19. ▸**b** The corporeal habitation of a soul. M19.

H. KELLER I thought the professors were the embodiment of wisdom. J. RABAN The city has always been an embodiment of hope.

2 The action of embodying; the process or state of embodying. **M19.**

F. HALL Souls . . condemned, by reason of sin, to repeated embodiment.

embody /ɪmˈbɒdi, ɛm-/ *verb*. Also (now *rare*) **im-** /ɪm-/. **M16.**
[ORIGIN from EM-[1], IM-[1] + BODY *noun*, after Latin *incorporare*.]
1 *verb trans.* Provide (a spirit) with a bodily form. **M16.**
2 *verb trans.* Unite into one body or mass; incorporate in a larger whole. **M16.** ▸**b** Include as a constituent part. **M19.**

J. MACKINTOSH Much of these treaties has been embodied into the general law of Europe. *New Scientist* When emulsion paints dry, the individual polymer particles must coalesce and embody the pigment. **b** H. MACMILLAN The various documents embodying the various agreements.

3 *verb trans.* Give a material or corporeal character to (what is spiritual). *rare*. **M17.**
4 *verb trans.* Give a material or discernible form to (an abstract principle, concept, etc.); express (such a principle etc.) *in* such a form. **M17.** ▸**b** Of a material or actual thing or person: be an embodiment of (an abstract concept, quality, etc.). **L19.**

J. E. T. ROGERS A popular notion, embodied in a rhyming couplet. W. S. CHURCHILL The Covenant . . embodied the . . resolve of a whole people to perish rather than submit. **b** G. BROWN Nobody embodied . . the whole outlook, attitude of the Communist machine bureaucrat as did Kruschev.

5 a *verb trans.* Form (people) into a body, esp. for military purposes. **M17.** ▸**b** *verb intrans.* Form or join a (military) body. **M17.**
†**6** *verb intrans. & refl.* Coalesce, form a homogeneous mass. **M17–E18.**
■ **embodier** *noun* **M17.**

embog /ɪmˈbɒɡ, ɛm-/ *verb trans.* Also †**im-**. Infl. **-gg-**. **E17.**
[ORIGIN from EM-[1], IM-[1] + BOG *noun*[1].]
Plunge into a bog; hamper (as) in a bog.

†**emboil** *verb trans. & intrans. rare* (Spenser). Only in **L16.**
[ORIGIN from EM-[1] + BOIL *verb*.]
(Cause to) boil with rage.

†**embold** *verb trans.* Also **im-**. **LME–E17.**
[ORIGIN from EM-[1], IM-[1] + BOLD *adjective*.]
Make bold, embolden.

embolden /ɪmˈbəʊld(ə)n, ɛm-/ *verb*. Also **im-** /ɪm-/. **L16.**
[ORIGIN from EM-[1], IM-[1] + BOLDEN.]
1 *verb trans.* Make bold or bolder; encourage, incite. **L16.**

SAKI You embolden one to make daring requests.

2 *verb intrans.* Use or change to a bold typeface. **L20.**
■ **emboldener** *noun* **M19.**

embolectomy /ɛmbəˈlɛktəmi/ *noun*. **E20.**
[ORIGIN from EMBOL(US + -ECTOMY.]
Surgical removal of an embolus; an instance of this.

emboli *noun* pl. of EMBOLUS.

embolia *noun pl.* see EMBOLIUM.

embolic /ɪmˈbɒlɪk, ɛm-/ *adjective*. **M19.**
[ORIGIN from EMBOLUS, EMBOLY + -IC.]
1 MEDICINE. Pertaining to or caused by an embolus. **M19.**
2 BIOLOGY. Characterized by emboly. **L19.**

embolisation *noun*, **embolise** *verb* vars. of EMBOLIZATION, EMBOLIZE.

embolism /ˈɛmbəlɪz(ə)m/ *noun*. **LME.**
[ORIGIN Late Latin *embolismus* from Greek *embolismos*, from *emballein* throw in, formed as EM-[2] + *ballein* throw: see -ISM.]
1 The periodic intercalation of days or a month in a calendar based on a non-solar year to correct the accumulating discrepancy between the calendar year and the solar year; the intercalated period. **LME.**
2 CHRISTIAN CHURCH. In some Eucharistic liturgies, a prayer following and based on the final petition of the Lord's Prayer. **E18.**
3 MEDICINE. The blocking of a blood vessel by something carried into it by the bloodstream (usu. a blood clot but sometimes a tumour, air, fat, etc.). **M19.** ▸**b** = EMBOLUS 2. **E20.**
■ **emboˈlismic** *adjective* of or pertaining to intercalation; intercalary: **M18.**

embolismus /ɛmbəˈlɪzməs/ *noun*. Pl. **-mi** /-mʌɪ, -miː/. **LME.**
[ORIGIN Late Latin: see EMBOLISM.]
†**1** = EMBOLISM 1. *rare*. **LME–L18.**
2 = EMBOLISM 2. **L19.**

embolium /ɪmˈbɒlɪəm, ɛm-/ *noun*. Pl. **-iums**, **-ia** /-ɪə/. **M19.**
[ORIGIN Latin from Greek *embolion* insertion, from *emballein*: see EMBOLISM, -IUM.]
The marginal part of the corium in some heteropteran insects.

embolization /ɛmbəlʌɪˈzeɪʃ(ə)n/ *noun*. Also **-isation**. **L17.**
[ORIGIN from EMBOLISM, EMBOLIZE: see -IZATION.]
†**1** Intercalation, embolism. *rare*. Only in **L17.**
2 MEDICINE. The introduction or occurrence of an embolus; the process of embolizing. **M20.**

embolize /ˈɛmbəlʌɪz/ *verb*. Also **-ise**. **E20.**
[ORIGIN from EMBOLUS, EMBOLISM + -IZE.]
MEDICINE. **1** *verb trans.* Introduce an embolus artificially into; cause embolism in. **E20.**
2 *verb intrans.* Develop into or form an embolus. **M20.**

embolus /ˈɛmbələs/ *noun*. Pl. **-li** /-lʌɪ, -liː/. **M17.**
[ORIGIN Latin = piston of a pump, from Greek *embolos* peg, stopper.]
†**1** MECHANICS. Something inserted or moving in another; *esp.* the piston of a syringe. **M17–M18.**
2 MEDICINE. The blood clot or other object or substance which causes embolism. **M19.**

emboly /ˈɛmbəli/ *noun*. **L19.**
[ORIGIN Greek *embolē* with assim. to -Y[3].]
BIOLOGY. Formation of a gastrula by invagination of the blastula. Cf. EPIBOLY.

embonpoint /ˌɒmbɒ̃ˈpwã, *foreign* ɑ̃bɔ̃pwɛ̃/ *noun & adjective*. **L17.**
[ORIGIN French phr. *en bon point* in good condition.]
▸**A** *noun*. Plumpness; the plump or fleshy part of a person's body. Also, a woman's bosom. **L17.**

G. CLARE A good paunch, or . . a bit of embonpoint, added dignity to a man.

▸**B** *adjective*. Plump. **E19.**

†**emborder** *verb trans.* Also **im-**. **M16–M17.**
[ORIGIN from EM-[1], IM-[1] + BORDER *noun*.]
Provide *with* a border; place or set as a border.

embosom /ɪmˈbʊz(ə)m, ɛm-/ *verb trans.* Also **im-** /ɪm-/. **L16.**
[ORIGIN from EM-[1], IM-[1] + BOSOM *noun*.]
1 Take to or cherish in one's bosom; embrace. Now *rare*. **L16.**
2 Enclose, conceal, shelter; envelop, surround. (Foll. by *in*, *with*.) Freq. in *pass.* **E17.**

P. EGAN A small snug country village embosomed in trees.

emboss /ɪmˈbɒs, ɛm-/ *verb*[1]. Also †**im-**. **LME.**
[ORIGIN from Old French base of French †*imbocer*, *embosser*, formed as EM-[1] + *boce* (mod. *bosse*) BOSS *noun*[1].]
▸**I** *verb trans.* **1** Cause to bulge or swell out; cover with protuberances. **LME.** ▸†**b** *fig.* Foll. by *out*: inflate (style, language). **M16–M17.**

SOUTHEY Its fretted roots Embossed the bank.

2 Carve, mould, or decorate with figures in relief; (of figures) stand out as ornaments upon. Also, represent (a subject) in relief. **LME.**

R. SUTCLIFF Look at the pattern embossed here on your dagger-sheath. V. AUSTIN The work is held face down . . and embossed with domed punches.

3 Ornament (as) with bosses; decorate sumptuously. **L16.**

W. COWPER Studs . . emboss his iron door. W. S. LANDOR Did we not . . Emboss our bosoms with the daffodils.

▸†**II** *verb intrans.* **4** Bulge, be convex. *rare*. **LME–L16.**
■ **embosser** *noun* **E17.** **embossing** *noun* (**a**) the action of the verb; (**b**) embossed ornamentation or lettering; †(**c**) a swelling, a protuberance: **LME.**

emboss /ɪmˈbɒs, ɛm-/ *verb*[2]. Also †**im-**. **LME.**
[ORIGIN Old French *emboscher* var. of *embuschier* AMBUSH *verb*.]
†**1** *verb intrans.* Of a hunted animal: plunge into a wood or thicket. **LME–L17.** ▸**b** *verb trans.* Drive (a hunted animal) to extremity. **L16–M18.**
2 *verb trans.* In *pass.* Be exhausted; foam at the mouth. Now *rare*. **L15.**
3 *verb trans.* Cover with foam. *arch.* **M16.**

†**emboss** *verb*[3] *trans.* **L16–E17.**
[ORIGIN Uncertain: perh. from EM-[1] + as BOSS *noun*[2].]
Encase *in* armour; plunge (a weapon) *in* an enemy's body. Also *fig.*, in *pass.*, be wrapped *in* ease.

embossed /ɪmˈbɒst, ɛm-/ *ppl adjective*. Also †**im-**. **LME.**
[ORIGIN from EMBOSS *verb*[1] + -ED[1].]
†**1** Humpbacked. Only in **LME.**
2 Carved or moulded in relief; decorated or ornamented in relief; (of figures, lettering, etc.) standing out in relief. **M16.**

R. COBB Lined notepaper headed with an embossed harp.

3 Covered with bosses; richly decorated. *rare*. **L16.**
†**4** Bulging, swollen; inflated (*lit. & fig.*). **L16–M17.**

embossment /ɪmˈbɒsm(ə)nt, ɛm-/ *noun*. Also †**im-**. **E17.**
[ORIGIN from EMBOSS *verb*[1] + -MENT.]
1 A swelling, a protuberance. Now *rare*. **E17.**
2 An embossed figure; embossed ornamentation. **E17.**
3 The action or process of embossing. *rare*. **E19.**

embosture /ɪmˈbɒstjʊə, ɛm-/ *noun*. *arch. rare*. Also †**im-**. **E17.**
[ORIGIN from EMBOSS *verb*[1] after *sculpture*.]
= EMBOSSMENT.

embothrium /ɪmˈbɒθrɪəm, ɛm-/ *noun*. **L19.**
[ORIGIN mod. Latin, from EM-[2] + Greek *bothrion* small pit, with ref. to the anthers.]
Any of various S. American evergreen shrubs of the genus *Embothrium* of the protea family, esp. *E. coccineum*, grown for its conspicuous scarlet flowers.

embouchement /ɪmˈbuːʃmənt, ɛm-; *foreign* ɑ̃buʃmɑ̃ (*pl. same*)/ *noun*. *rare*. **M19.**
[ORIGIN French, from *emboucher*: see EMBOUCHURE, -MENT.]
1 The mouth of a river. **M19.**
2 ANATOMY. The point at which one vessel leads into another. *rare*. **L19.**

embouchure /ɒmbʊˈʃʊə; *foreign* ɑ̃buʃyːr (*pl. same*)/ *noun*. **M18.**
[ORIGIN French, from *s'emboucher* refl., discharge itself by a mouth, from *emboucher* put in or to the mouth, formed as EM-[1] + *bouche* mouth: see -URE.]
1 MUSIC. The manner in which a player's mouth and lips are placed when playing a woodwind or brass instrument. **M18.** ▸**b** The mouthpiece of a musical instrument, esp. of a flute. **M19.**
2 The mouth of a river; the opening of a valley on to a plain. **L18.**

embound /ɪmˈbaʊnd, ɛm-/ *verb trans. poet. arch.* Also **im-** /ɪm-/. **LME.**
[ORIGIN from EM-[1], IM-[1] + BOUND *noun*[1].]
Set bounds to; confine.

embourgeoisé /ɑ̃burʒwaze/ *adjective*. **M20.**
[ORIGIN French, pa. pple of *embourgeoiser* make or become bourgeois, formed as EM-[1], BOURGEOIS *adjective & noun*[1].]
That has been bourgeoisified.

embourgeoisement /ɑ̃burʒwazmɑ̃/ *noun*. **M20.**
[ORIGIN French, from *embourgeoiser*: see EMBOURGEOISÉ, -MENT.]
= BOURGEOISIFICATION.

embourgeoisification /ɒmˌbʊəʒwɑːzɪfɪˈkeɪʃ(ə)n/ *noun*. **L20.**
[ORIGIN Blend of EMBOURGEOISEMENT and BOURGEOISIFICATION.]
= BOURGEOISIFICATION.

embow /ɪmˈbəʊ, ɛm-/ *verb trans. arch.* Also †**im-**. **LME.**
[ORIGIN from EM-[1], IM-[1] + BOW *noun*[1].]
1 Bend into a bow. *rare. obsolete* exc. in EMBOWED 2. **LME.**
2 ARCHITECTURE. Arch, vault, (a roof). (Earlier as EMBOWED 1.) **L15.**
†**3** Enclose as in a sphere; encircle. **E–M17.**
■ **embowment** *noun* (*rare*) **E17.**

embowed /ɪmˈbəʊd, ɛm-/ *ppl adjective*. Also **im-** /ɪm-/. **LME.**
[ORIGIN from EMBOW + -ED[1].]
1 ARCHITECTURE. Arched, vaulted; curved outwards. **LME.**
2 Bent into the form of a bow; convex. **L16.**
3 HERALDRY. Bent, *esp.* (**a**) (of an arm) bent at the elbow; (**b**) (of a dolphin) with the body arched. **E17.**

embowel /ɪmˈbaʊ(ə)l, ɛm-/ *verb trans.* Now *rare*. Also †**im-**. Infl. **-ll-**, ***-l-**. **E16.**
[ORIGIN In sense 1 from Old French *emboweler* alt. of *esbouele*r, from *es-* EX-[1] + *bouel* BOWEL. In sense 2 from EM-[1], IM-[1] + BOWEL.]
1 = DISEMBOWEL. **E16.**
†**2** Put or convey into the bowels or the depths. **L16–M17.**
■ **emboweller** *noun* (*rare*) **L16.**

embowelled /ɪmˈbaʊ(ə)ld, ɛm-/ *ppl adjective*. **L15.**
[ORIGIN from EMBOWEL + -ED[1].]
†**1** That has the bowels full. Only in **L15.**
2 Disembowelled. Now *rare* or *obsolete*. **L16.**
3 Concealed in the bowels or heart of something. **E17.**

embower /ɪmˈbaʊə, ɛm-/ *verb*. Also (*arch.*) **im-** /ɪm-/. **L16.**
[ORIGIN from EM-[1], IM-[1] + BOWER *noun*[1].]
1 *verb trans.* Shelter or enclose (as) in a bower; surround with foliage. **L16.**

B. TARKINGTON George . . stood . . embowered in the big red and gold drawing room.

†**2** *verb intrans.* Take shelter, lodge as in a bower. **L16–E17.**
■ **emberment** *noun* the action of embowering **M19.**

†**embowl** *verb trans. & intrans. rare*. **L16–L19.**
[ORIGIN from EM-[1] + BOWL *noun*[1].]
Make or grow into the form of a globe.

embox /ɪmˈbɒks, ɛm-/ *verb trans.* **E17.**
[ORIGIN from EM-[1] + BOX *noun*[2].]
Set (as) in a box.

embrace /ɪmˈbreɪs, ɛm-/ *verb*[1] *& noun*. Also †**im-**. **ME.**
[ORIGIN Old French *embracer* (mod. *embrasser*) from Proto-Romance base, from Latin IM-[1] + *bracchium* arm (cf. BRACE *noun*[1]).]
▸**A** *verb*. **1** *verb trans.* Encircle, surround; enclose. **ME.**

SHAKES. *Coriol.* You'll see your Rome embrac'd with fire. J. CONRAD The great waters which embrace the continents of this globe.

2 *verb trans.* & (usu. with pl. subj.) *intrans.* Hold (a person, each other) closely in the arms, usu. as a sign of affection; *euphem.* have sexual intercourse with. **LME.** ▸**b** *verb trans.* Kiss, esp. on the cheek. **M20.**

D. H. LAWRENCE Then the two men embraced. C. JACKSON She . . put her arms around him and embraced him passionately.

†**3** *verb trans.* Cultivate (a virtue, disposition, etc.). **LME–E17.**
4 *verb trans.* Take in with the eye or mind; perceive, comprehend. **LME.**

E. R. CONDER The infinite . . the intellect can seize though not embrace.

5 *verb trans.* Accept readily or with good grace; avail oneself of (an offer, an opportunity, etc.). **LME.**

E

▸†**b** Accept as a friend; welcome the services of (a person). M16–M17.

H. JAMES I don't embrace all my mother's quarrels.

†**6** *verb trans.* Take (a matter) in hand, undertake. LME–E19.
7 *verb trans.* Take up, adopt, (a doctrine, opinions, a course of action, a profession, etc.). M16.

E. A. FREEMAN The . . home of those . . who embraced the monastic life. W. LIPPMANN They turned away from liberalism and embraced collectivism as a method of ordering affairs.

8 *verb trans.* Include, contain; comprise. L16.

E. WILSON A system of law which should embrace all the different moral systems and thus be universally acceptable. C. C. TRENCH His military interests embraced a passion for uniforms, tactics, weapons and armies.

E

▸ **B** *noun.* An act of embracing; a clasp, a hug; *euphem.* an act of sexual intercourse. LME.

MILTON In embraces forcible and foule Ingendring with me. A. WILSON He put his arms around her and held her for a moment in a close embrace.

■ **embraceable** *adjective* able to be embraced; inviting an embrace: M19. **embracingly** *adverb* (*a*) in the manner of a person who embraces; (*b*) comprehensively: M17. **embracingness** *noun* comprehensiveness L19.

embrace /ɪm'breɪs, ɛm-/ *verb*[2] *trans. & intrans.* Now *rare* or *obsolete*. LME.
[ORIGIN App. back-form. from EMBRACER *noun*[2].]
LAW. Attempt to influence (a jury or juror) corruptly.

†**embrace** *verb*[3]. L15–L16.
[ORIGIN from EM-[1] + BRACE *noun*[1].]
Fasten with a brace or buckle. (Foll. by *to*.)

embracement /ɪm'breɪsm(ə)nt, ɛm-/ *noun.* Also †**im-**. L15.
[ORIGIN Old French, from *embracer*: see EMBRACE *verb*[1], -MENT.]
1 An embrace. *arch.* L15.
†**2** An undertaking. L15–M17.
3 A willing acceptance of a doctrine, something offered, etc. M16.
4 The action or an act of perceiving or comprehending. L16.
5 The action of clasping or encircling; the state of being clasped or encircled. E17.

embraceor *noun* var. of EMBRACER *noun*[2].

embracer /ɪm'breɪsə, ɛm-/ *noun*[1]. Also †**im-**. LME.
[ORIGIN from EMBRACE *verb*[1] + -ER[1].]
A person who embraces someone or something.

embracer /ɪm'breɪsə, ɛm-/ *noun*[2]. Also **-ceor**. LME.
[ORIGIN Anglo-Norman, Old French *embraseor* instigator, from Old French & mod. French *embraser* set on fire, formed as EM-[1] + *braise* live coals. For sense-development cf. ENTICE.]
LAW. A person who attempts to influence a jury or juror corruptly.
■ **embracery** *noun* the offence of an embracer; corruption of a jury or juror: LME.

embracive /ɪm'breɪsɪv, ɛm-/ *adjective.* M19.
[ORIGIN from EMBRACE *verb*[1] + -IVE.]
1 Given to or fond of embracing. *rare.* M19.
2 Embracing or tending to embrace all; inclusive. L19.
■ **embracively** *adverb* L19.

†**embraid** *verb trans.* Also **-bread**. L15–L16.
[ORIGIN from EM-[1] + BRAID *verb*[1].]
Plait, braid; interlace, intertwine.

embranchment /ɪm'brɑːn(t)ʃm(ə)nt, ɛm-/ *noun.* M19.
[ORIGIN French *embranchement*, formed as EM-[1], BRANCH *noun*, -MENT.]
A branching off or out, as of an arm of a river; a branch, an offshoot.

embrangle /ɪm'braŋg(ə)l, ɛm-/ *verb trans.* Also **im-** /ɪm-/. M17.
[ORIGIN from EM-[1], IM-[1] + BRANGLE.]
Entangle, perplex, confuse.

COLERIDGE The perplexities with which . . I have been thorned and embrangled.

■ **embranglement** *noun* E19.

†**embrasure** *noun*[1]. *rare* (Shakes.). Only in E17.
[ORIGIN from EMBRACE *verb*[1] + -URE.]
= EMBRACE *noun.*

embrasure /ɪm'breɪʒə, ɛm-/ *noun*[2] & *verb.* Also **-zure**. E18.
[ORIGIN French, from †*embraser* (now *ébraser*) widen (a door or window opening), of unknown origin: see -URE.]
▸ **A** *noun.* **1** *MILITARY.* An opening in a parapet that widens towards the outside, made to fire a gun through. E18.
2 A slanting or bevelling of the wall on each side of a door or window opening so as to form a recess; the area contained between such walls. M18.

A. GUINNESS We were ushered to a round table in a window embrasure.

3 *DENTISTRY.* The angle between adjacent teeth where their two surfaces curve inwards towards the line of contact. M20.
▸ **B** *verb trans.* Provide with an embrasure. E19.

embrave /ɛm'breɪv/ *verb trans.* L16.
[ORIGIN from EM-[1] + BRAVE *adjective.*]
†**1** Adorn, embellish. L16–M18.
2 Inspire with courage, make brave. M17.

embrazure *noun* & *verb* var. of EMBRASURE *noun*[2] & *verb.*

†**embread** *verb* var. of EMBRAID.

embreathe *verb* var. of IMBREATHE.

embrigade /ɛmbrɪ'geɪd/ *verb trans. rare.* L19.
[ORIGIN from EM-[1] + BRIGADE.]
Form into a brigade or into any organized body.

embrighten /ɪm'brʌɪt(ə)n, ɛm-/ *verb trans.* E17.
[ORIGIN from EM-[1] + BRIGHTEN.]
Make bright, brighten.
■ Also †**embright** *verb trans.* E17–M18.

embrittle /ɪm'brɪt(ə)l, ɛm-/ *verb trans. & intrans.* E20.
[ORIGIN from EM-[1] + BRITTLE *adjective.*]
Make or become brittle.
■ **embrittlement** *noun* the action or result of embrittling; loss of ductility: E20.

embrocado, **embroccata** *nouns* vars. of IMBROCCATA.

embrocate /'ɛmbrəkeɪt/ *verb trans.* Now *rare* or *obsolete.* E17.
[ORIGIN medieval Latin *embrocat-* pa. ppl stem of *embrocare*: see EMBROCATION, -ATE[3].]
MEDICINE. Bathe (a diseased or painful part of the body) with liquid.

embrocation /ɛmbrə'keɪʃ(ə)n/ *noun.* LME.
[ORIGIN Old French & mod. French, or medieval Latin *embrocatio(n-)*, from *embrocat-* pa. ppl stem of *embrocare*, from late Latin *embroc(h)a* from Greek *embrokhē* lotion: see -ATION.]
†**1** The bathing of a diseased or painful part of the body. LME–M17.
2 A liquid applied to a diseased or painful part of the body, now usu. by rubbing; a liniment. LME.

†**embroglio** *noun* var. of IMBROGLIO.

embroider /ɪm'brɔɪdə, ɛm-/ *verb.* LME.
[ORIGIN Anglo-Norman *enbrouder*, formed as EM-[1] + Old French *brouder*, *broisder* (mod. *broder*) from Germanic. The form *broid-* is partly due to blending with BROID *verb.*]
1 *verb trans. & intrans.* Decorate (cloth etc.) with needlework; produce (a design or motif) on cloth in this way. LME. ▸†**b** *gen.* Decorate, variegate; *iron.* smear with dirt, blood, etc. LME–M18.

J. BERGER A folded handkerchief with his monogram embroidered upon it. G. VIDAL Xerxes . . dried his lips with the back of an embroidered sleeve.

2 *verb trans. fig.* †**a** Make splendid, dignify; describe extravagantly. E–M17. ▸**b** Embellish (a narrative etc.) with rhetoric, exaggeration, or fictitious additions. E17.

b HOR. WALPOLE He had embroidered his own story with some marvellous legends.

■ **embroiderer** *noun* LME. **embroideress** *noun* a female embroiderer E18. **embroidering** *noun* (*a*) the action of the verb; (*b*) embroidered decoration: L15.

embroidery /ɪm'brɔɪd(ə)ri, ɛm-/ *noun.* LME.
[ORIGIN Anglo-Norman *enbrouderie*, formed as EMBROIDER: see -ERY.]
1 The art of embroidering. LME.
2 Embroidered work or material. L16.

M. PEAKE Laying down her embroidery on a table.

3 Any decoration likened in appearance to needlework; *spec.* (now *poet.*) the natural adornment of the ground by flowers; an adornment consisting of flowers. E17.
4 *fig.* Elaboration; inessential decoration or embellishment. M17.

embroil /ɪm'brɔɪl, ɛm-/ *verb*[1] & *noun.* Also †**im-**. E17.
[ORIGIN French *embrouiller*, formed as EM-[1], BROIL *verb*[2].]
▸ **A** *verb trans.* **1** Bring (affairs, a narrative, etc.) into a state of confusion. E17.
2 Involve in dissension or hostility (*with* someone); involve in or *in* difficulties, conflict, or intrigue. E17.

M. MEYER Although he enjoyed . . making speeches on controversial subjects, he disliked embroiling himself. J. M. COETZEE I did not mean to get embroiled in this.

3 Throw into uproar or tumult. E17.
▸ **B** *noun.* A state of dissension, perplexity, or confusion; an uproar. Now *rare* or *obsolete.* M17.
■ **embroiler** *noun* M17.

†**embroil** *verb*[2] *trans. rare.* M17–E18.
[ORIGIN from EM-[1] + BROIL *verb*[1].]
Burn up, set fire to.

embroilment /ɪm'brɔɪlm(ə)nt, ɛm-/ *noun.* E17.
[ORIGIN from EMBROIL *verb*[1] + -MENT.]
1 (An) uproar, (a) tumult. E17.
2 A state of conflict; a quarrel. M17.
3 The action or process of embroiling. M17.
4 A state of complication or confusion; a confused mixture. L17.

embrown /ɪm'braʊn, ɛm-/ *verb trans.* Also **im-** /ɪm-/. M17.
[ORIGIN from EM-[1], IM-[1] + BROWN *adjective.*]
1 Darken, make dusky. *poet.* M17.
2 Make brown. E18.

embrue, **embrute** *verbs* vars. of IMBRUE, IMBRUTE.

embrya *noun pl.* see EMBRYON.

embryo /'ɛmbrɪəʊ/ *noun & adjective.* LME.
[ORIGIN Late Latin *embryo*, *embrio*, mistaken form arising from taking Greek *embruon* as a noun in *-ōn*, *-ōnis*; *embruon* formed as EM-[2] + *bruein* swell, grow.]
▸ **A** *noun.* Pl. **-os**.
1 The entity which develops in a woman's womb until it is born as a baby. Now *esp.*, this entity prior to the time at which all the organs are developed, at about the eighth week after conception (cf. FETUS); in *MEDICINE* sometimes also distinguished from the conceptus or pre-embryo. LME. ▸**b** The unborn or unhatched offspring of an animal. M17.
2 *fig.* A thing in a rudimentary stage; a thing as yet no more than an idea. E17.
†**3** *CHEMISTRY.* A metal or compound prior to isolation from its natural state or matrix. M17–M18.
4 *BOTANY.* The part of the inside of a seed which develops into a plant, comprising in higher plants, when mature, a radicle, a plumule, and one or two cotyledons. E18.
– PHRASES: **in embryo** not yet developed or fully the thing specified.
– COMB.: **embryo sac** the cell inside the ovule of a seed plant within which fertilization occurs and which becomes the female gametophyte, containing the zygote and the endosperm nucleus.
▸ **B** *adjective.* = EMBRYONIC 2. M17.

embryo- /'ɛmbrɪəʊ/ *combining form* of EMBRYO: see -O-.
■ **embryo'genesis** *noun* the formation and development of the embryo M19. **embryoge'netic** *adjective* of or pertaining to embryogenesis L19. **embryoge'netically** *adverb* as regards embryogenesis E20. **embryo'genic** *adjective* = EMBRYOGENETIC M19. **embry'ogeny** *noun* = EMBRYOGENESIS M19. **embry'oma** *noun*, pl. **-mas**, **-mata** /-mətə/, *MEDICINE* a tumour (esp. a malignant one of childhood) composed of tissues resembling, or thought to arise from, those of the fetus or fetal remnants E20. **embry'otomy** *noun* (an instance of) surgical dissection of a fetus in order to remove it from the womb E18. **embryo'toxic** *adjective* poisonous to an embryo M20. **embryoto'xicity** *noun* the property of being embryotoxic; the degree to which something is embryotoxic: L20.

embryoid /'ɛmbrɪɔɪd/ *adjective & noun.* M20.
[ORIGIN from EMBRYO + -OID.]
▸ **A** *adjective.* Resembling an embryo. Chiefly in ***embryoid body*** below. M20.
embryoid body an aggregate of cells resembling an embryo, which develops when certain mouse tumours are injected into the peritoneal cavity of a mouse or grown in culture.
▸ **B** *noun.* An embryonic plant developed in a culture medium from a single cell. M20.

embryology /ɛmbrɪ'ɒlədʒi/ *noun.* M19.
[ORIGIN from EMBRYO- + -OLOGY.]
The branch of science that deals with the development of an organism up to the time of birth or hatching.
■ **embryo'logic** *adjective* = EMBRYOLOGICAL L19. **embryo'logical** *adjective* of or pertaining to embryology M19. **embryo'logically** *adverb* as regards embryology or embryonic development M19. **embry'ologist** *noun* an expert in or student of embryology M19.

embryon /'ɛmbrɪɒn/ *noun & adjective.* Now *rare* or *obsolete.* LME.
[ORIGIN medieval Latin from Greek *embruon*: see EMBRYO.]
▸ **A** *noun.* Pl. **-brya** /-brɪə/, **-ons**.
†**1 a** = EMBRYO *noun* 1A. LME–E19. ▸**b** = EMBRYO *noun* 1B. M17.
†**2** *fig.* = EMBRYO *noun* 2. L16–E19.
†**3** = EMBRYO *noun* 4. L18–L19.
▸ †**B** *adjective.* = EMBRYO *adjective.* E17–M19.

embryonal /ɪm'brʌɪən(ə)l, ɛm-/ *adjective.* M17.
[ORIGIN from late Latin *embryon-*, *embryo*, English EMBRYON + -AL[1].]
= EMBRYONIC 1.

embryonary /ɪm'brʌɪən(ə)ri, ɛm-/ *adjective.* M19.
[ORIGIN formed as EMBRYONIC + -ARY[1].]
Embryonic.

embryonate /'ɛmbrɪəneɪt/ *adjective.* L19.
[ORIGIN from EMBRYON(IC + -ATE[2], after EMBRYONATED.]
= EMBRYONATED 2.

embryonated /'ɛmbrɪəneɪtɪd/ *adjective.* M17.
[ORIGIN formed as EMBRYONAL + -ATE[3] + -ED[1].]
†**1** Of a mineral or chemical compound: occurring combined with or embedded in another material. M–L17.
2 Of an egg: containing an embryo. M18.

embryonic /ɛmbrɪ'ɒnɪk/ *adjective.* M19.
[ORIGIN from late Latin *embryon-*, EMBRYO *noun* + -IC.]
1 Of, pertaining to, or of the nature of an embryo. M19.
2 *fig.* Undeveloped, rudimentary; incipient. M19.
■ **embryonically** *adverb* in the embryo; as an embryo; as regards the embryo: L19.

embryoniferous /ˌɛmbrɪə'nɪf(ə)rəs/ *adjective.* E19.
[ORIGIN formed as EMBRYONIC + -I- + -FEROUS.]
BOTANY. Producing or bearing an embryo.

embryotic /ɛmbrɪ'ɒtɪk/ *adjective.* M18.
[ORIGIN from EMBRYO after *exotic*, *patriotic*, etc.]
1 = EMBRYONIC 2. M18.
2 = EMBRYONIC 1. M19.

embus /ɪmˈbʌs, ɛm-/ *verb*. Infl. **-ss-**. E20.
[ORIGIN from EM-[1] + BUS *noun*, after *embark*.]
Chiefly MILITARY. **1** *verb intrans*. Board a bus or other motor vehicle. E20.
2 *verb trans*. Transport by, or put on to, a bus etc. E20.

embusqué /ɑ̃byske/ *noun*. Pl. pronounced same. E20.
[ORIGIN French, pa. pple of *embusquer* from Old French *embuschier* AMBUSH *verb*.]
A person who avoids military service by obtaining a post in a government office or the like.

emcee /ɛmˈsiː/ *noun & verb*. *slang*. M20.
[ORIGIN Repr. pronunc. of the letters *MC*.]
▸ **A** *noun*. A master of ceremonies, a compère. Also, a person who provides entertainment by instructing a DJ and performing rap music; an MC. M20.
▸ **B** *verb trans. & intrans*. Act as master of ceremonies (for). M20.

eme /iːm/ *noun*[1]. *obsolete* exc. *dial*.
[ORIGIN Old English *ēam* = Old Frisian *ēm*, Middle Dutch *oem* (Dutch *oom*), Old High German *ōheim* (German *Oheim*).]
A friend. Formerly, an uncle.

eme *noun*[2] see EMU.

-eme /iːm/ *suffix*.
[ORIGIN Extracted from PHONEME.]
Used in LINGUISTICS to form nouns denoting units of structure, as ***grapheme***, ***morpheme***.

emend /ɪˈmɛnd/ *verb trans*. LME.
[ORIGIN Latin *emendare*, from *e-* E- + *menda* fault. Cf. AMEND *verb*.]
Alter (a text) to remove errors and corruptions; *gen*. free from faults, correct, rectify.
> E. BOWEN Miss Smith . . considered what she had said, but did not emend it.

■ **emender** *noun* L19.

emendate /ˈiːmɛndeɪt/ *verb trans*. L19.
[ORIGIN from Latin *emendat-* (see EMENDATOR) or back-form. from EMENDATION, EMENDATOR.]
= EMEND.

emendation /iːmɛnˈdeɪʃ(ə)n/ *noun*. LME.
[ORIGIN Latin *emendatio(n-)*, formed as EMENDATE: see -ATION.]
†**1** Reformation, improvement. LME–L17.
2 (An) improvement by alteration and correction; *esp*. (an) alteration of a text where it is presumed to be corrupt. L16.

†**emendative** *adjective*. *rare*. M17–E19.
[ORIGIN from Latin *emendat-*: see EMENDATOR, -IVE.]
Tending to emend.

emendator /ˈiːmɛndeɪtə/ *noun*. L17.
[ORIGIN Latin *emendator*, from *emendat-* pa. ppl stem of *emendare* EMEND: see -ATE[3], -OR.]
A person who emends something; a corrector.

emendatory /ɪˈmɛndət(ə)ri/ *adjective*. M17.
[ORIGIN Latin *emendatorius* corrective, formed as EMENDATE: see -ORY[2].]
†**1** Disciplinary. Only in M17.
2 Of or pertaining to emendation(s). L18.

emerald /ˈɛm(ə)r(ə)ld/ *noun & adjective*. Also †**-raude**. ME.
[ORIGIN Old French *e(s)meraude* (mod. *émeraude*), from Proto-Romance alt. of Latin SMARAGDUS.]
▸ **A** *noun*. **1** A bright green precious stone; now *spec*. one consisting of a particular variety of beryl. ME.
2 HERALDRY. The tincture gules in the fanciful blazon of arms of peers. Now *hist*. L16.
3 The colour of an emerald, emerald green. E18.
4 Type of a size (6½ points) larger than nonpareil and smaller than minion. L19.
▸ **B** *adjective*. **1** Bright green, like an emerald. E16.
2 Made of or containing an emerald. L19.
> W. JONES An emerald ring was thought to ensure purity.

– SPECIAL COLLOCATIONS & COMB.: **emerald cuckoo** an African cuckoo, *Chrysococcyx cupreus*, with green and gold plumage. **emerald-cut** (of a gem) cut in a square shape with stepped facets. **emerald green** (**a**) a bright green like that of an emerald; also, the pigment Paris green; the pigment viridian; (**b**) = EMERALD *adjective* 1. **emerald moth** any of various green geometrid moths of the family Geometridae. **the Emerald Isle** Ireland.
■ **emeraldine** /-ɪn, -ʌɪn/ *adjective & noun* (**a**) *adjective* = EMERALD *adjective* 1; (**b**) *noun* a green aniline dye: M19.

†**emeras** *noun*. M17–L19.
[ORIGIN Unknown.]
HERALDRY. An escutcheon on the shoulder of an armed knight.

†**emeraude** *noun & adjective* var. of EMERALD.

emerge /ɪˈməːdʒ/ *verb intrans*. L16.
[ORIGIN Latin *emergere*, from *e-* E- + *mergere* to dip, plunge.]
1 Of a fact, result, etc.: become known as the result of a discussion etc.; come into being with the passage of events. Of a problem: arise, esp. suddenly. L16.
> I. MURDOCH It emerged that Dora had never heard the cuckoo. W. S. CHURCHILL From the Restoration there emerged no national settlement.

2 Come up out of a liquid after being immersed. M17.
> T. BURNET The mountains emerged, and became dry land again.

3 Come into view from a place of darkness, concealment, confinement, etc. M17.
> E. TEMPLETON They saw Mr Parker emerge from the shadowy passage.

4 *fig*. Come out of a situation in a specified state; pass from a state of ignorance, obscurity, etc.; become publicly recognized or noticed. (Foll. by *from* the earlier state, *in* or *into* the later one.) M17.
> J. R. GREEN Florence emerged into communal greatness. A. PRICE He'll emerge whiter than white from Colonel Butler's enquiries. G. F. FIENNES Decisions are not made; they emerge.

emergence /ɪˈməːdʒ(ə)ns/ *noun*. M17.
[ORIGIN medieval Latin *emergentia*, from Latin *emergent-* pres. ppl stem of *emergere*: see EMERGE *verb*, -ENCE.]
†**1** An unforeseen occurrence; an emergency. M17–M19.
2 The process of emerging. E18.
3 BOTANY. An outgrowth from a stem or leaf composed of epidermal and subepidermal tissue. L19.

emergency /ɪˈməːdʒ(ə)nsi/ *noun & adjective*. M17.
[ORIGIN formed as EMERGENCE: see -ENCY.]
▸ **A** *noun*. **1** A situation, esp. of danger or conflict, that arises unexpectedly and requires urgent action; (a person with) a condition requiring immediate treatment. M17. ▸**b** Pressing need. Also, a condition of danger or disaster throughout a region. E18. ▸**c** SPORT. A substitute player. Now *Austral*. M19.
> J. T. STORY The distant clanging of an ambulance bell racing to an emergency. **b** DAY LEWIS A certain fund of calm within myself . . which I am able to draw upon in emergency. J. M. FLEMING Hose pipes to be used in case of emergency.

the Emergency *Irish* the Second World War. **b state of emergency**: in which a government suspends normal constitutional procedures.
†**2** The fact of happening or occurring suddenly or unexpectedly. M17–L18.
3 The action of rising out of the water. Now *rare* or *obsolete*. M17.
†**4** The process of emerging into view. M17–M18.
▸ **B** *attrib*. or as *adjective*. Used, called upon, or arising in an emergency. L19.
> D. LODGE The airport was on full emergency alert.

emergency exit, ***emergency landing***, ***emergency service***, etc.

emergent /ɪˈməːdʒ(ə)nt/ *adjective & noun*. LME.
[ORIGIN Latin *emergent-* pres. ppl stem of *emergere*: see EMERGE *verb*, -ENT. In sense 1 translating medieval Latin *emergens*.]
▸ **A** *adjective*. †**1** Designating a Jewish year beginning in May in commemoration of the Exodus. Only in LME.
2 Occurring unexpectedly; not specially provided for. *arch*. LME. ▸**b** Urgent, pressing. E18.
3 Occurring as a consequence of something. E17.
4 That is rising or has risen out of a surrounding medium. E17.
> W. D. THORNBURY An emergent shore line with offshore bar and lagoon.

5 In the process of coming out; emerging. M17.
> J. STRUTHERS The sun emergent smiled.

emergent evolution: in which new traits are regarded as emergents (see sense B.3 below) rather than as resultants.
6 Becoming noticed; coming into being; (of a nation) newly formed or independent. M17.
> *Amateur Photographer* The original Vogue contract . . made of him a cardinal amongst the emergent cockneys of the era.

▸ **B** *noun*. **1** A person who or thing which emerges; an outcome, a result. Now *rare*. E16.
†**2** An emergency. E16–E19.
3 An effect produced by a combination of causes but unable to be seen as the sum of their individual effects. Opp. ***resultant***. L19.
■ **emergently** *adverb* (*rare*) M17.

Emergicenter /ɪˈməːdʒɪsɛntə/ *noun*. *US*. L20.
[ORIGIN from EMERGENCY after SURGICENTER.]
(Proprietary name for) a clinic offering emergency treatment for minor illness or injury.

emerita /ɪˈmɛrɪtə/ *adjective*. M19.
[ORIGIN Latin, fem. of EMERITUS.]
Of a female former office-holder: retired but allowed to retain her title as an honour.

emerited /ɪˈmɛrɪtɪd, iː-/ *adjective*. *arch*. L17.
[ORIGIN formed as EMERITUS + -ED[1].]
Retired from active service; skilled through long experience.

emeritus /ɪˈmɛrɪtəs, iː-/ *adjective*. M18.
[ORIGIN Latin *emeritus* pa. pple of *emereri* earn (one's discharge) by service, from *e-* E- + *mereri* deserve: see MERIT *noun*.]
Honourably discharged from service; (of a former office-holder, esp. a professor) retired but allowed to retain his or her title as an honour.

emerods /ˈɛmərɒdz/ *noun pl*. *arch*. LME.
[ORIGIN Alt. of HAEMORRHOID + -S[1].]
Haemorrhoids.

emersed /ɪˈməːst/ *adjective*. *rare*. L17.
[ORIGIN from Latin *emersus* pa. pple of *emergere* EMERGE + -ED[1].]
Standing out from or above a medium; (of part of a plant) raised above the water.

emersion /ɪˈməːʃ(ə)n, iː-/ *noun*. M17.
[ORIGIN Late Latin *emersio(n-)*, from Latin *emers-* pa. ppl stem of *emergere* EMERGE: see -ION.]
1 ASTRONOMY. The reappearance of a celestial object after its eclipse or occultation. M17.
2 The process of appearing above the surface of water that previously hid the object. M17.
3 *gen*. The action of emerging from concealment or confinement. *rare*. M18.

Emersonian /ɛməˈsəʊnɪən/ *adjective & noun*. M19.
[ORIGIN from *Emerson* (see below) + -IAN.]
▸ **A** *adjective*. Of, pertaining to, or characteristic of the US author Ralph Waldo Emerson (1803–82) or his work. M19. E
▸ **B** *noun*. An admirer or student of Emerson. M19.
■ **Emersonianism** *noun* M19.

emery /ˈɛm(ə)ri/ *noun & verb*. L15.
[ORIGIN French *émeri* from Old French *esmeri(l)* from Italian *smeriglio* from Proto-Romance, from medieval Greek *smēri*, classical Greek *smiris*, *smuris* polishing powder. Cf. SMEAR *noun*.]
▸ **A** *noun*. **1** A naturally occurring mixture of corundum with an iron oxide or iron spinel, used as an abrasive and polishing material for metal, glass, and stone. L15.
2 In full ***emery bag***. A case containing emery, used for keeping needles bright. *US*. M19.
– COMB.: ***emery bag***: see sense 2 above; **emery board** a thin strip of emery-coated card or wood, used as a nail file; **emery cloth**, **emery paper**: coated with emery powder; **emery powder** ground emery; **emery wheel** an emery-coated grinding or polishing wheel.
▸ **B** *verb trans*. Polish with emery; coat with emery. *rare*. M19.

emesis /ˈɛmɪsɪs/ *noun*. L19.
[ORIGIN Greek, from *emein* to vomit.]
MEDICINE. Vomiting.

emetic /ɪˈmɛtɪk/ *noun & adjective*. M17.
[ORIGIN Greek *emetikos*, from *emetos* vomiting from *emein* to vomit: see -IC.]
▸ **A** *noun*. A substance that causes vomiting when ingested, *esp*. one given for this purpose. M17.
▸ **B** *adjective*. Causing vomiting; *fig*. sickening, revoltingly sentimental. L17.
emetic tartar = ***tartar emetic*** s.v. TARTAR *noun*[1].
■ **emetical** *adjective* = EMETIC *adjective* L17. **emetically** *adverb* (*rare*) M17.

emetine /ˈɛmɪtiːn/ *noun*. E19.
[ORIGIN from Greek *emetos*: see EMETIC, -INE[5].]
An alkaloid, $C_{29}H_{40}N_2O_4$, obtained from the roots of the ipecacuanha plant, *Cephaelis ipecacuanha*, and formerly used as an amoebicide.

†**emeu** *noun* var. of EMU.

émeute /eməːt/ *noun*. Pl. pronounced same. L18.
[ORIGIN French from Old French *esmote*, from *esmeu* (mod. *ému*) pa. pple of *esmovoir* (mod. *émouvoir*: see EMOTION), after *meute* crowd, uprising.]
A popular rising or disturbance.

EMF *abbreviation*. Also **emf**.
1 Electromagnetic field(s).
2 Electromotive force.
3 European Monetary Fund.

EMG *abbreviation*.
Electromyogram.

-emia *suffix* see -AEMIA.

emic /ˈiːmɪk/ *adjective*. M20.
[ORIGIN from PHONEMIC *adjective*.]
Describing the structure of a particular language or culture in terms of its internal elements and their functioning, rather than in terms of any existing external scheme. Cf. ETIC *adjective*.

emiction /ɪˈmɪkʃ(ə)n/ *noun*. M17.
[ORIGIN medieval Latin *emict-* pa. ppl stem of *emingere*, from *e-* E- + *mingere* urinate: see -ION.]
Urine.

emigrant /ˈɛmɪɡr(ə)nt/ *noun & adjective*. M18.
[ORIGIN Latin *emigrant-* pres. ppl stem of *emigrare*: see EMIGRATE *verb*, -ANT[1].]
▸ **A** *noun*. A person who emigrates; *spec*. (*hist*.) an émigré from the French Revolution. M18.
▸ **B** *adjective*. **1** That emigrates or has emigrated. L18.
2 Used by emigrants. Only *attrib*. M19.
emigrant road, ***emigrant ship***, ***emigrant train***, etc.

†**emigrate** *adjective*. Only in M17.
[ORIGIN Latin *emigratus* pa. pple of *emigrare*: see EMIGRATE *verb*, -ATE[2].]
That has migrated.

emigrate /ˈɛmɪɡreɪt/ *verb*. L18.
[ORIGIN Latin *emigrat-* pa. ppl stem of *emigrare*, from *e-* E- + *migrare* migrate: see -ATE[3].]
1 *verb intrans*. Leave one's country to settle in another. L18.
2 *verb trans*. Cause or assist to do this. L19.
■ **emigratory** *adjective* that is emigrating; pertaining to emigration: M19.

emigration /ɛmɪˈɡreɪʃ(ə)n/ *noun*. **M17**.
[ORIGIN Late Latin *emigratio(n-)*, formed as EMIGRATE *verb*: see -ATION.]
1 The action or an act of leaving a particular place or environment, permanently or temporarily. Now *rare* exc. as in sense 2. **M17**.
JER. TAYLOR Frequent Aspirations and Emigrations of his Soul after God.
2 The action or an act of emigrating. **L17**.
L. T. C. ROLT A sudden wave of emigration to what seemed a new promised land.
3 The group of people who emigrate from or to a particular place. **E19**.

émigré /ˈɛmɪɡreɪ/ *noun & adjective*. Also **e-**. **L18**.
[ORIGIN French, pa. pple of *émigrer* from Latin *emigrare*: see EMIGRATE *verb*.]
▸ **A** *noun*. Orig., a French emigrant, *esp*. one from the Revolution of 1789–99. Now, any emigrant, *esp*. a political exile. **L18**.
▸ **B** *adjective*. That is an émigré; composed of émigrés. **E20**.
V. NABOKOV Speeches she heard at émigré political meetings.

Emilian /ɪˈmɪlɪən/ *adjective & noun*. **M17**.
[ORIGIN from *Emilia* (see below) + -AN.]
▸ **A** *adjective*. Of or pertaining to Emilia, a district of northern Italy now part of the region of Emilia-Romagna, its inhabitants, or their dialect of Italian. **M17**.
▸ **B** *noun*. A native or inhabitant of Emilia; the Italian dialect of Emilia. **L19**.

†**emina** *noun* see HEMINA.

émincé /emɛ̃se/ *noun*. Pl. pronounced same. **E20**.
[ORIGIN French, use as noun of pa. pple of *émincer* slice thinly, from *é-* EX-¹ + *mincer*, formed as MINCE *verb*.]
A dish consisting of thinly sliced meat in sauce.

eminence /ˈɛmɪnəns/ *noun*. **ME**.
[ORIGIN Latin *eminentia*, formed as EMINENT: see -ENCE.]
▸ **I** *lit*. **1** An elevated or lofty position. **ME**.
K. WHITE Draw the fix'd stars from their eminence.
2 ANATOMY. A (rounded) projection on an organ or part, esp. on a bone. **ME**.
3 A piece of rising ground; a hill. **L17**.
W. S. CHURCHILL A large wooded eminence known . . as Hussar Hill.
▸ **II** *fig*. **4** Distinguished superiority in position, attainments, character, or the possession of any quality. **ME**. ▸†**b** Mastery, the upper hand. Only in **E16**.
B. RUSSELL The rise of men of science to great eminence in the State. **b** SHAKES. *Tr. & Cr.* You should not have the eminence of him.
†**5** Acknowledgement of superiority. *rare* (Shakes.). Only in **E17**.
6 An excellence; a distinction, an honour; superiority in degree, outstanding degree. *obsolete* exc. in ***by eminence***, ***by way of eminence*** below. **E17**.
J. PEARSON There must be . . some great eminence in the object worshipped.
by eminence, **by way of eminence** (now *rare*) *par excellence*; especially.
7 (Usu. **E-**.) A title of respect given to a cardinal or (formerly) any important person. Chiefly with possess. adjective **M17**. ▸**b** An important or eminent person. **M20**.

éminence grise /eminɑ̃ːs ɡriz/ *noun phr*. Pl. ***éminences grises*** (pronounced same). **M20**.
[ORIGIN French, lit. 'grey eminence', orig. applied to the Capuchin Père Joseph, confidential agent of Cardinal Richelieu (1585–1642). Cf. EMINENCE 7.]
A person who exercises power or influence though holding no official position. Also, a confidential adviser.

eminency /ˈɛmɪnənsi/ *noun*. **E17**.
[ORIGIN formed as EMINENCE: see -Y³.]
†**1** = EMINENCE. **E17–M18**.
†**2** Importance (of a place or requirement). Only in **17**.
3 Prominence or relative importance in one's thoughts. **M19**.

eminent /ˈɛmɪnənt/ *adjective*. **LME**.
[ORIGIN Latin *eminent-* pres. ppl stem of *eminere* project: see -ENT.]
1 High, lofty; towering above the surroundings. *arch*. **LME**. ▸**b** Protruding, projecting. *arch*. **M16**.
2 Remarkable in degree; important, noteworthy. **LME**.
H. P. BROUGHAM The reputation justly acquired by his eminent services.
3 Of a person: exalted, important; distinguished in position, attainments, or character. **L16**.
D. M. THOMAS The voice of such an eminent statesman earned instant respect. D. LESSING He . . early became eminent in his field.
†**4** Of a thing or place: principal, important; valuable. **E17–M18**.
†**5** [By confusion.] Imminent. **E17–E18**.

eminently /ˈɛmɪnəntli/ *adverb*. **LME**.
[ORIGIN from EMINENT + -LY².]
1 In or to a remarkable degree; notably, exceptionally. **LME**.
G. W. KNIGHT Cynicism is eminently logical to the modern . . mind. J. GALSWORTHY A task for which she was eminently qualified.
†**2** In a high or lofty position. Only in **17**.
†**3** Conspicuously. **M17–L18**.
4 PHILOSOPHY. In a superior manner (esp. of containment of an effect by a cause). **M17**.
†**5** [After EMINENT 5.] Imminently, urgently. **M–L17**.

emir /ɛˈmɪə/ *noun*. **L16**.
[ORIGIN French *émir* from Arabic *'amīr*: see AMIR.]
1 A male descendant of Muhammad. Now *rare*. **L16**.
2 A title of certain Muslim rulers; an Arab prince, governor, or commander. **M17**.
■ **emirate** /ˈɛmərət, ˈɛmɪərət, ɛˈmɪə-/ *noun* (*a*) the rank or position of an emir; (*b*) the region governed or ruled by an emir: **M19**.

emissary /ˈɛmɪs(ə)ri/ *noun*¹ *& adjective*. **E17**.
[ORIGIN Latin *emissarius*, from *emiss-* pa. ppl stem of *emittere* EMIT: see -ARY¹.]
▸ **A** *noun*. A person sent on a special mission, esp. to gain information, promote a cause, etc. Orig. usu. *derog*. **E17**.
H. JAMES Even if . . you are not Mr Cumnor . . they may still suspect you of being his emissary. H. KISSINGER If . . the Chinese accepted our proposal to send an emissary to Peking or receive theirs in Washington.
▸ **B** *adjective*. †**1** Emitted. Only in **M17**.
†**2** Sent on a special mission. **L17–M19**.
3 ANATOMY. Of a blood vessel: branching from a larger one; *spec*. designating veins that pass through the cranial wall and drain venous sinuses inside the skull into veins outside it. **M19**.

emissary /ˈɛmɪs(ə)ri/ *noun*². **E17**.
[ORIGIN Latin *emissarium*, from *emiss-*: see EMISSARY *noun*¹ *& adjective*, -ARY¹.]
1 An outlet, a channel. *obsolete* exc. *hist*. **E17**.
†**2** A duct of the body. **M17–M18**.

emissile /ɪˈmɪsɪl, -ʌɪl/ *adjective*. **M18**.
[ORIGIN from Latin *emiss-*: see EMISSARY *noun*¹ *& adjective*, -ILE.]
ZOOLOGY. Able to be protruded.

emission /ɪˈmɪʃ(ə)n/ *noun*. **LME**.
[ORIGIN Latin *emissio(n-)*, from *emiss-*: see EMISSARY *noun*¹ *& adjective*, -ION.]
1 Something emitted; an emanation. **LME**.
City Limits Experts monitor sea creatures for nuclear emissions.
2 The action or an act of emitting. Formerly also, the release of the soul at death; *fig*. the pouring out of affection. **E17**. ▸**b** Ejaculation of semen. **M17**.
LD RUTHERFORD The emission of these radiations from radioactive substances.
b ***nocturnal emission***: see NOCTURNAL *adjective* 1.
†**3** *gen*. The action of sending out something or someone. **E17–E19**.
HOBBES The emission of preachers to the infidels.
– COMB.: **emission nebula** ASTRONOMY: that shines with its own rather than reflected light; **emission spectrum**: showing the radiation from an emitting source; **emissions trading** a system whereby countries and organizations are given permits to produce a particular amount of carbon dioxide and other greenhouse gases, which they may trade with others; **emission theory** = *CORPUSCULAR* ***theory***.

emissive /ɪˈmɪsɪv/ *adjective*. **M17**.
[ORIGIN from Latin *emiss-*: see EMISSARY *noun*¹ *& adjective*, -IVE.]
†**1** That is emitted. **M17–M18**.
2 Of or pertaining to emission; *spec*. (HISTORY OF SCIENCE) designating the emission theory of light. **M19**.
R. JAKOBSON The classical distinction between . . emissive (or expressive) aphasia . . and receptive (or sensory) aphasia.
3 That emits or is capable of emitting. **L19**.
■ **emissivity** /ɛmɪˈsɪvɪti-, iːm-/ *noun* (PHYSICS) the relative ability of a surface to radiate heat; *spec*. the ratio of the rate at which it radiates heat to the rate at which a black body at the same temperature would radiate heat: **L19**.

emit /ɪˈmɪt/ *verb trans*. Infl. **-tt-**. **E17**.
[ORIGIN Latin *emittere*, from *e-* E- + *mittere* send.]
1 Give off, send out from oneself or itself, (something imponderable, as light, sound, scent, flames, etc.); discharge, exude, (a fluid). **E17**.
I. MURDOCH Gorse bushes . . emitted their strong coconut perfume. P. ACKROYD The strip lighting . . emitted a vague hum. *fig.*: A. POWELL She enjoyed emitting an impression of Cambridge severity.
†**2** Send out as an offshoot. **M17–M18**.
†**3** **a** Publish (a book or notice). **M17–M19**. ▸**b** Issue formally and with authority; *esp*. put (currency) into circulation. **L17**.
†**4** Discharge (a missile). Only in **E18**.
5 Utter, express, (an opinion etc.). **M18**.
JAS. MILL Complaints were . . emitted of the scarcity of money.
■ **emitter** *noun* a thing or substance which emits; *spec*. the part of a transistor where the charge carriers originate and from where they flow into the base: **L19**.

emma /ˈɛmə/. *noun*. **L19**.
Used for the letter *m* in spoken telephone communications and in the oral spelling of messages.
ack emma, ***pip emma***, ***toc emma***.

emmarble *verb* see ENMARBLE.

emmarvel /ɪˈmɑːv(ə)l/ *verb trans*. Now *rare*. Also (earlier) †**en-**. **M18**.
[ORIGIN from EN-¹, EM-¹ + MARVEL *noun*¹ or *verb*.]
Fill with wonder.

emmenagogue /ɪˈmiːnəɡɒɡ, ɛ-/ *adjective & noun*. **E18**.
[ORIGIN from Greek *emmēna* menses (from *em-* EM-² + *mēn-* month) + *agōgos* leading, eliciting, from *agein* to lead.]
MEDICINE. ▸†**A** *adjective*. = EMMENAGOGIC. **E18–M19**.
▸ **B** *noun*. An emmenagogic agent. **M18**.
■ **emmenagogic** /ɪˌmiːnəˈɡɒdʒɪk/ *adjective* promoting or increasing menstrual flow **L17**.

Emmental /ˈɛməntɑːl/ *noun*. Also **-thal**, **-t(h)aler** /-tɑːlə/. **E20**.
[ORIGIN German *Emmentaler* (formerly *-thaler*), from *Emmental* a region in Switzerland.]
A type of hard Swiss cheese with many holes, similar to Gruyère. Also ***Emmental cheese***.

emmer /ˈɛmə/ *noun*¹. **E20**.
[ORIGIN German from Old High German *amer*.]
A kind of tetraploid wheat, *Triticum dicoccon*, with two-grained spikelets that was eaten in prehistoric times and is now grown for fodder and breakfast cereals.

emmer *noun*² var. of EMBER *noun*².

emmet /ˈɛmɪt/ *noun*. Chiefly *dial*.
[ORIGIN Old English *ǣmete* weak fem. of *æmet(t)e*: see ANT.]
1 = ANT 1. **OE**.
2 In Cornwall: a holidaymaker, a tourist. **L20**.

emmetropia /ɛməˈtrəʊpɪə/ *noun*. **M19**.
[ORIGIN from Greek *emmetros* in measure (formed as EM-² + *metron* measure) + *ōp-*, *ōps* eye + -IA¹.]
The state of refraction of the normal eye, in which parallel light rays are focused on the retina when the eye is relaxed.
■ **emmetropic** /-ˈtrəʊpɪk, -ˈtrɒpɪk/ *adjective* **L19**.

Emmy /ˈɛmi/ *noun*. **M20**.
[ORIGIN Perh. from *Immy*, from *image* (*orthicon tube*) + -Y⁶.]
Any of the statuettes awarded annually by the American Academy of Television Arts and Sciences to an outstanding television programme or performer. Also ***Emmy award***.

emo /ˈiːməʊ/ *noun*. Also **emocore**. **L20**.
[ORIGIN Short for *emotional hardcore*.]
A style of rock music resembling punk but having more complex arrangements and lyrics that deal with emotional subjects.

emodin /ˈɛmədɪn/ *noun*. **M19**.
[ORIGIN from mod. Latin *emodi* former specific epithet of *Rheum australe* an Asian species of rhubarb, from Greek *Ēmōdos* Himalayas: see -IN¹.]
An orange anthraquinone, $C_{15}H_{10}O_5$, obtained from rhubarb, cascara, and some other plants and having cathartic properties.

emolliate /ɪˈmɒlɪeɪt/ *verb trans*. **E19**.
[ORIGIN Irreg. from Latin *emollire* (see EMOLLIENT) + -ATE³, after *emaciate* etc.]
Soften, make effeminate.
■ †**emolliative** *adjective* (*rare*) that tends to soften: only in **E17**.

emollient /ɪˈmɒlɪənt/ *adjective & noun*. **M17**.
[ORIGIN Latin *emollient-* pres. ppl stem of *emollire* make soft, from *e-* E- + *mollis* soft: see -ENT.]
▸ **A** *adjective*. That makes the skin soft or supple; *fig*. soothing; that makes more acceptable. **M17**.
R. HOGGART Working-class speech and manners . . are more abrupt, less provided with emollient phrases.
▸ **B** *noun*. An emollient agent. **M17**.
■ **emollience** *noun* **M20**.

†**emollition** *noun*. **E17–M18**.
[ORIGIN from Latin *emollit-* pa. ppl stem of *emollire*: see EMOLLIENT, -ITION.]
The action of making soft.

emolument /ɪˈmɒljʊm(ə)nt, ɛ-/ *noun*. **LME**.
[ORIGIN Old French & mod. French *émolument* or Latin *emolumentum*, *emoli-* gain, orig. prob. payment to a miller for the grinding of corn, from *emolere* grind up, from *e-* E- + *molere* grind: see -MENT.]
1 *sing*. & (usu.) in *pl*. Profit or gain arising from office or employment; reward, remuneration. **LME**.
N. FREELING A recommendation that you should have the rank and emoluments of a principal commissaire.
†**2** Benefit, comfort. **M16–M18**.
■ **emoluˈmentary** *adjective* profitable, beneficial **L18**.

†**emong** *preposition & adverb* var. of AMONG.

emony /ˈɛməni/ *noun*. **M16**.
[ORIGIN Aphet. from *anemone* (taken as *an emony*).]
= ANEMONE *noun* 1.

emote /ɪˈməʊt/ *verb intrans.* E20.
[ORIGIN Back-form. from EMOTION.]
Dramatize emotion; act emotionally or theatrically.
■ **emoter** *noun* M20.

emoticon /ɪˈməʊtɪkɒn, -ˈmɒtɪ-/ *noun.* L20.
[ORIGIN from EMOT(ION + ICON.]
A representation of a facial expression such as a smile or frown, formed by various combinations of keyboard characters and used in electronic communications to convey the writer's feelings or intended tone.
– NOTE: Examples are the sequences :-) and :-(representing a smile and a frown respectively.

emotion /ɪˈməʊʃ(ə)n/ *noun & verb.* M16.
[ORIGIN French *émotion*, from *émouvoir* excite, move the feelings of (after *mouvoir*, *motion*), ult. from Latin *emovere*, from *e-* E- + *movere* move.]
▸ **A** *noun.* †**1** A public disturbance; a commotion. M16–M18.
†**2** A migration; a change of position. Only in 17. ▸**b** A physical agitation or disturbance. L17–E19.

b SHELLEY The winds of heaven mix forever With a sweet emotion.

3 Agitation of mind; strong mental feeling. M17.

G. HUNTINGTON The colonel announced with emotion that this was the happiest day of his life.

4 Any of the natural instinctive affections of the mind (e.g. love, horror, pity) which come and go according to one's personality, experiences, and bodily state; a mental feeling. Also, mental feeling as distinguished from knowledge and from will. E19.

A. STORR Those who . . have had a relationship in which their emotions have not been deeply involved. M. AMIS Without a trace of hatred or anger or surprise or any emotion I have felt myself. J. HILTON He had shown so little emotion about anything.

▸ **B** *verb trans.* Make emotional; imbue with emotion. L18.
■ **emotionless** *adjective* M19. **emotionlessly** *adverb* E20. **emotionlessness** *noun* E20.

emotional /ɪˈməʊʃ(ə)n(ə)l/ *adjective.* M19.
[ORIGIN from EMOTION + -AL¹.]
1 Of or pertaining to the emotions; based on or appealing to the emotions. M19.

J. ROSENBERG A wide range of emotional expressions, from joy and surprise to horror and pain. F. WARNER My Mother . . forces herself on me by emotional blackmail. DAY LEWIS A woman . . capable of bitter resistance against domestic bullying or emotional exploitation.

2 Having the capacity for emotion; *esp.* easily affected by emotion. Also, full of emotion, showing strong emotion. M19.

T. HARDY The singer himself grew emotional, till she could imagine a tear in his eye. *Observer* It was assumed that women were too emotional to broadcast news bulletins.

TIRED *and emotional.*
■ **emotioˈnality** *noun* emotional character or temperament; the ability to feel or express emotion: M19. **emotionalize** *verb trans.* imbue with emotion; deal with emotionally: L19. **emotionally** *adverb* M19.

emotionalism /ɪˈməʊʃ(ə)n(ə)lɪz(ə)m/ *noun.* M19.
[ORIGIN from EMOTIONAL + -ISM.]
Emotional character; *esp.* a tendency to cultivate or give in weakly to emotion.

emotionalist /ɪˈməʊʃ(ə)n(ə)lɪst/ *noun & adjective.* M19.
[ORIGIN from EMOTIONAL + -IST.]
▸ **A** *noun.* **1** A person who bases a theory of conduct on the emotions. M19.
2 A person given to emotionalism. L19.
▸ **B** *adjective.* Based on or expressed in terms of the emotions. M20.

E. E. EVANS-PRITCHARD Emotionalist interpretations of religion.

emotive /ɪˈməʊtɪv/ *adjective.* M18.
[ORIGIN from Latin *emot-* pa. ppl stem of *emovere*: see EMOTION, -IVE.]
1 Arousing or able to arouse feeling or emotion; *spec.* in PHILOSOPHY & LITERARY CRITICISM expressing emotion, rather than descriptive. M18.

H. M. KENNEDY The emotive passionate quality of epic diction. C. S. LEWIS We use the highly emotive word 'stagnation' . . for what other ages would have called 'permanence'. K. CLARK The poet and painter . . both drew practically the whole of their emotive power from . . their boyhood.

emotive theory: that ethical and value judgements are expressions of feeling, not statements.
2 Having the capacity for (strong) emotion; of or pertaining to emotion. M19.

H. SPENCER Actions . . at once conscious, rational, and emotive.

■ **emotively** *adverb* L19. **emotiveness** *noun* L19. **emotivism** *noun* (adherence to) the emotive theory M20. **emoˈtivity** *noun* (**a**) the capacity for emotion; (**b**) emotional rather than descriptive quality or expression: M19.

emove /ɪˈmuːv/ *verb trans. rare.* E17.
[ORIGIN Latin *emovere*: see EMOTION.]
Affect with emotion.

EMP *abbreviation.*
Electromagnetic pulse.

empacket /ɪmˈpakɪt, ɛm-/ *verb trans. rare.* E19.
[ORIGIN from EM-¹ + PACKET *noun.*]
Pack up; put into packets.

†**empair** *verb* var. of IMPAIR *verb.*

empale *verb*, **empalement** *noun* vars. of IMPALE, IMPALEMENT.

empanada /ɛmpəˈnɑːdə, *foreign* empaˈnaða/ *noun.* M20.
[ORIGIN Spanish, use as noun of fem. pa. pple of *empanar* bake or roll in pastry, formed as EM-¹ + *pan* bread from Latin *panis*.]
COOKERY. A turnover with a filling of meat, cheese, or vegetables.

empanel /ɪmˈpan(ə)l, ɛm-/ *verb & noun.* Also **im-** /ɪm-/. Infl. **-ll-**, ***-l-**. LME.
[ORIGIN Anglo-Norman *empaneller*, formed as EM-¹, IM-¹, PANEL *noun*¹.]
▸ **A** *verb trans.* Enter (the names of a jury) on a panel or official list; enrol or constitute (a body of jurors). LME.
▸ †**B** *noun.* A list or panel of jurors. E16–L18.
■ **empanelment** *noun* the action of empanelling L19.

†**empannel** *verb trans. rare.* Infl. **-ll-**. E17–L19.
[ORIGIN from EM-¹ + PANEL *noun*¹.]
Put a packsaddle on.

emparadise *verb* var. of IMPARADISE.

†**emparl** *verb*, †**emparlance** *noun* vars. of IMPARL, IMPARLANCE.

†**empassion** *verb*, **empassioned** *ppl adjective* vars. of IMPASSION etc.

empathetic /ɛmpəˈθɛtɪk/ *adjective.* M20.
[ORIGIN from EMPATHY + *-etic*, after *sympathy*, *sympathetic*.]
= EMPATHIC *adjective.*
■ **empathetically** *adverb* M20.

empathize /ˈɛmpəθʌɪz/ *verb intrans.* & (*rare*) *trans.* Also **-ise.** E20.
[ORIGIN from EMPATHY + -IZE.]
Exercise or experience empathy *with* or with; sympathize.

empathy /ˈɛmpəθi/ *noun.* E20.
[ORIGIN Greek *empatheia*, formed as EM-² + *pathos* feeling: see -Y³; translating German *Einfühlung*.]
The power of mentally identifying oneself with (and so fully comprehending) a person or object of contemplation.

M. L. KING Pity is feeling sorry for someone; empathy is feeling sorry with someone.

■ **emˈpathic** *adjective* involving empathy; having empathy *to* or *with* a person, feeling, etc.: E20. **emˈpathically** *adverb* E20. **empathist** *noun* an adherent of a theory involving empathy E20.

†**empatron** *verb trans. rare* (Shakes.). Only in L16.
[ORIGIN from EM-¹ + PATRON *noun.*]
Act as patron to.

†**empeach** *verb & noun*, †**empeachment** *noun* vars. of IMPEACH *noun & verb*, IMPEACHMENT.

empearl *verb* var. of IMPEARL.

empennage /ɛmˈpɛnɪdʒ/ *noun.* E20.
[ORIGIN French = feathering (of an arrow), empennage, from *empenner* feather (an arrow), formed as EM-¹ + *penne* feather from Latin *penna*: see -AGE.]
The group of stabilizing and control surfaces at the tail of an aircraft.

†**empeople** *verb.* Also **im-**. L16–M19.
[ORIGIN from EM-¹ + PEOPLE *noun.*]
Fill with people, populate.

†**emperial** *adjective & noun* var. of IMPERIAL *adjective & noun.*

†**emperil** *verb* var. of IMPERIL.

emperor /ˈɛmp(ə)rə/ *noun.* ME.
[ORIGIN Old French *emperere*, *emperour* (mod. *empereur*), from Latin *imperator*, from *imperare* command, formed as IM-¹ + *parare* prepare, contrive: see -OR.]
1 The male monarch of an empire; orig., the title given to the monarch or head of the Roman Empire (in its various forms). ME.
2 *gen.* A title of sovereignty considered superior to that of king. LME.
†**3** A military leader or commander. LME–M18.
4 In full ***emperor penguin***. The largest species of penguin, *Aptenodytes forsteri*, found only in the Antarctic. L19.
5 In full ***emperor angelfish***, ***emperor fish***. A golden brown angelfish with yellow stripes, *Pomacanthus imperator*, found in parts of the Indian and Pacific Oceans. L19.
– PHRASES: ***purple emperor***: see PURPLE *adjective*. ***red emperor***: see RED *adjective*.
– COMB.: ***emperor angelfish***, ***emperor fish***: see sense 5 above; **emperor goose** a goose, *Anser canagica*, with variegated plumage, found in Alaska and NE Siberia; **emperor moth** any of several large Old World saturniid silk moths; *esp.* the European *Pavonia pavonia*, with prominent eyespots on all four wings; ***emperor penguin***: see sense 4 above.
■ **emperorship** *noun* the office, dignity, or reign of an emperor L16.

empery /ˈɛmp(ə)ri/ *noun. obsolete* exc. *poet.* ME.
[ORIGIN Old French *emperie*, *empirie* from Latin *imperium* EMPIRE.]
1 †**a** The status or dominion of an emperor. ME–L16. ▸**b** Absolute dominion. M16.
†**2** The legitimate authority of an officer or magistrate; legitimate government. LME–M17.
3 The territory of an emperor or a powerful ruler. LME.

empest *verb* var. of IMPEST.

emphasis /ˈɛmfəsɪs/ *noun.* Pl. **-ases** /-əsiːz/. L16.
[ORIGIN Latin from Greek, orig. = (mere) appearance, from *emphainein* to exhibit, formed as EM-² + *phainein* to show.]
†**1** A figure of speech in which more is implied than is actually said; a meaning conveyed by implication. (The sense in Greek & Latin.) L16–M18.
2 Vigour or intensity of statement or expression. L16. ▸†**b** An intense expression. *rare* (Shakes.). Only in E17.

E

J. MORLEY There is not a sentence of strained emphasis or overwrought antithesis.

3 Intensity or force of feeling, action, etc. L16.
4 Stress of voice laid on a word or phrase to indicate an implied extra meaning or to mark its importance. E17.

CONAN DOYLE 'If you think —' 'I *do* think,' said Holmes, with emphasis.

5 *transf.* Stress laid upon, or importance assigned to, a fact or idea. L17.

L. VAN DER POST The emphasis . . was on skill rather than violence.

6 Visual prominence, sharpness or clarity of contour, colouring, etc. L19.

F. HERBERT Dark hair swept back . . throwing emphasis on sharp cheekbones.

emphasize /ˈɛmfəsʌɪz/ *verb trans.* Also **-ise.** E19.
[ORIGIN from EMPHASIS + -IZE.]
Lay stress on (a word, phrase, etc.); add force to (an argument, action, etc.); bring (a fact, feature, etc.) into special prominence.

P. V. WHITE The slammed door emphasized the silence of the house. L. DEIGHTON He emphasized the lines of his cheek muscles by drawing his fingers down them. B. EMECHETA He . . banged at the kitchen table, just to emphasize his point.

■ **emphasizer** *noun* L19.

emphatic /ɪmˈfatɪk, ɛm-/ *adjective & noun.* E18.
[ORIGIN Late Latin *emphaticus* from Greek *emphatikos*, from Greek EMPHASIS: see -IC.]
▸ **A** *adjective.* **1** Of language, tone, gesture, etc.: forcibly expressive. E18. ▸**b** Of a word or syllable: bearing the stress. E19. ▸**c** GRAMMAR. Imparting emphasis. L19.

A. BROOKNER All her gestures were vigorous and all her interventions emphatic.

2 Of a person: expressing himself or herself with force or emphasis. M18.

GEO. ELIOT Mr. Lingon was equally emphatic.

3 Of an action or its result, or a state: forcible, pronounced; strongly marked. M19.

E. BOWEN Writing had dug through; the sheets were thin, her mother's pencil emphatic. N. SAHGAL The emphatic fullness of her bosom.

▸ **B** *noun.* A letter, word, phrase, etc., that is expressive or indicative of emphasis; *joc.* an expletive. Usu. in *pl.* E19.
■ **emphaticness** *noun* L20.

emphatical /ɪmˈfatɪk(ə)l, ɛm-/ *adjective.* Now *rare.* M16.
[ORIGIN formed as EMPHATIC: see -ICAL.]
†**1** Allusive, suggestive. M16–L18.
2 = EMPHATIC *adjective.* L16.
†**3** That is emphatically designated (such). M17–M18.
†**4** Of colour: illusory. M17–E18.

emphatically /ɪmˈfatɪk(ə)li, ɛm-/ *adverb.* L16.
[ORIGIN from EMPHATIC *adjective* or EMPHATICAL: see -ICALLY.]
1 In an emphatic way, with emphasis. L16.
†**2** In or as (mere) appearance. M–L17.
†**3** Allusively, suggestively. M–L17.

emphysema /ɛmfɪˈsiːmə/ *noun.* M17.
[ORIGIN Late Latin from Greek *emphusēma*, from *emphusan* puff up.]
MEDICINE. **1** Swelling caused by the abnormal presence of air in tissue. M17.
2 More fully ***pulmonary emphysema***, ***vesicular emphysema***. The enlargement and partial amalgamation of the air sacs of the lungs, resulting in breathlessness and wheezing. M19.
■ **emphysematous** *adjective* of the nature of or pertaining to emphysema M18.

emphyteusis /ɛmfɪˈtjuːsɪs/ *noun.* Pl. **-teuses** /-ˈtjuːsiːz/. L16.
[ORIGIN Late Latin from Greek *emphuteusis* lit. 'implanting', from *emphuteuein* to implant, formed as EM-² + *phuteuein* to plant, from *phuton* plant: see -PHYTE.]
In Roman law and many civil law jurisdictions: a long-term or perpetual lease, heritable and alienable; tenure under such a lease.
■ **emphyteutic** *adjective* of the nature of or held by emphyteusis M17.

E

emphyteuta /ɛmfɪˈtjuːtə/ *noun*. E18.
[ORIGIN Late Latin from Greek *emphuteutēs*, from *emphuteuein*: see EMPHYTEUSIS.]
A tenant holding land under emphyteusis.

empicture *verb* var. of IMPICTURE.

empiecement /ɪmˈpiːsm(ə)nt, ɛm-/ *noun*. L19.
[ORIGIN French *empiècement*, formed as EM-¹, PIECE *noun*: see -MENT.]
A piece of material inserted in a garment for decoration.

empierce /ɪmˈpɪəs, ɛm-/ *verb trans*. Now *rare*. Also **im-** /ɪm-/. L15.
[ORIGIN from EM-¹, IM-¹ + PIERCE *verb*.]
Pierce through; transfix.

†**empight** *verb*. Also **im-**. Pa. pple **-pight**. LME.
[ORIGIN from EM-¹, IM-¹ + *pight* (see PITCH *verb*²).]
1 *verb trans*. Implant, fix in. Only as **empight** pa. pple. LME–M18.
2 *verb intrans*. Become fixed. Only in L16.

empire /ˈɛmpʌɪə/ *noun & adjective*. ME.
[ORIGIN Old French & mod. French, earlier *emperie*, from Latin *imperium* rel. to *imperator* EMPEROR.]
▸ **A** *noun*. **I** Something under rule.
1 An extensive territory, esp. an aggregate of many states, under the ultimate authority of one person (an emperor or empress) or one sovereign state; *colloq*. a large group of companies controlled or owned by one company; a person's power or authority in an organization, esp. as represented by the number of his or her subordinates. ME.

F. FITZGERALD Siam was . . building an empire out of the territories of Laos and Cambodia. *Mail on Sunday* His multi-million dollar empire all began in Uncle Robert's garage in Kansas City. *Daily Telegraph* The management appears to be top heavy, . . caused by people reluctant to give up carefully nurtured empires. *fig*.: SHELLEY Scorn and despair—these are mine empire.

2 A sovereign state. Now *rare* or *obsolete*. M16.
▸ **II** Rulership.
3 Supreme and extensive political dominion, *esp*. that exercised by an emperor. LME. ▸**b** Absolute control; paramount influence. LME.

Spectator We have clung to the rhetoric of empire long after we have lost . . the ability to maintain its reality. **b** R. L. STEVENSON Long after that death yell was still ringing in my brain, silence had re-established its empire.

4 The position or dignity of an emperor. Now *rare*. E16.
5 A government in which the head of state is called an emperor or empress. Freq. as ***the Empire*** below. E19.
▸ **B** *attrib*. or as *adjective*. (Of furniture, dress, etc.) of the style fashionable in France during the Empire (or the Second Empire); (of wine) from the British Commonwealth. M19.

O. LOGAN Your new but ugly little Empire bonnet.

– COMB. & PHRASES: **empire builder** (*a*) *hist*. a person who added to the territory of the British Empire; a British overseas administrator; (*b*) a person who seeks to increase his or her authority or staff in an organization; **empire-building** the activity of an empire builder; **Empire City** *US* New York; **Empire Day** *hist*. the original name of Commonwealth Day; **empire-line** *adjective* (of a dress) having a high waist and a low neckline; **Empire State** *US* New York State; **Empire State of the South** *US colloq*. the American state of Georgia; ***Holy Roman Empire***, ***Roman Empire***: see ROMAN *adjective*; **Second Empire** the (period of) rule of Napoleon III as Emperor of the French, 1852–70; **the Empire** *hist*. (*a*) the Holy Roman Empire; (*b*) the British Empire; (*c*) the (period of) rule of Napoleon Bonaparte as Emperor of the French, 1804–15. ***the Flowery Empire***: see FLOWERY *adjective* 1.

empiric /ɛmˈpɪrɪk, ɪm-/ *adjective & noun*. LME.
[ORIGIN Latin *empiricus* noun from Greek *empeirikos*, from *empeiria* experience, from *empeiros* skilled, formed as EM-² + *peira* trial, experiment: see -IC.]
▸ **A** *adjective*. = EMPIRICAL. Now chiefly *US*. LME.
▸ **B** *noun*. **1** *hist*. Any of a sect of ancient physicians who drew their rules of practice only from experience. LME. ▸**b** *gen*. A scientist who relies solely on observation and experiment. *arch*. L16.
2 A person who practises medicine without scientific knowledge; a quack; a charlatan. *arch*. M16.

empirical /ɛmˈpɪrɪk(ə)l, ɪm-/ *adjective*. M16.
[ORIGIN from EMPIRIC + -AL¹.]
1 Based on, guided by, or employing observation and experiment rather than theory; (of a remedy, rule, etc.) used because it works, or is believed to. M16. ▸†**b** That practises medicine without scientific knowledge. L17–M19.

J. BARNES A co-operative farming venture . . left him with some empirical knowledge, but little understanding of horticultural principle.

2 Derived from or verifiable by experience, esp. sense experience. M17.

J. S. MILL An empirical law . . is an observed uniformity . . resolvable into simpler laws, but not yet resolved into them.

– SPECIAL COLLOCATIONS: **empirical formula** CHEMISTRY: giving the proportions of the various elements present in a molecule, not the actual number of atoms or their arrangement. **empirical psychologist** an exponent or adherent of empirical psychology.

■ **empirically** *adverb* M17. †**empiricalness** *noun*: only in M17.

empiricism /ɛmˈpɪrɪsɪz(ə)m, ɪm-/ *noun*. M17.
[ORIGIN from EMPIRIC + -ISM.]
1 Practice based on experiment and observation. Formerly, ignorant or unscientific practice, quackery. M17.
2 PHILOSOPHY. The doctrine or theory that all knowledge is based on experience derived from the senses; the doctrine or theory that concepts and statements have meaning only in relation to sense experience. Opp. RATIONALISM 3. Cf. SENSATIONALISM 1. L18. ***logical empiricism***: see LOGICAL *adjective*.
3 An assertion made on empirical grounds. M19.
■ **empiricist** *noun & adjective* (*a*) *noun* an exponent or adherent of empiricism; (*b*) *adjective* of, pertaining to, or characterized by philosophical empiricism: E18.

empirico- /ɛmˈpɪrɪkəʊ, ɪm-/ *combining form*. L19.
[ORIGIN from EMPIRICAL, EMPIRICISM + -O-.]
Used in sense 'empirical (and—)', as ***empirico-formalism***, ***empirico-psychological***.

†**empiricutic** *adjective*. *rare* (Shakes.). Only in E17.
[ORIGIN from EMPIRIC after *pharmaceutic*.]
Empirical.

empirio- /ɛmˈpɪrɪəʊ, ɪm-/ *combining form*.
[ORIGIN Alt.]
= EMPIRICO-.
■ **empirio-ˈcritical** *adjective* (PHILOSOPHY) of, pertaining to, or characterized by empirio-criticism E20. **empirio-ˈcriticism** *noun* PHILOSOPHY a form of positivism rejecting mind-body dualism and restricting knowledge to critically treated experience L19.

†**empirism** *noun*. E18–M19.
[ORIGIN French *empirisme*, from *empirique*, formed as EMPIRIC: see -ISM.]
Philosophical empiricism.

emplacement /ɪmˈpleɪsm(ə)nt, ɛm-/ *noun*. E19.
[ORIGIN French, formed as EM-¹ + *place* PLACE *noun*¹: see -MENT.]
1 MILITARY. A defended or protected position where a gun or missile is placed ready for firing. E19.
2 Situation, position; *spec*. that of a building. E19.
3 The action of putting or settling into place. M19.
■ **emplace** *verb trans*. [back-form.] put into a specified position or (MILITARY) an emplacement; situate: M19.

emplane /ɪmˈpleɪn, ɛm-/ *verb trans. & intrans*. E20.
[ORIGIN from EM-¹ + PLANE *noun*⁴.]
Take, put, or go on board an aircraft. (Foll. by *for* a destination.)

†**emplaster** *noun*. LME–E19.
[ORIGIN Old French *emplastre* (mod. *emplâtre*) from Latin *emplastrum* PLASTER *noun*.]
A plaster.

†**emplaster** *verb trans*. LME–M17.
[ORIGIN Old French *emplastrer* (mod. *emplâtrer*), formed as EMPLASTER *noun*.]
Cover with a plaster. Also, apply as a plaster.

†**emplastic** *adjective & noun*. LME.
[ORIGIN Late Latin *emplasticus* from Greek *emplastikos*, from *emplastron* PLASTER *noun*: see -IC.]
▸ **A** *adjective*. Suitable for use as a plaster; adhesive, glutinous. Also, that stops the pores. LME–M18.
▸ **B** *noun*. An adhesive or glutinous substance. M17–M18.

†**emplastration** *noun*. LME.
[ORIGIN Latin *emplastratio(n-)*, from *emplastrat-* pa. ppl stem of *emplastrare*, from *emplastrum* PLASTER *noun*: see -ATION.]
1 HORTICULTURE. A way of budding with a piece of bark surrounding the bud and attached like a plaster to a tree. LME–M18.
2 The application of a plaster. M16–M17.

emplastrum /ɪmˈplastrəm, -plɑːs-, ɛm-/ *noun*. *rare*. M16.
[ORIGIN Latin: see PLASTER *noun*.]
A plaster.

†**empleach** *verb* var. of IMPLEACH.

†**emplead** *verb* var. of IMPLEAD.

†**empledge** *verb* var. of IMPLEDGE.

empleomania /ˌɛmplɪəˈmeɪnɪə/ *noun*. L19.
[ORIGIN Spanish, from *empleo* employment + -MANIA.]
A mania for holding public office.

employ /ɪmˈplɔɪ, ɛm-/ *noun*. Also †**im-**. M17.
[ORIGIN from the verb.]
†**1** The action of employing a person or using a thing. M17–E19.
2 = EMPLOYMENT 2. Now *arch. & poet*. L17.
†**3** = EMPLOYMENT 2b. L17–L18.
†**4** An official position in public service. L17–E19.
5 The state or fact of being employed, esp. for payment. E18.

New Yorker Greene must have been in the employ of MI6.

employ /ɪmˈplɔɪ, ɛm-/ *verb trans*. Also †**im-**. LME.
[ORIGIN Old French & mod. French *employer* from Proto-Romance *implicare* for Latin *implicari* be involved (in) or attached (to), pass. of *implicare* enfold, involve: see IMPLICATE *verb*. Cf. IMPLY.]
1 Use for a particular purpose, make use of. (Foll. by *for*, *in*, *on*, †*to*.) LME.

SHAKES. *Merch. V.* Employ your chiefest thoughts to courtship. J. G. COZZENS She employed frequently all the improper words she knew. C. S. FORESTER They were going to take a leaf out of the Germans' book and employ poison gas. A. WILSON A complicated puzzle on which to employ his wit.

†**2** = IMPLY 1, 2, 4. E16–E17.
3 Use or retain the services of (a person), esp. in return for payment; pay (a person) to work for oneself or one's organization. L16.

A. BLOND If Thomas Chatterton had employed an agent he might not have starved to death.

4 Keep (a person, a person's senses or powers) occupied or busy; in *pass*., be engaged *in*, be at work *on* (also foll. by *about*). L16.

SWIFT He was imploy'd in drinking. G. BERKELEY Speculations to employ our curiosity. *refl*.: T. REID Castle-builders employ themselves . . in romance.

■ **employaˈbility** *noun* the character or quality of being employable E20. **employable** *adjective* L16.

employe /ɛmplɔɪˈiː, ɛmˈplɔɪiː, ɪm-/ *noun*. *US*. E20.
[ORIGIN Alt. of EMPLOYÉ, EMPLOYEE.]
= EMPLOYEE. Cf. EMPLOYÉ.

employé /ɒmˈplɔɪeɪ, *foreign* ɑ̃plwaje (*pl. same*)/ *noun*. Fem. **-ée**. E19.
[ORIGIN French, pa. ppl adjective of *employer* EMPLOY *verb*.]
= EMPLOYEE. Cf. prec.

employee /ɛmplɔɪˈiː, ɛmˈplɔɪiː, ɪm-/ *noun*. M19.
[ORIGIN from EMPLOY *verb* + -EE¹.]
A person who works for an employer. Cf. EMPLOYÉ, EMPLOYE.

employée *noun* fem. of EMPLOYÉ.

employer /ɪmˈplɔɪə, ɛm-/ *noun*. Also †**im-**. L16.
[ORIGIN from EMPLOY *verb* + -ER¹.]
A person who employs or who makes use (*of*); *esp*. a person or organization that pays someone to do work on a regular or contractual basis.

employment /ɪmˈplɔɪm(ə)nt, ɛm-/ *noun*. Also †**im-**. LME.
[ORIGIN from EMPLOY *verb* + -MENT.]
1 The action of employing; the state of being employed. LME. ▸†**b** The service of another person. L16–E17.

J. GALSWORTHY That public Museum of Art . . had given so much employment to officials. **b** SHAKES. *John* At your employment, at your service, sir!

full employment a situation in which all persons who wish to have a job can obtain one. **in the employment of** employed by (an employer).
2 Occupation, business; paid work; an activity in which a person is engaged; *arch*. a special errand or task. L16. ▸**b** A person's trade, profession, or occupation. M17. ▸†**c** = EMPLOY *noun* 4. M17–M18.

GOLDSMITH I . . went from town to town, working when I could get employment. H. T. LANE He completed the destruction of the book, and then turned to some other employment. J. BIRMINGHAM Colin . . was trying to work up some enthusiasm for the world of employment.

†**3** The use or purpose to which something is put. L16–M17.

SHAKES. *Rich. II* Eight thousand nobles . . The which he hath detain'd for lewd employments.

– COMB.: **employment agency** a business that finds employers or employees for those seeking them; **employment exchange**, **employment office** a state-run employment agency.

emplume /ɛmˈpluːm, ɪm-/ *verb trans*. Now *poet*. Also **im-** /ɪm-/. E17.
[ORIGIN Old French & mod. French *emplumer*, formed as EM-¹, PLUME *noun*.]
Adorn with or as with plumes.

†**emplunge** *verb* var. of IMPLUNGE.

†**emply** *verb* var. of IMPLY.

empocket *verb* var. of IMPOCKET.

empoison /ɪmˈpɔɪz(ə)n, ɛm-/ *verb*. *arch*. Also †**im-**. LME.
[ORIGIN Old French *empoisoner* (mod. *-nn-*), formed as EM-¹, POISON *noun*.]
▸ **I** †**1** *verb trans. & intrans*. Administer poison (to); *esp*. kill by poisoning. LME–L17.
2 *verb trans*. Put poison in (food or drink); affect (the body etc.) with poison; dip (a weapon) in poison, envenom. LME.

JOSEPH PARKER The serpent . . shows its empoisoned fang.

▸ **II** *fig*. **3** *verb trans*. Taint with sin or error; corrupt, spoil. LME.
4 *verb trans*. Make (a person's mind or feelings) bitter or virulent; destroy all pleasure in. L16.

J. HAWTHORNE His soul had been empoisoned against them and all the world.

■ **empoisoner** *noun* LME. **empoisonment** *noun* the action or act of empoisoning; the fact of being poisoned: M16.

empolder *verb* var. of IMPOLDER.

emporium /ɛmˈpɔːrɪəm, ɪm-/ *noun*. Pl. **-iums**, **-ia** /-ɪə/. L16.
[ORIGIN Latin from Greek *emporion*, from *emporos* merchant, formed as EM-² + verbal stem *por-*, *per-* to journey.]
1 A centre of commerce; a market. L16.

2 A shop, *esp.* one that sells unusual or fancy goods. Chiefly *joc.* M19.

M. MOORCOCK Kircheim's Café, a famous emporium of coffee and cream-cakes.

■ **emporial** *adjective* of or pertaining to an emporium; of the nature of an emporium: E17.

†**empory** *noun.* E17–L18.
[ORIGIN from EMPORIUM: see -Y³.]
= EMPORIUM 1.

†**empose** *verb* var. of IMPOSE *verb*.

†**empound** *verb* var. of IMPOUND.

†**empoverish** *verb*, **empoverishment** *noun* vars. of IMPOVERISH, IMPOVERISHMENT.

empower /ɪmˈpaʊə, ɛm-/ *verb trans.* Also †**im-**. M17.
[ORIGIN from EM-¹, IM-¹ + POWER *noun*.]
1 Invest formally with power; authorize, license (a person *to do*). M17.

City Limits It did not secure the necessary two-thirds that would have empowered the WI executive to campaign actively for it.

2 Endow with the ability or power required for a purpose or task; enable, permit. (Foll. by *to do*.) M17.

DEFOE Some have doubted whether the Devil is empowered to take up any human shape.

■ **empowerment** *noun* the action of empowering someone; the state of being empowered: M17.

empress /ˈɛmprɪs/ *noun.* ME.
[ORIGIN Old French *emperesse*, from *emperere* EMPEROR: see -ESS¹.]
1 The wife of an emperor; a woman with the power or rank of an emperor. ME.
2 A woman exercising absolute power. ME.

SHAKES. *Tit. A.* Tamora, the empress of my soul.

†**empress** *verb trans.* LME–E19.
[ORIGIN Old French & mod. French *empresser*: see EMPRESSÉ.]
Press (*lit.* & *fig.*); oppress.

empressé /ɑ̃prɛse/ *adjective.* Fem. **-ée**. M19.
[ORIGIN French, pa. ppl adjective of *empresser* urge, (refl.) be eager, (in Old French) press, crowd in, formed as EM-¹, PRESS *verb*¹: cf. IMPRESS *verb*¹.]
Eager, zealous; showing ***empressement***.

empressement /ɑ̃prɛsmɑ̃/ *noun.* E18.
[ORIGIN French, from *empresser*: see EMPRESSÉ, -MENT.]
Eagerness; effusive friendliness.

†**emprime** *verb & noun* var. of IMPRIME.

†**emprint** *noun, verb* see IMPRINT *noun, verb*.

emprise /ɪmˈprʌɪz, ɛm-/ *noun & verb.* ME.
[ORIGIN Old French & mod. French, use as noun of fem. pa. pple of Old French *emprendre* from Proto-Romance, from Latin EM-¹ + *prehendere, prendere* take. Cf. ENTERPRISE *noun*.]
▸ **A** *noun.* **1** An undertaking, *esp.* one of an adventurous or chivalrous nature. *arch.* ME.
2 Chivalry; martial prowess. *arch.* ME.
▸ †**B** *verb trans.* Undertake (a deed; *to do*). LME–M19.

†**emprison** *verb* see IMPRISON.

emprosthotonos /ɛmprɒsˈθɒtənəs/ *noun.* Now *rare.* LME.
[ORIGIN Greek, from *emprosthen* before + *tonos* a stretching.]
Tetanic spasm in which the head is drawn forwards on to the chest.

†**emprove** *verb*, †**emprovement** *noun* see IMPROVE *verb*², IMPROVEMENT.

Empsonian /ɛm(p)ˈsəʊnɪən/ *adjective & noun.* M20.
[ORIGIN from *Empson* (see below) + -IAN.]
▸ **A** *adjective.* Resembling or characteristic of the style of Sir William Empson (1906–84), English poet and critic. M20.

Times Lit. Suppl. Sonnets marked by a somewhat Empsonian obscurity.

▸ **B** *noun.* A devotee of Empson or his work. M20.

empt /ɛm(p)t/ *verb. obsolete* exc. *dial.*
[ORIGIN Old English *ǣmtian*, from *ǣmta, ǣmetta* leisure: see EMPTY *adjective & noun*.]
†**1** *verb intrans.* & *refl.* Be at leisure. Only in OE.
2 *verb trans.* Make empty, drain, exhaust. ME.
†**3** *verb trans.* Pour or clear out. Only in E17.

emptin *noun* see EMPTING.

emptiness /ˈɛm(p)tɪnɪs/ *noun.* LME.
[ORIGIN from EMPTY *adjective* + -NESS.]
1 The condition of being empty. LME. ▸**b** The condition of being empty *of* specified contents or a particular quality. L16.

L. DURRELL Behind lay the desert, its emptiness echoing like a seashell. D. ATHILL The area of emptiness in the emotional life of any childless woman.

2 (An) unoccupied space; a void, a vacuum. L16.

3 In *pl.* Trivialities. M19.

empting /ˈɛm(p)tɪŋ/ *noun.* In sense 2 also **-in** /-ɪn/. LME.
[ORIGIN from EMPT *verb* + -ING¹. In sense 2 partly alt. of EMPTYING.]
1 The action of making empty. *obsolete* exc. *dial.* LME.
2 In *pl.* Yeast; the yeasty lees of beer or cider. Cf. EMPTYING 2b. *US.* M17.

emption /ˈɛm(p)ʃ(ə)n/ *noun.* LME.
[ORIGIN Latin *emptio(n-)*, from *empt-* pa. ppl stem of *emere* buy: see -ION.]
†**1** A tax on the sale of plate and bullion in the King's Exchange. LME–L15.
2 In ROMAN LAW (now *hist.*), purchase in a contract of sale (correl. to VENDITION); *gen.* the action of buying. M16.

empty /ˈɛm(p)ti/ *adjective & noun.*
[ORIGIN Old English *ǣmtiġ, ǣmet(t)iġ*, from *ǣmta, ǣmetta* leisure, perh. from neg. *ā-* + *mōt* meeting (see MOOT *noun*¹).]
▸ **A** *adjective.* †**1** At leisure, unoccupied. Also, unmarried. Only in OE.
2 Of a receptacle: containing nothing. Opp. ***full***. OE. ▸**b** Foll. by *of*, †*in*: lacking, devoid of, (specified contents or a specified quality). L15.

A. NEWMAN Vicky put the empty suitcase on top of the wardrobe. **b** G. GREENE The air was empty of planes.

on an empty stomach: see STOMACH *noun*.

3 Of space, a place, a building, etc.: unoccupied, vacant; containing no furniture or occupants; uninhabited. OE. ▸**b** MATH. & LOGIC. Of a class or set: containing no members or elements. M20.

S. HAZZARD He lifted the folded mackintosh . . he had dumped on the empty seat alongside. S. NAIPAUL The office . . is empty and looks as if it has not been used for a long time.

4 Having no load or cargo; unladen. ME. ▸**b** Of the hand: not bringing or taking away anything. Of a person: empty-handed. E16.

b AV *Luke* 1:53 He hath filled the hungry with good things; and the rich he hath sent empty away.

return empty *arch.* (of a sword) come back without having been used in killing someone.

5 a Of a thing: lacking substance; meaningless, ineffectual; insincere. ME. ▸**b** Of a person: lacking knowledge and sense; frivolous, foolish. E17.

a ISAIAH BERLIN Progress and reaction, however much these words have been abused, are not empty concepts.

6 †**a** Of the body: shrunken, emaciated, weak. LME–E18. ▸†**b** Without money, destitute. L16–E18. ▸**c** Hungry. Now *colloq.* L16. ▸**d** Of a cow or other farm animal: not pregnant. E20.

– SPECIAL COLLOCATIONS & COMB.: **empty calories**: from food containing no nutrients. **empty-handed** *adjective* having or bearing nothing (***come empty-handed***, bring nothing, esp. no gift: ***go empty-handed***, leave having gained nothing). **empty-headed** *adjective* lacking common sense or intelligence, frivolous. **empty nest** *fig.* a household where the parents alone remain after the children have grown up and left home. **empty nester** *colloq.* a person whose children have grown up and left home. **Empty Quarter** the Rub' al-Kali, a desert region in the south of the Arabian peninsula. **empty suit** *US colloq.* a powerful or wealthy man regarded as lacking substance, ability, personality, etc. **empty word** GRAMMAR: having no meaning in itself but having a grammatical function.

▸ **B** *noun.* An empty vehicle, container, etc.; *esp.* one from which the contents have been removed. M19.

Time Out One can actually imagine him taking back the tavern empties.

empty /ˈɛm(p)ti/ *verb.* E16.
[ORIGIN from EMPTY *adjective*: cf. Old English *geǣmtiġian*.]
1 *verb trans.* Make empty; remove or clear out the contents of; deprive *of* specified contents or a specified quality. E16. ▸**b** Transfer the contents of (one receptacle) *into* another. L16. ▸**c** Remove (contents) from what contains them; transfer (contents) from one receptacle *into* another. Also foll. by *out* (*into*). L16.

D. HAMMETT Spade . . emptied his lungs with a long sighing exhalation. E. BOWEN The greengrocer's crates had been emptied of all but earth. **b** I. MCEWAN A second bar-hand came by to empty the ashtray into a bucket. **c** H. ROTH She . . emptied out the peelings that cluttered the sink into the garbage can.

2 *verb refl.* & (chiefly *N. Amer.*) *intrans.* Of a river etc.: discharge itself *into* another river, the sea, etc.; flow *into*. M16.

T. O'BRIEN Eisenhower Avenue emptied into a huge traffic circle.

3 *verb refl.* Chiefly THEOLOGY. of Christ: drain oneself of resources or *of* a particular attribute; efface oneself utterly. L16.
4 *verb intrans.* Become empty. M17.

J. BUCHAN The carriage had emptied, and I was left alone.

emptying /ˈɛm(p)tɪɪŋ/ *noun.* L16.
[ORIGIN from EMPTY *verb* + -ING¹.]
1 The action of making empty. L16.
2 What is emptied out of something. M17. ▸**b** In *pl.* = EMPTING 2. *US.* M19.

empurple /ɪmˈpəːp(ə)l, ɛm-/ *verb.* Also †**im-**. L16.
[ORIGIN from EM-¹, IM-¹ + PURPLE *adjective & noun*.]
1 *verb trans.* Make purple; *rare* clothe in purple. L16.
2 *verb intrans.* Become purple. L18.

Empusa /ɛmˈpjuːzə/ *noun.* Pl. **-sae** /-ziː/. Also †**Empuse**, **e-**. E17.
[ORIGIN Greek *Empousa*.]
1 CLASSICAL MYTHOLOGY. A hobgoblin supposed to be sent by Hecate. E17.
†**2** A spectre, a bogey. Only in 17.

empyema /ɛmpʌɪˈiːmə/ *noun.* LME.
[ORIGIN Late Latin from Greek *empuēma*, from *empuein* suppurate, formed as EM-² + *puon* pus.]
MEDICINE. A condition characterized by an accumulation of pus in a body cavity, esp. the pleural cavity.

empyreal /ɛmpʌɪˈriːəl, -pɪ-, ɛmˈpɪrɪəl/ *adjective. arch. & poet.* LME.
[ORIGIN medieval Latin *empyreus* (late Latin *empyrius*), from Greek *empurios*, formed as EM-² + *pur* fire: see -AL¹.]
1 = EMPYREAN *adjective*; *fig.* sublime, exalted. LME. ▸**b** Of or pertaining to the sky or heavens; celestial. M18.
2 Fiery; composed of or resembling the pure element fire. E17.
†**3** CHEMISTRY. Of a gas: able to support combustion. L18–E19.

empyrean /ɛmpʌɪˈriːən, -pɪ-, ɛmˈpɪrɪən/ *adjective & noun. arch. & poet.* LME.
[ORIGIN formed as EMPYREAL: see -EAN.]
▸ **A** *adjective.* Of or pertaining to the empyrean. LME.
▸ **B** *noun.* **1** The highest heaven, thought by the ancients to be the realm of pure fire and by early Christians to be the abode of God and the angels; *fig.* an exalted region, realm, or group. M17.

P. ZIEGLER Both men were members of that conjurors' empyrean, the Magic Circle.

2 The heavens, the sky; cosmic space. E19.

†**empyreum** *noun.* E17–L18.
[ORIGIN medieval Latin, use as noun (sc. *caelum*) of neut. of *empyreus*: see EMPYREAL.]
The empyrean.

empyreuma /ɛmpɪˈruːmə/ *noun.* M17.
[ORIGIN Greek *empureuma* live coal covered with ashes, from *empureuein* set on fire, formed as EM-² + *pur* fire.]
An empyreumatic smell or taste.

empyreumatic /ɛmˌpɪrʊˈmatɪk/ *adjective.* M17.
[ORIGIN Greek *empureumat-* stem of *empureuma*: see EMPYREUMA, -IC.]
Having or designating a foul smell or taste produced when organic matter is heated but prevented from burning.
■ **empyreumatical** *adjective* (*arch.*) M17.

EMS *abbreviation.*
European Monetary System.

EMU *abbreviation.*
Economic and (or European) Monetary Union.

emu /ˈiːmjuː/ *noun.* Also †**emeu**, (orig.) †**eme**. E17.
[ORIGIN Portuguese *ema*.]
†**1** A cassowary. E17–E18.
†**2** The greater rhea, *Rhea americana*. Only in L18.
3 A large shaggy flightless fast-running Australian bird, *Dromaius novaehollandiae*, related to the cassowary and ostrich. L18.

– COMB.: **emu-apple** (the succulent fruit of) an Australian tree, *Owenia acidula*, of the mahogany family; also called ***sour plum***, ***native peach***; **emu-bob** *verb intrans. & trans.* (*Austral.*) pick up small pieces of timber from (an area) after clearing or burning; **emu bush** any of several Australian shrubs, esp. of the genus *Eremophila* (family Myoporaceae), the fruits of which are eaten by the emu; **emu-wren** any of three very small Australian songbirds of the genus *Stipiturus* (family Maluridae), which have very long tail feathers with the sparse open structure seen in emu feathers.

e.m.u. *abbreviation.*
1 Electric multiple unit (railway vehicle).
2 Electromagnetic unit(s).

†**emulate** *adjective. rare* (Shakes.). Only in E17.
[ORIGIN Latin *aemulatus* pa. pple of *aemulari*: see EMULATE *verb*, -ATE².]
Ambitious.

emulate /ˈɛmjʊleɪt/ *verb.* L16.
[ORIGIN Latin *aemulat-* pa. ppl stem of *aemulari*, from *aemulus* rival: see -ATE³.]
1 *verb trans.* Compete with; rival or equal in some respect. L16.

SHAKES. *Merry W.* I see how thine eye would emulate the diamond. SIR W. SCOTT My royal nephew will soon emulate his father's wisdom.

†**2** *verb intrans.* Strive in a spirit of rivalry *to be* or *to do*. L16–M17.
3 *verb trans.* Imitate zealously; try to equal or excel. L16.

K. A. PORTER They were . . ideal characters and the first the children had ever admired and longed to emulate.

†**4** *verb trans.* Wish to rival (a person); be envious or jealous of. E–M17.

E

5 *verb trans.* (Of a computer etc. or its user) reproduce the action of (a different computer or software system) with the aid of hardware or software designed to effect this; run (a program etc.) on a computer other than that for which it was written. **M20.**

emulation /ɛmjʊˈleɪʃ(ə)n/ *noun.* **M16.**
[**ORIGIN** Latin *aemulatio(n-)*, formed as **EMULATE** *verb*: see **-ATION**.]
1 The desire or endeavour to equal or surpass others in some achievement or quality. **M16.**

Rolling Stone White, fond of writing suites in emulation of classical composers, continues to ignore his real strength.

†**2** Ambitious rivalry; contention or ill will between rivals. **M16–E18.**
†**3** Envy; resentment or disparagement of one's superiors. **M16–L18.**
4 The technique by which a computer or software system is enabled to execute programs written for a different type of computer, by means of special hardware or software. **M20.**

emulative /ˈɛmjʊlətɪv/ *adjective.* **L16.**
[**ORIGIN** from **EMULATE** *verb* + **-IVE**.]
1 Resulting from or characterized by emulation. **L16.**

J. HOOLE Emulative zeal.

2 Tending or disposed to emulate; imitative *of*. **M18.**

S. RICHARDSON Noble minds, emulative of perfection.

■ **emulatively** *adverb (rare)* **M18.** **emulativeness** *noun (rare)* **L19.**

emulator /ˈɛmjʊleɪtə/ *noun.* **L16.**
[**ORIGIN** Latin *aemulator*, formed as **EMULATE** *verb*: see **-OR**.]
1 A person who emulates. **L16.**
2 A piece of computer hardware or software used with one device to enable it to emulate another. **M20.**
■ †**emulatress** *noun (rare)* a female emulator **E17–M18.**

emulge /ɪˈmʌldʒ/ *verb trans.* Now *rare* or *obsolete*. **L17.**
[**ORIGIN** Latin *emulgere* milk out: see **EMULSION**.]
Drain (a bodily duct or secretory organ).

emulgent /ɪˈmʌldʒ(ə)nt/ *adjective & noun.* Now *rare*. **L16.**
[**ORIGIN** Latin *emulgent-* pres. ppl stem of *emulgere*: see **EMULSION**, **-ENT**.]
▸ **A** *adjective.* That strains or purifies; *spec.* designating a renal artery or vein. **L16.**
▸ **B** *noun.* A renal artery or vein. **E17.**
■ **emulgence** *noun (rare)* the action or an act of draining something of goodness or substance **L17.**

emulous /ˈɛmjʊləs/ *adjective.* **LME.**
[**ORIGIN** Latin *aemulus*: see **-ULOUS**.]
†**1 a** Of a thing: closely resembling, imitative *of*. Only in **LME.** ▸**b** Seeking to imitate or rival someone or something. (Foll. by *of*.) **M17.**

b D. M. DAVIN She was . . always emulous of the title and status of Professor.

2 Characterized or actuated by a spirit of rivalry. Formerly also, zealous; rival. **M16.**

LONGFELLOW Where every emulous scholar hears . . The rustling of another's laurels!

†**3** Covetous of praise or power; envious. **E–M17.**
■ **emulously** *adverb* **M17.**

emulsify /ɪˈmʌlsɪfʌɪ/ *verb trans.* **M19.**
[**ORIGIN** from Latin *emuls-* + (see **EMULSION**) + **-I-** + **-FY**.]
Convert into an emulsion.
■ **emulsifiaˈbility** *noun* the property of being emulsifiable **M20.** **emulsifiable** *adjective* **M20.** **emulsifiˈcation** *noun* **L19.** **emulsifier** *noun* an apparatus which emulsifies oils etc.; a substance which promotes the emulsification of two liquids: **L19.**

emulsion /ɪˈmʌlʃ(ə)n/ *noun & verb.* **E17.**
[**ORIGIN** French *émulsion* or mod. Latin *emulsio(n-)*, from Latin *emuls-* pa. ppl stem of *emulgere* milk out, from *e-* **E-** + *mulgere* to milk (cf. **MILK** *noun*): see **-ION**.]
▸ **A** *noun.* **1** Orig., a milky liquid obtained by crushing almonds in water. Later, any mixture of two immiscible liquids (e.g. oil and water) in which one is dispersed throughout the other in small droplets (though not as small as in a colloid). **E17.** ▸**b** In full ***emulsion paint***. A type of paint used for walls, consisting of an emulsion of resin in water. **M20.**
2 A light-sensitive coating on photographic films and plates, consisting of crystals of a silver halide dispersed in a medium such as gelatin. **E17.**
nuclear emulsion: see **NUCLEAR** *adjective*.
▸ **B** *verb trans.* **1** = **EMULSIFY**. Now *rare* or *obsolete*. **M18.**
2 Paint with emulsion paint. **M20.**

emulsive /ɪˈmʌlsɪv/ *adjective.* **M19.**
[**ORIGIN** from Latin *emuls-* (see **EMULSION**) + **-IVE**.]
Of the nature of an emulsion.

emulsoid /ɪˈmʌlsɔɪd/ *noun.* **E20.**
[**ORIGIN** from **EMULSION** + **-OID**.]
A colloidal system consisting of one liquid dispersed in another; a lyophilic sol.

emunctory /ɪˈmʌŋkt(ə)ri/ *noun & adjective.* **LME.**
[**ORIGIN** medieval Latin *emunctorius* adjective, *-ium* noun, from Latin *emunct-* pa. ppl stem of *emungere* wipe or blow the nose: see **-ORY**[2], **-ORY**[1].]
▸ **A** *noun.* A part of the body that serves to cleanse it or get rid of waste products. **LME.**
▸ **B** *adjective.* **1** Designating an emunctory. **M16.**
2 Pertaining to the blowing of the nose. **M19.**

†**emunge** *verb trans.* **M17–M19.**
[**ORIGIN** Latin *emungere*: see **EMUNCTORY**.]
Wipe, clean out; *fig.* cheat.

en /ɛn/ *noun.* **L18.**
[**ORIGIN** Repr. pronunc. of *N*, *n* as the letter's name: cf. **EM**.]
1 The letter N, n. **L18.**
2 *TYPOGRAPHY.* A unit of horizontal measurement in typesetting, equal to half the body of any size of metal type or half the nominal type-size in photosetting, used for calculating the extent of a line or text; half an em. **L18.**
– **COMB.**: **en dash** an en rule; **en quad**, **en quadrat** a spacing unit half as wide as an em quadrat; **en rule** a rule an en long, a short dash (as in *1914–18*).

en- /ɪn, ɛn/ *prefix*[1].
[**ORIGIN** Repr. Old French & mod. French *en-* from Latin **IN-**[2]. See also **EM-**[1].]
Used in words adopted from French and in English words modelled on these as a freely productive prefix, forming verbs (***a***) from nouns, with the sense 'put into or on', as ***enamour***, ***encurtain***, ***engulf***, ***enshroud***, ***entrust***; (***b***) from nouns or adjectives, with the sense 'bring into the condition or state denoted', as ***enrapture***, ***enslave***, sometimes combined with suffix **-EN**[5], as ***enlighten***, ***enliven***; (***c***) from verbs, with the sense 'in, into, on', as ***enfold***, or intensive, as ***entangle***. Often with parallel forms in **IN-**[2].
■ **enˈcentre** *verb trans.* place in the centre **E17.** †**endart** *verb trans.* (*rare*, Shakes.) direct swiftly, dart, (one's eye): only in **L16.** †**enfierce** *verb trans.* (*rare*, Spenser) make fierce: only in **L16.** †**enfree** *verb trans.* set free **L16–E17.** **enˈfreedom** *verb trans.* give freedom to **L16.** **enˈguard** *verb trans.* guard (carefully) **E17.** **enˈqueue** *verb trans.* *COMPUTING* add (an item of data awaiting processing) to a queue of such items **L20.** **enˈsaffron** *verb trans.* tinge with saffron-yellow colour **M17.** **enˈsulphur** *verb trans.* make sulphurous **E17.** **enˈverdure** *verb trans.* make verdurous, cover with verdure **L15.** †**enwallow** *verb intrans.* (*rare*, Spenser) wallow: only in **L16.** **enˈwood** *verb trans.* cover with trees **E17.**

en- /ɪn, ɛn/ *prefix*[2] (not productive).
Repr. Greek *en-* in, inside, as in *energy*, *enthusiasm*. See also **EM-**[2].

-en /ɪn, (ə)n/ *suffix*[1] (not productive).
[**ORIGIN** Old English from Germanic neut. of base of **-EN**[4].]
Forming dims. of nouns, as ***chicken***, ***maiden***.

-en /(ə)n/ *suffix*[2] (not productive).
[**ORIGIN** Old English from Germanic.]
Forming fem. nouns, as ***vixen***, and abstract nouns, as ***burden***.

-en /(ə)n/ *suffix*[3] (not productive).
[**ORIGIN** Old English *-an*, orig. part of the stem of weak nouns.]
The termination of the pl. of weak nouns, surviving in ***oxen***; later forming pl. nouns, as ***kine***, esp. added to other pls., as in ***brethren***, ***children***.

-en /(ə)n/ *suffix*[4] (not productive). After *r* in unstressed syllables **-n**.
[**ORIGIN** Old English from Germanic, = Greek *-inos*, Latin *-inus* **-INE**[1], **-INE**[2].]
Forming adjectives from nouns, with senses 'pertaining to, of the nature of, (*esp.*) made of', as ***earthen***, ***wheaten***, ***wooden***, ***woollen***. In other words now chiefly *arch.*, as ***silvern***, or metaphorical, as ***golden***, having been superseded in general by attrib. use of the noun.

-en /(ə)n/ *suffix*[5] (rarely productive).
[**ORIGIN** Old English *-nian* from Germanic. Most words are later and on the analogy of Old English verbs.]
1 Forming verbs with the sense 'make or become', from adjectives, as ***deepen***, ***fasten***, ***moisten***, or from nouns, as ***listen***, (later, on the analogy of verbs from adjectives) ***happen***, ***hearten***, ***strengthen***.
2 Occas. repr. Germanic formative of pres. stem in some strong verbs, as in ***waken***.

-en /(ə)n/ *suffix*[6] (not productive). After *r* & (*arch.*) *-l* **-n**.
[**ORIGIN** Old English *-en* = Old Saxon, Old High German *-an*, Old Norse *-inn*, *-enn*, Gothic *-ans*, from Germanic.]
Forming the pa. pple of strong verbs, also ppl adjectives from such pples (senses as for those in **-ED**[1]), as ***mistaken***, ***torn***, ***outspoken***, freq. now in restricted use, as ***bounden***, ***cloven***, ***drunken***, ***gotten***, ***proven***. Cf. **-ED**[1].

enable /ɪnˈeɪb(ə)l, ɛn-/ *verb.* Also †**in-**. **LME.**
[**ORIGIN** from **EN-**[1], **IN-**[2] + **ABLE** *adjective*: cf. **ABLE** *verb*.]
1 *verb trans.* **a** Give power to; strengthen; make adequate or competent. (Foll. by *for*, *to*.) Now *rare*. **LME.** ▸**b** Make able, give the means, *to be* or *to do* something. **M16.**

a *Church Times* The clergy are like joints in the Body of Christ, enabling the Church in its life and mission. **b** J. BUCHAN Oxford . . enabled me to discover what talents I had.

†**2** *verb intrans.* Become able, gain strength or power. **LME–M17.**
†**3** *verb trans.* Invest with legal status. **L15–E18.**
4 *verb trans.* Give legal power to; authorize, sanction. **L15.**

LD MACAULAY An act was . . passed enabling beneficed clergymen . . to hold preferment in England.

enabling act (***a***) a statute empowering a person or body to take certain action; (***b***) (chiefly *US*) a statute legalizing something otherwise unlawful.
†**5** *verb trans.* Regard as competent. **M–L16.**
6 *verb trans.* Make (an action) possible or effective; make (a device) operational, turn on. **E17.**

P. CASEMENT Psychoanalysis has the potential for enabling a re-birth of the . . personality.

■ **enablement** *noun* the action or a means of enabling **L15.** **enabler** *noun* a person who enables someone; *esp.* a person who helps others to achieve their potential or develop skills: **E17.**

enact /ɪˈnakt, ɛ-/ *verb trans.* Pa. pple **-ed**, (*rare*) **enact**. **LME.**
[**ORIGIN** from **EN-**[1] + **ACT** *noun*, *verb*, after medieval Latin *inactare*, *inactitare*.]
†**1** Enter in a public record; chronicle. **LME–M17.**
2 Make (a bill etc.) into an act; establish (a law, legal penalty, etc.); decree (a thing, *that*). **LME.** ▸†**b** Declare officially; appoint. **E17–E18.**

ADAM SMITH In 1463 it was enacted that no wheat should be imported. A. STORR There is little point in enacting savage penalties even for savage crime.

3 Represent (a scene, play, etc.) on or as on a stage; play (a part); take part in (a drama or scene in real life). **LME.**

H. JAMES The scene enacted in the great awe-stricken house. P. ROSE Marriages . . in which the two partners agree on the scenario they are enacting.

†**4** Accomplish (a deed). **L16–E17.**
†**5** Actuate, influence; inspire; implant (a feeling etc.) *into* a person. **E17–M19.**
■ **enactable** *adjective* **L19.** **enaction** *noun* (an) enactment **M17.** **enactive** *adjective* pertaining to or concerned with the enactment of law **M17.** **enactor** *noun* a person who enacts something **E17.** **enactory** *adjective* = **ENACTIVE** **M19.** †**enacture** *noun* (*rare*, Shakes.) a performance, fulfilment: only in **E17.**

enactment /ɪˈnaktm(ə)nt, ɛ-/ *noun.* **E19.**
[**ORIGIN** from **ENACT** + **-MENT**, superseding **ENACTION**.]
1 The action of enacting a law; the state or fact of being enacted. **E19.**
2 A thing which is enacted; an ordinance, a statute. **E19.** ▸**b** In *pl.* The provisions of a law. **M19.**

enaliosaur /ɪˈnalɪəsɔː/ *noun.* Now *rare* or *obsolete*. **M19.**
[**ORIGIN** from Greek *enalios* of the sea, formed as **EN-**[2] + *hali-* combining form of *halo-*, *hals* sea: see **-SAUR**.]
Any of various extinct marine reptiles of Mesozoic times, such as a plesiosaur or an ichthyosaur.
■ **enalioˈsaurian** *adjective & noun* **M19.**

enallage /ɪˈnalədʒi, ɛ-/ *noun.* Now *rare*. **E16.**
[**ORIGIN** Late Latin from Greek *enallagē*, from base of *enallassein* to exchange, formed as **EN-**[2] + *allassein* to change, from *allos* other.]
The substitution of one grammatical form for another, as of singular for plural, present for past tense, etc.

†**enaluron** *noun.* **M16–M18.**
[**ORIGIN** Uncertain: perh. from Anglo-Norman.]
HERALDRY. A bordure charged with birds, usu. eight in number.

enam /ɪˈnɑːm/ *noun.* **E19.**
[**ORIGIN** Urdu (Persian) from Arabic *ʼinʻām* favour, grant, verbal noun of *ʼanʻama* bestow a favour.]
In the Indian subcontinent: a grant of land free of the land tax due to the state; land so held.
■ ***enamdar*** /ɪˈnɑːmdɑː/ *noun* [Persian *-dār* holding, holder] a person who holds an *enam* **M19.**

enamel /ɪˈnam(ə)l/ *noun.* Also †**in-**. **LME.**
[**ORIGIN** from the verb: cf. **AMEL** *noun*.]
1 A glassy opaque or semi-transparent coating applied by fusion to metallic or other hard surfaces, either as ornamentation or as a protective coating. **LME.**

A. URE The enamel of these saucepans is quite free from lead. *fig.*: JER. TAYLOR Those Truths . . are the enamel and beauty of our Churches.

2 Smooth bright surface-colouring; verdure. Chiefly *poet.* **E17.**

W. GOLDING Not a crack in the sky, not a blemish on the dense blue enamel.

3 The very hard calcareous substance that occurs as a glossy coating on the crowns of teeth; any of several similar substances forming the outer layer of fish scales. **E18.**
4 A painting or other artistic work done in enamel. **M18.**
5 In full ***enamel paint***. A kind of paint which flows freely and gives a very smooth glossy finish. **M19.**
6 A cosmetic giving a smooth glossy appearance. **M20.**
– **COMB.**: ***enamel paint***: see sense 5 above; **enamel painting** the production of a picture by coating a hard surface with different colours of enamel; **enamelware** enamelled kitchenware; **enamelwork** a product made with the use of enamel.

enamel /ɪˈnam(ə)l/ *verb trans.* Also †**in-**. Infl. **-ll-**, ***-l-**. **LME.**
[**ORIGIN** Anglo-Norman *enameler*, *enamailler*, formed as **EN-**[1], **IN-**[2] + *amail*: see **AMEL**.]
1 Inlay, encrust, or coat (esp. metal) with enamel or a substance resembling enamel; apply a smooth hard coating to. **LME.** ▸**b** Apply make-up to (the face) to give an appearance of smoothness; apply nail polish to (a fingernail). **E19.**
2 Portray (figures etc.) with enamel. **L15.**

†**3** *fig.* Adorn magnificently; embellish superficially. L16–L17.
4 Variegate like enamelled work; adorn with rich and varied colours. *arch.* M17.

T. PRINGLE Millions of flowers of the most brilliant hues enamel the earth.

■ **enameller** *noun* a person who enamels something E17. **enamellist** *noun* an artist who works in enamel L19. **enamelling** *noun* (*a*) the action or technique of the verb; (*b*) enamel coating: LME.

enamelled /ɪˈnam(ə)ld/ *adjective.* Also †**in-**, ***-eled**. E16.
[ORIGIN from ENAMEL *verb* + -ED[1].]
†**1 a** Of literary style, a speaker, etc.: ornate, florid. E16–M17. ▸**b** Adorned with varied colours. E17.
2 Having naturally a hard polished surface, like enamel. L16.
3 Ornamented or coated with enamel; given a glossy coating. E17.

Punch An engraved invitation on enamelled paper. *Discovery* Enamelled kitchen stoves. G. VIDAL The walls . . are covered with enamelled tiles depicting lions.

enamor *verb* see ENAMOUR.

†**enamorado** *noun.* Pl. **-do(e)s**. E17–M18.
[ORIGIN Spanish use as noun of pa. pple of *enamorar* win the love of (cf. ENAMOUR).]
A lover.

†**enamorata** *noun* var. of INAMORATA.

†**enamorate** *verb* see INAMORATE *verb*.

†**enamorato** *noun* var. of INAMORATO.

enamour /ɪˈnamə, ɛ-/ *verb trans.* Also †**in-**, ***enamor**. ME.
[ORIGIN Old French & mod. French *enamourer* (cf. Italian *innamorare*, Spanish *enamorar*), formed as EN-[1], IN-[2] + AMOUR.]
1 Inspire or inflame with love. Usu. in *pass.* Foll. by *of*, *with*, †*on*. ME.

WELLINGTON He was much enamored of one of the Koorg Rajah's sisters.

2 Charm, delight, please. Usu. in *pass.* Foll. by *of*, †*on*, †*with*. L16.

N. SHUTE I take it that you aren't enamoured of the navy.

■ **enamouredness** *noun* (*rare*) = ENAMOURMENT L17. **enamourment** *noun* the state of being enamoured E18.

enanthema /ɛnənˈθiːmə/ *noun.* Also anglicized as **enanthem** /ɪˈnanθɪm/. M19.
[ORIGIN from EN-[2] + EX)ANTHEMA.]
MEDICINE. An eruption occurring on a mucus-secreting surface (e.g. the inside of the mouth).

enanthic *adjective* var. of OENANTHIC.

enantio- /ɪˈnantɪəʊ, ɛ-/ *combining form* of Greek *enantios* opposite: see -O-.
■ **enantioˈpathic** *adjective* (now *rare*) allopathic M19. **enantiˈopathy** *noun* (now *rare*) allopathy M19.

enantiodromia /ɪˌnantɪə(ʊ)ˈdrəʊmɪə, ɛ-/ *noun.* E20.
[ORIGIN Greek = running in contrary ways, formed as ENANTIO- + *dromos* running: see -IA[1].]
The process by which something becomes its opposite, and the effects of this; *esp.* the adoption of a set of beliefs which are opposed to those previously held.
■ **eˌnantiodroˈmiacal**, **enantiodromic** *adjectives* M20.

enantiomer /ɪˈnantɪə(ʊ)mə, ɛ-/ *noun.* M20.
[ORIGIN from ENANTIO- + -MER.]
CHEMISTRY. An enantiomorphous molecule or substance; an optical isomer.
■ **enantioˈmeric** *adjective* M20. **enantiˈomerism** *noun* the fact or condition of being enantiomeric M20.

enantiomorph /ɪˈnantɪə(ʊ)mɔːf, ɛ-/ *noun.* L19.
[ORIGIN from ENANTIO- + -MORPH.]
A form (*esp.* a crystal or molecule) related to another as an object is to its image in a mirror; a non-superposable mirror image.
■ **enantioˈmorphic** *adjective* = ENANTIOMORPHOUS E20. **enantioˈmorphically** *adverb* E20. **enantioˈmorphism** *noun* the fact or condition of being enantiomorphic; the occurrence of two enantiomorphic crystalline forms of a substance: L19. **enantioˈmorphous** *adjective* of or pertaining to an enantiomorph; of the nature of an enantiomorph or enantiomorphs: L19. **enantioˈmorphously** *adverb* L19.

enantiotropy /ɪˌnantɪˈɒtrəpi, ɛ-/ *noun.* E20.
[ORIGIN from ENANTIO- + -TROPY.]
CHEMISTRY. The existence of two forms of a substance, one stable above a certain transition temperature at which they are interconverted, the other stable below it.
■ **enantiotropic** /-ˈtrəʊpɪk, -ˈtrɒpɪk, ɛ-/ *adjective* E20.

enarch /ɛnˈɑːtʃ/ *verb*[1] *trans.* Now *rare*. Also **inarch** /ɪn-/. LME.
[ORIGIN formed as EN-[1], IN-[2] + ARCH *noun*[1]; perh. orig. from Old French *enarchier*.]
1 Build or draw in the form of an arch. LME.
2 Arch in, set or draw an arch over. M16.

†**enarch** *verb*[2] var. of INARCH *verb*[1].

enargite /ˈɛnɑːɡʌɪt/ *noun.* M19.
[ORIGIN from Greek *enargēs* clear (with ref. to its cleavage being evident) + -ITE[1].]
A sulphide of copper and arsenic that is an important copper ore and occurs as dark grey orthorhombic, usu. prismatic, crystals.

enarm /ɪnˈɑːm, ɛn-/ *verb*[1] *trans.* Now *rare* or *obsolete*. LME.
[ORIGIN Old French *enarmer* arm, equip, formed as EN-[1] + *armer* ARM *verb*[1].]
1 Equip with weapons. *obsolete* exc. *Scot.* LME.
2 *gen.* Equip, provide *with*, adorn *with*. LME.

enarm *verb*[2] var. of INARM.

†**enarration** *noun.* L16.
[ORIGIN Latin *enarratio(n-)*, from *e-* E- + *narratio(n-)*: see NARRATION.]
1 An exposition, a commentary. L16–M17.
2 A description, a detailed narrative. L16–E19.

enarthrodial /ɛnɑːˈθrəʊdɪəl/ *adjective.* Now *rare*. M19.
[ORIGIN from EN-[1] + ARTHRODIA + -AL[1].]
ANATOMY. Pertaining to or being an enarthrosis.

enarthrosis /ɛnɑːˈθrəʊsɪs/ *noun.* Pl. **-throses** /-ˈθrəʊsiːz/. L16.
[ORIGIN Greek *enarthrōsis*, from *enarthros* jointed: see -OSIS. Cf. EN-[2], ARTHROSIS.]
ANATOMY. A ball-and-socket joint; *esp.* one where the socket covers more than half of the ball.

enascent /ɪˈnas(ə)nt/ *adjective.* *rare*. M18.
[ORIGIN Latin *enascent-* pres. ppl stem of *enasci*: see ENATION, -ENT.]
That is just coming into being.

enation /ɪˈneɪʃ(ə)n/ *noun.* M19.
[ORIGIN Latin *enatio(n-)*, from *enasci* issue forth, be born, from *e-* E- + *nasci* be born: see -ATION.]
BIOLOGY. An outgrowth from the surface of an organ (e.g. from a leaf).

en attendant /ɑ̃n atɑ̃dɑ̃/ *adverbial phr.* M18.
[ORIGIN French.]
In the meantime, while waiting.

†**enaunter** *conjunction.* Also **in-**. LME–E17.
[ORIGIN Var. of *an*, *in*, *on aunter*, French *en aventure*: see ADVENTURE *noun*.]
In case, lest by chance.

en avant /ɑ̃n avɑ̃/ *adverbial phr. & interjection.* E19.
[ORIGIN French.]
Forward, onwards.

BYRON But never mind—*en avant!* live while you can.

en beau /ɑ̃ bo/ *adverbial phr.* E19.
[ORIGIN French.]
In a favourable manner; in the best light.

en bloc /ɑ̃ blɔk, ɒ̃ ˈblɒk/ *adverbial & adjectival phr.* M19.
[ORIGIN French.]
▸ **A** *adverbial phr.* As a whole; collectively, all together. M19.

B. BEAUMONT We would go en bloc to a film.

▸ **B** *adjectival phr.* Performed or made *en bloc*. E20.

en brosse /ɑ̃ brɔs/ *adverbial phr.* E20.
[ORIGIN French.]
Of hair: cut short and bristly.

en cabochon /ɑ̃ kabɔʃɔ̃/ *adverbial phr.* E19.
[ORIGIN French.]
With ref. to gem-cutting: as a cabochon; with curved surfaces rather than facets.

Encaenia /ɛnˈsiːnɪə/ *noun.* LME.
[ORIGIN Latin from Greek *egkainia* dedication festival, formed as EN-[2] + *kainos* new, recent.]
†**1** A renewal; a dedicatory festival. Only in LME.
2 The anniversary festival of the dedication of a place of worship, esp. (in Judaism) of the Temple at Jerusalem. Now *rare* or *obsolete*. LME.
3 The annual Commemoration of founders and benefactors at Oxford University. L17.

encage /ɪnˈkeɪdʒ, ɛn-/ *verb trans.* Also †**in-**. L16.
[ORIGIN from EN-[1], IN-[2] + CAGE *verb*.]
Confine (as) in a cage.

encamp /ɪnˈkamp, ɛn-/ *verb.* Also †**in-**. M16.
[ORIGIN from EN-[1], IN-[2] + CAMP *noun*[2].]
1 *verb trans. & intrans.* Lodge (soldiers) in a camp; establish a settled or fortified camp. M16.
2 *verb intrans.* Make camp; lodge in the open or in a temporary shelter. E18.

encampment /ɪnˈkampm(ə)nt, ɛn-/ *noun.* Also †**in-**. L16.
[ORIGIN from ENCAMP + -MENT.]
1 A place where troops are encamped; the temporary quarters of nomads, travellers, etc. L16.
2 The action or an act of encamping; the state of being encamped. L17.
3 A Masonic meeting. L18.

encapsidate /ɪnˈkapsɪdeɪt, ɛn-/ *verb trans.* L20.
[ORIGIN from EN-[1] + CAPSID *noun*[2] + -ATE[3].]
MICROBIOLOGY. Enclose in a capsid.
■ **encapsiˈdation** *noun* L20.

encapsulate /ɪnˈkapsjʊleɪt, ɛn-/ *verb trans.* Also **in-** /ɪn-/. L19.
[ORIGIN from EN-[1], IN-[2] + CAPSULE *noun* + -ATE[3].]
1 Enclose in or as in a capsule. L19.
2 *fig.* Exemplify the essential features of; epitomize, typify. M20.

V. GLENDINNING A story that encapsulates the confusion of social change.

■ **encapsuˈlation** *noun* M19.

encapsule /ɪnˈkapsjuːl, ɛn-/ *verb trans.* L19.
[ORIGIN from EN-[1] + CAPSULE *noun*.]
= ENCAPSULATE.

encaptivate /ɪnˈkaptɪveɪt, ɛn-/ *verb trans.* *rare*. Also †**in-**. E17.
[ORIGIN from EN-[1], IN-[2] + CAPTIVATE *verb*.]
Make captive, ensnare, (*lit.* & *fig.*); captivate.

encarnadine *verb* var. of INCARNADINE *verb*.

encarnalize /ɪnˈkɑːn(ə)lʌɪz, ɛn-/ *verb trans.* Also **in-** /ɪn-/, **-ise**. M19.
[ORIGIN from EN-[1], IN-[2] + CARNALIZE.]
Embody (a spirit, *fig.* an idea); make carnal or sensual.

encase /ɪnˈkeɪs, ɛn-/ *verb trans.* Also †**in-**. M17.
[ORIGIN from EN-[1], IN-[2] + CASE *noun*[2].]
1 Cover or surround like a case; in *pass.*, clad *in*. M17.

P. CAMPBELL The feet were encased in red woollen socks. G. VIDAL Clouds and smog encased Manhattan Island like a celluloid bell.

encased knot a knot of dead wood surrounded by, but not connected to, the living wood.
2 Put into or enclose within a case or receptacle. E18.

E. K. KANE The body was encased in a decent pine coffin.

encasement /ɪnˈkeɪsm(ə)nt, ɛn-/ *noun.* Also (*arch.*) **in-** /ɪn-/. M18.
[ORIGIN from ENCASE + -MENT.]
1 A thing that encases; a receptacle, a covering. M18.
2 The act of encasing; the state of being encased; *spec.* in BEE-KEEPING, the surrounding of a queen by worker bees; the mass of bees so produced. E19.

encash /ɪnˈkaʃ, ɛn-/ *verb trans.* M19.
[ORIGIN from EN-[1] + CASH *noun*[1].]
Convert (a draft, bill, cheque, etc.) into cash; obtain in the form of cash payments, realize.
■ **encashable** *adjective* E20. **encashment** *noun* the action of encashing; the amount of cash receipts: M19.

encaustic /ɛnˈkɔːstɪk/ *adjective & noun.* L16.
[ORIGIN Latin *encausticus* from Greek *egkaustikos*, from *egkaiein* burn in, formed as EN-[2] + *kaiein* to burn: see -IC.]
▸ **A** *adjective.* **1** Employing or involving strong heat to fix colours, *spec.* using pigments mixed with wax which is burnt in; (of a painting) produced in this way. L16.
2 Of a brick or tile: decorated with differently coloured clays that are inlaid and burnt in. M19.
▸ **B** *noun.* **1** [repr. Greek *egkaustikē tekhnē*] The art or process of encaustic painting. E17.
2 Encaustic work. M18.

encave /ɪnˈkeɪv, ɛn-/ *verb trans.* Also †**in-**. E17.
[ORIGIN from EN-[1], IN-[2] + CAVE *noun*[1].]
Enclose or shut up (as) in a cave.

encavern /ɪnˈkav(ə)n, ɛn-/ *verb trans.* *rare*. E17.
[ORIGIN from EN-[1] + CAVERN *noun*.]
Enclose or shut up (as) in a cavern.

-ence /(ə)ns/ *suffix.*
[ORIGIN French from Latin (i) *-entia*, from pres. ppl stems in *-ent-* -ENT, (ii) *-antia*: see -ANCE.]
Forming nouns of quality (or instances of it), as ***congruence***, ***impertinence***, ***sapience***, or of action, as ***reference***, ***reminiscence***. Since the 16th cent. many words ending in *-ance* from French have been altered back to *-ence* after Latin, and more recent words have taken *-ance* or *-ence* according to the Latin vowel (hence much inconsistency, as ***dependence*** or ***dependance***, ***resistance***, ***subsistence***). Cf. -ENCY.

enceinte /ɒ̃ˈsɑ̃t/ *noun.* Pl. pronounced same. E18.
[ORIGIN French from Latin *incincta* fem. pa. pple of *incingere* gird in from IN-[2] + *cingere* gird.]
The main enclosure or enclosing wall of a fortified place.

enceinte /ɒ̃ˈsɑ̃t/ *adjective.* *arch.* Also †**enseint**. See also ENSIENT. E17.
[ORIGIN French from medieval Latin *incincta* ungirded, from Latin IN-[3] + *cincta* fem. pa. pple of *cingere* gird.]
Of a woman: pregnant.

encell /ɪnˈsɛl, ɛn-/ *verb trans.* M17.
[ORIGIN from EN-[1] + CELL *noun*[1].]
Place in or as in a cell.

†**encense** *noun*, *verb* see INCENSE *noun*, *verb*[1], *verb*[2].

encentre /ɪnˈsɛntə, ɛn-/ *verb trans.* *rare*. Also ***-ter**. E17.
[ORIGIN from EN-[1] + CENTRE *noun*.]
Centre *in* something, place in the centre.

encephal- *combining form* see ENCEPHALO-.

encephalic /ɛnsɪˈfalɪk, ɛnˈkɛf(ə)lɪk/ *adjective.* E19.
[ORIGIN from Greek *egkephalos* brain (see ENCEPHALO-) + -IC.]
Of, pertaining to, or affecting the brain.

E

E

encephalisation *noun* var. of ENCEPHALIZATION.

encephalitis /ɛnˌsɛfəˈlʌɪtɪs, -ˌkɛf-/ *noun*. Pl. **-litides** /-ˈlɪtɪdiːz/. M19.
[ORIGIN from ENCEPHALO- + -ITIS.]
Inflammation of the brain, esp. sufficient to impair its function; a condition in which this is a dominant symptom.
encephalitis C = ST LOUIS ENCEPHALITIS.
■ **encephalitic** /-ˈlɪtɪk/ *adjective* L19. ˌ**encephaˈlitogen** *noun* an encephalitogenic agent M20. **enˌcephalitoˈgenic** *adjective* capable of causing encephalitis E20. **enˌcephalitogeˈnicity** *noun* the property of being encephalitogenic M20.

encephalization /ɛnˌsɛf(ə)lʌɪˈzeɪʃ(ə)n, -ˌkɛf/ *noun*. Also **-isation**. M20.
[ORIGIN from ENCEPHALO- + -IZATION.]
An evolutionary increase in the complexity or relative size of the brain; a shift of function from non-cortical parts of the brain to the cortex.

encephalo- /ɛnˈsɛf(ə)ləʊ, ɛnˈkɛf-/ *combining form* of Greek *egkephalos* brain, formed as EN-[2] + *kephalē* head: see -O-. Before a vowel **encephal-**.
■ **encephalocele** *noun* a congenital protrusion of part of the brain through a defect in the skull M19. **encephalogram** *noun* an X-ray photograph of the brain E20. **encephalograph** *noun* (*a*) = ENCEPHALOGRAM; (*b*) = ELECTROENCEPHALOGRAPH: M20. **encephaloˈgraphic** *adjective* of or pertaining to encephalography E20. **encephaˈlography** *noun* the radiological investigation of the brain E20. **encephalomyeˈlitis** *noun* inflammation of the brain and the spinal cord; any of several virus diseases (e.g. rabies) so characterized: E20. **encephaloˈpathic** *adjective* of, pertaining to, or causing encephalopathy L19. **encephaˈlopathy** *noun* (a) degenerative disease of the brain (*bovine spongiform encephalopathy*: see BOVINE *adjective* 1, *spongiform encephalopathy*: see SPONGIFORM 1) L19.

encephaloid /ɛnˈsɛf(ə)lɔɪd/ *adjective*. M19.
[ORIGIN French *encéphaloïde*, formed as ENCEPHALO-: see -OID.]
Of a cancerous tumour: having the soft consistency of brain tissue.

encephalon /ɛnˈsɛfəlɒn, -ˈkɛf-/ *noun*. M18.
[ORIGIN Greek *egkephalon* what is inside the head, formed as EN-[2] + *kephalē* head.]
ANATOMY. The brain.
■ Also **encephalos** *noun* (*rare*) E18.

enchafe /ɪnˈtʃeɪf, ɛn-/ *verb*. Now *rare* or *obsolete*. LME.
[ORIGIN Alt. of ESCHAUFE.]
1 *verb trans.* Make hot; *fig.* excite, anger. LME.
†**2** *verb intrans.* Grow hot. Only in LME.

enchain /ɪnˈtʃeɪn, ɛn-/ *verb trans.* LME.
[ORIGIN Old French & mod. French *enchaîner* from Proto-Gallo-Romance, formed as EN-[1] + Latin *catena* chain.]
†**1** Link together as in a chain. LME–M18.
2 Bind with chains; *fig.* restrain, impede the action of. LME.
ROBERT KNOX Ointments . . that stupefy and enchain our senses.
3 Engage, hold, (the attention, one's emotions, etc.). M17.
C. BRONTË Rachel's acting . . enchained me with interest.
■ **enchainment** *noun* the action of enchaining; the state of being enchained: M18.

enchaînement /ɑ̃ʃɛnmɑ̃/ *noun*. Pl. pronounced same. M19.
[ORIGIN French, lit. 'chaining up, concatenation'.]
A sequence of steps in ballet.

enchant /ɪnˈtʃɑːnt, ɛn-/ *verb trans.* Also †**in-**. LME.
[ORIGIN Old French & mod. French *enchanter* from Latin *incantare*, formed as IN-[2] + *cantare* sing: see CHANT *verb*.]
1 Put under a spell, bewitch. LME. ▸**b** Endow with magical powers or properties. L16.
b SHAKES. *Macb.* And now about the cauldron sing, . . Enchanting all that you put in.
†**2** Influence powerfully; delude; induce or compel *to do*. LME–L17.
3 Charm, delight, enrapture. Freq. in *pass.* L16.
J. A. MICHENER Glassware that would enchant all subsequent generations who loved beauty. R. CHURCH I was enchanted by the river and its activities.
■ **enchantedly** *adverb* in an enchanted manner L20. **enchanting** *adjective* (*a*) charming, delightful; (*b*) (now *rare* or *obsolete*) that puts someone under a spell: M16. **enchantingly** *adverb* L16.

enchanter /ɪnˈtʃɑːntə, ɛn-/ *noun*. Also †**in-**. ME.
[ORIGIN Old French *enchanteor*, -*our* (mod. -*eur*) from late Latin *incantator* from Latin *incantat-*: see INCANTATION, -ER[2].]
A person who uses magic, a sorcerer. Formerly also, a conjuror.
enchanter's NIGHTSHADE.

enchantment /ɪnˈtʃɑːntm(ə)nt, ɛn-/ *noun*. Also †**in-**. ME.
[ORIGIN Old French & mod. French *enchantement*, formed as ENCHANT: see -MENT.]
1 The use of magic or sorcery; an instance of this; the state of being under a spell. ME.
2 Great charm or fascination; the property of delighting; an enraptured condition. L17.
T. CAMPBELL Distance lends enchantment to the view.

enchantress /ɪnˈtʃɑːntrɪs, ɛn-/ *noun*. Also †**in-**. LME.
[ORIGIN Old French & mod. French *enchanteresse*, formed as ENCHANTER: see -ESS[1].]
1 A witch, a sorceress. LME.
2 *fig.* A charming or fascinating woman. E18.

encharge /ɪnˈtʃɑːdʒ, ɛn-/ *verb trans.* LME.
[ORIGIN Old French *enchargier* (mod. *encharger*), formed as EN-[1], CHARGE *noun*.]
†**1** Impose as a duty or responsibility; give (a thing) in charge. (Foll. by a person as indirect obj., *to*.) LME–E19.
†**2** Instruct or commission (a person) *to do* something. LME–L18.
3 Burden, entrust, or commission *with*. M17.

encharm /ɪnˈtʃɑːm, ɛn-/ *verb trans.* LME.
[ORIGIN Old French *encharmer*, formed as EN-[1], CHARM *noun*[1].]
Put under a spell, enchant; *fig.* delight. *obsolete* exc. *fig.*

†**enchase** *verb*[1] *trans.* LME–M18.
[ORIGIN Old French *enchacier*, formed as EN-[1], CHASE *verb*[1].]
Drive away, hunt, pursue.

enchase /ɪnˈtʃeɪs, ɛn-/ *verb*[2] *trans.* LME.
[ORIGIN Old French & mod. French *enchasser* enshrine, set (gems), encase, formed as EN-[1], *chasse*: see CASE *noun*[2].]
▸ **I** Ornament, adorn.
1 Adorn with figures in relief. Also, engrave; adorn (as) with engraved figures. LME. ▸**b** Engrave (figures) *on* or *in* a surface; portray by engraved figures. L16.
2 Set *in* gold or the like. Also (*fig.*), act as a setting for. M16.
3 Set (gold etc.) *with*, (as) with gems. L16.
4 Inlay or variegate *with* gold etc. M17.
▸ **II** Enclose.
†**5** Shut in, enclose. L16–E18.
6 Enshrine *in*, like a relic. E17.
fig.: T. KEN Thy bright Idea in my Heart Enchase.
7 Fit or place (a thing) into a space designed to receive it. E17.
■ †**enchasement** *noun* a frame, a setting M17–L18. **enchaser** *noun* a person who enchases or engraves metal M19.

encheer /ɪnˈtʃɪə, ɛn-/ *verb trans.* Also †**in-**. L16.
[ORIGIN from EN-[1], IN-[2] + CHEER *verb*.]
Gladden, make cheerful.

enchilada /ɛntʃɪˈlɑːdə/ *noun*. M19.
[ORIGIN Amer. Spanish, fem. of *enchilado* pa. pple of *enchilar* season with chilli, formed as EN-[1] + CHILLI.]
A usu. meat-filled tortilla served with chilli sauce.
the whole enchilada *N. Amer. colloq.* everything, everyone; the lot.

enchiridion /ɛnkʌɪˈrɪdɪən/ *noun*. LME.
[ORIGIN Late Latin from Greek *egkheiridion*, formed as EN-[2] + *kheir* hand + -*idion* dim. suffix.]
A handbook, a manual.

enchondroma /ɛnkɒnˈdrəʊmə/ *noun*. Pl. **-mas**, **-mata** /-mətə/. M19.
[ORIGIN mod. Latin, formed as EN-[2] + Greek *khondros* cartilage: see -OMA.]
Orig., a chondroma. Now *spec.*, one that arises inside a bone (cf. ECCHONDROMA), usu. in the hand or foot.
■ **enchondromatous** *adjective* M19. **enchondrosis** *noun*, pl. **-droses** /-ˈdrəʊsiːz/, a chondroma arising from cartilage L19.

enchorial /ɪnˈkɔːrɪəl, ɛn-/ *adjective*. Now *rare* or *obsolete*. E19.
[ORIGIN from Greek *egkhōrios* in or of the country, formed as EN-[2] + *khōra* country: see -AL[1].]
1 = DEMOTIC *adjective* 1. E19.
2 Belonging to or used in a particular country. M19.

encierro /ɛnˈθjɛrro/ *noun*. Pl. **-os** /-ɒs/. M19.
[ORIGIN Spanish, lit. 'shutting in', from *en-* (formed as IN-[2]) + *cierre* shutting.]
The driving of bulls through the streets of a Spanish town from a corral to the bullring.

encincture /ɪnˈsɪŋ(k)tʃə, ɛn-/ *verb* & *noun*. Chiefly *poet.* E19.
[ORIGIN from EN-[1] + CINCTURE *noun*.]
▸ **A** *verb trans.* = ENGIRDLE. E19.
▸ **B** *noun*. The fact of being surrounded; an enclosure. *rare*. M19.

encipher /ɪnˈsʌɪfə, ɛn-/ *verb trans.* Also **-cypher**, (earlier) †**in-**. L16.
[ORIGIN from EN-[1], IN-[2] + CIPHER *noun*.]
1 a Write (a message) in cipher. L16. ▸**b** Convert into coded form using a cipher; encrypt. L19.
2 Combine in a monogram *with*. M17.
■ **encipherment** *noun* the action of enciphering something M20.

encircle /ɪnˈsəːk(ə)l, ɛn-/ *verb trans.* Also †**in-**. L16.
[ORIGIN from EN-[1], IN-[2] + CIRCLE *noun*.]
1 Enclose in a circle; surround, encompass, (*with*). L16.
E. WAUGH Immense trees . . encircled Boot Magna Hall. B. HINES Latecomers climbed on to the dustbins, . . encircling each other's bodies with their arms.
2 Move in a ring around. Now *rare*. L16.
■ **encirclement** *noun* the act of encircling something; the fact or state of being encircled, esp. by hostile countries: E20. **encircler** *noun* (*rare*) M17.

encl. *abbreviation*.
Enclosed; enclosure.

en clair /ɑ̃ klɛːr/ *adverbial* & *adjectival phr.* L19.
[ORIGIN French.]
(Transmitted, written, etc.) in ordinary language, not in code or cipher.

enclasp /ɪnˈklɑːsp, ɛn-/ *verb trans.* Also †**in-**. L16.
[ORIGIN from EN-[1], IN-[2] + CLASP *noun*.]
Hold (as) in a clasp or embrace.

enclave /ˈɛnkleɪv/ *noun*. M19.
[ORIGIN French, from Old French & mod. French *enclaver* enclose, dovetail from popular Latin, from *in-* EN-[1] + *clavis* key.]
1 A region belonging to a country but surrounded by another country, as viewed by the latter (cf. EXCLAVE). M19.
2 A culturally or socially distinct minority group in a society or place. M20.

enclave *adjective* see ENCLAVÉ.

enclave /ɪnˈkleɪv, ɛn-/ *verb trans.* LME.
[ORIGIN Old French & mod. French *enclaver*: see ENCLAVE *noun*. In mod. use from ENCLAVE *noun*.]
Surround and isolate; make an enclave of.
— NOTE: Rare before L19.

enclavé /ɪnˈklɑːvi, ɛn-/ *adjective*. Also (earlier) **enclave**, **inclave**, /ɪnˈkleɪv, ɛn-/. M17.
[ORIGIN French, pa. ppl adjective of *enclaver*: see ENCLAVE *noun*.]
HERALDRY. Of the border of an ordinary: shaped like a dovetail joint.

†**enclinable** *adjective*, †**encline** *verb*, †**enclined** *ppl adjective* see INCLINABLE etc.

enclisis /ˈɛnklɪsɪs/ *noun*. L19.
[ORIGIN mod. Latin from Greek *egklisis*, from *egklinein* (see ENCLITIC).]
GRAMMAR. Pronunciation as an enclitic; the transfer of accentuation to a previous word.

enclitic /ɪnˈklɪtɪk, ɛn-/ *adjective* & *noun*. M17.
[ORIGIN Late Latin *encliticus* from Greek *egklitikos*, from *egklinein* lean on, formed as EN-[2] + *klinein* to lean, slope: see -IC.]
GRAMMAR. ▸**A** *adjective*. Designating a word so unemphatic as to be pronounced as if part of the preceding word, and sometimes attached to it (as English *of* in *piece of*, *not* in *cannot*, Latin *-que* and). M17.
▸ **B** *noun*. An enclitic word. M17.
■ †**enclitical** *adjective* (*a*) = ENCLITIC *adjective*; (*b*) *rare* that leans against something: E17–L18. **enclitically** *adverb* M19.

encloistered /ɪnˈklɔɪstəd, ɛn-/ *adjective*. Also (earlier) †**in-**. M16.
[ORIGIN from EN-[1], IN-[2] + CLOISTER *noun* + -ED[1].]
1 Shut up in a cloister; *fig.* imprisoned; isolated; sheltered. M16.
2 Surrounded by or provided with cloisters. E17.

enclose /ɪnˈkləʊz, ɛn-/ *verb trans.* Also **in-** /ɪn-/. ME.
[ORIGIN Old French & mod. French *enclos(e)*, pa. pple of *enclôre* from popular Latin from Latin *includere* INCLUDE.]
1 Orig., shut up in or *in* a room or building; imprison. Now only, seclude in a religious community from the outside world (chiefly as ***enclosed*** pa. pple). ME.
C. MARLOWE In the strongest tower Enclose him fast. O. SHIPLEY The nuns live in community, but are not enclosed.
2 Of things: surround; envelop; contain; MATH. (of two lines) form (an angle) at their intersection. ME.
R. L. STEVENSON A house with lawns enclosing it. G. GREENE The darkness had long enclosed them both.
3 Surround with or *with* a wall, fence, etc., to prevent free passage in and out. LME. ▸**b** Put hedges, walls, etc., on (waste or common land) for the purpose of cultivation or allocation to individual owners. LME. ▸**c** Of an army, a body of people, etc.: surround; hem in. Now *rare*. LME.
E. F. BENSON Parallel brick walls enclosing strips of garden belonging to neighbouring houses. **b** H. MARTINEAU An Act of Parliament is to be obtained for enclosing Brook common. **c** H. PHILLIPS Endeavor to enclose the British army and navy in the Delaware bay.
4 Insert in or *in* (a container etc.); cover completely; *esp.* place (a document) in the same envelope as a letter. LME.
P. MORTIMER Dear Mrs. Evans, I enclose a cheque for £10.
■ **enclosed** *ppl adjective* & *noun* (*a*) *ppl adjective* that is enclosed; (*b*) *noun* a thing that is enclosed with a letter (usu. preceded by *the*): L16. **encloser** *noun* †(*a*) a jeweller; (*b*) a person who encloses something, esp. common land: LME.

enclosure /ɪnˈkləʊʒə, ɛn-/ *noun*. Also **in-** /ɪn-/. LME.
[ORIGIN Legal Anglo-Norman, Old French, formed as ENCLOSE, -URE.]
1 The action of enclosing, *esp.* the enclosing of waste or common land. LME.
E. P. THOMPSON Wholesale enclosure, in which . . common rights are lost.
2 A thing that encloses; an encompassing barrier. M16.
3 A thing that is enclosed; a space marked off by boundaries, *spec.* at a racecourse; a document enclosed in the same envelope as a letter. L16.
members' enclosure, ***Royal Enclosure***, ***winners' enclosure***, etc.
4 The state of being enclosed, esp. in a religious community. E19.

O. SHIPLEY The nuns keep strict enclosure, and lead the contemplative life. T. KENEALLY Enclosure in the ghetto would be compulsory for all Jews.

enclothe /ɪnˈkləʊð, ɛn-/ *verb trans. rare.* **L15.**
[ORIGIN from EN-¹ + CLOTHE *verb*.]
Clothe, cover.

encloud /ɪnˈklaʊd, ɛn-/ *verb trans.* Also †**in-**. **L16.**
[ORIGIN from EN-¹, IN-² + CLOUD *noun*.]
Envelop in a cloud; overshadow.

†**encluse** *adjective & noun* var. of INCLUSE.

encode /ɪnˈkəʊd, ɛn-/ *verb trans.* **E20.**
[ORIGIN from EN-¹ + CODE *noun*.]
Write or represent in code or cipher; convert (information) into another form.
■ **encoder** *noun* a person who or thing which encodes something; *esp.* part of a computer that encodes data **M20.**

encoffin /ɪnˈkɒfɪn, ɛn-/ *verb trans.* Also †**in-**. **L16.**
[ORIGIN from EN-¹, IN-² + COFFIN *noun*.]
Put in or as in a coffin.

encoignure /ɑ̃kwaɲyːr/ *noun.* Pl. pronounced same. **M19.**
[ORIGIN French, formed as EN-¹ + *coin* corner: see COIN *noun*.]
A piece of usu. ornamental furniture made with an angle to fit into a corner.

encolour /ɪnˈkʌlə, ɛn-/ *verb trans.* Also ***-or**. **M17.**
[ORIGIN from EN-¹ + COLOUR *noun*.]
Tinge with colour.

encomia *noun pl.* see ENCOMIUM.

encomiast /ɛnˈkəʊmɪast/ *noun.* **E17.**
[ORIGIN Greek *egkōmiastēs*, from *egkōmiazein* to praise, from *egkōmion* ENCOMIUM.]
A composer or deliverer of an encomium; a flatterer, a eulogizer.

encomiastic /ɛnˌkəʊmɪˈastɪk/ *adjective & noun.* Now *rare.* **L16.**
[ORIGIN Greek *egkōmiastikos*, from *egkōmiazein*: see ENCOMIAST, -IC.]
▸ **A** *adjective.* Commendatory, eulogistic. **L16.**
▸ †**B** *noun.* An encomium. **M17–E19.**
■ **encomiastical** *adjective* (now *rare* or *obsolete*) = ENCOMIASTIC *adjective* **L16.** **encomiastically** *adverb* (*rare*) **M17.**

encomienda /ɛnˌkəʊmɪˈɛndə/ *noun.* **E19.**
[ORIGIN Spanish = commission, charge, from *encomendar* commit, charge, from *en-* (formed as IN-²) + *comendar* formed as COMMEND *verb*.]
hist. An estate granted to a Spaniard in America with powers of taxation and corvée over the Indian inhabitants; (the system derived from) such authority.
■ **encomendero** /-mɛnˈdɛːrəʊ/ *noun*, pl. **-os**, the holder of an encomienda **E19.**

encomium /ɛnˈkəʊmɪəm/ *noun.* Orig. anglicized as †**encomy**. Pl. **-iums**, **-ia** /-ɪə/. **M16.**
[ORIGIN Latin from Greek *egkōmion* eulogy, use as noun of neut. of adjective (sc. *epos* speech), formed as EN-² + *komos* revel.]
A formal or high-flown expression of praise; a panegyric.

encompass /ɪnˈkʌmpəs, ɛn-/ *verb trans.* Also †**in-**. **ME.**
[ORIGIN from EN-¹, IN-² + COMPASS *noun*.]
1 Surround, encircle; envelop, contain; include comprehensively, embrace. **ME.** ▸†**b** Outwit. *rare* (Shakes.). Only in **L16.**

GIBBON His throne was encompassed with domestic enemies. A. MOOREHEAD Living in a little capsule, encompassed by a huge unknown wilderness. V. F. WEISSKOPF Human experience encompasses much more than any given system of thought can express.

†**2** Make a circuit round, go all round. **M17–L18.**
3 = COMPASS *verb* 1. **L19.**

H. L. CAMERON What earthly reason could Captain Thistleby have for encompassing my destruction?

■ **encompassment** *noun* the action of encompassing; the state of being encompassed: **E17.**

†**encomy** *noun* see ENCOMIUM.

encoop /ɪnˈkuːp, ɛn-/ *verb trans. poet.* **M19.**
[ORIGIN from EN-¹ + COOP *noun*¹.]
Coop up.

encoppicement /ɪnˈkɒpɪsm(ə)nt, ɛn-/ *noun.* **M20.**
[ORIGIN from EN-¹ + COPPICE *noun* + -MENT.]
The promotion and preservation of coppices.

encore /ˈɒŋkɔː/ *interjection, noun, & verb.* **E18.**
[ORIGIN French = still, again, of disputed origin; not used in the English sense.]
▸ **A** *interjection.* Again, once more. **E18.**
▸ **B** *noun.* A spectators' or audience's demand for an item to be performed again, or for a further item to be performed after the nominal end of a concert etc. Also, an item performed in response to such a demand. **M18.**
▸ **C** *verb trans.* Call for the repetition of (an item) or a repetition by (a performer). **M18.**

encounter /ɪnˈkaʊntə, ɛn-/ *noun.* Also †**in-**. **ME.**
[ORIGIN Old French & mod. French *encontre*, formed as ENCOUNTER *verb*.]
1 a A meeting of adversaries in conflict; a duel, a battle. **ME.** ▸**b** *gen.* A meeting, esp. by chance or unexpectedly. **M17.** ▸**c** A session, or participation, in an encounter group. **M20.**

SIR W. SCOTT The Saxons . . and the Gael . . had many a desperate and bloody encounter. *fig.*: SHAKES. *Rich. III* This keen encounter of our wits. **b** HENRY MILLER As a result of that chance encounter on the street we met frequently thereafter. B. LOVELL The first encounter of a spacecraft with Saturn.

†**2** A lovers' meeting; an amatory approach. *rare* (Shakes.). Only in **L16.**
†**3** Manner, behaviour. *rare* (Shakes.). Only in **L16.**
– COMB.: **encounter group**: of people seeking emotional adjustment through close physical and emotional contact with one another.

encounter /ɪnˈkaʊntə, ɛn-/ *verb.* Also †**in-**. **ME.**
[ORIGIN Old French *encontrer* (mod. *rencontrer*) from Proto-Romance, from Latin IN-² + *contra* against.]
1 *verb trans.* Meet as an adversary; confront in battle. **ME.**

GIBBON The two kings encountered each other in single combat.

2 a *verb trans.* & (with pl. subj.) *intrans.* Meet, come upon, (a person or thing), esp. by chance or unexpectedly. **E16.** ▸**b** *verb trans.* Meet with, experience, (difficulties, opposition, etc.). **E19.**

a BYRON We never met before, and never . . may again encounter. T. HARDY The first person they encountered on entering the main street was the schoolmaster. **b** M. ESSLIN Ionesco encountered a rawer, more brutal world.

†**3** *verb trans. & intrans.* Express opposition (to); thwart; dispute. **M16–L18.**
†**4** *verb intrans.* Meet *with*; contend *with* as an adversary. **M16–L18.**
†**5** *verb trans.* Go to meet; approach. *rare* (Shakes.). Only in **E17.**

†**encounterer** *noun.* **E16.**
[ORIGIN from ENCOUNTER *verb* + -ER¹.]
1 An adversary; a contrary, an opposite. **E16–M17.**
2 A forward person; a flirt. *rare* (Shakes.). Only in **E17.**

encourage /ɪnˈkʌrɪdʒ, ɛn-/ *verb trans.* Also †**in-**. **LME.**
[ORIGIN Old French & mod. French *encourager*, formed as EN-¹ + *corage* COURAGE *noun*.]
1 Give courage, confidence, or hope to. **LME.**

J. RHYS You have . . encouraged me when I'd nearly given up.

2 Make sufficiently confident or bold *to do* a specified action. Also foll. by *to* a deed. **LME.**

D. M. FRAME The success of Montaigne's first two books encouraged him to write his third.

3 Urge, incite; recommend, advise. Foll. by *to do*. **L15.**

O. MANNING He had never encouraged Mrs. Trimmer to talk.

4 Stimulate (a person, personal activity) by help, reward, etc.; patronize; abet. **M17.**

M. W. MONTAGU No woman dares . . encourage two lovers at a time. R. LARDNER Rita's aunt had encouraged the romance.

5 Allow, promote, or assist (an activity or situation); foster, cherish. **L17.**

H. ACTON Reading was tolerated but not encouraged by her father.

■ **encourager** *noun* **M16.** **encouraging** *adjective* that encourages or tends to encourage **M17.** **encouragingly** *adverb* **M17.**

encouragement /ɪnˈkʌrɪdʒm(ə)nt, ɛn-/ *noun.* Also †**in-**. **M16.**
[ORIGIN Old French & mod. French, formed as ENCOURAGE: see -MENT.]
The action or process of encouraging; the fact of being encouraged; a fact or circumstance that encourages.

encover /ɪnˈkʌvə, ɛn-/ *verb trans. rare.* Also **in-** /ɪn-/. **LME.**
[ORIGIN from EN-¹, IN-² + COVER *verb*².]
Cover completely.

Encratite /ˈɛnkrətʌɪt/ *noun.* **L16.**
[ORIGIN Late Latin *encratita*, from patristic Greek *egkratitai* pl., from *egkratēs* self-controlled, continent, formed as EN-² + *kratos* strength: see -ITE¹.]
A member of any of several early Christian sects who carried ascetic practices to extremes.

†**encrease** *noun, verb,* †**-ment** *noun* vars. of INCREASE *noun, verb,* -MENT.

encrimson /ɪnˈkrɪmz(ə)n, ɛn-/ *verb trans.* Also **in-** /ɪn-/. **L16.**
[ORIGIN from EN-¹, IN-² + CRIMSON.]
Make or dye crimson.

encrinal /ˈɛnkrɪn(ə)l, ɛnˈkrʌɪn(ə)l/ *adjective.* **M19.**
[ORIGIN from ENCRINUS + -AL¹.]
= ENCRINITAL.

encrini *noun* pl. of ENCRINUS.

encrinite /ˈɛnkrɪnʌɪt/ *noun.* **E19.**
[ORIGIN from ENCRINUS + -ITE¹.]
PALAEONTOLOGY. **1** A crinoid, *esp.* a fossil crinoid. **E19.**
2 Limestone containing a large proportion of fossil crinoids. **M20.**
■ **encri'nital** *adjective* of, pertaining to, or of the nature of an encrinite; encrinitic: **M19.** **encrinitic** /-ˈnɪtɪk/ *adjective* containing fossil crinoids **M19.**

encrinus /ˈɛnkrɪnəs, ɛnˈkrʌɪnəs/ *noun.* Pl. **-ni** /-nʌɪ/. **M18.**
[ORIGIN mod. Latin, from Greek EN-² + *krinon* lily.]
A fossil crinoid; *spec.* one belonging to the extinct genus *Encrinus* of stalked crinoids.

encroach /ɪnˈkrəʊtʃ, ɛn-/ *verb & noun.* Also †**in-**. **LME.**
[ORIGIN Old French *encrochier* seize, fasten upon, formed as EN-¹ + *crochier* to crook, from *croc* hook formed as CROOK *noun*.]
▸ **A** *verb.* †**1** *verb trans.* Seize; obtain wrongfully. **LME–M17.**
2 *verb intrans.* Intrude usurpingly on another's territory, rights, etc.; make gradual inroads at the expense of something else. (Foll. by *on, upon.*) **M16.**

STEELE I shall not encroach upon your Time. W. S. CHURCHILL The jungle had already encroached avidly upon the track.

3 *verb intrans.* Advance gradually beyond due limits. **M16.**

G. GORDON The encroaching lines of spreading varicose veins at the back of her . . legs.

▸ **B** *noun.* Encroachment. **E17.**
■ **encroacher** *noun* **L16.** **encroachment** *noun* the action or an act of encroaching **LME.**

en croûte /ɒ̃ ˈkruːt, *foreign* ɑ̃ krut/ *adverbial phr.* **M20.**
[ORIGIN French.]
In a pastry crust.

encrown /ɪnˈkraʊn, ɛn-/ *verb trans.* Now *rare.* **L15.**
[ORIGIN from EN-¹ + CROWN *noun*.]
Put or form a crown on.

encrust /ɪnˈkrʌst, ɛn-/ *verb.* Also (earlier) **in-** /ɪn-/. **E17.**
[ORIGIN French *incruster* from Latin *incrustare*, formed as IN-² + *crusta* CRUST *noun*.]
1 *verb trans. & intrans.* (Cause to) form into a crust; (cause to) deposit a crust *on*. **E17.**
2 *verb trans.* Ornament or decorate (a surface) with an overlay of precious material. **M17.**

GIBBON The outside of the edifice was encrusted with marble.

3 *verb trans.* Cover with a crust or solid coating; form a crust or coating on. **L17.**

P. LIVELY Rose pink rock encrusted with a greyish green lichen.

4 *verb trans.* Enclose as *in* a crust. *rare.* **E18.**

encrustate *verb* var. of INCRUSTATE *verb*.

encrustation /ɛnkrʌˈsteɪʃ(ə)n, ɪn-/ *noun.* Also **in-** /ɪn-/. **E17.**
[ORIGIN French, or late Latin *incrustatio(n-)*, formed as INCRUSTATE *verb*: see -ATION.]
1 An outer layer or crust of fine material or ornamentation covering a rough substance; *esp.* a facing of marble etc. on a building. Formerly also *fig.*, an ornament or affectation. **E17.**

M. GIROUARD The extra diversion of a rich incrustation of sunflowers—in stone or wrought iron.

2 A crust formed naturally on the surface of an object; a scab; *esp.* a calcareous or crystalline deposit. **M17.** ▸**b** *fig.* An impenetrable layer of accumulated habits, vices, etc. **E19.**

P. H. JOHNSON Their salty incrustations sparkled in the gilding of the street lamps. **b** P. ZIEGLER Under an encrustation of traditional dogma a truth that . . seemed heretical but was soon accepted.

3 The formation of a crust; the fact or condition of being encrusted. **M17.**

encrypt /ɛnˈkrɪpt/ *verb trans.* **M20.**
[ORIGIN from EN-¹ + *crypt* in *cryptogram* etc.]
Convert into code, esp. to prevent unauthorized access; conceal *in* something by this means.
■ **encryption** *noun* the process of encrypting **M20.**

enculturation /ɪnˌkʌltjʊˈreɪʃ(ə)n, ɛn-/ *noun.* **M20.**
[ORIGIN from EN-¹ + CULTURE *noun* + -ATION.]
The process by which the values and norms of a society are passed on to or acquired by its members.
■ **en'culturate** *verb trans.* subject to enculturation; incorporate (a person) into a culture: **M20.** **en'culturative** *adjective* of, pertaining to, or constituting enculturation **M20.**

†**encumber** *noun.* Also **in-**. **ME–M17.**
[ORIGIN Old French & mod. French *encombre*, from *encombrer*: see ENCUMBER *verb*.]
The state of being encumbered; an encumbrance.

encumber /ɪnˈkʌmbə, ɛn-/ *verb trans.* Also **in-** /ɪn-/. **ME.**
[ORIGIN Old French & mod. French *encombrer* block up, formed as EN-¹ + Old French *combre* river barrage = medieval Latin *combrus* barricade of felled trees.]
†**1** Cause suffering or trouble to; harass; (of temptation, passions) overcome. **ME–M17.**
†**2** Involve or entangle *in*. **LME–E18.**
3 Hamper, impede (a person, movement, etc.); act as a check or restraint on. **LME.**

LD MACAULAY He could not be persuaded to encumber his feeble frame with a cuirass.

4 Fill or load with something obstructive or useless; block up. **LME.**

J. PRIESTLEY I have not . . encumbered my doctrine with . . difficulties. W. S. CHURCHILL The rest walked home across the corpses which encumbered the plain.

5 Burden with duties, debts, etc.; burden (an estate) with a mortgage. **L16.**

J. GALSWORTHY He had never committed the imprudence of . . encumbering himself . . with children.

†**6** Fold (the arms). *rare* (Shakes.). Only in E17.

encumberment /ɪnˈkʌmbəm(ə)nt, ɛn-/ *noun*. Now *rare*. Also **in-** /ɪn-/. ME.
[ORIGIN Old French *encombrement*, formed as ENCUMBER *verb*: see -MENT.]
1 The action of encumbering; the state or fact of being encumbered. ME.
†**2** Molestation, disturbance; Satanic temptation. ME–L16.
†**3** An encumbrance. E–M17.

encumbrance /ɪnˈkʌmbr(ə)ns, ɛn-/ *noun*. Also **in-** /ɪn-/. ME.
[ORIGIN Old French *encombrance*, from *encombrer*: see ENCUMBER *verb*, -ANCE.]
†**1** Encumbered state or condition; trouble, molestation. ME–M16.
2 A thing that encumbers; an impediment, a hindrance; a burden, a useless addition; an annoyance. LME.

R. MACAULAY I decided to get rid of the tent, which was a heavy encumbrance.

3 *LAW*. A right or interest in land possessed by someone other than the freeholder, as a lease, mortgage, etc. E17.

T. LUNDBERG The assets are free of any lien or encumbrances.

4 A person dependent on another for support; a dependant. M18.
without encumbrance having no children.
■ **encumbrancer** *noun* (*LAW*) a person who has an encumbrance on a piece of land M19.

†**encursion** *noun* var. of INCURSION.

encurtain /ɪnˈkəːt(ə)n, ɛn-/ *verb trans.* LME.
[ORIGIN Old French *enco(u)rtiner*, formed as EN-[1] + as CURTAIN *noun*.]
Surround with or as with a curtain; shroud, veil.

-ency /(ə)nsi/ *suffix*.
[ORIGIN from or after Latin *-entia* -ENCE. Cf. -ANCY.]
Forming nouns of quality, as ***efficiency***, or state, as ***presidency***, but not of action (cf. -ENCE).

encyclic /ɛnˈsʌɪklɪk, ɪn-, -ˈsɪk-/ *adjective & noun*. E19.
[ORIGIN formed as ENCYCLICAL: see -IC.]
= ENCYCLICAL.

encyclical /ɛnˈsɪklɪk(ə)l, ɪn-, -ˈsʌɪk-/ *adjective & noun*. M17.
[ORIGIN Late Latin *encyclicus*, from Greek *egkuklios* circular, general, formed as EN-[2] + *kuklos* circle: see -ICAL.]
▸ **A** *adjective*. Of an ecclesiastical letter, now esp. one issued by the Pope: intended for extensive circulation. M17.
▸ **B** *noun*. A papal letter sent to all bishops of the Roman Catholic Church. M19.

encyclopaedia *noun*, **encyclopaedian** *noun & adjective*, etc., vars. of ENCYCLOPEDIA etc.

encyclopedia /ɛnˌsʌɪkləˈpiːdɪə, ɪn-/ *noun*. Also **-paed-**. M16.
[ORIGIN mod. Latin from pseudo-Greek *egkuklopaideia* for *egkuklios* (cf. ENCYCLICAL) *paideia* general education.]
1 The circle of learning; a general course of instruction. Now *rare* or *obsolete*. M16.
2 A book or set of books containing extensive information on all branches of knowledge, or on one particular subject, usu. arranged alphabetically. M17.
the Encyclopedia *hist.* the French encyclopedia compiled in the 18th cent. by Diderot, d'Alembert, and others, and its successors. ***walking encyclopedia***: see WALKING *ppl adjective*.

encyclopedian /ɛnˌsʌɪkləˈpiːdɪən, ɪn-/ *noun & adjective*. Also **-paed-**. E17.
[ORIGIN from ENCYCLOPEDIA + -AN.]
▸ **A** *noun*. †**1** = ENCYCLOPEDIA 1. Only in E17.
2 An encyclopedist. *rare*. M19.
▸ **B** *adjective*. Encyclopedic. M19.

encyclopedic /ɛnˌsʌɪkləˈpiːdɪk, ɪn-/ *adjective*. Also **-paed-**. E19.
[ORIGIN formed as ENCYCLOPEDIAN + -IC.]
Of, pertaining to, or resembling an encyclopedia; embracing all branches of learning; full of information, comprehensive.

R. FRY His intellectual apprehension was . . heightened, and his knowledge . . became encyclopedic.

■ **encyclopedical** *adjective* M17. **encyclopedically** *adverb* M19.

encyclopedise *verb* var. of ENCYCLOPEDIZE.

encyclopedism /ɛnˌsʌɪkləˈpiːdɪz(ə)m, ɪn-/ *noun*. Also **-paed-**. M19.
[ORIGIN formed as ENCYCLOPEDIZE + -ISM.]
1 Encyclopedic learning or knowledge. M19.
2 The doctrines advocated by the French Encyclopedists. M19.

encyclopedist /ɛnˌsʌɪkləˈpiːdɪst, ɪn-/ *noun*. Also **-paed-**. M17.
[ORIGIN formed as ENCYCLOPEDIZE + -IST.]
1 A compiler of or contributor to an encyclopedia; *esp.* (usu. **E-**) any of the compilers of the French Encyclopedia. M17.
2 A person who attempts to deal with every branch of knowledge. L19.

encyclopedize /ɛnˌsʌɪkləˈpiːdʌɪz, ɪn-/ *verb trans.* Also **-paed-**, **-ise**. E19.
[ORIGIN from ENCYCLOPEDIA + -IZE.]
Arrange as an encyclopedia; describe in an encyclopedia.

encypher *verb* var. of ENCIPHER.

encyst /ɪnˈsɪst, ɛn-/ *verb*. Also **in-** /ɪn-/. E18.
[ORIGIN from EN-[1], IN-[2] + CYST.]
BIOLOGY. **1** *verb trans.* Enclose in a cyst. Chiefly as ***encysted*** *ppl adjective*. E18.
2 *verb intrans.* Become enclosed in a cyst; form a cyst. L19.
■ **encysˈtation** *noun* = ENCYSTMENT M19. **encystment** *noun* the process of becoming encysted M19.

end /ɛnd/ *noun*.
[ORIGIN Old English *ende* = Old Frisian *enda*, *-e*, Old Saxon *endi* (Dutch *einde*), Old High German *enti* (German *Ende*), Old Norse *endir*, *endi*, Gothic *andeis*, from Germanic, from Indo-European: cf. Sanskrit *anta* end, boundary, death.]
▸ **I** With ref. to space.
1 An extreme limit or outermost part of a portion of space or of something extended in space. *obsolete* exc. in ***the end of the earth***, ***the ends of the earth***, etc. below. OE. ▸†**b** A boundary. LME–L16.
2 A limit of size or quantity. Now usu. in neg. contexts. OE.

J. S. MILL There was no end to the advantages.

3 A division or region of a country, city, etc.; *obsolete* exc. in ***east end*** s.v. EAST *adjective*, ***west end*** s.v. WEST *adjective*. OE. ▸**b** An outlying part of a village or small town; an outlying property. Usu. preceded by a descriptive name. M19.

b E. M. FORSTER Howards End.

4 A proportion, a fraction. Only with adjectives of quantity. *obsolete* exc. *dial.* OE. ▸**b** A piece that has been detached or left; a fragment, a remnant. L15. ▸**c** A part, a portion; *esp.* (with possess. adjective) the part of an enterprise, activity, etc., with which a person is involved. E20.

b P. STUBBES Scraps or . . short ends of lace. **c** N. SHUTE Honey would have to come back to this country to tell us his end of it. *fig.*: S. BRILL Glich is the financial end, but policy comes from me.

b *CIGARETTE* ***end***.
5 Either of the two extremities of a line, or of the greatest dimension of any object; a part of anything which includes either of its two extremities. ME. ▸**b** *BOWLS & CURLING*. A portion of play in which all the bowls or stones are delivered from one particular end of the green or rink. L17. ▸**c** *ARCHERY*. The place at which a mark is set up; the number of arrows shot from one end of a range. E19. ▸**d** One half or side of a sports ground, a court, etc.; the part occupied by either of two opposing teams or players. M19. ▸**e** *AMER. FOOTBALL*. A player at the end of the line; a winger; the position occupied by such a player. L19.

J. WESLEY I was quickly wet to my toe's end. J. RATHBONE Mr. Curtis remained standing at the end of the bed. R. CAMPBELL We would corner him at the shallow end of the bath. L. GARFIELD There was a disturbance at the other end of the hall.
d D. L. SAYERS The slogger smote a vigorous ball from the factory end.

6 The surface which bounds an object at either extremity; the head of a cask. E16.
7 a A length of thread pointed with a bristle. Also more fully ***shoemaker's end***. L16. ▸**b** In full ***cable's end***. A short length of cable. M17. ▸**c** *N. Amer.* In full ***end of steel***. The limit to which a railway extends; a terminus. E20.
▸ **II** With ref. to time or serial order.
8 The limit of duration of a period of time; the termination or conclusion of an action, process, state, etc. OE. ▸**b** The latter or final part. LME.

Daily Telegraph Mr Benn did not speak beyond thanking the Chancellor at the beginning and end of the meeting. *attrib.*: *Scotsman* New annual premiums received . . totalled £16.41 million in the three months to end-September.

9 Termination of existence; destruction, downfall; a person's death. OE.

S. LEACOCK If I should meet my end here.

10 Ultimate state or condition. Chiefly in biblical quotations and allusions, often misinterpreted in sense 9. OE.
†**11** A termination of doubt or debate; a resolution, a settlement. ME–M16.
†**12** The completion of an action; the accomplishment of a purpose. ME–L17.
13 An intended result; an aim, a purpose. ME.

V. WOOLF Everybody in the crowded street . . had some end in view.

14 An outcome, a result. Now *rare*. LME.
15 A final cause or purpose; the object for which a thing exists. LME.

H. J. LASKI His love of liberty, which is the true end of government.

– PHRASES: **all ends over**, **all ends up** thoroughly. **and there's an end**, **and so an end** *arch.* and this is, or shall be, an end. ***at a loose end***: see LOOSE *adjective*. **at an end** finished, exhausted. ***at loose ends***: see LOOSE *adjective*. ***at one's wit's end***: see WIT *noun*. **at the end** at last. ***at the end of the day***: see DAY *noun*. ***be on the receiving end***, ***be at the receiving end***: see RECEIVING *adjective*. ***best end***: see BEST *adjective* etc. **be the end of** be the death or downfall of. ***big end***: see BIG *adjective*. ***bitter end***: see BITTER *adjective*, *noun*[2]. BUSINESS ***end***. ***cable's end***: see sense 7b above. **change ends** switch from occupying one half of a ground, court, etc., to the other, and change the direction of play. **choose ends** select the direction in which one wishes to play. ***come to a bad end***, ***come to an end***: see COME *verb*. ***deep end***: see DEEP *adjective*. ***defensive end***: see DEFENSIVE *adjective* 1. ***dirty end of the stick***: see DIRTY *adjective*. ***east end***: see EAST *adjective*. ***end of steel***: see sense 7c above. **end on** with the end facing one, or facing any object; with the end adjoining the end of the next object. **end to end** with the ends in contact, lengthways. †**for an end**, **for end** in conclusion, finally. **for this end** = ***to this end*** below. **from end to end** from one extremity to the other, throughout the length of something. ***get hold of the wrong end of the stick***: see STICK *noun*[1]. **go end for end** *NAUTICAL* (of a boat) be upset. **have at one's fingers' end**, **have at one's tongue's end** know by heart. **have the better end (of the staff)**, **have the worse end (of the staff)** get the best, or worst, of it. ***hinder end***: see HINDER *adjective*. **in the end** ultimately, in the long run. **keep one's end up** sustain one's part in an undertaking or performance; hold one's own. ***little end***: see LITTLE *adjective*. ***loose end***: see LOOSE *adjective*. **make an end of** put a stop to. **make both ends meet**, **make ends meet** live within one's income; maintain an adequate income. **no end** *colloq.* (***a***) a vast number or amount *of*, a remarkable example *of*; (***b***) *adverbial* very much. ***odds and ends***: see ODDS *noun* 2b. **on end** (***a***) in an upright position; (***b***) consecutively, continuously. **put an end to** stop, abolish, destroy. ***rear end***: see REAR *adjective*[1], *adverb & noun*. **right on end** consecutively, immediately. ***shallow end***: see SHALLOW *adjective*, *noun*, *& adverb*. ***sharp end***: see SHARP *adjective & adverb*. **shift end for end** *NAUTICAL* reverse (a rope, spar, etc.) so that one end is where the other used to be; upset (a boat). ***shoemaker's end***: see sense 7a above. ***small end***: see SMALL *adjective*. ***sticky end***: see STICKY *adjective*[2] 4b. **straight on end** = ***right on end*** above. ***the beginning of the end***: see BEGINNING *noun* 4. **the end** (***a***) *colloq.* the last straw, the limit of endurability; (***b***) *US slang* the best, the ultimate. ***the end of one's tether***: see TETHER *noun*. ***the end of the earth***: see ***the ends of the earth*** below. **the end of the line** (***a***) = ***the end of the road*** below; (***b***) the last goods in stock of a particular design or class. **the end of the road** *fig.* the point at which hope or endeavour has to be abandoned. **the end of the world** *fig.* a calamitous matter or situation (only in neg. contexts). **the ends of the earth**, **the end of the earth** the most distant regions of the earth. ***the right end of the stick***: see STICK *noun*[1]. ***the thin end of the wedge***: see WEDGE *noun*. ***the world's end***: see WORLD *noun*. ***the wrong end of the stick***: see STICK *noun*[1]. ***tight end***: see TIGHT *adjective*. ***to the end of the chapter***: see CHAPTER *noun*. †**to the end that** in order that. **to this end** for this purpose. **turn end for end** put each end of (a thing) where the other end used to be. ***west end***: see WEST *adjective*. **without end** endlessly, for ever. ***world without end***: see WORLD *noun*.

– COMB.: **end-around** *noun & adjective* (***a***) *noun* (*AMER. FOOTBALL*) an offensive play in which an end runs with the ball behind his or her own team's line and round the opposite end; (***b***) *adjective* (*COMPUTING*) involving the transfer of a digit from one end of a register to the other; **end-artery** *ANATOMY* an artery which supplies almost all the blood to a part of the body and does not anastomose with itself or other arteries; **endgame** the final stage of a game of chess, bridge, etc., when few men or cards remain; **endgate** *US* a tailboard; **end grain** the grain of wood seen when it is cut across the growth rings; **end-leaf** a usu. blank leaf inserted at one or other end of a bound book; **end line** (***a***) a boundary line marking the end of a field or court in various games; (***b***) a line forming a conclusion; **end-man** *US* (chiefly *hist.*) a man at the end of a line of blackface minstrels who engaged in comic repartee with the interlocutor; **endmember** the item at one end of a series; **end moraine**: formed or forming at the forward edge of a glacier; **endnote**: similar to a footnote but placed with others at the end of a book or chapter; **end organ** *ANATOMY* a specialized encapsulated ending of a sensory or motor nerve; **endpaper** a blank leaf placed at the beginning or end of a book (usu. in *pl.*); **end piece** a piece at the end of a structure or composition; **end plate** *ANATOMY* each of the discoidal expansions of a motor nerve where its branches terminate on a muscle fibre; **endplay** a method of play employed in the last few tricks of a game of bridge in order to force an opponent into making a disadvantageous discard or lead; **end point** (***a***) the final stage of a process, period, etc.; *CHEMISTRY* the point in a titration (usu. marked by a colour change) at which a reaction is complete; (***b***) a point at the end of a line; **end product** a final product, esp. of a radioactive decay series or a manufacturing process; **end result** the final outcome; **end run** *US* (***a***) *FOOTBALL* an attempt to run with the ball round one flank of the team; (***b***) an evasive tactic, esp. in war or politics; **end-scraper** *ARCHAEOLOGY* a flint scraper whose working edge is at one end of a blade or flake, transverse to the long axis; **end standard** a standard of length in the form of a metal bar or block, two of whose faces are the standard distance apart; **end-stopped** *adjective* (of verse) having a pause at the end of each line; **end user** the ultimate user of a product; **end zone** *N. Amer.* (***a***) the rectangular area at each end of a football field between the end line and the goal line; (***b***) in ice hockey, a section at each end of a rink extending from the neutral zone to the goal line.

end /ɛnd/ *verb*[1].
[ORIGIN Old English *endian* = Old Frisian *endia*, Old Saxon *endiōn* (Dutch *einden*), Old High German *entōn* (German *enden*), Old Norse *enda*.]
†**1** *verb trans.* Finish, complete. OE–M18.
2 *verb trans.* Put an end to, cause to cease; destroy. OE. ▸†**b** Kill. ME–E17.

SOUTHEY That merciful deed For ever ends thy suffering.

3 *verb intrans.* Come to an end. OE. ▸**b** Foll. by *in*: have as its result or conclusion; lead to. ME. ▸**c** Die. Now *rare*. ME. ▸**d** Come eventually to a specified state. Usu. foll. by *up*. L19.

J. BUCHAN Before the War ended I was travelling far and wide. **b** H. J. LASKI Political life, like human life, ends in death. **d** G. GREENE Englishmen who have started with the idea of attacking apartheid and ended trapped . . in a Bantu girl's bed. J. JOHNSTON Sometimes good people end up in prison.

4 *verb trans.* Bring to an end, conclude, (an action, speech, one's life, etc.). ME.

G. BERKELEY We ended the day with music at St. Agnes. R. BROOKE Night ends all things.

5 *verb intrans.* Of a portion of space, an object, etc.: terminate, have its end or extremity. LME.

SCOTT FITZGERALD There was a sharp line where my ragged lawn ended. J. FOWLES The beach ended in a fall of rocks.

— PHRASES, & WITH ADVERBS IN SPECIALIZED SENSES: **end by doing** come eventually to do. **end it (all)** *colloq.* commit suicide. ***end one's days***: see DAY *noun*. ***end or mend***, ***mend or end***: see MEND *verb*. **end up** put on end; (see also sense 3d above). ***war to end war(s)***: see WAR *noun*[1].

■ **ender** *noun* LME.

end /ɛnd/ *verb*[2] *trans. obsolete* exc. *dial.* E17.
[ORIGIN Uncertain: perh. dial. var. or corruption of IN *verb*, infl. by END *verb*[1].]
Put (corn etc.) into a barn; make into a haystack; get in.

end- *combining form* see ENDO-.

-end /ɛnd/ *suffix*.
Repr. Latin *-endus*, *-da*, *-dum*, of the gerundive of verbs in *-ere*, forming nouns usu. with the sense 'person (or thing) to be treated in a specified way', as ***addend***, ***dividend***. The neut. gerundial ending is sometimes retained as in ***addendum***, ***agendum***, etc.

end-all /ˈɛndɔːl/ *adjective & noun*. LME.
[ORIGIN from END *verb*[1] + ALL *pronoun*.]
▸ †**A** *adjective*. Ultimate, absolute. Only in LME.
▸ **B** *noun*. A thing that ends everything or is final; *the* supreme purpose or thing of significance. Chiefly in ***the BE-ALL and end-all***. E17.

endamage /ɪnˈdamɪdʒ, ɛn-/ *verb trans*. LME.
[ORIGIN from EN-[1] + DAMAGE *noun*.]
1 Affect adversely, harm. LME.
†**2** Inflict material injury or damage on; damage, spoil. L15–E19.
■ **endamagement** *noun* the action of endamaging; the state of being endamaged: L16.

endanger /ɪnˈdeɪn(d)ʒə, ɛn-/ *verb trans*. Also †**in-**. LME.
[ORIGIN from EN-[1], IN-[2] + DANGER *noun*.]
†**1** Expose (a person) to infringement of his or her rights; make liable to punishment by another person. Usu. in *pass.* (foll. by *to* the other person). LME–L16.
2 Put in danger. E16. ▸†**b** Make (a person) liable *to do*; put in peril *of doing*. M16–M18.

E. ROOSEVELT An epidemic that might endanger everybody in that area. F. HERBERT No woman wants her loved ones endangered.

endangered species: in danger of becoming extinct.
†**3** Subject (a person) to the will of another. M–L16.
†**4** Incur the risk of, chance. L16–L18.

ADDISON Unless they turned back quickly they would endanger being benighted.

†**5** Cause the danger of, make probable, (something untoward). E17–L18.

SOUTHEY So as to endanger setting it on fire.

■ **endangerer** *noun* L17. **endangerment** *noun* the action of endangering; the state of being endangered: L16.

endarch /ˈɛndɑːk/ *adjective*. E20.
[ORIGIN from ENDO- + Greek *arkhē* beginning, origin.]
BOTANY. Of xylem or its development: formed or occurring from the centre of a stem towards the periphery.

endarken /ɪnˈdɑːk(ə)n/ *verb trans*. Now *rare*. L16.
[ORIGIN from EN-[1] + DARKEN.]
Make dark, obscure (*lit.* & *fig.*).

†**endart** *verb* var. of INDART.

endarterectomy /ˌɛndɑːtəˈrɛktəmi/ *noun*. M20.
[ORIGIN from ENDO- + ARTERY + -ECTOMY.]
Surgical removal of part of the inner lining of an artery; an instance of this.

endarteritis /ˌɛndɑːtəˈrʌɪtɪs/ *noun*. L19.
[ORIGIN from ENDO- + ARTERITIS.]
MEDICINE. Inflammation of the inner lining of an artery.

endaspidean /ɛndəˈspɪdɪən/ *adjective*. L19.
[ORIGIN from mod. Latin *Endaspideae*, obsolete taxonomic name, formed as ENDO- + Greek *aspid-*, *aspis* shield: see -AN.]
Possessing or designating a bird's tarsal sheath with an anterior series of scutella on its outer side.

en daube /ɑ̃ doːb/ *adverbial phr*. E20.
[ORIGIN French.]
Stewed, braised.

endear /ɪnˈdɪə, ɛn-/ *verb trans*. Also †**in-**. L16.
[ORIGIN from EN-[1], IN-[2] + DEAR *adjective*[1], after French *enchérir* (from *en* + *cher* dear).]
†**1** Enhance the price or value of. L16–E19. ▸**b** Represent as valuable or important; exaggerate. E–M17.
†**2** Win the affection of; deepen (affection). L16–E18. ▸**b** Bind by obligation of gratitude. E–M17.
3 Make dear *to* someone; create affection for (a person or thing). E17.

H. KELLER The tenderness and sympathy which endeared Dr. Bell to so many hearts. P. USTINOV He immediately endeared himself to the liberal elements in his entourage.

†**4** Hold dear; treat affectionately. E17–E18.
■ **endearance** *noun* (*rare*) the action of endearing; the state of being endeared: M18. **endearing** *ppl adjective* inspiring or manifesting affection M17. **endearingly** *adverb* E18.

endearment /ɪnˈdɪəm(ə)nt, ɛn-/ *noun*. Also †**in-**. E17.
[ORIGIN from ENDEAR + -MENT.]
†**1** An enhancement; an exaggeration. Only in E17.
†**2** An obligation of gratitude. Only in 17.
3 The action of endearing; the fact of being endeared. Also, a thing that endears. M17.
4 An expression of love or fondness; a caress. E18.

D. LODGE Hero and heroine were exchanging husky endearments.

†**5** Affection, fondness. E18–E19.

endeavour /ɪnˈdɛvə, ɛn-/ *verb & noun*. Also ***-or**, †**in-**. LME.
[ORIGIN from ***put oneself in devoir*** S.V. DEVOIR 2: see -OUR.]
▸ **A** *verb*. †**1** *verb refl.* & *intrans.* Exert oneself. LME–M17.
†**2** *verb trans.* Exert (one's power, thoughts, etc.). *rare*. L16–M17.
3 *verb intrans.* Try, make an effort for a specified object; attempt strenuously (*to do*). L16.

J. S. MILL If we are endeavouring after more riches. T. HARDY Charlotte vainly endeavoured to hide her confusion.

4 *verb trans.* Use effort for; attempt (an action). Long *arch.* L16.
▸ **B** *noun*. The action of endeavouring; effort directed to attain an object; a strenuous attempt. LME.

COLERIDGE O Liberty! with profitless endeavour Have I pursued thee. T. E. LAWRENCE My determined endeavour is to scrape through with it. E. V. KNOX Fumbling with the screws of the windscreen, an endeavour which I have long proved to be vain.

do one's endeavour(s) do one's best, do all one can.
■ **endeavourer** *noun* †(**a**) a person who endeavours; (**b**) in full ***Christian Endeavourer***, a member of the Young People's Society of Christian Endeavour, a religious association begun in the US in 1881: L16.

†**endebted** *ppl adjective* var. of INDEBTED.

endeca- *combining form*, **endecasyllable** *noun*, etc., vars. of HENDECA- etc.

endeictic /ɛnˈdʌɪktɪk/ *adjective*. M17.
[ORIGIN Greek *endeiktikos* probative, indicative, from *endeiknunai* point out: see -IC. Cf. APODEICTIC, DEICTIC.]
Serving to show or demonstrate.

endemial /ɛnˈdiːmɪəl, ɪn-/ *adjective*. Now *rare* or *obsolete*. L17.
[ORIGIN from Greek *endēmios* (see ENDEMIC) + -AL[1].]
= ENDEMIC *adjective*.

endemic /ɛnˈdɛmɪk/ *noun & adjective*. M17.
[ORIGIN French *endémique* or mod. Latin *endemicus*, from Greek *endēm(i)os*, pertaining to a people, native, formed as EN-[2] + *dēmos* people: see -IC.]
▸ **A** *noun*. **1** An endemic disease. M17.
2 An endemic plant or animal. M20.
▸ **B** *adjective*. **1** (Of a disease, condition, etc.) habitually present in a certain area as a result of permanent local factors; of common occurrence; rife. E18.

J. G. COZZENS An occupational disease, endemic among social-service workers. L. NAMIER Hurricanes and slave troubles were endemic to the West Indies. G. STEINER Barbarism and political savagery are endemic in human affairs. D. ACHESON Curfews, 'roundups', and arrests became endemic.

2 Of a plant or animal: native to, and esp. restricted to, a certain country or area. M19.
■ **endemical** *adjective* = ENDEMIC *adjective* 1 M17. **endemically** *adverb* in an endemic manner; habitually: M17. **endemicity** /ɛndɪˈmɪsɪti/ *noun* the condition or fact of being endemic L19. **endemism** /ˈɛndɪmɪz(ə)m/ *noun* endemicity, esp. as regards the geographical distribution of plants and animals L19.

endenization /ɪnˌdɛnʌɪˈzeɪʃ(ə)n, ɛn-/ *noun*. Now *rare*. L16.
[ORIGIN from ENDENIZE + -ATION.]
The process of making someone a denizen; naturalization, enfranchisement; the fact of being endenizened.

†**endenize** *verb trans*. L16.
[ORIGIN Alt. of ENDENIZEN with assim. to verbs in -IZE.]
1 = ENDENIZEN. L16–M18.
2 Spirit away; change into superhuman form. E–M17.

endenizen /ɪnˈdɛnɪz(ə)n, ɛn-/ *verb trans*. L16.
[ORIGIN from EN-[1] + DENIZEN *noun*.]
Make a denizen or citizen; naturalize (*lit.* & *fig.*), enfranchise.

endergonic /ɛndəːˈɡɒnɪk/ *adjective*. M20.
[ORIGIN from ENDO- + Greek *ergon* work + -IC.]
SCIENCE. Accompanied by the absorption of energy.

endermic /ɛnˈdəːmɪk/ *adjective*. M19.
[ORIGIN from EN-[2] + Greek *derma* skin + -IC.]
MEDICINE. Acting on or through the skin.
■ **endermically** *adverb* M19.

en déshabillé /ɒ̃ deɪzaˈbiːjeɪ, *foreign* ɑ̃ dezabije/ *adjectival & adverbial phr.* Also anglicized as **in dishabille** /ɪn dɪsəˈbiːl/. L17.
[ORIGIN French, from *en* IN *preposition* + *déshabillé* DISHABILLE.]
In a state of undress or of partial dress.

endian /ˈɛndɪən/ *adjective*. L20.
[ORIGIN from Swift's *Gulliver's Travels*, in which *big-endians* and *little-endians* ate boiled eggs by breaking the 'big' end or 'little' end respectively.]
COMPUTING. ***Big-endian***, ***little-endian***, designating a system of ordering bytes in a word, or bits in a byte, in which the most significant (or least significant) item is put first.

ending /ˈɛndɪŋ/ *noun*. OE.
[ORIGIN from END *verb*[1] + -ING[1].]
1 The action of END *verb*[1]; an instance of this; termination, conclusion, completion, etc. OE.

E

W. MORRIS A fair ending crowned a troublous day.

2 A concluding or terminating part, esp. of a literary work, metrical line, or piece of music. Also, an inflectional or formative suffix. ME.
happy ending: see HAPPY *adjective*. ***weak ending***: see WEAK *adjective*.
■ **endingless** *adjective* M20.

ending /ˈɛndɪŋ/ *ppl adjective*. ME.
[ORIGIN from END *verb*[1] + -ING[2].]
1 That ends; final. ME.
†**2** Dying. *rare* (Shakes.). Only in L16.

en dishabille *adjectival & adverbial phr.* see EN DÉSHABILLÉ.

endite /ˈɛndʌɪt/ *noun*. L19.
[ORIGIN from ENDO- + -ITE[1].]
ZOOLOGY. An appendage on the inner side of a crustacean limb.

†**endite** *verb*[1] see INDICT *verb*[1].

†**endite** *verb*[2] see INDITE *verb*[1].

†**enditement** *noun* see INDICTMENT.

endive /ˈɛndʌɪv, -dɪv/ *noun*. LME.
[ORIGIN Old French & mod. French from medieval Latin *endivia* from medieval Greek *indibi* from Latin *intibum* from Greek *entubon*.]
†**1** A sowthistle; some similar yellow-flowered plant. Only in LME.
2 (The blanched leaves of) a blue-flowered plant of the composite family, *Cichorium endivia*, grown as a salad (chiefly in a form with curled much-dissected leaves) or as a vegetable (in a form with wavy undivided leaves, more fully ***Batavian endive***, ***broadleaved endive***). Also (in full ***wild endive***), the wild form of the related plant, chicory, *Cichorium intybus*. LME.
3 Blanched chicory crowns. Also ***French endive***. Chiefly *N. Amer.* M20.

endless /ˈɛndlɪs/ *adjective & adverb*. OE.
[ORIGIN from END *noun* + -LESS.]
▸ **A** *adjective*. **1** Having no end in (future) time, eternal. OE. ▸**b** Interminable, incessant. OE.

STEELE Death . . is a short Night, followed by an endless Day. **b** G. VIDAL A wild mountain clan, given to endless drinking bouts.

2 Having no end in space; boundless; of infinite length. LME.

W. BLACK The endless miles of moor. J. F. LEHMANN Airmen passed . . in endless streams.

3 Of an abstract thing, number, quality, etc.: boundless, infinite; *colloq.* innumerable, countless, unlimited. LME.

D. H. LAWRENCE He had brought them endless presents. A. THWAITE Her endless curiosity.

4 Of a belt, chain, etc.: made in the form of a loop, e.g. for continuous action round a set of wheels. E19.
▸ †**B** *adverb*. Infinitely, eternally. Only in ME.
■ **endlessly** *adverb* LME. **endlessness** *noun* (**a**) the quality of being endless; (**b**) a thing that has no end: ME.

endlong /ˈɛndlɒŋ/ *preposition, adverb, & adjective*. Now chiefly *N. English*.
[ORIGIN Old English *andlang* preposition (see ALONG *adjective*[2]), repl. in Middle English by forms partly from END *noun* + LONG *adjective*[1], partly from Old Norse *endlangr* adjective. Cf. -LONG.]
▸ **A** *preposition*. From end to end of; over the length of; along (as opp. to across). OE.
▸ **B** *adverb*. **1** From end to end, lengthwise. OE.
2 At full length; horizontally. *obsolete* exc. *N. English*. LME.
3 Straight on, straight through. *obsolete* exc. *N. English*. LME.
4 On end, vertically. E17.
▸ **C** *adjective*. **1** Extended lengthwise. *obsolete* exc. *N. English*. L15.
2 Set on end, perpendicular. *rare*. E18.

endmost /ˈɛndməʊst/ *adjective*. OE.
[ORIGIN from END *noun* + -MOST.]
Nearest to the end, furthest, most distant.

endo- /ˈɛndəʊ/ *combining form*. Before a vowel also **end-**.
[ORIGIN Repr. Greek *endon* within: see -O-.]
Internal, inner; inside.
■ **endoatmosˈpheric** *adjective* occurring or operating within the atmosphere L20. **endoˈcardial** *adjective* †(**a**) situated within the heart; (**b**) of or pertaining to the endocardium: M19.

endocar'ditic *adjective* affected with or suffering from endocarditis **M19**. **endocar'ditis** *noun* inflammation of the lining membrane of the heart, esp. that of the valves **M19**. **endo'cardium** *noun*, pl. **-dia**, the smooth membrane lining the cavities and valves of the heart **L19**. **endocarp** *noun* (BOTANY) the inner layer of the pericarp of a fruit, which lines the seed chamber **E19**. **endo'centric** *adjective* (LINGUISTICS) designating a compound or construction whose distribution is the same as that of one of its constituents **M20**. **endocervical** /-'sɜːvɪk(ə)l, -sə'vʌɪk(ə)l/ *adjective* situated or occurring within the cervix of the womb **E20**. **endo'cervix** *noun* (ANATOMY) the mucous membrane lining of the cervix of the womb **M20**. **endo'cranial** *adjective* of or pertaining to the cavity or inside of the skull (***endocranial cast***, a cast of this cavity, taken as a guide to the size and shape of the brain) **L19**. **endocuticle**, **-'ticula** *noun* (***a***) the flexible laminated inner part of the arthropod procuticle; (***b***) the inner part of the cuticle surrounding animal hairs: **E20**. **endo'cyclic** *adjective* (CHEMISTRY) situated inside a ring **E20**. **endocytose** /-'sʌɪtəʊz/ *verb trans.* (BIOLOGY) take in by endocytosis, engulf **L20**. **endocytosis** /-sʌɪ'təʊsɪs/ *noun* (BIOLOGY) the taking in of matter by a living cell by invagination of its membrane **M20**. **endocytotic** /-sʌɪ'tɒtɪk/ *adjective* of, pertaining to, or formed by endocytosis **L20**. **endo'dontal** *adjective* = ENDODONTIC **M20**. **endo'dontia** *noun* = ENDODONTICS **M20**. **endo'dontic** *adjective* of or pertaining to endodontics **M20**. **endo'dontically** *adverb* according to endodontic methods **M20**. **endo'dontics** *noun* the branch of dentistry that deals with the tooth pulp and its diseases **M20**. **endo'dontist** *noun* a practitioner or specialist in endodontics **M20**. **endoenzyme** *noun* (***a***) (now *rare*) an enzyme which acts within the cell producing it; (***b***) an enzyme which breaks bonds other than terminal ones in a long-chain molecule: **E20**. **endo'ergic** *adjective* (SCIENCE) = ENDERGONIC **M20**. **endo'glossic** *adjective* pertaining to or involving the use of a country's native language, esp. where this is not one of the world's major languages **L20**. **endo'lithic** *adjective* (***a***) containing a design on stone that extends inwards; (***b***) (BIOLOGY) living in or penetrating into stone: **L19**. **endolymph** *noun* the fluid in the membranous labyrinth of the ear **M19**. **endolym'phatic** *adjective* of, pertaining to, or containing endolymph **L19**. **endometrial** /-'miːt-/ *adjective* of or pertaining to the endometrium **M19**. **endometri'osis** /-miːt-/ *noun* (a condition marked by) the occurrence of endometrial tissue outside the womb **E20**. **endometriotic** /-miːtrɪ'ɒtɪk/ *adjective* of or pertaining to endometriosis **M20**. **endometritis** /-mɪ'trʌɪtɪs/ *noun* inflammation of the endometrium **L19**. **endometrium** /-'miːt-/ *noun* [Greek *mētra* womb] the mucous membrane lining the womb **L19**. **endomi'tosis** *noun*, pl. **-toses** /-'təʊsiːz/, BIOLOGY division of chromosomes in a cell nucleus without the subsequent division of the nucleus, giving rise to polyploidy **M20**. **endomitotic** /-'tɒt-/ *adjective* (BIOLOGY) pertaining to or involving endomitosis **M20**. **endo'mixis** *noun* (BIOLOGY) nuclear disintegration and re-formation without conjugation in some lower ciliates **E20**. **endo'normative** *adjective* (LINGUISTICS) drawing on usage within a language for models or standards **M20**. **endo'nuclease** *noun* (BIOCHEMISTRY) an enzyme which cleaves a polynucleotide chain by separating nucleotides other than the two end ones **M20**. **endonucleo'lytic** *adjective* (BIOCHEMISTRY) pertaining to or involving the removal of a nucleotide from a polynucleotide molecule other than from the end **M20**. **endonucleo'lytically** *adverb* (BIOCHEMISTRY) in an endonucleolytic manner **L20**. **endo'parasite** *noun* a parasite that lives in the internal organs of its host **L19**. **endopara'sitic** *adjective* of, pertaining to, or being an endoparasite **L19**. **endo'peptidase** *noun* (BIOCHEMISTRY) an enzyme which breaks peptide bonds other than terminal ones in a peptide chain **M20**. **endophyte** *noun* †(***a***) *rare* the part of a tree inside the bark; (***b***) a plant which lives inside another plant: **M19**. **endophytic** /-'fɪtɪk/ *adjective* of, pertaining to, or being an endophyte **L19**. **endopod**, **en'dopodite** *nouns* (ZOOLOGY) the inner branch of a biramous limb or appendage in some crustaceans **L19**. **endo'polyploid** *adjective* (GENETICS) exhibiting endopolyploidy **M20**. **endo'polyploidy** *noun* (GENETICS) polyploidy that is due to endomitosis **M20**. **endo'psychic** *adjective* contained or occurring in the mind **E20**. **endopterygote** /ɛndɒp'tɛrɪgəʊt/ *adjective & noun* (ZOOLOGY) (designating) an insect whose wings develop internally at first and which passes through a pupal stage **E20**. **endo'skeletal** *adjective* of or pertaining to an endoskeleton; of the nature of or having an endoskeleton: **L19**. **endoskeleton** *noun* a skeleton inside the body, as in vertebrates **M19**. **endosome** *noun* (***a***) *rare* the central part of some sponges; (***b***) a body of chromatin in the nucleus of some cells; a nucleolus: **L19**. **endosperm** *noun* nutritive material surrounding the embryo in some plant seeds **M19**. **endo'spermic** *adjective* of or pertaining to endosperm **L19**. **endospore** *noun* (***a***) the inner layer of the membrane or wall of some spores; (***b***) a spore formed in a case or theca; a naked spore before it develops a cell wall; (***c***) a resistant asexual spore that develops inside a vegetative bacterial cell: **L19**. **en'dosteal** *adjective* (***a***) of or pertaining to the endosteum; (***b***) situated in or derived from the inside of a bone: **M19**. **en'dosteally** *adverb* inside a bone **L19**. **en'dosteum** *noun*, pl. **-stea**, a layer of vascular tissue lining the cavity that is present in some bones **L19**. **endostyle** *noun* (ZOOLOGY) a groove in the pharynx of some lower chordates that secretes mucus that aids the ingestion of food particles **M19**. **endo'sulfan** *noun* a sulphur-containing compound used as an insecticide on fruit, vegetables, and forage **M20**. **endo'symbiont** *noun* an endosymbiotic organism **M20**. **endosymbi'osis** *noun* symbiosis in which one of the symbiotic organisms lives inside the other **M20**. **endosymbi'otic** *adjective* of or pertaining to endosymbiosis; (of an organism) living in such a relationship: **M20**. **endosymbi'otically** *adverb* in an endosymbiotic manner **L20**. **endo'toxic** *adjective* of, pertaining to, or caused by an endotoxin **E20**. **endo'toxin** *noun* a toxin present in a bacterial cell, *esp.* one that is released only when the cell disintegrates **E20**. **endotracheal** /-'treɪkɪəl, -trə'kiːəl/ *adjective* situated or occurring within the trachea; performed by way of the trachea: **L19**. **endotracheally** /-'treɪkɪəli, -trə'kiːəli/ *adverb* by way of the trachea **M20**. **endotrophic** /-'trəʊfɪk, -'trɒfɪk/ *adjective* BOTANY (of a mycorrhiza) penetrating into a root **L19**.

endocrine /'ɛndəkrʌɪn, -krɪn/ *adjective & noun*. **E20**.
[ORIGIN from ENDO- + Greek *krinein* to separate.]
PHYSIOLOGY. ▸**A** *adjective*. Designating a gland that secretes directly into the blood or lymph; of or pertaining to such glands or their secretions (hormones). Cf. EXOCRINE. **E20**.
▸**B** *noun*. An endocrine gland. **E20**.

■ **endocrino'logic** (chiefly *US*), **endocrino'logical** *adjectives* of or pertaining to endocrinology **M20**. **endocrino'logically** *adverb* as regards the endocrine glands or their activity **M20**. **endocri'nologist** *noun* an expert in or student of endocrinology **M20**. **endocri'nology** *noun* the branch of medicine that deals with the endocrine glands and hormones **E20**.

†**endoctrinate** *verb* see INDOCTRINATE.

†**endoctrine** *verb* see INDOCTRINE.

endoderm /'ɛndədɜːm/ *noun*. **M19**.
[ORIGIN from ENDO- + Greek *derma* skin.]
1 BIOLOGY. The inner germ layer of the embryo in early development; cells or tissue derived from this; such cells as forming the lining of the cavity of coelenterates. **M19**.
2 BOTANY. = ENDODERMIS. Formerly, a layer of cambium between phloem and xylem. **M19**.

endodermal /ɛndəʊ'dɜːm(ə)l/ *adjective*. **L19**.
[ORIGIN from ENDODERM and ENDODERMIS + -AL¹.]
Pertaining to or of the nature of endoderm or endodermis; derived from endoderm.
■ Also **endo'dermic** *adjective* **L19**.

endodermis /ɛndəʊ'dɜːmɪs/ *noun*. **L19**.
[ORIGIN from ENDODERM after *epidermis*.]
BOTANY. An inner layer of cells in the cortex of a root and of some stems, surrounding a vascular bundle.

endogamy /ɛn'dɒgəmi/ *noun*. **M19**.
[ORIGIN from ENDO- + -GAMY, after POLYGAMY.]
1 ANTHROPOLOGY. The custom of marrying only within the limits of a local community, clan, or tribe. **M19**.
2 BIOLOGY. The fusion of reproductive cells from related individuals. **E20**.
■ **endo'gamic** *adjective* of or pertaining to endogamy **L19**. **endogamous** *adjective* practising endogamy; of or pertaining to endogamy: **M19**.

endogen /'ɛndədʒ(ə)n/ *noun*. Now *rare* or *obsolete*. **M19**.
[ORIGIN French *endogène*, formed as ENDO-: see -GEN.]
BOTANY. A plant whose stem grows by the development of new material inside it, with no differentiation into wood and bark.

endogenetic /ˌɛndəʊdʒɪ'nɛtɪk/ *adjective*. **L19**.
[ORIGIN from ENDO- + -GENETIC.]
1 SCIENCE. Having an internal cause or origin. **L19**.
2 GEOLOGY. Formed or occurring inside the earth. **E20**.
■ **endo'genesis** *noun* = ENDOGENY **L19**.

endogenic /ɛndəʊ'dʒɛnɪk/ *adjective*. **M20**.
[ORIGIN from ENDO- + -GENIC.]
GEOLOGY. = ENDOGENETIC 2.

endogenous /ɛn'dɒdʒɪnəs, ɪn-/ *adjective*. **M19**.
[ORIGIN formed as ENDOGEN: see -GENOUS.]
1 BOTANY. Of, pertaining to, or designating a plant that grows by developing new material inside it. Now *rare* or *obsolete*. **M19**.
2 GEOLOGY. Formed or occurring within some structure or rock mass; *esp.* = ENDOGENETIC 2; BOTANY developing from deep rather than superficial tissue. **M19**.
3 Having an internal cause or origin; *spec.* (MEDICINE & PSYCHIATRY) having a cause inside the body or self, not attributable to any external or environmental factor. **L19**.

M. C. GERALD Endogenous depression is said to exist when the precipitating factors are not known.

■ **endogenously** *adverb* **M19**. **endogeny** *noun* growth or development from within **L19**.

endomorph /'ɛndə(ʊ)mɔːf/ *noun*. **L19**.
[ORIGIN from ENDO- + -MORPH.]
1 A mineral or crystal surrounded by a different mineral. **L19**.
2 A person whose build is soft and round (with noticeable development of tissue derived from embryonic endoderm, as viscera). **M20**.
■ **endo'morphic** *adjective* of, pertaining to, or characteristic of an endomorph; of the nature of an endomorph: **L19**. **endomorphy** *noun* the state or property of being an endomorph **M20**.

endomorphism /ɛndəʊ'mɔːfɪz(ə)m/ *noun*. **E20**.
[ORIGIN French *endomorphisme*, formed as ENDOMORPH: see -ISM.]
1 GEOLOGY. The alteration of cooling molten rock by reaction with the surrounding rock mass or assimilation of fragments of it. **E20**.
2 MATH. A homomorphism of a set into itself. **M20**.

endophora /ɛn'dɒfərə/ *noun*. **L20**.
[ORIGIN from ENDO- after *anaphora*.]
LINGUISTICS. An endophoric reference or relation.

endophoric /ɛndə'fɒrɪk/ *adjective*. **L20**.
[ORIGIN from ENDOPHORA + -IC.]
LINGUISTICS. Referring to something within the text.

endoplasm /'ɛndəplaz(ə)m/ *noun*. **L19**.
[ORIGIN from ENDO- + -PLASM.]
BIOLOGY. The inner, usu. granular, part of the cytoplasm of some cells, e.g. amoebae.
■ **endo'plasmic** *adjective* of, pertaining to, or occurring in endoplasm; chiefly in ***endoplasmic reticulum***, a network of membranes in the cytoplasm of a cell, involved in protein and lipid synthesis **M20**.

endorphin /ɛn'dɔːfɪn/ *noun*. **L20**.
[ORIGIN from END(OGENOUS + M)ORPHIN(E).]
Any of a group of peptides that occur in the brain and bind to the same receptors as morphine, thereby inhibiting pain.

endorsation *noun* see INDORSATION.

endorse /ɪn'dɔːs, ɛn-/ *noun*. **L16**.
[ORIGIN App. from the verb.]
HERALDRY. A vertical stripe borne on either side of a pale and having a width one-quarter (sometimes one-eighth) that of the pale.

endorse /ɪn'dɔːs, ɛn-/ *verb trans.* Also **in-** /ɪn-/. **L15**.
[ORIGIN medieval Latin *indorsare* from Latin IN-² + *dorsum* back. Superseded earlier ENDOSS.]
▸**I 1** Write a supplementary or official comment or instruction on (a document), esp. on the back, often to extend or limit its provisions; *spec.* sign (a bill of exchange) on the back to accept responsibility for paying it; sign (a cheque) on the back to make it payable to someone other than the stated payee. Also, write (a comment etc.) *on* a document; inscribe (a document) *with* (a comment etc.); make (a bill etc.) payable *to* another person by a signature on the back. **L15**.

SIR W. SCOTT Pointing out the royal warrant indorsed thereon. DICKENS We will indorse the parcel 'Pay the porter 2/6 extra for immediate delivery.' G. ORWELL For distances of less than a hundred kilometres it was not necessary to get your passport endorsed.

†**2** With double obj.: describe (a person) as; represent as being. **L16–M17**.
3 Confirm (a statement, opinion, etc.); declare one's approval of; vouch for. **M17**.

Time Green groups have endorsed methane as a cleaner-burning alternative to coal and oil.

4 Make a record of an offence on (a licence, esp. a driving licence). **M19**. ▸**b** *hist.* In *pass.* Of a black person in South Africa: be moved out of an urban area because of not satisfying the conditions that would qualify him or her to continue living there. Usu. foll. by *out of*. **M20**.
▸**II 5** HERALDRY. As **endorsed** pa. pple. ▸**a** = ADDORSED. **E16**. ▸**b** Of wings: turned back to back. **M18**. ▸**c** Of a pale: placed between two endorses. **M19**.
6 Load the back of (an animal) *with*. **L17**.

MILTON Elephants indorsed with towers.

■ **endorsable** *adjective* able to be endorsed; transferable by endorsement; (of an offence) incurring the endorsement of the offender's driving licence: **M18**. **endor'see** *noun* a person to whom a bill etc. is assigned by endorsement **M18**. **endorser** *noun* **L17**. **endorsible** *adjective* (now *rare*) = ENDORSABLE **E18**.

endorsement /ɪn'dɔːsm(ə)nt, ɛn-/ *noun*. Also **in-** /ɪn-/. **M16**.
[ORIGIN from ENDORSE *verb* + -MENT.]
1 A comment, signature, etc., with which a document is endorsed; the action or an act of endorsing. **M16**. ▸**b** A record of an offence entered on a licence, esp. a driving licence. **E20**.
2 Confirmation, ratification; approving testimony; an approving comment. **M17**.

R. L. STEVENSON I give the statement as Mackay's, without endorsement. D. BROWN The group enjoyed the full endorsement and blessing of the Vatican.

endoscope /'ɛndəskəʊp/ *noun*. **M19**.
[ORIGIN from ENDO- + -SCOPE.]
MEDICINE. An instrument that can be introduced into the body to give a view of the inside of an organ.
■ **endo'scopic** *adjective* **M19**. **endo'scopically** *adverb* **M20**. **en'doscopist** *noun* a person who uses an endoscope **M20**. **en'doscopy** *noun* the use of an endoscope **M19**.

endosmosis /ɛndɒz'məʊsɪs/ *noun*. Orig. (now *rare* or *obsolete*) **endosmose** /'ɛndɒzməʊz/. **E19**.
[ORIGIN French *endosmose*, formed as ENDO- + Greek *ōsmos* pushing: see -OSIS.]
Osmotic diffusion of solvent or solute into a vessel or cell.
■ **endos'motic** *adjective* **M19**. **endos'motically** *adverb* **L19**.

†**endoss** *verb trans.* **LME**.
[ORIGIN Old French & mod. French *endosser*, formed as EN-¹ + *dos* back. Repl. by ENDORSE *verb*.]
1 Write on the back of (a document); write (words) *on* a document. **LME–E17**.
2 Inscribe or portray on any surface. **LME–L16**.
3 Put (clothing) on one's back. *rare*. **LME–E19**.

endothelium /ɛndə(ʊ)'θiːlɪəm/ *noun*. Pl. **-ia** /-ɪə/. **L19**.
[ORIGIN mod. Latin, from ENDO- + Greek *thēlē* nipple + -IUM.]
ANATOMY. The layer of cells lining the blood vessels, the heart, and the lymphatic vessels. Also, the layer of cells lining serous cavities (cf. MESOTHELIUM).
■ **endothelial** *adjective* **L19**. **endotheli'oma** *noun*, pl. **-mas**, **-mata** /-mətə/, a tumour developing from endothelial tissue **L19**. **endotheli'omatous** *adjective* of or resembling an endothelioma **E20**.

endotherm /ˈɛndə(ʊ)θəːm/ *noun.* M20.
[ORIGIN from ENDO- after *homeotherm*.]
1 *ZOOLOGY.* An endothermic animal. M20.
2 *PHYSICAL CHEMISTRY.* A curve corresponding to an endothermic reaction. M20.

endothermic /ɛndəʊˈθəːmɪk/ *adjective.* L19.
[ORIGIN formed as ENDO- + THERMIC.]
1 *CHEMISTRY.* Accompanied by, or (of a compound) formed with, the absorption of heat. L19.
2 *ZOOLOGY.* Dependent on or capable of internal generation of heat. M20.

endothermy /ˈɛndəʊθəːmi/ *noun.* E20.
[ORIGIN from ENDO- + Greek *thermos* heat + -Y³.]
1 *MEDICINE.* = DIATHERMY. *rare.* E20.
2 *ZOOLOGY.* The internal generation of heat by the body of an animal as a means of controlling its temperature. M20.

endow /ɪnˈdaʊ, ɛn-/ *verb trans.* Also (earlier) †**in-**. LME.
[ORIGIN Legal Anglo-Norman *endouer*, formed as EN-¹ + Old French & mod. French *douer*, from Latin *dotare*, from *dot-*, *dos* dowry, rel. to *dare* give.]
1 Provide a dower for (a widow). Formerly also, give a dowry to (a woman). LME.
2 Enrich with property; bequeath or give a permanent income to (a person, institution, etc.); establish (a lectureship, annual prize, etc.) by providing the funds needed to maintain it. LME.

B. PYM Wealth could not be more nobly used than in . . endowing a number of fellowships.

3 Enrich or provide *with* an ability, talent, attribute, etc.; invest *with* a quality or (formerly) a privilege; in *pass.*, be possessed of or (*well* etc.) provided with talent or favourable qualities. Also foll. by †*in*, †*of*. LME.

R. L. STEVENSON Mentally, he was endowed above the average. J. I. M. STEWART The trade of playwright . . does endow one at times with something of the actor's assurance. A. STORR The patient endows the therapist with attributes which are predominantly parental. Q. BELL He was genial and well-endowed.

†**4** Of a personal attribute or quality: be inherent in (a person). *rare* (Shakes.). Only in E17.
■ **endower** *noun* L16.

endowment /ɪnˈdaʊm(ə)nt, ɛn-/ *noun.* Also †**in-**. LME.
[ORIGIN from ENDOW + -MENT.]
1 The action of endowing. LME.
2 An ability, talent, attribute, etc., with which a person is endowed. M16.

J. S. HUXLEY She was a person of great intellectual endowment.

3 The property or finance with which a person, institution, etc., is endowed. L16.

LD BRAIN Voluntary hospitals . . were supported by endowments and voluntary contributions.

– COMB.: **endowment assurance**, **endowment insurance** a form of life insurance providing for the payment of a sum to the insured on a specified date or to his or her estate on earlier death; **endowment mortgage**: in which the borrower pays interest only until an endowment policy matures, its proceeds then being used to repay the capital.

†**endrench** *verb* see INDRENCH.

endrin /ˈɛndrɪn/ *noun.* M20.
[ORIGIN from END(O- + DIELD)RIN.]
A chlorinated hydrocarbon insecticide, $C_{12}H_8Cl_6O$, a stereoisomer of dieldrin.

†**endship** *noun.* L16–E18.
[ORIGIN from END *noun* + -SHIP. Cf. *township*.]
A small suburb; a hamlet.

endsville /ˈɛn(d)zvɪl/ *noun. US slang.* Also **E-**. M20.
[ORIGIN from END *noun* + -S¹ + -VILLE.]
1 The greatest, the best; the imaginary home of good things or people. M20.
2 = *the end of the road* s.v. END *noun*. M20.

†**enduce** *verb* var. of INDUCE.

endue /ɪnˈdjuː, ɛn-/ *verb.* Also **in-** /ɪn-/. LME.
[ORIGIN Old French & mod. French *enduire*, partly from Latin *inducere* lead in (see INDUCE), partly formed as EN-¹ + *duire* from Latin *ducere* lead; assoc. in sense with Latin *induere* put on (clothes).]
†**1** *verb trans.* Induct into an ecclesiastical living or a lordship. Only in LME.
†**2** *verb trans.* & *intrans.* Orig. (of a hawk), pass (the contents of the crop), or the contents of (the crop), into the stomach. Later, digest (*lit.* & *fig.*). LME–E18.
3 *verb trans.* Orig., assume (a different form), take the form of. Later, put on (a garment). LME.

G. SANDYS Next, Phantasus . . indues a tree, Earth, water, stone. LYTTON Who had not yet endued his heavy mail.

4 *verb trans.* Clothe (a person). Usu. foll. by *with*. LME. ▸†**b** Overlay, cover. *rare.* M17–L18.
5 *verb trans.* †**a** = ENDOW 1, 2. LME–M17. ▸**b** Endow *with* an ability, talent, attribute, etc. Freq. in *pass.* LME. ▸†**c** Invest *with* an honour, dignity, etc. M–L16. ▸†**d** Supply *with* something. *rare* (Shakes.). L16–E17.

b J. BUTLER We know we are endued with capacities of action, of happiness and misery.

†**6** *verb trans.* Bring up, educate, instruct. Only in 16. ▸**b** Bring *to* a certain state or condition. *rare* (Shakes.). Only in E17.

endungeon /ɪnˈdʌndʒ(ə)n/ *verb trans. arch.* L16.
[ORIGIN from EN-¹ + DUNGEON *noun*.]
Put into or confine in a dungeon.

Endura /ɛnˈdjʊərə/ *noun.* L19.
[ORIGIN mod. Latin, from Old Provençal *endurar* endure, fast.]
ECCLESIASTICAL HISTORY. The physical privations (freq. fatal) undergone by the Cathars after consolamentum to prevent recontamination of the soul.

endurable /ɪnˈdjʊərəb(ə)l/ *adjective.* E17.
[ORIGIN from ENDURE + -ABLE.]
1 Capable of enduring, likely to endure; durable. Now *rare.* E17.

Blackwood's Magazine Rock-rooted castles, that seem endurable till the solid globe shall dissolve.

2 Able to be endured. E18.

J. UPDIKE Life . . was scarcely endurable—a torture of headaches, sleeplessness, . . and anxiety.

■ **endura'bility** *noun* (*rare*) M19. **endurableness** *noun* (*rare*) L18. **endurably** *adverb* (*rare*) E19.

endurance /ɪnˈdjʊər(ə)ns, ɛn-/ *noun.* Also †**in-**. L15.
[ORIGIN Old French & mod. French, from *endurer*: see ENDURE, -ANCE.]
1 Duration or continued existence in time; ability to last. L15. ▸†**b** Protraction of an existing condition. *rare* (Shakes.). Only in E17.

L. M. HAWKINS Sermons of four hours' endurance. M. ARNOLD This is why Byron's poetry had so little endurance in it.

2 Something which is endured; a hardship. M16.
3 The fact, habit, or power of enduring something unpleasant; long-suffering, patience. L16.

American Humorist Prolonging his visit beyond all endurance. F. KING He had a rare talent for endurance, bearing with insults and injuries . . with uncomplaining fortitude.

4 The ability of a thing to last or hold out; *esp.* the ability of a metal or other substance to withstand the repeated application of stress. L19.

Scientific American The spectacular endurance test . . when a Bellanca plane stayed aloft for 51 hours 11 minutes.

endure /ɪnˈdjʊə, ɛn-/ *verb.* Also †**in-**. ME.
[ORIGIN Old French & mod. French *endurer* from Latin *indurare* harden, from *in-* EN-¹ + *durus* hard.]
1 *verb trans.* & *intrans.* Undergo, bear, (pain, opposition, hardship, etc.), esp. without giving way. ME. ▸**b** Of a thing: withstand (strain, pressure, etc.) without being damaged; be subjected to. LME. ▸†**c** Withstand as an adversary; sustain. LME–E18.

G. GREENE So long as one is happy one can endure any discipline. M. L. KING A creature who could quietly endure, silently suffer and patiently wait. **c** DEFOE We were obliged to endure the whole weight of the imperial army.

†**2** *verb trans.* Harden (*lit.* & *fig.*); strengthen. LME–L16.
3 *verb intrans.* Remain in existence, last, persist. Formerly also, remain in a specified condition, place, etc. LME. ▸†**b** Be continued through space; extend from one point to another. Only in 16.

H. LATIMER So this great king endured a leper all the days of his life. H. KISSINGER Only those agreements endure which both sides have an interest in maintaining. R. SCRUTON Even at the point of death the will to live endures.

4 *verb trans.* Experience without resisting, submit to; bear, tolerate. Also foll. by *to do*, *that*. Freq. with neg. L15.

M. W. MONTAGU Men endure everything while they are in love. G. GREENE He longs to be off. He cannot endure this place.

†**5** *verb trans.* Permit of, be compatible with. L16–E19.
■ **endurant** *adjective* (*rare*) ready to endure; that endures or is capable of enduring: M19. †**endurement** *noun* the action of enduring; (a) hardship: E17–E18. **endurer** *noun* (*rare*) a person who endures something L16. **enduring** *ppl adjective* that lasts, that continues in existence or in the memory LME. **enduring** *preposition* (*obsolete* exc. *US dial.*) during LME. **enduringly** *adverb* M19. **enduringness** *noun* M19.

enduro /ɪnˈdjʊərəʊ, ɛn-/ *noun.* Pl. **-os**. M20.
[ORIGIN from ENDUR(ANCE + -O.]
A long-distance race for motor vehicles that is designed to test endurance rather than speed.

endways /ˈɛndweɪz/ *adverb.* Also (*rare*) **-way** /-weɪ/. LME.
[ORIGIN from END *noun* + -WAY, -WAYS.]
1 In the direction of the ends; end to end; lengthwise. LME.

J. SMEATON The stress upon the legs is always endways.

2 In a direct line, continuously. *obsolete* exc. *dial.* L16.
3 With the end foremost, uppermost, or towards the viewer. Also *endways on*. L17.

E. A. R. ENNION North Street, most of its . . houses endways on.

endwise /ˈɛndwʌɪz/ *adverb* & *adjective.* M17.
[ORIGIN from END *noun* + -WISE.]
▸ **A** *adverb.* **1** = ENDWAYS 3. M17.
2 = ENDWAYS 1. E19.
▸ **B** *adjective.* Acting or occurring endwise. L19.

ENE *abbreviation.*
East-north-east.

ene /iːn/ *adjective.* M20.
[ORIGIN from -ENE.]
CHEMISTRY. Designating a pericyclic reaction in which, in its simplest form, two alkene molecules rearrange to form one.

E

-ene /iːn/ *suffix.*
[ORIGIN Alt. of -INE⁵.]
1 *CHEMISTRY.* Forming the names of unsaturated hydrocarbons, as ***ethylene***, ***benzene***, ***naphthalene***; *spec.* denoting the presence of one double bond between carbon atoms (cf. DIENE, TRIENE).
2 Forming the names of synthetic or proprietary products, as ***corticene***.

en échelon /ɑ̃n eʃlɔ̃/ *adjectival & adverbial phr.* Also ***en e-***. E19.
[ORIGIN French.]
(Arranged) in an echelon. Cf. ***in echelon*** s.v. ECHELON *noun* 1.

enema /ˈɛnɪmə/ *noun.* Pl. **-mas**, **-mata** /-ˈmɑːtə/. LME.
[ORIGIN Late Latin from Greek, from *enienai* send or put in, inject, formed as EN-² + *hienai* send.]
MEDICINE. A quantity of liquid or gas forced into the rectum or colon, esp. to expel the contents; an act of introducing fluid in this way; a syringe or other appliance used for the purpose.
high enema: see HIGH *adjective*. ***low enema***: see LOW *adjective*.

enemy /ˈɛnəmi/ *noun* & *adjective.* ME.
[ORIGIN Old French *enemi* (mod. *ennemi*) from Latin *inimicus*, formed as IN-³ + *amicus* friend, friendly.]
▸ **A** *noun.* **1** A person who nurses hatred for or seeks to harm a person, group, or cause; an adversary, an antagonist. (Foll. by *of*, *to*.) ME. ▸**b** A thing which is prejudicial to something or counteracts its effect or influence. LME.

H. JAMES He had no enemies; he was an extremely amiable fellow, and universally liked. **b** W. PENN Vice, the Enemy of Religion.

2 A member of a hostile army or nation; an armed foe; a ship, aircraft, etc., of a hostile nation. ME.

G. BANCROFT All outside the family, tribe, or nation were usually held as enemies.

3 *The* hostile force; *the* army etc. of a nation at war with one's own. L16.

G. ORWELL Except at night, when a surprise attack was always conceivable, nobody bothered about the enemy.

4 ***the enemy***, time. Chiefly in ***how goes the enemy?*** *colloq.* M19.

– PHRASES: **be nobody's enemy but one's own** be responsible only for one's own misfortunes. **be one's own worst enemy** have the habit of bringing trouble upon oneself by one's own actions or behaviour. **enemy of the people**: a common form of indictment, esp. by Communist leaders, against a political opponent. **the enemy** (*a*) the Devil; (*b*) see sense 4 above. **the enemy of mankind** the Devil. **the great enemy**, **the last enemy** death. **the old enemy** the Devil.

▸ **B** *adjective.* †**1** Adverse, unfriendly, hostile. (Foll. by *to*, *with*.) ME–E18.

SWIFT Some evil genius, enemy to mankind.

2 Of or pertaining to a hostile force or nation. Now only *attrib.* LME.
enemy action, ***enemy hands***, ***enemy ship***, etc.

Eneolithic /iːnɪəˈlɪθɪk/ *adjective.* Also **Aen-**. E20.
[ORIGIN from Latin *aeneus* of copper or bronze + -O- + Greek *lithos* stone + -IC.]
ARCHAEOLOGY. = CHALCOLITHIC *adjective*.

energetic /ɛnəˈdʒɛtɪk/ *adjective.* M17.
[ORIGIN Greek *energētikos* active, from *energein* operate, effect, formed as EN-² + *ergon* work: see -IC.]
1 Powerfully operative or effective. *arch.* M17.

P. G. TAIT The most energetic chemicals.

2 Characterized by having much energy; strenuously active; forcible, vigorous. L18.

J. AUSTEN On the misery of what she had suffered . . she was energetic. G. B. SHAW Bursting into energetic action and shaking hands heartily. R. WEST An energetic woman, full of good sense and worldly wisdom.

3 *SCIENCE.* Of or pertaining to energy. E20.

energetical /ɛnəˈdʒɛtɪk(ə)l/ *adjective.* L16.
[ORIGIN formed as ENERGETIC + -AL¹.]
1 *PHILOSOPHY.* Operative, effective; active as opp. to passive. *arch.* L16.
†**2** = ENERGETIC 1. Only in M17.
3 = ENERGETIC 2. Now *rare.* M17.

energetically /ɛnəˈdʒɛtɪk(ə)li/ *adverb.* L18.
[ORIGIN from ENERGETIC or ENERGETICAL: see -ICALLY.]
1 In an energetic manner. L18.
2 SCIENCE. As regards energy; in terms of the energy released or required. M20.

Nature Membrane retrieval . . would be energetically a less costly process.

energetics /ɛnəˈdʒɛtɪks/ *noun.* M19.
[ORIGIN from ENERGETIC: see -ICS.]
1 The branch of science that deals with energy. M19.
2 The properties of a system as they concern its energy and its energy flows and changes. L19.

Nature Marsupials . . have acquired mammalian-type energetics.

E

energic /ɪˈnəːdʒɪk, ɛ-/ *adjective.* M17.
[ORIGIN from ENERGY + -IC.]
†**1** = ENERGETIC 1. M17–M18.
2 = ENERGETIC 2. Now *rare.* E18.
■ †**energical** *adjective* (*rare*) M16–E18.

energid /ˈɛnədʒɪd/ *noun.* Now *rare* or *obsolete.* L19.
[ORIGIN formed as ENERGY: see -ID².]
BIOLOGY. The nucleus of a cell and the cytoplasm with which it interacts.

energize /ˈɛnədʒʌɪz/ *verb.* Also **-ise**. M18.
[ORIGIN from ENERGY + -IZE.]
1 *verb trans.* Infuse energy into (a person, activity, etc.). M18. ▸**b** Supply energy, esp. by means of an electric current, for the operation of (a device). L19.

R. MAY You felt fear, and it energized you to rush for safety.

2 *verb intrans.* Expend energy, work; exercise one's powers. M18.
■ **energiˈzation** *noun* M20. **energizer** *noun* a person who or thing which energizes someone or something (*psychic energizer*: see PSYCHIC *adjective* 3) M18.

energumen /ɛnəˈgjuːmən/ *noun.* Also **-mene** /-miːn/. E18.
[ORIGIN Late Latin *energumenus*, from Greek *energoumenos* pa. pple of *energein* work in or upon, formed as EN-² + *ergon* work.]
1 A person believed to be possessed by the Devil or an evil spirit. E18.
2 A fanatic, a zealot. E18.
■ **eˌnerguˈmenical** *adjective* (*rare*) L17.

energy /ˈɛnədʒi/ *noun.* M16.
[ORIGIN French *énergie* or late Latin *energia* from Greek *energeia*, formed as EN-² + *ergon* work: see -Y³.]
1 Force or vigour of expression. M16.
2 The exercise of power; active operation, working. E17.
3 a *sing.* & in *pl.* Power actively and effectively used. M17. ▸**b** In *pl.* Individual powers in use; activities, exertions. M18.
4 (Latent) ability or capacity to produce an effect. L17.

J. R. LOWELL Institutions which could bear and breed such men as Lincoln and Emerson had surely some energy for good. A. KOESTLER A sparse, dark wiry figure, charged with nervous energy.

5 Vigour of action, utterance, etc.; a person's capacity for and tendency to strenuous exertion. E19.

L. HELLMAN The energy that had made us sprint into the zoo, running from monkey house to bird house. N. MITFORD They were eating up my time and energy in a perfectly shameless way.

6 SCIENCE. The ability to do work, i.e. move a body. Orig., that possessed by a body by virtue of its motion. E19. ▸**b** This ability provided in a readily utilized form, such as electric current or piped gas; resources that can be drawn on for this purpose. E20.

E. RUTHERFORD The enormous emission of energy from a radioactive substance. R. DAWKINS Energy such as ultraviolet light from the sun. **b** S. BELLOW The postwar prosperity of capitalism was based on cheap energy.

atomic energy, ***chemical energy***, ***electrical energy***, ***mechanical energy***, ***radiant energy***, ***solar energy***, etc. ***binding energy***: see BINDING *ppl adjective*.
– COMB.: **energy band** PHYSICS a group of states of a quantized system characterized by a continuous range of energy values which the system is capable of having; **energy gap** (**a**) PHYSICS a gap between adjacent energy bands, such that a particle cannot pass from the lower band to the higher without some minimum increase in its energy; (**b**) a national or global shortage of fuel and other sources of power; ***energy level***: see LEVEL *noun* 4c.

enervate /ˈɛnəveɪt/ *adjective.* E17.
[ORIGIN Latin *enervatus* pa. pple of *enervare*: see ENERVATE *verb*, -ATE².]
1 Lacking moral, literary, or artistic vigour; spiritless; effeminate. E17.
2 Lacking physical strength. E18.

enervate /ˈɛnəveɪt/ *verb trans.* E17.
[ORIGIN Latin *enervat-* pa. ppl stem of *enervare* extract the sinews of, weaken, from *e-* E- + *nervus* sinew: see -ATE³.]
1 Deprive of vigour or vitality; debilitate; weaken mentally, morally, or (formerly) physically. E17.

Q. BELL She was enervated and chafed by the excitements and disappointments of the previous months. JAN MORRIS A heavy, dank, enervating environment.

†**2** Destroy the force or authority of (an argument, doctrine, etc.); make ineffectual. E17–M19. ▸**b** Disparage. E–M17.
†**3** Cut the tendons of; *spec.* hamstring (a horse). M17–M18.
■ **enervatingly** *adverb* in an enervating manner L20. **enervative** *adjective* (*rare*) tending to enervate M19.

enervation /ɛnəˈveɪʃ(ə)n/ *noun.* LME.
[ORIGIN Late Latin *enervatio(n-)*, formed as ENERVATE *verb*: see -ATION.]
†**1** Impairment of a right or privilege. Only in LME.
2 The action of enervating; the state of being enervated. M16.

enerve /ɪˈnəːv/ *verb trans. obsolete* exc. *poet.* LME.
[ORIGIN Old French & mod. French *énerver* from Latin *enervare*: see ENERVATE *verb*.]
= ENERVATE *verb*.

†**enervous** *adjective.* M17–M18.
[ORIGIN from Latin *enervis* (from *e-* E- + *nervus* sinew) + -OUS.]
Lacking nerve or strength; powerless, futile.

Enets /ˈɛnɛts/ *noun & adjective.* M20.
[ORIGIN Russian.]
▸ **A** *noun.* Pl. same. A member of a Samoyedic people inhabiting north central Siberia; the Uralic language of this people (also called ***Yenisei*** (***Samoyed***)). Cf. NENETS. M20.
▸ **B** *attrib.* or as *adjective.* Of or pertaining to the Enets or their language. L20.

en évidence /ɑ̃n evidɑ̃ːs/ *adverbial phr.* E19.
[ORIGIN French.]
In or at the forefront; conspicuously.

†**enew** *verb trans.* LME–E17.
[ORIGIN Old French *enewer*, *eneauer*, formed as EN-¹ + *eau* water.]
Of a hawk etc.: drive (a waterbird) into the water.

enface /ɪnˈfeɪs, ɛn-/ *verb trans.* M19.
[ORIGIN from EN-¹ + FACE *noun*, after *endorse*.]
Write, print, or stamp something on the face of (a document); write, print, or stamp (something) on the face of a document.
■ **enfacement** *noun* something that is written, overprinted, etc., on a document M19.

en face /ɑ̃ fas/ *adverbial phr.* M18.
[ORIGIN French.]
With the face to the front, facing forwards; BIBLIOGRAPHY on the facing page. Cf. EN REGARD.

en famille /ɑ̃ famiːj/ *adverbial phr.* E18.
[ORIGIN French.]
At home, with one's family; as one of the family, informally.

enfant gâté /ɑ̃fɑ̃ gɑte/ *noun phr.* Pl. **-s -s** (pronounced same). E19.
[ORIGIN French = spoilt child.]
A person given undue flattery or indulgence.

enfantillage /ɑ̃fɑ̃tijaːʒ/ *noun.* Pl. pronounced same. E19.
[ORIGIN Old French & mod. French, from Old French *enfantil* from Latin *infantilis*: see INFANTILE, -AGE.]
A childish action or prank.

enfants gâtés, ***enfants terribles*** *noun phrs.* pls. of ENFANT GÂTÉ, ENFANT TERRIBLE.

enfant terrible /ɑ̃fɑ̃ tɛribl/ *noun phr.* Pl. **-s -s** (pronounced same). M19.
[ORIGIN French = terrible child.]
A person who causes embarrassment by ill-considered, or unorthodox behaviour or speech; an unconventional person.

enfeeble /ɪnˈfiːb(ə)l, ɛn-/ *verb trans.* ME.
[ORIGIN Old French *enfeblir*, *-lier*, formed as EN-¹ + *feble* FEEBLE *adjective*.]
Make feeble, weaken.
■ **enfeeblement** *noun* the action of enfeebling; the state of being enfeebled: M17. **enfeebler** *noun* (*rare*) E17.

†**enfelon** *verb trans.* L15–M19.
[ORIGIN Old French *enfelonner*, *-ir*, formed as EN-¹ + *felon* furious: see FELON *noun*¹ & *adjective*.]
Make furious, enrage.

enfeoff /ɪnˈfiːf, -ˈfɛf, ɛn-/ *verb trans.* Also †**in-**. See also INFEFT. LME.
[ORIGIN Anglo-Norman *enfeoffer* (Anglo-Latin *enfeoffare*), Old French *enfeffer*, formed as EN-¹ + *fief*: see FEE *noun*².]
1 LAW (now *hist.*). Put (a person) in possession of a fee or fief, under the feudal system; convey freehold property to by feoffment. (Foll. by *in*, *of*, *with*, †*on*.) LME.
2 *fig.* Hand over, give up possession of. L16.

enfeoffment /ɪnˈfiːfm(ə)nt, -ˈfɛf-; ɛn-/ *noun. obsolete* exc. *hist.* LME.
[ORIGIN from ENFEOFF + -MENT.]
LAW. The action of enfeoffing, feoffment; the state of being enfeoffed; a property conveyed or held by feoffment.

en fête /ɑ̃ fɛːt/ *pred. adjectival phr.* M19.
[ORIGIN French.]
Prepared for or engaged in holiday-making or celebration.

enfetter /ɪnˈfɛtə, ɛn-/ *verb trans.* L16.
[ORIGIN from EN-¹ + FETTER *noun*.]
Put in fetters (*lit.* & *fig.*); enslave *to* another.

enfever /ɪnˈfiːvə, ɛn-/ *verb trans.* M17.
[ORIGIN from EN-¹ + FEVER *noun*.]
Afflict with fever; *fig.* incense, enrage.

Enfield /ˈɛnfiːld/ *noun.* M19.
[ORIGIN An area of Greater London.]
In full ***Enfield rifle***. Any of various bolt-operated rifles made at the Royal Small Arms Factory, Enfield, or designed in imitation of them. Cf. LEE-ENFIELD.

enfilade /ɛnfɪˈleɪd/ *noun & verb.* E18.
[ORIGIN French, from *enfiler* thread on a string, pierce or traverse from end to end, formed as EN-¹ + *fil* thread: see FILE *noun*², -ADE.]
▸ **A** *noun.* **1** MILITARY. ▸†**a** The situation whereby a post commands the whole length of a line. Only in E18. ▸**b** Gunfire directed along a line from end to end (also ***enfilade fire***); an act of firing in this way. L18.
2 A suite of rooms with doorways in line with each other; a vista between rows of trees etc. E18.
▸ **B** *verb trans.* MILITARY. Subject to enfilade; cover the whole length of (a target) with a gun or guns. E18.

CLIVE JAMES The Germans installed concrete gun emplacements to enfilade the beaches.

enfile /ɪnˈfʌɪl, ɛn-/ *verb trans.* LME.
[ORIGIN French *enfiler*: see ENFILADE.]
†**1** Hang *up* or thread on a string. LME–L17.
2 HERALDRY. In *pass.* Of a charge: pierce or thread (another charge). (Foll. by *by*, *with*.) M19.

†**enfire** *verb trans.* L15.
[ORIGIN from EN-¹ + FIRE *noun*.]
1 Excite, arouse the passions of. L15–M19.
2 Set on fire. E16–E17.

enflame *verb* see INFLAME.

enflesh /ɪnˈflɛʃ, ɛn-/ *verb trans.* M16.
[ORIGIN from EN-¹ + FLESH *noun*.]
Chiefly THEOLOGY. Give bodily form to.
■ **enfleshment** *noun* the action or an act of enfleshing; (an) incarnation: M20.

enfleurage /ɒ̃fləˈrɑːʒ/ *noun.* M19.
[ORIGIN French, from *enfleurer* saturate with the perfume of flowers, formed as EN-¹ + *fleur* FLOWER *noun*: see -AGE.]
The extraction of perfumes from flowers by means of oils and fats.

enflower /ɪnˈflaʊə, ɛn-/ *verb trans.* E16.
[ORIGIN from EN-¹ + FLOWER *noun*.]
Adorn with flowers.

enflurane /ɛnˈflʊəreɪn/ *noun.* L20.
[ORIGIN from *en-* of unknown origin + FLU(O)R- + -ANE.]
PHARMACOLOGY. A liquid, $CHF_2{\cdot}O{\cdot}CF_2{\cdot}CHFCl$, used as an inhalational general anaesthetic similar to halothane but less potent.

†**enfold** *noun* see INFOLD *noun*.

enfold /ɪnˈfəʊld, ɛn-/ *verb*¹ *trans.* Also (*arch.*) **in-** /ɪn-/. LME.
[ORIGIN from EN-¹, IN-² + FOLD *noun*², *verb*¹.]
†**1** Involve; imply, entail; embroil *in*. LME–M17.
2 Wrap up *in* or *with* something; envelop, enclose. L16.

E. A. FREEMAN The royal robes in which the body had been enfolded.

3 Encompass, encircle; clasp, embrace. L16.

E. M. FORSTER He simply enfolded her in his manly arms.

4 Fold, shape into folds. Formerly also *fig.*, make involved or intricate. E17.
■ **enfolder** *noun* M16. **enfoldment** *noun* (**a**) *arch.* the action of enfolding; †(**b**) a thing that enfolds: L16.

enfold /ɪnˈfəʊld, ɛn-/ *verb*² *trans. rare.* Also **in-** /ɪn-/. E17.
[ORIGIN from EN-¹, IN-² + FOLD *noun*¹.]
Shut up (livestock) in a fold.

†**enforce** *noun.* LME–L17.
[ORIGIN from the verb.]
Effort, exertion.

enforce /ɪnˈfɔːs, ɛn-/ *verb.* Also (*arch.*) **in-** /ɪn-/. ME.
[ORIGIN Old French *enforcier*, (also mod.) *enforcir*, from Proto-Romance, from Latin IN-² + *fortis* strong.]
▸ **I** Put force or strength in.
†**1** *verb intrans.* & *refl.* Strive physically or mentally; exert oneself. (Foll. by *to do*.) ME–L16.
†**2** *verb trans.* Strengthen physically or morally; reinforce; encourage. (Foll. by *to do*.) LME–L17.
†**3** *verb intrans.* Grow stronger; become violent. Only in LME.
†**4** *verb trans.* Intensify, make more vigorous; strengthen (a feeling). LME–L18.

S. JOHNSON The temptations to do ill are multiplied and enforced.

5 *verb trans.* Urge, press home, (an argument, demand, etc.). Formerly also, emphasize. LME.

RUFUS ANDERSON Hoapile enforced his claim by an argument from a reciprocity of rights and duties.

▸ **II** Use force on.
†**6** *verb trans.* Drive or impel by physical or moral force (*to*, *from* a place, belief, etc.). ME–M17.
†**7** *verb trans.* Overcome by violence; conquer; rape. LME–M17.
†**8** *verb trans.* Exert force on, press hard on; *fig.* press or urge with arguments, pleas, etc. LME–M17.
9 *verb trans.* Compel, constrain, or oblige (*to do*). *arch.* LME.
▸ **III** Produce or impose by force.
†**10** *verb trans.* Produce or obtain by physical or other force; extort *from* a person. M16–L17.

ROBERT BURTON By the striking of a flint fire is inforced.

11 *verb trans.* Compel the occurrence or performance of; impose (a course of action) *on* a person. E17.

B. JOWETT To enforce the education of their children upon unwilling parents. *Observer* A telephone call from Moscow or Washington would be enough to enforce their withdrawal.

12 *verb trans.* Compel the observance of (a law, rule, practice, etc.); support (a demand, claim, etc.) by force. E17.

R. OWEN He called on party officials to enforce strict Marxist orthodoxy in the arts.

■ **enforcer** *noun* a person, organization, etc., that enforces something; *slang* a person who imposes his will on others by violence and intimidation, esp. as a member of a criminal gang: L16. **enforcingly** *adverb* forcibly; earnestly, impressively: L16.

enforceable /ɪnˈfɔːsəb(ə)l, ɛn-/ *adjective*. M19.
[ORIGIN from ENFORCE *verb* + -ABLE.]
Able to be enforced.
■ **enforceaˈbility** *noun* E20. **enforceableness** *noun* M19.

enforcedly /ɪnˈfɔːsɪdli, ɛn-/ *adverb*. LME.
[ORIGIN from ENFORCE *verb* + -ED[1] + -LY[2].]
†**1** Forcibly, violently. LME–L16.
2 Under compulsion. L16.

enforcement /ɪnˈfɔːsm(ə)nt, ɛn-/ *noun*. L15.
[ORIGIN Old French, formed as ENFORCE *verb*: see -MENT.]
1 Constraint, compulsion; a constraining or compelling influence. Now *rare*. L15.
†**2** The action or an act of assaulting or overcoming by violence. Only in L16.
3 The forceful pressing of an argument, demand, etc. L16.

S. SMILES It cost him many years of arguing, illustration, and enforcement.

4 The (forcible) extraction of payment; the process of compelling observance of a law, regulation, etc. L16.

SIR W. SCOTT The occasion seemed to require an enforcement of domestic discipline.

enforcement agency, *enforcement officer*, etc.
†**5** (A) reinforcement, esp. of an army etc. M17–M18.
– COMB.: **enforcement notice** ENGLISH LAW a notification issued by a local authority and requiring the recipient to remedy a breach of planning legislation.

enforcible /ɪnˈfɔːsɪb(ə)l, ɛn-/ *adjective*. Also †**in-**. L16.
[ORIGIN from ENFORCE *verb* + -IBLE.]
= ENFORCEABLE. Formerly, forcible, compelling.
■ **enforciˈbility** *noun* M20.

†**enform** *verb* see INFORM *verb*.

†**enfouldered** *adjective*. *rare* (Spenser). Only in L16.
[ORIGIN Uncertain: perh. from EN-[1] + Old French *fouldre* (mod. *foudre*) thundercloud + -ED[1].]
Full of thunderbolts; black as a thundercloud.

enframe /ɪnˈfreɪm, ɛn-/ *verb trans.* Also **in-** /ɪn-/. M19.
[ORIGIN from EN-[1], IN-[2] + FRAME *noun*.]
1 Frame, surround like a frame. M19.
2 Set in or as in a frame. L19.

†**enfranch** *verb*. L16–M17.
[ORIGIN Anglo-Norman *enfranchir*: see ENFRANCHISE.]
= ENFRANCHISE.

enfranchise /ɪnˈfran(t)ʃʌɪz, ɛn-/ *verb trans.* Also †**in-**. LME.
[ORIGIN Old French *enfranchiss-* lengthened stem of *enfranchir*, formed as EN-[1] + *franc*, *franche* free: see FRANK *adjective*[1].]
1 Invest (a town) with municipal rights, esp. the right of representation in parliament. LME.
2 Grant (a person) the rights of a citizen, esp. the right to vote. LME.
†**3** Admit to membership of a municipality, guild, corporation, etc. LME–M17.
4 **a** Give (a slave, serf, etc.) liberty. M16. ▸**b** Release from confinement. Chiefly *fig.* M16. ▸†**c** Free from political domination. E–M17.

b A. S. BYATT David . . talked excitedly too, enfranchised from the solitude of his fat and silence.

5 Release from obligatory payments or legal liabilities; convert (a leasehold or copyhold property) to freehold. L16.
■ **enfranchisable** *adjective* L19. **enfranchisement** /-ɪz-/ *noun* the action of enfranchising; the state of being enfranchised: L16. **enfranchiser** *noun* M17.

enfrenzy /ɪnˈfrɛnzi, ɛn-/ *verb trans.* Now *rare* or *obsolete*. M17.
[ORIGIN from EN-[1] + FRENZY *noun*.]
= FRENZY *verb*. Chiefly as ***enfrenzied*** *ppl adjective*.

ENG *abbreviation*.
Electronic news-gathering.

engage /ɪnˈɡeɪdʒ, ɛn-/ *noun*. Also †**in-**. L16.
[ORIGIN from the verb.]
†**1** Promise, agreement. Only in L16.
†**2** Entanglement, danger. Only in E17.
3 The engaging of swords. M19.

engage /ɪnˈɡeɪdʒ, ɛn-/ *verb*. Also †**in-**. LME.
[ORIGIN Old French & mod. French *engager* from Proto-Romance, formed as EN-[1], IN-[2] + base of WAGE *noun*.]
▸ **I** Pledge, secure.
1 *verb trans.* †**a** Make over as a pledge; pawn; mortgage. LME–M17. ▸**b** *fig.* Pledge (one's life, honour, etc.); put at risk, compromise. Now *rare*. M16. ▸†**c** Make (a person) security for a commitment. L16–M17.

b A. FRASER He would engage his soul for the reliability of all present.

2 *verb intrans.* Pledge oneself (*to do*, *that*); guarantee; enter into a contract or undertaking (*to do*; also *with* an employee or worker). M16. ▸**b** Foll. by *for*: answer for, guarantee; undertake to do, promise. M17. ▸**c** Take service with or *with* an employer. M18.

O. WILDE: I . . engage to have it done by September. **b** A. HAMILTON He could not engage for their safety.

3 *verb trans.* Bind by a legal or moral obligation (*to* a party or deed; *to do*). E17. ▸**b** *spec.* Bind by a promise of marriage, betroth. Usu. in *pass.* E18. ▸**c** In *pass.* Have a social or business engagement arranged; be occupied in a meeting. L19.

J. L. MOTLEY He declined engaging himself not to recall his foreign soldiery. P. G. WODEHOUSE Horace was engaged to marry . . Valerie. **b** M. PUZO Sonny was formally engaged to Sandra. **c** OED I am engaged for tomorrow, but could dine with you on Monday.

4 *verb trans.* Urge, persuade, induce. Now *rare*. M17.

T. KEIGHTLEY He engaged them to declare in his favour.

5 *verb trans.* Win over as an adherent or ally. *arch.* L17.
6 *verb trans.* Fascinate, charm. Now *rare*. E18.
7 *verb trans.* **a** Hire for work, take on as an employee; *refl.* take up employment (foll. by *to* the employer). M18. ▸**b** Secure for one's own use; arrange beforehand to occupy or use; book, reserve. M18.

a C. CHAPLIN We were able to engage a maid to come twice a week. J. CONRAD An American ship where . . he had dared to engage himself. **b** W. S. MAUGHAM She had offered to engage a room . . in the house of the woman. E. WAUGH The tables are all engaged.

▸ **II** Involve, entangle.
†**8** *verb trans.* Entangle physically; ensnare. L16–L17.
†**9** *verb trans.* & *intrans.* Involve, commit, (oneself) *in* an undertaking, quarrel, etc. Also foll. by other prepositions. L16–L18.
†**10** *verb intrans.* & *trans.* (Cause to) enter *into* or involve oneself *in* a place from which withdrawal is difficult. M17–M19.
11 *verb intrans.* Enter upon or occupy oneself *in* an activity, interest, etc. Formerly also foll. by *on*. M17.

J. BARZUN Nations where intellectuals engage . . in politics and state service.

12 *verb trans.* Keep occupied or busy, provide occupation for, (a person, a person's thoughts, etc.). Usu. in *pass.*, foll. by *in* (*on*, *with*). M17.

E. WAUGH The local police were engaged in directing all traffic . . to the course. W. S. CHURCHILL Colonisation . . was the task that engaged the Western pioneers.

13 *verb trans.* Attract and hold fast (a person's attention, interest, etc.). M18. ▸**b** Draw (a person) into a conversation. Usu. foll. by *in*. E20.

STEELE Her form . . engaged the eyes of the whole congregation in an instant. R. TRAVERS A mystery which engaged the attention of the press for some time. **b** A. POWELL Templar tried . . to engage the girl in conversation.

14 *verb trans.* ARCHITECTURE. Fasten, attach; let part of (a column) into a wall. Usu. in *pass.* M18.
15 *verb intrans.* & *trans.* Of part of a mechanism: come into contact with or fit into a corresponding part, so as to prevent or transmit movement; cause to do this; interlock (*with*). Also, put a motor vehicle into (gear, or a specified gear). M19.

V. NABOKOV Press home until you hear or feel the magazine catch engage. *Autosport* He could not engage third properly. W. BOYD Then the gears were engaged . . and the car slowly pulled away.

▸ **III** With ref. to combat.
16 **a** *verb intrans.* Enter into combat. Usu. foll. by *with*. M17. ▸**b** *verb trans.* Bring (forces) into battle (*with*). M19.

a SOUTHEY The mob . . did not venture to engage against musketry and cannon.

17 *verb trans.* Enter into combat with, attack. L17.

F. FITZGERALD American troops successfully engaged the enemy main forces and killed a great number.

18 *verb trans.* & *intrans.* Of combatants: bring (weapons) together preparatory to fighting. L17.

H. ALLEN Since there are no seconds . . I shall simply count three and engage.

■ **engager** *noun* a person who engages someone or *in* something, or enters into an engagement; *spec.* (*hist.*) a person who approved of the secret treaty made between Charles I and Scottish rulers in 1647: E17.

engagé /ɒŋɡaˈʒeɪ; *foreign* ɑ̃ɡaʒe (*pl. same*)/ *noun* & *adjective*. E19.
[ORIGIN French, pa. pple of *engager* ENGAGE *verb*.]
▸ **A** *noun*. N. AMER. HISTORY. = ENGAGEE. E19.
▸ **B** *adjective*. Of writers, artists, etc., or their works: showing social or political commitment. M20.

engageants /ɑ̃ɡaʒɑ̃, ɒŋɡəˈʒɑːnts/ *noun pl. obsolete* exc. *hist.* L17.
[ORIGIN French †*engageantes* use as noun of fem. pl. of †*engageant* enticing, pretty, pres. pple of *engager* ENGAGE *verb*: see -ANT[1].]
Double ruffles that fall over the wrists.

engaged /ɪnˈɡeɪdʒd, ɛn-/ *adjective*. E17.
[ORIGIN from ENGAGE *verb* + -ED[1].]
1 That has been engaged; *spec.* under a promise to marry; ARCHITECTURE (of a column) partly let into a wall. E17.
2 Of a telephone number or line, or a lavatory: unavailable because already in use. Of a tone: signifying that the telephone number called is engaged. L19.
3 = ENGAGÉ *adjective*. M20.
■ †**engagedness** *noun* L17–M18.

engagee /ɪŋɡeɪˈdʒiː, ɛŋ-/ *noun*. E19.
[ORIGIN from ENGAGE *verb* + -EE[1].]
A person engaged for service or work; *spec.* (N. AMER. HISTORY) a boatman hired by a fur-trader or explorer.

engagement /ɪnˈɡeɪdʒm(ə)nt, ɛn-/ *noun*. Also (earlier) †**in-**. E17.
[ORIGIN Old French & mod. French, formed as ENGAGE *verb*: see -MENT.]
†**1** A legal or moral obligation; a tie; an attachment. E17–L18.
2 The fact or state of being or becoming engaged, *spec.* to marry. M17. ▸**b** = COMMITMENT 5b. M20.

W. J. M. RANKINE Another method of effecting engagement . . by wheels in rolling contact. S. SPENDER Within three weeks of our engagement . . we were married. A. STORR He broke off his engagement.

3 A formal promise, agreement or undertaking. *arch.* M17. ▸**b** An appointment with another person; an agreement to meet. E19. ▸**c** In *pl.* Promises to pay; financial commitments. M19.

E. K. KANE An engagement was drawn up . . with the signatures of all the company. **b** B. TARKINGTON He . . apologized for having an engagement which made his departure necessary. **c** OED Mr. A. B. is unable to meet his engagements.

4 An encounter between parties at war; a battle. M17.

A. EDEN A big naval engagement with the German fleet.

†**5** The action of mortgaging property; a mortgage. Only in M17.
†**6** An inducement, a motive. M–L17.
7 A piece of business requiring a person's attention or presence; *esp.* a paid appointment, a job. L18.

W. COWPER From all his wearisome engagements freed. M. FONTEYN The season of 1910 was a limited summer engagement using dancers contracted to the Imperial Theatres.

– COMB.: **engagement ring**: given by a man to a woman when they agree to marry each other.

engaging /ɪnˈɡeɪdʒɪŋ, ɛn-/ *adjective*. L17.
[ORIGIN from ENGAGE *verb* + -ING[2].]
That engages; *esp.* charming, winning, attractive.

J. SCOTT Several most engaging views. F. BUNSEN She . . has always the same engaging manner.

■ **engagingly** *adverb* M17. **engagingness** *noun* E18.

engaol *verb* var. of ENJAIL.

en garçon /ɑ̃ ɡarsɔ̃/ *adverbial phr.* E19.
[ORIGIN French.]
As or in the manner of a boy or a bachelor.

en garde /ɑ̃n ɡɑːd/ *interjection*. L19.
[ORIGIN French = on guard.]
FENCING. A direction to prepare to fence, taking the opening position for action.

engarland /ɪnˈɡɑːlənd, ɛn-/ *verb trans.* Chiefly *poet.* L16.
[ORIGIN from EN-[1] + GARLAND *noun*.]
Encircle (as) with a garland.

engarrison /ɪnˈɡarɪs(ə)n, ɛn-/ *verb trans. obsolete* exc. *hist.* Also †**in-**. L16.
[ORIGIN from EN-[1], IN-[2] + GARRISON *noun*.]
Serve or station as a garrison in; protect by a garrison; *fig.* entrench or establish firmly (oneself).

†**engastrimyth** *noun*. L16–E18.
[ORIGIN French *engastrimythe* from Greek *eggastrimuthos*, formed as EN-[2] + *gastri* dat. of *gastēr* belly + *muthos* speech.]
A ventriloquist.
■ †**engastrimythic** *adjective*: only in M19.

E

E

Engelmann spruce /ˈɛŋɡ(ə)lmən ˈspruːs/ *noun phr.* Also **Engelmann's spruce** /-mənz/. **M19.**
[**ORIGIN** from George *Engelmann* (1809–84), US botanist + **SPRUCE** *noun*.]
A large alpine spruce, *Picea engelmannii*, of western N. America.

engem /ɪnˈdʒɛm, ɛn-/ *verb trans. rare.* Also **in-** /ɪn-/. Infl. **-mm-**. **E17.**
[**ORIGIN** from **EN-**[1], **IN-**[2] + **GEM** *noun*.]
Set (as) with gems; bejewel.

†**engeminate** *verb* see **INGEMINATE** *verb*.

engender /ɪnˈdʒɛndə, ɛn-/ *verb.* Also †**in-**. **ME.**
[**ORIGIN** Old French & mod. French *engendrer* from Latin *ingenerare*, formed as **IN-**[2] + *generare* **GENERATE** *verb*.]
1 *verb trans.* **a** Of a male: beget (offspring). *arch.* **ME.** ▸†**b** Of a female: conceive; bear. **ME–L17.** ▸**c** Of parents or ancestors, countries, situations, etc.: produce (living beings). **LME.**
2 *verb trans.* Give rise to, bring about, (a state of affairs, a quality, feeling, etc.). **ME.**

DRYDEN Immoderate Study engenders a grossness in the Mind. A. STORR A basic mistrust engendered by the circumstances of his early childhood.

†**3** *verb trans.* Produce in the course of nature; generate, develop, (a natural product). **LME–L18.**
†**4** *verb intrans.* Have sexual intercourse, copulate, (*with*); breed, procreate. **LME–E19.**
†**5** *verb intrans.* Come into being, arise, originate. **LME–M19.**

DRYDEN Thick clouds are spread, and storms engender there.

†**6** *verb trans.* Contract (a disease). **E16–E17.**
■ **engenderer** *noun* **LME.** **engenderment** *noun* †(*a*) development, origin; (*b*) the action of engendering: **L16.**

engendrure /ɛnˈdʒɛndrʊə, ɛn-/ *noun. arch.* Also **-dure** /-djʊə/, †**in-**. **ME.**
[**ORIGIN** Old French *engendr(e)ure*, formed as **ENGENDER**: see **-URE**.]
†**1** The action of engendering. **ME–M16.**
2 A person's parentage or origin. **LME.**

engild /ɪnˈɡɪld, ɛn-/ *verb trans. poet.* Pa. pple **-gilt** /-ˈɡɪlt/, **-gilded**. **LME.**
[**ORIGIN** from **EN-**[1] + **GILD** *verb*[1].]
= **GILD** *verb*[1].

engine /ˈɛndʒɪn/ *noun.* Also (*Scot.*, in senses 1 & 2) **ingine** /ɪnˈdʒʌɪn/. **ME.**
[**ORIGIN** Old French & mod. French *engin* from Latin *ingenium* natural quality, talents, clever device, formed as **IN-**[2] + *gen-* base of *gignere* beget.]
1 Natural talent, wit; genius. *obsolete* exc. *Scot.* **ME.** ▸†**b** A person's disposition. Chiefly *Scot.* **M16–E17.**

SIR W. SCOTT A man of quick ingine and deep wisdom.

†**2** Ingenuity; cunning. **ME–M17.**
†**3** An instance or product of ingenuity or cunning; an artifice, a plot; a snare. **ME–L18.**
4 An instrument; a tool. *arch.* **ME.** ▸**b** Orig., any offensive weapon. Later, a large weapon with some form of mechanism. Now *arch. & hist.* **ME.** ▸†**c** An instrument of torture, *esp.* the rack. **LME–L17.** ▸**d** A contrivance for catching game, fish, etc. **L15.**

H. POWER Our modern Engine the Microscope. **b** M. INNES A sling would . . be an engine to reckon with on bare ground. *fig.*: B. FRANKLIN The stage and the press . . became battering engines against religion.

†**5** The universe, or a particular division of the world, as a working entity. **E–M16.**
6 †**a** A person regarded as another's instrument or agent, a tool. **M16–M18.** ▸**b** A thing that is an agent or instrument (*of* an end or achievement). **L16.**

b *Times* We have been the engines of world growth.

7 A contrivance consisting of a number of moving parts that work together to produce a desired physical effect. Now *rare* exc. as below & as the 2nd elem. of comb. **M17.**

ADAM SMITH Engines for knitting gloves or stockings.

beer engine: see **BEER** *noun*[1].
8 A fire engine. *arch.* **M17.**
9 A stationary steam engine. **E19.**
atmospheric engine: see **ATMOSPHERIC** *adjective* 1.
10 A railway locomotive. **M19.**
11 A machine for producing energy of motion from some other form of energy, esp. heat that the machine itself generates. **M19.**
car engine, ***oil engine***, ***petrol engine***, ***rocket engine***, ***Wankel engine***, etc.
– **COMB.**: **engine driver** *spec.* a train driver; **engineman** a person who works on or operates an engine; **engine room** a room containing engines, esp. a ship's engines; **engine turning** the engraving of symmetrical patterns on metals by machine.

engine /ˈɛndʒɪn/ *verb.* **ME.**
[**ORIGIN** Old French *enginier* from medieval Latin *ingeniare*, from Latin *ingenium*: see **ENGINE** *noun*. In sense 4 from the noun.]
†**1** *verb trans.* Ensnare; deceive. Only in **ME.**
†**2** *verb trans. & intrans.* Contrive, devise; plan *to do*. **LME–E17.**
†**3** *verb trans.* Torture; assault (a place) with engines of war. **LME–E17.**
4 *verb trans.* Fit (a ship etc.) with an engine. **M19.**

engined /ˈɛndʒɪnd/ *adjective.* In sense 1 also †**in-**. **E17.**
[**ORIGIN** from **ENGINE** *noun* + **-ED**[2].]
†**1** Minded, disposed. *Scot. rare.* Only in **E17.**
2 Having an engine of a specified kind or position, or engines of a specified number. Only as 2nd elem. of comb., as ***rear-engined***, ***twin-engined***, etc. **M20.**

engineer /ɛndʒɪˈnɪə/ *noun.* Also †**in-**. **ME.**
[**ORIGIN** Orig. from Old French *engigneor* (mod. *ingénieur*) from medieval Latin *ingeniator*, from *ingeniare*: see **ENGINE** *verb*. Later from mod. French *ingénieur* or Italian *ingegnere*, from Proto-Romance, with suffix assim. to **-EER**.]
1 *hist.* A designer and constructor of military works. Formerly also, a builder of engines of war. **ME.** ▸**b** A soldier in a division of an army that specializes in engineering and (orig.) the design and construction of military works. **L18.**
b ***Royal Engineers***: see **ROYAL** *adjective*.
2 A designer or maker of engines. **L15.** ▸†**b** *fig.* An author or designer *of* something; a plotter. **L16–E18.**
3 a More fully ***civil engineer***. A person whose occupation is the design, construction, and maintenance of works of public utility, e.g. roads, bridges, and canals. **E17.** ▸**b** A person who works in any branch of engineering, esp. as a qualified professional. **M19.**
b ***chemical engineer***: see **CHEMICAL** *adjective*. ***electrical engineer***: see **ELECTRICAL** *adjective*. ***mechanical engineer***: see **MECHANICAL** *adjective*. ***SANITARY engineer***. ***STRUCTURAL engineer***.
4 A person in charge of an engine, now esp. a marine engine; *N. Amer.* a train driver. **E17.**
■ **engineership** *noun* the occupation or position of an engineer **M17.**

engineer /ɛndʒɪˈnɪə/ *verb.* **L17.**
[**ORIGIN** from the noun.]
1 *verb intrans.* Work as an engineer. **L17.**

R. W. EMERSON The grand tools with which we engineer.

2 *verb trans.* Design, make, or build as a work of engineering. **M19.**

M. HOWARD Margaret . . called in the electric company to engineer a heating system. *Scientific American* Gibson has . . engineered a bacterium capable of producing . . an enzyme that breaks down . . parathion.

3 *verb trans.* Arrange, contrive, or bring about, esp. artfully. **M19.**

G. GREENE I engineered a row on purpose and sacked him.

4 *verb trans.* Guide carefully, manoeuvre. *US.* **M19.**

engineering /ɛndʒɪˈnɪərɪŋ/ *noun.* **E18.**
[**ORIGIN** from **ENGINEER** *verb* + **-ING**[1].]
1 The work done by, or the occupation of, an engineer; the application of science for directly useful purposes, as construction, propulsion, communication, or manufacture. **E18.**
civil engineering the branch of engineering that deals with the design, construction, and maintenance of works of public utility. ***chemical engineering***: see **CHEMICAL** *adjective*. ***electrical engineering***: see **ELECTRICAL** *adjective*. ***mechanical engineering***: see **MECHANICAL** *adjective*. ***military engineering***: see **MILITARY** *adjective*. ***STRUCTURAL engineering***.
2 The action of working artfully to bring something about. **L18.**
3 A field of study or activity concerned with deliberate alteration or modification in some particular area. **E20.**
GENETIC engineering. ***human engineering***: see **HUMAN** *adjective*. ***planetary engineering***: see **PLANETARY** *adjective*. ***social engineering***: see **SOCIAL** *adjective*.
– **COMB.**: **engineering brick**: with high resistance to crushing, and low absorption of moisture; **engineering science** engineering as a field of study.

engineless /ˈɛndʒɪnlɪs/ *adjective.* **L19.**
[**ORIGIN** from **ENGINE** *noun* + **-LESS**.]
That is without an engine.

enginery /ˈɛndʒɪn(ə)ri/ *noun.* **E17.**
[**ORIGIN** from **ENGINE** *noun* + **-ERY**.]
†**1** The art of constructing engines; military engineering. Only in **17.**
2 Engines; machinery; *esp.* (*poet.*) engines of war, artillery. **M17.**

engird /ɪnˈɡəːd, ɛn-/ *verb trans.* Chiefly *poet.* Pa. t. & pple **-girt** /-ˈɡəːt/, **-girded**. **M16.**
[**ORIGIN** from **EN-**[1] + **GIRD** *verb*[1].]
= **ENGIRDLE**.

engirdle /ɪnˈɡəːd(ə)l, ɛn-/ *verb trans.* **L16.**
[**ORIGIN** from **EN-**[1] + **GIRDLE** *noun*[1].]
Form a girdle or ring round; encircle, surround.

†**engirt** *verb*[1] *trans.* **L16.**
[**ORIGIN** from **EN-**[1] + **GIRT** *verb*[1].]
1 Put a girdle or ring round; surround *with*. **L16–M17.**
2 = **ENGIRDLE**. **E17–M18.**

engirt *verb*[2] *pa. t. & pple* of **ENGIRD**.

†**engiscope** *noun* var. of **ENGYSCOPE**.

englacial /ɪnˈɡleɪʃ(ə)l, -sɪəl; ɛn-/ *adjective.* **L19.**
[**ORIGIN** from **EN-**[1] + **GLACIAL**.]
Situated, occurring, or formed inside a glacier.
■ **englacially** *adverb* **E20.**

Englander /ˈɪŋɡləndə/ *noun.* **E19.**
[**ORIGIN** from *England* + **-ER**[1], partly infl. by German *Engländer*. Earlier in **NEW ENGLANDER**.]
A native or inhabitant of England; an English person.
Little Englander: see **LITTLE** *adjective*.

English /ˈɪŋɡlɪʃ/ *adjective & noun.*
[**ORIGIN** Old English *englisc*, occas. *ænglisc*, formed as **ANGLE** *noun*[2]: see **-ISH**[1].]
▸ **A** *adjective.* **1** Of, pertaining to, or designating the group of Germanic peoples (Saxons and Jutes, as well as Angles) who invaded and settled in Britain in the 5th cent. AD, or (in post-Conquest times) the pre-Conquest Germanic inhabitants of England and their descendants. Long *obsolete* exc. *hist.* **OE.**
2 Designating the language of the English; written or spoken in English. **OE.**

R. W. EMERSON Our English Bible is a wonderful specimen of . . the English language.

3 Designating a person who is a native or inhabitant of England; of or pertaining to England or English people. **ME.**

H. HUNTER An English ship which had sailed round the world. J. D. SALINGER He drove over last Saturday with this English babe.

4 Marked by the characteristics of an English person. **M16.**

A. PHELPS A mind compact with sturdy and solid English elements.

▸ **B** *noun.* **1** Orig., the language spoken by the Germanic invaders of Britain in the 5th cent. AD. Now, the language descended from this, used in Britain, Ireland, Australia, New Zealand, the US, Canada, and many other countries. **OE.** ▸**b** The English language as used in a particular area or period or by a particular writer; a particular kind of English. **ME.** ▸**c** A person's facility in using English; the English language at a person's command. **LME.** ▸**d** The English word or expression equivalent in meaning to a given word etc. Foll. by *for*. **E20.**

G. ORWELL The fight against bad English is not frivolous. **b** *Caribbean Studies* The various Creoles and creolized Englishes of the Caribbean. **c** T. HARDY His English, though not good, was quite intelligible to her. **d** R. KEARTON I cannot remember the English for it.

b ***American English***, ***British English***, ***pidgin English***, ***Shakespeare's English***, etc.
2 (*The*) English people; (*the*) English soldiers or forces. Treated as *pl.* **L16.**

H. A. L. FISHER American divisions had fought with the French and English.

3 A size of type (equal to about 14 points) between great primer and pica. Now *hist.* **L16.**
4 In full ***plain English***. The sense expressed plainly in English; the plain sense. Usu. foll. by *of*. **M17.**

ADDISON An Oneirocritick, or, in plain English, an interpreter of dreams.

5 (Also **e-**.) = **SIDE** *noun* 18. *US.* **M19.**
6 English language or literature as a subject to be studied. **L19.**

J. I. M. STEWART I had always come first in . . English.

– **SPECIAL COLLOCATIONS & PHRASES**: ***Basic English***: see **BASIC** *adjective* 1. ***black English***: see **BLACK** *adjective*. ***Early English***: see **EARLY** *adjective*. **English basement** *US* a basement with windows and its own entrance. ***English bond***: see **BOND** *noun*[2] 9. **English breakfast** a substantial breakfast including hot cooked food. **English Canadian** an English-speaking Canadian (cf. ***French Canadian*** s.v. **FRENCH** *adjective*). **English disease** †(*a*) melancholia; (*b*) rickets; (*c*) = ***British disease*** s.v. **BRITISH** *adjective*. ***English elm***: see **ELM** 1. **English English** English as spoken by English people. ***English flute***: see **FLUTE** *noun*[1]. ***English galingale***: see **GALINGALE** 2. ***English maidenhair***: see **MAIDENHAIR** 2. ***English horn***: see **HORN** *noun*. **English Miss** a prim or prudish unmarried woman (cf. **MISS** *noun*[2]). ***English muffin***: see **MUFFIN** 1a. ***English mustard***: see **MUSTARD** *noun* 1. **English opening** *CHESS*: in which the queen's bishop's pawn is advanced two squares on the first move. **English rose** a typically attractive light-complexioned English girl. **English setter** a long-haired usu. white or partly white sporting dog. **English sickness** = ***English disease*** (c) above. ***English springer (spaniel)***: see **SPRINGER** 6. †**English treacle** the plant water germander, *Teucrium scordium*. ***English walnut***: see **WALNUT** 1. **Middle English** English as it was between Old English and 1470 or 1500 and the advent of printing, characterized particularly by a reduced system of grammatical inflections, an increased lexical borrowing from other languages, esp. French and Latin, and a highly varied orthography. **modern English** English as it has been since 1470 or 1500. ***Norman English***: see **NORMAN** *adjective* 1. **Old English** (*a*) English as it was before about 1150 or the Norman Conquest, a West Germanic inflected language (comprising four main dialects, Kentish, Mercian, Northumbrian, and West Saxon); also called ***Anglo-Saxon***; (*b*) *TYPOGRAPHY* a form of black letter resembling that used by early English printers; (*c*) ***Old English sheepdog***: see **OLD** *adjective & adverb*. **the English Channel**: see **CHANNEL** *noun*[1] 6. **the Queen's English**, **the King's English** the English language as written or spoken by educated people in Britain.
■ **Englishism** *noun* (*a*) an English idiom or form of speech; (*b*) English character or practices; attachment to what is English: **E19.** **Englishness** *noun* **E19.**

English /ˈɪŋglɪʃ/ *verb trans.* Also **e-**. LME.
[ORIGIN from the adjective.]
1 Translate into English; give the English equivalent of. LME.
†**2** Put into plain English, describe in simple terms. L16–L17.
3 = ENGLISHIZE 2. E19.

R. G. WHITE When a foreign word has been transplanted into our speech . . it should be thoroughly Englished.

Englisher /ˈɪŋglɪʃə/ *noun.* In sense 2 also **e-**. M17.
[ORIGIN from ENGLISH *adjective, verb* + -ER[1].]
1 An English subject; a native or inhabitant of England. Chiefly *Scot.* M17.
2 A person who translates a book etc. into English. E19.

Englishize /ˈɪŋglɪʃʌɪz/ *verb trans.* Also **-ise**. L18.
[ORIGIN from ENGLISH *noun & adjective* + -IZE.]
†**1** Bring to England, cause to live in England. *rare.* Only in L18.
2 Make English; give an English form or character to; Anglicize. M19.
■ **Englishiˈzation** *noun* L20.

Englishly /ˈɪŋglɪʃli/ *adverb.* LME.
[ORIGIN from ENGLISH *noun & adjective* + -LY[2].]
†**1** In English; by means of an English expression. LME–M16.
2 In the manner of English people or England. E17.

Englishman /ˈɪŋglɪʃmən/ *noun.* Pl. **-men**.
[ORIGIN Old English *Engliscmon*, formed as ENGLISH *adjective & noun*, MAN *noun*.]
A man who is English by birth or descent.

Englishry /ˈɪŋglɪʃri/ *noun.* LME.
[ORIGIN Anglo-Norman *englescherie*, Anglo-Latin *englescheria*, from ENGLISH *noun & adjective*: see -ERY.]
1 The fact of being English in character or (now *hist.*) by birth or descent. LME.

E. E. EVANS His objections to the system . . reveal his Englishry.

2 *hist.* The part of a population, esp. in Ireland, that is of English descent. L15.
3 English people. *rare.* M19.

M. TWAIN The Norman Conqueror came over to divert the Englishry.

Englishwoman /ˈɪŋglɪʃwʊmən/ *noun.* Pl. **-women** /-wɪmɪn/. LME.
[ORIGIN from ENGLISH *adjective & noun* + WOMAN *noun*.]
A woman who is English by birth or descent.

Englishy /ˈɪŋglɪʃi/ *adjective.* L19.
[ORIGIN from ENGLISH *noun & adjective* + -Y[1].]
Characteristically English.

Eng. Lit. /ɪŋ ˈlɪt/ *noun phr.* M19.
[ORIGIN Abbreviation.]
English literature, as a subject of academic study.

englobe /ɪnˈgləʊb, ɛn-/ *verb trans.* E17.
[ORIGIN from EN-[1] + GLOBE *noun*.]
1 Shape into a globe. E17.
2 Enclose in or as in a globe. Chiefly *fig.* M19.

englut /ɪnˈglʌt, ɛn-/ *verb trans. arch.* Also †**in-**. Infl. **-tt-**. L15.
[ORIGIN Old French *englotir* (mod. *engloutir*) from late Latin *inglut(t)ire*, formed as IN-[2] + *gluttire* swallow. In sense 2 directly from EN-[1], IN-[2] + GLUT *verb*[1].]
1 Swallow, gulp down. L15.
2 Glut, satiate. L15.

englyn /ˈɛŋlɪn/ *noun.* Pl. **englyns**, **englynion** /ɪŋləˈnɪən, ɛn-/. L16.
[ORIGIN Welsh.]
In Welsh poetry, a stanza (usu. a quatrain) having any of various strictly prescribed metrical structures.

engobe /ɑ̃gɔb/ *noun.* M19.
[ORIGIN French.]
A mixture of white clay and water applied as a coating to pottery to cover the natural colour or to provide a ground for decoration; = SLIP *noun*[1] 3.

engolden /ɪnˈgəʊld(ə)n, ɛn-/ *verb trans. & intrans.* E19.
[ORIGIN from EN-[1] + GOLDEN.]
Make or become golden.

engore /ɪnˈgɔː, ɛn-/ *verb*[1] *trans.* Now *rare* or *obsolete*. L16.
[ORIGIN from EN-[1] + GORE *noun*[1].]
Make gory, stain with blood.

†**engore** *verb*[2] *trans. rare* (Spenser). Only in L16.
[ORIGIN from EN-[1] + GORE *verb*[1].]
Gore, wound deeply; *fig.* enrage.

engorge /ɪnˈgɔːdʒ, ɛn-/ *verb.* Also (*rare*) **in-**. L15.
[ORIGIN Old French *engorgier* feed to excess (mod. *engorger* obstruct, congest), formed as EN-[1], GORGE *verb*.]
1 *verb trans. & intrans.* Gorge; feed greedily, fill to excess or to capacity. L15. ▸**b** In *pass.* Be filled to excess; be crammed *with*; MEDICINE be congested with fluid, esp. blood. Cf. GORGE *verb* 2a. L16.

Nature Ticks attach to the skin of their host . . , engorging on blood.

2 *verb trans.* Devour greedily; swallow up. M16.

Times Lit. Suppl. Enlarging the appetite of the consuming public so as to enable it to engorge a growing volume and variety of goods.

■ **engorgement** *noun* the action of engorging; the state of being engorged, *esp.* (MEDICINE) congestion of a tissue or organ with fluid, esp. blood: M16. **engorger** *noun* L16.

engouement /ɑ̃gumɑ̃/ *noun.* Pl. pronounced same. E19.
[ORIGIN French, lit. 'obstruction in the throat'.]
Unreasoning fondness; (an) infatuation.

engouled /ɪnˈguːld, ɛn-/ *adjective.* M19.
[ORIGIN from Old French & mod. French *engoulé* pa. pple of *engouler* gobble up, formed as EN-[1] + Old French *goule* (mod. *gueule*) throat: see -ED[1]]
HERALDRY. Of a bend, cross, etc.: entering the mouth of an animal.

engrace /ɪnˈgreɪs, ɛn-/ *verb trans.* Also †**in-**. L16.
[ORIGIN from EN-[1], IN-[2] + GRACE *noun*.]
†**1** Introduce into the favour of another. L16–M17.
2 THEOLOGY. Endow with grace. L19.

†**engraff** *verb trans.* Also **in-**. LME–M19.
[ORIGIN from EN-[1], IN-[2] + GRAFF *verb*.]
= ENGRAFT 1, 2.

engraft /ɪnˈgrɑːft, ɛn-/ *verb.* Also †**in-**. L16.
[ORIGIN from EN-[1], IN-[2] + GRAFT *verb*[1]. See also earlier ENGRAFF.]
1 *verb trans. & intrans.* = GRAFT *verb*[1] 1, 4. (Foll. by *into*, *upon*.) L16.
2 *verb trans.* Implant, incorporate, (*in* or *into* an already existing system etc.); add *on* to an already existing base; = GRAFT *verb*[1] 2a. L16.

HENRY FIELDING Acquiring solid lasting habits of virtue, and ingrafting them into our character. J. GRANT It had been added to, or engrafted on, the tall, old, square baronial tower.

†**3** *verb trans.* Add to the stock of a trading company. L17–L18.
†**4** *verb trans.* Introduce smallpox virus into (a person's system); inoculate. Only in E18.
5 *verb trans.* = GRAFT *verb*[1] 6. L19.
■ **engraftment** *noun* the action or an act of engrafting; a graft: M17.

engrail /ɪnˈgreɪl, ɛn-/ *verb trans.* LME.
[ORIGIN Old French *engresler* (mod. *engrêler*) make thin, formed as EN-[2] + *graisle*, *gresle* (mod. *grêle*) thin from Latin *gracilis*.]
1 Chiefly HERALDRY. Make small semicircular indentations in the edge of. Chiefly as ***engrailed*** *pa. pple.* LME.
2 Decorate *with* a border, metalwork, colours, etc. *obsolete* exc. *poet.* LME.
†**3** Indent, incise; sculpture in intaglio. M16–L18.
4 Give a serrated appearance to; roughen. L16.
■ **engrailed** *adjective* that has been engrailed; having the edge decorated with curvilinear indentations; (of a coin) having a series of such indentations or of raised dots around the margin: LME.

engrain *verb* see INGRAIN *verb*.

engram /ˈɛngram/ *noun.* E20.
[ORIGIN German *Engramm*, formed as EN-[2] + Greek *gramma* letter.]
A memory trace; *spec.* a permanent and physical change in the neuronal structure of the brain, postulated to represent a memory.
■ **engrammatic** /ɛngrəˈmatɪk/ *adjective* E20.

en grande tenue /ɑ̃ grɑ̃ːd təny/ *adverbial phr.* M19.
[ORIGIN French.]
In full dress.

†**engrandize** *verb trans.* Also **-ise**, **in-**. M17–L19.
[ORIGIN French *engrandiss-* lengthened stem of *engrandir*, from Italian *ingrandire*; assim. to verbs in -IZE. Cf. AGGRANDIZE.]
Make great; increase in importance, estimation, or rank.

en grand seigneur /ɑ̃ grɑ̃ sɛɲœːr/ *adverbial phr.* E19.
[ORIGIN French.]
In the manner of a nobleman.

engrasp /ɪnˈgrɑːsp, ɛn-/ *verb trans.* Now *rare* or *obsolete*. L16.
[ORIGIN from EN-[1] + GRASP *noun* or *verb*.]
Grasp (*lit.* & *fig.*); embrace, seize.

engrave /ɪnˈgreɪv, ɛn-/ *verb*[1]. Also †**in-**. Pa. pple **-graved**, (*arch.*) **-graven**. L15.
[ORIGIN from EN-[1], IN-[2] + GRAVE *verb*[1], after French †*engraver*.]
1 *verb trans.* Inscribe or ornament (a hard surface or object) with incised marks. L15.

S. SMILES To engrave spoons and forks with crests and ciphers.

2 *verb trans.* Carve (an inscription, figure, etc.) upon a surface or object; *fig.* fix indelibly *in* or *on* the memory, heart, etc. M16.

O. WISTER July third was to be engraved inside the wedding ring. W. S. MAUGHAM Isobel had a good memory and the various turns of the long discussion had engraved themselves upon it.

†**3** *verb trans.* Portray or represent by sculpture. M16–E17.
4 *verb trans. & intrans.* Produce a representation of (a picture, lettering, etc.) for printing by removal of part of the surface of a plate or block. M17.

WILKIE COLLINS I get my bread by drawing and engraving on wood for the cheap periodicals.

■ †**engravement** *noun* = ENGRAVING 1, 2 E17–E18.

†**engrave** *verb*[2] *trans.* Also **in-**. M16–L17.
[ORIGIN from EN-[1], IN-[2] + GRAVE *noun*[1] or *verb*[1].]
Put in a grave; entomb, bury.

†**engraven** *verb*[1] *trans.* Also **in-**. E17–L18.
[ORIGIN Perh. alt. of ENGRAVE *verb*[1], due to analogy of verbs with prefix EN-[1] and suffix -EN[5].]
= ENGRAVE *verb*[1].

engraven *verb*[2] *pa. pple*: see ENGRAVE *verb*[1].

engraver /ɪnˈgreɪvə, ɛn-/ *noun.* Also †**in-**. L16.
[ORIGIN from ENGRAVE *verb*[1] + -ER[1].]
1 A person who engraves something. L16.
2 An engraving tool. E19.
3 In full ***engraver beetle***. A bark beetle of the genus *Ips*, which makes channels in the surface of the sapwood of trees. L19.

engraving /ɪnˈgreɪvɪŋ, ɛn-/ *noun.* E17.
[ORIGIN from ENGRAVE *verb*[1] + -ING[1].]
1 The action of ENGRAVE *verb*[1]; the art of the engraver. E17.
2 An engraved figure or inscription. *rare.* E17.
3 A print made from an engraved plate. E19.

engrenage /ɑ̃grənaːʒ/ *noun.* Pl. pronounced same. E20.
[ORIGIN French, lit. 'gearing', from *engrener* feed corn into (a threshing machine), throw into gear, formed as EN-[1], GRAIN *noun*[1]: see -AGE.]
1 A set of circumstances that trap one; an organization or society regarded as full of snares. E20.
2 The process of preparing for effective joint action. M20.

engroove /ɪnˈgruːv, ɛn-/ *verb trans.* Also **in-** /ɪn-/. M19.
[ORIGIN from EN-[1], IN-[2] + GROOVE *noun* or *verb*.]
1 Work (something) into a groove. M19.
2 Form a groove in. L19.

en gros /ɑ̃ gro/ *adverbial phr.* E18.
[ORIGIN French.]
In general, in broad terms.

engross /ɪnˈgrəʊs, ɛn-/ *verb trans.* Also †**in-**. LME.
[ORIGIN Ult. formed as EN-[1], GROSS *adjective*. In branch I from Anglo-Norman *engrosser*, medieval Latin *ingrossare*, from Old French *grosse*, medieval Latin *grossa* large writing; in branch II from Old French *en gros*, medieval Latin *in grosso* in bulk, wholesale from late Latin *grossus* GROSS *adjective*; in branch III from Old French & mod. French *engrosser*.]
▸**I** Use large writing.
1 Write out in a large, clear hand; make a fair copy of. Now usu., express in legal form; produce (a legal document) in its final or definitive form. LME.
†**2** Settle or agree (a matter). LME–E16.
†**3** Make a written record of; enter in a formal document or list. LME–M17.
▸**II** Deal with on a large scale.
4 Orig. (now *hist.*), buy up wholesale; *esp.* corner the market in (a commodity) in order to control the price. Later (now *arch.*), concentrate (property, privileges, functions, etc.) in one's own possession; monopolize. LME. ▸†**b** Buy up large amounts of (land, tenements, etc.). M16–L18.

H. T. BUCKLE Seeing a single person engross the conversation.

†**5** Amass, collect from all quarters. LME–E17.
6 Require the entire use of, utilize all of. E17.

J. HARVEY The firm expanded . . . It came to engross every machine that had to do with building.

7 Of an object of thought or feeling: fully occupy (the mind, affections, time, etc.). M17.

W. COWPER My morning is engrossed by the garden.

8 Absorb the whole attention of (a person). Usu. in *pass.* (foll. by *in*, *with*). E18.

M. BARING Mademoiselle was engrossed in a French novel. A. HIGGINS He lost all interest in activities that had formerly engrossed him.

▸†**III** Make dense.
9 Thicken (a liquid); condense (a vapour). LME–L16.
10 Make (the body) gross or fat; coarsen (the mind). LME–E19.
11 Make thick or bulky; enlarge. L15–M17. ▸**b** Add to the numbers of (an army); draw up (troops) in a compact body. E16–M17.
■ **engrossedly** /-sɪdli/ *adverb* in an engrossed manner, with absorbed attention M19. **engrosser** *noun* (now *hist.*) LME. **engrossing** *ppl adjective* that engrosses; *spec.* that fully absorbs one's attention or interest: L16. **engrossingly** *adverb* M19. **engrossingness** *noun* M19. **engrossment** *noun* (*a*) the action of engrossing; the state of being engrossed; (*b*) a thing that is engrossed, *spec.* the definitive copy of a legal document: E16.

Eng. Tech. *abbreviation.*
Engineering Technician.

engulf /ɪnˈgʌlf, ɛn-/ *verb trans.* Also †**-gulph**, (*arch.*) **in-** /ɪn-/. M16.
[ORIGIN from EN-[1], IN-[2] + GULF *noun*.]
1 Swallow up (as) in a gulf or abyss; flow over and swamp. M16.

J. KOSINSKI I was hurled into . . the brown filth, which parted under my body to engulf me. D. BAGLEY The waters of Santego Bay arose to engulf the town. *fig.*: E. WELTY The ancient deck chair . . engulfed her like a hammock.

E

E

2 Affect powerfully, overwhelm; preoccupy, engross. L16.

> D. ACHESON A bitter debate engulfed the United States. W. S. CHURCHILL The loneliness and apathy which engulfed her after Albert's death.

3 *refl.* & in *pass.* Of a river: discharge itself into the sea; disappear underground. *arch.* M17.

■ **engulfment** *noun* the action of engulfing; the process of being engulfed: E19.

†**engyscope** *noun.* Also **engi-**. M17–M19.
[ORIGIN from Greek *eggus* near at hand + -SCOPE.]
A microscope; *spec.* a reflecting microscope.

†**enhabit** *verb* var. of INHABIT.

enhalo /ɪnˈheɪləʊ, ɛn-/ *verb trans.* M19.
[ORIGIN from EN-¹ + HALO *noun.*]
Surround (as) with a halo.

enhance /ɪnˈhɑːns, -hans, ɛn-/ *verb.* Also †**in-**. ME.
[ORIGIN Anglo-Norman *enhauncer* prob. alt. of Old French *enhaucier* from Proto-Romance, from Latin IN-² + *altus* high.]
†**1** *verb trans.* Lift, raise; raise the level of. ME–L16.
†**2** *verb trans.* Exalt in rank, wealth, etc.; elevate spiritually or morally; lift up with pride; praise. ME–M17.
3 *verb trans.* **a** Make appear greater; exaggerate. LME. ▸**b** Raise in degree; heighten, intensify, (a quality, attribute, etc.). L16.

> **a** G. DOWNES The satirist wished to enhance the infirmity of Philip. **b** GIBBON These delights were enhanced by the memory of past hardships.

4 a *verb trans.* Raise (a price or value); increase (a charge or cost). LME. ▸**b** *verb intrans.* Of property: rise in price. Formerly (of prices): rise. L15.
5 *verb trans.* Increase *in* (or formerly, in) price, value, importance, attractiveness, etc. Also, improve in quality, utility, or (formerly) beauty. E16.

> *Which Computer?* The ¼-inch tape streamer storage system . . has been enhanced to back-up the . . disc drives.

■ **enhancer** *noun* LME. **enhancive**, *-**sive** *adjective* tending to enhance M19.

enhancement /ɪnˈhɑːnsm(ə)nt, -hans-, ɛn-/ *noun.* M16.
[ORIGIN from ENHANCE + -MENT.]
1 Something that enhances; *esp.* an extra facility; a supplementary payment. M16.

> *Oxford Times* £2.48 per hour plus enhancements for evening and weekend work.

2 The action or process of enhancing; the fact of being enhanced. L16.

†**enhappy** *verb trans.* E17–M18.
[ORIGIN from EN-¹ + HAPPY *adjective.*]
Make happy or prosperous.

†**enharden** *verb trans.* E16–L19.
[ORIGIN from EN-¹ + HARDEN *verb.*]
Make (a person) hard.

enharmonic /ɛnhɑːˈmɒnɪk/ *adjective & noun.* E17.
[ORIGIN Late Latin *en(h)armonicus* from Greek *enarmonikos*, formed as EN-² + *harmonia* HARMONY: see -IC.]
MUSIC. ▸**A** *adjective.* **1** *hist.* Designating (ancient Greek music based on) a tetrachord divided into two quarter-tones and a major third. E17.
2 Pertaining to, involving, or designating musical intervals smaller than a semitone, esp. the relationship between notes which are equal only in a scale of equal temperament (e.g. C sharp and D flat); (of an instrument or keyboard) sounding more than 12 notes to an octave. L18.
▸**B** *noun.* **1** In *pl.* Enharmonic music. E17.
2 A note belonging to an enharmonic interval. L19.
■ **enharmonical** *adjective* = ENHARMONIC *adjective* M18. **enharmonically** *adverb* L19.

enhearse *verb* var. of INHEARSE.

enhearten /ɪnˈhɑːt(ə)n, ɛn-/ *verb trans.* Now *rare.* E17.
[ORIGIN from EN-¹ + HEARTEN *verb.*]
Encourage; embolden.

enheaven *verb* var. of INHEAVEN.

†**enherit** *verb* see INHERIT.

†**enheritable** *adjective*, †**enheritance** *noun* vars. of INHERITABLE, -ANCE.

enhungered /ɛnˈhʌŋgəd/ *adjective.* Now *rare.* L15.
[ORIGIN Alt. of AHUNGERED, ANHUNGERED by substitution of EN-¹ for the prefix.]
Hungry.

enhypostasia /ˌɛnhʌɪpəˈsteɪzɪə/ *noun.* L19.
[ORIGIN from EN-² + Greek *hupostasis* HYPOSTASIS + -IA¹.]
THEOLOGY. The personhood of Christ as existing through (and only through) the hypostasis.
■ **enhypostatic** /-ˈstat-/ *adjective* L19. **enhyˈpostatize** *verb trans.* (*rare*) unite in one hypostasis or person L19.

enigma /ɪˈnɪgmə/ *noun.* Also †**aen-**. Pl. **-mas**, **-mata** /-mətə/. M16.
[ORIGIN Latin *aenigma* from Greek *ainigma*, from base of *ainissesthai* speak allusively or obscurely, from *ainos* fable.]
1 A riddle, usu. one involving metaphor. Formerly also, an obscure or allusive speech. M16.
2 A perplexing, mysterious, or unexplained thing. E17.
3 An enigmatic person. E20.
■ **enigmatize** *verb* (now *rare*) †(**a**) *verb trans.* symbolize; (**b**) *verb trans. & intrans.* make or become enigmatic: M17.

enigmatic /ɛnɪgˈmatɪk/ *adjective.* E17.
[ORIGIN French *énigmatique* or late Latin *aenigmaticus*, formed as ENIGMA: see -ATIC.]
Of the nature of an enigma; perplexing, obscure; (of a person) baffling others' conjecture as to character, sentiments, identity, etc.; mysterious.

> J. THURBER As enigmatic as the face of Mona Lisa.

■ **enigˈmatical** *adjective* = ENIGMATIC M16. **enigˈmatically** *adverb* L16.

†**enigmatist** *noun.* E17–E18.
[ORIGIN Latin *aenigmatista* from Greek *ainigmatistēs*, from *ainigma* ENIGMA: see -IST.]
A person who writes enigmas or who speaks enigmatically.

enisle /ɛnˈʌɪl, ɪn-/ *verb trans.* Also **in-** /ɪn-/. E17.
[ORIGIN from EN-¹, IN-² + ISLE *noun*¹.]
1 Make into an island. E17.
2 Place or settle on an island; *fig.* isolate. M19.

> M. ARNOLD In the sea of life enisled . . we mortal millions live alone.

enjail /ɪnˈdʒeɪl, ɛn-/ *verb trans. arch.* Also **-gaol**, **in-** /ɪn-/. L16.
[ORIGIN from EN-¹, IN-² + JAIL *noun.*]
Shut up in, or as in, a jail.

enjamb /ɪnˈdʒam, ɛn-/ *verb.* E17.
[ORIGIN French *enjamber* stride over, go beyond, formed as EN-¹ + Old French & mod. French *jambe*: see JAMB.]
†**1** *verb intrans.* Encroach. Only in E17.
2 *verb trans.* PROSODY. Continue (a sentence) without a pause beyond the end of a line, couplet, or stanza. Chiefly as ***enjambed*** *ppl adjective.* L19.

enjambment /ɪnˈdʒam(b)m(ə)nt, ɛn-/ *noun.* Also **enjambement** /ɪnˈdʒam(b)m(ə)nt, ɛn-, *foreign* ɑ̃ʒɑ̃bmɑ̃/. M19.
[ORIGIN French *enjambement*, formed as ENJAMB: see -MENT.]
PROSODY. An instance of enjambing.

enjealous /ɪnˈdʒɛləs, ɛn-/ *verb trans. arch.* Also (earlier) †**in-**. E17.
[ORIGIN from EN-¹, IN-² + JEALOUS.]
Make jealous.

enjewel /ɪnˈdʒuːəl, ɛn-/ *verb trans.* Also †**in-**. Infl. **-ll-**, ***-l-**. E17.
[ORIGIN from EN-¹, IN-² + JEWEL *noun.*]
Adorn with jewels or like a jewel.

enjoin /ɪnˈdʒɔɪn, ɛn-/ *verb trans.* Also †**in-**. ME.
[ORIGIN Old French & mod. French *enjoi(g)n-* stem of *enjoindre* from Latin *injungere* join, attach, impose, formed as IN-² + *jungere* JOIN *verb.*]
1 Prescribe authoritatively (an action, conduct, etc.); *arch.* impose (a duty, penance, penalty, etc.). (Foll. by *on*, *upon*, †*to* a person.) ME. ▸**b** Command or call upon (a person) *to do*; order *that*. ME. ▸**c** Pledge *to* an observance. Formerly, sentence *to* a penalty. LME.

> A. J. AYER The sort of action that is enjoined or forbidden by some ecclesiastical authority. **b** SCOTT FITZGERALD 'Don't mention it,' he enjoined me. F. HERBERT I enjoin you to practice the meditation of peace.

†**2** Join together. LME–L17.
3 Prohibit, forbid; *esp.* (LAW) prohibit or restrain by an injunction. (Foll. by *from*.) L16.
■ **enjoiner** *noun* L16. **enjoinment** *noun* the action of enjoining; an injunction: M17.

enjoinder /ɪnˈdʒɔɪndə, ɛn-/ *noun.* M19.
[ORIGIN from ENJOIN after *rejoinder*.]
An imposition, a duty, an obligation.

enjoy /ɪnˈdʒɔɪ, ɛn-/ *verb.* LME.
[ORIGIN Old French *enjoier* give joy to, (refl.) enjoy, formed as EN-¹ + *joie* JOY *noun*, or Old French *enjoïr* enjoy, rejoice, formed as EN-¹ + *joïr* from Latin *gaudere*.]
1 *verb intrans.* †**a** Be in a state of joy; rejoice. LME–M16. ▸**b** Enjoy oneself. Only in imper. Orig. *N. Amer.* M20.
2 *verb trans.* Take delight or pleasure in; have, use, or experience with delight. LME. ▸**b** Have sexual intercourse with (usu. a woman). M16.

> E. M. FORSTER Don't pretend you enjoyed lunch, for you loathed it.

3 *verb trans.* Have the use or benefit of (something pleasant or advantageous). LME. ▸**b** Experience. L16.

> I. MURDOCH A guest bedroom, which also enjoyed a view of the lawn. **b** H. VENN At best, she enjoys poor health.

†**4** *verb trans.* Make happy, give pleasure to. L15–E17.
5 *refl.* Have a pleasant or delightful time. M17.

> OED He is enjoying himself at the seaside.

■ **enjoyaˈbility** *noun* the quality of being enjoyable; the degree to which something is enjoyable: L20. **enjoyable** *adjective* able to be enjoyed; delightful: M17. **enjoyableness** *noun* M19. **enjoyably** *adverb* L19. **enjoyer** *noun* L16. **enjoyingly** *adverb* (*rare*) with enjoyment. M19.

enjoyment /ɪnˈdʒɔɪm(ə)nt, ɛn-/ *noun.* M16.
[ORIGIN from ENJOY + -MENT.]
1 The action or state of enjoying something. M16.

> LD MACAULAY He would protect the Established Church in the enjoyment of her legal rights.

2 Pleasure; something that gives pleasure. M17.

†**enkennel** *verb trans. rare.* Infl. **-ll-**. L16.
[ORIGIN from EN-¹ + KENNEL *noun*¹.]
1 Lodge as in a kennel. L16–E17.
2 Contain like a kennel. Only in M19.

enkephalin /ɛnˈkɛf(ə)lɪn/ *noun.* M20.
[ORIGIN from Greek *egkephalos* brain: see ENCEPHALO-, -IN¹.]
BIOCHEMISTRY. Either of two pentapeptide endorphins occurring in the brain.

enkindle /ɪnˈkɪnd(ə)l, ɛn-/ *verb.* Also †**in-**. M16.
[ORIGIN from EN-¹, IN-² + KINDLE *verb*¹.]
1 *verb trans.* **a** Excite or inflame (strong feeling). M16. ▸**b** Cause (a flame, fire, etc.) to blaze up. L16.
2 *verb trans.* **a** Arouse strong feeling in. Formerly also foll. by *to* a purpose or object, *to do* an action. M16. ▸**b** Set on fire. Now *rare.* M16. ▸**c** Light up, illuminate (*lit.* & *fig.*). L19.

> **c** D. H. LAWRENCE He saw her face strangely enkindled.

†**3** *verb intrans.* Catch fire; burst into flame. M16–M18.
■ **enkindler** *noun* M19.

enknot *verb* var. of INKNOT.

enlace /ɪnˈleɪs, ɛn-/ *verb trans.* LME.
[ORIGIN Old French *enlacier* (mod. *enlacer*) from Proto-Romance, formed as IN-² + Proto-Romance alt. of Latin *laqueus* noose. Later taken as from EN-¹ + LACE *noun.*]
1 Encircle tightly; surround closely; embrace. LME.
2 Interlace, entwine, entangle. LME.
3 Pattern like lace. M19.

> N. FREELING Woodcutters' paths . . enlace every hill.

■ **enlacement** *noun* M19.

en l'air /ɑ̃ lɛːr/ *adverbial phr.* E18.
[ORIGIN French.]
In the air; BALLET while leaping vertically; MILITARY while unsupported.

enlarge /ɪnˈlɑːdʒ, ɛn-/ *verb.* Also †**in-**. ME.
[ORIGIN Old French *enlarger*, *-ir*, formed as EN-¹ + *large* LARGE *adjective*. In branch II after Old French *eslargir* (mod. *élargir*) set free.]
▸**I 1** *verb trans.* Make larger or wider; increase the size or extent of. Also (now *rare*) intensify, increase. ME. ▸**b** *verb trans.* Increase (esp. a person's thoughts or feelings) in range or scope; make more comprehensive. M16. ▸†**c** *verb trans.* Make appear larger; exaggerate. L16–M18. ▸**d** *verb trans.* LAW (now *hist.*). Extend (the time allowed for an action). M17. ▸**e** *verb trans. & intrans.* PHOTOGRAPHY. Reproduce on a larger scale. M19.

> D. CECIL The party . . was enlarged by a steady stream of friends and neighbours. *refl.*: SHAKES. *1 Hen. VI* Glory is like a circle in the water, Which never ceaseth to enlarge itself. **b** C. LAMB His fine suite of rooms . . were enough to enlarge a man's notions of himself.

2 *verb intrans.* Become larger, wider, or more comprehensive; expand, increase. L15. ▸†**b** Become stronger or more violent. E17–M18.

> B. JOWETT As our knowledge increases, our perception of the mind enlarges.

3 a *verb intrans.* & †*refl.* Speak or write in more detail; expatiate. Usu. foll. by *on*, *upon*. E17. ▸†**b** *verb intrans.* Foll. by *on*: add to (a plan); amplify (a hint). E18–E19.

> **a** B. PYM She had not enlarged on this bald statement.

▸**II 4** *verb trans.* Set free, release. *arch.* LME.
▸†**III 5** *verb trans. & intrans.* Give generously to or to; endow generously *with* gifts. L15–M17.
– PHRASES: **enlarge an estate** LAW convert an estate from a tenancy or leasehold to a freehold. **enlarge the heart** make a person's heart swell with gratitude or pride; increase a person's sympathies.
■ **enlarger** *noun* a person who or thing which enlarges; *spec.* an apparatus for producing photographic enlargements M16.

enlargement /ɪnˈlɑːdʒm(ə)nt, ɛn-/ *noun.* Also †**in-**. M16.
[ORIGIN from ENLARGE + -MENT.]
▸**I 1** (An) increase in size, extent, or scope; (an) increase in sympathies or understanding. M16. ▸**b** A photographic print that is larger than the negative from which it is produced, than an enprint, or than a print already made. M19.

> GEO. ELIOT An enlargement of the chapel . . absorbed all extra funds.

2 Expatiation on a subject; verbal amplification. *arch.* M17.
▸**II 3** Release from confinement. *arch.* M16.
†**4** (The right to) freedom of action; a privilege. E–M17.
5 Absence of inhibition in praying or preaching. *arch.* M17.

enleague /ɪnˈliːg, ɛn-/ *verb trans.* Now *rare.* Also (earlier) **in-** /ɪn-/. E17.
[ORIGIN from EN-¹, IN-² + LEAGUE *noun*² or *verb.*]
Unite in, or as in, a league.

enlèvement /ɑ̃lɛvmɑ̃; ɪnˈliːvm(ə)nt, ɛn-/ *noun*. Pl. pronounced same. M18.
[ORIGIN French, from *enlever* carry off: see -MENT.]
An abduction.

†**enlight** *verb trans. & intrans.* Also **in-**. OE–E19.
[ORIGIN Old English *inlīhtan* shine, from IN-¹ + *līhtan* (see LIGHT *verb*²). Later from EN-¹ + LIGHT *verb*².]
Shed light (on), *lit. & fig.*; light *up*.

enlighten /ɪnˈlʌɪt(ə)n, ɛn-/ *verb trans.* Also †**in-**. ME.
[ORIGIN Orig. from ENLIGHT + -EN⁵, later from EN-¹, IN-² + LIGHTEN *verb*² or LIGHT *noun* + -EN⁵.]
†**1** Make luminous. ME–E19.
2 Give spiritual knowledge or insight to. LME. ▸†**b** Remove blindness from (eyes). Freq. *fig.* LME–E18.
G. VIDAL Siddhartha became the enlightened one or Buddha.
3 Shed light on, illuminate, (*lit. & fig.*). Now *arch. & poet.* L16.
4 Instruct; inform (*on* a matter); (chiefly as ***enlightened*** pa. pple) make free from prejudice or superstition. M17.
ADDISON Before the World was enlightened by Learning and Philosophy. CONAN DOYLE I had no glimmer of what was in his mind, nor did he enlighten me.
†**5** Provide (a room, town, etc.) with light or lighting. M17–M19.
†**6** Revive, exhilarate. Only in M17.
■ **enlightenedness** *noun* the state or quality of being enlightened M19. **enlightener** *noun* a person who or thing which enlightens, esp. mentally or spiritually L16.

enlightenment /ɪnˈlʌɪt(ə)nm(ə)nt, ɛn-/ *noun*. M17.
[ORIGIN from ENLIGHTEN + -MENT.]
1 The action of mentally or spiritually enlightening; the state of being so enlightened. M17.
2 *the Enlightenment*, the philosophical movement that occurred in Europe, esp. France, in the 18th cent., in which reason and individualism came to be emphasized at the expense of tradition. M19.

enlink /ɪnˈlɪŋk, ɛn-/ *verb trans.* Also †**in-**. L15.
[ORIGIN from EN-¹, IN-² + LINK *noun*² or *verb*¹.]
Fasten together with links; connect closely. Chiefly *fig.*

enlist /ɪnˈlɪst, ɛn-/ *verb*. Also †**in-**. M16.
[ORIGIN from EN-¹, IN-² + LIST *noun*³ or *verb*⁴, perh. after Dutch *inlijsten* inscribe on a list.]
1 a *verb trans.* Enrol (another, (now *rare*) oneself) in one of the armed services. M16. ▸**b** *verb intrans.* Volunteer for and be accepted by one of the armed services. L18.
a enlisted man *US* a man in any of the armed services who ranks below a commissioned or warrant officer, *esp.* one ranking below a non-commissioned or petty officer.
2 *verb trans.* Engage or secure (a person, his or her services, etc.) as help or support. L16.
H. KELLER I wrote to my friends about the work and enlisted their sympathy.
■ **enlisˈtee** *noun* a person who is enlisted or who enlists for the armed services M20. **enlister** *noun* a person who enlists others for the armed services M19. **enlistment** *noun* the action or process of enlisting M18.

†**enlive** *verb trans.* Also **in-**. L16–M17.
[ORIGIN from EN-¹, IN-² + LIFE *noun*, after LIVE *verb*.]
= ENLIVEN.

enliven /ɪnˈlʌɪv(ə)n, ɛn-/ *verb trans.* Also †**in-**. M17.
[ORIGIN from ENLIVE + -EN⁵.]
†**1** Give life to; restore to life. M17–M18.
2 Give fuller life to, animate, invigorate; stimulate. M17.
3 Make lively or cheerful; relieve the monotony or dreariness of. E18.
■ **enlivener** *noun* M17. **enlivening** *noun* (*a*) the action of the verb; (*b*) a thing that enlivens someone or something: L17. **enliveningly** *adverb* in an enlivening manner M19. **enlivenment** *noun* the action of enlivening; the state of being enlivened; a thing that enlivens someone or something: L19.

enlock /ɪnˈlɒk, ɛn-/ *verb trans.* Also †**in-**. L16.
[ORIGIN from EN-¹, IN-² + LOCK *verb*¹.]
Lock up, shut in, enclose.

†**enlumine** *verb trans.* LME.
[ORIGIN Old French & mod. French *enluminer* from medieval Latin *inluminare* (Latin *illuminare*), formed as IN-² + *lumin-*, *lumen* light: cf. ILLUMINATE *verb*.]
1 Light up, illuminate; *fig.* enlighten, make clear; shed lustre upon. LME–E17.
2 Illuminate (a manuscript). LME–E16.

enmarble /ɪnˈmɑːb(ə)l, ɛn-/ *verb trans. rare*. Also (earlier) **emmarble** /ɪˈmɑːb(ə)l, ɛ-/. L16.
[ORIGIN from EN-¹, EM-¹ + MARBLE *noun*.]
Convert into marble; sculpture in or adorn with marble.

†**enmarvel** *verb* see EMMARVEL.

en masse /ɒ̃ ˈmas, *foreign* ɑ̃ mas/ *adverbial phr.* L18.
[ORIGIN French.]
In a mass; all together, as a group.

enmesh /ɪnˈmɛʃ, ɛn-/ *verb trans.* E17.
[ORIGIN from EN-¹ + MESH *noun*. Cf. IMMESH.]
Catch or entangle in, or as in, a mesh or net.
■ **enmeshment** *noun* entanglement L19.

enmity /ˈɛnmɪti/ *noun*. ME.
[ORIGIN Old French *enemi(s)tié* (mod. *inimitié*) from Proto-Romance, from Latin *inimicus*: see ENEMY, -ITY.]
1 The disposition or feelings of an enemy; ill will, hatred. ME.
M. MEYER To those who did not arouse his enmity, he could be charming.
2 The condition of being an enemy; a state of mutual hostility. LME.
P. H. GIBBS Old enmities and jealousies still smouldering across the frontiers.
†**3** (Something with) a harmful or prejudicial influence. LME–E17.
SHAKES. *Lear* To wage against the enmity o' th' air.

enmuffle /ɪnˈmʌf(ə)l, ɛn-/ *verb trans. rare*. E17.
[ORIGIN from EN-¹ + MUFFLE *verb*.]
Muffle up.

ennead /ˈɛnɪad/ *noun*. M16.
[ORIGIN Greek *ennead-*, *enneas*, formed as ENNEAGON: see -AD¹.]
A set of nine; *spec.* each of the six divisions in Porphyry's collection of Plotinus' works, each of which contains nine books.

enneagon /ˈɛnɪəgɒn, -g(ə)n/ *noun*. M17.
[ORIGIN from Greek *ennea* nine + -GON.]
A plane figure with nine straight sides and nine angles.

ennew /ɪˈnjuː, ɛn-/ *verb trans.* Long *rare*. Also †**in-**. LME.
[ORIGIN from EN-¹, IN-² + NEW *adjective*, after Latin *innovare* (see INNOVATE).]
Make new; renew. Formerly also, repeat, do again.

ennit /ˈɛnɪt/ *interjection*. *dial.* M20.
[ORIGIN Repr. a pronunc.]
Isn't it. Cf. INNIT.

ennoble /ɪˈnəʊb(ə)l, ɛn-/ *verb trans.* Also †**in-**. L15.
[ORIGIN Old French & mod. French *ennoblir*, formed as EN-¹, IN-², NOBLE.]
1 Make noble, impart nobility to; dignify; elevate or refine in character. L15.
R. W. EMERSON He who does a good deed, is instantly ennobled. H. ALLEN It was set with seed pearls . . and ennobled with a gilt pattern.
†**2** Make famous or illustrious. M16–L18.
3 Give the rank of a noble to (a person); make (a person) a peer or peeress. L16.
†**4** Of light: make conspicuous. *rare*. Only in 17.
■ **ennoblement** *noun* (*a*) the action of ennobling; the state or fact of being ennobled; †(*b*) a thing which ennobles: E17. **ennobler** *noun* L18.

en noir /ɑ̃ nwaːr/ *adverbial phr.* M19.
[ORIGIN French.]
On the black side; in the worst light.

ennui /ɒnˈwiː, *foreign* ɑ̃nɥi/ *noun & verb*. M18.
[ORIGIN French from Latin *in odio*: see ANNOY *noun*.]
▸ **A** *noun*. Mental weariness and dissatisfaction arising from lack of occupation or interest; boredom. M18.
R. HUGHES The ship's monkey, . . with no pig now to tease, nearly died of ennui. S. O'FAOLÁIN The long ennui of those empty days.
▸ **B** *verb trans.* As ***ennuied***, ***ennuyed*** pa. pple. = ENNUYÉ. E19.

ennuyant /ɑ̃nɥijɑ̃/ *adjective*. L18.
[ORIGIN French, pres. pple of *ennuyer*: see ENNUYÉ, -ANT¹.]
That gives rise to ennui; boring.

ennuyé /ɑ̃nɥije/ *adjective*. Fem. ***-ée***. M18.
[ORIGIN French, pa. ppl adjective of *ennuyer* bore, from *ennui*: see ENNUI.]
Affected with ennui; bored.
■ Also ***ennuyéd***, ***ennuyé'd*** *adjective* M19.

Eno /ˈiːnəʊ/ *noun*. L19.
[ORIGIN from J. C. *Eno* (c 1828–1915), English pharmacist.]
(Proprietary name for) a laxative and antacid preparation. Also ***Eno's (Fruit Salt)***.

eno- *combining form* see OENO-.

Enochic /iːˈnɒkɪk/ *adjective*. L19.
[ORIGIN from *Enoch* (see below) + -IC.]
Of, pertaining to, or characteristic of a person called Enoch, *spec.* the biblical son of Cain (*Genesis* 4:17), or the apocryphal Book of Enoch.
■ Also **Enochian** *adjective* E20.

enoki /ɪˈnəʊki/ *noun*. L20.
[ORIGIN Japanese *enoki-take*, from *enoki* nettle tree + *take* mushroom.]
In full ***enoki mushroom***. An edible Japanese mushroom, *Flammulina velutipes*, growing in clusters, with slender stems and small caps.

enol /ˈiːnɒl/ *noun*. M20.
[ORIGIN from -ENE + -OL, or back-form. from ENOLIC.]
CHEMISTRY. Any organic compound containing the unsaturated alcohol group ·CH=C(OH)· as a tautomeric form of a corresponding keto-compound.
KETO-ENOL.
■ **enolase** /ˈiːnəleɪz/ *noun* an enzyme involved in glycolysis and gluconeogenesis in the body M20. **enolate** /-nəl-/ *noun* (a compound containing) the carbanion of an enol M20. **eˈnolic** *adjective* L19. **enolization** /ˌiːnəlʌɪˈzeɪʃ(ə)n/ *noun* conversion into an enol or an enolic group M20.

enomotarch /ɪˈnɒmətɑːk/ *noun*. *rare*. E17.
[ORIGIN Greek *enōmotarkhēs*, from *enōmotia* (see ENOMOTY) + *-arkhēs* -ARCH.]
GREEK HISTORY. The commander of an enomoty.

enomoty /ɪˈnɒməti/ *noun*. *rare*. E17.
[ORIGIN Greek *enōmotia* band of sworn soldiers, formed as EN-² + *omnunai* swear: see -Y³.]
GREEK HISTORY. A division in the Spartan army.

enophthalmos /ɛnɒfˈθalmɒs/ *noun*. Also **-mus** /-məs/. L19.
[ORIGIN (mod. Latin *enophthalmus*) formed as EN-² + Greek *ophthalmos* eye.]
Abnormal retraction of the eyeball into the socket.

enorm /ɪˈnɔːm/ *noun & adjective*. LME.
[ORIGIN French *énorme* adjective or Latin *enormis*: see ENORMOUS.]
▸ †**A** *noun*. A monstrous act. Also, wickedness. LME–M16.
▸ **B** *adjective*. †**1** Of a sin, crime, etc.: monstrously wicked. L15–E18.
†**2** Abnormal; extravagant. E16–M18.
3 Vast; enormous. *arch.* L16.
– PHRASES: **enorm lesion**, †**enorm hurt** *SCOTS LAW* considerable damage in respect of property or rights.

†**enormious** *adjective*. LME–M17.
[ORIGIN from Latin *enormis* (see ENORMOUS) + -OUS.]
= ENORMOUS.

enormity /ɪˈnɔːmɪti/ *noun*. LME.
[ORIGIN Old French & mod. French *énormité* from Latin *enormitas*, from *enormis*: see ENORMOUS, -ITY.]
1 Orig., deviation from moral or legal rectitude. Now, the quality of being outrageous; monstrous wickedness. LME.
D. JACOBSON The enormity of the crime he wanted to commit.
2 Orig., a crime, a transgression. Now, a monstrous offence; a gross irregularity, a serious error. LME.
M. RENAULT He was committing an enormity by being out of bed in the middle of the night. JO GRIMOND Lawyers . . stride on, turning a blind eye to the enormities of their profession.
†**3** Abnormality, irregularity; an abnormal or irregular thing. L15–M19.
4 Enormous size, enormousness; daunting magnitude. Freq. considered *erron.* L18.
Times A wide-angle lens captures the enormity of the Barbican Centre. *Listener* People were not really aware of the enormity of that problem.

enormous /ɪˈnɔːməs/ *adjective*. M16.
[ORIGIN from Latin *enormis* (from *e-* E- + *norma* pattern) + -OUS.]
1 Excessive in size or intensity; very large, huge; very great. M16. ▸†**b** That has grown too much in power or importance. M17–M18.
G. S. FRASER *Cursor Mundi* is an enormous poem of 30,000 lines. A. THWAITE Kingsley went to enormous trouble for the son of his old companion.
†**2** Deviating from normality; abnormal, irregular; monstrous, shocking; outrageous, wicked. M16–E19.
■ **enormously** *adverb* E17. **enormousness** *noun* M17.

enosis /ɪˈnəʊsɪs, ˈɛnəsɪs/ *noun*. M20.
[ORIGIN mod. Greek *henōsis*, from *hena* one: see -OSIS.]
Political union, *esp.* that proposed between Greece and Cyprus.
■ **enotic** /-ˈnɒt-/ *adjective* M20. **enotist** *noun* /ɪˈnəʊtɪst/ an advocate of enosis M20.

enough /ɪˈnʌf/ *adjective, noun, & adverb*.
[ORIGIN Old English *genōg*, *genōh* = Old Frisian *enōch*, Old Saxon *ginōg* (Dutch *genoeg*), Old High German *genuog* (German *genug*), Old Norse *gnógr*, Gothic *ganōhs* from Germanic, rel. to Old English *genēah*, Old High German *ginah*, Gothic *ganah* it suffices. Cf. ˈNOUGH, NUFF.]
▸ **A** *adjective*. Sufficient in quantity, number, etc.; not less than what is needed. (Used in concord with a preceding or following noun, and predicatively.) OE.
J. CONRAD It has not soil enough . . to grow a single blade of grass. M. SINCLAIR Five weeks of it were enough to kill him. G. GREENE I've given her enough bromide to put her out of action till morning. J. IRVING If three or four people get stuffed into a car seat, nobody has enough room. *Country Life* There are enough hotels . . to suit any pocket.
▸ **B** *noun*. That which is sufficient; as much as is needed. OE.
A. P. HERBERT She could see enough of herself to be sure that she looked well. E. FROMM The greedy can never have enough, can never be 'satisfied'. *Proverb*: Enough is as good as a feast.
enough! stop!, say no more! **enough and to spare** plenty, a great deal. **enough of —** no more of — is wanted. **enough said** no more need be said. **have had enough (of something)** be satiated with or tired of something. **have enough to do (to achieve something)** have no easy task. **more than enough** = ***enough and to spare*** above.
▸ **C** *adverb*. (In mod. English ***enough*** normally follows the word it qualifies.)
1 Sufficiently; in a quantity or degree that satisfies or is effectual. OE.
J. M. COETZEE He felt strong enough to get up. B. GUEST He stayed long enough to drink eleven cups of tea.

E

2 (In vaguer sense.) With intensive force: fully, quite. Implying disparagement of what is conceded: tolerably, fairly. **E17.**

O. MANNING The quarrel began mildly enough. D. H. LAWRENCE She was intelligent enough, but not interested in learning.

aptly enough, ***oddly enough***, ***strangely enough***, etc. ***fair enough!***: see FAIR *adjective*. ***right enough***: see RIGHT *adverb*. ***sure enough*** undeniably, as was or might have been expected.

enounce /iːˈnaʊns, ɪ-/ *verb trans.* **E19.**
[ORIGIN French *énoncer* from Latin *enuntiare* ENUNCIATE after *announce*, *pronounce*.]
1 State in definite terms; enunciate. **E19.**
2 State publicly, proclaim. **E19.**
3 Utter, pronounce, (words etc.). **E19.**
■ **enouncement** *noun* **M19.**

E

enow /ɪˈnaʊ/ *adjective, noun, & adverb*[1]. Now *arch. & dial.*
[ORIGIN Old English *genōge*, nom. and accus. pl. of *genōg* ENOUGH.]
▸ **A** *adjective*. = ENOUGH *adjective*. (Orig. in concord with a pl. noun only.) **OE.**
▸ **B** *noun*. = ENOUGH *noun*. **ME.**
▸ **C** *adverb*. = ENOUGH *adverb*. **ME.**

enow /ɪˈnaʊ/ *adverb*[2]. **L18.**
[ORIGIN Contr. of *e'en* (= *even*) *now* or for *the now*.]
1 Just now, a moment ago. *Scot. & dial.* **L18.**
2 By and by, presently. *dial.* **L18.**

en pantoufles /ɑ̃ pɑ̃tufl/ *adverbial phr.* **E20.**
[ORIGIN French, lit. 'in slippers'.]
Relaxed, off guard; in a free and easy manner or atmosphere.

en passant /ɑ̃ pasɑ̃, ɒ paˈsɑːnt/ *adverbial phr.* **E17.**
[ORIGIN French.]
In passing, by the way.

J. JONES Then he writes *en passant* that his old landlady is dead.

take a pawn en passant CHESS take (with one's own pawn on the fifth rank) a pawn that has just made an initial move of two squares, as if that pawn had moved only one square.

en pension /ɑ̃ pɑ̃sjɔ̃/ *adverbial phr.* **E19.**
[ORIGIN French.]
In lodgings, as a boarder, esp. in France or another country in Continental Europe.

en permanence /ɑ̃ pɛrmanɑ̃ːs/ *adverbial phr.* **M19.**
[ORIGIN French.]
Permanently.

en place /ɑ̃ plas/ *adverbial phr.* **E19.**
[ORIGIN French.]
In place, in position.

enplane /ɪnˈpleɪn, ɛn-/ *verb trans. & intrans.* **M20.**
[ORIGIN from EN-[1] + PLANE *noun*[4].]
= EMPLANE.

en plein /ɑ̃ plɛ̃/ *adverbial phr.* **L19.**
[ORIGIN French = in full.]
GAMBLING. Entirely on one number or side; with the whole of one's bet.

en plein air /ɑ̃ plɛn ɛːr/ *adverbial phr.* **L19.**
[ORIGIN French, lit. 'in full air'.]
In the open air.

en poste /ɑ̃ pɔst/ *adverbial phr.* **M20.**
[ORIGIN French.]
In an official diplomatic position (at a specified place).

en prince /ɑ̃ prɛ̃ːs/ *adverbial phr.* **L17.**
[ORIGIN French.]
Like a prince; in a princely or luxurious manner.

en principe /ɑ̃ prɛ̃sip/ *adverbial phr.* **E20.**
[ORIGIN French.]
In principle.

enprint /ˈɛnprɪnt/ *noun.* **M20.**
[ORIGIN from *enlarged print*.]
A photographic print of the standard size produced by developing and printing companies, made by printing the whole of a negative to a moderate enlargement.

en prise /ɑ̃ priːz/ *adverbial phr.* **E19.**
[ORIGIN French.]
CHESS. In a position to be taken.

†**enquest** *noun* var. of INQUEST.

enquirable *adjective*, **enquiration** *noun* vars. of INQUIRABLE, INQUIRATION.

enquire *verb*, **enquiry** *noun* see INQUIRE, INQUIRY.

enrage /ɪnˈreɪdʒ, ɛn-/ *verb.* Also †**in-**. **L15.**
[ORIGIN Old French *enrager* become enraged (mod. also = enrage), formed as EN-[1], RAGE *noun*.]
†**1** *verb trans.* As ***enraged*** pa. pple. Maddened by anger, pain, etc.; frenzied. (Foll. by *by*, *with*.) **L15–E18.**
†**2** *verb intrans.* **a** Be distracted or maddened by hunger, thirst, etc. Foll. by *for*. **E–M16.** ▸**b** Become very angry. **M16–L18.** ▸**c** Prevail with violent or destructive effect. **M16–E17.**
3 *verb trans.* Make very angry. Chiefly as ***enraged*** pa. pple. **E16.**

Argosy Enraged at such treatment, the prince sprang up. JAMES CORBETT A titanic fight with an enraged tiger.

†**4** *verb trans.* Make violent; exacerbate; inflame (a wound etc.). **E16–M18.**
■ **enragedly** *adverb* in an enraged manner **L16.** **enragedness** *noun* the state of being enraged **E17.** **enragement** *noun* the action of enraging; the state of being enraged; (formerly) rapture: **L16.**

†**enrail** *verb* see INRAIL.

†**enrange** *verb trans. rare.* **LME.**
[ORIGIN from EN-[1] + RANGE *noun*[1], *verb*[1].]
1 Arrange; rank. **LME–L16.**
2 Range or ramble in (a forest). *rare* (Spenser). Only in **L16.**

enrank /ɪnˈraŋk, ɛn-/ *verb trans.* Now *rare* or *obsolete*. **L16.**
[ORIGIN from EN-[1] + RANK *noun*.]
Set (esp. soldiers) in a line or lines.

en rapport /ɑ̃ rapɔr, ɒn raˈpɔː/ *adverbial phr.* **E19.**
[ORIGIN French.]
In close and harmonious relation (*with*); in sympathy.

enrapt /ɪnˈrapt, ɛn-/ *adjective. poet.* **E17.**
[ORIGIN from EN-[1] + RAPT *adjective*.]
Enraptured; deeply absorbed in something.

enrapture /ɪnˈraptʃə, ɛn-/ *verb trans.* Also †**in-**. **M18.**
[ORIGIN from EN-[1] + RAPTURE.]
Delight intensely, ravish, entrance; inspire with poetic fervour.

enravish /ɪnˈravɪʃ, ɛn-/ *verb trans.* Now *rare*. **L16.**
[ORIGIN from EN-[1] + RAVISH.]
Delight intensely, enrapture.

en regard /ɑ̃ rəgaːr/ *adverbial phr.* **E20.**
[ORIGIN French.]
BIBLIOGRAPHY. On the facing page. Cf. EN FACE.

enregister /ɪnˈrɛdʒɪstə, ɛn-/ *verb trans.* Also (earlier) †**in-**. **LME.**
[ORIGIN Old French & mod. French *enregistrer*, formed as EN-[1] + *registre* REGISTER *noun*[1].]
Enter in a register or official record; put on record as law.
■ **enregiˈstration** *noun* registering, recording; *esp.* the mind's recording of actions that consequently become habitual or automatic **E20.**

en règle /ɑ̃ rɛgl/ *adverbial phr.* **E19.**
[ORIGIN French.]
In order, according to form.

en retraite /ɑ̃ rətrɛt/ *adverbial phr.* **M19.**
[ORIGIN French.]
In retirement.

en revanche /ɑ̃ rəvɑ̃ːʃ/ *adverbial phr.* **E19.**
[ORIGIN French.]
In return, as compensation; in revenge.

enrheum /ɪnˈruːm, ɛn-/ *verb trans. rare.* **M17.**
[ORIGIN Old French *enrheumer* (mod. *enrhumer*), formed as EN-[1], RHEUM *noun*[1].]
Affect with catarrh; give a cold to. Chiefly as ***enrheumed*** pa. pple.

enrich /ɪnˈrɪtʃ, ɛn-/ *verb.* Also †**in-**. **LME.**
[ORIGIN Old French & mod. French *enrichir*, formed as EN-[1] + *riche* RICH *adjective*.]
1 *verb trans.* Make rich or wealthy; *fig.* endow with mental or spiritual wealth. **LME.** ▸**b** Make splendid with (esp. costly) decoration. **L15.**
2 *verb intrans.* Increase one's wealth. *rare.* **E16.**
3 *verb trans.* Add to the wealth of; add something valuable or worthwhile to. **L16.** ▸**b** Make (soil, land) more productive; fertilize. **E17.**

R. W. EMERSON Owen has . . enriched science with contributions of his own. SAKI He had enriched her pantheon of personal possessions with a clever piece of work.

4 *verb trans.* Make richer in quality, colour, flavour, etc.; heighten, enhance. **E17.** ▸**b** Improve the nutritive quality of (food) by adding vitamins or nutrients. **M20.**

B. BAINBRIDGE Freda had hoped working in a factory would enrich Brenda's life.

5 *verb trans.* Increase the proportion of a particular constituent in (a substance); *spec.* increase the proportion of uranium-235 in (uranium). **E20.**

Nature Calcium salts enriched in the non-radioactive nuclides [46]Ca and [48]Ca are now available.

■ **enricher** *noun* a person who or thing which enriches someone or something **E17.** **enrichingly** *adverb* in a way that enriches someone or something **E19.**

enrichment /ɪnˈrɪtʃm(ə)nt, ɛn-/ *noun.* **E17.**
[ORIGIN from ENRICH + -MENT.]
1 The action or process of enrichment; the condition of being enriched. **E17.** ▸**b** SCIENCE. The proportion of a particular, usu. fissile, isotope in a quantity of an element (when greater than the natural proportion). Also, the increase in this proportion above the natural figure. **M20.**
2 Something that enriches; an ornament on a building, statue, etc. **M17.**

†**enridged** *adjective. rare* (Shakes.). Only in **E17.**
[ORIGIN from EN-[1] + RIDGE *noun*[1] + -ED[1].]
Ridged.

enring /ɪnˈrɪŋ, ɛn-/ *verb trans. poet.* **L16.**
[ORIGIN from EN-[1] + RING *noun*[1].]
Form a ring round, encircle; put a ring on.

enripen /ɪnˈrʌɪp(ə)n, ɛn-/ *verb trans. rare.* **M17.**
[ORIGIN from EN-[1] + RIPEN.]
Make ripe, mature (*lit. & fig.*).

enrobe /ɪnˈrəʊb, ɛn-/ *verb trans.* **L16.**
[ORIGIN from EN-[1] + ROBE *noun*[1].]
1 Dress in or cover with a robe. **L16.**
2 Coat (an item of food) in chocolate, a sauce, etc. **E20.**
■ **enrober** *noun* **L16.**

enrol /ɪnˈrəʊl, ɛn-/ *verb.* Also *-**ll**, †**in-**. Infl. -**ll**-. **LME.**
[ORIGIN Old French *enroller* (mod. *enrôler*), formed as EN-[1] + *rolle* ROLL *noun*[1].]
▸ **I 1** *verb trans.* **a** Write (a name) on a list, register, etc.; place (a person) on a list by adding a name. **LME.** ▸**b** Incorporate as an acknowledged member (*in* a group). **LME.** ▸**c** Place on the list of an army, make a member of an army; recruit (an army). **L16.**

b LYNDON B. JOHNSON Men and women were enrolled in classes of their choice. *fig.*: W. IRVING Determined . . to enrol myself in the fraternity of authorship.

a State Enrolled Nurse: see STATE *noun*.
2 *verb trans. hist.* Record in the documents of a court of justice; write (a deed etc.) on a roll or parchment; give legal form to. **LME.**
3 *verb trans.* Set down in a record. Also, commemorate, celebrate. **L15.**

G. HERBERT Small it is, in this poore sort To enroll thee.

4 *verb intrans.* Enter one's name on a list, register, etc., esp. as a commitment to membership of a society, class, etc. (foll. by *in*, *for*); join *as* a member, student, etc. **E20.**

P. ACKROYD He . . enrolled as a graduate student. M. FORSTER She enrolled for a six-month cookery course.

▸ **II 5** *verb trans.* Form into a roll or rolls; wrap or enfold *in* or *with*. Now *rare*. **LME.**
■ **enroˈllee** *noun* (*N. Amer.*) a person who has been enrolled **M20.** **enroller** *noun* **M17.** **enrolment** *noun* (**a**) the action of enrolling; the process of being enrolled; (**b**) the number of people who have been or may be enrolled, esp. in a school, university, etc.; (**c**) *hist.* a documentary record, esp. of a deed: **LME.**

enroot /ɪnˈruːt, ɛn-/ *verb trans.* Also **in-** /ɪn-/. **LME.**
[ORIGIN from EN-[1], IN-[2] + ROOT *noun*[1].]
Chiefly as ***enrooted*** ppl adjective.
1 Implant deeply in the mind; fix firmly as a custom. **LME.**
2 Fix by the root. **L15.**
†**3** Entangle like roots. *rare* (Shakes.). Only in **L16.**

enrough /ɪnˈrʌf, ɛn-/ *verb trans. poet.* **E17.**
[ORIGIN from EN-[1] + ROUGH *adjective*.]
Make (the sea) rough.

enround /ɪnˈraʊnd, ɛn-/ *verb trans.* Long *rare*. **LME.**
[ORIGIN from EN-[1] + ROUND *noun*[1].]
Surround.

en route /ɒ̃ ˈruːt/ *adverbial phr.* **L18.**
[ORIGIN French.]
On the way (*to*, *from*, etc.).

ens /ɛnz/ *noun.* Pl. **entia** /ˈɛntɪə, ˈɛnʃɪə/. **M16.**
[ORIGIN Late Latin *ens* use as noun of pres. pple formed from *esse* be, on the supposed analogy of *absens* ABSENT *adjective & noun*, to translate Greek *on* use as noun of pres. pple of *einai* be.]
1 PHILOSOPHY etc. Something which has existence; a being, an entity, as opp. to an attribute or quality. **M16.**
ens necessarium /nɛkɛˈsɑːrɪəm, nɛsɛˈsɛːrɪəm/ [mod. Latin = necessary being] a necessarily existent being; God. ***ens rationis*** /ratɪˈəʊnɪs, raʃɪ-/, pl. ***entia rationis***, [medieval Latin = being of the mind] an entity of reason; a being with no existence outside the mind. ***ens reale*** /reɪˈɑːli, rɪˈeɪli/, pl. ***entia realia*** /-lɪə/ [medieval Latin = real being] a being existing independently of any finite mind. ***ens realissimum*** /reɪəˈlɪsɪməm, rɪə-/ [mod. Latin] the most real being; God.
†**2** The essence; the essential part. **L16–M18.**

ENSA /ˈɛnsə/ *abbreviation. hist.*
Entertainments National Service Association, an organization which served to arrange entertainments for the British armed services during the Second World War.

ensaint /ɪnˈseɪnt, ɛn-/ *verb trans.* **L16.**
[ORIGIN from EN-[1] + SAINT *noun*.]
Make a saint, canonize; regard as a saint.

ensample /ɛnˈsɑːmp(ə)l/ *noun. arch.* **ME.**
[ORIGIN Anglo-Norman *ensa(u)mple* alt. of Old French *essample* EXAMPLE *noun*.]
= EXAMPLE *noun*.
– NOTE: The mod. arch. use is due chiefly to reminiscences of New Testament passages where the word occurs in AV and RV.

†**ensample** *verb trans.* **LME–M17.**
[ORIGIN from the noun.]
= EXEMPLIFY 2a, 3.

ensanguine /ɪnˈsaŋgwɪn, ɛn-/ *verb trans.* Also (earlier) †**in-**. **E17.**
[ORIGIN from EN-[1], IN-[2] + Latin *sanguin-*, *sanguis* blood.]
Stain with blood; make bloody or the colour of blood.

†**enschedule** *verb trans. rare* (Shakes.). Only in **L16.**
[ORIGIN from EN-[1] + SCHEDULE *noun*.]
Put in a schedule.

ensconce /ɪnˈskɒns, ɛn-/ *verb*. Also †**in-**. L16.
[ORIGIN from EN-[1], IN-[2] + SCONCE *noun*[2].]
†**1** *verb trans.* Provide with defensive earthworks; fortify. L16–M19.
†**2** *verb trans. & intrans.* Shelter within or behind a fortification. L16–M18.
3 *verb trans.* Establish or settle (esp. oneself) in a place for reasons of safety, security, or comfort. (*rare* before E19.) L16.

J. C. POWYS John and Mary had ensconced themselves on a small eighteenth-century sofa.

enscroll /ɪnˈskrəʊl, ɛn-/ *verb trans.* M19.
[ORIGIN from EN-[1] + SCROLL *noun*.]
1 HERALDRY. Depict together with a scroll. *rare*. M19.
2 Write, record in writing. E20.

enseal /ɪnˈsiːl, ɛn-/ *verb trans.* ME.
[ORIGIN Old French *enseeler*, formed as EN-[1] + *seel* SEAL *noun*[2].]
1 Fix a seal on; attest or confirm by sealing. Now *rare* or *obsolete*. ME.
2 Close with a seal, seal up. *arch.* ME.

†**enseam** *verb*[1] *trans.* L15–L18.
[ORIGIN Alt., through confusion with ENSEAM *verb*[2], of Old French *essaimer* (mod. *essimer*), formed as ES- + *saim* SEAM *noun*[3].]
Cause (a hawk, a horse) to lose superfluous fat.

†**enseam** *verb*[2] *trans. rare.* M16–E17.
[ORIGIN Old French *ensaimer* (mod. *ensimer*, †*ensémer*), formed as EN-[1] + *saim* SEAM *noun*[3]: cf. ENSEAM *verb*[1].]
Soil or load with grease.

†**enseam** *verb*[3] *trans. rare.* L16–E17.
[ORIGIN Unknown.]
Include; bring or contain together.

enseam /ɪnˈsiːm, ɛn-/ *verb*[4] *trans.* E17.
[ORIGIN from EN-[1] + SEAM *noun*[1], *verb*.]
1 Mark as with a seam. E17.
†**2** Sew or stitch up in. Only in E17.

†**ensear** *verb trans. rare.* L15–E17.
[ORIGIN from EN-[1] + SERE *adjective*.]
Dry up.

ensearch /ɪnˈsəːtʃ, ɛn-/ *verb. arch.* Also †**in-**. ME.
[ORIGIN Old French *encerchier*, *-serchier*, formed as EN-[1] + *cerchier* (mod. *chercher*) SEARCH *verb*[1].]
†**1** *verb trans.* Search into, investigate. ME–L16.
2 *verb trans.* Search; scrutinize, examine. LME.
†**3** *verb trans.* Search for, seek out. LME–M16.
†**4** *verb intrans.* Make a search; inquire. LME–L16.

†**enseint** *adjective* var. of ENCEINTE *adjective*.

ensemble /ɒ̃ˈsɒ̃b(ə)l, ɒnˈsɒmb(ə)l, *foreign* ɑ̃sɑːmbl (*pl. same*)/ *adverb & noun*. LME.
[ORIGIN Old French & mod. French from Proto-Romance, from Latin *insimul*, formed as IN-[2] + *simul* at the same time.]
▸ **A** *adverb*. Together; at the same time. Long *rare*. LME.
▸ **B** *noun*. **1** (The parts of) a thing viewed as a whole; the overall effect or appearance of something. Cf. earlier TOUT ENSEMBLE. M18.

J. BRODSKY They started to build, not separate buildings but whole architectural ensembles.

2 **a** The unity of performance achieved by two or more players, singers, or dancers performing together. E19. ▸**b** A group of stage artistes who perform together in a production; *esp.* the supporting actors or dancers as opp. to the stars or principals. E20. ▸**c** A scene on stage in which the ensemble or the whole cast appear; a piece of music performed by an ensemble. E20. ▸**d** A group of singers or musicians, esp. a small group of soloists, who perform together. M20.

a *Gramophone* There is just one spot of slightly poor ensemble where the castanets come in. **b** *attrib.*: *Flicks* The star . . is . . heading an ensemble cast of many familiar Allen regulars. **c** *Times* Lifar's opening *Noir et Blanc* . . put the company through its paces in a series of testing solos and ensembles.

d *vocal ensemble*, *wind ensemble*, etc.
3 A set of (usu. women's) clothes that harmonize and are worn together; an outfit. E20.
4 SCIENCE. A notional collection of systems of identical constitution but not necessarily in the same state; the family of possible outcomes or states of a given system; *spec.* a collection of particles large enough for its behaviour to be described statistically. E20.

R. C. TOLMAN The properties of a thermodynamic system . . may be studied with the help of the average properties of an appropriately chosen representative ensemble of systems.

– COMB.: **ensemble acting**, **ensemble playing**: in which all the roles are presented as contributing equally to a production.

†**ensense** *verb* see INSENSE.

ensepulchre /ɪnˈsɛpəlkə, ɛn-/ *verb trans.* Also ***-cher**. E19.
[ORIGIN from EN-[1] + SEPULCHRE.]
Swallow up and destroy; engulf.

enserf /ɪnˈsəːf, ɛn-/ *verb trans.* L19.
[ORIGIN from EN-[1] + SERF.]
Make a serf; deprive of political rights.
■ **enserfment** *noun* the action of enserfing M20.

ensete /ɛnˈsiːti/ *noun*. L18.
[ORIGIN Amharic.]
An Ethiopian tree of the banana family, *Ensete ventricosum*, with edible flower heads and seeds. Also called ***Abyssinian banana***.

enshadow /ɪnˈʃadəʊ, ɛn-/ *verb trans.* L15.
[ORIGIN from EN-[1] + SHADOW *noun*.]
Put in shadow, shade; conceal *from*.

ensheath /ɪnˈʃiːθ, ɛn-/ *verb trans.* Also **-sheathe** /-ˈʃiːð/. L16.
[ORIGIN from EN-[1] + SHEATH *noun*[1], SHEATHE *verb*.]
Enclose or conceal like a sheath.

enshell *verb* var. of INSHELL.

†**enshield** *adjective. rare* (Shakes.). Only in E17.
[ORIGIN Uncertain: perh. from EN-[1] + SHIELD *noun*[1], but cf. ENSHIELD *verb*.]
Shielded, concealed.

enshield /ɪnˈʃiːld, ɛn-/ *verb trans. rare.* M19.
[ORIGIN from EN-[1] + SHIELD *verb*. Cf. ENSHIELD *adjective*.]
Guard or screen as with a shield.

enshrine /ɪnˈʃrʌɪn, ɛn-/ *verb trans.* Also †**in-**. LME.
[ORIGIN from EN-[1], IN-[2] + SHRINE *noun*.]
1 Enclose (as) in a shrine; place in a receptacle appropriate for a precious or revered object. LME.

fig.: W. SPALDING Papal orthodoxy sat enshrined in the Escurial.

2 Contain as a shrine does; contain or embody in a way that protects or preserves. E17.

SAKI Her drawing-room . . enshrined the memorials or tokens of past and present happiness. R. A. KNOX It was necessary to enshrine Christian truths in a more exact, a more elaborate setting than of old. ANTHONY SMITH The rights of the ordinary individual, acquired over centuries and enshrined in law.

■ **enshrinement** *noun* the action of enshrining; a thing that enshrines; an embodiment: M19.

enshroud /ɪnˈʃraʊd, ɛn-/ *verb trans.* L16.
[ORIGIN from EN-[1] + SHROUD *noun*[1].]
Cover as with a shroud; completely envelop; hide from view.

G. BROWN Moscow was enshrouded in fog and my aircraft had to be diverted. *fig.*: W. H. DIXON The crimes . . were enshrouded in the deepest mystery.

ensialic /ɛnsʌɪˈalɪk/ *adjective*. M20.
[ORIGIN from EN-[2] + SIALIC *adjective*[1].]
GEOLOGY. Originating or occurring in or on sialic material; of or pertaining to structures or phenomena of this kind.

ensient /ɛnsɪˈɛnt/ *adjective*. E18.
[ORIGIN Alt. of ENSEINT *adjective*.]
LAW. Of a woman: pregnant.

ensiform /ˈɛnsɪfɔːm/ *adjective & noun*. M16.
[ORIGIN from Latin *ensis* sword + -FORM.]
▸ **A** *adjective*. Shaped like a sword blade; *spec.* (of a leaf) long and narrow with sharp edges and a pointed tip, like an iris leaf. M16.
ensiform cartilage = XIPHISTERNUM.
▸ **B** *noun*. An ensiform object; *spec.* = ***ensiform cartilage*** above. E20.

ensign /ˈɛnsʌɪn, -sɪn, -s(ə)n/ *noun*. LME.
[ORIGIN Old French & mod. French *enseigne* formed as INSIGNIA. Cf. ANCIENT *noun*[2].]
1 A signal, a rallying cry; a watchword, a slogan. Chiefly *Scot.* Long *rare*. LME.
2 A characteristic, a sign (*of* something). *arch.* LME.

R. L. STEVENSON If the Indian Empire, the trade of London, and all the . . ensigns of our greatness should pass away.

3 A conventional symbol, an emblem; *esp.* a badge of office; in *pl.*, heraldic bearings, as much of a heraldic achievement as is depicted. LME.

M. R. MITFORD Those ensigns of authority, the keys.

4 A military or naval standard; a flag; *spec.* a flag flown at the stern of a vessel to show its nationality; in Britain, each of three such flags with the union flag in one corner (see below). LME.
blue ensign orig. the ensign of the rear admiral's squadron, now that of naval auxiliary vessels. **red ensign** orig. the ensign of the admiral's squadron, now that of the British merchant navy. **white ensign** orig. the ensign of the rear admiral's squadron, now that of the Royal Navy and Royal Yacht Squadron.
†**5** A body of men serving under the same flag; a troop. M16–M17.
6 A standard-bearer (*hist.*); an infantry officer of the lowest commissioned rank, a second lieutenant, (*hist.* exc. in the Foot Guards); an officer in the Yeomen of the Guard. L16.
7 An officer of the lowest commissioned rank in the US navy. M19.
■ **ensigncy** *noun* (*hist.*) the rank or position of an ensign M18.

ensign /ˈɛnsʌɪn/ *verb*. *obsolete* exc. HERALDRY. L15.
[ORIGIN Old French *ensignier*, *enseigner* from medieval Latin *insignare* for Latin *insignire* mark, distinguish, formed as IN-[2] + *signum* SIGN *noun*.]
†**1** *verb trans. & intrans.* Indicate, point out. L15–L16.
†**2** *verb trans.* Teach, instruct. L15–L16.
3 *verb trans.* Mark with a sign or badge. Now only HERALDRY, distinguish or ornament (a charge) by depicting some object placed above it. L16.

†**ensignment** *noun*. LME.
[ORIGIN Old French & mod. French *enseignement*, formed as ENSIGN *verb*: see -MENT.]
1 Instruction; a lesson; a means of instruction, an example. LME–E17.
2 A badge of office. M16–E17.

ensilage /ˈɛnsɪlɪdʒ, ɛnˈsʌɪlɪdʒ/ *noun & verb*. L19.
[ORIGIN French, from *ensiler* from Spanish *ensilar*, from *en-* (formed as IN-[2]) + SILO: see -AGE.]
▸ **A** *noun*. **1** The process of making silage. L19.
2 Silage. L19.
▸ **B** *verb trans.* Treat (fodder) by ensilage; turn into silage. L19.

ensile /ɛnˈsʌɪl/ *verb trans.* L19.
[ORIGIN French *ensiler*: see ENSILAGE.]
= ENSILAGE *verb*.

ensimatic /ɛnsʌɪˈmatɪk/ *adjective*. M20.
[ORIGIN from EN-[2] + SIMATIC.]
GEOLOGY. Originating or occurring in or on simatic material; of or pertaining to structures or phenomena of this kind.

†**ensinew** *verb* var. of INSINEW.

ensky /ɪnˈskʌɪ, ɛn-/ *verb trans. poet.* E17.
[ORIGIN from EN-[1] + SKY *noun*.]
Place in the sky or in heaven. Usu. in *pass.*

enslave /ɪnˈsleɪv, ɛn-/ *verb trans.* Also †**in-**. E17.
[ORIGIN from EN-[1], IN-[2] + SLAVE *noun*[1].]
1 Make (a person) completely subject to or dominated by habit, superstition, passion, or the like. E17.

J. GLASSCO I was . . enslaved by the beauty of Paris.

2 Make a slave of, reduce to slavery; deprive of political freedom. M17.
■ **enslavement** *noun* the action of enslaving; the state of being enslaved: L17. **enslaver** *noun* E18.

ensnare /ɪnˈsnɛː, ɛn-/ *verb trans.* Also †**in-**. L16.
[ORIGIN from EN-[1], IN-[2] + SNARE *noun*.]
Catch in a snare. Chiefly *fig.*, beguile, lure; entangle in difficulties.
■ **ensnarement** *noun* (now *rare*) the action of ensnaring; the state or fact of being ensnared; a bait, a trap: E17. **ensnarer** *noun* (now *rare*) M17.

ensnarl /ɪnˈsnɑːl, ɛn-/ *verb trans.* Also (earlier) †**in-**. LME.
[ORIGIN from EN-[1], IN-[2] + SNARL *noun*[1].]
Entangle or catch as in a snarl or ravelled knot. Now only *fig.*

ensorcell /ɪnˈsɔːs(ə)l, ɛn-/ *verb trans.* Also **-el**, infl. **-ll-**, ***-l-**. M16.
[ORIGIN Old French & mod. French *ensorceler* alt. of Old French *ensorcerer*, formed as EN-[1] + *sorcier* SORCERER.]
Enchant, bewitch; fascinate.
■ **ensorcellment**, **-elment** *noun* magic, enchantment, a piece of magic M20.

ensoul /ɪnˈsəʊl, ɛn-/ *verb trans.* Also (earlier) **in-** /ɪn-/. E17.
[ORIGIN from EN-[1], IN-[2] + SOUL *noun*.]
1 Put or take into the soul; unite with the soul. Now *rare*. E17.
2 Infuse a soul into; fill effectually. E17.

C. GORE An organism ensouled by the indwelling word. *New Scientist* God would be more likely to ensoul the fetus at birth.

■ **ensoulment** *noun* the introduction of a soul into something M20.

ensphere /ɪnˈsfɪə, ɛn-/ *verb trans.* Also **in-** /ɪn-/. E17.
[ORIGIN from EN-[1], IN-[2] + SPHERE *noun*.]
1 Enclose (as) in a sphere; encircle. E17.
2 Shape into a sphere. M17.
■ **enspherement** *noun* (*rare*) M19.

†**enspire** *verb* see INSPIRE.

enstamp /ɪnˈstamp, ɛn-/ *verb trans.* Also (earlier) †**in-**. L16.
[ORIGIN from EN-[1], IN-[2] + STAMP *verb*.]
Stamp, imprint, (a mark etc.) *on* something; put a mark on, mark *with*.

†**enstate** *verb* var. of INSTATE.

enstatite /ˈɛnstətʌɪt/ *noun*. M19.
[ORIGIN from Greek *enstatēs* adversary (from its refractory nature) + -ITE[1].]
MINERALOGY. An orthorhombic magnesium silicate that is a member of the pyroxene group and occurs as translucent crystals of varying colours in igneous rocks and meteorites.

†**ensteep** *verb* var. of INSTEEP.

enstool /ɪnˈstuːl, ɛn-/ *verb trans.* L19.
[ORIGIN from EN-[1] + STOOL *noun*.]
Place on the stool of a W. African chief; enthrone (a chief).

enstyle *verb* var. of INSTYLE.

E

ensuant /ɪnˈsjuːənt, ɛn-/ *adjective*. L16.
[ORIGIN from ENSUE + -ANT¹.]
†**1** Appropriate *to* what has preceded. *rare*. Only in L16.
2 Ensuing, following; consequent (*on*). L19.

ensue /ɪnˈsjuː, ɛn-/ *verb*. Also †**in-**. LME.
[ORIGIN Old French *ensiw-*, *ensu-* stem of *ensivre* (mod. *ensuivre*) from Proto-Romance, from Latin *insequi*, formed as IN-² + *sequi* follow.]
†**1** *verb trans. & intrans.* Follow (a person); follow in (the steps of someone). LME–E17.
†**2** *verb trans.* Pursue, chase. LME–M16.
†**3** *verb trans.* Follow the guidance or example of; follow (one's inclination); take (advice). LME–L16.
4 **a** *verb intrans.* Be subsequent; occur or arise afterwards, esp. as a result or consequence; result *from* (also foll. by *on*, *upon*, †*by*, †*of*). LME. ▸†**b** *verb trans.* Succeed, come after, be subsequent to; result from. L15–M18.

> **a** T. HARDY One quarter of the trees would die away during the ensuing August. R. LYND Thereupon a long argument ensued.

†**5** *verb trans.* Correspond to. LME–E17.
6 *verb trans.* Seek after, aim at. *arch.* L15.
†**7** *verb trans.* Carry out (a plan); follow (an occupation); follow up; spend (a period of one's life). E16–E17.
■ **ensuer** *noun* (*rare*) M16.

en suite /ɒ̃ ˈswiːt, *foreign* ɑ̃ sɥit/ *adverbial, adjectival, & noun phr.* Also (esp. as adjectival & noun phr.) **ensuite** /ɒ̃ˈswiːt/. L18.
[ORIGIN French.]
▸ **A** *adverbial phr.* **1** In agreement or harmony (*with*). Now *rare* or *obsolete*. L18.
2 In a row, with one room leading into another; as part of the same set of rooms. (Foll. by *with*.) E19. ▸**b** As part of the same set of objects. (Foll. by *with*.) M20.

> *Cornish Guardian* 4 bedrooms (2 with shower rooms en suite).

▸ **B** *adjectival phr.* Of a room: that is en suite; forming part of the same set, immediately adjoining. M20.
▸ **C** *noun phr.* An en suite room, *esp.* an en suite bathroom. L20.

†**ensurance** *noun* see INSURANCE.

ensure /ɪnˈʃʊə, ɛn-/ *verb trans.* LME.
[ORIGIN Anglo-Norman *enseürer* alt. of Old French *asseürer* ASSURE. Cf. INSURE.]
1 Make sure, convince. Chiefly *refl.* & in *pass.* Long *rare*. LME.
†**2** Promise to (a person). (Foll. by *to do*, *that*.) LME–M17.
†**3** Engage, pledge, (a person); *esp.* become engaged to, espouse. LME–E17.
†**4** Guarantee, warrant. LME–M18.
5 Secure, make safe, (*against*, *from*, a risk etc.). LME. ▸†**b** Insure (a life, property, etc.). L17–M18.

> J. REYNOLDS Ensure us from all error and mistake.

6 Make certain the occurrence of (an event, situation, outcome, etc.). (Foll. by *that*.) M18.

> F. TUOHY Concessions had to be made, to ensure his silence. M. AMIS Everything has to be *just so*—and I . . ensure that it is.

7 Secure (a thing) *for* or *to* a person. Also foll. by double obj. L18.

> LEIGH HUNT It ensures us an intercourse with a nation we esteem.

— NOTE: *Ensure* and *insure* are often used with similar meaning, esp. in US English, but only *insure* now has the commercial sense of 'arrange for compensation in the event of damage to or loss of property'.
■ **ensurer** *noun* (*rare*) M17.

enswathe /ɪnˈsweɪð, ɛn-/ *verb trans.* Chiefly *poet.* L16.
[ORIGIN from EN-¹ + SWATHE *noun*¹ or *verb*.]
Wrap or bind (as) in a bandage; swathe.
■ **enswathement** *noun* a thing that enswathes or envelops; the state of being enswathed: L19.

ENT *abbreviation*.
Ear, nose, and throat.

ent- *combining form* see ENTO-.

-ent /(ə)nt/ *suffix*.
[ORIGIN French, or its source Latin *-ent-* pres. ppl stem of verbs of 2nd, 3rd, and 4th conjugations, or *-ant-* (see -ANT¹).]
Forming adjectives denoting existence of action, as ***effluent***, or state, as ***convenient***, or nouns denoting an agent, as ***president***, ***referent***, ***superintendent***, usu. from verbs. Conflicting English, French, & Latin analogies have produced much inconsistency of use of ***-ent*** and ***-ant***.

entablature /ɛnˈtablətʃə, ɪn-/ *noun*. Also †**in-**. E17.
[ORIGIN from Italian *intavolatura* boarding (partly through French ENTABLEMENT), from *intavolare* board up, formed as IN-² + *tavola* table: see -URE.]
1 ARCHITECTURE. The part of a classical building that is above and supported by the columns, comprising architrave, frieze, and cornice. E17.
2 A structure analogous to a classical entablature. M19.

> H. JAMES Fireplaces of white marble, the entablature of which was adorned with a delicate . . 'subject'.

■ **entablatured** *adjective* M19.

entablement /ɛnˈteɪb(ə)lm(ə)nt, ɪn-/ *noun*. M17.
[ORIGIN French, from *entabler*, formed as EN-¹ + *table*: see TABLE *noun*, -MENT.]
ARCHITECTURE. **1** = ENTABLATURE 1. Now *rare* or *obsolete*. M17.
2 The horizontal platform(s) supporting a statue, above the dado and the base. E19.

entail /ɪnˈteɪl, ɛn-/ *noun*. Also †**in-**. LME.
[ORIGIN from ENTAIL *verb*².]
1 LAW (now chiefly *hist.*). The settlement of the succession of land or other property on a designated class of descendants; the line of succession so prescribed. LME.
2 *fig.* Restriction to a prescribed succession of people; transmission as an inalienable inheritance; a secured inheritance. LME.

> J. MARTINEAU The natural entail of disease and character. J. BAYLEY Poets oppressed by the modern entail of the poet as self.

3 The fact of being necessarily consequent *upon*. M17.

> R. W. HAMILTON The entail of vice upon the circumstances of the present life.

†**entail** *verb*¹ LME.
[ORIGIN Old French *entaillier* (mod. *entailler*) from medieval Latin *intalliare*, formed as IN-² + *talliare* cut: see TAIL *verb*¹.]
1 *verb trans.* Carve; cut into; decorate with carvings. LME–M17.
2 *verb intrans.* Cut (*into*). *rare* (Spenser). Only in L16.

entail /ɪnˈteɪl, ɛn-/ *verb*² *trans.* Also †**in-**. LME.
[ORIGIN from EN-¹, IN-² + Anglo-Norman *taile* TAIL *noun*² or *taillé* TAIL *adjective*.]
1 LAW. Settle (land etc.) by entail; *fig.* confer as if by entail, bestow as an inalienable possession (*on*). LME.

> M. R. MITFORD The house and park . . were entailed on a distant cousin.

†**2** Attach inseparably *to*; attach, associate. Also foll. by *upon*. L16–E18.
3 Impose (inconvenience, expense, etc.) *on* or *upon* a person. M17.

> SIR W. SCOTT Which shall . . entail disgrace on all who have to do with it.

4 Necessitate as a consequence; have as an inevitable accompaniment, involve. E19.

> D. ATHILL He had no conception of what a real job . . entailed.

■ **entailable** *adjective* L17. **entailer** *noun* a person who entails property L18. **entailment** *noun* the action or an act of entailing something; PHILOSOPHY the strict or logically necessary implication of one proposition by another: M17.

†**entame** *verb*¹ *trans.* ME.
[ORIGIN Old French & mod. French *entamer* alt. of *atamer*: see ATTAME.]
1 Cut into, wound. ME–L15.
2 Make the first cut in; *fig.* begin. Only in L15.

entame /ɪnˈteɪm, ɛn-/ *verb*² *trans.* L15.
[ORIGIN from EN-¹ + TAME *adjective*.]
Tame; subdue.

entamoeba /ɛntəˈmiːbə/ *noun*. Also ***-meba**. Pl. **-bae** /-biː/, **-bas**. E20.
[ORIGIN mod. Latin, from ENTO- + AMOEBA.]
An amoeba of the parasitic genus *Entamoeba*, of which one species causes dysentery in humans and another is a harmless commensal in the colon.

entangle /ɪnˈtaŋg(ə)l, ɛn-/ *verb trans.* Also †**in-**. LME.
[ORIGIN from EN-¹, IN-² + TANGLE *noun*², *verb*.]
1 Cause to be held in something that is tangled or that impedes movement or extrication. LME.

> ADDISON Lest she should entangle her Feet in her Petticoat. *fig.*: BURKE Nets that entangle the . . silken wings of a tender conscience.

2 Involve (a person etc.) in difficulties, doubtful undertakings, etc. LME. ▸**b** Involve (a person) in a compromising relationship *with* another. L19.

> J. A. FROUDE The Pope . . had endeavoured to entangle his nephew in the conspiracy. **b** F. HUME He became entangled with a lady whose looks were much better than her morals.

3 Make tangled; interlace so that separation is difficult. M16.
4 Make complicated or intricate; complicate *with*. L17.

> L. STERNE Two other circumstances which entangled this mystery.

■ **entangler** *noun* L16.

entanglement /ɪnˈtaŋg(ə)lm(ə)nt, ɛn-/ *noun*. Also †**in-**. L16.
[ORIGIN from ENTANGLE + -MENT.]
1 The action of entangling; the condition or an instance of being entangled. L16.
2 A thing that entangles; a complication, an embarrassment. M17. ▸**b** MILITARY. An extensive barrier designed to impede an enemy's movements, now often made of stakes and tangled barbed wire. M19.
3 A compromising, usu. amorous, relationship. M19.

entasis /ˈɛntəsɪs/ *noun*. Pl. **-ases** /-əsiːz/. M17.
[ORIGIN mod. Latin from Greek, from *enteinein* to strain.]
ARCHITECTURE. A slight bowing of the shaft of a column (introduced to correct the visual illusion of concavity).

entelechy /ɛnˈtɛləki, ɪn-/ *noun*. LME.
[ORIGIN Late Latin *entelechia* from Greek *entelekheia*, formed as EN-² + *telei*, dat. of *telos* end, perfection + *ekhein* be in a (certain) state: see -Y³.]
PHILOSOPHY. **1** In Aristotle's use: the condition in which a potentiality has become an actuality; *spec.* the essential nature or informing principle of a living thing; the soul. LME. ▸**b** BIOLOGY. A supposed vital principle that guides the development and functioning of an organism. E20.
2 In Leibniz's use: a monad. L19.

entellus /ɪnˈtɛləs, ɛn-/ *noun*. M19.
[ORIGIN *Entellus*, an old man in Virgil's *Aeneid*.]
The hanuman monkey. Also ***entellus langur***, ***entellus monkey***.

entemple /ɪnˈtɛmp(ə)l, ɛn-/ *verb trans.* E17.
[ORIGIN from EN-¹ + TEMPLE *noun*¹.]
Enclose as in a temple; enshrine.

†**entend** *verb* see INTEND.

†**entender** *verb trans.* Also **in-**. L16–M18.
[ORIGIN from EN-¹, IN-² + TENDER *adjective*.]
Make tender; soften (the heart).

†**entendment** *noun* see INTENDMENT.

†**entent** *noun*, *verb* see INTENT *noun*, *verb*.

entente /ɑːnˈtɑːnt, *foreign* ɑ̃tɑ̃ːt (*pl. same*)/ *noun*. M19.
[ORIGIN French.]
A friendly understanding, esp. between states; a group of states sharing such an understanding.

entente cordiale /ɑ̃tɑ̃ːt kɔrdjal, ɑːnˌtɑːnt kɔːdɪˈɑːl/ *noun phr.* Pl. **-s -s** (pronounced same). M19.
[ORIGIN French.]
An entente, *spec.* (*hist.*) that arrived at by France and Britain in 1904.

†**entention** *noun* var. of INTENTION.

†**ententive** *adjective* see INTENTIVE.

entepicondylar /ˌɛntɛpɪˈkɒndɪlə/ *adjective*. L19.
[ORIGIN from ENTO- + EPICONDYLE + -AR¹.]
ANATOMY. ***entepicondylar foramen***, a foramen in the humerus of many vertebrates just above the medial epicondyle.

†**enter** *noun*. LME–L16.
[ORIGIN from the verb.]
The action, power, or right of entering; an entrance, a passage.

enter /ˈɛntə/ *verb*. ME.
[ORIGIN Old French & mod. French *entrer* from Latin *intrare*, from *intra* within.]
1 **a** *verb intrans.* Go or come in or (*arch.*) *in*; (as a stage direction, in 3 pres. subjunct.) come on stage. Also foll. by *into* a specified place, region, etc. ME. ▸**b** *verb trans.* Go or come into (a place, medium, etc.); go within the bounds of (a country etc.). ME. ▸†**c** *verb trans.* Seize (a crown, a throne). M16–M17. ▸**d** *verb trans.* Force an entrance into; break into. L16.

> **a** F. MARRYAT We . . entered into a noble forest. T. STOPPARD The door . . opens and two men enter. *transf.*: M. W. MONTAGU During these Excuses, enter Edgcombe. **b** D. H. LAWRENCE They had entered a wide river, from the narrow one. T. F. POWYS A flock of sheep all clamouring to enter a field.

a break and enter: see BREAK *verb*. **b enter one's head**, **enter one's mind** (of a thought, idea, etc.) occur to one, cross one's mind. ***enter the lists***: see LIST *noun*¹ 7b.
†**2** **a** *verb intrans.* Come or fall *into* a state or condition. ME–E18. ▸**b** *verb trans.* Come or pass into (a certain condition). Formerly also, take upon oneself (a position), take up (an occupation). Now *rare*. M16.
3 *verb intrans.* LAW. Take possession of land, esp. as an assertion of ownership. Also foll. by †*in*, *into*, (*up*)*on*. LME.
4 **a** *verb intrans.* Penetrate deeply into or *into* something. LME. ▸**b** *verb trans.* Pierce, penetrate; *spec.* (of a male) have sexual intercourse with; insert the penis into the vagina of (a woman). E17.

> **b** S. MARCUS He ejaculates without succeeding in entering her.

a the iron entered into his soul: see IRON *noun*.
5 **a** *verb intrans.* Become a member of an organization. (Foll. by *at*, *in*, *into*.) LME. ▸**b** *verb trans.* Become a member of; take up one's vocation in; begin to live, study, etc., in. E17.

> **a** BOSWELL He could not . . enter where . . he could not have an able tutor. **b** T. HARDY Your scheme was to be a University man and enter the church. J. BUCHAN In 1914 he entered the Cabinet as President of the Board of Agriculture.

6 *verb intrans.* Begin; make a beginning; engage in an activity. Now only *Scot. dial.*, begin work, *esp.* begin harvest. LME.
7 *verb trans.* Put *into*; insert, introduce. Now chiefly *techn.* LME.

DAVID POTTER The die is hardened and entered into a soft steel roller.

8 a *verb trans.* Record in a register, diary, account book, etc.; record particulars in (a journal), write up. Also foll. by *up*. LME. ▸**b** *verb trans.* Register (a vessel) entering or leaving a port; register with the authorities details of (goods being exported or imported). M17. ▸**c** *verb intrans. & trans.* Register as a competitor in a race, contest, etc.; submit (an animal, an inanimate object) for judging in a competition; become a competitor in (a race, contest, etc.). (Foll. by *for*, *in*.) L17. ▸**d** *verb trans.* US HISTORY. Get (public land) registered in one's name as the intending occupier or owner. L18. ▸**e** *verb trans.* Foll. by *up*: complete a series of entries in (an account book etc.). L19.

a J. STEINBECK The names were entered in the book. G. GREENE She hadn't entered the journal every day, and I had no wish to read every entry. *Personal Software* You must enter the coordinates of your shape as DATA in line 9000. **c** *Washington Post* Last year's winner . . did not enter this year. *Times* Davies . . has entered the French and Dutch open championships next month.

9 *verb trans.* **a** Give (an animal or bird) its first exercises or training; break in (a horse); (foll. by *at*, *to*) put (an untrained animal or bird) on the scent of a quarry. L15. ▸†**b** Instruct (a person) initially; initiate. (Foll. by *in*.) M16–M19.

a P. WAYRE After several weeks both birds would fly . . , and it was time to enter them to a lure.

10 *verb trans.* Formerly, take the first steps in, begin, (an activity). Now, begin (a period of time). E16.

G. B. SHAW I have now entered my 93rd year. C. ISHERWOOD George has felt himself entering a new phase. J. SIMMS The discussions . . entered a period of intense upheaval.

11 *verb trans.* Put or bring (a person) into something, esp. on to a ship. *arch.* E16.

12 *verb trans.* **a** Procure admission into or *into* a society or an employment for (a person); admit as a member. Formerly also, bring (a person) *into* a specified state or relationship. L16. ▸**b** Engage (an employee). M17.

a I. WALTON Having entred Edward into Queens Colledge. E. PEACOCK He therefore entered himself as a clerk to a solicitor.

13 *verb trans.* Record in due form in a court of law, a deliberative body, etc. Also foll. by *up*. L16.

A. PULLING The defendant failed to appear, and judgment was entered. *transf.*: J. L. AUSTIN Now we must enter two caveats.

14 *verb trans.* Look at or turn to a particular place in (a mathematical table). L16.

– WITH PREPOSITIONS IN SPECIALIZED SENSES: **enter into**, †**enter in** (*a*) take upon oneself (a commitment, duty, relationship, etc.); bind oneself by, subscribe to, (an agreement); (*b*) engage in the consideration of (a matter); (*c*) form part of, be an element of; be relevant to; (*d*) take an interest in; sympathize with; **enter on**, **enter upon** (*a*) take the first steps on; begin to travel on; †(*b*) begin an attack on; (*c*) begin to deal with or consider.

■ **enterable** *adjective* E18. **enterer** *noun* M16.

enter- /ˈɛntə/ *combining form*¹. Also **entre-** /ˈɛntrə/.

[ORIGIN Repr. Old French & mod. French *entre-* from Latin *inter-*: see INTER-.]

Forming compounds with the senses 'between', 'among', 'mutually'. Now repl. by INTER-. The compounds of English origin in which it occurs either are obsolete or have been refashioned with *inter-*.

enter- *combining form*² see ENTERO-.

entera *noun* pl. of ENTERON.

enteral /ˈɛntər(ə)l/ *adjective*. E20.

[ORIGIN Partly formed as ENTERIC + -AL¹, partly back-form. from *parenteral*.]

MEDICINE. Enteric; (of feeding, feeds, etc.) involving or passing through the intestine, either in the normal way (via the mouth etc.) or through an artificial opening (opp. PARENTERAL).

■ **enterally** *adverb* M20.

†**enterchange** *noun*, *verb* vars. of INTERCHANGE *noun*, *verb*.

enterclose /ˈɛntəkləʊs/ *noun*. *obsolete* exc. ARCHITECTURE. Also †**inter-**. LME.

[ORIGIN Old French *entreclos* (in medieval Latin *interclausum*), from *entre-* ENTER-¹ + *clos* CLOSE *noun*¹.]

A partition; a space partitioned off.

†**entercommon** *verb & noun* see INTERCOMMON.

†**entercommune** *verb* see INTERCOMMUNE.

†**entercommunicate** *verb*, **entercommunication** *noun* see INTERCOMMUNICATE etc.

†**entercourse** *noun* see INTERCOURSE.

†**enterdiction** *noun* see INTERDICTION.

†**enterfere** *verb* var. of INTERFERE.

†**enterfold** *verb* var. of INTERFOLD.

enteric /ɛnˈtɛrɪk/ *adjective & noun*. E19.

[ORIGIN Greek *enterikos*, formed as ENTERON: see -IC.]

ANATOMY & MEDICINE. ▸**A** *adjective*. **1** Of, pertaining to, or occurring in the intestines. E19.

enteric fever typhoid or paratyphoid fever.

2 = *enteric-coated* below. E20.

– COMB.: **enteric-coated** *adjective* (of a capsule) coated so that the contents are released in the intestine after passage through the stomach unaltered.

▸**B** *noun*. Enteric fever. E20.

entering /ˈɛnt(ə)rɪŋ/ *noun*. ME.

[ORIGIN from ENTER *verb* + -ING¹.]

1 The action of ENTER *verb*. ME.

†**2** An entrance; a door, a gate, etc.; an opening. LME–M16.

enteritis /ɛntəˈrʌɪtɪs/ *noun*. E19.

[ORIGIN from Greek ENTERON + -ITIS.]

MEDICINE. Inflammation of the intestine, esp. acute inflammation of the small intestine, usu. accompanied by diarrhoea.

†**enterlace** *verb* see INTERLACE *verb*.

†**enterlard** *verb* see INTERLARD.

†**enterline** *verb* see INTERLINE *verb*¹.

†**enterlude** *noun* see INTERLUDE.

†**entermarriage** *noun*, **entermarry** *verb* vars. of INTERMARRIAGE, INTERMARRY.

†**entermeddle** *verb* var. of INTERMEDDLE.

†**entermise** *noun*. Also **inter-**. L15.

[ORIGIN Old French *entremise*, from *entremetre* (mod. *-mettre*), repr. Latin *intermittere* and *intromittere*: see INTERMIT, INTROMIT.]

1 Business. Only in L15.

2 Interposition, intervention. E17–E18.

entero- /ˈɛntərəʊ/ *combining form* of Greek ENTERON intestine: see -O-. Before a vowel also **enter-**.

■ **enteroˈbiasis** *noun*, pl. **-ases** /-əsiːz/, infestation with or disease caused by pinworms of the genus *Enterobius* M20. **enterocele** *noun* [Greek *kēlē* tumour] a hernia or cyst containing part of the intestine E17. **enterochroˈmaffin** *adjective* (HISTOLOGY) designating chromaffin cells of the epithelium of the gastro-intestinal and respiratory tracts M20. **enteroˈcoccus** *noun*, pl. **-cocci** /-ˈkɒk(s)ʌɪ, -k(s)iː/, a streptococcus that occurs in the intestine E20. **enterocoel(e)** *noun* (ZOOLOGY) (part of) a coelom that is or has been in communication with the archenteron L19. **enteroˈcoelic**, **enteroˈcoelous** *adjectives* (ZOOLOGY) of or pertaining to an enterocoel L19. **enterocoely** *noun* (ZOOLOGY) development of a coelom by outpocketing of the archenteron M20. **enterocoˈlitis** *noun* inflammation of the small intestine and the colon M19. **enterocyte** *noun* a cell of the intestinal epithelium M20. **enteroˈcytic** *adjective* of, pertaining to, or involving enterocytes M20. **enteroˈgastrone** *noun* a hormone secreted by the small intestine that inhibits gastric secretion and peristalsis M20. **enteroheˈpatic** *adjective* of or pertaining to the intestine and the liver; *spec.* designating the circulation of bile salts etc. from their place of formation in the liver to the intestine, where they are reabsorbed into the blood and returned to the liver: M20. **enterohepaˈtitis** *noun* = *blackhead* (c) s.v. BLACK *adjective* L19. **enteroˈkinase** *noun* an enzyme secreted by the duodenum that converts trypsinogen to trypsin E20. **enterolith** *noun* a stone or a hardened lump of faeces that forms in the intestine L19. **enteˈropathy** *noun* (a) disease of the intestine L19. **enteropneust** /ˈɛntərə(ʊ)pnjuːst/ *noun* (ZOOLOGY) a hemichordate of the class Enteropneusta, comprising animals with gill slits that open into the pharynx, e.g. the acorn worm E20. **enteˈrostomy** *noun* (an instance of) the surgical formation of a permanent opening into the intestine through the abdominal wall, so as to bypass the stomach when feeding or the colon when eliminating waste L19. **enterotoˈxaemia** *noun* (VETERINARY MEDICINE) toxaemia due to an enterotoxin M20. **enterotoxiˈgenic** *adjective* (of bacteria) producing an enterotoxin M20. **enterotoxigeˈnicity** *noun* the property of being enterotoxigenic; the degree to which something is enterotoxigenic: L20. **enteroˈtoxin** *noun* a toxin produced in or affecting the intestine, such as those causing food poisoning and cholera E20. **Entero-ˈVioform** *noun* (proprietary name for) a preparation of clioquinol used to prevent and treat travellers' diarrhoea M20. **enteroˈviral** *adjective* of or pertaining to an enterovirus M20. **enterovirus** *noun* any of a group of picornaviruses which typically occur in the gastrointestinal tract, but including the poliovirus, Coxsackie virus, echovirus, and the virus of hepatitis A M20.

enteron /ˈɛntərɒn/ *noun*. Pl. **-ra** /-rə/. M19.

[ORIGIN Greek = intestine.]

An alimentary canal or cavity, esp. of an embryo or coelenterate.

†**enterplede** *verb* var. of INTERPLEAD.

enterprise /ˈɛntəprʌɪz/ *noun*. LME.

[ORIGIN Old French & mod. French *entreprise* use as noun of fem. pa. pple of *entreprendre*, later var. of *emprendre*: see EMPRISE.]

1 A piece of work taken in hand, an undertaking; *esp.* one that is bold, hazardous, or arduous. LME. ▸**b** A business firm, a company. L19.

G. F. KENNAN For a small country . . to launch an all-out military attack on Russia was a fantastic enterprise. J. W. KRUTCH The search for one kind of knowledge . . is the legitimate enterprise of science.

2 Disposition to engage in enterprises; initiative and imagination. L15.

E. F. BENSON American enterprise had already largely repaired the destruction caused by the earthquakes. C. P. SNOW The present generation hasn't got a scrap of enterprise.

†**3** The action of overseeing or managing. M16–E19.

4 The action of engaging in enterprises; *esp.* activity undertaken with an economic or commercial end in view. M18.

T. BENN All forms of enterprise, including nationalized industries . . the banks and insurance companies.

free enterprise: see FREE *adjective*. ***private enterprise***: see PRIVATE *adjective*.

– COMB.: **enterprise culture** a capitalist society in which entrepreneurs are given specific encouragement; **enterprise zone** an area in which a government seeks to stimulate enterprise by granting financial concessions to businesses operating there.

enterprise /ˈɛntəprʌɪz/ *verb*. Now *rare*. LME.

[ORIGIN Partly from ENTERPRISE *noun*; partly from French *entrepris* pa. pple of *entreprendre* (see ENTERPRISE *noun*).]

†**1** *verb trans.* Attack; make helpless or embarrassed. LME–E16.

2 *verb trans.* Take on (a work, a condition); attempt, undertake, (a challenging or arduous task). (Formerly foll. by *to do*.) L15.

3 *verb intrans.* Make an attempt, undertake an arduous task. E16.

■ **enterpriser** *noun* a person who engages in an enterprise; now *esp.* an entrepreneur: E16.

E

enterprising /ˈɛntəprʌɪzɪŋ/ *adjective*. E17.

[ORIGIN from ENTERPRISE *verb* + -ING².]

Orig., that undertakes; foolhardy; scheming. Now, showing initiative and imagination; resourceful.

SCOTT FITZGERALD An enterprising office-boy can make his way to the top.

■ **enterprisingly** *adverb* E19.

†**enterrogate** *verb* var. of INTERROGATE.

†**entersert** *verb* var. of INTERSERT.

†**entersole** *noun* var. of ENTRESOL.

†**entersparse** *verb* var. of INTERSPERSE.

†**entertain** *noun*. L16.

[ORIGIN from the verb.]

1 The action of entertaining a guest. Also, a formal meal or banquet. L16–L17.

2 Conversation; social behaviour. E–M17.

3 Pleasure; an amusement. Only in 17.

entertain /ɛntəˈteɪn/ *verb*. LME.

[ORIGIN Repr. tonic stem of Old French & mod. French *entretenir* from Proto-Romance base, from Latin *inter* among + *tenere* to hold.]

1 *verb trans.* **a** Keep up, maintain, (a state of things, a process, action, etc.). Now *arch. rare*. LME. ▸†**b** Keep in existence; keep in repair. L15–L17.

a H. H. MILMAN Entertaining a friendly correspondence with the orthodox Queen Theodelinda.

†**2** *verb trans.* Keep in a certain state or condition. L15–E18. ▸**b** Support, provide for, (a person). M17–L18.

†**3** *verb trans.* Hold mutually. L15–L16.

†**4** *verb trans.* Deal with; treat in a specified manner. L15–M17.

5 *verb trans. & intrans.* Have (a person) as a guest; show hospitality (to). L15.

J. BUCHAN He patronizes the drama and entertains lavishly. J. L. WATEN Mother was in the best room entertaining four ladies.

†**6** *verb trans.* Receive; allow to enter; accept. M16–E18. ▸**b** Receive and contain; accommodate. M17–E18.

7 *verb trans.* Keep (a person) in one's service; hire (a servant), take *into* one's service. Now *rare*. M16.

†**8** *verb trans.* Encounter, meet. *rare*. L16–M17.

†**9** *verb trans.* Take upon oneself; engage in. L16–E18.

10 *verb trans.* Keep or maintain in the mind; harbour, cherish; experience (a feeling). L16. ▸**b** Admit to consideration; receive (an idea). E17.

H. L. MENCKEN All the major religions . . entertain the concept of an infinite future. J. GLASSCO She entertained feelings of the purest and most venomous hatred. **b** G. F. KENNAN A new proposal was being entertained in the entourage of Colonel House. JOHN BROOKE It sounds fantastic that such beliefs could be seriously entertained.

11 *verb trans.* Occupy the attention, time, etc., of; converse with. *arch.* L16. ▸†**b** Occupy (time). L16–L17. ▸†**c** Engage (enemy forces). L16–M17.

CHESTERFIELD I have so often entertained you upon these important subjects.

12 *verb trans. & intrans.* Engage agreeably the attention (of); amuse. E17.

C. LAMB My favourite occupations . . now cease to entertain. K. A. PORTER When they entertain themselves at their numerous . . feasts. D. BAGLEY He entertained them with a hilarious account of some of his experiences.

■ **entertainable** *adjective* L17.

entertainer /ɛntəˈteɪnə/ *noun*. M16.

[ORIGIN from ENTERTAIN *verb* + -ER¹.]

A person who entertains; *spec.* a professional provider of amusement or entertainment.

Washington Post He . . had performed with such entertainers as Bob Hope.

entertaining /ɛntəˈteɪnɪŋ/ *adjective*. M17.
[ORIGIN formed as ENTERTAINER + -ING².]
†**1** Hospitable. *rare*. Only in M17.
†**2** Supporting life. *rare*. Only in L17.
3 Agreeable, interesting; *esp.* diverting, amusing. L17.

G. BERKELEY A part of knowledge both useful and entertaining.

■ **entertainingly** *adverb* E17. **entertainingness** *noun* E19.

entertainment /ɛntəˈteɪnm(ə)nt/ *noun*. LME.
[ORIGIN formed as ENTERTAINER + -MENT.]
†**1** Maintenance; support. LME–M18. ▸**b** *sing.* & in *pl.* Pay, wages. M16–E18.
†**2** Treatment (of people); manner of behaviour. M16–M17.
3 Occupation, occupying *of* time. Long *rare*. M16.
4 Hospitable provision for the wants of a guest. Now *rare*. M16. ▸**b** The action of receiving or providing for a guest. L16. ▸**c** A meal; *esp.* a formal or elegant meal, a banquet. Now *rare*. E17.

G. P. R. JAMES Take order that lodging and entertainment be prepared at York. **b** *Law Times* The proprietor . . undertakes to provide for the entertainment of all comers.

†**5** The action of keeping a person in, or of taking a person into, one's service; employment. L16–M17.
†**6** The action of receiving or accepting something, as information, a present, a proposal, etc. L16–E18.
†**7** Reception (of a person); manner of reception. L16–L17.
8 The action of occupying a person's attention agreeably; amusement. L16. ▸**b** A thing which entertains or amuses someone, *esp.* a public performance or exhibition designed to entertain people. M17.

H. CECIL The general atmosphere of colour and light-heartedness provide a good afternoon's entertainment. **b** A. J. P. TAYLOR The cinema threatened humbler forms of entertainment.

†**9** Accommodation, esp. of a ship in a harbour. L17–E18.
10 The action of harbouring or cherishing in the mind a feeling, idea, etc. M19. ▸**b** The consideration of an idea, proposal, etc. M19.

E. MIALL The deliberate entertainment of this selfish design.

†**entertake** *verb trans. rare* (Spenser). Only in L16.
[ORIGIN from ENTER-¹ + TAKE *verb*, as translation of French *entreprendre* (see ENTERPRISE *noun*).]
Entertain, receive.

†**entertangle** *verb* var. of INTERTANGLE.

†**entertissued** *adjective* var. of INTERTISSUED.

†**enterview** *noun, verb* vars. of INTERVIEW *noun, verb*.

†**enterweave** *verb* var. of INTERWEAVE.

enthalpy /ˈɛnθ(ə)lpi, ɛnˈθalpi/ *noun*. E20.
[ORIGIN from Greek *enthalpein* warm in, formed as EN-² + *thalpein* to heat: see -Y¹.]
PHYSICS. The total heat content of a system, expressed as a thermodynamic quantity obtained by adding its free energy to the product of its pressure and volume.

enthral /ɪnˈθrɔːl, ɛn-/ *verb trans.* Also †**in-**, *-**ll**. Infl. -**ll**-. LME.
[ORIGIN from EN-¹, IN-² + THRALL *noun*.]
1 Reduce to the condition of a thrall; make a slave. Long *arch*. LME.
2 Enslave mentally or morally; *esp.* fascinate and hold the attention of, captivate. Chiefly as ***enthralled*** pa. pple, ***enthralling*** *ppl adjective*. L16.

E. JENKINS He was enthralled by the . . spell of the orator. E. WAUGH Most of the subject matter was entirely new to me and I found it enthralling.

■ **enthraldom** *noun* (*rare*) the state or condition of being enthralled M17. **enthralment** *noun* the action of enthralling; the state or condition of being enthralled: E17.

enthrone /ɪnˈθrəʊn, ɛn-/ *verb trans.* Also †**in-**. E16.
[ORIGIN from EN-¹, IN-² + THRONE, repl. ENTHRONIZE.]
1 Set (a king, bishop, etc.) on a throne, esp. with ceremony; formally invest with the authority of a king, bishop, etc.; *fig.* give or ascribe supreme authority or honour to. E16.

M. E. BRADDON If she seem an angel to you, enthrone her in your heart of hearts.

2 Place in a high and prominent position. M19.

J. CONRAD The . . private office . . where old Heidig . . sat enthroned.

■ **enthronement** *noun* the action of enthroning; the fact of being enthroned: L17.

enthronize /ɪnˈθrəʊnʌɪz, ɛn-/ *verb trans.* Now *rare*. Also **-ise**, **in-** /ɪn-/. LME.
[ORIGIN Old French *introniser* from late Latin *intronizare* from Greek *enthronizein*, formed as EN-¹ + *thronos* THRONE *noun*: see -IZE.]
= ENTHRONE 1.
■ **enthroniˈzation** *noun* = ENTHRONEMENT E16.

enthuse /ɪnˈθjuːz, ɛn-/ *verb*. Orig. *US*. E19.
[ORIGIN Back-formation from ENTHUSIASM.]
1 *verb trans. & intrans.* Make enthusiastic; arouse enthusiasm. E19.
2 *verb intrans.* Show enthusiasm; gush. L19.

†**enthusian** *noun*. M17–E18.
[ORIGIN from Greek *enthousia* = *enthousiasmos*: see ENTHUSIASM, -AN.]
A person (seemingly) possessed by a god or in a prophetic frenzy.

enthusiasm /ɪnˈθjuːzɪaz(ə)m, ɛn-/ *noun*. E17.
[ORIGIN French *enthousiasme* or late Latin *enthusiasmus* from Greek *enthousiasmos*, from *enthousiazein* be inspired or possessed by a god, from *enthous*, *entheos* inspired, formed as EN-² + *theos* god.]
†**1** Possession by a god; supernatural inspiration; prophetic or poetic frenzy. Also, an occasion or manifestation of any of these. E17–L18.

H. HICKMAN Nothing made the Anabaptists so infamous as their pretended enthusiasms or revelations.

2 Extravagant religious emotion; imagined inspiration. *arch*. M17.
3 Strong intensity of feeling in favour of something or someone arising from a strong conviction of correctness, worthiness, effectiveness, etc.; passionate eagerness or interest. (Foll. by *for*, *to do*.) E18. ▸**b** An object of such feeling. E20.

C. MACKENZIE The health and happiness of George and his future wife were drunk with enthusiasm. A. POWELL There was not much enthusiasm for this suggestion. **b** M. SADLEIR Godwin, whose . . achievements in fiction were among Bulwer's youthful enthusiasms.

enthusiast /ɪnˈθjuːzɪast, ɛn-/ *noun & adjective*. E17.
[ORIGIN French *enthousiaste* or ecclesiastical Latin *enthusiastes* member of a heretical sect from Greek *enthousiastēs* person inspired, from *enthousiazein*: see ENTHUSIASM.]
▸ **A** *noun*. **1** A person who believes that he or she is the recipient of divine communications; a person of extravagant religious beliefs or emotions. *arch*. E17.
†**2** A person (seemingly) possessed by a god or in a prophetic frenzy. M17–E18.
3 A person full of enthusiasm about something or someone (foll. by *for*, *of*, †*to*). Also, a visionary, a self-deluded person. E18.
▸ **B** *adjective*. Enthusiastic. Now *rare*. L17.

enthusiastic /ɪnˌθjuːzɪˈastɪk, ɛn-/ *adjective & noun*. E17.
[ORIGIN Greek *enthousiastikos*, from *enthousiazein*: see ENTHUSIASM, -IC.]
▸ **A** *adjective*. †**1** Pertaining to or of the nature of extravagant religious emotion or divine possession. E17–M19.
†**2** Irrational, quixotic. L17–L18.
3 Full of enthusiasm, characterized by enthusiasm; of the nature of enthusiasm, rapturous. M18.

J. R. GREEN Enthusiastic joy hailed the accession of Elizabeth. D. H. LAWRENCE Over supper he became enthusiastic about Canada. J. F. LEHMANN Party Going . . received an early batch of enthusiastic reviews.

▸ †**B** *noun*. = ENTHUSIAST *noun* 1, 2. E17–E18.
■ **enthusiastical** *adjective* (*a*) *arch.* = ENTHUSIASTIC *adjective*; †(*b*) visionary; fanatically devoted to an idea or belief: L16. **enthusiastically** *adverb* L17.

enthymeme /ˈɛnθɪmiːm/ *noun*. Also †**-mem**, & in Latin form **enthymema** /ɛnθɪˈmiːmə/, pl. **-mas**, **-mata** /-mətə/. M16.
[ORIGIN Latin *enthymema* from Greek *enthumēma*, from *enthumeisthai* consider, infer, formed as EN-² + *thumos* mind.]
1 LOGIC. A syllogism in which one premiss is not explicitly stated. M16.
†**2** RHETORIC. An argument based on merely probable grounds. E17–M19.
■ **enthymematic** /-mɪˈmatɪk/ *adjective* of, pertaining to, or containing an enthymeme E19. †**enthymematical** *adjective* = ENTHYMEMATIC L16–L17.

entia *noun* pl. of ENS.

entice /ɪnˈtʌɪs, ɛn-/ *verb trans.* Also †**in-**. ME.
[ORIGIN Old French *enticier* prob. from Proto-Romance (lit. 'set on fire'), from Latin IN-² + alt. of *titio* firebrand.]
†**1** Incite (*to* a course of action); provoke (*to* anger etc.). ME–E17.
2 Persuade or attract by the offer of pleasure or advantage. (Foll. by *from*, *to* a place, course of action, etc.) ME.

EVELYN Beer mingled with Honey, to entice the Wasps. W. BLACK My Lady strove to entice him into the general talk. H. JAMES The English . . want to entice us away from our native land.

■ **enticer** *noun* LME. **enticingly** *adverb* in an enticing manner E17.

enticement /ɪnˈtʌɪsm(ə)nt, ɛn-/ *noun*. Also †**in-**. ME.
[ORIGIN Old French, formed as ENTICE: see -MENT.]
†**1** Incitement; something that incites. ME–L16.
2 The action of enticing; a means or method of enticing, an allurement. M16.

†**entierty** *noun* see ENTIRETY.

entify /ˈɛntɪfʌɪ/ *verb trans. rare*. E19.
[ORIGIN from late Latin *ent-* stem of ENS + -I- + -FY.]
PHILOSOPHY. Make into an entity; attribute objective reality to.

entincture /ɪnˈtɪŋ(k)tʃə, ɛn-/ *verb trans.* M18.
[ORIGIN from EN-¹ + TINCTURE *noun*.]
= TINCTURE *verb*.

entire /ɪnˈtʌɪə, ɛn-/ *adjective, adverb, & noun*. Also †**in-**. LME.
[ORIGIN Anglo-Norman *enter*, Old French & mod. French *entier*, fem. *-ière*, from Proto-Romance, from Latin *integrum* neut. of INTEGER.]
▸ **A** *adjective* **I 1** Whole; with no part excepted. LME.

J. TYNDALL Sufficiently strong to bear the entire weight of the body.

2 Complete in itself, constituting a whole; containing all essential parts. LME. ▸**b** Designating a kind of mixed beer. *arch*. M18.

J. A. SYMONDS In justice the whole of virtue exists entire.

3 Realized in its full extent; thorough, unqualified. LME. ▸**b** Of a person: wholehearted in belief etc.; uncompromising, confirmed. M16.

E. BOWEN Naomi's own good faith was so entire that it would never occur to her. **b** OED: He is an entire believer in Christianity.

4 Wholly of one piece; continuous, undivided. Now chiefly SCIENCE. LME. ▸**b** Having an unbroken outline; not indented. M18.
rank entire MILITARY (in) an unbroken formation.
5 Intact, unbroken; undiminished, unimpaired; *arch.* not fatigued or wounded. L16. ▸**b** Of a male animal: not castrated. L18.
6 Pure, unmixed, homogeneous. Now only in abstract sense, passing into sense 3. L16.
7 Wholly reserved (*to* a person), unshared, set apart. E17.
8 HERALDRY. Of a charge, esp. a cross: (having its extremities) attached to the sides of a shield. L17.
▸ †**II** Ethical senses.
9 Irreproachable, blameless. LME–L18.
10 Characterized by integrity; incorruptible, honest. LME–E18.
11 Of a feeling etc.: genuine, earnest, sincere. LME–E18.
12 Inward, intimate. *rare*. L15–L16.

SPENSER Casting flakes of lustful fire . . into their hearts and parts entire.

▸ †**B** *adverb*. Completely; sincerely. Only in LME.
▸ **C** *noun*. **1** The whole; the full extent. Now *rare*. L16.
2 Entirety. *rare*. E17.
3 Entire beer (see ENTIRE *adjective* 2b). *arch*. E19.
4 An uncastrated stallion. M19.
5 PHILATELY. A whole stamped envelope, wrapper, etc. (used or unused). L19.
■ **entirely** *adverb* & †*adjective* ME. **entireness** *noun* LME.

entirety /ɪnˈtʌɪərəti, -ˈtʌɪəti, ɛn-/ *noun*. Also (earlier) †**-tierty**. ME.
[ORIGIN Old French & mod. French *entièreté* from Latin *integritas*, from INTEGER: see -TY¹.]
1 Completeness; integrity; perfection. Freq. in ***in its entirety*** below. ME. ▸**b** LAW. The entire or undivided possession of an estate. ME.
in its entirety etc., in its etc. complete form; as a whole. **b by entireties** with husband and wife each deemed seised of a whole estate (now replaced in the UK by joint tenancy).
2 The whole, the sum total. Now *rare*. M19.

entisol /ˈɛntɪsɒl/ *noun*. M20.
[ORIGIN from ENTI(RE + -SOL.]
SOIL SCIENCE. A soil of an order comprising mineral soils that have not yet differentiated into distinct horizons.

entitative /ˈɛntɪtətɪv/ *adjective*. Now *rare*. E17.
[ORIGIN medieval Latin *entitativus* (in Scotist phr. *actus entitativus*), from *entitat-*: see ENTITY, -IVE.]
1 Pertaining to the mere existence of something. E17.
2 Having real existence. M19.
■ **entitatively** *adverb* L17.

entitle /ɪnˈtʌɪt(ə)l, ɛn-/ *verb trans.* Also †**in-**. LME.
[ORIGIN Anglo-Norman *entitler*, Old French *entiteler*, (also mod.) *intituler*, from late Latin *intitulare*, formed as IN-² + *titulus* TITLE *noun*.]
1 Give (a book, picture, composition, etc.) a title or (formerly) a heading or superscription. LME. ▸†**b** Dedicate (a book) *to* a person. LME–E17. ▸†**c** Ascribe (a book etc.) *to* an author. M16–E18.

B. COTTLE A clear . . way of entitling the tunes is to name them after their composers.

†**2** Write down under headings. LME–L16.
3 Give (a person) a title or designation indicating rank, office, etc. Now *rare*. LME.

W. FULBECKE The kings . . of England entitling themselues kings . . of Fraunce.

4 Orig., give (a person) the title *to* an estate. Now (chiefly of circumstances, qualities, etc.), confer on (a person or thing) a rightful claim *to* something or a right *to do*. LME. ▸†**b** Invest *with* an honour, office, etc. L16–M17.

W. HENRY The remaining salts . . have no properties sufficiently important to entitle them to a separate description. V. BRITTAIN A green card which entitled me to sit in the . . Press gallery. A. BRINK It's a free country and every man is entitled to his own views.

†**5** Regard or treat (a person) as having a title *to* something; represent as the agent, cause, or subject of a specified thing (foll. by *in*, *to*); *refl.* lay claim *to*. LME–E18. ▸**b** Impute *to*. Only in M17.

■ **entitlement** *noun* (**a**) *rare* a means of entitling, a name; (**b**) the fact of being entitled or qualified; (**c**) something to which a person is entitled, *esp.* a state benefit: **M19.**

†**entitule** *verb* var. of **INTITULE.**

entity /ˈɛntɪti/ *noun.* **L15.**
[**ORIGIN** French *entité* or medieval Latin *entitas*, *-tat-*, from late Latin *ent-* stem of **ENS**: see **-TY**[1].]
1 a Existence, being, as opp. to non-existence; the existence of a thing as opp. to its qualities or relations. **L15.** ▸**b** Essence, essential nature. **M17.**

V. SACKVILLE-WEST The one who had . . the strongest sense of his own entity.

2 All that exists. **E17.**
3 A thing that has a real existence, as opp. to a relation, function, etc. **E17.**

M. MUGGERIDGE I became aware of the British Empire . . as a geographical and political entity. G. F. KENNAN How could the people . . act as a collective entity . . unless they were . . organized.

ento- /ˈɛntəʊ/ *combining form.* Before a vowel also **ent-**.
[**ORIGIN** Repr. Greek *entos* within: see **-O-**.]
= **ENDO-**.
■ **entoblast** *noun* (**BIOLOGY**) †(**a**) *rare* a cell nucleolus; (**b**) endoderm, *esp.* that of an embryo: **M19.** **entoˈconid** *noun* (**ZOOLOGY**) a cusp on the posterior lingual corner of the tribosphenic lower molar **L19.** **entoderm** *noun* (**BIOLOGY**) = **ENDODERM** 1 **L19.** **entoˈdermal** *adjective* (**BIOLOGY**) = **ENDODERMAL** **L19.** **entoˈparasite** *noun* = **ENDOPARASITE** **L19.** **entoparaˈsitic** *adjective* = **ENDOPARASITIC** **L19.** **entophyte** *noun* = **ENDOPHYTE** (b) **M19.** **entophytic** /-ˈfɪtɪk/ *adjective* = **ENDOPHYTIC** **M19.** **entotymˈpanic** *adjective* (**ANATOMY**) situated within the tympanum **L19.** **entoˈzoal** *adjective* of, pertaining to, or designating an entozoon **M19.** **entozoon** /-ˈzəʊɒn/ *noun*, pl. **-zoa** /-ˈzəʊə/, an animal that lives inside another, esp. as a parasite **M19.**

entoil /ɪnˈtɔɪl, ɛn-/ *verb trans. arch. & poet.* **L16.**
[**ORIGIN** from **EN-**[1] + **TOIL** *noun*[2].]
Trap; ensnare. Chiefly *fig.*

entomb /ɪnˈtuːm, ɛn-/ *verb trans.* Also †**in-**. **LME.**
[**ORIGIN** Old French *entomber*, formed as **EN-**[1] + *tombe* **TOMB.**]
1 Place in a tomb; bury; enclose as in a tomb. **LME.**
2 Serve as a tomb for; receive like a tomb. **M17.**
■ **entombment** *noun* **M17.**

entomo- /ˈɛntəməʊ/ *combining form.*
[**ORIGIN** Repr. Greek *entomon* insect, neut. of *entomos* adjective, cut up, formed as **EN-**[2] + *temnein* to cut.]
Insect(s).
■ **entoˈmogenous** *adjective* (esp. of a fungus) living as a parasite in or on an insect **M19.** **entomoˈpathogen** *noun* an organism or other agent that causes disease in insects **L20.** **entomopathoˈgenic** *adjective* causing disease in insects **L20.** **entoˈmophagous** *adjective* that eats insects **M19.** **entoˈmophagy** *noun* the state of being entomophagous; the practice of eating insects: **M20.** **entoˈmophilous** *adjective* (of plants) fertilized by the agency of insects **L19.** **entoˈmostracan** *adjective & noun* (**ZOOLOGY**) (designating) any lower crustacean, i.e. one other than a malacostracan **M19.**

entomology /ɛntəˈmɒlədʒi/ *noun.* **M18.**
[**ORIGIN** French *entomologie* or mod. Latin *entomologia*, formed as **ENTOMO-**, **-LOGY.**]
The branch of zoology that deals with insects.
■ **entomoˈlogic** *adjective* **M20.** **entomoˈlogical** *adjective* **E19.** **entomoˈlogically** *adverb* **M20.** **entomologist** *noun* **L18.** **entomologize** *verb intrans.* practise entomology; collect or study insects: **E19.**

entone *verb* see **INTONE** *verb*.

entoproctan /ɛntə(ʊ)ˈprɒkt(ə)n/ *noun & adjective.* **E20.**
[**ORIGIN** from mod. Latin *Entoprocta* (see below), formed as **ENTO-** + Greek *prōktos* anus (as having the anus within the lophophoral ring): see **-AN.**]
ZOOLOGY. ▸**A** *noun.* A member of the phylum Entoprocta of acoelomate invertebrates. Cf. **BRYOZOAN**, **ECTOPROCTAN.** **E20.**
▸**B** *adjective.* Of, belonging to, or characteristic of Entoprocta. **E20.**
■ **ˈentoproct** *adjective & noun* = **ENTOPROCTAN** **M20.** **entoproctous** *adjective* = **ENTOPROCTAN** *adjective* **L19.**

entoptic /ɪnˈtɒptɪk, ɛn-/ *adjective.* **L19.**
[**ORIGIN** from **ENTO-** + **OPTIC** *adjective*.]
Of a visual phenomenon: originating inside the eye.
■ **entoptically** *adverb* **M20.**

entourage /ˈɒntʊrɑːʒ, ɒntʊ(ə)ˈrɑːʒ/ *noun.* **M19.**
[**ORIGIN** French, from *entourer* surround, from *entour* surroundings, use as noun of adverb = 'round about': see **-AGE.**]
A group of people in attendance on or accompanying someone important. Also, surroundings, environment.

en tout cas /ɑ̃ tu ka/ *noun phr.* **L19.**
[**ORIGIN** French = in any case or emergency.]
1 A parasol which also serves as an umbrella. **L19.**
2 (***En-Tout-Cas.***) (Proprietary name for) a type of hard tennis court. **M20.**

entr'acte /ˈɒntrakt, *foreign* ɑ̃trakt (*pl. same*)/ *noun.* **M19.**
[**ORIGIN** Obsolete French (now *entracte*), from *entre* between + *acte* act.]
The interval between two acts of a play; a performance or entertainment which takes place during an interval.

entrail /ˈɛntreɪl/ *noun*[1]. Also †**in-**. Usu. in *pl.* **ME.**
[**ORIGIN** Old French & mod. French *entraille(s)* (now only pl.) from medieval Latin *intralia* alt. of Latin *interanea* use as noun of neut. pl. of *interaneus* internal, from *inter*: see **INTERIOR.**]
▸**I** *sing.* †**1** *collect.* The intestines; the body's internal parts. **ME–M17.**
2 An internal organ, *esp.* an intestine. Now *rare.* **LME.**
▸**II** In *pl.*
3 The internal organs of a human or other animal; *spec.* the bowels, the intestines. **ME.**

A. C. CLARKE She was covered in blood . . hacking away at the entrails of a ten foot tiger shark.

†**4** The seat of the emotions; the heart, the soul. **LME–L18.**
5 *fig.* The innermost parts (*of* something). **LME.**

E. TEMPLETON He spent all his time probing into the entrails of their engines.

†**entrail** *verb & noun*[2]. **M16.**
[**ORIGIN** Old French *entreillier*, formed as **EN-**[1] + *treille* trelliswork.]
▸**A** *verb trans.* Entwine; interlace. **M16–M18.**
▸**B** *noun.* A coil. *rare* (Spenser). Only in **L16.**

entrain /ɑ̃trɛ̃/ *noun.* **M19.**
[**ORIGIN** French.]
Enthusiasm, animation.

entrain /ɪnˈtreɪn, ɛn-/ *verb*[1]. **M16.**
[**ORIGIN** Old French & mod. French *entraîner*, formed as **EN-**[1] + *traîner* drag: see **TRAIN** *verb*.]
1 *verb trans.* Draw away with or after oneself; *fig.* bring on as a consequence. Now *rare.* **M16.**

HENRY MILLER I entrained only my own ruin, my own bankruptcy.

2 *verb trans.* (Of a current or fluid) incorporate and sweep along in its flow; incorporate (air) in concrete. **L19.**

Nature As the melt water rises up the side of an iceberg, it entrains . . warmer, saltier water from the environment.

3 **BIOLOGY.** **a** *verb trans.* Of a rhythm or rhythmically varying thing: cause (another) gradually to fall into synchronism with it. **L20.** ▸**b** *verb intrans.* Fall into synchronism in such circumstances. (Foll. by *to.*) **L20.**

b *Scientific American* All sighted birds will entrain to the light from a single electroluminescent panel.

■ **entrainment** *noun*[1] the action or process of entraining or becoming entrained **L19.**

entrain /ɪnˈtreɪn, ɛn-/ *verb*[2]. **L19.**
[**ORIGIN** from **EN-**[1] + **TRAIN** *noun*[1].]
1 *verb trans.* Put (esp. troops) on a train. **L19.**
2 *verb intrans.* Go on board a train. **L19.**

H. NICOLSON We then go to the station and entrain for Detroit.

■ **entrainment** *noun*[2] (*rare*) the action or fact of entraining **L19.**

en train /ɑ̃ trɛ̃/ *adverbial phr.* **L18.**
[**ORIGIN** French.]
Afoot, under way; in or into the swing of something; occupied (*with*).

entrammel /ɪnˈtram(ə)l, ɛn-/ *verb trans.* Infl. **-ll-**, ***-l-**. **L16.**
[**ORIGIN** from **EN-**[1] + **TRAMMEL.**]
†**1** Bind or plait (the hair). **L16–E17.**
2 Fetter, hamper. **E17.**

entrance /ˈɛntr(ə)ns/ *noun.* **L15.**
[**ORIGIN** Old French, from *entrer* **ENTER** *verb*: see **-ANCE.**]
1 Power, right, or opportunity of entering; admission. **L15.** ▸**b** More fully ***entrance fee***. A charge made for being allowed to enter or join. **M17.**

J. GALSWORTHY One paid a shilling for entrance and another for the programme. C. S. FORESTER A door . . which gave entrance to a smaller room.

2 The action of coming or going in; **MUSIC** = **ENTRY** 1C. **E16.** ▸**b** The action of entering into an office, duty, etc. **M16.** ▸**c** An act of coming on stage by an actor or actress. **L16.**

A. RADCLIFFE La Motte was interrupted by the entrance of the ruffian. S. SPENDER The entrance of the whole orchestra at the end of a fugal introduction.

†**3** The beginning (of a period of time etc.); the first part (of a book etc.). **M16–M18.**
4 A means by which something is entered; a door, a gate, a passage, etc.; the mouth of a river; a point of entering something. **M16.**

G. M. TREVELYAN Gladstone . . made competitive examination the normal entrance to the Civil Service. J. WEIDMAN I walked in through the Broadway entrance . . then out the Thirty-Eighth Street side.

†**5** The action of entering or writing up in a record; something so entered. **L16–M19.**
6 The forward part of a ship's hull below the waterline. **L18.**
– **PHRASES**: **Great Entrance** in Orthodox Churches, the procession in which bread and wine are brought to the altar during the Liturgy. **Lesser Entrance**, **Little Entrance** in Orthodox Churches, the ceremony in which the book of the Gospels is laid on the altar during the Liturgy.
– **COMB.**: ***entrance fee***: see sense 1b above; **entrance form**: filled in by someone applying to be admitted to an organization, esp. a college or school; **entranceway** a door or corridor at the entrance to a building; **entrance wound**: made by a bullet etc. where it enters the body.

entrance /ɪnˈtrɑːns, ɛn-/ *verb trans.* Also †**in-**. **L16.**
[**ORIGIN** from **EN-**[1], **IN-**[2] + **TRANCE** *noun*.]
1 Affect with delight or wonder and seemingly put into a trance; captivate, delight. Usu. in *pass.* **L16.** ▸**b** Carry away in or as in a trance. **L16.**

A. P. HERBERT Engrossed, entranced, he forgot about time, and about humanity.

2 Put into a trance. **E17.**

ADDISON The Nine Days' Astonishment, in which the Angels lay entranced.

■ **entrancement** *noun* the action of entrancing; the state of being entranced: **M17.** **entrancing** *ppl adjective* captivating, delightful **M19.** **entrancingly** *adverb* **M19.**

entrant /ˈɛntr(ə)nt/ *noun & adjective.* **E17.**
[**ORIGIN** French, pres. pple of *entrer* **ENTER** *verb*: see **-ANT**[1]. Cf. earlier **INTRANT.**]
▸**A** *noun.* **1** A person who takes legal possession of land etc. Long *rare.* **E17.**
2 A person who enters a profession, becomes a member of an organization, etc. **E19.**
3 A person who comes or goes into a room, a place, etc. **M19.**
4 A competitor; a candidate in an examination. **M19.**

Washington Post Nearly two-thirds of the . . entrants will be competing in their first . . race.

▸**B** *adjective.* That enters. Long *rare* or *obsolete.* **M17.**

entrap /ɪnˈtrap, ɛn-/ *verb trans.* Also †**in-**. Infl. **-pp-**. **M16.**
[**ORIGIN** Old French *entrap(p)er*, formed as **EN-**[1] + *trappe* **TRAP** *noun*[1].]
1 Catch in or as in a trap; bring unawares into difficulty or danger. **M16.** ▸**b** Beguile *into*; *spec.* induce to commit a crime in order to secure a prosecution. **M19.**

Scientific American The filter . . would selectively entrap any magnetic particles. **b** *Times* He has acted as an agent provocateur to entrap people and implicate them in crimes which otherwise would not have been committed.

2 Involve in verbal contradiction. **E17.**
■ **entrapment** *noun* (**a**) the action or fact of entrapping; the condition of being entrapped; (**b**) a means of entrapping, a trap: **L16.** **entrapper** *noun* a person who entraps someone or something **L16.**

en travesti /ɒn ˌtravɪˈstiː/ *adverbial phr.* **M20.**
[**ORIGIN** Pseudo-Fr., from French *en* in + *travesti* pa. pple of *travestir* taken as noun: see **TRAVESTY** *adjective & noun*.]
Chiefly **THEATRICAL.** In the clothes or style of clothing of members of the opposite sex.

entre- *combining form* var. of **ENTER-**[1].

entreasure /ɪnˈtrɛʒə, ɛn-/ *verb trans.* **LME.**
[**ORIGIN** from **EN-**[1] + **TREASURE** *verb*.]
Store up (as) in a treasury.

entreat /ɪnˈtriːt, ɛn-/ *verb.* Also (now *rare*) **in-** /ɪn-/. **LME.**
[**ORIGIN** Old French *entraitier*, formed as **EN-**[1] + *traitier* **TREAT** *verb*.]
1 *verb trans.* Treat (a person etc.) in a specified way. *arch.* **LME.**

T. FULLER The pope ill entreated and imprisoned his messengers.

†**2** *verb intrans.* Enter into negotiations (*with* a person; *of*, *for* a thing). **LME–E17.**
†**3** *verb intrans.* Of a speaker, writer etc.: treat of or deal with a subject. (Foll. by *of*, *upon*.) **LME–L17.** ▸**b** *verb trans.* Deal with, handle, (a subject or question). **E16–L17.** ▸**c** *verb trans.* Occupy oneself with (a pastime etc.); pass (time). *rare.* Only in **L16.**
†**4** *verb intrans.* Plead *for* (a person, a favour, etc.). **LME–E19.**
†**5** *verb trans.* Persuade by pleading or supplication; (of circumstances etc.) induce *to do*. **LME–M17.**
6 *verb trans.* Request earnestly; beseech, implore, (a person). **E16.**

A. J. CRONIN I entreat you to give us shelter for the night. V. S. REID For the sake of your family, go away, I entreat you.

7 *verb trans.* Ask earnestly for (a thing). (Foll. by *of* a person.) **L16.**

JONATHAN MILLER To entreat of the gods what they will not give.

■ †**entreatable** *adjective* able to be handled; manageable; placable: **LME–E18.** †**entreatance** *noun* (**a**) treatment (of a person); (**b**) intercession: **M16–E17.** †**entreater** *noun* a negotiator, a mediator; a petitioner, a suitor: **E16–L17.** †**entreatful** *adjective* (*rare*, Spenser) full of entreaty, supplicating: only in **L16.** **entreatingly** *adverb* in an entreating way, pleadingly **M19.** †**entreative** *adjective* of the nature of or characterized by entreaty **E17–M18.**

entreatment /ɪnˈtriːtm(ə)nt, ɛn-/ *noun. arch.* **M16.**
[**ORIGIN** from **ENTREAT** + **-MENT.**]
†**1** Discussion, negotiation; a conversation. **M16–E17.**
2 Treatment (of a person). **E19.**

entreaty /ɪnˈtriːti, ɛn-/ *noun.* Also †**in-**. **LME.**
[**ORIGIN** formed as **ENTREATMENT** after **TREATY.**]
†**1 a** Treatment of a person; handling; management (of animals). **LME–L17.** ▸**b** Treatment of a subject; discussion, investigation. **LME–E17.**
†**2** Negotiation. **LME–E17.**

E

3 An earnest request, a supplication. L16.

E. B. BROWNING Refusing to give an ear to my husband's entreaties about seeing a physician.

entrechat /ɑ̃trəʃa (*pl. same*), ˈɑːntrəʃɑː/ *noun.* L18.
[ORIGIN French from Italian (*capriola*) *intrecciata* complicated (caper).]
A leap in which a ballet dancer strikes the heels together or crosses the feet a number of times while in the air.

entrecôte /ˈɒntrəkəʊt, *foreign* ɑ̃trəkoːt (*pl. same*)/ *noun.* M19.
[ORIGIN French, lit. 'between rib'.]
More fully ***entrecôte steak***. A boned steak cut off the sirloin.

entredeux /ɑ̃trədø/ *noun.* Pl. same. M19.
[ORIGIN French, lit. 'between two'.]
An insertion of lace, linen, etc., in sewing.

E

†**entredit** *noun* see INTERDICT *noun.*

†**entredite** *noun, verb* see INTERDICT *noun, verb.*

entrée /ˈɒntreɪ, *foreign* ɑ̃tre (*pl. same*)/ *noun.* E18.
[ORIGIN French: see ENTRY.]
1 *MUSIC.* **a** A piece of instrumental music, usu. resembling a march, forming the first part of a suite or divertissement, or introducing a character etc. on stage. E18. ▸**b** A group of dances on one theme in 17th- and 18th-cent. French ballet; an act of a 17th- or 18th-cent. French opera ballet. L18.
2 The action or manner of entering. M18. ▸**b** The entrance of the performers in a play, circus, or other large show. E19.

M. EDGEWORTH Nothing could be more awkward than our entrée.

3 The privilege or right of entrance; admission, esp. to a royal court. M18.

Q. BELL She certainly had the entrée to a feminine aristocratic circle. CLIVE JAMES For 50 cents I bought the entrée into the hard-core section of a big bookshop.

4 A dish served between the fish course and the main meat course; *N. Amer.* the main dish of a meal. M18.
– PHRASES: ***entrée en matière*** /ɑ̃ matjɛːr/ [lit. 'entry into the matter'] an opening remark or statement; the beginning of a literary work.

†**entremess** *noun.* Also **inter-**. ME–M18.
[ORIGIN Old French *entremes* (mod. *entremets*), from *entre* between + *mes* (mod. *mets*) MESS *noun.*]
Something served between the courses of a banquet.

entremet /ɑ̃trəmɛ/ *noun.* Pl. pronounced same, /-z/. L15.
[ORIGIN French *entremets*: see ENTREMESS.]
1 In *pl.* Side dishes. L15.
2 *sing.* & in *pl.* (treated as *sing.* or *pl.*). A sweet dish; a dessert; *rare* a side dish. M18.

entrench /ɪnˈtrɛn(t)ʃ, ɛn-/ *verb.* Also **in-** /ɪn-/. M16.
[ORIGIN from EN-¹, IN-² + TRENCH *noun, verb.*]
1 *verb trans.* Place within a trench; surround with a trench or trenches as fortification; establish firmly in a defensible position. M16.

WELLINGTON A camp which they had strongly entrenched.

2 *verb trans. fig.* Fortify as if in a trench; *spec.* (*POLITICS*) safeguard by constitutional provision; provide for the legal or political perpetuation of. L16.

Daily Telegraph What was proposed amounted to entrenching the political supremacy of the native Melanesian people at the expense of the Indians.

3 *verb intrans.* & *refl.* Establish a well-defended position. L16.

W. S. CHURCHILL He held all the Channel ports, and had entrenched himself from Namur through Antwerp to the sea.

†4 *verb trans.* Make (a wound) by cutting. *rare.* L16–E17.
5 *verb intrans.* Encroach, trespass, (*upon*); trench. M17.

J. WESLEY Let not the gentlewoman entrench upon the Christian.

entrenched /ɪnˈtrɛn(t)ʃt, ɛn-/ *ppl adjective.* Also **in-** /ɪn-/. L16.
[ORIGIN from ENTRENCH + -ED¹.]
1 Surrounded with or as with a trench; fortified; firmly established. L16. ▸**b** *POLITICS.* Of constitutional legislation, esp. a clause or provision: unable to be repealed except under more than usually stringent conditions. M20.

BURKE Their . . stations . . were strong intrenched camps. L. HUDSON Some assaults on previously entrenched beliefs have been so violent.

2 Dug out like a trench. L16.

entrenchment /ɪnˈtrɛn(t)ʃm(ə)nt, ɛn-/ *noun.* Also **in-** /ɪn-/. L16.
[ORIGIN formed as ENTRENCHED + -MENT.]
1 A position fortified by trenches; a fortification. L16.
2 Now chiefly *POLITICS.* The action or an instance of entrenching. M17.

entre nous /ɑ̃trə nu/ *adverbial phr.* L17.
[ORIGIN French.]
Between ourselves; in private.

entrepôt /ˈɒntrəpəʊ, *foreign* ɑ̃trəpo (*pl. same*)/ *noun.* E18.
[ORIGIN French (earlier †*entrepost*, †*-pos*), from *entreposer* store, from *entre* among + *poser* to place: see INTER-, POSE *verb*¹.]
1 A storehouse for the temporary deposit of goods, provisions, etc.; *rare* temporary deposit. E18.
2 A commercial centre to which goods are brought for import and export, and for collection and distribution. M18.

attrib.: *Times* Bahrain island was destined to become the centre of entrepôt trade for the Persian Gulf.

entrepreneur /ˌɒntrəprəˈnəː/ *noun.* E19.
[ORIGIN French, from *entreprendre* undertake + *-eur* -OR.]
1 **a** A director of a musical institution. E19. ▸**b** A person who organizes entertainments, esp. musical performances. M19.
2 A person who undertakes or controls a business or enterprise and bears the risk of profit or loss; a contractor who acts as an intermediary. M19.
■ **entrepreneurial** /-ˈn(j)ʊə-/ *adjective* of or pertaining to entrepreneurs or their activities; having the function or character of an entrepreneur: E20. **entrepreneurialism** /-ˈn(j)ʊə-/ *noun* = ENTREPRENEURSHIP M20. **entrepreneurially** /-ˈn(j)ʊə-/ *adverb* M20. **entrepreneurism** *noun* = ENTREPRENEURSHIP L20. **entrepreneurship** *noun* entrepreneurial activity or skills M20.

entresol /ˈɒntrəsɒl, *foreign* ɑ̃trəsɔl (*pl. same*)/ *noun.* Also †**entersole**, (*rare*) **intersole** /ˈɪntəsəʊl/. E18.
[ORIGIN French from Spanish *entresuelo*, from *entre* between + *suelo* storey.]
A low storey between the ground floor and the first floor of a building; a mezzanine storey.

entrism *noun* var. of ENTRYISM.

entropion /ɪnˈtrəʊpɪən, ɛn-/ *noun.* L19.
[ORIGIN from Greek EN-² after *ectropion*.]
Introversion of the eyelid.

entropy /ˈɛntrəpi/ *noun.* M19.
[ORIGIN from Greek EN-² + *tropē* transformation: see -Y³.]
1 *PHYSICS.* A thermodynamic quantity that represents numerically the extent to which a system's thermal energy is unavailable for conversion into mechanical work (the change of entropy of a system when it undergoes a reversible process is equal to the amount of heat it absorbs or emits divided by the absolute temperature of the system); *fig.* lack of order or predictability, gradual decline into disorder. M19.

fig.: *Observer* A busy mess-making inspector who spreads entropy wherever his inquiring hooter intrudes.

2 A logarithmic measure of the average information rate of a message or language. M20.
■ **enˈtropic** *adjective* of or pertaining to entropy; characterized by or resulting from entropy: M20. **enˈtropically** *adverb* as regards entropy; in an entropic manner: L20.

†**entrude** *verb* see INTRUDE.

entrust /ɪnˈtrʌst, ɛn-/ *verb trans.* Also **in-** /ɪn-/. E17.
[ORIGIN from EN-¹, IN-² + TRUST *noun.*]
1 Invest with a trust; give (a person etc.) the responsibility for a task, a valuable object, etc. Foll. by *with*; (arch.) *in, to do*; †*for*, formerly also *absol.* E17.

L. BRUCE I was entrusted with the unromantic job of weeding. G. GREENE He was going to entrust him with what amounted to his life.

2 Commit the safety of (a thing or person) or the execution of (a task) *to* a person, a thing, etc. E17.

N. MOSLEY You should not entrust the administration of details to subordinates. A. BROOKNER Sofka had paid a . . visit to Mr Cariani before entrusting the girls to his . . tuition.

■ **entrustment** *noun* (**a**) the action of entrusting; the fact of being entrusted; †(**b**) a position of trust; a duty with which one is entrusted: M17.

entry /ˈɛntri/ *noun.* ME.
[ORIGIN Old French & mod. French *entrée*, from Proto-Romance use as noun of Latin *intrata* fem. pa. pple of *intrare* ENTER *verb*: see -Y⁵.]
1 = ENTRANCE *noun* 2, 2c. ME. ▸**b** A ceremonial entrance (by a person of rank). M16. ▸**c** The start or resumption of a performer's part in a musical composition. L19. ▸**d** *BRIDGE.* (A card providing) an opportunity to transfer the lead to one's partner or one's dummy. L19.

b L. P. HARTLEY The landlord . . held the door open, so that Irma seemed to make a little entry.

make entry come or go in; come on stage.
2 = ENTRANCE *noun* 1. ME.

O. MANNING The manager warned him that, caught again, he would be forbidden entry . . to the hotel.

†3 = ENTRANCE *noun* 3. ME–E20.
4 = ENTRANCE *noun* 4. ME. ▸**b** A short passage between houses. Formerly also, an approach to a house. LME.

SHAKES. *Macb.* I hear a knocking At the south entry.

port of entry: see PORT *noun*¹, PORT *noun*³ 5b.
5 *LAW.* The actual taking possession of land etc. by entering or setting foot on it. LME.
6 = ENTRANCE *noun* 2b. Also, the action of becoming a member of an organization. LME.

H. WILSON Rockingham's entry into office . . marked a turning-point.

†7 A place used for lodgings or business. LME–M19.
8 Something entered in a register, diary, account book, etc.; an item in an index; a word, phrase, etc., defined in a dictionary, (such a word etc. and) the accompanying portion of text. LME. ▸**b** A record in a custom house of goods imported and exported. LME. ▸**c** A thing which has been entered for, or a person who has entered, a contest, race, etc.; the entrants for a contest, race, etc., collectively. L19.

V. WOOLF On a shelf were her diaries . . . And I made her read an entry. J. BARZUN A truly modern dictionary would add an entry under 'human': 'the opposite of admirable'. *Acorn User* To alter an entry, type in a new one. **c** B. PYM I have recently been judging entries for the Southern Arts Association Prize.

double-entry: see DOUBLE *adjective* & *adverb.* ***single-entry***: see SINGLE *adjective.* **c** ***new entry***: see NEW *adjective.*
†9 A dance between the parts of an entertainment; a musical entrée. M17–E18.
10 More fully ***young entry***: the hounds that are receiving their initial training in any one season; a single such hound. Orig. (now *rare*), the initial training of hounds. M19.
– COMB.: **entry form** an application form for a competition; **entry-level** (**a**) (of a product) suitable for a beginner or first-time user; basic; (**b**) (chiefly *US*) at the lowest level in an employment hierarchy; **entryman** *US* a person who enters upon public land with the intention of settling; **entry permit**: giving authorization for a foreigner to enter a country; **Entryphone** (proprietary name for) a telephonic link with a remote unlocking facility by which a caller can summon attention, identify himself or herself to a person inside a building or room, and be admitted; **entryway** *US* a way in to somewhere or something, an entrance.

entryism /ˈɛntrɪɪz(ə)m/ *noun.* Also **entrism** /ˈɛntrɪz(ə)m/. M20.
[ORIGIN from ENTRY + -ISM.]
The policy or practice of joining an organization, esp. a political one, with the intention of subverting its aims and activities.
■ **entryist** *noun & adjective* L20.

ents /ɛnts/ *noun pl. colloq.* L20.
[ORIGIN Shortened from *entertainments*.]
Social and leisure activities organized for the benefit of students, holidaymakers, etc.

Entscheidungsproblem /ɛntˈʃaɪdʊŋsproˌbleːm, ɛntˈʃʌɪdʊŋzˌprɒbləm/ *noun.* M20.
[ORIGIN German, from *Entscheidung* decision.]
MATH. & LOGIC = ***decision problem*** s.v. DECISION 3.

†**entune** *verb trans.* LME.
[ORIGIN Alt. of INTONE *verb*: cf. TUNE *noun.*]
1 = TUNE *verb* 2a. LME–E17.
2 = TUNE *verb* 3a. L15–M16.

entwine /ɪnˈtwʌɪn, ɛn-/ *verb.* Also †**in-**. L16.
[ORIGIN from EN-¹, IN-² + TWINE *verb*¹.]
1 **a** *verb trans.* & *intrans.* Twine or twist together; interweave. L16. ▸**b** *verb trans.* Make by twining. L17.

a SOUTHEY The Old Man Entwines the strong palm-fibres. **b** W. DE LA MARE The simplest bird entwines a nest.

2 *verb trans.* Clasp, enfold, embrace. M17.

TENNYSON True wife, Round my true heart thine arms entwine.

3 *verb trans.* Encircle (an object) *with* another; wind (an object) *around* or *about* another. L18.

C. BOUTELL A vine-branch entwined about a rod.

■ **entwinement** *noun* the action of entwining; the state of being entwined: M17.

entwist /ɪnˈtwɪst, ɛn-/ *verb trans. arch.* Also **in-** /ɪn-/. L16.
[ORIGIN from EN-¹, IN-² + TWIST *verb.*]
Clasp with or form into a twist; twist in *with*.

enubilate /ɪˈnjuːbɪleɪt/ *verb trans. rare.* M18.
[ORIGIN Latin *enubilat-* pa. ppl stem of *enubilare*, from *e-* E- + *nubilus* cloudy, from *nubes* a cloud: see -ATE³.]
Make clear.

enucleate /ɪˈnjuːklɪət/ *adjective.* L19.
[ORIGIN Latin *enucleatus*, formed as ENUCLEATE *verb*: see -ATE².]
BIOLOGY. Deprived of its nucleus.

enucleate /ɪˈnjuːklɪeɪt/ *verb trans.* M16.
[ORIGIN Latin *enucleat-* pa. ppl stem of *enucleare* extract the kernel from, make clear, from *e-* E-, NUCLEUS: see -ATE³.]
1 Clarify, explain. *arch.* M16.
2 *BIOLOGY.* Deprive (esp. a cell) of its nucleus. L16.
3 *SURGERY.* Remove (a tumour) from its capsule or (an eye) from its socket without rupturing it. M19.

enucleation /ɪˌnjuːklɪˈeɪʃ(ə)n/ *noun.* M17.
[ORIGIN French *énucléation* or medieval Latin *enucleatio(n-)*, formed as ENUCLEATE *verb*: see -ATION.]
The action or an instance of enucleating.

enumerate /ɪˈnjuːməreɪt/ *verb trans.* Pa. pple **-ated**, †**-ate**. E17.
[ORIGIN Latin *enumerat-* pa. ppl stem of *enumerare*, from *e-* E- + *numerus* number: see -ATE³.]
Specify as in a list, mention (a number of things) one by one; ascertain the number of.

■ **enumera'bility** *noun* the fact or quality of being enumerable M20. **enumerable** *adjective* = DENUMERABLE L19. **enumerative** *adjective* that enumerates; concerned with enumeration: M17. **enumeratively** *adverb* E20. **enumerator** *noun* a person who or thing which enumerates; *spec.* a person employed in taking a census: M19.

enumeration /ɪˌnjuːməˈreɪʃ(ə)n/ *noun*. M16.
[ORIGIN French *énumeration* or Latin *enumeratio(n-)*, formed as ENUMERATE: see -ATION.]
1 The action of enumerating; *spec.* the process of recording names and addresses etc. for a census. M16.
2 A list, a catalogue. E18.

enunciate /ɪˈnʌnsɪeɪt/ *verb*. E17.
[ORIGIN Latin *enuntiat-* pa. ppl stem of *enuntiare*, from *e-* E- + *nuntiare* ANNOUNCE: see -ATE³.]
1 *verb trans.* Express (an idea, theory, proposition, etc.) in definite terms. E17.
F. L. WRIGHT Although Laotse . . first enunciated the philosophy, it probably preceded him.
2 *verb trans.* & *intrans.* Pronounce, articulate, (a spoken word etc.). M18.
W. DE LA MARE Meticulously enunciating each syllable of each word.
3 *verb trans.* State publicly, proclaim. M19.
L. MACNEICE I listened to the voice of London enunciating facts for the masses.
■ **enunciable** *adjective* M17. **enunciator** *noun* E19.

enunciation /ɪˌnʌnsɪˈeɪʃ(ə)n/ *noun*. M16.
[ORIGIN Old French & mod. French *énonciation* or Latin *enuntiatio(n-)*, formed as ENUNCIATE: see -ATION.]
1 The action or manner of enunciating. M16.
†**2** A proposition, a statement. L16–M18.
3 The form of words in which a proposition is stated. L18.

enunciative /ɪˈnʌnsɪətɪv/ *adjective*. M16.
[ORIGIN Latin *enunciativus*, from *enuntiare*: see ENUNCIATE, -IVE.]
1 That serves to enunciate; declaratory (*of*). M16.
2 Pertaining to vocal utterance. M19.

enure *verb* var. of INURE *verb*¹.

enuresis /ɛnjʊəˈriːsɪs/ *noun*. E19.
[ORIGIN mod. Latin, from Greek *enourein* urinate in.]
Involuntary urination, *esp.* bedwetting.
■ **enuretic** /-ˈrɛt-/ *adjective* & *noun* (a person) affected with enuresis M20.

enurn *verb* var. of INURN.

enurny /ɪˈnəːni, ɛ-/ *adjective*. Now *rare*. M16.
[ORIGIN Anglo-Norman *eno(u)rné* from Old French *ao(u)rné* pa. pple of *ao(u)rner*: see ADORN *verb*.]
HERALDRY. Of a bordure: charged or decorated with animals.

envassal /ɪnˈvas(ə)l, ɛn-/ *verb trans.* Long *rare*. Infl. **-ll-**, ***-l-**. E17.
[ORIGIN from EN-¹ + VASSAL *noun*.]
Make a vassal of.

†**enveigh** *verb* var. of INVEIGH.

†**enveigle** *verb* var. of INVEIGLE.

enveil /ɪnˈveɪl, ɛn-/ *verb trans.* Also †**in-**. M16.
[ORIGIN from EN-¹, IN-² + VEIL *noun*.]
Cover (as) with a veil; place a veil on.

envein *verb* see INVEIN.

envelop /ɪnˈvɛləp, ɛn-/ *verb trans.* Also (now *rare*) **-ope**, †**in-**. LME.
[ORIGIN Old French *envoluper*, *-oper* (mod. *envelopper*), formed as EN-¹ + base repr. also by DEVELOP.]
1 Wrap up (as) in an outer covering or garment. LME.
M. DE LA ROCHE Wright . . brought his great coon coat, in which he enveloped himself on the platform.
2 Serve as a wrapping for; enclose, contain. L16.
DAY LEWIS The waters which envelop an embryo in the womb.
3 Surround and touch on all sides, esp. so as to conceal; cause to be so surrounded; *fig.* shroud, make obscure; affect deeply or overwhelmingly. (Foll. by *in*.) L16.
A. J. CRONIN The sun . . enveloped them in a bath of light. E. WAUGH A fog came up quite suddenly . . , enveloping men and quarry. J. HERRIOT A sudden misery enveloped me.
†**4** Cover on the inside, line. *rare* (Spenser). Only in L16.
5 Of troops: (partly) surround. L17.
■ **enveloping** *noun* (*a*) the action of the verb; (*b*) a wrapping; wrapping material: L17. **envelopment** *noun* (*a*) the action of enveloping something; the state of being enveloped; (*b*) a thing that envelops something: M18.

envelope /ˈɛnvələʊp, ˈɒn-/ *noun* & *verb*. Also (earlier) †**em-**. M16.
[ORIGIN French *enveloppe*, from *envelopper*: see ENVELOP.]
▸ **A** *noun*. **1** A wrapper, a covering; an enveloping layer or structure. M16.
H. WILLIAMSON Goodbye, brothers: your mortal envelopes lie here in Mother Earth.
floral envelope: see FLORAL *adjective*.
2 *spec.* The covering of a letter, now a piece of paper folded to form a packet, usu. with a flap that can be sealed, for completely enclosing a document etc. E18.
back-of-the-envelope *adjective* denoting calculations or plans of the sketchiest kind (typically, scribbled on a used envelope). ***stamped addressed envelope***: see STAMP *verb*.
3 FORTIFICATION. An earthwork in the form of a parapet or small rampart. E18.
4 a MATH. A curve or surface that is tangential to each of a family of curves or surfaces. L19. ▸**b** A curve passing through the maxima or minima of a sound wave or other oscillatory signal. E20.
5 The flexible gas container that gives a balloon or airship buoyancy. E20.
6 The sealed rigid outer covering of a vacuum tube. M20.
7 Orig. in AERONAUTICS: the limits within which an aircraft can safely operate as defined by the boundary of a graph of altitude against speed, altitude against range, etc. Now more widely, any operating or performance boundaries. M20.
D. J. CALVERT Subsequent trials explored the high-speed end of the envelope.
FLIGHT *envelope*. **push the envelope** go beyond established limits; innovate, pioneer.
▸ **B** *verb trans.* Put (a letter) in an envelope. *colloq.* M19.

envenom /ɪnˈvɛnəm, ɛn-/ *verb trans.* Also †**in-**. ME.
[ORIGIN Old French & mod. French *envenimer*, formed as EN-¹ + *venim* VENOM.]
†**1** Poison (a person or animal) by contact, bite, etc. ME–E18.
2 Put venom on or into (a weapon etc.); taint (the air etc.) with poison; make poisonous. ME.
Nature Several surgeon fishes appear to have envenomed spines.
3 Infuse venom or bitterness into (actions, feelings, words, etc.), embitter; corrupt morally, taint. ME.
A. P. HERBERT An envenomed old lady . . muttered maledictions on the Conservative Government.

en ventre sa mère /ɑ̃ vɑ̃ːtr sa mɛːr/ *adverbial phr.* Also ***en ventre sa mere***. L18.
[ORIGIN French = in its mother's womb.]
LAW. In the womb.

†**envermeil** *verb trans. rare*. ME–E19.
[ORIGIN Old French *envermeilli(e)r*, formed as EN-¹, VERMEIL *adjective* & *noun*.]
Tinge as with vermilion; make red.

enviable /ˈɛnvɪəb(ə)l/ *adjective*. E17.
[ORIGIN from ENVY *verb*¹ + -ABLE.]
That is to be envied; such as to arouse envy.
I. MURDOCH To sleep with a clear conscience every night is indeed enviable.
■ **envia'bility** *noun* E20. **enviableness** *noun* (*rare*) M19. **enviably** *adverb* E19.

envier /ˈɛnvɪə/ *noun*. LME.
[ORIGIN from ENVY *verb*¹ + -ER¹.]
A person who envies.

†**envigour** *verb* see INVIGOUR.

envious /ˈɛnvɪəs/ *adjective*. ME.
[ORIGIN Anglo-Norman = Old French *envieus* (mod. *-eux*), from *envie* ENVY *noun* after Latin *invidiosus* INVIDIOUS: see -OUS.]
▸ **I 1** Full of envy; showing or feeling envy (*of*). ME.
G. GISSING Cecily, whose powers of conversation and charms of manner made her bitterly envious. C. PETERS He was contemptuous of Bulwer's novels, but envious of their success.
†**2** Malicious, spiteful. ME–E18.
†**3** Grudging; parsimonious. L16–M17.
†**4** Enviable. L16–M17.
▸ †**II** [Infl. by ENVY *verb*².]
5 Emulous; full of emulation. ME–E19.
■ **enviously** *adverb* LME. **enviousness** *noun* LME.

enviro /ɪnˈvʌɪrəʊ/ *noun* & *adjective*. L20.
[ORIGIN Abbreviation.]
▸ **A** *noun*. Pl. **-os**. = ENVIRONMENTALIST *noun* 2. L20.
▸ **B** *adjective*. = ENVIRONMENTAL 2. L20.

environ /ɪnˈvʌɪrən, ɛn-/ *verb trans.* Also †**in-**. ME.
[ORIGIN Old French *environer* (mod. *-onner*), from *environ* surroundings, around, formed as EN-¹ + *viron* circuit, from *virer* VEER *verb*².]
1 Form a ring round, surround, encircle; beset, beleaguer, (*with*). ME.
T. TRAHERNE On every side we are environed with enemies. *Daedalus* The American lives in a society in which his successful manipulation of the environing conditions . . is crucial to his sense of himself.
2 Envelop, enclose. Formerly also, wrap up; conceal. LME.
J. TYNDALL We were environed with an atmosphere of perfect purity.
†**3** Go round in a circle, make a circuit round. LME–M17.
■ **environing** *noun* (*a*) the action of the verb; (*b*) a thing or things that environ; environment, surroundings; †(*c*) a circumference: LME.

environment /ɪnˈvʌɪrənm(ə)nt, ɛn-/ *noun*. E17.
[ORIGIN from ENVIRON *verb* + -MENT.]
1 The action of environing; the state of being environed. *rare*. E17.
2 The set of circumstances or conditions, esp. physical conditions, in which a person or community lives, works, develops, etc., or a thing exists or operates; the external conditions affecting the life of a plant or animal. Also, physical conditions viewed in relation to the possibility of life. E19.
A. KOESTLER Processes by which heredity and environment shape a man's character. J. D. WATSON I wished to remain in the stimulating environment of Copenhagen. ANTHONY HUXLEY Such alien environments as that of Jupiter. *Times* We offer highly competitive salaries, . . an environment receptive to new ideas.
the environment the totality of the physical conditions in which a human society lives.
3 The region surrounding a place. M19.
J. S. BLACKIE The environment of this loch put me in mind of Grasmere.
4 Context, setting, *spec.* (PHONETICS) that of a speech sound. M19.
5 A large artistic creation intended to be experienced with several senses while one is surrounded by it. M20.
6 COMPUTING. The structure and conditions within which a computer can operate; the combination of hardware, software, interfaces, etc., which enables a user to operate a system. M20.

environmental /ɪnˌvʌɪrənˈmɛnt(ə)l, ɛn-/ *adjective*. L19.
[ORIGIN from ENVIRONMENT + -AL¹.]
1 Of or pertaining to the (physical) environment. L19.
2 Concerned with the conservation of the environment; not harmful to the environment. L20.
■ **environmentally** *adverb* by means of the, or an, environment; as regards (the conservation of) the environment (***environmentally sensitive area***, an area designated as containing landscapes or wildlife threatened by unrestricted development or industrial use): L19.

environmentalist /ɪnˌvʌɪrənˈmɛnt(ə)lɪst, ɛn-/ *noun* & *adjective*. E20.
[ORIGIN from ENVIRONMENTAL + -IST.]
▸ **A** *noun*. **1** A person who holds or advocates the view that environment, esp. as opp. to heredity, has a dominant influence on the development of an individual or society. E20.
2 A person who is concerned about or seeks to protect the environment, esp. from pollution. L20.
▸ **B** *adjective*. Of or pertaining to environmentalism or environmentalists. M20.
■ **environmentalism** *noun* E20. **enˌvironmenta'listic** *adjective* M20.

environs /ɪnˈvʌɪrənz, ɛn-, ˈɛnvɪrənz/ *noun pl.* M17.
[ORIGIN French, pl. of *environ*: see ENVIRON *verb*.]
The district surrounding a place, esp. an urban area. (Foll. by *of*.)

envisage /ɪnˈvɪzɪdʒ, ɛn-/ *verb trans.* E19.
[ORIGIN French *envisager*, formed as EN-¹, VISAGE.]
1 Look straight at. Chiefly *fig.*, face up to (danger etc.). *arch.* E19.
KEATS To envisage circumstance, all calm, That is the top of sovereignty. R. MACAULAY Two pairs of . . eyes envisaged that remote wilderness.
2 Contemplate, regard, esp. in a particular way; imagine, esp. as a possibility or a future event; expect *that*. E19.
E. BOWEN Sickness not having been envisaged, there was no sickroom. W. GOLDING I drew in my breath . . as I envisaged the appearance I must have presented.
■ **envisagement** *noun* L19.

envision /ɛnˈvɪʒ(ə)n/ *verb trans.* E20.
[ORIGIN from EN-¹ + VISION *noun*.]
Foresee, envisage, visualize.

envoi /ˈɛnvɔɪ/ *noun*. Also (earlier) **-voy**. LME.
[ORIGIN Old French & mod. French, from *envoyer* send, from phr. *en voie* on the way.]
The concluding part of a literary work, *esp.* a short stanza concluding a ballade; *arch.* an author's concluding words, dedication, etc.

†**envolve** *verb* var. of INVOLVE.

envoy /ˈɛnvɔɪ/ *noun*¹. M17.
[ORIGIN French *envoyé* use as noun of pa. pple of *envoyer*: see ENVOI.]
1 A representative sent by one monarch or government to another on diplomatic business; a diplomat; now *spec.* an envoy extraordinary. M17.
envoy extraordinary †(*a*) a minister charged with a special or temporary mission; (*b*) a minister plenipotentiary, ranking below an ambassador and above a chargé d'affaires.
2 An agent, a messenger, a representative. L17.
■ **envoyship** *noun* the position or function of an envoy M18.

envoy *noun*² see ENVOI.

envy /ˈɛnvi/ *noun*. ME.
[ORIGIN Old French & mod. French *envie* from Latin *invidia*, from *invidere* look maliciously upon, grudge, formed as IN-² + *videre* see.]
†**1** Hostility; malice; enmity. ME–E18. ▸**b** Unpopularity, odium. L16–L17.
2 a A feeling of resentful or discontented longing aroused by another person's better fortune, situation, etc. (Foll. by *of*, †*at* the person, *at*, *of* a thing.) ME. ▸**b** The object or ground of envy. M19.

E

a E. O'BRIEN I noticed with envy that her legs were delicately tanned. b *Times* We had . . a musical education system that was the envy of the world.

†**3** [Infl. by French.] Longing, desire; enthusiasm. LME–E17.

■ **envyful** *adjective* (long *obsolete* exc. *Scot.*) full of envy or malice M16.

envy /ˈɛnvi/ *verb*¹. LME.
[ORIGIN Old French & mod. French *envier*, formed as ENVY *noun*.]
1 *verb trans.* Feel envy of (a person); wish to have the good fortune, possessions, etc., of (another person). Also, regard (the better fortune etc.) of another with resentment or discontent; wish to have (another person's good fortune etc.). Also with double obj. LME.

G. GREENE Daintry also envied him his wife; she was so rich, so decorative. C. JACKSON His many friends . . envied his popularity. B. PYM She wished she had a dog . . and envied two young men with a small mongrel.

†**2** *verb intrans. & trans.* Feel envious, grudging, or hostile; feel envious or resentful *that*. LME–L17.
†**3** *verb trans.* Give reluctantly or refuse to give (a thing) *to* a person; begrudge; treat (a person) grudgingly; regard with dislike or disapproval. M16–L18.

†**envy** *verb*² *trans. & intrans.* LME–E17.
[ORIGIN Old French *envier* from Latin *invitare* challenge: cf. VIE *verb*.]
Vie (with).

enwall /ɪnˈwɔːl, ɛn-/ *verb trans.* Now *rare*. Also **in-** /ɪn-/. LME.
[ORIGIN from EN-¹, IN-² + WALL *noun*¹.]
Enclose within a wall; act as a wall to.

enweave *verb* var. of INWEAVE.

enwheel /ɪnˈwiːl, ɛn-/ *verb trans. obsolete* exc. *poet.* E17.
[ORIGIN from EN-¹ + WHEEL *noun*.]
Encircle, surround.

enwiden /ɛnˈwʌɪd(ə)n, ɪn-/ *verb trans. rare.* L16.
[ORIGIN from EN-¹ + WIDEN.]
Widen, expand.

enwind /ɪnˈwʌɪnd, ɛn-/ *verb trans.* Chiefly *poet.* Also **in-**. Infl. as WIND *verb*¹; pa. t. & pple usu. **-wound** /-ˈwaʊnd/. L16.
[ORIGIN from EN-¹, IN-² + WIND *verb*¹.]
Wind itself around, surround with windings; make into a coil.

enwomb /ɪnˈwuːm, ɛn-/ *verb trans. arch. & poet.* Also †**in-**. L16.
[ORIGIN from EN-¹, IN-² + WOMB *noun*.]
1 Contain like a womb; bury *in* or shut up as in a womb. L16.
2 Make pregnant. Long *rare* or *obsolete*. L16.
3 Hold or place in a womb. Now *rare* or *obsolete*. E17.

enwound *verb pa. t. & pple*: see ENWIND.

enwrap /ɪnˈrap, ɛn-/ *verb trans. arch.* Also **in-** /ɪn-/. Infl. **-pp-**. LME.
[ORIGIN from EN-¹, IN-² + WRAP *verb*.]
1 Wrap, envelop, enfold, (*in*, *with*). LME.
†**2** Implicate, entangle, (*in*); involve in a common fate *with* another. LME–E19.
3 Involve, entail. LME.
4 Engross or absorb in thought, sleep, etc. L16.
■ **enwrapment** *noun* (*rare*) (**a**) the action of enwrapping; the state of being enwrapped; (**b**) a wrapping, a covering: M18. **enwrapping** *noun* (**a**) the action of the verb; (**b**) a fold: M16.

enwreathe /ɪnˈriːð, ɛn-/ *verb trans.* Now chiefly *literary*. Also **in-** /ɪn-/. L15.
[ORIGIN from EN-¹, IN-² + WREATHE *verb*.]
Surround as with a wreath; encircle like a wreath.

enwrought *adjective* var. of INWROUGHT *adjective*.

Enzed /ɛnˈzɛd/ *noun. Austral. & NZ colloq.* E20.
[ORIGIN Repr. pronunc. of *NZ* as abbreviation of *New Zealand*.]
New Zealand; a New Zealander.
■ **Enzedder** *noun* a New Zealander M20.

enzootic /ɛnzəʊˈɒtɪk/ *adjective & noun.* L19.
[ORIGIN from EN-² + Greek *zōion* animal + -IC.]
(Designating) a disease of animals that is prevalent in a particular locality.

enzyme /ˈɛnzʌɪm; *in sense 1 also* ɛnˈziːmi/ *noun.* M19.
[ORIGIN In sense 1 from EN-² + Greek *zumē* leaven; in sense 2 from German *Enzym*, from mod. Greek *enzumos* leavened.]
1 The leavened bread used for the Eucharist in the Greek Orthodox Church. M19.
2 A substance consisting largely or wholly of protein that is produced by a living organism and acts as a catalyst to promote a specific biochemical reaction. L19.
■ **enzyˈmatic** *adjective* E20. **enzyˈmatically** *adverb* M20. **enˈzymic** *adjective* L19. **enˈzymically** *adverb* M20.

enzymology /ɛnzʌɪˈmɒlədʒi/ *noun.* E20.
[ORIGIN from ENZYME + -OLOGY.]
The branch of biochemistry that deals with enzymes.
■ **en͵zymoˈlogical** *adjective* M20. **enzymologist** *noun* M20.

eo- /ˈiːəʊ/ *combining form.*
[ORIGIN from Greek *ēos* dawn: see -O-.]
Earliest, oldest; initial.

eoan /iːˈəʊən/ *adjective. poet.* E17.
[ORIGIN from Latin *eous* from Greek *ēōios*, from *ēos* dawn: see -AN.]
Of or pertaining to the dawn; eastern.

EOC *abbreviation.*
Equal Opportunities Commission.

Eocene /ˈiːə(ʊ)siːn/ *adjective & noun.* M19.
[ORIGIN from EO- + Greek *kainos* new, recent.]
GEOLOGY. ▸**A** *adjective.* Designating or pertaining to the second epoch of the Tertiary period or sub-era, following the Palaeocene and preceding the Oligocene, or (formerly) this together with the Palaeocene and Oligocene. M19.
▸**B** *noun. The* Eocene epoch; the series of rocks dating from this time, bearing evidence of an abundance of mammals, including early forms of horses, bats, and whales. M19.

EOG *abbreviation.*
Electro-oculogram.

eohippus /iːəʊˈhɪpəs/ *noun.* Pl. **-uses**. L19.
[ORIGIN mod. Latin (former genus name), from Greek *ēos* dawn + *hippos* horse.]
PALAEONTOLOGY. An extinct mammal of the Eocene epoch, ancestral to the horse; = HYRACOTHERIUM.

eo ipso /eɪəʊ ˈɪpsəʊ/ *adverbial phr.* L17.
[ORIGIN Latin, abl. of *idipsum* the thing itself.]
By that very act (or quality); through that alone; thereby. Cf. IPSO FACTO.

EOKA /eɪˈəʊkə/ *abbreviation. hist.*
Greek *Ethnikē Organōsis Kupriakou Agōnos* National Organization of Cypriot Struggle, an underground movement for furthering the Greek cause in Cyprus in the 1950s.

Eolian, **Eolic** *adjectives* see AEOLIAN, AEOLIC.

éolienne /ɪ͵əʊlɪˈɛn/ *noun.* Now *rare*. Also **aeol-**, **eol-**. E20.
[ORIGIN French, fem. of *éolien* of the wind, from *Éole* Aeolus, god of the winds, from Greek *aiolos* changeful: see -IAN.]
A fine dress fabric of silk and wool.

eolith /ˈiːə(ʊ)lɪθ/ *noun.* L19.
[ORIGIN from EO- + -LITH.]
ARCHAEOLOGY. Any of the roughly chipped stones found in Tertiary strata and orig. thought to be the earliest human artefacts, but now regarded as naturally formed; *loosely* any apparent artefact of natural origin.

Eolithic /iːə(ʊ)ˈlɪθɪk/ *adjective & noun.* L19.
[ORIGIN French *éolithique*, formed as EO- + -LITHIC.]
ARCHAEOLOGY. (Designating or pertaining to) the earliest period represented by worked flints with eoliths interpreted as being of artificial origin.

eon *noun* see AEON.

Eonism /ˈiːənɪz(ə)m/ *noun.* Also **e-**. E20.
[ORIGIN from Charles d'*Éon* (1728–1810), French adventurer who wore women's clothes + -ISM.]
Transvestism, esp. by a man.
■ **Eonist** *noun* a (usu. male) transvestite E20.

eo nomine /eɪəʊ ˈnəʊmɪni, ˈnɒmɪneɪ/ *adverbial phr.* E17.
[ORIGIN Latin, abl. of *id nomen* that name.]
Under that name; that is so called; explicitly.

eosin /ˈiːə(ʊ)sɪn/ *noun.* Also †**-ine**. L19.
[ORIGIN from Greek *ēos* dawn + -IN¹.]
A bromine derivative of fluorescein, obtained as a fluorescent red powder, or one of its red salts or other derivatives, used as dyes, biological stains, constituents of red inks, etc.

eosinophil /iːə(ʊ)ˈsɪnəfɪl/ *adjective & noun.* Also **-phile** /-fʌɪl/. L19.
[ORIGIN from EOSIN + -PHIL.]
▸**A** *adjective.* Readily stained by eosin. L19.
▸**B** *noun.* A kind of phagocytic granulocyte with large eosinophil granules in its cytoplasm. E20.
■ **͵eosinoˈphilia** *noun* an increased number of eosinophils in the blood, as in some allergic disorders and parasitic infections E20. **͵eosinoˈphilic** *adjective* (**a**) = EOSINOPHIL *adjective*; (**b**) of, pertaining to, or exhibiting eosinophilia: E20. **͵eosiˈnophilous** *adjective* = EOSINOPHIL *adjective* L19.

eotechnic /iːə(ʊ)ˈtɛknɪk/ *adjective.* M20.
[ORIGIN from EO- + Greek *tekhnikos*: see TECHNIC.]
Designating or pertaining to the first stage of industrial development.

-eous /ɪəs/ *suffix.*
[ORIGIN from Latin *-eus* + -OUS. Cf. -ACEOUS, -ANEOUS.]
Forming adjectives with the sense 'of the nature of, resembling', as ***erroneous***, ***gaseous***.

EP *abbreviation.*
1 Electroplate(d).
2 Extended-play (record).

ep- *prefix* see EPI-.

Ep. *abbreviation.*
Epistle.

e.p. *abbreviation.*
CHESS. En passant.

EPA *abbreviation. US.*
Environmental Protection Agency.

epacrid /ɛˈpakrɪd/ *noun.* L19.
[ORIGIN Partly from EPACRIS, partly from mod. Latin *Epacrideae* = Epacridaceae (see below): see -ID².]
Any shrub or small tree of the largely Australian family Epacridaceae, resembling the heaths but with usu. epipetalous stamens and anthers opening by slits; *spec.* any member of its type genus, *Epacris* (see EPACRIS).

epacris /ɛˈpakrɪs/ *noun.* E19.
[ORIGIN mod. Latin, from Greek *epi* on + *akron* summit, because chiefly alpine.]
Any of various Australian heathlike shrubs of the genus *Epacris* (family Epacridaceae: see EPACRID), with pink or white tubular flowers in the axils of the leaves.

epact /ˈiːpakt/ *noun.* M16.
[ORIGIN Old French & mod. French *épacte* from late Latin *epactae* pl., from Greek *epactai* intercalated (sc. *hēmerai* days) fem. pl. of *epaktos* brought in from *epagein* bring in, formed as EPI- + *agein* lead.]
1 The age of the moon in days at the beginning of a calendar year. M16.
2 The period of about 11 days by which the solar year is longer than the lunar year; any of these days. L16.
3 An intercalated day or period. *rare.* E17.

†**epaenetic** *adjective.* L17–M18.
[ORIGIN Greek *epainetikos*, from *epainein* to praise: see -IC.]
Expressing or containing praise, laudatory.

epagomenic /ɛpəgəˈmɛnɪk/ *adjective.* M19.
[ORIGIN from Greek *epagomenē* (sc. *hēmera* day) pa. pple of *epagein*: see EPACT, -IC.]
Intercalary; (of a god) worshipped on intercalary days.
■ **epaˈgomenal**, **epaˈgomenous** *adjectives* E20.

epana- /ˈɛpənə, ɛˈpanə/ *combining form.* Before a vowel **epan-**.
[ORIGIN from EPI- + Greek *ana* up, again.]
RHETORIC. Used in nouns and derived adjectives with the sense 'return, repetition'.
■ **eˈpanodos** *noun* (**a**) repetition of a sentence in an inverse order; (**b**) a return to the regular thread of discourse after a digression: L16.

epanalepsis /͵ɛpənəˈlɛpsɪs/ *noun.* M16.
[ORIGIN Greek *epanalēpsis* repetition, from *lēpsis* a taking: see EPANA-.]
The repetition of a word or clause following intervening matter.
■ **epanaleptic** *adjective & noun* (**a**) *adjective* characterized by epanalepsis; (**b**) *noun* an instance of epanalepsis: E20.

epanaphora /ɛpəˈnaf(ə)rə/ *noun.* M16.
[ORIGIN Greek = reference, from *phora* a carrying: see EPANA-.]
= ANAPHORA 1.
■ **epanaphoral** *adjective* E20.

épanchement /epɑ̃ʃmɑ̃/ *noun.* Pl. pronounced same. M19.
[ORIGIN French, lit. 'discharge, effusion', from *épancher* pour out (something) from late Latin alt. of classical Latin *expandere* EXPAND: see -MENT.]
An outpouring or disclosure of one's thoughts or feelings. Also, a relationship marked by mutual trust and the exchange of confidences.

eparch /ˈɛpɑːk/ *noun.* M17.
[ORIGIN Greek *eparkhos*, formed as EPI- + -ARCH.]
1 The governor of a civilian eparchy. M17.
2 The chief bishop of an ecclesiastical eparchy. L17.

eparchy /ˈɛpɑːki/ *noun.* L18.
[ORIGIN Greek *eparkhia*, from *eparkhos*: see EPARCH, -Y³.]
1 A province in the Orthodox Church. L18.
2 A province of ancient Greece; a smaller division (corresponding to a part of a present-day nomarchy) of modern Greece. L18.

eparterial /ɛpɑːˈtɪərɪəl/ *adjective.* L19.
[ORIGIN from EPI- + ARTERIAL.]
ANATOMY. Of a branch of a bronchus: situated above the pulmonary artery.

épatant /epatɑ̃/ *adjective.* E20.
[ORIGIN French, pres. ppl adjective of *épater* flabbergast.]
Shocking (to conventional persons); daring.

épater /epate/ *verb trans.* (*inf.*). E20.
[ORIGIN French = flabbergast.]
Startle, shock. Esp. as below.
épater les bourgeois, ***épater le bourgeois*** /lɛ burʒwa, lə/ shock the conventionally minded.

epaule /ɛˈpɔːl/ *noun.* E18.
[ORIGIN French *épaule*: see EPAULETTE.]
FORTIFICATION. The place where the face and flank of a bastion meet.

epaulement /ɛˈpɔːlm(ə)nt/ *noun.* Also †**esp-**. L17.
[ORIGIN French *épaulement* (earlier *esp-*), from *épauler* protect by an epaulement, from *épaule*: see EPAULETTE, -MENT.]
FORTIFICATION. A parapet or breastwork, esp. one protecting the flank.

épaulement /epolmɑ̃/ *noun.* Pl. pronounced same. M19.
[ORIGIN French: see EPAULEMENT.]
BALLET. A stance in which one shoulder is turned forward and the other drawn back, with the head facing over the forward shoulder; correct positioning of the shoulders.

epaulette /ˈɛpəlɛt, -pɔːl-, ɛpəˈlɛt/ *noun*. Also **-let**. L18.
[ORIGIN French *épaulette* dim. of *épaule* shoulder from Latin SPATULA, (in late Latin) shoulder blade: see -ET[1], -ETTE.]
1 An ornamental shoulder piece worn on a military or other uniform, usu. as a sign of rank. L18. ▸**b** A military officer; a commission. E19.

W. STYRON A blue jacket whose shoulders glittered with the epaulets of an army colonel.

2 A small shoulder-plate on a suit of armour. E19.
3 A loop or tab on the shoulder of a coat; a piece of trimming on the shoulder of a dress etc. M19.

D. BOGARDE Singh carefully removed the folded cap from his epaulette.

■ **epauletted** *adjective* having or wearing epaulettes E19.

epaxial /ɛˈpaksɪəl/ *adjective*. L19.
[ORIGIN from EPI- + AXIAL.]
ANATOMY. Situated on the dorsal side of an axis.

épée /ˈeɪpeɪ, *foreign* epe (*pl. same*)/ *noun*. L19.
[ORIGIN French = sword from Old French *espee*: see SPAY.]
A sharp-pointed duelling sword used (blunted) for fencing; the art of fencing with this.
■ **épéist** /ˈeɪpeɪɪst/, **épéiste** /epeist/ *noun* a fencer who uses or is proficient with an épée E20.

epeiric /ɛˈpʌɪrɪk/ *adjective*. E20.
[ORIGIN formed as EPEIROGENY + -IC.]
GEOLOGY. Of a sea: connected with the ocean but situated on a continent or continental shelf.

epeirogeny /ɛpʌɪˈrɒdʒəni/ *noun*. Also **epir-**. L19.
[ORIGIN from Greek *ēpeiros* mainland, continent + -GENY.]
The formation and alteration of continents by the (esp. vertical) movement of the earth's crust; an episode of this.
■ **epeirogenesis** /ɪˌpʌɪrə(ʊ)ˈdʒɛnɪsɪs/ *noun* = EPEIROGENY E20. **epeirogenetic** /ɪˌpʌɪrə(ʊ)dʒɪˈnɛtɪk/ *adjective* E20. **epeirogenic** /ɪˌpʌɪrə(ʊ)ˈdʒɛnɪk/ *adjective* L19. **epeiroˈgenically** *adverb* M20.

ependyma /ɛˈpɛndɪmə/ *noun*. L19.
[ORIGIN Greek *ependuma*, from *ependuein* put on over, formed as EPI- + EN-[2] + *duein* put.]
ANATOMY. The epithelial layer lining the cerebral ventricles and the central canal of the spinal cord in vertebrates.
■ **ependymal** *adjective* L19.

epenthesis /ɛˈpɛnθɪsɪs/ *noun*. Pl. **-eses** /-ɪsiːz/. M16.
[ORIGIN Late Latin from Greek, from *epenthe-* stem of *epentithenai* insert, formed as EPI- + EN-[2] + *tithenai* to place.]
The development of a sound or an unetymological letter in a word, e.g. the *b* in ***thimble***.
■ **epenthesize** *verb trans.* introduce or modify by epenthesis L19.

epenthetic /ɛpɛnˈθɛtɪk/ *adjective*. M19.
[ORIGIN Greek *epenthetikos*, from *epenthesis*: see EPENTHESIS, -IC.]
Of or pertaining to epenthesis; (of a sound or letter) that has come to be inserted in a word.

epeolatry /ɛpɪˈɒlətri/ *noun*. M19.
[ORIGIN from Greek *epeos*, *epos* word + -O- + -LATRY.]
The worship of words.

epergne /ɪˈpəːn/ *noun*. E18.
[ORIGIN Perh. from French *épargne* saving, economy.]
An ornament (often with branches) for the centre of a dinner table, for holding flowers, fruit, etc.

epexegesis /ɛˌpɛksɪˈdʒiːsɪs/ *noun*. Pl. **-eses** /-iːsiːz/. L16.
[ORIGIN Greek *epexēgēsis*, formed as EPI-, EXEGESIS.]
The addition of a word or words to clarify the meaning; the word(s) so added.
■ **epexegetic** /-ˈdʒɛt-/, **epexegetical** /-ˈdʒɛt-/ *adjectives* M19. **epexegetically** /-ˈdʒɛt-/ *adverb* L19.

eph- *prefix* see EPI-.

Eph. *abbreviation*.
Ephesians (New Testament).

ephah /ˈiːfə/ *noun*. LME.
[ORIGIN Hebrew *'ēpāh*, prob. from Egyptian.]
hist. An ancient Hebrew dry measure equivalent to the bath (of about 40 litres or 9 gallons).

ephebe /ɛˈfiːb, ɪ-, ˈɛfiːb/ *noun*. L19.
[ORIGIN Latin *ephebus* from Greek *ephēbos*, formed as EPI- + *hēbē* early manhood.]
A young man; *spec.* in ancient Greece, one from 18 to 20 years old undergoing military training.
■ **ephebic** *adjective* M19.

ephebeum /ɛfɪˈbiːəm/ *noun*. Pl. **-bea** /-ˈbiːə/. L17.
[ORIGIN Latin from Greek *ephēbeion*, from *ephēbos* EPHEBE.]
GREEK HISTORY. A palaestra court where young men could take exercise.

ephebiatrics /ɪˌfiːbɪˈatrɪks, ɛ-/ *noun*. M20.
[ORIGIN from Greek *ephēbos* (see EPHEBE) after *geriatrics*, *paediatrics*.]
The branch of medicine that deals with adolescents and their diseases.
■ **ephebiaˈtrician** *noun* an expert in or student of ephebiatrics M20.

ephectic /ɛˈfɛktɪk/ *noun & adjective*. M17.
[ORIGIN Greek *ephektikos* adjective, from *epekhein* hold back, reserve (judgement).]
▸ **A** *noun*. A member of the Sceptic school of philosophy in ancient Greece. M17.
▸ **B** *adjective*. Characterized by suspension of judgement. L17.

ephedra /ɛˈfɛdrə/ *noun*. E20.
[ORIGIN mod. Latin (see below) from Latin = equisetum, from Greek.]
Any of the trailing or scrambling evergreen gymnospermous shrubs of the genus *Ephedra* (family Ephedraceae), native to warm arid regions and with almost leafless stems like an equisetum.

ephedrine /ˈɛfədriːn/ *noun*. Also **-in** /-ɪn/. L19.
[ORIGIN from EPHEDRA + -INE[5], -IN[1].]
An alkaloid, $C_{10}H_{15}NO$, found in some ephedras and made as a sympathomimetic drug for use esp. as a bronchodilator for hay fever, asthma, etc.

ephelis /ɪˈfiːlɪs, ɛ-/ *noun*. Pl. **-lides** /-lɪdiːz/. M18.
[ORIGIN Latin from Greek *ephēlis*, (in pl.) rough facial spots.]
MEDICINE. A freckle; *collect.* any of various kinds of skin discoloration.

ephemera /ɪˈfɛm(ə)rə, -ˈfiːm-, ɛ-/ *noun*[1] *& adjective*. LME.
[ORIGIN medieval Latin, use as noun of fem. of late Latin *ephemerus* lasting only a day from Greek *ephēmeros*, formed as EPI- + *hēmera* day.]
▸ **A** *noun* (now treated as *pl.*). Pl. †**-ras**, †**-rae** /-riː/.
†**1** A fever lasting only one day. LME–E19.
2 Pl. **-ras**, **-rae** /-riː/. Orig. = EPHEMERON 2. Now, a winged insect of the genus *Ephemera* or the order Ephemeroptera, a mayfly. Cf. EPHEMERID *noun*. L17.
3 Orig., a person or thing of short-lived interest or use. Now, collectable items that were originally expected to have only short-term usefulness or popularity. M18.

S. JOHNSON These papers of a day, the Ephemerae of learning. A. NIFFENEGGER The Quigley Collection . . is over two thousand pieces of Victorian ephemera.

▸ †**B** *adjective*. Of a fever: lasting one day. LME–M16.
■ **ephemerist** *noun*[2] a person who collects (printed or written) ephemera L20.

ephemera *noun*[2] *pl.* see EPHEMERON.

ephemerae *noun pl.* see EPHEMERA *noun*[1].

ephemeral /ɪˈfɛm(ə)r(ə)l, -ˈfiːm-/ *adjective & noun*. L16.
[ORIGIN from Greek *ephēmeros* (see EPHEMERA *noun*[1] *& adjective*) + -AL[1].]
▸ **A** *adjective*. **1** Chiefly ZOOLOGY & MEDICINE. Beginning and ending in the same day; existing for one day or a few days only. L16.
2 In existence, or of interest or use, for a short time only; transitory. M17.

A. THWAITE Much of Gosse's energy was going into ephemeral journalism.

▸ **B** *noun*. **1** An insect that lives only one day. L16.
2 A thing or person of transitory existence or of short-lived interest or use. E19.
■ **ephemeralism** *noun* = EPHEMERALITY E20. **ephemeˈrality** *noun* ephemeral quality; in *pl.*, ephemeral matters: E19. **ephemerally** *adverb* M19. **ephemeralness** *noun* E20.

†**ephemeran** *adjective & noun*. M17–E18.
[ORIGIN from EPHEMERA *noun*[1] + -AN.]
= EPHEMERAL *adjective*, *noun* 1.

ephemerid /ɪˈfɛm(ə)rɪd, -ˈfiːm-/ *noun*. L19.
[ORIGIN mod. Latin *Ephemeridae* (see below), from *Ephemera* genus name: see EPHEMERA *noun*[1] *& adjective*, -ID[3].]
An insect of the order Ephemeroptera (cf. EPHEMERA *noun*[1] 2), *esp.* one of the family Ephemeridae.

†**ephemerid** *adjective*. E19–E20.
[ORIGIN Latin *ephemerid-* stem of *ephemeris*: see EPHEMERIS, -ID[2].]
= EPHEMERAL *adjective* 2.

ephemeris /ɪˈfɛm(ə)rɪs, -ˈfiːm-/ *noun*. Also (from the pl.) †**-rides**. Pl. **ephemerides** /ɛfɪˈmɛrɪdiːz/ E16.
[ORIGIN Latin from Greek, from *ephēmeros*: see EPHEMERA *noun*[1].]
1 A table giving the position of a celestial object at daily or other regular intervals throughout a period; a book containing such tables and other astronomical information, an astronomical almanac. E16.
2 *gen.* An almanac, a calendar. Now *rare* or *obsolete*. L16.
†**3** A diary, a journal. L16–L17.
4 = EPHEMERA *noun*[1] 2, 3. E19.
– COMB.: **ephemeris time** ASTRONOMY a timescale defined in terms of the orbital motion of the planets.
■ †**ephemerist** *noun*[1] a person who makes or uses an ephemeris M17–M18.

ephemeron /ɪˈfɛm(ə)rɒn, -ˈfiːm-/ *noun*. Pl. **-rons**, **-ra** /-rə/. See also EPHEMERA *noun*[1]. L16.
[ORIGIN Greek *ephēmeron* neut. of *ephēmeros*: see EPHEMERA *noun*[1] *& adjective*.]
†**1** A plant described by ancient writers as living only one day or causing death within one day. L16–M17.
2 An insect that lives only one day, or spends only one day in its winged form. Cf. EPHEMERA *noun*[1] 2. L16.
3 A short-lived person, institution, or production. L18.

T. SHARPE Of all ephemera he found television commentators the least to his liking.

■ **ephemerous** *adjective* = EPHEMERAL *adjective* M17.

Ephemeroptera /ɪˌfɛməˈrɒptərə, -ˌfiːm-/ *noun pl.* Also **e-**. E20.
[ORIGIN mod. Latin, from *Ephemera* (genus name) + Greek *pteron* wing: see EPHEMERA.]
(Members of) an order of insects that comprises the mayflies.
■ **ephemeropteran** *noun & adjective* M20.

Ephesian /ɪˈfiːʒ(ə)n/ *noun & adjective*. LME.
[ORIGIN from Latin *ephesius*, Greek *ephesios*, from Greek *Ephesos* Ephesus: see -AN.]
▸ **A** *noun*. **1** A native or inhabitant of Ephesus, an ancient Greek city on the west coast of Asia Minor. In *pl.* (treated as *sing.*), St Paul's Epistle to the Ephesians, a book of the New Testament. LME.
†**2** A close companion. *rare* (Shakes.). Only in L16.
▸ **B** *adjective*. Of or pertaining to Ephesus or its inhabitants. L19.

Ephesine /ˈɛfɪsɪn/ *adjective*. M16.
[ORIGIN Late Latin *Ephesinus*, from *Ephesus*: see EPHESIAN, -INE[1].]
Of or pertaining to Ephesus; chiefly ECCLESIASTICAL, referring to the Council of Ephesus in 431 or to liturgical uses believed to have originated in Ephesus.

ephialtes /ɛfɪˈaltiːz/ *noun*. Now *rare* or *obsolete*. LME.
[ORIGIN Greek *ephialtēs*.]
An evil spirit supposed to cause nightmares; a nightmare.

ephod /ˈiːfɒd, ˈɛfɒd/ *noun*. LME.
[ORIGIN Hebrew *'ēpōḏ*.]
1 *hist.* A sleeveless garment worn by priests in ancient Israel. LME.
2 A clerical garment. Formerly also, priestly office or influence. E17.

ephor /ˈɛfɔː/ *noun*. Also **E-**. Pl. **ephors**, **ephori** /ˈɛfərʌɪ/. L16.
[ORIGIN Latin *ephorus* or its source Greek *ephoros* overseer, formed as EPI- + base of *horan* see.]
1 GREEK HISTORY. In Sparta and other Dorian states, any of the magistrates with executive, judicial, and disciplinary power who came to have power over the king's conduct. L16.
2 In modern Greece: an overseer, a superintendent. E19.
3 A prefect at the Edinburgh Academy. L19.
■ **ephoral** /-f(ə)r(ə)l/ *adjective* M19. **ephorate** /-f(ə)rət/ *noun* the office of ephor; the body of ephors: M19.

Ephthalite /ˈɛfθəlʌɪt/ *noun & adjective*. L19.
[ORIGIN Late Greek *Ephthalitos*: see -ITE[1].]
hist. (Of, pertaining to, or designating) a white Hun.

ephyra /ˈɛfɪrə/ *noun*. Pl. **-rae** /-riː/. M19.
[ORIGIN mod. Latin from Greek *Ephura* a Nereid and an Oceanid.]
ZOOLOGY. A larval jellyfish, after separation from the scyphistoma.

epi- /ˈɛpi/ *prefix*. Usu. **ep-** /ɛp, *unstressed* ɪp/ before an unaspirated vowel, **eph-** /ɛf, *unstressed* ɪf/ before an aspirated one.
[ORIGIN Repr. Greek *epi* on, near to, above, in addition.]
1 Occurring, esp. in scientific words, with the senses 'on', as ***epicycle***, ***epigraph***, 'above, overlying', as ***epicotyl***, ***epidermis***, 'near to', as ***epipubis***, 'in addition', as ***epiphenomenon***.
2 CHEMISTRY, MINERALOGY, & GEOLOGY. In names of substances, denoting (***a***) analogy or similarity of composition, (***b***) a bridge in a molecule.
■ **epiˈcalyx** *noun*, pl. **-yces** /-ɪsiːz/, **-yxes**, BOTANY a whorl of small bracts like sepals surrounding the true calyx in certain plants, esp. members of the mallow family L19. **epicarp** *noun* (BOTANY) the outermost layer of the pericarp in a fleshy fruit; the peel, the skin: E19. **epichile** /-kʌɪl/ *noun* [Greek *kheilos* lip] BOTANY the flat projecting outer part of the hinged labellum found in some orchids M19. **epichlorˈhydrin** *noun* CHEMISTRY a cyclic epoxide, C_3H_5OCl, that is a toxic flammable volatile liquid used esp. in the manufacture of epoxy resins M19. **epiˈchordal** *adjective* (ZOOLOGY) situated or occurring on the dorsal side of the notochord L19. **epiˈclastic** *adjective* (GEOLOGY) (of rock) formed on the earth's surface by the alteration of pre-existing rocks L19. **epiˈcormic** *adjective* (BOTANY) [Greek *kormos* trunk (of a tree)] (of a shoot or branch) growing from a previously dormant bud on the trunk or a limb of a tree E20. **epicotyl** /-ˈkɒtɪl/ *noun* (BOTANY) the part of an embryo or seedling stem above the cotyledon(s) L19. **epiˈcranial** *adjective* of or pertaining to the scalp M19. **epicuticle**, **-ˈticula** *noun* (***a***) the thin waxy outer layer covering insects and other arthropods; (***b***) the thin membrane forming the outer part of the cuticle of animal hairs etc.: E20. **epicuˈticular** *adjective* of or pertaining to the epicuticle M20. **epiˈdiorite** *noun* (GEOLOGY) any rock formed from a basic igneous rock by metamorphism, with the original pyroxene transformed into amphibole L19. **epifluoˈrescence** *noun* fluorescence of an object in an optical microscope when irradiated from the viewing side L20. **epiˈfocal** *adjective* situated above the focus of an earthquake L19. **epiˈlithic** *adjective* (BOTANY) growing on stone E20. **epiˈotic** *adjective & noun* (ZOOLOGY) (***a***) *adjective* situated above the ear; *spec.* designating one of the five otic bones that may be present in vertebrates; (***b***) *noun* an epiotic bone: L19. **epipeˈlagic** *adjective* of, pertaining to, or designating the upper layer of the ocean, down to 100 or 200 metres M20. **epiˈpetalous** *adjective* (BOTANY) (of stamens) attached to petals M19. **epiˈpharynx** *noun* (ZOOLOGY) any of various structures developed from the roof of the mouth cavity in some insects and arachnids E19. **epiˈplankton** *noun* plankton in the upper layer of the sea, down to about 100 metres L19. **epiplankˈtonic** *adjective* of, pertaining to, or designating epiplankton M20. **epiplasm** *noun* the cytoplasm remaining in the ascus of a fungus after the dispersal of its

E

spores L19. **epipˈteric** *adjective & noun* (ANATOMY) (designating) a small Wormian bone sometimes found between the parietal and the greater wing of the sphenoid L19. **epipˈterygoid** *adjective & noun* (ZOOLOGY) (designating) a slender vertical bone situated above the pterygoid in the skull of some reptiles and primitive tetrapods L19. **epiˈpubic** *adjective* (ZOOLOGY) situated on the pubis; of the nature of an epipubis: L19. **epiˈpubis** *noun* (ZOOLOGY) a cartilage or bone in front of the pubis in amphibians, reptiles, and marsupials L19. **epiˈscleral** *adjective* (ANATOMY) of, pertaining to, or overlying the surface of the sclera of the eye M19. **epispore** *noun* (BOTANY) the outer covering of a spore of a lichen or fern M19. **epiˈstoma**, **epistome** *noun* (ZOOLOGY) a structure or region above or over the mouth in some invertebrates M19. **epiˈtheca** *noun* (*a*) a calcareous layer surrounding part of the theca of some corals; (*b*) the outer of the two overlapping halves of the cell wall of a diatom: M19. **epiˈthecium** *noun*, pl. **-ia** /-ɪə/, BOTANY the surface layer of the fruiting body in certain lichens and fungi L19. **epitope** *noun* [Greek *topos* place] MEDICINE the part of an antigen molecule to which an antibody molecule attaches itself M20. **epiˈtopic** *adjective* (MEDICINE) of or pertaining to an epitope M20. **epiˈtrochlear** *adjective* (ANATOMY) situated above or near the trochlea of the elbow joint M20. **epizone** *noun* (GEOLOGY) a metamorphic zone characterized by moderate temperature, low pressure, and high stress M20.

epibiont /ɛpɪˈbʌɪɒnt/ *noun*. M20.
[ORIGIN from EPI- + -BIONT.]
An organism living upon the surface of another, esp. non-parasitically.

epibiotic /ˌɛpɪbʌɪˈɒtɪk/ *adjective*. M20.
[ORIGIN from EPI- + Greek *biōtikos* pertaining to life: see BIOTIC.]
Pertaining to or designating an epibiont.

epiblast /ˈɛpɪblast/ *noun*. E19.
[ORIGIN from EPI- + -BLAST.]
1 BOTANY. A projection resembling a flap opposite the scutellum on the embryo of some grasses. E19.
2 BIOLOGY. The outermost layer of a young embryo before it differentiates into ectoderm and mesoderm. Also called ***ectoblast***. L19.
■ **epiˈblastic** *adjective* L19.

epiboly /ɛˈpɪbəli/ *noun*. Also **-le**. L19.
[ORIGIN Greek *epibolē* throwing or laying on, from *epiballein* throw on, formed as EPI- + *ballein* throw; assim. to -Y³.]
BIOLOGY. The process by which one set of cells spreads over and surrounds another by dividing more rapidly, as in gastrulation. Cf. EMBOLY.
■ **epiˈbolic** *adjective* L19.

epic /ˈɛpɪk/ *adjective & noun*. Also †**-ick**. L16.
[ORIGIN Latin *epicus* from Greek *epikos*, from *epos*: see EPOS, -IC.]
▸**A** *adjective*. **1** Narrating at length the adventures or achievements of one or more heroic figures, in the manner of the *Iliad* and *Paradise Lost*; of or pertaining to compositions of this kind. L16.
2 Of the kind described in epic poetry; grand and heroic; impressive in scope, grandeur, etc. M18.

N. MONSARRAT A survivor of what must have been an epic sea battle. D. HALBERSTAM He was . . as much a hero and a personage of that epic era as Eisenhower.

▸**B** *noun*. †**1** An epic poet. Only in M17.
2 An epic poem. E18.
3 a An imaginative work of any form seen as embodying a nation's conception of its past history. M19. ▸**b** A film or novel based on an epic narrative or heroic in type or scale; *colloq.* an exceptionally long, expensive, or lavish entertainment. E20.

b T. WOGAN On television I've endured the rigours of 'Miss World' . . and other epics.

4 Something in real life regarded as a fit subject for an epic. M19.

D. H. LAWRENCE Her life was the epic that inspired their lives.

5 The genre of epic literature. M20.

M. H. ABRAMS Epic and tragedy are the king and queen of poetic forms.

■ **epical** *adjective* = EPIC *adjective* E19. **epically** *adverb* M19.

epicanthus /ɛpɪˈkanθəs/ *noun*. M19.
[ORIGIN from EPI- + CANTHUS.]
A fold of skin from the upper eyelid that covers the inner angle of the eye, occurring in Mongolians and as a congenital anomaly in other people.
■ **epicanthic** *adjective* having or pertaining to an epicanthus E20.

epicardium /ɛpɪˈkɑːdɪəm/ *noun*. Pl. **-dia** /-dɪə/. M19.
[ORIGIN from EPI- + *-cardium*, after *pericardium*.]
1 ANATOMY. The visceral part of the serous pericardium, covering the heart. M19.
2 ZOOLOGY. Either of two hollow outgrowths from the pharynx in some ascidians. L19.
■ **epicardiac** *adjective* L19. **epicardial** *adjective* E20.

epicedium /ɛpɪˈsiːdɪəm/ *noun*. Pl. **-ia** /-ɪə/, **-iums**. Also (earlier, now *rare*) anglicized as **epicede** /ˈɛpɪsiːd/, (now *rare*) in Greek form as **epicedion** /ɛpɪˈsiːdɪən/. M16.
[ORIGIN Latin from Greek *epikēdeion* use as noun of neut. of *epikēdeios* funeral (adjective), formed as EPI- + *kēdos* care, grief, mourning.]
A funeral ode.
■ **epicedial** *adjective* M17. **epicedian** *adjective & noun* (*a*) *adjective* funereal, elegiac; †(*b*) *noun* = EPICEDIUM: E17.

epicene /ˈɛpɪsiːn/ *adjective & noun*. LME.
[ORIGIN Late Latin *epicœnus* from Greek *epikoinos*, formed as EPI- + *koinos* common.]
▸**A** *adjective*. **1** GRAMMAR. Of a noun or pronoun: that may refer to either sex without changing its grammatical gender; denoting both males and females. LME.
2 Of indeterminate sex; characteristic of both sexes. Also, effeminate. E17.

T. HARDY What had at first appeared as an epicene shape, the decreasing space resolved into a cloaked female.

3 For or used by both sexes. E17.

A. DUGGAN The men . . wore long epicene gowns.

▸**B** *noun*. **1** A person of indeterminate sex; an effeminate person. E17.
2 An epicene noun or pronoun. E17.

epicenter *noun* see EPICENTRE.

epicentral /ɛpɪˈsɛntr(ə)l/ *adjective & noun*. M19.
[ORIGIN Sense A.1 from Greek *epikentros* (see EPICENTRE); sense A.2 from EPICENTRE: see -AL¹.]
▸**A** *adjective*. **1** ZOOLOGY. Situated on a vertebral centrum. M19.
2 Of, pertaining to, or containing an epicentre. L19.
▸**B** *noun*. ZOOLOGY. An epicentral spine. M19.

epicentre /ˈɛpɪsɛntə/ *noun*. Also ***-ter**, & in sense 1 in mod. Latin form (now *rare*) **epicentrum** /ɛpɪˈsɛntrəm/, pl. **-ra** /-rə/. L19.
[ORIGIN Greek *epikentron* neut. of *epikentros* situated on a centre, formed as EPI- + *kentros* CENTRE *noun & adjective*.]
1 The point on the earth's surface directly above the focus of an earthquake. L19.
2 *fig.* The centre or heart of something, esp. something unpleasant. M20.

G. SWIFT At the very epicentre of the slaughter, on the infamous Western Front.

épicerie /episri/ *noun*. Pl. pronounced same. E20.
[ORIGIN French: see SPICERY.]
A grocer's shop in France.

epicheirema /ˌɛpɪkʌɪˈriːmə/ *noun*. L17.
[ORIGIN mod. Latin from Greek *epikheirēma* attempt, from *epikheirein* undertake, formed as EPI- + *kheir* hand.]
LOGIC. In Aristotle's use, an attempted proof that is not conclusive; (by misunderstanding, now *rare*) a syllogism in which one or both of the premisses is supported by a reason.

epicism /ˈɛpɪsɪz(ə)m/ *noun*. *rare*. M19.
[ORIGIN from EPIC + -ISM.]
The manner, style, etc., characteristic of epics.
■ **epicist** *noun* a writer of epic poetry M19.

†**epick** *adjective & noun* var. of EPIC.

epiclesis /ɛpɪˈkliːsɪs/ *noun*. Also **-kl-**. Pl. **-cleses** /-ˈkliːsiːz/. L19.
[ORIGIN Greek *epiklēsis*, from *epikalein* call on, formed as EPI- + *kalein* to call.]
CHRISTIAN CHURCH. The part of the Eucharistic prayer in which the descent of the Holy Spirit is invoked on the elements or the communicants.

epicondyle /ɛpɪˈkɒndɪl, -dʌɪl/ *noun*. M19.
[ORIGIN French *épicondyle*, mod. Latin *epicondylus*, from (the same root as) EPI- + CONDYLE.]
ANATOMY. A protuberance above or on the condyle of a long bone, *esp.* either of the two at the elbow end of the humerus.
■ **epicondylar** *adjective* M20. ˌ**epicondyˈlitis** *noun* a painful condition of an epicondyle or epicondylar region of the humerus; tennis elbow: M20.

epicontinental /ˌɛpɪkɒntɪˈnɛnt(ə)l/ *adjective*. E20.
[ORIGIN from EPI- + CONTINENTAL.]
GEOLOGY. Situated on a continent or continental shelf; *spec.* = EPEIRIC.

epicritic /ɛpɪˈkrɪtɪk/ *adjective*. E20.
[ORIGIN Greek *epikritikos* adjudicatory, from *epikrinein* decide, formed as EPI- + *krinein* to judge: see -IC.]
PHYSIOLOGY. Involving fine discrimination of sensory (esp. cutaneous) stimuli.

epicure /ˈɛpɪkjʊə/ *noun*. LME.
[ORIGIN medieval Latin *epicurus* appellative use of *Epicurus* from Greek *Epikouros* Epicurus: see EPICUREAN *noun* 1.]
†**1** (**E-**.) = EPICUREAN *noun* 1. LME–L18.
2 A person whose main concern is sensual pleasure, esp. eating; a glutton. *arch.* M16.
3 A person who cultivates a refined taste, esp. for food and drink. L16.
■ **epicurish** *adjective* (*rare*) M16.

epicurean /ˌɛpɪkjʊ(ə)ˈriːən/ *noun & adjective*. Also †**-ian**. LME.
[ORIGIN Old French & mod. French *épicurien* or Latin *epicureus*, *-ius* from Greek *epikoureios* from *Epikouros* Epicurus: see below, -EAN.]
▸**A** *noun*. **1** (Usu. **E-**.) A disciple or student of Epicurus (341–270 BC), a Greek philosopher who held that the highest good is pleasure (identified with the practice of virtue), that the gods do not concern themselves with human affairs, and that the world results from the chance combination of atoms; a person who holds similar views. LME.
2 A person devoted to pleasure, now esp. refined sensuous enjoyment. L16.
▸**B** *adjective*. **1** (Usu. **E-**.) Of or pertaining to Epicurus or his philosophy. L16.
2 Pertaining to or exhibiting a devotion to pleasure, esp. of a refined or sensuous kind; characteristic of or suited to such a person. E17.
■ Also †**epicureal**, **-ial** *adjective* M16–E18.

epicureanism /ɛpɪˈkjʊərɪənɪz(ə)m/ *noun*. M18.
[ORIGIN from EPICUREAN + -ISM.]
1 (Usu. **E-**.) The philosophical system of Epicurus. M18.
2 Adherence to the principles of Epicurus; devotion to a life of pleasure, esp. of a refined or sensuous kind. M19.

O. WELLES She knew how to eat, with the careful epicureanism of a woman who is used to having the best.

†**epicurian** *noun & adjective* var. of EPICUREAN.

†**epicurise** *verb* var. of EPICURIZE.

epicurism /ˈɛpɪkjʊ(ə)rɪz(ə)m/ *noun*. L16.
[ORIGIN Partly from Latin *Epicurus* (see EPICUREAN *noun* 1) after French *épicurisme*, partly from EPICURE + -ISM.]
1 (Usu. **E-**.) = EPICUREANISM 1. Now *rare*. L16.
†**2** The pursuit of pleasure; sensuality; gluttony. L16–L18.
3 The disposition and habits of an epicure; cultivated taste in food and drink. E17.

†**epicurize** *verb intrans*. Also **-ise**. L16–E18.
[ORIGIN from Latin *Epicurus* (see EPICUREAN *noun* 1) or EPICURE + -IZE.]
Live or behave as an epicure; feast daintily or luxuriously.

epicycle /ˈɛpɪsʌɪk(ə)l/ *noun*. LME.
[ORIGIN Old French & mod. French *épicycle* or late Latin *epicyclus* from Greek *epikuklos*, formed as EPI- + *kuklos* circle.]
A circle whose centre moves round the circumference of a larger circle; *spec.* (HISTORY OF SCIENCE) such a circle in the Ptolemaic system, in which the planets were regarded as moving in circles whose centres moved round larger circles (deferents) centred on the earth.
■ **epicyclic** /-ˈsʌɪk-, -ˈsɪk-/ *adjective & noun* (*a*) *adjective* of, pertaining to, or involving epicycles; designating a gear in which one wheel travels round the outside or the inside of another wheel with which it meshes; (*b*) *noun* an epicyclic gear: M19. **epicyclical** /-ˈsʌɪk-, -ˈsɪk-/ *adjective* = EPICYCLIC *adjective* M19.

epicycloid /ɛpɪˈsʌɪklɔɪd/ *noun*. L18.
[ORIGIN from EPICYCLE + -OID.]
A curve traced by a point on the circumference of a circle as it rolls round the outside of a fixed circle (or, formerly, round the inside: cf. HYPOCYCLOID).
■ **epicyˈcloidal** *adjective* E19.

Epidaurian /ɛpɪˈdɔːrɪən/ *noun & adjective*. M16.
[ORIGIN from Greek *Epidauros*, Latin *Epidaurus* (see below) + -IAN.]
GREEK HISTORY. ▸**A** *noun*. A native or inhabitant of Epidaurus, a city in ancient Greece in the NE Peloponnese which was a centre for the cult of Asclepius. M16.
▸**B** *adjective*. Of or pertaining to Epidaurus or Epidaurians. E17.

epideictic /ɛpɪˈdʌɪktɪk/ *adjective*. L18.
[ORIGIN Greek *epideiktikos*, formed as EPI- + *deiknunai* to show: see -IC.]
Using oratorical skill to praise or censure; characterized by a display of such skill.

†**epidemial** *adjective*. M16–E19.
[ORIGIN Old French, from *épidémie*: see EPIDEMIC, -AL¹.]
= EPIDEMIC *adjective* 1.

epidemic /ɛpɪˈdɛmɪk/ *adjective & noun*. E17.
[ORIGIN French *épidémique*, from Old French & mod. French *épidémie* from late Latin *epidemia* from Greek *epidēmia* prevalence of a disease, from *epidēmios* prevalent, formed as EPI- + *dēmos* people: see -IC.]
▸**A** *adjective*. **1** Of a disease: normally absent or infrequent in a population but liable to outbreaks of greatly increased frequency and severity; temporarily widespread. E17.

Scientific American One rickettsial disease, epidemic typhus, has been for centuries a great scourge of mankind.

2 Chiefly of something deprecated: widespread, prevalent, universal. M17.

Listener It is . . a type of character more than a political party. But it is epidemic enough . . to produce . . much damage.

▸**B** *noun*. A temporary but widespread outbreak of a particular disease; *fig.* a sudden marked increase in the extent or currency of something. M18.

V. BRITTAIN The ferocious influenza epidemic was already making us short of staff. *New Scientist* The epidemic of prejudice and discrimination towards HIV-infected people.

■ **epidemical** *adjective* (now *rare*) = EPIDEMIC *adjective* E17. **epidemically** *adverb* M17. **epidemicity** /-ˈmɪsɪti/ *noun* the quality of being epidemic L19.

epidemiology /ˌɛpɪdiːmɪˈɒlədʒi/ *noun*. L19.
[ORIGIN from Greek *epidēmia* (see EPIDEMIC) + -OLOGY.]
The branch of medicine that deals with the incidence and transmission of disease in populations, esp. with the aim of controlling it; the aspects of a disease relating to its incidence and transmission.

Listener The aetiology and epidemiology of the disease are not yet well understood.

■ **epidemioˈlogic** *adjective* (chiefly *US*) M20. **epidemioˈlogical** *adjective* M19. **epidemioˈlogically** *adverb* L19. **epidemiologist** *noun* L19.

†**epidemy** *noun.* L15–M19.
[ORIGIN Old French *ypidime, impidemie,* (also mod.) *épidémie*: see EPIDEMIC, -Y³.]
An epidemic; *spec.* the plague.

epidendrum /ɛpɪˈdɛndrəm/ *noun.* Also **-dron** /-drən/. L18.
[ORIGIN mod. Latin (see below), formed as EPI- + Greek *dendron* tree.]
Any orchid of the genus *Epidendrum* (or formerly included in it), comprising chiefly epiphytic plants of tropical America.

epiderm /ˈɛpɪdəːm/ *noun.* Now *rare* or *obsolete.* M19.
[ORIGIN French *épiderme* from late Latin EPIDERMIS.]
= EPIDERMIS.

epidermis /ɛpɪˈdəːmɪs/ *noun.* E17.
[ORIGIN Late Latin from Greek, formed as EPI- + *derma* skin.]
1 The surface epithelium of the skin of an animal, overlying the dermis. E17.
2 The outer animal integument of a shell. M18.
3 The outer layer of tissue in a plant, except where it is replaced by periderm. E19.
■ **epidermal** *adjective* E19. **epidermic** *adjective* M19. **epidermical** *adjective* (now *rare*) L17. **epidermically** *adverb* M19. **epidermoid**, ˌ**epiderˈmoidal** *adjectives* (composed of tissue) resembling epidermis; of the nature of epidermis: M19. ˌ**epiderˈmolysis** *noun* a condition in which the epidermis loosens and extensive blistering occurs, occurring esp. in babies L19.

epidiascope /ɛpɪˈdʌɪəskəʊp/ *noun.* E20.
[ORIGIN from EPI- + DIA-¹ + -SCOPE.]
An optical projector giving images of both opaque and transparent objects.

epididymis /ɛpɪˈdɪdɪmɪs/ *noun.* Pl. **epididymides** /ɛpɪdɪˈdɪmɪdiːz/. Cf. earlier DIDYMIS. E17.
[ORIGIN Greek *epididumis*, formed as EPI- + *didumos* testicle, twin, from *duo* two.]
ANATOMY. A convoluted duct on the posterior surface of the testis, where sperm are stored and along which they pass to the vas deferens.
■ **epididymal** *adjective* L17. **epididyˈmectomy** *noun* (an instance of) surgical removal of an epididymis E20. **epididyˈmitis** *noun* inflammation of an epididymis M19.

epididymo- /ɛpɪˈdɪdɪməʊ/ *combining form.* L19.
[ORIGIN from EPIDIDYMIS + -O-.]
MEDICINE. Of or pertaining to the epididymis and —, as *epididymo-orchitis* etc.

epidosite /ɪˈpɪdəsʌɪt/ *noun.* M19.
[ORIGIN Alt. of EPIDOTE: see -ITE¹. Cf. Greek *epidosis* an additional giving.]
GEOLOGY. A metamorphic rock composed chiefly of epidote and quartz.

epidote /ˈɛpɪdəʊt/ *noun.* E19.
[ORIGIN French *épidote*, from Greek *epididonai* give in addition, formed as EPI- + *didonai* give (with ref. to the great length of the crystals).]
MINERALOGY. A basic silicate of calcium, aluminium, and iron that occurs as monoclinic usu. green crystals in many metamorphic rocks. Also, any of several rock-forming silicates of analogous composition.
■ **epidotic** /-ˈdɒt-/ *adjective* M19. **epidotiˈzation** *noun* the process of becoming epidotized L19. **epidotized** *adjective* metamorphically altered into epidote M20.

epidural /ɛpɪˈdjʊər(ə)l/ *adjective & noun.* L19.
[ORIGIN from EPI- + DURA *noun*¹ + -AL¹.]
MEDICINE. ▸**A** *adjective.* Situated or administered in the spinal canal immediately outside the dura mater. L19.

Sun The painless-birth method is known as epidural anaesthesia.

▸**B** *noun.* A local anaesthetic administered into the epidural space of the spinal canal, used esp. in childbirth to produce a loss of sensation below the waist without affecting consciousness. L20.

epifauna /ˈɛpɪfɔːnə/ *noun.* E20.
[ORIGIN from EPI- + FAUNA.]
The animal life which lives on (rather than in) the seabed or on a marine animal or plant.
■ **epiˈfaunal** *adjective* M20.

epigamic /ɛpɪˈgamɪk/ *adjective.* L19.
[ORIGIN from EPI- + Greek *gamos* marriage + -IC.]
ZOOLOGY. Of the colours or behaviour of animals: having the property of attracting members of the opposite sex.

epigastrium /ɛpɪˈgastrɪəm/ *noun.* L17.
[ORIGIN Late Latin *epigastrion* from Greek use as noun of neut. sing. of *epigastrios* over the belly, formed as EPI- + *gastr-*, *gastēr* belly.]
ANATOMY. The upper central region of the abdomen.
■ **epigastric** *adjective* M17. †**epigastrical** *adjective* E–M17.

epigeal /ɛpɪˈdʒiːəl/ *adjective.* M19.
[ORIGIN formed as EPIGEOUS: see -AL¹.]
BOTANY. = EPIGEAN; (of germination) marked by an elongation of the hypocotyl so that the cotyledons are pushed above the ground.

epigean /ɛpɪˈdʒiːən/ *adjective.* L19.
[ORIGIN formed as EPIGEOUS: see -AN.]
BOTANY & ZOOLOGY. Growing or living on or close to the ground.

epigene /ˈɛpɪdʒiːn/ *adjective.* E19.
[ORIGIN French *épigène* from Greek *epigenēs*, formed as EPI- + -GENE.]
1 Of a crystal: chemically altered after its formation; pseudomorphic. Now *rare.* E19.
2 GEOLOGY. Occurring or formed at or near the earth's surface. L19.
■ **epigenic** /-ˈdʒɛn-/ *adjective* = EPIGENE 2 L19.

epigenesis /ɛpɪˈdʒɛnɪsɪs/ *noun.* M17.
[ORIGIN from EPI- + -GENESIS.]
BIOLOGY (now *hist.*). (A theory of) the development of an organism by progressive differentiation of an initially undifferentiated whole (freq. opp. ***preformation***). Also (earlier), formation by successive accretion of parts.

epigenetic /ˌɛpɪdʒɪˈnɛtɪk/ *adjective.* L19.
[ORIGIN from EPIGENESIS after *genetic.*]
1 BIOLOGY. Of, pertaining to, or of the nature of epigenesis. Also, resulting from external influences, not genetic. L19.
2 GEOLOGY. Of a deposit or feature: formed later than the rock etc. in which it is enclosed or situated. E20.
■ **epigenetically** *adverb* L19.

epigenetics /ˌɛpɪdʒɪˈnɛtɪks/ *noun.* M20.
[ORIGIN from EPIGENETIC: see -ICS.]
The branch of biology that deals with the effect of external influences on development.

epigeous /ɛpɪˈdʒiːəs/ *adjective.* M19.
[ORIGIN from Greek *epigeios*, formed as EPI- + *gē* earth: see -OUS.]
BOTANY & ZOOLOGY. = EPIGEAN.

epiglottis /ɛpɪˈglɒtɪs/ *noun.* Also (earlier) anglicized as †**epiglot.** LME.
[ORIGIN Greek *epiglōttis*, formed as EPI- + *glōtta* tongue. Cf. GLOTTIS.]
A thin leaf-shaped flap of cartilage, situated immediately behind the root of the tongue, which covers the entrance to the larynx during swallowing and prevents food from entering the windpipe.
■ **epiglottal** *adjective* M20. **epiglottic** *adjective* L19. ˌ**epiglottiˈditis** *noun* = EPIGLOTTITIS M19. ˌ**epigloˈttitis** *noun* inflammation of the epiglottis M19.

epigone /ˈɛpɪgəʊn/ *noun.* Pl. **epigones**, **epigoni** /ɪˈpɪgənʌɪ, ɛ-/. Also **-gon** /-gən/. M18.
[ORIGIN In pl. from French *épigones* from Latin *epigoni* from Greek *epigonoi*, pl. of *epigonos* offspring, formed as EPI- + *-gonos*, from *gignesthai* be born.]
A member of a succeeding (and less distinguished) generation.

A. BURGESS The generation of traitors—Alfred Adler, Carl Jung, and all their wretched epigones.

epigram /ˈɛpɪgram/ *noun.* LME.
[ORIGIN French *épigramme* or Latin *epigramma* from Greek, formed as EPI- + -GRAM.]
1 A short poem leading up to and ending in a witty or ingenious turn of thought. LME.
2 = EPIGRAPH 2. *obsolete* exc. *hist.* M16.
3 **a** A concise pointed saying. L18. ▸**b** Epigrammatic expression. M19.

a R. W. CHURCH He liked . . to generalize in shrewd and sometimes cynical epigrams.

■ **epigrammist** *noun* (*rare*) an epigrammatist M17.

epigrammatic /ˌɛpɪgrəˈmatɪk/ *adjective.* E17.
[ORIGIN Late Latin *epigrammaticus*, from Latin *epigrammat-* stem of *epigramma* EPIGRAM: see -IC, -ATIC.]
Of or pertaining to epigrams; of the nature or in the style of an epigram; concise, pointed.
■ **epigrammatical** *adjective* E17. **epigrammatically** *adverb* E19.

epigrammatise *verb* var. of EPIGRAMMATIZE.

epigrammatist /ɛpɪˈgramətɪst/ *noun.* L16.
[ORIGIN Late Latin *epigrammatista* from Greek *epigrammatistēs*, from *epigrammatizein*: see EPIGRAMMATIZE, -IST.]
A maker of epigrams.
■ **epigrammatism** *noun* epigrammatic style E19.

epigrammatize /ɛpɪˈgramətʌɪz/ *verb.* Also **-ise.** L17.
[ORIGIN Greek *epigrammatizein*, from *epigramma* (see EPIGRAM), or from Latin *epigrammat-* (see EPIGRAMMATIC) + -IZE.]
1 *verb trans.* Express in an epigrammatic style. L17. ▸**b** Make the subject of an epigram. M19.
2 *verb intrans.* Compose epigrams; write or speak in an epigrammatic style. E19.
■ **epigrammatizer** *noun* E19.

epigramme /ˈɛpɪgram/ *noun.* M18.
[ORIGIN French *épigramme*, app. a fanciful use of *épigramme* = EPIGRAM.]
COOKERY. A small piece of meat, usu. lamb, served as an entrée.

epigraph /ˈɛpɪgrɑːf/ *noun.* L16.
[ORIGIN Greek *epigraphē*, from *epigraphein* write on, formed as EPI- + *graphein* write.]
†**1** The superscription of a letter, book, etc.; the imprint on a title page. L16–E19.
2 An inscription, *esp.* one on a tombstone, building, statue, etc.; a legend on a coin. E17.

C. THIRLWALL The epigraph of the thousand citizens who fell . . at Chaeronea.

3 = MOTTO *noun* 2. M19.

Economist Towards the end of the book Mr Chevalier uses an epigraph from Daniel Halevy.

■ **epiˈgraphic** *adjective* of or pertaining to epigraphs or epigraphy M19. **epiˈgraphical** *adjective* = EPIGRAPHIC L19. **epiˈgraphically** *adverb* L19.

epigraphy /ɪˈpɪgrəfi, ɛ-/ *noun.* M19.
[ORIGIN from EPIGRAPH + -Y³: see -GRAPHY.]
1 Inscriptions collectively. M19.
2 The branch of knowledge that deals with the interpretation, classification, etc., of inscriptions; the palaeography of inscriptions. M19.
■ **epigrapher** *noun* an expert in or student of inscriptions L19. **epigraphist** *noun* an epigrapher M19.

E

epigyne /ˈɛpɪdʒʌɪn/ *noun.* Also in Latin form **epigynum** /ɛpɪˈdʒʌɪnəm/. L19.
[ORIGIN mod. Latin *epigynum*, from EPI- + Greek *gunē* woman, female.]
ZOOLOGY. The arachnid ovipositor; the external genital plate of spiders.

epigynous /ɪˈpɪdʒɪnəs, ɛ-/ *adjective.* M19.
[ORIGIN from mod. Latin *epigynus*, from EPI- + Greek *gunē* woman (used for 'pistil'): see -OUS.]
BOTANY. Of a flower: having the ovary completely enclosed in the receptacle and the stamens, sepals, etc., situated above it. Of stamens, sepals, etc.: so situated. Cf. HYPOGYNOUS, PERIGYNOUS.
■ **epigyny** *noun* epigynous condition L19.

epigynum *noun* see EPIGYNE.

epiklesis *noun* var. of EPICLESIS.

epiky /ˈɛpɪki/ *noun.* Long *obsolete* exc. *hist.* E16.
[ORIGIN medieval Latin *epikeia*, *epieikeia* from Greek *epieikeia*, formed as EPI- + *eikos* reasonable.]
Reasonableness, equity, esp. as a legal principle.

epilate /ˈɛpɪleɪt/ *verb trans.* L19.
[ORIGIN from French *épiler* (formed as ES- + Latin *pilus* hair) after *depilate.*]
Remove hair from.
■ **epiˈlation** *noun* L19.

epilepsy /ˈɛpɪlɛpsi/ *noun.* M16.
[ORIGIN French *épilepsie* or late Latin *epilepsia* from Greek *epilēpsia*, from *epilab-* stem of *epilambanein* seize, attack, formed as EPI- + *lambanein* take hold of.]
A condition in which a person has intermittent paroxysmal attacks of disordered brain function usu. causing a loss of awareness or consciousness and sometimes convulsions.

epileptic /ɛpɪˈlɛptɪk/ *adjective & noun.* E17.
[ORIGIN French *épileptique* from late Latin *epilepticus* from Greek *epilēptikos*, from *epilēpsia*: see EPILEPSY, -IC.]
▸**A** *adjective.* **1** Of, pertaining to, or of the nature of epilepsy. E17.

Financial Times An irate spasmodic fit bordering on the epileptic.

2 Affected with epilepsy. E17.
▸**B** *noun.* A person with epilepsy. M17.
■ **epileptical** *adjective* E17. **epileptically** *adverb* L19. **epileptiform** *adjective* resembling (the symptoms of) epilepsy M19. **epileptoˈgenic**, **epilepˈtogenous** *adjectives* producing epileptic attacks L19. **epileptoid** *adjective* resembling or of the nature of epilepsy M19.

epilimnion /ɛpɪˈlɪmnɪən/ *noun.* Pl. **-nia** /-nɪə/. E20.
[ORIGIN from EPI- + Greek *limnion* dim. of *limnē* lake.]
The upper, warmer layer of water in a stratified lake.

epilobium /ɛpɪˈləʊbɪəm/ *noun.* L18.
[ORIGIN mod. Latin, from EPI- + Greek *lobos* lobe, pod, with ref. to the insertion of the corolla at the end of the long ovary.]
Any of various plants constituting the genus *Epilobium* (family Onagraceae), with terminal racemes of pink or purplish flowers; a willowherb.

epilog *noun* see EPILOGUE *noun.*

epilogise *verb* var. of EPILOGIZE.

epilogist /ɪˈpɪlədʒɪst, ɛ-/ *noun.* E18.
[ORIGIN from EPILOG(UE + -IST.]
The writer or speaker of an epilogue.
■ **epilogistic** /ɛˌpɪləˈdʒɪstɪk/ *adjective* (*rare*) of the nature of an epilogue L18.

epilogize /ɪˈpɪlədʒʌɪz, ɛ-/ *verb.* Also **-ise.** E17.
[ORIGIN Greek *epilogizesthai*, from *epilogos*: see EPILOGUE, -IZE.]
1 *verb intrans.* Deliver an epilogue. E17.
2 *verb intrans.* Serve as an epilogue or ending. M17.
3 *verb trans.* = EPILOGUE *verb.* M19.

epilogue /ˈɛpɪlɒg/ *noun & verb.* LME.
[ORIGIN Old French & mod. French *épilogue* from Latin *epilogus* from Greek *epilogos*, formed as EPI- + *logos* saying, speech: see -LOGUE. Cf. PROLOGUE.]
▸**A** *noun.* Also *-**log.**
1 The concluding part of a literary work; a postscript. LME.

Financial Times The epilogue . . summarizes the lives of surviving children. *fig.*: *Economist* Oman's establishment of diplomatic relations with Russia is the epilogue to the Dhofar rebellion.

2 A speech or short poem addressed to the spectators by one of the actors at the end of a play. L16.

†**3** RHETORIC. The concluding part of a speech; a summary. Only in M17.

▸ **B** *verb trans.* Provide an epilogue to. E17.

■ **epilogical** /ɛpɪˈlɒdʒɪk(ə)l/ *adjective* (*rare*) pertaining to or resembling an epilogue L19. †**epiloguize** *verb intrans. & trans.* = EPILOGIZE M17–M18.

epiloia /ɛpɪˈlɔɪə/ *noun.* E20.
[ORIGIN from EPIL(EPSY after *paranoia*.]
MEDICINE. Tuberous sclerosis.

epimedium /ɛpɪˈmiːdɪəm/ *noun.* L18.
[ORIGIN mod. Latin (see below) from Greek *epimēdion*.]
Any of various low-growing creeping perennial herbs of the genus *Epimedium*, of the barberry family, which includes barrenwort, *E. alpinum*.

epimer /ˈɛpɪmə/ *noun.* E20.
[ORIGIN from EPI- + -MER.]
CHEMISTRY. Either of two stereoisomers differing in configuration about one asymmetric carbon atom when others are present in the molecule.
■ **epimerase** /ɪˈpɪm-, ɛ-/ *noun* an enzyme which catalyses inversion at an asymmetric carbon atom in a molecule containing more than one such atom M20. **epiˈmeric** *adjective* E20. **epimerism** /ɪˈpɪm-, ɛ-/ *noun* the fact or condition of having epimers E20. **epimerization** /ɪˌpɪmərʌɪˈzeɪ-, ɛ-/ *noun* the conversion of one epimer into another E20. **epimerize** /ɪˈpɪm-, ɛ-/ *verb trans.* convert (one epimer) into another M20.

epimera *noun* see EPIMERON.

epimere /ˈɛpɪmɪə/ *noun.* L19.
[ORIGIN from EPI- + -MERE.]
1 ZOOLOGY. = EPIMERON. L19.
2 EMBRYOLOGY. The part of the mesoderm that divides to form the dermatome, myotomes, and sclerotomes. L19.

epimerite /ɪˈpɪmərʌɪt, ɛ-/ *noun.* L19.
[ORIGIN from EPI- + Greek *meros* part + -ITE[1].]
ZOOLOGY. An anterior extension of the body in some protozoans that is used as an organ of attachment.

epimeron /ɛpɪˈmiːrən/ *noun.* Also †**-ra**, †**-rum**. Pl. **-ra** /-rə/. M19.
[ORIGIN from EPI- + Greek *mēros* thigh.]
ZOOLOGY. **1** Part of the lateral wall of a somite of a crustacean. M19.
2 The posterior sclerite of the thoracic pleuron of some insects. L19.
■ **epimeral** *adjective* M19.

epimorphic /ɛpɪˈmɔːfɪk/ *adjective.* M20.
[ORIGIN from EPI- + Greek *morphē* form + -IC.]
Of, pertaining to, or designating epimorphosis or an epimorphism.

epimorphism /ɛpɪˈmɔːfɪz(ə)m/ *noun.* M20.
[ORIGIN from EPI- + Greek *morphē* form + -ISM.]
MATH. A homomorphism of one set onto another.

epimorphosis /ˌɛpɪmɔːˈfəʊsɪs/ *noun.* E20.
[ORIGIN from EPI- + MORPHOSIS.]
ZOOLOGY. Regeneration in which a new part is produced by the growth of new tissue. Opp. MORPHALLAXIS.

epimysium /ɛpɪˈmɪsɪəm/ *noun.* M20.
[ORIGIN mod. Latin, from Greek EPI- + *mus* muscle.]
ANATOMY. A sheath of fibrous elastic tissue surrounding a muscle.

epimyth /ˈɛpɪmɪθ/ *noun.* M19.
[ORIGIN Greek *epimuthion* use as noun of neut. of *epimuthios* coming after the fable, formed as EPI- + *muthos* fable.]
The moral of a fable.

epinasty /ˈɛpɪnasti/ *noun.* L19.
[ORIGIN from EPI- + Greek *nastos* pressed together + -Y[3].]
BOTANY. A tendency in part of a plant to grow more rapidly on the upper side, so that it curves downwards.
■ **epiˈnastic** *adjective* L19.

-epine /ɪˈpiːn/ *suffix.*
[ORIGIN from EPI- + -INE[5].]
CHEMISTRY. Occurring in the names of compounds whose molecule includes an unsaturated seven-membered ring containing nitrogen.

epinephrine /ɛpɪˈnɛfrɪn, -riːn/ *noun.* Chiefly *US*. Also **-rin** /-rɪn/. L19.
[ORIGIN from EPI- + Greek *nephros* kidney + -INE[5], -IN[1].]
= ADRENALIN.

epineural /ɛpɪˈnjʊər(ə)l/ *adjective & noun.* M19.
[ORIGIN from EPI- + NEURAL.]
ZOOLOGY. ▸ **A** *adjective.* **1** Situated on a neural arch. M19.
2 Lying over and parallel to a nerve. E20.
▸ **B** *noun.* An epineural spine in a fish. M19.

epineurium /ɛpɪˈnjʊərɪəm/ *noun.* L19.
[ORIGIN from EPI- + Greek *neuron* nerve.]
ANATOMY. The outer sheath of connective tissue round a nerve trunk.

epinicia *noun* pl. of EPINICION.

epinician /ɛpɪˈnɪsɪən/ *adjective.* M17.
[ORIGIN from EPINICION + -AN.]
Celebrating victory.

epinicion /ɛpɪˈnɪsɪən/ *noun.* Now *rare*. Also **-cium** /-sɪəm/. Pl. **-cia** /-sɪə/. E17.
[ORIGIN Greek *epinikion* use as noun of neut. of *epinikios* of victory, formed as EPI- + *nikē* victory.]
A song of triumph.

Epipalaeolithic /ˌɛpɪpalɪə(ʊ)ˈlɪθɪk, -peɪl-/ *adjective & noun.* Also *-paleo-. E20.
[ORIGIN from EPI- + PALAEOLITHIC.]
ARCHAEOLOGY. (Designating or pertaining to) a period or culture that seems to show features of both the Palaeolithic and the Mesolithic periods and may be transitional between them.

epiphanous /ɪˈpɪf(ə)nəs, ɛ-/ *adjective.* E19.
[ORIGIN Sense 1 from Greek *epiphanēs*, formed as EPIPHANY, sense 2 from EPIPHANY: see -OUS.]
1 Resplendent. *rare*. E19.
2 = EPIPHANIC. L20.

epiphany /ɪˈpɪf(ə)ni, ɛ-/ *noun.* ME.
[ORIGIN Ult. from Greek *epiphainein* to manifest, formed as EPI- + *phainein* show: see -Y[3]. In sense 1 from Old French & mod. French *épiphanie* from ecclesiastical Latin *epiphania* pl. & sing. from ecclesiastical Greek *epiphania* pl.; in sense 2 partly from Greek *epiphaneia* manifestation.]
1 (Also **E-**.) A Christian festival observed on 6 January, in the Orthodox Church commemorating the baptism of Jesus and in the Western Church the manifestation of Jesus to the Gentiles in the persons of the Magi. ME.
2 A manifestation of some divine or superhuman being. E17.

E. IRVING The second coming . . the glorious Epiphany of God our Saviour. M. AYRTON Dionysus, whose apotheosis, or epiphany, . . was as a bull.

3 Any sudden and important manifestation or realization. M19.

T. EAGLETON *The Prelude* draws back from the tragic brink to which its isolated epiphanies allude. F. FERGUSSON The final perception or epiphany . . with which the play ends.

– COMB.: **Epiphanytide** the period of the Church's year beginning with and immediately following Epiphany.
■ **epiˈphanic** *adjective* of the nature of an epiphany M20. **epiphanize** *verb trans.* make manifest, reveal M20.

epiphenomenon /ˌɛpɪfəˈnɒmɪnən/ *noun.* Pl. **-mena** /-mɪnə/. E17.
[ORIGIN from EPI- + PHENOMENON.]
1 MEDICINE. A secondary symptom occurring with a disease but not necessarily regarded as its result or cause. E17.
2 PHILOSOPHY & PSYCHOLOGY. A concomitant or by-product of something; *spec.* consciousness or mental phenomena regarded as by-products of the physical activity of the brain and nervous system that do not influence behaviour. L19.
■ **epiphenomenal** *adjective* of the nature of or pertaining to epiphenomena L19. **epiphenomenalism** *noun* the doctrine that consciousness is an epiphenomenon L19. **epiphenomenalist** *adjective & noun* (*a*) *adjective* of or pertaining to epiphenomenalism; (*b*) *noun* an advocate of epiphenomenalism: E20.

epiphonema /ˌɛpɪfəˈniːmə/ *noun.* M16.
[ORIGIN Latin from Greek *epiphōnēma*, from *epiphōnein* call to.]
RHETORIC. An exclamatory sentence or striking reflection, which sums up or concludes a discourse or passage.

epiphora /ɪˈpɪf(ə)rə, ɛ-/ *noun.* L16.
[ORIGIN Latin from Greek = a bringing to or upon, formed as EPI- + *pherein* carry.]
1 RHETORIC. A figure in which one word is repeated impressively at the end of several sentences. Now *rare* or *obsolete*. L16.
2 MEDICINE. Excessive watering of the eye. M17.

epiphragm /ˈɛpɪfram/ *noun.* In sense 2 also in Latin form **epiphragma** /ɛpɪˈfragmə/. M19.
[ORIGIN mod. Latin *epiphragma* from Greek = lid, formed as EPI- + *phragma* fence.]
1 ZOOLOGY. The layer of hardened secretion with which a snail closes its shell before hibernation. M19.
2 BOTANY. A membrane closing the mouth of the spore case or fruiting body in some mosses and fungi. M19.

epiphyllous /ɛpɪˈfɪləs/ *adjective.* E19.
[ORIGIN from EPI- + Greek *phullon* leaf + -OUS.]
BOTANY. Growing or inserted on a leaf.

epiphyllum /ɛpɪˈfɪləm/ *noun.* M19.
[ORIGIN mod. Latin (see below), formed as EPI- + Greek *phullon* leaf, the flowers being borne on flattened leaflike branches.]
A cactus of the tropical American genus *Epiphyllum*, with flattened stems and large fragrant red or yellow flowers, *esp.* the night-flowering cactus *E. hookeri*.

epiphysis /ɪˈpɪfɪsɪs, ɛ-/ *noun.* Pl. **-physes** /-fɪsiːz/. M17.
[ORIGIN mod. Latin from Greek *epiphusis*, formed as EPI- + *phusis* growth.]
ANATOMY. **1** A part of a bone, esp. an extremity of a long bone, which during growth is separated from the main part by cartilage that eventually ossifies. M17.
2 The pineal gland. More fully ***epiphysis cerebri*** /ˈsɛrɪbrʌɪ/ [Latin *cerebrum* brain]. L19.
■ **epiphyseal** /ɛpɪˈfɪzɪəl/, **epiphysial** *adjectives* M19. **epiphysitis** /ɪˌpɪfɪˈsʌɪtɪs, ɛ-/ *noun* (MEDICINE) inflammation of an epiphysis or of the cartilage separating it from the main part of the bone L19.

epiphyte /ˈɛpɪfʌɪt/ *noun.* M19.
[ORIGIN from EPI- + -PHYTE.]
A plant (esp. one that is not parasitic) which grows on another plant.
■ **epiˈphytal** *adjective* (now *rare*) = EPIPHYTIC M19. **epiphytic** /-ˈfɪtɪk/ *adjective* of, pertaining to, or designating an epiphyte or epiphytes M19. **epiphytical** /-ˈfɪt-/ *adjective* (now *rare*) = EPIPHYTIC M19. **epiphytically** /-ˈfɪt-/ *adverb* M19. **epiˈphytous** *adjective* (now *rare*) = EPIPHYTIC M19.

epiphytotic /ˌɛpɪfʌɪˈtɒtɪk/ *adjective & noun.* L19.
[ORIGIN formed as EPIPHYTE after *epizootic*.]
(Designating) a plant disease that is temporarily prevalent over a large area.

epipleural /ɛpɪˈplʊər(ə)l/ *adjective.* M19.
[ORIGIN from Greek *epipleuros*, formed as EPI- + *pleura* rib: see -AL[1].]
ZOOLOGY. Situated on a rib.

epiplocele /ɪˈpɪpləsiːl, ɛ-/ *noun.* E17.
[ORIGIN Greek *epiplokēlē*, formed as EPIPLOON + -CELE.]
MEDICINE. A hernia in which part of the omentum protrudes.

epiploic /ɛpɪˈpləʊɪk/ *adjective.* M17.
[ORIGIN from EPIPLOON + -IC.]
ANATOMY. Of or pertaining to the omentum.
epiploic foramen an opening or passage connecting the two sacs of the peritoneum.

epiploon /ɪˈpɪpləʊɒn, ɛ-/ *noun.* Now *rare*. LME.
[ORIGIN Greek, from *epiplein* sail or float on.]
1 The omentum. LME.
2 The fat body of an insect. E19.

epipodite /ɪˈpɪpədʌɪt, ɛ-/ *noun.* M19.
[ORIGIN from EPIPODIUM + -ITE[1].]
ZOOLOGY. A process on the outer side of the protopodite of a limb in some crustaceans.
■ Also **epipod** /ˈɛpɪpɒd/ *noun* L19.

epipodium /ɛpɪˈpəʊdɪəm/ *noun.* Pl. **-ia** /-ɪə/. M19.
[ORIGIN mod. Latin from Greek *epipodion* use as noun of neut. of *epipodios* on the feet, formed as EPI- + *pod-*, *pous* foot.]
ZOOLOGY. A ridge running round the side of the foot in some molluscs.
■ **epipodial** *adjective* L19.

epirogeny *noun* var. of EPEIROGENY.

Epirot /ɪˈpʌɪrət, ɛ-/ *noun & adjective.* Also **-rote** /-rəʊt/. L16.
[ORIGIN Greek *ēpeirōtēs*, from *ēpeiros* land, mainland: see -OT[2], -OTE.]
▸ **A** *noun.* **1** A native or inhabitant of ancient or modern Epirus in NW Greece and southern Albania. L16.
†**2** (**e-**.) A person who lives inland. Only in M17.
▸ **B** *adjective.* Of or pertaining to Epirus or its people. M19.

episcopable /ɪˈpɪskəpəb(ə)l, ɛ-/ *adjective.* L17.
[ORIGIN from EPISCOPATE *verb* + -ABLE.]
Eligible to be made a bishop.

episcopacy /ɪˈpɪskəpəsi, ɛ-/ *noun.* M17.
[ORIGIN from ecclesiastical Latin *episcopatus* EPISCOPATE *noun* after *prelacy*: see -ACY.]
1 Government of a Church by bishops; the system of church government in which there is an order of bishops. M17.

ANTHONY WOOD He was never a cordial friend to Episcopacy, but rather a patron of the Non-conformists.

2 = EPISCOPATE *noun* 4. M17.

P. H. BLAIR Remaining at first at Lindisfarne, but removing to Hexham during the episcopacy of Cuthbert.

3 = EPISCOPATE *noun* 1. Now *rare*. L17.
4 = EPISCOPATE *noun* 3. Treated as *sing.* or *pl.* L18.

episcopal /ɪˈpɪskəp(ə)l, ɛ-/ *adjective & noun.* LME.
[ORIGIN Old French & mod. French *épiscopal* or ecclesiastical Latin *episcopalis*, from *episcopus* BISHOP *noun*: see -AL[1].]
▸ **A** *adjective.* **1** Of or pertaining to a bishop or bishops. LME.

W. JONES The episcopal ring . . was considered a symbol of sacerdotal authority. B. MOORE An Abbot with episcopal powers.

vicar episcopal: see VICAR 3.
2 Of or pertaining to episcopacy. Formerly also, advocating episcopacy. M17.

R. NELSON The Christian Church . . gives full Testimony in behalf of Episcopal Government.

3 (Of a Church) constituted on the principle of government by bishops, possessing bishops; belonging to such a Church. M18.

I. SHAW She was . . sending her . . son to an exclusive, all-boys' Episcopal school. *Christian Socialist* An episcopal priest.

Episcopal Church: *spec.* a Church of the Anglican Communion in the US, Scotland, and some other countries.
▸ **B** *noun.* = EPISCOPALIAN *noun.* E18.
■ **episcoˈpality** *noun* (*rare*) episcopal manner or bearing; episcopacy; an episcopate: E17. **episcopally** *adverb* as a bishop; at the hands of a bishop; as an episcopal Church: M17.

episcopalia /ɪˌpɪskəˈpeɪlɪə, ɛ-/ *noun pl.* M19.
[ORIGIN medieval Latin, neut. pl. of *episcopalis* EPISCOPAL.]
1 *hist.* Customary payments made by the clergy to the bishop of their diocese. M19.
2 Vestments, buildings, etc., belonging to a bishop. E20.

episcopalian /ɪˌpɪskəˈpeɪlɪən, ɛ-/ *adjective & noun*. L17.
[ORIGIN from EPISCOPAL + -IAN.]
▸ **A** *adjective*. (Usu. **E-**.) Belonging to or designating an episcopal Church or the Episcopal Church. L17.
▸ **B** *noun*. An adherent of episcopacy; (usu. **E-**) a member of an episcopal Church or the Episcopal Church. M18.
■ **episcopalianism** *noun* the principles of episcopal Churches or Episcopalians E19.

episcopate /ɪˈpɪskəpət, ɛ-/ *noun*. M17.
[ORIGIN ecclesiastical Latin *episcopatus*, from *episcopus* BISHOP *noun*: see -ATE¹.]
1 The position or office of a bishop. M17.
G. PRIESTLAND We do not believe the Church of England . . should play with the episcopate as if it were a privately-owned treasure.
2 An episcopal see, a bishopric. E19.
DISRAELI The Church Temporalities Bill in 1833 . . suppressed ten Irish episcopates.
3 Bishops collectively; *the* body of bishops in a Church. Treated as *sing.* or *pl.* M19.
4 The period during which a bishop holds office. L19.
E. A. FREEMAN In the third year of his episcopate he was driven out.

†**episcopate** *verb intrans. & trans.* M17–E18.
[ORIGIN Late Latin *episcopat-* pa. ppl stem of *episcopare* be (in medieval Latin also, make) a bishop, from ecclesiastical Latin *episcopus* BISHOP *noun*: see -ATE³. Cf. BISHOP *verb*¹.]
Act as or make a bishop.

episcope /ˈɛpɪskəʊp/ *noun*¹. E20.
[ORIGIN from EPI- + -SCOPE.]
An optical projector giving images of opaque objects.
■ **epiˈscopic** *adjective* E20.

episcope /ɪˈpɪskəpi, ɛ-/ *noun*². Also **-é** /-eɪ/. M20.
[ORIGIN Greek *episkopē* watching over, formed as EPI- + *skopē* watch.]
The pastoral supervision exercised by a bishop.

episcopicide /ɪˈpɪskəpɪsʌɪd, ɛ-/ *noun*. *rare*. L17.
[ORIGIN from ecclesiastical Latin *episcopus* BISHOP *noun* + -I- + -CIDE.]
†1 Murder of a bishop. L17–M18.
2 A person who or thing which causes the death of a bishop. *joc.* E20.

episcopize /ɪˈpɪskəpʌɪz, ɛ-/ *verb*. Also **-ise**. M17.
[ORIGIN from ecclesiastical Latin *episcopus* BISHOP *noun* + -IZE. Cf. EPISCOPATE *verb*.]
1 *verb trans.* Make (a person) a bishop. M17.
2 *verb intrans., & trans.* (with *it*). Rule as a bishop; assume the role of a bishop. Now *rare* or *obsolete*. L17.
3 *verb trans.* Bring under episcopal government; make episcopalian. M18.

episcotister /ɪˈpɪskətɪstə, ɛ-, ˌɛpɪskəˈtɪstə/ *noun*. E20.
[ORIGIN from Greek *episkotizein* throw a shadow or darkness over, formed as EPI- + *skotos* darkness: see -IST, -ER¹.]
A device used in experimental psychology for producing intermittent illumination of an object, consisting of a disc with a sector removed rotating in front of a light source.

episematic /ˌɛpɪsɪˈmatɪk/ *adjective*. L19.
[ORIGIN from EPI- + SEMATIC.]
ZOOLOGY. Of coloration, markings, etc.: serving to assist recognition by members of the same species.

episememe /ɛpɪˈsiːmiːm/ *noun*. M20.
[ORIGIN from EPI- + SEMEME.]
LINGUISTICS. The meaning of a tagmeme or of a grammatical construction.

episiotomy /ɪˌpɪsɪˈɒtəmi, ɛ-/ *noun*. L19.
[ORIGIN from Greek *epision* pubic region + -TOMY.]
Enlargement of the vulval orifice by incision into the perineum, performed to facilitate childbirth; an operation of this kind.

episode /ˈɛpɪsəʊd/ *noun*. L17.
[ORIGIN Greek *epeisodion* use as noun of neut. of *epeisodios* coming in besides, formed as EPI- + *eisodos* entrance, from *eis* into + *hodos* way, passage.]
1 *hist.* In Greek tragedy, an interpolated passage of dialogue between two choric songs. L17.
2 A scene or digression complete in itself but forming part of a continuous narrative; each of a series of connected incidents or scenes. L17. ▸**b** Each of the different successive broadcasts that go to make up a television or radio serial. E20.
G. S. FRASER Full of exciting episodes as it is . . *Beowulf* moves nevertheless with sad deliberate dignity. **b** A. ROAD To produce a single 25 minute episode of the show costs £44,000.
3 An incident or finite period in a person's life or the history of something, considered in isolation. L18.
N. CALDER Important episodes of mountain-building. I. MURDOCH A psychotic episode is sometimes of value in altering a pattern of consciousness.
4 *MUSIC*. A passage between successive statements of a subject or theme. M19.
transf.: N. FRYE The body of the poem is arranged in the form ABACA, a main theme repeated twice with two intervening episodes, as in the musical rondo.

episodic /ɛpɪˈsɒdɪk/ *adjective*. E18.
[ORIGIN from EPISODE + -IC.]
1 Of the nature of an episode; incidental. E18.
G. MAXWELL My earlier sojourn in the Hebrides . . in retrospect seemed episodic.
2 Occurring in or characterized by episodes; occasional, sporadic. E18.
GEO. ELIOT His episodic show of regard. *British Medical Journal* Episodic joint inflammation.
■ **episodal** /-ˈsəʊ-/ *adjective* (*rare*) = EPISODIC L19. **episodical** *adjective* = EPISODIC M17. **episodically** *adverb* M18. **episodicity** /ɛˌpɪsəˈdɪsɪti/ *noun* (*GEOLOGY*) episodic quality or character M20.

episome /ˈɛpɪsəʊm/ *noun*. M20.
[ORIGIN formed as EPI- + -SOME³.]
GENETICS. A genetic element inside some cells (as the DNA of some bacteriophages) able to replicate independently and also in association with a chromosome.
■ **epiˈsomal** *adjective* M20. **epiˈsomally** *adverb* M20.

epispastic /ɛpɪˈspastɪk/ *adjective & noun*. Now *rare*. M17.
[ORIGIN mod. Latin *epispasticus* from Greek *epispastikos*, from *epispan* attract, formed as EPI- + *span* to draw: see -IC.]
MEDICINE. ▸**A** *adjective*. Producing a blister or a serous discharge. M17.
▸ **B** *noun*. A blister; a substance for producing blisters. L17.

epistasis /ɪˈpɪstəsɪs, ɛ-/ *noun*. Pl. **-ases** /-əsiːz/. E19.
[ORIGIN Greek = a stoppage, from *ephistanai* to check, stop, formed as EPI- + *histanai* put.]
1 *MEDICINE*. A film that forms on urine after it has stood. *rare*. E19.
2 *MEDICINE*. The checking of a bodily discharge. *rare*. E19.
3 *GENETICS*. An interaction of genes that are not alleles; *esp.* the suppression of the effect of one such gene by another. E20.
■ Also **epistasy** /ɪˈpɪstəsi, ɛ-/ *noun* [Greek *epistasia* dominion] E20.

epistatic /ɛpɪˈstatɪk/ *adjective*. E20.
[ORIGIN from EPI- + STATIC, after *hypostasis*, *hypostatic*.]
GENETICS. Of, exhibiting, or caused by epistasis. (Foll. by *on*, *over*, *to*.)

epistaxis /ɛpɪˈstaksɪs/ *noun*. Pl. **-staxes** /-ˈstaksiːz/. L18.
[ORIGIN mod. Latin from Greek, from *epistazein* bleed at the nose, formed as EPI- + *stazein* drip.]
Bleeding from the nose; a nosebleed.

epistemic /ɛpɪˈstiːmɪk, -ˈstɛm-/ *adjective*. E20.
[ORIGIN from Greek *epistēmē*: see EPISTEMOLOGY, -IC.]
PHILOSOPHY & LINGUISTICS. Of or relating to (the extent of) knowledge or knowing, or its linguistic expression.
R. QUIRK We have epistemic modality expressing the degree of speaker's knowledge (e.g. *He may go* = 'I think it possible that he will').
■ **epistemically** *adverb* E20.

epistemics /ɛpɪˈstiːmɪks, -ˈstɛm-/ *noun*. M20.
[ORIGIN from EPISTEMIC: see -ICS.]
The branch of science that deals with knowledge and understanding.

epistemology /ɪˌpɪstɪˈmɒlədʒi, ɛ-/ *noun*. M19.
[ORIGIN from Greek *epistēmo-* combining form of *epistēmē* knowledge, from *epistasthai* know (how to do) + -OLOGY.]
The branch of philosophy that deals with the varieties, grounds, and validity of knowledge.
■ **eˌpistemoˈlogical** *adjective* L19. **eˌpistemoˈlogically** *adverb* in an epistemological manner; with reference to epistemology: L19. **epistemologist** *noun* L19.

episternum /ɛpɪˈstəːnəm/ *noun*. Pl. **-na** /-nə/, **-nums**. M19.
[ORIGIN from EPI- + STERNUM.]
ZOOLOGY. **1** The upper part of the sternum in mammals; an interclavicle in some other vertebrates. M19.
2 The anterior sclerite of the thoracic pleuron of some insects. M19.
■ **episternal** *adjective* situated on the sternum; of, pertaining to, or of the nature of an episternum: M19.

epistle /ɪˈpɪs(ə)l/ *noun*. OE.
[ORIGIN Orig. directly from Latin *epistola* from Greek *epistolē*, formed as EPI- + *stellein* send. In Middle English reintroduced from Old French (mod. *épître*).]
1 A letter, *esp.* one of a literary, formal, or public nature. Now freq. *joc.* or *rhet.* OE. ▸**b** A literary work in the form of a letter, usu. in verse. LME. ▸**c** A preface or letter of dedication at the beginning of a literary work. *obsolete* exc. in ***dedicatory epistle***, ***epistle dedicatory***. E17.
2 *CHRISTIAN CHURCH*. **a** Any of various books in the New Testament which originated as apostolic letters to Christian communities and individuals. ME. ▸**b** (**E-**.) *The* New Testament reading that precedes the Gospel in the Eucharist. LME.
a *CATHOLIC* ***Epistles***. ***pastoral epistles***: see PASTORAL *adjective*.
– COMB.: **Epistle side** *CHRISTIAN CHURCH* the south end of an altar, from which the Epistle is traditionally read.

epistle /ɪˈpɪs(ə)l/ *verb trans. & intrans. rare*. L16.
[ORIGIN from the noun.]
= EPISTOLIZE. Also, write in a letter.

epistler /ɪˈpɪs(t)lə/ *noun*. L16.
[ORIGIN from EPISTLE *noun*, *verb* + -ER¹.]
1 The writer of an epistle. L16.
2 *CHRISTIAN CHURCH*. = EPISTOLER 1. Now *rare* or *obsolete*. M17.

†**epistolar** *adjective*. LME–E18.
[ORIGIN Latin *epistolaris*: see EPISTOLARY, -AR¹.]
= EPISTOLARY.

epistolary /ɪˈpɪst(ə)l(ə)ri/ *adjective*. M17.
[ORIGIN French *épistolaire* or Latin *epistolaris*, from *epistola*: see EPISTLE *noun*, -ARY².]
1 Of or pertaining to (the writing of) epistles or letters. M17.
H. ACTON Some writers adapt themselves to their correspondents, even to the extent of changing their epistolary style.
2 In the form of a letter or letters; contained in or conducted by letters. M17.
T. JEFFERSON I recall . . the days of our former intercourse, personal and epistolary. *Notes & Queries* The year of the original epistolary form of the novel.
■ Also **epistolatory** *adjective* E18.

epistoler /ɪˈpɪst(ə)lə/ *noun*. M16.
[ORIGIN Sense 1 from Old French *epistelier* or medieval Latin *epistolaris*, *-arius* (see EPISTOLARY, -ER² 2); sense 2 from French †*épistolier* from Latin *epistolaris*, from *epistola* EPISTLE *noun*.]
1 *CHRISTIAN CHURCH*. The reader of the Epistle at the Eucharist. M16.
2 A letter-writer. M17.

†**epistolic** *adjective*. M18.
[ORIGIN Greek *epistolikos*, from *epistolē*: see EPISTLE *noun*, -IC.]
1 = EPISTOLOGRAPHIC. Only in M18.
2 = EPISTOLARY. Only in L18.
■ †**epistolical** *adjective* = EPISTOLARY M17–M18.

epistolise *verb* var. of EPISTOLIZE.

epistolist /ɪˈpɪst(ə)lɪst/ *noun*. M18.
[ORIGIN from Latin *epistola* EPISTLE *noun* + -IST.]
= EPISTLER 1.

epistolize /ɪˈpɪst(ə)lʌɪz/ *verb*. *arch.* Also **-ise**. M17.
[ORIGIN from Latin *epistola* EPISTLE *noun* + -IZE.]
1 *verb intrans.* Write a letter or letters. M17.
H. JAMES Be assured that the amount of thinking of you . . is out of all proportion to the amount of epistolizing.
2 *verb trans.* Write a letter to (a person), correspond with. M18.
BYRON St. Paul need not trouble himself to epistolize the present brood of Ephesians.
■ **epistolizer** *noun* M17.

epistolographic /ɪˌpɪst(ə)ləˈgrafɪk/ *adjective*. *arch.* L17.
[ORIGIN Greek *epistolographikos*, from *epistolē*: see EPISTLE *noun*, -O-, -GRAPHIC.]
(Of an alphabet or script) used in writing letters; *spec.* designating the demotic script of ancient Egypt.
■ **eˌpistoˈlography** *noun* letter-writing M19.

epistolophobia /ɪˌpɪst(ə)ləˈfəʊbɪə/ *noun*. E19.
[ORIGIN from (the same root as) EPISTOLOGRAPHIC + -PHOBIA.]
A marked reluctance to write letters.

epistrophe /ɪˈpɪstrəfi, ɛ-/ *noun*. L16.
[ORIGIN Greek *epistrophē*, from *epistrephein* turn about, formed as EPI- + *strephein* to turn.]
RHETORIC. Repetition of a word at the end of successive clauses.

epistyle /ˈɛpɪstʌɪl/ *noun*. Orig. in Latin form †**-stylium**, pl. **-ia**. M16.
[ORIGIN French *épistyle* or Latin *epistylium* from Greek *epistulion*, formed as EPI- + *stulos* column.]
ARCHITECTURE. = ARCHITRAVE 1.

episyllogism /ɛpɪˈsɪlədʒɪz(ə)m/ *noun*. M19.
[ORIGIN from EPI- + SYLLOGISM.]
LOGIC. A syllogism the major premiss of which is proved by a preceding syllogism.
■ ˌ**episylloˈgistic** *adjective* L19.

epitaph /ˈɛpɪtɑːf, -taf/ *noun & verb*. LME.
[ORIGIN Old French & mod. French *épitaphe* from Latin *epitaphium* funeral oration from Greek *epitaphion* use as noun of neut. of *epitaphios* over or at a tomb or burial, formed as EPI- + *taphos* obsequies, tomb.]
▸ **A** *noun*. An inscription upon a tomb; a brief composition characterizing a dead person. LME.
fig.: R. W. EMERSON The rolling rock leaves its scratches on the mountain . . the fern and leaf their modest epitaph in the coal.
▸ **B** *verb trans.* Describe in an epitaph; write an epitaph about. L16.
■ **epitapher** *noun* (*rare*) L16. **epiˈtaphic** *adjective* L19. †**epitaphical** *adjective*: only in L16. **epitaphize** *verb trans.* = EPITAPH *verb* M19.

epitaphial /ɛpɪˈtafɪəl/ *adjective*. *rare*. M19.
[ORIGIN from Greek *epitaphios*: see EPITAPH, -AL¹.]
Of, pertaining to, or contained in epitaphs.
■ **epitaphian** *adjective* †(*a*) delivered at a funeral; (*b*) = EPITAPHIAL: M17.

epitasis /ɪˈpɪtəsɪs, ɛ-/ *noun*. Pl. **-ases** /-əsiːz/. L16.
[ORIGIN mod. Latin from Greek, from *epiteinein* intensify, formed as EPI- + *teinein* stretch.]
The second part of a play, in which the action begins; the part of a play etc. where the plot thickens.

epitaxy /ˈɛpɪtaksi/ *noun*. M20.
[ORIGIN French *épitaxie*, formed as EPI-: see -TAXY.]
The growth of crystals on a crystalline substrate which determines their orientation.
■ **epiˈtaxial** *adjective* grown by or resulting from epitaxy M20. **epiˈtaxially** *adverb* so that epitaxy occurs; by an epitaxial process: M20. **epiˈtaxis** *noun* = EPITAXY M20.

epithalamium /ˌɛpɪθəˈleɪmɪəm/ *noun*. Also (earlier) **-ion** /-ɪən/. Pl. **-iums**, **-ions**, **-ia** /-ɪə/. L16.
[ORIGIN (Latin from) Greek *epithalamion* use as noun of neut. of *epithalamios* nuptial, formed as EPI- + *thalamos* bridal chamber.]
A song or poem in celebration of a wedding.
■ **epithalamial** *adjective* L19. **epithalamic** /-ˈlamɪk/ *adjective* M18. **epiˈthalamy** *noun* (now *rare* or *obsolete*) = EPITHALAMIUM L16.

epithalamus /ɛpɪˈθaləməs/ *noun*. Pl. **-mi** /-mʌɪ, -miː/. E20.
[ORIGIN from EPI- + THALAMUS.]
ANATOMY. The dorsal part of the diencephalon, which includes the pineal gland.

epithelia *noun* pl. of EPITHELIUM.

epitheliomuscular /ɛpɪˌθiːlɪə(ʊ)ˈmʌskjʊlə/ *adjective*. M20.
[ORIGIN from EPITHELIUM + -O- + MUSCULAR.]
Functioning as both epithelial and muscular tissue, as in some coelenterates; of or pertaining to such tissue.

epithelium /ɛpɪˈθiːlɪəm/ *noun*. Pl. **-lia** /-lɪə/. M18.
[ORIGIN mod. Latin, from EPI- + Greek *thēlē* teat, nipple + -IUM.]
1 *ANATOMY*. Tissue of the kind that covers the surface of the body and lines some hollow structures in humans and animals, consisting of sheets of cells bound closely together without intervening connective tissue; a particular kind or portion of such tissue. M18.
2 *BOTANY*. A layer of glandular cells such as those which line resin and gum canals. M19.
■ **epithelial** *adjective* of, pertaining to, or of the nature of epithelium M19. **epitheliaiˈzation** *noun* = EPITHELIZATION M20. **epithelioid** *adjective* resembling epithelium or epithelial cells L19. **ˌepitheliˈoma** *noun*, pl. **-mas**, **-mata** /-mətə/, a tumour of epithelial tissue, *esp.* a malignant tumour of squamous epithelium, a squamous-cell carcinoma L19. **ˌepitheliˈomatous** *adjective* affected with or of the nature of an epithelioma L19. **ˌepitheliˈosis** *noun* a condition marked by a proliferation of epithelial cells M20. **epithelization** /ˌɛpɪθiːlʌɪˈzeɪʃ(ə)n/ *noun* the process of becoming covered with or converted into epithelium M20.

epithem /ˈɛpɪθɛm/ *noun*. Also (earlier) †**-thima**. LME.
[ORIGIN Latin *epithema* from Greek *epithema*, *-thēma*, from *epitithenai*: see EPITHET.]
1 A liquid applied to the body externally, esp. as a compress or poultice; the application of this. *arch.* LME.
2 *BOTANY*. A group of water-secreting cells below the epidermis of the leaves of many plants. E20.
■ †**epithemation** *noun* = EPITHEM 1 LME–E18.

epithet /ˈɛpɪθɛt/ *noun & verb*. L16.
[ORIGIN French *épithète* or Latin *epitheton* use as noun of neut. of Greek *epithetos* attributed, pa. ppl adjective of *epitithenai* put on, add, formed as EPI- + *tithenai* to place.]
► **A** *noun*. **1** A word or phrase expressing a quality or attribute regarded as characteristic of the person or thing mentioned. L16.

> GEO. ELIOT Hollow, empty—is the epithet justly bestowed on Fame.

2 A significant appellation; a suitably descriptive term. L16.

> B. C. BRODIE We . . employ the French term of ennui, for want of an equally appropriate epithet in English.

transferred epithet: see TRANSFER *verb* 1b.
†**3** A term, an expression. *rare* (Shakes.). L16–E17.
4 An offensive or derogatory expression used of a person; a term of abuse, a profanity. L19.
5 Chiefly *BOTANY & MICROBIOLOGY*. In the binomial system of nomenclature: the element of a scientific name (typically in the form of an adjective in agreement with the generic name) indicating the species, variety, etc. E20.

> R. D. MEIKLE The willow was described by Smith as *Salix oleifolia* . . , an unfortunate choice of epithet since it was antedated by *S. oleifolia* of Villars.

specific epithet: see SPECIFIC *adjective*.
► **B** *verb trans*. Describe using an epithet, apply an epithet to. E17.

> G. MACDONALD Woeful Miss Witherspin, as Mark had epitheted her.

■ **epitheted** *adjective* (*a*) containing many epithets; (*b*) designated by an epithet, esp. one too coarse to mention: E19. **epiˈthetic** *adjective* †(*a*) = EPITHETED (a); (*b*) pertaining to or of the nature of an epithet: M18. **epiˈthetical** *adjective* = EPITHETIC E18. **epiˈthetically** *adverb* (*rare*) M19. **epithetize** *verb trans*. (*rare*) = EPITHET *verb* E18.

†**epitheton** *noun*. M16–E18.
[ORIGIN Latin: see EPITHET.]
An attribute; an epithet.

†**epithima** *noun* see EPITHEM.

†**epithumetic** *adjective* see EPITHYMETIC.

†**epithyme** *noun*. LME–E18.
[ORIGIN Latin *epithymon* from Greek *epithumon*, formed as EPI- + *thumon* thyme.]
A dodder, *Cuscuta epithymum*, parasitic on wild thyme.

epithymetic /ˌɛpɪθɪˈmɛtɪk/ *adjective*. Also (earlier) †**-thum-**. M17.
[ORIGIN Greek *epithumētikos*, from *epithumein* to desire, formed as EPI- + *thumos* soul, appetite: see -IC.]
Connected with desire or appetite.

epitomator /ɪˈpɪtəmeɪtə, ɛ-/ *noun*. E17.
[ORIGIN from Latin *epitomat-* pa. ppl stem of *epitomare*, formed as EPITOME: see -ATOR.]
A person who writes an epitome of a larger work.

epitome /ɪˈpɪtəmi, ɛ-/ *noun*. Also (*non-standard*) **-my**. E16.
[ORIGIN Latin from Greek *epitomē*, from *epitemnein* cut into, cut short, formed as EPI- + *temnein* to cut.]
1 A summary or abstract of a written work; a condensed account. E16.

> L. HUTCHINSON To number his virtues is to give an epitome of his life. *Daily Telegraph* Apply . . with an epitome of past commercial and engineering experience.

2 A thing that represents another in miniature; a person who or thing which embodies a quality etc.; a typical example. E16.

> W. HOLTBY Local government was an epitome of national government. J. FOWLES She was an epitome of all the most crassly arrogant traits of the . . British Empire.

– PHRASES: **in epitome** in miniature; in a summary.
■ **epiˈtomic** *adjective* of the nature of an epitome M17. **epiˈtomical** *adjective* = EPITOMIC E17. **epitomist** *noun* the writer of an epitome E17.

epitomize /ɪˈpɪtəmʌɪz, ɛ-/ *verb trans*. Also **-ise**. L16.
[ORIGIN from EPITOME + -IZE.]
1 Make an epitome of, abridge; give a condensed account of, summarize. L16. ►†**b** Reduce to a smaller scale. M17–E18.

> J. A. FROUDE I shall . . in a few pages briefly epitomize what passed.

2 Contain in a small compass; contain or express in brief the whole of; be a perfect example of, typify. E17.

> I. MURDOCH She epitomised everything he didn't care for about women.

■ **epitomiˈzation** *noun* the action of epitomizing; an epitome: E19. **epitomizer** *noun* E17.

epitomy *noun* see EPITOME.

epitrichium /ɛpɪˈtrɪkɪəm/ *noun*. L19.
[ORIGIN from EPI- + Greek *trikhion* dim. of *trikh-*, *thrix* hair.]
ANATOMY. A thin layer of cells covering the epidermis of an embryo, usu. disappearing before birth.
■ **epitrichial** *adjective* L19.

epitrite /ˈɛpɪtrʌɪt/ *noun*. E17.
[ORIGIN Latin *epitritos* from Greek = in the ratio of 4 to 3, formed as EPI- + *tritos* third.]
CLASSICAL PROSODY. A metrical foot consisting of one unstressed and three stressed syllables.

epitrochoid /ɛpɪˈtrɒkɔɪd, -ˈtrəʊ-/ *noun*. M19.
[ORIGIN from EPI- + Greek *trokhos* wheel + -OID.]
A curve traced by a point on a radius or extended radius of a circle that rolls outside another circle.
■ **ˌepitroˈchoidal** *adjective* E19.

epitrope /ɪˈpɪtrəpi, ɛ-/ *noun*. M16.
[ORIGIN Late Latin from Greek *epitropē*, from *epitrepein* yield, formed as EPI- + *trepein* to turn.]
RHETORIC. A figure of speech in which permission is given to an opponent, either seriously or ironically.

epizeuxis /ɛpɪˈzjuːksɪs/ *noun*. L16.
[ORIGIN Late Latin from Greek, formed as EPI- + *zeuxis* yoking, from *zeugnunai* to yoke.]
RHETORIC. The vehement or emphatic repetition of a word.

epizoon /ɛpɪˈzəʊɒn/ *noun*. Pl. **-zoa** /-ˈzəʊə/. M19.
[ORIGIN from EPI- + Greek *zōion* animal.]
An animal that lives on the surface of another, esp. as a parasite.
■ **epizoic** *adjective* living on the surface of an animal; of or pertaining to epizoa: M19.

epizootic /ˌɛpɪzəʊˈɒtɪk/ *adjective & noun*. L18.
[ORIGIN French *épizootique*, from *épizootie*, formed as EPI- + Greek *zōion* animal: see -OTIC.]
► **A** *adjective*. Of an animal disease: normally absent or infrequent in a population but liable to periods of greatly increased frequency; temporarily widespread. L18.
► **B** *noun*. A temporary but widespread outbreak of a particular disease among animals; an epizootic disease. M19.
■ **ˌepizootioˈlogic**, **ˌepizootioˈlogical**, **ˌepizooto-** *adjectives* of or pertaining to epizootiology M20. **ˌepizootiˈology**, **-zooˈtology** *noun* the branch of science that deals with the incidence and transmission of disease in animal populations, esp. with a view to controlling them; the aspects *of* an animal disease to do with its incidence and transmission: M20. **epiˈzooty** *noun* = EPIZOOTIC *noun* L18.

EPNS *abbreviation*.
Electroplated nickel silver.

EPO *abbreviation*.
1 Erythropoietin, esp. when isolated as a drug for medical use or for illegal use by athletes.
2 European Patent Office.

epoch /ˈiːpɒk/ *noun*. Also (earlier) †**-cha**. E17.
[ORIGIN mod. Latin *epocha* from Greek *epokhē* stoppage, fixed point of time, from *epekhein* stop, take up a position, formed as EPI- + *ekhein* hold, be in a certain state.]
► **I** A point in time.
1 The initial point in a system of chronology; a date from which succeeding years are numbered. Now *rare*. E17.
†**2** The date of origin of a situation, institution, etc.; an event marking such a date. M17–E19.
3 The beginning of a distinctive period in the history of something or someone. Cf. ERA 3. M17.

> L. M. MONTGOMERY I've had a splendid time . . . It marks an epoch in my life.

4 The date or time of an event. Now *rare* exc. as below. M17. ►**b** A point in time defined by the occurrence of particular events or by the existence of a particular state of affairs. E18. ►**c** *ASTRONOMY*. The point in time at which a particular phenomenon takes place; an arbitrarily fixed date relative to which planetary or stellar measurements are expressed. E18.

> T. JEFFERSON Inform him what . . you expect to deliver, with the epochs of delivery. **b** E. R. PITMAN It was an epoch never to be forgotten . . when she commenced labouring in Joppa.

► **II** A period of time.
5 Orig., a chronological period characterized by the numbering of years from a particular noteworthy event (cf. ERA 1a). Now = ERA 1b. E17.

> H. J. LASKI No man was so emphatically representative of his epoch as Adam Smith. D. LESSING Poor people lived there as the rich have done in previous epochs.

6 *GEOLOGY*. A division of geological time; *spec.* a subdivision of a period, corresponding to a stratigraphic series. E19.

> *Scientific American* The basis for dividing geologic time into eras, periods and epochs. W. C. PUTNAM The Pliocene Epoch, which merged with the Pleistocene, saw the rise of the living . . animals of the Earth.

7 *PHYSICS*. The time interval between the zero of time measurement and the zero of a simple harmonic motion; (also ***epoch angle***) the angular separation corresponding to this. L19.
– COMB.: ***epoch angle***: see sense 7 above; **epoch-making** *adjective* such as marks the beginning of a new epoch; historic, of major importance; remarkable.

epochal /ˈɛpɒk(ə)l, iːˈpɒk-/ *adjective*. L17.
[ORIGIN from EPOCH + -AL[1].]
1 Of or pertaining to an epoch or epochs. L17.
2 Forming or characterizing an epoch; epoch-making. M19.
■ **epochally** *adverb* M20.

epoché /ˈɛpɒki/ *noun*. E20.
[ORIGIN from Greek *epokhē* (see EPOCH) in sense 'suspension of judgement'.]
PHILOSOPHY. (In Greek Scepticism) refusal to adopt a judgement or belief, when the necessary knowledge is not attainable; (in Phenomenology) the setting aside of assumptions and known facts in order to perceive the essence of a phenomenon.

epode /ˈɛpəʊd/ *noun*. E17.
[ORIGIN French *épode* or Latin *epodos* from Greek *epōidos*, formed as EPI- + *ōidē* ODE.]
1 A Greek lyric poem composed of couplets in which a long line is followed by a shorter; a serious poem. E17.
2 The part of a Greek lyric ode following the strophe and antistrophe. L17.

éponge /epɔ̃ʒ/ *noun*. E20.
[ORIGIN French from Latin *spongia* SPONGE *noun*[1].]
Sponge cloth.

eponychium /ɛpəˈnɪkɪəm/ *noun*. L19.
[ORIGIN mod. Latin, from EPI- + Greek *onukh-*, *onux* nail.]
ANATOMY. The epidermis from which a nail develops in the fetus; the film of epidermis covering the root of a nail, the cuticle.

eponym /ˈɛpənɪm/ *noun*. M19.
[ORIGIN Greek *epōnumos* given as a name, giving one's name to a thing or person, formed as EPI- + -O- + -NYM.]
1 A person whose name has given rise (in fact or by repute) to the name of a people, place, institution, etc.; a personal name used as a common noun or used to form a common noun. M19. ►**b** A name or noun formed in this way. L19.

> G. GROTE Pelops is the eponym or name-giver of the Peloponnesus. A. BURGESS The eponym of H. G. Wells's *Christina Alberta's Father*, a retired laundry manager. **b** *Daily Telegraph* It would be absurd to compile a list of eponyms without mentioning . . 'malapropism' or 'stentorian'.

2 An Assyrian functionary who gave his name to his year of office. M19.
3 A person who is identified with something. L19.

C. MERIVALE Saturn becomes the eponym of all useful and humane discovery.

■ **epo'nymic** *adjective* of, pertaining to, or using eponyms; eponymous: M19. **epo'nymically** *adverb* M20. **e'ponymist** *noun* a person who is an eponym M19. **e'ponymous** *adjective* (of a person) giving his or her name to something; (of a thing) named after a particular person: M19. **e'ponymously** *adverb* L20.

eponymus /ɪˈpɒnɪməs, ɛ-/ *noun*. Pl. **-mi** /-mʌɪ, -miː/. M19.
[ORIGIN mod. Latin, formed as EPONYM.]
A historical or mythical person who is an eponym.

eponymy /ɪˈpɒnɪmi, ɛ-/ *noun*. M19.
[ORIGIN Greek *epōnumia* derived or significant name, formed as EPONYM: see -Y[3].]
1 Eponymic nomenclature; the practice of explaining names of peoples, places, etc., by referring them to the name of a historical or mythical person. M19.
2 The year of office of an Assyrian eponym. L19.

epoophoron /ɛpəʊˈɒf(ə)rɒn/ *noun*. L19.
[ORIGIN from EPI- + Greek *ōophoron* neut. of *ōophoros* bearing eggs, from *ōion* egg + *-phoros* bearing.]
ANATOMY. In the female, a group of vestigial tubules derived from the upper mesonephros, between an ovary and a Fallopian tube, corresponding to the male epididymis. Cf. PAROOPHORON.

epopee /ˈɛpəpiː/ *noun*. Now *rare*. L17.
[ORIGIN French *épopée* formed as EPOPOEIA.]
An epic poem, an epic; epic poetry.

epopoeia /ɛpəˈpiːə/ *noun*. *arch*. L16.
[ORIGIN Greek *epopoiia*, from *epos* (see EPOS) + *poiein* make.]
= EPOPEE.

epopt /ˈɛpɒpt/ *noun*. L17.
[ORIGIN Late Latin *epopta* from Greek *epoptēs*, formed as EPI- + *op-* see.]
GREEK HISTORY. A person fully initiated into the Eleusinian mysteries.

EPOS *abbreviation*.
Electronic point of sale.

epos /ˈɛpɒs/ *noun*. M19.
[ORIGIN Latin from Greek = word, song, from *ep-* stem of *eipein* say.]
1 Epic poetry; an epic poem; *esp.* narrative poetry embodying a nation's conception of its past history. M19.
2 = EPIC *noun* 4. M19.

epox- *combining form* see EPOXY-.

epoxide /ɪˈpɒksʌɪd/ *noun*. M20.
[ORIGIN from EPI- + OXIDE.]
CHEMISTRY. A compound whose molecule contains an oxygen atom linked to two carbon atoms as part of a ring; a cyclic ether.
– COMB.: **epoxide resin** an epoxy resin.
■ **epoxi'dation** *noun* the formation of an epoxide by addition of an oxygen atom to a carbon–carbon double bond M20. **epoxidize** *verb trans.* convert into an epoxide by epoxidation M20.

epoxy /ɪˈpɒksi, ɛ-/ *noun & verb*. M20.
[ORIGIN from EPOXY- as adjective.]
▸ **A** *noun*. (An) epoxy resin; (an) epoxy glue or cement. M20.
▸ **B** *verb trans*. Pa. t. & pple **epoxied**, **epoxyed**. Glue with epoxy glue or cement. L20.

epoxy- /ɪˈpɒksi, ɛ-/ *combining form*. Before a vowel also **epox-**. Also as attrib. adjective **epoxy**. E20.
[ORIGIN from EPI- + OXY-.]
1 CHEMISTRY. Designating or containing the group ·C·O·C· as it occurs in epoxides. E20.
epoxy-compound, *epoxy ring*, etc.
2 (Only as adjective) Pertaining to or derived from an epoxide; *esp.* designating thermosetting synthetic resins containing epoxy groups, and substances made from them, used esp. as coatings and adhesives. M20.
epoxy glue, *epoxy paint*, etc.

épris /epri/ *adjective*. Fem. **éprise** /epriz/. L18.
[ORIGIN French, pa. ppl adjective of *(s')éprendre* become attached or enamoured, formed as ES- + Latin *prehendere* seize.]
Enamoured (*of*); taken *with*.

EPROM /ˈiːprɒm/ *noun*. Also **eprom**. L20.
[ORIGIN from erasable programmable *ROM*.]
COMPUTING. A read-only memory whose contents can be erased by a special process (e.g. irradiation with ultraviolet light) and replaced.

eprouvette /ɛpruːˈvɛt/ *noun*. Also **é-**. L18.
[ORIGIN French *éprouvette*, from *éprouver* try, test: see -ETTE.]
hist. An apparatus for testing the strength of gunpowder.

epsilon /ˈɛpsɪlɒn, ɛpˈsʌɪlɒn/ *noun*. E18.
[ORIGIN Greek *e psilon* lit. 'bare e', short e written ε.]
1 The fifth letter (Ε, ε) of the Greek alphabet; ASTRONOMY (preceding the genitive of the Latin name of the constellation) the fifth brightest star in a constellation. E18.
2 An examiner's fifth-class mark; a person of low intelligence. E20.

Epsom /ˈɛpsəm/ *noun*. Also **e-**. M17.
[ORIGIN A town in Surrey, SE England.]
1 In full ***Epsom water***. The water of a mineral spring at Epsom. M17.
2 In full ***Epsom salt(s)***. Orig., salts (chiefly magnesium sulphate) obtained from Epsom water. Now, hydrated magnesium sulphate as used medicinally, as a purgative etc. M18.
3 The racecourse on Epsom Downs, where the Derby and the Oaks are run; the principal race meeting held there. E19.

epsomite /ˈɛpsəmʌɪt/ *noun*. E19.
[ORIGIN from EPSOM + -ITE[1].]
Hydrated magnesium sulphate, occurring as a white efflorescence in caves and near springs and as orthorhombic crystals.

Epstein–Barr virus /ɛpstʌɪnˈbɑː vʌɪrəs/ *noun phr.* M20.
[ORIGIN M. A. *Epstein* (b. 1921), Brit. virologist + Y. M. *Barr* (b. 1932), Irish-born virologist + VIRUS.]
A DNA herpesvirus which causes infectious mononucleosis and is associated with Burkitt's lymphoma and nasopharyngeal carcinoma.

ept /ɛpt/ *adjective*. M20.
[ORIGIN Back-form. from INEPT.]
Adroit, competent; appropriate, effective.
■ **eptitude** *noun* M20. **eptly** *adverb* L20.

epulary /ˈɛpjʊləri/ *adjective*. Now *rare*. L17.
[ORIGIN Latin *epularis*, from *epulum* banquet: see -ARY[2].]
Of or pertaining to a feast.

epulation /ɛpjʊˈleɪʃ(ə)n/ *noun*. Now *rare*. M16.
[ORIGIN Latin *epulatio(n-)*, from *epulat-* pa. ppl stem of *epulari* to feast, from *epulum* banquet: see -ATION.]
Feasting; a feast.

epulis /ɪˈpjuːlɪs, ɛ-/ *noun*. Pl. **-lides** /-lɪdiːz/. M19.
[ORIGIN mod. Latin from Greek *epoulis*, formed as EPI- + *oulon* gum.]
MEDICINE. A localized swelling of the gums.

epulotic /ɛpjʊˈlɒtɪk/ *noun & adjective*. Now *rare* or *obsolete*. M17.
[ORIGIN Greek *epoulōtikos*, from *epoulousthai* be covered with scars, formed as EPI- + *oulē* scar.]
MEDICINE. (A medicine or ointment) that induces cicatrization.
■ †**epulotical** *adjective* E–M17.

epurate /ˈɛpjʊreɪt/ *verb trans.* Now *rare* or *obsolete*. L18.
[ORIGIN from Old French & mod. French *épurer*, from *pur* PURE *adjective*: see -ATE[3].]
Purify, purge. Freq. *fig.*
■ **epu'ration** *noun* E19.

epyllion /ɪˈpɪlɪən, ɛ-/ *noun*. Pl. **-llia** /-lɪə/. L19.
[ORIGIN Greek *epullion* dim. of *epos*: see EPOS.]
A narrative poem resembling an epic in style or matter but of shorter extent.

EQ *abbreviation*.
Equalization or equalizer, adjustment of the levels of frequency response of an audio signal, or the controls that allow this adjustment.

equability /ɛkwəˈbɪlɪti/ *noun*. M16.
[ORIGIN Latin *aequabilitas*, formed as EQUABLE: see -ITY.]
1 The quality of being equable; freedom from fluctuation or variation. M16.
†**2** Ability to be regarded as equal; comparability. L16–E19.
†**3** Well-balanced condition. L16–E17.

equable /ˈɛkwəb(ə)l/ *adjective*. M17.
[ORIGIN Latin *aequabilis*, from *aequare* make level or equal, from *aequus* level, even, equal: see -ABLE.]
†**1** = EQUITABLE. Only in M17.
2 Of motion, temperature, the feelings, etc.: uniform, free from fluctuation or variation. L17.

A. T. THOMSON Mercury is . . adapted for thermometers; its expansion being most equable. M. F. MAURY The equable climates of Western Europe. P. H. JOHNSON He remained equable, sweet tempered and slow to anger.

3 Free from inequalities; uniform throughout; equally proportioned. L17.

C. THIRLWALL A new valuation . . with a view to a more equable system of taxation.

■ **equableness** *noun* M17. **equably** *adverb* E18.

equaeval /ɪˈkwiːv(ə)l, ɛ-/ *adjective*. Now *rare*. M19.
[ORIGIN from Latin *aequaevus*, from *aequus* equal + *aevum* age: see -AL[1].]
Of equal age; belonging to the same period.
■ Also †**equaevous** *adjective*: only in M17.

equal /ˈiːkw(ə)l/ *adjective, adverb, & noun*. LME.
[ORIGIN Latin *aequalis*, from *aequus* level, even, equal: see -AL[1].]
▸ **A** *adjective*. **1** Of a surface: even; level; on the same level. *arch.* LME.
2 Identical in amount, size, number, value, intensity, etc. LME.

E. HUXLEY The company employs about equal numbers of each, but . . Pakistanis are coming into the lead.

all things being equal, **other things being equal** circumstances being evenly balanced.
3 Possessing a (specified or implied) quality or attribute to the same degree; on the same level as regards rank, power, excellence, etc.; *spec.* (of voices) belonging to the same register. Also foll. by *to*, *with*. E16.

D. H. LAWRENCE No part should be subordinate to any other part: all should be equal. J. M. MURRY That was the excitement; but the dismay was equal. F. WELDON She had thought the Christian equal to the Jew; no more nor less.

†**4** Fair, just, impartial. E16–M18.
5 = EQUABLE 2. E17.

GIBBON He proceeded, in a firm and equal tone.

†**6** Uniform in appearance, size, or other property. M17–L18.
7 Evenly proportioned or balanced; uniform in effect or operation. M17.

GLADSTONE The Church contemplates with equal eye the whole of God's ordinances.

it is equal to me it makes no difference to me, it's all the same to me. ***separate but equal***: see SEPARATE *adjective*.
8 Adequate in ability, resources, quantity, etc. Now only foll. by *to*. L17.

ARNOLD BENNETT He had . . proved equal to the enormously difficult situation. B. BAINBRIDGE I was not in very good health then, and not equal to duty at all.

– SPECIAL COLLOCATIONS: **equal opportunity** the opportunity or right to be considered for employment or promotion without discrimination on certain grounds, as race, sex, or disability; the practice or policy of not discriminating in this way (freq. *attrib.* or in *pl.*). **equal pay** (the policy of giving) the same rate of pay for a particular job irrespective of the sex of the person doing it. **equal rights** (the policy of giving) the same rights for people of different races, both sexes, etc. ***equal temperament***: see TEMPERAMENT *noun* 9.
▸ †**B** *adverb*. Equally. L16–M17.
▸ **C** *noun*. **1** A person who is equal to another in rank, ability, etc., or (formerly) age. L16.

D. H. LAWRENCE She knew herself to be the social equal, if not the superior, of anyone she was likely to meet.

2 *an equal*, a state of equality, a par. *obsolete* exc. *dial.* L16.

equal /ˈiːkw(ə)l/ *verb*. Infl. **-ll-**, ***-l-**. L16.
[ORIGIN from EQUAL *adjective, adverb, & noun*.]
1 *verb trans.* Make equal; bring to the same level (*lit. & fig.*). *arch.* L16.

DRYDEN Rebellion equals all.

†**2** *verb trans.* Consider or represent as equal; liken, compare. L16–E19.
3 *verb trans.* Be or become equal to; match, rival. L16.

V. WOOLF Nothing on earth can equal this happiness. S. PLATH Let *a* equal acceleration and let *t* equal time.

4 †**a** *verb intrans.* Cope on equal terms *with*. *rare* (Shakes.). Only in L16. ▸**b** *verb trans.* Produce something equal to; reciprocate in equal measure. E17.

b DRYDEN Answer'd all her Cares, and equal'd all her Love.

– COMB.: **equal sign**, **equals sign** the symbol =, used to indicate mathematical or other equality.
■ **equalist** *noun* (*rare*) a person who asserts the equality of certain (indicated) persons or things M17.

equalise *verb*, **equaliser** *noun* vars. of EQUALIZE etc.

equalitarian /ɪˌkwɒlɪˈtɛːrɪən, iː-/ *adjective & noun*. L18.
[ORIGIN from EQUALITY + -ARIAN.]
= EGALITARIAN.
■ **equalitarianism** *noun* M19.

equality /ɪˈkwɒlɪti, iː-/ *noun*. LME.
[ORIGIN Old French *equalité* (mod. *égalité*) from Latin *aequalitas*, from *aequalis*: see EQUAL *adjective*, -ITY.]
1 a The condition of being equal in quantity, magnitude, value, intensity, etc. LME. ▸**b** MATH. A symbolic expression of the fact that two quantities are equal; an equation. M20.

C. V. WEDGWOOD Their votes . . would bring the supporters and the antagonists . . very nearly to an equality.

2 The condition of having equal rank, power, excellence, etc., with others. LME.

SOUTHEY Ye are all equal . . . Equality is your birth-right. S. UNWIN Her strong feelings about equality of the sexes.

†**3** Fairness, impartiality. LME–L17.
4 Evenness, uniformity. Now *rare*. LME. ▸†**b** Evenness of mind or temper; equability. L15–M18.
– COMB.: **Equality State** *US* Wyoming, the first state to give women the vote.

equalize /ˈiːkwəlʌɪz/ *verb*. Also **-ise**. L16.
[ORIGIN from EQUAL *adjective* + -IZE, partly after French *égaliser*.]
†**1** *verb trans.* = EQUAL *verb* 3. L16–E19.
†**2** *verb trans.* Consider to be equal, treat as equal; equate. Foll. by *to*, *with*. L16–M18.
†**3** *verb trans.* Bring to one level. L16–M17.
4 a *verb trans.* Make equal in magnitude, number, intensity, etc. E17. ▸**b** *verb intrans.* SPORT. Bring one's own side's score up to that of the other side. L19.
5 *verb trans.* Make equal in rank, power, etc. M17.

H. T. BUCKLE The invention of gunpowder equalised all men on the field of battle.

6 *verb trans.* Make uniform. E19.

K. JOHNSTON The rich forest lands . . which equalise the temperature.

E

E

7 *ELECTRICITY.* **a** *verb trans.* Correct or modify (a signal etc.) with an equalizer. **E20.** ▸**b** *verb intrans.* Compensate *for* by means of an equalizer. **M20.**
8 *verb intrans.* Become equal. **E20.**

Scientific American The salty water . . poured through the hole until the pressure equalized.

■ **equali'zation** *noun* **L18.**

equalizer /'iːkwəlʌɪzə/ *noun.* Also **-iser. L18.**
[ORIGIN from EQUALIZE + -ER[1].]
1 A person who aspires to be equal in rank, power, etc., to another. *rare.* **L18.**
2 A thing which makes equal. **L18.** ▸**b** *ELECTRICITY.* A passive network designed to modify a frequency response, esp. in such a way as to compensate for distortion. **E20.** ▸**c** *SPORT.* A goal, run, etc. that equalizes the score. **E20.** ▸**d** A revolver, a firearm; a weapon. *slang* (orig. *US*). **M20.**

equally /'iːkw(ə)li/ *adverb.* **LME.**
[ORIGIN from EQUAL *adjective* + -LY[2].]
1 To an equal degree or extent. **LME.**

V. WOOLF She . . sat there . . equally poised between gloom and laughter. *Oxfam Review* Equally, the new relationship . . offers new opportunities.

2 In equal shares or amounts. **LME.**

R. RENDELL There was two hundred thousand and she left it equally between her four kids.

3 Uniformly; in uniform degree or quantity. **LME.**

HUGH MILLER The population, formerly spread pretty equally over the country.

4 According to the same rule or measure. Formerly also, impartially, equitably. **E16.**
†**5** On a level; in a line *with.* **L16–E18.**

equalness /'iːkw(ə)lnɪs/ *noun.* **M16.**
[ORIGIN formed as EQUALLY + -NESS.]
1 = EQUALITY 1a, 2. **M16.**
†**2** Fairness, impartiality. Only in **M16.**
†**3** Uniformity, evenness. **M16–L18.**

equanimity /ɛkwə'nɪmɪti, iː-/ *noun.* **E17.**
[ORIGIN Latin *aequanimitas*, from *aequus* even + *animus* mind: see -ITY.]
†**1** Fairness, impartiality, equity. **E17–M18.**
2 Tranquillity of mind or temper; composure; resignation, acceptance of fate. **E17.**

V. BRITTAIN I refused to be . . impressed . . but such equanimity was difficult to achieve. S. SPENDER He faced adverse criticism with an equanimity which astonished me.

equanimous /ɪ'kwanɪməs, iː-/ *adjective.* **M17.**
[ORIGIN from Latin *aequanimus*, from *aequus* even + *animus* mind: see -OUS.]
Characterized by equanimity.
■ **equanimously** *adverb* **M17.** **equanimousness** *noun* (*rare*) **M18.**

equant /'iːkwənt/ *noun & adjective.* **M16.**
[ORIGIN Latin *aequant-* pres. ppl stem of *aequare*: see EQUATE, -ANT[1].]
▸ **A** *noun. HISTORY OF SCIENCE.* An imaginary circle introduced with the purpose of reconciling the planetary movements with the Ptolemaic hypothesis of uniform circular motion. **M16.**
▸ **B** *adjective.* **1** *HISTORY OF SCIENCE.* Designating an equant. **L16.**
2 *MINERALOGY.* Of a crystal: having its different diameters approximately equal in length. **E20.**

equate /ɪ'kweɪt, iː-/ *verb.* **LME.**
[ORIGIN Latin *aequat-* pa. ppl stem of *aequare* make equal, from *aequus* EQUAL *adjective*: see -ATE[3].]
†**1** *verb trans.* Make (bodies) equal; balance. *rare.* **LME–M18.**
†**2** *verb trans.* Take the average of. Only in **LME.**
3 *verb trans. ASTRONOMY.* Make a numerical adjustment to (an observation or calculation) in order to compensate for an irregularity or error. **M17.**
4 *verb trans.* Chiefly *MATH.* State the equality of (a thing) *to* or *with* another; put in the form of an equation. **L17.**
5 *verb trans.* Treat or regard as equivalent. Foll. by *with* (also *to*). **M19.**

ANTHONY SMITH It is no longer possible to equate death with the lack of a heart beat.

6 *verb intrans.* Be the equivalent of; be equal to; agree or correspond with. Foll. by *with* (also *to*). **M20.**

M. STOTT Cleanliness does not equate with godliness.

■ **equata'bility** *noun* the property of being equatable **M20.** **equatable** *adjective* able to be equated **L19.** **equative** *adjective & noun* (*LINGUISTICS*) (an expression, inflection, etc.) expressing equality, identity, or resemblance **E20.**

equation /ɪ'kweɪʒ(ə)n, *in sense 1 also* -ʃ(ə)n/ *noun.* **LME.**
[ORIGIN Old French & mod. French *équation* or Latin *aequatio(n-)*, formed as EQUATE: see -ATION.]
1 The action of making equal or equating; the state of being equal or in equilibrium; a balance. **LME.** ▸†**b** *ASTROLOGY.* Equal partition, esp. of the heavens into twelve houses. Only in **LME.**

J. W. KRUTCH Our characteristic equation of 'going to school' with 'getting an education'. A. F. DOUGLAS-HOME To establish an equation which would combine full employment with a steady level of prices.

†**2** *MATH.* The action of stating the identity in value of two quantities or expressions. **L16–L17.**
3 A mathematical formula affirming the equivalence of two symbolic or numerical expressions (indicated by the sign =); *fig.* (the relationship between) the factors to be taken into account when considering a matter. **L16.** ▸**b** *CHEMISTRY.* A formula indicating a reaction by means of the symbols for the elements or compounds involved in it. **E19.**

S. THEMERSON There are some exceptions to the equation 1 + 1 = 2. *Which?* There have been some changes to that equation which may tip the balance in favour of diesel.

Laplace's equation, Planck's equation, Schrödinger equation, etc. **equation of state** *SCIENCE*: showing the relationship between the values of the pressure, volume, and temperature of a substance at any one time.

4 *ASTRONOMY.* A numerical quantity added to or subtracted from an observed or calculated one to compensate for an irregularity or error; the action or an act of making such an adjustment. **M17.**
equation of time the difference between mean solar time (as shown by clocks) and apparent solar time (indicated by sundials), which varies with the time of year. **human equation** = ***personal equation*** (b) below. **personal equation** (*a*) *ASTRONOMY* an individual's time of reaction or habitual inaccuracy in making observations; a correction or allowance made for this; (*b*) personal prejudice or bias.

equational /ɪ'kweɪʒ(ə)n(ə)l/ *adjective.* **M19.**
[ORIGIN from EQUATION + -AL[1].]
1 Pertaining to or involving the use of equations. **M19.**

W. S. HATCHER An equational proof.

2 *BIOLOGY.* Pertaining to or designating a chromosome division in which the two chromatids of each reduplicated chromosome separate longitudinally, prior to being incorporated into two daughter nuclei. **E20.**
3 *GRAMMAR.* Of a sentence, phrase, etc.: that has a copula, expressed or understood; copular. **M20.**
■ **equationally** *adverb* in terms of equations; by means of equations or an equational division: **L19.**

equator /ɪ'kweɪtə/ *noun.* **LME.**
[ORIGIN (Old French & mod. French *équateur* from) medieval Latin *aequator*, in full *circulus aequator diei et noctis* circle equalizing day and night, formed as EQUATE: see -OR.]
1 *ASTRONOMY.* The great circle of the celestial sphere whose plane is perpendicular to the earth's axis and which is equidistant from the two celestial poles; when the sun is on it, the day is the same length as the night throughout the world. Also ***celestial equator.*** **LME.**
2 The great circle of the earth which is equidistant from the two poles and marks the division between the northern and southern hemispheres. **E17.** ▸**b** A circle on any spherical body that divides it into two equal parts; *esp.* one equidistant from two poles of rotation. **M18.**

Diver The Maldives are right on the Equator. **b** *New Yorker* Possible landing sites along the moon's equator.

3 **a** The part of a magnet midway between the poles, where its field is weakest. **M17.** ▸**b** ***magnetic equator***, the irregular line, passing round the earth in the neighbourhood of the geographical equator, on which the earth's magnetic field is horizontal. **M19.**
4 *BIOLOGY.* The plane of division of a cell or nucleus lying midway between the poles and at right angles to a line joining them. **L19.**
■ **equatorward** *adjective & adverb* (moving or facing) towards the equator **E20.** **equatorwards** *adverb* equatorward **L19.**

equatorial /ɛkwə'tɔːrɪəl/ *adjective & noun.* Also †**-eal. M17.**
[ORIGIN from EQUATOR + -IAL.]
▸ **A** *adjective.* **1** *gen.* Of or pertaining to an equator. **M17.**
equatorial plate *BIOLOGY* = ***METAPHASE plate.***
2 Of or pertaining to the earth's equator; situated, existing, or occurring on or near the equator. **E18.** ▸**b** Of the orbit of a satellite: lying in the plane of the equator. **M20.**

E. WAUGH Shading their eyes from the brilliant equatorial sun. *Discovery* This pull of the sun sets up equatorial bulge.

3 Of an astronomical telescope or its mounting: such that the telescope can be rotated about one axis in the plane of the equator and another parallel to the earth's axis, so that the diurnal motion of a celestial object anywhere in the sky can be followed by rotation about the latter axis only. **L18.**
▸ **B** *noun.* An equatorial telescope. **L18.**
■ **equatorially** *adverb* **E19.**

equerry /ɪ'kwɛri, 'ɛkwəri/ *noun.* Also †**esquiry**, †**querry. E16.**
[ORIGIN French †*escu(i)rie* (now *écurie* stable) from Old French *escurie, esquierie* company of squires, prince's stables, from *esquier* ESQUIRE *noun*; perh. assoc. with Latin *equus* horse. Sense 1 seems to be based on Old French *esquier d'esquierie* squire of stables.]
1 Orig., a groom, *spec.* an officer in the service of a royal or noble person charged with the care of the horses. Now, an officer in the British royal household whose duty is to attend on a particular member of the royal family. **E16.**

H. NICOLSON An . . equerry telephoned from the palace to warn them that H.M. was in a furious temper.

†**2** The stables belonging to a royal or princely household; the body of officers in charge of them. **M16–E19.**
■ **equerryship** *noun* the position of an equerry **E17.**

eques /'ɛkweɪz/ *noun.* Pl. **equites** /'ɛkwɪteɪz/. **L16.**
[ORIGIN Latin = horseman.]
= KNIGHT *noun* 4a.

equestrian /ɪ'kwɛstrɪən, ɛ-/ *adjective & noun.* **M17.**
[ORIGIN from Latin *equestr-*, *equester* belonging to a horseman, from *eques* horseman, knight, from *equus* horse: see -IAN.]
▸ **A** *adjective.* **1** Of or pertaining to horse-riding; (of a person) skilled in horse-riding. **M17.** ▸**b** On horseback; (of a portrait or statue) representing a person on horseback. **E18.**

J. G. EDGAR Their mettled palfreys and their equestrian grace. J. CHEEVER A statue of a man on horseback that displayed a suit of equestrian armor.

2 Of or pertaining to an order of knights in the Roman and Holy Roman Empires. **L17.**
▸ **B** *noun.* A rider or performer on horseback. **L18.**
■ **equestrial** *adjective* (now *rare*) = EQUESTRIAN *adjective* **M16.** **equestrianism** *noun* **M19.**

equestrienne /ɪˌkwɛstrɪ'ɛn/ *noun.* **M19.**
[ORIGIN Alt. of EQUESTRIAN after fem. nouns in *-enne*, as *Parisienne*.]
A female equestrian.

equi- /'iːkwi, ɛ-/ *combining form.* Also †**aequi-.**
[ORIGIN Repr. Latin *aequi-*, from *aequus* equal: see -I-.]
Used in words adopted from Latin, and in English words modelled on these, and as a freely productive prefix, with the sense 'equal(ly), in an equal degree'.
■ **equianal'gesic** *adjective* producing an equal analgesic effect **M20.** **equia'tomic** *adjective* (of an alloy or intermetallic compound) containing equal numbers of atoms of two particular constituent elements **M20.** **equiaxe** *adjective* [French *équiaxe*] = EQUIAXED **E19.** **equiaxed** *adjective* (of a crystal) having all its axes the same length **M19.** **equica'loric** *adjective* (of food) equivalent as regards content of calories **M20.** **equi'different** *adjective* (*MATH.*, now *rare* or *obsolete*) having equal differences, in arithmetic proportion **L17.** **equidi'mensional** *adjective* (of a particle) having approximately equal dimensions in each direction **M20.** **equi'final** *adjective* having the same result **M20.** **equifi'nality** *noun* the condition of being equifinal **E20.** **equiform** *adjective* having the same form **L19.** **equi'formity** *noun* uniformity **M17.** **equi'molar** *adjective* (*CHEMISTRY*) (*a*) containing an equal number of moles; (*b*) = EQUIMOLECULAR (a): **E20.** **equimo'lecular** *adjective* (*CHEMISTRY*) (*a*) containing an equal number of molecules; (*b*) = EQUIMOLAR (a): **E20.** **equi'multiple** *noun* any of a set of numbers each of which is the same multiple of a number in another set **M17.** **equi'numerous** *adjective* (*MATH. & LOGIC*) containing the same number of elements (foll. by *with*) **M20.** **equi'radial** *adjective* (*rare*) having equal radii **E19.** **equi-'signal** *adjective* designating the line or zone along which the signals from two radio beacons are equally strong, detection of this equality confirming position on the line; of or pertaining to a navigation system that works on this principle: **M20.** **equivalve** *adjective* (of a bivalve mollusc or its shell) having valves that are of similar size and shape **M19.** **equivo'luminal** *adjective* (of a wave) occurring without a change in the volume of each part of the medium through which it passes **L19.** **equivote** *noun* (*US*) a tied vote **M17.**

equiangular /iːkwɪ'aŋgjʊlə, ɛ-/ *adjective.* **M17.**
[ORIGIN from late Latin *equiangulus*, formed as EQUI- + *angulus* ANGLE *noun*[2]: see -AR[1].]
(Of a figure) having all its angles equal; having angles equal to those of something else (foll. by *with*).
equiangular spiral a spiral such that the angle between the tangent and the radius vector is the same for all points of the spiral; also called ***logarithmic spiral.***
■ **ˌequiangu'larity** *noun* the condition or fact of being equiangular **M17.**

equicrural /iːkwɪ'krʊər(ə)l/ *adjective.* **E17.**
[ORIGIN from late Latin *equicrurius* isosceles, formed as EQUI- + *crur-*, *crus* leg: see -AL[1].]
Of a triangle: isosceles. Of a cross: having limbs of equal length.

equid /'ɛkwɪd/ *noun.* **L19.**
[ORIGIN mod. Latin *Equidae* (see below), from Latin *equus* horse: see -ID[3].]
A mammal of the family Equidae of odd-toed ungulates, which includes horses, asses, and zebras.

equidistance /iːkwɪ'dɪst(ə)ns, ɛ-/ *noun.* **E17.**
[ORIGIN French *équidistance*, formed as EQUIDISTANT.]
The fact of being equidistant.
at equidistance at equal distances.

equidistant /iːkwɪ'dɪst(ə)nt, ɛ-/ *adjective.* **L16.**
[ORIGIN Old French & mod. French *équidistant* or medieval Latin *equidistant-*, formed as EQUI-, DISTANT.]
1 Separated by an equal distance or equal distances. **L16.**

ANTHONY SMITH Both the quick-witted and the dim-witted are equally exceptional, being equidistant from the central norm.

2 Of lines, linear features, etc.: everywhere the same distance apart, parallel. **L16.**

H. REPTON The banks of a natural river are never equidistant.

3 Pertaining to or possessing the property that distances on a map are correctly proportioned along all lines radiating from a particular point or all lines parallel to either a line of latitude or a line of longitude. **M19.**
■ **equidistantly** *adverb* **L16.**

†**equilater** *adjective*. L16–L18.
[ORIGIN Old French & mod. French *équilatère* or late Latin *aequilaterus*: see EQUILATERAL.]
= EQUILATERAL.

equilateral /iːkwɪˈlat(ə)r(ə)l, ɛ-/ *adjective*. L16.
[ORIGIN French *équilatéral* or late Latin *aequilateralis*, from *aequilaterus*, formed as EQUI- + Latin *later-*, *latus* side: see -AL¹.]
Having all its sides of equal length; (of a hyperbola) having axes of equal length and asymptotes at right angles.

†**equiliber** *noun* var. of EQUILIBRE.

equilibrant /ɪˈkwɪlɪbr(ə)nt, iː-/ *noun*. L19.
[ORIGIN French *équilibrant*, from *équilibrer* equilibrate, from *équilibre* formed as EQUILIBRIUM.]
MECHANICS. A force or system of forces capable of balancing another and producing equilibrium with it.

equilibrate /iːkwɪˈlʌɪbreɪt, ɪˈkwɪlɪ-, iː-/ *verb*. M17.
[ORIGIN Late Latin *aequilibrat-* pa. ppl stem of *aequilibrare*, formed as EQUI- + *libra* balance: see -ATE³.]
1 *verb trans.* Bring into or keep in equilibrium; cause to balance (*with*). M17.

DE QUINCEY To equilibrate the supply with the demand.

2 *verb intrans. & trans.* Be in equilibrium (with); balance. E19.
3 *verb intrans.* Approach a state of equilibrium. M20.

Journal of Endocrinology The Petri dishes were . . allowed to equilibrate for 24 h in an incubator.

■ **eˈquilibrator** *noun* a device for maintaining or restoring equilibrium E20.

equilibration /ˌiːkwɪlʌɪˈbreɪʃ(ə)n, ɪˌkwɪlɪ-, iː-/ *noun*. E17.
[ORIGIN Late Latin *aequilibratio(n-)*, formed as EQUILIBRATE: see -ATION.]
The action of bringing into or keeping in equilibrium; the state of being in equilibrium. Foll. by *to*, *with*.

†**equilibre** *noun*. Also **-ber**. E17–E19.
[ORIGIN French *équilibre* formed as EQUILIBRIUM.]
= EQUILIBRIUM.

equilibria *noun pl.* see EQUILIBRIUM.

equilibrial /iːkwɪˈlɪbrɪəl, ɛ-/ *adjective*. L18.
[ORIGIN from EQUILIBRIUM + -AL¹.]
Of or pertaining to equilibrium.

equilibriate /iːkwɪˈlɪbrɪeɪt, ɛ-/ *verb trans. & intrans.* M17.
[ORIGIN from EQUILIBRIUM + -ATE³.]
= EQUILIBRATE 1, 2.

equilibrio /iːkwɪˈlɪbrɪəʊ, ɛ-/ *noun*. Now *rare*. M17.
[ORIGIN Latin *aequilibrio*, abl. of *aequilibrium* EQUILIBRIUM.]
Equilibrium. Only in ***in equilibrio***.

equilibrious /iːkwɪˈlɪbrɪəs, ɛ-/ *adjective*. Now *rare*. M17.
[ORIGIN from EQUILIBRIUM + -OUS.]
In equilibrium; evenly balanced.

equilibrise *verb* var. of EQUILIBRIZE.

equilibrist /ɪˈkwɪlɪbrɪst, iː-; iːkwɪˈlɪb-, ɛ-/ *noun*. M18.
[ORIGIN from EQUILIBRIUM + -IST.]
A person who performs feats of balancing, *esp.* a tightrope walker.
■ **equiliˈbristic** *adjective* L19.

equilibrium /iːkwɪˈlɪbrɪəm, ɛ-/ *noun*. Pl. **-iums**, **-ia** /-ɪə/. E17.
[ORIGIN Latin *aequilibrium*, formed as EQUI- + *libra* balance.]
1 A well-balanced state of mind or feeling; equanimity, poise. E17. ▸**b** A state of indecision or neutrality produced by opposing influences of equal force. L17.

R. GITTINGS He was shaken by circumstances out of the philosophic and poetic equilibrium he had gained that winter. **b** W. PALEY That indifferency and suspense, that waiting and equilibrium of the judgement.

2 A condition of balance between opposing physical forces. M17.
3 A state in which the influences or processes to which a thing is subject cancel one another out and produce no overall change or variation. L17. ▸**b** ECONOMICS. A situation in which supply and demand are matched and prices stable. L19.

Scientific American At equilibrium the number of granules drifting down . . must be matched by the number of granules drifting up. T. LUPTON Interferences with the equilibrium between the individual and the social reality around him.

– PHRASES: ***dynamic equilibrium***: see DYNAMIC *adjective*. **neutral equilibrium**: in which a body remains in its new position after being disturbed. ***RADIATIVE equilibrium***. ***RADIOACTIVE equilibrium***. **stable equilibrium**: in which a body returns to its initial position after being disturbed. **unstable equilibrium**: in which a body continues to move in the direction given it by a disturbing force.

equilibrize /ɪˈkwɪlɪbrʌɪz/ *verb trans.* Also **-ise**. M19.
[ORIGIN from EQUILIBRIUM + -IZE.]
Bring into equilibrium; balance.

†**equinal** *adjective*. E17–M19.
[ORIGIN from Latin *equinus* (see EQUINE) + -AL¹.]
Equine.

equine /ˈiːkwʌɪn, ˈɛk-/ *adjective & noun*. L18.
[ORIGIN Latin *equinus*, from *equus* horse: see -INE¹.]
▸ **A** *adjective*. Of or pertaining to a horse or horses; resembling (that of) a horse; affecting horses. L18.
▸ **B** *noun*. A horse; an equid. L19.
■ **equinely** *adverb* in an equine manner; like a horse: L19.

equinoctial /iːkwɪˈnɒkʃ(ə)l, ɛ-/ *adjective & noun*. LME.
[ORIGIN Old French & mod. French *équinoctial* from Latin *aequinoctalis*, from *aequinoctium*: see EQUINOX, -AL¹.]
▸ **A** *adjective*. **1** Pertaining to a state of equal day and night. LME.
equinoctial circle, **equinoctial line** the celestial or terrestrial equator. **equinoctial point** = EQUINOX 2.
2 Pertaining to the period or point of an equinox; happening near the time of an equinox, *esp.* designating gales that prevail near the autumnal equinox. L16.
equinoctial armilla: see ARMILLA 1. **equinoctial day**: of 12 hours duration. **equinoctial month**: containing one or other of the equinoxes.
3 Equatorial. L16.
▸ **B** *noun* **1 a** The celestial equator. LME. ▸**b** The terrestrial equator. Now *rare*. L16.
†**2** = EQUINOX 1. LME–M17.
3 An equinoctial gale. M18.

equinox /ˈiːkwɪnɒks, ɛ-/ *noun*. LME.
[ORIGIN Old French & mod. French *équinoxe* or Latin *aequinoctium* (medieval Latin *equinoxium*), formed as EQUI- + *noct-*, *nox* night.]
1 Either of the two occasions in the year when the day is the same length as the night throughout the world, as the sun crosses the celestial equator. LME. ▸**b** The condition of having the days and nights of equal length. Now *rare*. LME.
autumnal equinox: see AUTUMNAL *adjective* 1. ***vernal equinox***: see VERNAL *adjective* 1.
2 ASTRONOMY. Either of the two points on the celestial sphere where the celestial equator intersects the ecliptic. LME.
†**3** The terrestrial equator. L16–E18.

equip /ɪˈkwɪp/ *verb trans.* Infl. **-pp-**. E16.
[ORIGIN French *équiper* (cf. Anglo-Norman *eskipeson* equipment, medieval Latin *eschipare* man (a vessel)), prob. from Old Norse *skipa* man (a vessel), fit up, arrange, from *skip* SHIP *noun*.]
1 Fit out or provide with what is necessary for action etc.; provide with arms or apparatus. (Foll. by *with*.) E16. ▸**b** Provide *with* money; finance. L17.

J. LONDON He had sought to equip himself with the tools of artistry. D. CARNEGIE The farm was equipped with a fine-looking dairy.

2 Array, dress; dress up or fit out (esp. oneself) for a journey, enterprise, etc. L17.

W. IRVING Chinook warriors . . equipped in warlike style. H. I. JENKINSON The tourist will do well to equip himself with good strong boots.

3 Provide with the physical or mental abilities for a task etc. Usu. in *pass*. L18.

R. FRAME Her character didn't equip her for the task of being a diplomat's wife.

equipage /ˈɛkwɪpɪdʒ/ *noun*. M16.
[ORIGIN French *équipage*, from *équiper*: see EQUIP, -AGE.]
▸ **I** Equipment.
†**1** The crew of a ship. *rare*. M16–M18.
†**2** The action of fitting out a ship, arming a soldier, etc. L16–L17.
†**3** The state or condition of being equipped. L16–M17.
4 Apparatus of war; all that an army requires for encampment, transport, etc.; the tackle of a ship. L16. ▸†**b** Clothing, costume, attire; *esp.* military uniform or trappings. L16–E19. ▸**c** Equipment for a journey, expedition, etc. E17. ▸†**d** Apparatus in general. M17–M18.

R. BEATSON With the guns, sails, rigging, and other equipage. **c** N. HAWTHORNE A few carpet-bags and shawls, our equipage for the night.

5 Small articles of domestic furniture, as china, glassware, etc. L17.
6 Articles for personal ornament or use; a case of these. E18.
▸ **II** The appurtenances of rank, social position, etc.
†**7** Formal state or order; style of living etc. L16–M18.

G. BURNET She made an equipage far above what she could support.

†**8** A retinue, a following. L16–E19.
†**9** The money required to maintain an official establishment. Also more fully ***equipage money***. M17–M18.
10 A carriage and horses with attendants; a carriage of this kind. E18.

J. FOWLES Horses being curried and groomed, equipages being drawn out.

▸ †**III** [As if from EQUI-.]
11 Equal step; equivalence. Chiefly in ***in equipage (with)***. E–M17.

†**equipage** *verb trans.* L16–L18.
[ORIGIN from the noun.]
Provide with an equipage, equip.

equiparate /ɪˈkwɪpəreɪt/ *verb trans.* *rare*. M17.
[ORIGIN Latin *aequiparat-* pa. ppl stem of *aequiparare* compare, liken, from *aequipar*, formed as EQUI- + *par* equal: see -ATE³.]
†**1** Reduce to a level. Only in M17.
2 Regard as equivalent; equate. (Foll. by *to*, *with*.) L17.

equiparation /ɪˌkwɪpəˈreɪʃ(ə)n/ *noun*. Now *rare*. LME.
[ORIGIN Latin *aequiparatio(n-)*, formed as EQUIPARATE: see -ATION.]
†**1** Impartial treatment. Only in LME.
2 The action of equating or (formerly) comparing. E17. ▸†**b** A comparison. E–M17.

equipartition /ˌiːkwɪpɑːˈtɪʃ(ə)n, ˌɛ-/ *noun*. E20.
[ORIGIN from EQUI- + PARTITION *noun*.]
PHYSICS. The equal distribution of the kinetic energy of a system among its various degrees of freedom; the principle that this exists for a system in thermal equilibrium.

équipe /ekip/ *noun*. Also **e-**. Pl. pronounced same. M20.
[ORIGIN French = group, team, formed as EQUIP.]
A motor-racing stable; a team, esp. of sports players.

E

equipendency /ɛkwɪˈpɛnd(ə)nsi/ *noun*. *rare*. M17.
[ORIGIN from EQUI- + PENDENCY.]
The state or condition of hanging in equipoise.
■ Also †**equipendence** *noun*: only in E17.

equipment /ɪˈkwɪpm(ə)nt/ *noun*. E18.
[ORIGIN French *équipement*, formed as EQUIP: see -MENT.]
1 Things used in equipping; articles used or required for a particular purpose; apparatus. E18. ▸**b** An item of equipment. Orig. only in *pl*. L18.

R. HOLMES A mass of carefully prepared equipment, including camp-beds, cutlery, Arabic guides.

2 The action of equipping; the state of being equipped; the manner in which a person or thing is equipped. M18.

R. W. EMERSON The admirable equipment of their Arctic ships carries London to the pole.

3 Intellectual resources. M19.

equipoise /ˈɛkwɪpɔɪz, iː-/ *noun & verb*. M17.
[ORIGIN from EQUI- + POISE *noun*¹, repl. the phr. *equal poise*.]
▸ **A** *noun*. **1** Equality or equal distribution of weight; equilibrium, esp. of intellectual, moral, or social forces or interests. M17.

W. S. CHURCHILL We had scored one goal and our opponents two, and there the struggle hung in equipoise for some time. A. G. GARDINER The swift transitions by which the mind in times of stress seeks to keep its equipoise.

2 A counterpoise; a balancing force. L18.
▸ **B** *verb*. **1** *verb trans.* Serve as an equipoise to; counterbalance. M17.

W. S. LANDOR No Praise Can equipoise his virtues.

†**2** *verb intrans.* Balance *with*. *rare*. Only in M17.
3 *verb trans.* Place or hold in equipoise; hold (the mind) in suspense. M18.

I. D'ISRAELI He had to equipoise the opposite interests of the Catholics and the Evangelists.

equipollence /iːkwɪˈpɒl(ə)ns, ɛ-/ *noun*. LME.
[ORIGIN Old French *equipolence* (mod. *équipollence*), from *equipolent*: see EQUIPOLLENT, -ENCE.]
1 Equality of power, authority, signification, etc. LME.
2 LOGIC. An equivalence between two or more propositions. LME.
■ Also **equiˈpollency** *noun* E17.

equipollent /iːkwɪˈpɒl(ə)nt, ɛ-/ *adjective & noun*. LME.
[ORIGIN Old French *equipolent* (mod. *équipollent*) from Latin *aequipollent-* of equal value, formed as EQUI- + *pollere* be strong.]
▸ **A** *adjective*. **1** Possessing equal power, authority, effectiveness, validity, etc. LME.

W. S. LANDOR A maritime power . . equipollent on the sea with France.

2 Identical in meaning or result; equivalent. L16. ▸**b** LOGIC. Of a proposition etc.: expressing the same thing as another, but in a different way. M17.
▸ **B** *noun*. Something that has equal power, effect, significance, etc.; an equivalent. E17.
■ **equipollently** *adverb* M17.

equiponderance /iːkwɪˈpɒnd(ə)r(ə)ns, ɛ-/ *noun*. Now *rare*. E18.
[ORIGIN from EQUIPONDERANT: see -ANCE.]
Equality of weight; equilibrium.
■ Also **equiˈponderancy** *noun* E18.

equiponderant /iːkwɪˈpɒnd(ə)r(ə)nt, ɛ-/ *adjective*. M17.
[ORIGIN medieval Latin *aequiponderant-* pres. ppl stem of *aequiponderare*, formed as EQUI- + *ponderare* weigh: see PONDER *verb*, -ANT¹.]
Of equal weight or (formerly) density; evenly balanced (now only *fig.*).

†**equiponderate** *adjective*. M16–E19.
[ORIGIN medieval Latin *aequiponderatus* pa. pple of *aequiponderare*: see EQUIPONDERANT, -ATE².]
Equal in weight; in equilibrium. (Foll. by *to*, *with*.)

equiponderate /iːkwɪˈpɒnd(ə)reɪt, ɛ-/ *verb*. M17.
[ORIGIN medieval Latin *aequiponderat-* pa. ppl stem of *aequiponderare* (see EQUIPONDERANT, -ATE³), or alt. of PREPONDERATE *verb*¹ by substitution of EQUI- for *pre-*.]
1 *verb trans.* Counterpoise, counterbalance. M17.

O. WALKER To equiponderate the prejudices of pleasure and interest.

E

†**2** *verb intrans.* Be in a state of equipoise. M17–E19.
■ **ˌequipondeˈration** *noun* balancing; balance: M17.

†**equiponderous** *adjective.* M17–E18.
[ORIGIN from EQUI- + Latin *ponder-, pondus* weight + -OUS.]
Of equal weight or density; of equal authority.

equipotent /iːkwɪˈpəʊt(ə)nt, ɛ-/ *adjective.* L19.
[ORIGIN from EQUI- + POTENT *adjective*[2].]
Chiefly PHARMACOLOGY. Equally powerful; having equal potencies.

equipotential /ˌiːkwɪpəˈtɛnʃ(ə)l, ˌɛ-/ *adjective & noun.* L17.
[ORIGIN from EQUI- + POTENTIAL.]
▸ **A** *adjective.* †**1** Of equal authority. Only in L17.
2 PHYSICS. (Of a line or surface) composed of points all at the same potential; having the same potential. M19.
3 BIOLOGY. Of embryonic tissue: having the same potentiality throughout for subsequent development. E20.
▸ **B** *noun.* PHYSICS. An equipotential line or surface. E20.
■ **ˌequipotentiˈality** *noun* (BIOLOGY) E20.

equipper /ɪˈkwɪpə/ *noun.* M19.
[ORIGIN from EQUIP + -ER[1].]
A person who or thing which equips.

equiprobability /ˌiːkwɪprɒbəˈbɪlɪti, ˌɛ-/ *noun.* E20.
[ORIGIN from EQUI- + PROBABILITY.]
The property of being equally probable.

equiprobable /iːkwɪˈprɒbəb(ə)l, ɛ-/ *adjective.* E20.
[ORIGIN from EQUI- + PROBABLE.]
Equally probable.

equirotal /iːkwɪˈrəʊt(ə)l, ɛ-/ *adjective.* M19.
[ORIGIN from EQUI- + Latin *rota* wheel + -AL[1].]
Having back and front wheels of equal diameter.

equisetum /ɛkwɪˈsiːtəm/ *noun.* Pl. **-ta** /-tə/, **-tums.** L17.
[ORIGIN mod. Latin (see below) from Latin *equisaetum*, from *equus* horse + *saeta* bristle.]
Any plant of the genus *Equisetum*, comprising rhizomatous herbaceous plants allied to the ferns and found worldwide except in Australasia, with hollow furrowed jointed stems freq. with whorled branches, and leaves reduced to nodal sheaths; a horsetail.

equitable /ˈɛkwɪtəb(ə)l/ *adjective.* M16.
[ORIGIN French *équitable*, from *équité* EQUITY, with active meaning of the suffix, as (e.g.) in *charitable*: see -ABLE.]
1 Characterized by equity or fairness; fair, just. Now chiefly of actions, arrangements, etc. M16.

> J. GATHORNE-HARDY How can it be equitable to exclude some of them from the benefits?

2 LAW. Pertaining to equity; (of a right, claim, etc.) valid or recognized in equity as opp. to common law. M17.

> *Times* Equitable mortgagees of a house in . . Hackney.

■ **equitaˈbility** *noun* L20. **equitableness** *noun* M17. **equitably** *adverb* M17.

equitant /ˈɛkwɪt(ə)nt/ *adjective.* L18.
[ORIGIN Latin *equitant-* pres. ppl stem of *equitare*: see EQUITATION, -ANT[1].]
BOTANY. Of a leaf: having its base folded and partly enclosing the leaf next above it, as in an iris.

equitation /ɛkwɪˈteɪʃ(ə)n/ *noun.* M16.
[ORIGIN French *équitation* or Latin *equitatio(n-)*, from *equitat-* pa. ppl stem of *equitare*, from *equit-*, *eques* horseman, from *equus* horse: see -ATION.]
1 The action or art of riding on horseback; horsemanship. M16.
2 A ride or outing on horseback. E18.

> J. BARTH Our daily equitations changed . . . Now we generally rode silently.

equites *noun* pl. of EQUES.

equity /ˈɛkwɪti/ *noun.* ME.
[ORIGIN Old French & mod. French *équité* from Latin *aequitas*, from *aequus* equal: see -ITY.]
1 Fairness, impartiality; even-handed dealing. ME.

> J. R. LOWELL There is a singular equity and absence of party passion.

2 That which is fair and right. Long *rare.* LME.
3 LAW. The recourse to general principles of justice to correct or supplement common and statute law; the part of a legal system based on this; *spec.* in England, the body of settled rules and principles originally administered by the Lord Chancellor and since 1873 by statute prevailing over any inconsistent rules of law. L16.
4 A right which is recognizable in a court of equity; an equitable right. E17.
equity of redemption the right of a mortgagor over the mortgaged property, *esp.* the right to redeem the property on payment of the principal, interest, and costs.
5 The value of a mortgaged property after deducting charges and claims against it. L19.
negative equity: see NEGATIVE *adjective*.
6 The issued share capital of a company (also ***equity capital***); the shareholders' interest in a company; in *pl.*, ordinary shares. E20.

> *Investors Chronicle* Bunzl now controls 24 per cent of the equity. *Times* The shift in portfolio preferences of . . investors from bonds to equities.

7 (**E-**.) (The name of) an actors' trade union in Britain and in the US and Canada. E20.

> Q. CRISP I know I am an actor because I have an Equity card.

– COMB.: ***equity capital***: see sense 6 above; **equity draftsman** *arch.* a barrister who composes pleadings in a court of equity.

equivalence /ɪˈkwɪv(ə)l(ə)ns/ *noun.* LME.
[ORIGIN Old French & mod. French *équivalence* from medieval Latin *aequivalentia*, from *aequivalent-*: see EQUIVALENT, -ENCE.]
1 The condition of being equivalent. LME.
principle of equivalence PHYSICS = ***equivalence principle*** below.
2 An instance of being equivalent. E20.
– COMB.: **equivalence class** MATH. the class of all members of a set that are in a given equivalence relation; **equivalence principle** PHYSICS a basic postulate of general relativity, stating that at any point of space-time the effects of a gravitational field cannot be experimentally distinguished from those due to an accelerated frame of reference; **equivalence relation** MATH. a reflexive, symmetric, and transitive relation between elements of a set.

equivalency /ɪˈkwɪv(ə)l(ə)nsi/ *noun.* M16.
[ORIGIN from medieval Latin *aequivalentia*: see EQUIVALENCE, -ENCY.]
1 = EQUIVALENCE 1. M16.
2 = EQUIVALENCE 2. M20.

equivalent /ɪˈkwɪv(ə)l(ə)nt/ *adjective & noun.* LME.
[ORIGIN Old French & mod. French *équivalent* from late Latin *aequivalent-* pres. ppl stem of *aequivalere*, formed as EQUI- + *valere* be strong: see -ENT.]
▸ **A** *adjective.* †**1** Of persons or things: equal in power, rank, authority, or excellence. (Foll. by *to, with, for.*) LME–L17.
2 Equal in value, significance, or meaning. (Foll. by *to*, †*with*, †*for.*) E16.

> H. ADAMS The minstrel, or *menestrier*, became very early a word of abuse, equivalent to blackguard. R. OWEN Speedboats and crystal chandeliers at prices equivalent to a lifetime's wages.

3 That is virtually the same thing; having the same effect. (Foll. by *to.*) M17.
equivalent circuit a notional electric circuit in which components such as resistors and capacitors are interconnected so as to reproduce the behaviour of a more complicated circuit or device and simplify its analysis.
4 Having the same relative position or function; corresponding. (Foll. by *to.*) M17.

> N. CHOMSKY We have the right to maintain missiles on the Russian border . . , but . . they do not have the equivalent right.

5 CHEMISTRY. Of a quantity of a substance: just sufficient to combine with or displace a specified quantity of another substance. M17.
equivalent weight the weight of a substance that is equivalent to 8 grams of oxygen or 1.0079 grams of hydrogen (formerly, to 1 gram of hydrogen).
6 MATH. Belonging to the same equivalence class. M20.
▸ **B** *noun.* **1** Something equal in value or worth. Also, something tantamount or virtually identical. E16.

> J. BRAINE Susan was a princess and I was the equivalent of a swine-herd. J. BARZUN The expert, the Ph.D. or his equivalent, is everywhere. I. MURDOCH She was used to doing things on the hunting field which seemed the equivalent of suicide.

2 A word, expression, sign, etc., of equivalent significance. M17.

> A. LURIE He . . made a neutral noise, the auditory equivalent of a shrug.

3 CHEMISTRY. An amount of a substance whose weight is the equivalent weight of the substance. E19.
– PHRASES: **mechanical equivalent of heat** the amount of mechanical energy that is equivalent to a standard amount of thermal energy, now 1 calorie (= 4.1868 joule).
■ **equivalently** *adverb* (**a**) to an equivalent extent or degree; (**b**) as an equivalent term; with equivalent significance; †(**c**) virtually, in effect: E16.

equivocacy /ɪˈkwɪvəkəsi/ *noun. rare.* M17.
[ORIGIN from late Latin *aequivocus* (see EQUIVOCAL) + -ACY.]
Equivocal character.

equivocal /ɪˈkwɪvək(ə)l/ *adjective & noun.* M16.
[ORIGIN from late Latin *aequivocus*, from Latin *aequus* equal + *vocare* to call: see -AL[1].]
▸ **A** *adjective* **1** **a** Of evidence, signs, etc.: of uncertain or doubtful significance. M16. ▸**b** Of sentiments, an attitude, etc.: undecided. L18.
2 Capable of more than one interpretation; ambiguous. L16. ▸†**b** Of a person: expressing himself or herself in equivocal terms. *rare* (Shakes.). Only in E17.

> K. A. PORTER Messages disguised in equivocal phrases.

3 Of uncertain nature. M17.

> SIR W. SCOTT The equivocal spirits called fairies.

†**4** Equal in name but not in reality. M17–M18.
5 Of a person, condition, tendency, etc.: questionable, suspicious; of doubtful merit or character. L18.

> R. ELLMANN His male friendships included some that were equivocal.

▸ †**B** *noun.* An equivocal term; a homonym. M17–M18.
■ **equivoˈcality** *noun* the quality or condition of being equivocal; something which is equivocal: M18. **equivocally** *adverb* †(**a**) nominally; (**b**) so as to admit of more than one application or interpretation; ambiguously: L16. **equivocalness** *noun* M17.

equivocate /ɪˈkwɪvəkət/ *noun. rare.* L17.
[ORIGIN from the verb.]
A word identical with another in form but not in meaning.

equivocate /ɪˈkwɪvəkeɪt/ *verb.* LME.
[ORIGIN Late Latin *aequivocat-* pa. ppl stem of *aequivocare*, from *aequivocus*: see EQUIVOCAL, -ATE[3].]
†**1** *verb trans. & intrans.* Use (a word) in more than one sense; apply (a word) to more than one thing. LME–L17.
2 *verb intrans.* Use ambiguous words or expressions in order to mislead; prevaricate. L16.

> D. HALBERSTAM Stevens ducked and faked and equivocated and finally, cornered, he admitted.

†**3** *verb trans.* Insinuate or evade (a point, oath, etc.) by equivocation. E–M17.
■ **equivocatingly** *adverb* in an equivocating manner M17. **equivocator** *noun* L16.

equivocation /ɪˌkwɪvəˈkeɪʃ(ə)n/ *noun.* LME.
[ORIGIN Late Latin *aequivocatio(n-)*, formed as EQUIVOCATE *verb*: see -ATION.]
†**1** = EQUIVOQUE *noun* 4; the use of words that are ambiguous. LME–E19.
2 LOGIC. A fallacy arising from the use of the same term in different senses in a syllogism. L16.
3 The use of ambiguous words or expressions in order to mislead; the use of an expression that is literally false but is true with the user's mental addition; an equivocal word or expression. E17.

> J. A. FROUDE The Bishop . . stooped to an equivocation too transparent to deceive any one. *fig.*: W. C. WILLIAMS Such resolves would lead . . to death, definitely and without equivocation.

equivoque /ˈiːkwɪvəʊk, ˈɛ-/ *adjective & noun.* Also **-voke.** LME.
[ORIGIN Old French & mod. French *équivoque* or late Latin *aequivocus*: see EQUIVOCAL.]
▸ †**A** *adjective.* = EQUIVOCAL. LME–M17.
▸ **B** *noun.* †**1** A thing which has the same name as something else. L16–M17.
2 An expression capable of more than one meaning; a pun; wordplay, punning. E17.

> T. F. DIBDIN Who mistook equivoque, abuse, and impudence, for wit. *Times Lit. Suppl.* Tony Augarde . . finds time for *bouts rimés*, echo poems and equivoques.

3 = EQUIVOCATION 3. *rare.* E17.
4 The fact of having more than one meaning or interpretation; ambiguity. E19.

> J. F. W. HERSCHEL Confusion, owing to the equivoque between the lunar and calendar month.

Equuleus /ɪˈkwʊlɪəs/ *noun.* E18.
[ORIGIN Latin = small horse, dim. of *equus* horse.]
(The name of) a small inconspicuous constellation that lies near the celestial equator between Aquarius and Delphinus; the Little Horse.

ER *abbreviation.*
1 Latin *Edwardus Rex* King Edward, or *Elizabetha Regina* Queen Elizabeth.
2 *N. Amer.* Emergency room.

Er *symbol.*
CHEMISTRY. Erbium.

er /əː, ə/ *interjection, verb, & noun.* M19.
[ORIGIN Imit.]
▸ **A** *interjection.* Expr. the inarticulate sound made by a speaker who hesitates or is uncertain what to say. M19.
▸ **B** *verb intrans.* Make this sound. M20.
▸ **C** *noun.* An utterance of this sound. M20.

-er /ə/ *suffix*[1].
[ORIGIN Old English *-ere* from Germanic.]
Forming nouns.
1 Forming nouns from nouns and adjectives with the senses (i) 'a person (orig. *spec.* a man) involved in or with, esp. as an occupation or profession', as ***hatter***, ***probationer***, ***tiler***, etc., some in adaptations of Latin words in *-graphus*, *-logus*, as ***geographer***, ***astrologer***, etc.; (ii) 'a person originating or resident in (a place)', as ***cottager***, ***foreigner***, ***Londoner***, ***New Yorker***, ***northerner***, ***villager***, etc.; (iii) 'a person or thing belonging to or connected with', as ***airliner***, ***old-timer***, ***sixth-former***, ***whaler***, etc.; (iv) 'a person who or thing which has or is', as ***double-decker***, ***fiver***, ***porker***, ***second-rater***, ***three-wheeler***, etc.; (v) 'a thing or action, done by or involving', as ***back-hander***, ***header***, etc.
2 Forming nouns from almost all verbs and some nouns with the senses (i) 'a person (orig. *spec.* a man) who or animal which does, an instrument, machine, occurrence, action, etc., which does', as ***blotter***, ***computer***, ***eye-opener***, ***lifer***, ***lover***, ***maker***, ***miler***, ***pointer***, ***poker***, ***shaker***, ***singer***, ***wheeler-dealer***, etc.; (ii) 'a thing suitable for', as ***broiler*** etc.; (iii) in ***fruiterer***, ***sorcerer***, etc., a pleonastic extension of words in -ER[2].

-er /ə/ *suffix*[2] (not productive).
1 Repr. Old French *-er* from Latin *-aris* -AR[1] (now usual) in nouns, as ***sampler*** etc.

2 Repr. Anglo-Norman *-er* (Old French *-ier*) from Latin *-arius*, *-arium* (see **-ARY**[1]) in nouns with the senses 'a person or thing connected with', as ***butler***, ***danger***, ***mariner***, etc., 'a receptacle for', as ***garner*** etc.
3 Repr. Old French *-eüre* from Latin *-atura* in nouns, as ***bracer*** etc., or Old French *-eör* (mod. *-oir*) from Latin *-atorium*, as ***laver*** etc.
4 Var. of **-OR** (repl. *-our*).

-er /ə/ *suffix*[3].
[**ORIGIN** Old English *-ra* (fem., neut. *-re*) adjective, *-or* adverbial, both from Germanic.]
Forming the compar. of adjectives and adverbs, now esp. of words of one syllable and occas. of two, as ***colder***, ***narrower***, etc.
– **NOTE**: Mod. spelling conventions are as follows: Words in *-e* drop the *e*, as *brave*: *braver*; a final single consonant other than *h*, *w*, or *x* is doubled if preceded by a single-letter vowel, as *grim*: *grimmer*; in most adjectives and a few adverbs in *-y* the *y* becomes *i*, as *early*: *earlier*, similarly in words in *-ey*, as *gooey*: *gooier*.

-er /ə/ *suffix*[4] (not productive).
[**ORIGIN** Repr. Anglo-Norman inf. ending of verbs.]
Forming nouns, freq. in **LAW**, with the sense '(a single instance of) the verbal action, a document effecting this', as ***cesser***, ***dinner***, ***disclaimer***, ***misnomer***, ***supper***, etc.

-er /ə/ *suffix*[5].
[**ORIGIN** Old English *-(e)rian* = Old Saxon, Old High German *-arōn*, Old Norse *-ra*, from Germanic.]
Forming frequentative and iterative verbs from (parts of) verbs or on sound-imitation, as ***clamber***, ***clatter***, ***mutter***, ***shudder***, ***slumber***, ***twitter***, etc.

-er /ə/ *suffix*[6]. Also **-ers** /əz/. **M19.**
Added to shortened forms of words to form slang & colloq. equivalents, as ***brekker***, ***footer***, ***rugger***, etc., among which ***soccer*** has passed into general use. As well as appearing in pls., as ***Divvers*** etc., the var. *-ers* is used esp. in proper names (e.g. ***Twickers*** = Twickenham) and to form adjectives, as ***bonkers***, ***crackers***, ***preggers***, ***starkers***, etc.
– **NOTE**: Orig. Rugby School slang, adopted at Oxford University, and then into wider use.

ERA *abbreviation*.
1 **BASEBALL**. Earned run average.
2 Equal Rights Amendment. *US*.

era /ˈɪərə/ *noun*. Also (earlier) †**ae-**. **M17.**
[**ORIGIN** Late Latin *aera* number used as basis of reckoning, item of account, epoch from which time is reckoned, from pl. of Latin *aer-*, *aes* copper, money, counter.]
1 a A system of numbering years from a particular noteworthy event; a period of years so numbered. Cf. **EPOCH** 5. **M17.** ▸**b** A period of history characterized by a particular state of affairs, series of events, etc.; a distinctive period in the history of something or someone. Cf. **EPOCH** 5. **M18.**
> **b** M. **HUNTER** Stone tools . . used well into the era of bronze. J. **BARZUN** The cataclysm of revolution . . opened a new era of art and thought called Romanticism.

2 = **EPOCH** 1. Now *rare*. **M17.**
3 = **EPOCH** 3; a date or event marking the beginning of a distinctive period. **E18.**
> W. H. **DIXON** The landing of this English Governor was an era in their lives.

4 A date or period to which an event is assigned. Now *rare*. **E18.**
5 **GEOLOGY**. A major division of geological time that is a subdivision of an eon and is itself divided into periods. **L19.**
> W. C. **PUTNAM** The Cenozoic, which is the contemporary Era, is a time of mammalian dominance.

– **PHRASES**: ***Christian Era***: see **CHRISTIAN** *adjective*. ***Common Era***: see **COMMON** *adjective*. **era of good feeling** (also with initial caps.) **US HISTORY** a period in the presidency of Monroe (1817–24) when there was virtually only one political party. ***vulgar era***: see **VULGAR** *adjective*.
– **COMB.**: **era-making** *adjective* = **EPOCH-*making***.

eradiation /ɪˌreɪdɪˈeɪʃ(ə)n/ *noun*. **M17.**
[**ORIGIN** from *e-* **E-** + **RADIATION**.]
1 The action of radiating. **M17.**
2 Something that is radiated; an emanation. **L17.**
■ **eˈradiate** *verb intrans. & trans.* (long *rare* or *obsolete*) **M17.**

eradicable /ɪˈradɪkəb(ə)l/ *adjective*. **M19.**
[**ORIGIN** from **ERADICATE** + **-ABLE**. Earlier in **INERADICABLE**.]
Able to be eradicated.

eradicate /ɪˈradɪkeɪt/ *verb trans.* **LME.**
[**ORIGIN** Latin *eradicat-* pa. ppl stem of *eradicare*, from *e-* **E-** + *radic-*, *radix* root: see **-ATE**[3].]
1 Pull up or out by the roots, uproot. **LME.**
2 Remove or destroy completely; extirpate, get rid of. **E17.**
> *New York Times* The Government has a fundamental . . interest in eradicating racial discrimination in education.

■ **eradicant** *adjective & noun* (a substance) intended to eradicate a particular pest or disease from a particular area **M20**. **eradicated** *ppl adjective* that has been eradicated; **HERALDRY** (of a tree) depicted with its roots exposed: **M17**. **eradicator** *noun* **M17.**

eradication /ɪˌradɪˈkeɪʃ(ə)n/ *noun*. **LME.**
[**ORIGIN** Latin *eradicatio(n-)*, formed as **ERADICATE**: see **-ATION**.]
The action of eradicating; total destruction.

eradicative /ɪˈradɪkətɪv/ *adjective*. **LME.**
[**ORIGIN** Old French *eradicatif*, *-ive*, formed as **ERADICATE** after *palliatif* **PALLIATIVE**: see **-IVE**.]
Tending or able to eradicate disease.

erasable /ɪˈreɪzəb(ə)l/ *adjective*. **M19.**
[**ORIGIN** from **ERASE** + **-ABLE**. Earlier in **INERASABLE**.]
Able to be erased; (of a medium or device) allowing what is on it or in it to be erased.
■ **erasaˈbility** *noun* **M20.**

erase /ɪˈreɪz/ *verb & noun*. **L16.**
[**ORIGIN** Latin *eras-* pa. ppl stem of *eradere*, from *e-* **E-** + *radere* to scrape.]
▸ **A** *verb trans.* **1** **HERALDRY**. Represent (the head or a limb of an animal) with a jagged or torn edge. Only as ***erased*** *ppl adjective*, ***erasing*** *verbal noun*. **L16.**
2 Rub out or obliterate (something written, typed, drawn, or engraved); remove *from* in this way; remove (a recorded signal) from magnetic tape etc. **L17.** ▸**b** Remove all traces of (something) from or *from* one's memory or mind. **L17.**
> **b** C. **CHAPLIN** I did my best to erase that night's horror from my mind. P. **ROSE** If it were possible to erase the past, to go back . . and try again.

3 Remove a recorded signal from (magnetic tape etc.). **M20.**
▸ **B** *noun*. The action of erasing a magnetic tape etc. Usu. *attrib.* **M20.**
erase facility, ***erase head***, etc.
■ **erasement** *noun* (now *rare*) **E18**. **eraser** *noun* a person who or thing which erases something; *spec.* a piece of (synthetic) rubber or plastic for erasing pencil or ink marks: **L18**. **erasion** *noun* (*rare*) the action or an act of erasing something **L18**. **erasive** *adjective* (*rare*) that tends to erase something **M17.**

Erasmian /ɪˈrazmɪən/ *adjective & noun*. **L19.**
[**ORIGIN** from *Erasmus* (see below) + **-IAN**.]
▸ **A** *adjective*. Pertaining to, characteristic of, or after the manner of Erasmus (*c* 1466–1536), Dutch humanist; designating the system of pronunciation he advocated for classical Greek. **L19.**
▸ **B** *noun*. A follower of Erasmus; a person who holds the views of Erasmus. **L19.**
■ **Erasmianism** *noun* (*rare*) **M18.**

erastes /ɛˈrasteɪs, -z/ *noun*. Pl. ***-tai*** /-tʌɪ/. **L20.**
[**ORIGIN** Greek *erastēs* lover, from *eran* be in love with.]
GREEK HISTORY. An older man who desires a younger man. Cf. **EROMENOS**.

Erastian /ɪˈrastɪən/ *noun & adjective*. **M17.**
[**ORIGIN** from *Erastus* (see below) + **-IAN**.]
▸ **A** *noun*. A follower of the (supposed) doctrines of Erastus (1524–83), Swiss physician and theologian; a person who maintains the ascendancy of the state over the Church in ecclesiastical matters, or the state's right to legislate on ecclesiastical matters. **M17.**
▸ **B** *adjective*. Characterized by, embodying, or designating the doctrine of Church and state held by Erastians. **E19.**
■ **Erastianism** *noun* **L17.**

erasure /ɪˈreɪʒə/ *noun*. **M18.**
[**ORIGIN** formed as **ERASE** + **-URE**.]
1 The action or an act of erasing something. **M18.**
2 The place where a letter etc. has been erased. **L19.**
> J. **BARNES** We use infra-red light to pierce erasures in the correspondence.

†**erber** *noun*[1] var. of **ARBER**.

†**erber** *noun*[2] see **ARBOUR**.

erbium /ˈəːbɪəm/ *noun*. **M19.**
[**ORIGIN** from *Ytterby*, Sweden (cf. **YTTERBIUM**) + **-IUM**.]
A soft malleable metallic chemical element of the lanthanide series, atomic no. 68, used in special alloys (symbol Er).
■ **erbia** *noun* erbium oxide, Er_2O_3, a pink powder **M19.**

erbswurst /ˈəːbzwəːst/ *noun*. **L19.**
[**ORIGIN** German, from *Erbse* pea + *Wurst* sausage.]
Seasoned pease-meal compressed into a sausage shape and used for making soup.

ere /ɛː/ *adverb*, *preposition*, *& conjunction*. Also (now *Scot.*) **ear**.
[**ORIGIN** Old English *ǣr* = Old Frisian, Old Saxon, Old High German *ēr* (Dutch *eer*, German *eher*), Gothic *airis* from compar. of Germanic base. Cf. **AIR** *adverb*, **OR** *adverb*, *preposition*, *& conjunction*[1].]
▸ **A** *adverb*. **1** Early; soon. Now only *Scot.* **OE.**
†**2 a** Sooner, earlier. **OE–M17.** ▸**b** Rather, in preference. **ME–M16.**
†**3** Formerly; on a former occasion; just now. **OE–M17.**
▸ **B** *preposition*. Before (in time). Freq. in ***ere then***, ***ere this***, etc. Now *arch. & poet.* **OE.**
> **SIR** W. **SCOTT** I trust the King is ere this out of their reach. M. **SKINNER** Eerie the hush in England ere the storm.

▸ **C** *conjunction*. **1** Of time: before. Also ***ere ever***, ***ere yet***, †***ere than***, †***ere that***. Now *arch. & poet.* **OE.**
> **TOLKIEN** I would give you a gift ere we go. E. **MUIR** Time seemed finished ere the ship passed by.

†**2** Of preference: rather than. **OE–LME.**

erect /ɪˈrɛkt/ *adjective*. **LME.**
[**ORIGIN** Latin *erectus* pa. pple of *erigere* set up, from *e-* **E-** + *regere* to direct.]
1 Upright; not bending or stooping; (of a line or surface) vertical; (of an optical image) having the same orientation as the object, not inverted. **LME.**
> J. **STEINBECK** As the sharp sun struck day after day, the leaves of the young corn became less stiff and erect. F. **KING** He walked briskly down the corridor . . , head erect and shoulders braced. *fig.*: C. **THIRLWALL** A spirit as erect as the King's tiara.

†**2** Of the mind or expression: uplifted; alert. **M16–L18.**
3 Of hair: standing up from the skin, bristling. Of a tail: standing out stiffly from the body. **M18.**
4 Of the penis or clitoris, or the nipples: enlarged and firm, esp. as a result of sexual arousal. **L19.**
■ **erectly** *adverb* **M17**. **erectness** *noun* **M17.**

E

erect /ɪˈrɛkt/ *verb*. **LME.**
[**ORIGIN** Latin *erect-* pa. ppl stem of *erigere*: see **ERECT** *adjective*.]
▸ **I** Elevate, raise.
1 *verb trans.* Set in an upright position; make erect. **LME.**
> A. **GORDON** The Charioteers . . bowed to the Ground, then erected themselves.

†**2** *verb trans.* Direct upwards; lift up (one's eyes, hands, or head); raise; set in a high position. **LME–E18.**
> E. **PAGITT** The Bishop . . erecting his hands stood . . with his face to the Altar.

†**3** *verb trans.* Raise in importance, dignity, etc.; elevate to an office, position, etc. **LME–E18.**
> **STEELE** We have seen . . Monarchs erected and deposed.

†**4** *verb trans.* Rouse, excite, embolden, (the mind, oneself). **M16–M18.**
▸ **II** Construct; establish.
5 a *verb trans.* Build, construct; set up (a statue, pole, etc.); *fig.* devise (a theory), form (a conclusion). **LME.** ▸**b** *verb intrans.* Be built. Only in ***be erecting***. **L17.**
> **a** **QUILLER-COUCH** A freshly-formed mound . . such as children erect over a thrush's grave. T. **CAPOTE** A barricade that state troopers had erected at the entrance. L. **DEIGHTON** Trestle tables . . had been erected in the garage.

6 *verb trans.* †**a** Raise (an army). **L15–L17.** ▸**b** Establish, found, (an office, corporation, institution, etc.); initiate (a project, scheme, etc.). Now *rare*. **M16.**
> **b** D. **HUME** The Jesuits, a new order of regular priests erected in Europe.

7 *verb trans.* **GEOMETRY**. Draw (a line) perpendicular to a given line; draw (a figure) with a given line as base. **M17.**
8 *verb trans.* **ASTROLOGY**. Construct (a horoscope, a chart of the sky). **M17.**
9 *verb trans.* Foll. by *into*: set up or present as; give the character or status of; form into. **L17.**
> G. **SAINTSBURY** The fallacy of erecting the practice of one . . style of literature into a code . . for all time.

■ **erectable** *adjective* **E19**. **erective** *adjective* †(**a**) tending to erect something; (**b**) pertaining to or involving erection of the penis: **E17.**

erectile /ɪˈrɛktʌɪl/ *adjective*. **M19.**
[**ORIGIN** French *érectile*, formed as **ERECT** *verb*: see **-ILE**.]
Able to be erected; (of tissue, an organ) able to become erect when suitably stimulated.
■ **erecˈtility** *noun* the quality of being erectile **M19.**

erection /ɪˈrɛkʃ(ə)n/ *noun*. **LME.**
[**ORIGIN** (Old French & mod. French *érection* from) Latin *erectio(n-)*, formed as **ERECT** *verb*: see **-ION**.]
1 The action or an act of erecting; an erect position. **LME.**
> **BURKE** Any . . innovation which may amount to the erection of a dangerous nuisance. H. H. **WILSON** Their respect for his memory was evinced by the erection of a monumental column.

2 An erect state of an organ, *spec.* the penis; an occurrence of this. **L15.**
3 A thing that is erected or built; a building. **E17.**
> D. **BREWSTER** A wooden erection said to have been Newton's private observatory.

erector /ɪˈrɛktə/ *noun*. **M16.**
[**ORIGIN** from **ERECT** *verb* + **-OR**.]
1 A person who erects something; a machine for assembling parts of buildings. **M16.**
2 A muscle which maintains an erect state of a part or an erect posture of the body. **M19.**
3 (**E-**.) (Proprietary name for) a construction toy consisting of components for making model buildings and vehicles. Chiefly in ***Erector set***. *N. Amer.* **E20.**

erelong /ɛːˈlɒŋ/ *adverb*. *arch.* Also **ere long**. **L16.**
[**ORIGIN** from **ERE** *preposition* + **LONG** *noun*.]
Before long; soon.

eremacausis /ˌɛrɪməˈkɔːsɪs/ *noun*. **M19.**
[**ORIGIN** from Greek *ērema* quietly + *kausis* burning, from *kaiein* to burn.]
The gradual decomposition of organic material into elements and simple compounds in the presence of air and moisture.

eremejevite *noun* var. of **JEREMEJEVITE**.

E

†**eremitage** *noun* var. of HERMITAGE.

eremite *noun* see HERMIT.

eremitic, **eremitical** *adjectives* see HERMITIC, HERMITICAL.

eremurus /ɛrɪˈmjʊərəs/ *noun*. Pl. **-ri** /-rʌɪ, -riː/, **-ruses**. E19.
[ORIGIN mod. Latin (see below), from Greek *erēmos* solitary + *oura* tail.]
Any of various hardy perennial plants of the Asiatic genus *Eremurus*, of the lily family, cultivated for their dense racemes of white, yellow, or reddish flowers; the foxtail lily.

erenach *noun* var. of HERENACH.

erenow /ɛːˈnaʊ/ *adverb*. *arch.* Also **ere now**. LME.
[ORIGIN from ERE *preposition* + NOW *noun*.]
Before this time.

erepsin /ɪˈrɛpsɪn/ *noun*. E20.
[ORIGIN from Latin *eripere* (see EREPTION) + PEPSIN.]
BIOCHEMISTRY. A proteolytic fraction in the intestinal juice, consisting of a mixture of peptidases.

ereption /ɪˈrɛpʃ(ə)n/ *noun*. E17.
[ORIGIN Latin *ereptio(n-)*, from *erept-* pa. ppl stem of *eripere*, from *e-* E- + *rapere* seize: see -ION.]
The action or an act of snatching or seizing.

erethism /ˈɛrɪθɪz(ə)m/ *noun*. E19.
[ORIGIN French *éréthisme* from Greek *erethismos*, from *erethizein* irritate: see -ISM.]
MEDICINE. Abnormally increased sensitivity or responsiveness in a part of the body; abnormal restlessness of mind and emotional sensitivity.
■ **eˈrethic**, **ereˈthistic** *adjectives* L19.

erewhile /ɛːˈwʌɪl/ *adverb*. *arch.* ME.
[ORIGIN from ERE *preposition* + WHILE *noun*.]
A while before, some time ago.

Erewhonian /ɛrɪˈwəʊnɪən/ *adjective* & *noun*. L19.
[ORIGIN from *Erewhon* (see below), a partial reversal of *Nowhere* + -IAN.]
▸ **A** *adjective*. Of, belonging to, or characteristic of the book *Erewhon* (1872) by Samuel Butler, or the Utopia it describes. L19.
▸ **B** *noun*. An inhabitant of Erewhon. E20.

erf /əːf/ *noun*. Chiefly *S. Afr.* Also †**erve**. Pl. **erfs**, **erven** /ˈəːv(ə)n/. L17.
[ORIGIN Dutch = land, yard.]
A piece of land; a building plot or site.

erg /əːg/ *noun*[1]. L19.
[ORIGIN Greek *ergon* work.]
PHYSICS. A unit of work or energy, equal to the amount of work done by a force of one dyne when its point of application moves one centimetre in the direction of the force; 10^{-7} joule.

erg /əːg/ *noun*[2]. Pl. **areg** /ˈarɛg/. L19.
[ORIGIN French from Arabic *ʿirq*, *ʿerg*.]
An area of shifting desert sand dunes, esp. in the Sahara.

ergastic /əːˈgastɪk/ *adjective*. L19.
[ORIGIN from Greek *ergastikos* capable of working, from *ergon* work: see -IC.]
CYTOLOGY. Pertaining to or designating the storage and waste products of metabolic activity in a cell.

ergastoplasm /əːˈgastə(ʊ)plaz(ə)m/ *noun*. E20.
[ORIGIN French *ergastoplasme*, from Greek *ergastikos*: see ERGASTIC, -O-, PLASM.]
CYTOLOGY. The ribosome-carrying components in the cytoplasm of a cell, part of the endoplasmic reticulum.
■ **ergastoˈplasmic** *adjective* E20.

ergastulum /əːˈgastjʊləm/ *noun*. Pl. **-la** /-lə/. E19.
[ORIGIN Latin from Greek *ergastērion* workshop.]
A building like a prison housing slaves on an estate (*ROMAN HISTORY*); any building for slaves or prisoners of war.

ergative /ˈəːgətɪv/ *adjective* & *noun*. M20.
[ORIGIN from Greek *ergatēs* worker + -IVE.]
LINGUISTICS. ▸ **A** *adjective*. Designating a case which is used to mark the subject of a transitive verb, as in Eskimo and Basque; possessing or belonging to such a case; functioning as such a case although not distinctively inflected as one. M20.
▸ **B** *noun*. (A word in) the ergative case. M20.
■ **ergaˈtivity** *noun* the state or condition of being ergative M20.

ergatocracy /əːgəˈtɒkrəsi/ *noun*. E20.
[ORIGIN from Greek *ergatēs* worker: see -O-, -CRACY.]
Government by workers; a government made up of workers.

-ergic /ˈəːdʒɪk/ *suffix*.
[ORIGIN from Greek *ergon* work + -IC.]
PHYSIOLOGY. Releasing, involving, or mimicking a specified substance as a neurotransmitter, as ***adrenergic***, ***cholinergic***, etc.

ergo /ˈəːgəʊ/ *adverb* & *noun*. LME.
[ORIGIN Latin.]
▸ **A** *adverb*. Therefore. LME.

Times I'm a writer, ergo I write.

▸ **B** *noun*. Pl. **-os**. A use of or occurrence of the word 'ergo'; a logical conclusion. Long *rare*. L16.

■ **ergoism** *noun* pedantic adherence to logically constructed rules E18.

ergo- /ˈəːgəʊ/ *combining form*.
[ORIGIN Greek *ergon* work: see -O-.]
Work, energy.
■ **ergosphere** *noun* (*ASTRONOMY*) a postulated region round a black hole, from which energy could escape L20.

ergocalciferol /ˌəːgə(ʊ)kalˈsɪfərɒl/ *noun*. M20.
[ORIGIN from ERGO(STEROL + CALCIFEROL.]
BIOCHEMISTRY. = CALCIFEROL.

ergocryptine /əːgəʊˈkrɪptiːn/ *noun*. M20.
[ORIGIN from ERGO(T + Greek *kruptos* hidden: see -INE[5].]
BIOCHEMISTRY & PHARMACOLOGY. An alkaloid extracted from ergot.

ergodic /əːˈgɒdɪk/ *adjective*. E20.
[ORIGIN from German *ergoden*, from Greek *ergon* work + *hodos* way: see -IC.]
Of, pertaining to, or possessing the property that in the limit all points in a space are covered with equal frequency, or that each sufficiently large selection of points is equally representative of the whole.
■ **ergoˈdicity** *noun* the quality or property of being ergodic M20.

ergogenic /əːgəˈdʒɛnɪk/ *adjective*. E20.
[ORIGIN from ERGO- + -GENIC.]
Intended to enhance physical performance, stamina, or recovery.

ergograph /ˈəːgə(ʊ)grɑːf/ *noun*. L19.
[ORIGIN from ERGO- + -GRAPH.]
An instrument for measuring and recording the work done by particular groups of muscles.
■ **ergogram** *noun* a record or tracing made by an ergograph E20. **ergoˈgraphic** *adjective* L19.

ergometer /əːˈgɒmɪtə/ *noun*. L19.
[ORIGIN from ERGO- + -METER.]
An instrument or machine which measures work or energy, esp. the work done in a spell of exercise.
■ **ergometry** *noun* the use of an ergometer M20.

ergometrine /əːgə(ʊ)ˈmɛtriːn, -ɪn/ *noun*. M20.
[ORIGIN from ERGOT + Greek *mētra* womb + -INE[5].]
PHARMACOLOGY. An oxytocic alkaloid in ergot that is an amide of lysergic acid and is given to control bleeding after childbirth. Cf. ERGONOVINE.

ergonomics /əːgəʊˈnɒmɪks/ *noun*. M20.
[ORIGIN from ERGO- after *economics*.]
The field of study that deals with the relationship between people and their working environment, as it affects efficiency, safety, and ease of action.
■ **ergonomic** *adjective* of or pertaining to ergonomics; (of an object or design) devised in accordance with the findings of ergonomics; (designed to be) conducive to efficient use: M20. **ergonomically** *adverb* M20. **erˈgonomist** *noun* an expert in or student of ergonomics M20.

ergonovine /əːgə(ʊ)ˈnəʊviːn/ *noun*. Chiefly *US*. M20.
[ORIGIN from ERGOT + Latin *novus* new + -INE[5].]
= ERGOMETRINE.

ergophobia /əːgə(ʊ)ˈfəʊbɪə/ *noun*. *joc.* E20.
[ORIGIN from ERGO- + -PHOBIA.]
Fear or dislike of doing work.

ergosterol /əːˈgɒstərɒl/ *noun*. E20.
[ORIGIN from ERGOT + -STEROL.]
BIOCHEMISTRY. A steroid alcohol, $C_{28}H_{44}O$, that is found in ergot and many other fungi and produces vitamin D_2 under ultraviolet irradiation.
■ Also †**ergosterin** *noun*: only in L19.

ergot /ˈəːgɒt/ *noun*. L17.
[ORIGIN French = cock's spur from Old French *ar(i)got*, *argoz* of unknown origin.]
1 A disease of rye, wheat, and certain other grasses in which the seeds become replaced by hard black sclerotia of a fungus of the genus *Claviceps*, esp. *C. purpurea*, giving the appearance of a cock's spur; a sclerotium, or sclerotia, of this kind; a fungus causing such a disease. L17.

Rolling Stone Her explanation was ergot poisoning. F. T. BROOKS Some of the ergots fall to the ground.

2 (A preparation or extract of) the dried sclerotia of this fungus used medicinally for the alkaloids they contain, esp. to induce contraction of the uterus. M19.
3 A small horny protrusion on the back of the fetlock of most horses. L19.
■ **ergoted** *adjective* affected with ergot M19. **ergotized** *adjective* = ERGOTED E19.

ergotamine /əːˈgɒtəmiːn/ *noun*. E20.
[ORIGIN from ERGOT + AMINE.]
PHARMACOLOGY. The pharmacologically active isomer of an alkaloid present in some kinds of ergot, chiefly used to treat migraine.

ergotism /ˈəːgətɪz(ə)m/ *noun*. M19.
[ORIGIN formed as ERGOTAMINE + -ISM.]
1 Acute or chronic poisoning by ergot alkaloids, with symptoms that may include vomiting, diarrhoea, itching, coma, or dry gangrene of the extremities. M19.
2 The occurrence of ergot in grasses. M19.

ergotoxine /əːgə(ʊ)ˈtɒksiːn, -ɪn/ *noun*. E20.
[ORIGIN from ERGOT + TOXIN + -INE[5].]
MEDICINE. An oxytocic mixture of three ergot alkaloids, used in obstetrics and to treat migraine; an alkaloid in such a mixture.

erhu /əːˈhuː/ *noun phr.* Also ***erh hu***. E20.
[ORIGIN Chinese *èrhú*, from *èr* two + *hú* bowed instrument.]
A Chinese two-stringed musical instrument played with a bow.

eria /ˈɪərɪə/ *noun*. Also **eri** /ˈɪəri/. M19.
[ORIGIN Assamese *eriyā* adjective, *eri* noun, from *erā* castor oil plant.]
(The cocoon of) an Indian saturniid silk moth, *Attacus ricini*. Usu. ***attrib.***
eria cocoon, ***eria moth***, ***eria silk***, etc.

eric /ˈɛrɪk/ *noun*. L16.
[ORIGIN Irish *éiric*.]
IRISH HISTORY. A blood fine or financial compensation which had to be paid by a murderer to the family or dependants of the victim.

erica /ˈɛrɪkə/ *noun*. E17.
[ORIGIN mod. Latin from Greek *ereikē*.]
Any of various shrubs of the genus *Erica* (family Ericaceae), characterized by narrow rigid revolute leaves and bell-shaped waxy purple or pink flowers; a heath.
■ **eriˈcaceous** *adjective* of or pertaining to the family Ericaceae, which comprises chiefly shrubs and small trees and includes the heaths, heather, rhododendron, and azalea M19.

ericetal /ɛrɪˈsiːt(ə)l/ *adjective* & *noun*. M19.
[ORIGIN from mod. Latin *ericetum* land dominated by erica, from Latin *erica* + -ETUM: see -AL[1].]
BOTANY. (A plant) that grows normally on heath or moorland.

ericoid /ˈɛrɪkɔɪd/ *adjective*. E20.
[ORIGIN from ERIC(A + -OID.]
Belonging to plants of the genus *Erica* and allied genera; resembling such plants, esp. in respect of their narrow revolute leaves.

Eridanus /ɛˈrɪdənəs/ *noun*. M16.
[ORIGIN Latin, a river in Greek mythol. in which Phaethon drowned.]
(The name of) a long winding constellation of the southern hemisphere that extends from near Orion to near Hydrus; the River.

†**eriff** *noun*. *rare*. L17–M18.
[ORIGIN Unknown.]
1 A two-year-old canary. L17–M18.
2 A newly initiated criminal. *slang*. Only in E18.

erigeron /ɪˈrɪdʒərɒn, ɛ-/ *noun*. E17.
[ORIGIN Latin = groundsel from Greek, from *ēri* early + *gerōn* old man (from its early flowering and hoary appearance or white pappus). In sense 2 mod. Latin from same source.]
†**1** Groundsel. E–M17.
2 Any of various plants of the genus *Erigeron*, of the composite family, resembling daisies, chiefly with white, pink, or mauve ray florets. Also called ***fleabane***. E19.

erineum /ɪˈrɪnɪəm, ɛ-/ *noun*. Pl. **-nea** /-nɪə/. L19.
[ORIGIN mod. Latin, formed as ERINOSE.]
†**1** A fungus supposed to be the cause of erinose. Only in L19.
2 = ERINOSE. E20.

erinnic /ɪˈrɪnɪk, ɛ-/ *adjective*. *rare*. E19.
[ORIGIN from Latin *Erinnys*, Greek *Erinus* a Fury + -IC.]
Characteristic of a Fury.
■ Also †**erinnical** *adjective* E17.

erinose /ˈɛrɪnəʊz, -s/ *noun*. E20.
[ORIGIN from Greek *erineos* woolly, from *erion* wool + *-ose* alt. of -OSIS.]
An area of a leaf densely covered with white hairs, caused by the presence of mites; the condition of having such an area. Freq. ***attrib.***

eriometer /ɛrɪˈɒmɪtə/ *noun*. E19.
[ORIGIN from Greek *erion* wool + -O- + -METER.]
An instrument for measuring the diameter of fine fibres by optical means.

†**Erisch** *adjective* & *noun* see ERSE.

eristic /ɛˈrɪstɪk/ *adjective* & *noun*. M17.
[ORIGIN Greek *eristikos*, from *erizein* wrangle, from *eris* strife.]
▸ **A** *adjective*. Of or pertaining to controversy or disputation; *spec.* (of an argument or arguer) aimed or aiming at victory rather than truth. M17.
▸ **B** *noun*. **1** A person given to disputation. M17.
2 The art of disputation. M19.
■ †**eristical** *adjective* E17–E18. **eristically** *adverb* M20.

Eritrean /ɛrɪˈtreɪən/ *adjective* & *noun*. E20.
[ORIGIN from *Eritrea* (see below) + -AN.]
▸ **A** *adjective*. Of or pertaining to Eritrea, a country in NE Africa on the Red Sea. E20.
▸ **B** *noun*. A native or inhabitant of Eritrea. M20.

erk /ɜːk/ *noun. slang.* Also **irk**. E20.
[ORIGIN Unknown.]
1 A naval rating; an aircraftman. E20.
2 A disliked person. M20.

erlang /ˈɜːlaŋ/ *noun.* M20.
[ORIGIN A. K. *Erlang* (1878–1929), Danish mathematician.]
A unit used to express the intensity of traffic in telephone lines, corresponding to that in one line continuously occupied.

Erlebnis /ɛrˈleːpnɪs/ *noun.* Pl. ***-nise*** /-nɪsə/. E20.
[ORIGIN German, lit. 'experience', from *leben* to live.]
A conscious experience undergone, as opp. to the content or the memory of one.

Erlenmeyer flask /ˈɜːlənmʌɪə flɑːsk/ *noun phr.* L19.
[ORIGIN E. *Erlenmeyer* (1825–1909), German chemist.]
A conical flat-bottomed laboratory flask with a narrow neck.

Erl King /ˈɜːlkɪŋ/ *noun.* L18.
[ORIGIN Partial translation of German *Erlkönig* lit. 'alder king', mistranslating Danish *ellerkonge* king of the elves.]
GERMANIC MYTHOLOGY. A bearded giant who lures little children to the land of death.

ERM *abbreviation.*
Exchange Rate Mechanism.

ermelin /ˈɜːm(ə)lɪn/ *noun.* Now *arch.* or *poet.* M16.
[ORIGIN Uncertain: cf. French *hermeline*, *armeline*, medieval Latin *armelinus*, and ERMINE.]
= ERMINE *noun* 1, 2.

ermine /ˈɜːmɪn/ *noun, adjective, & verb.* ME.
[ORIGIN Old French *ermine*, (also mod.) *hermine*, prob. from medieval Latin *(mus) Armenius* Armenian (mouse), equiv. to Latin *mus Ponticus* mouse of Pontus.]
▸ **A** *noun.* **1** A stoat; *esp.* one with white fur and black-tipped tail, the coat it has in winter in northern regions. ME.
2 The white fur of an ermine as used in clothing, often with the black tails displayed for the sake of effect. ME. ▸**b** In *pl.* Trimmings or garments made from this fur. L15.
3 HERALDRY. One of the two chief furs, consisting of a white field covered with distinctive black markings. Cf. VAIR. LME.
4 A symbol of purity or honour, esp. with ref. to the use of ermine in the robes of judges and peers. L18.

W. GODWIN Reluctant to fix an unnecessary stain upon the ermine of their profession.

5 In full ***ermine moth***. Any of various stout-bodied moths of the genus *Spilosoma*, having cream or white wings with black spots, and a very hairy caterpillar. M19.
▸ **B** *attrib.* or as *adjective.* **1** Made of or with ermine. LME.
2 White as ermine. *poet.* E17.
▸ **C** *verb trans.* Cause to have the appearance of ermine. E19.

ermined /ˈɜːmɪnd/ *adjective.* L15.
[ORIGIN from ERMINE *noun* + -ED[2].]
1 HERALDRY. Covered with the distinctive markings of ermine. L15.
2 Trimmed with ermine; resembling ermine. L15.
3 Robed in ermine; that has been made a judge or a peer. M18.

ermines /ˈɜːmɪnz/ *noun.* M16.
[ORIGIN Uncertain: perh. from Old French *hermines* pl. of *herminet*, dim. of *hermine* ERMINE *noun*.]
HERALDRY. A fur that is the reverse of ermine, with white markings on a black field.

erminites /ˈɜːmɪnʌɪts/ *noun.* M16.
[ORIGIN French *herminite*.]
HERALDRY. A fur resembling ermine but with markings that have a red hair on each side.

erminois /ɜːmɪˈnɔɪz/ *noun.* M16.
[ORIGIN Old French *(h)erminois*, from *hermine* ERMINE *noun*.]
HERALDRY. A fur resembling ermine but having black markings on a gold field.

erne /ɜːn/ *noun.* Also ***ern**.
[ORIGIN Old English *earn* = Middle Low German *arn*, *arnt* (Dutch *arend*), Old High German *arn*, Old Norse *ǫrn* from Germanic base.]
An eagle; *esp.* a sea eagle.

Ernestine /ˈɜːnɪstʌɪn/ *adjective.* M19.
[ORIGIN from *Ernest* (see below) + -INE[1].]
hist. Designating or pertaining to the elder of the two lines of the house of Frederick the Gentle, Elector of Saxony, which originated with his son Ernest (1441–86) and lost the electoral title to the Albertine line in 1547. Cf. ALBERTINE.

ERNIE /ˈɜːni/ *abbreviation.*
Electronic random number indicator equipment, the device used for drawing the prize-winning numbers of premium bonds.

erode /ɪˈrəʊd/ *verb.* E17.
[ORIGIN French *éroder* or Latin *erodere*, from *e-* E- + *rodere* gnaw.]
1 *verb trans.* Destroy imperceptibly, little by little; corrode; GEOLOGY (of rivers, wind, etc.) gradually wear away (soil, the land, etc.). E17. ▸**b** *fig.* Make gradually to be of less and less value, strength, etc. M20.

D. ATTENBOROUGH Rain and rivers eroded the soft sandstones. **b** *What Mortgage* Inflation erodes the real cost of repayments as time goes on.

2 *verb trans.* GEOLOGY. Form by erosion. M19.

J. S. HUXLEY The fantastic shapes into which wind, water, and ice had eroded the Alpine ranges.

3 *verb intrans.* Cause erosion. M19.
4 *verb intrans.* Undergo erosion, wear away; *fig.* diminish gradually in value, strength, etc. E20.

C. FREEMAN The earth . . had eroded so that the tree roots were exposed. *Daily Telegraph* The real value of the grant would erode through inflation.

■ **erodable** *adjective* = ERODIBLE L20. **erodible** *adjective* prone to erosion E20.

erogenic /ɛrəˈdʒɛnɪk/ *adjective.* L19.
[ORIGIN Irreg. from EROS + -GENIC.]
= EROGENOUS.

erogenous /ɪˈrɒdʒɪnəs, ɛ-/ *adjective.* L19.
[ORIGIN Irreg. from EROS + -GENOUS.]
Of a part of the body: sensitive to sexual stimulation; capable of giving sexual pleasure when touched or stroked. Esp. in ***erogenous zone***.

eromenos /ɛˈrəʊmɛnɒs/ *noun.* Pl. ***-noi*** /-nɔɪ/. L20.
[ORIGIN Greek *erōmenos* pa. pple of *eran* be in love with.]
GREEK HISTORY. A young man desired by an older man. Cf. ERASTES.

-eroo /əˈruː/ *suffix. colloq.* (chiefly *N. Amer., Austral., & NZ*).
[ORIGIN Fanciful.]
Forming nouns from verbs with the senses 'large of the type or class', 'overwhelming', 'remarkable', 'unexpected', as ***flopperoo***, ***peacheroo***, ***sockeroo***, etc.

Eros /ˈɪərɒs, ˈɛrəʊz/ *noun.* Pl. **Erotes** /ɪˈrəʊtɛz/, **Eroses** /ˈɪərɒsɪz, ˈɛrəʊzɪz/. Also **e-**. L17.
[ORIGIN Latin from Greek.]
1 Love; the god of love, Cupid; earthly or sexual love. L17.
2 FREUDIAN PSYCHOLOGY. The urge for self-preservation and sexual pleasure. Cf. THANATOS. E20.

erose /ɪˈrəʊs/ *adjective.* L18.
[ORIGIN Latin *erosus* pa. pple of *erodere*: see ERODE.]
BOTANY & ZOOLOGY. Having the margin irregularly denticulate, as if bitten by an animal.

erosion /ɪˈrəʊʒ(ə)n/ *noun.* M16.
[ORIGIN French *érosion* from Latin *erosio(n-)*, from *eros-* pa. ppl stem of *erodere*: see -ION.]
1 The action or process of eroding something; the state of being eroded. M16.
2 An instance of erosion. E18.
■ **erosional** *adjective* caused by or resulting from erosion E20. **erosionist** *noun* (GEOLOGY) a person who believes the contours of the land are due to erosion of the surface M19.

erosive /ɪˈrəʊsɪv/ *adjective.* M19.
[ORIGIN from Latin *eros-* (see EROSION) + -IVE.]
Having the property of eroding.
■ **erosiveness** *noun* M20. **eroˈsivity** *noun* E20.

erotema /ɛrəˈtiːmə/ *noun.* Long *rare.* M16.
[ORIGIN Late Latin from Greek *erōtēma*, from *erōtan* to question.]
RHETORIC. = EROTESIS.

Erotes *noun pl.* see EROS.

erotesis /ɛrəˈtiːsɪs/ *noun.* M16.
[ORIGIN Late Latin from Greek *erōtēsis*, from *erōtan* to question.]
RHETORIC. A figure of speech in which the speaker asks a question, with the confident expectation of a negative answer.
■ **erotetic** /-ˈtɛtɪk/ *adjective* interrogatory M19.

erotic /ɪˈrɒtɪk/ *adjective & noun.* M17.
[ORIGIN French *érotique* from Greek *erōtikos*, from *erōt-*, *erōs* sexual love: see -IC.]
▸ **A** *adjective.* Of or pertaining to sexual love; amatory, *esp.* tending to arouse sexual desire or excitement. M17.
▸ **B** *noun.* **1** An erotic poem. M19.
2 A doctrine or science of love. M19.
■ **erotical** *adjective* (*rare*) = EROTIC E17. **erotically** *adverb* L19. **eroticism** /-sɪz(ə)m/ *noun* erotic spirit or character; sexual excitement; the use of erotic material or practices: L19. **eroticist** /-sɪst/ *noun* a person given to the use of erotic material or practices M20.

erotica /ɪˈrɒtɪkə/ *noun pl.* M19.
[ORIGIN from Greek *erōtika* neut. pl. of *erōtikos*: see EROTIC.]
Orig., matters of love. Now, literature or art that is intentionally erotic.

I. MONTAGU My . . approach to literature included the pages in the bookseller's catalogue labelled 'Erotica'.

eroticize /ɪˈrɒtɪsʌɪz/ *verb trans.* Also **-ise**. E20.
[ORIGIN from EROTIC + -IZE.]
Make erotic, endow with an erotic quality; stimulate sexually.
■ **eroticiˈzation** *noun* M20.

erotise *verb* var. of EROTIZE.

erotism /ˈɛrətɪz(ə)m/ *noun.* M19.
[ORIGIN from Greek *erōt-*, *erōs* sexual love + -ISM.]
Sexual desire or excitement; eroticism.

erotize /ˈɛrətʌɪz/ *verb trans.* Also **-ise**. M20.
[ORIGIN formed as EROTISM + -IZE.]
= EROTICIZE.

eroto- /ɪˈrɒtəʊ/ *combining form* of Greek *erōt-*, *erōs* sexual love: see -O-.
■ **erotoˈgenic** *adjective* = EROGENOUS E20. **erotology** /ɛrəˈtɒlədʒi/ *noun* the description of sexual love and lovemaking; the field of study that deals with sexual love: L19. **erotoˈmania** *noun* excessive or morbid erotic desire; *spec.* de Clerambault's syndrome: M19. **erotoˈmaniac** *noun & adjective* (***a***) *noun* a person affected by erotomania; (***b***) affected by or symptomatic of erotomania: M19.

err /ɜː/ *verb.* ME.
[ORIGIN Old French *errer* from Latin *errare* from base rel. to Gothic *airzei* error, *airzjan* lead astray, Old Saxon, Old High German *irri* (German *irre*) astray.]
†**1** *verb intrans.* Roam, wander. ME–L17.
2 *verb intrans.* Go astray; stray *from* one's path or direction; deviate *from* a target or aim. *arch.* ME.
3 *verb intrans.* Go morally astray; sin. ME.

G. B. SHAW To come to the bosom of her Church as an erring but beloved child.

4 *verb intrans.* Make a wrong judgement, form a wrong opinion; make a mistake, blunder; (of a statement etc.) be incorrect. ME.

I. MURDOCH The Goncourt jury . . might sometimes err, but they would never make a crass or fantastic mistake.

err on the right side act so that the most likely error to occur is the least harmful one. **err on the side of** act with more rather than less of (a specified quality etc.).
†**5** *verb trans.* Do (something) wrongly or sinfully; make a mistake in. ME–M17.
■ **erraˈbility** *noun* (now *rare* or *obsolete*) liability to err, fallibility E18. **errable** *adjective* (now *rare* or *obsolete*) fallible LME. **erringly** *adverb* in an erring way E19.

errancy /ˈɛr(ə)nsi/ *noun.* E17.
[ORIGIN from ERRANT *adjective*: see -ANCY.]
The condition of erring or being in error.

errand /ˈɛr(ə)nd/ *noun.*
[ORIGIN Old English *ǣrende* = Old Frisian *ērende*, Old Saxon *ārundi*, Old High German *ārunti*, from Germanic base obscurely rel. to Old Norse *eyrindi*, *ǫrindi*, *erindi*: ult. origin unknown.]
1 †**a** A message, a verbal communication to be repeated to a third party. OE–M18. ▸**b** *spec.* in CHRISTIAN CHURCH. A petition or prayer presented through a saint. ME.

R. STANYHURST Tel your King, from me, this errand.

2 a A journey made for a special purpose; an expedition, a mission. Now *arch.* & *rhet.* OE. ▸**b** A short journey on which a person is sent to take a message, collect goods, or perform some similar small task. M17.

b V. GLENDINNING The oddest errand . . To buy a dressing-gown for a nun. C. CHAPLIN I was made to . . run errands and do odd jobs. I. COMPTON-BURNETT Can I write letters, or go on errands?

3 The business on which a person goes or is sent; the object of a journey. ME.

W. PALEY The errand which brought him to Jerusalem.

– PHRASES: **errand of mercy** a journey to give help or relieve distress. **fool's errand** a pointless undertaking. †**make an errand** (***a***) make a short journey; (***b***) find a pretext for going.
– COMB.: **errand boy**, **errand girl**: whose job is to run errands, esp. (formerly) for a shopkeeper.

errant /ˈɛr(ə)nt/ *adjective & noun.* See also ARRANT. ME.
[ORIGIN Branch I from Old French & mod. French *errant* pres. pple of *errer* ERR and of Old French *errer* travel (from late Latin *iterare*, from Latin *iter* journey). Branch II from Latin *errant-* pres. ppl stem of *errare* ERR: see -ANT[1].]
▸ **A** *adjective* & (*arch.*) as *pres. pple.*
▸ **I 1** Travelling, itinerant; (esp. of a knight) wandering in search of adventure. Freq. *postpositive.* Now *literary* exc. in KNIGHT ERRANT. ME.
errant polychaete ZOOLOGY any of various active carnivorous marine polychaete worms not confined to tubes or burrows.
†**2 a** = ARRANT 2. LME–L18. ▸**b** = ARRANT 3. M17–E18.
▸ **II 3** Astray, wandering; straying from the correct way; erratic. LME.

P. ZWEIG The errant boy returns, a prodigal son, to embrace his family. DICKENS With an errant motion of his hands as if he could have torn himself.

4 Erring in opinion, conduct, etc.; deviating from an accepted standard. E17.

G. F. WATTS Correcting errant taste in dress.

▸ **B** *noun.* A knight errant; a person who is errant. M17.
■ **errantly** *adverb* randomly; purposelessly: M19. **errantry** *noun* the condition of being errant; the condition, conduct, or ideas of a knight errant (cf. KNIGHT-ERRANTRY): M17.

errata /ɛˈrɑːtə, -ˈreɪt-/ *noun.* L16.
[ORIGIN Latin, pl. of ERRATUM.]
▸ **I 1** *pl.* of ERRATUM. L16.
▸ **II** *sing.* Pl. **-tas**, **-taes** /-təz/.
2 A list of errors in a text. M17.
†**3** = ERRATUM. M17–E18.

E

†**errate** *noun* see ERRATUM.

erratic /ɪˈratɪk/ *adjective & noun*. LME.
[ORIGIN Old French *erratique* from Latin *erraticus*, from *errat-* pa. ppl stem of *errare*: see ERR, -IC.]
▸ **A** *adjective*. **1** Irregular or uncertain in movement; having no fixed course or direction. LME. ▸†**b** Of a disease or pain: moving from one part of the body to another. M16–M18. ▸**c** Itinerant; nomadic; vagrant. *arch.* M17.

A. C. CLARKE The animal was moving in a curiously erratic path, . . making little darts to right or left.

2 Inconsistently variable in behaviour or habit; unpredictable; irregular or eccentric in opinion. M19.

M. E. BRADDON He did not appear at luncheon, but . . he is always erratic.

– SPECIAL COLLOCATIONS: **erratic block**, **erratic boulder**: that differs from the surrounding rock and is thought to have been brought from a distance by glacial action. †**erratic star** a planet.
▸ **B** *noun*. **1** An erratic person. E17.
2 = *erratic block* above. M19.
■ **erratical** *adjective* (now *rare* or *obsolete*) = ERRATIC *adjective* E17. **erratically** *adverb* E17. **erraticism** /-sɪz(ə)m/ *noun* erratic tendencies; an instance of erratic behaviour: L19. **erraticness** *noun* E20.

E

erratum /ɛˈrɑːtəm, -ˈreɪt-/ *noun*. Pl. **-ta** /-tə/. Earlier anglicized as †**-ate**. M16.
[ORIGIN Latin = error, use as noun of neut. pa. pple of *errare* ERR.]
An error in a printed or written text; *esp.* one noted in a list appended to a book or published in a subsequent issue of a journal.

errhine /ˈɛrʌɪn/ *noun*. Now *rare* or *obsolete*. E17.
[ORIGIN mod. Latin *errhinum* from Greek *errinon*, from *en* in + *rhin-*, *rhis* nostril.]
1 A medicinal preparation which induces sneezing when applied inside the nose. E17.
†**2** A pointed plug of lint steeped in such a substance for insertion in a nostril. E17–M18.

erroneous /ɪˈrəʊnɪəs, ɛ-/ *adjective*. LME.
[ORIGIN Old French or Latin *erroneus*, from Latin *erro(n-)* truant, vagabond, from *errare*: see ERR, -EOUS.]
1 Of an opinion, statement, doctrine, etc.: containing errors; mistaken, incorrect; (formerly) heretical. LME. ▸**b** Of a legal proceeding: faulty, irregular; rendered invalid by error. LME.

G. BUDD The erroneous impression that abscesses exist in the liver only.

†**2** Of a person, life, action, etc.: going astray morally or intellectually; criminal; misguided; heretical. LME–E19.

S. JOHNSON That erroneous clemency. BYRON The book which treats of this erroneous pair.

†**3** Wandering, moving aimlessly; vagrant. M17–L18.
■ **erroneously** *adverb* E16. **erroneousness** *noun* E17.

error /ˈɛrə/ *noun*. Also (earlier) †**-our**. ME.
[ORIGIN Old French *err(o)ur* (mod. *erreur*) from Latin *error*, from *errare* ERR: see -OR.]
▸ **I 1** The condition of erring in opinion or belief; a mistaken opinion or belief. ME.

C. LUCAS The general notion that springs are colder in summer and warmer in winter is but a vulgar error. V. KNOX This circumstance has led those into error. B. JOWETT Actions done in error.

2 Something done incorrectly because of ignorance or inadvertence; a mistake. ME. ▸**b** LAW. A mistake in matter of law appearing in the proceedings of a court of record. L15. ▸**c** BASEBALL. A mistake by a fielder. L19.

J. GALSWORTHY It was not her fault; it was her error of judgment. O. MANNING He was expected to pick up her errors of grammar and pronunciation.

clerical error: see CLERICAL *adjective* 2. **b** *writ of error*: brought to procure the reversal of a judgement, on the ground of error.
3 A mistake in moral behaviour, a transgression; wrongdoing. ME.
†**4** A flaw; a malformation. LME–L18.
5 The amount by which an observed or approximate numerical result differs from the true or exact one. E18.
probable error: see PROBABLE *adjective*. *random error*: see RANDOM *adjective*. *standard error*: see STANDARD *adjective*. *systematic error*: see SYSTEMATIC *adjective*.
6 PHILATELY. A postage stamp that differs from the usual form by having wrong wording, colour, etc. M19.
▸ **II 7** The action of wandering; a devious or winding course. *obsolete* exc. *poet.* E16.
– COMB.: **error bar** a line through a point on a graph, parallel to one of the axes, which represents the uncertainty or error of the corresponding coordinate of the point; **error box** ASTRONOMY a quadrilateral area of sky whose dimensions correspond to the uncertainty of a measured position inside it; **error circle** ASTRONOMY a circular area of sky with the same significance as an error box; **error message** COMPUTING an onscreen message indicating that the system has detected an error.
■ **errorist** *noun* a person who tends to make errors or who encourages error M17. **errorless** *adjective* M19.

-ers *suffix* var. of -ER[6].

ersatz /ˈəːsats, ˈɛː-, *foreign* ɛrˈzats/ *adjective & noun*. L19.
[ORIGIN German = compensation, replacement.]
▸ **A** *adjective*. Made or used as a (usually inferior) substitute for something else. L19.

New Yorker I stole packets of sugar and containers of ersatz cream. T. LEARY The external social drama which is as dehydrated and ersatz as TV.

▸ **B** *noun*. An ersatz thing. L19.

Erse /əːs/ *adjective & noun*. Now *arch.* or *derog.* Orig. †**Erisch**, †**Ersch**. LME.
[ORIGIN Early Scot. var. of IRISH.]
▸ **A** *adjective*. Orig., of or pertaining to Ireland or the Scottish Highlands; *spec.* of or pertaining to Highland Gaelic; written or spoken in Highland Gaelic. Later, of or pertaining to the Gaelic spoken in Ireland, Irish. LME.
▸ **B** *noun*. The Gaelic language; latterly *spec.* Irish Gaelic, Irish. L15.

erst /əːst/ *adverb & adjective*.
[ORIGIN Old English *ǣrest* superl. corresp. to *ǣr* ERE = Old Saxon *ērist* (Dutch *eerst*), Old High German *ērist* (German *erst*): see -EST[1].]
▸ **A** *adverb*. †**1** Earliest, first in order of time. OE–LME.
†**2** In the first place, in preference to doing something else. OE–E19.
†**3** At first, initially. OE–E17.
†**4** Sooner; before a specified time or event. ME–L16.
5 a Long ago, formerly, of old. *arch.* exc. *poet.* ME. ▸†**b** Recently; not long ago. L15–L18.
▸ †**B** *adjective*. Occurring first in time. OE–ME.
– PHRASES: †**at erst** (now, or then) and not before; at once.

erstwhile /ˈəːstwʌɪl/ *adverb & adjective*. L16.
[ORIGIN from ERST + WHILE *adverb*.]
▸ **A** *adverb*. Formerly; hitherto. *arch.* L16.

W. GOLDING His hair was frizzed and much lighter than erstwhile. R. SCRUTON The conservative will find the practice of politics as difficult as he has erstwhile found its theory.

▸ **B** *adjective*. Former. E20.

W. C. WILLIAMS The erstwhile chicken house has been a studio for years.

Ertebølle /ɜːtəˈbəːlə/ *adjective*. Also **-bölle**, **-bolle**. E20.
[ORIGIN Place in Jutland, Denmark.]
ARCHAEOLOGY. Designating or pertaining to a late Mesolithic culture in the western Baltic, the final phases of which show Neolithic influence.

erubescence /ɛrʊˈbɛs(ə)ns/ *noun*. *rare*. LME.
[ORIGIN Late Latin *erubescentia*, formed as ERUBESCENT: see -ESCENCE.]
Erubescent quality; blushing. Formerly, shame.

erubescent /ɛrʊˈbɛs(ə)nt/ *adjective*. M18.
[ORIGIN Latin *erubescent-* pres. ppl stem of *erubescere* blush, from *e-* E- + *rubescere* redden, from *rubere* be red: see -ESCENT.]
Reddening; blushing.

eruca /ɪˈruːkə/ *noun*. *rare*. Orig. anglicized as †**eruke**. LME.
[ORIGIN Latin: see ERUCIC.]
A caterpillar; a larva.

erucic /ɪˈruːsɪk/ *adjective*. M19.
[ORIGIN from Latin *eruca* rocket (the plant), caterpillar + -IC.]
erucic acid, a solid unsaturated fatty acid, $C_{21}H_{41}COOH$, present in mustard seeds and rape seeds.

eruciform /ɪˈruːsɪfɔːm/ *adjective*. L19.
[ORIGIN formed as ERUCIC + -I- + -FORM.]
Having the form of a caterpillar.

eruct /ɪˈrʌkt/ *verb intrans. & trans.* Now *rare*. M17.
[ORIGIN Latin *eructare*: see ERUCTATE.]
= ERUCTATE. Also, rise in the course of eructation.
■ **eruction** *noun* (*rare*) E17.

eructate /ɪˈrʌkteɪt/ *verb*. Now *rare*. M17.
[ORIGIN Latin *eructat-* pa. ppl stem of *eructare*, from *e-* E- + *ructare* to belch: see -ATE[3].]
1 *verb trans.* Expel or emit violently. Chiefly *fig.* M17.
2 *verb intrans.* Of a person: belch. L18.

eructation /iːrʌkˈteɪʃ(ə)n, ɪ-/ *noun*. LME.
[ORIGIN Latin *eructatio(n-)*, formed as ERUCTATE: see -ATION.]
1 a Belching; a belch. LME. ▸**b** (A) volcanic eruption; emission *of* something by a volcano. M17.
2 Material that is emitted. E17.

érudit /erydi, ɛrʊˈdiː/ *noun*. Pl. pronounced same. Also ***erudit*** /ˈɛrʊdɪt/. E19.
[ORIGIN French, formed as ERUDITE.]
A scholar.

erudite /ˈɛrʊdʌɪt/ *adjective & noun*. LME.
[ORIGIN Latin *eruditus* pa. pple of *erudire* instruct, train, from *e-* E- + *rudis* rude, untrained: see -ITE[2].]
▸ **A** *adjective*. **1** Learned, scholarly. Formerly, trained, instructed. LME.
2 Of writing etc.: that shows great learning. M16.
▸ **B** *noun*. An erudite person, a scholar. *rare*. M19.
■ **eruditely** *adverb* E16. **eruditeness** *noun* E19.

erudition /ɛrʊˈdɪʃ(ə)n/ *noun*. LME.
[ORIGIN Old French *érudition* or Latin *eruditio(n-)*, from *erudit-* pa. ppl stem of *erudire*: see ERUDITE, -ITION.]
†**1** Instruction, education; what is taught; a maxim. LME–M18.

HENRY FIELDING This gift Jenny had . . improved by erudition.

2 Orig., the state of being instructed or trained (foll. by *in*, *of*). Now, acquired knowledge, esp. in the humanities; learning, scholarship. M16.

G. B. SHAW This simple faith in my accomplishment as a linguist and my erudition as a philosopher.

■ **eruditional** *adjective* M17.

†**eruke** *noun* see ERUCA.

erump /ɪˈrʌmp/ *verb intrans. rare*. M17.
[ORIGIN Latin *erumpere*: see ERUPT.]
Break out; erupt; burst forth.

erumpent /ɪˈrʌmpənt/ *adjective*. M17.
[ORIGIN Latin *erumpent-* pres. ppl stem of *erumpere*: see ERUPT, -ENT.]
That bursts forth; *spec.* (BOTANY) projecting from a surface or substratum.

erupt /ɪˈrʌpt/ *verb*. M17.
[ORIGIN Latin *erupt-* pa. ppl stem of *erumpere*, from *e-* E- + *rumpere* burst forth.]
1 *verb intrans.* (Of volcanic material) be ejected in the course of an eruption; (of a rash, boil, etc.) appear on the skin; *gen.* (chiefly *fig.* exc. as below) come out of something (as if) with violence or rupture; burst forth. M17. ▸**b** *verb intrans. & trans.* (in *pass.*). Of a tooth: emerge through the skin of the gums in the course of development. M19.

W. OWEN Will toe-nails cease to grow; pimples to erupt? JO GRIMOND You could dangle a mussel . . over the water and suddenly a fish would erupt and seize it.

2 *verb trans.* Of a volcano, geyser, etc.: eject in an eruption. M18.

Nature On the lunar surface . . basalt magmas were erupted.

3 *verb intrans.* (Of a volcano, geyser, etc.) be in a state of eruption; suddenly become noisily active (foll. by *in*, *into*). L18.

J. IRVING When no strong leader emerged, the kingdom of Thak erupted in . . rebellion. S. BRETT The audience erupted into laughter and applause. R. FRAME After just a couple of hours . . my mother erupted, yelling at the guards.

eruption /ɪˈrʌpʃ(ə)n/ *noun*. LME.
[ORIGIN Old French *éruption* or Latin *eruptio(n-)*, formed as ERUPT: see -ION.]
1 The appearance on the skin of a rash or a collection of boils or the like; a rash; a pathological alteration of the appearance of the skin. LME.
2 The action or an act of bursting or breaking out from natural or artificial limits. M16. ▸**b** The emergence of a tooth through the skin of the gums in the course of development. M19.
3 a A sudden occurrence of something calamitous or noisy, as disease or laughter; an outbreak, an outburst. L16. ▸**b** A spell of activity in which a volcano ejects lava, ash, etc., usu. violently; a spell of activity in which a geyser ejects hot water. M18.

a HUGH WALPOLE Before the eruption of the civil war.

4 A thing that bursts out; a sudden rush of flame, water, or the like. L17.
■ **eruptional** *adjective* M19.

eruptive /ɪˈrʌptɪv/ *adjective & noun*. M17.
[ORIGIN from ERUPT + -IVE.]
▸ **A** *adjective*. Tending to erupt; of, pertaining to, or characterized by (an) eruption; (of rock) formed by the cooling and solidification of magma or (esp.) lava. M17.

BYRON The volcano's fierce eruptive crest. C. M. YONGE Illness of an eruptive kind.

▸ **B** *noun*. An eruptive rock. L19.

eruv /ˈɛrʊv/ *noun*. Pl. **-vim** /-vɪm/. L18.
[ORIGIN Hebrew *'ērūḇ*, from root *'rb* mixture (because the concept implies the mixing of public and private).]
Any of various symbolic arrangements which extend the private domain of Jewish households into public areas, thereby permitting activities in them that are normally forbidden in public on the Sabbath; *spec.* an urban area within which such an arrangement obtains, and which is symbolically enclosed by a wire boundary.

†**erve** *noun* var. of ERF.

erven *noun pl.* see ERF.

-ery /əri/ *suffix*.
[ORIGIN French *-erie*, partly from Proto-Romance, from Latin *-ario-* + *-ia* -Y[3]; partly from Old French *-ere*, *-eor* (mod. *-eur*) from Latin *-ator*, + *-ie* -Y[3].]
Forming nouns from nouns and verbs in which it denotes (*a*) things of a certain kind, as ***confectionery***, ***greenery***, ***machinery***, ***scenery***; (*b*) a place of work, as ***bakery***, ***brewery***; *US* a place where things can be bought, as ***bootery***, ***eatery***; a place where plants or animals live or are grown, as ***orangery***, ***piggery***, ***rockery***, ***rookery***, ***sealery***; (*c*) a state or condition, as ***bravery***, ***slavery***; an occupation, as ***archery***, ***midwifery***; (*d*) characteristic qualities, ideas, or actions (often *derog.*), as ***knavery***, ***popery***, ***tomfoolery***.

eryngium /ɪˈrɪndʒɪəm/ *noun*. L16.
[ORIGIN mod. Latin from Latin *eryngion* from Greek *ēruggion* dim. of *ēruggos* sea holly.]
Any of various umbelliferous plants of the genus *Eryngium*, with prickly leaves and blue or white flowers in thistle-like heads; *esp.* sea holly, *E. maritimum*.

eryngo /ɪˈrɪŋɡəʊ/ *noun*. Pl. **-o(e)s**. L16.
[ORIGIN Italian or Spanish *eringio* from Latin *eryngion* ERYNGIUM.]
†**1** The candied root of the sea holly, *Eryngium maritimum*, eaten as a sweet and considered an aphrodisiac. L16–E18.
2 Sea holly; any other plant of the genus *Eryngium*. M17.

erysipelas /ɛrɪˈsɪpɪləs/ *noun*. LME.
[ORIGIN Latin from Greek *erusipelas*, perh. from base of *eruthros* red + *pel-* in *pella* skin.]
An acute, sometimes recurrent, disease caused by a streptococcal infection and characterized by large raised red patches on the skin, esp. of the face and legs, with fever and severe general illness.
SWINE erysipelas.
■ ˌ**erysiˈpelatose** *adjective* = ERYSIPELATOUS E18.

erysipelatous /ˌɛrɪsɪˈpɛlətəs/ *adjective*. M17.
[ORIGIN from medieval Latin *erysipelatus* (from Greek *erusipelat-*, *erusipelas* ERYSIPELAS) + -OUS.]
Pertaining to or of the nature of erysipelas; affected with erysipelas.

erysipeloid /ɛrɪˈsɪpɪlɔɪd/ *noun*. L19.
[ORIGIN from ERYSIPELAS + -OID.]
Dermatitis of the hands due to infection with swine erysipelas.

erythema /ɛrɪˈθiːmə/ *noun*. L18.
[ORIGIN Greek *eruthēma*, from *eruthainein* be red, from *eruthros* red.]
Redness of the skin, usually in patches, as a result of injury or irritation.
■ **erythemal** *adjective* erythematous; causing erythema: M20. ˌ**erytheˈmatic** *adjective* erythematous L18. **erythematous** *adjective* of, pertaining to, or symptomatic of erythema M19.

erythr- *combining form* see ERYTHRO-.

erythraemia /ɛrɪˈθriːmɪə/ *noun*. Also ***-thremia**. M19.
[ORIGIN from ERYTHRO- + -AEMIA.]
†**1** The oxygenation of the blood in the lungs. *rare*. Only in M19.
2 An abnormally high concentration of red cells in the blood; a disease so characterized, *esp.* polycythaemia vera. E20.
■ **erythraemic** *adjective* characteristic of or characterized by erythraemia E20.

erythrasma /ɛrɪˈθrazmə/ *noun*. L19.
[ORIGIN from ERYTHRO- + Greek *-asma* (cf. CHLOASMA).]
A chronic skin disease caused by a corynebacterium and characterized by scaling discoloured patches on areas of moist skin in contact with each other.

erythremia *noun* see ERYTHRAEMIA.

erythrina /ɛrɪˈθriːnə/ *noun*. L18.
[ORIGIN mod. Latin, from Greek *eruthros* red.]
Any of various leguminous tropical trees and shrubs of the genus *Erythrina*; = ***coral tree*** (b) s.v. CORAL *noun*.

erythrine /ˈɛrɪθriːn, ɪˈrɪθriːn/ *noun*. Now *rare*. M19.
[ORIGIN formed as ERYTHRISM + -INE[5].]
= ERYTHRITE 2.

erythrism /ˈɛrɪθrɪz(ə)m/ *noun*. L19.
[ORIGIN from Greek *eruthros* red + -ISM.]
ZOOLOGY. Abnormal or excessive redness, as in the plumage or fur of a bird or animal; a red variety of a species.
■ **eryˈthristic** *adjective* exhibiting erythrism E20.

erythrite /ˈɛrɪθrʌɪt, ɪˈrɪθrʌɪt/ *noun*. M19.
[ORIGIN formed as ERYTHRISM + -ITE[1].]
1 A flesh-coloured variety of feldspar. Now *rare* or *obsolete*. M19.
2 *MINERALOGY*. A hydrated arsenate of cobalt and nickel occurring as a secondary mineral in red or pink translucent monoclinic crystals. Also called ***cobalt bloom***, ***red cobalt (ore)***, (earlier) ERYTHRINE. M19.
3 *CHEMISTRY*. = ERYTHRITOL. Now *rare*. M19.

erythritol /ɪˈrɪθrɪtɒl/ *noun*. L19.
[ORIGIN from ERYTHRITE + -OL.]
CHEMISTRY. An optically active tetrahydric alcohol, $C_4H_{10}O_4$, occurring in certain lichens and algae, the nitrate of which is used as a vasodilator.

erythro- /ɪˈrɪθrəʊ/ *combining form* of Greek *eruthros* red, and of ERYTHROCYTE: see -O-. Before a vowel **erythr-**.
■ **erythroblast** *noun* a nucleated cell which develops into an erythrocyte L19. **erythroˈblastic** *adjective* containing or involving erythroblasts E20. **erythroblasˈtosis** *noun* the presence of erythroblasts in the blood; *spec.* (more fully ***erythroblastosis fetalis***) = *HAEMOLYTIC* ***disease of the newborn***: M20. **erythroˈgenic** *adjective* causing redness, esp. of the skin E20. **erythroleuˈkaemia** *noun* (*MEDICINE*) a rare acute form of leukaemia with proliferation of erythroblasts and leucoblasts E20. **erythromeˈlalgia** *noun* [Greek *melos* limb] pain in the extremities, esp. the feet, with dilatation of the blood vessels and reddening of the skin L19. **erythroˈmycin** *noun* an antibiotic isolated from *Streptomyces erythreus*, similar in its effects to penicillin M20. **erythrophagocyˈtosis** *noun* the phagocytosis of erythrocytes M20. **erythroˈphobia** *noun* (*a*) fear of blushing; (*b*) a visual hypersensitivity to the colour red: L19. **erythrophore** *noun* a red pigment cell in an animal E20. **erythropoiesis** /-pɔɪˈiːsɪs/ *noun* the formation of red blood cells E20. **erythropoietic** /-pɔɪˈɛtɪk/ *adjective* pertaining to or characterized by erythropoiesis E20. **erythropoietin** /-pɔɪˈɛtɪn/ *noun* a hormone secreted by the kidneys that increases the rate of formation of red blood cells M20. **eryˈthropsia** *noun* [Greek *-opsia* seeing] a visual disorder in which everything appears red L19. **erythrosin** *noun* a brown powder, related to eosin, which gives a red colour in aqueous solution and is used as a biological stain and to colour food L19.

erythrocyte /ɪˈrɪθrəsʌɪt/ *noun*. L19.
[ORIGIN from ERYTHRO- + -CYTE.]
One of the principal cells in the blood of vertebrates, containing the pigment haemoglobin and transporting oxygen and carbon dioxide to and from the tissues. Also called ***red blood cell***, ***red cell***, ***red corpuscle***.
■ **erythrocytic** /-ˈsɪtɪk/ *adjective* of or pertaining to an erythrocyte; involving erythrocytes; (of malaria parasites etc.) occurring inside an erythrocyte: E20. **erythrocyˈtosis** *noun* an increased number of erythrocytes in the blood, esp. as a secondary symptom E20.

erythroid /ˈɛrɪθrɔɪd/ *adjective*. M19.
[ORIGIN from ERYTHRO- + -OID.]
1 Of a red colour. *rare*. M19.
2 Of or pertaining to erythrocytes or their precursors. E20.

erythrol /ˈɛrɪθrɒl/ *noun*. L19.
[ORIGIN from ERYTHRITE + -OL.]
CHEMISTRY. = ERYTHRITOL.

erythronium /ɛrɪˈθrəʊnɪəm/ *noun*. Pl. **-iums**, **-ia** /-ɪə/. E19.
[ORIGIN mod. Latin, from Greek *saturion eruthronion* red-flowered orchid.]
Any of various ornamental spring-flowering bulbs of the genus *Erythronium* of the lily family; = ***dog's tooth violet*** s.v. DOG'S TOOTH 1.

erythrose /ɪˈrɪθrəʊz, -s, ˈɛrɪ-/ *noun*. E20.
[ORIGIN from ERYTHRITE + -OSE[2].]
CHEMISTRY. A liquid tetrose sugar, $CHO{\cdot}(CHOH)_2{\cdot}CH_2OH$, existing as two optical isomers and differing from threose in having the hydroxyl groups on the second and third carbon atoms on the same side of the carbon chain.

Es *symbol*.
CHEMISTRY. Einsteinium.

es- /ɛs, *unstressed* ɪs/ *prefix* (not productive).
Repr. Old French *es-* (= Italian *s-*) from Latin *ex-* out, utterly (see EX-[1]), as ***escape***, ***escheat***. Cf. A-[7].

-es *suffix*[1] see -S[1].

-es *suffix*[2] see -S[2].

ESA *abbreviation*.
1 Environmentally sensitive area.
2 European Space Agency.

Esalen /ˈɛsələn/ *noun & adjective*. M20.
[ORIGIN Respelling of *Esselen*, an extinct N. Amer. Indian people of the Californian coast.]
(Designating) an alternative philosophy and technique aimed at increasing a person's self-awareness and potential by psychological and physiotherapeutic means.

Esau /ˈiːsɔː/ *noun*. M17.
[ORIGIN The biblical patriarch Isaac's elder twin son, who sold his birthright (*Genesis* 25:25 ff.).]
A person who prefers present advantage to permanent rights or interests.

escabeche /ˌɛskəˈbɛʃ, ˈɛskə-/ *noun*. Also (earlier) **escaveche**. E18.
[ORIGIN Spanish.]
A dish of fish that is fried then marinated in vinegar and spices and served cold.

escalade /ɛskəˈleɪd/ *noun*. L16.
[ORIGIN French, or Spanish *escalada*, *-ado*, = Italian *scalata*, from medieval Latin *scalare* SCALE *verb*[2]: see -ADE.]
The action or an act of scaling the walls of a fortified place by means of ladders.
■ Also **escalado** /ɛskəˈlɑːdəʊ/ *noun* (*arch.*), pl. **-oes**, L16.

escalade /ɛskəˈleɪd/ *verb trans*. E19.
[ORIGIN from the noun.]
Climb and get over (a wall) by means of ladders.

escalate /ˈɛskəleɪt/ *verb*. E20.
[ORIGIN Back-form. from ESCALATOR.]
1 *verb intrans*. Travel on an escalator. E20.
2 *verb trans. & intrans*. (Cause to) increase or develop, esp. by successive stages. M20.

M. L. KING The white liberal must escalate his support for the struggle for racial justice. M. EDWARDES A dispute . . escalated until some 14,000 employees . . went out on indefinite strike. N. MAILER It all escalated from car stealing up to armed robbery.

escalation /ɛskəˈleɪʃ(ə)n/ *noun*. M20.
[ORIGIN from ESCALATE + -ATION.]
The process or an act of increasing in scale, scope, etc., by successive stages; (a) step-by-step development, esp. of a war or dispute.

escalator /ˈɛskəleɪtə/ *noun*. Orig. *US*. E20.
[ORIGIN from ESCALADE *verb* + -ATOR, after *elevator*.]
A staircase consisting of an endless chain of steps driven by a motor and continuously ascending or descending.

fig.: *Economist* Prices and wages are fellow-travellers on the same upward escalator.

– COMB.: **escalator clause**, **escalator contract**, etc.: providing for a change in prices etc. to meet specified contingencies.

escalatory /ɛskəˈleɪt(ə)ri/ *adjective*. M20.
[ORIGIN from ESCALATE + -ORY[2].]
Tending to escalate; conducive of or constituting escalation.

escaline /ˈɛskəlɪn/ *noun*. Also **-in**. L17.
[ORIGIN French from Dutch *schelling*, German *Schilling*: see SHILLING.]
hist. Orig., a Flemish coin. Later, any of various coins used in South Africa and the southern states of the US.

escallonia /ɛskəˈləʊnɪə/ *noun*. L19.
[ORIGIN mod. Latin, from *Escallon*, 18th-cent. Spanish traveller + -IA[1].]
Any of various chiefly evergreen pink- or white-flowered shrubs of the S. American genus *Escallonia* (often included in the saxifrage family), used for hedging in mild coastal districts.

E

escallop /ɪˈskaləp, ɛ-, -ˈskɒl-/ *noun*. L15.
[ORIGIN Old French *escalope* shell. Cf. SCALLOP.]
1 = SCALLOP *noun* 2b. L15.
2 = SCALLOP *noun* 1. E17.
3 *HERALDRY*. A figure of a single valve of a scallop, borne as a charge. E17.
– COMB.: **escallop-shell** (*a*) = *SCALLOP* ***shell***; (*b*) an ornamental imitation of a scallop shell; (*c*) *HERALDRY* = sense 3 above.
■ **escalloped** *adjective* = SCALLOPED E17.

escalope /ɪˈskaləp, ɛ-, -ˈskɒl-, ˈɛskələʊp/ *noun*. Also **escalop**, **escallope**. E19.
[ORIGIN French from Old French = shell. Cf. ESCALLOP.]
A thin slice of boneless meat or (occas.) fish; *esp.* a special cut of veal from the leg.

escapable /ɪˈskeɪpəb(ə)l, ɛ-/ *adjective*. M19.
[ORIGIN from ESCAPE *verb* + -ABLE. Earlier in INESCAPABLE.]
Able to be escaped or avoided.

escapade /ˈɛskəpeɪd, ɛskəˈpeɪd/ *noun*. M17.
[ORIGIN French from Spanish or Provençal, from *escapar* to escape, from Proto-Romance: see ESCAPE *verb*, -ADE.]
†**1** An act of escaping from confinement or restraint; an escape. M17–M19.
2 An instance of irresponsible or unorthodox conduct. E19.

SIR W. SCOTT A youthful escapade, which might be easily atoned.

escape /ɪˈskeɪp, ɛ-/ *noun*. ME.
[ORIGIN Orig. from Old French *eschap*, from *eschaper* (see ESCAPE *verb*); later from the verb. Aphet. to SCAPE *noun*[1].]
1 The action or an act of escaping, or the fact of having escaped, from captivity, danger, etc. ME. ▸**b** (A) leakage of liquid, gas, electricity, etc. L19. ▸**c** The action of escaping from the gravitational force of a planet or other celestial object. M20.

JONSON What, has he made an escape! which way? **b** OED There is an escape of gas in the kitchen.

2 The possibility or a means of escaping; a way out; a fire escape. LME. ▸**b** An outlet for liquid; *esp.* a sluice etc. to convey surplus water from a canal. L19.

N. COWARD Nothing's any use. There's no escape, ever. K. AMIS For many of them, . . to be a priest is an escape from the poverty.

†**3** A breaking of rules or conventions; a transgression, an (amorous) escapade. LME–L17. ▸**b** A mistake; *esp.* a clerical or printer's error. L16–M19. ▸**c** An involuntary outburst of feeling; a shaft of wit. E17–L18.
4 (A means of) mental or emotional distraction from the realities of life. M19.

D. W. HARDING Readers who . . would turn to her . . for relief and escape.

5 A cultivated plant growing wild; an animal or bird which has escaped from captivity L19.
– COMB.: **escape clause**: specifying the conditions under which a contracting party is freed from an obligation; **escape code** *COMPUTING* = ***shift code*** s.v. SHIFT *noun* 15c; **escape committee** a group of prisoners that plans and coordinates escapes from a prison camp etc.; **escape hatch**: serving as an emergency exit in a submarine, ship, aircraft, etc.; **escape key** *COMPUTING*: that either terminates the current operating mode or changes the functions of other keys; **escape road** a slip road for the use of vehicles failing to negotiate a bend or hill; **escape shaft**: for the escape of miners if the ordinary shaft becomes blocked; **escape speed** = ***escape velocity*** below; **escape valve**: to allow the escape of steam etc. when the pressure gets too great; **escape velocity** the lowest velocity at which an unpowered body must be projected into space if it is not eventually to return by gravitational attraction; **escape wheel** a toothed wheel in the escapement of a watch or clock.

escape /ɪˈskeɪp, ɛ-/ *verb*. ME.
[ORIGIN Anglo-Norman, Old Northern French *escaper* (Old French *eschaper*, mod. *échapper*), from Proto-Romance, formed as EX-[1] + medieval Latin *cappa* cloak: see CAP *noun*[1]. Aphet. to SCAPE *verb*[1].]
1 *verb intrans*. Break free *from* captivity; free oneself by fleeing or struggling. Also foll. by *out of*. ME. ▸**b** Of a fluid,

E

powder, etc.: leak or seep out; pass out. Of an object: come out (as if) from confinement. LME.

C. HILL The King escaped from his captivity at Hampton Court. N. MONSARRAT Three hundred others escaped by means of ropes let down from these bastions. **b** J. L. WATEN From the darkness within a pungent odour escaped. W. GOLDING They had heaped up her.. hair out of the way on her head, though a curl or two had escaped.

†**2** *verb trans.* Escape from (prison, a person's control, etc.). ME–M17.

3 *verb trans.* Succeed in avoiding (something unwelcome); elude (a person's grasp). ME.

W. MAXWELL Very few families escape disasters of one kind or another. A. S. NEILL You can't escape becoming smug and dignified if you are an inspector.

4 *verb intrans.* Avoid capture, punishment, or something unwelcome; get off safely; go unpunished. ME. ▸†**b** Recover from serious illness. LME–L15.

AV *Acts* 27:44 They escaped all safe to land. DONNE He may escape with his life. G. B. SHAW We court the danger; but the real delight is in escaping. S. LEWIS His wife, his clamoring friends, sought to follow him, but he escaped.

5 *verb trans.* Elude (observation, search); fail to be noticed or recollected by (a person). ME.

E. M. FORSTER The name escaped her. What was the name? J. HERSEY He tried to escape her glance by keeping his back turned.

6 *verb trans.* Be uttered inadvertently by; issue involuntarily from (a person, a person's lips). LME.

T. HARDY The words had no sooner escaped her than an expression of unutterable regret crossed her face.

■ **escaper** *noun* E17.

escapee /ɛskeɪˈpiː, ɪˈskeɪpiː/ *noun*. M19.
[ORIGIN from ESCAPE *verb* + -EE¹.]
A person who has escaped, *esp.* an escaped prisoner.

escapeless /ɪˈskeɪplɪs, ɛ-/ *adjective*. M19.
[ORIGIN from ESCAPE *noun*, *verb* + -LESS.]
Unavoidable; impossible to escape (from).

escapement /ɪˈskeɪpm(ə)nt, ɛ-/ *noun*. See also SCAPEMENT (earlier). L18.
[ORIGIN French *échappement*, from *échapper*: see ESCAPE *verb*, -MENT.]
1 a A mechanism in a clock or watch that alternately checks and releases the train by a fixed amount and transmits a periodic impulse from the spring or weight to the balance wheel or pendulum; a mechanism in a typewriter that shifts the carriage a fixed amount when a key is pressed and released. L18. ▸**b** The mechanism in a piano which allows a hammer to move away after striking a string. L19.
duplex escapement: see DUPLEX *adjective* 1.
2 a The action of escaping. *rare*. E19. ▸**b** A means of escape; an outlet. *arch.* M19.

escapism /ɪˈskeɪpɪz(ə)m, ɛ-/ *noun*. M20.
[ORIGIN from ESCAPE *noun* + -ISM.]
The tendency to seek, or practice of seeking, distraction or relief from reality.

L. D. WEATHERHEAD Religion that was mere escapism.

escapist /ɪˈskeɪpɪst, ɛ-/ *noun & adjective*. M20.
[ORIGIN from ESCAPE *noun* + -IST.]
▸ **A** *noun*. **1** A person who escapes or tries to escape from captivity etc. M20.
2 A person who seeks distraction or relief from reality or who indulges in escapism. M20.

E. WAUGH Turning their backs on the world of effort and action ... Happy, drab escapists.

▸ **B** *adjective*. Providing distraction or relief from reality; involving or characteristic of escapism. M20.

A. STORR Escapist phantasies. W. STYRON The escapist euphoria of a tax dodger seeking to lose his past in Rio de Janeiro.

escapologist /ɛskeɪˈpɒlədʒɪst, ɛskəˈpɒl-/ *noun*. E20.
[ORIGIN from ESCAPE *noun* + -OLOGIST.]
A person, esp. a performer, skilled in freeing himself or herself from the constraints of knots, handcuffs, confinement, etc.
■ **es,capoˈlogical** *adjective* M20. **escapology** *noun* the methods and techniques of escaping, *esp.* those of an escapologist M20.

escarbuncle /ɪˈskɑːbʌŋk(ə)l, ɛ-/ *noun*. L15.
[ORIGIN Old French (mod. *escarboucle*) formed as ES-, CARBUNCLE.]
HERALDRY. A charge representing a carbuncle stone.

escargot /ɛˈskɑːgəʊ, ɪ-/ *noun*. Pl. pronounced same. L19.
[ORIGIN French from Old French *escargol* from Provençal *escaragol*.]
A snail as an article of food.

†**escarmouche** *noun*. LME–E19.
[ORIGIN Old French & mod. French: see SKIRMISH *noun*.]
A skirmish; *fig.* a fit of anger.

escarole /ˈɛskərəʊl/ *noun*. *N. Amer.* E20.
[ORIGIN French from Italian *scar(i)ola* from late Latin *(e)scariola*, from Latin *escarius* used as food, from *esca*: see ESCULENT.]
A variety of endive with broad undivided leaves, used in salads.

escarp /ɪˈskɑːp, ɛ-/ *noun*. L17.
[ORIGIN French *escarpe* from Italian *scarpa* slope. Cf. SCARP *noun*².]
1 FORTIFICATION. = SCARP *noun*² 1. L17.
2 *gen.* = SCARP *noun*² 2. M19.

escarp /ɪˈskɑːp, ɛ-/ *verb trans.* E18.
[ORIGIN French *escarper*, formed as ESCARP *noun*.]
Make into or provide with an escarp.

escarpment /ɪˈskɑːpm(ə)nt, ɛ-/ *noun*. E19.
[ORIGIN French *escarpement*, formed as ESCARP *noun*: see -MENT.]
1 FORTIFICATION. = ESCARP *noun* 1. E19.
2 A steep slope, *esp.* one at the edge of a plateau or separating areas of land at different heights; GEOGRAPHY the steep slope of a cuesta. E19.

escartelee /ɪˈskɑːtəliː, ɛ-/ *adjective*. Also **-ellé** /-əleɪ/. L17.
[ORIGIN Old French *escartelé* pa. pple of *escarteler* (mod. *écarteler*) divide into quarters, formed as ES- + *quartier* QUARTER *noun*.]
HERALDRY. Of a cross: quadrate. Of a line of partition: having a single square indentation. Usu. *postpositive*.

escaveche *noun* see ESCABECHE.

-esce /ɛs/ *suffix*.
[ORIGIN Repr. Latin *-escere*.]
In or forming verbs, usu. inceptive, as ***coalesce***, ***effervesce***, ***evanesce***, etc.

-escence /ˈɛs(ə)ns/ *suffix*.
[ORIGIN Repr. French *-escence* or Latin *-escentia*, formed as -ESCENT: see -ENCE.]
In or forming nouns corresp. to adjectives in -ESCENT, as ***deliquescence***, ***effervescence***, ***obsolescence***, etc.
■ Also **-escency** *suffix*.

-escent /ˈɛs(ə)nt/ *suffix*.
[ORIGIN Repr. French *-escent* or Latin *-escent-* pres. ppl stem of verbs in *-escere*: see -ESCE, -ENT.]
In or forming adjectives with the sense 'beginning to assume a particular state, variation of colour, etc.', as ***effervescent***, ***iridescent***, ***obsolescent***, ***phosphorescent***, ***putrescent***, etc.

eschalot /ˈɛʃəlɒt/ *noun*. E18.
[ORIGIN French *eschalotte* (now *échalotte*) alt. of Old French *esc(h)alo(i)gne*: see SCALLION. Cf. SHALLOT.]
A shallot onion.

eschar /ˈɛskɑː/ *noun*. LME.
[ORIGIN French *eschare* (now *escarre*) or late Latin *eschara*: see SCAR *noun*².]
A dry dark slough or scab, *esp.* one caused by burning.

escharotic /ɛskəˈrɒtɪk/ *adjective & noun*. E17.
[ORIGIN French *escharotique* (now *escar(r)otique*) or late Latin *escharoticus* from Greek *eskharōtikos*, from *eskhara*: see SCAR *noun*², -OTIC.]
▸ **A** *adjective*. Tending to produce eschars, caustic. E17.
▸ **B** *noun*. An escharotic substance. M17.

eschatocol /ˈɛskətəʊkɒl/ *noun*. L19.
[ORIGIN from Greek *eskhatos* last + *kolla* glue, after PROTOCOL.]
The concluding section of a charter, containing the attestation, date, etc.; a concluding clause or formula.

eschatology /ɛskəˈtɒlədʒi/ *noun*. M19.
[ORIGIN from Greek *eskhatos* last + -OLOGY.]
The branch of theology that deals with the four last things (death, judgement, heaven, and hell) and the final destiny of the soul and of humankind; a doctrine or belief about the Second Coming or the kingdom of God.
realized eschatology: see REALIZE 1.
■ **,eschatoˈlogical** *adjective* M19. **,eschatoˈlogically** *adverb* in relation to eschatology E20. **eschatologist** *noun* L19. **eschatologize** *verb trans.* give an eschatological character to E20.

eschaton /ˈɛskətɒn/ *noun*. M20.
[ORIGIN Greek *eskhaton* neut. of *eskhatos* last.]
THEOLOGY. The final event in the divine plan.

C. H. DODD The *eschaton*, the divinely ordained climax of history.

†**eschaufe** *verb trans.* LME–M16.
[ORIGIN Old French *eschaufer* (mod. *échauffer*) from Proto-Romance var. of Latin *excalefacere*, formed as EX-¹ + *calefacere*: see CHAFE *verb*.]
Heat, make warm; *fig.* excite.

escheat /ɪsˈtʃiːt, ɛ-/ *noun & verb*. ME.
[ORIGIN Old French *eschete* from Proto-Romance, ult. from Latin *excidere* fall away, escape, formed as EX-¹ + *cadere* fall.]
▸ **A** *noun*. **I** LAW.
1 Land that reverted to the feudal lord when the tenant died leaving no one eligible to succeed under the terms of the grant (*hist.*); (now *US* exc. *hist.*) property that reverts to the state or (formerly) the Crown when the owner dies intestate without heirs or (in Britain) who was attainted; *Scot.* property that is forfeited or confiscated. ME.
2 The reversion of an escheat by intestacy or (in Scotland) forfeiture. Now *Scot.* & *US* exc. *hist.* LME.
3 *hist.* The right of appropriating property that is subject to escheat. LME.
4 *hist.* A writ to obtain possession of such property. LME.
▸†**II 5** Forced contribution, plunder; in *pl.*, booty. L16–E17.
▸ **B** *verb*. LAW (now *Scot.* & *US* exc. *hist.*).
1 *verb trans.* Make an escheat of; hand over as an escheat *to* or *into*. LME. ▸**b** Forfeit. *Scot.* LME.
2 *verb intrans.* Revert by escheat *to* a lord, the Crown, or a state; become an escheat. LME.

H. KEMELMAN Without any other beneficiary the whole amount would escheat to the State.

■ **escheatable** *adjective* subject to escheat L16. **escheatage** *noun* (now *rare*) the right of succeeding to an escheat E17. **escheatment** *noun* forfeiture or lapsing by escheat M19. **escheator** *noun* an officer formerly appointed to deal with escheats in a county LME. **escheatorship** *noun* the office of escheator L16.

eschew /ɪsˈtʃuː, ɛ-/ *verb*. LME.
[ORIGIN Old French *eschiver* from Proto-Romance, from Germanic base of Old High German *sciuhen*, German *scheuen* shun. Cf. SHY *adjective*.]
†**1** *verb trans.* Avoid, escape, keep clear of (a danger, place, or person). LME–E18.

LD BERNERS To exchewe.. the displeasure of my lorde. ROBERT BURTON A woman a man may eschue, but not a wife.

2 *verb trans.* Carefully or deliberately abstain from, avoid, or shun (an action, indulgence, etc.). LME.

W. BEVERIDGE They must not only eschew evil but do good. H. JAMES She looked for a bench that was empty, eschewing a still emptier chair. E. WAUGH Old-fashioned people.. who today eschew the telephone. A. FRASER He eschewed equally the Roman Catholic tenets.. and the Puritan practices.

†**3** *verb intrans.* Get off, escape. LME–M16.
■ **eschewal** *noun* the action or an act of eschewing L16. **eschewer** *noun* L16. **eschewment** *noun* the action of eschewing M19.

eschscholtzia /ɪˈʃɒltsɪə, ɪsˈkɒlʃə, ɛ-/ *noun*. Also **-olzia**. L19.
[ORIGIN mod. Latin, from J. F. *Eschscholtz* (1793–1831), Russian-born naturalist and traveller + -IA¹.]
Any of various poppies of the Californian genus *Eschscholtzia*, of the poppy family; esp. *E. californica* (Californian poppy), much grown for its brilliant yellow or orange flowers and glaucous, finely divided leaves.

esclandre /ɛsklɑ̃dr/ *noun*. Pl. pronounced same. M19.
[ORIGIN French from ecclesiastical Latin *scandalum*: see SCANDAL *noun*.]
Unpleasant notoriety; a scandal, a scene.

esclavage /ɛsklavaːʒ/ *noun*. Now *rare* or *obsolete*. Pl. pronounced same. M18.
[ORIGIN French, lit. 'slavery', from Old French & mod. French *esclave* SLAVE *noun*¹: see -AGE.]
A necklace composed of chains, rows of beads, etc., supposed to resemble a slave's fetters.

escolar /ɛskəˈlɑːr/ *noun*. M19.
[ORIGIN Spanish, lit. 'scholar', orig. with ref. to the dark or black colouring of certain fishes of this family, seen as resembling an academic robe or gown.]
A member of the family Gempylidae of fast-swimming marine fishes found in warm and tropical seas worldwide, most of which have dark-coloured, elongated bodies and oily flesh.

escopette /ɛskə(ʊ)ˈpɛt/ *noun*. E19.
[ORIGIN Spanish *escopeta* (assim. to French *escopette* from Italian) from Italian *schioppetto* dim. of *schioppo* carbine from medieval Latin *sclop(p)us* harquebus: see -ETTE.]
hist. A kind of carbine formerly used in Mexico and the southern US.

escort /ˈɛskɔːt/ *noun*. L16.
[ORIGIN French *escorte* from Italian *scorta* use as noun of fem. pa. pple of *scorgere* guide, conduct from late or medieval Latin, ult. formed as EX-¹ + Latin *corrigere* set right, CORRECT *verb*.]
1 A body of armed men accompanying a traveller or travellers for protection, for surveillance, or as a mark of honour, or acting as a guard for baggage, provisions, treasure, etc. L16. ▸**b** A warship or warships accompanying merchant ships or other vessels for protection; a fighter aircraft accompanying bombers for protection. E20.

WELLINGTON Colonel Trant with his division attacked the escort of the military chest. **b** *attrib.*: W. S. CHURCHILL The First Cruiser Squadron.. had been.. employed on escort duties at sea.

2 A person or group of persons accompanying someone on a journey for courtesy's sake or for protection or guidance. M18. ▸**b** A person accompanying another socially; *esp.* a man accompanying a woman to a dance, party, etc. M20. ▸**c** A prostitute. *euphem.* L20.

G. VIDAL Because of our police escort, we did not have to go through the usual formalities. J. WAINWRIGHT I've organised a uniformed escort, for the coffin. **b** K. TENNANT Miss O'Shea was drinking ginger-beer and her escort had a shandy. **c** *attrib.*: E. JONG He had taken some.. businessmen there with girls from an escort service.

3 Attendance in the capacity of an escort; the protection or company of an escort. M19.

J. MARTINEAU The elder deities were compelled to.. attend in escort to the Eastern idol. C. S. FORESTER He usually had to leave Lady Emily to hunt.. under the escort of.. his aides-de-camp.

escort /ɪˈskɔːt, ɛ-/ *verb trans.* E18.
[ORIGIN French *escorter*, from *escorte*: see ESCORT *noun*.]
Act as an escort to; accompany for protection, guidance, courtesy, etc.

LD MACAULAY He was escorted by a bodyguard under the command of Sarsfield. J. AGATE She.. insisted on escorting me to the door herself.

■ **escortage** *noun* (*US*) the company or protection of an escort **L19**.

†**escot** *verb trans. rare* (Shakes.). Only in **E17**.
[ORIGIN Old French *escoter*, from *escot* (mod. *écot*): see SCOT *noun*[2].]
Pay a reckoning for, maintain.

escribe /ɪˈskrʌɪb, iː-, ɛ-/ *verb trans.* **M16**.
[ORIGIN from *e-* E- + Latin *scribere* write. Cf. EXSCRIBE.]
†**1** = EXSCRIBE 1. *rare*. Only in **M16**.
2 *GEOMETRY*. = EXSCRIBE 2. **L19**.

†**escript** *noun*. **LME–E18**.
[ORIGIN Old French: see SCRIPT *noun*[1].]
A written document; *spec.* a writ.

escritoire /ɛskriːˈtwɑː/ *noun*. **L16**.
[ORIGIN Old French = study, writing box (mod. *écritoire* writing desk) from medieval Latin SCRIPTORIUM.]
A writing desk with drawers, a bureau.

escrod /ɪˈskrɒd, ɛ-/ *noun*. *US* (now *rare*). **M19**.
[ORIGIN Unknown. Cf. SCROD.]
= SCROD.

escroll /ɪˈskrəʊl, ɛ-/ *noun*. Also (*Scot.*) **-ol**. **E17**.
[ORIGIN Old French *escroele* dim. of *escroe*: see ESCROW.]
†**1** = ESCROW *noun*. **E17–M18**.
2 *HERALDRY*. = SCROLL *noun* 4b. **E17**.

escrow /ɪˈskrəʊ, ɛ-/ *noun & verb*. **M17**.
[ORIGIN Anglo-Norman *escrowe*, Old French *escroe* scrap, scroll from medieval Latin *scroda* from Germanic base of SHRED *noun*.]
▸ **A** *noun*. **1** *LAW*. A bond, deed, etc. held by a third party and taking effect only when a stated condition is fulfilled. **M17**.
2 A deposit or fund held in trust or as a security. *N. Amer.* **L19**.

attrib.: *New Yorker* Banks began to advertise escrow services for drilling ventures.

in escrow in trust as an escrow.
▸ **B** *verb trans.* Place in escrow. *US*. **E20**.

escuage /ˈɛskjuːɪdʒ/ *noun*. *obsolete* exc. *hist.* **E16**.
[ORIGIN Anglo-Norman, Old French, from *escu* (mod. *écu*) shield (from Latin *scutum*) + -AGE. Cf. SCUTAGE.]
1 Personal service in the field for a period of forty days each year, the chief form of feudal tenure. **E16**.
2 = SCUTAGE. **L16**.

escudero /ɛskʊˈdɪərəʊ/ *noun*. *arch.* Pl. **-os**. **E17**.
[ORIGIN Spanish, formed as ESCUDO.]
A shield-bearer; an esquire; an attendant.

escudo /ɛˈskuːdəʊ/ *noun*. Pl. **-os**. **E19**.
[ORIGIN Spanish & Portuguese, from Latin *scutum* shield: cf. ÉCU, SCUDO.]
The basic monetary unit of Portugal (until the introduction of the euro in 2002) and the Cape Verde Islands.

esculent /ˈɛskjʊlənt/ *adjective & noun*. **E17**.
[ORIGIN Latin *esculentus*, from *esca* food, from *esse* eat: see -ULENT.]
▸ **A** *adjective*. Fit for food, eatable. **E17**.
▸ **B** *noun*. Something that is fit for food or eatable, *esp.* a vegetable. **E17**.

escutcheon /ɪˈskʌtʃ(ə)n, ɛ-/ *noun*. **L15**.
[ORIGIN Anglo-Norman, Old Northern French *escuchon* (Old French *escusson*, mod. *écusson*) from Proto-Romance from Latin *scutum* shield.]
1 *HERALDRY*. The shield or shield-shaped surface on which a coat of arms is depicted; the shield together with its armorial bearings; a representation of this, a coat of arms; a shield-shaped charge, an inescutcheon. **L15**. ▸†**b** A hatchment. Also ***funeral escutcheon***. **M17–E19**.
***escutcheon of* PRETENCE**.
2 A shield-shaped area or object; a protective plate, *spec.* one round a keyhole. **M17**. ▸**b** The middle of a ship's stern where the name is placed. **M19**.

Practical Wireless F. M. Tuner . . . Neat escutcheon and tuning dial.

3 *fig.* Reputation. Only in wider metaphors, esp. ***a blot on one's escutcheon***. **L17**.

P. G. WODEHOUSE It will undoubtedly tarnish the Ickenham escutcheon.

■ **escutcheoned** *adjective* **M18**.

Esd. *abbreviation*.
Esdras (Apocrypha).

ESE *abbreviation*.
East-south-east.

-ese /iːz/ *suffix*.
[ORIGIN Repr. Old French *-eis* (mod. *-ois*, *-ais*) from Proto-Romance from Latin *-ensis*.]
1 Forming adjectives and nouns (pl. same) from names of foreign countries and towns, with the sense '(a native or inhabitant) of', as ***Cantonese***, ***Japanese***, ***Portuguese***, ***Viennese***, etc.
2 Forming nouns from personal names and other nouns with the sense 'the language or style of', as ***Carlylese***, ***computerese***, ***Johnsonese***, ***officialese***, etc. Freq. *derog.*

esemplastic /ɛsɛmˈplastɪk/ *adjective*. **E19**.
[ORIGIN from Greek *hes* into + *hen* neut. of *heis* one + -PLASTIC, irreg. after German *Ineinsbildung* forming into one.]
Moulding into one, unifying.

C. N. MANLOVE No esemplastic imagination is at work to weld the particulars into a whole.

eserine /ˈɛsɛriːn/ *noun*. **M19**.
[ORIGIN French *ésérine*, from Efik *esere*: see -INE[5].]
= PHYSOSTIGMINE.

esker /ˈɛskə/ *noun*. Also **eskar**. **M19**.
[ORIGIN Irish *eiscir*.]
A long narrow sinuous ridge, usu. of sand and gravel, deposited by a stream flowing under a former glacier or ice sheet.

Eskimo /ˈɛskɪməʊ/ *noun & adjective*. Pl. same, **-os**. Also **Esquimau**, pl. **-aux** /-əʊ(z)/. **L16**.
[ORIGIN Danish from French *Esquimaux* pl. from Algonquian, perh. = 'people speaking a different language'.]
▸ **A** *noun*. **1** A member of a people inhabiting the Arctic coasts of eastern Siberia, Alaska, Canada, and Greenland. Cf. INUIT, YUIT. **L16**.
2 Either or both of the two main languages (Inupiaq and Yupik) of this people. **M18**.
3 = ***Eskimo dog*** below. **M19**.
– COMB.: **Eskimo-Aleut**, **Eskimo-Aleutian** *nouns & adjectives* (of) the language family comprising Eskimo and Aleut.
▸ **B** *attrib.* or as *adjective*. Of or pertaining to the Eskimo or their languages. **M18**.
Eskimo curlew a curlew, *Numenius borealis*, that breeds in northern Canada. **Eskimo dog** a sturdy dog used by Eskimos for pulling sledges and hunting, a husky. **Eskimo pie** (chiefly *N. Amer.*) (US proprietary name for) a bar of chocolate-coated ice cream. **Eskimo roll** a complete rollover in canoeing, from upright to capsized to upright.
– NOTE: The peoples inhabiting the regions from NW Canada to western Greenland prefer to call themselves *Inuit*. *Eskimo*, however, is the only term which applies to the people as a whole and is still widely used in anthropological and archaeological contexts.
■ **Eskimoid** *adjective* resembling (that of) an Eskimo, similar in racial type to the Eskimo **E20**.

Esky /ˈɛski/ *noun*. *Austral.* Also **e-**. **M20**.
[ORIGIN Uncertain: perh. from ESKIMO + -Y[6].]
A portable insulated container for keeping food and drink cool.
– NOTE: Proprietary name in Australia.

ESN *abbreviation*.
hist. Educationally subnormal.

esne /ˈɛzni/ *noun*. Long *obsolete* exc. *hist.*
[ORIGIN Old English *esne* = Old High German *asni*, Gothic *asneis* day-labourer.]
A serf, a hireling.

ESOL *abbreviation*.
English for speakers of other languages.

esophagus *noun* etc.: see OESOPHAGUS etc.

esophoria /ɛsəˈfɔːrɪə/ *noun*. **L19**.
[ORIGIN from Greek *esō* (see ESOTERIC) + -PHORIA.]
MEDICINE. A tendency for the visual axes to converge; latent convergent strabismus.

esoteric /ɛsəˈtɛrɪk, iːs-/ *adjective & noun*. **M17**.
[ORIGIN Greek *esōterikos*, from *esōterō* inner, compar. of *esō* within, from *es*, *eis* into: see -IC.]
▸ **A** *adjective*. **1** (Of a philosophical doctrine, mode of speech, etc.) designed for or appropriate to an inner circle of advanced or privileged disciples; communicated or intelligible only to the initiated; (of a person) initiated into or belonging to an inner circle. Opp. EXOTERIC *adjective* 1. **M17**.

M. HUNTER The magician is an esoteric figure—part priest, part philosopher, part artist. G. MURRAY Unless we are to interpret the word 'poetry' in some esoteric sense of our own. P. LARKIN The esoteric areas of Neoplatonic symbolism . . and the history of inner literary conventions. H. ACTON This passion for reading set her apart from her sisters though she shared their esoteric jokes.

Esoteric Buddhism a system of theosophical doctrines alleged to have been transmitted by an inner circle of Buddhists.
2 Not openly stated or admitted; confidential; secret. **M19**.

LD MACAULAY His esoteric project was the original project of Christopher Columbus. A. M. FAIRBAIRN Strauss had hardly the stuff in him to be an exoteric Conservative while an esoteric Radical.

▸ **B** *noun*. **1** A person initiated into esoteric doctrines. **M17**.
2 In *pl.* Esoteric doctrines or treatises. **E18**.
■ **esoterical** *adjective* esoteric **M19**. **esoterically** *adverb* **M18**.

esoterica /ɛsəˈtɛrɪkə, iːs-/ *noun pl.* **E20**.
[ORIGIN Greek *esōterika* neut. pl. of *esōterikos* ESOTERIC.]
Esoteric items or publications; esoteric details.

esotericism /ɛsəˈtɛrɪsɪz(ə)m, iːs-/ *noun*. **M19**.
[ORIGIN from ESOTERIC + -ISM.]
1 (Belief in) an esoteric doctrine. **M19**.

R. ADAMS Something . . beside which all older religious notions would appear . . an esotericism as shallow as the whispered secrets of children.

2 (A tendency towards) esoteric or obscure language or thought; an instance of this. **L19**.
■ **esotericist** *noun* an adherent of esoteric doctrines **L19**.

esoterism /ɪˈsɒtərɪz(ə)m/ *noun*. **M19**.
[ORIGIN from Greek *esōterō*: see ESOTERIC, -ISM.]
= ESOTERICISM.
■ **esotery** /ˈɛsət(ə)ri/ *noun* esoteric doctrine or knowledge **M18**.

esotropia /ɛsəˈtrəʊpɪə/ *noun*. **L19**.
[ORIGIN from Greek *esō* (see ESOTERIC) + *tropē* turning (noun) + -IA[1].]
MEDICINE. Convergent strabismus.

esox /ˈiːsɒks/ *noun*. **E16**.
[ORIGIN Latin from Gaulish.]
A large freshwater fish, *esp.* a pike. Now only as mod. Latin genus name.

ESP *abbreviation*.
1 English for special purposes.
2 Extrasensory perception.

espacement /ɪˈspeɪsm(ə)nt, ɛ-/ *noun*. **M19**.
[ORIGIN French, from *espacer* SPACE *verb*: see -MENT.]
1 The action of spacing, or of placing at suitable intervals. **M19**.
2 The distance at which trees or crops are set apart when planted. **M20**.

espada /eˈspaða, ɛˈspɑːdə/ *noun*. Pl. **-as** /-as, -əz/. **E18**.
[ORIGIN Spanish from Latin *spatha* sword, SPATHE.]
†**1** A Spanish sword. *rare*. Only in **E18**.
2 A matador. **L19**.

espadon /ɛspəˈdɒn/ *noun*. **M19**.
[ORIGIN French from Italian *spadone* augm. of *spada* sword from Latin *spatha* sword, SPATHE.]
hist. A large two-handled sword of the 15th to 17th cents.

espadrille /ɛspəˈdrɪl, ˈɛspədrɪl/ *noun*. **L19**.
[ORIGIN French from Provençal *espardi(l)hos*, from *espart* esparto.]
A light canvas shoe with plaited fibre sole, orig. worn in the Pyrenees; an alpargata.

espagnole /ɛspaɲɔl/ *noun*. **M19**.
[ORIGIN French (fem.), lit. 'Spanish', from Old French *espaignol*, *espaigneul*: see SPANIEL.]
In full ***espagnole sauce***. A simple brown sauce.

espagnolette /ɪˌspanjəˈlɛt, ɛ-/ *noun*. **E19**.
[ORIGIN French, from *espagnol* Spanish: see ESPAGNOLE, -ETTE.]
A kind of bolt used for fastening French windows, in which a single handle operates fasteners at the top and bottom of the window.

espalier /ɪˈspaljə, ɛ-/ *noun & verb*. **M17**.
[ORIGIN French from Italian *spalliera*, from *spalla* shoulder from Latin SPATULA, (in late Latin) shoulder blade.]
▸ **A** *noun*. **1** A fruit tree or ornamental shrub trained on a lattice or a framework of stakes. **M17**.
†**2** A row of trees or shrubs trained in this way. Only in **E18**.
3 A lattice or framework, or one of the stakes, on which a tree or shrub is trained. **M18**.
▸ **B** *verb trans.* Train as an espalier. **E19**.

esparcet /ɪˈspɑːsɪt, ɛ-/ *noun*. Long *rare*. **M17**.
[ORIGIN French *esparcette*, †*-et*, from Old French *espars* (mod. *épars*) from Latin *sparsus* SPARSE *adjective*: see -ETTE.]
A kind of sainfoin.

esparto /ɛˈspɑːtəʊ, ɪ-/ *noun*. Pl. **-os**. **M19**.
[ORIGIN Spanish from Latin *spartum* from Greek *sparton* rope.]
A tough grass, *Stipa tenacissima*, growing in Spain and N. Africa and used in paper-making. Also ***esparto grass***.

†**espaulement** *noun* var. of EPAULEMENT.

especial /ɪˈspɛʃ(ə)l, ɛ-/ *adjective*. **LME**.
[ORIGIN Old French (mod. *spécial*) from Latin *specialis*: see SPECIAL.]
1 Special as opp. to general. Formerly also, particular, individual, specific; provided for a particular purpose. *arch.* **LME**.

SHAKES. *Oth.* There is especial commission come from Venice. S. RICHARDSON I shall dispatch what I shall farther write . . by an especial messenger.

in especial in particular, especially, particularly.
2 Pre-eminent, exceptional. *obsolete* in *pred.* use. **LME**.

J. TYNDALL One fact of especial importance. I. MURDOCH He had always known and knew it now with an especial terror.

3 Pertaining chiefly to one particular person or thing. **M19**.

B. JOWETT I must repeat one thing . . for your especial benefit.

■ **especialness** *noun* (long *rare* or *obsolete*) **E17**.

especially /ɪˈspɛʃ(ə)li, ɛ-/ *adverb*. **LME**.
[ORIGIN from ESPECIAL + -LY[2].]
In an especial manner, to an especial degree; chiefly, more than in other cases.

†**espeler** *noun*. *rare*. **L15–E18**.
[ORIGIN Unknown. Cf. SPELLER *noun*[2].]
= SPILLER *noun*[2].

†**espelers** *noun pl.* see SPELLER *noun*[2].

E

E

esperance /ˈɛsp(ə)r(ə)ns/ *noun*. LME.
[ORIGIN Old French & mod. French *espérance*, from *espérer* to hope from Latin *sperare*: see -ANCE.]
Expectation, hope. *obsolete* exc. *hist.* as the motto of the Percy family, used as a battle cry.

SHAKES. *1 Hen. IV* Now Esperance! Percy! And set on.

Esperanto /ɛspəˈrantəʊ/ *noun & adjective*. L19.
[ORIGIN from Dr *Esperanto* (Esperanto for 'Hoping One'), pen name of its inventor (see below).]
(Of) an artificial language invented in 1887 for universal use by the Polish physician Dr L. L. Zamenhof (1859–1917), and based on roots common to the chief European languages with endings standardized.
■ **Esperantist** *noun* a person who knows Esperanto or advocates its use as a world language E20.

espial /ɪˈspʌɪ(ə)l, ɛ-/ *noun*. LME.
[ORIGIN Old French *espiaille* action of spying, (in pl.) spies, from *espier* ESPY: see -AL¹.]
1 a The action or an act of spying or keeping watch. *arch.* LME. ▸**b** The action of espying; the fact of being espied. L16.

a DICKENS The Captain . . cut a small hole of espial in the wall. **b** M. INNES She must slip to the other side and risk espial from the house.

†**2** A body of spies; a spy, a scout. LME–E19.

espiegle /ɪˈspjeɪg(ə)l, *foreign* ɛspjɛgl/ *adjective*. Now *rare*. E19.
[ORIGIN French *(Ul)espiegle* from Dutch *Uilenspiegel* (= German *Eulenspiegel*), from *uil* OWL *noun* + *spiegel* mirror from Latin *speculum*. Cf. *owlglass* s.v. OWL *noun*.]
Frolicsome, roguish.
■ **espieglerie** *noun* frolicsomeness, roguishness E19.

espionage /ˈɛspɪənɑːʒ, -ɪdʒ/ *noun*. L18.
[ORIGIN French *espionnage*, from *espionner* espy, from *espion* SPY *noun*: see -AGE.]
The practice of spying or using spies, esp. to obtain secret information.
INDUSTRIAL espionage.

esplanade /ɛspləˈneɪd, -ˈnɑːd/ *noun*. L16.
[ORIGIN French from Italian *spianata* from fem. of Latin *explanatus* flattened, levelled, pa. pple of *explanare*: see EXPLAIN, -ADE.]
1 *FORTIFICATION*. **a** The glacis of a counterscarp. Formerly, an area of flat ground on the top of a rampart. L16. ▸**b** A level open space separating a citadel from the town that it commands. E18.
2 *gen.* Any level open space, *esp.* one where the public may walk; a road along the seafront of a resort. L17.

F. MUIR Virginia Water . . had in its esplanade of shops a . . coin-operated drycleaners.

esplees /ɪˈspliːz, ɛ-/ *noun pl.* M17.
[ORIGIN Anglo-Norman *esple(t)z* pl. of Old French *espleit*, *esploit* revenue: see EXPLOIT *noun*.]
The crops, rents, services, etc., obtained from land; the land yielding these.

†**espontoon** *noun*. L18–M19.
[ORIGIN French *esponton*: see SPONTOON.]
= SPONTOON.

espousal /ɪˈspaʊz(ə)l, ɛ-/ *noun*. LME.
[ORIGIN Old French *espousaille* sing. of *espousailles* (mod. *épousailles*) from Latin *sponsalia* betrothal, use as noun of neut. pl. of *sponsalis* adjective, from *spons-*: see ESPOUSE, -AL¹. In sense 4 also infl. by ESPOUSE *verb*.]
1 In *pl.* & †*sing.* (The celebration of) a marriage or betrothal. *arch.* LME.
†**2** *sing.* & in *pl.* The marriage vows; the married state. Chiefly in ***break one's espousal***, ***hold espousal***. LME–L16.
†**3** An espoused person; a husband, a wife. L15–E17.
4 The action or an act of espousing a cause etc. Foll. by *of*. L17.

HOR. WALPOLE Political reasons forbid the open espousal of his cause.

espouse /ɪˈspaʊz, ɛ-/ *verb trans.* LME.
[ORIGIN Old French *espouser* (mod. *épouser*) from Latin *sponsare*, from *spons-* pa. ppl stem of *spondere* betroth. Cf. SPOUSE *verb*.]
1 Take (a person, esp. a woman) as spouse; marry. LME.

HOR. WALPOLE Before Edward had espoused the lady Grey, he had been contracted to the lady Eleanor Butler.

†**2** Join in marriage (*lit.* & *fig.*). *rare*. Only in L16.

SHAKES. *2 Hen. VI* In presence of . . twenty reverend bishops, I . . was espous'd.

†**3** Betroth (a person, esp. a woman); pledge, commit. (Foll. by *to*.) E–M17.

AV *Luke* 1:27 A virgine espoused to a man whose name was Ioseph.

4 Take to oneself or make one's own (a cause, quarrel, etc.); become a supporter of (a party); adopt, embrace (a doctrine, theory, profession, way of life). E17.

M. MUGGERIDGE They . . espouse all the right causes— . . divorce reform, raising the school age, abolition of capital punishment. P. ACKROYD A man . . who espoused the principles of classical order and hierarchy.

■ **espouser** *noun* (**a**) a person who espouses a cause etc.; a supporter; †(**b**) a person who brings about an espousal or espouses a woman: M17.

espressivo /ɛsprɛˈsiːvəʊ/ *adverb & adjective*. L19.
[ORIGIN Italian, from Latin *expressus*: see EXPRESS *adjective, adverb, & noun*².]
MUSIC. (Performed) with expression of feeling.

espresso /ɛˈsprɛsəʊ/ *noun*. Pl. **-os**. M20.
[ORIGIN Italian *(caffè) espresso*, from *espresso* squeezed, pressed out, from Latin *expressus*: see EXPRESS *adjective, adverb, & noun*².]
1 Coffee made by forcing steam through ground coffee beans. M20.
2 A coffee bar etc. where such coffee is sold. Also ***espresso bar***, ***espresso cafe***, etc. M20.

espringal /ɪˈsprɪŋg(ə)l, ɛ-/ *noun*. *obsolete* exc. *hist.* E17.
[ORIGIN Old French & mod. French *espringale*, from *espringuer* to spring, dance from Frankish *springan* SPRING *verb*¹.]
A medieval military machine for throwing stones, bolts, and other missiles.

esprit /ɛspri, ɛˈspriː, ˈɛspriː/ *noun*. L16.
[ORIGIN French from Latin *spiritus* SPIRIT *noun*.]
Vivacious wit.
esprit de corps /də ˈkɔː/ [see CORPS] regard for the honour and interests of the body to which one belongs; team spirit. ***esprit de l'escalier*** /də lɛskalje/ [lit. 'of the steps'] a clever remark that occurs to one after the opportunity to make it is lost. ***esprit fort*** /fɔːr/, pl. **-s -s** (pronounced same), [= strong] a strong-minded person, *esp.* one who claims independence of thought. ***point d'esprit***: see POINT *noun*².

espy /ɪˈspʌɪ, ɛ-/ *verb*. ME.
[ORIGIN Old French *espier* (mod. *épier*): see SPY *verb*.]
1 *verb trans.* Discover by looking out; catch sight of, esp. at a distance; descry, discern; detect (a flaw etc.). ME. ▸**b** Perceive by chance or unexpectedly. L15.

AV *Gen.* 42:27 As one of them opened his sack . . , he espied his money. SWIFT The seamen espied a rock within half a cable's length of the ship. J. WESLEY These skilful wrestlers espy the smallest slip we make.

2 *verb intrans.* & †*trans.* Act as a spy (on); keep a look out (for); make a close examination (of). *arch.* LME.

R. GREENE Espy her loves, and who she liketh best.

Esq. *abbreviation*.
Esquire.

†**esquadron** *noun*. L16–M18.
[ORIGIN Old French (mod. *escadron*), formed as SQUADRON.]
A squadron of cavalry.

-esque /ɛsk/ *suffix*.
[ORIGIN Repr. French *-esque* from Italian *-esco* from medieval Latin *-iscus*.]
In and forming adjectives with the sense 'resembling in style or characteristics', as ***arabesque***, ***burlesque***, ***Daliesque***, ***romanesque***, etc.

Esquimau *noun & adjective* var. of ESKIMO.

esquire /ɪˈskwʌɪə, ɛ-/ *noun*. Earlier as SQUIRE *noun*¹. LME.
[ORIGIN Old French *esquier* (mod. *écuyer*) from Latin *scutarius* shield-bearer, from *scutum* shield: see -ARY¹.]
1 Orig. (now *hist.*), a young nobleman who, in training for knighthood, acted as shield-bearer and attendant to a knight. Later, a man belonging to the higher order of English gentry, ranking next below a knight. LME. ▸**b** *hist.* Any of various officers in the service of a king or nobleman. L15. ▸**c** A landed proprietor, a country squire. *arch.* L16.

T. H. WHITE The exaggerated courtesy which was expected of pages before they became esquires on their way to knighthood. **b** *Notes & Queries* In 1536 Heneage took over Norris' post of esquire of the King's body.

2 A title of courtesy (now only in formal use and in addresses of letters) placed after the name of a man (orig. one with the rank of esquire, sense 1a or b) when no other title is used; *N. Amer.* a title appended to a lawyer's surname. Abbreviation **Esq.** LME.
3 A man who escorts a woman in public. Now *rare*. E19.
■ **esquireship** *noun* the rank of esquire; the service of an esquire: E17. **esquiress** *noun* a female armour-bearer or page L16.

esquire /ɪˈskwʌɪə, ɛ-/ *verb trans. rare*. M17.
[ORIGIN from the noun.]
1 Raise to the rank of esquire. M17.
2 Escort (a lady). L18.
3 Address as 'Esquire'. L19.

†**esquiry** *noun* var. of EQUERRY.

esquisse /ɛskis/ *noun*. Pl. pronounced same. M18.
[ORIGIN French from Italian *schizzo*: see SKETCH *noun*¹.]
A rough or preliminary sketch.

ESR *abbreviation*.
PHYSICS. Electron spin resonance.

esraj /ɛˈsrɑːdʒ/ *noun*. E20.
[ORIGIN Bengali *esrāj*.]
A three- or four-stringed Indian musical instrument with added sympathetic strings.

esrog *noun*, **esrogim** *noun pl.* see ETROG *noun*¹.

ess /ɛs/ *noun*¹. M16.
[ORIGIN Repr. pronunc. of *S*, *s* as the letter's name.]
The letter S, s; something S-shaped.
collar of esses: see COLLAR *noun*.

Ess /ɛs/ *noun*². M19.
[ORIGIN from French ESSENCE *noun*.]
In full ***Ess Bouquet***. A kind of perfume.

-ess /ɛs, ɪs/ *suffix*¹.
[ORIGIN Repr. French *-esse* from Proto-Romance from late Latin *-issa* from Greek.]
In and forming nouns denoting females, as ***actress***, ***adulteress***, ***countess***, ***goddess***, ***lioness***, etc., sometimes with the sense 'wife of', as ***ambassadress***, ***mayoress***, etc.
– NOTE: Nouns in *-er*, *-or*, etc., which are not sex-specific, where such exist, are now often preferred, and the forms ending in ***-ess*** may seem dated or sexist.

-ess /ɛs/ *suffix*² (not productive).
[ORIGIN Repr. Old French *-esse*, *-ece* from Latin *-itia*: cf. -ICE¹.]
In nouns of quality formed from adjectives, as ***duress***, ***largess***, etc.

essart /ɪˈsɑːt, ɛ-/ *noun*. M19.
[ORIGIN Old French, = Anglo-Norman ASSART *noun*.]
hist. = ASSART *noun* 1.

essart /ɪˈsɑːt, ɛ-/ *verb trans. & intrans. obsolete* exc. *hist.* E18.
[ORIGIN Old French *essarter*: see ASSART *verb*.]
= ASSART *verb*.

essay /ˈɛseɪ/ *noun*. L16.
[ORIGIN Old French & mod. French *essai*, from *essayer*: see ESSAY *verb*. Cf. ASSAY *noun*.]
▸ **I 1** A trial, a test; an experiment. L16.

A. BEVAN At this point an essay in collective action was tried.

2 = ASSAY *noun* 5. *obsolete* exc. *hist.* L16.
3 A trial specimen, a sample; an example; a rehearsal. Now only *spec.* in *PHILATELY*, a trial design of a stamp yet to be accepted. E17.
†**4** *HUNTING*. The breast of a deer, the part in which its fatness was tested; the testing of a deer's fatness. Only in 17.
▸ **II 5** An attempt, an endeavour. (Foll. by *at*, *in*; *to do*.) L16.

C. S. FORESTER The hand which he extended to the door missed its objective at the first essay.

6 A short prose composition on any subject. L16.

D. LODGE They . . handed in . . essays written in the style of F. R. Leavis.

†**7** A first tentative attempt at learning, composition, etc.; a first draft. M17–L18.

DRYDEN The first of Homer's Iliads (which I intended as an Essay to the whole work.)

■ **essay'ette** *noun* a short essay L19. **e'ssayical** *adjective* essayistic M19. **essayism** *noun* the writing of essays; essayistic quality: E19. **essaylet** *noun* = ESSAYETTE L19.

essay /ɛˈseɪ/ *verb*. L15.
[ORIGIN Alt. of ASSAY *verb* by assim. to Old French & mod. French *essayer* from Proto-Romance, from late Latin *exagium* weighing, a weight, from Latin *exag-* base of *exigere*: see EXACT *adjective*.]
1 *verb trans.* = ASSAY *verb* 1, 6. *arch.* L15.

POPE She . . No arts essay'd, but not to be admir'd.

2 *verb trans. & intrans.* Attempt to accomplish or perform (a deed, task, etc.); make an attempt (at); undertake or try *to do*. M16.

P. G. WODEHOUSE Valerie Twisleton was about to essay the mad task of defying this woman. G. GREENE Only Mrs Smith had essayed violence. A. BURGESS These pieces . . which essayed serious art, got nowhere. A. HAILEY They had even essayed some sex. E. BOWEN Several foreign firms, having essayed to set up factories in Dublin, decamped.

†**3** = ASSAY *verb* 4. L17–E19.
■ **essayer** *noun* (**a**) an assayer; †(**b**) a person who attempts to treat a certain subject or form of composition; an essayist: L16.

essayist /ˈɛseɪɪst/ *noun*. E17.
[ORIGIN from ESSAY *noun*, *verb* + -IST.]
1 A writer of essays. E17.
2 A person who carries out tests or trials. (Foll. by *of*.) Now *rare* or *obsolete*. M18.
■ **essay'istic**, **essay'istical** *adjectives* in the style of a literary essay; discursive, informal: M19.

esse /ˈɛsi/ *noun*. M16.
[ORIGIN Latin, use as noun of *esse* be.]
Essential nature, essence, esp. as opp. to BENE ESSE.

Listener No Anglican could possibly dream of claiming that Establishment . . is of the *esse* of the Church.

IN ESSE.

essence /ˈɛs(ə)ns/ *noun*. LME.
[ORIGIN Old French & mod. French from Latin *essentia*, irreg. from *esse* be + after Greek *ousia* being, from *ont-* pres. ppl stem of *einai* be: see -ENCE.]
1 *THEOLOGY*. The uniquely triune intrinsic nature of God, in respect of which the three persons of the Trinity are one. LME.
2 The substance of which something consists, *esp.* a celestial or elemental substance. LME.
3 The intrinsic nature or character of something; that which makes it what it is; the attributes, constituents, etc., that something must have for it not to be something

else and that serve to characterize it. LME. ▸**b** The most important or indispensable quality or element of anything. L16.

N. MITFORD The whole tradition is in its essence monastic. J. M. COETZEE He is neither cannibal nor laundryman, these are mere names, they do not touch his essence. **b** H. BELLOC He was carefully warned that surprise was the essence of this charming tradition. T. E. HULME The essence of poetry to most people is that it must lead them to a beyond of some kind. I. MURDOCH What goes on inwardly in the soul is the essence of each man, it's what makes us individual people.

nominal essence: of an abstract or conceptual entity. **real essence**: of something perceptible by the senses.
†**4** In ancient and medieval philosophy, an element additional to the four elements of the material world; = QUINTESSENCE 1. Chiefly in ***fifth essence***. LME–M19.
5 A distillate or extract from a plant or medicinal substance, having its active constituents or characteristic properties in a concentrated form; perfume, scent, etc., esp. as an alcoholic solution of volatile substances. E16.

J. GALSWORTHY The odour of flowers, . . of essences that women love, rose suffocatingly in the heat.

bath essence, ***coffee essence***, ***vanilla essence***, etc.
6 A spiritual or abstract entity. Formerly, anything (abstract or material) that exists. L16.

SHAKES. *Oth.* Her honour is an essence that's not seen.

7 The foundation of a thing's existence; the reality underlying phenomena. L16.

M. H. ABRAMS Art imitates the world of appearance and not of Essence. E. M. FORSTER It is unmanageable because it is a romance, and its essence is romantic beauty.

†**8** Existence regarded as a fact or as a property possessed by something. L16–L17.
†**9** Importance. E–M17.
– PHRASES & COMB.: **essence-peddler** *US* (*a*) a pedlar of medicines; (*b*) a skunk. **in essence** fundamentally, essentially. **of the essence (of)**, **the essence (of)** indispensable or important (to).

essence /ˈɛs(ə)ns/ *verb trans.* Now *rare*. M17.
[ORIGIN from the noun.]
Perfume with essence.

Essene /ˈɛsiːn/ *noun*. LME.
[ORIGIN Latin *Esseni* pl. from Greek *Essēnoi*, perh. from Aramaic.]
A member of a Jewish ascetic sect of the 1st cent. BC and the 1st cent. AD who lived communally and are widely regarded as the authors of the Dead Sea Scrolls.
■ **E'ssenian** *noun & adjective* †(*a*) *noun* = Essene; (*b*) *adjective* of, pertaining to, or resembling the Essenes: E18. **E'ssenic** *adjective* of the nature of Essenism M19. **E'ssenical** *adjective* (now *rare* or *obsolete*) = ESSENIC M17. **Essenism** *noun* the doctrine and practice of the Essenes; an Essenic tendency: M19.

essenhout /ˈɛs(ə)n(h)əʊt/ *noun*. *S. Afr.* E19.
[ORIGIN Afrikaans from Middle Dutch *eschenhout*, from *esch* ASH *noun*¹ + *hout* timber: see HOLT *noun*¹.]
= ESSENWOOD.

essential /ɪˈsɛnʃ(ə)l/ *adjective & noun*. ME.
[ORIGIN Late Latin *essentialis*, from Latin *essentia*: see ESSENCE *noun*, -IAL.]
▸ **A** *adjective*. **1** That is such in the absolute or highest sense. ME. ▸†**b** Thorough, complete. E17–E18.

W. SPARROW The love of God is essentiall happiness. **b** T. DEKKER He's a most essentiall gentleman.

2 Of or pertaining to a thing's essence. LME.
essential difference *LOGIC* = DIFFERENTIA.
3 †**a** Dependent on the intrinsic character of something. E16–L19. ▸**b** *MEDICINE*. Of hypertension or (formerly) any disease: of unknown cause. L19.
4 Absolutely indispensable or necessary. E16.

T. THOMSON Silica . . is an essential ingredient in mortar. I. MURDOCH It was . . essential that he should leave her alone. H. READ A certain complexity of experience is essential to eloquence. *Observer* It is not essential for our people to know everything.

essential amino acid, **essential fatty acid**: needed for growth but not synthesized by the body.
5 Constituting or forming part of a thing's essence; fundamental to its composition. M16. ▸**b** Affecting the essence of anything; significant, important. L18.

P. TILLICH It is a consequence of that which is not his essential being but is accidental in him. A. LURIE It's the essential part of my work, without which there wouldn't be . . any stories. M. HUNTER The mere fact of being human implies an essential loneliness in each of us. **b** N. PEVSNER The persistence over two hundred years of the Perpendicular style without any essential changes.

†**6** Having existence; real, actual. M16–M17.
7 Of the nature of or resembling an essence, extract, or perfume. M17.
essential oil a volatile oil obtained by distillation and having the characteristic odour of the plant etc. from which it is extracted.
8 *MUSIC*. (Of a note) belonging to the chord, as opp. to a passing note, appoggiatura, etc.; (of a sharp or flat) in the key signature, not accidental. E18.
▸ **B** *noun*. **1** An indispensable or fundamental characteristic, element, or thing. Usu. in *pl.* Formerly also (in *pl.*), the three vows of chastity, poverty, and obedience indispensable to monastic life. LME.

G. MAXWELL I had brought with me on my back the essentials of living for a day or two while I prospected.

†**2** Existence, being. *rare*. L15–M17.
■ **essentialize** *verb trans.* †(*a*) *rare* give essence or being to; (*b*) formulate in essential form, express the essential form of: M17. **essentialness** *noun* M17.

essentialism /ɪˈsɛnʃ(ə)lɪz(ə)m/ *noun*. M20.
[ORIGIN from ESSENTIAL + -ISM.]
1 *PHILOSOPHY*. A belief that things have a set of characteristics which make them what they are, and that the task of science and philosophy is their discovery and expression; the doctrine that essence is prior to existence (cf. EXISTENTIALISM). M20.
2 The view that all children should be taught on traditional lines the ideas and methods regarded as essential to the prevalent culture. M20.

essentialist /ɪˈsɛnʃ(ə)lɪst/ *noun & adjective*. E18.
[ORIGIN formed as ESSENTIALISM + -IST.]
▸ **A** *noun*. †**1** A nonjuror who believed that the usages omitted from the 1552 Prayer Book were essential. *rare*. Only in E18.
2 A person who follows or advocates essentialism. M20.
▸ **B** *adjective*. Of or pertaining to essentialism. M20.

essentiality /ɪˌsɛnʃɪˈalɪti/ *noun*. LME.
[ORIGIN Late Latin *essentialitas*, formed as ESSENTIAL: see -ITY.]
1 Essence, intrinsic nature. LME.
2 The quality or fact of being essential; necessity. M17.
3 An essential point or element. Formerly, an essential quality. Now only in *pl.* M17.

essentially /ɪˈsɛnʃ(ə)li/ *adverb*. LME.
[ORIGIN from ESSENTIAL + -LY².]
1 In essence or character. LME.

BARONESS ORCZY A cool, balmy, late summer's night, essentially English in its suggestion of moisture. A. S. BYATT We try to see things as they *are, essentially*, not as they first appear to be.

†**2** On the grounds of the actual nature of something or someone. L16–E17.
†**3** In fact, really. *rare* (Shakes.). Only in L16.
4 With respect to the essential points; substantially, fundamentally; indispensably. M18.

G. B. SHAW Joan was persecuted essentially as she would be persecuted today.

essenwood /ˈɛs(ə)nwʊd/ *noun*. L19.
[ORIGIN Partial translation of Afrikaans ESSENHOUT.]
Either of two large African evergreen trees of the mahogany family, *Ekebergia capensis* and *Trichilia emetica*, whose wood is used for furniture.

†**essera** *noun*. M16–E19.
[ORIGIN mod. Latin (whence French *essère*) from Arabic *aš-šarā* (the) dry scab, itch.]
A rash similar to that caused by nettles; a variety of nettle rash.

Essex /ˈɛsɪks/ *adjective & noun*. L16.
[ORIGIN A county in SE England.]
▸ **A** *adjective*. **1** ***Essex calf***, a calf reared in Essex; *derog.* (now *rare*), a person of that county. L16.
2 ***Essex pig***, a black pig with a white stripe round the body and white feet, of a kind formerly bred for pork and bacon; *US* a black pig of a kind bred for pork and bacon. M19.
3 ***Essex board***, a kind of fibreboard. M20.
4 ***Essex man*** (freq. *derog.*), a confident, affluent young businessman of the late 1980s, supposedly to be found esp. in the south-east of England and characterized as voting Conservative and benefiting from the entrepreneurial wealth created by Thatcherite policies. Also ***Essex girl***, a supposed type of young woman from the same milieu, variously characterized as unintelligent, promiscuous, and materialistic. L20.
▸ **B** *noun*. Pl. same. An Essex pig. L19.

essexite /ˈɛsɪksʌɪt/ *noun*. L19.
[ORIGIN from *Essex* County, Massachusetts, USA, where the first examples were found: see -ITE¹.]
GEOLOGY. A granular igneous rock typically containing labradorite and nepheline.

essive /ˈɛsɪv/ *adjective & noun*. L19.
[ORIGIN Finnish *essiivi*, from Latin ESSE: see -IVE.]
(Designating) a case in Finnish and certain other languages expressing a continuous state of being.

essoin /ɛˈsɔɪn/ *noun*. Orig. †**assoin**. ME.
[ORIGIN Old French *essoi(g)ne* (Anglo-Latin *essonium*), from *essoi(g)nier* ESSOIN *verb*.]
1 *LAW* (now *hist.*). (The offering of) an excuse for non-appearance in court at the appointed time, on grounds of illness, pilgrimage, etc. ME.
†**2** *gen.* An excuse; making of conditions, parleying, delay. ME–L16.

essoin /ɛˈsɔɪn/ *verb*. Orig. †**assoin**. ME.
[ORIGIN Old French *essoi(g)nier* from medieval Latin *exsoniare*, formed as EX-¹ + *sonia* lawful excuse, from Frankish: cf. Old High German *sunnia* hindrance = Old Saxon *sunnea* want, lack, Old Norse *syn* refusal, denial, Gothic *sunjon* to excuse.]
1 *verb trans. LAW* (now *hist.*). Excuse for non-appearance in court. Formerly also *gen.*, excuse. ME.
†**2** *verb trans. & intrans.* Avoid (a person); shun contact (with). Only in ME.
†**3** *verb intrans.* Excuse oneself, decline, refuse. LME–L15.

essoinee /ɛsɔɪˈniː/ *noun*. M17.
[ORIGIN from ESSOIN *verb* + -EE¹.]
LAW (now *hist.*). A person who had been essoined.

essoiner /ɛˈsɔɪnə/ *noun*. ME.
[ORIGIN Anglo-Norman *essoigniour*, from *essoignier*: see ESSOIN *verb*, -ER¹.]
LAW (now *hist.*). A person who offered an excuse for someone else's non-appearance in court.

essonite /ˈɛsənʌɪt/ *noun*. Also **he-** /ˈhɛ-/. E19.
[ORIGIN from Greek *hēssōn* less (as being less hard and heavy than other garnets) + -ITE¹.]
MINERALOGY. = CINNAMON ***stone***.

EST *abbreviation*.
1 Eastern Standard Time. *US*.
2 Electroshock (or electric shock) treatment.

est /ɛst/ *noun*. L20.
[ORIGIN Acronym, from Erhard Seminars Training, from the name of W. *Erhard* (b. 1935), who devised est in the US.]
A philosophy and technique aimed at developing self-awareness and a person's potential by means that include motivational methods from the world of business.

-est /ɪst/ *suffix*¹.
[ORIGIN Old English *-ost-*, *-ust-*, *-ast-*, and with umlaut *-est-*, *-st-*, both from Germanic. Cf. Greek *-isto-*, Sanskrit *iṣṭha-*.]
Forming the superl. of adjectives and adverbs, now esp. of words of one syllable and occas. of two, as ***hardest***, ***narrowest***, etc. The umlaut form survives in ***best***, ***eldest***.
– NOTE: Mod. spelling conventions are as follows: words in *-e* drop the *e*, as ***sore***: ***sorest***; a final single consonant other than *h*, *w*, or *x* is doubled if preceded by a single-letter vowel, as ***big***: ***biggest***; in most adjectives and a few adverbs in *-y* the *y* becomes *i*, as ***early***: ***earliest***, similarly in words in *-ey*, as ***gooey***: ***gooiest***.

-est /ɪst/ *suffix*². *arch.* Also **-st**.
[ORIGIN Old English *-est*, *-ast*, *-st* = Old High German *-ist* etc., Gothic *-is* etc.]
Forming the 2nd person sing. of verbs, as ***canst***, ***doest***, ***dost***, ***findest***, ***gavest***, etc.

establish /ɪˈstablɪʃ, ɛ-/ *verb*. LME.
[ORIGIN Old French *establiss-* lengthened stem of *establir* (mod. *établir*) from Latin *stabilire*, from *stabilis* STABLE *adjective*: see -ISH². See also STABLISH.]
▸ **I** *verb trans.* **1** Institute or ordain permanently by enactment or agreement; *spec.* give legal form and recognition to (a Church) as the official Church of a country. LME. ▸†**b** Secure or settle (property etc.) *on* or *upon* a person. LME–M17.

JOSEPH STRUTT This edict was established, for the regulation of the Christian army . . during the Crusade. J. SMEATON Having first established that they should quit the work at nights. **b** SHAKES. *Macb.* We will establish our estate upon Our eldest, Malcolm.

the Established Church *spec.* the Church of England or of Scotland.
2 Set up on a permanent or secure basis; bring into being, found, (a government, institution, business, etc.). LME.

W. S. CHURCHILL In 1851 the new colony of Victoria . . was established. ALDOUS HUXLEY Ask yourself what chance the loyalists ever had of establishing a liberal régime.

†**3** Make stable or firm; strengthen (*lit.* & *fig.*); ratify, confirm; restore (health). L15–E19.

J. AUSTEN Harriet's cheerful look and manner established hers.

4 Place (a person) in a secure position; put into residence or occupation; set up in business, appoint (esp. a civil servant) to a permanent post. L16. ▸†**b** Provide for the maintenance of (a dependant etc.). M17–L19.

B. TARKINGTON He expected to get his family established at the seashore by the Fourth of July. D. CECIL Recently ordained and established as a curate . . at Overton. A. POWELL The Pimleys had established themselves in a . . block of flats . . not far from Battersea Bridge.

5 Initiate and secure acceptance of (a custom, belief, etc.); gain and keep (a position, a reputation). L16. ▸**b** Introduce into a film or play and secure the identity or position of (a character, set, etc.). M20.

J. ROSENBERG Rembrandt's reputation as a portrait painter was very soon established. W. GOLDING Adults who tried to establish contact with him were never successful.

establish a suit *CARDS* play so that all one's remaining cards in a suit may take tricks.
6 Place beyond dispute; ascertain, demonstrate, prove. E18.

E

E. BOWEN This has been suspected; now it's established, known. A. FRASER It was up to him to establish who, if anyone, could help him.

▸ **II** *verb intrans.* **7** Take up residence, settle. L17.

■ **establishable** *adjective* able to be established M17. **establisher** *noun* L15.

establishment /ɪˈstablɪʃm(ə)nt, ɛ-/ *noun.* See also STABLISHMENT. L15.

[ORIGIN from ESTABLISH + -MENT.]

▸ **I** Something established.

†**1 a** A settled arrangement, an established practice; a settled constitution or government. L15–L18. ▸**b** *FRENCH HISTORY.* A code of law. E19.

2 An organized body maintained for a state purpose; the (number of) personnel of a regiment, ship, etc. L17. ▸**b** An institution or business; the premises or personnel of this. E19. ▸**c** A household; its members collectively, *esp.* the servants. E19.

b I. MURDOCH Miss Quentin was at the hairdresser . . an expensive Mayfair establishment **c** N. MONSARRAT Two maids, a chef, and an ancient gardener . . were all that was left of an establishment which had formerly numbered sixteen.

peace establishment reduced army etc. in time of peace. **war establishment** increased army etc. in time of war.

3 a (**E-**.) The ecclesiastical system established by law; the Established Church. Also ***Church Establishment.*** M18. ▸**b** (Usu. **E-**.) *The* group in society exercising authority or influence and seen as resisting change; any influential or controlling group. E20.

J. H. NEWMAN Keble, Rose, and Palmer, represented distinct parties in the Establishment. D. L. SAYERS Having been brought up in the odour of the Establishment, he was familiar with this odd dissenting peculiarity. **b** D. LODGE Radicals looking for an issue on which to confront the Establishment.

▸ **II** The action of establishing; the fact of being established.

4 A settled or stable condition, permanence; calmness of mind. M16. ▸**b** Settlement in life; *spec.* (now *rare*) marriage. L17. ▸**c** A settled income, a means of livelihood. E18.

C. MORGAN It gave her a sense of establishment to go continually to the same place. **b** J. AUSTEN He would willingly give up much wealth to obtain an early establishment. **c** W. COWPER It will afford me some sort of an establishment, at least for a time.

†**5** Something which strengthens, supports, or confirms. M16–M17.

†**6 a** The action of settling the constitution and practices of an established Church. M17–E18. ▸**b** The action of making a church an established Church; the fact or status of being an established Church. Formerly also, the legal recognition of a religious body. M17.

7 The length of time between the transit of a new or full moon across the meridian at a given place and the occurrence of the following high tide. M19.

establishmentarian /ɪˌstablɪʃm(ə)nˈtɛːrɪən/ *noun & adjective.* M19.

[ORIGIN from ESTABLISHMENT + -ARIAN.]

1 (A person) belonging to, or supporting the principle of, an established Church. M19.

2 (A person) belonging to or supporting the Establishment; (a person) having conservative views. M20.

■ **establishmentarianism** *noun* L19.

estacade /ɛstakad/ *noun.* Pl. pronounced same. E17.

[ORIGIN French from Spanish *estacada*: see STOCKADE.]

A dyke made of piles or stakes in water or marshy ground in order to impede an enemy.

estafette /ɛstafɛt/ *noun.* Pl. pronounced same. E17.

[ORIGIN French from Italian *staffetta* dim. of *staffa* stirrup, from Langobardic: see -ETTE.]

hist. A mounted courier.

estalagem /istaˈlaʒim/ *noun.* M19.

[ORIGIN Portuguese, from *estala* stable from Germanic base of STALL *noun*[1].]

A Portuguese inn.

†**estall** *verb trans.* Only in L16.

[ORIGIN Old French *estaler* place, fix, etc., in Anglo-Latin *estallare* assign terms for payment: see STALL *verb*[1], INSTALMENT *noun*[2].]

Arrange the payment of (a debt) in instalments.

†**estalment** *noun.* L16–M18.

[ORIGIN formed as STALMENT. Cf. INSTALMENT *noun*[2].]

(An) arrangement to pay by instalments; an instalment.

estamin /ˈɛstəmɪn/ *noun.* In sense 2 also **-mene**, **-mine** /-miːn/. E18.

[ORIGIN Old French *estamine* (mod. *étamine*) from Proto-Romance from Latin *staminea* use as noun of fem. of *stamineus* made of thread, from *stamen* thread.]

1 = ETAMINE. E18.

2 A twilled woollen dress fabric. M19.

estaminet /ɛstaminɛ/ *noun.* Pl. pronounced same, /-z/. E19.

[ORIGIN French from Walloon *staminé* byre, from *stamo* pole to which a cow is tethered in a stall, prob. from German *Stamm* stem, trunk.]

Orig., a cafe where smoking was allowed. Now, a small unpretentious cafe selling wine, beer, etc.

estampage /ɪˈstampɪdʒ, *foreign* ɛstɑ̃paːʒ (*pl. same*)/ *noun.* Now *rare.* L19.

[ORIGIN French, from Old French & mod. French *estamper* STAMP *verb*: see -AGE.]

ARCHAEOLOGY. An impression on paper of an inscription; *spec.* a squeeze, a rubbing.

estancia /ɛˈstansɪə; *foreign* estanˈθia, -ˈsia (*pl.*-s)/ *noun.* M17.

[ORIGIN Spanish, lit. 'station' = Old French *estance* dwelling from medieval Latin *stantia* from Latin *stant-* pres. ppl stem of *stare* to stand.]

A cattle ranch in Latin America or the southern US.

■ **estanciero** /ɛˌstansɪˈɛːrəʊ, *foreign* estanθiˈero/ *noun*, pl. **-os** /-əʊz, *foreign* -ɔs/, the keeper of an estancia, a cattle-rancher M19.

estate /ɪˈsteɪt, ɛ-/ *noun.* ME.

[ORIGIN Old French *estat* (mod. *état*), from Latin *status*: see STATE *noun*.]

▸ **I** Condition.

1 State or condition (material, moral, physical, etc.). *arch.* ME. ▸**b** A particular state, condition, or stage of life. *obsolete* exc. in certain phrs. ME.

E. A. FREEMAN The wall, in its first estate, seems to have been merely a dyke of earth and rough stones. BROWNING In prime of life, perfection of estate. F. NORRIS This was his final estate, a criminal. **b** *Book of Common Prayer* To live together . . in the holy estate of matrimony.

b man's estate manhood. **woman's estate** womanhood.

2 Condition as regards health, prosperity, etc. *arch.* LME. ▸†**b** Natural or normal condition; good condition, health, well-being. LME–L16.

H. A. L. FISHER The best and most permanent contribution which that age was able to make to the relief of man's estate.

▸ **II** Status, authority; a category of people with this.

3 Standing in the world, degree of rank or dignity; *esp.* high rank. *arch.* ME. ▸†**b** A person of high rank. LME–M17.

C. F. ALEXANDER The rich man in his castle, The poor man at his gate, God made them, high or lowly, And ordered their estate.

4 Grandeur, pomp, state. *obsolete* exc. *poet.* LME.

chair of estate, **cup of estate**, etc.: used on ceremonial or state occasions.

5 A particular class or category of people in a community or nation. Now *rare.* LME.

R. RECORDE This Rule is . . profitable for all estates of men. *Nature* The scientific estate is passing through a troubled period.

6 A class or order forming part of the body politic and sharing in government; *spec.* in Britain, each of the three estates of the Realm (see below). LME. ▸**b** In *pl.* An assembly of the governing classes or their representatives. E17.

GLADSTONE The concessions of the spiritual estate of the realm. **b** C. V. WEDGWOOD The meeting of the Dutch Estates at The Hague.

†**7** The authority of a monarch; governmental authority and administration. LME–L17.

†**8** Form of government, constitution. Only in 17.

†**9** A body politic, a state. E17–M18.

▸ **III** (A piece of) land; property.

10 Property, possessions, fortune, capital. *arch.* ME. ▸**b** The collective assets and liabilities of a person, esp. one deceased or bankrupt. M19.

b J. WAINWRIGHT A legacy . . from the estate of some uncle.

11 *LAW.* The interest that a person has in land or other property. LME.

estate in fee, ***estate tail***, etc.

12 A landed property, *esp.* a large one. M18. ▸**b** A property on which is grown a crop not native to Britain, as grapes, tea, coffee, or rubber. M19. ▸**c** A residential or industrial district planned as a whole by one owner or local authority; the aggregate of tied public houses belonging to one brewery. L19.

U. LE GUIN The family still owned an estate of seven thousand acres and fourteen villages. **b** P. V. PRICE The great wines are . . bottled at the estates where they are made. **c** C. PRIEST Now it was an estate, with thirty-six identical houses placed in a neat circular avenue.

c ***council estate***, ***housing estate***, ***industrial estate***, etc.

▸ **IV 13** In full ***estate car***, ***estate wagon***. A car designed to carry both passengers and goods, usu. with folding rear seats and a rear door in place of a boot. M20.

– PHRASES: †**after one's estate** according to one's means. ***cloth of estate***: see CLOTH *noun* 1. ***enlarge an estate***: see ENLARGE *verb*. †**make an estate of a thing** give an interest in or title to a thing *to* a person. **the estates of the realm**, **the three estates of the realm** (*a*) the three groups constituting Parliament, now the Lords Temporal (peers), the Lords Spiritual (bishops), and the Commons; (*b*) the Crown, the House of Lords, and the House of Commons. **Third Estate** (chiefly *hist.*) the English commons; the French bourgeoisie and working class before the Revolution. **fourth estate** orig., any group regarded as having power in the land; now *spec.* the press.

– COMB.: **estate agent** (*a*) a steward or manager of a landed estate; (*b*) a person who acts as agent and intermediary in the sale or lease of buildings and land; **estate-bottled** *adjective* = DOMAINE-*bottled*; ***estate car***: see sense 13 above; **estates bursar** a person in charge of the property that belongs to a college or university as endowment or investment; **estate duty** an estate tax levied in Britain between 1889 and 1975; **estate tax** a tax on the estate of a deceased person before it passes to the beneficiaries, such as inheritance tax in Britain; ***estate wagon***: see sense 13 above.

estate /ɪˈsteɪt, ɛ-/ *verb trans.* Now *rare* or *obsolete.* L16.

[ORIGIN from the noun.]

†**1** Bestow as an estate *on* or *upon*; let (land) *out.* L16–M17.

SHAKES. *Mids. N. D.* All my right of her I do estate unto Demetrius.

2 Establish (a person) in an estate; endow *with* possessions. E17. ▸†**b** Provide with an estate or property. E–M17.

JASPER MAYNE I have estated her in all I have.

†**3** Put into a particular state or condition; establish (*in*). E17–E18.

estated /ɪˈsteɪtɪd, ɛ-/ *adjective.* E17.

[ORIGIN from ESTATE *noun*, *verb* + -ED[2], -ED[1].]

Having wealth or (esp. landed) property.

esteem /ɪˈstiːm, ɛ-/ *noun.* ME.

[ORIGIN Old French & mod. French *estime*, from *estimer*: see ESTEEM *verb*.]

†**1** Value, worth; reputation. ME–E19.

W. IRVING All these were of precious esteem, being family reliques.

†**2** Estimate, valuation; estimated value. E16–L17.

J. BARGRAVE They put an esteem upon them, and I [was] made pay dear for them.

3 Estimation, opinion, judgement. *arch.* L16.

L. P. HARTLEY She sank in his esteem . . below the already lowly position occupied by women as a class.

4 Favourable opinion, regard, respect. E17.

M. MUGGERIDGE Something too banal to be taken seriously or held in esteem.

parity of esteem: see PARITY *noun*[1] 1.

esteem /ɪˈstiːm, ɛ-/ *verb.* LME.

[ORIGIN Old French & mod. French *estimer* from Latin *aestimare* estimate, assess.]

†**1** *verb trans.* Estimate the number, quantity, or magnitude of. (Foll. by *at*, *to*, *to be*.) LME–E18.

†**2 a** *verb trans.* Assign a value to; assess, appraise; *fig.* assess the merit of. LME–L18. ▸**b** *verb trans.* Judge, form an opinion of. M16–E17. ▸**c** *verb intrans.* Have a (specified) opinion *of*; be of the opinion *that*. M16–M18.

3 *verb trans.* Regard as being; consider *as*, *to be*. E16.

J. GALSWORTHY Black and mauve for evening wear was esteemed very chaste. SAKI The sort of secretary that any public man would esteem as a treasure.

4 *verb trans.* Hold in (favourable or unfavourable) estimation; think (highly, little) of. M16. ▸**b** Think highly of, respect. M16. ▸†**c** Regard as important. L16–M17.

G. GORER In a great many cases the presence or absence of a factor are quite differently esteemed. **b** D. CECIL A man she esteemed rather than loved. *Belfast Telegraph* Fellow workers . . regret the death of the brother of their esteemed colleague . . and tender deepest sympathy.

■ †**esteemable** *adjective* estimable, highly regarded E17–M18. **esteemer** *noun* M16.

ester /ˈɛstə/ *noun.* M19.

[ORIGIN German, prob. from *Essig* vinegar (from Latin *acetum*) + *Äther* ether.]

CHEMISTRY. Any organic compound in which a hydrogen atom in an acid is replaced by an alkyl, aryl, etc., group, as in fats and essential oils.

N. G. CLARK Lower, volatile esters are responsible for the fragrance and flavour of most fruits and flowers.

■ **esterase** /ˈɛstəreɪz/ *noun* an enzyme which hydrolyses an ester into an acid and an alcohol, phenol, etc. E20. **esterification** /ɪˌstɛrɪfɪˈkeɪʃ(ə)n, ɛ-/ *noun* the process of forming an ester; conversion of an acid into an ester: L19. **esterify** /ɪˈstɛrɪfʌɪ, ɛ-/ *verb trans.* convert into an ester E20.

Esth /ɛsθ, ɛst/ *noun & adjective.* Now *rare.* M19.

[ORIGIN German.]

= ESTONIAN.

Esth. *abbreviation.*

Esther (in the Bible & Apocrypha).

esthesis *noun*, **esthete** *noun*, **esthetic** *adjective & noun*, etc.

see AESTHESIS etc.

esthiomene /ɛsθɪˈɒmiːn/ *noun.* LME.

[ORIGIN medieval Latin *esthiomenus* from Greek *esthiomenos* pres. pple pass. or middle of *esthiein* eat.]

Orig., gangrene; a gangrenous sore. Now, (the ulcerated genital lesions of) the disease lymphogranuloma venereum.

†**Esthonian** *adjective & noun* var. of ESTONIAN.

estimable /ˈɛstɪməb(ə)l/ *adjective.* L15.

[ORIGIN Old French & mod. French from Latin *aestimabilis*, from *aestimare*: see ESTEEM *verb*, -ABLE. Earlier in INESTIMABLE.]

†**1** Able to be estimated, valued, or appraised. L15–E19.

†**2** Valuable; of great worth. L16–E19.

†**3** Important. L16–M18.

4 Worthy of esteem or regard. L17.

Discover Her views have put her at odds with the estimable Donald Johnson.

■ **estimableness** *noun* M18. **estimably** *adverb* M19.

estimate /ˈɛstɪmət/ *noun*. LME.
[ORIGIN from the verb, or perh. from Latin *aestimatus* verbal noun, from *aestimare*: see ESTEEM *verb*, -ATE[1].]
†1 Intellectual ability or comprehension. Only in LME.
†2 The action or an act of valuing or appraising; (a) valuation. M16–L17.
†3 Repute, reputation. L16–M17.
4 A judgement of the character or qualities of a person or thing, or of a state of affairs etc.; estimation, opinion. L16.

T. HARDY The journey was a fearfully heavy one . . at her own estimate. P. LARKIN He was mistaken if he expected her to be flattered by his estimate of her.

5 An approximate judgement of the number, quantity, position, etc., of something; the number etc. so assigned. M17. ▸b In *pl. The* statements of proposed public expenditure that the British Government presents to Parliament each year. M18.

G. BERKELEY The estimates we make of the distance of objects. LYNDON B. JOHNSON The police estimate of the total crowd . . was more than a quarter of a million.

6 A statement produced by a contractor or other tradesman of the price he or she expects to charge or will charge for doing a specified job; the price so stated. M18.

estimate /ˈɛstɪmeɪt/ *verb trans.* Pa. pple **-ated**, †**-ate**. L15.
[ORIGIN Latin *aestimat-* pa. ppl stem of *aestimare*: see ESTEEM *verb*, -ATE[3].]
†1 = ESTEEM *verb* 4. L15–M18.
†2 = ESTEEM *verb* 3. *rare*. M16–L18.
†3 Assign a value to; assess, appraise. L16–M18.
4 Form an opinion of; gauge. M17.

S. JOHNSON While an author is yet living, we estimate his powers by his worst performance.

5 Form a numerical estimate of or *that*; put *at* a specified number etc. by estimation; judge by estimation *to be* etc. M17.

A. CARNEGIE The loss . . was estimated at fully a third of the total quantity. B. RUSSELL Remains . . estimated to belong to a period about one million years ago. J. HILTON He pondered, . . calculating distances, estimating times and speeds. P. D. JAMES He estimated that Lampart would arrive in about five minutes. N. CHOMSKY An estimated 70,000 people took part.

estimation /ɛstɪˈmeɪʃ(ə)n/ *noun*. LME.
[ORIGIN Old French, or Latin *aestimatio(n-)*, formed as ESTIMATE *verb*: see -ATION.]
†1 Comprehension, intuition. Only in LME.
†2 The action of valuing or assessing; a statement of price or value; (a) valuation. LME–L18. ▸b Estimated value; a valuable. M16–L18.
3 The process of forming an approximate judgement of the number, quantity, position, etc., of something. LME.
4 Opinion, judgement, esp. as to the worth or character of a person or thing. LME. ▸†b Conjecture, guessing. *rare* (Shakes.). Only in L16.

J. LONDON Martin took a great slump in Maria's estimation.

5 Appreciation, esteem; repute; the importance of a place. *arch.* M16.

G. CANNING Wishing to know in what estimation he was held by mankind.

estimative /ˈɛstɪmətɪv/ *adjective*. Now *rare*. LME.
[ORIGIN Old French *estimatif*, *-ive* or medieval Latin *estimativus*, formed as ESTIMATE *verb*: see -IVE.]
1 Adapted for estimating; capable of estimating. LME.
†2 Estimated. E–M17.

estimator /ˈɛstɪmeɪtə/ *noun*. E17.
[ORIGIN Latin *aestimator*, formed as ESTIMATE *verb*: see -OR.]
1 A person who estimates. E17.
2 STATISTICS. A method for arriving at an estimate of a value; a quantity used or evaluated as such an estimate. M20.

estimatory /ɛstɪˈmeɪt(ə)ri/ *adjective*. M18.
[ORIGIN from ESTIMATOR or Latin *aestimatorius*, formed as ESTIMATOR: see -ORY[2].]
Involving or of the nature of an estimate.

estival *adjective*, **estivate** *verb*, **estivation** *noun*, etc. see AESTIVAL etc.

estoc /ˈɛstɒk/ *noun*. M19.
[ORIGIN Old French & mod. French, prob. from Old French *estochier* lunge (mod. *estoquer* wound (a bull) mortally) from Middle Dutch, Middle Low German *stoken*: see STOKER.]
hist. A short sword used for thrusting.

estocada /estoˈkaθa, ɛstəˈkɑːdə/ *noun*. E20.
[ORIGIN Spanish, from *estoque* sword (from Old French & mod. French ESTOC) + *-ada* -ADE.]
BULLFIGHTING. The thrust that finally kills the bull.

estoile /ɪˈstɔɪl, ɛ-/ *noun*. L16.
[ORIGIN Old French (mod. *étoile*) from Latin *stella* star.]
HERALDRY. A charge in the form of a star with (usu. six) wavy points or rays.

Estonian /ɪˈstəʊnɪən, ɛ-/ *adjective & noun*. Also †**Esthonian**. E18.
[ORIGIN from mod. Latin *Est(h)onia*, from ESTH after *Saxonia* etc.: see -AN.]
▸ **A** *adjective*. Of or belonging to Estonia, a country situated on the south side of the Gulf of Finland. E18.
▸ **B** *noun*. **1** A native or inhabitant of Estonia. E18.
2 The Finno-Ugric language of Estonia. M19.

estop /ɪˈstɒp/ *verb trans.* Infl. **-pp-**. LME.
[ORIGIN Anglo-Norman, Old French *estop(p)er*, *estouper* (mod. *étouper*) stop up, impede (medieval Latin *estoppare*) from late Latin deriv. of Latin *stuppa* oakum.]
1 Stop (as) with a dam, plug, etc. *arch.* LME.
2 LAW. Bar or preclude by estoppel. (Foll. by *from*, *to do*.) M16.

H. HALLAM The lord who had granted the charter of franchise was estopped from claiming him again.

■ **estoppage** *noun* stoppage; LAW the condition of being estopped: E18.

estoppel /ɪˈstɒp(ə)l/ *noun*. M16.
[ORIGIN Old French *estoup(p)ail* plug, stopper, formed as ESTOP: see -AL[1].]
1 LAW. The principle which precludes a person from asserting something contrary to what is implied by his or her previous action or statement or by a previous judicial determination concerning that person; an occasion on which this applies. M16.
estoppel in PAIS.
†2 An obstruction (to a watercourse). E–M17.

estouffade /ɛstufad/ *noun*. Pl. pronounced same. L19.
[ORIGIN French from Italian *stuf(f)ata* pa. pple of *stufare* to stew, from *stufa* stove from popular Latin, ult. from Greek *tuphos* smoke: cf. STEW *verb*.]
(A dish of) meat cooked very slowly in its own vapour.

estovers /ɪˈstəʊvəz, ɛ-/ *noun pl.* L15.
[ORIGIN Pl. of Anglo-Norman *estover* (Anglo-Latin *estoverium*) use as noun of *estover*, Old French *estoveir* be necessary, based on Latin *est opus* it is necessary: see -ER[4].]
LAW. **1** In full ***common of estovers***. The right to take wood for fuel, repairs, or other necessary purpose from land one does not own, esp. land of which one is the tenant or lessee. L15.
2 Wood to which a person is entitled by common of estovers; necessaries allowed by law. L16.

estrade /ɛˈstrɑːd/ *noun*. L17.
[ORIGIN French from Spanish ESTRADO.]
Orig., a slightly raised platform or dais for persons of rank to sit or recline on. Later, any dais.

estradiol *noun* see OESTRADIOL.

estrado /ɛˈstrɑːdəʊ/ *noun*. Now *rare*. Pl. **-os**. L16.
[ORIGIN Spanish from Latin STRATUM.]
1 A room or part of a room richly furnished and used for reclining; a drawing room. L16.
2 A platform. M19.

estral *adjective*, **estrane** *noun* see OESTRAL, OESTRANE.

estrange /ɪˈstreɪn(d)ʒ, ɛ-/ *verb trans.* L15.
[ORIGIN Anglo-Norman *estraunger*, Old French *estranger* (mod. *étranger*) from Latin *extraneare* treat as a stranger, from *extraneus*: see EXTRANEOUS. Cf. STRANGE *adjective*.]
1 Keep away or apart from or *from* an accustomed place, occupation, etc. *arch.* L15. ▸†b Withhold *from* a person's perception or knowledge. Only in 17. ▸†c Make (a person) a stranger *to*. E–M18.

I. D'ISRAELI Edward, long estranged from his native realm.

2 Destroy or divert the affection, trust, loyalty, etc., of (a person); destroy or divert (such a feeling); cause to turn away in feelings or affection (*from*). L15.

BURKE You are going to estrange his majestys confidence from me. W. S. CHURCHILL The Dutch rule of the conquered Belgian cities had estranged their inhabitants. *Morning Star* The murdered woman . . was identified . . as his estranged wife.

3 Cut off from a community; remove (a possession or subject) from the ownership or dominion of someone. (Foll. by *from*.) *arch.* E16.

J. HOOKER Infidels estranged from the house of God.

†4 Make unlike one's normal self; make insane; madden. M16–E17.
5 Make unfamiliar in appearance; disguise. *arch.* E17.
■ **estrangedness** /-(d)ʒdnɪs, -dʒɪdnɪs/ *noun* the state of being estranged M17.

estrangelo /ɪˈstraŋgələʊ, ɛ-/ *noun*. M18.
[ORIGIN Syriac *estrangēlō*, thought to be from Greek *stroggulos* rounded.]
An archaic form of Syriac script.

estrangement /ɪˈstreɪn(d)ʒm(ə)nt, ɛ-/ *noun*. M17.
[ORIGIN from ESTRANGE *verb* + -MENT.]
The action of estranging or becoming estranged; the state or an instance of being estranged; alienation.

E. JONES There were quarrels that led to lasting estrangements.

†**estranger** *noun*[1]. L15.
[ORIGIN Old French: see STRANGER *noun*.]
1 A person belonging to another family, nation, or district; a stranger; a foreigner. L15–M17.
2 LAW. = STRANGER *noun* 6b. L16–E18.

estranger /ɪˈstreɪn(d)ʒə, ɛ-/ *noun*[2]. E17.
[ORIGIN from ESTRANGE *verb* + -ER[1].]
A person who or thing which estranges.

estray /ɪˈstreɪ, ɛ-/ *noun*. E16.
[ORIGIN Anglo-Norman, from Anglo-Norman & Old French *estraier* STRAY *verb*[1].]
1 LAW. A valuable or domesticated animal found wandering and unclaimed by its owner. E16.
2 *gen.* Anything that has strayed or wandered. L16.

estray /ɪˈstreɪ, ɛ-/ *verb intrans.* *arch.* M16.
[ORIGIN Anglo-Norman & Old French *estraier* STRAY *verb*[2].]
Stray; go astray.

estreat /ɪˈstriːt, ɛ-/ *noun & verb*. See also EXTREAT. ME.
[ORIGIN Anglo-Norman *estrete*, Old French *estraite*, use as noun of fem. pa. pple of *estraire* extract from Latin *extrahere*.]
▸ **A** *noun*. LAW.
1 A copy of a legal record, *esp.* one of a fine or recognizance for use by an officer of the court. ME.
†2 In *pl.* Fines or other payments enforced by a court. LME–M17.
▸ **B** *verb trans.* Chiefly LAW. Extract a copy of the court record of (a fine, recognizance, etc.) for use in prosecution; enforce (a fine); enforce forfeiture of (bail, a recognizance, etc.). E16.

estrepement /ɪˈstriːpm(ə)nt, ɛ-/ *noun*. E16.
[ORIGIN Anglo-Norman, Old French, from *estreper* (whence Anglo-Latin *estrepare*) from Latin *extirpare* EXTIRPATE: see -MENT.]
LAW. Damage to an estate caused by a tenant.

estrich /ˈɛstrɪtʃ/ *noun*. Also **-idge** /-ɪdʒ/. LME.
[ORIGIN Old French *estruc(h)e* var. of *ostrusce* OSTRICH.]
†1 Var. of OSTRICH. LME–E18.
2 COMMERCE. The fine down of the ostrich. M19.

estriche /ˈɛstrɪtʃ/ *noun*.
[ORIGIN Old English *ēast-rīc*, formed as EAST + *rīc* kingdom.]
†1 Orig., the East Frankish kingdom. Later, any eastern kingdom. OE–ME.
2 In full ***estriche board***. Timber from Norway or the Baltic. *obsolete* exc. *hist.* LME.

estridge *noun* var. of ESTRICH.

estrin, **estriol** *nouns* vars. of OESTRIN, OESTRIOL.

estro /ˈɛstro/ *noun*. E17.
[ORIGIN Italian from Latin OESTRUS frenzy.]
Inspiration, impulse.

estrogen, **estrone** *nouns* see OESTROGEN, OESTRONE.

estropiated /ɪˈstrɒpɪeɪtɪd, ɛ-/ *adjective*. E20.
[ORIGIN from French *estropier* cripple, disfigure from Italian *stroppiare* alt. of *storpiare*, from Latin *turpis* ugly or *stuprare* defile, ravish: see -ATE[3], -ED[1].]
Disabled; disfigured.

estrous *adjective*, **estrum**, **estrus** *nouns* see OESTROUS *adjective* etc.

estuarial /ɛstjʊˈɛːrɪəl/ *adjective*. L19.
[ORIGIN formed as ESTUARINE + -AL[1].]
Of or pertaining to an estuary.
■ Also **estuarian** *adjective* L19.

estuarine /ˈɛstjʊ(ə)rʌɪn/ *adjective*. M19.
[ORIGIN from ESTUARY + -INE[1].]
Of or belonging to an estuary; *esp.* (of strata, organisms, etc.) formed, deposited, or occurring in an estuary.

P. LEVI How to drain a huge estuarine valley and make . . grazing land.

estuary /ˈɛstjʊ(ə)ri/ *noun*. Also †**ae-**. M16.
[ORIGIN Latin *aestuarium* tidal part of a shore, estuary, from *aestus* heat, swell, surge, tide: see -ARY[1].]
1 A tidal opening or inlet. Now *rare* exc. as in sense 2. M16.
2 *spec.* The tidal mouth of a large river, where the tide meets the stream. L16.
†3 A vapour bath. Only in M17.
†4 A place where liquid boils up; *fig.* mental turmoil. L17–E19.
– COMB.: **Estuary English** [with ref. to the estuary of the River Thames] a type of English accent identified as spreading outwards from London and containing features of both received pronunciation and London speech.

†**estuation** *noun* var. of AESTUATION.

estufa /eˈstufa/ *noun*. M19.
[ORIGIN Spanish, corresp. to Old French *estuve* (mod. *étuve*): see STEW *noun*[1].]
1 An underground chamber in which a fire is kept permanently alight, used as a place of assembly by the Pueblo Indians. M19.
2 A heated chamber in which Madeira is stored and matured. L19.

†**estuosity** *noun*. M17–M18.
[ORIGIN from Latin *aestuosus* full of heat, from *aestus* heat: see -OSITY.]
Heated condition.

e.s.u. *abbreviation.*
Electrostatic unit(s).

esurience /ɪˈsjʊərɪəns, ɛ-/ *noun.* E19.
[ORIGIN from ESURIENT: see -ENCE.]
The state of being esurient.
■ Also **esuriency** *noun* E19.

esurient /ɪˈsjʊərɪənt, ɛ-/ *adjective.* L17.
[ORIGIN Latin *esurient-* pres. ppl stem of *esurire* be hungry, desiderative verb from *es-* pa. ppl stem of *esse* eat: see -ENT.]
1 Hungry; impecunious and greedy. *arch. & joc.* L17.
2 Gastronomic. E19.
■ **esuriently** *adverb* L19.

ET *abbreviation.*
Extraterrestrial (being).

E

et /ɛt/ *conjunction.* ME.
[ORIGIN Latin.]
And. Only in medieval & mod. Latin phrs.: see below.
et al. /al/ (*a*) [abbreviation of Latin *alii, aliae, alia* masc., fem., & neut. pl. of *alius* other] and others; (*b*) [abbreviation of Latin ALIBI] and elsewhere. **et sequens** /ˈsɛkwɛnz/ [Latin, pres. pple of *sequi* follow] and the following (usu. abbreviated to ***et seq.***). **et sequentes** /sɛˈkwɛntiːz/ [Latin, masc. & fem. pl. of *sequens*], **et sequentia** /sɛˈkwɛntɪə/ [Latin, neut. pl. of *sequens*] and the following things (usu. abbreviated to ***et seq.***, ***et seqq.***). ET CETERA.

-et /ɪt/ *suffix*¹.
[ORIGIN Old French (fem. *-ete*, mod. *-ette*) = Italian *-etto, -etta*, from Proto-Romance *-itto, -itta*, perh. not of Latin origin.]
In nouns, orig. dims., mostly derived from French, as ***bullet***, ***fillet***, ***hatchet***, ***pullet***, ***tablet***, etc., but also from Italian, as ***nonet***.
– NOTE: Largely superseded in mod. word formation by the rel. -ETTE, -LET, exc. in words modelled on *duet, quartet*.

-et /ɪt/ *suffix*².
[ORIGIN Old English *-et, -ett* = Gothic *-iti*, Old High German *-izzi*.]
Forming neut. verbal and denominative nouns, as ***thicket*** etc.

ETA *abbreviation.*
1 Estimated time of arrival.
2 /ˈɛtə/ Basque *Euzkadi ta Azkatasuna* Basque Homeland and Liberty, a Basque separatist organization active in Spain from the 1960s.

eta /ˈiːtə/ *noun*¹. LME.
[ORIGIN Greek *ēta*.]
1 The seventh letter (H, η) of the Greek alphabet. LME.
2 Freq. written η. ▸**a** *attrib.* ASTRONOMY. (Preceding the genitive of the Latin name of the constellation) denoting the seventh brightest star in a constellation. L18. ▸**b** PHYSICS. In full ***eta meson***. A meson with zero isospin and spin and a mass of 549 MeV. M20.
b eta prime a meson like the eta meson except for having a mass of 958 MeV.
– COMB.: **eta patch** a large fan-shaped patch by which rigging can be attached to the envelope of an airship.

eta /ˈeɪtə/ *noun*². Pl. same. L19.
[ORIGIN Japanese, from *e* defile + *ta* much, many.]
A member of an outcast class in Japan. Cf. HININ.

eta *noun*³ var. of ITA.

etaerio /ɛˈtɪərɪəʊ/ *noun.* Pl. **-os.** M19.
[ORIGIN French *etairion, -ium* from Greek *hetaireia* association.]
BOTANY. An aggregate fruit, as a strawberry or raspberry.

etagere /ɛtəˈʒɛː/ *noun.* Also **étagère** /etaʒɛːr (*pl. same*), ɛtəˈʒɛː/. M19.
[ORIGIN French *étagère*, from *étage* shelf, STAGE *noun*.]
A piece of furniture with a number of open shelves on which to display ornaments etc.

étalage /etalaːʒ/ *noun.* Pl. pronounced same. E20.
[ORIGIN French, from *étaler* to display.]
A display, a show.

B. CAMPBELL The étalage of leaves at the entrance to many robins' nests.

etalon /ˈɛtəlɒn/ *noun.* Also **é-**. E20.
[ORIGIN French *étalon* lit. 'standard of measurement'.]
PHYSICS. A pair of half-reflecting flat plates of glass or quartz fixed parallel to one another a small distance apart, used to produce interference patterns.

etamine /ˈɛtəmiːn/ *noun.* Also **é-**. E18.
[ORIGIN French *étamine*: see ESTAMIN.]
A lightweight open-weave fabric of coarse yarn, now usu. cotton or worsted.

étang /etɑ̃/ *noun.* Pl. pronounced same. M19.
[ORIGIN French from Old French *estanc*: see STANK *noun*.]
A shallow pool or small lake, *esp.* one resulting from the blocking of streams by sand dunes along the French Mediterranean coast.

etaoin /ˈɛtəɔɪn/ *noun.* M20.
[ORIGIN See below.]
More fully ***etaoin shrdlu*** /ˈʃəːdluː/. (A slug containing) the letters *e, t*, etc. produced by running the finger down the first one or two vertical lines of keys on a Linotype machine, used as a temporary marker and sometimes printed by mistake; any absurd or unintelligible sequence of type. Cf. SHRDLU.

etatism /ɛˈtɑːtɪz(ə)m/ *noun.* Also ***étatisme*** /etatism/. E20.
[ORIGIN French *étatisme*, from *état* state: see ESTATE *noun*, -ISM.]
The extreme authority of the state over the individual citizen.
■ **etatist**, ***étatiste*** *adjective* characterized by or exhibiting etatism M20.

†**état-major** *noun.* L18–L19.
[ORIGIN French, from *état* (see ETATISM) + *major* MAJOR *noun*¹.]
The staff of an army, regiment, etc.; a managing or governing body.

etc. *abbreviation.*
Et cetera.

et cetera /ɛtˈsɛt(ə)rə, ɪt-/ *adverb, noun, & verb.* Also **etcetera**, **et caetera**. Abbrev. **etc.**, (now *rare*) **&c.** ME.
[ORIGIN Latin, from *et* and + *cetera* the rest, neut. pl. of *ceterus* remaining over.]
▸ **A** *adverb.* And the rest; and similar things; and so on; and the customary continuation. Also redupl. ME.

J. GRENFELL A long line of intellectuals—father, grandfather, etcetera. F. W. CROFTS Yours, etc., *Leon Felix*. *Shetland Times* Industries including agriculture, tourism, etc.

▸ **B** *noun.* 1 (An instance of) the adverb *et cetera*. L16.

New York Times Etcetera etcetera was followed by blah-blah-blah.

2 Something not mentioned explicitly, esp. for reasons of delicacy or propriety. Formerly *spec.*, (in *pl.*) trousers. L16.

J. CARY You don't know your etc. from an etc.

3 A number of unspecified things or persons. M17.
4 In *pl.* (The usual) additions; extras, sundries. E18.

E. BOWEN She began to pack her compact, comb and other etceteras.

▸ **C** *verb. euphem.* Pa. t. & pple **-a'd**, **-aed**. Replacing a suppressed verb. M19.

H. KINGSLEY I am etcetera'd if I stand it.

etch /ɛtʃ/ *noun*¹. L16.
[ORIGIN Contr.]
= EDDISH 2.

etch /ɛtʃ/ *noun*². L19.
[ORIGIN from the verb.]
1 The action or process of etching; an act or method of etching. L19.
deep-etch: see DEEP *adverb*.
2 PRINTING. A liquid applied to a lithographic stone so as to form a crust that protects some areas from ink. M20.
– COMB.: **etch figure**, **etch pit** a depression on the face of a crystal that is produced by the action of a solvent and is indicative of the crystal's microstructure.

etch /ɛtʃ/ *verb.* M17.
[ORIGIN Dutch *etsen* from German *ätzen* from Old High German *azzen, ezzen* from Germanic causative formed as EAT *verb*.]
1 *verb trans.* Engrave (metal, glass, or stone) by coating it with a protective layer, drawing in this with a needle, and then covering with acid or other corrosive that attacks the parts the needle has exposed; *esp.* engrave (a plate) in this way in order to print from it; use this process to produce (a picture) or a picture of (a subject). M17. ▸**b** Engrave by any method; SCIENCE selectively dissolve the surface of (a crystal or crystalline material) with a solvent. M18. ▸**c** *fig.* Produce or affect as if by etching; cause to stand out clearly or vividly. M19.

A. B. JAMESON All the Illustrations . . have been newly etched on steel. **c** J. BUCHAN The far mountains were etched in violet against a saffron sky. A. CARTER The dry air etched his face full of fine lines.

2 *verb intrans.* Engage in the art of etching. M17.
3 *verb trans.* Corrode; eat *out*, remove *from*, (with an acid or other solvent). M17.
■ **etchable** *adjective* able to be etched or to be made visible by etching M20. **etchant** *noun* a corrosive or dissolving agent used for etching M20. **etcher** *noun* a person who etches M17.

etching /ˈɛtʃɪŋ/ *noun.* M17.
[ORIGIN from ETCH *verb* + -ING¹.]
1 The action of ETCH *verb*; the art of the etcher. M17.
deep-etching: see DEEP *adverb*.
2 A copy or representation produced by the process of etching; an impression from an etched plate. M18.

HOR. WALPOLE His etchings for Aesop's fables.

– COMB.: **etching ground** the protective substance with which a surface is coated preparatory to etching.

ETD *abbreviation.*
Estimated time of departure.

Eteocretan /ˌiːtɪəˈkriːt(ə)n, ɛt-/ *noun & adjective.* E17.
[ORIGIN from Greek *Eteokrēt-, -krēs*, from *eteos* true + *Krēs* Cretan: see -AN.]
▸ **A** *noun.* 1 A member of a pre-Greek people of Crete. E17.
2 The language of this people. E20.
▸ **B** *adjective.* Of or pertaining to the Eteocretans or their language. L19.

eteostichon /ɛtɪˈɒstɪkɒn/ *noun. rare.* Also †**-stic.** M17.
[ORIGIN from Greek *eteos* genit. of *etos* year + *stikhos* row, rank.]
= CHRONOGRAM.

eternal /ɪˈtəːn(ə)l, iː-/ *adjective, noun, & adverb.* LME.
[ORIGIN Old French *eternal, -nel* (mod. *éternel*) from late Latin *aeternalis*, from Latin *aeternus* contr. of *aeviternus* eternal, from *aevum* age: see -AL¹.]
▸ **A** *adjective.* 1 That will always exist; that has always existed; without a beginning or an end in time; everlasting. LME. ▸**b** Pertaining to eternal things; having eternal consequences. E17. ▸**c** Not conditioned by time; not subject to time relations. M17.
eternal life: see LIFE *noun*.
2 Permanent; enduring. L15. ▸**b** Having a persistent resolve. *rare* (Shakes.). Only in E17. ▸**c** Tediously persistent; recurring, incessant. L18.

J. P. CURRAN The condition upon which God hath given liberty to man is eternal vigilance. A. ALISON Summits . . wrapped in eternal snow. O. MANNING He'd . . have wasted his life as a sort of eternal student. **c** C. MCCULLOUGH Their palates longed for a change from the eternal round of . . mutton chops, mutton stew.

the Eternal City: see CITY *noun*. **c eternal triangle** a relationship of three people involving sexual rivalry.
3 Infernal; extremely abhorrent. Now *slang* or *dial.* L16.
4 Of a truth, principle, etc.: valid for all time; immutable, unalterable. L17.
▸ **B** *noun.* 1 ***the Eternal***, God, the Deity. L16.
†2 Eternity, endless time. Chiefly in ***from eternal***. E17–M18.
3 In *pl.* Eternal things. M17.
▸ **C** *adverb.* Eternally, for ever. E17.
■ **eternalism** *noun* (*a*) eternalness; an eternal character or nature; (*b*) PHILOSOPHY the belief that the universe has no beginning and no end: L19. **eterˈnality** *noun* = ETERNALNESS L15. **eternally** *adverb* (*a*) throughout eternity, for ever; (*b*) continually, incessantly; (*c*) immutably: LME. **eternalness** *noun* the state or quality of being eternal M18.

eternalize /ɪˈtəːn(ə)lʌɪz/ *verb trans.* Also **-ise.** E17.
[ORIGIN from ETERNAL + -IZE.]
1 = ETERNIZE 2. E17.
2 = ETERNIZE 1. E19.

S. J. PERELMAN We eternalized baby shoes . . dipped them in bronze for ash trays.

3 = ETERNIZE 3. M19.

A. J. DAVIS It contains truth eternalised.

■ **eternaliˈzation** *noun* E20.

eterne /ɪˈtəːn, iː-/ *adjective, noun, & adverb. arch. & poet.* LME.
[ORIGIN Old French, from Latin *aeternus* ETERNAL *adjective*.]
▸ **A** *adjective.* Eternal. LME.
▸ **B** *noun.* †1 Eternity. Chiefly in ***from eterne***. LME–L15.
2 ***the eterne***, that which is eternal, *spec.* (with cap. initial) God. E17.
▸ †**C** *adverb.* Eternally. Only in 16.

eternise *verb* var. of ETERNIZE.

eternity /ɪˈtəːnɪti, iː-/ *noun.* LME.
[ORIGIN Old French *éternité* from Latin *aeternitas*, from *aeternus* ETERNAL *adjective*: see -ITY.]
1 The quality, condition, or fact of being eternal; eternal existence. LME. ▸**b** Perpetual or long-lasting continuance, esp. of fame. LME. ▸**c** In *pl.* *The* eternal truths or realities. M19.

D. BREWSTER An argument . . to prove the eternity of the world.

2 All of time past or time to come, or both jointly; infinite time, without a beginning or an end. LME. ▸**b** A very great or apparently endless length of time; a tediously long time. E18.

HOBBES 'Natural' are those which have been Lawes from all Eternity. **b** J. MOXON Those Grey Kentish Bricks . . will last to Eternity. D. H. LAWRENCE At last, after an eternity, Cicio came along the platform.

3 In *pl.* Eternity of time viewed as consisting of successive ages. LME.

E. B. BROWNING A clock Which strikes the hours of the eternities.

4 Timelessness; a state to which time has no application; the condition into which the soul enters at death; the afterlife. L16.

DAY LEWIS I had a vision of eternity in my sleep.

launch into eternity (cause to) die.
– COMB.: **eternity ring**: given as a symbol of lasting love and usu. set with an unbroken circle of stones.

eternize /ɪˈtəːnʌɪz, ˈiːtənʌɪz/ *verb trans.* Also **-ise.** M16.
[ORIGIN French *éterniser* or medieval Latin *eternizare*, from Latin *aeternus* ETERNAL *adjective*: see -IZE.]
1 Prolong indefinitely; make permanent; perpetuate (fame, memory, etc.). M16.

E. R. EDDISON Creatures . . eternized in amber.

2 Make eternally famous, immortalize. L16.
3 Make eternal in duration or character. L16.
■ **eterniˈzation** *noun* E17.

Etesian /ɪˈtiːʒɪən, ɪˈtiːz-, ɪˈtiːʒ(ə)n/ *adjective & noun.* Also **e-**. E17.
[ORIGIN from Latin *etesius* annual from Greek *etēsios*, from *etos* year: see -AN.]
(Designating) a dry north wind blowing over the Aegean and eastern Mediterranean in the summer.

eth /ɛð/ *noun*. Also **edh**. M19.
[ORIGIN Danish *edh*, perh. repr. the sound of the letter.]
The letter ð or đ, capital Đ, introduced in Old English to represent the voiced and voiceless dental fricatives /ð/ and /θ/; the letter in the form ð, ð, used in Old Norse and Icelandic to represent the voiced dental fricative /ð/. Also, the phonetic symbol ð, used *spec.* in the International Phonetic Alphabet to represent this voiced dental fricative.
– NOTE: Eth was used interchangeably with the letter thorn in Old and Middle English, and both were superseded by the digraph *th* with the advent of printing. In this dictionary eth is not used in early English forms, which are regularized with thorn.

eth- /ɛθ, iːθ/ *combining form* of ETHYL, as ***ethambutol***, ***ethene***, etc.

-eth /ɪθ/ *suffix*[1]. *arch.* Also **-th**.
[ORIGIN Old English *-eþ*, *-aþ*, *-þ* = Old High German *-it* etc., Gothic *-iþ* etc.]
Forming the 3rd person pres. sing. of verbs, as ***doeth***, ***doth***, ***findeth***, ***saith***.

-eth *suffix*[2] var. of -TH[2].

ethacrynic /ɛθəˈkrɪnɪk/ *adjective*. M20.
[ORIGIN from ETH- + ACRY(LIC + PHE)N(OXY- + ACET)IC.]
ethacrynic acid, a powerful diuretic drug used to treat oedema.

ethambutol /ɛˈθambjʊtɒl/ *noun*. M20.
[ORIGIN from ETH- + AMINE + BUT(AN)OL.]
A derivative of ethylenediamine used as a bacteriostatic agent to treat tuberculosis.

ethanal /ˈɛθ(ə)nal/ *noun*. M20.
[ORIGIN from ETHANE + -AL[2].]
CHEMISTRY. = ACETALDEHYDE.

ethanamide /ɪˈθanəmʌɪd/ *noun*. L20.
[ORIGIN from ETHAN(AL + AMIDE.]
= ACETAMIDE.

ethane /ˈiːθeɪn, ˈɛθ-/ *noun*. L19.
[ORIGIN from ETHER *noun*[1] + -ANE.]
CHEMISTRY. A colourless odourless flammable gas, C_2H_6, that is a simple alkane and a constituent of petroleum and natural gas.
– COMB.: **ethanediol** = *ETHYLENE* ***glycol***.

Ethanim /ˈɛθənɪm/ *noun*. M16.
[ORIGIN from Hebrew *yeraḥ hā-ʾēṯānīm* month of steady-flowing rivers, from *ēṯān* ever-flowing.]
In the Jewish calendar, = TISHRI.

ethanoic /ɛθəˈnəʊɪk/ *adjective*. L19.
[ORIGIN from ETHANE + -OIC.]
CHEMISTRY. = ACETIC 1.
■ **ethanoate** *noun* = ACETATE 1 M20. **ethanoyl** *noun* = ACETYL E20.

ethanol /ˈɛθənɒl/ *noun*. E20.
[ORIGIN from ETHANE + -OL.]
CHEMISTRY. A colourless volatile flammable liquid alcohol, C_2H_5OH, present in alcoholic drinks (cf. ALCOHOL 4), produced by the fermentation of hexose sugars, and used as a solvent, antifreeze, fuel, and intermediate; ethyl alcohol.
■ **ethanolamine** /-ˈnɒl-, -ˈnəʊl-/ *noun* each of three compounds which are derived from ammonia by successive replacement of hydrogen atoms with the group $\cdot C_2H_4OH$, melt near room temperature, and are used to form soaps by combination with fatty acids; *spec.* 2-aminoethanol, $H_2N{\cdot}C_2H_4OH$, used to purify gases: L19. **etha'nolic** *adjective* M20.

ethchlorvynol /ɛθklɔːˈvʌɪnɒl/ *noun*. M20.
[ORIGIN from ETH- + CHLOR-[1] + alt. of VIN(YL + -OL.]
PHARMACOLOGY. A short-acting sedative and hypnotic used to treat insomnia.
– NOTE: A proprietary name for this drug in the US and Canada is PLACIDYL.

ethel /ˈɛθ(ə)l/ *noun*[1]. Long *obsolete* exc. *hist.*
[ORIGIN Old English *æþel*, *ēþel*, *ōþel* = Old Saxon *ōþil*, Old High German *uodal*, Old Norse *óðal*, from Germanic: see UDAL. Cf. ATHEL, ATHELING.]
(An) ancestral land or estate; patrimony; (a) native land.

ethel *adjective* & *noun*[2] var. of ATHEL.

ethene /ˈɛθiːn/ *noun*. M19.
[ORIGIN from ETH- + -ENE.]
CHEMISTRY. = ETHYLENE.
■ **ethenoid** *adjective* = ETHYLENIC E20.

ether /ˈiːθə/ *noun*[1]. In senses 1–3 also (*arch.*) **aether**. LME.
[ORIGIN Old French *éther* or Latin *aether* from Greek *aithēr* upper air, from base of *aithein* kindle, burn, shine.]
1 *hist.* A substance formerly believed to occupy space beyond the sphere of the moon and to compose the stars and planets. LME.
2 The clear sky; the region above the clouds; the substance formerly believed to occupy this, above the air of the lower region. Now *literary*. L16. ▸**b** Air. E18.

A. UTTLEY Her voice floated . . through the silvery atoms of air and the mysterious ether to the great moon.

3 A very rarefied and highly elastic substance formerly believed to permeate all space, including the interstices between the particles of matter, and to be the medium whose vibrations constituted light (and radio waves); the notional medium of radio transmission; ***the ether*** (colloq.), radio as a medium or art form. M17. ▸†**b** Any hypothetical very rarefied fluid. L17–L18.

J. S. HUXLEY A . . request I made over the ether.

4 *CHEMISTRY*. **a** A pleasant-smelling colourless volatile liquid, $(CH_3CH_2)_2O$, made by the action of sulphuric acid on ethanol and used as a solvent, intermediate, and anaesthetic. M18. ▸†**b** A compound formed by the action of any other acid on ethanol. L18–M19. ▸**c** Any organic compound of the type ROR′, where R, R′ are alkyl, aryl, etc., groups. Formerly also (more fully ***compound ether***) = ESTER. M19.
c diethyl ether = sense 4a above.
■ **etherate** *noun* (*CHEMISTRY*) any compound whose molecule contains an ether molecule, esp. $(C_2H_5)_2O$ E20.

ether *verb* & *noun*[2] var. of EDDER.

ethereal /ɪˈθɪərɪəl/ *adjective* & *noun*. Also **-ial**, **aeth-**. E16.
[ORIGIN from Latin *aethereus*, *-ius* from Greek *aitherios*, from *aithēr*: see ETHER *noun*[1], -AL[1].]
▸ **A** *adjective*. **1** Of or pertaining to the region above the clouds (ETHER *noun*[1] 2); (chiefly *poet.*) heavenly, celestial. E16.

J. WILKINS The extreme Coldness of the Æthereal Air. MILTON Go, heavenly Guest, Ethereal Messenger.

2 Of the nature of or resembling the ether (ETHER *noun*[1] 1, 3); light, airy, attenuated; pertaining to or involving the ether. E16.

H. POWER The aetherial Medium (wherein all the Stars and Planets do swim). *Scientific American* Loudspeakers are . . used instead of headphones, so that the entire family can enjoy the etherial entertainment.

ethereal oil = ***essential oil*** s.v. ESSENTIAL *adjective* 7.
3 Resembling (a) spirit, impalpable; of unearthly delicacy and refinement. M17.

R. LEHMANN People said how ethereal she'd grown to look, how spiritual. S. SPENDER Music . . at once so ethereal and yet so earthly.

4 *CHEMISTRY*. Of or pertaining to ether (ETHER *noun*[1] 4a); resembling (that of) ether. E19.

N. G. CLARK Lower ketones have an ethereal or fruity odour.

▸ **B** *noun*. **1** The ethereal principle, the spirit or essence. Now *rare* or *obsolete*. M17.
2 An ethereal being, a spirit. M18.
■ **ethere'ality** *noun* the quality of being ethereal or beyond material analysis E19. **ethereali'zation** *noun* the action or process of etherealizing M19. **etherealize** *verb trans.* make ethereal in substance or appearance; spiritualize, refine: E19. **ethereally** *adverb* E17. **etherealness** *noun* M18.

etherean /ɪˈθɪərɪən/ *adjective*. *rare*. Also **-ian**. M17.
[ORIGIN formed as ETHEREAL + -AN.]
Heavenly, refined; (of a colour) soft, subdued.

ethereous /ɪˈθɪərɪəs/ *adjective*. Also **-ious**. M17.
[ORIGIN formed as ETHEREAL + -OUS.]
Composed of, or of the nature of, ether (ETHER *noun*[1] 1, 2, 3).

etherial *adjective* & *noun*, **etherian**, **etherious** *adjectives* vars. of ETHEREAL, ETHEREAN, ETHEREOUS.

etheric /ˈiːθ(ə)rɪk/ *adjective*. L19.
[ORIGIN from ETHER *noun*[1] + -IC.]
Of or pertaining to the ether (ETHER *noun*[1] 3).

Spiritualist What we carry over with us at death is our mind, and . . the etheric body.

■ Also **e'therical** *adjective* M17.

etherify /ˈiːθ(ə)rɪfʌɪ/ *verb trans.* M19.
[ORIGIN from ETHER *noun*[1] + -I- + -FY.]
CHEMISTRY. Convert into an ether.
■ **etherifi'cation** *noun* E19.

etherise *verb* var. of ETHERIZE.

etherism /ˈiːθ(ə)rɪz(ə)m/ *noun*. L19.
[ORIGIN from ETHER *noun*[1] + -ISM.]
Addiction to ether; the symptoms or state produced by taking ether as a stimulant or intoxicant.

etherize /ˈiːθ(ə)rʌɪz/ *verb trans.* Also **-ise**. M18.
[ORIGIN from ETHER *noun*[1] + -IZE.]
†**1** Electrify. *rare*. Only in M18.
2 Mix with ether, add ether to. Chiefly as ***etherized*** *ppl adjective*. E19.
3 *CHEMISTRY*. = ETHERIFY. *rare*. E19.
4 Administer ether to; anaesthetize with ether. M19.

T. S. ELIOT Like a patient etherized upon a table.

■ **etheri'zation** *noun* M19.

Ethernet /ˈiːθənɛt/ *noun*. L20.
[ORIGIN from ETHER *noun*[1] + NET(WORK *noun*.]
COMPUTING. A system of communication for local area networks by coaxial cable that prevents simultaneous transmission by more than one station; a network using this.

etheromania /ˌiːθ(ə)rə(ʊ)ˈmeɪnɪə/ *noun*. L19.
[ORIGIN from ETHER *noun*[1] + -O- + -MANIA.]
Addiction to ether.
■ **etheromaniac** *noun* a person so addicted L19.

ethic /ˈɛθɪk/ *noun*. LME.
[ORIGIN In branch I from Old French & mod. French *éthique*, Latin *ethice*, Greek (*hē*) *ēthikē* (sc. *tekhnē* art, science); in branch II from Old French *éthiques*, medieval Latin *ethica* pl. from Greek (*ta*) *ēthika*; fem. sing. and neut. pl of Greek *ēthikos*, formed as ETHOS: see -IC, -ICS.]
▸ **I** *sing.* **1** = sense 4 below. Now *rare* or *obsolete*. LME.
2 A set of moral principles, *esp.* those of a specified religion, school of thought, etc. L19.

P. MEDAWAR It is part of the puritan ethic that any activity so pleasurable must be harmful.

Protestant ethic: see PROTESTANT *adjective*. ***social ethic***: see SOCIAL *adjective*.
▸ **II** In *pl.*
3 A treatise on ethics (sense 4 below), *spec.* the one written by Aristotle. LME.
4 Usu. treated as *sing.* The science of morals; the branch of knowledge that deals with the principles of human duty or the logic of moral discourse; the whole field of moral science. L16.
SITUATION ***ethics***.
5 The moral principles or system of a particular leader or school of thought; the moral principles by which any particular person is guided; the rules of conduct recognized in a particular profession or area of human life. M17.

R. W. DALE The ethics of dining. G. B. SHAW The ethics of vivisectionists.

ethic /ˈɛθɪk/ *adjective*. LME.
[ORIGIN French *éthique* or Latin *ethicus* from Greek *ēthikos*, formed as ETHOS: see -IC.]
1 = ETHICAL *adjective* 1. LME.
2 = ETHICAL *adjective* 2. L16.

ethical /ˈɛθɪk(ə)l/ *adjective* & *noun*. E17.
[ORIGIN from ETHIC *adjective* + -AL[1].]
▸ **A** *adjective*. **1** Of or pertaining to morality or the science of ethics; pertaining to morals. E17.

J. MACKINTOSH The ethical principles of Hobbes, are completely interwoven with his political system. D. HALBERSTAM A woman with a strong ethical sense.

ethical *RELATIVISM*.
2 Dealing with the science of ethics or questions connected with it. M17.

J. RUSKIN Ethical and imaginative literature.

3 In accordance with the principles of ethics; morally correct, honourable; conforming to the ethics of a profession etc. L19.

C. BEATON Many buyers . . are eminently ethical and have a respect for the couturier's work. C. POTOK How ethical it was . . to give Danny books to read behind his father's back.

4 Of a medicine or drug: not advertised to the general public, and usu. available only on a doctor's prescription. M20.
5 *FINANCE*. Designating investment in enterprises whose activities do not offend against the investor's moral principles. L20.
▸ **B** *noun*. An ethical medicine or drug. M20.
■ **ethicalism** *noun* devotion to ethical ideals L19. **ethi'cality** *noun* ethical principles or behaviour; an ethical principle: L19. **ethically** *adverb* M17. **ethicalness** *noun* L17.

ethician /ɛˈθɪʃ(ə)n/ *noun*. *rare*. E17.
[ORIGIN from ETHIC *noun* + -IAN.]
= ETHICIST.

ethicise *verb* var. of ETHICIZE.

ethicist /ˈɛθɪsɪst/ *noun*. L19.
[ORIGIN from ETHIC *noun* + -IST.]
An expert in ethics; a writer on ethics; a person who is guided by or adheres to principles of ethics or morality in opposition to religion.
■ **ethicism** *noun* devotion to ethics or ethical ideals L19.

ethicize /ˈɛθɪsʌɪz/ *verb*. Also **-ise**. E19.
[ORIGIN formed as ETHICIST + -IZE.]
1 *verb intrans.* Discuss ethics; moralize. *rare*. E19.
2 *verb trans.* Make ethical, impart an ethical element to. L19.

ethico- /ˈɛθɪkəʊ/ *combining form*. E18.
[ORIGIN Repr. Greek *ēthiko-* combining form of *ēthikos*: see ETHIC *adjective*, -O-.]
Forming compound adjectives with the sense 'ethical and —', as in ***ethico-religious***, ***ethico-social***, etc.

ethide /ˈɛθʌɪd, ˈiːθ-/ *noun*. M19.
[ORIGIN from ETH- + -IDE.]
CHEMISTRY. Any binary compound of ethyl.

ethidium /ɛˈθɪdɪəm/ *noun*. M20.
[ORIGIN from ETH- + -IDE + -IUM.]
BIOCHEMISTRY. (The cation of) ethidium bromide.
– COMB.: **ethidium bromide** a purple derivative of phenanthridine used as a trypanocide, to stain DNA, and to destroy the superhelical structure of DNA.

E

ethine, **ethinyl** *nouns* vars. of ETHYNE, ETHYNYL.

ethionamide /ɛθɪˈɒnəmʌɪd/ *noun*. M20.
[ORIGIN from ETH- + THIO- + AMIDE.]
PHARMACOLOGY. An antibiotic, $C_8H_{10}N_2S$, which is active against mycobacteria and has been used to treat tuberculosis.

ethionic /ɛθʌɪˈɒnɪk/ *adjective*. M19.
[ORIGIN from ETHER *noun*[1] + THIONIC.]
CHEMISTRY. ***ethionic acid***, an acid, $HO_3S{\cdot}C_2H_4{\cdot}O{\cdot}SO_3H$, known only in solution and obtained by the action of water on ethionic anhydride; ***ethionic anhydride***, a crystalline cyclic compound, $C_2H_4S_2O_6$, formed by the action of sulphur trioxide on ethylene or ethanol.

ethionine /ɛˈθʌɪəniːn/ *noun*. M20.
[ORIGIN from ETH- after METHIONINE.]
BIOCHEMISTRY. An amino acid, $C_6H_{13}NO_2S$, that is the ethyl homologue of methionine and inhibits protein synthesis.

Ethiop /ˈiːθɪɒp/ *noun & adjective*. *arch*. Also †**Aeth-**. ME.
[ORIGIN Latin *Aethiops*, *Aethiop-* from Greek *Aithiops*, *Aithiop-* Ethiopian, from *aithein* to burn + *ōps* face.]
▸ **A** *noun*. = ETHIOPIAN *noun* 1. ME.
▸ **B** *attrib*. or as *adjective*. **1** Black. E17.
KEATS Ivy . . Shading its Æthiop berries.
†**2** Of or pertaining to Ethiopia. *rare*. Only in M17.

Ethiopian /iːθɪˈəʊpɪən/ *noun & adjective*. Also †**Aeth-**. ME.
[ORIGIN from *Ethiopia* (see below), *Aethiopia* (from Latin *Aethiops*: see ETHIOP, -IA[1]) + -AN.]
▸ **A** *noun*. **1** A native or inhabitant of Ethiopia, a country in NE Africa; *arch*. a black person. ME.
2 An advocate or supporter of Ethiopianism. E20.
▸ **B** *adjective*. **1** Of or pertaining to Ethiopia; *arch*. black, dark-skinned. L16.
Ethiopian serenader *arch*. a blackface minstrel.
2 Designating a zoogeographic region comprising Africa south of the Sahara. L19.
3 Of or pertaining to Ethiopianism. E20.
■ **Ethiopianism** *noun* a religious movement in sub-Saharan Africa which first appeared in the 1890s and was influenced by black nationalism E20.

Ethiopic /iːθɪˈɒpɪk/ *adjective & noun*. Also †**Aeth-**. M17.
[ORIGIN Latin *aethiopicus* from Greek *aithiopikos*, from *Aithiop-*: see ETHIOP, -IC.]
▸ **A** *adjective*. Orig. = ETHIOPIAN *adjective* 1. Now, designating the languages Ethiopic and Ge'ez; written in or employing one of these languages. M17.
▸ **B** *noun*. Any of several Semitic languages related to Arabic and spoken in Ethiopia and neighbouring areas. Also = GE'EZ. E18.
■ †**Ethiopical** *adjective*: only in L16.

†**Ethiops** *noun*. Also **Aeth-**. E18–M19.
[ORIGIN medieval Latin *aethiops* from Latin *Aethiops* ETHIOP *noun*.]
Any of various black or dark-coloured compounds of metals; *spec*. = ***Ethiops mineral*** below.
Comb.: **Ethiops martial** black iron oxide. **Ethiops mineral** black mercury sulphide.

ethisterone /ɛˈθɪst(ə)rəʊn/ *noun*. M20.
[ORIGIN from ETHYNYL + TESTOSTERONE.]
A synthetic progestogen derived from testosterone which is used to treat menstrual disorders.

ethmoid /ˈɛθmɔɪd/ *adjective & noun*. M18.
[ORIGIN Greek *ēthmoeidēs*, from *ēthmos* sieve: see -OID.]
ANATOMY. ▸ **A** *adjective*. Of, pertaining to, or designating a bone at the root of the nose forming part of the cranium, with perforations through which pass the olfactory nerves. M18.
▸ **B** *noun*. The ethmoid bone. M19.
■ Also **ethˈmoidal** *adjective* M18.

ethnarch /ˈɛθnɑːk/ *noun*. M17.
[ORIGIN Greek *ethnarkhēs*, from *ethnos* nation + *-arkhēs* -ARCH.]
A governor or leader of a nation or people; a ruler of a province.
■ **ethnarchy** *noun* (*a*) the province ruled by an ethnarch; (*b*) the position or post of an ethnarch: E17.

ethnic /ˈɛθnɪk/ *noun & adjective*. LME.
[ORIGIN ecclesiastical Latin *ethnicus* heathen from Greek *ethnikos*, from *ethnos* nation: see -IC.]
▸ **A** *noun*. †**1** A person who is not a Christian or a Jew; a pagan, a heathen. LME–E18.
2 *GREEK HISTORY*. An epithet that denotes nationality and is derived from or corresponds to the name of a people or city. E19.
3 A member of an ethnic group or minority. Chiefly *N. Amer*. M20.
▸ **B** *adjective*. **1** Pertaining to nations neither Christian nor Jewish; pagan, heathen. *arch*. L15.
2 Pertaining to national and cultural origins; designating origin by birth or descent rather than by present nationality. M19.
C. THUBRON Within a few years the ethnic Russians . . will be a minority in their own empire.
3 Pertaining to or designating a population subgroup (within a larger or dominant national or cultural group) with a common national or cultural tradition. M20. ▸**b** Characteristic of or belonging to a non-Western cultural tradition; *US colloq*. foreign, exotic. M20.
J. BAYLIS Deep-seated ethnic and national rivalries. **b** *Wall Street Journal* Indulge in a variety of ethnic cuisines.
ethnic cleansing the forcible removal of all members of a particular ethnic group from an area. **ethnic minority** a group differing physically or culturally from the rest of the community.
■ **ethnical** *adjective* †(*a*) pagan, heathenish; (*b*) of or pertaining to race; ethnological: LME. **ethnically** *adverb* L16. **ethnicism** /-sɪz(ə)m/ *noun* †(*a*) paganism, heathenism; a pagan superstition; (*b*) the pagan religions of antiquity; (*c*) consciousness of or emphasis on racial or national identity: E17. **ethnicist** /-sɪst/ *noun* (*a*) an ethnologist; (*b*) a supporter of one of more ethnic groups; (*c*) an enthusiast for the culture, food, dress, etc., of one or more ethnic groups: M19.

ethnicity /ɛθˈnɪsɪti/ *noun*. L18.
[ORIGIN from ETHNIC + -ITY.]
†**1** Paganism; pagan superstition. *rare*. Only in L18.
2 Ethnic character; the fact or sense of belonging to a particular ethnic group. M20.
Toronto Sun Kasparov . . is half-Jewish and half-American—an ethnicity more typical of the dominant Soviet players. *Times Educ. Suppl.* Those excluded on grounds of race, ethnicity, and social class.

ethno- /ˈɛθnəʊ/ *combining form*.
[ORIGIN from Greek *ethnos* nation: see -O-.]
Nation, people, culture.
■ **ethnoarchaeoˈlogical** *adjective* of or pertaining to ethnoarchaeology L20. **ethnoarchaeˈologist** *noun* an expert in or student of ethnoarchaeology L20. **ethnoarchaeˈology** *noun* the branch of knowledge that deals with the investigation of the social organization and other ethnological features of a present-day society on the basis of its material culture, in order to draw conclusions about past societies from their material remains M20. **ethnoboˈtanical** *adjective* of or pertaining to ethnobotany L19. **ethnoboˈtanically** *adverb* from an ethnobotanical point of view E20. **ethnoˈbotanist** *noun* an expert in or student of ethnobotany M20. **ethnoˈbotany** *noun* the traditional knowledge and customs of a people relating to plants; the branch of knowledge that deals with these: L19. **ethnocentred** *adjective* centred on one or more ethnic groups L20. **ethnoˈcentric** *adjective* centred on one's own race or ethnic group; based on or characterized by a tendency to evaluate other races or groups by criteria specific to one's own; having assumptions or preconceptions originating in the standards, customs, etc., of one's own race or group: E20. **ethnoˈcentricism** *noun* = ETHNOCENTRICITY L20. **ethnocenˈtricity** *noun* the fact of being ethnocentric; ethnocentric character: M20. **ethnoˈcentrism** *noun* = ETHNOCENTRICITY E20. **ethnocide** *noun* the deliberate and systematic destruction of the culture of an ethnic group, esp. within a larger community L20. **ethnoˈcultural** *adjective* pertaining to or having a particular ethnic group L20. **ethnoˈgenesis** *noun* the formation or emergence of an ethnic group within a larger community M20. **ethˈnogeny** *noun* the branch of anthropology that deals with the origin of races, peoples, and nations L19. **ethnohiˈstorian** *noun* an expert in or student of ethnohistory M20. **ethnohiˈstoric**, **ethnohiˈstorical** *adjectives* of or pertaining to ethnohistory M20. **ethnoˈhistory** *noun* the branch of knowledge that deals with the history of races and cultures, esp. non-Western ones M20. **ethnoˈlinguist** *noun* an expert in or student of ethnolinguistics M20. **ethnolinˈguistic** *adjective* pertaining to ethnolinguistics E20. **ethnolinˈguistics** *noun* the branch of linguistics that deals with the relations between linguistic and cultural behaviour E20. **ethnoˈmedicine** *noun* the branch of knowledge that deals with the traditional medical remedies and lore of a people L20. **ethnomethodoˈlogical** *adjective* of or pertaining to ethnomethodology M20. **ethnomethoˈdologist** *noun* an expert in or student of ethnomethodology M20. **ethnomethoˈdology** *noun* a method of sociological analysis that examines how individuals in everyday situations construct and maintain the social order of those situations M20. **ethnomusicoˈlogical** *adjective* of or pertaining to ethnomusicology M20. **ethnomusiˈcologist** *noun* an expert in or student of ethnomusicology M20. **ethnomusiˈcology** *noun* the branch of knowledge that deals with the music of cultures, esp. as an aspect of sociocultural behaviour M20. **ethnonym** *noun* a proper name by which a people or ethnic group is known; *spec*. a people's or group's own name for itself: M20. **ethnopharmaˈcology** *noun* the branch of knowledge that deals with the traditional drugs and medicinal substances of a people L20. **ethnophaulism** /-ˈfɔːlɪz(ə)m/ *noun* [Greek *phaulisma* disparagement] an expression that contains a disparaging reference to another people or ethnic group (e.g. ***Dutch courage***) or is a contemptuous name for them (e.g. ***Dago***) M20. **ethnoscience** *noun* the branch of knowledge that deals with the different ways the world is perceived and categorized in different cultures M20. **ethnoseˈmantic** *adjective* of or pertaining to ethnosemantics M20. **ethnoseˈmantics** *noun* the branch of knowledge that deals with the way members of a speech community categorize their experience, as inferred from the semantic organization of vocabulary M20.

ethnography /ɛθˈnɒgrəfi/ *noun*. E19.
[ORIGIN from ETHNO- + -GRAPHY.]
The scientific description of races and peoples with their customs, habits, and mutual differences; an example of this.
■ **ethnographer** *noun* a person who writes such descriptions; an expert in or student of ethnography: M19. **ethnoˈgraphic**, **ethnoˈgraphical** *adjectives* M19. **ethnoˈgraphically** *adverb* in an ethnographical manner; from an ethnographical point of view: M19.

ethnology /ɛθˈnɒlədʒi/ *noun*. M19.
[ORIGIN from ETHNO- + -LOGY.]
The branch of knowledge that deals with the characteristics of different peoples and the differences and relationships between them.
■ **ethnoˈlogic**, **ethnoˈlogical** *adjectives* M19. **ethnoˈlogically** *adverb* in an ethnological manner; from an ethnological point of view: M19. **ethnologist** *noun* M19.

ethogram /ˈiːθəgram/ *noun*. M20.
[ORIGIN from Greek *ēthos* nature or disposition of animals, (in pl.) customs + -GRAM.]
(A catalogue of) all the different kinds of behaviour or activity exhibited by an animal.

ethology /iːˈθɒlədʒi/ *noun*. M17.
[ORIGIN Latin *ethologia* from Greek, from *ēthos*: see ETHOS, -LOGY.]
†**1** The portrayal of character by mimic gestures, mimicry; an exposition of or treatise on manners. *rare*. M–L17.
2 The science of character formation. M19.
3 The branch of science that deals with animal behaviour, esp. in the wild. L19.
■ **ethoˈlogical** *adjective* M18. **ethologist** *noun* M18.

ethos /ˈiːθɒs/ *noun*. M19.
[ORIGIN Greek *ēthos* nature, disposition.]
The characteristic spirit of a culture, era, community, institution, etc., as manifested in its attitudes, aspirations, customs, etc.; the character of an individual as represented by his or her values and beliefs; the prevalent tone of a literary work in this respect.
M. SARTON The daring sense that anything could be said . . was surely one of the keys to the Bloomsbury ethos. R. FRY The general atmosphere—the ethos, which the works of art of a period exhale. D. L. EDWARDS Baptist congregations . . providing a . . popular alternative to an Anglicanism still aristocratic in its ethos.

ethosuximide /iːθəʊˈsʌksɪmʌɪd/ *noun*. M20.
[ORIGIN from ETH- + -O- + phonet. alt. of SUCCINIMIDE.]
3,3-Ethylmethylsuccinimide, a drug given orally to suppress petit mal seizures.

ethoxide /ɪˈθɒksʌɪd/ *noun*. L19.
[ORIGIN from ETHOXY- + -IDE.]
CHEMISTRY. A salt or simple compound containing the ethoxyl radical, as ***sodium ethoxide***, $NaOC_2H_5$.

ethoxy- /ɪˈθɒksi/ *combining form*. Also as attrib. adjective **ethoxy**. L19.
[ORIGIN from ETH- + OXY-.]
CHEMISTRY. Designating or containing an ethoxyl group.
■ **ethoxyˈethane** *noun* = ETHER *noun*[1] 4a L20.

ethoxyl /ɛˈθɒksʌɪl, -sɪl/ *noun*. M19.
[ORIGIN formed as ETHOXY- + -YL.]
CHEMISTRY. The radical $CH_3CH_2O{\cdot}$, derived from ethanol. Usu. in *comb*.
■ **ethoxylated** *adjective* containing an introduced ethoxyl group M20.

†**ethroclite** *adjective & noun* see HETEROCLITE.

ethrog *noun* see ETROG *noun*[1].

†**ethrogene** *adjective* see HETEROGENE.

ethyl /ˈɛθʌɪl, -θɪl, ˈiː-/ *noun*. M19.
[ORIGIN German, from *Äther* ether + -YL.]
CHEMISTRY. The radical $CH_3CH_2{\cdot}$ derived from ethane, present in ethanol, ether, etc. Usu. in *comb*.
– COMB.: **ethyl acetate** a colourless volatile liquid with a fruity smell, $CH_3COOC_2H_5$, used as a solvent; **ethyl alcohol** = ETHANOL; **ethylamine** a strongly basic liquid, $C_2H_5NH_2$; **ethylbenzene** *noun* a colourless liquid, $C_6H_5{\cdot}C_2H_5$, used in the manufacture of styrene; **ethyl chloride** a gas stored under pressure as a colourless flammable liquid and used as a solvent, anaesthetic, and intermediate; **ethyl ether** = ETHER *noun*[1] 4a.
■ **ethylate** *verb trans*. introduce an ethyl substituent into (a compound) M19. **eˈthylic** *adjective* M19.

ethylene /ˈɛθɪliːn, -θ(ə)l-/ *noun*. M19.
[ORIGIN from ETHYL + -ENE.]
A flammable gas, $CH_2{=}CH_2$, present in coal gas, natural gas, and crude oil, given off by ripening fruit, and used as an intermediate and to make polyethylene.
– COMB.: **ethylenediamine** a viscous liquid, $(NH_2{\cdot}CH_2{\cdot})_2$, used in making detergents and emulsifying agents (***ethylenediamine tetra-acetic acid*** = ***EDTA*** s.v. E, E); **ethylene glycol** a sweet-tasting liquid, $(HO{\cdot}CH_2)_2$, used esp. as an antifreeze; **ethylene oxide** a flammable toxic gas, $(CH_2)_2O$, used as an intermediate and fumigant.
■ **ethyˈlenic** *adjective* containing, derived from, or characteristic of ethylene; *spec*. designating a double bond between two carbon atoms: L19. **ethyˈlenically** *adverb* in the manner of the ethylene molecule, by virtue of an ethylenic bond M20.

ethylidene /iːˈθʌɪlɪdiːn, ɛˈθɪl-/ *noun*. M19.
[ORIGIN French *éthylydène*, from *éthylène* ETHYLENE + infixed *-yd-* from *aldéhyde* ALDEHYDE.]
CHEMISTRY. The radical $CH_3C{=}$. Usu. in *comb*.

ethyne /ˈiːθʌɪn, ˈɛθ-/ *noun*. Also **-ine**. L19.
[ORIGIN from ETH- + -INE[5], -YNE.]
= ACETYLENE.

ethynyl /ˈɛθɪnʌɪl, -nɪl/ *noun*. Also **-inyl**. M20.
[ORIGIN from ETHYNE + -YL.]
The radical CH:C·. Usu. in *comb*.
– COMB.: **ethynyloestradiol** a synthetic oestrogen with greater potency than oestradiol.

etic /ˈɛtɪk/ *adjective*. M20.
[ORIGIN from PHONETIC *adjective*.]
Designating a generalized non-structural approach to the description of a particular language or culture. Also (of language or behaviour), not serving to distinguish meaning but conveying information about the particular characteristics of a person. Cf. EMIC.

-etic /ˈɛtɪk/ *suffix*.
[ORIGIN from or after Greek *-etikos*, *-ētikos*: cf. -IC.]
Forming adjectives (and nouns), as ***paretic***, ***pathetic***, ***peripatetic***, ***prothetic***, etc. (often corresp. to nouns in ***-esis***).

†**etik** *adjective & noun* see HECTIC *adjective & noun*.

etin /ˈiːtɪn/ *noun*. Now *Scot.* (*arch.*).
[ORIGIN Old English *e(o)ten* = Old Norse *jǫtunn* (Swedish *jätte*, Danish *jette*).]
A giant.

-etin /ˈɛtɪn/ *suffix*.
[ORIGIN After QUERCETIN.]
Forming nouns denoting aglycones, usu. by replacing *-in* in the name of the glycoside from which the aglycone is obtained, as in ***phloretin***, ***quercetin***, etc.

etiolate /ˈiːtɪə(ʊ)leɪt/ *verb trans*. L18.
[ORIGIN French *étioler* from Norman French *(s')étieuler* grow into haulm, from *ét(i)eule* (Old French *esteule*, *estuble*, mod. *éteule*): see STUBBLE *noun*, -ATE³.]
Make (a plant) pale by excluding light; give a pale and sickly hue to (a person); *fig.* cause to lose vigour or substance. Chiefly as ***etiolated*** *ppl adjective*.

B. R. O. ANDERSON Marxist and liberal theory have become etiolated in a late Ptolemaic attempt to 'save the phenomena'.

■ **etioˈlation** *noun* L18.

etiology *noun* var. of AETIOLOGY.

etiquette /ˈɛtɪkɛt, ɛtɪˈkɛt/ *noun*. M18.
[ORIGIN French *étiquette* TICKET *noun*, etiquette.]
1 The conventional rules of personal behaviour in polite society; the prescribed ceremonial of a court; the formalities required in diplomacy; the order of procedure established by custom in the armed services, Parliament, etc.; the unwritten code governing the behaviour of professional persons. M18.

JAS. MILL It was to him that, in etiquette, the command of the expedition belonged. R. L. STEVENSON I consulted him upon a point of etiquette: if one should offer to tip the American waiter? DAY LEWIS My father was very much the professional clergyman, having a strong sense of clerical etiquette.

†**2** A rule of etiquette; an observance prescribed by etiquette. L18–E19.

M. B. KEATINGE Some of the etiquettes of his majesty's court are rather whimsical.

■ **etiˈquettical** *adjective* M19.

etna /ˈɛtnə/ *noun*. Also †**aetna**. M19.
[ORIGIN An active volcano in Sicily.]
A vessel (in the form of an inverted cone placed on a saucer) for heating a small quantity of liquid by burning spirit.

etoile /ɪˈtɔɪl, ˈɛtwaːl/ *noun*. M18.
[ORIGIN French: see ESTOILE.]
HERALDRY. = ESTOILE.

Eton /ˈiːt(ə)n/ *noun*. L19.
[ORIGIN *Eton* College, English public school founded by Henry VI on the Thames opposite Windsor.]
1 ***Eton blue***, a light blue used as the school colour at Eton. L19.
2 ***Eton collar***, a broad and stiff collar worn outside a coat collar. L19.
3 ***Eton jacket***, a short black open-fronted jacket, pointed at the back and cut square at the hips, formerly worn by the younger boys at Eton. L19.
4 In full ***Eton suit***, a suit of an Eton jacket with trousers or skirt. L19.
5 ***Eton fives***, a form of fives played by pairs in a three-walled court, the design of which is based on an area outside the chapel at Eton. L19.
6 ***Eton crop***, a close-cropped hairstyle worn by women in the 1920s. E20.
■ **Etonian** /-ˈtəʊnɪən/ *noun & adjective* (**a**) *noun* a person educated at Eton College; (**b**) *adjective* of, pertaining to, or characteristic of Eton College: M17.

etorphine /ɛˈtɔːfiːn/ *noun*. M20.
[ORIGIN from ET(HENE + M)ORPHINE.]
A synthetic derivative of morphine used esp. to immobilize large wild animals.

étourderie /eturdəri/ *noun*. Pl. pronounced same. M18.
[ORIGIN French, from ÉTOURDI.]
Thoughtlessness, carelessness; a thoughtless act, a blunder.

étourdi /eturdi/ *adjective & noun*. Also (fem.) ***-ie***. Pl. pronounced same. L17.
[ORIGIN French, pa. ppl adjective of *étourdir* stun, make dizzy.]
(A person who is) thoughtless or irresponsible.

étrenne /etrɛn/ *noun*. Pl. pronounced same. E19.
[ORIGIN French from Old French *estreine* ult. from Latin *strena*.]
A New Year's gift; a Christmas box.

etrier /ˈeɪtrɪeɪ; *foreign* etrije (*pl. same*)/ *noun*. Also **é-**. M20.
[ORIGIN French *étrier* stirrup, etrier.]
sing. & in *pl.* A short rope ladder with a few solid rungs, used by climbers.

etrog /ˈɛtrɒg/ *noun*¹. Also **eth-**, **es-** /ˈɛs-/. Pl. **-s**, **-im** /-ɪm/. L19.
[ORIGIN Hebrew *'eṯrōg*.]
A citron fruit as used ritually in the Jewish Feast of Tabernacles.

Etrog /ˈɛtrɒg/ *noun*². M20.
[ORIGIN See below.]
Any of the statuettes by the Canadian sculptor Sorel Etrog (b. 1933) formerly awarded annually for achievement in Canadian film-making.

Etrurian /ɪˈtrʊərɪən/ *noun & adjective*. E17.
[ORIGIN from Latin *Etruria*: see ETRUSCAN *adjective*, -AN.]
► **A** *noun*. = ETRUSCAN *noun* 1. E17.
► **B** *adjective*. = ETRUSCAN *adjective* 1. E17.

Etruscan /ɪˈtrʌsk(ə)n/ *adjective & noun*. E18.
[ORIGIN from Latin *Etruscus* + -AN.]
► **A** *adjective*. **1** Of or pertaining to (the people of) ancient Etruria, an area of Italy roughly corresponding to present-day Tuscany; of or in the language of ancient Etruria. E18.
2 Designating a kind of encaustic pottery made orig. in the 18th cent. by Josiah Wedgwood in imitation of ancient Etruscan pottery. M18.
3 Designating a style of decorative bookbinding with ornamentation based on the patterns on ancient Etruscan pottery. M19.
► **B** *noun*. **1** A native or inhabitant of ancient Etruria. M18.
2 The language of the Etruscans, not yet deciphered and of unknown affinities. L18.
■ **Etruˈscologist** *noun* an expert in or student of Etruscology L19. **Etruˈscology** *noun* the branch of knowledge that deals with Etruscan history and antiquities L19.

-ette /ɛt/ *suffix*.
[ORIGIN Repr. Old French fem. *-ette*: see -ET¹.]
Forming nouns with the senses 'small', as ***cigarette***, ***kitchenette***; 'imitation or substitute', as ***flannelette***, ***leatherette***; 'female', as ***suffragette***, ***usherette***.

ettle /ˈɛt(ə)l/ *verb & noun*. Chiefly & now only *Scot. & N. English*. ME.
[ORIGIN Old Norse *ætla* (also *etla*, *atla*) think, conjecture, purpose, destine, apportion, from Germanic (whence Old English *eaht*, Old High German *ahta*, German *Acht* consideration) from base also of Gothic *aha* mind, *ahma* spirit.]
► **A** *verb* **I 1** *verb trans*. Intend, purpose, plan, attempt, (a thing, *to do*). ME. ►†**b** Arrange; prepare. ME–E16.
2 *verb trans*. Destine, ordain, assign. ME.
3 *verb intrans*. Direct one's course; set out (*for*). ME. ►**b** Aim *at*, make an effort *at*; take aim (*at*, *for*). E18.
4 *verb trans*. Aim (a blow, a missile) *at* a person or target (*lit.* & *fig.*); direct (speech, actions) to an object. LME.
► **II 5** *verb trans*. Guess, conjecture; expect, anticipate. ME.
► **B** *noun*. **1** Chance, opportunity. M18.
2 Aim, intent, purpose. L18.

étude /ˈeɪtjuːd, eɪˈtjuːd; *foreign* etyd (*pl. same*)/ *noun*. M19.
[ORIGIN French: see STUDY *noun*.]
An instrumental piece, esp. for the piano, which concentrates on a particular aspect of technique or allows a display of virtuosity.

etui /ɛˈtwiː/ *noun*. Also **etwee**. E17.
[ORIGIN French *étui*, Old French *estui* prison, from Old French *estuier* shut up, keep, save. Cf. STEW *noun*², TWEE *noun*¹, TWEEZE *noun*, TWEEZER.]
A small usu. ornamental case for needles etc. Formerly also, a case for surgical instruments.

-etum /ˈiːtəm/ *suffix*. Pl. **-etums**, **-eta** /ˈiːtə/. L17.
[ORIGIN Latin *-etum* neut. of *-etus*.]
Forming nouns denoting: (***a***) a collection or plantation of different plants of a group, as ARBORETUM, PINETUM; (***b***) *ECOLOGY* an association dominated by the species or genus from which it is named.

etwee *noun* var. of ETUI.

-ety *suffix* see -ITY.

etymologicon /ˌɛtɪməˈlɒdʒɪkɒn/ *noun*. M17.
[ORIGIN mod. Latin from Greek *etumologikon* use as noun (sc. *biblion* book) of neut. sing. of *etumologikos* pertaining to etymology, from *etumologos*: see ETYMOLOGY, -IC.]
A book in which etymologies are traced and recorded; an etymological dictionary.

etymologize /ɛtɪˈmɒlədʒʌɪz/ *verb*. Also **-ise**. M16.
[ORIGIN medieval Latin *etymologizare*, from Latin *etymologia*: see ETYMOLOGY, -IZE.]
1 *verb trans*. Give or suggest an etymology or derivation for. M16.
2 *verb intrans*. Study etymology; search into the origins of words; give or suggest etymologies for words. M17.
■ **etymologiˈzation** *noun* (*rare*) L15.

etymology /ɛtɪˈmɒlədʒi/ *noun*. LME.
[ORIGIN Old French *ethimologie* (mod. *étymologie*) from Latin *etimologia* (medieval Latin *ethymologia*, *ethim-*) from Greek *etumologia*, from *etumologos* student of etymology, from *etumon*: see ETYMON, -OLOGY.]
1 An account of, or the facts relating to, the formation or development of a word and its meaning; the process of tracing the history of a word. LME. ►†**b** The original meaning of a word as shown by its etymology. L16–E18.
FOLK etymology.
2 The branch of grammar that deals with the way individual words are inflected. *arch.* L16.
3 The branch of linguistics that deals with the etymologies of words. M17.
■ **etymologer** *noun* = ETYMOLOGIST E17. **ˌetymoˈlogic** *adjective* = ETYMOLOGICAL E19. **ˌetymoˈlogical** *adjective* of or pertaining to etymology; in accordance with etymology: L16. **ˌetymoˈlogically** *adverb* in an etymological manner, according to the principles of etymology M18. **etymologist** *noun* M17.

etymon /ˈɛtɪmɒn/ *noun*. Pl. **-mons**, **-ma** /-mə/. L16.
[ORIGIN Latin from Greek *etumon* use as noun of neut. sing. of *etumos* true.]
†**1** The original form of a word; the word or combination of words from which a given word has been corrupted. L16–L18.
†**2** The original or primary meaning of a word. *rare*. E17–M19.
3 A word from which some given word is derived by borrowing, modification, etc. M17.

EU *abbreviation*.
European Union.

Eu *symbol*.
CHEMISTRY. Europium.

eu- /juː/ *prefix*.
[ORIGIN Repr. Greek *eu-*, from *eu* well, from *eus* good.]
Used chiefly in words derived from Greek or formed on Greek analogies with the senses 'good, well' or (*MEDICINE*) 'normal' (opp. DYS-).
■ **eubacˈterial** *adjective* of, pertaining to, or involving eubacteria L20. **eubacˈterium** *noun*, pl. **-ria** /-rɪə/, (***a***) a bacterium of the genus *Eubacterium*, which includes anaerobic rods occurring in the intestines of vertebrates, animal and plant products, tissue infections, and soil; (***b***) a true bacterium as distinct from an archaebacterium: M20. **eucaine** *noun* [after *cocaine*] a synthetic derivative of piperidine formerly used as a local anaesthetic L19. **eucaˈtastrophe** *noun* a happy ending in a story, a sudden or unexpected coming right of events M20. **euˈcentric** *adjective* (of an electron microscope stage) having the field and focus unchanged when the specimen is tilted L20. **euˈchlorine** *noun* an explosive gas composed of chlorine and chlorine dioxide E19. **euchroˈmatic** *adjective* (*BIOLOGY*) staining like euchromatin M20. **euˈchromatin** *noun* (*BIOLOGY*) chromosome material that stains normally, i.e. diffusely when the nucleus is not dividing, and is genetically active M20. **eucone** *adjective* (of the eyes of certain insects) having a crystalline cone L19. **eugeoˈclinal** *adjective* (*GEOLOGY*) = EUGEOSYNCLINAL L20. **eugeocline** *noun* (*GEOLOGY*) = EUGEOSYNCLINE L20. **eugeosynˈclinal** *adjective* (*GEOLOGY*) of or pertaining to a eugeosyncline M20. **eugeoˈsyncline** *noun* (*GEOLOGY*) a geosyncline containing volcanic rocks and a greater depth of sediment than a miogeosyncline M20. **euˈglobulin** *noun* (*BIOCHEMISTRY*) the fraction of serum globulin which is insoluble in pure water E20. **euˈhedral** *adjective* (of a mineral crystal in a rock) bounded by its proper faces, unrestrained by the proximity of adjacent crystals E20. **euˈphotic** *adjective* pertaining to or designating the upper layers of a body of water, where enough light penetrates for photosynthesis E20. **eupnoea** /juːpˈniːə/ *noun* [Greek *pnoē* breathing] natural or normal breathing E18. **eupnoeic** /juːpˈniːɪk/ *adjective* characterized by eupnoea; (of breathing) natural, normal: E20. **euˈsocial** *adjective* (*ZOOLOGY*) showing an advanced level of social organization, in which a single female or caste produces the offspring and non-reproductive individuals cooperate in caring for the young M20. **eustele** *noun* (*BOTANY*) a stele, characteristic of gymnosperms and dicotyledons, in which the vascular tissue is in separate strands in which the phloem occurs on one side or both sides of the xylem E20. **euˈstelic** *adjective* (*BOTANY*) having a eustele M20. **euˈthyroid** *adjective* (*MEDICINE*) having a normally functioning thyroid gland M20. **euˈthyroidism** *noun* (*MEDICINE*) euthyroid state E20.

eubages *noun pl.* var. of EUHAGES.

Euboic /juːˈbəʊɪk/ *adjective*. L16.
[ORIGIN Latin *Euboicus* from Greek *Euboikos*, from *Euboia* Euboea: see below, -IC.]
Of or belonging to Euboea, the largest of the Greek islands after Crete.
Euboic talent a weight in use at the time of the Persian war.
■ Also **Euboean** /juːˈbiːən/ *adjective* L17.

eucalypt /ˈjuːkəlɪpt/ *noun*. L19.
[ORIGIN Abbreviation.]
= EUCALYPTUS 1.

eucalyptus /juːkəˈlɪptəs/ *noun*. Pl. **-tuses**, **-ti** /-tʌɪ/. E19.
[ORIGIN mod. Latin, from Greek EU- + *kaluptos* covered, from *kaluptein* cover, conceal; so called from the unopened flower and its protective covering.]
1 Any of the genus *Eucalyptus* of flowering evergreen trees and shrubs, of the myrtle family, including species important as forest trees in Australia and grown elsewhere for their hardwood, oils, gums, and resins, and as ornamentals. E19.

2 In full *eucalyptus oil*. Any essential oil from eucalyptus leaves, used esp. in pharmacy, flavourings, and perfumery. L19.
■ **eucalyptian** *adjective* L19. **eucalyptic** *adjective* M19. **eucalyptol** *noun* a volatile essential oil, 1,8-cineole, present in the oils of eucalyptus, cajuput, wormseed, and lavender L19.

eucaryotic *adjective* var. of EUKARYOTIC.

eucharis /ˈjuːkərɪs/ *noun*. M19.
[ORIGIN Greek *eukharis* gracious, formed as EU- + *kharis* grace.]
Any of the Central and S. American genus *Eucharis* of evergreen bulbous plants, of the amaryllis family, grown in hothouses for their large white bell-shaped flowers.

Eucharist /ˈjuːk(ə)rɪst/ *noun*. Also e-. LME.
[ORIGIN Old French *eucariste* (mod. *eucharistie*) from ecclesiastical Latin *eucharistia* from ecclesiastical Greek *eukharistia* giving of thanks, (earlier) gratitude, from Greek *eukharistos* grateful, formed as EU- + *kharizesthai* show favour, give freely, from *kharis* grace.]
▸ I CHRISTIAN CHURCH. 1 One of the sacraments, the central act of Christian worship, in which bread and wine are consecrated and consumed as Christ's body and blood, to be a memorial of his sacrifice on the Cross; a service or rite in which this is done. LME.

Church Times Members.. want to supplement the conventional Eucharists with a service which will attract newcomers. G. WAINWRIGHT The volume.. lists some thirty Lutheran Eucharists.

†2 A pyx. LME–M16.
3 The consecrated Eucharistic elements, *esp.* the bread. M16.
▸ II *gen.* 4 (An act of) thanksgiving. E17.
■ **eucha'ristize** *verb trans.* consecrate (bread or wine) in a Eucharist E18.

Eucharistic /juːkəˈrɪstɪk/ *noun & adjective*. Also e-. E17.
[ORIGIN from EUCHARIST + -IC.]
▸ †A *noun*. = EUCHARIST 4. E17–E18.
▸ B *adjective*. 1 Of or pertaining to the Eucharist, or thanksgiving generally. M17.
2 Of the nature of or resembling the Eucharist. M19.
■ **Eucharistical** *adjective* = EUCHARISTIC *adjective* 1, 2 M16. **Eucharistically** *adverb* M17.

Euchite /ˈjuːkʌɪt/ *noun*. L16.
[ORIGIN Late Latin *euchita*, *eucheta* from Greek *eukhitēs*, *eukhētēs*, from *eukhē* prayer: see -ITE[1].]
A member of a 4th-cent. Christian sect which believed that salvation could be gained only through incessant prayer.

Euchologion /juːkəˈləʊdʒɪən, -ˈlɒdʒ-/ *noun*. Also **Euchology** /juːˈkɒlədʒi/, e-. M17.
[ORIGIN Greek *eukhologion*, from *eukhē* prayer: see -OLOGY.]
A book of prayers or religious rites; *spec.* a book of the Orthodox Church containing the Eucharistic rites and other liturgical matter.

euchre /ˈjuːkə/ *noun & verb*. E19.
[ORIGIN German dial. *Jucker(spiel)*.]
▸ A *noun*. 1 A card game for 2 to 4 players in which the highest cards are the joker (if used), the jack of trumps, and the other jack of the same colour in a pack with the lower cards removed, the aim being win at least three of the five tricks played. E19.
2 An instance of euchring or being euchred. M19.
▸ B *verb trans.* 1 Prevent (a bidder) from winning three or more tricks at euchre, thereby scoring points oneself. E19.
2 Cheat, trick, (*into*, *out of*); deceive, outwit. M19.

T. PYNCHON They have euchred Mexico into some such Byzantine exercise.

3 Exhaust; ruin, finish, do for, (a person). Usu. in *pass.* *Austral.* M20.

K. S. PRICHARD I've got to get water for me horses.. or we're euchred.

euclase /ˈjuːkleɪz/ *noun*. E19.
[ORIGIN French, from Greek EU- + *klasis* breaking (so called from its brittleness).]
MINERALOGY. A hydrated basic silicate of beryllium and aluminium occurring as pale monoclinic crystals sometimes valued as gems.

Euclid /ˈjuːklɪd/ *noun*. L16.
[ORIGIN Greek *Eukleidēs*, a mathematician of Alexandria, fl. 300 BC.]
(A copy of) the works of Euclid, esp. *The Elements*, long the principal textbook of geometry.

Euclidean /juːˈklɪdɪən/ *adjective*. Also -ian. E18.
[ORIGIN from Latin *Euclideus*, Greek *Eukleideios* (formed as EUCLID) + -EAN, -IAN.]
Of or pertaining to Euclid; that is according to the principles of Euclid.
Euclidean geometry the geometry of ordinary experience, based on the axioms of Euclid, esp. the one stating that parallel lines do not meet. **Euclidean space** the space of ordinary experience, for which Euclidean geometry holds.

eucomis /ˈjuːkəmɪs/ *noun*. E19.
[ORIGIN mod. Latin (see below), from Greek *eukomēs* beautiful-haired, formed as EU- + *komē* hair.]
Any of various bulbous African plants of the genus *Eucomis*, of the lily family, having the flower spike crowned by large leaflike bracts. Also called ***pineapple lily***.

eucrasia /juːˈkreɪsɪə, -zɪə/ *noun*. LME.
[ORIGIN medieval Latin from Greek *eukrasia* good temperament, formed as EU- + *krasis* CRASIS: see -IA[1].]
A good or normal state of health. Orig., a well-balanced mixture of bodily humours.

eucrasy /ˈjuːkrəsi/ *noun*. Long *rare* or *obsolete*. E17.
[ORIGIN from EUCRASIA: see -Y[3].]
= EUCRASIA.

†**eucratic** *adjective*. LME–L18.
[ORIGIN from Greek *eukratos*, from *eukrasia*: see EUCRASIA, -IC.]
Having good and bad points, with the good predominating.

eucrite /ˈjuːkrʌɪt/ *noun*. M19.
[ORIGIN from Greek *eukritos* easily discerned, formed as EU- + *kritos* separated, from *krinein* to separate: see -ITE[1].]
1 GEOLOGY. A highly basic gabbro containing anorthite or bytownite, together with augite. M19.
2 An achondritic stony meteorite composed principally of anorthite and augite. L19.

eucryphia /juːˈkrɪfɪə/ *noun*. L20.
[ORIGIN mod. Latin (see below), from Greek *eu* well + *-kruphos* hidden, with ref. to its joined sepals.]
A shrub or small tree of the genus *Eucryphia* (family Eucryphiaceae), with glossy dark green leaves and large white flowers, native to Australia and South America.

†**euctical** *adjective*. M17–M18.
[ORIGIN from Greek *euktikos* from *eukhesthai* pray from *eukhē* prayer, + -AL[1].]
Pertaining to prayer; supplicatory.

eudaemon *noun*, **eudaemonic** *adjective*, etc., vars. of EUDEMON etc.

eudaimonia /juːdʌɪˈmɒnɪə/ *noun*. E20.
[ORIGIN Greek, formed as EUDEMON: see -IA[1]. Cf. EUDEMONY.]
PHILOSOPHY. Happiness or well-being consisting in the full realization of human potential, esp. (in Aristotle's ethics) in rational activity exhibiting excellence.

eudaimonism *noun* var. of EUDEMONISM.

eudemon /juːˈdiːmən/ *noun*. Also -daem-. E17.
[ORIGIN Greek *eudaimōn* fortunate, happy, formed as EU- + *daimōn* genius, DEMON *noun*[1].]
1 = AGATHODEMON. E17.
2 The eleventh of the twelve astrological houses. L17.

eudemonic /juːdiːˈmɒnɪk/ *adjective*. Also -daem-. M19.
[ORIGIN Greek *eudaimonikos*, from EUDAIMONIA: see -IC.]
Conducive to happiness.

eudemonics /juːdiːˈmɒnɪks/ *noun pl.* (treated as *pl.* or *sing.*). Also -daem-. M19.
[ORIGIN formed as EUDEMONIC: see -ICS.]
The art of pursuing life with happiness as the ultimate goal.

eudemonism /juːˈdiːmənɪz(ə)m/ *noun*. Also -daem-, -daim-. E19.
[ORIGIN formed as EUDEMON + -ISM.]
An ethical system based on the view that the aim of moral action is personal fulfilment and well-being.
■ **eudemonist** *noun & adjective* (*a*) *noun* a believer in eudemonism; (*b*) *adjective* = EUDEMONISTIC: E19. **eudemo'nistic** *adjective* of or pertaining to eudemonism or eudemonists M19.

eudemony /juːˈdiːməni/ *noun*. *rare*. Also -daem-. M18.
[ORIGIN from Greek EUDAIMONIA: see -Y[3].]
Happiness; *spec.* = EUDAIMONIA.

eudiometer /juːdɪˈɒmɪtə/ *noun*. L18.
[ORIGIN from Greek *eudios* fine (of weather), formed as EU- + *dios* heavenly, genit. of *Zeus* god of the sky: see -OMETER. So called because an increase in the oxygen content of the air was formerly thought to accompany fine weather.]
Orig., an instrument for measuring the oxygen content of the air. Now, any instrument for measuring and analysing gases by volume; *spec.* a graduated glass tube in which gases are chemically combined by a spark between two terminals.
■ ˌ**eudio'metric** *adjective* M19. ˌ**eudio'metrical** *adjective* L18. ˌ**eudio'metrically** *adverb* E19. **eudiometry** *noun* E19.

Eudist /ˈjuːdɪst/ *noun & adjective*. L19.
[ORIGIN from *Eudes* (see below) + -IST.]
▸ A *noun*. A member of the Congregation of Jesus and Mary, founded for secular clergy by St Jean Eudes (1601–80), French missioner, and now concerned chiefly with secondary education in France, Canada, etc. L19.
▸ B *adjective*. Of, pertaining to, or designating the Eudists. E20.

eufunctional /juːˈfʌŋkʃ(ə)n(ə)l/ *adjective*. M20.
[ORIGIN from EU- + FUNCTIONAL *adjective*.]
That performs a function well.

Euganean /juːˈgeɪnɪən/ *adjective & noun*. E17.
[ORIGIN from Italian *Euganei* from Latin, a people of northern Italy: see -EAN.]
▸ A *adjective*. Designating a group of hills south-west of Padua. E17.
▸ B *noun*. In *pl.* The Euganean Hills. L19.

euge /ˈjuːdʒi/ *noun*. Now *rare* or *obsolete*. M17.
[ORIGIN Latin from Greek = well done!]
An expression of approval, a commendation.

eugenesis /juːˈdʒɛnɪsɪs/ *noun*. L19.
[ORIGIN from EU- + -GENESIS.]
The production of fit and healthy offspring, esp. by deliberate outbreeding or selection of individuals.
■ **euge'nesic**, **euge'netic** *adjectives* L19.

eugenia /juːˈdʒiːnɪə/ *noun*. L18.
[ORIGIN mod. Latin (see below), from Prince *Eugene* of Savoy (1663–1736), Austrian general.]
Any of various mostly tropical American trees of the genus *Eugenia*, of the myrtle family.

eugenic /juːˈdʒɛnɪk/ *adjective*. L19.
[ORIGIN formed as EUGENICS + -IC.]
Of or pertaining to eugenics.
■ **eugenically** *adverb* E20. **eugenicist** /-sɪst/ *noun* an expert in, or a student or advocate of, eugenics E20. **eugenist** *noun & adjective* (*a*) *noun* = EUGENICIST; (*b*) *adjective* = EUGENIC: E20.

eugenics /juːˈdʒɛnɪks/ *noun*. L19.
[ORIGIN from EU- + -GEN + -ICS.]
The science dealing with factors that influence the hereditary qualities of a race and with ways of improving these qualities, esp. by modifying the fertility of different categories of people.
negative eugenics: see NEGATIVE *adjective*. ***positive eugenics***: see POSITIVE *adjective*.

eugenol /ˈjuːdʒɪnɒl/ *noun*. L19.
[ORIGIN from EUGENIA + -OL.]
A liquid phenol, $C_{10}H_{12}O_2$, present in many essential oils, esp. clove oil; 4-allyl-2-methoxyphenol.

euglena /juːˈgliːnə/ *noun*. M19.
[ORIGIN mod. Latin (see below), from EU- + Greek *glēnē* eyeball, socket of joint.]
A single-celled freshwater flagellate of the genus *Euglena* (variously classed as a protozoan and an alga), which can form a green scum on stagnant water.
■ **euglenoid** *noun & adjective* (*a*) *noun* a flagellate of the order containing *Euglena*, comprising mostly green or colourless organisms with one or two flagella and a gullet reservoir; (*b*) *adjective* resembling or characteristic of *Euglena* or a euglenoid (***euglenoid movement***, a rhythmical movement in which waves of expansion and contraction pass along the body): L19.

euhages /juːˈheɪgiːz/ *noun pl.* Also ***-bages*** /-ˈbeɪgiːz/. E17.
[ORIGIN Latin, alt. of Greek *ouateis*: see OVATE *noun*[1]. Cf. VATES.]
Ancient Celtic priests or natural philosophers.

euhemerism /juːˈhiːmərɪz(ə)m/ *noun*. M19.
[ORIGIN from Latin *Euhemerus* from Greek *Euēmeros*, Sicilian writer (c 316 BC) who maintained that the gods and goddesses of Greek mythol. were deified men and women: see -ISM.]
The interpretation of myths as traditional accounts of real historical events and people.
■ **euhemerist** *noun & adjective* (*a*) *noun* a euhemeristic person; (*b*) *adjective* = EUHEMERISTIC: M19. **euheme'ristic** *adjective* inclined to euhemerism; exhibiting or characterized by euhemerism: M19. **euhemerize** *verb* (*a*) *verb trans.* subject to a euhemeristic interpretation; (*b*) *verb intrans.* follow the euhemeristic method of interpretation: M19.

eukaryotic /juːkarɪˈɒtɪk/ *adjective*. Also -cary-. M20.
[ORIGIN from EU- + Greek *karuon* nut, kernel + *-ōtēs* -OT[2].]
BIOLOGY. (Of a cell) characterized by a discrete nucleus with a membrane, and other organelles; (of an organism) composed of such cells, belonging to the group which includes most organisms other than bacteria; of or pertaining to a eukaryotic cell or organism.
■ '**eukaryote** *noun* a eukaryotic organism (opp. PROKARYOTE) M20.

eulachon /ˈjuːləkɒn/ *noun*. Also **oolichan** /ˈuːlɪkən/ and other vars. M19.
[ORIGIN Lower Chinook *ú̱txan*.]
A small oily food fish, *Thaleichthys pacificus*, of the Pacific coast of N. America, belonging to the smelt family. Also called ***candlefish***.

Euler /ˈɔɪlə/ *noun*. M19.
[ORIGIN L. *Euler* (1707–83), Swiss mathematician.]
Used *attrib.* and in *possess.* with ref. to Euler's discoveries in mathematics.
Euler's constant the limit as n tends to infinity of $1 + \frac{1}{2} + \frac{1}{3} + \ldots + \frac{1}{n} - \ln n$ (approximately 0.57715). **Euler's formula**, **Euler's theorem** any of various formulae and theorems arrived at by Euler, esp. $V + F - E = 2$, where V, F, and E are the numbers of vertices, faces, and edges of any simple convex polyhedron.
■ **Eulerian** /-ˈlɪərɪən/ *adjective* L19.

eulogia /juːˈləʊdʒɪə, ɛʌləˈgiːə/ *noun*. Pl. -iae /-ɪiː/. M18.
[ORIGIN Late (eccl.) Latin = consecrated bread from ecclesiastical Greek = blessing, praise, from Greek: see EULOGY.]
ECCLESIASTICAL. = ANTIDORON. Also, consecrated bread reserved for communicating those not present at the Eucharist.

eulogic /juːˈlɒdʒɪk/ *adjective*. *rare*. M18.
[ORIGIN from EULOGY + -IC.]
= EULOGISTIC.
■ **eulogically** *adverb* M17.

eulogise *verb* var. of EULOGIZE.

eulogium /juːˈləʊdʒɪəm/ *noun*. E17.
[ORIGIN medieval Latin = praise, app. blending of Latin *elogium* inscription on a tomb (see ELOGIUM) and medieval Latin *eulogia* (see EULOGY).]
= EULOGY 2.

eulogize /ˈjuːlədʒʌɪz/ *verb trans.* Also **-ise**. E19.
[ORIGIN from EULOGY + -IZE.]
Deliver or write a eulogy on; extol.

R. HAYMAN Lectures . . which tended to denigrate Czech achievements while eulogizing the primacy of German culture.

■ **eulogizer** *noun* a eulogist E19.

eulogy /ˈjuːlədʒi/ *noun*. LME.
[ORIGIN from medieval Latin *eulogium*, *eulogia* praise, from Greek *eulogia*, formed as EU-, -LOGY.]
1 High praise. LME.
2 A speech or piece of writing in praise of a person or thing, esp. a person who has recently died. L16.

P. G. WODEHOUSE He embarked forthwith on an eulogy of his late playmate.

†**3** ECCLESIASTICAL. = EULOGIA. Only in 18.
■ **eulogism** *noun* = EULOGY 2 M18. **eulogist** *noun* a person who delivers or writes a eulogy E19. **euloˈgistic** *adjective* of the nature of a eulogy, laudatory (foll. by *of*) E19. **euloˈgistically** *adverb* M19.

Eumenides /juːˈmɛnɪdiːz/ *noun pl.* L17.
[ORIGIN (Latin from) Greek, from *eumenēs* well-disposed, friendly, formed as EU- + *menos* spirit.]
The Greek Furies.

eunomia /juːˈnəʊmɪə/. *noun*. M19.
[ORIGIN Greek, formed as EU- + *-nomia*: see -NOMY. Cf. EUNOMY.]
A political condition of good law well administered.

Eunomian /juːˈnəʊmɪən/ *noun & adjective*. LME.
[ORIGIN from *Eunomius* (see below) + -AN.]
ECCLESIASTICAL. ▸**A** *noun*. A follower of Eunomius, 4th-cent. bishop of Cyzicus on the Sea of Marmara, who developed an extreme form of Arianism. LME.
▸ **B** *adjective*. Of or pertaining to Eunomius or Eunomians. L18.

eunomic /juːˈnɒmɪk/ *adjective*. M20.
[ORIGIN from EUNOMIA + -IC.]
Law-abiding; socially well ordered.

eunomy /ˈjuːnəmi/ *noun*. *rare*. E18.
[ORIGIN from Greek EUNOMIA: see -Y[3].]
= EUNOMIA.

eunuch /ˈjuːnək/ *noun & verb*. OE.
[ORIGIN Latin *eunuchus* from Greek *eunoukhos* lit. 'bedroom guard', from *eunē* bed + forms of *ekhein* keep.]
▸ **A** *noun*. **1** A castrated man; such a man employed as a harem attendant or (*hist.*) charged with important affairs of state in Mediterranean countries. OE.

GIBBON The private apartments of the palace were governed by a favourite eunuch.

2 *fig.* A person or thing with some kind of incapacity, specified or implied; an ineffectual person. L16.

BYRON The intellectual eunuch Castlereagh.

3 = CASTRATO. M18.
– COMB.: **eunuch flute** *hist.* a tubular musical instrument which produces notes from a membrane vibrated by the human voice.
▸ **B** *verb trans.* = EUNUCHIZE. Now *rare*. E17.
■ **eunuchism** *noun* the process or custom of making eunuchs; the condition of being a eunuch; emasculation: E17. **eunuchize** *verb trans.* castrate; reduce to the condition of a eunuch; emasculate (*lit.* & *fig.*): M17. **eunuchry** *noun* (*rare*) the state of being a eunuch M19.

eunuchoid /ˈjuːnəkɔɪd/ *adjective & noun*. L19.
[ORIGIN from EUNUCH + -OID.]
▸ **A** *adjective*. Resembling or having the characteristics of a eunuch; having reduced sexual characteristics. L19.
▸ **B** *noun*. A eunuchoid person. L19.
■ **eunuˈchoidal** *adjective* M20. **eunuchoidism** *noun* E20.

euonymus /juːˈɒnɪməs/ *noun*. M18.
[ORIGIN mod. Latin (Linnaeus) from Latin *euonymos* (Pliny) use as noun of Greek *euōnumos* having an honoured or auspicious name, formed as EU- + *onuma* name: see -NYM.]
Any of various shrubs and small trees of the genus *Euonymus* (family Celastraceae), which includes the spindle tree, *E. europaeus*.

Eupad /ˈjuːpad/ *noun*. E20.
[ORIGIN from Edinburgh University Pathological Department (where it was invented), with joc. ref. to EU- and PAD *noun*[3], as = good pad.]
PHARMACOLOGY. An antiseptic dry dressing of chlorinated lime mixed with boric acid.

eupathy /ˈjuːpəθi/ *noun*. E17.
[ORIGIN Greek *eupatheia* happy condition of the soul, formed as EU- + base of *pathos* feeling: see PATHOS, -Y[3].]
In Stoic philosophy, each of three rational dispositions of the mind (joy, caution, and will).

eupatorium /juːpəˈtɔːrɪəm/ *noun*. M16.
[ORIGIN mod. Latin from Greek *eupatorion* agrimony, *Agrimonia eupatoria*, from Mithridates *Eupator* (120–63 BC), king of Pontus: see -IUM.]
Any of various plants of the genus *Eupatorium*, of the composite family, largely of tropical America but including one British native, the hemp agrimony, *E. cannabinum*.

†**eupatory** *noun*. LME–M17.
[ORIGIN Latin *eupatoria* from Greek *eupatorion*: see EUPATORIUM, -Y[3].]
Hemp agrimony (see EUPATORIUM). Formerly also, wood sage, *Teucrium scorodonia*.

eupatrid /juːˈpatrɪd, ˈjuːpətrɪd/ *noun & adjective*. Pl. **eupatrids**, **eupatridai** /juːˈpatrɪdʌɪ/, **eupatridae** /juːˈpatrɪdiː/. M19.
[ORIGIN Greek *eupatridēs* person of noble ancestry, formed as EU- + *patēr* father.]
▸ **A** *noun*. In ancient Greece, a member of the hereditary aristocracy of Athens; *gen.* a person of noble descent. M19.
▸ **B** *adjective*. Of, pertaining to, or belonging to the eupatrids. M19.

eupepsia /juːˈpɛpsɪə/ *noun*. E18.
[ORIGIN Greek *eupepsia* digestibility, from *eupeptos*: see EUPEPTIC, -IA[1].]
Good digestion; absence of indigestion.

eupeptic /juːˈpɛptɪk/ *adjective*. L17.
[ORIGIN from Greek *eupeptos* easy to digest, having a good digestion, formed as EU- + *peptein* to digest: see -IC.]
†**1** Helping digestion. *rare*. Only in L17.
2 Having good digestion. M19.
3 Characteristic of or resulting from good digestion. M19.
▸**b** Cheerful, well-disposed, optimistic. M20.

CARLYLE A massiveness of eupeptic vigour.

■ **eupeptically** *adverb* M20. **eupepˈticity** *noun* the condition resulting from good digestion M19.

euphausiid /juːˈfɔːzɪɪd/ *noun & adjective*. Also **-sid** /-zɪd/. L19.
[ORIGIN from mod. Latin *Euphausia* genus name, from Greek EU- + *phainein* to show + *ousia* substance: see -ID[3].]
(Of, pertaining to, or designating) any of a group of marine shrimplike, planktonic, mostly luminescent, malacostracan crustaceans that includes krill.
■ **euphausiacean** *noun* a member of the order or suborder Euphausiaceae of euphausiids M20.

euphemious /juːˈfiːmɪəs/ *adjective*. *rare*. M19.
[ORIGIN from Greek *euphēmos*: see EUPHEMISM, -IOUS.]
1 = EUPHEMISTIC. M19.
2 Considered respectable. M19.
■ **euphemiously** *adverb* M19.

euphemise *verb* var. of EUPHEMIZE.

euphemism /ˈjuːfɪmɪz(ə)m/ *noun*. Also (now *rare*) in late Latin form **euphemismus** /juːfɪˈmɪzməs/. L16.
[ORIGIN Greek *euphēmismos*, from *euphēmizein* speak fair, from *euphēmos* fair of speech, formed as EU- + *phēmē* speaking: see -ISM.]
1 A figure of speech in which an offensive, harsh, or blunt word or expression is avoided and one that is milder but less precise or accurate is used instead. L16.
2 The milder word or expression used in an instance of euphemism. L18.

T. PYNCHON 'Foreign workers', a euphemism for civilian prisoners brought in from countries under German occupation.

■ **euphemist** *noun* a person who uses euphemisms M19.

euphemistic /juːfɪˈmɪstɪk/ *adjective*. M19.
[ORIGIN from EUPHEMISM: see -IST, -IC.]
Pertaining to euphemism; of the nature of a euphemism; containing a euphemism.
■ **euphemistical** *adjective* L19. **euphemistically** *adverb* by way of euphemism M19.

euphemize /ˈjuːfɪmʌɪz/ *verb trans. & intrans.* Also **-ise**. M19.
[ORIGIN Greek *euphēmizein*: see EUPHEMISM, -IZE.]
Speak or write (of) euphemistically.
■ **euphemizer** *noun* L19.

euphenics /juːˈfɛnɪks/ *noun*. M20.
[ORIGIN from EU- + PHEN(OTYPE + -ICS.]
The improvement of the bodily functioning or development of a person by medical or other means.
■ **euphenic** *adjective* M20.

euphonia /juːˈfəʊnɪə/ *noun*. Now *rare*. L16.
[ORIGIN Late Latin: see EUPHONY, -PHONIA.]
= EUPHONY.

euphonic /juːˈfɒnɪk/ *adjective*. M18.
[ORIGIN from EUPHONY + -IC.]
1 Of or pertaining to euphony. M18.
2 = EUPHONIOUS. E19.
■ **euphonical** *adjective* M17. **euphonically** *adverb* M19.

euphonious /juːˈfəʊnɪəs/ *adjective*. L18.
[ORIGIN formed as EUPHONIC + -IOUS.]
Full of or characterized by euphony; pleasing to the ear.

A. S. BYATT I want a name like Bowen, or Sackville . . ; euphonious but plain.

■ **euphoniously** *adverb* M19.

euphonise *verb* var. of EUPHONIZE.

euphonism /ˈjuːf(ə)nɪz(ə)m/ *noun*. Also in Latin form †**euphonismus**. L18.
[ORIGIN formed as EUPHONY + -ISM.]
The habit of using euphonious words; a euphonious expression.
■ **euphoˈnistic** *adjective* chosen with regard to euphony; aiming to be euphonious: M19.

euphonium /juːˈfəʊnɪəm/ *noun*. M19.
[ORIGIN from Greek *euphōnos*: see EUPHONY, -IUM.]
A valved brass wind instrument of tenor-bass pitch, used especially in brass and military bands.

euphonize /ˈjuːf(ə)nʌɪz/ *verb trans.* Also **-ise**. L18.
[ORIGIN from EUPHONY + -IZE.]
Make euphonious; alter (a word) for the sake of euphony.
■ **euphoniˈzation** *noun* L19.

euphonon /juːˈfəʊnɒn/ *noun*. E19.
[ORIGIN Greek *euphōnon* neut. of *euphōnos*: see EUPHONY.]
An obsolete musical instrument which resembled the upright piano in form and the organ in tone.

euphonous /ˈjuːf(ə)nəs/ *adjective*. E19.
[ORIGIN from EUPHONY + -OUS.]
= EUPHONIOUS.

euphony /ˈjuːf(ə)ni/ *noun*. LME.
[ORIGIN French *euphonie* from late Latin *euphonia* from Greek *euphōnia*, from *euphōnos* well-sounding, formed as EU-: see -PHONY. Cf. EUPHONIA.]
1 The quality, esp. of spoken words, of having a pleasant sound; the pleasing effect of sounds free from harshness. LME.

J. I. M. STEWART 'Albert Talbert' is lacking in euphony and even a shade ludicrous.

2 PHILOLOGY. The tendency to phonetic change giving easier pronunciation. L19.

euphorbia /juːˈfɔːbɪə/ *noun*. LME.
[ORIGIN Alt. (by assim. to -IA[1]) of Latin *euphorbea*, from *Euphorbus* (fl. 1st cent. BC), physician to Juba II, king of Mauretania.]
Any herb or shrub of the genus *Euphorbia* (family Euphorbiaceae); = SPURGE *noun*.
■ ˌ**euphorbiˈaceous** *adjective* of or pertaining to the family Euphorbiaceae M19.

euphorbium /juːˈfɔːbɪəm/ *noun*. ME.
[ORIGIN Latin *euphorbeum*, *-bium* from Greek *euphorbion*, from *Euphorbus*: see EUPHORBIA, -IUM.]
1 The resinous gum of certain succulent plants of the genus *Euphorbia*, formerly used as an emetic and purgative. ME.
†**2** = EUPHORBIA. E17–M18.

euphoria /juːˈfɔːrɪə/ *noun*. Also (now *rare*) **euphory** /ˈjuːf(ə)ri/. L17.
[ORIGIN mod. Latin from Greek, from *euphoros* borne well, healthy, formed as EU- + *pherein* to bear: see -IA[1], -Y[3].]
Orig., a state of well-being, esp. as produced in a sick person by a medicine. Now, a strong feeling of well-being, cheerfulness, and optimism, *esp.* one based on overconfidence or overoptimism; a mood marked by this, as symptomatic of a mental illness or the influence of drugs.

W. STYRON Cans of beer . . helped perpetuate my euphoria.

■ **euphoriant** *noun & adjective* (a drug) inducing euphoria M20. **euphoric** /-ˈfɒrɪk/ *adjective & noun* (**a**) *adjective* accompanied or characterized by euphoria; elated, ecstatic; (**b**) a euphoriant: L19. **euphorically** *adverb* M20.

euphrasia /juːˈfreɪzɪə/ *noun*. E18.
[ORIGIN medieval Latin from Greek, lit. 'cheerfulness', from *euphrainein* gladden, formed as EU- + *phrēn* mind.]
Any plant of the genus *Euphrasia*, of the figwort family; *esp.* = ***eyebright*** s.v. EYE *noun*.

euphrasy /ˈjuːfrəzi/ *noun*. *arch.* LME.
[ORIGIN Anglicized from medieval Latin EUPHRASIA.]
= ***eyebright*** s.v. EYE *noun*.

Euphratean /juːˈfreɪtɪən/ *adjective*. L19.
[ORIGIN from *Euphrates* (see below) + -AN.]
Of, pertaining to, or bordering on the River Euphrates, a long river of SW Asia that flows into the Persian Gulf.

euphuism /ˈjuːfjuːɪz(ə)m/ *noun*. L16.
[ORIGIN from *Euphues*, a fictional character (see below), from Greek *euphuēs* well-endowed by nature, formed as EU- + *phu-* (= be) in *phuē* growth: see -ISM.]
1 A literary and conversational style imitative of that found in John Lyly's *Euphues* (1578–80), which was fashionable in the late 16th and early 17th cents. and is characterized by an abundance of antitheses, alliteration, and similes referring to natural history and mythology; any artificial and affected style; high-flown language. L16.
2 An instance of euphuism; a euphuistic expression. L19.
■ **euphuist** *noun* a person who uses euphuism L16. **euphuˈistic**, **euphuˈistical** *adjectives* E19. **euphuˈistically** *adverb* M19.

eupione /ˈjuːpɪəʊn/ *noun*. Now *rare*. M19.
[ORIGIN Greek *eupiōn* very fat, formed as EU- + *piōn* fat; assim. to -ONE.]
A volatile oily liquid obtained by the distillation of wood, tar, etc.

euploid /ˈjuːplɔɪd/ *adjective*. E20.
[ORIGIN formed as EU- + -PLOID.]
GENETICS. Having an equal number of all the chromosomes of the haploid set.
■ **euploidy** *noun* euploid condition E20.

Eur- *combining form* see EURO-.

Eurafrican /jʊ(ə)rˈafrɪk(ə)n/ *adjective & noun*. Also (exc. in sense A.1) **Euro-African** /jʊərəʊ-/. L19.
[ORIGIN from EURO- + AFRICAN.]
▸ **A** *adjective*. **1** ANTHROPOLOGY. Designating a dark-skinned people supposed to have inhabited regions on both sides of the Mediterranean. L19.
2 Of or pertaining to both Europe and Africa, or countries or people of both continents. E20.
3 Of mixed European and (black) African descent; *spec.* designating Coloured people in South Africa. E20.
▸ **B** *noun*. A Eurafrican person (see sense A.3 above). E20.

euraquilo /jʊ(ə)rˈakwɪləʊ/ *noun*. Also **euroaquilo** /jʊ(ə)rəʊˈakwɪləʊ/. L16.
[ORIGIN Latin *euroaquilo* north-east wind, formed as EURUS + *aquilo* north wind.]
A stormy north-east or north-north-east wind blowing in the eastern Mediterranean. Cf. EUROCLYDON.

Eurasian /jʊ(ə)rˈeɪʃ(ə)n, -ʒ(ə)n/ *adjective & noun*. M19.
[ORIGIN Partly from EURO- + ASIAN, partly from *Eurasia* Europe and Asia together: see -AN.]
▸ **A** *adjective*. **1** Of mixed European and Asian (formerly esp. Indian) descent. M19.
2 Of or pertaining to Europe and Asia considered as one continent. M19.
▸ **B** *noun*. A person of mixed European and Asian (formerly esp. Indian) descent. M19.
– NOTE: In 19 *Eurasian* usu. referred to a person of mixed British and Indian parentage. It now more often denotes a person of mixed white American and SE Asian parentage.

Eurasiatic /jʊ(ə)rˌeɪʃɪˈatɪk, -eɪʒ-/ *adjective & noun*. Also **Euro-Asiatic** /ˌjʊərəʊeɪʃ-/. M19.
[ORIGIN from EURO- + ASIATIC.]
▸ **A** *adjective*. = EURASIAN *adjective* 2. M19.
▸ **B** *noun*. A person of Eurasiatic origin. M20.

Euratom /jʊ(ə)rˈatəm/ *noun*. M20.
[ORIGIN from *European Atomic* Energy Community.]
An international organization (now administratively part of the European Union) established in 1958 to coordinate the development and use of nuclear energy in some European countries.

eureka /jʊ(ə)ˈriːkə/ *interjection & noun*. E17.
[ORIGIN Greek *heurēka*, 1st person sing. pf. of *heuriskein* find: uttered by Archimedes when he hit upon a method of determining the purity of gold.]
▸ **A** *interjection*. Expr. exultation at a sudden discovery. E17.
▸ **B** *noun*. **1** A cry of ***eureka!*** M17.
2 A fortunate discovery. M19.
3 (**E-**.) (Proprietary name for) an alloy of copper and nickel used for electrical filament and resistance wire. E20.

eurhythmic /jʊ(ə)ˈrɪðmɪk/ *adjective*. In sense 2 also ***eury-**. M19.
[ORIGIN Partly from EURHYTHMY + -IC, partly back-form. from EURHYTHMICS.]
1 Of, pertaining to, or having harmonious proportions or regularity. M19.
2 Involving eurhythmics. E20.
■ **eurhythmical** *adjective* = EURHYTHMIC 2 E20. **eurhythmist** *noun* a person who practises or advocates eurhythmics E20.

eurhythmics /jʊ(ə)ˈrɪðmɪks/ *noun*. Also ***eury-**. E20.
[ORIGIN from EU- + RHYTHM + -ICS.]
A system of dance or rhythmical bodily movements, seeking to express the content of a piece of music or poetry, freq. used for educational and therapeutic purposes.

eurhythmy /jʊ(ə)ˈrɪðmi/ *noun*. In sense 2 also ***eury-**. L16.
[ORIGIN Latin *eur(h)ythmia* proportion from Greek *euruthmia*, formed as EU- + *rhuthmos* proportion, RHYTHM: see -Y³.]
1 Harmonious proportions, esp. in a building; symmetry; regularity. L16.
2 = EURHYTHMICS. M20.

euriballi *noun* var. of JURIBALLI.

Euripidean /jʊ(ə)ˌrɪpɪˈdiːən/ *adjective*. E19.
[ORIGIN from Latin *Euripideus* from Greek *Euripideios*, from *Euripidēs* (see below): see -AN.]
Of, pertaining to, or characteristic of the Athenian tragic poet Euripides (484–406 BC), or his works, style, etc.

euripus /jʊ(ə)ˈrʌɪpəs/ *noun*. Pl. **-pi** /-ʌɪ/. L16.
[ORIGIN Latin = strait (esp. that between Euboea and the mainland of Greece), canal from Greek *euripos*, formed as EU- + *rhipē* a rushing.]
†**1** Rapid inhalation and exhalation during the use of tobacco. *rare*. Only in L16.
2 A strait or sea channel with strong or irregular currents. E17.
3 An artificial channel; a canal. M18.

euro /ˈjʊərəʊ/ *noun*¹. *Austral.* Also **uroo**, **yuro**. Pl. **-os**. M19.
[ORIGIN Adnyamathanha (an Australian Aboriginal language of the Flinders Ranges region of South Australia) *yuru*.]
The wallaby *Macropus robustus*.

Euro /ˈjʊərəʊ/ *noun*² & *adjective*. *colloq.* L20.
[ORIGIN Abbreviation of EUROPEAN.]
▸ **A** *noun*. Pl. **-os**.
1 A European. Also, a Eurocommunist. L20.
2 = EUROBOND, EURODOLLAR. L20.
3 (**euro**) The single European currency unit (represented by the symbol €, divided into 100 cents), introduced in 1999 and replacing the national currencies of twelve European Union states in 2002. L20.
▸ **B** *adjective*. Of, pertaining to, or characteristic of (esp. Western) Europe or its inhabitants. L20.

Euro- /ˈjʊərəʊ/ *combining form*. Before a vowel also **Eur-** /jʊ(ə)r/.
[ORIGIN from *Europe*, EUROPEAN: see -O-.]
Forming nouns and adjectives with ref. to (***a***) Europe as a continent or a collection of countries; (***b***) the European Union or the European Parliament, as ***Euro-candidate***, ***Euro-election***, etc.; (***c***) money, securities, etc. held outside their country of origin or (later) expressed in Euros, as ***Euro-credit***, ***Eurofinance***.
■ **Euro-Aˈmerican** *adjective & noun* (***a***) *adjective* of or pertaining to both Europe and America; (***b***) *noun* a person with both European and American connections; a Westerner: E20. **Eurobabble** *noun* (*colloq.*) = EUROSPEAK L20. **Eurobond** *noun* an international bond issued outside the country in whose currency its value is stated M20. **Euroˈcentric** *adjective* = EUROPOCENTRIC M20. **Eurocenˈtricity**, **Euroˈcentrism** *nouns* = EUROPOCENTRISM L20. **Eurocheque** *noun* a collaborative banking arrangement enabling account holders from one European country to use their cheques in another; a cheque issued under this arrangement: M20. **Euroˈcommunism** *noun* a form of Communism in western European countries emphasizing acceptance of democratic institutions and independence of Soviet influence L20. **Euroˈcommunist** *noun & adjective* (***a***) *noun* an adherent of Eurocommunism; (***b***) *adjective* of or pertaining to Eurocommunism or Eurocommunists: L20. **Euˈrocracy** *noun* (*colloq.*) government by Eurocrats L20. **Eurocrat** *noun* (*colloq.*) a bureaucrat of any of various European organizations, esp. the European Union M20. **Eurocurrency** *noun* money held outside the country (usu. the US or Japan) in whose currency its value is stated M20. **Eurodollar** *noun* a US dollar deposited or held outside the US (not necessarily in Europe) L20. **Euroland** *noun* = ***eurozone*** below L20. **Euromarket** *noun* (***a***) the Common Market of the European Union; (***b***) the European money market; the market of a particular Eurocurrency: M20. **Euromissile** *noun* a medium-range nuclear weapon deployed in Europe L20. **Euro-MP** *noun* a Member of the European Parliament L20. **Euroˈparliament** *noun* the European Parliament L20. **Europarliamenˈtarian** *noun* = EURO-MP L20. **Europarliaˈmentary** *adjective* of or pertaining to the European Parliament L20. **Europhile** *noun* a person who admires Europe or who is in favour of participation in the European Union L20. **Europhobe** *noun* a person having a strong dislike of Europe or opposing participation in the European Union L20. **Europhobic** *adjective* of or designating a Europhobe L20. **Europop** *noun* pop music from continental Europe, often sung in English L20. **Euro-sceptic** *noun* a person who is not enthusiastic about increasing the powers of the European Union L20. **Eurospeak** *noun* the allegedly unattractive language used by Eurocrats L20. **Eurostar** *noun* (proprietary name for) the high-speed passenger rail service that links London with various European cities via the Channel Tunnel; a train operating this service: L20. **Eurostraˈtegic** *adjective* relating to defence strategy in Europe; *spec.* (of nuclear weapons) designed for deployment and use within Europe, having a strike capability limited to Europe: L20. **Euroˈsummit** *noun* a summit meeting of European Union heads of government L20. **Eurotrash** *noun* rich European socialites, esp. those living or working in the United States L20. **Eurovision** *noun* Europe-wide television provided by the collaboration of European broadcasting networks M20. **eurozone** *noun* the economic region formed by the member countries of the European Monetary Union that adopted a shared single currency, the euro, on 1 January 1999 L20.

Euro-African *adjective & noun* see EURAFRICAN.

euroaquilo *noun* var. of EURAQUILO.

Euro-Asiatic *adjective & noun* var. of EURASIATIC.

euroclydon /jʊ(ə)rˈɒklɪd(ə)n/ *noun*. E17.
[ORIGIN New Testament Greek *eurokludōn*, from Greek *Euros* (see EURUS) + *kludōn* wave, billow.]
= EURAQUILO; any tempestuous wind.

Europaeo- /jʊərəˈpiːəʊ/ *combining form*. Also **-peo-**.
[ORIGIN from Latin *Europaeus* European + -O-.]
Of or pertaining to Europe and —, as ***Europaeo-Asiatic*** etc.

European /jʊərəˈpiːən/ *noun & adjective*. L16.
[ORIGIN French *européen*, from Latin *europaeus*, from *Europa* Europe from Greek *Eurōpē*: see -EAN.]
▸ **A** *noun*. **1** A native or inhabitant of the continent of Europe. L16.
2 A person of European descent living outside Europe; a white person, esp. in a country with a non-white population. L17.
3 A person concerned with Europe as a whole; *spec.* an advocate of membership of the European Union. M20.

> A. F. DOUGLAS-HOME Harold Macmillan had always been a keen European.

▸ **B** *adjective*. **1** Of, pertaining to, or characteristic of the continent of Europe or its inhabitants. E17.

> J. CONRAD He had the pose of a Buddha preaching in European clothes.

European plan *N. Amer.* a method of charging for a hotel room exclusive of meals.
2 Occurring in or extending over Europe. M17.
3 Concerned with Europe as a whole rather than its individual countries, *spec.* designating various economic and defence organizations or unions of western Europe. L19.

> G. MEREDITH I am neither German nor French nor . . English. I am European and Cosmopolitan.

European Community the association of countries formed in 1967 from the European Economic Community, the European Coal and Steel Community, and Euratom. **European Court** (***a***) the European Court of Human Rights, set up by the Council of Europe to enforce its European Convention on Human Rights; (***b***) the Court of Justice of the European Union, compulsory in states which expressly accept it. ***European Currency Unit*** see ECU. **European Economic Community** an economic and political association of certain European countries as a unit with internal free trade and common external tariffs. **European Monetary System** a system by which the exchange rates of some European Union countries are kept within certain limits in relation to each other and to the average of all European Union currencies. **European monetary union** (a programme for) the phased introduction of a single monetary policy across Europe or (in later use) among the member states of the European Union; *spec.* the adoption of a shared single currency unit, the euro. **European Parliament** the principal representative and consultative body of the European Union. **European Union** an economic and political association of certain European states (incorporating the European Community), with internal free trade and common external tariffs, and whose members send representatives to the European Parliament.
■ **Europeanly** *adverb* M19.

Europeanise *verb* var. of EUROPEANIZE.

Europeanism /jʊərəˈpiːənɪz(ə)m/ *noun*. E19.
[ORIGIN from EUROPEAN + -ISM.]
1 Something peculiar to or characteristic of Europe or Europeans; European behaviour, culture, etc. E19.
2 (Advocacy of) the ideal of a unified Europe; *spec.* support for the European Union. M20.
■ **Europeanist** *noun & adjective* (a person) advocating a unified Europe or supporting the European Union M20.

Europeanize /jʊərəˈpiːənʌɪz/ *verb trans.* Also **-ise** L18.
[ORIGIN formed as EUROPEANISM + -IZE.]
Make European in appearance, form, manner, or extent.

> *Listener* These cards contain pictures of . . Europeanised biblical scenes.

■ **Europeaniˈzation** *noun* L19.

Europeo- *combining form* var. of EUROPAEO-.

europium /jʊ(ə)rˈəʊpɪəm/ *noun*. E20.
[ORIGIN from *Europe* + -IUM.]
A metallic chemical element of the lanthanide series, atomic no. 63 (symbol Eu).

Europocentric /jʊ(ə)ˌrəʊpə(ʊ)ˈsɛntrɪk/ *adjective*. M20.
[ORIGIN from *Europe* + -O- + -CENTRIC.]
Having or regarding Europe as its centre; presupposing the supremacy of Europe and Europeans in world culture etc.
■ **Europocenˈtricity**, **Europocentrism** *nouns* the condition of being Europocentric; a Europocentric doctrine: M20.

eurus /ˈjʊərəs/ *noun*. Long *rare*. LME.
[ORIGIN Latin from Greek *Euros*.]
The east or south-east wind; (**E-**) the god of the east or south-east wind.

eury- /ˈjʊəri/ *combining form* of Greek *eurus* wide. Opp. STENO-.
■ **euryˈbathic** *adjective* [Greek *bathos* depth] (of aquatic life) capable of living at varying depths E20. **euryhaline** /-ˈheɪlʌɪn, -ˈheɪliːn/ *adjective* [Greek *halinos* of salt] BIOLOGY tolerating a wide range of salinity L19. **euryˈhydric** *adjective* (BIOLOGY) tolerating a wide range of humidity M20. **euˈryphagous** *adjective* (ZOOLOGY) capable of feeding on a wide range of items E20. **eurytherm**, **euryˈthermal** *adjectives* (BIOLOGY) able to tolerate a wide range of temperature L19. **euryˈthermic** *adjective* = EURYTHERMAL E20. **euryˈthermous** *adjective* = EURYTHERMAL M20. **eurytope** *noun* (ECOLOGY) a eurytopic organism L19. **euryˈtopic** *adjective* (ECOLOGY) (of an organism) tolerating a wide range of types of habitat or ecological conditions M20.

eurypterid /jʊ(ə)ˈrɪptərɪd/ *noun*. L19.
[ORIGIN from mod. Latin *Eurypterus* genus name, from EURY- + Greek *pteron* wing: see -ID³.]
Any of the Eurypterida, extinct aquatic arthropods of Palaeozoic times, similar to scorpions but often larger and with a terminal pair of paddle-shaped appendages.

eurythmic *adjective*, **eurythmics** *noun*, etc. see EURHYTHMIC etc.

Eusebian /juːˈsiːbɪən/ *adjective & noun*. L17.
[ORIGIN from *Eusebius* (see sense 2 below) + -AN.]
▸ **A** *adjective*. †**1** Designating some kind of pear. Only in L17.
2 Of or pertaining to any of various early Christian saints and bishops called Eusebius; *spec.* designating the Arians of the 4th cent. AD, who included Eusebius of Nicodemia (d. *c* 342) and Eusebius of Caesarea (*c* 260–*c* 340). M19.
Eusebian canons tables compiled by Eusebius of Caesarea to illustrate the parallelism between corresponding passages in the different Gospels.
▸ **B** *noun*. *hist.* A member of the Eusebian Arians. M18.

Euskarian /juːˈskɛːrɪən/ *adjective & noun*. M19.
[ORIGIN from Basque *Euskara*, *Eskuara*, *Uskara* the Basque language + -IAN.]
▸ **A** *adjective*. Basque; *esp.* in ethnology, designating pre-Aryan characteristics in Europeans supposedly typified by the Basques. M19.
▸ **B** *noun*. A Basque person. L19.

eusol /ˈjuːsɒl/ *noun*. E20.
[ORIGIN from Edinburgh University *sol*ution, after EUPAD.]
PHARMACOLOGY. An antiseptic solution of chlorinated lime and boric acid.

Eustachian /juːˈsteɪʃ(ɪ)ən/ *adjective*. M18.
[ORIGIN from *Eustachius*, Latinized form of the name of Bartolomeo *Eustachio* (d. 1574) + -AN.]
Eustachian tube, the passage running through the temporal bone and connecting the middle ear and the nasopharynx, by virtue of which the air pressure is the same on both sides of the tympanum.

eustasy /ˈjuːstəsi/ *noun*. M20.
[ORIGIN Back-form. from EUSTATIC, after mod. Latin *-stasis* corresp. to *-static*: see -Y³.]
GEOGRAPHY. A uniform worldwide change of sea level.

eustatic /juːˈstatɪk/ *adjective*. E20.
[ORIGIN formed as EU- + STATIC.]
GEOGRAPHY. Accompanying or forming part of a worldwide change of sea level.
■ **eustatically** *adverb* M20.

Euston Road /juːstən ˈrəʊd/ *adjectival phr.* M20.
[ORIGIN A road in London, site of a former School of Drawing and Painting (1938–9).]
Designating a group of English post-Impressionist realistic painters of the 1930s and their type of art.

eustyle /ˈjuːstʌɪl/ *adjective & noun*. L17.
[ORIGIN Latin *eustylos* from Greek *eustulos* with pillars well placed, formed as EU- + *stulos* pillar.]
ARCHITECTURE. ▸**A** *adjective*. Of a building, colonnade, etc.: having the spaces between columns equal to 2¼ or 2½ times their diameters. L17.
▸**B** *noun*. The distance between columns in a eustyle structure. M19.

eusuchian /juːˈsjuːkɪən/ *noun & adjective*. L19.
[ORIGIN from mod. Latin *Eusuchia* (see below), formed as EU- + Greek *soukhos* crocodile: see -IAN.]
▸**A** *noun*. A crocodile of the suborder Eusuchia, which includes the only extant members of the order Crocodylia. L19.
▸**B** *adjective*. Of, pertaining to, or designating this suborder. L19.

eutaxitic /juːtakˈsɪtɪk/ *adjective*. L19.
[ORIGIN from EU- + Greek *taxis* arrangement + -ITE¹ + -IC.]
PETROGRAPHY. Having or designating a banded rock structure.

eutaxy /ˈjuːtaksi/ *noun*. Long *rare*. E17.
[ORIGIN French *eutaxie* from Greek *eutaxia*, formed as EU- + -TAXY.]
Good or established order or arrangement.

eutectic /juːˈtɛktɪk/ *noun & adjective*. L19.
[ORIGIN from Greek *eutēktos* easily melting, formed as EU- + *tēkein* melt: see -IC.]
▸**A** *noun*. **1** A mixture whose constituents are in such proportions that it melts and solidifies at a single temperature that is lower than the melting point of the constituents or any other mixture of them. L19.
2 A eutectic point. M20.
▸**B** *adjective*. Of, pertaining to, or designating a eutectic, its melting point, or the point representing its melting point in a phase diagram. L19.

> A. H. COTTRELL This is the ternary eutectic point at which the liquid is in equilibrium with all three solids.

■ **eutecˈtiferous** *adjective* giving rise to or having a eutectic E20. **eutectoid** *noun & adjective* (pertaining to or designating) a solid analogous to a eutectic, having a minimum transformation temperature between a solid solution and a mechanical mixture of solids E20.

euthanasia /juːθəˈneɪzɪə/ *noun*. E17.
[ORIGIN Greek, formed as EU- + *thanatos* death: see -IA¹.]
1 A gentle and easy death. E17.
2 A means of bringing about such a death (chiefly *fig.*, of something). M18.

> D. HUME Absolute monarchy . . is . . the true *Euthanasia* of the British constitution.

3 The action of bringing about such a death, esp. of a person who requests it as a release from incurable disease. M19.
■ **euthanasiac** *adjective* L20. **euthanasian** *adjective* L19. **euˈthanatize** *verb trans.* (*rare*) = EUTHANIZE L19. **ˈeuthanize** *verb trans.* subject to euthanasia; put (an animal) to death humanely: L20.

euthanasy /juːθəˈneɪzi/ *noun*. Now *rare*. M17.
[ORIGIN Anglicized from EUTHANASIA: see -Y³.]
= EUTHANASIA 1.

euthenics /juːˈθɛnɪks/ *noun*. E20.
[ORIGIN from Greek *euthēneein* thrive + -ICS.]
The science or art that deals with improving the conditions of life and the environment as an aid to human well-being.

eutherian /juːˈθɪərɪən/ *adjective & noun*. L19.
[ORIGIN from mod. Latin *Eutheria* (see below), formed as EU- + Greek *thēria* pl. of *thērion* wild animal: see -AN.]
(Pertaining to or designating) an animal of the infraclass Eutheria, comprising all mammals which develop a placenta (as opp. to marsupials and monotremes).

Eutopia /juːˈtəʊpɪə/ *noun*. M16.
[ORIGIN mod. Latin, from Greek EU- + *topos* place: see -IA¹. First used with a play on UTOPIA.]
A place of ideal happiness or good order.
– NOTE: Often wrongly regarded as the correct form of UTOPIA, which has largely superseded it.

eutrapelia /juːtrəˈpiːlɪə/ *noun*. M20.
[ORIGIN Greek, from *eutrapelos* pleasant in conversation, formed as EU- + *trepein* to turn: see -IA¹.]
Wit, repartee; liveliness; urbanity.
■ †**eutrapely** *noun* (*rare*) eutrapelia; reprehensible levity: L16–L17.

eutrophic /juːˈtrəʊfɪk, -ˈtrɒf-/ *noun & adjective*. L19.
[ORIGIN from (the same root as) EUTROPHY + -IC.]
▸**A** *noun*. A medicine that promotes good nutrition. *rare*. L19.
▸**B** *adjective*. Of a lake, swamp, etc.: rich in organic or mineral nutrients, *esp.* so rich that the resultant growth and decay of algae and other plants depletes the oxygen content significantly. M20.
■ **eutrophicate** *verb trans.* make (more) eutrophic M20. **ˌeutrophiˈcation** *noun* the process of becoming eutrophic M20.

eutrophy /ˈjuːtrəfi/ *noun*. E18.
[ORIGIN Greek *eutrophia*, formed as EU- + -TROPHY.]
1 Good nutrition. *rare*. Only in E18.
2 The state of being eutrophic. M20.

Eutychian /juːˈtɪkɪən/ *noun & adjective*. LME.
[ORIGIN ecclesiastical Latin *Eutychianus*, from *Eutyches*, Greek *Eutukhēs*: see -IAN.]
ECCLESIASTICAL HISTORY. ▸**A** *noun*. A follower of the doctrine of Eutyches (*c* 378–454), who held that the human nature of Christ was lost in the divine. LME.
▸**B** *adjective*. Of, pertaining to, or adhering to the doctrine of Eutyches. L16.
■ **Eutychianism** *noun* the Eutychian doctrine E17.

euxenite /ˈjuːksɪnʌɪt/ *noun*. M19.
[ORIGIN formed as EU- + Greek *xenos* stranger: see -ITE¹. So named from its containing many rare constituents.]
MINERALOGY. A niobate and tantalate of yttrium and other rare earth elements and uranium, occurring as brownish-black orthorhombic crystals in granite pegmatites.

eV *abbreviation*.
Electronvolt(s).

EVA *abbreviation*.
ASTRONAUTICS. Extravehicular activity.

evacuable /ɪˈvakjʊəb(ə)l/ *adjective*. M20.
[ORIGIN from EVACUATE + -ABLE.]
Able to be evacuated.

evacuant /ɪˈvakjʊənt/ *noun & adjective*. M18.
[ORIGIN Latin *evacuant-* pres. ppl stem of *evacuare*: see EVACUATE, -ANT¹.]
▸**A** *noun*. A medicine that induces some kind of bodily discharge, as defecation, vomiting, or sweating; *esp.* a purgative. M18.
▸**B** *adjective*. Having the property of an evacuant. E19.

evacuate /ɪˈvakjʊeɪt/ *verb*. Pa. pple **-ated**, †**-ate**. LME.
[ORIGIN Latin *evacuat-* pa. ppl stem of *evacuare* empty (bowels), (in late Latin) nullify, (in medieval Latin) remove (contents), from *e-* E- + *vacuus* empty: see -ATE³.]
1 *verb trans.* Empty, clear out the contents of (esp. the bowel or other bodily organ); produce a vacuum in (a vessel). Formerly, deplete (a person) of bodily humours or (the body) of blood, sweat, etc. LME. ▸**b** Empty *of* contents; *fig.* deprive *of* value or force. L16.

> E. LINKLATER They also chronicled . . a boil evacuated in October of the same year. **b** A. W. HADDAN To evacuate the sacraments of grace, and to regard them as merely acted prayers.

†**2** *verb trans.* Esp. of a medicine or a medical regimen: eliminate from the body (harmful matter, a disease). LME–L18.
†**3** *verb trans.* Chiefly THEOLOGY & LAW. Make void, annul. E16–L18.
4 *verb trans. & intrans.* Excrete (faeces); discharge (ingested material) through the bowel; *gen.* discharge, give off. Formerly, discharge (any matter) from the body or a part of it. E17. ▸†**b** *verb intrans.* Of air, water, etc.: escape, empty out. M17–E19.

> D. L. SAYERS Where arsenic was taken with . . a meal, nearly the whole of it would be evacuated within twenty-four hours.

5 *verb trans.* Clear (a building) of occupants. Formerly also, clear (a country or region) of or *of* inhabitants, troops, etc. E17.

> *New York Times* The warning calls had enabled the police to evacuate the building before the explosion.

6 *verb trans.* Remove (inhabitants, inmates, troops), esp. to a place of safety from a place that has become dangerous. M17.

> P. H. GIBBS I am in charge of a contingent of nurses and nuns just evacuated from the Belgian front. T. GUNN During the Blitz I was evacuated to a school in the country.

7 *verb trans. & intrans.* **a** MILITARY. (Cause to) relinquish the occupation of (a country, town, position, etc.). E18. ▸**b** *gen.* Withdraw from, leave, (premises etc.). E19.

> J. CONRAD He had had a lot to do with royalists . . after Toulon was evacuated. N. GORDIMER It had been forced to evacuate and was operating from some temporary hideout. **b** *Fortune* Flanders has evacuated her house to rent it to the Reagan staff for $5,500 a month. *Washington Post* 22 miles downstream, . . 1,200 of 3,600 residents have evacuated.

8 *verb trans.* Remove (fluid contents) so as to leave a void. *obsolete* exc. SURGERY. E18.
■ **evacuator** *noun* E17.

evacuation /ɪˌvakjʊˈeɪʃ(ə)n/ *noun*. LME.
[ORIGIN Late Latin *evacuatio(n-)*, formed as EVACUATE: see -ATION.]
1 The action or an act of evacuating; *spec.* (**a**) defecation; (**b**) the removal of the contents, esp. air, from a vessel; (**c**) the withdrawal of troops; the removal of occupants or inhabitants. LME.

> attrib.: *Arizona Daily Star* Nuclear refugees at an evacuation center.

†**2** The action of making invalid; cancelling, nullification; refutation. M16–M18.
3 A quantity of evacuated or excreted matter. E17.

evacuative /ɪˈvakjʊətɪv/ *adjective*. E17.
[ORIGIN French *évacuatif*, *-ive*, from *évacuer* from Latin *evacuare* EVACUATE: see -IVE.]
Tending to cause evacuation; of or pertaining to evacuation.

evacuee /ɪˌvakjuːˈiː/ *noun*. Orig. in French form ***évacué***, (fem.) **-*ée***, /evakɥe (*pl. same*)/. E20.
[ORIGIN French *évacué* pa. ppl adjective of *évacuer* from Latin *evacuare* EVACUATE: see -EE¹.]
A person who has been evacuated.

evade /ɪˈveɪd/ *verb*. L15.
[ORIGIN French *évader* from Latin *evadere*, from *e-* E- + *vadere* go.]
1 *verb trans.* Escape by contrivance from (attack, adverse designs, a pursuer, etc.); avoid, elude. L15.
2 *verb intrans.* Get away, escape. (Foll. by *from*, *out of*.) Now *rare*. E16.
3 *verb trans.* Contrive to avoid (esp. a duty; *doing*); avoid giving a direct answer to (a question, a questioner); escape yielding to (an argument, obligation, etc.) by means of sophistry; defeat the intention of (a law, stipulation, etc.). E17.

> C. IVES An opportunity for evading a question somewhat embarrassing to answer. G. GREENE Clues which point to James having evaded military service with insufficient excuse. A. BURGESS The novelist who lives abroad is trying to evade taxation or bad weather. C. P. SNOW Now he could evade talking about himself.

4 *verb intrans.* Practice evasion. E18.
5 *verb trans.* Of things: elude, baffle (efforts, power, etc.). E18.

> H. G. WELLS Emotion that evades definition.

■ **evadable** *adjective* M19. **evader** *noun* M18. **evadingly** *adverb* in an evading manner, evasively M19.

evagation /iːvəˈgeɪʃ(ə)n/ *noun*. L15.
[ORIGIN French *évagation* or Latin *evagatio(n-)*, from *evagat-* pa. ppl stem of *evagari*, from *e-* E- + *vagari* wander: see -ATION.]
†**1** Wandering of the thoughts, spirit, etc. L15–L17.
2 A digression in speech or writing. M17.
3 The action of wandering away or of departing from a locality, course, etc.; (an instance of) rambling, roving. E18.

evaginate /ɪˈvadʒɪneɪt/ *verb trans.* M17.
[ORIGIN Latin *evaginat-* pa. ppl stem of *evaginare* unsheath, from *e-* E- + *vagina* sheath: see -ATE³.]
1 Unsheath. *rare*. Only in M17.
2 MEDICINE. Turn (a tubular organ) inside out; evert. M17.
■ **evagiˈnation** *noun* (**a**) the action of evaginating; (**b**) an evaginated portion: M17.

evaluate /ɪˈvaljʊeɪt/ *verb trans.* M19.
[ORIGIN Back-form., after Old French & mod. French *évaluer*, from EVALUATION: see -ATE³.]
1 Work out the numerical value or equivalent of; find a numerical expression for. M19.
2 *gen.* Ascertain the amount or value of; appraise, assess. L19.

> J. S. HUXLEY To read all previous work on the subject, in order to evaluate one's own results correctly.

■ **evaluable** *adjective* L19. **evaluator** *noun* M20.

evaluation /ɪˌvaljʊˈeɪʃ(ə)n/ *noun*. M18.
[ORIGIN from Old French & mod. French *évaluation*, from *évaluer*, from *é-* (formed as ES-) + Old French *value*: see VALUE *noun*, -ATION.]
1 The action of valuing in monetary terms; a calculation or statement of value; (a) valuation. Now *rare*. M18.
2 The action or an act of evaluating; (an) assessment of worth. L18.

> E. BAKER My opinion of the manuscript can be accepted as a general evaluation of the writer's ability.

evaluative /ɪˈvaljʊətɪv/ *adjective*. E20.
[ORIGIN from EVALUATE + -IVE.]
Expressing, constituting, or providing a judgement as to the value of something; designed or serving to evaluate.

> *New York Times* Viewers have become increasingly evaluative, judgmental and critical of the programming. *English World-Wide* Pupils took part in an evaluative test.

E

E

evanesce /iːvəˈnɛs, ɛv-/ *verb intrans.* **M19.**
[**ORIGIN** Latin *evanescere*, from *e-* **E-** + *vanus* empty: see **-ESCE.**]
Pass out of existence, disappear.

C. P. SNOW I felt the burden of worry evanesce.

evanescent /iːvəˈnɛs(ə)nt, ɛv-/ *adjective.* **E18.**
[**ORIGIN** from Latin *evanescent-* pres. ppl stem of *evanescere*: see **EVANESCE, -ESCENT.**]
1 On the point of vanishing or becoming imperceptible; too small to perceive. **E18.**
2 That quickly vanishes or passes away; having no permanence. **M18.** ▸**b** *BOTANY.* Of a part of a plant: not permanent. **L18.**

L. EDEL Seeking to find words that would convey elusive and evanescent thought.

■ **evanescence** *noun* the process or fact of vanishing away; the quality of being evanescent: **M18.** **evanescently** *adverb* **M19.**

evangel /ɪˈvan(d)ʒɛl, -(d)ʒ(ə)l/ *noun*[1]. *arch.* Also **-gile** /-(d)ʒɪl/. **ME.**
[**ORIGIN** Old French & mod. French *évangile* from ecclesiastical Latin *evangelium* from Greek *euaggelion* (in eccl. use) good news, (in classical Greek) reward for bringing good news, from *euaggelos* bringing good news, formed as **EU-** + *aggelein* announce.]
1 The message of redemption of the world through Christ; the religious teaching contained in the New Testament; the Christian religion. **ME.**

SIR W. SCOTT That worthy man . . teacheth the Evangel in truth and sincerity.

2 a The record of Christ's life as contained in the four Gospels. **LME.** ▸**b** Any of the Gospels. **LME.**
3 A copy of the Gospels, esp. as used in taking an oath. Usu. in *pl.* **LME.**
†**4** Something confidently asserted or taken to be true. Only in **17.**
5 A political or social creed regarded as in some way analogous to a doctrine of salvation. **M19.**
6 A message of good news. **M19.**

evangel /ɪˈvan(d)ʒɛl, -(d)ʒ(ə)l/ *noun*[2]. **L16.**
[**ORIGIN** Greek *euaggelos*: see **EVANGEL** *noun*[1].]
An evangelist; *fig.* a person with a message to communicate.

New Yorker The people will take it as a 'message of solidarity' from the human-rights evangel.

Evangeliary /iːvanˈdʒɛlɪəri/ *noun.* Also in Latin form **Evangeliarium** /iːvandʒɛlɪˈɛːrɪəm/, pl. **-ria** /-rɪə/. **M19.**
[**ORIGIN** ecclesiastical Latin *evangeliarium*, from *evangelium*: see **EVANGEL** *noun*[1], **-ARY**[1].]
= **EVANGELISTARY.**

evangelic /iːvanˈdʒɛlɪk, ɛv-/ *adjective & noun.* **L15.**
[**ORIGIN** ecclesiastical Latin *evangelicus* from ecclesiastical Greek *euaggelikos*, from Greek *euaggelos*: see **EVANGEL** *noun*[1], **-IC.**]
▸ **A** *adjective* **1 a** = **EVANGELICAL** *adjective* 1b. **L15.** ▸**b** Of or pertaining to the Gospel narrative or the four Gospels. **L16.**
2 (Usu. **E-.**) ▸**a** = **EVANGELICAL** *adjective* 2a. **L16.** ▸**b** = **EVANGELICAL** *adjective* 2b. **E19.**
▸ †**B** *noun.* (Usu. **E-.**) = **EVANGELICAL** *noun.* **E17–E19.**

evangelical /iːvanˈdʒɛlɪk(ə)l, ɛv-/ *adjective & noun.* **M16.**
[**ORIGIN** from **EVANGELIC** + **-AL**[1].]
▸ **A** *adjective* †**1 a** = **EVANGELIC** *adjective* 1b. **M16–M18.** ▸**b** Of, pertaining to, or in accordance with the teaching of the gospel or the Christian religion. **M16.**

b G. BURNET Faith . . separated from the other Evangelical Graces.

b evangelical prophet Isaiah, viewed as prophesying the life of Christ and anticipating gospel doctrines in his writing.
2 (Usu. **E-.**) ▸**a** Protestant; *spec.* of or designating certain Churches in Europe (esp. that in Germany) which are, or were originally, Lutheran rather than Calvinistic. **M16.** ▸**b** Of, pertaining to, characteristic of, or designating the school of Protestants which lays particular stress on salvation by faith in the atoning death of Christ, and denies that good works and the sacraments have any saving efficacy. **L18.**

b G. PRIESTLAND Some evangelical papers . . profess to be speaking to the world, but do it in a language only intelligible to the converted. *Times* His . . piety was Evangelical rather than Modernist. *Christadelphian* Creationist writers from the Evangelical movement.

3 Of or pertaining to an evangelist or a preacher of the gospel. *rare.* **M17.**
4 a Eager to share an enthusiasm or belief with others. **E20.** ▸**b** = **EVANGELISTIC** 1b. **M20.**

a *Sunday Telegraph* Robin is evangelical about riding through France. **b** *Nature* An evangelical plea for the introduction of these difference equations into elementary mathematics courses.

▸ **B** *noun.* (Usu. **E-.**)
1 A Protestant; *spec.* a member of any Church called Evangelical. **M16.**
2 A member of the Evangelical school of Protestants, esp. within the Church of England. **E19.**

■ **evangelicalism** *noun* the doctrines or ethos of Evangelicals; adherence to the Evangelical school: **M19.** **evangelically** *adverb* **M16.**

evangelican /iːvanˈdʒɛlɪk(ə)n, ɛv-/ *adjective & noun.* Also **E-.** **M19.**
[**ORIGIN** formed as **EVANGELICAL** + **-AN.**]
▸ **A** *adjective.* = **EVANGELICAL** *adjective* 2b. **M19.**
▸ **B** *noun.* = **EVANGELICAL** *noun* 2. **L19.**
■ **evangelicanism** *noun* **M19.**

evangelicity /ɪˌvan(d)ʒəˈlɪsɪti/ *noun.* **M19.**
[**ORIGIN** from **EVANGELIC, EVANGELICAL** + **-ICITY.**]
The quality of being evangelical.

evangelise *verb* var. of **EVANGELIZE.**

evangelism /ɪˈvan(d)ʒ(ə)lɪz(ə)m/ *noun.* **E17.**
[**ORIGIN** from **EVANGEL** *noun*[2], **EVANGELIC** + **-ISM.**]
1 The preaching or promulgation of the gospel; activity as an evangelist. **E17.**
2 Adherence to or profession of Evangelical doctrines. **E19.**
3 Faith in the gospel. *rare.* **M19.**
4 Zealous advocacy of a cause or doctrine; proselytizing zeal. **E20.**

evangelist /ɪˈvan(d)ʒ(ə)lɪst/ *noun.* **ME.**
[**ORIGIN** Old French & mod. French *évangéliste* from ecclesiastical Latin *evangelista* from ecclesiastical Greek *euaggelistēs*, from *euaggelizesthai* **EVANGELIZE**: see **-IST.**]
1 Any of the writers of the four Gospels, Matthew, Mark, Luke, and John. **ME.**
2 a A person, esp. a layman, engaged in itinerant Christian missionary work. **LME.** ▸**b** A person who preaches the gospel or brings it to a non-Christian people. **M16.** ▸**c** A zealous advocate or promulgator of a cause or doctrine. **L20.**

c CARLYLE The French Revolution found its Evangelist in Rousseau.

†**3** A book or copy of the Gospels. **E16–E18.**

evangelistary /ɪˌvan(d)ʒəˈlɪstəri/ *noun.* Also in Latin form **evangelistarium** /ɪˌvan(d)ʒ(ə)lɪˈstɛːrɪəm/, pl. **-ria** /-rɪə/. **M17.**
[**ORIGIN** medieval Latin *evangelistarium* from ecclesiastical Latin *evangelista*: see **EVANGELIST, -ARY**[1].]
1 A book containing the portions of the Gospels that form part of the liturgy. **M17.**
2 A copy of the Gospels. **M19.**

evangelistic /ɪˌvan(d)ʒəˈlɪstɪk/ *adjective.* **M19.**
[**ORIGIN** from **EVANGELIST** + **-IC.**]
1 Of or pertaining to evangelists or evangelism; concerned with the spreading of the gospel. **M19.** ▸**b** Concerned with or aimed at communicating a belief or enthusiasm; hortatory. **L20.**
2 Of or pertaining to the four evangelists. **M19.**
3 Of or pertaining to the Evangelical school. **M19.**
■ **evangelistical** *adjective* (*rare*) **M17.** **evangelistically** *adverb* **E20.**

evangelium /iːvanˈdʒɛlɪəm/ *noun.* Now *rare* or *obsolete.* **M16.**
[**ORIGIN** ecclesiastical Latin: see **EVANGEL** *noun*[1].]
The gospel; a proclamation of the gospel.

evangelize /ɪˈvan(d)ʒ(ə)lʌɪz/ *verb.* Also **-ise.** **LME.**
[**ORIGIN** ecclesiastical Latin *evangelizare* from ecclesiastical Greek *euaggelizesthai*, from *euaggelos*: see **EVANGEL** *noun*[1], **-IZE.**]
1 *verb intrans.* Proclaim the gospel; act as an evangelist. **LME.**
†**2** *verb trans.* Proclaim as good news; preach about. **LME–L17.**

J. MARBECK From that time the kingdome of God was evangelized.

3 *verb trans.* Preach the gospel to; (seek to) convert to Christianity. **M17.**

Presbyterian Herald They are forbidden to evangelize the Malays, who are mostly Muslim.

4 Imbue with the spirit of the gospel; interpret in an evangelical sense. **L17.**
■ **evangeliˈzation** *noun* **M17.** **evangelizer** *noun* **LME.**

evangile *noun* var. of **EVANGEL** *noun*[1].

evanid /ɪˈvanɪd/ *adjective. arch.* **E17.**
[**ORIGIN** Latin *evanidus* rel. to *evanescere* **EVANESCE**: see **-ID**[1].]
1 Vanishing; of short duration; evanescent, fleeting. **E17.**
2 Faint, weak. **M17.**
†**3** Of a colour: merely apparent. **M17–M18.**

evanish /ɪˈvanɪʃ/ *verb intrans.* Now *rare.* **ME.**
[**ORIGIN** Old French *evaniss-* lengthened stem of *evanir* from Proto-Romance: see **E-**, **VANISH** *verb.*]
Vanish; die away or *away.*
■ **evanishment** *noun* **L18.**

Evans gambit /ˈɛv(ə)nz ˌɡambɪt/ *noun phr.* **M19.**
[**ORIGIN** from William Davies *Evans* (1790–1872), Welsh sea captain and chess player.]
CHESS. A gambit in which, following the Italian opening, White offers to sacrifice the queen's knight's pawn.

evaporable /ɪˈvap(ə)rəb(ə)l/ *adjective.* **M16.**
[**ORIGIN** French *évaporable* or medieval Latin *evaporabilis*, from *evaporare* **EVAPORATE** *verb*: see **-ABLE.**]
Able to be evaporated.
■ **evaporaˈbility** *noun* **M19.**

evaporate /ɪˈvapərɪt/ *noun. rare.* **E20.**
[**ORIGIN** from the verb.]
GEOLOGY. = **EVAPORITE.**

evaporate /ɪˈvapəreɪt/ *verb.* Pa. pple **-ated**, †**-ate.** **LME.**
[**ORIGIN** Latin *evaporat-* pa. ppl stem of *evaporare*, from *e-* **E-** + *vapor* steam: see **-ATE**[3].]
1 *verb trans.* Convert into vapour or gas; drive off in the form of vapour. Orig., drive out (bodily humours) in the form of vapour. (Foll. by *into*, *off*.) **LME.**

R. W. EMERSON The sun evaporates the sea.

2 *verb intrans.* Of a liquid or solid: give off or become vapour, pass off into the air etc. as vapour; decrease in bulk by evaporation. **M16.**

D. ATTENBOROUGH The more liquid part of it . . quickly evaporates.

†**3** *verb intrans.* Be emitted in the form of vapour; be exhaled. **M16–L18.**
4 *verb trans.* Emit in the form of vapour; lose by evaporation. **E17.**

ANTHONY HUXLEY The leaf would evaporate almost as much water as it would without its skin.

5 *verb trans. & intrans.* Reduce (a solution etc.) *to* a residuum by evaporation; subject to evaporation. **M17.**

LD RUTHERFORD The filtrate was evaporated to dryness.

evaporated milk: concentrated by partial evaporation of its liquid content.
6 *verb intrans.* Of an emotion, a situation, wealth, etc.: pass away like vapour; be wasted or dissipated. (Foll. by *into.*) **M17.**

E. J. HOWARD Her impatience to see him had evaporated. T. WINTON Their eyes widened and their businesslike boredom evaporated.

7 *verb intrans.* Of a person: disappear; leave; die. *joc.* **E18.**
■ **evaporator** *noun* a person who or thing which evaporates, *esp.* an apparatus in which things can be evaporated **E19.**

evaporation /ɪˌvapəˈreɪʃ(ə)n/ *noun.* **LME.**
[**ORIGIN** from Latin *evaporatio(n-)*, formed as **EVAPORATE** *verb*: see **-ATION.**]
1 The action or process of gradually turning from liquid or solid into vapour, or of passing away as vapour; an instance of this. **LME.**

D. ATTENBOROUGH Evaporation under the grilling sun has made the waters very salty.

2 The action or an act of evaporating a liquid or driving off the liquid part of something. **LME.**
3 Vapour given off by evaporation. Usu. in *pl.*, vapours, exhalations, fumes. **LME.**
4 Emission of vapour, esp. water vapour. Formerly also, emission of breath, fire, or sweat. **M16.**

ANTHONY HUXLEY Stomata control the evaporation from the leaf.

evaporative /ɪˈvap(ə)rətɪv/ *adjective & noun.* **LME.**
[**ORIGIN** Late Latin *evaporativus*, formed as **EVAPORATE** *verb*: see **-IVE.**]
▸ **A** *adjective.* Producing evaporation; employing or produced by evaporation. **LME.**
evaporative cooling: produced by the evaporation of a liquid.
▸ †**B** *noun.* A medicine that supposedly drew out bodily humours as vapour. Only in **LME.**
■ **evaporatively** *adverb* **M20.**

evaporimeter /ɪˌvapəˈrɪmɪtə/ *noun.* **E19.**
[**ORIGIN** from **EVAPOR(ATION** + **-IMETER.**]
An instrument for measuring the rate of evaporation.

evaporite /ɪˈvapərʌɪt/ *noun.* **E20.**
[**ORIGIN** Alt. of **EVAPORATE** *noun*: cf. **-ITE**[1].]
GEOLOGY. A sedimentary salt deposit left after the evaporation of a body of water; a rock produced in this way.
■ **evapoˈritic** *adjective* pertaining to or characteristic of an evaporite **M20.**

evapotranspiration /ɪˌvapəʊtranspɪˈreɪʃ(ə)n, -trans-/ *noun.* **M20.**
[**ORIGIN** from **EVAPO(RATION** + **TRANSPIRATION.**]
The loss of water from the land to the atmosphere by evaporation from the soil and transpiration from plants.
■ **eˌvapotranˈspirative** *adjective* **L20.** **eˌvapotranˈspire** *verb trans. & intrans.* lose (water) by evapotranspiration **M20.**

evasible /ɪˈveɪzɪb(ə)l/ *adjective.* **M19.**
[**ORIGIN** from Latin *evas-* (see **EVASION**) + **-IBLE.**]
Able to be evaded.

evasion /ɪˈveɪʒ(ə)n/ *noun.* **LME.**
[**ORIGIN** Old French *évasion* from Latin *evasio(n-)*, from *evas-* pa. ppl stem of *evadere* **EVADE**: see **-ION.**]
1 A means of evading a duty, question, etc.; an evasive argument, a prevaricating excuse. **LME.** ▸**b** The action or an act of evading; dodging, prevarication. **E17.**

E. BAKER Evasions often revealed more than direct statements. **b** H. T. BUCKLE I deem anonymous writing . . to be an evasion of responsibility.

b *tax evasion*: see **TAX** *noun.*
2 Escape from confinement or danger. Now *rare.* **LME.** ▸†**b** The possibility or a means of escape. **L16–M18.**
3 The action of avoiding or escaping a blow, pursuit, etc., by contrivance. **M17.**

4 The action of coming or going out. *rare*. M17.

evasive /ɪˈveɪsɪv/ *adjective*. E18.
[ORIGIN from Latin *evas-* (see EVASION) + -IVE.]
1 Of a person: exhibiting or given to evasion; tending to avoid direct or unambiguous replies. E18.
O. MANNING Clarence squirmed under these questions, shrugged and was evasive.
2 Of an action or utterance: constituting or containing evasion; equivocal. M18.
B. PLAIN He had given her an evasive answer.
evasive action: taken to avoid something unpleasant.
■ **evasively** *adverb* M18. **evasiveness** *noun* M18.

Eve /iːv/ *noun*[1].
[ORIGIN Old English *Ēfe* from late Latin *Eva* from Hebrew *Ḥawwāh*, perh. rel. to *hay* alive or Aramaic *hewyā* serpent.]
The first woman in Hebrew tradition.
daughter of Eve a woman, *esp.* one regarded as showing a typically feminine trait. **not know from Eve** have no knowledge of (a woman).
– COMB.: **(African) Eve hypothesis** the hypothesis (based on study of mitochondrial DNA) that modern humans have a common female ancestor who lived in Africa around 200,000 years ago.

eve /iːv/ *noun*[2]. ME.
[ORIGIN Orig. a two-syll. var. of EVEN *noun*[1]. For similar loss of *n* cf. CLEW *noun*, GAME *noun*, MAID *noun*.]
1 = EVENING 2. *arch.* exc. *poet.* ME.
2 The evening or day before a saint's day or church festival; *gen.* the evening or day before any date or event. ME. ***Christmas Eve***: see CHRISTMAS *noun*. ***Ember eve***: see EMBER *adjective*.
3 The time immediately preceding any event or action. L18.
V. BRITTAIN The poet's death on the eve of the Dardanelles campaign.
– COMB.: **eve-churr** †(*a*) the mole-cricket; (*b*) the nightjar; **eve-jar** the nightjar; **eve-of-poll** *adjective* of, pertaining to or occurring in the period immediately preceding the polling in an election.

evection /ɪˈvɛkʃ(ə)n/ *noun*. M17.
[ORIGIN Latin *evectio(n-)*, from *evect-* pa. ppl stem of *evehere* carry out, elevate, from *e-* E- + *vehere* carry.]
†1 A lifting up; elevation, exaltation (*lit.* & *fig.*). Only in M17.
2 A periodic inequality in the moon's motion manifested as a displacement in longitude, caused by the perturbing effect of the sun. E18.

even /ˈiːv(ə)n/ *noun*[1].
[ORIGIN Old English *ǣfen* rel. to synon. Old Frisian *ēvend*, Old Saxon *āband*, Middle Low German, Middle Dutch *āvont* (Dutch *avont*), Old High German *āband* (German *Abend*).]
1 The latter part of the day, the evening. *obsolete* exc. *poet.* & *dial.* OE.
R. KIPLING Bring it to my house this even.
2 = EVE *noun*[2] 2. *obsolete* exc. *dial.* ME.
– COMB.: **evenfall** the beginning of evening.

even /ˈiːv(ə)n/ *adjective* & *noun*[2].
[ORIGIN Old English *efen* = Old Frisian *even*, *iven*, Old Saxon *eben* (Dutch *even*, *effen*), Old High German *eban* (German *eben*), Old Norse *jafn*, Gothic *ibns*, from Germanic.]
► **A** *adjective*. **1** Of land, ground, etc.: level, flat, not hilly or sloping; of uniform height. OE. ►**b** Horizontal. *obsolete* exc. in phrs. below. LME.
b ***on an even keel*** see KEEL *noun*[1].
2 Of an action, movement, etc.: uniform, smooth; free from fluctuations; (of temper, the mind, etc.) equable, unruffled. OE.
T. H. HUXLEY The even rhythm of the breathing. R. KIPLING Every tale was told in the even, passionless voice of the native-born.
3 Orig., (of a weight or balance) true, accurate. Later, (of conduct, laws, etc.) equal, just, impartial. OE.
†4 (Of a path) straight, direct; (of speech or action) direct, straightforward; (of an object) straight ahead. ME–E17.
5 Equal in rank, power, etc.; on a par *with*, on equal terms *with*. ME.
BYRON I could not.. class My faults even with your own! W. S. CHURCHILL We worked together on even terms, more like brother and sister than mother and son.
honours are even: see HONOUR *noun*.
6 Equal in size, number, quantity, etc. ME. ►**b** Of a chance, bet, etc.: as likely to succeed as not; fifty-fifty. L16.
b BYRON Still their salvation was an even bet. *New York Times* Democrats believe they have a better-than-even chance at winning the seat.
of even date LAW & COMMERCE of the same date.
7 Of a surface or line: without bumps or hollows or other irregularities; smooth. ME.
J. M. NEALE When the snow lay round about, deep and crisp and even. A. PATON Kumalo would have stumbled, though the road was straight and even.
8 Medium, average; of proper magnitude. Now *rare* or *obsolete*. ME.
9 Level *with*; neither higher nor lower. *arch.* LME. ►**b** In the same plane or line (*with*); parallel. LME.
†10 Exact, precise. LME–E17.
11 Of a whole number: exactly divisible by two, without leaving a remainder. Of a thing in a series: numbered with or known by such a number. Opp. ***odd***. LME.
12 Accurately coincident or aligned. LME.
H. GARLAND His smile.. displayed fine, even teeth.
13 Uniform throughout in texture, colour, quality, etc. LME.
A. N. WILSON His face was scarlet.. so that flesh and acne blended into an even hue.
14 (Of a person) neither owing money nor owed; square, quits; (of accounts, affairs, etc.) having no balance or debt on either side. LME.
HARPER LEE Cecil had thirty cents, too, which made us even.
be even (with), **get even (with)** have one's revenge (on), retaliate (against). ***break even***: see BREAK *verb*.
15 Equally balanced. L16.
16 Of a sum of money, a number, etc.: not involving fractions; expressible in a round number. M17.
E. DICKINSON I wondered.. if Father'd multiply the plates—To make an even Sum. *Offshore* Discovery of the Sundari field .. brings the number of oil fields in the Natomas SE Sumatra territory to an even dozen.
– SPECIAL COLLOCATIONS & COMB.: ***even break***: see BREAK *noun*[1] 11b. **even hands** †(*a*) ***at even hands***, ***of even hands***, on equal terms; with neither gain nor loss; (*b*) ***be even hands*** *Scot.*, be even or quits *with*. **even money** (*a*) a sum expressible in a whole or a round number; (*b*) an even chance; betting odds of 1 to 1, offering a win equal to the stake. ***even parity***: see PARITY *noun*[1] 3d. **even Stephen(s)**, **even Steven(s)** /ˈstiːv(ə)n(z)/ *colloq.* even, equal, level; *esp.* an even chance. **even-toed** *adjective* having an even number of toes.
► **B** *noun*. †**1** ***on even*** = ANENT *preposition* (of which it is an early form). OE–ME.
†2 Nature, kind; *one's* like. Only in ME.
†3 Ability, resources. Only in ME.
†4 ***the even***, the plain truth *of* something. Only in L16.
5 SPORT. In *pl.* Something expressed in a whole or round number. L19.
in evens (run 100 yards or metres) in 10 seconds.

even /ˈiːv(ə)n/ *verb*.
[ORIGIN Old English *efnan* and *(ge)efnian*, formed as EVEN *adjective*.]
1 *verb trans.* Liken, compare, (*to*). *obsolete* exc. *dial.* OE. ►**b** Treat or represent as equal. (Foll. by *to*, *with*.) Now chiefly *Scot.* ME. ►†**c** Make equal in rank, dignity, etc. Only in ME.
C. READE Would ye even a beast to a man? **b** G. SAINTSBURY A touch of pathos,.. to be evened only to Shakespere's.
†2 *verb trans.* Level (*to* or *with* the ground etc.); raze. OE–M17.
3 *verb trans.* Make even, level, or straight; smooth. ME. ►†**b** Bring up to or restore to a level; bring into line. LME–M19. ►**c** Lower to a specified level (*lit.* & *fig.*); demean. *obsolete* exc. *dial.* M17.
†4 *verb intrans.* Be equal or comparable. (Foll. by *to*, *with*.) Only in ME.
5 *verb trans.* Match, equal. *rare*. LME. ►†**b** Keep pace with. *rare* (Shakes.). Only in E17.
6 *verb trans.* Make equal in magnitude; balance (an account), settle (a debt); come to agreement over (a point of difference). M16. ►†**b** Make (a person) even or quits *with* another. *rare* (Shakes.). Only in E17.
T. MAYNARD A wonderful chance to even old scores. *Billings (Montana) Gazette* Sheridan, Wyoming evened its record at 1-1.
†7 Cause to fit or match. M16.
†8 *verb trans.* Make (a balance) even. E17–E18.
– WITH ADVERBS IN SPECIALIZED SENSES: **even out** (*a*) make even or level; (*b*) become even or normal. **even up** compensate exactly; balance; make equal.

even /ˈiːv(ə)n/ *adverb*. Also (*arch.*, *dial.*, & *poet.*) **e'en** /iːn/.
[ORIGIN Old English *efne* = Old Frisian *efne*, Old Saxon *efno* (Dutch *even*), Old High German *ebano* (German *eben*), from West Germanic.]
► **I** In senses closely related to the adjective.
†1 Evenly, regularly, uniformly. OE–E18.
†2 Equally. OE–L16.
†3 In exact agreement. ME–M17.
4 Directly, straight; due (east etc.). *obsolete* exc. *dial.* ME.
► **II** As an intensive or emphatic particle.
5 With ref. to manner or time, or (formerly) position, shape, or quality: exactly, just, (*so*, *thus*, *as*, etc.); in the same way *as*; at the same time *as* (also foll. by *while*, †*with*, etc.). Formerly also, just now, just then; close at hand. *arch.* & *rhet.* OE.
SHAKES. *Sonn.* Let your love even with my life decay. YEATS The souls even while you speak Have slipped out of our bond. R. KIPLING He made his prayer (Even as you and I!). I. MURDOCH I looked back at Flora.. and even as I looked I saw that she was starting to cry.
6 Quite, fully, (esp. with following numeral). *obsolete* exc. foll. by *to*: right up to, as far as. *arch.* OE.
AV *Phil.* 2:8 He.. became obedient unto death, even the death of the cross.
7 Used to emphasize the identity or nature of a following person, thing, or circumstance. Also, namely, that is to say. *arch.* OE. ►**b** (Usu. **e'en**.) Before a verb: just, simply; nothing else but. *arch.* & *dial.* M16.
AV *Zech.* 11:10 I tooke my staffe, euen Beautie, and cut it. **b** J. BENTHAM Since it is begun, e'en let it take its course.
8 Implying an extremeness of the case mentioned in comparison with a weaker or more general one implied or expressed. Usu. preceding the word, phr., or clause emphasized. L16. ►**b** Emphasizing a compar.: still, yet. M18.
M. EDGEWORTH Even this stupid gardener.. is as useful to society as I am. D. H. LAWRENCE He was roughly, even cruelly received. A. LURIE He couldn't get her to listen, or even stand still. E. WAUGH Ludovic was not successful in the.. competition. His sonnet was not even commended. A. GUINNESS Actors were always close to her heart, even when she disapproved of them. J. FOWLES There's no lock on the door,.. you can't shut it even. *New York Times* I'm not sure, even if we tried, if we could put it out. **b** M. AMIS My position will be even stronger.
– PHRASES: ***even just***: see JUST *adverb*. **even now** (*a*) at this very moment; (*b*) now, as well as previously; (*c*) *poet.* a very short time ago. †**go even** agree (*with*).

even- /ˈiːv(ə)n/ *combining form* of EVEN *adjective*, *adverb*, orig. repr. a Germanic stem.
■ **even-ˈaged** *adjective* (of a forest) composed of trees that are of approximately the same age E20. †**even-Christian** *noun* a fellow Christian OE–E17. **even-ˈeven** *adjective* (NUCLEAR PHYSICS) (*a*) pertaining to nuclei of even mass number only; (*b*) designating nuclei containing even numbers of protons and neutrons: M20. **even-ˈhanded** *adjective* fair, impartial, balanced, E17. **even-ˈhandedly** *adverb* fairly, impartially L19. **even-ˈhandedness** *noun* fairness, impartiality M19. **even-ˈodd** *adjective* (of an atomic nucleus) having an even number of protons and an odd number of neutrons M20.

evendown /ˈiːv(ə)ndaʊn/ *adverb* & *adjective*. *Scot.* & *N. English*. Also **even down**. ME.
[ORIGIN from EVEN- + DOWN *adverb*.]
► **A** *adverb*. †**1** Straight down. Only in ME.
2 Downright; quite; completely. M19.
► **B** *adjective*. **1** Downright, sheer, out and out; (of a person, also) straightforward, direct. E18.
2 Straight, perpendicular; *esp.* (of rain) coming straight down. M18.

†**evene** *verb intrans.* M17–E18.
[ORIGIN French †*évenir* (Old French *esvenir*) from Latin *evenire*: see EVENT *noun*.]
Happen, result.

evener /ˈiːv(ə)nə/ *noun*. LME.
[ORIGIN from EVEN *verb* + -ER[1].]
A person who or thing which makes even; *spec.* something which distributes the load equally between two or more horses used for draught.

evening /ˈiːv(ə)nɪŋ/ *noun*.
[ORIGIN Old English *ǣfnung*, from *ǣfnian* grow towards night, formed as EVEN *noun*[1]: see -ING[1].]
†1 The process or fact of dusk falling; the time about sunset. OE–M16.
2 The close of day; *esp.* the time from about 6 p.m., or sunset if earlier, to bedtime. LME. ►**b** *fig.* The declining or closing period of life, or of anything compared to a day. Usu. foll. by *of*. E17. ►**c** Afternoon. *dial.* L18.
A. BLEASDALE It is early evening, going or just gone dark. A. YOUNG Long June evenings. **b** T. COLLINS Intending.. to spend the evening of his life indulging his hobby of chemistry.
3 An evening spent in a particular way. L18.
C. BEATON The wow of the evening was Carmen, the belly-dancer.
4 *ellipt.* As *interjection*. Good evening. *colloq.* E20.
5 *ellipt.* = ***evening paper*** below. *colloq.* M20.
– PHRASES: ***last evening***: see LAST *adjective*. **of an evening** *colloq.* habitually in the evening. ***social evening***: see SOCIAL *adjective*. **this evening** (during) the evening of today. ***TOMORROW evening***. ***YESTERDAY evening***.
– ATTRIB. & COMB.: In the senses 'of or pertaining to evening', 'existing, taking place, etc., during the evening', 'operating, acting, or on duty during the evening', as ***evening breeze***, ***evening flight***, ***evening meal***, ***evening train***, ***evening walk***. Special combs., as **evening class**: held in an evening for adults who wish to learn about a particular subject or interest or to acquire a particular skill; **evening dress** the clothes prescribed by fashion to be worn in the evening on formal occasions; **evening grosbeak** a N. American grosbeak, *Coccothraustes vespertinus*, with yellow colouring; ***evening LYCHNIS***; **evening paper** a newspaper published after about midday; **evening prayer** the Anglican service of evensong; **evening primrose** any plant of the genus *Oenothera* (see OENOTHERA) with flowers opening in the evening and wilting the next day (cf. ***sundrops*** s.v. SUN *noun*[1]); ***evening primrose oil*** an oil extracted from the seeds of *Oenothera lamarkiana*, which contains essential fatty acids and has been used in complementary medicine to treat premenstrual syndrome and other disorders. **evening school**: providing teaching in the evenings; **evening star** a planet, esp. Venus, when visible in the west after sunset; **evening suit** a man's formal suit worn in the evening.

evenings /ˈiːv(ə)nɪŋz/ *adverb*. *colloq.* & *dial.* (chiefly *N. Amer.*). M17.
[ORIGIN Pl. of EVENING: cf. DAYS, NIGHTS *adverbs* (earlier uses of -S[3] being identified with -S[1]).]
In the evening, every evening.

evenliness /ˈiːv(ə)nlɪnɪs/ *noun*. Long *obsolete* exc. *Scot.*
[ORIGIN Old English *efnlicnesse*, formed as EVENLY *adjective* + -NESS.]
The quality of being even; suitability; composure, equanimity.

evenly /ˈiːv(ə)nli/ *adjective*. Long *obsolete* exc. *Scot.* OE.
[ORIGIN from EVEN *adjective* + -LY[1].]
†**1** Equal; (of a date) the same. OE–E17.
2 (Of a person) fair, impartial; (of a surface) smooth, level. LME.

evenly /ˈiːv(ə)nli/ *adverb*. OE.
[ORIGIN from EVEN *adjective* + -LY[2].]
†**1 a** In an equal degree or proportion. OE–LME. ▸**b** In equal shares, equally; as much on one side as on the other. LME. ▸**c** To the same degree throughout. E17.

b E. FEINSTEIN We are evenly bad at the business of providing for one another's needs.

2 Without inclination or advantage to either side; impartially, equitably. ME.

T. ARNOLD A single battle, evenly contested.

†**3** Exactly; in exact agreement. ME.
4 So as to present an even or uniform surface, form, or line; without inequalities in level, colour, consistency, etc. LME.

B. PYM It is drying lighter, and quite evenly too. J. M. COETZEE He counted thirty tents evenly spaced over the camp terrain.

5 With equanimity; serenely, tranquilly; (of a movement or action) without variation, uniformly. LME.

J. STEINBECK He settled back and ate more slowly now, chewed evenly.

6 †**a** In a straight line, directly. *rare* (Shakes.). Only in L16. ▸**b** (On a) level *with*. L16.

evenness /ˈiːv(ə)nnɪs/ *noun*.
[ORIGIN Old English *efenniss*, from EVEN *adjective* + -NESS.]
1 Fairness in judicial matters. Formerly, equity, righteousness. OE.
2 The quality or state of being smooth or level, or exactly divisible by two. LME.
†**3** A balanced state or condition, equilibrium; equipoise. LME–M17.
4 Uniformity; regularity; calmness of mind, equanimity. L16.

A. J. ELLIS The evenness with which a Frenchman pronounces the syllables. P. G. WODEHOUSE The placid evenness of Kirk's existence began to be troubled. *Nature* This function . . compounds species richness . . and . . evenness (the apportionment of individuals among the species present).

evensong /ˈiːv(ə)nsɒŋ/ *noun*.
[ORIGIN Old English *æfensang*, from EVEN *noun*[1] + SONG *noun*[1].]
1 ECCLESIASTICAL. (Also E-.) Orig. (now *hist.*) the service of vespers in the pre-Reformation Western Church. Now, an Anglican service held in the afternoon or evening and having a set form, with prayers, psalms, canticles, Bible readings, and a recitation of the Creed. OE.
2 The time about sunset. *arch.* ME.
3 A song sung in the evening. LME.

event /ɪˈvɛnt/ *noun & verb*. L16.
[ORIGIN Latin *eventus*, from *event-* pa. ppl stem of *evenire* come out, result, happen, from *e-* E- + *venire* come.]
▸ **A** *noun*. **1** Something that happens or is thought of as happening; an occurrence, an incident; now *esp.* one that is significant or noteworthy. L16. ▸**b** *spec.* Each of a set of outcomes that are mutually exclusive and have a certain computable probability of occurrence. M19. ▸**c** An item in a programme of sport; an outcome held out as offering attractions to the public. M19. ▸**d** In *pl.* What is happening or has happened. M19. ▸**e** SCIENCE. A point of space-time. E20. ▸**f** PHYSICS. A single ionization, decay, or reaction of a subatomic particle. M20.

V. BRITTAIN The events reported in the newspapers seemed too incredible to be taken seriously. V. GLENDINNING The fountain playing was an event; it had been turned off all through the war. **c** P. ROTH His events were discus, shot, and javelin. *Western Morning News* Fund-raising events are being organised. *Observer* A three-day antique coin event starting on Tuesday. **d** E. MIALL Events have proved us right. G. B. SHAW I did not foresee this turn of events. **f** *Scientific American* The events yielding a positron and a neutral pion should be easier to identify.

2 The outcome of a course of proceedings; a consequence, a result. Now only in certain phrs. (see below). L16.

SIR W. SCOTT He then took his aim . . and the multitude awaited the event in breathless silence.

†**3** That which befalls a person or thing; fate. L16–L17.
4 The (actual or contemplated) fact of a thing's happening; the occurrence *of*. Now chiefly in ***in the event of*** below. E17.

P. G. WODEHOUSE Anonymous letters are too frequently traced to their writers, and the prospect of facing Kirk in such an event did not appeal to him.

– PHRASES: **after the event** afterwards rather than at the time or beforehand (***be wise after the event***, explain something after it occurs without having foreseen it; blame others for not having foreseen something). **at all events** in any case; whatever happens or happened. ***double event***: see DOUBLE *adjective & adverb*. ***happy event***: see HAPPY *adjective*. **in any event**, **in either event** = ***at all events*** above. **in the event** (**a**) as things turn(ed) out; (**b**) *US* = ***in the event of*** below. **in the event of** if (something specified) should happen; should (it) be the case.
– COMB.: **event horizon** ASTRONOMY a notional surface from beyond which no matter or radiation can reach an observer; *spec.* the Schwarzschild sphere of a black hole.
▸ **B** *verb intrans.* Take part in horse trials. Chiefly as ***eventing*** *verbal noun*. M20.
■ **eventer** *noun* a horse or rider that takes part in horse trials L20. **eventless** *adjective* without (noteworthy) events E19. **eventlessly** *adverb* L19. **eventlessness** *noun* L19.

eventful /ɪˈvɛntfʊl, -f(ə)l/ *adjective*. E17.
[ORIGIN from EVENT *noun* + -FUL.]
1 Full of striking events. E17.

LD MACAULAY The changes which fourteen eventful years had produced.

2 Fraught with important issues; momentous. L18.

SOUTHEY Thalaba . . waited calmly for the eventful day.

■ **eventfully** *adverb* E20. **eventfulness** *noun* M19.

eventide /ˈiːv(ə)ntʌɪd/ *noun*. *arch.*
[ORIGIN Old English *æfentid*, formed as EVEN *noun*[1], TIDE *noun*.]
The time of evening; evening.
– COMB.: **eventide home** a home for old people (orig. one maintained by the Salvation Army).

†**eventilate** *verb trans.* E17.
[ORIGIN Latin *eventilat-* pa. ppl stem of *eventilare*, from *e-* E- + *ventilare* VENTILATE.]
1 Expose to the wind or air; fan; winnow (corn); aerate (blood). Only in 17.
2 *fig.* Discuss. Only in M17.
■ †**eventilation** *noun* M17–M18.

eventration /iːvɛnˈtreɪʃ(ə)n/ *noun*. M19.
[ORIGIN French *éventration*, from *éventrer* eviscerate, from *é-* (formed as ES-) + *ventre* stomach: see VENTER *noun*[1], -ATION.]
1 MEDICINE. The extrusion outside the abdominal cavity of some of its contents. M19.
2 The action of opening an animal's belly. L19.

eventual /ɪˈvɛn(t)ʃʊəl/ *adjective*. E17.
[ORIGIN from Latin *eventus* EVENT *noun* + -UAL, after *actual*.]
†**1** Of or pertaining to events; of the nature of an event. Only in 17.
2 b Of the nature of a result; consequential. L17. ▸**b** Occurring as an end or result; ultimately resulting. E19.

b M. MEDVED The eventual fate of the killer.

†**3** Of a stipulation: conditional. Of an army: to be raised if required. L17–L18.
4 That will arise or happen under certain circumstances. *arch.* M18.
†**5** That happens to exist. M–L18.

eventuality /ɪˌvɛn(t)ʃʊˈalɪti/ *noun*. M18.
[ORIGIN from EVENTUAL + -ITY.]
1 A possible event; a contingency. M18.

C. RYAN Although he had been ordered not to destroy it, Harmel was prepared for the eventuality.

2 PHRENOLOGY. The faculty of observing and remembering the order of succession in events; the supposed organ of this faculty. E19.

eventually /ɪˈvɛn(t)ʃʊ(ə)li/ *adverb*. M17.
[ORIGIN formed as EVENTUALITY + -LY[2].]
†**1** In result, as distinct from by intention. M17–E18.
2 In the event, in the end, ultimately. L17.

J. N. ISBISTER The cancer that eventually killed him. J. KOSINSKI Eventually, he forgot about it.

†**3** To provide against a contingency; in conditional terms. M–L18.

eventuate /ɪˈvɛn(t)ʃʊeɪt/ *verb intrans.* Orig. *US*. L18.
[ORIGIN formed as EVENT *noun* + -ATE[3], after *actuate*.]
1 Have a (specified) result; turn out (well or badly); result *in*. L18.

A. J. ROSS The crisis had eventuated favourably. M. L. KING The bravery of the Indian . . had ultimately to eventuate in defeat.

2 Happen, result, come about. E19.

D. ACHESON Should this procedure eventuate it would be necessary for me to release . . a statement.

■ **eventuˈation** *noun* M19.

ever /ˈɛvə/ *adverb*. Also (*poet.*) **e'er** /ɛː/.
[ORIGIN Old English *æfre*; ult. origin unknown.]
▸ **I** Always, at all times.
1 Throughout all time, or all past or future time; eternally, perpetually; throughout one's life. Now usu. with sense limited by following adverb, preposition, or conjunction, as *after(ward)*, *before*, *since*. Also ***ever and ever***. OE.

Book of Common Prayer He liveth and reigneth ever one God. CARLYLE Ever must the Sovereign of Mankind be entitled King. LYTTON They would live happy ever after. A. BROOKNER Terrified of spiders ever since she was tiny.

2 On all occasions; whenever possible or appropriate; = ALWAYS 1. *N. English & literary*. OE.

GOLDSMITH He attacked the largest ships, and almost ever with success. SCOTT FITZGERALD The image of her mother, ever carried with her. P. G. WODEHOUSE It was ever her way to come swiftly to the matter in hand.

3 Constantly, incessantly; with continual recurrence. OE. ▸**b** With compar. or (usu. in *comb.*) pres. pple to denote a continued increase or decrease. ME.

H. GUNTRIP A fearless thinker whose mind was ever on the move. **b** M. MCLUHAN The ever more specialist activities of literate society. *Nature* The ever increasing number of synthetic chemicals in the environment.

†**4** Imparting a distrib. sense to following indef. pronoun or adverb; emphasizing the distrib. function of following distrib. word. Cf. EVERY, EVERYWHERE. OE–ME.
▸ **II** At any time. Chiefly with comparison, condition, negation, or question.
5 At any time. OE. ▸**b** Immediately following a superl.: that there has been at any time. E20.

J. BUCHAN The worst man I have ever known. M. LAVIN He won't give in, now or ever. I. MURDOCH The stream, more choked than ever with its debris. J. M. COETZEE Have you ever seen a doctor about your mouth? **b** *Guardian* The biggest ever postbag of telegrams.

6 On any supposition, by any chance, at all. OE. ▸**b** After interrog. pronoun, adverb, etc., to emphasize a question or an assertion of ignorance. Cf. HOWEVER, WHATEVER. *colloq.* L16.

G. W. DASENT To get above ground as fast as ever she could. J. STEINBECK If they ever know themselves, the land will be theirs. **b** T. TROLLOPE Where ever am I to find a girl that can pull me out of my chair in the way you do? O. MANNING I don't know why you ever started.

7 In any degree. Only in ***ever the*** followed by compar., & in ***ever so***, ***ever such*** below. M17.
– PHRASES: **as ever is**, **as ever was** (*postpositive*) *colloq.* nothing less than. **did you ever?** *colloq.* have you seen or heard the like? **ever and again**, **ever and anon** *arch.* occasionally. †**ever as** as long as; as often as; wherever. †**ever now and now**, †**ever now and then** every now and then. **ever so** (**a**) [from earlier *never so*] to any possible degree; (**b**) *colloq.* very; (**c**) *slang* very much. **ever such a —** (with following adjective & noun) *colloq.* a very —. **ever yours**, **yours ever**: in ending a letter to a close friend etc. ***for ever***: see FOREVER. **if ever there was one** & vars. (asserting that the person or thing just mentioned is a perfect or undoubted instance of its kind). **is he ever**, **is she ever** *N. Amer. slang* he or she is very. ***NEVER ever***. ***yours ever***: see ***ever yours*** above.
– COMB.: **ever-being** *adjective* that always is; **ever-blessed** *adjective* always blessed, always (to be) adored; **ever-blooming** *adjective* flowering throughout the growing season; **everdamp** a transfer paper with a hygroscopic coating to keep it moist; **ever-during** *adjective* (*arch.*) always enduring, everlasting; **ever-living** *adjective* that lives for ever, immortal (*lit.* & *fig.*); **ever-ready** *adjective & noun* (**a**) *adjective* permanently accessible, available, or prepared; (**b**) *noun* an ever-ready person or thing.

Everest /ˈɛv(ə)rɪst/ *noun*. E20.
[ORIGIN Mount *Everest* in Nepal and Tibet, the world's highest mountain, from Sir George *Everest* (1790–1866), Surveyor-General of India.]
1 The highest peak of attainment, difficulty, etc. E20.
2 A very large pile or heap. M20.

everglade /ˈɛvəgleɪd/ *noun*. *US*. E19.
[ORIGIN Prob. from EVER + GLADE *noun*[2].]
A marshy tract of land that is mostly under water and covered with tall grass. Usu. in *pl.* (with cap. initial), *the* marshes of this kind in S. Florida.

evergreen /ˈɛvəgriːn/ *noun & adjective*. M17.
[ORIGIN from EVER + GREEN *adjective*.]
▸ **A** *noun*. A tree or shrub that has green foliage all the year round. M17.
▸ **B** *adjective*. **1** Of a tree or shrub: having green foliage all the year round. Of a leaf: lasting until the following season of growth. Opp. DECIDUOUS 2. L17.
evergreen alkanet: see ALKANET 2. ***evergreen hazel***: see HAZEL *noun*[1]. **evergreen oak** = ***holm oak*** s.v. HOLM *noun*[2] 2. **the Evergreen State** *US* Washington State.
2 Of enduring freshness, success, or popularity. L18.

everlasting /ɛvəˈlɑːstɪŋ/ *adjective, noun, & adverb*. ME.
[ORIGIN from EVER + LASTING *adjective*.]
▸ **A** *adjective*. **1** Lasting for ever; infinite in future, or past and future, duration. ME.

AV *Isa.* 9:6 The mighty God, the everlasting Father. J. UPDIKE His soul has gone to everlasting fire!

everlasting DEATH. ***everlasting life***: see LIFE *noun*.
2 Lasting so long as to seem or be treated as eternal. ME. ▸**b** Lasting too long; repeated too often. M17.

POPE See Cromwell, damn'd to everlasting fame! DE QUINCEY Mighty gates of everlasting rock. **b** H. HALLAM The tedious descriptions of spring, and the everlasting nightingale.

3 Of a fabric, contrivance, etc.: almost infinitely durable, very slow to wear out. L16.
4 a Of a plant: perennial. Chiefly in ***everlasting pea*** below. L16. ▸**b** Of a flower: keeping its shape and colour when dried. L18.

a everlasting pea a leguminous plant, *Lathyrus latifolius*, with large ornamental coloured flowers. **b everlasting flower** = sense B.4 below.

▸**B** *noun*. **1** Eternity. Chiefly in ***for everlasting***, ***from everlasting***, ***to everlasting***. **LME**.

I. WATTS From everlasting thou art God To endless years the same.

2 ***the Everlasting***, God, the Eternal. **LME**.
3 A stout fabric; *spec.* a strong twilled woollen cloth. **L16**.
4 Any of various plants, chiefly of the composite family, with papery flower heads that keep their shape and colour when dried, *esp.* helichrysum; the flower of such a plant. Also called ***immortelle***. **L18**.

B. PYM Two wreaths of . . mauve everlastings and white chrysanthemums.

mountain everlasting = *cat's foot* (c) s.v. CAT *noun*[1]. **pearl everlasting**, **pearly everlasting** an ornamental N. American plant, *Anaphalis margaritacea*, with shiny white flower heads.

▸**C** *adverb*. †**1** For ever, throughout eternity. *rare*. Only in **L15**.
2 Very, exceedingly, excessively. *US slang*. **L17**.

K. D. WIGGIN She'd kick the ladder from out under her, everlastin' quick.

■ **everlastingly** *adverb* **LME**.

everlastingness /ɛvəˈlɑːstɪŋnɪs/ *noun*. **LME**.
[ORIGIN from EVERLASTING + -NESS.]
1 The quality or fact of being everlasting; endless or eternal existence. **LME**.
2 Endless future duration. Formerly also = ETERNITY 2. **LME**.
†**3** = ETERNITY 4. **LME–M19**.

everly /ˈɛvəli/ *adverb*. Long *obsolete* exc. *Scot.* **LME**.
[ORIGIN from EVER + -LY[2].]
Always, continually.

evermore /ɛvəˈmɔː/ *adverb*. **ME**.
[ORIGIN Orig. two words, from EVER + MORE *adverb*.]
1 For all future time. *arch.* **ME**.

WORDSWORTH A life of peace . . that hath been, is, and shall be evermore.

2 Always, constantly, continually. **ME**.

SOUTHEY Yonder roar . . evermore increasing, Still louder, louder, grows.

3 In expressed or implied neg. contexts: at any future time, ever again, any longer. Formerly also, in any degree. **LME**.

SHAKES. *Sonn.* I may not evermore acknowledge thee. E. B. BROWNING Not in England evermore.

eversible /ɪˈvəːsɪb(ə)l/ *adjective*. **L19**.
[ORIGIN Latin *evers-* pa. ppl stem of *evertere* EVERT: see -IBLE.]
Able to be everted.

eversion /ɪˈvəːʃ(ə)n/ *noun*. **LME**.
[ORIGIN French *éversion* or Latin *eversio(n-)*, from *evers-*: see EVERSIBLE, -ION.]
†**1** The action of overthrowing; the condition of being overthrown; an overthrow (*lit.* & *fig.*). **LME–E19**.
2 MEDICINE. The action of turning an organ or other structure outwards or inside out; the condition of being everted. **M18**.

eversive /ɪˈvəːsɪv/ *adjective*. **E18**.
[ORIGIN formed as EVERSIBLE + -IVE.]
Tending to the overthrow of or *of* something.

evert /ɪˈvəːt/ *verb trans.* **M16**.
[ORIGIN Latin *evertere*, from *e-* E- + *vertere* turn.]
1 Cast from power, overthrow (a government or regime); frustrate (a purpose); upset (a judgement, doctrine, etc.). *arch.* **M16**.
†**2** Cast down (a building); defeat (an enemy). **M–L16**.
†**3** Draw or turn aside (*lit.* & *fig.*). **L16–M17**.
†**4** Turn upside down; upset (*lit.* & *fig.*); disturb. *rare*. Only in **17**.

JONSON The very thought Everts my soul with passion.

5 Chiefly MEDICINE. Turn (an organ or other structure) outwards or inside out. Chiefly as ***everted*** *ppl adjective*. **L18**.

R. F. BURTON The lips are tumid and everted. S. BECKETT Her eyes, rolling now and everted.

evertebrate /ɪˈvəːtɪbrət/ *noun* & *adjective*. **L19**.
[ORIGIN from *e-* E- + Latin VERTEBRA + -ATE[2]. Cf. VERTEBRATE *adjective* & *noun*.]
ZOOLOGY. = INVERTEBRATE.

Everton toffee /ɛvət(ə)n ˈtɒfi/ *noun phr.* **M19**.
[ORIGIN *Everton*, a district of Liverpool in NW England.]
1 A brittle toffee orig. made in Everton, similar to butterscotch but containing cream or evaporated milk. **M19**.
2 Coffee. *arch. rhyming slang*. **M19**.

evertor /ɪˈvəːtə/ *noun*. **E20**.
[ORIGIN from EVERT + -OR.]
ANATOMY. A muscle that turns or rotates a part outwards.

every /ˈɛvri/ *adjective* (in mod. usage also classed as a *determiner*) & *pronoun*.
[ORIGIN Old English *ǣfre ǣlc* 'ever each': see EVER, EACH.]
▸**A** *adjective*. **1** Used before a sing. noun to give the same sense in relation to individuals as does *all* before the pl. noun in relation to the aggregate of them (almost = EACH *adjective*, but with a stronger connotation of generality or universality). Also, each of a merely notional aggregate. (Preceding the noun & all adjectives exc. possess. prons. Formerly also foll. by *a(n)* interposed before the noun; and preceding *the* + superl. adjective (now replaced by *even*).) **OE**. ▸**b** Used before a number or numeral adjective, or a period of time, to denote continued repetition or recurrence at the stated intervals. **LME**. ▸**c** Each (of two). *obsolete* exc. *dial.* **L16**.

SOUTHEY To see every person in his class at least once a week. T. HARDY Every spare minute of the following days he hovered round the house. J. C. POWYS They hide every sign of water. J. STEINBECK Every bit of electric wire had been requisitioned. S. J. PERELMAN The inescapable conviction that my every move is somehow being observed. **b** G. B. SHAW You shock me . . every second time you open your mouth. G. GREENE At each station on the Outer Circle a train stopped every two minutes.

at every turn: see TURN *noun*. ***every bit as***: see BIT *noun*[2]. **every inch** every bit (*of*); entirely, in every respect. **every last** *colloq.* absolutely every. ***every man jack***: see JACK *noun*[1]. **every now and again**, **every now and then** from time to time. ***every* ONCE *in a while***. **every penny** all one's money; all the money. **every so often** = *every now and again* above. **every time** *colloq.* on all occasions, without fail or exception, certainly (freq. as an affirmative exclam.). **every way** in every way, in every respect. **every which way** (chiefly *N. Amer.*) in every direction; *from* every direction. See also EVERYBODY, EVERYDAY, EVERYONE, etc. **b** ***every* FEW**. **every other** — every second —, every alternate —.

†**2** With *noun pl.* All severally. (Usu. with defining word interposed.) **M16–L17**.

SHAKES. *Temp.* I'll resolve you . . of every These happen'd accidents.

†**3** With *noun sing.* Any. **M16–M18**.

GOLDSMITH The weakness of the wall which every earthquake might overturn.

4 With *noun sing.* All possible —s; the utmost degree of. **L19**.

F. WELDON I . . showed her every kindness. *Guardian* Every effort should be made to sow the seed thinly.

▸**B** *pronoun*. †**1** Everybody. **ME–E16**.
†**2** Distributed to each member of an aggregate; = EACH *pronoun* 2. **ME–L15**.
3 Each, or every one, *of* several persons or things. (Formerly often treated as *pl.*). Now *obsolete* exc. *dial.*, *poet.*, & in ***all and every*** s.v. ALL *pronoun* & *noun* 4. **LME**.

DEFOE Every of the said chirurgeons is to have twelvepence a body. C. K. STEAD These words / spaced out between wave- / break in every of its modes.

— PHRASES: †**every other** each other.

everybody /ˈɛvrɪbɒdi/ *pronoun*. Orig. as two words. **M16**.
[ORIGIN from EVERY + BODY *noun*.]
Every person. Also as antecedent of pl. pronoun

BYRON Everybody does and says what they please. V. WOOLF Everybody in the house is sick of beef and mutton. J. STEINBECK Pilon knew everybody and everything about everybody.

everybody else all other persons.

everyday /ˈɛvrɪdeɪ; *as pred. adjective* ɛvrɪˈdeɪ/ *noun* & *adjective*. **LME**.
[ORIGIN from EVERY + DAY *noun*.]
▸**A** *noun*. †**1** Each day in continued succession. *rare*. Only in **LME**.
2 A weekday, a day other than Sunday. *dial.* **L19**.
▸**B** *attrib.* or as *adjective*. **1** Of or pertaining to every day, daily; pertaining to Sundays and weekdays alike. **M17**.

F. NIGHTINGALE The everyday management of a sick-room.

2 Worn or used on ordinary days. **M17**.

DICKENS Mr. Quilp invested himself in his every-day garments.

3 To be met with every day, unremarkable, ordinary; (of people and their attributes) commonplace, mediocre, inferior. **M18**.

COLERIDGE Persons of no every-day powers and acquirements. *Times* The everyday activity of shopping. G. SWIFT This sort of thing is not exactly everyday.

■ **everydayness** *noun* **M19**.

†**everydeal** *noun* & *adjective*. **ME**.
[ORIGIN from EVERY + DEAL *noun*[1].]
▸**A** *noun*. Every part, the whole. Following a noun or pronoun: every part (of it). **ME–M16**.
▸**B** *adverb*. In every part, in every respect; entirely, wholly. **ME–E18**.

everyhow /ˈɛvrɪhaʊ/ *adverb*. Also as two words. *rare*. **M19**.
[ORIGIN from EVERY + HOW *adverb*.]
In every way.

everylike /ˈɛvrɪlʌɪk/ *adverb*. Long *obsolete* exc. *dial.* **LME**.
[ORIGIN from EVER + obsolete var. of ALIKE *adverb*; later prob. regarded as from EVERY + LIKE *adjective*.]
†**1** Always in a similar fashion; continually. Only in **LME**.
2 From time to time, at intervals. *dial.* **M19**.

Everyman /ˈɛvrɪman/ *noun*. Pl. **-men**. **E20**.
[ORIGIN Name of the protagonist in a 15th-cent. morality play, from EVERY + MAN *noun*.]
The ordinary or typical person, 'the man in the street'.

everyone /ˈɛvrɪwʌn/ *pronoun*. Also as two words. **ME**.
[ORIGIN from EVERY + ONE *noun* & *pronoun*.]
= EVERYBODY. Also as antecedent of pl. pronoun.

C. P. SNOW She was loyal about him with everyone. I. MURDOCH Everyone has had their adventures.

everyone else = EVERYBODY *else*.

everyplace /ˈɛvrɪpleɪs/ *adverb*. *N. Amer.* Orig. as two words. **E20**.
[ORIGIN from EVERY + PLACE *noun*[1].]
In every place, everywhere.

everything /ˈɛvrɪθɪŋ/ *pronoun* & *noun*. Formerly as two words. **ME**.
[ORIGIN from EVERY + THING *noun*[1].]
▸**A** *pronoun*. **1** All things, all; all necessary or relevant things; (with following adjective) all that is —; *colloq.* a great deal. **ME**.

T. HARDY Everything had been done that could be done. H. JAMES In spite of everything these points had helped him. M. KEANE Perhaps everything would still be all right. E. J. HOWARD Everything possible was flush with the walls. O. MANNING I have lost everything. R. P. JHABVALA Everything is covered with mildew.

everything coming one's way, ***everything going one's way***: see WAY *noun*. **have everything** *colloq.* possess every attraction, advantage, or requirement. ***have everything one's own way***: see WAY *noun*.

2 *pred.* The thing of supreme importance. *colloq.* **L19**.

G. B. SHAW The idle pleasure of the moment is everything.

▸**B** *noun*. Something of every kind. Usu. in *pl. joc.* **L18**.

everyway /ˈɛvrɪweɪ/ *adverb*. Occas. as two words. **L16**.
[ORIGIN from EVERY + WAY *noun*: cf. ALWAY, ANYWAY.]
In every way, manner, or direction; in every respect.

everywhen /ˈɛvrɪwɛn/ *adverb*. Occas. as two words. **M19**.
[ORIGIN from EVERY + WHEN.]
At all times, always.

everywhere /ˈɛvrɪwɛː/ *adverb* & *noun*. Formerly also as two words. **ME**.
[ORIGIN Partly from EVER + YWHERE, partly from EVERY + WHERE.]
▸**A** *adverb*. **1** In every place or part. **ME**.

K. GRAHAME The Otters have hunted everywhere . . without finding the slightest trace. E. BOWEN The mist's muffling silence could be everywhere felt.

everywhere else in every other place.

2 In many places; of common occurrence. *colloq.* **E20**.

News Chronicle Lamé is everywhere. F. SWINNERTON Nothing in the room had been changed; newly gathered Talisman roses . . were everywhere.

▸**B** *noun*. All places or directions; *the* infinite. **LME**.

D. H. LAWRENCE Everywhere seemed silent.

here, there, and everywhere: see HERE *adverb*.
■ **everywhereness** *noun* (*arch.*) ubiquity, omnipresence **L17**.

everywheres /ˈɛvrɪwɛːz/ *adverb*. *US colloq.* & *dial.* **M19**.
[ORIGIN from EVERYWHERE + -S[3].]
= EVERYWHERE *adverb*.

everywhither /ˈɛvrɪwɪðə/ *adverb*. *arch.* Orig. as two words. **LME**.
[ORIGIN from EVERY + WHITHER *adverb*.]
In every direction.

Everywoman /ˈɛvrɪwʊmən/ *noun*. Pl. **-women**. **E20**.
[ORIGIN from EVERY + WOMAN *noun*, after EVERYMAN.]
The ordinary or typical woman.

Time Out New York Hester is a true hero, an honest-to-goodness Everywoman.

eve-star /ˈiːvstɑː/ *noun*. *obsolete* exc. *poet.* **LME**.
[ORIGIN from EVE *noun*[2] + STAR *noun*[1].]
= EVENING *star*.

eve-teasing /ˈiːvˌtiːzɪŋ/ *noun*. *Indian*. **M20**.
[ORIGIN from EVE *noun*[1] + TEASE *verb*.]
The making of unwanted sexual remarks or advances by a man to a woman in a public place.
■ **eve-teaser** *noun* **M20**.

Evian /ˈeɪvɪən, *foreign* evjɑ̃/ *noun*. Also **É-**. **M19**.
[ORIGIN See below.]
In full ***Evian water***. (Proprietary name for) a non-effervescent mineral water obtained from Évian (in full Évian-les-Bains), a spa town in eastern France.

evict /ɪˈvɪkt/ *verb trans.* **LME**.
[ORIGIN Latin *evict-* pa ppl stem of *evincere*, from *e-* E- + *vincere* conquer.]
1 LAW. Recover (property or the title to property) *from* a person by legal process. Also foll. by *of*. **LME**.
2 Expel (a person, esp. a tenant) from land or a building, usu. by legal process; drive out (a population). (Foll. by *from*, *out of*, †*of*.) **M16**.

E

E

Guardian A . . villainous landlord who goes to extreme lengths to evict his female lodger.

†**3** Conquer, overcome, (a country, adversary, etc.); obtain by conquest. M16–M17.
†**4** Defeat in argument or litigation; refute (an opinion); convince or convict (*of*). L16–M17.
†**5** Prove, settle by argument. L16–E18.
■ **evic'tee** *noun* an evicted tenant L19. **evictor** *noun* E19.

eviction /ɪ'vɪkʃ(ə)n/ *noun*. LME.
[ORIGIN Late Latin *evictio(n-)*, formed as EVICT: see -ION.]
1 *LAW* (now *hist.*). The recovery of property by legal process. LME.
2 The action of evicting a person, esp. a tenant. L16.
†**3** The action of conquering a country or of obtaining something by conquest. Only in E17.
†**4** The action of defeating a person in argument or of refuting an opinion; conviction of an accused person. E17–E18.
†**5** (A) proof, (a) demonstration. E17–L18.

evidence /'ɛvɪd(ə)ns/ *noun*. ME.
[ORIGIN Old French & mod. French *évidence* from Latin *evidentia*, from *evident-*: see EVIDENT, -ENCE.]
▸ **I** *gen.* †**1** An example. Only in ME.
2 An indication, a sign; indications, signs. ME.

M. E. HERBERT The country they were traversing gave evidence of careful cultivation. R. L. STEVENSON We were surrounded by so many evidences of expense and toil.

3 Facts or testimony in support of a conclusion, statement, or belief. (Foll. by *for*, *(in favour) of*, *against* the conclusion etc.; *of*, *from* the facts etc.) ME. ▸†**b** Something serving as a proof. LME–E18.

G. B. SHAW There is the same evidence for it as for anything else that happened millions of years before we were born. E. WAUGH I refuse to believe the evidence of my eyes . . . These creatures simply do not exist.

†**4** Manifestation, display. LME–E18.
5 The quality or condition of being evident; clearness, obviousness. M17.
▸ **II** *LAW*. **6** Information (in the form of personal or documented testimony or the production of material objects) tending or used to establish facts in a legal investigation; a piece of information of this kind. LME. ▸**b** Material admissible as testimony in a court of law. E19.

Daily Telegraph From the evidence given at the inquiry, certain breaches occurred of the Acts and regulations.

7 A document by means of which a fact is established; *esp.* (in *pl.*) title deeds. *obsolete* exc. *hist.* LME.
†**8** A person who provides testimony or proof; a witness. L16–E19.
– PHRASES: **bear evidence** give evidence in a court of law. **call in evidence** call (a person) as a witness in a court of law. ***circumstantial evidence***: see CIRCUMSTANTIAL *adjective* 1. ***external evidence***: see EXTERNAL *adjective* 4. *HEARSAY* ***evidence***. **in evidence** present; visible; conspicuous; (see also ***call in evidence*** above). ***internal evidence***: see INTERNAL *adjective*. ***rules of evidence***: see RULE *noun*. ***secondary evidence***: see SECONDARY *adjective*. **turn King's evidence**, **turn Queen's evidence**, (*US*) **turn state's evidence** testify for the prosecution in a trial for a crime in which one is an accomplice.

evidence /'ɛvɪd(ə)ns/ *verb*. E17.
[ORIGIN from the noun.]
1 *verb trans.* = EVINCE 6. E17.

L. M. MONTGOMERY Gilbert . . had evidenced no recognition whatever of the existence of Anne Shirley.

2 *verb trans.* Serve as or give evidence for; attest. E17.

R. V. JONES The Germans seemed to be taking it seriously as evidenced by their demands for heavy water.

†**3** *verb trans.* Establish by evidence; demonstrate, prove. M17–E19.
4 *LAW*. †**a** *verb trans.* Relate as a witness. M17–E19. ▸**b** *verb intrans.* Testify, appear as a witness. Now *rare*. M17.
■ †**evidencer** *noun* a witness L16–M18.

†**evidency** *noun*. M16.
[ORIGIN Latin *evidentia*: see EVIDENCE *noun*, -ENCY.]
1 = EVIDENCE *noun* 5. M16–E19.
2 = EVIDENCE *noun* 2. L16–E19.

evident /'ɛvɪd(ə)nt/ *adjective & noun*. LME.
[ORIGIN Old French & mod. French *évident* or Latin *evident-*, *-dens*, from *e-* E- + pres. pple of *videre* see: see -ENT.]
▸ **A** *adjective*. **1** Obvious (to the eye or mind); plain or clear to see or understand; apparent. Formerly also (of objects), conspicuous. LME.

E. F. BENSON The whole place, as could be seen at the most cursory glance, had been laid out with skill and care, but not less evident were the signs of subsequent neglect. N. MAILER It was evident to me that Yuriko was in love with him. I. MURDOCH Stagdon's evident assumption that most decisions . . were now taken by Miss Casement maddened Rainborough.

†**2** Of a sign, testimony, etc.: certain, indubitable. LME–M17.
▸ **B** *noun*. Something that serves as evidence; *spec.* in *SCOTS LAW*, a document proving a person's title to something; usu. in *pl.*, title deeds. LME.
■ **evidentness** *noun* M16.

evidential /ɛvɪ'dɛnʃ(ə)l/ *adjective*. E17.
[ORIGIN medieval Latin *evidentialis*, from Latin *evidentia*: see EVIDENCE *noun*, -AL[1].]
†**1** Resting on documentary evidence. *rare*. Only in E17.
2 Of the nature of or providing evidence; serving to attest. M17.

F. W. FARRAR That Paul should have passed . . from one direction of life to the very opposite is evidential of the power and significance of Christianity. *Times* The court had their written answer which had evidential value.

3 Of, pertaining to, or based on evidence. M17.

E. B. TYLOR The basis of theological science must be historical as well as evidential.

■ **evidentially** *adverb* M17.

evidentiary /ɛvɪ'dɛnʃ(ə)ri/ *adjective*. E19.
[ORIGIN from Latin *evidentia* EVIDENCE *noun* + -ARY[1].]
= EVIDENTIAL 2, 3.

evidently /'ɛvɪd(ə)ntli/ *adverb*. LME.
[ORIGIN from EVIDENT + -LY[2].]
1 So as to be distinctly visible or perceptible; without possibility of mistake or misunderstanding. Now *rare* or *obsolete*. LME.

GIBBON An act which evidently disclosed his intention of transmitting the empire to his descendants.

2 Plainly, obviously. Now usu. parenthetically or modifying a sentence: it is plain (that); it would seem (that); seemingly, apparently; (as a comment on a statement or a reply to a question) so it appears. L16.

D. HUME Reason was so evidently on their side. T. HARDY A frame of embroidered card-board—evidently the work of feminine hands. J. KOSINSKI The audience . . evidently approved his words. F. SWINNERTON Evidently they were brother and sister. *New York Times* Werblin does not speak to his former partners and, when asked why, will say curtly: 'Evidently, I don't like them.' R. RENDELL 'Were they old pals or something?' 'Evidently'

evil /'iːv(ə)l, -vɪl/ *noun*[1]. OE.
[ORIGIN from the adjective.]
1 Wickedness, moral depravity, sin; whatever is censurable, painful, malicious, or disastrous; the evil part or element of anything. OE.

G. B. SHAW Evil should not be countered by worse evil but by good.

†**2** A wrongdoing, a crime, a sin. OE–E17.
3 ***the evil***, (*collect. pl.*) people. ME.
†**4** A disaster, a misfortune. ME–L18.
5 A disease, a sickness. *obsolete* exc. *dial.* in *gen.* sense. ME. ▸†**b** *hist.* ***the evil***, ***the king's evil***, scrofula. LME.
6 Any particular thing that is physically or morally harmful. ME.

H. WILSON Whatever is decided will be wrong—it is a choice of evils. P. CAREY Honey Barbara submitted to the evils of alcohol with a guilty flush.

– PHRASES & COMB.: **evildoer** a person who does evil. **evildoing** wrongdoing. **lesser evil**, **lesser of two evils** the less harmful of two bad things; the alternative that has fewer drawbacks. ***speak evil of***: see SPEAK *verb*. ***the evil***: see senses 3, 5b above. ***the king's evil***: see sense 5b above. ***the social evil***: see ***social evil*** s.v. SOCIAL *adjective*.
■ **evilness** *noun* OE.

†**evil** *noun*[2]. *rare* (Shakes.). Only in E17.
[ORIGIN Unknown.]
A privy, a lavatory.

evil /'iːv(ə)l, -vɪl/ *adjective*.
[ORIGIN Old English *yfel* = Old Saxon *ubil*, Old Frisian, Middle Dutch *evel* (Du *euvel*), Old High German *ubil* (German *Übel*), Gothic *ubils*, from Germanic.]
1 Morally depraved, bad, wicked. OE.

AV *Gen.* 8:21 The imagination of mans heart is evil from his youth. *Christian Science Monitor* The villains are led by a freakishly evil woman.

2 Causing pain or trouble; unpleasant, offensive, disagreeable. OE. ▸†**b** Hard, difficult, (*to do*). ME–M16.

P. MATTHIESSEN Not once have I seen him downhearted or tired, nor has he responded . . to my own evil temper. J. STEINBECK The evil music filled the night.

†**3** Unsound; unwholesome; poor, unsatisfactory; defective. OE–E17. ▸**b** Of a workman, work, etc.: unskilful. E16–L18.
4 Harmful, prejudicial; malicious; (of an omen) boding ill; (of a reputation) unfavourable. ME.

W. S. CHURCHILL Adams spread evil rumours of their conduct.

5 †**a** Of conditions, fortune, etc.: unfortunate, miserable. ME–E17. ▸**b** Of a period of time: characterized by misfortune; unlucky, disastrous. LME.
– SPECIAL COLLOCATIONS: **evil day** = ***evil hour*** below. **evil days** a time when a person suffers misfortune. **evil eye** a malicious look; such a look superstitiously believed to do material harm; the ability to cast such looks. **evil hour** a time of ill luck, disaster, etc. **Evil One** *the* Devil. **evil spirit** a demon. **evil will** (now *rare*) malicious intention or purpose.

evil /'iːv(ə)l, -vɪl/ *adverb*. *obsolete* exc. in comb.
[ORIGIN Old English *yfele*, formed as EVIL *adjective*.]
= EVILLY.
– COMB.: †**evil-favoured** *adjective* having a repulsive appearance; **evil-liver** a person who lives a sinful life; **evil-looking**, **evil-smelling** *adjectives* having an unpleasant look, smell.

evilly /'iːvəli, -vɪli/ *adverb*. LME.
[ORIGIN from EVIL *adjective* + -LY[2].]
1 Wickedly; with evil purpose or result; unfavourably. LME.
†**2** Faultily; insufficiently; incorrectly; improperly. M16–L17.

evince /ɪ'vɪns/ *verb trans.* L16.
[ORIGIN Latin *evincere*: see EVICT.]
†**1** Prove by argument or evidence; establish; *rare* vindicate. L16–E19.

J. AUSTEN The pleasantness of an employment does not always evince its propriety.

†**2** Overcome, subdue. Only in 17.
†**3** **a** Convince. E17–L18. ▸**b** Confute. Only in 17.
†**4** Compel or extort by argument or persuasion. Only in M17.
5 Be an indication of; serve as evidence for; attest. M17.

E. BOWEN The two were typical in their point of view, as evinced by the lectures they gave.

6 Reveal the presence of (a feeling, quality, etc.); exhibit; give evidence of. E19.

S. BELLOW Leventhal, evincing neither anger nor satisfaction, though he felt both, rose.

■ †**evinceable** *adjective* = EVINCIBLE: only in L16. **evincible** *adjective* demonstrable L16. **evincive** *adjective* indicative E19.

Evipan /'ɛvɪpan/ *noun*. Also **e-**. M20.
[ORIGIN Unknown.]
PHARMACOLOGY. (Proprietary name for) the drug hexobarbitone.

evirate /'iːvɪreɪt, 'ɛ-/ *verb trans.* E17.
[ORIGIN Latin *evirat-* pa. ppl stem of *evirare* castrate, from *e-* E- + *vir* man: see -ATE[3].]
Castrate; emasculate.

eviration /iːvɪ'reɪʃ(ə)n, ɛv-/ *noun*. E17.
[ORIGIN Latin *eviratio(n-)*, formed as EVIRATE: see -ATION.]
Emasculation; the state of being emasculated.

evirato /ɛvɪ'rɑːtəʊ/ *noun*. Pl. **-ti** /-ti/. L18.
[ORIGIN Italian, use as noun of pa. pple of *evirare* from Latin: see EVIRATE.]
hist. = CASTRATO.

†**evirtuate** *verb*. M17.
[ORIGIN from Old French & mod. French *(s')évertuer*, from *é-* (formed as ES-) + *vertu* strength, VIRTUE: see -ATE[3].]
1 *verb trans.* Deprive of virtue, strength, or authority. M17–L18.
2 *verb refl.* Exert oneself. Only in M17.
3 *verb intrans.* Exert an influence. Only in L17.

eviscerate /ɪ'vɪsəreɪt/ *verb*. Pa. pple **-ated**, (now *poet.*) **-ate** /-ət/. L16.
[ORIGIN Latin *eviscerat-* pa. ppl stem of *eviscerare*, from *e-* E- + VISCERA: see -ATE[3].]
1 *verb trans.* Disembowel; gut (*lit.* & *fig.*). L16.

W. FAULKNER The house had not been damaged: merely eviscerated.

†**2** *verb trans.* Bring out the innermost secrets of. *rare*. E–M17.
3 *verb trans.* Elicit the essence of. *rare*. M17.
4 *verb trans.* Deprive *of* important or significant content; weaken, attenuate, emasculate. M19.

T. S. ELIOT The parched eviscerate soil Gapes at the vanity of toil.

5 *verb trans. SURGERY*. Remove the contents of (an eyeball). L19.
6 *verb intrans.* Of viscera: protrude through a surgical incision. M20.
■ **evisce'ration** *noun* M17. **eviscerator** *noun* a person who eviscerates something, or a device for eviscerating something, esp. carcasses M20.

evitable /'ɛvɪtəb(ə)l/ *adjective*. E16.
[ORIGIN Old French & mod. French *évitable* (from *éviter* from Latin *evitare*) or Latin *evitabilis*, from *evitare*: see EVITE, -ABLE.]
Avoidable. (Now usu. in neg. contexts.)

†**evitate** *verb trans. rare*. L16–E17.
[ORIGIN Latin *evitat-* pa. ppl stem of *evitare*: see EVITE, -ATE[3].]
= EVITE.

evitation /ɛvɪ'teɪʃ(ə)n/ *noun*. LME.
[ORIGIN Latin *evitatio(n-)*, from *evitare*: see EVITE, -ATION.]
Avoidance.

evite /ɪ'vʌɪt/ *verb trans. arch.* exc. *Scot.* E16.
[ORIGIN from Old French & mod. French *éviter* or Latin *evitare*, from *e-* E- + *vitare* shun.]
Avoid, shun.

eviternity *noun* var. of AEVITERNITY.

evocable /'ɛvəkəb(ə)l/ *adjective*. L19.
[ORIGIN French *évocable*, from *évoquer* from Latin *evocare*: see EVOKE, -ABLE.]
Able to be evoked.

evocate /ˈɛvə(ʊ)keɪt/ *verb trans.* **M17.**
[ORIGIN Latin *evocat-* pa. ppl stem of *evocare*: see EVOKE, -ATE[3].]
†1 Call forth. Only in **M17.**
2 Call up (spirits) from the dead or (events) from the past. **L17.**

evocation /ɛvə(ʊ)ˈkeɪʃ(ə)n/ *noun.* **LME.**
[ORIGIN from Latin *evocatio(n-)*, formed as EVOCATE: see -ATION.]
†1 GRAMMAR. A reduction of the third person to the first or second. **LME–M17.**
†2 **a** The calling of a person from a specified place or association; the summoning of a person's spirit from its abode. **L16–M17.** ▸**b** ROMAN HISTORY. The practice of calling upon the gods of a besieged city to forsake it and come over to the besiegers. **M17.**
3 The transfer of a legal case or action to a higher court. Now *hist.* **M17.**
4 The action or an act of evoking a spirit; a formula used for this purpose. **M17.**
5 In Platonic theory, the calling to mind or recollection of knowledge acquired in a previous state of existence. **M17.**
†6 = AVOCATION 3, 4. **M18–E19.**
7 The action or an act of calling into existence or activity something non-existent or latent; something that brings to mind a specified memory, image, or feeling. (Foll. by *of*.) **L18.**

W. FAULKNER The sum, the amount of the reward—the black, succinct evocation of that golden dream.

8 The action by which a chemical produced in one part of an embryo causes another part to develop in a particular way. **M20.**

evocative /ɪˈvɒkətɪv/ *adjective.* **M17.**
[ORIGIN Latin *evocativus*, formed as EVOCATE: see -ATIVE.]
Having the property of evoking; *esp.* bringing to mind some memory, image, or feeling; having imaginative associations. (Foll. by *of*.)

R. SCRUTON Whether music can actually describe the world or whether it is merely evocative. P. NORMAN 'Mummy', to Louis, was a vaguely thrilling word, evocative of someone young you could cuddle up to in bed.

■ **evocatively** *adverb* **M20.** **evocativeness** *noun* **M20.**

evocator /ˈɛvə(ʊ)keɪtə/ *noun.* **L18.**
[ORIGIN Latin, formed as EVOCATE: see -OR.]
1 A person who evocates or evokes something; *esp.* one who calls up a spirit. **L18.**
2 A chemical produced in one part of an embryo which causes another part to develop in a particular way; a morphogen. **M20.**

evocatory /ɪˈvɒkət(ə)ri, ɛvə(ʊ)ˈkeɪt(ə)ri/ *adjective.* **E18.**
[ORIGIN Late Latin *evocatorius*, formed as EVOCATE: see -ORY[2].]
Having the function or property of evoking spirits; evocative.

evoe /ɪˈvəʊi/ *interjection & noun.* Also **evohe**. **L16.**
[ORIGIN Latin *eu(h)oe* from Greek *euoi*.]
(An utterance of) a Bacchanalian exclamation expressing elation or boisterousness.

evoke /ɪˈvəʊk/ *verb trans.* **E17.**
[ORIGIN Latin *evocare*, from *e-* E- + *vocare* to call: perh. after French *évoquer*.]
1 Call forth; *esp.* call up (a spirit etc.) by the use of magic charms. **E17.**

T. WARTON To evoke the Queen of the Fairies.

2 Transfer (a legal case or action) to a higher court. Now *hist.* **M18.**
3 Call into being or activate (a memory, image, feeling, etc.); create in the imagination; produce (a response). **M19.**

H. J. LASKI The theory . . never produced in England the enthusiasm it evoked in France. C. MACKENZIE This statement evoked a murmur of agreement from the audience. V. S. PRITCHETT He had a loud, resonant voice and, being a fairish actor, could evoke the gallop of horses . . instantly.

■ **evoker** *noun* **M19.**

évolué /evɔlɥe/ *noun & adjective.* Pl. of noun pronounced same. **M20.**
[ORIGIN French, pa. pple of *évoluer* evolve.]
(Characteristic of or designating) an African who has had a European education or has adopted European ways or attitudes.

evolute /ˈiːvəluːt, ˈɛv-/ *noun & adjective.* **M18.**
[ORIGIN Latin *evolutus* pa. pple of *evolvere* EVOLVE.]
MATH. (Designating) a curve that is the locus of the centres of curvature of a given curve (its involute) and is the envelope of the normals; so called because a point on a taut string unwound from the evolute traces the involute.

evolute /ˈiːvəluːt, -ljuːt, ˈɛv-/ *verb.* **L19.**
[ORIGIN Back-form. from EVOLUTION.]
1 *verb intrans.* = EVOLVE 8. **L19.**
2 *verb trans.* = EVOLVE *verb* 1. *Journalists' slang.* **L19.**

evolution /iːvəˈluːʃ(ə)n, ˈljuː-, ˈɛv-/ *noun.* **E17.**
[ORIGIN Latin *evolutio(n-)* (unrolling and) reading of a papyrus roll, from *evolut-* pa. ppl stem of *evolvere* EVOLVE: see -ION.]
1 MILITARY & NAUTICAL. A movement of a body of troops or ships carried out to change their disposition. **E17.** ▸**b** *gen.* A wheeling about; each of a series of usu. ordered or deliberate movements, as of a dancer or a machine part. Usu. in *pl.* **L17.**

b P. G. WODEHOUSE 'Do you do Swedish exercises?' 'I go through a series of evolutions every morning.'

2 The action of opening out or unfolding; chiefly *fig.*, the orderly passage of a long train of events or of the time containing them. **M17.**
3 The process of developing in detail what is implicit in an idea or principle; the development of an argument; an outcome of such a process. **L17.**
4 The development of an animal or plant, or part of one, from a rudimentary to a mature state. **L17.** ▸**b** Any process of gradual change occurring in something, esp. from a simpler to a more complicated or advanced state; the passage of something through a succession of stages. Also, origination by natural development as opp. to production by a specific act. **E19.** ▸**c** A process by which different kinds of organism come into being by the differentiation and genetic mutation of earlier forms over successive generations, viewed as an explanation of their origins. **M19.**

J. T. NEEDHAM Nature . . ever exerting its Fecundity in a successive Evolution of organised Bodies. **b** *Times* The evolution of massive stars. J. PLAMENATZ They have quarrelled about the stage that capitalism has reached in the course of its evolution, how close it is to collapse. **c** G. M. TREVELYAN The whole idea of evolution and of 'man descended from a monkey' was totally incompatible with existing religious ideas. D. MORRIS At some point in the evolution of the squirrel family, the ancestors of this animal must have split off from the rest.

5 MATH. **a** The process of finding a root of some given quantity. *arch.* **E18.** ▸**b** The process of obtaining an involute from an evolute. Now *rare*. **E18.**
6 Chiefly BIOLOGY. Emergence or protrusion from an envelope, seed, vesicle, etc. **M18.**
7 The process of giving off gas, heat, light, or sound. **E19.**
– PHRASES: **theory of evolution** (*a*) *hist.* the hypothesis that an embryo or seed is a development of a pre-existing form which contains the rudiments of all the parts of the future organism; (*b*) the theory that present-day organisms have come into being through a process of evolution (sense 4c above).
■ **evolutional** *adjective* of, pertaining to, or produced by evolution **M19.** **evolutionally** *adverb* in an evolutional way **L19.**

evolutionary /iːvəˈluːʃ(ə)n(ə)ri, ˈljuː-, ɛ-/ *adjective.* **M19.**
[ORIGIN from EVOLUTION + -ARY[1].]
1 Of or pertaining to evolution or development; dealing with or assuming the theory of evolution. **M19.**

J. L. HARPER Species caught in different evolutionary pathways may face the same selective forces. E. C. MINKOFF Evolutionary biology. *London Review of Books* Taxonomists classify themselves as cladists or evolutionary systematists.

2 Of, pertaining to, or performing the evolutions or manoeuvres of troops or ships. **M19.**
■ **evolutionarily** *adverb* in an evolutionary way; from an evolutionary standpoint: **M20.**

evolutionise *verb* var. of EVOLUTIONIZE.

evolutionism /iːvəˈluːʃ(ə)nɪz(ə)m, -ˈljuː-, ɛ-/ *noun.* **M19.**
[ORIGIN from EVOLUTION + -ISM.]
The theory of evolution; evolutionary assumptions or principles. Opp. ***creationism***.

Times Lit. Suppl. The evolutionism inherent in Marx's general conception of history.

evolutionist /iːvəˈluːʃ(ə)nɪst, -ˈljuː-, ɛ-/ *noun & adjective.* **M19.**
[ORIGIN formed as EVOLUTIONISM + -IST.]
▸**A** *noun.* **1** MILITARY. A person skilled in evolutions. *rare.* **M19.**
2 A person who believes in or advocates the theory of evolution; an expert in or student of evolution. **L19.**
▸**B** *adjective.* Of or pertaining to evolutionism or an evolutionist. **L19.**
■ ˌ**evolutioˈnistic** *adjective* **L19.**

evolutionize /iːvəˈl(j)uːʃ(ə)nʌɪz, ɛ-/ *verb trans. & intrans.* Also **-ise**. **L19.**
[ORIGIN from EVOLUTION + -IZE.]
Develop in the course of evolution; change gradually.

evolutive /iːvəˈl(j)uːtɪv, ɛ-/ *adjective.* **L19.**
[ORIGIN from EVOLUT(ION + -IVE.]
Pertaining to, tending to, or promoting evolution.

evolvant /ɪˈvɒlv(ə)nt/ *noun.* **L20.**
[ORIGIN from EVOLVE + -ANT[1].]
BIOLOGY. An evolved or deliberately modified form of an organism, esp. a bacterium, or of an enzyme.

evolve /ɪˈvɒlv/ *verb.* **E17.**
[ORIGIN Latin *evolvere* unroll, unfold, from *e-* E- + *volvere* to roll.]
▸**I** *verb trans.* **1** Make more complicated or organized; bring to fuller development; develop. **E17.**

H. MOORE At some point you'd see something in the doodling, . . and from then on you could evolve the idea.

2 Disclose gradually to the mind; present in orderly sequence. **M17.**
3 Give off (gas, heat, etc.) as a result of internal processes. **E19.**
4 Bring out (something implicit or potential); deduce (a conclusion, law, etc.) from data; develop (a notion); work out (a theory). **M19.**

A. CARNEGIE Order was soon evolved out of chaos. W. GOLDING Roger Mason had evolved a method of dealing with Rachel.

5 Produce or develop in the course of evolution. Usu. in *pass.* **M19.**

H. T. LANE Teeth were first evolved not for purposes of mastication, but for attack and defence.

6 Produce (a condition, process, etc.) as a natural consequence. **M19.**
▸**II** *verb intrans.* **7** Gradually come into view or take shape; arise as a natural consequence; *spec.* (of an organism, part, or feature) come into being through evolutionary development. **E18.**

J. MCPHEE Gradually—as they added a room, razed a woodshed, . . —a new cabin evolved. J. GATHORNE-HARDY The British Nanny evolved out of . . a particular society. J. S. HUXLEY Leakey was convinced that early man had evolved in Africa.

8 Undergo evolution (*into*). **M19.**

L. MACNEICE They must . . have evolved late into sea-creatures. *Scientific American* The more massive a star is, the faster it evolves. F. SPALDING His [artistic] method evolved into a formula during the 1960s.

■ **evolvable** *adjective* **M19.** **evolvement** *noun* a process of evolving **M19.** **evolver** *noun* **E19.**

evolvent /ɪˈvɒlv(ə)nt/ *adjective & noun.* **E18.**
[ORIGIN Latin *evolvent-* pres. ppl stem of *evolvere* EVOLVE: see -ENT.]
▸†**A** *adjective.* MATH. ***evolvent line***, a tangent to an evolute. Only in **E18.**
▸**B** *noun.* **1** MATH. The involute of a curve. Now *rare* or *obsolete*. **E18.**
2 Something that gives rise to or evolves something else. Also, something that is evolved. **M19.**

†**evomit** *verb trans.* **LME–E18.**
[ORIGIN Latin *evomit-* pa. ppl stem of *evomere* spew out, from *e-* E- + *vomere* to vomit.]
Vomit, throw up, (the contents of the stomach).
■ †**evomition** *noun* **M17–E18.**

evulgate /ɪˈvʌlgeɪt/ *verb trans.* Now *rare* or *obsolete*. **L16.**
[ORIGIN Latin *evulgat-* pa. ppl stem of *evulgare*, from *e-* E- + *vulgare* spread among the multitude, from *vulgus* multitude: see -ATE[3].]
Make commonly known; divulge; publish.
■ **evulˈgation** *noun* **M17.**

evulse /ɪˈvʌls/ *verb trans.* **M18.**
[ORIGIN Latin *evuls-*: see EVULSION.]
Pull out, tear away.

evulsion /ɪˈvʌlʃ(ə)n/ *noun.* **LME.**
[ORIGIN Latin *evulsio(n-)*, from *evuls-* pa. ppl stem of *evellere* pluck out, from *e-* E- + *vellere* pluck.]
Forcible extraction.

evviva /ɛvˈviːva/ *noun.* **L19.**
[ORIGIN Italian, from *e* 'and' (from Latin *et*) used intensively + *viva*: see VIVA *noun*[1].]
A shout of applause or acclamation.

evzone /ˈɛvzəʊn, -ni/ *noun & adjective.* **L19.**
[ORIGIN mod. Greek *euzōnas*, *-os* noun from Greek adjective = dressed for exercise, formed as EU- + *zōnē* girdle.]
(Designating) a member of a select infantry regiment of the Greek army whose members wear a distinctive uniform that includes a fustanella.

ewe /juː/ *noun*[1].
[ORIGIN Old English *ēowu* = Old Frisian *ei*, Old Saxon *ewwi* (Middle Dutch *oie*, Dutch *ooi*), Low German *ouw (lamm)*, Old High German *ouwi*, *ou* (German *Aue*), Old Norse *ær*, from Germanic from Indo-European word repr. also by Latin *ovis*, Greek *o(w)is*. Cf. YOWE.]
A female sheep, *esp.* a fully grown one; a female of various related animals.
– COMB.: **ewe lamb** a female lamb; *fig.* one's most cherished possession (alluding to *2 Samuel* 12); **ewe neck** a horse's neck whose upper outline curves inwards instead of outwards; **ewe-necked** *adjective* (of a horse) having a ewe neck.

Ewe /ˈeɪweɪ/ *adjective & noun*[2]. **M19.**
[ORIGIN Ewe.]
▸**A** *adjective.* Of, pertaining to, or designating a Kwa language of Ghana, Togo, and Benin, or the people who speak this language. **M19.**
▸**B** *noun.* Pl. same. The Ewe language; a member of the Ewe people. **L19.**

ewer /ˈjuːə/ *noun*[1]. **LME.**
[ORIGIN Anglo-Norman *ewer*, *aiguer* from Old Northern French *eviere*, Old French & mod. French *aiguière*, from Proto-Romance from fem. of Latin *aquarius* pertaining to water, from *aqua* water: see -ER[2].]
A jug with a wide mouth, *esp.* a large water jug of the kind formerly used in bedrooms.

†**ewer** *noun*[2]. **LME–E17.**
[ORIGIN Old French from Latin *aquarius*: see EWER *noun*[1], -ER[2].]
= EWERER.

ewerer /ˈjuːərə/ *noun*. LME.
[ORIGIN from EWER *noun*[2] or EWERY: see -ER[1].]
hist. A servant who supplied those at table with water to wash their hands.

ewery /ˈjuːəri/ *noun*. Also **ewry** /ˈjuːri/. LME.
[ORIGIN from EWER *noun*[1] + -Y[3]: see -ERY.]
1 A place where ewers, towels, etc., were formerly kept; a department administratively responsible for this, esp. in the royal household. LME.
†**2** The ewers, towels, etc., that a ewerer looked after. LME–L15.

ewest /ˈjuːɪst/ *adverb*. *Scot.* E16.
[ORIGIN Unknown.]
Close at hand.

E

ewhow /ɛˈhwuː/ *interjection*. *Scot.* E19.
[ORIGIN from EH + *whow* var. of HOW *interjection*[1].]
Alas!

Ewigkeit /ˈeːvɪçkaɪt, ˈeɪvɪgkʌɪt/ *noun*. Also **e-**. L19.
[ORIGIN German = eternity.]
Eternity; infinity.
into the Ewigkeit *joc.* into thin air.

Ewing /ˈjuːɪŋ/ *noun*. E20.
[ORIGIN J. *Ewing* (1866–1943), US pathologist.]
Ewing's tumour, ***Ewing's sarcoma***, a rare malignant tumour of bone occurring in childhood and adolescence.

ewry *noun* var. of EWERY.

†**ewt** *noun* var. of EFT *noun*.

ex /ɛks/ *noun & adjective*. E19.
[ORIGIN EX-[1] 3.]
▸ **A** *noun*. Pl. **exes**, **ex's** /ˈɛksɪz/. A person who formerly occupied a position etc. denoted by the context; *spec.* a former husband or wife. E19.
▸ **B** *adjective*. Former, outdated. E19.

ex /ɛks/ *verb trans.* M20.
[ORIGIN Repr. pronunc. of *X*, *x*.]
Cross *out* with an X, = X *verb* 2.

ex /ɛks/ *preposition*. M19.
[ORIGIN Latin = out of.]
1 COMMERCE. Of stocks and shares: without, excluding. M19.

Daily Telegraph The shares were traded ex the one-for-one scrip issue.

ex dividend (with ref. to share prices) not including a dividend about to be paid.

2 Of goods: out of, sold direct from, (a ship, warehouse, etc.). Of an animal: out of (a specified dam). L19.

Lancet The standard hospital model costs £115 ex factory. *Horse & Hound* Malicious, Ch. 1961 by Helioscope ex Blackball by Shut out.

ex- /ɛks, ɪks, ɪgz/ *prefix*[1].
[ORIGIN Latin, formed as EX *preposition* Used before vowels, *c, f, h, p, q, s, t*: cf. E-, EF-.]
1 In verbs from Latin (directly or through Old & mod. French) with the senses 'out', as ***exclude***, 'upward', as ***extol***, 'thoroughly', as ***excruciate***, 'bring into a state', as ***exasperate***, 'remove, expel, relieve of', as ***expatriate***, ***exonerate***, ***excoriate***. Also in words (ult.) derived from such verbs, as ***exasperation***, ***exclusive***, ***excrescence***, ***extension***. Occas. forming nouns directly from English nouns, as ***exclosure***, ***exflagellation***, ***exsolution***.
2 Occas. (E- preferred) forming adjectives with the sense 'not having, deprived of', as ***exalbuminous***.
3 As a freely productive prefix forming nouns from titles of office, status, etc., with the sense 'former(ly)', as ***ex-convict***, ***ex-husband***, ***ex-president***, ***ex-Prime Minister***, ***ex-serviceman***, ***ex-servicewoman***.

ex- /ɛks/ *prefix*[2].
Repr. Greek *ex-* out (of), as ***exodus***, ***exorcism***. Occas. intensive, as ***exomologesis***.

exa- /ˈɛksə/ *combining form*.
[ORIGIN from H)EXA-, 10^{18} being $(10^3)^6$, suggested by the supposed analogy of *tera-*, *tetra-*: cf. PETA-.]
Used in names of units of measurement to denote a factor of 10^{18}, as ***exametre*** etc. Abbreviation *E*.

exacerbate /ɪgˈzasəbeɪt, ɛkˈsas-/ *verb trans.* M17.
[ORIGIN Latin *exacerbat-* pa. ppl stem of *exacerbare*, formed as EX-[1] 1 + *acerbare* make harsh or bitter, from *acerbus* harsh, bitter, grievous: see -ATE[3].]
Increase the sharpness of (a pain), the severity of (an illness), the bitterness of (a feeling), etc.; aggravate. Also, provoke the resentment of (a person).

J. BERGER The unfamiliar climate . . may have further exacerbated her nervous condition. J. MASTERS Such a step would merely exacerbate an already touchy situation. J. P. HENNESSY Trollope had been exacerbated by the noise of an itinerant German band.

■ **exacerbatingly** *adverb* in an exacerbating way M20.

exacerbation /ɪgˌzasəˈbeɪʃ(ə)n, ɛkˌsas-/ *noun*. LME.
[ORIGIN Late Latin *exacerbatio(n-)*, formed as EXACERBATE: see -ATION.]
1 The action of provoking to anger or bitterness; (an instance of) embittered feeling. LME.
2 (An) increase in the severity of a disease, punishment, etc.; *esp.* a paroxysm of a fever etc. E17.

British Medical Journal Several patients took 30–50 mg salbutamol a day during exacerbations.

exact /ɪgˈzakt, ɛg-/ *adjective & adverb*. M16.
[ORIGIN Latin *exactus* pa. pple of *exigere* complete, bring to perfection, examine, ascertain, formed as EX-[1] 1 + *agere* perform.]
▸ **A** *adjective*. **I** Precise, accurate.
1 Of a law or rule, discipline, etc.: permitting no deviation; strictly or punctiliously observed. M16.

JAS. MILL The troops were kept in . . exact discipline. W. BOYD He was excluded from the phenomenally exact social rankings which obtained in . . Nairobi society.

2 Of an action or process, knowledge, research, etc.: complete in every detail; minutely thorough. M16.

A. RADCLIFFE He gave an exact acquaintance with every part of elegant literature.

3 Of a person: marked by accuracy of knowledge, observation, workmanship, etc. Of a judge: strict, rigorous. L16.

C. BRONTË She was an exact, clever manager.

4 Of a result, numerical quantity, statement, etc.: not approximated in any way; completely accurate and precise. E17.

OED A is an exact multiple of B. J. CONRAD Get the exact bearings of his swag. E. O'NEILL Blow me if them warn't her exact words! P. BROOK The dosage is so subtle that it is impossible to establish the exact formula.

5 Of a likeness, representation, description, etc.: corresponding in every detail. M17.

W. S. MAUGHAM A word for which . . there is no exact equivalent in English. K. CLARK An exact replica.

6 Of a method, a scientific instrument, etc.: marked by precision, esp. of measurement; not allowing vagueness or uncertainty. M17.

F. MYERS No spoken language has yet been found exact enough to express the highest generalisations.

exact science a science (e.g. mathematics, chemistry) capable of absolute or quantitative precision.

▸ **II** Perfected, consummate.
†**7** Of a person: highly skilled or accomplished; refined as regards taste. L16–E18.

MILTON Eve, now I see thou art exact of taste.

†**8** Of a quality, condition, etc.: consummate, refined, perfect. L16–E18.

R. LOVELL The hearing is most exact in the hare.

†**9** Of an object: highly wrought, elaborate. Of a building: well designed. E17–E18.
▸ †**B** *adverb*. Exactly, precisely. L16–L18.

POPE There's a Rehearsal, Sir, exact at one.

■ **exactness** *noun* M16.

exact /ɪgˈzakt, ɛg-/ *verb*. LME.
[ORIGIN Latin *exact-* pa. ppl stem of *exigere*: see EXACT *adjective & adverb*.]
1 *verb trans.* Demand and enforce the payment of (a debt, penalty, etc.), the performance of (a task), the concession of (something desired), etc.; force to give or pay. (Foll. by *from*, (arch.) *of*.) LME. ▸†**b** Extort money from (a person). M–L16.

AV *2 Kings* 23:35 Iehoiakim . . exacted the siluer and the golde . . of euery one according to his taxation. E. JONES An indefatigable worker himself, he exacted the same standard from his assistants. H. J. LASKI William's advisers who exacted an oath of obedience from the clergy.

2 *verb trans.* Of circumstances etc.: make desirable or necessary; call for. L16.

R. BOYLE I must withhold my Beleef . . till their Experiments exact it.

†**3** *verb intrans.* Impose contributions *on* or *upon*. L16–E18.
4 *verb trans.* LAW. Call on (a defendant) to appear in court. Now *rare* or *obsolete*. E17.
5 *verb trans.* Extract forcibly. *arch.* M17.

T. FULLER It passeth my Chymistrie to exact any agreement herein out of the contrariety of writers.

6 *verb trans.* Inflict (vengeance) *against* or *from*. M19.
■ **exactable** *adjective* M19.

exacta /ɪgˈzaktə, ɛg-/ *noun*. *N. Amer.* M20.
[ORIGIN Amer. Spanish *quiniela exacta* exact quinella.]
BETTING. = PERFECTA.

exacter /ɪgˈzaktə, ɛg-/ *noun*. M16.
[ORIGIN from EXACT *verb* + -ER[1].]
1 = EXACTOR 4. M16.
2 = EXACTOR 1, 3. L16.

exacting /ɪgˈzaktɪŋ, ɛg-/ *adjective*. L16.
[ORIGIN from EXACT *verb* + -ING[2].]
Making excessive demands, esp. on one's strength, skill, attention, etc.; hard to satisfy.

A. E. STEVENSON His ability . . to fulfill the demands of his exacting office. A. HALEY The state of repair failed to measure up to their exacting standards.

■ **exactingly** *adverb* M19. **exactingness** *noun* M19.

exaction /ɪgˈzakʃ(ə)n, ɛg-/ *noun*. LME.
[ORIGIN French from Latin *exactio(n-)*, formed as EXACT *verb*: see -ION.]
1 The action or an act of exacting a payment, service, etc. LME. ▸**b** In *pl.* Pressing demands made (*on* a person's time etc.). M20.

b D. M. DAVIN I was . . wary of other people's drama and frugal of the exactions it makes on one's energy.

2 The action or an act of demanding more money etc. than is due; (an) extortion. LME.

F. HALL We may, without being chargeable with exaction, ask of him to remit . . the rigour of his requirements.

3 A sum of money (arbitrarily) exacted. LME.

BURKE The small balance . . remaining of the unjust exaction.

exactitude /ɪgˈzaktɪtjuːd, ɛg-/ *noun*. M18.
[ORIGIN French from *exact* formed as EXACT *adjective*: see -TUDE.]
Accuracy; attention to small details. Formerly also, perfect correctness (of a statement).

P. DE VRIES Dry martinis mixed with pharmaceutical exactitude.

exactly /ɪgˈzaktli, ɛg-/ *adverb*. M16.
[ORIGIN from EXACT *adjective* + -LY[2].]
†**1** To a perfect degree; completely. M16–E18.
2 With careful attention to detail or conformity to rule; meticulously. Now *rare*. M16.

H. MARTINEAU He paid for his lodging exactly and regularly.

3 Accurately, precisely; without discrepancy, vagueness, or uncertainty. M17. ▸**b** As a comment on a statement or a reply to a question: just so; I entirely agree. *colloq.* M19. ▸**c** Used with expressed or implied neg. when the statement denied is replaced by another of similar effect. L19.

H. JAMES It is exactly three months to a day since I left Northampton. M. SINCLAIR She didn't know what it was exactly. T. STOPPARD What exactly do you do in there? SCOTT FITZGERALD Exactly what it was she did not know. M. SINCLAIR He behaved exactly as if he had expected her. B. SPOCK At exactly 6 a.m., . . no earlier, no later. **c** OED Without exactly denying it, he led me to believe it was not true.

c not exactly (***a***) not quite, but close to (being); (***b***) *colloq. iron.* not at all, by no means.

exactor /ɪgˈzaktə, ɛg-/ *noun*. LME.
[ORIGIN Latin, formed as EXACT *verb* + -OR.]
1 A person who makes illegal or unreasonable demands; an extortioner. LME.
†**2** An officer of justice who extorted confessions and carried out sentences. LME–L16.
3 A person who collects taxes, dues, or customs. *arch.* L16.
4 A person who insists on a task, service, etc., as a matter of right; a person who makes demands. L16.
■ **exactress** *noun* (*rare*) a female exactor E17.

†**exaestuation** *noun*. Also **exest-**. M17–E18.
[ORIGIN Latin *exaestuatio(n-)*, from *exaestuat-* pa. ppl stem of *exaestuare* boil, foam, seethe, formed as EX-[1] 1 + *aestuare* boil etc., from *aestus* heat (noun): see -ATION.]
A boiling, an overheating, a fermentation.

exaggerate /ɪgˈzadʒəreɪt, ɛg-/ *verb*. M16.
[ORIGIN Latin *exaggerat-* pa. ppl stem of *exaggerare*, formed as EX-[1] 1 + *aggerare* heap up, from *agger* heap, mound: see -ATE[3].]
†**1** *verb trans.* Pile up, accumulate, (*lit.* & *fig.*). M16–L17.
†**2** *verb trans.* Emphasize the greatness of (a virtue, fault, etc.). M16–M18.

MONMOUTH It was . . praiseworthy in Bishop Jovius to exaggerate the praises of . . his Benefactors.

3 *verb trans.* & *intrans.* Represent (a thing) as greater than it really is; overstate, indulge in overstatement. (Earlier in EXAGGERATION 1.) E17.

G. GREENE One is inclined to exaggerate the value of another country's films. I. MCEWAN He exaggerates a lot, and turns his past into stories to tell at the bar.

4 *verb trans.* Enlarge or alter beyond normal proportions; make of abnormal size. (Earlier in EXAGGERATION 3.) M19.

LEIGH HUNT A nose exaggerated by intemperance. J. E. T. ROGERS The existing distress was exaggerated by this great social change.

■ **exaggeratedly** *adverb* to an excessive degree M19. **exaggeratingly** *adverb* in an exaggerating or hyperbolic manner E19. **exaggerative** *adjective* marked by or given to exaggeration L18. **exaggeratively** *adverb* M19. **exaggerativeness** *noun* L19. **exaggerator** *noun* a person who or thing which exaggerates E17. **exaggeratory** *adjective* = EXAGGERATIVE M18.

exaggeration /ɪgˌzadʒəˈreɪʃ(ə)n, ɛg-/ *noun*. M16.
[ORIGIN Latin *exaggeratio(n-)*, formed as EXAGGERATE: see -ATION.]
1 (A) representation of something as greater than it really is; (a) hyperbolic statement. M16. ▸**b** ART. (A) representation of a subject in which the features are emphasized or given excessive colouring. M18.

T. H. HUXLEY The exaggeration of the vertical height in the diagram. G. B. SHAW It is hardly an exaggeration to say that they discuss nothing else.

†**2** The action of dwelling on the greatness of a virtue, fault, etc.; emphasis. **L16–M18.**
3 (An) abnormal intensification of a condition. **M17.**

†**exagitate** *verb trans.* **M16.**
[**ORIGIN** Latin *exagitat-* pa. ppl stem of *exagitare*, formed as **EX-**[1] 1 + *agitare* **AGITATE** *verb*: see **-ATE**[3].]
1 Torment with pain; harass, persecute. **M16–L17.**
2 Debate, discuss. **M16–M18.**
3 Inveigh against. **L16–L17.**
4 Disturb, set in quicker motion, (the blood, breathing, etc.). **E17–M18.**

†**exagitation** *noun.* **E17.**
[**ORIGIN** Latin *exagitatio(n-)*, formed as **EXAGITATE**: see **-ATION**.]
1 Stirring up; (an) excitement. **E17–M18.**
2 Discussion. Only in **E17.**

exalbuminous /ɛksalˈbjuːmɪnəs/ *adjective.* **M19.**
[**ORIGIN** from **EX-**[1] 2 + Latin *albumin-*, **ALBUMEN** + **-OUS**.]
BOTANY. Having no albumen in the seed.

exalt /ɪɡˈzɔːlt, ɛɡ-/ *adjective. poet.* **E19.**
[**ORIGIN** from **EXALT** *verb* or its pa. pple.]
Exalted.

exalt /ɪɡˈzɔːlt, ɛɡ-/ *verb trans.* **LME.**
[**ORIGIN** Latin *exaltare*, formed as **EX-**[1] 1 + *altus* high.]
1 Raise aloft; elevate. Now *arch. & rhet.* **LME.** ▸**b** Raise (the voice) in speech or song; raise (a song); make (music). *arch.* **M16.**

J. BARLOW Exalt your heads, ye oaks.

2 Raise to a higher rank, station, etc.; *refl.* (*arch.*) assume a superior position. **LME.** ▸**b** Make (more) excellent or sublime; give a lofty character to; dignify. Chiefly as ***exalted*** *ppl adjective.* **E17.**

AV *1 Kings* 1:5 Then Adoniiah the sonne of Haggith exalted himselfe, saying, I wil be king. D. H. LAWRENCE Do away with the masters, exalt the will of the people. **b** DAY LEWIS Proud and poor, the Anglo-Irish exalted their snobbery into a tribal mystique. R. LEHMANN They parted in exalted peace of mind. W. CATHER That exalted serenity that sometimes came to her at moments of deep feeling.

exalted personage a person of high (usu. princely or royal) rank.

3 Praise highly, extol. **LME.**

J. BERGER Strong nations . . can only exalt and glorify their sons who . . sacrifice their life for . . an ideal.

4 Make rapturously excited. Formerly, elate with pride, joy, etc. Chiefly as ***exalted*** pa. pple. **LME.**

CLARENDON The covenanters . . were very reasonably exalted with this success. G. B. SHAW Lunatics, exalted by . . visions of a dawning millennium.

5 Intensify, heighten. Formerly, increase (a price). **LME.**

M. SCHAPIRO His [Van Gogh's] first aim was intensity, a firm . . image exalted by daring colour.

†**6** Raise (a substance) to a higher degree of purity or potency; refine, concentrate. Also, make (a physical effect) more powerful. **L15–E19.**

J. RAY Other stones being exalted to that degree of hardness. *fig.*: BURKE This is Jacobinism sublimed and exalted into its most pure essence.

7 *ASTROLOGY.* In *pass.* Of a planet: be in the sign of the zodiac where it exerts its greatest influence. **M17.**
8 Stimulate (a faculty) to greater activity. **M18.**

GEO. ELIOT Trivial causes had the effect of rousing and exalting the imagination.

■ **exaltedly** *adverb* in an exalted manner; with exaltation: **L18.** **exaltedness** *noun* exalted quality, rank, etc. **M17.** **exalter** *noun* **L15.**

exaltation /ɛɡzɔːlˈteɪʃ(ə)n, ɛks-/ *noun.* **LME.**
[**ORIGIN** Old French & mod. French, or late Latin *exaltatio(n-)*, from Latin *exaltat-* pa. ppl stem of *exaltare*: see **EXALT** *verb*, **-ATION**.]
1 The action of raising aloft; the state of being raised or elevated. Orig. only in ***Exaltation of the Cross*** below. **LME.** ▸**b** A group *of* larks in flight. (*rare* before **E19.**) **LME.**
Exaltation of the Cross a feast observed in the Roman and Orthodox Churches on 14 September in honour of the Cross of Christ, to commemorate either the exposition of the supposed True Cross in 629 after its recovery from the Persians, or the dedication by Constantine in 335 of the basilica built on the site of the Holy Sepulchre.
2 Elevation in rank, power, etc.; *esp.* the elevation of a monarch to a throne. Formerly also, elevated rank, culmination of fortune. **LME.** ▸**b** The raising of a thing to a high degree of excellence; exalted degree; an exalted manifestation. **M17.**

DEFOE Joseph . . told them the story of his exaltation in Pharaoh's court. **b** LD MACAULAY That chivalrous spirit . . was found in the highest exaltation among the Norman nobles.

3 *ASTROLOGY.* The position of a planet in the zodiac in which it exerts especially great influence. **LME.**
†**4** The action or an act of raising a substance to a higher degree of purity or potency. **L15–M18.**
5 Rapturous excitement; elation. **L15.**

G. ORWELL The exaltation, the lunatic enthusiasm, was still in his face.

6 Intensification. **M18.**

exalté /ɛɡzalte/ *adjective & noun.* Fem. **-ée**. Pl. of noun pronounced same. **M19.**
[**ORIGIN** French, pa. ppl adjective of *exalter* formed as **EXALT** *verb*.]
(A person who is) elated or impassioned.

exam /ɪɡˈzam, ɛɡ-/ *noun. colloq.* **M19.**
[**ORIGIN** Abbreviation.]
= **EXAMINATION** 2.

examen /ɛɡˈzeɪmɛn/ *noun.* **E17.**
[**ORIGIN** Latin = tongue of a balance, (fig.) examination, from *exigere* weigh accurately: see **EXACT** *adjective*.]
†**1** A critical dissertation or treatise, a disquisition. **E17–M18.**
2 (An) examination, (an) investigation. Now *rare.* **E17.** ▸**b** *ECCLESIASTICAL.* A formal examination of the soul or conscience. **M17.**
†**3** (An) investigation by experiment; a test. **M17–M18.**
4 The pointer of a balance. *rare.* **M19.**

examinable /ɪɡˈzamɪnəb(ə)l, ɛɡ-/ *adjective.* **L16.**
[**ORIGIN** from **EXAMINE** *verb* + **-ABLE**.]
1 *LAW.* Subject to examination; cognizable. **L16.**
2 *gen.* Able to be examined (in). **E17.** ▸**b** *ECCLESIASTICAL HISTORY.* Of a person: eligible to be examined for admission to Holy Communion. *Scot.* **E18.**

G. ADAMS The smallest examinable quantity of matter. *Times Lit. Suppl.* A subject which was both teachable (which . . partly meant examinable) and . . useful.

■ **examinaˈbility** *noun* **L19.**

examinant /ɪɡˈzamɪnənt, ɛɡ-/ *noun.* **L16.**
[**ORIGIN** Latin *examinant-* pres. ppl stem of *examinare*: see **EXAMINE** *verb*, **-ANT**[1].]
†**1** A person who is being examined as a witness; a person undergoing an examination as to fitness for church membership, ordination, etc. **L16–E19.**
2 A person who examines, an examiner. **E17.**

examinate /ɪɡˈzamɪnət, ɛɡ-/ *adjective & noun.* **LME.**
[**ORIGIN** Latin *examinatus* pa. pple of *examinare*: see **EXAMINE** *verb*, **-ATE**[2].]
▸ †**A** *adjective.* Examined; interrogated under torture. **LME–E19.**
▸ **B** *noun.* **1** A person under examination, either as a witness or as an accused person. **M16.**
2 A person who is examined for suitability or proficiency; an examination candidate. **L16.**

examination /ɪɡˌzamɪˈneɪʃ(ə)n, ɛɡ-/ *noun.* **LME.**
[**ORIGIN** Old French & mod. French from Latin *examinatio(n-)*, from *examinat-* pa. ppl stem of *examinare*: see **EXAMINE** *verb*, **-ATION**.]
1 a The action of judging or testing critically or by a standard, esp. one's conscience. **LME.** ▸**b** The action of inspecting or testing something in order to investigate its nature, condition, or qualities; the inspection or testing of a person in order to determine the state of his or her physical health or fitness. **M17.**

b M. HOCKING The doctor . . had given Janet a thorough examination.

2 (The action of conducting) a test of a person's knowledge or proficiency in which he or she is required to answer questions or perform tasks. **LME.**

JUDE COLLINS Some of you will pass your examination; more of you will not.

3 Formal interrogation, esp. of a witness or an accused person; a trial. **LME.** ▸**b** (A record of) the statements made by a witness or accused person when examined. **M16.**
examination-in-chief the questioning of a witness by the party which has called that witness to give evidence, in support of the case being made.
†**4** A testing, a trial, an assay, (*lit.* & *fig.*). **E–M16.**
5 The action of searching, investigating, or inquiring into a subject, statements, etc. **M16.**
– **COMB.:** **examination paper** a printed set of questions to be answered; a candidate's written answers.
■ **examinational** *adjective* **E19.**

examinator /ɪɡˈzamɪneɪtə, ɛɡ-/ *noun.* **M16.**
[**ORIGIN** Late Latin, from Latin *examinat-* pa. ppl stem of *examinare* **EXAMINE** *verb*: see **-ATOR**.]
1 = **EXAMINER** 3. Chiefly *Scot.* **M16.**
†**2** = **EXAMINER** 2. **M17–M19.**
†**3** = **EXAMINER** 1. *Scot.* **M18–M19.**

examinatorial /ɪɡˌzamɪnəˈtɔːrɪəl, ɛɡ-/ *adjective.* **M19.**
[**ORIGIN** from late Latin *examinatorius* + **-AL**[1].]
Of or pertaining to an examiner or an examination.

examine /ɪɡˈzamɪn, ɛɡ-/ *noun.* Now *hist.* exc. *Scot.* **L15.**
[**ORIGIN** from the verb.]
(An) examination.

examine /ɪɡˈzamɪn, ɛɡ-/ *verb.* **ME.**
[**ORIGIN** Old French & mod. French *examiner* from Latin *examinare* weigh accurately, from *examin-* **EXAMEN**.]
†**1** *verb trans.* Assay, prove, (precious metal); *fig.* put (a person) to the test. Only in **ME.**
2 *verb trans.* Investigate the nature, condition, or qualities of (something) by close inspection or tests; inspect closely or critically (*spec.* one's conscience); scrutinize; search (baggage); verify (calculations, account books); give (a person) a medical examination. Formerly also, judge or try by a standard. **ME.**

C. P. SNOW She examined the shelves, note-book in hand. L. HELLMAN The man in front was having his passport examined. LE ROI JONES He . . walks nervously around the room examining books and paintings.

3 *verb trans.* Inquire into, investigate, (a subject); consider or discuss critically; try to ascertain (*whether*, *how*, etc.). **ME.**

T. REID We shall examine this theory afterwards. G. B. SHAW We must examine why it occurred.

need one's head examined: see **HEAD** *noun.*
4 *verb trans. & intrans.* Test the knowledge or proficiency of (a person, esp. a pupil or candidate) by questioning (*in* or *on* a subject). **LME.**
5 *verb trans.* Interrogate formally (esp. a witness or an accused person). Formerly also, investigate the guilt or innocence of (an accused person). **LME.** ▸†**b** Interrogate under torture. **L16–E18.**
6 *verb intrans.* Look or inquire *into.* **M19.**
■ **examiˈnee** *noun* a person under examination; a person who is a candidate in an examination: **L18.** **examiningly** *adverb* in an examining manner; searchingly: **L19.**

examiner /ɪɡˈzamɪnə, ɛɡ-/ *noun.* **ME.**
[**ORIGIN** from **EXAMINE** *verb* + **-ER**[1].]
†**1** A person who examines or interrogates a witness or an accused person. **ME–L17.**
2 A person who inquires into facts or investigates the nature or condition of something; an investigator. **LME.**
medical examiner: see **MEDICAL** *adjective.*
3 A person appointed to examine a pupil, candidate, etc., or to set an examination. **E18.**
SATISFY ***the examiners***.
■ **examinership** *noun* the office or post of examiner **M19.**

examplar /ɪɡˈzɑːmplə, ɛɡ-/ *noun.* Now *rare.* **LME.**
[**ORIGIN** Old French *examplaire* var. of *exemplaire*: see **EXEMPLAR** *noun*.]
1 A model; a perfect specimen (of some quality); a person or thing to be imitated. **LME.**
2 Orig., a copy, a transcript. Now, a copy of a book. **LME.**
†**3** A needlework sampler. **M–L16.**

example /ɪɡˈzɑːmp(ə)l, ɛɡ-/ *noun.* **LME.**
[**ORIGIN** Old French (mod. *exemple*), alt. after Latin of *essample* (whence **ENSAMPLE** *noun*, aphet. **SAMPLE** *noun*) from Latin *exemplum*, from *eximere* take out (see **EXEMPT** *adjective*).]
1 A typical instance; a fact or thing illustrating a general principle; a person or thing illustrating a certain quality etc. **LME.** ▸**b** A specimen, an instance; a copy of a book, esp. a rare one. **M16.**

J. B. PRIESTLEY This is an admirable example of the public spirit of the Norwich citizens. M. TIPPETT Socrates thinks there are four common examples of divine madness. **b** H. NEMEROV The bison, Except for a few examples kept in cages, Is now extinct.

2 A person whose punishment is a warning or deterrent to others; an instance of such a punishment. **LME.**

D. CUSACK Should be expelled. Make an example of her.

3 A parallel case; a case with which comparison may be made. **LME.**

American Speech The name *Istanbul* replaced *Constantinople*. There are many similar examples.

4 A precedent appealed to for justification. Now *rare* or *obsolete.* **LME.**
5 Action or conduct regarded as something that ought to or may be imitated; a person whose conduct ought to be imitated. **LME.**

J. F. KENNEDY England's example in disarming unilaterally had not been followed by the other countries. A. C. BOULT Toscanini was an example to us all in his attitude of humble service to the composer and his music.

6 *LOGIC.* An argument in which a premiss is assumed from a particular instance. **M16.**
7 A problem or exercise designed to illustrate a principle or technique in mathematics etc. **L17.**
– **PHRASES:** **beyond example** surpassing or without comparison. **for example** by way of illustration. **give an example**, **give a good example**, **give a bad example** = *set an example* etc. below. **set an example**, **set a good example**, **set a bad example**, etc., act in such a (good, bad) manner as to induce imitation. **without example** having no comparable instance.

example /ɪɡˈzɑːmp(ə)l, ɛɡ-/ *verb trans.* **LME.**
[**ORIGIN** from the noun.]
†**1** Set a precedent for; justify by precedent. **LME–L16.**
2 Exemplify; provide a model of; find or give an instance of. Now only in *pass.* **LME.**

J. MORLEY A fervid assiduity that has not often been exampled.

3 Set an example to. Formerly also (of a thing), serve as an example or warning to. Now *rare.* **L16.**
†**4** Indicate (a person) as an example. **E–M17.**

†**exanguine** *adjective* var. of **EXSANGUINE**.

E

E

exanimate /ɪkˈsanɪmət, ɛk-/ *adjective*. M16.
[ORIGIN Latin *exanimatus* pa. pple of *exanimare* deprive of life, formed as EX-¹ 1 + *anima* breath of life: see -ATE².]
1 Dead; lifeless (in appearance); inanimate. M16.
2 Deprived of or lacking animation or courage. M16.

exanimate /ɪkˈsanɪmeɪt, ɛk-/ *verb trans*. Now *rare*. M16.
[ORIGIN Latin *exanimat-* pa. ppl stem of *exanimare*: see EXANIMATE *adjective*, -ATE³.]
†**1** Dishearten, dispirit. M16–M17.
†**2** Kill. L16–M17.
3 Make breathless or unconscious. L19.

ex animo /ɛks ˈanɪməʊ/ *adverbial phr*. E17.
[ORIGIN Latin = from the soul, formed as EX *preposition* + *animo* abl. of *animus* soul.]
Heartily, sincerely.

exannulate /ɪkˈsanjʊlət, ɛk-/ *adjective*. M19.
[ORIGIN from EX-¹ 2 + ANNULUS + -ATE².]
BOTANY. Having no annulus round the sporangium, as in certain ferns.

ex ante /ɛks ˈanti/ *adjectival & adverbial phr*. M20.
[ORIGIN mod. Latin, formed as EX *preposition* + Latin *ante* before.]
Chiefly ECONOMICS. ▸**A** *adjectival phr*. Based on prior assumptions or expectations; predicted, prospective. M20.
▸**B** *adverbial phr*. Before the event, in advance, beforehand. M20.

exanthema /ɪkˈsanθɪmə, ɛksanˈθiːmə/ *noun*. Pl. **exanthemata** /ɪksanˈθiːmətə, ɛk-/, **-themas**. Also **exanthem** /ɪkˈsanθɪm/. M17.
[ORIGIN Late Latin from Greek *exanthēma* eruption, formed as EX-² + *antheein* to blossom, from *anthos* flower.]
MEDICINE. The rash or skin signs of an acute, esp. febrile, disease; a disease characterized by this.
■ **exantheˈmatic** *adjective* E19. **exanˈthematous** *adjective* M18.

†**exantlate** *verb trans*. M–L17.
[ORIGIN Latin *exantlat-* pa. ppl stem of *exantlare* or *exanclare* draw out (a liquid): see -ATE³.]
Exhaust.
■ †**exantlation** *noun* (*a*) the action of drawing something out like water from a well; (*b*) exhaustion: M17–E18.

exaptation /ˌɛksapˈteɪʃ(ə)n/ *noun*. L20.
[ORIGIN from EX-¹ + *aptation* as in ADAPTATION.]
BIOLOGY. The process by which features acquire functions for which they were not originally adapted or selected. Also, a function which has evolved in this way.

exarate /ˈɛksəreɪt/ *adjective*. L19.
[ORIGIN Latin *exaratus* pa. pple of *exarare* plough up, write on a wax tablet, formed as EX-¹ 1 + *arare* to plough: see -ATE².]
ENTOMOLOGY. Of a pupa: having the appendages free from the body.

exaration /ɛksəˈreɪʃ(ə)n/ *noun*. Now *rare* or *obsolete*. M17.
[ORIGIN Late Latin *exaratio(n-)*, from *exarare*: see EXARATE, -ATE³.]
The action of writing or of engraving on stone; a composition.

exarch /ˈɛksɑːk/ *noun*. L16.
[ORIGIN ecclesiastical Latin *exarchus* from Greek *exarkhos* leader, chief, formed as EX-²: see -ARCH.]
1 *hist*. A governor or vicegerent of a distant province under the Byzantine emperors. L16.
2 In the Orthodox Church: any of certain bishops next in rank below a patriarch, with oversight of a province and (now or formerly) jurisdiction over a metropolitan; a primate of an autocephalous Church; a bishop appointed as a patriarch's representative in a distant part. L16.
■ **Exarchist** *noun* (*hist*.) a supporter of the Exarch of Bulgaria against the Patriarch of Constantinople during the schism of 1872–1945 E20.

exarch /ˈɛksɑːk/ *adjective*. L19.
[ORIGIN from EX-² + Greek *arkhē* beginning, origin.]
BOTANY. Of xylem or its development: formed or occurring from the periphery of a stem towards the centre.

exarchate /ˈɛksɑːkeɪt/ *noun*. M16.
[ORIGIN medieval Latin *exarchatus*, formed as EXARCH *noun*: see -ATE¹.]
1 The office or position of an exarch. M16.
2 The province under the jurisdiction or rule of an exarch. L16.

exasperate /ɪɡˈzasp(ə)reɪt, ɛɡ-/ *verb*. Pa. pple **-ated**, (*arch*.) **-ate** /-ət/. M16.
[ORIGIN Latin *exasperat-* pa. ppl stem of *exasperare*, formed as EX-¹ 1 + *asper* rough: see -ATE³.]
1 *verb trans*. & *intrans*. Irritate (a person) to annoyance or anger. (Formerly foll. by *to*, *to do*.) M16.

> E. F. BENSON This tender assurance served only to exasperate Aunt Catherine. E. WAUGH It was an exasperating moment when we landed at Rome . . and were told we could not proceed.

2 *verb trans*. Intensify (ill feeling, wickedness); increase the fierceness of (disease, pain, appetite, etc.); exacerbate. M16.
†**3** *verb trans*. Make more painful, aggravate; exaggerate (something unpleasant). M16–M18.
†**4** *verb trans*. Irritate physically; chafe. M16–L17.
†**5** *verb trans*. Make harsh or rugged; make (a law) more severe. L16–M18.
†**6** *verb intrans*. Become worse; (of a person) become enraged. M17–M18.
■ **exasperated** *adjective* that has been exasperated; (of a person) very irritable, mildly angry, esp. as a result of provocation or frustration: L16. **exasperatedly** *adverb* L19. **exasperatedness** *noun* M18. **exasperatingly** *adverb* in an exasperating manner M19. **exasperater** *noun* M17. **exasperator** *noun* M18.

exasperation /ɪɡˌzaspəˈreɪʃ(ə)n, ɛɡ-/ *noun*. M16.
[ORIGIN Latin *exasperatio(n-)*, from *exasperat-*: see EXASPERATE, -ATION.]
1 The condition of being exasperated; irritation; anger. Formerly also, an instance of this. M16.

> M. SPARK Mr. Lloyd looked round with offended exasperation.

2 The action or an act of exasperating; something that exasperates. E17. ▸**b** Exacerbation of a disease. M17.

> GEO. ELIOT He had made ties for himself which . . were a constant exasperation.

exaspidean /ɛksaˈspɪdɪən/ *adjective*. L19.
[ORIGIN from mod. Latin *Exaspideae*, formed as EX-¹ 1 + Greek *aspid-*, *aspis* shield: see -EAN.]
ZOOLOGY. Possessing or designating a bird's tarsal sheath with an anterior series of scutella on its outer side.

†**exauctorate** *verb trans*. Pa. pple **-ated**, **-ate**. L16.
[ORIGIN Latin *exauctorat-* pa. ppl stem of *exauctorare* dismiss from service, formed as EX-¹ 1 + *auctor*: see AUTHOR *noun*, -ATE³.]
1 Deprive (a law etc.) of authority. L16–L17.
2 Depose from office, deprive of rank. E17–E19.
■ †**exauctoration** *noun* E17–M19.

excalceate /ɪksˈkalsɪeɪt, ɛks-/ *verb trans*. Now *rare* or *obsolete*. E17.
[ORIGIN Latin *excalceat-* pa. ppl stem of *excalceare*, formed as EX-¹ 1 + *calceus* shoe: see -ATE³.]
Remove the shoes of, make barefoot, esp. as a symbolic gesture.
■ **excalceˈation** *noun* M18.

excamb /ɪkˈskamb, ɛk-/ *verb trans*. & *intrans*. L15.
[ORIGIN medieval Latin *excambiare*, formed as EX-¹ + late Latin *cambiare*: see CHANGE *verb*.]
SCOTS LAW. Exchange (land).
■ **excamber** *noun* E17.

excambion /ɪkˈskambɪən, ɛk-/ *noun*. LME.
[ORIGIN medieval Latin *ex(s)cambio(n-)*, formed as EXCAMB: see -ION.]
SCOTS LAW. An exchange of land.

excandescence /ɛkskanˈdɛs(ə)ns/ *noun*. Now *rare*. L17.
[ORIGIN Latin *excandescentia*, from *excandescere* grow white-hot, formed as EX-¹ 1 + *candescere* become light, white, or hot, from *candere* be white: see -ESCENCE.]
The state of being glowing hot. Chiefly *fig*., warmth of temper, spirits, etc.; passion; anger.
■ Also †**excandescency** *noun* E17–E19.

†**excantation** *noun*. *rare*. L16–M19.
[ORIGIN Alt. of *incantation* after Latin *excantare* bring out by enchantment, formed as EX-¹ 1 + *cantare* sing (see CHANT *verb*).]
The action of removing something by enchantment.

excarnate /ɪkˈskɑːnət, ɛk-/ *adjective*. M19.
[ORIGIN Late Latin *excarnatus*, from *excarnare*: see EXCARNATE *verb*, -ATE².]
Chiefly ARCHAEOLOGY. Stripped of flesh.

excarnate /ɪkˈskɑːneɪt, ɛk-/ *verb trans*. Now *rare*. M17.
[ORIGIN Late Latin *excarnat-* pa. ppl stem of *excarnare*, formed as EX-¹ 1 + *carn-*, *caro* flesh: see -ATE³.]
Remove the flesh from.
■ **excarˈnation** *noun* (*a*) the action of removing flesh; *spec*. the exposure of a corpse to let the flesh decay before it is buried; (*b*) loss of corporeal form, disembodiment: M19.

ex cathedra /ɛks kəˈθiːdrə, ˈkaθɪdrə/ *adverbial & adjectival phr*. E17.
[ORIGIN Latin = from the (teacher's) chair, formed as EX *preposition* + CATHEDRA.]
▸**A** *adverbial phr*. Authoritatively; as an official pronouncement; *esp*. (ROMAN CATHOLIC CHURCH) with the full weight of the Pope's office as divinely appointed guardian of Christian faith and morals. E17.

> *Redemption Tidings* The Pope . . claims to be infallible only when he speaks ex cathedra on faith and morals.

▸**B** *adjectival phr*. Authoritative, official; given ***ex cathedra***; dogmatic. E19.

excavate /ˈɛkskəveɪt/ *ppl adjective*. *rare*. L16.
[ORIGIN Latin *excavatus* pa. pple of *excavare*: see EXCAVATE *verb*, -ATE².]
Hollowed out.

excavate /ˈɛkskəveɪt/ *verb*. L16.
[ORIGIN Latin *excavat-* pa. ppl stem of *excavare*, formed as EX-¹ 1 + *cavare* make or become hollow, from *cavus* hollow: see -ATE³.]
1 *verb trans*. Make hollow by removing material from inside; make a hollow or hollows in; *esp*. remove material from (the ground) so as to make a hole. L16.

> DICKENS The foot of the cliff is excavated into a cavern.

2 *verb trans*. Make (a hole, channel, etc.) by removing material. M19.

> C. LYELL One of them began to excavate a hole.

3 *verb trans*. Uncover or investigate by digging; unearth (*lit*. & *fig*.); *esp*. make a systematic exploration of (an archaeological site) by this means. M19.

> J. A. MICHENER He had dreamed of excavating one of the silent mounds in the Holy Land. *American Notes & Queries* It excavates thousands of titles not found in the usual bibliographies.

4 *verb trans*. Extract by digging. M19.

> *Mining Magazine* About 60,000 t of gold ore had been excavated at the mine.

5 *verb intrans*. Make an excavation; take part in an archaeological excavation. M19.

> E. WILSON The deeper I have excavated, the more surely I have satisfied myself that the best was underneath.

excavation /ɛkskəˈveɪʃ(ə)n/ *noun*. E17.
[ORIGIN French, or Latin *excavatio(n-)*, formed as EXCAVATE *verb*: see -ATION.]
1 The action or an act of excavating, *spec*. as part of the archaeological investigation of a site. E17.

> B. TARKINGTON Excavations for the cellars of five new houses were in process. C. G. SELIGMAN The skeletal remains recovered from excavations during Archaeological Surveys.

2 An excavated space; a cavity, a hollow. L18.

> W. H. BARTLETT The wine-press was an oblong excavation in the rock.

■ **excavational** *adjective* L20.

excavator /ˈɛkskəveɪtə/ *noun*. E19.
[ORIGIN from EXCAVATE *verb* + -OR.]
1 A person who excavates; *esp*. one who excavates an archaeological site. E19.
2 A thing that excavates; *esp*. a machine (now usu. self-propelled) for removing soil from the ground. M19.
■ **exˈcavatory** *adjective* of or pertaining to excavation or the work of an excavator M19.

excave /ɪkˈskeɪv, ɛk-/ *verb intrans*. & †*trans*. *rare*. L16.
[ORIGIN Latin *excavare*: see EXCAVATE *verb*.]
Excavate.

†**excecate** *verb trans*. Pa. pple **excecated**, (earlier) **excecate**. E16–M17.
[ORIGIN Latin *excaecat-* pa. ppl stem of *excaecare*, formed as EX-¹ 1 + *caecus* blind: see -ATE³.]
Make blind (*lit*. & *fig*.).

excecation /ɛksɪˈkeɪʃ(ə)n/ *noun*. Now *rare* or *obsolete*. E16.
[ORIGIN from EXCECATE + -ATION.]
†**1** Mental or spiritual blindness; the action of bringing into this condition. E16–M17.
2 The action or an act of blinding, esp. as a punishment. E17.

excedent /ɪkˈsiːd(ə)nt, ɛk-/ *noun*. Now *rare* or *obsolete*. M17.
[ORIGIN Latin *excedent-* pres. ppl stem of *excedere*: see EXCEED, -ENT.]
An excess; something which exceeds.

exceed /ɪkˈsiːd, ɛk-/ *verb*. LME.
[ORIGIN Old French & mod. French *excéder* from Latin *excedere* go away or out, surpass, formed as EX-¹ 1 + *cedere* go.]
1 *verb trans*. Pass beyond or go over (a boundary, a specified point). *arch*. LME. ▸†**b** Transgress (a law). LME–L18. ▸**c** Go beyond the limit set by, do more than is warranted by, (a privilege, one's authority, etc.). M16.
2 *verb trans*. Be greater or more numerous than; be heavier than; go faster than. (Foll. by *by*.) LME. ▸†**b** Be too great or too much for. L16–M18.

> E. ROOSEVELT My actual expenses always exceeded these figures. M. MEYER The membership . . should not exceed nine. R. BRADBURY His gift . . exceeded the weight limit by no more than a few ounces. E. F. BENSON It was binding on drivers not to exceed such a speed.

3 *verb trans*. Surpass, outdo; be superior to. (Foll. by *in*.) LME.

> TENNYSON One whose rank exceeds her own. M. SCHORER In sheer clumsiness of style no living writer exceeds him.

†**4** *verb intrans*. Go beyond the bounds of propriety; go too far; be immoderate. LME–M18. ▸**b** Exaggerate. E18–E19.
5 *verb intrans*. Be pre-eminent; be greater or better; preponderate. L15.

> SHAKES. *Lucr*. The guilt being great, the fear doth still exceed. B. JOWETT Men always choose the life which exceeds in pleasure.

6 Chiefly at Cambridge University: have extra or special food at a meal; (of the food) be in extra quantity. L16.
■ **exceedable** *adjective* (*rare*) E17.

exceeding /ɪkˈsiːdɪŋ, ɛk-/ *verbal noun*. L15.
[ORIGIN from EXCEED + -ING¹.]
1 *gen*. The action of EXCEED *verb*. Formerly also, an instance of this, an unusual or excessive action or performance; the quality of surpassing others, excellence. L15.
2 a In *pl*. Chiefly at Cambridge University: extra food allowed on festival days. E17. ▸†**b** Usu. in *pl*. An amount in excess of calculation or what is usual; an excess, a surplus. E18–M19.

exceeding /ɪkˈsiːdɪŋ, ɛk-/ *adjective & adverb*. L15.
[ORIGIN formed as EXCEEDING *noun* + -ING².]
▸**A** *adjective*. †**1** Going beyond the bounds of propriety; going to extremes. L15–M18.

E. SANDYS Why was Anna so exceeding in craving children at the hands of God?

2 Surpassing; extremely great; pre-eminent in amount or degree. Chiefly *attrib.* M16.

LD MACAULAY The exceeding badness of the beer which he brewed. J. M. MURRY Recompensed for his exceeding suffering.

†**3** Supremely good. M–L16.

▸ **B** *adverb.* Exceedingly. *arch.* M16.

WORDSWORTH A virtuous household, though exceeding poor.

■ **exceedingly** *adverb* †(*a*) so as to outdo others; (*b*) extremely, very; very much: L15. **exceedingness** *noun* (long *rare*) L16.

excel /ɪkˈsɛl, ɛk-/ *verb.* Infl. **-ll-**. LME.

[ORIGIN Latin *excellere*, formed as EX-[1] 1 + *celsus* lofty.]

1 *verb intrans.* Be pre-eminent in the possession of some quality or the performance of some action. (Foll. by *at*, *as*, *in*.) LME.

J. A. SYMONDS How could a Spartan . . excel in any fine art? E. M. FORSTER They were . . deficient where she excelled. J. HILTON He . . excelled at games. J. P. HENNESSY Trollope excelled at evoking the spirit as well as the appearance of any place. N. MITFORD She excelled as a hostess.

2 *verb trans.* Be superior to (a person or thing) in the possession of some quality or the performance of some action; outdo, surpass. (Foll. by *in*.) LME. ▸**b** Surpass (another's qualities or work). *rare.* E17.

Z. GREY Sally wanted to look beautiful, to excell all the young ladies who were to attend. A. FRASER The coronation . . excelled in splendour anything he had conceivably expected. **b** S. JOHNSON He has excelled every composition of the same kind.

†**3** *verb trans.* Be greater than, exceed; be too much for, overpower. M17–E18.

excellence /ˈɛks(ə)l(ə)ns/ *noun.* LME.

[ORIGIN Old French & mod. French, or Latin *excellentia*, from *excellent-*: see EXCELLENT, -ENCE.]

1 The state or fact of excelling; the possession of good qualities or abilities to an eminent or unusual degree; surpassing merit, skill, or worth. LME.

N. ARNOTT The brightest examples have arisen of intellectual and moral excellence. D. HALBERSTAM The drive in television news was no longer for pure excellence, a drive to be better . . than the other two networks.

PAR EXCELLENCE.

2 Something in which a person or thing excels; an excellent feature, quality, or ability. LME.

A. P. STANLEY The great excellence of the eastern table-land was . . in pasture. J. H. NEWMAN Civilized nations allow that foreigners have their specific excellences.

†**3** **a** An excellent personality. LME–L18. ▸**b** = EXCELLENCY 3b. L16–L18.

excellency /ˈɛks(ə)l(ə)nsi/ *noun.* ME.

[ORIGIN Latin *excellentia*: see EXCELLENCE, -ENCY.]

1 = EXCELLENCE 1. Now *rare* or *obsolete.* ME. ▸†**b** Something that excels or takes the highest place; the best *of*. Only in 17.

2 (Usu. **E-**.) A designation of an important personage or dignitary; *spec.* the title of respect given to ambassadors, governors, and (*US*) Roman Catholic archbishops and bishops. Chiefly with possess. adjective M16.

W. WHISTON His Excellency the Muscovite Ambassador.

3 = EXCELLENCE 2. Now *rare.* E17. ▸†**b** *The* thing that makes something excellent. M17–E19.

excellent /ˈɛks(ə)l(ə)nt/ *adjective, adverb, & noun.* LME.

[ORIGIN Old French & mod. French from Latin *excellent-* pres. ppl stem of *excellere*: see EXCEL, -ENT.]

▸ **A** *adjective.* **1** That excels in some respect (either good or bad); (of a quality) existing in a greater degree; outstanding, supreme. Now *rare* or *obsolete* exc. as in sense 3. LME.

HENRY MORE The excellent usefulness of the Horse. D. HUME Elizabeth . . was an excellent hypocrite.

†**2** Excelling in rank or dignity; exalted, highly honourable. LME–E18.

AV *Ps.* 148:13 Let them praise the Name of the Lord, for his Name alone is excellent.

3 Pre-eminent; extremely good. E17.

M. INNES Folk with intelligences ranging from moderate through good to excellent. G. GREENE The Opera Society had given an excellent rendering of Patience.

▸ †**B** *adverb.* Excellently. LME–M18.

▸ **C** *noun.* **1** In *pl.* Excellences. *rare.* L15.

2 *the excellent*, (*collect. pl.*) excellent people. E17.

■ **excellently** *adverb* in an excellent manner or degree, extremely well LME.

excelsior /ɛkˈsɛlsɪɔː/ *interjection & noun.* L18.

[ORIGIN Latin, compar. of *excelsus*, formed as EX-[1] 1 + *celsus* lofty: see -IOR.]

▸ **A** *interjection.* Go higher! L18.

LONGFELLOW A voice replied, far up the height, Excelsior!

▸ **B** *noun.* **1** Curled shavings of soft wood for stuffing, packing, etc. Orig. *US.* M19.

V. NABOKOV A boy with hair like excelsior.

2 A person who or thing which reaches or aspires to reach higher. L19.

D. H. LAWRENCE Up he goes! Up like a bloomin' little Excelsior In his Sunday clothes!

3 (Usu. **E-**.) A very small size (3 points) of type. Chiefly *US.* E20.

excentral /ɪkˈsɛntr(ə)l, ɛk-/ *adjective. rare.* M19.

[ORIGIN from EX-[1] 1 + Latin *centrum* + -AL[1].]

= ECCENTRIC *adjective* 3.

excentric *noun & adjective* see ECCENTRIC.

excentricity *noun* see ECCENTRICITY.

except /ɪkˈsɛpt, ɛk-/ *ppl adjective, preposition, & conjunction.* LME.

[ORIGIN Latin *exceptus* pa. pple of *excipere*: see EXCENTRAL.]

▸ †**A** *ppl adjective.* Excepted, not included; exempted. LME–M17.

SHAKES. *Rich. III* Richard except, those whom we fight against Had rather have us win.

▸ **B** *preposition.* **1** Excepting, with the exception of, but. LME.

N. COWARD Nobody knows we're here except Freda. G. HOUSEHOLD No sign of life except swooping bats.

†**2** Leaving out of account; in addition to, besides. *rare.* L15–M18.

T. AMORY Except the hours of sleep, we were rarely from each other.

▸ **C** *conjunction.* **1** Used before a statement of fact that forms an exception to a statement just made. Usu. foll. by *that*: with the exception *that*. LME.

DAY LEWIS Irish nursemaids of whom I remember nothing except that one . . was called Eva. A. PRICE I thought he was you, at the door. Except he doesn't knock.

2 Unless. *arch.* exc. *poet.* L15.

W. OWEN Except you share With them in hell the sorrowful dark of hell.

3 Used before an adverb, phr., or clause expressing a respect in which a preceding statement is not applicable. L15.

L. BRUCE I wouldn't ever wear it, naturally—except maybe on Halloween. V. WOOLF There is no truth about life . . except what we feel. J. C. POWYS You can't break through life except by dying. E. WAUGH They . . left him in his room with no desire except to sleep. I. MURDOCH He never said this except jokingly to Harriet.

except for exception being made for, were it not for; = sense B.1 above.

except /ɪkˈsɛpt, ɛk-/ *verb.* LME.

[ORIGIN Latin *except-* pa. ppl stem of *excipere*, formed as EX-[1] 1 + *capere* take.]

▸ **I** **1** *verb trans.* Specify as not included in a category or group; exclude (*from*). As **excepted** pa. pple freq. *postpositive.* LME.

J. BRYCE The Church excepted, no agent did so much. K. TYNAN From their collective guilt I except Miss Zinkeisen alone.

2 *verb intrans.* Make objection (*against*), object or take exception (*to*). Now *rare.* LME.

†**3** *verb trans.* Offer or allege as an objection (*against*, *to*); object (*that*). L16–M18.

†**4** *verb trans.* Take exception to; protest against. *rare* (Shakes.). Only in L16.

▸ †**II** **5** Accept. LME–M17.

■ **exceptable** *adjective* M20.

excepting /ɪkˈsɛptɪŋ, ɛk-/ *preposition & conjunction.* L15.

[ORIGIN from EXCEPT *verb* + -ING[2].]

▸ **A** *preposition.* **1** If one excepts. L15.

2 With the exception of, except. M16.

GOLDSMITH This was received with great approbation by all, excepting my wife.

▸ **B** *conjunction.* **1** Unless. M17.

2 = EXCEPT *conjunction* 3. Now *rare.* M17.

exception /ɪkˈsɛpʃ(ə)n, ɛk-/ *noun.* LME.

[ORIGIN Old French & mod. French from Latin *exceptio(n-)*, formed as EXCEPT *verb*: see -ION.]

▸ **I** **1** The action of excepting someone or something from a group, the scope of a proposition, etc.; the state or fact of being so excepted. LME.

G. C. LEWIS This exception of women and children from the whole community.

2 A person who or thing which is excepted; *esp.* a particular case or individual that does not follow some general rule or to which a generalization is not applicable. Foll. by *to*, †*from*. LME.

B. RUSSELL 'Unsupported bodies in air fall' is a general rule to which balloons . . are exceptions. A. C. BOULT Sir Henry was most kind to younger musicians and I was no exception.

3 *LAW* (now *hist.*). A plea made by a defendant in bar of a plaintiff's action; *Scot.* a defence. Also, an objection made to the ruling of a court during the course of a trial; a plaintiff's objection to a defendant's affidavit or answer as insufficient. LME.

†**4** A plea tending to evade the force of an opponent's argument; a formal objection to a proceeding, a person's fitness for office, etc. LME–L17.

5 Objection, demur, cavil; a complaint, a criticism. Now *rare* or *obsolete* exc. in phrs. below. L15. ▸†**b** Dislike, dissatisfaction. *rare* (Shakes.). Only in E17.

S. PEPYS Sir C. Sedley's exceptions against both words and pronouncing were very pretty.

▸ †**II** **6** = ACCEPTION 1. LME–E17.

– PHRASES: **beyond exception** = *without exception* (b) below. **take exception (to)** object (to), take offence (at). **without exception** (*a*) with no one or nothing excepted (emphasizing the universality of a proposition etc.); (*b*) beyond reproach or suspicion. **with the exception of** except for.

■ **exceptionable** *adjective* (*a*) to which exception may be taken; (*b*) exceptional: L17. **exceptionableness** *noun* (*rare*) M17. **exceptionably** *adverb* (*rare*) in an exceptionable manner; exceptionally: E19. **exceptionary** *adjective* (*rare*) of, pertaining to, or indicative of an exception; exceptional: L18. **exceptionless** *adjective* without an exception; not admitting of an exception: L16.

exceptional /ɪkˈsɛpʃ(ə)n(ə)l, ɛk-/ *adjective.* M19.

[ORIGIN from EXCEPTION + -AL[1], after French *exceptionnel*.]

Of the nature of or forming an exception; unusual, out of the ordinary; special; (of a person) unusually good, able, etc.

I. MURDOCH The exceptional pallor of their skin . . put the onlooker . . in mind of Grecian marbles. J. BERGER The unusualness of both the things which were happening confirmed that the occasion was exceptional. R. JARRELL She herself was a very exceptional person.

■ **exceptionalism** *noun* the belief that a certain thing constitutes an exception in relation to others of its class, *spec.* (*POLITICS*) that the peaceful capitalism of the US is an exception to the Marxist law of the inevitability of violent class struggle E20. **exceptioˈnality** *noun* exceptional character or quality; an exceptional thing: M19. **exceptionally** *adverb* (*a*) unusually, outstandingly; (*b*) as an exception to rule or custom: M19. **exceptionalness** *noun* L19.

exceptious /ɪkˈsɛpʃəs, ɛk-/ *adjective.* Now *rare.* E17.

[ORIGIN from EXCEPTION + -OUS, after *captious*.]

Disposed to make objections; overcritical, petty.

■ **exceptiousness** *noun* L17.

exceptis excipiendis /ɛkˌsɛptɪs ɛksɪpɪˈɛndɪs/ *adverbial phr.* L19.

[ORIGIN Late Latin, from abl. pl. of Latin *exceptus* pa. pple, and of *excipiendus* gerundive, of *excipere*: see EXCEPT *verb*.]

With appropriate exceptions.

exceptive /ɪkˈsɛptɪv/ *adjective & noun.* L16.

[ORIGIN Late Latin *exceptivus*, formed as EXCEPT *verb*: see -IVE.]

▸ **A** *adjective.* **1** *GRAMMAR & LOGIC.* Introducing or making an exception; (of a proposition) having a subject that specifies an exception. L16.

2 Of people, their utterances, etc.: disposed or tending to take exception. E17.

▸ **B** *noun. GRAMMAR & LOGIC.* An exceptive proposition or word. L16.

†**exceptless** *adjective. rare* (Shakes.). Only in E17.

[ORIGIN Irreg. from EXCEPT *verb* + -LESS.]

Making no exception.

exceptor /ɪkˈsɛptə, ɛk-/ *noun.* M17.

[ORIGIN In sense 1 from EXCEPT *verb* + -OR; in sense 2 from late Latin, formed as EXCEPT *verb*.]

†**1** A person who objects or takes exception; an objector. M–L17.

2 A reporter or clerk; *spec.* a clerk under the later Roman Empire. *obsolete* exc. *hist.* L17.

†**excern** *verb trans. & intrans.* L16–M18.

[ORIGIN Latin *excernere* EXCRETE.]

Of a living organism or organ: separate (waste matter) preparatory to expelling it. Also, excrete.

excerpt /ˈɛksəːpt, ɪkˈsəːpt, ɛk-/ *noun.* Pl. **-s**, †**-a**. E17.

[ORIGIN Latin *excerptum* use as noun of neut. pa. pple of *excerpere*: see EXCERPT *verb*.]

1 An extract from a book, manuscript, musical work, etc. E17.

2 An offprint. *rare.* L19.

excerpt /ˈɛksəːpt, ɪkˈsəːpt, ɛk-/ *verb.* M16.

[ORIGIN Latin *excerpt-* pa. ppl stem of *excerpere*, formed as EX-[1] 1 + *carpere* pluck.]

1 **a** *verb trans. & intrans.* Reproduce (a chosen passage) from a text; choose (a passage) for this purpose. M16. ▸**b** *verb trans.* Take quotations or choose passages from. L19.

a O. SACKS 'The Man Who Fell out of Bed' is excerpted from *A Leg to Stand On.* **b** *American Speech* None of the volumes excerpted goes beyond 1967–68.

†**2** *verb trans.* Take out, remove. M16–E17.

excerption /ɪkˈsəːpʃ(ə)n, ɛk-/ *noun.* E17.

[ORIGIN Latin *excerptio(n-)*, formed as EXCERPT *verb*: see -ION.]

1 An excerpt. Formerly also, a collection of excerpts. E17.

2 The action of choosing or taking excerpts. M19.

■ **excerptor** *noun* (*rare*) L17.

E

excess /ɪkˈsɛs, ɛk-, attrib. ˈɛksɛs/ *noun, adjective, & verb.* LME.
[ORIGIN Old French & mod. French *excès* from Latin *excessus*, from *excess-* pa. ppl stem of *excedere* EXCEED.]
▸ **A** *noun* **I** †**1** The action of going out; adjournment. *rare.* LME–E17.
2 In full ***excess of mind***, ***excess of soul***. An ecstasy; a trance. LME–E17.
†**3** (A display of) extravagant emotion. LME–M18.
4 In *pl.* & †*sing.* Extravagant violation of law, decency, or morality; outrageous acts or conduct. LME.

P. WARNER He . . allowed his army to commit all the excesses that are particularly hateful.

5 The action or an act of exceeding the limits of moderation, esp. in eating or drinking; (an) indulgence. LME.

O. W. HOLMES What had he been doing to get his head in such a state?—had he . . committed an excess? H. ACTON Reading was Nancy's sole excess: in everything else she was moderate. B. BAINBRIDGE Liverish from the previous night's excess. N. ANNAN Walking . . to dispel the excesses of Christmas Eve dinner.

6 The state of being in greater quantity or degree than is usual, necessary, appropriate, or beneficial; superabundance; an extreme or excessive amount or degree *of* something. LME. ▸**b** *CHEMISTRY.* An amount of a substance greater than that needed to effect a given reaction or change. E19.

ISAIAH BERLIN All the criticisms directed against this or that writer for an excess of bias or fancy. K. AMIS Excess of energy was really her trouble. A. BURGESS Tired eyes, as from an excess of recent deskwork. **b** C. L. BLOXAM The carbonates of potash and soda are fused with an excess of arsenious acid.

to excess to an inappropriate or overindulgent extent, excessively.
7 The amount by which one number or quantity exceeds another; *spec.* a sum payable by an insured party in the event of a claim, the insurer paying the amount by which the claim exceeds this sum. LME. ▸†**b** Usury, interest. *rare* (Shakes.). Only in L16.
8 The fact of exceeding something else in amount or degree; preponderance. Formerly also, the fact of surpassing or excelling others. E17.
in excess of more than.
†**9** Departure *from* custom, reason, etc. E–M18.
10 The action or an act of exceeding one's authority, rights, etc. E19.
▸ †**II 11** = ACCESS *noun* 1b. M16–M17.
▸ **B** *adjective.* Constituting an excess; *esp.* exceeding the appropriate or stipulated amount. Usu. *attrib.* (After M17 *obsolete* until L19.) LME.

H. JAMES He was not absolutely simple, which would have been excess; he was only relatively simple, which was quite enough. B. SPOCK The body . . gets rid of excess water through the urine. B. TRAPIDO There is excess rubbish piling up . . beside the overflowing rubbish bin.

excess baggage baggage over the weight for which free carriage is permitted. **excess fare** payment due for travelling further or in a higher class than one's ticket allows. **excess postage** payment due when the stamps on a letter etc. are insufficient.
▸ **C** *verb trans.* **1** Subject to an excess fare. L19.
2 Declare (an employee) redundant. *US.* L20.

excessive /ɪkˈsɛsɪv, ɛk-/ *adjective & adverb.* LME.
[ORIGIN Old French & mod. French *excessif, -ive* from medieval Latin *excessivus*, from Latin *excess-*: see EXCESS, -IVE.]
▸ **A** *adjective.* †**1** Transgressing the bounds of law, decency, or morality. LME–M17.
2 Exceeding what is right, appropriate, or desirable; immoderate; given to excess. LME.

OED Avoid the company of excessive drinkers. ARNOLD BENNETT The doctor . . apparently saw nothing excessive in leaving two patients in charge of one unaided woman. J. M. MURRY An excessive and indiscriminating admiration of Wordsworth.

†**3** Exceeding what is usual; exceedingly great. L15–L17.
▸ †**B** *adverb.* Excessively. M16–L18.
■ **excessively** *adverb* (*a*) in an excessive amount, to an excessive degree; immoderately; †(*b*) wastefully, prodigally; greedily: LME. **excessiveness** *noun* L15.

exchange /ɪksˈtʃeɪn(d)ʒ, ɛks-/ *noun.* LME.
[ORIGIN Anglo-Norman *eschaunge*, Old French *eschange* (French *échange*), from *eschangier* (see EXCHANGE *verb*); *ex-* by assim. to Latin EX-[1].]
1 The action, or an act, of reciprocal giving and receiving (*of* goods, money, prisoners, blows, ideas, etc.). LME. ▸**b** *CHESS.* A capture first by one player and then by the other, as part of a single combination or manoeuvre. M18. ▸**c** A reciprocal arrangement in which two people in different countries but usu. in similar roles change places for a period. E20. ▸**d** A brief conversation, a discussion; an argument; a sequence of letters between correspondents. M20.

N. MONSARRAT A straight exchange, the veal loaf for the barrel. *Proverb:* (Fair) exchange is no robbery. **d** J. JONES This exchange of letters between a middle-aged clerk and a girl. P. L. FERMOR Her husband had come in a little while before and overheard our exchange. C. PRIEST Polite exchanges and pleasantries.

c *exchange professor*, *exchange student*, etc.
2 The giving and receiving of money for its equivalent in money of the same or another country; the trade of a money-changer. LME. ▸†**b** The profit obtained by a money-changer or moneylender. M16–M18.
3 a A building, office, institution, etc., used for the transaction of business or for monetary exchange. LME. ▸**b** In full ***telephone exchange***. A place where telephone calls are connected between different lines. L19. ▸**c** A Labour Exchange. L19.
4 a = ***bill of exchange*** s.v. BILL *noun*[3] 9. LME. ▸**b** The financial system by which commercial transactions, esp. between parties in different countries, are effected without the transmission of money, e.g. by bills of exchange; interconversion of different currencies; (in full ***rate of exchange***, ***exchange rate***) the value assigned to a currency for the purpose of interconversion with another. L15.
5 Replacement *of* one thing by another. Formerly also, alteration, variation, change. LME.
6 A person or thing offered or given in exchange or substitution for another. L15. ▸**b** A copy of a newspaper that is sent to another newspaper office in return for a copy of its newspaper; the newspaper received in return. Also more fully ***exchange paper***. L18.
7 *LAW* (now *hist.*). A mutual grant of equal interests. L16.
8 A bar or saloon. *US colloq.* M19.
9 *MEDICINE.* An amount of a foodstuff regarded as replacing an equivalent quantity of another that is not allowed in a diet. M20.
– PHRASES: ***bill of exchange***: see BILL *noun*[3] 9. ***foreign exchange***: see FOREIGN *adjective.* **in exchange** as a thing exchanged (*for*). ***labour exchange***: see LABOUR *noun.* ***local exchange***: see LOCAL *adjective.* ***lose the exchange***: see ***win the exchange*** below. ***medium of exchange***: see MEDIUM *noun.* ***par of exchange***: see PAR *noun*[1] 2a. ***post exchange***: see POST *noun*[4]. ***private branch exchange***: see PRIVATE *adjective.* ***rate of exchange***: see sense 4b above. ***stock exchange***: see STOCK *noun*[1] & *adjective.* ***telephone exchange***: see sense 3b above. **win the exchange**, **lose the exchange** *CHESS* capture, lose, a rook in exchange for a bishop or knight.
– COMB.: **exchange control** governmental control of currency exchange between countries; **exchange force**: between atoms or subatomic particles and involving an exchange of charge, spin, or other coordinates; ***exchange paper***: see sense 6b above; ***exchange rate***: see sense 3b above; **Exchange Rate Mechanism** a method of stabilizing exchange rates in the European Monetary System by giving each currency a fixed exchange rate with the ecu; **exchange transfusion** *MEDICINE* the simultaneous removal of some of a sick person's blood and replacement by normal blood; **exchange value** value when exchanged, exchangeable value.

exchange /ɪksˈtʃeɪn(d)ʒ, ɛks-/ *verb.* LME.
[ORIGIN Old French *eschangier* (mod. *échanger*), from *é-* EX-[1] + *changer* CHANGE *verb*.]
1 *verb trans.* Dispose of by exchange or barter; relinquish (something) and receive something else in return; give up (a prisoner) to the enemy in return for one taken by them. (Foll. by *for*, *against*, †*with* the thing received.) LME. ▸†**b** Obtain (something) in exchange *for*. L16–E17.

C. DAY They had exchanged their regular jackets for black alpaca coats.

†**2** *verb trans.* = CHANGE *verb* 4. LME–L16.
3 *verb trans.* Give and receive reciprocally; make an exchange of. Foll. by sing. or pl. obj. *with* a person. E17.

DAY LEWIS He was for ever buying, selling or exchanging books. W. CATHER Lou and Oscar exchanged outraged looks. J. WAIN They never passed each other without exchanging a word or two.

exchange contracts sign a legal contract with the vendor of a property or piece of land, making the purchase legally binding.
4 *verb intrans.* Of money, articles of trade, etc.: be receivable as an equivalent *for*. L18.
5 *verb intrans.* Undergo or take part in an exchange; be replaced in an exchange; *spec.* (of an officer) pass *out of* a regiment or ship (*into* another) by exchange with another officer. L18.

Good Housekeeping Daisy, a 14-year-old who exchanged with a 15-year-old French girl.

■ **exchanger** *noun* (*a*) a person who exchanges; *hist.* a money-changer, a money-dealer; (*b*) a device in which something is exchanged, *spec.* = ***heat-exchanger*** s.v. HEAT *noun*: LME.

exchangeable /ɪksˈtʃeɪn(d)ʒəb(ə)l, ɛks-/ *adjective.* L16.
[ORIGIN from EXCHANGE *verb* + -ABLE.]
†**1** = COMMUTATIVE 1. *rare.* Only in L16.
2 Able to be exchanged (*for*). M17.
3 Of value: estimated in terms of the value of the goods for which a thing may be exchanged. L18.
■ **exchangeaˈbility** *noun* L18.

exchequer /ɪksˈtʃɛkə, ɛks-/ *noun & verb.* ME.
[ORIGIN Anglo-Norman *escheker*, Old French *eschequier* (mod. *échiquier*) from medieval Latin *scaccarium* chessboard, from *scaccus* CHECK *noun*[1] (see CHECK *interjection*, -ER[2]); *ex-* by assoc. with EX-[1]. So called with ref. to the chequered tablecloth on which accounts were orig. kept by means of counters. Aphet. to CHEQUER *noun*[1].]
▸ **A** *noun.* In senses 2–4 usu. **E-**.
†**1** A chessboard; = CHEQUER *noun*[1] 1. ME–L15.
2 A department of state established under the Norman kings of England that dealt with the collection and administration of the royal revenues and with legal disputes about them. ME.
3 Orig. (now *hist.*), the Government department responsible for the receipt and custody of the money collected by the departments of revenue. Now, the Government's account at the Bank of England whose balance forms the Consolidated Fund. LME. ▸**b** ***the Exchequer***, the contents of the Exchequer. M17.
4 More fully ***Court of Exchequer***, ***Exchequer of Pleas***. A former court of law (merged in the High Court of Justice in 1873) which historically represented the Anglo-Norman Exchequer in its judicial capacity. L15. ▸**b** Either of the two analogous courts that formerly existed in Scotland and Ireland. E19.
5 A royal or national treasury. M16.
6 The monetary possessions of a private person, an institution, etc. E17.
– PHRASES: ***Chancellor of the Exchequer***: see CHANCELLOR 2. ***Court of Exchequer***, ***Exchequer of Pleas***: see sense 4 above. ***Marshal of the Exchequer***: see MARSHAL *noun*[1] 4. ***stop of the exchequer***: see STOP *noun*[2].
– COMB.: **exchequer bill** *hist.* a bill of credit with varying interest issued by authority of Parliament; **exchequer chamber** *hist.* the room in the Exchequer where judges and officials met; (also ***Court of Exchequer Chamber***) any of several former courts of appeal; a former forum of debate comprising all the judges.
▸ **B** *verb trans.* †**1** Place in an exchequer or treasury. *rare.* Only in E18.
2 *hist.* Proceed against (a person) in the Court of Exchequer. E19. ▸**b** Seize as contraband. E19.

excide /ɛkˈsʌɪd/ *verb trans.* M18.
[ORIGIN Latin *excidere* EXCISE *verb*[1].]
Cut out.

excimer /ˈɛksɪmə/ *noun.* M20.
[ORIGIN from EXCI(TED + DI)MER.]
CHEMISTRY. An exciplex, esp. formed from two identical atoms or molecules.

excipient /ɛkˈsɪpɪənt/ *adjective & noun.* E18.
[ORIGIN Latin *excipient-* pres. ppl stem of *excipere* take out, receive, formed as EX-[1] 1 + *capere* take: see -ENT.]
▸ †**A** *adjective.* That takes exception. Only in E18.
▸ **B** *noun.* **1** An inactive substance that serves as the vehicle or medium for a drug. M18.
2 The material or surface that receives the pigments in painting. M19.

exciplex /ˈɛksɪplɛks/ *noun.* M20.
[ORIGIN from EXCI(TED + COM)PLEX *noun*.]
CHEMISTRY. A molecule formed by a metastable bond between two atoms or molecules and existing only in an excited state.

excipulum /ɛkˈsɪpjʊləm/ *noun.* Pl. **-la** /-lə/. Also anglicized as **exciple** /ˈɛksɪp(ə)l/, **excipule** /ˈɛksɪpjuːl/. M19.
[ORIGIN Latin = receptacle, from *excipere*: see EXCIPIENT, -ULE.]
BOTANY. A layer of tissue underlying and containing the hymenium in the apothecium of a lichen.

excise /ˈɛksʌɪz/ *noun.* L15.
[ORIGIN Middle Dutch *excijs* (also *accijs*), perh. from Proto-Romance verbal noun from Latin *accensare* to tax, formed as AC- + *census* tax, CENSUS.]
1 A tax, a toll. L15.
2 *spec.* A duty levied on goods produced or sold within a country and on licences granted for certain activities. L16. *excise duty*, *excise officer*, etc.
†**3** Payment or imposition of excise duty. E–M18.
4 The government office responsible for the collection of excise duty. L18.
– COMB.: **excise law**: *spec.* (*US*) a licensing law; **exciseman** an officer employed to collect excise duty and prevent infringement of the excise laws; **excisemanship** the post of exciseman.

excise /ɪkˈsʌɪz, ɛk-/ *verb*[1] *trans.* L16.
[ORIGIN Latin *excis-* pa. ppl stem of *excidere*, formed as EX-[1] 1 + *caedere* to cut.]
1 Chiefly *BOTANY & ZOOLOGY.* Notch or hollow out some of the substance of. Chiefly as ***excised*** *pa. pple.* L16.
†**2** Circumcise (esp. a woman or girl). E–M17.
3 Remove or expunge (a passage) from or *from* a book etc. M17.

H. R. REYNOLDS Marcion excised other portions of the Gospel which contradict his views.

4 Cut out physically (a growth, organ, etc.); remove or take out as if by cutting. M19.

J. R. S. FINCHAM F can not only be integrated into the chromosome but can also be excised from it. *fig.:* W. H. AUDEN Where abnormal / growths of self-love are excised / by the crude surgery of a / practical joke.

■ **excisable** *adjective*[1] able or needing to be excised M19.

excise /ˈɛksʌɪz, ɪkˈsʌɪz, ɛk-/ *verb*[2] *trans.* M17.
[ORIGIN from EXCISE *noun*.]
1 Impose excise duty on (a thing). M17.
2 Force (a person) to pay excise duty; *arch.* overcharge. M17.
■ **exˈcisable** *adjective*[2] (of a person or thing) liable to (the imposition of) excise duty L17.

excision /ɪkˈsɪʒ(ə)n, ɛk-/ *noun*. **L15**.
[**ORIGIN** Old French & mod. French from Latin *excisio(n-)*, formed as **EXCISE** *verb*[1]: see **-ION**.]
1 The action of cutting off from existence; the condition of being so cut off; destruction. **L15**.
2 The action of excising a growth or organ from the body, a passage from a book, etc.; something so removed. **M16**.

A. POWELL Considerable excisions had been made.. but it had returned.. with orders for further expurgation.

3 The action of expelling a person from a religious society; excommunication. **M17**.
■ **excisional** *adjective* **M20**.

excitability /ɪkˌsʌɪtəˈbɪlɪti, ɛk-/ *noun*. **L18**.
[**ORIGIN** from **EXCITABLE** + **-ITY**.]
1 The property in plant and animal tissue of responding to a certain kind of stimulus. **L18**.
2 The quality in a person of being prone or susceptible to excitement. **E19**.

excitable /ɪkˈsʌɪtəb(ə)l, ɛk-/ *adjective*. **E17**.
[**ORIGIN** from **EXCITE** + **-ABLE**.]
Able to be excited; responsive to stimuli; prone or susceptible to excitement, easily excited. (Foll. by *to*.)

N. HAWTHORNE He is.. wonderfully excitable to mirth. E. BOWEN Keyed up by the sudden electric light, her manner was swaggering and excitable. *Scientific American* In excitable cells calcium channels open in response to the action potential.

■ **excitableness** *noun* **M19**.

excitant /ˈɛksɪt(ə)nt, ɪkˈsʌɪt(ə)nt, ɛk-/ *adjective & noun*. **E17**.
[**ORIGIN** from **EXCITE** + **-ANT**[1], perh. after French *excitant*.]
(An agent) that excites or stimulates.

A. JOHN The sea air is known to be an excitant. *Nature* The central excitant action of *d*-amphetamine.

■ ˈ**excitancy** *noun* the property of being (an) excitant **M19**.

†**excitate** *verb trans.* **M16–M17**.
[**ORIGIN** Latin *excitat-* pa. ppl stem of *excitare*: see **EXCITE**, **-ATE**[3].]
= **EXCITE** in senses current before **M17**.

excitation /ɛksɪˈteɪʃ(ə)n/ *noun*. **LME**.
[**ORIGIN** Old French & mod. French from late Latin *excitatio(n-)*, formed as **EXCITATE**: see **-ATION**.]
1 The state of being excited; an instance of this. Now chiefly with ref. to inanimate things: cf. **EXCITEMENT** 3b. **LME**.

J. MCPHEE He told the story without modulation, without a hint of narrative excitation. H. M. ROSENBERG The excitations associated with spin waves are also quantised.

2 The action or an act of exciting, esp. (in mod. use) tissue, electrical devices, atoms, etc. (see **EXCITE** 4, 5). **LME**.

T. H. HUXLEY The excitation of the retina proper. *Scientific American* The excitation of the electron from the valence band to the conduction band. *attrib.*: *Radio & Electronics World* The device reverts to its 'blank' state when the ac excitation voltage is removed.

3 Something that excites; a stimulus; an encouragement. *arch.* **E17**.

excitative /ɪkˈsʌɪtətɪv, ɛk-/ *adjective*. **L15**.
[**ORIGIN** French *excitatif*, *-ive*, from medieval Latin *excitativus*, formed as **EXCITATE**: see **-ATIVE**.]
Able or tending to excite. (Foll. by *of*.)

†**excitator** *noun*. *rare*. **L17–M19**.
[**ORIGIN** from **EXCITATE** + **-OR**.]
A person who or thing which excites; *spec.* in *ELECTRICITY*, an instrument for discharging a Leyden jar without giving the operator a shock.

excitatory /ɪkˈsʌɪtət(ə)ri, ɛk-/ *adjective*. **E19**.
[**ORIGIN** formed as **EXCITATE**: see **-ORY**[2].]
Producing or tending to produce excitation; produced by excitation.

excite /ɪkˈsʌɪt, ɛk-/ *verb*. **ME**.
[**ORIGIN** Old French & mod. French *exciter* or Latin *excitare* frequentative of *exciere* call out or forth, formed as **EX-**[1] 1 + *ciere* move, call.]
1 a *verb trans. & intrans.* Instigate, incite, move, stir up, (a person, God, the soul, etc.). (Foll. by *to*, *to do*, *into doing*.) **ME**. ▸†**b** *verb trans.* Provoke, challenge. **ME–L15**.

a P. KAVANAGH He looked like a spirited fellow who could be excited into doing two men's work.

2 *verb trans.* Call into being (a faculty, feeling, etc.); rouse (what is dormant or latent). **LME**. ▸†**b** Rouse from sleep, or unconsciousness; bring back to life. **LME–L15**. ▸†**c** Call up (a spirit). **LME–M17**.

T. HARDY The footman whose curiosity had been excited. W. S. MAUGHAM Her prettiness was not the sort that excites carnal desires.

3 *verb trans.* Induce or provoke (an action, a manifestation); bring about (an active condition). **LME**.

J. L. MOTLEY Fire-ships, intended only to excite a conflagration of the bridge. S. LEACOCK The very name 'Spy' excites a shudder of apprehension. P. ACKROYD Her behaviour was exciting more comment. J. HELLER He was distressed.. by how little attention his presence excited.

4 *verb trans.* Stimulate (living matter) so as to produce or increase its activity. **LME**.

5 *verb trans.* Magnetize or electrify (a substance or body); produce electrical activity in; produce (an electric current). Also, sensitize (a photographic film etc.). **M17**. ▸**b** *PHYSICS*. Cause to emit radiation; cause emission of (a spectrum); raise (an atom, electron, etc.) to a higher energy state. **E20**.

W. GARNETT The idea.. was to use.. the current produced by the armature to excite its own electro-magnet. **b** H. M. ROSENBERG The higher the temperature, the more electrons will be excited to the conduction band.

6 *verb trans. & intrans.* Arouse strong emotion (in); *esp.* make very interested or eager. **M19**.

E. WAUGH They let me up.. and said I wasn't to excite you. *Listener* Last week's legitimate television drama failed to excite.

excited /ɪkˈsʌɪtɪd, ɛk-/ *ppl adjective*. **M17**.
[**ORIGIN** from **EXCITE** + **-ED**[1].]
1 Of a substance, body, or device: that has been excited; magnetized; electrified; stimulated. **M17**. ▸**b** *PHYSICS*. Of an atom, electron, etc.: able to lose energy by emitting radiation. **M17**.
b excited state a state of a quantized system with more energy than the ground state.
2 Stirred by strong emotion, agitated; characterized by excitement. **M19**.

E. BOWEN Cecilia, strung-up, excited, not knowing where to begin. M. FRAYN The excited screaming of the children playing.

■ **excitedly** *adverb* **M19**. **excitedness** *noun* **E20**.

excitement /ɪkˈsʌɪtm(ə)nt, ɛk-/ *noun*. **LME**.
[**ORIGIN** from **EXCITE** + **-MENT**.]
1 The action of exciting; the fact of being excited. *rare*. **LME**.
2 †**a** A motive, an incentive, (*to* action); an exhortation (*to do*); something that tends to produce a specified feeling. **E17–M19**. ▸**b** An occasion of emotional excitement. **L19**.

b *Economist* No great excitements are expected from the last witnesses before the congressional committees.

3 a *MEDICINE*. A state of overactivity in an organ. Now *rare* or *obsolete*. **L18**. ▸**b** The state of being emotionally excited. Cf. **EXCITATION** 1. **M19**.

b S. MIDDLETON Fisher stood hot with excitement. M. TIPPETT I can remember the excitement when *Back to Methuselah* was first published.

exciter /ɪkˈsʌɪtə, ɛk-/ *noun*. **LME**.
[**ORIGIN** from **EXCITE** + **-ER**[1].]
1 A person who or thing which excites a person, feeling, event, etc. Formerly, an instigator. **LME**.
2 A device for producing excitation in another device; *spec.* (**a**) a small generator or battery that provides the energizing current for the field magnets of a main generator or motor; (**b**) *ELECTRONICS* part of a transmitter, radar, etc., that generates an internal constant-frequency signal. **L19**.

exciting /ɪkˈsʌɪtɪŋ, ɛk-/ *ppl adjective*. **E17**.
[**ORIGIN** from **EXCITE** + **-ING**[2].]
1 That excites a person; *esp.* arousing great interest or eagerness. **E17**.

J. T. STORY Beautiful girl; exciting too, rowing the river in her nightie. DAY LEWIS Sunday was the most exciting day of my week.

2 Of a cause, esp. that of a disease: immediately preceding the result. **E19**.
3 That excites something inanimate, as an electric current, radiation (see **EXCITE** 5). **L19**.

Nature The gel was stained.. and photographed using exciting light at 254 nm.

■ **excitingly** *adverb* **M19**. **excitingness** *noun* **E20**.

excitive /ɪkˈsʌɪtɪv, ɛk-/ *adjective*. **L18**.
[**ORIGIN** from **EXCITE** + **-IVE**.]
Tending to excite; productive *of*.

excitomotor /ɪkˈsʌɪtəʊməʊtə, ɛk-/ *adjective*. **L19**.
[**ORIGIN** from **EXCITOR** + **MOTOR** *noun & adjective*.]
PHYSIOLOGY. Producing or increasing motor activity.
■ Also **excitoˈmotory** *adjective* **M19**.

exciton /ˈɛksɪtɒn, ɪkˈsʌɪ-, ɛk-/ *noun*. **M20**.
[**ORIGIN** from **EXCIT(ATION** + **-ON**.]
PHYSICS. A mobile concentration of energy in a crystalline material consisting of an excited electron and an associated hole.
■ **exciˈtonic** *adjective* **M20**.

excitor /ɪkˈsʌɪtə, ɛk-/ *noun*. **E19**.
[**ORIGIN** from **EXCITE** + **-OR**, after *motor*.]
1 = **EXCITER** 1. **E19**.
2 *ANATOMY*. An efferent nerve whose stimulation increases the action of the part it supplies. **M19**.

excitory /ɪkˈsʌɪt(ə)ri/ *adjective*. **E19**.
[**ORIGIN** from **EXCITE** + **-ORY**[2].]
Producing or tending to produce excitation.

excitron /ˈɛksɪtrɒn/ *noun*. **M20**.
[**ORIGIN** from **EXCIT(ATION** + **-TRON**.]
ELECTRONICS. A kind of mercury-arc rectifier with a pool of mercury as the cathode and a grid to control the conduction from a hot spot maintained throughout the conduction cycle.

exclaim /ɪkˈskleɪm, ɛk-/ *noun*. *rare*. **L15**.
[**ORIGIN** from (the same root as) **EXCLAIM** *verb*.]
An exclamation, an outcry.

exclaim /ɪkˈskleɪm, ɛk-/ *verb intrans. & trans.* **L16**.
[**ORIGIN** French *exclamer* or Latin *exclamare*, formed as **EX-**[1] 1 + *clamare*: see **CLAIM** *verb*.]
Speak or say suddenly, excitedly, or forcefully, esp. in expression of anger, pain, delight, surprise, etc.; cry out. (Foll. by *that*.)

J. A. FROUDE The people exclaimed that they were betrayed by the gentlemen. D. H. LAWRENCE Men in the crowd exclaimed and groaned. L. M. MONTGOMERY 'Oh, do you really think so?' exclaimed Anne.

– WITH PREPOSITIONS IN SPECIALIZED SENSES: **exclaim against** *arch.* protest loudly against. **exclaim at** (**a**) *arch.* = ***exclaim against*** above; (**b**) cry out in admiration at. **exclaim on**, **exclaim upon** *arch.* (**a**) = ***exclaim against*** above; (**b**) apostrophize.
■ **exclaimer** *noun* **L17**.

exclamation /ɛkskləˈmeɪʃ(ə)n/ *noun*. **LME**.
[**ORIGIN** Old French & mod. French, or Latin *exclamatio(n-)*, from *exclamat-* pa. ppl stem of *exclamare*: see **EXCLAIM** *verb*, **-ATION**.]
1 The action of exclaiming; a sudden impassioned or emphatic utterance, a cry. **LME**.

E. F. BENSON Lucia suddenly gave a little exclamation of annoyance.

2 A loud protest or complaint (*against*). *arch.* **LME**.

J. PRIESTLEY What exclamation and abuse must he not expect?

3 *GRAMMAR*. An interjection. **M19**.
– COMB. & PHRASES: **exclamation mark**, (*US*) **exclamation point** a punctuation mark (!) used to show the exclamatory nature of the preceding phrase etc., and in *MATH.* to indicate a factorial; **note of exclamation** = ***exclamation mark*** above.

exclamative /ɪkˈsklamətɪv, ɛk-/ *adjective & noun*. *rare*. **M18**.
[**ORIGIN** formed as **EXCLAMATORY** + **-IVE**.]
▸ **A** *adjective*. = **EXCLAMATORY** 2. **M18**.
▸ **B** *noun*. An exclamatory expression. **M20**.

exclamatory /ɪkˈsklamət(ə)ri, ɛk-/ *adjective*. **L16**.
[**ORIGIN** from Latin *exclamat-*: see **EXCLAMATION**, **-ORY**[2].]
1 That exclaims; that gives rise to exclamation. **L16**.

DONNE An intemperate.. and exclamatory Sorrow.

2 Constituting or marking an exclamation. **E18**.

K. TYNAN Exclamatory titles like *Cheep!* and *Oh! Joy!*

■ **exclamatorily** *adverb* **M19**. **exclamatoriness** *noun* (*rare*) **L20**.

exclaustration /ɛksklɔːˈstreɪʃ(ə)n/ *noun*. **M20**.
[**ORIGIN** mod. Latin *exclaustratio(n-)*, formed as **EX-**[1] + Latin *claustrum* (see **CLOISTER** *noun*).]
Permission for a religious to live outside a religious community, dispensed from community obligations and the jurisdiction of the superior.
■ **exˈclaustrate** *verb trans.* grant exclaustration to **M20**.

exclave /ˈɛkskleɪv/ *noun*. **L19**.
[**ORIGIN** from **EX-**[1] + **EN)CLAVE** *noun*.]
A region belonging to a country but surrounded by another country, as viewed by the former (cf. **ENCLAVE** *noun*).

exclosure /ɪkˈskləʊʒə, ɛk-/ *noun*. **E20**.
[**ORIGIN** from **EX-**[1] + **CLOSURE**, after *enclosure*.]
An area from which unwanted animals are excluded.

exclude /ɪkˈskluːd, ɛk-/ *verb trans.* **LME**.
[**ORIGIN** Latin *excludere*, formed as **EX-**[1] 1 + *claudere* to shut.]
▸ **I** Keep out (what is outside).
1 Deny entry or access to; shut out from a place. (Foll. by *from*, †*out of*, †2nd obj.) **LME**.

EVELYN When Branches are so thick.. that they.. exclude the sun. G. MAXWELL A wire gate [was] fitted to the gallery stairs, so that he could.. be excluded from the studio.

2 Deny membership or participation to; debar from a right or privilege, prohibit from an activity, etc. (Foll. by *from*, †2nd obj.) **LME**.

W. S. CHURCHILL He excluded him from all share in the wars. J. R. ACKERLEY My father's decision to exclude me from his confidence.

3 Give no place to; prevent the occurrence or use of; make impossible, preclude. **LME**. ▸**b** Be incompatible with. **LME**.

A. RADCLIFFE The thick foliage excluded all view of the country. J. BARZUN It was decreed that politics and religion should be excluded from general conversation. **b** H. SPENCER Absolute indifference excludes the conception of will.

4 Omit from a category, series, etc., or from the scope of a statement, enactment, etc. Cf. **EXCLUDING**. **LME**. ▸**b** Of a term, statement, etc.: fail to include in its scope or meaning. **M16**.

E

J. B. PRIESTLEY These Lancashire towns—and this excludes industrial villages . . —have not the derelict look of some places elsewhere. **b** E. F. SCHUMACHER They [judgements] are based on a definition of cost which excludes all 'free goods'.

5 Reject from consideration, dismiss, rule out. **L16.**

G. B. SHAW In spite of the virginity she had vowed . . she never excluded the possibility of marriage for herself.

law of excluded middle, **law of excluded third**, **principle of excluded middle**, **principle of excluded third** *LOGIC*: that either a proposition or its negative must be true.

▸ **II** Thrust out (what is inside).

6 Banish, expel. **LME.**

7 Eject forcibly from a receptacle; *esp.* hatch from an egg. **LME.**

■ **excludable**, **excludible** *adjectives* **M20.**

excluder /ɪk'skluːdə, ɛk-/ *noun*. **M17.**
[ORIGIN from EXCLUDE + -ER[1].]
1 A person who excludes someone; *spec.* one who attempts to exclude a candidate from an office by voting against him or her; *hist.* a supporter of the Exclusion Bill. **M17.**
2 A device for keeping something out; *spec.* = ***queen excluder*** s.v. QUEEN *noun*. **M19.**
draught excluder: see DRAUGHT *noun*.

excluding /ɪk'skluːdɪŋ, ɛk-/ *preposition*. **M17.**
[ORIGIN Use of pres. pple of EXCLUDE *verb* 4: see -ING[2].]
If one does not take into account; apart from, except. Also, to the exclusion of.

C. DARWIN In all other respects, excluding fertility, there is a close general resemblance between hybrids and mongrels.

exclusion /ɪk'skluːʒ(ə)n, ɛk-/ *noun*. **LME.**
[ORIGIN Latin *exclusio(n-)*, from *exclus-* pa. ppl stem of *excludere*: see EXCLUDE, -ION.]
1 The action or an act of excluding; (an instance of) shutting out from a place, debarring from an office or society, rejecting from consideration, etc. **LME.**
2 Something that excludes or is excluded, esp. from the terms of a contract. **M17.**
– PHRASES: **Bill of Exclusion** = *Exclusion Bill* below. **method of exclusion(s)**, **process of exclusion(s)** the process of discovering the cause of a phenomenon or the solution of a problem by eliminating alternative hypotheses in turn. **to the exclusion of** so as to exclude.
– COMB.: **Exclusion Bill** *hist.* a bill of 1680 seeking to bar James Duke of York (the future James II) from the succession, on the grounds of his being a Roman Catholic; **exclusion clause** a clause disclaiming liability for something under a contract; **exclusion order** *LAW* (*a*) a statutory instrument preventing a suspected terrorist from entering Great Britain, or Northern Ireland, or the UK, (*b*) a court order barring a member of a household from the family home, usu. to protect others against domestic violence; **exclusion principle** *PHYSICS* the principle that no two fermions of the same kind can be in the same quantum state; also called ***Pauli exclusion principle***, ***Pauli's exclusion principle***; **exclusion zone** a zone into which entry is forbidden; *spec.* a delimited area which ships, aircraft, etc., of a given country (or foreign ships etc. in general) are warned not to enter.
■ **exclusionary** *adjective* of or pertaining to exclusion; having the effect of excluding; ***exclusionary rule***, a rule forbidding the use of certain types of evidence in court, esp. (*US*) that obtained in violation of a defendant's constitutional rights: **E19.** **exclusioner** *noun* (*obsolete* exc. *hist.*) a supporter of the Exclusion Bill **L17.**

exclusionist /ɪk'skluːʒ(ə)nɪst, ɛk-/ *noun & adjective*. **M18.**
[ORIGIN from EXCLUSION + -IST.]
▸ **A** *noun*. A person who favours excluding someone from a privilege, right, situation, etc.; *spec.* in *hist.*, (*a*) = EXCLUSIONER; (*b*) *Austral.* a free settler who opposed the granting of full civic rights to ex-convicts. **M18.**
▸ **B** *adjective*. Of, pertaining to, or designating an exclusionist or exclusionists; characterized by exclusionism. **E19.**
■ **exclusionism** *noun* the principles of an exclusionist **M19.**

exclusive /ɪk'skluːsɪv, ɛk-/ *noun & adjective*. **L15.**
[ORIGIN medieval Latin *exclusivus*, from Latin *exclus-*: see EXCLUSION, -IVE.]
▸ **A** *noun*. †**1** An excluding agent. Only in **L15.**
2 An exclusive proposition or word: see sense B.1 below. **M16.**
3 An exclusive person: see sense B.7 below. **E19.**
4 *hist.* An Australian exclusionist. **M19.**
5 An exclusive news item, article, etc.: see sense B.5b below. **E20.**
▸ **B** *adjective*. **1** Of a proposition: in which the predicate is asserted to apply to the subject specified and no other. Of a word: effecting such a restriction. **L16.**
2 Of a statement, enumeration, etc.: excluding something, *spec.* one or both of the specified terminal points. **M17.**
3 = EXCLUSORY. *rare*. **M17.**
exclusive voice the right of veto.
4 Not admitting of the simultaneous existence *of* something; incompatible. **E18.**

G. B. SHAW A confusion of the mutually exclusive functions of judge and legislator.

exclusive OR: see OR *noun*[2].
5 Of a right, privilege, quality, etc.: possessed or enjoyed by the individual(s) specified and no others; confined or restricted *to*. **M18.** ▸**b** Of a news item, article, etc.: published solely in one specified newspaper or periodical. Of a design, product, etc.: (stated to be) available from only one establishment or firm. (Foll. by *to*.) **M19.**

E. WAUGH There would be a sitting room for your exclusive use. **b** *Daily Telegraph* Furs from Grosvenor Canada . . are exclusive to Harrods.

6 Pursued, employed, etc., to the exclusion of all else; sole, only. **L18.**

C. DARWIN Natural Selection has been the main but not exclusive means of modification. H. SPENCER Exclusive devotion to work has the result that amusements cease to please.

7 Of a group, esp. a social circle, or a member of one: (excessively) reluctant to admit outsiders to membership. **E19.**

T. BENN An exclusive priestly caste claiming a monopoly right to speak on behalf of the Almighty.

Exclusive Brethren: see BROTHER *noun*.
8 Of an establishment etc.: used or patronized by a restricted (esp. aristocratic) social group; high-class, fashionable. **M20.**

J. CONRAD Her movements are commented on in the most exclusive drawing-rooms. *London Calling* Claridges, probably the most exclusive hotel in the world.

■ **exclusively** *adverb* (*a*) to the exclusion of all else; formerly (foll. by *of*, *to*), to the exclusion of specified persons or things; †(*b*) = EXCLUSIVE *adverb* 1: **LME.** **exclusiveness** *noun* **M18.** **exclusivism** *noun* a doctrine or policy of systematic exclusion, esp. of foreigners; the practice of excluding: **M19.** **exclusivist** *noun & adjective* (*a*) *noun* an advocate of exclusivism; also, a person who maintains the exclusive validity of a theory; (*b*) *adjective* advocating or practising exclusivism: **L19.** **exclusi'vistic** *adjective* exclusivist; exclusive: **M20.** **exclu'sivity** *noun* the quality of being exclusive; the right to exclusive use: **E20.**

exclusive /ɪk'skluːsɪv/ *adverb*. **LME.**
[ORIGIN medieval Latin, from *exclusivus* (see EXCLUSIVE *noun & adjective*) + adverbial ending *-e*.]
1 So as not to include the limits or extremes in a series. Opp. ***inclusive***. **LME.**

E. CHAMBERS He sent him all the Gazettes, from No. 195 to No. 300 exclusive.

2 Foll. by *of*: †(*a*) to the exclusion of; †(*b*) apart from, not to mention; (*c*) excluding, not counting. **L17.**

J. LOCKE To Inherit all . . exclusive . . of his brethren. F. SHERIDAN I . . should (exclusive of any other reasons) have thought myself bound. J. TYNDALL The châlet . . contained four men exclusive of myself and my guide.

exclusory /ɪk'skluːs(ə)ri, ɛk-/ *adjective*. **L16.**
[ORIGIN Late Latin *exclusorius*, from Latin *exclus-*: see EXCLUSION, -ORY[2].]
Having the power or function of excluding. (Foll. by *of*.)

†**excoct** *verb trans*. **LME.**
[ORIGIN Latin *excoct-* pa. ppl stem of *excoquere*, formed as EX-[1] 1 + *coquere* cook, melt.]
1 Purge away by heat. **LME–M17.**
2 Remove the moisture from; ripen, mature. **L16–E18.**
3 Extract (esp. a metal) by heat. Only in **17.**
■ †**excoction** *noun* (*rare*) the action of extracting by heat **E17–E18.**

excogitate /ɪks'kɒdʒɪteɪt, ɛks-/ *verb trans*. **E16.**
[ORIGIN Latin *excogitat-* pa. ppl stem of *excogitare* find out by thinking, formed as EX-[1] 1, COGITATE.]
Think out, devise, (something; *how*).
■ **excogitative** *adjective* concerned with or having the power of excogitating **M19.** **excogitator** *noun* **M19.**

excogitation /ˌɛkskɒdʒɪ'teɪʃ(ə)n/ *noun*. **M16.**
[ORIGIN Latin *excogitatio(n-)*, formed as EXCOGITATE: see -ATION.]
1 The action of devising in the mind. **M16.**
2 Something devised, a contrivance, a plan. **M17.**

excommunicable /ɛkskə'mjuːnɪkəb(ə)l/ *adjective*. **L16.**
[ORIGIN from EXCOMMUNICATE *verb* + -ABLE.]
Liable to be excommunicated; (of an offence) punishable by excommunication.

excommunicant /ɛkskə'mjuːnɪk(ə)nt/ *noun*. **L16.**
[ORIGIN ecclesiastical Latin *excommunicant-* pres. ppl stem of *excommunicare*: see EXCOMMUNICATE *verb*, -ANT[1].]
1 An excommunicated person. **L16.**
2 = EXCOMMUNICATOR. *rare*. **M17.**

excommunicate /ɛkskə'mjuːnɪkət/ *adjective & noun*. **E16.**
[ORIGIN ecclesiastical Latin *excommunicatus* pa. pple of *excommunicare*: see EXCOMMUNICATE *verb*, -ATE[2].]
(A person who is) excommunicated.

excommunicate /ɛkskə'mjuːnɪkeɪt/ *verb trans*. **LME.**
[ORIGIN ecclesiastical Latin *excommunicat-* pa. ppl stem of *excommunicare*, from EX-[1] 1 + Latin *communis* COMMON *adjective*, after *communicare* COMMUNICATE *verb*: see -ATE[3].]
Sentence to exclusion from the Christian sacraments or from communication with the faithful; expel from a religious society or community.
■ **excommunicative** *adjective* = EXCOMMUNICATORY **E19.** **excommunicator** *noun* a person who excommunicates **M17.** **excommunicatory** *adjective* expressing excommunication; (of a person) disposed to excommunicate: **E17.**

excommunication /ˌɛkskəmjuːnɪ'keɪʃ(ə)n/ *noun*. **LME.**
[ORIGIN ecclesiastical Latin *excommunicatio(n-)*, formed as EXCOMMUNICATE *verb*: see -ATION.]
1 The action of excommunicating. **LME.**
2 The sentence by which a person is excommunicated. **M17.**

excommunion /ɛkskə'mjuːnjən/ *noun*. **M17.**
[ORIGIN from COMMUNION after *excommunication*.]
= EXCOMMUNICATION.

ex-con /ɛks'kɒn/ *noun*. *slang*. **E20.**
[ORIGIN Abbreviation.]
= EX-CONVICT.

exconjugant /ɛks'kɒndʒʊg(ə)nt/ *noun*. **E20.**
[ORIGIN from EX-[1] 3 + Latin *conjugant-* pres. ppl stem of *conjugare* CONJUGATE *verb*.]
Each of a pair of micro-organisms that have recently been in conjugation.

ex-convict /ɛks'kɒnvɪkt/ *noun*. **M19.**
[ORIGIN from EX-[1] 3 + CONVICT *noun*.]
A person who has served a term in prison, esp. recently.

excoriate /ɪk'skɔːrɪeɪt, ɛks-/ *verb trans*. Pa. pple **-ated**, (*arch.*) **-ate** /-ət/. **LME.**
[ORIGIN Latin *excoriat-* pa. ppl stem of *excoriare*, formed as EX-[1] 1 + *corium* skin, hide: see -ATE[3].]
1 Remove portions of the skin (or analogous membrane) from, esp. by corrosive action or abrasion. **LME.**

M. BEERBOHM My wrists, my ankles, are excoriated.

2 Peel off (skin); remove (a lining membrane) by corrosion, abrasion, etc. **M16.**
†**3** Flay, skin, (a person or animal). **M16–E19.**
4 *fig.* Make a scathing attack on. **M20.**
■ **excori'ation** *noun* (*a*) the action or an act of excoriating; an excoriated place on the body, a sore; (*b*) scathing criticism, invective: **LME.**

excorticate /ɪk'skɔːtɪkeɪt, ɛks-/ *verb trans*. Pa. pple **-ated**, †**-ate**. **LME.**
[ORIGIN Late Latin *excorticat-* pa. ppl stem of *excorticare*, formed as EX-[1] 1, CORTEX: see -ATE[3].]
Remove the bark from (a tree) or the shell from (a nut).
■ **ˌexcorti'cation** *noun* **E18.**

excrement /'ɛkskrɪm(ə)nt/ *noun*[1] *& verb*. **M16.**
[ORIGIN French *excrément* or Latin *excrementum*, from *excre-* pa. ppl base of *excernere* EXCRETE: see -MENT.]
▸ **A** *noun*. **1** *sing.* & in *pl.* Faeces. Formerly, any matter excreted or given out by the body or a plant. **M16.**
†**2** In *pl.* Something which remains after a process of sifting or refining; dregs, lees, refuse. **M16–L17.**
▸ **B** *verb intrans.* Defecate. *rare*. **M17.**
■ **excre'mental** *adjective* pertaining to or consisting of excrement; of the nature of excrement: **L16.** **excremen'titial** *adjective* (*rare*) = EXCREMENTAL **E17.** **excremen'titious** *adjective*[1] = EXCREMENTAL **L16.** †**excrementitiously** *adverb* **M17–L18.** †**excrementitiousness** *noun*: only in **M17.**

†**excrement** *noun*[2]. **M16.**
[ORIGIN Latin *excrementum*, from *excrescere*: see EXCRESCENCE, -MENT.]
1 Something which grows out or forth, *esp.* hair, nails, or feathers; an outgrowth (*lit. & fig.*). **M16–E18.**
2 Growth, increase. Only in **E17.**
■ †**excrementitious** *adjective*[2] of the nature of or consisting of an outgrowth **M17–M18.**

†**excresce** *verb & noun*. **LME.**
[ORIGIN Latin *excrescere*: see EXCRESCENCE.]
▸ **A** *verb intrans.* & (*rare*) *trans.* Increase, esp. inordinately; exceed what is usual; grow out. **LME–L17.**
▸ **B** *noun*. An excess amount; an increase. Chiefly *Scot.* **M16–E19.**

excrescence /ɪk'skrɛs(ə)ns, ɛks-/ *noun*. **LME.**
[ORIGIN Latin *excrescentia*, from *excrescent-* pres. ppl stem of *excrescere* grow out, formed as EX-[1] 1 + *crescere* grow: see -ENCE.]
1 a An abnormal or diseased outgrowth on a person, animal, or plant; a disfiguring or unsightly addition (*lit. & fig.*). **LME.** ▸**b** Something that grows out naturally; an appendage. Now *rare*. **M17.**

a J. A. MICHENER The awful modern excrescences that monopolized the town—the hot-dog stands . . , the Moorish motels. **b** H. MOORE Sculpture had become overgrown with moss, weeds—all sorts of surface excrescences.

†**2** The action of growing out; immoderate growth, abnormal increase. **M16–M18.**
3 Exuberance; an exuberant outburst. Formerly, overblown pride, swagger. Now *rare*. **E17.**
■ **excrescency** *noun* (now *rare*) (*a*) the state or condition of being excrescent; (an) abnormal development; †(*b*) = EXCRESCENCE 3: **M16.**

excrescent /ɪk'skrɛs(ə)nt, ɛks-/ *adjective*. **L15.**
[ORIGIN Latin *excrescent-*: see EXCRESCENCE, -ENT.]
1 Increased by addition, greater; constituting more than the normal quantity. Now *rare*. **L15.**
2 That grows out naturally. Now *rare* or *obsolete*. **M17.**
3 Growing abnormally; forming or constituting an excrescence; redundant, superfluous. **M17.**
4 *PHILOLOGY*. Of a sound or letter in a word: due merely to euphony, not to derivation. **L19.**

■ **excre'scential** *adjective* of the nature of an excrescence; redundant, superfluous: M19.

†**excression** *noun*. E17–E18.
[ORIGIN Irreg. from Latin *excrescere* (see EXCRESCENCE) for EXCRETION *noun*[2].]
= EXCRESCENCE 1.

excreta /ɪk'skriːtə, ɛk-/ *noun pl.* M19.
[ORIGIN Latin, use as noun of neut. pl. of *excretus* pa. pple of *excernere* EXCRETE.]
Waste matter discharged from the body; *esp.* faeces, urine.
■ **excretal** *adjective* M19.

excrete /ɪk'skriːt, ɛk-/ *verb*. E17.
[ORIGIN Latin *excret-* pa. ppl stem of *excernere*, formed as EX-[1] 1 + *cernere* sift.]
†**1** *verb trans.* Of a drug, physician, etc.: cause the excretion of (matter). E–M17.
2 *verb trans. & intrans.* Separate and expel (esp. waste products of metabolism) from the body, an organ, a cell, etc. M17.

C. DARWIN Certain plants excrete sweet juice. P. PARISH Some drugs are . . quickly and easily excreted. C. RYCROFT Squids . . excrete their ink in order to repel predators.

■ **excreter** *noun* M19. **excretive** *adjective* able to excrete or promote excretion M17. **excretory** *adjective & noun* (*a*) *adjective* having the function of excreting; pertaining to the process of excretion; also, of the nature of excreta; (*b*) *noun* (now *rare*) an excretory vessel or duct: L17.

excretion /ɪk'skriːʃ(ə)n, ɛk-/ *noun*[1]. E17.
[ORIGIN French *excrétion* or Latin *excretio(n-)*, formed as EXCRETE: see -ION.]
1 The action or process of excreting; *spec.* emptying of the bowels. E17.
2 Material which is excreted. M17.

†**excretion** *noun*[2]. E17–E18.
[ORIGIN Late Latin *excretio(n-)*, from *excret-* pa. ppl stem of *excrescere*: see EXCRESCENCE, -ION.]
= EXCRESCENCE 1, EXCREMENT *noun*[2] 1.

†**excriminate** *verb trans. rare.* M16–L18.
[ORIGIN from EX-[1] 1 + (as) CRIMINATE.]
Clear of an imputation; shift an imputation from (one person) *upon* another.

excruciate /ɪk'skruːʃɪeɪt, ɛk-/ *verb trans.* L16.
[ORIGIN Latin *excruciat-* pa. ppl stem of *excruciare* torment, formed as EX-[1] 1 + *cruc-*, *crux* cross: see -ATE[3].]
1 Torment acutely (a person's senses). Formerly also, subject to physical torture; rack (one's brains). Now chiefly *hyperbol.* L16.
2 Torture mentally, inflict extreme mental anguish on. L16.

excruciating /ɪk'skruːʃɪeɪtɪŋ, ɛk-/ *adjective*. L16.
[ORIGIN from EXCRUCIATE + -ING[2].]
That excruciates; agonizing; *joc.* or *hyperbol.* (of a song, joke, etc.) so bad as to cause pain to the hearer.

B. TARKINGTON He . . was stabbed by excruciating pains in his legs. E. F. BENSON She sings the melody of the first movement of the 'Unfinished'. It is quite excruciating, but recognizable.

■ **excruciatingly** *adverb* E19.

excruciation /ɪkˌskruːʃɪ'eɪʃ(ə)n, ɛk-/ *noun*. E17.
[ORIGIN Latin *excruciatio(n-)*, formed as EXCRUCIATE: see -ATION.]
The action or an act of excruciating; the state of being excruciated.

excubitor /ɪk'skjuːbɪtə, ɛk-/ *noun*. L18.
[ORIGIN Latin, agent noun from *excubare* lie on guard, formed as EX-[1] 1 + *cubare* lie down: see -OR.]
1 A watchman, a sentinel. *rare.* L18.
2 ROMAN HISTORY. A member of one of the four companies into which the imperial guard was divided. M19.

exculpate /'ɛkskʌlpeɪt/ *verb*. M17.
[ORIGIN medieval Latin *exculpat-* pa. ppl stem of *exculpare*, formed as EX-[1] 1 + Latin *culpa* blame: see -ATE[3].]
1 *verb trans. & (rare) intrans.* Of a person, court, etc.: free (a person) from blame, clear from an accusation. (Foll. by *from*.) M17.

G. GROTE The latter stood exculpated on both charges. R. W. CLARK Freud's wish to exculpate himself from blame for the patient's treatment.

2 *verb trans.* Of a thing: provide grounds for exculpating; vindicate. Formerly also, justify. E18.
■ **excul'pation** *noun* (*a*) the action or an act of exculpating; (*b*) a ground for exculpating; an excuse: E18. **ex'culpatory** *adjective* serving or intended to exculpate L17.

excur /ɪk'skəː, ɛk-/ *verb intrans. rare.* Infl. **-rr-**. M17.
[ORIGIN Latin *excurrere*: see EXCURRENT.]
†**1** Stray, digress, (*lit. & fig.*); go to an extreme. M–L17.
2 = EXCURSE 2. M19.

excurrent /ɪk'skʌr(ə)nt, ɛk-/ *adjective*. E17.
[ORIGIN Latin *excurrent-* pres. ppl stem of *excurrere* run out, formed as EX-[1] 1 + *currere* run: see -ENT.]
1 Overflowing, superabundant. *rare.* Only in E17.
2 a That runs or flows out. E19. ▸**b** Serving as or providing an exit. M19.
3 BOTANY. Of a tree, trunk, etc.: having or designating an undivided main trunk. Of the midrib of a leaf: projecting beyond the tip or margin. M19.

excurse /ɪk'skəːs, ɛk-/ *verb intrans.* M18.
[ORIGIN Latin *excurs-*: see EXCURSION.]
1 Run off, wander, digress. Chiefly *fig.* M18.
2 Make or go on an excursion. L18.

excursion /ɪk'skəːʃ(ə)n, ɛk-/ *noun & verb*. L16.
[ORIGIN Latin *excursio(n-)*, from *excurs-* pa. ppl stem of *excurrere*: see EXCURRENT, -ION.]
▸ **A** *noun* **1** †**a** The action or an act of running out or of going beyond limits or to extremes. L16–M18. ▸**b** Extension, projection. Formerly, an extending or projecting part. Now *rare* or *obsolete*. M17.
2 MILITARY. A sally, a sortie, a raid. *obsolete* exc. in ***alarms and excursions, alarums and excursions*** s.v. ALARM *noun*. L16.
3 †**a** A digression in speech or writing. L16–E19. ▸**b** ASTRONOMY. A deviation from a regular path. E17.
†**4** An outburst of feeling; a sally of wit; an overstepping of the limits of propriety or custom; an escapade, a transgression; a vagary. E17–L18.
5 A journey or ramble made with the intention of returning to the starting point (*lit. & fig.*); *spec.* a pleasure trip taken esp. by a number of people to a particular place. L17.

J. BRYCE The only excursion into the historical domain which I shall have to ask the reader to make. B. CHATWIN Their first excursion into the outside world was a visit to the Flower Show. J. A. MICHENER Evening excursions to historic sites like . . the poetic ruins of Caesarea.

6 (The extent of) a movement to and fro of an oscillatory body or fluctuating quantity; (the extent of) a variation from an average value. L18. ▸**b** A sudden large increase in the output of a nuclear reactor. M20.

C. FORD The excursion of the bass strings is greater. *Scientific American* At higher levels . . there should be large temperature excursions caused by alternating layers of atmospheric gas heated by compression and cooled by expansion. *Wireless World* To limit the maximum excursion of the reference voltage.

— COMB.: **excursion fare**, **excursion ticket**, **excursion train**: for an excursion, usu. at a reduced rate.
▸ **B** *verb intrans.* Make or go on an excursion. *arch.* L18.
■ **excursional** *adjective* of or pertaining to an excursion M19. **excursionary** *adjective* of the nature of an excursion; going on an excursion: M18. **excursionist** *noun* a person (esp. one of a party) making or going on an excursion M19. **excursionize** *verb* (*a*) *verb trans.* (*rare*) explore (a district) by making excursions; (*b*) *verb intrans.* = EXCURSION verb: E19.

excursive /ɪk'skəːsɪv, ɛk-/ *adjective*. L17.
[ORIGIN formed as EXCURSE + -IVE, perh. after *discursive*.]
1 Of the nature of an excursion; consisting of excursions or digressions. L17.

W. IRVING We are wandering . . into excursive speculations.

2 Making or tending to make excursions; ranging widely; apt to stray, digressive; desultory. M18.

S. JOHNSON An intelligence perpetually on the wing, excursive, vigorous, and diligent. A. HELPS Do keep to the point, my excursive friends.

■ **excursively** *adverb* L18. **excursiveness** *noun* M18.

excursus /ɪk'skəːsəs, ɛk-/ *noun*. Pl. **excursuses**, **excursus** /-suːs/. E19.
[ORIGIN Latin = excursion, formed as EXCURSE.]
1 A fuller treatment in an appendix of some point in the main text of a book, esp. an edition of the classics. E19.
2 A digression within a narrative in which some point is discussed at length. M19.

excurvation /ɛkskəː'veɪʃ(ə)n/ *noun*. E19.
[ORIGIN from EX-[1] 1 + CURVATION.]
Outward curvature.

excusable /ɪk'skjuːzəb(ə)l, ɛk-/ *adjective*. LME.
[ORIGIN Old French from Latin *excusabilis*, from *excusare* EXCUSE *verb*: see -ABLE.]
1 Of a person: deserving or able to be excused or acquitted. (Foll. by †*of*.) Now *rare*. LME.
2 Of an action, conduct, etc.: admitting of excuse. LME. ***excusable homicide***: see HOMICIDE 1.
■ **excusa'bility** *noun* (*rare*) = EXCUSABLENESS E18. **excusableness** *noun* the quality of being excusable M17. **excusably** *adverb* E17.

excusal /ɪk'skjuːz(ə)l, ɛk-/ *noun*. L16.
[ORIGIN from EXCUSE *verb* + -AL[1]; cf. *refusal*.]
The action or fact of excusing or being excused, esp. from an official duty or requirement.

†**excusation** *noun*. ME.
[ORIGIN Old French from Latin *excusatio(n-)*, from *excusat-* pa. ppl stem of *excusare*: see EXCUSE *verb*, -ATION.]
1 A real or alleged ground for being released from an obligation or excused an action; an excuse; a pretext; a plea for forgiveness or leniency. ME–M17.
2 The action of offering an excuse, defence, or apology. LME–M19.
3 Release or freedom from an obligation, duty, etc. LME–M16.

excusator /ɪk'skjuːzətə, ɛk-/ *noun*. *obsolete* exc. *hist.* M17.
[ORIGIN Late Latin *excusator*, from Latin *excusat-* pa. ppl stem of *excusare*: see EXCUSE *verb*, -ATOR.]
A person who makes an excuse, defence, or apology; *spec.* one officially authorized to do so.

excusatory /ɪk'skjuːzət(ə)ri, ɛk-/ *adjective*. LME.
[ORIGIN medieval Latin *excusatorius*, formed as EXCUSATOR: see -ORY[2].]
Tending or meant to excuse; making or containing an excuse; apologetic.

excuse /ɪk'skjuːs, ɛk-/ *noun*. LME.
[ORIGIN Old French & mod. French, from *excuser*: see EXCUSE *verb*.]
1 The action of excusing a person or an action; now *esp.* indulgence, pardon. LME.

LYTTON The old woman gave me a note of excuse.

2 Something offered as a reason for being excused. LME.

A. LURIE I was so sure Kenneth wouldn't want to go that I . . gave an excuse for him. A. MOTION I make my excuses early, and lie on my unmade bed.

3 Something that serves to excuse or gives ground for excusing; a justification, a reason. LME.

D. DU MAURIER His wife was a scold, but that was no excuse to kill her. T. S. ELIOT I was glad of the excuse for coming up to London.

4 = APOLOGY *noun*[1] 4. *colloq.* M19.
■ **excuseless** *adjective* (long *rare*) without excuse M16.

excuse /ɪk'skjuːz, ɛk-/ *verb*. ME.
[ORIGIN Old French *escuser* (mod. *excuser*) from Latin *excusare* free from blame, formed as EX-[1] 1 + *causa* accusation.]
1 *verb trans. & intrans.* Seek to clear (a person) wholly or partially from blame without denying or justifying the action concerned; try to extenuate (an acknowledged fault). Formerly also, clear of blame by alleging *that*. ME.

I. WALTON I should rather excuse myself, then censure others. E. HAYWOOD She excused . . having made him wait.

†**2** *verb trans.* Maintain the innocence of (a person); defend from an accusation (*of*); seek to justify (an action). ME–L17.

R. HOLINSHED To excuse him of the death of the archbishop.

3 *verb trans.* Obtain exemption for (a person); give reasons for the exemption of (a person) *from* a duty or obligation. ME. ▸†**b** Decline (a deed, *to do*) with apologies. M16–M18.

V. WOOLF He went off laughing, excusing himself on the score of business. **b** J. HILDROP He prest me . . to dine with him, which I excused.

†**4** *verb trans.* Save (someone) from punishment or harm, esp. by taking someone's place; take the place of and so exempt from a duty. (Foll. by *of*, *from*.) ME–E18.
5 a *verb trans.* In *pass.* Have a sufficient excuse; be freed from blame. ME. ▸**b** *verb trans. & intrans.* Of a property, circumstance, etc.: serve as a justification (for). M16.

b G. GREENE The man looked sick and tired enough to excuse any artifice. TOLKIEN You speak evil of that which is fair . . , and only little wit can excuse you.

6 *verb trans.* Release from a task, duty, or obligation; dispense from payment, attendance, etc. (Foll. by *from*, 2nd obj.) ME.

OED The jury were excused from attendance for the rest of the week. D. ATHILL I had been excused games for all of one term.

7 *verb trans.* Judge leniently on the grounds of extenuating circumstances, forgive. LME. ▸**b** Admit apology for, overlook, condone, (a fault, offence, impropriety, etc.); regard (an action) indulgently. LME.

B. JOWETT The people may be excused for following tradition only. E. M. FORSTER You must excuse me if I say stupid things, but my brain has gone to pieces. **b** F. W. ROBERTSON The boldest heart may be excused a shudder. H. E. BATES Are you married? . . Excuse my asking a personal question.

8 *verb trans.* Refrain from exacting; dispense with. M17.

LYTTON From our royal court We do excuse your presence.

— PHRASES: **be excused** *colloq.* be allowed to leave the room (esp. to relieve oneself) or the table; urinate, defecate. **excuse me** an apology for interruption, lack of ceremony, etc.; an expression of polite or diffident dissent; (***excuse-me dance***, a dance in which one may take another person's partner). **excuse oneself** ask permission or apologize prior to leaving.
■ **excuser** *noun* †(*a*) *rare* a substitute, a deputy; (*b*) a person who offers or makes excuses: LME. **excusive** *adjective* tending to excuse; that excuses: L16.

†**excuss** *verb trans.* L16.
[ORIGIN Latin *excuss-* pa. ppl stem of *excutere*, formed as EX-[1] 1 + *quatere* shake.]
1 Investigate thoroughly; discuss; get (the truth) *from* a person. L16–E18.
2 Shake off, cast off, get rid of, (*lit. & fig.*). E–M17.
3 LAW. Seize (a debtor's goods) in execution of a warrant etc. Only in E18.

†**excussion** *noun*. E17.
[ORIGIN Latin *excussio(n-)*, formed as EXCUSS: see -ION.]
1 The action of shaking off or getting rid of something. Only in 17.
2 LAW. Seizure of goods for debt. E17–E18.

excyst /ɛkˈsɪst/ *verb intrans.* E20.
[ORIGIN from EX-[1] 1 + CYST, after *encyst*.]
BIOLOGY & MEDICINE. Emerge from a cyst.
■ **excystation**, **excystment** *nouns* (an instance of) emerging from a cyst. E20.

ex-directory /ɛksdɪˈrɛkt(ə)ri, -dʌɪ-/ *adjective*. M20.
[ORIGIN from EX *preposition* + DIRECTORY *noun*.]
Of a telephone number or subscriber: not listed in the directory through the subscriber's choice.

ex div /ɛks ˈdɪv/ *adverbial phr.* M19.
[ORIGIN Abbreviation.]
COMMERCE. = ***ex dividend*** s.v. EX *preposition* 1.

exeat /ˈɛksɪat/ *noun*. E18.
[ORIGIN Latin = let him or her go out, 3rd person sing. pres. subjunct. of *exire* EXIT *verb*[1].]

E

1 A permission for temporary absence from a college or other institution. E18.

P. ACKROYD He had been given a day's exeat from the hospital where he was being treated.

2 A permission granted by a bishop to a priest to move to another diocese. M18.

exec /ɪgˈzɛk, ɛg-/ *noun*. *colloq.* L19.
[ORIGIN Abbreviation.]
= EXECUTIVE *noun* 4.

execrable /ˈɛksɪkrəb(ə)l/ *adjective*. LME.
[ORIGIN Old French & mod. French *exécrable* from Latin *execrabilis* (in active and pass. senses), from *ex(s)ecrari*: see EXECRATE, -ABLE.]
†**1** Expressing or involving a curse; awful, fearful. LME–M17.
2 Of a person or thing: deserving to be cursed; detestable. L15.

New York Times The others who were wounded in the execrable attack on the synagogue.

†**3** Piteous, horrifying. L15–E19.
4 Of wretched quality; abominable, bad beyond description. M18.

D. MURPHY Some past tenant with execrable taste had left the whole place superficially hideous.

■ **execrably** *adverb* L16.

execrate /ˈɛksɪkreɪt/ *verb*. M16.
[ORIGIN Latin *execrat-* pa. ppl stem of *ex(s)ecrari* curse, formed as EX-[1] 1 + *sacrare* devote religiously, from *sacr-*, *sacer* holy: see -ATE[3].]
1 *verb intrans.* Utter curses. M16.
2 a *verb trans.* Invoke evil upon; express loathing for; abhor. M16. ▸†**b** *verb trans. & intrans.* Pronounce a curse (upon); declare accursed. *rare*. Only in L17.

a B. RUSSELL The symbol of a new order, admired by some, execrated by many.

†**3** *verb trans.* Make no longer holy; dedicate to evil. L16–M17.
■ **execrative** *adjective* of or pertaining to execration; characterized by or containing an execration: M19. **execrator** *noun* L16. **execratory** *adjective* of the nature of an execration; execrative: E17.

execration /ɛksɪˈkreɪʃ(ə)n/ *noun*. LME.
[ORIGIN Latin *execratio(n-)*, formed as EXECRATE: see -ATION.]
1 The action or an act of pronouncing a curse upon a person. *obsolete* exc. *hist.* LME.
2 Loathing, abhorrence. L16.

E. STILLINGFLEET The Indians, at naming the devil, did spit on the ground in token of execration.

3 An uttered curse, an imprecation; the uttering of curses, swearing. E17.

Harper's Magazine The infuriated multitude which surrounded him filling the air with menaces and execrations.

4 An object of cursing. *arch.* E17.

executable /ɛgˈzɛkjʊtəb(ə)l, ɪg-/ *adjective & noun*. L18.
[ORIGIN from EXECUTE + -ABLE.]
▸ **A** *adjective*. **1** That can be executed, performed, or carried out. L18.
2 COMPUTING. Designating instructions which can be executed, or the storage (directly accessible to the processor) in which they are held ready for execution; *spec.* designating files which can be loaded into memory and executed, i.e. program files as opposed to files containing data. M20.
▸ **B** *noun*. COMPUTING. An executable file. L20.

executant /ɪgˈzɛkjʊt(ə)nt, ɛg-/ *noun & adjective*. M19.
[ORIGIN French *exécutant* pres. pple of *exécuter*: see EXECUTE, -ANT[1].]
▸ **A** *noun*. A person who executes, carries out, or performs something, esp. music. M19.
▸ **B** *adjective*. That performs music. *rare*. M19.
■ **executancy** *noun* power and skill in performing music M19.

execute /ˈɛksɪkjuːt/ *verb*. Pa. pple **-cuted**, †**-cute**. LME.
[ORIGIN Old French & mod. French *exécuter* from medieval Latin *executare*, from Latin *ex(s)ecut-* pa. ppl stem of *ex(s)equi* follow up, carry out, pursue judicially, punish, formed as EX-[1] 1 + *sequi* follow.]
▸ **I** Carry out, perform, etc.
1 a *verb trans. & intrans.* Carry out, put into effect, (a plan, purpose, command, sentence, law, will, etc.). LME. ▸†**b** *verb trans.* Display or manifest (a sentiment or principle) with practical effect. LME–L17.

V. CRONIN To execute her plan Catherine needed the help of a friendly power. T. PYNCHON Oedipa had been named also to execute the will in a codicil dated a year ago.

2 a *verb trans.* Perform (a planned or skilled operation or movement). LME. ▸†**b** *verb trans. & intrans.* Perform or celebrate (a ceremony or religious service). LME–M18. ▸**c** *verb trans.* Perform acts of (justice, cruelty, etc.). *arch.* M16.

a G. BOYCOTT Richards . . executed his more aggressive strokes quite beautifully.

3 *verb trans.* Fulfil (a function), discharge (an office). LME.

S. KINGSLEY I do solemnly swear that I will faithfully execute the office of President of the United States.

4 *verb trans.* Go through the formalities required for (a legal act); make (a legal instrument) valid by signing, sealing, etc. M16.
execute an estate convey or confer an estate in property etc., esp. by some particular operation of law.
5 *verb trans.* Produce (a work of art or skill) from a design; perform (a piece of music). M18.

K. CLARK It is in one of Neumann's great buildings . . that Tiepolo executed his masterpiece.

▸ **II** Perform an execution on.
6 *verb trans.* Put to death as a judicial punishment for a crime; kill as a political act. LME.

L. DURRELL The authorities arrested and executed the Archbishop.

■ **executer** *noun* = EXECUTOR 2 M16.

execution /ɛksɪˈkjuːʃ(ə)n/ *noun*. LME.
[ORIGIN Old French & mod. French *exécution* from Latin *ex(s)ecutio(n-)*, from *ex(s)ecut-*: see EXECUTE, -ION.]
1 The action or an act of putting a person to death, esp. as a judicial punishment. Formerly also, any judicial, usu. corporal, punishment. LME.

N. MOSLEY His method of execution was to inflict innumerable small wounds so that his victims did not know that they were dying.

2 The action or an act of executing a plan, purpose, command, law, etc. LME. ▸**b** The enforcement by a public officer of the judgement of a court of law; *esp.* the seizure of the goods or person of a debtor in default of payment. E16. ▸†**c** The practical display or manifestation of a sentiment or principle. L16–M17.

H. JAMES There are a great many good ideas that are never put into execution. **c** SHAKES. *3 Hen. VI* Scarce I can refrain The execution of my big-swol'n heart Upon . . that cruel child-killer.

3 Destructive effect; infliction of damage or slaughter; destruction, esp. of a country refusing to pay a levy. Now chiefly in ***do execution***. E16.

fig.: THACKERAY Black eyes, which might have done some execution had they been placed in a smoother face.

†**4** Action, operation. M16–E18. ▸**b** Efficiency or excellence in action. M16–E17.
5 The carrying out of a planned or skilled operation or movement, the production of a work of art or skill; the (manner of) performance of a piece of music. Formerly, the performance of a ceremony or religious service. M16. ▸†**b** An act of executing a movement, work of art, etc.; a deed; a musical performance. Usu. in *pl.* L16–E18. ▸**c** Excellence in performance, esp. of music. L18.

S. BECKETT I managed a few steps of creditable execution and then fell. H. READ The charm of a great master's drawing is partly the extraordinary skill and sureness of its execution. *Personal Software* It has a speed of execution close to that of machine code.

6 The fulfilment or discharge of a function or office. L16.
7 The performance of the formalities required to validate a legal document. L18.
■ **executionary** *adjective* E20.

executioner /ɛksɪˈkjuːʃ(ə)nə/ *noun*. M16.
[ORIGIN from EXECUTION + -ER[1].]
1 An official who carries out a death sentence. M16.

fig.: SHAKES. *Rich. III* Though I wish thy death, I will not be thy Executioner.

2 *gen.* A person who carries out a judgement or sentence. L16.
3 A person who executes a plan, purpose, command, law, etc. Now *rare*. L16.
■ **executioneress** *noun* a female executioner M17.

executive /ɪgˈzɛkjʊtɪv, ɛg-/ *adjective & noun*. LME.
[ORIGIN medieval Latin *executivus*, from Latin *execut-*: see EXECUTE, -IVE.]
▸ **A** *adjective*. **1** Pertaining to execution; having the function of putting something into effect; *spec.* designating the branch of government that deals with putting into effect laws and judicial sentences. LME.

Gramophone Difficulties that appear to be as much executive as interpretational. *New York Times* This is the first time in the history of the Congress and the executive branch that we have worked out jointly an arms control proposal. *National Observer (US)* Executive editor of the Washington Post.

2 Of or pertaining to the executive of a government. E19.

Time Executive clemency if they were convicted was discussed with the President.

Executive Council *Austral.* & *NZ* a body presided over by the Governor General or Governor and consisting of ministers of the Crown, which gives legal form to Cabinet decisions etc. **executive officer** (**a**) an officer with executive power; (**b**) (in naval vessels and some other military contexts) the officer who is second in command to the captain or commanding officer. **executive privilege** the privilege, claimed by the President for the executive branch of the US Government, of withholding information in the public interest. **executive session** *US* a closed meeting of a governing body (orig. of the Senate for executive business). **executive toy** an object or device designed for the amusement or relaxation of executives in the office.
3 Apt or skilful in execution or performance. E19.
▸ **B** *noun*. **1** The executive branch of a government. L18.

Daily Telegraph Separation of powers between the legislature, the executive and the judiciary.

2 The person or persons in whom is vested the supreme executive authority of a country or state, esp. the US President (also called ***Chief Executive***) or the Governor of a state of the US. L18.
3 Any group or body concerned with administration or management; the executive committee of an organization. M19.

Times The executive of the Iron and Steel Trades Confederation . . voted 19 to 1 to back the . . pay-restraint package.

4 A person in an executive position in a business; a person skilled in executive or administrative work; a businessman, a businesswoman. E20.
■ **executively** *adverb* in execution, in performance; by the action of an executive: LME.

executor /ɪgˈzɛkjʊtə, ɛg-; *in sense 2* ˈɛksɪkjuːtə/ *noun*. ME.
[ORIGIN Anglo-Norman *execut(o)ur* from Latin *executor*, from *execut-*: see EXECUTE, -OR.]
1 A person appointed by a testator to execute his or her will. ME.
literary executor a person entrusted with responsiblity for a dead writer's unpublished works etc.
2 *gen.* A person who executes a plan, purpose, command, law, etc.; an agent, a performer; SCOTS LAW a person who executes a warrant. *arch.* LME.
†**3** = EXECUTIONER 1. L15–E17.
■ **executorship** *noun* the office or duty of an executor E16.

executorial /ˌɛksɪkjʊˈtɔːrɪəl/ *adjective & noun*. L15.
[ORIGIN medieval Latin *executorialis*, formed as EXECUTORY: see -AL[1].]
▸ **A** *adjective*. **1** ***executorial letters***, a papal mandate for the appointment of a designated person to a benefice. L15.
2 Of or pertaining to an executor; SCOTS LAW pertaining to the execution of a warrant. M18.
▸ †**B** *noun*. SCOTS LAW. A legal authority or instruction used to execute a decree or sentence. E16–E19.

executory /ɪgˈzɛkjuːt(ə)ri, ɛg-/ *adjective*. LME.
[ORIGIN Late Latin *executorius*, from Latin *executor*: see EXECUTOR, -ORY[2].]
1 Of a law: in force, operative. Now *rare*. LME.
2 Of a law, contract, etc.: not yet put into effect or performed; due to come into effect at a future date. L16.
3 Of or pertaining to execution or putting into effect. M17.
4 = EXECUTIVE *adjective* 1. M17.

executrix /ɪgˈzɛkjʊtrɪks, ɛg-/ *noun*. Pl. **-trices** /-trɪsiːz/, **-trixes**. LME.
[ORIGIN Late Latin *executrix*, from Latin EXECUTOR: see -TRIX.]
A female executor, esp. of a will.

executry /ɪgˈzɛkjʊtri, ɛg-/ *noun*. LME.
[ORIGIN from EXECUTOR + -Y[3].]
†**1** = EXECUTORSHIP. LME–L19.
2 *Scot.* The movable property of a deceased person. M17.

†**exede** *verb trans.* M17–M18.
[ORIGIN Latin *exedere*, formed as EX-[1] 1 + *ed-*, *esse* eat.]
Corrode, eat away.

exedra /ˈɛksɪdrə, ɪkˈsiːdrə, ɛk-/ *noun*. Also **exhedra** /ˈɛkshɪdrə, ɪksˈhiːdrə, ɛks-/. Pl. **-drae** /-driː/. E18.
[ORIGIN Latin from Greek, formed as EX-[2] + *hedra* seat.]
1 CLASSICAL HISTORY. A hall or arcade with seats, attached to a palaestra or a private house and used for conversation. E18. ▸**b** *gen.* An apse, a recess, a large niche. M19.
2 = CATHEDRA. E18.

†**exeem** *verb* var. of EXEME.

exegesis /ɛksɪˈdʒiːsɪs/ *noun*. Pl. **-geses** /-ˈdʒiːsiːz/. E17.
[ORIGIN Greek *exēgēsis*, from *exēgeisthai* interpret, formed as EX-[2] + *hēgeisthai* to guide.]
(An) exposition, esp. of Scripture; a gloss, an explanatory note or discourse.

M. ARNOLD A very small experience of Jewish exegesis will convince us. L. VAN DER POST He was to give me a long exegesis on the origin and meaning of tennis.

■ **exegesist** *noun* = EXEGETE 2 M19.

exegete /ˈɛksɪdʒiːt/ *noun*. M18.
[ORIGIN Greek *exēgētēs*, from *exēgeisthai*: see EXEGESIS.]
1 GREEK HISTORY. An interpreter or expounder of sacred lore. M18.

2 A person skilled in exegesis; an expositor (*of* a subject, doctrine, etc.). **M19.**

exegetic /ɛksɪˈdʒɛtɪk/ *adjective*. **M17.**
[**ORIGIN** Greek *exēgētikos*, from *exēgeisthai*: see **EXEGESIS**, **-IC**.]
= **EXEGETICAL**. (Foll. by *of*.)

exegetical /ɛksɪˈdʒɛtɪk(ə)l/ *adjective*. **E17.**
[**ORIGIN** formed as **EXEGETIC** + **-AL**[1].]
†**1** Of the nature of a gloss; explanatory. (Foll. by *of*, *to*.) **E17–E18.**
2 Of, pertaining to, or of the nature of exegesis; expository. **M19.**
exegetical theology exegetics.
■ **exegetically** *adverb* **M17.**

exegetics /ɛksɪˈdʒɛtɪks/ *noun*. **M19.**
[**ORIGIN** formed as **EXEGETIC**: see **-ICS**.]
The branch of theology that deals with the interpretation of Scripture.

exegetist /ɛksɪˈdʒiːtɪst/ *noun*. **M19.**
[**ORIGIN** from **EXEGETE** + **-IST**.]
= **EXEGETE** 2.

†**exeme** *verb trans*. Chiefly *Scot*. Also **exeem**. **E16.**
[**ORIGIN** Latin *eximere*: see **EXEMPT** *adjective & noun*.]
1 Free from pain, care, etc.; exempt from a payment, penalty, or obligation. (Foll. by *from*.) **E16–E20.**
2 Take away, remove; select or except *from*. Only in **17.**

exempla *noun* pl. of **EXEMPLUM**.

exemplar /ɪɡˈzɛmplə, ɛɡ-/ *noun*. **LME.**
[**ORIGIN** Old French & mod. French *exemplaire* from late Latin *exemplarium*, from *exemplum* **EXAMPLE** *noun*: see **-AR**[2].]
1 A model for imitation; an example. **LME.** ▸**b** The model, pattern, or original after which something is made; an archetype. **E17.**

R. FRY The exemplar which men put before themselves was the civilisation of Greece and Rome.

2 A typical instance; a specimen; a typical embodiment (*of* a quality etc.). **LME.**

V. S. PRITCHETT He seems a promising exemplar of the human being exposed to everything without the support of a settled society.

3 A copy of a book etc; a transcript. Formerly also, the original of a book from which copies are made. **LME.**
4 A parallel instance. **L17.**
■ **exemplarism** *noun* (*THEOLOGY*) (**a**) the doctrine that divine ideas are the source of finite realities; (**b**) the doctrine that Christ became incarnate as an exemplar to humankind: **L19.** **exemplarist** *adjective & noun* (*THEOLOGY*) (**a**) *adjective* of or pertaining to exemplarism; (**b**) *noun* a person who believes in or advocates exemplarism: **E20.**

†**exemplar** *adjective*. **LME–L18.**
[**ORIGIN** Late Latin *exemplaris*, perh. through Old French & mod. French *exemplaire* (adjective): see **EXEMPLAR** *noun*, **-AR**[1].]
= **EXEMPLARY** *adjective*
■ †**exemplarly** *adverb*: only in **17.**

exemplarity /ɪɛɡzɛmˈplarɪti/ *noun*. **E17.**
[**ORIGIN** medieval Latin *exemplaritas*, from late Latin *exemplaris*: see **EXEMPLARY** *adjective & adverb*, **-ITY**.]
The quality of being exemplary; exemplariness.

exemplary /ɪɡˈzɛmpləri, ɛɡ-/ *noun*. Now *rare*. **LME.**
[**ORIGIN** Late Latin *exemplarium*: see **EXEMPLAR** *noun*, **-ARY**[1].]
1 An example; a model, a pattern of conduct. **LME.**
†**2** A copy of a book; a transcript. **M16–E18.**

exemplary /ɪɡˈzɛmpləri, ɛɡ-/ *adjective & adverb*. **L16.**
[**ORIGIN** Late Latin *exemplaris*, from Latin *exemplum* **EXAMPLE** *noun*: see **-ARY**[2].]
▸ **A** *adjective*. **1** Of a person, quality, etc.: fit for imitation. **L16.**

A. KOESTLER Your behaviour remains exemplary and spotless. G. SWIFT I became a docile, dutiful, even an exemplary son.

2 Of a thing: serving as a model or pattern; archetypal. **L16.**
3 Of a kind liable to become an example; remarkable, signal, extraordinary. *arch.* **L16.**
4 Of a penalty, punishment, etc.: serving as a warning or deterrent. **E17.**
exemplary damages *LAW*: exceeding those necessary to compensate for actual loss and awarded to mark disapproval of the defendant's conduct.
5 Serving as a specimen or type; typical. **E17.**
†**6** Of or pertaining to an example; providing examples; illustrative. **E17–E19.**
▸ †**B** *adverb*. In an exemplary manner; to an exemplary degree. **E17–L18.**
■ **exemplarily** *adverb* **E17.** **exemplariness** *noun* the quality of being worthy of imitation **M17.**

exempli causa /ɪɡˌzɛmpli ˈkɔːzə; ɛɡ-, ˈkaʊzə/ *adverbial phr.* Now *rare*. **M16.**
[**ORIGIN** Latin, from genit. of *exemplum* **EXAMPLE** *noun* + abl. of *causa*: see **CAUSE** *noun*.]
= **EXEMPLI GRATIA**.

exemplification /ɪɡˌzɛmplɪfɪˈkeɪʃ(ə)n, ɛɡ-/ *noun*. **LME.**
[**ORIGIN** Anglo-Norman, and medieval Latin *exemplificatio(n-)*, from *exemplificat-* pa. ppl stem of *exemplificare*: see **EXEMPLIFY**, **-FICATION**.]
1 The action or an act of exemplifying or showing by example. **LME.**
2 An attested copy or transcript of a record, deed, etc. **LME.**
3 A thing that exemplifies; an example, an illustration. **L16.**
■ **exemplificational** *adjective* **E19.** **eˈxemplifiˌcative** *adjective* illustrative **E19.**

exemplify /ɪɡˈzɛmplɪfʌɪ, ɛɡ-/ *verb*. **LME.**
[**ORIGIN** medieval Latin *exemplificare*, from Latin *exemplum* **EXAMPLE** *noun*: see **-FY**.]
1 *verb trans*. Make an official or attested copy of (esp. a legal document). **LME.** ▸†**b** Copy (a document); quote in writing. **L16–E18.**
2 a *verb trans*. Illustrate by examples; find or provide an example of. **LME.** ▸**b** *verb intrans*. Quote examples by way of illustration. **L16.** ▸**c** *verb trans*. Be or serve as an example of. **L18.**

a D. CECIL Her stories do exemplify her moral point of view. **b** C. BROOKE-ROSE The professor exemplified with a vivid comparison from the animal kingdom. **c** W. STYRON Talk about your lovesick fool, how I exemplified such a wretch!

†**3** *verb trans. & intrans*. Set a (good) example (to). **LME–E16.**
†**4** *verb trans*. Adduce, quote, use as an example; compare *to* by way of example. **E16–L18.**
†**5** *verb trans*. Make after an example or model. **L16–L17.**
†**6** *verb trans*. Make an example of (a person). Only in **M17.**
†**7** *verb trans*. Manifest or display an example of (a quality etc.). **M–L17.**
■ **exemplifiable** *adjective* (*rare*) **E19.** **exemplifier** *noun* **M16.**

exempli gratia /ɪɡˌzɛmpli ˈɡreɪʃə; ɛɡ-/ *adverbial phr.* **M17.**
[**ORIGIN** Latin, from genit. of *exemplum* **EXAMPLE** *noun* + abl. of *gratia*: see **GRACE** *noun*.]
For example, for instance. Usu. abbreviated to ***e.g.***

exemplum /ɪɡˈzɛmpləm, ɛɡ-/ *noun*. Pl. **-pla** /-plə/. **L19.**
[**ORIGIN** Latin.]
An example; an illustrative or moralizing story.

exempt /ɪɡˈzɛm(p)t, ɛɡ-/ *adjective & noun*. **LME.**
[**ORIGIN** Latin *exemptus* pa. pple of *eximere* take out, deliver, free, formed as **EX-**[1] 1 + *emere* take.]
▸ **A** *adjective*. **1** Not exposed or subject to something unpleasant or inconvenient; not liable to a charge, tax, etc. (Foll. by *from*, †*of*.) **LME.** ▸**b** Free *from* a defect, weakness, etc. **L16.**

R. C. TRENCH They whom Christ loves are no more exempt than others from their share of earthly trouble and anguish. J. BERGER He is exempt on medical grounds from military service. **b** SHELLEY From custom's evil taint exempt and pure.

2 Independent of, not owing obedience to, a superior authority. Now *hist.* (of religious foundations). (Foll. by *from*.) **LME.** ▸**b** Not subject to influence or control. (Foll. by *from*.) **M17.**

A. P. STANLEY The Primate . . preferred to avoid the question of the exempt jurisdiction of Westminster. **b** GLADSTONE There is no European country in which ecclesiastical societies are exempt from civic control.

▸ **B** *noun*. **1** *ECCLESIASTICAL*. A person or establishment not subject to episcopal jurisdiction. *obsolete* exc. *hist.* **M16.**
†**2** An inferior cavalry officer in the French army who commanded in the absence of the captain and lieutenant and was exempt from ordinary military duty. **L17–E19.**
3 A French police officer. *obsolete* exc. *hist.* **L17.**
4 = **EXON** *noun*[1]. **E18.**
5 An exempted person; *esp.* one not liable to payment of tax or military service etc. **M19.**

exempt /ɪɡˈzɛm(p)t, ɛɡ-/ *verb trans*. Pa. pple **-ed**, (*arch.*) **exempt**. **LME.**
[**ORIGIN** formed as **EXEMPT** *adjective & noun*, orig. in pa. ppl form: see **-ED**[1].]
1 Grant immunity or freedom from or *from* a liability to which others are subject. **LME.**

J. A. FROUDE Clergy who committed felony were no longer exempted from the penalties of their crimes. R. D. LAING I was exempted from military service because of asthma. S. UNWIN My . . campaign to exempt books from Customs Clearance Charges.

2 Take or put away; remove, cut off; single out. (Foll. by *from*, *out of*.) Now *rare* or *obsolete*. **LME.**
†**3** Debar, exclude, *from*. **LME–L17.**
†**4** Omit from a category or enumeration; except. (Foll. by *from*, *out of*.) **LME–M18.**
■ **exemptible** *adjective* **E17.**

exemptile /ɪɡˈzɛm(p)tɪl, ɛɡ-/ *adjective*. Now *rare*. **E17.**
[**ORIGIN** Late Latin *exemptilis*, from *eximere*: see **EXEMPT** *adjective & noun*, **-IL**, **-ILE**.]
Removable.

exemption /ɪɡˈzɛm(p)ʃ(ə)n, ɛɡ-/ *noun*. **LME.**
[**ORIGIN** Old French & mod. French, or Latin *exemptio(n-)*, from *exempt-* pa. ppl stem of *eximere*: see **EXEMPT** *adjective & noun*, **-ION**.]
1 The action of exempting or the state of being exempted from something unpleasant or inconvenient; (granting of) immunity. **LME.** ▸**b** *ECCLESIASTICAL*. Freedom from control by one's normal superior, usu. the bishop of the diocese, and immediate subjection to either the superior of one's religious house or order, or the Pope. **LME.** ▸**c** Freedom from a defect or weakness. **M17.**
†**2** Removal; exception, exclusion. **M16–L17.**

exencephaly /ɛksɛnˈsɛf(ə)li, -ˈkɛf-/ *noun*. Also in mod. Latin form **-cephalia** /-sɪˈfeɪlɪə, -kɛ-/. **E20.**
[**ORIGIN** from **EX-**[2] + Greek *egkephalos* brain + **-Y**[3], **-IA**[1].]
A condition in which part of the brain protrudes through the skull.
■ **exenceˈphalic** *adjective* **E20.**

exenterate /ɪkˈsɛntəreɪt, ɛk-/ *verb trans*. **E17.**
[**ORIGIN** Latin *exenterat-* pa. ppl stem of *exenterare*, after Greek *exenterizein*, formed as **EX-**[2] + *enteron* intestine: see **-ATE**[3].]
Remove the contents of (part of the body, esp. the orbit); remove (an eyeball). Orig., disembowel.
■ **exenteˈration** *noun* **M17.**

exequatur /ɛksɪˈkweɪtə/ *noun*. **E17.**
[**ORIGIN** Latin, 3rd person sing. pres. subjunct. of *exequi* (see **EXECUTE**) = let him or her perform.]
1 *ROMAN CATHOLIC CHURCH*. A government's authorization for a bishop to exercise his office in its territory, or for any papal enactment to take effect there; a claim by a government that such authorization is required or can be withheld. **E17.**
2 An official recognition of a consul by a foreign government, authorizing him or her to exercise office. **L18.**

exequial /ɪkˈsiːkwɪəl, ɛk-/ *adjective*. **E17.**
[**ORIGIN** Latin *exsequialis*, from *exsequiae*: see **EXEQUY**, **-IAL**.]
Of or pertaining to a funeral.

exequy /ˈɛksɪkwi/ *noun*. Orig. †**exequies** (as *sing.*). **LME.**
[**ORIGIN** Old French *exequies*, from Latin accus. *exsequias* (nom. *-iae*) funeral procession or ceremonies, from *exsequi* follow after, accompany: see **EXECUTE**.]
1 In *pl.* & †*sing.* Funeral rites; a funeral ceremony. **LME.**
2 A funeral ode. *poet.* **L19.**

†**exerce** *verb*. Chiefly *Scot*. **LME.**
[**ORIGIN** Old French & mod. French *exercer* from Latin *exercere*: see **EXERCISE** *noun*.]
1 *verb trans*. Carry out or perform (a deed etc.); fulfil (a duty), exercise (a right or office); exert, wield, (justice, power, etc.). **LME–L18.**
2 *verb trans. & intrans*. Keep (a person) busy, engage the attention (of); train, discipline. **LME–L16.**
3 *verb trans*. Display, exhibit, (an emotion or quality). Only in **16.**

†**exercent** *adjective*. **M17–E18.**
[**ORIGIN** Latin *exercent-* pres. ppl stem of *exercere*: see **EXERCISE** *noun*.]
Exercising the duties of or practising one's profession or position, esp. that of an advocate.

exercise /ˈɛksəsʌɪz/ *noun*. **ME.**
[**ORIGIN** Old French & mod. French *exercice* from Latin *exercitium*, from *exercere* keep busy, practise, formed as **EX-**[1] 1 + *arcere* keep in, keep away.]
1 The employment or application of an organ, faculty, right, etc.; the exertion *of* influence or power; the practice *of* a virtue, function, profession, etc. **ME.** ▸†**b** The (method of) use *of* a weapon. **LME–L17.**

R. G. COLLINGWOOD Reconstructed historically, often not without the exercise of considerable historical skill. *New York Times* The exercise of the right of self-determination cannot be denied.

2 Practice for the sake of physical, mental, or spiritual training or improvement. **ME.** ▸**b** Disciplinary suffering; a trying experience; a state of distress or anxiety; a painful mental struggle. Now *rare*. **LME.** ▸†**c** Acquired skill. *rare* (Shakes.). Only in **E17.**
3 †**a** The action or an act of training or drilling troops, scholars, etc. **LME–E19.** ▸**b** A military drill or parade; in *pl.*, military training, athletics, etc. **M16.**
4 Exertion of the muscles, limbs, etc., esp. for the sake of strength or health. **LME.**

A. E. T. WATSON These horses have their own boys, who ride at exercise. JO GRIMOND She was much given to exercise, in her younger days chiefly golf, later long walks.

5 A task set or performed for training the body or mind, or as a test of proficiency, esp. in some particular skill. **M16.** ▸**b** A dissertation, composition, etc., submitted for a degree; a disputation, a viva voce. **M16.** ▸**c** Something written by a pupil; something designed to afford practice to a learner. **E17.** ▸**d** Any written composition; an essay, a sermon, a treatise. **E18.** ▸**e** In *pl.* Formal acts or ceremonies on some special occasion, esp. the conferment of a degree. *N. Amer.* **M19.**

P. G. WODEHOUSE Kirk . . was engaged on his daily sparring exercise with Steve Dingle. S. LEWIS He stood on the sleeping-porch and did his day's exercises. M. GIROUARD His stone-faced stables are an elaborate and convincing exercise in neo-Palladianism. *Times Educ. Suppl.* The damage limitation exercise meant that plans . . were put on ice. **c** E. BLISHEN If I gave the class an exercise he rarely got beyond writing the date.

†**6** A habitual occupation; a customary practice. **M16–M18.**
7 A religious observance or act of worship; a sermon; an act of preaching or prophesying. **M16.** ▸**b** The discussion

E

of a passage of Scripture; a meeting of a Presbytery for such a discussion; a Presbytery. *Scot.* **L16.** ▸**c** The practice and performance of religious ceremonies, worship, etc; the right to this. **M17.**

– PHRASES: ***five-finger exercise***. ***manual exercise***: see MANUAL *adjective*. **the object of the exercise** the essential purpose of an action or procedure.

– COMB.: **exercise book** a notebook in which to do school exercises; a book containing set exercises; **exercise bicycle**, (*colloq.*) **exercise bike** a stationary apparatus used for exercise, in which a person can sit and pedal against resistance, like a cyclist; **exercise price** *STOCK EXCHANGE* the price per share at which the owner of a traded option is entitled to buy or sell the underlying security; **exercise yard** an enclosed area used for physical exercise.

exercise /ˈɛksəsʌɪz/ *verb*. **LME.**
[ORIGIN from the noun.]
▸**I** *verb trans.* **1** Employ, put to practical effect, (a faculty, skill, right, etc.); exert, wield, (force, influence, justice, etc.); practise acts of (cruelty, duplicity, etc.); have (an effect). **LME.**

W. S. MAUGHAM He exercised great ingenuity in disguising old sets so that they looked new. G. F. KENNAN Kerensky's final defeat exercised a highly divisive effect on Western opinion. R. LYND Garrick and Kean exercise a spell on us.

2 Keep (a person) occupied or busy. Now only *refl.* & in *pass.* **LME.** ▸†**b** Till (the ground). **LME–L17.** ▸†**c** Use (an instrument or remedy); work (an animal). **E16–M18.**

J. P. MAHAFFY He and his fellows were all exercised as jurymen in deciding political and social disputes.

3 Train (a person) by practice; drill (soldiers); exert (the body, muscles, etc.) for the sake of strength or health; cause (an animal) to do this. Also, subject to ascetic discipline. **LME.** ▸†**b** Accustom, inure. **M16–E17.** ▸**c** Practise the use or deployment of (a weapon). **E18.**

G. B. SHAW I, with a bigger body to exercise and quite as much energy, must loaf and loll.

†**4** Perform, carry out, esp. habitually; take part in (an action, game, ceremony, religious service); play (a part); practise (a religion). **LME–E19.** ▸**b** Pursue or ply (an occupation or trade); practise (an art, language, etc.); carry out the functions of (an office). **LME–L18.**
5 Tax the powers of; engage the attention of; *esp.* vex, worry. **M16.**

C. RYCROFT Dreams are a continuation in sleep of thoughts which were exercising the sleeper while he was awake. ANTHONY SMITH Poe was much exercised by this thought.

▸**II** *verb intrans.* †**6** Perform or practise one's occupation (*on*); discourse *on* a subject. **E16–E18.**
7 Conduct or engage in a religious exercise or service; interpret Scripture. *obsolete* exc. *Scot.* **M16.**
8 Take exercise; go through exercises for practice; (of a soldier) drill. **E17.**

JONATHAN MILLER When you start to exercise, your heart automatically speeds up.

■ **exercisable** *adjective* able to be exercised, employed, or enforced **M18.** **exerciser** *noun* a person who or thing which exercises; *esp.* an apparatus for use in exercising the limbs etc.: **M16.**

exercitant /ɪɡˈzəːsɪtənt, ɛɡ-/ *noun*. **M19.**
[ORIGIN French from Latin *exercitant-* pres. ppl stem of *exercitare*: see EXERCITATION, -ANT¹.]
A person engaged in spiritual exercises.

exercitation /ɪɡˌzəːsɪˈteɪʃ(ə)n, ɛɡ-/ *noun*. **LME.**
[ORIGIN Latin *exercitatio(n-)*, from *exercitat-* pa. ppl stem of *exercitare* frequentative of *exercere*: see EXERCISE *noun*, -ATION.]
†**1** (Any particular form of) physical exercise. **LME–M17.**
2 The action or an act of exercising a faculty, skill, power, etc. **LME.** ▸**b** A display of (esp. literary or oratorical) skill; an essay, a composition. **M17.**
3 The action or an act of training by practice; a task undertaken for this purpose, an exercise. **L15.**
†**4** The practising of a trade; the habitual performance of actions. **L16–M17.**
5 (An act of) worship or religious observance. **M17.**

exercitor /ɪɡˈzəːsɪtə, ɛɡ-/ *noun*. **L17.**
[ORIGIN Latin, from *exercit-* pa. ppl stem of *exercere*: see -OR.]
ROMAN & SCOTS LAW (now *hist.*). A person to whom the daily profits of a ship belonged; a person who conducted a shipping business.
■ **exerciˈtorian** *adjective* **M19.**

Exercycle /ˈɛksəsʌɪk(ə)l/ *noun*. Orig. *US*. Also **e-**. **M20.**
[ORIGIN from EXER(CISE *noun* + BI)CYCLE *noun*.]
(Proprietary name for) an exercise bicycle.

exergonic /ɛksəːˈɡɒnɪk/ *adjective*. **M20.**
[ORIGIN from EX-² + Greek *ergon* work + -IC.]
SCIENCE. Accompanied by the release of energy.

exergue /ɪkˈsəːɡ, ɛkˈsəːɡ, ˈɛksəːɡ/ *noun*. **L17.**
[ORIGIN French from medieval Latin *exergum*, from Greek EX-² + *ergon* work.]
NUMISMATICS. A small space on a coin or medal, usu. on the reverse below the principal device, for the date, the engraver's initials, etc.; the inscription placed there.
■ **exergual** /-ɡ(ə)l/ *adjective* **M19.**

exergy /ˈɛksədʒi/ *noun*. **M20.**
[ORIGIN from EX-² after *energy*.]
PHYSICS & CHEMISTRY. The maximum amount of work that can be obtained from a process, or from a system by reversible processes.

exert /ɪɡˈzəːt, ɛɡ-/ *verb*. **M17.**
[ORIGIN Latin *ex(s)ert-* pa. ppl stem of *ex(s)erere* put forth, formed as EX-¹ 1 + *serere* bind, entwine, join. Cf. EXSERT.]
†**1** *verb trans.* Perform, practise, (an action or operation). **M17–M18.**
2 *verb trans.* Push out or up; discharge (a seed); emit (light). *obsolete* exc. *BOTANY*. **M17.**
†**3** *verb trans.* Bring to light, reveal. **L17–M18.**
4 *verb trans.* Exercise, apply, bring to bear, (a quality, force, etc.), esp. with considerable effort or effect. **L17.**

R. HAYMAN The teacher who probably exerted the most direct personal influence on him. M. SARTON It was finally hunger that exerted enough pressure to get Laura up.

5 *verb refl.* & †*intrans.* Use efforts or endeavours, strive, (*to do*; *for* a thing). **M18.**

M. SPARK He had a sense of having exerted himself a great deal.

■ **exertive** *adjective* tending to exert **M19.** †**exertment** *noun* (*rare*) the action or an act of exerting **L17–M19.**

exertion /ɪɡˈzəːʃ(ə)n, ɛɡ-/ *noun*. **M17.**
[ORIGIN from EXERT + -ION.]
†**1** The action or an act of displaying; (a) manifestation. **M17–L18.**

J. AUSTEN An exertion of spirits which increased with her increase of emotion.

2 The action or an act of exerting something, esp. a faculty, power, etc. (Foll. by *of*.) **L17.**
3 The action or an act of exerting oneself (physically or mentally); (an) effort; vigorous action. **L18.**

D. L. SAYERS She has, by her own exertions, made herself independent. N. MAILER The Filipinos jogged and panted from their exertion.

exes /ˈɛksɪz/ *noun pl. colloq.* **M19.**
[ORIGIN Abbreviation.]
Expenses.

†**exestuation** *noun* var. of EXAESTUATION.

Exeter /ˈɛksɪtə/ *noun*. **L18.**
[ORIGIN A city in SW England.]
1 ***Exeter carpet***, a type of rare hand-knotted carpet made in Exeter in the 18th cent. **L18.**
2 ***Exeter Hall***, a type of evangelicalism represented by gatherings which took place in a former building of this name in the Strand, London. **M19.**

exeunt /ˈɛksɪʌnt/ *verb intrans.* (*defective*). **L15.**
[ORIGIN Latin, 3rd person pl. pres. indic. of *exire*: see EXIT *verb*¹.]
A stage direction: (actors, or the characters whose names follow) leave the stage. Cf. EXIT *verb*¹.
exeunt omnes /ˈɒmniːz/ all leave the stage.

ex facie /ɛks ˈfeɪʃi/ *adverbial phr.* **M19.**
[ORIGIN from Latin *ex* out of + *facie* abl. of *facies* FACE *noun*.]
SCOTS LAW. On the face (of a document); so far as appears from a document.

exfiltrate /ˈɛksfɪltreɪt/ *verb trans. & intrans.* **L20.**
[ORIGIN Back-form. from EXFILTRATION.]
MILITARY. Remove (personnel or units) from behind enemy lines; covertly withdraw (an agent) from a dangerous position.

exfiltration /ɛksfɪlˈtreɪʃ(ə)n/ *noun*. **L19.**
[ORIGIN from EX-¹ 1 + FILTRATION; in sense 2 perh. after *infiltration*.]
1 The action or process of filtering or seeping out. *rare*. **L19.**
2 *MILITARY*. The action of exfiltrating. **M20.**

exflagellation /ˌɛksfladʒəˈleɪʃ(ə)n/ *noun*. **E20.**
[ORIGIN from EX-¹ 1 + FLAGELLATION.]
ZOOLOGY. The formation or shedding of flagella; the development of microgametes resembling flagella.
■ **exˈflagellate** *verb intrans.* undergo exflagellation **E20.**

exfoliate /ɪksˈfəʊlɪeɪt, ɛks-/ *verb*. **M17.**
[ORIGIN Late Latin *exfoliat-* pa. ppl stem of *exfoliare* strip of leaves, from Latin EX-¹ 1 + *folium* leaf: see -ATE³.]
1 *verb trans.* Cast off, shed, (the cuticle, the surface of a bone, etc.) in the form of thin layers or scales; *SURGERY* remove the surface of (a bone etc.) in this form. **M17.**
2 *verb intrans.* Of bone, skin, a mineral, etc.: separate or come off in thin layers or scales. Of a tree: throw off layers of bark. **L17.**
3 *verb trans. & intrans.* Unfold, develop. **E19.**

F. C. L. WRAXALL Questions exfoliated themselves. *New Yorker* Taking an active part in the exfoliating New York art scene.

4 *verb trans. & intrans.* Remove dead cells from (the skin) with a cosmetic product. **L20.**
■ **exfoliant** *noun & adjective* (designating) a cosmetic product designed to remove dead cells from the surface of the skin **L20.** **exfoliˈation** *noun* (*a*) the action or process of exfoliating; (*b*) a layer or scale produced by this: **L17.** **exfoliative** *noun & adjective* (*a*) *noun* (*rare*) something which produces exfoliation; (*b*) *adjective* causing or promoting exfoliation; involving or marked by exfoliation: **L17.**

ex gratia /ɛks ˈɡreɪʃə/ *adverbial & adjectival phr.* **M18.**
[ORIGIN Latin, from *ex* from + *gratia* GRACE *noun*.]
(Done, given, etc.) as a favour or without (esp. legal) compulsion.

exhalation /ɛksəˈleɪʃ(ə)n/ *noun*. **LME.**
[ORIGIN Latin *exhalatio(n-)*, from *exhalat-* pa. ppl stem of *exhalare* EXHALE *verb*¹: see -ATION.]
1 The action or an act of exhaling. **LME.**
2 *sing.* & in *pl.* Something which is exhaled; a mist, a vapour; an effluvium, a scent. **LME.**

S. O'FAOLÁIN The damp . . rose in curling exhalations from the pavements.

3 A body of (usu. ignited) vapour; a meteor. *arch.* **M16.**
4 *GEOLOGY*. An emission of volcanic or magmatic gases into the atmosphere. **E20.**
■ **exhalative** /ɛksˈhalətɪv, ɪks-/ *adjective* pertaining to exhalation **L16.** **exhalatory** /ɛksˈhalət(ə)ri, ɪks-/ *adjective* exhalative **E19.**

exhale /ɪksˈheɪl, ɛks-/ *verb*¹. **LME.**
[ORIGIN Old French & mod. French *exhaler* from Latin *exhalare*, formed as EX-¹ 1 + *halare* breathe.]
1 *verb intrans.* Be given off as vapour, evaporate. (Foll. by *from*.) **LME.**

R. W. EMERSON When flowers reach their ripeness, incense exhales from them.

2 *verb intrans.* & (in *pass.*) *verb trans.* Of blood etc.: pass or be passed slowly and in minute quantities through tissue. Now *rare*. **LME.**
3 *verb trans.* Draw up or drive off in the form of vapour; cause to evaporate. **L16.**

SIR W. SCOTT Bitumen and sulphur, which the burning sun exhaled from the waters of the lake.

4 *verb trans.* Expel from within by breathing; breathe out (life, words, a prayer, etc.). **L16.**

H. JAMES She exhaled a moan of relief. A. GRAY Tilting her head back to exhale smoke from her nostrils.

5 *verb trans.* Give off or send up (vapour, fumes, etc.) from the surface; give off like a vapour. **L16.**

J. CONRAD His whole person exhaled a charm. G. GREENE A white handkerchief . . exhaled as . . sweet an odour as a whole altar of lilies.

6 *verb trans.* Give vent to (anger, enthusiasm, etc.); dissipate (strong emotion). *arch.* **M18.**
7 *verb intrans.* Make an expiration, breathe out. **M19.**
■ **exhalable** *adjective* **L17.** **exhalant** *noun & adjective* †(*a*) *noun* an exhalant vessel or organ; (*b*) *adjective* that exhales; conveying blood etc. in minute quantities: **L18.** **exhalement** *noun* (an) exhalation **M17.**

†**exhale** *verb*². **L16.**
[ORIGIN from EX-¹ 1 + HALE *verb*¹.]
1 *verb trans. & intrans.* Draw (a thing) out of something, *spec.* (the sword) from the scabbard; drag (a person) away. **L16–E17.**
2 *verb trans.* Cause (blood, tears, etc.) to flow (*from*). **L16–E17.**
3 *verb trans.* Raise (a person) to a higher position; exalt. **L16–M17.**

exhaust /ɪɡˈzɔːst, ɛɡ-/ *noun*. **M19.**
[ORIGIN from EXHAUST *verb*.]
1 The exit or expulsion from an engine of steam, gas, or other motive fluid that has done its work of propulsion; the fluid so expelled; the pipework etc. through which this occurs, *esp.* the exhaust pipe of a motor vehicle. **M19.**

N. CALDER Lead injected into the air by car exhausts. J. COLVILLE The exhaust of our fighters streaked the blue sky with white lines.

2 (An apparatus for) the production of an outward current of air by creating a partial vacuum. **M19.**
– COMB.: ***exhaust manifold***: see MANIFOLD *noun* 5; **exhaust pipe**: by which gaseous combustion products are expelled from an engine into the air.

†**exhaust** *adjective*. **E16–E18.**
[ORIGIN Latin *exhaustus* pa. pple of *exhaurire*: see EXHAUST *verb*.]
Exhausted.

exhaust /ɪɡˈzɔːst/ *verb*. Pa. pple **exhausted**, †**exhaust**. **M16.**
[ORIGIN Latin *exhaust-* pa. ppl stem of *exhaurire*, formed as EX-¹ 1 + *haurire* draw (water), drain.]
1 *verb trans.* Draw out (air or other gas). Formerly, draw (anything) off or out (*lit.* & *fig.*). **M16.** ▸†**b** Take a draught of; drink or suck up. **L16–L17.**

G. BIRD Exhaust the air from beneath the bladder. M. EARBERY These things we have exhausted from the sacred Scriptures.

2 *verb trans.* Use up or consume completely; account for the whole of. **M16.**

J. S. MILL A sufficient number of drawings to exhaust all the possible combinations. A. BEVAN As time went on the iron ore was exhausted. J. CHEEVER The father's replies were short-tempered . . . His patience was exhausted.

3 *verb trans.* Empty by drawing the contents off or out; drain; empty *of* (specified contents). **E17.**

LD RUTHERFORD Sealed in an exhausted tube of hard glass.

4 *verb trans.* Drain (a person, country, etc.) of strength or resources, or (a soil) of nutritive ingredients; tire out. Freq. as ***exhausted***, ***exhausting*** *ppl adjectives* **M17.**

W. STUBBS The Thirty Years' War exhausted Germany. O. MANNING Harriet, suddenly exhausted, wished she were in bed.

5 *verb trans.* Draw out all that is essential or interesting in (an object of investigation or exposition); treat or study (a subject) so as to leave nothing further to be explained or discovered. **E18.**

A. NEWMAN They had quickly exhausted the . . topic.

6 *verb intrans.* Of steam: escape from an engine as exhaust. **M19.**

7 *verb intrans.* Of an engine or vehicle: discharge its exhaust (*into* etc.). **E20.**

Scientific American The Lockheed L1011 tail engine exhausts through the end of the fuselage.

■ **exhaustedly** *adverb* in an exhausted manner **M19.** **exhaustedness** *noun* exhausted state or condition **M19.** **exhauster** *noun* a person who or thing which exhausts; *esp.* a device for removing air or gas: **M18.** **exhausti'bility** *noun* the quality of being exhaustible **M19.** **exhaustible** *adjective* able to be exhausted **M17.** **exhaustingly** *adverb* in an exhausting manner **L19.** **exhaustless** *adjective* (*literary*) incapable of being exhausted, inexhaustible **E18.** †**exhaustment** *noun* (*rare*) the action or an act of exhausting something, esp. resources; the state of being exhausted: **E17–M19.** †**exhausture** *noun* the action of exhausting something; state of being exhausted; an instance of this: **L16–L18.**

exhaustion /ɪɡˈzɔːstʃ(ə)n, ɛɡ-/ *noun.* **E17.**
[ORIGIN Late Latin *exhaustio(n-)*, from Latin *exhaust-*: see EXHAUST *verb*, -ION.]

1 The action of draining something of a resource or emptying it of contents; the state of being so depleted or emptied. **E17.**

H. DAVY When cattle are fed upon land not benefited by their manure, the effect is always an exhaustion of the soil. *Nature* In the next tube the exhaustion has been carried further.

2 Total loss of strength or vitality in a person. **M17.**

A. KOESTLER Dance himself into a frenzy followed by exhaustion.

3 The removal or extraction *of* air from a vessel. **M17.**

4 The process or an act of establishing a conclusion by eliminating alternatives. (Earliest in ***method of exhaustions*** below.) **L17.**

method of exhaustions MATH. a way of proving the equality of two magnitudes by demonstrating the contradiction which occurs if one is greater or less than the other.

5 The action or process of consuming something or using it up completely. **M19.**

exhaustive /ɪɡˈzɔːstɪv, ɛɡ-/ *adjective.* **L18.**
[ORIGIN from EXHAUST *verb* + -IVE.]

1 Tending to exhaust a subject; leaving no part unexamined or unconsidered; thorough, complete, comprehensive. **L18.**

GLADSTONE I shall attempt in this limited work no exhaustive survey. L. GOULD She had made an exhaustive New York psychiatrist list.

2 Tending to drain of strength, energy, or resources; exhausting. **E19.**

M. KEANE Her day of exhaustive detective work.

■ **exhaustively** *adverb* **E19.** **exhaustiveness** *noun* **E19.**

exhedra *noun* var. of EXEDRA.

exheredate /ɪksˈhɛrɪdeɪt, ɛks-/ *verb trans.* Now *rare* exc. *Scot.* **M16.**
[ORIGIN Latin *exheredat-* pa. ppl stem of *exheredare*, formed as EX-[1] 1 + *hered-*, *heres* heir: see -ATE[3].]

Disinherit.

exheredation /ˌɛkshɛrɪˈdeɪʃ(ə)n/ *noun.* **LME.**
[ORIGIN Latin *exheredatio(n-)*, formed as EXHEREDATE: see -ATION. Cf. EXHEREDITATION.]

Disinheritance; an instance of this.

exhereditation /ˌɛkshɛrɛdɪˈteɪʃ(ə)n/ *noun. rare.* **L16.**
[ORIGIN Latin *exhereditat-* pa. ppl stem of *exhereditare*, from *exheredare*: see EXHEREDATE, -ATION.]

= EXHEREDATION.

exhibit /ɪɡˈzɪbɪt, ɛɡ-/ *noun.* **E17.**
[ORIGIN Latin *exhibitum* neut. sing. of pa. pple of *exhibere*: see EXHIBIT *verb*.]

1 a LAW. A document or object produced in a court as evidence or referred to and annexed to an affidavit. Formerly also, a document certified as having been attested by a witness. **E17.** ▸**b** A detailed and formal statement of particulars, esp. of debts, liabilities, etc. **E18.**

exhibit A the first exhibit in a case; *fig.* something regarded as evidence or the most important evidence.

2 In *pl.* The letters of orders and other documents which a beneficed or licensed Anglican priest may be required to produce at the first visitation after his admission; the fees payable on presenting these. **E17.**

3 A showing, a display; a production in evidence. **M17.** ▸**b** = EXHIBITION 6. *N. Amer.* **L19.**

Times The power to compel an exhibit of books of account. **b** S. BELLOW An exhibit of his pictures at a women's club.

4 An item on display in an exhibition, museum, etc.; the collection of items sent by any one contributor. **M19.**

J. BARNES Two exhibits in a side cabinet are easy to miss.

exhibit /ɪɡˈzɪbɪt, ɛɡ-/ *verb.* Pa. pple **-ited**, †**-it.** **LME.**
[ORIGIN Latin *exhibit-* pa. ppl stem of *exhibere*, formed as EX-[1] 1 + *habere* to hold.]

▸ **I** Show.

1 *verb trans.* Hold out or submit (a document) for inspection, esp. as evidence in a court of law. **LME.**

2 *verb trans.* Submit for consideration; present, prefer, (a petition, accusation, etc.). **LME.**

3 a *verb trans.* Manifest to the senses, esp. sight; present to view. **E16.** ▸†**b** *verb intrans.* Of a thing: reveal itself, be manifest. **M17–M18.**

a J. TYNDALL The lake . . exhibits the colour of pure water. G. ORWELL Big Brother is the guise in which the Party chooses to exhibit itself to the world. B. BAINBRIDGE These remarks seemed perfectly genuine, as really exhibiting the state of his mind.

4 *verb trans.* Set out in words or figures, detail. Now *rare.* **M16.**

5 *verb trans. & intrans.* Show (an item) publicly for entertainment, instruction, or in a competition; have (an item) on show in an exhibition. **E18.**

G. GISSING He exhibited one picture only. *Listener* There are twice as many nations exhibiting.

6 *verb trans.* Represent by a figure, drawing, etc. **L18.** ▸**b** Present a delineation or embodiment of in words or in actions. **M19.**

J. NICHOLSON One of these branches is exhibited in the figure. **b** LD MACAULAY In the power of exhibiting character by means of dialogue he was deficient.

7 *verb trans.* Indicate the presence of; give evidence of. **L18.**

O. HENRY He exhibited no signs of flinching. P. G. WODEHOUSE His employer had exhibited a disquieting disposition to blame him for everything.

▸ **II** Offer, administer.

†**8** *verb trans.* Offer, present, (sacrifice, praise, etc.); administer (an oath). **L15–M17.**

†**9** *verb trans.* Provide, grant, (*to*); defray (expense). **L15–M17.**

†**10** *verb intrans. & (rare) trans.* Provide maintenance *to* a student; support, maintain. **E17–M19.**

11 *verb trans.* Administer (medicine, a drug). Now *rare.* **E17.**

■ **exhibitable** *adjective* **M19.** **exhibitant** *noun* †(**a**) a person who preferred or presented an accusation; (**b**) *gen.* a person who exhibits something: **L17.** **exhibiter** *noun* (now *rare*) = EXHIBITOR **L16.** **exhibitor** *noun* a person who exhibits something, esp. in a show or exhibition **M17.**

exhibition /ɛksɪˈbɪʃ(ə)n/ *noun.* **LME.**
[ORIGIN Old French & mod. French from late Latin *exhibitio(n-)*, formed as EXHIBIT *verb*: see -ION.]

▸ **I** Provision.

†**1** Maintenance, support. **LME–E18.**

J. STRYPE To bestow £8 . . towards the use and exhibition of three grammar scholars.

†**2 a** *sing.* & in *pl.* An allowance of money for a person's support; a pension; a salary. **L15–M18.** ▸**b** A gift, a present. **L16–E17.**

a SWIFT He . . is driven to live in exile upon a small exhibition. **b** SHAKES. *Oth.* I would not do such a thing for . . petticoats, nor caps, nor any petty exhibition.

3 †**a** Financial assistance given to a student. Only in **16.** ▸**b** A monetary award given to a student for a fixed period from the funds of a school, college, etc., usu. after a competitive examination. **M17.**

b H. CARPENTER He also managed to win an Exhibition . . in Natural Science to Christ Church.

4 The administration of a medicine, drug, etc. Now *rare* or *obsolete.* **L18.**

▸ **II** Showing, a show.

5 The action or an act of exhibiting; manifestation; (a) visible show or display (of a feeling, quality, etc.). **L17.**

A. B. JAMESON Dunstan never would have dared such an exhibition of presumption. P. G. WODEHOUSE The exhibition of his virtues and the careful suppression of his defects. *attrib.*: A. CHRISTIE I do a couple of exhibition dances . . with Raymond . . he's the tennis and dancing pro.

make an exhibition of oneself behave in so ostentatious or conspicuous a manner as to appear ridiculous or contemptible.

6 A public display of items to give pleasure or instruction, or as a competition. **M18.** ▸**b** A public examination or display of the attainments of students. *US.* **L18.**

N. SHUTE An exhibition of Australian religious paintings at the National Gallery. *attrib.*: *New Yorker* Sumptuous exhibition catalogues proclaim their status as ideal gifts.

7 Something that is exhibited; a sight, a spectacle. Now *rare.* **L18.**

8 *N. Amer.* SPORT. A game whose outcome does not affect a team's standings, esp. one played before the start of a regular season. Usu. *attrib.* **M19.**

■ **exhibitional** *adjective* **M19.** **exhibitioner** *noun* †(**a**) *rare* a person who paid for another's maintenance; (**b**) a student who has been awarded an exhibition; (**c**) an exhibitor: **L16.**

exhibitionism /ɛksɪˈbɪʃ(ə)nɪz(ə)m/ *noun.* **L19.**
[ORIGIN from EXHIBITION + -ISM.]

1 (A psychosexual disorder characterized by) exposure of the genitals to strangers. **L19.**

2 A tendency towards display or extravagant behaviour. **E20.**

exhibitionist /ɛksɪˈbɪʃ(ə)nɪst/ *noun & adjective.* **E19.**
[ORIGIN formed as EXHIBITIONISM + -IST.]

▸ **A** *noun.* **1** A person who takes part in an exhibition or public performance. *rare.* **E19.**

2 A person who indulges in exhibitionism. **L19.**

▸ **B** *attrib.* or as *adjective.* Of, pertaining to, or displaying exhibitionism. **E20.**

■ **exhibitio'nistic** *adjective* characterized by or given to exhibitionism **M20.** **exhibitio'nistically** *adverb* **E20.**

E

exhibitive /ɪɡˈzɪbɪtɪv, ɛɡ-/ *adjective.* **L16.**
[ORIGIN mod. Latin *exhibitivus*, from Latin *exhibit-*: see EXHIBIT *verb*, -IVE.]

1 Having the property of exhibiting or showing; illustrative. (Foll. by *of*.) **L16.**

†**2** Having the function of imparting or communicating. (Foll. by *of*.) Only in **17.**

■ **exhibitively** *adverb* **E17.**

exhibitory /ɪɡˈzɪbɪt(ə)ri, ɛɡ-/ *noun & adjective.* **E17.**
[ORIGIN Late Latin *exhibitorius*, formed as EXHIBIT *verb*: see -ORY[1], -ORY[2].]

▸ †**A** *noun.* A procedure relating to the administration of a medicine, drug, etc. *rare.* Only in **E17.**

▸ **B** *adjective.* Intended to exhibit or to cause to be exhibited; of or pertaining to exhibition. **L18.**

exhilarant /ɪɡˈzɪlər(ə)nt, ɛɡ-/ *noun & adjective.* **E19.**
[ORIGIN French from Latin *exhilarant-* pres. ppl stem of *exhilarare*: see EXHILARATE, -ANT[1].]

▸ **A** *noun.* A medicine, drug, etc., that promotes exhilaration; a stimulant, a euphoriant. Now *rare.* **E19.**

▸ **B** *adjective.* That exhilarates; exhilarating. **M19.**

exhilarate /ɪɡˈzɪləreɪt, ɛɡ-/ *verb trans.* **M16.**
[ORIGIN Latin *exhilarat-* pa. ppl stem of *exhilarare*, formed as EX-[1] 1 + *hilaris* cheerful: see -ATE[3].]

Make cheerful or merry; enliven, gladden; thrill, invigorate.

DICKENS It seemed greatly to delight and exhilarate him to say so. A. WILSON The exhilarating weather of April with its lively south-east breezes. A. MCCOWEN I was also exhilarated by the sense of power that I felt on the stage.

■ **exhilaratingly** *adverb* in an exhilarating manner **M19.** **exhilarative** *adjective* tending to exhilarate **E19.** **exhilarator** *noun* (*rare*) a person who or thing which exhilarates **E19.**

exhilaration /ɪɡˌzɪləˈreɪʃ(ə)n, ɛɡ-/ *noun.* **E17.**
[ORIGIN Late Latin *exhilaratio(n-)*, formed as EXHILARATE: see -ATION.]

1 The action or means of exhilarating; an exhilarating influence. **E17.**

LONGFELLOW There was . . that wild exhilaration in the air.

2 The condition or feeling of being exhilarated. **E17.**

K. M. E. MURRAY Periods of great depression . . were . . outnumbered by his times of exhilaration.

exhorbitant *adjective & noun* var. of EXORBITANT.

exhort /ɪɡˈzɔːt, ɛɡ-/ *verb & noun.* **LME.**
[ORIGIN Old French & mod. French *exhorter* or Latin *exhortari*, formed as EX-[1] 1 + *hortari* encourage.]

▸ **A** *verb trans.* **1** Admonish earnestly; urge (a person) to praiseworthy conduct (foll. by *to* do, *to* a course of action). **LME.**

LD MACAULAY The people would be exhorted to liberality. P. KAVANAGH The Faithful were exhorted to receive Holy Communion. L. A. G. STRONG The referee was exhorting the pair.

2 Recommend (something) earnestly; insist upon. *arch.* **E16.**

J. A. FROUDE He . . again exhorted a reform.

▸ **B** *noun.* = EXHORTATION. Now *rare* or *obsolete.* **L15.**

■ **exhorter** *noun* a person who exhorts someone or something; *spec.* in some Christian Churches, a person appointed to give religious exhortation under the direction of a minister: **M16.**

exhortation /ɪɡzɔːˈteɪʃ(ə)n, ɛɡ-/ *noun.* **LME.**
[ORIGIN Old French & mod. French, or Latin *exhortatio(n-)*, from *exhortat-* pa. ppl stem of *exhortari*: see EXHORT, -ATION.]

1 The action or an act of exhorting. **LME.**

M. SPARK Exhortations to Freddy . . to come home from heathen posts to Christian Harrogate. R. F. HOBSON Punishment and exhortation had no effect and psychiatric help was sought.

2 A set speech delivered for the purpose of exhorting; *esp.* a formal or liturgical address. **LME.**

■ **exhortational** *adjective* **L20.**

exhortative /ɪɡˈzɔːtətɪv, ɛɡ-/ *adjective.* **LME.**
[ORIGIN Latin *exhortativus*, from *exhortat-*: see EXHORTATION, -IVE.]

= EXHORTATORY.

exhortatory /ɪɡˈzɔːtət(ə)ri, ɛɡ-/ *adjective*. LME.
[ORIGIN Late Latin *exhortatorius*, from Latin *exhortat-*: see EXHORTATION, -ORY².]
Of, pertaining to, or containing exhortation; intended to exhort.

exhumate /ɛksˈ(h)juːmeɪt, ɪɡˈzjuː-/ *verb trans*. Now *rare*. M16.
[ORIGIN medieval Latin *exhumat-*: see EXHUMATION, -ATE³.]
= EXHUME 1.

exhumation /ɛks(h)juːˈmeɪʃ(ə)n, ɪɡzjuː-/ *noun*. LME.
[ORIGIN medieval Latin *exhumatio(n-)*, from *exhumat-* pa. ppl stem of *exhumare*: see EXHUME, -ATION.]
The action or an act of exhuming.
■ ˈ**exhumator** *noun* an exhumer E19.

exhume /ɛksˈ(h)juːm, ɪɡˈzjuːm/ *verb trans*. LME.
[ORIGIN medieval Latin *exhumare*, from Latin EX-¹ 1 + *humus* ground.]
1 Dig out, unearth, (*lit. & fig.*); remove (something buried) from beneath the ground; *esp.* disinter a body with legal permission. LME.
2 GEOLOGY. Expose (a land surface) that was formerly buried. Chiefly as ***exhumed ppl adjective***. L19.
■ **exhumer** *noun* a person who exhumes something M19.

ex hypothesi /ɛks hʌɪˈpɒθəsʌɪ/ *adverbial phr*. E17.
[ORIGIN mod. Latin, from Latin *ex* by + abl. of late Latin HYPOTHESIS.]
According to the hypothesis (made); supposedly.

exies *noun pl.* var. of AIXIES.

exigeant /egziʒɑ̃/ *adjective*. Fem. ***-ante*** /-ɑ̃ːt/. L18.
[ORIGIN French, pres. ppl adjective of *exiger* from Latin *exigere*: see EXACT *adjective & adverb*.]
Exacting, demanding.

M. EDGEWORTH Those *exigeante* mothers who expect always to have possession of a son's arm.

exigence /ˈɛksɪdʒ(ə)ns, ˈɛɡzɪ-/ *noun*. LME.
[ORIGIN Old French & mod. French, or late Latin *exigentia*, from *exigent-*: see EXIGENT *adjective*, -ENCE.]
†**1** = EXIGENCY 1. LME–E19.
2 Urgent need or necessity. L16.

S. SPENDER Political exigence was never a justification for lies.

3 A situation calling for urgent measures; a crisis, an emergency. M17.

M. C. CLARKE Falstaff is equal to any exigence.

exigency /ˈɛksɪdʒ(ə)nsi, ˈɛɡzɪ-; ɪɡˈzɪdʒ(ə)nsi, ɛɡ-/ *noun*. L16.
[ORIGIN Late Latin *exigentia*: see EXIGENCE, -ENCY.]
1 What is demanded by a given situation; a requirement, a need. Now usu. in *pl.* L16.

A. POWELL His system of bookselling was designed to suit his own convenience, rather than the . . exigencies of the trade.

2 (An instance of) urgent need or necessity. In *pl.*, desperate straits. M17.

DRYDEN The Romans in great Exigency, sent for their Dictator from the Plow. ADDISON We . . complain of our want of bullion and must at last be reduced to the greatest exigencies.

3 Pressing or urgent quality; stringency (of requirements). M18.

W. ROBERTSON Such immediate . . assistance as the exigency of her affairs required. S. DONALDSON There had been a special timbre of exigency in Terrel's . . voice.

exigent /ˈɛksɪdʒ(ə)nt, ˈɛɡzɪ-/ *noun*¹. *obsolete* exc. *hist.* Also †**-end**. ME.
[ORIGIN Anglo-Norman *exigende* from medieval Latin *exigenda* neut. pl. of gerundive of Latin *exigere*: see EXACT *adjective & adverb*.]
LAW. A writ instructing a sheriff to summon a defendant to appear and answer the plaintiff, or else be declared an outlaw.

†**exigent** *noun*². LME.
[ORIGIN Old French, formed as EXIGENT *adjective*.]
1 A time or state of pressing need; a critical situation. Also, an end, a climax. LME–E18.
2 In *pl.* Needs, requirements. Only in 17.
3 A required amount. *rare*. Only in M19.

exigent /ˈɛksɪdʒ(ə)nt, ˈɛɡzɪ-/ *adjective*. E17.
[ORIGIN Latin *exigent-* pres. ppl stem of *exigere*: see EXACT *adjective & adverb*, -ENT.]
1 Urgent, pressing. E17.
2 Demanding more (*of* something) than is reasonable; exacting. E19.
■ **exigently** *adverb* L19.

exigenter /ˈɛksɪdʒ(ə)ntə, ˈɛɡz-/ *noun*. *obsolete* exc. *hist.* E16.
[ORIGIN Anglo-Norman, from *exigente*, *exigende*: see EXIGENT *noun*¹, -ER².]
LAW. An officer of the Court of Common Pleas (or, in the 18th and 19th cents., of the Court of King's or Queen's Bench) responsible for making out exigents.

exigible /ˈɛksɪdʒɪb(ə)l, ˈɛɡz-/ *adjective*. E17.
[ORIGIN French, from *exiger* from Latin *exigere*: see EXACT *adjective & adverb*, -IBLE.]
Of a duty, sum of money, etc.: able to be required; due; chargeable.

exiguity /ɛksɪˈɡjuːɪti, ɛɡzɪ-/ *noun*. E17.
[ORIGIN Latin *exiguitas*, from *exiguus*: see EXIGUOUS, -ITY.]
Exiguous quality; scantiness.

exiguous /ɪɡˈzɪɡjʊəs, ɛɡ-/ *adjective*. M17.
[ORIGIN Latin *exiguus*, from *exigere* weigh exactly: see EXACT *adjective & adverb*, -OUS.]
Scanty in size, amount, etc.; extremely small.

S. SASSOON My exiguous diary has preserved a few details of that . . march. J. I. M. STEWART An art-student living . . on some exiguous bursary.

■ **exiguously** *adverb* M20. **exiguousness** *noun* M18.

exilarch /ˈɛksɪlɑːk/ *noun*. L19.
[ORIGIN from EXILE *noun*¹ + -ARCH, translating Aramaic *rēš gālûṯā* chief of the exile.]
Any of the hereditary leaders of the Jewish community in Babylon from the 2nd to about the 10th cent., to whom Jews in other eastern countries paid homage.

exile /ˈɛksʌɪl, ˈɛɡz-/ *noun*¹. ME.
[ORIGIN Old French & mod. French *exil* Latinized alt. of earlier *essil* from Latin *exilium*, from *exul* banished person.]
1 Expulsion from one's own country to live abroad, imposed as a sentence or punishment; penal banishment; residence abroad enforced by law or political power. ME. ▸**b** Prolonged residence in a foreign country, either voluntary or imposed by circumstances; expatriation. LME.

M. M. KAYE You . . will be deposed and sent away to spend the remainder of your life in exile. **b** W. S. CHURCHILL Huguenots . . driven into exile by religious persecution.

b *internal exile*: see INTERNAL *adjective*. *tax exile*: see TAX *noun*. **the Exile** the captivity of the Jews in Babylon in the 6th cent. BC.
†**2** Devastation or wasteful destruction of property. LME–E17.

exile /ˈɛksʌɪl, ˈɛɡz-/ *noun*². ME.
[ORIGIN Prob. from Old French & mod. French *exilé* pa. pple of *exiler* EXILE *verb*, with muting of final syll., as in ASSIGN *noun*, infl. by Latin *exul*.]
1 A person obliged by law or compelled by circumstances to live abroad. Also, a person who does this from choice. ME.

D. ATHILL He was an Egyptian . . and had been living for some years as an exile in Germany.

tax exile: see TAX *noun*.
2 More fully ***exile-tree***, ***exile-oil-plant***. In the Indian subcontinent: a tree, *Thevetia peruviana* (family Apocynaceae), introduced from the W. Indies or tropical America. M19.

exile /ˈɛksʌɪl/ *adjective*. Now *rare* or *obsolete*. LME.
[ORIGIN from Latin *exilis*: see -ILE.]
†**1** Slender, shrunken, thin; diminutive. LME–L17.
2 Scantily endowed; poor; (of soil) meagre, barren. LME.
†**3** Thin in consistency; fine, tenuous, insubstantial. E17–L18.

exile /ˈɛksʌɪl, ˈɛɡz-/ *verb trans*. ME.
[ORIGIN Old French *exil(i)er* (mod. *exiler*) alt. of *essilier* from late Latin *exiliare*, from *exilium* EXILE *noun*¹.]
1 Banish (a person) from his or her native country or (*fig.*) a favourite place, environment, etc. (Foll. by *from*, *to*, †2nd obj.) ME.

J. AUSTEN You are fitted for society and it is shameful you should be exiled from it. J. R. GREEN The exiled Greek scholars were welcomed in Italy.

2 Discard, get rid of. Now *rare*. LME.

E. BOWEN For these . . occasions, ladies went tailormade; coaching, indeed, created its own fashions, exiling fussy, draped skirts.

†**3** Ravage, lay waste. LME–M16.
■ **exilement** *noun* (now *rare*) LME. †**exiler** *noun* LME–M17.

exilian /ɪɡˈzɪlɪən, ɪkˈsɪ-; ɛɡ-, ɛk-/ *adjective*. L19.
[ORIGIN from Latin *exilium* (see EXILE *noun*¹) + -AN.]
= EXILIC.

exilic /ɪɡˈzɪlɪk, ɪkˈsɪ-; ɛɡ-, ɛk-/ *adjective*. L19.
[ORIGIN from EXILE *noun*¹ + -IC.]
Of or pertaining to a period of exile, esp. that of the Jews in Babylon; in exile.

P. ACKROYD The isolation of an exilic writer like Turgenev.

†**exilient** *adjective*. M17–E18.
[ORIGIN Latin *ex(s)ilient-* pres. ppl stem of *ex(s)ilire*, formed as EX-¹ 1 + *salire* to jump, spring.]
Leaping up (as) with joy; exultant, rapturous.
■ †**exilience** *noun* E17–E18.

†**exilition** *noun*. M17–E18.
[ORIGIN Irreg. from Latin *ex(s)ilire* (see EXILIENT) + -ITION.]
A jumping up, a springing forth.

exility /ɪɡˈzɪlɪti, ɪkˈsɪ-; ɛɡ-, ɛk-/ *noun*. *arch.* LME.
[ORIGIN Latin *exilitas*, from *exilis*: see EXILE *adjective*, -ITY.]
1 Slenderness, thinness; smallness of size, extent, etc. LME.
†**2** Impoverishment. M16–L18.
3 Thinness of texture or consistency; fineness, tenuity. E17.

eximious /ɪɡˈzɪmɪəs, ɛɡ-/ *adjective*. Now *rare*. M16.
[ORIGIN Latin *eximius* set apart, select, from *eximere*: see EXEMPT *adjective*, -OUS.]
Distinguished, outstanding, pre-eminent.

exinanition /ɪkˌsɪnəˈnɪʃ(ə)n, ɛk-/ *noun*. Now *rare*. E17.
[ORIGIN Latin *exinanitio(n-)*, from *exinanire* make empty, formed as EX-¹ 1 + *inanis* empty.]
1 The action of emptying or draining (*lit. & fig.*); emptied or drained condition. E17.

JER. TAYLOR Fastings to the exinanition of spirits.

2 The action or an act of emptying of pride, self-will, or dignity; abasement, humbling, *spec.* (THEOLOGY) that taken upon himself by Christ. E17.

exine /ˈɛksɪn, -ʌɪn/ *noun*. L19.
[ORIGIN Perh. from EX-² + Greek *in-*, *is* fibre.]
BOTANY. The tough outer wall of a pollen grain. Opp. INTINE.

exist /ɪɡˈzɪst, ɛɡ-/ *verb intrans*. E17.
[ORIGIN Prob. back-form. from EXISTENCE. Cf. Latin *ex(s)istere* emerge, present oneself, come into being, (in late Latin) be (aux.), formed as EX-¹ 1 + *sistere* take a stand.]
1 Have objective reality or being. E17.

J. S. MILL The man called father might still exist though there were no child. G. SAINTSBURY Plays . . formed a large . . part of such literary pastime as existed.

2 Have being in a specified place or form or under specified conditions. Of a relation, circumstance, etc.: be found, subsist. (Foll. by adverbial phr., *as*, †noun or adjective compl.) E17.

N. ARNOTT Which substances . . usually exist as airs. R. H. MOTTRAM There was a stronger link between them than existed with the others of the family. G. ORWELL Similar slits existed in thousands . . throughout the building. P. W. ATKINS Ice-VII . . exists only when the pressure exceeds 25000 atm.

3 Continue alive or in being; maintain existence. Also, live, esp. under adverse conditions. L18.

V. BRITTAIN Love still existed . . in a world dominated by winter and death. N. SHUTE If the Geiger counter was correct, no life could exist there for more than a few days. R. P. GRAVES He would just be able to exist on his salary.

■ **exister** *noun* (*rare*) L19. **existing** *ppl adjective* that exists; *esp.* that exists now or existed at the time in question, current: M18.

existence /ɪɡˈzɪst(ə)ns, ɛɡ-/ *noun*. LME.
[ORIGIN Old French & mod. French, or late Latin *existentia*, from *ex(s)istent-* pres. ppl stem of *ex(s)istere*: see EXIST, -ENCE.]
†**1** Reality, as opp. to appearance. Only in LME.
2 The fact or state of existing; actual possession of being. LME. ▸**b** Continued being; *spec.* continued being as a living creature, life, esp. under adverse conditions. M17.

JAS. MILL It created some evils . . which previously had no existence. C. HILL Some men were questioning the existence of witches. **b** W. S. LANDOR I shall remember his [friendship] to the last hour of my existence.

bring into existence, ***come into existence***, etc. ***call into existence***: see CALL *verb*. **in existence** existing. ***b the struggle for existence***: see STRUGGLE *noun*.
3 a Something that exists; an entity, a being. E17. ▸**b** All that exists. M18.

a HENRY FIELDING I have heard of a man who believed there was no real existence in the world but himself.

4 A mode or kind of existing. M18.
– COMB.: **existence problem**, **existence theorem**, etc.: dealing with the existence of a mathematical or philosophical entity.
■ †**existency** *noun* = EXISTENCE 2, 3, 4 E17–E19.

existent /ɪɡˈzɪst(ə)nt, ɛɡ-/ *adjective & noun*. M16.
[ORIGIN Latin *ex(s)istent-*: see EXISTENCE, -ENT.]
▸ **A** *adjective*. **1** That exists or has being. Opp. ***non-existent***. M16.
2 Existing now or at the time in question; contemporary. L18.
▸ **B** *noun*. A person who or thing which exists. M17.

existential /ɛɡzɪˈstɛnʃ(ə)l/ *adjective*. L17.
[ORIGIN Late Latin *existentialis*, from *existentia*: see EXISTENCE, -AL¹.]
1 Of or relating to existence. L17.
2 LOGIC. Of a proposition etc.: predicating existence. E19. **existential import** the assumption made in a proposition that something denoted by it, esp. the subject term, exists. **existential quantifier**: asserting that something exists of which a related proposition is true.
3 PHILOSOPHY. Of or pertaining to existence, esp. human existence, as opp. to the essence of things; existentialist. M20.
■ **existentially** *adverb* E19.

existentialism /ɛɡzɪˈstɛnʃ(ə)lɪz(ə)m/ *noun*. M20.
[ORIGIN translating Danish *existents-forhold* (Kierkegaard) condition of existence, from EXISTENTIAL + -ISM.]
A modern philosophical trend, the leading tenet of which is that a person (unlike a thing) has no predetermined essence but forms his or her essence by acts of pure will. Cf. ESSENTIALISM.
■ **existentialist** *noun & adjective* (*a*) *noun* an advocate or adherent of existentialism; (*b*) *adjective* of, pertaining to, or characteristic of existentialism: M20. ˌ**existentiaˈlistic** *adjective* L20.

existible /ɪɡˈzɪstɪb(ə)l, ɛɡ-/ *adjective*. *rare*. E18.
[ORIGIN from EXIST *verb* + -IBLE.]
Capable of existing.
■ **existiˈbility** *noun* L17.

†**existimation** *noun.* M16–E18.
[ORIGIN Latin *existimatio(n-)*, from *existimat-* pa. ppl stem of *existimare*, formed as EX-¹ 1 + *aestimare* ESTEEM *verb*: see -ATION.]
Valuation of a person in respect of his or her qualities; public standing or reputation.

exit /ˈɛksɪt, ˈɛɡzɪt/ *noun.* L16.
[ORIGIN Latin EXITUS.]
1 A departure of an actor etc. from the stage during a scene; *fig.* a person's death. L16.
2 *gen.* A departure from any place or situation. Also, freedom or opportunity to depart. M17.

G. P. R. JAMES The man had just given admittance or exit to some one. J. LONDON Arthur was leaving the room, and Martin Eden followed his exit with longing eyes.

port of exit: see PORT *noun*³ 5b.
3 A means of egress, esp. from a public building; an outlet, a way out. L17. ▸**b** A place where traffic can leave a motorway etc.; a slip road provided at such a place. M20.

B. JOWETT An enclosure . . which was surrounded by a great ditch and had no exit. J. GASKELL We walked up the aisle . . and bunked out through the emergency exit.

4 CARDS (esp. BRIDGE). The action of deliberately losing the lead; a card enabling one to do this. M20.
– COMB.: **exit line** a line spoken by an actor or actress immediately before leaving the stage; **exit permit** = *exit visa* below; **exit poll** an unofficial poll, esp. for the media, in which voters leaving a polling station are asked how they voted; **exit visa** a visa enabling one to leave a country; **exit wound**: made by a bullet passing out of the body.

exit /ˈɛksɪt, ˈɛɡzɪt/ *verb*¹ *intrans.* (*defective*). M16.
[ORIGIN Latin, 3rd person sing. pres. indic. of *exire* go out, formed as EX-¹ 1 + *ire* to go.]
A stage direction: (the last speaker, or the character whose name follows) leaves the stage. Cf. EXEUNT.

transf.: COLERIDGE So exit Clotilda, and enter Bertram.

exit /ˈɛksɪt, ˈɛɡzɪt/ *verb*². E17.
[ORIGIN from EXIT *noun*.]
1 *verb intrans.* Make one's exit or departure, esp. from a stage; leave any place; *fig.* die. E17.

C. HAMPTON He exits . . into the bedroom, leaving the stage empty. F. SMYTH The bullet had . . exited just behind his right ear.

2 *verb intrans.* CARDS (esp. BRIDGE). Lose the lead deliberately. M20.
3 *verb trans.* Leave, get out of. L20.

exite /ˈɛksʌɪt/ *noun.* L19.
[ORIGIN from Greek *exō* outside + -ITE¹.]
ZOOLOGY. Each of the lateral lobes on the outer side of some crustacean limbs.

exitial /ɪɡˈzɪʃ(ə)l, ɛɡ-/ *adjective.* Long *rare.* LME.
[ORIGIN Latin *exitialis*, from *exitium* destruction: see -AL¹.]
Destructive to life, fatal.

exition /ɪkˈsɪʃ(ə)n, ɛk-/ *noun.* Now *rare* or *obsolete.* L17.
[ORIGIN Latin *exitio(n-)*, from *exit-* pa. ppl stem of *exire*: see EXIT *verb*¹, -ION.]
(A point of) exit or departure.

†**exitious** *adjective.* M16–E18.
[ORIGIN Latin *exitiosus*, from *exitium* destruction: see -OUS.]
= EXITIAL.

exitus /ˈɛksɪtəs/ *noun.* Pl. same. M17.
[ORIGIN Latin, from *exit-* pa. ppl stem of *exire*: see EXIT *verb*¹.]
A departure; an exodus. Now only MEDICINE, a fatal termination to an illness, a death.

ex libris /ɛksˈlɪbrɪs, -ˈliːb-, -ˈlʌɪb-, -ˈliːbriːs/ *noun.* Pl. same. L19.
[ORIGIN Latin, lit. 'out of the books or library (of —)'.]
An inscription, label, etc., indicating the owner of a book; *esp.* a bookplate.
■ **ex librism** *noun* the collecting of bookplates L19. **ex librist** *noun* L19.

ex-meridian /ɛksməˈrɪdɪən/ *adjective.* M19.
[ORIGIN from EX-¹ 1 + MERIDIAN *noun*.]
NAVIGATION. (Of an observation of the sun or other celestial object) not taken on the meridian, but close enough to it to be reducible to a meridian altitude; involving or calculated from such an observation.

Exmoor /ˈɛksmʊə, -mɔː/ *adjective & noun.* E19.
[ORIGIN *Exmoor*, SW England: see below.]
▸ **A** *adjective.* Designating (breeds of) livestock found in or originating from Exmoor, a hilly region on the Devon–Somerset border, *esp.* (**a**) a breed of horned short-woolled sheep; (**b**) a breed of small heavy-maned pony. E19.
▸ **B** *noun.* An Exmoor sheep or pony. E19.

ex nihilo /ɛks ˈniːhɪləʊ, ˈnʌɪ-/ *adverbial phr.* L16.
[ORIGIN Latin.]
Out of nothing.

exo- /ˈɛksəʊ/ *combining form.*
[ORIGIN Greek *exō* outside: see -O-.]
Outer, external.
■ **exoatmosˈpheric** *adjective* occurring or operating outside the atmosphere M20. **exobioˈlogical** *adjective* of or pertaining to exobiology or its subject matter M20. **exobiˈologist** *noun* an expert in or student of exobiology M20. **exobiˈology** *noun* the branch of science that deals with the possibility of life on other planets or in space M20. **exocarp** *noun* (BOTANY) the outer layer of the pericarp of a fruit M19. **exoˈcentric** *adjective* (LINGUISTICS) designating a compound or construction whose distribution is not the same as that of any of its constituents; not endocentric: E20. **exocuticle**, **-ˈticula**, pl. **-lae**, *noun* (**a**) the hard, chitinous outer part of the arthropod procuticle; (**b**) the middle part of the cuticle surrounding animal hairs etc.: E20. **exoˈcyclic** *adjective* (**a**) ZOOLOGY (of an irregular sea urchin) having the anus displaced from its usual apical position; (**b**) CHEMISTRY situated outside a ring: L19. **exocyˈtosis** *noun* (BIOLOGY) the release of matter by a living cell M20. **exocyˈtotic** *adjective* characterized by or subjected to exocytosis L20. **exoˈdontia** *noun* the extraction of teeth E20. **exoˈdontist** *noun* a specialist in exodontia E20. **exoelectron** *noun* an electron spontaneously emitted from a metal surface following abrasion or fracture M20. **exoenzyme** *noun* (**a**) an enzyme which acts outside the cell producing it; (**b**) an enzyme which breaks terminal bonds of long-chain molecules: E20. **exoˈergic** *adjective* (SCIENCE) = EXERGONIC M20. **exoˈergically** *adverb* (SCIENCE) with the release of energy L20. **exoerythroˈcytic** *adjective* (of malaria parasites etc.) occurring outside the red blood cells M20. **exoˈglossic** *adjective* pertaining to or involving the use of a language that is not native to the country concerned L20. **exo-ˈnarthex** *noun* the outer vestibule of an Orthodox church M19. **exoˈnormative** *adjective* (LINGUISTICS) drawing on foreign usage as a model for the native language M20. **exoˈnuclease** *noun* (BIOCHEMISTRY) an enzyme which removes successive nucleotides from the end of a polynucleotide molecule M20. **exonucleolytic** /-ˈlɪtɪk/ *adjective* (BIOCHEMISTRY) involving the removal of successive nucleotides from the end of a polynucleotide molecule L20. **exonucleoˈlytically** *adverb* (BIOCHEMISTRY) in an exonucleolytic manner L20. **exonym** *noun* a place name other than that used by the residents of the place concerned M20. **exoˈpeptidase** *noun* (BIOCHEMISTRY) an enzyme which breaks the terminal peptide bonds of peptide chains M20. **exoplanet** *noun* a planet which orbits a star outside the solar system L20. **exopod**, **eˈxopodite** *nouns* (ZOOLOGY) the outer branch of a biramous limb or appendage in some arthropods L19. **exopterygote** /ɛksɒpˈtɛrɪɡəʊt/ *adjective & noun* (ZOOLOGY) (designating) an insect whose wings develop externally and whose young usually resemble the adult, there being no real pupal stage E20. **exoˈskeletal** *adjective* of or pertaining to an exoskeleton; of the nature of or having an exoskeleton: L19. **exoskeleton** *noun* a hard outer layer of an animal body M19. **exosphere** *noun* the outermost part of a planet's atmosphere M20. **exoˈspheric** *adjective* of or pertaining to an exosphere; occurring in an exosphere: M20. **exospore** *noun* (**a**) the outer layer of the membrane or wall in some spores; (**b**) a spore formed by separation and release from a sporophore: M19. **exotoxin** *noun* a toxin released by a living micro-organism into its surroundings E20. **exotropia** /-ˈtrəʊpɪə/ *noun* [Greek *tropē* turning] MEDICINE divergent strabismus L19.

Exocet /ˈɛksəsɛt/ *noun.* L20.
[ORIGIN French = flying fish, from Latin *exocetus* from Greek *exōkoitos* sleeping out, fish that comes up on the beach, formed as EXO- + *koitos* bed.]
(Proprietary name for) a kind of rocket-propelled short-range guided missile used esp. in tactical sea warfare. Also *Exocet missile*.

exocrine /ˈɛksə(ʊ)krʌɪn, -krɪn/ *adjective.* E20.
[ORIGIN from EXO- + Greek *krinein* to separate.]
PHYSIOLOGY. Of, pertaining to, or designating a gland that secretes through ducts opening on to an epithelial surface. Cf. ENDOCRINE.

exoculation /ɛkˌsɒkjʊˈleɪʃ(ə)n/ *noun.* Now *rare* or *obsolete.* M17.
[ORIGIN medieval Latin *exoculatio(n-)*, from Latin *exoculat-* pa. ppl stem of *exoculare* deprive of eyes, formed as EX-¹ + *oculus* eye: see -ATION.]
The action of putting out a person's eyes; blinding.

Exod. *abbreviation.*
Exodus (in the Bible).

exode /ˈɛksəʊd/ *noun*¹. Also †**exod**. ME.
[ORIGIN Anglicized from EXODUS; in sense 1 through Old French & mod. French *Exode*.]
†**1** = EXODUS 1. ME–L16.
2 = EXODUS 2. *rare.* M18.

exode /ˈɛksəʊd/ *noun*². L17.
[ORIGIN French from Latin EXODIUM.]
CLASSICAL HISTORY. **1** In Roman drama, a comic interlude or farce following something more serious. L17.
2 In Greek drama, the end or catastrophe of a play. M18.

exoderm /ˈɛksə(ʊ)dəːm/ *noun.* L19.
[ORIGIN from EXO- + Greek *derma* skin.]
BIOLOGY. = ECTODERM.

exodermal /ɛksə(ʊ)ˈdəːm(ə)l/ *adjective.* E20.
[ORIGIN from EXODERM and EXODERMIS + -AL¹.]
Pertaining to or of the nature of exoderm or exodermis.

exodermis /ɛksə(ʊ)ˈdəːmɪs/ *noun.* E20.
[ORIGIN from EXO- after *endodermis*, *epidermis*.]
BOTANY. A specialized layer of a root beneath the epidermis or velamen.

exodium /ɪkˈsəʊdɪʌm, ɛk-/ *noun.* Pl. ***-dia*** /-dɪə/. E17.
[ORIGIN Latin from Greek *exodion* use as noun of neut. sing. of *exodios* pertaining to an exit, from *exodos*: see EXODUS.]
= EXODE *noun*².

exodus /ˈɛksədəs/ *noun.* Also (*rare*) **exody** /-di/. OE.
[ORIGIN ecclesiastical Latin *Exodus* from Greek *exodos*, formed as EX-² + *hodos* way.]
1 (**E-**.) (The name of) the second book of the Bible, relating the release of the Israelites from their bondage in Egypt and their journey to Canaan. OE.
2 A departure, usu. of many people; an emigration; *spec.* the departure of the Israelites from Egypt. E17.

S. BRETT Charles and Frances joined the exodus to the bar.

ex officio /ɛks əˈfɪʃɪəʊ/ *adverb, adjective, & noun.* As adjective usu. **ex-officio**. M16.
[ORIGIN Latin, from *officium* duty, OFFICE *noun*.]
▸ **A** *adverb & adjective.* (That is such) by virtue of one's office. M16.
ex-officio oath *hist.*: under which a person could be compelled to answer questions whose answers would expose him or her to censure or punishment.
▸ **B** *noun.* Pl. **-os**. A person or officer serving ex officio. E19.

exogamy /ɪkˈsɒɡəmi, ɛk-/ *noun.* M19.
[ORIGIN from EXO- + -GAMY.]
1 ANTHROPOLOGY. The custom by which a man is obliged to marry outside his own community, clan, or tribe. M19.
2 BIOLOGY. The fusion of reproductive cells from unrelated individuals. E20.
■ **exoˈgamic** *adjective* of or pertaining to exogamy L19. **exogamous** *adjective* practising exogamy; of or pertaining to exogamy: M19.

exogen /ˈɛksədʒ(ə)n/ *noun.* Now *rare* or *obsolete.* M19.
[ORIGIN French *exogène*, formed as EXO-: see -GEN.]
BOTANY. A plant whose stem grows by the development of new material on the outside.

exogenetic /ˌɛksə(ʊ)dʒɪˈnɛtɪk/ *adjective.* L19.
[ORIGIN from EXO- + -GENETIC.]
1 SCIENCE. Having an external cause or origin. L19.
2 GEOLOGY. Formed or occurring at the surface of the earth. E20.

exogenic /ɛksə(ʊ)ˈdʒɛnɪk/ *adjective.* E20.
[ORIGIN from EXO- + -GENIC.]
= EXOGENETIC.

exogenous /ɪkˈsɒdʒɪnəs, ɛk-/ *adjective.* M19.
[ORIGIN from mod. Latin *exogena* exogen (after classical Latin *indigena* native (noun & adjective)) + -OUS.]
1 BOTANY. Of, pertaining to, or designating a plant that grows by developing new material on the outside. Now *rare* or *obsolete.* M19.
2 GEOLOGY. Formed or occurring outside some structure or rock mass; *esp.* = EXOGENETIC 2; BOTANY developing from superficial rather than deep tissue. M19.
3 Having an external cause or origin; *spec.* (MEDICINE) caused by an organism, event, agent, etc., operating outside the body; environmental. L19.
■ **exogenously** *adverb* L19.

exolete /ˈɛksəliːt/ *adjective & noun.* E17.
[ORIGIN Latin *exoletus* pa. pple of *exolescere* become adult, fall out of use.]
▸ **A** *adjective.* Disused, obsolete; insipid, effete. Long *rare* or *obsolete.* E17.
▸ **B** *noun.* An effete person. *rare.* M20.

exolution /ɛksəˈluːʃ(ə)n/ *noun.* Now *rare.* E17.
[ORIGIN Latin *ex(s)olutio(n-)*, from *ex(s)olut-* pa. ppl stem of *ex(s)olvere* loosen, formed as EX-¹ + *solvere* loosen, let go: see -ION.]
†**1** The action of loosening or setting free; *esp.* (formerly) the emission of the principles called 'animal spirits', thought to be the cause of fainting. E17–M19.
2 Faintness, light-headedness; relaxation of the body's faculties. M17.

exomologesis /ˌɛksəmɒləˈɡiːsɪs/ *noun.* Pl. **-geses** /-ˈɡiːsiːz/. L16.
[ORIGIN Greek *exomologēsis*, from *exomologein* confess, formed as EX-² + *omologein* agree, admit.]
CHRISTIAN CHURCH. A full or public confession.

exomphalos /ɪkˈsɒmfələs, ɛk-/ *noun.* L16.
[ORIGIN Greek = prominent navel, formed as EX-² + *omphalos* navel.]
A protrusion of some of the contents of the abdomen through the umbilicus.

exon /ˈɛksɒn/ *noun*¹. M18.
[ORIGIN Repr. pronunc. /ɛɡzɔ̃/ of French EXEMPT *adjective & noun*.]
Each of the four officers acting as commanders of the Yeomen of the Guard. Cf. EXEMPT *noun* 4.

exon /ˈɛksɒn/ *noun*². L20.
[ORIGIN from *ex(pressed* pa. pple of EXPRESS *verb*¹ + -ON.]
GENETICS. A segment of a DNA or RNA molecule that contains coding information for a protein. Cf. INTRON.
■ **exonic** /ɪkˈsɒnɪk, ɛk-/ *adjective* L20.

exoner /ɪɡˈzəʊnə, ɛɡ-/ *verb trans.* *obsolete* exc. SCOTS LAW. E16.
[ORIGIN French *exonérer* from Latin *exonerare* EXONERATE.]
Relieve of a responsibility; free from or *from* blame or liability.

exonerate /ɪɡˈzɒnəreɪt, ɛɡ-/ *verb.* Pa. pple **-ated**, (*arch.*) **-ate** /-ət/. LME.
[ORIGIN Latin *exonerat-* pa. ppl stem of *exonerare*, formed as EX-¹ + *oner-*, *onus* burden: see -ATE³.]
1 *verb trans.* Free from or *from* blame or reproach; relieve from the blame or burden *of*. LME.

H. JAMES An affectionate farewell might help to exonerate him from the charge of neglect. Q. BELL The evidence . . tends to exonerate her.

2 *verb trans.* Take a burden from; relieve *of* a burden or possession; unload, make lighter, (a ship, one's conscience, etc.). Now *rare.* E16.

WELLINGTON Success would certainly exonerate our finances.

3 Relieve of a duty, obligation, payment, etc. Foll. by *from*, †*of.* M16.

†**4** *verb trans. & intrans.* Discharge the contents of (the body, bowels, etc.). M16–L19.

exonerate nature, **exonerate oneself** defecate.

†**5** *verb refl.* Of a river, sea, blood vessel, etc.: empty or flow *into.* L16–E18.

†**6** *verb trans.* Discharge, pour off, (a liquid, body of water, etc.) *into*; get rid of (people, a population). Only in 17.

▪ **exonerative** *adjective* tending to relieve of an obligation etc. E19.

exoneration /ɪɡˌzɒnəˈreɪʃ(ə)n, ɛɡ-/ *noun.* M16.
[ORIGIN Latin *exoneratio(n-)*, from *exonerare*: see EXONERATE, -ATION.]
1 The action or an act of freeing from blame or relieving of a duty or burden. M16.
†**2** Defecation. M17–L18.

†**exoneretur** *noun.* M18–M19.
[ORIGIN Latin = let him or her be discharged, 3rd person sing. pres. subjunct. pass. of *exonerare*: see EXONERATE.]
LAW. (The record of) the discharge of a bail when an action was withdrawn or settled or the prisoner taken to prison.

Exonian /ɪkˈsəʊnɪən, ɛk-/ *adjective & noun.* M19.
[ORIGIN from Latin *Exonia* Exeter + -IAN.]
▸ **A** *adjective.* Of or pertaining to Exeter, a city in SW England. M19.
▸ **B** *noun.* A native or inhabitant of Exeter. L19.

exonumia /ɛksə(ʊ)ˈnjuːmɪə/ *noun pl.* (also treated as *sing.*). M20.
[ORIGIN from EXO- + NUM(ISMATIC + -IA².]
Objects of historical interest that resemble coins or currency, such as medals and tokens.

exophora /ɛkˈsɒf(ə)rə/ *noun.* L20.
[ORIGIN from EXO- after *anaphora.*]
LINGUISTICS. An exophoric reference or relation.

exophoria /ɛksəˈfɔːrɪə/ *noun.* L19.
[ORIGIN from EXO- + -PHORIA.]
MEDICINE. A tendency for the visual axes to diverge; latent divergent strabismus.

exophoric /ɛksəˈfɒrɪk/ *adjective.* E20.
[ORIGIN from EXOPHORIA (& EXOPHORA) + -IC.]
1 MEDICINE. Having exophoria. E20.
2 LINGUISTICS. Referring to something outside the text. L20.

exophthalmos /ɛksɒfˈθalmɒs/ *noun.* Also **-mus** /-məs/. E17.
[ORIGIN (mod. Latin *exophthalmus* from) Greek *exophthalmos*, formed as EX-² + *ophthalmos* eye.]
Abnormal protrusion of the eyeball.
▪ **exophthalmia** *noun* = EXOPHTHALMOS E18. **exophthalmic** *adjective* characterized by exophthalmos L19.

exor *abbreviation.*
Executor.

exorable /ˈɛks(ə)rəb(ə)l/ *adjective.* Now *rare.* M16.
[ORIGIN Latin *exorabilis*, from *exorare* implore, formed as EX-¹ 1 + *orare* pray: see -ABLE.]
Able to be moved by entreaty.
▪ **exoraˈbility** *noun* (*rare*) L19.

exorbitance /ɪɡˈzɔːbɪt(ə)ns, ɛɡ-/ *noun.* LME.
[ORIGIN formed as EXORBITANCY: see -ANCE.]
1 (A) transgression of law or morality; an offence; misconduct, criminality. *arch.* LME.
2 The fact of being excessive or immoderate; extravagance; *esp.* gross excessiveness of a price, demand, etc. E17.
3 (An) eccentricity, (an) irregularity; (a) divergence from a prescribed track. Also, an attack of insanity. Now *rare* or *obsolete.* M17.

exorbitancy /ɪɡˈzɔːbɪt(ə)nsi, ɛɡ-/ *noun.* E17.
[ORIGIN from EXORBITANT: see -ANCY.]
†**1** = EXORBITANCE 1. E17–E18.
2 = EXORBITANCE 3. Now *rare* or *obsolete.* E17.
3 = EXORBITANCE 2. Formerly also, (a) disposition to exceed one's rights; excessive greed. M17.

exorbitant /ɪɡˈzɔːbɪt(ə)nt, ɛɡ-/ *adjective & noun.* Also **exhor-**. LME.
[ORIGIN Christian Latin *exorbitant-* pres. ppl stem of *exorbitare* go out of the track, formed as EX-¹ + *orbita* ORBIT *noun*: see -ANT¹.]
▸ **A** *adjective* **1 a** LAW. Of a case, offence, etc.: anomalous, outside the intended scope of a law. Of a power, privilege, or enactment: abnormal, irregular. LME. ▸†**b** *gen.* Abnormal, irregular; eccentric; frantic, wild. E17–E18.
2 Excessive, immoderate. Now chiefly of a price, demand, etc.: grossly excessive; far in excess of what is reasonable or appropriate. LME. ▸**b** Of an object, etc.: disproportionately or excessively large. *arch.* M17.

G. GREENE One resents being moved by so exorbitant an agony. *Times* These so-called bureaux de change are charging exorbitant rates of commission.

†**3** Deviating *from* a specified rule or principle; (of a remark etc.) irrelevant. LME–L17.
†**4** Transgressing the bounds of law, decency, or morality; M16–E18.
▸ †**B** *noun.* A person who or thing which exceeds proper bounds. *rare.* E17–E18.
▪ **exorbitantly** *adverb* M17.

exorbitate /ɪɡˈzɔːbɪteɪt, ɛɡ-/ *verb intrans.* Now *rare* or *obsolete.* E17.
[ORIGIN Late Latin *exorbitat-* pa. ppl stem of *exorbitare*: see EXORBITANT, -ATE³.]
Deviate or stray from the usual course (*lit.* & *fig.*).

exorbitation /ɪɡˌzɔːbɪˈteɪʃ(ə)n, ɛɡ-/ *noun.* Now *rare* or *obsolete.* E17.
[ORIGIN Late Latin *exorbitatio(n-)*, from *exorbitare*: see EXORBITATE, -ATION.]
(A) deviation from the usual course.

exorcise *verb* var. of EXORCIZE.

exorcism /ˈɛksɔːsɪz(ə)m, ˈɛksə-/ *noun.* LME.
[ORIGIN ecclesiastical Latin *exorcismus* from ecclesiastical Greek *exorkismos*, from *exorkizein* exorcize, formed as EX-² + *orkos* oath: see -ISM.]
1 The action or an act of exorcizing or expelling an evil spirit. LME.
†**2** The action of calling up spirits; the rites performed for this purpose. LME–M17.
3 A formula recited for the purpose of exorcizing. M16.

exorcist /ˈɛksɔːsɪst, ˈɛksə-/ *noun.* LME.
[ORIGIN ecclesiastical Latin *exorcista* from Greek *exorkistēs*, from *exorkizein*: see EXORCISM, -IST.]
1 A person who drives out evil spirits by invocation etc. LME. ▸**b** ECCLESIASTICAL HISTORY. The third of the four minor orders in the RC Church, one of whose functions was the exorcizing of evil spirits. M16.

b C. MACKENZIE Cassandra Batt . . was officially sexton, but acted as . . exorcist, doorkeeper, and subdeacon as well.

†**2** A person who seeks or purports to conjure up spirits. Only in E17.

SHAKES. *Jul. Caes.* Thou like an Exorcist, hast conjur'd up My mortified Spirit.

▪ **exorˈcistic** *adjective* of or pertaining to an exorcist or exorcism M20. **exorˈcistical** *adjective* = EXORCISTIC M17.

exorcize /ˈɛksɔːsʌɪz/ *verb trans.* Also **-ise**. LME.
[ORIGIN Old French & mod. French *exorciser* or ecclesiastical Latin *exorcizare* from Greek *exorkizein*: see EXORCISM, -IZE.]
1 Conjure up (an evil spirit); solemnly call upon (an evil spirit) *to do.* Now *rare* or *obsolete.* LME.
2 Drive away or expel (an evil spirit) by invocation or the use of some holy name. (Foll. by *from*, *out of.*) M16.

fig.: L. P. HARTLEY Wealth had not exorcised her fear of money.

3 Free or clear (a person or place) *of* evil spirits, malignant influences, etc. M17.

LYTTON Muttering hymns, monks huddled together . . as if to exorcize the land of a demon.

▪ **exorciˈzation** *noun* LME. **exorcizement** *noun* the action of exorcizing; exorcizing influence: L18. **exorcizer** *noun* E16.

exordium /ɪɡˈzɔːdɪəm, ɛɡ-/ *noun.* Pl. **-iums**, **-ia** /-ɪə/. L16.
[ORIGIN Latin, from *exordiri* begin, formed as EX-¹ 1 + *ordiri* begin.]
The beginning of anything; *esp.* the introductory part of a discourse or treatise.
▪ **exordial** *adjective* introductory; of or pertaining to an exordium: L17.

exosmosis /ɛksɒzˈməʊsɪs/ *noun.* Orig. (now *rare* or *obsolete*) **exosmose** /ˈɛksɒzməʊs/. E19.
[ORIGIN French *exosmose*, from Greek EX-² + *ōsmos* pushing: see -OSIS.]
Osmotic diffusion of solvent or solute out of a vessel or cell.

exossate /ɪkˈsɒseɪt, ɛk-/ *verb trans. rare.* E18.
[ORIGIN Latin *exossat-* pa. ppl stem of *exossare* to bone, formed as EX-¹ 1 + *oss-*, *os* bone: see -ATE³.]
Deprive of bones; bone.

†**exossation** *noun.* E17–E18.
[ORIGIN formed as EXOSSATE: see -ATION.]
The action or practice of causing fruit to grow without stones.

exostosis /ɛksɒsˈtəʊsɪs/ *noun.* Pl. **-toses** /-ˈtəʊsiːz/. L16.
[ORIGIN Greek *exostōsis* outgrowth of bone, formed as EX-² + *osteon* bone: see -OSIS.]
An outgrowth of bony tissue on a bone.
▪ **eˈxostosed** *adjective* affected with exostosis M18. **exostotic** /-ˈtɒtɪk/ *adjective* of, pertaining to, or of the nature of an exostosis M19.

exostracize /ɪkˈsɒstrəsʌɪz, ɛk-/ *verb trans.* Also **-ise**. M19.
[ORIGIN Greek *exostrakizein*, formed as EX-² + *ostrakizein* OSTRACIZE.]
Banish by ostracism.

exoteric /ɛksə(ʊ)ˈtɛrɪk/ *adjective & noun.* M17.
[ORIGIN Latin *exotericus* from Greek *exōterikos*, from *exōterō* outer, compar. of *exō* outside: see -IC.]
▸ **A** *adjective.* **1** (Of a philosophical doctrine, mode of speech, etc.) designed for or intelligible to outsiders; (of a disciple) not admitted to esoteric teaching; dealing with ordinary topics. Opp. ESOTERIC *adjective* 1. M17. ▸**b** Current among the general public; popular; ordinary. E19.

Times Lit. Suppl. A market surely exists for an exoteric study of Wittgenstein's notoriously recondite ideas.

2 Pertaining to the outside; external. Now *rare.* M17.
▸ **B** *noun.* **1** An uninitiated person; an outsider. L17.
2 In *pl.* Exoteric doctrines or treatises. M18.
▪ **exoterical** *adjective* M17. **exoterically** *adverb* M18. **exotericism** /-sɪz(ə)m/ *noun* (belief in) exoteric doctrines L19. **exotericist** /-sɪst/ *noun* a person who believes in exoteric doctrines M20.

exotherm /ˈɛksə(ʊ)θəːm/ *noun.* E20.
[ORIGIN from EXO- + Greek *thermē* heat.]
CHEMISTRY. **1** A substance that liberates heat during its formation and absorbs heat on decomposing. E20.
2 A sudden liberation of heat in a process. M20.
▪ **exoˈthermal** *adjective* = EXOTHERMIC E20. **exoˈthermally** *adverb* = EXOTHERMICALLY L19.

exothermic /ɛksə(ʊ)ˈθəːmɪk/ *adjective.* L19.
[ORIGIN French *exothermique*, formed as EXO-, THERMIC.]
CHEMISTRY. Accompanied by, or (of a compound) formed with, the liberation of heat.
▪ **exothermically** *adverb* in an exothermic manner M20. **ˌexotherˈmicity** *noun* the property of being exothermic; the quantity of energy liberated in an exothermic reaction: M20.

exotic /ɪɡˈzɒtɪk, ɛɡ-/ *adjective & noun.* L16.
[ORIGIN Latin *exoticus* from Greek *exōtikos*, from *exō* outside.]
▸ **A** *adjective.* **1** Of a word, fashion, plant, disease, etc.: introduced from abroad, not indigenous. Formerly also, belonging to another country, foreign, extrinsic, alien (*to*). L16.

G. W. TURNER Exotic pines now account for more than half of New Zealand's output of timber. *Times Lit. Suppl.* Minorities who have brought their exotic faiths from continents formerly under British domination.

2 Of behaviour, dress, a language, etc.: strikingly different, attractively unusual; glamorous. Formerly, outlandish, uncouth. E17. ▸**b** Of, pertaining to, or characteristic of a foreigner or something foreign. Now *rare.* M17.

H. INNES The cigarette was Turkish and the scent of it was an exotic intrusion in that solitude of snow and fir. W. CATHER Beside Alexandra lounged a strikingly exotic figure in a tall Mexican hat.

3 Of fuels, metals, etc.: of a kind not used for ordinary purposes or not ordinarily met with; specially produced or developed. M20.
– SPECIAL COLLOCATIONS: **exotic dancer** a striptease dancer.
▸ **B** *noun.* **1** A plant or animal that is not indigenous. M17.
2 A person of foreign origin. M17.
3 A striptease dancer. M20.
▪ †**exotical** *adjective* E17–E18. **exotically** *adverb* L17. **exoticism** /-sɪz(ə)m/ *noun* exotic character; something exotic: M19. **exoticness** *noun* M17.

exotica /ɪɡˈzɒtɪkə, ɛɡ-/ *noun pl.* L19.
[ORIGIN Latin, neut. pl. of *exoticus* EXOTIC.]
Exotic things.

exotism /ˈɛksətɪz(ə)m, ˈɛɡzə-/ *noun.* Also ***exotisme*** /ɛɡzɔtism/. E19.
[ORIGIN French *exotisme*, from *exotique*, formed as EXOTIC: see -ISM.]
Resemblance to what is foreign; a foreign air.

expand /ɪkˈspand, ɛk-/ *verb.* LME.
[ORIGIN Latin *expandere*, formed as EX-¹ 1 + *pandere* to spread.]
1 *verb trans.* Spread or stretch (a thing) out, esp. to its fullest extent; extend, open out. Formerly also, spread abroad, diffuse, (a report etc.). LME.

LEIGH HUNT Sicily then lay expanded like a map beneath our eyes. O. MANNING He . . expanded his mouth in a significant smirk.

2 *verb intrans.* Become extended; spread out, unfold. M16.

W. WITHERING Flowers . . expand at 6 or 7, and close at 2 in the afternoon.

3 *verb trans.* †**a** Give full expression to (a feeling), pour out. M17–E19. ▸**b** Express at greater length, develop, (an idea); write out (a contraction) in full; MATH. rewrite (a product, power, or function) as a sum, give the expansion of. E19.

b H. J. LASKI Priestley . . was encouraged by friends to expand his argument into a general treatise.

4 *verb trans.* Widen the boundaries of, increase the area, scope, etc., of; enlarge, dilate. M17.

I. WATT I . . believe that its use should be expanded rather than curtailed.

5 *verb intrans.* Become greater in area, bulk, capacity, etc.; become larger; *fig.* increase the scope of one's activity or the scale of operations of something; take in or go *into* a new area of activity. L18.

P. L. FERMOR Water is the one thing that expands when it freezes instead of contracting. S. NAIPAUL The sweat stains expanded across the back of his shirt. J. HARVEY The firm expanded and took in truck-mixers. *Marketing Week* Marks & Spencer is making a second attempt to expand into record sales. *fig.*: J. DICKEY My heart expanded with joy at the thought.

6 *verb intrans.* Throw off reserve; become expansive; expatiate *on*. **E19.**

D. H. LAWRENCE Dr Mitchell was beginning to expand. With Alvina he quite unbent.

■ **expanda'bility** *noun* the property of being expandable **M20.** **expandable** *adjective* able to be expanded **E20.** **expander** *noun* a person who or thing which expands; *esp.* something used to increase bulk or versatility (***chest-expander***: see CHEST *noun*). **M19.** **expandible** *adjective* = EXPANDABLE **L20.**

expanded /ɪk'spandɪd, ɛk-/ *ppl adjective.* **M17.**
[ORIGIN from EXPAND + -ED¹.]
1 That has expanded or has been expanded. **M17.**
expanded metal sheet metal slit and stretched into a lattice. **expanded plastic** lightweight cellular plastic used esp. for packaging and insulation.
2 GRAMMAR. Designating a tense in which a form of the verb *to be* is used with a present participle. **E20.**

expanding /ɪk'spandɪŋ, ɛk-/ *ppl adjective.* **L18.**
[ORIGIN formed as EXPANDED + -ING².]
That expands.
expanding bullet = DUMDUM. **expanding universe** the universe regarded as continually expanding, with the galaxies receding from one another.

expanse /ɪk'spans, ɛk-/ *noun.* **M17.**
[ORIGIN mod. Latin *expansum* firmament, use as noun of neut. of Latin *expansus* pa. pple of *expandere* EXPAND.]
1 An area of or *of* something presenting a wide unbroken surface; (*arch.*) *the* firmament. **M17.**

R. L. STEVENSON The bay was perfect—not a ripple . . upon its blue expanse. M. SPARK They were crossing the Meadows, a gusty expanse of common land.

2 The distance to which something expands or is expanded. **M19.**

expanse /ɪk'spans, ɛk-/ *verb trans. arch.* **L15.**
[ORIGIN formed as EXPANSIBLE.]
= EXPAND 1, 4.

expansible /ɪk'spansɪb(ə)l, ɛk-/ *adjective.* **L17.**
[ORIGIN from Latin *expans-* pa. ppl stem of *expandere* EXPAND: see -IBLE.]
1 Able to be enlarged or expanded, esp. by heat. **L17.**
2 Able to be opened or spread out. **M18.**
■ **expansi'bility** *noun* **E18.**

expansile /ɪk'spansʌɪl, ɛk-/ *adjective.* **M18.**
[ORIGIN formed as EXPANSIBLE + -ILE.]
Capable of causing or undergoing expansion; of or pertaining to expansion.

expansion /ɪk'spanʃ(ə)n, ɛk-/ *noun.* **E17.**
[ORIGIN Late Latin *expansio(n-)*, formed as EXPANSIBLE: see -ION.]
1 The action of spreading out or extending; the condition of being spread out or extended. **E17.**

POPE The gilded clouds in fair expansion lie. D. H. LAWRENCE The lotus . . opens with an expansion such as no other flower knows.

2 Something spread out, an expanse; (*arch.*) *the* firmament. **E17.** ▸†**b** The immensity of space. **L17–E18.**
3 The action or process of making or becoming greater in area, bulk, capacity, etc.; enlargement, dilatation; the amount or degree of this. **M17.** ▸**b** An increase in the scope of the activities or the scale of the operations of a company, country, etc. **M19.** ▸**c** Increase in the amount of territory ruled or controlled by a country. **L19.**

S. H. VINES Alternate expansion and contraction of the tissue. **b** *Times* Encouraging the expansion of exports. J. W. KRUTCH What we call prosperity depends upon continual expansion.

4 The detailed expression of what is implicit in a statement; the writing out in full of something abbreviated; MATH. the process of working out a product, power, or function and expressing it in simpler terms as a sum; the sum itself. **E19.**
5 An enlarged portion; something formed by the expansion of a thing. **M19.**

J. TYNDALL This lake is simply an expansion of the river Rhone.

– COMB.: **expansion bit** a drilling bit that can be adjusted to drill holes of different sizes; **expansion board** a circuit board that can be connected to or inserted in a computer to give extra facilities; **expansion bolt**: that expands when inserted, no thread being required; **expansion box** (**a**) a chamber to allow for expansion of a fluid or into which expansion occurs; (**b**) a unit that can be connected to a computer to give extra facilities; **expansion card** = ***expansion board*** above; **expansion engine** a steam engine in which expansion of the steam in the cylinder contributes to the force on the piston; **expansion joint**: made to allow for the thermal expansion of the parts that it joins; **expansion slot** a place in a computer where an expansion board can be added.
■ **expansional** *adjective* **E20.** **expansionary** *adjective* tending or directed towards (economic) expansion **M20.**

expansionist /ɪk'spanʃ(ə)nɪst, ɛk-/ *noun & adjective.* **M19.**
[ORIGIN from EXPANSION + -IST.]
▸ **A** *noun.* A person who advocates a policy or theory of (now usu. territorial or economic) expansion. **M19.**
▸ **B** *adjective.* Of, pertaining to, or advocating such a policy or theory. **L19.**
■ **expansionism** *noun* **E20.** **expansio'nistic** *adjective* = EXPANSIONIST *adjective* **M20.**

expansive /ɪk'spansɪv, ɛk-/ *adjective.* **M17.**
[ORIGIN formed as EXPANSIBLE + -IVE.]
1 Tending or able to expand, spread out, or occupy a larger space. **M17.** ▸**b** Of a force, movement, etc.: tending to cause expansion. **M17.** ▸**c** Of an engine, process, etc.: working by the expansion of steam or hot gases. **L18.**

fig.: C. SAGAN The human spirit is expansive; the urge to colonize new environments lies deep within many of us.

2 Free from reserve in feeling or speech; genially frank or communicative. **M17.**

JO GRIMOND In expansive moods they have gone further, asserting that they descend from Huguenot weavers.

3 Having wide bounds, broad, extensive; (of interests, sympathies, etc.) wide-ranging, comprehensive. **E19.**

Chicago Tribune The expansive residential districts of suburban Kansas City. W. H. AUDEN The expansive dreams of constricted lives.

■ **expansively** *adverb* **M19.** **expansiveness** *noun* **E19.** **expan'sivity** *noun* **M19.**

†**expansum** *noun.* **M17–L18.**
[ORIGIN mod. Latin (see EXPANSE *noun*): used to render Hebrew *rāqīa'* lit. 'beaten out'.]
The firmament (cf. EXPANSE *noun* 1).

ex parte /ɛks 'pɑːti/ *adverbial & adjectival phr.* As adjective freq. ***ex-parte***. **E17.**
[ORIGIN Latin = from a or the side.]
▸ **A** *adverbial phr.* **1** Orig., on the part *of*. Later (LAW), on behalf of. **E17.**
2 LAW. On behalf of or with reference to only one of the parties concerned (and without notice to the adverse party). **L17.**

Times The owners . . applied to the Divisional Court ex parte for leave to issue the . . writs.

▸ **B** *adjectival phr.* **1** LAW. Of an application, injunction, deposition, etc.: made, issued, etc., by or for only one party in a case. **L18.**
2 Of a statement etc.: one-sided, partial. **E19.**

expat /ɛks'pat/ *noun. colloq.* **M20.**
[ORIGIN Abbreviation.]
= EXPATRIATE *noun*.

expatiate /ɪk'speɪʃɪeɪt, ɛk-/ *verb.* Pa. pple **-ated**, (*arch.*) **-ate** /-ət/. **M16.**
[ORIGIN Latin *ex(s)patiat-* pa. ppl stem of *ex(s)patiari*, formed as EX-¹ 1 + *spatiari* to walk, from *spatium* space.]
1 *verb intrans.* & †*refl.* Wander about at will; roam unrestrained. Now *rare*. **M16.**

J. R. LOWELL Winter-flies . . crawl out . . to expatiate in the sun.

2 *verb intrans.* Speak or write at great length on a topic; dilate. Usu. foll. by *on*. **E17.**

D. CARNEGIE For the next hour he expatiated on the peculiar . . virtues of the plumbing market.

3 **a** *verb trans.* Extend or diffuse (a thing) so that it covers a wide area. Now *rare* or *obsolete*. **E17.** ▸†**b** *verb intrans. & refl.* Widen its scope or area; expand, extend. **M17–L18.**

T. ADAMS Princes expatiate their dominions.

■ **expatiater** *noun* a person who expatiates **M19.** **expatiative** *adjective* (**a**) having a tendency to expand; (**b**) given to roaming freely: **E19.** **expatiator** *noun* = EXPATIATER **M18.** **expatiatory** *adjective* marked by lengthy discourse; prone to talk at length: **E19.**

expatiation /ɪkˌspeɪʃɪ'eɪʃ(ə)n, ɛk-/ *noun.* **E17.**
[ORIGIN from EXPATIATE: see -ATION.]
†**1** Expansion, development; an extended portion. **E–M17.**
2 The action or an act of roaming at will. Also (*rare*), liberty to roam. **M17.**
3 (A) lengthy treatment of a topic. **E19.**

expatriate /ɪks'patrɪət, -'peɪt-, 'ɛks-/ *noun & adjective.* **E19.**
[ORIGIN formed as EXPATRIATE *verb*: see -ATE².]
▸ **A** *noun.* Orig., an exile. Now, a person who lives from choice in a foreign country. **E19.**

C. P. SNOW An American expatriate, corrupted by Europe in the Jamesian style.

▸ **B** *adjective.* Orig., exiled. Now, living in a foreign country from choice. Also, of or relating to an expatriate or expatriates. **E19.**

C. THUBRON Many of his contemporaries never forgave Turgenev for his expatriate life.

■ **expatriatism** *noun* the condition or fact of being an expatriate **L20.**

expatriate /ɪks'patrɪeɪt, -'peɪt-, ɛks-/ *verb.* **M18.**
[ORIGIN Latin *expatriat-* pa. ppl stem of *expatriare*, formed as EX-¹ 1 + *patria* native country: see -ATE³.]
1 *refl.* & (*rare*) *verb intrans.* Leave one's country voluntarily; emigrate, settle abroad. Also, renounce one's citizenship. **M18.**
2 *verb trans.* Expel (a person) from his or her native country; banish, exile. **E19.**
■ **expatri'ation** *noun* **L18.**

†**expect** *noun. rare.* **L16–E17.**
[ORIGIN from the verb.]
= EXPECTATION 3.

expect /ɪk'spɛkt, ɛk-/ *verb.* **M16.**
[ORIGIN Latin *ex(s)pectare*, formed as EX-¹ 1 + *spectare* to look.]
▸ **I** *verb intrans.* †**1** Defer action; wait. **M16–M18.**

HENRY MORE A Dog expects till his Master has done picking of the bone.

†**2** Foll. by *for*: look forward to. **L16–M17.**
3 Of a female: be pregnant. Chiefly & now always in ***be expecting***. Cf. sense 6b below. *colloq.* **E19.**

A. DESAI I was married, Sarla was expecting.

▸ **II** *verb trans.* †**4** Wait for, await. Of a destiny: be in store for. **L16–E19.** ▸**b** Wait to see or know (*what, how, when*, etc.). **L16–L18.**

GIBBON The . . king of the Goths, instead of expecting the attack of the Legions, boldly passed the Danube. W. COWPER Prisons expect the wicked. **b** W. GODWIN Mr. Tyrrel expected every moment when he would withdraw.

5 Regard as about or likely to happen; look forward to the occurrence of (an event). (Foll. by *that*, *to do*; someone or something *to do*.) **L16.**

M. EDGEWORTH They expected a visit in a few hours. J. TYNDALL The Mur . . was by no means so bad as we had expected. J. CONRAD You can't expect to have it always your own way. E. O'NEILL It's just as well to expect the worst and you'll never be disappointed. C. P. SNOW I expect I shall be able to manage. E. J. HOWARD She was always expecting something wonderful to happen to her.

6 Look forward to the arrival of (a person, esp. a guest) or the receipt of (something). **L16.** ▸**b** Be pregnant with (a child). Cf. sense 3 above. **E20.**

T. HARDY He expected a reply on the second morning . . but none came. G. B. SHAW Oh, Juggins, we're expecting Mr and Mrs Knox to tea. J. BUCHAN I . . may be absent for days. Expect me back when you see me. **b** J. HERRIOT Helen was expecting our baby this week-end.

7 Believe that it will prove to be the case that or *that*; suspect, suppose. **L16.**

S. O. JEWETT He's got too unwieldy to tackle a smart coon, I expect. B. PYM I expect your mother lies awake till you get in.

8 Look for as due or requisite from another. (Foll. by someone or something *to do*.) **E17.**

W. CATHER He seemed to expect his wife to do the talking. A. FRASER Much was traditionally expected of a royal prince in the way of benevolence.

■ **expected** *ppl adjective* that is expected, that one would expect; ***expected value*** (Math.), a value of a variable, calculated by adding all the possible values, each multiplied by the probability of its occurrence: **L16.** **expectedly** *adverb* (**a**) in the manner expected; (**b**) (introducing a sentence) it is to be expected that: **M18.** **expecter** *noun* **L16.** **expecting** *ppl adjective* †(**a**) expected; (**b**) expectant: **E17.** **expectingly** *adverb* **L17.**

expectable /ɪk'spɛktəb(ə)l, ɛk-/ *adjective.* **L16.**
[ORIGIN from EXPECT *verb* + -ABLE. In sense 1 after Spanish *espectable* from Latin *spectabilis*, from *spectare* look at.]
†**1** Distinguished, illustrious. Only in **L16.**
2 That ought to be or is expected. **M17.**

I. BARROW In that measure which is expectable from the natural infirmity . . of man. *Chambers's Journal* The machine . . can handle all expectable types of envelope.

■ **expectably** *adverb* **M20.**

expectance /ɪk'spɛkt(ə)ns, ɛk-/ *noun.* **E17.**
[ORIGIN formed as EXPECTANCY: see -ANCE.]
1 The state of waiting for something; esp. in ***after long expectance***. Formerly also, the state of waiting to know (*what, how, when*, etc.). *arch.* **E17.**

SHAKES. *Tr. & Cr.* There is expectance here from both the sides What further you will do.

2 The action or state of expecting the occurrence of something; expectation. Now *rare*. **E17.**

H. SLINGSBY Great expectance their is of a happy Parliament.

†**3** Grounds for expecting something; prospect, esp. of inheriting. **E17–L18.**

E. PARSONS An aunt . . from whom he has great expectances.

†**in expectance** in prospect.

expectancy /ɪk'spɛkt(ə)nsi, ɛk-/ *noun.* **E17.**
[ORIGIN Latin *ex(s)pectantia*, from *ex(s)pectant-*: see EXPECTANT, -ANCY.]
1 (An) expectation of a coming event; (an) expectant attitude. **E17.** ▸**b** An object of hope or expectation. *arch.* **E17.**

O. HENRY Sick with expectancy of the news he feared. D. PARKER There was an air of expectancy about them . . as of those who wait for a curtain to rise. **b** WORDSWORTH The Nation hailed Their great expectancy.

2 The extent to which an expectation may reasonably be entertained; the prospective chance of an event. **E17.**
life expectancy: see LIFE *noun*.
3 Chiefly LAW. The condition of being expected; the position of being entitled to a possession at some future

E

time, on the happening of a contingency or the termination of prior interests. Usu. in ***in expectancy*. M17.**

> BURKE A practical reputation, to do any good, must be in possession, not in expectancy.

4 The position of being a prospective heir. **E19.**
5 What a person is entitled to expect; *spec.* a prospective inheritance. **M19.**

expectant /ɪkˈspɛkt(ə)nt, ɛk-/ *adjective & noun.* **LME.**
[ORIGIN Latin *ex(s)pectant-* pres. ppl stem of *ex(s)pectare* EXPECT *verb*: see -ANT¹.]
▸ **A** *adjective.* **1** In an attitude of expectation; waiting to see what will happen, etc. **LME.**

> D. H. LAWRENCE A little group of expectant people, waiting to see the wedding.

2 Of a person: having or foreseeing the prospect of coming into a certain position, succeeding to an inheritance, etc. **LME.** ▸**b** Expecting the birth of a child. Chiefly in ***expectant mother*. M19.**

> LYTTON A pious Catholic, expectant of the cardinal's hat.

3 To be expected; *esp.* (LAW) due to come to a person in reversion. **E17.**

> A. TUCKER We encourage ourselves to any . . disagreeable task by prospect of the profit expectant therefrom.

expectant heir LAW a person with a reversionary right or hope of succession to a property.
4 Of a method (esp. a medical treatment), a policy, etc.: that leaves events to take their course. **E19.**
▸ **B** *noun.* **1** A person who is expecting an event, a benefit, etc.; *spec.* one who has the prospect of succeeding to property, a position, etc. **E17.**
2 A candidate for office. Formerly (*Scot.*), a candidate for the ministry who has not yet been licensed to preach. **M17.**
■ **expectantly** *adverb* **M19.**

expectation /ɛkspɛkˈteɪʃ(ə)n/ *noun.* **M16.**
[ORIGIN Latin *ex(s)pectatio(n-)*, from *ex(s)pectat-* pa. ppl stem of *ex(s)pectare* EXPECT *verb*: see -ATION.]
1 The action of waiting for someone or something. Now passing into sense 3: expectant waiting. **M16.** ▸**b** MEDICINE. The expectant method (see EXPECTANT *adjective* 4). **L17.**

> R. SOUTH A daily Expectation at the gate, is the readiest Way to gain Admittance into the House.

2 A preconceived idea of what will happen, what someone or something will turn out to be, etc.; the action of entertaining such an idea. **M16.**

> J. BUTLER Our expectations that others will act so and so in such circumstances. B. PYM Emma had so far failed to come up to her mother's expectations. J. LE CARRÉ Was Mundt to make a dramatic return to his home country, against all expectation?

3 The state or mental attitude of expecting something to happen; expectancy. **M16.**

> E. O'NEILL His face beams with the excited expectation of a boy going to a party.

4 A thing expected or looked forward to. **L16.**
†**5** Promise of future excellence. Esp. in ***of expectation***, ***of great expectation***, etc. **L16–L18.**
6 Grounds for expecting; *esp.* (in *pl.*) prospects of inheriting wealth. **E17.**

> AV *Ps.* 72:5 My soule waite thou onely vpon God; for my expectation is from him. J. R. ACKERLEY Mr. Burckhardt died . . intestate . . so that all my father's expectations came to nothing.

7 The condition of being expected. Only in ***in expectation*. M17.**

> T. REID Belief of good or ill either present or in expectation.

8 Degree of probability that something will occur, expressed numerically; MATH. = ***expected value*** s.v. EXPECTED. **E18.**
expectation of life, ***life expectation***: see LIFE *noun*.
9 Supposition with regard to the present or the past. **L18.**

expectative /ɪkˈspɛktətɪv, ɛk-/ *adjective & noun.* **L15.**
[ORIGIN medieval Latin *expectativus*, from Latin *ex(s)pectat-*: see EXPECTATION, -IVE.]
▸ **A** *adjective.* **1** ECCLESIASTICAL. Relating to the reversion of benefices etc.; reversionary. **L15.**
grace expectative, **expectative grace** *hist.* a mandate given by a king or pope conferring the right of succession to a benefice.
2 = EXPECTANT *adjective* 4. **E17.**
▸ **B** *noun.* †**1** A thing looked forward to; a prospective benefit. **E16–M18.**
2 = ***grace expectative*** (see sense A.1). **L16.**

expective /ɪkˈspɛktɪv, ɛk-/ *adjective. rare.* **M17.**
[ORIGIN from EXPECT *verb* + -IVE.]
= EXPECTATIVE *adjective*.

expectorant /ɪkˈspɛkt(ə)r(ə)nt, ɛk-/ *noun & adjective.* **M18.**
[ORIGIN Latin *expectorant-* pres. ppl stem of *expectorare*: see EXPECTORATE, -ANT¹.]
▸ **A** *noun.* An expectorant medicine. **M18.**
▸ **B** *adjective.* Of a medicine: causing increased production of sputum, and so facilitating clearance of the bronchial passages. **E19.**

expectorate /ɪkˈspɛktəreɪt, ɛk-/ *verb.* **E17.**
[ORIGIN Latin *expectorat-* pa. ppl stem of *expectorare*, formed as EX-¹ 1 + *pector-*, *pectus* breast: see -ATE³.]
†**1** *verb trans.* Of a medicine: enable (sputum) to be expelled from the chest or lungs. **E17–L18.**
2 *verb trans.* Eject from the throat or bronchial passages by coughing, hawking, etc. **M17.**

> E. B. BROWNING A woman expectorated blood violently as an effect of the experiment.

3 *verb refl. & intrans.* Relieve one's feelings. *arch.* **M17.**
4 *verb intrans.* Clear one's throat or bronchial passages of sputum; clear one's mouth of saliva, spit. **E19.**
■ **expectoˈration** *noun* the action or an act of expectorating or spitting; expectorated matter: **E17. expectorative** *noun & adjective* (*rare*) †(*a*) *noun* = EXPECTORANT *noun*; (*b*) *adjective* of or marked by expectoration: **M17. expectorator** *noun* †(*a*) = EXPECTORANT *noun*; (*b*) a person who expectorates or spits: **L17.**

expede /ɪkˈspiːd, ɛk-/ *verb trans. Scot.* Now *rare.* **M16.**
[ORIGIN Latin *expedire*: see EXPEDITE *verb*.]
†**1** Deal with; accomplish, complete, settle. **M16–L18.**
2 Send out or issue (a document) officially. **M16.**
†**3** Send, esp. quickly; dispatch. **L16–M17.**

ex pede Herculem /ɛks ˌpɛdɪ ˈhəːkjʊlɛm/ *adverbial phr.* **M17.**
[ORIGIN Latin = Hercules from his foot.]
Inferring the whole of something from an insignificant part, as Pythagoras supposedly calculated Hercules' height from the size of his foot.

expedience /ɪkˈspiːdɪəns, ɛk-/ *noun.* **LME.**
[ORIGIN formed as EXPEDIENCY: see -ENCE.]
1 = EXPEDIENCY 1. Now *rare* or *obsolete*. **LME.**
†**2** Haste, speed, dispatch. Also, something that requires this; an enterprise, an expedition. **L15–E17.**
3 = EXPEDIENCY 2. **E17.**

expediency /ɪkˈspiːdɪənsi, ɛk-/ *noun.* **E17.**
[ORIGIN Partly from late Latin *expedientia*, partly from EXPEDIENT: see -ENCY.]
1 The quality or state of being expedient; suitability to the circumstances or conditions of the case; fitness, advantage. **E17.**

> C. MIDDLETON In some perplexity . . about the expediency of the voyage.

2 The consideration of what is expedient, as a motive or rule of action; the consideration of what is politic as opp. to what is just and right. **E17.** ▸**b** In *pl.* Motives of expediency, the requirements of expediency. **M19.**

> I. D'ISRAELI Where political expediency seems to violate all moral right. B. BETTELHEIM His choice of work must not be due to mere convenience, chance or expediency. **b** J. S. MILL These reasons must arise from the special expediencies of the case.

expedient /ɪkˈspiːdɪənt, ɛk-/ *adjective & noun.* **LME.**
[ORIGIN Latin *expedient-* pres. ppl stem of *expedire*: see EXPEDITE *verb*, -ENT.]
▸ **A** *adjective* **I 1** Advantageous (in general or to a definite purpose); fit, proper; suitable to the circumstances of the case. Foll. by *for*, †*to*. Usu. *pred.* **LME.**

> T. BEDDOES These, if not necessary to the existence of vegetables, may be expedient to their flourishing state. W. TAYLOR The most expedient settlements for a trading country. F. L. WRIGHT To use our new materials . . in ways that were not only expedient but beautiful.

2 Useful or politic as opp. to right or just; advisable on practical rather than moral grounds. **L18.**

> J. MCPHEE Because everybody in Alaska hates Anchorage it is politically expedient to put the capital in a new place.

▸ †**II 3** Hasty, speedy; (of a march) direct. **L15–L16.**
▸ **B** *noun.* A means of attaining an end; a shift; a resource. **LME.**

> R. H. TAWNEY What is venial as an occasional expedient is reprehensible when carried on as a regular occupation. I. COLEGATE Her widely admired 'natural look' was achieved by the simple expedient of not taking much trouble over her clothes.

■ **expediently** *adverb* **LME. expedientness** *noun* (*rare*) **M18.**

expediential /ɪkˌspiːdɪˈɛnʃ(ə)l, ɛk-/ *adjective.* **M19.**
[ORIGIN from EXPEDIENCY + -AL¹.]
Of, pertaining to, or having regard to what is expedient.
■ **expedientially** *adverb* (*rare*) **L19.**

expeditate /ɪkˈspɛdɪteɪt, ɛk-/ *verb trans. obsolete* exc. *hist.* **E16.**
[ORIGIN medieval Latin *expeditat-* pa. ppl stem of *expeditare*, formed as EX-¹ 1 + *ped-*, *pes* foot, on the analogy of medieval Latin *excapitare* decapitate.]
Deprive (a dog) of claws or the ball of the foot to restrict free movement in hunting etc.
■ **expediˈtation** *noun* **E16.**

expedite /ˈɛkspɪdʌɪt/ *adjective.* Now *rare.* **M16.**
[ORIGIN Latin *expeditus* pa. pple of *expedire*: see EXPEDITE *verb*, -ITE².]
1 Prompt, speedy, expeditious. **M16.**
†**2** Clear of obstacles or impediments (*lit.* & *fig.*); free from difficulties. **L16–L17.**
†**3** Unencumbered; unrestricted in movement; active, nimble; (of a soldier) lightly equipped. **L16–L18.**
4 Of a thing: ready for immediate use; handy; serviceable. **E17.**
†**5** Of a person: prompt, alert, ready. Only in **17.**

expedite /ˈɛkspɪdʌɪt/ *verb trans.* **L15.**
[ORIGIN Latin *expedit-* pa. ppl stem of *expedire* extricate (orig. free the feet), put in order, formed as EX-¹ 1 + *ped-*, *pes* foot: see -ITE².]
1 Deal with, accomplish; dispatch, perform quickly. **L15.**

> B. TAYLOR Such is my wish: dare thou to expedite it.

2 Help forward, hasten the progress of. **E17.**

> K. M. E. MURRAY The Press would not agree to the extra expense . . without a guarantee that production would thereby be . . expedited.

3 Send out or issue (a document etc.) officially; dispatch (a message, a courier); send out (troops, munitions). Now *rare.* **E17.**
†**4** Clear of difficulties; clear up (confusion); facilitate (action or movement); disentangle, untie. Only in **17.**
■ **expediter** *noun* = EXPEDITOR **L19. expeditor** *noun* a person who expedites something; *spec.* a progress chaser: **M20.**

expedition /ɛkspɪˈdɪʃ(ə)n/ *noun.* **LME.**
[ORIGIN Old French & mod. French *expédition* from Latin *expeditio(n-)*, formed as EXPEDITE *verb*: see -ITION.]
†**1** The action of expediting something; prompt performance or supply of something; dispatch. **LME–M17.**
†**in expedition** in the condition of being expedited.
2 a A sending or setting forth with martial intentions; a warlike enterprise. **LME.** ▸**b** A journey, voyage, or excursion made for a specific purpose. **L16.**

> **a** R. HAKLUYT He conquered not in that expedition. **b** J. WYNDHAM There are notes of the places to which my expeditions took me.

b ***fishing expedition***: see FISHING *noun*.
†**3** The action of issuing official documents or other articles; a document so issued. **L15–L18.**
4 Quick movement; promptness, speed; dispatch. **L16.**

> MILTON With winged expedition, Swift as the lightning glance. W. PENN With all possible vigilance and expedition.

5 A body, esp. a military force, sent out for a specific purpose. **L17.**

> A. F. DOUGLAS-HOME The advance of a punitive expedition sent by King Henry.

■ **expeditioner** *noun* (*rare*) an expeditionist **M18. expeditionist** *noun* a person who makes, or takes part in, an expedition **M19. expeditionary** *adjective & noun* (*a*) *adjective* of or pertaining to an expedition; sent on an (esp. military) expedition; (*b*) *noun* an expeditionist: **E19.**

expeditious /ɛkspɪˈdɪʃəs/ *adjective.* **L15.**
[ORIGIN from EXPEDITION: see -ITIOUS¹.]
1 Speedily performed or given; conducive to speedy performance. **L15.**

> J. G. MURPHY Equipped for expeditious travelling.

2 Of a person: acting or moving with expedition; speedy. **L16.**

> J. A. FROUDE The German commission was as expeditious as the Spanish had been dilatory.

— NOTE: Rare before **17.**
■ **expeditiously** *adverb* **E17. expeditiousness** *noun* **E18.**

expel /ɪkˈspɛl, ɛk-/ *verb trans.* Infl. **-ll-**. **LME.**
[ORIGIN Latin *expellere*, formed as EX-¹ 1 + *pellere* to drive, thrust.]
1 Eject; cause to depart or emerge, esp. by the use of force; banish from a place; discharge (a bullet). (Foll. by *from*.) **LME.**

> E. HUXLEY In 1290 Edward I expelled the Jews. W. GOLDING She drew, puffed, expelled long coils of smoke. *Daily Telegraph* They were expelled on a flight leaving for Namibia later in the day. P. NORMAN He strove . . to expel even from his mind all that might be incriminating or unseemly.

2 Compel the departure of (a person) from a society, community, etc.; *esp.* enforce the departure of (a student) from an educational establishment as a punitive measure. (Foll. by *from*, †2nd obj.) **M16.**

> SOUTHEY Whoever acted contrary . . should be expelled the Society. M. MITCHELL They had just been expelled from . . the fourth university that had thrown them out in two years.

†**3** Reject from attention or consideration. **L16–M18.**
†**4** Keep off, exclude, keep out. *rare* (Shakes.). Only in **E17.**
■ **expellable** *adjective* **M17. expeˈllee** *noun* a person who has been expelled **L19. expeller** *noun* **M16.**

expellent /ɪkˈspɛlənt/ *noun & adjective.* Also **-ant**. **E19.**
[ORIGIN Latin *expellent-* pres. ppl stem of *expellere* EXPEL: see -ENT.]
▸ **A** *noun.* A medicine believed to expel unwholesome matter. *rare.* **E19.**
▸ **B** *adjective.* That expels or tends to expel. **M19.**

†**expence** *noun* var. of EXPENSE.

expend /ɪkˈspɛnd, ɛk-/ *verb trans.* **LME.**
[ORIGIN Latin *expendere*, formed as EX-¹ 1 + *pendere* weigh, pay. Cf. SPEND *verb*.]
▸ **I 1** Spend (money); devote (care, time, effort); employ for a given purpose. Formerly also, spend completely, consume (resources) in outlay. (Foll. by *on* an object, *in* an action, *doing*.) **LME.**

L. STEFFENS The promoter had expended nearly $300,000 in securing the legislation. P. G. WODEHOUSE He had expended much thought on the subject. C. RYCROFT Freud expended much ink and energy trying to prove that artists are neurotics.

2 Use up (material, strength, etc.) in any operation. Formerly also, consume (provisions). **M18.**

JOHN PHILLIPS After the currents had expended themselves. G. ORWELL A convenient way of expending labour power without producing anything that can be consumed.

3 *NAUTICAL*. Lose (spars, masts, etc.) in fighting, by storm, etc. Also, use up (spare rope) by winding it round a spar etc. **E19.**

F. MARRYAT Have you expended any boat's masts?

▸ †**II 4** Weigh mentally; consider, determine accurately. **M16–L17.**

■ **expender** *noun* **LME.**

expendable /ɪkˈspɛndəb(ə)l, ɛk-/ *adjective & noun*. **E19.**
[ORIGIN from EXPEND + -ABLE.]
▸ **A** *adjective*. That may be expended; regarded as not worth preserving or saving; not normally reused; unimportant, able to be sacrificed to achieve an object. **E19.**

W. L. WHITE In a war anything can be expendable—money or gasoline or equipment or most usually men.

▸ **B** *noun*. An expendable person or object. **M20.**
■ **expendaˈbility** *noun* **L20.** **expendably** *adverb* **L20.**

expenditor /ɪkˈspɛndɪtə, ɛk-/ *noun*. **L15.**
[ORIGIN medieval Latin, from *expenditus* irreg. pa. pple (after *venditus* sold) of *expendere*: see EXPEND, -OR.]
A person in charge of expenditure; *spec.* (now *hist.*) an officer appointed to disburse the money collected by tax for the repair of sewers.

expenditure /ɪkˈspɛndɪtʃə, ɛk-/ *noun*. **M18.**
[ORIGIN from EXPEND after EXPENDITOR: see -URE.]
1 a The action or practice of expending money, care, time, effort, etc. **M18.** ▸**b** The action or process of using up; consumption. **E19.**

a ADAM SMITH The collection and expenditure of the public revenue. GEO. ELIOT He disliked all quarrelling as an unpleasant expenditure of energy.

2 An amount expended. **L18.**

R. P. GRAVES The move had . . reduced his income and increased his expenditure. J. BRAINE My salary didn't allow for casual expenditures of nearly ten bob.

expense /ɪkˈspɛns, ɛk-/ *noun & verb*. Also †**-ence**. **LME.**
[ORIGIN Anglo-Norman, alt. of Old French *espense* from late Latin *expensa* (sc. *pecunia* money) fem. of pa. pple of Latin *expendere* EXPEND.]
▸ **A** *noun*. **1** The action or an act of expending something; the state of being expended; disbursement; consumption; loss; = EXPENDITURE 1. Now *rare*. **LME.**

S. JOHNSON This exuberance of money displayed itself in wantonness of expence. U. LE GUIN The protein issue . . was now insufficient for full normal expense of energy.

†**2** Money expended; an amount expended. **LME–M18.**

W. PETTY Where a People thrive, there the income is greater than the expence.

3 Burden of expenditure; the charge or cost involved in or required for something; in *pl.*, the charges etc. incurred by a person in the course of working for another or undertaking any enterprise; the amount paid in reimbursement. **LME.** ▸**b** A cause or occasion of expense. **L19.**

A. PARSONS Those who can afford the expence, usually go to . . the sea coast. *Daily Telegraph* The home eleven had got 52 at an expense of two wickets. V. WOOLF Nancy, dressed at enormous expense by the greatest artists in Paris. F. TUOHY Vince's fat cheque to cover the expenses of a prolonged stay in Paris. **b** OED His sons have been a great expense to him.

– PHRASES: **at a person's expense** causing a person to spend money or suffer injury, ridicule, etc. **at the expense of** so as to cause loss, damage, or discredit to; to the detriment of. **put to expense**, **put to great expense**, etc., cause to spend (much etc.) money.

– COMB.: **expense account** (*a*) an account in which are recorded other than capital payments made by a business; (*b*) a list of an employee's expenses payable by an employer.

▸ **B** *verb trans*. **1** Charge (a business) with expenses incurred. **E20.**
2 Offset (an expense) against taxable income. **M20.**
■ †**expenseful** *adjective* costly, expensive; extravagant: **E17–E18.** †**expenseless** *adjective* inexpensive; frugal: **M17–L18.**

expensive /ɪkˈspɛnsɪv, ɛk-/ *adjective*. **E17.**
[ORIGIN from Latin *expens-* pa. ppl stem of *expendere* EXPEND + -IVE. Assoc. early with EXPENSE.]
1 Given to profuse expenditure (of money, effort, etc.) or consumption (of time, health, etc.); lavish, extravagant. Now *rare*. **E17.**

STEELE Young Men . . are . . so expensive both of their Health and Fortune. J. GILCHRIST A regular arrangement of extracts . . is . . more expensive of time.

2 Causing much expense, costly; making a high charge; highly priced, dear. **M17.**

J. A. FROUDE The father . . was unable to give the child as expensive an education as he had desired. W. MAXWELL The two upstairs rooms are . . expensive to heat in winter.

■ **expensively** *adverb* **E17.** **expensiveness** *noun* **M17.**

expergefaction /ɪkˌspəːdʒɪˈfakʃ(ə)n, ɛk-/ *noun*. Now *rare* or *obsolete*. **M17.**
[ORIGIN Late Latin *expergefactio(n-)*, from Latin *expergefact-* pa. ppl stem of *expergefacere* awaken, arouse, from *expergere* awaken, arouse: see -FACTION.]
The action of awaking or rousing; the state, condition, or fact of being awakened or aroused.

experience /ɪkˈspɪərɪəns, ɛk-/ *noun*. **LME.**
[ORIGIN Old French & mod. French *expérience* from Latin *experientia*, from *experiri* try: see -ENCE.]
1 †**a** The action of putting to the test, trial. **LME–M17.** ▸**b** A procedure carried out to test or demonstrate something; an experiment. Now *rare* or *obsolete*. **LME.**

a J. SHIRLEY Make Experience of my loyalty, by some service.

2 Proof by actual trial; practical demonstration. *obsolete* exc. as passing into sense 3. **LME.**
3 Actual observation of or practical acquaintance with facts or events, considered as a source of knowledge. **LME.**

T. REID Experience informs us only of what has been, but never of what must be.

4 A state, condition, or event that consciously affects one; the fact or process of being so affected. **LME.** ▸**b** A state of mind or feeling forming part of the inner religious life; a state or phase of religious emotion. **L17.**

LD MACAULAY Both . . had learned by experience how soon James forgot obligation. J. BARZUN Boredom is not the trivial, harmless experience that common speech assumes. S. BARSTOW I'd never been involved in a wedding before . . it's what you might call an experience.

peak experience: see PEAK *noun*[1] & *adjective*.

5 The state of having been occupied in any branch of study or affairs; the extent or period of such an occupation; the aptitudes, skill, judgement, etc., thereby acquired. **L15.**

SHAKES. *Two Gent.* His years but young, but his experience old. G. GORER The belief that experience is unnecessary, because 'nature teaches'.

6 Knowledge resulting from actual observation or practical acquaintance, or from what one has undergone. **M16.** ▸†**b** A fact, maxim, or rule based on experience; something expertly fashioned. **L16–L17.**

J. TYNDALL I had had but little experience of alpine phenomena. G. GREENE My experience of diaries is they always give things away.

7 What has been experienced; the events that have taken place within the knowledge of an individual, a community, the human race, etc. **E17.**

A. P. HERBERT In all her experience as a model. J. HELLER To write about the Jewish experience in America.

experience /ɪkˈspɪərɪəns, ɛk-/ *verb trans*. **M16.**
[ORIGIN from the noun.]
†**1** Make trial or experiment of; test, try. **M16–L18.**
†**2** Ascertain or prove by experiment or observation. (Foll. by obj. clause, *that*.) **M16–M18.**
†**3** Give experience to; make experienced; train (soldiers); in *pass.*, be informed or taught by experience. **M16–M17.**
4 Have experience of; feel, suffer, undergo. **L16.**

SIR W. SCOTT The hottest weather I ever experienced. W. GOLDING Free-will cannot be debated but only experienced, like a colour or the taste of potatoes. D. MURPHY I experienced an almost hysterical elation. I. MURDOCH The most . . peaceful sleep that I had experienced for a long time.

experience RELIGION.

5 Learn (a fact) by experience; find (*how*, *what*, *that*). Now *rare*. **L16.**
■ **experienceable** *adjective* able to be experienced **E20.** **experiencer** *noun* †(*a*) *rare* an experimenter; (*b*) a person who experiences something: **M17.**

experienced /ɪkˈspɪərɪənst, ɛk-/ *adjective*. **M16.**
[ORIGIN from EXPERIENCE *noun*, *verb*: see -ED[2], -ED[1].]
1 Having experience; wise or skilful through experience. (Foll. by *in*.) **M16.**

H. MARTINEAU The stray sheep may come back experienced in pasturage. R. L. FOX A famous shield-to-shield rally by a battalion of Philip's most experienced veterans.

†**2** Tried, tested, approved; = EXPERT *adjective* 3. **M16–L18.**

S. JOHNSON To . . counteract by experienced remedies every new tendency.

3 = EXPERIENT *adjective* 2. Long *rare*. **E17.**

A. ALISON Experienced grievances.

experient /ɪkˈspɪərɪənt, ɛk-/ *adjective & noun*. **LME.**
[ORIGIN Latin *experient-* pres. ppl stem of *experiri*: see EXPERIENCE *noun*, -ENT.]
▸ **A** *adjective*. †**1** = EXPERIENCED 1. **LME–M17.**
2 Met with in the course of experience. *rare*. **E20.**
▸ **B** *noun*. †**1** Something experienced, tested, or tried. *rare*. Only in **E17.**
2 A person who experiences something or undergoes an experience. **L19.**

experiential /ɪkˌspɪərɪˈɛnʃ(ə)l, ɛk-/ *adjective*. **E19.**
[ORIGIN from EXPERIENCE *noun* + -IAL, after *inferential* etc.]
Of, pertaining to, or derived from experience or observation.
■ **experientialism** *noun* the theory or doctrine that all knowledge is based on experience **M19.** **experientialist** *noun* a supporter of or adherent of experientialism **L19.** **experientially** *adverb* with regard to experience, in or by experience **M17.**

experiment /ɪkˈspɛrɪmənt, ɛk-/ *noun*. **ME.**
[ORIGIN Old French, or Latin *experimentum*, from *experiri*: see EXPERIENCE *noun*, -MENT.]
▸ **I 1** The action of trying something or putting it to the test; a test, a trial. (Foll. by *of*.) *arch.* **ME.** ▸†**b** An expedient or remedy to be tried. **L16–E18.**
2 An action or procedure undertaken to make a discovery, test a hypothesis, or demonstrate a known fact. **LME.**

J. D. WATSON He . . visited other labs to see which new experiments had been done.

3 A procedure or course of action tentatively adopted without being sure that it will achieve its purpose. **L16.**

B. JOWETT The experiment had never been tried of reasoning with mankind.

4 The process or practice of conducting an experiment; experimentation. **L17.**

D. L. SAYERS She bought drugs in order to prove by experiment how easy it was . . to get hold of deadly poisons.

5 The equipment for a scientific experiment. **M20.**
▸ †**II 6** A practical proof; a specimen, an example. **ME–L17.**
7 Practical acquaintance with a person or thing; (an) experience. (Foll. by *of*.) **M16–M18.**

– PHRASES: ***Valsalva experiment***, ***Valsalva's experiment***: see VALSALVA 1.

■ †**experimentarian** *adjective & noun* (a philosopher) relying on experiment **M17–E19.** †**experimently** *adverb* by experience **LME–E19.**

experiment /ɪkˈspɛrɪmənt, ɛk-/ *verb*. **LME.**
[ORIGIN from the noun.]
†**1** *verb trans*. = EXPERIENCE *verb* 4. **LME–E18.**
†**2** *verb trans*. Ascertain or establish by trial. **L15–E19.**
3 *verb trans*. Make trial or experiment of; test, try. Now *rare*. **E16.**

S. LESLIE He had . . experimented their theories in his laboratory.

4 *verb intrans*. Perform an experiment or experiments (*on*, *with*). **L18.**

B. SPOCK You can experiment to see which precautions . . work best. E. BOWEN She experimented with the four-speed gear.

■ **experimenˈtation** *noun* the action or process of experimenting; a series of experiments: **L17.** **experiˈmentative** *adjective* of the nature of an experiment; inclined to make an experiment: **E19.** **experimenter** *noun* a person who experiments **M16.**

experimental /ɪkˌspɛrɪˈmɛnt(ə)l, ɛk-/ *adjective*. **L15.**
[ORIGIN medieval Latin *experimentalis*, from Latin *experimentum* EXPERIMENT *noun*: see -AL[1].]
†**1** Of a person: having actual or personal experience of something. Of a thing: coming within the range of experience; observed. **L15–M18.**
2 Based on experience as opp. to authority or conjecture; founded on experience only, empirical. Formerly also, discovered by experience. **E16.**

E. M. GOULBURN To bring myself and others to an experimental knowledge of God.

3 Based on, derived from, or making use of experiment; *esp.* designating (a specialist in) a branch of knowledge based on experiment. **L16.**

B. LOVELL Astronomical investigations are almost completely observational and not experimental.

experimental chemist, ***experimental physics***, ***experimental psychologist***, ***experimental psychology***, etc.

4 Of or pertaining to experiments; used in or for experiments. **L18.**

J. N. LOCKYER The spectrum of potassium . . varies very much under different experimental conditions.

5 Of the nature of an experiment; tentative; adopted or begun without assurance of success; *spec.* designating an educational establishment, artistic endeavour, etc., run or developed on non-traditional lines. **E19.**

JAS. MILL A first and experimental attempt. R. L. STEVENSON Wine in California is still in the experimental stage. M. GORDON Headmaster of an experimental school.

■ **experimentalism** *noun* (*a*) (adherence to) the principles of the empirical approach in philosophy or science; (*b*) *rare* experimental research, experimentation: **M19.** **experimentalist** *noun* (*a*) a scientist concerned with experimental research; a skilled experimenter; (*b*) a person given to experimenting with new methods of procedure etc.: **M18.** **experimentalize** *verb intrans*. perform or try experiments (*on*) **E19.** **experimentally** *adverb* (*a*) by or through experience; (*b*) by means of experiment: **L16.**

E

experimented /ɪk'spɛrɪmɛntɪd, ɛk-/ *ppl adjective.* Now *rare* or *obsolete.* **L15.**
[ORIGIN from EXPERIMENT *verb* + -ED[1].]
1 Experienced; versed or practised *in* a subject. **L15.**
†**2** Proved, tested, or known by experience or experiment; ascertained, authenticated. **M16–E19.**
†**3** = EXPERIENT *adjective* 2. **L17–E19.**

experimentum crucis /ɪk,spɛrɪmɛntəm 'kruːsɪs, 'kruːkɪs; ɛk-/ *noun phr.* **M17.**
[ORIGIN mod. Latin = crucial experiment.]
A decisive test showing which of several hypotheses is correct.

expert /'ɛkspəːt/ *noun.* **E19.**
[ORIGIN French, use as noun of Old French & mod. French *expert* adjective: see EXPERT *adjective.*]
1 A person with the status of an authority (*in* a subject) by reason of special skill, training, or knowledge; a specialist. Freq. *attrib.* **E19.**

W. BESANT My writing was well known; experts swore that the forgery was by me. I. A. RICHARDS A human relation between the expert and his lay audience must be created. *Essentials* The fitter will rely on keen eyes . . and expert knowledge. *Times* The court decides in the end, there are expert witnesses.

2 A person who is expert or who has gained skill from experience. (Foll. by *at, in, with.*) **M19.**

E. K. KANE Hans Christian . . an expert with the kayak and javelin.

3 A person who looks after or maintains machinery, esp. in a shearing shed; the manager of a team of shearers. *Austral. & NZ slang.* **E20.**

expert /'ɛkspəːt/ *adjective.* **LME.**
[ORIGIN Old French & mod. French, alt. of *espert* after Latin *expertus* pa. pple of *experiri* try.]
†**1** Experienced (*in*); having experience (*of*). **LME–L17.**

W. PETTY A Protestant Militia of 25,000, the most whereof are expert in war.

2 Trained by practice or experience; skilled, skilful, (*at, in, with*). **LME.**

E. E. HALE The Florentine was not expert in ecclesiastical matters. T. CAPOTE The expert execution of the crimes. R. WEST He was becoming an expert player of the administrative game. J. STEINBECK She was so expert with the rolling-pin that the dough seemed alive.

expert system a computer program into which has been incorporated the knowledge of experts on a particular subject so that non-experts can use it for making decisions, evaluations, or inferences.

†**3** Tried, proved by experience; = EXPERIENCED 2. **LME–E17.**
■ **expertly** *adverb* **LME. expertness** *noun* **M17.**

expert /'ɛkspəːt/ *verb.* **L19.**
[ORIGIN from EXPERT *noun.*]
1 *verb trans.* Examine as an expert. *N. Amer. colloq.* **L19.**
2 *verb intrans.* Look after or maintain the machinery and tools of a shearing shed. Chiefly as ***experting*** *verbal noun.* *Austral. & NZ slang.* **M20.**

expertise /ɛkspəː'tiːz/ *noun.* **M19.**
[ORIGIN French.]
Expert opinion or knowledge; know-how, skill, or expertness in something.

expertize /'ɛkspətʌɪz/ *verb intrans. & trans.* Also **-ise.** **L19.**
[ORIGIN from EXPERT *noun* + -IZE.]
Give an expert opinion (on); evaluate.

expiable /'ɛkspɪəb(ə)l/ *adjective.* Now *rare.* **L16.**
[ORIGIN French, or ecclesiastical Latin *expiabilis*, from *expiare*: see EXPIATE *verb*, -ABLE.]
Able to be expiated.

†**expiate** *adjective.* *rare* (Shakes.) Only in **L16.**
[ORIGIN Latin *expiatus* pa. pple of *expiare*: see EXPIATE *verb*, -ATE[2].]
Of an appointed time: fully come; past.

expiate /'ɛkspɪeɪt/ *verb.* **L16.**
[ORIGIN Latin *expiat-* pa. ppl stem of *expiare*, formed as EX-[1] 1 + *piare* seek to appease (by sacrifice), from *pius* PIOUS: see -ATE[3].]
†**1** *verb trans.* Put an end to (pain etc.) by death; extinguish (rage) by suffering to the full. **L16–E17.**
†**2** *verb trans.* Cleanse (a person or place) of or *of* guilt or pollution by religious ceremonies. **E–M17.**
3 *verb trans.* Avert (a predicted evil). *obsolete* exc. *hist.* **E17.**
4 *verb trans. &* †*intrans.* with *for.* Atone or make amends for. **E17.**

P. USTINOV His father's heresies . . would sooner or later have to be expiated.

5 *verb trans.* Extinguish the guilt arising from (a sin); constitute atonement for. **E17.**

H. JAMES His fault had been richly expiated by these days of impatience and bereavement. C. H. SISSON To be seen naked was a shame Which only death could expiate.

6 *verb trans.* Pay the penalty of (an offence). **M17.**

LD MACAULAY Some of the girls who had presented the standard to Monmouth at Taunton had cruelly expiated their offence.

expiation /ɛkspɪ'eɪʃ(ə)n/ *noun.* **LME.**
[ORIGIN Latin *expiatio(n-)*, formed as EXPIATE *verb*: see -ATION.]
1 The action or an act of making atonement for a crime etc.; the condition of being expiated. **LME.** ▸†**b** The action of ceremonially cleansing of guilt or pollution. **M16–M17.**

W. STYRON My crime was ultimately beyond expiation.

2 A means by which atonement is made. **M16.**

D. ATHILL The suffering was no expiation because it was of his own making.

– PHRASES: **day of expiation**, **feast of expiation** *arch.* the Day of Atonement. **in expiation** (**of**) for the purpose of expiating (for). **make expiation** atone.

expiator /'ɛkspɪeɪtə/ *noun.* **M19.**
[ORIGIN Latin, from *expiare*: see EXPIATE *verb*, -OR.]
A person who makes expiation for a sin, crime, etc.

expiatory /'ɛkspɪət(ə)ri/ *adjective.* **L15.**
[ORIGIN ecclesiastical Latin *expiatorius*, formed as EXPIATOR: see -ORY[2].]
Serving to expiate. (Foll. by *of.*)

expilation /ɛkspɪ'leɪʃ(ə)n/ *noun.* Now *rare.* **M16.**
[ORIGIN Latin *expilatio(n-)*, from *expilat-* pa. ppl stem of *expilare* plunder, formed as EX-[1] 1 + *pilare* fix firmly: see -ATION.]
The action of plundering.

expiration /ɛkspɪ'reɪʃ(ə)n/ *noun.* **LME.**
[ORIGIN Latin *ex(s)piratio(n-)*, from *ex(s)pirat-* pa. ppl stem of *ex(s)pirare*: see EXPIRE, -ATION.]
†**1 a** A vapour, an exhalation. **LME–M17.** ▸**b** Change into vapour, evaporation. **E16–M17.**
†**2** The action of breathing one's last; death. **M16–E19.**
3 = EXPIRY 1. **M16.**

W. S. MAUGHAM It was at the expiration of their term [of hard labour] that their real punishment began. *Los Angeles Times* The expiration date on a cottage cheese carton had passed.

4 The action or an act of breathing out. **L16.**

F. H. RAMADGE The impeded expiration . . caused . . the lower lobes of the lung to be exceedingly enlarged.

5 (An) emission *of* air, vapour, etc. **M17.**

T. HARDY There came . . an utter expiration of air from the whole heaven in the form of a slow breeze.

■ **expiratory** /ɛks'pʌɪrət(ə)ri/ *adjective* **M19.**

expire /ɪk'spʌɪə, ɛk-/ *verb.* **LME.**
[ORIGIN Old French & mod. French *expirer* from Latin *ex(s)pirare* breathe out, formed as EX-[1] 1 + *spirare* breathe.]
▸ **I** Die; come or bring to an end.
†**1** *verb trans.* Breathe out (the soul, one's last breath, etc.) in the act of dying. **LME–E18.**
2 *verb intrans.* Of a person or animal: breathe for the last time, die. Of a fire etc.: die out. **LME.**

S. KING A young man . . had remained in a coma for fourteen years before expiring. J. THURBER He tossed away his cigar and watched it expire in the damp night grass.

3 *verb intrans.* Of a period of time: come to an end; *rare* elapse, pass. Of an action, state, legal title, etc: cease, die out; become void or extinct through lapse of time. **LME.**

J. GALSWORTHY The agreement . . was for a period of five years, of which one only had expired. P. USTINOV At midnight . . a British ultimatum expired, and Britain was . . at war.

†**4** *verb trans.* Bring to an end; conclude; make (a charter, gift, etc.) invalid or void. **LME–E17.**
▸ **II** Exhale, emit.
5 *verb trans. & intrans.* Breathe out (air etc.). Opp. ***inspire.*** **L16.**
6 Pass out like a breath; be exhaled; (of a wind, flame, projectile, etc.) rush forth. Now *rare.* **E17.**
†**7** *verb trans.* Give off or emit (a perfume, vapour, etc.), exhale; (of a volcano) emit (flames). **E17–E19.**
■ **expi'ree** *noun* (*hist.*) a person sentenced to transportation to Australia whose term of punishment had expired **E19. expirer** *noun* **L18.**

expiry /ɪk'spʌɪri, ɛk-/ *noun.* **M18.**
[ORIGIN from EXPIRE + -Y[3].]
1 The end or termination of a period of time, a contract, a truce, etc. **M18.**
2 Dying, death. *rare.* **L18.**

episcate /ɪk'spɪskeɪt, ɛk-/ *verb trans.* Chiefly *Scot.* Now *rare.* **E17.**
[ORIGIN Latin *expiscat-* pa. ppl stem of *expiscare* fish out, formed as EX-[1] 1 + *piscare* to fish: see -ATE[3].]
Fish out, find out, (a fact etc.); investigate; elucidate.
■ **expis'cation** *noun* **E17.**

explain /ɪk'spleɪn, ɛk-/ *verb.* **LME.**
[ORIGIN Latin *explanare*, formed as EX-[1] 1 + *planus* flat, PLAIN *adjective*[1], to which the mod. spelling is assim.]
1 *verb trans. & intrans.* Make clear or intelligible (a meaning, difficulty, etc.); clear of obscurity or difficulty; give details of (a matter, *how*, etc.) **LME.** ▸†**b** Speak one's mind *against*, *upon.* **E–M18.** ▸**c** *verb trans., & intrans.* with subord. clause. Say in explanation. **M19.**

M. GRAY He took a card from his pocket . . . 'That will explain to Dr. Everard,' he said. J. A. MICHENER He was weary from trying to explain ideas to people who could not visualize them. C. P. SNOW Briers had been explaining to his superiors what he intended to do. *Daily Telegraph* The Blackfoot chief . . explained how the braves used to drive buffalo. **c** R. LANGBRIDGE Tears came into Susette's eyes . . . 'I have bitten my tongue,' Susette explained. R. H. MOTTRAM The nursing sister . . explaining that the occupants were more or less convalescent.

†**2** Make smooth (the forehead or face). **M16–M17.**
†**3** *verb trans. & intrans.* Open out, unfold (an object). **E17–E18.** ▸**b** *verb trans.* Make plainly visible. **E–M17.**
explain into, **explain itself into** develop into.
4 *verb trans.* State the meaning or significance of; interpret. **E17.**
explain away modify or remove the force of (esp. offensive language, awkward facts, etc.) by explanation.
5 *refl.* Make clear one's meaning; give an account of one's motives or conduct. **E17.**

Economist Mr Kitson, who has refused to withdraw his reported remarks, will be asked to explain himself.

6 *verb trans.* Account for; make clear the cause or origin of. **M18.**

A. LURIE Knowing about Roz explains a lot.

■ **explainable** *adjective* **E17. explainer** *noun* **L16.**

explanandum /ɛksplə'nandəm/ *noun.* Pl. **-da** /-də/. **L19.**
[ORIGIN Latin, neut. gerundive of *explanare* EXPLAIN.]
PHILOSOPHY. = EXPLICANDUM. Cf. EXPLANANS.

explanans /ɛksplə'nanz/ *noun.* Pl. **-nantia** /-'nantɪə/. **M20.**
[ORIGIN Latin, pres. pple of *explanare* EXPLAIN.]
PHILOSOPHY. = EXPLICANS. Cf. EXPLANANDUM.

explanate /'ɛkspləneɪt/ *adjective.* **M19.**
[ORIGIN Latin *explanatus* pa. pple of *explanare* EXPLAIN: see -ATE[2].]
ZOOLOGY. Spread out flat.

explanation /ɛksplə'neɪʃ(ə)n/ *noun.* **LME.**
[ORIGIN Latin *explanatio(n-)*, from *explanat-* pa. ppl stem of *explanare* EXPLAIN: see -ATION.]
1 The action or an act of explaining. **LME.**

G. B. SHAW An unfortunate child . . receiving an elaborate explanation of the figures on a clock dial.

2 A statement, circumstance, etc., which makes clear or accounts for something. **E17.**

A. RADCLIFFE La Motte now asked for an explanation of the scene. E. O'NEILL For there must be a cause and a rational explanation.

3 A declaration made with a view to mutual understanding and reconciliation. **M19.**

explanative /ɪk'splanətɪv, ɛk-/ *adjective.* **E17.**
[ORIGIN Late Latin *explanativus*, from Latin *explanat-*: see EXPLANATION, -IVE.]
Explanatory.

explanatory /ɪk'splanət(ə)ri, ɛk-/ *adjective.* **E17.**
[ORIGIN Late Latin *explanatorius*, from *explanat-*: see EXPLANATION, -ORY[2].]
Serving, or intended to serve, as explanation; (of a person) disposed to explain.

DICKENS He rendered himself as explanatory as he could.

■ **explanatorily** *adverb* **M19. explanatoriness** *noun* **M18.**

explant /'ɛksplɑːnt/ *noun.* **E20.**
[ORIGIN from the verb.]
A piece of tissue, an organ, etc., that has been explanted.

explant /ɪk'splɑːnt/ *verb trans.* **L16.**
[ORIGIN mod. Latin *explantare*, from Latin EX-[1] 1 + *plantare* to plant.]
†**1** Send out as an offshoot. Only in **L16.**
2 Remove (living tissue) from its original site, esp. to initiate a culture of it in a nutrient medium. **E20.**
■ **explan'tation** *noun* (**a**) the action of explanting; †(**b**) an offshoot: **L16.**

†**expletion** *noun.* **E17–E18.**
[ORIGIN Latin *expletio(n-)*, from *explere*: see EXPLETIVE, -ION.]
The action of filling; repletion; fulfilment.

expletive /ɪk'spliːtɪv, ɛk-/ *adjective & noun.* **LME.**
[ORIGIN Late Latin *expletivus*, from *explere* fill out, formed as EX-[1] 1 + *plere* fill: see -IVE.]
▸ **A** *adjective.* Introduced merely to make up a required quantity; *esp.* (of a word or phrase) serving to fill out a sentence or metrical line. Formerly also (of a conjunction), correlative. **LME.**
▸ **B** *noun.* **1** A word or phrase used to fill out a sentence or metrical line. **E17.** ▸**b** An oath; a meaningless exclamation. **E19.**

b A. GUINNESS Tony let fly a stream of expletives.

2 A person who or thing which serves merely to fill up space. **L17.**
■ **expletively** *adverb* **E17.**

expletory /ɪk'spliːt(ə)ri, ɛk-/ *adjective.* **L17.**
[ORIGIN from Latin *explet-* pa. ppl stem of *explere*: see EXPLETIVE, -ORY[2].]
= EXPLETIVE *adjective.*

explicable /ɪk'splɪkəb(ə)l, ɛk-, 'ɛksplɪkəb(ə)l/ *adjective*. M16.
[ORIGIN French, or Latin *explicabilis*, from *explicare*: see EXPLICATE, -ABLE.]
Able to be explained or accounted for.

ISAIAH BERLIN Everything is in principle explicable, for everything has a purpose.

■ **explicably** *adverb* M20.

explicandum /ɛksplɪ'kandəm/ *noun*. Pl. **-da** /-də/. M19.
[ORIGIN Latin, neut. gerundive of *explicare*: see EXPLICATE.]
PHILOSOPHY. The fact, thing, or expression to be explained or explicated. Cf. EXPLANANDUM, next.

explicans /ɛksplɪ'kans/ *noun*. Pl. **-cantia** /-'kantɪə/. L19.
[ORIGIN Latin, pres. pple of *explicare*: see EXPLICATE.]
PHILOSOPHY. The explaining part of an explanation; in the analysis of a concept or expression, the part that gives the meaning. Cf. EXPLANANS, prec.

explicate /'ɛksplɪkeɪt/ *verb*. M16.
[ORIGIN Latin *explicat-* pa. ppl stem of *explicare* unfold, formed as EX-¹ 1 + *plicare* to fold: see -ATE³.]
†**1** *verb trans.* Unfold, unwrap; open out (a bud, leaf, etc.); spread out, display. M16–E18. ▸**b** Make larger in area or volume. L16–M17.
2 *verb trans. & intrans.* Give details (of). Now *rare*. M16.
3 *verb trans.* Explain, make clear. M16. ▸†**b** *refl.* Make clear one's meaning. M16–M17.

M. AMIS I explicated a Donne sonnet.

4 *verb trans.* Develop the meaning or implication of (a principle, notion, etc.). E17.
†**5** *verb trans.* = EXPLAIN 6. E17–E18.
†**6** *verb trans.* Unravel, solve, (a difficulty etc.); disentangle, extricate *from* (a difficulty etc.). Also foll. by *out of*. E17–E18.
■ **explicatory** /ɛksplɪ'keɪt(ə)ri, ɛk'splɪkət(ə)ri/ *adjective* E17.

explication /ɛksplɪ'keɪʃ(ə)n/ *noun*. E16.
[ORIGIN French, or Latin *explicatio(n-)*, formed as EXPLICATE: see -ATION.]
1 The action or an act of stating or describing in detail. E16.
2 The action or an act of making clear the meaning of something; (an) interpretation. M16. ▸†**b** An exposition; a paraphrase. M17–L18.
3 (The result of) the process of developing the meaning or implication of a principle, notion, etc. E17.
†**4** The action of unfolding a flower, leaf, etc. Only in M17.
†**5** The action or an act of accounting for the cause or origin of a phenomenon etc. L17–M18.
†**6** = EXPLANATION 3. E–M18.

explication de texte /ɛksplikasjɔ̃ də tɛkst/ *noun phr.* Pl. ***explications de texte*** (pronounced same). M20.
[ORIGIN French.]
A detailed textual examination of a literary work; the making of such examinations.

explicative /ɪk'splɪkətɪv, ɛk-, 'ɛksplɪkətɪv/ *adjective & noun*. E17.
[ORIGIN French *explicatif*, from *expliquer* explain, from Latin *explicare*: see EXPLICATE, -IVE.]
▸ **A** *adjective*. †**1** Expansive. *rare*. Only in E17.
2 Explanatory, interpretative; *spec.* in *LOGIC* (of a judgement), that explains the predicate from analysis of the subject. M17.
▸ **B** *noun*. An explicative term or phrase. L18.
■ **explicatively** *adverb* M18.

explicator /'ɛksplɪkeɪtə/ *noun*. E17.
[ORIGIN Latin, from *explicare*: see EXPLICATE, -OR.]
An explainer.

explicit /ɪk'splɪsɪt, ɛk-/ *adjective*. E17.
[ORIGIN French *explicite*, or Latin *explicitus* pa. pple of *explicare*: see EXPLICATE.]
1 Distinctly expressing all that is meant; leaving nothing merely implied or suggested; unambiguous; clear. E17. ▸**b** Describing or portraying the naked body or intimate sexual activity. L20.

H. KISSINGER We had had communications from Chou En-Lai sufficiently explicit for our less supple minds to grasp. **b** *Times* A national newspaper carried explicit photographs of himself and his wife.

explicit faith *THEOLOGY* the acceptance of a doctrine with a clear understanding of all it involves.
2 Of a person, personal qualities, a book, etc.: outspoken; unreserved in expression. E18.

G. GREENE Her biography . . is a useful and sometimes explicit corrective to Mrs Cecil Chesterton's vulgar and inaccurate study.

3 *MATH.* Of a function: having the dependent variable defined directly in terms of the independent variable(s). E19.
■ **explicitly** *adverb* M17. **explicitness** *noun* M17.

explicit /'ɛksplɪsɪt/ *verb & noun*. ME.
[ORIGIN Late Latin; either 3rd person sing. = here ends, pl. *explicitunt*, or abbreviation of *explicitus est liber* the book is unrolled.]
▸ †**A** *verb intrans.* (*defective*). A statement placed at the end of a book, chapter, etc.: (the book etc.) ends here. ME–M19.
▸ **B** *noun*. The end; a conclusion. Cf. INCIPIT. M17.

explode /ɪk'spləʊd, ɛk-/ *verb*. M16.
[ORIGIN Latin *explodere* drive out by clapping, hiss off the stage, formed as EX-¹ 1 + *plaudere* clap the hands.]
1 *verb trans.* Reject with scorn (an opinion, proposal, etc.); discard. Now (*rare*) only in *pass.* M16. ▸**b** Discredit, bring into disrepute (a theory), show to be fallacious. M17.

C. G. B. DAUBENY As new views came into vogue, or old errors became exploded. **b** CONAN DOYLE One forms provisional theories and waits for time or fuller knowledge to explode them.

†**2** *verb trans.* Clap or hiss (a play etc.) off the stage; *gen.* drive away with disapproval; cry down. E17–E19.
†**3** *verb trans.* Force out, expel, esp. with violence and sudden noise. M17–E19.

DISRAELI The exploded cork whizzed through the air.

4 *verb intrans.* Expand, burst, or shatter with extreme violence and noise; *fig.* give vent suddenly to emotion; burst forth; appear suddenly, esp. as a success. L18. ▸**b** Increase suddenly or rapidly, esp. in size, numbers, amount, etc. M20.

E. PEACOCK 'Confound him!' or some stronger expletive exploded from the Earl's lips. J. UPDIKE The tires of planes touching down frequently explode from the heat. *Times* When it exploded six years ago alternative cabaret was unhampered by any precedent. **b** *Countryman* The problems of feeding the exploding world population. *Weekend Australian* Business-finance news has exploded . . in Australia and the US.

exploding wire a wire subjected to a sudden and very high electric current so that it explodes violently.
5 *verb trans.* Cause to expand, burst, or shatter with extreme violence and noise. L18.

P. G. WODEHOUSE It only needs a spark to explode a powder-magazine. E. L. RICE He inflates the bag and explodes it with a blow of his fist.

6 *verb trans.* Separate into its constituent parts; *spec.* show in or as a diagram with each component displaced outwards and separated from its neighbours but retaining its relative position. M20.

DAVID POTTER Booklets may be broken down or exploded into separate sheets.

exploded diagram, ***exploded drawing***, etc.
■ **explodable** *adjective* L19. **exploder** *noun* M17.

explodent /ɪk'spləʊd(ə)nt, ɛk-/ *noun*. M19.
[ORIGIN Latin *explodent-* pres. ppl stem of *explodere* EXPLODE.]
PHONETICS. = PLOSIVE *noun*.

exploit /'ɛksplɔɪt/ *noun*. ME.
[ORIGIN Old French *espleit*, *esploit*, fem. *esploite*, (mod. *exploit* achievement), from Latin *explicitum*, *-ta* neut. & fem. pa. pples of *explicare* EXPLICATE.]
†**1** Progress, speed; success; furtherance. ME–E16.
†**2** An attempt to gain advantage over or to subdue a person or place; a military enterprise. LME–M18.
3 An act, a feat, usu. of exceptional skill or bravery. M16.

G. SWIFT He wrote a book about his exploits, . . and for a few years he was one of the war-heroes.

exploit /ɪk'splɔɪt, ɛk-/ *verb*. LME.
[ORIGIN Old French *espleiter* (mod. *exploiter*) accomplish, enjoy, from Latin *explicare* EXPLICATE. In sense 4 from mod. French.]
†**1** *verb trans.* Accomplish, achieve, perform. LME–L18.
†**2** *verb intrans.* Act with effect; get on; prosper. LME–E17.
†**3** *refl.* Exert oneself. L15–M16.
4 *verb trans.* Work (a mine); make use of (natural resources); utilize for one's own ends, take advantage of, (a person, esp. an employee, etc.). M19.

T. BENN To make sure that the resources of the North Sea were exploited for the benefit of the nation. H. MACMILLAN My close ties with America . . could be usefully exploited. DAY LEWIS Like all children, I mercilessly exploited this kindness.

■ **exploita'bility** *noun* the property of being exploitable M20. **exploitable** *adjective* †(**a**) able to be accomplished; (**b**) able to be exploited: E17. **exploitage** *noun* exploitation M19. **exploitative** *adjective* of, pertaining to, or involving exploitation, esp. of people L19. **exploi'tee** *noun* a person who is exploited M20. **exploiter** *noun* L19. **exploitive** *adjective* = EXPLOITATIVE E20.

exploitation /ɛksplɔɪ'teɪʃ(ə)n/ *noun*. E19.
[ORIGIN French from Old French *expletation*, formed as EXPLOIT *verb*: see -ATION.]
The action or practice of exploiting something or someone.

exploration /ɛksplə'reɪʃ(ə)n/ *noun*. M16.
[ORIGIN French, or Latin *exploratio(n-)*, from *explorat-* pa. ppl stem of *explorare*: see EXPLORE, -ATION.]
†**1** **a** (An) examination, (an) investigation. *obsolete* exc. as in sense b. M16–L17. ▸**b** *MEDICINE*. A close examination of a wound, organ, etc., esp. for diagnostic purposes, with or without surgery. M19.
2 The action or an act of exploring a country, place, etc. E19.
■ **explorational** *adjective* E20.

explorative /ɪk'splɒrətɪv, ɛk-/ *adjective*. M18.
[ORIGIN from Latin *explorat-* (see EXPLORATION) + -IVE.]
= EXPLORATORY.
■ **exploratively** *adverb* M19.

explorator /'ɛkspləreɪtə/ *noun*. LME.
[ORIGIN Latin, formed as EXPLORATIVE: see -OR.]
†**1** A person employed to collect information; *esp.* a military scout, a spy. LME–L17.
†**2** A person who searches diligently. L16–L17.
3 = EXPLORER. M19.

exploratorium /ɪk,splɒrə'tɔːrɪəm, ɛk-/ *noun*. L20.
[ORIGIN from EXPLORAT(ION + -ORIUM.]
(Proprietary name for) a museum or similar centre where visitors may participate actively by handling exhibits, performing experiments, etc.

exploratory /ɪk'splɒrət(ə)ri, ɛk-/ *adjective & noun*. LME.
[ORIGIN Latin *exploratorius*, from *explorat-*: see EXPLORATION, -ORY².]
▸ **A** *adjective*. **1** Of or pertaining to exploration. LME.
2 Undertaken for purposes of exploration; built or used for such purposes. E17. ▸**b** Of a surgical operation or procedure: performed in order to ascertain the nature of a disorder or the scope for treatment; diagnostic. M19.

SOUTHEY Exploratory travels. *Offshore* Shell Oil Co. hit oil in an exploratory well.

3 Carrying out exploration, exploring. M19.
▸ **B** *noun*. = EXPLORATORIUM. L20.

explore /ɪk'splɔː, ɛk-/ *verb*. M16.
[ORIGIN French *explorer* from Latin *explorare* search out, formed as EX-¹ 1 + *plorare* utter a cry.]
1 *verb trans.* Investigate (a fact, a cause, *why*, etc.). M16. ▸†**b** Search for; search out. E17–E19.

S. WEINBERG In the late 1940's a 'big bang' cosmological theory was being explored by George Gamow.

explore every avenue investigate every possibility.
2 *verb trans.* Examine, scrutinize; *esp.* examine (a country, area, building, etc.) by going through it. L16. ▸**b** Examine by touch; probe (a wound). M18.

R. MACAULAY I went on exploring Jerusalem and the country round it. E. BOWEN Meggatt haunted her dressing-table, explored her cosmetics. **b** A. J. CRONIN She leaned forward and with the forefinger of one hand lightly explored the contours of his face.

exploring coil a flat coil of insulated wire connected to a galvanometer, used for finding the strength of a magnetic field from the current induced in the coil when it is quickly turned over or withdrawn.
3 *verb intrans.* Go on an excursion or exploration (*to*). E19.
4 *verb intrans.* Conduct a search *for*. L19.
■ **explorement** *noun* (*rare*) (an) exploration M17. **explorer** *noun* a person who explores; an apparatus or device for exploring: L17. **exploringly** *adverb* in an exploring manner M19.

explosion /ɪk'spləʊʒ(ə)n, ɛk-/ *noun*. E17.
[ORIGIN Latin *explosio(n-)*, from *explos-* pa. ppl stem of *explodere* EXPLODE: see -ION.]
1 The action or an act of forcing out or emitting something suddenly, esp. with violence and noise. E17. ▸**b** *PHONETICS*. = PLOSION. M19.

C. DARWIN The sudden explosion of viscid matter.

†**2** The action of scorning or rejecting an opinion, proposal, etc. M17–L18.
3 The action or an act of bursting or flying into pieces with extreme violence and noise; the loud noise accompanying this. M18. ▸**b** *GOLF*. More fully ***explosion shot***. A shot in which the ball is made to jump out of a bunker by striking the sand just behind the ball. E20.

N. MONSARRAT There was a shattering explosion as a bomb hit the water.

4 A sudden outbreak or show of emotion. E19.

SIR W. SCOTT Elspat was prepared for the first explosion of her son's passion.

5 A sudden or rapid increase, esp. in size, numbers, or amount. M20.

Time Latin America is in the midst of a 'population explosion'. M. KLINE The explosion of mathematical activity.

■ **explosi'bility** *noun* liability to explode L19. **explosible** *adjective* liable to explode L18.

explosive /ɪk'spləʊsɪv, ɛk-/ *adjective & noun*. M17.
[ORIGIN from EXPLOS(ION + -IVE.]
▸ **A** *adjective*. **1** Tending to force out with violence and noise. M17.

W. B. CARPENTER An expulsion of the offending particle by an explosive cough. C. G. WILLIAMS The explosive force will be less than it should be.

2 Forced out or produced by an explosion. M18.
explosive bolt: released by being blown out of position by an explosive charge. **explosive rivet**: containing an explosive charge by means of which it is fixed in place.
3 Tending to explode or to cause an explosion. L18.

M. BARING His relations with his two sisters were perpetually strained and often violently explosive. *Economist* Markings for detonators and other explosive material.

4 Of, or pertaining to, or of the nature of, an explosion. M19.

T. H. HUXLEY They combine with explosive violence, if exposed to sunshine. A. C. BENSON 'Art' . . is . . a snappish, explosive word.

5 PHONETICS. = PLOSIVE *adjective*. M19.
▸ **B** *noun*. **1** A substance that can be made to explode. L19. **high explosive** an explosive which detonates and is significantly more powerful than gunpowder, which merely burns rapidly.
2 PHONETICS. = PLOSIVE *noun*. L19.
■ **explosively** *adverb* E19. **explosiveness** *noun* E19.

Expo /'ɛkspəʊ/ *noun*. Also **e-**. Pl. **-os**. M20.
[ORIGIN Abbreviation of EXPOSITION.]
A large international exhibition.

expolitio /ɛkspə'lɪtɪəʊ, -'lɪʃ-/ *noun*. L16.
[ORIGIN Latin, from *expolit-* pa. ppl stem of *expolire* polish, embellish, formed as EX-¹ 1 + *polire* polish.]
RHETORIC. A figure of speech in which something is expressed in several different ways in order to give a fuller illustration.

E

expone /ɪk'spəʊn, ɛk-/ *verb trans*. Long chiefly *Scot*. LME.
[ORIGIN Latin *exponere*: see EXPOUND.]
1 Set forth in words, declare. LME.
2 Expound, explain, interpret. LME.
†**3** Expend (effort, money). L15–L16.
†**4** Expose *to* danger etc. M16–M17.

exponence /ɪk'spəʊn(ə)ns, ɛk-/ *noun*. L19.
[ORIGIN from EXPONENT: see -ENCE.]
1 The function of an exponent. *rare*. L19.
2 LINGUISTICS. The realization of a linguistic category or feature in speech or writing; the relation between categories etc. and exponents of them. M20.
■ Also **exponency** *noun* L19.

exponent /ɪk'spəʊnənt, ɛk-/ *adjective & noun*. L16.
[ORIGIN Latin *exponent-* pres. ppl stem of *exponere*: see EXPOUND, -ENT.]
▸ **A** *adjective*. That expounds or interprets. L16.
▸ **B** *noun*. **1** A number or symbol indicating a particular power of a quantity, usu. written above and to the right of the symbol representing that quantity; the power so indicated. L17.

M. KLINE Newton used.. fractional exponents, as in $x^{⅔}$.

2 A person who or thing which expounds, interprets, or illustrates; *esp.* a person who exemplifies something in his or her action. Also, an advocate or a supporter *of* something. E19.

A. C. BOULT He was the last great exponent of the rule that the right hand beats time while the left adds the expression. V. BROME A leading exponent of psychoanalysis. A. F. DOUGLAS-HOME If the exponents of snatch and grab were allowed to get away with their spoils. H. MACMILLAN Masses of statistics poured out by the eager exponents of Communist success.

3 A person who or thing which stands as a type, symbol, or index *of* something. E19.

H. MARTINEAU Price is the exponent of exchangeable value.

4 LINGUISTICS. An instance or realization in speech or writing of a linguistic category or feature. M20.
■ **expo'nentiate** *verb* (**a**) *verb trans*. (MATH.) make an exponent in an exponentiation; (**b**) *verb intrans*. increase exponentially: L20. ˌ**exponenti'ation** *noun* (MATH.) the operation of raising one quantity to the power of another E20.

exponential /ɛkspə(ʊ)'nɛnʃ(ə)l/ *adjective & noun*. E18.
[ORIGIN French *exponentiel*, formed as EXPONENT: see -IAL.]
MATH. ▸**A** *adjective*. (Of an equation or quantity) involving an independent variable as (part of) an exponent; represented by or pertaining to such an equation or quantity; *esp.* (of a process or phenomenon) proceeding with something multiplied by a constant factor in successive equal periods of time; increasingly rapid or steep. E18.

C. P. SNOW The income from Tolstoy's books rose in a steady exponential curve. J. ZIMAN The exponential growth of science.

exponential time COMPUTING the time required for a computer to solve a problem, where this time is an exponential function of the size of the input.
▸ **B** *noun*. An exponential quantity. L18.
■ **exponentially** *adverb* E20.

exponible /ɪk'spəʊnɪb(ə)l, ɛk-/ *noun & adjective*. M16.
[ORIGIN medieval Latin *exponibilis*, from *exponere*: see EXPOUND, -IBLE.]
(Designating) a proposition that admits of or requires explanation.

export /'ɛkspɔːt/ *noun & adjective*. L17.
[ORIGIN from the verb.]
COMMERCE. ▸**A** *noun*. **1** An article that is exported; usu. in *pl.*, (the amount or value of) exported goods. L17.

N. BARBER Exports from Egypt shot up.

invisible exports: see INVISIBLE *adjective*.
2 The action of exporting. E19.

J. R. GREEN The export of arms to Spain.

– COMB.: **export reject** an imperfect article withdrawn from export and sold on the home market; **export surplus** the amount by which a country's exports exceed its imports.
▸ **B** *adjective*. Designating an article of a (usu. high) quality suitable for exporting. L19.

H. CARMICHAEL A bottle of your export special.

export /ɪk'spɔːt, ɛk-, 'ɛkspɔːt/ *verb*. L15.
[ORIGIN Latin *exportare*, formed as EX-¹ 1 + *portare* carry.]
†**1** *verb trans*. Take away. L15–E18.
2 *verb trans. & intrans*. Send (esp. goods) to another country. M17.

fig.: W. COWPER Hast thou.. Exported slavery to the conquered East?

3 *verb trans*. COMPUTING. Transmit (data) from a system for use elsewhere. L20.
■ **exporta'bility** *noun* the quality of being exportable L19. **exportable** *adjective* able to be exported E18. **exporter** *noun* L17.

exportation /ɛkspɔː'teɪʃ(ə)n/ *noun*. E17.
[ORIGIN Latin *exportatio(n-)*, from *exportat-* pa. ppl stem of *exportare*: see EXPORT *verb*, -ATION.]
1 The action or practice of exporting. E17.
†**2 a** = EXPORT *noun* 1. Usu. in *pl*. M17. ▸**b** Something carried out. *rare*. E19.
3 LOGIC. The principle that if two propositions together imply a third, then the first of them on its own implies that the second implies the third. E20.

expose /ɪk'spəʊz, ɛk-/ *verb*. LME.
[ORIGIN Old French & mod. French *exposer*, based on Latin *exponere* (see EXPOUND) but re-formed on Latin pa. pple *expositus* and Old French & mod. French *poser*: see POSE *verb*¹.]
1 *verb trans*. Lay open *to* something undesirable, as danger, ridicule, censure, etc.; subject *to* risk. LME.

JOHN BROOKE On her western frontiers Hanover was exposed to attack from France.

2 *verb trans*. Place in an unsheltered position; leave without protection; uncover; put (a plant) out in the open air. Formerly also, risk, imperil. LME.

C. MILNE Up here we are now a little more exposed.

3 *verb trans*. Cause or allow to be seen; exhibit openly, display; disclose, reveal, show. LME. ▸**b** ECCLESIASTICAL. Exhibit (the Host, a relic) for adoration. M17.

B. JOWETT The dead are only to be exposed for three days. J. CONRAD Blunt had unbuttoned his.. jacket, exposing a lot of starched shirt-front. J. HAWKES A dreary expanse of blackened tree stumps exposed at low tide.

expose oneself display one's body indecently in public.
4 *verb trans*. Disclose (a secret, intention, etc.). Formerly (now *dial.*), explain, describe in detail. L15.
5 a *verb trans*. Foll. by *to*: lay open to the action or influence of. L16. ▸**b** In *pass*. Of something outdoors: be open *to* a particular quarter, be situated in a certain aspect. E18. ▸**c** *verb trans. & intrans*. Subject (a photographic film or plate) to light or the radiation to which it is sensitive. M19.

a A. DAVIS Once they had been exposed to the realities of the prison and judicial systems.

6 *verb trans*. Offer for or *for* sale. Also foll. by *to*. Now chiefly *Scot*. E17.
7 *verb trans*. Compel to be out of doors; *esp.* (*hist.*) leave an infant to perish for want of shelter. E17.
†**8** *verb trans*. Publish (a discourse); put (coin) in circulation. M17–M18.
9 *verb trans*. Unmask, show up, (an error, impostor, etc.); hold up to ridicule or reprobation (a misdeed, a wrongdoer). L17. ▸†**b** Hold up to ridicule (what is not a fault). L17–L18.

R. MACAULAY When I'm exposed I shall own up and admit it was a hoax. M. AMIS I didn't worry about the lies being exposed.

■ **exposable** *adjective* M20. **exposal** *noun* the fact of exposing or of being exposed E17. **exposedness** *noun* the state or condition of being exposed E17. **exposer** *noun* E17.

exposé /ɪk'spəʊzeɪ, ɛk-; *foreign* ɛkspoze (*pl. same*)/ *noun*. E19.
[ORIGIN French, pa. pple of *exposer*: see EXPOSE.]
1 An orderly statement of facts. E19.

A. S. BYATT A reasoned exposé of alternative courses of action.

2 A showing up or revelation of something discreditable. E19.

New York Review of Books The headline-making exposé of a nation's indifference to the Holocaust.

exposit /ɪk'spɒzɪt, ɛk-/ *verb trans*. L19.
[ORIGIN Latin *exposit-*: see EXPOSITOR.]
Reveal, show; expound.

exposita /ɪk'spɒzɪtə, ɛk-/ *noun*. Now *rare*. E19.
[ORIGIN Latin, fem. sing. (sc. *propositio*) of *expositus* pa. pple of *exponere*: see EXPOUND, PROPOSITION *noun*.]
LOGIC. = CONVERTEND.

exposition /ɛkspə'zɪʃ(ə)n/ *noun*. ME.
[ORIGIN Old French & mod. French, or Latin *expositio(n-)*, from *exposit-*: see EXPOSITOR, -ION.]
1 (An) interpretation, (an) explanation; an expository article or treatise, a commentary. ME.

W. SPARROW The exposition of the Bible. R. P. GRAVES The lectures were.. scholarly expositions of the classical text.

2 The action or process of stating or describing, in speech or writing; a detailed statement or description. LME. ▸**b** LOGIC. Formerly, any of various forms of argument. Now, the adducing of an empirically evident case in support of a general truth. L16. ▸**c** MUSIC. The first main section of a movement in sonata form; the opening section of a fugue. M19.

J. MORLEY Clear exposition was the only thing needed to convert him to the theory.

†**3** The action or practice of exposing infants. L16–L19.
4 The action or an act of exposing to view, esp. (ECCLESIASTICAL) the Host or a relic. Formerly also, (an) exposure of a misdeed. M17. ▸**b** An exhibition, a show, *esp.* a large or international one. M19.
†**5** = EXPOSURE 1b. L17–M19.
■ **expositional** *adjective* of the nature of an exposition, explanatory M19. **expositionally** *adverb* M20. **expositionary** *adjective* inclined to exposition; expositional: L19.

expositive /ɪk'spɒzɪtɪv, ɛk-/ *adjective & noun*. L15.
[ORIGIN from EXPOSITION + -IVE.]
▸ **A** *adjective*. Descriptive; explanatory; expository. L15.
▸ †**B** *noun*. An exposition; an argument. L15–L17.

expositor /ɪk'spɒzɪtə, ɛk-/ *noun*. ME.
[ORIGIN Old French & mod. French *expositeur* or late Latin *expositor*, from Latin *exposit-* pa. ppl stem of *exponere*: see EXPOUND, -OR.]
1 A person who or book which explains or interprets something. ME.
2 A person who describes something in detail; a narrator. LME.

expository /ɪk'spɒzɪt(ə)ri, ɛk-/ *noun & adjective*. LME.
[ORIGIN Late Latin *expositorius*, from Latin *exposit-*: see EXPOSITOR, -ORY².]
▸ **A** *noun*. A book which explains or interprets, *esp.* a written commentary. LME.
▸ **B** *adjective*. Of or pertaining to exposition; of the nature of or containing an exposition, explanatory. L16.
■ **expositorily** *adverb* M17.

ex post /ɛks 'pəʊst/ *adjectival & adverbial phr*. M20.
[ORIGIN mod. Latin, formed as EX *preposition* + Latin *post* after.]
Chiefly ECONOMICS. ▸**A** *adjectival phr*. Based on past events or actual results; occurring afterwards; actual rather than predicted; retrospective. M20.
▸ **B** *adverbial phr*. After the event; retrospectively. M20.

ex post facto /ɛks pəʊst 'faktəʊ/ *adverbial & adjectival phr*. M17.
[ORIGIN Erron. division of Latin *ex postfacto* in the light of subsequent events, from *ex* from, out of + abl. of *postfactum* that which is done subsequently.]
▸ **A** *adverbial phr*. After the event, after the fact; retrospectively. M17.
▸ **B** *adjectival phr*. Done after another thing; *esp.* (of a law) applied retrospectively. L18.

expostulant /ɪk'spɒstjʊlənt, ɛk-/ *adjective*. L19.
[ORIGIN Latin *expostulant-* pres. ppl stem of *expostulare*: see EXPOSTULATE, -ANT¹.]
Expostulating.

expostulate /ɪk'spɒstjʊleɪt, ɛk-/ *verb*. M16.
[ORIGIN Latin *expostulat-* pa. ppl stem of *expostulare*, from EX-¹ 1 + *postulare* demand.]
†**1** *verb trans*. Ask for; demand; ask *how* or *why*. M16–L17.
†**2** *verb intrans*. State a complaint. Only in M16.
†**3** *verb intrans*. Discourse. L16–L18.
4 *verb intrans*. Talk earnestly in order to protest at a person's action or to dissuade him or her. (Foll. by *with* the person, *about*, *on*, etc., a subject.) L16.

D. H. LAWRENCE Connie expostulated roundly, and was angry with both of them. W. GOLDING I began to expostulate at the wasted time. H. KISSINGER Semenov.. started expostulating on the dangers of accidental or unauthorized missile launches.

5 *verb trans*. †**a** Complain of (a grievance); remonstrate about (a matter) *with* someone. L16–E18. ▸†**b** Debate (a matter), esp. as an aggrieved person. L16–L18. ▸**c** Say in expostulation. Now only with spoken words as obj.: say as an expostulation. L16.

c V. WOOLF 'Tut-tut-tut,' Mrs Lynn-Jones expostulated.

■ **expostulative** *adjective* that expostulates M19. **expostulatively** *adverb* in an expostulating manner L19. **expostulator** *noun* E18. **expostulatory** *adjective* characterized by or of the nature of expostulation L16.

expostulation /ɪkˌspɒstjʊ'leɪʃ(ə)n, ɛk-/ *noun*. M16.
[ORIGIN Latin *expostulatio(n-)*, formed as EXPOSTULATE: see -ATION.]
1 The action or an act of expostulating. M16.
2 A spoken remonstrance, protest, or reproof. L16.

†**exposture** *noun*. *rare* (Shakes.). Only in E17.
[ORIGIN from EXPOSE after *posture* etc.]
= EXPOSURE 1.

exposure /ɪk'spəʊʒə, ɛk-/ *noun*. E17.
[ORIGIN from EXPOSE + -URE.]
1 The action of exposing; the fact or state of being exposed; *esp.* (**a**) the fact of being without shelter or protection from bad weather; (**b**) the unmasking of a wrongdoer. (Foll. by *to*.) E17. ▸**b** The way in which something is situated in relation to compass direction, wind, sunshine, etc. M17. ▸**c** A surface laid open to view, or to the operation of some agency. L19.

Nature Exposure to cigarette smoke during pregnancy. J. B. MORTON Hands that are . . red from exposure to sun and rain. B. BETTELHEIM Prisoners died . . as a result of exposure on the parade grounds. **b** M. MCCARTHY The back windows . . had a southern exposure. **c** *Scientific American* Fossiliferous exposures of middle Devonian rocks.

indecent exposure the intentional act of publicly displaying one's body in an indecent manner.

2 The action or an act of subjecting a photographic film or plate to light etc.; the length of time for which it is exposed; the combination of shutter speed and aperture; each of the sections of a film which can be or have been separately exposed. **M19.**

Photographer It takes . . 36 exposure 35mm films.

double exposure: see DOUBLE *adjective & adverb*. ***multiple exposure***: see MULTIPLE *adjective*.

3 The extent to which an insurance company is at risk from any particular contingency; orig. *spec.* (the risk of) the spread of fire from one property to another. **M19.** ▸**b** COMMERCE. The financial commitment of a bank or other company in any particular country, activity, or asset; the risk associated with this. **L20.**

4 MOUNTAINEERING. The openness or insecurity of a climber's position; the climber's awareness of this. **M20.**

5 The condition of being brought to the attention of the public; publicity achieved through broadcasting or advertising. **M20.**

6 Experience, esp. of a specified kind of work. **M20.**

City Limits At Lewisham theatre children are getting exposure to the Thespian arts.

– COMB.: **exposure meter** PHOTOGRAPHY: for measuring illumination and giving the exposure to use with a given film etc.

expound /ɪkˈspaʊnd, ɛk-/ *verb*. **ME.**
[ORIGIN Old French *espondre* from Latin *exponere* expose, publish, exhibit, explain, formed as EX-[1] 1 + *ponere* to place.]

1 *verb trans. & intrans.* Explain (what is difficult or obscure); comment on (a text or author); *esp.* comment on or interpret (a religious text). **ME.** ▸**b** *verb trans.* Give the significance or meaning of (a dream, symbol, riddle, etc.). *arch.* **LME.** ▸†**c** *verb trans.* Give the meaning of (a word or name), translate. **LME–M17.** ▸†**d** *verb trans.* Interpret the motives of (a person). Only in **17.** ▸†**e** *refl.* Explain one's meaning. **E–M17.**

E. ROOSEVELT He expounded at length the philosophy of Thomas Aquinas.

2 *verb trans.* Set out, declare, state in detail, (esp. a doctrine, opinion, idea, etc.). **LME.** ▸**b** MATH. Express in figures or symbols. Now *rare*. **E18.**

R. HAYMAN The doctor gave lectures expounding his theories.

3 *verb trans.* †**a** Foll. by *concerning*, *of*: explain (a statement) as referring to. **LME–E18.** ▸**b** Now chiefly LAW. Give a particular interpretation to, interpret in a particular way. **M16.** ▸†**c** Translate (in a specified way). **M16–E17.**

■ **expoundable** *adjective* **L19.** **expounder** *noun* **LME.**

†**express** *noun*[1]. **E16.**
[ORIGIN from EXPRESS *verb*[1].]

1 A graphic representation, an image; *fig.* a type, a model. **E16–M17.**

2 The action or an act of expressing or representing by words, signs, or actions; expression. **M17–E18.**

3 A condition or product in which something is expressed; a manifestation. **M17–M19.**

4 A mode of speech, a phrase; an utterance. **M–L17.** ▸**b** A specific mention, statement, or injunction. **M–L17.**

express /ɪkˈsprɛs, ɛk-; *as attrib. adjective also* ˈɛksprɛs/ *adjective, adverb, & noun*[2]. **LME.**
[ORIGIN Old French & mod. French *exprès* from Latin *expressus* distinctly or manifestly presented, pa. pple of *exprimere* (cf. EXPRESS *verb*[1]).]

▸ **A** *adjective* **I** †**1** Stated, explicitly recorded. **LME–L17.**

2 Definitely stated and not merely implied; definitely formulated; explicit; unmistakable in import. **LME.** ▸†**b** Outspoken; free from vacillation. **L16–L18.**

H. MARTINEAU Mr. Stanley's answer was express and clear. E. CALDWELL Evelyn Summerall had planned the cocktail party for the express purpose of having them meet. **b** HENRY MORE I love to feel myself of an express and settled judgment.

3 Specially designed for a particular object; done, made, or sent for a special purpose. **LME.**

J. MORLEY The social union is the express creation . . of the Deity.

4 Operating at high speed; designed for such operation; very fast. (Earliest in ***express train*** below; orig. so called as serving a particular destination.) **M19.**

DICKENS Going about the country at express pace. E. BOWEN Matchett is sending Anna's white velvet dress to the express cleaners.

▸ **II 5** Of an image, form, etc.: truly depicting the original, exact. *arch.* **E16.**

– SPECIAL COLLOCATIONS: **express delivery** a system for the immediate postal delivery of an item. **express lift**: which does not stop at every floor. **express messenger** a messenger specially dispatched; *spec.* one employed to convey items sent by express delivery. **express rifle**: discharging the bullet at high speed. **express train** a train running to a particular destination and stopping at few intermediate stations; a fast train.

▸ **B** *adverb*. †**1** Clearly, plainly, unmistakably; in distinct terms, positively. **LME–E18.**

†**2** Directly *against*; exactly; completely. **LME–L16.**

3 Specially, on purpose, for a particular end; at high speed; by express messenger or train. **LME.**

J. R. LOWELL A piece of news worth sending express.

▸ **C** *noun* **1 a** An express messenger. Freq. in titles of newspapers. **E17.** ▸**b** A message sent by an express messenger, a dispatch. **M17.**

2 A company undertaking the transport of parcels, money, etc., more rapidly and securely than routine freight; items so sent. Chiefly *US*. **M19.**

OED The books will be sent by express.

attrib.: ***express clerk***, ***express company***, ***express office***, ***express wagon***, etc. ***pony express***: see PONY *noun*.

3 a An express train. **M19.** ▸**b** An express rifle. **L19.**

a Orient Express: see ORIENT *noun*.

– COMB.: **expressman** *US* a man employed in transmitting parcels etc., esp. as an employee of an express company.

■ **expressage** *noun* (*US*) (the charge for) the sending of a parcel etc. by express **M19.** **expressness** *noun* **M17.**

express /ɪkˈsprɛs, ɛk-/ *verb*[1]. **LME.**
[ORIGIN Old French *expresser* from Proto-Romance, from Latin EX-[1] 1 + *pressare* PRESS *verb*[1]: repr. in use Latin *exprimere*.]

▸ **I** Press out.

1 *verb trans.* Get by pressing, squeezing, or wringing; *fig.* extort or elicit by pressure. Formerly also, expel or get rid of by force. (Foll. by *from*, *out of*.) **LME.** ▸**b** *verb trans. & intrans. spec.* Squeeze out (milk etc.) from the breast. **M20.**

2 *verb trans.* Emit or exude as if by pressure. *arch.* **E17.**

3 *verb trans.* Press or squeeze out the contents of. Now *rare*. **M17.**

▸ **II** Portray, represent.

4 *verb trans.* Orig., represent by sculpture, drawing, or painting; portray, depict. Now only, convey a notion of (a fact, characteristic, etc.) in a drawing etc. **LME.** ▸†**b** Be an image or likeness of; resemble. **L15–L17.**

HOR. WALPOLE Loggan used long strokes in expressing flesh. **b** DRYDEN Kids and Whelps their Sires and Dams express.

5 *verb trans.* Represent in language; put into words; give utterance to (a feeling, an intention). **LME.** ▸**b** Of a word, phrase, or statement: represent (a thought, sentiment, or state of affairs); denote, mean, signify. **E16.**

Law Reports The lease correctly expressed the bargain between the parties. N. SHUTE He expressed his thanks for all that they had done. J. CONRAD What he seemed mostly concerned for was the 'stride forward', as he expressed it. **b** S. BUTLER No words can express too strongly the caution which should be used. J. L. AUSTIN Sentences expressing commands or wishes.

express oneself say what one means or thinks (*on* a subject, *well*, *aptly*, etc.).

†**6** *verb trans.* Mention, specify; give an account of, describe; describe as. **LME–L18.** ▸**b** *verb intrans.* Make mention, give an account, *of*. **LME–E16.**

T. HEYWOOD Heardsman, thou hast exprest a monstrous beast. J. YORKE M. Milles in his Catalogue never expresseth him. W. COWPER I would express him simple, grave, sincere.

7 *verb trans.* Represent by a symbol or symbols, symbolize; MATH. represent (a number, relation, property, etc.) by a figure, symbol, or formula, esp. (a quantity) *in terms of* another. **LME.**

E. STILLINGFLEET A Child to express coming into the world, an old man for going out of it.

8 *verb trans.* Manifest by external signs, betoken, (esp. a personal feeling or quality). **LME.**

J. AUSTEN Never did tone express indifference plainer. M. GIROUARD The interior of each house expressed the artistic personality of its owners.

9 *verb trans.* State or mention explicitly. **L16.**

G. BERKELEY Hints and allusions, expressing little, insinuating much.

10 *verb trans.* GENETICS. Cause (an inherited characteristic or component, a gene) to appear in a phenotype. Usu. in *pass.* **E20.**

■ **expressedly** /-sɪdli/ *adverb* avowedly; explicitly, expressly: **M16.** **expresser** *noun* (*a*) a person who or thing which expresses; (*b*) a person with great powers of expression: **L16.** **expressible** *adjective* **E17.** **expressor** *noun* = EXPRESSER **E17.**

express /ɪkˈsprɛs, ɛk-/ *verb*[2] *trans.* Orig. *US*. **E18.**
[ORIGIN from EXPRESS *noun*[2].]

Send by express delivery or an express messenger.

expression /ɪkˈsprɛʃ(ə)n, ɛk-/ *noun*. **LME.**
[ORIGIN Old French & mod. French, or Latin *expressio(n-)*, from *express-* pa. ppl stem of *exprimere* (cf. EXPRESS *verb*[1]): see -ION.]

1 The action or an act of pressing or squeezing out. **LME.** ▸†**b** Something obtained in this way. Only in **17.**

2 The action of expressing something in words or symbols; the utterance of feelings, intentions, etc.; manifestation of a feeling or quality by an external sign or token. Formerly also, explicit mention, description. **LME.**

TENNYSON Adeline . . beyond expression fair. J. A. FROUDE To encourage the fullest expression of public feeling. M. TIPPETT He uses words as discourses and reserves the expression of artistic emotion for tone.

free expression: see FREE *adjective*.

3 A spoken utterance, a written declaration; an action, state, or fact whereby some feeling, quality, etc., is manifested or symbolized; a sign, a token. Now only foll. by *of*. **E17.**

J. GILBERT The death of Christ was the expression of Divine love. B. JOWETT Your words . . are the very expression of my own feelings.

4 Manner or means of expressing in language; wording, diction. **E17.** ▸**b** A word, a phrase, a form of speech. **M17.** ▸**c** MATH. A collection of symbols that jointly express a quantity. **L18.**

GEO. ELIOT He had not a great range of expression. **b** J. A. FROUDE Ambiguous expressions were explained away when challenged. B. PYM She was still 'under the doctor', as the expression was. D. LODGE She was brainwashed, if you'll pardon the expression. **c** A. S. EDDINGTON Simplifying the algebraic expressions.

5 In painting, sculpture, etc., the mode of expressing character, sentiment, action, etc. **E18.** ▸**b** MUSIC. Manner of performance that expresses the feeling of a passage. **L18.**

J. RUSKIN Masterpieces of expression. **b** M. E. BRADDON She played with brilliancy, and . . with expression.

6 Capacity of the face, voice, or attitude for expressing feeling or character; the appearance of the face, or the intonation of the voice, as indicating a person's feelings. **L18.**

J. MOORE There is more expression in the countenances of French women. DICKENS 'Can't I!' said Abbey, with infinite expression. M. FRAYN A quiet level voice without expression of any sort. A. SILLITOE An expression of anger spread over his face. R. WARNER He looked at me with a doubtful and cunning expression in his . . eyes.

7 GENETICS. The appearance in a phenotype of a character or effect attributed to a particular gene; the manner or degree of this; the process by which possession of a gene leads to the appearance in the phenotype of the corresponding character. **E20.**

R. R. GATES Families can differ greatly in the degree of expression of polydactyly.

– COMB.: **expression mark** MUSIC a sign or word indicating the expression required of a performer; **expression-stop** MUSIC a stop in a harmonium allowing expression by means of varied air pressure.

■ **expressional** *adjective* **E19.**

E

expressionism /ɪkˈsprɛʃ(ə)nɪz(ə)m, ɛk-/ *noun*. Also **E-**. **E20.**
[ORIGIN from EXPRESSION + -ISM.]

A style of painting, drama, music, etc., expressing the inner experience of the artist rather than impressions of the physical world.

■ **expressionist** *adjective & noun* (*a*) *adjective* practising expressionism; expressionistic; (*b*) *noun* an expressionist artist: **M19.** **expressioˈnistic** *adjective* of or produced by expressionists; characterized by expressionism: **E20.** **expressioˈnistically** *adverb* **E20.**

expressionless /ɪkˈsprɛʃ(ə)nlɪs, ɛk-/ *adjective*. **E19.**
[ORIGIN formed as EXPRESSIONISM + -LESS.]

1 That is not expressed. *rare*. **E19.**

2 Lacking expression. **M19.**

H. KINGSLEY A small man, with an impenetrable, expressionless face.

■ **expressionlessly** *adverb* **L19.** **expressionlessness** *noun* **M19.**

expressive /ɪkˈsprɛsɪv, ɛk-/ *adjective*. **LME.**
[ORIGIN French *expressif*, *-ive* or medieval Latin *expressivus*, from Latin *express-*: see EXPRESSION, -IVE.]

†**1** Tending to press out or expel. *rare*. Only in **LME.**

2 Of, pertaining to, or concerned with expression; having the function of expressing. **L15.**

J. JASTROW The receptive powers are in advance of the expressive ones.

3 Full of expression, characterized by expression; (of a word, gesture, etc.) expressing its meaning with striking force, significant. Formerly also (of a statement), explicit. **E17.**

R. W. CHURCH His Latin . . is singularly forcible and expressive. J. B. PRIESTLEY The instant look of horror on his expressive face.

4 Of a person: open or emphatic in expressing opinions, feelings, etc. (Foll. by *of*.) *rare*. **E17.**

C. LAMB We felt as we had been not enough expressive of our pleasure.

†**5** Expressing itself in action; tending to outward manifestation. **E17–M18.**

6 Serving to express, indicate, or represent. Foll. by *of*. **L17.**

S. WILLIAMS Tables expressive of this diurnal variation. M. EDGEWORTH An air of dignity which seemed expressive of conscious innocence.

E

■ **expressively** *adverb* L15. **expressiveness** *noun* M17. **expre'ssivity** *noun* (*a*) GENETICS the kind or degree of phenotypic expression of a gene; (*b*) the quality of being expressive: M20.

expressless /ɪk'sprɛslɪs, ɛk-/ *adjective. arch.* L16.
[ORIGIN from EXPRESS *adjective* + -LESS.]
That cannot be expressed; inexpressible.

expressly /ɪk'sprɛsli, ɛk-/ *adverb.* LME.
[ORIGIN from EXPRESS *adjective* + -LY[2].]
1 Distinctly, positively; in plain terms, explicitly. Formerly also, in full detail; with distinct enunciation. LME.
P. USTINOV Peasants were expressly forbidden to leave the estates.
†**2** Avowedly, directly. LME–L17.
3 For the express purpose; on purpose. E17.
J. BUCHAN Leithen . . has come here expressly to save the lady.

†**expressure** *noun.* LME.
[ORIGIN from Latin *express-* (see EXPRESSION) + -URE. Cf. Latin *pressura* pressure.]
1 Something which serves to press out or expel. *rare.* Only in LME.
2 An image, a picture. *rare* (Shakes.). Only in L16.
3 Expression by words or signs; manifestation, description. E17–M18.
4 The action of pressing or squeezing out; pressure. M17–M19.

expressway /ɪk'sprɛsweɪ, ɛk-/ *noun. N. Amer. & Austral.* M20.
[ORIGIN from EXPRESS *adjective* + WAY *noun*.]
A motorway through or bypassing a city.

†**exprobrate** *verb trans.* Also **-bate**. M16.
[ORIGIN Latin *exprobrat-* pa. ppl stem of *exprobrare*, formed as EX-[1] 1 + *probrum* shameful deed: see -ATE[3].]
1 Make (something) a subject of reproach. M16–M17.
2 Reproach (a person). M–L17.
3 Reprobate, censure. Only in M19.

exprobration /ɛksprə'breɪʃ(ə)n/ *noun.* Now *rare* or *obsolete*. LME.
[ORIGIN Latin *exprobratio(n-)*, from *exprobrat-*: see EXPROBRATE, -ATION.]
†**1** The action or an act of upbraiding or speaking reproachfully. LME–M19.
2 A reproachful utterance; reproachful language. M16.
†**3** Something which acts as a reproach. Only in L17.

ex professo /ɛks prə'fɛsəʊ/ *adverbial phr.* L16.
[ORIGIN Latin, formed as EX *preposition* + abl. of *professus*: see PROFESS.]
By profession; professedly.

expromission /ɛksprə'mɪʃ(ə)n/ *noun.* Now *hist.* E19.
[ORIGIN mod. Latin *expromissio(n-)*, from Latin *expromiss-*: see EXPROMISSOR, -ION.]
A legal arrangement in which a creditor allowed a third party to assume responsibility for a debt in place of the original debtor.

expromissor /ɛksprə'mɪsə/ *noun.* Now *hist.* L17.
[ORIGIN Late Latin, from Latin *expromiss-* pa. ppl stem of *expromittere* promise or agree to pay, formed as EX-[1] + *promittere*: see PROMISE *noun*, -OR.]
A person who agreed to pay; *esp.* one who took the place of a debtor in a case of expromission.

†**expropriate** *adjective. rare.* Only in LME.
[ORIGIN medieval Latin *expropriatus* pa. pple of *expropriare*: see EXPROPRIATE *verb*, -ATE[2].]
Expropriated; *spec.* debarred from owning property.

expropriate /ɪks'prəʊprɪeɪt, ɛks-/ *verb trans.* Pa. pple **-ated**, †**-ate**. L16.
[ORIGIN medieval Latin *expropriat-* pa. ppl stem of *expropriare*, formed as EX-[1] 1 + PROPRIUM property: see -ATE[3].]
1 Take out of the owner's hands, esp. for one's own use: *spec.* (of a public authority) take away (land) for public use or benefit. L16.
F. FITZGERALD The French had simply expropriated the village land to build their own farms. W. GOLDING A Royal Decree expropriated the land.
2 Dispossess (a person) of ownership; deprive of property. (Foll. by *from*.) E17.
M. B. BROWN The need of industrial capitalism for expropriated labourers.
†**3** Renounce control of; give up *to*. M17–L18.
■ **expropriator** *noun* M19.

expropriation /ɪks,prəʊprɪ'eɪʃ(ə)n, ɛks-/ *noun.* LME.
[ORIGIN Orig. from medieval Latin *expropriatio(n-)*, from *expropriat-* (see EXPROPRIATE *verb*); in mod. use directly from EXPROPRIATE *verb*: see -ATION.]
†**1** Renunciation (*of*). LME–M17.
2 The action or an act of expropriating. M19.

ex proprio motu /ɛks ,prəʊprɪəʊ 'məʊtuː, ,prɒ-/ *adverbial phr.* L17.
[ORIGIN Late Latin = by own motion.]
= MOTU PROPRIO; *spec.* in LAW (now chiefly *hist.*), by decision of a court without anyone's application.

†**expugn** *verb trans.* LME.
[ORIGIN Old French *expugner* or Latin *expugnare* take by storm, formed as EX-[1] 1 + *pugnare* to fight.]
1 Capture by fighting; take by storm; assault, attack, storm. LME–M17.
2 Overcome or expel by force of arms; conquer, overpower. LME–E18.

†**expugnable** *adjective.* L16–L18.
[ORIGIN Old French from Latin *expugnabilis*, from *expugnare*: see EXPUGN, -ABLE.]
Able to be captured or conquered.

†**expugnatory** *adjective.* E17–M18.
[ORIGIN Latin *expugnatorius* conquering, from *expugnat-* pa. ppl stem of *expugnare*: see EXPUGN, -ORY[2].]
Adapted for attack, offensive.

expulsatory /ɪk'spʌlsət(ə)ri, ɛk-/ *adjective.* L16.
[ORIGIN from Latin *expulsat-* pa. ppl stem of *expulsare*: see EXPULSE, -ORY[2].]
= EXPULSIVE 1.

expulse /ɪk'spʌls, ɛk-/ *verb trans.* LME.
[ORIGIN Latin *expulsare* frequentative of *expellere* EXPEL.]
Drive out, esp. with force, (*lit. & fig.*); eject, expel; evict.
■ **expulser** *noun* (now *rare*) M16.

expulsion /ɪk'spʌlʃ(ə)n, ɛk-/ *noun.* LME.
[ORIGIN Latin *expulsio(n-)*, from *expuls-* pa. ppl stem of *expellere* EXPEL: see -ION.]
The action or an act of expelling; the fact or condition of being expelled.
■ **expulsionist** *noun* a person who supports or advocates the expulsion of someone L19.

expulsive /ɪk'spʌlsɪv, ɛk-/ *adjective.* LME.
[ORIGIN Old French & mod. French *expulsif*, *-ive* from late Latin *expulsivus*, from *expuls-*: see EXPULSION, -IVE.]
1 Tending or having the power to expel, esp. from the body. LME.
†**2** Tending to repel. E–M17.

expulsory /ɪk'spʌls(ə)ri, ɛk-/ *adjective. rare.* LME.
[ORIGIN medieval Latin *expulsorius*, from Latin *expulsor* expeller, from *expuls-*: see EXPULSION, -OR, -ORY[2].]
Of or pertaining to expulsion; expulsive.

expunct /ɪk'spʌŋkt, ɛk-/ *verb trans.* L16.
[ORIGIN Latin *expunct-* pa. ppl stem of *expungere* EXPUNGE.]
Expunge, erase.

expunction /ɪk'spʌŋkʃ(ə)n, ɛk-/ *noun.* E17.
[ORIGIN Latin *expunctio(n-)*, formed as EXPUNCT: see -ION.]
1 The action of expunging; erasure. E17. ▸**b** PALAEOGRAPHY. The indication of an erasure or cancellation to be made in a manuscript by means of dots placed beneath the relevant letter or letters. M20.
†**2** A wiping out, a removal. E–M17.

expunctuation /ɛk,spʌŋktjʊ'eɪʃ(ə)n/ *noun.* M20.
[ORIGIN Blend of EXPUNCTION and PUNCTUATION.]
= EXPUNCTION 1b.

expunge /ɪk'spʌn(d)ʒ, ɛk-/ *verb trans.* E17.
[ORIGIN Latin *expungere* mark for deletion by points set above or below, formed as EX-[1] 1 + *pungere* to prick.]
1 Strike out, erase, omit, (a name or word) from a list, (a phrase or passage) from a text. E17.
2 *fig.* Wipe out, efface; annihilate, destroy; annul; put an end to. E17.
E. F. BENSON Certain moments she wanted to expunge completely from his mind. Y. MENUHIN A culture cannot be expunged from the face of the earth by political directive.
3 Get rid of, remove. E17.
H. E. MANNING To expunge God from Science.
■ **expunger** *noun* E17.

expurgate /'ɛkspəːgeɪt/ *verb.* E17.
[ORIGIN Latin *expurgat-* pa. ppl stem of *expurgare*, formed as EX-[1] 1 + *purgare*: see PURGE *verb*, -ATE[3].]
†**1** *verb trans.* Purge or cleanse (the body etc.) of excremental material. E–M17.
2 *verb trans. & intrans.* Remove from (a book) passages regarded as objectionable. L17.
■ **expurgator** *noun* a person who expurgates M17. **ex,purga'torial** *adjective* (*a*) of or pertaining to an expurgator; (*b*) tending to expurgate or purge: E19. **expurgatory** /ɪk'spəːgət(ə)ri, ɛk-/ *adjective* of or pertaining to expurgation; tending to expurgate or purge; ***Expurgatory Index***: see INDEX *noun* 6b: M17.

expurgation /ɛkspəː'geɪʃ(ə)n/ *noun.* LME.
[ORIGIN Partly from Latin *expurgatio(n-)* in medieval Latin sense of 'cleansing, freeing from impurities', formed as EXPURGATE; partly from EXPURGATE: see -ATION.]
†**1** The action or an act of cleansing from impurity (*lit. & fig.*). LME–M17.
2 The action or an act of removing impurities or objectionable elements. L16.
3 *spec.* The action or an act of removing from a book passages regarded as objectionable. E17.
†**4** ASTRONOMY. The reappearance of the sun after an eclipse; emersion. M18–M19.

expurge /ɪk'spəːdʒ, ɛk-/ *verb trans.* Now *rare.* L15.
[ORIGIN French *expurger* alt. of Old French *espurger* from Latin *expurgare* EXPURGATE.]
1 Cleanse, purify, (*from*, *of*). L15.
2 Remove (something offensive, excremental material). M16. ▸**b** Expunge from a book. M17.
3 = EXPURGATE 2. M17.

exquisite /'ɛkskwɪzɪt, ɪk'skwɪzɪt, ɛk-/ *adjective, adverb, & noun.* LME.
[ORIGIN Latin *exquisitus* pa. pple of *exquirere* search out, formed as EX-[1] 1 + *quaerere* search, seek.]
▸ **A** *adjective.* †**1** Carefully ascertained or adjusted; accurate, exact; careful, precise. LME–M18. ▸**b** Of a specified disease; accurately so named; typical, genuine. Only in 17.
MILTON Be not over exquisite To cast the fashion of uncertain evils.
†**2 a** Of language, expression, or terms: carefully or aptly chosen; uncommon; affected, overlaboured. L15–L17. ▸†**b** Of an expedient, explanation, or reason: ingeniously devised, far-fetched. Of studies: abstruse. L15–M17. ▸**c** Of food and drink: carefully chosen; choice; dainty, delicious. Now *rare* or *obsolete* exc. as passing into sense 5. M16.
b SHAKES. *Twel. N.* I have no exquisite reason for't, but I have reason good enough. G. HAVERS The English . . well understand all the most exquisite points of Navigation.
3 Elaborately devised or carried out, highly finished; carried to a high degree of perfection or completeness. *obsolete* (merged in sense 5). M16. ▸**b** Of a quality, disposition, or habit: cultivated to a high degree of intensity; consummate, extreme. M16.
W. CAVE Put to death with the most exquisite arts of torture. J. STRYPE Wherein he hath done such exquisite service to the Protestant cause. **b** JAS. MILL The exquisite ignorance and stupidity of the Mysoreans in the art of war.
†**4** Of a person: accomplished in a particular field; excellent, perfect. (Foll. by *at*, *in*, *to do*.) M16–E19.
B. FRANKLIN A most exquisite mechanic.
5 Of such consummate excellence, beauty, or perfection as to excite intense delight or admiration; of great delicacy or beauty. L16.
P. H. GIBBS The rose garden showed some exquisite blooms. *Times* Armed robbery, planned with exquisite skill by intelligent, determined men.
6 Of pain, pleasure, etc.: intense, acute; keenly felt. M17.
7 Of the power of (mental or physical) feeling, the senses, etc.: keenly sensitive to impressions; acutely susceptible to pain, pleasure, etc.; delicate, finely strung. M17.
LD MACAULAY He had an exquisite ear, and performed skilfully on the flute.
▸ **B** *adverb.* Exquisitely. Now *rare.* E16.
▸ **C** *noun.* A person (esp. a man) who is overnice in dress etc.; a fop, a dandy. E19.
■ **exquisitely** *adverb* LME. **exquisiteness** *noun* M16. **exquisitism** *noun* (*a*) foppishness, dandyism; (*b*) *rare* overprecision: M19. **ex'quisitively** *adverb* (*rare*) exquisitely M17.

ex rel. /ɛks 'rɛl/ *prepositional phr.* M19.
[ORIGIN Abbreviation.]
= EX RELATIONE.

ex relatione /ɛks rɪ,leɪʃɪ'əʊni/ *prepositional phr.* E17.
[ORIGIN Latin.]
LAW (now chiefly *hist.*). By relation of; according to the report of, as reported by.

exsangueous *adjective* var. of EXSANGUIOUS.

exsanguinate /ɪk'saŋgwɪneɪt, ɛk-/ *verb trans.* M19.
[ORIGIN Latin *exsanguinatus* drained of blood, formed as EX-[1] 2 + *sanguin-*, *-guis* blood: see -ATE[3].]
Drain of blood.
■ **exsangui'nation** *noun* the action of exsanguinating; severe loss of blood: E20.

exsanguine /ɪk'saŋgwɪn, ɛk-/ *adjective.* Also †**exang-**. M17.
[ORIGIN from EX-[1] 2 + SANGUINE *adjective*, after Latin *exsanguis* bloodless: see EXSANGUIOUS, -INE[1].]
Bloodless; without sufficient blood, anaemic; *fig.* lacking vigour or substance.
■ **exsan'guineous** *adjective* (*obsolete* exc. *hist.*) bloodless M17.

exsanguious /ɪk'saŋgwɪəs, ɛk-/ *adjective.* Also **-eous**. M17.
[ORIGIN from Latin *exsanguis* bloodless, formed as EX-[1] 2 + *sanguis* blood: see -IOUS, -EOUS.]
= EXSANGUINE.

exscind /ɪk'sɪnd, ɛk-/ *verb trans.* M17.
[ORIGIN Latin *exscindere* cut out, formed as EX-[1] 1 + *scindere* to cut.]
Cut out, excise, (*lit. & fig.*). Formerly also, destroy (a nation).

exscribe /ɪk'skrʌɪb, ɛk-/ *verb trans.* E17.
[ORIGIN Latin *exscribere*, formed as EX-[1] 1 + *scribere* write.]
†**1** Copy or write out, transcribe. E17–E18.
2 GEOMETRY. Draw (a circle) outside a triangle so that it touches one side and the lines obtained by producing the other two sides. L19.

†**exsculp** *verb trans. rare.* L16–M18.
[ORIGIN Latin *exsculpere*, formed as EX-[1] 1 + *sculpere* cut, carve.]
Cut out, hollow out by cutting.

exsect /ɪkˈsɛkt, ɛk-/ *verb trans.* M17.
[ORIGIN Latin *exsect-* pa. ppl stem of *exsecare* cut out, formed as EX-[1] 1 + *secare* to cut.]
Cut out (*lit. & fig.*), remove (as) by cutting.

exsection /ɪkˈsɛkʃ(ə)n/ *noun.* E17.
[ORIGIN Latin *exsectio(n-)*, formed as EXSECT: see -ION.]
Chiefly SURGERY. The action or an act of cutting out or away; (an) excision.

exsert /ɪkˈsəːt, ɛk-/ *verb trans.* M17.
[ORIGIN formed as EXERT.]
†**1** = EXERT 4. Only in M17.
2 BIOLOGY. Push out; cause to protrude. E19.
■ **exsertion** *noun* (*rare*) the action of exserting; the state or fact of being exserted: L19.

exsertile /ɪkˈsəːtɪl, ɛk-/ *adjective.* E19.
[ORIGIN French, from *exsert* exserted from Latin *ex(s)ertus* pa. pple of *ex(s)erere*: see EXERT, -ILE.]
BIOLOGY. Able to be exserted.

ex-service /ɛk(s)ˈsəːvɪs/ *adjective.* Also **-services** /-ˈsəːvɪsɪz/. E20.
[ORIGIN from EX-[1] 3 + SERVICE *noun*[1].]
Having belonged to one of the fighting services; pertaining to former servicemen or servicewomen.
– COMB.: **ex-serviceman** a former serviceman; **ex-servicewoman** a former servicewoman.

exsibilate /ɪkˈsɪbɪleɪt, ɛk-/ *verb trans.* Long *rare* or *obsolete.* E17.
[ORIGIN Latin *exsibilat-* pa. ppl stem of *exsibilare*, formed as EX-[1] 1 + *sibilare* hiss: see -ATE[3].]
Hiss off the stage; dismiss ignominiously.
■ ˌ**exsibiˈlation** *noun* M17.

exsiccate /ˈɛksɪkeɪt/ *verb trans.* Pa. pple **-ated**, †**-ate**. LME.
[ORIGIN Latin *exsiccat-* pa. ppl stem of *exsiccare*, formed as EX-[1] 1 + *siccare*, from *siccus* dry: see -ATE[3].]
Make dry; remove moisture from; drain of all water.

exsiccation /ɛksɪˈkeɪʃ(ə)n/ *noun.* LME.
[ORIGIN Latin *exsiccatio(n-)*, formed as EXSICCATE: see -ATION.]
The action of drying or draining; complete removal or absence of moisture.

exsiccative /ˈɛksɪkeɪtɪv, ɪkˈsɪkətɪv, ɛkˈsɪ-/ *adjective & noun.* Now *rare* or *obsolete.* LME.
[ORIGIN medieval Latin *exsiccativus*, formed as EXSICCATE: see -ATIVE.]
(A medicine or other substance) having the power of making dry.

ex silentio /ɛks sɪˈlɛntɪəʊ, -ˈlɛnʃ-/ *adverbial phr.* E20.
[ORIGIN Latin = from silence.]
By or from a lack of evidence to the contrary.
New York Review of Books Historians do not ordinarily go for the argument *ex silentio*.

exsolution /ɛksəˈluːʃ(ə)n/ *noun.* E20.
[ORIGIN from EX-[1] 1 + SOLUTION.]
GEOLOGY. The process by which a homogeneous solution, esp. a solid solution, separates into two or more distinct phases; the action or an act of passing out of solution.
■ **exˈsolve** *verb trans. & intrans.* (cause to) separate out from or be removed from a solution M20.

exspuition /ɛkspjʊˈɪʃ(ə)n/ *noun.* M17.
[ORIGIN Latin *exspuitio(n-)*, from *exspuere*, formed as EX-[1] 1 + *spuere* to spit: see -ITION.]
The action of spitting out; spittle.

†**exstacy**, **exstasy** *nouns & verbs* vars. of ECSTASY.

†**exstatic** *adjective & noun* var. of ECSTATIC.

†**exstillation** *noun* var. of EXTILLATION.

exstipulate /ɪkˈstɪpjʊlət, ɛk-/ *adjective.* E19.
[ORIGIN from EX-[1] 2 + STIPULA, STIPULE: see -ATE[2].]
BOTANY. Lacking stipules.

exstrophy /ˈɛkstrəfi/ *noun.* M19.
[ORIGIN from EX-[2] + Greek *stroph-* (see STROPHE) + -Y[3].]
MEDICINE. A congenital condition in which the wall of a hollow organ such as the bladder communicates with the exterior.

†**exstruct** *verb trans.* Also **extruct**. M16–M18.
[ORIGIN Latin *exstruct-* pa. ppl stem of *exstruere*, formed as EX-[1] 1 + *struere* build.]
Build or pile up.

exsuccous /ɪkˈsʌkəs, ɛk-/ *adjective.* Now *rare.* M17.
[ORIGIN Latin *exsuccus* without juice, formed as EX-[1] 2 + *succus* juice: see -OUS.]
Lacking juice, sapless; dry (*lit. & fig.*).

exsuction /ɪkˈsʌkʃ(ə)n, ɛk-/ *noun.* Long *rare* or *obsolete.* M17.
[ORIGIN from EX-[1] 1 + SUCTION.]
The action of sucking or drawing out something, esp. air.

exsufflate /ˈɛksʌfleɪt/ *verb trans.* M17.
[ORIGIN Late (esp. ecclesiastical) Latin *exsufflat-* pa. ppl stem of *exsufflare*, formed as EX-[1] 1 + Latin *sufflare*: see SUFFLATE.]
Orig., blow out, blow away. Now only *hist.*, do this as an exorcism or in token of renunciation of the devil.
■ **exsuˈfflation** *noun* (*a*) (*obsolete* exc. *hist.*) the action or an act of exsufflating; (*b*) MEDICINE the removal by blowing of material from a body cavity, esp. the respiratory tract: E16.

exsufflicate /ɪkˈsʌflɪkət, ɛk-/ *adjective. literary. rare.* E17.
[ORIGIN App. arbitrary from EXSUFFLATE.]
Puffed up, inflated; blown (*lit. & fig.*).

†**exsuperate** *verb trans.* L16–E18.
[ORIGIN Latin *exsuperat-* pa. ppl stem of *exsuperare*, formed as EX-[1] 1 + *superare* rise above, from *super* above: see -ATE[3].]
Overtop, surpass; overcome.

exsurge /ɪkˈsəːdʒ, ɛk-/ *verb intrans. rare.* L16.
[ORIGIN Latin *exsurgere*, formed as EX-[1] 1 + *surgere* rise.]
Rise up, start out.
■ **exsurgent** *adjective* †(*a*) arising, emerging; (*b*) rising above the rest: E17.

ext. *abbreviation.*
1 Exterior.
2 External.

exta /ˈɛkstə/ *noun pl.* M17.
[ORIGIN Latin.]
hist. The viscera; *spec.* the entrails of a victim from which omens were interpreted by a soothsayer.

†**extacy**, **extasy** *nouns & verbs* vars. of ECSTASY.

extant /ɪkˈstant, ɛk-, ˈɛkstənt/ *adjective.* M16.
[ORIGIN Latin *ex(s)tant-* pres. ppl stem of *ex(s)tare* be prominent or visible, exist, formed as EX-[1] 1 + *stare* stand: see -ANT[1].]
†**1** Able to be publicly seen, found, or reached; accessible. M16–M17.
2 Projecting or protruding from a surface. (Foll. by *above*, *from*, etc.) *arch.* M16.
3 Conspicuous, manifest. Now *rare.* M16.
4 In existence, *esp.* (of a document etc.) still existing, surviving. Formerly also, (of time) present; (of a fashion) current. M16.
G. L. HARDING There are scratched or hammered on some rocks outlines of various animals then extant. M. MEYER Gosse's reply is not extant.

†**extatic** *adjective & noun* var. of ECSTATIC.

extemporal /ɪkˈstɛmp(ə)r(ə)l, ɛk-/ *adjective.* Now *rare* or *obsolete.* L16.
[ORIGIN Latin *extemporalis* arising out of the moment, from *ex tempore*: see EXTEMPORE, -AL[1].]
1 Done or said without premeditation; impromptu, extempore. L16.
†**2** (Of a person) able to speak, or given to speaking, extempore; (of a faculty) pertaining to extempore speech or action. L16–M17.
■ †**extemporally** *adverb* L16–L17. †**extemporalness** *noun*: only in M17.

extemporaneous /ɪkˌstɛmpəˈreɪnɪəs, ɛk-/ *adjective.* M17.
[ORIGIN Late Latin *extemporaneus*, formed as EXTEMPORAL: see -ANEOUS.]
1 = EXTEMPORE *adjective* 1. M17.
2 = EXTEMPORARY 3. Of a medicine: requiring preparation at the time of prescription (opp. ***officinal***). E18.
■ **extemporaneously** *adverb* L18. **extemporaneousness** *noun* M18.

extemporary /ɪkˈstɛmp(ə)r(ə)ri, ɛk-/ *adjective.* L16.
[ORIGIN from EXTEMPORE + -ARY[1], after *temporary*.]
†**1** Sudden, unexpected; occasional, casual. L16–M18.
2 = EXTEMPORE *adjective* 1. E17.
3 Hastily built or prepared; makeshift. M17.
■ **extemporarily** *adverb* M17. **extemporariness** *noun* L17.

extempore /ɪkˈstɛmp(ə)ri, ɛk-/ *adverb, noun, & adjective.* M16.
[ORIGIN Latin *ex tempore* on the spur of the moment, formed as EX *preposition* + *tempore* abl. of *tempus* time.]
▸ **A** *adverb.* **1** Without premeditation or preparation; impromptu. (Now chiefly of speaking or of performing music.) M16.
†**live extempore**: for the present without regard for the future. **pray extempore**: without using a set form of prayer. **speak extempore**: without notes or other preparation.
†**2** At once, immediately. L16–M17.
▸ †**B** *noun.* An unprepared improvised speech, composition, or performance. L16–E19.
▸ **C** *adjective.* **1** Of a speech, musical performance, etc: spoken or done without preparation, esp. without written notes. Of a speaker or performer: performing without preparation. E17.
A. THWAITE His extempore lectures on Gray were particularly successful.
2 Occasional; sudden, unprepared for. (Now only of personal actions, with some notion of sense 1.) M17.
W. IRVING He was somewhat subject to extempore bursts of passion.
3 Makeshift, contrived for the occasion. L17.

extemporize /ɪkˈstɛmpərʌɪz, ɛk-/ *verb.* Also **-ise**. M17.
[ORIGIN from EXTEMPORE + -IZE.]
1 *verb intrans.* Speak extempore; compose or perform music extempore. M17.
E. HEATH I played the organ at which he had extemporized so often.
2 *verb trans.* Compose, perform, or produce extempore. E19.
W. H. AUDEN He amused himself / extemporising moral, / highly moral, iambics.
■ **extemporiˈzation** *noun* M19. **extemporizer** *noun* E19.

†**extempory** *adverb & adjective.* E17–L18.
[ORIGIN Anglicization.]
= EXTEMPORE *adverb & adjective.*

extend /ɪkˈstɛnd, ɛk-/ *verb.* ME.
[ORIGIN Latin *extendere* stretch out, formed as EX-[1] 1 + *tendere* stretch.]
▸ **I** Assess, value; take possession of.
1 *verb trans.* LAW (now *hist.*). Value (land); *esp.* value (the land of a debtor) in order to find by when the creditor will be paid from its rental. ME.
2 *verb trans.* **a** LAW (now *hist.*). Take possession of (land etc.) by a writ of extent or in payment of any other debt. L15. ▸**b** *gen.* Take possession of by force. Now *rare* or *obsolete.* E17.
▸ **II** Stretch, lengthen.
3 *verb trans. & †intrans.* Straighten or spread out (esp. the body, limbs, etc.) at full length. LME. ▸**b** Write out (notes, an abbreviation, etc.) in full; *esp.* transcribe (shorthand notes) in longhand. M17.
H. JAMES Elizabeth, whose august person had extended itself upon a huge . . bed.
4 †**a** *verb trans.* Stretch or pull out (something) to its full size; distend (a vessel etc.); hold or maintain in a stretched condition; *rare* train (a vine). LME–L18. ▸**b** *verb trans.* Cause (a horse) to lengthen its stride. E18. ▸**c** *verb refl.* (Of a horse) exert itself to the full, esp. in response to a challenge; (of an athlete etc.) use all one's efforts, exert oneself to the full. M19. ▸**d** *verb trans.* In *pass.* Of a horse, sportsman or sportswoman, etc.: be challenged into making maximum effort. E20. ▸**e** *verb intrans.* Of a horse: lengthen the stride. L20.
c E. WAUGH An indolent, humorous clergyman, who we did not think was extending himself fully in coaching us.
5 *verb intrans. & trans.* (Cause to) stretch or span over or *over* a period of time or a distance; (cause to) reach to or *to* a certain point. Also foll. by *into*, *through*, etc. LME.
STEELE His Troops are extended from Exilles to Mount Genevre. T. COLLINS On our right, the bare plain extended indefinitely. P. KAVANAGH Untrimmed hedges with briars extending well out into the fields.
6 *verb trans.* Prolong in duration. LME. ▸**b** Make longer, continue further in space. M16. ▸**c** Develop further; bring nearer to completion. E18.
SHAKES. *Macb.* You shall offend him, and extend his Passion. **b** W. BOYD The gleaming walnut dining table was fully extended to accommodate the family. A. BRIGGS During the fourth century . . some of the greatest Roman villas were built or extended. **c** ISAIAH BERLIN They consequently seek to extend historical knowledge to fill gaps in the past.
7 **a** *verb trans.* Spread out (*over*); cause to cover a space or area. LME. ▸**b** *verb intrans.* Cover an area; stretch out in various directions; (of a law, obligation, quality, etc.) have a certain range or scope. LME.
b G. GREENE The land belonging to it extended in a semi-circle three miles deep from the last cottage. F. O'BRIEN His knowledge of physics . . extended to Boyle's Law and the Parallelogram of Forces.
†**8** *verb trans.* Exaggerate. E16–E17.
9 *verb trans.* **a** Increase the scope or range of application of. L16. ▸**b** Increase the quantity or bulk of (a product) by the addition of another substance. M20.
a H. SPENCER The invention . . enabled men to extend the principles of mechanics to the atmosphere. G. VIDAL He merely used Christianity to extend his dominion over the world.
▸ **III** Stretch or hold out; offer.
10 *verb trans.* Stretch or hold out (the hand or something held in it). LME.
J. BERGER The hostess . . extends her arm in beckoning invitation.
11 *verb trans.* Grant (kindness, mercy, patronage, etc.) *to*; offer (a welcome, invitation, etc.). Formerly also, vent (malice), inflict (vengeance), issue (a legal process), *against*, *upon*. L15.
M. EDGEWORTH You should extend to me the same . . indulgence. D. CARNEGIE A man who has to refuse . . invitations extended by friends.
■ **extendaˈbility** *noun* = EXTENSIBILITY L20. **extendable** *adjective* = EXTENDIBLE M17. **extendiˈbility** *noun* the property of being extendible L15. **extendible** *adjective* able or (LAW, now *hist.*) liable to be extended L15.

extended /ɪkˈstɛndɪd, ɛk-/ *adjective.* LME.
[ORIGIN from EXTEND + -ED[1].]
1 Lengthened or prolonged in space or time; relatively long, extensive, or widespread. LME. ▸**b** Of an insurance policy: continuing to provide cover after the payment of premiums is discontinued. L19. ▸**c** BIBLIOGRAPHY. Of the page of a book: having had the inner margin restored. M20.

E

Catholic Herald A time for extended debate and reflection. *Independent on Sunday* The illegal use of solitary confinement for extended periods.

2 Stretched out, spread out. **M16.** ▸**b** Of a horse's gait: lengthened as far as possible without breaking. Cf. COLLECTED 2. **L18.**

3 *LAW* (now *hist.*). Of property: valued; taken possession of as payment of a debt. **E17.**

4 *PHILOSOPHY.* Having or possessing the quality of extension; occupying space. **M17.**

– SPECIAL COLLOCATIONS: **extended burial** *ARCHAEOLOGY:* with the body laid at full length (cf. ***crouched burial*** s.v. CROUCH *verb* 1). **extended family** *SOCIOLOGY:* comprising not only one couple and their children but also consanguineous and conjugal relatives living in the same household or near by. **extended-play** *adjective* (*a*) designating a record with more playing time than a single though of similar size; (*b*) designating a recording tape that is longer but thinner than the standard.

■ **extendedly** *adverb* **M17.** **extendedness** *noun* **L17.**

extender /ɪkˈstɛndə, ɛk-/ *noun.* **ME.**
[ORIGIN formed as EXTENDED + -ER¹.]
1 *gen.* A person who or thing which extends something. Formerly, *spec.* in *LAW*, a surveyor or valuer of property, esp. under a writ of extent. **ME.**
†**2** = EXTENSOR. **E17–L18.**
3 A substance added to a product to dilute the colour, increase the bulk, or vary some other property. **E20.**

extense /ɪkˈstɛns, ɛk-/ *noun & adjective.* Long *rare* or *obsolete.* **E17.**
[ORIGIN Old French, or Latin *extensus* pa. pple of *extendere* EXTEND.]
▸ †**A** *noun.* **1** An expanse. Only in **E17.**
2 Extension. Only in **M17.**
▸ **B** *adjective.* Extensive; extended. **M17.**

extensible /ɪkˈstɛnsɪb(ə)l, ɛk-/ *adjective.* **E17.**
[ORIGIN French, or medieval Latin *extensibilis*, from Latin *extens-* pa. ppl stem of *extendere*: see EXTEND, -IBLE.]
Able to be extended; extensile.
■ **extensiˈbility** *noun* **M17.** **extensibleness** *noun* **E18.**

extensile /ɪkˈstɛnsʌɪl, ɛk-/ *adjective.* **M18.**
[ORIGIN from Latin *extens-*: see EXTENSION, -ILE.]
Able to be extended; (of a tongue, tentacle, etc.) able to be protruded.

extension /ɪkˈstɛnʃ(ə)n, ɛk-/ *noun.* **LME.**
[ORIGIN Late Latin *extensio(n-)*, from Latin *extens-*, *extent-* pa. ppl stem of *extendere*: see EXTEND, -ION.]
1 The action of extending the body or a limb; the holding out or up of the hand or arm. **LME.** ▸**b** *SURGERY.* The application of axial traction to a fractured or dislocated limb or to an injured or diseased spinal column to restore it to its normal position. **E17.**
†**2** The action of stretching or straining something; a stretched or strained state; distension, swelling. **E16–E19.**
3 (An) increase in scope or range. **L16.** ▸**b** In full ***university extension***. Extramural teaching provided by a university or college. **M19.**

S. SONTAG The metaphor of the psychic voyage is an extension of the romantic idea of travel.

b attrib.: ***extension course***, ***extension lecture***, ***extension student***, etc.

4 The scope or range of an abstract thing. **E17.** ▸**b** *LOGIC.* The range of a term or concept as measured by the number of kinds of object which it denotes or contains. **L17.**

J. REYNOLDS The same extension of mind which gives the excellence of genius.

5 a Size, spatial extent. Now *rare.* **E17.** ▸**b** *PHYSICS & PHILOSOPHY.* The property of occupying space; spatial magnitude. **E17.** ▸**c** Something that occupies space. **M18.**
6 An increase in duration or in the time allowed for something, *spec.* the sale of alcoholic drinks. **M17.**
†**7** The fact of being spread out; an expanse (of country). **L17–L18.**
8 a (An) increase in length or area. **L18.** ▸**b** A part of something that extends or enlarges it; *esp.* one added for this purpose, e.g. to a building or a motorway. **M19.** ▸**c** (The number of) a subsidiary telephone distant from the main instrument or switchboard. **E20.**

b S. BECKETT His head is framed in headrest which is a narrower extension of backrest. B. PYM A cottage . . with that rather ugly 'extension' stuck on at the side.

9 The condition or fact of extending to a certain distance or in a certain direction. **L18.**

E. K. KANE Showing . . the former extension of the Esquimaux race to the higher north.

10 The action of adding up a horizontal line of figures or of computing a subtotal, as on an invoice; the figure thus obtained. **M19.**
11 *BALLET.* A position with the leg stretched at an angle from the body; the ability to hold such a position; the height above the waist that a dancer can raise one leg. **M20.**
12 The utmost lengthening of a horse's stride at a particular pace. **M20.**

– COMB.: **extension bellows**, **extension tube**: added to a camera between the body and lens to shorten the distance of closest focus of an object so that close-up pictures can be taken.
■ **extensionless** *adjective* (*PHILOSOPHY*) lacking extension in space or duration in time **E20.**

extensional /ɪkˈstɛnʃ(ə)n(ə)l, ɛk-/ *adjective.* **M17.**
[ORIGIN from EXTENSION + -AL¹.]
Of, pertaining to, or possessing extension; *spec.* (*LOGIC & PHILOSOPHY*) concerned with the objects denoted rather than the predicates applied; having the truth value unaltered if a constituent is replaced by another with the same denotation or extension.
■ **extensioˈnality** *noun* (*PHILOSOPHY*) the state or fact of being extensional **E20.** **extensionally** *adverb* by way of or in terms of extension **L19.**

extensity /ɪkˈstɛnsɪti, ɛk-/ *noun.* **M19.**
[ORIGIN from Latin *extens-*: see EXTENSION, -ITY.]
The quality of having (a certain) extension.

extensive /ɪkˈstɛnsɪv, ɛk-/ *adjective.* **LME.**
[ORIGIN French *extensif*, *-ive* or late Latin *extensivus*, formed as EXTENSITY: see -IVE.]
1 Possessing, characterized by, or pertaining to spatial extension; occupying space. Formerly, characterized by swelling. **LME.**

P. W. ATKINS The internal energy of a system depends on the amount of material it contains . . . This is an example of an extensive property.

†**2** Of metal: readily beaten into a thinner, more extensive form. Only in **17.**
3 Of an abstract thing (formerly also of a person or personal qualities): far-reaching, wide in scope, range, or application; comprehensive; lengthy. **E17.**

B. BETTELHEIM Our society seems to be . . expecting more extensive technology to solve the problems it creates.

4 Tending to cause extension; having the effect of extending. **M17.**
5 *LOGIC.* Of or pertaining to extension; denoting or applying to a number of different objects or kinds of object. **L17.**
6 Of a material thing: having a wide extent, occupying a large surface or space. **L18.**

A. BROOKNER A largish house set in extensive gardens.

7 *ECONOMICS.* Of a method of farming etc.: in which a relatively small crop is obtained from a large area with a minimum of attention and expense. **M19.**
■ **extensively** *adverb* **L16.** **extensiveness** *noun* **M17.**

extensometer /ɛkstɛnˈsɒmɪtə/ *noun.* **L19.**
[ORIGIN from Latin *extens-*: see EXTENSION, -OMETER.]
An instrument for measuring the extension or other deformation of a body under applied stress; an instrument using such deformations to record the elastic strain in metals, concrete, etc.

extensor /ɪkˈstɛnsə, ɛk-/ *noun.* **E18.**
[ORIGIN Late Latin, formed as EXTENSOMETER: see -OR.]
ANATOMY. A muscle which extends or straightens a limb etc. Also ***extensor muscle***. Cf. FLEXOR.

extent /ɪkˈstɛnt, ɛk-/ *noun.* **ME.**
[ORIGIN Anglo-Norman *extente* from medieval Latin *extenta* use as noun of fem. of Latin *extentus* pa. pple of *extendere* EXTEND.]
▸ **I** *LAW* (now *hist.*).
1 The action or an act of valuing property, esp. for the purpose of taxation; the value assigned in such a case. **ME.** ▸†**b** A tax levied on such a valuation; income from property so valued. **ME–M18.**
2 Seizure of property in execution of a writ; (a) sequestration. **L16.** ▸†**b** *fig.* An attack. **L16–E17.** ▸**c** A writ to recover debts adjudged by a court of record as due to the Crown, under which the body, lands, and goods of the debtor could all be seized at once to compel payment of the debt. Also ***writ of extent***. **M17.**

b SHAKES. *Twel. N.* In this uncivil and unjust extent Against thy peace.

▸ **II** *gen.* **3** The amount of space over which a thing extends; size, dimensions, amount. **L15.**

A. J. TOYNBEE The western pampa's vast extent can no longer be seen with the eye. J. HERSEY It was then that he first realised the extent of the damage.

4 Width or limits of application; scope; the limit to which something extends. **L16.** ▸†**b** Enlargement in scope or operation. **M17–E18.**

E. PAUL The drinks were watered to such an extent that temperance was automatically accomplished. L. DURRELL He was now alarmed at the extent to which it might become possible to hate her. J. GASKELL He can do what he likes with them to quite an extent. H. MACMILLAN I share to the fullest extent the responsibility of all the decisions.

†**5** The action of extending justice, kindness, etc. **L16–M17.**
6 A space or area of a specified kind; the whole *of* an area. **E17.**

R. GLOVER Th' imperial race That rul'd th' extent of Asia. C. WATERTON You may see a sloping extent of noble trees. G. P. MARSH They occupied only a small extent of England.

7 *LOGIC.* = EXTENSION 4b. **M17.**

8 *BELL-RINGING.* The total possible number of distinct changes in a given method. **E20.**

†**extent** *adjective.* **LME–M17.**
[ORIGIN Latin *extentus*: see EXTENT *noun*.]
= EXTENDED 1, 2, 4, 5.

extenuate /ɪkˈstɛnjʊeɪt, ɛk-/ *verb trans.* Pa. pple **-ated**, (earlier) †**-ate**. **LME.**
[ORIGIN Latin *extenuat-* pa. ppl stem of *extenuare* thin, reduce, diminish, formed as EX-¹ 1 + *tenuis* thin: see -ATE³.]
1 Make (a person, the body, etc.) thin; emaciate. *arch.* **LME.**
2 State at a low figure; disparage the magnitude or importance of; underrate. *arch.* **E16.** ▸**b** Treat (a crime, a fault, guilt) as of trifling importance; *esp.* (try to) lessen the seeming seriousness of (a crime etc.) by partial excuse; (of a circumstance) lessen the guilt of (a crime etc.). **L16.** ▸**c** Plead partial excuses for, try to justify. **M18.**

b B. BAINBRIDGE The prisoner's age and previous good character were extenuating circumstances. **c** A. RADCLIFFE She . . endeavoured to extenuate the conduct of Madame La Motte.

†**3** Diminish in size, number, or amount; lessen (a quality etc.) in degree; mitigate (a law). **M16–L18.**
4 Thin out in consistency, make less dense. Now *rare* or *obsolete.* **M16.**
†**5** Thin out (hair); make thin or narrow; beat (metal) into thin plates, draw into fine wire. **M16–L17.**
†**6** Disparage (a person, action, attribute, etc.); diminish in honour. **E17–E18.**
■ **extenuatingly** *adverb* in an extenuating manner **L19.** **extenuative** *adjective & noun* (a thing) tending to extenuate **L16.** **extenuator** *noun* **M18.** **extenuatory** *adjective* **E19.**

extenuation /ɪkˌstɛnjʊˈeɪʃ(ə)n, ɛk-/ *noun.* **LME.**
[ORIGIN Latin *extenuatio(n-)*, formed as EXTENUATE: see -ATION.]
1 a The action or an act of making or becoming emaciated. *arch.* **LME.** ▸†**b** The action or an act of diminishing in size or volume. **E17–L18.**
†**2** The action or an act of lessening a quality etc. in degree; (a) weakening; (an) impoverishment; mitigation of blame or punishment. **M16–E18.**
3 The action or an act of lessening or trying to lessen the guilt of a crime etc. by partial excuse. **L16.**

P. G. WODEHOUSE Some excuse, some theory in extenuation of his behaviour, is . . urgently needed.

4 The action or an act of belittling or underrating. **E17.**

exterior /ɪkˈstɪərɪə, ɛk-/ *adjective & noun.* **E16.**
[ORIGIN Latin, compar. of *exter* external: see -IOR.]
▸ **A** *adjective.* **1** Further from the centre, outer, (opp. ***interior***). Of an action etc.: manifested on the surface, outward, visible. **E16.**

C. CLARKE Beatrice possesses a fund of hidden tenderness beneath her exterior gaiety.

exterior angle: between a side of a triangle or polygon and the adjacent side produced. **exterior to** on the outer side or outside of.

2 Situated or coming from outside; external (*to*). **M16.**

F. L. WRIGHT It cannot be changed . . by the exterior pressures of any outward circumstances.

exterior BALLISTICS.

†**3** Concerned with externals. **M16–L18.**
4 *CINEMATOGRAPHY.* Outdoor. **L20.**
▸ **B** *noun.* **1** An outward part, feature, etc. Usu. in *pl.* **L16.**

SHAKES. *Merry W.* She did . . course o'er my exteriors with . . a greedy intention.

2 The outer surface of something. **L17.**

H. DOUGLAS Wooden frames, covered on the exterior with sheet copper.

3 An outward or visible aspect or demeanour, esp. as concealing a different one. **E19.**

J. CONRAD He was in reality of a timid disposition under his manly exterior.

4 An outdoor scene in a play or film; a film or film sequence shot outdoors. **L19.**
■ **exteriorly** *adverb* (*a*) with outward act; in externals; (*b*) on the surface; in an exterior position: **M16.**

exteriorise *verb* var. of EXTERIORIZE.

exteriority /ɪkˌstɪərɪˈɒrɪti, ɛk-/ *noun.* **E17.**
[ORIGIN from EXTERIOR + -ITY.]
1 The state of being outside or of having external existence; outwardness. **E17.**
2 Devotion to external instead of to inward and spiritual things. **L19.**

exteriorize /ɪkˈstɪərɪərʌɪz, ɛk-/ *verb trans.* Also **-ise**. **L19.**
[ORIGIN formed as EXTERIORITY + -IZE.]
Make exterior; *SURGERY* bring to the surface of the body or outside it. Also, give external form to, attribute external existence to.

R. HAYMAN He could exteriorize all his anxiety by writing.

■ **exterioriˈzation** *noun* **L19.**

exterminable /ɪkˈstəːmɪnəb(ə)l, ɛk-/ *adjective.* *rare.* **M17.**
[ORIGIN formed as EXTERMINATE + -ABLE.]
Able to be exterminated or destroyed.

exterminate /ɪkˈstəːmɪneɪt, ɛk-/ *verb trans.* Pa. pple **-ated**, †**-ate**. LME.

[ORIGIN Latin *exterminat-* pa. ppl stem of *exterminare* (in classical Latin only in sense 1, in Vulgate in sense 2), formed as EX-[1] 1 + *terminus* boundary: see -ATE[3].]

†**1** Drive beyond the boundaries of a state, community, etc.; banish. (Foll. by *from*, (*out*) *of*.) LME–L17.

2 Destroy utterly, kill, (a person or other living thing); kill all the members of (a race, sect, nation, etc.); make extinct; put a complete end to (an opinion). M16.

R. S. R. FITTER When the woods around Hampstead . . were grubbed up . . plants such as the tutsan . . were exterminated. A. BURGESS Jews had been . . tortured, sent to labour camps, exterminated.

†**3** Abolish, put an end to, (a thing). L16–L18.

†**4** MATH. Eliminate (an unknown quantity). M18–E19.

■ **exterminative** *adjective* = EXTERMINATORY L19. **exterminator** *noun* †(**a**) a person who banishes someone; (**b**) a person who exterminates or destroys someone or something; *spec.* (*N. Amer.*) a person employed to destroy vermin: LME. **exterminatory** *adjective* tending to exterminate L18.

extermination /ɪkˌstəːmɪˈneɪʃ(ə)n/ *noun*. LME.

[ORIGIN Late Latin *exterminatio(n-)*, formed as EXTERMINATE: see -ATION.]

†**1** Banishment, expulsion. LME–M17.

2 Total destruction, extinction. M16.

†**3** MATH. Elimination. M18–E19.

– COMB.: **extermination camp** a concentration camp for the mass killing of people, *esp.* one of those set up in Nazi Germany.

†**extermine** *verb trans.* LME–M17.

[ORIGIN Old French & mod. French *exterminer* from Latin *exterminare*: see EXTERMINATE.]

= EXTERMINATE 1, 2, 3.

extern /ɪkˈstəːn, ɛk-/ *adjective, noun, & verb*. Also **-erne**. M16.

[ORIGIN French *externe* or Latin *externus*, from *exter*: see EXTERIOR.]

▸ **A** *adjective*. **1** = EXTERNAL *adjective* 1. Now *rare* (*poet.*). M16.

2 = EXTERNAL *adjective* 4. Now *rare*. M16.

†**3** Situated in, belonging to, or designating a foreign country. M16–M17.

4 = EXTERNAL *adjective* 3a, c. (Foll. by *to*.) Now chiefly *poet.* L16.

5 Connected with a community but not resident in it. Cf. sense B.2 below. M19.

▸ **B** *noun*. †**1** Outward appearance. *rare* (Shakes.). Only in L16.

2 A person attached to a community or institution but not resident in it; *esp.*: (**a**) (in a strictly enclosed order of nuns) a sister who lives outside the enclosure and goes on outside errands; (**b**) (in a hospital) a non-resident doctor, worker, or patient; (in a school) a non-boarding pupil [French *externe*]. E17.

▸ **C** *verb trans*. Banish (a person considered politically undesirable) from a region or district. *SE Asian*. E20.

external /ɪkˈstəːn(ə)l, ɛk-/ *adjective & noun*. LME.

[ORIGIN from medieval Latin, from Latin *exter*: see EXTERN, -AL[1].]

▸ **A** *adjective*. **1** Outwardly visible or manifest; consisting of outward acts or observances. LME.

J. BUTLER The external worship of God. C. DARWIN Fertility in the hybrid is independent of its external resemblance to either pure parent.

2 Of or situated on the outside or visible part of something; ANATOMY situated towards the outer surface of the body (opp. *internal*). L16. ▸**b** Of a remedy or treatment: applied to the exterior of the body. E18.

T. HARDY The surgeon . . said that the external bruises were mere trifles.

external ear: see EAR *noun*[1].

3 **a** Situated outside or beyond the limits of a given object. (Foll. by *to*.) L16. ▸†**b** = EXTERN *adjective* 3. Only in L16. ▸**c** Of a thing presented in sense perception: (regarded as) existing independently of the mind perceiving it. M17.

a C. RYCROFT Hallucinations . . are experienced as though they were external to the person constructing them. **b** J. STEINBECK External realities . . she obliterated by refusing to believe in them.

a external RELATION. **b external world** the totality of external objects.

4 Originating or acting from outside. M17.

B. BETTELHEIM The need to ascribe inner conflict to some external force.

external evidence: derived from a source independent of the thing discussed.

5 Having an outside object or sphere of operation; *spec.* relating to foreign countries or foreign affairs. L18.

H. JAMES National questions . . of external as well as of domestic and of colonial policy.

6 Of a student or an examiner: taking or marking examinations of a university of which he or she is not a resident member. Of an examination or a degree: taken or obtained by an external student. L19.

7 COMPUTING. Not contained in the central processing unit. Also = PERIPHERAL *adjective* 3. M20.

▸ **B** *noun*. **1** In *pl.* Outward forms, observances, etc., as opp. to inner realities or substance. Also (*arch.*), outward features. M17.

R. SOUTH Adam was . . glorious in his externals; he had a beautiful body. M. M. FISKE Dwell in this artificial world [*sc.* the theatre], and you will know only the externals of acting.

2 External objects or circumstances; inessentials. M17.

M. L. KING What shall it profit a man, if he gain the whole world of externals . . and lose the internal—his own soul?

3 The exterior; an outward surface or aspect. *arch.* L18.

SOUTHEY Deformity and hollowness beneath The rich external.

■ **externally** *adverb* L16.

externalise *verb* var. of EXTERNALIZE.

externalism /ɪkˈstəːn(ə)lɪz(ə)m, ɛk-/ *noun*. M19.

[ORIGIN from EXTERNAL + -ISM.]

1 Excessive regard for outward form, esp. in religion. M19.

2 Devotion to the external world. L19.

■ **externalist** *noun & adjective* (a person) that manifests externalism L19.

externality /ɛkstəːˈnalɪti/ *noun*. L17.

[ORIGIN formed as EXTERNALISM + -ITY.]

1 The quality of being external; *esp.* (PHILOSOPHY) the fact of existing outside the perceiving subject. L17.

2 An external object or circumstance; an outward feature or characteristic. M19.

3 = EXTERNALISM. M19.

4 ECONOMICS. A side effect or consequence (of an industrial or commercial activity) which affects other parties without this being reflected in the cost or the price of the goods or services involved. M20.

externalize /ɪkˈstəːn(ə)lʌɪz, ɛk-/ *verb trans*. Also **-ise**. M19.

[ORIGIN from EXTERNAL *adjective* + -IZE.]

1 Make external; embody, give external form to; treat as existing or occurring in the external world. Also, reduce to external observances. M19.

2 ECONOMICS. Fail or choose not to incorporate (costs) as part of a pricing structure. M20.

■ **externaliˈzation** *noun* the action of externalizing; an embodiment: E19.

externat /ɛkstɛrna/ *noun*. Pl. pronounced same. M19.

[ORIGIN French, from *externe*: see EXTERN *noun*.]

A day school.

externate /ˈɛkstəneɪt, ɪkˈstəːneɪt, ɛk-/ *verb trans*. *rare*. L19.

[ORIGIN from EXTERN *adjective* + -ATE[3].]

= EXTERNIZE.

■ **exterˈnation** *noun* M19.

externe *adjective & noun* var. of EXTERN.

externise *verb* var. of EXTERNIZE.

externity /ɪkˈstəːnɪti, ɛk-/ *noun*. E18.

[ORIGIN from EXTERN *adjective* + -ITY.]

The quality of being external or outward; external characteristics.

externize /ɪkˈstəːnʌɪz, ɛk-/ *verb trans*. Also **-ise**. M19.

[ORIGIN formed as EXTERNITY + -IZE.]

Embody in external form; externalize.

■ **externiˈzation** *noun* M19.

exteroceptor /ˈɛkstərəʊˌsɛptə/ *noun*. E20.

[ORIGIN Perh. from EXTER(IOR or EXTER(NAL + -O- + RE)CEPTOR.]

PHYSIOLOGY. A sensory receptor which receives external stimuli.

■ **exteroˈceptive** *adjective* E20.

exterritorial /ˌɛkstɛrɪˈtɔːrɪəl/ *adjective*. L18.

[ORIGIN from EX-[1] 1 + TERRITORIAL, after EXTERRITORIALITY.]

= EXTRATERRITORIAL.

■ **exterritorially** *adverb* M19.

exterritoriality /ɛkstɛrɪˌtɔːrɪˈalɪti/ *noun*. L18.

[ORIGIN French *exterritorialité*, formed as EX-[1] 1, TERRITORIAL, -ITY.]

= EXTRATERRITORIALITY.

†**extill** *verb intrans. & trans*. M17–E19.

[ORIGIN Latin *exstillare*, formed as EX-[1] 1 + *stillare* to drop, from *stilla* drop.]

Come or send out in drops, exude.

†**extillation** *noun*. Also **exstill-**. E17–E18.

[ORIGIN from Latin *exstillat-* pa. ppl stem of *exstillare*: see EXTILL, -ATION.]

An act of coming out in drops; in *pl.*, matter that has come out thus.

extinct /ɪkˈstɪŋkt, ɛk-/ *adjective* (orig. *pa. pple*). LME.

[ORIGIN Latin *ex(s)tinctus* pa. pple of *ex(s)tinguere*, formed as EX-[1] 1 + *stinguere* quench.]

1 Of a fire, light, candle, etc.: extinguished; no longer burning. LME. ▸**b** Of life, hope, disease, or anything compared to a light or fire: ended, no longer existing; devoid of any brilliance or light. L15. ▸**c** Of a volcano: no longer erupting, having lost its capacity to erupt. M19.

R. BYFIELD It tooke fire . . but was quickly extinct. J. GALSWORTHY He would sit . . brooding . . , a cigar extinct between his lips. **b** R. LEHMANN His voice was flat . . and his eyes looked extinct.

c extinct volcano *fig.* a person who has lost the energy, reputation, etc., he or she once possessed.

†**2** Of a person: blotted out of existence; no longer living. L15–L17.

3 No longer used, recognized, etc.; discontinued, obsolete. Of a peerage or title: having no valid claimant. L15.

W. CRUISE Such a power, though extinct at law, would . . be enforced in equity.

4 That has died out: (**a**) (of a family, race, etc.) having no living representative; (**b**) (of a species etc.) no longer surviving in the world at large or in a given locality. L17.

C. DARWIN Megatherium, Toxodon, and other extinct monsters.

†**extinct** *verb*. LME–M17.

[ORIGIN Latin *ex(s)tinct-* pa. ppl stem of *ex(s)tinguere*: see EXTINCT *adjective*.]

= EXTINGUISH.

extincteur /ɛkstɛ̃ktœːr/ *noun*. Pl. pronounced same. L19.

[ORIGIN French from Latin *ex(s)tinctor*, formed as EXTINCT *verb*: see -OR.]

A fire extinguisher.

extinction /ɪkˈstɪŋkʃ(ə)n, ɛk-/ *noun*. LME.

[ORIGIN Latin *ex(s)tinctio(n-)*, formed as EXTINCT *verb*: see -ION.]

1 The action or process of making or becoming extinct; the state or fact of being extinct; destruction, annihilation; abolition, suppression. LME.

R. S. R. FITTER Londoners . . have uprooted some of the more striking plants of the London area almost to the point of extinction. T. S. ELIOT The progress of an artist is . . a continual extinction of personality. J. A. MICHENER Many times . . the Jews would be threatened with extinction.

2 PHYSICS. Reduction in the intensity of light or other radiation as it passes through a medium or object. L18. ▸**b** The appearance of darkness when a crystal is illuminated through a polarizer and viewed through another polarizer placed in a plane parallel to the first but oriented at right angles to it. L19.

attrib.: G. E. HUTCHINSON The transmission is low and the extinction coefficient high in the infrared.

extinctive /ɪkˈstɪŋktɪv, ɛk-/ *adjective*. LME.

[ORIGIN Orig. from medieval Latin *extinctivus*, formed as EXTINCT *verb*; in mod. use from EXTINCTION: see -IVE.]

Tending or having the power to extinguish. Formerly, tending to reduce inflammation.

†**extincture** *noun*. *rare* (Shakes.). Only in L16.

[ORIGIN from EXTINCT *verb* + -URE.]

Extinction, quenching.

extine /ˈɛkstɪn, -tʌɪn/ *noun*. M19.

[ORIGIN from Latin *ext(imus* outermost + -INE[1].]

BOTANY. = EXINE.

extinguish /ɪkˈstɪŋgwɪʃ, ɛk-/ *verb*. M16.

[ORIGIN from Latin *ex(s)tinguere*: see EXTINCT *adjective*, -ISH[2]. Cf. DISTINGUISH.]

▸ **I** *verb trans*. **1** Cause (a fire, light, etc.) to cease to burn or shine; quench, put out. M16.

W. TREVOR He extinguished the light and mounted the stairs in darkness. *fig.*: D. CECIL Nothing could wholly extinguish the flame of genius.

2 Do away with completely, put an end to; stifle, quench, (a feeling, faculty, etc.); nullify, make void, (a right, claim, etc.); suppress (an institution, office, etc.). M16. ▸**b** Wipe out (a debt) by full payment. M17.

J. YEOWELL Though the bishopric . . merged into the archbishopric . . it was not extinguished. C. S. FORESTER The rain . . extinguished the last chance of victory. E. F. SCHUMACHER Nationalisation extinguishes private proprietary rights. W. CATHER Something came up in him that extinguished his power of feeling and thinking.

3 Surpass by superior brilliance. *arch.* M16.

M. O. W. OLIPHANT The men . . were quite transcended and extinguished by their wives.

4 Exterminate, make extinct, (a family, race, etc.); *arch.* kill (a person). L16.

5 Reduce (an opponent) to silence. *colloq.* L19.

▸ **II** *verb intrans*. **6** Be extinguished, suppressed, etc.; become extinct. Now *rare*. L16.

■ **extinguishable** *adjective* E16.

extinguishant /ɪkˈstɪŋgwɪʃ(ə)nt, ɛk-/ *noun*. M20.

[ORIGIN from EXTINGUISH + -ANT[1]. Cf. *coolant*, *lubricant*, etc.]

A material used to put out fires.

extinguisher /ɪkˈstɪŋgwɪʃə, ɛk-/ *noun*. M16.

[ORIGIN from EXTINGUISH + -ER[1].]

1 *gen.* A person who or thing which extinguishes something. M16.

2 A hollow conical cap for extinguishing a candle. M17.

3 = ***fire extinguisher*** s.v. FIRE *noun*. E19.

extinguishment /ɪkˈstɪŋgwɪʃm(ə)nt, ɛk-/ *noun*. E16.

[ORIGIN formed as EXTINGUISHER + -MENT.]

1 The action of extinguishing a light, feeling, right, institution, etc.; the state of being extinguished. E16.

Daily Telegraph The end result is virtual extinguishment—for the footpath or bridleway . . has legally ceased to exist.

E

E

†**2** Extermination *of* a family, race, etc.; extinct condition. M16–M17.

extirp /ɪkˈstəːp, ɛk-/ *verb trans.* Long *arch.* LME.
[ORIGIN Old French & mod. French *extirper* Latin *ex(s)tirpare*: see EXTIRPATE.]
†**1** = EXTIRPATE 5. LME–M17.
2 = EXTIRPATE 1. L15.
†**3** = EXTIRPATE 4. L15–M17.
†**4** = EXTIRPATE 2, 3. M16–L17.

extirpate /ˈɛkstəpeɪt/ *verb trans.* Pa. pple **-ated**, (*obsolete* exc. *Scot.*) **-ate** /-ət/. M16.
[ORIGIN Latin *ex(s)tirpat-* pa. ppl stem of *ex(s)tirpare*, formed as EX-¹ 1 + *stirps* stem or stock of a tree: see -ATE³.]
1 Root out, eradicate, get rid of, (a heresy, vice, or other abstract thing). M16.

D. MURPHY Our antagonisms had become too deeply rooted for either of us to extirpate them.

2 Do away with as such (a specified category or grouping of people); break up (an organization). Formerly, expel (an individual). (Foll. by *from*, *out of*.) M16.

LD MACAULAY It is . . one of the first duties of every government to extirpate gangs of thieves. P. ACKROYD A small Anglican religious community . . which was extirpated by Parliamentary troops.

3 Kill all the members of (a race, sect, nation, etc.); make extinct. (Foll. by *out of*.) L16.

J. FERRIAR The Pygmies were extirpated by their wars. M. MCCARTHY Extinct and extirpated species, like the passenger pigeon.

4 Pull up by the roots, destroy totally, (a tree or plant). E17.
5 Chiefly SURGERY. Remove or excise completely from the body (something regarded as having roots). M17.

G. B. SHAW Operations which consist of amputating limbs and extirpating organs.

■ **extirpative** *adjective* (SURGERY) acting or tending to extirpate LME. **extirpator** *noun* a person who or thing which extirpates E18.

extirpation /ɛkstəˈpeɪʃ(ə)n/ *noun.* LME.
[ORIGIN French, or Latin *ex(s)tirpatio(n-)*, formed as EXTIRPATE: see -ATION.]
1 SURGERY. The complete removal or excision of an organ or diseased part. LME.
2 The action of expelling or destroying as undesirable; eradication of a vice or heresy; extermination of a race, species, etc. LME.
3 The action of pulling up by the roots. L17.

extispex /ɪkˈstɪspɛks, ɛk-/ *noun.* Pl. **-spices** /-spɪsiːz/. E18.
[ORIGIN Latin, from EXTA + *-spex*, from *specere* look at.]
ROMAN HISTORY. = HARUSPEX.

extispicy /ɪkˈstɪspɪsi, ɛk-/ *noun.* L17.
[ORIGIN Latin *extispicium*, formed as EXTISPEX: see -Y⁴.]
ROMAN HISTORY. Inspection of the entrails of sacrificial victims in order to predict the future; haruspicy.

extol /ɪkˈstəʊl, ɛk-/ *verb trans.* Also ***-oll**. Infl. **-ll-**. LME.
[ORIGIN Latin *extollere*, formed as EX-¹ 1 + *tollere* raise.]
†**1** Lift, raise. LME–M17.
†**2** Raise in rank or dignity; exalt. Also, uphold the authority of. LME–E18.
3 Praise enthusiastically. LME.

C. CHAPLIN She extolled the virtues of Joe, stressing how hard he had worked.

†**4** In a bad sense: make too much of, exaggerate. L15–M17.
†**5** Make swollen with pride, joy, etc. E16–M17.
■ **extoller** *noun* E17. **extolment** *noun* (*arch.*) the action or an act of praising; (a) eulogy: E17.

extorsion /ɪkˈstɔːʃ(ə)n, ɛk-/ *noun.* L19.
[ORIGIN medieval Latin *extorsio(n-)* var. of late Latin *extortio(n-)*: see EXTORTION.]
Rotation of the eyeballs in which the tops move away from each other and the bottoms approach each other.

extorsive /ɪkˈstɔːsɪv, ɛk-/ *adjective. rare.* M17.
[ORIGIN medieval Latin *extorsivus*, from *extors-* var. of Latin *extort-*: see EXTORT *verb*, -IVE.]
Tending to extort; obtained by extortion.

†**extort** *adjective.* LME–L16.
[ORIGIN Latin *extortus* pa. pple of *extorquere*: see EXTORT *verb*.]
Extorted, wrongfully obtained.

extort /ɪkˈstɔːt, ɛk-/ *verb.* E16.
[ORIGIN Latin *extort-* pa. ppl stem of *extorquere*, formed as EX-¹ 1 + *torquere* to twist.]
1 *verb trans.* Obtain (money, a promise, a concession, etc.) from a reluctant person by threat, force, importunity, etc. (Foll. by *from*, †*upon*.) E16. ▸**b** Of a circumstance, influence, etc.: compel, constrain, (a given reaction). M17.

W. S. CHURCHILL Adolescent ruffians who extorted pennies and apples from tradesmen in return for not breaking their windows. E. M. DELAFIELD Mary . . only finally married him when consent had been extorted from Mr. Ponsonby on his deathbed. **b** JAS. MILL A situation which extorted the compassion of Englishmen.

2 *verb trans.* Subject (a person) to extortion. Long *rare.* M16–E17.
3 *verb intrans.* Indulge in extortion. *arch.* L16.
4 *verb trans.* Extract (a meaning, an inference) *from* words, data, etc., in defiance of their natural interpretation. E17.

SHAKES. *Twel. N.* Do not extort thy reasons from this clause.

■ **extorter** *noun* L16.

extortion /ɪkˈstɔːʃ(ə)n, ɛk-/ *noun & verb.* ME.
[ORIGIN Late Latin *extortio(n-)*, formed as EXTORT *verb*: see -ION.]
▸ **A** *noun.* **1** The action or an act of extorting money etc.; (an) exaction. ME.

J. A. FROUDE By bribery and extortion he had obtained vast sums of money. J. S. BREWER The Dover boatmen, whose extortions may boast the prescription of three centuries.

2 *spec.* in LAW (now *hist.*). The unlawful taking of money by a public official under pretext of his or her office. L16.
3 *hyperbol.* An exorbitant demand. Also, an exorbitant sum. M18.
▸ **B** *verb.* **1** *verb intrans.* Indulge in extortion. L15.
2 *verb trans.* Charge exorbitantly. *obsolete* exc. *dial.* M17.
■ **extortionable** *adjective* (*rare*) = EXTORTIONARY M17. **extortionary** *adjective* given to or characterized by extortion E19. **extortioner** *noun* a person who indulges in or is given to extortion LME. **extortionist** *noun* = EXTORTIONER L19.

extortionate /ɪkˈstɔːʃ(ə)nət, ɛk-/ *adjective.* L18.
[ORIGIN from EXTORTION + -ATE².]
Characterized by extortion. Now chiefly in *hyperbol.* use: charging grossly excessive prices; (of a price or charge) grossly excessive, exorbitant.
■ **extortionately** *adverb* M20.

†**extortious** *adjective.* LME–L18.
[ORIGIN from EXTORTI(ON + -OUS, after *captious*.]
Characterized by or acquired through extortion.

extortive /ɪkˈstɔːtɪv, ɛk-/ *adjective.* M17.
[ORIGIN from EXTORT *verb* + -IVE. Cf. medieval Latin *extortivus*.]
Having a tendency to extort.

extra /ˈɛkstrə/ *adjective, noun, & adverb.* M17.
[ORIGIN Prob. from EXTRAORDINARY, after similar forms in French & German.]
▸ **A** *adjective.* Beyond or more than the usual, stipulated, or specified amount or number; additional; more than is necessary. M17.

T. JEFFERSON Money . . for any extra wants of our own troops. W. E. H. LECKY Soldiers were employed on extra pay to make the roads. L. P. HARTLEY Isabel hired the extra chairs and tea-things.

– SPECIAL COLLOCATIONS: **extra cover** CRICKET (the position of) a fieldsman between cover point and mid-off but further from the wicket. **extra time**: sometimes allowed for continued play after the normal finishing time of a football etc. match when the scores are then equal.

▸ **B** *noun.* **1** Something that is extra or additional; something given in addition or for which an extra charge is made; an extra charge or fee; an additional or special issue of a newspaper; in cricket, a run scored otherwise than by hitting the ball and running; *US* a coach specially hired or laid on. L18.

L. CARROLL 'With extras?' . . 'Yes . . we learned French and Music.' DICKENS 'What's the rent?' . . 'One pound per week . . . The boots and clothes are extras.' OED The builder took the contract very low, hoping to recoup himself by extras.

2 An additional person; *spec.* on the stage or in films, a person engaged temporarily for a minor part or to be present during a crowd scene. L18.
▸ **C** *adverb.* More than usually; additionally; in excess of the usual, specified, or expected amount. E19.

C. KINGSLEY He must be an extra good boy that day. M. DICKENS There will be two extra for dinner. N. BLAKE Packets of . . henbane and deadly nightshade, sixpence extra.

extra dry, **extra sec** (of champagne) very slightly sweetened. **extra virgin** (a particularly fine grade of olive oil) made from the first pressing of the olives and containing a maximum of one per cent oleic acid.

– COMB.: **extra-special** *noun & adjective* (**a**) *noun* the last edition of a London evening paper; an extra edition of a publication; (**b**) *adjective* designating such an edition; *fig.* (*colloq.*) very special; exceptionally good or fine.

extra /ˈɛkstrə/ *preposition. rare.* E17.
[ORIGIN Latin *extra* from *extera* abl. fem. of *exter* external.]
Outside, externally to.

extra- /ˈɛkstrə/ *prefix.*
[ORIGIN (chiefly medieval) Latin *extra-* from classical Latin *extra* outside, beyond: see EXTRA *preposition*. In classical Latin and late Latin in a few adjectives: see EXTRAMUNDANE, EXTRAORDINARY.]
Forming adjectives (usu. from adjectives) with the senses 'situated outside', 'not coming within the scope of'. Opp. INTRA-.
■ **extraˈcellular** *adjective* (BIOLOGY) situated or occurring outside a cell M19. **extraˈcellularly** *adverb* (BIOLOGY) outside a cell L19. **extrachomoˈsomal** *adjective* (BIOLOGY) existing or occurring independently of chromosomes E20. **extracorˈporeal** *adjective* (involving something) situated or occurring outside the body M19. **extracorˈporeally** *adverb* outside the body E20. **extraˈcranial** *adjective* situated or occurring outside the skull L19. **extracuˈrricular** *adjective* not coming within the scope of the normal curriculum; *fig.* outside the normal routine, *esp.* extramarital: E20. **extraˈdural** *adjective* (MEDICINE) = EPIDURAL *adjective* E20. **extra-eˈssential** *adjective* not included in the essence of something M17. **extra-eˈssentially** *adverb* as something extra-essential M17. **extra-Euroˈpean** *adjective* situated or occurring outside Europe; pertaining to matters outside Europe; (of a plant or animal) not found in Europe: E19. **extrafaˈmilial** *adjective* outside the family M20. **extraˈfloral** *adjective* (BOTANY) (of a nectary) situated outside a flower, esp. on a leaf or stem M19. **extragaˈlactic** *adjective* situated, occurring, or originating outside the Galaxy M19. **extraheˈpatic** *adjective* situated or occurring outside or beyond the liver M20. **extra-ˈillustrated** *adjective* (of a book) having pictures stuck into it from another source M20. **extra-illuˈstration** *noun* the action or practice of sticking pictures into a book from another source E20. **extra-ˈillustrator** *noun* a person who practises extra-illustration L19. **extraˈlegal** *adjective* that is beyond the province of law, not regulated by law M17. **extraˈlegally** *adverb* as an extralegal matter or act M20. **extraˈlimital** *adjective* situated, occurring, or derived from outside a particular area L19. **extralinˈguistic** *adjective* that is outside the field of linguistics or bounds of language E20. **extraˈliterary** *adjective* that is outside the province of literature M20. **extraˈlogical** *adjective* that lies outside the legitimate domain of logic M19. **extraˈmarital** *adjective* involving or constituting a (usu. sexual) relationship between a married person and someone other than his or her spouse E20. **extraˈmaritally** *adverb* in an extramarital way M20. **extra-ˈmetrical** *adjective* that represents a syllable additional to what the metre requires or will accommodate M19. **extraˈmusical** *adjective* that is outside the field of music, or not an intrinsic part of music E20. **extraˈnuclear** *adjective* situated outside the nucleus of an atom or cell L19. **extraˈocular** *adjective* situated or occurring outside the eyes E19. **extra-parliaˈmentary** *adjective* occurring or existing outside or independently of Parliament L19. **extra-paˈrochial** *adjective* that is outside the limits of a parish, or exempt from parish obligations (*lit.* & *fig.*) L17. **extraˈpunitive** *adjective* (PSYCHOLOGY) of, pertaining to, or designating a person who reacts aggressively to frustration, or unreasonably blames events or other people M20. **extraˈpunitively** *adverb* (PSYCHOLOGY) in an extrapunitive manner M20. **extraˈpunitiveness** *noun* (PSYCHOLOGY) extrapunitive quality M20. **extrapyraˈmidal** *adjective* (ANATOMY) involving or designating nerves concerned with motor activity that descend from the cortex to the spine and are not part of the pyramidal system E20. **extraˈsensory** *adjective* (regarded as) derived by means other than the known senses, e.g. by telepathy, clairvoyance, etc. (***extrasensory perception***, a person's supposed faculty of perceiving by such means) M20. **extrasoˈmatic** *adjective* deriving from events external to an individual M20. **extraˈsystole** *noun* (MEDICINE) a heartbeat outside the normal rhythm E20. **extrateˈrrestrial** *adjective & noun* (a being, esp. an intelligent one) existing or occurring beyond the earth's atmosphere M19. **extrateˈrrestrially** *adverb* elsewhere than on or in the earth or its atmosphere M20. **extraˈtropical** *adjective* situated, existing, or occurring outside the tropics L18. **extraˈuterine** *adjective* existing, formed, or occurring outside the uterus E18. **extraˈvascular** *adjective* situated or occurring outside the vascular system; not vascular in nature: E19. **extraˈvascularly** *adverb* outside the vascular system E20. **extraveˈhicular** *adjective* occurring outside a spacecraft in space M20.

extract /ˈɛkstrakt/ *noun.* LME.
[ORIGIN Latin *extractum* use as noun of neut. of *extractus* pa. pple to *extrahere*: see EXTRACT *verb*.]
†**1** A summary, an outline. LME–M17.
2 SCOTS LAW. A warrant empowering the performance of some judicial act; a properly authenticated copy of a legal or public record. M16.
†**3** Something drawn or taken out of a thing; *fig.* the essential part of a matter. L16–M17.

N. BACON The extract of all is, that he was chosen by the People and Parliament.

4 A substance extracted from another substance or a thing, e.g. by treating with solvents which are then evaporated; a preparation containing the active principle of a substance in concentrated form. L16.

L. VAN DER POST The designs were . . dyed ink-black with some vegetable extract.

malt extract, ***pituitary extract***, etc. ***fluid extract***: see FLUID *adjective*.
5 A passage from a book, manuscript, etc.; an excerpt, a quotation. M17.

L. C. KNIGHTS Place beside the extract quoted from Halifax a passage . . from *Love for Love*.

†**6** = EXTRACTION 2. M17–L18.

J. MORSE The first child of European extract, born in New England.

extract /ɪkˈstrakt, ɛk-/ *adjective* (orig. *pa. pple*). Long *obsolete* exc. *Scot.* See also EXTRAUGHT. LME.
[ORIGIN Latin *extractus* pa. pple of *extrahere*: see EXTRACT *verb*.]
1 Extracted; derived, descended. LME.
†**2** Distraught. M16–E17.

extract /ɪkˈstrakt, ɛk-/ *verb trans.* LME.
[ORIGIN Latin *extract-* pa. ppl stem of *extrahere*, formed as EX-¹ 1 + *trahere* draw.]
1 Draw out of a containing body or cavity, usu. with some degree of force, effort, dexterity, etc.; remove (something firmly fixed, esp. a tooth). LME. ▸**b** Get (money, consent, a confession, etc.) from a person in the face of initial unwillingness. LME.

SHAKES. *Meas. for M.* Putting the hand in the pocket and extracting it clutch'd. S. KINGSLEY Jacob . . extracts a horseshoe from the fire. E. J. HOWARD He extracted a battered packet of Gold Flake from the breast pocket of his shirt. **b** H. JAMES He extracted from Mrs Touchett a promise that she would bring her niece.

2 Obtain (constituent elements, juices, etc.) from a thing or substance by chemical or physical means. LME.

▸**b** Subject (a substance or thing) to a chemical or physical procedure in order to obtain a constituent. L19.

N. CALDER To extract vast quantities of metal from low-grade ores.

†**3** In *pass.* Be derived or descended (*from*). Also foll. by *of.* L15–L17.
4 Derive (happiness, amusement, understanding, etc.) from a specified source or situation; draw out (the sense of something); infer (a principle, right, etc.). L16.

GEO. ELIOT [He] means to extract the utmost possible amount of pleasure . . out of this life. J. BRAINE My brain . . began to extract the hard inescapable facts from the scrawled figures and abbreviations.

5 *MATH.* Calculate (a root of a number). L16.
6 *LAW.* Make a copy of (a recorded judgement), usu. in order to execute it or otherwise put it into effect. L16.
7 Take (a part) from a whole; *esp.* copy out (a passage in a book etc.). (Foll. by *from, out of.*) L16.

MILTON Woman is her Name, of Man Extracted. G. SAINTSBURY A great many maxims . . might be extracted from his works.

■ **extracta'bility** *noun* the quality of being extractable M20. **extractable** *adjective* able to be extracted L17. **extracted** *ppl adjective* derived, drawn out; *spec.* (of an animal) obtained by controlled breeding; (of honey) separated from the uncrushed comb by centrifugal force or gravity: L17. **extracting** *ppl adjective* †(*a*) *rare* (Shakes.) distracting; (*b*) that extracts: E17.

extractant /ɪk'strakt(ə)nt, ɛk-/ *noun.* M20.
[ORIGIN from EXTRACT *verb* + -ANT[1].]
A substance used to extract another from a solution, tissue, etc.

extraction /ɪk'strakʃ(ə)n, ɛk-/ *noun.* LME.
[ORIGIN Old French & mod. French from late Latin *extractio(n-)*, formed as EXTRACTANT: see -ION.]
1 The action or process of extracting; an act of extracting, esp. a tooth. LME.

J. E. T. ROGERS The extraction of gold from its ores.

2 Origin, lineage, descent. L15.

T. PAKENHAM A twenty-seven-year-old Adonis of Jewish extraction.

†**3** An extract. L16–L17.
†**4** An inference, a deduction. *rare.* E17–E19.

extractive /ɪk'straktɪv, ɛk-/ *noun & adjective.* LME.
[ORIGIN Partly from medieval Latin *extractivus* (formed as EXTRACT *verb*), partly from EXTRACT *verb*: see -IVE.]
▸ **A** *noun.* †**1** A plaster or medicine for drawing out harmful matter. Only in LME.
2 A substance left after the removal of vegetable extracts. E19.
3 A substance that can be extracted, an extract. M19.
▸ **B** *adjective.* †**1** Esp. of a plaster or medicine: tending to extract; capable of extracting. L16–M18.
2 Able to be extracted; of the nature of an extract. L18.
3 Concerned with the extraction of natural resources or products, esp. non-renewable ones. M19.

Arizona Daily Star A degree in Mineral Dressing or Extractive Metallurgy.

extractor /ɪk'straktə, ɛk-/ *noun.* E17.
[ORIGIN from EXTRACT *verb* + -OR.]
A person who or thing which extracts something; *spec.* (*a*) the part of a breech-loading gun which removes the cartridge; (*b*) an instrument for extracting honey from honeycombs.
– COMB.: **extractor fan** a ventilating fan in a window or wall to remove stale air.
■ **extractory** *adjective* E18.

extra dictionem /ˌɛkstrə dɪktɪ'əʊnɛm/ *adjectival phr.* E19.
[ORIGIN Latin, translating Greek *exō tēs lexeōs* outside the wording.]
Of a logical fallacy: not arising from the wording used to express it.

extradite /'ɛkstrədʌɪt/ *verb trans.* M19.
[ORIGIN Back-form. from EXTRADITION.]
1 Give up (a person) into the jurisdiction of another state in an action of extradition. M19.
2 Of a state: obtain the extradition of (a person) from another country. L19.

Daily Telegraph Grob . . had been extradited from France on charges alleging involvement with fraud.

■ **extraditable** *adjective* liable or making liable to extradition L19.

extradition /ɛkstrə'dɪʃ(ə)n/ *noun.* M19.
[ORIGIN French, formed as EX-[1] 1, TRADITION *noun.*]
The surrender or delivery of a person into the jurisdiction of another state in order that he or she may be tried by that state for a crime committed there.
– COMB.: **extradition treaty**: by which two states mutually bind themselves to extradite people to each other's jurisdiction in specified circumstances.

extrados /ɪks'treɪdɒs, ɛk-/ *noun.* L18.
[ORIGIN French, from Latin *extra* outside + French *dos* back.]
ARCHITECTURE. The upper or outer curve of an arch; *esp.* the upper curve of the voussoirs which form the arch. Cf. INTRADOS.

†**extraduce** *adjective. rare.* L16–E18.
[ORIGIN Latin *ex traduce*, from *ex* out of + *traduce* abl. of *tradux* vine-shoot trained for propagation.]
Derived (as) from a parent stock; hereditary.

extra-foraneous /ɛkstrəfə'reɪnɪəs/ *adjective. arch.* L18.
[ORIGIN from EXTRA- + Latin *foris* door + -ANEOUS.]
Outdoor.

extrajudicial /ɛkstrədʒuː'dɪʃ(ə)l/ *adjective.* M17.
[ORIGIN medieval Latin *extrajudicialis*, formed as EXTRA-, JUDICIAL.]
1 That is not part of the proceedings in court or of the case before a court; (of an opinion, confession, etc) not made in court, informal. M17.
2 That is outside the ordinary course of law or justice; not legally authorized; unwarranted. M17.
■ **extrajudicially** *adverb* L16.

extramission /ɛkstrə'mɪʃ(ə)n/ *noun.* M17.
[ORIGIN medieval Latin *extramissio(n)-*, formed as EXTRA-, MISSION *noun.*]
(An) emission. Now only *hist.*, the supposed emission of rays from the eyes as part of the visual process.

extramundane /ɛkstrə'mʌndeɪn/ *adjective.* M17.
[ORIGIN Late Latin *extramundanus*, from *extra mundum* outside the world or universe.]
1 (Pertaining to a region) situated beyond the earth. M17.
2 Situated outside or beyond the universe; pertaining to what is beyond the universe. E18.
3 *fig.* Remote, pertaining to things not of this world. E19.

extramural /ɛkstrə'mjʊər(ə)l/ *adjective.* M19.
[ORIGIN from Latin *extra muros* outside the walls + -AL[1].]
1 Situated or occurring outside the walls or boundaries of a town or city. M19.
2 Pertaining to or designating instruction given under the auspices of a university or college but intended for people other than its students. L19.
■ **extramurally** *adverb* E20.

extraneous /ɪk'streɪnɪəs, ɛk-/ *adjective.* M17.
[ORIGIN from Latin *extraneus* + -OUS.]
1 Of external origin; introduced or added from without; foreign *to* the object to which it is attached or which contains it. M17.

M. BAILLIE An extraneous body can be . . easily introduced into their bladder. G. P. MARSH The Low-German dialects were . . exposed to extraneous disturbing forces.

2 Not part of the matter in hand. (Foll. by *to.*) M17.
3 Of a person: not belonging to a specified group, family, etc. M17.
■ **extra'neity** *noun* (*rare*) the state or quality of being extraneous M19. †**extraneize** *verb trans.* (*rare*) make extraneous, remove M17–L18. **extraneously** *adverb* M18. **extraneousness** *noun* L19.

extranet /'ɛkstrənɛt/ *noun.* L20.
[ORIGIN from EXTRA- + NET *noun*[1], after INTRANET.]
COMPUTING. An intranet which can also be accessed, via the Internet, by a limited group of external users; a network comprising two or more intranets belonging to different organizations, linked via the Internet.

extraordinaire /ɪkˌstrɔːdɪ'nɛː, ɛk-, *foreign* ɛkstr(a)ɔrdinɛːr/ *postpositive adjective.* M20.
[ORIGIN French, formed as EXTRAORDINARY.]
Remarkable, outstanding; (of a person) unusually active or successful in a specified respect.

extraordinary /ɪk'strɔːd(ə)n(ə)ri, ɛk-, ɛkstrə'ɔːdɪn(ə)ri/ *adjective, noun, & adverb.* LME.
[ORIGIN Latin *extraordinarius*, from *extra ordinem* out of order, exceptionally, exceptionally.]
▸ **A** *adjective.* **1** Out of the usual or regular course or order; special. Formerly also, acting unusually, partial. LME. ▸†**b** *MUSIC.* = ACCIDENTAL *adjective* 2. L16–M18. ▸†**c** Not according to rule, out of order. M17–E18.

DEFOE Let him . . take some extraordinary measures to get in his debts.

extraordinary general meeting: of the members or shareholders of a club, company, or other organization, held at short notice, esp. in order to consider a particular matter. **extraordinary ray** *OPTICS* in double refraction, the ray that does not obey the ordinary laws of refraction. **extraordinary rendition** = RENDITION 1d.
2 Of an official etc.: outside or additional to the regular staff; specially employed. Freq. *postpositive* in titles, denoting secondary status. L16.

W. BLACKSTONE Another species of extraordinary juries, is the jury to try an attaint.

AMBASSADOR extraordinary. envoy extraordinary: see ENVOY *noun*[1].
3 Of a kind not usually met with, exceptional; now *esp.* so exceptional as to provoke astonishment, admiration, or disapproval. L16.

P. H. JOHNSON I thought how extraordinary it was that so kind a man could be so cruel. A. N. WILSON Extraordinary, isn't it, he was *eighty* when he wrote it.'

4 Exceeding what is usual in amount, degree, extent, or size, esp. to the point of provoking astonishment, admiration, or disapproval. L16.

J. TYNDALL The sun met us here with extraordinary power.

†**5** Additional to what is usual, extra. Freq. *postpositive.* M17–E19.

M. M. SHERWOOD Spending a few extraordinary shillings.

▸ **B** *noun.* **1** Something extraordinary; an extraordinary quality or bearing; an extraordinary action, incident, etc. Now only in *pl.* (*rare*). L16. ▸**b** In *pl.* Extraordinary receipts or payments. *arch.* L16.
†**2** An extraordinary envoy; a supernumerary official. Only in 17.
3 Orig., something extra; an additional or supplementary item. Now only, an extra allowance or expense. M17.

HOR. WALPOLE Munchausen . . presented an ample bill of extraordinaries for forage, etc.

▸ †**C** *adverb.* Extraordinarily. M17–L18.
■ **extraordinarily** *adverb* to an extraordinary degree, in an extraordinary manner M16. **extraordinariness** *noun* E17.

extrapolate /ɪk'strapəleɪt, ɛk-/ *verb.* M19.
[ORIGIN from EXTRA- + INTER)POLATE *verb.*]
†**1** *verb trans.* Remove (a passage) from written material. *rare.* Only in M19.
2 *verb trans. & intrans.* Extend (a range of values, a curve) on the assumption that the trend exhibited inside the given part is maintained outside it; assume the continuance of a known trend in inferring or estimating an unknown value; *gen.* predict on the basis of known facts or observed events. Also, obtain (an estimate, an extension of a given range etc.) by doing this; infer, or make an inference, *from.* L19.

S. WEINBERG Our calculations allow us to extrapolate the expansion of the universe backward in time. LD RUTHERFORD The effective straggling coefficient . . was calculated from this extrapolated curve. *Times Lit. Suppl.* His documents are . . comments on a particular colony at a particular time; . . it is hard work to extrapolate from them any general view about all the colonies.

3 *verb intrans.* Foll. by *to*: reach (a specified value) when extrapolated. E20.

Nature The line shown . . is a physical impossibility since it extrapolates to –666 at 4.599 Myr.

■ **extrapolable**, **extrapolatable** *adjectives* M20. **extrapo'lation** *noun* the action or process, or an act, of extrapolating L19. **extrapolative** *adjective* characterized by extrapolation; of the nature of extrapolation; employing or given to extrapolation: E20. **extrapolator** *noun* M20. **extrapolatory** *adjective* M20.

extraposition /ɛkstrəpə'zɪʃ(ə)n/ *noun.* E20.
[ORIGIN from EXTRA- + POSITION *noun.*]
GRAMMAR. The placing of a word or group of words outside or at the end of a clause instead of within, while retaining the sense, as in *the rain, it raineth every day.*
■ **extra'pose** *verb trans.* subject to extraposition; move *from* or *to*: M20.

extraprovincial /ɛkstrəprə'vɪnʃ(ə)l/ *adjective.* L17.
[ORIGIN medieval Latin *extraprovincialis*, from *extra provinciam* outside the province.]
Situated beyond the limits of a province; pertaining to travel outside a province.

extraterritoriality /ˌɛkstrətɛrɪtɔːrɪ'alɪti/ *noun.* M19.
[ORIGIN from mod. Latin *extra territorium* outside the territory + -AL[1] + -ITY.]
LAW. The freedom accorded to diplomatic officials from the jurisdiction of the territory in which they reside. Also, the right of or claim to jurisdiction of a country over individuals living abroad or companies operating abroad; the status of people living in a country but not subject to its laws.
■ ˌ**extraterri'torial** *adjective* M19.

†**extraught** *adjective* (orig. *pa. pple*). Only in 16.
[ORIGIN Var. of EXTRACT *adjective*; cf. *distraught.*]
= EXTRACT *adjective.*

extravagance /ɪk'stravəg(ə)ns, ɛk-/ *noun.* M17.
[ORIGIN French, formed as EXTRAVAGANT, -ANCE.]
†**1** A going out of the usual path (*lit. & fig.*); a digression; the position or fact of straying *from* a prescribed path. Only in M17.

MILTON A doctrine of that extravagance from the sage principles of piety.

2 An instance or kind of extravagant behaviour; an extravagant thing; *esp.* an absurd statement or action; a purchase or payment difficult to justify except as a whim or indulgence. M17.

M. MEYER Another of his lifelong extravagances, clothes. R. DAWKINS Extravagances such as the tails of male birds of paradise.

3 The quality of being extravagant, esp. in writing, speech, or thought. L17.
4 Prodigality or wastefulness in expenditure, household management, etc. E18.

E

M. EDGEWORTH Such extravagance, to give . . a silver penny, for what you may have for nothing.

extravagancy /ɪkˈstravəg(ə)nsi, ɛk-/ *noun*. E16.
[ORIGIN from EXTRAVAGANT: see -ANCY.]
†**1** The action or an act of wandering or departing from one's course. E16–M17.
2 = EXTRAVAGANCE 2. E16.
3 = EXTRAVAGANCE 3. Formerly also, eccentricity; impropriety, unbecomingness. Now *rare* or *obsolete*. M17.
†**4** = EXTRAVAGANCE 4. M17–E19.

extravagant /ɪkˈstravəg(ə)nt, ɛk-/ *adjective & noun*. LME.
[ORIGIN medieval Latin *extravagant-*, from Latin EXTRA- + *vagant-* pres. ppl stem of *vagari* wander: see -ANT[1]. Also infl. in gen. sense by French *extravagant*, Italian *(e)stravagante*.]
▸ **A** *adjective*. †**1** Widely divergent or discrepant; irrelevant. (Foll. by *from*, *to*.) LME–M17.
†**2** Varying widely from what is usual or proper; unusual, abnormal, strange; unbecoming, unsuitable. LME–E18.

T. FULLER Persons . . treacherously slain, which occasioned their hasty . . and extravagant interment.

3 ROMAN CATHOLIC CHURCH. Designating certain medieval papal decrees, orig. not collected in the decretals. LME.
4 Exceeding the bounds of reason; showing a lack of restraint or moderation; absurdly or astonishingly excessive or elaborate. L16.

W. H. IRELAND The extravagant panegyrist of various living characters. G. SAINTSBURY It is . . not in the least extravagant to regard Sir Thomas Browne as the greatest prose-writer in the English language. F. KING Her writing, backward-sloping and all extravagant loops and swirls.

5 That wanders out of bounds; straying, vagrant. *obsolete* exc. with allus. to Shakes. E17. ▸†**b** Of a soldier: not assigned to one place of duty; having a roving commission. Only in 17.

SHAKES. *Haml.* Th' extravagant and erring spirit hies To his confine.

†**6** Spreading or projecting beyond bounds; straggling. E–M17.

EVELYN Cutting the too thick and extravagant Roots a little.

7 Exceeding the bounds of economy or necessity in expenditure, way of life, etc.; profuse, prodigal, wasteful; (of a price) exorbitant. E18.

M. ROBERTS Madly extravagant and out of season, but I felt like having a treat.

▸ **B** *noun*. **1** ROMAN CATHOLIC CHURCH. An extravagant decree. E16.
†**2** A person who strays or wanders (*lit.* & *fig.*). L16–M17.
†**3 a** An exceptional or eccentric person; a fanatic. E17–E18. ▸**b** A person who is extravagant in expenditure, way of life, etc. M18–E19.
†**4** An extravagant act, statement, etc. E17–E18.
■ **extravagantly** *adverb* E17.

extravaganza /ɪkˌstravəˈganzə, ɛk-/ *noun*. M18.
[ORIGIN Alt. (after EXTRA-) of Italian *estravaganza* (usu. *strav-*), from *(e)stravagante* formed as EXTRAVAGANT.]
1 Extravagance of language or behaviour. Now *rare*. M18.
2 A literary, musical, or dramatic composition of an extravagant or fanciful character. L18.

extravagate /ɪkˈstravəgeɪt, ɛk-/ *verb intrans.* E17.
[ORIGIN from EXTRAVAGANT + -ATE[3].]
1 Stray *from* a right course, a text, *into* error, etc. E17.
2 Wander at large; roam at will. M18.
3 Exceed what is proper or reasonable. E19.
■ **extravaˈgation** *noun* E17.

†**extravage** *verb intrans.* L17–M18.
[ORIGIN from EXTRAVAGATE or EXTRAVAGANT.]
Go beyond the sphere of duty; digress; ramble.

extravasate /ɪkˈstravəseɪt, ɛk-/ *adjective*. *obsolete* exc. *poet.* M17.
[ORIGIN from EXTRAVASATE *verb* after adjectives in -ATE[2].]
That has extravasated; that is not contained inside a vessel.

extravasate /ɪkˈstravəseɪt, ɛk-/ *verb*. M17.
[ORIGIN from EXTRA- + Latin *vas* vessel + -ATE[3].]
Chiefly MEDICINE. **1** *verb trans.* Let or force out (a fluid, esp. blood) from the vessel that naturally contains it. M17.
2 *verb intrans.* Of blood, lava, etc.: flow out; undergo extravasation. L17.
■ **extravaˈsation** *noun* (chiefly MEDICINE) an escape or effusion of blood or other fluid, esp. from many small vessels into surrounding tissue; a quantity of blood etc. that has escaped: L17.

†**extravase** *verb trans. & intrans.* M17–M19.
[ORIGIN French *extravaser*, formed as EXTRA- + Latin *vas* vessel.]
= EXTRAVASATE *verb*.

extraversion /ɛkstrəˈvəːʃ(ə)n/ *noun*. L17.
[ORIGIN from EXTRA- + VERSION.]
†**1** A turning outwards (*lit.* & *fig.*); a making manifest. *rare*. L17–E18.
2 = EXTROVERSION 3. E20.
■ **extraversive** *adjective* = EXTROVERSIVE M20.

extravert /ˈɛkstrəvəːt/ *noun & adjective*. E20.
[ORIGIN from EXTRAVERSION. Cf. CONVERT *noun*.]
PSYCHOLOGY. = EXTROVERT *noun & adjective*.

extravert /ˈɛkstrəvəːt/ *verb trans.* M17.
[ORIGIN from EXTRA- + Latin *vertere* to turn.]
†**1** Make manifest. M–L17.
2 = EXTROVERT *verb*. M17.

†**extreat** *noun*. L15.
[ORIGIN Var. of ESTREAT, with *ex-* for *es-* after Latin.]
1 = ESTREAT *noun*. L15–E18.
2 Extraction. Only in L16.

extrema *noun pl.* see EXTREMUM.

extremal /ɪkˈstriːm(ə)l, ɛk-/ *noun*. E20.
[ORIGIN from EXTREMUM: see -AL[1].]
MATH. (A function represented by) a curve the integral along which has a maximum or minimum value; a surface the integral over which has such a value.

extremal /ɪkˈstriːm(ə)l, ɛk-/ *adjective*. LME.
[ORIGIN from EXTREME, (in sense 2) EXTREMUM + -AL[1].]
†**1** Outermost. Only in LME.
2 MATH. Of or pertaining to extreme qualities or configurations, or highest or lowest values. M20.

extreme /ɪkˈstriːm, ɛk-/ *adjective, noun, & adverb*. LME.
[ORIGIN Old French & mod. French *extrême* from Latin *extremus*, from *exter* outer.]
▸ **A** *adjective* **1 a** (Of a quality, condition, or feeling) existing in a very high degree, very great or intense; (of an action, measure, etc.) very severe or violent; (of a case or circumstance) having some characteristic in the utmost degree. LME. ▸†**b** Of a material agent: effective to a very high degree; very powerful. L15–M18. ▸**c** Of a person: going to great lengths; advocating severe or drastic measures; immoderate in opinion. Formerly also, strict, severe. M16. ▸**d** Of an opinion, fashion, etc.: immoderate, excessive. L19. ▸**e** Of a sport: performed in a hazardous environment and involving great physical risk. L20.

a J. BUCHAN Mr Craw's face showed extreme irritation. H. G. WELLS This is only a very extreme instance of the general state of affairs. V. WOOLF Here at college, where the stir and presence of life are so extreme.

2 Outermost, furthest from the centre; endmost, situated at an end. LME. ▸**b** Furthest; very far advanced in any direction; utmost, uttermost. L16.

R. WARNER Flats . . built at the extreme edge of the aerodrome. **b** B. BAINBRIDGE The extreme end of the corridor.

extreme and mean ratio MATH.: represented by a line divided according to the golden section, so that the ratio of its length to that of the longer part is the same as the ratio of the length of the longer part to that of the shorter (viz. 1.61803 . . .). †**extreme parts** the extremities of the body.

3 Last, latest. Cf. ***extreme unction*** below. Now *rare* or *obsolete*. L15.

extreme unction ROMAN CATHOLIC CHURCH (former name for) the sacrament of anointing the sick, esp. those thought to be near death.

▸ **B** *noun*. †**1** The utmost or terminating point or verge; an end, an extremity (in time or space). M16–E19.
2 A very high degree; *the* utmost degree. M16. ▸†**b** In *pl.* Straits, extremities, adversity. M16–M17.
3 a Something which is situated at one end of anything; either of two things as far as possible from each other in position, nature, or condition. M16. ▸**b** MATH. The first or last term of a series or proportion. Now *rare* or *obsolete*. L16. ▸**c** LOGIC. The subject or predicate in a proposition; the major or minor term in a syllogism. E17.

a G. GREENE It's strange how the human mind swings back and forth, from one extreme to another. *Proverb*: Extremes meet.

4 An excessive degree, a very great length; an extreme measure. L16.

MRS H. WOOD I never thought the masters would go to the extreme of a lock-out. J. ROSENBERG An enthusiastic temperament such as his easily led to extremes.

– PHRASES: **go to the other extreme** take a diametrically opposite course of action. **in extreme** = ***in the extreme*** below. **in one's extremes** = ***in the extremes*** below. **in the extreme** to an extreme degree, extremely. **in the extremes** in the last moments of life.

▸ †**C** *adverb*. To an extreme degree, extremely. L16–E19.
■ **extremely** *adverb* †(*a*) to the uttermost degree; with a very great degree of some quality, esp. severity; (*b*) to or in an extreme degree; very much: L15. **extremeness** *noun* M16.

extremism /ɪkˈstriːmɪz(ə)m, ɛk-/ *noun*. M19.
[ORIGIN from EXTREME + -ISM.]
1 Tendency to be extreme. M19.
2 The views or actions of extremists. E20.

extremist /ɪkˈstriːmɪst, ɛk-/ *noun & adjective*. M19.
[ORIGIN formed as EXTREMISM + -IST.]
▸ **A** *noun*. A person who holds extreme opinions or advocates extreme measures; a person who tends to go to extremes. M19.
▸ **B** *adjective*. Of or pertaining to extremists or extremism. E20.

extremity /ɪkˈstrɛmɪti, ɛk-/ *noun*. LME.
[ORIGIN Old French *extrémité* or Latin *extremitas*, from *extremus*: see EXTREME, -ITY.]
1 The terminal point or portion of anything; the very end. LME. ▸**b** In *pl.* The outermost parts of the body; the hands and feet. L15.

W. BECKFORD Both extremities of the cross aisles are terminated by altar-tombs.

†**2** = EXTREME *noun* 3a. Usu. in *pl.* LME–L16.
3 = EXTREME *noun* 2. LME.
4 A condition of extreme urgency or need; the utmost point of adversity. LME.

QUILLER-COUCH The man whom in his extremity I clothed and fed.

5 Great intensity of emotion or (formerly) action. Formerly also, a violent outburst. E16.

O. SACKS Those who are enduring extremities of suffering, sickness and anguish.

†**6** Extreme severity or rigour (of a reprimand, punishment, etc.). M16–M17. ▸**b** Extreme severity *of* weather. M16–E19.
†**7** (An) extravagance in opinion, behaviour, or expenditure. M16–E18.
8 The last moments of a person's life. *arch.* E17.
9 An extreme measure. Usu. in *pl.* *arch.* M17.
10 Extremeness. M19.

extremophile /ɛksˈtrɛməfʌɪl/ *adjective & noun*. M20.
[ORIGIN from EXTREME + -O- + -PHILE.]
▸ **A** *adjective*. BOTANY. Of a leaf canopy: having approximately equal numbers of leaves arranged horizontally and vertically. M20.
▸ **B** *noun*. BIOLOGY. A micro-organism, esp. an archaean, that lives in conditions of extreme temperature, acidity, alkalinity, or chemical concentration. L20.

extremum /ɪkˈstriːməm, ɛk-/ *noun*. Pl. **-mums**, **-ma** /-mə/. E20.
[ORIGIN Latin, use as noun of neut. of *extremus* extreme.]
MATH. A value of a function that is a maximum or a minimum (either relative or absolute).

extricable /ˈɛkstrɪkəb(ə)l, ɪkˈstrɪk-/ *adjective*. E17.
[ORIGIN from EXTRICATE: see -ABLE. Cf. earlier INEXTRICABLE.]
†**1** Able to be unravelled or solved. E17–E18.
2 Able to be set free or got out. L18.

extricate /ˈɛkstrɪkeɪt/ *verb trans.* E17.
[ORIGIN Latin *extricat-* pa. ppl stem of *extricare*, formed as EX-[1] 1 + *tricae* perplexities: see -ATE[3].]
1 Unravel; clear of tangles or (*fig.*) perplexities. Now *rare*. E17.
2 Get (a person) out of a difficulty, entanglement, etc.; remove, usu. with difficulty or dexterity, from what physically holds or contains someone or something. (Foll. by *from*, *out of*.) M17.

C. JACKSON After much embarrassed wriggling on her part he had extricated the offending garment. P. ACKROYD A foreigner who might extricate her from the world of Edwardian respectability. P. ROTH Suicide was the only way he might ever be able to extricate himself from his confusion and pain.

3 CHEMISTRY. Release (gas) during a reaction. Now *rare* or *obsolete*. L18.
■ **extriˈcation** *noun* (*a*) the action or an act of extricating; (*b*) hatching (from an egg): E17.

extrinsic /ɪkˈstrɪnsɪk, ɛk-/ *adjective*. M16.
[ORIGIN Late Latin *extrinsecus* outer, from Latin *extrinsecus* outwardly, from *exter* external + *-im* as in *interim* + *secus* alongside of: see -IC.]
†**1 a** Situated on the outside. *rare*. Only in M16. ▸**b** Pertaining to the outside, external. M18.

b K. AMIS You are denied visitors. . . And all extrinsic aids, like news.

2 Of a cause or influence: operating from outside, extraneous. E17.
3 Pertaining to an object in its external relations. Now *rare*. E17.
4 Due to external circumstances, not inherent. E17.

HAZLITT Without any extrinsic advantages of birth.

5 Not included, not forming part. Foll. by *to*. M17.
6 PHYSICS. Characteristic of or designating a semiconductor in which the electrical conduction is due chiefly to electrons or holes provided by an added dopant. M20.
– SPECIAL COLLOCATIONS: **extrinsic factor** vitamin B_{12}. **extrinsic muscle**: originating beyond a part and acting on it as a whole.
■ **extrinsical** *adjective* (now *rare*) = EXTRINSIC L16. **extrinsically** *adverb* L16. **extrinsicism** /-sɪsɪz(ə)m/ *noun* the view that the truth of religious dogma is received rather than demonstrated; an extrinsic thing: E20.

extrinsicate /ɪkˈstrɪnsɪkeɪt, ɛk-/ *verb trans.* *rare*. M17.
[ORIGIN from EXTRINSIC + -ATE[3].]
Exhibit outwardly, express.

extro- /ˈɛkstrəʊ/ *prefix*.
alt. of EXTRA- after INTRO-, used by way of antithesis to this.

extropy /ˈɛkstrəpi/ *noun*. **M20**.
[**ORIGIN** from **EX-**[1] + **EN)TROPY**.]
Human intelligence, culture, and technology viewed as a unified generative force (counteractive to that of entropy); a belief that by means of such a force human life will evolve indefinitely in an orderly, progressive manner, beyond its current form and limitations.
■ **exˈtropian** *noun & adjective* (*a*) *noun* a person who believes in or promotes extropy; (*b*) *adjective* of or relating to extropy, extropians, or their beliefs: **L20**. **exˈtropic** *adjective* **L20**.

extrorse /ɪkˈstrɔːs, ɛk-/ *adjective*. **M19**.
[**ORIGIN** Late Latin *extrorsus* adverb, in an outward direction, from Latin *extra* (see **EXTRA** *preposition*) + *versus* towards, pa. pple of *vertere* turn.]
BOTANY. Of an anther: releasing its pollen on the outside of the flower.

extrospective /ɛkstrəˈspɛktɪv/ *adjective*. **E20**.
[**ORIGIN** from **EXTRO-** after **INTROSPECTIVE**.]
Not introspective; regarding external objects rather than one's own thoughts and feelings.

extroversion /ɛkstrəˈvəːʃ(ə)n/ *noun*. **M17**.
[**ORIGIN** from **EXTRO-** + **VERSION**.]
1 Chiefly *MEDICINE*. The action of turning, or the condition of being turned, outwards or inside out. **M17**.
†**2** The diversion or wandering of a person's attention during a mystical experience. **M17–L18**.
3 *PSYCHOLOGY*. The fact or tendency of having one's thoughts and interests directed chiefly towards things outside the self. Opp. **INTROVERSION**. **E20**.
■ **extroversive** *adjective* (*PSYCHOLOGY*) characterized by or given to extroversion **E20**.

extrovert /ˈɛkstrəvəːt/ *noun & adjective*. **E20**.
[**ORIGIN** Var. of **EXTRAVERT** *noun* after **INTROVERT** *noun*: see **EXTRO-**.]
▸ **A** A person given to or characterized by extroversion; an outgoing, sociable person. **E20**.
▸ **B** Given to or characterized by extroversion; outgoing and sociable. **E20**.
■ **extroverted** *adjective* = **EXTROVERT** *adjective* **E20**. **extrovertish** *adjective* somewhat extrovert; like that of an extrovert: **M20**.

extrovert /ɛkstrəˈvəːt/ *verb trans. rare*. **L17**.
[**ORIGIN** from **EXTRO-** + Latin *vertere* to turn.]
Give an outward direction to.

†**extruct** *verb* var. of **EXSTRUCT**.

extrude /ɪkˈstruːd, ɛk-/ *verb*. **M16**.
[**ORIGIN** Latin *extrudere*, formed as **EX-**[1] 1 + *trudere* to thrust.]
1 *verb trans*. Thrust or force out; expel. (Foll. by *from*.) **M16**. ▸**b** Shape (metal, plastic, etc.) by forcing through dies. **E20**.

G. **VIDAL** Ticker-tape machines extruded tapes in code. E. **BOWEN** Still more ornate pieces have been extruded to the outlying wings.

2 *verb intrans*. Be extruded; protrude. **M19**.
■ **extrudable** *adjective* **L20**. **extruder** *noun* (*a*) a machine that shapes materials by forcing them through dies; (*b*) *TYPOGRAPHY* an ascender, a descender: **M20**.

extrusion /ɪkˈstruːʒ(ə)n, ɛk-/ *noun*. **M16**.
[**ORIGIN** medieval Latin *extrusio(n-)*, from Latin *extrus-* pa. ppl stem of *extrudere*: see **EXTRUDE**, **-ION**.]
1 Forceful expulsion from a place, position, privilege, etc. **M16**.
2 Expulsion by mechanical force, esp. of molten, fluid, or plastic material; *spec*. the shaping of metal or plastic by forcing through a die. **M17**.
3 An article made by extrusion. **E20**.

extrusive /ɪkˈstruːsɪv, ɛk-/ *adjective*. **E19**.
[**ORIGIN** from Latin *extrus-*: see **EXTRUSION**, **-IVE**.]
Tending to extrude; able to be extruded; *GEOLOGY* (of rock) having been extruded to the earth's surface as lava or ash.

extry /ˈɛkstri/ *adjective, adverb, & noun*. *colloq. & dial.* (chiefly *US*). **M19**.
[**ORIGIN** Alt.]
= **EXTRA** *adjective, adverb, & noun*.

extubation /ɛkstjʊˈbeɪʃ(ə)n/ *noun*. **L19**.
[**ORIGIN** from **EX-**[1] + **IN)TUBATION**.]
MEDICINE. The removal of tubes from an intubated patient.
■ **ˈextubate** *verb trans*. remove tubes from **L20**.

extuberant /ɪkˈstjuːb(ə)r(ə)nt, ɛk-/ *adjective*. Now *rare* or *obsolete*. **L16**.
[**ORIGIN** Latin *extuberant-* pres. ppl stem of *extuberare*: see **EXTUBERATE**, **-ANT**[1].]
Swelling out, protuberant.
■ †**extuberance** *noun* (*a*) the quality or condition of being extuberant; (*b*) a swelling, a projection: **E17–E19**. †**extuberancy** *noun* = **EXTUBERANCE** **M17–E18**.

†**extuberate** *verb intrans. & trans. rare*. **E17–M18**.
[**ORIGIN** Latin *extuberat-* pa. ppl stem of *extuberare* swell out, formed as **EX-**[1] 1 + *tuber* swelling: see **-ATE**[3].]
(Cause to) swell out or up.

extund /ɪkˈstʌnd, ɛk-/ *verb trans*. **E17**.
[**ORIGIN** Latin *extundere*, formed as **EX-**[1] 1 + *tundere* to beat.]
Produce with effort, hammer out.

exuberance /ɪgˈzjuːb(ə)r(ə)ns, ɛg-/ *noun*. **M17**.
[**ORIGIN** French *exubérance* from Latin *exuberantia*, from *exuberant-*: see **EXUBERANT**, **-ANCE**.]
1 A superabundance, esp. of something abstract. **M17**. ▸†**b** An abundance of good things. **L17–M18**.

J. **GALSWORTHY** This resentment expressed itself in . . an exuberance of family cordiality.

2 An overflow; a profuse outgrowth; a protuberance. Now *rare*. **M17**.
3 The quality or condition of being exuberant; luxuriance of growth in a plant; abundance of high spirits and good health in a person. **M17**. ▸**b** Copiousness or superfluity in expression. **E18**. ▸**c** An extravagance, an excessive outburst. **M19**.

Listener A man who had lost his youthful exuberance.

■ Also **exuberancy** *noun* **E17**.

exuberant /ɪgˈzjuːb(ə)r(ə)nt, ɛg-/ *adjective*. **LME**.
[**ORIGIN** French *exubérant* from Latin *exuberant-* pres. ppl stem of *exuberare*, formed as **EX-**[1] 1 + *uberare* be fruitful, from *uber* fruitful: see **-ANT**[1].]
1 **a** Of affection, joy, health, etc.: overflowing, abounding. **LME**. ▸**b** Of people or their actions etc.: effusive in display of feeling; *esp*. full of high spirits and good health. **E16**.

a E. F. **BENSON** She should be in the highest and most exuberant spirits at their little dinner. **b** A. **POWELL** He gave an exuberant greeting.

2 Growing luxuriantly; produced in excess. **E16**. ▸**b** Of speech or writing: copious, diffuse, lavishly ornamented. **M17**.

A. N. **WILSON** The exuberant frizz of hair which blew from the hood of her . . duffle coat.

3 Luxuriantly fertile; abundantly productive. **M17**.

D. G. **ROSSETTI** Love's exuberant hotbed.

4 Of a fountain, stream, etc.: overflowing. **L17**.
5 Of wealth, stores, display, etc.: lavish, abundant, profuse. **L17**.
■ **exuberantly** *adverb* **M17**.

exuberate /ɪgˈzjuːbəreɪt, ɛg-/ *verb*. **L15**.
[**ORIGIN** Latin *exuberat-* pa. ppl stem of *exuberare*: see **EXUBERANT**, **-ATE**[3].]
†**1** *verb trans*. *ALCHEMY*. Make (mercury) act effectively. **L15–L17**.
2 *verb intrans*. Be exuberant; abound, overflow. **E17**.
3 *verb intrans*. Develop *into*; indulge *in* with exuberant feeling. Now *rare*. **E18**.

Exucontian /ɛksjʊˈkɒntɪən/ *noun & adjective*. **M19**.
[**ORIGIN** from ecclesiastical Greek *exoukontios* (from phr. *ex ouk ontōn* out of non-being) + **-AN**.]
ECCLESIASTICAL. (Designating) an Arian.

exudate /ˈɛgzjʊdeɪt/ *noun*. **L19**.
[**ORIGIN** Latin *ex(s)udat-* pa. ppl stem of *ex(s)udare*: see **EXUDE**, **-ATE**[2].]
An exuded substance; a quantity of exuded material; *spec*. (*MEDICINE*) a mass of cells and fluid that has seeped out of blood vessels or an organ, e.g. in inflammation or malignancy. Cf. **TRANSUDATE**.

†**exudate** *verb trans. & intrans*. **M17–L18**.
[**ORIGIN** formed as **EXUDATE** *noun*: see **EXUDE**, **-ATE**[3].]
= **EXUDE**.

exudation /ɛgzjʊˈdeɪʃ(ə)n/ *noun*. **E17**.
[**ORIGIN** Late Latin *exsudatio(n-)*, formed as **EXUDATE** *noun*: see **-ATION**.]
1 The process of exuding. **E17**.
2 Something which is exuded; *esp*. something given off like a vapour. **E17**.

B. **MALAMUD** The cold rose like an exudation from the marble floor.

■ **eˈxudative** *adjective* (chiefly *MEDICINE*) pertaining to or characterized by exudation **M19**.

exude /ɪgˈzjuːd, ɛg-/ *verb*. **L16**.
[**ORIGIN** Latin *ex(s)udare*, formed as **EX-**[1] 1 + *sudare* to sweat.]
1 *verb intrans*. Ooze out; pass off slowly through pores, an incision, etc. **L16**.
2 *verb trans*. Give off (moisture, a smell, etc.) in this way. **M18**.
3 *verb trans*. (Of a person) show strongly (a personal characteristic or other abstract quality); (of a place) have a strong atmosphere of. **L19**.

D. H. **LAWRENCE** He seemed to exude pride . . as he walked about.

exulcerate /ɪgˈzʌlsəreɪt, ɛg-/ *verb*. *arch*. **M16**.
[**ORIGIN** Latin *exulcerat-* pa. ppl stem of *exulcerare*, formed as **EX-**[1] 1 + *ulcer-*, *ulcus*: see **ULCER** *noun*, **-ATE**[3].]
†**1** *verb trans. & intrans*. Cause ulcers (in). **M16–M18**.
†**2** *verb intrans*. Break out in ulcers or sores. **L16–E18**.
3 *verb trans*. Exasperate, irritate; wound (feelings); aggravate (a state). **L16**.
4 *verb intrans*. Act as an irritant or torment. **L17**.

exulceration /ɪgˌzʌlsəˈreɪʃ(ə)n, ɛg-/ *noun*. **M16**.
[**ORIGIN** Latin *exulceratio(n-)*, formed as **EXULCERATE**: see **-ATION**.]
1 Ulceration; the early stages of ulceration. Now *rare* or *obsolete*. **M16**.
2 An ulcer, a sore. **M16**.
3 Exasperation; embitterment. **L16**.

exult /ɪgˈzʌlt, ɛg-/ *verb*. **L16**.
[**ORIGIN** Latin *ex(s)ultare*, frequentative of *exsilire* leap up, formed as **EX-**[1] 1 + *salire* to leap.]
†**1** *verb intrans*. Spring or leap up; leap for joy. **L16–E18**.
2 *verb intrans*. Rejoice greatly, be elated. (Foll. by *in*, *at*, *on*, *over*; *to do*.) **L16**.
3 *verb trans*. Say exultingly. **E20**.
■ **exultingly** *adverb* in an exulting manner **M17**.

exultancy /ɪgˈzʌlt(ə)nsi, ɛg-/ *noun*. **E17**.
[**ORIGIN** Late Latin *ex(s)ultantia*, from Latin *ex(s)ultant-* pres. ppl stem of *ex(s)ultare*: see **EXULT**, **-ANCY**.]
(An) exultant state; exultation; a joyous rapture.
■ Also **exultance** *noun* **M17**.

exultant /ɪgˈzʌlt(ə)nt, ɛg-/ *adjective*. **M17**.
[**ORIGIN** Latin *ex(s)ultant-* pres. ppl stem of *ex(s)ultare*: see **EXULT**, **-ANT**[1].]
Triumphantly or rapturously joyful.
■ **exultantly** *adverb* **L19**.

E

exultation /ɛgzʌlˈteɪʃ(ə)n/ *noun*. **LME**.
[**ORIGIN** Latin *ex(s)ultatio(n-)*, from *ex(s)ultat-* pa. ppl stem of *ex(s)ultare*: see **EXULT**, **-ATION**.]
1 The action or a state of exulting; (the expression of) triumphant joy or rapture. **LME**.

J. R. **GREEN** The exultation of the Court over the decision of the judges. J. **BALDWIN** There arose in him an exultation and a sense of power.

2 An object exulted over, a cause of great joy. **L15**.
3 In *pl*. Shouts of joy. **L16**.

Exultet /ɪgˈzʌltɛt, ɛg-/ *noun*. **M19**.
[**ORIGIN** Latin = let it rejoice, 3rd person sing. pres. subjunct. of *ex(s)ultare* **EXULT**.]
ROMAN CATHOLIC CHURCH. The prose sung by the deacon at the blessing of the Paschal Candle on Easter Eve, of which *Exultet iam angelica turba* are the opening words.

exululate /ɛkˈsjʊljʊleɪt/ *verb intrans. rare*. **E17**.
[**ORIGIN** Latin *exululat-* pa. ppl stem of *exululare*, formed as **EX-**[1] 1 + *ululare* howl: see **ULULATE**.]
Howl, cry out.
■ **exuluˈlation** *noun* **E18**.

exumbrella /ɛksʌmˈbrɛlə/ *noun*. **L19**.
[**ORIGIN** from **EX-**[1] + **UMBRELLA**.]
ZOOLOGY. The outer, convex, side of the umbrella of a jellyfish.
■ **exumbrellar** *adjective* **L19**.

exundant /ɪkˈsʌnd(ə)nt, ɛk-/ *adjective*. **M17**.
[**ORIGIN** Latin *exundant-* pres. ppl stem of *exundare* gush forth, overflow, formed as **EX-**[1] 1 + *undare* rise in waves, from *unda* wave: see **-ANT**[1].]
Overflowing, superabundant.

exundation /ɛksʌnˈdeɪʃ(ə)n/ *noun*. Now *rare*. **L16**.
[**ORIGIN** Latin *exundatio(n-)*, from *exundare*: see **EXUNDANT**, **-ATION**.]
The action or an act of overflowing (by water).

exurb /ˈɛksəːb/ *noun*. Orig. *US*. **M20**.
[**ORIGIN** from Latin *ex* out of + *urbs* city, or back-form. from **EXURBAN**.]
A district outside a city or town, *esp*. a prosperous one beyond the suburbs.

exurban /ɛkˈsəːb(ə)n/ *adjective*. **E20**.
[**ORIGIN** from **EX-**[1] + **URBAN**, after **SUBURBAN**.]
Of or belonging to a district outside a city or town, esp. an exurb.
■ **exurbanite** *noun & adjective* (orig. *US*) (*a*) *noun* a person who lives in an exurb; (*b*) *adjective* = **EXURBAN**: **M20**.

exurbia /ɛkˈsəːbɪə/ *noun*. Orig. *US*. **M20**.
[**ORIGIN** from **EX-**[1] + *-urbia*, after **SUBURBIA**.]
Exurbs collectively; the region outside the suburbs of a city.

†**exust** *verb trans. rare*. **E17–E19**.
[**ORIGIN** Latin *exust-* pa. ppl stem of *exurere*, formed as **EX-**[1] 1 + *urere* burn.]
Burn up.

†**exustion** *noun*. **L16–E18**.
[**ORIGIN** Latin *exustio(n-)*, formed as **EXUST**: see **-ION**.]
Destruction by burning; the action of burning something.

exute /ɪgˈzjuːt, ɛg-/ *verb trans*. *obsolete* exc. *hist*. **M16**.
[**ORIGIN** Latin *exut-* pa. ppl stem of *exuere*: see **EXUVIAE**.]
Strip (a person) *of*; divest or deprive *of*.

exuviae /ɪgˈzjuːviiː, ɛg-/ *noun pl*. **M17**.
[**ORIGIN** Latin = clothing stripped off, skins of animals, spoils, from *exuere* divest oneself of.]
Cast skins, shells, or other shed outer parts of animals, whether recent or fossil; *spec*. (*ZOOLOGY*) sloughed skins; *fig*. remnants, remains.
■ **exuvial** *noun & adjective* †(*a*) *noun* in *pl*., spoils; (*b*) *adjective* pertaining to or of the nature of exuviae: **M17**. **exuviate** *verb trans. & intrans*. shed (as) exuviae, moult **M19**. **exuviˈation** *noun* **M19**.

ex vi termini /ɛks viː ˈtəːmɪniː/ *adverbial phr*. Now *rare* or *obsolete*. **E18**.
[**ORIGIN** mod. Latin = from the force of the term.]
By definition; by implication.

ex-voto /ɛksˈvəʊtəʊ/ *noun & adjective*. Pl. of noun **-os**. L18.
[ORIGIN Latin *ex voto* from *ex* out of, from + *voto* abl. sing. of *votum*: see VOTE *noun*.]
(Designating) something offered in fulfilment of a vow previously taken.
■ **ex-votive** *adjective* M19.

†**ey** *noun*. OE–M16.
[ORIGIN Old English *ǣg* = Old Saxon, Old High German (Dutch, German) *ei*, Crimean Gothic *ada*, from Germanic, prob. ult. rel. to Latin *ovum*, Greek *ōion*.]
= EGG *noun*.

†**ey** *interjection* var. of AY *interjection*[2].

-ey *suffix*[1] see -Y[1].

-ey *suffix*[2] see -Y[6].

E

eyalet /ɛˈjɑːlɛt/ *noun*. M19.
[ORIGIN Turkish from Arabic *iyāla(t)* management, administration, from *'āla* govern.]
= VILAYET.

eyas /ˈʌɪəs/ *noun & adjective*. Orig. †**nyas**. L15.
[ORIGIN Old French & mod. French *niais* (orig.) bird taken from the nest, (now) silly person, from Proto-Romance from Latin *nidus* nest. Initial *n* lost by misdivision as in ADDER *noun*[1]; spelling with *ey-* may be due to assoc. with EY *noun*.]
► **A** *noun*. **1** A young hawk in the nest, or taken from it for training; a hawk whose training is incomplete. L15.
2 A child, a youthful or immature person. L16.
► **B** *attrib.* or as *adjective*. Unfledged, youthful. L16.

eye /ʌɪ/ *noun*.
[ORIGIN Old English *ēage*, (Anglian) *ēge* = Old Frisian *āge*, Old Saxon *ōga* (Dutch *oog*), Old High German *ouga* (German *Auge*), Old Norse *auga*, Gothic *augo*, from Germanic. The Old English pl. *ēagan* survives in north. *een* and arch. *eyne* (Spenser); pl. *-s* dates from LME.]
► **I 1** The organ of sight in humans and animals; the region of the face surrounding this. OE. ▸**b** The imagined organ of sight as attributed to the heart, mind, or other quasi-personified things. OE. ▸**c** The (usu. human) eye as characterized by the colour of its iris. ME.

ALDOUS HUXLEY Behind their bifocal lenses his eyes were bright with excitement. J. STEINBECK Kino's eyes opened, and he looked first at the lightening square. G. B. SHAW Her eyes are red from weeping. **b** R. KIPLING Cities and Thrones and Powers Stand in Time's eye, Almost as long as flowers, Which daily die. **c** I. MURDOCH The light brown eyes gazed in her direction.

2 *sing.* & in *pl.* **a** A look, a glance, a gaze. OE. ▸**b** The aspect of a person's face as expressing his or her feelings. ME.

a W. COWPER Modestly let fall your eyes. **b** POPE View him with scornful, yet with jealous eyes.

3 The eye as possessing the power or faculty of vision. ME. ▸**b** A person or animal whose power of vision is used by another (usu. blind) person. LME. ▸**c** A detective, a detective agency, *esp.* a private one. *slang*. E20. ▸**d** A mechanical or electrical device resembling an eye in function. M20.

C. ISHERWOOD Her eyes no longer see him. *National Observer (US)* Right before your eyes on the wide screen. **b** WORDSWORTH Thou best Philosopher.. thou Eye among the blind. **d** W. H. AUDEN Let me pretend that I'm the impersonal eye of the camera Sent out.. to shoot on location.

4 a *sing.* & in *pl.* The sense of seeing; ocular perception. ME. ▸**b** An attentive look; attention, regard; observation, supervision. ME. ▸**c** *sing.* & in *pl.* Point of view, way of looking at a thing; opinion, judgement. ME. ▸**d** Range of vision, view, sight. Now *rare* or *obsolete* exc. *fig.* in ***one's mind's eye*** below. L16.

a J. LE CARRÉ It's for his eyes only. **b** T. MEDWIN I had.. fallen under the eye of the Government. G. F. KENNAN Lloyd George, with an eye to his political fortunes at home, chose to head the British delegation in person. **c** D. HUME Persons not lying under .. attainder were innocent in the eye of the law. R. DAHL Nanny .. in my eyes was filled with more wisdom than Solomon.

5 The faculty of visual perception, appreciation, or judgement, either in general or with some specific reference. M17.
► **II** An object resembling the eye in appearance, shape, function, or relative position.
6 a The small hole in a needle for taking the thread. OE. ▸**b** A small hole in bread or (now usu.) cheese. LME. ▸**c** A hole made in a tool for the insertion of a handle or some other object. M16. ▸**d** An opening or passage in a mill-stone, kiln, etc., for the introduction or withdrawal of substances; the entrance or exit of a fox's earth, a mine shaft, etc. M16.

a AV *Matt.* 19:24 It is easier for a camel to goe thorow the eye of a needle.

7 A mark or spot resembling an eye occurring on eggs, insect wings, etc.; *esp.* any of the marks near the end of the tail feathers of a peacock; each of the three spots on one end of a coconut. LME. ▸**b** GEOLOGY. A lens-shaped inclusion with a different texture from the surrounding rock. L19.
8 An object resembling an eye on a plant; *esp.* (*a*) an axillary bud or leaf bud; (*b*) the centre of a flower; (*c*) the remains of the calyx on a fruit. LME.

B. TRAPIDO Withered potatoes sprouting at the eyes.

9 In *pl.* Spectacles. Now *rare*. E16.
10 A loop, a ring; *esp.* a loop of thread in a hook and eye (see HOOK *noun* 1c); NAUTICAL a loop at the end of a rope, *esp.* one at the top end of a shroud or stay. L16.
11 *fig.* A place regarded as a centre of learning, culture, or the like. L16.
12 a ARCHITECTURE. The centre of any part, esp. of a volute. E18. ▸**b** The centre of a vortex or eddy; *esp.* the calm centre of a hurricane or storm. M19. ▸**c** The dense centre of a shoal of fish. M19. ▸**d** The brightest spot or centre of light; *esp.* the part of a furnace observed through the sight-hole. L19. ▸**e** The main mass of lean meat in a rasher of bacon, cutlet, etc. M20.
13 A prominent natural object, such as a hill or island. Only in place names. M19.
14 The opening through which the water of a fountain or spring wells up. M19.
15 A mass of ore left in a mine to be worked when other ore is becoming scarce or inaccessible; *fig.* (*Austral. & NZ*) the choicest portion, esp. of land. M19.
16 NAUTICAL. In *pl.* (in full ***eyes of her***, ***eyes of the ship***). The extreme forward part of a ship. M19.
► †**III 17** A slight shade, tinge, or hint *of* something. Only in 17.

– PHRASES ETC.: **a gleam in one's eye**, **a glint in one's eye** a barely formed idea; a child who has not yet been conceived. ***all my eye (and Betty Martin)***: see ***my eye (and Betty Martin)*** below. **an eye for an eye** [alluding to *Exodus* 21:24] revenge, retaliation in kind. APPLE ***of one's eye***. ***a smack in the eye***: see SMACK *noun*[2]. **a twinkle in one's eye** = ***a gleam in one's eye*** above. ***a wipe in the eye***: see WIPE *noun*. **be all eyes** watch attentively. BELIEVE ***one's eyes***. ***blue eye***: see BLUE *adjective*. ***cast an eye***: see CAST *verb*. **cast sheep's eyes at** = ***make sheep's eyes at*** below. ***catch the eye of***: see CATCH *verb*. †**change eyes** exchange amorous glances. ***clap eyes on***: see CLAP *verb*[1] 9. **close one's eyes to**, **close one's eyes against** ignore, refuse to recognize or consider. ***cock one's eye***: see COCK *verb*[1] 6. ***collect eyes***: see COLLECT *verb* 1. ***compound eye***: see COMPOUND *adjective*. ***cry one's eyes out***: see CRY *verb* 5d. ***damn my eyes!***, ***damn your eyes!***: see DAMN *verb*. ***deadeye***: see DEAD *adjective*. **do a person in the eye** defraud, thwart, or humiliate a person. ***easy on the eye(s)***: see EASY *adjective* 1b. ***electric eye***: see ELECTRIC *adjective*. ***evil eye***: see EVIL *adjective*. **eye of day** *poet.* the sun. **eyes down** *colloq.* the start of play at bingo. **eyes front**, **eyes left**, **eyes right** MILITARY (a command to) turn the head in the direction stated. **eyes on stalks**: widened in amazement, inquisitiveness, etc. ***eyes right***: see ***eyes front*** above. ***find favour in the eyes of***: see FAVOUR *noun*. ***Flemish eye***: see FLEMISH *adjective & noun*. **get one's eye in** SPORT accustom oneself to the prevailing conditions. ***glass eye***: see GLASS *noun & adjective*. **go eyes out** *Austral. & NZ colloq.* make every effort. ***green eye***: see GREEN *adjective*. ***green in one's eye***: see GREEN *noun*. ***grey eye***: see GREY *adjective*. **half an eye** a very slight degree of ocular perception (***see with half an eye***: at a glance, without effort). ***have a drop in one's eye***: see DROP *noun* 3b. **have an eye for** be quick to notice. **have an eye to** have as one's object; prudently consider. **have eyes bigger than one's belly**, **have eyes bigger than one's stomach** wish or expect to eat more than one can. **have eyes for** be interested in (***only have eyes for***, desire nothing or no one but). **have eyes in the back of one's head** know what is going on around one even when one cannot see it. **have eyes to see** be observant or discerning. **have one's eye on** (*a*) = ***keep an eye on*** below; (*b*) desire or hope to obtain. ***have one's eye on the ball***: see BALL *noun*[1] 2. ***here's mud in your eye!***: see MUD *noun*[1]. **hit one in the eye** (of a fact, object, etc.) be very obvious. ***in a pig's eye***: see PIG *noun*[1]. †**in eye** in sight or view. **in one's eye** in one's imagination; in mind. **in the eye of —**, **in the eyes of —** as far as — is concerned, in the view of. **in the public eye** receiving much public attention. ***in the*** TWINKLING ***of an eye***. **in the wind's eye** against the direction of the wind. †**into eye** into sight or view. ***jump to the eyes***: see JUMP *verb*. **keep an eye on** keep under observation. **keep an eye open**, **keep an eye out**, **keep an eye peeled**, **keep an eye skinned** be watchful; watch carefully *for*. ***keep a weather eye (on)***, ***keep one's weather eye (on)***, ***keep a weather eye open (for)***, ***keep one's weather eye open (for)***: see WEATHER *noun*. ***keep one's eye on the ball***: see BALL *noun*[1] 2. **keep one's eye(s) open**, **keep one's eye(s) out**, **keep one's eye(s) peeled**, **keep one's eye(s) skinned** = ***keep an eye open*** above. ***lay an eye on***, ***lay eyes on***: see LAY *verb*[1]. ***leap to the eye***: see LEAP *verb*. ***lift one's eyes***, ***lift up one's eyes***: see LIFT *verb*. **look a person in the eye** look directly or unashamedly at a person. **lose an eye** become unable to see with one eye. ***magic eye***: see MAGIC *adjective*. **make eyes at**, **make sheep's eyes at** look amorously at. ***meet the eye***: see MEET *verb*. ***mind one's eye***: see MIND *verb*. †**mingle eyes** = ***change eyes*** above. **my eye (and Betty Martin)** nonsense (freq. in ***all my eye (and Betty Martin)***). ***naked eye***: see NAKED *adjective*. ***needle's eye***: see NEEDLE *noun*. ***not bat an eye***: see BAT *verb*[2] 2. **one in the eye** a disappointment or setback *for* someone regarded as deserving it. **one's mind's eye** one's mental view or imagination. **open a person's eyes** (*a*) cause a person to stare in astonishment; (*b*) enlighten or undeceive a person. ***pass one's eye over***: see PASS *verb*. ***pipe one's eye(s)***: see PIPE *verb*[1] 4c. ***private eye***: see PRIVATE *adjective*. ***pull the wool over a person's eyes***: see WOOL *noun*. **run an eye over** examine cursorily. **see eye to eye** be of one mind, think alike. ***seeing eye***: see SEEING *ppl adjective*. **set eyes on** see, catch sight of. **shut one's eyes to**, **shut one's eyes against** = ***close one's eyes to*** above. ***spit in the eye of***: see SPIT *verb*[2]. ***straight eye***: see STRAIGHT *adjective*[1]. ***strong eye***: see STRONG *adjective*. ***tail of the eye***: see TAIL *noun*[1]. ***the glad eye***: see GLAD *adjective*. **the mind's eye** = ***one's mind's eye*** above. ***third eye***: see THIRD *adjective & noun*. ***throw dust in a person's eyes***: see DUST *noun*. ***turn a blind eye (to)***: see BLIND *adjective*. **up to one's eyes**, **up to the eyes** deeply or heavily (involved, engaged, etc.); to the limit. ***wash one's eyes***: see WASH *verb*. ***wipe one's eye***, ***wipe a person's eye***: see WIPE *verb*. **with one eye on** directing one's attention partly to. **with one's eyes open** in full awareness. **with one's eyes shut** (*a*) without full awareness; (*b*) with great ease. ***would give one's eyes***: see GIVE *verb*.

– COMB.: **eye bank** a stock of corneas taken from people soon after death and used for replacing defective corneas in blind people; **eyebath** a small cup-shaped vessel for applying lotion etc. to the eye; **eye-beam** a beam or glance of the eye; **eyeblack** mascara; **eye bolt** a bolt or bar with an eye at one end for a hook, ring, etc.; **eyebright** any of various plants of the genus *Euphrasia*, of the figwort family, many of which are valued by herbalists as a remedy for weak eyes (***red eyebright***: see RED *adjective*); **eye candy** *colloq.* visual images that are superficially attractive and entertaining but intellectually undemanding (cf. ***ear candy***); **eye-catcher** a person who or thing which catches the eye; **eye-catching** *adjective* striking; attractive; prominent; **eye contact** the state or practice of looking at another's eyes while he or she is looking at one's own; **eyecup** = ***eyebath*** above; **eye dialect** a form of writing in which spellings are altered in order to represent a dialectal pronunciation; **eye-drop** a tear; in *pl.*, a solution for applying to the eye; **eyehole** (*a*) *arch.* the eye socket; (*b*) a hole to look through; **eye language** interpersonal communication by means of the expression of the eyes; **eye-legible** *adjective* in a form that can be read by eye, without a magnifier or reader; **eye level** the level seen by eyes looking straight ahead; the height of the eyes; **eyeline** a person's line of sight; **eyeliner** a cosmetic applied in a line around the eye; **eye mask** a covering for the eyes; *spec.* one of soft material soaked with a lotion for refreshing the eyes; **eye-opener** (*a*) *US* a dram, *esp.* one taken in the morning; (*b*) a thing that enlightens or surprises; (*c*) a person who or thing which is outstandingly attractive; **eye-opening** *adjective* that enlightens or surprises; **eyepatch** = PATCH *noun*[1] 1c; **eye pencil** a pencil for applying lines of make-up around the eyes; **eyepiece** the lens or combination of lenses in a telescope or microscope by which the image is viewed or magnified; **eye-pit** (*a*) the eye socket; (*b*) the depression between the eye and the orbit; **eye rhyme** a correspondence (of words in a poem) in spelling but not in pronunciation; **eye-service** *arch.* the doing of work only when watched by an employer or master; **eyeshade** a visor for protecting the eyes from strong sunlight; **eyeshadow** make-up applied to the eyelids or around the eyes; **eyeshot** (*a*) seeing distance, range of sight; (*b*) a glance, a sudden look; **eye socket** the orbit of the eye; **eyes-only** *adjective* intended to be seen or read only by the person addressed; confidential; **eye splice** a splice made by turning back the strands at the end of a rope and interlacing them with the preceding part of the rope; **eyestalk** ZOOLOGY a movable stalk supporting the eye in some animals; **eye strain** weariness of the eyes resulting from excessive or incorrect use; †**eyestrings** the muscles, nerves, or tendons of the eye which were formerly supposed to break or crack at death or loss of sight; **eyestripe** a stripe on a bird's head which encloses or appears to run through the eye; **eye tooth** one of the canine teeth directly under or next to the eye, esp. in the upper jaw (***cut one's eye teeth***: see CUT *verb*; ***would give one's eye teeth***: see GIVE *verb*); **eyewash** (*a*) a lotion for the eye; (*b*) *slang* something said or done merely for appearance or effect; humbug; **eyewater** (*a*) tears; (*b*) lotion for the eye; (*c*) the aqueous or vitreous humour of the eye; **eyewear** spectacles, contact lenses, and other things worn on the eyes; **eye-wink** (*a*) a look or glance; (*b*) the time it takes to wink, an instant; **eyewitness** *noun & verb* (*a*) *noun* a person who can testify from his or her own observation; a person who has seen a particular thing done or happen; (*b*) *verb trans.* be an eyewitness of (an event); **eye worm** a filarial worm that infects the eye and subcutaneous tissue of humans and other primates in tropical Africa.
■ **eyelike** *adjective* resembling an eye E17.

eye /ʌɪ/ *verb*. Pres. pple & verbal noun **eyeing**, **eying**. M16.
[ORIGIN from the noun.]
1 *verb trans.* Fix the eyes upon, look at, observe. M16. ▸†**b** Regard or look upon *as*. M–L17.

W. GASS She sniffs the air and eyes a sailing cloud.

2 *verb trans.* Keep an eye on; watch closely. L16. ▸**b** Look at amorously or with sexual interest, ogle. Freq. as ***eye up***. L20.

R. COBB The two groups eyed one another, listlessly but without hostility. **b** S. NAIPAUL He eyed a shapely.. girl.

†**3** *verb trans.* See, perceive. L16–L18.

POPE The paths of gods what mortal can survey? Who eyes their motion?

†**4** *verb trans.* Have or keep in view; look to; aim at. L16–M17.
†**5** *verb intrans.* Appear to the eye, look. *rare* (Shakes.). Only in E17.

SHAKES. *Ant. & Cl.* My becomings kill me when they do not eye well to you.

6 *verb trans.* Pierce a hole in (a needle etc.). M19.
7 *verb intrans.* Of an egg: form an eye (see EYE *noun* 7). E20.
■ **eyeable** *adjective* (*a*) visible; (*b*) visually attractive: L18. **eyer** *noun* (*rare*) (*a*) an observer; (*b*) a maker of eyes in needles: LME.

eyeball /ˈʌɪbɔːl/ *noun & verb*. L16.
[ORIGIN from EYE *noun* + BALL *noun*[1].]
► **A** *noun*. **1** The globe of the eye, a firm white sphere within the eyelids that is formed by the sclera and the cornea. L16.
eyeball to eyeball confronting closely; with neither party yielding.
2 The pupil of the eye. Now *rare* or *obsolete*. L16.
► **B** *verb trans. & intrans.* Look (at), stare (at). *N. Amer. colloq.* E20.

A. MAUPIN He eyeballed me in a prim, chastising way.

eye-bree /ˈʌɪbriː/ *noun*. *obsolete* exc. *Scot. & dial.* OE.
[ORIGIN from EYE *noun* + BREE *noun*[1].]
†**1** The eyelid. OE–L18.
†**2** An eyelash. L16–E17.

3 = EYEBROW 1. L18.

eyebrow /ˈʌɪbraʊ/ *noun*. LME.
[ORIGIN from EYE *noun* + BROW *noun*¹; repl. EYE-BREE.]
1 The arch of short fine hair along the ridge above each eye; an artificial imitation of this. LME.
2 ARCHITECTURE. A fillet. E18.
– PHRASES: ***cock an eyebrow, cock one's eyebrows***: see COCK *verb*¹ 6. **raise an eyebrow**, **raise one's eyebrow(s)** show surprise or disbelief (*at*). **up to the eyebrows** = ***up to the eyes*** s.v. EYE *noun*.
– COMB.: **eyebrow pencil** a cosmetic pencil for drawing lines to accentuate the eyebrows; **eyebrow tweezers** tweezers for extracting unwanted hairs from the eyebrows.
■ **eyebrowed** *adjective* having eyebrows M19. **eyebrowless** *adjective* M19.

eyed /ʌɪd/ *adjective*. LME.
[ORIGIN from EYE *noun* + -ED².]
1 Having eyes. Usu. with preceding noun or adjective LME. ▸†**b** Gifted with sight; clear-sighted. L16–M17.
SCOTT FITZGERALD The owl-eyed man.
blue-eyed, ***green-eyed***, etc.
2 Of cheese, an implement, etc.: having a hole or holes. LME.
3 Ornamented with marks like eyes; spotted. E19.
KEATS Eyed like a peacock.
■ **eyedness** *noun* the fact of having one eye or a specified eye dominant, or of preferring to use it. M20.

eyeful /ˈʌɪfʊl, -f(ə)l/ *noun*. M19.
[ORIGIN from EYE *noun* + -FUL.]
1 As much as the eye can take in at once; a complete view, a good look at something. M19.
2 An exhilarating sight; *spec.* a strikingly attractive person. *colloq.* E20.

eyeglass /ˈʌɪɡlɑːs/ *noun* & *verb*. E17.
[ORIGIN from EYE *noun* + GLASS *noun*.]
▸ **A** *noun*. †**1** The lens of the eye. *rare* (Shakes.). Only in E17.
2 The lens of an optical instrument to which the eye is applied. M17.
3 A lens for assisting defective eyesight, a monocle; in *pl.*, a pair of these held in position by hand or supported on the bridge of the nose; *sing.* & in *pl.* (*N. Amer.*), (a pair of) spectacles. Formerly, a magnifying glass, a microscope. M18.
▸ **B** *verb trans.* & *intrans.* Look through an eyeglass (at). *rare*. E19.
■ **eyeglassed** *adjective* provided with an eyeglass or eyeglasses M19. **eye-glassy** *adjective* (*colloq.*) (supposedly) characteristic of one wearing an eyeglass; haughtily superior: L19.

eyelash /ˈʌɪlaʃ/ *noun*. M18.
[ORIGIN from EYE *noun* + LASH *noun*¹.]
1 Any of the hairs on the edge of the eyelid. Formerly, the line of such hairs. M18.
2 A hair's breadth, a minute distance. M20.

eyeless /ˈʌɪlɪs/ *adjective*. LME.
[ORIGIN from EYE *noun* + -LESS.]
1 That is without an eye or eyes. LME.
2 Deprived of the eyes. L16.
3 Blind. E17.

eyelet /ˈʌɪlɪt/ *noun* & *adjective*. LME.
[ORIGIN Old French *oillet* (mod. *œillet*), dim. of *oil* (mod. *œil*) eye from Latin *oculus*: see -ET¹.]
▸ **A** *noun*. **1** A small round usu. reinforced hole in leather, cloth, sailcloth, etc., for a lace, ring, or rope to pass through. LME.
2 A hole or slit in a wall, usu. for observation. LME.
3 A small eye, *esp.* one in a butterfly's wing. L16.
▸ **B** *attrib.* or as *adjective*. Of embroidery or fabric: composed of numerous small holes. E20.

eyelet /ˈʌɪlɪt/ *verb trans*. M19.
[ORIGIN from EYELET *noun*.]
Make eyelets in. Chiefly as ***eyeleted*** *ppl adjective*, ***eyeleting*** *verbal noun*.

eyelid /ˈʌɪlɪd/ *noun*. ME.
[ORIGIN from EYE *noun* + LID *noun*.]
Either of the upper and lower folds of skin that meet when the eye is closed.
hang on by the eyelids *fig.* have only a slight hold. ***not bat an eyelid***: see BAT *verb*² 2. ***third eyelid***: see THIRD *adjective* & *noun*.

eyesight /ˈʌɪsʌɪt/ *noun*. ME.
[ORIGIN from EYE *noun* + SIGHT *noun*.]
1 The power or faculty of seeing. ME.
J. MCPHEE His eyesight was not much better than what was required to see a blueberry inches away.
2 The action or an act of seeing; a look; observation. Now *rare* or *obsolete*. ME.
CARLYLE Things . . known to us by the best evidence, by eyesight.
†**3** The range of the eyes. ME–M17.

eyesome /ˈʌɪs(ə)m/ *adjective*. Now *poet*. L16.
[ORIGIN from EYE *noun* + -SOME¹.]
Attractive.

eyesore /ˈʌɪsɔː/ *noun*. ME.
[ORIGIN from EYE *noun* + SORE *noun*¹.]
†**1** Soreness of the eyes. ME–M16.
2 An ugly object or mark; something that is offensive to the eyes. M16.
3 A cause of annoyance, offence, or vexation. M16.
S. RUSHDIE This slum is a public eyesore, can no longer be tolerated.
†**4** A scar, flaw, or defect on a horse. L17–E18.

eyespot /ˈʌɪspɒt/ *noun*. E19.
[ORIGIN from EYE *noun* + SPOT *noun*.]
1 A kind of lily with a red spot in the middle of each leaf. E19.
2 A spot resembling an eye, esp. on a plant or animal. L19.
3 A small light-sensitive area of some invertebrates that serves in place of an eye. L19.
4 Any of several fungal diseases of sugar cane, cereals, and other grasses which causes yellowish oval spots on the leaves and stems. E20.
sharp eyespot: see SHARP *adjective* & *adverb*.
■ **eyespotted** *adjective* having spots resembling eyes L16.

Eyetalian /ʌɪˈtalɪən/ *adjective* & *noun*. *slang*. M19.
[ORIGIN Repr. non-standard or joc. pronunc. of ITALIAN.]
(An) Italian.

Eyetie /ˈʌɪtʌɪ/ *noun* & *adjective*. *slang*. *offensive*. E20.
[ORIGIN Rhyming abbreviation of EYETALIAN.]
(An) Italian.

eye view /ʌɪ ˈvjuː/ *noun phr*. Also **eye-view**. M18.
[ORIGIN from ***bird's eye view*** s.v. BIRD *noun*.]
Used after a possess. word or phr. to denote what is seen from the viewpoint of the person or thing specified.
ALDOUS HUXLEY How should one look at other people? . . Should one take the Freud's-eye view or the Cézanne's-eye view? *Listener* From his own eye-view Sir Compton has no lack of items to add to the history of his time.

eyot /eɪt, ˈeɪət/ *noun*. L17.
[ORIGIN Var. of AIT *noun*¹, infl. by *islet* and French *îlot*.]
= AIT *noun*¹.

eyra /ˈeɪrə/ *noun*. E17.
[ORIGIN Spanish from Tupi-Guarani (*e*)*irára*.]
In full ***eyra cat***. A wild cat, *Felis yagouaroundi*, in its red phase, found from Argentina and Paraguay to southern Texas.

eyre /ɛː/ *noun*. Now *hist*. ME.
[ORIGIN Old French *eire* from Latin *iter* journey.]
1 Itineration, circuit. Chiefly in ***justice in eyre*** below. ME.
justice in eyre an itinerant judge who rode from county to county to hold courts.
2 The circuit court held by a justice in eyre. LME.

eyrie /ˈɪəri, ˈʌɪəri, ˈɛːri/ *noun*. Also **aerie**, **aery**, **eyry**. L15.
[ORIGIN medieval Latin *area*, *aeria*, *eyria*, prob. from Old French & mod. French *aire* from Latin *area* level piece of ground, (in late Latin) nest of a bird of prey.]
1 The nest of a bird of prey, esp. an eagle, or of any other bird which builds high up; *fig.* a human residence built at a great height. L15.
†**2** A young bird of prey. L16–E17.

eyrir /ˈeɪrɪr/ *noun*. E20. Pl. **aurar** /ˈøɪrar/.
[ORIGIN Icelandic, from Old Norse, lit. 'ounce (of silver, etc.), money', prob. from Latin *aureus* golden, a gold coin.]
In Iceland, a monetary unit equal to one-hundredth of a króna; a coin worth this. Cf. ORE *noun*².

ezan /ɛˈzʌn/ *noun*. M18.
[ORIGIN Persian & Turkish pronunc. of Arabic *ʼaḏān*.]
= AZAN.

Ezek. *abbreviation*.
Ezekiel (in the Bible).

E

Ff

F, f /ɛf/.

The sixth letter of the modern English alphabet and of the ancient Roman one, corresp. to Greek digamma (Ϝ) (repr. /w/), Semitic waw (repr. the sounds of *w* (approx.) and *u*). The sound now normally represented by the letter is a voiceless labiodental fricative consonant, except in *of* where it is voiced. Pl. **F's**, **Fs**. Cf. EFF.

▸ **I 1** The letter and its sound.

F-word a euphemism for the word *fuck* and its derivs., esp. with reference to their use as expletives.

2 The shape of the letter.

f-hole either of a pair of soundholes resembling an ʃ or reversed ʃ in shape, in the belly of a musical instrument of the violin family. **F-shaped** *adjective* having a shape or cross-section like the capital letter F.

▸ **II** Symbolical uses.

3 Used to denote serial order; applied e.g. to the sixth group or section, sheet of a book, etc.

4 *MUSIC.* (Cap. F.) The fourth note of the diatonic scale of C major. Also, the scale of a composition with F as its keynote.

F clef the bass clef.

5 The sixth hypothetical person or example.

6 (Usu. cap. F.) Designating the sixth-highest class (of academic marks etc.).

7 *F-layer*, the highest, most strongly ionized stratum of the ionosphere. Also called ***Appleton layer***.

▸ **III 8** Abbrevs.: **F.** = Fahrenheit; Father (of a priest); Fellow of. **F** = (*PHYSICS*) farad(s); (*BACTERIOLOGY*) fertility; (*BIOLOGY*) filial generation; fine (pencil lead, or (*PHYSICS*) denoting the hyperfine quantum number, expressing the resultant of nuclear spin I and electronic angular momentum J); fibre (in ***F Plan***, (US proprietary name for) a type of high-fibre diet); (*CHEMISTRY*) fluorine; (*PHOTOGRAPHY*) focal length (prefixed to numbers indicating the ratio between the focal length of a camera lens and the diameter of the aperture, as *F*/2.8 or F2.8, *F*/4 or F4, etc.; cf. ***f-number*** below). **f.** = female; filly; folio; following page etc.; foreign; (*slang*) fuck, fucking (sometimes printed *f*—). **f** = (as *prefix*) femto-; (*PHOTOGRAPHY*) focal length (in ***f-number***, ***f/number***, a number indicating the ratio between the focal length of a camera lens and the diameter of the aperture; cf. ***F*** above); (*MUSIC*) forte; frequency; (*PHYSICS & CHEMISTRY*) fundamental (orig. designating one of the four main series (S, P, D, F) of lines in atomic spectra, now more frequently applied to electronic orbitals, states, etc., possessing three units of angular momentum (as ***f-electron***, ***f-orbital***, etc.)).

FA *abbreviation*.

1 Fanny Adams (freq. in ***sweet FA***).

2 Football Association.

3 Fuck all (freq. in ***sweet FA***). *slang*.

fa *noun* var. of FAH.

FAA *abbreviation*.

1 Federal Aviation Authority. *US*.

2 Fleet Air Arm.

faamafu /faaˈmafʊ/ *noun*. M20.

[ORIGIN Samoan.]

In Samoa, home-brewed liquor.

faa-Samoa /faa sɑːˈmɒʌ/ *noun*. M20.

[ORIGIN Samoan.]

The Samoan way of life.

fab /fab/ *noun & verb*. L20.

[ORIGIN Abbreviation of FABRICATION.]

ELECTRONICS. ▸**A** *noun*. A plant that manufactures microchips. L20.

▸ **B** *verb trans.* Produce (a microchip). L20.

fab /fab/ *adjective*. *colloq*. M20.

[ORIGIN Abbreviation of FABULOUS.]

Very good, wonderful.

JANE GREEN You looked completely fab the other night.

the Fab Four the Beatles.

■ Also **fabbo** *adjective* L20. **fabby** *adjective* L20.

faba bean *noun phr.* var. of FAVA BEAN.

Fabian /ˈfeɪbɪən/ *noun & adjective*. L16.

[ORIGIN Latin *Fabianus* of the Fabian gens of ancient Rome.]

▸ **A** *noun*. †**1** ***Flaunting Fabian***, a roistering swashbuckler. Only in L16.

2 A member of the Fabian Society, or a sympathizer with its ideals. L19.

▸ **B** *adjective*. **1** Of or pertaining to the Fabian gens of ancient Rome. M18.

2 After the manner of the cautious and delaying tactics employed by the Roman general Q. Fabius Maximus to wear out an enemy. L18. ▸**b** Designating or pertaining to a socialist society founded in 1884, which advocates a policy of cautious and gradual political change. L19.

■ **Fabianism** *noun* the doctrines of the Fabian Society L19. **Fabianist** *noun & adjective* E20.

fabism *noun* var. of FAVISM.

fable /ˈfeɪb(ə)l/ *noun*. ME.

[ORIGIN Old French from Latin *fabula* story, from *fari* speak.]

1 A fictitious narrative or statement. ME. ▸**b** A myth or legend; myths or legends in general. ME. ▸**c** A fiction invented to deceive. ME. ▸**d** A ridiculous or untrustworthy story; idle talk. LME. ▸**e** Something falsely claimed to exist, or having no existence outside popular legend. L16.

DRYDEN It seems a Fable, tho' the Fact I saw. **b** DAY LEWIS Like a queen of fable in rose-lamped gardens. **e** C. MARLOWE Come I think hell's a fable.

2 A short story, esp. one in which animals are the characters, which conveys a moral. ME.

M. GILBERT The Aesop fable in which a lion, caught in the toils of a net, is rescued by a mouse.

†**3** Talk, discourse. *rare*. LME–L16.

4 A person who or thing which has become proverbial. *arch.* M16.

5 The plot of a play or poem. Formerly also, a play. *arch.* M17.

fable /ˈfeɪb(ə)l/ *verb*. *arch.* LME.

[ORIGIN Old French *fabler* from Latin *fabulari* talk, discourse, formed as FABLE *noun*.]

†**1** *verb intrans.* Speak, converse. *rare*. LME–L16.

†**2** *verb intrans.* **a** Tell fictitious tales. LME–E19. ▸**b** Talk idly. L16–L19.

3 *verb intrans.* Tell lies. (Foll. by *with*.) M16.

4 *verb trans.* Talk about or relate fictitiously. M16.

■ **fabled** *ppl adjective* (**a**) having no real existence; (**b**) described or celebrated in fable: E17. **fabler** *noun* LME.

fabless /ˈfablɪs/ *adjective*. *US*. L20.

[ORIGIN from *fab* (shortened from FABRICATION) + -LESS.]

Of an electronics business: having no manufacturing plant; contracting out the manufacture of components (esp. microchips) to another company.

fabliau /ˈfablɪəʊ, fɑbljo/ *noun*. Pl. **-aux** /-əʊz, -o/. E19.

[ORIGIN French from Old French (Picard) *fablia(u)x* pl. of *fablel* dim. of *fable*: see FABLE *noun*.]

A verse tale, usu. burlesque in character, from the early period of French poetry.

fabric /ˈfabrɪk/ *noun*. L15.

[ORIGIN Old French & mod. French *fabrique* from Latin *fabrica* trade, manufactured object, workshop, forge, from *faber* worker in metal, stone, etc. Cf. FORGE *noun*.]

1 A building, an edifice. *arch.* L15.

†**2** A machine, an appliance. L16–M17.

3 The construction or designing of a building, an animal's body, a vehicle, etc.; *spec.* the construction and maintenance of a church. E17.

4 A building in which work or manufacture is carried on; a factory. M17.

5 A structure; a frame; the basic structure (walls, floor, and roof) of a building. M17.

H. G. WELLS The whole fabric of social life, conduct, law, property, confidence.

6 A type of construction or formation; texture. M17.

7 A manufactured textile, (a) woven, knitted, or felted material; a similar material made of chemically bonded fibres (also ***non-woven fabric***). Formerly also, a manufactured material generally. M18.

L. DEIGHTON I will buy new fabric for the front-room curtains.

8 The substance or structural material of something, *esp.* the woven tissue or fibre of a textile. E19.

fabric /ˈfabrɪk/ *verb trans.* Infl. **-ck-**. E17.

[ORIGIN from the noun.]

Construct, fashion, frame, make (a material or abstract object). (Foll. by *up*, *out*.)

fabricable /ˈfabrɪkəb(ə)l/ *adjective*. M20.

[ORIGIN Late Latin *fabricabilis*, from Latin *fabricare*: see FABRICATE, -ABLE.]

Able to be shaped; *spec.* able to be formed into the shape required for a finished product.

■ **fabricaˈbility** *noun* M20.

fabricant /ˈfabrɪk(ə)nt/ *noun*. Now *rare*. M18.

[ORIGIN French, pres. pple of Old French & mod. French *fabriquer* from Latin *fabricare*: see FABRICATE, -ANT[1].]

A maker, a manufacturer.

fabricate /ˈfabrɪkeɪt/ *verb trans.* LME.

[ORIGIN Latin *fabricat-* pa. ppl stem of *fabricari*, *-are*, from *fabrica*: see FABRIC *noun*, -ATE[3].]

1 Make with skill; manufacture; construct (something material or abstract). LME. ▸**b** Form into the shape required for a finished product. E20.

2 Invent (a lie, dishonest story, etc.); forge (a document). L18.

■ **fabricative** *adjective* L18.

fabrication /fabrɪˈkeɪʃ(ə)n/ *noun*. L15.

[ORIGIN from Latin *fabricatio(n-)*, formed as FABRICATE: see -ATION.]

1 The action or process of manufacturing or constructing something; a structure. L15.

2 The action of inventing a lie, dishonest story, etc., or of forging a document; a false statement, an invention, a forgery. L18.

T. WRIGHT The common account of his death is a mere fabrication.

fabricator /ˈfabrɪkeɪtə/ *noun*. E17.

[ORIGIN Latin, from *fabricare*: see FABRICATE, -OR.]

1 A person who or thing which fabricates. E17.

2 *ARCHAEOLOGY.* A rod-shaped flint implement, perh. used in the manufacture of other flint tools. L19.

Fabry–Pérot /fabrɪˈpɛrəʊ/ *noun*. E20.

[ORIGIN from C. *Fabry* (1867–1945) and A. *Pérot* (1863–1925), French physicists.]

PHYSICS. Used ***attrib.*** to designate devices invented by Fabry and Pérot.

Fabry–Pérot etalon = ETALON. **Fabry–Pérot interferometer** an interferometer incorporating an etalon.

fabular /ˈfabjʊlə/ *adjective*. L17.

[ORIGIN Latin *fabularis*, from *fabula* FABLE *noun*: see -AR[1].]

Pertaining to or of the nature of a fable; fabulous.

fabulate /ˈfabjʊleɪt/ *verb*. E17.

[ORIGIN Latin *fabulat-* pa. ppl stem of *fabulari*: see FABLE *verb*, -ATE[3].]

†**1** *verb intrans.* Narrate in fables. Only in E17.

†**2** *verb trans.* Relate as a fable or myth. Only in E17.

3 *verb trans.* Invent, fabricate. M19.

■ **fabuˈlation** *noun* M18. **fabulator** *noun* L15.

fabulist /ˈfabjʊlɪst/ *noun*. L16.

[ORIGIN French *fabuliste*, from Latin *fabula* FABLE *noun*: see -IST.]

1 A person who relates or composes fables or legends. L16. ▸†**b** A professional storyteller. Only in 17.

2 A person who invents dishonest stories; a liar. E17.

†**fabulize** *verb*. E17.

[ORIGIN from Latin *fabula* FABLE *noun* + -IZE.]

1 *verb intrans.* Invent fables. E17–E19.

2 *verb trans.* Concoct, invent; relate as legend *that*; make into a fable. M17–E19.

fabulosity /fabjʊˈlɒsɪti/ *noun*. E17.

[ORIGIN Latin *fabulositas*, from *fabulosus*: see FABULOUS, -ITY.]

1 The quality of being fabulous; fictitiousness, mythical character. E17.

†**2** A fabulous thing, a fable. E17–E19.

fabulous /ˈfabjʊləs/ *adjective*. LME.

[ORIGIN from French *fabuleux* or Latin *fabulosus*, from *fabula* FABLE *noun*: see -ULOUS.]

1 Of the nature of a fable; full of fables; unhistorical; known only or chiefly through fable. LME.

2 Given to relating fables. Now *rare*. M16. ▸†**b** Fond of listening to fables. L16–M17.

3 **a** Resembling a fable, absurd. *rare*. M16. ▸**b** Like things found only in fable; astonishing. E17. ▸**c** Excellent, marvellous, terrific. *colloq*. M20.

c ALAN ROSS Trueman puffed at a cigarette and said he felt fabulous.

4 Of alleged existences or facts: belonging to fable, legendary. L16. ▸†**b** Of a doctrine or notion: based on or arising in fable. E17–L18.

H. ADAMS On all the old churches you can see 'bestiaries' . . of fabulous animals, symbolic or not.

5 Celebrated in fable. E17.

■ **fabulously** *adverb* L16. **fabulousness** *noun* L16.

faburden /faˈbɜːd(ə)n/ *noun*. *obsolete* exc. *hist.* LME.

[ORIGIN Perh. from French *faux-bourdon* lit. 'false hum', assim. to FAH, BURDEN *noun*.]

1 A type of improvised polyphony, popular in England from the 15th cent. to the Reformation. LME.

2 The refrain or chorus of a song. L16.

facade /fəˈsɑːd/ *noun*. Also **façade**. **M17**.
[**ORIGIN** French *façade*, formed as FACE *noun*, after Italian *facciata*: see -ADE.]

1 The face or front of a building, *esp.* the principal front, looking on to a street or open space. **M17**.

R. MACAULAY The south façade has rounded arched windows and moulding and carving. JO GRIMOND One wing was a façade of gothic windows with nothing behind them.

2 An outward appearance or front, *esp.* one which is deceptive. **L19**.

Health Now Tormented individuals hiding behind a cheerful facade.

■ **facadism** *noun* (*a*) a style or practice in architecture which lays emphasis on the design and elegance of the facades of buildings; (*b*) the practice of preserving the facade of a building whose interior has been destroyed: **M19**. **facadist** *noun* a person who practices facadism **L20**.

face /feɪs/ *noun*. **ME**.
[**ORIGIN** Old French & mod. French from Proto-Romance alt. of Latin *facies* form, appearance, visage, aspect, prob. rel. to *fax* torch.]

▸ **I** The front of the head.

1 The front part of the head, from the forehead to the chin; the visage, the countenance; the corresponding part of the head of an animal, insect, or other creature. **ME**. ▸**b** A representation of a human countenance. **L15**. ▸**c** (A form of address to) a person, esp. one admired or despised to some degree. *slang*. **E20**.

E. BAKER Norma could see the criminal's face clearly, both full-front and in profile.

2 The countenance as a means of expressing feelings, character, etc.; what is shown by one's expression; a grimace. **ME**. ▸**b** Command of facial expression; composure, coolness, effrontery. **M16**.

N. MOSLEY She made a face as if there was something bitter on her tongue. **b** LONGFELLOW I wonder that any man has the face To call such a hole the House of the Lord.

3 Sight, presence. Chiefly in phrs. below. **ME**.

4 The front part of the head, as the part presented in encounters and confrontations; confrontation, opposition. **LME**.

5 The countenance with regard to beauty. **L16**. ▸**b** Make-up, cosmetics. *colloq.* **E20**.

▸ **II** The visible part or surface of a thing.

6 The surface or one of the surfaces of anything. **ME**. ▸†**b** ASTROLOGY. One third of a sign of the zodiac, extending over 10 degrees in longitude. **LME–E19**. ▸**c** An even or polished surface. **L19**.

7 Either side of a coin or medal, *esp.* the side bearing the effigy. Formerly also (*slang*), a coin. **E16**.

fig.: R. HOGGART The other side of the coin which has 'sincerity' on its face.

8 *gen.* The outer or upper side of a two-sided object; the front as opp. to the back. **E17**. ▸**b** The inscribed side of a document etc. **M17**. ▸**c** The marked or picture side of a playing card. **M17**.

G. R. PORTER Diagonal lines . . across the face of the cloth. E. BECKETT The face of a wheel which turns in a gear.

9 a ARCHITECTURE. The facade of a building; the exposed surface of a stone in a wall; the front of an arch. **E17**. ▸**b** *gen.* The principal side, often vertical or steeply sloping, presented by an object; *spec.* the front of a cliff, a geological fault, etc. **M17**. ▸**c** An open slope or hillside. *NZ*. **M19**.

b O. MANNING The snow was . . sliding wetly down from the rock faces above the houses.

10 Each of the surfaces of a solid. **E17**.

F. HOYLE A uniform cube . . resting on one of its faces on the ground.

11 The dial-plate of a clock or a watch. **L17**.

R. DAVIES The big clock's pallid face . . said it was a quarter to midnight.

12 The acting, striking, or working surface of an implement, tool, etc.; the striking surface of a golf club, cricket bat, hockey stick, etc. **E18**.

▸ **III** Outward appearance.

13 External appearance, look; semblance *of*. Now chiefly of abstract objects. **LME**.

J. BRYCE The problems of the world . . are always putting on new faces.

14 Outward show; disguise, pretence; a pretext. **LME**.

15 Visible state or condition; aspect. **L16**. ▸**b** The physical conformation of a country. **L17**.

▸ **IV** *techn.* **16** FORTIFICATION. The outer surface of a wall, esp. of one of the curtain walls of a bastion. **L15**. ▸**b** Either of two walls in a bastion which form a salient angle. **L17**.

17 TYPOGRAPHY. The printing surface of type or of a punch; a particular style of type. **L17**.
boldface, ***fat-face***, ***old-face***, etc.

18 MINING. The end of a tunnel, stope, etc., at which work is progressing; the principal surface from which coal is being removed. **E18**.

B. T. WASHINGTON It was . . a mile from the opening of the coal-mine to the face of the coal.

19 MILITARY. Each of the sides of a battalion when it is formed into a square. **M19**.

▸ **V** from the verb.

20 ICE HOCKEY & LACROSSE. More fully ***face-off***. The act of facing off (see FACE *verb* 8). **L19**.

– PHRASES: **before the face of** in the sight of. ***black in the face***: see BLACK *adjective*. ***blue in the face***: see BLUE *adjective* 1b. **do one's face** *colloq.* apply make-up to one's face. **face down**, **face downwards** having the face or front directed downwards. **face to face** looking one another in the face; directly; clearly. **face to faceness** directness, clearness. **face to face with** confronting. **face up**, **face upwards** having the face or front directed upwards. ***fling in a person's face***: see FLING *verb*. **fly in the face of** openly oppose or disobey. †**from face to foot** *rare* (Shakes.) from head to toe. ***grind the faces of***: see GRIND *verb*. ***have a face as long as a fiddle***: see FIDDLE *noun*. **have the face** be shameless enough. ***hide one's face***: see HIDE *verb*[1]. **in face of** = *in the face of* (a) below. **in one's face** directly at one, straight against one. **in the face of** (*a*) in front of; when confronted with; in spite of; (*b*) in the presence of. **in your face** (*a*) used as a derisive insult; (*b*) ***in-your-face*** *adjective*, blatantly aggressive or provocative; impossible to ignore or avoid. ***laugh in a person's face***: see LAUGH *verb*. ***laugh on the other side of one's face***, ***laugh on the wrong side of one's face***: see LAUGH *verb*. ***long face***: see LONG *adjective*[1]. **look a person in the face** confront a person with a steady gaze, implying courage, defiance, etc. **lose face** [translating Chinese *diū liǎn*] be humiliated, lose one's good name or reputation. **loss of face** humiliation, loss of reputation. **make a face** = *pull a face* below. **off one's face** *colloq.* drunk or under the influence of illegal drugs. **on the face of** in the words of. **on the face of it** *fig.* obviously, plainly; superficially, apparently. **open one's face** *US slang* speak. ***pull a face***: see PULL *verb*. **put a good face on**, **put a bold face on**, etc., make (a matter) look well, face with courage. **put a new face on** alter the aspect of. **put one's face on** *colloq.* apply make-up to one's face. **save face**, **save one's face** avoid public humiliation, save one's reputation. **set one's face against** steadfastly oppose. ***set one's face like a flint***: see FLINT *noun* & *adjective*. **set one's face to**, **set one's face towards** look or aim towards. ***show one's face***: see SHOW *verb*. **shut one's face** *slang* be quiet, stop talking. ***SUNDAY face***. **the acceptable face of** the tolerable or attractive manifestation or aspect of. **the face of the earth** the surface of the earth; anywhere. **the unacceptable face of** the intolerable or unattractive manifestation or aspect of. ***three faces under a hood***, ***three faces in a hood***: see THREE *adjective*. **to one's face** openly in one's sight or hearing; boldly, directly. ***turn one's face to the wall***: see WALL *noun*[1]. ***wash its face***: see WASH *verb*. ***wipe the — off a person's face***, ***wipe the — off one's face***: see WIPE *verb*.

– COMB.: **faceache** (*a*) neuralgia; (*b*) *slang* a mournful-looking person; **face-bone** the cheekbone; **face-brick** *US* a facing brick; **face card** = *court card* s.v. COURT *noun*[1]; **face-centred** *adjective* (of a crystal structure) in which an atom or ion occurs at each vertex and at the centre of each face of the unit cell; **facecloth** (*a*) a cloth for laying over and protecting the face; (*b*) a woollen fabric with a smooth surface; (*c*) a cloth for washing the face; **face cream** cream applied to the face to improve the complexion; **face flannel** = *facecloth* (c) above; **face-fungus** *colloq.* a man's facial hair, a beard; **face-glass** the glass window of a diver's helmet; **face guard** a mask for protecting the face; **facelift** the operation of facelifting; an improvement in appearance; **facelifting** (*a*) an operation to remove wrinkles by tightening the skin of the face; (*b*) *fig.* the refacing or redecoration of a building; **facemask** a mask covering the nose and mouth or the nose and eyes; ***face-off***: see sense 20 above; **facepack** a preparation designed to help the complexion, spread on the face and removed when dry; **face-painter** (*a*) a painter of portraits; (*b*) one who applies paint to the face; **face-painting** portrait painting; **face-piece** (*a*) a part of the rudder of a ship; (*b*) a diver's face-glass; (*c*) a facemask; **faceplate** (*a*) an enlarged end or attachment on the mandrel of a lathe, on which work can be mounted; (*b*) a plate protecting a piece of machinery; (*c*) a diver's face-glass; **face-play** facial movement in acting etc.; **face powder** a cosmetic powder for reducing the shine on the face; **face-saver** a thing or event that saves one's face or saves one from humiliation; **face-saving** *noun* & *adjective* preserving one's reputation, credibility, etc.; **face-symbol** CRYSTALLOGRAPHY a symbol designating the face or plane of a crystal; **face time** *N. Amer. colloq.* (*a*) time spent in face-to-face contact with someone, esp. one's employer; (*b*) time spent being filmed or photographed by the media; **face value** the nominal value as stated on a coin, note, etc.; apparent value or nature, esp. as opp. to actual value; **faceworker** a miner who works at the coalface.

face /feɪs/ *verb*. **LME**.
[**ORIGIN** from the noun.]

▸ **I** Confront, look at or towards.

1 *verb intrans.* Show a bold face; brag, swagger. *obsolete* exc. *dial.* **LME**. ▸†**b** Be false. Only in **L16**.

2 †**a** *verb trans.* Confront with assurance or impudence; bully. **LME–M17**. ▸**b** *verb trans.* Meet face to face; confront or oppose bravely or with confidence. **M17**. ▸**c** *verb trans.* & *intrans.* foll. by *up to*. Consider seriously (an idea, a fact, etc.); accept the inevitability, irrevocability of. **L18**.

b LYNDON B. JOHNSON India faced an important governmental crisis early in 1966. **c** M. L. KING My fears began to go . . . I was ready to face anything.

a face out of exclude shamelessly from; bully out of. **b face down** overcome (a person) by a show of determination or by browbeating. **face out** see (something) through with effrontery or impudence. **face the music** accept resolutely difficult or unpleasant consequences. **c face the facts** not shrink from or confront the truth, esp. when unwelcome. **let's face it** we must recognize an unwelcome fact.

3 *verb intrans.* **a** Look in a certain direction. (Foll. by *to*, *towards*.) **L16**. ▸**b** Be situated with the face or front in a specified direction. (Foll. by *on*, *to*.) **L18**.

a J. DICKEY I faced ahead . . and watched the rest of the light come.

4 *verb trans.* Look towards; be situated opposite to, front towards. **M17**. ▸**b** Of an engraving, illustration, etc.: stand on the opposite page to. **M18**.

H. JAMES He was one of the men who fully face you when they talk of themselves. S. GIBBONS The cowsheds faced the house.

5 *verb intrans.* Chiefly MILITARY. Turn around so as to be looking in a specified direction. Also foll. by *about*, *round*. **M17**.

F. A. GRIFFITHS Right or left about three-quarters face.

6 *verb trans.* †**a** Direct the looks of. Only in **M17**. ▸**b** MILITARY. Cause (soldiers) to turn and front in a certain direction. **M19**.

7 *verb trans.* Turn (a playing card etc.) face up. **L17**.

8 *verb intrans.* ICE HOCKEY & LACROSSE. Start or restart play by dropping the puck, or ball, between the sticks of two opposing players. Also foll. by *off*. **M19**. ▸**b** *verb trans.* Place (the puck or ball) in this way to start or restart play. Also foll. by *off*. **M19**.

▸ **II** Put a face or facing on.

9 *verb trans.* Provide (a garment) with facings. **M16**. ▸†**b** Trim, deck, adorn. **M16–L17**.

R. GRAVES His uniform was now the green tunic faced with red.

10 *verb trans.* Cover (a surface) with a layer of another material. **L17**.

A. GRAY The tenements were faced with grey stone instead of red.

11 *verb trans.* Smooth the face or surface of. Also foll. by *down*, *up*. **M19**.

12 *verb trans.* Coat (tea) with some colouring substance. Also foll. by *up*. **M19**.

faced /feɪst/ *adjective*. **E16**.
[**ORIGIN** from FACE *noun* + -ED[2].]
Having a face or expression of a specified kind; having a surface of a specified kind. Chiefly as 2nd elem. of comb., as ***fresh-faced*** etc.

faceless /ˈfeɪslɪs/ *adjective*. **M16**.
[**ORIGIN** from FACE *noun* + -LESS.]

†**1** Lacking face or courage; cowardly. **M–L16**.

2 Without a face; without identity; anonymous, characterless. **M19**.

C. THUBRON One of those faceless apartment blocks. S. MIDDLETON He had been faceless, a powerful name at the bottom of official orders.

■ **facelessly** *adverb* **L20**. **facelessness** *noun* **M20**.

facer /ˈfeɪsə/ *noun*. **E16**.
[**ORIGIN** from FACE *noun*, *verb* + -ER[1].]

†**1** A person who shows a bold face; a braggart, a bully. **E16–E17**.

2 A large cup or tankard, *esp.* one filled to the brim. *slang*. Now *rare* or *obsolete*. **E16**.

3 A blow in the face; a head-on blow. **E19**. ▸**b** *fig.* A great and sudden difficulty; a setback. **E19**.

facet /ˈfasɪt, -ɛt/ *noun* & *verb*. **E17**.
[**ORIGIN** French *facette* dim. of *face* FACE *noun*: see -ET[1].]

▸ **A** *noun*. **1** One side of a many-sided body, esp. when flat and smooth; *spec.* any of the cut and polished faces of a gem. **E17**. ▸**b** *fig.* A particular side or aspect of something. **E19**.

H. ADAMS The facets of the hexagon . . are more pleasing than the rounded surfaces of the cone. R. DAHL The different shades of green on the planes and facets of each clipped tree. **b** P. GALLICO An expert at every facet of the game. E. ROOSEVELT Certain sides of Franklin's character or particular facets of his personality.

2 ZOOLOGY. Any of the segments of a compound eye. **M19**.

▸ **B** *verb trans.* Cut or form facets upon. **L19**.

■ **faceted** *adjective* having facets; of a form which has many faces or aspects: **M19**. **faceting** *verbal noun* the action or process of cutting or forming facets **L19**.

facete /fəˈsiːt/ *adjective*. *arch.* **E17**.
[**ORIGIN** Latin *facetus* graceful, pleasant, witty.]

1 = FACETIOUS. **E17**.

†**2** Elegant, graceful, polished. Only in **M17**.

facetiae /fəˈsiːʃɪiː/ *noun pl.* **E16**.
[**ORIGIN** Latin *facetiae* pl. of *facetia* jest, from *facetus*: see FACETE.]

1 Pleasantries, witticisms. **E16**.

2 BOOKSELLING. Pornography. **M19**.

facetious /fəˈsiːʃəs/ *adjective*. **L16**.
[**ORIGIN** French *facétieux*, from *facétie* from Latin *facetia*: see FACETIAE, -OUS.]

†**1** Of manners etc.: polished, urbane. Only in **L16**.

2 Given to or characterized by pleasantry or joking, now esp. where inappropriate or trivializing; witty, humorous, amusing. **L16**.

J. CHEEVER The first was a facetious essay, attacking the modern toilet seat.

■ **facetiously** *adverb* **E18**. **facetiousness** *noun* **M16**.

F

facety /ˈfeɪsti/ *adjective. W. Indian.* **E20.**
[ORIGIN Prob. from FACY, perh. infl. by FEISTY.]
Rude, arrogant, excessively bold.

Fach /fax/ *noun.* Also ***f-***. **M19.**
[ORIGIN German = compartment, division, shelf.]
A line of work or business; a department of activity; ***métier***.

facia /ˈfeɪʃə/ *noun.* **M18.**
[ORIGIN Var. of FASCIA.]
1 = FASCIA 1. *rare.* **M18.**
2 = FASCIA 5. **L19.**
3 = FASCIA 6. **E20.**

facial /ˈfeɪʃ(ə)l/ *adjective & noun.* **E17.**
[ORIGIN medieval Latin *facialis*, from Latin *facies*: see FACE *noun*, -AL[1].]
▸ **A** *adjective.* †**1** *THEOLOGY.* Of vision etc.: face to face; open. **E17–E18.**
2 Of or pertaining to the face. **E19.**

A. N. WILSON Hugh was making a number of agonized facial gestures to Jen.

facial angle the angle formed by two lines, one running from the nostril to the ear and the other from the nostril to the forehead. **facial nerve** either of the seventh pair of cranial nerves, supplying the facial muscles and the tongue. ***facial sauna***: see SAUNA *noun*.
3 Of or belonging to the visible part or surface of something. **M19.**
▸ **B** *noun.* †**1** The facial angle. *rare.* Only in **E19.**
2 A beauty treatment for the face. **E20.**
■ **facially** *adverb* **M17.**

facialist *noun.* **L19.**
[ORIGIN from FACIAL + -IST.]
1 An actor, impersonator, etc. whose performance is noted for his or her exaggerated or humorous facial expressions. *US.* Now *rare.* **L19.**
2 A person who gives facials and other beauty treatments for the face. **E20.**

faciation /feɪsɪˈeɪʃ(ə)n/ *noun.* **E20.**
[ORIGIN from Latin *facies* (see FACE *noun*) + -ATION.]
ECOLOGY. A community containing more than one of the dominant species in an association.

faciendum /fakɪˈɛndəm, feɪʃɪ-/ *noun.* Pl. ***-da*** /-də/. **M19.**
[ORIGIN Latin = thing to be done, neut. gerundive of *facere* make, do.]
PHILOSOPHY. A thing that should be done.

facient /ˈfeɪʃ(ə)nt/ *noun. rare.* **M17.**
[ORIGIN Latin *facient-*: see -FACIENT.]
A person who does something; a doer.

-facient /ˈfeɪʃ(ə)nt/ *suffix.*
[ORIGIN Repr. Latin *facient-* making, pres. ppl stem of *facere* do, make.]
Forming adjectives and nouns with the sense '(substance etc.) producing an action or state' as ***abortefacient***, ***calefacient***, ***rubefacient***.

facies /ˈfeɪʃɪiːz/ *noun.* Pl. same. **E17.**
[ORIGIN Latin: see FACE *noun*.]
1 †**a** *joc.* The face. Only in **E17.** ▸**b** *MEDICINE.* The appearance or expression of the face, esp. when characteristic of a particular disease. **L19.**
2 *SCIENCE.* General aspect or appearance. **E18.** ▸**b** *spec. GEOLOGY.* The character of a rock formation as displayed by its composition, texture, fossil content, etc.; a formation or body presenting a unified set of properties. **M19.** ▸**c** *ECOLOGY.* The characteristic set of dominant species in a habitat. **E20.**

facile /ˈfasʌɪl, -sɪl/ *adjective.* **L15.**
[ORIGIN French, or Latin *facilis*, from *facere* do, make: see -ILE.]
1 a Easily done or won (esp. in a contemptible way); presenting few difficulties. **L15.** ▸†**b** Easy to use or understand. **M16–L18.** ▸**c** Superficial, without depth. **E20.**

a W. BEVERIDGE All other acts of piety will be facile and easy to him. **c** ALDOUS HUXLEY His models offered him facile consolations. J. UPDIKE The oracle spoke a great deal of facile, impudent, and traitorous nonsense.

2 Easily led; flexible, compliant, yielding; weak-minded. *arch.* exc. *SCOTS LAW.* **E16.**
3 Not harsh or severe; affable, courteous, relaxed. **L16.**
4 Working easily or freely; fluent, ready. **E17.**

D. HALBERSTAM The rewrite man turned reporter, very facile, very quick, a story banged out in ten minutes.

■ **facilely** *adverb* **L15.** **facileness** *noun* (now *rare*) **M16.**

facile princeps /ˌfasɪlɪ ˈprɪnsɛps/ *adjectival & noun phr.* **M19.**
[ORIGIN Latin.]
(A person who is) easily first; the acknowledged leader or chief.

facilitate /fəˈsɪlɪteɪt/ *verb trans.* **E17.**
[ORIGIN French *faciliter* from Italian *facilitare* from *facile* (from Latin *facilis*: see FACILE), after Latin *debilitare* DEBILITATE, etc.]
1 Make easy or easier; promote, help forward (an action, result, etc.). **E17.**

D. BAGLEY The revolving door had been taken away to facilitate passage in and out of the hotel. A. STORR They often used hypnosis to facilitate recall.

2 Lessen the labour of, assist (a person). Now *rare.* **M17.**
3 *PHYSIOLOGY.* Increase the likelihood of, strengthen (a response); bring about the transmission of (an impulse). **E20.**
■ **facilitative** *adjective* tending to facilitate something **M19.** **facilitator** *noun* a person who or thing which facilitates something **E19.**

facilitation /fəsɪlɪˈteɪʃ(ə)n/ *noun.* **E17.**
[ORIGIN formed as FACILITATE + -ATION.]
1 The action or an act of facilitating something. **E17.** ▸**b** A means of facilitating something, a help. Now *rare.* **M17.**
2 *PHYSIOLOGY.* The increased excitability of a neuron beyond a stimulated ganglion or synapse, resulting in an increased response to a stimulus. **L19.**

facilitatory /fəˈsɪlɪtət(ə)ri/ *adjective.* **M20.**
[ORIGIN from FACILITATE + -ORY[2].]
Of, pertaining to, or involved in facilitation; intended to facilitate.

facility /fəˈsɪlɪti/ *noun.* **LME.**
[ORIGIN French *facilité* or Latin *facilitas*, from *facilis*: see FACILE, -ITY.]
†**1** Gentleness, lightness. Only in **LME.**
2 a Unimpeded opportunity. Now also, an amenity or service which enables something to be done. **E16.** ▸**b** In *pl.* Favourable conditions for the easy or easier performance of something, *esp.* the physical means or equipment required in order to do something. **E19.**

a *Guardian* The bank should . . consider extending this survival facility to students' parents. *Times Educ. Suppl.* An edit facility so that the pupils can . . correct their work if they wish.
b C. FRANCIS Calcutta had few facilities . . no wharves, pontoons or landing stages. W. TREVOR There were full toilet and washing facilities.

3 The fact or condition of being easy or easily done; freedom from difficulty. **M16.**

BURKE The facility with which government has been overturned in France.

4 Aptitude, dexterity; ease or readiness of speech, action, etc. **M16.** ▸**b** Fluency of style. **L16.**

N. WEST The pleasures he received . . had decreased as his facility had increased.

†**5** Courtesy, affability. **M16–L18.**
6 Pliancy, readiness to be led or persuaded. *arch.* exc. *SCOTS LAW.* **M16.**
7 Ease, indolence. Now *rare* or *obsolete.* **E17.**

facing /ˈfeɪsɪŋ/ *noun.* **LME.**
[ORIGIN from FACE *verb* + -ING[1].]
1 The action of FACE *verb*. Also foll. by *about*, *off*, etc. **LME.**
2 Material covering part of a garment for contrast or strength; in *pl.*, the contrasting cuffs, collar, etc., of a military or military-style jacket. **M16.**

S. RICHARDSON I made robings and facings of a pretty bit of printed calico.

3 A superficial coating; the material of such a coating; *spec.* the outer layer of stone or brick which forms the face of a building, wall, bank, etc. **L16.**
– COMB.: **facing brick** a brick used in the outer wall of a building.

facinorous /fəˈsɪn(ə)rəs/ *adjective. arch.* **M16.**
[ORIGIN from Latin *facinorosus*, from *facinus*, *facinor-* (bad) deed, from *facere* do, make: see -OUS.]
Extremely wicked.
■ †**facinorious** *adjective* = FACINOROUS **E–M17.** **facinorousness** *noun* **E18.**

facio- /ˈfeɪʃɪəʊ/ *combining form* of Latin FACIES face: see -O-.
■ **facioˈplegic** *adjective* pertaining to paralysis of the face **E20.** **ˌfacioˌscapulo-ˈhumeral** *adjective* pertaining to the face, scapula, and arm **E20.**

fack *noun* see FACT.

façon de parler /fasɔ̃ də parle/ *noun phr.* Pl. ***façons de parler*** (pronounced same). **E19.**
[ORIGIN French.]
A way or manner of speaking; a mere phrase or formula.

façonné /fasɔne/ *adjective & noun.* Pl. of noun pronounced same. **L19.**
[ORIGIN French, pa. ppl adjective of *façonner* fashion.]
(Designating) a material into which a design has been woven.

façons de parler *noun phr.* pl. of FAÇON DE PARLER.

facsimile /fakˈsɪmɪli/ *noun, adjective, & verb.* Orig. †**fac simile**. **L16.**
[ORIGIN mod. Latin, from Latin *fac* imper. of *facere* do, make + *simile* neut. of *similis* SIMILAR.]
▸ **A** *noun.* †**1** The making of an exact copy, esp. of writing; imitation. **L16–M17.**
2 An exact copy, esp. of writing, printing, a picture, etc.; a reproduction. **L17.**

J. BRAINE My wife and I aren't exact facsimiles of that couple . . but we belong to the same world. B. MOORE A facsimile of an old chapter-house record book . . its original now destroyed.

in facsimile so as to be an exact reproduction.
3 *spec.* A system for producing a copy by radio etc. transmission of signals from scanning an original. **L19.**
– COMB.: **facsimile telegraphy** the transmission of copies of documents etc. by means of radio signals from which copies can be made using suitable receiving equipment.
▸ **B** *attrib.* or as *adjective.* That is a facsimile; exactly copied or like. **M18.**

F. H. A. SCRIVENER Elaborate facsimile editions of the chief codices.

▸ **C** *verb trans. & intrans.* Pres. pple & verbal noun **-leing**. Make or be a facsimile (of). **M19.**
■ **facsimilize** *verb trans.* (*rare*) reproduce exactly, make a facsimile of **E19.**

fact /fakt/ *noun.* Also (repr. dial. pronunc., now *US*) **fack** /fak/. **L15.**
[ORIGIN Latin *factum* use as noun of neut. pa. pple of *facere* do, make.]
1 †**a** (An) action, a deed; *esp.* a noble or brave action, an exploit, a feat. **L15–E19.** ▸**b** An evil or wrongful action; a crime. Now only in ***before the fact***, ***after the fact***, ***confess the fact***. **M16.**

a MILTON He who most excels in fact of Arms. J. AUSTEN Gracious in fact if not in word. **b** W. HARRISON He is . . hanged . . neere the place where the fact was committed. I. BANKS Will I agree to be an accomplice after the fact?

†**2** The act of making, doing, or performing. Chiefly in ***in the fact***, ***in the very fact***. **M16–E19.**

W. IRVING She was detected . . in the very fact of laughing.

3 Truth; reality. **L16.**

B. JOWETT Imagination is often at war with reason and fact.

4 A thing known for certain to have occurred or to be true; a datum of experience. **M17.**

E. M. FORSTER The facts are that she has been in England for three days and will not see us. C. ISHERWOOD You keep ignoring the fact that I *have* been back there.

5 A thing assumed or alleged as a basis for inference. **E18.**

OED The writer's facts are far from trustworthy.

6 *LAW. collect. sing.* & in *pl.* Events or circumstances as distinct from their legal interpretation. **E18.**

J. M. LELY A jury . . decides all the issues of fact.

– PHRASES: ***a matter of fact***: see MATTER *noun*. **as a matter of fact** actually. ***brute fact***: see BRUTE *adjective*. **fact of life** a thing (esp. unpleasant) the existence of which cannot be ignored. **facts and figures** precise information. **hard fact** inescapable truth. **in fact**, **in point of fact** in reality; (in summarizing) in short. ***issue of fact***: see ISSUE *noun*. ***Theatre of Fact***: see THEATRE *noun*. **the fact of the matter** the truth. **the facts of life** *colloq., euphem.* details of the human sexual functions.
– COMB.: **factfinder** a person engaged in fact-finding; **fact-finding** *noun & adjective* (**a**) *noun* the finding out of facts, the discovery and establishment of the facts of an issue; (**b**) *adjective* engaged in finding out facts; (esp. of a committee etc.) set up to discover and establish the facts of an issue; **fact sheet** a paper on which facts relevant to an issue are set out briefly.
■ **factful** *adjective* (*rare*) **L19.**

facta *noun pl.* see FACTUM.

factice /ˈfaktɪs/ *noun.* Also †**-is**. **L19.**
[ORIGIN German *Factis*, *Faktis*, from Latin *facticius* artificial, from *facere* make.]
A substance resembling rubber made by vulcanizing unsaturated vegetable oils and used chiefly as a compounding ingredient in rubber.

facticity /fakˈtɪsɪti/ *noun.* **M20.**
[ORIGIN from FACT + -ICITY.]
The quality or condition of being a fact; factuality.

faction /ˈfakʃ(ə)n/ *noun*[1]. **L15.**
[ORIGIN Old French & mod. French from Latin *factio(n-)*, from *fact-* pa. ppl stem of *facere* do, make: see -ION.]
†**1 a** The action of doing or making something; an instance of this. **L15–L17.** ▸**b** A way of behaving or acting. **M16–E17.**
2 A group or class of people; *spec.* a (self-interested or turbulent) party, esp. in politics. **E16.** ▸**b** *ROMAN HISTORY.* Any of the companies involved in chariot races in the circus. **E17.**

D. LODGE The membership quickly split into two factions, one . . respectful and conciliatory, the other determined to be bold.

3 Self-interested or turbulent party strife or intrigue; dissension; the prevalence of a partisan spirit. **M16.** ▸†**b** A quarrel. **L16–M17.**

W. S. CHURCHILL The religious passions of former years now flowed into the channels of political faction.

■ **factionary** *noun & adjective* (a) partisan **M16.** **factioˈneer** *noun & verb* (now *rare*) (**a**) *noun* = FACTIONIST; (**b**) *verb intrans.* promote faction or a faction: **E18.** **factionist** *noun* a promoter or member of a faction; a partisan: **E17.**

faction /ˈfakʃ(ə)n/ *noun*[2]. **M20.**
[ORIGIN Blend of FACT and FICTION *noun*.]
Fiction based on real events or characters, documentary fiction; an example of this.

-faction /fakʃ(ə)n/ *suffix*.
[ORIGIN Repr. Latin *-factio(n-)*: see FACTION *noun*[1].]
In and forming nouns of action related to verbs in **-FY**, as (*-fy* repr. Latin *facere*, French *faire*) ***satisfaction*** etc., (*-fy* repr. Latin *-ficare*, French *-fier*) ***petrifaction*** etc.

factional /ˈfakʃ(ə)n(ə)l/ *adjective*. M17.
[ORIGIN from FACTION *noun*[1] + -AL[1].]
Of or pertaining to a faction or factions; characterized by faction.

J. MASSON I was too . . junior . . to be involved in any psychoanalytic factional politics.

■ **factionalism** *noun* a state characterized by faction; tendency to factional differences; the factional spirit: E20. **factionalist** *adjective* of or pertaining to factionalism, factional M20. **factionalize** *verb trans. & intrans.* divide into factions, (cause to) become factional L20. **factionally** *adverb* L19.

factious /ˈfakʃəs/ *adjective*. M16.
[ORIGIN French *factieux* or Latin *factiosus*, from *factio(n-)*: see FACTION *noun*[1], -OUS.]
Characterized by or pertaining to faction or a faction.
■ **factiously** *adverb* (now *rare*) L16. **factiousness** *noun* L16.

†**factis** *noun* var. of FACTICE.

factitious /fakˈtɪʃəs/ *adjective*. M17.
[ORIGIN Latin *facticius*, from *fact-*: see FACTION *noun*[1], -ITIOUS[1].]
1 Made by human skill or effort, not naturally occurring or produced. Now *rare*. M17. ▸†**b** Of soil etc.: not original to an area. L17–E19.

J. BRYANT One was a natural eminence . . The other was a factitious mound.

2 Made for a special purpose; not genuine; not natural or spontaneous, artificial. L17.

R. WEST Stage plays . . arouse in the audience factitious emotion.

■ **factitiously** *adverb* L18. **factitiousness** *noun* M17.

factitive /ˈfaktɪtɪv/ *adjective & noun*. M19.
[ORIGIN mod. Latin *factitivus*, irreg. from Latin *factitare* frequentative of *facere* do, make: see -IVE.]
GRAMMAR. ▸**A** *adjective*. Of a verb: expressing the notion of making a thing to be of a certain character (e.g. *paint* the door green). Also designating the object etc. of such a verb. M19.
▸**B** *noun*. A factitive verb. L19.

factive /ˈfaktɪv/ *adjective*. E17.
[ORIGIN medieval Latin *factivus* creative, practical, from *fact-*: see FACTION *noun*[1], -IVE.]
†**1** Tending or able to make; concerned with making. E–M17.
2 GRAMMAR. Orig., factitive. Now usu., designating or pertaining to a verb taking an assumed fact as object (e.g. English *know, regret, resent*). L19.
■ **facˈtivity** *noun* M17.

factoid /ˈfaktɔɪd/ *noun & adjective*. L20.
[ORIGIN from FACT + -OID.]
▸**A** *noun*. An assumption or speculation that is reported and repeated so often that it becomes accepted as a fact; a simulated or imagined fact. L20.
▸**B** *adjective*. That is a factoid; having the character of a factoid; containing factoids. L20.

factor /ˈfaktə/ *noun*. LME.
[ORIGIN French *facteur* or Latin *factor*, from *fact-*: see FACTION *noun*[1], -OR.]
▸**I** †**1** A doer, a maker, a performer, a perpetrator. LME–M19.

CLARENDON An avow'd Factor and Procurer of that odious Judgement.

2 **a** An agent, a deputy, a representative. Now chiefly *Scot.* LME. ▸**b** An estate manager, a land agent; a bailiff. Also, a person appointed by a court to manage property. Now *Scot.* M16.
3 COMMERCE. A person buying and selling on commission for another; esp. a mercantile agent entrusted with goods with a view to their sale. LME. ▸**b** *hist.* Any of the third class of employees of the East India Company. L17. ▸**c** A person or agency that takes over and collects debts owed to other (esp. finance) companies. E20.

W. IRVING Mahomet . . was employed by different persons as . . factor in caravan journeys to Syria.

†**4** A partisan, an adherent. E16–E18.
5 US LAW. In certain states, a garnishee. *rare*. L19.
▸**II** **6** MATH. Each of the numbers or quantities that make up a given number or expression when multiplied together. L17.

C. HUTTON For that *zy* may be positive, the signs of the two factors *z* and *y* must be alike.

7 A circumstance, fact, or influence which tends to produce a result; an element or component of something; a measured or quantifiable property. E19. ▸**b** GENETICS. A gene or other heritable agent that determines a hereditary character. E20. ▸**c** BIOCHEMISTRY. Any of a number of substances in the blood (identified by numerals) which are involved in coagulation. E20.

E. F. BENSON The serene indulgence towards the doings of others which . . is . . a factor . . that makes for peace and pleasantness. M. M. KAYE Many factors . . prevented them from becoming friends: caste, upbringing and environment.

chill factor, *X factor*, etc. ***factor of safety***: see SAFETY *noun*. ***c factor VIII***, ***factor eight*** a beta globulin the congenital deficiency of which causes haemophilia.

– COMB.: **factor analysis** (*a*) statistical calculation of the relative importance of a number of factors regarded as influencing a set of values; **factor cost** the cost of an item of goods or a service in terms of the various factors which have played a part in its production or availability, and exclusive of tax costs. **factor group** MATH. a group G/H the elements of which are the cosets in a given group G of a normal subgroup H of G; **factor theorem** MATH.: that, given a polynomial $f(x)$, if $f(a) = 0$ then $(x - a)$ is a factor of $f(x)$, and vice versa.
■ **factorage** *noun* (*a*) the action or professional service of a factor; (*b*) commission or charges paid to a factor: E17. †**factoress** *noun* a female factor E17–E18. **factorship** *noun* the office or position of a factor or agent L16.

factor /ˈfaktə/ *verb*. E17.
[ORIGIN from the noun.]
1 *verb intrans.* Act as a factor or agent. E17. ▸**b** Sell (debts) to a factor. M20.
2 *verb trans.* Deal with (goods, money, etc.) as a factor or agent. E17.
3 *verb trans.* MATH. = FACTORIZE 2. M19.
4 *verb trans.* (Foll. by *in*, *into*) introduce as a factor; (foll. by *out*) exclude from an assessment. L20.

E. E. SMITH It was a contingency she always had to factor into her plans.

■ **factorable** *adjective* (MATH.) able to be factorized; expressible as a product of factors: M20.

factorial /fakˈtɔːrɪəl/ *noun & adjective*. E19.
[ORIGIN from FACTOR *noun* + -IAL.]
▸**A** *noun*. MATH. The product of a series of factors; *spec.* the product of an integer and all lower integers (expressed by !: 4! = 4 × 3 × 2 × 1). E19.
▸**B** *adjective*. Chiefly MATH. Of or pertaining to a factor or factors. M19.
■ **factorially** *adverb* by reference to factors E20.

factorize /ˈfaktərʌɪz/ *verb*. Also **-ise**. M19.
[ORIGIN from FACTOR *noun* + -IZE.]
1 *verb trans.* US LAW. In certain states: make (a third party) a garnishee. *rare*. M19.
2 *verb trans.* MATH. Resolve into factors; express as a product of factors. M19. ▸**b** *verb intrans.* Admit of being resolved into factors. E20.
■ **factorizable** *adjective* (MATH.) E20. **factoriˈzation** *noun* the operation of resolving a quantity into factors; a product of factors: L19.

factory /ˈfakt(ə)ri/ *noun*. M16.
[ORIGIN Ult. from (the same root as) FACTOR *noun* + -Y[3], (branch III) -Y[4]. In branch II repr. Portuguese *feitoria* (= Italian *fattoria*, Spanish *factoria*, French †*factorie*, later *factorerie*); in branch III after late Latin *factorium* (recorded in sense 'oil press').]
▸**I** **1** The employment, office, or position of a factor. *Scot.* M16.
▸**II** **2** *hist.* An establishment for traders doing business in a foreign country; a merchant company's foreign trading station. L16.
▸**III** **3** A building or buildings with equipment for manufacturing; a workshop; a works. E17.
4 A prison, orig. (*Austral.*) one for females; a police station. *slang*. E19.
– COMB.: **Factory Act(s)** an Act or Acts of Parliament regulating the operation of factories in the interest of the health and safety of employees; **factory farm** a farm using intensive methods of farming (esp. of livestock) usu. in an artificial environment, organized on industrial lines; **factory farming** running a factory farm, using the method of a factory farm; **factory floor** *fig.* the workers in an industry as opp. to the management etc.; **factory ship** a ship accompanying a fishing (orig. a whaling) fleet to process the catch; a fishing ship with facilities for immediate processing of the catch; **factory trawler** a trawler with facilities for processing its catch.

factotum /fakˈtəʊtəm/ *noun*. Also †**fac totum**. M16.
[ORIGIN medieval Latin *factotum*, from Latin *fac* imper. of *facere* do, make + *totum* the whole.]
1 Orig. †***dominus factotum***, †***magister factotum*** [Latin = master], †***Johannes factotum*** [= John]. A person who does all kinds of work; a jack of all trades; a person with delegated general powers; a servant who manages all his master's affairs. M16.

D. CECIL A general factotum, at one moment his personal attendant helping him to adjust his clothes, at another his confidential secretary.

2 TYPOGRAPHY. A decorative woodblock with a space in the centre for the insertion of an initial capital letter. *obsolete* exc. *hist.* L17.

factual /ˈfaktʃʊəl/ *adjective*. M19.
[ORIGIN from FACT after ACTUAL.]
Concerned with or of the nature of fact(s); actual, real, true.

W. LIPPMANN Factual knowledge of the social order . . statistics, censuses, reports. C. MILNE Story books and factual books—or as they are more usually called, fiction and non-fiction.

■ **factually** *adverb* M19. **factualness** *noun* E20.

factualism /ˈfaktʃʊəlɪz(ə)m/ *noun*. M20.
[ORIGIN from FACTUAL + -ISM.]
PHILOSOPHY. The theory maintaining that facts are pre-eminent and fundamental.
■ **factualist** *noun & adjective* (*a*) *noun* an adherent of factualism; (*b*) *adjective* of or pertaining to factualism or factualists: M20.

factuality /faktʃʊˈalɪti/ *noun*. L19.
[ORIGIN formed as FACTUAL + -ITY.]
The state or quality of being factual; realism of representation; truth to fact.

factum /ˈfaktəm/ *noun*. Pl. **facta** /ˈfaktə/, **factums**. M18.
[ORIGIN Latin: see FACT. In sense 2 through French legal usage.]
†**1** MATH. The product of two or more factors multiplied together. M18–E19.
2 LAW. An act, a deed; a statement of fact(s). L18.

facture /ˈfaktʃə/ *noun*. LME.
[ORIGIN Old French & mod. French from Latin *factura*: see FEATURE *noun*.]
1 The manner or style of making something; construction; workmanship. Now *rare*. LME.
2 The action or process of making something; manufacture. Now *rare*. L15.
3 ART. The quality of the execution of a painting, esp. of its surface. L19.

F

facty /ˈfakti/ *adjective*. *colloq.* L19.
[ORIGIN from FACT + -Y[1].]
Full of facts; (of a person) concerned primarily with facts, deficient in emotion or imagination.

facula /ˈfakjʊlə/ *noun*. Pl. **-lae** /-liː/. E18.
[ORIGIN Latin, dim. of *fac-*, *fax* torch: see -ULE.]
ASTRONOMY. A bright spot or streak on the sun's disc.
■ **facular** *adjective* of, pertaining to, or of the nature of a facula or faculae L19. **faculous** *adjective* = FACULAR M19.

facultate /ˈfak(ə)lteɪt/ *verb trans.* *rare*. M17.
[ORIGIN medieval Latin *facultare* make possible, from Latin *facultas* FACULTY: see -ATE[3].]
Authorize, empower.

facultative /ˈfak(ə)ltətɪv/ *adjective*. E19.
[ORIGIN French *facultatif*, *-ive*, from *faculté*: see FACULTY, -ATIVE.]
1 Permissive; optional; contingent. E19. ▸**b** *attrib.* in BIOLOGY. Capable of but not restricted to a particular (specified) function, mode of life, etc. Opp. OBLIGATE *adjective* 2. L19.
2 Of or pertaining to a faculty. M19.

faculty /ˈfak(ə)lti/ *noun*. LME.
[ORIGIN Old French & mod. French *faculté* from Latin *facultas*, from *facilis* FACILE: see -TY[1].]
▸**I** **1** An ability, aptitude, or competence for a particular kind of action (sometimes natural as opp. to acquired). Formerly also, ability in general. LME. ▸†**b** A personal quality; disposition. L15–E17.

D. H. LAWRENCE He had the faculty of making order out of confusion.

2 Means, resources; possessions, property. Now *rare* exc. in ***faculty theory*** below. LME.

A. YOUNG The prices . . are beyond their faculties.

†**3** A power or capacity of a thing; an active property. L15–E18.
4 An inherent power or property of the body or an organ; a physical capability. Freq. in *pl.* L15.

S. SASSOON One man had lost that necessary faculty . . his eyesight.

5 An inherent power or property of the mind, as reason, memory, etc.; a mental capability. Freq. in *pl.* L16.

H. JAMES His faculties—his imagination, his intelligence, his affections, his senses.

▸**II** †**6** *gen.* A branch of knowledge. LME–M18.
7 A branch of learning (orig. esp. theology, law, medicine, or arts) taught and studied at a university or (now) polytechnic or college; a department of a university etc. teaching a specific branch of learning; the staff and students of such a department; (chiefly *N. Amer.*) the teaching staff of a university or college. LME.

M. ARNOLD At Bonn there is a Protestant faculty of theology.

Dean of Faculty: see DEAN *noun*[1] 6.
8 An art, a trade, an occupation, a profession. *arch.* LME.

R. NEVE A . . Soap-boyler . . and another Gentleman of the same Faculty.

9 The members of a profession regarded as one body; *spec.* (*arch.*) *the* medical profession. E16.

T. HOOD Bacon . . was once in vogue amongst the Faculty for weak digestions.

Faculty of Advocates: see ADVOCATE *noun* 1.
▸**III** **10** The power, freedom, or right of doing something, given by law or by a superior. E16. ▸**b** An authorization, a licence; *esp.* (ECCLESIASTICAL) a dispensation to perform an action or hold a position otherwise illegal. M16.

M. ARNOLD Something . . anti-social which the State had the faculty to judge and the duty to suppress. **b** *Book of Common Prayer* None shall be . . a Deacon, except he be Twenty-three year of age, unless he have a Faculty.

– COMB.: **faculty psychology**: in which certain mental faculties are seen as accountable for the phenomena of mind; **faculty theory**: that each person should contribute to public taxation according to his or her ability.
▪ **facultied** *adjective* accredited by a faculty; endowed with a faculty: M19.

facund /ˈfak(ə)nd, fəˈkʌnd/ *noun & adjective. arch.* ME.
[ORIGIN As noun from Old French *faconde* from Latin *facundia*, from *facundus*, from *fari* speak. As adjective from Old French *facond* from Latin *facundus*.]
▸ †**A** *noun.* Eloquence. ME–L15.
▸ **B** *adjective.* Eloquent. LME.
▪ **faˈcundity** *noun* eloquence M16.

facy /ˈfeɪsi/ *adjective. dial. & slang.* E17.
[ORIGIN from FACE *noun* + -Y¹.]
Impudent, cheeky.

FAD *abbreviation.*
BIOCHEMISTRY. Flavin adenine dinucleotide.

fad /fad/ *noun. colloq.* (orig. *dial.*). M19.
[ORIGIN Prob. 2nd elem. of earlier FIDFAD. Cf. earlier FADDY.]
1 An individual's peculiar notion, rule of action, or preference; a whim, a crotchet. M19.
G. K. CHESTERTON A Socialist crank with some particular fad about public parks. D. WELCH It was one of Orvil's fads that he only liked bread in the form of toast.
2 Something briefly but enthusiastically taken up, esp. by a group; a craze. M19.
M. STOTT Odd how furnishing fads change as decisively . . as styles in dress.
– COMB.: **fadmonger** a faddist.

faddish /ˈfadɪʃ/ *adjective.* M19.
[ORIGIN from FAD *noun* + -ISH¹.]
Given to fads; marked by fads.
S. BRETT Alex was that very common theatrical type, a faddish actor.
▪ **faddishly** *adverb* E20. **faddishness** *noun* L19.

faddism /ˈfadɪz(ə)m/ *noun.* L19.
[ORIGIN formed as FADDISH + -ISM.]
Tendency to follow fads.
▪ **faddist** *noun* L19.

faddle /ˈfad(ə)l/ *verb & noun. dial. & colloq.* L17.
[ORIGIN Cf. FAD, FONDLE, etc. See also FIDDLE-FADDLE.]
▸ **A** *verb.* **1** *verb trans.* Fondle (a child). L17.
2 *verb intrans.* Spend time idly or in play. M18.
▸ **B** *noun.* Nonsense, trifling. M19.

faddy /ˈfadi/ *adjective. colloq.* (orig. *dial.*). E19.
[ORIGIN Prob. formed as FAD *noun* + -Y¹.]
Of a person: fussy about trifles, full of fads; *spec.* particular in matters of food. Of a thing: pursued as a fad.
▪ **faddiness** *noun* M19.

fade /feɪd/ *noun.* ME.
[ORIGIN from the verb.]
1 The action or an act of fading or losing freshness, vitality, or colour. Long *rare* in *gen.* use. ME.
2 A disappearance from the scene; a (quick or unobtrusive) departure. Chiefly in ***do a fade, take a fade***. *US slang.* E20.
3 CINEMATOGRAPHY, TELEVISION, & BROADCASTING. (An instance of) fading a picture or sound. Also, a gradual decrease or increase in the brightness of a picture or the volume of a sound. See also FADE-IN, FADE-OUT. E20.
4 Reduction in the effectiveness of a motor vehicle's braking system. M20.
5 A ball's swerved course, deviation of a ball from a straight course, esp. in golf; a (slice) stroke or shot causing this. M20.
▪ **fadeproof** *adjective* resistant to fading; retaining colour or brightness: E20.

fade /feɪd; *in sense 3 foreign* fad/ *adjective.* ME.
[ORIGIN Old French & mod. French: see FADE *verb.*]
1 Lacking in brilliance of colour; dull, pale, wan. Long *arch.* ME.
†**2** Lacking in freshness or vitality; withered, languishing. ME–M18.
3 That has lost its taste; *fig.* insipid, uninspiring. Now only as a Gallicism. LME.

fade /feɪd/ *verb.* ME.
[ORIGIN Old French *fader*, from *fade* vapid, dull, faded, prob. from Proto-Romance source blending Latin *fatuus* FATUOUS and *vapidus* VAPID.]
▸ **I** *verb intrans.* †**1** Lose strength or vitality; grow weak, waste away. ME–L16.
2 Lose freshness; droop, wither. LME.
A. UTTLEY Roses . . bloomed . . faded, and scattered their brown leaves on the grass. *fig.*: J. BRAINE One of those . . women whose good looks fade almost overnight.
3 Lose brightness or brilliance of colour; grow dim or pale. LME.
A. J. CRONIN The light began to fade and they looked for a shelter for the night. L. DEIGHTON The once red . . flags . . had faded to a light pink in the sunlight.
4 Become indistinct, disappear gradually. Also foll. by *away*. L16.
W. IRVING I saw the last blue of my native land fade away. J. LE CARRÉ As the morning dragged on her hopes faded, and she knew he would never come. E. REVELEY Tango faded from his mind as though she had never been.
5 Disappear from the scene mysteriously or unobtrusively; *slang* depart, go. Freq. foll. by *away, out*. M19.
J. B. PRIESTLEY 'My wife,' Mr. Rathbury muttered, fading out.
6 Of (esp. broadcast) sound: decrease gradually in volume, die away (usu. foll. by *out*). Foll. by *in, up*: (of broadcast sound) increase gradually in volume from an inaudible level. L19.
E. WELTY The whole sound of the sea faded behind the windbreak.
7 Of a radio signal: fluctuate in strength as a result of varying atmospheric conditions. Chiefly as ***fading*** *verbal noun.* E20.
8 CINEMATOGRAPHY & TELEVISION. Foll. by *out, in*: (of a picture etc.) gradually disappear from, become visible on, the screen. E20.
9 Of a motor vehicle's brake: become gradually less effective. M20.
10 Of a ball: deviate from a straight course, esp. in golf in a deliberate slice. M20.
▸ **II** *verb trans.* †**11** Deprive of freshness, strength, or vigour; *spec.* taint, corrupt. LME–L18.
12 Cause to lose colour or brightness; make dull or pale. Formerly, lose the brilliance of (a colour). M16.
E. O'NEILL Dungaree trousers faded by many washings. W. BOYD The sun has faded all the bright colours to grey and blue.
13 GAMBLING. Match the bet of (another player). *N. Amer. slang.* L19.
14 CINEMATOGRAPHY & TELEVISION. Cause (a picture etc.) to fade *out* or *in*: see sense 8 above. E20.
15 BROADCASTING. Foll. by *out (down), in (up)*: reduce, increase, (sound) gradually in volume. E20.
16 Cause (a ball) to fade or deviate from a straight course, esp. in golf. M20.
▪ **fadable** *adjective* (*rare*) liable to fade (earlier in UNFADABLE) M17. **faded** *ppl adjective* that has lost freshness, vitality, or colour; no longer fresh or bright: L15. **fadeless** *adjective* not subject to fading; perpetually fresh or bright: M17.

fade-in /ˈfeɪdɪn/ *noun.* E20.
[ORIGIN from FADE *verb* + IN *adverb*.]
1 CINEMATOGRAPHY, TELEVISION, & BROADCASTING. A gradual increase in the visibility of a picture or the volume of a sound. E20.
2 THEATRICAL. A gradual brightening of the stage. M20.

Fade-Ometer /feɪdˈɒmɪtə/ *noun.* Also **Fadeometer**. E20.
[ORIGIN from FADE *noun, verb* + -OMETER.]
(Proprietary name for) a machine for testing the fastness of colours by subjecting them to an accelerated weathering process.

fade-out /ˈfeɪdaʊt/ *noun.* E20.
[ORIGIN from FADE *verb* + OUT *adverb*.]
1 A (gradual or unobtrusive) disappearance or departure; *spec.* death. Chiefly *US slang.* E20.
2 CINEMATOGRAPHY, TELEVISION, & BROADCASTING. A gradual lessening in the visibility of a picture or the volume of a sound. E20.
3 THEATRICAL. A gradual dimming of the stage. M20.
4 A temporary interruption of radio communication; fading (see FADE *verb* 7). M20.

fader /ˈfeɪdə/ *noun.* E20.
[ORIGIN from FADE *verb* + -ER¹.]
An apparatus for controlling the volume of sound in a cinema film or the signal in sound or television broadcasting.

fadge /fadʒ/ *noun*¹. *Scot. & N. English.* LME.
[ORIGIN Unknown.]
A flat thick loaf or bannock.

fadge /fadʒ/ *noun*². *dial. & techn.* L16.
[ORIGIN Unknown.]
A bundle, a load; *esp.* (*Austral. & NZ*) a small bale or part-filled sack of wool.

fadge *noun*³ var. of FODGE.

fadge /fadʒ/ *verb.* Now chiefly *dial.* L16.
[ORIGIN Unknown.]
▸ **I** *verb intrans.* †**1** Be consistent, be suitable, be suited, (foll. by *with, to*); suit, agree, (foll. by *with*). L16–M18.
T. FULLER The Study of the Law did not fadge well with him.
2 Get on, thrive; (of an event) come off; (of a person) succeed in an enterprise. *obsolete* exc. *dial.* L16.
SIR W. SCOTT I shall be impatient to hear how your matters fadge.
3 Deal with a situation; manage, cope, (†*with*). *obsolete* exc. *dial. & W. Indian.* L16.
W. COWPER We . . have none but ourselves to depend on . . . Well, we can fadge.
†**4** Consent *to do*. L16–M17.
5 Get on well, hit it off, (*with* a person). Now *arch. & dial.* E17.
MILTON They shall . . be made, spight of antipathy, to fadge together.
▸ **II** *verb trans.* **6** Put the parts of (an object) together somehow. Now only foll. by *up*. L17.

fading /ˈfeɪdɪŋ/ *ppl adjective.* LME.
[ORIGIN from FADE *verb* + -ING².]
Subject to loss of colour or brightness; that fades.
▪ **fadingly** *adverb* M17. **fadingness** *noun* M17.

fado /ˈfaːdu, ˈfɑːdəʊ/ *noun.* Pl. **-os** /-uʃ, -əʊz/. E20.
[ORIGIN Portuguese, lit. 'fate'.]
A type of plaintive Portuguese song and dance, with a guitar accompaniment.

fady /ˈfeɪdi/ *adjective.* E18.
[ORIGIN from FADE *verb* + -Y¹.]
Tending to fade or become less bright.

faecal /ˈfiːk(ə)l/ *adjective.* Also ***fecal**. M16.
[ORIGIN formed as FAECES + -AL¹.]
Of the nature of or containing faeces.

faeces /ˈfiːsiːz/ *noun pl.* Also ***feces**. LME.
[ORIGIN Latin, pl. of *faex* dregs.]
1 Sediment, dregs. LME.
2 Waste matter discharged from the bowels; excrement. LME.

faecula *noun*, †**faeculent** *adjective* see FECULA, FECULENT.

faena /faˈena/ *noun.* E20.
[ORIGIN Spanish, lit. 'task'.]
BULLFIGHTING. A series of passes with cape and sword by a matador, preparatory to the kill.

Faenza /fɑːˈɛntsə/ *noun & adjective.* M19.
[ORIGIN A city in Emilia-Romagna province, northern Italy: cf. FAIENCE.]
(Designating) faience made at Faenza in the 16th cent.

faerie *noun & adjective* see FAERY.

Faeroese, **Faröese** *adjectives & nouns* vars. of FAROESE.

faery /ˈfeɪəri, ˈfɛːri/ *noun & adjective. arch.* Also (now chiefly in sense A.1) **faerie**. L16.
[ORIGIN Archaizing var. of FAIRY, introduced by Spenser.]
▸ **A** *noun.* **1** The enchanted world of fairies, esp. as portrayed in Spenser's *Faerie Queene*; fairyland. Also, the inhabitants of this world. L16.
YEATS The Land of Faery, where nobody gets old and godly and grave.
2 A supernatural being; a fairy. L16.
KEATS Zephyr, blue-eyed Faery, turn.
▸ **B** *adjective.* Belonging to or suggestive of the world of fairies; enchanted; beautiful but unreal. L16.
MILTON Faerie Elves. WORDSWORTH The Earth . . Again appears to be An unsubstantial faery place.

faff /faf/ *verb & noun.* L18.
[ORIGIN Cf. FAFFLE.]
▸ **A** *verb.* **1** *verb intrans. & trans.* Of a wind: blow in puffs (on). *dial.* L18.
2 *verb intrans.* Bustle *about* or *around* ineffectually, fuss. *dial. & colloq.* L19.
N. COWARD The Welfare Officers appeared, . . faffed about, . . and retired in due course.
▸ **B** *noun.* **1** A puff of wind. *dial.* L19.
2 *fig.* (An) ineffectual fussing, a dither. *colloq.* L19.
M. SAWYER Learner drivers never want to stop . . it took you all that faff to get into fourth gear.

faffle /ˈfaf(ə)l/ *verb intrans.* L16.
[ORIGIN Imit.]
1 Stutter, stammer. *dial.* L16.
2 Flap idly in the wind. Chiefly *dial.* L18.
3 Fuss, bustle ineffectually. *dial. & colloq.* L19.

fag /fag/ *noun*¹. LME.
[ORIGIN Unknown.]
1 A knot in cloth. LME.
2 A sheep tick. *Scot. & dial.* L18.

fag /fag/ *noun*². L15.
[ORIGIN Unknown. In sense 4 abbreviation of FAG END.]
†**1** Something that hangs loose; a flap. Only in L15.
2 A last remnant, a fag end (*lit. & fig.*); *spec.* the end of a cigarette. L16.
3 A leftover strip of land; also, tufts of last year's grass not grazed down. *dial.* L19.
4 A cigarette (orig. of a cheap sort). L19.

fag /fag/ *noun*³. L18.
[ORIGIN from FAG *verb*¹.]
1 A fatiguing or unwelcome task; drudgery. Also, exhaustion. *colloq.* L18.
A. WHITE It saves a lot of fag to have someone to scrub my back. J. R. ACKERLEY He can quite well . . find the journey up too much of a fag.
2 In a public school: a junior boy who performs menial tasks for a senior. Also *transf.*, a drudge. L18.

fag /fag/ *noun*[4]. *derog. slang* (chiefly *N. Amer.*). E20.
[ORIGIN Abbreviation.]
= FAGGOT *noun* 8.
– COMB.: **fag hag** a woman who consorts habitually with homosexual men.

fag /fag/ *verb*[1]. Infl. **-gg-**. M16.
[ORIGIN Unknown. Cf. FLAG *verb*[2].]
1 *verb intrans.* Grow weary or less eager, flag. Formerly also, swerve or turn aside *from*, *into*. *obsolete* exc. *dial.* M16. **2** *verb intrans.* Work until one is exhausted; toil, exert oneself. L18.

F. BURNEY All day I am fagging at business. JOYCE Hot day coming. Too much trouble to fag up the stairs.

3 *verb trans.* Make thoroughly weary; tire out, exhaust. Freq. foll. by *out*. Usu. in *pass.* E19.

D. LODGE I feel quite fagged after all that effort.

4 *verb trans.* In a public school, of a senior boy: use the services of (a junior) for menial tasks. E19. **5** *verb intrans.* In a public school, of a junior boy: perform menial tasks for a senior. Formerly (CRICKET), act as a fieldsman to a senior boy (usu. foll. by *out*). E19. **6** *verb trans.* NAUTICAL. Unravel the ends of (a rope). M19.

fag /fag/ *verb*[2] *trans. dial.* Infl. **-gg-**. M19.
[ORIGIN Unknown. Cf. BAG *verb*[2].]
= BAG *verb*[2].

fag end /'fagɛnd/ *noun*. E17.
[ORIGIN from FAG *noun*[2] + END *noun*.]
1 The last part of a piece of cloth, freq. of a coarser texture than the rest. Chiefly *transf.*, the last part or tail end of something, remaining after the best has been used up. E17.

W. GOLDING He was our lodger, hanging on to the fag-end of his life.

2 An untwisted end of a rope. L18. **3** A cigarette end. Cf. FAG *noun*[2] 4. *colloq.* E20.

fagger /'fagə/ *noun*. M19.
[ORIGIN from FAG *verb*[1] + -ER[1].]
1 A person who works hard. M19. **2** = FAGMASTER. M19.

faggot /'fagət/ *noun & verb*. Also ***fagot**. ME.
[ORIGIN Old French & mod. French *fagot* from Italian *fagotto* dim. of Proto-Romance back-form. from Greek *phakelos* bundle.]
▸ **A** *noun*. **1** A bundle of sticks or twigs tied together as fuel; *hist. spec.* one used in burning heretics alive. Hence, the punishment of being burnt alive for heresy. ME. ▸†**b** MILITARY. A fascine. LME–E18.

H. LATIMER Running out of Germany for fear of the fagot. A. E. COPPARD They had begun to make three faggots of the wood they had collected.

bear a faggot, **carry a faggot** *hist.*: in token of having renounced heresy.

2 A bunch (*of* herbs etc.); *fig.* a collection (*of* (esp. abstract) things). L15. **3** A bundle of iron or steel rods bound together for reheating, welding, and hammering into bars. M16. **4** As a term of abuse: an objectionable (old) woman, child, animal, etc. Chiefly *dial.* L16. †**5** A person engaged temporarily to fill another's place at the muster of a regiment or to keep up its strength. L17–E19. **6** *hist.* = ***faggot vote*** below. E19. **7** A kind of rissole or meatball made of minced pig's liver or other offal mixed with bread or suet, herbs, etc. Usu. in *pl.* Orig. *dial.* M19. **8** A male homosexual, esp. an effeminate one. *slang* (orig. *US*). *derog.* E20.
– COMB.: **faggot-iron**: in the form of bars or masses, produced by welding together a faggot of iron bars; **faggot stitch**, **faggot stitching**: resembling the faggoting of drawn-thread work, used to join two pieces of material; **faggot vote** *hist.* a vote manufactured by the nominal transfer to a person, not otherwise qualified, of sufficient property to enable him to vote.
▸ **B** *verb*. Infl. **-t(t)-**.
1 *verb trans.* Surround with or set on faggots (a person convicted of heresy). *rare*. M16. †**2** *verb intrans.* Of a former heretic: carry a faggot or wear an embroidered faggot in token of recantation. Only in M16. **3** *verb trans.* Tie together (as) in a faggot. L16.

fig.: J. C. HARE Things essentially . . different, bundled and fagoted together for the occasion.

4 *verb trans.* METALLURGY. Fasten or pile together (bars or rods of iron) for reheating and welding. Freq. as ***faggoted*** *ppl adjective*. M19. **5** *verb intrans.* Make faggots or bundles of sticks or twigs. L19. **6** *verb trans.* Ornament (needlework) with faggoting; join (pieces of material) by faggot stitch. E20.
■ **faggoter** *noun* (*rare*) a person who makes faggots or faggoting L15. **faggoting** *noun* (**a**) the action of the verb; (**b**) embroidery in which a number of threads are drawn out and a few cross-threads tied together in the middle (suggestive of faggots); the joining of materials in a similar manner: M19.

faggoty /'fagəti/ *adjective*. Also ***fagoty**. M19.
[ORIGIN from FAGGOT *noun* + -Y[1].]
1 Obsessed with faggots or the burning of heretics. *rare*. M19. **2** Of, resembling, or suggestive of a male homosexual or homosexuals. *slang* (orig. *US*). E20.

faggy /'fagi/ *adjective*. *slang* (chiefly *N. Amer.*). M20.
[ORIGIN from FAG *noun*[4] + -Y[1].]
= FAGGOTY 2.

Fagin /'feɪgɪn/ *noun*. M19.
[ORIGIN A character in Dickens's *Oliver Twist*.]
A trainer of thieves; a receiver of stolen goods; a thief.

fagioli /fa'dʒəʊli/ *noun pl.* M20.
[ORIGIN Italian, pl. of *fagiolo* bean.]
Beans (in Italian cookery).

fagmaster /'fagmɑːstə/ *noun*. L19.
[ORIGIN from FAG *noun*[3] + MASTER *noun*[1].]
In a public school: the senior boy for whom a junior fags.

fagot *noun & verb* see FAGGOT.

fagotto /fa'gɒtto, fə'gɒtəʊ/ *noun*. Pl. ***-tti*** /-t(t)i/, ***-ttos*** /-təʊz/. E18.
[ORIGIN Italian: see FAGGOT.]
MUSIC. A bassoon. Also, a primitive form of this, a curtal.

fagoty *adjective* see FAGGOTY.

fah /fɑː/ *noun*. Also **fa**. ME.
[ORIGIN from Latin *fa(muli)*: see UT.]
MUSIC. The fourth note of a scale in a movable-doh system; the note F in the fixed-doh system.

fahlerz /'fɑːlɛːts/ *noun*. L18.
[ORIGIN German, from *fahl* ash-coloured, gray + *Erz* ore.]
MINERALOGY. Any grey copper ore of the system whose typical forms are tetrahedrite and tennantite.

fahlore /'fɑːlɔː/ *noun*. E19.
[ORIGIN Partial translation.]
= FAHLERZ.

Fahr. *abbreviation*.
Fahrenheit.

Fahrenheit /'far(ə)nhʌɪt, 'fɑːr-/ *noun & adjective*. M18.
[ORIGIN Gabriel Daniel *Fahrenheit* (1686–1736), German physicist who invented the mercury thermometer.]
▸ **A** *noun*. The thermometric scale introduced by G. D. Fahrenheit, in which water freezes at 32° and boils at 212° under standard conditions. M18.
▸ **B** *adjective*. Designating or pertaining to this scale; *postpositive* (with a specified temperature) on this scale. E19.

faience /fʌɪ'ɒs, feɪ-, -'ɑːns/ *noun & adjective*. Also **faï-**, **fay-**. L17.
[ORIGIN French *faïence* from *Faïence* FAENZA.]
(Designating) tin-glazed or decorated earthenware or pottery (orig. that made at Faenza in northern Italy).

faik /feɪk/ *verb trans. Scot.* LME.
[ORIGIN Perh. aphet. from Scot. var. of DEFALK.]
1 Reduce (a total); deduct (a sum). LME. **2** Spare, excuse, let off. L18.

fail /feɪl/ *noun*[1]. ME.
[ORIGIN Old French *fai(l)le* (mod. *faille*), formed as FAIL *verb*.]
1 = FAILURE 1, 2. Now only in ***without fail***, definitely, for certain, irrespective of difficulties, (now only used to strengthen an injunction or promise, formerly also with statements of fact). ME.

SHAKES. *Wint. T.* What dangers, by his Highness' fail of issue, May drop upon his kingdom. S. BECKETT He won't come this evening . . But he'll come tomorrow Without fail.

2 = FAILURE 4. Long *rare* in *gen.* sense. L15. ▸**b** *spec.* A failure to achieve the required standard in an examination. M20.
†**for fail** as a precaution against failure.
†**3** Death. *rare* (Shakes.). Only in E17.

SHAKES. *Hen. VIII* How grounded he his title to the crown Upon our fail?

fail /feɪl/ *noun*[2]. *Scot.* Also **feal**. LME.
[ORIGIN Unknown.]
A thick sod or piece of turf, esp. as used for building walls etc.; such sods collectively.
fail and divot LAW (now *hist.*) a servitude conferring the right to remove sods for building, roofing, etc.
– COMB.: **fail-dyke** a wall built of sods.

fail /feɪl/ *verb*. ME.
[ORIGIN Old French & mod. French *faillir* be wanting, from Proto-Romance alt. of Latin *fallere* disappoint the expectations of, deceive.]
▸ **I** Be or become deficient.
1 *verb intrans.* & †*trans.* Be lacking (to). Now only, of something needed: be unavailable. See also FAILING *preposition*. ME. ▸†**b** *verb intrans.* Of a number: be wanting to complete a sum. Only in ME. ▸**c** *verb intrans. & trans.* Chiefly of time: be inadequate (for the needs of). *arch.* ME.

H. MAUNDRELL Shaded over head with Trees, and with Matts when the boughs fail. **c** AV *Heb.* 11:32 The time would faile mee to tell of Gideon.

2 *verb intrans. & trans.* Of supplies, resources, etc.: run low, become inadequate (for the needs of). ME.

SPENSER The breath gan him to fayle. J. LOCKE Where the credit and money fail, barter alone must do. H. BELLOC The grass was brown, our wells had failed.

3 *verb intrans.* Cease to exist; become extinct. ME. ▸†**b** Of a period of time: come to an end, expire. LME–E17.

AV *Ps.* 12.1 The faithfull faile from among the children of men. W. BLACKSTONE The blood of the Kempes shall not inherit till the blood of the Stile's fail.

4 *verb intrans.* Lose force or intensity; (of light etc.) grow dim or faint; (of a sound, a smell, etc.) die away, become indistinct; (of health, faculties, etc.) become weak or impaired, become too weak for one's needs. ME. ▸**b** *verb trans.* Of health, faculties, etc.: become too weak for the needs of. ME.

S. STURMY Let slip thine Anchor, the Wind fails. SHELLEY The Champak's odours fail Like sweet thoughts in a dream. G. ORWELL The light was failing, but there was no difficulty in recognizing her. **b** E. A. FREEMAN The heart of Eustace failed him. D. BLOODWORTH Rumours that Mao's health is failing have sent the Hong Kong stock exchange plummeting. B. UNSWORTH His eyes were failing, he could not see with any distinctness.

5 *verb intrans.* Of a person: decline in health or vigour, flag; *spec.* lose strength with the approach of death. ME. ▸**b** Die. *obsolete* exc. *dial.* E17.

W. S. CHURCHILL We shall not flag or fail We shall go on to the end. J. CARY She had . . been obliged to stay in bed, and the village said that she was failing at last. **b** SHAKES. *Hen. VIII* Had the King in his last sickness fail'd.

6 *verb trans. & intrans.* Not give due or expected service (to a person) at a time of need; prove unreliable as a resource or source of aid (to). ME.

G. GREENE Mr Opie had spoken rapidly . . and Dr Czinner found his knowledge of English failing him. E. CALDWELL To let a glance . . speak for them when words failed.

7 *verb intrans.* Prove defective when tested; (of a structure or other material thing) give way under pressure. Of machinery etc.: break down, cease to function. Formerly also, of soldiers: not stand up to the enemy. ME.

I. HAMILTON First the telephone failed, then the electricity.

▸ **II** Experience a deficiency.
8 *verb trans.* Be without, lack. Now *rare*. ME.

R. JEFFERIES I fail words to express my utter contempt.

9 *verb intrans.* Be lacking *in* an essential quality or part; *arch.* be destitute *of*. ME.

J. GAY A dancing-master . . seldom fails of the scarlet stocking. B. JOWETT The Dialogue fails in unity.

▸ **III** Fall short in performance or attainment.
10 *verb intrans.* Be remiss in the performance of a duty (foll. by *in*); neglect or omit *to do*. ME. ▸†**b** *verb trans.* Omit to perform (a customary or expected action). LME–E18. ▸**c** *verb trans.* Not keep (a promise, appointment, etc.). Formerly also, disappoint (a person's expectations). *arch.* E16.

S. HILL I cannot be said . . to have failed in carrying out my duty. J. LE CARRÉ Liz . . ignored her . . , failed to reply when she addressed her. **b** DEFOE My morning Walk with my Gun, which I seldom failed. **c** A. SEEGER I shall not fail that rendezvous.

11 *verb intrans.* Foll. by *of*: come short of hitting (a target), attaining (one's purpose or goal), achieving (an effect) etc. Formerly also, escape (a fate). ME. ▸**b** *verb trans.* Fall short of (a target), miss (one's footing); not succeed in obtaining (something sought). Long *arch.* LME.

GOLDSMITH A weak king . . seldom fails of having his authority despised. I. ASIMOV When our missing robot failed of location anywhere. **b** MILTON Though that seat of earthly bliss be fail'd, A fairer Paradise is founded now. J. CARROLL Several Celtic crosses . . failed the level of Colman's chin.

†**12** *verb intrans.* Deviate from what is true or correct; err, be at fault. (Foll. by *from*, *of*.) ME–L16.

T. STARKEY The ordur of our law . . in the punnyschment of theft . . faylyth much from gud cyvylyte.

13 *verb intrans.* Be unsuccessful in an attempt or enterprise. (Foll. by *in*, *to do*.) ME. ▸**b** Of an attempt, plan, etc.: meet with no success; miscarry. LME.

T. HARDY How could he succeed in an enterprise wherein . . Phillotson had failed? L. STEFFENS When tact and good humour failed, he applied force. L. VAN DER POST For once the charm of hot food . . failed to cheer me. **b** J. R. GREEN A revolt which failed . . through the desertion of their Head.

14 *verb intrans.* Of a crop etc.: give no return; prove unproductive. ME.

TENNYSON The year in which our olives fail'd.

15 *verb intrans.* Of a firm etc.: become insolvent. L17.

G. GREENE Racketeers who make money out of receiverships as the big firms fail.

16 *verb intrans. & trans.* Of a candidate: fall short of the required standard in (an examination or test). L19. ▸**b** *verb trans.* Of an examiner: adjudge (a candidate) to have failed. L19.

C. M. YONGE Almost all of them failed in arithmetic. ANTHONY SMITH He had failed a Cambridge exam owing to . . inadequacy in geometry.

▸ †**IV 17** *verb trans.* [After Latin *fallere*.] Deceive, cheat. *rare* (Spenser). Only in **L16**.

SPENSER So lively and so like that living sence it fayld.

– PHRASES & COMB.: †**fail little of doing** come close to experiencing (a given fate). **failover** COMPUTING a procedure by which a system automatically transfers control to a duplicate system when it detects a fault or failure. **fail safe** (of a mechanism) return to a danger-free position or state in the event of a breakdown. **fail-safe** *adjective* (of a mechanical or electrical device, procedure, etc.) returning or involving return to a danger-free position or state in the event of breakdown; *gen.* totally reliable or safe. ***words fail me***: see WORD *noun*.

■ **failed** *ppl adjective* (*a*) decayed; (of a person) infirm, decrepit; (*b*) that has been unsuccessful; (of a candidate for a degree) that has not passed: **L15**. **failer** *noun* **LME**.

failing /ˈfeɪlɪŋ/ *noun*. **LME**.
[ORIGIN from FAIL *verb* + -ING[1].]
1 The action of FAIL *verb*. **LME**.
2 A defect of character; a weakness. **L16**.

L. WOOLF Sharp ruined himself by drinking—a by no means uncommon journalistic failing.

F

failing /ˈfeɪlɪŋ/ *preposition*. **E19**.
[ORIGIN pres. pple of FAIL *verb*.]
In default of; in the absence of.

E. WAUGH We hoped Sebastian might give us luncheon . . . Failing him we can always try Boy Mulcaster.

faille /feɪl/ *noun*. **M16**.
[ORIGIN Old French & mod. French.]
†**1** A kind of hood or veil worn by women. **M16–L17**.
2 A light ribbed silk fabric. **M19**.

fáilte /ˈfɔːltʃə/ *noun*. *Scot. & Irish*. **L19**.
[ORIGIN Irish.]
An act or instance of welcoming someone. Usu. as an interjection.

failure /ˈfeɪljə/ *noun*. **M17**.
[ORIGIN Anglo-Norman (legal) *failer* for Old French *faillir* FAIL *verb*, inf. used as noun (see -ER[4]); assim. to -OR, (later) -URE. Cf. *leisure*, *pleasure*.]
1 (A) cessation in the existence or availability of something. **M17**.

M. ELPHINSTONE On the failure of issue . . an adopted son succeeds.

2 (An) omission to do or *to do* something due or requisite; default. **M17**.

T. LUNDBERG Failure to make returns . . could lead to prosecution.

†**3** A slight fault; a failing, a shortcoming. **M17–E18**.
4 (An instance of) failing to effect one's purpose; (a) lack of success. **M17**. ▸**b** A person who or thing which turns out unsuccessful. **M19**.

J. R. SEELEY We see efforts ending in feebleness and failure. **b** E. F. BENSON Minorca . . had been a dismal failure as far as she was concerned. D. CUSACK I feel such a failure I don't seem to get anywhere.

5 The process or fact of failing in health or strength, giving way under pressure, etc.; (a) cessation in the functioning of a mechanism, an organ of the body, etc. **L17**.

Happy Landings 106 [accidents] were attributable to engine failures. E. H. GOMBRICH An increasing failure of nerve.

heart failure, ***renal failure***, etc.

6 The process of becoming or the state of being insolvent. **E18**.

fain /feɪn/ *pred. adjective & adverb*. Now *arch. & dial.*
[ORIGIN Old English *fæg(e)n* corresp. to Old Saxon *fagan*, *-in*, Old Norse *feginn*, from Germanic, from base repr. by Old English *gefēon* rejoice. Cf. FAIN *verb*[1].]
▸ **A** *adjective*. **1** Happy, well-pleased. Freq. in ***full fain***, ***glad and fain***. Foll. by *of*, *to do*, *that*. **OE**.

SHAKES. *1 Hen. VI* Are glad and fain by flight to save themselves.

2 Glad or content under the circumstances *to do*. (Passing into sense 2b.) **ME**. ▸**b** Obliged, left with no alternative but *to do*. **E16**.

b I. D'ISRAELI Ascham, indeed, was fain to apologise for having written in English. E. BOWEN She was so blind to them down there that they were fain to stand pretending.

3 Disposed, inclined, eager. Foll. by †*of*, *for*, *to do*. **ME**. ▸†**b** Apt, wont, *to do*. **L16–M17**.
4 Fond. Formerly also, well-disposed, favourable. Long *obsolete* exc. *Scot.* **ME**.
▸ **B** *adverb*. Gladly, willingly. Now chiefly in ***would fain***. **ME**.

M. AMIS The boy . . had wrested from the girl some article . . which she would fain recover.

■ **fainly** *adverb* (*rare*) **M16**. **fainness** /-n-n-/ *noun* (chiefly *Scot. & N. English*) eagerness, gladness **ME**.

fain /feɪn/ *verb*[1]. Long *obsolete* exc. *Scot.*
[ORIGIN Old English *fæġnian* (formed as FAIN *adjective & adverb*) = Old Saxon, Old High German, Gothic *faginōn*, Old Norse *fagna*. See also FAWN *verb*[1]. Survival in Scot. prob. due to influence from Norwegian dial. *fegna* to welcome, from Old Norse *fagna*.]
†**1** *verb trans. & intrans.* (Cause to) be glad; rejoice. **OE–LME**.
†**2** *verb trans.* Welcome (a person). **ME–L15**.
3 *verb trans.* = FAWN *verb*[1] 1. **LME**.
4 *verb trans.* Like (a person or thing, *to do*); be fond of. **L16**.

fain /feɪn/ *verb*[2] *trans. & intrans. slang* (orig. *dial.*). Also (earlier) **fen** /fɛn/, infl. **-nn-**. **E19**.
[ORIGIN Uncertain: perh. formed as FEIGN *verb* 5 or alt. of FEND *verb*.]
Esp. among children: forbid the making of (some move or action) in a game, esp. marbles; claim exemption from (some unwelcome task or role) in a game. Freq. in ***fains I***, ***fain I***, ***fains it***, ***fain it***.

fainaigue /fɛˈneɪɡ, -iːɡ; fɪ-/ *verb*. *dial.* Now *rare* or *obsolete*. **M19**.
[ORIGIN Perh. from Old French *fornier* deny, ult. from Latin *foris* outside, away + *negare* deny. Cf. FINAGLE.]
1 *verb trans. & intrans.* Revoke (a suit etc.) at cards. **M19**.
2 *verb trans. & intrans.* Fail in a promise (to). **M19**.
3 *verb trans.* Cheat, deceive. **L19**.

fainéant /ˈfeɪnɪɒ̃; *foreign* fɛneɑ̃ (pl. of noun same)/ *noun & adjective*. **E17**.
[ORIGIN French, from *fait* 3rd person sing. of *faire* do + *néant* nothing.]
▸ **A** *noun*. A person who does nothing, an idler, an inactive official. **E17**.
▸ **B** *adjective*. Indolent, idle, inactive. **E19**.

■ **faineancy** /-ənsi/ *noun* = FAINÉANTISM **M19**. ***fainéantise*** /fɛneɑ̃tiːz, ˌfeɪneɪɒ̃ˈtiːz/ *noun* [French] = FAINÉANTISM **E17**. **fainéantism**, **-isme** /ˈfeɪneɪɒ̃tɪz(ə)m/ *noun* the state or quality of being a fainéant; indifference, idleness, inactivity: **L19**.

faint /feɪnt/ *noun*. See also FAINTS. **ME**.
[ORIGIN from FAINT *adjective*, *verb*.]
†**1** Faintness. **ME–M16**.
2 An act or state of fainting. **E19**.

E. CRISPIN Bent forward . . as though putting his head down to ward off a faint.

in a dead faint completely unconscious.

■ **faintless** *adjective* (now *rare*) unflagging **L16**.

faint /feɪnt/ *adjective*. Also (now only COMMERCE in sense 6b, formerly also in sense 1) **feint**. **ME**.
[ORIGIN Old French *faint*, *feint* pa. pple of *faindre*, *feindre* FEIGN.]
1 Feigned, simulated. Now *rare*. **ME**.

THACKERAY We wear feint smiles over our tears and deceive our children.

†**2** Shirking, lazy; sluggish. **ME–L17**.
3 Lacking in courage, cowardly. Now chiefly in ***faint heart***. **ME**.
4 Weak or dizzy through fear, hunger, exhaustion, etc.; inclined to faint. Foll. by †*of*, *with*. **ME**. ▸**b** Inducing faintness; (of a smell) sickly; (of an atmosphere) oppressive. *arch.* **E16**.

A. J. CRONIN From surprise and shock she actually turned faint. **b** WOODES ROGERS The Weather was very wet, hot and faint.

5 †**a** Esp. of a person or animal: weak, sickly, out of condition. **LME–M18**. ▸**b** Of an action, purpose, etc.: feeble, half-hearted. **L16**.

b J. F. LEHMANN The hopes still clung on, faint graspings at the idea that all might be well after all.

b ***damn with faint praise***: see DAMN *verb* 2.

6 Making a slight or feeble impression on the senses; hardly perceptible, dim, indistinct; (of a colour) pale. **LME**. ▸**b** *spec.* Designating the pale blue or neutral-tinted lines ruled on paper as a guide for handwriting. **M19**.

A. RANSOME A glimmer, faint at first, grew brighter. E. CALDWELL She whispered in a voice so faint that she could barely hear it herself. A. N. WILSON The very faint whiff of after-shave lotion he always exuded. R. C. HUTCHINSON I hadn't even the faintest idea what beauty was before I fell in love.

– SPECIAL COLLOCATIONS & COMB.: **faint heart** a cowardly spirit, cowardliness. **faint-heart** *adjective & noun* (*a*) *adjective* timid, cowardly; (*b*) *noun* a coward. **faint-hearted** *adjective* lacking courage, cowardly. **faint-heartedly** *adverb* in a faint-hearted manner. **faint-heartedness** the quality or state of being faint-hearted, cowardliness.

■ **faintest** *noun* (*colloq.*) *the* slightest idea or notion **M20**. **faintish** *adjective* somewhat faint **M17**. **faintishness** *noun* **M18**. **faintness** *noun* **LME**.

faint /feɪnt/ *verb*. **ME**.
[ORIGIN from the adjective.]
1 *verb intrans.* Grow or become faint; lose heart or courage, give way; decline, fade, flag, wilt. **ME**.

E. BOWEN The sky shone . . fainting down to the fretted line, but was being steadily drained by the dark below. J. COLVILLE The P.M. went to France to bolster up the fainting French morale. D. HALL Water its foliage as well as the soil, or you may . . find your basil has 'fainted.'

2 *verb intrans.* Lose consciousness, esp. temporarily through a fall in blood pressure; fall in a swoon. Also foll. by *away*. **LME**.

J. STEINBECK That big stupid horse fainted from the heat. E. FERBER For the first time in her healthy twenty-odd years Leslie Lynnton had fainted dead away.

fainting fit a faint, a swoon.

3 *verb trans.* Make faint, enfeeble. Now *rare*. **LME**.

SHAKES. *Hen. VIII* It faints me To think what follows.

■ **fainter** *noun* **E19**. **faintingly** *adverb* (now *rare*) in a fainting manner, like a person who is fainting **L16**.

faintly /ˈfeɪntli/ *adverb*. **ME**.
[ORIGIN from FAINT *adjective* + -LY[2].]
†**1** Feignedly, deceitfully. **ME–M18**.
2 In a faint manner; feebly, indistinctly; to an almost imperceptible degree, very slightly. **ME**.

STEELE To praise faintly the good Qualities of those below them. SCOTT FITZGERALD She . . heard them still singing faintly a song . . , very remote in time and far away. M. LAVIN The room . . was only faintly lit. G. GREENE His brother . . would be faintly surprised by this visit.

†**3** Hardly, scarcely. **E16–M17**.

faints /feɪnts/ *noun pl.* Also **feints**. **E18**.
[ORIGIN Pl. of FAINT *noun*.]
The impure spirit which comes over first and last in the process of distillation.

fainty /ˈfeɪnti/ *adjective*. *obsolete* exc. *poet. & dial.* **M16**.
[ORIGIN from FAINT *adjective* + -Y[1].]
1 Orig., faint, weak, languid. Later chiefly, inclined to faint. **M16**.
2 Causing faintness; sickly. **L16**.

fair /fɛː/ *noun*[1]. Also (now esp. in sense 2, *pseudo-arch.*) **fayre**. **ME**.
[ORIGIN Old French *feire* (mod. *foire*) from late Latin *feria* holiday, sing. of classical Latin *feriae* religious festivals, holy days.]
1 A regular gathering of buyers and sellers at a time and place ordained by charter, statute, or custom. Now *esp.* (a part of) such a gathering devoted entirely to amusements (also **funfair**). **ME**. ▸**b** An exhibition, esp. one designed to publicize a particular product or the products of one industry, country, etc. **E19**.

J. CARLYLE A mere cattle-fair; no booths with toys and sweeties. R. DAHL The fair came once a year with the swings and roundabouts and bumping cars. **b** A. CADE An annual pilgrimage to the Frankfurt Book Fair.

a day after the fair too late. ***Bartholomew fair***: see BARTHOLOMEW 2. ***mop fair***: see MOP *noun*[5].

2 = FÊTE *noun* 1b. **L19**.
– COMB.: **fairground** an outdoor area on which a fair is held.

fair /fɛː/ *adjective, adverb, & noun*[2].
[ORIGIN Old English *fæġer* = Old Saxon, Old High German *fagar*, Old Norse *fagr*, Gothic *fagrs*, from Germanic.]
▸ **A** *adjective*. **1** Pleasing to the sight; (of a person, esp. a woman) beautiful. *arch.* **OE**.

MILTON The fairest of her daughters Eve. J. RUSKIN A fair building is . . worth the ground it stands on.

†**2** Pleasing to the smell or hearing. **OE–LME**.
3 Of words, a speech, a promise, etc.: initially attractive or pleasing; specious; flattering. **OE**.

B. JOWETT The Sophists have plenty of brave words and fair devices.

†**4** Of speech, diction: elegant, fluent. **ME–L15**.
5 Of an amount, a fortune, etc.: considerable, handsome. **ME**.

A. SILLITOE A shrewdness that gained him a fair living from the small acreage of garden he cultivated.

†**6** *gen.* Desirable, pleasing; excellent. **ME–L17**.
7 (Of complexion, hair) light not dark, blonde; having a light complexion or light hair. **ME**.

J. GALSWORTHY The girl with the fair hair . . , the fair arms emerging from a skin-tight bodice.

8 Of weather: favourable; fine, bright, sunny. **ME**. ▸**b** Of the wind: favourable to a ship's course. **LME**.

C. RYAN The weather for the next three days would be fair with little cloud and virtually no winds. **b** C. FRANCIS The wind was still fair—that is, it was coming from a direction other than ahead.

9 Physically clean or sound. Latterly chiefly of water: pure, clear, clean. **ME**.
10 Of character, reputation, conduct: free from moral stain, unsullied, spotless. *arch.* **ME**.
11 Of a person, action, argument, etc.: just, unbiased, equitable, impartial; legitimate, in accordance with the rules or standards. **ME**. ▸**b** Of conditions, etc., esp. in sport: offering an equal chance of success. **E18**.

ISAIAH BERLIN We must seek to be fair, and not praise and blame arbitrarily. P. ANGADI Nanny . . can no longer deal with them all, it's not fair to ask it of her. **b** G. P. R. JAMES That would not matter if the ground were fair.

12 Of speech, behaviour, action, etc.: courteous, gracious, gentle. Formerly also, of a person's countenance: kindly. **ME**. ▸**b** In courteous address: kind, dear. *arch.* **LME**.

J. LOGAN I have used both fair and foul words.

13 Likely to succeed; promising; (of an omen) propitious. **ME**.

A. BURGESS If I kill you now and give myself up to the police, there's a fair chance that I may hang.

14 Unobstructed, clear, open; (now chiefly *dial.*) open to view, plainly to be seen. ME.

R. FORD The fairest though farthest way about is the nearest way home.

15 Now chiefly NAUTICAL. Of a line, surface, etc.: free from irregularities; smooth, even. L15.
16 Of handwriting: neat, legible. L17.

A. THWAITE Kindly copy My words in your fair hand.

17 (Of degree or quality) moderate, adequate, reasonable; (of an amount etc.) not excessive but sufficient. L19. ▸**b** Complete, utter, thorough. *colloq.* (esp. *Austral.* & *NZ*). L19.

H. JAMES The storm had given fair warning of its approach. J. GARDNER A pretty fair job to judge by the car and the paint on the house. **b** N. COWARD They can ramp about among obscure English essayists and have a fair beano.

▸ **B** *adverb*. **1** Beautifully, handsomely. Now *rare*. OE.

SHAKES. *1 Hen. IV* The moon shines fair.

2 Courteously, kindly. Now only in ***speak (a person) fair***, address civilly. OE. ▸†**b** In a proper or suitable manner; befittingly. ME–M17.
†**3** Gently, without haste or violence. Chiefly in ***fair and easily, fair and softly***. OE–E19.
4 Promisingly, auspiciously; favourably. *obsolete* exc. in ***bid fair***: see BID *verb* 6b. OE.
5 Honestly, impartially; according to the rules. ME.

P. DEMING He had tried so many times . . and so fair, and every time a failure.

6 Completely; fully; to a considerable degree. Now *dial.*, *N. Amer.*, *Austral.*, & *NZ*. ME. ▸†**b** Clearly, plainly. LME–L17. ▸**c** Directly, straight, due (north etc.). Now chiefly *Scot.* L15.

H. L. WILSON The thing fair staggered me.

7 Evenly, on a level. Chiefly *dial.* E18.
– SPECIAL COLLOCATIONS, PHRASES, & COMB. (of adjective & adverb): **a fair cop** a justifiable arrest. ***a fair crack of the whip***: see WHIP *noun*. ***a fair deal***: see DEAL *noun*[3] 3. **a fair field and no favour** equal conditions in a contest. ***a fair shake***: see SHAKE *noun*. **a fair treat** *colloq.* a very enjoyable or attractive thing or person. ***bid fair***: see BID *verb* 6b. **by fair means or foul** with or without violence or fraud. **fair and square** *adjectival & adverbial phr.* (*a*) *adjectival phr.* honest, above-board; (*b*) *adverbial phr.* honestly, justly, determinedly, straightforwardly, exactly. **fair copy** matter transcribed or reproduced after final correction. **fair-copy** *verb trans.* write out or reproduce after final correction. ***fair dinkum***: see DINKUM *adjective*. ***fair do(s)***: see DO *noun*[1] 1c. **fair enough!** *colloq.* that's reasonable. **fair-face**, **fair-faced** *adjectives* (*a*) having a fair complexion; (*b*) having a (usu. deceptively) attractive appearance; (*c*) (of brickwork etc.) not plastered. ***fair fall***: see FALL *verb*. ***fair game***: see GAME *noun*. **fair go** *Austral.* & *NZ colloq.* used for emphasis or to request someone to be reasonable or fair. **fair-haired** *adjective* (*a*) blonde; (*b*) (of a person) favourite, much loved. **fairlead**, **fairleader** NAUTICAL a device, usu. on deck or on a spur, for guiding a rope and preventing it from cutting or chafing. **fair maid** = FUMADO. **fair-minded** *adjective* just, unbiased. **fair-mindedly** *adverb* justly, without bias. **fair-mindedness** justness, absence of bias. **fair name** good reputation. **fair play** (*a*) honest, upright conduct; (*b*) equal conditions for all. **fair-spoken** *adjective* (of a person) courteous, bland. **fair-to-middling** *adjective* (*colloq.*) slightly above average. **fair trade** (*a*) trade carried on legally; (*b*) smuggling; (*c*) trade in which fair prices are paid to producers in developing countries. **fair trader** a smuggler. **fairway** (*a*) a navigable channel in a river etc.; the regular course or track of a ship; (*b*) the closely mown part of a golf course, excluding hazards, between the tee and the putting green. **fair-weather** *adjective* fit or suitable only for fine weather (***fair-weather friend***: not good in a crisis). **in a fair way to** likely to (succeed etc.). **keep fair**, **part fair** *arch.* remain, part, on good terms. ***play fair***: see PLAY *verb*. ***the fairer sex***, ***the fair sex***: see SEX *noun*. **write out fair** = *fair-copy* above.

▸ **C** *noun*. †**1** Beauty, good looks. In *pl.* points of beauty. OE–M17.
2 That which is fair; *the* fair aspect, etc.; fair play. LME.
3 A fair thing; *esp.* (*arch.* or *poet.*) a woman. LME.
– PHRASES ETC.: **fair's fair** *colloq.* (reciprocal) fairness is called for. **for fair** *US slang* completely, altogether.

fair /fɛː/ *verb*. OE.
[ORIGIN from FAIR *adjective*.]
1 *verb intrans.* †**a** Appear or become beautiful or clean. OE–LME. ▸**b** Of weather: clear. Also foll. by *away*, *off*, *up*. E19.
†**2** *verb trans.* Make fair, beautify. ME–L16.
3 *verb trans.* Make (the surface of a ship etc.) smooth and regular. M19.
– COMB.: **fairwater** a structure on a ship etc. for assisting its passage through water.

fairing /ˈfɛːrɪŋ/ *noun*[1]. L16.
[ORIGIN from FAIR *noun*[1] + -ING[1].]
A present, *esp.* one bought at a fair; *fig.* one's deserts.

fairing /ˈfɛːrɪŋ/ *noun*[2]. M19.
[ORIGIN from FAIR *verb* + -ING[1].]
The action of making the surface of a ship, aircraft, motor vehicle, etc., smooth and streamlined; a structure added for this purpose.

fairish /ˈfɛːrɪʃ/ *adjective & adverb*. E17.
[ORIGIN from FAIR *adjective*, *adverb* + -ISH[1].]
▸ **A** *adjective*. **1** Moderately good, passable; *dial.* tolerably well (in health). E17.
2 Considerable in amount, quite large. L19.
▸ **B** *adverb*. Quite, fairly. *colloq.* & *dial.* M19.

Fair Isle /ˈfɛːr ʌɪl/ *adjective* (chiefly *attrib.*). M19.
[ORIGIN One of the Shetland islands.]
Designating any of various traditional multi-coloured geometric designs for knitting or a woollen article knitted in such a design.

Fairlight Clay /ˈfɛːlʌɪt ˈkleɪ/ *noun phr.* L19.
[ORIGIN from *Fairlight* a town in Sussex + CLAY *noun*.]
A band of shales and clays of the Wealden series extending through Kent and East Sussex.

fairly /ˈfɛːli/ *adverb*. LME.
[ORIGIN from FAIR *adjective* + -LY[2].]
▸ **I 1** †**a** Beautifully, handsomely. LME–L19. ▸**b** Legibly, neatly. *rare*. L16.

a BYRON To make The skin . . appear more fairly fair.

2 Gently, peaceably, softly. Long only *Scot.* LME.

SHAKES. *Two Gent.* They parted very fairly in jest.

3 Properly, suitably. L16. ▸†**b** Courteously, respectfully. *rare* (Shakes.). L16–E17.
4 By proper means, legitimately; impartially, justly. M17.

DEFOE We came honestly and fairly by the ship. J. MITCHELL Miss Culhampton . . deserves more praise than I can fairly give her.

▸ **II 5** Completely, fully; actually. L16.

M. SINCLAIR Left to himself, the Vicar fairly wallowed in his gloom. L. GARFIELD The thin child whose sharp face is fairly shining with pleasure.

6 Clearly, plainly. M17.

SIR W. SCOTT [I] saw the bonny city lie stretched fairly before me.

7 Moderately, tolerably; to a considerable degree; acceptably. E19.

E. BOWEN You see well from here . . or at any rate, fairly. A. T. ELLIS She didn't look quite so odd . . but she still looked fairly odd. F. SWINNERTON They all left happy, and on the whole . . fairly sober.

– PHRASES: **fairly and squarely** = *fair and square* s.v. FAIR *adverb*.

fairness /ˈfɛːnɪs/ *noun*. OE.
[ORIGIN from FAIR *adjective* + -NESS.]
1 The quality or condition of being fair to look at; beauty. OE. ▸†**b** Fineness (of weather). LME–M18.
2 Honesty, impartiality, justice. LME.
†**3** Fair or peaceable means. LME–M16.
4 Lightness of complexion or hair; blondness. L16.

fairy /ˈfɛːri/ *noun & adjective*. See also FAERY. ME.
[ORIGIN Old French *faerie*, *faierie* (mod. *féerie*), formed as FAY *noun*[2]: see -ERY.]
▸ **A** *noun*. **1** The mythical land of fays, fairyland; the inhabitants of fairyland collectively; enchantment. Long *rare*. ME.
good fairy: see GOOD *adjective*.
2 A mythical small being with human form, popularly believed to possess magical powers and to interfere in human affairs (with either good or evil intent); now *esp.* such a being with the form of a delicate beautiful female, usu. with wings. LME.
3 *transf.* †**a** An enchantress. *rare* (Shakes.). Only in E17. ▸**b** A small graceful woman or child. M19. ▸**c** A male homosexual. *slang. derog.* L19.
▸ **B** *adjective*. **1** That is a fairy; of or pertaining to fairies; enchanted; fictitious. L16.
2 Fairylike; delicate, finely formed. L18.
– SPECIAL COLLOCATIONS & COMB.: **fairy armadillo** either of two very small furry burrowing armadillos, *Chlamyphorus retusus* and *C. truncatus*, having a series of plates attached to the spine and heavily armoured at the rear. **fairy cake** a small individual sponge cake, usu. iced and decorated. **fairy cycle** a low small-wheeled bicycle for a child. ***fairy flax***: see FLAX *noun* 2a. **fairy floss** *Austral.* candyfloss. **fairy godmother** a fairy who acts as a protector to a mortal child; *fig.* a benefactress. **fairyland** the home of the fairies; an enchanted region. **fairy lights** small coloured lights used for decoration, esp. on Christmas trees. **fairy martin** an Australian martin, *Petrochelidon ariel*, predominantly black and white with a red-brown crown. **fairy moss** = AZOLLA. **fairy penguin** the little (blue) penguin, *Eudyptula minor*, found on the south coasts of Australia and New Zealand. **fairy prion** a prion, *Pachyptila turtur*, which breeds on the coasts of SE Australia, New Zealand, and the Falkland Islands, and has a bluish bill and bluish feet. **fairy ring** a circular band of grass darker than that around it, caused by the growth of fungi, but popularly attributed to the dancing of fairies. **fairy rose** a miniature variety of China rose (*Rosa chinensis*). **fairy shrimp** any of various small transparent crustaceans, esp. *Chirocephalus diaphanus*, which typically swim on their backs and use their legs to filter food particles from the water. **fairy story** a fairy tale. **fairy tale** (*a*) a tale about fairies, or about a strange incident, coincidence, marvellous progress etc.; an unreal or incredible story, a fabrication; (*b*) the enchanted world of fairy tales, fairy tales as a genre. **fairy tern** (*a*) a small black-crowned Australasian tern, *Sterna nereis*; (*b*) the white tern, *Gygis alba*, of tropical oceans. ***fairy thimble(s)***: see THIMBLE *noun* 8. **fairy wren** any of various small Australasian songbirds of the genus *Malurus* (family Maluridae), with a long cocked tail and freq. with bright blue coloration in the male.
■ **fairyism** *noun* (*a*) the magical power of fairies; (*b*) fairylike conditions or characteristics: E18. **fairylike** *adjective* resembling (that of) a fairy L16.

faisandé /fɛzɑ̃de/ *adjective*. E20.
[ORIGIN French, pa. pple of *faisander* hang (game) up until it is high.]
Affected, artificial, theatrical; piquant, sensational, improper.

A. POWELL Orgies organised by *faisandé* party-givers in days by.

fait accompli /ˌfeɪt əˈkɒmpli, *foreign* fɛt akɔ̃pli/ *noun phr.* Pl. **faits accomplis**. M19.
[ORIGIN French = accomplished fact.]
A thing done and irreversible before those affected learn of it.

faith /feɪθ/ *noun & verb*. ME.
[ORIGIN Anglo-Norman *fed*, Old French *feid*, *feit* (/-θ/), from Latin *fides*, from var. of base also of *fidus* trustworthy, *fidere* to trust. Cf. FAY *noun*[1].]
▸ **A** *noun*. **I** Confidence, belief.
1 Confidence, reliance, belief esp. without evidence or proof. (Foll. by *in*.) ME. ▸**b** Belief based on testimony or authority. M16.

J. H. NEWMAN To have faith in God is to surrender oneself to God. *Encounter* Citizens who have lost faith in government and almost in democratic institutions too. **b** T. H. HUXLEY The absolute rejection of authority . . the annihilation of the spirit of blind faith.

2 What is or should be believed; a system of firmly held beliefs or principles; a religion. ME.

C. MCCULLOUGH Though she abandoned her faith for Paddy, she refused to adopt his in its stead. A. STORR Communism, . . although not a religion, is certainly a faith.

3 THEOLOGY. Belief in the doctrines of a religion, esp. such as affects character and conduct. LME. ▸**b** The spiritual apprehension of divine truth or intangible realities. LME.

SWIFT Faith is an entire Dependence upon the Truth, the Power, the Justice, and the mercy of God. R. D. LAING We are not satisfied with faith, in the sense of an implausible hypothesis irrationally held. **b** E. M. GOULBURN Faith . . the faculty by which we realize unseen things.

†**4** The power to convince; authority, credibility. LME–E19. ▸**b** Attestation, confirmation, assurance. LME–M18.
▸ **II** Fidelity.
†**5** A pledge, a solemn promise. ME–L17.

ROBERT WATSON Jane, here I geue to thee my faythe and truthe . . I wyll marrye thee.

6 The duty of fulfilling a trust or promise; allegiance, obligation. ME.

W. PHILLIP The Lords . . took their oaths of faith and allegiance unto Don Philip.

7 The fulfilment of a trust or promise; fidelity, loyalty. ME.

EVELYN Persons of great faith to his Majesty's cause.

– PHRASES: **act of faith** †(*a*) = AUTO-DA-FÉ; (*b*) an action demonstrating (religious) faith. ***article of faith***: see ARTICLE *noun* 9. **bad faith** treachery, intent to deceive. **breach of faith** (an act of) insincerity or treachery. **break faith**, **break one's faith** break one's word; be disloyal. **by my faith** *arch.* truly (in oaths). ***confession of faith***: see CONFESSION 7. ***Defender of the Faith***: see DEFENDER. ***explicit faith***: see EXPLICIT *adjective*. **give faith to** believe in, give credence to. **good faith** honesty of intention, sincerity. **i' faith** *arch.* = ***in faith*** below. ***implicit faith***: see IMPLICIT 2. **in faith** *arch.* truly (in oaths). **keep faith**, **keep one's faith** keep one's word; be loyal. **on faith** on trust. **on the faith of** relying on the security of. ***pin one's faith on***, ***pin one's faith to***: see PIN *verb*. **put one's faith in** = *pin one's faith on* s.v. PIN *verb*. **the faith** the true religion.
– COMB.: **faith cure**, **faith curer**, (*US*) **faith curist**, **faith healer**, **faith healing**: acting by faith and prayer, not drugs or other conventional medicine; **faith school** a school intended for students of a particular religious faith.
▸ †**B** *verb intrans.* (foll. by *in*, *on*) & *trans.* Believe, give credit to. LME–E17.
■ **Faithist** *noun & adjective* (*a*) *noun* a member of a sect whose religion is based on a text containing supposed revelations and on angelic communications; (*b*) *adjective* of or pertaining to this sect: L19. **faithworthy** *adjective* (*arch.*) worthy of belief, trustworthy M16.

faithful /ˈfeɪθfʊl, -f(ə)l/ *adjective, noun, & adverb*. ME.
[ORIGIN from FAITH *noun* + -FUL.]
▸ **A** *adjective*. **1** Full of (esp. religious) faith; believing, pious. *arch.* ME.
2 Loyal, constant, steadfast; true *to* (a person (esp. a sexual partner), one's word or beliefs). ME. ▸†**b** Of a promise etc.: containing a pledge of fidelity; binding. LME–E17.

DRYDEN Naturally good, and faithfull to his word. J. BARNES I may have discarded Christian sexual ethics, but I do believe in being faithful to one person at a time.

3 Thorough in performing one's duty; conscientious. LME.
4 Trustworthy, veracious; reliable. LME.
5 True to the fact or original; accurate. E16.

D. M. FRAME Handsome or ugly, he must paint a faithful likeness.

▸ **B** *noun*. **1** *The* true believers, *the* orthodox members of any religious community; esp. *the* Muslims; *the* loyal adherents of a (political) party. LME.

F

J. Priestley The faithful received the eucharist every Lord's day. Ld Macaulay A communion service at which the faithful might sit. A. J. P. Taylor The I.L.P. had only contributions from the faithful.

Commander of the Faithful: see COMMANDER 1.

2 A true believer; one of the faithful; a loyal follower. LME.

J. Archer He addressed the party faithfuls in twenty-three new members' constituencies.

▸ **C** *adverb*. = FAITHFULLY. Long *non-standard*. M16.

■ **faithfulness** *noun* LME.

faithfully /ˈfeɪθfʊli, -f(ə)li/ *adverb*. LME.
[ORIGIN from FAITHFUL *adjective* + -LY².]
†**1** With full faith, trust, or confidence. LME–E17.
2 With fidelity; loyally, conscientiously, sincerely. LME.

J. Conrad The duty had been faithfully and cleverly performed.

Yours faithfully: a customary formula for closing a business or formal letter.

3 In accordance with the facts; accurately, correctly. LME.

J. Mitchell My duty was to report as faithfully as possible on the life of people as I found them.

4 With binding assurances; solemnly, sincerely. LME.

E. O'Neill Promise me faithfully never to forget your father!

faithless /ˈfeɪθlɪs/ *adjective & noun*. ME.
[ORIGIN from FAITH *noun* + -LESS.]
▸ **A** *adjective*. **1** Without confidence or trust; lacking (religious) faith, unbelieving. ME.
2 Unfaithful, insincere, false to one's promises, perfidious, disloyal. LME.
3 Unreliable, unstable, delusive. Now *rare* or *obsolete*. E17.
▸ **B** *noun*. *The* non-believers, *the* people without faith. M16.
■ **faithlessly** *adverb* M17. **faithlessness** *noun* E17.

faitour /ˈfeɪtə/ *noun*. Long *arch. rare*. ME.
[ORIGIN Anglo-Norman (= Old French *faitor* doer, maker) from Latin FACTOR *noun*: see -OUR.]
An impostor, a cheat; *esp.* a vagrant shamming illness or pretending to tell fortunes.

faja /ˈfaxa/ *noun*. M19.
[ORIGIN Spanish.]
In Spain and Spanish-speaking countries: a sash, a girdle.

fajita /fəˈhiːtə, *foreign* faˈxita/ *noun*. Pl. **-as** /-əz, *foreign* -as/. L20.
[ORIGIN Mexican Spanish, lit. 'little strip or belt'.]
(A dish of) small strips of grilled spiced beef or chicken rolled in a tortilla with chopped vegetables, grated cheese, etc., and topped with sour cream. Usu. in *pl.*

fake /feɪk/ *noun*¹. E17.
[ORIGIN Unknown: rel. to FAKE *verb*¹.]
NAUTICAL. A single turn of a coiled rope or hawser.

fake /feɪk/ *adjective & noun*². Orig. *slang*. L18.
[ORIGIN Rel. to FAKE *verb*².]
▸ **A** *adjective*. Spurious, counterfeit, sham. L18.

Glasgow Herald Fake whisky . . . the symptoms following consumption are similar to those of gastric poisoning. G. Greene He gave her a bright fake smile.

▸ **B** *noun*. **1** A trick, a dodge: an act of pretence or deceit. E19. ▸**b** SPORT. A feint, a misleading movement to deceive an opponent. M20.
2 Something not genuine, a forgery, a sham. Orig. *spec.* (*slang*), a news story of questionable authenticity or that has been much embellished. M19. ▸**b** A person who is not genuine; a charlatan, an impostor. L19.

N. Freeling The big bronze bowl . . was not as he had hoped fourth-century Gallo-Roman, but a pretty impudent Italian fake.

3 Any of various substances used in manufacturing or furbishing; any substance used in a deception. M19.
– COMB.: **fake book** JAZZ a book of music containing the basic chord sequences of tunes.

fake /feɪk/ *verb*¹ *trans*. LME.
[ORIGIN Unknown: rel. to FAKE *noun*¹.]
NAUTICAL. Lay (a rope) in coils so that it runs clear; coil.

fake /feɪk/ *verb*². Orig. *slang*. E19.
[ORIGIN Uncertain: perh. var. of FEAGUE.]
1 *verb trans*. Do something to (a person or thing); *spec.* rob, steal, assault, kill. *slang*. Now *rare* or *obsolete*. E19.
2 *verb trans*. Make presentable or plausible; alter so as to deceive; contrive out of poor or sham materials. Also foll. by *up*. M19.

R. Boldrewood The horse-brand . . had been 'faked' or cleverly altered. G. B. Shaw What else could the poor old chap do but fake up an answer fit for publication.

3 *verb trans. & intrans.* Improvise (music); ad lib. *colloq.* E20.

Melody Maker One had to 'fake' saxophone and banjo parts from those of such other instruments as were catered for in the score.

4 *verb trans*. Imitate or counterfeit, esp. in order to deceive. E20.

J. Archer Stein . . had achieved notoriety in the art world by faking 300 paintings and drawings by well-known Impressionists.

poodle-fake: see POODLE *noun*.

5 *verb trans. & intrans.* Feign, simulate; pretend. M20. ▸**b** SPORT. Feint; deceive (an opponent) by a misleading movement. M20.

E. O'Neill I . . hid my face in my hands and faked some sobs. N. Algren The big boob lay pretending to sleep and anyone could see at a glance he was faking. **b** J. Lehane The . . player may begin to fake his opponent to force a defensive mistake.

6 *verb trans*. Foll. by *out*: trick or deceive (a person). *N. Amer. slang*. M20.

fakement /ˈfeɪkm(ə)nt/ *noun*. Orig. *slang*. E19.
[ORIGIN from FAKE *verb*² + -MENT.]
A dodge, a trick; an act of faking.

faker /ˈfeɪkə/ *noun*. Orig. *slang*. E19.
[ORIGIN formed as FAKEMENT + -ER¹. See also FAKIR 2.]
A person who fakes; a swindler.

fakery /ˈfeɪk(ə)ri/ *noun*. Orig. *slang*. L19.
[ORIGIN formed as FAKEMENT + -ERY.]
Deception, trickery; the practice of faking.

A. Clare The history of ESP, astrology, poltergeist phenomena is the history of charlatanry and fakery.

faki /ˈfeɪki, ˈfa-/ *noun*. L16.
[ORIGIN Arabic *faqīh* one learned in Islamic law. Cf. ALFAQUI.]
An expert in Islamic law; (in parts of Africa) a teacher in a Koran school.

fakir /ˈfeɪkɪə; *in sense 1 also* ˈfa-/ *noun*. In sense 1 also (*arch.*) **faquir**. E17.
[ORIGIN Arabic *faqīr* poor (man), partly through French *faquir*. Sense 2 alt. of FAKER by popular etym.]
1 A Muslim (or *loosely*. Hindu) religious mendicant or ascetic. E17.
2 = FAKER. *US*. L19.

fa-la /fɑːˈlɑː/ *noun*. L16.
[ORIGIN from a meaningless refrain.]
A kind of madrigal popular in the 16th and 17th cents.

Falabella /faləˈbɛlə/ *noun*. L20.
[ORIGIN Julio *Falabella* (d. 1981), Argentinian breeder.]
(An animal of) a breed of miniature horse, the adult of which does not usually exceed 75 cm in height.

falafel /fəˈlɑːf(ə)l/ *noun*. Also **fe-**. Pl. same. M20.
[ORIGIN Egyptian Arab. *falāfil*, pl. of Arabic *fulful*, *filfil* pepper.]
A ball or fritter of spiced minced pulses or other vegetables, eaten fried and usu. in bread.

Falange /fəˈlan(d)ʒ, fəˈlɑːn(d)ʒ/ *noun & adjective*. Also **Ph-**. M20.
[ORIGIN Spanish = PHALANX.]
(Designating or pertaining to) either of two political parties: (**a**) a Fascist and right-wing party in Spain; (**b**) a right-wing Christian (Maronite) party in Lebanon.
■ **Falangism** *noun* the principles of the (Spanish or Lebanese) Falange M20. **Falangist** *noun & adjective* (**a**) *noun* an adherent of the (Spanish or Lebanese) Falange; (**b**) *adjective* of or pertaining to Falangism or Falangists: M20.

Falasha /fəˈlɑːʃə/ *noun*. Pl. same, **-s**. E18.
[ORIGIN Amharic = exile, immigrant.]
A member of an Ethiopian group holding the Jewish faith (many of whom are now resident in Israel). Also called ***Black Jew***.

falbala /ˈfalbələ/ *noun*. E18.
[ORIGIN French, of unknown origin. See also FURBELOW *noun*.]
A trimming for women's petticoats, etc.; a flounce.

falcate /ˈfalkeɪt/ *adjective*. E19.
[ORIGIN Latin *falcatus*, from *falx*, *falc-* sickle: see -ATE².]
Chiefly BOTANY & ZOOLOGY. Bent or curved like a sickle; hooked.
■ †**falcation** *noun* a falcate condition or thing M17–E18.

falcated /ˈfalkeɪtɪd/ *adjective*. E18.
[ORIGIN formed as FALCATE + -ED¹.]
1 ASTRONOMY. Appearing crescent-shaped. E18.
2 = FALCATE Chiefly in ***falcated teal***, a duck, *Anas falcata*, native to China and NE Asia, named from the long sickle-shaped inner secondary feathers of the male. M18.

falces *noun* pl. of FALX.

falchion /ˈfɔːl(t)ʃ(ə)n/ *noun*. Also †**fau(l)ch-** & other vars. ME.
[ORIGIN Old French *fauchon*, from Proto-Romance, from Latin *falx*, *falc-* sickle. Latinized spelling with *-l-* from 16.]
1 A broad curved sword with the edge on the convex side. Later, a sword of any kind. ME.
†**2** A billhook. L15–M17.

Falcidian /falˈsɪdɪən/ *adjective*. M17.
[ORIGIN from *Falcidius*, Roman proconsul *c* 40 BC + -AN.]
ROMAN HISTORY. Designating or prescribed by a law which ordained that a Roman citizen must leave at least a quarter of his estate to his legal heirs.

falciform /ˈfalsɪfɔːm/ *adjective*. M18.
[ORIGIN from Latin *falx*, *falc-* sickle + -I- + -FORM.]
Chiefly ANATOMY. Sickle-shaped, curved, hooked.
falciform ligament a ligament separating the right and left lobes of the liver and joining the organ to the diaphragm and anterior abdominal wall.

falciparum /falˈsɪpərəm/ *noun*. M20.
[ORIGIN mod. Latin (see below), from Latin *falc(i)-* *falx* sickle + *-parum*: see -PAROUS.]
A protozoan, *Plasmodium falciparum*, which causes a severe form of malaria with tertian or subtertian fever. Chiefly in ***falciparum malaria***.

falcon /ˈfɔː(l)k(ə)n, ˈfɒlk(ə)n/ *noun*. ME.
[ORIGIN Old French & mod. French *faucon* oblique case of *fauc* from late Latin *falco*, *falcon-*, from *falx*, *falc-* sickle, or Germanic base of Old High German *falco*, whence Dutch *valk*, German *Falke* falcon. Latinized spelling with *-l-* from 15.]
1 Orig., any of the diurnal birds of prey used in falconry (cf. HAWK *noun*¹); *esp.* any of the smaller long-winged birds. In mod. use, any of numerous birds of prey, the majority belonging to the genus *Falco*, characterized by long, pointed wings. ME. ▸**b** FALCONRY *spec.* The female of this. Cf. TIERCEL. LME.
Eleonora's falcon, ***gyrfalcon***, ***lanner falcon***, ***peregrine falcon***, ***saker falcon***, etc. †**falcon-gentle** (the female of) the peregrine falcon.
2 A representation of a falcon. LME.
3 *hist.* A kind of light cannon used from the 15th to the 17th cent. L15.

falconer /ˈfɔː(l)k(ə)nə, ˈfɒlk(ə)nə/ *noun*. LME.
[ORIGIN Anglo-Norman *fauconer*, Old French *-ier* (mod. *fauconnier*), from *faucon*: see FALCON, -ER².]
A person who breeds, keeps, and trains falcons or other birds of prey; one who hunts with such birds, a follower of the sport of falconry.

falconet /ˈfɔː(l)k(ə)nɪt/ *noun*. M16.
[ORIGIN In sense 1 from Italian *falconetto* dim. of *falcone* FALCON; in sense 2 from FALCON: see -ET¹.]
1 *hist.* A light cannon used in the 16th and 17th cent. M16.
2 A small falcon or bird resembling a falcon; *spec.* any of various small falcons belonging to the genus *Microhierax* or a related genus. M19.

falconry /ˈfɔː(l)k(ə)nri, ˈfɒlk(ə)nri/ *noun*. L16.
[ORIGIN French *fauconnerie*, formed as FALCON: see -RY.]
The breeding, keeping, and training of falcons or other birds of prey; the sport or practice of hunting using such birds.

faldage /ˈfaldɪdʒ/ *noun*. Also †**fold-**. ME.
[ORIGIN Anglo-Latin *faldagium*, formed as FOLD *noun*¹ + *agium*: see -AGE. Var. after FOLD *noun*¹.]
hist. †**1** Rent paid for a fold or pen. Only in ME.
2 LAW. The right of the lord of a manor to graze a tenant's sheep in folds on his land, in order to manure it. LME.

faldetta /falˈdɛttə, falˈdɛtə/ *noun*. M19.
[ORIGIN Italian, dim. of *falda* fold of cloth, skirt.]
A combined hood and cape worn by women in Malta.

†**faldistory** *noun*. L17–M19.
[ORIGIN medieval Latin *faldistorium* var. of *faldistolium*: see FALDSTOOL.]
ECCLESIASTICAL. The seat or throne of a bishop within the chancel of a cathedral.

faldstool /ˈfɔːldstuːl/ *noun*.
[ORIGIN Late Old English *fældestōl*, *fyld(e)stōl* from Germanic, from base of FOLD *verb*¹, STOOL *noun*. Partly from medieval Latin *faldistolium* from West Germanic.]
ECCLESIASTICAL. **1** A seat (freq. folding) used by a bishop or other prelate when not occupying the throne or when officiating in any church other than his own. LOE.
2 A movable folding stool or desk at which worshippers kneel; *esp.* one used by a monarch at his or her coronation. E17.
3 A small desk at which the Litany is said or sung. E17.

fale /ˈfɑːle/ *noun*. E20.
[ORIGIN Samoan.]
A Samoan house with open sides and a thatched roof.

Falernian /fəˈləːnɪən/ *adjective & noun*. M17.
[ORIGIN from *Falernus* (see below) + -IAN.]
Chiefly *hist.* ▸**A** *adjective*. Of or pertaining to *Falernus ager*, an ancient district in Campania, Italy, famous for its wine. M17.
▸ **B** *noun*. Falernian wine. E18.
■ Also †**Falerne** *adjective & noun* E17–M18.

Faliscan /fəˈlɪsk(ə)n/ *noun & adjective*. L17.
[ORIGIN from Latin *Faliscus* + -AN.]
(A native or inhabitant) of the ancient Etrurian city of Falerii.
■ Also **Faliscian** *noun* (*rare*) E17.

Falklands /ˈfɔː(l)kl(ə)ndz/ *adjective*. Also **Falkland**. L19.
[ORIGIN The *Falklands*, informal name of the Falkland Islands in the S. Atlantic.]
Of or pertaining to the Falkland Islands.
■ **Falklander** *noun* a native or inhabitant of the Falkland Islands L19.

fall /fɔːl/ *noun*¹. Now *dial.*
[ORIGIN Old English *-fealle* = Old High German *falla* (German *Falle*), from the verb. Cf. FALL *noun*² V.]
A trapdoor, a trap.
– NOTE: Prob. the 2nd elem. of PITFALL, but there now usu. taken as FALL *noun*² or *verb*.

fall /fɔːl/ *noun*[2]. ME.

[ORIGIN Partly from Old Norse (= fall, death in battle, sin, downfall); partly from the verb. Cf. FELL *noun*[4].]

▸ **I** A falling from a height or to a lower level.

1 A dropping down from a height or relative height, esp. by the force of gravity. ME. ▸**b** A descent of rain, snow, etc.; the amount that falls. L16. ▸†**c** Shedding of blood. *rare* (Shakes.). Only in L16. ▸†**d** The downward stroke of a sword etc. *rare* (Shakes.). L16–E17. ▸**e** The descent or approach of night, twilight, winter, etc. *rare* exc. in ***nightfall***. M17. ▸**f** Birth of lambs etc. by dropping from the parents; the number born. L18.

F. SMITH One of them, by a fall from the Parapet . . , was killed.

rainfall, ***snowfall***, etc.

2 The time of year when leaves fall from trees; autumn. Now chiefly *N. Amer.* M16.

J. MCPHEE In early fall, towards the end of August, they gathered berries.

3 The manner in which something falls. M16.

4 Depreciation; a reduction in price, value, etc. M16.

Times There have been some quite remarkable price falls in the year.

5 Downward direction of a surface or outline; a slope, a declivity. M16. ▸**b** NAUTICAL. The slope of a ship's deck; the difference in level between decks. M17. ▸**c** The distance through which anything descends; the amount of the descent. L17.

T. GRAY A natural terrass . . with a gradual fall on both sides.

6 A sinking down (of waves, the sun, etc.); subsidence; *fig.* decline, decay. L16. ▸**b** The decline or closing part of a day, year, or life. E17.

W. MORRIS The wide sun reddened towards his fall.

7 The falling of a stream of water down a declivity; *sing.* & (freq.) in *pl.* a cascade, a waterfall. L16.

R. RAYMOND The roar of the falls is heard in the distance.

REVERSING ***falls***.

8 A lowering of the voice, a musical note, etc.; a cadence. E17.

SHAKES. *Twel. N.* That strain again. It had a dying fall.

9 A sinking of liquid in a measuring instrument; a lowering of pressure or temperature; a registering of this on an instrument. E19.

▸ **II** A falling over from an upright position.

10 A falling from an upright position to the ground; a controlled act of falling, esp. as a stunt or in judo. ME. ▸**b** CRICKET. The loss of a wicket. L19.

B. PYM She might have had a fall and be unable to move or get to the phone.

11 *fig.* A giving in to temptation; moral descent or ruin. ME. ▸**b** THEOLOGY. *The* lapse into a sinful state resulting from Adam's transgression. Also ***the Fall of Man***. ME. ▸†**c** The cause of a moral fall. M16–E17. ▸**d** An arrest; a period in prison. *criminals' slang*. L19.

12 Death, destruction, overthrow. ME.

B. HARRIS The fall of one of the greatest men in Europe . . Oliver Cromwell.

13 WRESTLING. A bout; a throw which keeps an opponent on the ground for a specified time. M16.

14 The surrender or capture of a city, fortress, etc. L16.

H. J. LASKI The . . vice which preceded the fall of Carthage and of Rome.

15 A felling of trees; the timber felled in one season. L16.

▸ **III** **16** A linear measure consisting of the 40th part of a furlong; the corresponding square measure. *obsolete* exc. *Scot.* & *N. English*. LME.

▸ **IV** **17** One's fortune, lot, or fate; what befalls one. *obsolete* exc. *Scot.* LME.

▸ **V** (Cf. FALL *noun*[1].)

18 An article of dress, *esp.* one which hangs from or lies over something, as a veil, a flat collar, etc. E16. ▸**b** Any item of material which hangs from something, *esp.* one which is decorative or ornamental. Also, a hairpiece or hairstyle in which the hair is long and falls down naturally. M17. ▸**c** The long hair hanging over the faces of certain terriers. E20.

S. E. FERRIER The Chantilly fall which embellished the front of her bonnet. **b** LADY BIRD JOHNSON Her hair simple but elegant with a fall.

19 a A rope in hoisting tackle, to which the power is applied. M17. ▸**b** NAUTICAL. In *pl.* The tackles by which lifeboats are hoisted or lowered from the davits. E19.

20 *gen.* Something which falls or has fallen. M18.

rainfall, ***rockfall***, ***windfall***, etc.

21 BOTANY. In *pl.* The parts or petals of a flower which bend downwards; *spec.* the outer perianth segments of an iris (cf. STANDARD *noun* 4). L18.

– PHRASES: ***break a fall***: see BREAK *verb*. **fall of the leaf** *rare* autumn. ***free fall***: see FREE *adjective*. ***ride for a fall***: see RIDE *verb*. ***take a fall***: see TAKE *verb*. ***the Fall (of Man)***: see sense 11b above. **try a fall** contend *with* (an opponent).

– COMB.: **fall-board** a shutter hinged at the bottom; **fall-breaker** a thing which breaks a fall; **fallfish** a N. American cyprinoid freshwater fish, *Semotilus corporalis*; **fall front** *noun* & *adjective* (having) a front part that drops or can be let down; **fall guy** *slang* an easy victim, a scapegoat; ***fall*** HERRING; **fall-leaf** *noun* & *adjective* (*US*) = DROP-LEAF; **fall line** (*a*) PHYSICAL GEOGRAPHY a narrow zone, distinguished by the occurrence of falls and rapids where rivers and streams cross it, marking the geological boundary between an upland region and a plain (*spec.* in *US*, between the Piedmont and the Atlantic coastal plain); (*b*) SKIING the natural route down a slope; **fall money** *criminals' slang* money set aside by a criminal for use in the event of arrest; **fall-rope** a rope used for lifting; **fall-trap** = FALL *noun*[1]; **fall zone** = ***fall line*** (a) above.

fall /fɔːl/ *verb*. Pa. t. **fell** /fɛl/; pa. pple **fallen** /ˈfɔːl(ə)n/.

[ORIGIN Old English *feallan*, *fallan* = Old Frisian, Old Norse *falla*, Old Saxon, Old High German *fallan* (Dutch *vallen*, German *fallen*) from Germanic. Cf. FELL *verb*[1].]

▸ **I** *verb intrans.* Descend from a height or to a lower level.

1 Drop or come down from a height or relative height, esp. by the force of gravity. OE. ▸**b** Of rain, hail, darkness, etc.: descend, come down (as) from the upper atmosphere. OE. ▸**c** *fig.* Of calamity, fear, sleep, etc.: come down *on*, *upon*. ME. ▸**d** Of the young of animals: be dropped or born. LME.

M. KEANE I unhooked my gold dress and let it fall . . round my feet. S. BRETT The curtain fell for the interval. **b** V. WOOLF Darkness fell as sharply as a knife in this climate.

free-fall: see FREE *adjective*.

2 Become detached and drop off. ME.

E. BOWEN The . . last leaves still clung to the trees, as though they would not fall.

3 Descend, sink; *esp.* (of water, flames, a storm, etc.) subside, ebb, abate. ME. ▸**b** Decline physically or morally. ME. ▸†**c** Of the sun etc.: go down, set. LME–L19.

P. S. BUCK A still grey day when the wind fell and the air was quiet and warm.

4 Of a river etc.: discharge itself, flow *into*. ME.

5 Of the face or facial expression: lose animation, assume a look of dismay or disappointment. LME. ▸**b** Of the eyes or glance: be cast down. L19.

6 Of sound, esp. the voice, a musical note, etc.: become lower or quieter. LME.

J. C. POWYS The names . . kept rising and falling like a musical refrain.

†**7** Reduce in size; become thinner or leaner; (of swelling) go down. M16–E19.

8 Decrease, become reduced; go down in price or value. L16.

H. WILSON Our majority . . had fallen to two when we lost Leyton. *Financial Times* Short sterling . . fell slightly to 87.79.

9 Of land: slope. L16.

A. PATON The ground falls away from one's feet to the valley below.

10 Of feathers, leaves, etc.: droop, hang down. L16.

11 Of speech etc.: issue or proceed *from*. E17.

12 (Of liquid in a measuring instrument) sink to a lower point; (of a measuring instrument) register a lowering of pressure or temperature. M17. ▸**b** Of temperature: become lower. L19.

A. CALDCLEUGH The thermometer in the winter seldom falls to freezing.

▸ **II** *verb intrans.* Lose an upright position.

13 Prostrate oneself in reverence or supplication. OE.

R. P. JHABVALA Realising who it was, they fell at the Nawab's feet.

14 Stumble or be drawn *into* (a trap, danger, error, etc.). OE.

15 Be brought or come suddenly to the ground. ME. ▸**b** CRICKET. Of a wicket: be knocked down by the ball to dismiss a batsman (also registering the dismissal of a batsman by any means). Of a batsman: be out *to* a catch, bowler, etc. L18.

Dogworld A dozen exhibitors slipped and fell in the mud.

16 Yield to temptation, sin; lose honour or moral standing. ME. ▸**b** Be arrested; be sent to prison. *criminals' slang*. L19.

D. LESSING It was because Adam ate the apple that he was lost, or fell.

17 *fig.* Of a fortification, empire, government, etc.: succumb to attack or opposition, be destroyed or overthrown. ME. ▸**b** CARDS. Be captured by a higher card. (Foll. by *to*.) E18.

L. NAMIER Lord North's government has fallen.

18 Drop down wounded or dead; die by violence. ME.

J. R. GREEN The greater part of the higher nobility had fallen in battle.

19 Of a building etc.: come down in fragments, tumble in ruins. ME.

▸ **III** *verb intrans.* Happen, occur, become.

20 (Of a lot, choice, etc.) chance *on*, light *on*; be allotted or apportioned *to*; come as a burden or duty *to*, devolve (*up*)*on*. ME.

C. THIRLWALL The suspicion of disaffection . . fell on a man of eminent talents. M. MEYER It fell to her to see to his personal needs.

†**21** Appertain, belong. Foll. by *to*, *for*. ME–M16.

22 Come into a specified state or position (by chance, naturally, in the course of events, or unawares); pass *into* (†*in*, †*to*) a specified state or position. ME. ▸†**b** Come as a consequence or result. ME–L17. ▸†**c** Change for the worse (*in*)*to*. LME–L16. ▸**d** Of light, the sight, a movement, etc.: have or take a specified direction, have a specified position, settle *on*. L16. ▸**e** Be (naturally) divisible *into*. M17.

AV *Luke* 10:30 A certaine man went downe from Hierusalem to Iericho, and fel among theeues. T. HARDY He fell into a heavy slumber and did not wake till dawn. A. HALEY Quiet fell when Tom made it clear he wished to speak. D. BARNES Before it fell into Nora's hands, the property had been in the . . family. **d** G. MACDONALD The sound of a closing door . . fell on my ear. E. M. FORSTER To the left fell the shadow of the embankment. J. RATHBONE I . . moved the candle, and its light fell on the red hair of Rubén. **e** A. EDEN The pictures at Windlestone fell naturally into three categories.

fall behind etc.

23 Occur, come to pass, happen; come at a specified time, have as date. ME.

W. HOLDER The Vernal Equinox, which . . fell upon the 21st of March. LONGFELLOW I am rather sorry that the Exhibition falls so late in the year.

24 With compl.: become. (Foll. by adjective, noun (now only *heir*), (now *dial.*) prepositional phr., (*arch.*) *to be*.) LME.

J. A. FROUDE All the offices fell vacant together. G. GREENE He fell silent . . as though aware of an indiscretion.

25 †**a** Of an office, living, etc.: become vacant. M16–L18. ▸**b** Of a benefice or its revenues: lapse. L16.

▸ **IV** *verb trans.* **26** †**a** Overthrow, bring down. ME–E17. ▸**b** Fell (trees). Now *dial.* exc. *US*, *Austral.*, & *NZ*. LME.

27 Have as one's share; get, obtain. *obsolete* exc. *dial.* LME.

28 Let fall, drop. Now only in BELL-RINGING. L15. ▸†**b** Give birth to (a lamb etc.). L16–M17.

†**29** Lower. E17–L18.

– PHRASES: ***bottom falls out of***: see BOTTOM *noun*. **fair fall** — *arch.* may good befall —. ***fall by the wayside***: see WAYSIDE *noun*. ***fall flat***: see FLAT *adjective*. ***fall foul of***: see FOUL *adverb*. ***fall from grace***: see GRACE *noun*. ***fall in love***: see LOVE *noun*. **fall into line** take one's place in a rank; collaborate with others, do as others. ***fall into place***: see PLACE *noun*[1]. ***fall into the habit of***: see HABIT *noun*. **fall in two** collapse, disintegrate. **fall on hard times**, **fall on evil times** suffer misfortune. **fall on one's face** (*a*) prostrate oneself in reverence; (*b*) fail ridiculously. **fall on one's feet** get out of difficulty or be successful, esp. unexpectedly or by good luck. **fall on one's sword** kill oneself with a sword. **fall over oneself** *colloq.* (*a*) be very clumsy; (*b*) be very hasty or eager (*to do*). **fall short** (*a*) be or become insufficient or inadequate; (*b*) (of a shot, missile, etc.) not go far enough; (foll. by *of*) fail to obtain or reach. ***fall to one's share***: see SHARE *noun*[2]. ***fall to pieces***: see PIECE *noun*. **fall to the ground** *fig.* (of a plan etc.) come to nothing, be abandoned, fail. ***fall to the lot of***: see LOT *noun*. **foul fall** — *arch.* may evil befall —.

– WITH ADVERBS IN SPECIALIZED SENSES: **fall aboard** (*a*) fall foul *of* (a ship, †a person); †(*b*) quarrel *with*. **fall about** *colloq.* be helpless, esp. with mirth; laugh uncontrollably. **fall apart** collapse, disintegrate. **fall astern** (of a ship) drop behind. **fall away** (*a*) withdraw one's support, desert, revolt, apostatize, (*from*); (*b*) become few or thin; decay, perish, vanish. **fall back** (*a*) give way, retreat; (*b*) ***fall back on***, ***fall back upon***, have recourse to, rely on when in difficulty. **fall behind** be outstripped, stop keeping up. **fall down** (*a*) (of a ship) travel down towards the sea; †(*b*) sicken; (*c*) ***fall down* (on)** come to grief (over), fail (in). **fall in** (*a*) (of a building) collapse inwards; †(*b*) make one's way in, (of a ship) take a course for land; (*c*) (now *rare*) happen, occur; (*d*) MILITARY (cause to) get into line; (*e*) agree; concur in an arrangement; †(*f*) make up a quarrel; (*g*) come to an end, terminate; (of a debt etc.) become due; (of land etc.) become available; (of a lease) run out; (*h*) ***fall in for***, come in for, get, incur; (*i*) ***fall in upon***, come upon or drop in upon by chance; (*j*) ***fall in with***, come upon by chance, happen to meet; agree with; accede to, go along with (views, plans); humour (an opinion etc.); harmonize with, coincide with. **fall off** (*a*) step aside, withdraw; (*b*) NAUTICAL (of a ship) fail to keep its head to the wind; deviate to leeward; (*c*) part company, become estranged; (*d*) decrease in size or number; deteriorate, decline. **fall on** (*a*) attack, join battle; (*b*) (now *rare*) begin, set to work. **fall out** (*a*) disagree, quarrel (*with*); (*b*) come to pass, occur; prove to be, turn out, *esp.* turn out well; (*c*) ***fall out of*** (MILITARY), leave or be dismissed from (the ranks). **fall over** †(*a*) go over *to* (an enemy); (*b*) *Scot.* fall asleep; (*c*) not stay upright, topple over; (***fall over backwards***: see BACKWARD *adverb* 1). **fall through** break down, fail, miscarry. **fall to** (*a*) close automatically; (*b*) set to, begin working, eating, fighting, etc. **fall together** †(*a*) close, collapse; (*b*) PHONETICS (of sounds) become identical.

– WITH PREPOSITIONS IN SPECIALIZED SENSES: **fall a** — *arch.* begin *doing*, †an action. **fall aboard** — fall foul of (a ship). **fall behind** — be outstripped by, stop keeping up with. **fall down** — *arch.* descend or travel down (a river etc.). **fall for** (*colloq.*, orig. *US*) be captivated or deceived by; yield to the attractions of; (see also sense 21 above). **fall from** — *arch.* forsake allegiance to; abandon; (see also Phrases above). **fall into** — †(*a*) come into or within; make a hostile approach to, make an inroad into; (*b*) engage in, begin, (esp. conversation, *with*); (*c*) comply with, accommodate oneself to; adopt (a habit etc.); (see also senses 4, 14, 22, & Phrases above). **fall on** — †(*a*) begin (an action or state, *doing*), set about; (*b*) attack, assault; (*c*) come across, light on; (*d*) have recourse to, make use of; (see also senses 1c, 20, 22d, & Phrases above). **fall to** — †(*a*) be drawn to, become a follower of; †(*b*) agree with, accede to; (*c*) *arch.* apply oneself to, begin, (an action, *doing*); (*d*) be killed or defeated by; (see also senses 15b, 17b, 20, 21, 22 above). **fall under** — (*a*) be classed among; (*b*) be subjected to.

fall upon — = *fall on* above; (see also senses 1c, 20 above). **fall within** — be included in, come within the scope of.

†**fallace** *noun*. ME–M17.

[ORIGIN Old French & mod. French formed as FALLACY.]

= FALLACY 1, 2.

fallacion /fə'leɪʃ(ə)n/ *noun*. Now *rare*. Also **-ian**. M16.

[ORIGIN Irreg. from FALLACY, or from FALLACIOUS after *suspicious*, *suspicion*.]

= FALLACY 2.

fallacious /fə'leɪʃəs/ *adjective*. E16.

[ORIGIN Old French & mod. French *fallacieux* from Latin *fallaciosus*, formed as FALLACY: see -ACIOUS.]

1 Containing a fallacy. E16.

2 †**a** Deceitful. M17–M18. ▸**b** Deceptive, misleading. M17.

3 Causing disappointment, delusive. M17.

■ **fallaciously** *adverb* M17. **fallaciousness** *noun* L17.

fallacy /'faləsi/ *noun*. L15.

[ORIGIN Latin *fallacia*, from *fallax*, *-ac-*, from *fallere* deceive: see -ACY. Cf. earlier FALLACE.]

1 †**a** Deception, guile, trickery; a deception; a lie. L15–M18. ▸**b** Deceptiveness, unreliability. L16.

2 A deceptive argument, a sophism; *spec.* in LOGIC, a flaw which vitiates a syllogism; one of the types of such flaws. Also, sophistry. M16.

JOHN GOODWIN I shall . . proceed to show the fallacies and other weaknesses of those pretences.

fallacy of accident the fallacy of arguing from one point to another where the two points agree, or do not agree, purely by accident. **fallacy of composition** the fallacy of assuming that what is true of a member of a group is true for the group as a whole. **fallacy of misplaced concreteness** the fallacy of considering an abstract entity to be more concrete than it actually is. PATHETIC *fallacy*.

3 An error, *esp.* one founded on false reasoning. Also, delusion, error. L16.

J. MARQUAND The fallacy that all Chinese look alike.

†**4** Fallibility. *rare*. M17–L18.

5 Unsoundness of opinion, an argument, etc.; delusiveness, disappointing character. L18.

fal-lal /fa'lal, fal'lal/ *noun*, *adjective*, & *verb*. *arch*. E18.

[ORIGIN Perh. suggested by FALBALA.]

▸ **A** *noun*. A piece of finery or frippery. Usu. in *pl*. E18.

▸ †**B** *adjective*. Affected, finicking, foppish. M18–M19.

▸ **C** *verb intrans*. Infl. **-ll-**. Behave or dress in an affected or finicking manner; idle, dally, procrastinate. M19.

■ **fallalery**, **-lallery** *noun* tawdry finery M19.

fall-away /'fɔːləweɪ/ *noun*. L17.

[ORIGIN from FALL *verb* + AWAY *adverb*.]

†**1** An apostate. Only in L17.

2 A falling off. L19.

fallback /'fɔːlbak/ *adjective* & *noun*. M18.

[ORIGIN from FALL *verb* + BACK *noun*[1] (sense A.1), BACK *adverb*.]

▸ **A** *adjective*. **1** Of a chaise etc.: having a back which can be let down. *US*. M18.

2 That may be used in an emergency; *spec.* (of a wage) comprising a minimum amount, paid when work is not available. M20.

Times 5000 dockers were without work and receiving 'fall-back' pay.

▸ **B** *noun*. **1** A reserve; something which may be used in an emergency, *esp.* a fallback wage. M19.

B. GUEST If that plan fell through, he had a fall-back in 'Lady E'.

2 A falling back, depression. L19.

fallen /'fɔːl(ə)n/ *ppl adjective* & *noun*. LME.

[ORIGIN pa. pple of FALL *verb*.]

▸ **A** *ppl adjective*. **1** That has fallen. Also ***fallen-in***, ***fallen-off***, etc. LME.

W. WITHERING The fallen branches of trees. J. JORTIN The Messiah was to restore fallen man. *New Republic* The miserable pensions that are being paid to the widows of fallen soldiers. D. H. LAWRENCE The grass plot was strewn with fallen leaves. G. GREENE This book . . should do much to raise Stevenson's . . fallen reputation.

fallen angel: see ANGEL *noun*. ***fallen arch***: see ARCH *noun*[1] 3b. **fallen woman** a woman who has lost her chastity, honour, or standing; a prostitute.

2 Of flesh etc.: shrunken, emaciated. E18.

▸ **B** *noun pl*. *The* people who have fallen, esp. in battle. M18.

W. D. NEWTON The corpses of the fallen were trodden . . beneath . . heedless soles.

■ **fallenness** /-n-n-/ *noun* L19.

faller /'fɔːlə/ *noun*. LME.

[ORIGIN from FALL *verb* + -ER[1].]

1 A person who or animal or thing which falls. Also ***faller-away***, ***faller-out***, etc. LME.

2 A person who fells trees. Chiefly *dial.*, *US*, *Austral.*, & *NZ*. M19.

fallibilism /'falɪbɪlɪz(ə)m/ *noun*. L19.

[ORIGIN formed as FALLIBLE: see -ISM.]

PHILOSOPHY. The principle that propositions concerning empirical knowledge cannot be proved.

■ **fallibilist** *adjective* maintaining or accepting fallibilism L19.

fallible /'falɪb(ə)l/ *adjective* & *noun*. LME.

[ORIGIN medieval Latin *fallibilis*, from Latin *fallere* deceive: see -IBLE.]

▸ **A** *adjective*. **1** Liable to err or to be deceived. LME.

H. H. MILMAN The papal power . . the representative of fallible man.

2 Liable to be erroneous; unreliable. LME.

W. HUBBARD Uncertain and fallible Reports.

▸ **B** *noun*. A person who is fallible. *rare*. E18.

■ **falli'bility** *noun* the state or fact of being fallible; an instance of this; (cf. earlier INFALLIBILITY): M17. **fallibly** *adverb* M16.

falling /'fɔːlɪŋ/ *noun*. ME.

[ORIGIN from FALL *verb* + -ING[1].]

1 The action of FALL *verb*; an instance of this. Also ***falling-off***, ***falling-out***, etc. ME.

SHAKES. *Haml.* O Hamlet, what a falling off was there. W. C. WELLS The falling of the mercury in the barometer. LONGFELLOW The silent falling of snow. F. D. DAVISON The business of falling, hauling and sawing pine logs. P. KURTH Their abrupt falling-out had done nothing to alter her conviction.

(as) easy as falling off a log *colloq.* very easy.

2 A thing which falls or has fallen. Now *rare*. LME.

†**3** A hollow, a declivity. M16–E18.

– COMB.: **falling sickness** *arch.* epilepsy.

falling /'fɔːlɪŋ/ *ppl adjective*. ME.

[ORIGIN from FALL *verb* + -ING[2].]

1 That falls. ME.

2 PROSODY & PHONETICS. Of a foot, rhythm, etc.: having the stress at the beginning, decreasing in stress. M19.

– SPECIAL COLLOCATIONS: **falling band** a collar which falls flat around the neck, fashionable during the 17th cent. ***falling diphthong***: see DIPHTHONG *noun* 1. **falling leaf** an aerobatic manoeuvre in which an aeroplane is stalled and side-slipped while losing height. **falling star** a meteor, a shooting star. **falling weather** *dial.* & *US* rain, snow, or hail.

fall-off /'fɔːlɒf/ *noun*. L19.

[ORIGIN from FALL *verb* + OFF *adverb*.]

A reduction, a withdrawal; diminution.

Fallopian /fə'ləʊpɪən/ *adjective*. E18.

[ORIGIN from *Fallopius* Latinized form of the name of Gabriello *Fallopio* (1523–62), Italian anatomist: see -AN.]

Designating any of various anatomical structures reputedly discovered by Fallopius; *esp.* in ***Fallopian tube***, (in a female mammal) either of the tubes that lead from the ovaries to the cavity of the uterus.

Fallot /'faləʊ, *foreign* falo/ *noun*. E20.

[ORIGIN Étienne Louis Arthur *Fallot* (1850–1911), French physician.]

MEDICINE. ***Fallot's tetralogy***, ***tetralogy of Fallot***, a condition in which four congenital cardiac abnormalities occur together, accompanied by cyanosis.

fallout /'fɔːlaʊt/ *noun*. M20.

[ORIGIN from FALL *verb* + OUT *adverb*.]

(The deposition of) airborne radioactive debris from a nuclear explosion. Also *fig.*, a consequence, esp. side effects, of an unexpected kind.

fallow /'faləʊ/ *noun*. ME.

[ORIGIN Prob. from FALLOW *verb*. Cf. Middle Low German *valge* (German *Felge*).]

†**1** (A piece of) ploughed land. ME–E18.

2 (A piece of) ground that is left uncultivated after being ploughed and harrowed, in order to restore its fertility. E16.

green fallow: planted with a green crop. ***summer fallow***: see SUMMER *noun*[1].

3 The state of lying fallow; an interval during which land is allowed to lie fallow. E16.

J. BILLINGSLEY Twelve successive crops of wheat, without an intervening fallow.

fallow /'faləʊ/ *adjective*[1].

[ORIGIN Old English *falu* (*fealu*), infl. *fealwe* etc. = Old Saxon *falu* (Dutch *vaal*), Old High German *falo* (German *fahl*, *falb*), Old Norse *fǫlr*, from Germanic.]

Of a pale brownish- or reddish-yellow colour.

fallow deer a Mediterranean deer, *Cervus dama*, widely naturalized in European parks and forests, which is smaller than the red deer and has a dappled fawn summer coat.

fallow /'faləʊ/ *adjective*[2]. LME.

[ORIGIN from FALLOW *noun*.]

1 Of land: left uncultivated for the current year or longer (esp. in ***lie fallow***, ***lay fallow***). Formerly also, ploughed in readiness for sowing. LME.

W. STYRON Great tracts of bramble-choked red earth gone fallow and worthless.

2 *fig.* Potentially useful but not put to use; inactive, uncreative. M17.

J. THURBER He had resumed work after a long fallow period. B. BETTELHEIM Decision-making is a function which . . tends to atrophy when it lies fallow.

3 *transf.* Esp. of an animal: not pregnant. M18.

■ **fallowness** *noun* E17.

fallow /'faləʊ/ *verb trans.* & (*rare*) *intrans.*

[ORIGIN Old English *fealgian*. Cf. Low German *falgen*, Middle High German *valgen*, *velgen*.]

1 Plough and break up (land) for sowing. OE.

2 Break up and leave fallow (land) with a view to destroying weeds, mellowing the soil, etc. LME.

falsary /'fɔːls(ə)ri, 'fɒls-/ *noun*. *arch*. LME.

[ORIGIN Latin *falsarius*, from *falsus*: see FALSE *noun*, *adjective*, & *adverb*, -ARY[1].]

1 A person who forges or fraudulently alters a document. LME.

†**2** A deceitful person. L16–L17.

false /fɔːls, fɒls/ *noun*, *adjective*, & *adverb*. OE.

[ORIGIN Latin *falsum* neut. of *falsus*, orig. pa. pple of *fallere* deceive; in Middle English reinforced by or newly formed from Old French *fals*, *faus*, fem. *false* (mod. *faux*, *fausse*) from Latin *falsus*.]

▸ **A** *noun*. †**1** Fraud, deceit; *esp.* counterfeiting of money. OE–LME.

†**2** A deceitful person. Only in ME.

3 Something which is untrue or deceptive; (a) falsehood. *arch.* LME.

R. GREENE Such reports more false than truth contain. TENNYSON Earth's falses are heaven's truths.

▸ **B** *adjective*. **I** Deceptive, misleading.

1 Of a statement etc.: deliberately asserting what is known to be untrue: ME. ▸**b** Of a person (esp. a witness), speech, etc.: deliberately untruthful; lying. ME.

R. MAUGHAM If we find your claim to be James Steede is false, if you're an impostor. D. M. WALKER It is an offence . . to apply a false or misleading trade description to any goods. *Oxford Mail* Roy Jenkins . . dismisses Labour's plans . . as a 'false prospectus'. **b** SHAKES. *Rich. III* The envious slanders of her false accusers.

2 Of a person, conduct, etc.: offering no firm basis for trust; disloyal, treacherous, (*to*). Also, insincere, affected. ME. ▸†**b** Of ground, a foundation, etc.: not firm, treacherous. L16–L17.

POPE They . . false to Phoebus, bow the knee to Baal. C. BRONTË Her promises are hollow—her offers false. O. WILDE The false friend coming close to him so as to betray him with a kiss. CONAN DOYLE He won her with his title . . and his false London ways. D. H. LAWRENCE They were all going about in a lugubrious false way, feeling they must not be natural or ordinary. **b** DRYDEN Graze not too near the Banks, my . . sheep, the Ground is false.

3 Of an appearance, indication, etc.: deceptive, illusory; apparent, not real. Of a medium of vision: that distorts the object viewed through it. ME.

G. B. SHAW The ghastliness of a beautiful thing seen in a false light. L. DURRELL Her gratitude . . creates the illusion that she communicates with her fellow, but this is false.

4 Of a weight, measure, etc.: dishonestly contrived to give an incorrect reading. Of dice: loaded. ME.

5 Not genuine; sham, spurious; (of a coin, jewel, etc.) made in fraudulent imitation from base materials; (of a document) forged. ME. ▸**b** Of a person: that pretends or is falsely claimed to be (what is denoted by the noun). ME. ▸**c** Of a quality, action, etc.: simulated, feigned. ME. ▸**d** Esp. of hair or other features of the body: worn as a disguise, to conceal a defect, for cosmetic reasons, etc. L16. ▸**e** Of a name or other personal attribute: adopted in place of the true one to disguise one's identity etc.; assumed. L19.

JOSEPH HALL Criples that pretend false soares. G. ALLEN A swindler has two sets [of diamonds]—one real, one false. J. LE CARRÉ The agent was given . . a false passport. **b** R. SOUTH All pretended false Messiahs vanish'd upon the Appearance of Christ the true one. **c** I. MURDOCH I could . . imagine her face, pulled into that false sadness with glee looking through. *Sunday Times* I don't like people who have this false modesty. I know that I am beautiful. **d** G. B. SHAW He claps on the false nose, and is . . grotesquely transfigured. G. GREENE A flashy and false blonde. **e** R. A. FREEMAN Now, a common thief, he was sneaking in under a false name. A. SILLITOE He joined [the army] too young by giving a false age.

6 Of a manoeuvre, signal, etc.: intended to mislead an opponent, pursuer, etc. LME.

W. DAMPIER Had we enter'd the Port upon the false signal, we must have been taken. W. BLACKSTONE Putting out false lights in order to bring any vessel into danger. A. AINGER Lamb had a love of . . putting his readers on a false scent.

7 Of something naturally occurring: superficially resembling the thing properly so called but lacking its essential qualities or functions. Used esp. in names of plants, animals, and gems. LME.

ST G. J. MIVART The superior or false vocal cords. G. H. WILLIAMS False planes, apparent crystal faces, whose position is not that of true crystal planes.

false acacia, ***false brome***, ***false cypress***, ***false hellebore***, ***false scorpion***, ***false topaz***, ***false vampire***, etc.

8 Of a structure etc.: supplementing or substituted for the one properly so called. LME.

E. WAUGH The dome was false . . Its dome was merely an additional storey full of segmental rooms.

▸ **II** Mistaken, wrong.

9 Of an opinion, proposition, etc.: not in accordance with the truth or the facts; erroneous, untrue. ME.

Book of Common Prayer From all false doctrine, heresie, and schism . . Good Lord, deliver vs. S. JOHNSON The same proposition cannot be at once true and false. LD MACAULAY It may perhaps correct some false notions. A. J. P. TAYLOR The cabinet acknowledged that its expectation of a short war had proved false.

10 Not conforming with orthodox practices or rules; incorrect, invalid. LME. ▸**b** Of a musical note: wrong in pitch, out of tune. L15.

SHAKES. *L.L.L.* I smell false Latin; 'dunghill' for unguem. LD MACAULAY The heralds tell us . . that to put colours on colours, or metals on metals, is false blazonry. A. POWELL You . . look at life with a false perspective. **b** M. KEANE His voice was as wrong to me as a false note in music.

11 Of a movement or manoeuvre: made at the wrong moment or in the wrong direction; misjudged. Freq. in ***false move***, ***false step***. E18.

F. CLISSOLD A false step might have swept us below into an immense crevasse. *Today* One false move could cost Sally her life. T. STOPPARD He tries to leave, the first of several false exits by him.

12 Of pride, a scruple, etc.: arising from mistaken notions; misguided. Also, of hope, confidence, etc.: having no substantial basis; unjustified. E18.

S. HILL Doctor Sparrow . . may toss his head with all the false confidence of a mistaken diagnosis. *Truck & Driver* Mantova . . had been lulled into a false sense of security. *Times* The facts should be spelled out . . without false regard for the prickliness of . . minorities.

– SPECIAL COLLOCATIONS & COMB.: **false alarm**: given without reason, either to mislead or under misapprehension of danger. **false arrest** *US* wrongful arrest. **false bedding** *GEOLOGY* = CROSS-BEDDING. ***false bittersweet***: see BITTERSWEET *noun* 4. **false bottom** a horizontal partition above the actual bottom of a vessel, box, etc., *esp.* one forming a secret compartment. ***false brome***: see BROME. **false card**: played (esp. in bridge) so as to give a misleading impression of one's strength in the suit led. **false-card** *verb intrans.* play a false card. **false ceiling** a dummy ceiling fixed below the actual one, e.g. to accommodate wires, conduits, etc. **false colours** *NAUTICAL* (freq. *fig.*) a flag to which one is not entitled, flown in order to deceive (esp. in ***under false colours***). **false conception** *MEDICINE* (**a**) = MOLE *noun*⁴; (**b**) pseudopregnancy. **false concord** *GRAMMAR* a breach of the rules governing the agreement of words within a sentence. **false dawn** a transient light which precedes the true dawn by about an hour, esp. in eastern countries; *fig.* a promising sign which comes to nothing. **false economy** a superficial saving that indirectly causes increased expenditure. **false face** (**a**) a mask; (**b**) a treacherous or two-faced person. **false fire** †(**a**) a discharge of blank shot; (**b**) *NAUTICAL* (*hist.*) a kind of flare used as a night signal, or to mislead an enemy. **false friend** *LINGUISTICS* a word or expression that has a similar form to one in one's native language, but a different meaning (e.g. English *magazine* and French *magasin* 'shop'). **false front** (**a**) see FRONT *noun* 8b; (**b**) a facade used to conceal the height of a building. ***false gallop***: see GALLOP *noun*. **false god**: falsely claimed to exist. **false imprisonment** *LAW* unlawful restriction placed on a person's liberty or movements. **false keel** an additional keel attached to the bottom of a ship's keel to strengthen it. **false key** a skeleton key. **false memory syndrome** *PSYCHOLOGY* the condition of apparently recollecting an event which did not actually occur, especially one of childhood sexual abuse arising from suggestion during psychoanalysis. ***false molar***: see MOLAR *noun* 1. **false point** a mistaken act of pointing by a game dog. **false-point** *verb intrans.* (of a game dog) point in error. **false position**: in which one is compelled to act in a manner inconsistent with one's true nature or principles. **false pretences** (orig. *LAW*) misrepresentations designed to create an erroneous impression, esp. in order to obtain money (*hist.*) or affection from someone. **false quantity** an incorrect use of a long for a short vowel or syllable, or vice versa (esp. in Latin verse). **false quarter** a horizontal crack in a horse's hoof, caused by injury to the coronet. **false relation** *MUSIC* the simultaneous or adjacent appearance in different voices of two conflicting notes, freq. the major and minor third of the same triad. **false start** (in racing) a wrong start, necessitating return to the starting point; *fig.* an unsuccessful attempt to begin something. **false teeth** removable artificial teeth made by or for a dentist to replace missing ones. ***false vampire***: see VAMPIRE 3a. **false whorl** *BOTANY* an arrangement simulating a whorl; *spec.* a verticillaster. **false witness** *arch.* perjury (esp. in ***bear false witness***, commit perjury). **falsework** temporary supports enabling the construction of a building etc. to proceed until it is self-supporting.

▸ **C** *adverb.* **1** Untruthfully. *arch.* ME.

SHELLEY If I speak false, then may my father perish.

2 Treacherously, deceitfully. Chiefly in ***play false*** s.v. PLAY *verb.* L16.

W. F. HARVEY Your . . wife has played false to you and has . . read that letter, and betrayed its contents to your enemy.

3 Improperly, wrongly. *arch.* L16.

T. MOORE False flew the shaft, though pointed well.

See also ***ring false*** s.v. RING *verb*¹..

■ **falsely** *adverb* ME. **falseness** *noun* the quality of being false; an instance of this: ME.

false /fɔːls, fɒls/ *verb trans.* ME.

[ORIGIN Old French *falser* (mod. *fausser*) from late Latin *falsare*, from *falsus*: see FALSE *adjective*.]

†**1** Counterfeit (money); forge (a document). ME–M16. ▸**b** Introduce falsehoods into; falsify. LME–L16. ▸**c** ***false a blow***, make a feint. Only in L16.

2 Break, violate, (one's word). Long *arch. rare.* ME.

T. HARDY Past regretting Loves who have falsed their vow.

†**3** Claim to be false. Esp. in ***false a doom*** (*Scot.*), impugn a judgement by appealing to a higher court. ME–E18.

4 Flatter or wheedle deceptively. *dial.* L19.

falsehood /ˈfɔːlshʊd, ˈfɒls-/ *noun.* Earlier (*obsolete* exc. *dial.*) **-head** /-hɛd/. ME.

[ORIGIN from FALSE *adjective* + -HEAD¹, -HOOD.]

†**1** Deceitfulness, treachery. ME–M16.

2 Lack of conformity with the truth; (intentional) falsity. ME. ▸**b** (An) untrue belief or doctrine. ME.

T. BEDDOES He has . . shewn the falsehood of the conclusion. S. NAIPAUL Truth and falsehood were inextricably intertwined in that statement. **b** A. HELPS Each age has to fight with its own falsehoods.

3 Fraudulent practice, deception; an instance of this, a counterfeit. Now *rare* or *obsolete.* ME.

MILTON Hee . . Artificer of fraud . . was the first That practised falshood under saintly shew.

4 An untruthful statement; a lie. ME.

R. L. STEVENSON Another man who never told a formal falsehood in his life may yet be himself one lie.

INJURIOUS ***falsehood***.

5 Untruthful speaking; lying. M17.

E. STILLINGFLEET Herodotus was . . suspected of falshood.

6 *SCOTS LAW.* = FALSET *noun*¹ 2. L17.

falset /ˈfɔːlsɛt, ˈfɒls-/ *noun*¹. Chiefly *Scot.* LME.

[ORIGIN Old French from late Latin *falsatum* neut. pa. pple of *falsare*: see FALSE *verb*.]

1 Falsehood, deceit. LME.

†**2** *SCOTS LAW.* (A) fraudulent transaction; (a) forgery etc. LME–M17.

†**falset** *noun*². Only in 18.

[ORIGIN Anglicization.]

= FALSETTO *noun*.

falsetto /fɔːlˈsɛtəʊ, fɒl-/ *noun & adjective.* L18.

[ORIGIN Italian, dim. of *falso* FALSE *adjective*. Cf. French *fausset*.]

▸ **A** *noun.* Pl. **-os**.

1 A high-pitched voice (esp. of an adult male) forced to notes above its natural register. L18.

2 A person who sings in such a voice. L18.

▸ **B** *attrib.* or as *adjective*. Above the natural register, high-pitched. E19.

■ **falsettist** *noun* = FALSETTO *noun* 2 L19.

falsies /ˈfɔːlsɪz, ˈfɒls-/ *noun pl.* M20.

[ORIGIN from FALSE *adjective* + -IE + -S¹.]

Shaped pads for increasing the apparent size of the female breasts.

falsification /ˌfɔːlsɪfɪˈkeɪʃ(ə)n, ˌfɒls-/ *noun.* M17.

[ORIGIN medieval Latin *falsificatio(n-)*, from *falsificat-* pa. ppl stem of *falsificare*: see FALSIFY, -ATION.]

1 The action of making false; *esp.* (**a**) the fraudulent alteration of a document, of weights and measures, etc.; (**b**) the misrepresentation of a fact. M17.

2 The action of showing to be false or erroneous; the proving of an item in an account to be wrongly inserted. Also, disappointment of a person's expectations. M19.

■ **falsificator** *noun* a person who falsifies E17.

falsify /ˈfɔːlsɪfʌɪ, ˈfɒls-/ *verb.* LME.

[ORIGIN (Old French *falsifier* from) medieval Latin *falsificare*, from Latin *falsificus* making false, from *falsus* FALSE *adjective*: see -FY.]

1 *verb trans.* Show to be false or erroneous. LME. ▸**b** Fail to fulfil (a prediction, expectation, etc.). L16.

T. JEFFERSON No man can falsify any material fact here stated. **b** WILKIE COLLINS The prognostications of our . . friends were pleasantly falsified.

2 *verb trans.* Alter (a document etc.) fraudulently. E16. ▸†**b** Debase with impurities; adulterate. M16–M17. ▸**c** Make incorrect or unsound; make (a balance or standard) untrue. L16. ▸**d** Misrepresent, distort, (a fact etc.). M17.

D. BREWSTER He . . falsified the document by the substitution of a paragraph. **c** AV *Amos* 8:5 Making the Ephah small, and the shekel great, and falsifying the balances by deceit. I. D'ISRAELI He falsified accentuation, to adapt it to his metre. **d** R. SCRUTON I shall try to show how the Marxist's picture . . falsifies the realities of politics.

†**3** *verb trans.* Break, violate, (a promise etc.). M16–L17.

R. GREENE Aeneas . . falsified his faith to Dido.

†**4** *verb trans.* Make in fraudulent imitation; counterfeit, fake. M16–L17.

M. LISTER They stampt and falsified the best ancient Medals so well.

†**5** *verb trans. & intrans.* *FENCING.* Pretend to aim (a blow); feint. L16–L17.

†**6** *verb intrans.* Make a false statement; deal in falsehoods (*with*). E17–L18.

SIR T. BROWNE His wisdome will hardly permit him to falsifie with the Almighty.

■ **falsiˌfiaˈbility** *noun* (*PHILOSOPHY*) the quality of being falsifiable M20. **falsifiable** *adjective* able to be falsified; *PHILOSOPHY* (of a proposition) that can be shown to be false: E17. **falsifier** *noun* M17.

falsism /ˈfɔːlsɪz(ə)m, ˈfɒls-/ *noun.* M19.

[ORIGIN from FALSE *adjective* + -ISM.]

A statement which is self-evidently false. Also, a platitude which is not even true. Opp. ***truism***.

falsity /ˈfɔːlsɪti, ˈfɒls-/ *noun.* ME.

[ORIGIN Latin *falsitas*, from *falsus*: see FALSE *adjective*, -ITY.]

1 Untruthfulness, insincerity. Formerly also, deceitfulness, treachery. ME.

2 A false doctrine, proposition, or statement; a falsehood, an error. Also, false doctrines or statements collectively. LME.

3 Incompatibility with the facts; lack of truth. L16.

falsobordone /ˌfalsoborˈdoːne/ *noun.* Also ***falso bordone***. Pl. **-ni** /-ni/. M18.

[ORIGIN Italian, from *falso* FALSE *adjective* + *bordone* BOURDON. Cf. French FAUX-BOURDON.]

MUSIC. A technique of singing psalms in harmony, following simple chord progressions.

Falstaffian /fɔːlˈstɑːfɪən, fɒl-/ *adjective.* E19.

[ORIGIN from *Falstaff* (see below) + -IAN.]

Characteristic of or resembling Sir John Falstaff, a fat, jolly, dissipated knight who features in Shakespeare's plays *Henry IV*, *Henry V*, and *The Merry Wives of Windsor*. Also, resembling the 'ragged regiment' recruited by Falstaff (2 *Hen. IV*).

faltboat /ˈfaltbəʊt/ *noun.* Also **-boot**. E20.

[ORIGIN (Partial translation of) German *Faltboot*, from *falten* to fold + *Boot* boat.]

A small collapsible boat.

falter /ˈfɔːltə, ˈfɒl-/ *verb*¹ & *noun.* Also †**faulter**. LME.

[ORIGIN Perh. from FOLD *verb*¹ (occas. used of the faltering of the legs and tongue) + *-ter*, as in TOTTER *verb*.]

▸ **A** *verb.* **1** *verb intrans.* Walk unsteadily; stumble, stagger. Of the limbs: give way, totter. LME. ▸**b** Of an inanimate thing: move spasmodically as if in hesitation; tremble, quiver. M19.

R. WISEMAN He felt his legs faulter. I. MCEWAN Like a newborn calf, the girl took a few aimless steps which faltered in embarrassment. **b** J. L. MOTLEY The . . Rhine as it falters languidly to the sea.

2 *verb intrans.* Speak in hesitant or broken tones; stammer. LME. ▸**b** *verb trans.* Utter in a hesitant voice. (Foll. by *forth*, *out*.) M18.

A. MOOREHEAD He faltered when he came to speak of . . Wills and fell back . . in tears. **b** H. H. MILMAN The Dean faltered out that he meant no harm. D. PAE 'Why would you have Ralph discharged?' she faltered.

3 *verb intrans.* Show indecision; hesitate. Also, of courage, hope, etc.: give way, flag. E16.

G. VIDAL Only once did I falter in the course of the ritual. A. BROOKNER She was oddly nervous, her earlier resolution faltering.

4 *verb intrans.* Show loss of energy, momentum, or functioning. Of a breeze: die away. M18.

N. MONSARRAT There was no more coal, so the power-stations faltered. C. FRANCIS Progress slowed down only when the wind faltered. A. WEST The conversation faltered for a moment.

5 *verb intrans.* Of a person: fail in strength; collapse. *obsolete* exc. *dial.* L18.

▸ **B** *noun.* An instance of faltering; an unsteadiness of voice, progress, etc. M19.

■ **falteringly** *adverb* in a faltering or hesitant manner E17.

falter /ˈfɔːltə, ˈfɒl-/ *verb*². E17.

[ORIGIN Perh. from var. of Old French *fautrer* to strike.]

Thresh (barley etc.) a second time in order to break off the awns.

Falun Gong /ˈfalən ˌɡɒŋ/ *noun phr.* Also **Falun Dafa** /ˈdaˌfə/. L20.

[ORIGIN Chinese = 'wheel of law', from *fǎ* law + *lún* wheel (+ *gōng* skill or *dàfǎ* great method).]

(A Taoist-Buddhist sect practising) a spiritual exercise and meditation regime with similarities to T'ai Chi.

falutin /fəˈluːtɪn/ *noun & adjective. colloq.* E20.

[ORIGIN Abbreviation.]

= HIGHFALUTIN.

falx /falks/ *noun.* Pl. **falces** /ˈfalsiːz/. E18.

[ORIGIN Latin = sickle.]

1 *ANATOMY.* In full ***falx cerebri*** /ˈsɛrəbrʌɪ/ [of the brain]. The sickle-shaped fold of the dura mater on the midline of the brain between the cerebral hemispheres. E18.

2 *ZOOLOGY.* = CHELICERA. Also = PATURON. Now *rare* or *obsolete.* M19.

fam /fam/ *noun & verb. slang.* Now *rare* or *obsolete.* L17.

[ORIGIN Abbreviation of FAMBLE *noun*.]

▸ **A** *noun.* = FAMBLE *noun.* L17.

▸ **B** *verb trans.* Infl. **-mm-**. Feel, handle. E19.

famatinite /faməˈtiːnʌɪt/ *noun.* L19.

[ORIGIN from Sierra de *Famatina*, mountain range in Argentina: see -ITE¹.]

MINERALOGY. A cubic sulphide of copper and antimony usu. occurring as grey metallic crusts or massive deposits.

F

F

famble /ˈfamb(ə)l/ *noun. slang.* Now *rare* or *obsolete.* M16.
[ORIGIN Perh. from the verb.]
1 A hand. M16.
†2 A ring. Only in L17.

famble /ˈfamb(ə)l/ *verb intrans. obsolete* exc. *dial.* LME.
[ORIGIN Perh. rel. to FUMBLE *verb.* Cf. Swedish *famla,* Danish *famle* grope.]
Speak imperfectly; stammer, stutter.

fame /feɪm/ *noun.* ME.
[ORIGIN Old French from Latin *fama* report, fame.]
▸ **I 1** Personal reputation, *esp.* good personal reputation. ME.
ill fame: see ILL *adjective & adverb.*
2 The condition of being much talked about, (esp. favourably); renown; reputation derived from great achievements. ME.

M. ESSLIN Ionesco's flowering into a dramatist of world-wide fame.

fame and fortune worldly success and riches as a goal or achievement. ***Hall of Fame***: see HALL *noun.* **of — fame** known or famous from —.
†**3** Infamy, bad repute. ME–L16.
▸ **II 4** Public report, rumour, (freq. personified); a report, a rumour. Now *rare.* ME.
■ **fameful** *adjective* (now *rare*) famous L16. **fameless** *adjective* L16.

fame /feɪm/ *verb*¹ *trans.* ME.
[ORIGIN Old French *famer,* formed as FAME *noun.* Cf. medieval Latin *famare.*]
1 Tell or spread as news, report. Now only in *pass.,* be currently reported *as, to be, to do. arch.* ME.

KEATS The fancy cannot cheat so well As she is fam'd to do.

2 Make famous, speak much of. Now chiefly as ***famed*** *ppl adjective,* famous, celebrated, (*for*). LME.

N. HAWTHORNE A corpulent, jolly fellow, famed for humour. *Country Quest* Edward I, the famed Hammer of the Scots.

†**fame** *verb*² *trans.* Only in ME.
[ORIGIN Aphet. from Old French *afamer* (mod. *aff-*), from Latin *ad* AF- + *fames* hunger. Cf. FAMISH.]
Starve, famish.

familia /fəˈmɪlɪə/ *noun.* Pl. **-iae** /-iiː/. E18.
[ORIGIN formed as FAMILY.]
ROMAN HISTORY. A household under one head regarded as a unit; the area of land regarded as sufficient to support one family.

familial /fəˈmɪljəl/ *adjective.* E20.
[ORIGIN French, from Latin *familia* FAMILY: see -AL¹.]
Of, pertaining to, or characteristic of (the members of) a family; MEDICINE occurring in several members of a family.

familiar /fəˈmɪlɪə/ *adjective & noun.* ME.
[ORIGIN Old French & mod. French *familier* from Latin *familiaris,* from *familia* FAMILY: see -AR¹.]
▸ **A** *adjective.* **1** On a family footing, extremely friendly, intimate, (*with*); *spec.* sexually intimate (*with*). ME. ▸**b** Unduly intimate (*with*). Long *rare.* LME.

S. JOHNSON Time and intercourse have made us familiar.

familiar angel a guardian angel. **familiar spirit** a demon attending and obeying a witch etc.
2 Of or pertaining to one's family or household. Now *rare.* LME.
†**3** Courteous, affable. LME–M18.
4 Informal, unceremonious; occas., excessively informal, impertinent, taking liberties *with.* LME.

L. STRACHEY The young visitor, ignorant of etiquette, began to make free with the toys on the floor, in a way which was a little too familiar. T. H. WHITE You must never be familiar, rude or vulgar with them.

5 Of an animal: domesticated, tame. Now *rare.* L15.
6 Well known, known from long or close association, recognized by the memory. (Foll. by *to.*) L15. ▸†**b** Homely, plain; easily understood. E16–L19. ▸**c** Common, current, habitual, usual. M16.

J. G. COZZENS The music was not familiar to Ernest. O. MANNING Relieved and delighted to see a familiar face.

7 Well or habitually acquainted *with.* E16.

W. MARCH She never saw him in person, and is familiar only with his photographs.

†**8** Of food etc.: congenial, suitable. E–M17.
▸ **B** *noun.* **1** A member of a person's family or household. Now only ROMAN CATHOLIC CHURCH, a person belonging to the household of the Pope or a bishop, who has domestic but not menial responsibilities. ME. ▸**b** An officer of the Inquisition, chiefly employed in arresting and imprisoning the accused. M16.
2 A close friend or associate; a close acquaintance *of.* LME.
3 A familiar spirit. L16.
■ **familiarism** *noun* (now *rare*) a colloquialism M18. **familiarly** *adverb* LME. **familiarness** *noun* (now *rare*) familiarity E17.

familiarise *verb* var. of FAMILIARIZE.

familiarity /fəmɪlɪˈarɪti/ *noun.* ME.
[ORIGIN Old French & mod. French *familiarité* from Latin *familiaritas,* from *familiaris*: see FAMILIAR, -ITY.]
1 The state of being extremely friendly; intimacy *with* (a person); *spec.* sexual intimacy (*with*). ME. ▸**b** Undue intimacy. LME. ▸†**c** A familiar person or friend; a circle of friends. Only in M17.
†**2** The quality proper to a member of a family; behaviour due from a close friend etc.; devotion, fidelity. LME–L16.
3 Informality, unceremoniousness, impertinence; the treatment of inferiors or superiors as equals. LME. ▸**b** An instance of familiar behaviour; something allowed only on the ground of intimacy; an act of sexual intimacy, a caress, kiss, etc. Usu. in *pl.* M17.

Proverb: Familiarity breeds contempt. **b** L. STRACHEY The Duchess had grown too fond of her major-domo. There were familiarities.

†**4** Suitableness (of food etc.). M16–M17.
5 Close or habitual acquaintance (*with*); the quality of being known from long or close association, recognizability. E17.

H. ACTON She could claim familiarity with the painters . . of the avant-garde. M. KEANE I did not want to know it so well that familiarity could dissolve my assurance.

familiarize /fəˈmɪlɪərʌɪz/ *verb.* Also **-ise.** E17.
[ORIGIN French *familiariser,* from *familiaire* FAMILIAR *adjective* + *-iser* -IZE.]
1 *verb trans.* Make habitual or well known (*to*). E17.
†**2** *verb trans.* Domesticate, tame (an animal). M–L17.
3 *verb trans.* Accustom, habituate, *to, to do.* Now *rare.* M17.
4 *verb trans.* Make (oneself, another, a person's mind, etc.) well acquainted or at ease *with.* L17.

J. A. FROUDE Wolsey . . familiarized Henry with the sense that a reformation was inevitable. A. GUINNESS Having arrived early in order to familiarise myself with my surroundings.

5 *verb refl. & intrans.* Adopt a familiar manner (*with*). Now *rare.* L17.
†**6** *verb trans.* Make (a person's manner) affable. E–M18.
7 *verb trans.* Bring into familiar use; popularize. Now *rare.* M18.
■ **familiariˈzation** *noun* M18. **familiarizer** *noun* L19.

Familist /ˈfamɪlɪst/ *noun.* Also **f-.** L16.
[ORIGIN from FAMILY + -IST.]
1 *hist.* A member of the sect called the Family of Love (see FAMILY). L16.
†**2** The head of a family, a family man. E–M17.
■ **Familism** *noun* (*hist.*) the doctrine and practice of the Familists M17.

familistère /familistɛːr/ *noun.* Now *rare.* Pl. pronounced same. L19.
[ORIGIN French, alt. of *phalanstère* PHALANSTERY after Latin *familia* FAMILY.]
The home of a group of people living together as one family.
■ Also ***familistery*** /famɪˈlɪst(ə)ri/ *noun* (*rare*) M19.

familistic /famɪˈlɪstɪk/ *adjective.* In sense 1 also **F-.** M17.
[ORIGIN from FAMILIST + -IC.]
†**1** Of or pertaining to the Familists or Familism. Only in M17.
2 Of or pertaining to a family. M17.
■ †**familistical** *adjective* M17–E18.

famille /famiːj/ *noun.* M19.
[ORIGIN French = family. See also EN FAMILLE.]
1 ***famille de robe*** /də rɔb/ [lit. 'of the robe'], a French family founded by a lawyer or with a legal tradition. M19.
2 ***famille jaune*** /ʒoːn/, ***famille noire*** /nwaːr/, ***famille rose*** /roːz/, ***famille verte*** /vɛrt/, Chinese enamelled porcelain of particular periods in the 17th and 18th cents., of which the predominant colour is, respectively, yellow, black, red, and green. L19.

family /ˈfamɪli, -m(ə)l-/ *noun & adjective.* LME.
[ORIGIN Latin *familia* household, from *famulus* servant: see -Y³.]
▸ **A** *noun.* **I** Of people or animals.
1 a The servants of a house or establishment; the retinue of a nobleman etc. Now *arch.* or *hist.* LME. ▸**b** The staff of a high-ranking military officer or state official. E19.
2 The descendants of a common ancestor; a house, a lineage. LME. ▸**b** A race; a people assumed to be descended from a common stock. L16.

DAY LEWIS I am of Anglo-Irish stock on both sides of my family.

3 A group of people living as one household, including parents and their children, boarders, servants, etc.; such a group as an organizational unit of society. E16.

A. POWELL The French family with whom I was to stay.

extended family, joint family, nuclear family, single-parent family, etc.
4 A group of individuals or nations bound together by political or religious ties or other ties of interest. L16. ▸**b** (The members of) a local organizational unit of the Mafia. *colloq.* M20.
5 The group of people consisting of one set of parents and their children, whether living together or not; any group of people connected by blood or other relationship; a pair of animals and their young. M17.

A. HECHT Though they mean only good, Families can become a sort of burden.

6 A person's children regarded collectively; a set of offspring. M17.

L. STRACHEY By her he had a large family of sons and daughters.

▸ **II** Of things.
7 *gen.* A group of things significantly connected by common features. E17.

Computing Equipment A family of hard disk sub-systems.

8 BIOLOGY. A basic taxonomic grouping ranking above genus and below order. M18.

ANTHONY HUXLEY Orchids from one of the largest of plant families.

9 A group of languages consisting of all those ultimately derived from one early language. M18.
10 MATH. A group of curves etc. obtained by varying one quantity. M18.
11 A group of musical instruments with the same fundamental method of sound production. M19.
– PHRASES: **Family of Love** *hist.* a sect which gained many adherents in England in the 16th and 17th cents., and which stressed the importance of love and held that absolute obedience was due to all governments. ***happy families, happy family***: see HAPPY *adjective.* ***Holy Family***: see HOLY *adjective.* **in a family way** in a domestic manner; informally. **in the family way** *colloq.* pregnant. **of family, of good family** descended from noble or worthy ancestors. ***start a family***: see START *verb.* †**the family** *slang* the criminal community.
▸ **B** *attrib.* or as *adjective.* Of or pertaining to the family or a particular family; intended for families; suitable for families or all the family. E17.

J. B. PRIESTLEY Without the impudent indecencies, and so entirely suitable for family entertainment. M. B. BROWN A general lack of initiative in third- and fourth-generation family firms. *Rolling Stone* Because I was Jewish, I was also family. A. CLARE A family history of alcoholism. *TV Guide (Canada)* The family dog disappears.

– COMB. & SPECIAL COLLOCATIONS: **family allowance, family benefit**: paid by the state or an employer to a parent or guardian of a child; **family bible** a bible used at family prayers and often having space for registering family births, deaths, etc., on its fly-leaves; **family butcher**: concentrating on supplying meat to families rather than to institutions etc.; **family circle** (*a*) the company of people making up a family and its closest friends; (*b*) a gallery in a theatre etc. above the dress circle; **family credit** = ***family income supplement*** below; **Family Division** a division of the High Court dealing with adoption, divorce, and other family matters; **family doctor** a general practitioner, normally consulted by, and often regarded also as a friend of, a family; **family hotel** a hotel with special facilities or terms for families; **family income supplement** in Britain, a regular payment by the state to a family with an income below a certain level; **family likeness** a resemblance between members of the same family; **family living** ECCLESIASTICAL a benefice in the gift of the head of a family; **family man** a man with a family; a man who spends much time with his family; **family name** a surname; a name traditionally given to members of a family; **family planning** birth control, contraception; **family portrait** a portrait of a member of a family; **family room** *N. Amer.* a living room commonly used by all members of a family; **family skeleton** a secret source of pain or shame to a family; **family therapy** a form of psychotherapy in which a patient is interviewed together with members of his or her family, some or all of whom may also subsequently be treated; **family tree** a genealogical diagram tracing the generations of a family; a diagram tracing the relationships of languages of the same family; **family values** values supposedly learned or reinforced within a traditional, close, family unit, typically those of high moral standards and discipline.

famine /ˈfamɪn/ *noun.* LME.
[ORIGIN Old French & mod. French, from *faim* hunger from Latin *fames.*]
1 Severe scarcity of food throughout a region; an instance or period of such scarcity. LME.
2 Lack of food, hunger; starvation. *arch.* LME.
3 Violent appetite, as of a famished person. Now *rare.* LME.
4 Extreme dearth of something specified, material or abstract. E17.

G. ORWELL This was one of the periods of tobacco famine and there was not a cigarette in the place.

– COMB.: **famine prices**: raised by scarcity.

famish /ˈfamɪʃ/ *verb.* LME.
[ORIGIN from FAME *verb*² + -ISH².]
1 *verb trans.* Reduce to the extremes of hunger; starve. LME.
2 *verb trans.* Kill with hunger, starve to death. LME.
3 *verb intrans.* **a** Suffer extreme hunger. M16. ▸†**b** Die of starvation. M16–L18.
■ **famished** *adjective* starved; *colloq.* very hungry: LME. **famishing** *adjective* starving; *colloq.* very hungry: L16. **famishment** *noun* the state, condition, or process of being famished L15.

famose /faˈməʊz/ *adjective & verb.* Long *arch.* LME.
[ORIGIN Latin *famosus*: see FAMOUS *adjective,* -OSE¹.]
▸ †**A** *adjective.* = FAMOUS *adjective.* LME–E17.
▸ **B** *verb trans.* = FAMOUS *verb.* L16.

famous /ˈfeɪməs/ *adjective*. LME.
[ORIGIN Anglo-Norman *famous*, Old French *fameus* (mod. *-eux*) from Latin *famosus*, from *fama* FAME *noun*: see -OUS.]
1 Celebrated, renowned, well-known, (*for*). LME.
R. JARRELL Is he really famous? . . I never heard of him before I got here. JAN MORRIS Oxford is chiefly famous for her University.
famous last words: see ***last words*** s.v. LAST *adjective*.
2 Notorious. *arch*. LME.
3 Of good repute; reliable, respectable. *Scot*. Now *rare*. LME.
†**4** Common, usual. E16–M18.
5 Excellent, splendid. *colloq*. L17.
■ **famousness** *noun* M16.

famous /ˈfeɪməs/ *verb trans. arch*. LME.
[ORIGIN from the adjective.]
Make famous, celebrate.

famously /ˈfeɪməsli/ *adverb*. LME.
[ORIGIN from FAMOUS *adjective* + -LY[2].]
†**1** Commonly, openly, notoriously. LME–E18.
2 In a famous or celebrated manner; notably; as is celebrated or well known; according to fame. L16.
SHAKES. *Rich. III* This land was famously enrich'd With politic grave counsel. C. M. J. MACCABE The eighteenth century is, famously, the great century of linguistic regulation.
3 Excellently, splendidly. *colloq*. E17.
THACKERAY Will any gentleman have some sherry and soda-water . . ? It clears the brains famously. C. BARRETT We got on famously . . Jim was as honest as they make them.

famulus /ˈfamjʊləs/ *noun*. Pl. **-li** /-lʌɪ, -liː/. M19.
[ORIGIN Latin = servant.]
An attendant, esp. on a scholar or a magician.

fan /fan/ *noun*[1]. OE.
[ORIGIN Latin *vannus* winnowing fan. See also VAN *noun*[1].]
1 a A basket or shovel used for separating grain from chaff by tossing in the air. *obsolete* exc. *hist*. OE. ▸**b** Any device or machine for winnowing grain. M17.
a AV *Matt*. 3:12 Hee . . whose fanne is in his hand . . will . . gather his wheat . . but . . burne vp the chaffe. B. JOWETT The grain shaken and winnowed by fans.
2 A device (usu. folding, and sector-shaped when spread out) for moving the air to cool one's face etc.; *esp*. one to be held in the hand. M16.
G. HUNTINGTON She opened her big feather fan . . and swept it slowly to and fro.
3 Something which, esp. when spread out, has the shape of a fan, as a bird's tail, a wing, a leaf, a tracery in a roof, etc. L16. ▸**b** A fan-shaped alluvial deposit formed esp. where a stream begins to descend a gentler slope. M19.
KEATS The fans Of careless butterflies. D. M. MULOCK The large brown fan of a horse-chestnut leaf. E. WAUGH The head-lamps . . spread a brilliant fan of light. C. CONRAN Slice the brains and spread them . . in a fan.
Rhenish fan: see RHENISH *adjective* 1.
4 NAUTICAL. (A blade of) a screw used in propelling vessels. L18.
5 A rotating apparatus usu. consisting of an axle or spindle with arms bearing flat or curved blades, esp. for producing a current of air as a means of ventilation etc. E19. ▸**b** A small sail for keeping the head of a windmill towards the wind. E19. ▸**c** An apparatus in a motor vehicle for sending a current of cold air over the radiator. E20.
J. MASTERS The fans in the ceiling whirred noisily, blowing hot air down on my head.
when the shit hits the fan: see SHIT *noun*.
– COMB.: **fan belt**: transmitting torque from the engine of a motor vehicle to the fan that cools the radiator; **fan dance**: in which the dancer is nude but partially concealed by fans; **fanfoot**, pl. **-feet**, **-foots**, (*a*) any of various noctuid moths of the family Hypeninae; (*b*) a gecko of the genus *Ptyodactylus*, with fan-shaped toes; **fan heater**: in which an electric fan drives air over an electric heater into a room etc.; **fan-jet** a jet engine with additional thrust from cold air drawn in by a fan; **fanlight** a (fan-shaped) window over a door or other window; **fan mussel** (the shell of) any of various large marine bivalve molluscs of the genus *Pinna* and family Pinnidae, with fragile elongate triangular shells; **fan palm** a palm tree of a kind having palmate leaves; **fan-tracery**, **fan-vaulting** ARCHITECTURE: composed of pendent semi cones covered with cusped panel work; **fan worm** a tube-dwelling marine polychaete of the families Sabellidae and Serpulidae, members of which have a fanlike crown of (usu. brightly coloured) filaments that project from the top of the tube, filtering the water for food particles. See also FANTAIL.
■ **fanlike** *adjective* resembling a fan E19. **fanwise** *adverb* in the manner of a fan L19.

†**fan** *noun*[2]. *rare* (Shakes.). Only in E17.
[ORIGIN from FAN *verb*.]
The action or result of fanning.

fan /fan/ *noun*[3]. L17.
[ORIGIN Abbreviation of FANATIC.]
†**1** A fanatic. *rare*. Only in L17.
2 A keen and regular spectator of a sport or supporter of a sports team; a devotee of a specified amusement, performer, etc.; *gen*. an enthusiast for a particular person or thing. Orig. *US*. L19.
H. V. MORTON The fight fans howling like a pack of hungry wolves. N. HORNBY The natural state of the football fan is bitter disappointment. E. CURRIE He's a big heavy-metal fan.
– COMB.: **fan base** the fans of a sports team, pop group, etc., considered as a distinct social grouping; **fanboy**, **fangirl** *colloq*. an obsessive fan of comics, music, science fiction, etc.; **fan club** an organized group of devotees of a theatrical etc. celebrity; **fan fiction** fiction written by a fan of, and featuring characters from, a particular TV series, film, etc.; **fan mail** the letters sent to a celebrity by his or her fans.
■ **fandom** *noun* E20.

Fan /fan/ *noun*[4] *& adjective*. Also **Fang**. Pl. of noun same. M19.
[ORIGIN French, app. from Fan *Pangwe*.]
A member of, of or pertaining to, an African people of the Ogowe basin in western equatorial Africa; (of) the Bantu language of this people.

fan /fan/ *verb*. Infl. **-nn-**. OE.
[ORIGIN from FAN *noun*[1]. See also VAN *verb*[1].]
1 *verb trans*. Winnow (grain etc.). OE. ▸**b** Winnow away (chaff); drive away or scatter like chaff. LME.
A. B. SOYER White oats . . are fanned, cleaned, and carried to a mill. **b** MILTON As chaff which, fanned, The wind drives.
2 *verb intrans*. Make a movement as with a fan; flap; flutter; (of the wind) blow. Now *rare*. LME. ▸**b** Be wafted gently along; move as by a gentle beating of the wings. *rare*. E17.
SHAKES. *Hen. V* Turn the sun to ice with fanning in his face with a peacock's feather. M. TWAIN To feel the . . night breezes fan through the place. **b** E. K. KANE We managed to fan along at a rate of two knots an hour.
3 *verb trans*. Move or drive (the air) with a fan. LME. ▸**b** Move like a fan, wave. *arch*. M17.
SOUTHEY The birds of heaven . . fann'd around him The motionless air of noon. **b** MILTON The willows . . Fanning their joyous leaves to thy soft lays.
4 *verb trans*. Blow gently and refreshingly on; cool by blowing gently on. L16.
COLERIDGE It fanned my cheek Like a meadow-gale of spring. C. MERIVALE Terraces, fanned by cool breezes from the sea.
5 *verb trans*. Drive a current of air (as) with a fan upon, so as to cool (a face etc.), to kindle (a flame etc.); *fig*. increase, foment, promote, (excitement etc.). E17. ▸**b** Sweep away (as) by the wind from a fan. E19.
H. WILLIAMSON To fan the embers in the hearth until the dry sticks burst into flame. J. S. HUXLEY The award fanned my poetic ambitions. A. T. ELLIS She . . plucked a large ivy leaf to fan herself. **b** SIR W. SCOTT To fan the flies from my ladie's face.
fan the flame *fig*. increase excitement etc.
6 *verb trans*. **a** Beat, rate soundly. Now chiefly *US*. L18. ▸**b** Feel, search by feeling; *esp*. search (a person) for weapons etc. M19.
b E. WALLACE No policeman has the right to 'fan' a prisoner until he gets into the police station.
7 *verb trans. & intrans*. Spread out or *out* in the shape of a fan. L19.
A. MOOREHEAD The creek fans out into innumerable channels. K. CROSSLEY-HOLLAND That ash soared and its branches fanned over gods and men.
8 *verb intrans. & trans*. BASEBALL. (Cause to) strike out. L19.

fana /fəˈnɑː/ *noun*. M19.
[ORIGIN Arabic *fanā'* annihilation.]
In Sufism, the obliteration of human attributes and of consciousness of self and their replacement by a pure consciousness of God.

Fanakalo /ˈfanəkaləʊ, ˈfanəkalɔː/ *noun*. Also **-galo** /-galəʊ, -galɔː/. M20.
[ORIGIN Nguni *fana ka lo*, from *fana* be like + *ka* possess. suffix + *lo* this.]
A lingua franca developed and used by the southern African mining companies, composed of frequently corrupted elements of the Nguni languages, English, and Afrikaans. Formerly called ***Kitchen Kaffir***.

fanal /ˈfeɪn(ə)l/ *noun*. Long *arch. rare*. Also **ph-**. M17.
[ORIGIN French from Italian *fanale*.]
A beacon, a lighthouse. Also, a (ship's) lantern.

fanam /fʌˈnɑːm/ *noun*. M16.
[ORIGIN Arabic from Malayalam *paṇam*.]
hist. A small coin, formerly current in southern India.

Fanar *noun* var. of PHANAR.

fanatic /fəˈnatɪk/ *adjective & noun*. M16.
[ORIGIN French *fanatique* or Latin *fanaticus* pertaining to a temple, inspired by a god, frenzied, from *fanum* temple: see FANE *noun*[2], -ATIC.]
▸ **A** *adjective*. **1** Of an action, speech: such as might result from possession by a god or demon. Of a person: frenzied, mad. Long *rare*. M16.
R. BAKER A fanatick fellow . . gave forth, that himselfe was the true Edward.
2 = FANATICAL 2. E17.
T. PENNANT The cloisters . . fell victims to fanatic fury. W. IRVING The Fanatic legions of the desert. C. POTOK What annoyed him was their fanatic sense of righteousness, their absolute certainty that . . they alone had God's ear.
▸ **B** *noun*. †**1** A mad person; a religious maniac. M17–E19.
M. CASAUBON One Orpheus, a mere fanatick.
2 A fanatical person, a person filled with excessive and mistaken enthusiasm, esp. in religion (orig. esp. Nonconformism). M17.
J. A. FROUDE The Jews . . were troublesome fanatics whom it was equally difficult to govern or destroy. R. MACAULAY They were both fanatics when they set their hearts on anything.

fanatical /fəˈnatɪk(ə)l/ *adjective*. M16.
[ORIGIN from FANATIC + -AL[1].]
†**1** = FANATIC *adjective* 1. M16–M17.
P. HOLLAND The men shaking & wagging their bodies . . after a fanaticall fashion.
2 Of a person, action, etc.: characterized by or filled with excessive and mistaken enthusiasm, esp. in religion. M16. ▸†**b** Extravagant. *rare* (Shakes.). Only in L16. ▸†**c** Nonconformist in religion. *derog*. L17–E18.
GEO. ELIOT I call a man fanatical when . . he . . becomes unjust and unsympathetic to men who are out of his own track. **c** ANTHONY WOOD Mr. John Fairclough . . a non-conforming minister, was buried in the fanatical burial place.
■ **fanatically** *adverb* L17. **fanaticalness** *noun* M17.

fanaticise *verb* var. of FANATICIZE.

fanaticism /fəˈnatɪsɪz(ə)m/ *noun*. M17.
[ORIGIN from FANATIC *adjective* + -ISM.]
The quality of being fanatical; excessive and mistaken enthusiasm, esp. in religion; an instance of this.

fanaticize /fəˈnatɪsʌɪz/ *verb*. Also **-ise**. E18.
[ORIGIN formed as FANATICISM + -IZE.]
1 *verb intrans*. Act in a fanatical manner. E18.
2 *verb trans*. Make fanatical; make a fanatic of. E19.

†**fanatism** *noun*. L17–E19.
[ORIGIN French *fanatisme*.]
Fanaticism.

fanchon /fɑ̃ʃɔ̃/ *noun*. Pl. pronounced same. L19.
[ORIGIN French, dim. of female name *Françoise*.]
hist. (A side piece or trimming of) a kerchief.

fanciable /ˈfansɪəb(ə)l/ *adjective*. M20.
[ORIGIN from FANCY *verb* + -ABLE.]
That may be fancied; *spec*. (of a person) sexually attractive.
C. DOLAN If you weren't fanciable . . the only option left was to be nice.

fancical /ˈfansɪk(ə)l/ *adjective*. Chiefly *dial*. L17.
[ORIGIN from FANCY *noun*: see -ICAL.]
Fanciful.

fancier /ˈfansɪə/ *noun*. M18.
[ORIGIN from FANCY *verb* + -ER[1].]
A person who fancies something; *spec*. a connoisseur or follower of something; an amateur breeder of plants or animals. Freq. with specifying word.
LD MACAULAY People who, in their speculations in politics, are not reasoners, but fanciers. *Observer* Unlike most mouse fanciers, he keeps detailed written records of the genetic background of all his strains.
pigeon-fancier, ***rose-fancier***, etc.

fanciful /ˈfansɪfʊl, -f(ə)l/ *adjective*. E17.
[ORIGIN from FANCY *noun* + -FUL.]
1 Characterized by or displaying fancy in design; fantastically designed, ornamented, etc.; odd-looking. E17.
SIR W. SCOTT She wears a petticoat . . I would it were . . of a less fanciful fashion. E. BOWEN She smiled at the memory . . as at any fanciful object, cameo or painted fan, . . valued once.
2 Suggested by fancy; imaginary, unreal. M17.
SAKI This chronicle of wonderful things, half fanciful, half very real.
3 Disposed to indulge in fancies, whimsical, capricious. Also (now *rare*), characterized by the possession of fancy. M17.
COLERIDGE Milton had a highly imaginative, Cowley a very fanciful mind. E. WAUGH You may think me fanciful . . but . . I feel sometimes I can see the old house smiling to itself.
■ **fancifully** *adverb* M17. **fancifulness** *noun* M17.

fancy /ˈfansi/ *noun & adjective*. LME.
[ORIGIN Contr. of FANTASY *noun*.]
▸ **A** *noun*. **1** Capricious or arbitrary preference; individual taste; an inclination (*to do*), a liking (*for*). LME. ▸†**b** *spec*. Inclination in love. M16–E18.
G. MACDONALD What could have made Miss Crowther take such a fancy to the boy? R. DAVIES I've always had a fancy for the name Mungo. B. PYM I've always had a fancy to go there.
catch the fancy (**of**), **take the fancy** (**of**) please, attract.
2 A supposition with no solid basis; an arbitrary notion. L15.

F

COLERIDGE As wild a fancy as any of which we have treated.

3 Caprice, changeful mood; a caprice, a whim. **L16.**

LD MACAULAY The antipathy of the nation to their religion was not a fancy that would yield to the mandate of a prince.

†**4** = FANTASY *noun* 1. **L16–E18.**

W. WOLLASTON We know matters of fact by the help of . . impressions made upon phansy.

5 Delusory imagination; unfounded belief; a delusion. **L16.**

A. P. STANLEY Which . . claims to be founded not on fancy . . but on Fact. J. WYNDHAM The . . childish fancies were on me again. I found myself waiting for . . horrible things.

6 Orig., imagination, *esp.* creative imagination. Later, the aptitude for the invention and development of illustrative or decorative imagery. **L16.**

M. PATTISON That ocean-horse in which the poetic fancy of the sea-roving Saxons saw an emblem of their . . vessels. G. HUNTINGTON Everyone in fancy . . went up those steps into the secret gardens.

F

7 Something pleasing or entertaining. Now usu., something fancied, as a horse to win a race. **L16.**
8 Inventive design; an invention, an original device, a contrivance. Formerly also *spec.*, a musical composition in an impromptu style. **L16.**

T. HERBERT Adorned with . . fancies of Arabic characters.

†**9** = FANTASY *noun* 2. **E–M17.**

P. HOLLAND Dreadfull spectres and fansies skreaking hideously round about him.

10 Taste, critical judgement. Now *rare*. **M17.**

ADDISON Palaces . . built with an excellent Fancy.

11 ***the Fancy***, those with a certain common hobby or interest, fanciers, *esp.* patrons of boxing; the art of boxing. **M18.**

R. L. STEVENSON A copy of *Boxiana*, on the fly-leaves of which a youthful member of the fancy kept a chronicle.

12 A fancy article; *esp.* a fancy cake. **M19.**

M. BRAGG A box of teacakes and fancies.

13 The art of breeding an animal etc. to develop particular points of conventional beauty or excellence; one of these points. **L19.**

▸ **B** *adjective* (usu. *attrib.*).
1 Involving or resulting from caprice; (of an action) capricious, whimsical; (of a price etc.) extravagant. **M17.**

DICKENS As a display of fancy shooting, it was extremely varied and curious. J. T. MICKLETHWAITE They will give a fancy price for a work by a Leighton.

2 Ornamental, not plain; (of foods etc.) of particularly fine quality; (of flowers etc.) particoloured. **M18.** ▸**b** Dealing in or selling fancy goods. **E19.**

b THACKERAY She buys a couple of begilt Bristol boards at the Fancy Stationers.

3 Added for ornament or extraordinary use. **L18.**
4 Based on fancy or imagination rather than fact. **E19.**

H. ROGERS We . . look at this wonderful character as a fancy portrait.

5 Of an animal etc.: bred to develop particular points of conventional beauty or excellence. **E19.**
6 Of a person: being an object of inclination or fancy. **E19.**

T. S. ELIOT One o' them fancy lads—a good soldier and fond o' the ladies.

— SPECIAL COLLOCATIONS & COMB.: **fancy bread** bread not of the ordinary texture, size, and weight. **fancy cake** a small iced cake. **fancy dress** (a) fanciful costume, esp. representing an animal, a character in history or fiction, etc. (***fancy-dress ball***, a dance at which fancy dress is worn). **fancy-free** *adjective* not in love (freq. in ***footloose and fancy-free***). **fancy franchise** *hist.*: based on complicated or arbitrary qualifications. **fancy man** (*a*) *slang, derog.* a man living on the earnings of a prostitute, a pimp; (*b*) *slang, derog.* a woman's lover; (*c*) in *pl.* = ***the fancy*** (see sense 11 above). **fancy-pants** *adjective & noun* (*colloq.*) (*a*) *adjective* superior or high-class in a pretentious way. (*b*) *noun* a fastidious, superior person; a dandy; **fancy piece** *slang, derog.* = **fancy woman** below. **fancy-sick** *adjective* (*arch.*) lovesick. **fancy woman** *slang, derog.* a kept mistress, a man's lover. **fancy-work** ornamental sewing etc.
■ **fanciless** *adjective* (*arch.*) **M18.** **fancily** *adverb* **M20.** **fanciness** *noun* **M20.**

fancy /ˈfansi/ *verb trans.* **M16.**
[ORIGIN Partly from FANCY *noun*, partly contr. of FANTASY *verb*.]
†**1** Please, attach by liking *to*. **M–L16.**

R. GREENE Fast fancied to the Keepers bonny Lasse.

2 Take a fancy to, like; be pleased with. Also, have an appetite for; be sexually attracted to. **M16.** ▸**b** Select (a horse) as the likely winner of a race. **M19.**

R. GRAVES Caligula sold him the sword-fighters whom nobody else seemed to fancy. C. P. SNOW I don't specially fancy having to deal with the old lady's kind of people. A. DRAPER I fancied a pie and chips. M. GEE She still looks quite a good lay. I think she fancies me a bit. **b** P. G. WODEHOUSE Ocean Breeze is fancied . . for a race . . at Goodwood.

3 Frame in fancy; conceive, imagine; suppose oneself to perceive. Freq. (*colloq.*) in imper. expr. surprise or incredulity. **M16.**

M. PATTISON We read Bingley, and fancy we are studying ecclesiastical history. R. L. STEVENSON You can fancy the excitement into which that letter put me. I. MURDOCH Fancy Bruno being interested in sex at his age.

†**4** Arrange fancifully or artistically; contrive, design, plan. **E17–M18.**

M. W. MONTAGU Furniture . . so well fancied and fitted up.

†**5** Liken in fancy *to*, transform in fancy *into*. **M17–M19.**

SOUTHEY Hast thou never . . fancied Familiar object into some strange shape?

†**6** Allot or ascribe in fancy. Only in **M17.**

N. BACON Fame hath fancied him that Title.

7 Believe without being able to prove; be inclined to suppose; rather think *that*. **L17.**

W. COBBETT The estate, I fancy, is theirs yet. A. S. NEILL I fancy that stern disciplinarians are men who hate to be irritated. D. MURPHY What I recollect, or fancy I recollect, is standing at the head of the stairs.

8 Have an unduly high opinion of, pride oneself on, (oneself, one's own actions, abilities, or qualities). **M19.**

H. CONWAY I was conceited and fancied my game at whist.

9 Breed (animals etc.) or grow (plants) to develop particular points of conventional beauty or excellence. **M19.**

H. MAYHEW Pigeons are 'fancied' to a large extent.

†**fand** *verb* var. of FOND *verb*[1].

fandangle /fanˈdaŋg(ə)l/ *noun.* **M19.**
[ORIGIN Perh. alt. of FANDANGO after *newfangle*.]
(A) fantastic ornament; nonsense, tomfoolery.

fandango /fanˈdaŋgəʊ/ *noun.* Pl. **-o(e)s. M18.**
[ORIGIN Spanish.]
1 A lively Spanish dance for two in 3/4 or 6/8 time, usu. accompanied by guitars and castanets; a piece of music for this dance. **M18.**
2 A social assembly for dancing, a ball. Now *rare* or *obsolete*. **M18.**
3 = FANDANGLE. **M19.**

fane /feɪn/ *noun*[1]. *obsolete* exc. *dial.*
[ORIGIN Old English *fana* = Old Saxon, Old High German *fano* (German *Fahne*), Old Norse *fani*, Gothic *fana*, from Germanic: rel. to Latin *pannus* (piece of) cloth. See also VANE.]
†**1** A flag, a banner, a pennant. **OE–E19.**
2 A weathercock. **LME.**

fane /feɪn/ *noun*[2]. *poet.* **LME.**
[ORIGIN Latin *fanum*.]
A temple.

fanega /fəˈneɪgə/ *noun.* **E16.**
[ORIGIN Spanish.]
A former Spanish dry unit of capacity usu. equal to a bushel or a bushel and a half.

fanfare /ˈfanfɛː/ *noun & verb.* **M18.**
[ORIGIN French, ult. of imit. origin.]
▸ **A** *noun.* **1** A short, showy, or ceremonious sounding of trumpets, bugles, etc.; a flourish; *fig.* an elaborate welcome. **M18.**

fig.: A. COOKE With very little fanfare Parliament passed a Clean Air Act.

2 A style of decoration for the bindings of books, developed in France in the 16th cent., in which each cover is divided into symmetrical compartments of varying shapes and sizes by a continuous interlaced ribbon. Freq. *attrib.* **L19.**
▸ **B** *verb intrans.* Sound a fanfare. **M19.**

fanfaron /ˈfanfərɒn/ *noun & adjective.* Now *rare*. **E17.**
[ORIGIN French, formed as FANFARE: see -OON.]
▸ **A** *noun.* **1** A blusterer, a braggart; a person who makes a parade *of* something. **E17.**
†**2** = FANFARE *noun* 1. Only in **M19.**
▸ **B** *adjective.* Braggart, boastful. **L17.**

fanfaronade /ˌfanfarəˈneɪd, -ˈnɑːd/ *noun & verb.* **M17.**
[ORIGIN French *fanfaronnade*, formed as FANFARE: see -ADE.]
▸ **A** *noun.* **1** Boisterous or arrogant talk, brag; ostentation; an instance of this. **M17.**
2 = FANFARE *noun* 1. **E19.**
▸ **B** *verb intrans.* Bluster, swagger. *rare.* **M19.**

fang /faŋ/ *noun*[1]. **LOE.**
[ORIGIN Old Norse *fang* capture, grasp, embrace, Old Frisian, Old Saxon, Old High German *fang*, from Germanic base repr. by FANG *verb*[1]. See also VANG.]
1 Something caught or taken; booty, spoils; the proceeds of a robbery etc. Long *obsolete* exc. *Scot.* **LOE.**
2 †**a** A capture, a catch; a tight grasp or grip. **LME–E17.** ▸**b** Power, ability (*lit. & fig.*); *esp.* the power of suction of a pump. *Scot. & N. English.* **L18.**
3 NAUTICAL. **a** = VANG. **E16.** ▸**b** In *pl.* The valves of a pump box. *rare.* **M19.**
4 A trap, a snare (*lit. & fig.*). *obsolete* exc. *Scot.* **M16.**
5 A canine tooth, esp. of a dog or wolf. In *pl.* also *gen.* the teeth of a dog, wolf, or other animal noted for strength of jaw. **M16.** ▸**b** The venom tooth of a snake. **E19.** ▸**c** A human tooth. *colloq.* **M19.**

R. CAMPBELL A huge male baboon, with razor-sharp fangs. *transf.*: BROWNING Fangs of crystal set on edge in his demesne. **b** C. DARWIN Each horn is tubular, like an adder's fang. **c** C. CHAPLIN The boss . . had . . no upper teeth except one fang.

c on the fang *Austral. slang* eating. **put in the fangs** *Austral. slang* demand money etc.
6 A claw, a talon. *obsolete* exc. *dial.* **M17.**
7 An embedded pointed tapering part; *esp.* (the prong of) the root of a tooth. Also, a spike, the tang of a tool. **M17.**

R. WEST Mamma had forgotten to put a hole for the fang of the buckle in the belt.

8 A passage etc. constructed for the conveyance of air in a mine. *dial.* **M17.**
■ **fangless** *adjective* **L16.**

Fang *noun*[2] *& adjective* see FAN *noun*[4] *& adjective*.

fang /faŋ/ *verb*[1]. Long chiefly *dial.*
[ORIGIN Old English *fōn*, superseded in Middle English by forms deriving from *fangen* pa. pple. Cf. Old Frisian *fā*, Old Saxon, Old High German *fahan*, Old Norse *fá*, Gothic *fāhan* rel. to Latin *pangere* fix. Cf. FANG *noun*[1].]
1 *verb trans.* Capture, seize; catch (fish etc.); lay hold of, grasp. **OE.** ▸†**b** Get (at), obtain; get together, collect. **LME–E17.**
2 *verb trans.* Receive, accept. **OE.**
†**3** *verb trans.* Take (arms, counsel, leave, a name, one's way, etc.); undertake (battle). Also foll. by *to* (*be*): take (a person or thing) for (a purpose). **OE–M16.**
4 *verb intrans.* Seize, take hold *on*; take *to*, turn *to*; proceed *to* or *against*; set on, attack. **OE.**
†**5** *verb intrans.* Set about, begin *on*; start *to do*. **OE–ME.**
6 *verb trans.* Promise, resolve, undertake. **ME.**
†**7** *verb intrans.* Take one's way, go; swerve *from*. **LME–M16.**

fang /faŋ/ *verb*[2] *trans.* **E19.**
[ORIGIN from FANG *noun*[1].]
1 Strike with a fang or fangs, bite. **E19.**
2 Prime (a pump) by pouring in sufficient water to start it. **E19.**

fang /faŋ/ *verb*[3] *& noun*[3]. *Austral. slang.* **M20.**
[ORIGIN from the name of the racing driver J. M. *Fangio* (1911–95).]
▸ **A** *verb intrans. & trans.* Drive at high speed. **M20.**
▸ **B** *noun.* A high-speed drive in a car. **M20.**

fanged /faŋd/ *adjective.* **E17.**
[ORIGIN from FANG *noun*[1] + -ED[2].]
Having fangs (of a specified kind).
back-fanged: see BACK-. ***front-fanged***: see FRONT *noun, adjective, & adverb*.

fangle /ˈfaŋg(ə)l/ *noun & verb.* **M16.**
[ORIGIN from NEWFANGLED.]
▸ **A** *noun.* **1** ***new fangle***, a new fashion, whim, or invention; a novelty. *derog.* Now *rare.* **M16.**
†**2** A fantastic, foppish, or silly contrivance; a piece of finery; foppery, fuss. **L16–L17.**
▸ **B** *verb trans.* Fashion, fabricate; trick out. *derog. obsolete* exc. *dial.* **M17.**
■ **fanglement** *noun* (*a*) the action of fashioning something; (*b*) something fashioned, an invention, a contrivance: **M17.**

fanglomerate /faŋˈglɒm(ə)rət/ *noun.* **E20.**
[ORIGIN from FAN *noun*[1] + CONGLOMERATE *noun*.]
GEOLOGY. A rock consisting of consolidated fragments originally deposited in an alluvial fan.

fango /ˈfaŋgəʊ/ *noun.* **E20.**
[ORIGIN Italian = mud, dirt.]
Mud of a kind obtained from thermal springs in Italy, used in curative treatment at spas etc.

fankle /ˈfaŋk(ə)l/ *verb & noun. Scot.* **LME.**
[ORIGIN from Scot. *fank* coil of rope + -LE[3].]
▸ **A** *verb trans.* Entangle. **LME.**
▸ **B** *noun.* A tangle, a muddle. Freq. in ***in a fankle***. **E19.**

C. DOLAN The clammy sheets and sticky nightgown that'd been getting into a fankle.

fannell /ˈfan(ə)l/ *noun. obsolete* exc. *hist.* **M16.**
[ORIGIN medieval Latin *fanula* or *fanonellus*, dim. rel. to FANON.]
= FANON 1.

fanner /ˈfanə/ *noun.* **E16.**
[ORIGIN from FAN *noun*[1], *verb* + -ER[1].]
†**1** A person who winnows grain etc. **E16–M17.**
2 (An appliance forming part of) a device for winnowing grain etc. **L18.**
3 = FAN *noun*[1] 5. *rare.* **M19.**
4 More fully ***wind-fanner***. The kestrel. (Cf. earlier ***wind-vanner*** s.v. VANNER *noun*[1] 2.) *dial.* **M19.**
5 A person who waves or operates a fan. **L19.**

Fannie Mae /fanɪ ˈmeɪ/ *noun phr. US slang.* **M20.**
[ORIGIN Alt. of abbreviation *FNMA* after the forenames *Fanny*, *Mae*.]
The Federal National Mortgage Association, a (now private) corporation which buys and sells mortgages.

fanny /ˈfani/ *noun*[1]. L19.
[ORIGIN Unknown.]
1 The female genitals. *coarse slang*. L19.
2 The buttocks. *N. Amer. slang*. E20.
– COMB.: **fanny belt**, **fanny pack** *N. Amer. slang* = ***bumbag*** s.v. BUM *noun*[1].

fanny /ˈfani/ *noun*[2]. E20.
[ORIGIN Perh. from female name *Fanny*. Cf. FANNY ADAMS 1.]
NAUTICAL. A tin container for drink.

fanny /ˈfani/ *verb*[1] *& noun*[3]. *slang*. M20.
[ORIGIN Unknown.]
▸ **A** *verb trans*. Deceive or persuade by glib talk. M20.
▸ **B** *noun*. Glib talk, a tall story. M20.

fanny /ˈfanɪ/ *verb*[2] *intrans*. *slang*. L20.
[ORIGIN from FANNY *noun*[1].]
Fool or mess *about*, *around*.

Fanny Adams /fanɪ ˈadəmz/ *noun*. *slang*. L19.
[ORIGIN Name of a girl who was murdered *c* 1867. In sense 2 sometimes interpreted as a euphemism for 'sweet fuck all'.]
1 NAUTICAL. Tinned meat; stew. L19.
2 More fully ***sweet Fanny Adams***. Nothing at all. Cf. ***FA***. E20.

fanon /ˈfanən/ *noun*. LME.
[ORIGIN Old French & mod. French from Frankish = Old Saxon, Old High German *fano*: see FANE *noun*[1]. Cf. GONFANON.]
1 = MANIPLE 1. LME.
2 A liturgical garment worn by the Pope when celebrating a solemn pontifical mass. M19.

fantabulous /fanˈtabjʊləs/ *adjective*. *slang*. M20.
[ORIGIN Blend of FANTASTIC *adjective* and FABULOUS *adjective*.]
Of almost incredible excellence.

fantad *noun* var. of FANTOD.

fantail /ˈfanteɪl/ *noun*. E18.
[ORIGIN from FAN *noun*[1] + TAIL *noun*[1].]
1 A fan-shaped tail or lower end. E18.
2 A broad-tailed variety of the domestic pigeon. Also ***fantail pigeon***, ***fantail dove***. M18.
3 Any of numerous monarch flycatchers of the largely SE Asian and Australasian genus *Rhipidura* (also ***fantail flycatcher***). L18.
4 The projecting part of the stern of a boat. L19.
5 The fan of a windmill. M20.
■ **fantailed** *adjective* E19.

fan-tan /ˈfantan/ *noun*. L19.
[ORIGIN Chinese *fān tān*, (Cantonese) *fāan tāan*.]
1 A Chinese gambling game in which the players try to guess the remainder, after division by four, of a number of coins etc. hidden under a bowl. L19.
2 A card game with a play of sevens and sequences on them. E20.

fantasia /fanˈteɪzɪə, fantəˈziːə/ *noun*. E18.
[ORIGIN Italian: see FANTASY *noun*.]
1 A musical or other composition in which the form is of minor importance, or which is based on a familiar tune or several familiar tunes. E18.
2 An Arab display involving horseback riding, dance, etc. M19.

fantasied /ˈfantəsɪd, -zɪd/ *adjective*. *arch*. Also **ph-**. M16.
[ORIGIN from FANTASY *noun*, *verb*: see -ED[2], -ED[1].]
Framed by the fancy; full of esp. strange or new fancies, imaginative; capricious, whimsical.

fantasise *verb* var. of FANTASIZE.

fantasist /ˈfantəsɪst/ *noun*. Also (in sense 1) **ph-**. M19.
[ORIGIN from FANTASY *noun* + -IST.]
1 = FANTAST. M19.
2 A person who fantasizes; a writer of fantasies. E20.

fantasize /ˈfantəsʌɪz/ *verb*. Also **ph-**, **-ise**. E20.
[ORIGIN formed as FANTASIST: see -IZE.]
1 *verb intrans*. Have a fantasy or fanciful vision; indulge in fantasy. E20.
2 *verb trans*. Visualize in fantasy, represent in the fancy. M20.

fantasque /fanˈtask/ *noun & adjective*. Now *rare*. L17.
[ORIGIN French, popular form of *fantastique* FANTASTIC.]
▸ †**A** *noun*. Fancy, whim. L17–E18.
▸ **B** *adjective*. Fanciful, fantastic; curious. E18.

fantassin /ˈfantasɪn/ *noun*. Now *rare*. M18.
[ORIGIN French from Italian *fantaccino*, from *fante* foot soldier. Cf. INFANTRY.]
A foot soldier.

fantast /ˈfantast/ *noun*. Also (*arch*.) **ph-**. L16.
[ORIGIN Orig. from medieval Latin from Greek *phantastēs* boaster; later through German *Phantast*.]
A visionary, a dreamer; a flighty impulsive person.

fantastic /fanˈtastɪk/ *adjective & noun*. Also (*arch*.) **ph-**. LME.
[ORIGIN Old French & mod. French *fantastique* from medieval Latin *fantasticus*, late Latin *phantasticus* from Greek *phantastikos*, from *phantazein* make visible, *phantazesthai* have visions, imagine, from *phantos* visible, from *phan-* base of *phainein* show: see -IC.]
▸ **A** *adjective*. **1** Existing only in the imagination; fabulous, unreal. Now *spec*. perversely or irrationally imagined. LME.

> D. L. SAYERS When people are very ill, they sometimes get fantastic ideas.

†**2** = FANTASTICAL *adjective* 2. LME–L18. ▸†**b** Of poetry: concerned with fantasy or illusory appearance. *rare*. L16–M17.
†**3** Pertaining to or of the nature of a phantasm. L15–E18.

> J. FLETCHER Is not this a fantastic house we are in, and all a dream we do?

4 Fanciful; capricious, arbitrary; *esp*. extravagantly fanciful, odd and irrational in behaviour. Formerly also, having a lively imagination. L15.

> G. WITHER Let no fantastique Reader now condemne Our homely Muse. R. W. EMERSON Great believers are always reckoned.. impracticable, fantastic, atheistic.

5 Eccentric, quaint, or grotesque in design, conception, construction, or adornment. Cf. earlier FANTASTICAL *adjective* 5. E17. ▸**b** Making light elaborate dance steps. Chiefly in phrs. below (after Milton *L'Allegro* 33). M17.

> W. SPALDING Vaulted halls adorned with the usual fantastic arches. B. TAYLOR The witch with fantastic gestures draws a circle. W. BOYD The sort of mad impossible fantastic lie a desperate man would dream up.

b the light fantastic (**toe**) *joc*. dancing. **trip the light fantastic** *joc*. dance.
6 Arbitrarily devised. Cf. earlier FANTASTICAL *adjective* 6. Now *rare*. M17.

> H. N. HUMPHREYS Occasionally fantastic variations of well-known inscriptions occur.

7 Unbelievable; incredibly great; extraordinary; excellent. *colloq*. M20.

> P. H. GIBBS You here too? It's fantastic really. T. STOPPARD Fantastic woman I took there—titian hair, green eyes, dress cut down to here. *Newbury Weekly News* Their support.. raised a fantastic sum.

▸ **B** *noun*. **1** A person who has fanciful ideas or indulges in wild notions. Now *arch. rare*. M16.
†**2** A person given to fine or showy dress; a fop. L16–L17.
■ **fantasticness** *noun* (now *rare*) M16.

fantastical /fanˈtastɪk(ə)l/ *adjective & noun*. Also (*arch*.) **ph-**. LME.
[ORIGIN from FANTASTIC + -AL[1].]
▸ **A** *adjective*. **1** = FANTASTIC *adjective* 1. LME.

> R. G. COLLINGWOOD The way in which we distinguish real from fantastical ideas.

2 Of or pertaining to fantasy as a product or faculty of the mind; imaginative. Now *rare*. E16.

> G. W. KNIGHT *Macbeth* is fantastical and imaginative beyond other tragedies.

†**3** = FANTASTIC *adjective* 3. M16–E18.
4 = FANTASTIC *adjective* 4. M16.

> D. L. SAYERS A man so slight and fantastical in manner.

†**5** = FANTASTIC *adjective* 5. M16–E17.
6 = FANTASTIC *adjective* 6. M16.
▸ **B** *noun*. = FANTASTIC *noun* 1. Now *arch. rare*. E17.
■ **fantastiˈcality** *noun* (*a*) fantastic character or quality, eccentricity, grotesqueness; (*b*) something that is fantastic, a whim: L16. **fantasticalness** *noun* †(*a*) *rare* the condition of being subject to phantasms; (*b*) fantasticality: M16.

fantastically /fanˈtastɪk(ə)li/ *adverb*. E16.
[ORIGIN from FANTASTIC *adjective* or FANTASTICAL *adjective*: see -ICALLY.]
†**1** Through the exercise of fancy or imagination. E16–L17.
2 In a fantastic manner; capriciously; eccentrically. M16.
3 To a fantastic degree; unbelievably; extremely. *colloq*. E20.

fantasticate /fanˈtastɪkeɪt/ *verb*. E17.
[ORIGIN from FANTASTIC *adjective* + -ATE[3].]
†**1** *verb trans*. Frame in fancy. Only in E17.
2 *verb intrans*. Frame fantastic notions, fantasize. Now *rare*. E17.
3 *verb trans*. Make fantastic. M20.
■ **fantastiˈcation** *noun* the action of fantasticating; (a) fantastic speculation; (a) fantastic display or show; ostentation, affection: L19.

fantastico /fanˈtastɪkəʊ/ *noun*. Pl. **-o(e)s**. L16.
[ORIGIN Italian = fantastic.]
An absurd or irrational person; an eccentric; a fantastically dressed person.

fantastry /ˈfantastri/ *noun*. Long *rare*. Also **ph-**. M17.
[ORIGIN formed as FANTAST + -RY.]
Fantastic creation or display; delusory or illusory character; a fantasy.

fantasy /ˈfantəsi, zi/ *noun*. Also **ph-**. LME.
[ORIGIN Old French *fantasie* (mod. *fantaisie*) = Italian *fantasia* from Latin *phantasia* from Greek = appearance (later phantom), faculty of imagination, etc., from *phantazein* make visible: see FANTASTIC, -Y[3]. See also FANCY *noun*.]
†**1 a** Mental apprehension of an object of perception; the faculty by which such apprehension is made. LME–M17. ▸**b** The image impressed on the mind by an object of sense. LME–L16.
†**2** A spectral apparition, a phantom; an illusory appearance. LME–L16.
3 Delusory imagination, hallucination; the fact or habit of deluding oneself by imaginary perceptions or reminiscences. Now *rare* or *obsolete*. LME.

> SMOLLETT He will.. be sometimes misled by his own phantasy.

4 (A product of) imagination; the process, faculty, or result of forming mental representations of things not actually present; (an) extravagant or visionary fancy. LME. ▸**b** An ingenious, tasteful, or fantastic invention or design; MUSIC a fantasia. LME. ▸**c** A mental image. E19. ▸**d** A daydream arising from conscious or unconscious wishes or attitudes. E20. ▸**e** A literary genre concerned with imaginary worlds and peoples; a composition in this genre. M20.

> J. R. LOWELL Fantasy, the image-making power common to all who have the gift of dreams. A. S. NEILL In dreams we have nightmares; but in fantasy, we have a certain control. M. SARTON We made up endless fantasies about what we would do when we were rich. P. DAVIES Release from gravity represents an unusually compelling fantasy. **b** DICKENS A monstrous fantasy of rusty iron. **d** P. LAFITTE The Rorschach test invites him to enact his very vaguest fantasies, as when he sees pictures in the fire. **e** F. BROWN Fantasy deals with things that are not and cannot be. *Which Micro?* A fully-animated televised fantasy.

5 A supposition resting on no solid grounds; whimsical or visionary speculation. LME.

> W. D. WHITNEY All that would be to them less than fancy—mere fantasy.

6 Caprice, changeful mood; an instance of this; a caprice, a whim. LME.

> G. BURNET It was.. out of no light fantasy.. that he thus refused it.

†**7** Inclination, liking, desire. LME–E17.

> R. HAKLUYT He fell into a fantasie and desire to.. know how farre that land stretched.

– COMB.: **fantasy football** a competition in which participants select imaginary teams from among the players in a league and score points according to the actual performance of their players; **fantasyland** a real or imaginary place full of wonderful or fantastic things.

fantasy /ˈfantəsi, -zi/ *verb*. Also **ph-**. LME.
[ORIGIN Old French *fantasier*, formed as FANTASY *noun*.]
1 *verb trans*. Imagine in a visionary manner. LME.
2 *verb intrans*. Indulge in fantasy; fantasize. M16.
†**3** *verb trans*. Take a fancy to, be favourably inclined to. M16–M17.

Fante /ˈfanti/ *noun & adjective*. Also **-ti**, **-tee** /-tiː/. E19.
[ORIGIN Fante.]
▸ **A** *noun*. **1** One of two main varieties of Akan spoken in Ghana, the other being the mutually intelligible Twi. E19.
2 Pl. **-s**, same. A member of a people inhabiting southern Ghana. L19.
▸ **B** *adjective*. Of or pertaining to the Fantes or their language. M19.
go Fante *arch*. = ***go native*** s.v. NATIVE *adjective*.

fantigue /fanˈtiːg/ *noun*. *dial*. E19.
[ORIGIN Unknown.]
A state of anxiety or excitement; an instance of this, *esp*. a fit of ill humour.

fantoccini /fantoˈtʃiːni, fantəˈtʃiːni/ *noun*. L18.
[ORIGIN Italian, pl. of *fantoccino* dim. of *fantoccio* puppet, from *fante* boy.]
1 *pl*. Mechanically worked puppets. L18.
2 *sing*. A marionette show. L18.

fantod /ˈfantɒd/ *noun*. *colloq*. Also **-tad** /-tad/. M19.
[ORIGIN Unknown.]
A state of fidgetiness, uneasiness, or unreasonableness; ***the fantods***, nervous depression or apprehension, the fidgets, 'the creeps'.

FANY *abbreviation*.
First Aid Nursing Yeomanry.

fanzine /ˈfanziːn/ *noun*. M20.
[ORIGIN from FAN *noun*[3] + MAGA)ZINE *noun*.]
A magazine for fans of a particular performer, group, etc.

FAO *abbreviation*.
Food and Agriculture Organization (of the United Nations).

†**fap** *adjective*. *slang*. L16–E19.
[ORIGIN Unknown.]
Drunk, intoxicated.

Fapesmo /fəˈpɛzməʊ/ *noun*. L16.
[ORIGIN A mnemonic of scholastic philosophers, A indicating a universal affirmative proposition, and E a universal negative proposition.]
LOGIC. The indirect mood of the first syllogistic figure, sometimes treated as the fourth-figure mood, = FESAPO.

FAQ *abbreviation*.
1 Fair average quality.
2 Frequently asked question(s).

F

F

faquir *noun* see FAKIR.

far /fɑː/ *adjective*. Compar. †**farrer**, FARTHER *adjective*, FURTHER *adjective*. Superl. †**farrest**, FARTHEST *adjective*, FURTHEST *adjective*; also FARMOST.
[ORIGIN Old English *feorr* = Old Frisian *fēr*, *fir*, Old Saxon *fer*, Old High German *fer*, from West Germanic; prob. from the adverb.]
1 Situated at a great distance; situated a long way off. OE. ▸**b** Remote in time, nature, or relationship. M16.

H. JAMES That's another of the things I love, living in far countries. **b** J. CONRAD In the far future gleamed . . the big mansion.

2 Extending to a great distance; long. ME.
3 More distant; being the further of two. LME.

G. GREENE It wasn't safe to cross the bridge . . for all the far side of the river was in the hands of the Vietminh.

– PHRASES ETC.: ***a far cry***: see CRY *noun*. **Far East** the extreme eastern countries of the Old World, *esp.* China and Japan. **Far Eastern** *adjective* of or pertaining to the Far East. **Far West** orig., the region to the west of early N. American settlements; now, the region west of the Great Plains (taking in the Rocky Mountains and the Pacific coast). **Far Wester** = *Far-Westerner* below. **Far Western** *adjective* of or pertaining to the Far West. **Far Westerner** a settler in or inhabitant of the Far West.
■ **farness** *noun* (*a*) remoteness; (*b*) *arch.* distant parts: LME.

far /fɑː/ *verb trans.* Long *obsolete* exc. *dial.* Infl. **-rr-**.
[ORIGIN Old English *feorran*, *fyrran* = Old High German *firren*, Old Norse *firra*, from Germanic, from base of FAR *adverb*.]
Put far off, remove.

E. GASKELL I wish the man were farred who plagues his brains wi' striking out new words.

far /fɑː/ *adverb & noun*. Compar. FARTHER *adverb*, FURTHER *adverb*; superl. FARTHEST *adverb*, FURTHEST *adverb*.
[ORIGIN Old English *feor(r)* = Old Frisian *fēr*, *fir*, Old Saxon *fer*, *ferro* (Dutch *ver*), Old High German *fer*, *ferro*, Old Norse *fjarri*, Gothic *fairra*, from Germanic compar. formation on Indo-European base repr. also by Sanskrit *para*, Greek *pera* further.]
▸ **A** *adverb*. **1** At a great distance, a long way off. OE.

K. GRAHAME A remote common far from habitation.

2 To a great distance; to a remote place. OE. ▸†**b** Over a large area, widely. ME–L17.

J. CONRAD They would have to go . . go far away.

3 By a great deal. (With a compar. or superl., verb, etc., indicating inequality; modifying an adjective, adverb, etc., implying variation from a standard.) OE. ▸**b** By a great interval or space. LME.

B. JOWETT They were not far wrong. C. P. SNOW It was far too good to miss. **b** J. THOMSON Far distant from their native soil.

4 To or at an advanced point in space or time; to a great length or degree. ME.

O. MANNING Her irritation did not carry her very far.

5 Preceded by *as*, *how*, *so*, *thus*, etc.: at or to a specific distance, to a specific extent. ME.
– PHRASES & COMB.: **as far as** (*a*) right to, not short of, (a place); (*b*) to whatever extent; ***as far as it goes***, within its limitations; (*c*) *N. Amer.* with regard to, as for; **by far** by a great amount. ***far and away***: see AWAY *adverb* 2. **far and near** in every part, everywhere. **far and wide** over a wide area, everywhere. **far be it from me to** — I would on no account —. **far-back** *adjective* remote, inaccessible, ancient. **far between** infrequent (***FEW and far between***). **far-come** *adjective* (*arch.*) come from a great distance. **far-down** *adjective* situated or existing far below. **far-famed** *adjective* widely known, celebrated. **far-flung** *adjective* (*rhet.*) widely extended, remote. **far forth** (*arch.*), †**farforth** *adverb* †(*a*) to a great distance or extent; (*b*) to a definite degree or (formerly) distance (in ***so far forth***, †***as far forth***, †***thus far forth***). **far from** *fig.* almost opposite to, anything but. **far gone** advanced in time; very ill, mad, tired, or drunk; much in debt; (foll. by *in*). **far-off** *adjective* remote, distant. **far or near** anywhere. **far out** *adjective* distant; *fig.* unconventional, avant-garde; (as *interjection*) excellent! **far-reaching** *adjective* widely applicable; carrying many consequences. **far-seeing** *adjective* prescient; prudent. **far-sighted** *adjective* (*a*) far-seeing; (*b*) seeing distant things more clearly than those close to. **far-sightedly** *adverb* in a far-sighted manner. **far-sightedness** the capacity to be far-sighted, far-sighted quality. ***go far***: see GO *verb*. **go too far** *fig.* go beyond the limits of reason, courtesy, etc. **how far** to what extent or distance. ***in so far (as)***: see IN *preposition*. ***not go far***: see GO *verb*. ***not trust X as far as one can see him or her***, ***not trust X as far as one can throw him or her***: see TRUST *verb*. **so far** to such an extent or distance; until now. **so far as** in so far as; as far as. **so far so good** progress has been satisfactory until now. **thus far** = *so far* above.
▸ **B** *noun*. Ellipt. after prepositions (chiefly *from*): a distant place, a considerable distance. ME.

farad /ˈfarad/ *noun*. M19.
[ORIGIN from FARADAY.]
PHYSICS. The SI unit of electrical capacitance, being the capacitance of a capacitor in which one coulomb of charge causes a potential difference of one volt between the plates. (Symbol F.)
– NOTE: Orig. proposed with different specifications, and as a unit of electrical charge.

faradaic /farəˈdeɪɪk/ *adjective*. L19.
[ORIGIN formed as FARADAISM + -IC.]
PHYSICS. Produced by or associated with electrical induction; inductive, induced.

faradaism /ˈfarədeɪɪz(ə)m/ *noun*. L19.
[ORIGIN from FARADAY + -ISM.]
= FARADISM.

Faraday /ˈfarədeɪ/ *noun*. In sense 2 **f-**. M19.
[ORIGIN Michael *Faraday* (1791–1867), English scientist.]
PHYSICS & CHEMISTRY **I 1** Used *attrib.* and in *possess.* to designate things discovered, invented, or explained by Faraday. M19.
Faraday cage an earthed metal screen surrounding a piece of equipment to protect it from external electrostatic interference. **Faraday constant** = sense 2 below. ***Faraday dark space***: see *Faraday's dark space* below. **Faraday effect** the rotation of the plane of polarization of electromagnetic waves when transmitted through certain substances in a magnetic field that has a component parallel to the direction of transmission. **Faraday's constant** = sense 2 below. **Faraday's dark space**, **Faraday dark space**: between the negative glow and the positive column in a low-pressure discharge tube. **Faraday's law** (*a*) a law stating that when the magnetic flux linking a circuit changes, an electromotive force is induced in the circuit proportional to the rate of change of the flux linkage; (*b*) a law stating that the amount of any substance deposited or liberated during electrolysis is proportional to the quantity of charge passed and to the equivalent weight of the substance.
▸ **II 2** That quantity of electric charge which is required to flow in order to deposit or liberate one gram-equivalent of any element during electrolysis (approx. equal to 96,490 coulomb). E20.

faradic /fəˈradɪk/ *adjective*. L19.
[ORIGIN from FARADAY + -IC.]
= FARADAIC.

faradism /ˈfarədɪz(ə)m/ *noun*. L19.
[ORIGIN formed as FARADIC + -ISM.]
Electrotherapy (using induced alternating currents).
■ **faradiˈzation** *noun* (now *rare*) treatment by faradism M19. **faradize** *verb trans.* (now *rare*) treat by faradism M19.

farandole /far(ə)nˈdəʊl, ˈfar(ə)ndəʊl/ *noun*. M19.
[ORIGIN French, from mod. Provençal *farandoulo*.]
A Provençal communal dance usu. in 6/8 time; a piece of music for this dance or in this time.

farang /faˈraŋ/ *noun*. M19.
[ORIGIN Thai from FRANK *noun*[1]: cf. FERINGHEE.]
Among Thais: a foreigner, *esp.* a European.

faraway /ˈfɑːrəweɪ, fɑːrəˈweɪ/ *adjective & noun*. E19.
[ORIGIN from FAR *adverb* + AWAY *adverb*.]
▸ **A** *adjective*. **1** Remote in time, space, or relationship. E19.
2 Of a look or expression: absent, dreamy. Of a voice: sounding faint, distant, or abstracted. L19.
▸ **B** *noun*. A remote place; the distance. *arch. & poet.* E19.
■ **farawayness** *noun* L19.

farce /fɑːs/ *noun*[1]. LME.
[ORIGIN Old French = stuffing, formed as FARCE *verb*.]
Forcemeat, (a) stuffing.

farce /fɑːs/ *noun*[2]. E16.
[ORIGIN French = FARCE *noun*[1], used metaphorically of comic interludes.]
1 A dramatic work intended only to excite laughter, often by presenting ludicrously improbable events. E16. ▸**b** The branch of drama consisting of such works. L17.

b A. S. NEILL Our school dramas tend toward comedy and farce rather than tragedy.

2 Anything fit only to be laughed at; a hollow pretence, a mockery. L17.

S. RAVEN He knows nothing and has taught nothing. The end of term exams were a mere farce.

■ **farcer** *noun* a person who writes or acts in a farce. E19. **farcify** *verb trans.* turn into a farce M19.

farce /fɑːs/ *verb trans*. ME.
[ORIGIN Old French *farsir* (mod. *farcir*), from Latin *farcire* stuff.]
1 Cram or stuff (*with*). Also foll. by *up*. Now *rare*. ME. ▸†**b** COOKERY. Stuff with forcemeat, herbs, etc. LME–M18.

W. DE LA MARE A mind Farced up with all I have learned and read.

†**2** Stuff or force *into*, *through*. LME–E17.
3 Lard, embellish, garnish. Also foll. by *up*. LME.
4 ECCLESIASTICAL. Amplify (a liturgical formula) by the insertion of certain words; interpolate a (vernacular) comment in (an epistle etc.). M19.

farceur /farsœːr (*pl. same*), fɑːˈsəː/ *noun*. L17.
[ORIGIN French, from †*farcer* act farces + *-eur* -OR.]
1 A joker, a wag. L17.
2 An actor or writer of farces. L19.

farcical /ˈfɑːsɪk(ə)l/ *adjective*[1]. E18.
[ORIGIN from FARCE *noun*[2] + -ICAL.]
Of, pertaining to, or resembling farce; extremely ludicrous or futile.

G. MURRAY The wild and farcical nature of the old comedy. A. FRASER The action would have been farcical if men's lives had not been at stake.

■ **farciˈcality** *noun* (an instance of) farcical quality M19. **farcically** *adverb* L18.

farcical /ˈfɑːsɪk(ə)l/ *adjective*[2]. Now *rare* or *obsolete*. M18.
[ORIGIN from FARCY + -ICAL.]
Of or pertaining to farcy.

farcy /ˈfɑːsi/ *noun*. Also (earlier) †**farcin**. LME.
[ORIGIN Old French *farcin* from late Latin *farciminum*, *farcimen*, from *farcire* to stuff.]
1 Glanders, esp. in chronic form. Also (*US*), a bacterial disease of cattle, marked by swelling and inflammation of lymph nodes. LME.
2 More fully ***farcy bud***, ***farcy button***. A small lymphatic growth characteristic of glanders. LME.
■ **farcied** *adjective* affected with farcy M19.

fard /fɑːd/ *noun*. Now *arch.* or *hist.* M16.
[ORIGIN Old French & mod. French, formed as FARD *verb*.]
Paint, esp. white paint, for the face.

fard /fɑːd/ *verb trans. arch.* LME.
[ORIGIN Old French & mod. French *farder*.]
1 Paint (the face) with cosmetics, orig. with fard. Freq. as ***farded*** *ppl adjective*. LME.
2 *transf. & fig.* Embellish, gloss over. M16.

fardel /ˈfɑːd(ə)l/ *noun*[1]. ME.
[ORIGIN Old French (mod. *fardeau*) bundle, load, from Proto-Romance: see -EL[2].]
1 A small pack, a parcel, a bundle. *arch.* ME.

fig.: H. ROGERS A fardel of myths.

2 A burden, esp. *fig.* of sin, sorrow, etc. LME.

BYRON These fardels of the heart.

†**3** A wrapping, *esp.* an item of clothing. LME–M17.
4 The omasum or third stomach of a ruminant. Also ***fardel-bag***. M19.

fardel /ˈfɑːd(ə)l/ *noun*[2]. *obsolete* exc. *hist.* LME.
[ORIGIN Contr., formed as FOURTH *adjective* + DEAL *noun*[1]. See also FARL.]
A fragment, a piece; *spec.* a quarter.

†**fardel** *verb trans.* Infl. **-l(l)-**. L15.
[ORIGIN from FARDEL *noun*[1]. In sense 2 perh. assoc. with FURL *verb*.]
1 Make into a bundle; bundle *up*. L15–E18.
2 NAUTICAL. = FURL *verb*. L16–E18.

fare /fɛː/ *noun*[1].
[ORIGIN Old English *fær* neut., *faru* fem., both from base of FARE *verb*.]
▸ **I** †**1** A coming or going; a course, a passage; a journey, a voyage. OE–M18. ▸**b** An expedition; *spec.* a fishing voyage. OE–M16.
†**2** A travelling company, a troop. ME–M17.
3 †**a** A road, a way, a path. LME–M18. ▸**b** A spoor or track, esp. of a rabbit or hare. *obsolete* exc. *dial.* L15.
4 Orig., a journey for which a price is paid. Later, the cost of conveyance of a passenger (formerly also of goods). LME.

O. MANNING He had not even the bus fare to and from his lodging.

5 A passenger (*occas.* passengers) paying to travel in a public vehicle, esp. a taxi. M16. ▸**b** A load, a cargo; *spec.* (*US*) a catch of fish. E17.

R. RENDELL I was driving the mini-cab, I'd just dropped a fare.

▸ **II 6** Mode of behaviour; bearing, demeanour, appearance. *obsolete* exc. *dial.* ME. ▸†**b** Display, pomp. Only in ME.
†**7** A course of action or events; proceedings, business. ME–M16. ▸**b** Noisy activity; fuss, commotion, uproar. ME–L15.
8 State of affairs; (good or bad) fortune. *obsolete* exc. *poet.* ME. ▸†**b** Good fortune, prosperity, success. ME–M18.
9 Food with regard to quality or quantity; food and drink provided. ME.

T. C. WOLFE The magic of strange foods and fruits was added to familiar fare.

bill of fare: see BILL *noun*[3].
– COMB.: **farebox** a locked receptacle on a bus or other public vehicle into which passengers drop their fares; **fare indicator** a device for registering the fares paid or due in a public vehicle; **fare stage** a part of the route of a public vehicle (esp. a bus) considered for the purpose of calculating the fare; the stop marking the limit of a stage.

†**fare** *noun*[2]. ME–M18.
[ORIGIN Italian *faro* from Latin *pharus*, Greek PHAROS.]
= PHARE *noun* 3.

fare /fɛː/ *noun*[3]. *obsolete* exc. *dial.* M16.
[ORIGIN Var. of FARROW *noun*.]
A young pig; a litter of pigs.

fare /fɛː/ *verb*.
[ORIGIN Old English *faran* = Old Frisian, Old Norse *fara*, Old Saxon, Old High German, Gothic *faran* (Dutch *varen*, German *fahren*), from Germanic from Indo-European.]
▸ **I 1** *verb intrans.* Journey, travel, make one's way. Foll. by *forth*: depart, set out. Now *arch. & literary*. OE.

M. ARNOLD Through the deep noontide heats we fare.
J. W. JOHNSON One puts on one's best clothes and fares forth.

†**2** *verb intrans.* Go, move, advance, proceed; flow, run. OE–M19.

SPENSER One knocked at the dore, and in would fare.

3 *verb trans.* Bear, carry, convey. *rare*. ME.
▸ **II 4** *verb intrans.* Get on in a specified manner (*well*, *ill*, etc.); have luck or treatment of a specified (*good*, *bad*,

etc.) kind. OE. ▸**b** Be entertained, be fed or feed oneself in a specified manner (*well* etc.). *arch.* LME.

P. KAVANAGH He did not care for his sisters, and was not worried how they fared in life. **b** E. K. KANE Our breakfast, for all fare alike, is hard tack.

fare thee well, **fare you well** *imper.* = FAREWELL *interjection*.

5 *verb intrans. impers.* in ***it fares***, ***it fared***, etc.: it happens, it happened, etc.; it turns out, it turned out, etc. ME.

SWIFT Beware . . that it fare not with you as with your predecessor.

†**6** *verb intrans.* Act, behave, conduct oneself; deal *with*, do *by*. ME–L17.

7 *verb intrans.* †**a** Seem or act *as though*, *as if*. LME–M17. ▸**b** Seem likely or incline *to do*, *to be*. *arch.* M19.

■ **farer** *noun* a traveller (chiefly as 2nd elem. of comb., as *seafarer*, *wayfarer*, etc.) LME.

farewell /fɛːˈwɛl; *as adjective usu.* ˈfɛːwɛl/ *interjection, noun, verb, & adjective.* LME.

[ORIGIN from imper. of FARE *verb* + WELL *adverb*.]

▸ **A** *interjection.* **1** As an expression of goodwill or a polite salutation on parting: goodbye. *arch.* LME.

2 *fig.*: As an expression of regret or an exclamation: goodbye to or *to*; no more of. *arch.* or *poet.* LME.

J. FORDYCE Farewel to real friendship, farewel to convivial delight.

▸ **B** *noun.* **1** An utterance of the word farewell; leave-taking, departure, parting good wishes. LME.

M. SPARK We had already said our farewells on the day before my departure.

sailor's farewell: see SAILOR *noun*. ***soldier's farewell***: see SOLDIER *noun*. ***take farewell***: see TAKE *verb*.

†**2** An aftertaste. M17–M18.

▸ **C** *verb trans.* **1** Bid or say goodbye to; take leave of. L16.

R. F. BURTON She farewelled me with her dying eyes.

2 Mark the departure or retirement of (a person) with a ceremonial occasion. L19.

▸ **D** *adjective.* Pertaining to, accompanying, or signifying a leave-taking. M17.

K. MOORE Are you going to give a farewell party?

fare-you-well /ˈfɛːjuwɛl/ *noun. US colloq.* Also **-thee-** /-ðɪ-/. L19.

[ORIGIN from *fare you well* s.v. FARE *verb* 4.]

to a fare-you-well, to the utmost degree, completely.

farfalle /fɑːˈfaleɪ, -li/ *noun pl.* M20.

[ORIGIN Italian *farfelle*, pl. of *farfalla*, lit. 'butterfly'.]

Small pieces of pasta shaped like bows or butterflies' wings.

farfel /ˈfɑːf(ə)l/ *noun.* Also **farfal**, **ferfel** /ˈfɜː-/. Pl. same, **-s**. L19.

[ORIGIN Yiddish *farfal*, *farfil*, *ferfel* (pl.), from Middle High German *varveln* noodles, noodle soup.]

Ground or granulated noodle dough; in *pl.*, granules or pellets of this.

†**far-fet** *ppl adjective.* ME–L17.

[ORIGIN from FAR *adverb* + pa. pple of FET.]

1 = FAR-FETCHED 1. ME–L17.

2 = FAR-FETCHED 2. M16.

far-fetched /fɑːˈfɛtʃt, ˈfɑːfɛtʃt/ *ppl adjective.* M16.

[ORIGIN from FAR *adverb* + pa. pple of FETCH *verb*. Cf. FAR-FET.]

1 Brought from far. *arch.* M16.

2 Of an idea, argument, simile, etc.: strained, unnatural, improbable. L16.

■ **far-fetchedness** *noun* M19.

farina /fəˈrʌɪnə, -ˈriːnə/ *noun.* LME.

[ORIGIN Latin, from *far* corn.]

1 Flour, meal. LME.

2 Any powdery substance or substance in powdered form. E18.

farinaceous /farɪˈneɪʃəs/ *adjective.* M17.

[ORIGIN Late Latin *farinaceus*, formed as FARINA: see -ACEOUS.]

1 Consisting of, made of, or characterized by flour or meal. M17.

2 Yielding flour or starch; starchy. M17.

3 Having a mealy nature or appearance. M17.

†**4** Covered with fine powder. M17–E19.

faring /ˈfɛːrɪŋ/ *noun.* M16.

[ORIGIN from FARE *verb* + -ING[1].]

1 The action of FARE *verb*. M16.

2 In *pl.* Made dishes. Now *rare*. M17.

farinha /fəˈriɲə, fəˈriːnjə/ *noun.* E18.

[ORIGIN Portuguese, formed as FARINA.]

= CASSAVA 2.

farinose /ˈfarɪnəʊs/ *adjective.* E18.

[ORIGIN Late Latin *farinosus*, from Latin FARINA: see -OSE[1].]

Covered with or yielding farina; of the nature of farina, finely powdered.

farkleberry /ˈfɑːk(ə)lb(ə)ri/ *noun.* M18.

[ORIGIN Prob. alt. of WHORTLEBERRY.]

A shrub or small tree, *Vaccinium arboreum*, bearing black berries, native to the south-eastern US.

farl /fɑːl/ *noun.* Chiefly *Scot.* L17.

[ORIGIN Contr. of FARDEL *noun*[2].]

Orig., a quarter of a thin cake of flour or oatmeal. Later, any such thin cake, whether quadrant-shaped or not.

farm /fɑːm/ *noun.* ME.

[ORIGIN Old French & mod. French *ferme* from medieval Latin *firma* fixed payment, from Latin *firmare* fix, settle, confirm, (in medieval Latin) contract for, from Latin *firmus* FIRM *adjective*.]

1 *hist.* **a** A fixed annual amount, in money or kind, payable as rent, tax, etc. ME. ▸**b** A fixed annual sum accepted as composition for taxes or other moneys collected. Also, a fixed charge imposed on a town, county, etc., to be collected within its limits. LME. ▸**c** The allowing of a person to collect and keep the revenues from taxes etc. in return for a fixed sum; the privilege of so collecting taxes etc. M17.

2 The condition or arrangement of being let at a fixed rent (in ***have in farm***, ***let in farm***, ***set to farm***, etc.). ME.

†**3** A lease. L15–M17.

4 A tract of land held (orig. on lease) under one management for the purposes of cultivation or the rearing of certain animals (for food or fur etc.). See also ***funny farm*** s.v. FUNNY *adjective*, *HEALTH* ***farm***. E16. ▸**b** A tract or tracts of water used for the breeding or rearing of fish or other animals (usu. of a specified kind). M19.

J. R. GREEN The farms of Lothian have become models of agricultural skill.

dairy farm, ***mink farm***, ***poultry farm***, etc. **bet the farm** *N. Amer. colloq.* risk all that one owns by backing a particular project, investment, etc. **buy the farm** *N. Amer. colloq.* die. ***collective farm***: see COLLECTIVE *adjective* 4. ***home farm***: see HOME *adjective*. *SEWAGE* ***farm***. **b** ***fish farm***, ***oyster farm***, ***trout farm***, etc.

5 A farmhouse. M16.

6 A place where children are farmed (see FARM *verb*[2] 4). *derog.* M19.

baby-farm etc.

7 A prison hospital. *arch. slang.* L19.

8 A storage installation for oil etc. M20.

– COMB.: **farm-gate** *adjective* relating to or denoting produce bought directly from the farm which produced it; **farmhand** a person who works on a farm; **farmhold** *arch.* a quantity of land held and cultivated as a farm; **farmland**: used or suitable for farming; **farmstead**, **farmsteading** a farm with the buildings on it; **farm team** *BASEBALL* a minor league team that provides players as needed to an affiliated major league team; **farmwife** (chiefly *N. Amer.*) a farmer's wife; **farmworker** a person who works on a farm.

farm /fɑːm/ *verb*[1] *trans.* Long *obsolete* exc. *dial.*

[ORIGIN Old English *feormian*, of unknown origin.]

Cleanse, empty.

farm /fɑːm/ *verb*[2]. LME.

[ORIGIN from FARM *noun*.]

†**1** *verb trans.* Rent (land etc.). LME–E18.

2 *verb trans.* Collect the fees or proceeds of (a tax, office, etc.) on payment of a fixed sum. M16.

M. PATTISON The Tidemann farmed . . the tin-mines belonging to the Duchy of Cornwall.

3 *verb trans.* **a** Let (land) to a tenant. Also foll. by *out*. Now *rare*. L16. ▸**b** Allow a person to collect and keep the revenues from (a tax) or the proceeds of (an undertaking etc.) in return for a fixed sum. Also foll. by *out*. E17. ▸**c** Hire out the labour of (a person etc.). Also foll. by *out*. E17.

4 *verb trans.* Take over, for a fee, the care of (a person, esp. (*derog.*) a child), maintenance of (an institution etc.), or performance of (a task etc.); (freq. foll. by *out*) arrange for another or others so to take over the care etc. of, delegate (work) to a subcontractor. M17.

DICKENS The parish authorities . . resolved, that Oliver should be 'farmed'. *New Statesman* One term 'farmed out' with a man tutor. *Globe & Mail (Toronto)* How could you get a strike going when the work can be so easily farmed out somewhere else?

5 *verb intrans.* Be a farmer, till the soil. E18.

6 *verb trans.* Cultivate, till. E19.

7 *verb trans. & intrans.* *CRICKET.* Of a batsman: contrive to receive most of (the bowling). M20.

■ **farmable** *adjective* that may be farmed or leased; suitable for farming: E17.

farman *noun* var. of FIRMAN.

farmer /ˈfɑːmə/ *noun.* LME.

[ORIGIN Anglo-Norman *fermer*, Old French & mod. French *fermier*, combining uses of medieval Latin *firmarius*, *firmator*, from *firma*: see FARM *noun*. In more mod. uses prob. from FARM *verb*[2] + -ER[1].]

1 A person who is allowed to collect and keep the revenues from taxes etc. in return for a fixed sum. LME.

H. AINSWORTH Speculators, farmers of revenues, and others.

†**2** A person who cultivates land for the owner; a bailiff, a steward. LME–L16.

3 Orig., a person who rents land for the purpose of cultivation. Now *gen.*, a person who cultivates a farm, as tenant or owner; one who farms land or rears certain animals (usu. of a specified kind). LME. ▸†**b** A person who leases a weir or mill. LME–E16.

dairy farmer, ***fish-farmer***, ***mink-farmer***, ***poultry-farmer***, ***trout-farmer***, etc.

4 A person who farms children (*derog.*), a task, etc. M19.

baby-farmer.

– COMB.: **farmer-general**, pl. **farmers-general**, [translating French *fermier général*] a person who collected taxes etc. in a district of France before the Revolution; **farmer's lung** a pulmonary disease caused by allergy to fungal spores from mouldy hay etc.; **farmers' market**: where produce of local farmers and growers is sold directly to the public.

■ **farmeress** *noun* (now *rare*) (**a**) a woman who farms land; (**b**) a farmer's wife: L16. **farmeˈrette** *noun* (chiefly *US*) a woman or girl who farms land E20. †**farmerly** *adjective* like a farmer M17–L18.

farmery /ˈfɑːməri/ *noun*[1]. M17.

[ORIGIN from FARM *noun* + -ERY.]

The buildings, yards, etc., belonging to a farm.

farmery *noun*[2] var. of FERMERY.

farmhouse /ˈfɑːmhaʊs/ *noun.* M16.

[ORIGIN from FARM *noun* + HOUSE *noun*[1].]

1 A house attached to a farm; *spec.* the chief such house. M16.

2 More fully ***farmhouse loaf***. A loaf of bread of an oval or rectangular shape with a curving top. M20.

farming /ˈfɑːmɪŋ/ *verbal noun.* L16.

[ORIGIN from FARM *verb*[2] + -ING[1].]

1 *gen.* The action of FARM *verb*[2]. L16.

2 *spec.* The business of cultivating land, raising stock, etc. M18.

dairy-farming, ***high farming***, ***organic farming***, ***sheep-farming***, etc.

farmost /ˈfɑːməʊst/ *adjective.* E17.

[ORIGIN from FAR *adjective* + -MOST.]

Furthest, most remote.

farmyard /ˈfɑːmjɑːd/ *noun & adjective.* M18.

[ORIGIN from FARM *noun* + YARD *noun*[1].]

▸ **A** *noun.* The yard or enclosure attached to a farmhouse. M18.

▸ **B** *attrib.* or as *adjective.* Coarse, disgusting, uncouth. E20.

farnesol /ˈfɑːnɪsɒl/ *noun.* E20.

[ORIGIN German, from mod. Latin (*Acacia*) *farnesiana* a plant that is a source of the alcohol, from Odoardo *Farnese* (1573–1626), Italian cardinal: see -OL.]

CHEMISTRY. A terpenoid alcohol, $C_{15}H_{25}OH$, that occurs in various essential oils and is used in the preparation of scents.

far niente /far nɪˈɛnte/ *noun phr.* E19.

[ORIGIN Italian = doing nothing.]

Idleness; ***dolce far niente***.

faro /ˈfɛːrəʊ/ *noun*[1]. Also (earlier) †**pharaoh**, †**pharo**. E18.

[ORIGIN French PHARAON, perh. as a name of the king of hearts. Cf. PHARAON 2.]

A gambling card game, in which the players bet on the order in which certain cards will appear when taken singly from the top of the pack.

– COMB.: **faro bank** (**a**) a gaming house where faro is played; (**b**) the banker's stake, against which the other players put their stakes.

faro /ˈfaro/ *noun*[2]. M19.

[ORIGIN French.]

A type of beer made in Belgium around Brussels.

Faroese /fɛːrəʊˈiːz/ *adjective & noun.* Also **Faeroese**, **Faröese**. M19.

[ORIGIN from *Faroes* (see below) + -ESE.]

▸ **A** *noun.* Of or pertaining to the Faroes, a group of islands in the N. Atlantic between the Shetland Islands and Iceland, and a semi-autonomous province of Denmark. M19.

▸ **B** *noun.* Pl. same.

1 A native or inhabitant of the Faroes. M19.

2 The Norse language of the Faroes. L19.

farol /faˈrol, fəˈrəʊl/ *noun.* Pl. ***faroles*** /faˈroles/, ***farols*** /fəˈrəʊlz/. M20.

[ORIGIN Spanish, lit. 'lantern'.]

BULLFIGHTING. A movement in which the bullfighter draws the bull by passing the cloak back rapidly over his own head.

farouche /fəˈruːʃ/ *adjective.* M18.

[ORIGIN French, alt. of Old French *faroche*, *forache* from medieval Latin *forasticus*, from Latin *foras* out-of-doors.]

Sullen, shy.

F. PARTRIDGE Her face has . . become less farouche, and her manner more confident. G. CHARLES He was not . . very articulate in discussion. Rather farouche.

■ **farouchely** *adverb* M20.

farraginous /fəˈreɪdʒɪnəs/ *adjective.* E17.

[ORIGIN from Latin *farrago*, *-gin-* (see FARRAGO) + -OUS.]

Hotchpotch, miscellaneous.

farrago /fəˈrɑːgəʊ, fəˈreɪgəʊ/ *noun.* Pl. **-os**, ***-oes**. M17.

[ORIGIN Latin = mixed fodder for cattle, (fig.) a medley, from *far* spelt, corn.]

A confused group; a medley, a mixture, a hotchpotch.

A. BURGESS Such a repetitive farrago of platitudes. M. GEE A farrago of madness and morals and murder of the language.

F

farrant /ˈfar(ə)nt/ *adjective*. *Scot. & N. English*. Also (earlier) **-and** /-(ə)nd/. LME.
[ORIGIN Perh. application of *farande* north. pres. pple of FARE *verb*.]
1 †**a** Comely, handsome. Only in LME. ▸**b** Proper, becoming, dignified. LME.
2 Having a specified appearance, disposition, or temperament, as ***evil-farrant***, ***well-farrant***, etc. LME.
■ **farrantly** *adverb* LME.

farrash *noun* var. of FERASH.

farrier /ˈfarɪə/ *noun & verb*. M16.
[ORIGIN Old French *ferrier* from Latin *ferrarius*, from *ferrum* horseshoe, iron: see -IER.]
▸**A** *noun*. **1** A smith who shoes horses; a person who treats the diseases and injuries of horses. M16.
2 An official with care of the horses in a cavalry regiment. M19.
▸**B** *verb*. **1** *verb intrans*. Practise farriery. E18.
2 *verb trans*. Treat (a horse) as a farrier does. E19.
■ **farriery** *noun* the art of the farrier; *spec*. veterinary surgery with regard to horses: M18.

farrow /ˈfarəʊ/ *noun*.
[ORIGIN Old English *fearh* (*fearh*) = Old High German *farah*, from West Germanic from Indo-European base also of Latin *porcus*, Greek *porkos*: see PORK. In sense 3 from the verb. See also FARE *noun*³.]
1 A young pig. OE.
2 A litter of pigs. L16.

R. D. BLACKMORE Two farrows of pigs ready for the chapman.

3 An act of farrowing. E17.

P. HOLLAND One sow may bring at one farrow twenty pigges.

farrow /ˈfarəʊ/ *adjective*. Chiefly *Scot*. L15.
[ORIGIN Flemish *verwe*, *varwe*, in *verwekoe*, *varwekoe*, †*verrekoe* cow that has become barren.]
Of a cow: not in calf, not having produced a calf.

farrow /ˈfarəʊ/ *verb trans. & intrans*. ME.
[ORIGIN from the noun.]
Of a sow: give birth to (young).

GOLDSMITH A sow . . farrowed fifteen pigs at a litter. M. WEBB When our sow farrowed, we were to keep all the piglets.

farruca /fəˈruːkə/ *noun*. E20.
[ORIGIN Spanish, fem. of *farruco* Galician or Asturian, from *Farruco* pet form of male forename *Francisco*.]
A type of flamenco dance.

†**farry** *verb trans. & intrans*. L17–E19.
[ORIGIN Back-form. from FARRIER *noun*.]
= FARRIER *verb*.

farsakh /ˈfɑːsak/ *noun*. L19.
[ORIGIN Persian & Arabic, rel. to FARSANG.]
= FARSANG.

farsang /ˈfɑːsaŋ/ *noun*. E17.
[ORIGIN Persian, rel. to PARASANG.]
An Iranian (Persian) unit of distance now equal to 6km (3.7 miles).

Farsi /ˈfɑːsiː/ *noun & adjective*. L19.
[ORIGIN from Arabic *fārsī*, from *Fārs* from Persian *Pārs* Persia, PARSEE.]
(Of or pertaining to) the (modern) Persian language.

fart /fɑːt/ *noun*. Now *coarse slang*. LME.
[ORIGIN from the verb.]
1 An emission of wind from the anus. (Used as a type of something worthless.) LME.

SNOO WILSON This process isn't working . . . It's not worth a fart.

2 A contemptible person. *slang*. M20.

M. GORDON Some old fart who should've been dead years ago.

fart /fɑːt/ *verb*. Now *coarse slang*.
[ORIGIN Old English (in *feorting* verbal noun) corresp. to Middle Low German *verten*, Old High German *ferzan*, Middle High German *verzen*, *vurzen* (German *farzen*, *furzen*), Old Norse (with metathesis) *freta*, from Germanic.]
1 *verb intrans*. Emit wind from the anus. OE.

J. P. DONLEAVY When someone farted in my house you could smell it in every room.

2 *verb trans*. Emit as wind from the anus. M17.
3 *verb intrans*. Fool *about* or *around*. E20.

J. WAINWRIGHT Look! It's important. Stop farting around.

■ **farter** *noun* L16.

farther /ˈfɑːðə/ *verb trans*. Now *rare*. LME.
[ORIGIN Var. of FURTHER *verb*.]
†**1** = FURTHER *verb* 3. *rare*. Only in LME.
2 = FURTHER *verb* 1. L16.
■ **fartherance** *noun* (*rare*) = FURTHERANCE L18.

farther /ˈfɑːðə/ *adverb & adjective*. ME.
[ORIGIN Var. of FURTHER *adverb*, *adjective*.]
▸**A** *adverb*. **1** More forward; to or at a more advanced point in space or time. ME.

V. WOOLF The gulls rose in front of him and . . settled again a little farther on.

2 To a greater extent; = FURTHER *adverb* 2. LME.
3 In addition, moreover; = FURTHER *adverb* 3. LME.
4 At a greater distance; = FURTHER *adverb* 4. LME.
▸**B** *adjective*. †**1** = FURTHER *adjective* 1. ME–M16.
2 More extended, additional; = FURTHER *adjective* 2. LME.
3 More distant or advanced, remoter; = FURTHER *adjective* 3. M16.

R. L. STEVENSON Where we have . . crossed a chain of mountains, it is only to find another . . upon the farther side. I. MURDOCH In the farther future, when you have made yourself right with the authorities.

Farther India = *Further India* s.v. FURTHER *adjective* 3.
– NOTE: The forms *farther*/*further* displaced *farrer*, the regular compar. of *far*. Until recently, *farther* was preferred in reference to physical distance, *further* in figurative contexts, but *further* is now usual in all contexts.
■ †**farthermore** *adverb & adjective* (**a**) *adverb* = FURTHERMORE; (**b**) *adjective* remoter: ME–E17.

farthermost /ˈfɑːðəməʊst/ *adjective*. L15.
[ORIGIN Var. of FURTHERMOST.]
Most distant or remote, furthest.

farthest /ˈfɑːðɪst/ *adjective & adverb*. LME.
[ORIGIN Var. of FURTHEST.]
▸**A** *adjective*. **1** Most distant or remote. LME.

W. JONES The farthest limits of the kingdom.

at farthest, **at the farthest** = *at furthest* s.v. FURTHEST *adjective*.
2 Longest. M17.
▸**B** *adverb*. To or at the greatest distance. L16.

farthing /ˈfɑːðɪŋ/ *noun*.
[ORIGIN Old English *fēorþing*, *-ung*, from *fēorþa* FOURTH, perh. after Old Norse *fjórðungr* quarter: see -ING³.]
1 *hist*. A quarter of an old penny; a British coin of this value (no longer legal tender). OE.

F. W. ROBERTSON A miser . . hoards farthings.

2 More fully ***farthing land***. A measure of land varying in extent from a quarter of an acre to thirty acres (approx. 0.1 to 12 hectares). Now *dial. rare*. OE.
†**3** In full ***farthing noble***, ***farthing of gold***. A quarter noble. LME–E17.
4 *fig*. A very little, the least possible amount. Usu. in neg. contexts. LME.

STEELE The gentleman . . has told her he does not care a farthing for her.

brass farthing: see BRASS *noun*.
■ **farthingsworth** *noun* as much as can be bought or sold for a farthing; a very small amount: ME.

farthingale /ˈfɑːðɪŋgeɪl/ *noun*. Also †**vardingale**. E16.
[ORIGIN Old French *verdugale*, *vertugalle*, alt. of Spanish *verdugado*, from *verdugo* rod, stick, from *verde* green.]
hist. A framework of hoops, or a hooped petticoat, formerly used to extend the skirts of women's dresses.
– COMB.: **farthingale chair** a 17th-cent. chair with a wide seat, a low straight back, and no arms.

†**farthingdeal** *noun*. LME–M19.
[ORIGIN Repr. Old English *fēorþan dǣl*, accus. of *fēorþa* FOURTH *adjective* + *dǣl* DEAL *noun*¹.]
A fourth part; *spec*. the fourth part of an acre.

fartlek /ˈfɑːtlɛk/ *noun*. M20.
[ORIGIN Swedish, from *fart* speed + *lek* play.]
A method of training for middle- and long-distance running, in which the athlete runs over country, mixing fast with slow work.

FAS *abbreviation*.
Fetal alcohol syndrome.

f.a.s. *abbreviation*.
Free alongside ship.

fasces /ˈfasiːz/ *noun pl*. L16.
[ORIGIN Latin, pl. of *fascis* bundle.]
1 *ROMAN ANTIQUITIES*. Rods in a bundle with an axe, carried by lictors before the superior magistrates as an emblem of power. L16.
2 (Symbols of) authority or power. E17.

fascet /ˈfasɪt/ *noun*. M17.
[ORIGIN Unknown.]
In glass-manufacturing, a tool used to introduce glass bottles into the annealing oven.

Fasching /ˈfaʃɪŋ/ *noun*. E20.
[ORIGIN German.]
In southern Germany and Austria: carnival, the carnival season, which lasts from Epiphany to Shrove Tuesday.

Fasci /ˈfaʃi/ *noun pl*. E20.
[ORIGIN Italian, pl. of *fascio*: see FASCISM.]
In Italy: groups of men organized politically, such as those in Sicily *c* 1895 or those of the Fascists.

fascia /ˈfaʃɪə, ˈfeɪ-, -ʃə/ *noun*. Pl. **-iae** /-iiː/, **-ias**. See also FACIA. M16.
[ORIGIN Latin = band, fillet, casing of a door etc., rel. to FASCES.]
1 *ARCHITECTURE*. A horizontal band of wood, stone, brick, or marble, esp. as used in an architrave. M16. ▸†**b** A ceiling coved on two opposite sides only. M17–E18.
†**2** A band for the hair or head. L16–E17.
3 Any object, or collection of objects, that gives the appearance of a band or stripe. E18.
4 *ANATOMY*. A thin sheet of connective tissue enclosing a muscle or other organ; the connective tissue forming this. L18.
5 The plate over a shop front on which is written the occupier's name, trade, etc. E20.
6 The instrument panel or dashboard of a motor vehicle. E20.
7 A covering, esp. a detachable one, for the front part of a mobile phone. L20.

fasciate /ˈfaʃɪeɪt, -ʃɪət/ *adjective*. L19.
[ORIGIN formed as FASCIATE *verb*: see -ATE².]
BOTANY. = FASCIATED *adjective* 3.

fasciate /ˈfaʃɪeɪt/ *verb trans*. Long *rare*. M17.
[ORIGIN Latin *fasciat-* pa. ppl stem of *fasciare* swathe, from FASCIA: see -ATE³.]
Bind with or as with a fascia.

fasciated /ˈfaʃɪeɪtɪd/ *adjective*. E18.
[ORIGIN from FASCIA + -ATE² + -ED¹. Cf. French *fascié*.]
†**1** *ARCHITECTURE*. Of a ceiling: coved on two opposite sides only. Only in E18.
2 Marked with bands or stripes. M18.
3 *BOTANY*. Exhibiting abnormal fusion of parts or organs normally separate, resulting in a flattened ribbon-like structure. Cf. FASCIATION 1. M19.

fasciation /faʃɪˈeɪʃ(ə)n/ *noun*. M17.
[ORIGIN formed as FASCIATE *verb*: see -ATION.]
1 The binding up of a limb etc. with bandages; a bandage. Long *rare* or *obsolete*. M17.
2 The growing together of contiguous parts; *esp*. (*BOTANY*) fasciated condition (FASCIATED 3). L17.

fascicle /ˈfasɪk(ə)l/ *noun*. L15.
[ORIGIN Latin *fasciculus* dim. of *fascis*: see FASCES, -CULE. Cf. FASCICULE, FASCICULUS.]
1 Chiefly *SCIENCE*. A small bundle, a bunch; *BOTANY* a cluster of short stalks, roots, etc.; *ANATOMY* a bundle of (muscle, nerve, etc.) fibres. L15.
2 Each part of a book published in instalments. M17.
■ **fascicled** *adjective* = FASCICULATE L18.

fascicular /faˈsɪkjʊlə/ *adjective*. M17.
[ORIGIN formed as FASCICULE + -AR¹.]
Chiefly *SCIENCE*. Of, pertaining to, or of the nature of a fascicle (FASCICLE 1).

fasciculate /faˈsɪkjʊleɪt, -lət/ *adjective*. L18.
[ORIGIN formed as FASCICULAR + -ATE².]
Chiefly *SCIENCE*. Arranged, growing, or occurring in a fascicle or fascicles (FASCICLE 1).
■ **fasciculated** *adjective* = FASCICULATE L18. **fascicuˈlation** *noun* the state of being fasciculate; *spec*. (*MEDICINE*) irregular spontaneous contraction of small groups of muscle fibres: L19.

fascicule /ˈfasɪkjuːl/ *noun*. L17.
[ORIGIN Latin *fasciculus* (see FASCICLE), after French *fascicule*. Cf. FASCICULUS.]
†**1** A handful. Only in L17.
2 = FASCICLE 1. *rare*. M18.
3 = FASCICLE 2. L19.

fasciculus /faˈsɪkjʊləs/ *noun*. Pl. **-li** /-lʌɪ, -liː/. E18.
[ORIGIN Latin: see FASCICLE. Cf. FASCICULE.]
1 Chiefly *SCIENCE*. = FASCICLE 1. E18.
2 = FASCICLE 2. M19.

fasciitis /fasɪˈʌɪtɪs, faʃɪ-/ *noun*. Also **fascitis** /fəˈsʌɪtɪs, -ʃʌɪ-/. L19.
[ORIGIN from FASCIA + -ITIS.]
MEDICINE. Inflammation of the fascia of a muscle etc.

fascinate /ˈfasɪneɪt/ *verb*. L16.
[ORIGIN Latin *fascinat-* pa. ppl stem of *fascinare*, from *fascinum* spell, witchcraft: see -ATE³.]
▸**I** *verb trans*. †**1** Bewitch, put under a spell. L16–M17.
2 Of a serpent etc.: deprive (a victim) of the power of escape or resistance by a look or by being in sight (formerly associated with witchcraft). M17.
3 Formerly, enslave (the faculties), paralyse (the judgement). Now, attract irresistibly, charm, enchant. M17.

P. SCOTT The range of Tusker's knowledge of the world had astonished him, fascinated him.

▸**II** *verb intrans*. **4** Be irresistibly attractive, charming, or enchanting. L19.
■ **fascinated** *adjective* that has been fascinated; irresistibly attracted (*by*), charmed (*by*, *with*): E18. **fascinatedly** *adverb* L19. **fascinating** *adjective* that fascinates; irresistibly attractive, charming: M17. **fascinatingly** *adverb* M19. **fascinative** *adjective* having power to fascinate, tending to fascinate M19.

fascination /fasɪˈneɪʃ(ə)n/ *noun*. E17.
[ORIGIN Latin *fascinatio(n-)*, formed as FASCINATE: see -ATION.]
1 The casting of a spell; sorcery; a spell. *obsolete* exc. *hist*. E17. ▸†**b** The state of being under a spell. M17–M18.
2 Fascinating quality; the power to fascinate; an irresistible attractiveness. L17. ▸**b** A serpent's power to fascinate a victim. L18.

M. TIPPETT He exercised a tyrannical fascination over them. R. F. HOBSON The luring fascination of the unknown.

3 The state of being fascinated; an instance of this, an irresistible feeling of attraction. (Foll. by *by*, *for*, *with*.) M19.

Christian Science Monitor Qaddafi doesn't reject Western technology, he has a fascination for it.

fascinator /ˈfasɪneɪtə/ *noun*. M18.
[ORIGIN Latin, formed as FASCINATE: see -OR.]
1 A magician. *arch.* M18.
2 An irresistibly attractive or charming person. M19.
3 A headscarf worn by women, either crocheted or made of a soft material. L19.

fascine /faˈsiːn/ *noun & verb trans.* L17.
[ORIGIN French from Latin *fascina*, from *fascis* bundle.]
▸ **A** *noun*. A long faggot used for engineering purposes and (esp. in war) for lining trenches, filling ditches, etc. L17.
▸ **B** *verb trans.* Fill up, protect, or strengthen with fascines. E19.

fasciola /fasɪˈəʊlə/ *noun*. Pl. **-lae** /-liː/. M19.
[ORIGIN Latin = small bandage.]
ANATOMY. In full ***fasciola cinerea*** /sɪˈnɪərɪə/, pl. ***fasciolae cinereae*** /-rɪiː/ [Latin *cinereus* = ash-coloured]. A thin layer of grey matter in the hippocampal formation of the brain.
■ **faˈsciolar** *adjective* of or pertaining to the fasciola; ***fasciolar gyrus*** = FASCIOLA: L19.

fascioliasis /fasɪəˈlʌɪəsɪs/ *noun*. Pl. **-ases** /-əsiːz/. L19.
[ORIGIN from mod. Latin *Fasciola* (see below), formed as FASCIOLA: see -IASIS.]
MEDICINE. Infestation (of humans or animals) with the liver fluke, *Fasciola hepatica*; the disease resulting from this.

Fascism /ˈfaʃɪz(ə)m, -sɪz(ə)m/ *noun*. Also **f-**. E20.
[ORIGIN Italian *fascismo*, from *fascio* bundle, group from popular Latin *fascium* for Latin *fascis* bundle: see -ISM.]
The principles and organization of the Italian Fascists, the Italian Fascist movement; a similar nationalist and authoritarian movement in another country; *loosely* right-wing authoritarianism.
■ Also ***Fascismo*** /faˈʃizmo/ *noun* [Italian] E20.

Fascist /ˈfaʃɪst, -sɪst/ *noun & adjective*. Also **f-**. E20.
[ORIGIN Italian *Fascista*, formed as FASCISM: see -IST.]
▸ **A** *noun*. A member of a body of Italian nationalists, which was organized in 1919 to oppose Communism in Italy and controlled the country from 1922 to 1943; a member of any similar nationalist and authoritarian organization in another country; *loosely* (usu **f-**), any person with right-wing authoritarian political views. E20.
▸ **B** *adjective*. Of, pertaining to, or characteristic of Fascism or Fascists. E20.
■ ***Fascisti*** /faˈʃisti/ *noun pl.* [Italian] the Italian Fascists E20. **Faˈscistic** *adjective* of or pertaining to Fascism or Fascists; having Fascist ideals: M20. **Faˈscistically** *adverb* E20. **faˈscistoid** *adjective* resembling (that of) a Fascist; tending towards Fascism: M20.

fascitis *noun* var. of FASCIITIS.

fash /faʃ/ *noun*[1]. *Scot. & N. English*. E18.
[ORIGIN from the verb.]
Trouble, vexation; bother; something that gives trouble.

fash /faʃ/ *noun*[2]. *slang*. L19.
[ORIGIN Abbreviation.]
Fashion.

fash /faʃ/ *adjective*. *slang*. L20.
[ORIGIN Abbreviation.]
Fashionable.

fash /faʃ/ *verb*. Chiefly *Scot. & N. English*. M16.
[ORIGIN Early mod. French *fascher* (now *fâcher*) from Proto-Romance, from Latin *fastus* disdain.]
1 *verb trans.* Annoy, trouble, bother, weary, (oneself, another). M16.
SIR W. SCOTT Never fash yoursel' wi' me . . but look to yoursel'.
2 *verb intrans.* Weary, be annoyed; trouble oneself; take trouble. (Foll. by *of*, *to do*.) L16.
■ **fashery** *noun* annoyance, worry; something that causes worry: M16.

fashion /ˈfaʃ(ə)n/ *noun*. ME.
[ORIGIN Anglo-Norman *fasun*, Old French & mod. French *façon* from Latin *factio(n-)*, from *fact-* pa. ppl stem of *facere* make, do: see -ION.]
1 Make, build, shape; appearance; characteristic form. In early use also, face, features. *arch.* ME.
2 A particular make, shape, style, or pattern; *spec.* a particular style of clothing. ME.
3 *gen.* (A) manner, (a) mode, (a) method, (a) way. LME.
H. JAMES He had never yet heard a young girl express herself in just this fashion. D. H. LAWRENCE He tried to talk to Alvina in a fatherly fashion. J. B. PRIESTLEY Nottingham seems gayer, in its own robust Midland fashion, than other provincial towns. N. SHUTE They bathed in leisurely fashion.
after a fashion not satisfactorily, but somehow or other. **after the fashion of** in the manner of, like. **in a fashion** = *after a fashion* above.
4 Mode of action, demeanour; in *pl.*, behaviour, manners, gestures. Now *rare*. LME.
†5 The action or process of making; workmanship as contributing to value. LME–L18.
6 Prevailing custom, a current or conventional usage, esp. of a particular period or place or among a particular class of society; *spec.* (a) current style in clothing, hairstyle. L15. ▸**b** *The* mode of dress, etiquette, furniture, speech, etc., prevalent at a particular time; *the* person who or thing which it is fashionable to admire or discuss. M16. ▸†**c** In *pl.* Manners and customs. Chiefly in ***know (the) fashions***, ***learn (the) fashions***, ***see (the) fashions***. M16–E18. ▸**d** Fashionable people; *the* fashionable world. E19.
B. PYM Dresses of the thirties and earlier, now coming back into fashion. W. BRONK Fashions in ornamental planting change. P. F. BOLLER At that time fashion dictated that women's skirts should be short. A. LURIE Fashions by and large imitated the clothes that little girls had worn. **b** B. TRAPIDO I wore it, as was then the fashion, well over half way up my thighs.
7 Social status; *spec.* high social status, esp. as shown by dress and behaviour. Chiefly in ***man of fashion***, ***woman of fashion***, etc. *arch.* L15.
8 Kind, sort. Now *rare*. M16.
9 A mere form, pretence. *obsolete* exc. *Scot.* in ***make fashion***, pretend. L16.
– COMB.: Forming adverbs from nouns and adjectives with the sense 'in the manner or fashion of, -wise', as ***crab-fashion***, ***Roman-fashion***, etc. With the sense 'fashionable, stylish', as ***fashion jewellery*** etc. Special combs., as **fashion-conscious** *adjective* aware of and concerned about fashion; **fashion-forward** *adjective* more modern than the current fashion; **fashion house** a business establishment displaying and selling high-quality clothes; **fashion-monger** a person who studies and follows fashion; **fashion paper** a journal dealing with fashionable life, esp. current fashions in dress; **fashion piece** NAUTICAL either of the two timbers in the underbody of a ship which form the shape of the stern; **fashion plate** a picture showing a fashion, esp. in dress; *fig.* a person who dresses in the current fashion; **fashion victim** *colloq.* a person who follows popular trends in dress and behaviour slavishly.
■ **fashionist** *noun* a follower of fashion E17. **fashionless** *adjective* L16.

fashion /ˈfaʃ(ə)n/ *verb trans.* LME.
[ORIGIN from the noun, after Old French & mod. French *façonner*.]
1 Make, create, form, mould. LME. ▸**b** Contrive, manage. Long *obsolete* exc. *dial.* M16. ▸†**c** Represent. *rare* (Spenser). Only in L16.
J. CLAVELL A cross . . that he fashioned out of two pieces of driftwood. H. KISSINGER The team the new President brought together to fashion a global strategy. J. M. COETZEE Whether he knew no way of fashioning a lamp or a candle.
2 Make into a specified shape; model *according to*, *after*, *like*; shape *into*, *to*. E16.
J. KOSINSKI The boys would . . fashion them into pistols.
3 Give a form suitable *to*, *to do*; accommodate, adapt *to*. Now *rare*. E16.
†4 Change the fashion of; modify, transform. Foll. by *to*. E16–M18. ▸†**b** Counterfeit, pervert. *rare* (Shakes.). Only in L16.
■ **fashioner** *noun* M16.

fashionable /ˈfaʃ(ə)nəb(ə)l/ *adjective & noun*. L16.
[ORIGIN from FASHION *verb*, *noun* + -ABLE.]
▸ **A** *adjective*. †**1** Able to be fashioned or shaped (*to*). L16–M17.
2 Dressing or behaving according to the current or best fashion. E17.
3 Conformable to fashion; in vogue, generally accepted; of, pertaining to, characteristic of, or frequented by fashionable people. E17. ▸†**b** Of a good fashion or appearance; stylish. M17–E18.
N. COWARD Funny how the South of France has become so fashionable in the summer, isn't it? L. HELLMAN My hair, . . straight in a time when it was fashionable to have curls.
†4 Merely formal. E–M17.
▸ **B** *noun*. A fashionable person. Usu. in *pl.* L18.
■ **fashionaˈbility** *noun* M19. **fashionableness** *noun* E17. **fashionably** *adverb* E17.

fashioned /ˈfaʃ(ə)nd/ *adjective*. LME.
[ORIGIN from FASHION *verb*, *noun*: see -ED[1], -ED[2].]
1 That has been fashioned, esp. in a specified way; (of a stocking) shaped to fit the contour of the leg. LME.
fully-fashioned: see FULLY *adverb*.
2 As 2nd elem. of comb.: of the specified description of fashion. Esp. in OLD-FASHIONED. L16.

fashionista /faʃəˈniːstə/ *noun*. *colloq.* L20.
[ORIGIN from FASHION *noun* + Spanish suffix *-ista* -IST (as in *Sandinista*, *turista*, etc.).]
A designer or follower of haute couture.

fashious /ˈfaʃəs/ *adjective*. *Scot. & N. English*. M16.
[ORIGIN French †*fascheux* (now *fâcheux*), from *fascher* (*fâcher*): see FASH *verb*, -IOUS.]
Causing anxiety or trouble; tiresome.

fasola /ˈfɑːsɒlɑː, -səʊl-/ *noun*. M20.
[ORIGIN from FA *noun* + SOL *noun*[1] + LA *noun*.]
MUSIC. A system of solmization in which the progression of syllables used is fa, sol, la, fa, sol, la, mi.

fast /fɑːst/ *noun*[1]. ME.
[ORIGIN Old Norse *fasta* = Old Saxon, Old High German *fasta*, from Germanic base of FAST *verb*.]
1 An act or instance of fasting. ME. ▸†**b** The action of fasting; abstinence from food. *rare*. E17–L18.
break one's fast stop fasting, take breakfast.
2 A day or season appointed for fasting. ME.
H. SEGAL She kept the yearly fast and went to the synagogue.
– COMB.: **fast day** a day appointed for fasting.

fast /fɑːst/ *noun*[2]. LME.
[ORIGIN Old Norse *festr*, from *festa* fasten, from *fastr* FAST *adjective*.]
NAUTICAL. A rope or chain for mooring.

†**fast** *noun*[3]. L17–M18.
[ORIGIN French *faste* from Latin *fastus*.]
Arrogance, pompousness.

fast /fɑːst/ *noun*[4]. M19.
[ORIGIN from the adjective.]
Something that is fast or fixed; *esp.* a body of rock or ice.

fast /fɑːst/ *adjective*.
[ORIGIN Old English *fæst* = Old Frisian *fest*, Old Saxon *fast* (Dutch *vast*), Old High German *festi* (German *fest*), Old Norse *fastr*, from Germanic.]
▸ **I 1** Firmly fixed in place; not easily moved; physically stable. *arch.* OE. ▸**b** Constant, steadfast. Now *rare*. OE. ▸**c** (Of sleep) deep, unbroken, sound; experiencing deep sleep. Now *dial.* L16. ▸**d** Of a colour: that will not quickly fade or wash out. M17. ▸**e** Of an organism: resistant to the stain-removing or toxic action of a (specified) agent. Usu. as 2nd elem. of comb. E20.
c R. MACAULAY A remarkably fast sleeper.
bedfast: see BED *noun*.
†2 Of a fortress or district: secure against attack. OE–M17.
3 Compact, solid, hard. *obsolete* exc. *dial.* OE. ▸**b** Frozen. *N. Amer.* Now *rare* or *obsolete*. E18.
4 Constipated. Long *obsolete* exc. *dial.* OE.
5 Firmly attached or tied; that cannot easily escape or be extricated. ME.
G. MAXWELL I had to make the rope fast to a stump.
6 †**a** Mean, niggardly. Only in ME. ▸**b** Tenacious. Foll. by *of*. Now *rare*. E16.
7 Closed firmly, bolted, locked. ME.
D. L. SAYERS He tried the handle, but the door was fast.
▸ **II 8** Rapid, swift, quick-moving; imparting quick motion. ME. ▸**b** Of a clock or watch: indicating a time more advanced than the true time. M19. ▸**c** PHOTOGRAPHY. (Of film etc.) needing only brief exposure; (of a lens) shortening the necessary exposure time, having a large aperture; (of a shutter) providing a brief exposure time. E20.
I. MURDOCH He did not run, he just walked at a fast steady pace.
9 Fashionable and hedonistic; dissipated, pleasure-loving; studiedly unconventional. M18.
J. S. HUXLEY He got into a fast set . . and took to gambling.
10 Suitable for or productive of quick movement; (of a cricket pitch, tennis court, putting green, etc.) on which a ball bounces or runs freely. M19.
– PHRASES: ***fast and* FURIOUS**. **fast and loose**, †**fast or loose** an old cheating game played with a stick and a belt or band; *fig.* inconstancy; ***play fast and loose***, ***play at fast and loose***, ignore one's obligations, be unreliable, trifle. ***hard and fast***: see HARD *adjective*. **make fast** bind, connect, fix firmly. **take fast hold of** hold or grasp tightly.
– SPECIAL COLLOCATIONS & COMB.: **fastback** (*a*) BOOKBINDING (a book with) a binding in which the backs of the sections adhere to the sheets; (*b*) (a car with) a back that slopes in a continuous line down to the bumper. **fastball** *N. Amer.* (*a*) a rapidly pitched ball in baseball; *fig.* a deception, an unfair action to gain an advantage; (*b*) a form of the game of softball. **fast-boat** a whaling boat which has attached itself to a whale by harpooning it. **fast bowler** CRICKET: employing fast bowling. **fast bowling** CRICKET: in which the ball travels at high speed. **fast break** in basketball, handball, etc., a swift attack from a defensive position. **fast-break** *verb intrans.* make a fast break. **fast breeder** (**reactor**) a breeder reactor in which fission is caused mainly by fast neutrons. ***fast buck***: see BUCK *noun*[8]. **fast foe** *arch.* a person who is unwaveringly hostile to one. **fast food**: wholly or partially prepared for quick sale or serving. **fast-food** *adjective* (*US*) produced without special effort or expense. **fast friend** a staunch or firm friend. **fast friendship** staunch or firm friendship. **fasthold** (now *rare*) a stronghold. **fast ice**: covering seawater but (usu.) attached to land. **fast land** *US* land lying above the high-water mark. **fast lane** a traffic lane on a motorway etc. intended for overtaking; *fig.* a means or route of rapid progress, a highly pressured lifestyle. **fast neutron** a neutron of high kinetic energy; *esp.* one released in nuclear fission and not slowed by any moderator. **fast one** *slang* an unfair action to gain an advantage (esp. in ***pull a fast one***, ***put over a fast one***). **fast reactor** a nuclear reactor in which fission is caused mainly by fast neutrons. **fast-talk** *verb trans.* (*N. Amer. colloq.*) persuade by rapid or deceitful talk. **fast track** a track for fast trains; *fig.* a means or route of rapid progress. **fast-track** *verb trans.* (*colloq.*) give priority to, treat as urgent. **fast train** an express train which stops at few intermediate stations. **fast-twitch** *adjective* (of a muscle fibre) that contracts rapidly, providing strength rather than endurance. **fast worker** *colloq.* a person who makes rapid progress, esp. in winning another's affections.
■ **fastish** *adjective* M19.

fast /fɑːst/ *verb*.
[ORIGIN Old English *fæstan* = Old Frisian *festia*, Middle Dutch & mod. Dutch *vasten*, Old High German *fastēn*, (German *fasten*), Old Norse *fasta*, Gothic *fastan*, from Germanic.]

F

1 *verb intrans.* Go without food (or formerly also drink), esp. as a religious observance or as a ceremonial expression of grief. OE. †**2** *verb trans.* Pass (time) fasting; observe (a day etc.) as a time of abstinence. ME–L17. **3** *verb trans.* Deprive of all or some kinds of food. M19.
▪ **faster** *noun* ME.

fast /fɑːst/ *adverb.*
[ORIGIN Old English *fæste* = Old Saxon *fasto* (Dutch *vast*), Old High German *fasto*, (German *fast* almost), Old Norse *fast*, from Germanic base of FAST *adjective*.]
1 With firm grasp or attachment; securely. OE. ▸†**b** With strict observance. ME–M16. ▸**c** So as to be unable to move. E16.

D. H. LAWRENCE The girl sat very insecurely, clinging fast.

2 So as not to be moved or shaken; so as to close firmly; fixedly. OE. ▸†**b** Earnestly, steadily. ME–M17. ▸†**c** Stoutly, strongly. ME–L16.

C. MEW We caught her, fetched her home at last And turned the key upon her, fast.

3 In a close-fitting manner; tightly. ME. **4** Close; very near. *arch.* ME. †**5** Soon, immediately. ME–L18. **6** Quickly, rapidly. ME. ▸**b** Readily, with alacrity. *obsolete* exc. in ***fast enough***. LME. ▸**c** In quick succession. L16.

A. P. HERBERT In truth the hare was travelling only half as fast as an express train. **c** SHELLEY My thoughts come fast.

7 In a dissipated manner, extravagantly, unconventionally, immorally. Chiefly in ***live fast***. L17.
– PHRASES: †**as fast as** as soon as. ***fast and* FURIOUS**. **fast asleep** sound asleep. **sleep fast** sleep soundly. **stick fast** be unable to move or make progress (*lit.* & *fig.*). ***thick and fast***: see THICK *adverb*.
– COMB.: **fast-forward** *noun, adjective, & verb* (**a**) *noun & adjective* (designating) a control on a machine using sound or videotape which enables the tape to be wound forward quickly; (**b**) *verb trans. & intrans.* (cause to) be wound forward quickly.

fasten /ˈfɑːs(ə)n/ *noun*. Long *obsolete* exc. *Scot. & N. English* in comb.
[ORIGIN Old English *fæsten* from Germanic, from base of FAST *verb*. Rel. to Old Saxon *fastunnia*, Gothic *fastubni*.]
= FAST *noun*[1].
– COMB.: **Fasten(s)-een**, **Fasten(s)-eve(n)**, **Fasten(s) Tuesday** the day before the beginning of the fast of Lent; Shrove Tuesday.

fasten /ˈfɑːs(ə)n/ *verb.*
[ORIGIN Old English *fæstnian* = Old Frisian *festna*, Old Saxon *fastnon*, Old High German *fastinōn*, *fest-*, from West Germanic, from base of FAST *adjective*: see -EN[5].]
▸ **I** *verb trans.* †**1** Make sure or stable; establish, confirm; ratify (an agreement). OE–M17. †**2** Make unable to move, immobilize. OE–M17. **3** Attach to something else; fix or hold securely in position; secure with a clasp, button, latch, bolt, seal, etc.; (now NAUTICAL) attach together the parts of. ME. ▸**b** *fig.* Direct (a look, thoughts, etc.) keenly (*up*)*on*; fix (a nickname, imputation, etc.) (*up*)*on*. ME. ▸†**c** Deliver effectively (a blow); imprint (a kiss). (Foll. by (*up*)*on*.) E16–L17.

J. AUSTEN The chaise arrived, the trunks were fastened on. E. M. FORSTER The rope that fastened Leonard to the earth. F. L. WRIGHT Three thicknesses of boards . . . the boards fastened together with screws. E. J. HOWARD He leaned out of the window to fasten back the shutter. **b** SAKI The character she had fastened on to him. A. J. CRONIN He felt Blodwen Page's eye fastened on him with a certain inquiry.

4 Secure as a means of connection (a clasp, button, tie, etc.); (foll. by *off*) secure (a thread etc.) with a knot, extra stitches, etc. ME.

P. D. JAMES He fastened his seat belt without speaking.

†**5** Make solid, strengthen, harden. ME–L16. **6** Join or bind in a contract (*with*), latterly *spec.* as an apprentice. Long *obsolete* exc. *dial.* LME. **7** Close with a grip (the hands, teeth). Long *obsolete* exc. *dial.* M16.
▸ **II** *verb intrans.* **8 a** Foll. by *on*, *upon*: lay hold of, seize on, single out for attack or attention, avail oneself eagerly of (a pretext etc.). ME. ▸**b** Foll. by *on to*, *to*: affix oneself to, take a grip of, seize; *spec.* harpoon (a whale). E19.

a M. DUFFY No delicious titbit of local information to fasten on. **b** J. A. MICHENER His hind quarters where two wolves had fastened onto him.

†**9** Without following preposition: take hold, attach oneself; take up a position. LME–M18. †**10** Become solid, harden, set. M17–M18. **11** Become unable to move, be immobilized. M18. **12** Admit of being fixed or secured. E19.

fastener /ˈfɑːs(ə)nə/ *noun*. L16.
[ORIGIN from FASTEN *verb* + -ER[1].]
A person who or thing which fastens something; a device for fastening.
zip fastener: see ZIP *noun*[1] 4.

fastening /ˈfɑːs(ə)nɪŋ/ *noun*. ME.
[ORIGIN formed as FASTENER + -ING[1].]
†**1** (Something which provides) strengthening, support. Only in ME. **2** The action of FASTEN *verb*. ME. **3** A device which fastens something. LME.

Fastext /ˈfɑːstɛkst/ *noun*. L20.
[ORIGIN Contr. of *fast teletext*.]
A facility in certain televisions to store some teletext pages in advance, displaying them instantly when requested by the user.

Fasti /ˈfastʌɪ, -tiː/ *noun*. Also **f-**. E17.
[ORIGIN Latin, pl. of *fastus* (*dies*), a lawful day, a day on which the courts sat.]
1 ROMAN HISTORY. A calendar or calendars showing the permitted days for legal and public business, festivals, games, anniversaries, etc. E17. **2** *transf.* A chronological register of events, lists of office-holders, etc. L17.

fastidious /faˈstɪdɪəs/ *adjective*. LME.
[ORIGIN Latin *fastidiosus*, from *fastidium* loathing: see -IOUS.]
†**1** Disagreeable, distasteful. LME–M18. †**2 a** Disgusted. M16–L17. ▸**b** Proud, disdainful, scornful. E17–L18. **3** Scrupulous or overscrupulous in matters of taste, cleanliness, propriety, etc.; squeamish. E17.

M. MEYER So fastidious in his tastes and so shy of human contact.

▪ **fastidiously** *adverb* E17. **fastidiousness** *noun* M16.

fastidium /faˈstɪdɪəm/ *noun*. *rare*. M18.
[ORIGIN Latin, from *fastus* FAST *noun*[3].]
Disgust; ennui.

fastigiate /faˈstɪdʒɪət, -ɪeɪt/ *adjective*. M17.
[ORIGIN from Latin *fastigium* tapering point, gable + -ATE[2].]
1 Sloping upwards or tapering to a point. *rare*. M17. †**2** Having a flat surface at the top; *esp.* corymbose. L18–M19. **3** BOTANY. Of a tree etc.: having the branches more or less parallel to the main stem. M19.

fastigium /faˈstɪdʒɪəm/ *noun*. L17.
[ORIGIN Latin: see FASTIGIATE.]
The apex, the summit; ARCHITECTURE the ridge or gable end of a roof, a pediment.

fasting /ˈfɑːstɪŋ/ *noun*. ME.
[ORIGIN from FAST *verb* + -ING[1].]
1 The action of FAST *verb*; an instance of this. ME. †**2** = FAST *noun*[1] 2. LME–M17.
– COMB.: **fasting blood sugar** the concentration of sugar in the blood after a period of fasting; **fasting day** a fast day.

fastly /ˈfɑːstli/ *adverb*. Now *arch. rare*. OE.
[ORIGIN from FAST *adjective* + -LY[2].]
= FAST *adverb*.

fastness /ˈfɑːs(t)nɪs/ *noun*. OE.
[ORIGIN from FAST *adjective* + -NESS.]
▸ **I 1** The quality or state of being firmly fixed; stability. Formerly also, firm attachment. OE. ▸†**b** Fidelity, loyalty, (*to*). L16–M17. †**2** Compactness, density, solidity; (of style) conciseness. M16–L17. †**3** Security, difficulty of access; safety, strength. L16–L17. **4** Rapidity, swiftness, quickness. M17. **5** Dissipation, extravagance, unconventionality, immorality. M19.
▸ **II 6** A stronghold, a fortress. OE.

C. HILL He lured the Scottish Army away from its fastness at Stirling. *fig.*: A. S. BYATT It never does the academic fastnesses real harm to be shaken.

†**7 a** Support, help. Only in LME. ▸**b** A fastening. L17–L19.

fastuous /ˈfastjʊəs/ *adjective*. Now *rare*. M17.
[ORIGIN Late Latin *fastuosus*, in classical Latin *fastosus*, from *fastus* FAST *noun*[3]: see -OUS, -UOUS.]
Haughty, arrogant, pretentious, ostentatious.
▪ **fastuously** *adverb* L17. **fastuousness** *noun* M17.

fat /fat/ *noun*[1]. See also VAT *noun*[1].
[ORIGIN Old English *fæt* = Middle Low German, Dutch *vat*, Old High German *faz* (German *Fass*), Old Norse *fat*, from Germanic.]
1 A vessel; *esp.* a large vessel for liquids, a tub, a cask. Long only *Scot.* OE. **2** A unit of capacity equal to eight bushels. *obsolete* exc. *hist.* LME. †**3** A cask for dry goods. M16–E19.

fat /fat/ *noun*[2]. LME.
[ORIGIN from the adjective.]
1 The fat part of something. LME. ▸**b** The richest or choicest part. *obsolete* exc. in ***the fat of the land*** below. LME. ▸**c** Fatness, corpulence. E18. ▸**d** THEATRICAL. A part which gives the player the opportunity of appearing to advantage. E19. **2** The oily or greasy substance of which the fat parts of animal bodies are largely composed; any variety of this, distinguished by its provenance. Also (more fully ***vegetable fat***), a similar substance made from plant products. M16. ▸**b** CHEMISTRY. Any of a class of compounds which are glyceryl esters of carboxylic acids and which include the compounds forming the typical constituents of animal fat. L19.
bacon fat, ***pork fat***, etc.
3 In *pl.* Fat cattle or sheep. *Austral. & NZ*. L19.
– PHRASES ETC.: **a bit of fat** *colloq.* a piece of good luck. ***chew the fat***: see CHEW *verb*. ***green fat***: see GREEN *adjective*. **the fat is in the fire** an explosion of anger is sure to follow. **the fat of the land** the best of everything (chiefly in ***live off the fat of the land***, ***live on the fat of the land***).
– COMB.: **fat body** ZOOLOGY an organ in the haemocoel of an insect which acts as a store of nutrients, esp. lipids and glycogen; **fat camp** a residential course with an emphasis on weight reduction, esp. for children; **fat-soluble** *adjective* soluble in fats or oils.
▪ **fatless** *adjective* E19. **fatlike** *adjective* resembling fat E18.

fat /fat, fa/ *noun*[3]. Now *rare*. M19.
[ORIGIN French, from Provençal *fat* stupid, ignorant, from Latin *fatuus* FATUOUS *adjective*.]
A presumptuous, conceited dandy; a fop.

fat /fat/ *adjective*. Compar. & superl. **-tt-**.
[ORIGIN Old English *fǣt(t)* = Old Frisian *fatt*, *fett*, Middle Dutch, Middle Low German *vett* (Dutch *vet*), Old High German *feizzet* (German *feist*), from West Germanic pa. pple formation on Germanic verb, from adjective.]
▸ **I 1** Well-fed, plump. Now chiefly, too plump, corpulent. OE. ▸**b** Of larger size than is usual; large in comparison with others of the same species. L19.

J. STEINBECK Ma was heavy, but not fat; thick with child-bearing and work. *fig.*: SHAKES. *Merch. V.* I will feed fat the ancient grudge I bear him.

2 Of an animal: made plump for slaughter, fattened up. OE. ▸**b** Of grain or fruit: well-developed; ripe, juicy. Now *rare*. LME.

DEFOE Whether he or she was fattest and fittest to kill first. **b** R. WEST If you roll the little withered ones between your fingers they taste sweet and rich like big fat ones.

3 Thick, full; TYPOGRAPHY characterized by thick strokes of abnormal width. ME.

J. RABAN Their briefcases were fat with glossy promotional literature.

▸ **II 4** Containing much fat or oil; greasy, oily, unctuous. OE.

J. DAVIES The Milk . . is so fat, that it makes a Cream two fingers thick.

5 Containing a high proportion of some particular component; (of wood) resinous; (of coal) bituminous; (of clay) sticky; (of limestone) nearly pure, slaking easily; *rare* (of air) thick, dense. Formerly also, (of water) thick, turbid; (of wine etc.) fruity, full-bodied. LME. **6** Of an actor's part etc.: offering abundant opportunity for skill and display; impressive. M18.

P. G. WODEHOUSE True acting part, the biggest in the piece, full of fat lines.

▸ **III 7** Rich, fertile; (of a benefice, job, lawsuit, etc.) yielding good returns, plentiful. Formerly also, (of a person) affluent, wealthy. ME.

J. FOWLES Incumbents of not notably fat livings do not argue with rich parishioners. P. S. BUCK They planted seed upon the earth that was fat with the richness of the dried water.

▸ **IV 8** Slow-witted, stupid; indolent, complacent. L16.

SHAKES. *Haml.* Duller shouldst thou be than the fat weed That roots itself in ease.

– SPECIAL COLLOCATIONS, PHRASES, & COMB.: **a fat chance** *slang* no or hardly any possibility. **a fat lot** *slang* a small amount (*of*), hardly any. **fat cat** *slang* a wealthy person, *esp.* a wealthy politician, civil servant, or businessman. **fat dormouse** = ***edible dormouse*** s.v. EDIBLE *adjective*. **fat-face** *adjective* (TYPOGRAPHY) designating a type characterized by thick strokes of abnormal width. **fat-faced** *adjective* having a fat face; TYPOGRAPHY = ***fat-face*** above. **fathead** a stupid person. **fat-headed** *adjective* stupid. **fat-headedness** stupidity. **fatmouth** *noun & verb* (*US slang*) (**a**) *noun* a loudmouth; (**b**) *verb intrans.* talk too much. **fatstock** livestock made fat for slaughter. **fat-witted** *adjective* dull, stupid. ***grease the fat pig***: see GREASE *verb*.
▪ **fatly** *adverb* †(**a**) plentifully; (**b**) to a great extent; (**c**) clumsily: L15.

fat /fat/ *verb*. *arch.* Infl. **-tt-**. OE.
[ORIGIN from the adjective.]
†**1** *verb trans.* [translating Hebrew *diššēn*.] Anoint (the head); load (an altar) with fat. OE–L17. ▸†**b** Cover with fat or grease; *gen.* cover thickly. LME–M17. **2** *verb trans. & intrans.* (Cause to) grow fat. ME.
kill the fatted calf [*Luke* 15] celebrate; *esp.* receive a returned prodigal with joy.
3 *verb trans.* Fertilize (soil etc.). LME.
▪ **fatter** *noun* (**a**) a person who (formerly also, a food which) fattens; †(**b**) an animal which grows fat (quickly etc.): E16.

fatal /ˈfeɪt(ə)l/ *adjective*. LME.
[ORIGIN Old French & mod. French, or Latin *fatalis*, from *fatum* FATE *noun*: see -AL[1].]
†**1** Allotted or decreed by fate. (Foll. by *to*.) LME–E18. ▸**b** Condemned by fate; doomed *to*. E16–M17.

R. BENTLEY It is fatal to our author ever to blunder when he talks of Egypt.

2 Of or concerned with destiny. Formerly also, prophetic, ominous. LME.
the Fatal Sisters the Fates. **the fatal thread**: supposedly spun by the Fates, determining the length of a person's life.
3 Fateful, decisive, important. LME.

M. GEE That fatal night when all her dreams came to a premature and bloody end.

4 Destructive; ruinous; resulting in death (*to*); (of a weapon, bait, etc.) deadly, sure to kill. **E16.** ▸**b** Causing serious harm, disastrous. **L17.**

V. WOOLF There is some flaw in me—some fatal hesitancy. J. A. MICHENER If the venom entered the bison anywhere near the head or face, it was invariably fatal. **b** T. HARDY It was a fatal omission of Boldwood's that he had never once told her she was beautiful. G. VIDAL The hairdresser had made the fatal error of using the wrong dyes.

5 Of the nature of fate; inevitable, necessary. **E17.**

N. HAWTHORNE What a hardy plant was Shakespeare's genius, how fatal its development.

■ **fatally** *adverb* (**a**) as predetermined by fate; (**b**) with fatal result: **LME.** **fatalness** *noun* **M17.**

fatalism /ˈfeɪt(ə)lɪz(ə)m/ *noun.* **L17.**
[ORIGIN from FATAL + -ISM, perh. after French *fatalisme*.]
1 Belief in fatality; the doctrine that all events are predetermined by fate. **L17.**
2 Submission to or compliance with this doctrine. **M18.**

fatalist /ˈfeɪt(ə)lɪst/ *noun & adjective.* **M17.**
[ORIGIN formed as FATALISM + -IST, perh. after French *fataliste*.]
▸ **A** *noun.* A person who believes or accepts that all events are predetermined by fate. **M17.**
▸ **B** *adjective.* Of or pertaining to fatalism or fatalists. **M19.**
■ **fata'listic** *adjective* of, pertaining to, or of the nature of fatalism **M19.** **fata'listically** *adverb* **M19.**

fatality /fəˈtalɪti, feɪ-/ *noun.* **L15.**
[ORIGIN French *fatalité* or late Latin *fatalitas*, from Latin *fatalis*: see FATAL, -ITY.]
1 The quality of causing death or disaster; a fatal influence. **L15.** ▸**b** A disastrous event, a calamity; *esp.* a death caused by an accident, in war, etc. **M19.**

B. R. O. ANDERSON He undermined all the racist fatalities that underlay Dutch colonial ideology.

2 = FATE *noun* 2. Now *rare*. **L16.**
3 The quality or condition of being predetermined, esp. doomed, by fate; the agency or supremacy of fate; subjection to fate. **M17.**

J. BUTLER A Fatality supposed consistent with what we certainly experience does not destroy the proof of an intelligent author and Governor of nature. J. A. SYMONDS The fatality attending an accursed house.

Fata Morgana /ˌfɑːtə mɔːˈɡɑːnə/ *noun.* **E19.**
[ORIGIN Italian = fairy Morgan, sister of King Arthur, whose legend was carried to Sicily by Norman settlers.]
A kind of mirage most frequently seen in the Strait of Messina between Italy and Sicily, attributed in early times to fairy agency; an illusion.

fate /feɪt/ *noun.* **LME.**
[ORIGIN Orig. from Italian *fato*, later from its source Latin *fatum* lit. 'that which has been spoken', neut. pa. pple of *fari* speak.]
1 The power or agency which, according to popular belief, predetermines all events from eternity. **LME.** ▸**b** MYTHOLOGY. A goddess of destiny, *esp.* each of the three Greek, Roman, or Scandinavian goddesses of destiny. **E16.**

A. LOOS Our paths seemed to cross each other and I told him . . a thing like that was nearly always the result of fate. P. BAILEY We did hope . . that everything would be for the best . . but Fate thought otherwise, didn't she? **b** H. ALLEN That Fate who sits at the gates of first beginnings and tangles the threads of life.

2 That which is destined to happen, esp. to a person; a person's or thing's appointed lot. **LME.** ▸**b** The ultimate condition of a person or thing. **M18.**

D. H. LAWRENCE He was expressionless, neutralized, possessed by her as if it were his fate. L. STRACHEY A curious fate awaited this young man. **b** N. MAILER The fate of the campaign was being determined elsewhere. S. HAZZARD A couple whose fates could not be predicted with confidence.

3 Death, destruction, ruin, downfall. **LME.**
– PHRASES: *a fate worse than* DEATH. **as sure as fate** quite certain(ly). *book of fate*: see BOOK *noun*. **decide a person's fate**, **fix a person's fate**, **seal a person's fate** determine what will become of a person. *tempt fate*: see TEMPT *verb*.

fate /feɪt/ *verb trans.* **L16.**
[ORIGIN from the noun.]
Preordain, predestine. Now only in *pass.* (foll. by *to be* or *do*); also *impers.* in ***it is fated***, ***it was fated***, etc. (foll. by *that*).

I. D'ISRAELI It was fated that England should be the theatre of the first of a series of Revolutions. J. CONRAD We knew we were fated . . to hear about one of Marlow's inconclusive experiences.

fated /ˈfeɪtɪd/ *adjective.* **L16.**
[ORIGIN from FATE *noun*, *verb*: see -ED[2], -ED[1].]
1 Preceded by an adverb or adjective: having a particular fate. *rare* exc. in ***ill-fated*** **L16.**
†**2** Fateful. *rare* (Shakes.). Only in **E17.**
3 Decreed, determined or controlled by fate. **E18.**

I. MURDOCH This was the moment, and Edward believed in fated moments.

4 Doomed to destruction. **E19.**

LD MACAULAY Cavalry . . were fast approaching the fated city.

fateful /ˈfeɪtfʊl, -f(ə)l/ *adjective.* **E18.**
[ORIGIN from FATE *noun* + -FUL.]
1 Of an utterance etc.: prophetic. **E18.**
2 = FATAL 4. **M18.**
3 Fraught with destiny, important, momentous, decisive. **E19.**

J. GALSWORTHY The confusion of patriotism and personalities left behind by the fateful gathering.

4 Controlled by or showing the influence of fate. **L19.**

E. PEACOCK As fateful as a Greek tragedy.

■ **fatefully** *adverb* **M19.** **fatefulness** *noun* **L19.**

Fatha *noun* var. of FATIHA.

fat hen /fatˈhɛn/ *noun phr.* **L18.**
[ORIGIN from FAT *verb* + HEN *noun*.]
Any of various weeds with succulent leaves, esp. the goosefoot *Chenopodium album* and (*dial.*) the oraches *Atriplex patula* and *A. prostrata*. Also (*Austral. & NZ*) any of various plants of these genera, sometimes eaten as vegetables.

father /ˈfɑːðə/ *noun & adjective.*
[ORIGIN Old English *fæder* = Old Frisian *feder*, Old Saxon *fadar* (Dutch *vader*), Old High German *fater* (German *Vater*), Old Norse *faðir*, Gothic *fadar*, from Germanic from Indo-European, whence also Latin *pater*, Greek *patēr*, Sanskrit *pitṛ*.]
▸ **A** *noun.* **1** A male parent of a human being (used as a form of address by a son or daughter, and sometimes a son- or daughter-in-law, and sometimes also familiarly by the mother of a man's child or children); a man who undertakes the responsibilities of a father towards a child; (now *rare*), any man who gives away a bride. Also, a male parent of an animal. **OE.**

I. MCEWAN Robert was desperate to be a father, desperate to have sons. *fig.*: B. F. TAYLOR Fox river, Rock river, Mississippi, the old Father of them all.

adoptive father, *biological father*, *birth father*, *foster-father*, *natural father*, etc.

2 A male ancestor, a forefather, a progenitor; *esp.* the founder of a race or family. **OE.** ▸**b** An originator, a founder, a designer; a man who gives the first influential example of something abstract. **LME.**

R. KIPLING Excellent herbs had our fathers of old. **b** R. V. JONES Hugo Meynell, known the world over as the father of English foxhunting.

3 A man who shows paternal care or kindness; a man to whom filial obedience and reverence are due; a patron (of literature etc.). **OE.** ▸**b** ECCLESIASTICAL. A man responsible for the spiritual care, guidance or instruction of a person (also ***spiritual father***); a confessor (in full (arch.) ***ghostly father***). **ME.** ▸**c** A priest belonging to a religious order; the superior of a monastic house. Later also used as a title preceding the name of any priest (abbreviation ***F.***, ***Fr.***). **ME.**

E. A. FREEMAN Scots . . owed no duty to Rome . . but only to their Father and Lord at Winchester.

4 CHRISTIAN CHURCH. (Usu. **F-**.) God; the first person of the Trinity. Formerly also, Christ. **OE.**
5 Used as a title of respect for an old and venerable man (or for something personified as such). **ME.**

T. GRAY Say, Father Thames . . Who foremost now delight to cleave With pliant arm thy glassy wave?

6 Each of the leading men or elders of a city or an assembly; *esp.* a senator of ancient Rome. Usu. in *pl.* **LME.** ▸**b** The oldest member, the doyen of a society etc.; the presiding member or president. **E17.**

A. DUGGAN He attended the Senate, and occasionally delivered a short speech to the assembled Fathers. **b** SMOLLETT I will take your place . . and think myself happy to be hailed 'Father of the Feast'.

7 COMPUTING. A tape of data from which the current version has been generated, retained for security reasons. **M20.**
– PHRASES: *Apostolic Fathers*: see APOSTOLIC *adjective* 1. *be gathered to one's fathers*: see GATHER *verb* 2. **Church Fathers** = *Fathers of the Church* below. CITY *fathers*. *conscript fathers*: see CONSCRIPT *adjective* 1. **Father of English poetry**: Chaucer. **Father of History**: Herodotus. **Father of lies**: the Devil. *father of the chapel*: see CHAPEL *noun*. **Father of the House of Commons**: the member with the longest continuous service. **Fathers of the Church** early Christian writers, esp. of the first five centuries. *Father Superior*: see SUPERIOR *adjective*. *founding father*: see FOUNDING *adjective*. *ghostly father*: see sense 3b above. *God the Father, God the Son, and God the Holy Spirit*, *God the Father, God the Son, and God the Holy Ghost*: see GOD *noun*. *Greek Fathers*: see GREEK *adjective*. **Holy Father**: the Pope. **Most Reverend Father in God** the title of a Church of England archbishop. *Our Father*: see OUR *adjective* 1b. *Pilgrim Father*: see PILGRIM *noun* 4. **Right Reverend Father in God** the title of a Church of England bishop. *Roman father*: see ROMAN *adjective*. *spiritual father*: see sense 3b above. **the father of a —**, **the father and mother of a —** *colloq.* a very severe (beating etc.); a very big (overdraft, row, etc.). *the Seraphic Father*: see SERAPHIC *adjective*. *White Father*: see WHITE *adjective*.
▸ **B** *attrib.* or as *adjective*. (Freq. with hyphen.) That is a father. **M17.**

– SPECIAL COLLOCATIONS & COMB.: *Father Christmas*: see CHRISTMAS *noun & interjection*. **father figure** an older man (esp. of influence) who is revered for paternal characteristics, and who may serve as an emotional substitute for a father. **father-in-law**, pl. **fathers-in-law**, (**a**) the father of one's wife or husband; (**b**) (now *rare*) a stepfather. **fatherland** a person's native country, now esp. Germany. **father-lasher** the short-spined sea scorpion, *Myoxocephalus scorpius*, found in N. Atlantic coastal waters. **father-long-legs** = DADDY-*long-legs*. **father right** the custom by which dynastic succession passes only in the male line. **Father's Day** a day on which fathers are conventionally honoured, usu. the third Sunday in June. *Father Time*: see TIME *noun*.

father /ˈfɑːðə/ *verb trans.* **LME.**
[ORIGIN from the noun.]
1 Procreate as a father; be or become the (biological) father of, beget. **LME.** ▸**b** Originate, found (a doctrine etc.). **M16.**

fig.: A. PRICE Arrogance that was fathered on pride by boredom.

2 Appear as, or acknowledge oneself as, the father of (a child) or (later) the author of (a book); take responsibility for. **LME.**

LD MACAULAY By these two distinguished men Paterson's scheme was fathered.

3 Act as a father to, look after. *arch.* **LME.**
4 Name the father of (a child); fix the paternity of (a child) or origin or source of (a thing); attribute (a piece of work etc.). Foll. by †*of*, *on*, *upon*. **M16.** ▸**b** *refl.* Indicate one's paternity. *obsolete* exc. *dial.* **L16.** ▸**c** Foist, impose *on*, *upon*. **E19.**

D. LIVINGSTONE And coolly fathered the traffic on the Missionaries.

fatherhood /ˈfɑːðəhʊd/ *noun.* Also †**-head**. **LME.**
[ORIGIN from FATHER *noun* + -HOOD, -HEAD[1].]
1 The quality or state of being a (real or spiritual) father. **LME.**
†**2** Paternal authority. **LME–L17.**
†**3** With possess. adjective: a title of respect esp. to a high-ranking clergyman, (rarely) to God, and to any man with a claim to respect. **LME–L17.**

fatherless /ˈfɑːðəlɪs/ *adjective & noun.* **LOE.**
[ORIGIN formed as FATHERHOOD + -LESS.]
▸ **A** *adjective.* **1** Without a father; having a dead, absent, or unknown father. **LOE.**
2 Of a book etc.: anonymous. *obsolete* exc. as *fig.* use of sense 1. **E17.**
▸ **B** *absol.* as *noun pl.* *The* people, esp. children, who are fatherless, as a class. **LOE.**
■ **fatherlessness** *noun* **E18.**

fatherlike /ˈfɑːðəlʌɪk/ *adjective & adverb.* **LME.**
[ORIGIN formed as FATHERHOOD + -LIKE.]
▸ **A** *adjective.* †**1** Resembling one's father. **LME–E17.**
2 Such as is proper to a father, fatherly. **L16.**
▸ **B** *adverb.* In a fatherly manner, as a father. **E16.**

fatherly /ˈfɑːðəli/ *adjective.* **LOE.**
[ORIGIN formed as FATHERHOOD + -LY[1].]
†**1** Ancestral. **LOE–M17.**
2 Of or pertaining to a (real or spiritual) father; paternal. Now only of feelings, conduct, or character. **LME.**
■ **fatherliness** *noun* **M16.**

fatherly /ˈfɑːðəli/ *adverb.* **LME.**
[ORIGIN formed as FATHERHOOD + -LY[2].]
In a fatherly manner.

fathership /ˈfɑːðəʃɪp/ *noun.* **LME.**
[ORIGIN formed as FATHERHOOD + -SHIP.]
Fatherhood, paternity.

fathogram /ˈfaðəɡram/ *noun.* **M20.**
[ORIGIN from FATHO(M *noun* + -GRAM.]
A tracing, made by an echo sounder, representing the varying depth of water beneath a moving vessel.

fathom /ˈfað(ə)m/ *noun.* Pl. **-s**, (with a number also) same.
[ORIGIN Old English *fæþm* corresp. to Old Frisian *fethem*, Old Saxon *faþmos* pl. two arms outstretched (Dutch *vadem*, *vaam* 6 feet), Old High German *fadum* cubit (German *Faden* 6 feet), Old Norse *faðmr* embrace, bosom, from Germanic.]
†**1** In *pl.*, the embracing arms; *sing.* that which embraces or contains, a lap, a bosom. Only in **OE.** ▸**b** *fig.* Grasp, power. **OE–E17.**
2 A measure of the length covered by the outstretched arms; this measure standardized to 6 feet (1.8288 m.), now chiefly used in soundings. Formerly also, a cubit. **OE.** ▸†**b** The stretching of the arms to their fullest extent. **E17–L18.** ▸**c** *fig.* (Breadth of) comprehension. *arch.* **E17.** ▸**d** In *pl.* Depths. **E17.**

J. MASEFIELD The swaying weeds ten fathom beneath the keel. R. BOLT Take anchor rope . . it's a penny a fathom. C. S. LEWIS His pictures . . plunged me a few fathoms deeper into my delight. **c** SHAKES. *Oth.* Another of his fathom they have none. **d** T. MIDDLETON Swallow up his father . . Within the fathoms of his conscience.

3 A quantity of esp. wood, coal, peat, etc., now usu. 6 ft square in cross-section, whatever the length. **M16.**

F

fathom /'faδ(ə)m/ *verb*.
[ORIGIN Old English *fæþmian*, formed as FATHOM *noun*.]
1 *verb trans.* Encircle with extended arms as in measuring. Formerly also, embrace, clasp, envelop. *arch.* OE.

SIR W. SCOTT Trees . . so thick that a man could not fathom them.

2 *verb trans.* Measure the depth of (water) with a sounding line; sound; *fig.* get to the bottom of, penetrate, comprehend fully; investigate (†*into*). L16.

E. LONGFORD Her insatiable desire to fathom people's characters. R. OWEN I spent a long time trying to fathom this puzzling line of thought.

3 *verb intrans.* Take soundings (*lit. & fig.*). Formerly also, enquire *into*. E17.
■ **fathomable** *adjective* (earlier in UNFATHOMABLE) M17. **fathomer** *noun* a person who or an instrument which fathoms L16.

fathomless /'faδ(ə)mlɪs/ *adjective*. E17.
[ORIGIN from FATHOM + -LESS.]
†**1** That cannot be encircled with the arms. *rare* (Shakes.). Only in E17.
2 Of measureless depth; incomprehensible. M17.
■ **fathomlessly** *adverb* E19.

fatidic /feɪ'tɪdɪk, fə-/ *adjective*. M17.
[ORIGIN Latin *fatidicus*, from *fatum* FATE *noun* + *-dicus*, from weak var. of base *dicere* say: see -IC.]
= FATIDICAL.

fatidical /feɪ'tɪdɪk(ə)l, fə-/ *adjective*. E17.
[ORIGIN formed as FATIDIC + -AL[1].]
Prophetic; gifted with prophetic power.

fatigable /'fatɪgəb(ə)l/ *adjective*. Also **fatiguable** /fə'ti:g-/. E17.
[ORIGIN Old French from late Latin *fatigabilis*, from Latin *fatigare*: see FATIGUE *verb*, -ABLE. Cf. earlier INFATIGABLE.]
Able to be fatigued; easily tired.
■ **fatiga'bility, fatigua'bility** *noun* susceptibility to fatigue E20.

fatigate /'fatɪgeɪt/ *verb trans.* *obsolete* exc. *dial.* M16.
[ORIGIN Latin *fatigat-* pa. ppl stem of *fatigare* FATIGUE *verb*: see -ATE[3].]
= FATIGUE *verb* 1.

†**fatigation** *noun*. LME–E18.
[ORIGIN Old French from Latin *fatigatio(n-)*, formed as FATIGATE: see -ATION.]
Weariness; (an) action causing weariness.

fatiguable *adjective* var. of FATIGABLE.

fatigue /fə'ti:g/ *noun*. M17.
[ORIGIN French, formed as FATIGUE *verb*.]
1 (An) action, task, or duty which causes weariness. M17.

D. M. FRAME The aim of Montaigne's retirement . . was to rest from the fatigues of court.

2 Weariness caused by bodily or mental exertion. E18. ▸**b** The condition of weakness in metals or other solid substances caused by cyclic variations in stress. Now esp. in ***metal fatigue***. M19. ▸**c** A condition of muscles, organs, cells, or (esp. luminescent) materials characterized by a (temporary) reduction in power, efficiency, or sensitivity following prolonged use or activity. L19. ▸**d** A lessening of the response to charitable appeals and situations of need as a result of overexposure to them. Usu. as 2nd elem. of comb. L20.

D. LESSING Anna was now so tired . . that fatigue was like heavy hands dragging down her legs and her arms. **c** J. BRONOWSKI This is what causes fatigue, and blocks the muscle action until the blood can be cleaned with fresh oxygen.

d ***aid fatigue, compassion fatigue, donor fatigue***, etc.
3 The non-military duty or duties of a soldier, sometimes allotted as punishment. L18. ▸**b** In *pl.* Garments worn by a soldier on fatigue. M19. ▸**c** = ***fatigue party*** below. L19.

H. WILLIAMSON One of the fatigues was the digging of ditches for the burying of water pipes. **b** E. JONG The kids buy . . war toys and child-sized fatigues.

– COMB.: **fatigue-dress** the dress of a soldier on fatigue; **fatigue party** a party of soldiers on fatigue.
■ **fatigueless** *adjective* E19. **fatiguesome** *adjective* (now *rare*) M18.

fatigue /fə'ti:g/ *verb trans.* L17.
[ORIGIN Old French & mod. French *fatiguer* from Latin *fatigare* exhaust as with riding or working, weary, harass, from *ad fatim, affatim* to satiety, to bursting, enough (cf. *fatiscare, -ari* burst open, gape open).]
1 Tire, weary, exhaust. L17.
2 Weaken (a material etc.) esp. by the application of stress; induce fatigue in (a muscle, organ etc.). L18.
■ **fatiguingly** *adverb* in a fatiguing manner, so as to cause fatigue E19.

Fatiha /'fɑ:tɪhə, 'fat-/ *noun*. Also **-hah**; **Fatha** /'fɑ:tə/. E19.
[ORIGIN Arabic *al-Fātiḥa* the opening (sura), use as noun of fem. pple *fātiḥa* opening, from *fataḥa* to open.]
The short first sura of the Koran, used by Muslims as an essential element of the ritual prayer.

fatiloquent /feɪ'tɪləkwənt/ *adjective*. *rare*. M17.
[ORIGIN from Latin *fatiloquus*, from *fati-* combining form of *fatum* FATE *noun* + *-loquus*, from *loqui* speak, after *eloquent*, etc.]
Prophetic; declaring fate.

Fatimid /'fatɪmɪd/ *noun & adjective*. Also **-ide** /-ʌɪd/. M19.
[ORIGIN from Arabic *Fāṭima* Fatima (see below) + -ID[3].]
(Designating or pertaining to) a descendant of Fatima, the daughter of Muhammad, and her husband Ali, cousin of Muhammad, esp. a member of the dynasty which ruled in parts of N. Africa, Egypt, and Syria from 909 to 1171.
■ Also **Fatimite** /-ʌɪt/ *noun & adjective* E18.

fatiscent /fə'tɪs(ə)nt/ *adjective*. E19.
[ORIGIN Latin *fatiscent-* pres. ppl stem of *fatiscere* yawn: see -ENT.]
Having chinks or clefts; cracked.

fatism *noun* var. of FATTISM.

fatling /'fatlɪŋ/ *noun*. *arch.* E16.
[ORIGIN from FAT *verb* + -LING[1].]
A calf, lamb, or other young animal fattened for slaughter.

fatness /'fatnɪs/ *noun*. OE.
[ORIGIN from FAT *adjective* + -NESS.]
1 The quality or state of being fat; plumpness, obesity. OE. ▸†**b** Oiliness. Only in LME.
†**2** A greasy or oily substance; an unctuous layer or deposit in soil. OE–E18.
3 Richness, abundance (of food); fertility (of land). Formerly also, (a) fertilizing property or substance; the richest part of land etc. *arch.* exc. *US*. OE.

T. HARDY The oozing fatness and warm ferments of the Var Vale.

fatso /'fatsəʊ/ *noun*. *slang* (*joc. & derog.*). Pl. **-oes**. M20.
[ORIGIN App. from pl. of FAT *noun*[2] fat person + -O.]
(A nickname for) a fat person.

fatten /'fat(ə)n/ *verb*. M16.
[ORIGIN from FAT *adjective* + -EN[5].]
1 *verb trans.* Make fat (esp. animals for slaughter). M16. ▸**b** *verb intrans.* Cause fatness. M17.

GIBBON The forest of Lucania, whose acorns fattened large droves of wild hogs. *fig.*: A. COOKE He tolerated, even fattened the newspaper myth of a locker-room tough guy. **b** T. COLLINS His cookery doesn't fatten, but it fills up.

2 *verb trans.* Fertilize, enrich, (soil etc.). M16.
3 *verb intrans.* Grow or become fat. (Foll. by †*in*, *on*, *with*.) L17.

V. S. PRITCHETT Bertie's pink face fattened with delight.

■ **fattener** *noun* a person who or thing which fattens; *esp.* an animal which fattens (early, slowly, etc.): E17. **fattening** *ppl adjective* (**a**) causing fatness or increase in weight; (**b**) that grows fat: L17.

fattish /'fatɪʃ/ *adjective*. LME.
[ORIGIN from FAT *adjective* + -ISH[1].]
Somewhat fat; plump.

fattism /'fatɪz(ə)m/ *noun*. Also **fatism**. L20.
[ORIGIN from FAT *adjective* + -ISM.]
Prejudice or discrimination against fat people.
■ **fattist** *noun & adjective* (**a**) *noun* a person who practises fattism; (**b**) characterized by fattism: L20.

fattoush /fa'tu:ʃ/ *noun*. Also **fatoush**. M20.
[ORIGIN Arabic.]
A Middle Eastern salad dish consisting of tomatoes, cucumber, etc. with croutons made from toasted pitta bread.

†**fattrels** *noun pl.* *Scot.* L18–E20.
[ORIGIN French †*fatraille* trumpery, things of no value.]
Ribbon-ends; a loose, trailing piece of cloth etc.

fatty /'fati/ *adjective & noun*. LME.
[ORIGIN from FAT *adjective, noun*[2] + -Y[1].]
▸ **A** *adjective*. **1** Resembling or of the nature of fat; oily, greasy. LME.
†**2** (Of a plant) full of sap, juicy; (of an animal) plump. LME–E17.
3 Of soil: fertile, rich. LME.
4 Consisting of or containing fat; adipose. L15.
5 Marked by abnormal deposition of fat. M19.
– SPECIAL COLLOCATIONS: **fatty acid** CHEMISTRY any of the series of open-chain carboxylic acids including those found as esters in fats and oils. **fatty degeneration** tissue degeneration, e.g. of the liver or heart, marked by the deposition of fat in the cells of the tissue.
▸ **B** *noun*. (A nickname for) a fat person. L18.
■ **fattiness** *noun* L16.

fatuitous /fə'tju:ɪtəs/ *adjective*. M18.
[ORIGIN from FATUITY + -OUS.]
Characterized by fatuity.

fatuity /fə'tju:ɪti/ *noun*. M16.
[ORIGIN French *fatuité* or Latin *fatuitas*, from *fatuus* foolish: see -ITY.]
The state or condition of being fatuous; (an instance of) folly or (crass) stupidity; (now *rare* exc. SCOTS LAW) imbecility, dementia.

E. WAUGH The endless succession of Hollywood films, the slick second-rateness of the best of them, the blank fatuity of the worst.

fatuoid /'fatjʊɔɪd/ *noun*. E20.
[ORIGIN from mod. Latin *fatua* (see below) fem. of Latin *fatuus* (see FATUOUS) + -OID.]
A mutant form of the cultivated oat, prob. representing a partial reversion to the wild oat, *Avena fatua*.

fatuous /'fatjʊəs/ *adjective*. E17.
[ORIGIN from Latin *fatuus* foolish, silly, insipid + -OUS.]
†**1** Tasteless, vapid. Only in E17.
2 Of a person, personal action, feeling, etc.: vacantly silly, purposeless, idiotic. M17.

E. PERKINS They're all fatuous, self-obsessed, undirected, confused, emotional retards.

3 In a state of dementia or imbecility. Now *rare* exc. SCOTS LAW. M18.
■ **fatuously** *adverb* L19. **fatuousness** *noun* L19.

fatwa /'fatwɑ:/ *noun*. Also **fetwa**. E17.
[ORIGIN Arabic *fatwā*, from *'aftā* decide a point of law: see MUFTI *noun*[1].]
A (usu. written) decision on a point of Islamic law given by a mufti.

faubourg /fobu:r (*pl. same*), 'fəʊbʊəg/ *noun*. L15.
[ORIGIN French: cf. medieval Latin *falsus burgus* not the city proper.]
A part of a town or city lying outside the gates, a suburb, *esp.* a suburb of Paris.

faucal /'fɔ:k(ə)l/ *adjective*. M19.
[ORIGIN from FAUCES + -AL[1].]
= FAUCIAL; *spec.* in PHONETICS (now *rare*), guttural.

fauces /'fɔ:si:z/ *noun pl.* LME.
[ORIGIN Latin = throat.]
ANATOMY. The cavity at the back of the mouth from which the larynx and the pharynx open out.

faucet /'fɔ:sɪt/ *noun*[1]. LME.
[ORIGIN Old French & mod. French *fausset* from Provençal *falset*, from *falsar* bore (= Old French & mod. French *fausser* damage, break into).]
†**1** A peg or spigot to stop the vent hole in a cask etc. LME–M18.
2 A tap for drawing liquor from a barrel etc. Now *dial.* & *US*. LME.
3 A tap for drawing any liquid or gas from a pipe or vessel; *spec.* one providing access to a supply of piped water for household etc. *US*. M19.
4 The enlarged section of a pipe made to receive the spigot end of the next section. *US*. L19.

†**faucet** *noun*[2]. L17–E18.
[ORIGIN Alt. of FACET.]
A facet; a faceted stone.

†**fauchion** *noun* var. of FALCHION.

faucial /'fɔ:ʃ(ə)l/ *adjective*. E19.
[ORIGIN from Latin *fauci-*, *fauces* FAUCES + -AL[1]. Cf. FAUCAL.]
Of, pertaining to, or proceeding from the fauces.

faugh /fɔ:/ *interjection*. Also **foh**. M16.
[ORIGIN Natural exclam.]
Expr. disgust.

†**faulchion** *noun* var. of FALCHION.

Faulknerian /fɔ:k'nɪərɪən/ *adjective*. M20.
[ORIGIN from William *Faulkner* (see below) + -IAN.]
Of or pertaining to the American novelist William Faulkner (1897–1962) or his writings.

fault /fɔ:lt, fɒlt/ *noun*. ME.
[ORIGIN Old French *faut(e)* (mod. *faute*) from Proto-Romance use as noun of fem. and neut. of pa. pple of Latin *fallere* FAIL *verb*.]
1 Deficiency, lack, or want *of*. Formerly also *absol.*, lack of food or necessities of life. Now *arch.* or *poet.* ME.

R. W. EMERSON And, fault of novel germs, Mature the unfallen fruit.

†**2** Default, failing, neglect. ME–L16.
3 A defect, imperfection, or blemish of character, constitution, structure, workmanship, appearance, etc. ME.

D. LIVINGSTONE His independence and love of the English were his only faults.

c ***foot-fault***: see FOOT *noun*.
4 Something wrongly done; (a) transgression; (an) offence. LME. ▸**b** A failure in an attempt; a slip, an error, a mistake. E16. ▸**c** TENNIS etc. A violation of the rules; a stroke or move which incurs a penalty; *esp.* a service in which the ball falls outside prescribed limits. L16. ▸**d** SHOWJUMPING. A penalty point incurred for an error in performance. E20.

F. W. ROBERTSON A restless, undefinable sense of fault. B. JOWETT A fault which is most serious . . ; the fault of telling a lie. **b** I. WATTS There must be some fault in the deduction.

5 Responsibility for something wrong, culpability. Also, a defect causing something wrong or undesirable. LME.

TENNYSON Creatures voiceless through the fault of birth. G. ORWELL It won't be my fault if old Victory Mansions doesn't have the biggest outfit of flags in the whole street.

†**6** An unsound or damaged place; MILITARY a gap in the ranks. E16–L17.

SHAKES. *John* Patches set upon a little breach Discredit more in hiding of the fault.

7 *HUNTING.* A break in the line of scent; loss of scent; a check caused by this. L16.
8 *GEOLOGY.* A fracture in a rock formation, marked by the relative displacement and discontinuity of strata on either side of the plane of the fracture. L18.
normal fault, ***overthrust fault***, ***reverse fault***, ***strike-slip fault***, ***thrust fault***, ***transform fault***, ***wrench fault***, etc.
9 A break or other defect in an electric circuit. M19.

– PHRASES: **at fault** (**a**) *HUNTING* having lost the scent; (**b**) puzzled, unsure what to do; (**c**) culpable, to blame. ***double fault***: see DOUBLE *adjective & adverb*. **find fault (with)** make an adverse criticism (of), complain (of). **in fault** *arch.* culpable, at fault. **to a fault** (usu. of a commendable quality etc.) excessively. **with all faults** at the buyer's risk.

– COMB.: **fault block** a mass of displaced rock bounded by or between faults; **fault breccia**: consisting of compacted rock fragments produced by the mechanical stress of faulting and usu. lying along the line of the fault; **fault-finder** a person who (esp. habitually) finds fault; **fault-finding** *noun & adjective* (**a**) *noun* the action or habit of finding fault, petty criticism; (**b**) *adjective* that finds fault, esp. habitually; **fault line** *GEOLOGY* the line of intersection of a fault with the earth's surface or with a horizontal plane (***fault-line scarp***, ***fault-line valley***: produced secondarily along a fault line by erosion).
■ **faultful** *adjective* (*arch.*) faulty, culpable L16.

fault /fɔːlt, fɒlt/ *verb*. LME.
[ORIGIN from the noun. Perh. also infl. by Old French *fauter*.]
†**1** *verb intrans.* Be wanting or absent. LME–E16.
2 *verb intrans.* Come short of an accepted standard, fail. Long *rare*. LME.
3 *verb intrans.* Commit a fault; go or do wrong; offend. (Foll. by *against, to, toward*.) *arch.* LME.

T. CARTWRIGHT He that marrieth another, faulteth against the former wife. BROWNING Had I died for thee I had faulted more.

4 *verb trans.* Find fault with, blame, censure. LME. ▸**b** Declare to be or mark as faulty. L16.

American Speech Of all the productions of the publishing world, dictionaries are . . the most likely to be faulted by reviewers. **b** *Spectator* His final conclusion at least cannot be faulted.

†**5** *verb trans.* Stand in need of, lack. LME–L15.
†**6** *verb intrans.* Be deficient or lacking *in*. E16–E17.
†**7** *verb intrans.* Make a mistake, blunder. M16–M18.

CHESTERFIELD His tongue stammering and faulting.

8 *verb trans. GEOLOGY.* Cause a fault or faults in; break the continuity of (a stratum etc.). Chiefly as ***faulted*** *ppl adjective*, ***faulting*** *verbal noun*. M19.
■ **faulting** *noun* (**a**) the action of the verb; (**b**) *GEOLOGY* an instance of causing a fault or faults, a break in the continuity of a stratum etc.: LME. **faulture** *noun* (*rare*) something blemished or imperfect, a failing, (the commission of) an error E19.

faulter /ˈfɔːltə, ˈfɒlt-/ *noun*. *Scot. & N. English*. LME.
[ORIGIN from FAULT *verb* + -ER¹.]
A person who commits a fault; a culprit, an offender.

†**faulter** *verb* var. of FALTER *verb*¹.

faultless /ˈfɔːltlɪs, ˈfɒlt-/ *adjective*. LME.
[ORIGIN from FAULT *noun* + -LESS.]
1 Without defect, imperfection, or blemish; irreproachable. LME.

E. A. FREEMAN The faultless model of a ruler. M. BARING Her French accent was perfect, her diction faultless.

2 Guiltless, innocent. Long *obsolete* exc. as passing into sense 1. E16.
■ **faultlessly** *adverb* E17. **faultlessness** *noun* L16.

faulty /ˈfɔːlti, ˈfɒlti/ *adjective*. LME.
[ORIGIN Partly from FAULT *noun* + -Y¹, partly after French *fautif*.]
1 Defective, imperfect, blemished. LME.

W. DAMPIER They made a new Boltsprit . . our old one being very faulty. I. MURDOCH Homer is imperfect. Science is imperfect. Any high thinking of which we are capable is faulty.

2 Guilty; to blame. Long *rare* or *obsolete*. LME.
3 Of the nature of a fault; censurable, wrong. M16.

E. M. GOULBURN A faulty habit of mind.

4 Having imperfections or failings. L16.

J. BUTLER To forgive injuries . . so peculiarly becomes an imperfect, faulty creature. S. RICHARDSON His reputed faulty morals.

■ **faultily** *adverb* M16. **faultiness** *noun* M16.

faun /fɔːn/ *noun*. LME.
[ORIGIN Old French & mod. French *faune* or Latin *Faunus* an ancient Italian god worshipped by shepherds and farmers and identified with Greek Pan.]
CLASSICAL MYTHOLOGY. A member of a class of ancient Italian rural deities in human form with goat's ears and tail (and later with goat's legs), characterized by lustfulness.
■ **faunal** *adjective*¹ (*rare*) L16.

fauna /ˈfɔːnə/ *noun*. Pl. **-nas**, **-nae** /-niː/. L18.
[ORIGIN mod. Latin application of *Fauna*, an ancient Italian rural goddess, sister of *Faunus* (see FAUN). Cf. FLORA.]
1 *collect. sing.* & in *pl.* The animals or animal life of a given area, habitat, or epoch. Cf. FLORA. L18.
2 A treatise or list of these. L19.
■ **faunal** *adjective*² L19. **faunally** *adverb* L19. **faunist** *noun* an expert in or student of fauna M18. **fauˈnistic** *adjective* of or pertaining to a faunist or fauna: L19. **fauˈnistical** *adjective* faunistic L19. **fauˈnistically** *adverb* in a faunistic manner L19.

Fauntleroy /ˈfɔːntlərɔɪ/ *noun*. L19.
[ORIGIN from the novel *Little Lord Fauntleroy* (1885) by Frances Hodgson Burnett.]
More fully ***Little Lord Fauntleroy***.
1 ***Fauntleroy suit***, ***Fauntleroy costume***, a boy's velvet suit with a lace collar. L19.
2 A boy resembling 'Little Lord Fauntleroy'; a gentle-mannered or elaborately dressed boy (freq. *iron.*). E20.

faunule /ˈfɔːnjuːl/ *noun*. E20.
[ORIGIN from FAUNA + -ULE.]
ECOLOGY. The fauna of a specified small habitat, *esp.* a group of fossils from one small area.

fausen /ˈfɔːz(ə)n/ *noun*. Long *obsolete* exc. *dial.* M16.
[ORIGIN Unknown.]
An eel. Also ***fausen-eel***.

faussebraie /ˈfɔːsbreɪ/ *noun*. Also **-braye**. L15.
[ORIGIN French, from *fausse* fem. of *faux* false + *braie* = medieval Latin *braca* dyke, embankment.]
FORTIFICATION. An artificial mound or wall thrown up in front of the main rampart. Formerly also, a covered way.

faust /fɔːst/ *adjective*. *rare*. L17.
[ORIGIN Latin *faustus*, from base of *favere* favour.]
Happy.
■ †**faustity** *noun* E17–E18.

Faustian /ˈfaʊstɪən/ *adjective*. L19.
[ORIGIN from Johann *Faust* (see below) + -IAN.]
Of, pertaining to, or characteristic of Johann Faust (Johannes Faustus) a wandering astrologer and necromancer who lived in Germany *c* 1488–1541, who was reputed to have sold his soul to the Devil.

faute de mieux /fot də mjø/ *adverbial & adjectival phr*. M18.
[ORIGIN French.]
(Used) for want of a better alternative.

†**fauter** *noun* var. of FAUTOR.

fauterer /ˈfɔːt(ə)rə/ *noun*. Now *rare* or *obsolete*. M17.
[ORIGIN Extended from FAUTE DE MIEUX: see -ER¹. Cf. *caterer*.]
= FAUTOR 1.

fauteuil /fotœːj/ *noun*. Pl. pronounced same. M18.
[ORIGIN French from Old French *faudestuel*, *faldestoel*: see FALDSTOOL.]
1 An armchair. *arch.* M18.
2 A theatre stall, seat in a bus, etc., resembling an armchair. M19.

fautor /ˈfɔːtə/ *noun*. Now *rare*. Also †**-er**. ME.
[ORIGIN Old French & mod. French *fauteur* from Latin *fautor*, from *favere* favour: see -OR.]
1 An adherent, a partisan, a supporter. ME.
†**2** A protector, a patron. LME–L17.
■ **fautorship** *noun* the fact or condition of being a fautor M19. †**fautress** *noun* a female fautor L16–E18.

fauve /fəʊv/ *noun & adjective*. E20.
[ORIGIN French, lit. 'wild animal'.]
▸ **A** *noun*. = FAUVIST *noun*. E20.
▸ **B** *adjective*. = FAUVIST *adjective*. Also, vividly coloured. M20.

fauvism /ˈfəʊvɪz(ə)m/ *noun*. E20.
[ORIGIN French *fauvisme*, formed as FAUVE + -ISM.]
A style of painting with vivid use of colour, orig. that of the school of Henri Matisse (1869–1954).

fauvist /ˈfəʊvɪst/ *noun & adjective*. Also ***fauviste*** /fovist (pl. of noun same)/. E20.
[ORIGIN French *fauviste*, formed as FAUVE + -IST.]
▸ **A** *noun*. An adherent of fauvism. E20.
▸ **B** *adjective*. Of or pertaining to fauvism or fauvists. E20.

faux /fəʊ/ *adjective*. L17.
[ORIGIN French.]
(Of a material) made in imitation, artificial; (esp. of behaviour) not genuine, false, fake.

Time Not the real thing, of course, but thick faux furs. J. WATERMAN The faux friendliness of people on the street.

– NOTE: Rare before L20.

faux bonhomme /fo bɔnɔm/ *noun phr*. Pl. ***faux bonshommes*** /fo bɔ̃zɔm/. E20.
[ORIGIN French = false good-natured man.]
A sly and shifty person who assumes an open and good-natured manner.

faux-bourdon /foburdɔ̃/ *noun*. Pl. pronounced same. L19.
[ORIGIN French.]
= FABURDEN.

faux-naïf /fonaif, fəʊnʌɪˈiːf/ *noun & adjective*. Pl. pronounced same. M20.
[ORIGIN French, formed as *faux* false + NAÏF.]
▸ **A** *noun*. A person who pretends to be ingenuous or naive. M20.
▸ **B** *adjective*. **1** Of a work of art: self-consciously or meretriciously simple and artless. M20.
2 Of a person: pretendedly ingenuous or naive. M20.

faux pas /fəʊ ˈpɑː, *foreign* fo pa/ *noun phr*. Pl. same, /ˈpɑːz, *foreign* pa/. L17.
[ORIGIN French, from *faux* false + *pas* step.]
A false step; an act that compromises one's (esp. a woman's) reputation; an offence against social convention; an indiscreet remark or action.

fav. *abbreviation*.
Favourite (esp. in horse-racing).

fava bean /ˈfɑːvə/ *noun phr*. *N. Amer.* Also **faba bean** /ˈfɑːbə/. E19.
[ORIGIN from Italian *fava* from Latin *faba* bean.]
= ***broad bean*** s.v. BEAN *noun* 1a.

fave /feɪv/ *noun & adjective*. *slang*. M20.
[ORIGIN Abbreviation.]
▸ **A** *noun*. = FAVOURITE *noun* 1. M20.
▸ **B** *adjective*. = FAVOURITE *adjective*. M20.

†**favel** *noun*. ME.
[ORIGIN Old French *fauvel*, from *fauve* fallow-coloured: see -EL².]
1 (The name of) a fallow-coloured or chestnut horse, *esp.* one proverbial as the type of fraud, cunning, or duplicity. Chiefly in ***curry favel*** (see CURRY *verb*¹ 1). ME–E17.
2 (The personification of) cunning or duplicity. LME–L16.

favela /faˈvela/ *noun*. M20.
[ORIGIN Portuguese.]
A Brazilian shack, shanty, or slum.

Faverolle /ˈfavərɒl, -ˈrəʊl/ *noun*. E20.
[ORIGIN Prob. from *Faverolles* in the department of Seine-et-Oise, France.]
(A bird of) a breed of domestic fowl originated in France by crossing light Brahmas or Dorkings with Houdans.

favic /ˈfeɪvɪk/ *adjective*. L19.
[ORIGIN from FAVUS + -IC.]
MEDICINE. Of or pertaining to favus.

favism /ˈfeɪvɪz(ə)m/ *noun*. Also **-bism** /-bɪz(ə)m/. E20.
[ORIGIN from Italian *favismo*, from *fava* broad bean from Latin *faba* bean: see -ISM.]
MEDICINE. An allergic syndrome involving haemolytic anaemia, manifested after eating or exposure to broad beans and associated with an inherited enzyme deficiency.

favonian /fəˈvəʊnɪən/ *adjective*. M17.
[ORIGIN Latin *favonianus*, from *Favonius* the west wind: see -IAN.]
Of or pertaining to the west wind; gentle, propitious.

favor *noun, verb*, **favorable** *adjective*, etc., see FAVOUR *noun* etc.

favour /ˈfeɪvə/ *noun*. Also ***favor**. ME.
[ORIGIN Old French *favour*, *-or* (mod. *faveur*) from Latin *favor*, *-oris*, from *favere* regard with good will, rel. to *fovere* cherish.]
1 Propitious or friendly regard; esteem, liking. Formerly also, a liking, a preference. ME. ▸**b** Approving disposition towards a thing; inclination to commend, sanction, or adopt. E19.

SIR W. SCOTT His young Life-guardsman, for whom he seemed to have taken a special favour. LD MACAULAY Rochester . . stood high in the favour of the King.

curry favour: see CURRY *verb*¹ 5. **find favour (in the eyes of)** be liked (by), prove acceptable (to).
2 Kindness beyond what is due or usual; gracious or friendly action arising from special goodwill. LME. ▸**b** An instance of this; an act of exceptional kindness as opp. to one of duty or justice; *euphem.* in *pl.*, a woman's allowing of sexual intercourse with her. L16. ▸**c** *COMMERCE.* A letter. *arch.* M17.

SIR W. SCOTT I have a friend . . who will . . do me so much favour. **b** TENNYSON I came to ask a favour of you. N. MARSH Do me a favour and get the hell out of this, will you?

3 †**a** Lenity, mitigation of punishment; a lenient act. Also, an indulgence, a privilege. LME–L18. ▸**b** Leave, permission, pardon. *arch.* L16.

a SHAKES. *Merch. V.* That, for this favour, He presently become a Christian.

b under favour if one may venture to say so.
4 Partiality towards a litigant etc., too lenient or too generous treatment. LME.

P. MASSINGER Not swayed or by favour or affection.

a fair field and no favour: see FIELD *noun*. ***without fear or favour***: see FEAR *noun*¹.
5 Aid, support, furtherance. LME.

J. S. C. ABBOTT He begged permission, under favor of the night, to surprise the Bellerophon.

in favour of on behalf of, in support of, on the side of, to the advantage of. **in one's favour** to a person's advantage.
6 Something which draws affection or goodwill; attraction, beauty; an attraction, a charm. *arch.* LME.

AV *Ecclus* 40:21 Thine eye desireth fauour and beautie. A. HELPS It takes away much of the favour of life.

F

7 Appearance, aspect, look. *arch.* **L15.** ▸**b** The countenance, the face. *arch.* **E16.** ▸†**c** A feature. **L16–M17.**

T. FULLER *Palestine* . . tricked and trimmed with many new Cities, had the favour thereof quite altered. W. RAND To learn the favour of his Countenance from his Picture. **b** J. RAY By their virtuous behaviour compensate the hardness of their Favour.

8 Something given or worn as a mark of favour, celebration, or allegiance, as a knot of ribbons, a rosette, a cockade, etc. **L16.**

W. HOLTBY Paper caps bearing the favours of the Kingsport team. T. H. WHITE The great champion would fight under a favour of her own.

▪ **favourless** *adjective* (long *rare*) **E16.**

favour /ˈfeɪvə/ *verb*. Also ***favor**. **LME.**
[ORIGIN Old French *favorer* from medieval Latin *favorare*, from Latin *favor*: see FAVOUR *noun*.]

1 *verb trans.* Regard with favour; have a liking or preference for; approve. **LME.**

E. STILLINGFLEET Josephus seems to favour the division of the City into three parts.

2 *verb trans.* Show favour to, treat kindly; countenance, encourage. **LME.** ▸**b** Indulge or oblige (a person) *with*. **LME.**

S. BUTLER A strong bias within . . to favour the deceit. Q. BELL To be, if not spoiled, outrageously favoured. **b** LYTTON Fielding twice favoured me with visits.

†**3** *verb intrans.* Show favour (*un*)*to*. **LME–M16.**

4 *verb trans.* Treat with partiality; side with, take the part of. **LME.**

OED The examiner was accused of having favoured his own pupils.

5 *verb trans.* Aid, support; show oneself propitious to. **LME.** ▸**b** Of a circumstance, fact, etc.: lend confirmation or support to (esp. a belief, doctrine, etc.); point in the direction of. **M16.**

BURKE If Providence should . . favour the allied arms. *absol.*: BROWNING Had but fortune favored. **b** C. C. ABBOTT Every indication favored rain.

6 *verb trans.* Deal gently with; avoid putting too much strain on (a limb etc.); ease, save, spare. *colloq.* **E16.**

DICKENS This habit . . favours my infirmity.

7 *verb trans.* Resemble in face or features; occas., have a look of. *colloq.* **E17.**

E. WELTY Becky's the one she takes after . . . You don't favor him.

8 *verb trans.* Of circumstances, weather, etc.: prove advantageous to (a person); be the means of promoting (an operation or process); facilitate. **M17.**

W. THOMSON The darkness of the night favoured the enterprise.

▪ **favourer** *noun* **LME.**

favourable /ˈfeɪv(ə)rəb(ə)l/ *adjective*. Also ***favorable**. **ME.**
[ORIGIN Old French & mod. French *favorable* from Latin *favorabilis*, from *favor*: see FAVOUR *noun*, -ABLE.]

1 That regards with favour; inclined to countenance or help; well-disposed, propitious. **ME.** ▸**b** Gracious; kindly, obliging. Now *arch. rare.* **E16.**

SHAKES. *Tam. Shr.* Happier the man whom favourable stars Allots thee for his lovely bedfellow. E. A. FREEMAN King Swegen was lending a favourable ear to their prayers. **b** SHAKES. *2 Hen. IV* Unless some dull and favourable hand will whisper music to my weary spirit.

†**2** Winning favour; pleasing; comely. **LME–L16.** ▸**b** Admissible, allowable. *rare.* Only in **M17.**

†**3** Showing undue favour, partial, (*to*). Only in **LME.**

4 Advantageous, convenient; facilitating one's purpose or wishes; helpful, suitable. **LME.**

CLARENDON A place very favourable for the making Levies of Men. T. PENNANT Sail with a favourable breeze.

5 That is in favour of, approving, commendatory. **M17.** ▸†**b** Tending to palliate or extenuate. **L17–L18.**

DEFOE Giving a favourable account of the place.

6 That concedes what is required or requested; auspicious, promising; giving consent. **M18.** ▸**b** Of a patient's condition, progress, etc.: satisfactory, favouring recovery. **E20.**

GIBBON The eunuch . . soon returned with a favourable oracle.

▪ **favourableness** *noun* **M16.** **favourably** *adverb* **LME.**

favoured /ˈfeɪvəd/ *adjective*[1]. Also ***favored**. **LME.**
[ORIGIN from FAVOUR *noun* + -ED[2].]

Having a favour or favours of a specified kind; *esp.* having a specified sort of appearance or features. Chiefly as 2nd elem. of comb., as ***well-favoured*** etc.

▪ **favouredly** *adverb* **M16.** **favouredness** *noun* **M16.**

favoured /ˈfeɪvəd/ *adjective*[2]. Also ***favored**. **M17.**
[ORIGIN from FAVOUR *verb* + -ED[1].]

Having been favoured.

G. GREENE The favoured few who visited him at Rye.

most favoured nation: to which a state has granted by treaty etc. the greatest political or commercial privileges, *esp.* to which a state accords the lowest scale of import duties.

favourite /ˈfeɪv(ə)rɪt/ *noun & adjective*. Also ***favorite**. **L16.**
[ORIGIN French †*favorit* (now *favori*, *-ite*) from Italian *favorito* pa. pple of *favorire*, from *favore* FAVOUR *noun*.]

▸ **A** *noun*. **1** A person or thing regarded with particular favour and preferred above others. **L16.** ▸**b** A competitor generally expected to win; *esp.* a racehorse etc. at the shortest odds. **E19.**

DAY LEWIS She sang . . 'Kathleen Mavourneen' and other popular favourites of the time. S. BELLOW An older brother was the favourite; she was neglected. **b** H. CECIL The favourite for the Oaks is My Conscience and the betting on it is 2 to 1 against.

2 A chosen intimate companion of a monarch or other person in power, esp. when unduly favoured. **L16.**

S. SPENDER D— . . behaved to me like a spoiled favourite towards a mad prince.

†**3** A supporter, a well-wisher, a friend, a follower. Only in **L16.**

SHAKES. *1 Hen. VI* This factious bandying of their favourites.

4 A curl or lock of hair hanging loose on the temple (as fashionable during the 17th and 18th cents.). *obsolete* exc. *hist.* **L17.**

J. GAY Sooner I would . . with immodest fav'rites shade my face.

▸ **B** *adjective*. Regarded with especial favour or liking, preferred above others. **E18.**

S. KAUFFMANN A bottle of their favourite wine, sparkling Burgundy. A. THWAITE They treated him like a favourite nephew—sharing his interests, listening to his poems.

favourite son *US* a person who has endeared himself particularly to his country or state; *esp.* a candidate for presidential or other high office who has the support of the constituency or the political leaders of his own state.

favouritism /ˈfeɪv(ə)rɪtɪz(ə)m/ *noun*. Also ***favoritism**. **M18.**
[ORIGIN from FAVOURITE + -ISM.]

1 Undue partiality; the unfair favouring of one person or group at the expense of another. **M18.**

I. D'ISRAELI Truth will always prevail over literary favouritism.

2 The state or condition of being a favourite. **E19.**

Times Grattan continued to enjoy its favouritism with the analysts, rising another 6p.

favus /ˈfeɪvəs/ *noun*. **M16.**
[ORIGIN Latin = honeycomb.]

MEDICINE. A contagious skin disease affecting the face and scalp, characterized by yellow crusts made up of the threads of the fungus *Trichophyton schoenleini* and skin debris; a similar disease affecting fowls. Also called ***honeycomb ringworm***.

fawn /fɔːn/ *noun*[1] *& adjective*. **LME.**
[ORIGIN Old French & mod. French *faon* (†*foun*, †*feon*) from Proto-Romance, from Latin *fetus* offspring, FETUS.]

▸ **A** *noun*. **1** A young deer, esp. a fallow deer; a buck or doe of the first year. **LME.**

in fawn (of a deer) pregnant.

†**2** *gen.* A young animal, a cub. **L15–E17.**

3 A light yellowish brown. **L19.**

– COMB.: **fawn-colour** the colour fawn; **fawn-coloured** *adjective* of the colour fawn.

▸ **B** *adjective*. Of a light yellowish brown. **M20.**

†**fawn** *noun*[2]. **L16–M18.**
[ORIGIN from FAWN *verb*[1].]

An act of fawning; a servile cringe.

fawn /fɔːn/ *verb*[1]. **ME.**
[ORIGIN Var. (repr. Old English *fagnian*) of FAIN *verb*[1].]

1 *verb intrans.* Of an animal, esp. a dog: show affection or pleasure esp. by tail-wagging, grovelling, or whining. **ME.**

†**2** *verb trans.* Fawn on; caress. **ME–L15.**

3 *verb intrans.* Behave servilely or abjectly; affect a cringing pleasure or fondness. **ME.**

– WITH PREPOSITIONS IN SPECIALIZED SENSES: **fawn on**, **fawn upon** (*a*) show delight at the presence of; lavish caresses on; (*b*) affect a servile fondness for, behave cringingly to.

▪ **fawner** *noun* a person who fawns, cringes, or flatters, a toady **LME.**

fawn /fɔːn/ *verb*[2]. **LME.**
[ORIGIN from FAWN *noun*[1].]

1 *verb trans.* Of a deer: give birth to (a fawn). Long *rare* or *obsolete*. **LME.**

2 *verb intrans.* Give birth to a fawn. **L15.**

fawning /ˈfɔːnɪŋ/ *adjective*. **LME.**
[ORIGIN from FAWN *verb*[1] + -ING[2].]

1 Showing affection or pleasure by tail-wagging etc.; fondling. **LME.**

2 Showing servile deference, flattering. **L16.**

▪ **fawningly** *adverb* **L16.** **fawningness** *noun* a fawning disposition or demeanour, cringing behaviour, servility **L17.**

fax /faks/ *noun*[1]. Long *obsolete* exc. *dial.*
[ORIGIN Old English *feax* = Old Frisian *fax*, Old Saxon, Old High German *fahs*, Old Norse *fax* (Norwegian *faks*).]

The hair of the head.

– NOTE: The final element in the names *Fairfax*, *Halifax*.

▪ **faxed** *adjective* having hair, hairy; ***faxed star***, a comet: **OE.**

fax /faks/ *noun*[2] *pl. colloq.* **M19.**
[ORIGIN Repr. pronunc.]

Facts.

fax /faks/ *noun*[3] *& verb*. **M20.**
[ORIGIN Repr. abbreviation of FACSIMILE.]

▸ **A** *noun*. **1** Facsimile; facsimile telegraphy; *esp.* a message etc. sent or a copy obtained by such a method. **M20.**

2 A fax machine. **L20.**

– COMB.: **fax machine**: for sending and receiving faxes.

▸ **B** *verb trans.* Transmit by facsimile telegraphy. **L20.**

▪ **faxable** *adjective* **L20.** **faxer** *noun* **L20.**

fay /feɪ/ *noun*[1]. Long *arch. rare.* **ME.**
[ORIGIN Old French *fei* (mod. *foi*), earlier *feit*, *feid*: see FAITH.]

Faith.

G. P. R. JAMES By my fay, the place seems a fortress instead of an abbey.

fay /feɪ/ *noun*[2]. *literary.* **LME.**
[ORIGIN Old French *fa(i)e* (mod. *fée*) from Latin *fata* the Fates (pl. of *fatum* FATE *noun*) taken as fem. sing. in Proto-Romance.]

A fairy.

fay /feɪ/ *noun*[3]. **M18.**
[ORIGIN from FAY *verb*[2].]

Surface soil, esp. containing loose stones etc. and needing to be cleared; dross.

fay /feɪ/ *noun*[4]. **E20.**
[ORIGIN Abbreviation.]

= OFAY.

fay /feɪ/ *verb*[1].
[ORIGIN Old English *fēgan* = Old Saxon *fogian* (Dutch *voegen*), Old High German *fuogen* (German *fügen*) from West Germanic.]

†**1** *verb trans.* Fit, adapt, or join (*lit. & fig.*); put together; fix in position. **OE–ME.**

2 *verb intrans.* Suit, do, go on favourably, succeed. *obsolete* exc. *dial.* **ME.**

3 **a** *verb trans.* Fit (a piece of timber) closely and accurately *to* (another). **M18.** ▸**b** *verb intrans.* Of a piece of timber: fit closely to another, so as to leave no intervening space. **M18.**

4 *verb intrans.* Fit *in*, fit. *US.* **M19.**

fay /feɪ/ *verb*[2] *trans.* Now *dial.* **ME.**
[ORIGIN Old Norse *fægja*.]

Cleanse; cleanse and polish; clean out; clear away.

fayalite /ˈfeɪəlʌɪt/ *noun*. **M19.**
[ORIGIN from *Fayal*, an island in the Azores: see -ITE[1].]

MINERALOGY. An orthorhombic iron silicate which is an endmember of the olivine family of minerals.

fayence *noun & adjective* var. of FAIENCE.

fayre *noun* see FAIR *noun*[1].

faze /feɪz/ *verb*[1] *trans.* Orig. *US.* Also **phase**. **M19.**
[ORIGIN Var. of FEEZE *verb*.]

Disconcert, perturb. (Usu. in neg. contexts.)

F. ROBB Although Cope might be only a fishing skipper no gilded plutocrat was going to faze him.

†**faze** *verb*[2] see FEAZE *verb*.

fazenda /fəˈzɛndə/ *noun*. **E19.**
[ORIGIN Portuguese = Spanish HACIENDA.]

In Portugal, Brazil, and other Portuguese-speaking countries: an estate, a large farm; the homestead belonging to such an estate etc.

▪ **fazendeiro** /fazɛnˈdɛːrəʊ/ *noun*, pl. **-os**, a person who owns or occupies a fazenda **E19.**

†**fazle** *verb intrans.* **LME–M17.**
[ORIGIN Rel. to German *faselen*, Dutch *vezelen*.]

Ravel (*out*).

FBA *abbreviation*.
Fellow of the British Academy.

FBI *abbreviation*. *US.*
Federal Bureau of Investigation.

FC *abbreviation*.
Football Club.

FCC *abbreviation*. *US.*
Federal Communications Commission.

FCL *abbreviation*.
Full container load.

FCO *abbreviation*.
Foreign and Commonwealth Office.

fcp. *abbreviation*.
Foolscap.

FD *abbreviation*.
Latin *Fidei Defensor* Defender of the Faith.

FDA *abbreviation*. *US.*
Food and Drugs Administration.

FDC *abbreviation*.
1 First-day cover.
2 *Fleur-de-coin*.

FDI *abbreviation*.
Foreign direct investment.

Fe *symbol.*
[ORIGIN Latin *ferrum*.]
CHEMISTRY. Iron.

†**feague** *verb trans.* Also **feak**. See also FIG *verb*[3]. L16.
[ORIGIN Perh. formed as FEAK *verb*[1]. Cf. FAKE *verb*[2].]
1 Beat, whip; punish; bring down. Foll. by *away*: set going briskly, work hard at. L16–E19.
2 = FIG *verb*[3] 2. Only in L18.

feak /fiːk/ *verb*[1]. Also (earlier) **feat** /fiːt/. E16.
[ORIGIN German *fegen* cleanse, sweep.]
FALCONRY. **1** *verb trans.* Wipe (the beak); wipe the beak of. E16.
2 *verb intrans.* Of a hawk: wipe the beak after feeding. L16.

feak *verb*[2] var. of FEAGUE.

feal *noun* var. of FAIL *noun*[2].

feal /fiːl/ *adjective. arch.* M16.
[ORIGIN Old French, alt. of *feil* from Latin *fidelis*: see FEALTY.]
Faithful, constant, loyal.

fealty /ˈfiːəlti/ *noun.* ME.
[ORIGIN Old French *feau(l)te*, *fealte* (mod. *féauté*) from Latin *fidelitas*, from *fidelis* faithful, from *fides* FAITH: see -TY[1].]
1 A feudal tenant or vassal's (acknowledgement of the obligation of) fidelity to his lord. ME.
> G. BURNET The Bishops were also obliged to swear fealty to the Prince. SIR W. SCOTT Each bent the knee To Bruce in sign of fealty.

2 *gen.* Allegiance, fidelity. M16.

fear /fɪə/ *noun*[1].
[ORIGIN Old English *fǣr* corresp. to Old Saxon *vār* ambush, Middle Dutch *vare* fear (Dutch *gevaar* danger), Old High German *fāra* ambush, stratagem, danger, deceit (German *Gefahr* danger), from Germanic.]
†**1** A sudden calamity; danger. Only in OE.
2 The painful emotion caused by the sense of impending danger or evil; an instance of this. ME. ▸**b** A state of alarm or dread. ME.
> A. N. WILSON Fear gripped him, a quite physical sensation, a tightening of the lungs, a weak fluttering in the stomach. F. WELDON 'Cows kill four people a year . .' said Bella, who always had a statistic to back up a fear. *personified*: COLERIDGE Pale Fear Haunted by ghastlier shapings. **b** E. GRIFFITH I set out . . in fear and trembling.

3 Apprehension or dread *of*, *to do*, *that*, *lest*. Esp. in ***for fear (of)***, in order to avoid the risk (of). ME. ▸**b** A feeling of mingled dread and reverence towards God or (formerly) any rightful authority. ME.
> H. KELLER I could not suppress an inward fear . . lest I should fail. J. GARDNER The fear that every minute detail might not go perfectly. L. DEIGHTON Extension phones that a servant could use to eavesdrop without fear of discovery. **b** AV *Ps.* 111:10 The feare of the Lord is the beginning of wisedome.

4 Reason for alarm. Also formerly, something that is to be dreaded. Now *rare*. LME. ▸†**b** Ability to inspire fear. E–M17.
> COVERDALE *Ps.* 53:5 They are afrayed, where no feare is.

5 Solicitude, anxiety for the safety of a person or thing. Now chiefly in ***for fear of one's life***, ***in fear of one's life***. L15.
– PHRASES: ***for fear (of)***: see sense 3 above. **put the fear of God into** terrify. **without fear or favour** impartially. **no fear** *colloq.* no chance, not likely, certainly not.

fear *noun*[2] var. of FIAR *noun*.

fear /fɪə/ *verb.*
[ORIGIN Old English *fǣran* = Old Saxon *fāron* lie in wait (Middle Dutch *vaeren* fear), Old High German *fārēn* plot against, lie in wait, Old Norse *fǣra* taunt, slight: cf. Gothic *ferjans* pl., liers-in-wait.]
▸ **I 1** *verb trans.* Inspire with fear, frighten. Now *arch. & dial.* OE.
†**2** *verb trans.* Drive (*away*, *to*, *into*) by fear. LME–M17. ▸**b** Deter *from* (a course of conduct etc.). LME–M17.
> SHAKES. *Meas. for M.* A scarecrow . . to fear the birds.

▸ **II 3** *verb trans.* Revere (esp. God). OE.
> DEFOE If you fear God . . as your father.

4 *verb intrans. & (arch.) refl.* Be afraid (*lest*, †*of*). LME.
> C. MARLOWE I fear me he is slain.

never fear, **never you fear** *colloq.* there is no danger of that.
5 *verb trans.* Be afraid of (a person, thing, or anticipated event); hesitate *to do*; shrink from *doing*. LME.
> DRYDEN He would have spoke, but . . fear'd Offence. E. CLODD What man cannot understand he fears.

6 *verb intrans.* Be apprehensive *for*. LME. ▸†**b** *verb trans.* Be apprehensive about. M16–M17.
> DRYDEN Let the greedy merchant fear for his ill-gotten gain.

7 *verb trans.* Have an uneasy sense of the probability of, be afraid *that*; apprehend or anticipate (something unpleasant). L15.
> A. TROLLOPE I fear we are all in your black books. M. PATTISON London had ceased to fear a foreign foe.

†**8** Regard with distrust; doubt. L16–M18.

■ **feared** *ppl adjective* (*a*) (now *dial.*) frightened, afraid; timid (*of*, *for*, *to do*); (*b*) regarded with fear: ME. **fearer** *noun* M16. **fearingly** *adverb* †(*a*) in a terrifying manner; (*b*) timidly: M16.

fearful /ˈfɪəfʊl, -f(ə)l/ *adjective & adverb.* ME.
[ORIGIN from FEAR *verb* + -FUL.]
▸ **A** *adjective* **I 1** Causing fear or terror; dreadful, terrible; inspiring reverence. ME.
> W. FULKE A flying Dragon . . very fearefull to looke upon.

2 Notable of its kind, esp. in badness; annoying; exceedingly bad, long, boring, etc. *colloq.* M17.
> DAY LEWIS As a result of . . arriving a whole day late . . I got into a fearful fluster.

▸ **II 3** Frightened; timid, apprehensive, nervous. (Foll. by *of*, *that*, *lest*, *to do*.) LME. ▸†**b** Anxious *about*, *of* (something). M–L16.
> ADDISON Th' impatient Greyhound . . Bounds . . to catch the fearful Hare.

†**4** Cautious, wary. E16–L18.
5 Of a look, word, etc.: showing signs of fear. M16.
> SOUTHEY Hasty, yet faltering in his fearful speech.

6 Full of reverence. L16.
▸ **B** *adverb.* Exceedingly, excessively. Now *dial.* M17.
■ **fearfully** *adverb* (*a*) dreadfully, terribly; to a fearful extent; *colloq.* exceedingly, excessively; (*b*) timidly, nervously, anxiously, cautiously: LME. **fearfulness** *noun* the quality or state of being affected by fear; the capacity of inspiring fear: LME.

fearless /ˈfɪəlɪs/ *adjective.* L16.
[ORIGIN from FEAR *noun*[1] + -LESS.]
1 Unaffected by fear, bold; showing no sign of fear. L16.
†**2** Not regarded with fear; giving no cause for fear. L16–M18.
■ **fearlessly** *adverb* L16. **fearlessness** *noun* E17.

fearnought /ˈfɪənɔːt/ *noun & adjective.* M18.
[ORIGIN from FEAR *verb* (in imper.) + NOUGHT.]
(Of) a strong thick kind of woollen cloth used for weather-resistant clothes, porthole covers, etc. Cf. DREADNOUGHT *noun* 1.
■ Also **fearnothing** *noun & adjective* E18.

fearsome /ˈfɪəs(ə)m/ *adjective.* M18.
[ORIGIN from FEAR *verb*, *noun*[1] + -SOME[1].]
Fear inspiring; frightful, dreadful; appalling, esp. in appearance.
■ **fearsomely** *adverb* L19. **fearsomeness** *noun* L19.

†**feasance** *noun.* M16–M18.
[ORIGIN Anglo-Norman *fesa(u)nce*, Old French & mod. French *faisance*, from *fais-* pres. stem of *faire* do: see -ANCE.]
The execution of a condition, obligation, feudal service, etc.

feasibility /fiːzɪˈbɪlɪti/ *noun.* E17.
[ORIGIN from FEASIBLE: see -ITY.]
1 The quality or state of being feasible. E17.
2 A feasible thing. *rare.* M17.
– COMB.: **feasibility report**, **feasibility study**: on or into the practicability of a proposed plan.

feasible /ˈfiːzɪb(ə)l/ *adjective.* LME.
[ORIGIN Old French & mod. French *faisable*, †*faisible*, from *fais-* pres. stem of *faire* do: see -IBLE.]
1 Practical, possible; manageable, convenient, serviceable. LME.
> D. LODGE Christian unity is now a feasible objective for the first time since the Reformation.

2 Likely, probable, plausible. M17.
> *Vanity Fair* The only feasible explanation for Pacelli's silence.

– NOTE: Sense 2 is well established and is supported by considerable literary authority. However, some traditionalists object to the use, regarding it as not justifiable on etymological grounds.
■ **feasibleness** *noun* M17. **feasibly** *adverb* M17.

feast /fiːst/ *noun.* ME.
[ORIGIN Old French *feste* (mod. *fête*), from Latin *festa* neut. pl. (taken as fem. sing. in Proto-Romance) of *festus* festal, joyous. Cf. FÊTE *noun*.]
1 A religious anniversary observed with rejoicing. ME. ▸**b** An annual village festival (orig. held on the feast day of the saint to whom the parish church is dedicated). M16.
2 A sumptuous meal or entertainment; a banquet, esp. public, for many guests. Also formerly, a series of such entertainments. ME.
> BUNYAN Mr. Carnal Security did again make a feast for the town of Mansoul.

†**3** Rejoicing, festivity. ME–M17.
4 An ample and delicious meal; *fig.* delight or gratification to the mind or senses. LME.
> T. GRAY Voices, that were a perfect feast to ears that had heard nothing but French operas. TOLKIEN The evening meal seemed a feast . . wine . . bread and butter, and salted meats, and dried fruits, and good red cheese.

– PHRASES: ***double feast***: see DOUBLE *adjective & adverb*. ***feast of EXPIATION***. **feast of reason** intellectual talk. ***Feast of Weeks***: see WEEK *noun*. **immovable feast** a religious feast celebrated on the same date every year. **make feast** (*a*) *arch.* make merry; feast; †(*b*) show honour or respect to, make much of (a person); fête. **movable feast** a religious feast of which the date varies from year to year; *joc.* a meal etc. taken at no regular time.
– COMB.: **feast day**: on which a feast is held.

feast /fiːst/ *verb.* ME.
[ORIGIN Old French *fester* (mod. *fêter*), formed as FEAST *noun* Cf. FÊTE *verb*.]
1 *verb intrans. & (arch.) trans.* with *it*. Partake of a feast; feed sumptuously *on*, *upon*; *fig.* regale or gratify oneself *on*, *upon*. ME. ▸†**b** *verb intrans.* Enjoy oneself. *rare* (Shakes.). Only in E17.
> LYTTON I have . . feasted upon the passions. V. CRONIN Feasting late at night on oysters, champagne and spiced dishes.

2 *verb trans.* Provide a feast for; entertain sumptuously; pass (time etc.) *away* in feasting; *fig.* regale, gratify. ME.
> DEFOE Our men . . feast themselves here with fresh provisions. E. L. DOCTOROW She . . feasted her eyes on the little girl.

■ **feaster** *noun* †(*a*) a provider of a feast; (*b*) a partaker of a feast; a person who lives luxuriously: LME.

feastful /ˈfiːstfʊl, -f(ə)l/ *adjective. arch.* LME.
[ORIGIN from FEAST *verb* + -FUL. Perh. suggested by FESTIVAL.]
Of or pertaining to feasting; given to feasting; festive.

feat /fiːt/ *noun.* LME.
[ORIGIN Old French *fet*, (also mod.) *fait* from Latin *factum* FACT.]
†**1** An action, a deed, a course of conduct; overt action. LME–M18. ▸**b** = FACT 1b. L15–M16.
> SIR W. SCOTT He changed his mortal frame By feat of magic mystery.

2 A noteworthy act or achievement; an action showing dexterity or strength; a surprising trick. Formerly esp. a noble or brave deed. LME.
> J. B. MORTON The feat of remaining under water for half an hour in a steel casket has been performed by an Egyptian. M. HUNTER A leader, who outdid them all in feats of daring. D. FRASER He speared a wolf . . a rare feat.

feat of arms an achievement in battle or tournament, esp. in single combat.
†**3** A kind of action; a pursuit, an employment, an art, a profession. LME–M17.
†**4** The art or knack of doing something. LME–L17.
†**5** Fact; actuality. LME–E16.

feat /fiːt/ *adjective & adverb.* Now *arch. & dial.* ME.
[ORIGIN Old French *fet* (mod. *fait*) from Latin *factus* lit. 'made (for something)': see FACT.]
▸ **A** *adjective.* **1** Fitting, suitable, *for*, *to*; becoming; elegant; neat. ME.
> SHAKES. *Temp.* Look how well my garments sit upon me, Much feater than before.

2 Apt; smart, adroit; deft; dexterous, nimble. LME.
> J. GAY The featest maid That e'er . . delightsome gambol play'd.

†**3** Affected. M16–E18.
▸ **B** *adverb.* Featly. Now *rare* or *obsolete*. LME.
■ **featness** *noun* L16.

†**feat** *verb*[1] *trans.* LME.
[ORIGIN from FEAT *adjective*.]
1 Equip, make fit. LME–L17.
2 Show as elegant. *rare* (Shakes.). Only in E17.

feat *verb*[2] see FEAK *verb*[1].

feather /ˈfɛðə/ *noun.*
[ORIGIN Old English *feþer* = Old Frisian *fethere*, Old Saxon *feþara* (Dutch *veer*), Old High German *fedara* (German *Feder*), Old Norse *fjǫðr* from Germanic, from Indo-European base repr. also by Sanskrit *patra* wing, Greek *pteron*, *pterux* wing, Latin *penna* PEN *noun*[2].]
▸ **I** As an appendage.
1 Any of the appendages growing from a bird's skin, consisting of a partly hollow horny shaft or midrib, fringed with vanes of barbs; in *pl.*, plumage. OE.
> N. TINBERGEN Fighting Cranes preen their feathers in between fights.

†**2** In *pl.* Wings. OE–E17.
> W. RALEIGH Josephus gave all Noah's children feathers, to carry them far away.

3 Plumage; *fig.* attire. ME. ▸**b** (A) type of plumage; (a) species (of bird). L16.
> THACKERAY I saw him in full clerical feather. **b** S. RUTHERFORD Fowls of a feather flock together.

4 A bird; *collect.* game birds. E17.
▸ **II** As a detached object.
5 A feather as a detached object; in *pl.* or *collect.*, feathers as a material. OE.
†**6** A pen. OE–L18.
7 A piece or pieces of feather attached to the base of an arrow, to direct its flight; a flight. LME.
> R. BOYLE The Feathers that wing our Arrows.

8 A plume worn as a decoration or crest. LME.
9 A very light object; a trivial thing. M16. ▸**b** = FEATHERWEIGHT 1. M18.
> SHAKES. *All's Well* You boggle shrewdly; every feather starts you.

▸ **III** Something resembling a feather.

10 a A tuft of hair, *esp.* one standing upright on a person's head or growing in a different direction to the rest of a horse's coat. **M16.** ▸**b** A fringe of long hair on the legs etc. of a dog, horse, etc. **L16.** ▸**c** The foamy crest of a wave; the wake left by a submarine periscope. **M19.**
11 A projecting rib or tongue on an implement, piece of machinery, etc.; *esp.* one intended to fit into a groove. Also, a longitudinal strengthening rib on a shaft. **M18.**
12 One of the degrees in boiling sugar. Now *rare.* **E19.**
13 A blemish or flaw resembling a feather (in an eye, a precious stone, etc.). **M19.**
▸**IV** [from the verb.]
14 *ROWING.* The action of feathering. **M19.**
– PHRASES: **a feather in one's cap**, **a feather in one's hat**, etc., (*fig.*) an achievement to be proud of. ***birds of a feather***: see BIRD *noun.* CONTOUR *feather. fine feathers*: see FINE *adjective & adverb.* **in fine feather**, **in full feather**, **in high feather**, etc., in good spirits, health, or condition. ***fur and feather***: see FUR *noun*[1] 2c. **of the same feather**, **of that feather**, **of every feather** of the same etc. kind or character. ***Prince of Wales' feathers***: see PRINCE *noun.* **smooth a person's ruffled feathers** restore a person's equanimity, appease a person. ***spit feathers***: see SPIT *verb*[1]. **you could have knocked me down with a feather** I was astonished. **the white feather** cowardice (a white feather in a game bird's tail being a mark of bad breeding); freq. in ***show the white feather***, display cowardice.
– COMB.: **feather-brain** a foolish, dim-witted person or intelligence; **feather-brained** *adjective* foolish, dim-witted; **feather-cut** a hairstyle in which hair is cut to be thin and wispy like a feather; **feather duster** a brush made of feathers for dusting; **feather-foil** water violet, *Hottonia palustris*; **feather-grass** a Eurasian perennial grass, *Stipa pennata*, grown as an ornamental for its feathery inflorescences; **feather-footed** *adjective* having feet covered with feathers; *fig.* moving silently and quickly; **feather-head** = *feather-brain* above; **feather-headed** *adjective* = *feather-brained* above; *feather* HYACINTH; **featherman** (*obsolete* exc. *hist.*) a dealer in feathers; **feather ore** jamesonite or a similar native sulphide of lead and antimony occurring in fibrous or capillary form; **feather palm** a palm tree of a kind having pinnate leaves; **feather-pate** = *feather-brain* above; **feather-pated** *adjective* = *feather-brained* above; **feather star** a crinoid echinoderm of the order Comatulida having a small disc-like body, long feathery arms for feeding and movement, and short appendages for grasping the surface; **feather-stitch** *noun & verb* (**a**) *noun* an ornamental zigzag stitch; (**b**) *verb trans. & intrans.* sew (with) this stitch; **feathertail** *adjective* = *feather-tailed* below; ***feathertail glider*** = ***flying mouse*** s.v. FLYING *ppl adjective*; **feather-tailed** *adjective* (of a small marsupial) having a tail with a row of long stiff hairs along each side; ***feather-tailed possum***, a small arboreal possum, *Distoechurus pennatus*, found in New Guinea; **feather-tongue** *verb trans.* (*CARPENTRY*) provide with a tongue or projection for fitting into a groove; **feather-top grass** a grass with a feathery inflorescence, *esp.* one of the genus *Calamagrostis* or *Pennisetum*; **feather-topped** *adjective* (*hist.*) (of a wig) frizzed at the top; **featherwife** (*obsolete* exc. *hist.*) a woman who prepares and deals in feathers; **feather-work** the art of working in feathers.
■ **feather-like** *adjective* resembling (that of) a feather **L16.**

feather /ˈfɛðə/ *verb.*
[ORIGIN Old English *gefiþrian*; re-formed (in pa. pple) in Middle English from the noun.]
▸**I** Cover or provide with feathers.
†**1** *verb trans.* Give wings to (*lit.* & *fig.*). **OE–E19.**

T. L. BEDDOES Blessings of mine Feather your speed!

2 *verb trans.* Provide, clothe, or adorn, (as) with feathers; *spec.* fit (an arrow) with a feather. **ME.** ▸†**b** Wound with an arrow. **LME–L16.**
†**3** *verb intrans.* & *refl.* Grow or get feathers; become fledged. **LME–L18.**

D. PELL The Vulture . . beholds her young to thrive and feather.

†**4** *verb trans.* Of a cock: cover with outspread feathers; mate with (a hen). *rare.* **LME–E18.**
5 *verb trans.* **a** Line with feathers. **M16.** ▸**b** Coat with feathers. Chiefly in ***tar and feather***. **M18.**
a feather one's nest, **feather one's own nest** appropriate things for oneself, enrich oneself when opportunity occurs.
▸**II** Give the appearance of feathers.
6 *verb trans.* = FEATHER-EDGE *verb.* **E17.**
7 *verb trans.* & *intrans.* *ROWING.* Turn (an oar) so as to pass through the air edgeways. **M18.** ▸**b** Rotate (propeller blades) about their axes so that they offer minimal resistance to forward motion through air or water; vary the angle of incidence of (helicopter rotors etc.). **M19.**
8 *verb intrans.* Move or float like a feather or feathers; grow in a feathery shape or form. **L18.** ▸**b** Of cream: rise on the surface of coffee etc. like small feathers. Orig. *US.* **M19.**

R. D. BLACKMORE The wave and dip of barley feathering to a gentle July breeze.

9 *verb intrans.* *HUNTING.* Of a dog: make a quivering movement with the tail and hindquarters while searching for a scent. **E19.**

feather bed /ˈfɛðəbɛd, fɛðəˈbɛd/ *noun phr.* & *verb.* As verb usu. **feather-bed**. **OE.**
[ORIGIN from FEATHER *noun* + BED *noun.*]
▸**A** *noun.* **1** A bed or mattress stuffed with feathers. **OE.**
2 *fig.* Something (esp. a job, situation, etc.) comfortable or easy. Freq. *attrib.* **L17.**
3 In *pl.*, treated as *sing.* A stonewort of the genus *Chara*; a bed of stoneworts. **E19.**
▸**B** *verb trans.* Infl. **-dd-**. Provide with, esp. economic, advantages or comforts; pamper, make things easy for. **M20.**
■ **feather-bedding** *noun* making or being made comfortable by favourable (esp. economic) treatment; *spec.* the employment of superfluous staff: **E20.**

feathered /ˈfɛðəd/ *adjective.* **OE.**
[ORIGIN from FEATHER *noun, verb*: see -ED[2], -ED[1].]
1 Having feathers; provided or fitted with a feather or feathers. **OE.** ▸**b** Pertaining to or consisting of animals with feathers. **E17.**
feathered friend (*colloq.* or *iron.*) a bird.
2 (Apparently) having wings; winged, fleet. Chiefly *poet.* **L16.**
3 Formed or arranged like feathers; like a feather or feathers; having markings resembling a feather or feathers. **L16.**

feather edge /ˈfɛðərɛdʒ/ *noun & verb.* **E17.**
[ORIGIN from FEATHER *noun* + EDGE *noun.*]
▸**A** *noun.* The fine edge of a wedge-shaped board or plank. Freq. *attrib.* **E17.**
▸**B** *verb trans.* Cut to a feather edge; produce a feather edge on. **M17.**

featherfew /ˈfɛðəfjuː/ *noun.* **ME.**
[ORIGIN Alt.]
= FEVERFEW.

feathering /ˈfɛð(ə)rɪŋ/ *noun.* **M16.**
[ORIGIN from FEATHER *verb* + -ING[1].]
1 The action of FEATHER *verb.* **M16.**
2 Plumage; the feathers of an arrow; structure or markings like a feather or feathers. **M16.**
3 *ARCHITECTURE.* Cusping in tracery. **E19.**

featherless /ˈfɛðəlɪs/ *adjective.* **LME.**
[ORIGIN from FEATHER *noun* + -LESS.]
Without feathers.
■ **featherlessness** *noun* **E18.**

featherlet /ˈfɛðəlɪt/ *noun.* **M19.**
[ORIGIN from FEATHER *noun* + -LET.]
A small feather.

featherweight /ˈfɛðəweɪt/ *noun & adjective.* **E19.**
[ORIGIN from FEATHER *noun* + WEIGHT *noun.*]
▸**A** *noun.* **1** A weight at which boxing etc. matches are made, intermediate between bantamweight and lightweight, in the amateur boxing scale now being between 54 and 57 kg, though differing for professionals, wrestlers, and weightlifters, and according to time and place; a boxer etc. of this weight. Also formerly, the lightest weight allowed to be carried by a horse in a handicap race. **E19.**
2 A very light person or thing. **M19.**
▸**B** *adjective.* Very light in weight; (of a boxer etc.) that is a featherweight, of or pertaining to featherweights. **L19.**

feathery /ˈfɛð(ə)ri/ *adjective & noun.* **M16.**
[ORIGIN from FEATHER *noun* + -Y[1].]
▸**A** *adjective.* Having or covered with feathers; resembling feathers in appearance or lightness; tipped or fringed (as) with feathers; stuffed with feathers. **M16.**
▸**B** *noun.* A golf ball stuffed with feathers. **L19.**
■ **featheriness** *noun* **L17.**

featly /ˈfiːtli/ *adjective. arch.* **E19.**
[ORIGIN from FEAT *adjective* + -LY[1].]
Graceful, neat.

featly /ˈfiːtli/ *adverb. arch.* **LME.**
[ORIGIN from FEAT *adjective* + -LY[2].]
In a feat manner; gracefully, neatly, nimbly, deftly.

featural /ˈfiːtʃ(ə)r(ə)l/ *adjective.* **L19.**
[ORIGIN from FEATURE *noun* + -AL[1].]
Of or pertaining to a feature or the features.
■ **featurally** *adverb* **E19.**

feature /ˈfiːtʃə/ *noun.* **LME.**
[ORIGIN Old French *feture*, *faiture* form from Latin *factura* formation, creature, from *fact-* pa. ppl stem of *facere* do: see -URE.]
1 Form, shape; proportions, esp. of the body. Long *arch.* **LME.** ▸†**b** A form, a shape, a creation; a creature. **LME–M17.** ▸†**c** Good shape or looks. Only in **L16.**

T. FULLER The king fell much enamoured of her feature.

†**2** A part of the body; an element of bodily form. **LME–M18.**

SWIFT I agreed in every Feature of my Body with other Yahoos.

3 A part of the face; in *pl.* freq. (the proportions or lineaments of) the face. **LME.**

A. C. CLARKE His features relaxed into a slight smile.
D. M. THOMAS Her face, in which the eyes were the best feature.

4 A distinctive or characteristic part of a thing; a part that arrests attention by its prominence etc.; *LINGUISTICS* a distinct quality of a linguistic element which may have contrastive value. **L17.** ▸**b** A distinctive or prominent article or item in a newspaper, magazine, etc. **M19.** ▸**c** A feature film or programme. **E20.**

R. L. STEVENSON A world almost without a feature; an empty sky, an empty earth. H. PEARSON His after-dinner snooze was still a regular feature of his day. R. P. GRAVES A feature of the house was the impressive hallway. **c** C. JACKSON The movie over . . to be replaced with the next feature, Charlie Chaplin in *The Gold Rush*.

distinctive feature: see DISTINCTIVE *adjective* 1. **c *double feature***: see DOUBLE *adjective & adverb*.
– COMB.: **feature film** a film of some length intended to form the main item in a cinema programme; **feature-length** *adjective* of the length of a typical feature film or programme; **feature programme** a broadcast based on one specific subject; **feature writer**: who writes a feature or features in a magazine etc.

feature /ˈfiːtʃə/ *verb.* **M18.**
[ORIGIN from the noun.]
1 *verb trans.* Resemble in features, favour. Now chiefly *dial.* **M18.**

J. HAWTHORNE She featured her mother's family more than her father's.

2 *verb trans.* Affect the features of; be a feature of. Now *rare.* **E19.**

A. W. KINGLAKE Knolls and ridges which featured the landscape.

3 *verb trans.* Outline or portray the features of; picture. **E19.**

J. GALSWORTHY He lay awake, featuring Fleur . . recalling her words.

4 *verb trans.* Make a special display, attraction, or feature of; give prominence to, esp. in play, film, etc. **L19.**

C. CHAPLIN I was to have my name featured . . at the top of the bill. B. BAINBRIDGE Bernard's first appearance on television, in a programme featuring his work.

5 *verb intrans.* Be a feature or special attraction; participate or play an important part *in*. **M20.**

Times Libraries . . feature prominently in many of the local authority cuts.

featured /ˈfiːtʃəd/ *adjective.* **L15.**
[ORIGIN from FEATURE *noun, verb*: see -ED[2], -ED[1].]
1 Fashioned, formed, shaped; having features (of a specified kind). **L15.** ▸†**b** Well-formed; comely. **M16–L18.**

JOSEPH HALL Thy nose . . is . . featured like some curious Turret.

2 Shaped into or expressed by features or form. Now *rare.* **M18.**
3 Made a feature or special attraction. **L19.**

Globe & Mail (Toronto) The featured artists were Paula Robinson, flute; James Campbell, clarinet.

featureless /ˈfiːtʃəlɪs/ *adjective.* **L16.**
[ORIGIN from FEATURE *noun* + -LESS.]
1 Without good features, ugly. *rare.* **L16.**
2 Without features; having no prominent features; uninteresting, uneventful. **E19.**

Punch The month will be so featureless. I. COLEGATE The house is square and more or less featureless.

■ **featurelessness** *noun* **L19.**

featurely /ˈfiːtʃəli/ *adjective.* Now *rare.* **E19.**
[ORIGIN from FEATURE *noun* + -LY[1].]
Having strongly marked features; characteristic, typical.
■ **featureliness** *noun* **E19.**

featurette /fiːtʃəˈrɛt/ *noun.* **M20.**
[ORIGIN from FEATURE *noun* + -ETTE.]
A short feature film or programme.

†**featy** *adjective.* **E17–L19.**
[ORIGIN from FEAT *adjective* + -Y[1]. Cf. FITTY *adjective.*]
Neat, pretty; clever.

feaze /fiːz/ *verb. obsolete* exc. *NAUTICAL.* Also (earlier) †**faze**. **M16.**
[ORIGIN Prob. from Low Dutch naut. term: cf. Middle Low German, Middle Dutch *vēse* fringe, frayed edge, rel. to Old English *fæs*, *fas*, Old High German *faso*, *fasa* fringe (German *Faser* fibre, filament, *fasern* fray out).]
1 *verb intrans.* Of a rope etc.: unravel or fray at the end. **M16.**
2 *verb trans.* Unravel or fray (a rope etc.). **L16.**

Feb. *abbreviation.*
February.

febricitant /fɪˈbrɪsɪt(ə)nt/ *noun & adjective.* Long *rare.* **M16.**
[ORIGIN Latin *febricitant-* pres. ppl stem of *febricitare* have a fever, from *febris* fever: see -ANT[1].]
(A person) affected with fever.

febricula /fɪˈbrɪkjʊlə/ *noun.* Now *rare* or *obsolete.* **M18.**
[ORIGIN Latin, dim. of *febris* fever: see -CULE.]
MEDICINE. A slight fever of short duration.

febrifacient /fɛbrɪˈfeɪʃ(ə)nt/ *adjective & noun. rare.* **E19.**
[ORIGIN from Latin *febris* fever + -FACIENT.]
MEDICINE. ▸**A** *adjective.* Producing fever. **E19.**
▸**B** *noun.* A substance that causes fever. **E19.**

febrific /fɪˈbrɪfɪk/ *adjective.* Earlier in ANTIFEBRIFIC. **E18.**
[ORIGIN French †*fébrifique*, from Latin *febris* fever: see -FIC.]
Producing fever; feverish.

febrifugal /fɛˈbrɪfjʊg(ə)l, fɛbrɪˈfjuːg(ə)l/ *adjective.* **M17.**
[ORIGIN from (the same root as) FEBRIFUGE + -AL[1].]
Serving or intended to reduce fever, anti-febrile.

febrifuge /ˈfɛbrɪfjuːdʒ/ *noun & adjective*. L17.
[ORIGIN French *fébrifuge*, from Latin *febris* fever: see -FUGE.]
▸ **A** *noun*. A medicine to reduce fever; a cooling drink. L17.
▸ **B** *adjective*. = FEBRIFUGAL. E18.

febrile /ˈfiːbrʌɪl/ *adjective*. M17.
[ORIGIN French *fébrile* or medieval Latin *febrilis*, from Latin *febris* fever: see -ILE.]
Of or pertaining to fever; produced by or indicative of fever; feverish.

fig.: M. LASKI Her continued febrile chatter about the evening obscurely troubled Roy.

■ **febrility** /fɪˈbrɪlɪti/ *noun* feverishness L19.

Febronian /fɛˈbrəʊnɪən/ *adjective & noun*. L19.
[ORIGIN from *Febronius* (see below) + -IAN.]
ECCLESIASTICAL HISTORY. ▸**A** *adjective*. Of or pertaining to 'Justinus Febronius' (J. N. von Hontheim of Trier, Germany) or his doctrine (published in 1763) that national Roman Catholic Churches should be as far as possible independent of Rome. L19.
▸ **B** *noun*. An adherent of Febronius or his views. L19.
■ **Febronianism** *noun* the doctrine of Febronius M19.

February /ˈfɛbrʊəri, ˈfɛbjʊəri/ *noun*. ME.
[ORIGIN Old French *feverier* (mod. *février*), from late Latin (Proto-Romance) *febrarius* for Latin *februarius*, from *februa* (neut. pl.) a Roman festival of purification held on 15 February. Later refashioned after Latin.]
The second month of the year in the Gregorian calendar, containing twenty-eight days, except in a leap year when it has twenty-nine. Also *fig.*, with allusion to the rain and melting snows considered characteristic of the month in Britain and elsewhere in the northern hemisphere. Also (*popularly*) called ***February fill-dyke*** (referring to its rain and snows).

attrib.: SHAKES. *Much Ado* What's the matter, That you have such a February face, So full of frost, of storm and cloudiness?

februation /fɛbrʊˈeɪʃ(ə)n/ *noun*. Now *rare*. M17.
[ORIGIN Latin *februatio(n-)*, from *februare* purify (cf. FEBRUARY): see -ATION.]
A ceremonial purification.

fecal *adjective* see FAECAL.

feces *noun pl.* see FAECES.

Fechner's law /ˈfɛxnəz lɔː/ *noun phr.* L19.
[ORIGIN Gustav Theodor *Fechner* (1801–87), German psychologist.]
PSYCHOLOGY. A law stating that the strength of a sensation is a logarithmic function of the strength of the stimulus. Also called ***Weber–Fechner law***.

fecial *adjective & noun* var. of FETIAL.

feck /fɛk/ *noun*. *Scot. & N. English*. L15.
[ORIGIN Aphet. from var. of EFFECT *noun*.]
1 The greater or better part; a great quantity. L15.

R. BURNS I hae been a devil the feck o' my life.

†**2** The purpose, the intended result; the point (of a statement etc.). L15–E17.
3 Efficacy, efficiency, value. M16.

J. GALT Your laddie there's owre young to be o' ony feck in the way o' war.

■ **feckful** *adjective* efficient M16. **feckfully** *adverb* E17. **feckly** *adverb* †(**a**) indeed; (**b**) mostly; almost: L17.

feck /fɛk/ *verb*[1] *trans. slang* (chiefly *Irish*). E19.
[ORIGIN Perh. var. of FAKE *verb*[2].]
Steal.

feck /fɛk/ *verb*[2] *Irish* (*coarse slang*). L20.
[ORIGIN Euphem. alt. of FUCK *verb*.]
1 *verb trans.* = FUCK *verb* 2, 3.
2 *verb intrans.* ***feck off*** = ***fuck off*** s.v. FUCK *verb*.

fecket /ˈfɛkɪt/ *noun*. *Scot.* L18.
[ORIGIN Unknown.]
An under waistcoat or vest.

feckless /ˈfɛklɪs/ *adjective*. Orig. *Scot. & N. English*. L16.
[ORIGIN from FECK *noun* + -LESS.]
Feeble, futile, ineffective, aimless; irresponsible.

A. SILLITOE We'd left our topcoats at home, but kids are ever feckless.

■ **fecklessly** *adverb* M19. **fecklessness** *noun* M17.

fecula /ˈfɛkjʊlə/ *noun*. Also **faec-**. Pl. **-lae** /-liː/. L17.
[ORIGIN Latin *faecula* crust of wine, dim. of *faex* dregs, sediment: see -CULE.]
1 Sediment resulting from infusion of crushed vegetable matter; *esp.* starch obtained in this way. Also *gen.*, sediment, dregs. L17.
2 Faecal matter of insects or other invertebrates. E20.

feculence /ˈfɛkjʊl(ə)ns/ *noun*. M17.
[ORIGIN Old French & mod. French *féculence* or late Latin *faeculentia*, from *faeculentus*: see FECULENT, -ENCE.]
1 Feculent matter; filth; scum. M17.
2 The quality or state of being feculent; foulness. M19.
■ Also †**feculency** *noun* E17–E19.

feculent /ˈfɛkjʊl(ə)nt/ *adjective*. Also †**faec-**. L15.
[ORIGIN French *féculent* or Latin *faeculentus*, formed as FAECES: see -ULENT.]
1 Containing or of the nature of faeces or dregs; filthy; turbid; foul, fetid. L15.
†**2** Covered with faeces. *rare* (Spenser). Only in L16.

fecund /ˈfɛk(ə)nd, ˈfiːk-/ *adjective*. LME.
[ORIGIN French *fécond* or Latin *fecundus*.]
1 Highly productive, esp. of offspring; prolific, fertile. LME.

A. BROOKNER Fecund and beaming, Evie found motherhood the easiest thing in the world.

2 Producing fertility, fertilizing. L17.
3 DEMOGRAPHY. Capable of bearing children. Cf. FECUNDITY 3, FERTILE 1b. E20.

fecundability /fɪˌkʌndəˈbɪlɪti/ *noun*. E20.
[ORIGIN from FECUND + -ABILITY, after Italian *fecondabilità*.]
The probability of becoming pregnant within a given period of time, esp. a month or a menstrual cycle.

fecundate /ˈfɛk(ə)ndeɪt, ˈfiːk-/ *verb trans.* M17.
[ORIGIN Latin *fecundat-* pa. ppl stem of *fecundare*, from *fecundus* fecund: see -ATE[3].]
1 Make productive. M17.

J. R. LOWELL Even the Trouvères . . could fecundate a great poet like Chaucer.

2 = FERTILIZE 2. E18.

fecundation /fɛk(ə)nˈdeɪʃ(ə)n, fiːk-/ *noun*. M16.
[ORIGIN formed as FECUNDATE: see -ATION.]
Fertilization; impregnation.

fecundify /fɪˈkʌndɪfʌɪ/ *verb trans.* Long *rare* or *obsolete*. E18.
[ORIGIN from FECUND + -I- + -FY.]
= FECUNDATE.

fecundity /fɪˈkʌndɪti/ *noun*. LME.
[ORIGIN French *fécondité* or Latin *fecunditas*, from *fecundus* fecund: see -ITY.]
1 The capacity to reproduce, fertility, productiveness, esp. in abundance. LME.

A. BURGESS Why . . complain of fecundity when god commanded us to be fruitful?

2 The capacity for making productive or fertile. M17.
3 DEMOGRAPHY. Reproductive capacity; the maximum number of live births calculated to be possible in a given population. Cf. FERTILITY 3. M19.

fed /fɛd/ *noun*. *US*. Also (esp. in sense 3) **F-**. L18.
[ORIGIN Abbreviation of FEDERAL, FEDERALIST.]
1 = FEDERALIST *noun*. L18.
2 An official of the US federal government; *esp.* a member of the US Federal Bureau of Investigation. *slang*. E20.

T. LEARY He starts out like a fed, and now he's offering me acid.

3 = ***Federal Reserve Bank*** or ***Federal Reserve Board*** s.v. FEDERAL *adjective*. M20.

fed /fɛd/ *adjective*. LME.
[ORIGIN pa. pple of FEED *verb*[1].]
1 Supplied with food; nourished. LME.
†**2** Fattened. M16–E17.
3 ***fed up***, surfeited, disgusted, extremely bored or tired, (*with*). E20.
– PHRASES: **fed to death**, **fed to the teeth**, **fed to the back teeth** = sense 3 above.

fed *verb pa. t. & pple* of FEED *verb*[1].

fedai /fəˈdɑːiː/ *noun*. Pl. (in sense 1) same, **-s**, (in sense 2) **fedayeen** /fɛdʌɪˈjiːn/. L19.
[ORIGIN Arabic & Persian *fidā'ī* one who gives his life for another, from *fadā* ransom (someone with something).]
1 *hist.* An Ismaili Muslim assassin. L19.
2 In *pl.* (***fedayeen***). Guerrillas in Muslim countries; *esp.* (**a**) Arab guerrillas operating against the Israelis; (**b**) Marxist paramilitary groups operating in Iran. M20.

fedan *noun* var. of FEDDAN.

fedayeen *noun pl.* see FEDAI.

feddan /fɛˈdɑːn/ *noun*. Also ***fedan***. E19.
[ORIGIN Arabic *faddān* a yoke of oxen, an acre.]
A measure of land used in Egypt and some other Arab countries, equivalent to 0.405 hectare (about one acre) or more in certain areas.

federacy /ˈfɛd(ə)rəsi/ *noun*. Now *rare*. M17.
[ORIGIN from FEDERATE *adjective* (see -ACY) or abbreviation of CONFEDERACY.]
1 The state of being joined by a treaty; an alliance. M17.
2 = CONFEDERACY 3. E19.

federal /ˈfɛd(ə)r(ə)l/ *adjective & noun*. Also (esp. in senses A.3, B.) **F-**. M17.
[ORIGIN from Latin *foedus*, *foeder-* covenant: see -AL[1]. Cf. French *fédéral*.]
▸ **A** *adjective*. **1** Of or pertaining to a covenant or treaty. Now only *spec.* in THEOLOGY, pertaining to or based on the doctrine of God's Covenant with Adam as representing humankind and with Christ as representing the Church. M17.
2 Of, pertaining to, or of the nature of a system of government in which several states form a central political unity but remain independent in internal affairs. Cf. UNITARY *adjective* 2. M17. ▸**b** Of or pertaining to the central government as distinguished from the separate units constituting it. L18.

A. F. DOUGLAS-HOME Ways . . which would give to the three territories a Federal structure. **b** A. E. STEVENSON Some of the federal aid might take the form of . . grants to the states.

3 *US HISTORY*. (Usu. **F-**.) Favouring a central or federal government; *esp.* of or pertaining to the Federalist party or the northern states and their supporters or troops in the Civil War. L18.
4 Comprising an association of largely independent units. E20.

Times Lit. Suppl. The geography and diverse character of Wales made a federal university of scattered colleges a necessity.

– SPECIAL COLLOCATIONS: **federal district** the district used as the seat of federal government. ***federal land bank***: see LAND BANK 2. **Federal Reserve Bank** *US* each of twelve regional banks which regulate and serve the member banks of the Federal Reserve System. **Federal Reserve Board** *US* the board regulating the Federal Reserve System and consisting of governors appointed by the US President with Senate approval. **Federal Reserve System** the US national banking system of reserve cash available to banks. **federal territory** the territory used as the seat of federal government.
▸ **B** *noun*. *US HISTORY*. (Usu. **F-**.) A supporter of the Union government or (esp.) a soldier in Union armies in the American Civil War. M19.
■ **federally** *adverb* (**a**) THEOLOGY on the basis of a covenant; (**b**) in the manner of a federation: M17.

federalise *verb* var. of FEDERALIZE.

federalism /ˈfɛd(ə)rəlɪz(ə)m/ *noun*. L18.
[ORIGIN French *fédéralisme*, from *fédéral* FEDERAL *adjective*: see -ISM.]
(The principle of) a federal system of government; advocacy of this; *spec.* in *US HISTORY* (usu. **F-**) the principles of the Federalists.

federalist /ˈfɛd(ə)rəlɪst/ *noun & adjective*. L18.
[ORIGIN French *fédéraliste*, from *fédéral*: cf. FEDERAL & see -IST.]
▸ **A** *noun*. A person who supports federalism; *spec.* in *US HISTORY* (usu. **F-**) a member or supporter of the Federalist party. L18.
▸ **B** *adjective*. Of, pertaining to, or favouring federalism or federalists; *spec.* in *US HISTORY* (usu. **F-**) designating or pertaining to the party advocating a federal union of American colonies after the War of Independence. E19.
■ **federaˈlistic** *adjective* inclined to federalism, somewhat federalist M19.

federalize /ˈfɛd(ə)rəlʌɪz/ *verb trans.* Also **-ise**. E19.
[ORIGIN French *fédéraliser*, from *fédéral* FEDERAL *adjective*: see -IZE.]
Unite in a federal union or government; place under federal jurisdiction.

federate /ˈfɛd(ə)rət/ *noun & adjective*. L17.
[ORIGIN Latin *foederatus* pa. ppl formation on *foedus*, *foeder-* covenant + *-atus* -ATE[2]. Cf. French *fédéré*.]
▸ **A** *noun*. **1** A party to a covenant. *rare*. L17.
2 FRENCH HISTORY. [translating French *fédéré*.] A deputy to the Fête of the Federation, 14 July 1790; a member of one of the armed associations formed during the first French Revolution, or during the Hundred Days; a member of the Commune in 1871. L18.
▸ **B** *adjective*. Federated, confederate. E18.

federate /ˈfɛdəreɪt/ *verb trans. & intrans.* E19.
[ORIGIN Late Latin *foederat-* pa. ppl stem of *foederare*, from *foedus*, *foeder-*: see FEDERATE *noun & adjective*, -ATE[3].]
Unite in or form into a league or federation.

A. J. AYER All the factories in a given industry should be federated into a Guild. P. SCOTT There had been an attempt to get the rulers of the Tradura agency states to federate.

federation /fɛdəˈreɪʃ(ə)n/ *noun*. E18.
[ORIGIN French *fédération* from late Latin *foederatio(n-)*, formed as FEDERATE *verb*: see -ATION.]
1 The action of federating; *esp.* the union of several states etc. under a federal government, each remaining independent in internal affairs. E18.
2 A federated society; a federal group of states etc. L18.
■ **federationist** *noun* a supporter of federation M19.

federative /ˈfɛd(ə)rətɪv/ *adjective*. L17.
[ORIGIN from Latin *foederat-* (see FEDERATE *verb*) + -IVE; perh. partly from French *fédératif*.]
1 Of or pertaining to the formation of a covenant or alliance. Now *rare*. L17.
2 Of, pertaining to, or of the nature of a federation; forming part of a federation; inclined to federation. L18.

†**fedity** *noun*. M16–M18.
[ORIGIN Latin *foeditas*, from *foedus* foul: see -ITY.]
Foulness, loathsomeness; in *pl.*, foul or loathsome practices.

fedora /fɪˈdɔːrə/ *noun*. Orig. *US*. L19.
[ORIGIN from *Fédora*, title of a drama (1882) by Victorien Sardou (1831–1908).]
A low soft felt hat with a curled brim and the crown creased lengthways.

F

F

†**fee** *noun*[1].
[ORIGIN Old English *feoh, fioh, fēo* = Old Frisian *fia*, Old Saxon *fehu* cattle, property (Dutch *vee* cattle), Old High German *fihu, fehu* cattle, property, money (German *Vieh* cattle), Gothic *faihu* from Germanic var. of Indo-European base, repr. by Sanskrit *paśu*, Latin *pecu* cattle (cf. Latin *pecunia* money).]
1 Livestock, cattle. OE–M16.
2 Movable property. OE–L16.
3 Money. OE–L17.

fee /fiː/ *noun*[2]. ME.
[ORIGIN Anglo-Norman = Old French *feu, fiu, fieu*, (also mod.) *fief*, pl. *fiez* from Proto-Romance var. of medieval Latin *feodum, feudum*, derived from Frankish base, rel. to Old High German *fehu*, Old English *fēo*, etc.: see FEE *noun*[1].]
1 *LAW*. **a** *hist.* (Tenure of) an estate in land (in England always a heritable estate) in return for homage and service to a superior lord by whom it is granted; an estate so held, a fief, a feudal benefice. ME. ▸**b** (Tenure of) a heritable estate in land. See also earlier FEE SIMPLE, FEE TAIL. M16.
a in fee by a heritable right subject to feudal obligations. *in one's* DEMESNE *as of fee*. **b at a pin's fee** *arch.* at the value of a pin, at very little value. **hold in fee** *fig. (arch.)* hold as one's absolute and rightful possession.
†**2** Homage paid by a vassal to a superior; service, employment. ME–L16.
3 A territory held in fee; a lordship. Now *arch.* or *hist.* LME.
†**4** The heritable right to an office of profit, held feudally, or to a pension or revenue. LME–E19.
†**5** A tribute to a superior. LME–E17.
†**6** A perquisite, an incidental benefit attaching to employment etc. LME–M18. ▸**b** Any allotted portion. L16–M17.
7 †**a** A prize, a reward. LME–M17. ▸†**b** A bribe. M16–M17. ▸**c** A gratuity, a tip. L16.
8 A fixed salary or wage. Also in *pl.*, wages. *obsolete* exc. *hist.* LME.

R. SIMPSON The post of King's standard-bearer, with the fee of six shillings . . a day.

9 The sum payable to a public officer in return for the execution of relevant duties. LME.

R. L. FOX Aristotle did receive a handsome fee for his services, and . . died a rich man.

10 The sum paid for admission to an examination, a society, a public building, etc. LME.

J. K. JEROME There is a grotto in the park which you can see for a fee.

11 The remuneration due to a lawyer, physician, or other professional person, for consultation etc. L16.

V. PACKARD His standard fee for offering advice is $500 a day.

12 In *pl.* Regular payment for tuition at school, university, etc. E17.
13 More fully ***transfer fee***. The money paid to an employer for the transfer of an employee, esp. for the transfer of a footballer. L19.

fee /fiː/ *verb*. Pa. t. & pple **feed, fee'd**. LME.
[ORIGIN from FEE *noun*[2].]
†**1** *verb trans.* Grant (a person) a fief or feudal estate. LME–L15.
2 *verb trans.* Engage for a fee; *Scot.* hire (a servant etc.). LME. ▸†**b** Bribe. LME–E19.
3 *verb trans.* Give a fee or payment to. E16.

W. CATHER It wasn't necessary to fee porters or waiters. E. JONG They are Whores fer hire to anyone that fees 'em.

4 *verb intrans.* Take service *with*, hire oneself *to*. M17.
– COMB.: **feeing market** *hist.* a twice-yearly hiring market at which farmhands hired themselves out for the next six months.

feeb /fiːb/ *noun*. *US slang*. E20.
[ORIGIN Abbreviation of FEEBLE *adjective & noun*.]
A stupid or mentally disabled person.

feeble /ˈfiːb(ə)l/ *adjective & noun*. ME.
[ORIGIN Anglo-Norman, Old French *feble*, var. of *fieble* (mod. *faible*), later forms of *fleible*, from Latin *flebilis* that is to be wept over, from *flere* weep: see -BLE.]
▸**A** *adjective*. **1** Lacking physical strength, frail, weak, (now only of living things). ME.

G. M. FRASER He was still in shocking pain and entirely feeble.

2 Lacking intellectual or moral strength. ME.
†**3** Poor, mean, scanty. Foll. by *of*: poorly supplied. ME–L16.
4 Lacking energy, force, or effect. ME.

C. WILSON The feeble argument fails to do justice to Jung's basic conception.

5 Faintly perceived; indistinct, dim. M19.

J. RHYS Amélie brought out candles . . but the night swallowed up the feeble light.

– COMB.: **feeble-minded** *adjective* of very low intelligence, stupid; (now *offensive*) having a mental disability. **feeble-mindedness** the state of being feeble-minded.
▸**B** *noun*. **1** A weak, frail, or ineffectual person. ME.
2 *FENCING*. The blade of a sword from the middle to the point. Cf. FOIBLE *noun* 1, FORTE *noun*[1] 1. M17.
3 A weakness, a foible. *rare*. L17.
■ **feebleness** *noun* ME. **feebling** *noun* a feeble person, a weakling L19. **feeblish** *adjective* L17. **feebly** *adverb* ME.

feeble /ˈfiːb(ə)l/ *verb*. ME.
[ORIGIN from the adjective.]
1 *verb intrans.* Become feeble. Now *rare* or *obsolete*. ME.
2 *verb trans.* Make feeble; weaken. *arch.* ME.

A. E. COPPARD The illness feebled him.

feebless /ˈfiːblɪs/ *noun*. Long *arch. rare*. ME.
[ORIGIN Old French *feblesse* (mod. *faiblesse*), from *feble* FEEBLE *adjective*: see -ESS[2].]
Weakness, infirmity; poor health.

feed /fiːd/ *noun*. L16.
[ORIGIN from the verb.]
1 The action or an act of eating or feeding; the taking or giving of food. L16.
2 Grazing; pasturage, pasture. L16.
3 Food for animals, fodder. L16. ▸**b** Food for humans. *US colloq.* E19.

M. SHADBOLT Turnips for next year's winter feed.

4 A meal of corn, oats, etc. given to a horse or other animal. M18.
5 A (large or sumptuous) meal; a feast. *colloq.* E19.

B. BEHAN They're all bloody big fellows . . from eating bloody great feeds and drinking cider.

6 The action or process of supplying something, as fuel or material to a machine etc.; the mechanism or means of supply. M19. ▸**b** The (amount of) material supplied. M19.

P. BENJAMIN Graduating the feed of the paper to the exact speed of the machine. D. L. SAYERS A commercial vehicle with a leaking feed.

7 *THEATRICAL*. An actor etc. who provides lines or cues for another to react to; a comedian's straight man. Cf. earlier FEEDER 11. E20.

S. BRETT Wilkie was a grand feed, but that's all he was. I was the funny one.

8 A facility whereby a radio or television programme, set of Internet data, etc. is transmitted or made available from a central source to a studio or user; a programme etc. so transmitted. L20.
– PHRASES: **on the feed** (of fish) feeding or seeking food. **off one's feed** having no appetite. **out at feed** turned out to graze.
– COMB.: **feed bag** a nosebag; **feed check (valve)** a valve between a feed-pipe and a boiler to prevent return of feed-water; **feed cock**: which regulates the flow of water to a boiler etc.; **feed crop** barley, beans, wheat, etc., grown for animal food; **feed crusher**, **feed cutter** a machine for processing feed; **feed dog** the mechanism in a sewing machine which feeds the material under the needle; **feed floor** *US* a floor off which cattle etc. can eat food; **feedlot** an area or building where livestock are fed or fattened up; **feed pipe**: which takes water etc. from a feed-tank to a boiler or other machine; **feed pump**: which supplies water, fuel, etc., to a machine; **feed room** *US & NZ* a room in which animal feed is stored; **feedstock** raw material to supply a machine or industrial process; **feedstuff** fodder; **feed tank** a tank containing a supply of water for a steam locomotive, a boiler, etc., or for drinking; a tank containing liquid for a machine or industrial process; **feed trough** (*a*) a trough between railway lines from which a steam locomotive scoops up water; (*b*) *US* a trough in which food for animals is placed; **feed water** a supply of water for a boiler etc.

feed /fiːd/ *verb*[1]. Pa. t. & pple **fed** /fɛd/.
[ORIGIN Old English *fēdan* = Old Frisian *fēda*, Old Saxon *fōdean* (Dutch *voeden*), Old High German *fuoten*, Old Norse *fœða*, Gothic *fōdjan*, from Germanic.]
▸**I** *verb trans.* **1** Give food to, supply with food; suckle. OE. ▸**b** Put food into the mouth of. LME. ▸†**c** Graze, pasture, (cattle etc.). LME–M18.

E. M. FORSTER Tom shall feed us on eggs and milk.
b *refl.*: H. D. TRAILL His meal might be served up to him on costly dishes, but he fed himself with his fingers.

2 Provide with nourishment or sustenance; support. OE.

I. WATTS God . . feeds the strength of every Saint.

3 Serve as food or sustenance for. ME.
4 Fill with food, pamper; fatten *up* (cattle etc.). ME.
5 Keep continuously supplied (with water, fuel, working material, etc.); insert further coins etc. into (a meter) for continued functioning. ME. ▸**b** Relay or supply electrical signals or power to, esp. as part of a larger network or system. L19. ▸**c** *FOOTBALL* etc. Give a pass or passes to. L19. ▸**d** *THEATRICAL*. Supply (an actor etc.) with lines or cues to react to; act as straight man to (a comedian). Cf. earlier FEEDER 11. E20. ▸**e** *JAZZ*. Play an accompaniment for (a soloist); provide as an accompaniment. Orig. *US*. M20.

P. THEROUX There was a swimming pool nearby, fed by a waterfall.

6 Gratify, seek to satisfy (an appetite, passion, etc.); sustain (a person) *with* hope etc. ME.

J. MARSTON This morne my vengeance shall be amply fed.
R. KNOLLES Craftily feeding him with the hope of libertie.

7 Cause to be eaten or grazed by cattle etc.; use (land) as pasture; give as food (*to*). M17.

A. SILLITOE He wanted fish to . . feed to the cat.

8 Of cattle etc.: eat, feed on, graze. Also foll. by *down, off*. E18.
9 Foll. by *through*: cause to pass gradually and steadily through a confined space. E20.

M. BELSON The person who fed the sheets of paper through the machine.

10 Foll. by *back*: return by feedback. E20.
▸**II** *verb intrans.* **11** Take food, eat; (of a baby etc.) suckle. Foll. by *off, on*: consume, be nourished by. ME.

POPE Devouring dogs . . fed on his trembling limbs. A. UPFIELD Cows feeding off the same grass as myxomatized rabbits. *Lancet* The baby fed well and gained weight.

12 Of material: pass continuously *to, into* a machine, reservoir, etc. M17. ▸**b** Begin to be effective or influential; have an impact, esp. on the economy. L20.
13 Foll. by *back*: return as feedback. M20.
– PHRASES: ***bite the hand that feeds one***: see BITE *verb*. **feed a part** *THEATRICAL* fill out a part with trivial details etc. **feed high**, **feed full and high** supply with rich and abundant food. **feed the fishes** (*a*) be drowned; (*b*) be seasick.
– COMB.: **feedforward** the modification or control of a process by its anticipated or predicted results or effects (cf. FEEDBACK).
■ **feedable** *adjective* M17.

feed, **fee'd** *verb*[2] *pa. t. & pple* of FEE *verb*.

feedback /ˈfiːdbak/ *noun*. E20.
[ORIGIN from FEED *verb*[1] + BACK *adverb*.]
1 The return of a fraction of the output signal from one stage of an electric circuit, amplifier, etc., to the input of the same or a preceding stage; the signal so returned. E20.
2 *BIOLOGY, PSYCHOLOGY*, etc. Modification or control of a process or system by its results or effects, esp. by the difference between a desired and actual result. M20.
3 Information about the result of an experiment, performance, etc.; response. M20.
– PHRASES: **negative feedback** feedback which tends to cause a decrease in the output signal, or, more widely, which tends to attenuate the effect of which it is part. **positive feedback** feedback which tends to cause an increase in the output signal, or which tends to amplify the effect of which it is part.

feeder /ˈfiːdə/ *noun*. LME.
[ORIGIN from FEED *verb*[1] + -ER[1].]
1 A person who supports, sustains, or supplies food for another, an animal, etc. LME. ▸†**b** The host of a parasite; *derog.* a person who keeps another as a sycophant or spy. L16–E19.
2 A person who fattens up livestock for market. LME. ▸**b** A person who attends to the feeding of a flock, a shepherd, (*lit. & fig.*). LME. ▸**c** A person who supervises the feeding or training of horses, hounds, fighting cocks, etc. L18.
3 A consumer of food (esp. in a specified manner). M16. ▸†**b** A person dependent on another for sustenance; a servant. Only in E17. ▸**c** An animal (being) fattened for market. Now chiefly *US*. L18.
4 A person who or thing which supplies material to a machine in regulated quantities. M17.
5 *MINING*. A smaller lode falling into the main lode or vein. E18. ▸**b** An underground spring; an escape of water or gas. E18.
6 A natural or artificial water course which flows into another body of water; a tributary (*lit. & fig.*). L18. ▸**b** A branch road, railway line, air service, etc., linking outlying districts with the main lines of communication. M19.

b *attrib.*: *Modern Railways* Feeder services to smaller terminals.

7 A device used in feeding; a baby's bottle or bib; a receptacle from which animals etc. may feed. E19.

A. TYLER Morgan invented an elaborate sort of . . device to tip squirrels off the bird feeder.

8 The bowler in certain ball games. Also, a game resembling rounders. E19.
9 A reservoir of liquid metal to be supplied to a casting; a channel or means of supply of liquid metal. M19.
10 *ELECTRICAL ENGINEERING*. A heavy untapped main for carrying electrical energy to a distribution point or system. L19. ▸**b** An electrical connection between an aerial and a transmitter or receiver of electromagnetic waves. E20.
11 *THEATRICAL*. = FEED *noun* 7. L19.

feeding /ˈfiːdɪŋ/ *noun*. OE.
[ORIGIN from FEED *verb*[1] + -ING[1].]
1 The action of FEED *verb*[1]; an instance of this. OE.
2 Food, diet. Now *rare*. LME.
3 Grazing land, pasturage. *obsolete* exc. *dial.* LME.
– COMB.: **feeding bottle** a bottle fitted with a teat from which a baby can suck milk; **feeding cup** a small vessel with a spout for feeding liquid to an invalid lying down; **feeding frenzy** (*a*) an aggressive and competitive group attack on prey by sharks or other voracious predators; (*b*) *fig.* an episode of frantic competition or rivalry for something, esp. among journalists covering a story, personality, etc.; **feeding time** the time at which captive animals are fed.

fee farm /ˈfiːfaːm/ *noun phr.* LME.
[ORIGIN Anglo-Norman *fee-ferme*, Old French *feuferme, fiofferme*: see FEE *noun*[2], FARM *noun*. Cf. FEU FARM.]
LAW. **1** Tenure by which land is held in fee simple subject to a perpetual fixed rent, without other services; the estate or the land so held. LME.

2 More fully ***fee farm rent***. The rent paid for an estate so held. LME.

■ **fee farmer** *noun* a person who holds a fee farm E16.

fee-faw-fum /ˌfiːˌfɔːˈfʌm/ *noun*. Now *rare*. L17.
[ORIGIN The first line of doggerel spoken by the giant in the fairy tale 'Jack the Giant Killer' ('Jack and the Beanstalk') on seeing Jack.]
1 A bloodthirsty person. L17.
2 Nonsense, such as might terrify children. E19.

feel /fiːl/ *noun*. ME.
[ORIGIN from the verb.]
†**1** Perception, consciousness, understanding, knowledge. *Scot. & N. English*. ME–E18.
2 Sensory awareness; the sense of touch. Now only in ***to the feel***. ME.
3 The action or an act of feeling or testing by touch. LME. ▸**b** An instance of fondling someone without their permission. *colloq.* M20.

> **b** *Cosmopolitan* Kerry, 26, took control when a stranger tried to cop a feel in a packed train.

4 The feeling or sensation given by an object or material when touched. LME.

> J. MARQUAND The feel of cold water on the body.

5 The impression characteristically produced by something. M18.

> A. AIRD The cosy feel of a moorland pub.

– PHRASES: **have a feel for** have a natural talent for or understanding of (a subject etc.). ***raw feel***: see RAW *adjective*.

feel *adjective* var. of FIEL.

feel /fiːl/ *verb*. Pa. t. & pple **felt** /fɛlt/.
[ORIGIN Old English *fēlan* = Old Frisian *fēla*, Old Saxon *gifōlian* (Dutch *voelen*), Old High German *fuolen* (German *fühlen*), from West Germanic.]
▸ **I 1** *verb trans.* Touch, esp. with the hand or finger(s); examine or explore by touching. OE. ▸**b** *verb intrans.* Use the hand, finger, or other part of the body to touch. L16. ▸**c** *verb trans.* Fondle (a person) without their consent, for one's own sexual stimulation. Freq. foll. by *up*. *colloq.* M20.

> W. TREVOR He felt the leaves of the rubber plant, taking them in turn between thumb and forefinger. **b** M. LEITCH He began to feel with his hands along the edges of the door. **c** J. KEROUAC We used to get next to pretty young daughters and feel them up in the kitchen.

2 *verb trans.* Test, discover, or ascertain by handling or touching; try to ascertain by touch *whether*, *if*, *how*. ME. ▸**b** *fig.* Test or discover by cautious trial; sound out a person, the strength of an enemy, etc. Also foll. by *out*. ME.

> OED The surgeon felt if any bones were broken. **b** D. ACHESON Relations with him became easier . . as we felt one another out.

3 *verb intrans.* Grope about; search *in*, *for*, etc., by touch. LME. ▸**b** *verb trans.* Ascertain the presence or nature of anything by or as by touch. Freq. foll. by *out*. M19.

> E. J. HOWARD He . . felt hopefully in his pockets for pennies, but there were none. **b** H. R. MILL The form of the floor of the ocean has thus been gradually felt out point by point.

▸ **II 4** *verb trans.* Perceive through physical sensation, esp. the sense of touch. OE. ▸**b** Perceive by taste or smell. *obsolete* exc. *dial.* ME. ▸**c** *verb intrans.* Have or be capable of having sensations of touch. ME.

> J. STEINBECK She could feel his warm breath against her skin. **b** E. B. RAMSAY I feel a smell of tea.

†**5** *verb trans.* Perceive mentally, become aware of. OE–E17.
6 *verb trans.* Be conscious of (a sensation, emotion, etc.); experience, undergo. Foll. by simple obj., obj. with inf. or (esp. adjective) compl., *that*. ME. ▸**b** *verb trans.* Be physically affected or injured by; be emotionally affected by; behave as if conscious of. LME. ▸**c** *verb intrans.* with compl. Be conscious of being, regard oneself as. E19. ▸**d** *verb intrans.* Be inclined *to do*. *US*. M19.

> C. MARLOWE I feel Thy words to comfort my distressed soul! POPE You . . Shall feel your ruling passion strong in death. T. HARDY Not having exerted myself . . I felt no sleepiness whatever. A. CARNEGIE I had never . . felt the power and majesty of music to such a high degree. **b** HARPER LEE Our mother died when I was two, so I never felt her absence. S. BELLOW On my way home, feeling the vodka I've drunk. **c** J. HERRIOT I felt rather a lout in my working clothes among the elegant gathering.

7 *verb intrans.* with compl. Have a particular notion; be in a particular frame of mind; have a sensation or experience *as if*, *as though*. ME.

> G. B. SHAW I feel as if I were sitting on a volcano. C. P. SNOW Sometimes I felt anxious about what was being said in there.

8 *verb trans.* †**a** Think, hold as an opinion. LME–M16. ▸**b** Have an impression or conviction of; believe *that*; consider *to be*. E17.

> **b** H. JAMES I was certain you would come—I have felt it all day. D. H. LAWRENCE I feel you don't love him, dear. I'm almost sure you don't.

9 *verb intrans.* with compl. Be consciously perceived (esp. through the sense of touch) as; produce the sensation of being, give the impression of being; seem *as if*, *as though*. L16.

> A. CALDCLEUGH The air felt chilly. M. ROBERTS It feels as though they've only been together for a little while.

10 *verb intrans.* Have one's sensibilities aroused; experience emotion; have sympathy *with*, have compassion *for*. E17.

> LD MACAULAY A moderate party . . had always felt very kindly towards the Protestant Dissenters. Y. WINTERS The insane, who sometimes perceive and feel with great intensity.

– PHRASES & COMB.: ***feel a person's collar***: see COLLAR *noun*. ***feel good***: see GOOD *adjective*. **feel-good** (*colloq.*, orig. *US*) *adjective & noun* (causing) a feeling of happiness and well-being; ***feel in one's bones***: see BONE *noun*. **feel like** (*a*) feel as though, feel similar to; (*b*) desire (a thing), have an inclination towards *doing*. **feel no pain** *slang* be insensibly drunk. **feel oneself** be fit, confident, etc. **feel oneself into** enter imaginatively into, bring oneself to identify or empathize with. **feel one's feet** = ***find one's feet*** s.v. FIND *verb*. **feel one's legs** be conscious of one's powers, be at one's ease. ***feel one's oats***: see OAT *noun*. **feel one's way** find one's way by groping; proceed cautiously. **feel one's wings** = ***feel one's legs*** above. ***feel small***: see SMALL *adjective*. **feel the draught**, **feel the pinch** *colloq.* feel the adverse effects of changed (esp. financial) conditions. **feel the pulse of** feel an artery to ascertain the heartbeat rate (and so the state of health) of; *fig.* ascertain the intentions or sentiments of. ***feel the weight of***: see WEIGHT *noun*. **feel up to** feel capable of or ready to face. ***feel wretched***: see WRETCHED *adjective* 1a. **make one's presence felt** have an effect on others, influence proceedings.

■ **feelable** *adjective* that can or may be felt LME.

feeler /ˈfiːlə/ *noun*. LME.
[ORIGIN from FEEL *verb* + -ER[1].]
1 A person who feels an emotion; a person who understands or experiences something. LME.

> P. THOMPSON We are to be the main feelers of the consequences. J. R. LOWELL He was not a strong thinker, but a sensitive feeler.

2 A person who perceives by the senses, esp. by touch. E16.

> N. FAIRFAX All hearers deaf, all feelers numb.

3 ZOOLOGY. An organ in certain animals for testing things or searching for food by touch, as an antenna or a palpus. M17.

> R. F. CHAPMAN Elongation, such as occurs in the cockroach, is possibly associated with the use of antennae as feelers.

4 A tentative hint or proposal put out to test opinion. M19.

> *Sun (Baltimore)* The Germans also were making peace feelers both to Britain and the United States and to Russia with the object of splitting the Allies.

5 More fully ***feeler gauge***. A thin (usu. metal) strip of a known thickness, used to measure narrow gaps or clearances; a device with such strips. M20.

feeling /ˈfiːlɪŋ/ *noun*. ME.
[ORIGIN from FEEL *verb* + -ING[1].]
1 The action of FEEL *verb*. ME.
2 Physical sensibility other than sight, hearing, taste, or smell; the sense of touch. ME. ▸**b** (A) physical sensation; a perception due to this. ME.

> ADDISON The Sense of Feeling can indeed give us a Notion of . . Shape. **b** R. G. COLLINGWOOD A hundred people . . may all feel cold, but each person's feeling is private to himself.

3 The condition of being emotionally affected or committed; an emotion (*of* fear, hope, etc.). ME. ▸**b** In *pl.* Emotions, susceptibilities, sympathies. L18.
4 Consciousness; an emotional appreciation or sense (*of* a condition etc.). LME.

> J. T. MICKLETHWAITE The feeling of perfect equality inside the church.

5 A belief not based solely on reason; an attitude, a sentiment. LME.

> B. JOWETT They have the feelings of old men about youth.

6 Capacity or readiness to feel (esp. sympathy or empathy); sensibility. LME.

> D. HUME The delicacy of his feeling makes him sensibly touched.

†**7** Knowledge of something through experience of its effects. E16–M17.
8 The quality felt to belong to a thing; the general emotional effect produced (esp. by a work of art) on a spectator or hearer. L16.

> R. WARNER There was a feeling of space about the room.

– PHRASES: **bad feeling** animosity. ***better feelings***: see BETTER *adjective* etc. **good feeling** benevolence, amity, the avoidance of unkindness. **hurt the feelings of** upset, offend. **ill feeling** bad feeling, malice, animosity. ***MIXED feelings***.

■ **feelingless** *adjective* E19. **feelingful** *adjective* E20.

feeling /ˈfiːlɪŋ/ *adjective*. LME.
[ORIGIN from FEEL *verb* + -ING[2].]
1 Capable of sensation; sentient. LME.
2 Fully realized; vivid, acute, heartfelt. M16.
3 Of language etc.: expressing or indicating emotion. L16.
4 Affected by emotion; sensitive, sympathetic, compassionate. E17.

feelingly /ˈfiːlɪŋli/ *adverb*. LME.
[ORIGIN from FEELING *adjective* + -LY[2].]
†**1** With accurate perception, sensibly; appropriately. LME–M17.
2 So as to be felt or leave an impression behind. LME.
3 By or from personal feeling or knowledge; in a heartfelt manner; with emotion. M16.
†**4** Sensitively. L18–E19.

feelthy /ˈfiːlθi/ *adjective*. *slang*. M20.
[ORIGIN Joc. imitation of foreign pronunc. of FILTHY *adjective*.]
Obscene.

feely /ˈfiːli/ *noun*. M20.
[ORIGIN from FEEL *verb* + -Y[1]. Cf. MOVIE.]
A (hypothetical) film augmented by tactual effects. Freq. in ***the feelies***.

feer /fɪə/ *verb trans.* Also **pheer**, **veer**. LME.
[ORIGIN Perh. from Old English *fyrian* make a furrow, from *furh* FURROW *noun*.]
Mark off (land) for ploughing.

■ **feering** *noun* (*a*) the action of the verb; (*b*) = LAND *noun*[1] 6a: M18.

feerie *adjective* var. of FEIRIE.

fee simple /fiː ˈsɪmp(ə)l/ *noun phr.* Pl. **fees simple**. LME.
[ORIGIN Anglo-Norman: see FEE *noun*[2], SIMPLE *adjective*.]
LAW. Tenure of a heritable estate in land etc. for ever and without restriction to any particular class of heirs; an estate so held.

fees tail *noun* pl. of FEE TAIL.

feet *noun* pl. of FOOT *noun*.

fee tail /fiː ˈteɪl/ *noun phr.* Pl. **fees tail**. LME.
[ORIGIN Anglo-Norman *fee taile* = Anglo-Latin *feudum talliatum*: see FEE *noun*[2], TAIL *adjective*.]
LAW. (Tenure of) a heritable estate entailed or restricted to some particular class of heirs of the person to whom it is granted.

feetless /ˈfiːtlɪs/ *adjective*. Now *rare*. E17.
[ORIGIN from FEET + -LESS.]
Without feet, footless.

feeze /fiːz/ *noun*. LME.
[ORIGIN from FEEZE *verb*. See also VEASE.]
1 A rush; a violent impact. Also, a rub. Now *dial. & US*. LME.
2 A state of alarm. *US dial.* M19.

feeze /fiːz/ *verb trans.* *obsolete* exc. *dial.* Also †**pheeze**.
[ORIGIN Old English *fēsian*, of unknown origin. Cf. FAZE *verb*[1].]
†**1** Drive; drive off or away; put to flight. OE–L17.
2 Frighten. LME.
3 a Do for (a person). Esp. in threat ***I'll feeze you***. L16. ▸**b** Beat, flog. E17.

fegary /fɪˈgɛːri/ *noun*. *dial. & colloq.* Now *rare*. E17.
[ORIGIN Alt. of VAGARY.]
Usu. in *pl.* **1** A vagary, a prank; a whim, an eccentricity. E17.
2 A gewgaw, a trifle; finery in dress. E18.

fegs /fɛgz/ *noun & interjection*. *obsolete* exc. *Scot. & dial.* Also **fecks**. L16.
[ORIGIN Perh. from FAY *noun*[1] or FAITH + -KIN(S).]
(A meaningless noun) expr. solemn conviction or astonishment.
i' fegs = ***i' faith*** s.v. FAITH *noun*.

fehi *noun* var. of FEI.

Fehling /ˈfeɪlɪŋ/ *noun*. L19.
[ORIGIN Hermann von *Fehling* (1812–85), German chemist.]
Fehling reaction, ***Fehling test***, ***Fehling's reaction***, ***Fehling's test***, the reaction of Fehling's solution with aldehydes, used as an analytical test esp. for aldose sugars. ***Fehling solution***, ***Fehling's solution***, an alkaline solution of copper(II) sulphate and a tartrate.

Fehm *noun*, **Fehmgericht** *noun*, vars. of VEHME, VEHMGERICHT.

fei /ˈfeɪi/ *noun*. Also **fehi**, **fe'i**. E19.
[ORIGIN Tahitian.]
(The fruit of) a type of banana widely grown in Polynesia and Melanesia, which is characterized by violet sap and erect inflorescences.

feign /feɪn/ *verb*. ME.
[ORIGIN Old French & mod. French *feign-* pres. stem of *feindre* from Latin *fingere* form, conceive, contrive.]
1 *verb trans.* Fashion materially. *rare*. ME.
2 *verb trans.* Invent (a story, excuse, etc.); forge (a document); counterfeit. *arch.* ME.
3 *verb trans.* Allege, maintain fictitiously. ME.
†**4 a** *verb refl. & intrans.* Disguise one's sentiments; dissemble. ME–M16. ▸**b** *verb trans.* Disguise, conceal. ME–L16.
†**5** *verb intrans. & refl.* Avoid duty by false pretences, shirk; be reluctant *to do*. ME–M16.
6 *verb trans.* Make a show of, simulate, pretend to. ME. ▸**b** *verb intrans.* Practise simulation. E17.

> P. PEARCE Tom could not feign interest in what seemed so far away in time. A. SCHLEE Charlotte . . feigned a weakness she did not entirely feel.

F

7 *verb refl.* & (now usu.) *intrans.* with compl. Pretend to be; pretend *to be*, *to do*. ME.

DEFOE Satan made David feign himself mad. Q. CRISP The only method . . by which one can survive one's emotions is to feign not to have them.

8 *verb trans.* Represent in fiction. Now *rare*. LME. ▸†**b** *verb intrans.* Make fictitious statements. LME–M17.

9 *verb trans.* Imagine (what is unreal). Now *rare*. LME. ▸†**b** Believe erroneously and arbitrarily. M16–E18. ▸**c** Assume fictitiously for purposes of calculation. *arch.* L17.

†**10** *verb trans.* Adulterate. *rare*. LME–E17.

†**11** *verb trans.* & *intrans.* Pretend to deal (a blow etc.). LME–M17.

†**12** *verb intrans.* & *trans.* MUSIC. Sing softly, hum; sing with due regard to the accidentals not indicated by old notation. LME–E17.

■ **feignedly** /ˈfeɪnɪdli/ *adverb* in a feigned manner. LME. **feignedness** /ˈfeɪnɪdnɪs/ *noun* the quality of being feigned LME. **feigner** *noun* LME. **feigning** *noun* (*a*) the action of the verb; †(*b*) an assumption, a fiction: LME. **feigningly** *adverb* in a feigning manner LME.

F

feijão /feɪˈ(d)ʒãuː/ *noun*. M19.
[ORIGIN Portuguese from Latin *phaseolus* bean.]
Any of various edible beans, *esp.* a form of haricot bean, *Phaseolus vulgaris*, used as a staple item of diet in Brazil. Cf. FEIJOADA.

feijoa /feɪˈ(d)ʒəʊə; fɛ-, fiː-, -ˈjəʊə/ *noun*. L19.
[ORIGIN mod. Latin (see below), from J. da Silva *Feijó* (1760–1824), Brazilian naturalist.]
An evergreen shrub or small tree of the tropical S. American genus *Feijoa*, of the myrtle family; the edible green fruit of this, which resembles the guava.

feijoada /feɪˈ(d)ʒwaðə, -də/ *noun*. M20.
[ORIGIN Portuguese, from FEIJÃO.]
A Brazilian stew made with black beans and pork, sausage, etc., served with rice.

Feinne /ˈfeɪnjə/ *noun pl.* Also **Fein**. L18.
[ORIGIN Irish *féinne* genit. sing. (taken as pl.) of FIAN.]
The Fenian warriors of Irish history and legend.

feint /feɪnt/ *noun*. L17.
[ORIGIN Old French & mod. French *feinte* use as noun of fem. of pa. pple of *feindre* FEIGN.]
1 a FENCING & BOXING etc. A blow, cut, or thrust intended to deceive and distract the opponent. L17. ▸**b** MILITARY. A movement made in order to deceive an enemy. L17.
2 An assumed appearance; a pretence. L17.

feint *adjective* see FAINT *adjective*.

feint /feɪnt/ *verb intrans*. ME.
[ORIGIN Sense 1 from French *feint* (see FAINT *adjective*); sense 2 from FEINT *noun*.]
†**1** Deceive. ME–L17.
2 Make a sham attack. Foll. by *at*, *on*, *upon*. M19.

feints *noun pl.* var. of FAINTS.

feirie /ˈfɪəri/ *adjective*. *Scot.* Also **feerie**. LME.
[ORIGIN Perh. rel. to FERE *adjective*.]
Fit to travel; nimble, vigorous.
■ **feirily** *adverb* M16.

feis /fɛʃ, feɪʃ/ *noun*. In sense 1 also **fes(s)**. Pl. **feiseanna** /-ʃənə/. L18.
[ORIGIN Irish = wedding feast, feast, festival.]
1 An assembly of kings, chiefs, etc., formerly believed to be a kind of early Celtic parliament. L18.
2 An Irish or Scottish festival of the arts, resembling the Welsh Eisteddfod. L19.

feist *noun* see FIST *noun*².

feisty /ˈfʌɪsti/ *adjective*. *colloq.* (orig. *N. Amer.*). L19.
[ORIGIN from FEIST + -Y¹.]
Aggressive, excitable, touchy; plucky, spirited.

SCOULAR ANDERSON [King] David . . was defeated by the English led by the feisty old Archbishop of York. *Sunday Times* Maria is a feisty, ferociously protective mother.

■ **feistily** *adverb* L20. **feistiness** *noun* L20.

felafel *noun* var. of FALAFEL.

Felapton /fəˈlaptɒn/ *noun*. M18.
[ORIGIN A mnemonic of scholastic philosophers first used in medieval Latin, E indicating a universal negative proposition, A a universal affirmative proposition, and O a particular negative proposition.]
LOGIC. The fourth mood in the third syllogistic figure, in which the major premiss is a universal negative, the minor premiss a universal affirmative, and the conclusion a particular negative.

Feldenkrais /ˈfɛld(ə)nkrʌɪs/ *noun*. M20.
[ORIGIN Moshe *Feldenkrais* (1904–84), Russian physicist and mechanical engineer.]
Feldenkrais method, a system designed to promote bodily and mental efficiency and well-being by conscious analysis of neuromuscular activity, via exercises which improve flexibility and coordination and increase ease and range of motion.

feldgrau /ˈfɛltgraʊ/ *noun* & *adjective*. M20.
[ORIGIN German = field grey.]
(Of) a dark grey, = ***field grey*** s.v. FIELD *noun*.

feldsher /ˈfɛldʃə/ *noun*. Also **-scher**. L19.
[ORIGIN Russian *fel'dsher* from German *Feldscher* field surgeon.]
In Russia and the former USSR: a person with practical training in medicine and surgery, but without professional medical qualifications; a physician's or surgeon's assistant; a local medical auxiliary.

feldspar /ˈfɛl(d)spɑː/ *noun*. Also **felspar** /ˈfɛlspɑː/. M18.
[ORIGIN Alt. of German *Feldspat(h)*, from *Feld* FIELD *noun* + *Spat(h)* SPATH with substitution of synonym. SPAR *noun*³; *fels-* by false etym. from German *Fels* rock.]
MINERALOGY. Any of a large class of monoclinic or triclinic aluminosilicate minerals which are mostly colourless or pink and include many common rock-forming minerals.
aventurine feldspar: see AVENTURINE 2.

feldspathic /fɛl(d)ˈspaθɪk/ *adjective*. Also **felspathic** /fɛlˈspaθɪk/. M19.
[ORIGIN formed as FELDSPAR + -IC.]
MINERALOGY. Of the nature of feldspar; containing (much) feldspar.

feldspathoid /ˈfɛl(d)spəθɔɪd/ *noun*. Also **felspath-** /ˈfɛlspəθ-/. L19.
[ORIGIN formed as FELDSPAR + -OID.]
MINERALOGY. Any of a group of minerals chemically similar to the feldspars, but containing less silica.
■ **feldspaˈthoidal** *adjective* M20.

Félibre /felibr/ *noun*. Pl. pronounced same. L19.
[ORIGIN French from Provençal *felibre* any one of the teachers in the temple whom the child Jesus questioned, from late Latin *fellibris* var. of *fellebris* nursling from Latin *fellare* to suck.]
A member of a society founded in 1854 by Provençal writers to maintain and purify Provençal as a literary language and to promote the artistic interests of the South of France.

Félibrism /ˈfeɪlɪbrɪz(ə)m/ *noun*. E20.
[ORIGIN from FÉLIBRE + -ISM.]
(The principles of) the movement instituted by the Félibres.

felicide /ˈfiːlɪsʌɪd/ *noun*. M19.
[ORIGIN from Latin *feles* cat + -CIDE.]
The killing of a cat or cats.

felicific /fiːlɪˈsɪfɪk/ *adjective*. M19.
[ORIGIN Latin *felicificus*, from *felix* happy: see -FIC.]
Making or tending to make happy.

felicitate /fɪˈlɪsɪteɪt/ *verb*. E17.
[ORIGIN Late Latin *felicitat-* pa. ppl stem of *felicitare* make happy, from *felix* happy: see -ATE³.]
1 a *verb intrans.* Cause happiness. *rare*. E17. ▸**b** *verb trans.* Make happy. Now *rare*. M17.
2 *verb trans.* Regard as or pronounce to be happy or fortunate. Now *spec.* congratulate (a person, *on*). M17.

felicitation /fɪˌlɪsɪˈteɪʃ(ə)n/ *noun*. E18.
[ORIGIN from FELICITATE: see -ATION.]
1 Congratulation. E18.
2 A congratulatory speech or message, a congratulation. Usu. in *pl.* L18.

felicitous /fɪˈlɪsɪtəs/ *adjective*. M18.
[ORIGIN from FELICITY + -OUS.]
1 Happy; showing or marked by great happiness. Formerly also, fortunate, prosperous, successful. (Earlier in FELICITOUSLY 1.) M18.

J. RUSKIN In the refinement of their highly educated . . benevolent and felicitous lives.

2 a Of an action, manner, etc.: very apt, well suited to the occasion. L18. ▸**b** Of a person: happy or pleasantly apt in expression, manner, or style. E19.

a O. WILDE Your poems are most charming, and your choice of epithets exquisite and felicitous.

3 Pleasing, delightful. L19.

J. ROSENBERG There is something particularly felicitous about this painting, which has aroused the highest enthusiasm.

felicitously /fɪˈlɪsɪtəsli/ *adverb*. M16.
[ORIGIN from FELICITOUS + -LY².]
1 Happily, prosperously, successfully. *rare*. M16.
2 Aptly; with striking appropriateness or grace. E19.

felicity /fɪˈlɪsɪti/ *noun*. LME.
[ORIGIN Old French & mod. French *félicité* from Latin *felicitas*, from *felix*, *felic-* happy: see -ITY.]
1 The state or an instance of being happy; happiness, bliss. LME.
2 A cause or source of happiness. LME.
3 Prosperity, good fortune, success. Now *rare*. LME. ▸†**b** In *pl.* Prosperous circumstances; successful enterprises; successes. LME–M18. ▸**c** A stroke of fortune; singular fortunateness (of an occurrence); a fortunate trait. M18.
4 An appropriateness in invention or expression. E17. ▸**b** A happy inspiration; a well-chosen expression. M17.

felid /ˈfiːlɪd/ *noun*. L19.
[ORIGIN mod. Latin *Felidae* (see below), from Latin *feles* cat: see -ID³.]
ZOOLOGY. An animal of the family Felidae, which includes the cats, lion, tiger, leopard, etc.

feline /ˈfiːlʌɪn/ *adjective* & *noun*. L17.
[ORIGIN Latin *felinus*, from *feles* cat: see -INE¹.]
▸ **A** *adjective*. Of or pertaining to cats; characteristic of a cat; resembling a cat in any respect. L17.

LYTTON The feline care with which he stepped aside from any patches of mire.

▸ **B** *noun*. A cat (chiefly *joc.*); *gen.* any felid. M19.
■ **felinely** *adverb* M19. **felinity** /fɪˈlɪnɪti/ *noun* M19.

felix culpa /ˌfiːlɪks ˈkʌlpə, ˌfeɪlɪks, ˈkʊlpɑː/ *noun phr.* M20.
[ORIGIN Latin, lit. 'happy fault', from the Exultet in the liturgy for Holy Saturday.]
THEOLOGY. The Fall of Man or the sin of Adam as resulting in the blessedness of the Redemption; *transf.* an apparent error or tragedy with happy consequences.

fell /fɛl/ *noun*¹.
[ORIGIN Old English *fel(l)* = Old Frisian, Old Saxon *fel* (Dutch *vel*), Old High German *fel* (German *Fell*), Old Norse *ber-fjall* bear-skin, Gothic *þruts-fill* 'swelling skin', from Germanic from Indo-European base repr. also by Latin *pellis*, Greek *pella* skin.]
1 The skin or hide of an animal, usu. with the hair, wool, etc. OE. ▸**b** Human skin. OE.

R. GRAVES A lion of tawny fell. **b** P. HOLLAND That kind of dropsy wherein water runneth between the fell and the flesh.

flesh and fell: see FLESH *noun*.
2 A covering of hair, wool, etc., esp. when thick or matted; a fleece. L16.

J. R. LOWELL The surly fell of Ocean's bristled neck.

– COMB.: **fellmonger** a person who prepares skins for leather-making; *arch.* a dealer in hides and skins; **fell-wool** wool pulled from sheepskins as opp. to that shorn from the living animal.

fell /fɛl/ *noun*². Now chiefly *Scot.* & *N. English*. ME.
[ORIGIN Old Norse *fjall* and *fell* hill, mountain, prob. rel. to Old Saxon *felis*, Old High German *felis*, *felisa* (German *Fels*) rock.]
1 A hill, a mountain. *obsolete* exc. in proper names as ***Bowfell***, ***Scafell***, etc. ME.
2 A stretch of high moorland, a ridge, a down. ME.
– COMB.: **fell-field** ECOLOGY (an area of) a habitat characteristic of tundra, with scattered low-lying vegetation and stony soil; **fell hound** (an animal of) a variety of foxhound orig. bred for hunting in hill country; **fellside** the sloping side of a fell.

†**fell** *noun*³. *rare* (Spenser). Only in L16.
[ORIGIN Latin *fel* (*fell-*) gall.]
Gall; rancour.

fell /fɛl/ *noun*⁴. E17.
[ORIGIN from FELL *verb*¹. Cf. FALL *noun*².]
1 A fall of lambs (see FALL *noun*² 1f). E17.
2 A cutting down of timber; the amount of timber cut down in one season. M17.
3 The sowing down of the edge of a seam to form a smooth surface. L19.

fell /fɛl/ *adjective* & *adverb*. ME.
[ORIGIN Old French *fel* from Proto-Romance, whence also (from oblique case) FELON *noun*¹ & *adjective*.]
▸ **A** *adjective*. **1** Fierce, cruel, ruthless; terrible, destructive. Now *poet.* & *rhet.* ME.

F. O'BRIEN Fell adders hiss and poisonous serpents roll.

2 Keen, piercing; intensely painful or destructive. Now *dial.*, *poet.*, & *rhet.* ME.

G. TURBERVILLE Small arrowis, cruel heads, that fel and forked be.

†**3** Hot, angry, enraged. ME–L16.
4 Full of spirit, doughty. *obsolete* exc. *dial.* ME. ▸**b** Eager *for*, *on*, †*to*. *obsolete* exc. *dial.* M17.
5 Shrewd, clever, cunning. *obsolete* exc. *Scot.* & *dial.* ME.
6 Exceedingly great, mighty. *obsolete* exc. *Scot.* E16.
– PHRASES: ***at one fell swoop***, ***in one fell swoop***: see SWOOP *noun* 2b.
▸ **B** *adverb*. In a fell manner; cruelly, fiercely; eagerly; greatly. ME.

L. G. GIBBON Mistress Melon was a fell good worker.

■ **fellness** *noun* (*obsolete* exc. *dial.* or *poet.*) the quality of being fell; cruelty; fierceness; keenness: LME.

fell /fɛl/ *verb*¹ *trans.*
[ORIGIN Old English *fellan*, *fyllan* = Old Frisian *falla*, *fella*, Old Saxon *fellian* (Dutch *vellen*), Old High German *fellen* (German *fällen*), Old Norse *fella* from Germanic base, causative of FALL *verb*.]
1 Cause to fall; knock or strike down (a person or animal, formerly a building etc.); cut down (a tree). OE. ▸**b** Lay low, kill. OE.

R. GRAVES The Tiger then felled him with a . . blow on the side of his head. L. K. JOHNSON Let no more trees be felled or else the forest will be bare. **b** J. HELLER Gold was positive he would be . . felled by a heart attack.

†**2** Bring or let down, lower. ME–E17.
3 Stitch down (the edge of a seam) so that it lies flat over the other edge and leaves a smooth surface. M18.
■ **fellable** *adjective* (of a tree etc.) that may be felled L16.

fell *verb*² *pa. t.* of FALL *verb*.

fella /ˈfɛlə/ *noun*. Also **fellah**. M19.
[ORIGIN Repr. an affected or non-standard pronunc. of FELLOW *noun*. Cf. FELLER *noun*².]
= FELLOW *noun* 8.

fellah /ˈfɛlə/ *noun*¹. Pl. **-aheen**, **-ahin**, /-əhiːn/, **-ahs**. M18.
[ORIGIN Arabic *fallāḥ*, colloq. pl. *fallāḥīn*, tiller of the soil, from *falaḥa* split, till the soil.]
A peasant in an Arabic-speaking country, esp. in Egypt.

fellah *noun*² var. of FELLA.

fellaheen, **fellahin** *nouns* pls. of FELLAH *noun*¹.

fellate /fɛˈleɪt/ *verb trans. & intrans.* L19.
[ORIGIN Latin *fellat-* pa. ppl stem of *fellare* suck: see -ATE³.]
Perform fellatio (on).
■ **fellator** *noun* a person who performs fellatio L19. **fellatrix** *noun* a female who performs fellatio L19.

fellatio /fɛˈleɪʃɪəʊ, -ˈlɑːt-/ *noun*. L19.
[ORIGIN mod. Latin, from Latin *fellatus* pa. pple, formed as FELLATE.]
Sucking or licking of a sexual partner's penis.

fellation /fɛˈleɪʃ(ə)n/ *noun*. L19.
[ORIGIN from (the same root as) FELLATIO: see -ION.]
= FELLATIO.

feller /ˈfɛlə/ *noun*¹. LME.
[ORIGIN from FELL *verb*¹ + -ER¹.]
1 A person who fells a person, animal, or (esp.) timber. LME.
2 An attachment on a sewing machine for felling seams etc.; a person who fells seams etc. L19.

feller /ˈfɛlə/ *noun*². E19.
[ORIGIN Repr. an affected or non-standard pronunc. of FELLOW *noun*. Cf. FELLA.]
= FELLOW *noun* 8.
feller-me-lad, **feller-my-lad**, **young feller-me-lad**, **young feller-my-lad** a frivolous or irresponsible young man; esp. used as a disapproving form of address.

felloe /ˈfɛləʊ/ *noun*. Also **felly** /ˈfɛli/.
[ORIGIN Old English *felg*, pl. *felga*, corresp. to Middle Low German, Middle Dutch *velge* (Dutch *velg*), Old High German *felga* (German *Felge*), of unknown origin.]
The outer rim or a part of the rim of a wheel, supported by the spokes; each of the curved pieces which join together to form a wheel rim.

fellow /ˈfɛləʊ/ *noun & adjective*. LOE.
[ORIGIN Old Norse *félagi*, from *fé* (= Old English *feoh* FEE *noun*¹) + Germanic base of LAY *verb*¹.]
▸ **A** *noun*. **1** A person who shares with another in anything; a partner, a colleague, an ally. Now *rare*. LOE. ▸†**b** In a bad sense: an accomplice. LME–M19. ▸†**c** A partaker or sharer *of*. LME–M17.
2 A companion, an associate, a comrade. Now usu. in *pl.* ME. ▸†**b** *spec.* A female companion. ME–E17.
H. COGAN Brave men, their fellows in arms.
3 Either of a pair; a partner, a counterpart, a match. ME.
JOYCE One boot stood upright.. the fellow of it lay upon its side.
4 An equal in rank, ability, or kind. ME. ▸**b** A contemporary. Usu. in *pl.* L19.
E. FAIRFAX His fellowes late shall be his subjects now. BYRON Danger levels man and brute, And all are fellows in their need.
5 A member of a company or party with common interests. ME.
6 a Any of the incorporated senior members of a college or collegiate foundation. LME. ▸**b** A member of the governing body in certain universities. M19. ▸**c** An elected graduate holding a stipendiary position in a college for a period of research. L19.
7 A member, or sometimes a privileged member, of certain learned societies. LME.
Fellow of the British Academy, *Fellow of the Royal Society*, etc.
8 A man, a boy. *colloq.* LME.
J. CARLYLE He looked dreadfully weak still, poor fellow! G. STEIN Rose had lately married Sam Johnson a decent honest kindly fellow. P. H. GIBBS All very innocent, he thought... A fellow must amuse himself now and then.
9 †**a** (Used as form of address to) a servant or other person of low station. LME–L16. ▸**b** A despised person. LME. ▸†**c** A black person. *US*. M18–M19.
– PHRASES ETC.: **fellow-me-lad**, **fellow-my-lad** = *feller-me-lad* s.v. FELLER *noun*² (cf. *young fellow-me-lad* below). **good fellow** an agreeable or convivial companion. *hail-fellow(-well-met)*: see HAIL *interjection*. **jolly fellow** = *good fellow* above. **my dear fellow**, **my good fellow**: used as forms of address, now sometimes implying censure. *stout fellow*: see STOUT *adjective*. *teaching fellow*: see TEACHING *ppl adjective*. **young fellow-me-lad**, **young fellow-my-lad** = *feller-me-lad* s.v. FELLER *noun*² (cf. *fellow-me-lad* above).
▸ **B** *attrib.* or as *adjective*. **1** (Sometimes hyphenated.) Belonging to the same class; associated in joint action; in the same relation to the same object. M16.
fellow Christian, *fellow guest*, *fellow man*, *fellow member*, *fellow prisoner*, *fellow student*, *fellow sufferer*, etc.
2 Equivalent *to*. Now *rare*. E17.
H. BUSHNELL They.. have nothing fellow to God in their substance.
– COMB. & SPECIAL COLLOCATIONS: **fellow citizen** a citizen of the same city as another; **fellow citizenship** the state of being fellow citizens; **fellow-commoner** †(**a**) a joint-partaker with others, *esp.* a person who eats at the same table; (**b**) *hist.* any of a privileged class of undergraduates at Oxford, Cambridge, or Dublin, entitled to dine at the fellows' table; (**c**) a person who has a right of common with others; **fellow countryman** a person who belongs to the same country as another; a compatriot; **fellow creature** a person or animal made by the same creator, *spec.* by God; **fellow-heir** a joint heir; **fellow soldier** a soldier who fights under the same standard or on the same side as another; **fellow subject** a subject of the same monarch; **fellow-travel** *verb intrans.* sympathize with the aims and general policy of the Communist Party or other party or movement; **fellow-traveller** (**a**) a person who travels with another; (**b**) a non-Communist who sympathizes with the aims and general policy of the Communist Party; *transf.* a person who sympathizes with but is not a member of another party or movement.
■ **fellowess** *noun* (*rare*) a female fellow, a woman L15.

fellow /ˈfɛləʊ/ *verb trans.* Now *rare*. ME.
[ORIGIN from the noun.]
1 †**a** Join in partnership or companionship *with*, *to*. ME–L16. ▸**b** Make an equal *with*, *to*. LME.
†**2** Accompany, be associated with; be a partner in. LME–M17.
3 Equal, match. M17.
P. HEYLIN It will be a palace.. not fellowed in Europe.

†**fellow-feel** *verb intrans.* (*inf. & pres. trans.*). E17–E18.
[ORIGIN Back-form. from FELLOW FEELING.]
Share the feelings of others; sympathize *with*.

fellow feeling /fɛləʊˈfiːlɪŋ/ *noun*. E17.
[ORIGIN from FELLOW *noun* + FEELING *noun*, translating Latin *compassio*, Greek *sympatheia* SYMPATHY.]
1 Sympathy. E17.
2 A sense of common interest. Now *rare*. E18.

fellowless /ˈfɛləʊlɪs/ *adjective*. LME.
[ORIGIN from FELLOW *noun* + -LESS.]
1 Without a partner or companion. *rare*. LME.
2 Without an equal, matchless. L16.

fellowlike /ˈfɛləʊlʌɪk/ *adjective & adverb*. *obsolete* exc. *poet.* L15.
[ORIGIN from FELLOW *noun* + -LIKE.]
▸ **A** *adjective*. †**1** Companionable, sympathetic. L15–M17.
2 Like a partner or companion. E16.
▸ †**B** *adverb*. **1** Like one's fellows, similarly. Only in M16.
2 Sociably. L16–L17.

fellowly /ˈfɛləʊli/ *adjective & adverb*. *obsolete* exc. *poet. & rhet.* ME.
[ORIGIN formed as FELLOWLIKE + -LY¹.]
▸ **A** *adjective*. †**1** Pertaining to or befitting friends or companions. ME–L16.
2 Companionable, sociable. LME.
▸ **B** *adverb*. On equal terms; sociably; familiarly. ME.

fellowship /ˈfɛlə(ʊ)ʃɪp/ *noun & verb*. ME.
[ORIGIN from FELLOW *noun* + -SHIP.]
▸ **A** *noun*. **1** Participation, sharing; community of interest, sentiment, or nature. ME. ▸†**b** Partnership, (a) membership in a society. LME–E17.
SWIFT Joining with us here in the fellowship of slavery.
2 Companionship, company, society. ME.
J. LOCKE To have fellowship with those of his own kind.
3 Intimate personal communion; intercourse. ME. ▸†**b** Communication. M16–E17.
4 Friendliness; the spirit of comradeship; an instance of this. ME.
R. L. STEVENSON Life forces men apart and breaks up the goodly fellowships for ever. R. H. TAWNEY A band of comrades, where fellowship should be known for life.
5 A body of fellows or equals; a company. Now *rare*. ME.
6 = COMMUNION 4. LME.
the right hand of fellowship admission or entitlement to communion.
7 A guild, a corporation, a company. LME. ▸†**b** The members of a guild or corporation. LME–M17. ▸**c** An association of any kind; a society, a club, a fraternity. M16.
c J. P. DONLEAVY The Student Christian Movement is a fellowship of students who desire to understand the Christian faith.
8 †**a** The body of fellows in a college or university; the society constituted by the fellows. L15–L18. ▸**b** The status or emoluments of a fellow in a college, learned society, etc.; a post as a fellow in a college etc. E16.
b S. SPENDER If they.. obtained fellowships, generally they became absorbed into the Oxford hierarchy.
9 MATH. The process of calculation by which gain or loss is divided among partners. M16.
▸ **B** *verb*. Infl. **-pp-**, ***-p-**.
†**1** *verb trans.* Unite in fellowship; associate *with*, *to*. LME–M16.
†**2** *verb trans.* Accompany. LME–L15.
3 *verb trans.* Admit to fellowship; enter into participation or comradeship with. Now only in religious use. LME.
4 *verb intrans.* Join in fellowship; associate *with*. Now only in religious use & chiefly *US*. LME.

felly *noun* var. of FELLOE.

felly /ˈfɛli/ *adverb*. ME.
[ORIGIN from FELL *adjective* + -LY².]
1 Fiercely, cruelly; destructively. ME. ▸†**b** Bitterly, keenly; terribly. LME–L16. ▸**c** Exceedingly. *dial.* E19.
†**2** Craftily, cunningly. Only in LME.

felo de se /ˌfiːləʊ dɪ ˈsiː, ˌfɛ-, ˈseɪ/ *noun phr.* Pl. ***felones de se*** /fɪˌləʊniːz/, ***felos de se*** /ˌfiːləʊz/. E17.
[ORIGIN Anglo-Latin *felo* FELON *noun*¹ & *adjective*, *de se* of himself.]
1 A person who commits suicide (formerly a criminal act in the UK) or any malicious act which leads to his or her own death; *fig.* a self-destructive person or thing. E17.
2 Suicide. L18.

felon /ˈfɛlən/ *noun*¹ & *adjective*. ME.
[ORIGIN Old French & mod. French (noun & adjective), oblique case of *fel* (see FELL *adjective*) = Provençal *fel(on)* from medieval Latin *fel(l)o*, *fel(l)on-*, of unknown origin.]
▸ **A** *noun*. **1** A person who has committed felony. ME.
†**2** A wicked person, a villain; the Devil; an evil spirit. ME–E19.
– COMB.: **felon-setting** *Irish* informing on or otherwise helping to catch a criminal.
▸ **B** *adjective*. **1** Cruel, fierce, terrible, wild; wicked; murderous. *arch.* ME. ▸†**b** Angry, sullen. LME–M16.
†**2** Brave, sturdy. LME–L16.
†**3** Impressively large. *Scot.* LME–E17.

felon /ˈfɛlən/ *noun*². ME.
[ORIGIN App. spec. use of FELON *noun*¹ & *adjective*: cf. medieval Latin *fel(l)o* in same sense.]
A whitlow; an abscess, boil, or inflamed sore; inflammation (of a part of an animal).
– COMB.: **felon-grass** *Scot. & N. English* any of several plants reputed to cure felon in cattle; esp. masterwort, *Peucedanum ostruthium*.

felones de se *noun phr. pl.* see FELO DE SE.

felonious /fɛˈləʊnɪəs, fɪ-/ *adjective*. LME.
[ORIGIN from FELONY + -OUS.]
1 Of or pertaining to felony; of the nature of felony. Earliest in FELONIOUSLY. LME. ▸**b** Of a person: that has committed felony. M19.
2 Wicked, atrociously criminal. Now chiefly *poet.* L16.
■ **feloniously** *adverb* LME. **feloniousness** *noun* E18.

†**felonous** *adjective*. LME.
[ORIGIN from FELON *noun*¹ + -OUS.]
1 Wicked. LME–L16.
2 Fierce, cruel, violent; bold, sturdy. LME–L16.

felonry /ˈfɛlənri/ *noun*. M19.
[ORIGIN from FELON *noun*¹ + -RY.]
The class of felons; *hist.* the convict population in Australia.

felony /ˈfɛləni/ *noun*. ME.
[ORIGIN Old French & mod. French *félonie*, formed as FELON *noun*¹ & *adjective*: see -Y³.]
†**1** Wickedness; anger; deceit, treachery. ME–M16.
†**2** A crime, a misdeed, a sin. ME–E16.
3 FEUDAL LAW. An act committed by a vassal which involved the forfeiture of his fee. ME.
4 Crime regarded by the law as grave, and usu. involving violence; an instance of this. (In the US and formerly in England distinguished from, and regarded as more serious than, ***misdemeanour***.) ME.
felony de se /dɪ ˈseɪ/ [Latin = of himself] = FELO DE SE 2.

felos de se *noun phr. pl.* see FELO DE SE.

Felsenmeer /ˈfɛlzənmiːr/ *noun*. Pl. **-e** /-ə/. E20.
[ORIGIN German, lit. 'rock-sea'.]
PHYSICAL GEOGRAPHY. An expanse of angular frost-riven rocks which may develop on a flat terrain in arctic and alpine climates; a boulder field.

felsic /ˈfɛlsɪk/ *adjective*. E20.
[ORIGIN Contr. of FELDSPAR and SILICA: see -IC.]
GEOLOGY. Of, pertaining to, or designating a group of light-coloured minerals including feldspars, feldspathoids, quartz, and muscovite; (of rock) containing a high proportion of such minerals. Cf. MAFIC.

felsite /ˈfɛlsʌɪt/ *noun*. L18.
[ORIGIN from *fels-* in FEL(D)SPAR + -ITE¹.]
GEOLOGY. Any fine-grained igneous rock consisting mainly of feldspar and quartz.
■ **felsitic** /fɛlˈsɪtɪk/ *adjective* L20.

felspar *noun* var. of FELDSPAR.

felspathic *adjective*, **felspathoid** *noun* vars. of FELDSPATHIC, FELDSPATHOID.

felstone /ˈfɛlstəʊn/ *noun*. M19.
[ORIGIN Partial translation of German *Felsstein*, from *Fels* rock + *Stein* stone.]
GEOLOGY. = FELSITE.

felt /fɛlt/ *noun & adjective*¹.
[ORIGIN Old English *felt* = Old Saxon *filt* (Dutch *vilt*), Old & mod. High German *filz*, from West Germanic base rel. to that of FILTER *noun*.]
▸ **A** *noun*. **1** A fabric made of wool or other fibrous materials consolidated by heat and mechanical action so that the fibres are matted together. OE.
2 A piece of felt; something made of felt, *esp.* a felt hat. Formerly also, a filter made of felt or other material. LME.

F

F

▸**b** *PAPER-MAKING.* A piece of woven cloth with a felted nap. **M18.**

3 A thickly matted mass of hair or other fibrous substance; *dial.* couch grass. **LME.**

▸ **B** *attrib.* or as *adjective.* Made of felt. **LME.**

felt pen, **felt tip**, **felt-tip pen**, **felt-tipped pen** a pen with a felt point.

■ **feltlike** *adjective* resembling felt **E17.** **felty** *adjective* feltlike **M19.**

felt /fɛlt/ *ppl adjective*[2]. **L16.**

[**ORIGIN** pa. pple of **FEEL** *verb.*]

That is or has been felt; of which one is aware.

■ **feltness** *noun* **L19.**

felt /fɛlt/ *verb*[1]. **ME.**

[**ORIGIN** from the noun.]

1 *verb trans.* Make of felt. Chiefly as ***felted*** *ppl adjective.* **ME.**

2 *verb trans.* Make into felt; bring to a feltlike consistency; press together. **E16.**

3 *verb intrans.* Form into feltlike masses, become matted together. **L18.**

4 *verb trans.* Cover with felt. **L19.**

felt *verb*[2] *pa. t. & pple* of **FEEL** *verb.*

felter /ˈfɛltə/ *noun*[1]. **ME.**

[**ORIGIN** from **FELT** *verb*[1] + **-ER**[1].]

A person who makes or works with felt.

felter /ˈfɛltə/ *noun*[2]. Long *obsolete* exc. *dial.* **E17.**

[**ORIGIN** from **FELTER** *verb.*]

A tangle, a matted mass.

felter /ˈfɛltə/ *verb trans. obsolete* exc. *dial.* **LME.**

[**ORIGIN** Old French *feltrer* (mod. *feutrer*), from *feltre* (mod. *feutre*) from medieval Latin *feltrum*, *filtrum*: see **FILTER** *noun.*]

1 Tangle (hair etc.); mat together. **LME.**

2 Entangle; encumber. **M16.**

†**3** Filter. **M16–E17.**

felting /ˈfɛltɪŋ/ *noun.* **L17.**

[**ORIGIN** from **FELT** *verb*[1] + **-ING**[1].]

1 The action of **FELT** *verb*[1]. **L17.**

2 Felted cloth. **E19.**

felucca /fɛˈlʌkə/ *noun.* **E17.**

[**ORIGIN** Italian *feluc(c)a* prob. from Spanish †*faluca* perh. from Arabic word of uncertain origin; cf. Moroccan Arab. *flūka.*]

A small vessel propelled by lateen sails or oars, or both, formerly used in the Mediterranean area for coastal transport or trading, and still in use on rivers, esp. the Nile.

felwort /ˈfɛlwəːt/ *noun.*

[**ORIGIN** Old English *feldwyrt*, formed as **FIELD** *noun* + **WORT** *noun*[1].]

The autumn gentian, *Gentianella amarella*, a plant with dull purple flowers found esp. in chalk and limestone grassland. Formerly also, any of several gentians grown in gardens, esp. *Gentiana lutea.*

fem /fɛm/ *noun*[1]. *slang. derog.* **L20.**

[**ORIGIN** Abbreviation.]

An effeminate man.

fem *noun*[2] see **FEMME.**

FEMA /fiːmə/ *abbreviation. US.*

Federal Emergency Management Agency.

female /ˈfiːmeɪl/ *adjective & noun.* **ME.**

[**ORIGIN** Old French & mod. French *femelle* from Latin *femella* dim. of *femina* woman. The present form is due to assoc. with *male.*]

▸ **A** *adjective.* **1** Of, pertaining to, or designating the sex which can bear offspring or produce eggs; in organisms which undergo sexual reproduction, designating, pertaining to, or producing gametes (ova) that can be fertilized by male gametes. **ME.** ▸**b** Of a plant, flower, etc.: bearing pistils but lacking stamens; fruit-bearing. **L18.**

female child, ***female dog***, ***female ostrich***, ***female salmon***, etc.

2 Of a plant, mineral, or other object: having a colour or other property associated with femaleness, esp. as being inferior to a corresponding male property etc. Now *rare* exc. in certain collocations (see below). **LME.**

3 Composed or consisting of women or girls or of female animals or plants. **M16.**

MILTON That fair femal Troop.. that seemd of Goddesses.

4 Of, pertaining to, or characteristic of, women or girls or female animals. Formerly also, effeminate; weak. **L16.**

G. GREENE It lacks the female touch. A man's den. A. S. BYATT She began to feel very female, an attendant servant-cum-girl-friend, his woman.

5 Of a mechanical instrument etc.: hollowed or moulded in order to receive a corresponding or male part. **M17.**

▸ **B** *noun.* **1** A female person, animal, or plant; (the member(s) of) the female sex. **ME.**

F. MARRYAT The stag.. was.. acting as a sentinel for the females. H. G. WELLS The female of the species.. by the age of fifteen has a clearer sense of reality in these things than most men have to the doddering end of their days.

2 A woman or girl as distinguished from a man or boy; *gen.* (now only *derog.* or *joc.*) a woman, a girl. **ME.**

– **SPECIAL COLLOCATIONS & COMB.:** **female circumcision** incision or removal of some of the genitals of a girl or woman (sometimes including infibulation). ***female condom***. **female fern** = ***lady fern*** s.v. **LADY** *noun.* **female hemp** (*obsolete* exc. *hist.*) = ***fimble hemp*** s.v. **FIMBLE** *noun.* **female impersonator** a male performer dressed and acting as a woman. **female rhyme** a feminine rhyme (see **FEMININE** *adjective* 3b). ***female screw***: see **SCREW** *noun*[1] 1.

■ **femalely** *adverb* (*rare*) **M19.** **femaleness** *noun* the quality of being female **L19.** **femality** /fiˈmalɪti/ *noun* female nature or characteristics **M17.** **femalize** *verb* †(**a**) *verb intrans.* become effeminate; (**b**) *verb trans.* give a feminine ending to (a word): **L17.**

feme /fiːm, fɛm/ *noun.* **M16.**

[**ORIGIN** Anglo-Norman, Old French (mod. **FEMME**), from Latin *femina* woman.]

1 A woman. *obsolete* (–**M17**) exc. in phrs. below. **M16.**

2 *LAW.* A wife. **L16.**

– **PHRASES:** **feme covert** /ˈkʌvət/ [see **COVERT** *adjective* 5] *LAW, hist.* a married woman. **feme sole** /səʊl/ *LAW, hist.* (**a**) an unmarried woman, *esp.* a divorcee; (**b**) a married woman who trades etc. alone or independently of her husband.

femerell /ˈfɛm(ə)rɪl/ *noun.* **LME.**

[**ORIGIN** Old French *fumeril* louvre (in medieval Latin *fumerillum*, *-ellum*).]

Chiefly *hist.* A louvre or covered aperture on the roof of a kitchen, hall, etc., for ventilation or escape of smoke.

femic /ˈfɛmɪk/ *adjective.* **E20.**

[**ORIGIN** Contr. of **FERROMAGNESIAN**: see **-IC.**]

PETROGRAPHY. Designating, belonging to, or characteristic of a large category of igneous rocks whose chemical composition (broadly non-aluminous and ferromagnesian) can be expressed as a combination of certain normative minerals (notably pyroxene and olivine). Cf. **SALIC** *adjective*[2].

femicide /ˈfɛmɪsʌɪd/ *noun.* **E19.**

[**ORIGIN** Irreg. from Latin *femina* woman + **-CIDE**, after *homicide.*]

The killing of a woman.

feminal /ˈfɛmɪn(ə)l/ *adjective.* **LME.**

[**ORIGIN** medieval Latin *feminalis*, from Latin *femina* woman: see **-AL**[1]. Cf. Old French *feminal.*]

Of or pertaining to women; womanly, feminine.

■ **feminality** /fɛmɪˈnalɪti/ *noun* (**a**) female nature; (**b**) a female trait or peculiarity (usu. in *pl.*): **M17.**

femineity /fɛmɪˈniːɪti/ *noun.* **E19.**

[**ORIGIN** from Latin *femineus* womanish (from *femina* woman) + **-ITY.**]

Womanliness; womanishness.

feminie /ˈfɛmɪni/ *noun. arch.* **LME.**

[**ORIGIN** Old French *femenie*, from Latin *femina* woman.]

Womankind. In early use *spec.* the Amazons; also, their land.

feminine /ˈfɛmɪnɪn/ *adjective & noun.* **LME.**

[**ORIGIN** Old French & mod. French *féminin*, *-ine* or Latin *femininus*, *-ina*, from *femina* woman: see **-INE**[1].]

▸ **A** *adjective.* **1** Of a person or animal: female. Now *rare.* **LME.** ▸†**b** Of an object to which sex is attributed, esp. a celestial body: female. **L16–M19.**

SHAKES. *L.L.L.* A soul feminine saluteth us.

2 Of or pertaining to women; characteristic of or regarded as characteristic of women; womanly. **LME.** ▸**b** Womanish; effeminate. *derog.* Long *rare* or *obsolete.* **LME.**

A. WILSON Women scholars were primarily women and should not disregard the demands of feminine fashion. M. AMIS Men are often urged, by women, to recognize the feminine side of their nature.

3 *GRAMMAR.* Designating the gender to which belong words classified as female on the basis of sex or some arbitrary distinction, such as form; (of a word) belonging to this gender; (of a suffix, inflection, etc.) used with or to form words of this gender. **LME.** ▸**b** *PROSODY & MUSIC.* [Orig. in French verse, of feminine words ending in mute *-e* (used as a feminine suffix).] Of a rhyme or the ending of a verse or phrase: having the final syllable or note unaccented. **E17.**

J. STODDART Every noun denoting a female animal is feminine. **b** J. A. WESTRUP The feminine endings in the melody are similar to those found in early eighteenth-century instrumental music.

b feminine caesura: not immediately following a stress.

▸ **B** *noun.* **1** A woman. Formerly also, woman, women. Now *rare.* **L15.**

2 *GRAMMAR.* A word classified as feminine; the feminine gender. **M16.**

■ **femininely** *adverb* **M17.** **feminineness** *noun* **M19.**

femininist /ˈfɛmɪnɪnɪst/ *noun. rare.* **L19.**

[**ORIGIN** from **FEMININE** + **-IST.**]

= **FEMINIST** *noun*

■ **feminiˈnistic** *adjective* **E20.**

femininity /fɛmɪˈnɪnɪti/ *noun.* **LME.**

[**ORIGIN** formed as **FEMININIST** + **-ITY.** Cf. **FEMINITY.**]

1 The characteristic quality or qualities of woman; womanliness; the state or fact of being female. **LME.** ▸**b** Effeminacy. **M19.**

M. FONTEYN Tamara Karsavina.. is seductive, enchanting, coquettish, demure, innocent, or haughty.. She captures every aspect of femininity. **b** T. P. O'CONNOR Features delicate almost to femininity.

2 Womankind. *rare.* **LME.**

feminise *verb* var. of **FEMINIZE.**

feminism /ˈfɛmɪnɪz(ə)m/ *noun.* **M19.**

[**ORIGIN** from Latin *femina* woman + **-ISM**; in sense 2 from French *féminisme.*]

1 The qualities of a female; *spec.* in *MEDICINE*, the development of female secondary sexual characteristics in a male. **M19.**

2 Advocacy of equality of the sexes and the establishment of the political, social, and economic rights of women; the movement associated with this. **L19.**

L. WOOLF The kind of fact which made—and makes—feminism the belief or policy of all sensible men.

feminist /ˈfɛmɪnɪst/ *adjective & noun.* **L19.**

[**ORIGIN** French *féministe*, from Latin *femina* woman: see **-IST.**]

▸ **A** *adjective.* Of or pertaining to feminism or the advocacy of women's equality and rights. **L19.**

▸ **B** *noun.* An advocate of feminism or women's equality or rights. Cf. earlier **FEMININIST. E20.**

■ **femiˈnistic** *adjective* **E20.**

feminity /fɪˈmɪnɪti/ *noun.* **LME.**

[**ORIGIN** Old French & mod. French *féminité* from medieval Latin *feminitas*, from Latin *femina* woman: see **-ITY.**]

1 = **FEMININITY** 1. **LME.** ▸**b** = **FEMININITY** 1b. **M17.**

2 = **FEMININITY** 2. **LME.**

feminize /ˈfɛmɪnʌɪz/ *verb.* Also **-ise. M17.**

[**ORIGIN** from Latin *femina* + **-IZE.** Cf. French *féminiser.*]

1 *verb trans.* Make feminine or female; make characteristic of or associated with women. **M17.** ▸**b** Induce female physiological characteristics in. **E20.**

2 *verb intrans.* Become or grow feminine. *rare.* **M19.**

■ **feminiˈzation** *noun* the action of feminizing; the process of becoming feminized; the state of being feminized (***testicular feminization***: see **TESTICULAR** 1): **M19.**

feminoid /ˈfɛmɪnɔɪd/ *adjective.* **E20.**

[**ORIGIN** from Latin *femina* woman + **-OID.**]

Feminine (but not female); of female form or appearance.

femme /fam; *in senses 8, 9 also* fɛm/ *noun.* In sense 9 also ***fem*** /fɛm/. Pl. ***femmes*** /fam, famz; fɛmz/. **L17.**

[**ORIGIN** French: see **FEME.**]

▸ **I** In phrases.

1 ***femme couverte*** /kuvɛrt, kʊˈvəːt/, pl. ***couvertes*** /-vɛrt, -ˈvəːts/ [see **COVERT** *adjective* 5], = ***FEME covert*. L17.**

2 ***femme de chambre*** /də ʃɑ̃ːbr, ˈʃɑːmbrə/ [lit. 'of the (bed)room'], a lady's maid. **M18.**

3 ***femme incomprise*** /ɛ̃kɔ̃priːz/, pl. ***incomprises*** /-priːz/, a woman who is misunderstood or unappreciated. **M19.**

4 ***femme de ménage*** /də menaːʒ, meɪˈnɑːʒ/ [lit. 'of the household'], a charwoman, a domestic help. **L19.**

5 ***femme du monde*** /dy mɔ̃ːd, duː mɔːnd/, a woman of the world. **L19.**

6 ***femme fatale*** /fatal, faˈtɑːl/, pl. *fatales* /-tal, -ˈtɑːl/, a dangerously attractive woman. **E20.**

▸ **II** Simply.

7 *gen.* A woman, a wife. *rare.* **E19.**

8 A girl. *US slang.* **E20.**

9 A lesbian taking a traditionally feminine role. *slang.* **M20.**

femora *noun pl.* see **FEMUR.**

femoral /ˈfɛm(ə)r(ə)l/ *adjective & noun.* **L18.**

[**ORIGIN** from Latin **FEMUR**, *femor-* + **-AL**[1].]

Chiefly *ANATOMY.* ▸**A** *adjective.* Of or pertaining to the femur or thigh. **L18.**

femoral artery: running down the front of the upper thigh and the rear of the lower thigh, continuing into the popliteal artery.

▸ **B** *noun.* The femoral artery. **M19.**

femoro- /ˈfɛmərəʊ/ *combining form.*

[**ORIGIN** formed as **FEMORAL** + **-O-.**]

Used in *ANATOMY & MEDICINE* to form words in senses 'of the femur', 'femoral and —', as ***femoro-fibular***, ***femoro-popliteal.***

femto- /ˈfɛmtəʊ/ *combining form.*

[**ORIGIN** from Danish or Norwegian *femten* fifteen: see **-O-.**]

Used in names of units of measurement to denote a factor of 10^{-15}, as ***femtosecond*** etc. Abbreviation ***f.***

femur /ˈfiːmə/ *noun.* Pl. **femurs**, **femora** /ˈfɛm(ə)rə/. **L15.**

[**ORIGIN** Latin = thigh.]

1 The thigh bone in vertebrates. Formerly also, the thigh. **L15.**

2 The third articulated segment of the leg in insects and some other arthropods. **M19.**

fen /fɛn/ *noun*[1].

[**ORIGIN** Old English *fen(n)* = Old Frisian *fen(n)e*, Old Saxon *fen(n)i* (Dutch *veen*), Old High German *fenna*, *fenni* (German *Fenn*), Old Norse *fen*, Gothic *fani* clay, from Germanic.]

1 (A tract of) low land covered wholly or partly with shallow water or subject to frequent flooding; *ECOLOGY* wet land with alkaline, neutral, or only slightly acid peaty soil (cf. **BOG** *noun*[1]). **OE.**

the Fens low-lying districts of Cambridgeshire, Lincolnshire, and neighbouring counties in eastern England, which were formerly marshland but have been drained for agriculture since the 17th cent.

2 Mud, filth, excrement. Long *obsolete* exc. *dial.* **OE.**

– **COMB.:** **fenberry** the cranberry; **fen-fire** a will-o'-the-wisp; **fenman** a native or inhabitant of the Fens; **fen-runners** long

skates for skating on fens; ***fen sedge***: see SEDGE 1; ***fen tiger***: see TIGER *noun* 4a.
■ **fenner** *noun* a native or inhabitant of the Fens M19.

fen /fɛn/ *noun*². Long *obsolete* exc. *dial.*
[ORIGIN Old English *fyne*. The mod. form (with *e* for Old English *y*) is Kentish. Cf. VINNY.]
†**1** Mould, mildew, moisture. Only in OE.
2 A mould that attacks the hop plant. M18.

fen /fʌn/ *noun*³. Pl. same. M19.
[ORIGIN Chinese *fēn* a hundredth part.]
A monetary unit of China, equal to one-tenth of a jiao.

fen *verb* see FAIN *verb*².

fence /fɛns/ *noun*. ME.
[ORIGIN Aphet. from DEFENCE *noun*.]
†**1** The action of defending. ME–E16.
†**2** Means or method of defence. LME–M18.
3 A railing or barrier constructed of posts of any of various materials connected by wire, planks, etc., used to enclose and prevent entry to and exit from a field, yard, etc.; *arch.* a bulwark, a defence. LME. ▸**b** A structure for a horse to jump over in a competition, race, etc. M19.
R. CAMPBELL The corrugated iron fence which separated our two gardens.
4 The action or art of fencing. M16.
A. DUGGAN Our enemies would use the same tricks of fence.
5 A person who or an establishment which deals in stolen goods. L17.
6 A guard, guide, or gauge designed to regulate the movements of a tool, machine, etc. E18.
– PHRASES: ***electric fence***: see ELECTRIC *adjective*. ***live fence***: see LIVE *adjective*. **mend one's fences** (*a*) *US* (of a member of Congress) renew contact with the electors, improve political relationships; (*b*) *gen.* renew contact or make peace with a person. **over the fence** *Austral. & NZ colloq.* unreasonable, unjust. ***rush one's fences***: see RUSH *verb*² 8. **sit on the fence** remain neutral in a contest, not take sides, not commit oneself. **sunk fence**: placed along the bottom of a ditch, or formed by a ditch. ***zigzag fence***: see ZIGZAG *adjective*.
– COMB.: **fence lizard** a N. American spiny lizard, *Sceloporus undulatus*; **fence-mending** the action of mending one's fences, renewal of contact, improving of (political) relationships; **fence-month** (*a*) the period (about 30 days) of fawning for deer, during which hunting was forbidden; (*b*) the close season for fishing; **fencerow** *US* an uncultivated strip of land on each side of and below a fence; **fence-shop**: selling stolen goods; **fence-sitter** a person who sits on the fence, a person who will not commit himself or herself; **fence-sitting** the action of sitting on the fence, refusal to commit oneself.
■ **fenceful** *adjective* (now *rare* or *obsolete*) protecting, shielding E17.

fence /fɛns/ *verb*. LME.
[ORIGIN from the noun.]
1 **a** *verb trans.* Protect, shield, screen, (*from, against*); fortify, surround (as) with a fence (foll. by *about, in, round, up*); keep *off* with a fence. LME. ▸**b** *verb trans.* Repel, keep *out* or *off*. *arch.* L16. ▸†**c** *verb intrans.* Provide defence or protection *against*. L17–M18.
a E. BIRNEY Lieutenant Smith began to write rapidly, his arm fencing the paper from Turvey's gaze. R. C. HUTCHINSON The houses were formidably fenced off with barbed wire. **b** SIR W. SCOTT A cup of sack shall fence the cold.
2 *verb trans. SCOTS LAW.* Open the proceedings of (a court of law, *hist.* the Parliament) by the use of a form of words forbidding the unnecessary interruption or obstruction of the proceedings. LME.
3 *verb intrans.* Practise the art or sport of fencing. L16. ▸**b** Engage in skilful argument; parry, evade answering (a question). (Foll. by *with*.) M17.
a J. D. WATSON Afternoons were spent at a gymnasium learning how to fence. **b** B. UNSWORTH In all our conversations I was fencing with him, scoring off him all the time.
4 *verb trans. & intrans.* Deal in (stolen goods). E17.
5 *verb intrans.* Of a horse etc.: jump fences. L19.

fencer /ˈfɛnsə/ *noun*. L16.
[ORIGIN from FENCE *verb* + -ER¹.]
1 A person who practises the art or sport of fencing. Formerly also, a professional sword-fighter; a gladiator. L16.
2 A receiver of stolen goods. L17.
3 A horse which jumps fences (*well, badly*, etc.). E19.
4 A person who puts up or mends fences. E19.

fenchone /ˈfɛntʃəʊn/ *noun*. L19.
[ORIGIN German *Fenchon*, from *Fenchel* fennel: see -ONE.]
CHEMISTRY. A fragrant liquid terpenoid ketone, $C_{10}H_{16}O$, found esp. in fennel and thuja oils.
■ **fenchane** *noun* a liquid saturated bicyclic hydrocarbon, $C_{10}H_{18}$, from which fenchone and the fenchenes are formally derived E20. **fenchene** *noun* any of a series of isomeric liquid terpenes of formula $C_{10}H_{16}$, obtained by reducing fenchone L19.

fencible /ˈfɛnsɪb(ə)l/ *adjective & noun*. ME.
[ORIGIN Aphet. from DEFENSIBLE.]
▸ **A** *adjective*. **1** Of a person: fit and liable for defensive military service. Formerly also, of arms or armour: able to be used for defence. Chiefly *Scot. obsolete* exc. *hist.* ME. ▸**b** *hist.* Of a military force: composed of soldiers liable only for Home Service. L18.
†**2** Of a fortress, town, etc.: able to be defended; well-fortified. L16–E19.
SPENSER No fort so fencible.. But that continuall battery will rive.
†**3** Able to serve as a fence or enclosure. E18–E19.
SIR W. SCOTT The thorn hedges are nearly fencible.
▸ **B** *noun. hist.* A soldier liable only for Home Service. L18.

fencing /ˈfɛnsɪŋ/ *noun*. LME.
[ORIGIN from FENCE *verb* + -ING¹.]
1 The action of protecting or setting up a defence *against* something. Long *rare* or *obsolete*. LME.
2 *SCOTS LAW.* The formal opening of a court of law or (*hist.*) the Parliament. M16.
3 The practice, art, or sport of engaging in combat with swords, esp. according to a set of rules using foils, épées, or sabres to score points. L16. ▸**b** The action of engaging in skilful argument or evading questions. E17.
4 A fence, an enclosure, a railing; fences collectively; material for fences. L16.
5 The action of putting up a fence. E17.
6 The action (by a horse) of jumping a fence. E19.
7 The action or practice of dealing in stolen goods. M19.

fend /fɛnd/ *noun*. *Scot. & dial.* M17.
[ORIGIN from the verb.]
1 Defence, protection. M17.
2 An effort; an attempt; the action or activity of making an effort or efforts. E18.

fend /fɛnd/ *verb*. ME.
[ORIGIN Aphet. from DEFEND.]
1 *verb trans. & intrans.* = DEFEND. Now *arch. & poet.* ME.
fend and prove (now *dial.*) argue, wrangle.
2 *verb trans.* Keep from or away, ward off. Now usu. foll. by *off*. LME.
C. RYCROFT Go to bed with hot Horlick's malted milk to fend off night starvation.
3 *verb trans.* Forbid; prevent (*from*). Cf. FAIN *verb*². *obsolete* exc. *dial.* LME.
4 *verb intrans.* Make an effort, strive, struggle. M16. ▸**b** Foll. by *for*: look after, provide for (usu. oneself). E17. ▸**c** Fare, manage. *Scot. & dial.* E18.
D. H. LAWRENCE A man has to fend and fettle for the best. **b** G. SWIFT We don't need him any more.. we can fend for ourselves.
5 *verb trans.* Support, maintain. Chiefly *Scot. & dial.* M17.
SIR W. SCOTT They are puirly armed, and warse fended wi' victual.
■ **fendy** *adjective* (*dial.*) resourceful, managing; active: E18.

Fendant /fɑ̃dɑ̃/ *noun*. E20.
[ORIGIN Swiss French.]
(The grape producing) a dry white wine of SW Switzerland.

fender /ˈfɛndə/ *noun*. ME.
[ORIGIN from FEND *verb* + -ER¹.]
▸ **I** **1** **a** *NAUTICAL.* A piece of old cable, matting, rubber, etc., hung over a vessel's side to protect it against chafing or impact. ME. ▸**b** A large piece of timber fixed as a guard to protect a pier or dock wall. L16. ▸**c** A low metal frame fitted to a fireplace to prevent coals from rolling outside the hearth. M17. ▸**d** A sluice(-gate). M19. ▸**e** A mudguard; a wing or bumper of a motor vehicle. *N. Amer.* E20.
a V. SACKVILLE-WEST Those little fenders which prevent a ship from bumping too roughly against the quay. **c** G. ORWELL To sit in a room like this, in an armchair beside an open fire with your feet in the fender.
2 *gen.* Anything used to keep something off or prevent collision. E17.
▸ **II** **3** = DEFENDER. *obsolete* exc. *dial.* LME.
– COMB.: **fender bender** *slang* (chiefly *N. Amer.*) a (usu. minor) collision between vehicles; **fender stool** a long footstool placed close to the fender of a fireplace.

†**feneration** *noun*. L16–L18.
[ORIGIN Latin *faeneratio(n-)*, from *faenerare, -ari* lend on interest, from *faenus, faenor-* interest: see -ATION.]
Usury.

fenestella /fɛnɪˈstɛlə/ *noun*. LME.
[ORIGIN Latin, dim. of *fenestra* window: see -EL².]
1 *ARCHITECTURE.* A small window or opening in a wall, esp. in the side of an altar or confessio, enabling the relics inside to be seen. LME. ▸**b** A small niche in the wall on the south side of the altar in a church, containing the piscina and often the credence. L18.
2 *PALAEONTOLOGY.* A fossil bryozoan of Palaeozoic age. Chiefly as mod. Latin genus name. M19.

†**fenester** *noun*. ME–E19.
[ORIGIN Old French *fenestre* (mod. *fenêtre*) formed as FENESTRA.]
A window.

fenestra /fɪˈnɛstrə/ *noun*. Pl. **-trae** /-triː/. E19.
[ORIGIN Latin = window.]
1 *BOTANY.* A small mark or scar left by the separation of the seed from the ovary. *rare*. E19.
2 *ANATOMY.* A small hole or opening in a bone; *esp.* either of two openings, covered by membranes, in the inner ear (see below). M19.
fenestra ovalis /əʊˈvɑːlɪs, -ˈveɪl-/ [Latin = oval window] the opening between the middle ear and the vestibule. **fenestra rotunda** /rəˈtʌndə/ [Latin = round window] the opening between the cochlea and the middle ear.
3 *MEDICINE.* **a** A perforation in a surgical instrument other than in the handle. Also, an opening in a dressing. L19. ▸**b** A hole cut surgically in any structure of the body; *esp.* one made by fenestration. M20.

fenestral /fɪˈnɛstr(ə)l/ *adjective*. Now *rare*. L17.
[ORIGIN formed as FENESTRA + -AL¹.]
Of or pertaining to a window.

fenestrate /fɪˈnɛstrət, ˈfɛnəstrət/ *adjective*. M19.
[ORIGIN Latin *fenestratus* pa. pple of *fenestrare* provide with openings or windows, formed as FENESTRA; see -ATE².]
Having an opening. Now *spec.* in *BOTANY & ZOOLOGY*, having small perforations or transparent areas.

fenestrate /fɪˈnɛstreɪt, ˈfɛnəstreɪt/ *verb trans*. L19.
[ORIGIN Latin *fenestrat-* pa. ppl stem of *fenestrare*: see FENESTRATE *adjective*, -ATE³.]
Provide with small holes or openings; perforate.

fenestrated /fɪˈnɛstreɪtɪd, ˈfɛnəstreɪtɪd/ *adjective*. E19.
[ORIGIN formed as FENESTRATE *adjective* + -ED¹.]
= FENESTRATE *adjective*. Also, (of a surgical instrument) having one or more fenestrae.

fenestration /fɛnɪˈstreɪʃ(ə)n/ *noun*. M19.
[ORIGIN formed as FENESTRATE *verb* + -ION.]
1 *ARCHITECTURE.* The arrangement of windows in a building. M19.
2 *BOTANY & ZOOLOGY.* The condition of being fenestrate. L19.
3 *SURGERY.* (The operation of cutting) an artificial opening into the labyrinth of the ear, used to restore hearing in cases of otosclerosis. L19.

fenfluramine /ˌfɛnˈfluːrəmiːn/ *noun*. M20.
[ORIGIN from *fen-* (alt. of PHENYL) + FLUOR- + AMINE *noun*, elems. of the systematic name (see below).]
A drug related to amphetamines but causing less stimulation of the central nervous system, formerly used clinically as an appetite suppressant.

feng shui /ˈfɛŋʃuːi, ˈfʌŋ-/ *noun*. L18.
[ORIGIN Chinese, from *fēng* wind + *shuǐ* water.]
In Chinese thought, a system of laws considered to govern spatial arrangement and orientation in relation to the flow of energy (chi), and whose favourable or unfavourable effects are taken into account when siting and designing buildings.

Fenian /ˈfiːnɪən/ *noun & adjective*. E19.
[ORIGIN from Old Irish *féne* one of the names of the ancient population of Ireland, confused with *fiann* FIAN the guard of legendary kings: see -IAN.]
▸ **A** *noun*. **1** Any of the band of mercenary warriors of Irish history and legend who acted as permanent guard of the high king of Ireland. E19.
2 A member of a 19th-cent. league among the Irish in the US and Ireland for promoting revolution and the overthrow of the British Government in Ireland; *offensive* a Catholic. M19.
▸ **B** *adjective*. Of or pertaining to the Fenians or Fenianism. M19.
■ **Fenianism** *noun* the principles, purposes, or methods of the 19th-cent. Fenians M19.

fenks /fɛŋks/ *noun pl.* E19.
[ORIGIN Unknown.]
The fibrous parts of a whale's blubber, which contain the oil; the refuse of blubber when melted.

fennec /ˈfɛnɛk/ *noun*. L18.
[ORIGIN Arabic *fanak* from Persian *fanak, fanaj*.]
More fully ***fennec fox***. A small fox, *Vulpes zerda*, which inhabits deserts from Morocco to Arabia and is notable for its very large ears.

fennel /ˈfɛn(ə)l/ *noun*.
[ORIGIN Old English *finugl, finule* fem., *fenol, finul* masc., and Old French *fenoil*, from Latin *faeniculum* dim. of *faenum* hay.]
An aromatic yellow-flowered umbelliferous herb, *Foeniculum vulgare*, with feathery leaves used to flavour fish sauces, salad dressings, etc. Also, any of various similar or related plants (see below).
– PHRASES & COMB.: ***dog fennel***: see DOG *noun*. **fennel flower** any of various plants of the genus *Nigella*, of the buttercup family; esp. *N. sativa* (black cumin), the seeds of which are used as a flavouring. **fennel-giant** *arch.* = ***giant fennel*** below. **Florence fennel** = FINOCCHIO. **giant fennel** any of various large Mediterranean umbellifers of the genus *Ferula*, related to fennel. ***hog's fennel***: see HOG *noun*. **sweet fennel** = ***Florence fennel*** above.

fennish /ˈfɛnɪʃ/ *adjective*. L16.
[ORIGIN from FEN *noun*¹ + -ISH¹.]
1 = FENNY *adjective*¹ 1. L16.
2 Belonging to or produced from a fen. L16.

Fennoscandian /fɛnəʊˈskandɪən/ *adjective*. E20.
[ORIGIN from German *fennoskandisch* adjective, from Latin *Fenni* the Finns + -O-: see SCANDIAN *adjective*.]
GEOLOGY. Designating or pertaining to the ancient land mass in NW Europe comprising most of Scandinavia, Finland, and adjacent parts of Russia.

F

fenny /ˈfɛni/ *adjective*[1]. OE.
[ORIGIN from FEN *noun*[1] + -Y[1].]
1 Of the nature of a fen; boggy, swampy. OE. ▸†**b** Muddy, dirty. OE–M17.
Watsonia Crowinstown Lake.. has a fenny margin.. but is becoming acid on the west side.
2 Inhabiting, growing, or produced in a fen. Now only of plants. M16.
SHAKES. *Macb.* Fillet of a fenny snake, In the cauldron boil and bake.

fenny *adjective*[2] see VINNY.

fenoterol /fɛnəˈtɛrɒl/ *noun*. L20.
[ORIGIN from *feno-* repr. PHENO- + *-ter-* arbitrary elem. + -OL.]
PHARMACOLOGY. A sympathomimetic agent used esp. as a bronchodilator in the treatment of asthma.

fenster /ˈfɛnstə/ *noun*. E20.
[ORIGIN German = window.]
GEOLOGY. An opening eroded through a stratum in a region of overfolding or overthrusting, exposing a younger stratum beneath.

fent /fɛnt/ *noun* & *verb*. LME.
[ORIGIN Old French & mod. French *fente* slit, from use as noun of fem. pa. pple of Latin *findere* cleave, split. See VENT *noun*[1].]
▸ **A** *noun*. **1** A short slit or opening in a robe, *esp.* the opening at the throat; a placket. Now chiefly *dial.* LME.
fig.: L. DURRELL Rumours.. had begun to scuttle about the fents and warrens of the old town.
2 A remnant of cloth. M19.
attrib.: H. MITCHELL I hunted the fent shops for remnants of gay prints.
▸ **B** *verb trans.* Make slits in. *rare*. L16.

fentanyl /ˈfɛntənʌɪl, -nɪl/ *noun*. M20.
[ORIGIN from *fen-* (representing PHEN-) + *-t-* + *an-* (in ANILIDE) + -YL.]
MEDICINE. A synthetic opiate drug which is a powerful pain-killer and tranquillizer.

fenugreek /ˈfɛnjʊɡriːk/ *noun*.
[ORIGIN Old English *fenogrecum*, superseded in Middle English by forms from Old French & mod. French *fenugrec*, from Latin *faenugraecum*, for *faenum Graecum* 'Greek hay': the Romans used the dried plant for fodder.]
A leguminous plant, *Trigonella foenum-graecum*, with aromatic seeds used to flavour curries etc. Also *gen.*, any plant of the genus *Trigonella*.
bird's-foot fenugreek: see BIRD *noun*. **sweet fenugreek** = *Darling clover* s.v. DARLING *noun*[2].

feod *noun* see FEUD *noun*[2].

†**feodal** *adjective* var. of FEUDAL *adjective*[1].

feodary *noun* var. of FEUDARY.

feoff /fiːf, fɛf/ *verb trans.* Now *rare* or *obsolete*. ME.
[ORIGIN Anglo-Norman *feoffer*, Old French *fieuffer*, *fieffer*, formed as FIEF *noun*.]
1 LAW. Put in legal possession; = ENFEOFF *verb* 1. ME.
†**2** Confer (a heritable possession) *on*, *upon*. L16–M17.

feoffee /fɛˈfiː/ *noun*. *obsolete* exc. *hist.* LME.
[ORIGIN Anglo-Norman *feoffé* pa. pple of *feoffer*: see FEOFF, -EE[1].]
LAW. **1** More fully ***feoffee in trust***, ***feoffee of trust***. A trustee invested with a freehold estate in land, latterly esp. for charitable or other public purposes. LME.
2 The person to whom a feoffment is made. M16.

feoffer *noun* var. of FEOFFOR.

feoffment /ˈfiːfm(ə)nt, ˈfɛf-/ *noun*. *obsolete* exc. *hist.* ME.
[ORIGIN Anglo-Norman, formed as FEOFF *verb*: see -MENT.]
LAW. **1** The action of putting a person in possession of property, rents, etc., under the feudal system; the mode of conveying freehold property by livery of seisin. ME. ▸**b** More fully ***feoffment of trust***, ***feoffment upon trust***, ***feoffment to uses***. A conveyance of land to one person in trust for another, or for certain uses. L15.
charter of feoffment, **deed of feoffment**: recording or (later) effecting a feoffment.
†**2** Possession of property as a result of feoffment; the property itself. Only in ME.
†**3** A deed of feoffment. LME–L17.

feoffor /ˈfiːfə, ˈfɛfə/ *noun*. *obsolete* exc. *hist.* Also **-er**. LME.
[ORIGIN Anglo-Norman *feoffour*, formed as FEOFF *verb*: see -OUR, -OR.]
LAW. **1** A person who makes a feoffment to another. LME.
†**2** = FEOFFEE. LME–E17.

-fer /fə/ *suffix*. Also (see below) **-ifer**.
[ORIGIN Latin = carrying, bearing, from *ferre* carry, bear.]
Forming (usu. with intermediate -I-) nouns with the sense 'a person or thing having, containing, or carrying', as ***aquifer***, ***crucifer***, ***rotifer***, etc.

féra /fera/ *noun*. Pl. pronounced same. Also ***ferra***. E19.
[ORIGIN Swiss French.]
A whitefish from any of certain Alpine lakes.

feracious /fəˈreɪʃəs/ *adjective*. Now *rare*. M17.
[ORIGIN from Latin *ferac-*, *ferax* from *ferre* to bear: see -ACIOUS.]
Bearing abundantly; fruitful, prolific.
CARLYLE A world so feracious, teeming with endless results.

feracity /fəˈrasɪti/ *noun*. Now *rare*. LME.
[ORIGIN Latin *feracitas*, formed as FERACIOUS: see -ACITY.]
The quality of being feracious.

ferae naturae /ˌfɪəriː nəˈtʃʊəriː, ˌfɛrʌɪ nəˈtjʊərʌɪ/ *pred.* & *postpositive adjectival* & *noun phr.* M17.
[ORIGIN Latin = of wild nature.]
Chiefly LAW. Undomesticated or wild (animals).

Feraghan /ˈfɛrəɡɑːn/ *noun*. E20.
[ORIGIN Persian, from *Ferghana*, a region in central Asia.]
A costly handmade Persian rug, usu. of cotton.

feral /ˈfɪər(ə)l/ *adjective*[1]. E17.
[ORIGIN Latin *feralis* pertaining to funeral rites or to the dead.]
1 Deadly, fatal. Now *rare* or *obsolete*. E17.
2 Funereal, gloomy. Now *arch.* or *poet.* M17.

feral /ˈfɪər(ə)l, ˈfɛr(ə)l/ *adjective*[2] & *noun*. E17.
[ORIGIN from Latin *fera* wild animal, use as noun (sc. *bestia*) of *ferus* wild + -AL[1].]
▸ **A** *adjective*. **1** Of, pertaining to, or resembling, a wild animal; savage, fierce, brutal. E17.
I. MURDOCH Her intense animal face was blazing with health and vitality and feral curiosity.
2 Wild, untamed, uncultivated. M17. ▸**b** Chiefly of animals: belonging to or forming a wild population ultimately descended from individuals which escaped from captivity or domestication; born of such an animal in the wild. M19.
b *Watsonia* The fact that a plant can maintain itself.. where it was planted, without further care.. is not sufficient to justify calling it feral.
b feral pigeon the common pigeon of town and city centres and elsewhere, that is descended from domesticated forms of the rock dove, *Columba livia*.
▸ **B** *noun*. A wild beast; a domesticated animal living wild. M17.

ferangi *noun* var. of FERINGHEE.

ferash /fɛˈraʃ/ *noun*. Also **farrash**. E17.
[ORIGIN Persian & Urdu *farrāš* from Arabic = a person who spreads out bedding, carpets, etc.]
A servant in some Muslim countries; *spec.* a menial performing heavy domestic tasks.

ferberite /ˈfəːbərʌɪt/ *noun*. E19.
[ORIGIN from surname *Ferber* (see below) + -ITE[1].]
†**1** [J. J. *Ferber* (1743–90), Swedish mineralogist.] GEOLOGY. A variety of gneiss. Only in E19.
2 [Rudolph *Ferber*, 19th-cent. German mineralogist.] MINERALOGY. A monoclinic ferrous tungstate (isostructural with wolframite) usu. occurring as black elongated prisms. M19.

fer de lance /fɛː də ˈlɑːns/ *noun*. Pl. **fers de lance** (pronounced same), **fer de lances**. L19.
[ORIGIN French = iron (head) of lance.]
A highly venomous tropical American pit viper, *Bothrops atrox*.

fer-de-moline /fɛːdəməˈlʌɪn/ *noun*. Pl. ***fers-*** (pronounced same). LME.
[ORIGIN French *fer de moulin* lit. 'iron of mill'.]
HERALDRY. A charge resembling the iron support of a millstone.

fere /fɪə/ *noun*. *arch.* Also †**yfere**.
[ORIGIN Old English *ġefēra*, from Germanic base of Y- + (ult.) ablaut var. of base of FARE *verb* (Northumbrian *fǣra*).]
1 A comrade, a partner; a friend or companion of either sex. OE.
TENNYSON The lamb.. raceth freely with his fere.
2 A husband or wife; the mate of an animal etc. ME.
B. TAYLOR Paris.. Took thee, the widow, as his fere.
†**3** An equal, a peer. ME–E19.

fere /fɪə/ *adjective*. Long only *Scot.* ME.
[ORIGIN Old Norse *fœrr* ult. from Germanic ablaut var. of base of FARE *verb*. Cf. FEIRIE.]
Sound, strong; in good health.

feretory /ˈfɛrət(ə)ri/ *noun*. ME.
[ORIGIN Old French *fiertre* from Latin *feretrum* from Greek *pheretron* bier, from *pherein* bear, assim. to words in *-tory*.]
1 A (portable) shrine containing the relics of a saint. ME.
2 A small room or chapel in which shrines were deposited. LME.
3 A bier. LME.

feretrum /ˈfɛrətrəm/ *noun*. *rare*. Pl. ***-tra*** /-trə/. L15.
[ORIGIN Latin: see FERETORY.]
= FERETORY 1.

feretto /fəˈrɛtəʊ/ *noun*. Now *rare* or *obsolete*. M17.
[ORIGIN Italian *ferretto* (*di spagna* 'of Spain'), dim. of *ferro* iron from Latin *ferrum*.]
Copper calcined with sulphur or zinc sulphate, used to colour glass.

ferfel *noun* var. of FARFEL.

fergusonite /ˈfəːɡəs(ə)nʌɪt/ *noun*. E19.
[ORIGIN from Robert *Ferguson* (1799–1865), Scot. physician + -ITE[1].]
MINERALOGY. A tetragonal niobate and tantalate of iron, cerium, yttrium, and other elements, usu. occurring as grey, yellow, or brown prisms.

feria /ˈfɪərɪə, ˈfɛ-/ *noun*. LME.
[ORIGIN Latin = holiday: see FAIR *noun*[1]. In sense 2 through Spanish.]
1 ECCLESIASTICAL. A weekday, *esp.* one on which no festival falls. LME.
2 In Spain and Spanish-speaking America: a fair. M19.
■ †**ferie** *noun* [Old French] = FERIA 1 LME–E17.

ferial /ˈfɪərɪəl, ˈfɛr-/ *adjective*. LME.
[ORIGIN Old French & mod. French *férial* or its source medieval Latin *ferialis*, formed as FERIA: see -AL[1].]
1 ECCLESIASTICAL. Designating or pertaining to an ordinary weekday as opp. to a day appointed for a festival or fast. LME.
†**2** SCOTS LAW. Designating a day or time when courts of law were closed and legal process was invalid. LME–E18.
3 Of or pertaining to a holiday. L15.

†**feriation** *noun*. E17–E19.
[ORIGIN medieval Latin *feriatio(n-)*, from Latin *feriat-* pa. ppl stem of *feriari* make holiday, formed as FERIA: see -ATION.]
The keeping of a holiday; cessation of work.

ferine /ˈfɪərʌɪn/ *adjective*. M17.
[ORIGIN Latin *ferinus*, from *fera*: see FERAL *adjective*[2], -INE[1].]
1 Bestial. M17. ▸**b** Of, pertaining to, or resembling, a wild animal; untamed, savage. L17.
J. NORRIS To.. suffer the ferine and brutish part to get the Ascendant over that which is Rational and Divine. **b** J. S. BLACKIE Dogs and cocks.. and other ferine combatants.
2 Of a disease: malignant. *rare*. M17.

feringhee /fəˈrɪŋɡi/ *noun*. *Indian*. Also **ferangi** /fəˈraŋɡi/. E17.
[ORIGIN Urdu from Persian *firangī* from base of FRANK *noun*[1].]
1 In India and parts of the Middle East, a European. Freq. *derog.* E17.
2 A Eurasian of Portuguese-Indian descent. *obsolete* exc. *hist.* M18.

Ferio /ˈfɛrɪəʊ/ *noun*. M16.
[ORIGIN Latin = to strike dead, taken as a mnemonic of scholastic philosophers, E a universal negative proposition, I a particular affirmative proposition, and O a particular negative proposition.]
LOGIC. The fourth mood of the first syllogistic figure, in which a universal negative major premiss and a particular affirmative minor yield a particular negative conclusion.

Ferison /fɛˈrʌɪs(ə)n/ *noun*. E16.
[ORIGIN A mnemonic of scholastic philosophers: see FERIO.]
LOGIC. The sixth mood of the third syllogistic figure, in which a universal negative major premiss and a particular affirmative minor yield a particular negative conclusion.

ferity /ˈfɛrɪti/ *noun*. M16.
[ORIGIN Old French *ferite* or Latin *feritas*, from *ferus* wild: see -ITY.]
1 The quality or state of being wild or savage; wildness, ferocity. M16.
2 Barbarity; savage cruelty or inhumanity. Now *rare* or *obsolete*. E17.
3 Primitive or barbarous condition. M17.

ferk *verb* var. of FIRK.

ferlie *adjective*, *noun*, & *verb* var. of FERLY.

ferling /ˈfəːlɪŋ/ *noun*. *obsolete* exc. *hist.*
[ORIGIN Old English *fēorþling*, from *fēorþa* FOURTH + -LING[1].]
†**1** A quarter of a penny; a farthing. OE–E18.
2 The fourth part of a piece of land; each of four wards of a borough etc. E17.

ferly /ˈfəːli/ *adjective*, *noun*, & *verb*. Now chiefly *Scot.* & *dial.* Also **ferlie**.
[ORIGIN Old English *fǣrlić*, formed as FEAR *noun*[1] + -LY[1].]
▸ **A** *adjective*. †**1** Sudden, unexpected. OE–LME.
†**2** Dreadful, frightful, terrible. ME–L16.
3 Strange, wondrous; remarkable, surprising. ME.
▸ **B** *noun*. †**1** Wonder, astonishment. ME–L15.
2 Something strange or wonderful, a marvel; a curiosity, a novelty. ME. ▸**b** A strange, unpleasant, or monstrous person or animal. L18.
DAY LEWIS Those ferlies you'll not behold Till the guardians of that valley have crossed Your hand with fairy gold.
▸ **C** *verb intrans.* Wonder, marvel *at*. LME.
R. BURNS They'll.. ferlie at the folk in Lon'on.

fermail /ˈfəːmeɪl/ *noun*. L15.
[ORIGIN Old French & mod. French, (Old French also *-aille*), from medieval Latin *firmaculum*, *ferm-* clasp, brooch, buckle, from *firmare* fix: see FIRM *verb*, -AL[1].]
Chiefly HERALDRY. A buckle, a clasp.

Fermat /ˈfəːmɑː/ *noun*. E19.
[ORIGIN Pierre de *Fermat* (1601–65), French mathematician.]
MATH. Used in *possess.* and *attrib.* to designate concepts introduced by Fermat.
Fermat number any number of the form $2^{2^n} + 1$, where n is a positive integer. **Fermat's last theorem** a conjecture (of which Fermat noted that he had 'a truly wonderful proof'), that if n is an integer greater than 2, $x^n + y^n = z^n$ has no positive integral solutions. **Fermat's theorem** (*a*) a theorem that if p is a prime and a an integer not divisible by p, then $a^{p-1} - 1$ is divisible by p; (*b*) = ***Fermat's last theorem*** above.

fermata /fəːˈmɑːtə/ *noun*. Pl. **-tas**, **-te** /-teɪ/. **L19**.
[ORIGIN Italian.]
MUSIC. (A sign indicating) an unspecified prolongation of a note or rest.

ferment /ˈfəːmɛnt/ *noun*. **LME**.
[ORIGIN Old French & mod. French, or Latin *fermentum* from *fervere* boil: see -MENT.]
1 Leaven, yeast; a fermenting agent; *arch.* an enzyme. **LME**.

> J. GRIGSON To make the ferment, cream the yeast and sugar . . and whisk in the water.

2 = FERMENTATION 1. **E17**. ▸**b** *fig.* Agitation, excitement, tumult. **L17**.

> G. BERKELEY The first ferment of new wine. **b** E. MANNIN He had thought to sleep but the ferment of his thoughts did not permit of it.

ferment /fəˈmɛnt, fəː-/ *verb*. **LME**.
[ORIGIN Old French & mod. French *fermenter* from Latin *fermentare*, from *fermentum*: see FERMENT *noun*.]
1 *verb intrans.* Undergo fermentation. **LME**. ▸**b** *transf.* & *fig.* Become excited or agitated; be exacerbated. **L17**.

> **b** I. COMPTON-BURNETT It is a good thing to speak of things openly . . . Then nothing can ferment and fester underneath.

2 *verb trans.* Subject to fermentation; cause fermentation in. **L15**. ▸**b** *transf.* & *fig.* Excite, stir up; exacerbate, foment. **M17**.

> **b** R. W. EMERSON The Christianity which fermented Europe.

■ **fermentaˈbility** *noun* the quality of being fermentable **L18**. **fermentable** *adjective* able to be fermented **M18**. **fermenter**, **-or** *noun* (**a**) a vessel in which fermentation takes place; (**b**) an organism which causes fermentation: **E20**.

fermental /fəˈmɛnt(ə)l/ *adjective*. **M17**.
[ORIGIN from FERMENT *noun* + -AL[1].]
Pertaining to or of the nature of a ferment or fermentation.

fermentate /ˈfəːmɛnteɪt/ *verb trans.* Now *rare* or *obsolete*. **L16**.
[ORIGIN Latin *fermentat-* pa. ppl stem of *fermentare* FERMENT *verb*: see -ATE[3].]
Cause to ferment; leaven.

fermentation /fəːmɛnˈteɪʃ(ə)n/ *noun*. **LME**.
[ORIGIN Late Latin *fermentatio(n-)* formed as FERMENTATE: see -ATION.]
1 A biochemical process of the nature of that involved in the action of yeast on sugars or dough, involving effervescence, evolution of heat, and chemical breakdown of the substance acted on. **LME**.
alcoholic fermentation, ***bottom fermentation***, ***lactic fermentation***, ***saccharine fermentation***, etc.
2 *fig.* (A state of) excitement or agitation. **M17**.
– COMB.: **fermentation lock** a valve placed on top of a vessel of fermenting wine etc. to enable gas to escape.

fermentative /fəˈmɛntətɪv/ *adjective*. **M17**.
[ORIGIN formed as FERMENTATE + -IVE.]
1 Pertaining to or of the nature of fermentation; developed by fermentation. **M17**.
2 Tending to cause or undergo fermentation. **M17**.

fermentescible /fəːmɛnˈtɛsɪb(ə)l/ *adjective*. **L17**.
[ORIGIN from FERMENT *verb*: see -ESCE, -IBLE.]
Capable of causing or undergoing fermentation.

fermentive /fəˈmɛntɪv/ *adjective*. **M17**.
[ORIGIN from FERMENT *noun*, *verb* + -IVE.]
Tending to produce fermentation.

fermentum /fəˈmɛntəm, fəː-/ *noun*. **E18**.
[ORIGIN medieval Latin use of Latin = yeast: see FERMENT *noun*.]
ROMAN CATHOLIC CHURCH (now *hist.*). A portion of the Eucharistic oblation sent from the papal mass to a neighbouring presbyter.

fermery /ˈfəːm(ə)ri/ *noun*. Also **farm-** /ˈfɑːm-/. **LME**.
[ORIGIN Aphet. from Old French *enfermerie* from medieval Latin *infirmaria* INFIRMARY.]
hist. An infirmary, esp. of a monastery.

Fermi /ˈfəːmi/ *noun*. **E20**.
[ORIGIN Enrico *Fermi* (1901–54), Italian-born physicist.]
▸ **I 1** Used *attrib.* to denote principles and concepts arising from Fermi's work. **E20**.
Fermi energy, **Fermi level** the energy of the Fermi surface. **Fermi statistics** = FERMI–DIRAC STATISTICS. **Fermi surface** a surface in momentum space representing the maximum energy, at absolute zero, of the electrons in a crystal lattice with respect to their direction of motion.
▸ **II 2** (**f-**.) A unit of length used in nuclear physics, equal to 10^{-15} m. **M20**.

Fermi–Dirac statistics /ˌfəːmɪdɪˈrak stəˌtɪstɪks/ *noun phr.* **E20**.
[ORIGIN FERMI + P. A. M. *Dirac* (1902–84), English physicist.]
PHYSICS. A type of quantum statistics, introduced by Fermi and Dirac, used to describe systems of identical particles which obey the exclusion principle.

fermion /ˈfəːmɪɒn/ *noun*. **M20**.
[ORIGIN from FERMI + -ON.]
PHYSICS. A particle that has an antisymmetric wave function, and hence half-integral spin, and can be described by Fermi–Dirac statistics. Cf. BOSON.

fermium /ˈfəːmɪəm/ *noun*. **M20**.
[ORIGIN from FERMI + -IUM.]
A radioactive metallic chemical element of the actinide series, atomic no. 100, which is produced artificially (symbol Fm).

fern /fəːn/ *noun*.
[ORIGIN Old English *fearn* = Middle Dutch *væren* (Dutch *varen*), Old High German *farn* (German *Farn*), from West Germanic.]
Any of the numerous vascular cryptogams of the order Filicopsida, which reproduce by means of spores borne usu. on the underside of the fronds, which are typically pinnately divided (freq. repeatedly); *collect.* a quantity of ferns.
beech fern, ***flowering fern***, ***lady fern***, ***male fern***, ***royal fern***, ***tree fern***, ***walking fern***, etc.
– COMB.: **fern ally** a member of various orders of vascular cryptogams related to the ferns, e.g. the clubmosses, horsetails, and quillworts; **fernbird** a warbler, *Bowdleria punctata*, with spiny tail feathers, found only in New Zealand; ***fernbrake***: see BRAKE *noun*[1] 1; **fern crushing** *NZ* the inhibition of fern growth, chiefly by grazing with cattle etc.; **fern-house** a conservatory in which ferns are grown; **fern-owl** the nightjar; **fernland** (**a**) *NZ* land covered with fern; (**b**) (**F-**) (*Austral.*, *arch.*) New Zealand; **Fernleaf** *slang*. New Zealander; **fern-seed** the supposed seed of the fern, believed before the reproduction of ferns was understood to be invisible and to render the possessor invisible.
■ **fernery** *noun* a place where ferns are grown; a glass case, planter, or conservatory for growing ferns: **M19**. **fernless** *adjective* **L19**. **fernlike** *adjective* resembling (that of) a fern or fern frond **M17**. **ferny** *adjective* of, pertaining to, or resembling, fern; having abundant ferns: **E16**.

fern /fəːn/ *adjective* & *adverb*. Long *obsolete* exc. *dial.* in FERNYEAR.
[ORIGIN Old English *fyrn* cogn. with Old Saxon *furn*, *forn* formerly, Old Norse *forn* (adjective) ancient.]
▸ **A** *adjective*. Former, ancient, past, of old. **OE**.
▸ †**B** *adverb*. Formerly, long ago, a long time. **OE–LME**.

fern /fəːn/ *verb*. **LME**.
[ORIGIN from the noun.]
1 *verb trans.* Cover with fern. *rare*. **LME**.
†**2** *verb intrans.* Feed on fern. **L16–L17**.

†**fernambuck** *noun*. **L16–E18**.
[ORIGIN Alt. of *Pernambuco*, a seaport in Brazil, now Recife.]
= BRAZIL *noun*[1] 1.

ferntickle /ˈfəːntɪk(ə)l/ *noun*. Long *obsolete* exc. *dial.* **LME**.
[ORIGIN Unknown.]
A freckle; a small mark or blemish on the skin.

fernyear /ˈfəːnjɪə/ *noun* & *adverb*. Long *obsolete* exc. *dial.* As noun also **fern year**. **OE**.
[ORIGIN from FERN *adjective* + YEAR *noun*[1].]
▸ **A** *noun*. †**1** A past year; olden times. **OE–L18**.
2 Last year. **LME**.
▸ †**B** *adverb*. In past years; in the course of last year. **OE–E19**.

ferocious /fəˈrəʊʃəs/ *adjective*. **M17**.
[ORIGIN from Latin *feroc-*, *ferox* fierce: see -IOUS.]
1 Savage, bloodthirsty; fierce, destructive. **M17**.

> S. LEWIS The ferocious Colonel bellowed 'What the hell would I do that for?'

2 Indicative of or characterized by ferocity. **E18**.

> C. MACKENZIE His scowl became absolutely ferocious.

3 Very great, extreme; very unpleasant. *colloq.* **L19**.

> M. ALLINGHAM I say, there's a ferocious draught somewhere.

■ **ferociously** *adverb* **L18**. **ferociousness** *noun* **M18**.

ferocity /fəˈrɒsɪti/ *noun*. **M16**.
[ORIGIN Old French & mod. French *férocité* or its source Latin *ferocitas*, formed as FEROCIOUS: see -ITY.]
The quality or state of being ferocious; habitual fierceness or savageness; a ferocious act.

> E. WAUGH The charity of religion tempered her ferocity as an antagonist.

-ferous /f(ə)rəs/ *suffix*. Also (see below) **-iferous**.
[ORIGIN Repr. French *-fère* or Latin *-fer* carrying, bearing (see -FER) + -OUS.]
Forming (usu. with intermediate -I-) adjectives with the sense 'having, containing, or carrying', as ***auriferous***, ***fructiferous***, ***pestiferous***, etc.

ferox /ˈfɛrɒks/ *noun*. **M19**.
[ORIGIN from mod. Latin *Salmo ferox*, lit. 'fierce salmon', former name of the variety.]
More fully ***ferox trout***. A brown trout of a very large variety, occurring in large deep lakes in NW Europe.

ferra *noun* var. of FÉRA.

ferrament /ˈfɛrəm(ə)nt/ *noun*. Also in Latin form **ferramentum** /fɛrəˈmɛntəm/, pl. **-ta** /-tə/. **LME**.
[ORIGIN Old French *ferrement* from Latin *ferramentum* implement of iron, from *ferrum* iron: see -MENT.]
An iron instrument or tool (usu. in *pl.*); in *pl.* *esp.* ironwork on windows etc.

Ferrarese /fɛrəˈriːz/ *noun* & *adjective*. **L16**.
[ORIGIN Italian, from *Ferrara* (see below) + -ESE.]
▸ **A** *noun*. Pl. same, †**-s**. A native or inhabitant of Ferrara, a city in Emilia-Romagna in northern Italy. **L16**.
▸ **B** *adjective*. Of or pertaining to Ferrara. **L19**.

ferrate /ˈfɛreɪt/ *noun*. **M19**.
[ORIGIN from Latin *ferrum* iron + -ATE[1].]
CHEMISTRY. A salt formed (as) from ferric oxide, Fe_2O_3, and a base; a salt containing oxyanions of trivalent iron.

ferredoxin /fɛrɪˈdɒksɪn/ *noun*. **M20**.
[ORIGIN from Latin *fer(rum* iron + REDOX + -IN[1].]
BIOCHEMISTRY. Any of certain iron-containing proteins which participate in intracellular electron-transfer processes.

Ferrel /ˈfɛr(ə)l/ *noun*[1]. **E20**.
[ORIGIN W. *Ferrel* (1817–91), US meteorologist.]
METEOROLOGY. **1** ***Ferrel's law***: that winds are deflected by Coriolis forces, to the right and left in the northern and southern hemispheres respectively. **E20**.
2 ***Ferrel cell***, an atmospheric convection cell in which air rises at latitude 60° N. or S. and sinks at latitude 30°. **E20**.

ferrel *noun*[2] & *verb* var. of FERRULE *noun* & *verb*.

ferreous /ˈfɛrɪəs/ *adjective*. *rare*. **M17**.
[ORIGIN from Latin *ferreus*, from *ferrum* iron: see -EOUS.]
1 Of or pertaining to iron; consisting of or containing iron. **M17**.
2 Like iron in hardness or colour. **E19**.

†**ferrer** *noun*. Also **-our**. **LME–L18**.
[ORIGIN Old French *fereor*, *ferour* (mod. *ferreur*), from medieval Latin *ferrator*, from *ferrare* shoe horses, from Latin *ferrum* iron, (in medieval Latin) horseshoe: see -ER[2].]
A blacksmith; *esp.* a farrier.

ferret /ˈfɛrɪt/ *noun*[1]. **LME**.
[ORIGIN Old French *fuiret*, (also mod.) *furet*, by suffix substitution from Old French *fu(i)ron*, from Proto-Romance, from late Latin *furo*, *furon-* thief, ferret, from Latin *fur* thief: see -ET[1].]
1 A half-tamed variety of polecat, freq. with white or pale fur, kept for driving rabbits from burrows, killing rats, etc. **LME**.
black-footed ferret a rare mammal, *Mustela nigripes*, resembling the polecat and native to N. American prairies.
2 *fig.* A detective; a person who searches assiduously. **E17**.
■ **ferrety** *adjective* resembling (that of) a ferret **E19**.

ferret /ˈfɛrɪt/ *noun*[2]. **L16**.
[ORIGIN Prob. from Italian *fioretti* floss silk, pl. of *fioretto* dim. of *fiore* FLOWER *noun*.]
†**1** ***ferret silk***, floss silk. **L16–E17**.
2 A stout cotton or silk tape. *arch.* **M17**.

ferret /ˈfɛrɪt/ *verb*. **LME**.
[ORIGIN from FERRET *noun*[1]. Cf. French *fureter*.]
1 a *verb intrans.* Hunt with ferrets. Chiefly as ***ferreting*** *verbal noun*. **LME**. ▸**b** *verb trans.* Clear (a burrow etc.) by means of a ferret. **L15**.

> **b** R. JEFFERIES Even if the burrows be ferreted, in a few weeks this great hole shows signs of fresh inhabitants.

2 *verb trans.* Drive out (as) with a ferret. (Foll. by *about*, *away*, *forth*, *off*, *out*.) **L16**.

> D. H. LAWRENCE Ferretted the rats from under the barn.

3 a *verb trans.* Bother, worry, (a person); hunt or search *out* (also foll. by *up*). **L16**. ▸**b** *verb intrans.* Worry, be concerned (*about*); search or rummage about. **L16**.

> **a** L. DEIGHTON Does he sniff round to see what he can ferret out? **b** A. SILLITOE I'll just nip round to see your dad, and tell him you're here, in case he should ferret about you. E. BOWEN Eva . . ferreted under a gauntlet, laid bare her wristwatch.

■ **ferreter** *noun* **ME**.

ferreting /ˈfɛrɪtɪŋ/ *noun*. *arch.* **L17**.
[ORIGIN from FERRET *noun*[2] + -ING[1].]
= FERRET *noun*[2].

ferri- /ˈfɛri/ *combining form*.
[ORIGIN from Latin *ferrum* iron: see -I-.]
Of or containing iron, esp. in the ferric (trivalent) state. Cf. FERRO-.
■ **ferricrete** *noun* (GEOLOGY) a breccia or conglomerate cemented by iron compounds **E20**. **ferricyˈanic** *adjective* (CHEMISTRY): ***ferricyanic acid***, an unstable brown solid acid, $H_3Fe(CN)_6$ **M19**. **ferriˈcyanide** *noun* (CHEMISTRY) a salt containing the anion $Fe(CN)_6^{3-}$ **M19**.

ferriage /ˈfɛrɪɪdʒ/ *noun*. Also **ferryage**. **ME**.
[ORIGIN from FERRY *noun*, *verb* + -AGE.]
1 The fare paid for the use of a ferry. **ME**.
2 The action or means of ferrying a person or thing across water. **LME**.

ferrian /ˈfɛrɪən/ *adjective*. **M20**.
[ORIGIN from FERRIAGE + -AN.]
MINERALOGY. Having a constituent element partly replaced by ferric iron. Cf. FERROAN.

ferric /ˈfɛrɪk/ *adjective*. **L18**.
[ORIGIN from Latin *ferrum* iron + -IC.]
1 *gen.* Of, pertaining to, or containing iron. **L18**.
2 CHEMISTRY. Of or containing iron in the trivalent state. Cf. FERROUS. **M19**.
ferric acid a hypothetical parent acid of the ferrates.

ferrier /ˈfɛrɪə/ *noun*. Now *rare*. Also **ferryer**. **ME**.
[ORIGIN from FERRY *verb* + -ER[1].]
A person who operates a ferry, a ferryman.

ferriferous /fɛˈrɪf(ə)rəs/ *adjective*. **E19**.
[ORIGIN from Latin *ferrum* iron + -FEROUS.]
Producing or yielding iron.

F

F

ferrimagnetism /fɛrɪˈmagnɪtɪz(ə)m/ *noun*. M20.
[ORIGIN from FERRI- + MAGNETISM.]
A form of magnetism resembling but weaker than ferromagnetism, that is associated with antiparallel alignment of neighbouring atoms or ions having unequal magnetic moments.
■ **ferrimagnet** *noun* a ferrimagnetic solid M20. **ferrimagˈnetic** *adjective & noun* (*a*) *adjective* pertaining to or exhibiting ferrimagnetism; (*b*) *noun* = FERRIMAGNET: M20.

Ferris wheel /ˈfɛrɪs wiːl/ *noun phr*. L19.
[ORIGIN G. W. G. *Ferris* (1859–96), Amer. engineer + WHEEL *noun*.]
A giant, vertical revolving wheel with passenger cars on its periphery, used at amusement parks etc.

ferrite /ˈfɛrʌɪt/ *noun*. M19.
[ORIGIN from Latin *ferrum* iron + -ITE[1].]
1 A mixed oxide of ferric iron and another metal or metals; *spec.* a compound of formula MFe_2O_4 (where M is a divalent metal), many examples of which have magnetic and electrical properties which make them suitable for use in high-frequency electrical components. M19.
2 METALLURGY. An allotrope of pure iron which has a body-centred cubic crystal structure and is present as a solid solvent in low-carbon steels. L19.
3 PETROGRAPHY. A microscopic particle of amorphous iron oxide present in a rock. L19.
■ **ferritic** /fəˈrɪtɪk/ *adjective* (METALLURGY) containing, composed of, or characteristic of ferrite E20.

ferritin /ˈfɛrɪtɪn/ *noun*. M20.
[ORIGIN from FERRI- + -*t*- + -IN[1].]
BIOCHEMISTRY. A water-soluble protein containing ferric iron, involved in storing iron in mammalian metabolism.

ferro- /ˈfɛrəʊ/ *combining form*.
[ORIGIN from Latin *ferrum* iron: see -O-.]
Of, connected with, or containing iron; (in alloy names) containing iron and (another metal), as ***ferrochromium***, ***ferromanganese***, ***ferrovanadium***, etc.; CHEMISTRY of iron in the ferrous (divalent) state (cf. FERRI-).
■ **ferro-ˈalloy** *noun* an alloy of iron and one or more other metals, esp. as used in metallurgical processing E20. **ferroˈconcrete** *noun & adjective* (of) reinforced concrete E20. **ferrocyˈanic** *adjective* (CHEMISTRY): ***ferrocyanic acid***, a white solid acid, $H_4Fe(CN)_6$ E19. **ferroˈcyanide** *noun* (CHEMISTRY) a salt containing the anion $Fe(CN)_6^{4-}$ E19. **ferroˈprussiate** *noun* (chiefly PHOTOGRAPHY) = FERRICYANIDE; *attrib.* designating a blueprint process involving potassium ferricyanide and ferric ammonium citrate: L19.

ferroan /ˈfɛrəʊən, fəˈrəʊən/ *adjective*. M20.
[ORIGIN from FERRO- + -AN.]
MINERALOGY. Having a constituent element partly replaced by ferrous iron. Cf. FERRIAN.

ferrocene /ˈfɛrəsiːn/ *noun*. M20.
[ORIGIN from FERRO- + -*cene* from *cyclopentadiene*.]
CHEMISTRY. An orange crystalline compound, $Fe(C_5H_5)_2$, having a molecule in which two parallel planar aromatic cyclopentadiene ligands enclose an iron atom in a sandwich structure.

ferroelectric /ˌfɛrəʊɪˈlɛktrɪk/ *adjective & noun*. M20.
[ORIGIN from FERRO- + ELECTRIC.]
PHYSICS. ▸**A** *adjective*. Of, relating to, or having the property of exhibiting a permanent electric polarization and hysteresis when subjected to an electric field. M20.
▸**B** *noun*. A ferroelectric body or substance. M20.
■ **ferroelectrically** *adverb* M20. **ferroelecˈtricity** *noun* the quality of being ferroelectric; the phenomena exhibited by ferroelectric substances M20.

ferromagnesian /ˌfɛrə(ʊ)magˈniːʒ(ə)n, -zjən/ *adjective*. L19.
[ORIGIN from FERRO- + MAGNESIAN.]
Of a rock or mineral: containing iron and magnesium as major components.

ferromagnetic /ˌfɛrə(ʊ)magˈnɛtɪk/ *adjective & noun*. M19.
[ORIGIN from FERRO- + MAGNETIC.]
▸**A** *adjective*. †**1** = PARAMAGNETIC *adjective* 1. M–L19.
2 Of, pertaining to, or exhibiting ferromagnetism. L19.
▸**B** *noun*. A ferromagnetic (orig. = paramagnetic) body or substance. M19.
■ **ferroˈmagnet** *noun* a ferromagnetic body or substance M20. **ferromagnetically** *adverb* M20.

ferromagnetism /fɛrə(ʊ)ˈmagnɪtɪz(ə)m/ *noun*. M19.
[ORIGIN from FERRO- + MAGNETISM.]
Orig., paramagnetism. Now, the form of magnetism shown by metallic iron, cobalt, and nickel, which is characterized by a large magnetic permeability and the phenomenon of hysteresis, and is associated with parallel alignment of the magnetic moments of neighbouring atoms.

ferronnerie /fɛrɔnri, fɛˈrɒnəriː/ *noun & adjective*. Also ***ferronerie***. E20.
[ORIGIN French = iron work, wrought iron.]
(Designating) decoration with a motif of arabesques and scrolls, used on pottery etc.

ferronnière /fɛrɔnjɛːr (*pl. same*); fɛˌrɒnɪˈɛː/. *noun*. Also ***ferronière***. M19.
[ORIGIN French = frontlet, coronet worn on the forehead: after Leonardo da Vinci's portrait *La belle ferronnière*.]
An ornamental chain with a central jewel, worn around the head.

ferrosoferric /fɛrəʊsə(ʊ)ˈfɛrɪk/ *adjective*. M19.
[ORIGIN from mod. Latin *ferrosus* ferrous + -O- + FERRIC.]
CHEMISTRY. Of both ferrous and ferric iron. Only in ***ferrosoferric oxide***, magnetite, magnetic iron oxide, Fe_3O_4.

†**ferrour** *noun* var. of FERRER *noun*.

ferrous /ˈfɛrəs/ *adjective*. M19.
[ORIGIN from Latin *ferrum* iron + -OUS.]
1 CHEMISTRY. Of or containing iron in the divalent state. Cf. FERRIC 2. M19.
2 Of iron; (chiefly of an alloy) containing iron in significant quantities. Orig. & freq. in ***non-ferrous***. L19.

ferrugineous /fɛrʊˈdʒɪnɪəs/ *adjective*. M17.
[ORIGIN from Latin *ferrugineus* (see FERRUGINOUS) + -OUS: see -EOUS.]
= FERRUGINOUS.

ferruginous /fɛˈruːdʒɪnəs/ *adjective*. M17.
[ORIGIN from Latin *ferrugo*, *-gin-* iron rust, dark red (from *ferrum* iron) + -OUS. Cf. French *ferrugineux*.]
1 Of the nature of or containing iron or its compounds (orig. iron rust). M17.
2 Of the colour of rust; reddish-brown. M17.
ferruginous duck a diving duck, *Aythya nyroca*, with predominantly dark rust-brown plumage; also called ***white-eyed pochard***.

ferrule /ˈfɛruːl, ˈfɛr(ə)l/ *noun & verb*. Also **ferrel** /ˈfɛr(ə)l/ (verb infl. **-ll-**). E17.
[ORIGIN Alt. (prob. by assim. to Latin *ferrum* iron, and -ULE) of earlier VERREL. Cf. VIRL.]
▸**A** *noun*. A (usu.) metal ring or cap for strengthening, *esp.* one for preventing the end of a stick, tube, etc., from splitting or wearing. E17.

> H. ALLEN The ferrule of a cane was heard clicking on the mosaics in the vestibule.

▸**B** *verb trans*. Provide or fit with a ferrule. L17.
■ **ferruled** *adjective* provided with a ferrule M19.

ferruminate /fɛˈruːmɪneɪt/ *verb trans*. Long *rare* or *obsolete*. E17.
[ORIGIN Latin *ferruminat-* pa. ppl stem of *ferruminare* to cement, from *ferrumen*, *-min-* cement, from *ferrum* iron: see -ATE[3].]
Cement, solder, unite.
■ **ferrumiˈnation** *noun* E17.

ferry /ˈfɛri/ *noun*. ME.
[ORIGIN Old Norse *ferja* ferryboat, or *ferju* as in *ferjukarl*, *-maðr* ferryman, *ferjuskip* ferryboat = Dutch *veer*, Middle High German *vër(e)* (German *Fähre*), from Germanic, from base of FARE *verb*.]
1 A passage or place where a boat etc. regularly transports passengers, vehicles, or goods across a stretch of water. ME.
2 A boat etc. for transporting passengers, vehicles, or goods across a stretch of water. ME. ▸**b** A module for transporting an astronaut from the surface of a planet etc. to the spacecraft. M20.
3 A service for transporting passengers, vehicles, or goods, across a stretch of water by boat etc.; LAW the right to operate and to levy a toll for such a service. E18. ▸**b** A service for delivering aircraft to the user by flying, esp. across a sea or a continent. E20. ▸**c** A service carrying passengers and goods usu. short distances by air. M20.
– COMB.: **ferryboat** = sense 2 above; **ferry-bridge** a type of ferryboat in which a train is transported across a river or bay; **ferryman** a person who keeps or looks after a ferry.

ferry /ˈfɛri/ *verb*.
[ORIGIN Old English *ferian* reinforced by forms from cognate Old Norse *ferja* = Old Saxon *ferian*, Old High German *ferren* (Middle High German *vern*), Gothic *farjan*, from Germanic, from base of FARE *verb*.]
1 *verb trans*. Carry, transport, take from one place to another, esp. across a stretch of water (formerly also, the sea) by boat. (Foll. by *over*, *across*.) OE. ▸**b** Work (a boat) across a stretch of water. L18. ▸**c** Fly (an aircraft) to a delivery point. E20.

> R. CAMPBELL He ferried the stone across on rafts. M. MUGGERIDGE They would ferry my father about from meeting to meeting.

2 *verb intrans*. Go across water by boat. Formerly also, go, depart. (Foll. by *over*.) OE.

> R. BURNS When death's dark stream I ferry o'er.

■ **ferryable** *adjective* (*rare*) (of a river etc.) that may be crossed in a boat etc. L19.

ferryage *noun* var. of FERRIAGE.

ferryer *noun* var. of FERRIER.

fers de lance *noun pl.* see FER DE LANCE.

fers-de-moline *noun* pl. of FER-DE-MOLINE.

fertile /ˈfəːtʌɪl/ *adjective*. LME.
[ORIGIN French from Latin *fertilis*, from *ferre* to bear: see -ILE.]
1 (Of soil) rich in the materials needed to support vegetation; fruitful; (of an animal or plant) able to produce offspring; (of a seed or egg) able to develop into a new individual; *fig.* (of the mind) inventive, productive of ideas. LME. ▸**b** DEMOGRAPHY. Productive of (live-born) children. Cf. FECUND 3. E20. ▸**c** NUCLEAR PHYSICS. Able to be transformed into a fissile isotope by the capture of a neutron. M20.

> A. J. TOYNBEE The soil . . was fertile and needed only water to make it productive. A. BEVAN The sense of injustice arising from gross inequalities . . is a fertile source of discontent. *Lancet* The number of children that a fertile couple have depends on . . the efficiency of the contraceptive methods they use.

Fertile Crescent a semicircular region stretching from the eastern Mediterranean to the Persian Gulf.
2 Tending to assist productiveness. L16.
†**3** Abundant. E–M17.
■ **fertilely** *adverb* L16. **fertileness** *noun* L16.

fertilisation *noun*, **fertilise** *verb*, **fertiliser** *noun* vars. of FERTILIZATION etc.

fertility /fəˈtɪlɪti/ *noun*. LME.
[ORIGIN French *fertilité* from Latin *fertilitas*, from *fertilis* FERTILE: see -ITY.]
1 The quality of being fertile; fruitfulness; productiveness. LME.
2 In *pl.* Productive powers. Now *rare*. E17.
3 DEMOGRAPHY. Productiveness; the actual number of (live) births. Cf. FECUNDITY 3. M19.

fertilization /ˌfəːtɪlʌɪˈzeɪʃ(ə)n/ *noun*. Also **-isation**. M19.
[ORIGIN from FERTILIZE + -ATION.]
The action or process of fertilizing.
double fertilization: see DOUBLE *adjective & adverb*.

fertilize /ˈfəːtɪlʌɪz/ *verb trans*. Also **-ise**. M17.
[ORIGIN from FERTILE + -IZE. Cf. French *fertiliser*.]
1 Make (esp. soil) fertile or productive. M17.

> H. ACTON The fortunes of England depended on the use of natural manure in fertilizing the soil.

2 BIOLOGY. Cause (a female individual, plant, egg, etc.) to develop a new individual by the introduction of male reproductive material. M19.

> S. SPENDER Fertilized another master's wife and left the school under a pregnant cloud.

■ **fertilizable** *adjective* M19.

fertilizer /ˈfəːtɪlʌɪzə/ *noun*. Also **-iser**. M17.
[ORIGIN from FERTILIZE + -ER[1].]
1 A substance which fertilizes soil etc.; manure, *esp.* an artificially prepared substance containing nitrogen, phosphorus, or potassium added to soil in order to fertilize it. M17.
2 An agent of fertilization in plants. M19.

ferula /ˈfɛrjʊlə/ *noun*. LME.
[ORIGIN Latin = giant fennel, rod.]
1 An umbelliferous plant of the genus *Ferula*; giant fennel. LME.
2 A long splint. Now *rare* or *obsolete*. LME.
3 = FERULE 2. L16.
■ **feruˈlaceous** *adjective* (now *rare*) resembling the giant fennel M17.

ferule /ˈfɛruːl/ *noun & verb trans*. LME.
[ORIGIN Latin FERULA.]
▸**A** *noun*. **1** = FERULA 1. Now *rare* or *obsolete*. LME.
2 A rod, cane, or other instrument of punishment; *esp.* a flat ruler with a widened end. L16.
▸**B** *verb trans*. Beat or strike with a ferule. L16.

fervency /ˈfəːv(ə)nsi/ *noun*. L15.
[ORIGIN from Old French *fervence* or its source late Latin *ferventia*, from *fervent-* pres. ppl stem of *fervere*: see FERVENT, -ENCY.]
1 Intensity of heat. Now *rare*. L15.
2 Intensity of feeling; ardour; zeal. M16.
■ Earlier †**fervence** *noun* LME–L16.

fervent /ˈfəːv(ə)nt/ *adjective*. ME.
[ORIGIN Old French from Latin *fervent-* pres. ppl stem of *fervere* boil, glow: see -ENT.]
1 Of a person, personal feeling, etc.: ardent, intense; earnest. ME. ▸**b** (Of a sea, storm, uproar, etc.) violent; (of a pestilence) raging. Now *rare* or *obsolete*. LME.

> C. P. SNOW His interest was as fervent, as vivid and factual, as it must have been when he was a young man. D. M. THOMAS Madame Serebryakova even claimed to be a fervent admirer of Frau Erdman's voice.

2 Hot, burning, boiling. Formerly also in MEDICINE (of a bodily humour or a disease) hot, violent; (of a medicine) of violent effect. LME. ▸†**b** Of cold: severe, intense. LME–M17.
■ **fervently** *adverb* †(*a*) burningly, severely; (*b*) ardently, intensely: LME. **ferventness** *noun* (now *rare*) LME.

fervid /ˈfəːvɪd/ *adjective*. L16.
[ORIGIN Latin *fervidus*, from *fervere*: see FERVENT, -ID[1].]
1 Burning, glowing, hot. Now *poet.* L16.

> QUILLER-COUCH It was so pleasing to find a breeze up there allaying the fervid afternoon.

2 Intense; impassioned. M17.

> P. G. WODEHOUSE In a situation which might have stimulated another to fervid speech, George Pennicut contented himself with saying 'Goo!'

■ **fervidly** *adverb* M19. **fervidness** *noun* L17.

fervor *noun* see FERVOUR.

fervorous /ˈfəːv(ə)rəs/ *adjective*. Now *rare*. E17.
[ORIGIN from FERVID + -OUS.]
Full of fervour.

fervour /ˈfəːvə/ *noun*. Also ***-or**. ME.
[ORIGIN Old French *fervo(u)r* (mod. *ferveur*) from Latin *fervor*, from *fervere*: see FERVENT, -OR.]
1 (An instance of) intense feeling, ardour, passion, zeal. ME.
E. F. BENSON Her heart had remained, indeed, most inconveniently young, its sympathies were all with youth and its fervours. B. PLAIN A sudden brightness came into the little face, a fervor so glowing.
2 (A condition of) intense heat. Formerly also, seething or turbulence in water. LME.
SHELLEY Those deserts.. whose.. fervors scarce allowed A bird to live.

fes *noun* see FEIS.

Fesapo /ˈfɛsəpəʊ/ *noun*. E19.
[ORIGIN A mnemonic of scholastic philosophers, E indicating a universal negative proposition, A a universal affirmative proposition, and O a particular negative proposition.]
LOGIC. The fourth mood of the fourth syllogistic figure, in which a particular negative conclusion is drawn from a universal negative major premiss and a universal affirmative minor premiss. Cf. FAPESMO.

Fescennine /ˈfɛsɪnʌɪn/ *adjective*. E17.
[ORIGIN Latin *Fescenninus* pertaining to Fescennia: see below, -INE¹.]
Of or pertaining to Fescennia in Etruria, known for scurrilous dialogues in verse; licentious, obscene, scurrilous.

fescue /ˈfɛskjuː/ *noun & verb*. Also (earlier) †**festu**. LME.
[ORIGIN Old French *festu* (mod. *fétu*) from Proto-Romance, from Latin *festuca* stalk, stem, straw.]
▸ **A** *noun*. †**1** A straw, a twig; something small or trivial. LME–E17.
2 A small stick etc. for pointing out the letters to children learning to read; a pointer. Now *rare*. E16.
3 Any of various perennial freq. wiry and tufted grasses constituting the genus *Festuca*; any of several slender annual grasses constituting the genus *Vulpia*. Also ***fescue-grass***. M18.
Chewings fescue, ***rat's tail fescue***, ***red fescue***, ***sheep's fescue***, etc.
▸ †**B** *verb trans*. Direct or assist in reading, using a fescue. M17–M18.

fess /fɛs/ *noun*¹. Also **fesse**. L15.
[ORIGIN Old French *fesse* alt. of *faisse* from Latin FASCIA.]
HERALDRY. An ordinary consisting of a broad horizontal stripe across the middle of the field, usu. occupying one-third of the shield.
in fess (of more than one charge) in the position of a fess, arranged horizontally.
– COMB.: **fess point** a point at the exact centre of a shield.

fess *noun*² see FEIS.

fess /fɛs/ *verb intrans. colloq.* Also **'fess**. E19.
[ORIGIN Aphet. from CONFESS.]
Confess, own *up*.
L. M. ALCOTT I shall tell them myself.. and "fess' to mother how silly I've been. J. BIRMINGHAM Nobody will fess up to it now, so I guess that link is going to have to stay lost.

fesse *noun* var. of FESS *noun*¹.

fest /fɛst/ *noun*. Orig. *US*. M19.
[ORIGIN German = festival.]
A festival, a special occasion. Chiefly as 2nd elem. of comb., as ***filmfest***, ***songfest***. Cf. GABFEST.

festa /ˈfɛstə/ *noun*. E19.
[ORIGIN Italian from Latin: see FEAST *noun*.]
In Italy, a feast, a festival, a holy day.

festal /ˈfɛst(ə)l/ *adjective & noun*. L15.
[ORIGIN Old French from late Latin *festalis*, from *festum*, (pl.) *festa*: see FEAST *noun*, -AL¹.]
▸ **A** *adjective*. Of, pertaining to, or given up to, a feast or festivity; in holiday mood, joyous. L15.
DE QUINCEY The ball-room wore an elegant and festal air.
▸ **B** *noun*. A feast, a festivity. *poet*. E19.
– NOTE: Rare before M18.
■ **festally** *adverb* M19.

fester /ˈfɛstə/ *noun*. Now *rare*. LME.
[ORIGIN Old French *festre* from Latin FISTULA.]
1 Orig. = FISTULA. Later, a sore, an ulcer; a suppurating place. LME.
†**2** A cicatrice or scar (over a festering wound). L15–M16.

fester /ˈfɛstə/ *verb*. LME.
[ORIGIN from the noun, or Old French *festrir*, formed as FESTER *noun*.]
1 *verb intrans*. Of a wound or sore: (orig.) gather or produce pus, ulcerate; (now usu.) suppurate. LME. ▸**b** Of poison etc.: infect surrounding parts, rankle. Foll. by *into*: become by festering. Now chiefly *fig*. of grief etc. LME.
C. ISHERWOOD I had cut it on a piece of tin.. and now it had suddenly festered and was full of poison. **b** H. WOTTON Ancient quarrels.. festering in his breast. BURKE Smitten pride smarting from its wounds, festers into new rancour.
2 *verb intrans*. Putrefy, rot. LME.
SHAKES. *Sonn*. Lilies that fester smell far worse than weeds.
3 *verb trans*. Cause to ulcerate or suppurate; *fig*. allow (malice etc.) to rankle. LME. ▸†**b** Cicatrize. LME–M16.
J. MARSTON I.. festred rankling malice in my breast. R. ESTCOURT Take heed, lest your ungentle Hand shou'd fester what you mean to heal.
■ **festerment** *noun* (*rare*) the process or state of festering; *dial*. something that festers: M19.

†**festial** *noun*. L15–E18.
[ORIGIN medieval Latin *festialis* perh. error for *festivalis*: see FESTIVAL.]
= FESTIVAL *noun* 1.

festilogy /fɛˈstɪlədʒi/ *noun*. Also **-ology** /-ɒlədʒi/. M19.
[ORIGIN medieval Latin *festilogium*, from Latin *festum* feast: see -LOGY.]
A treatise on ecclesiastical festivals.

†**festin** *noun*. Also **-ine**. E16–M19.
[ORIGIN French, Spanish *festin*, Italian FESTINO *noun*².]
= FESTINO *noun*².

festinate /ˈfɛstɪnət, -eɪt/ *adjective*. Now *rare*. E17.
[ORIGIN Latin *festinatus* pa. pple, formed as FESTINATE *verb*: see -ATE².]
Hasty, hurried.
■ **festinately** *adverb* L16.

festinate /ˈfɛstɪneɪt/ *verb trans. & †intrans*. *rare*. L16.
[ORIGIN Latin *festinat-* pa. ppl stem of *festinare* hurry: see -ATE³.]
Hasten, speed.

festination /fɛstɪˈneɪʃ(ə)n/ *noun*. M16.
[ORIGIN Latin *festinatio(n-)*, formed as FESTINATE *verb*: see -ATION.]
1 Haste, speed. Now *rare*. M16.
2 *MEDICINE*. A gait with short fast tottering steps that occurs in some cases of Parkinson's disease. L19.

†**festine** *noun* var. of FESTIN.

Festino /fɛˈstʌɪnəʊ/ *noun*¹. M16.
[ORIGIN A mnemonic of scholastic philosophers, E indicating a universal negative proposition, I a particular affirmative proposition, and O a particular negative proposition.]
LOGIC. The third mood of the second syllogistic figure, in which a particular negative conclusion is drawn from a universal negative major premiss and a particular affirmative minor premiss.

†**festino** *noun*². Pl. **-o(e)s**. M18–M19.
[ORIGIN Italian, dim. of FESTA.]
An entertainment, a feast.

festival /ˈfɛstɪv(ə)l/ *adjective & noun*. LME.
[ORIGIN Old French from medieval Latin *festivalis*, formed as FESTIVE: see -AL¹.]
▸ **A** *adjective*. **1** Of or befitting a feast or feast day. Now only *attrib*. & usu. taken as noun. LME.
†**2** Joyful, merry. L16–L17.
▸ **B** *noun*. †**1** A book containing an exhortation for each feast day. L15–E17.
2 A (time of) festive celebration or merrymaking; a feast day. L16. ▸**b** A (usu. periodic) series of theatrical or musical performances, films, etc., of special importance. E19.
B. TARKINGTON People were gayest on New Year's Day; they made it a true festival. **b** *Publishers Weekly* The annual Shakespeare festival at Stratford-on-Avon.
3 = FÊTE *noun* 1b. *US*. M19.

festive /ˈfɛstɪv/ *adjective*. M17.
[ORIGIN Latin *festivus*, from *festum*, (pl.) *festa*: see FEAST *noun*, -IVE.]
1 Of or befitting a feast or festival; joyous, cheerful. M17.
G. HUNTINGTON Order something festive, perhaps champagne.
the festive season *spec*. the period around Christmas.
2 Of a person: fond of feasting, jovial; (of a place, season, etc.) devoted to a feast or feasting. M18.
■ **festively** *adverb* E19.

festivity /fɛˈstɪvɪti/ *noun*. LME.
[ORIGIN Old French & mod. French *festivité* or Latin *festivitas*, formed as FESTIVE: see -ITY.]
1 A festive celebration, a feast; (an occasion of) rejoicing or gaiety. In *pl*., festive proceedings. LME.
E. SUMMERSKILL Weddings, golden weddings, funerals, and other festivities.
†**2** Festive quality or condition; suitability for a festival; cheerfulness. M16–L17.
■ **festiveness** *noun* M20. **festivous** *adjective* (now *rare* or *obsolete*) = FESTIVE M17.

festology *noun* var. of FESTILOGY.

festoon /fɛˈstuːn/ *noun*. M17.
[ORIGIN French *feston* from Italian *festone* festal ornament, from Latin *festa*: see FEAST *noun*, -OON.]
1 A chain or garland of flowers, leaves, ribbons, drapery, etc. (suspended in a curve between two points). M17. ▸**b** *transf*. Something hanging like a festoon. M19.
J. RUSKIN The curved rock from which the waterfall leaps into its calm festoons.
festoon blind a window blind consisting of vertical rows of horizontally gathered fabric that may be drawn up into a series of ruches.
2 *ARCHITECTURE*. A carved or moulded ornament representing a festoon. M17.
3 A small brown moth of oak woods, *Apoda limacodes*. L19.
■ **festoonery** *noun* something arranged in festoons, arrangement in festoons M19.

festoon /fɛˈstuːn/ *verb trans*. L18.
[ORIGIN from the noun.]
Adorn (as) with or form into festoons; hang up in festoons; cover, drape.
G. SANTAYANA A gold watch-chain heavily festooning a big paunch. T. GUNN Ivy-festooned statues of Greek gods.

Festschrift /ˈfɛs(t)ʃrɪft/ *noun*. Also **f-**. Pl. **-en** /-ən/, **-s**. E20.
[ORIGIN German, lit. 'celebration-writing'.]
A volume of writings collected in honour of a scholar, freq. presented to mark an occasion in his or her life.

†**festu** *noun* see FESCUE.

†**festual** *adjective*. E16–M19.
[ORIGIN from Latin *festum*, (pl.) *festa* FEAST *noun* after *spiritual* etc.]
Festal, festival.

festucine /ˈfɛstjʊsʌɪn/ *adjective*. *rare*. M17.
[ORIGIN from Latin *festuca* stalk, straw + -INE¹.]
Straw-coloured.

FET *abbreviation*.
ELECTRONICS. Field-effect transistor.

fet /fɛt/ *verb trans. obsolete* exc. *dial*. Infl. **-tt-**. Pa. t. & pple **fet**.
[ORIGIN Old English *fetian*: see FETCH *verb*.]
Fetch (in various senses).

feta /ˈfɛtə/ *noun*. Also **fetta**. M20.
[ORIGIN mod. Greek *pheta*.]
A white salty Greek ewe's-milk cheese.

fetal /ˈfiːt(ə)l/ *adjective*. Also **foet-**. E19.
[ORIGIN from FETUS + -AL¹.]
Of, pertaining to, or of the nature of a fetus; in the condition of a fetus.
fetal alcohol syndrome *MEDICINE* a congenital syndrome associated with excessive consumption of alcohol by the mother during pregnancy, and characterized by retardation of mental development and of physical growth, microcephaly, and a characteristic pattern of facial features (abbreviation ***FAS***). **fetal distress** evidence of deteriorating condition of a fetus during labour.

fetalization /fiːt(ə)lʌɪˈzeɪʃ(ə)n/ *noun*. Also **foet-**, **-isation**. M20.
[ORIGIN from FETAL + -IZATION.]
The retention into adult life of bodily characteristics which earlier in evolutionary history were only infantile.
■ **'fetalized** *adjective* characterized by or manifesting fetalization M20.

fetation /fiːˈteɪʃ(ə)n/ *noun*. Also **foet-**. M17.
[ORIGIN from Latin *fetat-* pa. ppl stem of *fetare* (*foet-*) bring forth, breed, from *fetus*: see FETUS, -ATION.]
The formation of a fetus or embryo.

fetch /fɛtʃ/ *noun*¹. M16.
[ORIGIN from the verb.]
1 An act of fetching, a reach, a sweep, (*arch*.); *spec*. a sheepdog's bringing of sheep back to the handler by the most direct route (the third stage of sheepdog trials). M16.
J. C. SHAIRP A great fetch of imaginative power.
2 A contrivance, a stratagem, a trick. Now *arch*. *rare*. M16.
H. BUSHNELL No ingenious fetches of argument.
3 *NAUTICAL*. **a** An act of tacking. Now *rare*. M16. ▸**b** The line of a continuous stretch of water from point to point, e.g. of a bay or of open sea, or traversed by wind or waves. M19.
4 An indrawn or caught breath; a sigh. *dial*. M19.

fetch /fɛtʃ/ *noun*². L17.
[ORIGIN Unknown.]
The apparition or double of a (usu. living) person.
M. LEADBEATER She believed she had seen his fetch as a forerunner of his death.

†**fetch** *noun*³ see VETCH.

fetch /fɛtʃ/ *verb*.
[ORIGIN Old English *feċċ(e)an* alt. of *fetian* FET *verb*, prob. rel. to Old English *fatian*, Old Frisian *fatia*, Old High German *fazzōn* (German *fassen*) grasp, perh. orig. 'put in a vessel', from base of FAT *noun*¹, VAT *noun*.]
1 *verb trans. & intrans*. Go in search of and bring back (a person or thing); collect (a person or thing). OE.
R. L. STEVENSON 'Rum,' he repeated, 'Rum! rum!' I ran to fetch it. M. DRABBLE Do let me come and fetch you, because look, it's raining outside. E. ALBEE Fetch,.. puppy, go fetch.
deep-fetched: see DEEP *adverb*. FAR-FETCHED.
†**2** *verb trans*. Obtain, get, come by. ME–M17. ▸**b** *CRICKET*. Score (a specified number of runs). M18–E20.
H. LATIMER Christ sent this man unto the priest to fetch there his absolution.
3 *verb trans*. Cause to come; succeed in bringing; elicit. LME.
Y. MENUHIN They could fetch such extraordinary sounds from primitive instruments.

F

4 *verb trans.* Deal (a blow); make (a stroke). Usu. with indirect obj. Now *colloq.* LME. ▸**b** Strike (a person). Now chiefly *US.* M16.

P. BARKER She fetched me such a swipe across the face.

5 *verb trans.* Derive, deduce, infer, borrow. Now *rare* or *obsolete.* M16.

E. STILLINGFLEET Many great Families . . fetched their pedegree from the Gods.

6 *verb trans.* Draw (breath); heave (a sigh); utter (a groan etc.). Now *arch. rare.* M16.

T. BEDDOES The child . . was still fetching deep sobs.

7 *verb trans.* Make, perform, (a movement); take (a walk etc.). *arch.* exc. *US.* M16.

THACKERAY Mr. Warrington . . was gone to fetch a walk in the moonlight.

8 Orig. NAUTICAL. ▸**a** *verb trans.* Arrive at, reach; come up with (a boat etc.). M16. ▸**b** *verb intrans.* Take a course; bring a boat etc. up. L16. ▸†**c** *verb trans.* Get into (the wake of a boat etc., the course of the wind). E17–M18.

a B. STOKER With the wind blowing from its present quarter . . she should fetch the entrance of the harbour.

9 *verb trans.* Of a commodity: realize, sell for (a price). Formerly also (of money) purchase (a commodity). E17.

D. J. ENRIGHT Artichokes fetch a good price in France.

10 *verb trans.* Move to interest, admiration, or delight; attract. *colloq.* E17.

J. K. JEROME To say that the child has got its father's nose . . fetches the parents.

– PHRASES, & WITH ADVERBS & PREPOSITIONS IN SPECIALIZED SENSES: **fetch about** (*a*) (esp. NAUTICAL) make a movement, a turn, etc.; (*b*) swing round (the arm, a weapon) to gather impetus; †(*c*) contrive, devise, plan. *fetch a gutser*: see GUTSER *noun*. **fetch and carry** (orig. of a dog) run backwards and forwards with things, be a mere servant. **fetch around** = *fetch round* below. **fetch away** = *fetch way* below. **fetch down** bring or force down. †**fetch in** surround, enclose; take in (*lit.* & *fig.*). †**fetch off** get the better of, make an end of. **fetch out** draw out, develop, display. **fetch round** revive, recover; (cause to) regain consciousness. **fetch up** (*a*) (orig. NAUTICAL) reach, come in sight of, get to (a place etc.); come to a stop, end up (*at*, *in*, etc.); (*b*) vomit; †(*c*) raise, elevate; (*d*) overtake, come up (*with*); (*e*) make up (lost ground etc.); (*f*) *US* bring up, rear (children). **fetch way** NAUTICAL move or shift from its proper place; break loose.

– COMB.: **fetch-and-carry** the action of fetching and carrying; a person who fetches and carries; **fetch-up** a coming to a standstill; stopping.

■ **fetcher** *noun* LME.

fetching /ˈfɛtʃɪŋ/ *adjective.* L16.
[ORIGIN from FETCH *verb* + -ING².]
†**1** Contriving, scheming, crafty. Only in L16.
2 Alluring, fascinating, delightful, attractive. *colloq.* L19.
■ **fetchingly** *adverb* L19.

fetch-light /ˈfɛtʃlʌɪt/ *noun.* L17.
[ORIGIN from FETCH *verb*, *noun*² + LIGHT *noun*.]
A corpse candle, *esp.* one supposedly seen before a death moving from the person's house to his or her grave.

fête /feɪt, fɛt/ *noun.* Also **fete**. LME.
[ORIGIN French from Old French *feste* FEAST *noun*. See also EN FÊTE.]
1 A festival, an entertainment, a fair. LME. ▸**b** A sale or bazaar, esp. out of doors, designed to raise money for charity. L19.
2 A religious festival, a saint's day. E19.

fête /feɪt, fɛt/ *verb trans.* Also **fete**. E17.
[ORIGIN from the noun, after French *fêter*.]
Entertain (a person) with a fête or feast, make much of (a person); give a fête in honour of, commemorate or celebrate by a fête.

V. CRONIN Alexis Orlov, then being feted . . as the victor of Chesme Bay.

fête champêtre /fɛt ʃɑ̃pɛːtr/ *noun phr.* Pl. **-s -s** (pronounced same). L18.
[ORIGIN French, formed as FÊTE *noun* + *champêtre* rural.]
An outdoor or pastoral entertainment, a rural festival.

fête galante /fɛt galɑ̃t/ *noun phr.* Pl. **-s -s** (pronounced same). E20.
[ORIGIN French, formed as FÊTE *noun* + *galante* fem. of *galant* GALLANT *adjective*.]
A ***fête champêtre***, esp. as depicted in an 18th-cent. French genre of painting; a painting in this genre.

fêtes champêtres, ***fêtes galantes*** *noun phrs.* pls. of FÊTE CHAMPÊTRE, FÊTE GALANTE.

fetial /ˈfiːʃ(ə)l/ *adjective & noun.* *obsolete* exc. *hist.* Also **fecial**. M16.
[ORIGIN Latin *fetialis* (erron. *fec-*), of unknown origin.]
▸ **A** *noun.* In ancient Rome: a member of a group of priests who acted as heralds and performed the rites connected with the declaration of war and conclusion of peace. M16.
▸ **B** *adjective.* Of or pertaining to a fetial; heraldic, ambassadorial. M16.

fetich(e) *noun* var. of FETISH.

fetichism *noun* var. of FETISHISM.

feticide /ˈfiːtɪsʌɪd/ *noun.* Also **foet-**. M19.
[ORIGIN from FETUS: see -CIDE.]
The action of destroying a fetus or causing abortion.
■ **feti'cidal** *adjective* of or pertaining to feticide L19.

fetid /ˈfɛtɪd, ˈfiːt-/ *adjective.* Also **foetid**. LME.
[ORIGIN Latin *fetidus* (erron. *foet-*) from *fetere* to stink: see -ID¹.]
Foul-smelling, stinking.

M. MITCHELL The smell of sweat, of blood, of unwashed bodies, of excrement rose up in waves . . until the fetid stench almost nauseated her.

■ **fetidly** *adverb* M19. **fetidness** *noun* E18.

fetiferous /fiːˈtɪf(ə)rəs/ *adjective.* Also **foet-**. M17.
[ORIGIN from Latin *fetifer*, from *fetus*: see FETUS, -FEROUS.]
Producing offspring.

fetish /ˈfɛtɪʃ/ *noun.* Also **-ich(e)**. E17.
[ORIGIN French *fétiche* from Portuguese *feitiço* charm, sorcery, use as noun of adjective 'made by art', from Latin *facticius* FACTITIOUS.]
1 Orig., an object used by peoples of W. Africa as an amulet or means of enchantment. Later more widely, an inanimate object reverenced as having magical powers or as being animated by a spirit. E17. ▸**b** An object, principle, etc., irrationally reverenced, esp. in an obsessive manner. M19. ▸**c** PSYCHOLOGY. A non-sexual part of the body, object, action, etc. acting as a focus for sexual desire. L19.

H. ALLEN The witch-doctor's horrible little manikin, a fetish with . . a blind, silly face. G. GORER The lucky mascot, the fetish which will preserve its owner from misfortune. **b** E. FIGES I made a fetish of being always punctual, always punctilious and conscientious.

†**2** In representations of black people's speech: incantation, worship; an oath. E18–E19.

fetisheer /fɛtɪˈʃɪə/ *noun.* Now *rare.* Also **fetisher** /ˈfɛtɪʃə/. E17.
[ORIGIN Portuguese *feiticeiro*, from *feitiço* (see FETISH), later infl. by French *fétiche* or English FETISH.]
1 A person believed to have power over fetishes; a witch doctor, a priest. E17.
2 = FETISH 1. *rare.* M17.

fetishise *verb* var. of FETISHIZE.

fetishism /ˈfɛtɪʃɪz(ə)m/ *noun.* Also **fetich-**. E19.
[ORIGIN from FETISH + -ISM.]
(A religion, lifestyle, psychological condition, etc., involving) devotion to or reverence for a fetish or fetishes.
■ **fetishist** *noun & adjective* (*a*) *noun* a person who has a fetish or who worships a fetish or fetishes; (*b*) *adjective* fetishistic M19. **feti'shistic** *adjective* of, pertaining to, or characteristic of, fetishism; of the nature of a fetish M19.

fetishize /ˈfɛtɪʃʌɪz/ *verb trans.* Also **-ise**. M20.
[ORIGIN from FETISH + -IZE.]
Make a fetish of; pay undue respect to, overvalue.
■ **fetishi'zation** *noun* M20.

fetlock /ˈfɛtlɒk/ *noun.* ME.
[ORIGIN Corresp. to Dutch *vetlok*, Flemish *vitlok*, Middle High German *vizzeloch*, *-lach* (German *Fissloch*) rel. to German *Fessel* fetlock, deriv. of Germanic var. of base of FOOT *noun*.]
1 The part of a horse's leg where the tuft of hair grows behind the pastern joint. ME.
2 = FETTERLOCK 1. Now *rare.* L17.
■ **fetlocked** *adjective* (*rare*) hobbled or fastened by the fetlock; shackled: E18.

fetor /ˈfiːtə/ *noun.* Also **foetor**. L15.
[ORIGIN Latin *fetor* (erron. *foet-*), from *fetere*: see FETID; -OR.]
A foul or offensive smell; a stench.

fetta *noun* var. of FETA.

fetter /ˈfɛtə/ *noun.*
[ORIGIN Old English *feter* corresp. to Old Saxon pl. *feteros* (Dutch *veter* lace), Old High German *fezzera* (early mod. German *Fesser*), Old Norse *fjoturr*, from Germanic, from Indo-European base of FOOT *noun*.]
1 A chain or shackle (orig. for the feet); a bond; a handcuff. Usu. in *pl.* OE. ▸**b** In *pl.* Captivity. E18.
2 Anything that confines or impedes; a restraint. OE.

J. LONDON His neck chafed against the starched fetter of a collar. O. NASH A dinner engagement . . is no longer a fetter, Because liars can just . . lie their way out of it.

■ **fetterless** *adjective* E17.

fetter /ˈfɛtə/ *verb trans.*
[ORIGIN Old English *gefeterian*, *-fetran* formed as FETTER *noun* or from Old Norse *fjotra*.]
1 Bind (as) with fetters; chain, shackle. OE.

W. IRVING I now fettered my horse to prevent his straying.

2 Impose restraint on; confine, impede. E16.

J. PRIESTLEY The best faculties . . may be sunk and fettered by superstition.

■ **fetterer** *noun* (*rare*) E17.

fetterlock /ˈfɛtəlɒk/ *noun. arch.* LME.
[ORIGIN from FETTER *noun* + LOCK *noun*².]
1 A portable lock for a shackle or hobble; a padlock. LME. ▸**b** The padlock as a heraldic or symbolic badge or device. LME.
†**2** = FETLOCK 1. L16–M19.

fettle /ˈfɛt(ə)l/ *noun*¹. *obsolete* exc. *Scot. & N. English.*
[ORIGIN Old English *fetel* = Old High German *fezzil* (German *Fessel*) chain, band, Old Norse *fetill* bandage, strap, from Germanic base meaning 'grasp, hold'.]
A strip or band of material; a belt, a bandage, a handle on a pannier etc.

fettle /ˈfɛt(ə)l/ *noun*². Orig. *dial.* M18.
[ORIGIN from the verb.]
Condition, state, trim. Now chiefly in ***in good fettle***, ***in fine fettle***, etc.

J. AGATE The old lady was in tremendous fettle and looking as imposing as ever.

fettle /ˈfɛt(ə)l/ *verb.* Now *dial. & techn.* LME.
[ORIGIN from FETTLE *noun*¹.]
1 *verb trans.* Make ready, arrange, put to rights, tidy; groom (a horse etc.). LME. ▸**b** Hit (a person). *dial.* M19. ▸**c** *techn.* Prepare, clean, trim, (the rough edge of a metal casting, pottery before firing, a furnace, etc.). L19.
2 *verb refl. & intrans.* Get oneself ready, prepare, (for battle etc.). Long *obsolete* exc. *dial.* LME. ▸**b** *verb intrans.* Busy oneself, fuss. M18.
■ **fettler** *noun* a person who fettles; *esp.* a repairer of railway lines: L19.

fettuccine /fɛtʊˈtʃiːni/ *noun pl.* Also **fettucine**. E20.
[ORIGIN Italian, pl. of *fettuccina* dim. of *fetta* slice, ribbon.]
Ribbons of pasta; an Italian dish consisting largely of this and usu. a sauce.

fetus /ˈfiːtəs/ *noun.* Also **foetus**. Pl. **-uses**. LME.
[ORIGIN Latin *fetus* pregnancy, giving birth, young offspring, abstract noun parallel to adjective *fetus* pregnant, productive.]
An unborn viviparous animal in the womb, an unhatched oviparous animal in the egg; *esp.* an unborn human more than eight weeks after conception.
– NOTE: The spelling *foetus* has no etymological basis but is recorded from 16 and until recently was the standard British spelling. In technical usage *fetus* is now the standard spelling throughout the English-speaking world, but *foetus* is still found in British English outside technical contexts.

fetwa *noun* var. of FATWA.

feu /fjuː/ *noun & verb.* L15.
[ORIGIN Old French: see FEE *noun*².]
SCOTS LAW. ▸**A** *noun.* **1** Orig., a feudal tenure in which land is granted by one person to another in return for an annual payment in place of military service. Now, a perpetual lease for a fixed sum. L15. ▸**b** A piece of land held in feu. L18.
in feu, **upon feu** (of tenured land) subject to certain payments or services.
2 *hist.* = FEE *noun*² 1a. E17.
– COMB.: **feu duty** the annual sum payable on a feudal tenure.
▸ **B** *verb trans.* Grant (land) on feu. L16.

feu /fø/ *adjective.* E19.
[ORIGIN French.]
Of a person: deceased, late.

†**feuage** *noun.* E17–E18.
[ORIGIN Old French, from *feu* FIRE *noun*: see -AGE.]
= FUMAGE.

feuar /ˈfjuːə/ *noun.* L16.
[ORIGIN from FEU *noun* + -AR².]
SCOTS LAW. = FIAR.

feud /fjuːd/ *noun*¹ *& verb.* ME.
[ORIGIN Old French *fede*, *feide* from Middle Low German, Middle Dutch *vēde*, Middle Low German *veide*, corresp. to Old High German *fēhida* (German *Fehde*) = Old English *fǣhþu* enmity, Old Frisian *fāithe*, *fēithe*, from Germanic base of FOE.]
▸ **A** *noun.* **1** Active hatred, hostility, ill will. *obsolete* exc. *dial.* ME.
2 A state of bitter and lasting mutual hostility, esp. between two families, tribes, or individuals, marked by murderous assaults in revenge for previous injury. LME.

E. A. FREEMAN Carrying out an ancestral deadly feud. F. FITZGERALD The Catholics . . and old-fashioned political parties continued their fierce blood feuds.

3 A quarrel, contention. M16.

C. S. FORESTER Jimmy and Doris quarrelled ceaselessly . . continuing a feud that . . originated some time back.

▸ **B** *verb intrans.* Conduct a feud. L17.

K. CROSSLEY-HOLLAND If . . feuding families could not settle a dispute . . it was brought before a court.

feud /fjuːd/ *noun*². Also (now *rare*) **feod**. ME.
[ORIGIN medieval Latin *feudum*, *feodum*: see FEE *noun*².]
hist. = FEE *noun*² 1a, 3.

feudal /ˈfjuːd(ə)l/ *adjective*¹. Also †**feodal**. E17.
[ORIGIN medieval Latin *feudalis*, *feodalis*, formed as FEUD *noun*²: see -AL¹.]
1 Of or pertaining to a feud or fief. E17.

M. HALE Wales, that was not always the feudal Territory of . . England.

2 Of or pertaining to the holding of land in feud; designating or pertaining to a medieval European system of administration, jurisdiction, land tenure, etc. (or similar system elsewhere), based on the relationship between a vassal and his superiors, the highest lord of which was often the king, and by which land was granted (ultimately to a vassal who worked the land) in return for homage, military service, and other duties. M17.

GIBBON The first rudiments of the feudal tenures. T. BENN The feudal nonsense of a hereditary title.

■ **feudally** *adverb* in a feudal manner; under feudal conditions: M19. **feudalism** *noun* the feudal system or its principles M19. **feudalist** *noun* a representative or a supporter of the feudal system E19. **feudalistic** *adjective* of the nature of or inclined to feudalism L19.

feudal /ˈfjuːd(ə)l/ *adjective*². *rare*. E19.
[ORIGIN from FEUD *noun*¹ + -AL¹.]
Of or pertaining to a feud or state of bitter hostility.

feudalise *verb* var. of FEUDALIZE.

feudality /fjuːˈdalɪti/ *noun*. E18.
[ORIGIN French *feudalité*, *féod-*, from *feudal*, *féodal*, formed as FEUDAL *adjective*¹: see -ITY.]
†**1** *LAW*. Fealty. Only in Dicts. E18–M19.
2 Feudal quality or state; the principles and practice of the feudal system. L18.

J. S. MILL The very essence of feudality was . . the fusion of property and sovereignty.

3 A feudal regime; a power like that of feudalism; a feudal holding or fief. E19.

feudalize /ˈfjuːd(ə)lʌɪz/ *verb trans*. Also **-ise**. E19.
[ORIGIN from FEUDAL *adjective*¹ + -IZE.]
Make feudal, bring under the feudal system; convert (lands) into feudal holdings; reduce (persons) to the position of feudal vassals.
■ **feudaliˈzation** *noun* M19.

feu d'artifice /fø dartifis/ *noun phr*. Pl. ***feux d'artifice*** (pronounced same). L17.
[ORIGIN French, lit. 'fire of artifice'.]
A firework show; a firework.

feudary /ˈfjuːdəri/ *noun & adjective*. Now *arch.* or *hist.* Also **feod-**. LME.
[ORIGIN medieval Latin *feodarius*, formed as FEUD *noun*²: see -ARY¹.]
▸ **A** *noun*. **1** A person who holds lands of an overlord on condition of homage and service; a feudal tenant, a vassal. LME. ▸**b** A subject, a dependant, a servant. E17.

T. FULLER Accepted of the Jewish King to be honourary feodaries unto him.

†**2** An officer responsible for receiving the revenues of wards of court. L15–M18.
▸ **B** *adjective*. Feudally subject (*to*). L16.

†**feudatary** *noun & adjective*. L16.
[ORIGIN medieval Latin *feudatarius*, from *feudat-*: see FEUDATORY, -ARY¹.]
▸ **A** *noun*. = FEUDATORY *noun* 2. L16–E19.
▸ **B** *adjective*. = FEUDATORY *adjective* Only in 17.

feudatory /ˈfjuːdət(ə)ri/ *adjective & noun*. L16.
[ORIGIN medieval Latin *feudatorius*, from *feudat-* pa. ppl stem of *feudare* enfeoff, formed as FEUD *noun*²: see -ATE³, -ORY².]
▸ **A** *adjective*. Owing feudal allegiance *to*, subject *to*; under overlordship. L16.

P. F. TYTLER The petty chiefs . . had for a long period been feudatory to the Norwegian crown.

▸ **B** *noun*. **1** A feud, a fief, a fee; a dependent lordship. M17.
2 A person who holds lands by feudal tenure; a feudal vassal. M18.

feu de joie /fø də ʒwa/ *noun phr*. Pl. ***feux de joie*** (pronounced same). E17.
[ORIGIN French, lit. 'fire of joy'.]
▸ **I** †**1** A bonfire. E17–L18.
2 A salute fired by rifles etc. on occasions of ceremony or public rejoicing. E18.
▸ **II 3** *fig.* A joyful thing or occasion; a celebration. M17.

feudist /ˈfjuːdɪst/ *noun*¹. Now *US*. L16.
[ORIGIN from FEUD *noun*¹ + -IST.]
A person who has a feud with another.

feudist /ˈfjuːdɪst/ *noun*². E17.
[ORIGIN French *feudiste* or mod. Latin *feudista*, formed as FEUD *noun*²: see -IST.]
1 A writer on feuds or fiefs; an authority on feudal law. E17.
†**2** A person living under the feudal system. E17–M18.

feu farm /ˈfjuːfɑːm/ *noun*. LME.
[ORIGIN Old French *feuferme*: see FEE FARM.]
SCOTS LAW. Tenure by which land is held of a superior on payment of an annual sum.

feu follet /fø fɔlɛ/ *noun phr*. Pl. ***feux follets*** (pronounced same). M19.
[ORIGIN French, lit. 'frolicsome fire'.]
A will-o'-the-wisp, an ignis fatuus, (*lit. & fig.*).

feuillemorte /fœjmɔrt/ *adjective*. L16.
[ORIGIN French = dead leaf. Cf. FILEMOT.]
Of the colour of a dead leaf; brown or yellowish brown.

†**feuillet** *noun*. Only in 18.
[ORIGIN French *feuillette* from medieval Latin *folietta* a measure of wine.]
A half hogshead.

feuilleté /fəːjəˈteɪ/ *noun*. M20.
[ORIGIN French = flaky.]
A puff pastry case with a sweet or savoury filling.

feuilleton /ˈfəːɪtɒ̃, *foreign* fœjtɔ̃ (*pl. same*)/ *noun*. M19.
[ORIGIN French, from *feuillet* dim. of *feuille* leaf: see -ET¹, -OON.]
(A part of a newspaper etc. devoted to) fiction, criticism, light literature, etc.; an article or work suitable for or printed in that part.

E. JONES He earned part of his living by writing regular feuilletons for the local press.

feuilletonist /ˈfəːɪtɒnɪst/ *noun*. Also ***feuilletoniste*** /fœjtɔnist (*pl. same*)/. M19.
[ORIGIN French *feuilletoniste*, formed as FEUILLETON + *-iste* -IST.]
A writer of feuilletons.
■ **feuilletoˈnistic** *adjective* characteristic of feuilletonists L19.

Feulgen /ˈfɔɪlg(ə)n/ *noun*. E20.
[ORIGIN R. J. *Feulgen* (1884–1955), German biochemist.]
Used *attrib.* to denote a technique devised by Feulgen for preferentially staining chromosomes or other bodies containing DNA.

feux d'artifice, feux de joie, feux follets *noun phrs*. pls. of FEU D'ARTIFICE etc.

fever /ˈfiːvə/ *noun & verb*. OE.
[ORIGIN Latin *febris*; reinforced in Middle English by Anglo-Norman *fevre*, Old French & mod. French *fièvre* from Latin.]
▸ **A** *noun*. **1** An abnormally high temperature of the body as a whole; any of various diseases characterized by this. OE.

I. MURDOCH Jealousy inhabited her like a fever making her shake and sweat.

blackwater fever, Lassa fever, relapsing fever, scarlet fever, yellow fever, etc. **fever and ague** (now *US*) malaria. ***hay fever***: see HAY *noun*¹.

2 A state of intense nervous excitement or agitation. ME.

W. EMPSON The fever and multiplicity of life . . are contrasted with the calm of the external space.

– COMB.: **fever heat** the high temperature of the body in fever; *fig.* fever pitch; **fever pitch** a state of abnormal excitement; **fever therapy** the treatment of disease by induced fever.
▸ **B** *verb*. **1** *verb trans*. Affect (as) with a fever. E17.

R. L. STEVENSON The stir and speed of the journey . . fever him, and stimulate his dull nerves.

2 *verb intrans*. Be seized with a fever. M18.
■ **feveret** *noun* (now *rare*) a slight fever E18.

feverfew /ˈfiːvəfjuː/ *noun*. OE.
[ORIGIN Latin *febrifuga*, *-fugia*, formed as FEVER + *fugare* drive away; forms from Latin superseded in Middle English by those from Anglo-Norman *feiverfue*.]
An aromatic white-flowered herb of the composite family, *Tanacetum parthenium*, used to treat migraine and formerly as a febrifuge.

feverish /ˈfiːv(ə)rɪʃ/ *adjective*. LME.
[ORIGIN from FEVER *noun* + -ISH¹.]
1 (Of food, climate, etc.) causing or tending to cause fever; (of a country etc.) infested with fever. LME.

G. CAMPBELL Tracts which are exceedingly feverish in summer.

2 Having symptoms (resembling those) of a fever. Formerly also, ill of a fever. M17. ▸**b** Of the nature or indicative of a fever. L17.

J. AUSTEN Though heavy and feverish . . a good night's rest was to cure her. **b** J. STEINBECK His face was puffed and feverish.

3 Excited; restless; hectic. M17.

B. RUBENS Rabbi Zweck frantically opened every drawer, rummaging through their contents with feverish fingers.

■ **feverishly** *adverb* †(**a**) with the symptoms of fever; (**b**) excitedly, restlessly: M17. **feverishness** *noun* M17.

feverous /ˈfiːv(ə)rəs/ *adjective*. LME.
[ORIGIN from FEVER *noun* + -OUS.]
1 = FEVERISH 2. LME.
2 = FEVERISH 1. E17.
3 = FEVERISH 3. E17.
■ **feverously** *adverb* M17.

few /fjuː/ *adjective* (in mod. usage also classed as a *determiner*), *pronoun*, & *noun*.
[ORIGIN Old English *fēawe*, *fēawa* contr. *fēa* = Old Frisian *fē*, Old Saxon *fa(o)* Old High German *fao*, *fō*, Old Norse *fár*, Gothic pl. *fawai* from Germanic from Indo-European base also of Latin *paucus*, Greek *pauros* small.]
▸ **A** *adjective*. **1** With *noun pl.* Not many, hardly any; a small number (with *compar. & superl.*). (Preceding the noun and other adjectives but following any determiners (the def. article, demonstratives, possessives, etc.) or ordinal numerals (also *last*, *next*); also pred. after *be* etc.) OE.

J. CONRAD Packing his few belongings. P. G. WODEHOUSE He was a man of few words. R. S. THOMAS After the few people have gone. P. SCOTT Marriages and christenings, of which there seemed . . to be fewer than there were funerals. *Times* They have few, if any, close friends. W. BOYD Temple spent the next few days in an . . attempt to find someone who would admit he was a 'problem'. *Economist* There are very few openings in universities at the moment.

2 With *noun pl. A* small number of. (Preceding the noun and other adjectives.) ME. ▸**b** *A* small quantity of. Long *obsolete* exc. *dial.* LME.

J. CONRAD In a very few hours I arrived. A. UTTLEY The leaves had gone, all but a few odd ones.

3 Of a company or number: small. Now *rare*. LME.

New York Times The fewest number of firemen in the history of the city.

▸ **B** *pronoun & noun*. **1** *absol.* Few people or things understood contextually; not many *of*, hardly any *of*. (Also modified by adverb as *very*, *many*.) OE.

SHAKES. *Hen. V* We few, we happy few, we band of brothers. A. HELPS How few of your fellow-creatures can have the opportunity. G. B. SHAW Very few of them are fortunate enough to enjoy this advantage. G. GREENE Few . . drank anywhere else.

2 *A* small number (*of*). ME. ▸**b** *A* good bit, *a* considerable extent. *arch. slang*. M18.

C. ISHERWOOD Most of the boys looked up and grinned . . , only a few were sullen. J. C. POWYS Courtly travellers, a few of whom were bound for Oxford. **b** W. IRVING Determined to astonish the natives a few!

3 *The* small company (specified or understood). Now usu. *the* minority, *the* elect; *spec.* (**F-**) *the* Royal Air Force pilots who took part in the Battle of Britain. M16.
– PHRASES: **a good few** *colloq.* a considerable number (of). ***catch a few z's, get a few z's***: see Z, Z 1b. **every few** once in every small group of (days, miles, etc.), at intervals of a few (days, miles, etc.). **few and far between** neither numerous nor frequent. **have a few** *spec.* (*colloq.*) have a few alcoholic drinks. **in few** *arch.* in few words, in short, briefly. **no fewer than** as many as (a specified number). **not a few, quite a few** *colloq.* a considerable number (of or *of*). ***of few words***: see WORD *noun*. **some few** some but not at all many (*of*).
■ **fewness** *noun* small number or quantity OE.

fewmet /ˈfjuːmɪt/ *noun*. Also **fumet**. LME.
[ORIGIN (from Anglo-Norman var. of) Old French *fumees* (pl.), from *fumer* (repr. Latin *fimare*) to dung.]
sing. & (usu.) in *pl.* The excrement of a deer.

fewter /ˈfjuːtə/ *noun & verb*. Long *obsolete* exc. *hist.* LME.
[ORIGIN Old French *feutre*, *fautre* from medieval Latin *filtrum*: see FILTER *noun*.]
▸ **A** *noun*. A support or rest for a spear attached to a saddle or side of a breastplate and lined with felt to absorb the shock of impact. LME.
▸ **B** *verb trans*. Put (a spear) in a fewter. LME.

T. H. WHITE They fewtered their spears again, and thundered into the charge.

†**fewterer** *noun*. ME–E19.
[ORIGIN Anglo-Norman *veutrier* (= Anglo-Latin *veltrarius*) from Old French *veutre*, *v(e)autre*, *veltre* (mod. *vautre*) boar-hound, from Proto-Romance contracted and dissimilated form of Latin *vertragus* greyhound, of Gaulish origin.]
A keeper of greyhounds. More widely, an attendant.

fewtrils /ˈfjuːtrɪlz/ *noun pl. dial.* M18.
[ORIGIN Cf. FATTRELS.]
Little things, trifles.

DICKENS I ha' gotten decent fewtrils about me agen.

fey /feɪ/ *adjective*. Long chiefly *Scot.*
[ORIGIN Old English *fǣġe* = Old Saxon *fēgi* (Dutch *veeg*), Old High German *feigi* (German *feige* cowardly), Old Norse *feigr* from Germanic.]
1 Fated to die, at the point of death (as manifested by strange exultant behaviour supposedly portending death). Formerly also, accursed, unlucky; weak, feeble. OE. ▸**b** Disordered in mind, behaving strangely like a person about to die; possessing or displaying magical or supernatural powers. Now freq. *iron.*, affected. L18.

R. BURNS Thro' they dash'd, and hew'd, and smash'd, Till fey men died awa. **b** J. LE CARRÉ His interlocuter was whimsical if not downright fey.

†**2** Leading to or portending death; fatal. ME–L18.
■ **feyly** *adverb* M20. **feyness** *noun* L19.

Feynman /ˈfʌɪnmən/ *noun*. M20.
[ORIGIN Richard Phillips *Feynman* (1918–88), US theoretical physicist.]
PHYSICS. ***Feynman diagram***, a space-time graph that represents an interaction between two or more elementary particles, *spec.* each of a set of such diagrams that represent possible ways in which a particular process can occur.

fez /fɛz/ *noun*. Pl. **fezzes**. E19.
[ORIGIN Turkish *fes*, perh. through French *fez*, named after *Fez* (now *Fès*) in Morocco, once the chief place of manufacture.]
A flat-topped conical red hat with a tassel worn by men in some Muslim countries, and formerly the national headdress of the Turks.
■ **fezzed** *adjective* wearing a fez M19.

ff *abbreviation.*
Fortissimo.

ff. *abbreviation.*
1 Folios.
2 Following pages etc.

fff *abbreviation.*
Fortissimo.

FFV *abbreviation. US.*
First family or families of Virginia.

Fg Off. *abbreviation.*
Flying Officer.

FHB *abbreviation.*
Family hold back (when guests are sharing a meal).

FHSA *abbreviation.*
Family Health Services Authority.

FIA *abbreviation.*
[ORIGIN French *Fédération Internationale de l'Automobile*.]
The international governing body for motor-racing events.

F

fiacre /fiˈɑːkrə; *foreign* fjakr (*pl. same*)/ *noun.* L17.
[ORIGIN French, from the Hôtel de St *Fiacre*, rue St Antoine, Paris, where such vehicles were first hired out.]
A small four-wheeled horse-drawn carriage.

†**fial** *noun* var. of PHIAL.

Fian /fiːn/ *noun.* Also **Fiann**. Pl. **Fianna** /ˈfiːənə/, **Fians**. L18.
[ORIGIN Irish *fian* (pl. *fianna*), orig. 'band of warriors and hunters'. Cf. FEINNE.]
= FENIAN *noun* 1.

fiancé /fiˈɒnseɪ, -ˈɑːns-, -ˈɒs-/ *noun.* Fem. **-ée**. M19.
[ORIGIN French, from Old French & mod. French *fiancer* betroth, from Old French *fiance* a promise.]
A man or woman engaged to be married to another; the person to whom one is engaged.

fianchetto /fɪənˈtʃɛtəʊ, -ˈkɛtəʊ/ *noun & verb.* M19.
[ORIGIN Italian, dim. of *fianco* FLANK *noun*.]
CHESS. ▶**A** *noun.* Pl. **-oes**. The development of a bishop by moving it one square to a long diagonal of the board. M19.
▶ **B** *verb trans.* Develop (a bishop) in this way. E20.

Fiann *noun* var. of FIAN.

Fianna Fáil /fɪˌanə ˈfɔɪl/ *noun phr.* E20.
[ORIGIN Irish from *fianna* (see FIAN) + *Fáil* genit. of *Fál* an ancient name for Ireland.]
An Irish Republican Party founded in 1926 by De Valera, in opposition to the Anglo-Irish treaty of 1921.

fiant /ˈfʌɪənt/ *noun.* M16.
[ORIGIN Latin, first word in formula *fiant literae patentes* 'let letters patent be made out'.]
hist. A warrant addressed to the Irish Chancery for a grant under the Great Seal.

fiants /ˈfɪənts/ *noun pl.* Long *arch.* Also †**fuants**. L16.
[ORIGIN Old French *fient*, (also mod.) *fiente* dung, repr. popular Latin development of Latin *fimus*. The specialization of sense seems to be English.]
HUNTING. The excrement of certain animals, e.g. the fox and the badger.

fiar /ˈfiːə/ *noun. Scot.* Also **fear**. L15.
[ORIGIN from FEE *noun*² + -AR². Cf. FEUAR.]
LAW. A person who has the reversion of a property and is its ultimate owner.

fiasco /fɪˈaskəʊ, *in sense 1 foreign* ˈfjasko/ *noun.* Pl. **-scos**, (sense 1) **-schi** /-ski/. M19.
[ORIGIN Italian; in sense 2 from phr. *far fiasco* lit. 'make a bottle', with unexpl. allus.]
1 A bottle, a flask. (Not anglicized.) M19.
2 A complete and ignominious failure, orig. of a dramatic or musical performance; an ignominious result. M19.

H. JAMES One of the biggest failures that history commemorates, an immense national *fiasco*.

fiat /ˈfʌɪat/ *noun & verb.* LME.
[ORIGIN Latin, 3rd person sing. pres. subjunct. of *fieri* = let it be done, let there be made. In sense A.2 short for *fiat lux* (Vulgate Genesis 1:3) = let there be light.]
▶ **A** *noun.* **1** A formal authorization (orig. expressed by the Latin word *fiat* or a formula containing it) for a proposed arrangement, a request, etc.; *gen.* an authoritative pronouncement, a decree, an order. LME.

F. FITZGERALD Japan took over French Indochina by diplomatic fiat. R. C. A. WHITE The unsatisfactory procedure of the writ of error on the fiat of the Attorney-General.

2 A command by which something is brought into being. L16.

J. TYNDALL Was space furnished at once, by the fiat of Omnipotence, with these burning orbs?

— COMB.: **fiat money** *US* inconvertible paper money made legal tender by Government decree.
▶ **B** *verb trans.* Sanction by (official) pronouncement. M19.

J. S. LE FANU My uncle fiated the sexton's presentment, and the work commenced forthwith.

fib /fɪb/ *noun. colloq.* M16.
[ORIGIN Perh. short for FIBLE-FABLE.]
1 A person who tells (trivial or venial) lies. M16.
2 A (trivial or venial) lie. E17.

H. JAMES They are very sincere; they don't tell fibs.

fib /fɪb/ *verb*¹ *intrans. colloq.* Infl. **-bb-**. E17.
[ORIGIN from the noun.]
Tell a (trivial or venial) lie.
■ **fibber** *noun* E17. **fibbery** *noun* falsehood, lying M19.

fib /fɪb/ *verb*² *trans. & intrans. slang.* Infl. **-bb-**. M17.
[ORIGIN Unknown.]
Administer a pommelling (to), esp. in boxing.

fiber, **fiberglass** *nouns* see FIBRE, FIBREGLASS.

fible-fable /ˈfɪb(ə)lfeɪb(ə)l/ *noun.* Long *obsolete* exc. *dial. rare.* L16.
[ORIGIN Redupl. of FABLE *noun*.]
Nonsense.

Fibonacci /fiːbəˈnɑːtʃi/ *noun.* L19.
[ORIGIN Name given to Leonardo of Pisa (fl. 1200), Tuscan mathematician.]
MATH. ***Fibonacci numbers***, ***Fibonacci series***, ***Fibonacci's numbers***, ***Fibonacci's series***, the series of numbers, 1, 1, 2, 3, 5, 8, . . . , in which each number is the sum of the two preceding ones.

fibre /ˈfʌɪbə/ *noun.* Also ***fiber**. LME.
[ORIGIN Old French & mod. French from Latin *fibra*.]
†**1** A lobe of the liver; in *pl.*, the entrails. LME–E17.
2 ANATOMY & ZOOLOGY. Any threadlike structure forming part of the muscular, nervous, connective, or other tissue in an animal body. M16.

T. HOLCROFT In cold countries the fibres of the tongue must be less flexible. B. BAINBRIDGE Straining in every fibre I crouched there, panting.

yellow fibre: see YELLOW *adjective*.
3 BOTANY. A threadlike element in plant tissue; *spec.* an elongated thick-walled cell lacking protoplasm. M17.

W. HAMILTON The vascular fibres of the bark.

4 A slender subdivision of a root. M17.
5 A thread or filament forming part of a textile. Also, a thread formed from glass, metal, etc. E19.

F. SMYTH Smith set to work on the rest of the fluff, and found . . fibres of wool, cotton, . . and jute.

carbon fibre, *glass fibre*, etc.
6 *collect.* Any material consisting of animal, vegetable, or man-made fibres; *esp.* one that can be spun, woven, or felted. Also, fibrous structure. E19.

HUGH MILLER Pieces of coal which exhibit the ligneous fibre. *Wall Street Journal* The company entered the man made fiber field with rayon.

7 *fig.* Essential character or make-up. M19.

N. MONSARRAT We are not all made of the same stern fibre.

moral fibre: see MORAL *adjective*.
8 METALLURGY. A structure characteristic of wrought metal in which there is a directional alignment or elongation of crystals or inclusions. M19.
9 The part of a foodstuff that cannot be digested or absorbed; roughage. Also ***dietary fibre***. E20.
— COMB.: **fibreboard** (a sheet of) compressed wood or other plant fibre, used as a building material; **fibrefill** material made of synthetic fibres, used for padding garments, cushions, etc.; **fibre-optic** *adjective* relating to or used in fibre optics; **fibre optics** the transmission of light by total internal reflection through fibres of glass or other transparent solids; **fibre tip** *adjective & noun* (*a*) *adjective* fibre-tipped; (*b*) *noun* a fibre-tipped pen; **fibre-tipped** *adjective* (of a pen) having a tip made of tightly packed capillary fibres which hold the ink.
■ **fibred** *adjective* having fibres (chiefly as 2nd elem. of comb.). M17. **fibreless** *adjective* having no fibres or strength M19. **fibrescope** *noun* a fibre-optic device for viewing inaccessible internal structures, esp. in the human body M20.

fibreglass /ˈfʌɪbəglɑːs/ *noun.* Also ***fiberglass**, (US proprietary name) **Fiberglas**. M20.
[ORIGIN from FIBRE + GLASS *noun*.]
Any material consisting of glass filaments woven into a textile or paper, or embedded in plastic etc., for use as a construction or insulation material.

fibriform /ˈfʌɪbrɪfɔːm/ *adjective.* M19.
[ORIGIN from FIBRE + -I- + -FORM.]
Having the form of a fibre or fibres.

fibril /ˈfʌɪbrɪl/ *noun.* M17.
[ORIGIN mod. Latin *fibrilla*: see FIBRILLA.]
1 BOTANY. The ultimate subdivision of a root. M17.
2 A small or delicate fibre; *spec.* a constituent strand of an animal, vegetable, or man-made fibre. Also, a threadlike molecular formation such as occurs in some colloidal systems and proteins. L17.

fibrilla /fʌɪˈbrɪlə, fɪ-/ *noun.* Pl. **-llae** /-liː/. M17.
[ORIGIN mod. Latin, dim. of *fibra* FIBRE.]
= FIBRIL 2.
■ **fibrillar** *adjective* of, relating to, or of the nature of a fibrilla M19. **fibrillary** *adjective* = FIBRILLAR L18. **fibrilliform** *adjective* having the form of a fibril M19. **fibrillose** *adjective* (marked with fine lines as if) composed of or covered with fibrils E19.

fibrillate /ˈfʌɪbrɪleɪt, ˈfɪ-/ *verb.* M19.
[ORIGIN from FIBRILLA + -ATE³.]
1 *verb intrans.* Of blood: turn into fibrillae (in clotting). M19.
2 *verb intrans.* Of the muscles of the heart: contract irregularly fibril by fibril. E20.
3 *verb trans.* PAPER-MAKING. Beat (vegetable fibre) down into its constituent fibrils. E20. ▸**b** *verb intrans.* Of fibre: split up into fibrils. M20.
■ **fibrillated** *ppl adjective* having a fibrillar structure M19.

fibrillation /fʌɪbrɪˈleɪʃ(ə)n, fɪ-/ *noun.* M19.
[ORIGIN formed as FIBRILLATE: see -ATION.]
1 Arrangement into fibrils; formation of fibrillae; a fibrillated mass. M19.
2 MEDICINE. Irregular spontaneous contraction in the individual fibres of a muscle, esp. of the auricles or ventricles of the heart. L19.
3 PAPER-MAKING. The beating of vegetable fibre into its component fibrils. E20.

fibrin /ˈfʌɪbrɪn, ˈfɪ-/ *noun.* E19.
[ORIGIN from FIBRE + -IN¹.]
A protein forming fibres. Now only *spec.* an insoluble protein formed by enzyme action from fibrinogen when blood coagulates, which forms a fibrous network round the clot.

fibrinogen /fɪˈbrɪnədʒ(ə)n/ *noun.* L19.
[ORIGIN from FIBRIN + -GEN.]
A soluble protein present in blood plasma, from which fibrin is formed during coagulation.

fibrinoid /ˈfʌɪbrɪnɔɪd/ *adjective & noun.* E20.
[ORIGIN German, formed as FIBRIN + -OID.]
MEDICINE. (Of the nature of or involving) a granular material, resembling fibrin in its staining properties, which is found in the placenta during pregnancy, as well as in various diseased tissues.

fibrinolysis /fʌɪbrɪˈnɒlɪsɪs/ *noun.* E20.
[ORIGIN from FIBRIN + -LYSIS.]
The breakdown of fibrin in blood clots.
■ **fibrinolysin** *noun* any of various enzymes which dissolve blood clots by breaking down the fibrin; *spec.* plasmin: E20. ˌ**fibrinoˈlytic** *adjective* pertaining to or causing fibrinolysis E20.

fibrinous /ˈfʌɪbrɪnəs/ *adjective.* M19.
[ORIGIN from FIBRIN + -OUS.]
Composed of, containing, or of the nature of fibrin.
■ **fibriˈnosity** *noun* fibrinous quality L19.

fibro /ˈfʌɪbrəʊ/ *noun. Austral. & NZ colloq.* Pl. **-os**. M20.
[ORIGIN Abbreviation.]
= FIBRO-CEMENT. Also, a house composed mainly of this.

fibro- /ˈfʌɪbrəʊ/ *combining form.*
[ORIGIN Latin, from *fibra* FIBRE: see -O-.]
ANATOMY & MEDICINE. Forming nouns and adjectives with the sense 'fibrous, of fibre', chiefly in terms referring to fibrous tissue.
■ **fibroadeˈnoma** *noun*, pl. **-mas**, **-mata** /-mətə/, a tumour (esp. a benign tumour of the breast) formed of mixed fibrous and glandular tissue L19. **fibroadeˈnomatous** *adjective* of the nature of a fibroadenoma L19. **fibroblast** *noun* any of the fibre-secreting cells in connective tissue L19. **fibroˈblastic** *adjective* of, involving, or relating to fibroblasts L19. **fibrocartilage** *noun* fibrous cartilage, containing bundles or networks of fibres M19. **fibrocartiˈlaginous** *adjective* of the nature of fibrocartilage M19. **fibroceˈment** *noun* a mixture of asbestos and cement, used in sheets for building E20. **fibroˈcystic** *adjective* characterized by the development of fibrous tissue and cystic spaces M19. **fibrocyte** *noun* an inactive form of fibroblast found in mature fibrous tissue E20. **fibroˈgenesis** *noun* formation of (fibrous) connective tissue M20. **fibroˈgenic** *adjective* causing fibrogenesis M20. **fibromyˈalgia** *noun* a rheumatic condition characterized by muscular or musculoskeletal pain with stiffness and localized tenderness at specific points on the body L20. **fibroˈplasia** *noun* proliferation of fibrous tissue, esp. in the process of healing E20. **fibrosarˈcoma** *noun*, pl. **-mas**, **-mata** /-mətə/, a sarcoma in which the predominant cell is a malignant fibroblast L19. **fibroˈvascular** *adjective* (BOTANY) consisting of a mixture of fibrous and vascular tissue M19.

fibroid /ˈfʌɪbrɔɪd/ *adjective & noun.* M19.
[ORIGIN from FIBRE + -OID.]
▶ **A** *adjective.* Resembling, composed of, or characterized by fibrous tissue. M19.
▶ **B** *noun.* MEDICINE. A tumour containing much fibrous tissue; *esp.* a fibrous myoma of the uterus. L19.

fibroin /ˈfʌɪbrəʊɪn/ *noun.* M19.
[ORIGIN from FIBRO- + -IN¹.]
A protein forming the main component of raw silk filaments, spiders' webs, etc.

fibrolite /ˈfʌɪbrəlʌɪt/ *noun.* E19.
[ORIGIN from FIBRO- + -LITE.]
MINERALOGY. = SILLIMANITE.

fibroma /fʌɪˈbrəʊmə/ *noun.* Pl. **-mas**, **-mata** /-mətə/. M19.
[ORIGIN from Latin *fibra* FIBRE + -OMA.]
MEDICINE. A benign tumour of fibrous tissue.

fibrose /ˈfʌɪbrəʊs/ *adjective.* Now *rare.* L17.
[ORIGIN mod. Latin *fibrosus*: see FIBRE, -OSE¹.]
= FIBROUS.

fibrose /fʌɪˈbrəʊs/ *verb intrans.* L19.
[ORIGIN Back-form. from FIBROSIS.]
Form fibrous tissue. Chiefly as ***fibrosed***, ***fibrosing*** *ppl adjectives*.

fibrosis /fʌɪˈbrəʊsɪs/ *noun*. Pl. **-broses** /-ˈbrəʊsiːz/. L19.
[ORIGIN from Latin *fibra* FIBRE + -OSIS.]
MEDICINE. (An) abnormal increase of fibrous tissue within an organ.
cystic fibrosis a hereditary disorder of the exocrine glands, in which the production of thick mucus leads to the blocking of the pancreatic ducts, intestines, bronchi, etc.

fibrositis /fʌɪbrəˈsʌɪtɪs/ *noun*. E20.
[ORIGIN from FIBROSE *adjective* + -ITIS.]
MEDICINE. Any rheumatic disorder of uncertain origin believed to involve the fibrous tissue; *esp.* painful inflammation of the back and shoulder muscles.
■ **fibrositic** /fʌɪbrəˈsɪtɪk/ *adjective* relating to or affected with fibrositis E20.

fibrotic /fʌɪˈbrɒtɪk/ *adjective*. L19.
[ORIGIN formed as FIBROSIS: see -OTIC.]
Affected with or characterized by fibrosis.

fibrous /ˈfʌɪbrəs/ *adjective*. E17.
[ORIGIN from FIBRE + -OUS. Cf. French *fibreux*.]
1 Formed from or full of fibres. E17.
fibrous protein any of a class of proteins having an elongated freq. helical molecular structure with little folding. **fibrous tissue** the common connective tissue of mammals, consisting of fibrous collagen with fibroblasts or fibrocytes, forming ligaments, fasciae, etc.
2 Resembling fibre or fibres. E18.
■ **fibrously** *adverb* L19. **fibrousness** *noun* E18.

fibry /ˈfʌɪbri/ *adjective*. E19.
[ORIGIN from FIBRE + -Y[1].]
Resembling a fibre; having many fibres.

fibster /ˈfɪbstə/ *noun*. E19.
[ORIGIN from FIB *verb*[1] + -STER.]
A person who tells fibs; a petty liar.

fibula /ˈfɪbjʊlə/ *noun*. Pl. **-lae** /-liː/, **-las**. L16.
[ORIGIN Latin *fibula* brooch, perh. from base of *figere* to fix.]
1 *ANATOMY*. The outer of the two bones between the knee and the ankle, articulating at its upper end with the tibia. L16.
2 *ANTIQUITIES*. A clasp, a buckle, a brooch. L17.
■ **fibular** *adjective* of, pertaining to, or (formerly) resembling the fibula of the leg E18.

-fic /fɪk/ *suffix*. Also (see below) **-ific**.
[ORIGIN Repr. (French *-fique* from) Latin *-ficus* making, doing, from weakened base of *facere* make, do.]
Forming (usu. with intermediate **-I-**) adjectives corresp. to Latin adjectives in *-ficus* or modelled on them, (1) from nouns, with the sense 'making, producing', as ***calorific***, ***pacific***, ***prolific***; (2) from adjectives, with the sense 'performing actions of a specified kind', as ***magnific***, or, later, 'bringing into a specified state', as ***beatific***; (3) from verbs, with the sense 'causing to', as ***horrific***; (4) from adverbs, with the sense 'acting in a specified way', as ***malefic***.

-fication /fɪˈkeɪʃ(ə)n/ *suffix*. Also (see below) **-ific-**.
[ORIGIN Repr. (French *-fication* from) Latin *-ficatio(n-)* corresp. to verb stems in *-fica(t-)*.]
Forming (usu. with intermediate **-I-**) the regular nouns of action corresp. to verbs in **-FY** which represent or are modelled on Latin verbs in *-ficare*, as ***glorification***, ***purification***, ***transmogrification***.

fice *noun* see FIST *noun*[2].

ficelle /fisɛl (*pl. same*), fɪˈsɛl/ *noun*. L19.
[ORIGIN French = string.]
1 The off-white colour of much string. Only *attrib.* or in *comb.*, as ***ficelle-colour***, ***ficelle-coloured***. L19.
2 A (stage) device, an artifice. L19.
G. MURRAY Raids on women were a real cause of war, but they were also a . . favourite *ficelle* of fiction.

fiche /fiʃ (*pl. same*), fiːʃ/ *noun*[1]. M20.
[ORIGIN French, short for *fiche de voyageur*.]
The registration form filled in by foreign guests in French hotels.

fiche /fiːʃ/ *noun*[2]. Pl. same, **-s**. M20.
[ORIGIN Abbreviation.]
= MICROFICHE.

Fichtean /ˈfɪxtɪən/ *adjective*. E19.
[ORIGIN from *Fichte* (see below) + -AN.]
Of or connected with the German idealist philosopher Johann Gottlieb Fichte (1762–1814) or his views.

fichu /ˈfiːʃuː/ *noun*. M18.
[ORIGIN French, of unknown origin.]
A triangular piece of muslin, lace, or the like, worn by women round the neck and shoulders, and formerly also over the head.

fickle /ˈfɪk(ə)l/ *adjective*.
[ORIGIN Old English *ficol* rel. to *ġefic* deceit, *befician* deceive, and further to *fǣcne* deceitful, *fācen* deceit(ful), corresp. to Old Saxon *fēkan*, Old High German *feihhan*, Old Norse *feikn* portent.]
1 Deceitful, false. Now only (*Scot.*) of a place: treacherous, unsafe. OE.
M. O. W. OLIPHANT It's a fickle corner in the dark.
2 Of a person, feelings, etc.: changeable in disposition, loyalty, affections, etc.; inconstant. ME.
S. NAIPAUL A . . lover fighting to keep to himself the affections of a fickle mistress. M. IGNATIEFF They were dependent on the fickle mercy of their sons.
3 Of a thing, esp. the weather: changeable, inconstant. LME.
F. CHICHESTER The wind was unusually fickle, changing speed and direction every few minutes.
■ **fickleness** *noun* LME. **fickly** *adverb* ME.

fickle /ˈfɪk(ə)l/ *verb trans. Scot. & dial.* M16.
[ORIGIN from the adjective.]
Baffle, perplex.
S. SMILES Other questions were put to 'fickle' him.

fico /ˈfiːkəʊ/ *noun. arch.* Pl. **-os**. L16.
[ORIGIN Italian from Latin *ficus* FIG *noun*[1]. Cf. FIGO.]
†**1** = FIG *noun*[1] 1C. L16–M17.
2 = FIG *noun*[1] 3. L16.
SHAKES. *Merry W.* 'Steal' foh! A fico for the phrase!

fictile /ˈfɪktʌɪl, -tɪl/ *adjective & noun*. E17.
[ORIGIN Latin *fictilis*, from *fict-*: see FICTION *noun*, -ILE.]
▸ **A** *adjective*. **1** Made of earth, clay, etc., by a potter. E17.
2 Of or pertaining to pottery or pottery manufacture. M19.
▸ **B** *noun*. A piece of pottery. Now *rare*. M19.

fiction /ˈfɪkʃ(ə)n/ *noun*. LME.
[ORIGIN Old French & mod. French from Latin *fictio(n-)*, from *fict-* pa. ppl stem of *fingere* fashion: see -ION. Cf. FEIGN.]
1 *gen.* A thing feigned or imaginatively invented; an invented statement or narrative; an untruth. LME.
GIBBON Such an anecdote may be rejected as an improbable fiction.
2 *gen.* The action of feigning or of inventing imaginary events etc. (orig. *spec.* for the purpose of deception); imaginative invention as opp. to truth or fact. L15.
C. THIRLWALL The scene may . . have afforded temptation for fiction. F. WELDON How much is fiction and how much is true?
3 *spec.* Literature consisting of the narration of imaginary events and the portrayal of imaginary characters; (the genre comprising) novels and stories collectively. L16. ▸**b** A work of fiction, a novel or story. L19.
LYTTON Old people like history better than fiction. **b** G. ORWELL He's supposed to publish my next three fictions.
4 *spec.* A conventionally accepted falsehood or pretence. L16.
DICKENS By a . . pleasant fiction his single chamber was always mentioned in the plural.
legal fiction: see LEGAL *adjective*.
†**5** Fashioning, imitating; arbitrary creation; a device, a thing created. L16–L18.
■ **fictionary** *adjective* (*rare*) = FICTIONAL L19. **fictioˈneer** *noun* a writer or inventor of fiction E20. **fictionist** *noun* a narrator or writer of fiction E19. **fictionize** *verb* (**a**) *verb trans.* = FICTIONALIZE; (**b**) *verb intrans.* invent a fictional version of events etc.: M19.

fiction /ˈfɪkʃ(ə)n/ *verb. rare.* E19.
[ORIGIN from the noun.]
1 *verb trans.* Feign; fictionalize. E19.
2 *verb intrans.* Admit of being fictionalized. M20.

fictional /ˈfɪkʃ(ə)n(ə)l/ *adjective*. M19.
[ORIGIN from FICTION *noun* + -AL[1].]
Of, pertaining to, or of the nature of fiction; imaginatively invented.
■ **fictioˈnality** *noun* the quality or state of being fictional M20. **fictionaliˈzation** *noun* the action or process of fictionalizing; a fictionalized version: M20. **fictionalize** *verb trans.* make into fiction, give a fictional form to; give a fictional version of (an actual event etc.): E20. **fictionally** *adverb* L19.

†**fictious** *adjective*. E17–L19.
[ORIGIN from Latin *fict-* (see FICTION *noun*) + -IOUS.]
Fictitious; characterized by fiction.

fictitious /fɪkˈtɪʃəs/ *adjective*. E17.
[ORIGIN from Latin *ficticius*, from *fict-*: see FICTION *noun*, -ITIOUS[1].]
1 Artificial, arbitrarily devised; counterfeit, imitation, sham. E17.
H. CROOKE Distinguish betweene natural and fictitious precious Stones.
2 Imaginary, invented; unreal, false; (of a name or character) assumed. E17.
N. ROWE The fictitious Justice of the Gods. POPE Make use of Real Names and not of Fictitious Ones.
3 Of, pertaining to, or characteristic of literary fiction. L18.
E. WAUGH How to invent names for fictitious characters without fear of prosecution.
4 Regarded as or called such by a legal or conventional fiction. M19.
H. J. S. MAINE Adoption, as a method of obtaining a fictitious son.
■ **fictitiously** *adverb* M17. **fictitiousness** *noun* M17.

fictive /ˈfɪktɪv/ *adjective*. L15.
[ORIGIN French *fictif*, *-ive* or medieval Latin *fictivus*, from Latin *fict-*: see FICTION *noun*, -IVE.]
†**1** Given to feigning in order to deceive. Only in L15.
2 Originating in fiction, created by the imagination; fictitious; unreal, sham. E17.
W. H. AUDEN Into what fictive realms can imagination/translate you.
3 Concerned with the creation of fiction; imaginatively creative. M19.
– NOTE: Rare before 19.
■ **fictively** *adverb* L19. **fictiveness** *noun* L20.

ficus /ˈfiːkəs, ˈfʌɪkəs/ *noun*. LME.
[ORIGIN Latin *ficus* fig tree, fig.]
1 *MEDICINE*. A type of condyloma resembling a fig. Long *rare* or *obsolete*. LME.
2 A tree or shrub of the large genus *Ficus*, of the mulberry family, which includes the fig, *F. carica*, and the rubber plant, *F. elastica*. M19.

fid /fɪd/ *noun & verb*. E17.
[ORIGIN Unknown.]
Chiefly *NAUTICAL*. ▸**A** *noun*. **1** A conical pin used to open the strands of rope in splicing. E17.
2 A plug of oakum for the vent of a gun. E17.
3 A square wooden or metal bar to support a topmast or topgallant; a bar used to support or steady anything. M17.
4 A small thick piece of anything; a bundle, a heap, a pile. In *pl.*, lots. *dial. & colloq.* M19.
▸ **B** *verb trans.* Infl. **-dd-**. Fix (a topmast etc.) with a fid. E18.

-fid /fɪd/ *suffix*.
[ORIGIN Latin *-fidus* split: see TRIFID.]
Forming adjectives with the sense 'divided into a specified number of parts', as ***quadrifid***, or (in *BOTANY*) 'divided in a specified way', as ***palmatifid***.

fidalgo /fɪˈdalgəʊ/ *noun. obsolete* exc. *hist.* Pl. **-os**. M17.
[ORIGIN Portuguese, contr. of *filho de algo* son of something. Cf. HIDALGO.]
A Portuguese noble.

Fid. Def. *abbreviation*.
Latin *Fidei Defensor* Defender of the Faith.

fiddle /ˈfɪd(ə)l/ *noun*.
[ORIGIN Old English *fiþele* = Middle Dutch & mod. Dutch *vedel* (*veel*), Old High German *fidula* (German *Fiedel*), Old Norse *fiðla* from Germanic from Proto-Romance, from Latin *vitulari* celebrate a festival, be joyful (cf. *Vitula* goddess of victory and jubilation).]
▸ **I 1** A stringed musical instrument of the violin family; *spec.* a violin. Now chiefly *colloq.* or *derog.* OE.
2 A person who plays a fiddle; *transf.* (now *rare*) a person to whose music others dance, a jester, an entertainer. L16.
F. MARRYAT He was . . the fiddle of the ship's company.
3 Something resembling a fiddle in shape; *esp.* (*NAUTICAL*) a contrivance to stop things sliding off a flat surface in rough weather. M19.
4 Fiddling, fussing; a fuss, an inconvenience. L19.
J. S. BLACKIE The eternal whirl and fiddle of life.
5 A swindle, a fraud; a piece of cheating. *colloq.* L19.
J. T. STORY This little harmless horse-racing racket and fiddle.
▸ **II 6** As *interjection*. Nonsense! Fiddlesticks! M19.
– PHRASES: ***fit as a fiddle***: see FIT *adjective*. **hang up one's fiddle** (chiefly *US*) retire from business, give up an undertaking. **hang up one's fiddle when one comes home** (chiefly *US*) cease to be cheerful or entertaining when in the company of one's family. **have a face as long as a fiddle** look miserable. **on the fiddle** engaged in a swindle or piece of cheating. **play first fiddle** take a leading role. **play second fiddle**, **play third fiddle** take a subordinate role.
– COMB.: **fiddle-back** (a chair with) a back shaped like the body of a fiddle; a chasuble similarly shaped; **fiddle-bow** the stringed bow with which a fiddle is played, a fiddlestick; **fiddle-case**: in which a fiddle is kept; **fiddle dock** a dock, *Rumex pulcher*, with fiddle-shaped leaves; **fiddle-fish** the monkfish, *Squatina squatina*; **fiddlehead** (**a**) = *scroll-head* s.v. SCROLL *noun* 2(b); (**b**) (in full ***fiddlehead greens***) the new leaf of certain ferns, considered a delicacy; **fiddleheaded** *adjective* having a fiddlehead or a fiddle-patterned handle; **fiddle pattern**: in the shape of the body of a fiddle; **fiddle-patterned** *adjective* (of cutlery) having the handle shaped like the body of a fiddle; **fiddle-string** any of the strings on a fiddle; **fiddlewood** (the timber of) any of various neotropical trees of the genus *Citharexylum*, of the verbena family, esp. the W. Indian *C. fruticosum* and *C. spinosum*.

fiddle /ˈfɪd(ə)l/ *verb*. LME.
[ORIGIN from the noun.]
1 *verb intrans.* Play the fiddle. LME.
V. WOOLF An old Spaniard who fiddled . . so as to make a tortoise waltz.
2 *verb trans.* Play (a tune etc.) on the fiddle. LME.
3 *verb intrans.* Be idle or frivolous; make aimless movements, toy or play *with*, *about*, *at*, etc.; fritter *away*. M16.
SWIFT He took a pipe in his hand, and fiddled with it till he broke it. H. SMART They've had him fiddling about so long in the school, he's most likely forgot how to gallop.

F

4 a *verb trans.* Cheat, swindle, falsify; get by cheating. *slang.* **E17.** ▸**b** *verb intrans.* Cheat; intrigue. **M19.**

G. CLARE He . . found out that the books had been fiddled, and how the fiddling had been done.

fiddlededee /fɪd(ə)ldɪˈdiː/ *interjection & noun.* **L18.**
[ORIGIN from FIDDLE *noun, verb* with a meaningless redupl. addition.]
▸ **A** *interjection.* Nonsense! **L18.**
▸ **B** *noun.* Nonsense, absurdity. **M19.**

fiddle-faddle /ˈfɪd(ə)lfad(ə)l/ *noun, adjective, verb, & interjection.* **L16.**
[ORIGIN Redupl. of FIDDLE *noun, verb.* Cf. GIBBLE-GABBLE.]
▸ **A** *noun.* **1** Trifling talk or action; a trifling or trivial matter (usu. in *pl.*). **L16.**
2 A trifler, a gossip. Now *dial.* **E17.**
▸ **B** *adjective.* Trifling, petty, fussy. **E17.**
▸ **C** *verb intrans.* Fuss, trifle, mess about. **M17.**
▸ **D** *interjection.* Nonsense! **L17.**

F

fiddler /ˈfɪdlə/ *noun.*
[ORIGIN Old English *fiþlere* (= Old Norse *fiðlari*), formed as FIDDLE *noun*: see -ER[1].]
1 A person who plays the fiddle. **OE.**
drunk as a fiddler: see DRUNK *adjective.*
2 A trifler. Now *spec.* a person who makes aimless movements or who toys or plays with something. **L16.**
3 a In full ***fiddler crab***. Any of various small crabs of the genus *Uca*, the males of which have one claw larger than the other and held in position like a violinist's arm. **E18.** ▸**b** = ***fiddle-fish*** s.v. FIDDLE *noun.* Also, the shovel-nosed ray, *Trygonorhina fasciata*, of Australian waters (more fully ***fiddler ray***). **L19.**
4 A cheat, a swindler, a falsifier. *slang.* **M19.**
5 A sixpence. *slang. obsolete* exc. *hist.* **M19.**
– COMB.: **fiddler-back**, **fiddler beetle**, an Australian black scarab beetle, *Eupoecila australasiae*, with green fiddle-shaped markings; ***fiddler crab***: see sense 3a above; ***fiddler ray***: see sense 3b above; **Fiddler's Green** *NAUTICAL* the sailor's Elysium, a place of wine, women, and song.

fiddlestick /ˈfɪd(ə)lstɪk/ *noun.* **LME.**
[ORIGIN from FIDDLE *noun* + STICK *noun*[1].]
1 A bow with which a fiddle is played. **LME.**
2 An insignificant thing, a triviality. *colloq.* Now *rare.* **E17.**

W. IRVING We do not care a fiddlestick . . for . . public opinion.

3 *sing.* & (usu.) in *pl.* As *interjection.* Nonsense! **E17.**

THACKERAY Do you suppose men so easily change their natures? Fiddlestick! THOMAS HUGHES Fiddlesticks! it's nothing but the skin broken.

fiddley /ˈfɪdli/ *noun.* **L19.**
[ORIGIN Unknown.]
NAUTICAL. An iron framework (usu. covered by a grating) round the deck opening leading to the engine room and stokehold of a steamer; the space it encloses.

fiddling /ˈfɪdlɪŋ/ *adjective.* **L16.**
[ORIGIN from FIDDLE *verb* + -ING[2].]
1 That fiddles. **L16.**
2 Petty; futile, contemptible, inconsiderable; *colloq.* fiddly. **M17.**

fiddly /ˈfɪdli/ *adjective. colloq.* **E20.**
[ORIGIN from FIDDLE *verb* + -Y[1].]
Requiring time or dexterity; pernickety.

fidei-commissum /ˌfʌɪdɪʌɪkɒˈmɪsəm/ *noun.* Pl. **-ssa** /-sə/. **E18.**
[ORIGIN Latin, neut. pa. pple of *fidei-committere* entrust a thing to a person's good faith, from *fidei* dat. of *fides* FAITH + *committere* entrust, commit.]
ROMAN LAW. A bequest in which an heir or legatee is instructed to transfer the legacy in whole or part to a third party.
■ **fideicommissary** *adjective* [Latin *fidei commissarius*: see -ARY[1]] of, pertaining to, or of the nature of a fidei-commissum **L19.**

fideism /ˈfʌɪdiːɪz(ə)m/ *noun.* **L19.**
[ORIGIN from Latin *fides* FAITH + -ISM.]
The doctrine that knowledge depends on faith or revelation.
■ **fideˈistic** *adjective* **E20.**

fidejussor /fʌɪdɪˈdʒʌsə/ *noun.* **E16.**
[ORIGIN Latin, from *fide-jubere*, from *fide* abl. of *fides* FAITH + *jubere* to order: see -OR 2.]
ROMAN LAW. A person who authorizes the bail of or goes bail for another; a surety.
■ **fidejussory** *adjective* [Latin *fidejussorius*] of or pertaining to surety or bail **M18.**

Fidelism /fɪˈdɛlɪz(ə)m/ *noun.* Also in Spanish form **Fidelismo** /fɪdɛˈlɪzməʊ/. **M20.**
[ORIGIN from Spanish *Fidelismo*, from *Fidel* Castro Ruz: see CASTROISM, -ISM.]
= CASTROISM.
■ **Fidelist** *adjective* of or pertaining to Fidel Castro or Fidelism **M20.**

fidelity /fɪˈdɛlɪti/ *noun.* **LME.**
[ORIGIN French *fidélité* or Latin *fidelitas*, from *fidelis* faithful, from *fides* FAITH: see -ITY.]
1 Loyalty, faithfulness, unswerving allegiance (*to* a person, spouse, cause, etc.). **LME.** ▸†**b** One's word of honour, one's pledge. **M–L16.** ▸**c** *ECOLOGY.* The degree of association of a species with a plant community. **M20.**

G. BURNET They serve those that hire them . . with . . great Fidelity. R. DAWKINS Kittiwakes form monogamous pair-bonds of exemplary fidelity.

2 Trustworthiness, veracity, accuracy (of a thing, †a person); correspondence with an original, *spec.* the degree to which a reproduced or transmitted sound, picture, etc., resembles the original. **M16.**

R. HOOKER The principall thing required in a witnesse is fidelitie. POPE Be very free of your Remarks . . in regard . . to the Fidelity of the Translation. G. STEINER Ancient literature . . was handed down with great fidelity.

high fidelity: see HIGH *adjective.*
– COMB.: **fidelity bond**, **fidelity insurance**, etc.: taken out by an employer to indemnify him or her against losses incurred through an employee's dishonesty etc.

fidepromissor /ˌfʌɪdɪprɒˈmɪsə/ *noun.* **L19.**
[ORIGIN Latin, from *fidepromittere*, from *fides* FAITH + *promittere* to promise: see -OR.]
ROMAN LAW. A person who pledges himself as security for another; a bail, a surety.

fidfad /ˈfɪdfad/ *noun & adjective.* Now *rare.* **M18.**
[ORIGIN Contr. of FIDDLE-FADDLE.]
▸ **A** *noun.* A person who gives attention to trifles, a fusspot; a trifle, a petty matter of detail. **M18.**
▸ **B** *adjective.* = FIDDLE-FADDLE *adjective.* **M19.**

fidge /fɪdʒ/ *verb & noun. dial. & colloq.* **L16.**
[ORIGIN Perh. rel. to FIG *verb*[2], FYKE *verb.*]
▸ **A** *verb intrans.* Move about restlessly or uneasily; be eager and restless; (of a limb) twitch. **L16.**
▸ **B** *noun.* The action of fidgeting; the state of being fidgety; a fidgety person. **M18.**

fidget /ˈfɪdʒɪt/ *noun.* **L17.**
[ORIGIN Sense 1 prob. from FIDGE *verb*; senses 2 & 3 from FIDGET *verb.*]
1 *sing.* & (usu.) in *pl.* Vague physical uneasiness, seeking relief in continual spasmodic movements; uneasiness, restlessness. Freq. ***the fidgets***. **L17.**
2 A person who fidgets or causes others to fidget. **E19.**
3 The action or habit of fidgeting. **M19.**

fidget /ˈfɪdʒɪt/ *verb.* **L17.**
[ORIGIN from the noun.]
1 *verb trans.* Cause to fidget; make uncomfortable, trouble, worry. **L17.**

J. AUSTEN She says I fidget her to death. ALBERT SMITH The heat fidgetted them all by day.

2 *verb intrans.* Make spasmodic movements indicative of restlessness, uneasiness, or impatience; move restlessly. **M18.** ▸**b** Be uneasy, worry. **M19.**

J. HATTON The chairman fidgetted uneasily in his seat. S. HILL His hands, which usually fidgeted with papers or cigar tin, were folded. **b** J. H. EWING Mother fidgetted because I looked ill.

■ **fidgeter** *noun* **E20.** **fidgetingly** *adverb* in a fidgeting manner **L19.**

fidget pie /fɪdʒɪt ˈpʌɪ/ *noun phr.* Also (earlier) **fitchet pie** /fɪtʃɪt/. **L18.**
[ORIGIN Unknown.]
A savoury pie containing onions, apples, and bacon.

fidgety /ˈfɪdʒɪti/ *adjective.* **M18.**
[ORIGIN from FIDGET *verb* + -Y[1].]
Inclined to fidget; uneasy, restless, impatient.
■ **fidgetily** *adverb* **L19.** **fidgetiness** *noun* **L18.**

fidibus /ˈfɪdɪbəs/ *noun.* **E19.**
[ORIGIN German: ult. origin unknown.]
A paper spill for lighting a pipe etc.

Fido /ˈfʌɪdəʊ/ *noun.* Also **FIDO.** **M20.**
[ORIGIN Acronym, from Fog Investigation Dispersal Operation.]
A device enabling aircraft to land by dispersing fog by means of petrol burners on the ground.

fiducial /fɪˈdjuːʃ(ə)l/ *adjective.* **L16.**
[ORIGIN Late Latin *fiducialis*, from Latin *fiducia* trust, from *fidere* to trust: see -AL[1], -IAL.]
1 *SURVEYING, ASTRONOMY*, etc. Designating a line, point, etc., assumed as a fixed basis of comparison. **L16.**
2 *THEOLOGY.* Of, pertaining to, or of the nature of trust or reliance. **E17.**
■ **fiducially** *adverb* **M17.**

fiduciary /fɪˈdjuːʃ(ə)ri/ *noun & adjective.* **L16.**
[ORIGIN Latin *fiduciarius*, from *fiducia*: see FIDUCIAL, -ARY[1].]
▸ **A** *noun.* †**1** Something that secures trust. Only in **L16.**
2 A person who holds a position of trust with respect to someone else, a trustee or someone subject to comparable obligations. **M17.**
▸ **B** *adjective* **1 a** Holding something in trust, acting as trustee. *obsolete* exc. *ROMAN LAW.* **M17.** ▸**b** Held or given in trust. **M17.** ▸**c** Of or pertaining to a trust, trustee, or trusteeship. **M18.**
†**2** Resembling or proceeding from trust. **M–L17.**
3 Of a paper currency: depending for its value on public confidence or securities. **L19.**
■ **fiduciarily** *adverb* †(*a*) trustfully; (*b*) under the conditions of a trust: **M17.**

fidus Achates /fʌɪdəs əˈkeɪtiːz/ *noun phr. literary.* **E17.**
[ORIGIN Latin = faithful Achates: see ACHATES.]
= ACHATES.

fie /fʌɪ/ *interjection & noun.* **ME.**
[ORIGIN Old French & mod. French *fi* from Latin *fi* exclam. of disgust at a stench. Cf. Old Norse *fý*.]
▸ **A** *interjection.* Expr. disgust, reproach, or (a pretence or assumption of) outraged propriety. *arch.* **ME.**

C. M. YONGE 'For shame, Viola! Oh fie! Oh Vi!' I said, in accordance with an ancient formula.

▸ **B** *noun.* An utterance of the word 'fie', a reproach, a protest. Now *rare.* **M16.**

fief /fiːf/ *noun & verb.* **E17.**
[ORIGIN Old French & mod. French: see FEE *noun*[2]. Cf. FEOFF *verb.*]
▸ **A** *noun.* = FEE *noun*[2] 1a. Also, one's sphere of operation or control. **E17.**

J. CLAVELL I served Lord Yoshi Chikitada . . when the clan's fief was no bigger than this village. H. WILSON It is his fief, an appointive bureaucracy.

▸ †**B** *verb trans.* Grant as a fief. Only in **L18.**
■ **fiefdom** *noun* a fief **E19.**

fie-fie /ˈfʌɪfʌɪ/ *adjective & verb. arch.* or *joc.* **E19.**
[ORIGIN Redupl. of FIE.]
▸ **A** *adjective.* Improper, of an improper or shocking character, causing (pretended) outrage. **E19.**
▸ **B** *verb intrans. & trans.* Say 'fie' (to). **M19.**

fiel /fiːl/ *adjective.* Long *obsolete* exc. *Scot.* Also **feel.**
[ORIGIN Old English *fǣle* = Old High German *feili* (German *feil*). Sense 2 may be a different word.]
†**1** Excellent, proper, good. **OE–LME.**
2 Comfortable, pleasant, cosy; soft, smooth. *Scot.* **L18.**

field /fiːld/ *noun & adjective.*
[ORIGIN Old English *feld*, corresp. to Old Frisian, Old Saxon *feld* (Dutch *veld*), Old High German, German *Feld*, from West Germanic.]
▸ **A** *noun.* **I** (A piece of) ground.
†**1** (A stretch of) open land. **OE–L17.**

C. MARLOWE Hilles and vallies, dales and fields. AV *Gen.* 2:5 Euery plant of the field.

2 (A piece of) land appropriated to pasture or tillage or some particular use, and usu. bounded by hedges, fences, etc. (Freq. with specifying word.) **OE.**

J. RUSKIN The fields! . . All spring and summer is in them. R. BRAUTIGAN The older children . . had to work in the fields . . picking beans.

cornfield, ***turnip-field***, etc.
3 The ground on which a battle is fought; a battlefield. Freq. ***the field***. **ME.**

LD MACAULAY These three chiefs . . fled together from the field of Sedgemoor. *fig.*: B. L. FARJEON I bade her good-day, and left Captain Bellwood in possession of the field.

4 A battle. *arch.* **LME.** ▸†**b** Order of battle. **E16–L17.**

MILTON What though the field be lost?

5 The country as opp. to a town or village. Now *arch. & dial.* **LME.**

SHAKES. *Mids. N. D.* In the town, the field, You do me mischief.

6 A piece of ground put to a (usu. specified) use other than pasture or tillage. **L16.**
airfield, ***bleachfield***, ***playing field***, etc.
7 Country which is, or is to become, the scene of a campaign; the scene of military operations. Chiefly ***the field***. **E17.**

J. A. MICHENER Days when a force of four hundred well-armed men could be put into the field.

8 a An enclosed piece of ground for playing a game, as cricket, football, etc., or for athletic events; part of this as an area of attack or defence. **M18.** ▸**b** *collect.* Field events (in athletics). Orig. *US.* **E20.**
infield, ***outfield***, etc.
9 *collect.* The players or partakers in an outdoor contest or sport; all competitors except a specified one or specified ones. **M18.** ▸**b** *CRICKET.* The side not batting. **M19.**

J. ARCHER They're into the straight mile—Minnow leads the field around the bend. *Horse & Hound* We had a large field out . . and hounds . . put on a spectacular performance.

10 In *CRICKET* etc., (the position of) a player stationed in a particular area of the field. **E19.**

M. R. MITFORD That exceedingly bad field . . caught him out.

11 A tract of ground abounding with some (usu. specified) natural product. **M19.**

C. CORNWALLIS Bowls filled with the precious metal, and . . labelled with the name of the field from which it was taken.

coalfield, ***diamond field***, ***goldfield***, ***oilfield***, etc.
▸ **II** An area of operation.
12 An area or sphere of action, operation, or investigation; a (wider or narrower) range of opportunities. **ME.** ▸**b** Scope, opportunity, extent of material for action or operation. Now *rare* or *obsolete.* **M17.** ▸**c** *MATH.* An algebraic system with two operations that satisfy certain axioms analogous to those for the multiplication and addition of

real numbers; a commutative ring that contains a unit element for multiplication and an inverse for each non-zero element. L19. ▸**d** COMPUTING. A set of one or more characters in a record which together represent a single item of information; an item that is or can be represented in this way. M20.

T. THOMSON A very interesting field of investigation. **b** SWIFT The matter . . will afford field enough for a divine to enlarge on.

13 The space or range within which objects are visible from a particular viewpoint, or through an optical instrument, the eye, etc., in a given position. Freq. ***field of observation, field of view, field of vision***, etc. M18.

A. BAIN The eye can take in a wide field at once. J. TYNDALL Organisms . . shooting rapidly across the microscopic field. R. HILLARY I noticed how small was my field of vision. H. READ As the mind perceives, it automatically selects and organizes the field of perception.

14 PHYSICS. A region in which some condition prevails, *esp.* a region of electric, gravitational, magnetic, etc., influence; the presence of such influence; the force exerted by such influence on a standard object. M19. ▸**b** EMBRYOLOGY. A region of an embryo capable of developing into a particular organ or part of one. E20. ▸**c** PSYCHOLOGY. An environment or situation regarded as a system of psychological forces with which an individual interacts. M20.

▸ **III** An extended surface.

15 The surface on which something is portrayed; *esp.* (HERALDRY) the surface of an escutcheon or of one of its divisions. Also, the groundwork of a picture, coin, flag, etc. LME.

TENNYSON Sir Lancelot's azure lions . . Ramp in the field.

16 A large stretch, an expanse, of sea, sky, ice, snow, etc. L16.

SHAKES. *Per.* Without covering, save yon field of stars. J. RUSKIN The snows round . . are the least trodden of all the Mont Blanc fields. *fig.*: A. BARRY The whole field of English history.

– PHRASES: ***a fair field and no favour***: see FAIR *adjective*. **a good field** a large number of good competitors, a group of strong candidates. ***back the field***: see BACK *verb* 5. ***common field***: see COMMON *adjective*. ***deep field***: see DEEP *adjective*. **depth of field** the distance between the nearest and the furthest objects that give an image judged to be in focus in a camera etc. ***electric field***: see ELECTRIC *adjective*. **field of honour** the ground where a duel or battle is fought. ***flood and field***: see FLOOD *noun*. **hold the field** avoid being superseded. **in the field** on campaign; in the natural environment as opp. to headquarters, a laboratory, etc. **keep the field** continue a campaign. ***long field***: see LONG *adjective*[1]. ***magnetic field***: see MAGNETIC *adjective*. ***open field***: see OPEN *adjective*. **play the field** *colloq.* avoid exclusive commitment to one person etc. ***potter's field***: see POTTER *noun*[1]. ***short field***: see SHORT *adjective*. **take the field** begin a campaign. ***track and field***: see TRACK *noun*.

▸ **B** *attrib.* or as *adjective*. **1** Of an animal, plant, etc.: having the open country as a natural habitat. LME.

C. CONRAN It might be easier to substitute ordinary field mushrooms.

2 Of military equipment: light and mobile for use with armies in the field. L16.

3 Of a test, piece of research, work, etc.: carried out or achieved in the natural environment. L18.

A. PRICE Aske needs more field experience, at the sharp end.

– COMB. & SPECIAL COLLOCATIONS: **field artillery** light ordnance fitted for travel and use in active operations; **field battery** a battery of light guns for use on a battlefield; **field bean** a variety of bean plant, *Vicia faba*, closely related to the broad bean but with smaller seeds, grown to improve soil fertility and for stockfeed; **field bed** (*a*) a camp bed, *esp.* one for use on active service; (*b*) a bed made in the open; ***field bindweed***: see BINDWEED 1; **field book**: used in the field by a surveyor for technical notes; **field boot** a military boot that is knee-length and close-fitting; **field character** a visible character that can be used in identifying a bird etc. in the field; **field-conventicle** an open-air conventicle; **field corn** *N. Amer.* corn grown to feed livestock; **field cornet** *hist.* a minor magistrate in charge of a district of the Cape Colony; **fieldcraft** the techniques involved in living, travelling, or making military or scientific observations in the field, especially while remaining undetected; **field day** (*a*) MILITARY (a day on which troops are drawn up for) a manoeuvring exercise, a review; (*b*) a day spent in the field for the purpose of hunting, exploration, etc.; (*c*) *fig.* a great occasion, a day noted for brilliant or important events, a triumph; **field dressing** bandage, ointment, etc., for dressing a wound on the battlefield; **field-effect transistor** a semiconductor device in which the majority carriers flow along a channel whose effective resistance is controlled by a transverse electric field produced by a reverse bias applied to a gate region surrounding the channel; **field emission** the emission of electrons from the surface of a conductor under the influence of a strong electrostatic field as a result of the tunnel effect; ***field emission microscope***, a device which utilizes this effect to produce an enlarged image of the emitting surface on a fluorescent screen; **field equation** any equation describing a field; *spec.* any of a series of equations relating to electromagnetic and gravitational fields established by J. C. Maxwell and Einstein respectively. **field event** an athletic event other than a race, such as weight-putting, jumping, discus-throwing, etc. (cf. ***track event*** s.v. TRACK *noun*); ***field fleawort***: see FLEA *noun*; **field general** AMER. FOOTBALL = QUARTERBACK *noun* 1; **field glass**, **field glasses** a (usu. binocular) telescope for outdoor use; **field goal** in American football and basketball, a goal scored when the ball is in normal play; in American football also, a goal scored from a drop kick or place kick direct from a scrimmage; in rugby football, a goal scored from a drop kick; **field grey** *noun & adjective* [translating German *Feldgrau*] (of) a shade of grey, the regulation colour of the uniform of a German infantryman; **field guide** a book for the identification of birds, flowers, etc., in the field; **field hand** (orig. *US*, now chiefly *hist.*) a person, esp. a slave, employed as a farm labourer; ***field hockey***: see HOCKEY *noun*[1] 1; **field hospital** a temporary military hospital esp. near a battlefield; **field madder** a Eurasian cornfield weed, *Sherardia arvensis*, of the madder family, with small pink flowers and whorled leaves; **field mark** a visible mark that can be used in identifying a bird etc. in the field; **field magnet**: providing magnetic flux in an electric generator or motor; **Field Marshal** an army officer of the highest rank; **field-meeting** †(*a*) a duel; (*b*) *hist.* a religious meeting held in the open air; (*c*) an outdoor meeting of naturalists, archaeologists, etc.; **field mouse** = ***wood mouse*** s.v. WOOD *noun*[1] (also ***long-tailed field mouse***); **field mushroom** a common edible mushroom, *Agaricus campestris*; **field mustard** charlock; **field notes** notes made by a surveyor, scientist, sociologist, etc., while engaged in fieldwork; **field officer** an army officer ranked above a captain and below a general; ***field pea***: see PEA *noun*[1] 2; **field-preacher** a person who preaches in the open air; **field-preaching** the action or an act of preaching in the open air; **field rank** the rank of a field officer; **field scabious** a scabious of dry grassy places, *Knautia arvensis*; **field spaniel** a spaniel trained to retrieve; a spaniel closely allied to but larger than the cocker; **field sports** outdoor sports, *esp.* hunting, shooting, and fishing; **fieldstone** stone used in its natural form, esp. for building; **field strength** the intensity of an electric, magnetic, or other field (***field-strength meter*** a device for measuring this); **field system** the system by which cultivated ground is subdivided into areas of arable, meadow, and pastureland; **field telegraph** a movable kind of telegraph for use on campaign; **field-test** *verb trans.* test (a device) in the environment in which it is to be used; **field theory** a theory about a field of operation, investigation, or influence, or in which the idea of such a field is the dominant concept; ***field vole***: see VOLE *noun*[2]; **fieldwork** (*a*) work carried out in the natural environment by a surveyor, collector of scientific data, sociologist, etc.; (*b*) MILITARY a temporary fortification; (*c*) (now *hist.*) the work of a field hand; **fieldworker** a person engaged in fieldwork.

■ **fieldful** *noun* as much or as many as a field will hold L19. **fieldward(s)** *adverb* towards the fields, in the direction of the fields E19.

field /fiːld/ *verb*. E16.

[ORIGIN from the noun.]

†**1** *verb intrans.* Take the field, fight. Only in 16.

2 *verb intrans.* Act as a fielder or fieldsman in cricket, baseball, etc. E19.

3 *verb trans.* Stop and return (the ball) in cricket, baseball, etc. M19. ▸**b** Deal competently with (a succession of questions etc.). E20.

b *Independent* Assistants have been fielding abusive phone calls ever since.

4 *verb intrans.* Bet on the field against the favourite. L19.

5 *verb trans.* Put (a sports team or army) into the field; select (a team or individual) to play. E20.

Time The Soviets fielded a huge conventional army that could have overrun Western Europe.

fielded /ˈfiːldɪd/ *adjective*. E17.

[ORIGIN from FIELD *noun*, *verb*: see -ED[2], -ED[1].]

1 Engaged on a battlefield, fighting in the open field. Long *arch. rare.* E17.

2 Of a ball in cricket, baseball, etc.: stopped (and returned). Of a succession of questions etc.: dealt (competently) with. L19.

3 Designed to form a field or fields; CABINETMAKING designating a panel of wood etc. made to project slightly beyond the surface of its frame. E20.

fielden /ˈfiːld(ə)n/ *adjective & noun*. Long *dial. rare*. M16.

[ORIGIN from FIELD *noun* + -EN[4].]

▸ **A** *adjective*. Level and open; consisting of fields. Formerly also, rural, rustic. M16.

▸ †**B** *noun*. Open land, cultivated land. E17–E18.

fielder /ˈfiːldə/ *noun*. ME.

[ORIGIN from FIELD *noun*, *verb* + -ER[1].]

1 A person who or animal which works in the fields. Long *rare* or *obsolete*. ME.

2 A person who backs the field against the favourite. M19.

3 In cricket, baseball, rounders, etc.: a member of the side that is not batting, a player on the side trying to get the other out, esp. one other than the bowler. M19.

fieldfare /ˈfiːldfɛː/ *noun*.

[ORIGIN Late Old English *feldefare*, perh. formed as FIELD *noun* + the stem of FARE *verb*.]

A thrush, *Turdus pilaris*, with a grey head and rump, known in Britain chiefly as a winter visitor.

fieldsman /ˈfiːldzmən/ *noun*. Pl. **-men**. E19.

[ORIGIN from FIELD *noun* + -'S[1] + MAN *noun*.]

In cricket, baseball, etc.: a member of the side that is not batting, a fielder.

fiend /fiːnd/ *noun*.

[ORIGIN Old English *fēond* = Old Frisian *fiand*, Old Saxon *fiond* (Dutch *vijand*), Old High German *fiant* (German *Feind*), Old Norse *fjándi*, Gothic *fijands*, from pres. pple of Germanic verb whence Old English *fēoġan*, Old Norse *fía*, Goth *fijan* hate. Cf. formation of FRIEND *noun*.]

†**1** An enemy, a foe. OE–ME.

2 = DEVIL *noun* 1. OE.

MILTON The Gates . . belching outrageous flame . . since the Fiend pass'd through. SIR W. SCOTT What the foul fiend can detain the Master so long?

fiend a haet, fiend haet: see HAET. ***fiend's limb***: see LIMB *noun*[1].

3 An evil spirit; a demon, devil, or diabolical being. OE.

F. BRAGGE Revenge . . makes a man a fiend incarnate. J. WESLEY Inflam'd with Rage like Fiends in Hell.

4 A person of superhuman wickedness, esp. cruelty or malignity. ME. ▸†**b** A monster; the personification of a baleful or destructive influence. LME–L18. ▸**c** A mischievous or annoying person; *esp.* (usu. with specifying word) a devotee, an addict. Freq. *joc.* E17.

SPENSER That cursed man, that cruel feend of hell. **b** W. COWPER He calls for famine, and the meagre fiend Blows mildew from between his shrivel'd lips. **c** ROBERT KNOX If religion, as Lenin said, is the opium of the people, he . . has done his best to make drug-fiends of us all. J. D. SALINGER Old Brossard was a bridge fiend, and he started looking around the dorm for a game.

■ **fiendlike** *adjective* resembling a fiend, characteristic of a fiend L16. **fiendly** *adjective* (*arch.*) †(*a*) hostile, unfriendly; (*b*) fiendish: OE.

F

fiendish /ˈfiːndɪʃ/ *adjective & adverb*. E16.

[ORIGIN from FIEND + -ISH[1].]

▸ **A** *adjective*. Resembling or characteristic of a fiend; superhumanly cruel and malignant; *colloq.* notably unpleasant, intractable, exasperating, etc. E16.

▸ **B** *adverb*. Excessively, horribly. *rare*. M19.

■ **fiendishly** *adverb* in a fiendish manner; excessively, horribly L19. **fiendishness** *noun* E17.

fierasfer /fʌɪəˈrasfə/ *noun*. M19.

[ORIGIN mod. Latin *Fierasfer* former genus name from Provençal *fieras-fer*, *fielat-fer*, from Old Provençal *filat* thread, net (from Latin *filum* FILE *noun*[2]) + *fer* fierce, wild (from Latin *ferus* wild).]

= ***pearlfish*** (b) s.v. PEARL *noun*[1] *& adjective*.

fierce /fɪəs/ *adjective & adverb*. ME.

[ORIGIN Anglo-Norman *fers*, Old French *fiers* nom. of *fer*, *fier* (mod. *fier* proud) from Latin *ferus* untamed.]

▸ **A** *adjective*. **1** Esp. of a wild animal: having or displaying a violent aggressiveness; of a violent and intractable temper. ME. ▸**b** Full of violent desire; furiously zealous; ardent. †Foll. by *for*, *to*, *upon*, and *to* with *inf.* LME. ▸**c** Of a mechanism: violent, not smooth or easy in action, forceful in effect. E20.

MILTON Moloc . . The fiercest Spirit That fought in Heav'n; now fiercer by despair. W. COWPER Poetry disarms The fiercest animals with magic charms. P. F. BOLLER A blooded brood stallion with a fierce and ungovernable nature. **b** E. NICHOLAS He is . . fierce for the Duke of Gloucesters returne. POPE Vengeful slaughter, fierce for human blood. J. COE They're fierce nationalists, all of them. **c** D. HALLIDAY The brake was fiercer than I expected, but the thing was stable enough.

†**2** High-spirited, brave, valiant. ME–L17.

†**3** Proud, haughty. ME–L16.

SHAKES. *2 Hen. VI* He is fierce and cannot brook hard language.

4 Esp. of emotions or natural forces: violently raging; unpleasantly strong or intense. ME.

POPE Music the fiercest grief can charm. W. S. CHURCHILL A vessel which . . could ride out the fiercest storms of the Atlantic ocean. J. STEINBECK The fierce light of the burning house.

▸ **B** *adverb*. In a fierce manner. Now *rare*. ME.

SHAKES. *1 Hen. VI* Mid-day sun fierce bent against their faces.

■ **fiercely** *adverb* ME. **fierceness** *noun* LME.

fieri facias /ˌfʌɪərʌɪ ˈfeɪʃɪas/ *noun phr.* LME.

[ORIGIN Latin = cause to be made, from *fieri* be made, come into being + *facias* 2nd person sing. pres. subjunct. of *facere* do, make.]

LAW (now *hist.*). A writ to a sheriff for executing judgement.

fierté /fjɛrte/ *noun*. Now *rare*. L17.

[ORIGIN French, after *fier*: see FIERCE, -TY[1].]

Haughtiness; high spirit.

fiery /ˈfʌɪəri/ *adjective*. ME.

[ORIGIN from FIRE *noun* + -Y[1].]

1 Consisting of fire; flaming with fire; fire-bearing. ME.

AV *Dan.* 3:23 These three men . . fell downe bound into the midst of the burning fierie furnace. DRYDEN He deals his fiery Bolts about.

fiery cross (*a*) *hist.* a wooden cross, charred and dipped in blood, used as a battle rallying signal among Scottish clans; (*b*) a burning cross used as a symbol of intimidation by the Ku Klux Klan.

2 Looking like fire; brightly glowing or flaming; blazing red. ME. ▸**b** Of eyes: flashing, ardent. M16.

A. RADCLIFFE The sun threw a fiery gleam athwart the woods.

3 Hot as fire; burning, red hot. ME. ▸**b** Acting like fire; producing a burning sensation; inflaming. M16. ▸**c** CRICKET. Making the ball rise dangerously. L19.

R. HOOKER The sword which is made fierie doth not only cut . . but also burne. **b** A. BAIN The fiery taste of alcoholic liquors.

4 Made, tested, or performed by the agency of fire. LME.

AV *1 Pet.* 4:12 The fiery triall which is to trie you.

5 Ardent, eager, fierce, spirited; pugnacious, irritable. LME. ▸**b** Of a horse: mettlesome. L16.

LD MACAULAY Adventures irresistibly attractive to his fiery nature. C. M. YONGE Charles, in his fiery petulance, declared that he would go. E. A. FREEMAN Such fiery zeal implies the firmest belief. **b** SHAKES. *Rich. II* The Duke . . Mounted upon a hot and fiery steed.

6 Of gas: liable to take fire, highly flammable. Of a mine etc.: containing such gas, liable to explosions. M18.

■ **fierily** *adverb* E17. **fieriness** *noun* LME.

fiesta /fɪˈɛstə/ *noun*. M19.
[ORIGIN Spanish = feast.]
In Spain or Spanish America: a religious festival; *gen.* any festivity or holiday.

FIFA /ˈfiːfə/ *abbreviation*.
French *Fédération Internationale de Football Association* International Association Football Federation.

fi. fa. *abbreviation*.
Fieri facias.

F

fife /fʌɪf/ *noun & verb*. M16.
[ORIGIN German *Pfeife* PIPE *noun*[1] or French *fifre* from Swiss German *Pfifre* (German *Pfeifer* PIPER).]
▶ **A** *noun*. **1** A kind of small shrill flute, used chiefly along with drums in military music. M16.
2 A player of this instrument. M16.
3 The sound of this instrument. E17.
▶ **B** *verb*. **1** *verb intrans.* Play the fife. L16.
2 *verb trans.* Play (an air etc.) on the fife. L19.

fifer /ˈfʌɪfə/ *noun*[1]. M16.
[ORIGIN from FIFE *verb* + -ER[1].]
A player of the fife.

Fifer /ˈfʌɪfə/ *noun*[2]. L19.
[ORIGIN from *Fife* (see below) + -ER[1].]
A native or inhabitant of Fife, a local government region of east central Scotland (formerly a county and also known as 'the kingdom of Fife').

fife rail /ˈfʌɪfreɪl/ *noun*. E18.
[ORIGIN Unknown.]
NAUTICAL. A rail round the mainmast of a sailing ship, with belaying pins for running rigging. Formerly also a rail forming the upper fence of the bulwarks on each side of the quarterdeck and poop in a man-of-war.

FIFO /ˈfʌɪfəʊ/ *abbreviation*.
Chiefly COMPUTING. First in, first out.

fifteen /fɪfˈtiːn, ˈfɪftiːn/ *adjective & noun* (*cardinal numeral*).
[ORIGIN Old English *fīftēne* (-*tiene*) = Old Frisian *fiftīne*, Old Saxon *fīftein* (Dutch *vijftien*), Old High German *fimfzehan* (German *fünfzehn*), Old Norse *fimtán*, Gothic *fimftaihun*, from Germanic base of FIVE, -TEEN.]
▶ **A** *adjective*. **1** One more than fourteen (a cardinal numeral represented by 15 in arabic numerals, xv, XV in roman). OE.

R. L. STEVENSON Fifteen men on the dead man's chest.

fifteen minutes (of fame) [with ref. to Andy Warhol's statement (1968), 'In the future everybody will be world famous for fifteen minutes'] a brief period of fame enjoyed by an ordinary person.

†**2** = FIFTEENTH *adjective*. LME–E17.

LD BERNERS The fyftene day of May.

▶ **B** *noun*. **1** Fifteen persons or things identified contextually, as years of age, chances (in giving odds), minutes, shillings (now *hist.*), pence, etc. OE.
The Fifteen the Jacobite rebellion of 1715.
2 One more than fourteen as an abstract number; the symbols or figures representing this (15 in arabic numerals, xv, XV in roman). LME.
†**3** Each of fifteen parts into which something was or might have been divided; *esp.* a tax of one-fifteenth formerly imposed on personal property. L15–M17.
4 The fifteenth of a set or series with numbered members, the one designated fifteen, (usu. ***number fifteen***, or with specification, as ***book fifteen***, ***chapter fifteen***, etc.); a size etc. denoted by fifteen, a garment etc. of such a size, (also ***size fifteen***). E16.
5 A set of fifteen; a thing having a set of fifteen as an essential or distinguishing feature; *spec.* (**a**) CRIBBAGE the exact sum of fifteen made by the face value of two or more cards (a court card being reckoned as ten), by which a player scores two points; (**b**) a team of fifteen in rugby football. M17.

R. KIPLING You're as good as in the First Fifteen already.

– COMB.: Forming compound numerals with multiples of a hundred, as **915** (read ***nine hundred and fifteen***, US also ***nine hundred fifteen***), etc. In dates used for one thousand five hundred, as **1512** (read ***fifteen twelve***), ***fifteen-nineties***, etc. With nouns + -ER[1] forming nouns with the sense 'something (identified contextually) being of or having fifteen —s', as ***fifteen-tonner*** etc. Special combs., as **fifteen-pounder** a gun throwing a shot that weighs fifteen pounds.

fifteenth /fɪfˈtiːnθ, ˈfɪftiːnθ/ *adjective & noun* (*ordinal numeral*).
[ORIGIN Old English *fīftēoþa*, repl. in Middle English by forms from FIFTEEN + -TH[2].]
▶ **A** *adjective*. Next in order after the fourteenth, that is number fifteen in a series, (represented by 15th). OE.

HENRY FIELDING And here we put an end to the fifteenth book. J. RUSKIN Dull inventions of the fifteenth century.

fifteenth part *arch.* = sense B.2 below.
▶ **B** *noun*. **1** The fifteenth person or thing of a category, series, etc., identified contextually, as day of the month, (following a proper name) person, esp. monarch or pope, of the specified name, etc. OE.

N. TORRIANO She having had a very bad Night from the Fourteenth to the Fifteenth.

2 Each of fifteen equal parts into which something is or may be divided (*hist.* a tax equal to one such part formerly imposed on personal property), a fraction which when multiplied by fifteen gives one, (= ***fifteenth part*** above). LME.

W. BLACKSTONE Tenths and fifteenths were temporary aids . . granted to the king by Parliament.

3 MUSIC. An interval embracing fifteen notes on the diatonic scale; a note a fifteenth above another given note; a chord of two notes a fifteenth apart. Also, an organ stop sounding fifteen notes above the open diapason. LME.
– COMB.: Forming compound numerals with multiples of a hundred, as ***five-hundred-and-fifteenth*** (**515th**) etc.
■ **fifteenthly** *adverb* in the fifteenth place M17.

fifth /fɪfθ/ *adjective, noun, & adverb* (*ordinal numeral*).
[ORIGIN Old English *fīfta* = Old Frisian *fifta*, Old Saxon *fifto* (Dutch *vijfde*), Old High German *fimfto* (German *fünfte*), Old Norse *fimti*, from Germanic from Indo-European, whence also Latin *quintus*, Greek *pemptos*: see -TH[2].]
▶ **A** *adjective*. Next in order after the fourth, that is number five in a series, (represented by 5th). OE.

W. COWPER Just made fifth chaplain of his patron lord.

fifth column [translating Spanish *quinta columna*] *hist.* an extra body of supporters claimed by General Mola as being within Madrid when he besieged the city with four columns of Nationalist forces in 1936; *gen.* an organized body sympathizing with and working for the enemy within a country at war etc. **fifth columnist** a member of a fifth column, a traitor, a spy. **fifth gear** the fifth in a sequence of forward gears in a motor vehicle, bicycle, etc. **fifth-generation** *adjective* (of a computer) belonging to a proposed new class of computer employing artificial intelligence. **Fifth Monarchy** the last of the five great empires referred to in the prophecy of Daniel (*Daniel* 2:44); ***Fifth-Monarchy-man***, a member of a 17th-cent. sect who expected the immediate coming of Christ and advocated the repudiation of all other government and the establishment of his reign by force. **fifth part** *arch.* = sense B.3 below. **fifth position** BALLET the position, esp. when starting or finishing a step, in which the feet are placed turned outwards one immediately in front of but touching the other, so that the toe of the back foot just protrudes beyond the heel of the front foot; the corresponding position of the arms. **fifth wheel** (**a**) the extra wheel of a coach; (**b**) the horizontal turntable over the front axle of a carriage etc. as an extra support to prevent its tipping; (**c**) *colloq.* a superfluous person or thing. **smite under the fifth rib** *arch.* strike to the heart, kill. **take the Fifth (Amendment)** *US* appeal to Article V of the ten original amendments (1791) to the Constitution of the US, which states that 'no person . . shall be compelled in any criminal case to be a witness against himself'; (in extended use) decline to incriminate oneself.

▶ **B** *noun*. **1** The fifth person or thing of a category, series, etc., identified contextually, as day of the month, (following a proper name) person, esp. monarch or pope, of the specified name, forward gear, etc. OE.

SHELLEY Each fifth shall give The expiation for his brethren here. W. ROBERTSON The spoil . . after setting apart the king's fifth, was divided.

2 MUSIC. An interval embracing five consecutive notes in the diatonic scale; a note a fifth above another given note; a chord of two notes a fifth apart. LME.
3 Each of five equal parts into which something is or may be divided, a fraction which when multiplied by five gives one, (= ***fifth part*** above). M16.
4 In *pl.* Articles of the fifth degree in quality; fifth-rate material. L19.
5 (A bottle containing) a fifth of a gallon of liquor. *US colloq.* M20.
– COMB.: Forming compound ordinal numerals with multiples of ten, as ***forty-fifth*** (**45th**), ***five-thousand-and-fifth*** (**5005th**), etc.
▶ **C** *adverb*. Fifthly. E16.
■ **fifthly** *adverb* in the fifth place E16.

fiftieth /ˈfɪftɪɪθ/ *adjective & noun* (*ordinal numeral*).
[ORIGIN Old English *fīftigeoþa*, corresp. to Old Norse *fimmtugandi*, from FIFTY on the analogy of TENTH *adjective & noun*: see -TH[2].]
▶ **A** *adjective*. Next in order after the forty-ninth, that is number fifty in a series, (represented by 50th). OE.

AV *Lev.* 25:11 A Iubile shall that fiftieth yeere be vnto you.

fiftieth part *arch.* = sense B.2 below.
▶ **B** *noun*. **1** The fiftieth person or thing of a category, series, etc., identified contextually. OE.
2 Each of fifty equal parts into which something is or may be divided, a fraction which when multiplied by fifty gives one, (= ***fiftieth part*** above). E19.
– COMB.: Forming compound numerals with multiples of a hundred, as ***one-hundred-and-fiftieth*** (**150th**) etc., and (*arch.*) with numerals below ten, as ***three-and-fiftieth*** etc.

fifty /ˈfɪfti/ *adjective & noun* (*cardinal numeral*).
[ORIGIN Old English *fīftiġ* = Old Frisian, Old Saxon *fiftich* (Dutch *vijftig*), Old High German *fimfzug* (German *fünfzig*), Old Norse *fimmtigr*, Gothic *fimftigjus*: see FIVE, -TY[2].]
▶ **A** *adjective*. **1** Five times ten (a cardinal numeral represented by 50 in arabic numerals, l, L in roman). OE.

BROWNING The new edition fifty volumes long. TENNYSON Better fifty years of Europe than a cycle of Cathay.

2 A large indefinite number of. E19.

H. S. BLACKWOOD I'll not forget old Ireland, Were it fifty times as fair.

▶ **B** *noun*. **1** Fifty persons or things identified contextually, as years of age, points, runs, etc., in a game, chances (in giving odds), etc. OE.

LEIGH HUNT A corpulent man of fifty.

2 A set of fifty; a thing having a set of fifty as an essential or distinguishing feature; *spec.* a fifty-pound note or fifty-dollar bill. OE.

AV *2 Kings* 1:13 Hee sent againe a captaine of the third fiftie, with his fiftie.

3 Five times ten as an abstract number; the symbols or figures representing this (50 in arabic numerals, l, L in roman). LME.
4 The fiftieth of a set or series with numbered members, the one designated fifty, (usu. ***number fifty***, or with specification, as ***chapter fifty***, ***verse fifty***, etc.); a size etc. denoted by fifty (also ***size fifty***). E16.
5 In *pl.* *The* numbers from 50 to 59 inclusive, esp. denoting years of a century or units of a scale of temperature; *one's* years of life between the ages of 50 and 59. L19.

R. B. ANDERSON A series of works published in the fifties and sixties.

– COMB.: Forming compound numerals (cardinal or ordinal) with numerals below ten, as ***fifty-nine*** (**59**), ***fifty-ninth*** (**59th**), etc., and (cardinals) with multiples of a hundred, as **350** (read ***three hundred and fifty***, US also ***three hundred fifty***), etc. Special combs., as **fifty-fifty** *adverb & adjective* (*colloq.*, orig. *US*) (on a basis of) fifty per cent, with equal shares, half-and-half; **fifty-year rule** a rule that public records should normally become open to inspection fifty years after their compilation.
■ **fiftyfold** *adjective & adverb* (**a**) *adjective* fifty times as great or as numerous; having fifty parts, divisions, elements, or units; (**b**) *adverb* to fifty times the number or quantity: OE. **fiftyish** *adjective* about fifty (in age, measurements, etc.) E20.

fig /fɪg/ *noun*[1]. ME.
[ORIGIN Old French & mod. French *figue* from Provençal *fig(u)a* from Proto-Romance alt. of Latin *ficus* fig tree, fig.]
1 A soft pear-shaped many-seeded fruit, eaten fresh or dried, which is borne by the widely cultivated Mediterranean tree *Ficus carica*; (more fully ***fig tree***) the tree which bears this fruit, a member of the mulberry family. Also, with specifying word, any of several other plants of the genus *Ficus* or unrelated plants having similar fleshy fruits; the fruit of such a plant. ME. ▸**b** A banana, *esp.* a small one. Chiefly *W. Indian.* L16. ▸†**c** More fully ***fig of Spain***, ***Italian fig***. A poisoned fig, used to kill a person secretly. L16–L17. ▸**d** A raisin. *dial.* L18.
Hottentot fig, ***Indian fig***, ***Moreton Bay fig***.
†**2** **a** *sing.* & in *pl.* Haemorrhoids, piles. LME–M16. ▸**b** An excrescence on the frog of a horse's hoof resembling a fig. L16.
3 A small, valueless, or contemptible thing. LME. ▸**b** A small piece of tobacco. *US.* M19.
– PHRASES: **not care a fig for**, **not give a fig for** regard as worthless or of no importance. **not worth a fig** of no value.
– COMB.: **figbird** (**a**) = BECCAFICO; (**b**) any of various Australasian orioles of the genus *Sphecotheres*, feeding on fruit; **fig-marigold** = MESEMBRYANTHEMUM; **fig parrot** = LORILET; **fig-pecker** = BECCAFICO; ***fig tree***: see sense 1 above; **figwort** any of various plants of the genus *Scrophularia* (family Scrophulariaceae), which bear dull, usu. purplish-brown flowers and were formerly thought useful against tuberculosis of the lymph nodes of the neck (scrofula).
■ **figged** *adjective* = FIGGY E18. **figgy** *adjective* (**a**) resembling figs; (**b**) (of a pudding) made with raisins: M16.

fig /fɪg/ *noun*[2]. Now *rare* or *obsolete*. L16.
[ORIGIN French *figue* (in phr. *faire la figue*) from Italian *fica*.]
An insulting gesture in which the thumb is thrust between two of the closed fingers or into the mouth.

fig /fɪg/ *noun*[3]. M19.
[ORIGIN from FIG *verb*[3].]
1 Dress, equipment. Only in ***in full fig***. M19.
2 Condition, form. Esp. in ***in fine fig***, ***in great fig***. L19.

fig /fɪg/ *verb*[1] *trans.* Now *rare* or *obsolete*. Infl. **-gg-**. L16.
[ORIGIN from FIG *noun*[2].]
Insult by giving the fig to.

fig /fɪg/ *verb*[2] *intrans.* *obsolete* exc. *dial.* Infl. **-gg-**. L16.
[ORIGIN Var. of FYKE *verb*. Cf. FIDGE *verb*.]
Move briskly and restlessly; jog to and fro.

fig /fɪg/ *verb*[3] *trans.* Infl. **-gg-**. L17.
[ORIGIN Var. of FEAGUE.]
†**1** Fill (the head) with nonsense etc. Only in L17.
2 Cause (a horse) to be lively and carry its tail well by applying ginger to its anus. Also foll. by *out*, *up*. E19.
3 Foll. by *out*, *up*: dress, get up; make smart. E19.

fig. *abbreviation*.
Figure.

Figaro /ˈfɪɡərəʊ/ *noun. arch. slang.* Pl. **-os.** M19.
[ORIGIN The hero of *Le barbier de Séville* and *Le mariage de Figaro* by Beaumarchais (1732–99), and later in operas by various composers.]
A barber.

figh /fiːk/ *noun.* L19.
[ORIGIN Arabic, lit. 'understanding'.]
The theory or philosophy of Islamic law, based on the teachings of the Koran and the traditions of the Prophet.

fight /fʌɪt/ *noun.*
[ORIGIN Old English *feohte*, *feoht*, *ġefeoht*, from base of the verb. Cf. Old Frisian *fiuht*, Old Saxon, Old High German *fehta* (Dutch *gevecht*), Old High German *gifeht* (German *Gefecht*).]
1 The action of fighting. *arch.* OE.
2 a A hostile encounter between (esp. large organized) opposing forces, = BATTLE *noun* 1. Now *arch.* or *rhet.* OE. ▸**b** A combat, esp. unpremeditated, between two or more people, animals, or other parties. Now also *spec.*, a boxing match. ME.

a P. HOLLAND The conflicts and fights at sea, in the first Punick warre.

3 *fig.* Strife, struggle for victory; a conflict against an opposing force. OE.

SHELLEY What secret fight Evil and good . . Waged thro' that silent throng. P. SCOTT His old man's dream of a fight to the bitter end.

†**4** A kind of screen used during naval encounters to conceal and protect the combatants. L16–L17.
5 Appetite or ability for fighting; pugnacity. E19.

D. WELCH Great walls of fight and resistance.

– PHRASES: **make a fight of it**, **put up a fight** offer resistance. *running fight*: see RUNNING *ppl adjective.* **sham fight** an imitation battle held as a training exercise or for display. **show fight** not give in tamely.
■ **fighty** *adjective* warlike, pugnacious ME.

fight /fʌɪt/ *verb.* Pa. t. **fought** /fɔːt/, pa. pple **fought**, (*arch.*) **foughten** /ˈfɔːt(ə)n/.
[ORIGIN Old English *feohtan* = Old Frisian *fiuhta*, Old Saxon *fehtan* (Du *vechten*), Old High German *fehtan* (German *fechten*) from West Germanic.]
1 *verb intrans.* Contend in war or battle or single combat. (Foll. by *against*, *with*, an opponent, *for* a person or thing supported or desired.) OE. ▸**b** *verb refl.* Bring (oneself) *into*, *out of*, *to* a certain condition etc. by fighting. M17.

J. WOLCOT He . . is ready to fight up to his knees in blood for her Majesty. I. MURDOCH She fought like a maniac. C. ISHERWOOD When they fought . . it was with fists and bottles and furniture.

2 *verb intrans. transf.* & *fig.* Contend, struggle, strive for victory; campaign or strive determinedly to achieve something. (With constructions as sense 1.) OE.

E. CALAMY Men that fight against a Reformation. S. SPENDER He fought in the General Election . . in the Liberal cause. A. PRICE The trailing blackberry shoots . . were fighting with the vigorous crop of stinging nettles.

3 *verb trans.* Engage in or conduct (a battle, duel, etc.). ME. ▸**b** Maintain (a cause, suit at law, quarrel, etc.) against opposition; contend over, contest (a question or election). E17. ▸**c** Contend with (a horse etc.) for mastery. *US.* M19. ▸**d** Win or make (one's way) by fighting. M19.

T. HARDY A midnight battle had been fought on the moors. **b** ADDISON He fights the cause Of honor, virtue, liberty, and Rome. **d** J. DIDION Maria tried to . . fight her way out of sleep.

4 *verb trans.* Engage or oppose in war, battle, or a duel, or with fists; war against. L17. ▸**b** Strive to overcome, contend against (disease, fire, fear, etc.). L18.

DAY LEWIS The scene of a battle . . when the boys of Wexford had fought the oppressors. **b** TENNYSON She cannot fight the fear of death. J. DICKEY The whole search party have to fight rapids after rapids for hour after hour.

5 *verb trans.* Cause (cocks, dogs, etc.) to fight. L17.
6 *verb trans.* Handle (troops, a ship, gun, etc.) in battle. L18.

R. L. STEVENSON He told Captain Hotham to . . fight his vessel till she sank.

7 *verb trans.* Contend in single combat for (a prize). *rare.* E19.
– PHRASES, & WITH ADVERBS IN SPECIALIZED SENSES: *fight a person with his or her own weapons*: see WEAPON. **fight back** (*a*) *verb phr. trans.* & *intrans.* resist; (*b*) *verb phr. trans.* suppress (one's feelings). **fight down** overcome, suppress (one's feelings). *fight fair*: see FAIR *adjective.* **fight off** (*a*) *verb phr. trans.* strive to defend oneself against, repel with effort; (*b*) *verb phr. intrans.* try to back out of something. **fight out** pursue (a fight etc.) to the end, settle by fighting (freq. in *fight it out*). **fight shy of** avoid, be unwilling to approach (a person, task, etc.). *fight tooth and nail*: see TOOTH *noun.* **fight up against** (now *rare* or *obsolete*) struggle against being overwhelmed by. *fight windmills*: see WINDMILL *noun* 1.
– COMB.: **fightback** a retaliation, a rally, a recovery; **fight-off** a contest to decide a tie, *spec.* in a fencing match.
■ **fightable** *adjective* E19.

fighter /ˈfʌɪtə/ *noun.*
[ORIGIN Old English *feohtere* = Old High German *fehtāri*. Later from FIGHT *verb* + -ER[1].]
1 A person, animal, etc., who fights. OE.
2 A high-speed military aircraft designed mainly for aerial combat. E20.
– ATTRIB. & COMB.: In the sense 'designating or pertaining to a fighter (aircraft) or fighters', as *fighter cover*, *fighter machine*, *fighter pilot*, *fighter plane*, *fighter squadron*, etc. Special combs., as **fighter bomber** an aircraft serving as both a fighter and a bomber.

fighting /ˈfʌɪtɪŋ/ *verbal noun.* ME.
[ORIGIN from FIGHT *verb* + -ING[1].]
The action of FIGHT *verb.*
– COMB.: **fighting chair** *US* a fixed chair on a boat used by a person trying to catch large fish; **fighting chance** an opportunity of succeeding by great effort; *fighting cock*: see COCK *noun*[1] 1; **fighting drunk** *adjective* (*colloq.*) drunk and quarrelsome; **fighting fit** *adjective* fit enough to fight; at the peak of fitness; **fighting fund** a sum of money raised to finance a cause or campaign; **fighting mad** *adjective* (*colloq.*) furiously angry; **fighting sails** (chiefly *hist.*) the sails retained by a ship going into action, formerly the courses and topsails only; **fighting talk** *colloq.* talk indicating a willingness to fight, talk likely to provoke a fight; **fighting top** NAUTICAL a circular gun platform placed high on the mast of a warship; **fighting trim** the state of readiness of a ship for battle; *fig.* excellent health or condition, readiness for action, (chiefly in *in fighting trim*); **fighting weight** the specified weight or weight range within which a boxer etc. must come to be eligible to fight in a certain class; an individual's ideal weight for fitness; **fighting words** *colloq.* words indicating a willingness to fight, words likely to provoke a fight.

fighting /ˈfʌɪtɪŋ/ *ppl adjective.* ME.
[ORIGIN formed as FIGHTING *noun* + -ING[2].]
That fights, able and ready to fight; militant, warlike.
Siamese fighting fish: see SIAMESE *adjective.*
■ **fightingly** *adverb* M17.

fig leaf /ˈfɪɡliːf/ *noun.* Pl. **leaves** /-liːvz/. M16.
[ORIGIN from FIG *noun*[1] + LEAF *noun*[1].]
1 The leaf of a fig tree, *spec.* (with ref. to *Genesis* 3:7) when used as a covering to conceal the genitals. M16.
2 *fig.* A means of concealing something shameful or indecorous. Usu. in *pl.* M16.

C. KINGSLEY They tore off . . even the fig-leaves of decent reticence.

■ **fig-leafed**, **-leaved** *adjective* (*a*) made of fig leaves; (*b*) (of the genitals etc.) covered by fig leaves: E18.

figment /ˈfɪɡm(ə)nt/ *noun.* LME.
[ORIGIN Latin *figmentum*, from base of *fingere* to fashion: see -MENT.]
1 a An invented statement, story, doctrine, etc. LME. ▸**b** A thing which has no existence other than in the imagination. E17.

b P. PEARCE Neither a silly figment of her imagination nor a flesh-and-blood man.

†**2** Something moulded or fashioned; an image, model, etc. L16–M17.
■ **figmental** /fɪɡˈmɛnt(ə)l/ *adjective* of the nature of a figment, fictitious, imaginary M17.

†**figo** *noun.* Pl. **-os.** L16–M17.
[ORIGIN Old Spanish & Portuguese.]
= FICO.

SHAKES. *Hen. V* The Figo for thee then.

figuline /ˈfɪɡjʊlɪn, -ʌɪn/ *adjective* & *noun.* Now *rare.* M17.
[ORIGIN Latin *figulinus*, from *figulus* potter: see -INE[1].]
▸ **A** *adjective.* **1** Made of earthenware. M17.
2 Of earth: suitable for pottery. L17.
▸ **B** *noun.* **1** Potter's clay. M19.
2 An earthen vessel. L19.

figura /fɪˈɡjʊərə/ *noun.* Pl. ***-rae*** /-riː/, ***-ras***. M20.
[ORIGIN Latin: see FIGURE *noun.*]
1 THEOLOGY. A type of a person. Cf. FIGURE *noun* 8. M20.
2 A person who represents a higher or supervening reality. *literary.* M20. ▸**b** An act or deed that is representative or symbolic. M20.

figurable /ˈfɪɡjʊrəb(ə)l/ *adjective.* E17.
[ORIGIN Old French & mod. French, formed as FIGURE *verb*: see -ABLE.]
Able to receive a definite figure or form; able to be represented figuratively.
■ **figuraˈbility** *noun* M18.

figurae *noun pl.* see FIGURA.

figural /ˈfɪɡjʊr(ə)l/ *adjective.* LME.
[ORIGIN Old French, or late Latin *figuralis*, from *figura* FIGURE *noun*: see -AL[1].]
1 = FIGURATIVE 1, 2. LME.
†**2** MATH. = FIGURATE *adjective* 3. M16–E18.
3 a *gen.* Pertaining to figures or shapes. Now *rare* or *obsolete.* M17. ▸**b** *spec.* Of sculpture: consisting of human or animal figures, usu. in relief. M20.
4 MUSIC. Florid, embellished with a rapid repetitive accompaniment. L19.
■ **figurally** *adverb* LME.

figurant /fiɡyrɑ̃ (*pl. same*), ˈfɪɡjʊr(ə)nt/ *noun.* Fem. ***-ante*** /-ɑ̃ːt (*pl. same*), -(ə)nt/. L18.
[ORIGIN French, pres. ppl adjective of *figurer* FIGURE *verb*: see -ANT[1].]
1 A ballet dancer. Now *rare* or *obsolete.* L18.
2 A supernumerary actor in a play; a (freq. non-dancing) performer with a supporting role in a ballet. L18.

figurante /fɪɡʊˈrante, fɪɡjʊˈranti/ *noun*[1]. Now *rare* or *obsolete.* Pl. ***-ti*** /-ti/, ***-tes*** /-tɪz/. L18.
[ORIGIN Italian, verbal adjective of *figurare* FIGURE *verb.*]
= FIGURANT 1.

figurante *noun*[2] see FIGURANT.

figuranti *noun pl.* see FIGURANTE *noun*[1].

figurate /ˈfɪɡjʊreɪt/ *ppl adjective* & *noun.* L15.
[ORIGIN Latin *figuratus* pa. pple, formed as FIGURATE *verb*: see -ATE[2].]
▸ **A** *ppl adjective.* **1** Formed into or represented by a figure; having definite form or shape. L15.
†**2** Based on figures or metaphors; figurative. M16–E18.
3 MATH. Capable of representation by geometrical figures. Now only in ***figurate numbers***, (series of) numbers, such as polygonal numbers, that can be represented as occupying a simple geometrical figure. E17.
4 MUSIC. = FIGURAL 4. E18.
▸ **B** *noun.* A figurate thing, *esp.* a figurate number. Now *rare* or *obsolete.* E17.

figurate /ˈfɪɡjʊreɪt/ *verb trans.* L15.
[ORIGIN Latin *figurat-* pa. ppl stem of *figurare* form, fashion, from *figura* FIGURE *noun*: see -ATE[3].]
†**1** Liken *to*, compare *to*. Only in L15.
†**2** Represent by a figure or emblem. M16–M17.
†**3** Give figure or shape to; present in visible shape. E17–E18.
4 Speak of or treat figuratively; represent by a figure or metaphor. M17.

figuration /fɪɡəˈreɪʃ(ə)n, -ɡjʊ-/ *noun.* LME.
[ORIGIN Old French & mod. French, or Latin *figuratio(n-)*, formed as FIGURATE *verb*: see -ATION.]
1 The form, shape, outline, or contour of a thing. LME. ▸**b** The action or process of giving shape to; assignment to a certain form. M16.

THOMAS SMITH The different shapes and figurations of letters in several ages of the world.

†**2** MATH. The making of arithmetical figures; the multiplying of a number into itself. LME–L17.
3 Allegorical representation. M16.

W. FULKE The sacrament is not a bare figuration of the flesh of Christ.

4 MUSIC. Use of florid counterpoint; alteration by the introduction of passing notes, rapid figures, etc. L16.

Listener Short skirling woodwind figurations and languid dying falls on the solo cello.

5 Ornamentation by means of figures or designs. M17.

figurative /ˈfɪɡərətɪv, -ɡjʊ-/ *adjective.* LME.
[ORIGIN Late Latin *figurativus*, formed as FIGURATE *verb*: see -ATIVE.]
1 Emblematic, typical. LME.
2 Based on or using figures or metaphors; metaphorical, not literal. LME.

COVERDALE By a figurative . . speech he declareth the horror . . of the damned.

3 Containing or using many figures of speech. L16.

W. BELSHAM Shakespeare . . is the most figurative writer in our language.

†**4** Pertaining to the use of graphic symbols or numbers. L16–E19.
5 Pertaining to or of the nature of pictorial or sculptural representation. E17. ▸**b** *spec.* Of an artist, a style of painting, etc.: creating forms which are recognizably derived from objective sources without necessarily being clearly representational. M20.

b *Listener* Figurative painters today undoubtedly owe much to abstract expressionism.

6 MUSIC. = FIGURAL 4. E18.
■ **figuratively** *adverb* LME. **figurativeness** *noun* E18.

figure /ˈfɪɡə/ *noun.* ME.
[ORIGIN Old French & mod. French from Latin *figura*, from base of *fingere* to fashion: see -URE.]
▸ **I** Form, shape.
†**1 a** The proper or distinctive form of a person or thing. ME–E17. ▸**b** *gen.* The external form or shape of something. LME.
2 GEOMETRY. A definite form consisting of a two-dimensional space enclosed by a line or lines or a three-dimensional space enclosed by a surface or surfaces; any of the classes of these, as the triangle, circle, cube, etc. ME.

A. KOESTLER A geometrical figure on the blackboard.

3 A person considered as a visible form. ME. ▸**b** A person as an object of mental contemplation. M18.

L. HELLMAN A figure in the distance running up and down the beach. R. ELLISON A figure in a nightmare which the sleeper tries . . to destroy. **b** ISAIAH BERLIN Its most venerated figure, a cultivated, fastidious, and morally sensitive scholar. K. ISHIGURO All groups of pupils tend to have a leader figure.

4 The bodily shape or bodily frame of a person etc. LME.

T. DREISER Her rather slim and as yet undeveloped figure. DAY LEWIS Nor can I recall his face or figure.

F

F

5 a Style of living, *esp.* ostentatious living. *arch.* **E17.** ▸**b** Importance, distinction; personal rank or standing. Now chiefly in ***man of figure***, ***woman of figure***. *arch.* **L17.**
▸ **II** Represented form, likeness.
6 The image or representation of something material or abstract. **ME.** ▸†**b** An imaginary form. **LME–L16.**

BURKE He is their standard figure of perfection.

7 A representation of the human form in sculpture, painting, etc.; a statue, a portrait. **ME.**

K. CLARK Round the merchants' church . . are life-size figures of the saints. J. BERGER The porcelain figure of the shepherdess.

8 An emblem, a type. **ME.**

C. CARTWRIGHT The Rock . . was a Type and a Figure of Christ.

†**9 a** A person acting a part. Only in **LME.** ▸**b** A part enacted, a represented character. Also, a position, capacity. **E17–E18.**
▸ **III** A written character.
10 A numerical symbol, esp. each of the ten used in Arabic notation. **ME.** ▸**b** A number, amount of money, or value, expressed in figures. **M19.** ▸**c** In *pl.* Arithmetical calculations. **E20.** ▸**d** *CRICKET.* In *pl.* A bowler's average. **M20.**

L. P. HARTLEY He felt disinclined to go on totting up figures. S. WEINBERG Wavelengths given . . to eight significant figures. **b** J. F. KENNEDY The tremendous figures that the Germans were spending.

†**11** *gen.* A letter of the alphabet, a symbol for a musical note, a mathematical symbol, or other written character. **L16–M17.**
▸ **IV** Devised form; design.
12 A diagram, an illustrative drawing. (Freq. abbreviated to ***fig.***) **LME.**
13 *ASTROLOGY.* A diagram of the aspects of the astrological houses; a horoscope. **LME.**
14 An ornamental arrangement of lines or other markings; a decorative pattern. **L16.** ▸**b** *spec.* The pattern formed by the grain and knots in wood. **L19.**
15 An evolution or set of evolutions in dancing. Also, one of the divisions of a set dance. **M19.**

F. NORRIS A square dance was under way, the leader of the city band calling the figures.

16 *SKATING.* A movement or series of movements following a prescribed pattern and often beginning and ending at the same point. **M19.** ▸**b** A movement in formation flying or swimming following a prescribed pattern. **M20.**
▸ **V** Repr. Greek *skhēma* form.
17 *LOGIC.* The form of a syllogism as determined by the position of the middle term. **LME.**
18 *MUSIC.* A short succession of notes which produce a single impression; a brief melodic or rhythmic motif out of which longer passages are developed. **LME.**
19 More fully ***figure of speech***. A form of rhetorical expression which gives beauty, variety, force, etc., to a composition, as metaphor or hyperbole. **LME.** ▸**b** A metaphor, a metaphorical expression. **LME.**

S. SONTAG My subject is not physical illness itself but the uses of illness as a figure or metaphor.

20 (Usu. **F-**.) In *pl.* (The name of) a class in a Roman Catholic school, college, or seminary, now only *spec.* the second class, immediately above Elements and below Rudiments, in certain Jesuit Schools. **E17.**
21 *GRAMMAR.* Any of the standard deviations from the normal forms of words, as elision, or from the rules of construction, as ellipsis. **E17.**

– PHRASES ETC.: **cut a figure** = *make a figure* below. ***double figures***: see DOUBLE *adjective & adverb*. ***facts and figures***: see FACT. ***father figure***: see FATHER *noun*. **figure four (trap)** an animal trap with a trigger set in the shape of a figure 4. ***figure of EIGHT***. **figure of four (trap)** = *figure four trap* above. **figure of fun** a grotesque or ridiculous person. **figure of merit** a numerical expression taken as representing the performance or efficiency of a given device or material. ***four-figure***: see *two-figure* below. ***four figures***: see *two figures* below. **go the whole figure** *US* do something thoroughly, go the whole hog. **keep one's figure** not grow stout. **make a figure** (*a*) (with qualifying adjective) present a specified appearance, create a particular impression; (*b*) play a prominent or important part. ***mother-figure***: see MOTHER *noun*[1]. ***parent-figure***: see PARENT *noun*. ***public figure***: see PUBLIC *adjective & noun*. ***significant figure***: see SIGNIFICANT *adjective* 1c. ***three-figure***: see *two-figure* below. ***three figures***: see *two figures* below. **two-figure**, **three-figure**, **four-figure**, etc. *adjectives* designating or involving (*a*) numbers respectively between 10 and 99, 100 and 999, 1000 and 9999, etc.; (*b*) numbers expressed to two, three, four, etc., significant figures. **two figures**, **three figures**, **four figures**, etc., a total between 10 and 99, 100 and 999, 1000 and 9999, etc.
– COMB.: **figure-caster** (*a*) (now *rare*) a person who casts horoscopes; (*b*) a person who performs numerical calculations; **figure-casting** the action or practice of casting horoscopes; **figure-dance** a dance consisting of several distinct figures or divisions; **figure-dancer** a performer in a figure-dance; **figure-flinger** (long *rare*) = *figure-caster* (a) above; **figure-floating** the formation of set patterns by a group of swimmers floating in the water; **figure-hugging** *adjective* (of a woman's garment) fitting closely to the contours of the wearer's body; **figure skater** a person who practises figure skating; **figure skating** a type of ice skating in which the skater combines a number of movements including steps, jumps, and turns; **figure weaving** weaving of cloth with individual patterns or figures in it.
■ **figureless** *adjective* **E17.**

figure /ˈfɪɡə/ *verb*. **LME.**
[ORIGIN Old French & mod. French *figurer* from Latin *figurare*, from *figura* FIGURE *noun*.]
†**1** *verb trans.* Give figure to; form, shape. **LME–L18.**
2 *verb trans.* Represent in a diagram or picture. **LME.** ▸**b** Trace (a design, letter, etc.). **E16.**

R. L. STEVENSON The Greeks figured Pan . . stamping his foot. H. ADAMS There are two series of windows, one figuring the . . followers of Louis VIII.

3 *verb trans.* Be an image or type of; represent typically. Now *rare*. **LME.**

H. COGAN This boy leaned on his elbow upon the . . chair and figured mercy.

†**4** *verb trans.* Liken *to*. **LME–E16.** ▸**b** Resemble. *rare*. **M16–L18.**
5 *verb trans.* Express in a metaphorical sense; express by means of a metaphor or other image. **LME.** ▸†**b** Adorn with figures of speech. **M17–E18.**
6 *verb trans.* Ornament or adorn with a design or pattern; *MUSIC* embellish with an accompaniment in quicker time. **LME.**

F. NORRIS A white paper figured with knots of pale green leaves.

†**7** *verb trans.* Prefigure, foretell. **LME–L16.**
8 *verb trans.* Represent by speech or action. **L15.**
9 *verb trans.* Picture in the mind; imagine. **E17.**

E. L. LINTON All the pains and grief his imagination had ever figured.

10 *verb intrans.* †**a** Stand for, lay claim to. Foll. by *for*. **E–M17.** ▸**b** Appear, feature, make an appearance. Also, be conspicuous. **M17.** ▸**c** Show off. (Foll. by *away*, *off*.) **L18.** ▸**d** Foll. by *as*: appear in the character of, resemble. **E19.**

b E. M. FORSTER She was expected to figure at this function, and to figure largely. J. P. DONLEAVY There's the garden that's figured so prominently in my dreams. J. DIDION Maria tried to remember in which of the woman's stories Lee had figured.

11 a *verb trans.* Mark with numerical figures; express in figures. **L17.** ▸**b** *verb trans.* *MUSIC.* Mark (esp. the bass) with numbers in order to indicate the proper harmony. **L17.** ▸**c** *verb intrans.* Use figures in arithmetic. **M19.**
12 *verb intrans. & trans.* *DANCING*, *SKATING*, etc. Perform (a figure or set of evolutions). Also foll. by *down*, *away*, *out*. **M18.**
13 *verb trans.* Reckon, calculate; understand, ascertain. *colloq.* (orig. & chiefly *N. Amer.*). **M19.**

J. D. SALINGER Even though I was pretty loaded, I figured I could . . use a few extra bucks. L. BRUCE It didn't work out the way I had figured it.

14 *verb intrans.* Foll. by *on*, *upon*: think over, consider; count on, expect. *colloq.* (chiefly *US*). **M19.** ▸**b** (Of information received, an event, etc.) be understandable, make sense. Freq. with impers. *it* (foll. by *that*). **M20.**
– WITH ADVERBS IN SPECIALIZED SENSES: **figure out** (*a*) work out, esp. by arithmetic or logic; (*b*) (chiefly *US*) understand, estimate; (see also sense 13 above). **figure up** reckon up with figures.
■ **figurer** *noun* **M16.**

figured /ˈfɪɡəd/ *adjective*. **LME.**
[ORIGIN from FIGURE *verb*, *noun*: see -ED[1], -ED[2].]
1 Having a particular figure or shape. **LME.** ▸†**b** Having a definite shape, structured. **E17–L18.**

T. DWIGHT Its summits are finely figured, and richly diversified.

2 Shaped into or represented by a figure or figures; *MATH.* = FIGURATE *adjective* 3. **L15.**
3 Adorned with patterns or designs. **L15.**

T. SHERIDAN A pretty figured linen gown.

4 Adorned with rhetorical figures; figurative. **E16.**
5 Of a dance: consisting of figures. **E18.**
6 *HERALDRY.* Of the sun, moon, or other charge: drawn with a human face. **M19.**
7 *MUSIC.* = FIGURAL 4. **L19.**
– SPECIAL COLLOCATIONS: ***figured bass***: see BASS *noun*[2].

figurehead /ˈfɪɡəhɛd/ *noun*. **M18.**
[ORIGIN from FIGURE *noun* + HEAD *noun*.]
1 An ornamental carving, usually a bust or full-length figure, placed over the cutwater of a ship. **M18.**
2 A nominal leader, president, etc., who has little or no authority or influence. **L19.**

figurette /fɪɡjʊˈrɛt/ *noun*. *rare*. **M19.**
[ORIGIN from FIGURE *noun* + -ETTE.]
= FIGURINE.

figurine /ˈfɪɡəriːn, -ɡjʊ-/ *noun*. **M19.**
[ORIGIN French from Italian *figurina* dim. of *figura* FIGURE *noun*: see -INE[4].]
A small modelled or sculpted figure; a statuette.

figurist /ˈfɪɡjʊrɪst/ *noun*. *obsolete* exc. *hist.* **L16.**
[ORIGIN from FIGURE *verb* + -IST.]
A believer in the figurative nature of something, e.g. of the presence of Christ in the Eucharist.

Fijian /fiːˈdʒiːən/ *noun & adjective*. **E19.**
[ORIGIN from *Fiji* (see below) + -AN.]
▸ **A** *noun*. **1** A native or inhabitant of the Fiji archipelago or the state of Fiji in the S. Pacific. **E19.**
2 The Austronesian language of the Fijians. **M19.**
▸ **B** *adjective*. Of, pertaining to, or designating the Fiji archipelago, the Fijians, or their language. **M19.**

fike *verb* var. of FYKE *verb*.

†**filace** *noun*. Also **-aze**. **LME–M16.**
[ORIGIN Anglo-Norman *filaz* file of documents from medieval Latin *filacium*, either from Latin *filum* thread, FILE *noun*[2], or abbreviation of late Latin *chartophylacium* chest for papers, from Greek *khartophulakion*, from *khartēs* paper, CHART *noun* + *phulak-* (*phulassein*) to keep, guard.]
LAW. = FILE *noun*[2] 1.

filacer /ˈfɪləsə/ *noun*. *obsolete* exc. *hist.* Also **-zer** /-zə/. **E16.**
[ORIGIN Law French, formed as FILACE: see -ER[2].]
LAW. An officer of the superior courts at Westminster who filed original writs and issued processes.

filagree *noun* var. of FILIGREE.

filament /ˈfɪləm(ə)nt/ *noun*. **L16.**
[ORIGIN French, or mod. Latin *filamentum*, from late Latin *filare* spin, from Latin *filum* thread: see -MENT.]
1 A fine flexible length of some material, esp. in a plant or animal, or produced artificially from glass, metal, etc.; *spec.* (*a*) a thin stream of light or wisp of smoke etc.; (*b*) a thread of man-made fibre. **L16.** ▸**b** *ASTRONOMY.* A narrow threadlike streamer from the sun's chromosphere or in its corona. **M19.** ▸**c** A heat-resistant conducting wire, now usu. made of tungsten, in an electric bulb or thermionic valve which is heated or made incandescent by the electric current. **L19.**

J. GASKELL These aren't spiderwebs: . . they're mycelium filaments, the start of my mushrooms. F. KING Filaments of mist were beginning to curl over the sides of the island.

2 a *BOTANY.* The slender stalk which supports the anther. **M18.** ▸**b** *ZOOLOGY.* The barb of a down feather. **M19.**
■ **filamentary** /fɪləˈmɛnt(ə)ri/ *adjective* of, pertaining to, or of the nature of a filament or filaments **M19.** **filamented** *adjective* having filaments **L19.** **filamentose** /fɪləˈmɛntəʊs/ *adjective* = FILAMENTOUS **M19.** **filamentous** /fɪləˈmɛntəs/ *adjective* (*a*) composed of or containing filaments; (*b*) resembling a filament; threadlike: **L17.**

filander /fɪˈlandə/ *noun*[1]. Now *rare*. **L15.**
[ORIGIN Old French & mod. French *filandre* rel. to Old French *filandrier*, *-iere* (mod. *filandière* fem.) spinner, ult. from *filer* spin, from late Latin *filare*: see FILAMENT.]
A threadlike intestinal worm afflicting hawks; *sing.* & (usu.) in *pl.*, a disease caused by such worms.

filander *noun*[2] see PHILANDER *noun*.

filar /ˈfʌɪlə/ *adjective*. **L19.**
[ORIGIN from Latin *filum* thread + -AR[1].]
Of or pertaining to (a) thread; *esp.* (of an optical instrument) having threads or wires across its field of view.

filaree /fɪləˈriː/ *noun*. *US*. **L19.**
[ORIGIN Alt. of ALFILARIA.]
= ALFILARIA.

filaria /fɪˈlɛːrɪə/ *noun*. Pl. **-iae** /-ɪiː/, **-ias**. **M19.**
[ORIGIN mod. Latin *Filaria* former genus name, from Latin *filum* thread + *-aria* -ARY[1].]
A parasitic nematode worm of the superfamily Filarioidea, which includes a number of organisms responsible for diseases in humans.
■ **filarial** *adjective* pertaining to, caused by, or of the nature of filariae **L19.**

filariasis /fɪˌlɛːrɪˈeɪsɪs, fɪləˈrʌɪəsɪs/ *noun*. Pl. **filariases** /fɪˌlɛːrɪˈeɪsiːz, fɪləˈrʌɪəsiːz/. **L19.**
[ORIGIN from FILARIA + -IASIS.]
MEDICINE. Any of a group of tropical diseases resulting from infection with filariae; *spec.* a disease, transmitted by mosquitoes, in which worms of the genera *Wuchereria* or *Brugia* are present in the lymph vessels, leading to elephantiasis.
■ Also **filariˈosis** *noun*, pl. **-oses** /-ˈəʊsiːz/, **L19.**

filature /ˈfɪlətʃə, -tjə/ *noun*. **M18.**
[ORIGIN French from Italian *filatura*, from *filare* spin from late Latin *filare*: see -URE.]
(An establishment for) the reeling of silk from cocoons.

filaze, **filazer** *nouns* vars. of FILACE, FILACER.

filbert /ˈfɪlbət/ *noun*. **LME.**
[ORIGIN Anglo-Norman *philbert*, dial. French *noix de filbert* a nut ripe about St Philibert's day (20 or (Old Style) 22 August).]
1 A cultivated hazelnut, *esp.* one of a relatively elongated kind. Also, a tree producing these, esp. *Corylus maxima*. **LME.** ▸**b** The head. *slang*. **L19.**
2 *ART.* In full ***filbert brush***. A flat oval bristle brush used in oil painting. **M20.**

filch /fɪltʃ/ *verb & noun*. **ME.**
[ORIGIN Unknown.]
▸ **A** *verb*. **1** *verb trans.* Steal, pilfer, snatch, (esp. things of small value); carry off furtively. (Foll. by *away*, *off*.) **ME.**

HENRY MILLER If Curley didn't have the money he would filch it from his mother's purse.

2 *verb intrans.* Engage in stealing or pilfering. **M16.**

GEO. ELIOT If I don't lie and filch somebody else will.

3 *verb trans.* Rob (*of* something). *rare.* **M16.**

▸ **B** *noun.* †**1** A staff with a hook at one end, used to steal articles from hedges, open windows, etc. **E17–E18.**

2 A thing which has been filched. Now *rare.* **E17.**

■ **filcher** *noun* **L16.** **filching** *noun* (*a*) the action of the verb; (*b*) = FILCH *noun* 2: **M16.**

file /fʌɪl/ *noun*[1].

[ORIGIN Old English (Anglian) *fīl* = Old Saxon *fīla* (Dutch *vijl*), Old High German *fīhala*, *fīla* (German *Feile*), from West Germanic.]

1 An instrument (now usu. of steel) with small raised cutting edges or teeth on its surface(s), used for smoothing or shaping objects. **OE.** ▸**b** *fig.* Discipline or hardship imposed for the benefit or cleansing of the soul etc.; a person who or thing (personified) which imposes this. **ME.**

2 A person, *esp.* an artful person; a fellow, a chap. *slang.* **E19.**

– COMB.: **filefish** any of numerous, chiefly tropical, fishes of the family Balistidae with rough skin suggesting the surface of a file; **file shell** any of various bivalve molluscs belonging to the genus *Lima* and related genera, with rough shells; **file snake** any of various snakes that resemble a file in shape or texture; *spec.* (*a*) a wart snake; (*b*) *S. Afr.* a non-venomous colubrid snake of the genus *Mehelya*.

file /fʌɪl/ *noun*[2]. **E16.**

[ORIGIN from FILE *verb*[3] reinforced by French *fil* thread (from Latin *filum*) & *file* (from *filer* FILE *verb*[3]).]

▸ **I** Repr. French *fil*.

1 A string, wire etc., on which documents etc. are run for keeping; a folder etc. for preserving papers, documents, etc., esp. arranged in a particular order for easy reference; a collection of papers so kept, esp. in an office, or in a court of law referring to a cause. Formerly also, a list, a catalogue. **E16.** ▸**b** COMPUTING. A collection of related records stored for use by a computer. **M20.**

D. LODGE He nodded at a manilla file reposing on his otherwise immaculate desk.

2 HERALDRY. Each of the dependent points of a label. Formerly also, a label. **M16.**

†**3** The thread, drift, or course of a story etc. **M16–M17.**

4 (More fully ***file in the foot***) a disease in cattle and sheep characterized by lines or cracks in the hoofs. Formerly also, a disease in trees. Now *dial.* **E17.**

▸ **II** Repr. French *file*.

5 A line of people (esp. soldiers) or things one behind the other. **L16.** ▸**b** MILITARY. A small detachment of soldiers etc. (now usu. only two). **E17.**

6 CHESS. Each of the eight lines of squares extending across the board from player to player. **E17.**

– PHRASES: ***file in the foot***: see sense 4 above. **in file** one behind the other. ***Indian file***: see INDIAN *adjective*. **on file** in a file or filing system. **open file** CHESS: on which there is no pawn of either colour (***seize the open file***, place a rook or the queen on an open file in a position such that that piece cannot immediately be driven from the file). ***single file***: see SINGLE *adjective & adverb*.

– COMB.: **filename** an identifying name given to a computer file. **file server** a device which manages access to one or more separately stored files of data.

file /fʌɪl/ *noun*[3]. *slang* (long *obsolete* exc. *US*). Now *rare.* **L17.**

[ORIGIN Unknown.]

Earlier †***file-cloy***. A pickpocket.

file *noun*[4] var. of FILI.

file /fʌɪl/ *verb*[1].

[ORIGIN Old English *fȳlan* = Middle Low German *vülen*, Middle High German *viulen*, from West Germanic, from Germanic base also of FOUL *adjective*.]

1 *verb trans.* = DEFILE *verb*[1] 2. *arch.* **OE.**

2 a *verb trans.* = DEFILE *verb*[1] 1. *obsolete* exc. *dial.* **ME.** ▸†**b** *verb intrans.* = DEFILE *verb*[1] 6. **ME–E17.**

†**3** *verb trans.* **a** Defame, dishonour. **ME–M17.** ▸**b** Accuse, blame; condemn, find guilty. **ME–M18.**

†**4** *verb trans.* = DEFILE *verb*[1] 3. Only in **ME.**

file /fʌɪl/ *verb*[2]. **ME.**

[ORIGIN from FILE *noun*[1].]

1 *verb trans. & intrans.* Smooth or shape (an object) with a file. **ME.**

C. MCCULLERS His . . wife sat filing her fingernails.

2 *verb trans.* Remove (roughness etc.) with a file. Now only with *away*, *off*, *out*. **ME.**

fig.: TENNYSON So grated down and filed away with thought.

3 *verb trans.* Polish or elaborate (esp. a literary work) to perfection. **LME.**

SHAKES. *Sonn.* Precious phrase by all the Muses fil'd.

■ **filer** *noun*[1] **ME.**

file /fʌɪl/ *verb*[3]. **LME.**

[ORIGIN French *filer* string on a thread, from late Latin *filare* spin, from Latin *filum* thread.]

▸ **I** Corresp. to FILE *noun*[2] I.

1 a *verb trans.* Arrange (now only documents etc.) in a particular order for preservation and easy reference; place (a document etc.) on file; put away in a file. Formerly also, string on a thread. **LME.** ▸**b** *verb trans. & intrans.* Place (a document) on file among official records by formal procedures of registration; submit (an application for a patent, a petition for divorce, etc.) to the appropriate authority. **E16.** ▸**c** *verb trans. & intrans.* Assert a title to (a piece of land or a mining claim). *N. Amer.* **L19.**

a A. BURGESS I sent the silly thing to headquarters, but they will have filed it among the other missives of madmen. **b** J. BARTH I petitioned for permission to file an amended complaint. T. LUNDBERG The company must file with Companies House . . a copy of the company's audited accounts. *Guardian* She filed successfully for divorce.

a filing cabinet: with drawers for storing documents.

2 *verb trans.* Of a newspaper reporter: transmit (a story, information, etc.) to a newspaper for publication. **M20.**

A. CARTER He filed copy to a New York newspaper for a living.

▸ **II** Corresp. to FILE *noun*[2] II.

†**3** *verb trans.* Arrange (soldiers) in a file or files. **L16–M17.**

4 *verb intrans.* March or walk (*away*, *off*, etc.) in file. **E17.** ▸†**b** *fig.* Keep pace with. *rare.* Only in **E17.**

J. GALSWORTHY The coffin was borne into the chapel, and, two by two, the mourners filed in behind it. G. W. TARGET If the bell does not ring for Assembly, I want you to file out and go into the hall quietly. **b** SHAKES. *Hen. VIII* My endeavours, Have ever come too short of my desires, Yet fil'd with my abilities.

■ **filer** *noun*[2] **L19.**

†**file** *verb*[4] *intrans. slang.* **L17–M18.**

[ORIGIN from FILE *noun*[3].]

Pick pockets.

■ †**filer** *noun*[3] **L17–E18.**

filé /ˈfiːleɪ/ *noun. US.* **M19.**

[ORIGIN French, pa. pple of *filer* twist.]

Pounded or powdered sassafras leaves used to flavour and thicken soup, esp. gumbo. Earliest in ***GUMBO filé***.

filemot /ˈfɪlɪmɒt/ *adjective & noun. arch.* **M17.**

[ORIGIN Alt. of FEUILLEMORTE.]

(Of) a yellowish-brown or dead-leaf colour.

filet /ˈfiːleɪ, ˈfɪlɪt; *foreign* filɛ (*pl. same*)/ *noun*[1]. **M19.**

[ORIGIN French: see FILLET *noun*.]

1 = FILLET *noun* 9. Chiefly in phrs. below. **M19.**

filet de boeuf /ˌfiːleɪ də ˈbəːf, *foreign* filɛ də bœf/ a fillet of beef. **filet mignon** /ˌfiːleɪ ˈmiːnjɔ̃, *foreign* filɛ miɲɔ̃/, pl. **mignons** (pronounced same) [see MIGNON] a slice cut from the small end of the tenderloin of beef.

2 A kind of net or lace with a square mesh. **L19.**

filet design, ***filet lace***, ***filet net***, etc.

fili /ˈfiːli/ *noun.* Also ***file***. Pl. **-*d*(*h*)**. **L19.**

[ORIGIN Irish *fileadha*, *filidh*, pl. forms of *file* poet.]

In medieval Irish legal tradition, a poet seer, ranking above a bard.

filial /ˈfɪlɪəl/ *adjective & noun.* **LME.**

[ORIGIN Old French & mod. French, or ecclesiastical Latin *filialis*, from Latin *filius* son, *filia* daughter: see -AL[1].]

▸ **A** *adjective.* **1** Of a child; (esp. of sentiment, duty, etc.) due from a child. **LME.** ▸**b** That is due to a child. **M16.**

A. BURGESS She fell in love with an older man . . filial deprivation had something to do with it.

2 Having the character or relationship of a child or offspring; *spec.* in BIOLOGY, designating the offspring of a cross. **LME.**

first filial generation BIOLOGY the immediate offspring of individuals selected for crossing. **second filial generation** BIOLOGY: produced by interbreeding of individuals of a first filial generation.

▸ †**B** *noun.* An offshoot. **M16–M18.**

■ **fili'ality** *noun* filial quality or relation **E17.** **filially** *adverb* **E17.** **filialness** *noun* (*rare*) **E18.**

filiate /ˈfɪlɪeɪt/ *verb trans.* **L18.**

[ORIGIN medieval Latin *filiat-* pa. ppl stem of *filiare* acknowledge as one's child, from Latin *filius* son, *filia* daughter: see -ATE[3].]

= AFFILIATE *verb* 3.

filiation /fɪlɪˈeɪʃ(ə)n/ *noun.* **LME.**

[ORIGIN Old French & mod. French from eccl. & medieval Latin *filiatio(n-)* relationship as a child, (esp.) sonship, from Latin *filius* son, *filia* daughter: see -ATION.]

1 The relationship (as) of a child (esp. a son) to his or her father; *spec.* in THEOLOGY, the relationship (as) of a son to God; adoption (as a son) by God. **LME.**

2 = AFFILIATION 3. **M16.**

3 Descent or derivation *from*; the genealogical relation of one language, area of study, etc., to another. **L18.**

H. KURATH The relationships between the Indo-European dialects and their filiation in prehistoric times.

4 Formation of branches or offshoots; a branch or offshoot of a society or language. **L18.**

filibeg /ˈfɪlɪbɛg/ *noun. Scot.* Also **fillebeg**, **philabeg**, & other vars. **M18.**

[ORIGIN Gaelic *feileadh-beag* little kilt, from *feileadh* plaid + *beag* little.]

The gathered and belted lower part of a plaid; a kilt.

filibuster /ˈfɪlɪbʌstə/ *noun & verb.* Earlier †**flibutor**, †**flibustier**. **L16.**

[ORIGIN Orig. from Dutch *vrijbuiter* FREEBOOTER; then (**L18**) from French *flibustier*; finally (**M19**) from Spanish *filibustero*, from French.]

▸ **A** *noun.* †**1** *gen.* A freebooter. *rare.* Only in **L16.**

2 Any of a class of pirates who pillaged the Spanish colonies in the W. Indies in the 17th cent. **L18.**

3 A member of an American band of adventurers who incited revolution in various Latin American states in the mid 19th cent.; *gen.* a person who engages in unauthorized warfare against a foreign state. **M19.**

4 An act of obstruction in a legislative assembly, esp. by prolonged speaking; a person who engages in such an act. Chiefly *N. Amer.* **L19.**

D. HALBERSTAM It was not a short spiel, but a genuine filibuster, and it went on and on, reactionary and embarrassing.

▸ **B** *verb.* **1** *verb intrans.* Act as a filibuster or adventurer. **M19.** ▸**b** *verb trans.* Subject to the methods of a filibuster or adventurer. **M19.**

2 *verb intrans. & trans.* Practise obstruction (against) in a legislative assembly. Chiefly *N. Amer.* **L19.**

H. WILSON Even if ministers were not filibustering to ensure that the Prime Minister's Questions were not reached. *New Scientist* Marcus Kimble MP . . was prepared to filibuster any attempts to give the offer statutory protection.

■ **filibusterer** *noun* **M19.** **filibusterism** *noun* the practice of, or inclination to, filibustering **M19.**

filices *noun* pl. of FILIX *noun*.

filicic /fɪˈlɪsɪk/ *adjective.* **M19.**

[ORIGIN from German *Filixsäure* filicic acid, from Latin *filic-* *filix* fern: see -IC.]

CHEMISTRY. ***filicic acid***, a mixture of phenolic compounds, with anthelmintic properties, obtained from the rhizome of the male fern, *Dryopteris filix-mas*, and other ferns.

■ **filicin** *noun* filicic acid, or a crude extract containing it **L19.**

filicide /ˈfɪlɪsʌɪd/ *noun.* **M17.**

[ORIGIN from Latin *filius* son, *filia* daughter + -CIDE.]

1 The action of killing a son or daughter. **M17.**

2 A person who kills a son or daughter. **E19.**

***filid*(*h*)** *nouns* pls. of FILI.

filiform /ˈfʌɪlɪfɔːm/ *adjective.* **M18.**

[ORIGIN from Latin *filum* thread + -I- + -FORM. Cf. French *filiforme*.]

Having the form of a thread; threadlike.

J. MCPHEE The filiform leaves of the sundews were spread out like the spines of umbrellas.

filigrane /ˈfɪlɪgreɪn/ *noun.* Also †**filigreen**. **M17.**

[ORIGIN French from Italian *filigrana*, from Latin *filum* thread + *granum* seed. Cf. FILIGREE.]

= FILIGREE *noun*.

filigree /ˈfɪlɪgriː/ *noun & verb.* Also **fila-** /ˈfɪlə-/. **L17.**

[ORIGIN Alt. of FILIGREEN.]

▸ **A** *noun.* Ornamental work, orig. with beads or precious stones, of fine (usu. gold or silver) wire, twisted, plaited, and soldered into a delicate openwork design; anything delicate resembling this. **L17.**

Scientific American A filigree of gold inlaid inscriptions details each bell's musical properties. *attrib.*: A. RADCLIFFE Enclosed within a filigree screen of gold, lay the image of the saint.

▸ **B** *verb trans.* Work in or ornament with filigree. Chiefly as ***filigreed*** *ppl adjective.* **L18.**

J. A. MICHENER He had Texas-style boots, filigreed with silver.

†**filigreen** *noun* var. of FILIGRANE.

filing /ˈfʌɪlɪŋ/ *noun.* **LME.**

[ORIGIN from FILE *verb*[2] + -ING[1].]

1 The action of FILE *verb*[2]. **LME.**

2 A particle rubbed off by a file. Usu. in *pl.* **LME.**

filio-pietistic /ˌfɪlɪəʊpʌɪəˈtɪstɪk/ *adjective.* **L19.**

[ORIGIN from Latin *filius* son, *filia* daughter + -O- + PIETISTIC.]

Marked by excess of filial piety.

Filipino /fɪlɪˈpiːnəʊ/ *noun & adjective.* Also (fem.) **-na** /-nə/. **L19.**

[ORIGIN Spanish, from (*las Islas*) *Filipinas* the Philippines.]

▸ **A** *noun.* Pl. **-os**, fem. **-as**.

1 A native or inhabitant of the Philippines in SE Asia, *esp.* one of Spanish or mixed descent. **L19.**

2 The national language of the Philippines, based on Tagalog. (Orig. called ***Pilipino***.) **M20.**

▸ **B** *adjective.* Of or pertaining to Filipinos or the Philippines, or their language. **E20.**

filix /ˈfʌɪlɪks, ˈfɪ-/ *noun.* Pl. **-*lices*** /-lɪsiːz/. **M18.**

[ORIGIN Latin.]

BOTANY. A fern. Usu. in pl. *Filices*, the group of ferns as a whole.

filix mas /mɑːs/ [= male] an anthelmintic preparation obtained from the rhizome of the male fern, *Dryopteris filix-mas*.

fill /fɪl/ *noun*[1].

[ORIGIN Old English *fyllu* = Old High German *fullī* (German *Fülle*), Old Norse *fyllr*, Gothic *ufarfullei*, from Germanic, from base of FULL *adjective*. In senses 2–5 from the verb.]

1 Enough to satisfy or sate; as much as one wants (*of* food etc.). **OE.**

DRYDEN Away, my goats, away: for you have browz'd your fill. *fig.*: A. SETON She had had her fill of the cloisters and the hovering nuns, kindly as most of them were.

F

2 A quantity sufficient to fill a space or container; a single charge. M16.

R. L. STEVENSON If there is a fill of tobacco among the crew . . pass it round.

3 The action or an act of filling. *rare.* M18. ▸**b** *POKER.* The act of filling one's hand. M19.

4 An embankment to fill or traverse a gully or hollow. M19.

5 Material used to fill a space or cavity. L19. ▸**b** Auxiliary or secondary material inserted to ensure continuity in music, literature, etc. M20. ▸**c** *ARCHAEOLOGY.* The body of material found in a pit etc. during excavation, of a later period than the feature itself. M20.

J. S. FOSTER The fill is poorly compacted. **b** C. WATSON He knew . . what would tickle a sub-editor's fancy and help meet the insatiable demand for short 'fills'. **c** *World Archaeology* This layer . . accounted for most of the fill in the excavated portions of the site.

F

fill *noun*² see THILL *noun*¹.

fill /fɪl/ *verb.*

[ORIGIN Old English *fyllan* = Old Frisian *fullia*, Old Saxon *fullian* (Dutch *vullen*), Old High German *fullen* (German *füllen*), Old Norse *fylla*, Gothic *fulljan*, from Germanic, from base of FULL *adjective.*]

▸ **I** Make or become full.

1 *verb trans.* Make full; put as much into (a receptacle etc.) as can be held; stock abundantly; populate densely. (Foll. by *with*.) OE. ▸†**b** Impregnate. E–M17.

J. L. WATEN She filled the kettle and placed it on the stove. J. CONRAD The . . brutality . . filled him with a despairing desire to escape.

2 *verb intrans.* Become full (*with*). E17. ▸**b** Of the eyes: brim with tears. L19.

TENNYSON Twice a day the Severn fills. W. GASS Big Hans began pouring whiskey in the kid's mouth but the mouth filled without any getting down his throat.

3 *NAUTICAL.* **a** *verb trans.* (Of the wind) cause (sails) to swell; cause (sails) to be swelled by the wind. E17. ▸**b** *verb intrans.* Have sails distended by the wind; (of a sail) become distended by the wind. L17.

▸ **II** Occupy completely.

4 *verb trans.* Occupy the whole capacity or extent of; spread over, pervade. OE.

G. VIDAL Smoke filled the room. J. THURBER A detailed recital . . would fill a large volume.

5 *verb trans.* Hold (a position); discharge the duties of (an office or post). LME.

G. GREENE He filled with perfect tact a part which combined assistant, secretary and male nurse.

6 *verb trans.* Replace the emptiness of (space or time), occupy (a vacant space or time). M16.

B. JOWETT Amusements which fill a vacant hour.

7 *verb trans.* Appoint a person to occupy (a vacant place or position). L16.

E. A. FREEMAN The people at large claimed a voice in filling the episcopal chair.

8 *verb trans.* Plug (a hole or gap) with material; *spec.* in *DENTISTRY*, stop (a hollow tooth) with cement, amalgam, gold, etc. M19.

▸ **III** Satisfy, fulfil, complete.

9 *verb trans.* Satisfy, satiate, glut. OE. ▸†**b** *verb intrans.* Become sated. ME–L16.

S. PEPYS I sat before Mrs. Palmer . . and filled my eyes with her. **b** SHAKES. *Ven. & Ad.* Glutton-like she feeds, yet never filleth.

10 *verb trans.* Execute (a command), perform (a duty), fulfil (a promise, a prophecy). Now *rare* or *obsolete.* OE.

†**11** Make perfect, accomplish, complete (a task, a period of time, one's days). OE–E17.

12 *verb trans.* Make up as an order or prescription. Chiefly *N. Amer.* M19.

13 *POKER* etc. ▸**a** *verb intrans.* Complete a flush etc. by drawing the necessary cards. Of a flush etc.: be completed. M19. ▸**b** *verb trans.* Improve (one's hand) or complete (a flush etc.) by drawing the necessary cards. M19.

▸ **IV** With the introduced contents as obj.

14 *verb trans.* Put into or *into* a receptacle with the intention of filling it; pour out or (now usu.) *out* (a drink etc.); load (corn etc.) on to a ship. ME.

W. DAMPIER Having fill'd our Water, cut our Wood, and got our Ship in a sailing posture. R. L. STEVENSON The other immediately filled some of the spirit into a tumbler.

– PHRASES: ***back and fill***: see BACK *verb* 9. ***fill a gap***: see GAP *noun.* ***fill one's boots***: see BOOT *noun*². ***fill the bill***: see BILL *noun*³.

– WITH ADVERBS IN SPECIALIZED SENSES: **fill in** (*a*) add material to occupy the space within (a cavity, outline, etc.); (*b*) add what is wanted to complete (an unfinished document, blank cheque, etc.); (*c*) *slang* thrash, beat up; (*d*) find occupation during (a period of inactivity); (*e*) *colloq.* inform (a person) more fully (foll. by *on* a subject); (*f*) act as a substitute, stand in, (*for*). **fill out** (*a*) enlarge, become enlarged or plumper, to a desired or proper limit; (*b*) (chiefly *US*) = ***fill in*** (a) above; (see also sense 13 above). **fill up** (*a*) make or become full to capacity, fill completely; (*b*) provide what is needed to occupy the vacant parts or places in or deal with the deficiencies of; fill in (a document etc.); do away with (a pond etc.) by filling; stop up; (*c*) fill the tank of a motor vehicle with petrol etc.; †(*d*) complete or come up to the measure of, equal, satisfy.

– COMB.: **fill-in** (*a*) a person or thing put in as a substitute or to fill a vacancy; (*b*) a briefing; **fill-up** a thing that fills something up; an act of filling up a petrol tank etc.

■ **fillable** *adjective* L15.

filled /fɪld/ *ppl adjective.* L16.

[ORIGIN from FILL *verb* + -ED¹.]

1 That has been filled (freq. as 2nd elem. of comb.); made full; containing filling. Also ***filled-in***, ***filled-up***, etc. L16.

2 *spec.* Made up or extended by the use of foreign material; adulterated. L19.

fille de chambre /fij də ʃɑ̃ːbr/ *noun phr. arch.* Pl. ***filles de chambre*** (pronounced same). L17.

[ORIGIN French.]

A chambermaid; a lady's personal maid.

fille de joie /fij də ʒwa/ *noun phr.* Pl. ***filles de joie*** (pronounced same). E18.

[ORIGIN French, lit. 'girl of pleasure'.]

A prostitute.

filler /ˈfɪlə/ *noun*¹. L15.

[ORIGIN from FILL *verb* + -ER¹.]

1 A person who or thing which fills something or brings about fullness; a machine or device for filling. Also ***filler-in***, ***filler-up***, etc. L15.

BYRON The fifteen hundred fillers of hot rooms, called the fashionable world.

2 Something used to fill a cavity, stop a gap, complete a load, make bulk, etc.; *spec.* (*a*) a substance used to fill cracks etc. in a surface before painting; (*b*) extraneous material inserted to avoid a gap in an utterance, a newspaper column, a broadcast, etc.; (*c*) an inert substance added to chemical compounds to give the desired bulk, texture, strength, etc. L16.

M. A. K. HALLIDAY Exclamations and 'fillers' such as *oh, ah, quoi! Which?* Many outdoor fillers . . lack the flexibility to cope with the movement of timber as it gets wet and dries out again.

– COMB.: **filler cap** a cap closing the pipe leading to the petrol tank of a motor vehicle; **filler hose** the hose of a petrol pump at a garage etc.

filler /ˈfɪlɛː/ *noun*². Also **fillér**. Pl. same. E20.

[ORIGIN Hungarian *fillér*.]

A monetary unit of Hungary, equal to one-hundredth of a forint.

filles de chambre, ***filles de joie*** *noun phrs.* pls. of FILLE DE CHAMBRE, FILLE DE JOIE.

fillet /ˈfɪlɪt/ *noun.* ME.

[ORIGIN Old French & mod. French *filet* from Proto-Romance dim. of Latin *filum* thread: see FILE *noun*², -ET¹.]

▸ **I 1** A ribbon, string, or narrow band worn around the head to keep the hair in place or for ornament. ME.

†**2** An ornamental border or edging on a cloth, garment, furniture, etc. LME–E17.

3 A thin narrow band of anything; *ARCHITECTURE* a narrow flat band separating two mouldings, a band between the flutes of a column. L15. ▸**b** A strip of wood; *esp.* one fastened to a surface to serve as a support, to strengthen a joint, etc. M16. ▸**c** *HERALDRY.* A horizontal division of a shield, a quarter of the depth of a chief. *rare.* L16. ▸**d** A narrow band of painted, gilded, etc., decoration. In *BOOKBINDING*, a line impressed into a book cover; a wheeled tool for producing such lines. M17. ▸**e** A ribbon of metal from which coin blanks are punched. M18.

†**4** A thread, a string; a thing resembling a thread or string, as a root fibre, the stamen of a plant, etc. M16–M18.

5 A strip of material for binding; a band, a bandage. M17.

6 A raised rim or ridge on any surface. E18.

7 A curve inside an angle serving to prevent concentration of stress. E20. ▸**b** *AERONAUTICS.* A fairing at the junction of two surfaces to smooth the flow of air. M20.

▸ **II 8** A band of nerve or muscle fibre, a tendon, the frenum of the tongue. In *pl.*, the loins. LME.

9 A fleshy boneless piece of meat from near the loins or ribs of an animal; the undercut of a sirloin of beef. LME. ▸**b** A boned side of a fish; a boneless cut from a fowl. E18. ▸**c** The middle part of a leg of veal boned, rolled, and tied with string; a piece of beef, fish, etc., prepared in this way. E18.

b *Good Housekeeping* Place one salmon fillet in the centre of the pastry.

– COMB.: **fillet steak** the undercut of a sirloin of beef; **fillet weld** a weld of roughly triangular section joining two surfaces at right angles to each other.

fillet /ˈfɪlɪt/ *verb trans.* E17.

[ORIGIN from the noun.]

1 Bind with or as with a fillet; encircle with an ornamental band. E17.

D. M. MOIR Her golden tresses . . Were filleted up with roses.

2 Now chiefly *BOOKBINDING.* Mark or ornament with a fillet. E17.

B. FRANKLIN A book whose covering is filleted with gold.

3 Divide (meat, fish) into fillets; remove the bones from. M19.

fig.: *Times* Officers reporting to the general were sometimes called into the Colonel's office first and . . could have their information filleted.

■ **filleter** *noun* L19.

filleting /ˈfɪlɪtɪŋ/ *noun.* L16.

[ORIGIN from FILLET *verb* + -ING¹.]

1 The action of FILLET *verb*; an instance of this. L16.

2 Binding tape, a piece of this; a band, a bandage. M17.

fillette /fijɛt/ *noun.* Pl. pronounced same. M19.

[ORIGIN French.]

A young girl.

filling /ˈfɪlɪŋ/ *noun.* ME.

[ORIGIN from FILL *verb* + -ING¹.]

1 The action of FILL *verb.* Also ***filling-in***, ***filling-up***, etc. ME.

T. CHALMERS Such a filling up of the time as will keep you away from the evil communications.

2 Something which fills or is used to fill a space or hole, stop up a gap, etc.; *spec.* (*a*) stones and rubble used to make up a bank or wall; (*b*) (chiefly *US*) weft; (*c*) (a quantity of) material used to fill a sandwich etc.; (*d*) cement, gold, etc., used to fill a cavity in a tooth; (a tooth filled with) a quantity of such material. LME. ▸**b** Extraneous or inferior material used to add bulk or fill space. M17.

D. JACOBSON She will make pancakes, with a filling of hot, spiced quince. F. SMYTH The teeth . . were in perfect condition apart from a single amalgam filling. **b** SWIFT The prefaces of Dryden . . meerly writ at first for filling To raise the volume's price a shilling.

– COMB.: **filling station** an establishment selling petrol etc. to motorists.

filling /ˈfɪlɪŋ/ *adjective.* L16.

[ORIGIN from FILL *verb* + -ING².]

That fills; *spec.* that makes the stomach feel full.

fillip /ˈfɪlɪp/ *noun.* E16.

[ORIGIN Imit.]

1 A smart blow (with the fist etc.). Now *rare.* E16.

J. STILL There was a knave not far, Who caught one good fillip on the brow with a door-bar.

2 A movement made by bending the last joint of the finger against the thumb and suddenly releasing it; a smart stroke or tap given in this way. M16.

BOSWELL The Prince . . by a fillip, made some of it [wine] fly in Oglethorpe's face.

3 A trifle; a moment. E17.

BYRON Eat, drink, and love; the rest's not worth a fillip.

4 A stimulus, an incentive. E18.

J. N. ISBISTER The interest from abroad . . was a great fillip to Freud.

fillip /ˈfɪlɪp/ *verb.* LME.

[ORIGIN Imit.]

1 *verb intrans.* Make a fillip with the fingers. LME. ▸**b** *verb trans.* Flip or flick (the fingers). E18.

2 *verb trans.* Propel (a small missile, a coin, etc.) with or as with a fillip. M16. ▸**b** Strike smartly; tap or flick with the finger. L16.

A. FONBLANQUE Our aforesaid merchant filliped a nut sharply against his bullying giant.

3 *verb trans.* Urge, stimulate. M16.

SHELLEY Pour: that the draught may fillip my remembrance.

fillis /ˈfɪlɪs/ *noun.* Also **ph-**. E20.

[ORIGIN French *filasse* tow.]

HORTICULTURE. A loosely twisted hemp or jute string, used for tying up plants etc.

fillister /ˈfɪlɪstə/ *noun.* E19.

[ORIGIN Perh. from French *feuilleret* in same sense.]

A rabbet plane used in making window sashes (also ***fillister plane***); a rabbet on the outer edge of a window-sash bar.

filly /ˈfɪli/ *noun.* LME.

[ORIGIN Old Norse *fylja* (corresp. to Old High German *fuli(n)*, *fulihha*, Middle High German *vülhe*), from Germanic base of FOAL *noun.*]

1 A young female horse or other equid, *spec.* from the time of weaning to the age of 4 or 5. Cf. COLT *noun*¹, FOAL *noun.* LME.

2 *transf.* A lively girl or young woman. *colloq.* E17.

– COMB.: **filly-foal** a female foal.

film /fɪlm/ *noun.*

[ORIGIN Old English *filmen* = Old Frisian *filmene* skin, from West Germanic, ult. from base of FELL *noun*¹.]

†**1** A membrane. OE–M18.

EVELYN A Wallnut . . the Shell lin'd with Films.

2 A thin skin, sheet, coating, or layer, of some material. L16.

D. WELCH The light film of dust on the laurels. M. ATWOOD Sandwiches wrapped in plastic film.

3 A fine thread or filament, as of gossamer, silk, etc. **L16.**

C. DARWIN Like films of silk blown by the wind.

4 Dimness or an abnormal opacity affecting the eye. **E17.**

L. MORRIS O'er his glaring eyes the films of death Crept.

5 A thin mist; a haze. **M19.**

E. L. DOCTOROW She saw everything through a film of salt tears.

6 A coating of light-sensitive emulsion on a photographic plate etc. **M19.** ▸**b** Plastic material coated with one or more layers of light-sensitive emulsion used in photography, cinematography, etc.; a roll of this. **L19.**

C. WALLACE Loading by touch is quite simple . . . The photographer should try it with an old film.

7 A drama, episode, event, etc., recorded on cinematographic film, magnetic tape, etc., for subsequent viewing. **E20.** ▸**b** (The making of) films (esp. cinematographic) considered as an art form. **E20.** ▸**c** In *pl.* The cinema industry. **E20.**

A. GRAY He watched a cowboy film in the staff club cinema. **b** T. BARR Film presents . . elements . . which are peculiar to itself and are not part of the theater. **c** I. MURDOCH Anna never tried to get into films.

– COMB.: **film badge** a device containing photographic film which registers the wearer's exposure to radiation; **film buff** a person enthusiastic or knowledgeable about the cinema; ***film clip***: see CLIP *noun*[1] 2b; **film colour** PSYCHOLOGY colour perceived as an opaque mist, unattached to a distinct surface; **filmcraft** the art or technique of making cinematographic films; **filmfest** a festival of films; **filmgoer** a frequenter of the cinema; **film pack** a pack of sheets of photographic film for use in a plate camera; **filmset** *verb trans.* set (matter for printing) by filmsetting; **filmsetter** an organization or person who does filmsetting; **filmsetting** PRINTING the setting of matter to be printed by projecting it on to a photographic film from which the printing surface is prepared; **film speed** (*a*) the degree of sensitivity to light of a photographic film; (*b*) the speed at which a cinematographic film passes through a camera or projector; **film star** a celebrated cinema actor or actress; **film stock** unexposed film; **film strip** a series of transparencies for projection, esp. as a teaching aid; **film unit** the actors, technicians, and equipment involved in recording (a part of) a film for the cinema, television, etc.

■ **filmdom** *noun* the world of cinema; (those involved in) the cinema industry: **E20.** **filmic** *adjective* of, pertaining to, or resembling cinematography or the cinema; suitable for reproduction on film: **M20.** **filmically** *adverb* **E20.** **fil'mography** *noun* a list of cinematographic films by a particular director, actor, etc., or on a particular subject **M20.**

film /fɪlm/ *verb.* **E17.**
[ORIGIN from the noun.]
1 *verb trans.* Cover with or as with a film. Also foll. by *over*. **E17.** ▸**b** *verb intrans.* Become covered with a film; grow dim or hazy. Also foll. by *over*. **M19.**

A. DESAI The dust filming the window pane. **b** D. LESSING The bird's eyes are filming, and blood wells from its open beak.

2 *verb trans.* Record (a scene, person, etc.) on cinematographic film or magnetic tape; make a film of (a book, play, etc.). **L19.** ▸**b** *verb trans.* & *intrans.* Make (a film etc.) for the cinema, television, etc.; take part in the making of (a film etc.). **M20.**

Daily Telegraph Cameras were allowed for the first time to film their Lordships inside their red-carpeted sanctum. A. S. NEILL I have seen *Hamlet* filmed. **b** *Daily Telegraph* The bear . . was filming a commercial in the Western Isles when he swam off.

3 *verb intrans.* Be (well or ill) suited for reproduction on film. **E20.**

W. SAROYAN The sort of face that would film well and look good on the screen.

■ **filmable** *adjective* able to be filmed; suitable for reproduction on film: **E20.**

film noir /fɪlm ˈnwɑː, *foreign* film nwaːr/ *noun phr.* Pl. **-s -s** (pronounced same). **M20.**
[ORIGIN French, lit. 'black film'.]
A film of a gloomy or fatalistic nature; the branch of film consisting of such works.

filmy /ˈfɪlmi/ *adjective.* **E17.**
[ORIGIN from FILM *noun* + -Y[1].]
1 Forming a thin sheet or coating. **E17.**
2 Resembling a film; gauzy, resembling gossamer. **E17.**

S. KAUFFMANN Her filmy negligee heightening the illusion that she floated.

filmy fern any of various small ferns of the genera *Hymenophyllum*, *Trichomanes*, and related genera, with thin translucent fronds, forming sheets on moist rocks etc.; (***Tunbridge filmy fern***: see TUNBRIDGE 3).

†**3** Of a membranous structure. Only in **M17.**
4 Covered (as) with a film; dim, hazy. **E19.**

G. SWIFT All I ever see in his eyes is a filmy gaze, fixed on the distance.

■ **filmily** *adverb* **L19.** **filminess** *noun* **E18.**

filo /ˈfiːləʊ/ *noun.* Also **phyllo**. **M20.**
[ORIGIN mod. Greek *phullo* leaf.]
Dough that can be stretched into very thin leaves and layered so as to make sweet and savoury pastries; pastry made from this dough.

Filofax /ˈfʌɪlə(ʊ)faks/ *noun.* **M20.**
[ORIGIN Alt. after FILE *noun*[2], pl. of FACT *noun* (cf. FAX *noun*[2].)]
(Proprietary name for) a loose-leaf notebook or portable filing system, including a diary.

filoplume /ˈfʌɪlə(ʊ)pluːm/ *noun.* **L19.**
[ORIGIN mod. Latin *filopluma*, from Latin *filum* thread + *pluma* feather: see -O-.]
ORNITHOLOGY. A thin hairlike feather.

filopodium /fʌɪlə(ʊ)ˈpəʊdɪəm/ *noun.* Pl. **-ia** /-ɪə/. **E20.**
[ORIGIN from Latin *filum* thread + PODIUM.]
ZOOLOGY. A threadlike pseudopodium.
■ **filopodial** *adjective* **L20.**

filoselle /ˈfɪləsɛl/ *noun.* Also †**-sella**. **M16.**
[ORIGIN French from Italian *filosello*.]
1 (Silk thread similar to) floss silk. Also ***filoselle silk***. **M16.**
†**2** A kind of material, prob. of silk and wool. Only in **17.**

filovirus /ˈfiːləʊvʌɪrʌs/ *noun.* **L20.**
[ORIGIN from Latin *fil(um* thread, filament + -O- + VIRUS.]
Any of a family of filamentous RNA viruses (including the Ebola and Marburg viruses) which cause severe haemorrhagic fevers in humans and primates.

fils /fis/ *noun*[1]. **L19.**
[ORIGIN French = son.]
The son, junior: appended to a name to distinguish between a father and son of the same name. Cf. PÈRE 2.

House & Garden Russell *père* had been in banking . . . Russell *fils* . . thought this a bit-too-cramping project.

fils /fɪls/ *noun*[2]. Pl. same. **L19.**
[ORIGIN Colloq. pronunc. of Arabic *fals* a small copper coin: see FLOOSE.]
1 *hist.* Any of various small copper coins in the Middle East. **L19.**
2 A monetary unit of Iraq, Bahrain, Jordan, Kuwait, and formerly various other Arab countries, equal to one-thousandth of a dinar. Also, a monetary unit of Yemen equal to one-hundredth of a riyal. **M20.**

filter /ˈfɪltə/ *noun.* **LME.**
[ORIGIN Old French *filtre* var. of *feltre* (mod. *feutre* felt) from medieval Latin *filtrum*, from West Germanic base rel. to that of FELT *noun*.]
†**1** (A piece of) felt. Only in **LME.**
2 A piece of felt, woollen cloth, or (now esp.) unsized paper, freq. in the shape of a conical funnel, etc., through which liquid may be passed to free it of suspended matter; any device with this function, as one with a stratum of sand, charcoal, or other porous material. **M16.**

fig.: A. ALISON The whole information . . was strained through the imperial filters.

3 A material used for filtering. *rare.* **E19.**
4 Any device or arrangement which removes or separates out constituents, as (***a***) a device for removing impurities from the air (also ***air filter***); (***b***) a screen for absorbing light of some or all colours (also ***colour filter***, ***light filter***); (***c***) a pad of absorbent material fitted at the mouth end of a cigarette to reduce harmful ingredients in the smoke; also, a cigarette with such a filter; (***d***) a sheet or block of material placed in the path of a beam of X-rays etc. in order to absorb radiation of certain wavelengths; (***e***) ELECTRONICS a circuit that attenuates all signals except those within one or more frequency bands; (***f***) an arrangement for the filtering of traffic; (***g***) COMPUTING a piece of software that processes data before passing it to another application: **M19.**

P. SCOTT The box . . that had a filter on the lid to keep the contents dry.

– COMB.: **filter aid** any substance added to a liquid or to a filtering medium to prevent the formation of an impervious filter cake; **filter bed** a pond or tank with a false bottom covered with sand or gravel, acting as a filter; **filter cake** a deposit of insoluble material on a filter; **filter-feeder** an animal that obtains its nourishment by filter-feeding; **filter-feeding** the filtering and ingestion by an organism of nutrient matter suspended in water; **filter paper** porous paper used for filtering; **filter-passing** *adjective* (of a virus) filterable; **filter tip** a filter fitted at the mouth end of a cigarette; a cigarette with such a filter; **filter-tipped** *adjective* having a filter tip.

filter /ˈfɪltə/ *verb.* **L16.**
[ORIGIN from the noun.]
1 *verb trans.* Pass (a liquid, air, electrical signal, light, etc.) through a filter; pass as through a filter; remove constituents from. **L16.** ▸**b** *verb intrans.* Engage in filtering liquid etc. **L16.**

LD RUTHERFORD The precipitate of lead sulphide was filtered off. D. ATTENBOROUGH Cilia around their mouths created a current of water and from it they filtered their food. B. A. FARRELL The patient had already been filtered through psychiatric and psychological interviews.

2 *verb intrans.* Flow through a filter; pass as through a filter; percolate; move slowly, trickle; (of news etc.) leak *out*, come *through*. **L18.** ▸**b** *spec.* Of road traffic: join traffic coming from another direction at a junction, esp. when other traffic from the same direction has to stop. **E20.**

E. BOWEN Restrictions were being relaxed and Catholics were now filtering back again. P. GOODMAN The prosperous well-paying jobs do not filter down evenly to the poorest groups. A. GUINNESS A pale greenish light filtered through the window-panes.

3 *verb trans.* Obtain (as) by passing through a filter. **L18.** ▸**b** Foll. by *out*: separate or prevent the passage of (as) by a filter. **E20.**
4 *verb trans.* Act as a filter to. **M19.**

K. WATERHOUSE The roller blind filtering a green, dead light over the empty desks.

■ **filterer** *noun* **E19.**

filterable /ˈfɪlt(ə)rəb(ə)l/ *adjective.* Also **filtrable**. **E20.**
[ORIGIN from FILTER *verb* + -ABLE.]
Able to be filtered; *spec.* (of a virus) able to pass through a filter that retains bacteria.
■ **filtera'bility** *noun* **E20.**

filth /fɪlθ/ *noun & verb.*
[ORIGIN Old English *fȳlþ* = Old Saxon *fūlipa* (Dutch *vuilte*), Old High German *fūlida*, from Germanic base of FOUL *adjective*: see -TH[1].]
▸ **A** *noun* **1** †**a** Rotting or purulent matter; rottenness. **OE–L17.** ▸**b** Dirt, esp. of a disgusting kind. **ME.**

b J. MANN Even common folk seemed to understand the link between filth and disease.

2 *fig.* Moral defilement, vileness; corruption; obscenity. **OE.** ▸**b** Foul or obscene language; obscene literature. **M18.** ▸**c** *The* police. *slang. derog.* **M20.**

c *Times* 'It's the filth,' cried one of the robbers.

†**3** The quality or state of being foul; filthiness. **ME–L16.**
4 In *pl.* Types of dirt. Formerly also, foul acts (done or suffered), moral transgressions. Now *rare*. **ME.**
5 A disreputable, disliked, or promiscuous person. *obsolete* exc. *dial.* **ME.**
▸ **B** *verb trans.* Make foul, defile. *rare.* **LME.**

filthy /ˈfɪlθi/ *adjective & adverb.* **ME.**
[ORIGIN from FILTH *noun* + -Y[1].]
▸ **A** *adjective.* **1** Corrupt; morally foul; obscene. **ME.**

JILLY COOPER Telling such filthy stories at dinner that the great industrialist . . left the table in high dudgeon.

2 Full of filth; covered with filth; dirty, foul. **LME.** ▸†**b** Of air or clouds: murky, thick. **L16–E17.**

M. MOORCOCK I must have been utterly filthy. I had not . . properly washed for at least six weeks. G. M. FRASER The whole place was filthy with refuse. **b** SHAKES. *Macb.* Hover through the fog and filthy air.

3 Disgraceful, contemptible, low, disgusting. **LME.**

N. COWARD If he told you that, he's a filthy liar.

filthy lucre [from *Titus* 1:11] dishonourable gain; *loosely* money.

4 Delighting in filth. Now *rare*. **E16.**
5 Of weather, a mood, etc.: extremely unpleasant. **L19.**

P. BOOTH Don't take any notice of him. He's been in a filthy mood all day.

▸ **B** *adverb.* Filthily; to a disgusting extent. Now chiefly in ***filthy rich***. **E17.**
■ **filthify** *verb trans.* make filthy **L18.** **filthily** *adverb* **M16.** **filthiness** *noun* **L15.**

filthy /ˈfɪlθi/ *verb trans.* **E20.**
[ORIGIN from the adjective.]
Make filthy.

filtrable *adjective* var. of FILTERABLE.

filtrate /ˈfɪltreɪt/ *noun.* **M19.**
[ORIGIN formed as FILTRATE *verb*: see -ATE[1].]
The liquid that has passed through a filter.

filtrate /ˈfɪltreɪt/ *verb.* **E17.**
[ORIGIN mod. Latin *filtrat-* pa. ppl stem of mod. Latin *filtrare* filter: see -ATE[3].]
1 *verb trans.* = FILTER *verb* 1. **E17.**
2 *verb intrans.* = FILTER *verb* 2. **E18.**

filtration /fɪlˈtreɪʃ(ə)n/ *noun.* **E17.**
[ORIGIN French, from *filtrer* to filter: see -ATION.]
1 The action or process of filtering. **E17.**
2 Movement (as) through a filter; percolation. **E17.**

filtre /filtr/ *noun.* Pl. pronounced same. **M20.**
[ORIGIN French.]
A filtering appliance for making coffee, which allows boiling water to pass through ground coffee into a cup or pot; coffee made with such an appliance.

fimble /ˈfɪmb(ə)l/ *noun.* **L15.**
[ORIGIN Dutch *femel*, Low German *fimel* from French *(chanvre) femelle* female (hemp).]
More fully ***fimble hemp***. The male plant of the hemp. Cf. ***carl hemp*** s.v. CARL *noun* 3.

fimble /ˈfɪmb(ə)l/ *verb intrans.* & *trans.* Long *obsolete* exc. *dial.* **L16.**
[ORIGIN App. var. of FUMBLE *verb*, with vowel suggesting lighter movement.]
Move the fingers lightly and frequently over (something).

FIMBRA /ˈfɪmbrə/ *abbreviation.*
Financial Intermediaries, Managers, and Brokers Regulatory Association.

fimbria /ˈfɪmbrɪə/ *noun.* Pl. **-iae** /-ɪiː/. **M18.**
[ORIGIN Late Latin = border, fringe.]
Chiefly ANATOMY & BOTANY. A fringe; any of the threads or other projections forming a fringe; *spec.* any of a number of finger-like projections surrounding the ovarian end of a Fallopian tube.

fimbriate /ˈfɪmbrɪeɪt/ *adjective.* **E19.**
[ORIGIN Latin *fimbriatus* fringed, formed as FIMBRIA: see -ATE².]
1 Chiefly BOTANY & ZOOLOGY. = FIMBRIATED 2. **E19.**
2 HERALDRY. = FIMBRIATED 1. **L19.**

fimbriated /ˈfɪmbrɪeɪtɪd/ *adjective.* **L15.**
[ORIGIN formed as FIMBRIA + -ED¹.]
1 HERALDRY. Of a charge: bordered with a narrow band or edge. **L15.**
2 Chiefly BOTANY & ZOOLOGY. Fringed, bordered with hairs or hairlike processes. **L17.**

fimbriation /fɪmbrɪˈeɪʃ(ə)n/ *noun.* **M19.**
[ORIGIN formed as FIMBRIATE: see -ATION.]
HERALDRY. The condition of being fimbriated; a border, a narrow edge.

fin /fɪn/ *noun*¹.
[ORIGIN Old English *fin(n)* = Middle Low German *finne*, Middle Dutch *vinne* (Dutch *vin*), prob. ult. rel. to Latin *pinna* feather, wing.]
► **I 1** An organ attached to various parts of the body in fishes and cetaceans, which serves for propulsion and steering in the water; a similar organ in some other animals. **OE.**

> J. WAIN Wicked sharks . . were swimming just below the surface, their fins poking out.

adipose fin, anal fin, dorsal fin, pectoral fin, ventral fin, etc.
2 A finned animal; a fish. Now *rare.* **M16.**
► **II** A thing resembling a fin.
†**3** The lid (of the eye). Only in **E17.**
4 The baleen of a whale; a blade or thin strip of whalebone. Now *rare* or *obsolete.* **M17.**
5 A sharp lateral projection on the share or the coulter of a plough. **M17.**
6 A person's arm and hand; a hand. *slang.* Now *rare.* **L18.**
7 A small projecting surface on an aircraft or rocket, esp. for ensuring stability; a similar projection on other devices to improve heat transfer etc. **M19.**
8 A finlike appendage to a ship's bottom; a keel shaped like a dorsal fin inverted; a centreboard. **L19.**
9 A projecting attachment on a motor vehicle, esp. on the tail. **M20.**
10 An underwater swimmer's flipper. **M20.**
– COMB.: **finback** = *fin whale* below; **finfoot**, pl. **-s**, any of a number of tropical aquatic birds of the family Heliornithidae, superficially resembling grebes but belonging to the same order as the cranes and rails; **fin-footed** *adjective* having feet adapted for swimming by being webbed or lobate; **fin ray** ZOOLOGY each of the long slender bony processes supporting the fins of a fish; **fin-toed** *adjective* having lobate toes; **fin-weed** *dial.* restharrow; **fin whale** a large baleen whale, *Balaenoptera physalus*, which has a prominent dorsal fin (also called ***common rorqual***).
■ **finlike** *adjective* resembling a fin **M17.**

fin /fɪn/ *noun*². *slang.* **M19.**
[ORIGIN from FINNIP.]
A five-pound or (*N. Amer.*) five-dollar note.

Fin *noun*³ see FINN.

fin /fɪn/ *verb.* Infl. **-nn-**. **E16.**
[ORIGIN from FIN *noun*¹.]
1 *verb trans.* Cut off the fins from (a fish); cut up (a chub). **E16.**
2 a *verb trans.* Swim in or along, as a fish; make (one's way etc.) by swimming under water. **M19.** ►**b** *verb intrans.* Swim under water. **M20.**
3 *verb trans.* Provide (an aircraft, motor vehicle, etc.) with fins. **M20.**

finable /ˈfʌɪnəb(ə)l/ *adjective.* Also **fineable**. **L15.**
[ORIGIN from FINE *verb*² + -ABLE.]
Liable for or subject to a fine; for which a fine may be imposed.

finagle /fɪˈneɪɡ(ə)l/ *verb. colloq.* (orig. *US*). Also **phe-**. **E20.**
[ORIGIN from FAINAIGUE: see -LE³.]
1 *verb intrans.* Use dishonest or devious means to bring something about; fiddle. **E20.**
2 *verb trans.* Secure by dishonest or devious means. **M20.**
■ **finagling** *verbal noun* the action of the verb; an instance of this: **E20.**

final /ˈfʌɪn(ə)l/ *adjective & noun.* **ME.**
[ORIGIN Old French & mod. French *final* or Latin *finalis*, from *finis* end: see -AL¹.]
► **A** *adjective.* **1** Putting an end to something, *spec.* to uncertainty or conflict; not to be altered; conclusive. **ME.**

> CONAN DOYLE Some . . were complete failures, and as such will hardly bear narrating, since no final explanation is forthcoming.

2 Marking the last stage of a process; ultimate. **LME.**
3 Having regard to end or purpose. **LME.**
4 Coming at the end (of a series, a word, etc.). **M16.**

> J. BETJEMAN I put my final shilling in the meter. G. GREENE That final 'e' which so neatly distinguishes the artiste from the artist.

– SPECIAL COLLOCATIONS & PHRASES: ***final cause***: see CAUSE *noun.* **final clause** GRAMMAR a clause expressing purpose or intention (e.g. in English one introduced by *in order that* or *lest*). **final demand** an account which is a creditor's last attempt to procure money owed, before taking punitive measures. **final drive** the last part of the transmission in a motor vehicle. **final process** LAW (now *hist.*) process of execution. **final proof** US LAW the process observed in paying for pre-empted land after six months' occupancy. **final solution** [translating German *Endlösung*]: the German policy, from 1941, of exterminating Jewish people in Europe; the process of massacring these victims. ***in the final analysis***: see ANALYSIS 1.
► **B** *noun* **1** †**a** ***for final***, finally, conclusively; ***in final***, in conclusion. Only in **LME.** ►**b** Completion, an end. Now *rare.* **L16.**
2 A final thing; *spec.* (***a***) the final letter or sound of a word; (***b***) MUSIC the principal note in any mode; (***c***) the last or deciding heat or game in a sports or other competition; (***d***) the last series of examinations; in *pl.*, the examinations of the last series, esp. at university etc.; (***e***) the edition of a newspaper published latest in the day. **E17.**

finale /fɪˈnɑːli/ *noun.* **M18.**
[ORIGIN Italian, as noun of adjective from Latin *finalis*: see FINAL.]
1 The last movement or section or (formerly) note of a musical composition; the closing section of an act in an opera; the closing part of a drama or other public entertainment. **M18.**
2 The conclusion. **L18.**

finalise *verb* var. of FINALIZE.

finalism /ˈfʌɪn(ə)lɪz(ə)m/ *noun.* **L19.**
[ORIGIN from FINAL + -ISM.]
1 The belief that an end or limit has been reached. *rare.* **L19.**
2 The doctrine that natural processes such as evolutionary changes are directed towards some end or goal. **E20.**

finalist /ˈfʌɪn(ə)lɪst/ *noun.* **L19.**
[ORIGIN from FINAL + -IST.]
1 A person who believes that an end or limit has been reached. *rare.* **L19.**
2 A competitor who has qualified for a final; a candidate in the last of a series of examinations. **L19.**

finalistic /fʌɪnəˈlɪstɪk/ *adjective.* **E20.**
[ORIGIN from FINALISM: see -ISTIC.]
Of or pertaining to the doctrine that natural processes such as evolutionary changes are directed towards some end or goal.

finality /fʌɪˈnalɪti/ *noun.* **M16.**
[ORIGIN French *finalité* from late Latin *finalitas*, from Latin *finalis*: see FINAL, -ITY.]
†**1** An end in view; a guiding object. Only in **M16.**
2 The quality, condition, or fact of being final; the condition of being at the limit; the belief that something is final. **M19.** ►**b** A thing that is final; a final act, state, or utterance. **M19.**
3 The relation of being an end or final cause; the principle of final cause viewed as operative in the universe. **M19.**

finalize /ˈfʌɪn(ə)lʌɪz/ *verb.* Also **-ise**. **E20.**
[ORIGIN from FINAL *adjective* + -IZE.]
1 *verb trans.* Complete, bring to an end, put in final form; approve the final form of. **E20.**
2 *verb intrans.* Bring something to completion, conclude. **M20.**
■ **finaliˈzation** *noun* **M20.**

finally /ˈfʌɪn(ə)li/ *adverb.* **LME.**
[ORIGIN from FINAL *adjective* + -LY², after Old French *final(e)ment*, late Latin *finaliter*.]
1 In the end; lastly; at last. **LME.** ►**b** As a final point or conclusion (of a speech or piece of writing etc.). **LME.**

> V. WOOLF Finally, . . he retired to Hampstead. J. M. COETZEE Sitting upright with his back to the wall, he finally fell asleep. **b** AV *2 Cor.* 13:11 Finally, brethren, farewell.

2 Once for all, irreversibly, decisively, conclusively. **LME.**

> O. MANNING I suggest you see it before finally making up your mind to finance this venture.

finance /fʌɪˈnans, fɪ-; ˈfʌɪnans/ *noun.* **LME.**
[ORIGIN Old French & mod. French = †end, †payment, money, from *finer* make an end, settle, etc., from *fin* end. The senses now current are from mod. French.]
†**1** Ending, an end. *rare.* **LME–E17.**
†**2** Payment of a debt; compensation; a ransom. **LME–L16.**
†**3** Supply (of goods); stock of money. **L15–E16.**
†**4** A tax; taxation; revenue. **L15–L17.**
†**5** Borrowing of money at interest. **M16–E18.**
6 In *pl.* The monetary resources of a monarch, state, company, or individual. **M18.**

> F. OWEN My finances are in a most pitiable state.

7 The management of (esp. public) money; the science of levying and applying revenue. **L18.**

> *Times* Those who understand the intricacies of public finance.

high finance: see HIGH *adjective.*
– COMB.: **finance company**, **finance house** a company mainly concerned with providing money for hire-purchase transactions.
■ **financist** *noun* = FINANCIER *noun* 1 **L19.**

finance /fʌɪˈnans, fɪ-; ˈfʌɪnans/ *verb.* **L15.**
[ORIGIN from the noun.]
†**1** *verb intrans. & trans.* Pay or put to ransom. Only in **L15.**
2 *verb intrans.* Engage in or manage financial operations; provide oneself with capital. **E19.**
3 *verb trans.* Provide with money, esp. capital; provide money for. **M19.**

> L. NAMIER The factor had to finance his West Indian correspondents—lend them money for the sake of consignments. M. GIROUARD School boards financed by a local school rate were to be set up in the towns.

■ **fiˈnanceable** *adjective* **L20.** †**financer** *noun* = FINANCIER *noun* 2 **M17–M18.**

financeer *verb* var. of FINANCIER *verb.*

financial /fʌɪˈnanʃ(ə)l, fɪ-/ *adjective & noun.* **M18.**
[ORIGIN from FINANCE *noun* + -IAL.]
► **A** *adjective.* **1** Of or pertaining to revenue or money matters. **M18.**

> G. GORER By financial difficulties I do not mean absolute poverty.

financial modeller a person engaged in financial modelling; a computer program for financial modelling. **financial modelling** computer-assisted construction of abstract models for financial calculations, projections, etc. **financial year** a year as reckoned for taxing or accounting (e.g. the British tax year, reckoned from 6 April). ***financial wizard***: see WIZARD *noun* 2b.
2 In possession of money. *Austral. & NZ slang.* **E20.**
► **B** *noun.* In *pl.* Shares in companies dealing in money. **L20.**
■ **financialist** *noun* = FINANCIER *noun* 1 **M19.** **financially** *adverb* **L18.**

financier /fʌɪˈnansɪə, fɪ-/ *noun.* **E17.**
[ORIGIN French, formed as FINANCE *noun*: see -IER.]
1 A person who is concerned with or skilled in finance, esp. establishing and managing public funds; a capitalist. **E17.**
†**2** FRENCH HISTORY. An administrator, collector, or farmer of taxes before the Revolution. **L17–M18.**

financier /fʌɪnanˈsɪə, fɪn-/ *verb intrans.* Usu. *derog.* Also **financeer**. **E19.**
[ORIGIN from the noun.]
Conduct financial operations; swindle.

finasteride /fɪˈnastərʌɪd/ *noun.* **L20.**
[ORIGIN from *fina-* of unknown origin + *ster-* (in STEROID *noun*) + -IDE.]
A drug which inhibits the production of dihydrotestosterone, used to treat benign prostate hyperplasia and male-pattern baldness.

finca /ˈfɪŋka, ˈfɪŋkə/ *noun.* **E20.**
[ORIGIN Spanish, from *fincar* cultivate, perh. from Latin *figere* fix, fasten, plant.]
In Spain and Spanish America: landed property; a country estate; a ranch.

finch /fɪn(t)ʃ/ *noun.*
[ORIGIN Old English *finč* = Middle Dutch *vinke* (Dutch *vink*), Old High German *finc(h)o* (German *Fink*), from West Germanic.]
Any of numerous small passerine birds, typically having short, stout beaks adapted for seed eating, belonging to the family Fringillidae and certain related families.
bullfinch, chaffinch, goldfinch, greenfinch, hawfinch, etc.
■ **finchlike** *adjective* resembling (that of) a finch **L19.**

find /fʌɪnd/ *noun.* **E19.**
[ORIGIN from the verb.]
1 An act or instance of finding; a discovery (of a fox, treasure, minerals, etc.). **E19.**
2 A thing which is found. **M19.** ►**b** A person who comes usefully to notice (public or one's own). **L19.**

> J. LUBBOCK Bronze weapons are entirely absent from the great finds of the Iron Age. **b** R. DAVIES I'm sure this boy is a lucky find Do let's have him.

– PHRASES: **sure find** (***a***) HUNTING a place where a fox etc. is sure to be found; (***b***) a person who or thing which is sure to be found.
– COMB.: **find-place**, **find-spot** ARCHAEOLOGY the place where an object was found.

find /fʌɪnd/ *verb.* Pa. t. & pple **found** /faʊnd/.
[ORIGIN Old English *findan* = Old Frisian *finda*, Old Saxon *findan*, *fiþan* (Dutch *vinden*), Old High German *findan* (German *finden*), Old Norse *finna*, Gothic *finþan*, from Germanic.]
► **I** Meet with or come upon by chance or in the course of events.
1 *verb trans.* Become aware of or get possession of by chance; come across, meet with. **OE.** ►**b** *euphem.* Steal. *slang.* **M19.**

> M. PATTISON In 1276, we find the Emperor and the King of England in constant communication. OED I found a shilling on the floor. W. STAFFORD Travelling through the dark I found a deer/dead on the edge of the Wilson River road. H. ROTH I found her sitting very quietly, as usual, in her large arm-chair.

2 *verb trans.* Come to have, obtain, receive, experience. **OE.**

> J. M. NEALE Ye who now do bless the poor Shall yourselves find blessing. F. W. NEWMAN I . . despair of finding readers among those who seek solely for amusement.

3 *verb trans.* Discover or perceive on inspection or consideration. ME. ▸b *refl.* Come to be, or perceive oneself to be, in a specified state or position. LME.

> E. HEMINGWAY I found I was quite drunk. H. L. MENCKEN I have found nothing in it save nonsense. **b** SCOTT FITZGERALD He found himself increasingly in a position to do as he wished. G. GREENE Myatt found himself alone.

4 *verb trans.* Learn through experience or trial; regard as, prove (something) to be. ME.

> T. HARDY I've tried to keep it from you, but have found I cannot. M. KEANE Joan did not find him amusing.

†5 *verb trans.* Detect; discover the identity or true character of. ME–L18.
6 *verb trans.* Feel, suffer from; perceive (a taste, smell, etc.). *obsolete* exc. *dial.* LME.
7 *verb trans.* Gain or recover the use of (one's limbs, powers, etc.). M16.
▸II Discover or attain (as if) by search or effort.
8 *verb trans.* Discover or obtain by searching; rediscover (something lost). OE. ▸b *verb trans. & intrans.* Discover (game, a scent) in hunting. ME. ▸c *verb refl.* Discover one's niche or vocation. M17. ▸d *verb trans.* Of an address: be adequate to enable a letter etc. to reach (a person). E20.

> AV *Luke* 15:6 Reioyce with me, for I have found my sheepe which was lost. E. WAUGH Find another glass.. if you can. **b** *Field* Archen Hills was blank.. but hounds found at once in Woodend. **c** A. MILLER Not finding yourself at the age of thirty-four is a disgrace!

9 *verb trans.* Ascertain by mental effort or calculation; discover by study or inquiry. OE.
10 *verb trans.* Contrive, devise, invent; be the discoverer of (a scientific fact etc.). OE.
11 LAW. †a *verb intrans.* Determine. Only in OE. ▸b *verb trans.* Authoritatively determine and declare (a person) to be *guilty, innocent*, etc., (an issue, offence, etc.) to be that specified, *that*; determine and deliver (a verdict). LME. ▸c *verb trans.* Ascertain the validity of (an indictment etc.). L15. ▸d *verb intrans.* Determine and deliver a verdict (*against, for*, etc., the accused or a party in a dispute). E17.

> **b** J. BUCHAN The jury found it a case of suicide while of unsound mind. **d** M. RICHLER The jury found in favour of the insurance company.

12 *verb trans.* Arrive at, reach; reach by a natural or normal process; *arch.* reach the conscience or understanding of. ME.

> SOUTHEY Yet may a dagger find him. COLERIDGE Whatever *finds* me, bears witness for itself that it has proceeded from a Holy Spirit. I. MURDOCH A letter to the theatre finds me.

13 *verb trans.* Succeed in obtaining; procure (money, sureties, bail, etc.); make or arrange to have (time, opportunity, etc.). ME. ▸b Summon up (courage, resolution, strength, etc.). LME.

> HOR. WALPOLE I just found a moment to write you a line. **b** OED At last he has found courage to speak.

▸III Provide.
14 *verb trans.* Supply, provide. ME.

> E. A. FREEMAN The government required each county to find its quota of ships.

15 *verb trans.* Provide for (a person, oneself); support, maintain. Foll. by *in*: supply with. ME. ▸†b Serve to maintain. L15–L16.
– PHRASES: **all found** (of servants' wages) with board and lodging provided. ***find fault (with)***: see FAULT *noun*. ***find favour (in the eyes of)***: see FAVOUR *noun*. **find God** experience religious conversion. **find in one's heart to, find it in one's heart to** (*a*) *arch.* desire to; (*b*) bring oneself to, be hard-hearted enough to, (usu. in neg. contexts). **find its way** be brought or get *into* etc. **find Jesus** experience conversion to Christianity. ***find mean(s)***: see MEAN *noun*[1]. **find one's feet** learn to stand or walk, get the use of one's feet; *fig.* grow in ability or confidence, develop one's powers, acquire knowledge or capability in a new job etc. ***find one's match***: see MATCH *noun*[1]. **find one's way** to contrive to reach, arrive at. ***find RELIGION***. **find the lady** = THREE-*card trick*. ***find the mean(s)***: see MEAN *noun*[1]. **how do you find yourself?** how are you? **know where to find** understand (a person), know the views of. **take us as you find us** accept us as we are.
– WITH ADVERBS IN SPECIALIZED SENSES: **find out** (*a*) seek out, detect, discover; detect in an offence, discover the identity or true character of; (*b*) make a discovery, discover a fact, the truth, etc. **find up** (now *dial.*) discover by searching, seek out.
– COMB.: **find-fault** a person who finds fault, a fault-finder.
■ **findable** *adjective* able to be found LME.

finder /ˈfʌɪndə/ *noun*. ME.
[ORIGIN from FIND *verb* + -ER[1].]
1 A person who finds something or someone. Also ***finder-out*** etc. ME. ▸b A person whose occupation it is to find something, a prospector; *slang* a thief. M18.
finders keepers *colloq.* whoever finds something is entitled to keep it.
†2 A dog trained to seek out or retrieve game. LME–M19.
3 A thing which finds something; a contrivance or instrument for finding something. L16. ▸b *spec.* A small telescope attached to a large one to help locate the object to be viewed. L18. ▸c A part of a camera showing the extent of the picture, = ***viewfinder*** s.v. VIEW *noun*. L19.

fin de siècle /fɛ̃ də sjɛkl/ *noun & adjectival phr.* L19.
[ORIGIN French = end of century.]
(Designating or characteristic of) the end of a century, *spec.* the nineteenth century; decadent.

†**findhorn** *noun* see FINNAN.

finding /ˈfʌɪndɪŋ/ *noun*. ME.
[ORIGIN from FIND *verb* + -ING[1].]
1 The action or an instance of finding or discovering. ME.
†2 The action of inventing or devising; a device. ME–M17.
3 The action of maintaining or supporting (a person etc.). ME. ▸†b Keep, maintenance, support. LME–M16.
†4 The action of providing or supplying. LME–L16.
5 A thing found; a discovery, a find. LME.

> R. CARSON The full scope of the dangerous interaction of chemicals is.. little known, but disturbing findings now come regularly.

6 The result of a judicial or other formal inquiry; a verdict. Freq. in *pl.* M19.

> J. LANG The court-martial still adheres to its finding of murder.

7 In *pl.* A craftsman's tools and sundries. *US*. M19.
– COMB.: **finding list** a list of books in a particular location or category in a library; **finding store** *US* a shop selling craftsmen's findings.

†**findon** *noun* see FINNAN.

findrinny /ˈfɪndrɪni/ *noun*. L19.
[ORIGIN Old Irish *findruine* from early Old Irish *findbruine*, from *find* (mod. *fionn*) white + elem. prob. from base of *bruth* heat.]
White bronze.

fine /fʌɪn/ *noun*[1]. ME.
[ORIGIN Old French & mod. French *fin* from Latin *finis* end, (in medieval Latin) a sum to be paid on concluding a lawsuit.]
▸I End.
1 Cessation, termination, conclusion. Now only in ***in fine*** below. ME.
in fine †(*a*) in the end, at last; (*b*) finally, to sum up, in short.
†2 The end of life, death. ME–M16.
†3 The limit; extremity, an extreme case. LME–M19.
†4 The end in view; an aim, a purpose. LME–E17.
†5 A consequence, a result. E16–E17.
▸II 6 LAW. The final agreement or settlement of a suit; *spec.* the compromise of a fictitious or collusive suit for the possession of land, formerly used as a form of conveyance. *obsolete* exc. *hist.* ME.
▸III A fee, a penalty.
7 a A penalty of any kind. *arch.* ME. ▸b A sum of money imposed as the penalty for breaking the law or a regulation. LME.

> **a** J. S. BLACKIE We stood for our faith, when our life was the fine. **b** H. HALLAM Fines to the amount of £85,000.. were imposed on the Covenanters.

†8 A sum of money offered or paid for exemption from punishment or as compensation for injury. ME–E17.
†9 A fee paid for any privilege. LME–M18.
10 *hist.* A fee paid to a feudal landlord by the tenant or vassal on the transfer or alienation of the tenancy. LME. ▸b A sum of money paid by an incoming tenant in consideration of a low rent. E16.
– COMB.: **fine rolls** *hist.* rolls recording payments made to the Crown for the granting of privileges, land, etc.

fine /fʌɪn/ *noun*[2]. E17.
[ORIGIN from FINE *adjective*.]
†1 A fine woman. E–M17.
2 Fine weather. M19.

> C. LAMB You go about, in rain or fine, at all hours.

3 A fine thing; *spec.* (in *pl.*), very small particles. L19.

> *New Yorker* There's no shale upstream.. No fines to contaminate it.

fine /ˈfiːnə/ *noun*[3]. L19.
[ORIGIN Irish.]
IRISH HISTORY. An ancient family or sept.

fine /fin/ *noun*[4]. Pl. pronounced same. E20.
[ORIGIN French, abbreviation of FINE CHAMPAGNE.]
(A) French brandy; *spec.* = FINE CHAMPAGNE.
fine de la maison, fine maison /(də la) mɛzɔ̃/ a house brandy.

fine /fʌɪn/ *adjective & adverb*. ME.
[ORIGIN Old French & mod. French *fin* from Proto-Romance from Latin *finire* FINISH *verb*.]
▸A *adjective* I 1 Of superior quality; very good of its kind. ME.

> S. RAVEN He drank half a bottle of very fine claret.

2 Free from dross or impurity; clear, pure, refined. ME. ▸b Of gold or silver: containing a specified (high) proportion of pure metal. LME. ▸c Of a liquid: pure, clear, transparent. Now chiefly *dial.* L15.
†3 Sheer, absolute, perfect; *iron.* consummate, egregious. ME–E18.
4 Virtuous, morally upright; honourable, noble. ME.
5 Very skilful, highly accomplished. ME.

> N. MITFORD He was said to be the finest billiards player in the British Isles.

6 Excellent, of striking merit, admirable; (amongst collectors of coins, books, etc.) in a good but not excellent state of preservation. ME. ▸b Good, enjoyable; (in weakened sense) satisfactory, acceptable, all right. M19.

> G. SAINTSBURY The greatest artist could have done nothing finer. *iron.*: BROWNING A fine way to paint soul, by painting body So ill. **b** C. KINGSLEY He thought of the fine times coming when he would be a man. K. AMIS 'You don't mind, do you?'.. 'Fine with me.'

7 Remarkably good-looking, handsome, beautiful; imposing, dignified. LME. ▸b Of good size; large, well-grown. L16.

> D. H. LAWRENCE He was a fine fellow, big, straight and fearless-looking. E. MANNIN A fine big house with a pillared porch, like a Greek temple. **b** MRS H. WOOD He is not a fine child, for he is remarkably small; but he is a very pretty one.

8 Of dress etc.: ornate, showy, smart. E16.

> *Proverb*: Fine feathers make fine birds.

9 Characterized by or affecting refinement or elegance. M16.

> W. BESANT He's only a working man, you see. He hasn't got your fine ways.

10 Of a thought, saying, etc.: admirably conceived or expressed. L17. ▸b Of speech, writing, etc.: ornate, elegant, affected. L18. ▸c Flattering, complimentary; euphemistic. M19.

> HOBBES Two or three fine sayings are not enough to make a wit. **b** H. CHAPONE Idle gallantry and unmeaning fine speeches. **c** J. MORLEY Hardly.. more than a fine name for self-indulgence.

11 Of the weather, a day, etc.: bright, clear; free from rain or fog, and with some sunshine. E18.

> A. AYCKBOURN It is a fine evening, the sun streams through the french windows.

12 In good health or spirits; well. L18.

> H. HOOD There's nothing wrong with my heart... I'm fine, just fine.

▸II Delicate, subtle.
13 Delicately beautiful; exquisitely fashioned. LME. ▸b Of emotion etc.: elevated, refined. E17.
14 Delicate in structure; thin, filmy. LME. ▸b Very small; in small particles. M16.

> I. MCEWAN His hair was unnaturally fine, like a baby's. **b** J. STEINBECK A fine sandy dust arose from the land.

15 Extremely thin or slender. LME. ▸b CRICKET. Behind the wicket and near the line of flight of the ball. M19.

> SPENSER Like a crane his neck was long and fyne.

16 Of a weapon, tool, etc.: having a sharp point or edge. LME.
†17 Clever, subtle, ingenious; cunning, artful. LME–M18.
18 Capable of delicate perception or discrimination. M16.

> A. BAIN The part endowed with the finer tactile power feels the other.

19 Not easily perceptible; subtle, minute, precise. M16.

> T. STOPPARD I was just explaining one or two of the finer points.

▸B *adverb*. Now chiefly *colloq. & dial.*
1 Well, very well; completely, thoroughly. ME.

> D. MACDONALD Most of the tricks were good tricks and they worked fine.

2 In a fine manner; elegantly. E16.

> SWIFT The neighbours who come here to dine Admire to hear me speak so fine.

3 Delicately, subtly; precisely. L16.
– SPECIAL COLLOCATIONS, PHRASES, & COMB. (of adjective & adverb): ***as fine as fivepence***: see FIVE *adjective & noun*. **cut it fine** allow very little margin, time, space, etc. **fine and dandy** *colloq.* first-rate; (of a person) well. **fine-axe** *verb trans.* face (stone) to a smooth surface by tapping with a mason's axe. ***fine chemicals***: see CHEMICAL *noun*. **fine cut** a kind of finely shredded tobacco. **fine-cut** *adjective* finely cut or shredded. **fine-draw** *verb trans.* (*a*) sew together (two pieces of cloth, the edges of a rent, etc.) so that the join is barely perceptible; (*b*) draw out to extreme thinness or subtlety. **fine-drawn** *adjective* (*a*) subtle, extremely thin; (*b*) SPORT (now *rare*) reduced in weight by training. **fine feathers** gaudy plumage (*lit. & fig.*). **fine gentleman** a man characterized by refined manners and tastes; *derog.* a man of fashion, a dandy, a man who thinks himself above working. **fine-grain** *adjective* fine-grained; PHOTOGRAPHY of or capable of producing an image which may be considerably enlarged without appearing grainy. **fine-grained** *adjective* having a fine grain; consisting of small particles. **fine-hair** *verb trans.* remove fine hairs or down from (a pelt). **fine-hand** *adjective* written in a fine or delicate hand. **fine lady** a woman of quality or refinement; *derog.* a woman of fashion, a woman who thinks herself above working. **fine print** = ***small print*** s.v. SMALL *adjective*. **fine-spun** *adjective* spun or drawn out to a fine thread, delicate, flimsy; *fig.* excessively subtle or refined, unpractical. **fine structure** small-scale or detailed variation in structure, texture, appearance, etc., *esp.* (PHYSICS) the presence of closely spaced lines in spectra (cf. HYPERFINE); ***fine-structure constant***, a fundamental (and dimensionless) physical constant, equal to approximately 1/137, which occurs in expressions describing the fine structure of the atomic spectra of hydrogen, helium, etc. **fine-tooth comb** a comb with narrow close-set teeth; ***go over with a fine-tooth comb, go through with***

F

a fine-tooth comb, search or examine thoroughly. **fine-tooth-comb** *verb trans.* comb (a person's hair) with a fine-tooth comb; *fig.* search or examine thoroughly. **fine-tune** *verb trans.* make delicate adjustments to. **fine tuner** a device for fine tuning. **fine tuning** the process of making delicate adjustments (to an instrument etc., *fig.* the economy etc.). **fine-weather** *adjective* fit or suitable only for fine weather. ***fine weather for ducks***: see DUCK *noun*[1]. **not put too fine a point on it**, **not put too fine a point upon it**, **not put too fine an edge on it**, **not put too fine an edge upon it** speak bluntly. **one fine day** once upon a time. **one of these fine days** some day in the future. **one's finest hour** the time of one's greatest success. **run it fine** = *cut it fine* above.

†fine *verb*[1] *intrans. & trans.* ME–L16.
[ORIGIN Old French *finer* from Proto-Romance from Latin *finis* end.]
Bring or come to an end; finish.

fine /fʌɪn/ *verb*[2]. ME.
[ORIGIN from FINE *noun*[1].]
▸ **I** †**1** *verb trans. & intrans.* Pay (as) a penalty, ransom, or composition. ME–M18.
2 *verb intrans.* Pay for a privilege or appointment. *obsolete* exc. *hist.* M16.
3 †**a** *verb intrans.* Pay a sum on renewal of tenure. Only in L17. ▸**b** *verb trans.* Foll. by *down*, *off*: secure the reduction of (rent) by paying a lump sum. *obsolete* exc. *hist.* E18.
▸ **II 4** *verb trans.* Impose a fine on, punish by a fine. Formerly also *gen.*, punish. M16.

Independent He was subsequently convicted of drink-driving . . and fined $150.

fine /fʌɪn/ *verb*[3]. ME.
[ORIGIN from FINE *adjective*. Cf. French *finer*, medieval Latin *finare* refine.]
1 *verb trans.* Make clear or pure, refine, (now only beer and wine). Also foll. by *down*. ME.

fig.: BROWNING Fined and thrice refined I' the crucible of life.

†**2** *verb trans.* Make beautiful, embellish; smarten *up*. LME–M17.
3 *verb trans.* Break into small particles; make less coarse. M16.
4 *verb intrans.* Of liquid: become clear, clarify. Also foll. by *down*. M16.
5 *verb trans. & intrans.* Make or become more slender or attenuated; slim *down*, dwindle or whittle *away*. E19.

EDWARD THOMAS Twilight has fined to naught. N. FREELING Hard work and fresh air had fined her down so much that she suddenly found herself far too thin.

6 *verb intrans.* Of the weather: become clear, brighten *up*. Now chiefly *Austral. & NZ*. L19.

fineable *adjective* var. of FINABLE.

fine art /fʌɪn ˈɑːt/ *noun phr.* M18.
[ORIGIN from FINE *adjective* + ART *noun*[1], translating French *beaux-arts* (pl.).]
1 In *pl.* Those arts which appeal to the intellect or the sense of beauty, as literature, music, and esp. painting, sculpture, and architecture. M18. ▸**b** *sing.* Any one of these arts; *transf.* a thing requiring a high degree of skill, a high accomplishment. L19.
2 These arts collectively, esp. as constituting a branch of practice or study. M19.

fine champagne /fin ʃɑ̃paɲ/ *noun phr.* Pl. **-s -s** (pronounced same). M19.
[ORIGIN French = fine (brandy from) Champagne.]
Old liqueur brandy from the Grande Champagne and Petite Champagne vineyards in the Charente, France; an example, glass, or drink of this. Cf. FINE *noun*[4].

†fineer *verb* var. of VENEER *verb*.

Fine Gael /fiːnə ˈɡeɪl/ *noun phr.* M20.
[ORIGIN Irish, lit. 'tribe of Gaels'.]
An Irish political organization and party which entered the Dáil in 1937 in succession to the United Ireland Party.

fineish /ˈfʌɪnɪʃ/ *adjective.* L16.
[ORIGIN from FINE *adjective* + -ISH[1].]
†**1** Affecting refinement, fastidious. L16–M17.
2 Rather fine. M17.

fineless /ˈfʌɪnlɪs/ *adjective.* *rare.* E17.
[ORIGIN from FINE *noun*[1] + -LESS.]
Boundless, infinite, unlimited.

finely /ˈfʌɪnli/ *adverb.* ME.
[ORIGIN from FINE *adjective* + -LY[2].]
1 Perfectly, completely, thoroughly. Long *obsolete* exc. *Scot.* ME.
2 Superbly, excellently, beautifully; with great skill, to great effect. LME.
†**3** Cleverly, shrewdly, with cunning. M16–M17.
4 With delicacy or sensitivity. M16.
5 To a fine point or edge; minutely, precisely. M16.
6 Ornately, showily, smartly. M17.

fineness /ˈfʌɪnnɪs/ *noun.* LME.
[ORIGIN from FINE *adjective* + -NESS.]
1 *gen.* The quality or state of being fine. LME.

LEIGH HUNT He wrote to the Prince of Orange upon the fineness of his troops. W. S. LANDOR As little as a silkworm knows about the fineness of her thread.

2 Purity of a metal, degree of freedom from alloy. Now *spec.* the number of parts per thousand of gold or silver in an alloy. L15.
3 Astuteness, cunning; an artifice, a stratagem. Now *rare*. E16.
– COMB.: **fineness ratio** the ratio of length to width in a ship's hull, aircraft fuselage, etc.

finer /ˈfʌɪnə/ *noun.* Now *rare* or *obsolete*. LME.
[ORIGIN from FINE *verb*[3] + -ER[1].]
A person who or thing which refines; a refiner.

finery /ˈfʌɪn(ə)ri/ *noun*[1]. L16.
[ORIGIN French *finerie*, from Old French *finer* refine: see -ERY.]
Chiefly *hist.* A hearth where cast iron is made malleable or in which wrought iron or steel is made from pig iron.

finery /ˈfʌɪn(ə)ri/ *noun*[2]. L17.
[ORIGIN from FINE *adjective* + -ERY, after BRAVERY.]
1 Showy dress or decoration; an example of this. L17.

M. J. FRIEDMAN Members of both factions had festooned themselves with all manner of finery.

2 Looks, beauty; affected or ostentatious elegance or splendour. Now *rare*. E18.

fines herbes /finz ɛrb, fiːnz ˈɜːb/ *noun phr. pl.* M19.
[ORIGIN French = fine herbs.]
Chopped mixed herbs used in cooking.
aux fines herbes /o, əʊ/ flavoured with chopped mixed herbs.

finesse /fɪˈnɛs/ *noun & verb.* LME.
[ORIGIN French, from Proto-Romance, from base of *fin* FINE *adjective*: see -ESS[2].]
▸ **A** *noun.* **1** Clarity, purity (esp. of metals); slenderness, delicacy. Now *rare*. LME.

P. GALLICO The finesse and delicacy of her wristbones.

2 Delicacy of manipulation or discrimination; refinement. M16.

J. CHEEVER She could wave a hornet away from her wineglass with great finesse.

3 Artfulness, cunning; subtle strategy. M16.

J. AUSTEN She was not experienced in the finesse of love.

4 An artful stratagem; a ruse, a trick. M16. ▸**b** CARDS. An attempt to take a trick with a card lower than but not in sequence with a card of the same suit also held. M19.
▸ **B** *verb.* **1** CARDS. ▸**a** *verb intrans.* Attempt to take a trick by a finesse. M18. ▸**b** *verb trans.* Play (a card) in a finesse. M18.
2 *verb intrans.* Use artifice or stratagem. L18. ▸**b** *verb trans.* Achieve by artifice; bring about or manage by delicate handling. E19.

M. E. BRADDON She diplomatized and finessed with them as if she had been canvassing the county. **b** D. EDGAR The wheeling and dealing, the brinkmanship and finessing of opponents, the whole elaborate political game.

finew *adjective, verb, & noun* see VINNY.

finewed *adjective* see VINNIED.

fingan *noun* var. of FINJAN.

finger /ˈfɪŋɡə/ *noun.*
[ORIGIN Old English *finger* = Old Frisian *finger*, Old Saxon, Old High German *fingar* (Dutch *vinger*, German *Finger*), Old Norse *fingr*, Gothic *figgrs*, from Germanic.]
▸ **I 1** Each of the five terminal members of the hand, or each of the four, excluding the thumb. OE.
2 Formerly *gen.*, the breadth of a finger as a measure, ¾ inch. Now *spec.* (*slang*) an amount of liquor one finger-breadth deep in a glass, a small measure of liquor. LME.

J. D. SALINGER I brought my glass over and poured myself out . . at least four fingers of Scotch.

3 A digit of an animal. Now *rare*. LME.
4 A part of a glove etc. which is made to receive a finger. M16.
5 Skill in fingering a musical instrument etc.; touch. Now *rare*. M18.
▸ **II** Something which resembles a finger.
6 A finger-like projection, esp. on a plant. LME. ▸**b** A banana. L19. ▸**c** A long narrow pier or other structure. M20.

BROWNING Our fig tree . . has furled Her five fingers. **c** *Times* Aircraft can taxi to the . . 900 ft. long glazed pier, or 'finger', which stretches out from the terminal to provide completely enclosed passenger access.

7 Any small projecting rod etc. with a mechanical function; the pointer of a clock or watch (now *dial.*). L15.

T. HARDY On the clock's dull dial a foggy finger, Moving to set the minutes right.

8 A short and narrow object or piece of material, e.g. an item of food. M19.

J. JOHNSTON A plate of thin fingers of hot buttered toast.

fish finger etc.
9 *slang.* **a** A police officer, a detective. L19. ▸**b** An informer. E20. ▸**c** A pickpocket. E20. ▸**d** A person who indicates victims to criminals. M20.
– PHRASES ETC.: **all fingers and thumbs** clumsy, awkward. ***as easy as kiss your fingers***: see KISS *verb*. ***auricular finger***: see AURICULAR *adjective* 4. ***burn one's fingers***: see BURN *verb* 10. ***clean fingers***: see CLEAN *adjective*. ***cross one's fingers***: see CROSS *verb*. ***easy as kiss your fingers***: see KISS *verb*. FIRST ***finger***. ***five finger***: see FIVE *adjective & noun*. FOREFINGER. ***fourth finger***: see FOURTH *adjective*. **get one's finger out**, **get the finger out** *slang* hurry up, begin work in earnest, take action, (freq. in *imper.*). **give the finger to** *slang* make an obscene gesture to (a person etc.) with the middle finger raised. ***green fingers***: see GREEN *adjective*. **have a finger in the pie** be (esp. officiously) concerned in the matter. ***index finger***: see INDEX *noun*. ***keep one's fingers crossed***: see CROSS *verb*. ***lady's finger***: see LADY *noun & adjective*. **lay a finger on** touch, however slightly (usu. in neg. & hypothetical contexts). **lay one's finger on** = *put one's finger on* below. **let slip through one's fingers** lose by letting go one's hold of, *fig.* miss the opportunity of. **lift a finger** make the slightest effort (usu. in neg. contexts). ***little finger***: see LITTLE *adjective*. ***long finger***: see LONG *adjective*[1]. ***middle finger***: see MIDDLE *adjective*. **move a finger** = *lift a finger* above. **one's fingers itch** one is longing or impatient (*to do*). **point a finger at**, **point the finger at** (*a*) throw scorn on; (*b*) identify as responsible, accuse. **pull one's finger out** *slang* = *get one's finger out* above. **put a finger on** = *lay a finger on* above. **put one's finger on** point to or identify with precision (a cause of trouble etc.). **put the finger on** *slang* inform against; identify as a victim. **raise a finger** = *lift a finger* above. ***ring finger***: see RING *noun*[1]. ***second finger***: see SECOND *adjective*. **shake one's finger at** *fig.* = *wag one's finger at* below. ***snap one's fingers at***: see SNAP *verb* 7. **stir a finger** = *lift a finger* above. **take one's finger out** *slang* = *get one's finger out* above. ***third finger***: see THIRD *adjective & noun*. **turn round one's little finger**, **turn round one's finger**, **twist round one's little finger**, **twist round one's finger** = *wrap round one's little finger* below. ***two fingers***: see TWO *adjective* 1. **wag one's finger at** *fig.* reprove, rebuke. ***white finger(s)***: see WHITE *adjective*. **wind round one's little finger**, **wind round one's finger** = *wrap round one's little finger* below. ***with a wet finger***: see WET *adjective*. ***work one's fingers to the bone***: see BONE *noun*. **wrap round one's little finger**, **wrap round one's finger** easily exert one's will over (a person), persuade without difficulty.
– COMB.: **finger alphabet** a system of manual signs for communicating with deaf people; **fingerboard** a flat strip of wood etc. at the top end of a stringed musical instrument, against which the strings are pressed to determine notes; **finger bowl** a bowl for water etc. for rinsing the fingers at table, esp. after dessert; **finger-breadth** the width of the finger used as a measure; **finger buffet** a buffet consisting of food that may be eaten with the fingers; **finger-dry** *verb trans. & intrans.* dry and style (hair) with the fingers; **finger food** food so served that it can conveniently be eaten without cutlery; **finger-glass** a glass for water etc. for rinsing the fingers at table, esp. after dessert; **finger hole** one of a series of holes in a wind instrument which are opened and closed by the fingers in playing; **finger lake** a long narrow lake in a glaciated valley; **finger language** = *finger spelling* below; **finger-lickin'**, **-licking** *adverb & adjective* (*colloq.*, orig. *US*) [from proprietary slogan 'it's finger lickin' good'] (*a*) *adverb* to the extent that one licks one's fingers; (*b*) *adjective* tasty, appetizing; **fingermark** a mark left on a surface by the touch of a (dirty) finger; **finger millet** a tropical cereal grass, *Eleusine coracana*, with digitate spikes; **fingernail** each of the nails of the fingers (***to one's fingernails***, completely, thoroughly); **finger-paint** *noun & verb intrans.* (use) a paint that can be applied with the fingers; **fingerpick** *noun & verb* (*a*) *noun* a plectrum worn on a finger; (*b*) *verb intrans. & trans.* play (a guitar etc., music, esp. country and western) using a fingerpick; **fingerplate** a plate fastened on a door to protect it from fingermarks; **finger-pointing** *verbal noun & adjective* (of or pertaining to) accusation; **fingerpost** *noun & verb* (*a*) *noun* a signpost at a crossroads or junction; (*b*) *verb trans.* indicate the direction of by means of a fingerpost; **fingerprint** *noun & verb* (*a*) *noun* an impression made on a surface by a person's finger, esp. as used for identifying a criminal etc.; *fig.* any sign identifying a person, a distinctive characteristic; (*b*) *verb trans.* record the fingerprint(s) of (a person); **finger puppet** a small puppet made to fit on a finger; **finger-ring** a ring worn on the finger; **finger's-breadth** = *finger-breadth* above; **finger-snap** a snap of the fingers; **finger spelling** manual signs for communicating with deaf people; **fingerstall** a sheath to protect a finger when injured or in a handicraft etc.; **finger-stone** †(*a*) a stone sufficiently small to be thrown by the hand; (*b*) a convexly tapering cylindrical stone; a belemnite; **finger-tight** *adverb* as tight as can be made by the hand; **finger-wagging** *verbal noun & adjective* (of or pertaining to) reprimand or warning; **finger wave** a wave set in wet hair with the fingers.
■ **fingered** *adjective* (*a*) having fingers (esp. of a specified kind); (*b*) resembling a finger: E16. **fingerful** *noun* as much as can be held on one finger or between two fingers; a small quantity: L19. **fingerless** *adjective* without fingers E16. **finger-like** *adjective* resembling (that of) a finger or fingers L18. **fingery** *adjective* branching into fingers or finger-like divisions E19.

finger /ˈfɪŋɡə/ *verb.* LME.
[ORIGIN from the noun.]
†**1** *verb trans.* Point at with a finger; point *out* (as) with a finger. LME–M18.
2 *verb trans.* Play on (a musical instrument) with the fingers; play (a passage of music) with the fingers used in a particular way. LME. ▸**b** Mark (written music) with signs or figures indicating the fingers with which the notes are to be played. E19.
3 *verb trans.* Lay the fingers on with the intention to steal, pilfer, (*from*). M16.
4 *verb trans.* Hold or turn about in one's fingers; put one's fingers on, touch with the fingers; do this repeatedly or restlessly. L16. ▸**b** *verb trans. & intrans.* Handle (money) with unworthy motives. L16.
5 *verb intrans.* Make restless or repeated movements (*at*) with the fingers; toy *with*. Formerly also *fig.*, long or grope *for*. M17.
6 *verb trans.* Manipulate with the fingers; *fig.* elaborate, work up with minute labour. *rare*. E19.

7 *verb trans.* Indicate (a victim) or supply (information) to criminals; inform on or identify (a criminal) to the police. *N. Amer. slang.* **M20.**
■ **fingerer** *noun* **M16.**

finger-end /fɪŋgər'ɛnd/ *noun.* Pl. **finger-ends.** Also **finger's end**, pl. **fingers' ends. ME.**
[ORIGIN from FINGER *noun* (+ -'S[1]) + END *noun*.]
The end or tip of a finger. Cf. FINGERTIP *noun*.
at one's finger-ends = *at one's fingertips* s.v. FINGERTIP *noun*. **have at one's finger-ends** = *have at one's fingertips* s.v. FINGERTIP *noun*. **to the finger-ends**, **to one's finger-ends** = *to the fingertips* s.v. FINGERTIP *noun*.

fingering /'fɪŋg(ə)rɪŋ/ *noun*[1]. **LME.**
[ORIGIN from FINGER *verb* + -ING[1].]
The action of FINGER *verb*; *MUSIC* (the marking of written music to indicate) the method of using the fingers to play an instrument or a particular passage. See also CROSS-FINGERING.

fingering /'fɪŋg(ə)rɪŋ/ *noun*[2]. Orig. †**fingram. E17.**
[ORIGIN Perh. alt. of Old French *fin grain* fine grain: cf. GROGRAM.]
†**1** (An example of) a kind of woollen cloth. *Scot.* **E17–M18.**
2 A kind of fine wool or yarn used for knitting. **L17.**

fingerling /'fɪŋgəlɪŋ/ *noun & adjective.* **LME.**
[ORIGIN from FINGER *noun* + -LING[1].]
▸ **A** *noun.* †**1** Each of the fingers of a glove; a fingerstall. **LME–L16.**
2 A parr; any very young fish. **E18.**
3 A very small being. **M19.**
▸ **B** *attrib.* or as *adjective.* Of a fish or other animal: small because still very young. **L19.**

fingertip /'fɪŋgətɪp/ *noun & adjective.* **M19.**
[ORIGIN from FINGER *noun* + TIP *noun*[1].]
▸ **A** *noun.* The tip of a finger. (Cf. earlier FINGER-END.) **M19.**
at one's fingertips ready at hand. **have at one's fingertips** be thoroughly conversant with, have ready knowledge of. **to the fingertips**, **to one's fingertips** through and through, in every way, completely.
▸ **B** *attrib.* or as *adjective.* **1** *ARCHAEOLOGY.* Of ornament: made with the fingertips. **E20.**
2 Of a garment: reaching to the fingertips. **M20.**
3 That can be controlled by a light movement of the fingers. **M20.**

fingle-fangle /'fɪŋg(ə)lfaŋg(ə)l/ *noun. arch.* **M17.**
[ORIGIN Redupl. of FANGLE *noun*. Cf. FIDDLE-FADDLE.]
A trifle; something whimsical or fantastic.

Fingo /'fɪŋgəʊ/ *noun.* Pl. **-os. E19.**
[ORIGIN Xhosa *mfengu* destitute wanderer.]
A member of a people of South Africa made up of various groups driven from Natal in the early 19th cent. and now largely living in the Eastern Cape province.

†**fingram** *noun* see FINGERING *noun*[2].

fingrigo /'fɪŋgrɪgəʊ/ *noun.* Pl. **-os. L17.**
[ORIGIN Jamaican creole, perh. from FINGERY *adjective* + GO *noun*[1], *verb*.]
A W. Indian climbing shrub with large prickles, *Pisonia aculeata*, of the bougainvillea family.

finial /'fɪnɪəl, 'fʌɪn-/ *adjective & noun.* **LME.**
[ORIGIN from unrecorded Anglo-Norman or Anglo-Latin, from Old French & mod. French *fin*, Latin *finis* end: see -AL[1].]
▸ †**A** *adjective.* Final. **LME–L15.**
▸ **B** *noun.* **1** *ARCHITECTURE.* An ornament which surmounts the apex of a roof, pediment, gable, tower corner, canopy, etc.; the topmost part of a pinnacle. **LME.**
2 An ornamental knob or extremity on a piece of silverware, cutlery, etc. **M20.**
■ **finialled** *adjective* having finials **M19.**

finical /'fɪnɪk(ə)l/ *adjective.* **L16.**
[ORIGIN Prob. from FINE *adjective* + -ICAL, & orig. university slang; perh. suggested by Middle Dutch *fijnkens* accurately, neatly, prettily.]
Overparticular, precise, fastidious; *arch.* excessively delicate in workmanship or elaborate in detail.
■ **finically** *adverb* **M17.** **finicalness** *noun* **L17.** **finicality** /fɪnɪ'kalɪti/ *noun* (a) finical quality **L16.**

finicism /'fɪnɪsɪz(ə)m/ *noun.* **M19.**
[ORIGIN from FINICK *noun* + -ISM.]
Finical affectation.

finick /'fɪnɪk/ *noun.* **E18.**
[ORIGIN Prob. back-form. from FINICAL.]
A finical person.

finick /'fɪnɪk/ *verb intrans.* Chiefly *dial.* **M19.**
[ORIGIN Prob. back-form. from FINICKING.]
Perform work or act finically.

finicking /'fɪnɪkɪŋ/ *adjective & noun.* Also **finikin** /'fɪnɪkɪn/. **M17.**
[ORIGIN from FINICAL, with suffix-substitution of -ING[2].]
▸ **A** *adjective.* = FINICAL. Also, trifling. **M17.**
▸ †**B** *noun.* (Usu. **finikin**.)
1 A variety of the domestic pigeon. **E18–M19.**
2 A finicking person. Only in **M18.**
■ **finickingly** *adverb* **L19.**

finicky /'fɪnɪki/ *adjective.* **E19.**
[ORIGIN from FINICAL, with suffix-substitution of -Y[1], or from FINICK *verb* + -Y[1].]
= FINICAL. Also, needing much attention to detail.

> D. HEWETT All sorts of . . delicacies to tempt Gwennie's finicky appetite. A. GUINNESS His rehearsals . . never became stodgy or finicky.

■ **finickiness** *noun* **M19.**

finif *noun* var. of FINNIP.

finify /'fʌɪnɪfʌɪ/ *verb trans. obsolete* exc. *US & dial.* **L16.**
[ORIGIN from FINE *adjective* + -I- + -FY.]
Make fine; adorn, decorate.

finikin *adjective & noun* see FINICKING.

fining /'fʌɪnɪŋ/ *noun.* **LME.**
[ORIGIN from FINE *verb*[3] + -ING[1].]
1 The action of FINE *verb*[3]. **LME.**
2 *sing.* & (usu.) in *pl.* A substance used for clarifying liquid, now *spec.* beer or wine. **L18.**

finis /'fiːnɪs, 'fɪnɪs, 'fʌɪnɪs/ *noun.* **LME.**
[ORIGIN Latin = end.]
1 At the end of a book: the end. **LME.**
2 The conclusion, the end, the finish; the end of life, death. **L17.**

finish /'fɪnɪʃ/ *noun.* **L18.**
[ORIGIN from the verb.]
1 The last stage, the termination, the conclusion, the end; *spec.* (*a*) the end of a hunt, race, or other contest or event; the death of a fox; the point at which a race etc. ends; (*b*) the final taste impression of a wine etc. **L18.**

> A. M. JOHNSON To look upon death . . as the finish of your sorrows! L. W. MEYNELL They were pieces in a game that still had to be played to a grim finish.

fight to the finish a contest which lasts until one party is defeated. **from start to finish** throughout.
2 A thing which finishes, or gives completeness or perfection to something; *spec.* the last coat of paint or plaster laid on a surface; a veneer or other material added to something, usu. to enhance its appearance; a mode of finishing furniture etc. **L18.**

> R. V. JONES The standard of finish was terrible, and . . no one who was doing a decent job would leave his work in that state.

3 A place of entertainment open late (a possible last call on a night out). *arch. slang.* **L18.**
4 The condition or quality of being finished or perfected. **E19.**
5 Methylated spirit. *colloq.* Now *rare.* **L19.**
– COMB.: **finish line** = *finishing line* s.v. FINISHING *noun*.

finish /'fɪnɪʃ/ *verb.* **ME.**
[ORIGIN Old French *feniss-* (mod. *finiss-*) lengthened stem of *fenir* (mod. *finir*) from Latin *finire*, from *finis* end: see -ISH[2].]
▸ **I** *verb trans.* **1** Bring to an end, come to the end of, go through the last stage of, (a thing, *doing*). **ME.** ▸**b** Foll. by *off*: provide with an ending. **M19.**

> SCOTT FITZGERALD When Jordan Baker had finished telling all this. E. WAUGH The colonel finished the last war as a brigadier.

2 Bring to completion; make or do completely; complete. Also foll. by *off*. **LME.**

> S. BELLOW He was still finishing his work well within the deadlines.

3 Perfect finally or in detail, put the final and completing touches to, (also foll. by *off*, *up*); complete or perfect the education of (a person, esp. a girl), the fattening of (cattle etc.), the manufacture of (woodwork, cloth, etc.) by surface treatment. **LME.** ▸†**b** Make (*into*) by a final operation. **E18–E19.**
4 Deal with or dispose of the whole or the remainder of (an object); complete the consumption of (food, one's stock of something), the reading of (a book etc.). **E16.** ▸**b** Kill, destroy; reduce to utter exhaustion or helplessness. Also foll. by *off*. Now chiefly *colloq.* **E17.**

> **b** V. BRITTAIN Why couldn't a torpedo have finished me? R. INGALLS That just about finished the place for us.

▸ **II** *verb intrans.* **5** Come to an end, reach the end, (also foll. by *up*); cease, leave *off*; end *in* (a thing), *by* (*doing*), *up* (in a particular state or place, (*by*) *doing*. **LME.** ▸†**b** Die. **LME–E17.** ▸**c** *SPORT.* Come to the end of a course or race (in a particular condition or place). **L19.**

> B. FRANKLIN Partnerships often finish in quarrels. D. DU MAURIER Yawning a little as they waited for the sermon to finish. E. BOWEN The girl finished up with a rush. *Heritage Outlook* This was unfortunately denied to us at the last moment so we finished up in the Public Library. **c** D. FRANCIS Treetops broke down and finished last, limping.

6 Foll. by *with*: complete one's use of or association with. **L18.**
■ **finishable** *adjective* (earlier in UNFINISHABLE) **M19.**

finished /'fɪnɪʃt/ *ppl adjective.* **L16.**
[ORIGIN from FINISH *verb* + -ED[1]. Earlier in UNFINISHED.]
1 That has been finished; ended, completed. **L16.**
2 Consummate, perfect, accomplished. **E18.**

finisher /'fɪnɪʃə/ *noun.* **E16.**
[ORIGIN formed as FINISHED + -ER[1].]
1 A person who or thing which finishes (something). **E16.**
finisher of the law *joc.* (*arch.*) a hangman, an executioner.
2 *spec.* ▸**a** A worker or machine performing the final operation in a manufacturing process. **L17.** ▸**b** A discomfiting thing, a decisive or crushing blow (*lit.* & *fig.*). *colloq.* **L18.**

finishing /'fɪnɪʃɪŋ/ *noun.* **LME.**
[ORIGIN formed as FINISHED + -ING[1].]
1 The action of FINISH *verb*. Also ***finishing-off***. **LME.**
2 A thing which gives a finished appearance; decoration, ornamental work. **M17.**
– COMB.: **finishing line**, **finishing post** a (real or imaginary) line, post, which marks the end of a race etc.; **finishing school** a school for completing the education, esp. of girls, with an emphasis on the social graces.

finishing /'fɪnɪʃɪŋ/ *ppl adjective.* **E18.**
[ORIGIN formed as FINISHED + -ING[2].]
That finishes (something).
finishing stroke, **finishing touch** a last action or added effect in the preparation or production of something (usu. in *pl.*).

finishment /'fɪnɪʃm(ə)nt/ *noun.* Now *US.* **LME.**
[ORIGIN formed as FINISHED + -MENT.]
End, finishing; death.

finitary /'fʌɪnɪt(ə)ri/ *adjective.* **M20.**
[ORIGIN from FINITE *adjective & noun* after UNITARY.]
MATH. Of a proof, relation, etc.: involving a finite number of steps or other entities.

finite /'fʌɪnʌɪt/ *adjective & noun.* **LME.**
[ORIGIN from Latin *finitus* pa. pple of *finire* FINISH *verb*.]
▸ **A** *adjective.* **1** Having bounds, ends, or limits; not infinite or infinitesimal. **LME.** ▸**b** Having an existence subject to limitations and conditions. **M17.**

> C. P. SNOW Not in the vague future, but in finite time. E. L. DOCTOROW You will be left with a finite amount of money.

†**2** Fixed, determined, definite. **L15–L17.**
3 *MATH.* (Of a line) having two ends; (of a numerical quantity) neither infinitely large nor infinitesimally small; corresponding to or represented by a finite number or a finite number of items. **L16.**
finite difference, ***finite group***, etc.
4 *GRAMMAR.* (Of a verb part) limited by number and person, not in the infinitive; (of a clause) containing a finite verb part. **L18.**
5 *MUSIC.* Of a canon: with a separately composed ending. **M19.**
▸ **B** *noun.* A finite being or thing; *GRAMMAR* a finite verb part or form. Also, that which is finite. **E17.**
■ **finitely** *adverb* **M17.** **finiteness** *noun* **E17.**

finite /'fʌɪnʌɪt/ *verb trans.* **E17.**
[ORIGIN from the adjective.]
Make finite.

finitise *verb* var. of FINITIZE.

finitism /'fʌɪnʌɪtɪz(ə)m/ *noun.* **E20.**
[ORIGIN from FINITE *adjective* + -ISM.]
1 *PHILOSOPHY & THEOLOGY.* The belief that the world, or some realm, or God, is finite. **E20.**
2 A view of mathematics that rejects the validity of actual infinities; *spec.* the doctrine that every proof should involve only a finite number of steps. **M20.**
■ **finitist** *noun & adjective* (*a*) *noun* an adherent of finitism; (*b*) *adjective* characterized by or relating to finitism: **L19.** **fini'tistic** *adjective* **M20.**

finitize /'fʌɪnʌɪtʌɪz/ *verb trans.* Also **-ise. E20.**
[ORIGIN formed as FINITISM + -IZE.]
Make finite.

finitude /'fɪnɪtjuːd/ *noun.* **M17.**
[ORIGIN formed as FINITISM + -TUDE.]
The condition or state of being finite; finiteness.

finity /'fɪnɪti/ *noun.* **L17.**
[ORIGIN Old French *finité*, from *fini* pa. pple of *finir* to bound, from Latin *finire* FINISH *verb*.]
Finiteness, finitude; an instance of this.

finjan /fɪn'dʒaːn/ *noun.* Also ***-gan*** /-'gaːn/. **E17.**
[ORIGIN Arabic *finjān* from Persian *pingān* cup.]
A small porcelain coffee cup, used in the eastern Mediterranean region.

fink /fɪŋk/ *noun*[1]. *N. Amer. slang. derog.* **L19.**
[ORIGIN Unknown.]
An unpleasant contemptible person; *spec.* (*a*) an informer; (*b*) a detective; (*c*) a strikebreaker. Cf. ***ratfink*** s.v. RAT *noun*[1].

fink *noun*[2] var. of VINK.

fink /fɪŋk/ *verb*[1] *intrans. non-standard.* **L19.**
[ORIGIN Repr. a pronunc.]
Think.

fink /fɪŋk/ *verb*[2] *intrans. N. Amer. slang.* **E20.**
[ORIGIN from FINK *noun*[1].]
1 Inform (*on*). **E20.**
2 Back *out* (*on*). **M20.**

F

finkle /ˈfɪŋk(ə)l/ *noun*. *obsolete* exc. *dial*. ME.
[ORIGIN Latin *faeniculum*: see FENNEL.]
Fennel.

Finlander /ˈfɪnləndə/ *noun*. Now *rare*. E18.
[ORIGIN from *Finland* (see FINN) + -ER[1].]
= FINN.

Finlandization /fɪnləndʌɪˈzeɪʃ(ə)n/ *noun*. Also **-isation**. M20.
[ORIGIN from *Finland* (see FINN) + -IZATION, translating German *Finnlandisierung*.]
hist. A policy of benevolent neutrality towards the Soviet Union, such as was allegedly pursued by Finland from 1944; the adoption of such a policy.
■ **ˈFinlandize** *verb trans*. induce (a country) to adopt a policy of benevolent neutrality towards the Soviet Union L20.

finless /ˈfɪnlɪs/ *adjective*. L16.
[ORIGIN from FIN *noun*[1] + -LESS.]
Without fins.

F

finlet /ˈfɪnlɪt/ *noun*. L19.
[ORIGIN from FIN *noun*[1] + -LET.]
A small fin.

Finn /fɪn/ *noun*. Also (now *rare*) **Fin**.
[ORIGIN Old English *Finnas* pl., corresp. to German *Finne*, Old Norse *Finnr*; recorded as Latin *Fenni* (Tacitus), Greek *phinnoi* (Ptolemy).]
A member of a people of Scandinavia and NE Europe speaking a Finno-Ugric language; a native or inhabitant of Finland.
– NOTE: *Finn* and *Finland* do not correspond to terms used by the Finns themselves (who use *Suomi* & derivs.).

finnack *noun* var. of FINNOC.

finnan /ˈfɪnən/ *noun*. Also †**findhorn**, †**findon**. E18.
[ORIGIN from *Findon*, a fishing village near Aberdeen (confused with *Findhorn*, place and river).]
More fully ***finnan haddock***, (*Scot.*) ***finnan haddie***. A haddock cured with the smoke of green wood, turf, or peat.

finned /fɪnd/ *adjective*. ME.
[ORIGIN from FIN *noun*[1] + -ED[2].]
Having a fin or fins (of a specified kind).

finner /ˈfɪnə/ *noun*. L18.
[ORIGIN from FIN *noun*[1] + -ER[1].]
= ***fin whale*** s.v. FIN *noun*[1].

finnesko /ˈfɪnəskəʊ/ *noun*. Also **fin(n)sko**. Pl. same. L19.
[ORIGIN Norwegian *finnsko*, from *Finn* FINN + *sko* shoe.]
A boot made of tanned reindeer skin with the hair left on the outside.

Finnic /ˈfɪnɪk/ *adjective*. M17.
[ORIGIN from FINN + -IC.]
Of or pertaining to the Finns, the group of peoples ethnically allied to the Finns, or the group of languages allied to Finnish.
■ **Finnicize** /ˈfɪnɪsʌɪz/ *verb trans*. (*rare*) give a Finnish form to E19.

finnied *adjective* see VINNIED.

finnip /ˈfɪnɪp/ *noun*. *slang*. Also **fin(n)if** /ˈfɪnɪf/. M19.
[ORIGIN Uncertain: perh. repr. Yiddish *finef* five.]
A five-pound or five-dollar note.

Finnish /ˈfɪnɪʃ/ *adjective & noun*. L17.
[ORIGIN from FINN + -ISH[1].]
▸ **A** *adjective*. Of or pertaining to the Finns or (occas.) the group of peoples ethnically allied to the Finns. L17.
Finnish spitz a small stocky kind of spitz with a coarse reddish-brown coat.
▸ **B** *noun*. The Finno-Ugric language of the Finns. L18.

Finno- /ˈfɪnəʊ/ *combining form*.
[ORIGIN from FINN + -O-.]
Finnish or Finnic and —.
■ **Finno-Ugrian** /-ˈuːgrɪən, -ˈjuː-/ *adjective & noun* = FINNO-UGRIC L19. **Finno-Ugric** /-ˈuːgrɪk, -ˈjuː-/ *adjective & noun* (belonging to) the group of Uralic languages including Finnish, Estonian, Lappish, and Hungarian L19.

finnoc /ˈfɪnək/ *noun*. *Scot*. (now *dial*.). Also **-ack**, **ph-**. E17.
[ORIGIN Gaelic *fionnag*, from *fionn* white.]
An immature sea trout or salmon.

finnow *adjective, verb, & noun* see VINNY.

finnowed *adjective* see VINNIED.

finnsko *noun* var. of FINNESKO.

finny /ˈfɪni/ *adjective*[1]. L16.
[ORIGIN from FIN *noun*[1] + -Y[1].]
1 Having a fin or fins. L16.
2 Of the nature of or like a fin. E17.
3 Teeming with fish; of or pertaining to fish. *literary*. M18.

finny *adjective*[2], *verb, & noun* see VINNY.

fino /ˈfiːnəʊ/ *noun*. Pl. **-os**. M19.
[ORIGIN Spanish = FINE *adjective*.]
A type of light-coloured dry sherry; a glass or drink of such sherry.

finocchio /fɪˈnɒkɪəʊ/ *noun*. Also **-ochio**. E18.
[ORIGIN Italian from popular Latin var. of Latin *faeniculum*: see FENNEL.]
A form of fennel with swollen leaf bases, *Foeniculum vulgare* var. *azoricum*, eaten as a vegetable.

Finsen /ˈfɪns(ə)n/ *adjective*. E20.
[ORIGIN N. R. *Finsen* (1860–1904), Danish physician.]
Designating (apparatus used for) the treatment of skin diseases by ultraviolet light.

finsko *noun* var. of FINNESKO.

fiord *noun* var. of FJORD.

fiorin /ˈfʌɪərɪn/ *noun*. E19.
[ORIGIN App. from Irish *fiorthann* long coarse grass.]
More fully ***fiorin grass***. A tufted perennial grass, *Agrostis stolonifera*, that sends up stalks from a rooting decumbent base. Also called ***creeping bent***.

fiorite /fɪˈɔːrʌɪt/ *noun*. E19.
[ORIGIN from Santa *Fiora* in Tuscany, western Italy, where first described: see -ITE[1].]
MINERALOGY. A siliceous sinter that occurs as a pearly encrustation near hot springs and fumaroles.

fioritura /fɪˌɔːrɪˈtʊərə/ *noun*. Pl. **-re** /-ri, -reɪ/. M19.
[ORIGIN Italian, from *fiorire* to flower.]
MUSIC. A decoration or embellishment of a melody.

fip /fɪp/ *noun*. *arch*. *US slang*. E19.
[ORIGIN Abbreviation.]
= ***fippenny bit*** s.v. FIPPENNY *adjective*.

fipenny *adjective & noun* var. of FIPPENNY.

fippence /ˈfɪp(ə)ns/ *noun*. *colloq*. Now *rare* or *obsolete*. E17.
[ORIGIN Repr. a pronunc.]
Fivepence.

fippenny /ˈfɪp(ə)ni/ *adjective & noun*. *arch*. Also **fipenny**. E19.
[ORIGIN Repr. a pronunc. of *fivepenny*: see FIVE.]
▸ **A** *adjective*. = ***fivepenny*** s.v. FIVE. E19.
fippenny bit *US* a Spanish half-real piece; a silver coin used in the Eastern US before 1857 and worth about six cents.
▸ **B** *noun*. A clasp knife. *slang*. E19.

fipple /ˈfɪp(ə)l/ *noun*. E17.
[ORIGIN Cf. Icelandic *flipi* lip of a horse.]
A complete or partial plug at the head of a wind instrument, *esp*. a partial plug at the head of a recorder, whistle, etc., leaving a narrow channel for air; the narrow channel itself.
– COMB.: **fipple flute** a flute which is played by blowing endwise.

fir /fəː/ *noun*. LME.
[ORIGIN Prob. from Old Norse *fyri-* (in *fyriskógr* fir-wood etc.) from Germanic, from base also of Old English *furhwudu* fir-wood, Old High German *forha* (German *Föhre*), Old Norse *fura*. See also VAR *noun*.]
1 An evergreen coniferous tree; now *esp*. one belonging to the genus *Abies* of the pine family, characterized by upright cones and flat needles usu. arranged in two rows. Also, a Douglas fir; a Scotch fir. Also ***fir tree***. LME.
balsam fir: see BALSAM *noun*. ***Douglas fir***: see DOUGLAS *noun*[1]. ***red fir***: see RED *adjective*. ***Scotch fir***: see SCOTCH *adjective*. **silver fir** a fir whose needles are white or silvery underneath, spec. *Abies alba*, a timber tree of central and southern Europe. ***white fir***: see WHITE *adjective*.
2 The wood of a fir. LME.
– COMB.: **fir balsam** = ***balsam fir*** above; **fir clubmoss** a European clubmoss, *Huperzia selago* (family Lycopodiaceae), with a branching form resembling a miniature tree; **fir cone** a cone of a fir or pine.

Firbolg /fɪəˈbɒlg, *foreign* fɪrˈbɔləg/ *noun*. M18.
[ORIGIN Irish: ult. origin unknown.]
A member of a legendary early colonizing people of Ireland.

fire /ˈfʌɪə/ *noun*.
[ORIGIN Old English *fȳr* = Old Frisian, Old Saxon *fiur* (Dutch *vuur*), Old High German *fiur*, *fūir* (German *Feuer*) from West Germanic base, corresp. to Greek *pur*.]
1 The active principle operative in combustion, manifested as a hot bright shifting body of gas or as incandescence; such gas or incandescence. (One of the four elements of the ancients.) OE. ▸**b** *spec*. The burning flame(s) of hell or purgatory. OE. ▸**c** Volcanic heat; a flow of lava. Formerly also, a volcanic eruption. L16.

J. MABBE A face as red as fire.

2 Fuel in a state of combustion; a mass of burning material in a grate, furnace, etc.; a heater with a flame or incandescent element. OE. ▸**b** Fuel as a means of making a fire or setting something alight, *esp*. fuel that is already burning. *obsolete* exc. *dial*. OE. ▸**c** In full ***Greek fire***. A flammable composition for setting light to enemy ships, works, etc., first used by the Greeks of Constantinople. *obsolete* exc. *hist*. ME.

F. M. FORD The fire . . was burning brightly; she must have just put coals on. *fig*.: POPE Some spark of your celestial fire.

electric fire, ***gas fire***, ***open fire***, etc.
3 Destructive burning, esp. of a large mass or area; a conflagration. As *interjection*, warning of a fire. ME.

S. JOHNSON Now a rabble rages, now a fire.

4 Lightning; a flash of lightning; a thunderbolt. ME.
5 Fever, inflammation; disease as a consuming agency. *arch*. ME.
6 a A burning passion or emotion. ME. ▸**b** Ardour of temperament; zeal, fervour, enthusiasm. E17. ▸**c** Liveliness of imagination; vivacity; poetic inspiration. M17.

a SHAKES. *Merry W.* The wicked fire of lust. **b** M. AYRTON She's got no fire, Estelle, no go, no zing.

7 State of combustion. Chiefly in ***on fire*** below. LME.
8 Luminosity; a glowing or flashing appearance resembling that of fire. M16.

W. BLACK A great fire of sunset spread over the west.

9 The action of firing guns etc. L16.

J. G. FARRELL Rifle and revolver fire was almost continuous during . . the night.

10 A flare, a firework; the flammable composition used in a firework or other combustible device. Orig. & now only in ***false fire*** s.v. FALSE *adjective*. E17.
11 Torture or death by burning. Now *rare*. M17.
12 The heating quality in liquors etc.; *joc*. a warming drink of liquor etc. M18.
13 CRICKET. The tendency of a ball to fly up erratically, or of a wicket etc. to cause the ball to fly up. L19.
– PHRASES ETC.: ***ball of fire***: see BALL *noun*[1] 3. **between two fires** shot at or attacked from two directions. BONFIRE. ***catch fire***: see CATCH *verb*. ***cease fire***, ***ceasefire***: see CEASE *verb*. ***coal of fire***: see COAL *noun* 1. **fire and brimstone** torment in hell. **fire and sword** burning and slaughter, esp. by an invading army. **fire in one's belly**, **fire in the belly** ambition, driving force, initiative. **fires of heaven** *poet*. the stars. **give fire (to)** set alight, kindle. **go on fire** (chiefly *Scot*. & *Irish*) begin to burn. **go through fire (and water)** encounter or face all dangers, submit to the severest ordeal. ***Great Fire***: see GREAT *adjective*. ***Greek fire***: see sense 2c above. ***hang fire***: see HANG *verb*. ***heap coals of fire on a person's head***: see COAL *noun*. **heavenly fires** *poet*. the stars. ***holy fire***: see HOLY *adjective*. ***indirect fire***: see INDIRECT *adjective*. ***Kentish fire***: see KENTISH *adjective*. ***line of fire***: see LINE *noun*[2]. ***miss fire***: see MISS *verb*[1]. **no smoke without fire** no rumour without some basis in fact. **on fire** ignited, burning, (***like a house on fire***: see HOUSE *noun*[1]); *fig*. inflamed with passion, anger, zeal, etc. ***open fire***: see OPEN *adjective*. ***out of the frying pan into the fire***, ***out of the pan into the fire***: see PAN *noun*[1]. **play with fire** trifle with dangerous matters. **pull out of the fire** = ***snatch out of the fire*** below. ***pull the chestnuts out of the fire***: see CHESTNUT *noun*. ***Ring of Fire***: see RING *noun*[1]. ***running fire***: see RUNNING *adjective*. **save out of the fire** preserve as a remnant from a disaster. **set fire to**, †**set fire in**, †**set fire on** apply fire to, cause to start burning, kindle, ignite. **set on fire** ignite, kindle; *fig*. inflame. **set the Thames on fire**, **set the world on fire** do something remarkable, make an impact, (usu. in neg. contexts). **snatch out of the fire** rescue from disaster or ruin. ***St Anthony's fire***, ***St Elmo's fire***: see SAINT *noun & adjective*. **strike fire** elicit sparks by friction or by a blow. **take fire** begin to burn. ***the fat is in the fire***: see FAT *noun*[2]. **under fire** being shot at; *fig*. being adversely criticized etc. ***wandering fire***: see WANDERING *ppl adjective*. **where's the fire?** *joc*. what's the hurry? WILDFIRE.
– COMB.: **fire alarm** a device for or means of giving warning of fire; **fire ant** a tropical American ant of the genus *Solenopsis*, having a painful and sometimes dangerous sting; esp. *S. invicta*, which has become a serious pest in the south-eastern US; **fireback** (*a*) (a metal plate for) the back wall of an open hearth; (*b*) (also ***fireback pheasant***) either of two pheasants of SE Asia, *Lophura ignita* and *L. erythrophthalma*; **fire balloon** a hot-air balloon whose buoyancy is derived from a fire burning at its mouth; **fire-bird** any of various small birds with bright orange or red plumage, *esp*. (*US*) the Baltimore oriole; **fire blanket** a sheet of usu. fireproof material with which to smother a fire in an emergency; **fireblight**: see ***pear-blight*** s.v. PEAR *noun*; **fireboard** a board used to close up a fireplace; *US* a mantelpiece; **firebomb** *noun & verb* (*a*) *noun* an incendiary bomb; (*b*) *verb trans*. attack or destroy with a firebomb or firebombs; **firebrat** a bristletail, *Thermobia domestica*, which frequents warm places in houses; **firebreak** an obstacle preventing the spread of (esp. grass or forest) fires, as an area of cleared or ploughed land; **firebrick** a brick capable of standing intense heat without burning, used in grates etc.; **fire brigade** an organized body of people trained and employed to extinguish fires; **firebug** *colloq*. an incendiary, an arsonist; **fire certificate**: confirming that current statutory fire regulations have been complied with at a particular premises; **fireclay** clay of a kind used for making firebricks; **fire company** (*a*) a section of a fire brigade; (*b*) a fire-insurance company; **fire control** a system of regulating the firing of guns from a ship or fort; the station from which such control is exercised; **fire coral** a branched stinging coral of the genus *Millepora* and suborder Milleporina; **fire crack** a crack caused by heat, *esp*. one which occurs in metal being reheated or annealed; **firecracker** (chiefly *N. Amer*.) an explosive firework; **firecrest** a kinglet, *Regulus ignicapillus*, with a golden crest, found in woods and forests in central and southern Europe and Asia Minor; **fire cross** = ***fiery cross*** s.v. FIERY *adjective*; **fire-cure** *verb trans*. cure (esp. tobacco or leather) over a fire; **fire curtain** (*a*) a fireproof curtain in a theatre etc.; (*b*) MILITARY = CURTAIN *noun* 7; **firedamp** (a miner's name for) gas, esp. methane, that forms an explosive mixture with air in coal mines; **fire department** *N. Amer*. a fire brigade; **fire discipline** MILITARY the training of soldiers to fire exactly as commanded, so that their actions are coordinated; ***firedog***: see DOG *noun* 7; **fire door** a fireproof door to inhibit or prevent the spread of fire; **fire drill** (*a*) a simple device for kindling fire consisting of a pointed stick and a piece of wood; (*b*) a rehearsal of the procedure to be used in case of fire; **fire engine** (*a*) a vehicle carrying equipment to fight and extinguish fires; (*b*) (*obsolete* exc. *local*) a steam engine; **fire escape** an emergency staircase, esp. on the outside of a building, enabling people to escape should fire break out; an apparatus serving the same purpose; **fire exit** a passage or door to go through to escape from fire; **fire extinguisher** an apparatus with a jet for discharging liquid chemicals, foam, etc., in order to extinguish fire; **fire-eyed** *adjective* (*poet*.) having eyes glowing as with fire; **firefight** MILITARY a struggle to establish superiority of firepower over an enemy; a fight involving fire or firearms; **firefighter** a person whose task

is to extinguish fires; a member of a fire brigade; **firefighting** (*a*) the extinguishing of fires; (*b*) (in business) the action of dealing with problems as they arise rather than responding in a more systematic way; **firefinch** any of various small African songbirds of the genus *Lagonosticta*, of the waxbill family, the males of which have mainly pink or reddish plumage; **firefish** any of several scorpionfishes with venomous spines, esp. of the genera *Pterois* and *Dendrochirus*; **firefly** a winged nocturnal beetle that emits light, usu. in flashes, found esp. in the tropics; *spec.* one of the family Lampyridae; **fire-fork** (*obsolete* exc. *dial.* or *hist.*) a fork-shaped instrument for stirring up a fire, putting on fuel, etc.; **fireguard** (*a*) a protective (usu. meshed) framework or grating, placed in front of an open fire in a room; (*b*) *N. Amer.* = ***fire-watcher*** below; (*c*) *N. Amer.* = ***firebreak*** above; **firehall** *N. Amer.* a fire station; **fire hearth** (*a*) a brick or stone area on which a fire is made; the hearth in front of a fireplace; (*b*) a cooking range or stove on a ship; **fire hose** a hosepipe for extinguishing fires; **firehouse** (*a*) (*obsolete* exc. *dial.* or *hist.*) a house with a fireplace in it; the room in a house where the family fire was; (*b*) *US* a fire station; **fire-hunting** *US* (*a*) the firing of timber to drive out game; (*b*) hunting at night with lights; ***fire hydrant***: see HYDRANT; **fire insurance** insurance against losses by fire; **firelight** †(*a*) lightning; (*b*) the light given by a fire or fires; **firelighter** (*a*) a person who kindles a fire; (*b*) material for lighting fires, *esp.* a piece of flammable material used to help start a fire in a grate; **fire line** (*a*) a firebreak; (*b*) a fire station telephone line for operation (not administrative) use; **firelit** *adjective* illuminated by firelight; **firemaster** †(*a*) an officer of artillery who superintended the manufacture of explosives or fireworks; (*b*) (chiefly *Scot.*) the chief officer of a fire brigade; **fire-new** *adjective* (*arch.*) brand-new; **fire office** an office or company dealing in fire insurance; **fire opal** a girasol; **fire-pan** a receptacle for holding or carrying fire; a brazier, a portable grate; **fire pink** a N. American campion, *Silene virginica*, with narrow scarlet petals; **fire-plough** a simple device for making fire, similar to a fire drill; ***fireplug***: see PLUG *noun* 2; **fire policy** a certificate from a fire office guaranteeing compensation in case of fire; **fire position** MILITARY the position from which an attacking force opens fire during an advance; **firepower** (*a*) MILITARY the ability of the guns and missiles of a military force to inflict destruction; (*b*) *fig.* financial, emotional, or intellectual strength; **fire practice** = ***fire drill*** (b) above; **fireproof** *adjective & verb trans.* (make) able to resist fire or great heat; **fireproofing** (*a*) making proof against fire; (*b*) material used to make something fireproof; **fire raid** an air raid with incendiary bombs; **fire-raiser** an arsonist; **fire-raising** arson, incendiarism; **fire ranger** *N. Amer.* an official who keeps watch against the occurrence of forest fires; **fire-red** *adjective & noun* (*a*) *adjective* red like fire; reddened by fire; (*b*) *noun* (COMMERCE) a brilliant red pigment with a strong resistance to oil and light; **fire risk** (*a*) the risk of loss by fire; (*b*) the obligation of a fire-insurance company to make good loss by fire; (*c*) a property insured against fire, *esp.* one which is likely to go on fire; an object, state of affairs, etc., conducive to the outbreak of a fire; **fire room** (*a*) a room containing a fireplace; (*b*) the furnace room of a building or stokehold of a ship; **fire salamander** a robust short-tailed salamander, *Salamandra salamandra*, that has black skin with bright red, orange, and yellow markings, native to upland forests of Europe, NW Africa, and SW Asia; **fire sale** a sale of goods (freq. at low prices) remaining after the destruction of commercial premises by fire; **fire screen** (*a*) a movable screen to keep off the direct heat of a fire; (*b*) = ***fireguard*** (a) above; (*c*) an ornamental screen placed in front of a fireplace when the fire is unlit; **fireship** (*a*) *hist.* a ship loaded with combustibles etc. and set adrift among enemy ships etc. to ignite and destroy them; (*b*) *arch. slang* a person with venereal disease; a prostitute; **fire-shovel**: for putting coal etc. on a fire or for removing coal or ashes; **fire station** a building where a fire brigade is based, housing fire engines; **fire step** = ***FIRING step***; **fire-stick** (*a*) a burning brand; (*b*) = ***fire drill*** (a) above; (*c*) an implement for stirring up a fire; **firestorm** (*a*) *poet.* a storm of fire; (*b*) an intense conflagration into which surrounding air is drawn with great force, esp. resulting from incendiary or nuclear bombing; **fire-swallower** = FIRE-EATER 1; **firethorn** = PYRACANTHA; **fire tongs**: for grasping coal etc.; **fire trap** a building without proper fire exits and in which a fire, once started, would spread easily; **fire-tree** *NZ* = POHUTUKAWA; **fire-vessel** (*a*) a receptacle for fire; (*b*) *hist.* = ***fireship*** (a) above; **fire-walk** the ceremony of fire-walking; **fire-walker** a person who takes part in a fire-walk; **fire-walking** walking barefoot over hot stones, ashes, etc., a religious rite in Fiji and elsewhere, and formerly an ordeal in European countries; **firewall** (*a*) a fireproof wall to inhibit or prevent the spread of fire; (*b*) COMPUTING a part of a computer system or network which is designed to block unauthorized access while permitting outward communication; **fire warden** *N. Amer.* an official employed to prevent or extinguish fires; **fire-watcher** a person engaged in fire-watching; **fire-watching** (*a*) tending a fire; (*b*) keeping watch for fires, esp. those caused by bombs; **firewater** *colloq.* strong alcoholic liquor; **fireweed** any of several plants that spring up on burnt land; *spec.* rosebay willowherb; **firewoman** a female firefighter; **firewood** wood prepared for burning, fuel; **fire worship** the treatment of fire as a god; *popularly* Zoroastrianism; **fire worshipper** a person who treats fire as a god; *popularly* a Zoroastrian.

fire /ˈfʌɪə/ *verb.*

[ORIGIN Old English *fȳrian*, from FIRE *noun*.]

†**1** *verb trans.* Supply with material for a fire. Only in OE.

2 *verb trans.* Inspire, inflame; stimulate (the imagination); fill (a person) with enthusiasm. ME.

> R. K. NARAYAN Dead and decaying things seemed to . . fire his imagination. M. MOORCOCK To fire me with a sense of wonder at the marvels of science and technology.

3 *verb trans.* Set fire to with the intention of damaging or destroying. LME. ▸**b** Light, kindle, burn, (a beacon, an explosive, waste vegetation, etc.). LME.

> F. O'BRIEN They made an attempt to fire the complete building by igniting a number of armchairs. **b** A. UTTLEY Hedges were trimmed and the cuttings fired in numerous little bonfires.

4 *verb trans.* Light (gunpowder); discharge or let off (a gun, firework, etc.); explode (a mine). E16. ▸**b** Eject or propel (a shot, bullet, or other missile) from or as from a gun etc. L16. ▸**c** Produce or deliver (a broadside, salute, etc.) by discharge of guns. M19. ▸**d** *fig.* Deliver (a speech, question, look, etc.) in a sharp explosive manner. M19.

> F. MARRYAT Edward fired his gun into the body of the man. **b** D. CARNEGIE Crowley . . grabbed the . . revolver, and fired another bullet into the prostrate body. P. CAMPBELL The shots had . . been fired near Portobello Bridge. **d** F. TUOHY Nor were the questions he now fired at the girl evidence of any real curiosity.

5 *verb intrans.* **a** Of a gun etc.: go off. M16. ▸**b** Discharge a gun or other firearm; shoot. M17.

> **b** E. HEMINGWAY The pistol did not fire. F. FITZGERALD Nhu's own troops were refusing to fire on the crowds.

b fire into the brown (of them): see BROWN *noun* 1.

6 *verb trans.* Drive away or out by or as if by fire. (Foll. by *out*.) Now *rare* or *obsolete*. M16.

7 a *verb intrans.* Become excited or inflamed. M16. ▸**b** *verb trans. & intrans.* Make or become hot or inflamed. *rare*. L17.

> **a** W. IRVING She fired up at the arrogance of the squire.

8 *verb trans. & intrans.* (Cause to) glow or redden as if on fire. L16.

> A. LANG Watching . . the dawn as it fired.

9 *verb intrans.* Of an explosive etc.: catch fire, be ignited. E17. ▸**b** Of (a cylinder in) an internal-combustion engine: undergo ignition of its fuel. L19.

b fire on all cylinders: see CYLINDER 3.

10 *verb trans.* FARRIERY. Burn, cauterize. E17.

11 *verb trans.* Subject to the action or effect of fire; bake (pottery etc.); dry or cure (tea or tobacco) by artificial heat. M17.

12 a *verb trans.* Supply (a furnace, engine, boiler, power station) with fuel. M18. ▸**b** *verb intrans.* Make up a fire; light the fire of a furnace. Also foll. by *up*. M19. ▸**c** *verb intrans.* Light a pipe, cigar, etc. Also foll. by *up*. *colloq.* M19.

> **a** H. FAST She's built to be fired by coal.

13 *verb trans. & intrans.* Of flax: be or become covered with black spots as if burnt. L18.

14 PHOTOGRAPHY. **a** *verb trans.* Release (the shutter of a camera). L19. ▸**b** *verb intrans.* Take a photograph. Also foll. by *away*, *off*. L19.

> **a** *Diver* All you have to do is load the film . . frame your subject, and fire the shutter.

15 *verb trans.* Expel (a person) forcibly; dismiss, discharge. Also (*US*) foll. by *out*. L19.

> A. MILLER When a man gets old you fire him, you have to, he can't do the work. P. MORTIMER He resigned before Reuters fired him.

hire and fire: see HIRE *verb* 1.

– WITH ADVERBS IN SPECIALIZED SENSES: **fire away** begin or go ahead (esp. speaking), in a rapid and energetic manner; (see also sense 14b above). **fire up** (*a*) show sudden anger; (*b*) *N. Amer. colloq.* stimulate, fill with enthusiasm; (see also senses 12b, c above).

■ **fireable** *adjective* able to be fired or set on fire M17.

firearm /ˈfʌɪərɑːm/ *noun*. M17.

[ORIGIN from FIRE *noun* + ARM *noun*[2].]

A portable weapon from which a missile is propelled by means of an explosive charge; a rifle, gun, pistol, etc. Usu. in *pl.*

fireball /ˈfʌɪəbɔːl/ *noun*. LME.

[ORIGIN from FIRE *noun* + BALL *noun*[1].]

1 MILITARY HISTORY. A ball filled with combustibles or explosives used as a projectile to damage an enemy or enemy fortifications. LME.

2 A ball of flame or fire; *spec.* (*a*) a large meteor; (*b*) a ball of lightning; (*c*) a ball of flame resulting from a nuclear explosion. M16.

3 HERALDRY. A bomb or grenade with fire issuing from the top, bottom, and both sides. M19.

4 *fig.* A very energetic person; a person with a fiery temper. M20.

■ **fireballer** *noun* (BASEBALL) a pitcher who throws a very good fastball L20. **fireballing** *adjective* (BASEBALL) L20.

fire-boot /ˈfʌɪəbuːt/ *noun*. *obsolete* exc. *hist.* Also †**-bote**. L15.

[ORIGIN from FIRE *noun* + BOOT *noun*[1].]

LAW. The supplying of fuel to a fire; wood used for this purpose; the right of a tenant to take firewood from the landlord's estate.

firebox /ˈfʌɪəbɒks/ *noun*. M16.

[ORIGIN from FIRE *noun* + BOX *noun*[2].]

†**1** A tinderbox. M16–M19.

†**2** A kind of firework. Only in M17.

3 The fuel chamber of a steam boiler. L18.

firebrand /ˈfʌɪəbrand/ *noun*. ME.

[ORIGIN from FIRE *noun* + BRAND *noun*.]

1 A piece of burning wood. ME.

2 *fig.* A person who or thing which kindles strife, inflames passion, etc. LME.

> W. HOLTBY Astell . . was a firebrand, a troubler of the peace.

†**3** = ***brand mark*** (a) s.v. BRAND *noun*. L17–E18.

firedrake /ˈfʌɪədreɪk/ *noun*. OE.

[ORIGIN from FIRE *noun* + DRAKE *noun*[1].]

1 GERMANIC MYTHOLOGY. A fiery dragon. OE.

†**2** A fiery meteor. M16–M19.

†**3** A person with a fiery red nose. *rare* (Shakes.). Only in E17.

fire-eater /ˈfʌɪəriːtə/ *noun*. L17.

[ORIGIN from FIRE *noun* + EATER.]

1 An entertainer who eats or pretends to eat fire. L17.

2 A person who is fond of fighting or quarrelling; (now *rare*) a duellist. E19.

■ **fire-eating** *ppl adjective* that eats fire E19.

fire-fang /ˈfʌɪəfaŋ/ *verb & noun*. *obsolete* exc. *dial.* & *US*. E16.

[ORIGIN from FIRE *noun* + FANG *verb*[1].]

▸ **A** *verb trans.* Scorch; damage (esp. barley, oats) by overheating; burn. Chiefly as ***fire-fanged*** *ppl adjective*. E16.

▸ **B** *noun*. The state of being fire-fanged; damage from overheating. M18.

fire-flaught /ˈfʌɪəflɔːt, -flaxt/ *noun*. Orig. *Scot.* Now *rare*. LME.

[ORIGIN from FIRE *noun* + FLAUGHT *noun*[1].]

1 Lightning, a flash of lightning. LME.

2 *transf.* A sudden burst or rush; a fiery glance. M17.

fire-iron /ˈfʌɪərʌɪən/ *noun*. ME.

[ORIGIN from FIRE *noun* + IRON *noun*.]

†**1** An implement of iron etc. for striking a light. ME–M16.

2 In *pl.* Implements for tending a domestic fire, usu. tongs, poker, and shovel. M17.

fireless /ˈfʌɪəlɪs/ *adjective*. L16.

[ORIGIN from FIRE *noun* + -LESS.]

1 Without energy, life, or imagination. L16.

2 Without a fire; devoid of fire. M17.

– COMB.: **fireless cooker** an insulated chamber able to be brought to and maintained at a temperature high enough for cooking in; a haybox.

firelock /ˈfʌɪəlɒk/ *noun*. M16.

[ORIGIN from FIRE *noun* + LOCK *noun*[2].]

hist. **1** A gunlock in which sparks were produced by friction or percussion to ignite the priming. M16.

2 A musket having this type of lock. L16.

3 A soldier armed with such a weapon. M17.

fireman /ˈfʌɪəmən/ *noun*. Pl. **-men**. E17.

[ORIGIN from FIRE *noun* + MAN *noun*.]

1 A person who uses firearms. E17.

2 A person who attends to a furnace or to the fire of a steam engine, steamship, etc.; a stoker. M17.

> R. P. WARREN The fireman . . bent to heave a shovelful of coal into the firebox door.

3 A person whose task is to extinguish fires, a firefighter. E18.

> S. SPENDER A few scores of firemen . . relieved of fire-fighting duties.

visiting fireman: see VISITING *ppl adjective*.

4 MINING. A person whose duty is to check mines for firedamp, supervise blasting, etc. M19.

fireplace /ˈfʌɪəpleɪs/ *noun*. L17.

[ORIGIN from FIRE *noun* + PLACE *noun*[1].]

A place for a fire, *esp.* a partially enclosed place at the base of a chimney where a domestic fire is situated; the structure surrounding or area in front of this.

firer /ˈfʌɪərə/ *noun*. E17.

[ORIGIN from FIRE *verb* + -ER[1].]

1 An incendiary, an arsonist. Now *rare* or *obsolete*. E17.

2 A person who sets anything on fire; a person who fires clay etc. E19.

3 A person who discharges a firearm; a gun etc. that fires in a specified way. M19.

fireside /ˈfʌɪəsʌɪd/ *noun & adjective*. M16.

[ORIGIN from FIRE *noun* + SIDE *noun*.]

▸ **A** *noun*. **1** Orig., the space under a chimney to the right and left of a domestic fire, occupied by two seats. Now, the space around a fireplace. M16.

2 *collect.* Those who sit around one's fire; one's household. *arch.* E18.

3 One's home, home life. M19.

▸ **B** *adjective*. **1** Situated beside or pertaining to a domestic fire. M18.

2 Intimate, relaxed; *esp.* designating an informal political talk broadcast to the nation. Orig. *US*. E19.

> *Observer* Fireside chats from Number 10 Downing Street. *New Yorker* He talked of his private meetings with Gorbachev . . the 'fireside summit'.

fire stone /ˈfʌɪəstəʊn/ *noun*. OE.

[ORIGIN from FIRE *noun* + STONE *noun*.]

1 A stone used in striking fire, *esp.* iron pyrites. Also, the flint of a firelock. *arch.* OE.

2 A stone that resists the action of fire, used for lining furnaces, ovens, etc. L15. ▸**b** Any of certain soft calcareous sandstones. *local*. E18.

3 A hearthstone. Now *rare*. E17.

F

FireWire /ˈfʌɪəˌwʌɪə/ *noun.* L20.
[ORIGIN from FIRE *noun* + WIRE *noun*.]
COMPUTING. (Proprietary name for) a standard high-speed data connector for connecting different kinds of digital device; the international standard governing this.

firework /ˈfʌɪəwəːk/ *noun.* M16.
[ORIGIN from FIRE *noun* + WORK *noun*.]
▸ **I 1** A combustible or explosive composition for use in war; a machine charged with such a composition. Now *rare* or *obsolete*. M16.
2 A device producing spectacular effects by the use of combustibles; a rocket, squib, etc.; in *pl.* & †*sing.*, a colourful and spectacular display of such devices. L16.
Times Crowds gathered to ooh and aah at the riverboat procession and fireworks.
†**3** A set arrangement of such devices, forming a pictorial or ornamental design. L16–L18.
4 In *pl.* A display of wit, passion, anger, etc. L17.
Today Ward was appointed manager of York City . . with the brief to produce a few fireworks on the pitch.
▸ †**II 5** Work done by, in, or with fire. Only in 17.
6 A place where fuel is obtained; an apparatus for working with fire. Only in 17.
■ **fireworker** *noun* †(*a*) an artillery officer or other person who is concerned with explosives in war; (*b*) a person who makes fireworks: E17.

firing /ˈfʌɪərɪŋ/ *noun.* LME.
[ORIGIN from FIRE *verb* + -ING¹.]
1 The action of setting something on fire. LME. ▸**b** The action of catching fire. *rare*. L16. ▸**c** The ignition of the fuel in a cylinder of an internal-combustion engine. L19.
W. COBBETT Those meetings led . . to the firing and pulling down of houses.
2 Material for a fire, fuel. L15.
3 The discharging of a firearm etc. E16. ▸**b** BELL-RINGING. The ringing of all the bells in a peal at once. L18.
R. BEATSON Night coming on, the firing on both sides ceased.
4 FARRIERY. Cauterizing. M17.
5 The sudden drying and death of the leaves of a plant. L17.
6 The action of subjecting something to heat or fire; baking, curing. L18.
7 The action of supplying a furnace, boiler, etc. with fire or fuel. L19.
– COMB.: **firing line** the front line of troops in a battle; *fig.* the forefront in any conflict; **firing party** a firing squad; **firing point** (*a*) the temperature at which a flammable oil is liable to spontaneous combustion; (*b*) in target shooting, the position from which the shots are fired; **firing squad** a group of soldiers detailed to fire a salute at a military funeral or to shoot a condemned person; **firing step** a board or ledge in a trench on which a soldier stands to fire.

firk /fəːk/ *verb.* Also **ferk**.
[ORIGIN Old English *fercian*, *færcian*, prob. from *fær*: see FARE *noun*¹.]
†**1** *verb trans.* Bring, carry, conduct. OE–LME.
2 †**a** *verb refl.* & *intrans.* Urge oneself forward; move quickly, hasten. ME–L16. ▸**b** *verb intrans.* Move about briskly; dance, frisk about, fidget. *obsolete* exc. *Scot.* & *dial.* L16.
3 *verb trans.* Urge, press hard; drive, drive away. Now only foll. by *off*, *out*, *up*. LME.
4 *verb trans.* Beat, whip, trounce. *arch.* M16.
G. A. SALA A poor rogue soundly firked at the post.
†**5** *verb trans.* Cheat, rob; get (money, a living) by cheating. E17–E18.
T. DEKKER As from poor clients lawyers firk money.
■ **firker** *noun* M17.

firkin /ˈfəːkɪn/ *noun.* LME.
[ORIGIN Prob. from Middle Dutch dim. of *vierde* fourth: see -KIN.]
1 A small cask for liquids, fish, butter, etc., originally containing a quarter of a barrel. LME.
2 A unit of capacity equal to half a kilderkin. LME.

firlot /ˈfəːlɒt/ *noun. Scot.* Now *rare* or *obsolete*. L15.
[ORIGIN Anglo-Latin *firlota*, *ferlota*, *ferthelota* (13) prob. from Old Norse *fjórði hlotr* fourth part: see FOURTH, LOT *noun*.]
(A container used as) a measure of capacity for corn etc. equal to a quarter of a boll.

firm /fəːm/ *noun.* L16.
[ORIGIN Spanish & (in senses 2, 3) Italian *firma*, from medieval Latin (cf. FARM *noun*), from Latin *firmare* strengthen, (in late Latin) confirm by one's signature, from *firmus* FIRM *adjective*.]
†**1** One's autograph signature. L16–M18.
†**2** The name under which the business of a commercial enterprise is transacted. M18–M19.
C. E. RIDDELL Trading under the firm of 'Grant & Co.'
3 A partnership or company for carrying on a business; a group of people working together, orig. (*derog.*) to further their own interests; a (criminal) organization or gang; a group of hospital doctors and their assistants. L18.
R. KIPLING Wressley was the working-member of the Foreign Office firm. M. GIROUARD The house was . . decorated by the newly founded firm of Watts and Company.
long firm a group of swindlers obtaining goods without paying. **old firm** *colloq.* the or an established and reliable partnership; (**O-F-**) a name for Celtic and Rangers Football Clubs.

firm /fəːm/ *adjective & adverb.* ME.
[ORIGIN Old French & mod. French *ferme* from Latin *firmus*.]
▸ **A** *adjective.* **1** Securely fixed; not easily moved; steady, stable. ME.
OED Try whether the post is firm in the ground. C. S. LEWIS All the knots which you wished to be firm would come untied.
†**firm land** dry land, solid earth; the mainland; *terra firma*. **on firm ground**: see GROUND *noun*.
2 Not shaking or wavering; steady or controlled (esp. in motion). LME.
W. C. BRYANT O aged man, would that thy knees were firm As is thy purpose. R. L. STEVENSON He took my hand in his large firm grasp.
3 Fixed, settled, established; (of a decree, law, etc.) immutable; (of an offer) not liable to cancellation after acceptance. LME. ▸†**b** Assured, secure (as a possession etc.). LME–M18. ▸†**c** Certain, sure; valid. LME–L17.
H. MACMILLAN In spite of some misunderstandings, the old alliance remained firm.
4 Of a person, personal attribute, or action: not easily moved or swayed; steadfast; unwavering; resolute, determined. LME.
M. EDGEWORTH 'I am the count', replied he, in a firm tone. T. S. ELIOT Be firm with her . . Assert your right to a little privacy. J. RATHBONE They remained firm in the Catholic faith suffering persecution . . and like misfortunes.
5 Of solid or compact structure or texture; resistant to pressure or impact; hard, sound, undecayed. LME.
L. DEIGHTON Its subsoil is firm enough to take the weight of a bombing plane. U. BENTLEY He had a firm, well-disciplined body.
†**6** Healthy, robust. Cf. INFIRM *adjective*. L16–L18.
POPE Lamented youth! in life's firm bloom he fell.
7 Of a price, commodity, etc.: maintaining a level or value. M19.
J. ARCHER Gold was still climbing and the Deutschmark . . remained firm, while the dollar was on the retreat.
– COMB.: **firmware** COMPUTING a permanent form of software built into certain kinds of computers.
▸ **B** *adverb.* Firmly; so as to be or remain firm. Now chiefly in ***hold firm***, ***stand firm***. ME.
■ **firmish** *adjective* somewhat firm M19. **firmly** *adverb* LME. **firmness** *noun* M16.

firm /fəːm/ *verb.* ME.
[ORIGIN Partly (either through French *fermer* or directly) from Latin *firmare* (see FIRM *noun*); partly a new formation on FIRM *adjective*.]
▸ **I** *verb trans.* **1** †**a** Establish, confirm, encourage (a person etc.); ratify, settle, strengthen (an agreement, title, etc.). ME–E19. ▸†**b** Make (a document) valid by seal, signature, etc.; sign (one's name). E16–L17. ▸**c** Foll. by *up*: make immutable or not liable to cancellation, confirm. *colloq.* L20.
DRYDEN Jove has firm'd it with an Awfull Nod. **b** DRYDEN Your Father's hand, Firm'd with his Signet. **c** SNOO WILSON We'll firm up the deal later.
2 Make firm or fast; fix securely (esp. plants *in* soil); hold firmly. LME.
Practical Gardening Firm the plant well in but don't over compact the soil.
3 Make compact or resistant to pressure; solidify. Also foll. by *up*. L16.
W. FOLKINGHAM Boggie and spungie grounds are . . firmed by frequent ouer-flowing them with Fords.
▸ **II** *verb intrans.* **4** Become firm; (of prices etc.) stabilize, improve after a decline. Also foll. by *up*. L19.
Timber Trades Journal The Scandinavian market, . . weak over recent months, is now showing signs of firming. R. WILLIAMS The whole picture was beginning to firm up in my mind.

firmament /ˈfəːməm(ə)nt/ *noun.* Now *literary*. ME.
[ORIGIN Old French & mod. French from Latin *firmamentum*, from *firmare*: see FIRM *adjective*, -MENT.]
1 The arch or vault of heaven with its clouds and stars; the sky, the heavens. Also formerly, heaven as God's dwelling place. ME.
J. G. FARRELL A low bank of cloud . . was slowly mounting over the entire firmament, concealing the stars.
†**2** A celestial sphere in Ptolemaic astronomy, *spec.* that of the fixed stars. ME–M17.
†**3** Anything which strengthens or supports; a substratum, a foundation. LME–E18.

firmamental /fəːməˈmɛnt(ə)l/ *adjective.* M16.
[ORIGIN from FIRMAMENT + -AL¹.]
1 Of or pertaining to the firmament. M16.
2 Of the nature of a supporting framework or substratum. Now *rare* or *obsolete*. L17.

firman /ˈfəːmən, fəːˈmɑːn/ *noun.* Also **farman** /ˈfɑːmən, fəˈmɑːn/. E17.
[ORIGIN Persian *firmān* = Sanskrit *pramāṇa* (right) measure, standard, authority.]
An edict or order issued by an Ottoman or Middle Eastern ruler or official, esp. a grant, licence, or permit.

†**firmitude** *noun.* M16–E18.
[ORIGIN Latin *firmitudo*, from *firmus* FIRM *adjective*: see -TUDE.]
Firmness, solidity, strength, resolution.

†**firmity** *noun.* LME–E18.
[ORIGIN Old French & mod. French *fermeté*, formed as FIRM *adjective*. Later refashioned after Latin *firmitas*: see -ITY.]
Firmness, solidity, stability; allegiance.

†**firmless** *adjective. poet.* L16–M18.
[ORIGIN from FIRM *adjective* + -LESS.]
Unsteady, shifting.

firn /fɪən/ *noun.* M19.
[ORIGIN German from Old High German *firni* old, rel. to Old Saxon *fern* past, *forn* formerly, Old Norse *forn* ancient (Swedish *forn* former).]
= NÉVÉ.

firry /ˈfəːri/ *adjective.* E19.
[ORIGIN from FIR + -Y¹.]
Having many firs; of or pertaining to the fir.

first /fəːst/ *adjective, adverb, & noun* (*ordinal numeral*).
[ORIGIN Old English *fyr(e)st* = Old Frisian *ferost*, *-est*, *ferst*, Old High German *furist* (*furisto* prince, whence German *Fürst*), Old Norse *fyrstr*, from Germanic superl., from Indo-European base also of Latin *primus*, Greek *prōtos*, Sanskrit *prathama*.]
▸ **A** *adjective.* **1** Preceding all others in time, order, series, succession, etc.; earliest in occurrence, existence, etc.; basic; that is number one in a series; (represented by 1st). OE. ▸**b** Occurring or presenting itself next after a given point of time (expressed or implied). E17.
S. JOHNSON Each of the six first lines of the *Iliad* might lose two syllables. T. HARDY Mr Clare . . whose first wife had died . . married a second late in life. SCOTT FITZGERALD I thought of the first sheep I ever remember seeing. I. MURDOCH An April evening . . the big trees in first leaf. DAY LEWIS Memories from my first two years. G. GORDON For the first few years of his working life . . he had had to work every second Saturday. **b** MORTIMER COLLINS I shall get back to London by the first train.
first conjugation, ***first declension***, etc.
2 Foremost or most advanced in position. OE.
OED The first horse in the race.
3 Foremost in rank, importance, or excellence. ME. ▸**b** In official titles: having precedence over all others. M18.
J. OZELL Courage, a General's first Quality. H. MARTINEAU I was told a great deal about 'the first people in Boston'.
b ***first cellist***, ***first lieutenant***, ***First Lord of the Treasury***, ***First Sea Lord***, ***first violin***, etc.
▸ **B** *adverb.* **1** Before anyone or anything else, in time, rank, serial order, etc. OE. ▸†**b** Originally. OE–E18.
SCOTT FITZGERALD After greeting Rosemary and her mother he waited for them to speak first. *Proverb*: First come, first served.
2 Before another specified or implied thing, time, event, etc.; as the first point in a topic, argument, etc., in the first place. ME. ▸**b** In preference to something else; rather; more likely. LME.
A. R. PENNINGTON It is impossible for the priest to remit the sins of any unless they are first remitted by Christ. J. BUCHAN She could scarcely refuse to give him breakfast first. J. STEINBECK He . . slipped off first one shoe and then the other. **b** BROWNING Die? He'll bribe a gaoler or break prison first.
3 For the first time, then and not earlier. ME.
T. HARDY He . . surveyed people up and down when first making their acquaintance. G. GREENE In this story of . . Hunca-Munca . . the unmistakable Potter style first appears.
4 *ellipt.* Travelling first class. L19.
▸ **C** *noun* **I 1** The first person or thing of a category, series, etc., identified contextually, as day of the month, (following a proper name) person, esp. monarch or pope, of the specified name, base in baseball, etc. ME.
OED He is always the first to find fault. S. BECKETT I was stopped by a second policeman, similar in all respects to the first.
2 *The* first part, *the* beginning. LME.
F. MARRYAT We shall be able to stem the first of the flood. D. H. LAWRENCE It was wrong from the first It was wrong to begin with.
3 HERALDRY. *The* tincture first mentioned in a blazon. M16.
▸ **II 4** *gen.* A person who or thing which is first. L16.
5 MUSIC. The highest part of a duet, trio, etc. L18.
6 In *pl.* Goods of the best quality. E19.
7 (A person having) a place in the first class of an examination; (the winner of) first place in a race etc. M19.
S. SPENDER To gain a First, a Scholarship, . . seemed as difficult as scaling some great height. J. DIDION She took all the jumping firsts at the . . horse show.
8 A first-class compartment, carriage, or section, on a train etc. E20.
9 A first edition (of a book). E20.

10 = *first gear* below. E20.

11 The first known or discovered example of a thing; a first instance or occurrence, esp. of something notable. M20.

> J. F. STRAKER 'I'm sorry about that, Paul.' That made another first: they had not used Christian names before.

– PHRASES ETC.: *after first brush*: see BRUSH noun[2] 1. **at first** at the beginning. *at first blush*: see BLUSH noun 1. *at first brush*: see BRUSH noun[2] 1. *at the first blush*: see BLUSH noun 1. **come in first** win a race. *double first*: see DOUBLE adjective & adverb. **feet first** (a) with the feet in front; (b) colloq. in a coffin, dead. **first and foremost** first(ly) and most important(ly). **first and last** taking one thing with another, all in all, from start to finish. **first in, first out** (a) (of a system of accounting) in which the goods first acquired by a company are valued as though they are the first to be sold; (b) COMPUTING (designating or pertaining to) a procedure in which the item removed from a buffer, queue, etc., is always the one that has been in the longest. **first of all** before anyone or anything else, firstly. **first off** colloq. (orig. US) at first, to begin with. **first or last** sooner or later. **first past the post** (designating) the winner of an election by virtue of receiving the most votes though perhaps not having an absolute majority. **first up** colloq. first of all, at the first attempt. *first-wicket partnership*: see WICKET 3b. **from first to last** throughout. **from the first** from the beginning. *for the first time*: see FOR preposition. **head first** with the head in front. *in the first flight*: see FLIGHT noun[1]. *in the first instance*: see INSTANCE noun. **in the first place** first, firstly; to begin with. *of the first head*: see HEAD noun. **of the first order** [French *du premier ordre*] outstanding, excellent. *of the first water*: see WATER noun 10b. *on first blush*, *on the first blush*: see BLUSH noun 1. **the first** the beginning; even one elementary thing (about).

– SPECIAL COLLOCATIONS & COMB.: (As ordinal.) Forming compound ordinal numerals with multiples of ten, as *forty-first* (*41st*), *five-thousand-and-first* (*5001st*), etc. (As adjective.) **first aid** help given to an injured person (until medical treatment is available); *first-aid post*, a place where first aid is available. **first-aider** a person trained or skilled in first aid. *first base*: see BASE noun[1]. *first blood*: see BLOOD noun. *first blush*: see BLUSH noun 1. **firstborn** adjective & noun (a) adjective that is born first, eldest; (b) noun one's first or eldest child. *first brush*: see BRUSH noun[2] 1. *First Cause*: see CAUSE noun. *first chop*: see CHOP noun[3]. **first coat** a first layer of paint etc. **first comer** a first or earliest arrival. *First Consul*: see CONSUL 2. **first cost** = *prime cost* s.v. PRIME adjective. *first cousin*: see COUSIN noun 1. **first cross** the crossing of two pure breeds; an offspring of such a cross. **first day** (a) Sunday, esp. among the Society of Friends; (b) the first day of issue of stamps etc.; (*first-day cover*: see COVER noun[1]). **first degree** spec. (a) the least serious category of burn; (b) the most serious category of crime (*principal in the first degree*: see PRINCIPAL noun 2a). **first-degree** adjective (a) (of a burn) affecting only the epidermis; (b) US (of murder) premeditated and without mitigating circumstances. *first derivative*: see DERIVATIVE noun 3. **first edition** the first printed form in which a book etc. is published; the whole number of copies in this form; one copy in this form. **first finger** the finger next to the thumb. **first floor** the floor immediately above the ground floor; N. Amer. the ground floor. *First Folio*: see FOLIO noun. **first-foot** noun & verb (chiefly Scot.) (a) noun the first person to cross the threshold in the New Year; (b) verb intrans. be such a person; go on a round of visits as a New Year begins (chiefly as *first-footing* verbal noun). **first-footer** a person who first-foots or goes first-footing. **first fruits** (a) the first products of agriculture for the season, esp. as offered to God, fig. the first results of work etc.; (b) hist. a payment to a superior by the new holder of an office, esp. an ecclesiastical office. **first gear** the lowest or bottom forward gear in a motor vehicle, bicycle, etc. **first-generation** adjective (of a computer) distinguished by the use of vacuum tubes and belonging essentially to the period 1945–55. *first good*: see GOOD noun. *first* INTENTION. **first lady** the most important lady; US spec. the wife of the President, or another appointed woman acting as hostess for him. **first language** one's native language. *first lesson*: see LESSON noun 2. *first* LIEUTENANT. **first light** the time when light first appears in the morning. **first line** (orig. MILITARY) the line of fighting forces or fig. the group of people who are most advanced or of the highest quality. *First Lord of the Treasury*: see TREASURY. **first love** (the emotion felt) the first time one falls in love; the person with whom one falls in love for the first time; one's favourite occupation, possession, etc. *first* MOVER. **first name** a person's personal given or Christian name, as opp. to his or her surname (*on first-name terms*, sufficiently friendly to address each other by first names). **first-name** verb trans. address by first name, be on first-name terms with. **First Nation** (in Canada) an indigenous American Indian community officially recognized as an administrative unit, or functioning as such. **first night** the first public performance of a play etc. **first-nighter** a person who attends a first night or first nights. **first offender** an offender against the law against whom no previous conviction is recorded. **first officer** (a) the mate on a merchant ship; (b) the second in command to the captain on an aircraft. *first person*: see PERSON noun. **first position** (a) MUSIC the lowest possible position of the hand on the fingerboard of a stringed instrument; (b) BALLET a disposition of the body in which the legs are together with heels touching, and the toes are turned out at a right angle. *first post*: see POST noun[6]. *first quarter*: see QUARTER noun 7b. **first reading** the first of three successive occasions on which a bill must have been presented to a legislature before it becomes law, permitting its introduction. *first refusal*: see REFUSAL 2. **first responder** N. Amer. a person whose job entails being the first on the scene of an emergency, e.g. a firefighter or police officer. **first school** a primary school intended for children between the ages of 5 and 8 or 9. *First Sea Lord*: see SEA. *First Secretary*: see SECRETARY noun. **first sergeant** US the highest ranking non-commissioned officer in a company. *first sound*: see SOUND noun[2]. *first storey*: see STOREY noun. **first strike** an aggressive attack with nuclear weapons before their use by the enemy. *first string*: see STRING noun. **first thing** (a) the most elementary or rudimentary thing (freq. in *not know the first thing about*); (b) adverb (colloq.) before anything else; (c) *first things first*, the most important things before any others. **first-time buyer** a person seeking to buy a home who has not previously owned one and so has none to sell. **first-timer** a person who does or is something for the first time. **First War** = *First World War* s.v. WORLD. *first water*: see WATER noun 10. **First World** (a) hist. the US and USSR; (b) the developed countries apart from the (former) Communist bloc. *First World War*: see WORLD noun.

■ **firstness** noun LME.

first class /fəːs(t) ˈklɑːs; *as adjective also* ˈfəːs(t)klɑːs/ *noun phr., adjective, & adverb.* As adjective & adverb usu. **first-class**. L18.

[ORIGIN from FIRST adjective + CLASS noun.]

▸ **A** *noun phr.* The first (usu. the highest) of a series of classes into which people or things are grouped; a set of people or things grouped together as better than others; the best accommodation in a train, boat, aircraft, etc.; mail given preferential treatment; a compartment of a train etc. offering the best accommodation; (a person with) a place in the highest division of an examination list. L18.

▸ **B** *adjective.* Belonging to, achieving, travelling by, etc., the first class; of the best quality, very good; of the highest order. M19.

> R. K. NARAYAN This threatened to develop into a first-class crisis. F. FORSYTH Harcourt-Smith was of the university intake, with a first-class degree. *Times* The price of the first class stamp has remained at 17p since September 1984.

– COMB.: **first-classman** a person with a first-class degree.

▸ **C** *adverb.* By first-class accommodation in a train, boat, aircraft, etc.; by first-class mail; colloq. excellently. L19.

first hand /fəːstˈhand; *as adjective also* ˈfəːsthand/ *noun phr., adjective, & adverb.* As adjective & adverb (now usu.) **first-hand**. M18.

[ORIGIN from FIRST adjective + HAND noun.]

▸ **A** *noun phr.* **at first hand**, directly from the first source, without intermediate agency. M18.

▸ **B** *adjective.* Of or pertaining to the first source, original; coming direct from the first source, derived from personal experience. M18.

> INA TAYLOR She had no first-hand knowledge of the subject.

▸ **C** *adverb.* Directly from the first source, at first hand. M19.

> www.fictionpress.com She knew first-hand how dangerous Ellen's temper could be.

firstling /ˈfəːs(t)lɪŋ/ *noun & adjective.* M16.

[ORIGIN from FIRST adjective + -LING[1].]

▸ **A** *noun.* The first product or result of something; the first offspring of a season. Usu. in *pl.* M16.

▸ **B** *attrib.* or as *adjective.* That is the first product or result; firstborn. E17.

firstly /ˈfəːs(t)li/ *adverb.* M16.

[ORIGIN from FIRST adjective + -LY[2].]

As the first point in a topic, argument, etc.; in the first place.

first-rate /fəːs(t)ˈreɪt; *as adjective also* ˈfəːs(t)reɪt/ *noun, adjective, & adverb.* Also (usual form in sense A.1) **first rate**. M17.

[ORIGIN from FIRST adjective + RATE noun[1].]

▸ **A** *noun.* **1** hist. The highest of the rates or classes by which warships were distinguished according to the number of guns they carried. M17.

2 A warship of the first rate (*hist.*); a person or thing of the highest class or rank (now *rare*). L17.

▸ **B** *adjective.* **1** hist. Of a warship: of the first rate. L17.

2 Of the highest class or excellence; extremely good, excellent. colloq. M18.

> M. E. G. DUFF As long as France remained a first-rate power. M. GORDON Her misfortune was to be a merely first-rate painter in an age of geniuses.

▸ **C** *adverb.* Excellently, very well. colloq. M19.

> B. W. ALDISS 'You're looking first-rate' 'And you, Sicily evidently agrees with you'.

■ **first-rater** noun a first-rate person or thing E19.

firth /fəːθ/ *noun*[1]. Chiefly N. English poet. Now *rare* or *obsolete*. LME.

[ORIGIN Metath. var. of FRITH noun[2].]

A (hunting) forest; a coppice, a small wood.

firth /fəːθ/ *noun*[2]. Orig. Scot. LME.

[ORIGIN Old Norse *fjǫrðr* FJORD: cf. FRITH noun[3].]

An arm of the sea; a river estuary.

fisc /fɪsk/ *noun.* Also (SCOTS LAW) **fisk**. L16.

[ORIGIN French, or Latin FISCUS rush-basket, purse, treasury.]

1 hist. Orig. the private treasury of the Roman emperors, later developing into a public treasury but retaining considerable imperial control. L16. ▸**b** An exchequer. Now *rare*. L16.

2 SCOTS LAW. The public treasury or Crown to which estates lapse by escheat; the revenue to the Crown by escheat. Formerly also, the right of the Crown to the estate of a rebel. *obsolete* exc. *hist.* L17.

fiscal /ˈfɪsk(ə)l/ *adjective & noun.* M16.

[ORIGIN French, or Latin *fiscalis*, from *fiscus* treasury: see FISC.]

▸ **A** *adjective.* **1** Of or pertaining to a treasury. Now chiefly, of or pertaining to governmental financial matters. M16.

2 Of or pertaining to financial matters in general. Chiefly US. M19.

– SPECIAL COLLOCATIONS: **fiscal agent** a bank or trust company appointed by a corporation etc. to act as its financial representative. **fiscal drag** ECONOMICS (a deflationary effect on economic growth caused by) the tendency of tax yields to increase at a higher rate than inflation when tax allowances remain fixed. **fiscal engineer** US a specialist in fiscal engineering. **fiscal engineering** US management of the finances of a firm so as to take maximum advantage of tax exemptions etc. **fiscal year** (chiefly N. Amer.) a financial year (for the US Government, beginning 1 October (before 1976, 1 July)).

▸ **B** *noun.* **1** A legal official in any of various countries, having the function of public prosecutor and (in the Netherlands and formerly in Dutch Colonies) esp. concerned with revenue. Formerly also, an official of the treasury. M16. ▸**b** *Scot.* = *procurator fiscal* s.v. PROCURATOR 3. L16.

2 [Afrikaans *fiskaal* = public official (cf. sense 1), hangman, from the birds' habit of impaling prey on thorns.] Any of a number of largely black and white African shrikes of the genus *Lanius*, spec. *L. collaris*. Freq. *fiscal shrike*, *fiscal bird*. Orig. *S. Afr.* L18.

3 A stamp given as a receipt for a payment of tax etc. M19.

4 A fiscal year (specified by a following date). Chiefly US. M20.

> *National Observer (US)* Both houses . . approved a preliminary budget resolution setting forth targets . . for fiscal 1977, which begins Oct. 1.

■ **fiscality** /fɪˈskalɪti/ *noun* (a) exclusive or excessive regard to fiscal matters; (b) in *pl.*, fiscal matters: E19. **fiscally** adverb from a fiscal point of view M19.

Fischer-Tropsch /fɪʃəˈtrɒpʃ/ *noun.* M20.

[ORIGIN from F. J. E. *Fischer* (1877–1948), and H. *Tropsch* (1889–1935), German chemists.]

CHEMISTRY. Used *attrib.* to designate a process which produces hydrocarbons etc. through the catalytic hydrogenation of carbon monoxide.

fiscus /ˈfɪskəs/ *noun.* Pl. **fisci** /ˈfɪskʌɪ/. M17.

[ORIGIN Latin: see FISC.]

= FISC 1, 1b.

> H. ALLEN Coined silver dollars were lying idle in the Mexican fiscus.

fisgig *noun & adjective* var. of FIZGIG *noun*[1] *& adjective.*

fish /fɪʃ/ *noun*[1]. Pl. same, **-es** /-ɪz/.

[ORIGIN Old English *fisc* = Old Frisian *fisk*, Old Saxon, Old High German *fisc* (Dutch *visch*, German *Fisch*), Old Norse *fiskr*, Gothic *fisks*, cogn. with Latin *piscis*, from Indo-European.]

1 Orig., any animal living exclusively in water (now only as 2nd elem. of comb., as *crayfish*, *cuttlefish*, *jellyfish*, *shellfish*, and in COOKERY). Now, any of a large and varied group of cold-blooded aquatic vertebrates possessing gills and fins. OE. ▸**b** In full *tin fish*. A torpedo. *nautical slang.* E20. ▸**c** A dollar. US slang. E20.

> c R. JESSUP Would a hundred fish do you? . . Would it be enough for the bus?

angelfish, *anglerfish*, *bluefish*, *catfish*, *codfish*, *dogfish*, *hagfish*, *monkfish*, etc.

2 (Usu. **F-**.) In *pl.* *The* constellation and zodiacal sign Pisces. OE.

> L. MACNEICE We all know you were born under the Fish.

3 The flesh of fish, esp. as food (opp. *flesh*, *fowl*). ME.

4 Usu. with preceding (derog.) adjective A person. colloq. M18.

> P. SCOTT Her family . . were cold fish to a man.

– PHRASES: **a fish out of water** a person not in accustomed or preferred surroundings. *a nice kettle of fish*, *a pretty kettle of fish*: see KETTLE noun 1. **be food for fishes**. *blind fish*: see BLIND adjective. *bony fish*: see BONY adjective. *cartilaginous fish*: see CARTILAGINOUS 1. *cry stinking fish*: see STINKING adjective. **drink like a fish** drink (esp. alcohol) excessively. *feed the fishes*: see FEED verb[1]. **fish and chips** fried fish with fried chipped potatoes. *Flying Fish*: see FLYING ppl adjective. **have other fish to fry** have more important business to attend to. *kettle of fish*: see KETTLE 1. **neither fish, nor flesh, nor good red herring** of indefinite character. *queer fish*: see QUEER adjective & noun. **royal fish** whales, porpoises, and sturgeon, if caught near the coast or cast ashore belonging to the Crown, or in the Duchy of Cornwall to the Prince of Wales. *soup and fish*: see SOUP noun. *Southern Fish*: see SOUTHERN. *stinking fish*: see STINKING adjective. *walking fish*: see WALKING ppl adjective. *wet fish*: see WET adjective. *ye gods and little fishes*: see GOD noun.

– COMB.: **fish basket** (a) a basket for carrying fish; (b) US a creel for catching fish; **fishbowl** a (usu. glass) bowl in which to keep live (esp. ornamental) fish; **fishcake** a small cake of flaked or minced fish and mashed potato, often coated in batter or breadcrumbs and fried; **fish-carver** a knife for serving fish; **fish-day** (now *arch.* or *hist.*) a day on which fish is eaten; a fast day; **fish eagle** any eagle or other large bird of prey that feeds on fish; spec. any of certain eagles of the genus *Haliaetus*; **fish-eaters** a knife and fork for eating fish; **fisheye** noun & adjective (a) noun a variety of moonstone; a diamond, an imitation diamond; (b) adjective (of a lens) wide-angled with a curved front; **fish farm** a place where fish are bred for food; **fish-farmer** a person engaged in fish-farming; **fish-farming** the breeding of fish for food; **fish finger** an

F

oblong piece of flaked or minced fish coated in batter or breadcrumbs; **fish-fork** a small four-tined fork for eating fish; a large broad four-tined fork for serving fish; **fish-fry** (*a*) *US* a picnic where fish is fried and eaten; (*b*) = FRY *noun*[1] 3; **fishgarth** (now *arch. & dial.*) an enclosure on a river or the seashore for keeping or catching fish; **fish-glue** isinglass; **fish hawk** the osprey; **fish hook** (*a*) a bent piece of wire, usu. barbed, used for catching fish; (*b*) NAUTICAL a hook forming part of the tackle used to raise an anchor; ***fish kettle***: see KETTLE 1; **fish knife** a small broad bluntedge knife for eating fish; a similar large knife for serving fish; **fish ladder** a series of pools built like steps to enable fish to ascend a fall or dam; **fish louse** any of numerous small crustaceans of the class Branchiura, esp. of the genus *Argulus*, temporary parasites of fish; **fishmeal** ground dried fish used as fertilizer etc.; **fishmonger** a dealer in fish; **fishnet** *adjective & noun* (*a*) *adjective* (of a garment or fabric, esp. of tights or stockings) open-meshed; (*b*) *noun* in *pl.*, fishnet tights or stockings; **fish plate** the perforated draining plate of a fish kettle; **fish poison** (*a*) a substance toxic to fish; (*b*) any of certain plants, extracts of which have an intoxicating effect on fish; *esp.* Jamaican dogwood, *Piscidia piscipula*, and (*US*) buckeye; **fish pond** a pond in which live fish are kept; *joc.* the sea, the ocean; **fish pool** a pool in which live fish are kept; **fishpot** a wicker trap for eels, lobsters, etc.; **fish sauce** a sauce made to be eaten with fish; **fish slice** (*a*) a carving knife for fish; (*b*) a cook's implement for turning or taking out fish or other (fried) food; **fish-sound** the swimming bladder of a fish; **fish stick** *N. Amer.* a fish finger; **fish supper** a dish of fried fish and chips to be eaten for supper; **fish tank** a tank in which live (esp. ornamental) fish are kept; **fishwife** a woman who sells fish; a foul-mouthed abusive woman; **fishworm** *US* an earthworm; a worm used as bait for fish.

– NOTE: The normal pl. is *fish*, but the older form *fishes* is still used when referring to different kinds of fish (e.g. 'freshwater fishes of the British Isles').

■ **fishful** *adjective* containing many fish M16. **fishless** *adjective* L16. **fishlike** *adjective* E17. **fishling** *noun* (*rare*) a young or small fish M19.

fish /fɪʃ/ *noun*[2]. Pl. **-es** /-ɪz/, same. E16.
[ORIGIN Senses 1 & 2 prob., sense 3 certainly from French *fiche*, from *ficher* fix, from Proto-Romance intensive of Latin *figere* fix.]
1 A flat plate of iron, wood, etc. laid on a beam, rail, etc., or across a joint, to protect or strengthen it. E16.
2 NAUTICAL. A long piece of wood, concave on one side and convex on the other, lashed to a spar that has fractured or been weakened in order to strengthen it. M17.
3 A small flat piece of bone, ivory, etc., sometimes fish-shaped, used instead of money in card games. E18.
– COMB.: **fish-beam**: comprising an iron plate sandwiched between two beams; **fish-bolt** a bolt for fastening fishplates and rails together; **fishplate** either of two plates holding rails together.

fish /fɪʃ/ *noun*[3]. Pl. **-es** /-ɪz/, same. M17.
[ORIGIN from FISH *verb*[1].]
1 NAUTICAL. The purchase used in fishing an anchor. Earliest in *comb.* M17.
2 An act of fishing. *colloq.* L19.
3 An object accidentally left or dropped down the borehole of an oil well, hindering further drilling. M20.

fish /fɪʃ/ *verb*[1].
[ORIGIN Old English *fiscian* = Old Frisian *fiskia*, Old Saxon *fiskon* (Dutch *vissen*), Old High German *fiskōn* (German *fischen*), Old Norse *fiska*, Gothic *fiskōn*, from Germanic, from base of FISH *noun*[1].]
▸ **I** *verb intrans.* **1** Catch or try to catch fish, esp. by using a net or hook and line etc. (Foll. by *for*.) OE. ▸**b** *fig.* Try to convert other individuals to Christianity. LME.

> C. STEAD This waterside, where he had fished for gudgeon as a child.

2 Try to obtain or elicit a compliment, secret, etc., by indirect means or artifice. (Foll. by *for*.) M16.

> J. AUSTEN I am not fishing; don't compliment me. RODDY DOYLE She told us that . . she wasn't showing off and fishing for gratitude.

3 Search for something in or under water; grope or feel in search for or *for* something concealed. M17. ▸**b** (Try to) clear the borehole of a well of extraneous obstacles. E20.

> M. SHADBOLT Reg tossed the gun in the harbour. The police are still fishing for it. S. KING The pitchman sighed and fished inside his shirt.

4 Of water: provide (good or bad) sport for anglers. L19.

> J. BUCHAN Sim had always declared that it [a tarn] only fished well after rain.

▸ **II** *verb trans.* **5** Catch or try to catch (fish); collect (coral etc.) from the seabed. LME.
6 Try to catch fish in (a stretch of water); search (something) *for* (information, papers, etc.). LME.

> J. BUCHAN Remote glens where I could fish unfrequented streams.

7 Draw or pull (as) from water (foll. by *from*, *out*, *out of*, *up*); elicit, get *out* esp. by artifice, (a fact, opinion or secret). LME. ▸**b** NAUTICAL. Draw the flukes of (an anchor) up close to the gunwale. L15. ▸**c** Pull (a wire) through a conduit or between floors or walls by means of a stiff looped wire or other device pushed in from the nearer end. L19.

> J. G. COZZENS The sodden body fished out of dirty water. R. CHANDLER He fished a match out of his pants.

8 Use as a bait in fishing; use (a boat etc.) for fishing. L19.
9 Compete as a fisherman in (a fishing competition). L19.
– PHRASES: **fish for oneself** rely on one's own efforts. **fish in troubled waters** make one's profit out of disturbances. **fish out** exhaust the fish from (a pool etc.).
■ **fisha'bility** *noun* the property or condition of being fishable M20. **fishable** *adjective* (of water) able to be fished in, suitable for fishing in E17.

fish /fɪʃ/ *verb*[2] *trans.* E17.
[ORIGIN from FISH *noun*[2].]
1 Mend or strengthen (a spar etc.) with a fish or fishes. E17.
2 Join (rails) with a fish or fishes. M19.

fisher /'fɪʃə/ *noun*.
[ORIGIN Old English *fiscere* = Old Frisian *fisker*, Old Saxon *fiskari* (Dutch *visser*), Old High German *fiscāri* (German *Fischer*), Old Norse *fiskari*, from Germanic, from base of FISH *noun*[1]: see -ER[1].]
1 A person employed in catching fish, a fisherman. *arch.* OE. ▸**b** *fig.* More fully ***fisher of men*** [*Matthew* 4:19]. An evangelist. OE.
2 An animal that catches fish for food. M16. ▸**b** *spec.* A large N. American arboreal carnivore of the weasel family, *Martes pennanti*; the fur of this animal. L17.
3 A fishing boat. M19.

fisherman /'fɪʃəmən/ *noun*. Pl. **-men**. LME.
[ORIGIN from FISHER + MAN *noun*.]
1 A person who catches fish for a living or for sport; an angler. LME.
fisherman's bend NAUTICAL a knot tied by making a full turn round usu. the ring of an anchor and making one half hitch through the turn and a second round the standing part of the rope. **fisherman's knit** a type of thick ribbed knitting. **fisherman's knot**: used to join two small lines by tying an overhand knot in the end of each and around the opposite standing part. **fisherman's rib** = ***fisherman's knit*** above. **fisherman's story**, **fisherman's tale** = ***fishing story*** s.v. FISHING *noun*.
2 A fishing boat. E17.
3 An animal that catches fish. *rare*. M17.
4 A person who retrieves objects left or dropped down the borehole of an oil well. E20.
■ **fisherwoman** *noun* M18.

fishery /'fɪʃ(ə)ri/ *noun*. E16.
[ORIGIN from FISH *verb*[1] + -ERY, or from FISHER + -Y[3].]
1 The business, occupation, or industry of catching fish or other products from the sea, rivers, etc. E16.
2 (An establishment in) a place or district where fish are caught. L17.
3 LAW. The right of fishing in certain waters. M18.

fishgig /'fɪʃgɪg/ *noun*. Now *rare*. M17.
[ORIGIN Alt., after FISH *noun*[1].]
= FIZGIG *noun*[2].

fishify /'fɪʃɪfʌɪ/ *verb trans.* L16.
[ORIGIN from FISH *noun*[1] + -I- + -FY.]
Cause (flesh) to become like fish or insubstantial or wasted.

> SHAKES. *Rom. & Jul.* O flesh, flesh, how art thou fishified!

fishing /'fɪʃɪŋ/ *noun*. ME.
[ORIGIN from FISH *verb*[1] + -ING[1].]
1 The action of FISH *verb*[1]. ME.
coarse fishing, ***fly-fishing***, ***line-fishing***, ***pearl-fishing***, etc.
2 = FISHERY 3. *obsolete* exc. *hist.* LME.
3 = FISHERY 2. LME.
– ATTRIB. & COMB.: Esp. in the sense 'used for or concerned with fishing', as ***fishing boat***, ***fishing net***, ***fishing port***, ***fishing smack***, ***fishing tackle***, ***fishing village***. Special combs., as **fishing expedition** *fig.* (*a*) a legal investigation with the purpose of discovering information on which to base a later proceeding; (*b*) a search undertaken not with the stated purpose but in the hope of discovering incriminating evidence; **fishing line** a thin thread of silk, nylon, cord, etc. to which a baited hook, sinker, float, etc. are attached, used for catching fish; **fishing rod** a long thin tapering rod, usu. jointed, to which a line is attached for angling; **fishing story** an exaggerated account of an incident.

fishing /'fɪʃɪŋ/ *ppl adjective*. M17.
[ORIGIN from FISH *verb*[1] + -ING[2].]
1 Of an animal: that catches fish. M17.
fishing frog an anglerfish.
2 Of a question: asked in order to elicit information indirectly. E19.

fishtail /'fɪʃteɪl/ *noun & verb*. M19.
[ORIGIN from FISH *noun*[1] + TAIL *noun*[1].]
▸ **A** *noun*. The tail of a fish; anything resembling this in shape or lateral movement; *esp.* an arrow unsteady in flight. M19.
– COMB.: **fishtail burner** a gas burner producing a spreading flame.
▸ **B** *verb intrans.* Swing the tail of an aircraft or the back of a vehicle from side to side (in aircraft to reduce the landing speed); move with the tail so swinging. E20.

> *fig.*: R. CHANDLER A large black and gold butterfly fishtailed in and landed on a hydrangea bush.

fishy /'fɪʃi/ *adjective*. L15.
[ORIGIN from FISH *noun*[1] + -Y[1].]
1 Resembling a fish or some characteristic of a fish; *esp.* (of the eye) dull, vacant-looking. L15.

> E. M. FORSTER Adams was whiskiefied and fishy-faced, and obviously a bully.

2 Smelling or tasting like fish. M16.
3 Containing many fish. Now only *poet.* or *joc.* M16.
4 Consisting of fish. L17.

> POPE Watery fowl, that seek their fishy food.

5 Of dubious character, questionable. *colloq.* M19.

> O. MANNING Poor old Yaki, innocently involved in this fishy business.

■ **fishily** *adverb* M19. **fishiness** *noun* M18.

fisk *noun* see FISC.

fisk /fɪsk/ *verb intrans.* Long *arch. rare*. LME.
[ORIGIN Perh. frequentative (with *-k* suffix as in *walk*, *talk*) of Old English *fȳsan* hurry, or of *fēsian*, *fȳsian* FEEZE *verb*. Cf. synon. Swedish *fjäska* frequentative of *fjäsa* bustle, make a fuss.]
Move briskly, frisk or whisk (*about*).

> R. KIPLING Take *me* from Pevensey to fisk and flyte through fern and forest.

fissibility /fɪsɪ'bɪlɪti/ *noun*. *rare*. L18.
[ORIGIN from Latin *fiss-* (see FISSILE) + -IBILITY.]
The quality of being easily split.

fissile /'fɪsʌɪl/ *adjective*. M17.
[ORIGIN Latin *fissilis*, from *fiss-* pa. ppl stem of *findere* split: see -ILE.]
1 Inclined or tending to split; able to be split. M17.

> GODFREY SMITH The plain fact is that the Labour Party is historically, fundamentally and . . irrevocably fissile.

2 *spec.* Able to undergo nuclear fission. M20.
■ **fissility** /fɪ'sɪlɪti/ *noun* the quality of being fissile L17.

fission /'fɪʃ(ə)n/ *noun & verb*. E17.
[ORIGIN Latin *fissio(n-)*, from *fiss-*: see FISSILE, -ION.]
▸ **A** *noun*. **1** The action of splitting or dividing into pieces. E17.

> C. RYCROFT The absence of a native genius for compromise has led to complete fission.

2 BIOLOGY. The division of a cell or organism into new cells or organisms, as a mode of reproduction. M19.
BINARY ***fission***. ***multiple fission***: see MULTIPLE *adjective*.
3 PHYSICS. The splitting of a heavy atomic nucleus into (usu.) two nuclei spontaneously or under the impact of another particle, with resulting release of energy. M20.
– COMB.: **fission bomb** an atomic bomb.
▸ **B** *verb intrans. & trans.* (Cause to) undergo fission. E20.

> G. R. KEEPIN Those heavy nuclides which can be fissioned by thermal neutrons. G. SAMPSON When Latin lost its role and cultures began to fission along national lines in the Renascence.

– NOTE: Rare before M19.
■ **fissiona'bility** *noun* the quality of being fissionable M20. **fissionable** *adjective* able to undergo fission; tending to undergo fission: M20.

fissiparous /fɪ'sɪp(ə)rəs/ *adjective*. M19.
[ORIGIN Irreg. from Latin *fissus* pa. pple of *findere* to split, after *viviparous* etc.]
1 BIOLOGY. Reproducing by fission; of or pertaining to reproduction by fission. M19.
2 Tending to split or divide; pertaining to splitting or division. L19.

> R. QUIRK The fissiparous tendencies that local needs and nationalist susceptibilities are fostering.

■ **fissiparity** /fɪsɪ'parɪti/ *noun* (*a*) the quality of being fissiparous; (*b*) the process of fissiparous reproduction: L19. **fissiparously** *adverb* L19. **fissiparousness** *noun* M20.

fissiped /'fɪsɪpɛd/ *adjective & noun*. Also **-pede** /-piːd/. M17.
[ORIGIN Late Latin *fissipes*, *-ped-*, from Latin *fissus* (see FISSIPAROUS) + *pes*, *ped-* foot.]
ZOOLOGY. ▸ **A** *adjective*. Having the toes separated. Now *spec.* designating those mammals of the order Carnivora other than the pinnipeds. M17.
▸ **B** *noun*. A fissiped animal. Cf. PINNIPED. M17.

fissive /'fɪsɪv/ *adjective*. L19.
[ORIGIN from Latin *fiss-*: (see FISSILE) + -IVE.]
Pertaining to or of the nature of fission.

fissle /'fɪs(ə)l/ *noun & verb*. *Scot. & dial.* Also **fistle**. E18.
[ORIGIN Imit.: cf. FIZZLE.]
▸ **A** *noun*. **1** A rustling noise. Formerly also, a fuss. E18.
▸ **B** *verb*. **1** *verb trans. & intrans.* Rustle. E18.

> W. MCILVANNEY Straw fissled, inventing shapes in the darkness.

†**2** *verb intrans.* Move about restlessly; fidget. L18–L19.

fissural /'fɪʃ(ə)r(ə)l/ *adjective*. LME.
[ORIGIN from FISSURE *noun* + -AL[1].]
Of or pertaining to a fissure or fissures; like a fissure; having fissures.
– NOTE: In isolated use before L19.

fissuration /fɪʃər'eɪʃ(ə)n/ *noun*. M19.
[ORIGIN French, from *fissurer*, formed as FISSURE: see -ATION.]
The action or process of fissuring; the state of being fissured.

fissure /'fɪʃə/ *noun & verb*. LME.
[ORIGIN Old French & mod. French, or Latin *fissura*, from *fiss-*: see FISSILE, -URE.]
▸ **A** *noun*. **1** An opening, usu. long and narrow, made by cracking, splitting, or separation of parts. Orig. esp. in MEDICINE, a linear wound or ulceration; now chiefly, a long cleft in rock or ice. LME.

E. HEATH The Rift Valley, that great fissure in the earth which extends for a thousand miles. *fig.*: E. GELLNER Not *any* genetically transmitted trait will have the effect of producing a fissure in society.

2 HERALDRY. A diminutive of the bend sinister. L15.
3 The action of fissuring; the state of being fissured; sharp division. M17.

R. D. LAING The fissure into self and ego, inner and outer, good and bad occurs.

– COMB.: **fissure eruption** GEOLOGY a steady emission of lava along a fissure in the earth's crust; **fissure vein** MINERALOGY a fissure in the earth's crust filled with valuable mineral.
▸ **B** *verb*. **1** *verb trans.* Make a fissure or fissures in; split. M17.
2 *verb intrans.* Develop a fissure or fissures; crack. M19.
■ **fissured** *adjective* having a fissure or fissures; broken up by fissures: L18.

fist /fɪst/ *noun*[1].
[ORIGIN Old English *fȳst* = Old Frisian *fest*, Middle Low German *füst* (Dutch *vuist*), Old High German *fūst* (German *Faust*), from West Germanic.]
1 The hand clenched with the fingers bent into the palm (so esp. in striking a blow and in holding something); grasp, grip. OE.

R. L. STEVENSON The blind man clung close to me, holding me in one iron fist. E. BAKER He was sure Shillitoe would swing his right fist and tensed, ready to block the blow.

2 The hand. Now only *joc.* ME. ▸**b** TYPOGRAPHY. A hand-shaped symbol with a pointing finger used to draw attention to a note etc. Also called ***index***. Cf. HAND *noun* 8b. L19.

T. PYNCHON She was near the door with an unidentifiable drink in her fist.

3 One's handwriting (now only *joc.*); *transf.* the style of transmitting by telegraph peculiar to an individual operator. L15.
– PHRASES: **give us your fist** shake hands. ***hand over fist***: see HAND *noun*. **make a fist at**, **make a fist of** *colloq.* bungle, be unsuccessful at. **make a good fist at**, **make a good fist of** *colloq.* make a good attempt at, succeed in doing well. **make a poor fist at**, **make a poor fist of** *colloq.* make a poor attempt at, fail to do well.
– COMB.: **fist fight** a fight with bare fists, *esp.* a spontaneous one; **fist-fucking** *coarse slang* (**a**) male masturbation; (**b**) the sexual act or practice of inserting one's hand into another's vagina or rectum.
■ **fistful** *noun* the quantity held by a fist, a handful E17. **fisti'ana** *noun pl.* [-ANA] publications or other items concerning or associated with boxing M19.

fist /fʌɪst/ *noun*[2]. Also (*Scot. & US*) **feist** /fʌɪst/, (*US*, esp. in sense 3) **fice** /fʌɪs/, **fiste** /fʌɪst/, (*obsolete* exc. *dial.*) **foist** /fɔɪst/. ME.
[ORIGIN Rel. to FIST *verb*[2], from West Germanic base. In branch II abbreviation of *fisting cur, dog*, etc.]
▸ **I 1** An act of breaking wind. Formerly also, a foul smell. Now *rare* or *obsolete*. ME.
2 A puffball fungus. Long *obsolete* exc. *dial.* L16.
▸ **II** *US* (forms other than ***fist*** usual).
3 A small dog, a cur. L18.
4 A person of little worth; a bad-tempered person. M20.

fist /fɪst/ *verb*[1] *trans.* L16.
[ORIGIN from FIST *noun*[1].]
1 Strike with the fist, punch. L16.

Daily Chronicle The latter unobserved by the referee fisted the ball into the net. W. GOLDING He danced, fisted the air a bit, then gave an ejaculatory laugh.

2 Grasp with the fist. Now chiefly NAUTICAL, handle (a sail, oar, etc.). E17.

SHAKES. *Coriol.* We have been down together in my sleep, Unbuckling helms, fisting each other's throat.

3 Clench (the hand, the fingers) into a fist. M20.

S. PLATH Then I fisted my fingers together and smashed them at his nose.

†**fist** *verb*[2] *intrans.* Also **foist**. OE–L17.
[ORIGIN Rel. to FIST *noun*[2], from West Germanic base.]
Break wind.
fisting cur, **fisting dog**, **fisting hound** a small pet dog.

fiste *noun* see FIST *noun*[2].

fisted /ˈfɪstɪd/ *adjective*. L16.
[ORIGIN from FIST *noun*[1] + -ED[2].]
1 As 2nd elem. of comb.: having a fist or hand of the specified kind. L16.
close-fisted, ***ham-fisted***, etc.
2 Having or using fists. *rare*. E19.

†**fistic** *noun*. M16–E18.
[ORIGIN medieval Latin *fisticum* from Arabic *fustuq*, *-aq*, *fistiq* ult. from Greek *pistakion* PISTACHIO.]
A pistachio. Also ***fistic nut***, ***fistic tree***.

fistic /ˈfɪstɪk/ *adjective*. *colloq.* E19.
[ORIGIN from FIST *noun*[1] + -IC.]
Pugilistic.
■ **fistical** *adjective* M18.

fisticuff /ˈfɪstɪkʌf/ *verb*. Also (now *rare*) **fisty-**. M17.
[ORIGIN from FISTICUFFS.]
1 *verb trans.* Strike with the fists. M17.
2 *verb intrans.* Fight with the fists. M19.

fisticuffs /ˈfɪstɪkʌfs/ *noun pl.* Also (now *rare*) **fisty-**. E17.
[ORIGIN Prob. from FISTY + CUFF *noun*[2] + -S[1].]
Fighting with the fists.

B. CHATWIN Fifty years of fisticuffs had flattened his nose.

fistle *noun & verb* var. of FISSLE.

fistmele /ˈfɪstmiːl/ *noun*. E17.
[ORIGIN from FIST *noun*[1] + MELE measure.]
The distance from the end of the extended thumb to the opposite side of the hand, about 15 cm or 6 inches, used *spec.* in ARCHERY to gauge the correct height of the string from the braced bow. Cf. SHAFTMENT *noun*[1].

fistula /ˈfɪstjʊlə/ *noun*. Pl. **-lae** /-liː/, **-las**. LME.
[ORIGIN Latin = pipe, flute; partly through Old French *fist(u)le*, *festre* FESTER *noun*.]
1 A reed instrument or pipe of the ancient Romans. LME.
2 A long pipelike ulcer; an abnormal passage between two internal structures of the body or between one such and the surface of the body. L15. ▸**b** A passage in the body made for surgical purposes. L19.
3 A whale's spout; a slender tube in certain invertebrates. M17.
4 ECCLESIASTICAL (now *hist.*). A tube through which communicants, esp. the Pope, received the consecrated wine. L17.

fistular /ˈfɪstjʊlə/ *adjective*. LME.
[ORIGIN Old French *fistulaire* or Latin *fistularis*, formed as FISTULA: see -AR[1].]
1 = FISTULOUS 1. LME.
2 = FISTULOUS 2. E18.

fistulate /ˈfɪstjʊleɪt/ *verb*. E17.
[ORIGIN Latin *fistulat-* pa. ppl stem of *fistulare*, from FISTULA: see -ATE[3].]
†**1** *verb intrans.* Form or grow into a fistula. Only in 17.
†**2** *verb trans.* Make tubular. *rare*. Only in M18.
3 *verb trans.* VETERINARY MEDICINE. Provide with an artificial fistula. M20.

fistulose /ˈfɪstjʊləʊs/ *adjective*. LME.
[ORIGIN formed as FISTULOUS: see -OSE[1].]
= FISTULOUS.

fistulous /ˈfɪstjʊləs/ *adjective*. LME.
[ORIGIN from Latin *fistulosus*, formed as FISTULA: see -ULOUS.]
1 MEDICINE. Pertaining to or of the nature of a fistula; having a fistula. LME.
2 Esp. BOTANY. Naturally tubular or pipelike in form; having or containing a tube or tubes. L16.

fisty /ˈfɪsti/ *adjective*. Now *rare*. L17.
[ORIGIN from FIST *noun*[1] + -Y[1]. Prob. repr. earlier in FISTICUFFS.]
Of or pertaining to fists or their use in fighting.

fistycuff *verb* see FISTICUFF.

fistycuffs *noun pl.* see FISTICUFFS.

fit /fɪt/ *noun*[1]. Also **fytte**.
[ORIGIN Old English *fitt*, perh. identical with Old High German *fizza* border of cloth (German *Fitze* skein of yarn, †thread with which weavers mark off a day's work) and Old Norse *fit* hem, but cf. FIT *noun*[2].]
1 A section of a poem or song; a canto. *obsolete* exc. *hist.* OE.
2 A piece of music; a strain. *arch.* LME.

fit /fɪt/ *noun*[2].
[ORIGIN Old English *fitt*. Orig. meaning perh. 'juncture', 'meeting', 'match', which might relate this word to, or identify it with, FIT *noun*[1]: cf. FIT *adjective*, *verb*[1].]
▸ †**I 1** Conflict, struggle. Only in OE.
2 A position of danger or excitement; a (painful, pleasant, etc.) experience or fate. LME–E17. ▸**b** A mortal crisis. Only in L16.

CHAUCER This noble king . . The firste night had many a mery fitte With eche of hem. **b** SPENSER The life did flit away . . And all his senses were with deadly fit opprest.

▸ **II 3** A short period. Now only (*dial.*), a spell of weather of a specified kind. ME.

D. DYKE Which is not . . rooted, but onely for a fitte. SWIFT A fit of good weather would tempt me a week longer.

4 Orig., one of the paroxysms of a recurrent disease. Later, a short sudden attack of illness, now usu. one marked by convulsions or loss of consciousness. Also, a sudden uncontrollable outbreak of a symptom. M16. ▸†**b** *spec.* An outbreak of madness (formerly viewed as a recurrent disease). L16–E18. ▸**c** *spec.* An epileptic fit. Formerly, a fainting fit; an attack of hysteria. E18. ▸**d** *hyperbol. sing.* & in *pl.* A violent emotional reaction, as of shock or displeasure; esp. in ***have fits***, ***have a fit***, (orig. *US*) ***throw a fit***. *colloq.* M19.

SHAKES. *Jul. Caes.* He had a fever . . And when the fit was on him, I did mark How he did shake. SMOLLETT I expect to be laid up with another fit of the gout. M. SPARK Sandy affected to have a fit of spluttering coughs. **b** SHAKES. *Tit. A.* Unless some fit or frenzy do possess her. **c** B. MACDONALD He . . begun to foam . . and I seen he was in a fit. **d** DAY LEWIS You'd better not tell your Auntie or she'd have a fit.

apoplectic fit, ***epileptic fit***, ***fainting fit***, etc.
5 A sudden brief spell of (a given) activity, of inaction, of a specified feeling, etc. Also, a sudden impulse to action; a mood. L16.

H. B. STOWE When the fit was on him, he would shoe a horse better than any man. CONAN DOYLE Now he has got an energetic fit and intends to do it. P. G. WODEHOUSE He had developed fits of absent-mindedness. N. MITFORD Her attitude of . . vagueness alternating with sudden fits of severity.

6 A sudden violent outburst of laughter, tears, anger, etc. Usu. foll. by *of*. M17.

D. LESSING Maryrose and I . . burst into fits of helpless laughter. R. TRAVERS Ashe . . in a fit of temper flung it overboard.

7 HISTORY OF SCIENCE. Either of two alternating states of a light wave at any given point in its path, characterized respectively by a tendency to be reflected by a transparent body and a tendency to be transmitted by it; the coming into being of either state, as a property of the wave. E18.
– PHRASES: **beat into fits**, **beat to fits** *colloq.* defeat or excel thoroughly. **by fits**, **by fits and starts**, **in fits and starts** with irregular bursts of activity, spasmodically. **give a fit** surprise or outrage (a person). **give fits** *colloq.* defeat (a person) crushingly; *US* rebuke (a person) soundly. **in fits** in a state of hysterical amusement. ***in fits and starts***: see ***by fits and starts*** above. **into fits** into a state of hysterical amusement. ***lick into fits***: see LICK *verb*. ***throw a fit***: see THROW *verb*.

fit /fɪt/ *noun*[3]. L17.
[ORIGIN from FIT *verb*[1]. See also FIT-OUT, FIT-UP.]
1 The process of making a person fit for something. Now only *spec.* (*US*), the training of a person for college. L17.
2 The fitting or adjustment of one thing to another, esp. a garment to the body; the way in which a garment, machine part, etc., fits. E19. ▸**b** A garment etc. in respect of its fit. M19.

J. KOSINSKI The . . words meshed with each other like oiled millstones ground to a fine fit. A. LURIE The . . superb fit of their clothes. **b** CONAN DOYLE The dress . . could not have been a better fit if I had been measured for it.

fit /fɪt/ *adjective & adverb*. Compar. & superl. **-tt-**. LME.
[ORIGIN Unknown.]
▸ **A** *adjective*. †**1** Of an object: possessing the right measurements or size; fitting exactly. (Foll. by *to*.) LME–E18.

J. HARINGTON You must have a hollow key with a worm fit to that screw.

2 Adapted to the requirements of the case; appropriate, suitable. (Foll. by *for*, *to do*, *to be done*.) LME. ▸**b** BIOLOGY. Possessing or conferring the ability to survive and reproduce in a particular environment. LME.

H. PRIDEAUX What is the fittest portion of our Substance to be set apart. E. O'NEILL Is that banshee schreeching fit music for a sick man? D. CUSACK A . . divergence of opinion regarding the fit penalty to be meted out.

b ***survival of the fittest***.
3 Befitting the person or circumstances; right, proper. Now only *pred.* foll. by *to do*, *to be done*. LME. ▸†**b** Needful *to be done*. E17–M18.

W. CONGREVE 'Tis fit Men should be coy, when Women woo.

see fit, **think fit** decide or choose (*to do*, esp. an arbitrary or foolish thing).
4 In a suitable condition; prepared, ready. Exc. *dial.* now only foll. by *for*, *to do*, *to be done*. M16.

H. GLASSE They will be fit to eat in two or three days. J. CONRAD We felt . . fit for nothing but placid staring.

5 Inclined, disposed. Now usu. (*colloq. & dial.*), angry, desperate, exhausted, etc., enough *to do*. L16. ▸**b** Of a thing: likely or calculated *to do*. *colloq.* L18.

DEFOE I am fit to hang myself because I can't find it out. J. H. NEWMAN He . . keeps you standing till you are fit to sink. **b** J. CONRAD Beastly beer . . rotten stuff fit to make an old he-goat yell if you poured it down its throat.

fit to be tied in a very angry mood.
6 Of an adequate standard, sufficiently good; (of a person) qualified, competent, or worthy. (Foll. by *for*, *to do*, *to be done*.) L16.

SHAKES. *Jul. Caes.* Let's carve him as a dish fit for the gods. B. FRANKLIN This is a business I am not fit for. SCOTT FITZGERALD He wasn't fit to lick my shoe. F. L. WRIGHT The dwelling became more fit for human habitation. M. EDWARDES He came to the conclusion that my activities . . were beyond reproach and that I was a fit person to join the NEB.

7 In a suitable state for strenuous physical activity; *gen.* in good health. *colloq.* E18.

S. HILL Your digestive and nervous systems are perfect, you are fit and well. A. HAILEY He . . kept himself fit with a rigid daily exercise schedule.

fighting fit: see FIGHTING *verbal noun*. **fit as a fiddle**, **fit as a flea** extremely fit.
8 Sexually attractive, good-looking. *slang*. L20.

FHM I . . hit the jackpot and retired with my fit flatmate to her room.

▸ **B** *adverb*. **1** With a close correspondence or fit. Now *rare* or *obsolete*. LME.

W. RAND One cup would go fit into the other.

2 In a manner calculated or likely *to do*. *colloq. & dial.* E19.

F

J. C. HARRIS Clarence Bullard was there, dressed up fit to kill. W. GASS Pa laughed fit to shake the house.

fit /fɪt/ *verb*[1]. Infl. **-tt-**. Pa. t. & pple **fitted**, (*dial. & US*) **fit**. LME.
[ORIGIN from FIT *adjective* exc. in sense 1, of unknown origin.]
▸ **I** *verb trans.* †**1** Marshal, deploy, (troops). Only in LME.
2 Be suited to or appropriate for; befit. Usu. *impers.* in ***(it) fits, it is fitting***, etc. LME.

N. ROWE This Boldness does not fit a Stranger. H. SIDDONS What the contents of Middleton's letter were it fitted me not to inquire.

3 Meet the requirements of; suit. *obsolete* exc. *dial.* L16. ▸**b** In *pass.*, be suited (*dial.*). Formerly also (*refl.*), suit oneself. M17.

A. HORNECK A temptation which will fit one, will not fit another.

4 Esp. of a garment: be of the right measurements or proper shape and size for. Also (*fig.*), correspond to or accord with exactly. L16.

W. S. GILBERT To let the punishment fit the crime. QUILLER-COUCH The bullets in the . . body do not fit your pistols, but came from a larger pair. D. HAMMETT He wore . . a black overcoat that fitted him very snugly.

fit the bill: see BILL *noun*[3].
5 Bring into a suitable condition; make ready, fit, or competent. Exc. *dial.* now only foll. by *for*, *to*, *to do*. L16.

AV *Rom.* 9:22 Vessels of wrath fitted to destruction. J. BRYCE It . . does not completely fit him to weigh the real merits of statesmen. R. MACAULAY Nature had not fitted her for learning.

6 Provide (now esp. a thing) *with* what is suitable or necessary; equip. L16.

I. WALTON I wil fit him to morrow with a Trout for his breakfast. DICKENS Apartments . . which were richly fitted with a polished wood. G. B. SHAW A small kitchen table . . fitted as a writing table with an old canister full of pens.

7 Make (a thing) correspond or conform to something else, adapt, adjust, (usu. foll. by *to*); find room for. L16.

R. W. EMERSON Nature has a magic by which she fits the man to his fortunes.

8 Adjust (an object) to the contours of its receptacle or counterpart; fix, apply, etc., (an object) so that it exactly occupies a given position; try the fit of (a garment etc.). E17.

H. HUNTER The tyrant . . who fitted the unhappy traveller to his bed of iron. J. CONRAD Shades . . fitted low over all the lights imparted to the room something of a forest's deep gloom. A. J. CRONIN He took the key . . and fitted it in the lock. M. FRAYN To fit all the pieces of the jig-saw together.

9 a Give (a person) a deserved punishment; avenge oneself on, requite. Now *dial.* & *Austral.* E17. ▸**b** Secure enough (genuine or false) evidence to convict, frame. Also foll. by *up*. Orig. *Austral.* L19.

F. BURNEY With a look that implied—I'll fit you for this!

10 Provide or adapt a garment etc. to suit the measurements of (a person). L17.

L. DURRELL At the dressmaker's, being fitted for a shark-skin costume.

▸ **II** *verb intrans.* **11 a** Be proper or suitable. Usu. *impers.* in ***it fits, it is fitting***, etc. Now *rare* or *obsolete*. L16. ▸**b** Be in accord or harmonize *with*. Now *arch. rare*. L16.

a SPENSER Sometimes I joy when glad occasion fits. MILTON To appear as fits before th' illustrious lords. **b** SHAKES. *Tit. A.* Why dost thou laugh? It fits not with this hour.

12 Be of the right shape and size to occupy a given position; *fig.* be in harmony or accord with facts, circumstances, one's companions, etc. Usu. foll. by *in* (adverb & preposition), *into*, (fig.) *in with*. L17.

OED This peg fits into this hole. K. AMIS My ideas work. Because they fit in with the way life's lived. *Woman's Illustrated* How would they fit in, in this new land?

13 Esp. of a garment in relation to its wearer: be of the correct measurements. L18.

G. GREENE The doors no longer quite fitted and had to be propped at night. T. CAPOTE His suits fitted as though he had borrowed them from a stout friend.

fit like a glove: see GLOVE *noun*. ***the cap fits***: see CAP *noun*[1].
– WITH ADVERBS & PREPOSITIONS IN SPECIALIZED SENSES: **fit in** (*adverb & preposition*), **fit into** accommodate within a given space or (*fig.*) a schedule etc.; (see also sense 12 above). **fit on** adjust (a garment) to the body so that it fits exactly. **fit out** (chiefly NAUTICAL) equip with all that is necessary in the way of stores, clothing, etc. **fit up** (**a**) equip, esp. with suitable furniture or appliances; (**b**) *slang* conceal or place incriminating evidence on; (see also sense 10b above).

fit /fɪt/ *verb*[2] *trans. & intrans. Scot.* Infl. **-tt-**. L16.
[ORIGIN Var. of FOOT *verb*.]
= FOOT *verb*.
fit fair, **fit the tee** CURLING position oneself to deliver a shot at the proper distance from the far tee.

fit /fɪt/ *verb*[3]. Infl. **-tt-**. L16.
[ORIGIN from FIT *noun*[2].]
†**1** *verb trans.* Force (a thing) by paroxysms *out of* its usual position. *rare* (Shakes.). Only in L16.

SHAKES. *Sonn.* How have mine eyes out of their spheres been fitted In the distraction of this madding fever!

2 *verb intrans.* Have an epileptic fit, be seized by a fit. M20.

fitch /fɪtʃ/ *noun*[1]. *obsolete* exc. *dial.* LME.
[ORIGIN Var. of VETCH.]
A vetch, any of various plants of the genus *Vicia* and allied genera; spec. *V. sativa*, grown for fodder (usu. in *pl.*).
– NOTE: In AV *fitches* is used to render the Hebrew name of two non-leguminous cultivated plants: black cumin, *Nigella sativa* (*Isaiah* 28:25), and spelt, *Triticum spelta* (*Ezekiel* 4:9).

fitch /fɪtʃ/ *noun*[2]. LME.
[ORIGIN Early Dutch *fisse*, *visse*, *vitsche*: cf. FITCHEW.]
1 The fur or hair of the polecat. LME.
2 A polecat. Now *dial.* L15.
3 In full ***fitch-brush***. A brush made of polecat hair or hog's or other similar hair. M19.

fitch /fɪtʃ/ *noun*[3]. E20.
[ORIGIN Unknown.]
BASKET-MAKING. A kind of plait in which two canes are twisted together in the same direction so as to enclose a crossing weft at each half-turn.

fitch /fɪtʃ/ *verb*. *Scot. & N. English.* L15.
[ORIGIN App. intermediate between FYKE *verb* and FIDGE *verb*.]
1 *verb trans.* Change the place of; shift. L15.
2 *verb intrans.* Move in small spurts from place to place. E17.

fitché /ˈfɪtʃeɪ/ *adjective*. Also **-ée**, **-y**. L16.
[ORIGIN French *fiché*, *-ée* pa. ppl adjective of *ficher* to fix.]
HERALDRY. Of a cross: having its lower limb tapered to a point.

fitched /fɪtʃt/ *adjective*. M16.
[ORIGIN from FITCHÉ + -ED[1].]
HERALDRY. = FITCHÉ.

fitchée *adjective* var. of FITCHÉ.

fitchet /ˈfɪtʃɪt/ *noun*. M16.
[ORIGIN Dim. of FITCH *noun*[2]: see -ET[1].]
1 = FITCHEW. Also, a dark-coloured ferret resulting from a cross between a polecat and a ferret; a polecat-ferret. M16.
2 A weasel. *dial.* L17.

fitchet pie *noun phr.* see FIDGET PIE.

fitchew /ˈfɪtʃuː/ *noun*. LME.
[ORIGIN Old French *ficheau* dial. var. of *fissel* (pl. *fissiaulx*), later *fissau*, dim. of a word appearing in early Dutch as *fisse*, *visse*, *vitsche*, whence ult. also FITCH *noun*[2].]
1 A polecat. LME.
2 The fur of the polecat. LME.

fitchy *adjective* var. of FITCHÉ.

fitful /ˈfɪtfʊl, -f(ə)l/ *adjective*. L16.
[ORIGIN from FIT *noun*[2] + -FUL.]
†**1** Of a fever etc.: marked by fits or paroxysms. *rare*. L16–M18.

SHAKES. *Macb.* After life's fitful fever he sleeps well.

2 Marked by irregular bursts of activity or strength; spasmodic; capricious. E19.

E. MIALL The fitful and convulsive energy they have at times displayed. A. HALEY He dozed off into a fitful sleep.

■ **fitfully** *adverb* L18. **fitfulness** *noun* E19.

fitly /ˈfɪtli/ *adjective*. *rare*. L16.
[ORIGIN from FIT *adjective* + -LY[1].]
= FIT *adjective*.

fitly /ˈfɪtli/ *adverb*. M16.
[ORIGIN from FIT *adjective* + -LY[2].]
1 Suitably, appropriately. M16.
†**2** At an opportune moment. Only in E17.

AV *Prov.* 25:11 A word fitly spoken is like apples of gold.

fitment /ˈfɪtm(ə)nt/ *noun*. E17.
[ORIGIN from FIT *verb*[1] + -MENT.]
†**1** The action of making fit or ready for something. *rare* (Shakes.). Only in E17.
†**2** That which is fitting; duty. *rare* (Shakes.). Only in E17.
3 A piece of fitted or fixed furniture; a part fitted to a machine etc. Usu. in *pl.* M19.

N. BLAKE The cottage was snug enough, if somewhat austere in its fitments.

4 The process of fitting or attaching in a given position. L19.

fitna /ˈfɪtnə/ *noun*. Also **-ah**. E20.
[ORIGIN Arabic, lit. 'rebellion, strife'.]
ISLAM. Unrest or rebellion, esp. against a rightful ruler.

fitness /ˈfɪtnɪs/ *noun*. L16.
[ORIGIN from FIT *adjective* + -NESS.]
1 The quality of being suitable, qualified, or morally fit for something. L16. ▸**b** BIOLOGY. (A numerical measure of) ability to survive and reproduce in a particular environment. L16.

Time Our nominee's character or fitness for the job.

warrant of fitness: see WARRANT *noun*[1].
2 Conformity with what circumstances require; propriety. L16.
the fitness of things, **the eternal fitness of things** [orig. with ref. to the ethical theories of Samuel Clarke (1675–1729)] the natural appropriateness of the existing order of things; what is fitting or appropriate.
†**3** Readiness, inclination. *rare* (Shakes.). Only in E17.
†**4** The quality of having exactly the right measurements. M17–L18.
5 The quality or state of being physically fit. M20.

S. RUSHDIE He developed a passionate interest in fitness and gymnastics.

fit-out /ˈfɪtaʊt/ *noun*. E19.
[ORIGIN from FIT *verb*[1] + OUT *adverb*.]
The action of equipping with all that is necessary, esp. in dress; an outfit.

fitted /ˈfɪtɪd/ *ppl adjective*. E17.
[ORIGIN from FIT *verb*[1] + -ED[1].]
1 Suitable or qualified *for*, *to do*; calculated or likely *to do*. E17.

ROBERT WATSON How much . . Philip's power and character were fitted to excite jealousy. J. CAREY Being fifteen stone . . he was not well fitted for a career in ballet.

2 That has been fitted; (of a covering etc.) shaped so as to fit exactly; (of a cupboard) designed to fit a given space; (of a room, esp. a kitchen) equipped with (matching) units specially designed to fit their positions. E19.
fitted carpet: cut to cover the whole floor of a room. **fitted sheet** a bedsheet with box ends fitting closely round the mattress.
■ **fittedness** *noun* M17.

fitten /ˈfɪt(ə)n/ *noun*. Long *obsolete* exc. *dial.* Also **fitton**. LME.
[ORIGIN Unknown.]
A lie, an invention.

fitten /ˈfɪt(ə)n/ *adjective*. Now *dial.* (chiefly *US*). M17.
[ORIGIN from FIT *verb*[1] + -EN[6].]
Suitable, fit.

W. FAULKNER He would see fitten to reveal it.

fitter /ˈfɪtə/ *noun*. M17.
[ORIGIN from FIT *verb*[1] + -ER[1].]
1 *gen.* A person who or thing which fits or adapts something. M17.
2 *spec.* A person who supervises the fitting, alteration, etc., of garments. M19.
3 A mechanic who assembles or repairs machine or engine parts. M19.
4 A person employed to fix installations or appliances of any kind. M19.
gas-fitter, ***pipe-fitter***, etc.

†**fitter** *verb intrans. & trans.* LME–E17.
[ORIGIN Perh. rel. to Middle High German *vetze* (German *Fetzen*) rag, scrap: see -ER[5]. Cf. FRITTER *verb*.]
Break into very small pieces; shred.

fitters /ˈfɪtəz/ *noun pl.* *obsolete* exc. *dial.* M16.
[ORIGIN from FITTER *verb* See also FLITTERS, FRITTER *noun*[2].]
Very small pieces; fragments, smithereens.

fitting /ˈfɪtɪŋ/ *noun*. E17.
[ORIGIN from FIT *verb*[1] + -ING[1].]
1 The action of FIT *verb*[1]; *spec.* (**a**) the action or an act of fitting a garment to the wearer by a tailor or dressmaker; (**b**) the assembling and adjusting of machine parts. E17.
2 Something fitted; a piece of apparatus or furniture, a fixture. Usu. in *pl.* E19.

S. DELANEY The landlady pointed it out to me as part of the furniture and fittings.

– COMB.: **fitting room**: in which a garment etc. is fitted to the wearer; **fitting shop** a place where machine parts are put together.

fitting /ˈfɪtɪŋ/ *ppl adjective*. LME.
[ORIGIN from FIT *verb*[1] + -ING[2].]
1 Becoming, proper, appropriate. LME.

B. T. WASHINGTON In order that the distinguished visitor might have a fitting reception.

2 Adjusted exactly to the contours of something. Now only with prefixed adverb, as ***close-fitting***. M16.
■ **fittingly** *adverb* M17. **fittingness** *noun* M17.

fitton *noun* var. of FITTEN *noun*.

fitty /ˈfɪti/ *adjective*. *obsolete* exc. *dial.* L16.
[ORIGIN Prob. from FIT *adjective*, *verb*[1] or + -Y[1], but perh. partly alt. of FEATY.]
Fitting, becoming; neat, trim.

fit-up /ˈfɪtʌp/ *noun*. *slang*. M19.
[ORIGIN from FIT *verb*[1] + UP *adverb*[1].]
1 A stage or other theatrical accessory that can be fitted up for the occasion. M19. ▸**b** In full ***fit-up company***. A touring company which carries such properties with it. L19.
2 An act of concealing or placing incriminating evidence on a person. L20.

fitz /fɪts/ *noun. obsolete* exc. *hist.* **ME.**
[**ORIGIN** Anglo-Norman spelling of Old French *fiz*, earlier *filz* (mod. *fils*), from Latin *filius* son.]
A son. Chiefly in patronymic designations, surviving as an elem. in surnames, e.g. ***Fitzherbert***, ***Fitzwilliam***, latterly sometimes bestowed on the illegitimate sons of princes.

J. WEST The contentions of Henry Fitz-empress with Eleanora of Guienne.

FitzGerald /fɪts'dʒɛr(ə)ld/ *adjective.* **E20.**
[**ORIGIN** G. F. *FitzGerald* (1851–1901), Irish physicist.]
SCIENCE. ***FitzGerald contraction***, ***FitzGerald effect***, ***FitzGerald–Lorentz contraction***, ***FitzGerald–Lorentz effect*** [**LORENTZ**], the relativistic foreshortening, in the direction of motion, of a body moving relative to the observer.

fiumara /fjuː'mɑːrə/ *noun.* **E19.**
[**ORIGIN** Italian.]
(The dried bed of) a mountain torrent, esp. in Italy.

five /fʌɪv/ *adjective & noun* (*cardinal numeral*).
[**ORIGIN** Old English *fīf* = Old Frisian, Old Saxon *fīf* (Dutch *vijf*), Old High German *fimf*, *finf* (German *fünf*), Old Norse *fimm*, Gothic *fimf*, from Germanic from Indo-European, whence also Latin *quinque*, Greek *pente*, Sanskrit *pañca*.]
▸ **A** *adjective.* One more than four (a cardinal numeral represented by 5 in arabic numerals, v, V in roman). **OE.**

G. GREENE A hand . . with five pennies in the palm.

five orders: see **ORDER** *noun*. **five positions** *BALLET* the five basic positions of the feet, with one of which most steps begin and end; the five corresponding positions of the arms. ***the five K's***: see **K**, **K** 1. ***the Five Nations***: see **NATION** *noun*[1]. ***the five senses***: see **SENSE** *noun* 8. ***the five wits***: see **WIT** *noun*. ***the Five Wounds***: see **WOUND** *noun*.
▸ **B** *noun.* **1** Five persons or things identified contextually, as parts or divisions, years of age, points, runs, etc., in a game, chances (in giving odds), minutes, inches, shillings (now *hist.*), pence, etc. **OE.**

E. BLYTON The five in the little cart all talked at once.

know how many beans make five: see **BEAN** *noun*. **take five** *colloq.* take a five-minute break; take a short break, relax.
2 One more than four as an abstract number; the symbol or figure representing this (5 in arabic numerals, v, V in roman). **OE.**

L. EGAN What else looks like an S except a five?

3 A set of five; a thing having a set of five as an essential or distinguishing feature; *spec.* (**a**) a playing card, domino, or face of a die marked with five pips or spots; (**b**) a five-pound note, a five-dollar bill. **LME.**

A. TYLER 'How would you like that, sir?' . . 'Fives and ones.'

bunch of fives *slang* a hand, a fist.
4 The fifth of a set or series with numbered members, the one designated five, (usu. ***number five***, or with specification, as ***book five***, ***chapter five***, etc.); a size etc. denoted by five, a shoe, glove, garment, etc., of such a size, (also ***size five***). **E16.**

R. KIPLING Number Five was unpacking.

Radio Five: see **RADIO** *noun* 3.
5 The time of day five hours after midnight or midday (on a clock, watch, etc., indicated by the numeral five displayed or pointed to). Also ***five o'clock***. **M16.**

R. L. STEVENSON Where all the children dine at five.

– **COMB.**: Forming compound cardinal numerals with multiples of ten from twenty to ninety, as ***thirty-five***, (arch.) ***five-and-thirty***, etc., and (*arch.*) their corresponding ordinals, as ***five-and-thirtieth***, etc., and with multiples of a hundred, as ***205*** (read ***two hundred and five***, US also ***two hundred five***), etc. With nouns + **-ER**[1] forming nouns with the sense 'something (identified contextually) being of or having five —s', as ***five-seater*** etc. Special combs., as **five-and-dime (store)**, **five-and-ten (cent store)** *N. Amer.* a cheap store (orig. one where all the articles were priced at five or ten cents); **five-corner** *sing.* & (usu.) in *pl.*, (the fruit of) any of several shrubs of the Australian coast of the genus *Styphelia*; **five-eighth** in Austral. & NZ rugby football, a player between the halfback and the three-quarter; **five finger** (*a*) *sing.* & in *pl.*, any of various plants, *esp.* cinquefoil (also ***five-finger grass***); (*b*) a starfish with the usual five arms; (*c*) ***five-finger exercise***, an exercise on the piano for all the fingers; *fig.* an easy task; (*d*) ***five-finger discount*** (US slang), (the proceeds of) stealing or shoplifting; **five hundred** a form of euchre in which 500 points make a game; **five-leaf** (long *rare*) cinquefoil; **five-lined** *adjective* consisting of or marked with five lines; **five o'clock shadow** beard growth which is visible on a man's face after about 5 p.m.; ***five o'clock tea***: see **TEA** *noun* 5(a); **fivepence** (*a*) five pence, esp. of the old British currency before decimalization; ***as fine as fivepence*** (arch. colloq.), very smart; (cf. **FIPPENCE**); (*b*) (usu. two words) since 1968, a coin worth five (new) pence; **fivepenny** *adjective* worth or costing fivepence; (cf. **FIPPENNY**); **Five Pillars of Islam** the five foundations upon which the religion of Islam rests, shahada, salat, zakat, sawm, and hajj. **fivepin bowling**, **fivepins** a game in which five pins or skittles are set up and bowled at to be knocked down; **five-spice mix**, **five-spice powder** a mixture of ground sweet spices, used esp. in Chinese cookery; **five-star** *adjective* (*a*) given five stars in a grading, esp. where this indicates the highest quality; (*b*) having or being a military rank that is distinguished by five stars on the shoulder piece of the uniform; **fivestones** jacks played with five stones; **five-year plan** a plan for the economic development of a country spread over five years, *esp.* the plan for the economic development of the former USSR, inaugurated in 1928.
■ **fivefold** *adjective & adverb* (*a*) *adjective* five times as great or as numerous; having five parts, divisions, elements, or units; (*b*) *adverb* to five times the number or quantity: **OE. fiver** *noun* (*colloq.*) a five-pound note, a five-dollar bill: **M19. fivesome** *noun* a set of five persons or things; a game (esp. of golf) for five players: **LME.**

fives /fʌɪvz/ *noun*[1]. **M17.**
[**ORIGIN** Pl. of **FIVE** treated as sing.: ult. significance unkn.]
A game in which a ball is struck by a gloved hand or a bat against one wall of a court.
Eton fives: see **ETON** 5. ***Rugby fives***: see **RUGBY** 2. ***Winchester fives***: see **WINCHESTER** *noun* 1.

†**fives** *noun*[2] *pl.* var. of **VIVES**.

fix /fɪks/ *noun.* **E19.**
[**ORIGIN** from the verb.]
1 A position from which it is difficult to escape, a predicament. *colloq.* **E19.**

TOLKIEN To find ourselves in the same fix or a worse one. G. M. FRASER Our little party was in an appalling fix.

2 Condition, state; (working) order. *US colloq.* **E19.**

H. WOODRUFF In getting a whole stable of horses into fix to trot races.

3 The material used for lining a puddling furnace. **L19.**
4 (A reliable indication of) the position of an aircraft, a ship, etc., found by bearings or astronomical observation; the action of obtaining such an indication; *transf.* an assessment or identification (of location, size, price, etc.). **E20.**

F. CHICHESTER I got a sun fix with the sextant. M. AMIS Five days of London time and still no fix on Selina.

radio fix the position of a ship, aircraft, etc., found by radio. ***running fix***: see **RUNNING** *ppl adjective*.
5 A bribe, bribery; an illicit arrangement. *slang.* **E20.**

E. D. SULLIVAN It's impossible to scare tough hombres who can get $55 a barrel for beer that costs them $7. There's plenty leeway for the 'fix'. M. KINGTON The Peruvians have always claimed that the result was a fix and demanded a replay.

6 A dose of a narcotic drug, *esp.* one (to be) taken by an addict. *slang.* **M20.**

J. KEROUAC Bull was . . taking his fix . . jabbing with the needle into his . . arm. I. MURDOCH He needed her as a drug addict needs his fix.

7 The action of fixing or determining something, *spec.* the price of gold; the time at which such fixing takes place. **L20.**

†**fix** *adjective.* **LME–L17.**
[**ORIGIN** Old French (mod. *fixe*) or its source Latin *fixus*: see **FIX** *verb*.]
Fixed.

fix /fɪks/ *verb.* **LME.**
[**ORIGIN** Partly from **FIX** *adjective*, partly from medieval Latin *fixare*, from Latin *fixus* pa. pple of *figere* fix, fasten.]
▸ **I 1** *verb trans.* Fasten, make firm or stable in position; place; attach (a bayonet) to the muzzle of a rifle etc.; secure against displacement; implant (principles, memory, etc.). Freq. foll. by *in*, *on*, *to*. **LME.** ▸**b** *verb intrans.* Become firmly attached or implanted; adhere *to*. Now *rare* or *obsolete*. **L17.** ▸**c** *verb trans. GENETICS.* Establish (a character, or the gene responsible for it) as a permanent property of subsequent generations. **E20.**

E. HALL His head to be fixed on a pole. E. BUDGELL I resolved . . to fix his face in my memory. **b** S. RICHARDSON Prejudices in disfavour . . fix deeper . . than prejudices in favour.

2 *verb trans.* Direct steadily and unwaveringly; set (the eyes, gaze, affections, attention) *on*, *upon*. Also attract and hold (the eyes, gaze, attention, etc.). **LME.** ▸**b** Make motionless with astonishment etc., hold spellbound. Now *rare*. **M16.** ▸**c** Make (the eyes, features, etc.) rigid, as in death. **E19.**

T. HERBERT Could but these Idolaters fix their mind upon Heaven. BYRON A shrine would fix The eye upon its seeming crucifix. **c** SHELLEY Fix those tortured orbs in peace and death.

3 *verb trans.* Deprive of volatility or fluidity. Orig. *spec.* in *ALCHEMY*, cause (a volatile spirit or essence) to combine with a tangible solid or liquid. **L15.** ▸**b** (Of a plant or bacterium) assimilate (nitrogen or carbon dioxide) by converting it into a non-gaseous compound; *gen.* cause (an element) to form a compound. **M19.** ▸**c** Preserve and harden (tissue etc.), esp. for microscopic examination. **L19.**
4 *verb intrans.* Lose volatility or fluidity; congeal. Now *rare* or *obsolete*. **E17.**
5 *verb trans.* Secure from change, vacillation, or wandering; give stability or constancy to (the mind, thoughts, affections, purposes). **E17.** ▸**b** Settle immovably the purposes or convictions of. Foll. by *against*, *for*, *on*, *to do*. Now only in *pass.* **L17.** ▸**c** Make constant in devotion. (Foll. by *in*, *to*.) Now *rare* or *obsolete*. **E18.**

BACON Images are said by the Roman church to fix the cogitations . . of them that pray before them. **c** J. AUSTEN If a woman conceals her affection . . from the object of it, she may lose the opportunity of fixing him.

6 *verb trans.* Make (a colour, a drawing, a photographic image, etc.) fast and permanent. **M17.**
7 *verb trans.* Hold engaged or occupied, corner (*lit.* & *fig.*). Also, single out *with* one's eyes etc. **M17.**

S. RICHARDSON As I entered one Room he went into another . . At last I fixed him speaking to Rachel.

▸ **II 8** *verb trans.* Place definitely or more or less permanently; station, establish; locate; set *up*. *colloq.* **M16.** ▸**b** Foll. by *up*: arrange the accommodation of (a person); attend to the wants of; provide *with*. **L19.**

T. TWINING The dining-table was fixed in the middle of the room. SOUTHEY We are fixed here for some time. **b** R. C. PRAED He'd . . fix up Mr. Sabine comfortably for the night.

9 *verb intrans.* **a** Take up one's position mentally. Now *rare* or *obsolete*. **E17.** ▸**b** Foll. by *on*, *upon*: settle one's choice on, choose, select. **M17.** ▸**c** Decide, determine, *to do*, arrange *for doing*. **L18.**

b H. J. BROOKE Our choice would probably fix on that which was most predominant. **c** J. KEBLE I have fixed to go to London.

10 *verb intrans.* Settle, esp. permanently, take up one's position or abode. *arch.* **E17.**

GOLDSMITH Where luxury once fixes, no art can either lessen or remove it.

11 *verb trans.* Appoint or assign the precise position or time of; refer (a thing) to a definite place, time, etc. Formerly also, attribute exclusively *to*. **M17.** ▸**b** Allocate or determine the incidence of (a responsibility, liability, etc.). Also, burden (a person) *with* costs, liability, etc. **M19.**

S. JOHNSON Here will I fix the limits of transgression. J. H. NEWMAN The full moon is not fixed to any certain day in either month.

12 *verb trans.* Settle definitely; specify, determine, (a thing, *that*); settle or determine the form of, give a permanent form to, arrest changes or development in (language, literature, etc.). **M17.**

SWIFT Some Method . . for ascertaining and fixing our Language for ever. SOUTHEY It was . . fixed that the brigadier should go. E. A. PARKES The War Office authorities have fixed the daily supply . . at 8 gallons.

fix a person's fate: see **FATE** *noun*.
13 *verb trans.* Adjust, make ready for use, arrange in proper order, organize. Also get ready, put in order, tidy; prepare (food or drink); apply cosmetics to. Also foll. by *up*. **M17.** ▸**b** Mend, repair; redecorate; alter with the purpose of improvement. Also foll. by *up*. **M18.** ▸**c** Obtain the support of (a person) by illegal or dubious means, esp. bribery; arrange (the result of a match etc.) fraudulently. **L18.** ▸**d** Arrange favourably for oneself; deal with, silence, kill (a person). *slang.* **M19.** ▸**e** Castrate or spay (an animal). **M20.**

B. HARTE Mother'll fix you suthin' hot. G. VIDAL She . . fixed her face in a compact mirror. **b** G. STEIN The smell of paint when they were fixing up the kitchen. **c** J. BETJEMAN I fix the Planning Officer . . and the Mayor. *Guardian* The mere suspicion that matches were being 'fixed' would be disastrous for the game. **d** O. W. HOLMES If you can't fix it so as to be born here [Boston], you can come and live here. P. G. WODEHOUSE 'Don't you worry. I'll fix him.' . . 'You wouldn't croak him?' **e** D. H. LAWRENCE Is he a gentleman or a lady?—Neither, . . I had him fixed.

14 *verb intrans.* **a** Intend, arrange, make preparations *to do*. Also foll. by *up*. **E18.** ▸**b** Put oneself in proper trim; dress up, smarten up. Also foll. by *up*. **L18.**

a J. B. PRIESTLEY I may be able to fix up for you both to go out to supper afterwards. E. WELTY I think she was fixing to pull him out of that bed. **b** W. FAULKNER You better go to the bathroom and fix up.

15 *verb trans.* Fettle, line (a puddling furnace) with a fix. **L19.**
16 *verb intrans.* & *refl.* Inject oneself with a narcotic drug. *slang.* **M20.**
■ **fixable**, **-ible** *adjective* **L15.**

fixate /fɪk'seɪt/ *verb.* **L19.**
[**ORIGIN** from Latin *fixus* (see **FIX** *adjective*) + **-ATE**[3].]
1 *verb trans.* Fix, make stable. Now *rare*. **L19.**
2 *verb intrans.* Be or become fixed. **L19.**

O. SACKS Their eyes roll for a moment, and then fixate.

3 *verb trans.* Direct one's eyes on, concentrate one's gaze directly on. **L19.**

D. MORRIS The baby's eyes can now fixate objects.

4 *PSYCHOLOGY.* Arrest (part of one's libido) at an immature stage, causing an abnormal attachment to persons or things and abnormal emotional responses; cause (a person) to undergo this. Also *loosely*, in *pass.*, be or become obsessed with. Freq. foll. by *on*. **E20.**

W. McDOUGALL The *libido* . . of every child normally becomes fixated upon the parent of the opposite sex. R. QUIRK We mustn't get fixated on the reception of contemporary fiction.

F

fixation /fɪkˈseɪʃ(ə)n/ *noun*. LME.
[ORIGIN medieval Latin *fixatio(n-)*, from *fixat-* pa. ppl stem of *fixare*: see FIX *verb*, -ATION.]
1 SCIENCE & MEDICINE. The action or process of fixing; *spec.* conversion, now esp. of nitrogen, to a non-gaseous form; immobilization of a limb, a fractured bone, a joint, or a displaced or floating organ. LME.
†**2** The quality or condition of being non-volatile or able to resist the action of fire. E17–E18.
3 A fixed proportion or standard. Formerly also, a fixed habitation or location. Now *rare*. E17.
T. FULLER Far . . from Ipswich his first fixation. B. FRANKLIN No . . invariable fixation for coining can be made.
4 *gen.* The action or an act of fixing; the fact or condition of being fixed. M17.
J. BENTHAM The fixation of the punishment not lying within the province of the jury. CARLYLE Yet it had attained no fixation or consistency.
5 The action or an act of concentrating the gaze directly on an object. L19.
G. F. STOUT The fixation of images is not accompanied by overt movement.
6 PSYCHOLOGY. The arresting of part of the libido at an immature stage, causing an abnormal attachment to persons or things and abnormal emotional responses; *loosely* an obsession, concentration on one idea. (Foll. by *on*.) E20.
M. HUNTER Publishers with fixations on stories of English boarding-school life.

fixative /ˈfɪksətɪv/ *adjective & noun*. M17.
[ORIGIN from FIX *verb* + -ATIVE.]
▸ **A** *adjective*. Tending to set or fix something, used for fixing. M17.
▸ **B** *noun*. A substance used to set or fix something, as colours or drawings, hair, biological material before microscopic examination, volatile components of perfumes, etc. L19.

fixature /ˈfɪksətʃə/ *noun*. Now *rare*. M19.
[ORIGIN from FIX *verb* after *curvature* etc.]
A preparation used to hold hair in position.

fixed /fɪkst/ *ppl adjective*. Also (*arch.*) **fixt**. LME.
[ORIGIN from FIX *verb* + -ED[1].]
1 Definitely and permanently placed or assigned; stationary or unchanging in relative position; definite, permanent, lasting. LME.
MILTON In which of all these Orbes hath Man His fixed seat. C. THIRLWALL A fixt and uniform rent. M. PATTISON Every Hanse town was in its turn represented, according to a fixed cycle. B. JOWETT Colours which are dyed in this way become fixed. P. CAREY To . . disappear like the image on an improperly fixed photograph.
2 **a** Directed steadily or intently towards an object. M16. ▸**b** Made rigid or immobile (as in strong emotion or by death). M17.
a A. RADCLIFFE He regarded her with a fixed attention. R. WEST Under Kitty's fixed gaze I had to open a letter. **b** H. MARTINEAU The papers in his hand shook; but his countenance was fixed.
3 Placed or attached firmly (*lit. & fig.*); made firm or stable in position. Also (now *rare*), resolved, intent, or set on something. L16. ▸**b** HERALDRY. Of a cross: having the limbs attached to the edges of the escutcheon. *rare*. L17.
LD MACAULAY For all persecution he felt a fixed aversion.
4 **a** Not easily volatilized; deprived of volatility. M17. ▸**b** Unable to be distilled or evaporated without decomposition. E19.
5 Prepared, put in order. Now *rare*. M17.
6 *pred.* Situated (*well, badly*, etc.) in material or financial terms; (foll. by *for*) situated with regard to. *colloq.* M19.
M. LAURENCE Not wealthy, perhaps, but certainly nicely fixed.
7 Corrupted, bribed; having the result fraudulently prearranged. *slang*. L19.
L. STEFFENS Being in with the stables, I soon began to hear about 'fixed races'.
– SPECIAL COLLOCATIONS & COMB.: *fixed capital*: see CAPITAL *noun*[2] 2; **fixed focus** a camera focus at a distance from the lens that is not adjustable; **fixed idea** = IDÉE FIXE. **fixed income** income from a pension, investment, etc., that is set at a particular figure and does not rise with the rate of inflation; **fixed odds** odds in betting that are predetermined; **fixed oil** a non-volatile oil; **fixed point** (*a*) PHYSICS a well-defined reproducible temperature, usu. that of a change of phase, used for calibration or for defining a temperature scale; (*b*) MATH. a point that is unchanged by a given transformation or by each of a given set of transformations; (*c*) a time of day at which a particular item is always broadcast, the rest of the programme schedule being devised so as to accommodate it; (*d*) COMPUTING, used *attrib.* to designate a mode of representing a number by a single sequence of digits whose values depend on their location relative to a radix point in a predetermined position in the sequence; **fixed star** a star as now commonly understood, with a seemingly unchanging position relative to the other stars (in contrast to planets, comets, and meteors); **fixed-wing** *adjective* designating aircraft of the conventional type as opp. to rotating-wing aircraft such as helicopters.
■ **fixedly** /ˈfɪksɪdli/ *adverb* L16. **fixedness** /ˈfɪksɪdnɪs/ *noun* E17.

†**fixen** *noun* var. of VIXEN.

fixer /ˈfɪksə/ *noun*. E17.
[ORIGIN from FIX *verb* + -ER[1].]
1 A person who fixes something; *spec.* a person who makes (esp. illicit) arrangements or bargains. E17.
2 A thing which fixes something; *spec.* a substance for fixing photographic images etc. M19.
– COMB.: **fixer-upper** *N. Amer. colloq.* a house in need of repairs, esp. one that is for sale.

fixidity /fɪkˈsɪdɪti/ *noun*. Now *rare*. M18.
[ORIGIN from FIX *adjective* or FIXED after *fluidity*: see -ITY.]
Fixity.

fixing /ˈfɪksɪŋ/ *noun*. E17.
[ORIGIN from FIX *verb* + -ING[1].]
1 *gen.* The action of FIX *verb*; a thing which fixes something. E17. ▸**b** A method or means of fixing. *rare*. M17.
2 In *pl.* Apparatus, equipment; the trimmings of a dress or dish; adjuncts. E19.

fixit /ˈfɪksɪt/ *noun*. E20.
[ORIGIN from FIX *verb* + IT *pronoun*.]
1 = FIXER 1. Esp. as a pseudo-surname in ***Miss Fixit***, ***Mr Fixit***, etc. E20.
2 The action or an act of fixing something. M20.

fixity /ˈfɪksɪti/ *noun*. M17.
[ORIGIN Partly from FIX *adjective* + -ITY, partly through French *fixité*.]
1 The property of a substance of not evaporating or losing weight when heated. Now *rare* or *obsolete*. M17.
2 *gen.* The condition of not being liable to displacement or change; the quality of being fixed; stability, permanence; an instance of this, a permanent thing. L18.

fixt *ppl adjective* see FIXED.

fixture /ˈfɪkstʃə, -tjə/ *noun*. L16.
[ORIGIN Alt. of FIXURE after *mixture*.]
1 The action of fixing; the process of becoming fixed. Now *rare* or *obsolete*. L16. ▸**b** The condition of being fixed; fixedness, fixity. E19.
SHAKES. *Merry W.* The firm fixture of thy foot would give an excellent motion to thy gait.
2 LAW. In *pl.* Accessory articles annexed to a house or piece of land and regarded as legally part of it. M18.
3 In *pl.* Appendages, adjuncts; apparatus. *N. Amer.* M18.
J. C. OATES It had . . swivel-type reading lamps and mahogany fixtures.
4 Anything fixed or securely fastened in position; anything made firm, stable, or immobile. L18.
5 A person or thing confined to or established in one place. Chiefly *pred.* L18.
L. AUCHINCLOSS For twenty-five years I've been a fixture in her home.
6 A (date agreed for a) meeting, appointment, etc.; *esp.* (the date appointed for) a sporting event, as a match, race, etc. E19.
CLIVE JAMES My afternoon fixture in Hiroshima, the Toyo Kogyo plant. *Football Monthly* West Ham still have a third of their home fixtures remaining.

fixure /ˈfɪkʃə, -sjʊə/ *noun*. Long *arch. rare*. E17.
[ORIGIN Late Latin *fixura*, from Latin *figere* FIX *verb*: see -URE.]
Fixed condition, position, or attitude; fixedness, stability.

fiz *noun, verb* see FIZZ *noun, verb*.

fizgig /ˈfɪzɡɪɡ/ *noun*[1] *& adjective*. Also **fis-**, (in sense 5) **phiz-**. E16.
[ORIGIN Prob. from FIZZ *verb* + GIG *noun*[1].]
▸ **A** *noun*. **1** A flighty or flirtatious young woman. *arch.* E16.
2 A kind of whirligig or spinning top. *rare*. M17.
3 A kind of small firework, a cracker. *arch.* M17.
4 A piece of tawdry finery. Also, a silly notion. *arch.* E19.
5 An informer. *Austral. slang*. L19.
▸ **B** *adjective*. Flighty. *arch.* E20.

fizgig /ˈfɪzɡɪɡ/ *noun*[2]. Long *rare*. See also FISHGIG. M16.
[ORIGIN Prob. ult. from Spanish *fisga* harpoon.]
A kind of harpoon.

fizz /fɪz/ *noun*. Also (now *rare*) **fiz**. M18.
[ORIGIN from the verb.]
1 A disturbance, a fuss. Long *rare* or *obsolete*. M18.
2 A hissing or spluttering sound. E19.
3 High spirits, dash, animation. *arch.* M19.
4 An effervescent drink, *esp.* champagne. *colloq.* M19.
– COMB.: **fizz-boat** *NZ* a motor boat, a speedboat.

fizz /fɪz/ *verb*. Also (now *rare*) **fiz**, infl. **-zz-**. M17.
[ORIGIN Imit.]
†**1** *verb trans.* Cause to make a fizz. Only in M17.
2 *verb intrans.* Make a hissing or spluttering sound; move with a fizzing sound. L17.
3 *verb intrans.* Foll. by *out*: fade or die away. M19.

fizzer /ˈfɪzə/ *noun*. M19.
[ORIGIN from FIZZ *verb, noun* + -ER[1].]
1 An excellent or first-rate thing. M19.
2 = FIZZ *noun* 4. *rare*. L19.
3 CRICKET. A very fast ball; a ball that deviates with unexpected speed after pitching. *colloq.* E20.
4 A charge sheet. *military slang*. M20.
5 A disappointing failure, a fiasco. *Austral. & NZ slang*. M20.

fizzle /ˈfɪz(ə)l/ *verb & noun*. LME.
[ORIGIN Imit.: see FIZZ *verb*, -LE[3]. Cf. FISSLE.]
▸ **A** *verb intrans.* †**1** Break wind quietly. LME–M18.
2 Make a feeble hissing or spluttering sound. M19.
3 Fail, end in a fiasco; reach a lame conclusion. Freq. foll. by *out*. M19.
▸ **B** *noun*. †**1** The action of breaking wind quietly. L16–M18.
2 (The action of making) a feeble hissing or spluttering sound. M19.
3 A failure, a fiasco, a lame conclusion. Also foll. by *out*. M19.

fizzy /ˈfɪzi/ *adjective*. M19.
[ORIGIN from FIZZ *verb* + -Y[1].]
(Given to) fizzing; effervescent.
■ **fizzily** *adverb* L20. **fizziness** *noun* L20.

fjeld /fjɛld/ *noun*. M19.
[ORIGIN Norwegian (Bokmål) *fjeld* from Old Norse *fjall*: see FELL *noun*[2].]
A high barren rocky plateau, esp. in Scandinavia.

FJI *abbreviation*.
Fellow of the Institute of Journalists.

fjord /fjɔːd/ *noun*. Also **fiord**. L17.
[ORIGIN Norwegian from Old Norse *fjǫrðr*. Cf. FIRTH *noun*[2], FORD *noun*.]
A long, narrow, deep inlet of the sea between steep cliffs, as on the Norwegian coast (now ascribed to erosion by glaciers).

FL *abbreviation*.
Florida.

fl. *abbreviation*.
1 Latin *floruit* he or she flourished.
2 Fluid.

Fla *abbreviation*.
Florida.

flab /flab/ *noun*. E19.
[ORIGIN Sense 1 alt. of FLAP *noun*; sense 2 back-form. from FLABBY.]
1 = FLAP *noun* 6b. *dial.* E19.
2 Flabbiness; bodily fat. *colloq.* M20.
K. GILES She looks pretty good . . no flab round the thighs yet.

flabbergast /ˈflabəɡɑːst/ *verb trans. colloq.* L18.
[ORIGIN Unknown.]
Dumbfound, confound, astonish. Freq. as ***flabbergasted*** *ppl adjective*.
R. PARK She gave a screech of astonishment and flopped into a chair, completely flabbergasted.

flabby /ˈflabi/ *adjective*. L17.
[ORIGIN Expressive alt. of FLAPPY.]
1 Chiefly of flesh: hanging down, through its own weight; flaccid, limp. Of a person etc.: overweight. L17.
J. GALSWORTHY Thanks to abstemious habits, he had not grown fat and flabby.
2 Of language, character, etc.: weak, lacking vigour. L18.
3 Damp, clammy. Now *rare*. L18.
■ **flabbily** *adverb* M19. **flabbiness** *noun* E18.

flabellate /fləˈbɛleɪt/ *adjective*. E19.
[ORIGIN from Latin *flabellum* fan + -ATE[2].]
BOTANY & ZOOLOGY. Fan-shaped.

flabelliform /fləˈbɛlɪfɔːm/ *adjective*. L18.
[ORIGIN formed as FLABELLATE + -I- + -FORM.]
= FLABELLATE.

flabellum /fləˈbɛləm/ *noun*. Pl. **-lla** /-lə/. M19.
[ORIGIN Latin, from *flabrum* gust, from *flare* to blow: see -ELLUM.]
A fan; *esp.* one carried in religious ceremonies.

flaccid /ˈflaksɪd, ˈflasɪd/ *adjective*. E17.
[ORIGIN French *flaccide* or Latin *flaccidus*, from *flaccus* flabby: see -ID[1].]
1 Of flesh etc.: lacking stiffness, hanging or lying loose or in wrinkles, flabby, limp. E17. ▸**b** BOTANY. Bending without elasticity; relaxed from lack of moisture, drooping. E17.
H. WILLIAMSON Further exercises brought the aching flaccid muscles back into tension.
2 Of an abstract thing: lacking vigour, feeble. M17.
F. W. FARRAR His resolutions have been feeble, and his purposes flaccid. R. C. HUTCHINSON The flaccid voice of one whose reserves are long overdrawn.
■ **flaccidity** /flәkˈsɪdɪti, fləˈsɪ-/ *noun* L17. **flaccidly** *adverb* M19. **flaccidness** *noun* E18.

flacherie /ˈflaʃ(ə)riː/ *noun*. L19.
[ORIGIN French = flaccidity.]
An infectious disease of silkworms marked by digestive disorders and bodily flaccidity.

Flacian /ˈfleɪʃɪən/ *noun & adjective*. M16.
[ORIGIN from *Flacius* (see below) + -AN.]
▸ **A** *noun*. A follower of Matthias Flacius (1520–75), a Lutheran theologian, who opposed the adiaphorist views advocated by Melanchthon; an anti-adiaphorist. M16.

▸ **B** *adjective*. Of or pertaining to Matthias Flacius or his followers. L19.
■ **Flacianist** *noun* L19.

flack /flak/ *noun*[1]. *slang* (chiefly *US*). M20.
[ORIGIN Unknown.]
A press agent; a publicity man. Also ***flackman***.
■ **flackery** *noun* public relations, promotion, hype M20.

flack *noun*[2] var. of FLAK.

flack /flak/ *verb*[1]. *obsolete* exc. *dial.* LME.
[ORIGIN Imit.; = Middle Dutch *vlacken*, Old Norse *flaka* (of a wound) gape, Icelandic *flaka* to flap, hang loose.]
1 *verb intrans.* Flap, flutter; flap the wings; palpitate. LME.
2 *verb trans.* Move or shake intermittently; flap, flick. M18.
3 *verb trans.* Beat with a flail; rake (hay). M18.
4 *verb intrans.* Hang loosely. *dial.* E19.

flack /flak/ *verb*[2]. *N. Amer. colloq.* M20.
[ORIGIN from FLACK *noun*[1].]
1 *verb intrans.* Act as a flack, disseminate favourable publicity. M20.
2 *verb trans.* Speak in favour of, promote (a person or thing); disseminate (information etc.). L20.

flacker /ˈflakə/ *verb intrans.* & (*rare*) *trans.* Now chiefly *dial.* LME.
[ORIGIN Prob. rel. to Old English *flacor* adjective (of arrows) flying, from imit. base repr. also by Middle High German *vlackern* flicker (German *flackern*), Old Norse *flǫkra*, *flǫkta* flutter. Cf. FLICKER *verb*.]
Flap (the wings), flutter.

flacket /ˈflakɪt/ *noun*. *obsolete* exc. *dial.* ME.
[ORIGIN Old Northern French *flasquet*, dim. of *flasque*: see FLASK *noun*, -ET[1].]
A flask, bottle, or vessel; *esp.* a barrel-shaped liquor vessel.

flacon /flakɔ̃/ *noun*. Pl. pronounced same. E19.
[ORIGIN French: see FLAGON.]
A small stoppered bottle; *esp.* one for scent or smelling salts.

fladge /fladʒ/ *noun*. *slang*. M20.
[ORIGIN Abbreviation.]
= FLAGELLATION 2b.

flag /flag/ *noun*[1]. LME.
[ORIGIN Rel. to Dutch *flag*, Danish *flæg*: ult. origin unknown.]
1 Any of various plants, *esp.* irises, with sword-shaped leaves; *esp.* (more fully ***water flag***, ***yellow flag***) a yellow-flowered Eurasian iris, *Iris pseudacorus*, common in streams and pools. LME. ▸**b** In *pl.* or *collect.* A kind of coarse grass. L16.

AV *Job* 8:11 Can the rush growe vp without myre? can the flag growe without water?

sweet flag: see SWEET *adjective & adverb*.
2 The blade or long slender leaf of a cereal or other plant. L16.

R. JEFFERIES The wheat was then showing a beautiful flag.

– COMB.: **flag-root** *N. Amer.* (the root of) sweet flag, *Acorus calamus*.

flag /flag/ *noun*[2]. LME.
[ORIGIN Prob. of Scandinavian origin: cf. Icelandic *flag* spot where a turf has been cut out, Old Norse *flaga* slab of stone.]
1 A piece of turf; a sod; a slice of earth turned over by the plough. Also *collect.*, turf; ploughed earth. Long *dial.* LME.
2 A flat slab of any fine-grained rock which may be split into flagstones; a flagstone; (in *pl.*) a pavement or floor of flagstones. LME.

G. JONES The sound of his boots on the kitchen flags. *comb.*: W. J. LOCKE A narrow flag-paved street.

flag /flag/ *noun*[3]. L15.
[ORIGIN Unknown.]
A quill feather of a bird's wing. Usu. in *pl.* or as ***flag-feather***.

flag /flag/ *noun*[4]. M16.
[ORIGIN Perh. orig. an application of the adjective.]
1 A piece of bunting or other material, usu. oblong or square, attachable by one edge to a staff or halyard, and used as a standard, ensign, or signal, or for decoration or display. M16.
2 *spec.* NAUTICAL. A flag carried by a vessel to show that an admiral is in command. Hence, the emblem of an admiral's rank afloat; the admiral himself; a flagship. M17.
3 *spec.* A flag raised, dropped, waved, etc., to indicate the start or finish of a race. Hence, the moment so indicated. Also, a device on a chess clock which falls when the time limit is reached. M19.
4 The tail of an animal, *esp.* of a setter. M19.
5 An apron. *slang*. M19.
6 A small object or device resembling a flag; *esp.* a visible part of the mechanism in a taxi's meter etc., used to indicate availability. E20.
7 A statement of the name (and sometimes other details) of a newspaper or other publication, as printed on the page. M20.
8 COMPUTING. A symbol or symbols used to indicate some property of the data in a record, *spec.* the truth of a statement. M20.

– PHRASES: **black flag** (*a*) a pirate's ensign; (*b*) a flag formerly hoisted outside a prison to announce the execution of a criminal. ***chequered flag***: see CHEQUERED *adjective* 1. **flag of convenience** a foreign flag under which a ship is registered in order to avoid financial charges etc. **flag of truce** a white flag used to signal the wish for a truce. **give the honour of the flag** make etc. an acknowledgement of supremacy by lowering the flag to another. **hoist one's flag** (of an admiral) take up command. **hoist the flag** make a claim to discovered territory by raising one's national flag. **keep the flag flying** refuse to haul down one's flag and surrender; continue the fight (chiefly *fig.*). **lower one's flag**, **strike one's flag** take one's flag down, esp. as a token of respect, submission, or surrender; (of an admiral) relinquish command. **put the flag out**, **put the flags out** celebrate a victory or other event. ***rally round the flag***: see RALLY *verb*[1]. ***red flag***: see RED *adjective*. **show the flag** (esp. of a naval vessel) make an official visit to a foreign port or elsewhere; *fig.* ensure that notice is taken of oneself, one's country, etc. ***strike one's flag***: see ***lower one's flag*** above. **white flag** a flag of truce, a flag disclaiming hostile intention. ***yellow flag***: see YELLOW *adjective*.
– COMB.: **flag boat** a boat serving as a mark in sailing matches; **flag captain** the captain of a flagship; **flag day** a day on which a charity holds a street collection, and donors are given small paper badges as tokens; **Flag Day** *US* the anniversary (14 June) of the adoption of the Stars and Stripes in 1777; **flag fall** the dropping of a flag to indicate the start of a race; **flag-flying** the flying of flags; *fig.* (*colloq.*) (*a*) (deliberate) overbidding at bridge; (*b*) = ***kite-flying*** (c) s.v. KITE *noun*; **flag football** *N. Amer.* a form of touch football in which the ball-carrier's advance is halted when an opponent snatches a flag from his or her pocket or belt; **flag lieutenant** an admiral's aide-de-camp; **flag list** the roll of flag officers; **flagman** †(*a*) an admiral, a flag officer; (*b*) a person who has charge of, carries, or signals with a flag; **flag officer** an admiral, vice admiral, or rear admiral; a yacht-club commodore; **flagpole** a flagstaff; **flag rank** the rank of flag officer; **flagstaff**, pl. **-staffs**, **-staves**, a pole or staff on which a flag is hoisted; **flag station**: where trains stop only if signalled; **flag-wagging** *slang* (*a*) signalling with hand-held flags; (*b*) = ***flag-waving*** below; **flag-waver** a chauvinist, a political agitator; **flag-waving** trying to arouse popular enthusiasm, jingoism.
■ **flagless** *adjective* not bearing a flag or flags M19. **flaglet** *noun* a small flag L19.

†**flag** *adjective*. L16–M18.
[ORIGIN Unknown.]
Hanging down, drooping (esp. of hair, an animal's tail).

flag /flag/ *verb*[1] *trans.* Infl. **-gg-**. E16.
[ORIGIN from FLAG *noun*[2].]
Pave with flagstones. Also, (of a stone) form the paving of.
■ **flagging** *noun* (*a*) the action of the verb; (*b*) the material used in paving; the pavement: E17.

flag /flag/ *verb*[2]. Infl. **-gg-**. M16.
[ORIGIN Rel. to FLAG *adjective*.]
1 *verb intrans.* Hang down; flap about loosely. M16. ▸†**b** *verb trans.* Allow to droop; drop (the head, ears, tail, etc.). M17–M18.

SHELLEY Its sails were flagging in the breathless noon.

†**2** *verb intrans.* (Of wings) move feebly; (of a bird) move its wings feebly; fly unsteadily or near the ground. L16–M18.

SPENSER My Muse, whose fethers . . Doe yet but flagg and slowly learn to fly.

3 *verb intrans.* Become limp or flaccid; (of a plant) droop, fade. E17.
4 *verb trans.* †**a** (Of a bird etc.) relax the efforts of (its wings) from fatigue; (of conditions etc.) impede (the wings). E17–E18. ▸**b** Allow or cause to become languid; enfeeble. E17.

b J. M. FAULKNER Famine and fever flagged their forces.

5 (The predominant sense.) *verb intrans.* Become feeble or unsteady in flight or motion; be unable to maintain one's speed, strength, or interest; lag through fatigue; become languid. M17. ▸**b** Of an author, book, pleasure, conversation, etc.: wane in vigour or interest, grow dull. L17.

E. BOWEN He never flagged in his wish that they should continue to learn. J. M. COETZEE The work was hard; by mid-morning K was flagging. **b** THOMAS HUGHES By degrees the cricket flagged, and most of the men went off.

flag /flag/ *verb*[3] *trans.* Infl. **-gg-**. L17.
[ORIGIN from FLAG *noun*[1].]
†**1** Plant *about* with flags or reeds. Only in L17.
2 Tighten (the seams of a barrel) by means of flags or rushes. M18.
3 Cut off the flag or blade of (wheat). M19.

flag /flag/ *verb*[4] *trans.* Infl. **-gg-**. L18.
[ORIGIN from FLAG *noun*[4].]
1 Provide with, decorate, or mark out (as) with flags; place a flag on or over. L18. ▸**b** Mark with a small flag or tag so that relevant items may be readily found. M20. ▸**c** COMPUTING. Assign a flag (FLAG *noun*[4] 8) or flags to (information). M20.

Times In honour of the day all the official buildings . . were flagged. *Scientific American* The presence of a transposon simultaneously generates a mutation . . . identifies itself . . and flags its location.

2 Inform or communicate (as) by means of a flag or flags; *esp.* (also foll. by *down*) stop (a driver, vehicle, etc.) by waving or signalling; obtain (a lift) by such means. M19.

S. BELLOW He went into the middle of the street and flagged a cab. C. THUBRON I was flagged down for breaking one of the . . traffic laws. *absol.*: J. DIDION Mr McClellan met them . . . flagging wildly when he caught sight of the truck.

flagella *noun* pl. of FLAGELLUM.

flagellant /ˈfladʒ(ə)l(ə)nt, fləˈdʒɛl(ə)nt/ *noun & adjective*. L16.
[ORIGIN Latin *flagellant-* pres. ppl stem of *flagellare* to whip, from FLAGELLUM: see -ANT[1].]
▸ **A** *noun*. **1** A person who scourges himself or herself as a religious discipline or penance; *esp.* a member of one of the bands of such people common in Europe in the 13th cent. and later. Usu. in *pl.* L16.
2 *gen.* A person who flagellates (himself or herself, or others) from cruelty, for sexual gratification, etc. L18.
▸ **B** *adjective*. Given to flagellation, flagellating. L19.
■ **flagellantism** *noun* M19.

flagellar /fləˈdʒɛlə/ *adjective*. L19.
[ORIGIN from FLAGELLUM + -AR[1].]
BIOLOGY. Of or pertaining to a flagellum or flagella.

flagellate /ˈfladʒ(ə)lət, -eɪt/ *adjective & noun*. M19.
[ORIGIN from FLAGELLUM + -ATE[2].]
▸ **A** *adjective*. Having flagella; *esp.* of the nature of a flagellate, pertaining to flagellates. Also, flagelliform. M19.
▸ **B** *noun*. Any member of the subphylum Mastigophora (formerly the class Flagellata) of microscopic protozoans, characterized by the possession of flagella (used for locomotion). L19.
■ **flagellated** *adjective* provided with flagella L19.

flagellate /ˈfladʒ(ə)leɪt/ *verb trans.* Pa. pple **-ated**, (*rare*) **-ate** /-ət/. E17.
[ORIGIN Latin *flagellat-* pa. ppl stem of *flagellare*: see FLAGELLANT, -ATE[3].]
Scourge, whip.
■ **flagellator** *noun* a person who flagellates M16. **flagellatory** *adjective* pertaining to flagellation M19.

flagellation /fladʒəˈleɪʃ(ə)n/ *noun*. LME.
[ORIGIN ecclesiastical Latin *flagellatio(n-)*, formed as FLAGELLATE *verb*: see -ATION. Sense 3 from FLAGELLATE *adjective & noun*.]
1 (**F-**.) The scourging of Jesus; a picture representing this. LME.
2 *gen.* The action of scourging or flogging; a flogging. L15. ▸**b** Beating as a means of sexual gratification. L19.
3 ZOOLOGY. = EXFLAGELLATION. Also, the arrangement of flagella on an organism. L19.
■ ˈ**flagellative** *adjective* pertaining to flagellation M19.

flagelliform /fləˈdʒɛlɪfɔːm/ *adjective*. E19.
[ORIGIN from FLAGELLUM + -I- + -FORM.]
BIOLOGY. Having the form of a flagellum.

flagellin /fləˈdʒɛlɪn/ *noun*. M20.
[ORIGIN from FLAGELL(UM + -IN[1].]
BIOCHEMISTRY. A fibrous protein isolated from bacterial flagella.

flagellist /ˈfladʒ(ə)lɪst/ *noun*. M19.
[ORIGIN from FLAGELLUM + -IST.]
A flagellator.

flagellomania /ˌfladʒ(ə)lə(ʊ)ˈmeɪnɪə/ *noun*. L19.
[ORIGIN from FLAGELLUM + -O- + -MANIA.]
Enthusiasm for flogging (as a punishment); abnormal desire for flagellation of oneself or others.
■ **flagellomaniac** *noun & adjective* L19.

flagellum /fləˈdʒɛləm/ *noun*. Pl. **-lla** /-lə/. E19.
[ORIGIN Latin, dim. of *flagrum* scourge.]
1 A whip, a scourge. Chiefly *joc.* E19.
2 BIOLOGY. A motile whiplike projection from a cell. Also, (BOTANY) a runner, a creeping shoot. M19.

flageolet /fladʒəˈlɛt, ˈfladʒəlɪt/ *noun*[1]. M17.
[ORIGIN French, dim. of Old French *flag(e)ol*, *flajol* from Provençal *flaujol*, of unknown origin: see -ET[1].]
1 A small wind instrument resembling the recorder, having six principal holes, including two for the thumb, and sometimes keys. M17.
2 An organ stop having a tone similar to that of this instrument. M19.

flageolet /fladʒəˈlɛt, *foreign* flaʒɔlɛ (*pl. same*)/ *noun*[2]. L19.
[ORIGIN French, ult. from Latin *phaseolus* bean: see -ET[1].]
A small kind of (esp. French) kidney bean. Also ***flageolet bean***.

flagger /ˈflagə/ *noun*[1]. M19.
[ORIGIN from FLAG *verb*[1], *noun*[2] + -ER[1].]
1 A person who lays down flagstones. M19.
2 A streetwalker. *slang*. Now *rare* or *obsolete*. M19.

flagger /ˈflagə/ *noun*[2]. *obsolete* exc. *hist.* L19.
[ORIGIN from FLAG *noun*[4] + -ER[1].]
A person who carries a flag before a traction engine to warn of its approach.

flaggy /ˈflagi/ *adjective*[1]. LME.
[ORIGIN from FLAG *noun*[1] + -Y[1].]
1 Having many flags or reeds. LME.
2 Resembling a flag or reed. L16.
3 Consisting or made of flags or reeds. E17.
4 Of corn, straw, etc.: having a large blade (cf. FLAG *noun*[1] 2). M19.

F

F

flaggy /ˈflaɡi/ *adjective*². *obsolete* exc. *dial.* M16.
[ORIGIN from FLAG *verb*² + -Y¹.]
1 Soft and flabby, flaccid. M16.
2 Hanging down limply or lankly, drooping, pendulous. L16.
■ **flagginess** *noun* M17.

flaggy /ˈflaɡi/ *adjective*³. M19.
[ORIGIN from FLAG *noun*² + -Y¹.]
Of stone: readily split into flags, laminate.

flagitate /ˈfladʒɪteɪt/ *verb trans. rare.* E17.
[ORIGIN Latin *flagitat-* pa. ppl stem of *flagitare* demand earnestly: see -ATE³.]
Entreat, importune.
■ **flagiˈtation** *noun* M17.

flagitious /fləˈdʒɪʃəs/ *adjective.* LME.
[ORIGIN from Latin *flagitiosus*, from *flagitium* importunity, shameful crime, from *flagitare*: see FLAGITATE, -IOUS.]
Extremely wicked, criminal, villainous.
■ **flagitiously** *adverb* E17. **flagitiousness** *noun* L17.

flagon /ˈflaɡ(ə)n/ *noun.* LME.
[ORIGIN Old French & mod. French *flacon* from late Latin *flasco*, *-on-* FLASK *noun*.]
1 A large bottle for holding liquor; *spec.* (*a*) in early use, a metal bottle with a screw top, such as was carried by pilgrims; (*b*) a flattened globular glass bottle for wine or cider, holding nearly twice as much as an ordinary bottle (now usu. 1.13 litres). LME.
2 a A vessel used to hold the wine at the Eucharist. L15. ▸**b** A large vessel containing drink for use at table, usu. with a handle, spout, and lid. E16.
3 The amount of liquid held by a full flagon; a flagon and its contents. E17.

flagrance /ˈfleɪɡr(ə)ns/ *noun. rare.* E17.
[ORIGIN (Old French) formed as FLAGRANCY; in mod. use from FLAGRANT: see -ANCE.]
1 = FLAGRANCY 1. E17.
2 = FLAGRANCY 2. M19.

flagrancy /ˈfleɪɡr(ə)nsi/ *noun.* L16.
[ORIGIN Latin *flagrantia*, from *flagrant-*: see FLAGRANT, -ANCY.]
1 Glaring shamefulness; outrageousness, scandalousness, notoriety. L16.
2 *lit.* Blazing or glowing condition. *rare.* E17.

flagrant /ˈfleɪɡr(ə)nt/ *adjective.* L15.
[ORIGIN French, or Latin *flagrant-* pres. ppl stem of *flagrare* burn, blaze, be inflamed: see -ANT¹.]
1 †**a** Resplendent, glorious. Only in L15. ▸**b** Blazing, burning, glowing; gaudy. *arch.* L15. ▸†**c** Of a fluid: fiery, hot. Only in 17. ▸†**d** Burning red from a flogging. E18–M19.

> **b** SOUTHEY The crackling hearth, Where heath and cistus gave their flagrant flame. CARLYLE A.. Dowager (who dresses .. in flagrant colours). *fig.*: DE QUINCEY Flagrant health, health boiling over in fiery rapture.

†**2** Of a feeling, passion, etc.: ardent, burning. E16–L18.
3 Of an offence, an offender: glaring, notorious, scandalous, blatant. E18.

> T. F. DIBDIN An indifferent General, and a flagrant traitor. ALDOUS HUXLEY Surprised in flagrant inattention, Jeremy started guiltily. W. C. WILLIAMS A flagrant miscarriage of justice in our local courts.

4 Actually in progress; (of war etc.) raging. E19.
in flagrant delict = IN FLAGRANTE DELICTO.
■ **flagrantly** *adverb* M18. **flagrantness** *noun* (*rare*) E18.

flagrante delicto /fləˌɡrantɪ dɪˈlɪktəʊ/ *adverbial phr.* E19.
[ORIGIN Latin = (in) the heat of the crime.]
= IN FLAGRANTE DELICTO.

flagship /ˈflaɡʃɪp/ *noun.* L17.
[ORIGIN from FLAG *noun*⁴ + SHIP *noun*.]
1 A ship bearing an admiral's flag, *esp.* one in a fleet or squadron. L17.
2 Something considered a leader or superior example of its kind; *spec.* the major product, model, etc., in a company's range. M20.

flagstone /ˈflaɡstəʊn/ *noun.* M16.
[ORIGIN from FLAG *noun*² + STONE *noun*.]
1 A flat stone suitable for paving etc.; (in *pl.*) a pavement or paved floor. M16.
2 Sandstone that can be split up into flags. E19.
■ **flagstoned** *adjective* paved with flagstones L19.

flail /fleɪl/ *noun & adjective.*
[ORIGIN Old English (assumed), = Old Saxon *flegil*, Middle Dutch & mod. Dutch *vlegel*, Old & mod. High German *flegel*, from West Germanic, prob. from Latin *flagellum* scourge, flail. In Middle English prob. from Old French *flaiel* or Middle Dutch *vlegel*.]
▸ **A** *noun.* **1** A threshing implement consisting of a wooden handle attached to a heavy free-swinging pole or club. OE.
2 Something resembling this; a whip, a scourge. LME.
Protestant flail a short staff weighted with lead carried by Protestants at the time of the 'Popish Plot' (1678–81).
†**3** Something which swings on a pivot, as the clapper of a bell, the lever of a press, etc. LME–L17.
4 A medieval weapon consisting of a (usu. iron) handle with a spiked club or lengths of chain attached. L15.
▸ **B** *attrib.* or as *adjective.* MEDICINE. Of a part of the body: abnormally movable, hanging loosely. L19.
– COMB. & SPECIAL COLLOCATIONS: **flail chest** a condition in which multiple rib fractures cause excessive flexibility of the chest wall, sufficient to interfere with breathing; **flail harvester**, **flail mower**, etc., a harvesting, mowing, etc., machine having free-swinging cutters mounted on a horizontal rotor; **flail-joint** MEDICINE a joint showing grossly excessive mobility; ***flail mower***: see ***flail harvester*** above; **flail-tank** a tank with flails attached, used to detonate mines.

flail /fleɪl/ *verb.* L15.
[ORIGIN from the noun.]
1 *verb trans.* Scourge, beat; strike with or as with a flail. L15. ▸**b** Thresh (corn etc.) with a flail. E19.

> P. BAILEY She flailed the ancient carpet as if it contained demons instead of dust.

2 *verb intrans. & trans.* Thrash about (with); wave or swing (an object) wildly or erratically. L19.

> I. MCEWAN Clawing at their throats, retching, flailing their arms and falling to the grass. J. MONTAGUE Windshield wipers flail helpless against the rain.

flair /flɛː/ *noun*¹. Also **flare**. M17.
[ORIGIN Old French = a kind of flatfish.]
A ray or skate.

flair /flɛː/ *noun*². L19.
[ORIGIN French, from *flairer* to smell from Proto-Romance from Latin *fragrare*: see FRAGRANT.]
1 An instinct for selecting or performing what is excellent or useful; instinctive discernment. Also, originality, stylishness. L19.

> U. LE GUIN He seemed to have lost the flair .., the sense for where the really important problem lay. C. FREEMAN To wear an inexpensive dress with such flair that her friends were under the impression that she dressed extravagantly.

2 Special aptitude, ability, or enthusiasm *for*. E20.

> D. CARNEGIE With his Irish geniality, he had a flair for making people like him.

flair /flɛː/ *verb trans.* E20.
[ORIGIN from FLAIR *noun*².]
Sniff, smell out, scent; *fig.* detect.

> *Glasgow Herald* We flair survivals of phrase and intonation lurking in the speech .. of very aged persons. *absol.*: J. MASEFIELD The fox .. flaired with his muzzle.

flaith /flɑː/ *noun.* M19.
[ORIGIN Irish.]
IRISH HISTORY. The chief of an ancient family or *fine*.

flak /flak/ *noun.* In sense 2 also **flack**. M20.
[ORIGIN German, abbreviation of *fliegerabwehrkanone* lit. 'aviator-defence-gun'.]
1 Anti-aircraft fire (*spec.* German, in the Second World War). M20.

> J. BRAINE The bomb-aimer got a faceful of flak.

2 *fig.* Strong adverse criticism; hostile reactions. M20.

> *Times* When someone left the office lights on during a power crisis, they .. got a good deal of flak in the morning.

– COMB.: **flak-catcher** a person or organization whose job it is to deal with criticism on behalf of another; **flak jacket** a protective jacket of heavy fabric reinforced with metal.

flake /fleɪk/ *noun*¹. ME.
[ORIGIN Perh. from Old Norse *flaki*, *fleki* wicker shield (Danish *flage* hurdle).]
1 A (wattled) hurdle, sometimes used as a temporary gate. Now *dial.* ME.
2 A frame or rack for storing provisions, esp. oatcakes, or drying produce, esp. fish. LME.
3 MINING. A framework of boards used as a shelter from the weather. *obsolete* exc. *dial.* M17.
4 NAUTICAL. A small stage or workmen's cradle hung over the side of a ship. M19.

flake /fleɪk/ *noun*². ME.
[ORIGIN Immediate source unkn.: perh. senses of different origins. Cf. Norwegian *flak* patch, flake, *flake* form into flakes, Swedish *isflak* ice floe, Old Norse *flakna* flake off, split, Dutch *vlak* spot, fleck, prob. from Germanic. Cf. FLAW *noun*¹, FLAUGHT *noun*¹.]
1 = SNOWFLAKE 1. ME. ▸**b** A small piece of down or fluff; something resembling this. M17.
†**2** A spot, a fleck, a blemish. LME–M16.
3 An ignited fragment thrown off by a fire; an isolated tongue of flame. LME.
4 A stratum or lamina; a thin sheet; *spec.* a (loose) sheet of ice, a floe. LME.
5 A small flattish fragment. E16.
6 A thin piece peeled or split off from a surface. L16. ▸**b** ARCHAEOLOGY. A piece of stone detached from a larger block, esp. by human action in the course of the manufacture of implements. M19.
7 A bundle of parallel threads; a loose lock of hair. Cf. FLAKE *noun*³. *arch.* L16.
8 One of the natural divisions of the flesh, *esp.* of certain fishes. E17. ▸**b** Dogfish or other shark, as food. E20.
9 (A plant of) a variety of carnation with striped petals. Cf. BIZARRE *noun* 1, PICOTEE *noun*. E18.
10 In *pl.* Any of various kinds of breakfast cereal; *esp.* cornflakes. E20.
– COMB.: **flake culture** a primitive culture characterized by the use of stone implements made from flakes struck for the making of implements; **flake-stand** a cooling tub for the worm of a still; **flake white** a pigment made from flakes of white lead; **flake tool** ARCHAEOLOGY a tool made from a flake struck for the making of a tool (***flake-tool culture*** = ***flake culture*** above).

flake /fleɪk/ *noun*³. E17.
[ORIGIN Cf. FAKE *noun*¹ and German *Flechte* of same meaning.]
= FAKE *noun*¹. Cf. FLAKE *noun*² 7.

flake /fleɪk/ *verb*¹. LME.
[ORIGIN from FLAKE *noun*².]
1 *verb intrans.* Fall as flakes. Orig., now only *occas.*, of snow. LME.

> D. M. MOIR Butterflies .. Down flaking in an endless stream.

2 *verb trans.* Cover with or as with flakes (of snow etc.). E17.

> LONGFELLOW His russet beard was already Flaked with patches of snow, as hedges sometimes in November.

3 *verb trans.* Mark with flecks or streaks. E17.
4 *verb trans.* Break flakes from; break or rub off in flakes. M17. ▸**b** *verb intrans.* Come away or off in flakes; separate as flakes. M18.

> E. B. TYLOR Most stone knives of the kind seem to have been used, as they were flaked off. W. RYE Watermen .. are believed to flake off their dirt .. by rubbing themselves against the sharp angles of square flint church towers. **b** B. BAINBRIDGE The plaster was flaking off the ceiling.

5 *verb intrans. & trans.* Break into small pieces; separate into flakes. M17.
■ **flaked** *ppl adjective*¹ (*a*) arranged in flakes or layers; (*b*) marked with flecks or streaks: L16. **flaker** *noun* a person who or thing which flakes; *spec.* an implement for flaking flint: L19. **flaking** *noun* the action of the verb; the condition of being flaked or flecked; a flecked appearance: E19.

flake /fleɪk/ *verb*². L15.
[ORIGIN Var. of FLACK *verb*¹, FLAG *verb*².]
†**1** *verb intrans.* Become languid or flabby; flag; (of a garment) fall in folds. L15–L16.
2 *verb intrans.* Lie about, laze, bask. *dial.* M17.
3 *verb intrans.* Faint or fall asleep (from exhaustion, drunkenness, etc.). Usu. foll. by *out*. *colloq.* M20.

> K. HULME When you flaked, I didn't know whether to get a doctor or not.

■ **flaked** *ppl adjective*² tired *out*, exhausted, unconscious, asleep M20.

flake /fleɪk/ *verb*³ *trans.* L19.
[ORIGIN from FLAKE *noun*³. Cf. FAKE *verb*¹.]
NAUTICAL. Lay (a rope) on the deck in coils so that it will run out freely when required; lay out (a chain cable) on the forecastle deck for examination; lay (a sail) down in folds on either side of the boom. Also foll. by *down*. Cf. FAKE *verb*¹.

flaky /ˈfleɪki/ *adjective.* L16.
[ORIGIN from FLAKE *noun*² + -Y¹.]
1 Consisting of or resembling flakes. L16.
2 Separating easily into flakes; (of pastry) consisting of thin flakes when baked. L17.
3 Full of locks or tufts of hair. Now *rare*. E19.
4 Crazy, eccentric. *N. Amer. slang.* M20.
■ **flakily** *adverb* M19. **flakiness** *noun* M18.

flam /flam/ *noun*¹, *verb*, *& adjective.* E17.
[ORIGIN Perh. abbreviation of FLIMFLAM or FLAMFEW.]
▸ **A** *noun.* †**1** A fanciful notion, a whim. Only in 17.
†**2** A fanciful composition of verse. M17–M18.
3 A fabrication or falsehood; (a piece of) deception; flattery, blarney. M17.
▸ **B** *verb trans.* Infl. **-mm-**. Deceive by a fabrication or trick, or by flattery. *obsolete* exc. *dial.* & *US.* M17.
▸ †**C** *adjective.* Counterfeit, fabricated, fictitious. Only in L17.

flam /flam/ *noun*². L18.
[ORIGIN Prob. imit.]
A type of stroke in side drum playing, made by striking both sticks against the parchment leaving a slight interval between them.

> R. GRAVES Could I call a double-flam From the drums.

flamant *adjective* var. of FLAMMANT.

†**flamb** *verb trans. Scot.* LME–M19.
[ORIGIN Anglo-Norman *flaum(b)er*, French *flamber* singe; orig. a var. of *flam(m)er* FLAME *verb*.]
Baste.

†**flambant** *adjective.* L16–L19.
[ORIGIN French, from *flamber* FLAME *verb*.]
Flaming.

flambé /ˈflɒmbeɪ, *foreign* flɑ̃be/ *adjective & verb.* L19.
[ORIGIN French, pa. pple of *flamber* singe, pass through flame.]
▸ **A** *adjective.* **1** (Of a copper-based glaze) iridescent from the effects of a special firing process; (of a type of Chinese porcelain) characterized by such a glaze. L19.

2 Of food: covered with spirit and served alight. E20.
▸ **B** *verb trans.* Pa. t. & pple **-béed**. Cover (food) with spirit and set alight. M20.

flambeau /ˈflambəʊ/ *noun*. Pl. **-s**, **-x** /-z/. M17.
[ORIGIN Old French & mod. French, dim. of *flambe*, †*flamble*, from Latin *flammula*, dim. of *flamma* FLAME *noun*.]
1 A flaming torch, *esp.* one made of several thick waxed wicks. M17.
fig.: A. E. HOUSMAN The chestnut casts his flambeaux.
2 A large (branched) candlestick. L19.

flamboyant /flamˈbɔɪənt/ *noun*. Also **-boyan** /-ˈbɔɪən/, **-boyante**. L19.
[ORIGIN Prob. French, use as noun of FLAMBOYANT *adjective*.]
The royal poinciana, *Delonix regia*. Also more fully ***flamboyant tree***.

flamboyant /flamˈbɔɪənt/ *adjective*. M19.
[ORIGIN French, pres. pple of *flamboyer* to blaze, flame, from *flambe*: see FLAMBOYANT *noun*, -ANT[1].]
1 a ARCHITECTURE. Of a style: characterized by wavy flame-like lines. M19. ▸**b** Resembling a flame in form; wavy. L19.
a *absol.*: N. PEVSNER French Flamboyant . . is compared unfavourably with English Perpendicular. **b** F. WILKINSON A so-called flamboyant blade, on which the edge was scalloped.
2 Gorgeously (flame-)coloured; (of a person, behaviour, etc.) florid, ostentatious, showy. M19.
CONAN DOYLE His brilliant necktie, shining pin, and glittering rings were flamboyant in their effect. S. J. PERELMAN A young lady in flamboyant theatrical make-up appeared.
■ **flamboyance**, **flamboyancy** *nouns* the quality of being flamboyant L19. **flamboyantly** *adverb* L19.

flamdoodle *noun* see FLAPDOODLE.

flame /fleɪm/ *noun*. ME.
[ORIGIN Anglo-Norman *flaum(b)e*, Old French & mod. French *flam(m)e*, from Latin *flamma*.]
1 (A portion of) ignited gas, typically incandescent and often tongue- or spire-shaped. ME. ▸**b** The state of visible combustion; in *pl.* (with *the*), fire, esp. with ref. to death or destruction by burning. LME.
DRYDEN Thrice to the vaulted Roof the Flames aspire. M. AMIS The flabby blue flame from the gas-ring. *fig.*: A. S. BYATT An atmosphere of smothered conflagration . . —not visible flame, but the uneasy smouldering . . of a bonfire. **b** E. O'NEILL Their cities shall vanish in flame, their fields shall be wasted.
2 A burning intense emotion; passion; *esp.* love. Formerly also, genius, talent, esp. in writing. ME. ▸**b** A lover; now usu. (*joc.*) in ***old flame*** a former lover. M17.
MABEL COLLINS This flame of ardent ambition kept her alive. J. FOWLES Her eyes were all flame as she threw a passionate look back at Charles.
3 A bright beam of light; *fig.* brilliance, brilliant colouring. LME.
W. C. BRYANT The northern lights . . cold, wandering flames.
4 Something resembling a flame in shape or esp. in colour. E17. ▸**b** The red-orange colour of flame. E18.
M. E. BRADDON The yellow stonecrop made a flame of colour on the top. **b** *attrib.*: *Vogue* His [a designer's] back-baring flame dress.
5 A pale noctuid moth, *Axylia putris*. E19.
6 COMPUTING. A vitriolic or abusive email message, typically sent in quick response to another message. L20.
– PHRASES: **burst into flame(s)** ignite. ***fan the flame***: see FAN *verb*. **in flames** on fire (***shoot down in flames***: see SHOOT *verb*). ***oil on the flames***, ***oil to the flames***: see OIL *noun*. ***old flame***: see sense 2b above.
– COMB.: **flame-cell** ZOOLOGY a ciliated cell at the end of a protonephridium which creates a water current in the tubule; **flame gun** a flame-throwing gun used to destroy weeds, etc.; **flame nettle** any of various labiate plants of the genus *Solenostemon*, with variegated leaves, grown as house plants; = COLEUS; **flame-projector** = ***flame-thrower*** below; **flameproof** *adjective & verb trans.* (make) able to resist flames; **flame-retardant**, **flame-resistant** *adjectives* (of fabric etc.) not readily flammable; **flame test**: for detecting certain chemical elements by the characteristic colour they give to a flame; **flame-thrower** a weapon for throwing a spray of ignited fuel; **flame-trap** a device fitted to prevent the passage of flame through a system esp. in an internal-combustion engine; **flame tree** any of various trees with brilliant red or yellow flowers; *esp.* a bottle tree, *Brachychiton australis*, native to Australia; **flame-ware** cooking equipment, esp. of glass, that can withstand the heat of an open flame.
■ **flameless** *adjective* burning without flame; devoid of flame: E17. **flamelet** *noun* a small flame M19. **flamelike** *adjective* resembling (that of) a flame M16.

flame /fleɪm/ *verb*. ME.
[ORIGIN Anglo-Norman *flaum(b)er*, Old French *flam(m)er*, (also mod.) *flamber*, from *flam(m)e* FLAME *noun*.]
1 *verb intrans.* Burn with a flame or flames; emit flames. ME. ▸**b** *verb trans.* Burn, set on fire, consume or destroy with flames. Long *rare*. L16. ▸**c** *verb trans.* Subject to the action of flame. L19.
b *fig.*: T. S. ELIOT The brief sun flames the ice, on pond and ditches. **c** *American Speech* Allowing my loop wire to cool sufficiently after flaming it.
flame out (of a jet engine) lose power through extinction of the flame in the combustion chamber; **flameout** (an instance of) loss of power through this cause.
2 *verb intrans.* Shine or glow (red) like flame. ME.
C. MACKENZIE A crimson spot flaming now on both of his cheekbones.
3 †**a** *verb trans.* Kindle, excite (emotion etc.). LME–M17. ▸**b** *verb intrans.* (Of a person) be consumed *with* fury, passion, etc.; burst out into anger etc.; (of passion etc.) burst out. Also foll. by *out*, *up*. M16.
b LD MACAULAY He flamed with indignation. E. WAUGH Love, patriotism, zeal for justice, and personal spite flamed within him. A. LURIE It is years since she flamed out like that at anyone.
4 a *verb trans.* Send forth or convey by means of a flame. LME. ▸**b** *verb intrans.* Move like flame. *poet.* M17.
a T. A. COOK Beacon fires . . which flamed messages along the valley. **b** TENNYSON Once again thou flamest heavenward.
5 *verb trans. & intrans.* COMPUTING. Send (someone) a vitriolic or abusive email message, usu. in response to another message. L20.
■ **flamer** *noun* a person who or thing which flames; *arch. slang* something or someone glaringly conspicuous: L16.

flamen /ˈfleɪmɛn, ˈflɑː-/ *noun*. Pl. **flamens**, **flamines** /ˈflamɪniːz/. ME.
[ORIGIN Latin.]
Chiefly ROMAN HISTORY. A priest serving a particular god.
flamen dialis /dɪˈeɪlɪs, dɪˈɑːlɪs/ the flamen of Jupiter.

flamenco /fləˈmɛŋkəʊ/ *noun & adjective*. Pl. **-os**. L19.
[ORIGIN Spanish = Fleming.]
(Designating or pertaining to) a style of music played (esp. on the guitar) and sung by Spanish Gypsies; (a song or dance) to music in this style.

flamfew /ˈflamfjuː/ *noun*. Long *rare*. L16.
[ORIGIN French †*fanfelue* (now *fanfreluche*) from medieval Latin *famfaluca* bubble, lie, app. from Greek *pompholux* bubble.]
A bauble, a showy trifle.

flamines *noun pl.* see FLAMEN.

flaming /ˈfleɪmɪŋ/ *ppl adjective & adverb*. LME.
[ORIGIN from FLAME *verb* + -ING[2].]
▸ **A** *adjective*. **1** That flames; in flames, on fire. LME. ▸**b** Burning hot, fiery. M17.
DAY LEWIS Like flaming swords they barred my way. **b** D. FRANCIS Flaming June had come and gone: it was raining again.
2 Glowing, brilliant; (with ref. to colour) bright, vivid. LME. ▸**b** *fig.* Highly coloured; exaggerated; extravagant; (of an argument etc.) passionate. E17.
M. E. BRADDON The flaming poppies among the ripening corn. **b** SHAKES. *Tr. & Cr.* He having colour enough, and the other higher, is too flaming a praise for a good complexion.
3 Blasted, damned, bloody. *colloq.* L19.
ALAN BENNETT That flaming dog has messed on our steps again.
▸ **B** *adverb*. Damn, bloody. *colloq.* M20.
M. KINGTON Then flaming well think of something better.
■ **flamingly** *adverb* E17.

flamingo /fləˈmɪŋɡəʊ/ *noun*. Pl. **-o(e)s**. M16.
[ORIGIN Spanish †*flamengo*, FLAMENCO flamingo, Fleming, from Middle Dutch *Vlaminc* Fleming.]
1 Any of a number of wading birds of the family Phoenicopteridae, with pink or scarlet plumage, long slender legs and neck, and a heavy bent bill which is held upside down in the water when feeding. M16.
2 A deep pink colour. L19.
attrib.: V. WOOLF Lovely evenings, with . . flamingo clouds.

flammability /flaməˈbɪlɪti/ *noun*. M17.
[ORIGIN from (the same root as) FLAMMABLE: see -ABILITY.]
= INFLAMMABILITY.
– NOTE: Formerly obsolete (M17 only) but revived in M20: cf. FLAMMABLE.

flammable /ˈflaməb(ə)l/ *adjective*. E19.
[ORIGIN from Latin *flammare*, from *flamma* flame: see -ABLE.]
Easily set on fire, inflammable.
– NOTE: Often preferred to avoid the possible ambiguity of ***inflammable***.

flammant /ˈflam(ə)nt/ *adjective*. *obsolete* exc. HERALDRY. Also **flamant**. L15.
[ORIGIN Old French *flam(m)ant*, from *flam(m)er* to FLAME *verb*.]
Flaming.

flammeous /ˈflamɪəs/ *adjective*. Now *rare*. M17.
[ORIGIN from Latin *flammeus* (from *flamma* flame) + -OUS: see -EOUS.]
Of the nature of, or resembling, flame, esp. in colour; shining, resplendent.

flammiferous /flaˈmɪf(ə)rəs/ *adjective*. *rare*. M17.
[ORIGIN from Latin *flammifer* + -OUS: see -FEROUS.]
Bearing flame.

flammivomous /fləˈmɪvəməs/ *adjective*. *rare*. M17.
[ORIGIN from late Latin *flammivomus* (from *flamma* flame + *-vomus* vomiting) + -OUS.]
Vomiting out flame.

flammulated /ˈflamjʊleɪtɪd/ *adjective*. L19.
[ORIGIN from mod. Latin *flammulatus*, from Latin *flammula* dim. of *flamma* flame: see -ED[1].]
Of a reddish colour, ruddy. Chiefly in ***flammulated owl***, a small owl, *Otus flammeolus*, native to western N. and Central America.
■ **flammuˈlation** *noun* (*rare*) a small flamelike marking M19.

flamy /ˈfleɪmi/ *adjective*. LME.
[ORIGIN from FLAME *noun* + -Y[1].]
1 Consisting of flames; flaming. LME.
2 Resembling flame, esp. in colour. LME.

flan /flan/ *noun*. M19.
[ORIGIN French, orig. = a round cake, from Old French *flaon*: see FLAWN.]
1 An open pastry or sponge case containing a (sweet or savoury) filling. Cf. earlier FLAWN. M19.
2 A disc of metal from which a coin is made. M19.

flancard /ˈflaŋkɑːd/ *noun*. Also **flanchard** /ˈflantʃɑːd/. L15.
[ORIGIN Old French, from *flanc* FLANK *noun*.]
hist. A piece of armour for the thigh, or for the flank of a horse.

flanch /flɑːn(t)ʃ/ *noun*[1] & *verb*. Also **flaunch** /flɔːn(t)ʃ/. E18.
[ORIGIN Uncertain: perh. from FLAUNCH *noun*[1].]
▸ **A** *noun*. = FLANGE *noun* 2. E18.
▸ **B** *verb*. [Cf. Old French *flanchir* bend.]
1 *verb intrans.* Spread *out*; slope outwards towards the top. L18.
2 *verb trans.* Foll. by *up*: slope (esp. the outside of a chimney shaft) inwards towards the top. M19.
■ **flanching** *noun* (**a**) the action or state of spreading outwards; (**b**) the sloping fillet of cement or mortar embedding the base of a chimney pot: M19.

flanch *noun*[2] var. of FLAUNCH *noun*[1].

flanchard *noun* var. of FLANCARD.

flanconade /ˈflaŋkəneɪd/ *noun*. M17.
[ORIGIN French, from *flanc* FLANK *noun*: see -ADE.]
FENCING. A thrust in the side.

Flanders /ˈflɑːndəz/ *noun*. LME.
[ORIGIN Dutch *Vlaanderen* pl.: a region and former principality in the south-west of the Low Countries, now divided between Belgium, the Netherlands, and France.]
Used ***attrib.*** to designate things originating in or associated with Flanders.
Flanders brick = ***Bath brick*** s.v. BATH *noun*[1]. **Flanders poppy** a red corn poppy used as the emblem of the Allied soldiers who fell in the First World War; an artificial red poppy sold on behalf of the ex-service community and worn in Britain on Remembrance Day and the period directly preceding it (cf. POPPY *noun* 1c).
■ **Flanderkin** *noun* (*arch.*) a native or inhabitant of Flanders E16. **Flandrian** *adjective* (**a**) (now *rare*) of or pertaining to Flanders or its inhabitants; (**b**) GEOLOGY of, pertaining to, or designating the period following the end of the last glaciation in NW Europe: M17. **Flandrish** *adjective* (*arch.*) Flemish ME.

flane /fleɪn/ *noun*. Long only *Scot. arch.*
[ORIGIN Old English *flān* masc. and fem. = Old Norse *fleinn* masc., cogn. with Old English *flā* FLO.]
An arrow.

flane /flɑːn/ *verb intrans.* L19.
[ORIGIN Back-form. from FLÂNEUR.]
Laze, saunter.

flânerie /flɑnri/ *noun*. L19.
[ORIGIN French, from *flâner* lounge, saunter idly.]
Idling.

flâneur /flɑnœːr/ *noun*. Pl. pronounced same. M19.
[ORIGIN French, from *flâner* (see FLÂNERIE) + *-eur* -OR.]
An idler.
R. HOLMES Paris . . celebrated the idea of the *flâneur*, the man who drifts round the streets, gazing at everything.

flange /flan(d)ʒ/ *noun & verb*. L17.
[ORIGIN Uncertain: rel. to FLANCH *noun*[1] & *verb*.]
▸ **A** *noun*. **1** A part that widens out (now only in a vein of ore). L17.
2 A projecting flat rim, collar, or rib, serving esp. for strengthening, attachment, or (on a wheel) maintaining position on a rail. Also, a rim or fan standing out from the main part of a natural object. M18.
M. KINGSLEY The brown water . . striking a ridge of higher rock . . flew up in a lovely flange. J. MASTERS The wheels' flanges ground against the inside of the rail.
blank flange: see BLANK *adjective*.
▸ **B** *verb*. [Cf. Old French *flangir* bend.]
1 *verb trans.* Provide with a flange. Chiefly as ***flanged*** *ppl adjective*. L18.
2 *verb intrans.* Widen out or *out*. E19.
3 *verb intrans.* Alter a sound recording by removing sound of a particular but varying frequency (orig. by pressing alternately on the flanges of the tape reels playing two copies of the recording simultaneously, now by means of a flanger). Usu. as ***flanging*** *verbal noun*. L20.
■ **flangeless** *adjective* E20. **flanger** *noun* (**a**) *US* a vertical scraper for clearing snow from railway tracks to allow room for the

F

wheel flanges; (**b**) a device that alters a sound signal by introducing a cyclically varying phase shift into one of two identical copies of the signal and recombining them: L19.

flank /flaŋk/ *noun*. LOE.
[ORIGIN Old French & mod. French *flanc*, from Frankish base meaning 'a side'.]
1 The fleshy or muscular part of the side of a person or animal, strictly that between the ribs and the hip. Formerly also, the belly; the womb. LOE. ▸**b** A cut of meat, or a piece of hide, from the flank of an animal. M18.

T. A. COWARD The Redwing . . can be distinguished by its long pale eye-stripe and reddish flanks. G. ORWELL From the hip to the knee her flank was against his.

2 The side part of anything, esp. a building, mountain, etc. E17.

A. MILLER They drive . . up a steep gorge whose flanks almost blot out the sky.

3 The extreme right or left side of (esp.) an army or other body of people in military formation; a wing. M17. ▸**b** FORTIFICATION. A part of a work so disposed as to defend another by flanking fire. L17.

C. S. FORESTER A company commander then had to get his men forward again, watching his flanks. *fig.*: R. MAY To fight on both flanks—to oppose totalitarianism . . and to recover our . . belief in the worth and dignity of the person.

in flank at the side.
4 The side of the tooth of a gearwheel, or of a screw thread, which makes effective contact with another surface. M19.
– COMB.: **flank forward** RUGBY UNION a wing forward.

flank /flaŋk/ *verb*[1]. M16.
[ORIGIN from the noun. Cf. French *flanquer*.]
†**1** *verb intrans.* Deliver a raking fire. Only in M16.
2 *verb trans.* Guard, strengthen, or defend, on the flank; attack or threaten the flank of; (of artillery) fire sideways on, rake. L16.

SIR W. SCOTT An advanced angle . . with shot-holes for flanking the door-way.

3 *verb trans.* Be situated at the side of; *esp.* be situated on either side of. M17.

E. GLASGOW A red brick house flanked by a stony hill. F. HERBERT She saw Paul approaching flanked by two small boys.

4 *verb trans.* Dodge, evade. *arch. US slang.* M19.

flank /flaŋk/ *verb*[2] *trans.* M19.
[ORIGIN Imit.: cf. *flick*, *spank*.]
Flick; crack (a whip).

flanker /ˈflaŋkə/ *noun & verb*. M16.
[ORIGIN from FLANK *verb*[1] + -ER[1].]
▸ **A** *noun*. **1** A fortification for protecting or threatening a flank. M16.
2 One of a detachment of soldiers sent to guard the flanks of a military formation. L16. ▸**b** A trick or swindle. Chiefly in ***pull a flanker***, ***work a flanker***, etc. *slang* (orig. MILITARY). E20. ▸**c** In RUGBY UNION etc., a flank forward, a wing forward. In AMER. FOOTBALL, a player who lines up in a position to the outside of an end. M20.
3 A thing which flanks anything. E17.
▸ **B** *verb*. [Cf. Dutch *flankeren* from French *flanquer* FLANK *verb*[1].]
1 *verb trans.* Protect on the flanks; protect or threaten from a flanker. *arch.* L16.
2 *verb intrans.* Make an attack on the flank. Now *rare* or *obsolete*. E17.

flannel /ˈflan(ə)l/ *noun & adjective*. Also (*obsolete* exc. *dial.*) **-en** /-ən/. ME.
[ORIGIN Prob. from Welsh *gwlanen* woollen article, from *gwlân* wool.]
▸ **A** *noun*. **1** Any of various loose-textured soft woollen or man-made fabrics of plain or twilled weave and slightly napped on one side. ME. ▸†**b** A Welshman. *rare* (Shakes.). Only in L16.
2 In *pl.* Underwear or other garments, *esp.* trousers, made of flannel. E17.

H. FAST He was . . dressed in gray flannels and a blue blazer.

3 A small piece of (usu. cotton towelling) fabric for washing the face, hands, etc. E19.
4 Nonsense; flattery; bragging. *slang*. E20.
– COMB.: **flannelboard** = FLANNELGRAPH; **flannel-cake** a kind of thin wheat griddle cake; **flannel flower** an Australian umbelliferous plant, *Actinotus helianthi*, the involucre of which resembles a snipped piece of white flannel; **flannelmouth** *US slang* a flatterer, a braggart.
▸ **B** *attrib.* or as *adjective*. Made of flannel. L16.

J. D. SALINGER There was this very Joe Yale-looking guy, in a grey flannel suit.

■ **flanneˈlette** *noun* a napped cotton fabric imitating the texture of flannel L19. **flannelgraph** *noun* a sheet of flannel to which paper or cloth cut-outs will adhere, used esp. as a teaching aid M20. **flannelled** *adjective* wrapped in flannel; wearing flannel trousers: L18. **flannelly** *adjective* resembling flannel M19.

flannel /ˈflan(ə)l/ *verb*. Infl. **-ll-**, *** -l-**. M19.
[ORIGIN from the noun.]
1 *verb trans.* Rub with a flannel; *rare* wrap in flannel. M19.

I. MCEWAN Steered him to the washbasin, was filling it with warm water and flanneling his face.

2 *verb trans. & intrans.* Use flattery (on); bluff, mislead. *slang*. M20.

J. BRAINE I managed to flannel him into the belief that I approved of his particular brand of efficiency.

flannen *noun & adjective* see FLANNEL *noun & adjective*.

flanque *noun* var. of FLAUNCH *noun*[1].

flap /flap/ *noun*. ME.
[ORIGIN from the verb.]
▸ **I** The action of FLAP *verb*.
1 A light blow or slap (with something broad and flexible). ME.

SWIFT Give him a soft Flap on his Eyes.

2 (The noise produced by) the motion of something broad and loose, *esp.* the up-and-down movement of a wing. L18. ▸**b** PHONETICS. A consonantal sound produced by a single fast flapping motion of the tongue or other organ. M19. ▸**c** A state of anxiety, agitation, or excitement; a fuss; MILITARY an alert. *colloq.* E20.

C. KINGSLEY I can hear the flap and snort of the dogs' nostrils. J. TYNDALL A gnat can execute many thousand flaps of its little wings in a second. **c** *Punch* There is a flap because the price of bread is going up.

c be in a flap be anxious, agitated, or excited. **get in a flap**, **get into a flap** become anxious, agitated, or excited.
▸ **II** Something that flaps.
†**3** Something broad and flat to strike with; *esp.* a fly swatter. LME–E18.
4 Something broad and flat hinged or attached on one side only, as a trapdoor, the cover of a pocket, the seal of an envelope, etc. E16. ▸**b** A hanging or pendent portion of a garment, hat, etc. M16. ▸**c** A valve which opens and shuts on one hinged side. Also ***flap valve***. E19. ▸**d** The gill cover of a fish. E19. ▸**e** The pendent portion(s) of a saddle. M19. ▸**f** A hinged or sliding section of a wing or tailplane used to control lift etc.; an aileron. E20.

J. STEINBECK Casy spread the tent flaps with his hands and stepped out. **b** C. T. DENT Tying the flaps of his hat over his ears.

cat flap: see CAT *noun*[1].
5 In *pl.* (A disease marked by) swollen glands in the mouth of a horse. L16.
6 Something broad and loose, irrespective of connection with anything else. E17. ▸**b** A large, broad mushroom; an open mushroom top. Cf. FLAB *noun* 1. M18. ▸**c** A loose covering for the lower part of the abdomen. *US*. E19.

THACKERAY The flap of a shoulder of mutton.

7 A girl or woman of light or loose character. *slang* (now *dial.*). M17.

J. MABBE Fall to your flap, my Masters, kisse and clip.

8 SURGERY. A portion of skin or flesh separated from the underlying tissue, but remaining attached at the base while being transplanted to another site. Also, a piece of skin used as a graft. E19.
– COMB.: **flapmouthed** *adjective* (*slang*, *derog.*) having a mouth with broad hanging lips; **flap-sight** a hinged sight on a rifle; **flap-table** a table with one or more hinged leaves; ***flap valve***: see sense 4c above.
■ **flapped** *adjective* formed like a flap, pendulous; having a flap or flaps: M17. **flapless** *adjective* E20.

flap /flap/ *verb*. Infl. **-pp-**. ME.
[ORIGIN Prob. imit.: cf. CLAP *verb*[1].]
1 *verb trans. & intrans.* Strike with a sudden blow. Long *obsolete* exc. *dial.* ME.

J. SKELTON I shall flappe hym as a fole to fall at my fete.

2 a *verb trans.* Cause to swing or sway about, flutter, or flop, esp. with accompanying noise. ME. ▸**b** *verb intrans.* Of something attached at one point or side or loosely fastened: swing or sway about, flutter, flop (freq. making a noise); *fig.* (of ears) open wide, strain to hear something. E16. ▸**c** Toss (esp. a pancake) smartly. M19.

a SOUTHEY I hear the wind, that flaps The curtain of the tent. J. STEINBECK Lennie flapped his big hands helplessly. **b** DICKENS The . . curtains flapped . . idly in the wind. P. PEARCE He unbuttoned his pyjama jacket and let it flap open. M. ERSKINE You get on and explain them . . Harris . . has his ears positively flapping.

3 *verb trans.* Strike with something flexible and broad; (of a bird) strike with the flat of the wing; drive *away* or *off* in such a way. LME. ▸**b** *verb intrans.* Make a flap or stroke. L16.

J. H. WIFFEN Night's shrieking bird Flaps the friezed window with her wing. G. W. LE FEVRE Two men would run before me to flap away the flies.

4 a *verb trans.* Move up and down, beat (the wings). LME. ▸**b** *verb intrans.* (Of wings, flippers, arms, etc.) beat, move up and down; beat the wings etc. L17.

a J. G. WOOD The Swift does not flap its wings so often as the Swallow. **b** R. L'ESTRANGE 'Tis common for a duck to run flapping and fluttering away.

5 *verb intrans.* Of a bird, ship, etc.: travel with wings, sails, etc., flapping. L18.

C. KINGSLEY A slate-blue heron . . flapped fifty yards up the creek.

6 *verb intrans.* Be upset, become agitated; fuss; panic. *colloq.* E20.

flapdoodle /ˈflapduːd(ə)l/ *noun*. *colloq.* Also ***flam-** /ˈflam-/. M19.
[ORIGIN Arbitrary.]
Nonsense, rubbish.

F. MARRYAT The gentleman has eaten no small quantity of flapdoodle . . it's the stuff they feed fools on.

flap-dragon /ˈflapdrag(ə)n/ *noun & verb*. Long *rare* or *obsolete*. L16.
[ORIGIN from FLAP *verb* + DRAGON.]
▸ **A** *noun*. (A raisin etc. as caught and eaten in) the game of snapdragon. L16.
▸ **B** *verb trans.* Swallow as one would a snapdragon. *rare* (Shakes.). Only in E17.

flapjack /ˈflapdʒak/ *noun*. E17.
[ORIGIN from FLAP *verb* + JACK *noun*[1].]
1 A flat cake or pancake; an apple turnover. E17.
2 A sweet biscuit made with rolled oats. M20.
3 A powder compact. M20.

flapper /ˈflapə/ *noun*. L16.
[ORIGIN from FLAP *verb* + -ER[1].]
1 Something flat to strike with, esp. to make a noise; a fly swatter. L16.
2 A person who flaps or strikes another, esp. to get his or her attention. Hence, a reminder. Now *rare* or *obsolete*. E18.
3 A newly fledged wild duck or partridge. Chiefly *dial.* M18.
4 Something hanging by one side or working on a hinge; *esp.* the striking part of a flail, a swingle. L18. ▸**b** A fin or flipper; a crustacean's tail; (*slang*) the hand. Now *rare*. M19. ▸**c** An irregular race meeting (cf. FLAPPING 2). *slang*. E20.
5 [Perh. from FLAP *noun* 7, or a fig. use of sense 3.] ▸†**a** A young prostitute; a promiscuous young girl. *slang*. L19–E20. ▸**b** Orig., a young girl nearing maturity. Later, a young woman (esp. an unconventional or flighty one). *colloq.* L19. ▸**c** *spec.* A fashionable young woman of the 1920s and 1930s. *colloq.* E20.
– COMB.: **flapper vote** (*derog.*, now *hist.*) the parliamentary vote granted to women of 21 and over in 1928.
■ **flapperdom**, **flapperhood** *nouns* the condition of being a flapper (sense 5b, c) E20. **flapperish** *adjective* characteristic of or like a flapper E20.

†**flappet** *noun*. L16–E18.
[ORIGIN from FLAP *noun* + -ET[1].]
A little flap.

flapping /ˈflapɪŋ/ *verbal noun*. LME.
[ORIGIN from FLAP *verb* + -ING[1].]
1 The action of FLAP *verb*. LME. ▸**b** *spec.* AERONAUTICS. The angular up-and-down oscillation of the blade of a helicopter about its hinge. M20.
2 A form of racing not subject to the rules of an official body. *slang*. E20.

flappy /ˈflapi/ *adjective*. L16.
[ORIGIN from FLAP *verb* + -Y[1].]
†**1** Flabby. *rare*. Only in L16.
2 That flaps, or has a tendency to flap. M19.

flare /flɛː/ *noun*[1]. E19.
[ORIGIN from the verb.]
1 The action or quality of flaring; a dazzling irregular light; a sudden outburst of light or flame. E19. ▸**b** *fig.* A dazzling display; a sudden outburst of emotion etc.; a sudden or loud noise. M19. ▸**c** ASTRONOMY. A sudden outburst of radiation from the sun (freq. ***solar flare***) or a star. M20.

TOLKIEN Many of them carried torches, and in the flare I could see their faces. **b** H. E. BATES She got up with a flare of energy . . almost running. *Daily Telegraph* Amid a flare of trumpets, the procession returned.

2 PHOTOGRAPHY. Extraneous illumination of the film, due to internal reflections etc. M19.
3 A gradual swell or bulging outward (orig. in SHIPBUILDING); a gradual widening or spreading outward (esp. of a skirt etc.); that part which widens or spreads; (in *pl.*) flared trousers. M19. ▸**b** AERONAUTICS. A lessening of the steepness of the glide path of an aircraft about to land. Also ***flare-out***. M20.

J. AGEE A woman . . her face narrow beneath her flare of sunbonnet.

4 (A device giving off) a bright flame, used as a signal or as illumination of a target etc.; a flame of burning waste gas from an oil well etc. L19.

S. GIBBONS The wickering hissing of the gas flares which lit the hall and cast sharp shadows. *Lifeboat* His yacht . . was now in distress and firing flares.

– COMB.: **flarepath** an area illuminated to guide aircraft in landing or taking off; **flare star** ASTRONOMY a star in which flares occur from time to time.
■ **flareless** *adjective* M20.

flare /flɛː/ *noun*[2]. *dial.* M19.
[ORIGIN Unknown.]
The fat about a pig's kidney.

flare *noun*[3] var. of FLAIR *noun*[1].

flare /flɛː/ *verb.* M16.
[ORIGIN Uncertain (perh. Scandinavian).]
1 †**a** *verb trans.* Spread out, display (one's hair). Only in M16. ▸**b** *verb intrans.* Of hair etc.: spread out, stream (as if) in the wind. Now *rare.* L16.
2 *verb trans. & intrans.* Spread out or display (oneself) conspicuously. Now *rare.* E17.

GOLDSMITH A flaming torch, if flared round in a circle . . appears as a ring of fire.

3 *verb intrans.* Of a ship's sides, a wine glass, a skirt, trousers, etc.: widen gradually in an upward or downward direction. E17. ▸**b** *verb trans.* Cause to spread or widen gradually outwards. Freq. as ***flared*** *ppl adjective.* M19. ▸**c** *verb trans. & intrans.* AERONAUTICS. Reduce the steepness of the glide path of (an aircraft) about to land. M20.

b T. MORRISON Jadine flared her nostrils. W. GOLDING His white trousers were flared at the bottom.

4 *verb intrans.* Burn with a spreading, unsteady flame; blaze or glow (as) with flame; *fig.* burst into sudden (usu. temporary) activity, emotion, etc. Freq. foll. by *out, up.* M17. ▸**b** *verb trans.* Light up with a flare; cause a candle to burn with an unsteady light; send by means of a flare. Also, burn off (waste gas) at an oil well etc. M18.

K. MANSFIELD Blue flowers and red flowers . . flared in the roadside hedges. E. WELTY The log shifted . . and light flared all over in the room. U. LE GUIN She was . . easily upset, and her temper flared at a word. *Times* Jeers and insults which flared into scattered stone-throwing. **b** J. R. GREEN The English beacons flared out their alarm along the coast.

– COMB.: **flare-out** (*a*) = *flare-up* (a) below; (*b*) AERONAUTICS = FLARE *noun*[1] 3b; **flare-up** (*a*) a sudden bursting out into flame, anger, excitement, etc.; (*b*) NAUTICAL a signal flare.

flary /ˈflɛːri/ *adjective.* Now *rare.* M19.
[ORIGIN from FLARE *noun*[1] + -Y[1].]
Having or resembling a flare or flares; *esp.* gaudy, showy.

flaser /ˈflɑːzə/ *noun.* L19.
[ORIGIN German, dial. form of *Flader* streak, vein.]
GEOLOGY. Used *attrib.* and in *comb.* to denote (the presence of) a streaky structure characterized by lenses of little-altered parent rock in a rock metamorphosed by shearing, as ***flaser-gabbro***, ***flaser structure***, etc.

flash /flaʃ/ *noun*[1]. Now *local.* In sense 1 also **flosh** /flɒʃ/. See also FLUSH *noun*[1]. ME.
[ORIGIN Old French & mod. French *flache*, central form of Picard and Norman dial. *flaque* from Middle Dutch *vlacke.*]
1 A pool, a marshy place. ME.
2 A water-filled hollow formed by subsidence due to rock salt extraction (esp. in Cheshire). L19.

flash /flaʃ/ *noun*[2]. M16.
[ORIGIN from FLASH *verb.*]
▸ **I** A burst of light. Cf. FLASH *verb* II.
1 A sudden, transitory burst or blaze of flame or light. M16. ▸**b** A flashlight, an electric torch. E20. ▸**c** A photographic flashlight; a photograph taken using this. M20.

K. CLARK The dark landscape is lit only by terrific flashes of lightning.

flash in the pan: see PAN *noun*[1]. **c *electronic flash***: see ELECTRONIC *adjective.*
2 A brief period of time (during which a flash is visible); an instant. Usu. in ***in a flash*** immediately, instantaneously. E17.
3 A brief outburst or transient display of something (seen as resembling a flash of light); *esp.* a sudden access of feeling or knowledge. E17. ▸**b** A brief news dispatch or bulletin (orig. by telegraph, now on radio or television). M19. ▸**c** A brief scene on film or television. E20.

SHAKES. *Haml.* Your flashes of merriment that were wont to set the table on a roar. J. CONRAD He gave us a flash of his white teeth. ALDOUS HUXLEY To some people . . there come little flashes of illumination—momentary glimpses into the nature of the world.

hot flash: see HOT *adjective.*
4 †**a** A piece of showy talk; an empty phrase. E17–M18. ▸**b** Superficial brilliance; ostentation. L17. ▸**c** [from FLASH *adjective.*] Thieves' slang, cant. Now chiefly *hist.* M18.

b CLIVE JAMES The man was all artist, humble under the flash.

c *patter flash*: see PATTER *verb*[1] 3.
†**5** A superficially brilliant or showy person. E17–E19.
6 a A coloured patch of cloth on a uniform or other clothing, esp. on the upper arm or shoulder and with the distinguishing device of a regiment, country, etc. M19. ▸**b** A patch of or *of* bright colour on a darker background. L20.

b C. PHILLIPS Leila's mother had large flashes of grey in her hair.

7 Excess metal, plastic, etc., forced between facing surfaces as two halves of a mould close up, forming a thin projection on the final object. E20.
8 A thin layer (of glass, chrome, etc.). E20.
▸ **II** A sudden movement of water. Cf. FLASH *verb* I.
9 †**a** A splash of water; a large wave. E17–E18. ▸**b** A sudden rush of water let down from a weir to increase the depth of the river temporarily. Also, a contrivance for producing this. L17.
†**10** A sudden burst of rain, wind, etc. M17–E19.
– COMB.: **flashbulb**: producing a flash of light used for photography under conditions of low light; **flash burn**: caused by sudden intense heat, esp. from a nuclear explosion; **flash card**: with words etc., shown briefly to a child by a teacher as an aid to learning; **flashcube** a set of (four) flashbulbs arranged as a cube and operated in turn; **flash-dry** *verb trans.* dry in a very short time; **flash flood** a sudden, destructive flood; **flash-freeze** *verb trans.* freeze (food etc.) very rapidly so as to prevent the formation of ice crystals; **flash-fry** *verb trans.* fry at a high temperature for a short time; **flashgun** a device to hold and operate a camera flashlight; **flash lamp** (*a*) a portable flashing electric lamp, *esp.* an electric torch; (*b*) = ***flashlight*** (b) below; **flashlight** (*a*) a flashing light used in signalling, lighthouses, etc.; (*b*) a device which provides a burst of intense illumination for photography in dark conditions; (*c*) = ***flash lamp*** (a) above; **flash photolysis** CHEMISTRY the use of a very brief intense flash of light to bring about gas-phase decomposition or dissociation, usu. as a means of studying short-lived molecules etc.; **flashpoint** (*a*) the lowest temperature at which the vapour from an oil etc. will ignite in air; (*b*) *fig.* a point of climax at which violent action (as loss of temper, active hostility, etc.) begins; **flash powder** a powder which burns rapidly with a bright flash, esp. as formerly used in photography; **flash tube** a gas-discharge tube used to provide an electronic flash when a current is suddenly passed through it.
■ **flashless** *adjective* without a flash, emitting no flash; (of gunpowder etc.) emitting no flash when ignited: E20.

flash /flaʃ/ *noun*[3]. *rare.* L16.
[ORIGIN Unknown.]
= FLASHING *noun*[2].

flash /flaʃ/ *adjective.* Chiefly *colloq.* L17.
[ORIGIN from FLASH *noun*[2].]
1 a Of or pertaining to thieves or prostitutes; *spec.* of thieves' slang, cant. *arch.* L17. ▸**b** Of, pertaining to, or resembling sporting and betting men as a class, esp. patrons of boxing and racing. E19.
2 Gaudy, showy, superficially attractive; too smart. L18.

W. PLOMER A flash flat in Chelsea of a bogus elegance.

3 Counterfeit, sham. Now *rare* or *obsolete.* E19.
4 Knowing, fly, cheeky. *slang.* E19.

DOUGLAS STUART Some flash young coot, to tell him how to shoe a horse!

– SPECIAL COLLOCATIONS & COMB.: ***Flash Harry***: see HARRY *noun*[2]. **flash-house** *arch.* a brothel.
■ **flashly** *adverb* E19. **flashness** *noun* M19.

flash /flaʃ/ *verb.* ME.
[ORIGIN App. imit.: cf. PLASH *verb*[2], DASH *verb*[1], SPLASH *verb*[1], SLASH *verb.*]
▸ **I** Expr. movement of water.
1 *verb trans.* Splash (water) *about, (up)on. obsolete* exc. as passing into sense 6. ME.

T. HERBERT The wave flashing upon our decks . . much salt water.

2 *verb intrans.* Of the sea, a wave, a river, etc.: dash, break, flow swiftly. (Passing into sense 5.) LME.

M. SCOTT The roaring surf was flashing up over the clumps of green bushes.

3 *verb trans.* Send a flash or rush of water down (a river, millstream, etc.). L18.
▸ **II** With ref. to light or fire. Freq. with adverbs.
4 *verb intrans.* Burst suddenly into flame or light; give out flame or sparks. LME.

J. TYNDALL Lightning flashed about the summits of the Jungfrau. J. BARNES Every third street-lamp flickered and flashed into life.

5 *verb intrans.* Move swiftly, like a flash of light; burst suddenly into view or perception. LME.

R. L. STEVENSON It flashed into my mind . . that . . the powder for the gun had been left behind. E. GLASGOW A bird and its shadow flashed over the winter fields. G. HEYER Often the answer to a problem will flash upon one in the night.

6 *verb trans.* (Cause to) emit or reflect (light, fire, etc.) like a flash or in flashes; cause to gleam or shine; send out swiftly. L16. ▸**b** *verb trans. & intrans. spec.* Signal to (other traffic) by causing one's vehicle's (head)lights to shine briefly or intermittently. M20.

C. KINGSLEY Turning round I had a lantern flashed in my face. W. S. MAUGHAM A light was flashed and in that heavy darkness the sudden glare was terrifying.

7 *verb intrans.* Break out *into* sudden action, words, etc. E17. ▸**b** Burst into sudden anger or excitement. Foll. by *out, up.* E19.

A. H. GREEN The imprisoned steam flashes forth in repeated explosions.

8 Chiefly *slang.* ▸**a** *verb intrans.* Make a flash or display, show off. Now *rare.* E17. ▸**b** *verb trans.* Make a great display of, exhibit ostentatiously, show off. L18. ▸**c** *verb trans. & intrans.* Exhibit or expose (part of one's body, esp. the genitals) briefly and indecently. *slang.* M19.

a SHAKES. *Timon* A naked gull, which flashes now a phoenix. **b** A. CARTER The blonde . . flashed a pair of vast, blue, indecorous eyes at the young reporter.

9 *verb intrans.* Emit or reflect light suddenly or intermittently; gleam. L18.

SHELLEY Like wingèd stars the fireflies flash and glance. R. MACAULAY Fierce black eyes that flashed while he spoke.

10 *verb trans.* Express or communicate by a flash or flashes; *esp.* send (a message, news, etc.) by radio, telegraph, etc. L18. ▸**b** *verb trans. & intrans.* CINEMATOGRAPHY. Show or be shown briefly on the screen. E20.

J. A. FROUDE The cannon . . flashed their welcome through the darkness. *Listener* Electronic indicators which flash train times and platform numbers momentarily.

11 *verb trans.* Cover (glass etc.) with a thin layer or film of some material. M19.
– WITH ADVERBS IN SPECIALIZED SENSES: **flash over** (*a*) make an (accidental) electric circuit by sparking across a gap; (*b*) (of a fire) spread instantly across a gap because of intense heat.
– COMB.: **flashback** (*a*) a flame moving rapidly back through a combustible vapour; (*b*) a scene in a film, novel, etc., which returns or changes to an earlier time; **flashboard** a board set up on a mill dam to increase the flow of water through the mill; **flashover** an accidental electrical discharge across a gap, esp. where the voltage is too great for the insulation on a conductor.

F

flasher /ˈflaʃə/ *noun.* E17.
[ORIGIN from FLASH *verb* + -ER[1].]
†**1** A person who splashes water. *rare.* E17–M18.
2 Something emitting flashes of light. Now *esp.* (a sign or signal using) an automatic device which switches a light or lights rapidly on and off. L17.
†**3** A flash person; *spec.* an attendant at a gaming table. M–L18.
4 CRICKET. A batsman inclined to play forcefully at balls wide of the off stump. *colloq.* M20.
5 A person who exposes himself indecently. *colloq.* L20.

flashing /ˈflaʃɪŋ/ *noun*[1]. L16.
[ORIGIN from FLASH *verb* + -ING[1].]
The action of FLASH *verb*; an act or instance of this.
– COMB.: **flashing point** = ***flashpoint*** (a) s.v. FLASH *noun*[2].

flashing /ˈflaʃɪŋ/ *noun*[2]. L18.
[ORIGIN from FLASH *noun*[3] + -ING[1].]
A strip of non-porous material (esp. flexible metal) that excludes water from the junction of a roof covering with another surface; material used for this.

flashy /ˈflaʃi/ *adjective.* L16.
[ORIGIN from FLASH *noun*[2], *verb* + -Y[1].]
†**1** Splashing. L16–E17.
†**2** Watery; insipid; trifling, insubstantial. L16–M19.
3 Flashing, sparkling, brilliant. Hence, showy, of fine appearance, gaudy, cheaply attractive. Also, momentary. E17.

H. BUSK One ruby glitter'd like the flashy Mars. C. J. LEVER The splendour of a very flashy silk waistcoat. C. LASSALLE The storm, flashy and loud, began as they ran downstairs.

†**4** Excited, eager. M17–L18.
5 Of a person, an attribute, etc.: superficially brilliant; given to showing off; vain, conceited. L17.

G. COLMAN A young flashy Englishman will sometimes carry a whole fortune on his back. DE QUINCEY The secondhand report of a flashy rhetorician. A. TYLER Those black-haired, flashy, beauty-queen types.

■ **flashily** *adverb* M18. **flashiness** *noun* E17.

flask /flɑːsk/ *noun.*
[ORIGIN Old English *flasce*, *flaxe* (in sense 2 from French *flasque* from Old French *flasche*, *flaske*) from medieval Latin *flasca*. In sense 3 prob. from Italian *fiasco* from medieval Latin *flasco*, *flascon*. Ult. origin unknown. Cf. FLAGON.]
†**1** A (wooden, skin, etc.) container for liquor. OE–LME.
2 a FOUNDING. A frame used to hold a mould for casting. M17. ▸**b** DENTISTRY. A sectional metal container for holding a denture during vulcanization. M19.
3 A bottle, usu. of bulbous or conical shape, with a narrow neck; *esp.* a glass vessel used in chemistry, or (in a covering of wickerwork or plaited grass) for wine or oil. Now fig. *ellipt.*, a vacuum or Thermos flask. L17.
hip flask, ***powder flask***, ***Thermos flask***, ***vacuum flask***, etc.

flask /flɑːsk/ *verb trans.* E18.
[ORIGIN from the noun.]
†**1** Protect with wickerwork etc., as a flask is protected. Only in E18.
2 Put in a flask; *spec.* in DENTISTRY, place (a denture) in a flask and enclose with plaster prior to vulcanizing. M19.

flasket /ˈflɑːskɪt/ *noun. arch.* ME.
[ORIGIN from Old Northern French *flasquet* FLACKET.]
1 A container; *esp.* a (small) flask. ME.
2 A long shallow basket. LME.

flasque /flɑːsk/ *noun.* M16.
[ORIGIN French *flasque* FLASK *noun* or alt. of *flanque* var. of FLAUNCH *noun*[1].]
HERALDRY. A bearing resembling a flanch, but smaller, esp. in width.

flat /flat/ *noun*[1]. ME.
[ORIGIN from the adjective.]
1 A piece of level ground; a plain; the low ground through which a river flows. Freq. in *pl.* ME. ▸**b** A tract of low-lying marshy ground; a swamp. E17.

SHAKES. *Haml.* Till of this flat a mountain you have made. A. B. EDWARDS The river widens away before us; the flats are green on either side. **b** SHAKES. *Temp.* All the infections that the sun sucks up From bogs, fens, flats.

2 (Without *pl.*) ▸**a** That which is flat, the flat part of something; *spec.* (*a*) the broad surface of a sword etc. as opp. to the edge; (*b*) the inside *of* the open hand. LME. ▸**b** Level country; *esp.* level ground without hedges or ditches for horse-racing; *the* season or occupation of flat-racing. M19.

a W. SNELGRAVE He gave me a slight blow . . with the flat of his Cutlace. DICKENS Here's old Bill Barley on the flat of his back. **b** J. WILSON Sic a . . body . . could never have been bred or born on the flat.

3 A nearly level tract over which the tide flows or which is covered by shallow water; a shallow, a shoal. Usu. in *pl.* L15.

G. C. DAVIES At low water, the muds or flats are dry.

mudflat, ***sandflat***, etc.
4 A tract of arable land, a ploughed section of a field; *esp.* each of the larger portions into which the common field was divided, a square furlong. *obsolete* exc. *dial.* or *hist.* E16.
5 †**a** A die loaded by being shaved on one or more surfaces. M16–E18. ▸**b** *gen.* Something of a broad thin shape, as a disc, a coin, a strip of wood, a piece of metal, etc. M16.
6 MUSIC. A note lowered a semitone below natural pitch; a sign (♭) indicating this lowering. L16.
double flat: see DOUBLE *adjective & adverb*. **sharps and flats** *loosely* the black keys of a piano.
7 A horizontal plane; a level. Formerly also, a plane figure. L16. ▸**b** A flat space or flattened surface; *esp.* a worn patch on a tyre. L19. ▸**c** In full ***optical flat***. A block or lamina (usu. made of glass) with one or more surfaces made accurately plane and smooth, any unevenness etc. being small compared with the wavelength of light. L19.

J. BENTHAM A declivity is . . preferable by far to a dead flat.

8 a A broad flat-bottomed receptacle; a flat-bottomed boat. M17. ▸**b** A relatively long or broad and low article of dress, as a low-heeled shoe, *US* a low-crowned hat. E19.
9 A horizontal upper surface; *esp.* the horizontal part of a roof. Formerly also, a landing on a staircase, the tread of a stair. E18.
10 MINING. A horizontal (part of) a bed, stratum, or vein. M18.
11 A simpleton; someone who is (easily) taken in, a dupe. Freq. contrasted with ***sharp***. *arch. slang.* M18.

THACKERAY You wouldn't be such a flat as to let three thousand a year go out of the family.

12 THEATRICAL. A section of scenery mounted on a frame. L18.
join the flats *fig.* make a thing into a coherent whole; preserve the appearance of a consistent attitude.
13 NAUTICAL. **a** In *pl.* Timbers in the midships of a vessel. E19. ▸**b** The partial deck or floor of a particular compartment. M19.
14 (The paint used for) a surface painted with a uniform matt finish. E19.
15 A flat tyre; a puncture. E20.

J. M. CAIN I was in the filling station, fixing flats.

flat /flat/ *noun*[2]. E19.
[ORIGIN Alt. of FLET *noun*[1] by assoc. with FLAT *adjective*.]
1 A floor or storey in a house. Now *rare*. E19.
2 A dwelling comprising a room or rooms forming a unit (esp. self-contained) within a house or larger building, and freq. wholly or chiefly on one floor. E19.
– COMB.: **flatmate** a person who shares a flat with another.
■ **flatlet** *noun* a small flat E20. **flatted** *adjective* divided into, constructed as, or consisting (partly) of flats E20.

flat /flat/ *adjective & adverb*. Compar. & superl. **-tt-**. ME.
[ORIGIN Old Norse *flatr* = Old High German *flaz* from Germanic: ult. relationship uncertain.]
▸ **A** *adjective* **I 1** Horizontally level; without inclination. ME.

J. GWILT In India . . all buildings of any importance have flat roofs.

2 Spread out, stretched, lying at full length. ME. ▸**b** Of a building etc.: levelled with the ground; overthrown, razed. M16. ▸**c** Lying in close apposition; with the whole length and breadth evenly in contact with a surface. M16.

E. K. KANE The hunter is flat and motionless. R. KIPLING A big wind blew . . the tents flat. **b** SHAKES. *Coriol.* To lay the city flat, To bring the roof to the foundation. **c** H. J. STONOR The ladder was standing flat against the wall.

3 Even, smooth, unbroken, without projection; (of the face, features, etc.) without prominence, not projecting; (of land) not undulating; (of a surface) smooth, level. ME. ▸**b** Deflated, punctured. E20. ▸**c** ELECTRONICS. Uniform in behaviour over a given range of frequencies; responding equally to signals of all frequencies. E20.

I. MURDOCH Flat cornlands where . . miles away against the sky one could perhaps see a silo. M. SPARK Miss Brodie's chest was flat, no bulges at all. **b** E. BOWEN My tyre . . went really flat.

4 Having a broad level surface and little depth; *esp.* (of a foot) touching the ground with most or all of the lower surface in walking or standing, having little or no arch. LME. ▸**b** Of a vessel: wide and shallow. L15.

W. DAMPIER The Booby is a Water-fowl . . her Feet are flat like a Ducks Feet. D. LARDNER This ruler consists of a flat piece of wood with a straight edge.

(***as***) ***flat as a pancake***: see PANCAKE *noun* 1.
5 (Of a tint etc.) of uniform depth and shade; PHOTOGRAPHY lacking contrast; (of paint etc.) not glossy. M18.

W. M. CRAIG Throwing every mass of shadow into a flat tint. P. CAREY She uses a flat plastic paint.

▸ **II 6** Unrelieved by condition or qualification; absolute, downright, unqualified, plain. M16. ▸**b** Impecunious, penniless, broke. Cf. ***flat broke***. *US slang*. M19.

T. JEFFERSON In flat contradiction to their Arret of December last. T. KEIGHTLEY He claimed to be put in possession . . but met with a flat refusal. G. SAINTSBURY Such hints at rebellion . . were . . regarded as flat heresy.

leave flat go away from (a person) without warning, drop suddenly and completely. **that's flat** let there be no doubt about it.
7 Completely lacking in attraction or interest; dull, lifeless; monotonous, insipid. L16.

M. PATTISON A rather flat treatment of trite themes. E. GASKELL It seems so flat to be left behind.

fall flat prove a failure, fail to win applause, response, etc.
8 Deficient in sense or mental vigour; stupid, dull, slow-witted. *arch.* L16.

J. R. SEELEY I look for nothing from empty, slow, flat people.

9 a MUSIC. Relatively low in pitch; *esp.* (of a note or singer) below true pitch; (of a key) having a flat or flats in the signature. L16. ▸**b** Of a sound, voice, etc.: not clear and sharp, dead, dull. E17.

b F. WELDON Annie had a flat, nasal telephone voice.

a B flat, **E flat**, etc., a semitone lower than B, E, etc.
10 †**a** Of an accent, syllable, etc.: unstressed. L16–E17. ▸**b** GRAMMAR. Of a word, esp. an adverb: not distinguished by an ending characteristic of its part of speech. Now *rare*. L19. ▸**c** PHONETICS. Of a sound: characterized by the downward shift of higher frequencies. M20.
11 Lacking energy or spirits, lifeless, dejected; depressed. E17. ▸**b** Of trade etc.: depressed, inactive, sluggish. M19. ▸**c** Of an electric battery: run down, discharged. M20.

C. LAMB I am now calm, but sadly taken down and flat.

12 Of drink etc.: lacking in flavour, stale; *esp.* having lost effervescence. E17.
13 a Of a loan etc.: without interest. *US*. M19. ▸**b** COMMERCE. Unvarying, fixed, uniform; not varying with changed conditions or in particular cases. L19.
– SPECIAL COLLOCATIONS & COMB.: **flat arch** an arch with a flat intrados. **flatbed** *noun & adjective* (denoting) something with a flat working surface, esp. (*a*) a truck with a flat load-carrying area; (*b*) a scanner, plotter, etc. which keeps paper flat during use. **flatboat** (*a*) a broad flat-bottomed boat; (*b*) *US* a large roughly made boat formerly used for floating goods etc. down western rivers. **flat bottom** (*a*) = ***flatboat*** above. **flat-bottom**, **flat-bottomed** *adjectives* (esp. of a boat) having a flat bottom. **flatbread** flat, thin, typically unleavened bread. **flat-cap** (the wearer of) a cap with a low crown, *esp.* (now *hist.*) a round cap worn in the 16th and 17th cents. by citizens of London. **flatcar** *N. Amer.* a railway wagon without raised sides or ends. **flatfish** any of numerous flat-bodied, bottom-dwelling bony fishes forming the order Heterosomata and including sole, plaice, turbot, etc. **flat foot** (*a*) a foot with an arch that is lower than usual; (*b*) (***flatfoot***) *slang* a police officer. **flat-footed** *adjective* (*a*) having flat feet; (*b*) *colloq.* downright, resolute; unready, unprepared; clumsy, uninspired. **flat-four** *adjective* (of an engine) having four cylinders all horizontal, two on each side of the crankshaft. **flat-headed** *adjective* (*a*) having or appearing to have a flat head; (*b*) ***flat-headed borer*** (US), the wood-boring larva of any of various beetles of the family Buprestidae. **flat iron** (*a*) a domestic iron for pressing linen etc., heated by external means and usu. triangular in shape; (*b*) *colloq.* a boat, building, etc., like a flat iron in shape. **flatland** (*a*) a hypothetical land in space of two dimensions; (*b*) (orig. *US*) a region of flat land. **flat-leaf parsley**, **flat-leaved parsley** parsley of a variety with large, flat leaves, popular in southern Europe. **flat-nosed** *adjective* having a flat nose. **flat-pack** (*a*) a piece of furniture or other equipment that is sold in pieces packed flat in a box for easy transport and is assembled by the buyer; (*b*) ELECTRONICS a package for an integrated circuit consisting of a rectangular sealed unit with a number of horizontal metal pins protruding from its sides. **flat parsley** = ***flat-leaf parsley*** above. **flat-pea** *Austral.* a leguminous shrub of the genus *Platylobium*, with flat pods. **flat race**: run over level ground, as opp. to a hurdle race or a steeplechase. **flat-racing** the racing of horses in flat races. **flat rate** a rate of payment etc. that is the same in all cases, not proportional or otherwise variable. **flat spin** (*a*) AERONAUTICS a nearly horizontal spin; (*b*) *colloq.* a state of agitation, panic. **flat-tail mullet** an Australian mullet, *Liza argentea*. **flat-top** *slang* (*a*) an aircraft carrier; (*b*) a man's short flat haircut. **flat tyre** (*a*) a deflated or punctured tyre; (*b*) *N. Amer. colloq.* a dull and spiritless person. **flatware** (*a*) crockery such as plates, saucers, etc. (opp. ***hollow ware***); (*b*) *N. Amer.* cutlery. **flatwater** *N. Amer.* slowly moving water in a river etc., as opp. to rapids. **flatwoods** *US* low-lying wooded country, esp. in Ohio, Alabama and Florida.
▸ **B** *adverb*. †**1** Directly, exactly; due (*east* etc.). M16–M17.
2 Downright, absolutely, positively, plainly; completely, quite. L16. ▸**b** Exactly, precisely. Orig. *US*. E20.

C. JENNER Sir Harry contradicted him flat. W. S. MAUGHAM You haven't turned it down flat? **b** JOHN CLARKE It took her about two minutes flat to step into jeans and sweater.

flat out at top speed, using all one's strength and resources.
3 MUSIC. In a flat manner; a semitone below natural pitch. L17.

OED She has a tendency to sing flat.

■ **flattish** *adjective* E17.

flat /flat/ *verb*[1]. Infl. **-tt-**. L16.
[ORIGIN from the adjective.]
1 *verb trans.* = FLATTEN 1. Now *rare*. L16.
†**2** *verb trans.* Lay flat or level, raze, throw down. E–M17.

O. FELTHAM She hath . . flatted their strongest Forts.

3 NAUTICAL. †**a** *verb intrans.* Of a ship: turn its head from the wind. Only in E17. ▸**b** *verb trans.* Force (the sail) flat or close against the mast. M17. ▸**c** *verb intrans.* = FLATTEN 3b. M18.

b W. MONSON He hears the Seamen cry . . flat a Sheet.

†**4** *verb trans.* = FLATTEN 2. E17–E18. ▸**b** *verb intrans.* = FLATTEN 2b. M17–E18.

BACON An Orenge, Limon and Apple . . fresh in their Colour, But their Iuyce somewhat flatted. G. BURNET So great a length does . . flat the Hearers, and tempt them to sleep. **b** T. FULLER Their loyalty flatteth and deadeth by degrees.

5 *verb intrans.* = FLATTEN 3. Now *rare* or *obsolete* exc. in ***flat off***, ***flat out*** below. L17.
flat off *US* (*rare*) slope gradually to a level. **flat out** *US* become gradually thinner; *fig.* fail (esp. in business), collapse.
6 *verb trans.* MUSIC. = FLATTEN 4. Now chiefly *US*. L17.

W. APEL Variants in which some of the original tones are flatted.

7 *verb trans.* = FLATTEN 5. M19.
8 *verb trans. & intrans.* Saw lengthwise through the thickness of (a plank etc.), so reducing the width. L19.
– COMB.: **flat-out** *US* a failure, a fiasco.
■ **flatter** *noun* (*a*) a worker who makes something flat; (*b*) a tool used in making things flat, esp. a blacksmith's broad-faced hammer: E18. **flatting** *noun* (*a*) = FLATTENING; *esp.* the process of rolling out sheet metal; (*b*) (paint used for) a uniform matt coat: E17.

flat /flat/ *verb*[2] *intrans.* *Austral.* Infl. **-tt-**. L20.
[ORIGIN from FLAT *noun*[2].]
Live in or share a flat (*with*).

flathead /ˈflathɛd/ *noun*. E18.
[ORIGIN from FLAT *adjective* + HEAD *noun*.]
1 (A member of) any of various peoples, esp. (**Flathead**) certain N. American Indian peoples such as Chinook, Choctaw, and Salish, who customarily practised head-flattening or (in the case of the Salish) were erroneously credited with so doing. E18.
2 A fish with a flattened head; *spec.* any of numerous marine fishes of the family Platycephalidae. L18.
3 A fool, a simpleton. *dial. & slang*. M19.
4 A hognose snake. *US*. L19.
– COMB.: **flathead catfish** a large N. American catfish, *Pylodictis olivaris*, with long slender body and flattened head.

flatline /ˈflatlʌɪn/ *noun & verb*. *colloq.* M20.
[ORIGIN with ref. to the line displayed on a heart monitor (sense 2).]
▸ **A** *noun*. **1** A horizontal line on a graph, or the horizontal portion of a curve, esp. when indicating lack of change or variation. M20.
2 A horizontal line on an electrocardiogram etc., usu. indicating absence or marked reduction of function (esp. cardiac arrest or brain death). L20.
▸ **B** *verb intrans.* **1** Die. L20.
2 Fail to increase. L20.

Guardian Their share of the vote has flatlined at about 33–34 per cent.

■ **flatliner** *noun* a person who has had a cardiac arrest or who is brain-dead L20.

flatling /ˈflatlɪŋ/ *adverb*. *arch. & dial.* Also **-lings** /-z/. LME.
[ORIGIN from FLAT *adjective* + -LING[2].]
1 In a prostrate position, at full length, flat. LME.
2 With the flat side (esp. of a sword). LME.

†**flatlong** *adverb*. L16–M17.
[ORIGIN from FLAT *adjective* + -LONG.]
1 In or into a prostrate position. L16–M17.
2 With the flat side; with flat sides in contact. L16–M17.

flatly /ˈflatli/ *adverb*. LME.
[ORIGIN from FLAT *adjective* + -LY[2].]
1 In a flat or prostrate position. Long *rare* or *obsolete*. LME.
2 In a plain, blunt, or decisive manner; without hesitation, ambiguity, or qualification; absolutely, completely. M16.

H. MANTEL 'They're doubling my salary,' he said flatly.

3 In a dull or spiritless manner; without zest, insipidly; prosaically. **M17.**
4 With a small degree of curvature. Also, as on a flat surface; without relief. **L18.**

flatness /ˈflatnɪs/ *noun.* **LME.**
[**ORIGIN** from **FLAT** *adjective* + **-NESS.**]
1 The quality or condition of being flat or level. **LME.**
2 Absoluteness, unqualified condition. Also, outspokenness, plainness (of speech). **L16.**
3 Lack of sharpness and clarity in a sound; deadness of tone, voice, etc. **E17.**
4 Lack of spirit or energy; apathy, dejectedness; lack of mental acuteness or alertness. **M17.**
5 The quality in speech or writing of lacking animation, brilliance, or pointedness; prosaic dullness. **M17.**
6 The quality of having a small degree of curvature; reduced convexity. **L17.**
7 Lack of relief or prominence; the quality or state of having an even and unbroken surface. **E18.**
8 Deficiency in flavour; insipidity, vapidity. **E18.**
9 Lack of incident or interest, monotony; sluggishness of commercial activity. **E19.**
10 The condition of having great breadth or length in proportion to height or depth. **L19.**

flatten /ˈflat(ə)n/ *verb.* Cf. **FLAT** *verb*[1]. **M17.**
[**ORIGIN** from **FLAT** *adjective* + **-EN**[5].]
1 *verb trans.* Make flat in shape; reduce to a plane surface; make broad and thin; reduce the thickness or height of, esp. by pressure; squeeze or beat flat. **M17.**

D. L. SAYERS Bunter, like a steam-roller, had passed over everything, flattening out all traces of upheaval. F. O'CONNOR Flattening themselves against the side to let . . people through. W. GOLDING The water was smoother today as though the dead air were flattening it.

2 *verb trans.* Make flat, vapid, or insipid; make dull or spiritless; deprive of interest; deaden, depress. **M17.** ▸**b** *verb intrans.* Become insipid or dull; lose spirit, droop. **L17.**

G. BURNET The odiousness of the crime grew at last to be so much flatten'd by the frequent executions. BURKE So far from endeavouring to excite this spirit, nothing has been omitted to flatten and lower it. **b** R. L'ESTRANGE Satisfactions that . . flatten in the very tasting.

3 *verb intrans.* Be or become flat or flatter; lose convexity or protuberance; grow broad at the expense of thickness. Also foll. by *out.* **E18.** ▸**b** *NAUTICAL.* Of the wind etc.: decrease in force. **M18.**

b G. ANSON The storm at length flattening to a calm.

4 *verb trans. MUSIC.* Lower in pitch by a semitone. **E19.**
5 *verb trans.* Paint (a surface) with a matt finish; deprive (paint) of lustre. **E19.**
6 *verb trans.* Knock down. Also, defeat crushingly, humiliate. *colloq.* **L19.**

M. GEE We would have flattened them, me and my mates in the army.

– **PHRASES**: **flatten in** *NAUTICAL* extend a sail more nearly fore and aft of the vessel. **flatten out** *AERONAUTICS* bring an aircraft into a position parallel with the ground; (of an aircraft) assume such a position.
■ **flattener** *noun* **M18.** **flattening** *verbal noun* the action or process of making or becoming flat; the condition of being flattened: **E18.**

flatter /ˈflatə/ *verb*[1]. **ME.**
[**ORIGIN** Origin unkn., perh. back-form. from **FLATTERY.**]
1 *verb trans.* Try to please or win the favour of by obsequious speech or conduct; pay obsequious attention to. **ME.**

SHAKES. *Rich. II* I mock my name, great king, to flatter thee.

2 *verb trans.* Compliment unduly or insincerely, overpraise. **ME.**

OED 'Your beautiful voice—' 'Ah! you are flattering me.' L. STEFFENS I did not flatter anybody: I told the truth as near as I could get it.

†**3** *verb intrans.* Of an animal, esp. a dog: display (apparent) pleasure or affection by tail-wagging, making a pleased sound, etc. **LME–E17.** ▸**b** *verb trans.* Touch or stroke lightly and caressingly. *rare.* **L16–E18.**

E. TOPSELL Dogges . . who would fawn & gently flatter vpon all those which came . . there.

4 *verb trans.* Gratify the vanity or self-esteem of; make (a person) feel honoured; gratify (a person's vanity). **LME.**

W. H. PRESCOTT Others he flattered by asking their advice. P. ACKROYD A very clever young man who flattered her self-regard by becoming infatuated with her.

5 *verb trans.* Encourage or cheer (a person) with hopeful or pleasing manifestations; inspire with (esp. unfounded) hope. **LME.** ▸**b** Please or delude with the belief, idea, or suggestion *that.* Chiefly *refl.* **L16.**

W. H. PRESCOTT Men had flattered themselves . . with the expectation of some change for the better. *absol.*: *Field* Two furlongs from home Maiden Erlegh looked dangerous, but he flattered only to deceive. **b** H. JAMES She flattered herself that she was a very just woman.

6 *verb trans.* Play upon the vanity or susceptibilities of (a person); beguile or persuade by blandishments; coax, wheedle. **E16.**

T. FULLER Or did he hope . . to flatter Heaven into a consent?

7 *verb trans.* Beguile, charm away (sorrow etc.); charm *to* (tears etc.). *arch.* **L16.**

SHAKES. *Rich. III* Flatter my sorrows with report of it.

8 *verb trans.* Of a painter, portrait, etc.: represent too favourably, exaggerate the good looks of. **L16.** ▸**b** Show to the best advantage, make effective, emphasize the good points of. **E20.**

HOR. WALPOLE Oliver . . said to him ' . . I desire you . . to paint my picture truly like me, and not flatter me.' *absol.*: CONAN DOYLE A good-looking woman, too, if the photograph does not flatter. **b** J. CHEEVER A grey silk dress—a cloth and a color that flattered her.

9 *verb trans.* Gratify (the eye, ear, etc.). **L17.**

R. L. STEVENSON The beauty of the stone flattered the young clergyman's eyes.

– **PHRASES**: **flatter to deceive** appear promising but ultimately disappoint.
■ **flatterer** *noun* **ME.** **flattering** *ppl adjective* that flatters; ***flattering unction*** [Shakes. *Haml.*], a salve that one administers to one's own conscience or self-esteem: **LME.** **flatteringly** *adverb* **LME.**

†**flatter** *verb*[2] *intrans.* **LME–E19.**
[**ORIGIN** Imit.: cf. *flacker, flutter, flitter.*]
Float, flutter.

flattery /ˈflat(ə)ri/ *noun.* **ME.**
[**ORIGIN** Old French *flaterie* (mod. *flatterie*), from *flater* verb = flatter, prob. ult. from Germanic base of **FLAT** *adjective* with meaning 'pat, smooth, caress'.]
1 The action or practice of flattering; undue or insincere praise; adulation; cajolery, blandishment. **ME.**

GOLDSMITH Tyranny over his inferiors, and flattery to the queen. C. P. SNOW It sounded like flattery, like the kind of extravagant compliment he used to give her.

2 Gratifying deception, delusion. *rare* (chiefly Shakes.). **L16.**

SHAKES. *Oth.* She is persuaded I will marry her, out of her own love and flattery.

3 An act or instance of flattering. Now *rare.* **L16.**

R. BOYLE Your Custome to look ev'n upon Smal Praises as Flatteries.

flattie /ˈflati/ *noun. colloq.* Also **-y.** **L19.**
[**ORIGIN** from **FLAT** *adjective* + **-IE**, **-Y**[6].]
1 A flatfish. **L19.**
2 A flat-bottomed boat. **L19.**
3 A police officer. Cf. ***flatfoot*** s.v. **FLAT** *adjective.* **L19.**
4 A flat-heeled shoe. Orig. *US.* **M20.**

flatulence /ˈflatjʊl(ə)ns/ *noun.* **E18.**
[**ORIGIN** formed as **FLATULENCY** + **-ENCE.** Cf. **FLATULENCY.**]
1 Inflated or puffed-up condition, windiness, vanity; pomposity, pretentiousness. **E18.**
2 a The condition of being charged with gas. *rare* exc. as below. **E19.** ▸**b** *spec.* The state or condition of having the stomach or other part of the alimentary canal charged with gas. **M19.** ▸**c** The tendency of a food to produce flatus. **M19.**

flatulency /ˈflatjʊl(ə)nsi/ *noun.* **L16.**
[**ORIGIN** from **FLATULENT** + **-ENCY.**]
1 a = **FLATULENCE** 2c. **L16.** ▸**b** = **FLATULENCE** 2b. **M17.**
2 *fig.* = **FLATULENCE** 1. **M17.**

flatulent /ˈflatjʊl(ə)nt/ *adjective.* **L16.**
[**ORIGIN** French from mod. Latin *flatulentus*, from Latin *flatus* blowing, blast, from *flare* to blow: see **-ULENT.**]
▸ **I 1** Causing or apt to cause the formation of gas in the alimentary canal. **L16.**

M. DONOVAN Eaten in quantity it [beet-root] often proves flatulent.

2 Caused by, accompanied by, or troubled with an accumulation of gas in the alimentary canal. **M17.**

G. BIRD Occasional attacks of indigestion, with flatulent eructations.

3 *fig.* Inflated, puffed up, windy, pretentious. **M17.**

DRYDEN How many of those flatulent Writers have I known. K. AMIS Some flatulent work on textile trades in the time of the Tudors.

▸ **II 4** †**a** Of a windy nature, full of air or wind. **E17–M18.** ▸**b** Liable to, or prolific in, windy blasts. Long *rare* or *obsolete.* **L17.**

b R. BOHUN The Spring and Autumn . . are the most Flatulent Seasons of the yeere.

■ **flatulently** *adverb* **M19.** **flatulentness** *noun* (*rare*) flatulence **M16.**

flatuosity /flatjʊˈɒsɪti/ *noun.* Long *rare* or *obsolete.* **L16.**
[**ORIGIN** from **FLATUOUS** + **-ITY.**]
†**1** A quantity of wind, air, or gas. **L16–E17.**
2 = **FLATULENCE** 2b. **E17.** ▸**b** A tendency to cause flatulence. *rare.* **E18.**

†**flatuous** *adjective.* **L16.**
[**ORIGIN** medieval Latin *flatuosus*, from Latin *flatus*: see **FLATUS**, **-OUS.**]
1 = **FLATULENT** 4. **L16–E18.**
2 = **FLATULENT** 1. Only in **17.**
3 = **FLATULENT** 2. **E17–E18.**
4 = **FLATULENT** 3. **M17–E18.**

flatus /ˈfleɪtəs/ *noun.* **M17.**
[**ORIGIN** Latin, from *flare* to blow.]
1 Gas accumulated in the alimentary canal, or expelled from the anus; wind. **M17.**
2 A blowing, a blast; a breath, a puff of wind. Now *rare.* **L17.**
†**3** A morbid inflation or swelling (*lit.* & *fig.*). **E–M18.**

flatwise /ˈflatwʌɪz/ *adverb.* Also **-ways** /weɪz/, (*rare*) **-way** /-weɪ/. **E17.**
[**ORIGIN** from **FLAT** *adjective* + **-WISE**, **-WAYS.**]
With the flat side (esp. as opp. to the edge) uppermost, foremost, or applied to another surface.

flatworm /ˈflatwəːm/ *noun.* **M18.**
[**ORIGIN** from **FLAT** *adjective* + **WORM** *noun.*]
Any worm of the phylum Platyhelminthes, characterized by a flattened body with three cell layers, a blind gut, and no other body cavity, and including trematodes (flukes), cestodes (tapeworms), and turbellarians.

Flaubertian /fləʊˈbɛːtɪən, -ˈbəːt-/ *adjective.* **E20.**
[**ORIGIN** from *Flaubert* (see below) + **-IAN.**]
Of, pertaining to, or characteristic of the French novelist Gustave Flaubert (1821–1880), or his writings.

flaucht *noun* var. of **FLAUGHT** *noun*[2].

flaught /flɔːt/ *noun*[1]. Chiefly *Scot.* **ME.**
[**ORIGIN** Prob. Old English or Old Norse from Germanic, from parallel bases of **FLAKE** *noun*[2], **FLAW** *noun*[1]. Cf. also **FLIGHT** *noun*[3].]
1 A flash of light, lightning, or fire; a tongue of flame. See also **FIRE-FLAUGHT.** **ME.**
2 A flake of snow. **LME.**
3 Turf, greensward; a turf. Cf. **FLAG** *noun*[2] 1. **LME.**
4 A lock of hair. **L18.**
5 A sudden blast of wind (and rain). **E19.**

flaught /flɔːt/ *noun*[2]. Chiefly *Scot.* Also **-cht.** **L16.**
[**ORIGIN** Var. of **FLOCHT.**]
1 = **FLOCHT** 1. **L16.**
2 A spreading out, as of wings for flight. **E19.**
3 A flock of birds, a flight. **E19.**
4 The action of fleeing, flight. **L19.**

flaughter /ˈflaxtə/ *verb. Scot.* & *N. English.* **M18.**
[**ORIGIN** from **FLAUGHT** *noun*[2]. Cf. **FLICHTER** *verb.*]
1 *verb trans.* Flutter. Of a light: flicker. **M18.**
2 *verb trans.* & *intrans.* Make or become angry, excited, or afraid. **L18.**
3 *verb trans.* & *intrans.* Spread open, sprawl; knock down. **M19.**

flaunch /flɔːn(t)ʃ/ *noun*[1]. Also **flanque** /flɑːŋk/, **flanch** /flɑːn(t)ʃ/. **LME.**
[**ORIGIN** Perh. from Old French *flanche* (fem.) = *flanc* (masc.) **FLANK** *noun.*]
HERALDRY. A subordinary formed on each side of the shield by a line convex towards the centre, always borne double.
■ **flaunched** *adjective* having flaunches **L17.**

flaunch *noun*[2] & *verb* var. of **FLANCH** *noun*[1] & *verb.*

flaunt /flɔːnt/ *noun.* Now *rare.* **L16.**
[**ORIGIN** from the verb.]
†**1** In *pl.* Showy dress, finery. **L16–E17.**
2 The action or a habit of making a display. **E17.**

flaunt /flɔːnt/ *verb.* **M16.**
[**ORIGIN** Unknown.]
1 *verb intrans.* & *trans.* (with *it*). Display oneself ostentatiously or impudently; show off. **M16.** ▸**b** *verb trans.* (Now the usual sense.) Parade or flourish (oneself, one's possessions, abilities, etc.) provocatively or defiantly. **E19.**

W. IRVING The Miss Lambs might now be seen flaunting along the streets in French bonnets. **b** O. WILDE They flaunt their conjugal felicity in one's face, as if it were the most fascinating of sins. G. GREENE The little man . . flaunting his cane and battered bowler along the endless road out of the screen.

2 *verb intrans.* Flutter or wave proudly. **L16.**

T. HOOD No pennons brave Flaunted upon the mast.

3 *verb trans.* Flout. Usu. considered *erron.* **E20.**
– **NOTE**: The use of *flaunt* to mean *flout* is a common error, first recorded in the 1920s.
■ **flaunter** *noun* **L16.** **flaunting** *ppl adjective* (**a**) showy, gaudy, ostentatious; (**b**) waving gaily or proudly: **M16.** **flauntingly** *adverb* **L16.** **flaunty** *adjective* given to ostentation or show; impudent, vain: **L18.**

flautando /flaʊˈtandəʊ/ *noun* & *adverb.* **E19.**
[**ORIGIN** Italian, pres. pple of *flautare* play the flute, from *flauto* flute.]
MUSIC. (A direction: with) a flutelike violin tone, produced either by playing harmonics or by bowing lightly over the fingerboard.
■ Also ***flautato*** /flaʊˈtɑːtəʊ/ *noun* & *adverb* **M19.**

F

flautino /flaʊˈtiːnəʊ/ *noun.* Pl. **-os.** In sense 2 also **-na** /-nə/. E18.
[ORIGIN Italian, dim. of *flauto* flute.]
1 A small flute or flageolet. E18.
2 A gemshorn organ stop of 2-ft length and pitch. M19.

flautist /ˈflɔːtɪst/ *noun.* M19.
[ORIGIN Italian *flautista*, from *flauto* flute. Cf. earlier FLUTIST.]
A person who plays the flute.

flauto /ˈflauto, ˈflaʊtəʊ/ *noun.* Pl. ***-ti*** /-ti/, ***-tos*** /-təʊz/. E18.
[ORIGIN Italian = FLUTE *noun*[1].]
1 Orig., a recorder. Later, a flute. Also, the part played by such an instrument. E18.
flauto piccolo /ˈpikkolo, ˈpɪkələʊ/, pl. ***-li*** /-li/, ***-los*** /-ləʊz/, [= small] †(*a*) a small recorder; (*b*) a piccolo. ***flauto traverso*** /traˈverso, trəˈvəːsəʊ/, pl. ***-si*** /-si/, ***-sos*** /-səʊz/, a side-blown flute.
2 An organ stop of flute scale. L19.

flavanthrone /fleɪˈvanθrəʊn, flə-/ *noun.* Also **-ene** /-iːn/. E20.
[ORIGIN German *Flavanthren*, formed as FLAVO- + ANTHRA(QUINONE: see -ONE, -ENE.]
CHEMISTRY. A yellow synthetic dye, $C_{28}H_{12}N_2O_2$, derived from anthraquinone. Also ***flavanthrone yellow***.

flavescent /fləˈvɛs(ə)nt/ *adjective.* M19.
[ORIGIN Latin *flavescent-* pres. ppl stem of *flavescere*, from *flavus* yellow: see -ESCENT.]
Turning a pale yellow; yellowish.

Flavian /ˈfleɪvɪən/ *adjective & noun.* L16.
[ORIGIN Latin *Flavianus*, from *Flavius* (see below): see -AN.]
ROMAN HISTORY. ▸**A** *adjective.* Of or pertaining to any of several distinguished Romans of the name of Flavius or the gens to which they belonged (among whose members were the emperors Vespasian, Titus, and Domitian). L16.
▸**B** *noun.* A member of the Flavian gens. M20.

flavin /ˈfleɪvɪn/ *noun.* Also **-ine** /-iːn, -ɪn/. M19.
[ORIGIN from Latin *flavus* yellow + -IN[1], -INE[5].]
1 CHEMISTRY. = QUERCETIN. M19.
2 BIOCHEMISTRY. Any of a group of naturally occurring pigments which have a tricyclic molecular structure based on fused benzene, pyrazine, and pyrimidine rings, and include a number of biologically important substances such as riboflavin. M19.
– COMB.: **flavin adenine dinucleotide**, **flavin mononucleotide** coenzymes derived from riboflavin (cf. FLAVOPROTEIN).

flavine /ˈfleɪviːn, -ɪn/. *noun.* M19.
[ORIGIN formed as FLAVIN: see -INE[5].]
1 See FLAVIN. M19.
2 Any of a group of yellow derivatives of acridine having antiseptic properties, e.g. acriflavine. E20.

flavivirus /ˈfleɪvɪvʌɪrəs/ *noun.* L20.
[ORIGIN from Latin *flavus* yellow + VIRUS.]
Any of a genus of RNA viruses which include the causative agents of a number of arthropod-borne diseases such as yellow fever, dengue, and several forms of encephalitis.

flavo- /ˈfleɪvəʊ/ *combining form* of Latin *flavus* yellow: see -O-.
Used esp. in CHEMISTRY, sometimes with the sense 'containing flavin'.
■ **flavoˈprotein** *noun* (BIOCHEMISTRY) any of a group of conjugated proteins having flavin mononucleotide or flavin adenine dinucleotide as cofactor, involved in oxidation-reduction reactions in the cell M20.

flavone /ˈfleɪvəʊn/ *noun.* L19.
[ORIGIN from FLAVO- + -ONE.]
A colourless crystalline tricyclic compound, 2-phenylbenzo-1,4-pyrone, $C_{15}H_{10}O_2$. Also, any derivative of this, many examples of which are yellow plant pigments.
■ **flavonoid** *noun* any of a large class of plant pigments having a structure based on or similar to that of flavone, including anthocyanins, anthoxanthins, etc., besides flavones M20. **flavonol** *noun* a hydroxy derivative of flavone, 3-hydroxyflavone, $C_{15}H_{10}O_3$; any derivative of this, many examples of which are yellow plant pigments: L19.

flavor *noun, verb* see FLAVOUR *noun, verb.*

flavorous /ˈfleɪv(ə)rəs/ *adjective.* L17.
[ORIGIN from FLAVOUR *noun* + -OUS.]
Full of flavour; pleasing to the taste and smell.

flavour /ˈfleɪvə/ *noun.* Also ***-or.** LME.
[ORIGIN Old French *flaor* (infl. by *savour*) perh. from Proto-Romance blending of Latin *flatus* blowing, breath and *foetor* stench.]
1 Fragrance, smell; an aroma; a trace of a particular odour. *arch.* LME.
> J. MASEFIELD The strong ammonia flavour Of horses' stables.

2 The quality perceived by the sense of taste (aided by smell); a distinctive taste. L17. ▸**b** A substance added to food etc. to impart a specific taste. L18.
> J. STEINBECK Doc was frying sausages, sprinkling a little chocolate over them. It gave them an odd and oriental flavour, he thought. **b** M. PYKE Should a really convincing raspberry flavour be developed, will its use be wrong in the absence of raspberries?

flavour of the month a short-lived fashion; a person who or thing which is very popular for a short time.
3 *fig.* An indefinable characteristic quality; a slight admixture *of* a (usu. undesirable) quality. L17.
> H. L. MENCKEN There is always a flavour of doubt . . a feeling . . that, after all, the scoundrel *may* have something up his sleeve. *Company* Amsterdam . . is compared with Venice, but the flavour is totally different.

4 PARTICLE PHYSICS. A quantized property of quarks which differentiates them into at least six varieties (up, down, charmed, strange, top, bottom). Also, an analogous property of leptons. L20.
■ **flavourful** *adjective* E20. **flavourist** *noun* a person who creates flavourings for drinks, perfumes, etc. L20. **flavourless** *adjective* M18. **flavourlessness** *noun* M19. **flavoursome** *adjective* M19. **flavoury** *adjective* E18.

flavour /ˈfleɪvə/ *verb.* Also ***-or.** LME.
[ORIGIN from the noun.]
1 *verb intrans.* †**a** Be odorous, savour, smell. Only in LME. ▸**b** Have the flavour *of.* L19.
> **b** M. CORELLI A strange sickening sense of unrest that flavoured of despair.

2 *verb trans.* Give flavour, taste, or scent to; season. M16.
> S. RUSHDIE Water flavoured with freshly squeezed limes.

■ **flavoured** *adjective* (*a*) mixed with a flavouring agent; (*b*) having a (usu. specified) flavour: M18. **flavouring** *noun* (*a*) the action of the verb; (*b*) a perfume or flavour; *spec.* something used to give flavour to food or drink: LME.

flaw /flɔː/ *noun*[1]. ME.
[ORIGIN Perh. from Old Norse *flaga* slab of stone, prob. from Germanic base parallel to that of FLAKE *noun*[2].]
▸**I** A detached piece (cf. FLAKE *noun*[2], FLAUGHT *noun*[1]). Now chiefly *dial.*
1 A flake of snow; a spark or tongue of fire. ME.
2 A fragment, a splinter: *obsolete* exc. *Scot.*, the point of a horseshoe nail which is snapped off after passing through the hoof; hence, something worthless. LME.
3 Turf; a single turf. Cf. also FLAG *noun*[2] 1. E18. ▸**b** The quantity of peats cut in a season. E19.
▸**II** A broken or faulty place. (Perh. earliest in WHITLOW.)
4 A defect, imperfection, or blemish. L15. ▸**b** In a legal document, title, etc.: an invalidating defect or fault. E17. ▸**c** A failure or shortcoming; a fault. M18.
> E. WHARTON Two little lines near her mouth, faint flaws in the smooth curve of the cheek. **b** G. BURNET A Prince who knew there was a flaw in his title would always govern well. **c** J. G. COZZENS Now he could see it well enough as the flaw that it was, a defect in self-control.

5 A crack, fissure, or breach. E17.
> SWIFT He that would keep his house in repair, must attend every little breach or flaw.

6 A lie, a falsehood. *Scot.* E18.
■ **flawless** *adjective* without crack, defect, or imperfection M17. **flawlessly** *adverb* L19. **flawlessness** *noun* L19.

flaw /flɔː/ *noun*[2]. E16.
[ORIGIN Prob. from Middle Low German *vlāge*, Middle Dutch *vlāghe* (Dutch *vlaag*), the primary sense perh. being 'stroke'.]
1 A sudden blast or gust of wind. E16. ▸**b** A short spell of rough weather. L18.
†**2** A sudden onset; a burst of feeling or passion; a sudden uproar. L16–L17.

flaw /flɔː/ *verb*[1] *intrans. & trans.* E17.
[ORIGIN from FLAW *noun*[1].]
Make or become faulty; break, crack.
> P. COLQUHOUN Elm is very apt to flaw and splinter. *Times Lit. Suppl.* A fallacy that flaws the entire book.

■ **flawed** *ppl adjective* imperfect, blemished; faulty, damaged. LME.

flaw /flɔː/ *verb*[2]. *rare.* E19.
[ORIGIN from FLAW *noun*[2].]
1 *verb intrans.* Blow in gusts. E19.
2 *verb trans.* Ruffle as a gust of wind does. L19.

flaw *verb*[3] see FLAY *verb*[1].

flawn /flɔːn/ *noun. arch.* ME.
[ORIGIN Old French *flaon* (mod. FLAN) from medieval Latin *flado*, *fladon-*, from Frankish (Dutch *vlade*, *vla* custard), from West Germanic.]
A custard or cheesecake. Also, a pancake. Cf. FLAN.

flax /flaks/ *noun.*
[ORIGIN Old English *flæx* (*fleax*) = Old Frisian *flax*, Middle Dutch & mod. Dutch *vlas*, Old High German *flahs* (German *Flachs*), from West Germanic, prob. from Indo-European base repr. also by Greek *plekein*, Latin *plectere*, German *flechten* to plait.]
▸**I 1** A blue-flowered plant, *Linum usitatissimum* (family Linaceae) cultivated for its seed (linseed), and for textile fibre made from its stalks. OE.
2 a With specifying word: any of various related or similar plants. LME. ▸**b** More fully ***New Zealand flax***. A New Zealand plant, *Phormium tenax*, of the agave family, the leaves of which yield a fibre used for baskets etc. M19.
a fairy flax *Linum catharticum*, bearing small white flowers and formerly used in laxative preparations. **pale flax** *L. bienne*, bearing pale blue flowers. **purging flax** = *fairy flax* above.
TOADFLAX.
▸**II 3** The fibre of the plant *Linum usitatissimum*, whether dressed or not; cloth made from this fibre, linen. OE. ▸†**b** *spec.* The fibre as a material for making candle or lamp wicks; a wick. OE–M17.
4 A material resembling the fibres of the flax plant or similarly used. M16.
– COMB.: **flax-blue** (of) the blue of the flax flower; **flax-brake**, **flax-break**, **flax-breaker** a device or machine to thresh out the fibres of flax; **flax-bush**, **flax-lily** NZ = sense 2b above; **flax comb** an instrument for cleaning and straightening flax fibres; **flax-flower blue** = *flax-blue* above; **flax-hackle** = *flax comb* above; ***flax-lily***: see *flax-bush* above; **flaxseed** (*a*) linseed; (*b*) US a pupa of the Hessian fly, which resembles a seed of flax.
■ **flaxy** *adjective* made of flax; like flax: M17.

flax /flaks/ *verb.* US *colloq.* M19.
[ORIGIN from the noun.]
1 *verb trans.* Beat severely. Usu. foll. by *out.* M19.
2 *verb intrans.* Foll. by *out*: tire, become exhausted. L19.
3 *verb intrans.* Foll. by *(a)round*: bestir oneself, bustle about. L19.

flaxen /ˈflaks(ə)n/ *adjective.* LME.
[ORIGIN from FLAX *noun* + -EN[4].]
1 Made of flax, linen. LME.
2 Of hair etc.: coloured like dressed flax, pale yellow. E16.
3 Of or pertaining to flax as a commercial product. E18.

flay /fleɪ/ *verb*[1] *trans.* Also (*dial.*) **flaw** /flɔː/, †**flea.**
[ORIGIN Old English *flēan* = Middle Dutch *vlae(gh)en* (Dutch *vlaen*), Old Norse *flá*, from Germanic.]
1 Strip or pull off the skin or hide of; skin. OE.
> U. LE GUIN The tanned skins of rebels flayed alive.

2 Strip, peel *off* (the skin). ME. ▸†**b** Tear off (a man's beard) together with the skin. ME–L15.
> F. M. FORD Those two women pursued that poor devil and flayed the skin off him.

3 Strip off or severely damage portions of the skin from; excoriate. ME.
> LD MACAULAY The prospect of dying in Newgate, with a back flayed and an eye knocked out.

4 Remove or strip *off* (an outer covering, as peel, bark, etc.). Now chiefly *dial.* ME. ▸**b** Pare (*off*) thin slices of (turf). L16.
> F. FORSYTH She was rusty, her paint blistered by the sun in many places, flayed off by salt spray in others.

5 Strip an outer covering from; peel. L16. ▸†**b** Strip (a person) of clothing; undress. *rare* (Shakes.). Only in E17. ▸**c** Strip (a building etc.) of its exterior covering or ornament. M17.
6 Rob or cheat (a person); pillage, plunder. *arch.* L16.
> J. A. FROUDE Plundering cities and temples and flaying the people with requisitions.

7 Subject to acute pain or torture; *fig.* criticize severely, abuse. L18.
> W. SAFIRE The antisloppiness brigade . . has flayed the cliché users.

– COMB.: **flay-flint** a skinflint.
■ **flayer** *noun* LME.

flay *verb*[2] *& noun* var. of FLEY.

flea /fliː/ *noun & verb*[1].
[ORIGIN Old English *flēa(h)*, corresp. to Middle Low German, Middle Dutch *vlō* (Dutch *vloo*), Old High German *flōh* (German *Floh*), Old Norse *fló*, from Germanic.]
▸**A** *noun.* Any of various small wingless parasitic insects of the order Siphonaptera, which live on the skin of mammals and birds, feeding on blood, and are noted for their agility in jumping. Also (with specifying word), any of various invertebrates which jump or move jerkily like a flea. OE.
bat flea, ***cat flea***, ***dog flea***, ***human flea***, etc. ***fit as a flea***: see FIT *adjective* 7. **go away with a flea in one's ear**, **send away with a flea in his or her ear**, etc., go away, send (a person) away, discomfited by a reproof or rebuff.
– COMB.: **fleabag** *slang* (*a*) a sleeping bag; (*b*) a shabby place, esp. lodgings; a shabby, unkempt person; **fleabane** any of various plants, esp. of the genera *Pulicaria* and *Erigeron* (family Compositae), reputed to drive away fleas; *spec.* (more fully ***common fleabane***) *P. dysenterica*, a marsh plant bearing yellow flowers; **flea beetle** any of numerous small jumping beetles of the family Chrysomelidae, many of which are serious plant pests; **flea bite** (*a*) (the red spot caused by) the bite of a flea; MEDICINE a petechial haemorrhage into the skin resembling this; (*b*) *fig.* a trifling inconvenience or discomfort; (*c*) a small reddish, brown, or black spot in the coloration of a horse, dog, or other animal; **flea-bitten** (*a*) bitten by or infested with fleas; (*b*) (of the coloration of an animal) sprinkled with flea bites on a lighter ground; **flea bug** US = *flea beetle* above; **flea circus** a show of performing fleas; **flea collar** a collar (for a dog or cat) impregnated with a substance that kills fleas; **flea-dock** butterbur; **flea-hopper** US a small jumping hemipteran insect of the family Miridae, harmful to plants; esp. *Halticus bracteatus* (garden flea-hopper) and *Psallus seriatus* (cotton flea-hopper); **flea-louse** a jumping plant louse of the hemipteran family Psyllidae; **flea market** a street market; **fleapit** *slang* an allegedly verminous place of public assembly; *esp.* a cinema; **fleawort** any of several plants of the genus *Tephroseris*, related to the ragworts; *esp.* (more fully ***field fleawort***) *T. integrifolia*, a Eurasian plant of calcareous grassland.
▸**B** *verb trans.* Rid of fleas. E17.

W. H. Auden The dog fleaing itself in the hot dust.

■ **fleasome** *adjective* (*joc.*) full of fleas (usu. assoc. with GLEESOME) M19. **fleay** /ˈfliːi/ *adjective* E17.

†**flea** *verb*² var. of FLAY *verb*¹.

flead *noun* var. of FLEED.

fleadh /ˈflɑː/ *noun*. M20.
[ORIGIN from Irish Gaelic *fleadh ceoil* music festival, from *fleadh* feast, drinking bout + *ceoil* music.]
A festival of Irish or Celtic music, dancing, and culture.

fleam /fliːm/ *noun*¹ & *verb*. Now *dial.* ME.
[ORIGIN Alt. of FLUME *noun*.]
▸ **A** *noun*. Orig., a stream or river. Now, a mill stream, an artificial channel. ME.
▸ **B** *verb intrans.* Flow, stream (*away*). LME.

fleam /fliːm/ *noun*². LME.
[ORIGIN Old French *flieme* (mod. *flamme*) from Proto-Romance alt. of late Latin *phlebotomus* (medieval Latin *fledomum*, *fletoma*), from Greek *phlebotomon* use as noun of neut. adjective (see PHLEBOTOMY).]
MEDICINE (now chiefly *hist.*). A lancet used for blood-letting; latterly *esp.* one for the bleeding of horses.

flebile /ˈfleɪbɪleɪ/ *adjective*. E17.
[ORIGIN Italian from Latin *flebilis* that is to be wept for; plaintive: see FEEBLE *adjective*.]
MUSIC. Mournful, plaintive.

flèche /flɛʃ, fleɪʃ/ *noun*. Pl. pronounced same. ME.
[ORIGIN Old French & mod. French = arrow.]
†**1** An arrow. Only in ME.
2 FORTIFICATION. A work in communication with the covered way, placed at the salient angle of the glacis. E18.
3 ARCHITECTURE. A slender spire, usu. of wood and rising from a roof. M19.
4 Any of the twenty-four points on a backgammon board. M19.
5 FENCING. In full ***flèche attack***. A running attack. E20.

flechette /fleɪˈʃɛt/ *noun*. Also **fléchette**. E20.
[ORIGIN French *fléchette*, dim. of *flèche* arrow: see -ETTE.]
MILITARY. A missile resembling a dart, dropped from an aircraft.

fleck /flɛk/ *noun*¹. L16.
[ORIGIN Rel. to FLECK *verb*¹.]
1 A blemish, freckle, or spot in the skin. L16. ▸**b** A patch of colour, light, etc. E19.

E. Figes Everything is different about old people . . . Those little brown flecks on the skin. **b** P. H. Johnson She smiled at the flecks of sunlight fluttering like moths about the ceiling.

2 A small particle; a flake, a speck. M18.

C. Lassalle There were little flecks of cork in her glass.

■ **fleckless** *adjective* M19. **flecklessly** *adverb* L19.

fleck *noun*² var. of FLICK *noun*².

fleck *noun*³ var. of FLICK *noun*³.

fleck /flɛk/ *verb*¹ *trans.* LME.
[ORIGIN Uncertain; cf. Old Norse *flekkr* noun, *flekka* verb, or Middle Low German, Middle Dutch *vlecke* (Dutch *vlek*) = Old High German *flec*, *fleccho* (German *Fleck*, *flecken*), of unknown origin.]
Spot, streak; mark with flecks; dapple, variegate. Freq. as ***flecked*** *ppl adjective*.

G. Swift Little orange spots of mud flecked her stockings. S. King Deep green eyes flecked with hazel.

fleck /flɛk/ *verb*². Long *obsolete* exc. *dial.* M16.
[ORIGIN Perh. var. of FLAG *verb*². Cf. FLEG *verb*².]
Fly low; flit, flutter about.

fleck *verb*³ see FLICK *verb*².

fleckered /ˈflɛkəd/ *adjective*. L15.
[ORIGIN from FLECK *verb*¹ + -ER⁵ + -ED¹.]
Marked with flecks; dappled; scattered in flecks.

Geo. Eliot Seated . . in the fleckered shade of the ash tree.

fleckled /ˈflɛk(ə)ld/ *adjective*. L16.
[ORIGIN from FLECK *noun*¹ + -LE¹ + -ED².]
Dappled; freckled.

flection *noun* var. of FLEXION.

fled *verb pa. t. & pple* of FLEE *verb*.

fledge /flɛdʒ/ *adjective*. *obsolete* exc. *dial.* LME.
[ORIGIN Prob. repr. base of Old English *unfligge*, glossing Latin *implumes* unfledged; corresp. to Middle Dutch *vlugghe* (Dutch *vlug*), Old High German *flucchi* (German *flügge* is from Low German), from West Germanic, from base of FLY *verb*.]
1 Of a young bird: fit to fly, fledged. LME. ▸†**b** *fig.* High-spirited. LME–M17.
2 Provided *with* feathers for flight. M17.

fig.: Milton All the fond hopes, which forward Youth and Vanitie are fledge with.

■ **fledgeless** *adjective* unfledged M18.

fledge /flɛdʒ/ *verb* & *noun*. M16.
[ORIGIN from the adjective.]
▸ **A** *verb*. **1** *verb intrans.* Of a young bird: develop feathers large enough for flight; become fully plumed. M16.

Bird Watching Young ravens take about six weeks to fledge.

2 *verb trans.* Bring up (a young bird) until its feathers are developed enough for flight. L16.
3 *verb trans.* Provide (a bird, an arrow) with feathers; adorn with feathers; cover (as) with feathers or down. L16.

L. P. Hartley Low hills rose behind the town, green hills already fledged with autumn yellow.

▸ **B** *noun*. A feather or downlike covering. *rare.* E20.

D. H. Lawrence He had now a black fledge on his upper lip, a black finely-shaped line.

■ **fledged** *ppl adjective* able to fly; *fig.* mature, independent: L16.

fledgling /ˈflɛdʒlɪŋ/ *noun* & *adjective*. Also **fledgeling**. M19.
[ORIGIN from FLEDGE *adjective* + -LING¹, after *nestling*.]
▸ **A** *noun*. A young bird just fledged; *fig.* an inexperienced person. M19.
▸ **B** *attrib.* or as *adjective*. Inexperienced; raw. M19.

E. Johnson He gave fledgling authors a chance to appear in print.

fledgy /ˈflɛdʒi/ *adjective*. *rare.* L16.
[ORIGIN formed as FLEDGLING + -Y¹.]
†**1** Fledged; ready to fly. Only in L16.
2 Covered with feathers, feathery. E19.

flee /fliː/ *verb*. Pa. t. & pple **fled** /flɛd/.
[ORIGIN Old English *flēon* = Old Frisian *flia*, Old Saxon *fliohan* (Middle Dutch *vlien*, Dutch *vlieden*), Old High German *fliohan* (German *fliehen*), Old Norse *flý(j)a*, Gothic *þliuhan* from Germanic. Already in Old English confused with FLY *verb*.]
▸ **I** *verb intrans.* **1** Run away from or as from danger; take flight; hasten or run for safety or protection. (Foll. by *from*, *out of*; *to*, *into*.) OE. ▸**b** Get safely away, make one's escape. ME.

E. Bowen She fled to the back of the house and hid in a box-room. W. S. Churchill The Marquis, brokenhearted, fled into exile. E. Blishen They fled, to be caught round the next corner. **b** G. Orwell Goldstein had fled and was hiding no one knew where.

2 Withdraw hastily, go away, leave. Foll. by *from*, *out of*. OE.

A. B. Jameson Two years later he fled from society.

3 = FLY *verb* I. Now only *poet.* OE.

Shelley The dark arrow fled In the noon.

4 Vanish, cease, pass away. ME.

Gibbon The animating health and vigour were fled.

▸ **II** *verb trans.* **5** Run or hasten away from (a person, place, etc.); forsake. OE.

B. Malamud Hundreds of Jews are leaving the city as if fleeing the plague. *Bird Watching* Continental birds . . fleeing food failures.

6 Avoid with dread or distaste; shun. OE. ▸**b** Contrive to avoid; evade. Now *rare.* ME.

fleece /fliːs/ *noun*.
[ORIGIN Old English *flēos*, *flēs*, (West Saxon) *flīes* = Dutch *vlies*, Middle High German *vlies* (German *Vlies*), from West Germanic base; prob. ult. rel. to the base of Latin *pluma* feather.]
1 The woolly covering or pelt of a sheep or similar animal. OE. ▸**b** HERALDRY. A charge representing a sheep-skin with its wool suspended by a ring. E16. ▸**c** A sheep; *collect.* sheep. L18.
Golden Fleece (*a*) GREEK MYTHOLOGY a fleece of gold sought and won by Jason; (*b*) (in full ***Order of the Golden Fleece***) an order of knighthood instituted in 1430 by Philip the Good, Duke of Burgundy. ***double fleece***: see DOUBLE *adjective* & *adverb*.
2 The body or quantity of wool shorn from a sheep at one time. LME. ▸**b** An act of robbery or cheating. Formerly also, a share of booty. E17.

Sir W. Scott Thou shalt have a necklace of jet at next shearing-feast, if our fleeces bear any price in the market.

3 A thing resembling a sheep's fleece in appearance or in consistency; *esp.* a rough abundant head of hair. E16. ▸**b** Fabric with a fleecy consistency; a soft silky nap, esp. as a lining. M19. ▸**c** A jacket or other garment made from or lined with fleece or a fleece-like material. L20.

Pope Soft as the fleeces of descending snow.

– COMB.: **fleece-picker** *Austral.* & *NZ* a person who picks up fleeces in a shearing shed; **fleece-wool** wool from the main part of a fleece obtained at the annual shearings.
■ **fleecelike** *adjective* resembling (that of) a fleece E18.

fleece /fliːs/ *verb*. M16.
[ORIGIN from the noun.]
1 *verb trans.* & *intrans.* Obtain (money etc.) *from* a person by unfair means. Now *rare.* M16.

Carlyle To divide what they fleeced from these poor drudges.

2 *verb trans.* Strip (a person, city, etc.) of or *of* money, property, etc.; rob; charge an excessive amount. L16.

A. Sillitoe They aren't going to fleece an old salt like me and get away with it.

3 *verb trans.* Clip or shear the fleece from (a sheep). Now *rare.* E17.
4 *verb trans.* Dapple or fleck with fleecy masses; cover (as) with a fleece. M18.

J. Fowles The sky half blue, half fleeced with white clouds.

■ **fleeceable** *adjective* M19. **fleeced** *adjective* (*a*) provided with a fleece (of a specified kind); (*b*) that has been fleeced: L16. **fleecer** *noun* E17.

fleech /fliːtʃ/ *verb*. *Scot.* & *N. English*. LME.
[ORIGIN Uncertain: cf. Old High German *flēhōn*, *flēhen* flatter, beseech, Middle High German *vlēhen*, German *flehen* beseech, Dutch *vleien* flatter.]
1 *verb trans.* Coax, cajole, wheedle; beseech, entreat. LME.
2 *verb intrans.* Speak coaxingly or beseechingly; fawn. LME.

fleecy /ˈfliːsi/ *adjective* & *noun*. As noun also **-ie**. M16.
[ORIGIN from FLEECE *noun* + -Y¹.]
▸ **A** *adjective*. **1** Consisting of fleeces; woollen. M16.
2 Covered with a fleece; fleeced. L16.
3 Resembling a fleece in colour or consistency; woolly; (of the sky) flecked with white clouds. M17.
▸ **B** *noun*. A fleece-picker. *Austral.* & *NZ slang*. L19.
■ **fleecily** *adverb* L19. **fleeciness** *noun* M20.

fleed /fliːd/ *noun*. Chiefly *dial.* Also **flead**. M19.
[ORIGIN Unknown.]
= FLICK *noun*³.

fleer /ˈfliːə/ *noun*¹. Now *rare.* ME.
[ORIGIN from FLEE *verb* + -ER¹.]
A person who flees.

fleer /flɪə/ *verb* & *noun*². LME.
[ORIGIN Prob. of Scandinavian origin; cf. Norwegian and Swedish dial. *flira*, Danish dial. *flire* grin, laugh derisively.]
▸ **A** *verb*. †**1** *verb intrans.* Grin, grimace; make a wry face as if about to cry. LME–L18.
2 *verb trans.* & *intrans.* (with *at*, †*upon*). Jibe, jeer, sneer at; laugh at mockingly or scornfully. LME.

I. Gurney Three jeering, fleering spectres, That walked abreast and talked of me.

3 *verb intrans.* Laugh in a coarse, impudent, or fawning manner. Formerly foll. by *on*, *upon*. M16.

Daily Telegraph Impudent-looking wenches . . leering and fleering and chuckling *con amore*.

▸ **B** *noun*. A mocking look or speech; a sneer. E17.

Shakes. *Oth.* And mark the fleers, the gibes, and notable scorns, That dwell in every region of his face.

■ **fleerer** *noun* E17. **fleeringly** *adverb* in a fleering manner E17.

fleet /fliːt/ *noun*¹.
[ORIGIN Old English *flēot* (once) ship or ships collect., from *flēotan* float, swim: see FLEET *verb*¹.]
1 A naval force; a number of warships under one commander-in-chief. More widely, a number of ships or boats sailing in company. OE. ▸**b** *The* navy. E18.
2 A number of persons, birds, or other objects moving in company. Now *esp.* a group of vehicles or aircraft having the same proprietor or otherwise forming a unit. LME.

R. Hoggart Buses . . from a big town fleet. K. Waterhouse A fleet of electric trollies piled high with newspaper parcels.

3 A set or row of drift nets fastened together end to end. L18.

– PHRASES & COMB.: ***Admiral of the Fleet***: see ADMIRAL 3. **First Fleet**, **Second Fleet**, **Third Fleet** AUSTRAL. HISTORY groups of convict ships arriving in 1788, 1790, 1791 respectively. ***Fleet Admiral***: see ADMIRAL 3. **Fleet Air Arm** *hist.* the aviation service of the Royal Navy. **fleet in being** (chiefly *hist.*) a fleet of warships considered as exerting a strategic influence by their mere existence. **flogging round the fleet** *hist.* the punishment of being flogged alongside each vessel in the fleet.

fleet /fliːt/ *noun*².
[ORIGIN Old English *flēot* (also *flēote* or *-a*), corresp. to Old Frisian *flēt*, Middle Dutch & mod. Dutch *vliet*, Middle High German *vlieʒ*, Old Norse *fljót*, from Germanic base of FLEET *verb*¹.]
1 A place where water flows; a creek, an inlet. Now *dial.* or in proper names. OE.
2 ***the Fleet***, (the name of) a stream (now covered) flowing into the Thames between Ludgate Hill and Fleet Street; *hist.* the prison that stood near it. LME.

– COMB.: **Fleet marriage** *hist.* a wedding performed clandestinely by a Fleet parson (see below) in the Fleet; **Fleet parson** *hist.* any of a number of disreputable clergymen to be found in or around the Fleet ready to perform clandestine marriages; **Fleet Street** [name of a street in London formerly devoted largely to the production and publication of daily newspapers] the British press; British journalism or journalists collectively.

fleet /fliːt/ *adjective*¹. Now *dial.* Also **flet** /flɛt/. LME.
[ORIGIN pa. pple of FLEET *verb*².]
Of milk: skimmed.

fleet /fliːt/ *adjective*² & *adverb*¹. *poet.* or *literary*. E16.
[ORIGIN Prob. from Old Norse *fljótr*, from Germanic base of FLEET *verb*¹.]
▸ **A** *adjective*. **1** Swift in movement; nimble. Cf. FLEET *verb*¹ 7. E16.

Shakes. *L.L.L.* Their conceits have wings, Fleeter than arrows. K. Crossley-Holland Even Thialfi, as fleet of foot as any man in Midgard, was hard put to keep up with him.

2 Evanescent; transient. Cf. FLEET *verb*¹ 6. E19.

Baroness Orczy A bright smile, fleet and sweet, illumined her dainty face.

▸ **B** *adverb*. Quickly, swiftly. L16.

F

L. G. GIBBON Tired though he was he came to her side right fleet enough.

■ **fleetly** *adverb* = FLEET *adverb*[1] L16. **fleetness** *noun* E17.

fleet /fliːt/ *adjective*[3] & *adverb*[2]. Now chiefly *dial.* E17.
[ORIGIN Perh. from Old English cognate of Dutch *vloot* shallow, from Germanic base of FLEET *verb*[1].]
▸ **A** *adjective*. Of water: shallow. E17.
▸ **B** *adverb*. At or to a small depth. Esp. in ***plough fleet***, ***sow fleet***. M17.

fleet /fliːt/ *verb*[1].
[ORIGIN Old English *flēotan* float, swim = Old Frisian *fliāta*, Old Saxon *fliotan* (Dutch *vlieten*), Old High German *fliozan* (German *fliessen*), Old Norse *fljóta* float, flow, from Germanic.]
▸ **I** Float.
1 *verb intrans.* Rest on the surface of the water; be buoyed up; (of a vessel) be or get afloat. *obsolete* exc. *dial.* OE.
†**2** *verb intrans.* Drift or float in water or air. OE–M18. ▸**b** Move unsteadily, as if floating; sway; fluctuate, waver. LME–M17.
3 *verb intrans.* Swim. Long *obsolete* exc. *hist.* OE.
†**4** *verb intrans.* Travel by water, sail. ME–E18.
▸ **II** Flow, slip away, etc.
5 *verb intrans.* Of water, a river, etc.: flow. Long only *Scot.* ME.
6 a *verb intrans.* Glide away or *away*; vanish, fade (*away*). Now only of abstract things: *esp.* (of time) pass rapidly, slip *away*. Formerly also, waste *away*, disintegrate. Cf. FLEET *adjective*[2] 2. *arch.* ME. ▸**b** *verb trans.* Pass, while away (time). *rare.* E17.
7 *verb intrans.* Move swiftly; flit, fly (*away*). Cf. FLEET *adjective*[2] 1. *arch.* LME.
▸ **III 8** *verb trans.* NAUTICAL. Change the position of, shift (a block, rope, etc.). L17.

fleet /fliːt/ *verb*[2] *trans.* Now *dial.* Pa. pple **-ed**, †**fleet**. Cf. FLEET *adjective*[1]. LME.
[ORIGIN Prob. from Old English *flēt* cream, from base of *flēotan* FLEET *verb*[1]; but cf. also Dutch *vlieten* (= FLEET *verb*[1]) used in this sense.]
Remove the scum from the surface of (a liquid); *esp.* skim (milk, the cream from milk).
■ **fleeting** *noun* (*a*) the action of the verb; (*b*) in *pl.*, skimmings, curds: LME.

fleeting /ˈfliːtɪŋ/ *ppl adjective*. OE.
[ORIGIN from FLEET *verb*[1] + -ING[2].]
†**1** Floating; swimming. OE–L16.
†**2** Shifting, unstable; (of a person, an attribute) fickle, inconstant. ME–M17.

MILTON Of such a variable and fleeting conscience what hold can be tak'n?

†**3** Flowing; fluid. ME–L17.
4 Passing or gliding swiftly away; (esp. of time, life) passing by rapidly; brief; transient; not permanent or enduring. M16.

E. H. GOMBRICH The Impressionist preoccupation with the fleeting moment. A. N. WILSON All those girls had been fleeting presences in his life.

■ **fleetingly** *adverb* L19. **fleetingness** *noun* E18.

fleg /flɛɡ/ *noun*[1]. *Scot.* E18.
[ORIGIN from FLEG *verb*[1].]
A fright, a scare.

fleg /flɛɡ/ *noun*[2]. *Scot.* Now *rare* or *obsolete*. E18.
[ORIGIN Unknown.]
A random blow or kick, a stroke.

fleg /flɛɡ/ *verb*[1] *trans.* *Scot.* Infl. **-gg-**. E17.
[ORIGIN Unknown. Cf. FLEY.]
Frighten, scare.

fleg /flɛɡ/ *verb*[2] *intrans.* *Scot.* Infl. **-gg-**. L18.
[ORIGIN Uncertain: perh. var. of FLAG *verb*[2], FLECK *verb*[2].]
Flee, run off; fly away. (Foll. by *off*.)

†**flegm** *noun* var. of PHLEGM.

flehmen /ˈfleɪmən/ *noun*. L20.
[ORIGIN German (verb), (of a horse) curl the lip in sexual excitement.]
A behavioural response found in many male mammals when they detect particular smells from females, characterized by a curling of the upper lip and a raising of the head.

Flem /flɛm/ *noun*. *colloq.* E20.
[ORIGIN Abbreviation.]
= FLEMING *noun*[1] 1.

†**fleme** *verb trans.* OE–E19.
[ORIGIN Old English *flīeman*, from *flēam* flight from Germanic from ablaut var. of base of FLEE *verb*.]
Cause to flee; banish, exile.
– NOTE: Only in isolated Scottish use after 16.

Fleming /ˈflɛmɪŋ/ *noun*[1].
[ORIGIN Late Old English *Flæmingi*, partly from Old Norse and partly from Middle Dutch *Vlaminc* (whence Old Norse), from *Vlām-* base of *Vlaanderen* Flanders: see -ING[3].]
1 A native or inhabitant of Flanders. LOE.
†**2** A Flemish ship. *rare.* Only in L16.

Fleming /ˈflɛmɪŋ/ *noun*[2]. E20.
[ORIGIN Sir John Ambrose *Fleming* (1849–1945), English electrical engineer.]
PHYSICS. **1** ***Fleming's left-hand rule***, a mnemonic which represents the direction of the force exerted on a current-carrying conductor in a magnetic field by the second finger of the left hand, the directions of the current and the field being indicated by the first finger and thumb held perpendicularly to it and to each other. Also called ***left-hand rule***. E20.
2 ***Fleming's right-hand rule***, a mnemonic concerning the behaviour of a conductor moving in a magnetic field, according to which the directions of the magnetic field, the induced current, and the motion of the conductor are indicated respectively by the first finger, second finger, and thumb of the right hand when these are held out perpendicular to each other. Also called ***right-hand rule***. E20.

Flemish /ˈflɛmɪʃ/ *adjective & noun*. ME.
[ORIGIN Middle Dutch *Vlāmisch* (Dutch *Vlaamsch*) = Old Frisian *Flamsk*, assim. to FLEMING *noun*[1]: see -ISH[1].]
▸ **A** *adjective*. **1** Of or pertaining to Flanders in the Low Countries, its people, or its language. ME.
2 Resembling a Fleming in habits and behaviour. *rare.* L16.
▸ **B** *noun*. The West Germanic language of Flanders, comprising a group of Dutch dialects, now one of the two official languages of Belgium. E18.
– SPECIAL COLLOCATIONS & COMB.: ***Flemish bond***: see BOND *noun*[2]. **Flemish coil** NAUTICAL a rope coiled down flat with the end coming to the centre and each coil closely packed within the preceding coil. **Flemish-coil** *verb trans.* (NAUTICAL) = FLEMISH *verb*. **Flemish eye** NAUTICAL a kind of eye splice in which the ends are scraped down, tapered, passed oppositely, marled, and served over with spun yarn. **Flemish horse** NAUTICAL a short foot rope at the yardarms of a square-rigged ship.

flemish /ˈflɛmɪʃ/ *verb trans.* M19.
[ORIGIN from the adjective.]
NAUTICAL. Coil or lay up (a rope) in a Flemish coil. Freq. foll. by *down*.

flense /flɛns/ *verb trans.* Also **flench** /flɛn(t)ʃ/, **flinch** /flɪn(t)ʃ/. E19.
[ORIGIN Danish *flensa* = Norwegian *flinsa*, *flunsa* flay.]
1 Cut up and slice the fat from (a whale or seal). E19.
2 Flay or skin (a seal); strip off (the skin of a seal). L19.

flesh /flɛʃ/ *noun*.
[ORIGIN Old English *flǣsc* = Old Frisian *flask*, Old Saxon *flēsk* (Dutch *vlees*), Old High German *fleisc* (German *Fleisch*), Old Norse *flesk* pork, bacon, from Germanic.]
▸ **I 1** The soft substance of animal bodies, esp. the muscular part; the tissue which covers the bones and is enclosed by the skin. OE.

BUNYAN His . . sins, that stick as close to him as the flesh sticks to the bones.

2 The tissue of animal bodies regarded as food (esp. as excluding fish and sometimes fowl); meat. Now chiefly in phrs. below or preceded by specifying word. OE.

T. NASHE The puffin that is halfe fish, halfe flesh. S. BARING-GOULD When a wolf has once tasted human flesh, he desires to taste it again.

3 Quantity or excess of flesh in proportion to bone; plumpness, fat. Formerly also, good condition. M16.

E. GARRETT Its [a face's] once noble outlines were blurred by too much flesh.

4 The soft pulpy substance of a fruit or plant; the part which is enclosed by the rind and which encloses the core or kernel, esp. as regarded as an article of food. L16.

ANTHONY HUXLEY A large pumpkin with bright orange flesh.

5 The visible surface of the human body, with reference to its colour and appearance. E17. ▸**b** = FLESH COLOUR. M19.

b *attrib.*: F. H. BURNETT A flesh silk stocking.

6 More fully ***flesh side***. The side of a hide that adjoined the flesh. M17.
▸ **II 7** People of the same kindred or descent collectively; (one of) one's family. Now *rare* exc. in ***one flesh***, ***flesh and blood*** below. OE.

SHELLEY What, if we . . were his own flesh, His children and his wife?

8 That which has corporeal life; the animal kingdom; humankind. Now chiefly in ***all flesh*** below. OE.

SHAKES. *Much Ado* As pretty a piece of flesh as any is in Messina. R. W. EMERSON He . . visits worlds which flesh cannot enter.

9 The physical or material frame of a human; the body. Now chiefly in biblical allusion or in ***in the flesh*** below. OE. ▸**b** = BODY *noun* 3. OE.

AV *Job* 19:26 Though . . wormes destroy this body, yet in my flesh shall I see God. W. HABINGTON My frighted flesh trembles to dust.

10 The animal or physical nature of humans; human nature as subject to material needs and limitations. OE.

J. A. FROUDE The archbishop retired to his see to afflict his flesh with public austerities.

11 The sensual appetites and inclinations as opp. to those of mind and soul; carnal nature. ME.

F. W. FARRAR Things which tend to the gratification of the flesh.

– PHRASES: **all flesh** whatever has bodily life. ***a thorn in one's flesh***, ***a thorn in the flesh***: see THORN *noun* 1b. **flesh and blood** *noun* (*a*) humankind; the body or its material; human nature with its emotions and infirmities; (*b*) *one's* (*own*) near relatives, descendants, or ancestors. **flesh-and-blood** *adjective* actually living, not supernatural or imaginary. **flesh and fell** *noun & adverb* (*arch.*) (*a*) *noun* the whole substance of the body; (*b*) *adverb* entirely. ***go the way of all flesh***: see GO *verb*. **in flesh** *arch.* corpulent, well-fed, in good condition. **in the flesh** in bodily form, in life. **lose flesh** grow thinner. **make a person's flesh creep**, **make a person's flesh crawl** frighten, horrify, or disgust, esp. with dread of the supernatural. ***neither fish, nor flesh*** (***nor good red herring***): see FISH *noun*[1]. **one flesh** [*Genesis* 2:24] intimately united, esp. by virtue of marriage. ***piece of flesh***: see PIECE *noun*. ***pound of flesh***: see POUND *noun*[1]. ***press flesh***, ***press the flesh***: see PRESS *verb*[1]. ***proud flesh***: see PROUD *adjective* 8. **put on flesh** grow fatter. **sins of the flesh** sins related to sensual temptation, esp. unchastity. ***the world, the flesh, and the devil***: see WORLD *noun*.
– COMB.: **flesh-brush** a brush used to stimulate the circulation by rubbing the skin; **flesh fly** a fly which deposits its eggs or larvae in dead flesh, a meat fly; *esp.* the black and grey fly *Sarcophaga carnaria*; **flesh-hook** (long *rare* or *obsolete*) (*a*) a hook for removing meat from a pot; (*b*) a hook on which meat is hung; **flesh-meat** (*obsolete* exc. *dial.*) flesh (occas. excluding pork or bacon) as an article of food; **fleshmonger** †(*a*) a butcher; †(*b*) a pander, a fornicator; (*c*) *arch. rare* a slave-dealer; **fleshpot** (*a*) *arch.* a pot in which flesh is cooked; (*b*) in *pl.* (with ref. to *Exodus* 16:3), places providing luxurious or hedonistic living; **flesh-quake** *arch.* a trembling of the body; ***flesh side***: see sense 6 above; **flesh tint** (*a*) = FLESH COLOUR; (*b*) in *pl.*, a painter's rendering of flesh colours; **flesh-worm** a worm that feeds on flesh; **flesh wound** a wound which does not penetrate the bone or any vital organ.
■ **fleshen** *adjective* (long *rare* or *obsolete*) made of flesh (*lit.* & *fig.*); covered with flesh: LME. **flesher** *noun* (*a*) (chiefly *Scot.*) a butcher; (*b*) *US* a fleshing knife: ME. **fleshhood** *noun* (*arch.*) the state or condition of being in the flesh, incarnation: LME. **fleshless** *adjective* L16.

flesh /flɛʃ/ *verb*. LME.
[ORIGIN from the noun.]
1 †**a** *verb trans.* & *intrans.* MEDICINE. Grow new tissue in (a wound); heal over. Only in LME. ▸**b** *verb trans.* Make fleshy, fatten (*lit.* & *fig.*). Long *rare.* E17. ▸**c** *verb trans.* Cover (bones etc.) with flesh; embody in flesh. M17. ▸**d** *verb trans.* & *intrans.* Foll. by *out*. Make or become (more) substantial. L19.

b H. G. WELLS We've fleshed ourselves a bit, eh? **c** T. FULLER This bare Sceleton of Time, Place, and Person must be fleshed with some pleasant passages. **d** J. LE CARRÉ The extra work that fleshed out his pension.

2 *verb trans.* Give (a hound etc.) a piece of the flesh of the game killed in order to incite it; make (an animal) eager for prey by the taste of blood. M16.
3 *verb trans.* **a** Initiate in or inure to bloodshed or warfare. M16. ▸†**b** Initiate *in* or inure or habituate *to* any practice; harden (in wrongdoing). L16–E18. ▸**c** Arouse or excite (a person) by a foretaste of success or gratification. Now *rare* or *obsolete*. L16.

a A. W. KINGLAKE He fleshed his troops . . with enterprises against the enemy's posts. **c** DRYDEN Him, flesh'd with slaughter, and with conquest crown'd.

4 *verb trans.* Plunge (a weapon) into flesh; use (a sword etc.) for the first time on flesh, 'blood'. L16. ▸**b** Gratify (lust, rage, etc.). Long *rare* or *obsolete*. E17.

SHAKES. *2 Hen. IV* The wild dog shall flesh his tooth on every innocent. *fig.*: J. R. LOWELL The poor youth, just fleshing his maiden pen in criticism. **b** SHAKES. *All's Well* This night he fleshes his will in the spoil of her honour.

5 *verb trans.* Remove the flesh adhering to (a skin or hide). L18.
6 *verb trans.* Paint flesh colour. *rare.* M19.
■ **fleshment** *noun* (*rare*, Shakes.): only in E17.

flesh colour /ˈflɛʃkʌlə/ *noun & adjective*. Also *****color**. L16.
[ORIGIN from FLESH *noun* + COLOUR *noun*.]
▸ **A** *noun*. A light brownish pink, supposedly the colour of the flesh of a Caucasian seen through the skin. L16.
▸ **B** *attrib.* or as *adjective*. Of this colour. E18.
■ **flesh-coloured** *adjective* = FLESH COLOUR *adjective* M18.

fleshed /flɛʃt/ *adjective*. LME.
[ORIGIN from FLESH *noun*, *verb*: see -ED[2], -ED[1].]
1 Having or covered with flesh. (Freq. preceded by specifying word.) LME.

C. DARWIN A yellow or purple fleshed fruit.

2 Inured to or eager for battle or bloodshed. L16. ▸†**b** Bent *upon* the destruction or injury of (a person). E–M17.

SHAKES. *Rich. III* They were flesh'd villains, bloody dogs.

fleshing /ˈflɛʃɪŋ/ *noun*. LME.
[ORIGIN from FLESH *verb*, *noun*: see -ING[1].]
1 a In *pl.* The pieces of flesh scraped from a hide. LME. ▸**b** The action of scraping pieces of flesh from a hide. L18.
2 The action of FLESH *verb* 2. L16.
3 In *pl.* Flesh-coloured tights, esp. as part of a stage costume. M19.
– COMB.: **fleshing knife** a large two-handled implement with a blunt edge used in fleshing hides.

fleshly /ˈflɛʃli/ *adjective & adverb*. OE.
[ORIGIN from FLESH *noun* + -LY[1].]
▸ **A** *adjective*. **1** Of or pertaining to desire or bodily appetites; lascivious, sensual. OE.
J. BANVILLE The paroxysms of fleshly pleasure.
†**2** Connected by or based on ties of flesh and blood, natural. OE–L16.
3 Unredeemed, unregenerate. Long *rare*. OE.
4 Of or pertaining to the material body; mortal; material as opp. to divine or spiritual. ME.
5 Pertaining to, concerned with, or influenced by (considerations concerning) life in this world; worldly. ME.
†**6** Fat, plump; fleshy. LME–L17.
7 Consisting of flesh (*lit.* & *fig.*); *esp.* (of the heart) soft and tender as opp. to hard. Now *rare* or *obsolete*. LME.
▸ †**B** *adverb*. **1** Bodily; materially. ME–M17.
2 Carnally, sensually, sexually. ME–L16.
■ **fleshliness** *noun* †(*a*) *rare* incarnate condition; (*b*) carnality; †(*c*) fleshiness, plumpness: OE.

fleshy /ˈflɛʃi/ *adjective*. LME.
[ORIGIN from FLESH *noun* + -Y[1].]
1 Well covered with flesh; fat, plump. LME.
G. GREENE The fleshy and porky figure of the actor.
2 Of or pertaining to flesh; *esp.* consisting of flesh, without bone. Also *fig.* (now *rare*), of a heart etc.: soft, tender. LME. ▸**b** Of plant or fruit tissue: pulpy, not fibrous. L16. ▸**c** Corporeal, bodily. E17.
TINDALE The pistle of Christ . . written . . not in tables of stone, but in fleshy tables of the herte. **c** MILTON He, sovran priest . . Poor fleshy tabernacle entered.
†**3** = FLESHLY 4. LME–M16.
COVERDALE *Job* 10:4 Hast thou fleszshy eyes then, or doest thou loke as man loketh?
4 Resembling flesh, like flesh. LME.
J. ABERNETHY An increase of bulk, and a fleshy feel.
■ **fleshiness** *noun* LME.

flet /flɛt/ *noun*[1].
[ORIGIN Old English *flet(t)* = Old Norse *flet*, ult. from Germanic base of FLAT *adjective*.]
†**1** The floor or ground beneath one's feet. OE–LME.
2 †**a** A dwelling, house, or hall. OE–LME. ▸**b** The inner part of a house. *Scot.* LME.
– PHRASES: **fire and flet** *arch.* fire and houseroom.

flet /flɛt/ *noun*[2]. *Scot.* L18.
[ORIGIN App. repr. Old Norse *flétta* plait, from *flétta* = German *flechten* to plait.]
A mat of plaited straw; *esp.* one placed on the back of a packhorse.

flet *adjective* var. of FLEET *adjective*[1].

fletch /flɛtʃ/ *verb trans.* M17.
[ORIGIN Alt. of FLEDGE *verb*, prob. infl. by FLETCHER.]
Provide (an arrow) with feathers for flight (*lit.* & *fig.*).
■ **fletching** *noun* (*a*) the action of the verb; (*b*) the feathers of an arrow: M20.

fletcher /ˈflɛtʃə/ *noun*. ME.
[ORIGIN Old French *flech(i)er*, from *fleche* arrow, ult. origin unknown: see -ER[2].]
A person who makes or trades in arrows (and occas. bows).

Fletcherian /flɛˈtʃɪərɪən/ *adjective*. M19.
[ORIGIN from *Fletcher* (see below) + -IAN.]
Of, pertaining to, or characteristic of (the work of) the English dramatist John Fletcher (1579–1625).

Fletcherism /ˈflɛtʃərɪz(ə)m/ *noun*. *obsolete* exc. *hist.* E20.
[ORIGIN from Horace *Fletcher* (1849–1919), US author + -ISM.]
The practice of thorough mastication as advocated by Fletcher.
■ **Fletcherite** *noun* a follower of Fletcher E20. **fletcherize** *verb trans.* masticate thoroughly E20.

fletton /ˈflɛt(ə)n/ *noun*. Also **F-**. E20.
[ORIGIN *Fletton*, a village in Cambridgeshire, southern England.]
A type of brick made by a semi-dry process, orig. from the Oxford clay near Fletton. Also ***fletton brick***.

fleur-de-coin /flœːrdəkwɛ̃/ *noun*. L19.
[ORIGIN French = bloom of the minting die.]
NUMISMATICS. Mint or perfect condition of a coin.

fleur-de-lis /flɜːdəˈliː/ *noun*. Pl. **fleurs-** (pronounced same). Also **-lys**; (*arch.* or *poet.*) **flower-de-luce** /flaʊədɪˈluːs/, pl. **-luces** /-ˈluːsɪz/. ME.
[ORIGIN Old French *flour de lys*, formed as *flour* FLOWER *noun* + *de* of + *lys* LILY, also assoc. with a fanciful Latin *flos deliciae* flower of delight.]
1 (The flower of) any of various plants of the genus *Iris*, of the iris family. ME.
2 The heraldic lily, composed of three petals bound together near their bases and traditionally supposed to have represented an iris, the head of a sceptre, or the top of a battleaxe or other weapon; *esp.* (*sing.* & in *pl.*) the former royal arms of France (characterized by this device). Also, the former royal family of France or (before 1789) the French standard, nation, or government. ME.
3 The representation or figure of the heraldic fleur-de-lis. Also (*hist.*), a brand of such a form with which convicted criminals were branded under the French penal code. LME.

fleuret /ˈflɔːrɛt/ *noun*[1]. Now *rare* or *obsolete*. M17.
[ORIGIN French (from *fleur* flower) = Italian *fioretto* dim. of *fiore* flower: see -ET[1].]
A fencing foil.

fleuret /flʊəˈrɛt, flɔː-/ *noun*[2]. E19.
[ORIGIN French *fleurette* dim. of *fleur* FLOWER *noun*: see -ET[1].]
An ornament resembling a small flower.

fleurettée /ˈflɔːrəteɪ/ *adjective*. M16.
[ORIGIN French *fleuretté(e)*, from *fleurette*: see FLEURET *noun*[2].]
HERALDRY. = FLORY.

fleuron /ˈflʊərɒn, ˈflɔː-, *foreign* flœːrɔ̃ (*pl. same*)/ *noun*. LME.
[ORIGIN Old French *floron* (mod. *fleuron*), from *flour* FLOWER *noun*.]
1 A flower-shaped ornament, used esp. in architecture or printing, as a device on coins, etc. LME.
2 A small pastry puff used for garnishing. Long *rare* or *obsolete*. M17.
†**3** = FLORET *noun* 1. *rare*. Only in E18.

fleury *adjective* var. of FLORY *adjective*.

flew *noun* var. of FLUE *noun*[1].

flew *adjective*[1], *adjective*[2] vars. of FLUE *adjective*[1], *adjective*[2].

flew *verb pa. t.* of FLY *verb*.

flewet /ˈfluːɪt/ *noun*. *obsolete* exc. *Scot.* & *N. English*. L16.
[ORIGIN Unknown.]
A hard blow or stroke, a buffet.

flews /fluːz/ *noun pl.* L16.
[ORIGIN Unknown.]
The thick hanging lips of a bloodhound or similar dog.
■ **flewed** *adjective* (long *rare*) having flews (of a specified kind) L16.

flex /flɛks/ *noun*[1]. M19.
[ORIGIN Latin *flexus*, from *flex-*: see FLEX *verb*.]
MATH. A point of inflection.

flex /flɛks/ *noun*[2]. E20.
[ORIGIN Abbreviation of FLEXIBLE.]
(A length of) flexible insulated wire for carrying low-current electricity, esp. to portable domestic appliances.

flex /flɛks/ *verb*. E16.
[ORIGIN Latin *flex-* pa. ppl stem of *flectere* bend.]
1 *verb trans.* Cause to bend; *esp.* in ANATOMY, bend (a joint or limb), move or contract (a muscle) to bend a joint. E16. ▸**b** GEOLOGY. Distort (strata). L19. ▸**c** ARCHAEOLOGY. Place (a corpse) with the legs drawn up under the chin. Chiefly as ***flexed*** *ppl adjective*. E20.
J. STEINBECK He flexed his muscles against his back. B. CHATWIN Young rooks were learning to flex their wings.
flex one's muscles *fig.* give a show of aggression or strength.
2 *verb intrans.* Be or become bent; be capable of bending; (of a muscle etc.) contract. E20.
Scientific American The arrow . . must flex slightly as it is launched. J. BERGER He saw the muscles . . down its haunches flex as it zigzagged.
■ **flexed** *ppl adjective* that has been flexed, bent; (HERALDRY) ***flexed and reflexed***, having two extremities curved in opposite directions, as the letter S: L16. **flexing** *noun* the action of the verb; an instance of this, a bending: E20.

flexibility /flɛksɪˈbɪlɪti/ *noun*. E17.
[ORIGIN French *flexibilité* or late Latin *flexibilitas*, from Latin *flexibilis*: see FLEXIBLE, -ITY.]
1 Ability to be bent, pliancy. E17.
2 Readiness to yield to influence or persuasion; pliancy of mind or disposition. M17.
3 Susceptibility of modification or alteration; capacity for ready adaptation. L18. ▸**b** Chiefly MUSIC. Capacity of the voice or fingers for free, rapid, or varied execution or delivery. L18.

flexible /ˈflɛksɪb(ə)l/ *adjective & noun*. LME.
[ORIGIN Old French & mod. French, or Latin *flexibilis*, formed as FLEX *verb* + -IBLE.]
▸ **A** *adjective*. **1** Orig., able to be inclined or made favourable *to*. Now, willing or disposed to yield to influence or persuasion; able to be guided or easily led; manageable. LME.
SHAKES. *3 Hen. VI* Women are soft, mild, . . and flexible.
2 Able to be bent; admitting of change in figure without breaking; yielding to pressure, pliable, pliant. LME.
ALDOUS HUXLEY Mitsima rolled out another piece of clay into a long flexible cylinder. ANTHONY HUXLEY Flexible garage doors composed of metal strips.
flexible friend *joc.* [from an advertising slogan] a credit card.
†**3** Of a fluid: not rigid, yielding. Of a wind: variable in direction, shifting. Only in 17.
4 Able to be modified or adapted to various purposes or uses; supple; versatile. M17.
SYD. SMITH Some have been selected for flexible politics. LYTTON His voice was so deep and flexible. M. HUNTER So variable are the uses of language, so infinitely flexible their application.
flexible response a strategy based on a spectrum of possible military responses to any threat.
▸ **B** *noun*. = FLEX *noun*[2]. L19.
■ **flexibleness** *noun* (now *rare*) = FLEXIBILITY E17. **flexibly** *adverb* E17.

flexile /ˈflɛksʌɪl/ *adjective*. *arch.* M17.
[ORIGIN Latin *flexilis*, from *flex-*: see FLEX *verb*, -ILE.]
1 Easily bending or bent; supple, pliant; (of the features) mobile. M17.
2 a Easily directed or influenced; yielding. M17. ▸**b** Capable of varied adaptation, versatile. M18.
■ **fleˈxility** *noun* M17.

flexion /ˈflɛkʃ(ə)n/ *noun*. Also (*rare*) **flection**. E17.
[ORIGIN Latin *flexio(n-)*, from *flex-*: see FLEX *verb*, -ION.]
1 The action or an act of bending, curvature; *esp.* the bending of a limb or joint by action of the flexor muscles. E17.
2 †**a** *gen.* Alteration, change, modification. E–M17. ▸**b** A modification of the sound or tone of the voice; inflection. M18.
3 The bent part of anything, a bend, a curve. E17.
4 GRAMMAR. Modification of the form of a word; *esp.* the change of ending in conjugation, declension, etc.; inflection. E17.
5 MATH. = FLEXURE 6. E18.
■ **flexional** *adjective* (*a*) of, pertaining to, or of the nature of flexion; (*b*) (of a language) based on flexions: M19. **flexionless** *adjective* M19.

flexitime /ˈflɛksɪtʌɪm/ *noun*. Also **flextime** /ˈflɛkstʌɪm/. L20.
[ORIGIN from FLEXIBLE + TIME *noun*.]
An arrangement whereby employees are free to vary their starting and finishing times (within prescribed limits), while working a contracted number of hours; working time so arranged.

†**flexive** *adjective*. E17–L18.
[ORIGIN from Latin *flex-*: see FLEX *verb*, -IVE.]
Tending to bend, flexible.

flexography /flɛkˈsɒgrəfi/ *noun*. M20.
[ORIGIN from Latin *flexus*, from *flex-*: see FLEX *verb*, -OGRAPHY.]
A rotary printing method using rubber or plastic plates moulded in relief and special inks for printing esp. on packaging materials.
■ **flexoˈgraphic** *adjective* M20.

flexor /ˈflɛksə/ *noun*. E17.
[ORIGIN mod. Latin, from Latin *flex-*: see FLEX *verb*, -OR.]
ANATOMY. More fully ***flexor muscle***. A muscle whose function is to bend a joint or limb. Cf. EXTENSOR.

flextime *noun* var. of FLEXITIME.

flexuous /ˈflɛksjʊəs/ *adjective*. E17.
[ORIGIN from Latin *flexuosus*, from *flexus* a bending, from *flex-*: see FLEX *verb*, -OSE[1], -OUS.]
1 Full of bends and curves; winding, sinuous. E17.
2 Moving in bends or waves, undulating. *rare*. E17.
■ **flexuose** *adjective* (chiefly BOTANY) = FLEXUOUS 1 E18. **flexuˈosity** *noun* (*a*) the state or quality of being flexuous; (*b*) an instance of this, a winding: E17. **flexuously** *adverb* M17.

flexure /ˈflɛkʃə/ *noun*. L16.
[ORIGIN Latin *flexura*, from *flex-*: see FLEX *verb*, -URE.]
1 The action or an act of flexing or bending; curvature. L16.
2 Flexed or bent condition; bent figure or posture; bending or winding form. E17.
3 Something that is bent; a bend, a curve; *spec.* the inner surface of a flexed joint. E17.
†**4** A tendency to bend or be bent; a strain. Only in M17.
†**5** Ability to bend or be bent. M17–E19.
6 SCIENCE. The curving of a line or surface or solid, esp. from or towards a straight line, plane, etc. L17.
7 GEOLOGY. The bending of strata under pressure. M19.
■ **flexural** *adjective* of or relating to flexure L19.

fley /fleɪ/ *verb & noun*. *obsolete* exc. *Scot.* & *N. English*. Also **flay**. ME.
[ORIGIN Old Norse *fleygja* ult. from West Germanic causative of FLY *verb*.]
▸ **A** *verb*. **1** *verb trans.* Put to flight, frighten *away*. ME.
2 *verb trans.* Frighten, scare, terrify. ME.
3 *verb intrans.* Be afraid; take fright. Long *rare* or *obsolete*. M18.
▸ **B** *noun*. A fright, a scare. L18.
■ **fleysome** *adjective* frightful, dreadful L18.

flibbertigibbet /flɪbətɪˈdʒɪbɪt/ *noun*. LME.
[ORIGIN Prob. imit. of meaningless chatter.]
1 Orig., a gossip or chatterer. Now usu. a flighty, irresponsible, or frivolous person. LME.
E. BOWEN I'd always been the bright one, Victor the quiet one; I'd been the flibbertigibbet, he'd been the steady.
2 a (A name for) a devil or fiend. *rare*. E17. ▸**b** [After a character in Sir Walter Scott's novel *Kenilworth*.] An impish, mischievous child; a restless person, usu. grotesque in appearance. E19.
b O. HENRY Some venomous kobold or flibbertigibbet, whining, complaining, cursing.
■ **flibbertygibbety** *adjective* (*rare*) irresponsible, frivolous L19.

†**flibutor** *noun* see FILIBUSTER.

flic /flɪk, *foreign* flik (*pl. same*)/ *noun*. **L19**.
[**ORIGIN** French.]
A French police officer.

flicflac /ˈflɪkflak/ *noun*. **M19**.
[**ORIGIN** French; imit. of a succession of sharp sounds.]
BALLET. A lashing movement of the leg related to the fouetté.

flichter /ˈflɪxtə/ *verb*. *Scot*. (now *local*). Also **flighter**. **LME**.
[**ORIGIN** Prob. imit.; see -ER[5]. Var. form prob. infl. by FLIGHT *verb*.]
1 *verb intrans*. Flutter, move irregularly or feebly; (of a light) flicker. **LME**.

SIR W. SCOTT A branch of ivy flightering awa frae the wa'.

2 *verb intrans*. Struggle; tremble, quiver. **E16**.

ALLAN RAMSAY My flighteren heart gangs pittie-pattie.

3 *verb trans*. Alarm, startle. **E18**.

flick /flɪk/ *noun*[1]. **LME**.
[**ORIGIN** Imit.]
1 A light, sharp, blow, esp. one given with something pliant, a whip, the fingernails, etc. **LME**. ▸**b** A sudden movement, a jerk; *esp*. a snap or click of the fingers. **M19**. ▸**c** (A stroke played with) a quick turn of the wrist, esp. in throwing or playing a ball; a turn of the ball. **L19**.

b P. H. GIBBS Waiters scurried about at the flick of Robin's fingers.

2 A slight, sharp, sound (produced by a light blow or sudden movement). **M19**.

ALBERT SMITH The only . . sound . . being . . the flick of the driver's whip.

3 Something that is flicked; a fleck (of light etc.). **M19**.

THACKERAY Flicks of yellow that the rushlight threw on the . . ceiling.

4 (A showing of) a motion picture; (in *pl*.) the cinema. Cf. FLICKER *noun*[2] 3. *slang*. **E20**.

F. SWINNERTON Take her to the theatre, the ballet, the flicks. J. BRAINE Tea at the Raynton, then a flick.

– **COMB**.: **flick knife**: with a blade springing out when a button is pressed.
■ **flicky** *adjective* characterized by flicks or flicking **L19**.

flick /flɪk/ *noun*[2]. Chiefly *dial*. Also **fleck** /flɛk/. **LME**.
[**ORIGIN** Alt. of FLIX *noun*[1].]
The fur of a hare or rabbit; hence *collect*., hares and rabbits.

flick /flɪk/ *noun*[3]. *obsolete* exc. *dial*. Also **fleck** /flɛk/. **L16**.
[**ORIGIN** Uncertain: perh. same word as FLICK *noun*[5], FLITCH *noun*.]
The fat around a pig's kidney.

flick /flɪk/ *noun*[4]. *colloq*. (now *rare*). **L19**.
[**ORIGIN** Unknown.]
A fellow, a chap.

flick *noun*[5] see FLITCH *noun*.

†**flick** *verb*[1] *trans*. *criminals' slang*. **L17–M19**.
[**ORIGIN** Prob. from FLICK *noun*[5]. Cf. FLITCH *verb*.]
Cut.

flick /flɪk/ *verb*[2] & *adverb*. Also ***fleck** /flɛk/. **E19**.
[**ORIGIN** from FLICK *noun*[1].]
▸ **A** *verb*. **1** *verb trans*. Strike or propel lightly and smartly with something flexible; jerk or flip *away*, *off*, etc. **E19**. ▸**b** *spec*. Play or deliver (a ball) with a flick of the wrist etc. **L19**.

A. R. HOPE Flicking each other with our towels. S. GIBBONS She . . flicked the reminders of dinner off the table with Adam's drying-up towel.

2 *verb intrans*. Move or go with quick, smart movements or vibrations; esp. riffle or look rapidly *through*, *over*, etc., (pages, a book, etc.). **M19**.

J. GARDNER The porch lights flicked on and off. P. NORMAN The white label of the gramophone record flicks round and round. J. SIMMS He flicked through the notebook he always carried.

3 *verb trans*. Make a light stroke or movement with (a whip etc.); move or shake with a flick. **M19**.

F. HERBERT A smile flicked the corners of the wrinkled old mouth. B. HINES She still swiped at him, and . . he still flicked his head back.

▸ **B** *adverb*. With a flick. *rare*. **M19**.

flicker /ˈflɪkə/ *noun*[1]. **E19**.
[**ORIGIN** Imit. of the bird's call.]
Any of various American woodpeckers of the genus *Colaptes*; esp. *C. auratus* (more fully ***common flicker***, ***northern flicker***).

flicker /ˈflɪkə/ *verb* & *noun*[2].
[**ORIGIN** Old English *flicorian*, *flycerian* (cf. Low German *flickern*, Dutch *flikkeren*), orig. synon. with FLACKER.]
▸ **A** *verb*. **1** *verb intrans*. Of a bird: flutter. Now *rare*. **OE**.
†**2** *verb intrans*. Make caressing or fondling movements; act or look in a coaxing or affectionate manner; dally (*after*). **ME–E19**.

DRYDEN Lavinia . . looks a little flickering after Turnus.

†**3** Waver, vacillate, act unreliably. **ME–M18**.

W. SHENSTONE A race of flickering knaves.

4 *verb intrans*. & (*rare*) *trans*. (Cause to) flutter rapidly, quiver, undulate; wave to and fro. **LME**.

TENNYSON Nor cared the serpent . . to flicker with his double tongue. R. WARNER The beginnings of a smile flickered at the corners of her mouth.

5 *verb intrans*. Flash up and die away rapidly (and repeatedly); (of flame) burn fitfully; (of light) vary rapidly in brightness. **E17**.

C. MERIVALE A gleam of hope still flickered in their bosoms. M. DE LA ROCHE A gust came down the chimney and the night-light flickered.

flicker out die away after a final flicker.

6 *verb trans*. Cause to move rapidly or fitfully like a flicker of light; indicate by a flicker. **M19**.

R. LANGBRIDGE He watched her eye-lashes flicker dismissal. D. H. LAWRENCE He . . flickered his two-forked tongue from his lips.

▸ **B** *noun*. **1** An act of flickering, a flickering movement. **M19**.

D. BAGLEY The flame which burned without a flicker in the still air. *fig*.: A. S. BYATT She looked at him with a flicker of interest.

2 A wavering, unsteady light or flame. **M19**. ▸**b** A rapid, rhythmic variation in illumination or sound; the visual or aural sensation caused by this. **L19**. ▸**c** *spec*. A succession of abrupt changes in the image on a television etc. screen (esp. with an overlap between them), causing visual confusion. **L19**.

P. G. WODEHOUSE A flicker of lightning came and went in the darkness.

3 = FLICK *noun*[1] 4. *slang*. Now *rare*. **E20**.
– **COMB**.: **flicker fusion frequency** OPTICS the frequency of flicker above which the eye perceives a light source as constant; **flicker photometer**, **flicker photometry** a photometer, a photometric technique, used for comparing the intensities of two light sources (esp. of different colours), which works by measuring the flicker produced when the same visual field is illuminated alternately by the two sources; **flickertail** *N. Amer*. = ***Richardson's ground squirrel*** s.v. RICHARDSON *noun*[1].
■ **flickering** *verbal noun* the action of the verb; an instance of this: **LME**. **flickeringly** *adverb* in a flickering manner **M19**. **flickery** *adjective* that flickers, flickering **L19**.

flickermouse /ˈflɪkəmaʊs/ *noun*. *obsolete* exc. *dial*. Pl. **-mice** /-mʌɪs/. **M17**.
[**ORIGIN** Alt. of FLITTER-MOUSE.]
= BAT *noun*[3].

flier *noun* var. of FLYER.

flight /flʌɪt/ *noun*[1].
[**ORIGIN** Old English *flyht* corresp. to Old Saxon *fluht*, Middle Dutch & mod. Dutch *vlucht* from West Germanic, from Germanic base of FLY *verb*.]
1 The action or manner of flying or moving through the air with or as with wings. **OE**. ▸†**b** The power of flying. Only in **ME**.

DAY LEWIS The butterflies whose dithering flight was no more erratic than my aunts' talk. D. ATTENBOROUGH Their wings were so small . . that they had lost the power of flight.

2 Swift movement, esp. of a projectile through the air; *spec*. the passage of a projectile from a gun to a target. **ME**. ▸**b** Swift passage *of* time. **M17**. ▸**c** In games, the trajectory and pace of a ball through the air; the control or variation of this in order to deceive an opponent. **L19**.

SHELLEY Ships, whose flight is swift along the wave. **b** MILTON The never-ending flight Of future days. **c** *Squash World* I tried . . to slow the ball down and put a bit of flight on it.

3 †**a** The wing of a bird. Only in **ME**. ▸**b** *collect*. The flight feathers. **M18**.
4 A flock of things passing through the air, *esp*. a flock of birds or insects. **ME**. ▸**b** A volley of missiles, esp. arrows. Chiefly *hist*. **M16**. ▸**c** The young birds that take wing at one time. **L16**. ▸**d** A company *of* angels. **E17**. ▸**e** A migration or migrating body of birds or insects. **E19**.

HARPER LEE Watching flights of martins sweep low over the . . rooftops. **b** W. OWEN Sudden successive flights of bullets streak the silence. **e** P. MATTHIESSEN The numerous dead red-starts . . —a whole migratory flight—that must have perished.

5 A flight arrow. Also, flight-shooting. **LME**. ▸**b** The tail of a dart, by which it is balanced when in flight. **M20**.
†**6** A state of agitation or trembling. **E–M16**.
7 FALCONRY. The pursuit of game etc. by a hawk; the quarry being pursued. **M16**.
8 The distance which a bird, aircraft, missile, etc., can or does fly. **E17**.
9 A mounting, soaring, or excursion of the imagination, fancy, ambition, etc. **M17**.

C. JOHNSTON A silence more expressive . . than all the flights of eloquence.

10 A series of stairs running between two landings. **E18**. ▸**b** A series of locks on a canal in graduated steps. **M19**. ▸**c** A series of hurdles or rails usu. for racing over. **M19**.

R. MACAULAY They climbed a steep, winding flight of stone stairs. J. S. FOSTER A landing serves as a rest between flights.

11 The action or technique of travelling through the air or through space in an aircraft, spacecraft, etc. **L18**. ▸**b** An instance of air or space travel; a timed journey by an airline from one place to another; a journey or voyage through the air or through space. **L18**. ▸**c** A Royal Air Force unit consisting of about six aircraft; the members of such a unit. **E20**.

b R. BRADBURY It was the boy's first flight into space, his very first time in a rocket. E. WELTY She had come on a night flight from Chicago.

12 The husk or glume of oats. **M19**.
13 The lower part of the clapper of a bell. **L19**.
– **PHRASES**: **in flight** flying, travelling through the air (see also IN-FLIGHT). **in the first flight**, **in the top flight** taking a leading place. †**of the same flight** *rare* (arrows) having the same power of flight; of equal size and weight. **take a flight**, **take one's flight** fly, move swiftly through the air.
– **COMB**.: **flight arrow** a light, well-feathered arrow for long-distance shooting; **flight attendant** a passenger attendant in an aircraft; **flight bag** a small zipped bag with a shoulder strap, as carried by air travellers; **flight call** (*a*) the cry made by a bird in flight; (*b*) an announcement at an airport, informing passengers that they may board their aircraft; **flight control** a system for directing the movement of aircraft, located either on the ground or in the aircraft itself; **flight crew** a team of people who ensure the effective operation and safety of an aircraft during its flight; **flight deck** (*a*) the deck of an aircraft carrier on which aircraft take off and land; (*b*) the part of an aeroplane accommodating the pilot, navigator, etc.; **flight envelope** AERONAUTICS the possible combinations of speed and altitude, speed and range, etc., of a particular kind of aircraft or aeroengine; **flight feather** any of the feathers which support a bird in flight, comprising the primary and secondary feathers; **flight lieutenant** a rank in the Royal Air Force, immediately below squadron leader; **flightline** (*a*) the course taken by (esp. migrating) birds; (*b*) a general area in an airfield including hangars, ramps, etc., where aircraft are parked and serviced; **flight net** a net used for catching birds; **flight-number** the identifying number of a scheduled aircraft flight; **flight officer** a rank in the Women's Royal Air Force, equivalent to flight lieutenant; an officer in the US air forces; **flight path** the planned or actual course of an aircraft or spacecraft; **flight plan** AERONAUTICS the prearranged scheme for a particular flight; **flight recorder** a device in an aircraft which records the technical details of each flight, for use in the event of an accident; **flight refuelling** the refuelling of an aircraft while in flight; **flight sergeant** a rank in the Royal Air Force, next above sergeant; **flight-shaft** = ***flight arrow*** above; **flight-shooting** (*a*) ARCHERY distance-shooting with flight arrows; (*b*) shooting wildfowl in flight; **flight-shot** (*a*) the distance to which a flight arrow is shot; a bowshot; (*b*) a shot taken at wildfowl in flight; **flight-test** *verb trans*. test (an aircraft, rocket, etc.) during flight.
■ **flightless** *adjective* (of birds, insects, etc.) lacking the power of flight **L19**.

flight /flʌɪt/ *noun*[2]. **ME**.
[**ORIGIN** Corresp. to Old Frisian *flecht*, Old Saxon, Old High German *fluht* (Dutch *vlucht*, German *Flucht*), Old Norse *flótti* from Germanic, from base of FLEE *verb*. Prob. already in Old English.]
1 The action or manner of fleeing or running away from or as from danger etc.; hasty retreat. **ME**.

H. DOOLITTLE My trip to Greece . . might have been interpreted as a flight from reality. C. CONNOLLY As escapes from the problem, as flights from guilt, they may be welcome.

put to flight cause to flee, rout. **take flight**, **take to flight** run away, flee.

2 ECONOMICS. The selling of currency or withdrawal of investments etc. in anticipation of a fall in value. Foll. by *from*. **E20**.

flight /flʌɪt/ *noun*[3]. *obsolete* exc. *dial*. **L15**.
[**ORIGIN** Var. of FLAUGHT *noun*[1].]
A flake of snow; a snowstorm.

flight /flʌɪt/ *verb*. **E16**.
[**ORIGIN** from FLIGHT *noun*[1], *noun*[2].]
†**1** *verb intrans*. Flutter; fluctuate. Cf. FLICHTER. *Scot*. *rare*. Only in **E16**.
2 *verb trans*. Put to flight, rout; frighten. *obsolete* exc. *dial*. **L16**. ▸**b** Set flying, start in flight. **E19**.
3 *verb intrans*. †**a** Migrate. **E17–M18**. ▸**b** Fly in flights. **L19**.
4 *verb trans*. Feather (an arrow). **M19**.
5 *verb trans*. Shoot (wildfowl) in flight. **L19**.
6 *verb trans*. Vary the trajectory and pace of (a cricket ball etc.). **E20**.

flighted /ˈflʌɪtɪd/ *ppl adjective*. **L16**.
[**ORIGIN** from FLIGHT *noun*[1] + -ED[2].]
1 Having a certain flight or speed. *rare*. **L16**.
2 Feathered. **M18**.
3 Of steps: arranged in flights. **E20**.

flighter *verb* var. of FLICHTER.

flighty /ˈflʌɪti/ *adjective*. **M16**.
[**ORIGIN** from FLIGHT *noun*[1] + -Y[1].]
1 Swift, fleet. *rare*. **M16**.

P. MATTHIESSEN The animals are flighty now, and so I stalk them with more care.

2 Guided by whim or fancy rather than by judgement or common sense; fickle, frivolous. **M18**.

H. G. WELLS Your wits might be flighty, but . . your character was sound. A. THWAITE Edmund, though young, was certainly not flighty.

3 Insane, crazy. Now *rare*. **E19**.

■ **flightily** *adverb* L18. **flightiness** *noun* M18.

flim /flɪm/ *noun. slang.* L19.
[ORIGIN Abbreviation of FLIMSY *noun*.]
A £5 note.

flimflam /ˈflɪmflam/ *noun, adjective, & verb.* Also **flim-flam**. M16.
[ORIGIN Symbolic redupl. formation with vowel variation: cf. WHIM-WHAM.]
▸ **A** *noun.* **1** A trifle, a conceit. Now usu. *collect.*, nonsense. M16.

W. A. WALLACE The wanderings of his dotage, and flim-flam after all.

2 A contemptible trick. Now usu. *collect.*, humbug, deception. M16.

Times No amount of public relations flim-flam can disguise the fact that extremists win.

3 A confidence trick; confidence trickery. *slang.* L19.
▸ **B** *adjective.* Frivolous, nonsensical; fictitious, sham. L16.

R. HOLINSHED His slanderous reports are vnderpropt with flim-flam surmises.

▸ **C** *verb trans.* Infl. **-mm-**. Humbug, beguile (*into* something); *spec.* (*slang*) cheat (by a confidence trick). M17.

Punch Marketing practices that smacked of flimflamming the public.

■ **flimflammer**, **flimflammery** *nouns* L19.

flimmer /ˈflɪmə/ *noun.* Pl. same. M20.
[ORIGIN German = tinsel.]
BIOLOGY. A mastigoneme, *esp.* a slender one.

flimmer /ˈflɪmə/ *verb intrans.* L19.
[ORIGIN Imit.: cf. German *flimmern*.]
Flicker, move unsteadily.

flimsy /ˈflɪmzi/ *adjective & noun.* E18.
[ORIGIN Prob. based on FLIMFLAM: see -SY.]
▸ **A** *adjective.* **1** Frail, slight, insubstantial; easily destroyed, poorly put together. E18.

J. CHEEVER The walls were flimsy—part frosted glass and part plywood.

2 Trivial, paltry; frivolous, superficial. M18.

T. T. LYNCH The flimsy individual who has read fifty novels in a year, but nothing else. ISAIAH BERLIN A historical and emotional atmosphere for which the evidence is flimsy, but which is artistically indispensable.

▸ **B** *noun.* **1** A banknote. *slang.* Now *rare* or *obsolete.* E19.
2 A flimsy thing or material; *esp.* (a document on) thin paper (as used for taking copies on a typewriter etc.). M19.

D. L. SAYERS She . . shook the top sheet, carbons, and flimsies together.

■ **flimsily** *adverb* L18. **flimsiness** *noun* E18.

flinch /ˈflɪn(t)ʃ/ *verb*[1] *& noun.* M16.
[ORIGIN Old French *flenchir*, *flainchir* turn aside, from West Germanic, whence also Middle & mod. High German *lenken* to bend, turn.]
▸ **A** *verb.* †**1** *verb intrans.* Slink, sneak *off*, *away*. M16–E17.
2 *verb intrans.* Give way, draw back, turn aside, now esp. through a failure in courage or endurance; shrink *from* anything. L16. ▸†**b** *verb trans.* Withdraw (from), lose. L17–M19.

G. SANTAYANA Oliver never flinched in his determination to pursue higher things. C. MCCULLOUGH Too much of a land person . . to flinch from doing what had to be done.

3 *verb intrans.* Shrink under pain, trouble, etc.; wince; blench. L17.

E. BOWEN Rupert's wife . . stood . . breathing hard and flinching away from the lightning. J. HERRIOT The skin isn't broken, but he flinches if you press here.

▸ **B** *noun.* An act or instance of flinching. E19.
■ **flincher** *noun* L16. **flinchingly** *adverb* (*rare*) with flinching L19.

flinch *verb*[2] var. of FLENSE.

flinder /ˈflɪndə/ *noun.* Long *obsolete* exc. *dial.* ME.
[ORIGIN Corresp. to Dutch *vlinder* butterfly.]
A moth or butterfly.

flindermouse /ˈflɪndəmaʊs/ *noun. obsolete* exc. *dial.* Pl. **-mice** /-mʌɪs/. L15.
[ORIGIN from FLINDER + MOUSE *noun*: cf. FLICKERMOUSE, FLITTERMOUSE.]
= BAT *noun*[3].

flinders /ˈflɪndəz/ *noun*[1] *pl.* LME.
[ORIGIN Prob. of Scandinavian origin: cf. Norwegian *flindra* thin chip or splinter.]
Fragments, small pieces, splinters. Cf. FLITTERS, FITTERS.

Flinders /ˈflɪndəz/ *noun*[2]. L19.
[ORIGIN Capt. Matthew *Flinders* (1774–1814), English navigator.]
1 ***Flinders bar***, a soft iron bar placed vertically near a ship's compass to correct deviation due to magnetic induction. L19.
2 ***Flinders grass***, any of various grasses esp. of the genus *Iseilema*, giving valuable forage. *Austral.* L19.

flindosa /flɪnˈdəʊzə/ *noun. Austral.* Also **-sy** /-zi/. M19.
[ORIGIN Alt. of mod. Latin *Flindersia* (see below), from FLINDERS *noun*[2].]
(The timber of) an Australian hardwood rainforest tree, *Flindersia australis* (family Rutaceae). Also called ***Australian teak***.

fling /flɪŋ/ *noun.* ME.
[ORIGIN from the verb.]
1 An attempt at or attack upon something; now *spec.* a sarcastic remark, a jibe. ME.

C. JOHNSTON A fling at the clergy never fails to raise a laugh.

have a fling at (*a*) make an attempt at; (*b*) make a (verbal) attack on.
2 A hasty or reckless movement; a violent movement, a flinging about of the body. M16. ▸**b** A dance involving vigorous movement; chiefly in ***Highland fling*** below. E19.

H. N. COLERIDGE The furious jerks and flings which . . [the shark] made.

Highland fling a type of vigorous Scottish reel. **take the fling(s)** *Scot.* become bad tempered or unmanageable.
3 An act of flinging; a throw. L16.

W. DE LA MARE After a few lasso-like flings of it, he had run the rope . . over one of a few large hooks.

4 A period of self-indulgence or pleasure; a good time; *spec.* a brief (usu. extramarital) affair. E19.

Y. MENUHIN It was our fling, our time of freedom, of unconcern, of letting duty slide. A. LURIE Rosemary isn't looking for a fling She's looking for an undying passion.

fling /flɪŋ/ *verb.* Pa. t. & pple **flung** /flʌŋ/. ME.
[ORIGIN Perh. rel. to Old Norse *flengja* (Swedish *flänga*, Danish *flænge*) flog.]
▸ **I** *verb intrans.* **1** Rush; go angrily or violently. ME.

LD MACAULAY The Chancellor . . flung away in a rage. S. MIDDLETON He flung back the way he had come. V. WOOLF Are we to fling off in a new direction?

†**2** Come *together* in fighting; aim a blow (*at*). ME–L15.
3 (Of a horse etc.) kick and plunge violently; be unruly; (of a person) be restive or violent, struggle; freq. *fig.*, burst into invective or complaint. LME.

SHAKES. *Macb.* Duncan's horses . . Turn'd wild in nature, broke their stalls, flung out. J. PAYN I had rather she had flung out at me.

4 Dance, caper. *Scot.* E16.
▸ **II** *verb trans.* **5** Throw (*lit.* & *fig.*), hurl, cast, toss, propel, esp. with violence, malice, or recklessness. Freq. with adverbs. LME. ▸**b** Put suddenly or violently *into* prison etc. LME.

EDWARD WARD Fling dirt enough, and some will stick. T. HARDY She flung a cloak round her. QUILLER-COUCH I flung a short glance downward at the birches and black water. S. LEWIS The February city, where lorries flung up a spattering of slush. J. BUCHAN They would fling me a question or two about South Africa. **b** LD MACAULAY Laud was flung into the Tower.

6 Spread out or extend (the arms etc.) suddenly; kick *up* (the heels). M17.

E. FEINSTEIN She flung her arms round me, and sobbed.

7 Send out, emit (light, sound, etc.). *arch.* M17.

MILTON The sun begins to fling His flaring beams.

8 Throw (oneself) *at*, *down*, *into*, *on*, etc.; *fig.* throw (oneself, one's efforts) *into* an activity etc. E18.

LYTTON I flung myself into his arms and wept. J. RATHBONE He flung himself back in his chair. J. MCCARTHY She had flung all her energies into the rebellion.

†**9** Get the better of; cheat, swindle. *slang.* M18–M19.

C. JOHNSTON He cannot fling his worthy associate out of the whole spoil.

10 Throw down to the ground; *esp.* (of a horse) throw (a rider). L18.

HOR. WALPOLE His horse started, flung him, and fell upon him. TENNYSON Never a man could fling him; for Willy stood like a rock.

– PHRASES, & WITH ADVERBS IN SPECIALIZED SENSES: **fling aside** disregard; reject. **fling down** throw to the ground; overthrow; demolish. **fling off** abandon, disown; throw off the scent. **fling open** open suddenly or violently. **fling in a person's face** refer reproachfully to (a previous action, statement, etc., of that person). ***fling in a person's teeth***: see TOOTH *noun*. **fling to** shut suddenly or violently. ***fling to the winds***, ***fling to the four winds***: see WIND *noun*[1]. **fling up** (*a*) throw up (a defensive mound etc.); (*b*) relinquish. **fling wide** = ***fling open*** above.
■ **flinger** *noun* E16.

flint /flɪnt/ *noun & adjective.*
[ORIGIN Old English *flint* = Middle Dutch *vlint* rel. to Old High German (German dial.) *flins* and perh. to Greek *plinthos* tile (see PLINTH).]
▸ **A** *noun.* **1** A hard stone which consists of nearly pure silica and occurs as nodules which are grey within and have a white crust. OE. ▸**b** Anything hard and unyielding. ME.

b SIR W. SCOTT Callum, flint to other considerations, was penetrable to superstition.

2 (A piece of) this stone or, in modern devices, a metal (usu. a hard alloy containing misch metal), struck against iron or steel in order to produce sparks for ignition, e.g. in a flintlock gun, a cigarette lighter, etc. OE.
3 Any piece of flint; freq. a piece flaked or ground into a tool or weapon by prehistoric humans. ME.

J. DYER Ancient roads, o'er whose broad flints Such crowds have roll'd. J. A. MICHENER Flints . . sharpened to a glistening sheen on one serrated edge.

set one's face like a flint be steadfast. ***skin a flint***: see SKIN *verb*.
4 a In full ***flint glass***. A pure lustrous glass made from lead oxide, sand (orig., ground flint), and alkali. L17. ▸**b** In full ***flint corn***. Any of various varieties of maize having very hard kernels. Chiefly *US*. E18.
5 A journeyman tailor who refuses to submit to an employer's terms. Cf. DUNG *noun* 3. *slang. obsolete* exc. *hist.* M18.
▸ **B** *attrib.* or as *adjective.* Of flint. ME.
– COMB.: ***flint corn***: see sense A.4b above; ***flint glass***: see sense A.4a; **flint-hearted** *adjective* hard-hearted; **flintlock** [LOCK *noun*[2] 3] *hist.* (the lock of) a gun discharged by a spark from the flint igniting the primer; **flint paper** (*a*) a paper burnished or glazed to a high gloss; (*b*) an abrasive paper; **flintstone** = senses A.1, 2, 3 above; **flintwood** = ***blackbutt*** s.v. BLACK *adjective*.
■ **flintless** *adjective* E19.

F

flinty /ˈflɪnti/ *adjective.* M16.
[ORIGIN from FLINT + -Y[1].]
Of or full of flint; resembling flint in colour, texture, hardness, or impenetrability.

J. L. WATEN The sun glared at us through flinty clouds. S. KING Her eyes were flinty, proud, and unbelieving.

– COMB.: **flinty-hearted** *adjective* having a hard heart or centre, hard-hearted.
■ **flintily** *adverb* L19. **flintiness** *noun* E17.

flip /flɪp/ *noun*[1]. L17.
[ORIGIN Perh. from FLIP *verb* with the sense of 'whip up' into froth.]
Orig., a mixed drink of beer and spirits heated with a hot iron. Now, a drink of spirits or wine beaten with egg and sugar, served either warm or iced.
egg-flip: see EGG *noun*.
– COMB.: **flip-dog**, (*US*) **flip-iron** a poker used to heat flip.

flip /flɪp/ *noun*[2]. L17.
[ORIGIN from the verb.]
1 A sharp blow. L17.

W. BESANT The . . flips which we poor women have to endure from harsh masters.

2 A sudden jerk or movement, a flick; a turning over, a somersault. E19. ▸**b** The springing of the barrel of a gun at the moment of discharge. L19.

G. C. DAVIES A derisive flip of their white tails. H. JAMES He gave a flip with a finger-nail to his cigarette. F. ASTAIRE They tossed Zenzo . . across the full length of the stage with a few double flips thrown in.

3 A (short) flight in an aircraft; a quick trip or tour in any conveyance. *colloq.* E20.

P. FIDDICK His pre-Easter flip to the Berlin Wall.

– COMB.: **flip jump** a toe jump in figure skating; **flip side** the reverse or less important side of a gramophone record.

flip /flɪp/ *adjective. colloq.* (orig. *dial.* & *US*). M19.
[ORIGIN from the verb.]
Nimble, now usu. of tongue; glib, flippant.

Times The word 'schizophrenia' is flung about today with flip facility. J. LE CARRÉ He's too damn flip with his alibi.

flip /flɪp/ *verb.* Infl. **-pp-**. M16.
[ORIGIN Prob. contr. FILLIP *verb* but cf. FLIP-FLAP.]
1 *verb intrans.* Make a flip (*at*) with the fingers etc. M16.

S. GRAND Viciously flipping at the flowers . . with the stick he carried.

2 *verb trans.* Strike smartly with the fingers, a whip, etc.; flick. L16.

J. PYCROFT Minnie laughed and flipped her old friend with her glove.

3 *verb trans. & intrans.* Put (something) into motion with a flip or jerk; move (something) with a flip or jerk; toss (a coin etc.). E17.

M. BARING The boys . . began making pellets and flipping them at each other. J. STEINBECK They had to flip for who would go to the party first. B. BAINBRIDGE Freda kept flipping ash on the carpet. *Listener* The Ambassador flipped the switch: the lights went on.

4 *verb intrans.* Fly in a (small) aircraft; make a short trip. *colloq.* E20.
5 *verb intrans.* Be or become wildly excited or enthusiastic; lose one's self-control; go mad. Also ***flip one's lid***, (chiefly US) ***flip one's wig***. *colloq.* M20.

Boston Globe Our food and service are great . . Your club treasurer will flip over our rates. G. SWIFT He'd flipped, he'd gone bananas.

– COMB. & PHRASES: **flip chart** (orig. *US*) a large pad erected on a stand and bound so that one page can be turned over at the top to reveal the next; **flip chip** COMPUTING a chip on one side of which all the connections are in the form of contacts which can be made simultaneously by pressing the chip against the matching substrate and applying heat or pressure; **flip one's lid**, **flip one's wig**: see sense 5 above.; **flip through** look rapidly through (a book, index, etc.), flick through; **flip-top** *adjective* (of a table) having additional sections at either end that can be drawn or folded outwards to increase the surface area; (of a package) that can be flipped open, usu. by pulling the top upwards and back.

■ **flipping** *ppl adjective & adverb* (colloq.) damned(ly), bloody E20. **flippy** *adjective* (of a skirt) flared and short, so as to flick up as the wearer walks M20.

flipe *noun, verb* vars. of FLYPE *noun, verb*.

flip-flap /ˈflɪpflap/ *noun, adverb, verb, & adjective*. E16.
[ORIGIN Redupl. of FLAP *noun* with vowel variation: cf. FLIP-FLOP.]
▸ **A** *noun*. **1** Something that flaps. Now *rare* or *obsolete*. E16.
2 A kind of somersault. L17.
▸ **B** *adverb*. With a repeated flapping movement. L16.
▸ **C** *verb trans. & intrans.* Infl. **-pp-**. Flap. L16.
▸ **D** *adjective*. That flaps. *rare*. M19.

F

flip-flop /ˈflɪpflɒp/ *noun, verb, & adverb*. M17.
[ORIGIN Redupl. of FLOP *noun* with vowel variation: cf. FLIP-FLAP.]
▸ **A** *noun*. **1** Something that flaps or flops. Now *esp*. a sandal consisting of a flat sole and straps. M17.
2 A (backward) somersault. Cf. FLIP-FLAP *noun* 2. *N. Amer.* E20.
3 ELECTRONICS. A switching circuit that changes from one stable state to another, or via an unstable state back to its stable state, in response to a triggering pulse. M20.
▸ **B** *verb trans. & intrans.* Infl. **-pp-**. Flip or flap. L19.
▸ **C** *adverb*. In a flapping manner. E20.

flippancy /ˈflɪp(ə)nsi/ *noun*. M18.
[ORIGIN from FLIPPANT: see -ANCY.]
The quality or an instance of being flippant.

flippant /ˈflɪp(ə)nt/ *adjective & noun*. E17.
[ORIGIN from FLIP *verb* + -ANT[1], perh. in imitation of heraldic adjectives, as *couchant*, *trippant*.]
▸ **A** *adjective*. **1** Nimble; pliant. *obsolete* exc. *dial*. E17.
†**2** Talkative, voluble, fluent. E17–L18.
†**3** Sportive, playful. Only in 18.
4 Lacking in seriousness; treating serious matters lightly; disrespectful. E18.

E. M. FORSTER I should never have talked in this flippant, superficial way. G. A. BIRMINGHAM He resents the flippant mirth of those whom he regards as his inferiors.

▸ **B** *absol*. as *noun*. A flippant person. Now *rare*. L18.

W. COWPER The flippant and the scold.

■ **flippantly** *adverb* M18. **flippantness** *noun* E18.

flipper /ˈflɪpə/ *noun & verb*. E19.
[ORIGIN from FLIP *verb* + -ER[1].]
▸ **A** *noun*. **1** A limb adapted for swimming, as the limb of a turtle, the (fore)limb of a seal, the wing of a penguin, etc. E19. ▸**b** A flexible attachment to the foot used for underwater swimming, esp. by frogmen. M20.
2 The hand. *slang*. M19.
3 CRICKET. A topspinner given an extra flip of the fingers. M20.
▸ **B** *verb intrans*. Move by means of flippers. M20.

flirt /flɜːt/ *noun*. M16.
[ORIGIN App. imit.: cf. FLICK *noun*[1], SPURT *noun*.]
▸ **I 1** †**a** A smart stroke of wit, a joke; a jibe. M16–E18. ▸**b** A smart tap or blow. *obsolete* exc. *dial*. L16.
2 A sudden jerk or movement; a quick throw or flick; a darting movement. L16.

G. WHITE Hedge-sparrows have a remarkable flirt with their wings.

3 HOROLOGY. A lever etc. for causing sudden movement. L18.
▸ **II 4** A person who behaves in a flirtatious manner; someone to flirt with. Formerly *esp*. a flighty young woman. M16. ▸†**b** A promiscuous woman. E17–E18.

OUIDA Sabretasche had an universal reputation as a most unscrupulous flirt. E. J. HOWARD She wasn't a flirt; she never edged up to sex and backed off giggling.

■ **flirtish** *adjective* resembling or characteristic of a flirt M17. **flirty** *adjective* of, pertaining to, or characterized by, flirtation M19.

flirt /flɜːt/ *verb*. M16.
[ORIGIN formed as the noun.]
†**1** **a** *verb intrans. & trans.* Sneer, jibe, scoff, *at* or at; turn up one's nose *at* or at. Formerly also, flare (the nostrils). M16–M18. ▸**b** *verb trans.* Give (a person) a sharp sudden blow. M16–M17.
2 *verb trans.* Propel or throw with a jerk or sudden movement; give sudden motion to; flip, flick; spread (a bird's wing, tail, etc.) quickly; open and close (a fan) smartly. L16. ▸**b** Blurt *out*. Now *rare* or *obsolete*. M17.

T. DEKKER Tis thy fashion to flirt inke in everie mans face.

3 *verb intrans.* Move with a jerk, spring, dart. Now *rare*. L16.

R. L. STEVENSON The tails of his night-shirt flirting as he turned.

4 *verb intrans.* Behave in a superficially amorous manner, dally. E17. ▸**b** Toy *with* (an idea etc.); deal lightly or frivolously *with* (a serious matter). M19.

N. MITFORD He had danced and flirted.. with other people. **b** N. PODHORETZ The notion I had been flirting with of staying in England forever was out.

■ **flirter** *noun* E19.

flirtation /fləːˈteɪʃ(ə)n/ *noun*. E18.
[ORIGIN formed as FLIRT *noun* + -ATION.]
The action or an instance of flirting (sense 4).

attrib.: SAKI If he got as far as the flirtation stage.. sheer perversity.. might carry him on to more definite courtship.

■ **flirtational** *adjective* (*rare*) M19.

flirtatious /fləːˈteɪʃəs/ *adjective*. M19.
[ORIGIN Irreg. from FLIRTATION + -OUS on the analogy of *ambition*, *ambitious*: see -TIOUS.]
Given to or of the nature of flirtation.

EDMUND WHITE He had a big, thin-lipped mouth.. that condescended once in a while to be flirtatious.

■ **flirtatiously** *adverb* M19. **flirtatiousness** *noun* L19.

†**flirt-gill** *noun*. L16–E17.
[ORIGIN from FLIRT *noun, verb* + GILL *noun*[4].]
A promiscuous woman. Cf. GILL-FLIRT.

flisk /flɪsk/ *verb*. *obsolete* exc. *dial*. L16.
[ORIGIN Imit.: cf. WHISK *verb*.]
1 *verb intrans.* Frisk about; be restless. L16.
2 *verb trans.* Make restless or angry. L18.
3 *verb trans.* Flick. L18.
■ **flisky** *adjective* (Scot.) frisky E19.

flit /flɪt/ *noun*. M19.
[ORIGIN from the verb.]
1 A removal, a (secret) change of abode, esp. in order to avoid a creditor. M19.
do a flit decamp. ***moonlight flit***: see MOONLIGHT *noun & adjective*.
2 A light movement or touch; a flutter. L19.
3 (**F-**.) (Proprietary name for) an insecticide used esp. in the form of a spray. E20.
4 A homosexual. *US slang*. M20.

†**flit** *adjective*. *poet*. L16–M17.
[ORIGIN Var. of FLEET *adjective*[2], infl. by FLIT *verb*.]
Swift, nimble; fleeting, unsubstantial.

SPENSER Now, like a stag; now, like a faulcon flit.

flit /flɪt/ *verb*. Infl. **-tt-**. ME.
[ORIGIN Old Norse *flytja* from weak grade of base of *fljóta*: see FLEET *verb*[1].]
1 *verb trans.* Remove to another place. Now chiefly *Scot. & N. English*. ME. ▸†**b** Get rid of, drive *away*. LME–L16. ▸**c** Shift (a tethered animal) to fresh grazing. E16.

G. W. DASENT They flitted home their goods and laid up the ship.

†**2** *verb trans.* Change the condition or direction of. Only in ME.
3 *verb intrans.* Depart, migrate; move or pass away. Also foll. by *away*, *from*, *to*. ME. ▸**b** Of time: pass away. L16.

R. BURNS Like the Borealis race, That flit ere you can point their place. N. HAWTHORNE Our spirits must have flitted away unconsciously.

4 *verb intrans.* †**a** Change in state, condition, or direction; alter, shift about. LME–E19. ▸**b** Of a flame: flicker, die down. M19.
5 *verb intrans.* Pass lightly, softly, or rapidly. Freq. with *about*, *by*, *off*, *to and fro*, etc. LME. ▸**b** Of a bird, bat, or other flying thing or creature: fly lightly and swiftly, make short flights. M16.

TENNYSON Unawares they flitted off, Busying themselves about the flowerage. W. H. AUDEN A shadow-train flitted foreshortened through fields. A. AYCKBOURN Flitting from woman to woman as the mood takes you. **b** T. CAMPBELL The bat flits to and fro. L. M. MONTGOMERY Fireflies were flitting over in Lovers' Lane. B. ENGLAND The helicopter flitted about with such dainty ease.

6 *verb intrans.* Move house; change one's abode, esp. secretly (cf. FLIT *noun* 1). Chiefly *Scot. & N. English*. E16.

A. GUINNESS My mother and I flitted, leaving behind.. a wake of unpaid bills.

flitch /flɪtʃ/ *noun*. Also (now *dial*.) **flick** /flɪk/.
[ORIGIN Old English *flicce*, corresp. to Middle Low German *vli(c)ke*, Old Norse *flikki* (whence dial. *flick*) from Germanic, as in Old Norse *flik* rag.]
1 The side of an animal, salted and cured. Now only, a side of bacon. OE.

B. CHATWIN A flitch of bacon was rammed into a rack in the rafters.

Dunmow flitch a side of bacon presented periodically at Dunmow in Essex to any couple proving conjugal harmony for a year and a day.

2 A lengthwise slice of timber from a tree trunk, esp. an outside slice. M18. ▸**b** Any of several planks fastened together to form a compound beam. Also (in full ***flitch plate***), a strengthening plate added to a beam, girder, or any woodwork. L19.
3 **a** A square piece of blubber from a whale. L18. ▸**b** A steak cut from a halibut. L19.

– COMB.: **flitch beam** a compound beam, esp. one consisting of a metal plate between two slabs of wood; ***flitch plate***: see sense 2b above.
■ Also **flitchen** *noun* (*obsolete* exc. *dial*.) LME.

flitch /flɪtʃ/ *verb trans*. M19.
[ORIGIN from the noun. Cf. earlier FLICK *verb*[1].]
Cut into flitches; cut as a flitch is cut.

flite *noun, verb* vars. of FLYTE *noun, verb*.

fliting *verbal noun* var. of FLYTING.

flitter /ˈflɪtə/ *noun*[1]. M16.
[ORIGIN from FLIT *verb* + -ER[1].]
A person who or thing which flits.

flitter /ˈflɪtə/ *noun*[2]. *rare*. M17.
[ORIGIN German.]
A small thin metal square used in decoration.

flitter /ˈflɪtə/ *noun*[3]. E19.
[ORIGIN from the verb.]
A flittering or fluttering motion.
– COMB.: **flitter-winged** *adjective* having wings that flutter.

flitter /ˈflɪtə/ *verb*. LME.
[ORIGIN from FLIT *verb* + -ER[5]. Cf. FLITTERS.]
1 *verb intrans.* Flit about; fly quickly, flutter. LME.
†**2** *verb intrans.* Fly all about, fly *into* dust or pieces. M16–L17.
†**3** *verb intrans.* Wither, droop. *rare*. L16–M19.
4 *verb trans.* Cause to flit; shuffle (cards). *rare*. M19.
■ **flittery** *adjective* (*rare*) (of ideas, feelings, etc.) uncertain, flitting about, wavering M19.

flitter-mouse /ˈflɪtəmaʊs/ *noun*. Pl. **-mice** /-mʌɪs/. M16.
[ORIGIN from FLITTER *verb* + MOUSE *noun*, after Dutch *vledermuis* or German *Fledermaus*. Cf. FLICKERMOUSE, FLINDERMOUSE.]
= BAT *noun*[3].

flittern /ˈflɪt(ə)n/ *noun*. Chiefly *dial*. L17.
[ORIGIN Perh. rel. to FLITTERS.]
(A strip of wood from) an oak sapling.

flitters /ˈflɪtəz/ *noun pl*. Chiefly *dial. & US*. E17.
[ORIGIN Alt. of FITTERS, assoc. with FLITTER *verb*. Cf. FLINDERS.]
Fragments; splinters, tatters.

flitting /ˈflɪtɪŋ/ *noun*. ME.
[ORIGIN from FLIT *verb* + -ING[1].]
1 The action of FLIT *verb*: an instance of this. ME.
2 *spec*. The action of moving house, a removal. Now chiefly *Scot. & N. English*. ME. ▸**b** The goods, furniture, etc., which are moved in a flitting; baggage. ME.
moonlight flitting: see MOONLIGHT *noun & adjective*.

flivver /ˈflɪvə/ *noun*. *US slang*. E20.
[ORIGIN Unknown.]
A cheap car or aeroplane; a 'banger'.

flix /flɪks/ *noun*[1]. M17.
[ORIGIN Unknown.]
Fur (of an animal). Cf. FLICK *noun*[2].

†**flix** *noun*[2] see FLUX *noun*.

flixweed /ˈflɪkswiːd/ *noun*. L16.
[ORIGIN from †*flix* var. of FLUX *noun* + WEED *noun*[1]: the plant was a supposed remedy for dysentery.]
A Eurasian cruciferous plant, *Descurainia sophia*, with small yellow flowers and finely divided leaves.

†**flo** *noun*. Pl. **flon**. OE–E17.
[ORIGIN Old English *flā* weak fem., rel. to *flān* FLANE *noun*.]
An arrow.

float /fləʊt/ *noun*. Also †**flote** (see also FLOTE-GRASS). OE.
[ORIGIN Partly from Old English, Old Norse *flot* floating state, Old English *flota*, Old Norse *floti* ship, fleet; partly from the verb.]
▸ **I 1** **a** The action or an act of floating. Formerly also, the condition of floating or being on the water; esp. in †***on float*** afloat. Now *rare*. OE. ▸**b** An operation of floating a currency. L20.

A. THACKERAY A romantic float in a gondola.

†**2** A stream, a river; the sea; a wave. ME–M17.

SHAKES. *Temp.* Upon the Mediterranean flote Bound sadly home for Naples.

†**3** The flood of the tide; an overflow from a river, a flood; esp. in ***on float*** in flood, at high water. E16–L18.

fig.: A. M. BENNETT With all her animal spirits in the fullest float of exhilaration.

▸ **II** A floating object.
4 A cork or other buoyant object used on a fishing line to indicate by movement when a fish bites, or on a fishing net to support the edge. ME. ▸**b** A hollow or inflated part or organ supporting an organism in the water. M19. ▸**c** A buoyant device used to help an inexperienced swimmer remain afloat. L19. ▸**d** A structure fitted to the alighting gear of an aircraft to enable it to float on water. L19.

L. MACNEICE The handsome glass balls which are used as floats for nets.

5 A mass of weeds, ice, etc., floating on the surface of water. Now *rare*. M16.
6 Any of the boards or paddles of a water wheel or paddle wheel. E17.

7 A hollow ball or other similar device for regulating the water level in a boiler, cistern, etc., or the petrol level in the carburettor of a petrol engine. M18.
8 THEATRICAL. *sing.* & in *pl.* The footlights. E19.
9 A soft drink with a scoop of ice cream floating in it. Also ***ice-cream float***. E20.

> J. DIDION She was also attracted to happy endings . . the Coke float that followed the skinned knee.

▸ **III** A broad, level, shallow means of transportation.
10 A raft, a flat-bottomed boat. LME.

> P. V. WHITE The saplings were soon bound together, and upon floats of hollow logs, by means of thongs.

11 A low-bodied cart or vehicle; *esp.* a low-bodied battery-powered vehicle for delivering milk or other goods (also ***milk float***). M19.
12 A platform on wheels with a display on it, used in processions. L19.

> A. BURGESS Behind him came floats with young people's tableaux—The Jazz Age, . . Prison Reform.

▸ **IV** Misc. uses corresp. to senses of the verb.
13 A tool used in the making of archers' bows. *obsolete* exc. HERALDRY. LME.
14 Any of various tools used for smoothing or levelling; *esp.* (*a*) a single-cut file; (*b*) a plasterer's trowel; (*c*) a marble-worker's polishing block. M17.
15 Chiefly MINING. Loose rock or ore brought by water from its original formation. Also, particles of ore which do not settle readily in water. Also ***float-ore*** etc. L17.
16 A trench used for floating or irrigating land. L18.
17 WEAVING. The passing of weft threads over a section of the warp without being interwoven; a thread or group of threads so passed. M19.
18 A government warrant confirming a prospective settler's claim to a part of a tract of public land put up for sale. *US*. M19.
19 a A sum of money in a shop etc. made available for change-giving or minor expenditures. E20. ▸**b** The amount of money represented by cheques etc. in transit. Chiefly *US*. E20.
20 In critical path analysis, the period of time by which the duration of an activity may be extended. M20.
– COMB.: **float-board** = sense 6 above; **float chamber** a small chamber in a carburettor from which petrol, maintained at a constant level by the action of a float, is supplied to the jets; **float-cut** *adjective* (of a file) single-cut; **float glass**: manufactured by the float process (see below); **float-light** a lightship; ***float-ore***: see sense 15 above; **floatplane** a seaplane equipped with floats; **float process**: for making plate glass by drawing it in a continuous sheet from the melting tank and on to the surface of molten metal for hardening.

float /fləʊt/ *verb*. Also †**flote**.
[ORIGIN Late Old English *flotian* = Old Saxon *floton* (Middle Dutch *vlōten*), Old Norse *flota*, from Germanic weak grade of base of FLEET *verb*[1]. Reinforced in Middle English by Old French *floter* (mod. *flotter*) from Proto-Romance, prob. also from Germanic.]
▸ **I** *verb intrans.* **1** Rest or move on the surface of a liquid without sinking; be or become buoyant; (of a stranded ship) get afloat. LOE.

> W. COWPER Her timbers yet are sound, And she may float again. T. H. HUXLEY Ice floats readily on water.

2 Move gently, drift, on or as on the surface of a moving liquid; move or be suspended freely (*in* a liquid or gas etc.). Formerly also, (of a fish) swim. ME. ▸**b** Move or depart in a casual or leisurely way; wander from place to place. *slang*. E20. ▸**c** Of a currency: fluctuate in international exchange value according to market forces. M20. ▸**d** ELECTRONICS. Of a part of an electric circuit: be unconnected to a source of fixed potential. M20.

> J. STEINBECK Any dead fish or sea bird that might have floated in on a rising tide. M. INNES A murmur of voices floated briefly down. A. POWELL Dark fumes floated above the houses.

3 †**a** Undulate, oscillate, be unsteady; spread in an undulating form; *fig.* waver. L16–E19. ▸**b** Move or hover dimly before the eye or in the mind. L17.

> **b** B. PLAIN Her face floats over the pages . . and no matter what else I'm thinking, part of me is always thinking of her.

4 COMMERCE. Of an acceptance: be in circulation. L18.
5 WEAVING. Of a thread: pass over or under several threads either of the warp or weft, instead of being interwoven with them. L19.
▸ **II** *verb trans.* **6** Cover with a liquid; irrigate (land); flood, drench, saturate. L16.

> J. AUSTEN He thought . . I should find the near way floated by this rain.

7 a Of water, the tide, etc.: support, set afloat, or bear along by the force of the current, (a buoyant object). E17. ▸**b** Cause to be borne along on the surface of water, or to move gently in or through the air; transport by water. M18. ▸**c** Bring into favour, launch (a company, scheme, etc.); put (shares in a company) up for sale on the stock market; air (an idea, theory, etc.); circulate (a rumour). M19. ▸**d** Allow (a currency) to have a fluctuating exchange rate. L20.

> **b** E. WAUGH Exquisite private jokes which they wrote on leaves and floated downstream. C. RYAN Makeshift ferries composed of rubber rafts were slowly floating trucks across the river. *Daily Telegraph* Barnes . . floated over a high cross and Lineker was there to nod it into the net. **c** F. FORSYTH Bormac was . . floated with an issue of half a million ordinary shares. H. KISSINGER Brezhnev . . floated the concept of 'a system of collective security in Asia.'

8 Make smooth or level; *esp.* (*a*) PLASTERING level (the surface of plaster) with a trowel; (*b*) FARRIERY (now *rare*) file the teeth (of a horse). E18.
– COMB.: **float-boat** †(*a*) a ship's longboat; (*b*) a raft; **float-stone** (*a*) a bricklayer's stone for smoothing bricks used in curved work; (*b*) a light porous stone that floats.
■ **floatative** *adjective* tending to or producing flotation M19. **floating** *noun* (*a*) the action of the verb; an instance of this; (*b*) PLASTERING the second of three coats of plaster: M16.

floatable /ˈfləʊtəb(ə)l/ *adjective*. E19.
[ORIGIN from FLOAT *verb* + -ABLE.]
1 Of a river: capable of supporting floating objects, that can be floated on. Chiefly *US*. E19.
2 Capable of floating; buoyant. M19.
■ **floata'bility** *noun* L19.

floatage /ˈfləʊtɪdʒ/ *noun*. Also **flot-**. E17.
[ORIGIN from FLOAT *noun*, *verb* + -AGE.]
1 The action or state of floating. E17.
2 (The right of appropriating) flotsam; floating masses. E17.
3 a *collect.* Ships etc. afloat on a river. M19. ▸**b** The part of a ship above the waterline; freeboard. M19.
4 Floating power, buoyancy. L19.

floatation *noun* var. of FLOTATION.

floatel /fləʊˈtɛl/ *noun*. Also **flotel**. M20.
[ORIGIN Blend of FLOAT *verb* and HOTEL.]
A hotel that floats (*esp.* a boat used as a hotel) or that is built over water; a floating accommodation block.

floater /ˈfləʊtə/ *noun*. L16.
[ORIGIN from FLOAT *verb* + -ER[1].]
1 A person who or thing which floats; *spec.* (*a*) *US slang* a dead body found floating in water; (*b*) *Austral.* a meat pie floating in pea soup; (*c*) a piece of float-ore (see FLOAT *noun* 15). L16.
2 A voter who is not committed to any political party; *US*, *derog.* one whose vote may be bought. M19.
3 A person who frequently changes jobs or place of residence. *US*. M19. ▸**b** An official order to leave a town, district or state; a sentence suspended on condition that the offender leaves the area. *US slang*. E20.
4 STOCK EXCHANGE. A government stock certificate etc. recognized as security. L19.
5 A mistake, a gaffe. *slang*. E20.

float-grass *noun* var. of FLOTE-GRASS.

floating /ˈfləʊtɪŋ/ *ppl adjective*. L16.
[ORIGIN from FLOAT *verb* + -ING[2].]
1 That floats. L16.
2 Variable, unstable; (now esp. of a population) not fixed in a definite place. L16.
3 (Of financial capital) not fixed or permanently invested; (of a debt) short-term and unfunded; (of a currency or its exchange rate) fluctuating. E19. ▸**b** COMMERCE. (Of a cargo) at sea; *esp.* (of a marine insurance policy) providing cover for any ship and its cargo used by a shipping company on specified journeys. M19.
4 Having little or no attachment; disconnected. E19.
– SPECIAL COLLOCATIONS: **floating anchor** a sea anchor. **floating bridge** (*a*) a bridge made of two small bridges with the uppermost able to be extended beyond the lower by means of pulleys, formerly used for crossing moats; (*b*) a bridge supported by a caisson or pontoon; (*c*) a ferry working on chains. ***floating dock***: see DOCK *noun*[3]. **floating island** (*a*) a detached floating mass of vegetation; (*b*) COOKERY a dessert of custard with meringues etc. floating in it. **floating kidney** an abnormal condition in which the kidneys are movable; such a kidney. **floating light** (*a*) a lightship; (*b*) a lifebuoy with a light. **floating mill** *US* a mill constructed so as to float in a river and be worked by the current. **floating point** COMPUTING a decimal point that does not occupy a fixed position in the numbers processed, part of the representation of a given number specifying the position of the point for that number; usu. *attrib.* as ***floating-point***; **floating rib** each of the last two pairs of ribs, which have no anterior connection to each other or to the sternum. **floating voter**: not committed to any political party.
■ **floatingly** *adverb* M17.

floatsome *noun* see FLOTSAM.

floaty /ˈfləʊti/ *adjective*. LME.
[ORIGIN from FLOAT *noun*, *verb* + -Y[1].]
†**1** Well-watered. Only in LME.
2 Capable of floating, buoyant. E17.
3 Of a garment or fabric: light and airy. L20.

floc /flɒk/ *noun*. E20.
[ORIGIN from FLOCCULUS.]
In *pl.* & *collect. sing.* A flocculent mass of fine particles and colloidal material.

flocci *noun* pl. of FLOCCUS.

floccillation /flɒksɪˈleɪʃ(ə)n/ *noun*. *rare*. M19.
[ORIGIN mod. Latin *floccillus* dim. of Latin FLOCCUS: see -ATION.]
= CARPHOLOGY.

floccinaucinihilipilification
/ˌflɒksɪˌnɔːsɪˌnɪhɪlɪˌpɪlɪfɪˈkeɪʃ(ə)n/ *noun*. *rare*. M18.
[ORIGIN from Latin *flocci*, *nauci*, *nihili*, *pili*, words denoting 'at little value' + -FICATION.]
The action or habit of estimating as worthless.

floccipend /ˈflɒksɪpɛnd/ *verb trans.* Long *rare* or *obsolete*. M16.
[ORIGIN from Latin *flocci pendere* hold at little value.]
Regard as insignificant; make no account of.

floccose /ˈflɒkəʊs/ *adjective*. M18.
[ORIGIN Late Latin *floccosus*, from Latin FLOCCUS: see -OSE[1].]
1 Covered with or consisting of woolly tufts. Now *rare* or *obsolete*. M18.
2 Covered with or composed of flocci. M19.

flocculate /ˈflɒkjʊleɪt/ *verb trans.* & *intrans.* L19.
[ORIGIN formed as FLOCCULUS: see -ATE[3].]
Form into flocculent masses.
■ **flocculant** *noun* a substance which promotes the clumping of particles, esp. one used in treating waste water E20. **floccu'lation** *noun* L19.

floccule /ˈflɒkjuːl/ *noun*. M19.
[ORIGIN formed as FLOCCULUS: see -ULE.]
A small portion of matter like a flock or tuft of wool.

flocculent /ˈflɒkjʊl(ə)nt/ *adjective*. E19.
[ORIGIN from Latin FLOCCUS + -ULENT.]
1 Resembling tufts or flocks of wool; consisting of loose woolly masses. E19.
2 Covered with a short woolly substance; downy. L19.
■ **flocculence** *noun* the state or condition of being flocculent; the condition of containing flocci: M19.

flocculus /ˈflɒkjʊləs/ *noun*. Pl. **-li** /-lʌɪ, -liː/. L18.
[ORIGIN mod. Latin, dim. of Latin FLOCCUS: see -ULE.]
1 A floccule; *esp.* one held in suspension in or precipitated from a fluid. L18.
2 ANATOMY. A small lobe on the undersurface of the cerebellum. M19.
3 ASTRONOMY. A small cloudy wisp on the surface of the sun, revealed by the spectroheliograph. E20.

floccus /ˈflɒkəs/ *noun*. Pl. **flocci** /ˈflɒksʌɪ/. M19.
[ORIGIN Latin = FLOCK *noun*[2].]
Something resembling a flock of wool; a tuft of woolly hairs or filaments.

flocht /flɒxt/ *noun*. *Scot.* L15.
[ORIGIN App. repr. Old English base parallel with FLIGHT *noun*[1]. Cf. also FLAUGHT *noun*[2].]
1 A state of agitation or excitement; a flutter. L15.
†**2** The action of fleeing, flight. *rare*. Only in E16.

flock /flɒk/ *noun*[1].
[ORIGIN Old English *flocc* = Middle Low German *vlocke*, Old Norse *flokkr*: ult. origin unknown.]
1 A band, body, or company of people. Now *obsolete* exc. as in *transf.* from senses 2 and 3. OE. ▸**b** In *pl.* Great numbers, 'swarms'. M16.

> LD BERNERS They parceyued a flocke of men of armes commynge togyder. **b** COVERDALE *2 Macc.* 14:14 The Heithen which fled out of Iewry . . came to Nicanor by flockes.

2 A number of animals of one kind, esp. birds, feeding or travelling together. ME.

> J. RATHBONE Flocks of larks and fieldfares rose ahead of me.

3 A number of domestic animals of one kind, now usu. sheep, goats, or geese, kept together. ME.

> POPE He . . sitting down, to milk his flocks prepares.

flocks and herds sheep and cattle.
4 a The Christian body, esp. in relation to Christ as the Good Shepherd; a congregation, esp. in relation to its pastor. ME. ▸**b** A group of people, as children, pupils, etc., under the charge or guidance of one or more persons as parents, teachers, etc. L19.

> **a** AV *1 Pet.* 5:2 Feede the flocke of God which is among you. R. HOGGART Like the relationship laid down as proper between the minister and his flock.

– COMB.: **flock-book** a list of pedigrees of sheep; **flockmaster** a sheep-farmer; **flock pigeon** an Australian bronzewing pigeon, *Phaps histrionica*, forming large flocks.
■ **flockless** *adjective* L16.

flock /flɒk/ *noun*[2]. ME.
[ORIGIN Old French & mod. French *floc* from Latin FLOCCUS.]
1 A lock or tuft of wool, cotton, etc. Formerly also, the type of something worthless. ME.

> W. FULKE They look white, like flocks of wooll. J. LYLY I will never care three flocks for his ambition.

2 In *pl.* & *collect. sing.* A material for quilting or stuffing made of wool refuse or torn-up cloth. ME.

> W. CONGREVE Put more flocks in her bed.

3 In *pl.* & *collect. sing.* Powdered wool or cloth, formerly used in thickening cloth and now in making flock paper. L15.
4 CHEMISTRY. In *pl.* Light loose masses precipitated. L16.
– COMB.: **flock-bed**, **flock-mattress**: stuffed with flock; **flock paper** wallpaper that has been sized and then sprinkled with powdered wool.
■ **flocky** *adjective* (*a*) resembling flock; (*b*) floccose: LME.

flock /flɒk/ *verb*[1]. ME.
[ORIGIN from FLOCK *noun*[1].]
†**1** *verb trans.* Gather (individuals) into a company; muster (troops); bring (crowds) *in*. ME–L16.

J. HOOKER So had he flocked in Englishmen to ouerrun his countrie.

2 *verb intrans.* Congregate, go in great numbers, troop. Freq. with adverbs. ME.

G. GREENE Hundreds of women were flocking into the capital for market. J. M. COETZEE Who would not flock to see the entertainment?

†**3** *verb trans.* Lead *away* to another flock. L16–L17.
4 *verb trans.* Crowd or throng round (a person). Long *obsolete* exc. *dial.* E17.

JOHN TAYLOR Good fellowes trooping, flock'd me so.

flock /flɒk/ *verb*[2] *trans.* M16.
[ORIGIN from FLOCK *noun*[2].]
1 Stuff with flock. Also, cover (a prepared surface of cloth, paper, etc.) with flock. M16.
†**2** *fig.* Treat with contempt, regard as worthless. M–L16.

flockmeal /ˈflɒkmiːl/ *adverb.* Long *arch. rare.*
[ORIGIN Old English *floccmǣlum*: see FLOCK *noun*[1], -MEAL.]
By or in flocks, flock by flock.

floe /fləʊ/ *noun.* E19.
[ORIGIN Prob. from Norwegian *flo* from Old Norse *fló* layer, stratum. Cf. FLAW *noun*[1].]
A sheet of floating ice; a detached portion of an ice field. Also ***ice floe***.
floe ice ice floating in sheets.

flog /flɒg/ *verb.* Orig. *slang.* Infl. **-gg-**. L17.
[ORIGIN Prob. imit. or from Latin *flagellare* FLAGELLATE *verb*.]
1 *verb trans.* Beat, whip; punish with repeated blows of a birch, cane, whip, etc.; drive (laziness etc.) out of or (learning etc.) into a person by beating. L17. ▸**b** Urge (a horse etc.) on with a whip. L18.

F. E. SMEDLEY I have not forgotten the Greek and Latin flogged into us at Westminster. G. GORER Six women were publicly flogged . . till the blood ran down their backs. **b** G. P. R. JAMES Take off the bridles . . and flog them down the valley.

flog to death *colloq.* talk about, promote, etc., *ad nauseam*. ***b flog a dead horse***: see DEAD *adjective* etc.

2 *verb trans.* Beat, lash, strike (an object etc.), esp. for a particular purpose; ANGLING cast a fly line over (a stretch of water) repeatedly; CRICKET punish (a bowler, the bowling). E19. ▸**b** *verb intrans.* Of a sail: beat or flap heavily. M19.

J. F. W. HERSCHEL Trees were seen to flog the ground with their branches. **b** F. MARRYAT The storm-staysail . . flogged and cracked with a noise louder than the gale.

3 *verb trans.* **a** Defeat; excel. *slang.* M19. ▸**b** Tire (*out*). Usu. in *pass. dial.* L19.

a E. A. FREEMAN I think for position it flogs every place I know. **b** R. KIPLING I went to bed; for I was fair flogged out.

4 *verb trans.* Sell, offer for sale (esp. worthless or shoddy goods or those illicitly obtained). Also, steal. *slang.* E20.

M. DRABBLE Let's go and look at the ghastly thing that Martin flogged us. *Listener* He was . . flogging quack remedies to innocents who needed protecting from him.

5 *verb intrans.* Proceed by violent, painful, or exhausting effort. E20.

M. BINCHY It would be nicer than flogging all the way to Clarence Gardens.

■ **flogger** *noun* (*a*) a person who flogs; *colloq.* an advocate of corporal punishment; (*b*) *slang* a riding whip; (*c*) a tool for removing the stoppers of casks, bottles, etc.: E18. **flogging** *verbal noun* the action of the verb, esp. the practice of corporal punishment; an instance of this; ***flogging round the fleet***: see FLEET *noun*[1]: L17.

flokati /flɒˈkɑːti/ *noun.* M20.
[ORIGIN mod. Greek *phlokatē* peasant's blanket.]
More fully ***flokati rug***. A Greek woven woollen rug with a thick loose pile.

†**flon** *noun* pl. of FLO.

flong /flɒŋ/ *noun.* L19.
[ORIGIN French FLAN.]
Prepared paper for making stereotype moulds.

flood /flʌd/ *noun.*
[ORIGIN Old English *flōd* corresp. to Old Frisian, Old Saxon *flōd* (Dutch *vloed*), Old High German *fluot* (German *Flut*), Old Norse *flóð*, Gothic *flōdus*, from Germanic from Indo-European (as in Greek *plōein* swim, *plōtos* navigable).]
1 The flowing in of the tide. Also ***flood tide***. OE.

R. DONNELLY The young flood making close in shore. *fig.*: SHAKES. *Jul. Caes.* There is a tide in the affairs of men Which, taken at the flood, leads on to fortune.

2 A body of flowing water; a river, a stream. *obsolete* exc. *poet.* OE.

W. SOMERVILLE Ev'ry . . hollow Rock, that o'er the dimpling Flood Nods pendant.

3 Water as opp. to land; the sea. *obsolete* exc. *poet.* OE.

W. COWPER Swiftly dividing the flood, To a slave-cultured island we came.

flood and field sea and land.

4 An overflowing or irruption of (a great body of) water over land not usually submerged, an inundation, a deluge. OE.

LD MACAULAY When the floods were out, he exposed his life to imminent risk. P. THEROUX The river . . was in full flood. *fig.*: TENNYSON His passions all in flood And masters of his motion.

Noah's Flood: see NOAH 1. **the Flood** = ***Noah's Flood*** s.v. NOAH 1.

5 A profuse and violent outpouring (as) of water or other liquid; a swollen stream; a torrent, a downpour. ME.

Times Karen Barber's flood of tears . . was all too understandable. J. ARCHER Andrew was surprised and touched by the flood of letters.

6 In *pl.* Uterine haemorrhage. Long *rare* or *obsolete*. M17.
7 A floodlight. Freq. in *pl. colloq.* M20.

M. AYRTON Estelle switches on the big floods and the strips.

– COMB.: **flood-hatch** a framework of boards sliding in grooves, to be raised in time of flood; a sluice, a floodgate; **flood-lamp** a floodlight; **floodlight** *noun & verb* (*a*) *noun* (a lamp providing) intense artificial light which eliminates all shadows on the surface illuminated; (*b*) *verb trans.* illuminate with a floodlight or floodlights, esp. with the light projected from several directions; **floodlit** *ppl adjective* illuminated by a floodlight or floodlights; **flood-mark** the high-water mark; **flood plain** a tract of low-lying ground which is often flooded by a river etc.; ***flood tide***: see sense 1 above.

■ **floody** *adjective* (long *rare*) of, pertaining to, or of the nature of a flood LME.

flood /flʌd/ *verb.* E17.
[ORIGIN from the noun.]
1 *verb trans.* Cover with a flood, inundate (*lit.* & *fig.*). E17.

E. WAUGH The domestic hot water machine has burst and flooded the kitchen quarters. E. PAUL When rationing ends and beef begins flooding the market. B. MALAMUD The river overflowed its banks, flooding the lower reaches of the city.

flooded box *Austral.* coolibah. **flooded gum** *Austral.* any of several eucalypts growing in damp soil.

2 *verb intrans.* Come (*in*) in great quantities; overflow; be or become flooded. M18.

L. EVANS If it floods early, it scarce retires within its Banks in a Month. K. MOORE Thoughts of Rollo came flooding back.

3 *verb intrans.* Have a uterine haemorrhage. L18.
4 *verb trans.* Pour (*out, away, back*) in a flood. Chiefly *fig. rare.* E19. ▸**b** Drive *out* (of one's home etc.) by a flood or floods. Usu. in *pass.* E20.

C. MERIVALE The lifeblood of the provinces is flooded back upon Paris.

5 *verb trans.* Cover or fill with water, irrigate; deluge (a burning house, a mine, etc.) with water; (of rain) fill (a river) to overflowing; overfill (a carburettor) with petrol. M19.

A. BAIN A violent storm has flooded the rivers. R. DAVIES He'll be drowned same as when the Cambrian pit was flooded!

■ **floodable** *adjective* liable to flood, subject to inundation E19. **flooding** *noun* (*a*) in *pl.*, floods, *fig.* fullness, superabundance; (*b*) *gen.* the action of the verb; an instance of this; (*c*) a uterine haemorrhage: L17.

floodgate /ˈflʌdgeɪt/ *noun.* ME.
[ORIGIN from FLOOD *noun* + GATE *noun*[1].]
1 A gate that may be opened or closed to admit or exclude (esp. flood) water; *spec.* the lower gate of a lock. ME. ▸**b** *fig.* A restraint, barrier, or check, esp. on the emotions. ME.

b SHAKES. *Ven. & Ad.* Through the floodgates breaks the silver rain. THACKERAY The floodgates were opened, and mother and daughter wept.

†**2** A stream that was closed by or passed through a floodgate; a strong stream, a torrent (*lit.* & *fig.*). LME–M17.
3 A sluice. Also (*dial.*), a gate suspended over a stream so as to rise with the water in flood time but prevent the passage of cattle etc. at low water. M16.

fig.: C. CARTWRIGHT My Lord, you let a flood-gate of Arguments out. *attrib.*: SHAKES. *Oth.* My particular grief Is of so flood-gate and o'erbearing nature.

flookan /ˈfluːk(ə)n/ *noun.* Also (earlier) **flooking** /ˈfluːkɪŋ/. E18.
[ORIGIN Unknown.]
MINING. A transverse vein of clayey material; the material forming this.

floor /flɔː/ *noun.*
[ORIGIN Old English *flōr*, corresp. to (M)Du *vloer*, Middle High German *vluor* (German *Flur*), Old Norse *flórr*, from Germanic.]
▸ **I** A level structure in a house or other building.
1 The layer of boards, bricks, tiles, stones, etc., covering the base of a room or other compartment; the lower surface of a room. Also in extended usage, the base of a cavity, etc. OE. ▸**b** *fig.* A minimum, esp. of prices or wages. M20.

J. TYNDALL The stone floor was dark with moisture. G. STEIN The parlour had a thick and flowered carpet on the floor. **b** *Economist* A floor of only £12 a week on the wages of British artists.

2 The lower surface of a set of rooms etc. extending on one level through a building; the set of rooms etc. on such a level; a storey. LME.

M. GIROUARD The second and third floors overhung the lower half of the house.

3 **a** The framework or underside of the ceiling of a room etc., considered in relation to the compartment above. L16. ▸**b** The framework or structure of joists etc. supporting the flooring of a room. E18.

a *fig.*: C. BOWEN Then Caesar . . Bounding his throne by Ocean, his fame by the firmament floor. **b** P. NICHOLSON Floors in which bridging joists are used.

4 NAUTICAL. †**a** The deck. Only in 17. ▸**b** The bottom of a vessel on either side of the keelson. Also, a floor timber. E19.
5 *spec.* (passing into branch II). ▸**a** The part of a legislative assembly which members sit in and speak from; the right to speak next in a debate. M18. ▸**b** (The floor of) the part of a hall etc. used for dancing. M19. ▸**c** (The floor of) a film or television studio where a programme etc. is shot. M20.

a J. T. STORY I remember my maiden speech on the floor of the House. **c** MARGARET KENNEDY I'll make a shooting script . . . It'll be something you can go on the floor with.

▸ **II** A level space.
6 An artificial platform or levelled space designed for a particular activity (and freq. with specifying word). OE. ▸**b** *transf.* The corn etc. laid on such a space for threshing; in the malting process, a batch of grain etc. laid at one time for steeping. LME.

fig.: W. COWPER Where flails of oratory thresh the floor.

threshing floor: see THRESHING *noun*.

7 A naturally level space or extended surface. Also (*colloq.* or *dial.*), the ground. LME.

L. STEPHEN Forests of pine rise steeply from the meadow floor. *Times* With the field drawn tight around the bat and catches being snapped up off the floor. N. CALDER They lowered a camera to the ocean floor.

†**8** An area or region. *rare.* LME–E17.

BACON Both of them . . fill a whole Floare or Orbe vnto certaine Limits.

▸ **III** A surface as a foundation.
9 A surface on which something rests, a foundation. OE.

J. SMEATON The arches are . . 6 feet from the floor to the springer.

10 The stratum immediately beneath a seam of coal etc. M19.

T. H. HUXLEY Vegetable remains are also met with in rocks beneath the coal, forming what is called the floor.

▸ **IV** A layer.
11 A layer, a stratum; a horizontal course. E18.

J. RAY Many Beds or Floors of all kinds of Sea-Shells.

12 A unit of measurement used in embankment work, usu. equal to a volume 18 or 20 feet square by one foot deep. Now *rare* or *obsolete*. E18.

– PHRASES: **cross the floor** join the opposing side of an assembly. ***first floor***: see FIRST. **from the floor** (of a question, statement, etc.) given by an individual member at a meeting etc., as opp. to a representative of the platform etc. ***ground floor***: see GROUND *noun*. **mop the floor with** *slang* = ***wipe the floor with*** below. PELVIC ***floor***. ***second floor***: see SECOND *adjective*. **take the floor** (*a*) begin to dance on a dance floor etc.; (*b*) *N. Amer.* speak in a debate. ***third floor***: see THIRD *adjective & noun*. **wipe the floor with** *slang* inflict a humiliating defeat on, crush.

– COMB.: **floorboard** *noun & verb* (*a*) *noun* a board forming a section of the floor of a room etc.; (*b*) *verb trans.* (*US slang*) press (the accelerator pedal) down as far as possible, drive fast; **floorcloth** a cloth used for washing floors; **floor lamp** *N. Amer.* a standard lamp; **floor leader** *US* the leader of a party in a legislative assembly; **floor-length** *adjective* reaching to the floor; **floorman** a person who supervises the gaming tables in a casino; **floor manager** (*a*) a person in charge of a floor; *esp.* a shopwalker; (*b*) the stage manager of a television production; ***floor mop***: see MOP *noun*[3] 1; **floor plan** the diagram of a floor, *esp.* one showing the rooms etc. on one storey of a building; **floor polish** a manufactured substance for making floors glossy; **floor show** an entertainment presented on the floor of a restaurant, nightclub, etc., as opp. to on a stage; **floor timber** NAUTICAL each of the parts of the ship's timbers which are placed immediately across the keel; **floorwalker** *US* a shopwalker.

■ **floorage** *noun* (*rare*) a number of floors, an amount of flooring M18. **floorless** *adjective* M19.

floor /flɔː/ *verb.* LME.
[ORIGIN from the noun.]
1 *verb trans.* Cover or provide with a floor or floors; form or serve as the floor of. LME.

S. PEPYS Looking over the joiners, flooring my dining-room. C. VANCOUVER The . . sleeping place floored with flat stones. J. BUCHAN A cup in the hills, floored . . with short, crisp pasture.

2 *verb trans.* Bring to the floor or ground; knock down; cause to fall. M17.

BYRON The usual excuse of floored equestrians. B. MALAMUD The Deputy Warden floored the Fixer with a blow.

3 *verb trans.* Overcome, get the better of; defeat; confound, nonplus, baffle. Also (*arch. colloq.*), get through (a piece of work) successfully. **E19.** ▸**b** *verb intrans.* Commit a fatal blunder, fail. Long *rare* or *obsolete*. **M19.**

DISRAELI I was the only man who could floor O'Connell. R. CHURCH Any word of more than one syllable floored me. N. ANNAN A . . first-class man . . could be expected to *floor* the bookwork in the early papers.

4 *verb trans.* Place *upon* (something) as a floor. *rare.* **L19.**

E. B. TYLOR The doctrine of a Heaven, floored upon a firmament.

5 *verb trans.* Hang (a picture) low on the wall. *rare.* **L19.**

■ **floorer** *noun* a person or thing which floors; esp. (**a**) a knock-down blow; (**b**) a confounding or baffling thing: **L18.** **flooring** *noun* (**a**) the action of the verb; (**b**) a floor of a room etc.; the materials of which it is made; (**c**) in the malting process, the operation of spreading the grain on the malt floor and treating it there: **LME.**

floose /fluːs/ *noun.* Also **flus**, †**fluce**, & other vars. **L16.**
[ORIGIN Arabic *fulūs* money, pl. of *fals* a small copper or bronze coin from Greek *phollis* FOLLIS. Cf. FILS *noun*[2].]
A small coin of N. Africa, Arabia, India, and neighbouring countries; *collect.* money.

floozie /ˈfluːzi/ *noun. colloq.* Also **-sie**, **-zy**. **E20.**
[ORIGIN Uncertain: perh. rel. to FLOSSY *adjective*.]
A girl or woman, *esp.* one of disreputable character.

flop /flɒp/ *noun.* **E17.**
[ORIGIN from the verb.]
1 *gen.* The action of FLOP *verb*; an instance of this; a flopping motion; the heavy dull sound produced by this. **E17.** ▸**b** Something loose and pendulous, a flap. **E20.**

b P. ARROWSMITH David . . pushed a flop of hair back off his forehead.

2 A mass of thin mud or other viscous fluid. *dial.* **M19.**
3 **a** A successful act of trickery; an act of cheating. *US slang.* Now *rare* or *obsolete*. **M19.** ▸**b** A reversal of attitude or behaviour; a sudden change of party or policy. *US colloq.* **L19.**
4 A dismal failure, a collapse; a person who or thing (esp. an enterprise) which fails; something unable to fulfil a role adequately. *colloq.* **L19.**

ROBERT ANDERSON That's a terrible thing . . to make a flop of the first job you've got. I. HAMILTON As a social event the party was a flop.

5 A flabby or soft person. *slang.* **E20.**

F. O'CONNOR She was a great flop of a woman.

6 A bed; somewhere to spend the night. Also, a safe house for criminals. *slang.* **E20.**

S. BELLOW The flop I found was in a tall clapboard hotel.

– COMB.: **flop-eared** *adjective* having pendulous ears; **flophouse** *slang* (orig. *US*) a dosshouse.
– NOTE: Rare before 19.

flop /flɒp/ *verb.* Infl. **-pp-**. **E17.**
[ORIGIN Var. of FLAP *verb*.]
1 *verb intrans.* Swing or sway about heavily and loosely. **E17.**

R. JARRELL His fair hair kept flopping in his face. *fig.*: T. E. LAWRENCE A miserable squad flops like a wet dishcloth.

2 *verb intrans.* Move heavily, clumsily, or in an ungainly way; sit, kneel, lie, fall, etc., *down* awkwardly or suddenly. Also, make the dull sound of a soft body falling or a flat thing slapping the water. **L17.** ▸**b** *verb intrans. & trans.* (Cause to) change one's attitude or behaviour; (cause to) change sides; bring or come over. *US colloq.* **L19.**

P. H. JOHNSON She flopped over like a rag doll. **b** C. R. COOPER Hurriedly lawmakers who had been opposed to it 'flopped' to the other side.

3 *verb trans.* Throw (*down*) suddenly, cause to fall heavily and noisily. **E19.**

T. HOOD In bolts our bacon-hog . . And flops him down in all the muck.

4 *verb trans.* Move (a wing, limb, etc.) heavily and loosely up and down. **M19.**

J. E. TENNENT Cawing and flopping his wings in the sky.

5 *verb trans.* Strike with a sudden blow; close *up* with a blow. *dial.* (now *rare*). **M19.**
6 *verb trans.* Achieve (success in an examination, good marks, etc.) by cheating. *US colloq.* Now *rare.* **M19.**
7 *verb intrans.* Fail dismally, collapse, disappoint expectations, prove inadequate. *colloq.* **E20.**

Observer If the play 'flops' after a run of . . three or four nights. M. REYNOLDS Lenin supposedly tried to apply the teachings of Marx to Russia—and flopped.

8 *verb intrans.* Sleep; spend the night. *slang.* **E20.**

M. SHADBOLT It's only tucker I need . . and a place to flop at nights.

■ **flopper** *noun* (*US slang*) (**a**) a fraudster; (**b**) a person who deserts to the opposing political side or party: **L19.**

flop /flɒp/ *adverb.* **E18.**
[ORIGIN from the verb.]
With a flop, or flopping noise.

flopperoo /flɒpəˈruː/ *noun. N. Amer. slang.* Also **floperoo**. **M20.**
[ORIGIN from FLOP *verb* + -EROO.]
A flop, a failure.

floppy /ˈflɒpi/ *adjective & noun.* **M19.**
[ORIGIN from FLOP *verb* + -Y[1].]
▸ **A** *adjective.* **1** Having a tendency to flop (*lit. & fig.*); limply flexible, flaccid. **M19.**
2 *floppy disk*, a flexible disk with a magnetic coating, used to store machine-readable data; this together with its protective envelope. **L20.**
▸ **B** *noun.* A floppy disk. **L20.**
■ **floppily** *adverb* **L19.** **floppiness** *noun* **L19.**

flor /flɒr, flɔː/ *noun.* **L19.**
[ORIGIN Spanish, lit. 'flower'.]
A film of yeast allowed to develop on the surface during the making of fino sherry.

flor. *abbreviation.*
Latin *floruit* he or she flourished.

flora /ˈflɔːrə/ *noun.* Pl. **-ras**, **-rae** /-riː/. **E16.**
[ORIGIN Latin, from *flor-*, *flos* flower.]
1 (**F-**.) An ancient Italian goddess of fertility and flowers. Hence, the personification of nature's power to produce flowers. **E16.**
2 A catalogue of the plants of a defined area, with descriptions of them and/or stations for the more unusual species. **L18.**
3 The plants or plant life of a given area, habitat, or epoch. Cf. FAUNA. **L18.**
INTESTINAL *flora*.
– COMB.: **Flora dance** *dial.* [see *floral dance* s.v. FLORAL *adjective*] = *furry dance* s.v. FURRY *noun*; **Flora day**, **Flora's day** *dial.* = FURRY *noun*.

floral /ˈflɔːr(ə)l/ *adjective & noun.* **M17.**
[ORIGIN Latin *Floralis* or directly from Latin *flor-* (see FLORA): see -AL[1].]
▸ **A** *adjective.* **1** (**F-**.) Pertaining to or in honour of the goddess Flora. **M17.**
2 Of or pertaining to a flower or flowers. **M18.**
3 Pertaining to a flora or floras. **L19.**
– SPECIAL COLLOCATIONS: **floral dance** [alt. of FURRY *noun*] = *furry dance* s.v. FURRY *noun*. **floral diagram**: showing a cross-section of a flower, with the relative positions of petals, sepals, stamens, ovary, etc. **floral envelope** the perianth of a flower; the corolla and/or calyx. **floral formula**: expressing concisely the structure of a flower (the number and arrangement of parts), by means of letters, numerals, and symbols. **floral leaf** any of the modified leaves occurring in an inflorescence (bracts) or forming part of a flower (petals, sepals). **floral tribute** an offering of flowers at a funeral. *floral whorl*: see WHORL *noun* 3.
▸ **B** *noun.* †**1** (**F-**.) A dancer at a Roman festival in honour of Flora. Only in **M17.**
2 A fabric with a floral design. **L19.**
■ **florally** *adverb* **E19.**

Floréal /ˈflɔːrɪəl, *foreign* flɔreal/ *noun.* **E19.**
[ORIGIN French, from Latin *floreus* flowery, from *flor-*, *flos* flower: see -AL[1].]
The eighth month of the French Republican calendar (introduced 1793), extending from 20 April to 19 May.

floreated *ppl adjective* var. of FLORIATED.

Florence /ˈflɒr(ə)ns/ *noun & adjective.* **ME.**
[ORIGIN Old French & mod. French, name of the chief city of Tuscany, western Italy, = early Italian *Fiorenze* (now *Firenze*), from Latin *Florentia*.]
▸ **A** *noun.* †**1** A gold florin. **ME–L16.**
2 Any of several fabrics, *esp.* (**a**) *hist.* a woollen cloth; (**b**) a lightweight silk dress fabric. **L15.**
†**3** = *Florence wine* below. **E–M18.**
▸ **B** *attrib.* or as *adjective.* Made in or obtained from Florence. **M16.**
Florence fennel: see FENNEL *noun*. **Florence flask** a long-necked glass flask, used to hold Florence oil. **Florence oil** a superior kind of olive oil. **Florence wine** *arch.* a red wine from Tuscany.

†**florent** *adjective.* **L15–E18.**
[ORIGIN Latin *florent-* pres. ppl stem of *florere* FLOURISH *verb*: see -ENT.]
Putting out flowers or leaves and shoots; *fig.* flourishing.

Florentine /ˈflɒr(ə)ntʌɪn; *in senses A.5, B.2 also* -tiːn/ *noun & adjective.* **ME.**
[ORIGIN Old French & mod. French *Florentin*, *-ine* or Latin *Florentinus*, from *Florentia*: see FLORENCE, -INE[1]. See also *À LA Florentine*.]
▸ **A** *noun.* **1** A native or inhabitant of Florence in NW Italy. **ME.**
2 A fabric of silk or (formerly) cotton or worsted, used for garments. Cf. FLORENCE *noun* 2. **M16.**
3 A kind of pie; *esp.* meat etc. baked on a plate with a cover of pastry. Now *rare* or *obsolete*. **L16.**
4 The Italian dialect spoken in Florence. **L16.**
5 A kind of biscuit packed with nuts, glacé cherries, and other preserved fruit, coated on one side with chocolate. **M20.**
▸ **B** *adjective.* **1** Of, obtained from, or associated with the city of Florence. **L16.**
Florentine iris a bearded iris with almost white flowers, *Iris × germanica* var. *florentina*, the chief source of orris root. **Florentine mosaic**: composed of pieces of semi-precious stone embedded in marble etc. to form patterns or pictures. **Florentine pie** *rare* = sense A.3 above. **Florentine stitch** EMBROIDERY: worked in zigzag patterns on canvas.
2 COOKERY. Of eggs, fish, etc.: served on a bed of spinach or with spinach sauce. Usu. *postpositive*. **M18.**
3 EMBROIDERY. Using Florentine stitch. **E20.**

flore pleno /ˌflɔːrɪ ˈpleməʊ, ˈpliːn-/ *adjectival phr.* **L19.**
[ORIGIN Latin, lit. 'with a full flower'.]
Double-flowered.

florescence /flɔːˈrɛs(ə)ns/ *noun.* **L18.**
[ORIGIN mod. Latin *florescentia*, from Latin *florescent-* pres. ppl stem of *florescere* inceptive of *florere* to flower: see -ENCE. Earlier in REFLORESCENCE.]
The process of flowering or bursting into flower; the period of flowering. Now chiefly *fig.* Also (now *rare* or *obsolete*), an inflorescence.

Scientific American The imported culture did not reach full florescence until the sixth century.

■ **florescent** *adjective* (*rare*) bursting into flower, flowering (*lit. & fig.*) **E19.**

F

floret /ˈflɒrɪt, ˈflɔː-/ *noun.* **L17.**
[ORIGIN from Latin *flor-*, *flos* flower + -ET[1].]
1 A small flower forming part of an inflorescence; *spec.* (BOTANY) (**a**) any of the individual small flowers making up the ray or disc of a composite flower; (**b**) (in a grass) an individual lemma and palea, together with the flower they enclose. **L17.**
2 A tiny blossom or flowering plant; a floweret. **L18.**

P. MATTHIESSEN A rock garden . . set about with strap fern, edelweiss, and unknown alpine florets.

3 Any of the segments into which a cauliflower or broccoli head may be divided. **M20.**
■ **floreted** *adjective* covered or adorned with tiny flowers **M19.**

floriated /ˈflɔːrɪeɪtɪd/ *adjective.* Also **-eated**. **M19.**
[ORIGIN Irreg. from Latin *flor-*, *flos* flower + -I- + -ATE[2] + -ED[1].]
Decorated with floral ornaments; *fig.* highly exaggerated.
■ **floriate** *adjective* = FLORIATED **L19.** **flori'ation** *noun* a floral decoration; a musical flourish: **M19.**

floribunda /flɒrɪˈbʌndə, flɔː-/ *noun.* **L19.**
[ORIGIN mod. Latin, use as noun of fem. of *floribundus* flowering profusely, from Latin *flor-*, *flos* flower + *-bundus* (as in *moribundus*), infl. by *abundus* copious.]
A plant, esp. a type of garden rose (also *floribunda rose*), bearing its flowers in dense clusters.

florican /ˈflɔːrɪkan/ *noun.* Also **-ikan**. **L18.**
[ORIGIN Unknown.]
Either of two small bustards native to the Indian subcontinent, (more fully *Bengal florican*) *Houbaropsis bengalensis*, and (more fully *lesser florican*) *Sypheotides indica*.

floriculture /ˈflɒrɪkʌltʃə, ˈflɔː-/ *noun.* **E19.**
[ORIGIN from Latin *flor-*, *flos* flower + CULTURE *noun*, after *horticulture*.]
The growing of (ornamental) flowers.
■ **floricultural** *adjective* **E19.** **floriculturist** *noun* a person who practises or is skilled in floriculture **M19.**

florid /ˈflɒrɪd/ *adjective.* **M17.**
[ORIGIN (French *floride* from) Latin *floridus*, from *flor-*, *flos* flower or *florere* to flower: see -ID[1].]
1 Having many or (formerly) consisting of flowers; flowery. *arch.* **M17.**

GOLDSMITH In florid beauty groves and fields appear.

2 *fig.* Profusely decorated as with flowers; highly (usu. excessively) ornate. Chiefly of speech or writing, or a speaker or writer: having or using many rhetorical ornaments or flowery words and phrases. **M17.** ▸**b** ARCHITECTURE. Esp. of 15th- and 16th-cent. buildings: enriched with elaborate decoration. **E18.** ▸**c** Of music: in which a simple theme is varied and embellished with melodic figures; figurate. Of counterpoint: consisting of a combination of different kinds. **E18.**

R. FRY A lover of all that was rich, exuberant and even florid. P. ACKROYD My French is . . somewhat florid and literary.

†**3** Glowing with beauty; highly attractive. Of a colour: bright, glaring. **M17–L18.**

J. BUTLER Florid and gaudy Prospects and Expectations.

4 Having a ruddy or highly coloured complexion. Also, flushed *with* an emotion. **M17.** ▸†**b** Of blood: bright red, i.e. from the arteries. **M17–L18.**

N. MAILER The sort of heavy florid man who seems boyish at forty. E. L. DOCTOROW Morgan was now florid with excitement.

5 In the bloom of health; flourishing, vigorous. *arch.* **M17.**

STEELE I . . attribute the florid old age I now enjoy, to my . . walks up Hedington-Hill.

6 Of a disease or its manifestations: occurring in a fully developed form. **L20.**

Lancet Patients . . whose florid symptoms had not remitted with major tranquillisers.

■ **flo'ridity** *noun* florid quality **E18.** **floridly** *adverb* **M17.** **floridness** *noun* **M17.**

F

Florida /ˈflɒrɪdə/ *noun*. **M18**.
[**ORIGIN** A region (since 1845 a state) in the extreme south-east of the US.]
Used *attrib.* to designate things found in, obtained from, or associated with Florida.
Florida moss an epiphytic bromeliad, *Tillandsia usneoides*, resembling lichen, distributed from the southern US to S. America. **Florida room** *N. Amer.* a kind of sun lounge or sheltered porch. ***Florida snapping turtle***: see **SNAPPING** *ppl adjective* 3. **Florida water** a toilet water resembling eau de cologne, frequently containing orange-water.

Floridan /ˈflɒrɪd(ə)n/ *noun & adjective*. **M18**.
[**ORIGIN** from **FLORIDA** + **-AN**.]
= **FLORIDIAN**.

floridean /fləˈrɪdɪən/ *adjective*. Also **F-**. **E20**.
[**ORIGIN** from mod. Latin *Florideae* (see below) + **-AN**.]
Belonging to the Florideae, a subclass of the Rhodophyceae (red algae); ***floridean starch***, a reserve polysaccharide found in many red algae.
■ Also **florideous** *adjective* (now *rare* or *obsolete*) **L19**.

Floridian /fləˈrɪdɪən/ *noun & adjective*. Cf. **FLORIDAN**. **L16**.
[**ORIGIN** from **FLORIDA** + **-IAN**.]
► **A** *noun*. An inhabitant (formerly, a N. American Indian) of Florida. **L16**.
► **B** *adjective*. Of, pertaining to, or associated with Florida. **E19**.

floriferous /flɒˈrɪf(ə)rəs, flɔː-/ *adjective*. **M17**.
[**ORIGIN** from Latin *florifer* (from *flori-* combining form of *flos* flower) + **-OUS**: see **-FEROUS**.]
Bearing (numerous) flowers.
■ **floriferousness** *noun* **E18**.

florigen /ˈflɔːrɪdʒ(ə)n, ˈflɒ-/ *noun*. **M20**.
[**ORIGIN** from Latin *flori-* combining form of *flos* flower + **-GEN**.]
A hypothetical hormone in plants, not yet isolated but thought to induce flowering.

florikan *noun* var. of **FLORICAN**.

florilegium /flɒrɪˈliːdʒɪəm, flɔː-/ *noun*. Also †**-legy**. Pl. **-gia** /-dʒɪə/, **-giums**. **E17**.
[**ORIGIN** mod. Latin, lit. 'bouquet', from Latin *flori-* combining form of *flos* flower + *legere* to gather, translating Greek *anthologion* **ANTHOLOGY**.]
A collection of choice extracts from literature; an anthology. Also (*rare*), with ref. to etymological sense: a book describing choice flowers.

florin /ˈflɒrɪn/ *noun*. **ME**.
[**ORIGIN** Old French & mod. French from Italian *fiorino*, from *fiore* flower: the coin orig. so named bore a lily (fleur-de-lis) on the reverse: see **FLORENCE**.]
1 A gold coin first issued at Florence in 1252. *obsolete* exc. *hist.* **ME**.
2 An English gold coin issued by Edward III, equivalent to six shillings or six shillings and eightpence in the currency of the day. *obsolete* exc. *hist.* **L15**.
3 Any of various (orig. gold or silver) coins current at various times on the Continent. Now only, the monetary unit of the Netherlands; a guilder. **E17**.
4 In modern British pre-decimal coinage: the silver, later cupro-nickel, two-shilling piece, first minted in 1849. **M19**.
GODLESS ***florin***.

floripondio /flɔːrɪˈpɒndɪəʊ/ *noun*. **E17**.
[**ORIGIN** Spanish from mod. Latin *floripondium*, app. from Latin *flori-* combining form of *flos* flower + *pondus* weight.]
Either of two S. American plants of the nightshade family, *Brugmansia arborea* and *B. sanguinea*, allied to the thorn apple.

florist /ˈflɒrɪst/ *noun*. **E17**.
[**ORIGIN** from Latin *flor-*, *flos* flower + **-IST**, after French *fleuriste* or Italian *florista*.]
A person who cultivates or breeds (ornamental) flowers, now esp. for sale. Also (now usu.), a dealer in (cut) flowers.

floristic /fləˈrɪstɪk/ *adjective & noun*. **L19**.
[**ORIGIN** from **FLORA** + **-ISTIC**.]
► **A** *adjective*. Of or pertaining to floristics. **L19**.
► **B** *noun*. In *pl.* (treated as *sing.*). The branch of phytogeography that deals with the distribution of plants. **L19**.
■ **floristically** *adverb* **E20**.

floristry /ˈflɒrɪstri/ *noun*. **E19**.
[**ORIGIN** from **FLORIST** + **-RY**.]
The art, study, or business of a florist. Formerly, garden flowers collectively.

floruit /ˈflɒrʊɪt, ˈflɔːr-/ *noun*. **M19**.
[**ORIGIN** Latin, 3rd person sing. perf. indic. of *florere* to flourish.]
The period during which a person etc. flourished.

H. W. WATKINS Professor de Groot puts his life at A.D. 65–135, and his *floruit* in the reign of Trajan.

florula /ˈflɔːrʊlə/ *noun*. Pl. **-lae** /-liː/, **-las**. **M19**.
[**ORIGIN** mod. Latin, dim. of Latin *Flora*: see **FLORA**, **-ULE**.]
A small or circumscribed flora (**FLORA** 2, 3). Also, a small collection of plants from an area.

florulent /ˈflɔːrʊl(ə)nt, ˈflɒ-/ *adjective*. *rare*. **L16**.
[**ORIGIN** Latin *florulentus*, from *flor-*, *flos* flower: see **-ULENT**.]
Covered with flowers or representations of flowers.

flory /ˈflɔːri/ *adjective*. Also **fleury** /ˈflʊəri/. **LME**.
[**ORIGIN** Old French *flo(u)ré* (mod. *fleuré*), from *fleur* **FLOWER** *noun*: see **-Y**[5].]
HERALDRY. Decorated with a fleur-de-lis or fleurs-de-lis; *esp.* (of a cross) having limbs tipped with fleurs-de-lis.

floscular /ˈflɒskjʊlə/ *adjective*. **L18**.
[**ORIGIN** from Latin *flosculus* (see **FLOSCULE**) + **-AR**[1].]
BOTANY. = **FLOSCULOUS** 2.

floscule /ˈflɒskjuːl/ *noun*. **M17**.
[**ORIGIN** French, or Latin *flosculus* dim. of *flos* flower.]
†**1** Something resembling a small flower. Only in **M17**.
2 *BOTANY*. Any of the florets in a composite flower. Now *rare*. **L18**.

flosculous /ˈflɒskjʊləs/ *adjective*. **M17**.
[**ORIGIN** formed as **FLOSCULE** + **-OUS**.]
†**1** Having the nature or flavour of a flower or flowers. **M–L17**.
2 *BOTANY*. Composed of florets (**FLORET** *noun* 1(a)); *spec.* consisting entirely of disc florets. Of a floret: belonging to the disc, tubular. **M18**.

flos ferri /flɒs ˈfɛrʌɪ/ *noun phr.* **M18**.
[**ORIGIN** Latin, lit. 'flower of iron'.]
MINERALOGY. A branching coral-like variety of aragonite, often occurring with haematite.

flosh *noun* see **FLASH** *noun*[1].

floss /flɒs/ *noun*[1]. Chiefly *Orkney & Shetland*. **E17**.
[**ORIGIN** Cf. Norwegian dial. *flos*, *flus* a strip peeled off, *flysja* to peel.]
The stems of the soft rush, *Juncus effusus*, esp. as used for thatch or woven into ropes.

floss /flɒs/ *noun*[2]. **M18**.
[**ORIGIN** Old French *flosche* down, pile on velvet, mod. *floche*, as in *soie floche* floss silk; ult. origin unknown.]
1 The rough silk surrounding a silkworm's cocoon; *transf.* the silky down in maize and certain other plants. Also = ***floss silk*** below. **M18**.
2 A downy or fluffy surface. Also, an accumulation of flossy particles; fluff. **L18**.

F. NORRIS Overlaying the flush of rose in her cheeks . . was a faint sheen of down, a lustrous floss.

3 In full ***dental floss***. Floss silk or similar thread used to clean between the teeth. **E20**.
4 Usu. ***candyfloss***. A (usu. pink or white) mass of fluffy spun sugar. **M20**.

fig. (*attrib.*): R. HOGGART Invitations to a candy-floss world: the newer mass art.

– **COMB.**: **floss silk** (*a*) the rough silk broken off in winding a cocoon, esp. as carded and used in the manufacture of common silk; (*b*) untwisted silk fibres used in embroidery and crewel work.

floss /flɒs/ *noun*[3]. **M19**.
[**ORIGIN** German *Floss*, cogn. with **FLOAT** *noun*.]
METALLURGY. The molten slag floating on the iron in a puddling furnace.

floss /flɒs/ *verb*. **M20**.
[**ORIGIN** from **FLOSS** *noun*[2].]
1 *verb intrans.* Behave in a flamboyant manner; show off. *US black slang*. **M20**.
2 *verb trans. & intrans.* Clean between (the teeth) with dental floss. **L20**.

flossy /ˈflɒsi/ *adjective*. **M19**.
[**ORIGIN** from **FLOSS** *noun*[2] + **-Y**[1].]
1 Resembling or consisting of floss (**FLOSS** *noun*[2]). **M19**.
2 Excessively grand or stylish; fancy, showy. Also, cheeky, forward. *N. Amer. colloq.* **L19**.

S. TUROW Dixon still had the flossy gleam of a cheap suit . . and . . he was if anything more brash.

■ **flossied** *ppl adjective* (*colloq.*) dressed *up* in a showy style **M20**.

flot /flɒt, *foreign* flo (*pl. same*)/ *noun*. **L19**.
[**ORIGIN** French, lit. 'wave'.]
A trimming of lace or loops of ribbon, arranged in overlapping rows.

flota /ˈfləʊtə/ *noun*. **L17**.
[**ORIGIN** Spanish = fleet.]
hist. The Spanish fleet which used to cross the Atlantic and bring back the products of America and the W. Indies. Formerly also *gen.*, a fleet.

flotage *noun* var. of **FLOATAGE**.

flotant /ˈfləʊt(ə)nt/ *adjective*. **E17**.
[**ORIGIN** French *flottant* pres. pple of *flotter* to float.]
HERALDRY. Of a banner, ship, etc.: floating (in the wind, water, etc.).

flotation /fləʊˈteɪʃ(ə)n/ *noun*. Also **float-**. **E19**.
[**ORIGIN** from **FLOAT** *verb* + **-ATION**, after French *flottaison*. The spelling *flot-* adopted to conform with *flotilla*.]
1 The action or process of floating in a liquid etc.; the condition of keeping afloat. **E19**.
centre of flotation: see **CENTRE** *noun*. **line of flotation**, **plane of flotation**: in which the horizontal surface of a fluid intersects a body floating in it.
2 The action of floating a company or enterprise. **L19**.
3 The separation of the components of crushed ore etc. by their different capacities to float on a given liquid. **E20**.
froth flotation: in which a frothing agent is added to the liquid used, causing the valuable particles to collect in the surface bubbles.
– **COMB.**: **flotation tank** a lightproof, soundproof tank of salt water in which one may float as a form of deep relaxation.

†**flote** *noun, verb* vars. of **FLOAT** *noun, verb*.

flote-grass /ˈfləʊtgrɑːs/ *noun*. Also **float-grass**. **LME**.
[**ORIGIN** from *flote* obsolete var. of **FLOAT** *noun, verb* + **GRASS** *noun*.]
Any of various grasses or (formerly) sedges of marshy or watery places; now usu. floating sweetgrass, *Glyceria fluitans*.

flotel *noun* var. of **FLOATEL**.

flotilla /fləˈtɪlə/ *noun*. **E18**.
[**ORIGIN** Spanish, dim. of *flota* = Provençal *flota*, Old French *flote* (mod. *flotte*) fleet: see **FLOTA**.]
A small fleet; a fleet of boats or small vessels.

flotsam /ˈflɒts(ə)m/ *noun*. Also (*dial.*) **floatsome** /ˈfləʊt-/, (*arch.*) **flotson** /ˈflɒts(ə)n/. **E17**.
[**ORIGIN** Anglo-Norman *floteson*, from *floter* **FLOAT** *verb*. For the form cf. **JETSAM**; cf. also **LAGAN**, **WAVESON**.]
1 *LAW*. Wreckage of a ship or its cargo found floating on the surface of the sea. Usu. assoc. with **JETSAM**. **E17**.
2 Timber etc. washed down by a stream. Orig. *dial.* **E19**.
3 *transf. & fig.* Things (or persons) discarded as worthless. **M19**.

R. BUCHANAN A mania for buying all sorts of flotsam and jetsam. P. GALLICO The flotsam of bums, drifters and down-and-outers.

4 Newly ejected oyster spawn. **L19**.

flounce /flaʊns/ *noun*[1]. **L16**.
[**ORIGIN** from **FLOUNCE** *verb*[1].]
A sudden fling or jerk of the body or of a limb or limbs; a plunging or flopping movement; usu. such a movement as an expression of annoyance, impatience, or disdain.

flounce /flaʊns/ *noun*[2]. **E18**.
[**ORIGIN** Alt. of earlier **FROUNCE** *noun*[1], prob. by assim. to **FLOUNCE** *verb*[1].]
A wide ornamental strip of material gathered and sewn by its upper edge, esp. round a woman's skirt, so that its lower edge hangs full and free.

H. JAMES She was dressed in white muslin, with a hundred frills and flounces.

flounce /flaʊns/ *verb*[1] *& adverb*. **M16**.
[**ORIGIN** Uncertain: perh. connected with Norwegian *flunsa* hurry, Swedish dial. *flunsa* fall with a splash, or perh. of imit. origin, as *bounce*, *pounce*.]
► **A** *verb*. **1** *verb intrans.* Dash, flop, plunge; go with agitated or violent motion, esp. as an expression of anger or annoyance. (Foll. by *in*, *off*, *out*, etc.) **M16**.

T. FULLER He commanded them all at once to flounce into the river. A. BROOKNER She flounces into the bathroom and does not speak to him. R. COBB Adopting his high-and-mighty manner and flouncing out in a fury.

†**2** *verb trans.* Dash, drive, or fling violently. **L16**.
3 *verb intrans.* Of a person or animal: make abrupt or jerky movements with the body or limbs; throw the body about. **E17**.

J. SHUTE When one hath struck a great fish, he plungeth and flounceth.

► **B** *adverb*. With a flounce. Now *rare*. **L16**.

flounce /flaʊns/ *verb*[2] *trans.* **L17**.
[**ORIGIN** Alt. of earlier **FROUNCE** *verb*: cf. **FLOUNCE** *noun*[2].]
1 Curl, frizz, trim. *rare*. **L17**.
2 Adorn or trim with a flounce or flounces. **E18**.

M. R. MITFORD Striped muslin to flounce my gowns.

■ **flouncing** *noun* (*a*) the action of putting a flounce on a garment; (*b*) a flounce, the material of which a flounce is made: **M18**.

flouncy /ˈflaʊnsi/ *adjective*. Also **-ey**. **E19**.
[**ORIGIN** from **FLOUNCE** *noun*[2] + **-Y**[1].]
Having flounces, flounced.

flounder /ˈflaʊndə/ *noun*[1]. **ME**.
[**ORIGIN** Anglo-Norman *floundre* (Anglo-Latin *flundra*), Old French (and mod. Norman French) *flondre*, prob. of Scandinavian origin (cf. Old Swedish *flundra*, Danish *flynder*, Old Norse *flyðra*).]
1 A small flatfish, *Platichthys flesus*, found in European coastal waters and rivers. Also (with specifying word), any of numerous small flatfishes of the families Pleuronectidae and Bothidae. **ME**.
witch flounder: see **WITCH** *noun*[3]. ***yellowtail flounder***: see **YELLOWTAIL**.
2 A thing resembling a flounder in appearance: (*a*) *dial.* a liver fluke; (*b*) a tool formerly used to shape the front of a boot. **M19**.

flounder /ˈflaʊndə/ *verb & noun*[2]. **L16**.
[**ORIGIN** Imit. (perh. blend of **FOUNDER** *verb* and **BLUNDER** *noun, verb*) on the basis of the frequency of *fl-* in words expressing impetuous, clumsy, or rough movement, as *fling*, *flounce*.]

▸**A** *verb.* **1** *verb intrans.* Orig., stumble. Later, plunge or tumble about, move clumsily, struggle along, as or as if in mud or deep water. L16.

V. WOOLF She would jump straight into a stream and flounder across. A. UTTLEY She floundered along, bumping into outstretched boughs, tripping over stones.

†**2** *verb trans.* Cause to stumble or struggle; confound. M–L17.

3 *verb intrans. transf.* Make mistakes; struggle or show confusion in thoughts or words; manage something badly or with difficulty. L17.

L. P. HARTLEY To flounder for ever in these cruel uncertainties. P. BARKER Knowing how to cope with situations that left other people floundering.

▸**B** *noun.* The action of the verb; an instance of this. M19.

■ **flounderer** *noun* M19. **flounderingly** *adverb* in a floundering manner M20.

flour /ˈflaʊə/ *noun.* Also †**flower**. See also FLOWER *noun.* ME.

[ORIGIN Orig. form of FLOWER *noun*, becoming differentiated in the sense 'the finest part of meal'; the spelling *flower* was also used in this sense until early 19.]

▸**I 1** Orig., the finest quality of meal. Hence, the finer part of the meal of wheat or other grain, obtained by bolting. Now *esp.* wheatmeal. ME.

E. RAFFALD Rub a little of the butter into the flour.

plain flour, ***self-raising flour***, ***wholemeal flour***, etc. ***cornflour***: see CORN *noun*[1].

2 Any fine soft powder, *esp.* that obtained by the grinding of seeds, farinaceous roots, etc. LME.

SOUTHEY A vessel laden with manioc flour. *Science* Turbid water . . charged with comminuted rock debris or 'glacial flour'.

▸†**II** See FLOWER *noun.*

– COMB.: **flour beetle** a small beetle of the genus *Tribolium*, the larvae of which feed on flour; **flour-bolt**, **flour-bolter** a sieve for flour.

flour /ˈflaʊə/ *verb.* LME.

[ORIGIN from the noun.]

1 *verb trans.* Sprinkle or cover with flour. LME.

A. CARTER The morning sky . . was as white as if it had been floured. P. BARKER Her arms were floured half-way to the elbow.

2 *verb trans.* Grind into flour. *US.* E19.

flouring mill a mill for making flour, as distinct from a gristmill.

3 *verb trans. & intrans.* MINING. Break up (a metal, esp. mercury), be broken up, into small sulphide-coated particles. M19.

flourish /ˈflʌrɪʃ/ *noun.* LME.

[ORIGIN from the verb.]

1 The blossom on a fruit tree. *Scot. & N. English.* LME. ▸†**b** The condition of being in blossom. L16–E19. ▸**c** *fig.* Prosperity, vigour; perfection, prime. L16.

c SIR W. SCOTT The flourish of his powerful relative's fortunes had burst forth in the finery of his dress. *Times* Shares retreat after early flourish.

†**2** A prolusion; a piece of ornamental preamble, preliminary to serious discussion or business. M16–E17.

3 Ostentatious embellishment; gloss. Now *rare.* L16.

4 MUSIC. **a** A fanfare of horns, trumpets, etc. L16. ▸**b** A florid passage or style of composition; a short extemporized prelude or ornamental addition. M17.

a A. SETON There was a great flurry and a flourish of trumpets. *fig.* (*collect.*): J. ARCHER An oil rig which, with much flourish and advance publicity, he had towed out to the Prospecta Oil site. **b** ALLAN RAMSAY The fine flourishes of new musick imported from Italy.

5 An ostentatious gesture made with a weapon or other instrument; *spec.* a graceful sweeping movement made with a weapon at the start of a fencing match. E17. ▸**b** *gen.* A showy or extravagant gesture. M18.

STEELE Before he applied his weapon to my chin, he gave me a flourish with it. **b** W. VAN T. CLARK She . . got back into the coach with a flourish of her skirts. C. HAMPTON With a flourish, he produces a cauliflower from the paper bag.

6 A literary or rhetorical embellishment; a florid expression. E17.

7 An ornament of flowing curves about a letter or word in handwriting. M17. ▸**b** A florid decoration; scrollwork, tracery. L17.

A. DESAI She wrote in long, spidery flourishes. **b** A. ALVAREZ An ornamental iron gateway, painted black, its flourishes picked out in gold.

■ **flourishy** *adjective* L19.

flourish /ˈflʌrɪʃ/ *verb.* ME.

[ORIGIN Old French & mod. French *floriss-* lengthened stem of *florir* (now *fleurir*) from Proto-Romance alt. of Latin *florere*, from *flos*, *flor-* FLOWER *noun*: see -ISH[2].]

▸**I** Blossom, thrive.

1 *verb intrans.* Of a plant or tree: grow vigorously, thrive. ME. ▸**b** Flower, blossom. *obsolete* exc. *Scot.* ME.

N. MOSLEY It was a marvel so many flowers could flourish near a desert. B. PLAIN Like weeds in . . rain it had flourished, spreading roots and . . tentacles.

2 *verb intrans.* Thrive, prosper, be successful. ME.

G. GREENE I doubt . . whether a lion would flourish on green things. M. HOLROYD Old pagan festivals, long-forgotten elsewhere, still flourished. D. M. THOMAS As her playing improved . . her career began to flourish.

†**3** *verb intrans.* Display vigour *in*, *with*; abound *in*, overflow *with*. ME–E18.

4 *verb intrans.* **a** Spend one's life or be active during a specified period. Foll. by *in*, *at*, *about*, etc. LME. ▸**b** Be at the height of fame or excellence, be in one's prime. Also (*colloq.*), be in good health. M16.

a W. IRVING James flourished nearly about the time of Chaucer and Gower. **b** N. BALCHIN He said, 'How's Marcia?' . . I just said, 'Oh, flourishing.'

▸**II** Adorn.

†**5** *verb trans.* Adorn with flowers or verdure; cause to bloom. ME–E17.

†**6** *verb trans. gen.* Adorn, embellish, decorate. ME–E18. ▸**b** Embellish (a book or writing); decorate, illuminate. LME–M17.

7 †**a** *verb trans.* Embellish (words, a speech) with rhetorical phrases or flowery expressions. ME–L17. ▸**b** *verb intrans.* Speak floridly and copiously *on* or *upon*; use florid language. Now *rare.* E18.

▸**III** Display ostentatiously.

8 a *verb trans.* Wave (something) about ostentatiously; brandish (a weapon etc.). Also, move (the limbs) about vigorously. LME. ▸**b** *verb intrans.* Of a weapon: be brandished. Long *rare.* LME.

DICKENS Looking at the dwarf . . as he flourished his arms and legs about. C. MORGAN When he recognized her, he would clutch at the handkerchief . . and flourish it in the air. J. MONTAGUE He flourished a sabre to rally troops and plunge across the Somme.

9 a *verb trans.* Make a display or parade of; show ostentatiously. LME. ▸**b** *verb intrans.* Make a flourish or parade; show off, brag, swagger. Now *rare.* M16.

a W. GOLDING A huge hoarding which was flourishing beans . . ten feet in the air. D. M. THOMAS She stormed in . . . She flourished before me two photographs.

†**10** *verb intrans.* MUSIC. Play a short extemporized prelude before the real performance. M16–E19. ▸**b** Of trumpets: sound a fanfare. L16–E18.

†**11** *verb intrans.* Move with a flourish; make sweeping movements. *rare.* E–M18.

■ **flourisher** *noun* LME. **flourishing** *noun* the action of the verb; an instance of this; a decoration, ornamental detail: ME. **flourishingly** *adverb* L15. **flourishment** *noun* (*rare*) prosperity, thriving E18.

floury /ˈflaʊəri/ *adjective.* LME.

[ORIGIN from FLOUR *noun* + -Y[1].]

Covered with flour or powder; of or resembling flour.

floury miller an Australian cicada, *Abricta curvicosta*, whose body is covered with white down.

flout /flaʊt/ *verb & noun.* M16.

[ORIGIN Perh. from Dutch *fluiten* whistle, play the flute, hiss (*uitfluiten*); cf. synon. German colloq. *pfeifen auf* pipe at.]

▸**A** *verb.* **1** *verb trans.* Treat with disdain; mock, express contempt for. Now usu., openly disregard (a law, opinion, etc.). M16.

G. SAINTSBURY Locke . . had expressly flouted (or rather . . denounced) poetry as idle and pernicious. R. MACAULAY Those who live loosely and flout the laws. M. FRAYN If one is flouting the generally accepted rules of behaviour one must exercise discretion.

†**flouting stock** (*a*) an object of mockery; (*b*) = FLOUT *noun.*

2 *verb intrans.* Scoff, jeer; express contempt. L16.

BROWNING Ah, you may flout and turn up your faces.

▸**B** *noun.* A mocking speech or action. L16.

■ **flouter** *noun* L16. **floutingly** *adverb* L16.

flow /fləʊ/ *noun*[1]. LME.

[ORIGIN from the verb.]

1 The action or fact of flowing. LME. ▸**b** The quantity that flows; rate of flowing. E19. ▸**c** That which flows; flowing liquid. E19.

SHELLEY The flow Of sudden tears. H. READ The natural flow of water towards the lower level of the sea. R. L. BRUCKBERGER All networks of radio and television and the flow of their waves. **b** L. DEIGHTON At first the flow was no faster than a kitchen tap. **c** J. WILSON The still flow of this majestic river.

2 †**a** A deluge, a flood. LME–L16. ▸**b** An overflowing; *spec.* a periodical overflow of the Nile or other river. E17.

3 The incoming or rise of the tide. (Opp. *ebb.*) L16.

J. RUSKIN The Thames tide, with its tossing wherries at the flow.

4 Any continuous movement resembling the flow of a river and connoting a copious supply; an outpouring, a stream. M17. ▸**b** The loose or undulating way in which a garment, outline, etc., flows or hangs. M19.

N. MITFORD There were no more big house parties, but a continual flow of people. D. LODGE I tried to stem her flow of intimate reminiscence. C. PRIEST My creative energy was undiminished . . there was nothing that could . . obstruct the flow. **b** J. RUSKIN In the folds of the drapery . . is a flow like that of waves.

5 More fully ***plastic flow***. A gradual permanent deformation of a solid under stress, without fracture or loss of cohesion. L19.

– PHRASES: **flow of soul** genial conversation (as complement to *feast of reason*). **flow of spirits** sudden or (now usu.) habitual cheerfulness. †**set one's eyes at flow** *rare* (Shakes.) (cause to) weep.

– COMB.: **flow-blue** a blue colour applied to pottery or porcelain which diffuses readily through the glaze; **flow chart**, **flow diagram** a diagram showing the movement or action of persons or things in any complex system, as an industrial plant or a computer program; **flow line** (*a*) PHYSICS an imaginary curve drawn in a fluid such that at each point the direction of motion of the fluid is along the tangent to the curve at that point; (*b*) (in *pl.*) the lines that appear on the surface of wrought metal when polished or etched, indicating the direction of flow of the metal during working; (*c*) any of the related routes followed by goods, materials, etc., in the various stages of manufacture or treatment; a path depicted on a flow chart; ***flow-line production*** = ***flow production*** below; **flowmeter** an instrument for measuring the rate of flow of gas, liquid fuel, etc.; **flow pipe** the pipe by which hot water leaves the boiler in a heating or hot water system; **flow production** the continual passage of goods from one piece of equipment to another in the successive stages of production; **flow sheet** = ***flow chart*** above; **flowstone** GEOLOGY rock deposited by water flowing in a thin sheet; a rock formation so formed; **flow structure** GEOLOGY the structure in igneous rock produced by the flow of the molten mass before solidification.

F

flow /fləʊ/ *noun*[2]. Chiefly *Scot.* L17.

[ORIGIN Perh. from Icelandic (Old Norse) *flói* of the same meaning, rel. to *flóa* FLOW *verb.*]

1 In full ***flow moss***. A watery swamp, a morass. L17.

attrib.: *Daily Telegraph* The 'flow' country of Caithness and Sutherland, an open peat bog.

2 A quicksand. E19.

flow /fləʊ/ *verb.* Pa. t. **flowed** /fləʊd/; pa. pple **flowed** /fləʊd/, †**flown**.

[ORIGIN Old English *flōwan*, cogn. with Old Norse *flóa* flood, Middle Low German *vlōien*, Dutch *vloeien* flow, from Germanic base of FLOOD *noun.*]

▸**I** Glide along as a stream.

1 *verb intrans.* Of fluids, a stream, etc.: glide or run along, move along in a current. (Foll. by *along*, *down*, *out*, etc.) OE. ▸**b** Of blood or other bodily fluid: circulate within the vessels of the body. ME. ▸**c** Foll. by *over*: overflow. Long *rare.* E16.

H. ALLEN The water . . was soon seen and heard to be flowing away at a rapid rate. I. MCEWAN Usually the canal flows north, but today it was completely still. O. HENRY A little iron bridge . . under which the small tortuous river flows. *fig.*: G. GREENE The stream of the unconscious continues to flow undisturbed. **c** SHAKES. *Ant. & Cl.* My lord Who is so full of grace that it flows over On all that need.

†**2** *verb intrans.* Become liquid, melt. OE–M18.

3 *verb intrans.* **a** Of people: come or go as a stream, move smoothly or in a crowd. LME. ▸**b** Of things: move as a stream, run smoothly and easily. Of electricity: move as a current, circulate. Of money: circulate within the economy, be transferred. LME.

a T. S. ELIOT A crowd flowed over London Bridge, so many. **b** A. BEVAN Investment flowed freely from Europe to America. A. MILLER The emotion flowing between them prevents anyone from speaking. G. GREENE Along the route to Tanyin flowed a fast stream of . . cars. *Acorn User* Data can flow between computers . . in two directions simultaneously.

4 Of hair, a garment, etc.: hang easily and gracefully, lie in undulating curves, stream. LME.

G. MILLAR Wavy, brown hair flowing glossily over his round head.

†**5** *verb trans.* Cause to flow or run; make fluid. LME–M17.

6 *verb intrans.* Of talk, literary style, etc.: proceed smoothly. L16.

A. S. BYATT The conversation . . flowed easily enough. S. BRETT I think my version flows better . . sounds more poetic.

7 *verb intrans.* MATH. Increase or diminish continuously by infinitesimal quantities. *arch.* E18.

8 *verb intrans.* Of a solid: undergo plastic flow (see FLOW *noun*[1] 5). L19.

▸**II** Stream forth.

9 *verb intrans.* Gush out, well forth, spring; (of blood) be shed. OE. ▸**b** Issue *from*, *out of*; result *from*. ME. ▸**c** Of a person: pour out one's feelings. L17.

D. CARNEGIE The blood flowing from his wounds left a crimson trail. *transf.*: B. PLAIN Ferns flowed out of hanging baskets at the windows. **b** H. G. WELLS The broad principles of action that flow from this wide conception of socialism. **c** TENNYSON The mother flow'd in shallower acrimonies.

10 *verb intrans.* Of the sea or a tidal river: rise and advance, be in flood. Freq. in ***ebb and flow***. Cf. EBB *verb* 1. OE. ▸†**b** Of a river, esp. the Nile: overflow. Cf. FLOWN *ppl adjective*[1] 1. ME–E17. ▸†**c** Of the eyes: become overfull, run (with tears). ME–E18.

fig.: E. M. FORSTER Waves of emotion broke, as if a tide of passion was flowing through the . . air.

11 *verb intrans.* †**a** Of wealth etc.: abound. Only in OE. ▸**b** Of wine etc.: run abundantly, be poured out unstintingly. L15.

12 *verb intrans.* Foll. by *with*: abound in, be plentifully supplied with. Now *rare* exc. in allusion to biblical phr. below. ME.

AV *Exod.* 3:8 A lande flowing with milke and hony.

13 *verb trans.* Cover or fill with water, flood. Now *rare*. LME. ▸**b** Cover with any liquid, as varnish or glaze. Now *rare*. M19.

14 *verb trans.* Produce (a liquid or stream of liquid). *rare*. M16.

– COMB.: **flow-on** *noun & adjective* (*Austral.* & *NZ*) (*a*) consequences; (*b*) (designating or pertaining to) a wage or salary adjustment made for certain workers as a consequence of adjustments already made for other related workers.

■ **flowage** *noun* (*a*) the act of flowing; flooded state; (*b*) plastic flow: M19.

flower /ˈflaʊə/ *noun*. Also (earlier) †**flour**. See also FLOUR *noun*. ME.

[ORIGIN Anglo-Norman *flur*, Old French *flor*, *flour* (mod. *fleur*), from Latin *flos flor-*. The orig. sp. *flour* was disused by L17 exc. in its specialized sense (see FLOUR *noun*).]

▸**I 1** The seed-bearing part of a plant, consisting botanically of reproductive organs (stamens and/or carpels) typically surrounded by a (usu. coloured) corolla and a (usu. green) calyx (or sometimes by a calyx alone). In popular use, such an organ when brightly coloured and conspicuous; a blossom, a bloom. ME.

N. E. HICKIN Damp hedges . . golden with the yellow daisy-like flowers of fleabane.

2 A blossom (and usu. its stalk) considered independently of the growing plant, esp. as used in groups for decoration or as a mark of honour or respect. ME.

E. O'NEILL And me still goin' every day to put flowers on Maw's grave. S. HILL Dorothea . . went out into the garden to cut some flowers for Eleanor.

flower of an hour *US* a plant of the mallow family, *Hibiscus trionum*, which has short-lived pale yellow flowers with a purple eye and is native in warmer parts of the Old World (and naturalized in N. America). ***language of flowers***: see LANGUAGE *noun*[1]. ***the Hundred Flowers***: see HUNDRED *adjective*.

3 A representation of a flower in painting, embroidery, architecture, etc.; *esp.* = FLEUR-DE-LIS 3. ME. ▸**b** *TYPOGRAPHY*. A stylized ornament, often based on the shape of a flower, printed in rows to form a decorative border, heading, etc. L18.

4 *fig.* Formerly, virginity. Now, a precious possession, an adornment. ME.

LD MACAULAY A precious prerogative which . . even the Whigs allowed to be a flower properly belonging to the Crown.

5 *fig.*. *The* finest individual(s) out of a number of persons or things; the pick. ME. ▸**b** *The* finest embodiment *of* a quality. ME. ▸**c** *The* choicest part *of* something; *the* essential part *of* a matter. Cf. FLOUR *noun*. LME.

L. VAN DER POST The generation which lost its finest flower in the First World War. R. H. MORRIESON Yuh were the flower of the district, Natalie. **b** TENNYSON Lancelot, the flower of bravery. **c** J. GAY I sip the tea's delicious flower. CARLYLE The flower of the matter is . . that they sit in secret.

6 In *pl.* Rhetorical embellishments; fine phrases. LME.

R. BOYLE Discourses not tricked up with Flowers of Rhetorick.

7 A flowering plant; *esp.* one grown for its flowers. LME. **flower of Jove** a woolly campion, *Lychnis flos-jovis*, cultivated for its bright pink flowers. ***bellflower***, ***passion flower***, ***sunflower***, ***wallflower***, etc.

8 *fig.* The most active or vigorous period of a person's life; one's prime. Formerly also, the period of a person's greatest prosperity. LME.

J. WEBB Jeffery Monmouth was in his Flower Anno 1156. SIR W. SCOTT He is a man in the flower of life, about thirty. J. B. PRIESTLEY We looked like the affluent society in full flower.

9 *CHEMISTRY*. The powdery form *of* a substance, esp. one obtained by sublimation. In later use only in *pl.* *arch.* LME. ▸**b** Of a plant: the state of being in bloom. Chiefly as ***in flower***, ***into flower***. E17.

flowers of sulphur: see SULPHUR *noun*. ***flowers of zinc***: see ZINC *noun*.

10 [After French *fleurs*, perh. alt. of *flueurs*: see FLUOR.] In *pl.* The menstrual discharge. Now *rare* or *obsolete*. LME.

11 Any of various fungoid growths. M16.

flower of wine a scum formed by certain yeasts on fermenting wine. **flowers of tan** a mould, *Fuligo varians*, found on tanbark, dead wood, etc.

▸†**II** See FLOUR *noun*.

– COMB.: **flower arrangement** the art of arranging flowers in vases etc. for artistic effect; **flower bed** a garden bed in which flowers are grown; **flower-bug** (orig. *US*) any of various predatory hemipteran insects of the family Anthocoridae, occurring in flowers, on foliage, etc.; **flower children** = *flower people* below; **flower-fence** a W. Indian leguminous shrub, *Caesalpinia pulcherrima*, used for hedging in the tropics; **flower-fly** a dipteran insect which frequents flowers, *esp.* one of the family Syrphidae (hoverflies); **flower girl** (*a*) a woman selling flowers, *esp.* in the street; (*b*) a small girl carrying or scattering flowers in front of the bride at a wedding; **flower head** *BOTANY* a dense compact inflorescence; *spec.* = CAPITULUM (b); **flowerpecker** any of various oriental and Australasian passerine birds of the family Dicaeidae; **flower people** a class of hippies, prominent in the late 1960s, who carried flowers as emblems of peace and love; **flower-piece** a picture or arrangement of flowers; **flowerpot** a small vessel, typically of red earthenware or plastic and tapering downwards, for holding soil in which a plant or plants may be grown; **flower power** the ideas of flower people, regarded as an instrument for changing the world; **flower spike** = SPIKE *noun*[1] 2.

■ **flowerful** *adjective* having many flowers M19. **flowerless** *adjective* not flowering or adorned with flowers; ***flowerless plant*** (*BOTANY*), a cryptogam: L15. **flowerlessness** *noun* M19. **flower-like** *adjective* & *adverb* (*a*) *adjective* resembling (that of) a flower; (*b*) *adverb* in the manner of a flower: E17.

flower /ˈflaʊə/ *verb*. ME.

[ORIGIN from the noun, prob. after Old French *florir*, *flourir* FLOURISH *verb*.]

▸**I** *verb intrans.* **1** Come into or be in flower; blossom, bloom. ME. ▸**b** *fig.* Foll. by *into*, *to*: develop into. M19.

b E. J. HOWARD A contentment that flowered . . almost to ecstasy. *Philadelphia Inquirer* She has flowered into young womanhood.

2 *fig.* Be in or attain one's fullest perfection, the highest stage in one's development, etc. Formerly, foll. by *in*, *of*: thrive in respect of, abound in. ME.

DAY LEWIS We who 'flowered' in the Thirties/were an odd lot.

†**3** Of beer or wine: froth, mantle. LME–M18.

▸**II** *verb trans.* **4** Cover (as) with flowers. Also foll. by *over*. Now *rare*. LME.

W. BARTRAM Its thick foliage . . is flowered over with large milk-white . . blossoms.

5 Decorate with (esp. embroidered) representations of flowers or with floral patterns. E16.

transf.: M. ARNOLD The frost flowers the whiten'd window-panes.

6 *HORTICULTURE*. Induce (a plant) to flower. M19.

■ **flowering** *noun* (*a*) in *pl.*, figures of flowers; †(*b*) *sing.* blossoms collectively; (*c*) the action of the verb, the process of coming into flower: ME.

flowerage /ˈflaʊərɪdʒ/ *noun*. L17.

[ORIGIN from FLOWER *noun*, *verb* + -AGE.]

†**1** The hanging up of bunches of flowers. Only in L17.

2 The process or result of flowering; flowers collectively. M19.

flower-de-luce *noun* see FLEUR-DE-LIS.

flowered /ˈflaʊəd/ *adjective*. LME.

[ORIGIN from FLOWER *noun*, *verb*: see -ED[2], -ED[1].]

1 Covered with flowers; decorated with (esp. embroidered) representations of flowers. LME.

2 Bearing flowers of a specified kind or number. L16.

†**3** In flower. M17–L18.

flowerer /ˈflaʊərə/ *noun*. L18.

[ORIGIN from FLOWER *verb* + -ER[1].]

1 A person who decorates china etc. with floral patterns. L18.

2 A plant that flowers in a specified manner or at a specified time. M19.

floweret /ˈflaʊərɪt/ *noun*. LME.

[ORIGIN from FLOWER *noun* + -ET[1].]

1 A small flower. Chiefly *literary*. LME.

2 = FLORET *noun* 3. E20.

flowering /ˈflaʊərɪŋ/ *ppl adjective*. LME.

[ORIGIN from FLOWER *verb* + -ING[2].]

†**1** At the height of one's vigour, beauty, prosperity, etc.; flourishing. LME–E17.

flowering age, **flowering youth** the prime of life or youth.

2 Of a plant: that is in bloom. E16.

3 = FLOWERY *adjective* 1. L16.

4 That bears (conspicuous) flowers. Chiefly in names of plants contrasted with similar or allied species in which the flowers are inconspicuous or absent. L17.

flowering cherry any of several species of *Prunus* grown for their ornamental flowers (and not their fruit). ***flowering*** CURRANT. ***flowering*** DOGWOOD. **flowering fern** = ***royal fern*** s.v. ROYAL *adjective*. **flowering raspberry** an American bramble, *Rubus odoratus*, with large rose-purple flowers and leaves resembling those of the maple. **flowering rush** a tall monocotyledonous aquatic plant, *Butomus umbellatus* (family Butomaceae), with umbels of pinkish flowers and rushlike triquetrous leaves. ***flowering willow***: see WILLOW *noun* 3.

flowery /ˈflaʊəri/ *adjective & noun*. LME.

[ORIGIN from FLOWER *noun* + -Y[1].]

▸**A** *adjective*. **1** Having many flowers, covered with flowers. LME. ▸**b** Composed of flowers, of the nature of flowers. M17.

flowery dell *rhyming slang* a cell. **the Flowery Empire**, **the Flowery Land** China.

2 Ornamented with figures of flowers or floral designs. LME. ▸**b** *HERALDRY*. = FLEURY *adjective*. Now *rare* or *obsolete*. L17.

3 Characterized by flowers of speech; full of fine words and phrases. E17.

B. TAYLOR Smyrna is . . called, in the flowery tongue of the East, the 'Ornament of Asia'.

▸**B** *noun*. [Abbreviation of *flowery dell* above.] A (prison or police) cell. E20.

■ **flowerily** *adverb* L19. **floweriness** *noun* M18.

flowing /ˈfləʊɪŋ/ *noun*. OE.

[ORIGIN from FLOW *verb* + -ING[1].]

1 The action of FLOW *verb*. OE.

2 †**a** An overflowing, a flood. ME–M17. ▸**b** That which flows or streams out; a stream, a wave. Now *rare*. LME.

flowing /ˈfləʊɪŋ/ *ppl adjective*. OE.

[ORIGIN from FLOW *verb* + -ING[2].]

1 That flows; gliding or running along. OE.

2 Rising like the tide; brimming, abundant, copious. E16.

R. BURNS All-cheering Plenty, with her flowing horn.

3 Of language or style: gliding easily or smoothly, fluent. M16. ▸**b** Of manner or demeanour: easy, graceful, smooth. E17.

G. HAKEWILL A great wit, and flowing eloquence.

4 Of hair, a garment, etc.: hanging easily and gracefully, streaming, unconfined. E17.

5 Of lines or contours: smoothly continuous, not rigid or abrupt. E18.

JAMES SMITH Tracery is . . flowing, where the lines branch out into leaves, arches, &c.

– SPECIAL COLLOCATIONS: **flowing sail** *NAUTICAL* a full unconfined sail. ***flowing sheet***: see SHEET *noun*[2].

■ **flowingly** *adverb* E17. **flowingness** *noun* E18.

flown /fləʊn/ *ppl adjective*[1]. *arch.* E16.

[ORIGIN Obsolete pa. pple of FLOW *verb*.]

1 In flood; *fig.* swollen (*with*), puffed up. Now only in allusion to Milton (see below). E16.

MILTON Then wander forth the Sons of Belial, flown with insolence and wine.

†**2** *NAUTICAL*. Of a sheet: slackened to allow free movement in the wind. E17–M18.

flown /fləʊn/ *ppl adjective*[2]. E16.

[ORIGIN pa. pple of FLY *verb*.]

That has flown or been flown. Also foll. by *out* and preceding adjective as ***far-flown***, ***new-flown***.

flown cover *PHILATELY* an envelope or cover dispatched by airmail.

flown *verb*[1] *pa. pple* of FLY *verb*.

†**flown** *verb*[2] *pa. pple* of FLOW *verb*.

FLQ *abbreviation*.

French *Front de Libération de Quebec* Quebec Liberation Front.

Flt Lt *abbreviation*.

Flight Lieutenant.

Flt Off. *abbreviation*. *hist.*

Flight Officer.

Flt Sgt *abbreviation*.

Flight Sergeant.

flu /fluː/ *noun*. Also **'flu**, †**flue**. M19.

[ORIGIN Abbreviation.]

Influenza or any similar, milder infection.

G. BARKER She's in bed, she's got the 'flu.

Asian flu: see ASIAN *adjective*. ***French flu***: see FRENCH *adjective*. GASTRIC ***flu***.

■ **fluey** *adjective*[1] suffering from flu L20. **flu-like** *adjective* M20.

†**fluate** *noun & verb*. L18.

[ORIGIN French, from *fluor* FLUORINE + -ATE[1].]

▸**A** *noun*. **1** = FLUORIDE. L18–M19.

2 A fluosilicate applied as a solution to building stone to make it harder and more durable. Only in L19.

▸**B** *verb trans.* Treat (stone) with fluate. Only in L19.

flub /flʌb/ *verb & noun*. *N. Amer. colloq.* E20.

[ORIGIN Unknown.]

▸**A** *verb trans.* & *intrans.* Infl. **-bb-**. Botch, bungle, mess *up*; perform badly. E20.

▸**B** *noun*. Something badly or clumsily done; a slip-up. M20.

flubdub /ˈflʌbdʌb/ *noun*. Chiefly *US*. L19.

[ORIGIN Unknown.]

Nonsense, undue fuss; bombastic or inept language.

R. KIPLING Any God's quantity of fuss and flubdub to bury a man.

†**fluce** *noun* var. of FLOOSE.

fluctuant /ˈflʌktjʊənt/ *adjective*. M16.

[ORIGIN Old French & mod. French, pres. pple of Old French *fluctuer* from Latin *fluctuare*: see FLUCTUATE, -ANT[1].]

1 Moving like waves. Chiefly *fig.*, unstable, wavering. M16.

R. L'ESTRANGE How is it possible for any man to be at rest in this fluctuant wandering humour and opinion?

2 Floating (as) on waves; buoyant. *rare*. E17.

BACON Fluctuant as the ark of Noah.

fluctuate /ˈflʌktʃʊeɪt, -tjʊ-/ *verb*. M17.

[ORIGIN Latin *fluctuat-* pa. ppl stem of *fluctuare* undulate, from *fluctus* current, flow, wave, from stem of *fluere* flow: see -ATE[3].]

1 *verb intrans.* Undulate; move like or (as) on waves. Now *rare* or *obsolete*. M17. ▸**b** *verb trans.* Unsettle; cause to undulate. *rare*. L18.

2 *verb intrans.* Vary irregularly, be unstable or unsettled; vacillate, waver. M17.

J. JAY The Committee . . fluctuates, new members constantly coming in, and old ones going out. V. WOOLF She fluctuated between irritation and interest.

fluctuation /flʌktʃʊˈeɪʃ(ə)n, -tjʊ-/ *noun*. LME.
[ORIGIN Old French & mod. French, or Latin *fluctuatio(n-)*, formed as FLUCTUATE: see -ATION.]
1 Vacillation, wavering; an instance of this. LME.
L. MURRAY We should be plunged into a state of uncertainty and fluctuation.
2 The action or condition of passing irregularly between one state and another; repeated variation. E17. ▸**b** An alternate rise and fall in amount or degree. E19.
I. D'ISRAELI Every modern language has always existed in fluctuation and change. **b** R. OWEN Fluctuations in the electricity supply . . render digital clocks inaccurate.
3 MEDICINE. Of a swelling: a consistency indicating the presence of fluid. E17.
4 *lit.* A wavelike motion. Now *rare*. M17.
■ **fluctuational** *adjective* of, pertaining to, or of the nature of fluctuation E20.

fluctuous /ˈflʌktjʊəs/ *adjective*. Now *rare* or *obsolete*. L16.
[ORIGIN Latin *fluctuosus* full of waves from *fluctus* wave: see -OUS.]
Full of, or resembling, waves.

flue /fluː/ *noun*[1]. Also **flew**. LME.
[ORIGIN Middle Dutch *vluwe* fishing net (Dutch *flouw* snipe net).]
A kind of fishing net, either fixed or towed. Also ***flue net***.

flue /fluː/ *noun*[2]. LME.
[ORIGIN Unknown.]
†**1** The mouthpiece of a hunting horn. Only in LME.
2 Orig., a chimney. Now, a smoke duct in a chimney, a duct allowing the exit of hot gases from a furnace etc.; a channel for conveying heat, esp. a hot-air passage in a wall; a tube for heating water in some kinds of boiler. L16.
N. GORDIMER Like torn paper drawn up a flue by the draught of flames.
3 The spout in a pawn shop. *slang*. E19.
in flue in pawn. **up the flue** (*a*) in pawn; (*b*) in a bad way, lost, dead.
4 The airway of a flue pipe in an organ. L19.
– COMB.: **flue-boiler** a boiler whose water space is traversed by flues; **flue-brush** a round or cylindrical brush of stiff bristle or wire for cleaning the inside of a chimney or flue; **flue-cure** *verb trans.* cure (tobacco) by artificial heat from flues; **flue-dust** dust which collects in the flue of a furnace; *spec.* metalliferous dust collected in the flue of a metallurgical furnace; **flue-gas** any mixture of gases from the flues of chemical or smelting factories; **flue pipe** an organ pipe into which air enters directly, i.e. without striking a reed; **flue-stop** an organ stop controlling a flue register; **flue-work** the flue-stops of an organ collectively.
■ **flued** *ppl adjective* having a flue or duct E19. **flueless** *adjective* E20.

flue /fluː/ *noun*[3]. L16.
[ORIGIN App. from Flemish *vluwe* of same meaning: cf. FLUFF *noun*[1].]
1 A woolly or downy substance; down, nap. L16.
Observer Nabokov . . wrote about the flue of a nymphet's arm.
2 Soft light particles, fluff. L18.
DICKENS Its old-established flue under its old-established four-post bedsteads.
■ **fluey** *adjective*[2] covered in flue E19.

†**flue** *noun*[4] var. of FLU.

flue /fluː/ *adjective*[1]. *obsolete* exc. *dial.* Also **flew**. LME.
[ORIGIN Unknown.]
1 Shallow. LME.
2 Having a wide opening, splayed. L17.

flue /fluː/ *adjective*[2]. *obsolete* exc. *dial.* Also **flew**. E17.
[ORIGIN Unknown.]
Weak, sickly, delicate.

flue /fluː/ *verb trans. & intrans.* L18.
[ORIGIN App. from FLUE *adjective*[1].]
Make or become wider or divergent; splay.

fluellen /flʊˈɛlɪn/ *noun*. Also **-in**. M16.
[ORIGIN Alt. of Welsh *llysiau Llywelyn* Llewelyn's herbs: cf. the personal name *Fluellen* (= Llewellyn) in Shakes.]
†**1** Any of several kinds of speedwell; *esp.* heath speedwell, *Veronica officinalis*. Also ***male fluellen***. M16–M18.
2 Either of two creeping yellow-flowered cornfield weeds allied to the snapdragon, *Kickxia spuria* (more fully ***round-leaved fluellen***), and *K. elatine* (more fully ***sharp-leaved fluellen***). Also †***female fluellen***. L16.

†**fluence** *noun*[1]. E17.
[ORIGIN formed as FLUENCY: see -ENCE.]
1 A stream. Only in E17.
2 A smooth and easy flow (of words etc.); readiness of utterance. Only in 17.

fluence /ˈfluːəns/ *noun*[2]. *colloq.* Also **'f-**. E20.
[ORIGIN Aphaeretic form of INFLUENCE *noun*.]
A mysterious, magical, or hypnotic power. Chiefly in ***put the fluence on*** (a person or thing).
M. PROCTER If ever I saw a girl trying to put the 'fluence on a fellow it was Tess.

fluency /ˈfluːənsi/ *noun*. E17.
[ORIGIN from FLUENT + -ENCY.]
†**1** Copiousness, abundance. E17–E18.
2 A smooth and easy flow (of words, wit, etc.); ready utterance; ease and readiness in speech etc. M17.
J. W. EBSWORTH The genuine sweetness and musical fluency of his best lyrics. J. BARZUN Thanks to his fluency in French and German he was able . . to make his ideas known.

fluent /ˈfluːənt/ *adjective & noun*. L16.
[ORIGIN Latin *fluent-* pres. ppl stem of *fluere* flow: see -ENT.]
▸ **A** *adjective* **1** †**a** Flowing freely or abundantly; abounding *in*. L16–L17. ▸**b** Giving freely; generous. Long *obsolete* exc. *dial.* E17. ▸**c** Of hair: abundant, flowing. *arch. & poet.* E17.
2 Articulate, expressing oneself quickly and easily; *esp.* able to speak a (specified) foreign language easily and without hesitation. L16. ▸**b** Of speech, style, etc.: flowing easily and readily. Of language: used with skill; *esp.* (of a foreign language) spoken with facility. E17. ▸**c** Of movement etc.: easy, graceful; not rigid or stiff. M19.
A. G. GARDINER Fluent talkers are not necessarily good conversationalists. **b** GEO. ELIOT A soft voice with a clear fluent utterance. R. GRAVES Criccieth's mayor addressed them First in good Welsh and then in fluent English. **c** E. HEMINGWAY He . . played a smoothly fluent game of billiards that contrasted with his own ninety-four-year-old brittleness.
3 Of a liquid, stream, etc.: that flows; flowing. Now chiefly *transf. & fig.* E17.
J. S. C. ABBOTT Masses of cavalry, in fluent and refluent surges.
4 (Of a substance) ready to flow, fluid; *fig.* not settled, liable to change. *arch.* E17.
WORDSWORTH His quick hand bestowed On fluent operations a fixed shape. E. B. BROWNING The broad, fluent strata of pure air.
5 MATH. Continuously increasing or decreasing infinitesimally. *arch.* M18.
▸ **B** *noun*. †**1** A current of water, a stream. L16–E18.
2 MATH. A fluent quantity (see sense A.5 above). *arch.* M18.
■ †**fluential** *adjective* (MATH.) = FLUENT *adjective* 5 L18–E19. **fluently** *adverb* E17.

fluff /flʌf/ *noun*[1]. L18.
[ORIGIN Prob. dial. var. of FLUE *noun*[3]. Cf. Flemish *vluwe* fluff, Dutch *fluweel* velvet.]
1 Any light, loosely adhering, or flocculent material, such as that which separates from blankets etc. L18. ▸**b** Soft fur or down. L19.
E. O'BRIEN I saw fluff and dust . . under the bed.
2 A piece of downy or feathery material; a soft or downy mass or bunch. M19.
J. R. LOWELL Tiny fluffs of feathered life. T. HARDY All this fluff of muslin about you.
3 A mistake made in speaking, playing music, a game, etc.; orig. & freq. THEATRICAL, a mistake in delivering one's lines. *colloq.* L19.
Daily Telegraph In spite of a surprising number of fluffs, there was some excellent playing.
4 Something unimportant, a trifle; *collect.* trivia. E20.
American Notes & Queries The more immediate monetary rewards to be gained by starring in a piece of unchallenging romantic fluff.
– PHRASES: ***bit of fluff***: see BIT *noun*[2] 6.

fluff /flʌf/ *verb*[1] *& noun*[2]. *Scot. & N. English*. L18.
[ORIGIN Imit.]
▸ **A** *verb*. **1** *verb intrans. & trans.* (in *pass.*) (Cause to) puff, pant. L18. ▸**b** *verb trans.* Blow *out* (a candle etc.). E20.
2 *verb intrans.* Flutter; move in the wind. E19.
3 *verb intrans.* Make a fuss. M19.
▸ **B** *noun*. A puff, a whiff; a short blast, a small explosion. E19.

fluff /flʌf/ *verb*[2]. E19.
[ORIGIN from FLUFF *noun*[1].]
1 *slang*. **a** *verb trans.* Falsify, disguise the defects of, obscure. E19. ▸**b** *verb intrans.* Bluff, lie. E20.
H. WILSON To reach a clear decision, with nothing fluffed or obscure. **b** M. GILBERT Watch him . . he's fluffing . . . He's acting. Dangerous man.
2 *verb intrans.* Obtain money by devious means; give short change, solicit tips. *Railway slang*. L19.
3 *verb intrans. & trans.* Make or become fluffy; shake or be shaken *up* or *out* into a soft fluffy mass. L19.
N. BLAKE Birds huddled in the snow-laden hedges, their plumage fluffed out. K. HOM There is no need to 'fluff' the rice before serving it.
4 *verb trans.* Make into fluff. L19.
5 *verb trans.* Put a soft surface on (the flesh side of leather). L19.
6 *verb intrans.* Move or float softly; settle *down* like a ball of fluff. L19.
W. C. RUSSELL A fog . . fluffing thick and soft as feathers about the ship.
7 *verb trans. & intrans.* Make a mistake esp. in a game or performance; blunder, bungle, fail. *colloq.* L19.
Daily Telegraph The very best the Minister can hope for is that he will not fluff lines given to him by his officials. DAY LEWIS I kept fluffing when I practised them [songs].

fluffy /ˈflʌfi/ *adjective*. E19.
[ORIGIN from FLUFF *noun*[1] + -Y[1].]
1 Consisting of or resembling fluff; soft, downy. E19.
2 Covered with fluff, down, fur, or the like. M19.
3 Frivolous, silly, feather-brained; *spec.* (THEATRICAL) unsure of one's lines. *colloq.* L19.
C. SHIELDS Only deeply fluffy people have romances.
■ **fluffily** *adverb* E20. **fluffiness** *noun* M19.

flugelhorn /ˈfluːg(ə)lhɔːn/ *noun*. M19.
[ORIGIN German *Flügelhorn*, from *Flügel* wing + *Horn* HORN *noun*.]
A brass wind instrument with a cup-shaped mouthpiece and a wide conical bore.

F

fluid /ˈfluːɪd/ *adjective & noun*. LME.
[ORIGIN Old French & mod. French *fluide* or Latin *fluidus* from *fluere* flow: see -ID[1].]
▸ **A** *adjective*. **1** Flowing or moving readily, not solid or rigid; PHYSICS (of a substance) that consists of particles moving freely among themselves, has no fixed shape, and yields easily to external pressure; *fig.* changing readily, not settled or stable. LME.
C. LUCAS The salt fuses readily, and runs very fluid. H. ARENDT Shifting and fluid cliques of society. W. S. CHURCHILL A moment of great hesitancy . . , when everything was fluid and uncertain.
†**2** Of speech etc.: fluent. L17–L18.
3 Operating by means of a liquid; that uses a liquid to transmit power. M19.
fluid clutch, ***fluid coupling***, ***fluid drive***, ***fluid flywheel***, etc.
▸ **B** *noun*. **1** A fluid substance; a liquid, a gas; *esp.* a liquid preparation having a specified purpose. M17.
brake fluid, ***cleaning fluid***, etc. ***ideal fluid***: see IDEAL *adjective*.
2 *spec.* A liquid constituent or secretion of a living organism. E18.
cerebrospinal fluid, ***seminal fluid***, ***synovial fluid***, etc.
3 Any of various all-pervading substances postulated to account for physical phenomena. Chiefly *hist.* M18.
– SPECIAL COLLOCATIONS & COMB.: **fluid amplifier** a device in which small changes in a low-energy flow of fluid produce corresponding changes in a much larger flow. **fluid dram**, **fluid drachm** a unit of liquid capacity: in Britain, equal to ⅛ fluid ounce (0.217 cu. in., 3.56 cc); in the US equal to 0.225 cu. in., 3.69 cc (see also FLUIDRAM). **fluid extract**, (*US*. **fluidextract**) a concentrated solution (usu. in alcohol) of the active principle of a vegetable drug prepared to a standard strength. **fluid gram** a unit of liquid capacity equal to 1 cm³: see also FLUIGRAM. **fluid mechanics** the branch of mechanics that deals with the flow of fluids and the way they respond to and exert forces. **fluid ounce**, (*US*. **fluidounce**) a unit of liquid capacity: in Britain equal to 1/20 imperial pint (1.734 cu. in., 28.42 cc), in the US equal to 1/16 US pint (1.804 cu. in., 29.56 cc).
■ **fluidly** *adverb* L17. **fluidness** *noun* (*rare*) M17.

fluidal /ˈfluːɪd(ə)l/ *adjective*. L19.
[ORIGIN from FLUID + -AL[1].]
Of or pertaining to fluids or flowing; *spec.* (of rocks) showing evidence of a former fluid state.

fluidible /ˈfluːɪdɪb(ə)l/ *adjective*. E20.
[ORIGIN from FLUID + -IBLE.]
Capable of changing shape like a fluid under pressure.

fluidic /fluːˈɪdɪk/ *adjective*. L19.
[ORIGIN from FLUID + -IC.]
1 Of the nature of a fluid. L19.
2 SPIRITUALISM. Of or pertaining to the astral body. L19.
3 Of or pertaining to fluidics. M20.

fluidics /fluːˈɪdɪks/ *noun pl.* (usu. treated as *sing.*). M20.
[ORIGIN from FLUID + -ICS: see -IC.]
The technique of using small interacting flows and fluid jets to perform functions or operate systems; the branch of technology that deals with this.

fluidify /fluːˈɪdɪfʌɪ/ *verb trans.* M19.
[ORIGIN from FLUID + -I- + -FY.]
Make (a substance) fluid.
■ **fluidifiˈcation** *noun* M20.

fluidise *verb* var. of FLUIDIZE.

fluidism /ˈfluːɪdɪz(ə)m/ *noun*. M19.
[ORIGIN from FLUID + -ISM.]
1 The theory which refers all diseases to the state of the bodily fluids. *obsolete* exc. *hist.* M19.
2 SPIRITUALISM. The hypothesis of the existence of supersensible fluidic bodies. L19.
■ **fluidist** *noun* a believer in fluidism (either sense) L19.

fluidity /fluːˈɪdɪti/ *noun*. E17.
[ORIGIN from FLUID + -ITY.]
1 The quality, condition, or degree of being fluid. E17.
2 The quality (of speech, movement, etc.) of flowing smoothly, fluency. E17.
3 *transf. & fig.*: The ability or tendency to change; flexibility, instability. E19.

fluidize /ˈfluːɪdʌɪz/ *verb.* Also **-ise**. E19.
[ORIGIN from FLUID + -IZE.]
1 *verb intrans.* & *trans.* Make or become fluid. E19.
2 Cause (a mass of finely divided solid) to acquire the characteristics of a fluid by the upward passage of gas etc. through it. M20.
■ **fluidiˈzation** *noun* the process of fluidizing; the state of being fluidized: M20. **fluidizer** *noun* an apparatus in which fluidization is carried out M20.

fluidram /ˈfluːɪdram/ *noun. US.* Also **-drachm**. M19.
[ORIGIN Contr.]
= ***FLUID dram***.

fluigram /ˈfluːɪgram/ *noun. US.* Also **-gramme**. L19.
[ORIGIN Contr.]
= ***fluid gram*** s.v. FLUID.

fluke /fluːk/ *noun*[1].
[ORIGIN Old English *flōc*, corresp. to Old Norse *flóki*, rel. by ablaut to Middle Low German, Middle Dutch *flac*, Old High German *flah* (German *flach*) flat.]
1 A flatfish; *esp.* a flounder. Now chiefly *dial.* OE.
2 Any of various parasitic flatworms (trematodes); *esp.* (also ***liver fluke***) *Fasciola hepatica*, which occurs in the livers of affected sheep and has an intermediate stage in snails of the genus *Limnaea*. M17.
3 A variety of kidney potato. M19.
■ **fluked** *adjective* = FLUKY *adjective*[1] M19.

fluke /fluːk/ *noun*[2]. M16.
[ORIGIN Perh. from FLUKE *noun*[1], from the shape.]
1 Either of the broad triangular plates on the arms of an anchor. M16. ▸**b** A barb or the barbed head of an arrow, lance, harpoon, etc. E17.
2 Either of the two lobes of a whale's tail. E18.

fluke /fluːk/ *noun*[3]. M19.
[ORIGIN Uncertain: perh. of dial. origin.]
1 Orig. in BILLIARDS and other games: a chance lucky stroke. Now more widely: a piece of luck, an unexpected success, an unlikely chance occurrence. M19.

> CLIVE JAMES A swimming pool which by some fluke did not contain a floating body. ***attrib.***: *Daily Chronicle* It was no fluke victory.

2 A puff *of* wind, a chance breeze. L19.

> QUILLER-COUCH Swaying this way and that . . as corn is swayed by flukes of summer wind.

fluke /fluːk/ *verb*[1]. M19.
[ORIGIN from FLUKE *noun*[2].]
1 *verb intrans.* Of a whale: use the flukes in swimming, dive showing the flukes. M19.
2 *verb trans.* Secure (a whale carcass) by a rope or chain around the tail. L19.

fluke /fluːk/ *verb*[2] *trans.* & *intrans.* M19.
[ORIGIN from FLUKE *noun*[3].]
Orig. in BILLIARDS and other games: achieve by or make a lucky stroke. Now more widely: do, get, etc., (something) by luck rather than skill.

> *Times* Bennett . . tried for a cannon, but fluked the white. N. GOULD Even if he managed to fluke home in this trial. J. I. M. STEWART If I did fluke a place at Oxford.

fluky /ˈfluːki/ *adjective*[1]. Also **-ey**. M19.
[ORIGIN from FLUKE *noun*[1] + -Y[1].]
Infested with parasitic flukes.

fluky /ˈfluːki/ *adjective*[2]. Also **-ey**. M19.
[ORIGIN from FLUKE *noun*[3] + -Y[1].]
Lucky, obtained by chance rather than skill. Of wind etc.: erratic, uncertain.
■ **flukily** *adverb* L19. **flukiness** *noun* L19.

flume /fluːm/ *noun.* ME.
[ORIGIN Old French *flum*, *flun* from Latin *flumen* river, from *fluere* to flow.]
†**1** A river, a stream; water. ME–M17.
2 An artificial channel conveying water etc. for industrial use, esp. for the transport of logs or timber. M18. ▸**b** A water chute used as a fairground ride etc.; a water slide. L20.

> B. TAYLOR Wooden flumes, raised on tall tressels, brought water . . to the diggings.

3 A deep narrow channel or ravine with a stream running through it. Orig. *US.* L18.
– PHRASES: **be up the flume** *US slang* have come to grief, be dead. **go up the flume** *US slang* come to grief, die.

flume /fluːm/ *verb.* M19.
[ORIGIN from the noun.]
1 *verb intrans.* Build flumes for a watercourse. M19.
2 *verb trans.* Convey in a flume. L19.
3 Take water from (a river etc.) by means of a flume. L19.

flummadiddle /ˈflʌmədɪd(ə)l/ *noun. US.* Also **flummer-**, **fum(m)a-** /ˈfʌmə-/, & other vars. M19.
[ORIGIN Prob. from FLUMMERY *noun*.]
1 A dish made with stale bread, pork fat, molasses, and spices, baked in the oven. M19.
2 Nonsense, humbug; something trivial or ridiculous. M19.

flummer /ˈflʌmə/ *verb trans.* Now *rare* or *obsolete*. In sense 2 also **flummery** /flʌm(ə)ri/. M16.
[ORIGIN Sense 1 prob. imit.; in sense 2 perh. back-form. from FLUMMERY *noun*.]
†**1** Repeat indistinctly, mumble. Only in M16.
2 Flatter; deceive by flattery. M18.

flummerdiddle *noun* var. of FLUMMADIDDLE.

flummery /ˈflʌm(ə)ri/ *noun.* E17.
[ORIGIN Welsh *llymru*, perh. rel. to *llymrig* bare, soft, slippery.]
1 A dish made with boiled, jellied oatmeal or wheatmeal. E17. ▸**b** Any of various sweet dishes made with milk, flour, eggs, gelatin, etc. L17.
2 Flattery, empty compliment; nonsense, humbug. M18. ▸**b** *collect.* Trifles, useless trappings or ornaments. L19.

> THACKERAY These petitioners . . begin with a fine flummery about the . . eminent genius of the person whom they are addressing. **b** A. FRASER Even the celebration of Christmas was denounced as being a piece of Popish flummery.

flummery *verb* see FLUMMER.

flummox /ˈflʌməks/ *verb. colloq.* Also **-ux**. M19.
[ORIGIN Prob. dial., imit.]
1 *verb trans.* Bewilder, confuse, confound, perplex, disconcert. M19.

> M. AMIS I sat flummoxed and muttering like a superannuated ghost. ***absol.***: L. MACNEICE Voices that flummox and fool.

2 *verb intrans.* Give in, give up, collapse. *US.* M19.

> D. P. THOMPSON If he should flummox at such a chance, I know of a chap . . who'll agree to take his place.

flump /flʌmp/ *noun.* M18.
[ORIGIN from the verb.]
The action or sound of flumping; a heavy dull thud.

flump /flʌmp/ *verb.* E17.
[ORIGIN Imit.]
1 *verb intrans.* Fall or move heavily, flop *down*, with a dull noise. E17.
2 *verb trans.* Set or throw *down* with a soft thud. E19.

flung *verb pa. t.* & *pple* of FLING *verb*.

flunk /flʌŋk/ *verb* & *noun.* Orig. *US.* E19.
[ORIGIN Uncertain: cf. FUNK *noun*[3] & *verb*[2].]
▸ **A** *verb.* **1** *verb intrans.* Give up, back down, fail utterly (also foll. by *out*). E19. ▸**b** *spec.* Fail in an examination; (foll. by *out*) leave or be dismissed from school etc. because of academic failure. M19.

> **b** M. J. BRUCCOLI Fitzgerald came close to flunking out . . when he failed three of his six courses.

2 *verb trans.* Fail (an examination); reject (an examination candidate). M19.

> *Times* I was utterly . . depressed and flunked my A levels. A. MILLER If you don't start studyin' math he's gonna flunk you, and you won't graduate.

▸ **B** *noun.* A complete failure, esp. in an examination. M19.
■ **flunker** *noun* a person who fails an examination L19.

flunkey /ˈflʌŋki/ *noun*[1]. Orig. *Scot.* Also **-ky**. M18.
[ORIGIN Perh. rel. to FLANKER 'a person who stands at one's flank': see -Y[6].]
1 A liveried manservant, a footman; a menial attendant. Usu. *derog.* M18.

> A. CARTER A braided, bewigged flunkey brought us a silver bucket of iced champagne. H. ROBBINS Now he wants me to buy him some flowers for a dame . . . I'm nothing but a flunkey around here.

2 An obsequious or fawning person; a toady, a snob. M19.
3 A cook, kitchen-hand, or waiter. *US.* E20.
■ **flunkeydom** *noun* the domain of flunkeys; flunkeys collectively; the spirit of a flunkey: M19. **flunkeyiˈana** *noun collect.* the sayings or characteristics of flunkeys M19. **flunkeyism** *noun* the manner, speech, etc., of a flunkey M19.

flunkey /ˈflʌŋki/ *noun*[2]. *US.* M19.
[ORIGIN from FLUNK + -Y[6].]
A person who fails, esp. in an examination; one who comes to grief through ignorance, a mug.

fluo- /ˈfluːəʊ/ *combining form* of FLUORINE: see -O-. Cf. FLUORO-.
■ **fluoˈborate** *noun* a salt of fluoboric acid, containing the anion BF_4^- E19. **fluoˈboric** *adjective* containing fluorine and boron; esp. in ***fluoboric acid***, a strong acid, HBF_4, known only in aqueous solution: E19. **fluoˈcerite** *noun* (MINERALOGY) a hexagonal fluoride of cerium, lanthanum, and related elements, usu. occurring as colourless to pink prisms or tabular crystals M19. **fluoˈphosphate** *noun* a mineral or other substance that is both a fluoride and a phosphate L19. **fluoˈsilicate** *noun* a salt of fluosilicic acid, containing the anion SiF_6^{2-} M19. **fluosiˈlicic** *adjective*: ***fluosilicic acid***, a strong acid, H_2SiF_6, known in aqueous solution or as hydrates E19.

fluor /ˈfluːə/ *noun.* E17.
[ORIGIN Latin = flow, from *fluere* to flow: see -OR. Cf. French †*flueur*.]
†**1** In *pl.* The menstrual discharge. Cf. FLOWER *noun* 10. E–M17.
†**2** A flow, a flowing; a stream; an effluvium. M–L17.
†**3** A fluid state; a fluid mass; (in *pl.*) 'the humours' of the body. M17–E18.
4 MINERALOGY. **a** [translating German *Fluss*.] Any mineral of a kind less hard and more fusible than gems. Long *obsolete* exc. *hist.* M17. ▸**b** A fluorine-containing mineral of this kind. Now *spec.* = FLUORSPAR. *arch.* L18.

fluor- *combining form* see FLUORO-.

fluoranthene /flʊəˈranθiːn/ *noun.* L19.
[ORIGIN from FLUORO- (the compound fluoresces) + PHEN)ANTH(R)ENE.]
CHEMISTRY. A crystalline tetracyclic aromatic hydrocarbon, $C_{16}H_{10}$, obtained from coal tar; any derivative of this.

fluorated /ˈflʊəreɪtɪd/ *adjective.* L18.
[ORIGIN from FLUOR- + -ATE[2] + -ED[1].]
CHEMISTRY. Combined with fluorine or hydrofluoric acid.

fluorene /ˈflʊəriːn/ *noun.* L19.
[ORIGIN from FLUORO- (the compound fluoresces) + -ENE.]
CHEMISTRY. A crystalline tricyclic aromatic hydrocarbon, $C_{13}H_{10}$, obtained from coal tar; any derivative of this.

fluoresce /flʊəˈrɛs/ *verb intrans.* L19.
[ORIGIN Back-form. from FLUORESCENCE.]
Exhibit fluorescence, be fluorescent.
■ **fluorescer** *noun* a fluorescent substance E20.

fluorescein /ˈflʊərəsiːn, -sɪn/ *noun.* L19.
[ORIGIN from FLUORESCENCE + -EIN.]
CHEMISTRY. An orange-red crystalline solid, $C_{20}H_{12}O_5$, obtained by reaction of resorcinol and phthalic anhydride, which exhibits greenish-yellow fluorescence in visible light, is often used in solution as a marker or indicator, and has antiseptic properties.

fluorescence /flʊəˈrɛs(ə)ns, flɔː-/ *noun.* M19.
[ORIGIN from FLUORSPAR (which exhibits this property) + -ESCENCE.]
Electromagnetic radiation emitted by certain substances when they are subject to incident radiation (esp. violet or ultraviolet light or X-rays), electrons, or other particles; the property of absorbing light of short (freq. invisible) wavelength and emitting light of longer (visible) wavelength. Cf. PHOSPHORESCENCE.

fluorescent /flʊəˈrɛs(ə)nt, flɔː-/ *adjective.* M19.
[ORIGIN formed as FLUORESCENCE + -ESCENT.]
Having the property of or emitting fluorescence; pertaining to, resulting from, or of the nature of fluorescence.
fluorescent lamp, **fluorescent light**, etc.: in which light is produced by fluorescence; *esp.* a discharge tube in which a phosphor on the inside of the tube is made to fluoresce by ultraviolet light from mercury vapour. **fluorescent screen** a screen coated with fluorescent material for displaying images produced by incident X-rays, electrons, or other radiation.
■ **fluorescently** *adverb* M20.

fluorian /ˈflʊərɪən/ *adjective.* M20.
[ORIGIN from FLUORINE + -IAN.]
MINERALOGY. Having a constituent element partly replaced by fluorine.

fluoric /ˈflʊərɪk/ *adjective.* L18.
[ORIGIN French †*fluorique*, from *fluor* FLUOR: see -IC.]
Of fluorine or fluorspar; †***fluoric acid***, hydrofluoric acid.

fluoridate /ˈflʊərɪdeɪt, ˈflɔː-/ *verb.* M20.
[ORIGIN Back-form. from FLUORIDATION.]
1 *verb trans.* & *intrans.* Add traces of a fluoride or other source of fluoride ions to (water, toothpaste, food, etc.) in order to reduce or prevent tooth decay. M20.
2 *verb trans.* Treat (teeth) with a preparation containing fluoride. M20.

fluoridation /flʊərɪˈdeɪʃ(ə)n, flɔː-/ *noun.* E20.
[ORIGIN from FLUORIDE + -ATION.]
1 The process by which a mineral absorbs fluorine. E20.
2 The addition of traces of a fluoride to drinking water to prevent or reduce tooth decay. M20.
3 = FLUORIDIZATION 2. M20.
■ **fluoridationist** *noun* a person who advocates the fluoridation of public water supplies M20.

fluoride /ˈflʊərʌɪd, flɔː-/ *noun.* E19.
[ORIGIN from FLUORINE + -IDE.]
CHEMISTRY. A compound of fluorine with a less electronegative element or radical; a salt or ester of hydrofluoric acid.

fluoridization /ˌflʊərɪdʌɪˈzeɪʃ(ə)n, ˌflɔː-/ *noun.* Also **-isation**. M20.
[ORIGIN from FLUORIDE + -IZATION.]
1 = FLUORIDATION 2. M20.
2 The application of a fluoride to the teeth to prevent or reduce decay. M20.
■ **fluoridize** *verb trans.* M20.

fluorimeter /flʊəˈrɪmɪtə/ *noun.* E20.
[ORIGIN from FLUOR(ESCENCE + -IMETER.]
= FLUOROMETER 2.
■ **fluoriˈmetric** *adjective* L20. **fluoriˈmetrically** *adverb* M20. **fluoˈrimetry** *noun* E20.

fluorinate /ˈflʊərɪneɪt, ˈflɔː-/ *verb trans.* M20.
[ORIGIN from FLUORINE + -ATE[3].]
Treat with fluorine; CHEMISTRY introduce one or more fluorine atoms into (a compound or molecule), usu. in place of hydrogen. Also, fluoridate. Freq. as ***fluorinated*** *ppl adjective*.
■ **fluoriˈnation** *noun* M20.

fluorine /ˈflʊəriːn, ˈflɔː-/ *noun*. E19.
[ORIGIN from FLUOR + -INE[5].]
An extremely reactive pale yellow gaseous chemical element, atomic no. 9, belonging to the halogen group (symbol F).

fluorite /ˈflʊərʌɪt, ˈflɔː-/ *noun*. M19.
[ORIGIN from FLUOR + -ITE[1].]
MINERALOGY. = FLUORSPAR.

fluoro- /ˈflʊərəʊ, ˈflɔː-/ *combining form* of FLUORINE (less commonly FLUORIDE) or FLUORESCENCE: see -O-. Before a vowel also **fluor-**. Cf. FLUO-.
■ **fluoˈrapatite** *noun* (*MINERALOGY*) a variety of apatite containing a substantially higher proportion of fluorine than of chlorine M19. **fluoroˈcarbon** *noun* any of a large class of synthetic, chemically stable compounds of carbon and fluorine M20. **fluorochrome** *noun* a chemical that fluoresces, esp. one used as a label in biological research M20. **ˈfluoroform** *noun* an unreactive gas, CHF_3, that is the fluorine analogue of chloroform L19. **fluorophoˈtometer** *noun* a fluorometer (sense 2) incorporating a photometer E20. **fluorophotoˈmetric** *adjective* of or pertaining to fluorophotometry M20. **fluorophoˈtometry** *noun* the use of the fluorophotometer M20. **fluoroˈpolymer** *noun* an organic polymer containing fluorine atoms, such as PTFE M20. **fluoroˈquinolone** an antibiotic used esp. in the treatment of systemic infections L20. **fluoˈrosis** *noun* (a diseased state due to) poisoning by a fluorine compound E20.

fluorometer /flʊəˈrɒmɪtə, flɔː-/ *noun*. L19.
[ORIGIN from FLUORO- + -METER.]
1 A device used to measure the intensity of a fluoroscopic image. L19.
2 An instrument for measuring the intensity or other property of fluorescence. E20.
■ **fluoroˈmetric** *adjective* of or pertaining to the fluorometer (sense 2) or fluorometry E20. **fluoroˈmetrically** *adverb* M20. **fluorometry** *noun* the use of a fluorometer (sense 2) E20.

fluoroscope /ˈflʊərəskəʊp, ˈflɔː-/ *noun*. L19.
[ORIGIN from FLUORO- + -SCOPE.]
An instrument with a fluorescent screen which is used with an X-ray source to give a visible X-ray image of an object.
■ **fluoroˈscopic** *adjective* of or pertaining to a fluoroscope or fluoroscopy L19. **fluoroˈscopically** *adverb* M20. **fluoˈroscopy** *noun* the use of a fluoroscope L19.

fluorspar /ˈflʊəspɑː/ *noun*. L18.
[ORIGIN from FLUOR + SPAR *noun*[3].]
Calcium fluoride, CaF_2, occurring as a transparent or translucent mineral (colourless when pure but often variously coloured by impurities) which crystallizes in the cubic system and is used ornamentally and as a metallurgical flux. Cf. FLUOR *noun* 4b.

fluoxetine /fluːˈɒksətiːn/ *noun*. L20.
[ORIGIN from FLU(ORO- + OX(Y- + -*etine* (perh. from *e-* + *t-* (in TOLYL) + AM)INE).]
PHARMACOLOGY. A synthetic compound which selectively inhibits the uptake of serotonin in the brain and is given orally for the treatment of depression; *N*-methyl-3-(*p*-trifluoromethylphenoxy)-3-phenylpropylamine, $C_{17}H_{18}F_3NO$.
– NOTE: A proprietary name for this drug is PROZAC.

fluphenazine /fluːˈfɛnəziːn/ *noun*. M20.
[ORIGIN from FLU(ORO- + PHEN(OTHI)AZINE.]
PHARMACOLOGY. A phenothiazine derivative, $C_{22}H_{26}F_3N_3OS$, used as a tranquillizer.
– NOTE: A proprietary name for this drug in the US is PROLIXIN.

flurazepam /flʊəˈreɪzɪpam, -ˈraz-/ *noun*. M20.
[ORIGIN from FLU(O)R(O- after DIAZEPAM.]
PHARMACOLOGY. A benzodiazepine widely used as a hypnotic.

flurr /flɜː/ *verb*. Now *rare* or *obsolete*. M17.
[ORIGIN Imit.]
1 *verb trans.* Scatter, throw about. M17.
2 *verb intrans.* Fly up; whirr, flutter. L17.

flurry /ˈflʌri/ *noun & verb*. L17.
[ORIGIN from FLURR, prob. after HURRY *noun*, *verb*.]
▸ **A** *noun*. **1** A sudden agitation of the air; a gust or squall. L17. ▸**b** A sudden shower (*of* snow, rain, etc.); a rush (*of* birds etc.). Orig. *US*. L17.

SWIFT The boat was overset by a sudden flurry from the north. **b** P. G. WODEHOUSE A scrambling flurry of blows at close quarters, and then . . they fell together. V. BRITTAIN An icy wind drove flurries of snow into my face.

2 A sudden commotion or excitement; nervous agitation or hurry; a sudden burst of activity. E18.

W. IRVING How happy I was to . . leave behind me the hurry and worry and flurry of the city.

▸ **B** *verb*. **1** *verb trans.* Confuse or agitate (as) by haste, noise, etc. M18.

F. BURNEY This flurried me violently, insomuch that my memory failed me.

2 *verb intrans.* Agitate the air; come down in flurries. L19.

E. P. ROE The petals of the cherry were flurrying down like snow in every passing breeze.

■ **flurriedly** *adverb* in a flurried manner M19.

flus *noun* var. of FLOOSE.

flush /flʌʃ/ *noun*[1]. LME.
[ORIGIN Var. of FLASH *noun*[1].]
A pool, a marshy place; = FLASH *noun*[1] 1. Now chiefly *ECOLOGY*, a piece of wet ground over which water flows but not in a definite channel.

flush /flʌʃ/ *noun*[2]. E16.
[ORIGIN Rel. to FLUSH *verb*[1].]
▸ **I 1** A sudden rush of water, esp. as caused for a specific purpose. E16. ▸**b** The stream from a mill wheel. E19.
2 A (sudden) abundance or rush (*of* anything); *esp.* (**a**) a rush of emotion, elation produced by success, victory, etc., (**b**) a fresh growth (of grass etc.), freshness, vigour. Freq. ***in the first flush***, ***in full flush***. E16. ▸**b** A flight of birds suddenly started up. L16.

J. T. STORY You do things in the early flush of marriage that you prefer to forget later on. P. V. WHITE Let me bring you the roses . . There's such a flush. D. ATTENBOROUGH The frogs feast on the great flush of insects that have . . come with the rain.

3 The action of or a device for cleansing a drain, water closet, etc., by flushing. L19.

C. BEATON Her lavatory . . equipped with a gold handle which one pulled . . to bring about a discreetly gurgling flush of water.

attrib.: ***flush lavatory***, ***flush toilet***, etc.

▸ **II 4** A glow of light or colour; *esp.* (a rush of blood causing) a reddening of the face, neck, etc. M17.

A. GUINNESS I felt an angry flush beginning to rise to my face.

hectic flush: occurring in some wasting diseases. ***hot flush***: see HOT *adjective*.

flush /flʌʃ/ *noun*[3]. E16.
[ORIGIN French †*flus*, *flux* (whence Flemish *fluys* and Spanish *flux*, Italian †*flusso*) from Latin *fluxus* FLUX *noun*.]
CARDS. A hand of cards all of one suit, or including a prescribed number of one suit.
royal flush, **royal straight flush** *POKER* a straight flush headed by an ace. **straight flush** a flush that is also a sequence.

flush /flʌʃ/ *adjective*[1]. M16.
[ORIGIN Prob. rel. to FLUSH *verb*[1].]
1 †**a** Lacking nothing, perfect. Only in M16. ▸**b** Full to overflowing; *esp.* (of a stream etc.) in flood. E17. ▸**c** Full of life or enthusiasm; vigorous. Now *rare* or *obsolete*. E17.

c H. BROOKE Both appeared quite flush and confident of victory.

2 Plentifully supplied, esp. with money (foll. by *with*, *of*); prosperous; (of money) plentiful. L16. ▸**b** Lavish, generous. *dial.* E18.

P. KAVANAGH Money was flush in those days and flowed . . freely. N. MAILER If . . you are flush and have a few dollars to spare, I'm sure my mother could use it.

3 Blushing; flushed. *arch.* L16.

M. DRAYTON Thy Cheeke, now flush with Roses.

4 Even, level, in the same plane (*with* the adjacent surface); *spec.* (of a ship's deck) on one level. E17. ▸**b** *TYPOGRAPHY*. Not indented or protruding. E20.

J. GRANT The original castle starts flush from the edge of the rock. B. COTTLE The one high-walled mansion not flush with the line of the town street.

– COMB.: **flush-decker** a ship with a flush deck.
■ **flushness** *noun* M17. **flushy** *adjective* (now *rare*) E18.

flush /flʌʃ/ *adjective*[2]. L16.
[ORIGIN from FLUSH *noun*[3].]
CARDS. Orig., (of a player) holding a flush. Now usu. (of a hand or sequence) forming or including a flush.

flush /flʌʃ/ *verb*[1]. ME.
[ORIGIN Prob. imit. Perh. infl. by FLASH *verb*.]
1 *verb intrans.* Move rapidly, dart, spring; *esp.* (of a bird) fly up suddenly, start up. ME. ▸†**b** Of people: rush, swarm. LME–M17.

F. NORRIS With a startling rush of wings, a covey of quail flushed from the brush.

2 *verb trans.* Cause (esp. a game bird) to fly or start up; put up. L15. ▸**b** Reveal; bring into the open; drive *out*. M20.

P. SCOTT A plan for flushing the tiger and driving it . . on to the guns. **b** R. H. MORRIESON The enthralled hush . . flushed a still sulking Herbert out of the bedroom.

3 *verb intrans.* & *trans.* (Cause to) spurt, rush out or flow with sudden violence. Now *rare*. M16.

J. RAY Milk . . heated to such a degree doth suddenly . . flush up and run over.

4 *verb intrans.* Of blood: rush into and redden the face etc.; (of the face etc.) become red or hot, blush. L16. ▸**b** *verb trans.* Make red or ruddy; cause to blush or colour. Chiefly as ***flushed*** *ppl adjective*. L17.

DRYDEN What means . . That blood, which flushes guilty in your face? H. JAMES She thrilled, she consciously flushed, and all to turn pale again. **b** W. COWPER Flushed with drunkenness.

5 *verb intrans.* & *trans.* (Cause to) glow *with* colour, light, etc. M17.

J. R. LOWELL A meadow flushed with primroses.

6 *verb trans.* Inflame with pride or passion; encourage. Chiefly as ***flushed*** *ppl adjective*. M17.

BURKE Flushed with the insolence of their first inglorious victories.

7 *verb trans.* Fatten *up* (sheep); stimulate (ewes) with a good diet in the breeding season. M18.
8 *verb trans.* Cleanse (a drain, lavatory, etc.) by a flow of water; dispose of anything thus (foll. by *away*, *down*). L18. ▸**b** Flood (a meadow etc.). M19.
9 *verb intrans.* Of a plant: send out shoots. E19. ▸**b** *verb trans.* Cause (a plant) to send out shoots. L19.
■ **flushable** *adjective* able to be flushed or flushed away M20. **flusher** *noun* (also ***flusherman***) a person employed to flush sewers M19. **flushing** *noun* the action of the verb; an instance of this: LME.

flush /flʌʃ/ *verb*[2] *trans.* M19.
[ORIGIN from FLUSH *adjective*[1] 4.]
Make flush or level; fill in (a joint etc.) level with a surface; point.

flush /flʌʃ/ *adverb*. E18.
[ORIGIN from FLUSH *adjective*[1].]
With direct force or full effect; squarely. Also, level; (formerly) directly, straight.

Flushing /ˈflʌʃɪŋ/ *noun*. M19.
[ORIGIN A port in the Netherlands (Dutch *Vlissingen*).]
A type of rough, thick, woollen cloth. Freq. *attrib.*

Flushinger /ˈflʌʃɪŋə/ *noun*. L17.
[ORIGIN formed as FLUSHING + -ER[1].]
hist. A ship or sailor from Flushing.

flusker /ˈflʌskə/ *verb*. *obsolete* exc. *dial.* M17.
[ORIGIN Prob. imit.: cf. FLUSH *verb*[1].]
1 *verb intrans.* Flutter, fly erratically. M17.
2 *verb trans.* In *pass.* Be flustered, confused. M19.

fluster /ˈflʌstə/ *verb & noun*. E17.
[ORIGIN Uncertain; perh. rel. to Icelandic *flaustur* hurry, *flaustra* to bustle.]
▸ **A** *verb*. **1** *verb trans.* Confuse with drink, render slightly intoxicated. Passing into sense 3. E17.

THACKERAY His head is flustered with burgundy.

2 *verb intrans.* Be excited, eager, or agitated; bustle. Now *rare*. E17.

P. KAVANAGH The mother flustered around the returned son, helping him off with his coat.

3 *verb trans.* Flurry, confuse, make nervous. Cf. sense 1 above. E18.

I. WALLACE The degree to which the news had flustered him was a surprise.

▸ **B** *noun*. Flurry, flutter, agitation; a confused or agitated state. Formerly also, an impressive bustle or show of activity. L17.

DAY LEWIS As a result of . . arriving a whole day late . . I got into a fearful fluster.

■ **flustered** *ppl adjective* fuddled; confused, agitated, flurried: E17.

flustrate /ˈflʌstreɪt/ *verb trans. arch. colloq.* E18.
[ORIGIN from FLUSTER *verb* + -ATE[3].]
= FLUSTER *verb* 1, 3.
■ **fluˈstration** *noun* M18.

flute /fluːt/ *noun*[1]. ME.
[ORIGIN Old French *flahute*, *fleüte*, *flaüte* (mod. *flûte*), prob. from Provençal *flaüt*, perh. blend of *flaujol* (see FLAGEOLET *noun*[1]) and *laüt* LUTE *noun*[1].]
1 A woodwind instrument of cylindrical shape without a reed, having holes along it stopped by fingers or keys, orig. with the mouthpiece at one end, now in the side near one end. ME. ▸**b** A player of this instrument. M16.
English flute a recorder. ***nose-flute***: see NOSE *noun*. ***transverse flute***: see TRANSVERSE *adjective*. ***whistle and flute***: see WHISTLE *noun* 1c.
2 An organ stop similar in tone to this instrument. Also ***flute stop***. E17.
3 A tall slender wine glass used esp. for sparkling wine. M17.
4 A semi-cylindrical (longitudinal) groove: *spec.* (*ARCHITECTURE*) in a column. M17.
■ **flutelike** *adjective* resembling (that of) a flute E18. †**flutenist** *noun* = FLUTIST M17–E18. **flutist** *noun* a flute player (cf. FLAUTIST) E17.

flute /fluːt/ *noun*[2]. M16.
[ORIGIN Sense 1 from Dutch *fluit* lit. = FLUTE *noun*[1]; sense 2 from French *flûte*, of unknown origin.]
NAUTICAL (now *hist.*).
1 A Dutch sailing vessel with a rounded stern. M16.
2 A warship serving as a transport, with part of her armament removed. M17.

flute /fluːt/ *verb*. LME.
[ORIGIN from FLUTE *noun*[1].]
▸ **I 1** *verb intrans.* Play a flute or pipe. LME. ▸**b** *verb trans.* Play (a tune etc.) on a flute or pipe. M19.
2 *verb intrans.* & *trans.* Whistle, sing, or speak, in flutelike tones. E19.

F

TENNYSON Some . . swan . . fluting a wild carol ere her death. S. O'FAOLÁIN The doves fluting long and slow in the deep woods. S. J. PERELMAN 'Too too divine having you,' she fluted.

▸ **II 3** *verb trans.* Make flutes or grooves in; provide with or arrange in flutes. **L16.** ▸**b** *verb intrans.* Hang or jut *out* in flutes. **L19.**

■ **fluted** *ppl adjective* (*a*) having grooves or flutes; arranged in flutes; (*b*) having the tonal quality of a flute: **E17.** **fluter** *noun* (now *rare*) a flute player **ME.**

flutey *adjective* var. of **FLUTY.**

fluting /ˈfluːtɪŋ/ *noun.* **L15.**
[ORIGIN from FLUTE *verb* + -ING[1].]
1 The action of playing on the flute or making flutelike sounds; an instance of this. **L15.** **2** = FLUTE *noun*[1] 4. **E17.** **3** The action of making flutes in columns etc.; ornamentation with flutes; fluted work. **E18.**

flutter /ˈflʌtə/ *noun.* **M17.**
[ORIGIN from the verb.]
1 The action or state of fluttering; vibration; an instance of this. **M17.** ▸**b** MEDICINE. Abnormal rapid rhythmic contractions, esp. of the atrium of the heart. **E20.** ▸**c** An (undesirable) oscillation of a wing or other part of an aircraft under stress. **E20.** ▸**d** A rapid variation in the pitch or loudness of a sound, not audible as such but heard as distortion; a property in a reproducer that gives rise to this. Cf. **WOW** *noun*[1] 2. **E20.**

ADDISON An infinite Variety of Motions to be made use of in the flutter of a Fan. G. K. CHESTERTON The fine French kings came over in a flutter of flags and dames.

cause a flutter among the dovecotes: see DOVECOTE.

†**2** Ostentatious display or fuss. **M17–E19.**

R. BENTLEY They . . make a mighty flutter and triumph.

3 (A state of) tremulous excitement or agitation; esp. in ***in a flutter***, (*colloq.*) ***all of a flutter***. **M18.**

J. W. CROKER The flutter of her nerves . . makes her very miserable. DICKENS He immediately . . fell into a great flutter.

4 A small bet or speculation. *slang.* **L19.**

P. G. WODEHOUSE Here we all are—you with the money, me with the book— . . let's have a little flutter.

– COMB.: **flutter-mill** *US* a mill worked by a flutter wheel; **flutter-tongue** *noun & verb* (*a*) *noun* rapid tonguing used in playing wind instruments (freq. *attrib.*); (*b*) *verb trans. & intrans.* perform or play (with) rapid tonguing; **flutter wheel** a small water wheel worked by the impact of a rapid stream of water from a chute.

flutter /ˈflʌtə/ *verb.*
[ORIGIN Old English *floterian*, *-orian* frequentative of Germanic base of FLEET *verb*[1]: see -ER[5]. Cf. synon. German *flattern*, †*flotteren*, †*flutteren*.]
†**1** *verb intrans.* Float about on water. **OE–L18.**
2 *verb intrans.* Of a bird, insect, etc.: flap the wings in a quivering manner in short flights or while stationary; fly in quick irregular movements. **OE.** ▸**b** *verb trans.* Move (something) *away* etc. by a quivering action (of the wings). **E17.**

J. MCCOSH The moth fluttering about the light which is to consume it. **b** ALBERT SMITH Seeds, which the bird had fluttered from his cage.

3 *verb intrans.* Move (downwards, to and fro, etc.) with quick light vibrations; quiver; (of the heart or pulse) beat rapidly (and weakly). **M16.**

GEO. ELIOT Here and there a leaf fluttered down. D. WELCH Her silk scarves fluttered in the wind. J. L. WATEN He saw a little smile flutter on Mother's lips and then disappear.

4 *verb trans.* Flap (wings etc.) in a quivering manner; move or wave (a flag etc.) lightly; agitate, ruffle. **E17.** ▸**b** *verb trans.* Throw into confusion or excitement. **M17.**

J. HERVEY The gay butterfly flutters her painted wings. W. STYRON She . . fluttered her eyelids and turned her gaze demurely down. B. BAINBRIDGE Nina fluttered her fingers at him. **b** E. WHARTON Young Mr Gryce's arrival had fluttered the maternal breasts of New York.

b ***flutter the dovecotes***: see DOVECOTE.

5 *verb intrans.* Quiver with excitement; be agitated. **M17.**

THACKERAY Fluttering with her own audacity.

6 *verb intrans.* Move about aimlessly or restlessly; hover. **L17.**

W. BLACK She . . kept fluttering about the hall, bothering the patient clerks with inquiries.

■ **flutteˈration** *noun* (now chiefly *US*) the action or state of fluttering; an instance of this; *esp.* confusion, bustle: **M18.** **flutterer** *noun* **LME.** **fluttering** *verbal noun* the action of the verb; an instance of this: **LME.** **flutteringly** *adverb* in a fluttering manner **E19.** **fluttery** *adjective* liable to flutter, fluttering **LME.**

fluty /ˈfluːti/ *adjective.* Also **-ey.** **E19.**
[ORIGIN from FLUTE *noun*[1] + -Y[1].]
Flutelike in tone; piping.

fluvial /ˈfluːvɪəl/ *adjective.* **LME.**
[ORIGIN Latin *fluvialis*, from *fluvius* river, from *fluere* to flow: see -AL[1].]
Of or pertaining to a river or rivers; found or living in rivers.

■ **fluvialist** *noun* a person who explains geological features as being due to the action of existing rivers **E19.**

fluviatile /ˈfluːvɪətʌɪl/ *adjective.* **L16.**
[ORIGIN French from Latin *fluviatilis*, from *fluviatus* moistened, wet, from *fluvius*: see FLUVIAL, -ILE.]
Of or pertaining to a river or rivers; found or living in rivers; formed or produced by the action of rivers.

fluvio- /ˈfluːvɪəʊ/ *combining form* of Latin *fluvius* river: see -O-.

■ **fluvioˈglacial** *adjective* (*a*) pertaining to or produced by the action of streams originating in glacial ice; (*b*) of, pertaining to, or produced by the combined action of, both rivers and glaciers: **L19.** **fluviolaˈcustrine** *adjective* of, pertaining to, or produced by the combined agency of, both rivers and lakes **M19.**

fluviology /fluːvɪˈɒlədʒi/ *noun.* **E20.**
[ORIGIN from FLUVIO- + -LOGY.]
The branch of science that deals with rivers; a body of knowledge concerning a river or rivers.

fluviometer /fluːvɪˈɒmɪtə/ *noun.* **M19.**
[ORIGIN formed as FLUVIOLOGY + -METER.]
An instrument for measuring the rise and fall of rivers.

fluvoxamine /fluːˈvɒksəmiːn/ *noun.* **L20.**
[ORIGIN from FLU(ORO- + V(ALERIAN + OX(Y- + AMINE.]
PHARMACOLOGY. A synthetic compound, $C_{15}H_{21}F_3N_2O_2$, that selectively inhibits the reuptake of serotonin and is used to treat depression and some compulsive disorders.

flux /flʌks/ *noun.* In sense 1 also †**flix.** **LME.**
[ORIGIN Old French & mod. French, or Latin *fluxus*, from *flux-* pa. ppl stem of *fluere* to flow.]
1 A flowing out (from the bowels, an organ, etc.) of fluid material; *esp.* an abnormal or excessive discharge of blood or excrement; (*arch.*) diarrhoea, dysentery. **LME.**

bloody flux: see BLOODY *adjective & adverb.* ***white flux***: see WHITE *adjective.*

2 The action of flowing; the flowing in of the tide (esp. in ***flux and reflux***). **LME.** ▸**b** A stream, a flood: esp. *fig.*, of people, talk, etc. **E17.**

fig.: C. THIRLWALL The flux and reflux of the nations which fought and wandered in the countries. **b** J. CHEEVER I heard thunder, and a second later a flux of summer rain inundated the county. P. L. FERMOR The vehicle threaded its way through a flux of traffic.

3 A continuous succession of changes of condition, composition, or substance. **LME.** ▸**b** The passing away of life, time, etc. **E17.**

L. EDEL The flux of the mind, its continuity and yet its continuous change. **b** J. THOMSON Thus to remain, Amid the flux of many thousand years.

in a state of flux in an unstable condition.

4 MATH. Continued motion of a point etc. Later also = FLUXION 3. Now *rare* or *obsolete.* **M17.**
†**5** A liquid or molten state. **L17–L18.**
6 Any substance which is mixed with a metal etc. in order to facilitate melting; a substance used to make colours fusible in enamelling, pottery, etc. **E18.**
7 PHYSICS. **a** The rate of flow of any fluid, or of radiant energy, particles, etc., across a given area; the amount of this crossing a given area in a given time. **M19.** ▸**b** (The number of) lines of magnetic induction or electric displacement passing through an area; the integral over the area of the component of the field strength normal to the area. Also ***magnetic flux***, ***electric flux***. **L19.**

a *New Scientist* The thermal neutron flux . . will be . . 2×10^{13} neutrons per square centimetre per second. *Nature* The flux of hydrogen atoms in the solar wind. **b** J. A. FLEMING If . . a disc of iron is placed in a uniform field of magnetic force, the flux concentrates itself in the iron.

– COMB.: **flux density** the quantity of (magnetic, electric, etc.) flux passing through unit area; **flux-gate (magnetometer)** a kind of magnetometer (used esp. in aerial surveys) consisting of one or more soft iron cores each surrounded by primary and secondary windings, the characteristics of the external magnetic field being determined from the signals produced in the secondary windings; **flux-line** any of a set of lines representing by their direction and density the direction and rate of flow of a fluid etc. or the direction and strength of a magnetic or electric field; **fluxmeter**: for measuring (changes in) magnetic etc. flux.
– NOTE: The var. *flix* survives in FLIXWEED.

†**flux** *adjective.* **LME–L18.**
[ORIGIN Latin *fluxus* ppl adjective, from *fluere* to flow.]
In a state of flux, flowing, fluctuating.

flux /flʌks/ *verb.* **LME.**
[ORIGIN from the noun.]
1 *verb trans.* Purge; cause a flux in (a person). Now *rare* or *obsolete.* **LME.** ▸†**b** *verb intrans.* Undergo a flux. **LME–M18.**
2 *verb trans. & intrans.* Make or become fluid; fuse, melt. **L15.**
3 *verb trans.* Treat or heat with a flux (FLUX *noun* 6). **L18.**
4 *verb intrans.* Flow copiously. Now *rare.* **E19.**

†**fluxible** *adjective.* **L15.**
[ORIGIN Old French, or late Latin *fluxibilis* liquid, from Latin *flux-* pa. ppl stem of *fluere* to flow: see -IBLE.]
1 Able to be melted, fusible. **L15–M18.**
2 Fluid. Also, pliable. **M16–E18.**
3 Liable to flux or change, variable. **M16–L17.**

■ †**fluxibility** *noun* **L16–M18.**

†**fluxile** *adjective.* **E17–M19.**
[ORIGIN Late Latin *fluxilis* from *flux-*: see FLUXIBLE, -ILE.]
= FLUXIBLE 2, 3.

■ †**fluxility** *noun* **M17–E18.**

fluxion /ˈflʌkʃ(ə)n/ *noun.* **M16.**
[ORIGIN Old French & mod. French, or from Latin *flux-*: see FLUXIBLE, -ION.]
1 = FLUX *noun* 1. Now *rare* or *obsolete.* **M16.**
2 The action of flowing (out); continuous motion; continual change. **L16.** ▸†**b** = EFFLUVIUM 2. **E17–M18.**
3 MATH. Increase or decrease of a continuously varying quantity; the rate of this. Now chiefly *hist.*, in ***method of fluxions***, the Newtonian calculus. **L17.**

■ **fluxional** *adjective* (*a*) MATH. of or pertaining to fluxions; (*b*) resulting from or subject to flux; flowing, variable: **M18.** **fluxionary** *adjective* (now *rare*) = FLUXIONAL **M18.** **fluxionist** *noun* (MATH., *hist.*) a person who uses (the method of) fluxions **M18.**

†**fluxive** *adjective.* **L16–E18.**
[ORIGIN medieval Latin *fluxivus* fleeting, transitory, from *flux-*: see FLUXIBLE, -IVE.]
Liable to flow; fluid; fluctuating, variable.

fly /flʌɪ/ *noun*[1]. Pl. **flies.**
[ORIGIN Old English *flȳġe*, *flēoge* = Old Saxon, Old High German *flioga* (Dutch *vlieg*, German *Fliege*), from West Germanic, from Germanic base of FLY *verb*.]
1 Any winged insect, as a bee, locust, moth, etc. Now usu. restricted to small winged insects of any group not popularly identifiable, or falling under sense 2 as below or as the 2nd elem. of comb. **OE.** ▸**b** Any of various winged insects harmful to crops or animals; a disease caused by such an insect. **E18.**

alderfly, ***caddis fly***, ***damselfly***, ***firefly***, ***greenfly***, ***ichneumon fly***, ***mayfly***, ***sawfly***, ***stonefly***, etc. **b** ***hop-fly***, ***potato-fly***, ***sheep fly***, etc.

2 A dipteran or two-winged insect; an insect of the order Diptera (comprising the true flies). **OE.** ▸**b** *ellipt.* The tsetse fly. *S. Afr.* **M19.**

blowfly, ***crane fly***, ***horsefly***, ***housefly***, ***hoverfly***, ***sandfly***, ***warble fly***, etc.

3 *fig.* (A type of) something insignificant. **ME.**

HAZLITT He would not hurt a fly.

4 ANGLING. A natural fly or an imitation of this consisting of a hook dressed with silk and feathers, etc., used as fishing bait. **L16.**

R. BRAUTIGAN I cast . . and let my fly drift.

dry fly, ***watchet fly***, ***wet fly***, etc.

†**5** A familiar demon; *transf.* a spy, a flatterer. **L16–M17.**
6 PRINTING. **a** A printer's devil. *rare.* **L17.** ▸**b** The person who or machine which takes the printed sheets from the press. **M18.**
7 (Usu. **F-**.) *The* constellation Musca. **L17.**

– PHRASES: **drink with the flies** (*Austral. & NZ slang*) drink alone. **fly in amber** *fig.* a curious relic. **fly in the ointment** [after *Ecclesiastes* 10:1] a trifling circumstance that spoils the enjoyment or agreeableness of a thing. **fly on the wall** (*a*) an unperceived observer; (*b*) CINEMATOGRAPHY a film-making technique whereby events are observed realistically with minimum interference rather than acted out under direction. **fly on the wheel** a person who overestimates his or her own influence. **like flies** in large numbers or quantities. ***Lord of the Flies***: see LORD *noun*. **no flies on** *slang* no lack of astuteness in (a person); nothing shady or underhand about (a deal etc.). ***squashed fly*** (***biscuit***): see SQUASH *verb* 1.

– COMB.: **fly agaric** a poisonous mushroom, *Amanita muscaria*, with a white-spotted scarlet cap; **flybane** (*a*) any of various supposedly insecticidal plants, *esp.* catchfly; (*b*) *rare* poison for flies; **fly-bird** a hummingbird; **fly-bitten** *adjective* †(*a*) flyspecked; †(*b*) = FLYBLOWN (a); (*c*) stung by flies; **fly-book** a book-shaped case in which anglers keep fishing flies; †**fly-cap** a kind of headdress, shaped like a butterfly; **fly-cast** *verb intrans.* (in fly-fishing) cast a line with a fly rod; **fly-dope** *N. Amer.* insect repellent; **fly-eater** an eater of flies; *spec.* any of several small Australasian warblers constituting the genus *Gerygone* (family Muscicapidae); **fly-fan** an instrument or motor-driven fan for driving away flies; **fly-fish** *verb intrans.* fish with a fly as bait; **fly-fishing** fishing with a fly; **fly-flap** *noun & verb* (*a*) *noun* an instrument for driving away flies; (*b*) *verb trans.* strike with a fly-flap, beat, whip; **fly-flapper** (*a*) a person who drives away flies with a fly-flap; (*b*) a fly-flap; **fly fungus** (*a*) = ***fly agaric*** above; (*b*) a parasitic fungus, *Entomophthora muscae*, which infests and kills houseflies and other insects; ***fly honeysuckle***: see HONEYSUCKLE 2; **fly-hook** a hook baited with a fly; **fly line** *noun*[1]: for fly-fishing; **fly-mould** = ***fly fungus*** (b) above; **fly net** a net for keeping flies away; **fly orchid** an orchid, *Ophrys insectifera*, with small dark-purple flowers resembling flies; **flypaper** paper treated with a sticky substance for catching and poisoning flies; **fly rod**: for fly-fishing; **fly screen** a screen for keeping flies away; **flyspeck** (*a*) a small stain produced by the excrement of an insect; (*b*) a disease of apples etc., with small black surface specks, caused by the fungus *Leptothyrium pomi*; **flyspecked**, **flyspeckled** *adjectives* marked with flyspecks; **fly spray** a spray, usu. an aerosol, containing a liquid for killing flies; **fly strike** infestation of the skin of sheep with the maggots of blowflies; **fly-strip** an impregnated plastic strip for poisoning flies; **fly swatter** a device for killing flies by hitting them; **fly-swish** = ***fly whisk*** below; **flyweight** a weight in boxing and other sports below bantamweight, in the amateur boxing scale now being below 52 kg, though differing for professionals and in other sports, and according to time and place; (designating) a boxer etc. of this weight; ***light flyweight***, (of) a weight in amateur boxing of below 49 kg, (designating) a boxer of this weight; **fly whisk** an instrument for driving away flies; **fly-wire** screening designed to keep out flies.

fly /flʌɪ/ *noun*². Pl. **flies**, (in sense 3 also) **flys**. OE.
[ORIGIN from the verb.]
1 The action or an act of flying. OE. ▸**b** The course of a ball, or the ball itself, as it travels through the air. M19.

b J. T. FARRELL A long high fly which was easily caught.

2 a The 32 points of a mariner's compass; a compass card. L16. ▸**b** A speed-regulating device in a clockwork mechanism. L16. ▸**c** A flywheel or other similar speed-regulating device in machinery. M17.
3 *hist.* **a** A stagecoach. E18. ▸**b** A lightweight covered carriage drawn by one horse. E19.

b P. V. WHITE The Bonners drove, in the family carriage and a hired fly.

4 THEATRICAL. In *pl.* The space above the front part of the stage. E19.

H. ROSENTHAL The three rooms . . high up in the opera house on the level with the 'flies.'

5 Orig., the sloping walls or roof of a tent. Now, the flap at the entrance of a tent. Also = ***flysheet*** (b) below. E19.

P. MATTHIESSEN The others have rigged a fly over the fire and are making tea . . in this downpour.

6 Waste cotton. E19.
7 A strip on a garment which contains or covers the fastening; *sing.* & (freq.) in *pl.*, the flap that hides the fastening at the front of a pair of trousers; the fastening itself. M19.

G. GREENE The flies of his grey flannel trousers gaped from a lost button.

8 The breadth of a flag from the staff to the end. M19. ▸**b** The part of a flag which is furthest from the staff. M19.
– PHRASES: **give it a fly** *Austral. & NZ slang* make an attempt, have a go. **have a fly at** *Austral. & NZ slang* make an attempt at, have a go at. **on the fly** (*a*) while in motion through the air; (*b*) *transf.* while active, busy, or on the move.
– COMB.: **fly ash** ash resulting from the burning of powdered coal; **fly ball** BASEBALL a ball hit so as to be catchable; **fly boy** *US slang* a member of the Air Force, esp. a pilot; **flybridge** an open deck with duplicate controls situated above the main bridge of a ship; a flying bridge; **fly camp** a temporary camp; **fly-cruise** a holiday starting with an air journey to the place where a sea cruise begins; **fly-drive** a holiday or a journey involving both flying and driving; **fly frame** in spinning, a flyer frame; **fly half** RUGBY a stand-off half; **fly-kick** a kick, esp. in rugby, made while the ball is in the air; **flyleaf** a blank leaf at the beginning or end of a book; the blank leaf of a circular etc.; **flyline** *noun*² the regular line of flight followed by a migrating bird; **flyman** (*a*) *hist.* a person who drives a fly (sense 3b above); (*b*) THEATRICAL a person positioned in the flies to work the ropes etc.; **fly-nut** a screw nut with wings or projections enabling it to be tightened by hand; **fly page** either side of a flyleaf; **fly-post**, **fly-poster** *verbs trans. & intrans.* display (handbills etc.) rapidly in unauthorized places; **flysheet** (*a*) a two- or four-page leaflet or circular; (*b*) a protective cover pitched outside and over a tent; **fly stitch** an embroidery stitch similar to chain stitch but open-ended; **fly-tip** *verb trans.* carry out the fly-tipping of (rubbish etc.); **fly-tipping** the unauthorized dumping of building rubble or other waste; **flyway** (*a*) = ***flyline*** above; (*b*) a vast area occupied by bird populations containing both winter and breeding grounds linked by migratory routes; **flywheel** a heavy-rimmed wheel attached to a revolving shaft to store momentum, usu. so as to regulate machinery.

fly /flʌɪ/ *adjective. slang.* E19.
[ORIGIN Uncertain: perh. rel. to the verb.]
1 Knowing, sharp, wide awake. E19.

A. PRICE He was too fly to let anyone pin so much as a charity flag on him. P. ACKROYD Are you fly to what's going on?

put fly inform, tell, (a person).
2 Of the fingers: nimble, skilful. Now *rare.* M19.
3 Stylish, sophisticated, fashionable. *N. Amer.* L19.

P. BAKER A super fly pimp jumped out of a gold limousine that had white-wall tires and TV antennas in the back.

– SPECIAL COLLOCATIONS: **fly cop** *US slang* a detective, a plain-clothes police officer. **fly-flat** *slang* a person who is or thinks he or she is wise, but is or gives the impression of being a fool. **fly-pitch** *slang* a street pitch. **fly-pitcher** *slang* a person who operates a fly-pitch; a street trader.
■ **flyness** *noun* L19.

fly /flʌɪ/ *verb.* Pa. t. **flew** /fluː/; pa. pple **flown** /fləʊn/.
[ORIGIN Old English *flēogan* = Old Frisian *fliāga*, Old Saxon (Dutch *vliegen*), Old High German *fliogan* (German *fliegen*), Old Norse *fljúga*, from Germanic.]
▸ **I 1** *verb intrans.* Move through the air with wings. (Foll. by *about, away, off, out*, etc.) OE. ▸**b** *verb intrans. fig.* Of fame, a report, etc.: spread, become known. Also, (of words, thoughts, emotions, etc.) shift, change, or be exchanged swiftly and animatedly. ME. ▸**c** *verb intrans.* Of a fish: spring from the water, rise into the air. Cf. ***flying fish*** s.v. FLYING *ppl adjective.* L16. ▸**d** *verb trans.* Cover by flying (a course or distance). E17.

J. STEINBECK A pigeon flew in through the open hay door. **b** T. HARDY That young man's feelings had flown hither and thither between minister and lady. S. MIDDLETON Conversation and laughter were flying. **d** SHAKES. *Macb.* Ere the Bat hath flowne His Cloyster'd flight.

2 *verb intrans.* Pass or rise quickly through the air. (Foll. by *away, off, up*, etc.) OE. ▸**b** Of stairs: go straight up or down without change of direction. Now *rare.* L17. ▸**c** Spring lightly, jump *over.* E18.

DRYDEN Golden stars flew up to light the skies.

3 *verb intrans.* Move or travel swiftly, pass rapidly, rush along. (Foll. by *along, away, back*, etc.) ME. ▸**b** *spec.* Of time: pass quickly, rush by. M16.

J. TYNDALL The velocity with which the earth flies through space. D. H. LAWRENCE She flew along the terrace and up the steps to the roof. **b** S. MIDDLETON The first three days had passed slowly, but by Thursday time flew.

4 *verb intrans.* Move with a start or rush; spring, hasten; depart hurriedly. ME.

J. I. M. STEWART Mabel has to fly . . But she did so very much want to meet you.

5 *verb intrans.* Be forced or driven off or away suddenly and quickly. (Foll. by *from, out of.*) ME. ▸**b** More fully ***fly in pieces***. Break up suddenly, split up. L15. ▸**c** Of a door or window: be thrown suddenly *open, up*, etc. E17. ▸**d** Of money: be rapidly spent. M17. ▸**e** BASEBALL. Hit a fly ball. (Foll. by *out.*) L19.

LD BERNERS His hede flewe fro hys sholders. DAY LEWIS The squawking hens bouncing up and down . . straw and feathers flying. **c** G. GREENE Suddenly the door which I had pushed against so often before flew open.

6 FALCONRY. **a** *verb intrans. & trans.* Of a hawk: fly (*at*) and attack. LME. ▸**b** *verb trans. & intrans.* Send (a hawk) to fly and attack. E16. ▸**c** *verb trans.* Chase or attack with a hawk. L16.
7 *verb trans.* Release (a bird) to fly; keep (birds) for racing, hunting, etc. E17. ▸**b** Make (a kite) rise and stay aloft in the air. See also ***fly a kite*** below. M17.

J. CLAVELL It's one of my few rules: only to fly the falcons that I've trained. **b** *fig.*: TENNYSON O Madam, You fly your thoughts like kites.

8 *verb intrans.* Of a flag, garment, or other partially attached object: flutter, wave. M17. ▸**b** *verb trans.* Set or keep (a flag) flying. M17.

R. BROOKE And the moon came down and danced to me, And her robe was white and flying. V. BRITTAIN The flags flying in the streets . . for Queen Victoria's Diamond Jubilee.

9 *verb intrans.* NAUTICAL. Of the wind: shift or veer suddenly. L17.
10 *verb intrans.* Of an aircraft or spacecraft: travel through the air or space at speed. M19. ▸**b** Of a person: travel by aircraft, pilot an aircraft. E20.

B. MOORE That's a helicopter, it could not fly all the way from Rome. **b** W. S. MAUGHAM When I said I wanted to learn to fly he said he'd fix it for me. DAY LEWIS The womb-like sensation of flying in an air-liner.

11 *verb trans.* Of an aircraft or its occupant(s): cover, traverse, or perform, by flying. L19. ▸**b** Conduct or pilot (an aircraft). E20. ▸**c** Convey or transport by aircraft. E20.

Captain The machine which flew the channel. N. SHUTE He was flying a courier service. **b** C. POTOK He flies big planes that drop bombs.

▸ **II 12** *verb intrans. & trans.* = FLEE (exc. sense 3). OE.
– PHRASES: ***as the crow flies***: see CROW *noun*¹. **fly a kite** *fig.* (*a*) raise money by an accommodation bill; (*b*) try something out; make an announcement or take a step in order to test public opinion; (*c*) ***go fly a kite*** (*colloq.*, chiefly *N. Amer.*), go away. **fly at higher game** *fig.* have nobler ambitions. **fly high** *fig.* (*a*) be ambitious, aim high; (*b*) prosper, flourish. ***fly in pieces***: see sense 5b above. ***fly off the handle***: see HANDLE *noun*¹. **fly past** make a ceremonial aircraft flight past some person or place. ***fly the coop***: see COOP *noun*¹. **fly the track** (*US colloq.*) turn from the usual or expected course. **fly to arms** take up arms eagerly or suddenly. ***go fly a kite***: see ***fly a kite*** (c) above. **let fly** (*a*) *verb phr. trans.* discharge (a missile), utter (an oath, strong words, etc.); (*b*) *verb phr. intrans.* make a physical or verbal attack; fire, shoot, (*at*); (*c*) *verb phr. trans.* NAUTICAL allow (a sail or sheet) to fly loose; hoist (colours). **make the money fly** spend money quickly. ***pigs might fly***: see PIG *noun*¹. ***sparks will fly***: see SPARK *noun*¹.
– WITH ADVERBS & PREPOSITIONS IN SPECIALIZED SENSES: **fly at**, **fly on**, **fly upon** spring upon violently, attack with fury. **fly in** (*a*) (adverb) arrive by aircraft; (*b*) (preposition) = ***fly into*** below. **fly into** fall or pass suddenly into (a passion, raptures, etc.). **fly off** (*a*) start away, leave suddenly; (*b*) *fig.* take another course, break away *from*. ***fly on***: see ***fly at*** above. **fly out** (*a*) spring out, rush out suddenly; (*b*) burst out or explode in conduct, temper, etc.; (*c*) depart by aircraft. ***fly upon***: see ***fly at*** above.
– COMB.: **flyback** (*a*) the return of the hands of a stopwatch or chronograph to zero; (*b*) the return of the scanning spot in a cathode-ray tube to the starting point; (*c*) the portion of each cycle of a sawtooth waveform in which the signal diminishes; **fly-by** (*a*) = ***fly-past*** (a) below; (*b*) a close approach of a spacecraft to a planet etc.; **fly-by-night** *noun & adjective* (*a*) *noun* a person who makes night excursions or decamps by night in order to avoid debts; (*b*) *adjective* unreliable, dishonest; superficial, short-lived; **fly-by-wire** *adjective & noun* (designating) a semi-automatic (freq. computer-regulated) system for controlling the flight of an aircraft, spacecraft, etc. **fly-in** (*a*) the action or an act of delivering troops, goods, etc., by air to a specified place; (*b*) a service or entertainment provided for people who have arrived by air; **fly-off** *noun & adjective* (*a*) *noun* the action of flying off; (*b*) *adjective* (of a motor-vehicle brake) requiring a manual operation to put it on or off but not to keep it on; **flyover** (*a*) a road or rail bridge which crosses over a road or railway; (*b*) = ***fly-past*** (a) below; **fly-past** (*a*) the action of flying past, or of forming part of a procession of aircraft; (*b*) = ***fly-by*** (b) above; **fly-the-garter** a game in which players leap from one side of a 'garter' or line of stones over the back of another player; **fly-through** a computer-animated simulation of what would be seen if one were flying through a particular real or imaginary region; **flyunder** a road or railway which runs under another; **fly-up-the-creek** *US* (*a*) the green heron, *Butorides virescens*; (*b*) a flighty person; (*c*) a native or inhabitant of Florida.

flyable /ˈflʌɪəb(ə)l/ *adjective.* L16.
[ORIGIN from FLY *verb* + -ABLE.]
†**1** Flying; that flies. Only in L16.
2 Able to be leapt over (on horseback). *colloq.* L19.
3 (Of weather) suitable for flying; (of goods) transportable by air; (of an aircraft) capable of flying, able to be flown. M20.

flyaway /ˈflʌɪəweɪ/ *adjective & noun.* Also **fly-away**. L18.
[ORIGIN from FLY *verb* + AWAY.]
▸ **A** *adjective.* **1** Apt to fly away; *spec.* sudden, impulsive, volatile, flighty. L18.

Daily Mirror Spurned by her fly-away husband, Mick, Bianca Jagger dances alone.

2 Of a garment: loose, streaming. Of a person's hair: fine and difficult to control. M19.

She Added body to my fine, flyaway hair without leaving it stiff and sticky.

▸ **B** *noun.* A person who or thing which flies away. E19.

flyblow /ˈflʌɪbləʊ/ *noun & verb.* M16.
[ORIGIN from FLY *noun*¹ + BLOW *noun*², *verb*¹.]
▸ **A** *noun.* A fly's egg deposited in meat, carrion, etc.; a maggot hatched from this. M16.
▸ **B** *verb trans.* Infl. as BLOW *verb*¹; pa. t. **-blew** /-bluː/, pa. pple usu. **-blown** /-bləʊn/.
1 Of a fly etc.: deposit eggs on or in (meat etc.). Cf. earlier BLOW *verb*¹ 18. E17.
2 *fig.* Corrupt secretly, taint. E17.
■ **flyblown** *adjective* (*a*) full of flyblows; tainted, impure, corrupt; (*b*) *Austral. & NZ slang* without any money, broke: E16.

fly-boat /ˈflʌɪbəʊt/ *noun.* L16.
[ORIGIN Dutch *vlieboot* a boat used orig. on the *Vlie*, a channel off the north coast of the Netherlands; later assoc. with FLY *noun*¹: see BOAT *noun*.]
1 *hist.* A fast sailing vessel, *esp.* a Dutch flat-bottomed boat, used for coastal trade or for warfare, exploration, etc. L16.
†**2** A small boat; *esp.* a ship's boat. L16–E19.
†**3** A fishing boat used in Shetland, a buss. E17–L18.
4 A swift boat used on canals. M19.

flycatcher /ˈflʌɪkatʃə/ *noun.* L16.
[ORIGIN from FLY *noun*¹ + CATCHER.]
1 Any of numerous birds that feed on insects, typically catching their prey by short flights from a perch, *esp.* (*a*) a member of the Old World family Muscicapidae; (*b*) = ***monarch flycatcher*** s.v. MONARCH *noun*; (*c*) = ***tyrant flycatcher*** s.v. TYRANT *noun* 5. L16.
fantail flycatcher, ***least flycatcher***, ***paradise flycatcher***, ***pied flycatcher***, ***spotted flycatcher***, etc.
2 A person who or thing which catches flies. E17. ▸**b** An insectivorous plant. M19.

flyer /ˈflʌɪə/ *noun.* Also **flier**. LME.
[ORIGIN from FLY *verb* + -ER¹.]
1 Something which flies; a creature or thing that flies or is carried through the air. LME.

C. DARWIN Birds breeding on precipices, and good fliers, are unlikely to be exterminated.

2 A person who runs away, a fugitive; a fleer. LME.
3 Each of a series of rectangular steps forming a straight flight. M17.
4 A mechanism which has a regular and fast-moving revolution, as: an appliance for regulating the motion of a roasting jack; a sail of a windmill; the part of a spinning wheel which twists the thread as it leads it to and winds it on the bobbin. L17.
5 A person, animal, vehicle, train, etc., which moves with exceptional speed. L18. ▸**b** A flying jump or leap. L19. ▸**c** CRICKET. A ball pitched short that flies up sharply. E20.

E. WALLACE Fifty-Five is a flyer . . He did the five furlongs in fifty-eight and a fifth seconds.

6 A speculative venture, *esp.* a speculative financial investment. *US.* M19.
7 A small handbill or flysheet, *esp.* one issued by the police or used for advertising purposes. *N. Amer.* L19.

New Yorker The police . . put out flyers asking witnesses . . to come forward.

8 An aircraft. L19. ▸**b** An aviator. M20.

H. G. WELLS The most efficient heavier-than-air fliers that had ever appeared.

9 An ambitious or outstanding person; an excellent or outstanding thing. *colloq.* E20.

T. PARKER People of higher rank . . say he's something of what's called a 'flyer'.

– PHRASES: **take a flyer** take a chance.

F

F

flying /ˈflʌɪɪŋ/ *verbal noun*. ME.
[ORIGIN from FLY *verb* + -ING[1].]
The action of FLY *verb*; *spec.* the action of guiding, piloting, or travelling in an aircraft or spacecraft.
– COMB. (not all clearly separable from collocations of the ppl adjective): **flying boat** (*a*) a boat-shaped car on a funfair roundabout; (*b*) a form of seaplane with a fuselage that resembles a boat; **flying corps** an aircraft unit for military or naval purposes; **flying field** an airfield; **flying jacket** a short jacket similar to a bomber jacket, typically made of leather and with a warm lining or collar and several pockets; **flying machine** (now *arch.* or *hist.*) a machine that can be flown in the air, *esp.* one that is heavier than air and depends on its motors for propulsion and lift; **Flying Officer** a rank in the Royal Air Force, immediately below Flight Lieutenant; **flying school** a place where people are taught to fly aircraft; **flying speed** the speed of an aircraft at take-off or in normal level flight; **flying squadron** a Royal Air Force unit or formation made up of several flights; (see also s.v. FLYING *ppl adjective*); **flying suit** (*a*) a suit worn by someone piloting an aircraft; (*b*) a kind of one-piece trouser suit worn as a casual fashion garment.

flying /ˈflʌɪɪŋ/ *ppl adjective*. OE.
[ORIGIN from FLY *verb* + -ING[2].]
1 That flies. OE.

A. WINCHELL A menagerie of curious beasts, and crawling and creeping and flying things.

2 That flies about; *fig.* circulating, shifting about, itinerant, volatile. LME.

BUNYAN I hope they are but flying stories. W. SAUNDERS Flying pains and weaknesses of the limbs.

3 That passes through the air esp. quickly. M16.
4 That passes or travels swiftly, that passes by rapidly; (of a vehicle etc.) designed for rapid movement. M16. ▸**b** Esp. of a trip or visit: passing, hasty, transient. Also, temporary. M16.

POPE Earth rolls back beneath the flying steed. **b** H. WILSON He paid me a flying visit.

5 That flees, fleeing. L16.
6 Hanging loose; fluttering, waving. E17.
– PHRASES: *come off with flying colours*, *come through with flying colours*: see COLOUR *noun*. †**under a flying seal**, †**with a flying seal** (of a letter) having a seal but not closed, so that it can be read while in transit.
– SPECIAL COLLOCATIONS (not all clearly separable from combs. of the verbal noun): **flying bomb** an unmanned aircraft with an explosive warhead. **flying bridge** †(*a*) a drawbridge; (*b*) a temporary bridge constructed for military purposes; (*c*) an auxiliary bridge situated higher than the main bridge of a yacht or other ship. **flying buttress** a buttress, usu. on an arch, which slants upwards to a wall from a pier or other support. **flying change** an equestrian movement in which the leading leg in the canter position is changed without loss of speed while the horse is in the air. *flying circus*: see CIRCUS *noun* 8. †**flying coach** a swift stagecoach. **flying coffin** *colloq.* a hazardous or vulnerable aeroplane. **flying column** a military force capable of rapid movement and independent operation. **flying doctor** a doctor who habitually visits patients in remote areas by aircraft. **flying dragon** = *flying lizard* below. *Flying* DUTCHMAN. **flying facade** a facade that rises above the level of the roof of a building. **flying fish** (*a*) any of various tropical fishes of the family Exocoetidae, capable of gliding considerable distances above the water by means of winglike pectoral fins; (*b*) ***the Flying Fish***, (the name of) the constellation Volans. **Flying Fortress** the Boeing B-17, a US long-range heavy bomber developed in the late 1930s. **flying fox** (*a*) any of numerous fruit-eating bats, mainly of the genus *Pteropus*, found in India, Madagascar, SE Asia, and Australia; (*b*) (*Austral.* & *NZ*) a carrier operated by cables across a gorge etc. **flying frog** a nocturnal Asian tree frog, *Polypedates leucomystax*, which is able to make long gliding jumps using the large webs between its extended toes. **flying gurnard** any of various tropical benthic marine fishes of the family Dactylopteridae, with greatly enlarged pectoral fins, able to leap out of the water. **flying horse** (*a*) a throw in wrestling, similar to the flying mare; (*b*) ***the Flying Horse*** (now *rare* or *obsolete*), (the name of) the constellation Pegasus. **flying jenny** (chiefly *US*) a merry-go-round. **flying jib** (*a*) NAUTICAL a light sail set on an extension of a jib boom; (*b*) *slang* a loud-mouthed talker. **flying jump**, **flying leap**: made with a running start. *flying kites*: see KITE *noun* 5a. *flying leap*: see *flying jump* above. **flying lemur** either of two SE Asian nocturnal arboreal mammals of the genus *Cynocephalus*, order Dermoptera, which resemble lemurs and can glide hundreds of feet by means of a membrane between the fore and hind limbs and the tail; also called ***colugo***. **flying lizard** any arboreal agamid lizard of the SE Asian genus *Draco* able to glide short distances by means of skin membranes supported by elongated ribs. **flying mare** a throw in wrestling, in which one wrestler throws the other over his or her back using the other's arm as a lever. **flying mouse** the smallest gliding marsupial, *Acrobates pygmaeus* (family Burramyidae), of eastern Australia; also called ***feathertail glider***, ***pygmy glider***. **flying phalanger** any of various small Australasian marsupials of the genera *Petaurus* and *Petauroides* (family Petauridae), that are able to make gliding leaps by means of furred skin membranes between fore and hind limbs; also called ***glider***. **flying picket** (a member of) a group of striking workers who move from place to place picketing premises and companies other than those at which they are employed. †**flying post** a post travelling by relays of horses. **flying ring** each of a number of rings suspended in pairs or rows by swinging ropes, used in acrobatics and gymnastics. **flying saucer** a disc- or saucer-shaped unidentified flying object. *Flying Scotsman*: see SCOTSMAN 2. **flying shear** a device for shearing a long continuous length of metal into short pieces. **flying shore** a horizontal shore used to provide temporary support between two buildings. **flying spot** a small spot of light that moves rapidly over an object, the reflected or transmitted light from the spot being used to reproduce an image of the object. **flying squad** a division of a police force or other body organized for rapid movement. **flying squadron** a military detachment or other body organized for rapid movement; (see also s.v. FLYING *verbal noun*). **flying squid** any of various squid that are able to leap out of the water, esp. of the family Ommastrephidae. **flying squirrel** (*a*) any of various mainly Asian nocturnal squirrels able to make gliding leaps between trees by means of furred skin membranes between fore and hind limbs; (*b*) = ***flying phalanger*** above. **flying start** (*a*) a start in which the competitors pass the starting point at full speed; (*b*) *fig.* an initial advantage, an excellent start. **flying tackle** a tackle in football etc. made while running or jumping. **flying trapeze** a trapeze on or from which acrobats swing to and fro. **flying wing** a type of aircraft designed without a fuselage or a tailplane.

Flynn /flɪn/ *noun*. *colloq.*, chiefly *N. Amer.* & *Austral.* M20.
[ORIGIN prob. from the name of the actor Errol Flynn (1909–59), known for his wild behaviour.]
be in like Flynn, be immediately and emphatically successful, esp. in a romantic or sexual context.

flype /flʌɪp/ *noun*. Chiefly *N. English*. Also **flipe**. M16.
[ORIGIN Cf. Dutch *fleb*, *flep* a woman's forehead cloth, Danish *flip* flap, FLYPE *verb*.]
A fold, a flap; *esp.* a hat brim.

flype /flʌɪp/ *verb trans.* Chiefly *Scot.* Also **flipe**. ME.
[ORIGIN Cf. Middle Danish *flippe* to skin, FLYPE *noun*.]
1 Strip off (the skin etc.), peel, flay. ME.
2 Turn up or down, fold back; turn inside out. M16.

flysch /flɪʃ/ *noun*. M19.
[ORIGIN Swiss German.]
GEOLOGY. A thinly bedded sedimentary deposit consisting of shales and marls alternating with coarser strata such as sandstones and conglomerates. Orig. *spec.* (**F-**), such a deposit of late Cretaceous to Oligocene age in the Alps.

flyte /flʌɪt/ *noun*. *obsolete* exc. *Scot.* & *dial.* Also **flite**.
[ORIGIN Old English *flīt*, from *flītan*: see FLYTE *verb*.]
†**1** Contention, strife; abuse. OE–E17.
2 A scolding match. M18.

flyte /flʌɪt/ *verb*. *obsolete* exc. *Scot.* & *dial.* Also **flite**.
[ORIGIN Old English *flītan* = Old Saxon *andflītan* contend, Old High German *flīz(z)an* strive (German *sich befleissen* busy oneself).]
†**1** *verb intrans.* Contend, strive; argue noisily; chide. (Foll. by *against*, *on*, *with*.) OE–E18.
2 a *verb trans.* Chide, scold, (a person). LME. ▸**b** *verb intrans.* Scold. (Foll. by *at*.) E16.
▪ **flyter** *noun* a person who disputes or scolds OE. **flyting** *noun* (*a*) the action of the verb; contention, scolding, rebuking; (*b*) a contest of poetical invective, esp. as practised by 16th-cent. Scottish poets: ME.

flytrap /ˈflʌɪtrap/ *noun*. L18.
[ORIGIN from FLY *noun*[1] + TRAP *noun*[1].]
1 A plant which catches flies; *esp.* (in full ***Venus flytrap***, ***Venus's flytrap***), a N. American marsh plant, *Dionaea muscipula* (family Droseraceae), which has hinged leaves able to spring shut and trap insects which touch sensitive trigger hairs. L18.
2 The mouth. *slang*. L18.
3 A trap for catching flies. E19.

FM *abbreviation*[1].
1 Field Marshal.
2 Frequency modulation.

fm *abbreviation*[2].
Fathom(s).

Fm *symbol*.
CHEMISTRY. Fermium.

FMCG *abbreviation*.
Fast-moving consumer goods.

FMV *abbreviation*.
Full-motion video.

FNMA *abbreviation*. *US*.
Federal National Mortgage Association (see FANNIE MAE).

FO *abbreviation*.
1 Flying Officer.
2 Foreign Office.

fo. *abbreviation*.
Folio.

FOAF *abbreviation*. Also **FOF**.
Friend of a friend (as the unidentifiable source of a story, rumour, opinion, etc.).

foal /fəʊl/ *noun & verb*.
[ORIGIN Old English *fola* = Old Frisian *fola*, Old Saxon *folo*, Middle Dutch *volen*, (also mod.) *veulen*, Old High German *folo* (German *Fohlen*), Old Norse *foli*, Gothic *fula*, from Germanic, rel. to synon. Latin *pullus*, Greek *pōlos*; cf. FILLY.]
▸ **A** *noun*. **1** A horse or other equid before or soon after birth; a colt or filly, *esp.* one under one year of age. OE. ▸**b** An elephant or camel of similar age. *rare*. LME.
in foal, **with foal** (of a mare, she-ass, etc.) pregnant.
†**2** A horse. ME–E16.
3 MINING. A young boy employed in the transporting of coal from the working face to the tramway. *obsolete* exc. *hist.* L18.
– COMB.: **foalfoot** (now *dial.*) the plant coltsfoot, *Tussilago farfara*; **foal-tooth** each of the first teeth of a horse etc.
▸ **B** *verb trans.* & *intrans.* Of a mare, she-ass, etc.: give birth to (a foal). LME.

foam /fəʊm/ *noun*.
[ORIGIN Old English *fām* = Old & mod. High German *feim*, from West Germanic from Indo-European, rel. to Latin *pumex* PUMICE *noun* and *spuma* SPUME *noun*.]
1 A mass of small bubbles formed on the surface of water or another liquid by agitation, fermentation, etc. OE. ▸**b** Foaming saliva issuing from the mouth; froth of perspiration on the coat of an animal. OE. ▸**c** Foam for smothering fire, produced by adding a chemical agent to water or by other means; a chemical agent used in producing such foam. E20.

L. DURRELL The sighing of the waves as they thickened into roundels of foam. I. MCEWAN The white foam burst from the bottle's neck.

2 Foaming water, the sea. *arch.* OE.
3 Rubber or plastic solidified in a lightweight cellular mass with many small gas bubbles. Also ***foam rubber***, ***foam plastic***, etc. M20.
– COMB.: **foamback** *adjective & noun* (a fabric etc.) backed by a thin layer of synthetic foam; **foam extinguisher** a fire extinguisher generating a mass of foam; **foam flower** any of various N. American plants of the genus *Tiarella*, of the saxifrage family; esp. *T. cordifolia*, grown for its feathery racemes of small white or reddish flowers; ***foam plastic***, ***foam rubber***: see sense 3 above.
▪ **foamless** *adjective* E19.

foam /fəʊm/ *verb*.
[ORIGIN Old English *fǣman* = Old High German *feimen*, from West Germanic; superseded in Middle English by a new formation from the noun.]
1 *verb intrans.* Emit foam; froth at the mouth; be covered in foamy perspiration; *colloq.* be very angry. OE.

W. IRVING Fall down in convulsions [and] foam at the mouth. E. A. FREEMAN Still urging on his foaming horse.

†**2** *verb trans.* Cover (as) with foam. *rare*. ME–M16.
†**3** *verb intrans.* Emerge as foam. Only in LME.
4 *verb intrans.* Of a liquid: froth, gather foam; run foaming *along*, *down*, etc.; pass off or away in foam. LME.

T. C. WOLFE Below him a mountain stream foamed down its rocky bed.

5 *verb trans.* Emit in or like foam; pour *out* with rage and violence. LME.

W. COWPER They roam the earth . . foaming out their own disgrace.

6 a *verb trans.* Fill with foaming liquor. *poet.* E18. ▸**b** *verb intrans.* Of a cup etc.: be filled with foaming liquor. E19.
▪ **foamingly** *adverb* while foaming E17.

foamed /fəʊmd/ *adjective*. E20.
[ORIGIN from FOAM *verb*, *noun*: see -ED[1], -ED[2].]
1 Covered with foam. E20.
2 Having or made to a cellular structure like that of foam. M20.
foamed slag a lightweight cellular building material made by solidifying a foam of molten blast furnace slag.

foamy /ˈfəʊmi/ *adjective*.
[ORIGIN Old English *fāmig*, *fǣmig*, formed as FOAM *noun* + -Y[1].]
1 Covered with foam, full of foam, frothy. OE.
2 Consisting or of the nature of foam; of, pertaining to, or resembling foam. LME.
▪ **foaminess** *noun* L19.

fob /fɒb/ *noun*[1]. LME.
[ORIGIN from FOB *verb*[1].]
†**1** A cheat, an impostor. *rare*. Only in LME.
2 A trick, an artifice. Now *arch. slang*. E17.

fob /fɒb/ *noun*[2]. L15.
[ORIGIN Unknown.]
1 *gen.* Froth, foam. *dial.* L15.
2 The scum or froth produced during the manufacture of soap. M19.

fob /fɒb/ *noun*[3]. M17.
[ORIGIN Prob. of German origin (cf. German dial. *Fuppe* pocket): orig. a cant term.]
1 A small pocket in the waistband of trousers, for carrying a watch, money, or other valuables. M17.
2 The contents of the fob, cash. *rare*. L17.
3 In full ***fob chain***. A chain attached to a watch carried in the fob; an ornamental attachment to a fob chain; a tab on a key ring. L19.
– COMB.: *fob chain*: see sense 3 above; **fob watch** a pocket watch suitable for carrying in the fob.

fob /fɒb/ *verb*[1] *trans.* Infl. **-bb-**. LME.
[ORIGIN Cf. German *foppen* cheat, deceive, quiz, banter.]
1 Cheat, deceive. (Foll. by *of*, *out of*.) LME.

HENRY FIELDING While everyone else he is fobbing, He still may be honest to me.

2 Foll. by *off*: ▸**a** Put off deceitfully, put off *with* (something inferior); attempt to satisfy with an excuse or pretence; palm (something inferior) off *on*, pass off (something fraudulent) *as*. L16. ▸†**b** Remove by deceit. E–M17.

a H. JAMES She was the girl his mother would have fobbed off on him. G. HEYER How could I hope to fob myself off as Evelyn at such a gathering. E. TAYLOR You wouldn't be fobbed off or coaxed away from a subject. G. PRIESTLAND Let nobody try to fob them off with fairy tales about appropriate technology.

†**3** Bring *into* or bestow *on* by trickery; pass off *on*; get up, procure, or promote, by trickery. M17–E19.

fob /fɒb/ *verb*[2] *trans.* Infl. **-bb-**. E19.
[ORIGIN from FOB *noun*[3].]
Put into one's fob; pocket.

fob /fɒb/ *verb*[3] *intrans. dial. & techn.* Infl. **-bb-**. M19.
[ORIGIN from FOB *noun*[2].]
Froth, foam.

f.o.b. *abbreviation.*
Free on board.

focaccia /fəˈkatʃə/ *noun.* M20.
[ORIGIN Italian.]
A kind of flat savoury Italian bread made with oil and usually seasoned with herbs etc.

focal /ˈfəʊk(ə)l/ *adjective.* L17.
[ORIGIN (mod. Latin *focalis*) from FOCUS *noun*: see -AL[1].]
1 Of or pertaining to a focus; collected or situated at a focus. L17.
2 MEDICINE. Of a disease etc.: occurring at discrete foci; localized. L19.
– SPECIAL COLLOCATIONS: **focal distance**, **focal length** the distance between the centre of a lens or mirror and the focus. **focal plane** the plane perpendicular to the axis of a lens or mirror and containing the focus. **focal point** a focus (of a lens etc. or *fig.*).
■ **focally** *adverb* at a focus M19.

focalize /ˈfəʊk(ə)lʌɪz/ *verb.* Also **-ise**. M19.
[ORIGIN from FOCAL + -IZE.]
1 *verb trans.* Bring (rays of light, heat, etc.) to a focus; focus. M19.
2 *verb trans. & intrans.* Adjust or arrange the focus of (the eye). L19.
3 *verb trans.* MEDICINE. Confine (a disease etc.) to a focus or foci. Chiefly as ***focalized*** *ppl adjective.* E20.
■ **focaliˈzation** *noun* L19.

foci *noun pl.* see FOCUS *noun.*

†**focile** *noun.* LME–E18.
[ORIGIN medieval Latin *focile* lit. 'steel for striking fire', FUSIL *noun*[2].]
Either of the bones of the forearm or of the lower leg: the ulna or tibia (***greater focile***), the radius or fibula (***lesser focile***).

fo'c's'le *noun* see FORECASTLE.

focus /ˈfəʊkəs/ *noun.* Pl. **foci** /ˈfəʊsʌɪ/, **focuses**. M17.
[ORIGIN Latin = fireplace, domestic hearth.]
1 GEOMETRY. Any of a number of points from which the distances to any point of a given curve or solid obey a simple arithmetic relation, as (***a***) (of an ellipse) either of two points from which the distances to any point on the curve have a constant sum; (***b***) (of a parabola) a point whose distance from any point on the curve equals the distance from the directrix to the same point on the curve; (***c***) (of a hyperbola) either of two points from which the distances to any point on the curve have a constant difference. M17.

J. BRONOWSKI The orbit of a planet . . is a broad ellipse in which the sun is . . at one focus.

2 a PHYSICS. A point at which rays or waves (of light, heat, sound, etc.) meet after reflection or refraction, or (more fully ***virtual focus***) from which divergent rays appear to proceed. M17. ▸**b** The distance from a lens etc. to this point (= ***focal length***); the position at which an object must be situated for the image of it given by a lens or mirror to be sharply defined; the adjustment (of a lens, the eye, etc.) necessary to produce a well-defined image; the state of producing a clear image thus. L17. ▸**c** *fig.* A state of (unity and) clear definition. L18.

a J. F. W. HERSCHEL A far greater heat than can be produced in the focus of any burning-glass. H. D. THOREAU We were exactly in the focus of many echoes. **b** F. T. PALGRAVE Rapid alteration of the eye's focus in looking at the landscape. R. MACAULAY The distant prospect . . neared and acquired focus and clarity. W. BOYD His headache wouldn't allow him to bring the small print into focus. **c** W. S. JEVONS The transactions of many different individuals . . are brought to a focus.

a ***principal focus***: see PRINCIPAL *adjective.* **b** ***short focus***: see SHORT *adjective.*
3 MEDICINE. The primary or principal site in the body of an infection, malignant growth, or other disease. L17.
4 The centre of attention, activity, or greatest energy; the place of origin of an earthquake, a storm, a volcanic eruption, etc.; LINGUISTICS an element of a sentence that is given prominence by intonation etc. M18.

W. FAULKNER The courthouse the center, the focus, the hub. M. H. ABRAMS To shift the focus of critical interest from audience to artist. A. HAILEY Nim remained in the witness chair, the focus of attention. R. P. GRAVES He became the focus for romantic stories.

– PHRASES & COMB.: ***conjugate focus***: see CONJUGATE *adjective.* **depth of focus** (***a***) = ***depth of field*** s.v. FIELD *noun*; (***b***) the distance between the two extreme axial points behind a lens at which an image is judged to be in focus. ***FIXED focus***. **focus group** a group of people chosen to be representative of the population as a whole or of a specific subset of the population, and brought together to take part in guided discussions about consumer products, political policies, etc., so that their attitudes and opinions can be studied. **focus puller** an assistant to a film or television cameraman, who is responsible for keeping the lens focused during filming. **in focus**, **out of focus** giving, not giving, a sharply defined image as seen through a lens, the eye, etc. ***virtual focus***: see sense 2a above.
■ **focusless** *adjective* L19.

focus /ˈfəʊkəs/ *verb.* Infl. **-s-**, **-ss-**. L18.
[ORIGIN from the noun.]
1 *verb trans.* Make converge to or as to a focus; bring into focus; adjust the focus of (the eye, a lens, etc.); concentrate *on*. L18. ▸**b** *verb intrans.* Focus the eye, a lens, etc. M19.

R. BRADBURY I raised the beam of my flashlight . . , I focused it . . on the hole in the yellow ceiling. O. MANNING Guy tilted forward his glasses and tried to focus the spectacle before him. C. ACHEBE He took a little time to focus his eyes properly and decide who I was. H. M. ROSENBERG Electrons can be focussed into narrow beams by electrostatic or magnetic lenses. C. PRIEST I focused much of my distemper on London: I noticed only its bad qualities.

2 *verb intrans.* Converge to or as to a focus; come into focus; come to a focus; concentrate or be concentrated *on*. M19.

I. MURDOCH My eyes were dazed by the change of light and could not focus. H. KISSINGER Our concerns were still focusing on Iraq. A. BLEASDALE Miss Sutcliffe looks around the room, focuses finally on a big . . wardrobe. *Times* The DTI would not say whether the inspectors . . would focus on specific cases.

■ **focusable** *adjective* L19. **focuser** *noun* a device for focusing; *spec.* an electrostatic or magnetic device for focusing particles: L19.

fodder /ˈfɒdə/ *noun & verb.*
[ORIGIN Old English *fōdor* = Middle Low German *vōder*, Middle Dutch & mod. Dutch *voeder*, Old High German *fuotar* (German *Futter*), Old Norse *fóðr*, from Germanic, from base rel. to that of FOOD.]
▸ **A** *noun.* †**1** Food in general. OE–M17.
2 Food for cattle, horses, etc. Now *spec.* dried food, as hay, straw, etc., for stall-feeding. See also ***cannon fodder*** s.v. CANNON *noun.* OE.
– COMB.: **fodder-cheese** cheese made from the milk of cows being foddered on hay.
▸ **B** *verb trans.* Give fodder to; feed *with* as fodder. In early use also *gen.*, feed. LME.
■ **fodderer** *noun* E17. **fodderless** *adjective* M19.

fodge /fɒdʒ/ *noun. Scot. & N. English.* Also **fadge** /fadʒ/. M18.
[ORIGIN Unknown. Cf. FODGEL (earlier).]
A short fat person.

fodgel /ˈfɒdʒ(ə)l/ *adjective. Scot.* E18.
[ORIGIN Prob. from FODGE: see -EL[2].]
Plump, buxom.

fodient /ˈfəʊdɪənt/ *adjective & noun. rare.* L17.
[ORIGIN Latin *fodient-* pres. ppl stem of *fodere* dig: see -ENT.]
▸ **A** *adjective.* Digging, burrowing. L17.
▸ **B** *noun.* A burrowing animal. L19.

FoE *abbreviation.*
Friends of the Earth.

foe /fəʊ/ *adjective & noun.* Now *poet. & rhet.* OE.
[ORIGIN Repr. two distinct Old English words: (i) *fāh* adjective = Old Frisian *fāch*, (ii) *ġefā* noun, orig. use as noun of adjective = at feud (with), both = Old High German *gifēh* at feud, odious, from West Germanic. After the prefix *ge-* Y- was lost in early Middle English, the simple adjective and the orig. compound noun became coincident.]
▸ **A** *adjective.* At feud *with*; hostile, inimical (*to*). Long *obsolete* exc. in FOEMAN. OE.
▸ **B** *noun.* **1** Orig., an adversary in a feud or in mortal combat. Now more widely, a personal enemy or opponent, an ill wisher, *fig.* a thing inimical to one's well-being. OE.

POPE Embrace, embrace, my sons! be foes no more!

2 A member of a hostile army or nation, an enemy in battle or war. ME.

C. BOWEN Trojans eye me in wrath, and demand my life as a foe! C. DAY Aside from colds, . . his only foes were sick headaches.

3 *collect.* A hostile force, the enemy. L16.

C. RYAN A foe most of them remember as the fiercest soldiers they had ever encountered.

foehn *noun* see FÖHN.

foeman /ˈfəʊmən/ *noun. arch. & literary.* Pl. **-men**. OE.
[ORIGIN from FOE *adjective* + MAN *noun.*]
An enemy in war, an adversary.

foetal *adjective* var. of FETAL.

foetalisation, **foetalization** *nouns* vars. of FETALIZATION.

foetation *noun* var. of FETATION.

foeticide *noun* var. of FETICIDE.

foetid *adjective* var. of FETID.

foetiferous *adjective* var. of FETIFEROUS.

foetor *noun* var. of FETOR.

foetus *noun* var. of FETUS.

FOF *abbreviation* var. of FOAF.

fog /fɒg/ *noun*[1]. LME.
[ORIGIN Uncertain: cf. Norwegian *fogg.*]
1 The grass which springs up after hay has been cut; the aftermath. Also, long grass left standing in a pasture or among stubble and used as winter grazing. LME.
under fog with the long grass left standing. ***YORKSHIRE fog***.
2 Moss. *Scot. & N. English.* LME.

fog /fɒg/ *noun*[2]. M16.
[ORIGIN Perh. back-form. from FOGGY *adjective.*]
1 A thick cloud of minute water droplets suspended in the atmosphere at or near the earth's surface, esp. when combined with dust or smoke; the obscurity produced by this. M16. ▸**b** *transf.* Any abnormal darkened state of the atmosphere; an opaque mass *of* smoke. E17.

J. MASEFIELD Then fog came down . . and hid the seas.

2 *fig.* A state of perplexity. Esp. in ***in a fog***. E17.

J. GARDNER He wandered . . in a mental fog, unable to recognize his car when he saw it.

3 PHOTOGRAPHY. A deposit of silver on a negative or print etc., obscuring the image; an unwanted clouding. M19.
– COMB.: **fog bank** a dense haze at sea; **fogbound** unable to proceed because of fog; **fogbow** a phenomenon like a rainbow, produced by the action of light on fog; **fog-dog** = DOG *noun* 10; **foghorn** *noun & verb* (***a***) *noun* a sounding instrument (on a ship or on shore) warning ships in a fog; *fig.* (*colloq.*) a loud penetrating voice; (***b***) *verb trans. & intrans.* (*colloq.*) utter or talk in a loud penetrating voice; **fog lamp**: for improving visibility in fog; **fogman** a railwayman who places fog signals; **fog signal** (***a***) a detonator placed on a railway line in foggy weather to warn drivers; (***b***) (the signal given by) a foghorn.
■ **fogless** *adjective* M19.

fog /fɒg/ *verb*[1]. Infl. **-gg-**. L16.
[ORIGIN from FOG *noun*[2].]
▸ **I** *verb trans.* **1** Surround or choke with fog; cover with fog or condensed vapour, steam or mist *up*. L16.

W. BARLOW Somtimes by clouds it [the sun] is enueloped, and by mists fogged. A. HIGGINS Hot steam drifted about her, fogging up the window.

2 Put in a mental fog; bemuse, perplex. Also, make (an idea) confused. E19.

R. MACAULAY This reply had . . so fogged the poor reporter's mind that he had written no more.

3 PHOTOGRAPHY. Affect with an obscuring deposit of silver, make cloudy. M19.
4 *verb trans.* Treat with something in the form of a spray, esp. an insecticide. Chiefly as ***fogging*** *verbal noun.* M20.
▸ **II** *verb intrans.* **5** HORTICULTURE. Of a plant: damp *off*. M19.
6 Become covered or filled with fog; become covered with condensed vapour, steam or mist *up*. L19.

T. O'BRIEN When his glasses fogged he did not bother to wipe them.

7 Place fog signals on a railway line. Chiefly as ***fogging*** *verbal noun.* L19.

fog /fɒg/ *verb*[2]. Infl. **-gg-**. E18.
[ORIGIN from FOG *noun*[1].]
1 *verb intrans.* Become overgrown with moss. *Scot.* E18.
2 *verb trans.* AGRICULTURE. Leave (land) under fog. Also, feed (animals) on fog or foggage. E19.

fogey /ˈfəʊgi/ *noun & adjective.* Also **fogy**, (*Scot.*) **foggie** /ˈfɒgi/. L18.
[ORIGIN Rel. to FOGRAM.]
▸ **A** *noun.* **1** An elderly or decrepit person, *esp.* one with old-fashioned or conservative ideas. Chiefly ***old fogey***. *derog.* (orig. *Scot.*). L18.

J. RAE Some old fogey they have dragged out of retirement.

young fogey a young person with markedly conservative tastes or ideas.
2 An invalid or garrison soldier. *Scot.* (*obsolete* exc. *hist.*). L18.
▸ **B** *adjective.* Antiquated in ideas or outlook; fogeyish. *derog.* M19.

Sunday Telegraph The reactionary and Fogey elements at the Vatican.

■ **fogeydom** *noun* the condition of a fogey M19. **fogeyish** *adjective* resembling or characteristic of a fogey L19. **fogeyism** *noun* the ideas or condition of a fogey M19.

foggage /ˈfɒgɪdʒ/ *noun. Scot.* L15.
[ORIGIN medieval Latin *fogagium*, from FOG *noun*[1]: see -AGE.]
1 = FOG *noun*[1]. L15.
2 (The right of) pasturing cattle on fog. *obsolete* exc. *hist.* L15.

fogger /ˈfɒgə/ *noun.* L16.
[ORIGIN Perh. from *Fugger*, surname of a family of merchants and financiers of Augsburg in the 15th and 16th cents.]
1 A person given to underhand practices for the sake of gain; *esp.* a low-class lawyer. Long *obsolete* exc. in PETTIFOGGER. L16.
2 A petty chapman; a pedlar. *dial.* E19.

F

3 A middleman between a nail-maker and a wholesale nail-merchant. *obsolete* exc. *hist.* **M19.**

foggy /ˈfɒgi/ *adjective.* **L15.**
[ORIGIN In branch II certainly, and perh. in branch I also, from FOG *noun*[1].]
▸ **I 1** Of air, mist, etc.: thick and murky. Also, having the consistency of or filled with fog or thick mist. **L15.** ▸**b** *fig.* Esp. of the understanding: confused, muddled. Of an idea or perception: indistinct. **E17.**

b K. ISHIGURO My memory's so foggy these days.

2 Of flesh etc.: spongy in consistency, flabby. Of a person or animal: unwholesomely fat or bloated. *obsolete* exc. *dial.* **M16.**
†**3** Marshy, boggy. **M16–M17.**
†**4** Of beer: thick with floating particles. **E17–M18.**
5 PHOTOGRAPHY. Obscured by a deposit of silver, cloudy. **M19.**
– SPECIAL COLLOCATIONS & PHRASES: **Foggy Bottom** *US colloq.* Washington DC. **not have the foggiest**, **not have the foggiest idea**, **not have the foggiest notion** *colloq.* not have the slightest idea.
▸ **II 6** Resembling, consisting of, or covered with fog or rank grass; *Scot.* mossy. **M17.**
■ **foggily** *adverb* **L16.** **fogginess** *noun* **M16.**

F

fogle /ˈfəʊg(ə)l/ *noun. arch. slang.* **E19.**
[ORIGIN Unknown.]
A (silk) handkerchief.

fogou /ˈfəʊguː/ *noun.* **L19.**
[ORIGIN Cornish *fogo*, *fougo*.]
ARCHAEOLOGY. A Cornish form of souterrain.

fogram /ˈfəʊgrəm/ *noun & adjective. arch. slang.* **M18.**
[ORIGIN Unknown.]
▸ **A** *noun.* An old-fashioned person; a fogey. **M18.**
▸ **B** *adjective.* Old-fashioned or antiquated in outlook. **L18.**

fogy *noun* var. of FOGEY.

foh *interjection* var. of FAUGH.

föhn /fəːn/ *noun.* In sense 2 freq. **foehn.** **M19.**
[ORIGIN German, in Old High German *phōnno*, Middle High German *foenne*, ult. from Latin (*ventus*) *Favonius* mild west wind.]
1 A warm dry south wind which blows down the valleys on the north side of the Alps. **M19.**
2 METEOROLOGY. A warm dry katabatic wind developing on the lee side of a mountain range in response to air moving across the range. Also ***föhn wind***. **L19.**

foible /ˈfɔɪb(ə)l/ *adjective & noun.* **L16.**
[ORIGIN French, obsolete var. of *faible*: see FEEBLE *adjective*.]
▸ †**A** *adjective.* Weak, feeble. **L16–E18.**
▸ **B** *noun.* **1** FENCING. = FEEBLE *noun* 2. Cf. FORTE *noun*[1] 1. **M17.**
2 A special defect or peculiarity in a person's character etc., *esp.* one forming a source of misguided pride. **L17.**

THACKERAY A foible of Mr. Holt's . . was omniscience. A. FRATER He had flown with the emir . . and was familiar with his foibles at the controls.

foiblesse /fwablɛs/ *noun.* Now *rare* or *obsolete*. Pl. pronounced same. **L17.**
[ORIGIN French, obsolete var. of *faiblesse*, from *faible* FEEBLE *adjective*.]
A weakness of character; a failing; a liking or weakness *for*.

foie gras /fwɑː ˈgrɑː/ *noun phr. colloq.* Also **foie-gras.** **E19.**
[ORIGIN Abbreviation.]
= ***PÂTÉ de foie gras***.

foil /fɔɪl/ *noun*[1]. **ME.**
[ORIGIN Partly from Old French *foil* masc. from Latin *folium* leaf, partly from Old French *foille* fem. (mod. *feuille*) from Latin *folia* neut. pl. of *folium* treated as fem. sing. Cf. CINQUEFOIL, MILFOIL, TREFOIL.]
1 Metal (or †other substance) hammered or rolled into a thin sheet. Now also, metallized plastic film. **ME.**

K. AMIS To take the foil off the roasting capon and put it higher in the gas-oven.

aluminium foil, ***tin foil***, etc.
†**2** A leaf; a heraldic representation of a leaf. **LME–M16.**
3 †**a** *gen.* A thin layer of any material; a paring. **LME–E17.** ▸**b** A counterfoil. Now *rare* or *obsolete*. **L15.**
4 A thin leaf of metal placed under a precious stone to increase its brilliance or under a transparent substance to give it the appearance of a precious stone. Formerly also, the setting of a precious stone. **LME.**

HENRY FIELDING The finest brilliant requires a foil.

5 A sheet of metal foil (now usu. of a tin amalgam) placed behind the glass of a mirror as a reflector; *gen.* a backing, a backing. **L16.**
6 A thing which or person who sets off another by contrast. **L16.**

HAZLITT Real excellence does not seek for a foil in inferiority.

7 ARCHITECTURE. Each of the small arcs between the cusps of a Gothic window or arch. **M19.**

foil /fɔɪl/ *noun*[2]. *arch.* **L15.**
[ORIGIN from FOIL *verb*[1] III.]
1 A setback or check in an enterprise; a repulse, a defeat. **L15.**

C. MARLOWE Never had the . . Emperor So great a foil by any foreign foe. R. SOUTH It may give a man many a . . foil and many a disheartening blow.

†**2** WRESTLING. A throw not resulting in a complete fall. **M16–L17.**

foil /fɔɪl/ *noun*[3]. **L16.**
[ORIGIN from FOIL *verb*[1] I. Cf. Old French *foulis*, Old French & mod. French *foulée* in same sense.]
HUNTING. **1** The track or scent of a hunted animal. **L16.**
run the foil, **run upon the foil** (of a hunted animal) run over the same track a second time (and so baffle hounds).
2 A scent obliterating that of a hunted animal. **M20.**

foil /fɔɪl/ *noun*[4]. **L16.**
[ORIGIN Unknown.]
A light blunt-edged fencing sword with a button on the point; in *pl. & sing.*, the exercise of fencing with such weapons.

foil /fɔɪl/ *noun*[5]. **M20.**
[ORIGIN Abbreviation.]
= HYDROFOIL.
– COMB.: **foil-borne** (of a boat) lifted out of the water by means of hydrofoils; (of the motion etc. of a boat) taking place while the boat is so supported.

foil /fɔɪl/ *verb*[1]. **ME.**
[ORIGIN Perh. from Anglo-Norman var. of Old French & mod. French *fouler* full cloth, trample, ult. from Latin *fullo* FULLER *noun*[1]. The development in branch II is paralleled in DEFOIL, DEFOUL.]
▸ **I** In sense of French *fouler*: cf. FULL *verb*[1].
1 *verb trans.* Trample, tread down. *obsolete* exc. *dial.* **ME.**

R. KNOLLES King Richard . . caused the ensignes of Leopold . . to be puld downe, and foiled under foot.

2 *verb trans. & intrans.* HUNTING. Cross (ground, a scent or track), or, formerly, travel *down* a stream, in such a way as to obliterate the scent. **LME.**
▸ **II** Infl. by FOUL *adjective*, *verb*.
3 *verb trans.* Foul, pollute. *obsolete* exc. *dial.* **LME.**

N. UDALL A man hath no honour to foile his handes on a woman.

†**4** *verb trans.* Violate the chastity of (a woman). **LME–L16.**
▸ **III** (Cf. earlier FOIL *noun*[2].)
5 *verb trans.* Defeat or repulse (an opponent); beat off (an attack). Formerly also (in wrestling), inflict a foil or incomplete fall on. **M16.** ▸†**b** *verb intrans.* Suffer defeat or discomfiture. **L16–M17.** ▸**c** *verb trans.* Outdo, surpass. **L17.**

POPE Not fiercer woes thy fortitude could foil.

6 *verb trans.* Render ineffectual, frustrate, (a plan, attempt, etc.); frustrate the efforts or designs of (a person etc.). **M16.**

A. HOPKINS With enchanting waywardness he . . foils expectations. P. L. FERMOR Nets over the . . currant bushes foiled starlings but not us.

foil /fɔɪl/ *verb*[2] *trans.* **L16.**
[ORIGIN from FOIL *noun*[1].]
Chiefly as ***foiled*** *ppl adjective*.
1 Place foil under (a crystal etc.) to accentuate its brilliance; *fig.* set off by contrast. **L16.**
†**2** Coat (glass, a mirror) with metal foil on one side as a reflector. Also, cover *over* (as) with foil. **E17–E19.**
3 ARCHITECTURE. Ornament with foils. **M19.**

foiling /ˈfɔɪlɪŋ/ *noun*[1]. **M16.**
[ORIGIN from FOIL *verb*[1] + -ING[1].]
The action of FOIL *verb*[1]; *esp.* the treading of a deer or other animal. Also, an animal's trail.

foiling /ˈfɔɪlɪŋ/ *noun*[2]. **L16.**
[ORIGIN from FOIL *verb*[2] + -ING[1].]
The action or process of FOIL *verb*[2]; ARCHITECTURE ornamentation in the form of foils.

foilist /ˈfɔɪlɪst/ *noun.* **E20.**
[ORIGIN from FOIL *noun*[4] + -IST.]
A person who fences with a foil.

†**foillage** *noun* see FOLIAGE *noun*.

†**foin** *noun*[1]. **ME–E18.**
[ORIGIN Old French *foine* (mod. *fouine*) from Proto-Romance deriv. of Latin *fagus* beech.]
(The fur of) the beech marten, *Martes foina*; in *pl.*, garments or trimmings of this fur.

foin /fɔɪn/ *noun*[2]. *arch.* **ME.**
[ORIGIN Old French *foine*, *foisne* (mod. *fouine*) three-pronged fish spear, from Latin *fuscina* trident; partly from FOIN *verb*.]
†**1** A kind of spear. Only in **ME.**
2 A thrust made with a pointed weapon. **LME.**

M. TWAIN Arthur smote . . Mordred with a foin of his spear.

†**3** = FOIL *noun*[4]. **M17–E18.**

foin /fɔɪn/ *verb. arch.* **LME.**
[ORIGIN from FOIN *noun*[2].]
1 *verb intrans.* Make a thrust with or *with* a pointed weapon; lunge. Freq. foll. by *at* a person. **LME.**

transf.: G. CAVENDISH The boare continually foining at him with his great tuskes.

†**2** *verb trans.* Thrust at, stab. **LME–M16.**

foison /ˈfɔɪz(ə)n/ *noun.* **ME.**
[ORIGIN Old French & mod. French from Proto-Romance from Latin *fusio(n-)* outpouring: see FUSION, PROFUSION.]
▸ **A** *noun.* **1** A plentiful supply, an abundance, (*of*); *esp.* a plentiful harvest. Formerly also (in *pl.*), abundant resources. *arch.* **ME.**

R. W. HAMILTON We anticipate the foison of an unknown husbandry. J. R. LOWELL He has a perennial foison of sappiness.

2 Inherent vigour, strength, or vitality. Now chiefly *Scot.* **ME.**

HENRY SMITH Such a foison hath your alms that . . it increases, like the widow's meal.

3 Sustaining power; nutriment. Now *Scot. & dial.* **LME.**

J. GEE The Liturgie . . is but dry meat, and hath no foison in it.

▸ **B** *verb trans.* Supply generously (*with*). Long *arch.* **LME.**

Maclean's Magazine Mr. Boyczuk won ribbons for his tray foisoned with grapes and apples.

■ **foisonless** *adjective* (chiefly *Scot.*) (**a**) lacking strength, weak, exhausted; (**b**) not nutritious: **E18.**

foist /fɔɪst/ *noun*[1]. **LME.**
[ORIGIN formed as FUST *noun*[1].]
†**1** A wooden cask for wine etc. **LME–M16.**
2 A fusty smell. **E19.**

†**foist** *noun*[2]. **L15.**
[ORIGIN Old French & mod. French *fuste* from Italian *fusta*, from *fusto* stem, trunk or from Latin *fustis* cudgel.]
1 A vessel propelled both by sails and oars; a light galley. **L15–L18.**
2 A river barge. **M16–E17.**

†**foist** *noun*[3]. **L16.**
[ORIGIN from FOIST *verb*[1].]
1 A cheat or dishonest person; *spec.* a pickpocket. **L16–L17.**
2 An act of deception, a trick. **E–M17.**
3 A fraudulent insertion. **M18–E19.**

foist *noun*[4] see FIST *noun*[2].

foist /fɔɪst/ *verb*[1]. **M16.**
[ORIGIN Dutch dial. *vuisten*, from *vuist* FIST *noun*[1].]
†**1** *verb trans. & intrans.* Palm (a false die) so as to be able to produce it at the right moment. Only in **M16.** ▸**b** *verb intrans.* Practise deception, cheat; *spec.* pick a pocket. **L16–L18.**
2 *verb trans.* Introduce *in*, *into* surreptitiously or unwarrantably. **L16.**

LYTTON The . . interpolations . . supposed to be foisted into the Odyssey.

3 *verb trans.* Impose (an unwelcome person or thing) *on*, *upon*; palm off or *off* (something worthless). Also, falsely fix the authorship of (a composition) *on*, *upon*. **L16.**

MILTON The unskilfull fraud of him that foisted this Epistle upon Ignatius. G. A. SALA You have inferior articles foisted on you while being charged for the best. W. VAN T. CLARK Men . . only too willing to foist the burden . . on to others. G. GREENE God knows what Foreign Office type they might foist on us.

foist /fɔɪst/ *verb*[2]. *obsolete* exc. *dial.* **L16.**
[ORIGIN from FOIST *noun*[1]. Cf. FUST *verb*.]
Become fusty.

†**foist** *verb*[3] var. of FIST *verb*[2].

foisty /ˈfɔɪsti/ *adjective.* **E16.**
[ORIGIN from FOIST *noun*[1] + -Y[1]. Cf. FUSTY.]
Having a stale musty smell; fusty.

fol. *abbreviation.*
Folio.

folacin /ˈfəʊləsɪn/ *noun.* **M20.**
[ORIGIN from FOL(IC + AC(ID *noun* + -IN[1].]
= ***FOLIC acid***.

folate /ˈfəʊleɪt, ˈfɒl-/ *noun.* **M20.**
[ORIGIN from FOLIC + -ATE[1].]
BIOCHEMISTRY. A salt or ester of folic acid.

fold /fəʊld/ *noun*[1].
[ORIGIN Old English *fald* contr. of *falæd*, *falod*, *-ud*, corresp. to Old Saxon *faled*, Middle Low German *valt*, Dutch *vaalt*.]
1 A pen or enclosure for livestock, esp. sheep. **OE.** ▸**b** An enclosed piece of ground forming part of a farm. Now *rare.* **LME.** ▸**c** The animals enclosed in a fold (now *rare*); *spec.* in *Scot.*, a herd of Highland cows used for breeding. **M17.**
2 *fig.* The Church, the body of Christian believers; *the* group of people who share a particular set of values etc. **ME.**

W. S. MAUGHAM He met an abbé who was celebrated for his success in bringing infidels and heretics back to the fold.

– COMB.: **fold-course** *hist.* the right of faldage; the land subject to this right.
■ **foldless** *adjective*[1] having no fold or pen **E19.**

fold /fəʊld/ *noun*[2]. **ME.**
[ORIGIN from FOLD *verb*[1].]
1 (Either of) the two parts of an object which are brought together in folding; the hollow between two such parts. **ME.** ▸**b** A leaf of a book; each side of a double door. Now

chiefly, a layer or thickness of cloth etc. E16. ▸c A coil of a serpent's body or of string etc. L16. ▸d An undulation or gentle curve of the ground; a slight hill or hollow. M19. ▸e *GEOLOGY*. A bending or curvature in rock strata. M19.

A. GRAY The thick woollen stockings . . would not stay up but hung in folds round her ankles. G. HEYER Her crooked fingers worked amongst the folds of her silken skirt. **d** H. BELLOC That kind of landscape in which hills seem to lie in a regular manner, fold on fold, one range behind the other.

2 The action of folding. Formerly also, an embrace. E17. ▸b A manner or way of folding paper etc. L19.

SHAKES. *Tr. & Cr.* And the weak wanton Cupid Shall from your neck unloose his amorous fold.

3 A line or crease made by folding. M19.
■ **foldless** *adjective*[2] having no fold or crease M19.

fold /fəʊld/ *noun*[3]. ME.
[ORIGIN from -FOLD in *manifold*, *threefold*, etc.]
†**1** A time, a repetition. Chiefly in ***many a fold***. ME–L17.
2 (A specified number of) times. L17.

N. ARNOTT The effect was found to be several fold greater than of steam from the same quantity of fuel.

3 Each portion of a manifold thing. *rare*. E19.

fold /fəʊld/ *verb*[1].
[ORIGIN Old English *faldan*, *fealdan* = Middle Dutch *vouden* (*vouwen*), Old High German *faltan* (German *falten*), Old Norse *falda*, Gothic *falþan*, from Germanic redupl. strong verb.]
1 *verb trans.* Double or bend (a flexible thing) over on itself (also foll. by *in*, *over*, *together*); bend (a portion of a thing) *back*, *down*. OE. ▸b *verb trans. GEOLOGY*. Cause (rock strata etc.) to undergo bending or curvature. L19.

W. H. AUDEN He envies those who have learned, / when reading newspapers, / how to fold them.

2 *verb trans.* Lay (the arms etc.) together so as to overlap or intertwine; clasp (the hands) together or (now usu.) *together*. OE. ▸†b Plait; mat (hair). LME–L16.

R. COBB Even if they had had wings, they would have kept them prudently folded. C. P. SNOW His hands, folded on his blotting-paper, stood out heavy-knuckled.

3 *verb trans. & intrans.* Coil, wind. Now only with *about*, *round*. ME.
4 *verb trans.* Enclose (as) in a fold or folds, swathe, envelop (foll. by *in*, †*with*); embrace, clasp *in* one's arms or *to* one's breast. ME.

TENNYSON Shadows of the silver birk Sweep the green that folds thy grave. E. WHARTON Mrs Fisher . . had folded her in a demonstrative embrace.

5 *verb intrans.* Yield to pressure so as to become folded, admit of being folded. Formerly also *fig.*, falter, lose courage; yield, succumb. Now chiefly as ***folding*** *ppl adjective*. ME. ▸b *GEOLOGY*. Of rock strata etc.: undergo bending or curvature. M19. ▸c Collapse; cease to function, go bankrupt. Also foll. by *up*. E20.

c A. BURGESS His trick cycle folded under him. S. BELLOW Competitors are trying to steal my chemist from me. Without him I'll have to fold.

†**6** *verb trans. & intrans.* Bend (oneself, a limb, etc.), bow. ME–E17.
7 *verb intrans. BIOCHEMISTRY*. Of a polypeptide or polynucleotide chain: adopt a specific three-dimensional structure. M20.
– WITH ADVERBS IN SPECIALIZED SENSES: **fold away** make more compact by folding. **fold in** *COOKERY* add (an ingredient) gently with a spoon, fork, etc., so as to mix it in without stirring or beating. **fold out** admit of being unfolded. **fold up** = *fold away* above; (see also sense 5c above).
– COMB.: **foldaway** *adjective* adapted to be folded away; **foldboat** [translating German *Faltboot*] = FALTBOAT; **fold-out** *noun & adjective* (an oversize page in a magazine etc.) which has to be unfolded by the reader; **fold-up** *adjective* adapted to be folded up.
■ **foldable** *adjective* L19.

fold /fəʊld/ *verb*[2] *trans.* OE.
[ORIGIN from FOLD *noun*[1].]
1 Enclose (sheep etc.) in a fold; *fig.* bring into the body of Christian believers. Also foll. by *up*. OE.

I. MURDOCH There was the distant sound of folded sheep.

2 Place sheep in a fold or folds on (a piece of land) to manure it. L17.

-fold /fəʊld/ *suffix*.
[ORIGIN Old English *-fald*, *-feald* = Old Frisian, Old Saxon *-fald* (Dutch *-voud*), Old & mod. High German *-falt*, Old Norse *-faldr*, Goth *-falþs*, cogn. with FOLD *verb*[1] and with Greek *-paltos*, *-plasios*, also with *plo-* in *haplos*, and prob. with Latin (*sim*)*plex*.]
Forming adjectives and adverbs from cardinal numerals and adjectives meaning 'many' with the senses 'multiplied by', 'in an amount multiplied by', 'having so many parts', as in ***threefold***, ***manifold***, etc., and parallel nouns used with *a* with the sense 'a specified number or amount of times' (cf. FOLD *noun*[3]).

†**foldage** *noun* var. of FALDAGE.

folder /ˈfəʊldə/ *noun*[1]. Now *rare*. L16.
[ORIGIN from FOLD *verb*[2] + -ER[1].]
A person who folds sheep, a shepherd.

folder /ˈfəʊldə/ *noun*[2]. M17.
[ORIGIN from FOLD *verb*[1] + -ER[1]. Earlier in UNFOLDER.]
1 *gen.* A person who folds or doubles over something. Also foll. by *up*. M17.
2 A machine which folds paper etc. M19.
3 A folded pamphlet, circular, etc. *US*. L19.
4 A folding cover or holder for loose papers. E20.

folderol /ˈfɒldərɒl/ *noun*. Also **falderal** /ˈfaldəral/. E19.
[ORIGIN from a meaningless refrain in songs.]
A showy but useless item, a trifle; nonsense, trivial display.

E. GARRETT That his darling might never want for fal-de-rals. *Nation* The brochure for the seminar is chock-full of motivational folderol.

folding /ˈfəʊldɪŋ/ *noun*. LME.
[ORIGIN from FOLD *verb*[1] + -ING[1].]
1 The action of FOLD *verb*[1]; an instance of this. LME.
2 A point or place of folding; a hill, a hollow; a group of hills or hollows; a fold of a garment. LME.

SIR W. SCOTT The foldings of his mantle green.

– COMB.: **folding strength** the capacity of paper to withstand continuous alternate folding without tearing.

folding /ˈfəʊldɪŋ/ *ppl adjective*. E17.
[ORIGIN from FOLD *verb*[1] + -ING[2].]
That folds; that is or can be folded.
folding door(s): consisting of two or more sections which can be folded against each other. **folding money** *colloq.* paper money.

foley /ˈfəʊli/ *noun*. Also **F-**. L20.
[ORIGIN The name of Jack *Foley* (1891–1967), US film sound technician, who pioneered the technique.]
Used *attrib.*, as ***foley artist***, ***foley editing***, etc., with ref. to a cinematographic technique for adding recorded sound effects after the shooting of a film.

folia /fəˈliə/ *noun*[1]. L18.
[ORIGIN Portuguese, lit. 'madness', from Provençal. Cf. FOLLY *noun*.]
A wild dance of Portuguese origin. Also, a special tune associated with this dance, esp. as a theme for instrumental variations.

folia *noun*[2] pl. of FOLIUM.

foliaceous /fəʊlɪˈeɪʃəs/ *adjective*. M17.
[ORIGIN Latin *foliaceus*, from *folium* leaf: see -ACEOUS.]
1 a *BOTANY*. Having the form or appearance of a leaf; (of a lichen) = FOLIOSE. Formerly, of a flower: having petals. M17. ▸b Of or pertaining to a leaf or leaves; consisting of leaves. E19.
2 *GEOLOGY*. Consisting of, or of the nature of, thin leaflike plates. E18.
3 *ZOOLOGY*. Shaped or arranged like leaves. E19.

foliage /ˈfəʊlɪɪdʒ/ *noun & verb*. Also (earlier) †**foillage**. LME.
[ORIGIN Alt. (after Latin *folium*) of Old French & mod. French *feuillage*, †*foillage*, from *feuille* leaf: see FOIL *noun*[1], -AGE.]
▸ **A** *noun*. **1** Ornamental representation of leaves. Also (now *rare* or *obsolete*), an instance of this. LME.
2 The leaves of a tree, plant, etc., collectively. E17.

J. HAWKES Every leaf gleams dully in the . . sun, and yet all are merged in the mass of heavy foliage.

– COMB.: **foliage leaf** a normal green leaf (opp. petals and other modified leaves); **foliage plant**: grown for its decorative leaves rather than for its flowers.
▸ **B** *verb trans.* Decorate with foliage (real or representational). Chiefly as ***foliaged*** *ppl adjective*. M18.

foliar /ˈfəʊlɪə/ *adjective*. L19.
[ORIGIN mod. Latin *foliaris*, from Latin *folium* leaf: see -AR[1].]
Of, pertaining to, or of the nature of a leaf.
foliar feed nutrients supplied to the leaves of a plant.

foliate /ˈfəʊlɪət, -eɪt/ *adjective*. E17.
[ORIGIN Latin *foliatus* leaved, from *folium* leaf: see -ATE[2].]
†**1** Of metal: beaten into foil. E17–E19.
2 Resembling a leaf; leaflike. M17.
3 Having leaves. Also, decorated with representations of foliage. L17.
4 *BOTANY*. = FOLIOLATE. Cf. TRIFOLIATE. M19.

foliate /ˈfəʊlɪeɪt/ *verb*. M17.
[ORIGIN from Latin *folium* leaf + -ATE[3]. With second part of sense 1 cf. medieval Latin *foliare*.]
1 *verb trans.* Apply foil or tin amalgam to (glass). Formerly also, beat (metal) into foil. M17.
2 *verb intrans.* Send out leaves. L18.

fig.: A. BURGESS These [euphemisms] are foliating like triffids.

3 *verb intrans.* Split into thin leaflike sheets or laminae. L18.
4 *verb trans. ARCHITECTURE*. Decorate (an arch etc.) with foils or leaf shapes. E19.
5 *verb trans.* Mark the leaves of (a book or manuscript) with consecutive numbers. Cf. PAGINATE. M19.

foliated /ˈfəʊlɪeɪtɪd/ *adjective*. M17.
[ORIGIN from FOLIATE *adjective*, *verb* + -ED[1].]
1 Chiefly *GEOLOGY & MINERALOGY*. Composed of thin leaflike sheets or laminae. M17.
2 Having or consisting of leaves. E18.
3 Chiefly *ZOOLOGY & CONCHOLOGY*. Shaped like a leaf or leaves; having leaflike processes. E19.
4 Decorated with carved foliage or with architectural foils. M19.

foliation /fəʊlɪˈeɪʃ(ə)n/ *noun*. E17.
[ORIGIN from FOLIATE *adjective*, *verb*: see -ATION.]
1 The process of bursting into leaf; the state of being in leaf. Also, a leaflike process or (formerly) scale. E17. ▸†b The petals of a flower. L17–M18. ▸c *BOTANY*. Arrangement of leaves in bud; vernation. L18.
2 Decoration of an arch etc. with foils; tracery made up of foils. E19. ▸b An arrangement of carved foliage. L19.
3 *GEOLOGY*. The process or property of splitting into leaflike sheets or laminae; the laminae into which a crystalline rock divides. M19.
4 The consecutive numbering of the leaves in a book or manuscript. M19.

foliator /ˈfəʊlɪeɪtə/ *noun*. M19.
[ORIGIN from FOLIATE *verb* + -OR.]
A person who numbers the leaves of a book etc.

foliature /ˈfəʊlɪətʃə/ *noun*. L17.
[ORIGIN Latin *foliatura*, from *foliatus* FOLIATE *adjective*: see -URE.]
(A cluster of) foliage. Also, carved foliage.

folic /ˈfəʊlɪk, ˈfɒl-/ *adjective*. M20.
[ORIGIN from Latin *folium* leaf + -IC.]
folic acid, a vitamin of the B complex found in leafy green vegetables, liver, and kidney, whose deficiency causes pernicious anaemia and which is chemically a pteroylglutamic acid with one glutamic acid residue. Also called ***folacin***, (chiefly *US*) ***vitamin M***.

folie /ˈfɒli; *foreign* fɔli (*pl. same*)/ *noun*. E19.
[ORIGIN French: see FOLLY *noun*.]
Mental illness, mania, madness. Chiefly in names of pathological conditions: see below.
folie à deux /ɑː ˈdəː, *foreign* a dø/ an identical delusion or mental disorder affecting two people living in close association. **folie de grandeur** /də ɡrɒ̃ˈdəː, *foreign* ɡrɑ̃dœːr/ delusions of grandeur. **folie du doute** /duː ˈduːt, *foreign* dy dut/ obsessive self-doubt.

foliferous *adjective* var. of FOLIIFEROUS.

foliicolous /fəʊlɪˈɪkələs/ *adjective*. L19.
[ORIGIN from Latin *folii-* combining form of *folium* leaf + -COLOUS.]
Of a liverwort or fungus: growing or parasitic on leaves.

foliiferous /fəʊlɪˈɪf(ə)rəs/ *adjective*. Also **foliferous** /fə(ʊ)ˈlɪf-/. E19.
[ORIGIN formed as FOLIICOLOUS + -FEROUS.]
Bearing leaves or leaflike appendages.

folio /ˈfəʊlɪəʊ/ *noun*, *adjective*, & *verb*. LME.
[ORIGIN In sense A.I, a generalization of medieval Latin use of abl. of Latin *folium* leaf, in references 'at leaf so-and-so', or a Latinization of Italian *foglio*. In sense A.II, developed from phr. *in folio*, from Italian *in foglio*.]
▸ **A** *noun*. Pl. **-os**.
▸ **I** With ref. to numbering.
1 An individual leaf of paper, parchment, etc. (either loose as one of a series, or forming part of a bound volume) which is numbered on the recto or front side only. LME.
2 *BOOKKEEPING*. The two opposite sides of a ledger or account book when they are used concurrently. Also, a single page of a ledger etc. showing both sides of an account. L16.
3 The page number in a printed book. L17.
4 A fixed number of words (in British legal documents etc. 72 or, in parliamentary proceedings, 90, in the US 100) used as a unit in reckoning the length of a document. M19.
▸ **II** With ref. to size.
5 A size of book in which each leaf is half a standard printing sheet. Usu. ***in folio***. L16.
6 A sheet of paper folded once to form two leaves (four pages). E17.
7 A book or manuscript made up of sheets of paper folded once; a volume of the largest size. E17.
First Folio the first collected edition of Shakespeare's works, published in folio format in 1623.
▸ **B** *adjective*. Formed of sheets (or a sheet) folded once; (of a book) of the largest standard size. E17.
▸ **C** *verb trans.* Number the pages of. Chiefly as ***folioing*** *verbal noun*. M19.

foliolate /ˈfəʊlɪələt, -eɪt/ *adjective*. M19.
[ORIGIN from FOLIOLE + -ATE[2].]
BOTANY. Consisting of leaflets; (with numerical prefix) having the specified number of leaflets, as ***3-foliolate***.

foliole /ˈfəʊlɪəʊl/ *noun*. M18.
[ORIGIN French from Latin *foliolum* dim. of *folium* leaf: see -OLE[1].]
1 *BOTANY*. Each of the divisions of a compound leaf; a leaflet. M18.
2 *ZOOLOGY*. A small leaflike appendage. M19.

foliose /ˈfəʊlɪəʊz/ *adjective*. E18.
[ORIGIN Latin *foliosus*, from *folium* leaf: see -OSE[1].]
Leafy; *spec.* (***a***) (of a liverwort) having the plant body differentiated into a stem and leaves (opp. ***thalloid***); (***b***) (of a lichen) in which the thallus is lobed and leaflike and

attached to the substrate by rhizoids (opp. ***crustose***, ***fruticose***).

foliot /ˈfɒlɪət/ *noun*. ME.
[ORIGIN Old French = fowler's snare, (also mod.) foliot of a clock, prob. from *folier* play the fool, from *fol* foolish. In sense 2 cf. Italian *folletto* = French (*esprit*) *follet*, dim. of *fol*.]
†**1** Foolish or deluding talk. Only in ME.
†**2** A kind of goblin. Only in E17.
3 *ANTIQUITIES*. The earliest form of escapement in clocks, consisting of a bar with adjustable weights on the ends. L19.

folium /ˈfəʊlɪəm/ *noun*. Pl. **-ia** /-ɪə/. M18.
[ORIGIN Latin.]
1 A leaf. Also, a leaflike process. Usu. in *pl*. M18.
2 *GEOLOGY*. A thin leaflike sheet, as of a schistose rock. Usu. in *pl*. L18.
3 *MATH*. ***folium of Descartes***, a cubic curve with a single node at which a single loop begins and ends. M19.
4 = FOLIO *noun* 6. *rare*. L19.

F

folivore /ˈfəʊlɪvɔː/ *noun*. L20.
[ORIGIN from Latin *foli(i)*- combining form of *folium* leaf: see -VORE.]
ZOOLOGY. An animal that feeds primarily on leaves.
■ **folivorous** /fə(ʊ)ˈlɪv(ə)rəs/ *adjective* (of an animal) feeding primarily on leaves; (of diet) consisting of leaves: L20.

folk /fəʊk/ *noun*. Pl. same, **-s**.
[ORIGIN Old English *folc* = Old Frisian *folk*, Old Saxon, Old High German *folc* (Dutch *volk*, German *Volk*), Old Norse *folk* people, army, detachment, from Germanic. Cf. VOLK.]
1 A people, a nation, a race; (of animals) a species, a kind. *arch*. OE.
2 In *pl*. (***folk***, †***folks***) & †*sing*. (A group of) people in relation to a superior, as the subjects of a king, the retainers or workpeople of a lord etc. *arch*. OE.

G. PETTIE The maister of the house . . ought . . to shewe himself more seuere towards his owne folke, then towards others.

3 In *pl*. (***folk(s)***) & (now *arch*. & *dial*.) *sing*. People in general. Freq. with qualifying adjective designating people of a certain group or class. Now chiefly *colloq*. OE.

S. JOHNSON Folks want me to go to Italy. J. B. PRIESTLEY The working folk of Lancashire have much in common, of course, with their Yorkshire neighbours. I. SHAW I don't have a rich father, like some folks I know.

the wee folk: see WEE *adjective*.
4 In *pl*. (***folk(s)***). Relatives, members of one's family; (*dial*. & *US*) friends, neighbours. M17.

C. BROWN My folks didn't come up too much. Dad would never come any place to see me.

5 *ellipt*. = ***folk music*** below. M20.
– ATTRIB. & COMB.: Esp. in the sense 'of the (common) mass of people, traditional, popular', as ***folk art***, ***folk belief***, ***folk culture***, ***folk hero***, ***folk legend***, ***folk literature***, ***folk myth***, ***folk remedy***, ***folk wisdom***, etc. Special combs., as **folk-blues** the original blues of the black Americans of the southern US, as opp. to composed imitations; **folk club** a club where folk music is performed; **folk dance** a dance of popular or traditional origin; a piece of music for such a dance; ***folk epic***: see EPIC *noun*; **folk-etymologize** *verb trans*. & *intrans*. alter by folk etymology; **folk etymology** the popular modifying of the form of a word to make it seem to be derived from familiar words, as ***sparrowgrass*** for ***asparagus***; **folkfest** (chiefly *N. Amer*.) a festival of folk music or other elements of folk culture; ***folk guitar***: see GUITAR *noun*; **folkland** *hist*. land which was the property of the common people; **folk medicine** medicine of a traditional kind employing herbal remedies etc.; **folk memory** (a) recollection of the past persisting among a (group of) people; **folkmoot**, **folkmote** *hist*. a general assembly of the people of a town, city, etc.; **folk music** music of popular or traditional origin; modern music composed in the style of this; **folk psychology** the psychology of races or peoples; **folk rock** folk music incorporating the stronger beat of rock music and usu. also electric stringed instruments; **folksay** *US* traditional speech, the speech, proverbs, etc., of an oral tradition; **folk singer** a singer of folk songs; **folk song** a song of popular or traditional origin; a modern composition in this style; **folk tale** a tale of popular or traditional origin; **folkway(s)** the traditional behaviour of a (group or class of) people; **folkweave** a rough loosely woven fabric.
■ **folkie** *noun* (*colloq*.) a folk singer; a devotee of folk music: M20. **folkish** *adjective* characteristic of the (common) people or traditional culture etc.; unsophisticated: M20. **folknik** *noun* [-NIK] a devotee of folk music M20.

folklore /ˈfəʊklɔː/ *noun*. M19.
[ORIGIN from FOLK + LORE *noun*[1].]
1 The traditional beliefs, customs, songs, tales, etc., preserved in oral tradition among a (group of) people; the branch of knowledge that deals with these. M19.
2 Popular fantasy or belief. M20.
■ **folkloric** *adjective* of or pertaining to folklore L19. **folklorish** *adjective* resembling folklore E20. **folklorist** *noun* a person who studies folklore M19. **folkloˈristic** *adjective* of or pertaining to folklore, of the character of folklore L19. **folkloˈristics** *noun* folklore as a branch of knowledge or a subject of research M20.

folksy /ˈfəʊksi/ *adjective*. M19.
[ORIGIN from FOLK + -SY.]
1 Friendly, sociable, informal. M19.

D. MORGAN His folksy, direct style, uncomplicated . . values, and support for social legislation . . resonated with the Okies.

2 Having the characteristics of folk art or culture; *esp*. ostensibly or artificially folkish. M20.

R. SCARCE The music twangs folksy and with a heavy heaping from a hymnal.

■ **folksiness** *noun* M20.

folky /ˈfəʊki/ *adjective*. E20.
[ORIGIN from FOLK + -Y[1].]
= FOLKSY 2.
■ **folkiness** *noun* M20.

folles *noun* pl. of FOLLIS.

follicle /ˈfɒlɪk(ə)l/ *noun*. Also (*rare*) **-cule** /-kjuːl/. LME.
[ORIGIN Latin *folliculus* little bag, dim. of *follis* bellows: see -CULE.]
1 *ANATOMY*. Any of various small rounded saclike or vesicular structures, often having a secretory function; *esp*. (***a***) (also ***hair follicle***) a secretory gland or cavity containing a hair root; (***b***) any of the cavities in the ovary in which ova form. LME.
GRAAFIAN ***follicle***.
2 *BOTANY*. **a** A capsular fruit. Now *spec*. a single-carpelled fruit opening on one side only. E18. ▸**b** An air-filled vesicle. L18.
– COMB.: **follicle-stimulating hormone** a pituitary hormone which promotes ripening of the follicles in the ovary and sperm formation in the testes; abbreviation ***FSH***.

follicular /fɒˈlɪkjʊlə/ *adjective*. L17.
[ORIGIN Latin *follicularis*, formed as FOLLICLE: see -AR[1].]
1 Of the nature of or resembling a follicle; consisting of follicles. L17.
2 Of or pertaining to a follicle or follicles; affecting follicles of a particular kind. M19.
■ **follicularly** *adverb* L20.

folliculated /fɒˈlɪkjʊleɪtɪd/ *adjective*. L18.
[ORIGIN formed as FOLLICLE + -ATE[2] + -ED[1].]
Provided with a follicle or follicles.

follicule *noun* var. of FOLLICLE.

folliculitis /fəlɪkjʊˈlʌɪtɪs/ *noun*. M19.
[ORIGIN formed as FOLLICLE + -ITIS.]
Inflammation of (esp. hair) follicles.

folliculose /fɒˈlɪkjʊləʊs/ *adjective*. E19.
[ORIGIN Latin *folliculosus*, formed as FOLLICLE: see -OSE[1].]
= FOLLICULAR 1.

folliful /ˈfɒlɪfʊl, -f(ə)l/. *adjective*. Long *obsolete* exc. *dial*. M16.
[ORIGIN from FOLLY *noun* + -FUL.]
Foolish.

follis /ˈfɒlɪs/ *noun*. Pl. **folles** /ˈfɒliːz/. L19.
[ORIGIN Latin.]
hist. A bronze or copper coin introduced by Diocletian in AD 296 and again used in Byzantine currency *c* 800.

follow /ˈfɒləʊ/ *noun*. L19.
[ORIGIN from the verb. See also FOLLOW-ON, FOLLOW-THROUGH, FOLLOW-UP.]
1 The action of FOLLOW *verb*. L19.
2 *BILLIARDS & SNOOKER* etc. A stroke in which the cue ball is struck above the centre in order to cause it to roll forward after the object ball which it has set in motion; the impulse or spin given to the ball by such a stroke. L19.

follow /ˈfɒləʊ/ *verb*.
[ORIGIN Old English *folgian* corresp. to Old Frisian *fol(g)ia*, *fulgia*, Old Saxon *folgon* (Dutch *volgen*), Old High German *folgēn* (German *folgen*), beside Old English *fylgan*, Old Norse *fylgja* accompany, help, lead, follow, pursue, from Germanic.]
▸ **I** Go or come after; accompany; succeed.
1 *verb trans*. & *intrans*. (foll. by *after*). Go or come after (a person or object in motion). OE.

J. R. GREEN One of the Norman strangers who followed in the wake of the Conqueror. E. BOWEN One by one they had followed each other out. J. CHEEVER The smell of fresh earth that follows a plow.

2 a *verb trans*. & (now *rare*) *intrans*. with *after*, †*on*, †*upon*. Go after with intent to keep up, overtake, or catch; go in pursuit, chase, (a person or object in motion). OE. ▸**b** *verb trans*. & (now *rare*) *intrans*. with *after*. Pursue (an object of desire); strive after, aim at. ME. ▸†**c** *verb trans*. Pursue (an affair) to its conclusion or accomplishment; prosecute; enforce (a law). Also foll. by *on*, *upon*, *against*. M16–L17.

a G. GREENE The chap who was following him had to queue up at the ordinary entrance and lost him. **b** T. GUNN The blue jay scuffling in the bushes follows some hidden purpose. **c** SHAKES. *2 Hen. IV* O, such a day, so fought, so followed, and so fairly won.

3 *verb trans*. Go after or along with (a person) as an attendant or companion; accompany; *fig*. be a (necessary) accompaniment to, be consequent upon. OE. ▸**b** *verb trans*. Go after as an admirer, suitor, etc. E17. ▸**c** *verb trans*. & *intrans*. Attend (the body of a deceased person) to the grave; *colloq*. attend (a person's funeral). E19.

S. C. HALL The rheumatic . . creature who had 'followed' the family for more than forty years. **b** SHAKES. *Haml*. Do they hold the same estimation they did when I was in the city? Are they so followed?

4 a *verb trans*. & *intrans*. Come after (something else) in sequence, order of time, etc. ME. ▸**b** *verb intrans*. Happen or occur after something else; ensue. Formerly also, proceed, continue. (Foll. by *on*.) LME. ▸**c** *verb trans*. Provide (a thing) *with* a sequel or a successor. L17.

a E. BOWEN He went off to order the supper—just supper, they said, fish or something, with coffee to follow. W. TREVOR The Whitsun visitors would follow the Easter ones. **b** I. MURDOCH He had, since his retirement . . had no opportunities for self-indulgence, since Fanny's death had followed so soon after.

5 a *verb intrans*. Result, be deducible, occur as a consequence. (Foll. by *from*, †*of*.) ME. ▸**b** *verb trans*. Come after or succeed (something) as a consequence. L16.

a M. HOLROYD If friends were God's apology for families, it followed they should be as unlike one's own family as possible. **b** ANTHONY SMITH Fits can follow many of the ordinary vicissitudes of life, such as fright.

▸ **II** Keep to or trace the course of.
6 *verb trans*. Treat or take (a person) as a guide, leader, etc.; accept the authority or example of; espouse the opinions or cause of. OE.

ISAIAH BERLIN Kant insisted, following Rousseau, that a capacity for rational self-direction belonged to all men.

7 *verb trans*. Conform to, comply with, obey, or act upon or in accordance with (advice, command, fashion, etc.). OE. ▸†**b** Conform to in likeness, resemble, take after; imitate. OE–L17.

I. MURDOCH I . . followed my rule of never speaking frankly to women in moments of emotion. R. S. THOMAS And he writes there/in invisible handwriting the instructions/the genes follow.

8 *verb trans*. Pursue or practise (a way of life, a hobby, etc.); engage in or apply oneself to (work etc.); *esp*. earn a living at (a profession). OE.

G. GREENE The career of an *hôtelier* was not . . the one which the Jesuits had expected me to follow.

9 *verb trans*. Go forward along, keep to the track or course of, (a path etc.). ME.

E. M. FORSTER Her track through the dew followed the path that he had turfed over. R. BRAUTIGAN I walked down . . from Steelhead, following the Klamath River.

10 *verb trans*. & *intrans*. Keep track of mentally, understand, grasp the meaning of, (an argument, a speaker, etc.). L17. ▸**b** *verb trans*. Watch the progress or course of (a person or object in motion); take a close interest in the present state or progress of (events, a football team, etc.). L17.

J. GASKELL It is a bit difficult . . to follow technicalities in a foreign tongue. R. MACDONALD I don't quite follow. I'm very stupid today. **b** R. DAVIES I don't suppose he made a move without you following him with your eyes. F. JOHNSON We are following with concern events in Germany.

– PHRASES: ***follow in a person's footsteps***: see FOOTSTEP *noun* 1. ***follow one's nose***: see NOSE *noun*. ***follow suit***: see SUIT *noun*. ***follow the crowd***: see CROWD *noun*[2]. **follow the drum** *arch*. be a soldier. **follow the hounds** go hunting. ***follow the plough***: see PLOUGH *noun* 3. **follow the sea** be a sailor. **follow the string** *ARCHERY* (of a bow) take on a permanent curve from use.
– WITH ADVERBS IN SPECIALIZED SENSES: **follow on** (***a***) continue moving in the same direction as an object moving in front; provide continuation; (***b***) *CRICKET* (of a team) go in to bat for a second innings immediately after failing in their first innings to reach a score a prescribed number of runs fewer than that of their opponent's first innings. **follow out** pursue to a conclusion; carry out (instructions) precisely. **follow through** continue to completion; *spec*. (*GOLF*, *CRICKET*, etc.) continue a stroke or action (esp. to the full extent of the swing), after the ball has been struck or (in bowling) released. **follow up** pursue steadily or closely; make further investigation of; reinforce by further action or support.
– COMB.: **follow-me-lads** *arch*. [cf. French *suivez-moi-jeune-homme*] curls or ribbons hanging loosely over the shoulder; **follow-my-leader**, (*N. Amer*.) **follow-the-leader** a game in which each player must do as the leader does, or pay a forfeit; **follow-spot** a spotlight that follows a performer on the stage.
■ **followable** *adjective* LME.

follower /ˈfɒləʊə/ *noun*. OE.
[ORIGIN from FOLLOW *verb* + -ER[1].]
1 a An attendant, a servant, a companion. OE. ▸**b** An adherent, a disciple; a person who follows an example, rule of conduct, etc. ME. ▸**c** An admirer; *esp*. a man courting a maidservant who calls at the house to see her. *arch*. M19.

a F. FERGUSSON He meets an old man with his servants . . and kills him and all his followers.

2 a A thing that comes after or succeeds something else. *rare*. LME. ▸**b** A person who goes or comes after a person or object in motion; a pursuer. L16.

b SHAKES. *3 Hen. VI* Ah hark! The fatal followers do pursue.

3 A young cow, horse, or hen. Chiefly *Scot*. & *N. English*. LME.
4 A mechanical part whose motion or action is derived from that of another part to which force is applied; *spec*. (***a***) a block or plate through which the pressure of a press, piledriver, etc., is applied; (***b***) a wheel etc. deriving its motion from a driving wheel, cam, etc. L17.
■ **followership** *noun* E20.

following /ˈfɒləʊɪŋ/ *noun*[1]. ME.
[ORIGIN from FOLLOW *verb* + -ING[1].]
1 The action of FOLLOW *verb*. Also foll. by adverb. ME.

Joseph Strutt Queen Elizabeth . . frequently indulged herself in following of the hounds. W. D. Whitney The following-up of a series of acts.

2 A body of followers, attendants, or adherents. LME.

B. T. Bradford The bartender . . was something of a character and had a large following.

following /ˈfɒləʊɪŋ/ *adjective, noun*[2], *& preposition*. ME.
[ORIGIN formed as FOLLOWING *noun*[1] + -ING[2].]
▸ **A** *adjective*. **1** That follows. ME. ▸**b** *esp*. In introducing a statement etc.: now to be mentioned. ME.

Shakes. *Lucr.* What following sorrow may on this arise. Pope His following shield the fallen chief o'erspread. *New Yorker* The following year, a grand jury . . questioned him. **b** A. Thwaite The son sent his father the following account of a visit.

2 *NAUTICAL*. Of a wind or sea: blowing or moving in the direction of the ship's course. E16.
▸ **B** *absol*. as *noun*. *The* fact(s), person(s), thing(s), etc., now to be mentioned. L18.
▸ **C** *preposition*. As a sequel to or consequence of; coming after in time. M20.

H. Gardner He had . . become the idol of the West End stage, following the sensational success of a rather sentimental historical play.

follow-on /ˈfɒləʊɒn, fɒləʊˈɒn/ *noun & adjective*. L19.
[ORIGIN from *follow on* s.v. FOLLOW *verb*.]
▸ **A** *noun*. The action or an act of following on. L19.

Cricket World In the first three hours of the follow-on came just 77 runs.

▸ **B** *attrib*. or as *adjective*. That follows on. L19.

Financial Times A large follow-on order . . for engines.

follow-through /fɒləʊˈθruː/ *noun & adjective*. L19.
[ORIGIN from *follow through* s.v. FOLLOW *verb*.]
▸ **A** *noun*. The action or an act of following through. L19.

P. Metzler He rolled his drives with long contact between ball and strings, and finished them with a full follow-through. *Times* Dealers reported that best levels could not be maintained because of a lack of follow-through.

▸ **B** *attrib*. or as *adjective*. That follows through. E20.

follow-up /ˈfɒləʊʌp/ *noun & adjective*. E20.
[ORIGIN from *follow up* s.v. FOLLOW *verb*.]
▸ **A** *noun*. The action or an act of following up; a continuation or repetition of an initial action; *esp*. (**a**) a second advertisement, letter, etc., referring to an earlier one; (**b**) *MEDICINE* a renewal or continuation of contact with, or a re-examination of, a patient at an interval or intervals after treatment. E20.

Listener There was no evidence . . that the whole operation was planned . . as a follow-up to the occupation of Southern Thule. O. Sacks His wife became virtually exempt from migraine and in a six-month follow-up had suffered only two attacks.

▸ **B** *attrib*. or as *adjective*. That follows up; of or pertaining to (a) renewed or repeated action. E20.

folly /ˈfɒli/ *noun & verb*. ME.
[ORIGIN Old French & mod. French *folie* madness, from *fol* mad, foolish: see FOOL *noun*[1] *& adjective*, -Y[3]. In sense 2b cf. also French *folie* delight, favourite abode.]
▸ **A** *noun*. **1** The quality or state of being foolish or deficient in understanding; lack of good sense; unwise conduct. ME.

T. Gray Where ignorance is bliss, 'Tis folly to be wise. H. Carpenter *The Tale of Tom Kitten* deals with the folly of forcing children into tidy clothes.

2 An instance of foolishness; a foolish act, idea, practice, etc.; a ridiculous thing. ME. ▸**b** A costly ornamental building (considered as) serving no practical purpose. L16.

John Brooke To avoid the follies and weaknesses of his grandfather. **b** P. Levi The Monument was a Gothic folly, a carved stone tower standing alone in a field.

†3 Evil, wickedness; harm; (a) crime, (a) sin; *esp*. (an act of) lechery or fornication. ME–M17.
†4 Madness; rage. ME–L17.
5 *THEATRICAL*. In *pl*. (A revue with) glamorous female performers. E20.
Ziegfeld Follies etc.
▸ **B** *verb intrans*. Act foolishly. *arch*. M18.

Folsom /ˈfəʊls(ə)m/ *adjective*. E20.
[ORIGIN See below.]
Designating or pertaining to a prehistoric culture first found near Folsom in NE New Mexico, USA, or its remains, esp. a type of fluted lanceolate projectile point.

foment /ˈfə(ʊ)mɛnt/ *noun*. LME.
[ORIGIN Latin *fomentum*: see FOMENT *verb*. In sense 3 prob. infl. by FERMENT *noun*.]
1 = FOMENTATION 1b. Now *rare*. LME.
2 A thing that foments something; a stimulus, an encouragement. *obsolete* exc. as passing into sense 3. E17.

Henry More The foments of strife and palliations of hypocrisy.

3 = FERMENT *noun* 2b. L18.

T. Jefferson Should the present foment in Europe not produce republics everywhere.

foment /fə(ʊ)ˈmɛnt/ *verb trans*. LME.
[ORIGIN Old French & mod. French *fomenter* from late Latin *fomentare*, from Latin *fomentum* lotion, poultice, from *fovere* heat, cherish.]
1 Bathe or poultice with fomentations; apply a fomentation to. LME.
2 a Foster, stimulate, or instigate (a sentiment, a course of conduct, sedition, etc.). E17. ▸**b** Promote the growth, development, effect, or spread of (something physical). *arch*. M17.

a E. Longford Strong hostility to Wellington was being fomented in the House of Lords. V. Glendinning She . . orchestrated and fomented the quarrels and alliances of her . . young men.

†**3** Excite, irritate. M17–E18.
†**4** Warm. Only in M17.
■ **fomenter** *noun* E16.

fomentation /fəʊmɛnˈteɪʃ(ə)n/ *noun*. LME.
[ORIGIN Old French & mod. French, or late Latin *fomentatio(n-)*, from *fomentat-* pa. ppl stem of *fomentare*: see FOMENT *verb*, -ATION.]
1 a The action or an act of applying a fomentation (sense 1b). LME. ▸**b** A preparation of hot moist material or a warm or medicated lotion for application to the body. LME.
2 The action of fostering, stimulating, or instigating; an influence, a stimulus. E17.
†**3** The action of warming. Only in M17.

fomites /ˈfəʊmɪtiːz/ *noun pl*. In sense 1 also sing. †**fomes**. M17.
[ORIGIN Latin = tinder.]
†**1** The cause or source of a disease or *fig*. of sin etc. M17–L18.
2 Inanimate carriers of infection; *spec*. the clothes, bedding, etc., of a person with a communicable disease. E19.

Fomorian /fəˈmɔːrɪən/ *adjective & noun*. L19.
[ORIGIN from Old Irish *fomoir*, later *fomhóir*, with 2nd elem. possibly rel. to either Irish *muir* sea or Old English *mære* nightmare (see MARE *noun*[2]), + -IAN.]
IRISH MYTHOLOGY. (A member) of a race of pirates or giants.

†**fon** *noun*[1], *adjective, & verb*. ME.
[ORIGIN Origin & exact interrelations unkn. See also FOND *adjective*, FUN *verb*.]
▸ **A** *noun*. A fool. ME–L16.
▸ **B** *adjective*. Foolish. LME–L16.
▸ **C** *verb*. Infl. **-nn-**.
1 *verb intrans*. Be foolish or infatuated; act the fool. LME–M16.
2 *verb trans*. Make a fool of. Only in LME.

Fon /fɒn/ *noun*[2] *& adjective*. M19.
[ORIGIN Fon.]
▸ **A** *noun*. Pl. same, **-s**.
1 A member of a W. African people inhabiting the southern part of Benin. M19.
2 The Kwa language of this people, a close relative of Ewe. M19.
▸ **B** *attrib*. or as *adjective*. Of or pertaining to the Fon or their language. M19.

fond /*in sense 3* fɒnd; *in senses 1 & 2 foreign* fɔ̃ (*pl. same*)/ *noun*. Also †**fonds**. M17.
[ORIGIN French *fond*, *fonds* (now differentiated in sense) from Old French *fonz*, *fons* ult. from Latin *fundus* bottom: cf. FUND *noun*. See also AU FOND.]
1 Foundation, ground, groundwork. Now *rare*. M17.
2 = FUND *noun* 3. Now *rare*. L17.
3 = FUND *noun* 4. *obsolete* exc. *Scot. dial*. L17.

fond /fɒnd/ *adjective*. LME.
[ORIGIN from FON *noun*[1], *verb*: see -ED[2], -ED[1].]
†**1** Insipid, flavourless; sickly. LME–E19.
2 Infatuated, foolish. Now *esp*. foolishly credulous or confident. LME.

T. Fuller Never more to fright Children with fond tales of Bugbears.

3 Imbecile; mad. *obsolete* exc. *dial*. LME.
4 Eager, glad, inclined. Foll. by *to do*, †*of*. *obsolete* exc. *Scot*. M16.

I. Watts We are so fond to appear always in the right.

5 Foll. by *of*, †*on*: having a strong affection or liking for; (formerly) proud of. L16.

C. Connolly He was fond of wine and very partial to grapes and figs. E. Templeton She worries about Father . . I didn't know she was so fond of him. P. Rose The melodramas in which he was fond of acting.

6 a Of a person, an action, or attribute: overaffectionate, foolishly doting; tender, loving. L16. ▸**b** Of an opinion, a sentiment, etc.: held with strong or unthinking affection, foolishly optimistic. M17.

a J. Buchan Every letter he wrote was treasured by a fond mother. D. Welch She shook her head and smiled with fond reproach. **b** W. H. Auden Our fondest hopes were granted. E. P. Thompson It was the fond belief of the English people that the employment of spies . . was un-British.

†**7** Trifling, trivial. E–M17.
■ **fondish** *adjective* M19.

†**fond** *verb*[1]. Also **fand**.
[ORIGIN Old English *fandian* corresp. in form to Old Frisian *fandia*, Old Saxon *fandon*, Old High German *fantōn*.]
1 *verb trans*. Put to the proof, try, test; tempt. OE–LME.
2 *verb trans*. Attempt, undertake (*to do*, a deed). OE–L16.
3 *verb trans*. Seek, look for. Only in ME.
4 *verb intrans. & refl*. Go, travel. ME–M17.

†**fond** *verb*[2]. M16.
[ORIGIN from FOND *adjective*.]
1 *verb intrans*. Dote *on*, *upon*, *over*. M16–E17.
2 *verb trans*. Make a fool of; beguile. M16–L17.
3 *verb trans*. Caress, fondle; be fond of. L17–E18.

fonda /ˈfɒndə, ˈfɒndə/ *noun*. E19.
[ORIGIN Spanish, formed as FONDUK.]
In Spain and Spanish-speaking countries: an inn, a hotel.

fondaco /ˈfɒndəkəʊ, *foreign* ˈfondako/ *noun*. Now *rare*. Pl. **-chi** /-ki/. L16.
[ORIGIN Italian, formed as FONDUK.]
In Italy etc.: a warehouse; formerly also, an inn, a hotel.

F

fondant /ˈfɒnd(ə)nt/ *noun*. L19.
[ORIGIN French, use as noun of pres. pple of *fondre* melt: see FOUND *verb*[2], -ANT[1].]
A sweet made of a soft paste of flavoured (and usu. coloured) sugar; (more fully ***fondant paste***) such a paste.
– COMB.: **fondant icing**: made of fondant paste; ***fondant paste***: see above.

fondle /ˈfɒnd(ə)l/ *verb & noun*. L17.
[ORIGIN Back-form. from FONDLING.]
▸ **A** *verb*. †**1** *verb trans*. Treat indulgently; pamper. L17–L18.
2 *verb trans*. Handle or treat with fondness; caress, stroke lovingly or amorously. L18.

A. Paton Kumalo lifted him up, and wiped his nose clean, and kissed and fondled him. J. Osborne She puts out her hand, and runs it over his head, fondling his ear and neck. *Daily Express* Optician Geoffrey Wilson who fondled a young woman patient in his darkened consulting room was yesterday struck off.

3 *verb intrans*. Behave or speak fondly or amorously (*with*, *together*, etc.). E19.

Dickens 'Foolish Nell', said the old man fondling with her hair.

▸ **B** *noun*. An act of fondling. E19.
■ **fondler** *noun* M18.

fondling /ˈfɒndlɪŋ/ *noun*. Now *rare*. LME.
[ORIGIN from FOND *adjective* + -LING[1].]
†**1** A foolish person. LME–L18.
2 A much loved person; a person much caressed or fondled; a pet. L16.

fondly /ˈfɒndli/ *adjective*. *rare*. L16.
[ORIGIN from FOND *adjective* + -LY[1].]
= FOND *adjective* 2, 6.

fondly /ˈfɒndli/ *adverb*. LME.
[ORIGIN from FOND *adjective* + -LY[2].]
†**1** Foolishly, ignorantly. LME–M17.
2 Affectionately, tenderly, lovingly. L16.

Coleridge Fondly in his arms he took Fair Geraldine. E. Waugh She . . asked fondly about his injuries.

3 With self-deceiving, affectionate, or foolish credulity. M18.

W. Irving I will henceforth . . endeavour to be all that she fondly imagined me.

fondness /ˈfɒndnɪs/ *noun*. LME.
[ORIGIN from FOND *adjective* + -NESS.]
1 (An instance of) foolishness or folly. *obsolete* exc. *dial*. LME.
2 Foolish or unreasoning affection or tenderness. L16.

J. Gay By partial fondness shown . . we doat upon our own.

3 Affection, tenderness; a strong (and unreasoning) inclination, partiality, propensity, or desire *for*. E17.

Hannah More A mother's fondness reigns Without a rival. B. Bainbridge Some people thought of foxgloves as weeds, but she had a fondness for them.

†**fonds** *noun* see FOND *noun*.

fondue /ˈfɒnd(j)uː/ *noun*. M19.
[ORIGIN French, fem. pa. pple of *fondre* melt: see FOUND *verb*[2].]
A dish of flavoured melted cheese. Also, any dish in which small pieces of food are dipped into a hot or boiling liquid.

fonduk /ˈfɒndʊk/ *noun*. E18.
[ORIGIN Arabic *funduq* from Greek *pandokeion*, *pandokheion* inn.]
In N. Africa: an inn, a hotel; a warehouse.

fons et origo /fɒnz ɛt ˈɒrɪgəʊ, ɒˈrʌɪgəʊ/ *noun phr*. E19.
[ORIGIN Latin.]
The source and origin (*of*). Earliest in ***fons et origo mali*** /ˈmɑːliː/, the source and origin of evil.

A. N. Wilson The *fons et origo* of his devotion to Catholicism was that it was the ancient faith of Europe.

font /fɒnt/ *noun*[1]. LOE.
[ORIGIN Latin *fons*, *font-* spring, fountain, in specialized eccl. use *fons* or *fontes baptismi* water(s) of baptism.]
1 A receptacle, usu. of stone and free-standing, for the water used in baptism. Also ***baptismal font***. LOE. ▸**b** A

receptacle for holy water. M16. ▸c The reservoir for oil in a lamp. L19.
2 A spring, a fountain; the fount or source (of something). LOE.
– COMB.: **font-name** (one's) baptismal name; †**font-stone** = sense 1 above.
■ **fontful** *noun* (*rare*) as much as a font will hold LME.

font /fɒnt/ *noun*[2]. L16.
[ORIGIN French *fonte*, from *fondre* melt: see FOUND *verb*[2]. See also FOUNT *noun*[2].]
1 The action or process of casting or founding. Also, cast iron. *rare*. L16.
2 PRINTING. A complete set of type of a particular face and size; a set of characters of a consistent design (esp. as bought from a particular supplier) for the composition of text; a typeface. Also ***font of type***. L17.
– COMB.: **fontware** COMPUTING typesetting software designed to enable special printing fonts to be used.

F

fontal /ˈfɒnt(ə)l/ *adjective & noun*. L15.
[ORIGIN Old French, or medieval Latin *fontalis*, from Latin *fons*, *font-*: see FONT *noun*[1], -AL[1].]
▸ **A** *adjective* **1 a** Of or pertaining to a fountain or spring. *rare*. L15. ▸**b** Of or pertaining to the source or fountainhead of something; original, primary. L17.
> **b** COLERIDGE The fontal truths of natural religion.

2 Of or pertaining to a baptismal font; baptismal. L15.
▸ **B** *noun*. HERALDRY. A shell or urn (usu. supported by a mythological figure) from which a stream of water flows, symbolizing a river. L17.

fontanelle /fɒntəˈnɛl/ *noun*. Also *-**el**. M16.
[ORIGIN French from mod. Latin *fontanella* Latinization of Old French *fontenelle* dim. of *fontaine* FOUNTAIN *noun*: see -EL[2].]
†**1** A hollow of the skin between muscles. Only in M16.
†**2** A natural or artificial outlet for bodily secretions, morbid fluids, or the like; *fig.* a source, an outlet. E17–M19.
3 Any of a number of soft areas of incomplete ossification in the skull of an infant, lying at junctions of more than two sutures. M18.

fontange /fɔ̃tɑ̃ːʒ/ *noun*. Pl. pronounced same. L17.
[ORIGIN French, from the Duchesse de *Fontanges*, a mistress of Louis XIV.]
hist. (A hairstyle requiring the front hair to be curled into a high dressing on a wire frame, topped by) a topknot of ribbon or lace.

fontina /fɒnˈtiːnə/ *noun*. M20.
[ORIGIN Italian.]
A mild pale yellow Italian cheese.

food /fuːd/ *noun*.
[ORIGIN Late Old English *fōda*, from Germanic: no exact counterparts in other Germanic langs. Cf. FEED *verb*[1], FODDER *noun*.]
1 Substance(s) (to be) taken into the body to maintain life and growth, nourishment; provisions, victuals. LOE. ▸†**b** One's livelihood. LOE–E17. ▸**c** An article of food; a type of food. LME. ▸**d** Solid nourishment, as opp. to drink. E17.
> T. R. MALTHUS Want of food . . the most efficient cause of the three immediate checks to population. SCOTT FITZGERALD After a day without food he began to grow hungry.

2 *fig.* Something providing spiritual, emotional, or mental sustenance. Now *spec.* matter or material to discuss or dwell on. LOE.
> STEELE Praise is the Food of a great Soul. SOUTHEY A lively tale, and fraught With . . food for thought. L. RITCHIE There the reflective will find food for their meditations.

†**3** The act of eating. ME–L16.
†**4** That which is fed or nurtured; a child, a creature, a person. ME–L15.
5 Nutriment absorbed by a plant from the earth or air. M18.
– PHRASES: **be food for fishes** be drowned. **be food for powder** be fit only to die in battle; be a soldier or soldiers. **be food for worms** be dead. ***fast food***: see FAST *adjective*. ***junk food***: see JUNK *noun*[2]. ***skin food***: see SKIN *noun*.
– COMB.: **food bank** *N. Amer.* a place supplying food to poor or destitute people; **food chain** ECOLOGY a series of organisms each dependent upon the next for food, esp. by direct predation; **food chemistry** the branch of science that deals with the chemical constitution of foods; **food cycle** ECOLOGY the system of interdependent food chains in a community; **food fish** a fish used as food by humans; **foodgrain** any of a variety of grains that are grown for human consumption; ***food-pass***: see PASS *noun*[2] 14; **food poisoning** illness due to bacteria or toxins in food consumed; **food processor** a kitchen appliance or other machine for processing food by chopping, mixing, shredding, etc.; **food stamp** *US* a stamp exchangeable for food, issued cheaply to the needy; **foodstuff** an item of food, a substance used as food; **food value** the relative nourishing power of a food, nutritional value; **food web** ECOLOGY = *food cycle* above.
■ **foodful** *adjective* (chiefly *poet.*) rich in food; nutritious: M17. **foodless** *adjective* LME.

foodaholic /fuːdəˈhɒlɪk/ *noun*. *colloq.* M20.
[ORIGIN from FOOD + -AHOLIC.]
A person with an inordinate craving for or obsession with food; a compulsive eater.

foodie /ˈfuːdi/ *noun*. *colloq.* Also **foody**. L20.
[ORIGIN from FOOD + -IE, -Y[6].]
A person with a particular interest in food; a gourmet.

foody *noun* var. of FOODIE.

foody /ˈfuːdi/ *adjective*. E17.
[ORIGIN from FOOD + -Y[1].]
Full of food (*rare*); of or pertaining to food.

foofaraw /ˈfuːfərɔː/ *noun*. *N. Amer. colloq.* M19.
[ORIGIN from French *fanfaron* boastful, boastful person; in later use prob. infl. by French *frou-frou* frill.]
1 Trinkets or showy apparel; trappings. M19.
2 A great deal of fuss or attention. M20.
> *Time* You've gotta love Halloween and all the foofaraw that goes along with it.

foo fighter /ˈfuː fʌɪtə/ *noun*. M20.
[ORIGIN from 'Where there's foo there's fire', a nonsense catch-phrase from the US *Smoky Stover* cartoon strip.]
An unidentified flying object, orig. one of a kind reported by US pilots during the Second World War, usu. described as a bright light or ball of fire.

foo-foo *noun* var. of FUFU.

fool /fuːl/ *noun*[1] *& adjective*. ME.
[ORIGIN Old French *fol* noun & adjective (mod. *fol*, *fou* mad, madman) from Latin *follis* bellows, inflated ball, (later, fig.) windbag, empty-headed person. See also TOMFOOL.]
▸ **A** *noun*. **1** A person who behaves or thinks imprudently or unwisely; a silly person. ME.
> T. DEKKER Fooles by lucky Throwing, oft win the Game. QUILLER-COUCH When first I met you . . I thought you a fool To-day you have grown into an unmitigated ass. *Proverbs*: A fool and his money are soon parted. A fool at forty is a fool indeed. A fool may give a wise man counsel. There's no fool like an old fool. Fools rush in where angels fear to tread.

2 A jester or clown, esp. as formerly retained in a great household. ME.
3 A person who is fooled or imposed on, a dupe. *arch.* exc. in ***make a fool of***. LME.
4 A person with a mental disability or mental illness. *obsolete* exc. in ***born fool***, ***natural fool*** (now only as gen. terms of abuse). LME.
> R. LASSELS The Pazzorella, where they keep madmen and fools.

– PHRASES & COMB.: **act the fool** act foolishly; indulge in buffoonery or ridiculous behaviour. ***All Fools' Day***: see ALL *adjective* 2. *APRIL fool*. **be a fool for** be unable to resist the appeal or attractions of. **be a fool for one's pains** have one's trouble for nothing. **be a fool to** *arch.* be nothing in comparison with. **Feast of Fools** *hist.* a burlesque festival sometimes celebrated in churches in the Middle Ages on New Year's Day. **fool's coat** the motley or particoloured coat of a fool or jester. **fool's cress** = *fool's watercress* below. *fool's* ERRAND. **fool's gold** any yellow mineral, *esp.* pyrite or chalcopyrite; *fig.* something deceptively attractive, profitable, etc., in appearance. **fool's mate** CHESS: in which the first player is checkmated by the opponent's second move. **fool's paradise** a state of illusory happiness. **fool's parsley** an umbelliferous garden weed, *Aethusa cynapium*, with finely divided leaves, superficially resembling parsley. **fool's watercress** an aquatic umbelliferous plant, *Apium nodiflorum*, with pinnate leaves resembling those of watercress. **nobody's fool**, **no fool** a sensible person, not easily deceived. **play the fool** = ***act the fool*** above. ***ship of fools***: see SHIP *noun* 1.
▸ **B** *adjective*. Foolish, silly, stupid. Now *colloq.* (chiefly *N. Amer.*). ME.
> S. COLVIL Fighting is a fool thing. W. N. HARBEN He's goin' to ruin us with his fool notions.

fool hen *US colloq.* a spruce grouse or similar bird, esp. when young or tame.
■ **foolship** *noun* (now *rare*) (*a*) the quality or state of being a fool; foolishness; (*b*) (with possess. pronoun, as ***your foolship*** etc.) a mock title of respect for a fool: L15.

fool /fuːl/ *noun*[2]. L16.
[ORIGIN Perh. transf. use of FOOL *noun*[1].]
Orig. a confection of clotted cream, a custard trifle. Now, a purée of fruit (esp. gooseberries) mixed or served with cream or custard.

fool /fuːl/ *verb*. LME.
[ORIGIN from FOOL *noun*[1] *& adjective*.]
†**1** *verb intrans.* Be or become foolish or insane. LME–L15.
2 *verb intrans.* Behave like a fool; play the fool, idle, trifle. L16. ▸**b** Act as a clown or jester. E17.
> W. WYCHERLEY My heart is too much in earnest to be fooled with. THOMAS HUGHES You and I . . go fooling about with him, and get rusticated. **b** C. STEAD His weakness for playground leadership led him to cavort and fool.

3 *verb trans.* Make a fool of; impose upon; dupe or trick (*out of*, *into*); deprive *of* or put *off* by trickery. L16.
> ANTHONY SMITH As every sense can be fooled, every sensation can, therefore, be wrong.

you could have fooled me *colloq.*: expr. scepticism or contradiction.
4 *verb trans.* Make foolish, infatuate. Now *rare* or *obsolete*. E17.
– WITH ADVERBS IN SPECIALIZED SENSES: **fool about** play the fool. **fool along** *US* go slowly or aimlessly. **fool around** play the fool; *US* hang about aimlessly; *colloq.* flirt, have an affair. **fool away** fritter or squander foolishly. **fool round** = *fool around* above.

foolery /ˈfuːləri/ *noun*. M16.
[ORIGIN from FOOL *noun*[1] + -ERY. See also TOMFOOLERY.]
The practice of fooling or acting foolishly; a foolish action or thing.
> W. WARNER With . . Fooleries more than few I courted her.

foolhardy /ˈfuːlhɑːdi/ *adjective*. ME.
[ORIGIN Old French *folhardi* from *fol* foolish (see FOOL *noun*[1] *& adjective*) + *hardi* HARDY *adjective*.]
Foolishly adventurous or bold; reckless; delighting in needless risks.
> F. CHICHESTER It was a crazy, dangerous flight . . the most foolhardy I had ever attempted.

■ **foolhardily** *adverb* LME. **foolhardiness** *noun* ME.

foolish /ˈfuːlɪʃ/ *adjective*. ME.
[ORIGIN from FOOL *noun*[1] + -ISH[1].]
1 Lacking good sense or judgement; like or befitting a fool; indicative of or proceeding from folly; ridiculous. ME.
> G. GREENE It was foolish, . . but one cannot always be logical. S. RAVEN You'd have a very good chance of a first if you tried. But . . you settle for what's just good enough to keep you from looking foolish.

2 Humble, insignificant, trifling. Now *arch. & dial.* L16.
> R. BOLDREWOOD A hundred miles is . . no foolish ride.

■ **foolishly** *adverb* L15. **foolishment** *noun* foolishness E20. **foolishness** *noun* the quality or state of being foolish; a foolish act or thing: L15.

foolometer /fuːlˈɒmɪtə/ *noun*. *joc.* M19.
[ORIGIN from FOOL *noun*[1] + -OMETER.]
A standard for the measurement of fools or folly.

foolproof /ˈfuːlpruːf/ *adjective*. E20.
[ORIGIN from FOOL *noun*[1] + PROOF *adjective*.]
Safeguarded against any kind of accident; so straightforward as to be incapable of misuse or mistake.
> *Times* The cost of making nuclear reactors absolutely foolproof would outweigh their economic advantages.

foolscap /ˈfuːlzkap, *in sense 2 also* -lsk-/ *noun*. Also (earlier) **fool's cap**. E17.
[ORIGIN from FOOL *noun*[1] + -'S[1] + CAP *noun*[1].]
1 A fool's or jester's cap, usually hung with bells. Also, a dunce's cap. E17.
2 A former size of paper for printing, 13½ × 17 inches (about 340 × 430 mm). Also, a former size of writing paper, 13 × 8 inches (about 330 × 200 mm). L17.
3 An illustration of a fool's cap used as a watermark. L18.

foot /fʊt/ *noun*. Pl. **feet** /fiːt/, (sense 7 also) **foot**, (sense 18) **foots**.
[ORIGIN Old English *fōt*, pl. *fēt* = Old Frisian *fōt*, Old Saxon *fōt*, *fuot* (Dutch *voet*), Old High German *fuoȥ* (German *Fuss*), Old Norse *fótr*, Gothic *fōtus*, from Germanic from Indo-European base repr. also by Sanskrit *pad*, *pāda*, Greek *pous*, *pod-*, Latin *pes*, *ped-* foot.]
▸ **I 1** The terminal part of the leg below the ankle joint. OE. ▸†**b** The leg and foot. LME–M17. ▸**c** A diseased condition of the foot. Only with specifying word. M19.
> J. STEINBECK His feet did not stamp the clods or feel the warmth . . of the earth. I. MURDOCH He lightly stroked the feet, probing between the long separated toes.

c ***Madura foot***, ***trench foot***, etc.
2 Step, pace, tread. Freq. with specifying word. OE.
> F. MARRYAT I was not aware of your presence. Your foot is so light. B. JOWETT Dogs . . swift of foot.

†**3** Power of walking or running. ME–M18.
> H. BRACKEN Horses may alter as to their Speed or Foot.

4 a The end of a bed, couch, grave, etc., towards which the feet of an occupant are placed; the lower end of a table etc. LME. ▸**b** The portion of a sock, stocking, etc., which covers the foot of the wearer. L16.
> **a** D. DUNNETT At the foot of the bed stood Thorfinn. **b** W. HARRISON He will carrie his hosen . . to save their feet from wearing.

5 *hist.* Infantry. Also †***men of foot***. M16.
> STEELE Their Foot repulsed the same Body of Horse in three successive Charges.

▸ **II 6** PROSODY. A metrical unit with a varying number of syllables, one of which bears a main stress; a similar unit of speech. OE.
▸ **III 7** (Pl. also ***foot***.) A unit of length; *esp.* one of one-third of a yard, equal to 30.48 centimetres. Also (with specifying word), an area or volume equal to that of a square or cube whose edges are one foot long. OE. ▸**b** A distance or space of the least size. ME.
> P. MASSINGER A room of eight feet square. R. HODGSON Spiders big as bladders lie Under hemlocks ten foot high. **b** SHAKES. *1 Hen. IV* I'll starve ere I'll rob a foot further.

cubic foot, ***square foot***.
8 Any of various measures relating to specified commodities, *esp.* a measure used in tin-mining. Now chiefly *dial.* E17.
▸ **IV 9** An adjustable piece of wood or iron fastened to the front of the beam of a wheelless plough and used to

regulate the depth of ploughing. Also ***plough-foot***. *obsolete* exc. *hist.* **ME.**

10 The lower (usu. projecting) part of an object which serves as a support; the base. **LME.**

D. L. SAYERS Three cut-glass goblets (one with a chipped foot).

11 The terminal point of the leg of a chair, table, pair of compasses, etc. **LME.**

D. BREWSTER Place one foot of the compasses in the quadrant *NF.*

12 a *BOTANY.* The part by which a petal is attached; the root of a hair. **L17.** ▸**b** *ZOOLOGY.* A locomotive or adhering organ of an invertebrate. **M19.**

13 *PRINTING.* Either of the two plane surfaces, divided by a groove, at the base of a type. **L17.**

14 *MUSIC.* The terminal portion of an organ pipe. **M19.**

15 The plate in a sewing machine which holds the material steady. **L19.**

▸**V 16** The lowest part or bottom of a hill etc., or of any structure in an erect or sloping position, as a wall, ladder, staircase, etc. **ME.** ▸**b** The beginning or end of the slope of a bridge. **LME.** ▸**c** *NAUTICAL.* The lower edge of a sail. **L17.**

G. BERKELEY A town situate at the foot of Vesuvius.

†**17** Something written at the end of a document etc.; *spec.* (**a**) the sum or total of an account; (**b**) the refrain or chorus of a song. **LME–E18.**

DRYDEN A trifling sum of Misery, New added to the foot of thy Account.

18 *sing.* & (usu.) in *pl.* (*foots*). Dregs; refuse of oil etc.; coarse sugar. **M16.**

B. RANDOLPH They raise the foot of the oyl, so that thick and thin goes together.

19 The lower end or bottom of (a page of) a document, list, etc. **M17.**

W. WOLLASTON At the foot of the page.

▸†**VI 20** = FOOTING 7. **M16–E19.** ▸**b** Ground, reason. **L17–L18.**

B. FRANKLIN I wish all correspondence was on the foot of writing and answering when one can. **b** HOR. WALPOLE The Prince excused his own inapplication on the foot of idleness.

21 Foothold, standing ground. **L16–M17.**

F. KIRKMAN Hinder new love from getting foot in her heart.

22 Standard rate of calculation or valuation. **L16–M18.**

J. LOCKE He must pay twenty per Cent. more for all the commodities he buys with the Money of the new Foot.

– PHRASES: ***a foot in both camps***: see CAMP *noun*[2] 5. **at foot** (of a foal etc.) accompanying its mother. ***athlete's foot***: see ATHLETE 1. **at the feet of** in the position of a disciple or subject of, or a supplicant to. ***bind hand and foot***: see HAND *noun.* ***change one's feet***: see CHANGE *verb.* ***cold feet***: see COLD *adjective.* ***cover one's feet***: see COVER *verb*[2] 1. ***cut the grass from under a person's feet***: see GRASS *noun.* ***cut the ground from under a person's feet***: see GROUND *noun.* **drag one's feet** be deliberately uncooperative or slow to act. ***fall on one's feet***: see FALL *verb.* ***feel one's feet***: see FEEL *verb.* ***feet FIRST.*** ***feet FOREMOST.*** **feet of clay** (cf. *Daniel* 2:33) fundamental weakness in a person who has appeared to be of great merit. ***find one's feet***: see FIND *verb.* ***FIRST-foot.*** †**foot and hand** stepping forward and striking simultaneously (***come in foot and hand***, attack an opponent by so doing). **foot in the door** a chance of ultimate success, an opportunity to progress, esp. in ***have a foot in the door***, ***have one's foot in the door***; cf. ***toe in the door*** s.v. TOE *noun.* **foot to foot** *arch.* with one foot against an opponent's; in close combat. ***from head to foot***: see HEAD *noun.* **get one's feet under the table** establish oneself securely in a situation. **get one's feet wet** *fig.* begin to take an active part. **have one foot in the grave** be or appear to be near death. **have one's feet on the ground** be practical and sensible. ***have the ball at one's feet***: see BALL *noun*[1] 2. **keep one's feet** avoid falling, remain upright. ***land on one's feet***: see LAND *verb* 3. **my foot!** *colloq.*: contradicting contemptuously. ***not let the grass grow under one's feet***: see GRASS *noun.* **not put a foot wrong** not make a single mistake in behaviour or speech. ***off one's feet***: see OFF *preposition & adjective.* **on foot** (**a**) walking or running as opp. to riding, driving, etc.; (**b**) (of an action etc.) afoot, in motion; ***set on foot***, start (an action etc.). **on one's feet** standing or walking, *esp.* standing to make a speech; well enough to walk about. **on the right foot** at an advantage, in a favourable position, (esp. in ***get off on the right foot***, make a good start). **on the wrong foot** at a disadvantage, in an awkward position, (esp. in ***get off on the wrong foot***, make a bad start). ***put one's best foot forward***: see BEST *adjective.* **put one's feet up** take a rest, esp. sitting or lying with one's feet propped up. **put one's foot down** (**a**) be firmly insistent or repressive; (**b**) accelerate a motor vehicle. **put one's foot in it** *colloq.* blunder, *esp.* inadvertently say or do something to cause offence or embarrassment. ***run a person off his feet or her feet***: see RUN *verb.* **set foot in**, **set foot on** enter, go to, (a place etc.). ***shake the dust off one's feet***: see DUST *noun.* ***shoot oneself in the foot***: see SHOOT *verb.* ***sit at the feet of***: see SIT *verb.* **stand on one's own feet**, **stand on one's own two feet** be independent or self-reliant. ***take the weight off one's feet***: see WEIGHT *noun.* **to one's feet** to a standing position (in ***get to one's feet***, ***jump to one's feet***). **tread under foot** *fig.* oppress. **under foot** on the ground, with regard to conditions for walking etc. **under one's feet** in one's way, obstructing one's actions or progress. ***vote with one's feet***: see VOTE *verb.* ***walk a person off his feet or her feet***: see WALK *verb*[1]. **with one's foot on the neck of** *arch.* completely dominating.

– COMB.: **foot-and-mouth (disease)** a contagious virus disease of cattle etc. with ulceration of hoofs, around the mouth, etc.; **foot-bank** = BANQUETTE; **footbath** (**a**) an act of washing the feet; (**b**) a small shallow bath used for this; **footboard** a board, esp. in or on a vehicle, to support the foot or feet or to stand on; **foot bone** the tarsus; **foot boy** †(**a**) a boy attendant; (**b**) *arch.* a pageboy; **footbrake** a brake in a vehicle operated by pressure of the foot; **foot breadth** *arch.* the breadth of a foot (as a measure); **footbridge** a bridge for pedestrians; **foot-candle** a disused unit of illumination equal to the illumination given by a source of one candela at a distance of one foot (equivalent to one lumen per square foot, 10.764 lux); **foot-cloth** †(**a**) a large richly ornamented cloth laid over the back of a horse; (**b**) *arch.* a carpet; **foot-drop** *MEDICINE* a permanently downward position of the foot, due to paralysis of the dorsiflexor muscles; **footfall** (**a**) *arch.* the sound of a footstep; (**b**) (in marketing) the number of people entering a shop or shopping area at a given time; **foot-fault** *noun & verb* (*TENNIS*) (**a**) *noun* a fault consisting in overstepping the baseline or running etc. while serving; (**b**) *verb intrans.* make a foot-fault; **foot-folk** *arch.* foot soldiers, infantry; **footgear** footwear; **foot guards** infantrymen with a special guarding function; now *spec.* (with cap. initials) in the British army, the Grenadier, Coldstream, Scots, Irish, and Welsh Guards; **foothill** a hill lying at the base of a mountain or mountain range; **foothold** a place giving support for the feet, a surface for standing on, (*lit. & fig.*); an established place; a basis from which advantage may be gained or influence or support increased; cf. ***toe-hold*** s.v. TOE *noun*; **foot-lambert** a (disused) unit of surface brightness corresponding to the emission or reflection of one lumen per square foot; †**foot-land-raker** a footpad; **foot-licker** *arch.* a slave, a humble or fawning suppliant; **footlights** screened lights in front of a stage at the level of the actors' feet; (*fig.*) *the* acting profession; **footlocker** *N. Amer.* a small trunk or chest; **foot log** *US* a log used as a footbridge; **footloose** *adjective* free to act or acting as one pleases, having no ties; **footmark** (**a**) *rare* a mark on the foot; (**b**) a footprint; **foot muff** a covering of fur or similar material in which the feet are placed for warmth; **foot pace** (**a**) a walking pace; (**b**) a raised portion of a floor, a dais; (**c**) a hearthstone; (**d**) a half landing; **footpad** [PAD *noun*[2]] *hist.* a highway robber operating on foot; **foot page** *arch.* a boy servant or attendant; **foot passenger** a person who walks as opp. to riding or driving, a pedestrian; **footpath** a path for walkers; a pavement for pedestrians at the side of a road; **footplate** a driver's and fireman's platform in a locomotive; **foot plough** a swing plough; **foot-pound** the quantity of energy expended when a force of one pound moves through a distance of one foot; ***foot-POUNDAL***; **foot-pound-second** *adjective* designating or pertaining to a system of measurement in which these form the basic units of length, mass, and time respectively; **foot-race** a race between competitors on foot; **footrest** a bench, stool, rail, etc., used to support the feet of a seated person; **foot rope** *NAUTICAL* (**a**) a bolt rope to which the lower edge of a sail is sewn; (**b**) a rope below a yard, for sailors to stand on while furling or reefing; **foot rot** (**a**) a bacterial disease of the foot in animals, esp. sheep; (**b**) a fungal disease of plants, affecting the base of the stem; **foot rule** a rigid measure one foot long; **foot soldier** an infantryman; **footsore** *adjective* having sore feet, esp. from walking; **footstalk** *BOTANY & ZOOLOGY* a small supporting stalk; a petiole, peduncle, or the like; **foot's pace** = ***foot pace*** (a) above; **footstall** the base or pedestal of a pillar or statue; **footstone** †(**a**) a base, a pedestal; (**b**) the foundation stone of a building; (**c**) a (commemorative) stone at the foot of a grave; **footstool** (**a**) a stool for resting the foot or feet on while sitting (*lit. & fig.*); †(**b**) a stool on which to stand to reach a higher position; **footsure** *adjective* sure-footed; **foot-tapping** *adjective* having a strong rhythmic musical beat; **footwall** *GEOLOGY* the fault block which lies below an inclined fault; **footwarmer** a contrivance or covering for keeping the feet warm; **foot-washing** the action or an act of washing the feet, esp. as a religious rite; **footway** a way or path for walkers or pedestrians; **footwear** what is worn on the feet; boots, shoes, socks, etc., collectively; **footwork** use of the feet in sports (esp. football), dancing, etc.; agility, adroitness; **footworn** *adjective* (*arch.*) (**a**) worn by the feet; (**b**) footsore.

▪ **footless** *adjective* **LME.** **footlike** *adjective* resembling a foot **E20.**

foot /fʊt/ *verb.* **LME.**

[ORIGIN from the noun.]

▸**I 1** *verb intrans.* & (esp.) *trans.* with *it.* ▸**a** Step, or tread to music or in time; dance. **LME.** ▸**b** Walk, go on foot. **L16.**

a DRYDEN A Quire of Ladies . . That featly footing seem'd to skim the Ground. **b** S. E. FERRIER He footed away as fast as his short legs . . permitted. G. GREENE The taxi drew up at the corner of a city street. 'We foot it from here.'

2 *verb trans.* Set foot on; walk, dance, etc., on or over. **M16.**

J. HENRY The ground we footed within the last three days is a very rugged isthmus. R. L. STEVENSON It was good to foot the grass.

3 *verb trans.* Settle or establish (a person, esp. oneself) in or *in* a specified place. Now *rare.* **L16.**

4 *verb trans.* **a** Strike or push with the foot or feet; kick; spurn (*lit. & fig.*). Now *rare.* **L16.** ▸**b** Of a bird, esp. a hawk: seize with the talons. **L16.**

a SHAKES. *Merch. V.* You that did . . foot me as you spurn a stranger cur Over your threshold.

5 *verb trans.* Follow the tracks of; trace. **L18.**

▸**II 6** *verb trans.* Make a foot for, add or attach a foot to. **LME.**

SMOLLETT The stockings which his wife footed for me.

7 a *verb trans.* Write the total at the foot of, add up (an account, bill, etc.). Freq. foll. by *up.* **L15.** ▸**b** *verb trans.* Pay or settle (a bill). *colloq.* **E19.** ▸**c** *verb intrans.* Mount or total *up* to or *to* a particular sum. **M19.**

a H. B. STOWE The wall-paper was . . garnished with chalk memorandums, and long sums footed up. **b** T. C. WOLFE Tell him . . to spare no expense. I'll foot the bills.

footage /ˈfʊtɪdʒ/ *noun.* **L19.**

[ORIGIN from FOOT *noun* + -AGE.]

1 Payment of miners by the linear foot of work; the amount paid or mined. **L19.**

2 A length in linear feet, esp. of cinematographic or television film used; material recorded on a length of such film. **E20.**

New York Times Some of the footage looked as though it had been filmed in Paris. *Broadcast* Close-up footage of the beetles, ants and worms.

football /ˈfʊtbɔːl/ *noun & verb.* **LME.**

[ORIGIN from FOOT *noun* + BALL *noun*[1].]

▸**A** *noun.* **1** A large round or elliptical inflated ball, usu. of leather or (now) plastic. **LME.**

2 A primarily open-air game played with such a ball by two sides each seeking to move it across the opponents' goal line by kicking or other permitted means; (manner or style of) the playing of this game. **LME.**

Listener Most of the impressive football came from Real Madrid.

American football, ***Association football***, ***Australian Rules football***, ***five-a-side football***, ***Gaelic football***, ***rugby football***, etc. ***football boot***, ***football club***, ***football ground***, ***football helmet***, ***football match***, ***football pitch***, ***football player***, etc.

3 *fig.* A person or thing continually kicked or tossed or bandied about. **M16.**

L. ADAMIC The Yugoslav peoples were once again a football in international power politics.

– COMB.: **football coupon** a coupon used in an entry for a football pool; **football hooligan** a person who engages in hooliganism while attending or travelling to or from a football match; ***football pool(s)***: see POOL *noun*[2] 5b.

▸**B** *verb.* **1** *verb trans.* Kick or treat like a football. **L16.**

2 *verb intrans.* Play football. **L19.**

– NOTE: Without specification usu. understood as Association football in Britain, American football in the US, Canadian football in Canada, Australian Rules football in Australia, rugby football in NZ, or whatever form of the game is most commonly played in the particular country or area.

▪ **footballer** *noun* a football player **L19.**

footed /ˈfʊtɪd/ *adjective.* **LME.**

[ORIGIN from FOOT *noun*, *verb*: see -ED[2], -ED[1].]

1 Having a foot or feet; having footlike appendages; (as 2nd elem. of comb.) having feet of a specified kind or number. **LME.**

A. C. SWINBURNE Fair as the snow and footed as the wind.

bare-footed, ***cat-footed***, ***flat-footed***, ***four-footed***, ***sure-footed***, etc.

2 Composed in metrical feet. Long *rare.* **M16.**

footer /ˈfʊtə/ *noun*[1]. **E17.**

[ORIGIN from FOOT *noun*, *verb* + -ER[1].]

1 A person who goes on foot, a pedestrian. Now *rare* exc. in ***FIRST-footer.*** **E17.**

2 *BOWLS.* A small mat on which a player stands when delivering the ball. **M19.**

3 With numeral prefixed: a person or thing having a height or length of the specified number of feet. **M19.**

4 A bird, esp. a hawk, which is skilful in seizing prey in the talons. **L19.**

5 A line of information appearing at the foot of each page of a document, containing the date, chapter heading, etc. **L20.**

footer /ˈfuːtə/ *noun*[2] & *verb. dial.* & *slang.* Now *rare.* **M18.**

[ORIGIN Var. of FOUTRE.]

▸**A** *noun.* A worthless or idle person. **M18.**

▸**B** *verb intrans.* Trifle, potter about, dawdle. **M19.**

footer /ˈfʊtə/ *noun*[3]. *slang.* **M19.**

[ORIGIN from FOOTBALL *noun*: see -ER[6].]

Football.

footie *noun* var. of FOOTY *noun.*

footing /ˈfʊtɪŋ/ *noun.* **LME.**

[ORIGIN from FOOT *verb* + -ING[1].]

▸**I 1** The action of placing the feet, esp. so as not to slip or stumble; stable position of the feet, foothold. **LME.**

SIR W. SCOTT Unless he climb, with footing nice, A far projecting precipice. TOLKIEN He missed his footing on a round stone and fell into the cold water.

2 The action of walking, pacing, stepping, or dancing; a step, a tread. Formerly also, a dance. Now *rare.* **M16.** ▸†**b** The action of setting foot on land. *rare* (Shakes.). Only in **E17.**

GOLDSMITH A squire from the country . . desirous of learning the new manner of footing. KEATS To him they bent their footing through the dews. **b** SHAKES. *Oth.* Whose footing here anticipates our thoughts A se'nnight's speed.

3 A mark or impression left by the foot or feet. Now *rare.* **L16.**

▸**II 4** †**a** The foundation, ground, or basis on which something rests or from which it rises. **LME–L17.** ▸**b** A projecting course or number of courses at the base of a wall etc. for support. **E17.**

5 Support for the foot; surface (of a specified kind) for walking or standing on. **L16.**

F

Sir W. Scott Where scarce was footing for the goat. J. Steinbeck The bottom of the gulch levelled off, and the footing was sand.

6 *gen.* A firm or secure position, an established place, a foothold. L16.

A. Trollope She had made good her footing in her aunt's house.

7 The basis on which or conditions under which an enterprise is established or operates; the position or status of a person in relation to others; a degree of intimacy etc. M17.

H. James Ask them to take you in on the footing of a lodger. V. Sackville-West Once we have finished all our business we may meet upon an equal footing. *Times* The stimulation of enterprise is best organized on a regional footing.

8 One's entrance on a new position, one's admittance to a trade, society, etc.; a fee required for this. E18. **pay for one's footing**, **pay one's footing** pay the customary fee for admittance to a trade, society, etc.

▸ **III 9** The action of adding up a column of figures; a sum total. L15.

F

10 The action of making a foot for or attaching a foot to a stocking etc.; (a) material used for this. E16.

11 The attached edge of a lace trim. L17.

12 A piece of hard wood dovetailed to the end of an arrow nearest the pile. M19.

footle /ˈfuːt(ə)l/ *verb & noun. slang.* L19.

[ORIGIN Perh. from FOOTER *verb* with suffix substitution of -LE³.]

▸ **A** *verb intrans.* Trifle (*about*), play the fool. L19.

▸ **B** *noun.* Nonsense, twaddle; something trifling and silly. L19.

▪ **footler** *noun* E20.

footling /ˈfuːtlɪŋ/ *adjective.* L19.

[ORIGIN from FOOTLE *verb* + -ING².]

Trivial, silly.

G. B. Shaw Paraphrases of great works, made by footling people. J. Carey Making up plots and complications, which he always found a bit footling.

footling /ˈfʊtlɪŋ/ *adverb.* M18.

[ORIGIN from FOOT *noun* + -LING².]

MEDICINE. Of a birth, presentation, delivery, etc.: with the feet foremost.

footman /ˈfʊtmən/ *noun.* Pl. **-men**. ME.

[ORIGIN from FOOT *noun* + MAN *noun*.]

1 An infantryman. ME.

2 A pedestrian; a (good, fast, etc.) walker or runner. *obsolete* exc. *dial.* LME.

3 A servant or attendant accompanying a rider or carriage on foot. Also ***running footman***. *obsolete* exc. *hist.* LME.

4 A liveried servant whose chief duties include attending to the employer's carriage and door and waiting at table. E18.

5 A trivet to hang on grate bars. M18.

6 Any of a number of moths belonging to the tiger moth family Arctiidae. E19.

▪ **footmanship** *noun* (now *rare* or *obsolete*) (***a***) the action of, or skill in, running or walking; (***b***) the occupation or office of a footman: M16.

footnote /ˈfʊtnəʊt/ *noun & verb.* E19.

[ORIGIN from FOOT *noun* + NOTE *noun*².]

▸ **A** *noun.* A note printed or written at the foot of a page etc.; *fig.* a piece of additional or incidental information. E19.

▸ **B** *verb trans.* Supply with a footnote or footnotes; comment on in a footnote. M19.

footprint /ˈfʊtprɪnt/ *noun.* M16.

[ORIGIN from FOOT *noun* + PRINT *noun*.]

1 An impression left by the sole of the foot in walking, standing, etc. M16.

2 a The ground area beneath a vehicle or aircraft that is affected by noise, blast, etc.; the area of contact between a tyre and the ground. M20. ▸**b** The area within which a broadcast signal from a particular source can be received. L20. ▸**c** The area of desk space occupied by a computer or other piece of equipment. L20.

3 The impact on the environment of human activity in terms of pollution, damage to ecosystems, and the depletion of natural resources. Cf. ***carbon footprint*** s.v. CARBON *noun*. L20.

footsie /ˈfʊtsi/ *noun*¹. *colloq.* M20.

[ORIGIN Joc. dim. of FOOT *noun*: see -IE. Cf. FOOTY *noun*.]

Amorous play with the feet.

G. Fowler I played footsie with her during Don José's first seduction by Carmen. *fig.*: *Economist* Pakistan is . . despite recent games of footsie with Peking, a staunchly anti-communist ally.

Footsie /ˈfʊtsi/ *noun*². *colloq.* L20.

[ORIGIN Alt. of ***FT–SE*** s.v. F, F, after FOOTSIE *noun*¹.]

(Proprietary name for) the Financial Times–Stock Exchange 100 share index.

footslog /ˈfʊtslɒg/ *verb & noun. colloq.* L19.

[ORIGIN from FOOT *noun* + SLOG *verb*.]

▸ **A** *verb intrans.* Infl. **-gg-**. March or tramp laboriously. L19.

▸ **B** *noun.* A laborious march or tramp. E20.

▪ **footslogger** *noun* a person who footslogs; an infantryman: L19.

footstep /ˈfʊtstɛp/ *noun.* ME.

[ORIGIN from FOOT *noun* + STEP *noun*¹.]

1 An impression made by a foot, a footprint. Now chiefly *fig.* in ***follow in a person's footsteps***, ***walk in a person's footsteps***, follow a person's example, take the same course of action as a person. ME.

Sun The teenage daughter . . decides she does not want to follow in the footsteps of her mother.

2 A step or tread of the foot. M16. ▸**b** A distance covered in a step. Now *rare*. L18.

R. Kenan She thought she heard footsteps.

3 A step on which to place the foot to ascend or descend. L16. ▸**b** Chiefly *hist.* A footboard for a printing press operator. L17. ▸**c** A bearing to sustain the foot of a vertical shaft or spindle. Also ***footstep bearing***. M19.

†**4** A vestige, a trace. L16–L18.

footy /ˈfʊti/ *noun. colloq.* Also **-ie**. E20.

[ORIGIN Joc. dim. of FOOT *noun*: see -Y⁶, -IE. Cf. FOOTSIE *noun*¹.]

1 Football. Chiefly *Austral. & NZ.* E20.

2 Also redupl. **footy-footy**. = FOOTSIE *noun*¹. M20.

footy /ˈfuːti/ *adjective. dial. & colloq.* Also (earlier, *obsolete* exc. *Scot.*) **fouty**. E18.

[ORIGIN Var. of FOUGHTY.]

Paltry, worthless, little and insignificant.

footy-footy *noun* see FOOTY *noun* 2.

foo yong /fuː ˈjɒŋ/ *noun phr.* Also **fu yung** /fuː ˈjʌŋ/. M20.

[ORIGIN Chinese (Cantonese) *foò yung*, lit. 'hibiscus'.]

A Chinese dish or sauce made with eggs mixed and cooked with other ingredients.

foozle /ˈfuːz(ə)l/ *noun. slang.* M19.

[ORIGIN Rel. to FOOZLE *verb*.]

1 A fogey; a stupid person, a bungler. Now *rare*. M19.

2 A clumsy failure, a botched attempt; *esp.* a bungled golf stroke. L19.

foozle /ˈfuːz(ə)l/ *verb trans. slang.* M19.

[ORIGIN German dial. *fuseln* work badly: cf. FUSEL OIL.]

Do clumsily, botch, bungle, (esp. a golf stroke).

▪ **foozler** *noun* L19.

fop /fɒp/ *noun.* LME.

[ORIGIN Unknown.]

†**1** A foolish person. LME–E18.

2 A dandy, an exquisite. L17.

†**3** A conceited person. M18–E19.

▪ **fopling** *noun* a petty fop L17.

†**fop** *verb.* Infl. **-pp-**. E16.

[ORIGIN App. from German *foppen* cheat, deceive: prob. orig. thieves' cant.]

1 *verb intrans.* Act foolishly, play the fool. Only in E16.

2 *verb trans.* Make a fool of, cheat, dupe. Also, fob *off*. Only in 17.

foppery /ˈfɒp(ə)ri/ *noun.* M16.

[ORIGIN from FOP *noun* + -ERY.]

†**1 a** A foolish action, practice, idea, or statement; a thing foolishly esteemed. M16–M18. ▸**b** Foolishness, stupidity. L16–E18.

2 The behaviour or manner characteristic of a fop; dandyism; an instance of this. L17. ▸**b** (An example of) foppish finery. E18.

foppish /ˈfɒpɪʃ/ *adjective.* E17.

[ORIGIN from FOP *noun* + -ISH¹.]

†**1** Resembling or befitting a fool. E17–E18.

2 Resembling or befitting a fop or dandy. L17.

G. Steinem The foppish fashions . . all proudly announced a distance from physical labour. B. Unsworth Erasmus had always been . . careful of his appearance and was now at a foppish age.

▪ **foppishly** *adverb* M17. **foppishness** *noun* E17.

for /fɔː, *unstressed* fə/ *preposition, conjunction, & noun.*

[ORIGIN Old English *for* = Old Frisian, Old Saxon *for*, Gothic *faur*, prob. reduced form of Germanic preposition meaning 'before (of place and time)', repr. by Old English FORE *preposition* = Old Frisian, Old Saxon, Old High German *fora*, beside Old Saxon, Old High German forms with *-i*, viz. *furi* (German *für*) and Old Norse *fyrir*.]

▸ **A** *preposition.* †**I** Before. Cf. FORE *preposition*.

1 In front of, in or into the presence of; (in oaths) before. OE–LME.

2 Before in time. OE–ME.

3 In preference to. OE–E16.

▸ **II** Of representation, substitution, or exchange.

4 Representing, as a representative of. OE.

I. Murdoch A fear not exactly of James but of something that James stood for.

5 In place of, instead of; on behalf of. OE.

H. James You can see for yourself—she has got half the place down. G. Greene He kept in the dusky background . . and let the ladies fight for him. V. S. Pritchett She had no one left to pray for. B. Bainbridge She wasn't afraid of him; she was afraid for him.

6 Introducing that with which something is (to be) exchanged: in exchange for; as the price or penalty of; in requital of. OE. ▸**b** At the cost of, to the amount of. L18.

T. Hardy There was to be one execution—only one—for arson. I. Murdoch I bought up the entire stock for less than a pound. W. Golding I offer them the idea for free. **b** Thomas Hughes The Lord's men were out, by half-past twelve o'clock for ninety-eight runs. A. Alpers He sent them a cheque for £5.

▸ **III 7** In defence or support of; on the side of; in favour of. Also *ellipt.*, in favour. Opp. ***against***. OE. ▸**b** In honour of; after. Chiefly in ***name for*** (now chiefly *N. Amer., Austral., & Scot.*). E18.

T. Hardy Tupcome was for sleeping in Bristol that night, but Dornell . . insisted upon mounting and getting back. E. Templeton In the Bible, one can find quotations for and against any human activity. J. Grenfell She's always been one for sailors ever since she can remember. H. Wilson A tally of those for and against. **b** C. McCullough There are streets named for him all over New Zealand.

▸ **IV** Of purpose, result, or destination.

8 With the object or purpose of; with a view to; as preparatory to, in anticipation of; conducive to; leading to, giving rise to, with the result or effect of. OE. ▸**b** With the purpose or result of benefiting; as a service to. Also, (chiefly following adjectives, nouns, or adverbs of quality) as affecting beneficially or the reverse. OE. ▸**c** With the purpose of being, becoming, or serving as. L15.

T. Hardy Seeing . . that somebody was there cleaning for Sunday he entered. M. Keane I supposed you had been out for a healthy brisk walk. I. Murdoch Now I must find Miranda and tell her to change for church. J. Wainwright The sexual assault in each case is motive enough for the murder. W. Golding Thackeray keeps us in suspense and ignorance for our own good. M. Roberts What are you doing that for? asks Beth, puzzled. **b** T. Hardy A bad job for thee, Christian, that you should have showed your nose then. V. Woolf Nobody lives for himself alone. I. Murdoch After all, it is for Clement that I am here. J. Simms Kiyoko was there; I would play for her. **c** Dickens [He] went for a soldier, and never came back. G. Ewart Had an egg for breakfast every morning. P. Ackroyd He . . slices two pieces of bread for toast.

9 Used pleonastically before *to* and an infinitive with the sense 'in order to do' or simply 'to do' (now *arch. & dial.*). Also (*US*) introducing a noun or pronoun followed by an infinitive after verbs of wanting, liking, etc. ME.

G. Washington You must ride round ye back of ye Mountain for to get below them. A. Tyler His mother hated for Cody to mix with outsiders. A. F. Loewenstein You used to like for me to touch you, Billy.

10 In order to obtain, win (money etc.), save (one's life), etc. ME. ▸**b** Indicating the object of a feeling or a faculty. L16.

Ld Macaulay Charles fled for his life. V. Woolf Then she went to him for assurance. J. Cheever He was rude to his friends when they stopped in for a drink. A. White I have worked for my living since I was 16. M. Procter They had phoned for their wheel man like calling for a taxi. **b** E. Bowen He did not care for her looks or her clothes. M. Keane He had a long briar in his hand and examined its point carefully for hairs. I. Murdoch Why wantonly destroy one's palate for cheap wine? V. S. Pritchett One discovers a gift for saying things with two meanings. F. Tuohy I had developed a grudging admiration for him.

11 In order to arrive at or reach; with the purpose of going to or towards, in the direction of. LME.

T. Hardy He made straight for the point whence proceeded the low roar. I. Murdoch He wondered where Miranda was going, and concluded that she was bound for the village shop. J. Wainwright I was starting for home the next day.

12 To be received by, to belong to; to be used by, with, or in connection with. LME.

T. Hardy He is . . a perfect match for her. E. Waugh Details of the costumes for a charity ballet. G. Greene I've some bad news for all of you. I. Murdoch I wear small oval rimless spectacles for reading.

13 Following a verb, adjective, or noun of quality denoting suitability, appropriateness, appointment, purpose, or design; following a noun or as a predicate indicating the possession of such a quality. LME. ▸**b** Following an adjective or adverb qualified by *too*, *enough*, etc. with the sense 'to require', 'to allow', 'to constitute', etc. E19.

T. Hardy Tell him flatly that you are not for him? R. Macaulay It wasn't for me to question her. R. Hardy They were hunters and they were built for nothing else. G. Greene I had the impression that the party was for tonight? G. Household There was nothing for it but to go. A. Carter You'll find a full account of the operation in *The Lancet* for June 1898. **b** A. Carter His teeth were chattering too much for him to speak coherently. H. Carpenter She has grown too big for the White Rabbit's house.

14 Introducing a noun or pronoun followed by an infinitive with the sense 'that he, she, etc. may, might, should, etc.' E16.

E. Bowen And it would be a shame for you all to go, added Doreen. D. Abse It took a long time for the dust to settle. V. S. Pritchett It was exciting for her to drive the old man dangerously fast.

▸ **V** Of attributed or assumed character.

15 As being, as equivalent to, as; in the character of; (now *dial.*) as a type of. OE.

R. MACAULAY Anyhow, Hobart I knew for an ignorant person. S. O'FAOLÁIN Norah cursed him and all of us for a pack of cowards. T. E. LAWRENCE They'd have taken for granted I was too soft for man's work. W. STAFFORD We stood with wet towels over our heads for shade.

▸ **VI** Of cause or reason.

16 By reason of, under the influence of (a feeling). OE.

17 Because of, on account of (a person or thing); on account of one's regard for. Also (*arch.*) in adjurations or exclamations: for the sake of. OE. ▸**b** In consequence of, due to the effect of. Now chiefly after comparatives (otherwise usu. replaced by *from*, *of*, *through*). ME.

R. MACAULAY The artist's spirit, which loved beauty for what it was. V. WOOLF He had been arrested three times for attending seditious meetings. L. BRUCE I sort of felt sorry for the damned flies. I. MURDOCH Emily told him that he had married Harriet for snobbish reasons. **b** T. COOPER He lacketh teeth for age. G. GREENE Two young officers, who were obviously the worse for drink.

18 Indicating the presence or operation of something usu. as an obstacle or hindrance. OE. ▸**b** In spite of, notwithstanding (*rare* exc. in ***for all***, ***for any***, with noun or *that*). Also in conjunction phr. ***for all*** (***that***), notwithstanding that, although (now *rare* in literary use). OE. ▸†**c** As a precaution against, so as to prevent; against, from, of. ME–E18.

T. HARDY If it had not been for our Betty I should have gone long ago! M. SINCLAIR You can't see the text for the footnotes. D. WELCH I could not sleep for the squeaking of the crickets. A. CARTER There was hardly room to move for large chairs and cupboards. I. MURDOCH A clever face if it were not for a kind of childish timidity. **b** LEIGH HUNT I am not a very bad play-fellow . . for all I am so much bigger. W. GOLDING Somehow for all his apparent amiability a note that can only be called patronizing creeps in. W. H. AUDEN The flirtatious male . . never doubting That for all his faults he is loved. **c** J. MOXON That may hinder the Corner of the edge of the Chissel for coming at the Work.

▸ **VII** Of correspondence or correlation.

19 Preceded and followed by the same noun indicating equality in number or quantity between objects compared or contrasted. ME.

W. OWEN Faces that used to curse me, scowl for scowl. *Listener* The difference, programme for programme, is fully three million.

20 Preceding a designation of number or quantity to which another is stated to correspond proportionally. LME.

J. BERESFORD It contains . . for one inch of lean four or five of stringy fat. *Times* In Britain and West Germany there are 1.3 murders a year for every 100,000 people.

▸ **VIII** Of reference.

21 So far as concerns, with regard or respect to, concerning. ME.

G. GREENE For all he knew he was surrounded by friends. D. ABSE For my part I felt a righteous pride. G. HOUSEHOLD For the rest of the route there were enough old footprints. E. FEINSTEIN I could be a pile of clothes or papers for all the attention she gives me.

22 Considering, or making the allowance required by, the usual nature of. L17.

W. S. MAUGHAM He was talkative, forward for his age, a great reader, and clever.

▸ **IX** Of duration and extension.

23 Marking actual or intended duration: during, throughout. LME.

M. KEANE It was really in her power to endure Nurse for a few days. F. TUOHY He shouted continuously for about four minutes.

24 Marking distance: over, to the extent of. M16.

M. G. LEWIS After travelling for five and twenty miles. R. HARDY At night you can see a fire on the plain for twenty miles.

– PHRASES & COMB.: (A selection of cross-refs. only is included: see esp. other nouns) ***all for***: see ALL *adverb* 1. ***as for***: see AS *adverb* etc. **be for it** *slang* (orig. MILITARY) be in or due for trouble or punishment. ***for all*** (***that***): see ALL *pronoun & noun* 3. ***for because***. ***for ever***: see FOREVER. ***for free***: see FREE *adjective*. ***for one thing***: see THING *noun*[1]. **for-profit** *adjective* profit-making. ***for sale***: see SALE *noun*. **for the first time**, **for the second time**, etc., as a first, second, etc., instance. **I for one**, **she for one** I etc. as one, I etc. as a unit in an aggregate. **now for —**: indicating desire for or anticipation or expectation of.

▸ **B** *conjunction*. **1** Introducing a clause containing the cause of a fact, the statement of which precedes or follows; because. *arch.* ME.

DRYDEN Why comes not he? . . for he's a puling sprite.

2 Introducing a new clause or series of clauses containing the proof(s) of or reason(s) for believing what has previously been stated: seeing that, since. ME.

M. KEANE He did not know—how could he, for nobody told him? J. STEINBECK Do not touch it, for if you do . . . it will blind you.

†**3** In order that. ME–L16.

SHAKES. *3 Hen. VI* And, for the time shall not seem tedious, I'll tell thee what befell me.

†**4** ***for and***, and moreover. E16–E17.

SHAKES. *Haml.* A pick-axe and a spade, a spade, for and a shrouding sheet.

▸ **C** *noun*. An argument or reason in favour of something. Chiefly in ***the fors and againsts***. Cf. PRO *noun*[2]. E19.

for- /fɔː, *unstressed* fə/ *prefix*[1] (no longer productive).

[ORIGIN Old English *for-*, *fær-* = Old Frisian *for-*, *fir-*, Old Saxon *for-*, Old High German *fir-*, *far-* (Dutch, German *ver-*), Gothic *fair-*, *faur-*, corresp. to Greek *peri-*, *para-*, Latin *per-*, *por-*, Sanskrit *pari*, *parā*, from Indo-European prefix with variation of form and meaning esp. (i) rejection, exclusion, prohibition, (ii) destruction, (iii) exhaustion.]

▸ **I** Forming verbs.

1 Forming verbs from verbs, with intensive privative sense 'away, off', as †***forthrow***.

2 Forming verbs from verbs, with the sense 'prohibit or exclude by —', as ***forbid***.

3 Forming verbs from verbs, with the sense 'abstain, neglect, renounce', as ***forbear***, ***forgo***, ***forgive***, ***forget***, ***forsake***, ***forswear***.

4 Forming verbs from verbs, with the sense '— wrongly or pervertedly', as †***forworship***.

5 Forming verbs from verbs, with the sense 'with destructive or painful effect', as ***fordo***, ***forhunger***, or 'asunder, in pieces', as †***forburst***. ▸**b** Forming verbs from nouns, used only in pa. pple, with the sense 'overpowered or troubled by', as †***forstormed***.

6 Forming verbs from verbs, with the sense 'excessively, so as to overwhelm', chiefly in pa. pple as †***forfrighted***, †***forpampered***, or 'so as to exhaust (oneself) by —', as ***forwander***.

7 Forming trans. verbs from intrans. or trans. verbs, with the sense 'all over, extensively, thoroughly', as †***forbruise***.

8 Forming verbs from verbs, with intensive force, as †***fordread***.

9 Forming trans. verbs from adjectives or nouns, with the sense 'make or give —', as †***forfeeble***, †***forlength***.

▸ **II** Forming adjectives.

10 Forming adjectives from adjectives with intensive force, as †***forblack***, ***forlorn***, †***forweary***.

for- /fɔː, *unstressed* fə/ *prefix*[2] (not productive).

[ORIGIN Repr. Old French *for-*, *fors-*, identical with *fors* adverb (mod. *hors*) from Latin *foris*, *foras* outside.]

In words adopted from French, as ***forfeit*** etc.

for- *prefix*[3] see FORE-.

f.o.r. *abbreviation*.

Free on rail.

forage /ˈfɒrɪdʒ/ *noun*. ME.

[ORIGIN Old French & mod. French *fourrage*, from Old French *fuerre* (mod. *feurre* straw) from Frankish from Germanic base of FODDER: see -AGE.]

1 Fodder for horses or cattle, now esp. for army horses. ME. ▸**b** Food which animals etc. find for themselves. L17.

b T. HOOPER Flowers producing forage for the honeybee.

2 The action of foraging or providing forage; a raid or search for food or supplies. L15. ▸†**b** The action of raging or ravening. L16–M17.

†**3** In *pl.* Foragers. E16–E17.

– COMB.: **forage cap** a cloth undress cap worn esp. by the infantry in the British army; **forage crop**: grown for animal feed; **forage fish**: of interest to humans chiefly as food for more valuable fish; **forage harvester** a machine for harvesting forage crops.

forage /ˈfɒrɪdʒ/ *verb*. LME.

[ORIGIN Old French & mod. French *forrag(i)er*, formed as FORAGE *noun*.]

▸ **I** *verb trans*. **1** Obtain forage or supplies from; plunder, pillage. LME.

CARLYLE Noble and Peasant had been pillaged, ransomed, foraged, eaten-out by so many different Armies.

2 Supply with forage or food. M16.

DISRAELI He foraged their pony . . and supplied them from his dairy.

3 Obtain by foraging or rummaging; search *out*. M17.

THACKERAY His valet . . went out and foraged knowledge for him.

▸ **II** *verb intrans*. **4** Seek out food or provisions; go out in search of food. M16.

J. K. JEROME Bread and butter, and jam, and bacon and eggs, and other things we foraged around the town for. R. MACDONALD Blackbirds were foraging under the trees and around a feeder.

†**5** Gorge oneself; revel *in*. L16–L17.

SHAKES. *Hen. V* His most mighty father . . smiling to behold his lion's whelp Forage in blood of French nobility.

6 Make inroads *on*, *upon*; raid. M17.

CHARLES I He permitteth his Souldiers to . . forrage upon the Countrey.

7 Make a search (*for*); rummage. M18.

W. IRVING He passed many an hour foraging among the old manuscripts.

forager /ˈfɒrɪdʒə/ *noun*. LME.

[ORIGIN Old French *forragier*, from *forrage* FORAGE *noun*; also Old French *forrageour* (mod. *fourrageur*) from *forragier* FORAGE *verb*: see -ER[2].]

†**1** A harbinger, a messenger. LME–E17.

2 A person (*spec.* a soldier) who forages; a member of a foraging party. L15.

3 An animal etc. which seeks its own food. E17. ▸**b** An ant or other insect searching for food; an army ant. M19.

foralite /ˈfɔːrəlʌɪt/ *noun*. M19.

[ORIGIN from Latin *forare* to bore + -LITE.]

GEOLOGY. A tubelike marking in sandstones etc. resembling a worm burrow.

foram /ˈfɔːrəm/ *noun*. E20.

[ORIGIN Abbreviation.]

A foraminifer.

foramen /fəˈreɪmɛn/. *noun*. Pl. **foramina** /fəˈramɪnə/. L17.

[ORIGIN Latin *foramen*, *foramin-* from *forare* to bore.]

Esp. ANATOMY. An opening, an orifice, a hole; a short passage.

EPIPLOIC foramen. **foramen magnum** /ˈmagnəm/ [Latin = large] a large hole in the occipital bone by which the spinal cord enters the skull. ***STENSEN's foramen***.

foraminate /fəˈramɪneɪt/ *verb trans*. L16.

[ORIGIN formed as FORAMINIFER + -ATE[3].]

Bore, pierce, perforate.

foraminifer /fɒrəˈmɪnɪfə/ *noun*. Pl. **foraminifera** /fɒrəmɪˈnɪf(ə)rə/, **foraminifers**. M19.

[ORIGIN from Latin *foramin-* (see FORAMEN) + -I- + -FER.]

ZOOLOGY. A rhizopod of the chiefly marine order Foraminiferida, typically having a calcareous shell with perforations (foramina) through which pseudopodia extend, the fossils forming a major constituent of chalk and many marine oozes.

■ **foramiˈniferal** *adjective* of or pertaining to foraminifera; containing or consisting of foraminifera: M19. **foramiˈniferan** *noun & adjective* (**a**) *noun* = FORAMINIFER; (**b**) *adjective* of or pertaining to foraminifera: L20. **foramiˈniferous** *adjective* having foramina; foraminiferal: M19.

†**foraminous** *adjective*. E17–E19.

[ORIGIN formed as FORAMINIFER + -OUS.]

Full of holes, perforated, porous.

forasmuch /fərəzˈmʌtʃ/ *adverb*. *arch*. ME.

[ORIGIN Orig. 3 words *for as much*, translating Old French *por tant que* for so much as.]

forasmuch as, seeing that, since.

forastero /fɒrəˈstɛːrəʊ/ *noun*. Pl. **-os**. M19.

[ORIGIN Spanish = foreign.]

Any of various medium-quality varieties of the cacao tree, orig. ones imported to Venezuela from the W. Indies. Cf. CRIOLLO.

foray /ˈfɒreɪ/ *noun*. LME.

[ORIGIN Prob. from the verb.]

1 A hostile or predatory incursion; a raid; *gen.* an (adventurous) expedition. LME.

D. LESSING They make frequent forays southwards to raid and plunder crops and livestock. A. POWELL Occasional forays into upper-crust life, spending a weekend at some country house.

†**2** Plunder, prey. LME–L16.

†**3** The advance guard of an army. LME–L16.

foray /ˈfɒreɪ/ *verb*. LME.

[ORIGIN Back-form. from FORAYER.]

1 *verb trans*. Raid in search of forage or booty; plunder. Now *rare* or *obsolete*. LME.

2 *verb intrans*. Go on or make a foray. LME.

forayer /ˈfɒreɪə/ *noun*. ME.

[ORIGIN Old French *forrier* (Anglo-Norman *forreiour*) forager (mod. *fourrier* quartermaster) from Proto-Romance.]

1 A person who forays; a forager, a raider. ME.

†**2** A person who goes on ahead; a messenger. ME–M16.

forb /fɔːb/ *noun*. E20.

[ORIGIN Greek *phorbē* fodder, forage, from *pherbein* to feed.]

Any herbaceous plant other than a grass.

forbad(e) *verb pa. t.*: see FORBID *verb*.

forbear *noun* var. of FOREBEAR.

forbear /fɔːˈbɛː/ *verb*. Pa. t. **-bore** /-ˈbɔː/; pa. pple **-borne** /ˈ-bɔːn/.

[ORIGIN Old English *forberan* = Old High German *farberan* restrain, abstain, Gothic *frabairan* endure, from base of FOR-[1], BEAR *verb*[1].]

†**1** *verb trans*. Bear, endure, submit to. OE–L16.

CHAUCER I may not . . Forbere to ben out of your compagnie.

2 *verb trans*. Bear with, have patience with, tolerate. Now chiefly *Scot*. OE.

CAPT. J. SMITH I have forborne your insolencies.

†**3** *verb trans. & intrans*. Bear up against, control (oneself, one's emotions). OE–LME.

4 *verb trans*. †**a** Dispense with, do without. OE–E17. ▸†**b** Give up, part with, lose. ME–L16. ▸**c** Keep away from, leave alone. Now chiefly *Scot*. ME.

a W. BULLEIN He is the best bonde slave . . and least can be forborne. b LYDGATE She hath forbore Her maydenhead. c SIR W. SCOTT I know all his haunts, and he cannot forbear them long.

5 *verb trans. & intrans.* Abstain or refrain from or *from* (an action etc.); cease or decline *to do*. ME.

E. B. BROWNING I forbore involving you in such a responsibility. J. K. JEROME His aspect was too wretched to invite conversation, and we forbore, therefore, to ask him questions. R. GRAVES Forbearing from the jealousy that . . he was convinced that she must feel.

6 *verb trans.* Refrain from using or uttering; hold back. ME. ▸b *refl.* Restrain oneself. *rare*. M16.

POPE Forbear that dear, disastrous name. b AV 2 *Chron.* 35:21 Forebeare thee from medling with God.

7 *verb trans.* Show mercy or indulgence to; spare. Now *rare*. ME. ▸b *verb intrans.* Be patient; show forbearance. L16.

C. BOWEN May the splinters icy thy delicate feet forbear! b W. COWPER The kindest and the happiest pair Will find occasion to forbear.

F

8 *verb trans.* Give up (a claim, a lawsuit); refrain from enforcing or demanding, esp. the payment of (a debt). Now *rare*. LME.

■ **forbearant** *adjective* tolerant, indulgent, patient M17. **forbearer** *noun* LME. **forbearing** *ppl adjective* †(*a*) abstinent; (*b*) patient, long-suffering: LME.

forbearance /fɔːˈbɛːr(ə)ns/ *noun*. L16.
[ORIGIN from FORBEAR *verb* + -ANCE.]
1 Abstinence from enforcing what is due, esp. the payment of a debt. L16.

Proverb: Forbearance is no quittance.

2 The action or habit of forbearing; an instance of this. L16.

T. JEFFERSON Laws which rendered criminal . . the forbearance of repairing to church. G. GROTE The various acts and forbearances which a man supposes to constitute the sum of his duty.

3 Forbearing conduct or spirit; patient endurance, lenity. L16.

D. BREWSTER The man of the world treats the institutions of religion with more respect and forbearance. A. POWELL He behaved with great forbearance when I let his fire out.

– COMB.: †**forbearance money** money paid to a creditor, in addition to interest, for allowing late payment of a debt.

†**forbid** *noun*. *rare*. E17–M18.
[ORIGIN from the verb.]
A forbidding, a prohibition.

forbid /fəˈbɪd/ *verb*. Pa. t. **-bade** /-ˈbad, -ˈbeɪd/, **-bad** /-ˈbad/; pa. pple **-bidden** /-ˈbɪd(ə)n/, (*arch.*) **-bid**; pres. pple & verbal noun **-bidding**.
[ORIGIN Old English *forbēodan* = Old Frisian *forbiāda*, Dutch *verbieden*, Old High German *farbiotan* (German *verbieten*), Gothic *faurbiudan*, from base of FOR-[1], BID *verb*.]
▸ I *verb trans.* 1 Command not to do, have, or use; not allow to exist or happen. Foll. by double obj. of the person commanded (orig. dat.) and the thing prohibited; a person, a thing, *that*, †*to do*; a person *from* (now *rare*), *to do*; a thing *to* a person; a thing *being done*, *to be done*. OE.

LYTTON When strength and courage are forbid me. E. W. LANE He forbade both men and women from entering them. DICKENS Will you forbid him the house where I know he is safe? J. STEINBECK A law that requires you to pull your blinds down after sundown, and forbids you to pull them down before. G. GREENE The law that forbade the evidence in divorce cases being published. C. HILL Cromwell's first action on reaching Ireland was to forbid any plunder or pillage.

2 Exclude, keep back, hinder, restrain; make impossible or undesirable. With constructions as sense 1. OE.

R. B. SHERIDAN The state I left her in forbids all hope. I. MURDOCH Hugo suggested that I should come and live with him, but some instinct of independence forbade this.

†3 Ban, exile, debar. E17–E19.
▸ II *verb intrans.* 4 Not allow it, prevent it. Chiefly in exclams. LME.

SHAKES. 1 *Hen. VI* I may not open; The Cardinal of Winchester forbids.

– PHRASES: *forbid the* BANNS. **God forbid (that)** may it not happen (that).
■ **forbiddal** *noun* (*rare*) = FORBIDDANCE M19. **forbiddance** *noun* the action or an act of forbidding; (a) prohibition: E17.

forbidden /fəˈbɪd(ə)n/ *adjective*. ME.
[ORIGIN from FORBID *verb* + -EN[6].]
1 That has been forbidden; prohibited, banned; out of bounds. ME.

J. CONRAD It is deadly because of its forbidden treasures. O. MANNING Harriet was doubtful about this essay into forbidden territory.

forbidden degrees: see DEGREE *noun*. **forbidden fruit** (*a*) the fruit forbidden to Adam (*Genesis* 2:17); *fig.* illicit pleasure; (*b*) any of several varieties of citrus fruit, *esp.* the shaddock, *Citrus maxima*. *forbidden ground*: see GROUND *noun*.

2 PHYSICS. Designating or involving a transition between two quantum-mechanical states that does not conform to some selection rule, esp. for electric dipole radiation. E20.
■ **forbiddenly** *adverb* (*rare*) E17. **forbiddenness** /-n-n-/ *noun* M17.

forbidding /fəˈbɪdɪŋ/ *adjective*. L16.
[ORIGIN formed as FORBIDDEN + -ING[2].]
1 That forbids. L16.
2 Repellent, of uninviting appearance; formidable, stern. E18.

E. K. KANE We saw the same forbidding wall of belt-ice. L. DEIGHTON A forbidding figure: distant and cold and expert.

■ **forbiddingly** *adverb* M19. **forbiddingness** *noun* M18.

forbore *verb pa. t.*, **forborne** *pa. pple*: see FORBEAR *verb*.

forbye /fəˈbʌɪ, fɔːˈbʌɪ/ *preposition & adverb*. Now chiefly *Scot. & dial.* Also **-by**. ME.
[ORIGIN from FOR-[3] + BY *preposition, adverb*. Cf. German *vorbei*.]
▸ A *preposition*. 1 Of motion: past, close by. ME. ▸b Of position: hard by, near. L16.

SPENSER A goodly Lady did foreby them rush.

†2 In preference to, before, beyond. Only in ME.
3 Beside, in comparison with. ME.
4 Besides, not to mention. M16.

S. R. CROCKETT No doubt he had many a sin on his soul, forbye murder.

†5 Through the means of, by. *rare* (Spenser). Only in L16.
▸ B *adverb*. 1 Aside; nearby. ME. ▸b Of motion or time: along, past. ME.

P. BUCHAN The blacksmith stood a little forby, wi' hammer in his hand. b W. STORY That time has been long forby.

2 Besides, in addition. L16.

SIR W. SCOTT But . . there was another reason forby. I. BANKS There's plenty of bread . . and plenty of soup forbye, if you get hungry again.

force /fɔːs/ *noun*[1]. ME.
[ORIGIN Old French & mod. French from Proto-Romance, from Latin *fortis* strong. In branch II from FORCE *verb*[1].]
▸ I 1 Physical strength as an attribute of living beings. Now *rare*. ME.

Daily News As soon as his recovered forces will justify the voyage and journey he will make the passage.

2 Strength, energy, violence, intense effect, as an attribute of physical action or movement; effort; *spec.* the strength or speed of a wind, as represented by numbers in the Beaufort scale. ME.

J. BRAINE She gave me a blow on my chest with more force than playfulness behind it. M. LEITCH His palms burned—they had taken the force of his tumble on the gritty road. B. MOORE The wind force increased, sending a great slap of water over the edge of the pier.

3 Strength or power of a ruler, nation, etc.; *esp.* military strength or power. Formerly also, the strength of a fortress etc.; the fighting strength of a ship. ME.

SHAKES. 3 *Hen. VI* And lo where George of Clarence sweeps along, of force enough to bid his brother battle.

4 A body of armed men, ships, etc., an army; in *pl.*, troops, the fighting strength of a nation or commander. ME. ▸b *A* large part, number, or quantity (formerly also without preceding article); *the* majority. *obsolete* exc. *Scot. & dial.* LME. ▸c An organized body of workers etc. Also (US HISTORY), the number of slaves in the service of a plantation owner etc. E19. ▸d *The* police; a body of police. M19.

B. PLAIN A large force of Japanese planes attacked the United States naval facilities at Pearl Harbor. *fig.*: B. BETTELHEIM The story of Faust is that of a battle for his soul between the forces of light and darkness. b DEFOE Her maid, with a force of crying, said her master was dead. d G. GORER The Metropolitan Police is on a different footing to the numerous other forces in Britain. *Belfast Telegraph* If the Government expects members of the force and the Army to risk injuries . . it has got to pay up.

5 Physical strength exerted on an object or person, esp. in order to compel or constrain action; violence; (moral or physical) coercion, esp. in *by force*, by violent means, by compulsion. Formerly also, (a) constraint, (a) compulsion. ME. ▸b *spec.* in LAW. Unlawful violence against a person or thing. Formerly also, an act of this. M16.

K. WHITE I have very little society and that is quite a force on my friends. *New York Times* The problem in Central America is not the show of force, it is the use of force.

6 Mental or moral strength. Now only, power of effective action in overcoming resistance etc. ME.
7 Value, importance. Now only, the real import, significance, or effect in context, of a word, statement, etc. ME.
8 Power (of a non-material thing) to control, influence, or produce an effect; efficacy; *esp.* power to convince or sway judgement. LME. ▸b Legal validity, binding power of a law. LME. ▸c Power of an artistic medium, as writing, painting, etc., to convey an impression or idea with vividness or effect. M19. ▸d The ability of a dog to move sheep. *Austral. & NZ*. M20.

L. P. HARTLEY It had the overwhelming force of any new obsession. D. JACOBSON He had no more to say, perhaps because he felt the force of my argument. c C. CLARKE Slender comes out in this play with extraordinary force.

9 a PHYSICS. (The intensity of) an agency or influence that produces or tends to produce a change in the motion of a moving body, or produces motion or stress in a stationary body. M17. ▸b Orig., the cause of motion, heat, electricity, etc., conceived as a principle or power. Now only *transf. & fig.*, an agency, influence, or source of power likened to a physical force; often in *pl.*, as ***forces of nature***, ***economic forces***. L18.
10 (Usu. F-.) *The* life force supposedly harnessed by Jedi knights in the *Star Wars* films; *transf.* any unseen but powerful influence on a person or situation. L20.
▸ II †11 The plunger of a force pump. L16–M18.
12 TENNIS etc. A powerful stroke played with the purpose of forcing an error from the opponent; *spec.* in REAL TENNIS, such a shot aimed at the dedans. M17.
13 BRIDGE etc. A bid to which one's partner must reply, an act of forcing. M19.
14 BILLIARDS. A stroke in which the cue ball is struck off-centre causing it to stop or recoil at a particular angle. M19.

– PHRASES ETC.: **armed forces** (the people constituting) the fighting strength of a nation etc. *brute force*: see BRUTE *adjective*. *by force*: see sense 5 above. **by force of** by virtue of, by means of. **come into force** come into operation, take effect. *electromotive force*: see ELECTROMOTIVE *adjective*. *from force of habit*: see HABIT *noun*. **in force** (*a*) in large numbers; (*b*) LAW operative, binding, valid. **join forces** combine efforts. *life force*: see LIFE *noun*. **put in force** enforce. *task force*: see TASK *noun*. **with force and arms** LAW (now *hist.*) = VI ET ARMIS.
– COMB.: **force cup** a rubber cup attached to a handle which clears a blocked drain by creating a vacuum in it; a plunger; **force-feed** *noun & verb* (*a*) *noun* a supply, esp. of lubricant, maintained under applied force or pressure; (*b*) *verb trans.* feed (a prisoner, animal, etc.) by force; **force field** (chiefly SCIENCE FICTION) a region or barrier of (usu. invisible) force; **force-land** *verb intrans. & trans.* [after FORCED *landing*] (cause to) make a forced landing; **forceout** BASEBALL a putting out of a base runner by necessitating an advance to the next base when it is not possible to do so safely; **force pump** (*a*) a pump that forces water beyond the range of atmospheric pressure; (*b*) a kind of stomach pump used for force-feeding; **force stroke** = sense 12 above.

force /fɔːs/ *noun*[2]. *N. English*. Also **foss** /fɒs/. LME.
[ORIGIN Old Norse *fors* (Swedish *fors*, Danish *fos*).]
A waterfall.

force /fɔːs/ *verb*[1]. ME.
[ORIGIN Old French & mod. French *forcer*, formed as FORCE *noun*[1].]
▸ I Apply force.
1 a *verb trans.* Compel or oblige (a person, oneself, etc.) *to do*, *into doing*, or *to* or *into* a course of action; *spec.* rape (esp. a woman). ME. ▸b *verb trans. &* (now only *dial.*) *intrans.* Urge or push to the limits; strain or strive (*to do*). ME. ▸c *verb trans. & intrans.* CARDS. Compel (a player) to trump or reveal the strength of a hand; compel a player to play (a certain card). M18. ▸d *verb trans.* BASEBALL. Put out (a base runner) by necessitating an advance to the next base when it is not possible to do so safely. Usu. foll. by *out*. M19. ▸e *verb intrans.* TENNIS etc. Use a force stroke. L19.

a D. H. LAWRENCE She tried to force her mind to the contemplation of the new state of things. R. H. MOTTRAM He lay in bed until hunger forced him to rise. W. C. WILLIAMS He was insistent and forced her against her will to get into his car.

2 a *verb trans.* Compel or constrain by physical, mental, moral, or circumstantial means; PHYSICS modify by external action. LME. ▸b *verb trans. & intrans.* Of a sheepdog: move (sheep) in a certain direction. *Austral. & NZ*. E20.

a W. S. CHURCHILL The President's . . use of the patronage at his disposal to force the repeal of the Silver Purchase Act. J. CHEEVER Her wicked sisters had got pregnant in order to force their marriages.

3 *verb trans.* Cause, bring about, or produce, by effort. M16.

L. VAN DER POST I thought it useless to waste the energies of the whole party forcing a way through. A. MACLEAN He looked at me, forced a pale smile that was half apology, half recognition.

4 a *verb trans.* Overpower, capture, take by force, (a stronghold, defence, †troops); obtain by force, extort. L16. ▸b *verb trans.* Make a way by force through, break through, (a pass, enemy lines, etc.); break open (a lock, door, etc.). E17. ▸c *verb intrans.* Make one's way *in*, *out*, *through*, or *up*, by force. Now *rare*. M17.

a T. JEFFERSON The people . . forced the prison of Saint Lazare. G. STEIN Sometimes it hurt so in him, . . it would force some slow tears from him. A. WILSON If he had forced from the public and the critics respect and hearing. b J. T. STORY I watched her open a locker, using a hatpin to force the lock. R. RENDELL It appears she was shot by someone who forced an entry to this house. c DRYDEN For Love they force thro' Thickets.

5 *verb trans.* Drive, push, or propel violently or against resistance. Chiefly with prepositions or adverbs. L16.

C. S. FORESTER The lower the brig would settle, . . the greater would be the pressure forcing water through the hole. E. BOWEN Had she been left alone . . life might yet have forced her on to her own feet. N. MOSLEY I thought I should force her mouth open by pressing my fingers between her teeth.

6 *verb trans.* Foll. by *on, upon*: impose or press (a thing) forcibly on (a person); oblige (a person) to turn or resort to (a thing). **E17.** ▸†**b** Enforce (a law). *rare* (Shakes.). Only in **E17.** ▸**c** Impose an unnatural or unusual sense or context on (a word, analogy, etc.). **M17.**

R. LANGBRIDGE Her lack of money had forced her back upon the most respectable costume which she had. N. MITFORD She gets a hold over people . . with her charm and her prestige and then forces her own values on them. **c** EDWARD WHITE This is manifestly to force the Scripture.

7 *verb trans.* Hasten artificially the growth, development, or maturity of (a plant, farm animal, child, etc.). **E17.**

ANTHONY HUXLEY Hyacinths and other bulbs we force in winter. K. M. E. MURRAY Regular schooling should not be begun too young, early 'forcing' being . . the cause of many boys of promise proving disappointments.

▸ †**II** Give, have force.

8 *verb trans.* Strengthen, reinforce; fortify. **LME–E19.** ▸**b** Season, spice. **LME–L15.** ▸**c** *verb trans.* Clarify (wine) by a short process. **M18–M19.**

9 *verb trans. & intrans.* Be concerned, attach importance to, care (*for, of, to do*). Usu. in neg. contexts. **LME–E17.**

SHAKES. *Lucr.* I force not argument a straw.

10 *verb intrans.* Be of importance; matter, signify. **LME–E17.**

– PHRASES: **force a card** make a person choose a particular card unconsciously in a conjuring trick. **force a person's hand** compel a person to act prematurely or to adopt a policy unwillingly. **force a smile** make oneself smile, smile in spite of one's feelings. **force down** compel (an aircraft) to land. **force one's voice** strain to get notes beyond one's usual range or a degree of loudness beyond what is easy or natural. **force the bidding** raise the price rapidly at an auction. **force the game** (CRICKET etc.) run risks to increase the rate of scoring. **force the issue** compel a decision. **force the pace** adopt a fast pace in a race in order to tire out one's adversary or adversaries quickly.

force /fɔːs/ *verb*² *trans. obsolete* exc. *Scot. dial.* **LME.**
[ORIGIN Anglo-Norman *forcer*, from Old French *forces*, from Latin *forfices*, FORFEX pair of scissors, clipping shears.]
Clip or shear (a fleece, a beard); *esp.* clip off the coarser upper part of (a fleece).

†**force** *verb*³ *trans.* **LME–L18.**
[ORIGIN Alt. of FARCE *verb* by confusion with FORCE *verb*¹. Surviving in FORCEMEAT.]
= FARCE *verb* 1, 1b.

fig.: SHAKES. *Tr. & Cr.* Wit larded with malice, and malice forced with wit.

forceable /ˈfɔːsəb(ə)l/ *adjective.* **LME.**
[ORIGIN Old French *forçable*, formed as FORCE *verb*¹: see -ABLE. Cf. FORCIBLE.]
1 = FORCIBLE. Now *rare.* **LME.**
2 Able to be forced. **L16.**
■ **forceably** *adverb* **LME.**

forced /fɔːst/ *ppl adjective.* **L15.**
[ORIGIN from FORCE *verb*¹ + -ED¹.]
1 Compelled, imposed, or obtained by force; compulsory. **L15.**

I. MURDOCH A forced marriage which her free nature would resent and soon detest.

2 Produced or maintained with effort; strained; (of a gesture etc.) affected, unnatural. **L16.**

G. GORDON The forced, indeed intense, jollity he found himself . . assuming when conversing with certain members of the company.

3 Artificially made or prepared; *esp.* (of soil) disturbed by digging, having the topsoil raised. Long *obsolete* exc. *dial.* **E17.**
4 Of a plant, crop, etc.: made to bear, or produced, out of the proper season. **L17.**

E. BOWEN She thought they looked like forced roses, magnetized into being.

5 Of (a draught of) air: produced or supplied by artificial means, as a blower etc. **M19.**

– SPECIAL COLLOCATIONS & COMB.: **forced-choice** *adjective* (of a question, technique, etc.) requiring a choice to be made by the participant between a number of prearranged answers or alternatives. **forced labour** compulsory labour, usu. under rigorous conditions. **forced landing** an unavoidable landing by an aircraft in an emergency. **forced march**: requiring a special effort by troops etc. **forced move** a move in chess etc. to which there is no reasonable alternative.
■ **forcedly** /ˈfɔːsɪdli/ *adverb* **M16.** **forcedness** /ˈfɔːsɪdnɪs/ *noun* **M17.**

force de frappe /fɔrs də frap/ *noun phr.* Pl. ***forces de frappe*** (pronounced same). **M20.**
[ORIGIN French = striking force.]
MILITARY. A striking force; *spec.* the French independent nuclear striking force.

forceful /ˈfɔːsfʊl, -f(ə)l/ *adjective & adverb.* **M16.**
[ORIGIN from FORCE *noun*¹ + -FUL.]
▸ **A** *adjective.* **1** Full of force, powerful, strong; (of a speech etc.) impressive, effective. **M16.**

P. G. WODEHOUSE One of those forceful characters which monopolize any stage on which they appear.

2 Acting with force, violent; (now *rare*) driven or propelled with force. **L16.**

N. CHOMSKY An end to any forceful interference in the internal affairs of Vietnam or any other nation.

▸ **B** *adverb.* Forcefully. *rare.* **E18.**
■ **forcefully** *adverb* **L18.** **forcefulness** *noun* **E19.**

forceless /ˈfɔːslɪs/ *adjective.* **M16.**
[ORIGIN from FORCE *noun*¹ + -LESS.]
Without force; feeble.

force majeure /fɔrs maʒœːr/ *noun phr.* **L19.**
[ORIGIN French = superior strength.]
Irresistible force, overwhelming power; *spec.* an unforeseeable course of events excusing fulfilment of a contract.

forcemeat /ˈfɔːsmiːt/ *noun.* **L17.**
[ORIGIN from FORCE *verb*³ + MEAT *noun*.]
A mixture of finely chopped meat or vegetables etc., seasoned and spiced, and chiefly used for stuffing or garnish.

forcené /fɔrsəne/ *adjective.* **E18.**
[ORIGIN French, pa. pple of *forcener, forsener*, be or become mad or enraged, from Old French *fors* (mod. *hors*) + *sen* sense.]
HERALDRY. Of a horse: rearing or standing on its hind legs.

forceps /ˈfɔːsɛps, -sɪps/ *noun sing. & pl.* **L16.**
[ORIGIN Latin.]
1 Also ***pair of forceps***. A pair of pincers, usually held in one hand to obtain a firm grip on a small object, esp. in surgery or anatomical dissection, or in entomology. Also, in obstetrics, a large two-bladed instrument designed to encircle and pull upon the baby's head to assist delivery. **L16.**
2 ZOOLOGY. An organ or part of the body that has the shape of, or may be used as, a forceps, e.g. the cerci of earwigs. Formerly also, either of the two branches of this. **M17.**

forcer /ˈfɔːsə/ *noun*¹. Long *obsolete* exc. *hist.* **ME.**
[ORIGIN Old French *forc(i)er*.]
A chest, a coffer.

forcer /ˈfɔːsə/ *noun*². **M16.**
[ORIGIN from FORCE *verb*¹ + -ER¹.]
1 A person who or thing which forces. Now *esp.* a person who produces forced crops. **M16.**
2 An instrument or means of forcing; *esp.* (the plunger of) a force pump. **M17.**

forces de frappe *noun phr.* pl. of FORCE DE FRAPPE.

forcible /ˈfɔːsɪb(ə)l/ *adjective & adverb.* **LME.**
[ORIGIN Legal Anglo-Norman, Old French, formed as FORCE *verb*¹: see -IBLE. Cf. FORCEABLE.]
▸ **A** *adjective.* **1** Done by or involving the use of force or violence. Esp. in LAW in ***forcible detainer***: see DETAINER *noun*² 1. **LME.**

P. SCOTT They ate it in different ways, a few eagerly, most reluctantly, some by forcible feeding.

2 Having force; now chiefly (of a person, action, speech, etc.) producing a powerful effect, convincing; formerly also, (of a person, material thing, or natural agency) strong, powerful. **M16.**

L. STEPHEN One man sees everything in the forcible light and shade of Rembrandt.

▸ **B** *adverb.* Forcibly. **L16.**
– COMB.: **forcible-feeble** *noun & adjective* [after Shakes. *2 Hen. IV*] (a person) disguising feebleness under a show of force.
■ **forci'bility** *noun* **L18.** **forcibleness** *noun* **M16.** **forcibly** *adverb* **L15.**

forcing /ˈfɔːsɪŋ/ *verbal noun.* **LME.**
[ORIGIN from FORCE *verb*¹ + -ING¹.]
The action of FORCE *verb*¹.
– COMB.: **forcing frame**, **forcing house** a frame, a building, where the growth or maturity of a plant, fruit, etc. is artificially hastened; **forcing pen** *Austral. & NZ* a pen into which sheep are forced or driven in order to guide them to a certain point.

forcipate /ˈfɔːsɪpeɪt/ *adjective.* **M17.**
[ORIGIN from Latin *forcip-* FORCEPS + -ATE².]
Chiefly BOTANY & ZOOLOGY. Shaped like forceps; deeply forked.
■ Also **forcipated** *adjective* **M17.**

forcy /ˈfɔːsi/ *adjective.* Chiefly *Scot. & N. English.* **LME.**
[ORIGIN from FORCE *noun*¹ + -Y¹.]
Full of force, strong, active; (of weather) propitious for speedy growth or ripening of crops.

ford /fɔːd/ *noun.*
[ORIGIN Old English *ford* = Old Frisian *forda*, Old Saxon *-ford* in place names (Dutch *voorde*), Old & mod. High German *furt*, from West Germanic, Germanic base of FARE *verb*.]
1 A shallow place where a river or other stretch of water may be crossed by wading or with a vehicle. **OE.**
2 A tract of water; a stream; the sea. *obsolete* exc. *dial.* **M16.**

ford /fɔːd/ *verb.* **E17.**
[ORIGIN from the noun.]
1 *verb trans.* Cross (water) by means of a ford. **E17.**
2 *verb intrans.* Cross (*over*) water by means of a ford. **L17.**
■ **fordable** *adjective* **E17.** **fording** *noun* (*a*) the action of the verb; (*b*) a ford: **M18.**

fordeal /ˈfɔːdiːl/ *noun & adjective.* Long *obsolete* exc. *Scot.* **L15.**
[ORIGIN from FOR-² + DEAL *noun*¹ (part).]
▸ **A** *noun.* **1** Precedence; *arch.* advantage. **L15.**
2 A store, a reserve. **E19.**
▸ **B** *adjective.* In reserve, in hand. **E19.**

Fordism /ˈfɔːdɪz(ə)m/ *noun.* **E20.**
[ORIGIN from the name of Henry *Ford* (1863–1947), US motor manufacturer + -ISM.]
The use in manufacturing industry of the methods pioneered by Henry Ford, esp. large-scale mechanized mass production.
■ **Fordist** *noun & adjective* **L20.**

fordo /fɔːˈduː/ *verb trans. arch.* Also **fore-**. Pa. t. **-did** /-ˈdɪd/; pa. pple **-done** /-ˈdʌn/.
[ORIGIN Old English *fordōn* = Old Saxon *fardōn* (Dutch *verdoen*), Old High German *fartuon* (German *vertun*), from base of FOR-¹, DO *verb*.]
1 Kill; put an end to (life). **OE.**

SHAKES. *Haml.* This doth betoken The corse they follow did with desperate hand fordo it own life.

2 Destroy, ruin, spoil, (a place, thing, †person); lay waste to (land). **OE.**
3 †**a** Abolish (an institution); annul (a law). **OE–M19.** ▸**b** Do away with, remove, (an abstract object, esp. sin). **ME.**
†**4** Undo; make powerless, counteract, (poison, temptation, etc.). **ME–E17.**
5 As ***fordone*** *pa. pple.* Exhausted, tired out. **M16.**

M. ARNOLD With Indian heats at last fordone.

fordrunken /fɔːˈdrʌŋk(ə)n/ *ppl adjective.* Long *arch.*
[ORIGIN Old English *fordruncen*, from FOR-¹ + DRUNKEN *adjective* (= Middle Low German *verdrunken*).]
Drunk, overcome with drink.

fore /fɔː/ *adjective & noun.* **L15.**
[ORIGIN Independent use of FORE-.]
▸ **A** *adjective.* †**1** Anterior in time, previous, former. **L15–E18.**
2 Situated in front. Freq. opp. ***back***, ***hind***, ***aft***. **E16.**

J. SPOTTISWOOD The Cannon having made great breaches in the fore and back walls.

▸ **B** *noun.* The forepart of something, the front; the bow of a ship. (Earliest in ***to the fore*** below.) **M17.**
to the fore (*a*) (of a person) present, on the spot, alive, surviving; (*b*) (of money etc.) ready, available; (*c*) in full view, conspicuous; (*d*) ***come to the fore***, come to the front, come into prominence, take a leading part.

fore /fɔː/ *adverb, preposition, & conjunction.* Also **'fore**.
[ORIGIN Old English *fore* = Old Frisian *for(e)*, *fara*, Old Saxon, Old High German *fora* (Dutch *voor*, German *vor*), Gothic *faura*, from Germanic, rel. to Sanskrit *pra*, *purā*, Greek *pro*, *para*, Latin *pro*, *prae*, *per*. From 16th cent. often regarded as abbreviation of *before*.]
▸ **A** *adverb.* **1** Before in time, previously. Long *obsolete* exc. *dial.* **OE.**
†**2** Forward, forth. **ME–M17.**
3 See FORE AND AFT.
▸ **B** *preposition.* **1** Before in place, in the presence of. **OE.**

SHAKES. *Wint. T.* Contract us fore these witnesses.

2 Before in time, previous to. *obsolete* exc. *dial. & US.* **OE.**
†**3** In support of; on account of. **OE–LME.**
†**4** Before in order, in preference to. **ME–M17.**
▸ **C** *conjunction.* Before. *US.* **E19.**

American Speech My two boys died 'fore they was ten.

fore /fɔː/ *interjection.* **M19.**
[ORIGIN Prob. aphet. from BEFORE, AFORE.]
GOLF. As a warning to anyone in the probable line of flight of a ball: look out!

fore- /fɔː/ *prefix.* Also (not productive) **for-**. **OE.**
[ORIGIN Repr. FORE *adverb & preposition*, *adjective*.]
1 Forming verbs and their derivs. in senses 'before, in front', as ***foreshorten***, 'beforehand, in advance', as ***forecast***, ***foreordain***.
2 Forming nouns in senses 'in front (of), front-', as ***forecourt***, ***forelimb***, 'that is the front part of', as ***forearm***, 'of, near, or towards the bow of a ship or connected with the foremast, forward', as ***forecastle***, ***forehold***, 'that is in advance (of), anticipatory, precedent', as ***forefather***, ***forenoon***.
3 Formerly occas. forming prepositions, as ***fore-against***.
■ **fore'act** *verb trans. & intrans.* (now *rare*) act beforehand **E17.** **fore-a'gainst**, **-a'gain** *preposition* (long *obsolete* exc. *Scot.*) over against, directly opposite **L15.** †**fore-alleged** *ppl adjective* previously alleged **L16–E18.** **forebay** *noun* a reservoir or channel from which water is discharged to run a mill wheel **LME.** †**forebell** *noun* the first of a peal of bells **L15–E19.** **forebitter** *noun* (NAUTICAL) a sea-song, esp. sung for recreation **E20.** **forebody** *noun* †(*a*) the front part of a dress; (*b*) NAUTICAL the forward part of the hull of a ship: **E17.** **forebow** *noun*¹ (*obsolete* exc. *dial.*) [from BOW *noun*¹] (*a*) in *pl.*, the shoulders of an animal; (*b*) the prow of a ship: **E16.** †**forebow** *noun*² [from BOW *noun*³] an arched frame on the front of a saddle **E18–M19.** **forebrain** *noun* (ANATOMY) the anterior part of the brain, including the cerebrum and diencephalon **L19.** **forebreast** *noun* (*a*) (now only *Scot.*) the forepart of something; orig. *spec.* the vanguard of an army; (*b*) MINING = FOREFIELD: **LME.** **forecabin** *noun* a cabin in the forward part of a vessel **E19.** **forecaddie** *noun* a

F

caddie who goes ahead of golfers to see where the balls fall L18. **fore'call** *verb trans.* call or ordain beforehand M17. **forecar** *noun* (now *rare*) an early kind of motorcycle having a passenger's seat in front E20. **forecarriage** *noun* the front part of the framework of a carriage M16. **fore-'cited** *ppl adjective* previously cited L16. **forecon'ceive** *verb trans.* (long *rare*) preconceive M16. **foredawn** *noun* the time preceding the dawn L19. **foreday** *noun* †(*a*) in *pl.*, preceding days, past life; (*b*) (chiefly *Scot.* & *US*) the early part of the day, before or around dawn: ME. **foredeck** *noun* the deck at the forward part of a ship; the forward part of the deck: E16. **fore'destine** *verb trans.* (*rare*) predestine ME. **fore'destiny** *noun* (*rare*) destiny, fate M16. **foredoor** *noun* (now *rare*) a front door M16. **foredune** *noun* the part of a dune system nearest to the sea E20. **fore-elders** *noun pl.* (chiefly *N. English*) ancestors, progenitors ME. **foreface** *noun* the front part of something, *esp.* the face of an animal; an iron framework forming the front part of a fireplace: M16. **forefield** *noun* (MINING) a coalface, *esp.* the most advanced part of a coalface currently being worked L17. **forefighter** *noun* (*rare*) a fighter in the front ranks LME. **fore'gainst, -gain** *preposition* (long *obsolete* exc. *Scot.*) over against, directly opposite LME. **foregame** *noun* (now *rare*) a preliminary game L16. **foreganger** *noun* †(*a*) a forerunner, a predecessor; (*b*) NAUTICAL a short piece of rope connecting a line to a harpoon in whale-fishing etc.; (*c*) NAUTICAL a 15-fathom length of strong anchor chain which ran between an anchor and the rest of the cable, and could withstand extra wear and tear: ME. **foregate** *noun* a front gate LME. **foregift** *noun* (LAW) a premium for a lease E18. **foreglance** *noun* (*a*) the action of glancing forward; (*b*) a glance beforehand: M19. **fore'guess** *verb trans.* guess beforehand; anticipate, conjecture: LME. **foregut** *noun* (ANATOMY & ZOOLOGY) the anterior part of the gut L19. **forehammer** *noun* (*Scot.* & *N. English*) a large hammer used by a blacksmith; a sledgehammer: LME. **fore'hear** *verb trans.* & *intrans.* (now *rare*) hear beforehand L16. †**forehent** *verb trans.* (*rare*) overtake, take in advance: only in L16. **forehock** *noun* a foreleg cut of pork or bacon E20. **forehold** *noun* (NAUTICAL) (a section of) a hold in the forward part of a ship M17. **forehorse** *noun* the foremost horse in a team L15. **forein'tend** *verb trans.* intend beforehand L16. **forelady** *noun* (chiefly *US*) = FOREWOMAN 2 L19. †**forelend** *verb trans.* (*rare*, Spenser) grant previously: only in L16. †**forelie** *verb intrans.* (*rare*, Spenser) lie across the front of: only in L16. †**forelift** *verb trans.* lift up in front L16–M18. **fore'live** *verb trans.* & *intrans.* live before (another); exist previously: LME. **foreloader** *noun* a loader mounted on the front of a tractor etc. M20. **fore'mean** *verb trans.* intend beforehand E17. †**foremention** *verb trans.* mention beforehand L16–M18. **forenamed** *ppl adjective* (*arch.*) named or mentioned before, aforesaid ME. **foreoath** *noun* (LAW, now *hist.*) in Anglo-Saxon England, an oath required of the party bringing a suit unless the fact complained of was manifest OE. **fore'order** *verb trans.* order beforehand; preordain: L19. **fore'plan** *verb trans.* plan beforehand L18. **foreplane** *noun* a carpenter's plane used for preliminary smoothing E18. **forepleasure** *noun* pleasure induced by sexual stimulation E20. **forepurpose** *noun* (now *rare* or *obsolete*) a previous intent or design L16. **fore'purpose** *verb trans.* (now *rare* or *obsolete*) intend or resolve beforehand: M16. **forerank** *noun* the front rank, the most prominent place L16. †**fore-recited** *ppl adjective* previously recited; aforesaid: E–M17. **forerib** *noun* a rib of beef for roasting, cut from just in front of the sirloin (freq. in *pl.*) M19. **forerider** *noun* a person who rides ahead; a scout, a messenger: L15. **foreseat** *noun* (now *Scot.* & *US*) a seat or position in front, esp. in church; the front part of a box pew: L16. **fore'seize** *verb trans.* (*rare*) take (something one is destined to receive) prematurely L17. **fore'shine** *verb intrans.* (*arch.*) shine forth; throw light forward: L16. **foreshock** *noun* a lesser shock preceding the main shock of an earthquake E20. †**foreshop** *noun* (chiefly *Scot.*) a shop fronting a street M17–E19. **foreside** *noun* the forepart; the front or upper side: LME. **fore'signify** *verb trans.* prefigure, typify; foretell: M16. †**foreskirt** *noun* the front or a front part of a coat or robe below the waist M16–M17. **foresleeve** *noun* the part of a sleeve which covers the forearm; a loose ornamental sleeve formerly worn over an ordinary sleeve: LME. **fore'spent** *ppl adjective* (now *rare*) spent previously L16. †**fore-spurrer** *noun* (*rare*, Shakes.) a person who spurs or presses on ahead: only in L16. **forestick** *noun* (*US*) the front stick lying on the andirons in a wood fire L18. **forestone** *noun* (*a*) a mass of rock which interrupts a vein of ore; (*b*) the front crosspiece of a blast furnace: M17. **forestroke** *noun* a forward stroke in bell-ringing, sword-fighting, etc. L17. **fore'suffer** *verb trans.* & *intrans.* suffer beforehand M19. **foretack** *noun* (NAUTICAL) a rope by which the weather corner of a foresail is kept in place L15. **fore'teach** *verb trans.* (*rare*) teach (a person, something) beforehand M16. **foretime** *noun* (*arch.*) the past, early days, old times L15. **foretooth** *noun* a front tooth (usu. in *pl.*) OE. **fore-understanding** *noun* (*rare*) instinctive knowledge or understanding; intuition: M16. **fore'utter** *verb trans.* (*rare*) foretell L16. **forewheel** *noun* either of the front wheels of a four-wheeled carriage E18. **forewing** *noun* either of the anterior wings of an insect M19. **foreworld** *noun* the prehistoric or primeval world L18. **fore'write** *verb trans.* write beforehand (chiefly as ***forewritten*** *ppl adjective.*) LME.

fore and aft /fɔːr (ə)nd ˈɑːft/ *adverbial & adjectival phr.* As adjective usu. **fore-and-aft**. E17.
[ORIGIN Perh. translating phr. of Low German origin: cf. Dutch *van voren en van achteren*.]
Chiefly NAUTICAL. ▸**A** *adverb*. **1** From stem to stern, lengthwise. E17.
2 Of position: in or at both bow and stern, all over the ship. E17.
3 Of motion or direction: backwards and forwards. E18.
▸**B** *adjective*. Placed or directed lengthwise. E19.
– COMB. & SPECIAL COLLOCATIONS: **fore-and-aft cap** a cap with a peak at each end; **fore-and-aft rigged** *adjectival phr.* (of a vessel) having sails set lengthwise as opp. to on yards; opp. ***square-rigged*** s.v. SQUARE *adjective*.
■ **fore-and-after** *noun* (*a*) a vessel, esp. a schooner, which is fore-and-aft rigged; (*b*) a fore-and-aft cap: E19.

fore-appoint /fɔːrəˈpɔɪnt/ *verb trans. arch.* M16.
[ORIGIN from FORE- + APPOINT.]
Appoint beforehand.
■ **fore-appointment** *noun* previous appointment, preordination L16.

forearm /ˈfɔːrɑːm/ *noun*. E18.
[ORIGIN from FORE- + ARM *noun*[1].]
The part of the arm from the elbow to the wrist or fingertips; the corresponding part in the foreleg of an animal or the wing of a bird.

A. GRAY His sleeves were rolled well above his elbows exposing robust hairy forearms.

forearm /fɔːrˈɑːm/ *verb trans.* L16.
[ORIGIN from FORE- + ARM *verb*[1].]
Arm beforehand (freq. *fig.*).

E. M. GOULBURN We are forearmed against surprises. *Bird Watching* Forwarned is forearmed, for such knowledge alerts you to the . . likely species in the . . habitat you are visiting.

forebear /ˈfɔːbɛː/ *noun*. Orig. *Scot.* Also **forbear**. L15.
[ORIGIN from FORE- + var. of BEER *noun*[2].]
An ancestor, a forefather, (freq. in *pl.*).

W. MAXWELL Their forebears had perhaps come on a later wave of European migration.

forebode /fɔːˈbəʊd/ *verb*. E17.
[ORIGIN from FORE- + BODE *verb*[1].]
1 **a** *verb trans.* Have a presentiment of (a thing, esp. something evil), *that*; anticipate. E17. ▸**b** *verb intrans.* Conjecture, forecast. E18.

POPE My soul foreboded I should find the bower Of some fell monster.

2 *verb trans.* Betoken, portend. M17.
3 *verb trans.* Announce beforehand, predict. M17.

W. H. DIXON Old men foreboded evil days to come.

■ **forebodement** *noun* (*rare*) (a) foreboding M18. **foreboder** *noun* a person who or thing which forbodes L17. **forebodingly** *adverb* in a foreboding manner, predictively E19.

foreboding /fɔːˈbəʊdɪŋ/ *noun*. LME.
[ORIGIN from FOREBODE + -ING[1].]
1 A prediction, a presage. LME. ▸**b** A portent, an omen. LME.

J. TYNDALL Heedless of the forebodings of many prophets of evil weather.

2 A presentiment of coming evil. E17.

R. SUTCLIFF There was a queer superstitious feeling in him . . a queer foreboding of trouble to come. D. ACHESON The army, against the deepest forebodings of General Walker, moved forward.

forecame *verb pa. t.* of FORECOME.

forecast /ˈfɔːkɑːst/ *noun*. LME.
[ORIGIN from the verb.]
†**1** **a** A plan, a plot. LME–M18. ▸**b** A design, a purpose, an aim. M16–L17.
2 The action or faculty of forecasting; forethought, prudence. Now *rare*. M16.

CARLYLE The doctrine, which Swift, with the keen forecast of genius, dimly anticipated.

3 A conjectural estimate, based on present indications, of something in the future, esp. of coming weather; a prediction. L17.

C. LAMB A forecast of the wearisome day that lies before me. *Observer* The previous forecast of no serious gale.

forecast /ˈfɔːkɑːst/ *verb*. Pa. t. & pple **-cast**, **-casted**. LME.
[ORIGIN from FORE- + CAST *verb*.]
1 **a** *verb trans.* & *intrans.* Contrive or plan beforehand; foreordain, predestine. *obsolete* exc. *dial.* LME. ▸**b** *verb trans.* Consider beforehand. M16.

a A. GOLDING At the first sight the thing which was forecast by good order, seemeth to happen by adventure.

2 *verb trans.* & *intrans.* Estimate or conjecture beforehand (future events or conditions, esp. the weather); predict. L15.

MILTON If it happen as I did forecast. M. E. G. DUFF I am quite unable to forecast the future. E. O'BRIEN The weather bureau forecast sun.

■ **forecastable** *adjective* L19. **forecaster** *noun* a person who forecasts M17. **forecastingly** *adverb* (now *rare* or *obsolete*) with prior planning or consideration M16.

forecastle /ˈfəʊks(ə)l/ *noun*. Also **fo'c's'le**. LME.
[ORIGIN from FORE- + CASTLE *noun*[1].]
NAUTICAL. **1** *hist.* A short raised deck at the front of a ship, orig. raised like a castle to command the enemy's decks. LME.
2 *hist.* The forward part of the upper deck of a ship. L15.
3 The forward part of a ship, below the deck, where the sailors live. M19.

foreclose /fɔːˈkləʊz/ *verb*. ME.
[ORIGIN Old French & mod. French *forclos* pa. pple of *forclore*, formed as FOR-[2] + *clore* CLOSE *verb*: assoc. with FOR-[1], FORE-.]
▸**I** *verb trans.* †**1** Bar from escaping, prevent the passage or leaving of. Only in ME.
2 Exclude, bar, shut out completely. LME.

D. NEAL The Puritans being thus foreclosed and shut out of the Church.

3 Hinder or prohibit (a person) *from*, *to do*; hinder the action or activity of. LME. ▸**b** Prevent the performance or occurrence of (an action or event). M16. ▸**c** Debar (a person) from enjoyment (*of*). M19.

G. BERKELEY A mind not hardened by impenitency, nor foreclosed by pride. **b** W. LIPPMANN One career excluding others, one course foreclosing its alternatives.

†**4** Close fast, stop up, block up (an opening, way, etc.). L15–M18.
5 Establish an exclusive claim to. L16.

R. W. EMERSON And finding . . even virtue and truth foreclosed and monopolized.

6 Settle (an arguable point) by anticipation. E18.
7 LAW. Bar (a person entitled to redeem a mortgage) upon non-payment of the money due; deprive of the equity of redemption. E18. ▸**b** Bar (a right of redemption); take away the power of redeeming (a mortgage). E18.

b G. SANTAYANA Tenants must occasionally be evicted and mortgages foreclosed.

▸**II** *verb intrans.* **8** Revoke the power of redeeming a mortgage. Freq. foll. by *on*. E18.

A. TROLLOPE A . . notice . . from the duke's lawyer, saying that he meant to foreclose.

foreclosure /fɔːˈkləʊʒə/ *noun*. E18.
[ORIGIN from FORE- + CLOSURE.]
LAW. The action of foreclosing a mortgage or depriving a mortgagor of the right of redemption; a proceeding to bar the right of redeeming mortgaged property.

forecome /fɔːˈkʌm/ *verb*. *rare*. Pa. t. **-came** /-ˈkeɪm/; pa. pple **-come**. OE.
[ORIGIN from FORE- + COME *verb*.]
1 *verb trans.* Come before, anticipate. OE.
2 *verb trans.* Gain the advantage of, overcome. OE.
†**3** *verb intrans.* Come before the usual time. Only in ME.

foreconscious /fɔːˈkɒnʃəs/ *adjective* & *noun*. E20.
[ORIGIN from FORE- + CONSCIOUS *adjective*, translating German *vorbewusst*.]
PSYCHOLOGY. (Of or pertaining to) that part of the mind below the threshold of immediate conscious attention, whose memories can be brought into the conscious field. Cf. PRECONSCIOUS.

forecourt /ˈfɔːkɔːt/ *noun*. M16.
[ORIGIN from FORE- + COURT *noun*[1].]
1 An enclosed space in front of a building, an outer court. M16. ▸**b** *spec.* The part of a filling station where petrol is supplied. M20.

E. METEYARD The ivy-clad cottage, with its forecourt or garden standing to the front. K. ISHIGURO We sat on a bench in the forecourt of the . . station.

2 The front part of a court used for sports or games, *esp.* the part of a tennis court between the service line and the net. E20.

foredge *noun* var. of FORE-EDGE.

foredo *verb* var. of FORDO.

foredoom /ˈfɔːduːm/ *noun*. M16.
[ORIGIN from FORE- + DOOM *noun*[1].]
A doom or judgement pronounced beforehand; destiny.

foredoom /fɔːˈduːm/ *verb trans.* L16.
[ORIGIN from FORE- + DOOM *verb*.]
1 **a** Forecast, foreshadow. *rare*. L16. ▸**b** Foreordain, predestine. L17.
2 Doom or condemn beforehand (*to*). E17.

BOSW. SMITH His efforts were . . foredoomed to failure.

fore-edge /ˈfɔːrɛdʒ/ *noun*. Also **foredge**. M17.
[ORIGIN from FORE- + EDGE *noun*.]
The front or outer edge, esp. the outer vertical edge of a page or a book.
– COMB.: **fore-edge painting** a picture or decoration on the fore-edge of a book.

fore-end /ˈfɔːrɛnd/ *noun*. LME.
[ORIGIN from FORE- + END *noun*.]
1 Now chiefly NAUTICAL. The front or front part of a place. LME. ▸**b** In *pl.* The forward space in a submarine used for storing torpedoes and as living quarters for the crew. Also, the submarine ratings quartered there. M20.
2 The beginning or early part of a period of time. Now *Scot.* & *dial.* E17.
3 The front part of the stock of a gun, supporting the barrel. L19.
4 The hock of a foreleg of pork or bacon. E20.
– COMB.: **fore-end loader** AGRICULTURE a loader attached to the front of a tractor or other vehicle.

forefather /ˈfɔːfɑːðə/ *noun*. ME.
[ORIGIN from FORE- + FATHER *noun*: cf. Old Norse *forfaðir*.]
A person from whom one's father or mother is descended, an ancestor; a member of the past generations of a family or race. Usu. in *pl.*

J. W. KRUTCH Modern man has far more knowledge . . than his forefathers had.

Forefathers' Day *US.* 21 December, the anniversary of the landing of the first settlers at Plymouth, Massachusetts.
■ **forefatherly** *adjective* of or pertaining to one's forefathers, ancestral M19.

forefeel /fɔːˈfiːl/ *verb trans.* Pa. t. & pple **-felt** /-ˈfɛlt/. L16.
[ORIGIN from FORE- + FEEL *verb*.]
Feel beforehand, have a presentiment of.
■ **forefeeling** *noun* (*a*) the action of the verb; (*b*) a presentiment: M16.

forefend *verb* var. of FORFEND.

forefinger /ˈfɔːfɪŋɡə/ *noun*. LME.
[ORIGIN from FORE- + FINGER *noun*.]
The finger next to the thumb, the index finger.

forefoot /ˈfɔːfʊt/ *noun*. Pl. **-feet** /-fiːt/. LME.
[ORIGIN from FORE- + FOOT *noun*, perh. after Dutch *voorvoet* (cf. German *Vorderfuss*).]
1 Either of the front feet of a quadruped. LME. ▸†**b** The hand. *joc. rare* (Shakes.). Only in L16.
H. McMURTRIE The long claws of their fore-feet enable them to dig with great effect.
2 *NAUTICAL*. The foremost piece of the keel of a ship. L18.
B. GREENHILL The . . 'long' ship . . had a projecting forefoot, which came to be developed . . as a ram.

forefront /ˈfɔːfrʌnt/ *noun*. LME.
[ORIGIN from FORE- + FRONT *noun*.]
1 The principal face or foremost part, esp. of a building. Now *rare*. LME. ▸**b** The front rank or vanguard of an army. L15.
2 *fig.* The very front; the leading or most important part or place. L16.
J. R. GREEN The great statutes which stand in the forefront of our laws. G. M. TREVELYAN They were in the forefront of progress and invention.
3 The beginning of a book, document, or literary work. Long *arch.* L16.

foregather *verb* var. of FORGATHER.

forego /fɔːˈɡəʊ/ *verb*[1] *trans.* & *intrans.* Pa. t. **-went** /-ˈwɛnt/; pa. pple **-gone** /-ˈɡɒn/. OE.
[ORIGIN from FORE- + GO *verb*.]
Go before, precede in place or time.
A. D. T. WHITNEY Sublimely unaffected by all that had foregone. J. PAYNE His head forewent his feet and he fell to the ground.

forego *verb*[2] var. of FORGO.

foregoer /fɔːˈɡəʊə, ˈfɔː-/ *noun*[1]. LME.
[ORIGIN from FORE- + GOER.]
†**1** A messenger sent before, a forerunner; *spec.* a purveyor. LME–M18.
2 A person who or thing which goes in front; a leader. Also, an example, a pattern. LME.
R. BAXTER The promised Glory, and the future blessings that are its necessary Foregoers.
3 A predecessor. M16.
4 *NAUTICAL*. = FOREGANGER (b). L17.

foregoer *noun*[2] var. of FORGOER.

foregoing /ˈfɔːɡəʊɪŋ/ *adjective*. LME.
[ORIGIN from FOREGO *verb*[1] + -ING[2].]
That goes or has gone before; preceding; previously mentioned.
T. HARDY Instead of new articles . . those that had been rejected in the foregoing summer were brought out again. *absol.*: HOR. WALPOLE Besides the foregoing, Lord Breadalbane has . . eleven portraits.

foregone /ˈfɔːɡɒn, fɔːˈɡɒn/ *ppl adjective*[1]. L16.
[ORIGIN pa. pple of FOREGO *verb*[1].]
That has gone before or gone by; (of time) past.
foregone conclusion (*a*) a decision or opinion come to in advance of the evidence or necessary facts; (*b*) a result that can be or could have been foreseen.

foregone *ppl adjective*[2] var. of FORGONE.

foreground /ˈfɔːɡraʊnd/ *noun* & *verb*. L17.
[ORIGIN from FORE- + GROUND *noun* after Dutch *voorgrond*: cf. German *Vordergrund*.]
▸**A** *noun*. **1** The part of a view which is in front and nearest the observer, esp. as represented in a picture. L17.
K. CLARK The composition is divided into a foreground with figures, and a very distinct landscape.
2 *fig.* The most conspicuous or prominent position. E19.
J. A. SYMONDS The Aeolians occupied the very foreground of Greek literature.
– COMB.: **foreground music** music played in the foreground, which dominates over any other sound.
▸**B** *verb trans.* Place in the foreground, make prominent; *spec.* (LINGUISTICS) draw attention to (a particular feature or message in a piece of writing) by means of esp. striking or unexpected linguistic devices. L19.
M. EATON This description tends to foreground narrative and script at the expense of other factors. *Fremdsprachen* In any informative text, the purpose should be foregrounded.
■ **foregrounding** *verbal noun* the action of the verb; *spec.* (LINGUISTICS) the action of emphasizing something by means of linguistic devices: M20.

forehand /ˈfɔːhand/ *noun* & *adjective*. M16.
[ORIGIN from FORE- + HAND *noun*.]
▸**A** *noun*. †**1** An arrow for shooting straight in front of one. Only in M16.
2 The position in front or above; the upper hand, the advantage. *obsolete* exc. *Scot.* M16. ▸†**b** That which holds the front position; the vanguard. *rare* (Shakes.). Only in E17.
3 The part of a horse which would be in front of a rider. E17.
4 *TENNIS & BADMINTON* etc. A forehand stroke. E20.
Tennis World Her killer forehand is now supported by a . . top spin backhand.
on the forehand (on the side on which one must strike a ball etc.) forehanded.
▸**B** *adjective*. †**1** Designating an arrow for shooting straight before one. Only in L16.
2 Done or given at some earlier time; (of a payment) made in advance. *obsolete* exc. *Scot.* L16.
3 Foremost, leading. *obsolete* exc. *Scot.* M17.
4 *TENNIS & BADMINTON* etc. Designating a stroke played with the arm extended away from the body and the palm of the hand facing one's opponent. Also, designating an area of a court in which such a stroke is usually played. L19.
J. BARRINGTON The most efficient forehand volley is built up on a relatively short back-swing.
■ **forehander** *noun* (TENNIS & BADMINTON etc.) a forehand stroke E20.

forehanded /ˈfɔːhandɪd/ *adjective* & *adverb*. L16.
[ORIGIN from FOREHAND + -ED[2].]
▸**A** *adjective*. †**1** (Of a horse) *well* etc. built in the forehand; (of a person) *well* etc. built. L16–L18.
2 Looking to the future; prudent, thrifty. Now *Scot.* & *US.* M17. ▸**b** That has made provision for the future; comfortable, well-to-do. Now *US.* M17.
J. R. LOWELL They were . . a thrifty forehanded race.
3 *TENNIS & BADMINTON* etc. Of a stroke: forehand. Now *rare*. L19.
▸**B** *adverb*. *TENNIS & BADMINTON* etc. With a forehand stroke. L19.
■ **foreˈhandedness** *noun* (*US*) the action of looking to the future; prudence, foresight: M19.

forehead /ˈfɒrɪd, ˈfɔːhɛd/ *noun*.
[ORIGIN Old English *forhēafod*, from FOR-[3], FORE- + *hēafod* HEAD *noun*. Cf. Old Frisian *forhāfd*, Middle Low German *vorhōved*, Dutch *voorhoofd*, German *Vor(der)haupt*.]
1 That part of the face which extends from the level of the eyebrows up to the natural line of the hair. Also, the corresponding part of the face of an animal. OE.
E. HEMINGWAY Their helmets came low down over their foreheads and the side of their faces.
†**2** A feeling or attitude able to be expressed in a person's countenance; *spec.* innocence, modesty, assurance. LME–L18.
T. SHERIDAN No body . . could have the forehead or folly to turn it into ridicule.
3 The front part, the forefront. L15.
■ **foreheaded** *adjective* (now *rare*) having a forehead L16. **foreheadless** *adjective* (now *rare* or *obsolete*) having no forehead, lacking in shame or assurance E17.

foreign /ˈfɒr(ə)n, -ɪn/ *adjective*, *noun*, & *adverb*. ME.
[ORIGIN Old French *forein*, *forain* from Proto-Romance, from Latin *foras*, from *fores* door. For the spelling with *-eign* cf. *sovereign*.]
▸**A** *adjective*. **I** Of another place.
†**1** Out of doors, outside; ***chamber foreign***, a privy, a lavatory. Only in ME. ▸**b** Concerned with matters outside one's home, manor, etc. E17–E18.
2 Belonging to, coming from, or characteristic of, another country or nation. ME. ▸**b** Belonging to or coming from another district, county, society, etc. LME.
H. BELLOC He fell, crying and howling in a foreign tongue to gods of his own in the northland.
3 Situated outside the country; not in one's own land. LME. ▸**b** Situated outside an estate, district, county, etc. LME.
C. ISHERWOOD I am in a foreign city, alone, far from home.
4 Carried on or taking place abroad, into or with another country. M16.
5 Dealing with matters concerned with other countries. L16.
▸**II** Alien, not one's own.
6 Alien in character; extraneous, dissimilar, inappropriate, irrelevant. (Foll. by *to*.) LME. ▸**b** Unfamiliar, strange. L19.
H. MOORE Culture remains a foreign element, something outside the desires and necessities of everyday life.
7 Belonging to or coming from other persons or things; not one's own. LME. ▸†**b** Of a possession: other than personal. L16–E18. ▸†**c** Not of one's household or family. *rare* (Shakes.). Only in E17.
R. BLACKMORE Machines . . Move by a foreign impulse, not their own.
8 Esp. of matter in tissue etc.: introduced from outside. E17.
– PHRASES: ***chamber foreign***: see sense 1 above. ***of foreign growth***: see GROWTH *noun*.
▸**B** *noun*. †**1** [Short for *chamber foreign*.] A privy. ME–L16.
†**2** A person or thing from another place; a foreigner, an outsider. ME–M17.
3 *ellipt.* Foreign language, foreign parts, etc. E17.
P. O'DONNELL He was a foreigner and he babbled in foreign.
4 That part of a town which lies outside the borough or parish proper; in *pl.*, the outer court of, or the land immediately outside the precincts of, a monastery. *obsolete* exc. in local place names. M17.
▸**C** *adverb*. *NAUTICAL*. To or for foreign parts, abroad. Chiefly in ***go foreign***, ***sail foreign***, etc. E19.
– SPECIAL COLLOCATIONS & COMB.: **foreign affairs** matters abroad; *spec.* those concerning the interests of the home country. **foreign aid** money or goods given by one state to another. **Foreign and Commonwealth Office** (the building used for) the British government department dealing with foreign affairs. **foreign body** a piece of extraneous matter, esp. in tissue. **foreign devil** *derog.* [see KWAI-LO] in China, a foreigner, *esp.* a European. **foreign exchange** (dealings in) the currency of other countries. **foreign-going** *adjective* (of a ship) going to foreign countries. ***foreign legion***: see LEGION *noun*. **Foreign Minister** a government minister responsible for foreign affairs (an equivalent of the British Foreign Secretary in many other countries). **Foreign Office** (the building used for) a government department dealing with foreign affairs; *spec.* (*hist.* & *colloq.*) = ***Foreign and Commonwealth Office*** above. **Foreign Secretary** the head of the British Foreign and Commonwealth Office. ***foreign trade***: see TRADE *noun*.
■ **foreignism** *noun* (*a*) the imitation of what is foreign; (*b*) a phrase, idiom, etc., of foreign origin: M19. **foreignize** *verb trans.* & *intrans.* make or become (as if) foreign M17. **foreignly** *adverb* L19. **foreignness** /-n-n-/ *noun* E17.

foreigner /ˈfɒrənə, -ɪnə/ *noun*. LME.
[ORIGIN from FOREIGN *adjective* + -ER[1].]
1 A person born in or belonging to another country, esp. one whose language and culture differ from one's own. LME.
A. LURIE Some foreigner who knows only a few words of your language.
2 A person not belonging to a particular place or society; a stranger, an outsider. Now chiefly *dial.* LME.
F. WELDON She was reckoned a foreigner: she came from Crossley, five miles away. C. RAINE Children . . are foreigners in our world until they become naturalised.
3 Something originating abroad, *spec.* a foreign vessel; an imported animal or article. L17. ▸**b** In *pl.* Foreign stocks and shares. L19.
ADDISON The lemons, the brandy, the sugar, and the nutmeg, were all foreigners.
4 Something done or made at work by an employee for his or her own benefit; a piece of paid work not declared to the relevant authorities. *slang*. M20.
A. BLEASDALE We're both goin' t' get prosecuted f' doin' a foreigner while we're on the dole.

forejudge /fɔːˈdʒʌdʒ/ *verb*[1]. M16.
[ORIGIN from FORE- + JUDGE *verb*, after French *préjuger*, Latin *praejudicare* PREJUDGE.]
1 *verb trans.* Judge or determine beforehand or without a fair trial; prejudge. M16.
†**2** *verb trans.* & *intrans.* with *of*. Form an opinion of beforehand. E17–L18.
■ **forejudgement** *noun* a judgement made in advance M16.

forejudge *verb*[2] var. of FORJUDGE.

fore-kamer *noun* see VOORKAMER.

foreknow /fɔːˈnəʊ/ *verb*. Pa. t. **-knew** /-ˈnjuː/; pa. pple **-known** /-ˈnəʊn/. LME.
[ORIGIN from FORE- + KNOW *verb*.]
1 *verb trans.* Know (of) in advance, foresee. LME.
2 *verb intrans.* Have previous knowledge *of*. E18.

foreknowledge /fɔːˈnɒlɪdʒ/ *noun*. M16.
[ORIGIN from FORE- + KNOWLEDGE *noun*.]
Prior knowledge of an event etc., prescience.
G. GROTE Money lent with the foreknowledge that the borrower will be unable to pay it. SAKI Elaine felt a sudden foreknowledge of something disagreeable about to happen.

foreknown *verb pa. pple* of FOREKNOW.

forel /ˈfɒr(ə)l/ *noun* & *verb*. Also **-rr-**. ME.
[ORIGIN Old French (mod. *fourreau*) sheath, from *fuerre*, from Frankish = Old High German *fōtar*, *fuotar* case, cover (German *Futter* lining), Gothic *fōdr* sheath, from Germanic, rel. to Sanskrit *pātra* receptacle, from *pāti* protects.]
▸**A** *noun*. †**1** A scabbard. Only in ME.
2 A case or covering for a book or manuscript. Now *dial.* LME.
3 A kind of parchment resembling vellum, used to cover books, esp. account books. M16.
4 A selvedge, a border of cloth. Now *dial.* L17.

F

▸ **B** *verb trans.* Infl. **-ll-**. Cover (a book) with forel. *obsolete* exc. *dial.* M17.

forelaid *verb pa. t. & pple* of FORELAY.

foreland /ˈfɔːlənd/ *noun.* ME.
[ORIGIN from FORE- + LAND *noun*¹. Cf. Old Norse *forlendi* land between hills and sea, Dutch *voorland*.]
†**1** Land other than that customarily granted to tenants of a manor; such land granted temporarily on special terms. Only in ME.
2 A cape, a headland, a promontory. LME. ▸**b** Land deposited by the action of the sea in front of a coast. L19.

R. RECORDE The great forlonde of Affrike, commonly called the cape of Good hope.

†**3** A piece of land adjoining a street; a house or tenement facing a street. *Scot.* L15–L18.
4 A strip of land in front of something; a strip of land left between the foot of a wall or embankment and an adjacent moat or ditch. L16.
5 A stretch of borderland. M19.

F

J. KITTO I looked towards the west, and beheld the forelands of Carmel.

6 GEOLOGY. A stable unyielding block of the earth's crust, against which compression produces a folded mountain range. E20.

forelay /fɔːˈleɪ/ *verb trans.* Pa. t. & pple **-laid** /-ˈleɪd/. M16.
[ORIGIN from FORE- + LAY *verb*¹.]
1 Lie in wait for, waylay. *obsolete* exc. *dial.* M16. ▸†**b** Lie in ambush around or near (a place). M16–L17.
2 Plot or take action against; frustrate, hinder. Long *rare.* L16.
3 Lay down or plan beforehand; prearrange. *obsolete* exc. *dial.* E17.

foreleg /ˈfɔːlɛg/ *noun.* LME.
[ORIGIN from FORE- + LEG *noun*.]
Either of the front legs of a quadruped.

forelimb /ˈfɔːlɪm/ *noun.* L18.
[ORIGIN from FORE- + LIMB *noun*¹.]
Either of the anterior limbs of a vertebrate animal; a foreleg, wing, flipper, etc.

forelock /ˈfɔːlɒk/ *noun*¹. OE.
[ORIGIN from FORE- + LOCK *noun*¹.]
1 A lock of hair growing just above the forehead. OE.
take time by the forelock, **take occasion by the forelock**, **take opportunity by the forelock**, etc., [cf. *Father Time* s.v. TIME *noun*] not let a chance slip away.
2 The part of the mane of a horse etc. growing from the poll and hanging over the forehead. E18.
– COMB.: **forelock-touching**, **forelock-tugging** the action or an act of touching or plucking at one's hair as at the peak of a cap; *fig.* obsequiousness, servility.

forelock /ˈfɔːlɒk/ *noun*² *& verb.* ME.
[ORIGIN from FORE- + LOCK *noun*².]
Chiefly NAUTICAL. ▸**A** *noun.* A wedge or pin passed through a hole in a bolt etc. to keep it in place; a cotter. ME.
– COMB.: **forelock bolt** a bolt with a hole for a forelock; **forelock hook** a hook by which a bunch of three yarns is twisted into a strand.
▸ **B** *verb trans.* Fasten with a forelock or cotter. LME.

forelook /ˈfɔːlʊk/ *noun.* Now *US.* ME.
[ORIGIN from FORE- + LOOK *noun*.]
†**1** Foresight, foreknowledge; providence. Only in ME.
2 A look ahead. L16.

forelook /fɔːˈlʊk/ *verb.* ME.
[ORIGIN from FORE- + LOOK *verb*.]
†**1** *verb trans.* Have foreknowledge of, foresee; provide for. Only in ME.
2 *verb intrans.* Look ahead or to the future. L15.
†**3** *verb trans.* Bewitch by a look. L16–E17.

foreman /ˈfɔːmən/ *noun.* Pl. **-men**. ME.
[ORIGIN from FORE- + MAN *noun*, perh. after Old Norse *formaðr* leader, or immed. from Dutch *voorman* (cf. German *Vormann*).]
1 a A chief servant; an overseer, a steward, a bailiff. ME. ▸**b** A principal workman supervising other workers. L16.

a J. Q. ADAMS I sometimes think I must come to this—to be the foreman upon my own farm. **b** J. SMEATON One of the masons . . offered himself as foreman over the stone-cutters.

†**2** A man who goes in front, a leader; a soldier in the front rank. LME–L17.
3 The appointed leader and spokesperson of a jury. E17.
4 The most prominent and influential person in an organization or society. *obsolete* exc. *local* as a title of a municipal officer. E17.
■ **foremanship** *noun* the office or position of a foreman; supervision (as) by a foreman: M19.

foremast /ˈfɔːmɑːst/ *noun.* L15.
[ORIGIN from FORE- + MAST *noun*¹.]
1 The mast of a ship (with two or more masts) nearest the bow. L15.
2 The station of being before the mast. Only *attrib.*, as ***foremast man***, ***foremast seaman***, a sailor below the rank of petty officer. E17.

foremen *noun* pl. of FOREMAN.

foremilk /ˈfɔːmɪlk/ *noun.* E20.
[ORIGIN from FORE- + MILK *noun*.]
1 Colostrum. E20.
2 The first milk drawn from a cow etc. at each milking; the first part of the milk from a breast at a feed. E20.

foremost /ˈfɔːməʊst/ *adjective & adverb.*
[ORIGIN Old English *formest*, *fyrmest*, from *forma* first with additional superl. suffix (see -EST¹): later assim. to FORE- + -MOST.]
▸ **A** *adjective* **1** †**a** First in a series. OE–M16. ▸**b** First in time. Long *obsolete* exc. *Scot.* ME.
2 Most notable or prominent; best, chief. OE.

W. S. CHURCHILL Marlborough stood forth, even above his comrade, the great Eugene, as the foremost soldier of the age. A. FRASER The situation was naturally inimical to many of the Scots, foremost among them the Highlanders.

3 Most advanced in position; (in) front. ME.

GOLDSMITH The giant . . was foremost now; but the Dwarf was not far behind. DICKENS The boat drove stern foremost before it [the tide].

▸ **B** *adverb.* Before anything else; in the first place. Now chiefly in ***FIRST and foremost***. OE.
– PHRASES: **feet foremost**, **head foremost**, etc., with the feet etc. in front, feet etc. first.
■ **foremostly** *adverb* (*rare*) E17.

foremother /ˈfɔːmʌðə/ *noun.* L15.
[ORIGIN from FORE- + MOTHER *noun*¹, after *forefather*.]
A female ancestor or predecessor. Usu. in *pl.*

M. STOTT A modern mother is spared much of the toil of her foremothers.

forename /ˈfɔːneɪm/ *noun.* M16.
[ORIGIN from FORE- + NAME *noun*, after French *prénom*, Latin *praenomen*, Dutch *voornam*, etc.]
A personal name which precedes the surname, a first name; in ROMAN HISTORY = PRAENOMEN.

forenight /ˈfɔːnʌɪt/ *noun.* Long *obsolete* exc. *Scot.* ME.
[ORIGIN from FORE- + NIGHT *noun*.]
The early part of the night; the evening.

forenoon /ˈfɔːnuːn/ *noun.* Chiefly *arch.* exc. NAUTICAL. LME.
[ORIGIN from FORE- + NOON *noun*.]
The day until noon; the morning.

L. G. GIBBON As though it were nine o'clock in the forenoon and the sun shining bravely.

forensic /fəˈrɛnsɪk/ *adjective & noun.* M17.
[ORIGIN from Latin *forensis*, formed as FORUM: see -IC.]
▸ **A** *adjective.* **1** Of, pertaining to, or used in a court of law, now *spec.* in relation to the detection of crime. M17.

DICKENS In an imposing and forensic manner. F. FORSYTH Scotland Yard, among the copious facilities of its forensic science department, has a section devoted to voice analysis.

forensic accountancy the application of accountancy to investigating fraud. **forensic medicine** the application of medical knowledge to legal problems.
2 Of, pertaining to, or employing forensic medicine. M20.

P. D. JAMES We can be sure of nothing until we have . . the forensic reports.

▸ **B** *noun.* **1** A speech or written thesis setting out one side of a question. *US.* E19.
2 Forensic science (esp. as the designation of a department, laboratory, etc.). *colloq.* M20.

Independent I wonder what forensic would find under your fingernails.

■ **forensically** *adverb* M19.

foreordain /fɔːrɔːˈdeɪn/ *verb trans.* LME.
[ORIGIN from FORE- + ORDAIN.]
Ordain or appoint beforehand, predestinate.

foreordination /ˌfɔːrɔːdɪˈneɪʃ(ə)n/ *noun.* E17.
[ORIGIN from FORE- + ORDINATION.]
Ordination or appointment beforehand, predestination; an instance of this.
■ Also **foreˈordinance** *noun* (*rare*) M16.

forepart /ˈfɔːpɑːt/ *noun.* LME.
[ORIGIN from FORE- + PART *noun*.]
1 The foremost part, the front; *spec.* the bow of a ship. LME.

W. DAMPIER The head or fore-part is not altogether so high as the Stern.

2 *hist.* A stomacher. E17.
3 The earlier part. E17.

A. HAMILTON In the Forepart of the seventeenth Century.

forepassed /fɔːˈpɑːst/ *ppl adjective.* Now *rare.* Also **-past**. M16.
[ORIGIN from FORE- + *passed*, *past* pa. ppl adjective of PASS *verb*.]
Already past; bygone, erstwhile.

forepaw /ˈfɔːpɔː/ *noun.* E19.
[ORIGIN from FORE- + PAW *noun*¹.]
Either of the front paws of an animal.

forepeak /ˈfɔːpiːk/ *noun.* L17.
[ORIGIN from FORE- + PEAK *noun*¹. Cf. Dutch *voorpiek*.]
NAUTICAL. The front end of a hold or cabin in the angle of the bows of a ship.

foreperson /ˈfɔːpəːs(ə)n/ *noun.* L20.
[ORIGIN from FORE- + PERSON *noun*.]
A foreman, a forewoman. (Used to avoid sexual distinction.)

forepiece /ˈfɔːpiːs/ *noun.* M16.
[ORIGIN from FORE- + PIECE *noun*.]
The foremost or front piece of something; THEATRICAL a curtain-raiser.

foreplay /ˈfɔːpleɪ/ *noun.* E20.
[ORIGIN from FORE- + PLAY *noun*.]
Sexual stimulation preceding intercourse.

foreprise, **foreprize** *verbs* vars. of FORPRISE.

forequarter /ˈfɔːkwɔːtə/ *noun.* LME.
[ORIGIN from FORE- + QUARTER *noun*.]
A front quarter of something, *spec.* of a carcass (of beef, lamb, etc.). In *pl.*, the front part of the body of a quadruped.

foreran *verb pa. t.* of FORERUN.

forereach /fɔːˈriːtʃ/ *verb.* M17.
[ORIGIN from FORE- + REACH *verb*¹.]
Chiefly NAUTICAL. **1** *verb intrans.* Make way into wind whilst tacking; shoot ahead, gain ground *on*. M17.
2 *verb trans.* Gain ground on, overtake: *fig.* get the better of. E19.

foreright /fɔːˈrʌɪt/ *adverb, adjective, preposition, & noun. obsolete* exc. *dial.* Also (*rare*) **-rights** /-ˈrʌɪts/. LME.
[ORIGIN from FORE- + RIGHT *adjective, adverb*.]
▸ **A** *adverb.* Directly forward, in or towards the front, straight ahead. LME.
▸ **B** *adjective.* **1** Of a path, current, etc.: direct; straight in front. E17. ▸†**b** Of a wind: in one's favour. E–M17.
2 Of a branch: growing straight out. M18.
3 a Rash, reckless, headstrong, stubborn. M18. ▸**b** Honest, straightforward; blunt, plain-spoken. E19.
▸ **C** *preposition.* †**1** Straight along. Only in M17.
2 Opposite, over against, right in front of. M19.
▸ **D** *noun.* **1** Something straightforward; direct or blunt speech. M18. ▸**b** A branch growing straight out. L19.
2 Coarse wholemeal bread. L18.

foreroom /ˈfɔːruːm/ *noun.* L15.
[ORIGIN from FORE- + ROOM *noun*¹.]
1 A compartment in the bow of an open boat. *obsolete* exc. *Scot.* L15.
2 A front room, a parlour. Now *US.* E18.

forerun /fɔːˈrʌn/ *verb.* Infl. **-nn-**. Pa. t. **-ran** /-ˈran/; pa. pple **-run**. OE.
[ORIGIN from FORE- + RUN *verb*.]
†**1** *verb intrans.* Run on in front. OE–M17.
2 *verb trans.* †**a** Run in front of, precede; act as herald of. ME–M18. ▸**b** Be the precursor of (a future event etc.), indicate the coming of, foreshadow. L16.
3 *verb trans.* Outrun, outstrip, (now only *fig.*). E16.

R. W. CHURCH Even genius . . cannot forerun the limitations of its day.

4 *verb trans.* Anticipate, forestall. L16.

Times Lit. Suppl. Akenside who foreran e. e. cummings by using lower case 'i' for the first person pronoun.

forerunner /ˈfɔːrʌnə/ *noun.* ME.
[ORIGIN from FORERUN + -ER¹.]
1 A person who runs ahead, *esp.* one who prepares or shows the way; a precursor, a herald, a guide. Now chiefly *fig.* ME. ▸**b** *spec.* A skier who runs over the course as a preliminary to a skiing race in order to check for possible hazards and clear spectators from the course. M20.

M. MEYER The forerunners of Impressionism—Delacroix, Courbet, Corot and, especially, Turner and Constable.

2 In *pl.* The members of the advance guard of an army. M16.
3 A predecessor, an ancestor. L16.

L. STERNE My . . observations will be altogether of a different cast from any of my forerunners.

4 A thing which precedes, prepares for, or foreshadows another. L16.

M. DE LA ROCHE Bright red-gold wavelets of cloud . . forerunners of the strong tide of day. V. BROME The highly successful London visit was the forerunner of many such visits.

5 NAUTICAL. **a** = FOREGANGER (b). L17. ▸**b** A piece of cloth attached to a log line to mark the end of the stray line. E19.

foresaid /ˈfɔːsɛd/ *adjective & noun. obsolete* exc. *Scot.* OE.
[ORIGIN from FORE- + SAID *ppl adjective*.]
▸ **A** *adjective.* Previously mentioned, aforesaid. OE.
▸ **B** *noun.* Chiefly LAW. A person or matter previously mentioned. Usu. in *pl.* M16.

foresaid *verb pa. t. & pple* of FORESAY.

foresail /ˈfɔːseɪl/ *noun.* L15.
[ORIGIN from FORE- + SAIL *noun*[1].]
In a square-rigged vessel, the lowest sail on the foremast. In a fore-and-aft rigged vessel, a sail on the after side of the foremast. In a single-masted vessel, any triangular sail before the mast.

foresaw *verb pa. t.* of FORESEE.

foresay /fɔːˈseɪ/ *verb trans.* Now *rare* or *obsolete.* Pa. t. & pple **-said** /-ˈsɛd/. OE.
[ORIGIN from FORE- + SAY *verb*[1].]
Say beforehand, predict.

foresee /fɔːˈsiː/ *verb.* Pa. t. **-saw** /-ˈsɔː/; pa. pple **-seen** /-ˈsiːn/.
[ORIGIN Old English *foresēon*, from FORE- + *sēon* SEE *verb.* In 16 perh. partly a new formation.]
1 *verb trans.* Be aware of beforehand; predict (a thing, *that*). OE.
V. BRITTAIN Few prophets foresaw . . an even more profound clash nearly ten years later.
†**2** *verb trans.* Prepare; provide for or against in advance. OE–M17.
†**3** *verb intrans.* Exercise foresight; make provision. LME–E17.
4 *verb intrans.* Foresee events. *rare.* M17.
■ **foreseer** *noun* M16.

foreseeable /fɔːˈsiːəb(ə)l/ *adjective.* E19.
[ORIGIN from FORESEE + -ABLE. Earlier (L17) in UNFORESEEABLE.]
Able to be foreseen.
foreseeable future the period during which the general course of events can reasonably be predicted.
■ **foreseeaˈbility** *noun* E20. **foreseeably** *adverb* M20.

foreset /ˈfɔːsɛt/ *adjective.* E20.
[ORIGIN from FORE- + SET *ppl adjective.*]
GEOLOGY. Of layers of sediment: deposited on the inclined, advancing, forward slope of a delta.

foreset /fɔːˈsɛt/ *verb trans.* Now *rare.* Infl. **-tt-**. Pa. t. & pple **-set**. OE.
[ORIGIN from FORE- + SET *verb*[1].]
†**1** Place in front, put first. OE–LME.
2 Arrange or settle beforehand; predetermine. M16.

foreshadow /ˈfɔːʃadəʊ/ *noun.* M19.
[ORIGIN from FORE- + SHADOW *noun*, after FORESHADOW *verb.*]
An indication or imperfect representation of something to come.
J. M. LUDLOW A truce is often the foreshadow of a peace.

foreshadow /fɔːˈʃadəʊ/ *verb trans.* L16.
[ORIGIN from FORE- + SHADOW *verb.*]
Serve as a type or presage of, prefigure; suggest or indicate (something to come).
J. L. MOTLEY The surrender of Ghent foreshadowed the fate of Flanders.

foresheet /ˈfɔːʃiːt/ *noun.* M17.
[ORIGIN from FORE- + SHEET *noun*[2].]
NAUTICAL. **1** A rope by which the lee corner of a foresail is kept in place. M17.
2 In *pl.* The inner part of the bows of a boat having gratings on which the bowman stands. E18.

foreshew *verb* see FORESHOW.

foreship /ˈfɔːʃɪp/ *noun.* OE.
[ORIGIN from FORE- + SHIP *noun.*]
The foremost part of a ship; the prow.

foreshore /ˈfɔːʃɔː/ *noun.* M18.
[ORIGIN from FORE- + SHORE *noun*[1].]
The part of a shore between high- and low-water marks, or between the water and land cultivated or built on.
P. NORMAN Miles of sand, the foreshore . . like some dark, wet ocean, with the real sea . . in the distance.

foreshorten /fɔːˈʃɔːt(ə)n/ *verb trans.* L16.
[ORIGIN from FORE- + SHORTEN, prob. after Dutch *verkorten.*]
Show or portray (an object) with the apparent shortening due to visual perspective; *fig.* shorten, curtail, abridge.
J. REYNOLDS The best of the painters could not even foreshorten the foot. V. WOOLF Little men and women, foreshortened from this height, hurried along by the railings.

foreshot /ˈfɔːʃɒt/ *noun.* Chiefly *Scot.* L17.
[ORIGIN from FORE- + SHOT *noun*[1].]
1 A projecting part of a building. L17.
2 DISTILLING. The first spirits obtained. L18.

foreshow /fɔːˈʃəʊ/ *verb trans. arch.* Pa. pple **-shown** /-ˈʃəʊn/, **-showed**. Also **-shew**, pa. pple **-shewn**, **-shewed**. OE.
[ORIGIN from FORE- + SHOW *verb.*]
†**1** Look out for; provide. OE–ME.
2 Foretell, give promise or warning of, prefigure. LME.
POPE Astrologers, that future fates foreshow. J. IMISON The falling of the mercury forshews thunder.
†**3** Show, display, betoken. L16–E17.
SHAKES. *Per.* Your looks foreshow You have a gentle heart.
■ †**foreshower** *noun* a person who foretells; a thing which prefigures or portends: M16–M18. **forshowing** *noun* (*a*) the action of the verb; (*b*) a prognostication, a sign or token of a future event: OE.

foresight /ˈfɔːsʌɪt/ *noun.* ME.
[ORIGIN from FORE- + SIGHT *noun*, prob. after Old Norse *forsjá, -sjó.*]
1 The action or faculty of foreseeing; prescience. ME.
JOSEPH HALL Want of foresight makes thee more merry. J. GALSWORTHY She had no foresight, and never went to meet trouble.
2 Care or provision for the future; providence, prudence. ME.
H. T. BUCKLE In hot climates, nature being bountiful, man is not obliged to use foresight.
3 A view forward; a prospect. LME. ▸**b** The action or an act of looking forward (*lit.* & *fig.*). L16.
J. B. MOZLEY The perpetual foresight of death.
4 The front sight of a gun. E19.
5 SURVEYING. A sight taken looking forwards. M19.
■ **foresighted** *adjective* having or using foresight; prescient, prudent: M17. **foresightedly** *adverb* M20. **foresightedness** *noun* E20. **foresightful** *adjective* full of foresight L16.

foreskin /ˈfɔːskɪn/ *noun.* M16.
[ORIGIN from FORE- + SKIN *noun*, after German *Vorhaut.*]
The loose skin covering the end of the penis, the prepuce.

foreslack *verb* var. of FORSLACK.

foreslow *verb* var. of FORSLOW.

forespeak /fɔːˈspiːk/ *verb*[1]. Pa. t. **-spoke** /-ˈspəʊk/, (*arch.*) **-spake** /-ˈspeɪk/; pa. pple **-spoken** /-ˈspəʊkən/, (*arch.*) **-spake**. ME.
[ORIGIN from FORE- + SPEAK *verb.*]
1 †**a** *verb intrans.* Speak beforehand; make predictions, prophesy. ME–M17. ▸**b** *verb trans.* Say or speak of beforehand; foretell. Now *rare.* LME.
2 *verb trans.* Order or reserve beforehand; bespeak. *obsolete* exc. *Scot.* M17.
■ **forespeaker** *noun* (*obsolete* exc. *Scot.*) a person who speaks for another; an advocate, a spokesman: ME.

forespeak *verb*[2] var. of FORSPEAK.

forespend *verb* var. of FORSPEND.

forespoke *verb*[1], *verb*[2] *pa. t.*, **forespoken** *verb*[1], *verb*[2] *pa. pple*: see FORESPEAK *verb*[1], FORSPEAK.

forest /ˈfɒrɪst/ *noun & verb.* ME.
[ORIGIN Old French (mod. *forêt*) from late Latin *forestis* (*silva*) 'outside wood', a royal forest reserved for hunting, from *foris* out of doors, outside; in Anglo-Latin *foresta, forestum.*]
▸ **A** *noun.* **1** A large tract of land covered with trees and undergrowth sometimes mixed with pasture (in proper names also a district formerly forest but now cultivated); the trees growing in such a tract. ME. ▸**b** *transf.* & *fig.* A large number, a dense mass. E17.
U. LE GUIN The trees went on and on, . . endless, a forest all over the world. **b** ARNOLD BENNETT A forest of pillars stood planted on the ground floor.
New Forest, *Sherwood Forest*, etc. *rainforest*: see RAIN *noun*[1].
2 a *hist.* A (woodland) area, esp. owned by the monarch, kept for hunting and having its own laws and officers. ME. ▸**b** A tract of wild land reserved for the stalking of deer. Also *deer-forest*. E18.
†**3** A wild uncultivated place; a wilderness. ME–M17.
D. PELL Away she betakes her self into the great and wide Forrest of the Sea.
– COMB.: **forest-bed** GEOLOGY a stratum originating from a primeval forest; **forest devil** *Austral.* a device for removing tree stumps; **forest falcon** an American hawk of the genus *Micrastur*; **forest fire** an uncontrolled fire in woodland; **forest floor** the ground in a forest; *spec.* the layer of more or less decayed organic debris forming the upper soil of a forest; **forest fly** a parasitic fly of the genus *Hippobosca*; esp. *H. equina*, which is troublesome to horses, cattle, etc., and in Britain is found chiefly in the New Forest; **forest-green** *adjective & noun* (of) any of various shades of green associated with forests, *esp.* Lincoln green; **forest kangaroo** = FORESTER 3a(b); **forest laws** *hist.* laws enacted by Norman kings relating to the royal forests; **forest mahogany** *Austral.* (the timber of) any of several eucalypts, esp. *Eucalyptus resinifera*; **forest marble** an argillaceous oolitic limestone found in SW England, having conspicuous dendritic markings; also called *landscape marble*; **forest oak** *Austral.* casuarina; **forest park** an area of forest land open to the public and having recreational facilities; **forest ranger** an official who patrols, manages, and protects a (public) forest; **forest red gum** (the timber of) an Australasian tree, *Eucalyptus tereticornis*; **forest tree** a tree of any large species suitable for or growing in a forest; **forest wallaby** any of several wallabies of the genus *Dorcopsis*, that inhabit the forests of New Guinea.
▸ **B** *verb trans.* **1** Place in a forest. *rare.* E19.
2 Make into a forest; plant with trees. M19.
■ **forested** *adjective* covered with forest; thickly planted with trees: E17. **forestful** *noun* as much or as many as a forest will hold M19. **forestless** *adjective* L19.

forestage /ˈfɔːsteɪdʒ/ *noun.* LME.
[ORIGIN from FORE- + STAGE *noun.*]
†**1** The forecastle of a ship; a ship having a forecastle. LME–L15.
2 THEATRICAL. The front part of a stage, esp. an apron stage. E20.

forestal /ˈfɒrɪst(ə)l/ *adjective.* E19.
[ORIGIN from FOREST *noun* + -AL[1].]
Of or pertaining to a forest.

forestall /ˈfɔːstɔːl/ *noun.*
[ORIGIN Old English *for(e)steall*, from FORE- + *steall* (app.) a position taken up. In sense 2 from FORE- + STALL *noun*[1], in Anglo-Latin *forstallum* a piece of land in front of a building.]
†**1** An ambush. In LAW, the offence of waylaying a traveller on the highway; the jurisdiction of this. OE–E17.
2 *hist.* A piece of armour attached to a horse's bridle to protect the face. E16.
3 Something at or facing the front; *spec.* the space in front of a farmhouse or the approach to it from a road. Long *obsolete* exc. *dial.* M16.

forestall /fɔːˈstɔːl/ *verb trans.* ME.
[ORIGIN from the noun. Earliest in Anglo-Latin *for(e)stallare* forestall the market, waylay, Anglo-Norman *forstallour* forestaller of markets.]
1 *hist.* Intercept or buy up (goods etc.) before they come to market, esp. to force up the price (formerly an indictable offence). ME. ▸**b** Spoil the trade of (a fair or market) by buying up goods beforehand or by dissuading sellers from bringing them. LME.
fig.: SWIFT To confine, forestall, and monopolize the beams of the sun.
†**2** Lie in wait for, intercept, cut off. LME–M18.
†**3** Obstruct (a road, the entrance to a house, etc.) by armed force. LME–E17.
4 Hinder, obstruct, or prevent by anticipation. L16. ▸†**b** Bar or deprive (a person) *from*, *of*, *out of* by prior action. L16–M17.
R. MACAULAY She must get down to her . . book quickly, or she would be forestalled by all these tiresome people.
†**5** Preoccupy, secure beforehand; influence, prejudice. L16–L17.
6 Act before; anticipate (and make ineffective). L16.
A. STORR Carefully and neatly dressed, in order to forestall any possible criticism of their appearance.
7 Think of or deal with before the appropriate time. M17.
MILTON What need a man forestall his date of grief.
■ **forestaller** *noun* ME.

forestalment /fɔːˈstɔːlm(ə)nt/ *noun.* Also ***-ll-**. E17.
[ORIGIN from FORESTALL *verb* + -MENT.]
The action or result of forestalling; an instance of forestalling.

forestation /fɒrɪˈsteɪʃ(ə)n/ *noun.* E20.
[ORIGIN from FOREST *noun* + -ATION.]
The planting or establishing of a forest, afforestation.

forestay /ˈfɔːsteɪ/ *noun.* ME.
[ORIGIN from FORE- + STAY *noun*[1].]
1 NAUTICAL. A stay from the head of the foremast to a ship's deck or bowsprit to support the foremast. ME.
2 PRINTING. A leg supporting the frame or ribs of a hand press. M19.

forester /ˈfɒrɪstə/ *noun.* ME.
[ORIGIN Old French & mod. French *forestier*, formed as FOREST *noun*: see -ER[2]. Cf. Anglo-Latin *forestarius.*]
1 An officer in charge of a forest or of growing timber. ME.
2 A person who lives in a forest. E16.
3 a A bird or animal of the forest; *spec.* (*a*) a New Forest pony; (*b*) *Austral.* the Eastern grey kangaroo, *Macropus giganteus.* M17. ▸**b** Any of various Palaearctic zygaenid moths of the genus *Ino*, having bright metallic green wings. Also (*N. Amer.*), any of various moths of the family Agaristidae. E19.
4 A forest tree. M17.
5 (**F-**.) A member of any of various friendly societies known as the (Ancient, Independent, etc.) Order of Foresters. M19.

forestial /fəˈrɛstɪəl/ *adjective.* L17.
[ORIGIN from FOREST *noun* + -IAL.]
Of or pertaining to a forest, forestal.

forestry /ˈfɒrɪstri/ *noun.* L17.
[ORIGIN formed as FORESTIAL + -RY.]
1 SCOTS LAW (now *hist.*). The privileges of a royal forest; the estate to which these privileges are attached. L17.
2 Wooded country; a vast extent of trees. E19.
3 The art or science of planting and managing forests. M19.

foresty /ˈfɒrɪsti/ *adjective.* E17.
[ORIGIN formed as FORESTIAL + -Y[1].]
Like a forest; covered in forest.

foretaste /ˈfɔːteɪst/ *noun.* LME.
[ORIGIN from FORE- + TASTE *noun*[1].]
A taste beforehand, a partial enjoyment or suffering (*of*) in advance; an anticipation.
Review of English Studies This volume . . can offer only a foretaste of the riches that are promised when the whole project is complete.

F

foretaste /fɔːˈteɪst/ *verb trans.* LME.
[ORIGIN from FORE- + TASTE *verb*.]
1 Have a foretaste of, anticipate. LME.

T. KEN Saints thus Celestial Joys fore-taste.

2 Taste before another. *rare*. M17.

MILTON Foretasted Fruit Profan'd first by the Serpent.

foretell /fɔːˈtɛl/ *verb*. Pa. t. & pple **-told** /-ˈtəʊld/. ME.
[ORIGIN from FORE- + TELL *verb*.]
1 *verb trans.* Tell of (an event etc.) before it takes place; predict, prophesy. ME. ▸**b** Foreshadow, presage, be the precursor of. L16.

E. M. FORSTER It is impossible to foretell the future with any degree of accuracy. **b** C. MCCULLERS The clouds . . grew steadily denser, and foretold a heavy summer rain.

†2 *verb intrans.* Speak *of* beforehand, prophesy *of*. ME–M17.

MILTON To introduce One greater, of whose day he shall foretell.

†3 *verb trans.* Inform or enjoin (a person) beforehand; state in advance. ME–L17.

HOBBES A Man is free to fore-tell, or not, what points he will insist upon.

■ **foretellable** *adjective* E20. **foreteller** *noun* L16.

forethink /fɔːˈθɪŋk/ *verb*[1]. Pa. t. & pple **-thought** /-ˈθɔːt/. OE.
[ORIGIN from FORE- + THINK *verb*[2].]
1 *verb trans.* Think out beforehand, premeditate; contrive, plan. *obsolete* exc. *dial.* OE.

N. ROWE My brain forethought And fashion'd every action of my life.

2 *verb trans.* Think of or contemplate beforehand; anticipate. ME.

W. BALDWIN Rather of a friend hope the best, then forethinke the worst.

†3 *verb intrans.* Think beforehand *of*. L16–E18.

J. NORRIS He could not make it without forethinking of it.

■ **forethinker** *noun* M19.

forethink *verb*[2] var. of FORTHINK *verb*[1].

forethought /ˈfɔːθɔːt/ *noun*. ME.
[ORIGIN from FORE- + THOUGHT *noun*[1].]
1 Previous consideration; anticipation, premeditation. ME.

GEO. ELIOT The title which she had never given him before came to her lips without forethought.

†2 An idea or design previously thought out; an anticipation. ME–E18.
3 Care or thought for the future. LME.

B. JOWETT Just so much forethought as is necessary to provide for the morrow.

■ **foreˈthoughtful** *adjective* full of forethought; provident: E19. **foreˈthoughtfully** *adverb* L19. **foreˈthoughtfulness** *noun* M17.

forethought *verb*[1] *pa. t. & pple*: see FORETHINK *verb*[1], FORTHINK *verb*[1].

forethought *verb*[2] *pa. t. & pple*: see FORTHINK *verb*[1].

foretoken /ˈfɔːtəʊk(ə)n/ *noun*. OE.
[ORIGIN from FORE- + TOKEN *noun*.]
A sign of something to come.

foretoken /fɔːˈtəʊk(ə)n/ *verb trans.* OE.
[ORIGIN from FORE- + TOKEN *verb*; later from the noun.]
Indicate beforehand; portend.

B. MALAMUD Inspired by the change in her, hoping it might foretoken better luck for him.

foretold *verb pa. t. & pple* of FORETELL.

foretop /ˈfɔːtɒp, NAUTICAL -təp/ *noun*. ME.
[ORIGIN from FORE- + TOP *noun*[1].]
1 **a** A lock of hair growing above or arranged on a person's forehead, a forelock; a similar part of a wig. Now *rare* or *obsolete*. ME. ▸**b** A tuft of hair growing on or hanging over the forehead of an animal. Now chiefly *US*. E17.
†2 (The front part of) the top of the head. LME–L18.
3 NAUTICAL. The top of a foremast, the platform around the head of the lower foremast. L15.
4 The front seat on top of a horse-drawn vehicle. *US*. M19.

fore-topgallant /fɔːtɒpˈgal(ə)nt, -təˈgal-/ *adjective*. E16.
[ORIGIN from FORE- + TOPGALLANT.]
NAUTICAL. Designating or pertaining to a part of a mast above the foretopmast.
fore-topgallant mast, ***fore-topgallant sail***, ***fore-topgallant yard***, etc.

foretopmast /fɔːˈtɒpmɑːst, -məst/ *noun*. L15.
[ORIGIN from FORE- + TOPMAST.]
NAUTICAL. The mast above the lower foremast.

foretopsail /fɔːˈtɒps(ə)l, -seɪl/ *noun*. L15.
[ORIGIN from FORE- + TOPSAIL.]
NAUTICAL. The sail above the foresail.
pay with the foretopsail: see PAY *verb*[1].

forever /fəˈrɛvə/ *adverb & noun*. Also (now esp. in sense A.1) **for ever**. ME.
[ORIGIN Orig. two words, from FOR *preposition* + EVER.]
▸ **A** *adverb*. **1** For all future time, in perpetuity, (also ***for ever and ever***, ***for ever and a day***, (arch.) ***for ever and ay***); *colloq.* for a very long time. ME.

J. MORLEY Hitherto certainly, and probably it will be so for ever. E. FEINSTEIN Do people recover from such pain, or are they damaged forever? *Look Now* We felt that we'd known each other forever.

— **for ever!** may — flourish!

2 Continually, incessantly, repeatedly. *colloq.* L18.

Daedalus He is forever telling us what he will do and why.

▸ **B** *noun*. **1** (An) eternity, perpetuity. M19.

M. ANDERSON This is forever, here where we stand . . how does one spend a forever?

2 After verbs: a very long time. *colloq.* M20.

J. AIKEN They always take for ever to change. A. CARTER It seemed forever before he got to the centre of the stage.

■ **foreverness** *noun* the state or condition of lasting for ever, permanence E19.

for evermore /fərɛvəˈmɔː/ *adverb phr.* Also **forevermore**. ME.
[ORIGIN from FOR *preposition* + EVERMORE.]
For all future time, in perpetuity.

forewarn /fɔːˈwɔːn/ *verb*[1] *trans.* ME.
[ORIGIN from FORE- + WARN *verb*[1].]
1 Warn, caution, or admonish beforehand. ME.

SHAKES. *3 Hen. VI* We were forewarned of your coming And shut the gates. *Proverb*: Forewarned is forearmed.

2 Announce beforehand, prophesy. *rare*. L16.

Daily Telegraph Nuns . . are worried that a holy relic is forewarning a world catastrophe.

■ **forewarner** *noun* LME. **forewarning** *noun* (**a**) the action of the verb; (**b**) a warning beforehand; prior notice or admonition: LME.

forewarn *verb*[2] var. of FORWARN.

forewent *verb*[1], *verb*[2] *pa. t.*: see FOREGO *verb*[1], FORGO.

forewoman /ˈfɔːwʊmən/ *noun*. Pl. **-women** /-wɪmɪn/. E18.
[ORIGIN from FORE- + WOMAN *noun*.]
1 A woman appointed as leader and spokesperson of a jury. E18.
2 A female worker supervising other workers. M19.

foreword /ˈfɔːwəːd/ *noun*. M19.
[ORIGIN from FORE- + WORD *noun*, after German *Vorwort*.]
A preface; a section of introductory remarks, esp. by a person other than the author of the main work.

forex /ˈfɒrɛks/ *noun*. L20.
[ORIGIN Abbreviation.]
COMMERCE. The foreign exchange market; foreign exchange.

foreyard /ˈfɔːjɑːd/ *noun*[1]. LME.
[ORIGIN from FORE- + YARD *noun*[1].]
A yard or court in front of a building.

foreyard /ˈfɔːjɑːd/ *noun*[2]. L15.
[ORIGIN from FORE- + YARD *noun*[2].]
NAUTICAL. The lowest yard on a foremast.

forfare /fɔːˈfɛː/ *verb*. Long *obsolete* exc. *Scot.* OE.
[ORIGIN from FOR-[1] + FARE *verb*.]
1 *verb intrans.* †**a** Pass away, perish, decay. OE–L16. ▸**b** As ***forfared*** pa. pple. Worn out with travel, age, etc. LME.
2 *verb trans.* Cause to perish, destroy. OE.

forfeit /ˈfɔːfɪt/ *noun*. ME.
[ORIGIN Old French *forfet*, (also mod.) *forfait* crime, from pa. pple of *for(s)faire* transgress (medieval Latin *forisfacere*), formed as FOR-[2] + *faire* do: in sense 3 also infl. by the verb.]
†1 A transgression, a crime, an offence; wilful injury. Also, breach or violation *of*. ME–E19.
2 Something to which the right is lost by the commission of a crime or fault; a penal fine; a penalty for breach of contract or neglect of duty. LME.
3 The losing of something by way of penalty, forfeiture. LME.
4 A penalty for a breach of contract, neglect, etc., a fine, *esp.* a trivial fine for a breach of the rules of a club, game, etc.; an article surrendered as a penalty in a game. E17.

forfeit /ˈfɔːfɪt/ *adjective*. LME.
[ORIGIN Old French *forfet*, *-fait* pa. pple of *forfaire*: see FORFEIT *noun*.]
(To be) given up as a penalty for an offence, a breach of agreement, etc. (Foll. by *to*.)

J. G. FARRELL The saying of prayers and sewing-up in bedding of those whose lives had been forfeit.

forfeit /ˈfɔːfɪt/ *verb*. ME.
[ORIGIN from FORFEIT *noun*.]
1 †**a** *verb intrans.* Do wrong, sin, transgress. ME–M16. ▸**b** *verb trans.* Transgress against, violate (one's faith or oath). *rare*. LME.
2 **a** *verb trans.* Lose the right to, be deprived of, have to pay, as a penalty for crime, neglect, etc. LME. ▸**b** *verb trans.* Lose or give up, as a necessary consequence. LME. ▸**c** *verb intrans.* Incur the penalty of forfeiture. Long *rare*. E18.

DEFOE My life and effects were all forfeited to the English government. B. CHATWIN He ran away three times and three times forfeited his wages. **b** E. WAUGH In their austere trade they had forfeited the arts of leisure.

forfeit bail, ***forfeit one's bail***: see BAIL *noun*[1].

3 *verb trans.* Of a governing power: subject (land, goods) to forfeiture; (chiefly *Scot.*) subject (a person) to forfeiture, deprive *of* estates. *obsolete* exc. *hist.* LME.
†4 *verb trans.* Exact a forfeit or fine from. L16–M18.
†5 *verb trans.* Cause the forfeiture, loss, or ruin of. E17–E18.
■ **forfeitable** *adjective* liable to be forfeited, subject to forfeiture LME. **forfeiter** *noun* LME.

forfeiture /ˈfɔːfɪtʃə, -tjʊə/ *noun*. LME.
[ORIGIN Old French *forfaiture*, formed as FORFEIT *noun* + -URE.]
†1 Transgression of a law; crime; sin. LME–E17.
2 The fact of losing or becoming liable to deprivation of or *of* an estate, life, an office, right, etc., in consequence of an offence or breach of agreement. LME.

A. FRASER The penalty for high treason was death, as well as the forfeiture of titles and offices.

†3 The penalty for an offence. LME–M17.
4 That which is forfeited; a fine. Now *rare* or *obsolete*. LME.

forfend /fɔːˈfɛnd/ *verb*. Also **fore-**. LME.
[ORIGIN from FOR-[1] + FEND *verb*.]
†1 *verb trans.* Forbid, prohibit. (Foll. by *to do*.) LME–L19.

E. PAGITT Anselme . . forfended Priests to have Wives. J. BADCOCK This ingenious veterinarian forefends the practice of mixing clay in the stuffing.

2 *verb trans. & intrans.* Avert, keep away, prevent, (esp. evil). Freq. in ***Heaven forfend!*** etc. *arch.* LME.

C. S. LEWIS Heaven forfend I should be taken to mean that Wyvern is the same to-day.

3 *verb trans.* Secure or protect by precautionary measures. Now chiefly *US*. L16.

forfex /ˈfɔːfɛks/ *noun*. E18.
[ORIGIN Latin.]
1 A pair of scissors. *joc.* E18.
2 ENTOMOLOGY. A pair of anal organs shaped like scissors, which cross when closed. E19.

forficate /ˈfɔːfɪkeɪt/ *adjective*. E19.
[ORIGIN from Latin *forfex*, *forfic-* pair of scissors + -ATE[2].]
Shaped or functioning like a pair of scissors; deeply forked.
■ Also **forficated** *adjective* M18.

forficulate /fɔːˈfɪkjʊlət/ *adjective*. L19.
[ORIGIN from Latin *forficula* dim. of *forfex* pair of scissors + -ATE[2].]
Chiefly BOTANY & ZOOLOGY. Shaped like a (small) pair of scissors.

forfoughten /fɔːˈfɔːt(ə)n/ *ppl adjective*. *obsolete* exc. *Scot. & N. English*. ME.
[ORIGIN from FOR-[1] + FOUGHTEN.]
Wearied, worn-out, esp. with fighting.

forgather /fɔːˈgaðə/ *verb intrans.* Also **fore-**. L15.
[ORIGIN Dutch *vergaderen* meet, assemble (= German *vergattern*) assim. to FOR-[1], GATHER *verb*.]
1 Gather together, assemble. L15.

E. JONES They used to forgather regularly once a week in the Café.

2 Meet (*with*). E16. ▸**b** Associate *with*, take *up* with. L18.

R. FERGUSSON When I again Auld Reikie see, And can forgether, lad, with thee. S. R. CROCKETT The outsailed *Seahorse* and the deceived *Ariel* had forgathered off the Isle of Man.

forgave *verb pa. t.*: see FORGIVE.

forge /fɔːdʒ/ *noun*. ME.
[ORIGIN Old French & mod. French from Proto-Romance from Latin *fabrica* trade, workshop, fabric.]
1 A smithy. ME.

JO GRIMOND A blacksmith's forge in which the smith in leather apron hammered out red-hot horse-shoes.

†2 Manufacture, construction; style of construction, make, workmanship. LME–L17.
3 A blacksmith's hearth or fireplace with attached bellows, used for heating iron to make it malleable. L15.

fig.: W. M. PRAED In laboured phrase and polished lie Wrought by the forge of flattery.

4 A hearth or furnace for melting or refining metals; a workshop etc. where this is done. L15.
– COMB.: **forge-man** a worker in a forge, a blacksmith; **forge-master** the manager or owner of a forge.

forge /fɔːdʒ/ *verb*[1]. ME.
[ORIGIN Old French & mod. French *forger* from Latin *fabricare* FABRICATE.]
1 *verb trans.* Make, fashion, construct, (a material thing). *obsolete* exc. as passing into sense 4. ME.
2 *verb trans.* Make (something) in fraudulent imitation of something else; imitate fraudulently, counterfeit, (esp. a document, a signature, a banknote, etc.) in order to pass the fraudulent imitation off as genuine. ME.

R. BUCHANAN As if I had . . forged the laird's name. R. GRAVES He had forged a document purporting to be a testimonial.

3 *verb trans.* Fabricate, invent, (a tale, a lie). Formerly also, coin (a word etc.). LME.

W. CAMDEN Some thinke it to be no ancient name, but forged by the writer of King Arthurs historie. C. KINGSLEY A charge . . forged by that villain.

4 *verb trans.* Shape by heating in a forge and hammering; beat into shape. LME.

H. ALLEN The smith spent the afternoon forging two heavy chains. *fig.*: B. PYM A link might have been forged between two solitary people.

5 *verb intrans.* Work at a forge; do a blacksmith's work. LME.
6 *verb intrans.* Commit forgery. Now *rare*. L16.
■ **forgea'bility** *noun* ability to be forged L19. **forgeable** *adjective* able to be forged LME. †**forgeful** *adjective* apt to forge, creative M18–E19. **forger** *noun* a person who forges something, esp. fraudulently LME. †**forgerer** *noun* a forger L16–E19.

forge /fɔːdʒ/ *verb*[2] *intrans. & trans.* M18.
[ORIGIN Perh. alt. of FORCE *verb*[1].]
1 *verb intrans.* Of a ship: make way esp. by momentum or pressure of wind or tide. M18.
forge ahead take the lead esp. in a race, move forward rapidly.
2 *verb trans.* Make *one's way* by momentum, esp. gradually and steadily. L19.

forge /fɔːdʒ/ *verb*[3] *intrans.* M19.
[ORIGIN Perh. from FORGE *verb*[1] 4, with ref. to the sound.]
= CLICK *verb*[1] 1b.

forgery /'fɔːdʒ(ə)ri/ *noun.* L16.
[ORIGIN from FORGE *verb*[1] + -ERY.]
1 The making of a thing in fraudulent imitation of something else; *esp.* the forging of a document. L16. ▸**b** Something that has been forged or counterfeited; *esp.* a forged document. L16. ▸**c** The fact of being forged. *rare.* M17.

SHAKES. *Lucr.* Guilty of treason, forgery, and shift. **b** B. JOWETT That . . one of the most excellent writings bearing the name of Plato should be a forgery.

2 Orig., deception, a deceit. Later, fictitious invention. Now only *poet.* L16.
†**3** The action or craft of forging metal. Only in 17.

forget /fə'gɛt/ *noun*[1]. Chiefly *colloq.* M19.
[ORIGIN from FORGET *verb.*]
An instance of forgetting; a lapse of memory.

forget *noun*[2] var. of FORGETT.

forget /fə'gɛt/ *verb.* Infl. **-tt-**. Pa. t. **-got** /-'gɒt/; pa. pple **-gotten** /-'gɒt(ə)n/, (*US, arch., & poet.*) **-got**.
[ORIGIN Old English *forġietan* = Old Frisian *forjeta*, Old Saxon *fargetan* (Dutch *vergeten*), Old High German *firgezzan* (German *vergessen*), from West Germanic, from base of FOR-[1] + GET *verb.*]
1 *verb trans.* Lose remembrance of; cease to retain in one's memory. (Foll. by simple obj., obj. clause.) OE. ▸**b** *verb intrans.* Lose or cease to retain remembrance of something. LME. ▸**c** *verb trans.* Fail to recall to mind; not recollect. L18.

E. M. FORSTER I had forgotten we were dining out. S. SASSOON Why should I remember that and forget so much else? **c** TOLKIEN There is another danger . . which he does not see . . . He has forgotten Treebeard.

2 *verb trans.* Omit or neglect through inadvertence. Usu. foll. by *to do.* OE. ▸**b** *verb trans.* Omit to take, leave behind inadvertently. ME. ▸**c** *verb trans.* Omit to mention, leave unnoticed, pass over inadvertently. M16.

T. F. POWYS This order—that Mr. Pix never forgot to give. **b** SHAKES. *1 Hen. IV* A plague upon it! I have forgot the map . . . No, here it is.

3 *verb trans.* Cease or omit to think of, let slip out of the mind, leave out of sight, take no note of. OE. ▸†**b** *verb trans.* Drop the practice of (a duty, virtue, etc.); lose the use of (one's senses). LME–L17. ▸**c** *verb intrans.* Foll. by *about*: not recall the facts concerning; not remember to take action in the matter of. *colloq.* L19.

J. CONRAD He was nearly forgotten. *absol.*: R. C. TRENCH God may forgive, man is not therefore to forget. **c** N. GOULD He had forgotten about that, it was such a long time ago. I. MURDOCH He had completely forgotten about his son and was not pleased to be reminded.

4 *verb trans.* Neglect wilfully, disregard, slight. ME.

A. RADCLIFFE Why should I be in danger of forgetting what is due to my father?

– PHRASES ETC.: **don't you forget it** *emphatic colloq.* remember it, keep it in mind. **forget about it**, **forget it** *imper.* (*colloq.*) take no more notice of it, there is no need for apology or thanks. **forget oneself** (*a*) neglect one's own welfare; (*b*) *arch.* lose consciousness; (*c*) act unbecomingly or unworthily.
■ **forgetness** *noun* (*rare*) forgetfulness LME. **forgettable** *adjective* (earlier in UNFORGETTABLE) M19. **forgetter** *noun* LME. **forgetting** *verbal noun* (*a*) the action of the verb; †(*b*) the state of being unconscious, oblivion: ME.

forgetful /fə'gɛtfʊl, -f(ə)l/ *adjective.* LME.
[ORIGIN from FORGET *verb* + -FUL.]
1 Apt, inclined, or liable to forget. (Foll. by *of.*) LME.
2 Heedless, neglectful. Foll. by *of, to do.* E16.
3 Inducing forgetfulness or oblivion. Chiefly *poet.* M16.
■ **forgetfully** *adverb* E18. **forgetfulness** *noun* LME.

forgetive /'fɔːdʒɪtɪv/ *adjective.* L16.
[ORIGIN Perh. from FORGE *verb*[1].]
Skilled at making; inventive, creative.

forget-me-not /fə'gɛtmɪnɒt/ *noun.* M16.
[ORIGIN translating Old French *ne m'oubliez mie*: cf. Middle High German *vergiz min nicht* (German *Vergissmeinnicht*). In the 15th cent. worn as a lover's token.]
1 Any of various low-growing plants of the genus *Myosotis*, of the borage family; esp. *M. scorpioides*, which has bright blue flowers with a yellow centre; a flowering stem of such a plant. Also (locally or with specifying word), any of various (cultivated ornamental) plants resembling these, usu. with small, bright blue flowers. M16.
Alpine forget-me-not (*a*) any of various mountain plants of the genus *Myosotis*, esp. *M. alpestris*; (*b*) *N. Amer.* any of several plants of the Rocky Mountains of the genus *Eritrichium*, of the borage family. **Cape forget-me-not** a plant of the borage family native to southern Africa, *Anchusa capensis*. **Chinese forget-me-not** a hound's tongue, *Cynoglossum amabile*, native to eastern Asia.
†**2** The ground pine, *Ajuga chamaepitys*. Only in L16.
– COMB.: **forget-me-not blue** (of) a clear bright blue.
– NOTE: Rare before E19.

forgett /'fɔːdʒɪt/ *noun.* Also **forget**. L17.
[ORIGIN French FOURCHETTE.]
A side piece for a finger or thumb of a glove.

forgettory /fə'gɛt(ə)ri/ *noun. joc. colloq.* Also **-ery**. E20.
[ORIGIN Blend of FORGET *verb* and MEMORY.]
The faculty of forgetting; faultiness of memory.

forgivable /fə'gɪvəb(ə)l/ *adjective.* Also **-giveable**. M16.
[ORIGIN from FORGIVE + -ABLE.]
Able to be forgiven.
■ **forgivableness** *noun* the quality of being forgivable L19. **forgivably** *adverb* in a manner that is excusable or deserves forgiveness (earlier in UNFORGIVABLY) E20.

forgive /fə'gɪv/ *verb.* Pa. t. **-gave** /-'geɪv/; pa. pple **-given** /-'gɪv(ə)n/.
[ORIGIN Old English *forġiefan* corresp. to Old Saxon, Old High German *fargeban* (Dutch *vergeven*, German *vergeben*), Old Norse *fyrirgefa* forgive, Gothic *fragiban* grant, from Germanic, from base of FOR-[1] + GIVE *verb.*]
†**1** *verb trans.* Give, grant. OE–L15.
2 *verb trans.* Pardon (an offence); cease to resent or claim requital for; remit (a debt). (Foll. by indirect obj. or *to* a person.) OE.

T. MOORE Clonmell never forgave this to Grattan. *Time* A scheme that would forgive all debt.

3 *verb intrans.* Pardon an offence or an offender; give up resentment against a person etc. OE.

POPE To err is human, to forgive, divine.

4 *verb trans.* Give up resentment against, pardon, (an offender) (foll. by *for*); (now *rare*) give up one's claim against (a debtor). ME.

ARNOLD BENNETT He had forgiven his father for having thwarted his supreme ambition.

†**5** *verb trans.* Give up (resentment, anger); give up one's resolve *to do.* ME–M16.
6 *verb trans.* Make excuse or apology for, regard indulgently. M17.

J. HIGGINS Forgive me for asking, Father, but are you American or Irish?

■ **forgiver** *noun* ME. **forgiving** *ppl adjective* that forgives; inclined to forgive; indicating forgiveness: L17. **forgivingly** *adverb* M17. **forgivingness** *noun* M18.

forgiveness /fə'gɪvnɪs/ *noun.* OE.
[ORIGIN from *forgiven* pa. pple of FORGIVE + -NESS.]
1 The action of forgiving; the state of being forgiven. Formerly also, indulgent permission. OE.

M. MILNER The trespasses that the prayer book says we also need forgiveness for. *Time* He advocates complete forgiveness of interest payments.

2 Readiness to forgive. ME.

E. F. BENSON That higher power of forgiveness which is to forget.

forgo /fɔː'gəʊ, fə-/ *verb.* Also **forego**. Pa. t. **-went** /-'wɛnt/; pa. pple **-gone** /-'gɒn/. OE.
[ORIGIN from FOR-[1] + GO *verb.*]
†**1** *verb intrans.* Go away, go past, pass away. OE–M16.
2 *verb trans.* Go by, pass over; leave alone or undone, overlook, slight. Long *arch. rare.* OE.
3 *verb trans.* Abstain or refrain from (an action, a procedure). OE.

E. A. FREEMAN We forego any comparison between the two men.

†**4** *verb trans.* Let go (involuntarily); lose, forfeit. OE–L16.
5 *verb trans.* Go from, forsake, leave. *arch.* ME.
6 *verb trans.* Go without, deny to oneself; let pass, omit to take or use; give up, renounce. ME.

B. PYM They did not consider that it was necessary for them to forgo any of the pleasures.

†**7** *verb trans.* Only as **forgone** pa. pple. Exhausted, esp. from travelling; faint with emotion. ME–L16.

forgoer /fɔː'gəʊə/ *noun.* Also **fore-**. E17.
[ORIGIN from FORGO + -ER[1].]
A person who forgoes something.

forgone /fɔː'gɒn/ *ppl adjective.* Also **fore-**. L19.
[ORIGIN pa. pple of FORGO.]
That has been forgone.

forgot *verb pa. t. & pple*: see FORGET *verb.*

forgotten *verb pa. pple*: see FORGET *verb.*

forinsec /fə'rɪnsɪk/ *adjective. obsolete* exc. *hist.* M18.
[ORIGIN medieval Latin (*servitium*) *forinsecum*, from Latin *forinsecus* (adverb) out of doors.]
forinsec service, service due to the superior from whom one's lord held land.

†**forinsecal** *adjective.* M16–M18.
[ORIGIN from Latin *forinsecus* (see FORINSEC) + -AL[1].]
Foreign; alien, extrinsic.

forint /'fɒrɪnt/ *noun.* M20.
[ORIGIN Hungarian from Italian *fiorino*: see FLORIN.]
The basic monetary unit of Hungary, equal to 100 filler.

forisfamiliate /ˌfɔːrɪsfə'mɪlɪeɪt/ *verb trans.* L16.
[ORIGIN medieval Latin *forisfamiliat-* pa. ppl stem of *forisfamiliare*, from *foris* outside + *familia* family: see -ATE[3].]
CIVIL & SCOTS LAW. Liberate (a child) from family tutelage by giving him or her possession of part of his or her inheritance.
■ **forisfamili'ation** *noun* E17.

forjeskit /fə'dʒɛskɪt/ *adjective. Scot.* L18.
[ORIGIN Uncertain: cf. FOR-[1], DISJASKIT.]
Jaded, tired out.

forjudge /fɔː'dʒʌdʒ, fə-/ *verb trans.* Also **fore-**. LME.
[ORIGIN Old French *forjugier*, formed as FOR-[2] + JUDGE *verb*: in medieval Latin *for(is)judicare* dispossess.]
1 LAW. Dispossess, oust, or exclude by a judgement. Foll. by *from, of*, or with double obj. Now *rare.* LME.
†**2** Condemn judicially (*to* a penalty). LME–M18.
■ **forjudger** *noun* [-ER[4]] a judgement of sentence of deprivation, expulsion, or banishment L15.

fork /fɔːk/ *noun.*
[ORIGIN Old English *forca*, *force* corresp. to Old Frisian *forke*, Old Saxon *furka*, Old High German *furcha* (Dutch *vork*, German (dial.) *Furke*), Old Norse *forkr*, from Germanic from Latin *furca* pitchfork, forked stake, whence Old French & mod. French *fourche*, Old Northern French *fourque* (which reinforced the word in Middle English).]
▸ **I** A pronged implement.
1 A pronged agricultural implement, usu. with a long straight handle, used for digging, lifting, carrying, or throwing, and formerly as a weapon. Cf. PITCHFORK *noun*[1]. OE. ▸†**b** The forked tongue of a snake. *rare* (Shakes.). Only in E17.
2 A (usu. metal) implement with two, three, or four prongs, used for holding food while it is cut, conveying food to the mouth or plate, and as a cooking utensil. (Freq. with specifying word.) LME.

J. JOHNSTON People were eating cream cakes with tiny silver forks.

carving fork, ***fish fork***, ***toasting fork***, etc. ***silver-fork***: see SILVER *adjective.*
3 A prong, *esp.* the prong of a fork. Usu. in *pl.* L17. ▸**b** A pickpocket; in *pl.*, the fingers, esp. as used in picking a pocket. *arch. slang.* L17.
4 In full ***tuning fork***. A two-pronged steel instrument designed to give a particular note (esp. middle C) when struck. L18.
▸ **II** An object with two or more branches.
†**5** In *pl.* (usu. treated as *sing.*) or *sing.* A gallows. ME–E19. ▸†**b** ROMAN ANTIQUITIES. The yoke under which defeated enemies had to pass as a token of submission; a whipping post. Only in 17.
6 A stake, stick, etc., with a forked end (used as a support for vines etc.). LME.
7 ARCHITECTURE. A pair of timbers supporting a roof-tree. LME.
8 A bifurcation or division into branches; the point at which something forks; each of the branches, prongs, etc., into which something forks. LME. ▸**b** A person's leg (usu. in *pl.*). Also, the part of the human body at which the legs join the trunk. E17. ▸**c** CHESS. A simultaneous attack by one piece, esp. a knight, on two opposing pieces. M17. ▸**d** The point at which one river divides or two rivers join; a branch, a tributary. Chiefly *N. Amer.* M18. ▸**e** A flash (of forked lightning); a tongue (of flame). M19.

G. MEREDITH Torches were struck in . . the trees, or in the fork of the branches. A. AYCKBOURN Turn left . . through the village, then take the right fork past the pub. **d** W. IRVING The fork of the Nebraska, where it divides itself into two . . beautiful streams.

†**9** A barbed arrowhead. *rare* (Shakes.). Only in E17.
10 A part of any machine or device having two or more prongs; *esp.* the part of a bicycle frame in which the (front or back) wheel revolves. M19.
– PHRASES: MORTON'S FORK.
– COMB.: **forkball** BASEBALL a pitch in which the ball is held with the thumb, index finger, and middle finger spread; **fork-lift (truck)** a vehicle with a pronged device for lifting and carrying heavy items; **fork lunch**, **fork luncheon**, **fork supper**, etc.: consisting

F

of food suitable for eating with a fork alone, so that it can be eaten standing; **forktail** any of various animals with forked tails; *spec.* (*a*) a salmon in the fourth year of its growth; (*b*) any of several chiefly black and white thrushlike birds constituting the genus *Enicurus*, native to SE Asia; **fork-tailed** *adjective* (esp. in names of birds etc.) having a forked tail.

■ **forkful** *noun* as much as may be lifted on a fork **M17.** **forklike** *adjective* resembling (that of) a fork **E17.**

fork /fɔːk/ *verb.* **ME.**
[**ORIGIN** from the noun.]
1 *verb intrans.* Form a fork; have or divide into branches, bifurcate; diverge, esp. in a specified direction. **ME.** ▸**b** *verb trans.* CHESS. Attack (two pieces) simultaneously with one piece. **E18.**

J. SYLVESTER The Tree, In two faire branches forking fruitfully. M. REID The lightning forked and flashed. C. MACKENZIE They came to where the track forked to their respective crofts.

2 *verb trans.* Make or form into the shape of a fork. **M17.**
3 *verb trans.* Pick a pocket. *arch. slang.* **L17.**
4 *verb trans.* MINING. Pump (a mine) dry; remove (water) by pumping. **E18.**
5 *verb trans.* Move (as) with a fork; dig, throw, scoop *in*, *out*, *over*, etc., with a fork. **E19.**

T. BERGER He forked up a plump piece of meat and put it between his lips. *Amateur Gardening* Fork a little peat into the soil. *absol.*: W. HOLTBY On the stacks beyond the chestnut trees, labourers were forking.

6 *verb trans.* & *intrans.* Foll. by *out*, *over*, *up*: hand over (esp. money), pay, give up. *colloq.* **M19.**

J. BARNES They had to . . fork out at Christmas, and fork out money.

■ **forker** *noun* **L16.**

forked /fɔːkt/ *adjective.* **ME.**
[**ORIGIN** from **FORK** *noun*, *verb*: see **-ED**[2], **-ED**[1].]
1 Having a fork or forks or a forklike end; shaped like a fork, bifurcate, divergent, cleft. **ME.** ▸**b** Of a road: making or having a fork or forks; branching. **E16.** ▸**c** Having (a specified number of) prongs or forks. **M16.** ▸**d** Of an arrow: having a fork-shaped arrowhead; (of an arrowhead) fork-shaped. **M16.** ▸**e** Of a mountain: cleft at the summit. *poet.* **E17.**
†**2** Of an argument: ambiguous, equivocal. **M16–L17.**
3 Horned; *fig.* cuckolded. Now *rare* or *obsolete.* **L16.**
4 Having the lower part of the trunk divided; two-legged. *rare.* **E17.**

– **SPECIAL COLLOCATIONS**: **forked head** a forked arrow(head). **forked lightning**: in the form of a zigzag or a branching line. **forked tongue** a lying or deceitful tongue (freq. in ***with a forked tongue***, ***with forked tongue***).

■ **forkedly** *adverb* **E17.** **forkedness** *noun* **E17.**

forky /ˈfɔːki/ *adjective.* **L17.**
[**ORIGIN** from **FORK** *noun* + **-Y**[1].]
Forked, fork-shaped.
■ **forkiness** *noun* **E17.**

†**forlese** *verb trans.* Pa. t. **-lore**; pa. pple **-lorn**. See also **FORLORN** *adjective.*
[**ORIGIN** Old English *forlēosan* = Old Frisian *forliāsa*, Old Saxon *far-*, *forliosan* (Dutch *verliezen*), Old High German *firliosan* (German *verlieren*), Gothic *fraliusan*, from Germanic, from bases of **FOR-**[1], **LOSE** *verb.*]
1 Lose. **OE–M17.**
2 Destroy; kill. **OE–M17.** ▸**b** Ruin; put to shame; lead astray. Usu. in *pass.* **ME–L16.**
3 Leave, abandon, forsake. **ME–E17.**

†**forloff** *noun* see **FURLOUGH.**

forlorn /fəˈlɔːn/ *adjective & noun.* **OE.**
[**ORIGIN** pa. pple of **FORLESE.**]
▸ **A** *adjective.* †**1** Morally lost; abandoned, depraved. **OE–L17.**
2 a Foll. by *of*, *from*: forsaken by (a person); bereft of (a thing). Chiefly *poet.* **ME.** ▸**b** Abandoned, forsaken, deserted; left alone, desolate. **M16.**

a TENNYSON Mournful Œnone wandering forlorn Of Paris once her playmate. **b** E. BOWEN The stretch of forlorn marsh and sad sea-line.

3 †**a** Ruined, doomed to destruction. **LME–E18.** ▸**b** Desperate, hopeless. **E17.**
4 In pitiful condition; of a wretched appearance. **L16.**

E. F. BENSON Lucia had looked so tired, so forlorn, so young to be visited with such hopeless trouble.

▸ †**B** *noun.* **1** A forlorn person. **E16–E19.**
2 = **FORLORN HOPE. M17–L18.**

■ **forlornity** *noun* (*US*) forlornness **M19.** **forlornly** *adverb* **M17.** **forlornness** /-n-n-/ *noun* the state or quality of being forlorn **OE.**

forlorn hope /fəˌlɔːn ˈhəʊp/ *noun phr.* **M16.**
[**ORIGIN** Dutch *verloren hoop* lost troop, from *verloren* pa. pple of *verliezen* (see **FORLESE**) and *hoop* company (see **HEAP** *noun*).]
1 MILITARY. A picked troop sent to the front to begin an attack; a storming party, a body of skirmishers. In *pl.* also, the people composing such a troop; adventurers. **M16.** ▸**b** A dangerous or desperate enterprise. **M18.**
†**2** The losers at a gaming table collectively. Also, a gambler's last stake. *slang.* **E17–L18.**
3 A faint hope; an enterprise unlikely to succeed. **M17.**

form /fɔːm/ *noun.* Also (now only in sense 18) **forme. ME.**
[**ORIGIN** Old French & mod. French *forme* from Latin *forma* mould, shape, beauty.]
▸ **I** Shape, arrangement of parts.
1 The visual aspect, esp. the shape or configuration, of a thing; the shape of a body. **ME.** ▸†**b** Beauty, comeliness. **LME–M17.** ▸**c** Shape and structure considered abstractly as an element in the arts. **M19.** ▸**d** CRYSTALLOGRAPHY. More fully ***crystal form***. A set of crystal faces all of which have the same relation to the symmetry elements. **L19.**

A. MACLEAN The Schloss Adler was built in the form of a hollow square. J. S. FOSTER The fabric . . gives character and form to the spaces within it. **c** O. N. ROOD In painting . . colour is subordinate to form. *Dance Theatre Journal* Everything she had to say . . was right there in the dancing . . . She expressed everything through form.

†**2** An image, a likeness, a representation. **ME–E17.**
3 A person or animal as visible or tangible. **ME.**

D. WELCH I did not notice the dark form on the bench. I. MURDOCH Felix stood . . his tall form blotting out the evening star.

4 The particular mode in which a thing exists or manifests itself. **ME.** ▸**b** A species, a kind, a variety; an artistic or literary genre. **LME.** ▸**c** LINGUISTICS. Any of the ways in which a word may be pronounced, inflected, or spelled; the external characteristics of a word or other unit as distinct from its meaning. **M18.** ▸**d** BOTANY. A taxonomic grouping ranking below a variety, which contains organisms differing from a given variety, subspecies, etc., in some trivial, freq. impermanent, character, e.g. a colour variant. **L19.**

D. L. SAYERS The arsenic was taken in liquid form. B. MOORE God was there . . in the form of a wafer of bread and a chalice of wine. **b** A. S. BYATT A form is as good as the writer who chooses it. JO GRIMOND Traces of a primitive form of barley . . have been found. **c** MAX-MÜLLER The Chinese sound *ta* means, without any change of form, great, greatness, and to be great.

†**5** The way in which something is done or made; method, fashion. **ME–M17.**
6 A set, customary, or prescribed way of doing something; correct or usual procedure. **ME.** ▸**b** The present state of affairs; what is happening or going on, what is to be done. *colloq.* **M20.**

b B. BAINBRIDGE What's the form tonight? You are coming, I take it.

†**7** A model, a type, a pattern, an example. **LME–L17.**
8 PHILOSOPHY. **a** In Platonic philosophy, the transcendent idea or archetype which serves as the pattern for a created thing. **LME.** ▸**b** In Aristotelian and scholastic philosophy, the essential determinant principle of a thing; that which makes something (***matter***) a determinate species or kind of being. **LME.** ▸**c** In Kantian philosophy, that element of knowledge which is supplied by the mind and gives reality and objectivity to the thing known, as distinct from the element (***matter***) supplied by feeling. **E19.**
9 Arrangement and expression of ideas esp. in the arts; style in musical or literary composition. **LME.**

J. R. LOWELL Form . . is the artistic sense of decorum controlling the coordination of parts.

10 A set or fixed order of words; the customary or legal method of drawing up a document etc. Also, a regularly drawn document. **LME.** ▸†**b** A recipe, a prescription. **LME–E17.** ▸**c** A document with blanks to be filled up. **M19.**

D. L. SAYERS They were married in the old . . Prayer Book form, and the bride said 'Obey'. **c** L. VAN DER POST There was no filling in of forms in triplicate.

11 a Behaviour according to prescribed or customary rules; observance of etiquette, decorum, etc. Also *derog.*, outward observance or conformity without intrinsic sincerity. **LME.** ▸**b** Orig., a way of behaving oneself; an instance of a specified kind of behaviour; in *pl.*, manners. Later, a mode of behaviour or procedure in accordance with prescribed usage, etiquette, etc., a ceremony. Freq. *derog.*, a ritual without intrinsic meaning. **L16.**

a J. GRAHAME Giving thanks to God—not thanks of form, A word and a grimace, but reverently. **b** M. MITCHELL The old usages went on, must go on, for the forms were all that were left to them.

12 †**a** A grade or degree of rank, eminence, or quality. **LME–E18.** ▸**b** Any of the classes in which schoolchildren may be placed according to age or ability. **M16.**

a S. PEPYS Thinking is working, though many forms beneath what my Lady and you are doing. **b** MORTIMER COLLINS He was in the fifth form at Eton.

13 Orderly arrangement of parts; regularity, good order. **L16.**

P. SCOTT My passion for form and order . . everything used but with care and kept clean.

14 Of a racehorse, an athlete, etc.: condition of health and training, fitness. Also, record of previous performances by a racehorse, an athlete, etc. **M18.** ▸**b** Liveliness, good spirits. *colloq.* **L19.** ▸**c** Criminal activity on public record. *slang.* **M20.**

S. L. ELLIOTT A bloke might try and get some form up and get in the football team next winter. *Observer* On 1984 form, there are eight drivers who stand a good chance of winning today. **b** P. BOOTH 'Dad's sure in good form today,' she yelled. **c** P. LAURIE The boy's elder brother had form for doping greyhounds.

▸ **II** A material object.
15 A mould, frame, or block in or on which something is shaped. **ME.** ▸**b** *spec.* A temporary structure for holding fresh concrete in shape while it sets. **E20.**

Daily Telegraph You warm a small amount of metal, put it in the scroll form and gradually pull it round to the shape.

16 The lair of a hare. **ME.**

M. BURTON A slight depression in the long grass known as a 'form', where the hare habitually crouches during the day.

17 A long seat without a back, a bench. **LME.**

A. UTTLEY They sat outside . . on long low forms.

18 PRINTING. (Usu. **forme.**) Type set and locked in a chase ready for printing; a quantity of film arranged for making a plate etc. **L15.**

F. NORRIS We begin to set Saturday's paper at about four Friday afternoon, and the forms are locked about two in the morning.

– **PHRASES**: **a matter of form** a point of correct procedure; *colloq.* mere routine. **bad form**: offending against current social conventions. ***common form***: see **COMMON** *adjective.* ***crystal form***: see sense 1d above. **good form**: complying with current social conventions. ***in any shape or form***: see **SHAPE** *noun*[1]. **in due form**, **in proper form**, etc., according to the conventions, (merely) formally. **in form** (*a*) = ***in due form*** above; (*b*) = ***in good form*** below. **in good form** etc., playing or performing well, in good spirits. ***in no shape or form***: see **SHAPE** *noun*[1]. ***in proper form***: see ***in due form*** above. **off form** not performing well, not at one's best. **on form** = ***in good form*** above. ***true to form***: see **TRUE** *adjective, noun, & adverb.*

– **COMB.**: **form-board** a board with spaces to take blocks of various shapes and sizes, used in intelligence tests; **form book** a record of the performances of a racehorse etc.; **form catalogue** a library catalogue in which books of a certain kind or literary genre are listed together; **form class** (*a*) FORESTRY a group of trees having a similar form factor (see below); (*b*) LINGUISTICS a class of linguistic forms with grammatical features in common; **form critic** a person who engages in form criticism; **form criticism** textual analysis of the Bible etc. by tracing the history of its content of proverbs, myths, and other forms; **form drag** the drag on a moving body resulting from its shape; **form factor** FORESTRY the ratio of the volume of a tree to that of a regularly shaped body of the same height and base; **form-fitting** *adjective* (of clothing) fitting the body closely; **form genus** (chiefly MYCOLOGY & PALAEONTOLOGY) a collective group of (parts of) organisms showing morphological similarities but not necessarily a genetic relationship; a group of similar trace fossils; **form historian** = ***form critic*** above; **form history** = ***form criticism*** above; **form letter** a standardized letter to deal with frequently occurring matters; **form-line** CARTOGRAPHY a line drawn on a map to show the estimated configuration or elevation between the contour lines (usu. in *pl.*); **form-master**, **form-mistress**, a teacher who has particular responsibility for a class of schoolchildren; **form quality** a quality of the whole of something rather than of its constituent parts; **form-room** the room where a class of schoolchildren is based; **form-species** a subdivision of a form genus; **form sheet** (orig. *US*) = ***form book*** above; **form word** a word with a formal or grammatical function; **formwork** = sense 15b above.

■ **formful** *adjective* (now *rare* or *obsolete*) full of form or forms; shapely; imaginative: **M18.** **formless** *adjective* shapeless, having no determinate or regular form **L16.** **formlessly** *adverb* **L19.** **formlessness** *noun* **E18.**

form /fɔːm/ *verb*[1]. **ME.**
[**ORIGIN** Old French *fourmer*, (also mod.) *former* from Latin *formare*, from *forma* **FORM** *noun.*]
1 *verb trans.* Give form or shape to; fashion, mould. **ME.** ▸†**b** *verb trans.* Formulate; state formally. **ME–L17.** ▸**c** *verb trans.* Give a specified form to; fashion *into* a certain shape, *after*, *by*, *from*, *on*, a pattern. **ME.** ▸†**d** *verb trans.* Express by form, embody. *rare* (Spenser). Only in **L16.** ▸**e** *verb intrans.* Orig., agree in form, fit *with*. Later, take a (specified) shape, be shaped *into*. **E18.** ▸**f** *verb trans.* ELECTRICITY. Convert (a semiconductor device, the plates of a lead-acid accumulator, etc.) into a particular state by the application of a current or voltage. **L19.**

MILTON The Rib he formd and fashond with his hands. **c** C. MCCULLOUGH A little silver brooch formed into the rising sun emblem. **e** L. STEPHEN A ridge of rocky peaks, forming into two ridges about its centre.

2 *verb trans.* Mould (a person, the mind, a faculty, etc.) by discipline, experience, or education. **ME.**

A. JESSOPP Rudely scrawled by some one whose hand is not yet formed. J. BAYLEY The inescapable burden of being formed by parents and by early traumas.

3 *verb trans.* Construct, frame, make, produce, (something); articulate (a word). **ME.** ▸**b** *verb trans.* Frame in the mind, conceive, (an idea, a judgement, etc.). Also (*obsolete* exc. *dial.*), imagine. **L16.** ▸**c** *verb intrans.* Come into being. **E19.**

M. CONNELLY A large rustic table formed by driving four stakes into the ground and placing planks on top. A. CARNEGIE We had before this formed a small debating club. **b** G. GREENE She was forming a plan. Q. CRISP I formed no positive opinion of him whatsoever. **c** W. BRONK The stars . . form and evolve, . . explode in novae.

4 *verb trans.* Go to make up; compose. LME. ▸**b** Serve as, constitute; be one or a part *of*. E19.

H. JAMES The two houses together formed a single dwelling. DAY LEWIS The simple fishermen who formed the greater part of his congregation. **b** E. A. FREEMAN A realm of which Northumberland constitutionally formed a part. G. VIDAL His statistics would form the basis of a report.

5 *verb trans.* LINGUISTICS. Construct (a word) by derivation etc.; have (a case etc.) expressed by an inflection etc. LME.

RICHARD MORRIS The verbs of the strong conjugation form the past tense by a change of the root-vowel.

6 *verb trans.* Place in order, arrange; organize (persons or things) *into* a society, system, etc. LME.

J. R. GREEN The Clerks of the Royal Chapel were formed into a body of secretaries.

7 *verb trans. & intrans.* MILITARY. Arrange or draw up or *up* in order; assume or take up an arrangement in a (specified) formation. E18.

C. C. TRENCH They formed in squadron column. I. HAY On the command 'form fours', odd numbers will stand fast.

8 *verb trans.* Develop or acquire (a habit); enter into or contract (a friendship, an alliance, etc.). M18.

J. BUTLER Active habits are to be formed by exercise. T. HARDY I have never loved anybody . . I have not even formed a strong friendship.

form /fɔːm/ *verb*[2] *intrans.* Now *rare*. LME.
[ORIGIN from FORM *noun*.]
Of a hare: have its form (*in* a particular place), be placed.

-form /fɔːm/ *suffix*. Also (see below) **-iform**.
[ORIGIN Repr. French *-forme*, Latin *-formis*, from *forma* FORM *noun*.]
Forming (usu. with intermediate **-i-**) adjectives with the sense 'having the form of', as ***cruciform*** etc., and referring to the number of forms, as ***uniform***, ***multiform***, etc.

forma /ˈfɔːmə/ *noun*. Pl. **-mae** /-miː/, **-mas**. E20.
[ORIGIN Latin: see FORM *noun*.]
BOTANY. = FORM *noun* 4d.

formable /ˈfɔːməb(ə)l/ *adjective*. LME.
[ORIGIN from FORM *verb*[1] + -ABLE.]
1 Able to be created or formed; workable, plastic. LME.
2 Properly formed; formal, shapely. Long *obsolete* exc. *dial.* LME.
■ **formaˈbility** *noun* E19.

formal /ˈfɔːm(ə)l/ *noun*. E17.
[ORIGIN from the adjective.]
1 In *pl.* Things which are formal. *rare*. E17.
2 (An) evening dress; an occasion on which evening dress is worn. Chiefly *N. Amer.* M20.

M. BEADLE Young ladies . . wear short formals, and old ladies wear floor-length evening dresses. A. YORK She looked sufficiently virginal to be attending her first formal.

formal /ˈfɔːm(ə)l/ *adjective*. LME.
[ORIGIN Latin *formalis*, from *forma*: see FORM *noun*, -AL[1].]
1 a PHILOSOPHY. Of or pertaining to the form or constitutive essence of a thing; essential. LME. ▸†**b** Pertaining to the specific form of an animal or plant. LME–L17. ▸**c** Of or pertaining to the outward form, shape, appearance, arrangement, or external qualities of a thing. Formerly also, (of knowledge) theoretical. M17. ▸**d** LOGIC. Concerned with the form, not the matter, of reasoning. M19.

a R. SOUTH Deceit is the formal, constituent reason of hypocrisy. **c** F. W. ROBERTSON All living unity is spiritual, not formal.

2 Of, pertaining to, or in accordance with recognized rules or conventions, esp. of art. LME. ▸†**b** Of a story: elaborately constructed; circumstantial. L16–E18. ▸†**c** Made in proper form, complete; veritable, unmistakable. M17–E18.

U. BENTLEY We've done away with formal grammar and parsing and all that rubbish. W. S. CHURCHILL The Treaty . . bound Louis, not only in formal terms, but by a gentleman's agreement, to recognise . . William III as King.

†**3** Having a definite principle; regular, methodical. LME–E18. ▸**b** Well-formed, regular, shapely. LME–L16. ▸**c** Sound in mind; sane. *rare* (Shakes.). Only in L16.
4 Of a person, action, etc.: rigorously observant of etiquette, convention, etc.; prim; (unduly) precise or ceremonious. E16.

S. HILL Her voice was cool, formal. A. BROOKNER Her manners were charming and formal.

5 Valid or correctly so called in virtue of its form; explicit and definite, not merely tacit or accepted as equivalent. M16.
6 Connected with or accompanied by form or ceremony; (of dress) suitable for a polite or ceremonial occasion. L16.

E. ROOSEVELT The President . . gave a formal reception for me: all were seated according to protocol.

†**7** That is so merely in outward form or appearance. L16–M18.
8 (Excessively) regular or symmetrical; stiff, methodical. L16.

M. GIROUARD The formal Italianate garden, with . . parterres patterned with bedded-out flowers.

9 Merely a matter of convention; routine, perfunctory; having the form without the spirit. M17.

G. GREENE The papers which might just get him past a formal cursory examination.

– SPECIAL COLLOCATIONS: ***formal cause***: see CAUSE *noun*. **formal concept** [translating German *formaler Begriff*] a concept of logic free from the descriptive content that would restrict it to any particular subject matter. **formal education** education in an academic institution. ***formal operations***: see OPERATION 6b. **formal sin** a forbidden or sinful action done with evil intent.
■ **formalness** *noun* L17.

formaldehyde /fɔːˈmaldɪhʌɪd/ *noun*. L19.
[ORIGIN from FORMIC + ALDEHYDE.]
A colourless, pungent, toxic gaseous aldehyde, HCHO, usu. prepared by oxidation of methanol and used as formalin or in the manufacture of plastics etc.; methanal. Cf. FORMALIN.

formalin /ˈfɔːm(ə)lɪn/ *noun*. L19.
[ORIGIN from FORMALDEHYDE + -IN[1].]
An aqueous solution of formaldehyde (37 per cent by weight), used as a disinfectant, preservative for biological specimens, etc.
■ **formaliniˈzation** *noun* treatment with formalin M20. **formalinize** *verb trans.* treat with formalin E20.

formalise *verb* var. of FORMALIZE.

formalism /ˈfɔːm(ə)lɪz(ə)m/ *noun*. E19.
[ORIGIN from FORMAL *adjective* + -ISM.]
1 Strict or excessive adherence to prescribed forms; an instance of this. E19.

C. MERIVALE Completely enchained by their dogmatic formalisms.

2 The use or observance of prescribed forms (esp. of worship) without regard to their inner significance. M19. ▸**b** THEOLOGY. The basing of ethics on the form of the moral law without regard to intention or consequences. M20.

J. MORLEY The cant and formalism of any other degenerate form of active faith.

3 MATH. **a** (The conception of pure mathematics as) the manipulation according to certain rules of intrinsically meaningless symbols. E20. ▸**b** A particular mathematical theory or mode of description of a physical situation or effect. M20.
4 THEATRICAL. A movement away from naturalism, originating in Russia *c* 1890; a symbolic and stylized manner of production. E20.

A. NICOLL We are here [in the Nō plays] confronted with a theatre in which formalism is dominant.

5 The theory held by an early 20th-cent. Russian literary group that form and technique are the means to and the goal of artistic creation; (excessive) concern with form and technique rather than content. M20.

formalist /ˈfɔːm(ə)lɪst/ *noun & adjective*. E17.
[ORIGIN French *formaliste* or medieval Latin *formalista*: see FORMAL *adjective*, -IST.]
▸ **A** *noun*. †**1** A person supporting the religious group currently holding power; a time-server. E–M17.
2 A person excessively attached to forms; a stickler for etiquette, ceremony, or rules. M17.
3 An adherent or student of formalism. E20.
▸ **B** *adjective*. Of or pertaining to formalism; formalistic. E20.

formalistic /fɔːməˈlɪstɪk/ *adjective*. M19.
[ORIGIN from FORMALIST + -IC.]
Characterized by formalism.

formality /fɔːˈmalɪti/ *noun*. M16.
[ORIGIN French *formalité* or medieval Latin *formalitas*, from *formalis*: see FORMAL *adjective*, -ITY.]
†**1** Literary or artistic form or style. M16–L17.
2 Accordance with legal form. *rare*. M16.
3 Conformity to rules, propriety; rigid or merely conventional observance of forms. L16.

F. ATTERBURY Nor was his Attendance on Divine Offices a matter of Formality and Custom, but of Conscience.

†**4** The formal or essential nature of something; the defining characteristic, a formal category. L16–M18.

J. GOAD Motion is the Formality of Wind. JER. TAYLOR If it be propounded as evil, the will that chooses it under that formality is criminal.

5 The quality of being formal; precision of manners; stiffness of design. L16.

R. FRAME He bows. I'm rather taken aback by his courtly formality.

6 In *pl.* & *collect. sing.* Robes or insignia of office or dignity. *obsolete* exc. *hist.* L16. ▸†**b** Ceremonial or distinctive dress. L17–E18.
†**7** Outward form; the appearance or semblance (*of* something). E–M17.

MILTON Sacred things not perform'd sincerely . . are no way acceptable to God in their outward formality.

†**8** Method, regularity; uniform procedure. E–M17.
9 †**a** Ceremonious attention (paid to a person). E17–M18. ▸**b** A requirement of etiquette, regulation, or custom, (esp. with an implied lack of real significance). M17.

a R. KNOLLES Entertaining him with all the formalities that feigned friendship could deuise. **b** G. ORWELL The confession was a formality, though the torture was real.

10 Ceremony, elaborate procedure. M17.

S. PEPYS A great deal of do and formality in choosing of the Council and officers.

11 A formal or ceremonial act; a legal, authorized or customary procedure. L17.

E. HEMINGWAY We would have to be married under Italian law and the formalities were terrific.

formalize /ˈfɔːm(ə)lʌɪz/ *verb*. Also **-ise**. L16.
[ORIGIN from FORMAL *adjective* + -IZE, partly through French *formaliser*.]
†**1** *verb trans.* Impart or constitute the form or essence of. L16–L17.
†**2** *verb trans. & intrans.* (foll. by *upon*). Raise scrupulous objections (to); cavil (at). L16–L18.
†**3** *verb trans.* Cause to take sides, declare *oneself* for or against. L16–M17.
4 *verb trans.* Give a formal or definite shape to; state or establish formally. M17.

M. O. W. OLIPHANT The gates . . shut against him, did no more than formalize that sentence of banishment.

5 *verb intrans.* Act with formality; be formal or ceremonious. Now *rare*. M17.

J. HALES They turned . . their true Fasting into Formalizing and partial abstinence.

6 *verb trans.* Make formal; make ceremonious, precise, or rigid; give legal formality to (a document etc.); imbue with formalism. L18.

New York Times We have reached an agreement on the disability bill and we hope to have it formalized by Monday.

■ **formalizable** *adjective* able to be formalized M20.

formally /ˈfɔːm(ə)li/ *adverb*. LME.
[ORIGIN from FORMAL *adjective* + -LY[2].]
1 In formal respects; as regards form. LME.

F. BOWEN What is formally correct may be materially false.

†**2** According to logical form; according to the principles of art or science. LME–L16.
3 Explicitly, expressly. E16.

W. BLACKSTONE Perhaps in no instance it has ever been formally expressed at the first institution of a state.

4 In prescribed or customary form; with the formalities required to make an action valid or definite; in set form. M16.

W. RAEPER MacDonald accepted the invitation formally after being presented with the official documents.

†**5** Regularly; in the normal or usual manner; with exact correspondence. Only in 17.
6 With formality of manner, ceremoniously. E17.

A. MASSIE Willy addressed Colette formally as '*vous*' while she called him '*tu*'.

7 As a matter of form; as a formality. L19.

formamide /ˈfɔːməmʌɪd/ *noun*. M19.
[ORIGIN from FORMIC + AMIDE.]
CHEMISTRY. A colourless liquid amide, $HCONH_2$, derived from formic acid.

formant /ˈfɔːm(ə)nt/ *noun*. E20.
[ORIGIN German, from Latin *formant-* pres. ppl stem of *formare* FORM *verb*[1]: see -ANT[1].]
LINGUISTICS. **1** Orig., the characteristic tone of a vowel sound; now, any of several characteristic bands of resonance which together determine the sound quality of a vowel. E20.
2 A morpheme occurring only in combination in a word or word stem. M20.

forma pauperis /fɔːmə ˈpɔːpərɪs/ *noun phr.* L16.
[ORIGIN Latin, lit. 'the form of a poor person'.]
LAW (now *hist.*). (The condition of) a poor person, in respect of being able to bring a legal action without payment. Freq. in ***in forma pauperis***, ***sub forma pauperis***, as a poor person; *transf.* & *fig.* humbly, in supplication.

format /ˈfɔːmat/ *noun*. M19.
[ORIGIN French from German, from Latin *formatus* (*liber*) shaped (book) pa. pple of *formare* FORM *verb*[1].]
1 The physical characteristics of a book or other object, esp. the shape and size. M19.
2 A style or manner of arrangement or procedure. M20.

V. PACKARD The over-all format . . was: 'Basic pattern of 'good guys' versus 'bad men'.' *Which Computer?* Entering the date in the . . American format (month, day, year).

3 A defined structure for the processing, storage, or display of computer data. Also, the medium in which a sound recording is made available. **M20.**

Q A double album in its original vinyl format.

format /ˈfɔːmat/ *verb trans.* Infl. **-tt-**. **M20.**
[ORIGIN from the noun.]
Chiefly COMPUTING. Arrange or put into a format; impose a format on.

Times There are dot matrix printers . . which format each character as required. *QL User* The program formats a disk in such a fashion that equal amounts of storage are used for each record.

formate /ˈfɔːmeɪt/ *noun.* Also †**formiate**. **E19.**
[ORIGIN from FORMIC + -ATE¹.]
CHEMISTRY. A salt or ester of formic acid.

F

formate /fɔːˈmeɪt/ *verb intrans.* **E20.**
[ORIGIN Back-form. from FORMATION.]
Of an aircraft or pilot: take up formation *with*, fly in formation.

formation /fɔːˈmeɪʃ(ə)n/ *noun.* **LME.**
[ORIGIN Old French & mod. French, or Latin *formatio(n-)*, from *format-* pa. ppl stem of *formare* FORM *verb*¹: see -ATION.]
1 The action of forming, the process of being formed; creation, production. **LME.** ▸**b** The action or process of forming an accumulator plate, semiconductor device, etc. Cf. FORM *verb*¹ 1f. **L19.**

J. ROSENBERG The atmosphere at home played an even greater role in the formation of his character.

2 A thing formed. **M17.**
3 The arrangement of the parts of something; structure, conformation. **L18.** ▸**b** The disposition of fibres in a sheet of paper. **E20.**
4 Orig. MILITARY. A formal arrangement of persons or things (ships, aircraft, etc.) acting together as a unit. **L18.**

J. A. FROUDE The usual Roman formation in battle was in triple line.

in formation (of aircraft etc.) together, in a set pattern or configuration.
5 GEOLOGY. An assemblage of rocks or series of strata having some common characteristic. **E19.**
6 ECOLOGY. A mature community of plant species adapted to particular conditions. **L19.**
– COMB.: **formation dancing** a variety of (competitive) ballroom dancing in which a team of couples dances a prepared routine; **formation flying** flying in formation; **formation-rule** LOGIC each of a set of rules together specifying permissible combinations of signs in a given system.
■ **formational** *adjective* of or pertaining to a formation or formations **L19.** **formationally** *adverb* **L19.**

formative /ˈfɔːmətɪv/ *adjective & noun.* **L15.**
[ORIGIN Old French *formatif, -ive* or medieval Latin *formativus*, from *format-*: see FORMATION, -ATIVE.]
▸ **A** *adjective.* **1** Capable of forming or creating; serving to fashion. **L15.** ▸**b** Of or pertaining to formation; *spec.* (ARCHAEOLOGY, usu. **F-**) = PRECLASSIC. **M19.**

C. DARWIN The formative organs themselves are perfect in structure. **b** D. ARKELL The formative years of his life, between the ages of five and twelve. N. HORNBY I emerged from all these formative experiences completely unformed.

2 LINGUISTICS. Of an inflectional or derivative affix: used in forming words. **E18.**
3 Of tissue: capable of growth and development. **L19.**
▸ **B** *noun.* A formative element or agent. **M18.**

L. BLOOMFIELD Any unanalyzable word or formative is a morpheme. J. GALSWORTHY That essential formative of character, east wind.

■ **formatively** *adverb* **M17.** **formativeness** *noun* **M19.**

formatore /formaˈtoːre/ *noun.* Pl. **-ri** /-ri/. **M19.**
[ORIGIN Italian, agent noun from *formare* to form.]
A modeller in wax or plaster; a technical assistant who repairs or restores pottery, metalwork, etc.

forme *noun* see FORM *noun*.

†**forme** *adjective.*
[ORIGIN Old English *forma* = Old Frisian *forma*, Old Saxon *formo*, Gothic *fruma*, superl. from base of FORE *adverb*.]
1 Earliest or earliest in time or serial order; the first of two, former. **OE–LME.**
2 Foremost, first, in position, rank, etc. **ME–E16.**

formé, **formée** *adjectives* see FORMY.

formedon /ˈfɔːmɪdən/ *noun.* obsolete exc. *hist.* **L15.**
[ORIGIN Anglo-Norman from Anglo-Latin *forma doni*, *forma donationis* form of gift.]
LAW. A writ of right formerly used to claim entailed property.

formée, **formé** *adjectives* see FORMY.

former /ˈfɔːmə/ *noun*¹. **LME.**
[ORIGIN from FORM *verb*¹ + -ER¹.]
1 A person who forms something; a maker, a creator, a shaper. **LME.**

R. CUDWORTH The Framer and Former of the Vniverse.

2 A tool, mould, or other device used to form articles or shape material. **M17.** ▸**b** ELECTRICITY. A frame or core about which a coil is wound. **L19.** ▸**c** AERONAUTICS. A transverse member that strengthens and gives shape to a wing or fuselage. **E20.**

T. HOOPER The wax cups are prepared by dipping a wooden or glass former into molten beeswax.

†**former** *noun*². **M16–E18.**
[ORIGIN Old French *formoir* chisel (mod. *fermoir*): see -ER².]
A kind of chisel or gouge.

former /ˈfɔːmə/ *adjective & noun*³. **ME.**
[ORIGIN from FORME *adjective* + -ER³: cf. FOREMOST.]
▸ **A** *adjective.* **1** Orig., earlier in time. Now chiefly, of the past, belonging to or occurring in an earlier period. **ME.** ▸†**b** First, foremost. **LME–E16.** ▸**c** Previously owned, occupied, frequented, etc. **LME.** ▸**d** Designating a previous holder of an office etc.; sometime, ex-. Orig. *US.* **E20.**

B. MOORE The last thing . . I want is to reopen our disagreements of former days. **c** S. LEWIS From the Babbitts' former house had come two much-carved rocking chairs. **d** *Daily Telegraph* Former Army Major, Brian Hart, had sued for wrongful dismissal.

Former Prophets: see PROPHET.
†**2** At or towards the front. **LME–L17.**
3 The first or first mentioned of two (opp. ***latter***). **E17.**

A. WINCHELL The former locality . . has for many years been a favourite collecting-ground of geologists.

▸ **B** *noun.* *The* first or first mentioned of two people or things (opp. ***latter***). **L16.**

C. FORD The former may be made by several methods.

-former /ˈfɔːmə/ *suffix.* **M19.**
[ORIGIN from FORM *noun* + -ER¹.]
A member of a specified class or form in a school.

DENNIS POTTER The choice of grammar school sixth-formers would be Oxford or Cambridge first.

formeret /ˈfɔːm(ə)rɛt/ *noun.* **L19.**
[ORIGIN French, from *forme* FORM *noun*.]
ARCHITECTURE. A rib-moulding at the junction of a vault with the vertical wall; a wall rib.

formerly /ˈfɔːməli/ *adverb.* **L16.**
[ORIGIN from FORMER *adjective* + -LY².]
†**1** Before another or something else; first. **L16–M17.**
2 At some past time, in former days. **L16.**

E. WAUGH Now . . he found a naughty relish in what he had formerly shunned.

†**3** A short time ago, just now. **L16–M18.**

Formgeschichte /ˈfɔːmgəʃɪxtə/ *noun.* **E20.**
[ORIGIN German, from *Form* form + *Geschichte* history.]
= ***form criticism*** s.v. FORM *noun*.

†**formiate** *noun* var. of FORMATE *noun*.

formic /ˈfɔːmɪk/ *adjective.* **L18.**
[ORIGIN formed as FORMICA *noun*¹: see -IC.]
1 CHEMISTRY. ***formic acid***, a colourless irritant volatile liquid carboxylic acid, HCOOH, produced by various insects (esp. ants) and plants, and used in tanning and dyeing; methanoic acid. **L18.**
2 Of or pertaining to ants. *rare.* **E19.**

formica /fɔːˈmʌɪkə/ *noun*¹. **LME.**
[ORIGIN Latin = ant.]
†**1** A disease characterized by small pustules and a burning and itching of the skin. **LME–M16.**
2 An ulcer, abscess, or excrescence, occurring esp. in a hawk's bill or a dog's ears. **E17.**
3 An ant. Now only as mod. Latin genus name. **M19.**

Formica /fɔːˈmʌɪkə/ *noun*². Also **f-**. **E20.**
[ORIGIN Unknown.]
(Proprietary name for) a hard, durable plastic laminate used esp. as a decorative heat-resistant surfacing material.

formicarioid /fɔːmɪˈkɛːrɪɔɪd/ *adjective & noun.* Also **-caroid** /-ˈkɛːrɔɪd/, **-cariid** /-ˈkɛːrɪɪd/. **L19.**
[ORIGIN from mod. Latin *Formicarius* genus name from medieval Latin *formicarium*: see FORMICARY, -OID.]
ORNITHOLOGY. Of or pertaining to, a bird of, the large neotropical passerine family Formicariidae, comprising the insectivorous antbirds.

formicary /ˈfɔːmɪk(ə)ri/ *noun.* **E19.**
[ORIGIN medieval Latin *formicarium*, formed as FORMICA *noun*¹: see -ARY¹.]
An ants' nest; an anthill.

formicate /ˈfɔːmɪkeɪt/ *verb intrans. rare.* **L17.**
[ORIGIN Latin *formicat-* pa. ppl stem of *formicare* crawl like an ant (said of the pulse or skin), from *formica* ant: see -ATE³.]
Crawl like an ant; crawl (as if) *with* ants.

J. R. LOWELL An open space, which formicated with peasantry.

formication /fɔːmɪˈkeɪʃ(ə)n/ *noun.* **E18.**
[ORIGIN Latin *formicatio(n-)*, formed as FORMICATE: see -ATION.]
Chiefly MEDICINE. A sensation as of insects crawling over or under the skin.

formicid /ˈfɔːmɪsɪd/ *adjective & noun.* **L19.**
[ORIGIN mod. Latin *Formicidae* (see below), from *formica* ant: see -ID³.]
ENTOMOLOGY. (Of, pertaining to, or designating) an insect of the hymenopteran family Formicidae, which comprises the ants.

formicine /ˈfɔːmɪsʌɪn/ *adjective.* **L19.**
[ORIGIN Latin *formicinus*, from *formica* ant: see -INE¹.]
Of or pertaining to ants; *spec.* designating ants (related to and resembling those) of the genus *Formica*.

formidable /ˈfɔːmɪdəb(ə)l, fɔːˈmɪd-/ *adjective.* **LME.**
[ORIGIN French, or Latin *formidabilis*, from *formidare* to fear: see -ABLE.]
To be dreaded or viewed with respect; likely to be hard to overcome, resist, or deal with.

J. S. HUXLEY Giant nettles with a formidable sting. A. STORR A formidable lady, rich, beautiful, energetic and self-willed.

■ **formidaˈbility** *noun* **M18.** **formidableness** *noun* **M17.** **formidably** *adverb* **L17.**

†**formidolous** *adjective. rare.* **M17–L18.**
[ORIGIN from Latin *formidolosus* causing or feeling dread, from *formido* dread: see -OUS.]
Causing fear, terrible; feeling fear, timorous.

forming /ˈfɔːmɪŋ/ *verbal noun.* **LME.**
[ORIGIN from FORM *verb*¹ + -ING¹.]
1 The action of FORM *verb*¹; the fact or process of being formed. **LME.**
2 ELECTRICITY. = FORMATION 1b. Cf. FORM *verb*¹ 1f. **E20.**

formol /ˈfɔːmɒl/ *noun.* **L19.**
[ORIGIN from FORMALDEHYDE + -OL.]
= FORMALIN.
■ **formolize** *verb trans.* = FORMALINIZE **M20.**

Formosan /fɔːˈməʊs(ə)n/ *adjective & noun. hist.* **M17.**
[ORIGIN from *Formosa*, former (orig. Portuguese) name of Taiwan, from Latin *formosa* (sc. *insula* island) fem. of *formosus* beautiful: see -AN.]
▸ **A** *adjective.* Of or pertaining to Formosa (now Taiwan), a large island off the SE coast of China. **M17.**
▸ **B** *noun.* A native or inhabitant of Formosa; the language of Formosa, a dialect of Chinese. **E18.**

formose /ˈfɔːməʊs, -z/ *noun.* **L19.**
[ORIGIN from FORMALDEHYDE + -OSE².]
CHEMISTRY. A mixture of hexose sugars formed from formaldehyde by a condensation reaction in the presence of weak alkali.

formosity /fɔːˈmɒsɪti/ *noun.* Now *rare* or *obsolete.* **LME.**
[ORIGIN Old French *formosité* from Latin *formositat-*, from *formosus* beautiful, from *forma* FORM *noun*: see -ITY.]
Beauty; a beautiful thing.

formula /ˈfɔːmjʊlə/ *noun.* Pl. **-lae** /-liː/, **-las**. **E17.**
[ORIGIN Latin, dim. of *forma* FORM *noun*: see -ULE.]
1 A set form of words prescribed by authority or custom for use on ceremonial or social occasions; also (freq. *derog.*), a rule unintelligently or slavishly followed, a traditional or conventional belief or established method. **E17.** ▸**b** A set form of words as a definition or an enunciation of a principle or (religious) doctrine; *esp.* a statement or method intended to reconcile different aims or opinions. **E18.** ▸**c** LITERARY CRITICISM. A stock epithet, phrase, or line, repeated for various effects in literary composition, esp. epic poetry. **L19.**

K. CLARK All art is to some degree symbolic and recognition depends on certain long accepted formulae. D. MACDONALD The formula for a best seller now includes a minimum of 'outspoken' descriptions of sexual activities. C. V. WEDGWOOD The executioner did not go through the usual formula of asking for, and receiving the forgiveness of his victim. **b** H. H. WILSON Forcing the Brahmins . . to repeat the Mohammedan formula of faith. P. G. WODEHOUSE It was plain that this girl and he were poles apart and could never hope to find a formula. **c** *transf.*: E. M. FORSTER He enters crying 'Revenge!' or 'My heart bleeds for humanity!' or whatever his formula is.

2 A prescription; a list of ingredients, a recipe; *N. Amer.* baby food made up from a recipe. **E18.**

T. MORRISON She was a wet-nurse . . and made her living from white babies. Then formula came and she almost starve to death.

3 a MATH. & PHYSICS etc. A general rule, principle, or relationship expressed in symbols, often as an equation. **L18.** ▸**b** CHEMISTRY. An expression of the atomic constituents of a compound by means of symbols and figures. **M19.** ▸**c** In general scientific use, a group of symbols or figures condensing a set of facts. **M19.**
b *empirical formula*: see EMPIRICAL. **c *dental formula***: see DENTAL *adjective*. ***floral formula***: see FLORAL *adjective*.
4 MOTOR RACING. The class or specification of a racing car, usu. expressed in terms of engine capacity. **E20.**
Formula One (proprietary name for) an international form of motor racing, whose races are called Grands Prix.

formulable /ˈfɔːmjʊləb(ə)l/ *adjective.* **L19.**
[ORIGIN from FORMUL(ATE + -ABLE.]
Able to be formulated.

formulae *noun pl.* see FORMULA.

formulaic /fɔːmjʊˈleɪɪk/ *adjective*. L19.
[ORIGIN from FORMULA + -IC.]
Of the nature of a formula.
■ **formuˈlaically** *adverb* M20.

formular /ˈfɔːmjʊlə/ *noun*. Long *rare*. LME.
[ORIGIN formed as FORMULARY *noun*: see -AR[2].]
= FORMULARY *noun*.

formular /ˈfɔːmjʊlə/ *adjective*. *rare*. L18.
[ORIGIN from FORMULA + -AR[2].]
1 Formal, correct in form. L18.
2 = FORMULARY *adjective*. L19.
■ **formularize** *verb trans*. = FORMULATE M19. **formulariˈzation** *noun* the action or an act of formularizing L19.

formularism /ˈfɔːmjʊlərɪz(ə)m/ *noun*. E20.
[ORIGIN from FORMULARY *noun* + -ISM.]
Rigid adherence to or dependence on formularies.
■ **formularist** *noun* L19.

formulary /ˈfɔːmjʊləri/ *noun*. M16.
[ORIGIN French *formulaire* or medieval Latin *formularius* (*liber* book), formed as FORMULA: see -ARY[1].]
1 A collection or system of formulae; a document or book containing the set or prescribed form or forms, esp. of religious belief or ritual; *gen*. a formula. M16.
2 PHARMACOLOGY. A listing of medicinal drugs with their uses, methods of administration, etc. E19.

formulary /ˈfɔːmjʊləri/ *adjective*. E18.
[ORIGIN from FORMULA + -ARY[1].]
Of the nature of a formula; of or pertaining to a formula or formulae; using formulae.

formulate /ˈfɔːmjʊleɪt/ *verb trans*. M19.
[ORIGIN from FORMULA + -ATE[3], after Old French & mod. French *formuler* from medieval Latin *formulare*, formed as FORMULA.]
Reduce to or express (as) in a formula; express in a concise or systematic way.

H. ARENDT Romantic intellectuals who had formulated the main tenets of a conservative ideology.

■ **formuˈlation** *noun* (*a*) the action of formulating; (*b*) a material or mixture prepared according to a particular formula: L19. **formulator** *noun* E20.

formule /ˈfɔːm(j)uːl/ *noun*. *rare*. L17.
[ORIGIN Old French & mod. French from Latin FORMULA.]
= FORMULA.

formulise *verb* var. of FORMULIZE.

formulism /ˈfɔːmjʊlɪz(ə)m/ *noun*. M19.
[ORIGIN from FORMULA + -ISM.]
Adherence to or dependence on conventional formulas.
■ **formulist** *noun* M19.

formulize /ˈfɔːmjʊlʌɪz/ *verb trans*. Also **-ise**. M19.
[ORIGIN from FORMULA + -IZE.]
Formulate; construct a formula for.
■ **formuliˈzation** *noun* M19.

formy /ˈfɔːmi/ *adjective*. Also (earlier) **-é**, **-ée**. LME.
[ORIGIN French *formé* pa. ppl adjective of *former* FORM *verb*[1].]
HERALDRY. Of a cross: = PATTÉE.

formyl /ˈfɔːmʌɪl, -mɪl/ *noun*. M19.
[ORIGIN from FORMIC + -YL.]
CHEMISTRY. The radical ·CHO. Usu. in *comb*.
■ **formylate** *verb trans*. introduce one or more formyl groups into (a compound or molecule) by chemical reaction M20. **formyˈlation** *noun* M20.

Fornax /ˈfɔːnaks/ *noun*. E19.
[ORIGIN Latin *fornax* FURNACE *noun*.]
Orig. †*Fornax Chemica*. (The name of) a small inconspicuous constellation of the southern hemisphere, south-west of Cetus; the Furnace.

fornent /fɔːˈnɛnt, fə-/ *preposition*. *Scot., Irish, & N. English*. Also **-nst** /-nst/. LME.
[ORIGIN from FORE *adverb* + ANENT.]
1 Opposite to, facing; alongside. LME.

SIR W. SCOTT King Ahasuerus . . sate upon his royal throne fornent the gate of his house.

2 With regard to, concerning. LME.

fornicate /ˈfɔːnɪkət/ *adjective*. E19.
[ORIGIN Latin *fornicatus* vaulted, arched, formed as FORNIX: see FORNICATE *verb*, -ATE[2].]
Arched, bending over.

fornicate /ˈfɔːnɪkeɪt/ *verb intrans*. M16.
[ORIGIN ecclesiastical Latin *fornicat-* pa. ppl stem of *fornicari*, from Latin FORNIX, *fornic-* brothel, (orig.) arch, vaulted chamber: see -ATE[3].]
Commit or indulge in fornication.

fornication /fɔːnɪˈkeɪʃ(ə)n/ *noun*[1]. ME.
[ORIGIN Old French & mod. French from ecclesiastical Latin *fornicatio(n-)*, formed as FORNICATE *verb*: see -ATION.]
1 Voluntary sexual intercourse between esp. unmarried persons; (esp. in biblical use) adultery. ME.

R. GRAVES Unjust that our mistress, . . a married woman, should commit adultery and yet unmercifully whip her for mere fornication.

2 *fig*. Idolatry. ME.

fornication /fɔːnɪˈkeɪʃ(ə)n/ *noun*[2]. *rare*. E18.
[ORIGIN Latin *fornicatio(n-)*, formed as FORNICATE *adjective*: see -ATION.]
ARCHITECTURE. An arching, a vaulting.

fornicator /ˈfɔːnɪkeɪtə/ *noun*. LME.
[ORIGIN Late Latin, from *fornicatio(n-)*: see FORNICATION *noun*[1], -OR.]
A person who commits or indulges in fornication.
■ **fornicatress** *noun* = FORNICATRIX L16.

fornicatrix /ˈfɔːnɪkeɪtrɪks/ *noun*. Pl. **-trices** /-trɪsiːz/, **-trixes**. L16.
[ORIGIN Late Latin, fem. of FORNICATOR: see FORNICATOR, -TRIX.]
A woman who commits or indulges in fornication.

J. UPDIKE The hero throws Jo, the third of his willing fornicatrices, onto the bed full of guests' wraps.

fornix /ˈfɔːnɪks/ *noun*. Pl. **-nices** /-nɪsiːz/. L17.
[ORIGIN Latin = arch, vaulted chamber.]
A thing resembling an arch. Chiefly ANATOMY, an arched organ or structure; *spec*. (*a*) (more fully ***fornix cerebri*** /ˈsɛrɪbrʌɪ/) a band of white fibres at the base of the brain; (*b*) any of the uppermost recesses of the vagina.

forold /fɔːrˈəʊld, fər-/ *verb intrans*. Long *dial*.
[ORIGIN Old English *forealdian*, from FOR-[1] + *ealdian* grow old, from *eald* OLD *adjective*. Cf. Old High German *faralten* (German *veralten*).]
Grow old, wear out with age. Now only as ***forolded*** *ppl adjective*.

†**forpass** *verb*. LME.
[ORIGIN Old French *fo(u)rpasser*, from *fors* FOR-[2] + *passer* PASS *verb*.]
1 *verb trans*. Surpass, excel; *rare* exceed (a time limit). LME–E17.
2 *verb intrans*. Pass beyond; *rare* go past, pass. L15–L16.

SPENSER One day as hee forpassed by the plaine With weary pace.

forpet /ˈfɔːpɪt, -pɛt/ *noun*. *Scot. & N. English*. Also **-pit** /-pɪt/. M17.
[ORIGIN Alt. of *fourth part*.]
A quarter of a peck.

forpine /fɔːˈpʌɪn, fə-/ *verb trans*. & (*rare*) *intrans*. *arch*. ME.
[ORIGIN from FOR-[1] + PINE *verb*.]
(Cause to) pine or waste away; torture.

forpit *noun* var. of FORPET.

forprise /fɔːˈprʌɪz, fə-/ *verb trans*. Now *rare*. Also **fore-**, **-prize**. LME.
[ORIGIN Anglo-Norman *forpris(e)* pa. pple of *for(s)prendre* to except, from *for(s-* FOR-[2] + *prendre* take.]
Chiefly LAW. Take out, except, exempt.

forrader *adjective & adverb* see FORWARDER *adjective & adverb*.

forrel *noun & verb* var. of FOREL.

†**forridden** *adjective*. E16–E19.
[ORIGIN from FOR-[1] + *ridden* pa. pple of RIDE *verb*.]
Exhausted by (excessive) riding.

forrit /ˈfɒrɪt/ *adverb*. *Scot. & N. English*. E18.
[ORIGIN Alt. of FORWARD *adverb*.]
Forward(s), ahead.

†**forsado** *noun*. Pl. **-os**. E17–M18.
[ORIGIN Spanish *forçado* (now *forzado*). Cf. FORSARY.]
A galley slave.

forsake /fəˈseɪk/ *verb trans*. Pa. t. **-sook** /-ˈsʊk/; pa. pple **-saken** /-ˈseɪk(ə)n/.
[ORIGIN Old English *forsacan* = Old Saxon *forsakan* (Dutch *verzaken*), Old High German *firsahhan*, from West Germanic, from base of FOR-[1] + Old English *sacan* quarrel, accuse: see SAKE *noun*[1].]
†**1** Decline or refuse (something offered, *to do*). OE–E17. ▸**b** Avoid, shun, refuse to undertake or have to do with. ME–L16. ▸**c** Deny (an accusation, oneself, etc.); deny or renounce allegiance to (God, a lord, etc.). ME–L16.
2 Give up, surrender, (esp. something valued). Passing into sense 3. OE. ▸**b** Break off from or renounce (a task, plan, doctrine, or belief, or (esp.) a sin). Formerly also with inf. as obj. ME.

SHAKES. *Lucr.* And for himself himself he must forsake. **b** J. T. FOWLER The southern Picts . . had forsaken idolatry.

3 Abandon, withdraw from; *esp*. withdraw one's help, friendship, or companionship from, desert. ME.

G. ORWELL His nerve so forsook him that he began shouting for mercy even before the beating began. B. PYM It was as if a monk should forsake his cloister to embrace the riches of the world.

■ **forsaken** *ppl adjective* deserted, left solitary or desolate LME. **forsakenly** *adverb* L16. **forsakenness** /-n-n-/ *noun* E17. **forsaker** *noun* LME.

†**forsary** *noun*. M16–E18.
[ORIGIN French †*forsaire*, *-çaire* (now *forçat*). Cf. FORSADO.]
A galley slave.

forset /fəˈsɛt/ *verb trans*. Now *dial*. Infl. **-tt-**. Pa. t. & pple **-set**.
[ORIGIN Old English *forsettan*, formed as FOR-[1] + SET *verb*[1]: = Middle High German *versetzen*.]
Beset; bar (a way); waylay, entrap, (a person).

forshape /fəˈʃeɪp/ *verb trans*. Long *rare* or *obsolete*. OE.
[ORIGIN from FOR-[1] + SHAPE *verb*.]
Transform; *rare* disfigure.

†**forslack** *verb*. Also **fore-**. ME.
[ORIGIN from FOR-[1] + SLACK *verb*.]
1 *verb intrans*. Slacken. *rare*. ME–L16.
2 *verb trans*. Be slack in, neglect; lose or spoil by slackness or delay. L16–M17.

forslow /fəˈsləʊ/ *verb*. *arch*. Also **fore-**. OE.
[ORIGIN formed as FOR-[1] + *slāwian* be slow, from *slāw* SLOW *adjective*.]
1 *verb trans*. Be slow about; lose or spoil by sloth; delay, neglect. OE.

W. HUBBARD They were resolved to foreslow no opportunity.

2 *verb trans*. Hinder, obstruct. L16.

R. C. SINGLETON What delay foreslows the laggard nights.

†**3** *verb intrans*. Be slow or dilatory. Only in L16.

SHAKES. *3 Hen. VI* Forslow no longer; make we hence amain.

■ **forsook** *verb* pa. t. of FORSAKE.

forsooth /fəˈsuːθ/ *adverb*. *arch., iron.*, or *derog*.
[ORIGIN Old English *forsōþ*: see FOR *preposition*, SOOTH *noun*.]
In truth, indeed; truly.

forspeak /fɔːˈspiːk, fə-/ *verb trans*. Also **fore-**. Pa. t. **-spoke** /-ˈspəʊk/; pa. pple **-spoken** /-ˈspəʊkən/. OE.
[ORIGIN from FOR-[1] + SPEAK *verb*.]
†**1** Deny. Only in OE.
†**2** Renounce; *rare* forbid. OE–L16.
†**3** Speak against, speak ill of. LME–E17.

SHAKES. *Ant. & Cl.* Thou hast forspoke my being in these wars, And say'st it is not fit.

4 Bewitch or charm, esp. by excessive praising. Now only *Scot*. LME.

SIR W. SCOTT To obviate the risque of forspeaking . . add some little ejaculation expressive of deference to heaven or fortune.

■ **forspeaker** *noun* (now only *Scot*.) a witch, an enchanter LME.

forspend /fəˈspɛnd/ *verb trans*. Also **fore-**. Pa. t. & pple **-spent** /-ˈspɛnt/. OE.
[ORIGIN from FOR-[1] + SPEND *verb*.]
†**1** Spend, squander. OE–ME.
2 Exhaust, tire out. Chiefly as ***forspent*** *ppl adjective*. L16.

forspoke, **forspoken** *verbs* see FORSPEAK.

†**forstand** *verb trans*. Pa. t. & pple **-stood**. OE.
[ORIGIN from FOR-[1] + STAND *verb*.]
1 Oppose, withstand. OE–E18.
2 [Cf. German *verstehen*.] Understand. OE–L19.

forsterite /ˈfɔːstərʌɪt/ *noun*. E19.
[ORIGIN from J. R. *Forster* (1729–98), German naturalist + -ITE[1].]
MINERALOGY. An orthorhombic magnesium silicate mineral of the olivine group forming white, yellow, or green crystals.

Forstner bit /ˈfɔːstnə bɪt/ *noun phr*. E20.
[ORIGIN Benjamin *Forstner* (1834–97), inventor.]
A type of wood-drilling bit.

†**forstood** *verb pa. t. & pple* of FORSTAND.

forswear /fɔːˈswɛː, fə-/ *verb*. Pa. t. **-swore** /-ˈswɔː/; pa. pple **-sworn** /-ˈswɔːn/. OE.
[ORIGIN from FOR-[1] + SWEAR *verb*.]
1 *verb trans*. Renounce or abandon on oath, abjure, (a cause, one's country, *to do*, etc.). OE.

ANTHONY SMITH The kind of self-denial which forswears virtually every sort of proven aid.

2 *verb intrans. & trans*. (*refl.* & in *pass.*). Swear falsely, commit perjury. OE.

J. S. BLACKIE I have sworn to obey the laws, and I cannot forswear myself.

3 *verb trans*. †**a** Swear by (a thing) falsely or profanely. Only in ME. ▸**b** *verb trans*. Swear (something) falsely; break, forsake, or go back on (an oath, sworn allegiance, etc.). *arch*. L16.
4 *verb trans*. Deny or repudiate on oath or with strong protestation. LME.
■ **forswearer** *noun* a perjurer LME. **forsworn** *ppl adjective* perjured OE. **forswornness** /-n-n-/ *noun* (*rare*) OE.

forsythia /fɔːˈsʌɪθɪə, fə-/ *noun*. M19.
[ORIGIN mod. Latin (see below), from William *Forsyth* (1737–1804), English botanist: see -IA[1].]
Any of various chiefly Chinese shrubs of the genus *Forsythia*, of the olive family, grown for their yellow bell-shaped flowers which appear in spring before the leaves.

fort /fɔːt/ *noun*. LME.
[ORIGIN Old French & mod. French, or Italian *forte*, use as noun of *fort*, *forte* strong: see FORT *adjective*.]
▸ **I 1** MILITARY. A building or place fortified for defensive or protective purposes, usu. surrounded with a ditch, rampart, and parapet, and garrisoned with soldiers; *fig*. a strong position, a stronghold. LME.
hold the fort act as temporary substitute, cope with an emergency.
2 *hist*. A trading station (orig. fortified). *N. Amer*. L18.
▸ **II** See FORTE *noun*[1].

†**fort** *adjective*. LME–L18.
[ORIGIN Old French & mod. French from Latin *fortis* strong.]
Strong, powerful.

F

fort /fɔːt/ *verb*. Chiefly *US*. M16.
[ORIGIN from the noun.]
1 *verb trans.* Defend or protect (a place) with a fortification; enclose or station (people) in or *in* a fort. M16.
2 *verb intrans.* Build a fort or a fortification. E18.

fortalice /ˈfɔːtəlɪs/ *noun*. Also †**fortilage**. LME.
[ORIGIN medieval Latin *fortalitia*, *-itium*, from Latin *fortis* strong.]
Orig., a fortress. Now chiefly, a small fort or outwork of fortification.

forte /ˈfɔːteɪ, ˈfɔːti, fɔːt/ *noun*¹. Orig. †**fort**. M17.
[ORIGIN French *fort*, use as noun of *fort* (see FORT *noun*); the French fem. form was substituted for the masc. in English, as in *locale*, *morale*. Pronunc. latterly infl. by FORTE *adverb, adjective, & noun*².]
1 FENCING. The stronger part of a sword blade, from the hilt to the middle. Cf. FEEBLE *noun* 2, FOIBLE *noun* 1. M17.
2 The strong point of a person; the thing in which one excels. L17.
W. TREVOR He, as though repetition were his forte, repeated the words.

F

forte /ˈfɔːti/ *adverb, adjective, & noun*². E18.
[ORIGIN Italian = strong, loud, from Latin *fortis* strong.]
MUSIC. ▶**A** *adverb & adjective*. A direction: loud(ly). (Abbreviation *f.*) E18.
forte forte very loudly; abbreviation *ff*. ***mezzo forte***: see MEZZO *adverb*.
▶**B** *noun*. A loud tone or passage. M18.

Fortean /ˈfɔːtɪən/ *noun & adjective*. M20.
[ORIGIN from the name of Charles H. *Fort* (1874–1932), US journalist and student of paranormal phenomena + -EAN.]
▶**A** *noun*. A follower of Charles Fort; an investigator of paranormal phenomena. M20.
▶**B** *adjective*. Of, relating to, or designating paranormal phenomena. L20.
■ **Forteˈana** *pl. noun* such phenomena collectively L20.

fortepiano /ˌfɔːtɪpɪˈanəʊ/ *noun, adverb, & adjective*. M18.
[ORIGIN Italian: see FORTE *adverb & adjective* and PIANO *adverb & adjective*.]
MUSIC. ▶**A** *noun*. Pl. **-os**. An early form of the pianoforte. M18.
▶**B** *adverb & adjective*. (**forte piano**.) A direction: loud(ly) and then immediately soft(ly). (Abbreviation *fp.*) L19.

fortes *noun pl.* see FORTIS.

Fortescue /ˈfɔːtɪskjuː/ *noun*. *Austral.* Also **f-**. L19.
[ORIGIN Perh. from FORTY + SKEWER (with ref. to the abundant spines of the fish), alt. after the surname *Fortescue*.]
A small scorpionfish, *Centropogon australis*, having poisonous spines.

forth /fɔːθ/ *adverb, preposition, & noun*.
[ORIGIN Old English *forþ* = Old Saxon *forþ*, Old Frisian *forth* (Dutch *voort*), Middle High German *vort* (German *fort*), from Germanic (repr. by Gothic *faurþis* further), from Indo-European base repr. by FORE-.]
▶**A** *adverb*. **1** Of movement or direction: forwards, onwards. Formerly also used ellipt.: go forwards. *obsolete* exc. in ***back and forth*** s.v. BACK *adverb*. OE.
2 Forward, into view. Only with such verbs as ***bring forth***, ***come forth***, ***show forth***, etc. Formerly also with certain verbs where *out* is now used, as ***lay forth***, ***single forth***. OE. ▸†**b** Used ellipt.: go or come forward, into view; come out *with*, utter. LME–M16.
E. BOWEN Forth into the midst stepped Hermione. A. CARTER Blackened statues stretched their arms forth, as if attempting to flee the fire.
3 Of movement: away or out from a place of origin, (temporary) residence, or confinement. Formerly also with certain verbs where *out* is now used, as ***lend forth***, ***lock forth***. OE. ▸**b** Used ellipt.: go away or out from. *arch.* ME. ▸†**c** Of position: away; abroad; not at home. ME–E17.
I. MURDOCH The hilarious excitement which Christian had been holding in check throughout our interview burst wildly forth. R. GRAVES The seven years' curse is ended now That drove me forth from this kind land. **c** SHAKES. *Com. Err.* Say he dines forth, and let no creature enter.
4 Of extent in time: onwards, following immediately and continuously on from a specified point in time. *arch.* OE. ▸†**b** Of action: continuously, persistently. OE–E19.
AV *Ps.* 113:2 Blessed be the name of the Lord: from this time forth. **b** SIR W. SCOTT Now, men of death, work forth your will.
†**5** Of extent in space: onwards from a specified point or place, continuously in one direction without deviation. OE–M16.
COVERDALE *Ezek.* 6:14 From the wildernesse off Deblat forth.
†**6** At or to an advanced point in time, position, or progress. ME–L15.
– PHRASES: ***and so forth***: see SO *adverb, conjunction, & adjective*. **forth of** (now only *poet.*) out of. †**forth with** along with, at the same time as. ***hold forth***: see HOLD *verb*.
▶**B** *preposition*. †**1** Forward, up to, to the extent of (chiefly with *even*). Also in conjunction phr. ***forth that***: until. OE–LME.
2 Out or away from; (from) out of. Now *rare*. M16.
H. F. CARY Never fire, With so swift motion, forth a stormy cloud, Leap'd downward.
▶†**C** *noun*. Free course. *rare* exc. in ***have one's forth***, have outlet, have free course. LME–E17.

forth- /fɔːθ/ *combining form*. OE.
[ORIGIN from FORTH *adverb*.]
Forming ppl adjectives (rarely verbs) and nouns of action and (*rare*) agent, as ***forthgoing***, ***forthspeaker***, ***forthtell***, etc.
†**forthbring** *verb trans.* (*a*) bear (offspring, fruit); (*b*) bring forward; utter. **forthˈbringing** *verbal noun* (*a*) the action of *forthbring verb* above; (*b*) *esp.* the carrying forth of a body for burial. **forthˈfare** *verb intrans.* †(*a*) die; (*b*) go away, depart. †**forthgo** *verb intrans.* (*a*) go forth, depart; (*b*) come forth, proceed. **forthˈgoing** *noun & adjective* (*a*) *noun* a going forth, a departure; (*b*) *adjective* that goes forth; *esp.* enthusiastic. **forthˈputting** *noun* (*a*) the action of putting forth; (*b*) *US* obtrusive behaviour. **forthˈputting** *adjective* (now chiefly *US*) forward, obtrusive. †**forthset** *verb trans.* set forth, display. **forthˈsetting** *noun* a display, an exhibition.

for that /fɔː ˈðat/ *conjunction*. *arch.* LOE.
[ORIGIN See FOR *preposition* 17, THAT *conjunction*.]
1 For the reason that, because. LOE.
SHAKES. *Merry W.* For that I love your daughter.. I must advance the colours of my love.
†**2** For the purpose that; in order that. LOE–L16.

forthcome /fɔːθˈkʌm/ *verb & ppl adjective*. Now *rare*. OE.
[ORIGIN Orig. from FORTH- + COME *verb*. In mod. use verb back-form. from the pa. ppl adjective.]
▶**A** *verb intrans.* Pa. t. **-came** /-ˈkeɪm/, pa. pple **-come**. Come forth. OE.
▶**B** *ppl adjective*. That has come forth or been issued. E19.
■ **forthcomer** *noun* E19.

forthcoming /fɔːθˈkʌmɪŋ/ *verbal noun*. In sense 2 also **furthcoming**. M16.
[ORIGIN from FORTH- + COMING *noun*.]
1 A coming forward or out. Formerly *esp.* an appearance in court. M16.
2 SCOTS LAW. An action brought by the arrester of property in order to make the proceeds of arrestment available. M17.

forthcoming /fɔːθˈkʌmɪŋ, *esp. attrib.* ˈfɔːθkʌmɪŋ/ *ppl adjective*. L15.
[ORIGIN from FORTH- + COMING *adjective*.]
1 About or likely to come forth or appear; approaching (in time); (ready to be) produced when wanted, at one's disposal. L15.
H. KISSINGER I informed his Cabinet members that a final decision would be forthcoming within twenty-four hours. P. FULLER My reflections on these two great thinkers will be expanded.. in a forthcoming book.
2 Of a person: ready to make or meet advances; responsive, informative. M19.
Punch The War Minister.. was not very forthcoming on the question of dive bombers.
■ **forthcomingness** *noun* E19.

forthink /fɔːˈθɪŋk, fə-/ *verb*¹. Long chiefly *Scot.* Also **fore-**. Pa. t. & pple **-thought** /-ˈθɔːt/.
[ORIGIN Old English *forþencan* (from FOR-¹ + *þencan* THINK *verb*²) = Old High German *fordenchen* (German *verdenken*).]
†**1** *verb trans.* Despise, distrust. Only in OE.
†**2** *verb refl. & intrans.* Repent (*of*), be sorry (*for*, *that*, *to do*). ME–M17.
G. WHETSTONE Forthinke of thy forepassed faultes. W. WARNER Wel may I fore think mee so to haue done.
3 *verb trans.* Think of with pain or regret; repent of, be sorry for. ME.
R. BOLT If you will even now forthink and repent of your obstinate opinions, you may still taste his gracious pardon.

†**forthink** *verb*². Pa. t. & pple **-thought**. ME.
[ORIGIN from FOR-¹ + THINK *verb*¹.]
1 *verb trans.* Displease, cause regret to. ME–M16.
2 *verb trans.* Cause regret or repentance in (a person). Foll. by *of*, *for*, *that*. ME–L16.
A. KING It forthinkes me sore that I haue sinned.

†**forth on** *adverb*. Also **forthon** OE.
[ORIGIN from FORTH *adverb* + ON *adverb*.]
1 Straight away, forthwith. OE–ME.
2 Of time or space: onwards, forwards. L15–E17.
A. GOLDING From the beginning foorthon, Moyses and the Prophets gaue it you. SHAKES. *Timon* My free drift.. flies an eagle flight.. forth on.

forthought *verb pa. t. & pple*: see FORTHINK *verb*¹, *verb*².

forthright /ˈfɔːθrʌɪt, fɔːθˈrʌɪt/ *adverb, adjective, & noun*. OE.
[ORIGIN from FORTH *adverb* + -RIGHT.]
▶**A** *adverb*. **1** Straight forward, in a direct manner. OE.
KEATS Until impatient in embarrassment he forthright pass'd.
2 Straight away, immediately. ME.
SPENSER Whose dore forthright To him did open as it had beene taught.
▶**B** *adjective*. **1** Proceeding in a straight course. *arch.* OE.
R. L. STEVENSON A headlong, forth-right tide.
2 Straightforward, outspoken; decisive, unhesitating; unswerving. M19.
J. A. MICHENER He was an attractive man, forthright and generous in his impulses. M. FORSTER She was forthright and daring and could not stand artifice of any kind.
▶**C** *noun*. A straight course. E17.
SHAKES. *Temp.* Here's a maze trod, indeed, through forth-rights and meanders!
■ **forthrightly** *adverb* M20. **forthrightness** *noun* straightforwardness L19.

forthward /ˈfɔːθwəd/ *adverb & adjective*. *arch.*
[ORIGIN Old English *forþweard*, from FORTH *adverb* + -WARD. Cf. FORWARD *adverb, adjective, & noun*.]
▶**A** *adverb*. †**1** Continually. Only in OE.
2 From a specified time onwards, hereafter. ME.
3 Forward, onward, ahead; out, away (from a place). ME.
▶**B** *adjective*. = FORWARD *adjective*. *rare*. L15.

forthwith /fɔːθˈwɪθ, -ð/ *adverb*. ME.
[ORIGIN Partly abbreviation of FORTHWITHAL, but partly from *forth with* s.v. FORTH *adverb*, used absol.]
†**1** Along with, at the same time. Only in ME.
2 Immediately, at once, without delay. LME.
R. COBB She would write forthwith to my parents and let them know how I had behaved.

†**forthwithal** *adverb*. ME–M16.
[ORIGIN from FORTH *adverb* + WITH *preposition* + ALL *pronoun*. Cf. WITHAL.]
= FORTHWITH 2.

†**for-thy** *conjunction*. OE–M19.
[ORIGIN Old English *forþi*, *forþȳ*, from FOR *preposition* + *þȳ*, instr. of THE: see THE *adverb*.]
For this reason, therefore.

fortieth /ˈfɔːtɪɪθ/ *adjective & noun* (*ordinal numeral*).
[ORIGIN Old English *fēowertigoþa*, formed as FORTY + -TH².]
▶**A** *adjective*. Next in order after the thirty-ninth; that is number forty in a series, (represented by 40th). OE.
fortieth part *arch.* = sense B.2 below.
▶**B** *noun*. **1** The fortieth person or thing of a category, series, etc., identified contextually. M18.
2 Each of forty equal parts into which something is or may be divided, a fraction which when multiplied by forty gives one, (= ***fortieth part*** above). E19.
– COMB.: Forming compound numerals with multiples of a hundred, as ***two-hundred-and-fortieth*** (**240th**) etc., and (*arch.*) with numerals below ten, as ***five-and-fortieth*** etc.

fortification /ˌfɔːtɪfɪˈkeɪʃ(ə)n/ *noun*. LME.
[ORIGIN French from late Latin *fortificatio(n-)*, from *fortificat-* pa. ppl stem of *fortificare*: see FORTIFY, -ATION.]
▶**I** The action of fortifying.
1 MILITARY. The action of fortifying or providing with defensive works. LME. ▸**b** The art or science of fortifying or providing with defensive works. M17.
W. RALEIGH Much common good.. likely to arise with mutual fortification of both those kingdoms.
†**2** Strengthening, corroboration, ratification. L15–E17.
3 The strengthening of wine with alcohol, esp. a spirit. L19. ▸**b** The addition of nutrients, such as vitamins, to food. M20.
▶**II 4** MILITARY. A defensive work; a wall, tower, earthwork, etc. Usu. in *pl.*, such works collectively. LME. ▸**b** *transf. & fig.* A means of defence. L16.
C. LYELL Extensive fortifications to protect them from their enemies.
5 †**a** GUNNERY. The additional thickness of metal serving to strengthen parts of a cannon. E–M17. ▸†**b** *gen.* A means of strengthening. M–L17. ▸**c** *spec.* The strengthening timbers etc. of a ship, esp. a whaling vessel. *rare*. E19.
– COMB.: **fortification spectra** MEDICINE (the shimmering lights seen in) teichopsia.

fortified /ˈfɔːtɪfʌɪd/ *ppl adjective*. L15.
[ORIGIN from FORTIFY *verb* + -ED¹.]
1 Strengthened; provided with means of defence; protected with fortifications. L15.
2 **a** Of wine: strengthened with alcohol, esp. a spirit. E20. ▸**b** Of food: given an increased nutritive value, esp. by the addition of vitamins. E20.

fortify /ˈfɔːtɪfʌɪ/ *verb*. LME.
[ORIGIN Old French & mod. French *fortifier* from late Latin *fortificare*, from Latin *fortis* strong: see -FY.]
▶**I** Make strong.
1 *verb trans.* Strengthen the structure of. LME. ▸**b** *spec.* Strengthen (a gun) by additional thickness of metal; strengthen (a ship) by additional timbers etc. E17. ▸**c** Cover or bind with some protective material or appliance. Now passing into senses 7 and 8. E17.
DRYDEN The.. Bee.. Employ'd at home.. to fortify the Combs. **c** WELLINGTON Kegs.. well fortified with iron hoops.
2 *verb trans.* Impart strength or vigour to; give (a person, oneself) strength or endurance for some effort. LME.
B. BAINBRIDGE To fortify herself for the task ahead she allowed herself a little more brandy.

3 *verb trans.* **a** Strengthen mentally or morally; cheer, encourage. **LME.** ▸**b** Confirm, add support to (a statement etc.). *arch.* **LME.**

a S. LEWIS The assurance of Tanis Judique's friendship fortified Babbitt's self-approval. **b** H. MARTINEAU A distinct charge is brought against you, fortified by particulars.

†**4** *verb trans.* Make more powerful or effective; reinforce with additional resources; garrison (a fortress). **LME–E18.**

E. HALL He fortified Burdeaux with Englishmen.

†**5** *verb intrans.* Gain strength, grow strong. **E–M17.**
6 *verb trans.* **a** Strengthen (wine) with alcohol, esp. a spirit. Freq. as ***fortified*** *ppl adjective.* **L19.** ▸**b** Increase the nutritive value of (food), esp. with vitamins. **M20.**

b *Which?* Instant potato contains no vitamin C, unless it has been fortified.

▸ **II** Strengthen against attack.
7 *verb trans.* Provide (a town etc.) with defensive works; protect with fortifications. **LME.**

W. ROBERTSON These were . . commanded to fortify Leith.

8 *verb trans.* Surround (an army etc.) with defences; put in a state of defence. **L15.**

F. FITZGERALD The Vietnamese would have to fortify Vietnamese hamlets against other Vietnamese.

9 *verb intrans.* Erect fortifications; establish a defensive position. **L16.**

U. S. GRANT The enemy was fortifying at Corinth.

■ **fortifiable** *adjective* **E17.** **fortifier** *noun* **M16.**

†**fortilage** *noun* var. of **FORTALICE.**

Fortin barometer /ˈfɔːtɪn bəˈrɒmɪtə/ *noun phr.* Also **Fortin's barometer.** **L19.**
[ORIGIN from J. N. *Fortin* (1750–1831), French instrument-maker.]
A barometer with an adjustable reservoir of mercury.

fortis /ˈfɔːtɪs/ *noun & adjective.* **L19.**
[ORIGIN Latin = strong.]
▸ **A** *noun.* Pl. (in sense 2) **-tes** /-tiːz/.
1 A variety of dynamite. **L19.**
2 PHONETICS. A fortis consonant. **M20.**
▸ **B** *adjective.* PHONETICS. Of a consonant: strongly articulated; *spec.* designating the more or most strongly articulated of two or more homorganic consonants. **E20.**
– NOTE: In PHONETICS opp. ***lenis***.

fortissimo /fɔːˈtɪsɪməʊ/ *adverb, adjective, & noun.* **E18.**
[ORIGIN Italian, superl. of **FORTE** *adverb, adjective, & noun*².]
MUSIC. ▸**A** *adverb & adjective.* A direction: very loud(ly). (Abbreviation ***ff.***) **E18.**
▸ **B** *noun.* Pl. **-mos, -mi** /-mi/. A very loud tone or passage. **M19.**

fortitude /ˈfɔːtɪtjuːd/ *noun.* **ME.**
[ORIGIN Old French & mod. French from Latin *fortitudo, -din-*, from *fortis* strong: see **-TUDE.**]
1 Moral strength or courage, esp. in the endurance of pain or adversity. (One of the four cardinal virtues.) **ME.**

C. C. TRENCH She bore with fortitude her husband's absence. J. BUCHAN To go tandem-driving with him at Oxford required fortitude, for he was very blind.

†**2** Physical or structural strength. **LME–E18.**

R. EDEN A beast . . excelling all other beastes in fortitude and strength.

3 ASTROLOGY. A dignity. Long *rare* or *obsolete.* **M16.**
■ **fortiˈtudinous** *adjective* endowed with or characterized by fortitude **M18.**

fortlet /ˈfɔːtlɪt/ *noun.* **ME.**
[ORIGIN from **FORT** *noun* + **-LET.**]
A small fort.

fortnight /ˈfɔːtnʌɪt/ *noun.*
[ORIGIN Old English *fēowertiene niht*: see **FOURTEEN, NIGHT** *noun.*]
A period of two weeks.

Financial Times The Islamic year . . has less than a fortnight to run.

a fortnight from today, a fortnight today, a fortnight from Monday, a fortnight last Tuesday, Monday fortnight, etc. **TODAY** ***fortnight.***

fortnightly /ˈfɔːtnʌɪtli/ *adjective & noun.* **E19.**
[ORIGIN from **FORTNIGHT** + **-LY**¹.]
▸ **A** *adjective.* Produced or occurring fortnightly; paid etc. fortnightly. **E19.**
▸ **B** *noun.* A newspaper or magazine published fortnightly. (In earliest use spec. ***The Fortnightly Review.***) **E20.**

fortnightly /ˈfɔːtnʌɪtli/ *adverb.* **E19.**
[ORIGIN formed as **FORTNIGHTLY** *adjective & noun* + **-LY**².]
Every fortnight, by the fortnight.

Fortran /ˈfɔːtran/ *noun.* Also **f-**, **FORTRAN.** **M20.**
[ORIGIN from *for(mula tran(slation.*]
(The name of) a programming language used esp. for scientific calculations.

fortravail /fɔːˈtraveɪl, fə-/ *verb trans. obsolete* exc. *Scot.* Also **-travel** /-ˈtrav(ə)l/. **ME.**
[ORIGIN from **FOR-**¹ + **TRAVAIL** *verb.*]
Exhaust with labour. Usu. in *pass.*

fortress /ˈfɔːtrɪs/ *noun.* **ME.**
[ORIGIN Old French & mod. French *forteresse* strong place from Proto-Romance, from Latin *fortis* strong. Cf. **FORT** *noun.*]
A military stronghold, *esp.* a strongly fortified town fit for a large garrison.

K. CLARK His palace began as a fortress built on an almost impregnable rock. *fig.*: *Guardian* I have never seen a European policy as a policy of withdrawal into a fortress Europe.

fortress /ˈfɔːtrɪs/ *verb trans. arch.* **L15.**
[ORIGIN from the noun.]
Fortify; protect (with or as with a fortress); serve as a fortress to.

fortuitism /fɔːˈtjuːɪtɪz(ə)m/ *noun.* **L19.**
[ORIGIN from **FORTUIT(OUS** + **-ISM.**]
The belief that adaptation in nature is due to mere chance.
■ **fortuitist** *noun* a person who believes in fortuitism **L19.**

fortuitous /fɔːˈtjuːɪtəs/ *adjective.* **M17.**
[ORIGIN Latin *fortuitus*, from *forte* by chance, from *fors* chance, luck + **-OUS.**]
That is due to or produced by chance; accidental, casual. Now also, happening by a lucky chance, fortunate.

A. BRINK His presence is not fortuitous. He has a role to play. F. POPCORN Was it a master plan or just fortuitous timing?

– NOTE: The traditional, etymological meaning is 'happening by chance'. In modern English, however, *fortuitous* tends to be used to refer to fortunate outcomes, and has become more or less a synonym for 'lucky' or 'fortunate'.
■ **fortuitously** *adverb* **M17.** **fortuitousness** *noun* the quality of being fortuitous, accident, chance **M17.**

fortuity /fɔːˈtjuːɪti/ *noun.* **M18.**
[ORIGIN Irreg. formed as **FORTUITOUS**: see **-ITY.**]
Fortuitousness; accident; a chance occurrence.

fortunate /ˈfɔːtʃ(ə)nət/ *adjective & noun.* **LME.**
[ORIGIN Latin *fortunatus*, from *fortuna*: see **FORTUNE** *noun*, **-ATE**².]
▸ **A** *adjective.* **1** Favoured by fortune; lucky, prosperous. (Foll. by *to, to do.*) **LME.**

DAY LEWIS I was singularly fortunate to spend these summers of childhood among such people. *absol.*: *Scientific American* An armchair reader, envious of the fortunate who will visit the sites.

2 Bringing or presaging good fortune, auspicious, favourable. **LME.**

LD MACAULAY It ought to be considered as a most fortunate circumstance.

▸ **B** *noun.* A fortunate person or thing. Long *rare.* **E17.**
■ **fortunateness** *noun* **M16.**

†**fortunate** *verb trans.* **LME–L18.**
[ORIGIN Latin *fortunat-* pa. ppl stem of *fortunare*, from *fortuna*: see **FORTUNE** *noun*, **-ATE**³.]
Make fortunate, give good fortune to, prosper.

fortunately /ˈfɔːtʃ(ə)nətli/ *adverb.* **M16.**
[ORIGIN from **FORTUNATE** *adjective* + **-LY**².]
In a fortunate manner, luckily, successfully; (modifying a sentence) it is fortunate that.

W. S. MAUGHAM Bertha fortunately detested such festivities as did Miss Ley herself. G. VIDAL Fortunately, there were no ruins in sight.

fortune /ˈfɔːtʃuːn, -tʃ(ə)n/ *noun.* **ME.**
[ORIGIN Old French & mod. French from Latin *fortuna* chance as a divinity, (esp. good) luck.]
1 (Also **F-**.) Chance or luck as a power in human affairs; this power personified as a goddess. **ME.**

LD MACAULAY When fortune changed . . his real propensities began to show themselves.

†**2** A chance, an accident; an adventure. **ME–E18.** ▸**b** A mishap, a disaster. **L15–E17.**

T. STANLEY Many other good Fortunes happening to the Athenians . . are recorded.

3 *sing.* & in *pl.* The good or bad luck that befalls a person or an enterprise. **LME.** ▸**b** A person's destiny. Chiefly in ***tell a person's fortune*** below. **LME.**

J. R. GREEN On the fortunes of Philip hung the fortunes of English freedom. A. C. BOULT It has not been my good fortune to see inside many of the great London homes.

4 Good luck; success, prosperity. **LME.**

J. HARINGTON A herald by great fortune found out his pedigree.

5 Position as determined by wealth; wealth; a substantial amount of money etc. **M16.**

D. CARNEGIE George Eastman . . amassed a fortune of a $100 million. D. CAUTE A leather shoulder bag that had cost a fortune.

6 *sing.* & in *pl.* A person's condition or standing in life; a prosperous condition. **E17.**

JANET MORGAN The Millers . . looked equally prosperous . . but their fortunes, too, were imperceptibly growing shakier.

7 A wealthy woman, an heiress. *obsolete* exc. in ***marry a fortune*** below. **M17.**
8 ASTROLOGY. A planet, esp. in a favourable aspect; *spec.* the planet Saturn, the planet Jupiter. **L17.**
– PHRASES: **a small fortune** a large amount of money. †**by fortune** by chance. ***Fortune's wheel***: see **WHEEL** *noun* 8. ***hostage to fortune***: see **HOSTAGE** *noun*¹. **make a fortune, make one's fortune** become rich (other than by inheritance). **man of fortune, woman of fortune,** etc., a person possessing great (usu. inherited) wealth. **marry a fortune** *arch.* marry a rich heiress. ***push one's fortune***: see **PUSH** *verb.* **seek one's fortune, try one's fortune** pursue, make trial of, one's luck, esp. in the hope of achieving wealth and position. **soldier of fortune** an adventurous person ready to take service under any person or state in return for money; a mercenary. **tell a person's fortune** supposedly foretell a person's future by palmistry etc. ***tempt fortune***: see **TEMPT** *verb.* ***try one's fortune***: see ***seek one's fortune*** above. ***wheel of fortune***: see **WHEEL** *noun.* ***woman of fortune***: see ***man of fortune*** above.
– COMB.: **fortune cookie** *N. Amer.* a baked dough cake containing a prediction etc. on a slip of paper; **Fortune 500, Fortune 1000** *US* (an annual list of) the five hundred (from 1970 the one thousand) largest US industrial corporations; **fortune-hunter** a person who indulges in fortune-hunting; **fortune-hunting** attempting to secure a fortune for oneself, esp. by marrying a wealthy woman; **fortune-teller** a person who practises fortune-telling; **fortune-telling** supposedly foretelling a person's future by palmistry etc.
■ **fortuneless** *adjective* **L16.**

F

fortune /ˈfɔːtʃuːn, -tʃ(ə)n/ *verb.* **LME.**
[ORIGIN Old French *fortuner* from Latin *fortunare* make fortunate, from *fortuna*: see **FORTUNE** *noun.*]
†**1** *verb trans.* Assign a (specified) fortune to (a person etc.); control the fortunes of. **LME–E17.** ▸**b** Destine (a person) *to do* something; ordain (something) *to* happen. **LME–E17.**
2 *verb intrans.* Happen, chance, occur. Usu. *impers.* in ***it fortuned that.*** Now *arch.* or *poet.* **LME.**
3 *verb intrans.* †**a** Happen, chance, *to be, to do.* **LME–L18.** ▸**b** Come by chance *on. rare.* **M17.**
4 *verb trans.* Orig. (foll. by *off, out*), find a husband for (a girl) by providing a dowry. Later, endow with wealth or fortune, dower. Cf. earlier **FORTUNED** 2. Now *rare.* **M18.**

fortuned /ˈfɔːtʃ(ə)nd/ *adjective.* Now *rare.* **LME.**
[ORIGIN from **FORTUNE** *noun, verb*: see **-ED**², **-ED**¹.]
1 Having or characterized by a (specified) fortune. Formerly also, fortunate. **LME.**
2 Possessed of a fortune or portion, wealthy. **M17.**

†**fortunize** *verb trans. rare.* Also **-ise.** **L16–M17.**
[ORIGIN from **FORTUNE** *noun* + **-IZE.**]
Regulate the fortunes of; make fortunate.

forty /ˈfɔːti/ *adjective & noun (cardinal numeral).*
[ORIGIN Old English *fēowertig* = Old Frisian *fiuwertich*, Old Saxon *fiwartich* (Dutch *veertig*), Old High German *fiorzug* (German *vierzig*), Old Norse *fjórir tigir*, Gothic *fidwor tigjus*: see **FOUR, -TY**².]
▸ **A** *adjective.* **1** Four times ten (a cardinal numeral represented by 40 in arabic numerals, xl, XL in roman). **OE.** ▸**b** A large indefinite number. **E17.**

C. READE Dietrich's forty years weighed him down like forty bullets. **b** G. HERBERT I have forty businesses in my hands.

forty hours in the Roman Catholic Church the continuous exposition of the Host for forty hours, used as an occasion of special devotion or intercession. **forty winks** *colloq.* a short sleep, *esp.* one taken after a meal; a nap.
▸ **B** *noun.* **1** Forty persons or things identified contextually, as years of age, points, runs, etc., in a game, chances (in giving odds), minutes, etc. **OE.**

G. BERKELEY Alciphron is above forty.

2 A set of forty; a thing having a set of forty as an essential or distinguishing feature. **ME.** ▸**b** One fourth of a quarter section of land, comprising forty acres (approx. 16.2 hectares). *US.* **M19.**
3 Four times ten as an abstract number; the symbols or figures representing this (40 in arabic numerals, xl, XL in roman). **ME.**
4 The fortieth of a set or series with numbered members; the one designated forty, (usu. ***number forty***, or with specification, as ***chapter forty, verse forty,*** etc.); a size etc. denoted by forty, a garment etc. of such a size, (also ***size forty***). **E16.**
5 In *pl.* The numbers from 40 to 49 inclusive, esp. denoting years of a century or units of a scale of temperature; *one's* years of life between the ages of 40 and 49. **L19.**

GEORGIANA HILL What were called half-caps were worn in the early forties.

HUNGRY ***forties.*** **roaring forties** stormy ocean tracts between latitude 40° and 50° south. **the Forties, the Long Forties** the sea area between the NE coast of Scotland and the SW coast of Norway (from its depth of over 40 fathoms).
6 A crook, a thief, a sharper. *Austral. slang.* **L19.**
– COMB.: Forming compound numerals (cardinal or ordinal) with numerals below ten, as ***forty-nine (49), forty-first (41st),*** etc., and (cardinals) with multiples of a hundred, as ***340*** (read ***three hundred and forty,*** *US* also ***three hundred forty***), etc. With nouns + **-ER**¹ forming nouns with the sense 'something (identified contextually) being of or having forty —s', as ***forty-seater*** etc. Special combs., as **forty acre** *US & NZ* a section of land comprising forty acres; **forty-eight** (*a*) a plant pot of which forty-eight are formed from one cast of clay; (*b*) in *pl.*, forty-eight leaves to the sheet in a printed book; (*c*) the forty-eight preludes and fugues of J. S. Bach; **forty-five** (*a*) ***the Forty-five,*** the Jacobite rebellion of 1745; (*b*) a card game in which each trick counts five and the game is forty-five; (*c*) *N. Amer.* a revolver of .45 calibre; (*d*) a 45-rpm 7-inch microgroove gramophone record; **forty-footer** a forty-foot yacht; **forty-niner** a gold-digger who settled in California during the gold fever of 1849.

■ **fortyfold** *adjective & adverb* (**a**) *adjective* forty times as great or as numerous; having forty parts, divisions, elements, or units; (**b**) *adverb* to forty times the number or quantity: OE. **fortyish** *adjective* about forty (in age, measurements, etc.) E19.

forum /ˈfɔːrəm/ *noun*. Pl. **-rums**, **-ra** /-rə/. LME.
[ORIGIN Latin, rel. to *fores* (outside) door, orig. an enclosure surrounding a house.]
1 ROMAN ANTIQUITIES. The public place or marketplace of a city; the place of assembly for judicial and other business, esp. at Rome. LME. ▸**b** A place of or meeting for public discussion; a periodical etc. which provides an opportunity for conducting a debate. M18.

GIBBON The principal Forum; which appears to have been of a circular, or rather elliptical form. **b** L. NKOSI During its . . run to town the bus becomes a great forum for the airing of political views.

2 A court, a tribunal (*lit. & fig.*). L17.

fig.: J. MORLEY It is truth that in the forum of conscience claims an undivided allegiance.

– COMB.: **forum shopping** (orig. *US*) the practice by a plaintiff of seeking out the court felt most likely to give a sympathetic hearing to his or her case.

forwander /fɔːˈwɒndə, fə-/. *verb intrans.* Now *arch.* exc. *Scot.* ME.
[ORIGIN from FOR-[1] + WANDER *verb*.]
Weary oneself with wandering; wander far and wide. Usu. in *pass.*

forward /ˈfɔːwəd/ *verb trans.* L16.
[ORIGIN from FORWARD *adverb*.]
1 Orig., put forward, set on foot. Later, help forward, promote. L16.

E. A. FREEMAN To protect its rights and to forward its interests. M. DE LA ROCHE George Fennel . . came to see him, and still further forwarded his recovery.

2 Accelerate the growth of (a plant etc.). E17.

SWIFT I forward the grass, and I ripen the vine.

3 †**a** Pass on, make known widely. Only in E18. ▸**b** Send forward; send (a letter etc.) on to a further destination; COMMERCE dispatch (goods etc.). M18.

b W. GOLDING Forwarding address: Rinderpest, Bloemfontein, SA. J. N. ISBISTER His name was forwarded, and he was duly elected.

b forwarding agent, **forwarding merchant** a person whose business is the receiving and shipment or transmission of goods.
4 BOOKBINDING. Prepare (a book) for finishing by putting a plain cover on. L19.

forward /ˈfɔːwəd/ *adverb, adjective, & noun*. As adverb also **-wards** /-wədz/.
[ORIGIN Old English *forweard* var. of *forþweard*: see FORTHWARD.]
▸ **A** *adverb*. **1** Towards the future, continuously onwards. Now chiefly in ***from this day forward***, ***look forward to***, below. OE. ▸**b** COMMERCE. For future delivery or payment. L19.

S. SMILES The elder student from that time forward acted as the Mentor of the younger one. **b** *Farmers Weekly* He sold 300t of feed barley forward in August for January collection.

from this day forward etc., from this day etc. onwards. ***look forward to***: see LOOK *verb*.
†**2** Further on in a series; onwards from a specified point. LME–M17.

MARVELL I am this day beginning my long journey to Archangel, and so forward.

3 Towards what is in front, onwards. LME.

M. SINCLAIR She hurled herself forward and he caught her. E. WAUGH The crowds . . shuffled forward towards the Abbey.

backward and forward, ***backwards and forwards***: see BACKWARD *adverb* 4. ***fast-forward***: see FAST *adverb*. ***Great Leap Forward***: see GREAT *adjective*. ***leap forward***: see LEAP *noun*[1]. ***put one's best foot forward***: see BEST *adjective* etc.
4 Towards the front, in the direction in which one is facing. E16.

E. BOWEN Lilian wore her hair forward over her shoulders in two . . braids. J. M. COETZEE His mother sat with . . her head drooping forward.

play forward: see PLAY *verb*.
5 At an advanced point; in advance; ahead; at a point beyond another. E16.

AV *Num.* 32:19 Wee will not inherite with them on yonder side Iordane, or forward.

6 *fig.* Onward, so as to make progress. E16.

F. SWINNERTON Determination spurred her forward.

go forward be going on, progress.
7 To the front (from being behind); to the foreground (from being in the background); into view. E17.

A. RADCLIFFE Dorothee, who had lingered far behind, was called forward.

bring forward: see BRING *verb*. ***carry forward***: see CARRY *verb*. **come forward** offer oneself for a task, post, etc. ***put forward***: see PUT *verb*[1]. ***set forward***: see SET *verb*[1].
8 NAUTICAL & AERONAUTICS. In, near, to, or towards, the bow or nose. M17.

F. ASTAIRE To lie down in his bunk up forward just outside the cockpit.

– COMB.: **forward-looking** *adjective* (of a person etc.) progressive; **forward scatter** = *forward scattering* below; **forward-scatter** *verb trans.* scatter (radiation etc.) through an angle of less than 90 degrees with respect to the original direction; **forward scattering** scattering of radiation etc. involving a change of direction of less than 90 degrees; radiation etc. so scattered; *esp.* propagation of high-frequency radio waves beyond the horizon by scattering or reflection from the ionosphere.
▸ **B** *adjective*. †**1** Belonging to a front part or to the earliest part. Only in OE.
2 Situated in the forepart. Long *rare* or *obsolete* in *gen.* sense. ME. ▸**b** Orig., that lies in front. Later, that lies in the direction towards which one is moving. M17. ▸**c** NAUTICAL & AERONAUTICS. Belonging to the forepart of a ship etc.; that is in or near or to or towards the bow or nose. L19.

SHAKES. *All's Well* Let's take the instant by the forward top. **b** A. W. KINGLAKE Out of the forward horizon. **c** F. CHICHESTER The forward half of *Gipsy Moth* was in smooth water. D. LODGE Taking one's place in the forward passenger cabin of a wide-bodied jet.

3 That is in an advanced state or condition; progressing towards maturity or completion. Chiefly *pred.* E16. ▸**b** Of a plant, a crop, the season: well advanced, early. L16. ▸**c** Of a pregnant animal: *in* or *with* foal etc. L17.

MRS H. WOOD A sturdy little fellow . . sufficiently forward in walking to get about the room. *Landscape* The two wines at their best . . are fruity and forward, with a charm that develops early.

4 Ready, prompt, eager, (*to do*). Formerly also, inclined *to* or *for*. *arch.* E16. ▸**b** Ardent, spirited, zealous. Now *rare* or *obsolete*. E17.

M. PATTISON Authors were always forward to send him copies of their learned publications. **b** WELLINGTON He is a gallant, forward officer.

5 Presumptuous, bold, overfamiliar. M16.

W. S. MAUGHAM There was nothing saucy in her manner, forward or pert.

6 Well advanced for one's years, precocious. L16.

PRINCESS ALICE My children . . are so forward, clever, and spirited.

7 Directed towards a point in advance, onward, towards the front. E17. ▸**b** CRICKET. Designating or pertaining to a stroke made in playing forward (see ***play forward*** s.v. PLAY *verb*). L19. ▸**c** FOOTBALL etc. Of a pass: towards one's opponents' goal line. L19.

H. H. WILSON General Wood was compelled . . to undertake a forward movement.

8 Of opinions etc.: advanced, extreme; *esp.* favouring or advocating vigorous aggressive action. E17.

Pall Mall Gazette Denouncing outrage and dynamite, and what are generally known as 'forward' measures.

9 a COMMERCE. Of a business transaction, contract, etc.: relating to future produce, delivery, etc. L19. ▸**b** Prospective; advanced; with a view to the future. M20.

a *Daily News* Consumers will not pay this price for forward contracts. **b** *Financial Times* Elridge's forward planning was aggressive and ambitious.

▸ **C** *noun*. †**1** The fore or front part; the first part. OE–ME.
2 (The position of) an attacking player in football, hockey, etc. L19.
■ **forwardly** *adverb* in a forward manner; *US* in a forward direction: M16. **forwardness** *noun* E16.

forwarder /ˈfɔːwədə/ *noun*. M16.
[ORIGIN from FORWARD *verb* + -ER[1].]
A person who or thing which forwards something.

forwarder /ˈfɔːwədə/ *adjective & adverb*. Also (*non-standard & joc.*) **forrader** /ˈfɒrədə/. L18.
[ORIGIN Compar. of FORWARD *adjective & adverb*: see -ER[3].]
Further forward.
can't get any forwarder, (*non-standard & joc.*) **can't get no forwarder** can make no progress.

forwards *adverb* see FORWARD *adverb, adjective, & noun*.

†**forwarn** *verb trans.* Also **fore-**. OE–E19.
[ORIGIN from FOR-[1] + WARN *verb*[2].]
Prohibit, forbid.

†**forwaste** *verb trans.* M16–M17.
[ORIGIN from FOR-[1] + WASTE *verb*.]
Waste; use up, exhaust; lay waste; make feeble.

†**forwear** *verb trans.* Pa. t. **-wore**; pa. pple **-worn**. See also FORWORN *adjective*. ME–E17.
[ORIGIN from FOR-[1] + WEAR *verb*[1].]
Wear out, wear away, exhaust.

forwearied /fɔːˈwɪərɪd/ *adjective*. *arch.* M16.
[ORIGIN pa. pple of FORWEARY: see -ED[1].]
Tired out.

forweary /fɔːˈwɪəri/ *verb trans.* *arch.* ME.
[ORIGIN from FOR-[1] + WEARY *verb*.]
Weary, tire out.

forwent *verb pa. t.* of FORGO.

forwhy /fəˈwʌɪ/ *adverb & conjunction*. Also as two words. OE.
[ORIGIN from FOR *preposition* + WHY.]
▸ **A** *adverb*. **1** *interrog.* For what reason, why? OE.

W. KETHE For why? The Lord our God is good. K. HULME She is surprised by that, although she can't say for why.

†**2** *rel.* On account of which, wherefore. ME–E17.
▸ **B** *conjunction*. **1** Because. ME.
†**2** = FOR *conjunction* 2. ME–E17.

†**forwore** *verb pa. t.* of FORWEAR.

forworn /fɔːˈwɔːn/ *adjective*. *arch.* E16.
[ORIGIN pa. pple of FORWEAR.]
Tired out.

†**forworn** *verb pa. pple* of FORWEAR.

foryield /fɔːˈjiːld, fə-/ *verb trans.* *obsolete* exc. *Scot.*
[ORIGIN Old English *forgieldan* = Old High German *fargeltan* (German *vergelten*), formed as FOR-[1] + YIELD *verb*.]
Pay, recompense, requite.

forzando /fɔːtˈsandəʊ/ *adverb & adjective*. E19.
[ORIGIN Italian, from *forzare* to force.]
MUSIC. (A direction:) with force or emphasis; = SFORZANDO.

Fosbury flop /fɒzb(ə)ri ˈflɒp/ *noun phr.* M20.
[ORIGIN from Richard (Dick) *Fosbury* (b. 1947), US athlete and 1968 Olympic gold-medallist + FLOP *noun*.]
A method of high jumping in which the athlete leaps head first and arches the back in attempting to clear the bar.

foss *noun*[1] var. of FOSSE.

foss *noun*[2] var. of FORCE *noun*[2].

fossa /ˈfɒsə/ *noun*[1]. Pl. **fossae** /ˈfɒsiː/. M17.
[ORIGIN Latin = ditch, from fem. pa. pple of *fodere* dig.]
ANATOMY. A shallow depression or cavity.

fossa /ˈfɒsə/ *noun*[2]. M19.
[ORIGIN Malagasy *fosa*. Cf. FOSSANE.]
A red-brown catlike viverrid mammal, *Cryptoprocta ferox*, the largest carnivore of Madagascar.

fossane /ˈfɒseɪn/ *noun*. L18.
[ORIGIN French, formed as FOSSA *noun*[2].]
The Malagasy civet, *Fossa fossa*, a foxlike brown spotted nocturnal viverrid mammal of Madagascar.

fosse /fɒs/ *noun*. Also **foss**. LOE.
[ORIGIN Old French & mod. French from Latin *fossa*: see FOSSA *noun*[1].]
1 A canal, a ditch, a trench; *esp.* one serving as a barrier or defence, a moat. Earliest as a name (now ***the Fosse***, ***Fosse Way***) of one of the four great Roman roads in Britain, so called from the ditch on each side, and probably running from Axminster to Lincoln. LOE.

R. GRAVES Strengthening the ancient City ramparts, clearing and deepening the choked fosse.

†**2** A deep hole or pit; a grave or place for sacrifice. L15–M19.

F. FAWKES A deep round foss he made, And on the kindling wood the victim laid.

3 ANATOMY. = FOSSA *noun*[1]. M18.
■ **fossed** *adjective* (*rare*) surrounded (as) by a fosse L17.

fossé /ˈfɒseɪ/ *noun*. Also (earlier, *Scot.*) **foussie** /ˈfuːsi/. E16.
[ORIGIN French, from late Latin *fossatum* neut. pa. pple of Latin *fossare* frequentative of *fodere* dig.]
= FOSSE 1.

fossette /fɒˈsɛt/ *noun*. M19.
[ORIGIN French, dim. of *fosse*: see -ETTE.]
Chiefly ZOOLOGY. A small hollow or depression, as in a bone or shell.

fossick /ˈfɒsɪk/ *verb*. Chiefly *Austral. & NZ*. M19.
[ORIGIN Unknown: sense 3 is almost certainly the earliest.]
1 *verb intrans.* In MINING, search for gold in abandoned workings, or by digging out crevices etc.; *gen.* search, rummage about or *about*. M19.

C. BARRETT An Arab fossicking among potsherds on a low mound, held up a verdigrised copper coin. H. P. TRITTON Most were fossicking in the creeks and gullies and the old workings. P. CAREY The Joys were seen . . fossicking out at the tip for their neighbours' rejected furniture.

2 *verb trans.* Search (a place etc.); dig *out* or *up*. M19.

B. CRONIN No one will get to fossicking those tents while Pup's there. F. CHICHESTER I felt hungry and fossicked out the remains of the excellent jam and egg sandwiches.

3 *verb trans.* Obtain by asking, ferret out. *dial.* L19.
■ **fossicker** *noun* M19.

fossil /ˈfɒs(ə)l, -sɪl/ *noun & adjective*. M16.
[ORIGIN French *fossile*, from Latin *fossilis* dug up, from *foss-* pa. ppl stem of *fodere* dig: see -ILE.]
▸ **A** *noun*. †**1** A fossilized fish found, and believed to have lived, underground. Only in M16.
2 Orig., any rock or mineral dug out of the earth. Later, anything preserved in the strata of the earth and recog-

nizable as the remains or vestiges of a plant or animal of a former (usu. prehistoric) geological period. E17.

JAN MORRIS The Dawn Redwood nearby was rediscovered .. in 1945, after centuries in which it was known only as a fossil. *attrib.*: D. ATTENBOROUGH Anyone can date many rocks .. and by doing so put into order the major events of fossil history.

zonal fossil, zonal guide fossil: see ZONAL *adjective*.

3 A person, thing, or idea belonging to the past or incapable of development or change; a fossilized person or thing. M19.

4 A word or linguistic form preserved only in isolated regions or in set phrases or forms, as ***hue*** in ***hue and cry***. M20.

▸ **B** *adjective*. **1** Found buried in the earth, dug up. Now chiefly, of the nature of a fossil (sense A.2 above). M17.

P. MATTHIESSEN Close by one print an imprint of lost ages, a fernlike fossil brachiopod in a broken stone.

fossil fuel any fuel, as coal or petroleum, formed below ground from the remains of plants and animals during the geological past.

2 Belonging to the past, antiquated; fixed; incapable of change or development. M19.

ALDOUS HUXLEY But in practice and emotionally he was a child, a fossil mid-Victorian child.

■ **fossilate** *verb trans. & intrans.* (cause to) become a fossil E19. **fossiˈlation** *noun* L19. **fossildom** *noun* the condition or character of being a fossil L19. **fossiled** *adjective* fossilized M19. **fossiˈliferous** *adjective* containing fossils or organic remains L19. **fossilist** *noun* (now *rare*) a palaeontologist M18. †**fossilogy** *noun* palaeontology L18–M19.

fossilize /ˈfɒs(ə)lʌɪz, -sɪl-/ *verb trans. & intrans.* Also **-ise**. L18.
[ORIGIN from FOSSIL *noun* + -IZE.]

1 (Cause to) become a fossil. L18.

T. O'BRIEN He could .. imagine himself finally stopping and freezing and fossilizing. D. ATTENBOROUGH It is difficult to believe that .. a jellyfish could retain its shape long enough to be fossilized.

2 (Cause to) become antiquated, fixed, or incapable of change or development. M19.

A. CARNEGIE Long years of peace had fossilized the service. B. M. H. STRANG Fossilised survivals of the old pattern of prenegation (*nill* = *won't*).

■ **fossilizable** *adjective* E20. **fossiliˈzation** *noun* E19.

fossor /ˈfɒsə/ *noun*. M19.
[ORIGIN Latin = digger, miner, (in late Latin) gravedigger, from *foss-*: see FOSSIL, -OR.]

1 *ECCLESIASTICAL HISTORY*. An officer of the early Christian Church charged with the burial of the dead. M19.

2 [mod. Latin *Fossores* former taxonomic division.] Any of various sphecoid or other hymenopteran insects with legs adapted for digging or nest-building; a digger wasp. L19.

fossorial /fɒˈsɔːrɪəl/ *adjective*. M19.
[ORIGIN from medieval Latin *fossorius* (formed as FOSSOR) + -IAL.]

1 Of an animal: that habitually burrows or digs. M19.

2 Of or pertaining to burrowing animals; *esp.* (of a limb etc.) adapted for burrowing. M19.

fossula /ˈfɒsjʊlə/ *noun*. Pl. **-lae** /-liː/. M19.
[ORIGIN Latin, dim. of *fossa*: see FOSSA *noun*[1], -ULE.]
Chiefly *ZOOLOGY*. A small fossa or depression.

foster /ˈfɒstə/ *noun*[1] & *adjective*.
[ORIGIN Old English *fōster* from Germanic base of FOOD + instr. suffix. In branch A.II from the adjective.]

▸ **A** *noun* †**I** **1** Food, nourishment. OE–L17.

2 Care, keeping, fostering. *rare*. ME–M19.

▸ **II** **3** A foster-parent; a nurse. *arch*. OE.

4 A foster-child. Formerly also, offspring. Long only *Scot*. ME.

▸ **B** *attrib.* or as *adjective*. (Freq. with hyphen.)

1 Having a specified familial relationship not by blood or adoption, but by virtue of nursing, bringing up, or care, as ***foster-brother***, ***foster-daughter***, ***foster-sister***, ***foster-son***. OE.

M. FORSTER My idea of happiness was to have a family ... Even an adoptive or foster family would have sufficed.

2 Concerned with the care of orphans, or children in need of a temporary but stable home. L19.

T. KENEALLY When I was twelve I went to a foster-home, a childless couple in Connecticut.

– COMB. & SPECIAL COLLOCATIONS: **foster-child** a child nursed or brought up as their own by people other than his or her biological or adoptive parents; **foster-father** a man who brings up a child as his own; the husband of a wet nurse; **foster-mother** (*a*) a woman who nurses and brings up a child as her own, or on behalf of the child's natural mother; (*b*) an apparatus for rearing chickens hatched in an incubator; **foster-nurse** a nurse who brings up a child as her own.

†**foster** *noun*[2]. LME–L17.
[ORIGIN Contr.]
= FORESTER.

foster /ˈfɒstə/ *verb*.
[ORIGIN Old English *fōstrian* (= Old Norse *fóstra*), formed as FOSTER *noun*[1] & *adjective*.]

1 *verb trans.* Nourish, feed. Now chiefly *fig.* OE.

SHAKES. *Cymb.* One bred of alms and foster'd with cold dishes.

2 a *verb trans. & intrans.* Raise (a child). Now only, nurse or bring up (a child) as a foster-child, be a foster-parent (to). ME. ▸†**b** *verb trans.* Teach or train *in* (beliefs, habits, etc.). LME–L16. ▸**c** *verb trans.* Of an authority etc.: assign (a child) to be fostered. Also foll. by *out*. L20.

S. JOHNSON A Laird, a man of wealth and eminence, sends his child .. to a tacksman or tenant to be fostered. *Sunday Telegraph* A West Indian friend who fosters and I had a party together with all our children.

3 *verb trans.* Encourage, harbour, or nurse (a feeling); (of circumstances) be conducive to; promote the development of; (now only with mixture of sense 4) encourage or help the growth of (a plant etc.). (Foll. by *up*.) ME. ▸†**b** *verb trans.* Encourage *in* a habit etc. M16–M17.

A. STORR Teachers hope to detect and foster creativity in their pupils. K. CROSSLEY-HOLLAND If you want a friend whom you can wholly trust, foster his friendship.

4 *verb trans.* Tend with affectionate care, cherish; keep warm. *arch*. LME.

GOLDSMITH What a viper have I been fostering in my bosom!

■ **fosterable** *adjective* M19.

fosterage /ˈfɒst(ə)rɪdʒ/ *noun*. E17.
[ORIGIN from FOSTER *verb* + -AGE.]

1 The action of fostering a child; responsibility for fostering a child. E17.

2 *hist.* The custom among the Scottish and Irish nobility of employing a tenant as a foster-mother. L18.

3 The action of encouraging or promoting something. E19.

fosterer /ˈfɒst(ə)rə/ *noun*. LME.
[ORIGIN formed as FOSTERAGE + -ER[1].]

1 A person who fosters a child, a foster-parent. LME.

2 A person who or thing which encourages or promotes something or someone; a patron. L16.

3 A foster-brother; a foster-child. *Irish*. M18.

fosterling /ˈfɒstəlɪŋ/ *noun*. OE.
[ORIGIN from FOSTER *noun*[1] & *adjective* + -LING[1].]
A foster-child, a nursling; a protégé.

fostress /ˈfɒstrɪs/ *noun*. E17.
[ORIGIN formed as FOSTERLING + -ESS[1].]
A female fosterer.

fother /ˈfɒðə/ *noun*.
[ORIGIN Old English *fōþer* = Old Saxon *fōþar* (Dutch *voer*), Old High German *fuodar* (German *Fuder*), from West Germanic base, prob. from ablaut var. of base meaning 'stretch out', as in FATHOM *noun*.]

1 A cartload; *fig.* an enormous quantity (of gold or money). *obsolete* exc. *dial.* OE. ▸**b** A mass; a quantity (of people etc.). ME.

2 A specific weight (latterly usu. 19½ hundredweight, approx. 990 kg) used for lead or (rarely) coal. ME.

fother /ˈfɒðə/ *verb*. L18.
[ORIGIN Prob. from Dutch *voederen* (now *voeren*), or Low German *fodern* = German *füttern* to line.]
NAUTICAL. **1** *verb trans.* Cover (a sail) with oakum and draw it over a leak with the intention of stopping it. L18.

2 *verb intrans.* Stop a leak by this method. E19.

fou /fuː/ *adjective*. *Scot.* M16.
[ORIGIN Var. of FULL *adjective*.]
Inebriated, drunk.

Foucault /ˈfuːkəʊ, *foreign* fuko/ *noun*. M19.
[ORIGIN J. B. L. *Foucault* (1819–68), French physicist.]
Used ***attrib.*** and in ***possess.*** to designate things discovered, devised, or worked on by Foucault.

Foucault current an eddy current. **Foucault pendulum**, **Foucault's pendulum** a pendulum designed to demonstrate the earth's rotation by the rotation of its plane of oscillation.

foudroyant /fuːˈdrɔɪənt, *foreign* fudrwajɑ̃/ *adjective*. M19.
[ORIGIN French, pres. pple of *foudroyer* strike (as) with lightning, from *foudre* from Latin *fulgur* lightning: see -ANT[1].]

1 Thunderous, noisy. Also, dazzling. M19.

2 Of a disease: beginning suddenly and in a very severe form. L19.

fouetté /fwete (*pl. same*), ˈfwɛteɪ/ *noun*. M19.
[ORIGIN French, pa. pple of *fouetter* to whip.]
BALLET. A step in which a dancer stands on one *pointe* and executes a rapid sideways movement with the free leg.

fougade /fuːˈgɑːd/ *noun*. Now *rare*. M17.
[ORIGIN French from Italian *fogata*, from †*fogare* flee, fly: see -ADE.]
= FOUGASSE.

fougasse /fuːˈgɑːs/ *noun*. E19.
[ORIGIN French, alt. of FOUGADE.]
MILITARY. A landmine filled with pieces of rock, metal, etc., designed to fly in a given direction when the explosive is lit.

fought /fɔːt/ *ppl adjective*. M16.
[ORIGIN pa. pple of FIGHT *verb*.]
That has been fought. Chiefly with specifying adverb, as ***well fought***.

fought *verb pa. t. & pple* of FIGHT *verb*.

foughten /ˈfɔːt(ə)n/ *ppl adjective*. *arch*. M16.
[ORIGIN pa. pple of FIGHT *verb*.]
Designating a field on which a battle has been fought.

foughty /ˈfaʊti/ *adjective*. *dial.* See also FOOTY *adjective*. E17.
[ORIGIN Corresp. to Dutch *vochtig*, Swedish *fuktig*, Danish *fugtig* damp: prob. already in Old English.]
Musty.

foujdar /ˈfaʊdʒdɑː/ *noun*. L17.
[ORIGIN Persian *fawjdār* military commander, from Arabic *fawj* troop + Persian *-dār* holding, holder.]
In the Indian subcontinent: a police officer; formerly also, a criminal judge in Bengal.

foul /faʊl/ *noun*. OE.
[ORIGIN from FOUL *adjective*. In sense 3 partly from FOUL *verb*.]

1 That which is foul. Opp. FAIR *noun*[2]. OE.

foul befall *arch.* may evil befall.

2 *sing.* & (occas.) in *pl.* A disease in the feet of cattle. Now usu. ***foul-in-the-foot***, ***foul of the foot***. E16.

3 A collision or entanglement, esp. in rowing or running. M18.

4 A violation of the rules of a game, *esp.* one involving interference with play by an opponent; *BOXING* an illegal punch (one below the belt, etc.). L19.

Today He could have broken Myler's ribs, it was a blatant foul.

foul /faʊl/ *adjective*.
[ORIGIN Old English *fūl* = Old Frisian, Old Saxon, Old High German *fūl* (Dutch *vuil* dirty, German *faul* rotten, lazy), Old Norse *fúll*, Gothic *fūls* stinking, from Germanic, from Indo-European base also of Latin PUS, *putere* to stink, Greek *puon*, *puos*, *puar* pus.]

▸ **I** Not wholesome, clean, or attractive.

1 Highly offensive to the senses; *esp.* smelling of decay. OE. ▸**b** Of a disease, sore, etc.: marked by festering or gangrene. OE.

N. SHUTE The whole city was becoming foul and beginning to smell. J. LE CARRÉ The foul stench of decaying fish oil. **b** SHAKES. *A.Y.L.* I will .. Cleanse the foul body of th' infected world.

2 Not clean; dirty, soiled. Now *arch. & dial.*, exc. with mixture of sense 1: disgustingly dirty, filthy. OE. ▸**b** Of a road etc.: muddy. LME.

C. S. LEWIS A hamper full of his foul linen for your wife to wash. D. DAVIE Pavements foul with miners' spittle.

3 *fig.* Of a person, action, etc.: repugnant to the moral sense; revoltingly or detestably wicked, vile. Chiefly *rhet.* OE. ▸†**b** Guilty of a charge; implicated in a crime. ME–E17.

AV *Mark* 9:25 Iesus .. rebuked the foule spirit. C. THIRLWALL Aristophanes must stand convicted .. of the foulest motives. LD MACAULAY A court foul with all the vices of the Restoration. E. O'NEILL It is a foul sin in the sight of Jehovah.

4 Of speech etc.: indecent, obscene. Also, disgustingly abusive. OE.

P. H. GIBBS 'I believe you've got a German mistress.' 'You have a foul mind.' G. B. SHAW I called her the foulest names until she gave in. A. SILLITOE He cursed them in foul, well-polished language.

5 Shameful, discreditable. ME.

MILTON The dire event, That with sad overthrow and foul defeat Hath lost us Heav'n.

6 Not attractive in appearance; ugly, unsightly. Now *arch. & dial.* ME. ▸**b** Of a sound: not pleasing to the ear. Now *dial.* LME.

AV *Job* 16:16 My face is fowle with weeping. R. W. EMERSON There is no object so foul that .. light will not make beautiful.

7 Of weather: wet and windy. ME. ▸**b** *NAUTICAL*. Of wind or tide: unfavourable to sailing. E18.

J. BUCHAN It's a foul day, so you'd better stop indoors.

8 Of a misfortune etc.: wretchedly bad, grievous. LME.

MILTON Eadbald, vext with an evil Spirit, fell .. into foul fits of distraction.

9 Of manner, conduct, etc.: marked by violence, rough, harsh. Also, of a method: unscrupulous, dishonest; (esp. in ***by fair means or foul***). LME. ▸**b** *SPORTS & GAMES*. Not (acting) according to the rules. L16.

R. W. EMERSON War is a foul game. **b** *Times* A foul shot on the pink cost him six points.

10 Of air, water, etc.: filled with impurities or (now chiefly) noxious matter. M16. ▸**b** Dull, discoloured. *arch.* L16.

JOYCE The very air .. becomes foul and unbreathable when it has been long enclosed.

11 Of a diet or eater: consisting of or eating coarse food or (now chiefly) carrion. E18.

12 *hyperbol.* Extremely unpleasant or disagreeable. *dial. & colloq.* L18.

C. CONNOLLY I had a foul journey. CLIVE JAMES He was foul to his children because by growing up they reminded him that he would .. die. *Balance* I was in a foul temper and in no mood for the delights ahead.

▸ **II** Not clear, obstructed.

F

13 Clogged or impeded with foreign matter. (Now chiefly of a gun barrel or (*dial.*) of land overgrown with weeds.) L15.

F. NIGHTINGALE If your chimney is foul, sweep it.

14 NAUTICAL. Of a coast or sea bottom: rocky. Of a ship: having its keel overgrown with seaweed, barnacles, etc. E17.

15 NAUTICAL. Entangled with or impeded by something, and thus not having free movement. (Foll. by *of*.) E17.

G. W. MANBY A small axe to cut away the line, in case of its getting foul when running out.

– SPECIAL COLLOCATIONS & COMB.: **foul anchor** (*a*) an anchor which has become caught in some impediment; (*b*) *spec.* an anchor which has got its cable twisted round the stock or flukes; a representation of this, used as the seal of the Lord High Admiral of Britain. **foul ball** BASEBALL a ball struck so that it falls outside the lines drawn from the home base through the first and third bases. **foul brood** any of several bacterial diseases of larval bees, marked by a sickly unpleasant smell in the hive. **foul copy** (now *rare*) a first copy, defaced by corrections (opp. *fair copy*). †**foul disease**, †**foul evil** (*a*) epilepsy; (*b*) syphilis. **foul Fiend** the Devil. **foul line**: marking the boundary of a playing area etc. **foul mouth** a person who uses foul language. **foul-mouthed** *adjective* using foul language. **foul-mouthedness** foul-mouthed quality. **foul papers** pages of a first copy, defaced by corrections. **foul play** (*a*) unfair play in a game; (*b*) *transf.* dishonest or unscrupulous dealings; *spec.* violent crime resulting in another's death. **foul proof** a proofreader's marked proof (opp. to the clean or corrected copy which succeeds it). ***foul strike***: see STRIKE *noun*[1] 11a. ***foul tip***: see TIP *noun*[2].

▪ **foully** *adverb* ME. **foulness** *noun* foul quality or state; a foul substance or deposit: OE.

F

foul /faʊl/ *verb*.

[ORIGIN Old English *fūlian* = Old High German *fūlōn* (German *faulen*). In Middle English prob. a new formation from the adjective.]

1 *verb intrans.* Be or become foul, dirty, or clogged. Now freq. foll. by *up*. OE.

G. DURRELL The water fouled very quickly, so that it had to be changed three times a day.

2 *verb trans.* Make foul or dirty, esp. with excrement. ME. ▸**b** *verb intrans.* Of an animal: defecate. L15.

N. MONSARRAT Grand Harbour . . was fouled by scum . . and dead fish. Q. BELL A stray dog . . having fouled the carpets beyond bearing.

foul one's nest, **foul one's own nest** *fig.* (*a*) bring discredit on one's family etc. by one's actions; (*b*) speak disparagingly of one's family etc.

3 *verb trans. fig.* Pollute with guilt; dishonour, disgrace. ME.

CHESTERFIELD Your *Commensaux*, who . . foul themselves with . . scoundrel gamesters.

4 *verb trans.* Make ugly, deface. Long *arch.* ME.

Daily News Passing . . to the main line the engine fouled the points.

5 *verb trans.* Chiefly NAUTICAL. Cause to become entangled. Also, make immovable; block, obstruct (a sea bottom etc.). E18. ▸**b** *verb intrans.* Become entangled. M19. ▸**c** *verb trans.* Run foul of, collide with. M19.

b F. FRANCIS He will be perpetually fouling in the branches. **c** THOMAS HUGHES He managed . . to get into Iffley lock . . without fouling the gates.

fouled anchor = ***foul anchor*** s.v. FOUL *adjective*.

6 *verb trans. & intrans.* SPORT. Be guilty of foul play against (an opponent or member of an opposing team). L19.

7 *verb intrans.* BASEBALL. Hit a foul ball. L19.

– WITH ADVERBS IN SPECIALIZED SENSES: **foul off** *verb phr. trans.* (in *pass.*) = ***foul out*** (b) below; **foul out** (*a*) *verb phr. intrans.* (of a baseball batter) be made out by hitting a foul ball which is caught on the fly by one of the opposing team; (*b*) *verb phr. trans.* (in *pass.*) & *intrans.* (in basketball) be put out of the game for exceeding the permitted number of fouls; **foul up** *verb phr. trans. & intrans.* (*fig.*) throw or be thrown into confusion, mess or be messed up.

▪ **fouling** *noun* (*a*) the action of the verb; (*b*) a foul deposit: LME.

foul /faʊl/ *adverb*. OE.

[ORIGIN from the adjective.]

†1 In a loathsome or stinking manner. OE–M16.

†2 Shamefully, disgracefully. ME–L16.

SHAKES. *Rich. III* I'll have this crown of mine cut from my shoulders Before I'll see the crown so foul misplaced.

†3 Grievously, sorely. ME–L16.

SPENSER Two of . . her nephews are so fowle forlorne.

†4 In an ugly manner. Only in LME.

5 Not in the correct or regular manner. L17.

6 NAUTICAL. Into a state of entanglement, into collision. L17.

fall foul of (*a*) come into collision with; (*b*) quarrel with; (*c*) make an attack on. **run foul of** = ***fall foul of*** (a) above.

7 In a manner contrary to the rules of a game or of fair play. E18.

play a person foul *fig.* behave treacherously to a person.

– COMB.: **foul-hook** *verb trans.* hook (a fish) elsewhere than in the mouth.

Foulah *noun & adjective* var. of FULAH.

foulard /ˈfuːlɑː, -ɑːd/ *noun*. M19.

[ORIGIN French, of unknown origin.]

1 A thin printed or checked material of silk or of silk and cotton. M19.

2 A handkerchief of this material. L19.

foulé /fule/ *noun*. L19.

[ORIGIN French = pressed (cloth), pa. pple of *fouler* FULL *verb*[1].]

A light woollen dress material with a fibrous appearance.

foulmart *noun* var. of FOUMART.

foul-up /ˈfaʊlʌp/ *noun*. *colloq.* (orig. *US*). M20.

[ORIGIN from FOUL *verb* + UP *adverb*[1].]

A confused situation; a muddle, a mess.

foumart /ˈfuːmət, -mɑːt/ *noun*. Now chiefly *dial.* Also **foul-** /ˈfaʊl-/. ME.

[ORIGIN from FOUL *adjective* + unstressed form of Old English *mearþ*: see MARTEN. Cf. MART *noun*[4].]

The polecat, *Mustela putorius*. Also as a term of contempt.

found /faʊnd/ *noun*[1]. M16.

[ORIGIN from FOUND *verb*[2].]

The process of founding metal or material for glass.

†**of found** *Scot.* made of cast metal.

found /faʊnd/ *noun*[2]. *Scot.* E17.

[ORIGIN from FOUND *verb*[1].]

sing. & in *pl.* The foundations of a building.

found /faʊnd/ *ppl adjective*. LME.

[ORIGIN pa. pple of FIND *verb*.]

1 That has been found or discovered. Chiefly with preceding adverb, as ***new-found*** LME.

2 Chiefly NAUTICAL. That is equipped or supplied. Only with preceding adverb etc., as ***well found***. L18.

3 Obtained without effort or searching; *spec.* (*a*) (of a stone) taken from the surface of the ground, not quarried; (*b*) (of an artist's materials) taken from the natural environment and used unaltered to form artistic works [cf. French *objet trouvé*]; (of art) based on such materials; (*c*) (of poetry) formed by taking an existing piece of prose and breaking it up into rhythmical units: L19.

found /faʊnd/ *verb*[1]. ME.

[ORIGIN Old French & mod. French *fonder* from Latin *fundare*, from *fundus* bottom, foundation.]

▸ **I** *verb trans.* **1** Lay the base or foundation of (a building). Sometimes simply, build, construct. Usu. in *pass.* Now *rare*. ME.

AV *Matt.* 7:25 The windes . . beat vpon that house: and it fell not, for it was founded vpon a rocke.

2 Be the original builder of (an edifice, town, etc.); establish (an institution) for the first time, esp. with provision for its future maintenance. ME.

C. THIRLWALL His son Lycaon founds the first city, Lycosura. L. STEPHEN De Foe founded the modern school of English novelists. H. FAST Thomas Seldon presided over the bank his father founded.

3 Establish (something abstract) on a firm basis, support, principle, etc.; base, ground. Of a thing: serve as a basis for. ME. ▸**b** Ground (a person) *in* a subject of instruction. Long *arch.* LME.

J. LUBBOCK A classification of insects founded on larvae. OED This novel is believed to be founded on fact. G. F. KENNAN His success at home had been founded . . on his appeal to common people. **b** H. ALLEN That you will undertake the instruction of the young clerk . . with the end in view of founding him in . . *Penmanship*.

▸ **II** *verb intrans.* **4** Base one's opinion, (of an opinion etc.) be based, *on*, *upon*. Chiefly *Scot.* M19.

T. M. COOPER The rather inconclusive fact on which Innes founds.

▪ **founded** *adjective* (*a*) (with qualifying adverb) having a (good, bad, etc.) basis; (*b*) (without adverb, *arch.*) having a firm foundation, well-justified: L15.

found /faʊnd/ *verb*[2] *trans.* LME.

[ORIGIN Old French & mod. French *fondre* from Latin *fundere* pour, melt.]

†1 Dissolve (ingredients) together. Only in LME.

2 Melt and mould (metal); cast or form (an article) by this process. E16.

3 Fuse to make glass; make (glass, a glass article) by fusing. L18.

found *verb*[3] *pa. pple* of FIND *verb*.

foundation /faʊnˈdeɪʃ(ə)n/ *noun*. LME.

[ORIGIN Old French & mod. French *fondation* from Latin *fundatio(n-)*, from *fundat-* pa. ppl stem of *fundare*: see FOUND *verb*[1], -ATION.]

1 The action of building on a firm substructure; the state of being so built. Now *rare*. LME.

2 *fig.* The action of establishing or constituting on a permanent footing; *esp.* the establishing of an institution with provision for its future maintenance. LME. ▸†**b** The charter establishing a society, institution, etc., with rules for its maintenance. LME–M16.

of the New Foundation, **of the Old Foundation** (of a cathedral) in which the chapter was reconstituted, left intact, by Henry VIII at the Reformation.

3 A fund devoted to the permanent maintenance of an institution; an endowment. LME. ▸**b** An institution (e.g. a college, hospital, monastery, etc.) maintained by an endowment. E16. ▸**c** An organization with a permanent fund devoted to financing research, the arts, and other charitable causes. E20.

b M. MEYER Sweden then boasted two universities, both ancient foundations.

on the foundation, †**of the foundation** entitled to enjoy the funds of an endowed institution, i.e. by being a member of it. **c** ***Gulbenkian Foundation***, ***Rockefeller Foundation***, etc.

4 The solid ground or base (natural or artificial) on which a building rests. Also *sing.* & (usu.) in *pl.*, the lowest part of a building, constructed below ground level and supporting the weight of the whole. LME.

fig.: P. G. WODEHOUSE A hearty laugh that rocked me to my foundations.

5 *fig.* That on which an abstract thing is based or depends; an underlying principle or source, the basis of a report or belief, etc. LME. ▸†**b** A basis of agreement. M17–L18. ▸**c** In *pl.* The fundamental principles *of* a subject, esp. as a separate object of study. E19.

B. RUSSELL In all social animals . . cooperation . . has some foundation in instinct. R. HOGGART Girls who were . . the foundation of Leeds' predominance as a centre for ready-made clothing. M. MUGGERIDGE My mother's suspicions . . were quite without foundation.

6 *transf.* Something on which other parts are overlaid; *esp.* (*a*) a basic underpart or backing of a hat, skirt, etc.; (*b*) (in knitting etc.) the first set of stitches, to which the rest are secured. M19. ▸**b** A base for cosmetics. Usu. *attrib.*, as ***foundation cream***. E20. ▸**c** = ***foundation garment*** below. M20.

7 BEE-KEEPING. Sheets of beeswax placed in a frame for the bees to build their combs on. M19.

– COMB.: **foundation garment** a woman's corset or other supporting undergarment; **foundation member** = ***founder member*** s.v. FOUNDER *noun*[1]; **foundation-school** an endowed school; **foundation stone** a stone forming part of the foundations of a building, *esp.* one laid at a public ceremony to mark the beginning of the building; *fig.* a basis; **foundation stop** an organ stop sounding only a note and its octaves.

▪ **foundational** *adjective* forming a foundation; basic, fundamental: L17. **foundationary** *adjective* of or relating to a foundation M18. **foundationer** *noun* a person who is on the foundation of an endowed school or college M19. **foundationless** *adjective* having no foundation or basis M17. **foundationlessness** *noun* L19.

founder /ˈfaʊndə/ *noun*[1]. ME.

[ORIGIN from FOUND *verb*[1] + -ER[1].]

1 The original builder of a city or edifice. ME.

2 A person who sets up or establishes something for the first time; *esp.* a person who establishes an institution with an endowment for its future maintenance. ME.

†3 A person who supports or maintains another. M16–E17.

– COMB.: **founder effect** BIOLOGY the reduced genetic diversity which results when a population is descended from a small number of colonizing ancestors; **founder member** a member of an organization from the time when it was founded; **founder's kin** relatives of the founder of a school etc. who are thereby entitled to preferential treatment; **founder's shares** special shares issued to the founders or original subscribers of a public company, who receive a dividend only after the ordinary and preference share dividends have been paid.

▪ **foundership** *noun* M16.

founder /ˈfaʊndə/ *noun*[2]. ME.

[ORIGIN from FOUND *verb*[2] + -ER[1], perh. after Old French & mod. French *fondeur*.]

1 A person who casts metals or makes articles of cast metal. ME.

bell-founder, ***iron-founder***, etc.

2 A person who founds glass. M19.

founder /ˈfaʊndə/ *noun*[3]. LME.

[ORIGIN from FOUNDER *verb*. In sense 1 cf. French *fondrilles*.]

†1 In *pl.* Sediment, dregs. Only in LME.

2 Inflammation of a horse's foot from overwork. Also, a similar disease in dogs. M16.

3 In full ***body-founder***, ***chest-founder***. Rheumatism of the chest muscles in a horse. M18.

4 A landslip. L19.

founder /ˈfaʊndə/ *verb*. ME.

[ORIGIN Old French *fondrer*, *esfondrer* send to the bottom, submerge, collapse, from Proto-Romance verbs from alt. of Latin *fundus* bottom: cf. medieval Latin *fundora* bottom, *funderare* to founder.]

▸ **I** *verb trans.* **1** Knock to the ground; fell. Long *obsolete* exc. *Scot.* ME.

2 Cause to fall with lameness, fatigue, or (*fig.*) shock, dismay, etc.; *esp.* affect (a horse) with the founder. L16.

S. BECKETT Like an old hack foundered in the street, struggling no more. E. BOWEN Shock foundered Eric, sent him silly all over.

3 Cause (a ship) to fill with water and sink. M17.

▸ **II** *verb intrans.* **4** Chiefly of a horse or its rider: fall to the ground, esp. from lameness. Also, stick fast in a bog. LME.

B. ENGLAND Ansell staggered, foundered dully.

5 Of a structure: collapse, give way. L15.

C. LYELL The cliffs of Bawdsey . . are foundering slowly.

6 Of a ship: fill with water and sink to the bottom. E17. ▸**b** *fig.* Of a plan, hope, relationship, etc.: come to grief, fail. E17.

W. C. WILLIAMS Their ship . . had foundered in a storm at sea. **b** T. SHARPE Sir Godber's ideals had . . foundered on the rocks of financial necessity. GODFREY SMITH The development plans nearly foundered . . for lack of capital.

founderous /ˈfaʊnd(ə)rəs/ *adjective*. Chiefly *dial.* & *LAW*. Also **foundrous**. L17.
[ORIGIN from FOUNDER *verb* + -OUS.]
Causing a person or horse to founder; miry, full of pot-holes.

S. WEYMAN The road was deep and foundrous, and . . I was obliged to leave it . . to pass the worst places.

†**foundery** *noun* var. of FOUNDRY.

founding /ˈfaʊndɪŋ/ *noun*. M17.
[ORIGIN from FOUND *verb*² + -ING¹.]
1 (The casting of metal in) the manufacture of articles of cast metal. M17.
bell-founding, *iron-founding*, etc.
2 (The fusing of materials in) the manufacture of glass. L18.

founding /ˈfaʊndɪŋ/ *ppl adjective*. E20.
[ORIGIN from FOUND *verb*¹ + -ING².]
Associated in the foundation of an institution.
founding father *spec.* an American statesman at the time of the Revolution, esp. a member of the Federal Constitutional Convention of 1787. **founding member** = *founder member* s.v. FOUNDER *noun*¹.

foundling /ˈfaʊndlɪŋ/ *noun*. ME.
[ORIGIN from pa. pple of FIND *verb* + -LING¹, perh. after Middle Dutch & mod. Dutch *vondeling*.]
An abandoned child of unknown parentage.
– COMB.: **foundling hospital**, †**foundling house** *hist.* an institution caring for foundlings.

foundress /ˈfaʊndrɪs/ *noun*. LME.
[ORIGIN from FOUNDER *noun*¹ + -ESS¹.]
1 A female founder; *esp.* a woman who founds an institute. LME.
2 *ZOOLOGY*. A female which founds a colony. L19.

foundrous *adjective* var. of FOUNDEROUS.

foundry /ˈfaʊndri/ *noun*. Also †**foundery**. E17.
[ORIGIN from FOUND *verb*² + -RY, perh. after Old French & mod. French *fonderie*.]
1 The art or business of founding or casting metal; metal castings. E17.
2 A building where metal or glass is founded. M17.
– COMB.: **foundryman** a worker in a foundry.

fount /faʊnt/ *noun*¹. L16.
[ORIGIN Prob. back-form. from FOUNTAIN *noun* after *mount*, *mountain*.]
A source of water; a spring. Now chiefly *fig.*

R. P. GRAVES Housman . . seems to have been a fount of amusing anecdotes.

■ **fountful** *adjective* (chiefly *poet.*) full of springs E17.

fount /faʊnt/ *noun*². L17.
[ORIGIN Alt.]
PRINTING. = FONT *noun*² 2.
– NOTE: Until the advent of computer typesetting the usual form in Britain, and still common in British English.

fountain /ˈfaʊntɪn/ *noun*. ME.
[ORIGIN Old French & mod. French *fontaine* from late Latin *fontana* use as noun (sc. *aqua* water) of *fontanus* adjective of *fons*, *font-* a spring.]
1 A natural spring; the source of a river, stream, etc. Now chiefly *poet.* & *arch.* exc. *S. Afr.* ME. ▸**b** *fig.* A principal origin or source. LME.

H. M. BRACKENRIDGE The greatest objection to this country is the want of fountains and running streams. **b** W. BLACKSTONE The French law, which is derived from the same feodal fountain.

2 A jet or number of jets of water made to spout artificially; a structure built for such a jet or jets to rise and fall in. Also = *drinking fountain* s.v. DRINKING *verbal noun*. E16. ▸**b** = *SODA fountain*. M19.
3 *HERALDRY*. A roundel barry wavy argent and azure, representing water. E17.
4 A small reservoir for holding liquid, esp. oil in a lamp or ink in a pen or printing press. E18.
– COMB.: **fountainhead** the headwaters or source of a stream etc.; *fig.* an original source, esp. of information; **fountain pen**: in which the nib is constantly replenished with ink from a reservoir inside the pen.
■ **fountained** *adjective* supplied with fountains or springs E19. **fountaineer** *noun* (now *rare*) a person who operates or has charge of a fountain E17. **fountainless** *adjective* devoid of springs or fountains L17. **fountainous** *adjective* of the nature of a source; full of springs: M17.

fountain /ˈfaʊntɪn/ *verb intrans. & trans.* L19.
[ORIGIN from the noun.]
(Cause to) rise like the waters of a fountain.

four /fɔː/ *adjective & noun* (*cardinal numeral*).
[ORIGIN Old English *fēower* = Old Frisian *fiūwer*, *fiōr*, Old Saxon *fiwar*, *fiuwar*, *fiori*, Old High German *fior*, *fier* (Dutch, German *vier*), Old Norse *fjórir*, Gothic *fidwōr*, from Germanic from Indo-European, whence Sanskrit *catvārah*, *catur-*, Greek *tessares*, Latin *quattuor*.]
▸ **A** *adjective*. One more than three (a cardinal numeral represented by 4 in arabic numerals, iv, IV, rarely iiii, IIII, in roman). OE.

P. THOMAS They fired four Guns as Signals of Distress. E. L. LINTON He . . was the safest confidant to be found within the four seas. M. WEBB The meeting lasted four hours. DAY LEWIS Four tall windows on the ground floor.

four figures: see FIGURE *noun*. *the four freedoms*: see FREEDOM *noun*. **four walls** the walls of a room or a house, in extended usage the symbol of confinement within a restricted space. *to the four winds*: see WIND *noun*¹. *within the four corners*: see CORNER *noun* 3.

▸ **B** *noun*. **1** Four people or things identified contextually, as parts or divisions, years of age, points, runs, etc., in a game, chances (in giving odds), minutes, inches, shillings (now *hist.*), pence, horses in hand, etc. ME.

AV *2 Sam.* 21:22 These foure . . fell by the hand of Dauid. L. SIMOND An elegant post-chaise and four stopped at the door.

2 One more than three as an abstract number; the symbol(s) or figure(s) representing this (4 in arabic numerals, iv, IV, rarely (exc. on clock faces) iiii, IIII, in roman). ME.

W. WHEWELL Four . . was held to be the most perfect number.

3 The time of day four hours after midnight or midday (on a clock, watch, etc., indicated by the numeral four displayed or pointed to). Also *four o'clock*. LME.

SWIFT If you'll be sure to come at four.

4 A set of four; a thing having a set of four as an essential or distinguishing feature; *spec.* (*a*) a playing card, domino, or side of a die marked with four pips or spots; (*b*) a crew of four in a rowing boat; in *pl.*, boat races between such crews; (*c*) in *pl.*, four leaves to the sheet in a printed book; (*d*) an engine or motor vehicle with four cylinders; (*e*) *CRICKET* a hit to the boundary for which four runs are scored (cf. SIX *noun* 4(e)); (*f*) four playing cards of the same rank as a scoring combination (also in *pl.*). L15.

C. MACKENZIE Cosway was called away to make up a four at Bridge. J. ARCHER A four for Harvey . . and a six for the dealer.

5 The fourth of a set or series with numbered members, the one designated four (usu. *number four*, or with specification, as *book four*, *chapter four*, etc.); a size etc. denoted by four, a shoe, glove, garment, etc., of such a size, (also *size four*). E16.

E. WALLACE He had . . rowed 'four' in his boat.

Radio Four: see RADIO *noun* 3.

6 Each of a set of four; *spec.* (*a*) a large plant pot of which four are formed from a cast of clay; (*b*) a candle of which four constitute a pound in weight. E19.

– COMB.: Forming compound cardinal numerals with multiples of ten from twenty to ninety, as *thirty-four*, (*arch.*) *four-and-thirty*, etc., and (*arch.*) their corresponding ordinals, as *four-and-thirtieth* etc., and with multiples of a hundred, as *204* (read *two hundred and four*, US also *two hundred four*), *5004* (read *five thousand and four*, US also *five thousand four*), etc. With nouns + -ER¹ forming nouns with the sense 'something (identified contextually) being of or having four —s', as *four-seater*, *four-wheeler*, etc. Special combs., as **four-ale** *hist.* ale sold at fourpence a quart; a bar selling such ale; **four-ball** a golf match between two pairs with each player using a separate ball, the best ball on each side counting at each hole; **four-by-four** (*a*) (also **4 × 4**) a vehicle having four-speed transmission and four-speed auxiliary transmission; (*b*) *N. Amer.* a post or batten measuring four inches by four in cross-section; **four-by-two** (*a*) *military slang* the cloth attached to a pull-through; (*b*) *slang*, *derog.* a Jew; (*c*) *N. Amer.*, *Austral.*, & *NZ* a post or batten measuring four inches by two in cross-section; also called *two-by-four*; **four-channel** *adjective & noun* (designating) any of various systems for recording and playing back sound signals whereby, through the placing of four loudspeakers, the original front-to-back sound distribution may be reproduced as well as the side-to-side one of stereophony; **four-colour** *adjective* having or pertaining to four colours; *four-colour problem*, a problem to prove that any plane map can be coloured with only four colours so that no two same-coloured regions have a common boundary; **four-cycle** *adjective* = *four-stroke* below; **four-dimensional** *adjective* having a fourth dimension in addition to length, breadth, and depth; **four-eyes** *slang*, *derog.* (a nickname for) a bespectacled person; *four-figure*: see FIGURE *noun*; **four-flush** *noun & verb* (*a*) *noun* an almost worthless poker hand having four (not five) cards of the same suit; (*b*) *verb intrans.* (*US*) bluff, brag; **four-flusher** *US* a bluffer, a humbug; **four-foot** *adjective* (*obsolete* exc. *poet.*) four-footed; **four-footed** *adjective* having or using four feet (*esp.* opp. to biped); quadruped; **four-four** *adjective & noun* (*MUSIC*) (designating) time or rhythm consisting of four crotchets in a bar; **Four-H club** *N. Amer.* a club for the instruction of young people in citizenry and agriculture (from supposedly improving head, heart, hands, and health); **four-handed** *adjective* (*a*) (of a mammal) quadrumanous; (*b*) having or using four hands; (of a card game etc.) for four players; (of a piece of keyboard music) for two players; **four hundred** *US* the highest social group in a locality; **four-in-hand** (*a*) a vehicle with four horses driven by one person on the box; (*b*) *US* a necktie (to be) worn tied in a loose knot with two hanging ends; *four last things*: see LAST *adjective*; *four-leaf clover*: see CLOVER *noun*; **four-letter** *adjective* consisting of four letters; *esp.* designating any of several coarse English monosyllabic words referring to sexual or excretory functions; *four-letter man*, an obnoxious person; **four o'clock** (*a*) (more fully *four o'clock flower*) = *marvel of Peru* s.v. MARVEL *noun*¹; (*b*) the Australian friarbird; (*c*) a light meal taken at about four o'clock; **four-oh-four** (also **404**, **404 error**) *COMPUTING* an error message displayed by a browser indicating that an Internet address cannot be found; **four-part** *adjective* (*MUSIC*) composed for four parts or voices; **fourpence** four pence, esp. of the old British currency before decimalization; **fourpenny** *adjective* (*a*) worth or costing fourpence; *fourpenny nail*, a nail 1½ inches long of which a thousand add up to four pounds in weight; (*b*) *fourpenny one* (*colloq.*), a hard blow, esp. to the face; **four-post** *adjective* (of a bed) having four posts to support a canopy overhead; **four-poster** (**bed**) a four-post bed; **four pounder** a gun that throws a shot that weighs four pounds; **four-rowed** *adjective* having four rows; *four-rowed barley*, a form of six-rowed barley, *Hordeum vulgare*, having four longitudinal rows of fertile spikelets; **fourscore** *arch.* eighty; **four-square** *adjective*, *adverb*, & *noun* (*a*) *adjective* square-shaped, solidly based; resolute; (*b*) in a square form or position, resolutely; (*c*) *noun* (*arch.*) a figure having four equal sides; **four-star** *adjective & noun* (*a*) *adjective* given four stars in a grading in which this denotes the highest standard or the next standard to the highest, excellent; having or designating a military rank distinguished by four stars on the shoulder piece of the uniform; (*b*) *noun* something given a four-star grading, esp. petrol; **four-stroke** *adjective* (of an internal-combustion engine) having a cycle of four strokes (intake, compression, combustion, and exhaust); **four-vector** [German *Vierervektor*] *MATH.* a vector defined by four scalar components; *esp.* a space–time vector in relativity theory; **four-went(-ways)** (*obsolete* exc. *dial.*) a point where four ways meet, a crossroads; **four wheel** a four-wheeled vehicle; **four-wheel drive** (*a*) a transmission system which provides power directly to all four wheels of a vehicle; (*b*) a vehicle with four-wheel drive; **four-wheeler** a four-wheeled vehicle, *spec.* (*hist.*) a four-wheeled hackney carriage.
■ **fourfold** *adjective*, *adverb*, & *noun* (*a*) *adjective* four times as great or as numerous; having four parts, divisions, elements, or units; (*b*) *adverb* to four times the number or quantity; (*c*) *noun* (*rare*) a fourfold amount: OE. †**fourscorth** *adjective* eightieth L16–E18.

†**fourbe** *noun*. M17.
[ORIGIN French, lit. (masc.) 'cheat, impostor', (fem.) 'imposture' in thieves' cant, (from (fem.) *fourber* cheat,) from *fourbe* adjective, from Italian *furbo* (adjective) astute, (noun) a cunning person.]
1 A cheat, an impostor. M17–M18.
2 A trick, an imposture. M–L17.

†**fourbery** *noun*. Also **fur-**. M17–M19.
[ORIGIN French *fourberie*, from *fourber*: see FOURBE, -ERY.]
A piece of deception; a fraud, a trick, an imposture. Also (*rare*), deceit, trickery.

Fourcault /ˈfʊəkəʊ/ *noun*. E20.
[ORIGIN Émile *Fourcault* (1862–1919), Belgian inventor.]
Used *attrib.* to designate (apparatus used in) a continuous process for making sheet glass in which glass is drawn vertically upwards through a slot in a floating trough.

fourché /ˈfɔːʃeɪ/ *adjective*. Also **-ée**. L16.
[ORIGIN French *fourchée* forked, from *fourche* (pitch)fork.]
HERALDRY. Forked.

fourchette /fʊəˈʃɛt/ *noun*. M18.
[ORIGIN French, dim. of *fourche*: see FORK *noun*, -ETTE. See also *À LA fourchette*.]
1 *ANATOMY*. Something forked or resembling a fork; *spec.* the fold of skin at the posterior edge of the vulva. M18.
2 A forked object, instrument, or device; *spec.* the forked piece between two adjacent fingers of a glove. M19.
3 In any of several card games, a combination of cards immediately above and below the card led. L19.

Fourdrinier /fʊəˈdrɪnɪə, -ɪeɪ/ *noun*. M19.
[ORIGIN Henry (d. 1854) and Sealy (d. 1847) *Fourdrinier*, Brit. paper-makers and patentees of such a machine.]
In full *Fourdrinier machine*, †*Fourdrinier's machine*. A machine for making paper as a continuous sheet by drainage on a wire mesh belt.

fourgon /furgɔ̃/ *noun*. Pl. pronounced same. M19.
[ORIGIN French.]
A baggage wagon, a luggage van.

Fourier /ˈfʊrɪə, -rɪeɪ/ *noun*. M19.
[ORIGIN J. B. J. *Fourier* (1768–1830), French mathematician.]
MATH. & PHYSICS. Used *attrib.* and (less usu.) in *possess.* to designate various expressions etc. arising from the work of Fourier.
Fourier analysis the analysis of a complex waveform into a set of sinusoidal functions the frequencies of which form a harmonic series. **Fourier series** an infinite series of the form $\frac{1}{2}a_0 + (a_1 \cos x + b_1 \sin x) + (a_2 \cos 2x + b_2 \sin 2x) + \ldots$, (where the *a*s and *b*s are constants), used to represent or approximate a periodic function in Fourier analysis. **Fourier transform**, a function derived from another function and representing it by a spectrum of sinusoidal functions.

Fourierism /ˈfʊrɪərɪz(ə)m/ *noun*. M19.
[ORIGIN French *Fouriérisme*, from *Fourier* (see below) + -ISM.]
A system for the reorganization of society in accordance with the phalansterian principles of the French socialist Charles Fourier (d. 1837).
■ **Fourierist** *noun & adjective* (*a*) *noun* an adherent or student of Fourierism; (*b*) *adjective* of or pertaining to Fourierism: M19. **Fourieˈristic** *adjective* = FOURIERIST *adjective* L19.

fou rire /fu riːr/ *noun phr.* E20.
[ORIGIN French, lit. 'mad laughter'.]
(A fit of) wild or uncontrollable laughter.

Fournier /ˈfʊənɪə/ *noun*. E20.
[ORIGIN P. S. *Fournier* (see below).]
A typeface modelled on types made by the French punch-cutter P. S. Fournier (d. 1768).

fourniture /furnityːr/ *noun*. Pl. pronounced same. L19.
[ORIGIN French, lit. 'furniture'.]
= FURNITURE 7.

fourreau /ˈfʊərəʊ/ *noun*. **L19.**
[**ORIGIN** French, lit. 'sheath, scabbard'.]
A close-fitting dress; an underskirt forming part of a dress.

fourrier /ˈfʊərɪə/ *noun*. Long *obsolete* exc. *hist*. Also †**furrier**. **LME.**
[**ORIGIN** French, from Old French *forrier*: see **FORAYER**.]
A person going in advance of an army etc. to secure accommodation or other requirements; a purveyor, a quartermaster. Also, a harbinger, a courier.

foursome /ˈfɔːs(ə)m/ *pronoun, noun, & adjective*. **ME.**
[**ORIGIN** from **FOUR** + **-SOME**[2].]
▸ **A** *pronoun & noun*. **1** Formerly, four in all. Now, a group of four. **ME.**
2 *GOLF*. A match for four people, with two playing on each side. **M19.**
▸ **B** *attrib*. or as *adjective*. For four; *esp*. (of a dance) performed by four people together. **E19.**

F

fourteen /fɔːˈtiːn, ˈfɔːtiːn/ *adjective & noun* (*cardinal numeral*).
[**ORIGIN** Old English *fēowertīene* = Old Frisian *fiuwertīne*, Old Saxon *fiertein* (Dutch *veertien*), Old High German *fiorzehan* (German *vierzehn*), Old Norse *fjórtán*, Gothic *fidwōrtaihun*: see **FOUR**, **-TEEN**.]
▸ **A** *adjective*. One more than thirteen (a cardinal numeral represented by 14 in arabic numerals, XIV in roman). **OE.**
▸ **B** *noun*. **1** One more than thirteen, as an abstract number; the symbols or figures representing this (14 in arabic numerals, xiv, XIV in roman). **OE.**
2 Fourteen people or things identified contextually, as years of age, chances (in giving odds), minutes, shillings (now *hist*.), pence, etc. **LME.**
3 The fourteenth of a set or series with numbered members, the one designated fourteen, (usu. ***number fourteen***, or with specification, as ***book fourteen***, ***chapter fourteen***, etc.); a size etc. denoted by fourteen, a garment etc. of such a size, (also ***size fourteen***). **LME.**
4 A set of fourteen; a thing having a set of fourteen as an essential or distinguishing feature. **M20.**
5 Any of a set of fourteen; *spec*. (***a***) a plant pot of which fourteen are formed from one cast of clay; (***b***) a candle of which fourteen add up to a pound in weight. **L20.**
– **COMB.**: Forming compound numerals with multiples of a hundred, as **514** (read ***five hundred and fourteen***, US also ***five hundred fourteen***), etc. In dates used for one thousand four hundred, as **1485** (read ***fourteen eighty-five***), ***fourteen-twenties***, etc. With nouns + **-ER**[1] forming nouns with the sense 'something (identified contextually) being of or having fourteen —s', as ***fourteen-tonner*** etc.
■ **four'teener** *noun* something comprising fourteen parts; *esp*. (***a***) *rare* a poem of fourteen lines; (***b***) a line of fourteen syllables: **E19.**

fourteenth /fɔːˈtiːnθ, ˈfɔːtiːnθ/ *adjective & noun* (*ordinal numeral*).
[**ORIGIN** Old English *fēowertēoþa*, repl. in Middle English by forms from **FOURTEEN** + **-TH**[2]. Cf. Old Norse *fjórtándi*.]
▸ **A** *adjective*. Next in order after the thirteenth, that is number fourteen in a series, (represented by 14th). **OE.**
fourteenth part *arch*. = sense B.3 below.
▸ **B** *noun*. **1** The fourteenth person or thing of a category, series, etc., identified contextually, as day of the month, (following a proper name) person, esp. monarch or pope, of the specified name, etc. **OE.**
2 *MUSIC*. An interval embracing fourteen consecutive notes in the diatonic scale; a note a fourteenth above another given note; a chord of two notes a fourteenth apart, or based around the fourteenth of a note. **L16.**
3 Each of fourteen equal parts into which something is or may be divided, a fraction which when multiplied by fourteen gives one, (= ***fourteenth part*** above). **E19.**
– **COMB.**: Forming compound numerals with multiples of a hundred, as ***three-hundred-and-fourteenth*** (***314th***) etc.
■ **fourteenthly** *adverb* in the fourteenth place **M17.**

fourth /fɔːθ/ *adjective, noun, & adverb* (*ordinal numeral*).
[**ORIGIN** Old English *fēo(we)rþa* = Old Saxon *fiortho* (Dutch *vierde*), Old High German *fiordo* (German *vierte*), Old Norse *fjórði*, from Germanic from Indo-European, whence also Latin *quartus*, German *tetartos*, Sanskrit *caturtha*.]
▸ **A** *adjective*. Next in order after the third, that is number four in a series, (represented by 4th). **OE.**
fourth day Wednesday. **fourth dimension** a property of bodies that would make them be to solids as solids are to surfaces; *PHYSICS* time viewed as a quality resembling a length. ***fourth estate***: see **ESTATE** *noun*. **fourth finger** the finger fourth from the thumb, the little finger. **fourth gear** the fourth in a sequence of forward gears in a motor vehicle, bicycle, etc. **fourth-generation** *adjective* (of a computer) distinguished by large-scale integrated-circuit technology and very large rapid-access memory and belonging essentially to the post-1970 period. **fourth part** *arch*. = sense B.3 below. **fourth position** *BALLET* the position, esp. when starting or finishing a step, in which the feet are placed turned outwards one in front of the other, separated by the distance of one step; the corresponding position of the arms. **fourth wall** *THEATRICAL* a proscenium opening through which a stage is seen. **Fourth World** those countries considered to be the poorest and most underdeveloped of the Third World.
▸ **B** *noun*. **1** The fourth person or thing of a category, series, etc., identified contextually, as day of the month, (following a proper name) person, esp. monarch or pope, of the specified name, etc. **ME.** ▸**b** A person making up a foursome for a game, social event, etc. **E19.** ▸**c** (A person having) a place in the fourth class in an examination list. **E20.** ▸**d** = ***fourth gear*** above. **E20.**

S. **STURMY** Three Right Lines being given, To find a fourth in proportion to them. J. **O'HARA** He .. had three quick drinks and was on his fourth. J. **GARDNER** Selecting the Mahler Fourth. **b** T. S. **ELIOT** Wanting a fourth at bridge. **c** C. L. **WRENN** The consciousness in the minds of the Oxford authorities that Sweet had obtained a 'fourth' in greats.

Fourth of July, **Glorious Fourth**: the anniversary of the Declaration of Independence of the United States (1776).
2 *MUSIC*. An interval embracing four consecutive notes in the diatonic scale; a note a fourth above another given note; a chord of two notes a fourth apart, or based around the fourth of a note. **L16.**
3 Each of four equal parts into which something is or may be divided, a fraction which when multiplied by four gives one, a quarter, (= ***fourth part*** above). **L16.**

Scientific American Mortality during pregnancy and delivery may account for a fourth of the deaths.

third-and-fourth, ***thirds-and-fourths***: see **THIRD** *noun* 2.
– **COMB.**: Forming compound ordinal numerals with multiples of ten, as ***fifty-fourth*** (***54th***), ***five-thousand-and-fourth*** (***5004th***), etc.
▸ **C** *adverb*. Fourthly. **L15.**
■ **fourthly** *adverb* in the fourth place **E16.**

4WD *abbreviation*.
Four-wheel drive.

foussie *noun* see **FOSSÉ**.

fouter *noun* var. of **FOUTRE**.

fouth /fuːθ/ *noun*. *Scot*. **LME.**
[**ORIGIN** Var. of **FULTH**.]
Fullness, plenty.

foutre /ˈfuːtə/ *noun*. Now *rare* or *obsolete*. Also **fouter**. **L16.**
[**ORIGIN** Old French, use as noun of inf. from Latin *futuere* have sexual intercourse with (a woman).]
1 A valueless thing; the slightest amount. Esp. in ***a foutre for —***, ***not a foutre***. (Cf. **FUCK** *noun* 3.) *slang*. **L16.**
2 A worthless or contemptible person. **E18.**

fouty *adjective* see **FOOTY** *adjective*.

fovea /ˈfəʊvɪə/ *noun*. Pl. **-eae** /-ɪiː/. **L17.**
[**ORIGIN** Latin = small pit.]
ANATOMY. A small depression or pit; *esp*. the shallow pit in the retina at the back of the eye, which consists of cones and is the site of highest visual acuity (cf. ***macula lutea*** s.v. **MACULA** 2).
fovea centralis /sɛnˈtrɑːlɪs/ [= central] the fovea of the retina.
■ **foveal** *adjective* of, pertaining to, or situated in a fovea **L19.** **foveate**, **foveated** *adjectives* having or distinguished by a fovea or foveae; pitted: **M19.**

foveola /fəʊˈviːələ/ *noun*. Pl. **-lae** /-liː/. **M19.**
[**ORIGIN** Latin, dim. of **FOVEA**.]
ANATOMY. A small fovea.
■ **foveolate** *adjective* having or distinguished by a foveola or foveolae; pitted: **M19.** **foveolated** *adjective* = **FOVEOLATE** *adjective* **E19.**

fovilla /fəˈvɪlə/ *noun*. Now *rare* or *obsolete*. **L18.**
[**ORIGIN** mod. Latin, perh. alt. of *favilla*.]
BOTANY. The substance contained in pollen cells.

fowl /faʊl/ *noun*. Pl. same, **-s**.
[**ORIGIN** Old English *fugol* = Old Frisian *fugel*, Old Saxon *fugal*, Old High German *fogal* (Dutch *vogel*, German *Vogel*), Old Norse *fugl*, Gothic *fugls*, from Germanic, from base of **FLY** *verb*.]
1 A bird. *arch*. exc. as 2nd elem. of comb. (see below). **OE.** ▸†**b** *spec*. A game bird. **M17–M18.**

E. **TOPSELL** To defend them from Eagles, and other ravening Fowls. **MILTON** Beasts of chase, or fowl of game In pastry built. **b** **EVELYN** Sometimes we shot at fowls and other birds.

domestic fowl: see **DOMESTIC** *adjective* 2. ***game-fowl***: see **GAME** *noun*. ***guinea fowl***: see **GUINEA** 1. **WATERFOWL**. **WILDFOWL**.
2 A domestic cock or hen; any of various gallinaceous birds chiefly kept for eggs and flesh. Also *US*, a domestic duck or turkey. **ME.**

D. L. **SAYERS** I had half a dozen fowls to kill and pluck.

Surrey fowl: see **SURREY** *noun*[1] 2.
†**3** In *pl*. Winged creatures. **LME–M17.**

T. **GAGE** Battes, or Rear-mice and other fowle.

4 a *gen*. The flesh of fowl, esp. as food. Now only in ***fish, flesh, and fowl***. **L16.** ▸**b** *spec*. The flesh of a domestic cock or hen considered as food. **M19.**

b I. M. **BEETON** The remains of cold roast fowl.

– **COMB.**: ***fowl cholera***; ***fowl leucosis***: see **LEUCOSIS** 2; **fowl-paralysis** = **MAREK'S DISEASE**; **fowl pest** (***a***) = ***fowl plague*** below; (***b***) = ***NEWCASTLE disease***; **fowl plague** an acute, highly contagious, and usually fatal virus disease affecting poultry; **fowl pox** a virus disease of poultry in which lesions appear on the feather-free parts of the body, or on the mucous membranes of the mouth, nose, or throat; **fowl-run** an enclosure for fowls; a breeding establishment for fowls.

fowl /faʊl/ *verb intrans*. **OE.**
[**ORIGIN** from the noun.]
Catch, hunt, shoot, or snare wild birds, esp. wildfowl.

fowler /ˈfaʊlə/ *noun*. **OE.**
[**ORIGIN** from **FOWL** *verb* + **-ER**[1].]
1 A person who hunts birds, esp. wildfowl, for sport or food; a bird-catcher. **OE.**
†**2** A kind of light cannon, esp. for use on board ship. **LME–M17.**

fowling /ˈfaʊlɪŋ/ *noun*. **LME.**
[**ORIGIN** formed as **FOWLER** + **-ING**[1].]
The action of **FOWL** *verb*; the practice of catching, hunting, shooting, or snaring wild birds, esp. wildfowl.
– **COMB.**: **fowling piece** a light gun for shooting wildfowl.

fox /fɒks/ *noun*.
[**ORIGIN** Old English *fox* = Old Saxon *vuhs* (Dutch *vos*), Old High German *fuhs* (German *Fuchs*), from Germanic.]
▸ **I 1** Any of various sharp-snouted bushy-tailed carnivorous canids distinguished by a flattened skull and erect triangular ears; *esp*. the red-furred *Vulpes vulpes* (also ***red fox***), an important beast of the chase in England and proverbial for its cunning. **OE.**

R. **BURNS** Foxes and statesmen, subtile wiles ensure. W. **HOLTBY** Hounds .. lost their fox in Lipton Sticks. N. **TINBERGEN** Repeated raids by a fox in the egg-season.

Arctic fox: see **ARCTIC** *adjective* 1b. ***crazy like a fox***, ***crazy as a fox***: see **CRAZY** *adjective* 3. **fox and geese** a game played on a board with pegs, draughtsmen, etc. **fox and hounds** a game in which one player is pursued by the other players. **play the fox** (***a***) act cunningly; (***b***) sham (illness etc.). ***white fox***: see **WHITE** *adjective*.
2 *fig*. **a** A cunning, sly, or crafty person. **OE.** ▸**b** A freshman at a college etc. *arch*. *US slang*. **M19.** ▸**c** An attractive woman. *N. Amer. slang*. **M20.**

J. **ARBUTHNOT** Don't you see how that old fox steals away your customers?

3 The fur of the fox, esp. as dressed and used for clothing. **LME.**
POINTED fox.
4 Any of various animals related to the fox or considered to resemble it in appearance or habits. Usu. with specifying word. **L16.**
flying fox, ***sea fox***, etc.
5 (Usu. **F-**.) Orig. ***the Fox and Goose***. *The* constellation Vulpecula. **L18.**
▸ **II** Senses of obscure development.
†**6** A kind of sword. **L16–E18.**
7 A sourness in fermented beer caused during the brewing process. Long *rare* or *obsolete*. **M18.**
8 *NAUTICAL*. A strand formed by twisted rope yarn and used as seizing. **M18.**
– **COMB.**: **fox bane** a yellow-flowered aconite, *Aconitum vulparia*, native to central and southern Europe; **foxberry** the cowberry; **fox-chase** (***a***) *arch*. a fox-hunt; (***b***) a game in imitation of this; **fox-coloured** *adjective* of a reddish-brown or -yellow colour; **foxfire** *US* the phosphorescent light emitted by certain fungi on decaying timber; **fox-fur** (***a***) the dressed coat of a fox; (***b***) a garment lined or trimmed with such fur; **foxglove** (***a***) a tall woodland plant of the figwort family, *Digitalis purpurea*, which has tall spikes of purple or white bell-shaped flowers and is the source of digitalis; (***b***) any of various similar plants; *esp*. (formerly) mullein; **fox grape** any of various N. American wild grapes, esp. *Vitis labrusca*, from which originate many cultivated varieties; **foxhole** (***a***) *MILITARY* a hole in the ground used as a shelter against missiles or as a firing point; (***b***) *fig*. a place of refuge or concealment; **foxhound** a kind of hound bred and trained to hunt foxes; **fox-hunt** *noun & verb* (***a***) *noun* a hunt for a fox or foxes with hounds; a meeting or association for this; (***b***) *verb intrans*. go fox-hunting; **fox-hunter** a person who takes part in a fox-hunt; **fox-hunting** *noun* the sport or action of hunting a fox or foxes with hounds; **fox-hunting** *ppl adjective* that goes fox-hunting; fond of fox-hunting; **fox mark** a brown spot or stain in the leaves of a book, a print, etc., caused by damp affecting impurities in the paper; **fox moth** a reddish-brown European eggar moth, *Macrothylacia rubi*, with black-and-yellow woolly larvae; **fox-red** *adjective & noun* (of) a bright reddish brown; **fox shark** the thresher shark; **fox skin** the skin of a fox; **fox snake** a large harmless colubrid snake of N. America, *Elaphe vulpina*; **fox sparrow** a red-tailed N. American sparrow, *Zonotrichia iliaca*; **fox squirrel** a squirrel, *Sciurus niger*, of the eastern US; **fox terrier** a short-haired terrier bred for the unearthing of foxes, but kept chiefly as a pet.
■ **foxery** *noun* the characteristics or behaviour of a fox; craftiness, cunning: **LME.** **foxlike** *adjective* resembling (that of) a fox; *esp*. crafty, cunning: **L16.** **foxship** *noun* (***a***) *rare* the character or qualities of a fox, foxiness; (***b***) (with possess. adjective, as ***your foxship*** etc.) *joc*. a title or form of address given to a fox: **E17.**

fox /fɒks/ *verb*. **M16.**
[**ORIGIN** from the noun.]
†**1** *verb trans*. Pierce with a sword, stab. **M–L16.**
2 †**a** *verb trans*. Achieve by crafty means. *rare*. Only in **E17.** ▸**b** *verb intrans*. Act craftily, dissemble; sham illness etc. **M17.**
3 *verb trans*. Intoxicate, make drunk, befuddle. Chiefly as ***foxed*** *ppl adjective*. *arch*. **E17.** ▸†**b** Daze or stupefy (fish); make (fish) easy to catch by this means. **M17–E19.**
4 *verb trans*. Deceive, puzzle, trick. **M17.**

A. B. **LONGSTREET** Has he foxed you? U. **BENTLEY** I was foxed as how to cross the gulf that separated our two chairs.

5 *verb intrans*. Of beer: turn sour in the fermenting process. **M18.**
6 *verb trans*. Repair (a boot or shoe) by renewing the upper leather; ornament (the upper of a shoe) with a strip of leather. **L18.**

7 *verb trans.* Discolour (the leaves of a book, an engraving, etc.) with fox marks; *transf.* discolour with spots or blotches. Chiefly as ***foxed** ppl adjective*. **M19.**

foxie /ˈfɒksi/ *noun. Austral. & NZ.* **E20.**
[ORIGIN Abbreviation of *fox terrier*: see FOX noun, -IE.]
A fox terrier.

foxing /ˈfɒksɪŋ/ *noun.* **ME.**
[ORIGIN from FOX verb, noun + -ING[1].]
†**1** A fox's trick, a clever ruse or deceit. Only in **ME.**
2 The action of FOX verb. **M18.**
3 A strip of leather or other material used to ornament the upper of a boot or shoe. **M18.**
4 Discoloration, esp. of the leaves of a book etc. by fox marks. **L19.**

Foxite /ˈfɒksʌɪt/ *noun & adjective. hist.* **L18.**
[ORIGIN from C. J. *Fox* (see below) + -ITE[1].]
▸**A** *noun.* A political supporter or adherent of the Whig politician Charles James Fox (1749–1806), opponent of the younger Pitt. **L18.**
▸**B** *adjective.* Of or pertaining to Fox or the Foxites. **L18.**

foxtail /ˈfɒksteɪl/ *noun.* **LME.**
[ORIGIN from FOX noun + TAIL noun[1].]
1 A fox's brush (formerly a badge of a fool or jester). **LME.**
2 Any of several grasses of the genus *Alopecurus*, with a soft spikelike panicle; esp. *A. pratensis*, a common grass of meadows. Also ***foxtail-grass***. **M16.**
– COMB.: ***foxtail-grass***: see sense 2 above; **foxtail lily** = EREMURUS; **foxtail millet** the grass *Setaria italica*, with a dense spikelike panicle, grown as a cereal in warm countries and as fodder in the US.

foxtrot /ˈfɒkstrɒt/ *noun & verb.* **L19.**
[ORIGIN from FOX noun + TROT noun[1].]
▸**A** *noun.* **1** A pace with short steps, as in changing from trotting to walking. **L19.**
2 A ballroom dance with slow and quick steps; a piece of music for this dance. **E20.**
▸**B** *verb intrans.* Infl. **-tt-**. Dance a foxtrot. **E20.**
■ **foxtrotter** *noun* **E20.**

foxy /ˈfɒksi/ *adjective.* **E16.**
[ORIGIN from FOX noun + -Y[1].]
1 Foxlike; of the nature or appearance of a fox; *esp.* crafty, cunning. **E16.**

TENNYSON Modred's narrow foxy face. M. GEE He's . . foxy in his dealings with his elders.

2 a Of a painting: marked by an excessive predominance of reddish tints. **L18.** ▸**b** *gen.* Fox-coloured; reddish-brown or -yellow. **M19.**
3 Discoloured or defective through atmospheric conditions, improper treatment, etc.; *spec.* (of the leaves of a book etc.) discoloured by fox marks. **E19.**
4 Of a woman: sexually attractive. *colloq.*, orig. *N. Amer.* **E20.**

Details You spot a female who interests you. She's foxy beyond belief.

■ **foxily** *adverb* **M20.** **foxiness** *noun* **L19.**

foy /fɔɪ/ *noun. obsolete* exc. *dial.* **L15.**
[ORIGIN Dutch *fooi* tip, gratuity, Middle Dutch *foye*, *voye* from French *voie* way, journey.]
A parting entertainment, present, or drink, given by or to a person setting out on a journey.

foyaite /ˈfɔɪəʌɪt, ˈfəʊjəʌɪt/ *noun.* **L19.**
[ORIGIN from *Foya* locality in Portugal + -ITE[1].]
GEOLOGY. A type of nepheline-syenite rock, typically of trachytoid texture and containing orthoclase.

foyer /ˈfɔɪeɪ; *foreign* fwaje (*pl. same*)/ *noun.* **L18.**
[ORIGIN French = hearth, home from Proto-Gallo-Romance, from Latin *focus* fire: see -ER[2].]
1 = FOCUS *noun* 4. **L18.**
2 A large room in a theatre or concert hall for the use of the audience during intervals. Also, the entrance hall of a hotel, theatre, or other public building. **M19.**

FP *abbreviation*[1].
1 Former pupil.
2 Freezing point.

fp *abbreviation*[2].
Forte piano.

FPA *abbreviation.*
Family Planning Association.

FPS *abbreviation*[1].
Fellow of the Pharmaceutical Society.

fps *abbreviation*[2].
1 Feet per second.
2 Foot-pound-second.
3 Frames per second.

FPU *abbreviation.*
COMPUTING. Floating-point unit, a processor that performs arithmetic operations.

Fr *symbol.*
CHEMISTRY. Francium.

Fr. *abbreviation*[1].
1 Father.
2 French.

fr. *abbreviation*[2].
Franc(s).

†**fra** *preposition, adverb, & conjunction* see FRO.

frab /frab/ *verb trans. dial.* Infl. **-bb-**. **M19.**
[ORIGIN Unknown: cf. CRAB verb[1].]
Harass, worry.

frabjous /ˈfrabdʒəs/ *adjective. joc. colloq.* **L19.**
[ORIGIN Nonsense word invented by Lewis Carroll.]
Delightful, joyous.
■ **frabjously** *adverb* **L19.**

fracas /ˈfrakɑː/ *noun.* Pl. same /-kɑːz/. **E18.**
[ORIGIN French, from *fracasser* from Italian *fracassare* make an uproar.]
A disturbance, a row, an uproar.

R. MACAULAY An unseemly fracas with the police.

†**frache** *noun.* **M17–M19.**
[ORIGIN Unknown.]
A metal tray for holding glassware in the annealing process.

†**fracid** *adjective.* **M17–M19.**
[ORIGIN Latin *fracidus* soft, mellow (of olives), from *frax*, pl. *fraces* lees of oil: see -ID[1].]
Rotten from overripeness.

frack *adjective* var. of FRECK *adjective*.

fractal /ˈfrakt(ə)l/ *noun & adjective.* **L20.**
[ORIGIN French, from Latin *fract-*: see FRACTION, -AL[1].]
MATH. ▸**A** *noun.* A curve or surface having the property that any small part of it, enlarged, has the same statistical character as the whole. **L20.**
▸**B** *adjective.* Of the nature of a fractal; of or relating to fractals. **L20.**

fracted /ˈfraktɪd/ *adjective.* **M16.**
[ORIGIN from Latin *fract-* (see FRACTION) + -ED[1].]
†**1** Broken; *MATH.* fractional. **M16–E18.**
2 *HERALDRY.* Having a part displaced as if broken. **E19.**

fractile /ˈfraktʌɪl/ *noun.* **M20.**
[ORIGIN from FRACTION noun + -ILE.]
STATISTICS. = QUANTILE.

fractile /ˈfraktʌɪl, -tɪl/ *adjective. rare.* **E18.**
[ORIGIN from Latin *fract-* (see FRACTION) + -ILE.]
Fragile; of or relating to breakage.

fraction /ˈfrakʃ(ə)n/ *noun.* **LME.**
[ORIGIN Old French & mod. French from Christian Latin *fractio(n-)* breaking (as of bread), from Latin *fract-* pa. ppl stem of *frangere* break: see -ION.]
1 *MATH.* A numerical quantity that is not a whole number; one or more aliquot parts of a unit or whole number; any quantity expressed as a numerator (written above a horizontal line) divided by a denominator (written below the line); a small proportion or (*loosely*) amount. **LME.**

L. A. G. STRONG Walter tried a massé shot, and missed by the fraction of an inch. B. BAINBRIDGE It skimmed the air a fraction above Adolf's head.

continued fraction, ***decimal fraction***, ***improper fraction***, ***proper fraction***, ***vulgar fraction***, etc.
2 a The dividing of bread in the Eucharist. **LME.** ▸**b** *gen.* The action of breaking or disrupting; (formerly) refraction. Now *rare* or *obsolete*. **M16.**

b O. FELTHAM When the Affections are glewed to the world, Death makes not a Dissolution, but a Fraction.

†**3** The result of breaking; the state of being broken; a fracture, a breach, a fissure. **LME–L18.**
†**4** An interruption of harmony; discord; a breach of the peace; a rupture. **E16–L18.**
5 A thing broken off; a disconnected portion; a small piece. Now *rare*. **E17.**
6 A portion of a one-square-mile section of undeveloped land. *US.* **L18.**
7 Each of the portions, differing in physical or chemical properties, into which a mixture may be separated by distillation or another process. **M19.**
8 An organized group of Communists within a non-Communist body such as a trade union; any deviant or schismatic group. **E20.**

fractional /ˈfrakʃ(ə)n(ə)l/ *adjective.* **L17.**
[ORIGIN from FRACTION + -AL[1].]
1 Of, pertaining to, or dealing with a fraction or fractions; comprising or being a fraction; of the nature of a fraction; incomplete, partial, insignificant. **L17.**

Financial Times Fractional early gains were eventually replaced by equally minor falls.

2 Pertaining to or involving separation of a mixture into fractions. **M19.**
3 Of or pertaining to a (Communist) fraction. **E20.**
– SPECIAL COLLOCATIONS: **fractional crystallization** the separation of fractions of different chemical composition from a solution or liquid mixture by crystallization under varying physical conditions. **fractional currency**, **fractional note** *N. Amer.*: of less value than the basic monetary unit. **fractional distillation** separation, by means of distillation usu. with a fractionating column, of a liquid mixture into fractions differing in boiling point (and hence chemical composition). ***fractional note***: see ***fractional currency*** above.
■ **fractionalism** *noun* the doctrine or policy of a (Communist) fraction; factionalism, schism: **M20.** **fractionalist** *noun & adjective* (**a**) *noun* an adherent of fractionalism; (**b**) *adjective* of or pertaining to fractionalists or fractionalism: **M20.** **fractionally** *adverb* **L19.**

fractionalize /ˈfrakʃ(ə)n(ə)lʌɪz/ *verb trans.* Also **-ise**. **M20.**
[ORIGIN from FRACTIONAL + -IZE.]
Break up or separate into distinct parts or fractions.
■ **fractionaliˈzation** *noun* **M20.**

fractionary /ˈfrakʃ(ə)n(ə)ri/ *adjective.* **L17.**
[ORIGIN from FRACTION + -ARY[1].]
1 = FRACTIONAL 1. **L17.**
2 Dealing with or carried on by fractions or fragments; tending to divide into fractions. **M19.**

fractionate /ˈfrakʃəneɪt/ *verb.* **M19.**
[ORIGIN from FRACTION + -ATE[3].]
1 *verb trans. CHEMISTRY* etc. Separate into fractions by distillation or another method. **M19.** ▸**b** *gen.* = FRACTIONALIZE. **M20.**
fractionating column a tall vessel with horizontal subdivisions and inert packing, in which vapour from a still passes upwards through descending condensate, the vapour becoming progressively enriched in more volatile components as it ascends, and the less volatile components becoming concentrated in the descending liquid.
2 *verb intrans.* Break up into fractions. **M20.**
■ **fractioˈnation** *noun* **L19.**

fractionize /ˈfrakʃənʌɪz/ *verb trans.* Also **-ise**. **L17.**
[ORIGIN from FRACTION + -IZE.]
Break up into fractions.
■ **fractioniˈzation** *noun* **M20.**

fractious /ˈfrakʃəs/ *adjective.* **M17.**
[ORIGIN from FRACTION + -OUS, prob. after *faction*, *factious*. Sense 1 perh. from Latin *fract-* (see FRACTION) + -IOUS.]
†**1** Accompanied by breakage or rupture of parts. Only in **M17.**
2 Refractory, unruly; quarrelsome; cross, peevish. **L17.**

K. JONES Christina was the more fractious of the two, passionate and given to terrible tantrums. C. MCCARTHY The horse was fractious and scared and it skittered about in the street.

■ **fractiously** *adverb* **M18.** **fractiousness** *noun* **E18.**

fracto- /ˈfraktəʊ/ *combining form.* **L19.**
[ORIGIN from Latin *fractus* broken + -O-.]
METEOROLOGY. Prefixed to names of cloud types, with the sense 'broken, fragmentary' (***fracto-cumulus***, ***fracto-nimbus***).

fracture /ˈfraktʃə/ *noun.* **LME.**
[ORIGIN Old French & mod. French, or Latin *fractura*, from *fract-*: see FRACTION, -URE.]
1 The action of breaking; the fact of being broken; breakage; *esp.* the breaking of a bone. **LME.**
2 The result of breaking, esp. of a bone, or (*GEOLOGY*) of a stratum or strata under deformational stress; a crack, a division, a split. Formerly also, a broken part, a splinter. **LME.**
comminuted fracture, ***compound fracture***, ***greenstick fracture***, ***open fracture***, ***simple fracture***.
3 The way in which a rock or mineral breaks when subjected to a blow (as opp. to ***cleavage***); the characteristic appearance of the freshly broken surface of a rock or mineral. **L18.**
4 *PHONOLOGY.* = BREAKING 1b. **L19.**

fracture /ˈfraktʃə/ *verb.* **L16.**
[ORIGIN from the noun.]
1 *verb trans.* Cause a fracture in (esp. a bone). **L16.** ▸**b** Impress, excite, amuse greatly. *US slang.* **M20.**

M. CUTLER I fell upon a large round timber and fractured two ribs.

2 *verb intrans.* Break, suffer fracture. **L19.**

H. M. ROSENBERG What determines the point at which the specimen will fracture?

3 *verb trans. PHONOLOGY.* = BREAK *verb* 1f. **L19.**
■ **fracturable** *adjective* **L19.**

frae *preposition, adverb, & conjunction* see FRO.

fraenum *noun* var. of FRENUM.

frag /frag/ *noun & verb. US military slang.* **L20.**
[ORIGIN Abbreviation of *fragmentation grenade*.]
▸**A** *noun.* A hand grenade.
▸**B** *verb trans.* Attack or kill (someone, esp. an unpopular senior officer) with a hand grenade.

fragile /ˈfradʒʌɪl/ *adjective.* **L15.**
[ORIGIN Old French & mod. French, or Latin *fragilis*, from base of *frangere* break: see -ILE.]
†**1** Morally weak or vulnerable; liable to sin. **L15–M16.**
2 Liable to break or be broken; weak, perishable, easily destroyed. **M16.** ▸**b** Of a person: delicate in frame, constitution, or physique. **M19.**

BACON Of Bodies, some are Fragile; and some are Tough. *fig.*: G. VIDAL My own position here is fragile. **b** A. NEWMAN She looked . . young and fragile.

fragile X syndrome *MEDICINE* an inherited condition characterized by an X chromosome that is abnormally susceptible to

F

damage, especially by folic acid deficiency, tending to cause mental disability.
▪ **fragilely** *adverb* M19. **fragileness** *noun* E18.

fragility /frəˈdʒɪlɪti/ *noun*. LME.
[ORIGIN Old French & mod. French *fragilité* or Latin *fragilitas*, from *fragilis*: see FRAGILE, -ITY.]
†**1** Moral weakness. LME–E17.
2 The quality of being fragile. L15.

fig.: S. JOHNSON The fragility of beauty.

fragment /ˈfragm(ə)nt/ *noun*. LME.
[ORIGIN French, or Latin *fragmentum*, from base of *frangere* break; see -MENT.]
1 A broken off, detached, or incomplete part (*lit. & fig.*); a (comparatively) small (detached) portion; a broken piece; a part remaining when the rest is lost or destroyed. LME. ▸**b** An extant portion of a written work which as a whole is lost; a portion of work left uncompleted by its author; a part of anything uncompleted. L16.

CONAN DOYLE He held our cards in his hand, and he tore them up and stamped on the fragments. B. TARKINGTON It seemed to him that the last fragment of his familiar world had disappeared.

†**2** As a term of contempt. *rare* (Shakes.). Only in E17.

F

fragment /fragˈmɛnt, ˈfragm(ə)nt/ *verb trans. & intrans.* E19.
[ORIGIN from the noun.]
Break or separate into fragments (*lit. & fig.*).

H. FAST The population of the car was fragmented by language and origin. V. GLENDINNING The family began to fragment; sisters died or married and moved away.

▪ **fragmented** *adjective* broken or separated into fragments; disjointed, fragmentary: E19.

fragmental /fragˈmɛnt(ə)l, ˈfragm(ə)nt(ə)l/ *adjective*. E19.
[ORIGIN from FRAGMENT *noun* + -AL[1].]
= FRAGMENTARY.
▪ **fragmentally** *adverb* E19.

fragmentary /ˈfragm(ə)nt(ə)ri/ *adjective*. E17.
[ORIGIN from FRAGMENT *noun* + -ARY[1].]
1 Of the nature of, or composed of, fragments; not complete or entire; disconnected or disjointed. E17.

E. K. KANE Becoming embarrassed in fragmentary ice. B. JOWETT His knowledge is fragmentary and unconnected.

2 GEOLOGY. Composed of fragments of previously existing rock or other substances. M19.
▪ **fragmentarily** *adverb* M19. **fragmentariness** *noun* M19.

fragmentation /fragmɛnˈteɪʃ(ə)n/ *noun*. L19.
[ORIGIN from FRAGMENT *noun* + -ATION.]
The action of breaking or separating into fragments; the state of being fragmented; *spec.* in BIOLOGY, separation into parts which form new individuals or units.
– COMB.: **fragmentation bomb**, **fragmentation grenade**: designed to disintegrate into small fragments on explosion.

fragmentize /ˈfragm(ə)ntʌɪz/ *verb trans.* Also **-ise**. E19.
[ORIGIN from FRAGMENT *noun* + -IZE.]
Break into fragments.
▪ **fragmentiˈzation** *noun* M20. **fragmentizer** *noun* a machine for breaking up scrap metal L20.

†**fragor** *noun*. E17–E18.
[ORIGIN Latin, from base of *frangere* break: see -OR.]
A loud harsh noise, a crash, din.

fragrance /ˈfreɪgr(ə)ns/ *noun & verb*. M17.
[ORIGIN Old French & mod. French, or Latin *fragrantia*, from *fragrant-*: see FRAGRANT, -ANCE.]
▸ **A** *noun*. Sweetness of smell; sweet or pleasing scent; (in COSMETICS) a scent; *fig.* a pleasing emotional association. M17.

KEATS To . . share The inward fragrance of each other's heart. J. C. POWYS There was a faint fragrance of sap-filled grass in the air.

▸ **B** *verb trans.* Supply or fill with fragrance. *rare*. M19.

fragrancy /ˈfreɪgr(ə)nsi/ *noun*. L16.
[ORIGIN Latin *fragrantia*: see FRAGRANCE, -ANCY.]
The quality of being fragrant; sweetness of smell.

fragrant /ˈfreɪgr(ə)nt/ *adjective*. LME.
[ORIGIN French, or Latin *fragrant-* pres. ppl stem of *fragrare* smell sweet: see -ANT[1].]
Emitting a pleasant odour; sweet-smelling.

R. BROOKE From the inland meadows, Fragrant of June and clover, floats the dark. E. WAUGH Dust hung in the cool air, fragrant as crushed herbs.

fragrant orchid an orchid, *Gymnadenia conopsea*, with fragrant lilac flowers, frequent in calcareous grassland.
▪ **fragrantly** *adverb* E16.

'fraid /freɪd/ *adjective*. *colloq.* L19.
[ORIGIN Aphet. from AFRAID.]
Expr. regret: (I'm) afraid.

R. KIPLING Wish I could, Lizzie. 'Fraid I can't. D. GRAY 'So you won't go on working here?' 'No. 'Fraid not.'

frail /freɪl/ *noun*[1]. LME.
[ORIGIN Old French *fraiel*, of unknown origin.]
A kind of basket made of rushes, used for packing figs, raisins, etc.; the quantity of fruit contained in this. Also ***frail-basket***.

frail /freɪl/ *noun*[2]. *dial.* E19.
[ORIGIN Dissimilated form of FLAIL *noun*.]
A flail.

frail /freɪl/ *noun*[3]. *slang* (chiefly *US*). E20.
[ORIGIN from the adjective.]
A woman.

frail /freɪl/ *adjective*. ME.
[ORIGIN Old French *fraile*, *frele* (mod. *frêle*) from Latin *fragilis* FRAGILE.]
1 Morally weak; unable to resist temptation; (of a woman, *arch.*) immoral. Now *literary*. ME.

W. IRVING The leniency of one who felt himself to be but frail. E. A. FREEMAN A child of the frail Abbess of Leominster.

2 Liable to break or be broken; easily crushed or destroyed; fragile, transient. ME.

J. MARTINEAU A profounder but a frailer bliss. J. F. LEHMANN The sun burnt more fiercely through the frail shield of the willow leaves.

3 Weak in constitution or health; susceptible to illness; weakened by illness. ME.

P. H. GIBBS She looked thin, frail, and over-worked. W. BOYD The shock was too much for his frail body and he died in . . the morning.

†**4** Tender. *rare* (Spenser). Only in L16.
▪ **frailly** *adverb* ME. **frailness** *noun* (now *rare*) ME.

frail /freɪl/ *verb trans.* *US dial.* M19.
[ORIGIN Prob. from FRAIL *noun*[2].]
Beat, thrash.

frailty /ˈfreɪlti/ *noun*. ME.
[ORIGIN Old French *fraileté* from Latin *fragilitas*, from *fragilis* FRAGILE: see -ITY.]
1 Moral weakness; instability of mind; liability to yield to temptation. ME. ▸**b** A fault arising from moral weakness, a foible. E17.

SHAKES. *Oth.* Is't frailty that thus errs? **b** J. CHEEVER They quarreled like adults, with a cunning knowledge of each other's frailties.

2 Physical weakness, perishableness, infirmity, susceptibility to damage or destruction; an instance of this. Formerly also, a frail feature, a flaw. LME.

J. UPDIKE A man whose increasing physical frailty compelled retreat from social excitements.

fraise /freɪz/ *noun*[1]. E17.
[ORIGIN French = mesentery of a calf, in transf. use.]
1 A ruff such as was worn in the 16th cent. and was again fashionable in the 19th cent. E17.
2 A defensive palisade round a fortification, placed near the berm. L18.

fraise /freɪz/ *noun*[2]. L19.
[ORIGIN French, from *fraiser* enlarge a circular hole.]
A tool used for enlarging a circular hole; HOROLOGY a tool with several cutting edges.

fraise *noun*[3] var. of FROISE.

fraise /freɪz/ *verb trans.* E18.
[ORIGIN French *fraiser*, formed as FRAISE *noun*[1].]
FORTIFICATION. Fence or defend with or as with a fraise.

Fraktur /ˈfraktʊə/ *noun*. L19.
[ORIGIN German.]
TYPOGRAPHY. A German style of black letter, the normal type used for printing German from the 16th to the mid 20th cent.

framable /ˈfreɪməb(ə)l/ *adjective*. Also **frameable**. L16.
[ORIGIN from FRAME *verb* + -ABLE.]
Able to be framed. Formerly also, conformable.

framboesia /framˈbiːzɪə/ *noun*. Also ***-bes-**. E19.
[ORIGIN mod. Latin, formed as FRAMBOISE: see -IA[1].]
The disease yaws.

framboise /frɑːmˈbwɑːz/ *noun & adjective*. L16.
[ORIGIN Old French & mod. French from Proto-Gallo-Romance, conflation of Latin *fraga ambrosia* ambrosian strawberry.]
▸ **A** *noun*. †**1** The raspberry. L16–M17.
2 A shade of pink: raspberry colour. M20.
▸ **B** *adjective*. Of raspberry colour. E20.

frame /freɪm/ *noun*. ME.
[ORIGIN from the verb.]
▸ †**I 1** Advantage, benefit, profit. Only in ME.
▸ **II** Action or manner of framing.
2 †**a** A large body of people, an array. Only in LME. ▸**b** An established order or system, esp. of government. L16. ▸†**c** An arrangement of words; a formula in logic. E17–M18.

b SHAKES. *Macb.* But let the frame of things disjoint, both the worlds suffer.

b frame of reference (*a*) a system of coordinate axes in relation to which position may be defined and motion conceived of as taking place; (*b*) a set of standards governing perceptual or logical evaluation or social behaviour.
†**3** Adapted or adjusted condition; definite form, regular procedure; order. L15–E19.

SHAKES. *Haml.* Good my lord, put your discourse into some frame.

4 The action of framing or constructing; a contrivance, a plan. *obsolete* exc. *N. Amer. slang*, a frame-up. M16.
5 Mental or emotional disposition or state. More fully ***frame of mind***. M16.

DEFOE In this thankful frame I continued. T. DREISER Short . . was in an exceedingly jovial frame of mind.

6 The manner of framing; structure; constitution, nature. L16.

SPENSER The goodly frame . . of Castle Joyeous.

▸ **III** A framed work, a structure.
7 a The universe, the heavens, the earth, or any part of it, regarded as a structure. ME. ▸†**b** Any structure, device, or machine constructed of parts fitted together. LME–E18. ▸**c** The animal, esp. the human body, with reference to its build or constitution. L16. ▸**d** In Newfoundland, a string of nets for catching seals. E19. ▸**e** An emaciated animal (*Austral. & US*); in *pl.* (*Austral.*), draught cattle. L19.

c A. FRASER For all her slight frame, she was not unathletic.

8 A supporting structure; a structure of which the outline or skeleton is not filled in; a framework. LME. ▸**b** *spec.* A structure of wood, steel, or concrete, which supports and forms an integral part of a building. LME. ▸**c** A building, *esp.* a wooden one. Now only *spec.* (*US*), a frame house etc. (see below). LME. ▸**d** A supporting structure used in embroidery. Formerly also, a loom. E16. ▸**e** PRINTING. A piece of furniture carrying cases of type and other equipment, at which a compositor works. L17. ▸**f** That part of a pair of spectacles which encloses the lenses and holds them in position. M19. ▸**g** The rigid part of a bicycle. L19. ▸**h** In SNOOKER etc., the triangular form used in setting up the red balls; these balls as set up; a round of play in which all the balls (or a sufficient number for a victory) are pocketed in order; in SKITTLES & TENPIN BOWLING, each of the several innings forming a game. L19. ▸**i** The supporting skeleton of a motor vehicle, aircraft (cf. ***airframe*** s.v. AIR *noun*[1]), etc. E20.

P. S. BUCK The door was hung loosely upon a warped wood frame.

climbing frame: see CLIMB *verb* 1. ***mainframe***: see MAIN *adjective*. ***walking frame***: see WALKING *noun*. ***X-frame***: see X, X. ***ZIMMER frame***.
9 A surrounding structure, such as a case or border, in which something such as a picture or a pane of glass is set or let in. L16. ▸**b** HORTICULTURE. A portable or fixed structure covered with transparent material, used to protect seeds and young plants. L17. ▸**c** An open box of slats in which bees build and which can be removed from the hive. L17. ▸**d** Any of various utensils of which the outer case or border is an important part. E18. ▸**e** CINEMATOGRAPHY. Any of the series of separate pictures on a film. E20. ▸**f** TELEVISION. A single complete image or picture built up from a series of lines. M20.

T. S. ELIOT A photograph in a silver frame. *fig.*: H. CARPENTER Its opening and closing passages provide a frame to the narrative.

in the frame under consideration, in the spotlight. **b** ***cold frame***: see COLD *adjective*.
10 COMPUTING. **a** A complete or self-identifying message in a data communication system; a section of a recording on magnetic tape that comprises a single bit in each track. L20. ▸**b** A graphic panel in a display window, *spec.* in an Internet browser, enclosing a self-contained section of data and permitting multiple, independent document viewing. L20.
– COMB.: **frame aerial** a radio aerial composed of a rectangle or loop of wire, adapted for directional reception; **frame-breaker** *hist.* a Luddite; **frame drum**: with its head(s) stretched over a frame or hoop; **frame dwelling**, **frame house**, etc.: built of wood, supported by a framework of timbers; **frame saw** a thin saw stretched in a frame; **frameset** the frame and front fork of a bicycle; **frame story**: that serves as a framework within which a number of other stories are told; **frame work** work done on or with a frame (cf. FRAMEWORK).
▪ **frameless** *adjective* M19.

frame /freɪm/ *verb*.
[ORIGIN Old English *framian*, from base of FROM. Cf. Old Norse *frama* to further, advance, & related Old Norse *fremja* to further, advance, perform, which prob. infl. the sense-development.]
†**1** *verb intrans.* Profit, be of service. OE–ME.
2 *verb intrans.* Make progress; prosper, succeed; fare. *obsolete* exc. *dial.* OE.
†**3** *verb trans.* Make ready for use; equip or adorn *with*. Only in ME.
†**4** *verb trans.* Prepare (timber) for use in building; hew out; perform the carpenter's work for (a building). ME–E18.
5 *verb trans.* **a** Contrive, devise, invent (a plot, rule, story, etc.); compose; express. LME. ▸**b** Conceive, imagine. *arch.* L16. ▸†**c** Cause, produce. Only in L16. ▸**d** Form, articulate, utter (words, sounds). E17.

a M. McCarthy She . . stood looking out into the garden, endeavouring to frame an apology. R. P. Graves The motion was framed in anti-conservative terms. **b** Geo. Eliot He could frame to himself no probable image of love-scenes between them. **c** Shakes. *2 Hen. VI* Fear frames disorder.

a frame up *N. Amer. slang* prearrange (an event) surreptitiously and with sinister intent; plan in secret; fake the result of.

6 *verb trans.* Make, construct. LME.

B. Jowett The things in heaven are framed by the Creator in the most perfect manner.

†**7 a** *verb trans.* Give shape to, form (with material object); compose, give expression to (the face). L15–E18. ▸**b** *verb trans.* Shape, direct (one's thoughts, actions, etc.) to a certain purpose; *arch.* dispose, lead, (a person). Foll. by *for*, *to*, *to do*. M16. ▸**c** *verb trans. & intrans.* Direct (one's steps); set out upon (a journey); shape one's course, go. *obsolete* exc. *dial.* L16. ▸**d** *verb intrans. & trans.* Prepare, attempt, or pretend to do something; contrive *to* do something. Also, show promise in an activity. Now chiefly *dial.* E17.

a Shakes. *3 Hen. VI* I can . . frame my face to all occasions. **b** S. Pepys We were as merry as I could frame myself to be. J. Keble Thy silent grace, framing aright our lowly orisons. **c** E. Brontë Frame upstairs, and make little din. **d** Mrs H. Ward He frames well in speaking.

8 *verb trans.* Adapt, adjust, fit (chiefly an abstract object) *to* or *into* (something). M16. ▸†**b** *verb intrans.* Adapt oneself, conform. Of things: suit, fit. M16–M17.

Wordsworth Unto this he frames his song.

9 *verb trans.* Set or enclose in a frame; serve as a frame for. E18.

J. Carlyle I have your . . Villa framed and hung up. D. M. Thomas Her long straight black hair framed a somewhat heavy face.

10 *verb trans.* Concoct a false charge or accusation against; devise a scheme or plot with regard to; make the victim of a frame-up. *slang* (orig. *US*). E20.

C. E. Mulford Honest men framed, and guilty men let off for political reasons.

– COMB.: **frame-up** (*colloq.*, orig. *US*) something that has been prearranged or concocted, esp. with a sinister intent; a conspiracy or plot, e.g. to incriminate a person on false evidence.

▪ **framed** *adjective* that has been framed; provided with a frame: LME. **framer** *noun* a person who frames something LME. **framing** *verbal noun* (**a**) the action of the verb; (**b**) a framework; a frame or set or system of frames: LME.

frameable *adjective* var. of FRAMABLE.

framework /ˈfreɪmwəːk/ *noun*. See also ***frame work*** s.v. FRAME *noun*. L16.

[ORIGIN from FRAME *noun* + WORK *noun*.]

A structure made of parts joined to form a frame; *esp.* one designed to enclose or support; a frame, a skeleton.

F. C. Burnand The old arm-chair, whose framework had been made any number of years ago. *fig.*: H. I. Ansoff A large majority of decisions must be made within the framework of a limited total resource. *Tribune* A legal framework for individual workers' rights.

framework of reference = ***frame of reference*** s.v. FRAME *noun* 2b.

frampold /ˈframp(ə)ld/ *adjective*. *obsolete* exc. *dial.* L16.

[ORIGIN Unknown.]

1 Peevish, cross. L16.

2 Of a horse: fiery, spirited. E17.

franc /fraŋk/ *noun*. LME.

[ORIGIN Old French & mod. French, derived from the legend *Francorum rex* king of the Franks, on gold coins first struck in the reign (1350–64) of Jean le Bon.]

Orig., a gold coin used in medieval France; later, a silver coin used in France. Now, the basic monetary unit of Switzerland and certain other (formerly) French-speaking countries (and of France, Belgium, and Luxembourg until replaced by the euro in 2002). Cf. CENTIME, RAPPEN.

franc-archer /frɑ̃karʃe/ *noun*. Pl. ***franc-archers*** (pronounced same), ***francs-archers*** /frɑ̃zarʃe/. L17.

[ORIGIN French, lit. 'free archer'.]

FRENCH HISTORY. A member of a body of archers established by Charles VII, and exempted from taxes in consideration of their services.

franchise /ˈfran(t)ʃʌɪz/ *noun*. ME.

[ORIGIN Old French & mod. French, from *franc*, fem. *franche* free, FRANK *adjective*[1] + *-ise*, repr. Latin *-itia*, -ESS[2].]

†**1** Nobility of mind; liberality, magnanimity. ME–M17.

†**2** Freedom; exemption from servitude or subjection. ME–M17.

3 A legal immunity or exemption from a particular burden or jurisdiction, granted to an individual, a corporation, etc. Now chiefly *hist.* ME. ▸**b** A percentage specified in a marine insurance policy below which the underwriter incurs no responsibility. M19.

P. Holland A most famous towne . . with the franchises and right of a Colonie.

4 A right or privilege granted by the power of the monarch to any individual or group of people. LME. ▸**b** The powers granted by a governing body to any company set up for the public interest. *US*. E19. ▸**c** The authorization granted to a sports club, certifying its existence and ownership. *N. Amer.* E20. ▸**d** The authorization granted by a company to sell its products or services in a particular area. M20. ▸**e** An outstanding player in a team sport. *US colloq.* M20.

J. E. T. Rogers The right of having a watermill was a franchise. **c** S. Bellow The politics surrounding cable-TV franchises in Chicago. *Times* Liverpool is probably the only major city in England without a McDonald's franchise.

†**5** Freedom from arrest, granted to fugitives in certain privileged places; right of asylum or sanctuary. Also, an asylum, a sanctuary. LME–E17.

6 The freedom or full membership of a corporation or state; citizenship. LME.

C. Thirlwall Those citizens who had been deprived of their franchise for lighter offences.

†**7** The area over which a privilege extends; a territory, domain. LME–L19.

8 The right of voting at public elections. L18. ▸**b** Any one of the principles of qualification for the right to vote. L19.

V. S. Naipaul First election with universal adult franchise.

b *fancy franchise*: see FANCY *noun & adjective*.

▪ **franchisal** *adjective* of or belonging to franchises L19. **franchiˈsee** *noun* a holder of a franchise (FRANCHISE *noun* 4d) M20. **franchiser** *noun* (**a**) *rare* a person who is entitled to vote; (**b**) a company which or person who grants franchises: M19. **franchisor** *noun* = FRANCHISER (b) M20.

franchise /ˈfran(t)ʃʌɪz/ *verb trans.* LME.

[ORIGIN Old French & mod. French *franchiss-* lengthened stem of *franchir*, from *franc*, fem. *franche* free: see FRANK *adjective*[1]. Cf. AFFRANCHISE, ENFRANCHISE.]

Now chiefly as ***franchised*** *ppl adjective*, ***franchising*** *verbal noun*.

1 Make or set free; invest with a franchise or privilege; = ENFRANCHISE. Now *rare*. LME.

2 a Confer certain powers on (a company set up for the public interest). *US*. E20. ▸**b** Grant a franchise to; authorize (an individual) to sell certain products or services in a particular area. M20.

▪ †**franchisement** *noun* [Old French] = ENFRANCHISEMENT M16–E19.

†**Francic** *adjective*. L17–M19.

[ORIGIN medieval Latin *Francicus*, from *Francus* FRANK *noun*[1]: see -IC.]

Of or pertaining to the ancient Franks or their language.

francisc /franˈsɪsk/ *noun*. Also in Latin form **-cisca** /-ˈsɪskə/. E19.

[ORIGIN (French *francisque* from) medieval Latin *francisca*.]

hist. A kind of battleaxe used by the ancient Franks.

Franciscan /franˈsɪsk(ə)n/ *noun & adjective*. L16.

[ORIGIN French *franciscain* from mod. Latin *Franciscanus*, from *Franciscus* Francis: see below, -AN.]

▸ **A** *noun*. A friar or nun of the order founded by St Francis of Assisi in 1209. L16.

▸ **B** *adjective*. Of or belonging to the order of St Francis; pertaining to the Franciscans. L16.

▪ **Franciscanism** *noun* (*rare*) the system and practice of the Franciscans M19.

francise *verb* var. of FRANCIZE.

francium /ˈfransɪəm/ *noun*. M20.

[ORIGIN from *France* country of the element's discoverer + -IUM.]

A radioactive chemical element, atomic no. 87, which is the heaviest member of the alkali metal group and occurs as a decay product in uranium ores (symbol Fr). Cf. VIRGINIUM.

francize /ˈfransʌɪz/ *verb trans.* Also **-ise**. M17.

[ORIGIN French *franciser*, from *français* French.]

Make French; *spec.* (in Quebec) cause to adopt French as an official or working language.

▪ **franciˈzation** *noun* the action of making something French; the status thus conferred; *spec.* (in Quebec) the adoption of French as an official or working language: M17.

Franck–Condon /fraŋkˈkɒnd(ə)n/ *adjective*. E20.

[ORIGIN J. *Franck* (1882–1964) and E. U. *Condon* (1902–74), US physicists.]

PHYSICS. Designating or associated with the principle that an electronic transition leaves the nuclear configuration of a molecule unchanged.

franco /ˈfraŋko/ *adjective & adverb*. L19.

[ORIGIN Italian (*porto*) *franco* free (carriage).]

Of a foreign business transaction: free of any postal or delivery charge.

Franco- /ˈfraŋkəʊ/ *combining form*.

[ORIGIN from medieval Latin *Francus* FRANK *noun*[1] + -O-.]

Forming adjective and noun combs. with the meaning 'French, Frankish or French and —', as ***Franco-Canadian***, ***Franco-German***, ***Franco-Prussian***, ***Franco-Roman***. Cf. GALLO-[1].

▪ **Francoˈmania** *noun* a craze or excessive liking for France and French things L19. **Francophil(e)** *adjective & noun* (a person who is) friendly towards France or fond of France and French things L19. **Francoˈphilia** *noun* friendliness towards France; excessive fondness for France and French things: M20. **Francophobe** *adjective & noun* (a person who is) affected with Francophobia L19. **Francoˈphobia** *noun* dread or dislike of France and French things L19.

François Premier /frɑ̃swa prəmje/ *adjectival phr.* M19.

[ORIGIN French = Francis I (see below).]

Designating the styles of architecture, furniture, etc., characteristic of the reign of Francis I, King of France 1515–47.

Francoist /ˈfraŋkəʊɪst/ *noun & adjective*. M20.

[ORIGIN from *Franco* (see below) + -IST.]

▸ **A** *noun*. A supporter of (the policies of) General Francisco *Franco* y Bahamonde (1892–1975), Spanish Nationalist leader and later dictator of Spain. M20.

▸ **B** *adjective*. Of, pertaining to, or supporting the regime, policies, or principles of Franco. M20.

francolin /ˈfraŋkəlɪn/ *noun*. M17.

[ORIGIN French from Italian *francolino*, of unknown origin.]

Any of numerous African or Asian partridges belonging to the genus *Francolinus*.

Franconian /fraŋˈkəʊnɪən/ *adjective & noun*. E19.

[ORIGIN from *Franconia* (see below) + -AN.]

▸ **A** *adjective*. Of or pertaining to (the inhabitants of) Franconia, a region of Germany, formerly a duchy, bordering the River Main. E19.

▸ **B** *noun*. **1** A native or inhabitant of Franconia. M19.

2 *collect.* A group of medieval West Germanic dialects, combining features of Low and High German; the group of modern German dialects of Franconia. M20.

francophone /ˈfraŋkə(ʊ)fəʊn/ *noun & adjective*. Also **F-**. E20.

[ORIGIN from FRANCO- + Greek *phōnē* voice.]

(A person who is) French-speaking.

francs-archers *noun pl.* see FRANC-ARCHER.

franc tireur /frɑ̃ tirœːr/ *noun phr.* Pl. **-s -s** (pronounced same). E19.

[ORIGIN French = free shooter.]

An irregular soldier, a guerrilla fighter; *hist.* a member of an irregular French light-infantry corps, originating in the Revolutionary wars.

frangible /ˈfrandʒɪb(ə)l/ *adjective*. LME.

[ORIGIN Old French, or medieval Latin *frangibilis*, from Latin *frangere* break: see -IBLE.]

Able to be broken, breakable, fragile.

▪ **frangiˈbility** *noun* L18.

frangipane /ˈfrandʒɪpeɪn/ *noun*. L17.

[ORIGIN French, formed as FRANGIPANI.]

1 = FRANGIPANI 1. L17.

2 = FRANGIPANI 2. M19.

3 An almond-flavoured cream or paste. M19.

frangipani /frandʒɪˈpani, -ˈpɑːni/ *noun*. Also (now *rare*) **-panni**. M19.

[ORIGIN *Frangipani*, 16th-cent. Italian marquis, inventor of a perfume for scenting gloves.]

1 A perfume resembling jasmine. Now *spec.* the scent of the blossom of the frangipani plant, or an imitation of it. M19.

2 A fragrant ornamental shrub or tree of the neotropical genus *Plumeria*, of the dogbane family, *esp.* red jasmine, *P. rubra*. L19.

franglais /ˈfrɒ̃gleɪ, *foreign* frɑ̃glɛ/ *noun*. M20.

[ORIGIN French, blend of *français* French and *anglais* English.]

A corrupt version of the French language marked by the indiscriminate use of words and phrases of British and American origin.

franion /ˈfranɪən/ *noun*. Long *arch. rare*. M16.

[ORIGIN Unknown.]

A gallant, a lover. Also (Spenser), a promiscuous woman.

Frank /fraŋk/ *noun*[1].

[ORIGIN Old English *Franca* = Old High German *Franko*, perh. named after a weapon: cf. Old English *franca* javelin. Reinforced in Middle English by medieval Latin *Francus*, Old French & mod. French *Franc*, from Germanic. Cf. SAXON.]

1 A member of the Germanic nation or nations that conquered Gaul in the 6th cent., and from which the country received the name France. OE.

2 In the eastern Mediterranean region: a person of Western nationality. Cf. FERINGHEE. L17.

†**frank** *noun*[2]. LME–E19.

[ORIGIN Old French *franc* sty, from Germanic.]

An enclosure, *esp.* one for feeding hogs or other animals in, a sty.

frank /fraŋk/ *noun*[3]. E18.

[ORIGIN from FRANK *verb*[2].]

1 *hist.* The superscribed signature of a person entitled to send letters free of charge. E18. ▸**b** A letter bearing such a signature. M18.

2 The mark or impression made on an envelope etc. by franking it; a franked cover. M20.

frank /fraŋk/ *noun*[4]. *dial.* E19.

[ORIGIN Imit. of the bird's cry.]

The heron.

frank /fraŋk/ *noun*[5]. *colloq.* (chiefly *N. Amer.*). M20.

[ORIGIN Abbreviation.]

A frankfurter.

F

frank /fraŋk/ *adjective*[1]. ME.
[ORIGIN Old French & mod. French *franc*, *franche* from medieval Latin *francus* free. Orig. identical with the ethnic name *Francus* (see FRANK *noun*[1]).]
1 †**a** Free; not in slavery or captivity. ME–M17. ▸**b** Free from restriction, obligation, or anxiety. Long *obsolete* exc. *hist.*, in (chiefly legal) collocations as FRANK-FEE, FRANK-PLEDGE, etc. ME.
2 Liberal, bounteous, generous. Now *rare*. ME.

CARLYLE He.. set about improvements.. on a frank scale.

†**3** Of a plant, tree, etc.: of superior quality, producing good or abundant fruit, flowers, etc. Also of a drug or remedy: of high quality, valuable. Cf. FRANKINCENSE. L15–M17.
†**4** Luxuriant in growth, vigorous. M16–E17.
5 Ingenuous, open, sincere; candid, outspoken. M16. ▸**b** Undisguised, avowed. M18. ▸**c** MEDICINE. Unmistakable, obvious. L19.

E. LINKLATER His scowl had vanished, and he smiled in a large, frank, and genial way. L. DURRELL Though she was evasive with the doctors she was perfectly frank with her friends. A. THWAITE Before they had even met, they were frank critics of each other's poetry. **b** A. WILSON He leaned his head back against the chair and gave way to frank laughter. **c** R. D. LAING Schizoid manifestations.. perilously close to frank psychosis. *Lancet* Foul-smelling infected urine often containing frank blood.

†**Frank** *adjective*[2]. M16–L17.
[ORIGIN from FRANK *noun*[1].]
Native to or characteristic of the Western nations of Europe.

frank /fraŋk/ *verb*[1] *trans.* LME.
[ORIGIN from FRANK *noun*[2].]
1 Enclose and feed (*up*) in an enclosure. Long *rare*. LME.
†**2** Feed *up*, cram. M16–M17.

frank /fraŋk/ *verb*[2] *trans.* E18.
[ORIGIN from FRANK *adjective*[1].]
1 a *hist.* Sign (a letter etc.) to ensure transmission free of charge. E18. ▸**b** Put an official sign or mark on (a letter etc.), by mechanical means, to record payment of postage. Also *gen.*, put any official sign on (an envelope etc.). E20. ▸**c** Put a postmark on (a letter etc.) or on top of (a postage stamp). M20.

b F. RAPHAEL The envelopes... were franked 'STUDENT'S EXERCISE'. DAVID POTTER Letters and packets are franked with a handstamp or machine impression.

b franking machine: for officially marking letters with a sign in lieu of a postage stamp and recording the cost of postage incurred.
2 *fig.* Facilitate the coming and going of (a person); provide with a social entrée to. *arch.* E19.

T. COLLINS I have enough money to frank myself in a frugal way for some weeks.

3 Pay the passage of (a person); convey gratuitously. *arch.* E19.

J. H. BURTON An opportunity of being franked to Poland.

4 Exempt, make immune; *esp.* (*hist.*) exempt from future payment of tax etc. L19.
■ **franker** *noun* (**a**) a person who franks a letter; (**b**) a machine or device for franking letters: L18.

frankalmoign /ˈfraŋk(ə)lmɔɪn/ *noun*. E16.
[ORIGIN Anglo-Norman *fraunke almoigne*. Cf. FRANK *adjective*[1], ALMOIGN.]
LAW (now *hist.*). A feudal tenure in England by which a religious body could hold land perpetually, usu. in return for praying for the soul of the donor and his descendants.

Franken- /ˈfraŋk(ə)n/ *noun*. *colloq. derog.* L20.
[ORIGIN from FRANKENSTEIN.]
Forming nouns with the sense 'genetically modified'.
■ **Frankenfood** *noun* genetically modified food. L20.

Frankenstein /ˈfraŋk(ə)nstʌɪn/ *noun*. M19.
[ORIGIN The title of a novel (1818) by Mary Shelley whose eponymous main character constructed and gave life to a human monster. Often wrongly used as the name of the monster itself.]
A terrible creation; a thing that becomes terrifying to its creator. Also ***Frankenstein monster***, ***Frankenstein's monster***.
■ **Frankenˈsteinian** *adjective* M20.

Frankenthal /ˈfraŋk(ə)ntɑːl/ *noun*. M19.
[ORIGIN A town in the Palatinate, Germany.]
In full ***Frankenthal porcelain***, ***Frankenthal ware***, etc. A porcelain made at Frankenthal from the middle to the end of the 19th cent.

frank-fee /ˈfraŋkfiː/ *noun*. LME.
[ORIGIN from FRANK *adjective*[1] + FEE *noun*[2].]
LAW. A tenure of land in fee simple; land so held.

frankfold /ˈfraŋkfəʊld/ *noun*. *obsolete* exc. *hist.* E17.
[ORIGIN from FRANK *adjective*[1] + FOLD *verb*[2].]
LAW. = FALDAGE 2.

frankfurter /ˈfraŋkfəːtə/ *noun*. Also *__frankfurt__. L19.
[ORIGIN German *Frankfurter Wurst* Frankfurt sausage.]
A seasoned smoked beef and pork sausage, originally made at Frankfurt am Main in Germany.

frankincense /ˈfraŋkɪnsɛns/ *noun*. LME.
[ORIGIN Old French *franc encens* lit. 'high-quality (see FRANK *adjective*[1]) incense'.]
An aromatic gum resin used esp. for burning as incense, obtained from trees of the genus *Boswellia* (family Burseraceae), native to Somalia. Also, a similar resin obtained from fir or pine trees. Also, a tree yielding such a resin.

Frankish /ˈfraŋkɪʃ/ *adjective & noun*. ME.
[ORIGIN from FRANK *noun*[1] + -ISH[1].]
▸ **A** *adjective*. †**1** Of or pertaining to France or the French. Only in ME.
2 Of or pertaining to the ancient Franks. LME.
3 Of or pertaining to the Western nations of Europe. (Cf. FRANK *noun*[1] 2.) *rare*. L16.
▸ **B** *noun*. †**1** The language or people of France. Only in ME.
2 †**a** *collect. pl.* The ancient Franks. Only in ME. ▸**b** The language of the ancient Franks. M19.

franklin /ˈfraŋklɪn/ *noun*[1]. ME.
[ORIGIN Anglo-Latin *francalanus*, from *francalis* held without fees, from *francus* free: see FRANK *adjective*[1], -AL[1], -AN.]
†**1** A freeman. Only in ME.
2 A freeholder; *spec.* in the 14th and 15th cents., a member of a class of landowners of free but not noble birth, ranking below the gentry. *obsolete* exc. *hist.* ME.

LYTTON His dress was that of a substantial franklin.

†**3** A liberal host. L16–E18.

Franklin /ˈfraŋklɪn/ *noun*[2]. L18.
[ORIGIN Benjamin *Franklin* (1706–1790), US statesman, inventor, and scientist.]
1 In full ***Franklin stove***. A free-standing stove for heating a room. Also, a kind of iron fireplace. *N. Amer.* L18.
2 More fully ***Franklin's rod***. A lightning conductor. *US. arch.* E19.
■ **Franˈklinian** *adjective & noun* (**a**) *adjective* of, pertaining to, or characteristic of Benjamin Franklin; (**b**) *noun* a follower of Franklin: M18. **frankliniˈzation** *noun* (MEDICINE, *arch.*) the therapeutic use of static electricity L19.

franklinite /ˈfraŋklɪnʌɪt/ *noun*. E19.
[ORIGIN from *Franklin*, borough in New Jersey (ult. formed as FRANKLIN *noun*[2]) + -ITE[1].]
MINERALOGY. An oxide of zinc and iron, often with some manganese, which is a mineral of the magnetite group and usu. occurs as black octahedral crystals.

frankly /ˈfraŋkli/ *adverb*. M16.
[ORIGIN from FRANK *adjective*[1] + -LY[2].]
†**1** Freely; without restriction or restraint. M16–E17.
2 Generously, bountifully; unconditionally, unreservedly. Now *rare*. M16.

C. BRONTË The power of meriting the kindness.. so frankly offered.

3 Without concealment or reserve; avowedly, openly, plainly. M16.

E. BOWEN Quite frankly, the country gives me the creeps. J. BARTH Wingate told me frankly I was a damn fool. A. T. ELLIS The tourist haunts were.. frankly bent on commerce and communication.

4 With freedom of artistic expression. M19.

frankmarriage /ˈfraŋkmarɪdʒ/ *noun*. ME.
[ORIGIN Anglo-Norman *franc mariage*: see FRANK *adjective*[1], MARRIAGE.]
LAW (now *hist.*). A tenure by which a man and his wife held lands granted to them by the father or other blood relative of the wife, which were heritable for four generations, in return for no other service than fealty.

frankness /ˈfraŋknɪs/ *noun*. M16.
[ORIGIN from FRANK *adjective*[1] + -NESS.]
1 Freedom of manner or approach; candour, ingenuousness, openness; *spec.* outspokenness. M16.

J. TYNDALL I shall offend them.. by my frankness in stating this.

†**2** Bounteousness, generosity. L16–M18.
3 Freedom of artistic expression. L18.

frank-pledge /ˈfraŋkplɛdʒ/ *noun*. ME.
[ORIGIN Law Latin *franciplegium*, Latinization of Anglo-Norman *fraumcplege*, from Anglo-Norman *fraunc*, Old French & mod. French *franc* FRANK *adjective*[1] + *plege* PLEDGE *noun*, mistranslation of ***frithborh*** s.v. FRITH *noun*[1], through the altered forms *freoborg*, *friborg*, in which the 1st elem. was identified with *free*.]
LAW (now *hist.*).
1 Each of the mutually responsible members of a tithing etc. Also (occas.) the tithing itself. ME.
2 The system by which each member of a tithing was responsible for the good conduct of, or damage done by, every other member. LME.
view of frank-pledge a court held periodically for the production of the members of a tithing or later of a hundred or a manor.

frantic /ˈfrantɪk/ *adjective, noun, & adverb*. Also †**fren-**, †**phren-**. LME.
[ORIGIN Old French & mod. French *frénétique* from Latin *phreneticus* FRENETIC. The early change from -*e*- to -*a*- is unaccounted for.]
▸ **A** *adjective*. **1** Of a person. ▸**a** Mentally deranged, insane; violently or ragingly mad. Now *rare* or *obsolete*. LME. ▸**b** Wildly excited; distraught with rage, pain, grief, or other emotion. E17.

a A. B. JAMESON His father, believing him frantic, shut him up.. in his chamber. **b** J. K. JEROME Little mishaps, that.. drive you nearly frantic with rage, when they occur on the water.

2 Of an action, quality, etc.: pertaining to or displaying frenzy, uncontrolled, violent. E16. ▸†**b** Of a disease: accompanied by delirium or frenzy. L16–E18.

H. KELLER I felt as if invisible hands were holding me, and I made frantic efforts to free myself.

3 Extreme, very great. *colloq.* E20.

I. MURDOCH He felt a.. frantic desire for a drink.

▸ †**B** *noun*. A person who is frantic; a lunatic, a delirious patient. LME–M18.
▸ †**C** *adverb*. In a frantic manner. *rare*. L16–M17.
■ **frantically** *adverb* M18. **franticly** *adverb* (now *rare*) M16. **franticness** *noun* E16.

frap /frap/ *noun*. *rare*. L16.
[ORIGIN Imit.: cf. RAP *noun*[1].]
A noise made by knocking.

frap /frap/ *verb*. Infl. **-pp-**. ME.
[ORIGIN Old French *fraper* (mod. *frapper*).]
1 *verb trans.* & †*intrans.* (with *at*, *on*). Strike, beat. *obsolete* exc. *dial.* ME.
2 *verb trans.* NAUTICAL. Tie or bind together (esp. halyards) to increase tension or to prevent from blowing loose. M16.
■ **frapping** *verbal noun* (**a**) the action of the verb; (**b**) NAUTICAL a rope for binding or lashing: E19.

†**frape** *noun*[1]. ME–E18.
[ORIGIN App. from Old French *frap* multitude, of unknown origin.]
A crowd; a mob, a rabble.

frape /freɪp/ *noun*[2]. E18.
[ORIGIN Prob. from FRAP *verb*.]
1 In full ***frape-boat***. A type of boat with much frapping. *rare*. E18.
2 A rope used for mooring a boat. E20.

†**fraple** *verb intrans.* L16–E17.
[ORIGIN Perh. from Old French *frapillier* grow angry or indignant.]
Dispute, wrangle, bluster.

frapler /ˈfraplə/ *noun*. *arch.* L16.
[ORIGIN from FRAPLE + -ER[1].]
A blusterer, a bully.

frappant /frapɑ̃/ *adjective*. L18.
[ORIGIN French, pres. pple of *frapper* strike.]
Striking, impressive.

frappé /ˈfrapeɪ, *foreign* frape/ *adjective & noun*. M19.
[ORIGIN French, pa. pple of *frapper* in sense of 'to ice (drinks)'.]
▸ **A** *adjective*. (Chiefly of wine) iced, cooled; (of a drink) served with crushed ice. M19.
▸ **B** *noun*. A drink served with crushed ice or frozen to a slushy consistency. E20.

Frascati /fraˈskɑːti/ *noun*. M20.
[ORIGIN A district in Latium, Italy, SE of Rome.]
A wine, usu. white, produced in the Frascati region.

frass /fras/ *noun*. M19.
[ORIGIN German, from *fressen* devour (see FRET *verb*[1]).]
The excrement of larvae; the refuse left behind by boring insects.

frat /frat/ *noun*[1]. *N. Amer. slang*. L19.
[ORIGIN Abbreviation.]
(A member of) a students' fraternity.

frat /frat/ *noun*[2] & *verb*. *slang*. M20.
[ORIGIN Abbreviation.]
▸ **A** *noun*. **1** Fraternization by troops. M20.
2 A woman with whom a soldier fraternizes. M20.
▸ **B** *verb intrans.* Infl. **-tt-**. Fraternize (*with*). M20.
■ **fratter** *noun* M20.

fratch /fratʃ/ *verb & noun*. Also **thratch** /θratʃ/. LME.
[ORIGIN Prob. imit.]
▸ **A** *verb intrans.* †**1** Make a harsh or strident noise; creak. LME–L15.
2 Disagree, quarrel; scold. Now chiefly *dial.* E18.
▸ **B** *noun*. A disagreement, a quarrel. E19.
■ **fratchety**, **fratchy** *adjectives* scolding, quarrelsome L19.

frate /ˈfrɑːti, *foreign* ˈfraːte/ *noun*. Pl. **-ti** /-ti/. E18.
[ORIGIN Italian, lit. 'brother'.]
An Italian friar.

frater /ˈfreɪtə/ *noun*[1]. ME.
[ORIGIN Old French *fraitur* aphet. from *refreitor*, from late Latin *refectorium* REFECTORY.]
hist. The dining room of a monastery; a refectory.

frater /ˈfreɪtə/ *noun*[2]. M16.
[ORIGIN Latin = brother.]
†**1** An Abraham-man. (See ABRAHAM). M16–L17.
†**2** A friar. L16–M17.
3 A brother; a comrade. L18.

fraternal /frəˈtəːn(ə)l/ *adjective & noun*. LME.
[ORIGIN medieval Latin *fraternalis*, from Latin *fraternus*, from *frater* brother: see -AL[1].]
▸ **A** *adjective*. Of, pertaining to, or characteristic of, a brother or brothers; brotherly. LME.
fraternal order *US* a brotherhood or friendly society. **fraternal polyandry**: in which a woman married to one man is also wife

to that man's brother(s). **fraternal twin**: developed from a separate ovum and not necessarily closely similar to its sibling.
▶ **B** *noun. MEDICINE.* A fraternal twin. E20.
■ **fraternally** *adverb* E17.

fraternise *verb* var. of FRATERNIZE.

fraternity /frəˈtəːnɪti/ *noun.* ME.
[ORIGIN Old French & mod. French *fraternité* from Latin *fraternitas*, from *fraternus*: see FRATERNAL, -ITY.]
1 A group or order of men organized for religious or devout purposes. ME.
2 A group of men associated by some common interest, or of the same class, occupation, etc.; a guild or company. LME. ▸**b** A male students' society at a college or university, usu. with a name consisting of three letters of the Greek alphabet; a student association for academic and extracurricular activities. *N. Amer.* L18.
A. J. CRONIN Emmy.. preferred always to stop at those cafés likely to be frequented by the sporting fraternity.
3 The relationship between brothers; brotherhood. LME.
4 The state or quality of being fraternal; brotherliness. LME.
Observer Too much fratricide, too little fraternity.

fraternize /ˈfratənʌɪz/ *verb.* Also **-ise**. E17.
[ORIGIN French *fraterniser* from medieval Latin *fraternizare*, from *fraternus*: see FRATERNAL, -IZE.]
1 *verb intrans.* Form a friendship or associate (*with*), as a brother or brothers. E17. ▸**b** *spec.* Enter into friendly relations or associate socially with or *with* troops of an occupying power or civilians of an occupied country, usu. in contravention of military orders; *esp.* (of a soldier) have sexual relations with a woman of an occupied country. L19.
SIR W. SCOTT Too little of a democrat to fraternize with an affiliated society of the *soi-disant* Friends of the People. **b** *transf.*: F. TRUEMAN It was made clear by Len Hutton that we should not fraternize with the West Indian cricketers.
2 *verb trans.* Bring into fraternal association; unite as brothers. Now *rare.* M17.
COLERIDGE To know ourselves Parts and proportions of one wondrous whole! This fraternizes man.
■ **fraterniˈzation** *noun* [French *fraternisation*] the action of fraternizing; fraternal association: L18. **fraternizer** *noun* L18.

fratery *noun* var. of FRATRY *noun*[1].

frati *noun* pl. of FRATE.

fratricide /ˈfratrɪsʌɪd/ *noun.* L15.
[ORIGIN Old French & mod. French, or (in sense 1) Latin *fratricida*, (in sense 2) late Latin *fratricidium*, from Latin *fratr-*, *frater* brother: see -CIDE.]
1 A person who kills his or her brother or sister. L15.
2 The action of killing one's brother or sister. M16.
■ **fratriˈcidal** *adjective* E19.

fratry /ˈfreɪtri/ *noun*[1]. Now *rare.* Also **-tery** /-t(ə)ri/. LME.
[ORIGIN App. from FRATER *noun*[1] + -Y[3].]
= FRATER *noun*[1].

fratry /ˈfreɪtri/ *noun*[2]. *obsolete* exc. *hist.* M16.
[ORIGIN medieval Latin *fratria*, *fratreia* fraternity, app. infl. by Greek *phratria*.]
A fraternity or brotherhood; a friary.

Frau /fraʊ/ *noun.* Pl. **-en** /-ən/, **-s**. E19.
[ORIGIN German: cf. FROW *noun*[1].]
A German or Austrian woman. Freq. as a title, corresponding to ***Mrs***.

fraud /frɔːd/ *noun.* ME.
[ORIGIN Old French & mod. French *fraude* from Latin *fraud-*, *fraus* deceit, injury.]
1 The use of false representations to gain unjust advantage; criminal deception. ME. ▸**b** The quality of being deceitful; insincerity. Now *rare.* LME. ▸†**c** A state of delusion. *rare* (Milton). M–L17.
SWIFT They look upon fraud as a greater crime than theft. **b** LD MACAULAY Vices.. which are the natural defence of weakness, fraud and hypocrisy. **c** MILTON So glister'd the dire Snake, and into fraud Led Eve.
2 An act or instance of deception; a dishonest artifice or trick. LME.
M. TWAIN It was a base fraud—a snare to trap the unwary.
3 A method or means of deceiving; now *esp.* a person or thing not fulfilling expectation or description, an impostor. M17.
W. COWPER Not all.. Can.. Discern the fraud beneath the specious lure. R. COBB He's a bit of a fraud.. well, let us say, he exaggerates.
– PHRASES: **in fraud of** so as to defraud. ***pious fraud***: see PIOUS *adjective*.
– COMB.: **fraudsman** a cheat, an impostor, a fraud; **fraud squad** a division of a police force appointed to investigate fraud.
■ **fraudful** *adjective* fraudulent, treacherous LME. **fraudfully** *adverb* LME. **fraudless** *adjective* (now *rare*) free from fraud L16. **fraudster** *noun* a person who commits fraud, *esp.* in business dealings L20.

fraudulence /ˈfrɔːdjʊl(ə)ns/ *noun.* L15.
[ORIGIN Old French, or ecclesiastical Latin *fraudulentia*, from Latin *fraudulentus*: see FRAUDULENT, -ENCE.]
The quality or fact of being fraudulent; deceit.
■ Also **fraudulency** *noun* (now *rare*) M17.

fraudulent /ˈfrɔːdjʊl(ə)nt/ *adjective.* LME.
[ORIGIN Old French, or Latin *fraudulentus*, from *fraud-*: see FRAUD, -ULENT.]
1 Guilty of or given to fraud; deceitful, dishonest. LME.
2 Characterized by, of the nature of, or accomplished by, fraud. LME.
fraudulent preference: see PREFERENCE 4.
†**3** *MEDICINE.* Putrefying, gangrenous. LME–E17.
■ **fraudulently** *adverb* with intent to deceive, dishonestly LME.

Frauen *noun pl.* see FRAU.

fraughan /frɔːn/ *noun. Irish.* E18.
[ORIGIN Irish *fraochán*.]
= BILBERRY.

fraught /frɔːt/ *noun. obsolete* exc. *Scot.* ME.
[ORIGIN Middle Dutch, Middle Low German *vracht* (whence German *Fracht*) beside *vrecht* FREIGHT *noun*.]
†**1** = FREIGHT *noun* 2. ME–L17.
2 = FREIGHT *noun* 1. LME.
3 = FREIGHT *noun* 2b. LME.
J. M. BARRIE To carry a fraught of water to the manse.

fraught /frɔːt/ *ppl adjective.* LME.
[ORIGIN pa. pple of FRAUGHT *verb*.]
1 Of a ship: laden. *arch.* LME.
2 Supplied, provided, equipped, *with*. Now *poet.* LME.
SHAKES. *Lear* I would you would make use of your good wisdom, Whereof I know you are fraught.
3 Foll. by *with*. Involving, attended *with*, full of, (meaning etc.); destined to produce, threatening or promising, (danger, difficulty, etc.). L16.
P. G. WODEHOUSE A meeting with Oofy Prosser at this moment might be fraught with pain and embarrassment. K. CLARK An imaginary world, vaster, more dramatic and more fraught with associations.
4 Causing or suffering anxiety or distress. M20.
D. FRANCIS Don't look so fraught... They said it was clear there now. V. GLENDINNING Poor Georgina died after only four years of fraught marriage.

fraught /frɔːt/ *verb trans. arch.* Pa. t. & pple **fraught**, **fraughted**. See also FRAUGHT *ppl adjective*. LME.
[ORIGIN Middle Dutch *vrachten* load (a ship), formed as FRAUGHT *noun*.]
1 = FREIGHT *verb* 1. *obsolete* exc. as FRAUGHT *ppl adjective*. LME.
†**2** = FREIGHT *verb* 2. *Scot.* LME–L16.
3 Supply, provide, equip *with*. LME.
■ **fraughtage** *noun* †(*a*) = FREIGHTAGE 1; (*b*) = FREIGHT *noun* 2: LME. †**fraughter** *noun* (*Scot.*) = FREIGHTER 1 E16–L17.

Fräulein /ˈfrɔɪlʌɪn, *foreign* ˈfrɔylaɪn/ *noun.* L17.
[ORIGIN German, dim. of FRAU.]
An unmarried German woman; a German governess. Freq. as a title, corresponding to ***Miss***.

Fraunhofer /ˈfraʊnhəʊfə/ *noun.* M19.
[ORIGIN Joseph von *Fraunhofer* (1787–1826), Bavarian optician and physicist.]
1 ***Fraunhofer lines***, ***Fraunhofer's lines***, dark (absorption) lines in solar and stellar spectra. M19.
2 ***Fraunhofer diffraction***, ***Fraunhofer's diffraction***, diffraction in which the pattern is a linear function of the phase variation across the diffracting aperture or object. Cf. FRESNEL ***diffraction***. L19.

fraxetin /ˈfraksɪtɪn/ *noun.* M19.
[ORIGIN formed as FRAXIN + -ETIN.]
CHEMISTRY. A hydroxy derivative, $C_{10}H_8O_5$, of coumarin, the aglycone of fraxin.

fraxin /ˈfraksɪn/ *noun.* M19.
[ORIGIN from Latin *fraxinus* ash (tree) + -IN[1].]
CHEMISTRY. A coumarin glycoside found in the bark of ash, horse chestnut, and other trees. Cf. FRAXETIN.

fraxinella /fraksɪˈnɛlə/ *noun.* M17.
[ORIGIN mod. Latin, dim. of Latin *fraxinus* ash tree, with allus. to the pinnate leaves.]
A Eurasian plant of the rue family, *Dictamnus albus*, with showy white flowers and fragrant leaves which secrete a volatile flammable oil. Also called ***burning bush***, ***gas plant***.

fray /freɪ/ *noun*[1]. LME.
[ORIGIN from FRAY *verb*[1].]
†**1** An assault, an attack. LME–L16.
2 A disturbance, a stir; a noisy quarrel, a brawl; a fight, conflict (*lit.* & *fig.*). LME.
W. S. CHURCHILL The South African Armoured division.. was very forward in the fray. A. UTTLEY Susan was drawn in the fray to dust and polish. P. USTINOV It was time for the clergy to enter the fray against the Catholics in the Kremlin.
3 A feeling of fear; alarm, fright. *obsolete* exc. *Scot.* LME.

fray /freɪ/ *noun*[2]. M17.
[ORIGIN from FRAY *verb*[2].]
The result of fraying; a frayed place.

fray /freɪ/ *verb*[1]. ME.
[ORIGIN Aphet. from AFFRAY *verb*, EFFRAY.]
1 a *verb trans.* Affect with fear, frighten. *obsolete* exc. *poet.* & *dial.* ME. ▸†**b** *verb intrans.* Be afraid, fear; tremble, shudder with fear. LME–M17.
a *absol.*: SPENSER Instead of fraying they themselves did feare.
2 a *verb intrans.* Quarrel; make a disturbance, fight. *arch.* LME. ▸†**b** *verb trans.* Assault, attack; attack and drive *off*. LME–L16.
3 *verb trans.* Frighten or scare away. (Foll. by *away*, *off*, *out*.) *arch.* E16.
SIR W. SCOTT It is enough to fray every hawk from the perch.

fray /freɪ/ *verb*[2]. LME.
[ORIGIN French *frayer*, earlier *freiier*, *froiier*, from Latin *fricare* rub.]
1 *verb trans.* & *intrans.* Of a deer: rub (its head) against something to remove the velvet from its newly formed horns. LME.
2 a *verb trans.* Wear through by rubbing; ravel out the edge or end of (something woven or twisted); *fig.* strain (the nerves or temper). Formerly also, bruise. LME. ▸**b** *verb intrans.* (Of material) become ragged at the edge, unravel; *fig.* (of nerves or temper) become strained. E18.
a E. BOWEN The.. situation more and more frayed the young men's already battle-strained nerves. D. LODGE O'Shea's suit was baggy and threadbare, his shirts were frayed. **b** G. GREENE The cuffs had frayed and been repaired.
3 *verb trans.* Clear, force, (a path, way, etc.). L18.
J. G. FARRELL Think of.. the camel! Adapted.. for the desert regions through which it frays its diurnal passage.
■ **fraying** *verbal noun* (*a*) the action of the verb; (*b*) an abrasion on a tree, or the discarded velvet, resulting from a deer's fraying: LME.

F

frayn /freɪn/ *verb.*
[ORIGIN Old English *freġnan*, *frīnan* = Old Saxon *fregnan*, Old Norse *fregna*.]
1 *verb trans.* & *intrans.* Ask. *obsolete* exc. *dial.* OE.
†**2** *verb trans.* Ask for, request. Only in ME.

frazil /ˈfreɪz(ə)l, frəˈzɪl/ *noun. N. Amer.* L19.
[ORIGIN Canad. French *frasil* snow floating on water. Cf. French *fraisil* cinders.]
Slush consisting of small ice crystals formed in water too turbulent to freeze solid. Also ***frazil ice***.

frazzle /ˈfraz(ə)l/ *verb* & *noun. colloq.* (orig. *dial.* & *US*). E19.
[ORIGIN Uncertain: perh. blend of FRAY *verb*[2] and FAZLE.]
▶ **A** *verb trans.* & *intrans.* Fray, wear out, exhaust; *fig.* burn, char, shrivel up with burning. Freq. as ***frazzled*** *ppl adjective.* E19.
▶ **B** *noun.* The state of being frazzled; a frazzled thing. Chiefly in ***burnt to a frazzle***, ***worn to a frazzle***, ***beaten to a frazzle***, etc. E19.

FRCS *abbreviation.*
Fellow of the Royal College of Surgeons.

freak /friːk/ *noun* & *adjective.* M16.
[ORIGIN Prob. of dial. origin.]
▶ **A** *noun.* **1** A caprice, a whim, a vagary. *arch.* M16.
R. L. STEVENSON You should be able to stop and go on, and follow this way or that, as the freak takes you.
2 Capriciousness. *arch.* L17.
C. BRONTË A decent quiescence under the freak of manner, gave me the advantage.
3 A capricious prank or trick. *arch.* E18.
A. TROLLOPE Expelled from Harrow for some boyish freak.
4 Something fanciful or extravagant; (more fully ***freak of nature***) an abnormal or irregular occurrence, an abnormally developed person or thing, a monstrosity. L18. ▸**b** A person regarded as strange because of their unusual appearance or behaviour. *colloq.* L19.
b T. C. BOYLE They'd always looked at him as if he were a freak.. some kind of subspecies.
5 a A person obsessed with a specified activity, thing, etc., an enthusiast. *colloq.* E20. ▸**b** A hippy or other unconventional person; a person who uses or is addicted to drugs, esp. hallucinogenic or other specified drugs. *slang.* E20.
a B. W. ALDISS I was up early. I am a yoga freak.
– COMB.: **freak show** (at a fair) a sideshow featuring abnormally developed individuals.
▶ **B** *attrib.* or as *adjective.* Abnormal or capriciously irregular, freakish. Also, of or pertaining to freaks, unconventional. L19.
C. MCCULLERS A freak plant, a zinnia with six bronze petals and two red. K. M. E. MURRAY Unfortunately freak weather for August occurred and he arrived.. in snow. J. O'FAOLAIN He might have been ready to.. join some freak sect.
■ **freakdom** *noun* freakishness L19.

freak /friːk/ *verb*. **M17.**
[ORIGIN from FREAK *noun*; sense 1 perh. alt. of FRECK *verb* by assoc. with STREAK *verb*[2].]
1 *verb trans.* Fleck or streak randomly; variegate. Chiefly as ***freaked*** pa. pple. **M17.**

R. GRAVES A wan winter landscape, Hedges freaked with snow.

2 *verb intrans.* Gambol, frolic. *rare.* **M17.**
3 *verb trans. & intrans.* (Cause to) undergo narcotic hallucinations or a powerful emotional experience; (cause to) become angry. Chiefly foll. by *out*. *slang.* **M20.**

D. ADAMS 'It's the wild colour scheme that freaks me,' said Zaphod. L. ALTHER When she was first doing therapy, it freaked her out.

– COMB.: **freak-out** an intense emotional experience, *esp.* one resulting from the use of hallucinatory drugs.

freakish /'friːkɪʃ/ *adjective*. **L17.**
[ORIGIN from FREAK *noun* + -ISH[1].]
Capricious, whimsical; irregular, unpredictable; curious, grotesque.
■ **freakishly** *adverb* **L19.** **freakishness** *noun* **L17.**

freaky /'friːki/ *adjective*. **E19.**
[ORIGIN from FREAK *noun* + -Y[1].]
Freakish; *esp.* unconventional, weird.
■ **freakily** *adverb* **M20.** **freakiness** *noun* **L19.**

freath /friːð/ *verb trans. & intrans. Scot.* **E18.**
[ORIGIN Unknown: cf. FROTH *noun*.]
(Cause to) froth or foam.

freck /frɛk/ *adjective*. *obsolete* exc. *Scot. & N. English.* Also **frack** /frak/.
[ORIGIN Old English *frec*, *fric*, *fræc* = Old High German *freh* covetous, greedy (German *frech* bold, insolent), Old Norse *frekr* greedy, Gothic *faihufriks* avaricious.]
1 Eager, prompt, ready. **OE.**
2 Strong, vigorous. **E16.**
■ **freckly** *adverb* **ME.**

freck /frɛk/ *verb trans.* **E17.**
[ORIGIN Orig. pa. pple *freckt*, abbreviation of *freckled*: see FRECKLE, and cf. FREAK *verb*.]
Mark with spots or freckles; dapple.

freckle /'frɛk(ə)l/ *noun & verb*. Orig. (long *obsolete* exc. *dial.*) **frecken** /'frɛk(ə)n/. **LME.**
[ORIGIN Old Norse *freknur* pl. (Swedish *fräkne*, Danish *fregne*).]
▸ **A** *noun*. **1** A light brown patch on the skin, usu. produced by exposure to the sun. **LME.**
2 *gen.* A small spot or discoloration. **L15.**
▸ **B** *verb*. **1** *verb intrans.* Become marked with freckles. **M16.**
2 *verb trans.* Mark with freckles. **E17.**
■ **freckled** *adjective* (**a**) marked with freckles; spotted, dappled; †(**b**) (*rare*) resembling a freckle: **LME.** **freckly** *adjective* covered with freckles **E18.**

free /friː/ *adjective, noun, & adverb*.
[ORIGIN Old English *frēo* = Old Frisian, Old Saxon, Old High German *frī* (Dutch *vrij*, German *frei*), Gothic *freis*, from Germanic from Indo-European, repr. by Sanskrit *priya* dear, from base meaning 'to love'.]
▸ **A** *adjective* **I 1** Of a person: not or no longer in bondage, servitude, or subjection to another, having personal rights and social and political liberty as a member of a society or state. **OE.**

B. RUSSELL Sympathy not only for free Greeks, but for barbarians and slaves. *Country Life* She wanted to be an artist and a free woman, refusing to be called 'Mrs'. *fig.*: J. DENHAM Who . . free from Conscience, is a slave to Fame.

†**2** Noble, honourable, of gentle birth and breeding. Also, (of character and conduct) noble, honourable, generous, magnanimous. **OE–M17.**

SHAKES. *Oth.* I would not have your free and noble nature Out of self-bounty be abus'd. MILTON Thou Goddess fair and free.

3 Of a state, its citizens, and institutions: enjoying national and civil liberty, not subject to foreign domination or despotic or tyrannous government. **ME.** ▸**b** *spec.* Designating (freq. with cap. initial) a political or racial group actively opposed to an invading, occupying, or hostile power; *esp.* denoting those who continued resistance to Germany in the Second World War after the capitulation of their respective countries. **M20.**

SHAKES. *Cymb.* Till the injurious Romans did extort This tribute from us, we were free. S. SMILES Holland . . became the chief European centre of free thought, free religion, and free industry. **b** C. GRAVES The scattered remnants of the Free French, Free Dutch, Free Polish, and Free Norwegian fleets.

▸ **II 4** Acting from one's own will or choice and not compelled or constrained; determining one's own action or choice without outside motivation. **OE.**

E. A. FREEMAN The choice of the electors would be perfectly free.

5 Ready to do or grant something; acting willingly or spontaneously; (of an act) done of one's own accord; (of an offer or agreement) readily given or made, made with good will. **ME.** ▸**b** Of a horse: ready to go, willing. **L15.** ▸**c** Ready *to do* something; eager, willing, prompt. *obsolete* exc. in ***free to confess*** below, where the adjective is now understood as sense 16b. **M17.**

c J. CLARE Mark . . his generous mind; How free he is to push about his beer.

6 Ready to give, liberal, lavish. Foll. by *of*. **ME.** ▸**b** (Of a gift) given out of liberality or generosity, not in return or requital for something; unrequested, unsolicited. **LME.**

S. BUTLER For Saints themselves will sometimes be Of Gifts that cost them nothing, free.

7 (Of speech) characterized by liberty in the expression of sentiments or opinions; uttered or expressed without reserve; plain-spoken. **ME.** ▸**b** Not observing due bounds, licentious, loose. **M19.**

H. NELSON Gave Lord Hood my free opinion that 800 troops . . would take Bastia. L. J. JENNINGS Men used rather free expressions to each other . . in the days of the Regency. **b** TENNYSON Earl Limours Drank till he jested with all ease, and told Free tales.

8 Acting without restriction or limitation; allowing oneself ample scope *in* doing something. **L16.** ▸**b** Unstinted as to supply or quantity; coming forth in profusion; administered without stint; abundant, copious. **M17.**

POPE How free the present age is in laying taxes on the next. H. BRACKEN He gives us a Caution not to be too free with such Preparations. G. BERKELEY The free use of strong fermented liquors. **b** S. BARING-GOULD A monthly rose that was a free bloomer.

9 Frank and open in conversation or dealings; ingenuous, unreserved. Also, forward, familiar, impudent. **M17.**

DEFOE I pressed him to be free and plain with me. R. B. SHERIDAN Not so free, fellow!

▸ **III 10 a** Usu. foll. by *from*, *of*: released or exempt from, not liable to (a rule, penalty, or payment). **OE.** ▸**b** Exempt from, having immunity from, not subject to (something regarded as hurtful or undesirable). **ME.**

a LD MACAULAY Free from all the ordinary rules of morality. **b** J. FERRIAR Our own writers are not free from this error. N. LINDLEY The point . . appears to me . . free from any real difficulty.

11 Exempt from, or not subject to, some particular jurisdiction or lordship. Also, possessed of particular rights and privileges. **ME.**
12 Of real property: held without obligation on rent or service, freehold. *arch.* **ME.**
13 Given or provided without charge or payment, gratuitous. Also, admitted, carried, or placed without charge or payment. **ME.**

DRYDEN Lazy Drones, without their Share of Pain, In winter Quarters free, devour the Gain.

14 Invested with the rights or immunities of or *of*, admitted to the privileges of or *of* (a chartered company, corporation, city, or the like). **LME.** ▸**b** Allowed the use or enjoyment *of* (a place etc.). **L17.**

J. LOCKE Is a Man under the Law of England? What made him Free of that Law? J. ENTICK The shop-keepers are obliged to be free of the city. **b** KEATS And I was free of haunts umbrageous.

15 Exempt from restrictions with regard to trade; not subject to tax, toll, or duty; allowed to trade in any market. **M17.**
▸ **IV 16** Not impeded, restrained, or restricted in actions, activity, or movement; unhampered, unfettered. **ME.** ▸**b** At liberty, allowed, or permitted *to do* something. **LME.** ▸**c** Unbiased, open-minded. Long *rare* or *obsolete*. **M17.**

A. RADCLIFFE Her dress . . was loosened for the purpose of freer respiration. B. JOWETT The various passions are allowed to have free play. **b** DICKENS She was free to come and go.

17 Clear of obstruction; not blocked; open, unobstructed. **ME.**

J. NARBOROUGH They did meet with no Ice, but a free and open Sea. SIR W. SCOTT And quickly make the entrance free.

18 Clear of something regarded as objectionable or an encumbrance. Foll. by *of*, *from*. **ME.**

R. HOLME A Woman all Hairy, no part of her Face free. C. LUCAS There is hardly any mine . . free from pyrite.

19 Guiltless, innocent, acquitted. Now *rare* or *obsolete*. **ME.**
20 At liberty; able to move about or range at will; *esp.* not kept in confinement or custody, released from confinement or imprisonment; liberated. **LME.**

LD MACAULAY Deer, as free as in an American forest. J. MORLEY Calvin . . set free all those souls. *Times* He wanted the accused to be allowed to go free.

21 Of a material: yielding easily to operation; easily worked; loose and soft in structure. **E16.** ▸**b** Of wood: without knots. **L17.**

J. SMEATON This stone was capable of being thus wrought, and was so free to the tool.

22 Not fixed, fastened, or held in one particular place. **L16.**

MILTON The tawny lion, pawing to get free His hinder parts.

23 Released from ties, obligations, and restraints. **L16.** ▸**b** Released or exempt from work or duty; clear of engagements; (of a room, table, etc.) not occupied or in use. **E17.**

SHAKES. *Ant. & Cl.* Free, madam! no . . He's bound unto Octavia. **b** G. BURNET Coleman had a whole day free to make his escape. E. WAUGH There is no table free. K. AMIS What about lunch today? Are you free?

24 Allowable or allowed (*to* or *for* a person *to do* something); open or permitted *to*. *arch.* **L16.** ▸**b** LINGUISTICS. Designating a form that can occur in isolation. **E20.** ▸**c** *PHONETICS*. Of a vowel: occurring in a syllable not ended by a consonant. **M20.**

J. JACKSON It was free to everyone to bastinado a Christian where he met him.

25 Disengaged from contact or connection with some other body or surface; relieved from the pressure of an adjacent or superincumbent body. **E18.**

ROBERT KNOX At the free surface of the mucous membrane.

26 Of a literary or artistic style: not observing strict laws of form. Of a translation: not adhering strictly to the original, not literal. **E19.**
27 *CHEMISTRY*. Not combined. **E19.**
28 *PHYSICS*. Of a source of power: disengaged, available to do work. **E19.**
29 *NAUTICAL*. Of the wind: not adverse. **M19.**

R. H. DANA We had the wind free . . sail after sail the captain piled on her.

– PHRASES: ***be free with***: see ***make free with*** below. **free and easy** *adjectival, adverbial, & noun phr.* (***a***) *adjectival phr.* unconstrained, natural, unaffected; unceremonious; careless, slipshod; morally lax, permissive; ***free and easiness***, a state or manner of being free and easy; (***b***) *adverbial phr.* (*rare*) in a free and easy manner; (***c***) *noun phr.* (*arch. slang*) a convivial gathering. **free on board**, **free on rail**, etc., without charge for delivery to a ship, a railway wagon, etc. **free to confess** ready and willing to make a confession. **free, white, and over twenty-one** *colloq.* not subject to another person's control or authority, independent. **it's a free country** *colloq.* the (course of) action proposed is not illegal or forbidden. **make free with**, **be free with** take liberties with. ***set free***: see SET *verb*[1]. ***Wee Free Kirk***: see WEE *adjective*.
▸ **B** *absol.* as *noun*. †**1** A person of noble birth or breeding; a knight or lady. **OE–M16.**
2 A free person. Long only as *collect. pl.*, *the* class of free people. **ME.**
Land of the Free: see LAND *noun*[1].
3 (**F-**.) ▸**a** *The* Free Church of Scotland, (later) *the* United Free Church. *Scot. colloq.* **M19.** ▸**b** A member of the Free Church of Scotland or (later) the United Free Church; ***Wee Free***: see WEE *adjective*. *Scot. colloq.* **L19.**
4 *FOOTBALL*. A free kick. **M19.**
5 A free thing; *esp.* something for which no charge is made. **E20.**
6 ***for free***, (provided) without cost or payment. *colloq.* (orig. *US*). **M20.**
▸ **C** *adverb*. **1** In a free manner; freely; *esp.* without cost or payment. **ME.**

DRYDEN Achitophel . . Disdain'd the golden Fruit to gather free. G. SEMPLE The Middle of the Current of the River, runs the freest.

free, gratis, and for nothing *colloq.* absolutely without charge.
2 *NAUTICAL*. Not close-hauled. **E19.**

F. MARRYAT We were going about four knots and a half free.

– SPECIAL COLLOCATIONS & COMB.: ***free agent***: see AGENT *noun* 4. **free alms** = FRANKALMOIGN. **free-associate** *verb intrans.* (*PSYCHOLOGY*) engage in free association. **free association** *PSYCHOLOGY* the statement, by a person under test, of ideas evoked by those specified by the tester, without further suggestion or control by the tester; an idea or feeling so evoked. **free ball** *SNOOKER* the right to nominate any ball as the object ball, as a result of being snookered by a foul stroke; a ball so nominated. **freebase** *noun & verb* (***a***) *noun* cocaine purified by heating with ether, and taken by inhaling the fumes or smoking the residue; (***b***) *verb trans.* purify (cocaine) thus. ***free bench***: see BENCH *noun* 6. **freeborn** *adjective* (***a***) born to the rights and liberty of a citizen, not born to slavery; (***b***) of, pertaining to, or befitting a freeborn person. **Free Church** (***a***) *gen.* a Church free from state control, *esp.* the Nonconformist as opp. to the Established Church; (***b***) *spec.* (*hist.*, more fully ***Free Church of Scotland***) the Church formed by ministers seceding from the Scottish Presbyterian establishment (1843), which amalgamated with the United Presbyterian Church to form the United Free Church in 1900. **free city** (***a***) *hist.* a medieval sovereign city state in Germany; (***b***) a semi-autonomous city under the authority of an international body. **free electron** an electron not bound in an atom or molecule. **free energy** *spec.* a thermodynamic property of a system that represents ability to do work. **free enterprise** the freedom of private business from state control. **free expression** the uninhibited expression of one's thoughts, feelings, and creative capacities. **free fall** motion under the force of gravity only, ballistic flight; unpowered motion in space; *esp.* the part of a parachute descent occurring before the parachute opens. **free-fall** *verb intrans.* move in a free fall. **free fight**: in which all present may join. **free float** (in critical path analysis) a float that can be utilized with no adverse effect on the timing of subsequent processes. **free-for-all** *adjective & noun* (designating or pertaining to) a fight that is open to all, an unrestricted contest or discussion. **free gift**: made not in return for anything; *esp.* an object given away by a firm in order to promote sales of a product. **free grace** the unmerited favour of God. **free hand** the right of acting completely at one's own discretion, *esp.* in relation to a particular undertaking (chiefly in ***give a free hand***, ***have a free hand***). **freehand** *adjective* (of a drawing) made without artificial aid to the hand. **free-handed** *adjective* generous, *esp.* with money. **free-handedly** *adverb* generously. **free-handedness** open-handedness, generosity. **free-hearted** *adjective* having a free heart; frank, open, unreserved; not burdened by anxiety, guilt, or suspicion; impulsive; generous, liberal. **free house** a public house or inn that does not belong to a brewery and may thus sell any brewer's liquor. **free kick** FOOTBALL a kick which the opposing team are not allowed to hinder or block (under different rules for different forms of the game), as one allowed against a team committing an infringement or in other defined circumstances. **Free Kirk** (***a***) *hist.* the Free Church of Scotland; (***b***) the minority of the Free Church of Scotland which stood apart when the main body amalgamated with the United Presbyterian Church to form the United Free Church in 1900. **free labour** (***a***) labour of people who are free, not slaves; (***b***) labour of people who are not members of a trade union. **free library**: available for use without payment. **free list**: of persons or things to be admitted free of payment, duty, etc. **free-liver** a person who gives free indulgence to the appetites, esp. eating. **free-living** *adjective* (***a***) (of a person) that is a free-liver; (***b***) BIOLOGY living freely and independently, not attached to a substrate; *esp.* not parasitic or symbiotic. **freeload** *verb intrans.* (*slang*) behave as a freeloader. **freeloader** *slang* a person who eats or drinks or is accommodated free of charge, a sponger. **free love** (the doctrine permitting) sexual relations irrespective of marriage. **free lunch** (orig. *US*) a lunch given gratis, *esp.* by barkeepers to attract custom; *fig.* (with allusion to the proverb ***there's no such thing as a free lunch***) something for nothing. **free market**: in which prices are determined by unrestricted competition. ***free pardon***: see PARDON *noun* 4b. **free pass** (a document giving the holder) the right to travel on a railway etc. or to enter a place of entertainment without paying. **free path** PHYSICS (***a***) the distance which a molecule or other particle traverses without encountering another particle or colliding with a containing wall; (***b***) the distance a sound wave travels between successive reflections from the walls of an enclosure; (in both senses chiefly in ***mean free path*** s.v. MEAN *adjective*[2]). **free period** a period in the regular timetable of an educational establishment during which a particular teacher or student has no definitely assigned duties. **free place** a place in a secondary fee-paying school awarded without charge to a particular student. **free port** (***a***) a port open to all traders; (***b***) a port area where goods are exempt from customs duty during loading and unloading. ***Free Presbyterian Church***: see PRESBYTERIAN *adjective* 1. **free-quarter** *hist.* (***a***) the obligation or impost of having to provide free board and lodging for troops; (***b***) the right of troops to be billeted in free quarters; the necessity for troops of having to find free quarters. **free radical** CHEMISTRY an uncharged atom or group of atoms having one or more unpaired electrons available for bonding. **free range** *US* open pastureland. **free-range** *adjective* designating (eggs or meat from) hens or other domestic fowl, or other animals raised for food, given some freedom of movement in seeking their own food. ***free rein***: see REIN *noun*[1]. **freeride** *noun & verb* (***a***) *noun* a type of snowboard designed for all-round use on and off piste; (***b***) *verb intrans.* ride such a snowboard, especially when not competing in races or performing tricks. **free school** (***a***) (chiefly *hist.*) a school at which no fees are charged; (***b***) an independent school run on the basis of freedom from restriction for the pupils. **free selection** AUSTRAL. HISTORY = SELECTION 4. **free skating** a competitive programme of variable skating figures performed to music. **free soil** US HISTORY territory in which slavery was prohibited; *attrib.* pertaining to or designating a 19th-cent. political party opposing the extension of slavery beyond the original slave states. **free space** PHYSICS: unoccupied by matter or by any electromagnetic or gravitational fields. **free speech** the right to express opinions of any kind without incurring a penalty. **free-spoken** *adjective* not concealing one's opinions, frank, blunt. **free-standing** *adjective* not attached or connected to another structure, not supported by a structural framework. **free state** (***a***) a state not subject to another; *rare* a republic; (***b***) US HISTORY a state of the US in which slavery did not exist. **Free Stater** a native, inhabitant, or supporter of a particular free state, *esp.* (*hist.*) of the Orange Free State or of the Irish Free State. **free stock** plants grown from seed to be used as rootstocks in grafting. **freestyle** *adjective* (***a***) *gen.* (of movement) unrestricted; (***b***) *spec.* (of a swimming race) in which any style of stroke may be used; (of wrestling) with few restrictions on the holds permitted. **free-tailed** *adjective*: ***free-tailed bat***, a molossid, *spec.* one of the genus *Tadarida*. **freethinker** a person who refuses to submit the reasoning process to the control of authority in religious belief; a rationalist. **freethinking** *noun & adjective* (***a***) *noun* free thought; (***b***) *adjective* holding the principles of freethinkers. **free thought** the free exercise of reason in matters of religious belief, rationalism. **free-to-air** (of television programmes) broadcast on standard public or commercial networks rather than on satellite, cable, or digital ones. **free trade** (***a***) an open and unrestricted trade; (***b***) trade or commerce left to follow its natural course without restriction on imports etc.; (***c***) *arch.* trade which evades the lawful customs duties, smuggling. **free-trader** a person who takes part in free trade; an adherent of free trade. **free vector** MATH. a vector of which only the magnitude and direction are specified, not the position or line of action. **free verse** = VERS LIBRE. **free vote** a parliamentary vote not made subject to party discipline. ***free warren***: see WARREN *noun*[1] 1b. **freeware** COMPUTING software that is available without charge. **freeway** (orig. *US*) an express highway, esp. with restricted access; a toll-free highway. **free wheel** the driving wheel of a bicycle able to revolve with the pedals at rest; a wheel or propeller that can run free of a clutch or other connection with motive power. **freewheel** *verb intrans.* ride a bicycle without pedalling, coast; *fig.* move or act without effort or constraint. **free world** the non-Communist countries collectively (as referred to by them).

free /friː/ *verb trans.* Pa. t. & pple **freed**.

[ORIGIN Old English *frēon*, *frēog(e)an* = Old Norse *fría*, *friá*, from Germanic, from base of FREE *adjective*.]

1 Make free (*from*, †*of*); set at liberty; release or deliver from bondage or constraint. OE.

> C. KINGSLEY Then he freed one of these four men. B. JOWETT A philosophy which could free the mind from the power of abstractions.

2 Relieve or deliver *from*, rid or ease *of* (a burden, obligation, inconvenience); exempt *from* (payment, tribute), confer immunity on. Formerly also, exempt (a church or similar foundation) from feudal services or exactions. OE. ▸**b** Clear from blame or stain; show or declare to be guiltless; absolve, acquit. Long *obsolete* exc. *Scot.* L16. ▸**c** Relieve or rid of the presence of a person. Foll. by *from*, *of*. L16. ▸†**d** Grant immunity *from* the operation of a thing; make safe and secure *from*. E–M17.

> D. HUME He freed their subjects from all oaths of allegiance. J. R. GREEN The towns had long since freed themselves from all payment of the dues . . exacted by the King. **b** AV *Rom.* 6:7 He that is dead, is freed from sinne. **c** H. MARTINEAU The gentleman soon chose to free the family of his presence. **d** D. PELL There are but few Trees . . that are free'd from the Thunder, save the Lawrel.

†**3** Remove so as to leave the place clear, banish, get rid of. L16–M17.

> S. DANIEL Free thine owne torment, and my griefe release.

†**4** Leap or get clear over (a ditch or other obstacle). L16–L18.
5 Clear, disengage, or disentangle (a thing) from some obstruction or encumbrance; get (oneself) loose, extricate. Formerly also, open so as to allow free passage. E17. ▸**b** NAUTICAL. Bail out water from (a ship). E17.

> DRYDEN Nor cou'd their tainted Flesh with Ocean Tides Be freed from Filth. *fig.*: C. M. YONGE Having freed himself from his difficulties.

6 MINING. Register (a new mine, vein, etc.) by making the customary payment. E17.

†**7** Frank (a letter). L18–E19.

> S. JOHNSON Please to free this letter to Miss L. Porter.

■ **freer** *noun* a person or agent who frees or sets free someone or something E17.

-free /friː/ *suffix*.

[ORIGIN from FREE *adjective*, *noun*, & *adverb*.]

Forming adjectives and adverbs with the sense 'free of or from (the first element)', as ***carefree***, ***dust-free***, ***lead-free***, ***rent-free***.

freebie /ˈfriːbi/ *adjective & noun*. *colloq.* (orig. *US*). M20.

[ORIGIN Arbitrary expansion of FREE *adjective*.]

▸ **A** *adjective*. Free, provided without charge. M20.

▸ **B** *noun*. Something free, provided without charge; *esp.* a free gift, free hospitality, or the like. M20.

freeboard /ˈfriːbɔːd/ *noun*. L17.

[ORIGIN formed as FREE *adjective* + BOARD *noun*; in sense 1 translating Anglo-Norman *franc bord*, in Anglo-Latin *francum bordum*: see FRANK *adjective*[1], BOARD *noun*.]

1 LAW (now *hist.*). The right of claiming a certain portion of land outside the fence of a park or forest; the land thus claimed. L17.

2 NAUTICAL. The height of a ship's side between the waterline and the lowest part of the deck. E18.

freeboot /ˈfriːbuːt/ *verb intrans.* L16.

[ORIGIN Back-form. from FREEBOOTER.]

Act as a freebooter, plunder.

freebooter /ˈfriːbuːtə/ *noun*. L16.

[ORIGIN Dutch *vrijbuiter*, formed as FREE *adjective* + BOOTY + -ER[1]. See also FILIBUSTER.]

A person who goes in search of plunder; a pirate; a piratical adventurer (*lit.* & *fig.*).

†**free-booty** *noun*. E17.

[ORIGIN formed as FREE *adjective* + BOOTY after FREEBOOTER.]

1 Plunder or spoil (to be) taken by force. E17–M18.
2 Taking of booty, plundering. *rare*. Only in M17.

freedman /ˈfriːdmən/ *noun*. Pl. **-men**. E17.

[ORIGIN from *freed* pa. pple of FREE *verb* + MAN *noun*.]

An emancipated (male) slave.

freedom /ˈfriːdəm/ *noun*.

[ORIGIN Old English *frēodōm*: see FREE *adjective*, -DOM.]

1 Exemption or release from slavery or imprisonment (*lit.* & *fig.*); personal liberty. OE.

> R. GRAVES I became your slave . . and it was you who gave me my freedom.

2 The quality of being free from the control of fate or necessity; the power of self-determination attributed to the will. OE.

> J. LOCKE In this then consists Freedom, (*viz.*) in our being able to act . . according as we shall choose, or will.

†**3** The quality of being free or noble; nobility, generosity, liberality. ME–L16.

4 The state of being able to act without hindrance or restraint; liberty of action; the right *of*, *to do*. ME.

> O. SITWELL The septs of Ireland . . fighting for their personal ideal of freedom—the freedom to fight.

5 Exemption *from* a specific burden, charge, or service; an immunity. ME. ▸**b** An immunity, privilege, or right possessed by a city, corporation, university, or other institution. Formerly also, a body possessing such an immunity etc.; the district over which a particular immunity etc. extended. L16.

> T. KEIGHTLEY Freedom from arrest, a privilege at that time necessary for the cause of liberty.

6 Exemption from arbitrary, despotic, or autocratic control; independence; civil liberty. LME.

> SWIFT Freedom consists in a people's being governed by laws made with their own consent.

†**7** Readiness or willingness to act. LME–E19.

> BACON We found . . such a freedome and desire to take strangers . . into their bosom.

8 The right of participating in the privileges attached to citizenship *of* a town or city (often given as an honour to distinguished people), or to membership *of* a company or trade. Also, the document or diploma conferring such freedom. LME. ▸**b** Foll. by *of*: unrestricted access to or use of. M17. ▸**c** The liberty or right to practise a trade; the fee paid for this. *obsolete* exc. *hist.* E18.

> J. WESLEY They presented me with the freedom of the city. **b** J. H. BURTON Having conferred on you the freedom of the library, he will not concern himself by observing how you use it.

F

9 Foll. by *from*. The state of not being affected by (a defect, disadvantage, etc.); exemption. E17.

> M. R. MITFORD There is a freedom from cant about the authoress.

10 Orig., the overstepping of due customary bounds in speech or behaviour, undue familiarity. Now also, frankness, openness, familiarity; outspokenness. E17.

> R. BOYLE This Love, I have taken the freedom to style 'Seraphic Love'. BURKE I talked . . with the freedom I have long used to him on this and other subjects.

11 Facility or ease in action or activity; absence of encumbrance. E17.

> J. TYNDALL The sun's rays penetrate our atmosphere with freedom.

12 Boldness or vigour of conception or execution. M17.

> J. HOWELL I alwaies lov'd you for the freedom of your genius.

13 A piece of common land allotted to a freeman. *Scot.* M18.

– PHRASES: ***Bird of Freedom***: see BIRD *noun*. **degree of freedom** (***a***) PHYSICS each of the independent modes in which motion or displacement of a body can occur; (***b***) CHEMISTRY (in *pl.*) properties which can vary independently in a system of given composition; (***c***) STATISTICS (in *pl.*) independent quantities contributing to a distribution. ***freedom of* CONSCIENCE**. ***freedom of* RELIGION**. ***freedom of speech*** = ***free speech*** s.v. FREE *adjective*, *noun*, & *adverb*. ***freedom of the press***: see PRESS *noun*[1]. **Freedom of the Rule** *Scot.* liberty granted to a Scottish advocate to plead at the English bar. **the four freedoms** freedom of speech, freedom of religion, freedom from want or fear, and freedom of the will.

– COMB.: **freedom fighter** a person who takes part in a resistance movement to an established political system; **freedom ride**, **freedom rider** *US* (a person taking part in) an organized challenge to racial laws in the American South during the 1960s, orig. a refusal to abide by the laws governing segregated seating in buses.

Freefone *noun* var. of FREEPHONE.

freehold /ˈfriːhəʊld/ *noun & adjective*. LME.

[ORIGIN translating Anglo-Norman *fraunc tenement* 'free holding'.]

▸ **A** *noun*. **1** A tenure by which an estate is held in fee simple, fee tail, or for term of life; a similar tenure of a dignity or office. LME.

2 An estate or office held by such a tenure. LME.

▸ **B** *attrib.* or as *adjective*. Held by freehold; of the nature of or pertaining to freehold. E16.

freeholder /ˈfriːhəʊldə/ *noun*. LME.

[ORIGIN translating Anglo-Norman *fraunc tenaunt* 'free tenant', in Anglo-Latin *francus tenans*.]

A person who possesses a freehold estate; SCOTS LAW (now *hist.*) a person who held land directly from the monarch, and who acquired by this the right to vote and to be elected to Parliament.

freelage /ˈfriːlɪdʒ/ *noun*. *obsolete* exc. *dial.* ME.

[ORIGIN from FREE *adjective* + alt. of -LOCK.]

1 Freedom; a franchise, a privilege. Long *rare*. ME.
2 A heritable property. *Scot.* E19.

freelance /ˈfriːlɑːns/ *noun*, *verb*, *adjective*, & *adverb*. Orig. two words. E19.

[ORIGIN from FREE *adjective* + LANCE *noun*.]

▸ **A** *noun*. **1** *hist.* A (medieval) mercenary, a *condottiere*. E19.

2 A person operating without permanent commitments in a particular sphere of activity; *spec.* a person who works, usu. in a specialist area, for no fixed employer. M19.

▸ **B** *verb intrans.* Act or work as a freelance. Freq. as ***freelancing*** *verbal noun*. E20.

▸ **C** *attrib.* or as *adjective*. Working as or done by a freelance or freelances. E20.

▸ **D** *adverb*. As or by a freelance or freelances. M20.

■ **freelancer** *noun* a freelance M20.

freely /ˈfriːli/ *adverb*. OE.

[ORIGIN from FREE *adjective* + -LY[2].]

1 Of one's own accord, spontaneously; without constraint or reluctance; unreservedly, without stipulation;

readily, willingly. OE. ▸b With freedom of will or choice. ME.

R. W. DALE He freely forgives the penitent. H. JAMES She told fibs as freely as she applied trimmings. b MILTON Because we freely love, as in our will To love or not.

2 Without restraint or reserve with regard to speech; unreservedly, frankly, openly, plainly. ME.

LD MACAULAY She well knew that she was not handsome, and jested freely on her own homeliness. C. P. SNOW He began to talk more freely among strangers.

3 Without restraint or restriction on action or activity; without hindrance or interference. ME. ▸b Without observance of or conformity to strict rule; loosely. M19.

J. MORLEY The right of thinking freely and acting independently. J. CONRAD He moved freely. I. MURDOCH Caverns or grottos through which, bending double, one could freely pass. b MAX-MÜLLER Translate it somewhat freely.

BREATHE freely.

4 Without stint; plentifully, abundantly; generously, liberally. ME.

DEFOE We ate very freely.

†5 In freedom; with the rights of free birth; without servitude; with absolute possession. ME–M17.

SHAKES. *Twel. N.* Thou shalt live as freely as thy lord To call his fortunes thine.

†6 Nobly; excellently, beautifully. ME–L15.
†7 Without payment or cost, gratis. Also, without punishment. ME–M18.
8 Entirely, completely; very. *Scot.* E16.

freeman /ˈfriːmən/ *noun*. Pl. **-men**. OE.
[ORIGIN from FREE *adjective* + MAN *noun*.]
1 A man who is personally free, with the rights and liberty of a citizen, not a slave or serf or subject to a tyrannical or occupying power. OE.
2 A person who possesses the freedom of a city, borough, or company. ME.

freemartin /ˈfriːmɑːtɪn/ *noun*. L17.
[ORIGIN Unknown: cf. Irish, Gaelic *mart* cow (fattened for the market).]
A hermaphrodite or imperfect female twin calf.

Freemason /ˈfriːmeɪs(ə)n/ *noun*. Also **f-**. LME.
[ORIGIN from FREE *adjective* + MASON *noun*.]
1 A skilled worker in stone, a mason; *esp.* a member of a class of such workers who customarily moved from place to place to work on any great building project and who possessed a system of secret signs and passwords for recognition among themselves. Now only *hist.* exc. as passing into sense 2. LME.

E. TOPSELL The master work-men, free masons, and carpenters.

2 A member of a society for mutual help, called the *Free and Accepted Masons* and having elaborate secret rituals. Formerly & orig. also, an honorary member accepted into a society of Freemasons (sense 1). M17.

Times He managed to keep his cool . . giving another officer a freemason's handshake.

■ **Freemaˈsonic** *adjective* M19.

Freemasonry /ˈfriːmeɪs(ə)nri/ *noun*. LME.
[ORIGIN from FREEMASON + -RY.]
†1 The craft or occupation of a skilled mason. Only in LME.
2 The system and institution of Freemasons. L18.
3 (Often **f-**.) Secret or tacit brotherhood; instinctive sympathy and understanding. E19.

V. GLENDINNING There was a sort of Freemasonry among those who . . stayed on in London during the worst of the war.

freeness /ˈfriːnɪs/ *noun*. Now *rare*. LME.
[ORIGIN from FREE *adjective* + -NESS.]
1 The quality or state of being free; freedom. LME.
2 Readiness; generosity. LME.
3 Unreservedness, frankness. M16.
4 Something free, provided without charge, esp. free hospitality. *W. Indian.* M20.

Freephone /ˈfriːfəʊn/ *noun*. Also **-fone**, **f-**. M20.
[ORIGIN from FREE *adjective* + alt. of PHONE *noun*[2].]
A telephone service whereby an organization pays the cost of certain incoming calls.
– NOTE: Proprietary name in the US.

Freepost /ˈfriːpəʊst/ *noun*. Also **f-**. L20.
[ORIGIN from FREE *adjective* + POST *noun*[2].]
A postal service whereby an organization pays the postage costs for certain incoming letters.

freesia /ˈfriːzɪə/ *noun*. L19.
[ORIGIN mod. Latin (see below), from Friedrich H. T. *Freese* (d. 1876), German physician: see -IA[1].]
Any of various plants (freq. hybrids) of the southern African genus *Freesia*, of the iris family, much grown for their fragrant tubular flowers of varied colours; a flowering stem of such a plant.

freestone /ˈfriːstəʊn/ *noun*. ME.
[ORIGIN formed as FREE *adjective* + STONE *noun*; in sense 1 translating Old French *franche pere*, Anglo-Latin *lapis liber* lit. 'stone of superior quality': see FRANK *adjective*[1].]
1 Any of various fine-grained sandstones or limestones that can be cut or sawn easily. Also, a slab or piece of such stone. ME.
2 In full ***freestone peach***, ***freestone nectarine***. A kind of peach or nectarine in which the stone becomes loose when the fruit is ripe. E19.

free will /friː ˈwɪl/ *noun & adjectival phr.* Also **free-will**. ME.
[ORIGIN from FREE *adjective* + WILL *noun*[1], translating late (eccl.) Latin *liberum arbitrium*, whence French *libre arbitre*.]
▸A *noun*. 1 Spontaneous will, inclination to act without suggestion from others. ME.

AV *Ezra* 7:13 All they . . which are minded of their owne free-will to goe vp to Ierusalem.

2 The power of directing one's own actions unconstrained by necessity or fate. ME.

HOBBES The third way of bringing things to pass, distinct from necessity and chance, namely freewill.

▸B *attrib.* or as *adjective*. (Usu. **free-will**.) Given readily or spontaneously, voluntary. M16.

BOSW. SMITH The free-will offerings of their golden ornaments by the Libyan women.

– COMB.: **Free Will Baptist** a member of a N. American sect, of Welsh origin, of Arminian Baptists.
■ **freewiller** *noun* (*arch.*, *derog.*) a believer in the doctrine of free will, *esp.* an Arminian L17.

freeze /friːz/ *noun*[1]. LME.
[ORIGIN from the verb.]
1 The action of FREEZE *verb*; *esp.* a state, coming, or period, of severe frost. LME. ▸b *spec.* The fixing or stabilization of prices, wages, etc., at a certain level or figure; the prevention of assets, credits, etc., from being realized. M20.

K. FIELD During a freeze there is no comfort in a southern house. *fig.*: J. D. SALINGER She gave me the big freeze when I said hello. b *New Statesman* A Socialist government should actively support a new nuclear freeze in Europe.

b ***wage freeze***: see WAGE *noun*.
2 A film shot in which movement is arrested by the repetition of a frame; a facility for stopping a film or videotape at a particular frame. M20.

M. EATON The credits come up . . on a freeze of Fletch's face.

– COMB.: **freeze-frame**, **freeze-shot** = sense 2 above.

†**freeze** *noun*[2]. M17–E18.
[ORIGIN Unknown.]
Water used for diluting wine.

freeze /friːz/ *verb*. Pa. t. **froze** /frəʊz/; pa. pple **frozen** /ˈfrəʊz(ə)n/, (*colloq.*) **froze**. See also FRORE.
[ORIGIN Old English *frēosan* = Middle Low German, Middle Dutch *vrēsen* (Dutch *vriezen*), Old High German *friosan* (German *frieren*), Old Norse *frjósa*, from Germanic from Indo-European base repr. by Latin *pruina* hoarfrost, Sanskrit *pruṣvā*.]
▸I *verb intrans.* 1 impers. in ***it freezes***, ***it is freezing***, etc.: the local temperature is such that water becomes solid through loss of heat; there is frost; *colloq.* it is bitterly cold. OE.

F. SMITH It snowed all night, and froze very hard.

2 Of (a body of) water: be converted into or become covered with ice through loss of heat. Of any liquid: solidify through loss of heat. Also, (esp. of an object containing moisture) become hard and rigid in this way. ME.

J. MCPHEE With the arrival of cold, they [fruit] freeze on the vine, and when they thaw . . they are . . sweeter. R. V. JONES His transport was immobilized because the engine oil had frozen solid.

3 Be or become fastened *to* or *together* by frost. LME.

C. FRY He should stand in the winter sea Till his clothes freeze to his flesh.

4 Be affected by or have the sensation of extreme cold; be or feel very cold. Also, suffer the loss of vital heat; be brought *to death* in this way (freq. *hyperbol.*); die by frost. LME. ▸b Have the feelings quenched or powers paralysed, esp. through experiencing an intensity of fright, shock, horror, or the like; be appalled, be terrified. M16. ▸c Become rigid or motionless; stop abruptly and hold one's position. Also, (of a movement in a film) be arrested by the repetition of a frame. M19.

COLERIDGE Her limbs did creep and freeze. C. LAMB His kitchen chimney was never suffered to freeze. J. D. SALINGER I wished I knew who'd swiped my gloves . . because my hands were freezing. b POPE Pale, trembling, tired, the sailors freeze with fears. J. P. MAHAFFY If I behold the tiny fish on which they put such a price I freeze with horror. c C. BRONTË The smile on his lips froze. *Listener* Whenever a sentry appeared, they froze.

▸II *verb trans.* 5 Affect with frost; make hard or rigid, injure or kill, by extreme loss of heat; bring *to death* in this way (usu. in *pass.*; freq. *hyperbol.*). ME.

J. KOSINSKI The frost came, freezing everything solid under the snow. *transf.*: C. KINGSLEY Will she not freeze me too into stone?

6 a Congeal or inhibit the flow of (blood) as if by loss of heat; now chiefly *fig.* in ***freeze someone's blood*** below. Also, cause to experience an intensity of fright, shock, horror, or the like, appal, terrify; chill (the feelings); paralyse (powers). LME. ▸b Cause (a liquid) to solidify by removal of heat; form ice on the surface of (a river, lake, etc.). Also = DEEP-FREEZE *verb*. L15.

a S. RICHARDSON I should have melted her by love, instead of freezing her by fear. b JOHN ROSS We froze oil of almonds in a shot-mould.

7 Make (assets, credits, etc.) temporarily or permanently unrealizable; fix or stabilize (prices, wages, etc.) at a stated level. E20.

J. D. MACDONALD The Feds . . froze the accounts balances. Money can come in. Nothing goes out. R. GERVAIS & S. MERCHANT He's frozen any wage increases, he's put a stop on all overtime.

8 Arrest at a certain stage of development or progress; make immobile; fix in a particular position. Also, arrest (a movement in a film) by repeating a frame. M20.

G. ORWELL To arrest progress and freeze history at a chosen moment. A. COOKE Chaplin . . froze his stance and very slowly raised his elbows.

– PHRASES, & WITH ADVERBS IN SPECIALIZED SENSES: **freeze someone's blood** terrify someone. **freeze on to** *slang* take or keep tight hold of (*lit.* & *fig.*). **freeze out** *US slang* exclude from business, society, or other activity, by competition, boycotting, etc. **freeze over** *verb phr. intrans.* & *trans.* (usu. in *pass.*) become covered, cover, with a coating of ice. **freeze up** (*a*) set fast in ice; (*b*) obstruct by the formation of ice. ***till hell freezes*** (***over***), ***until hell freezes*** (***over***), ***when hell freezes*** (***over***): see HELL *noun*.
– COMB.: **freeze-dried** *adjective* preserved by freeze-drying; **freeze-dry** *verb trans.* preserve (foodstuffs, blood plasma, pharmaceuticals, etc.) by freezing followed by subjecting to a high vacuum which removes ice by sublimation; **freeze-out** (*a*) ***freeze-out poker***, a variety of poker in which the players, as fast as they lose their staked capital, drop out, all the money going to the player last remaining; (*b*) an act of freezing or forcing out; the exclusion of someone from business, society, or the like, by competition, boycotting, etc.; **freeze-thaw** *attrib. adjective* (GEOLOGY) designating the alternate freezing and thawing of water around rocks etc. as a mechanism for erosion; **freeze-up** the condition of being obstructed by the formation of ice; a period during which land or water is frozen, esp. so as to prevent travel; an area so affected; a frozen condition.
■ **freezable** *adjective* L19. **freezy** *adjective* (*rare*) chilled almost to freezing, bitterly cold LME.

freezer /ˈfriːzə/ *noun*. M19.
[ORIGIN from FREEZE *verb* + -ER[1].]
1 A thing that freezes; *spec.* a refrigerated room or compartment designed to keep food frozen, a deep-freeze. M19.
2 An animal bred for export as a frozen carcass. *Austral.* & *NZ.* L19.
3 A punch used in chasing metal to produce a frosted groundwork. L19.

freezing /ˈfriːzɪŋ/ *verbal noun*. LME.
[ORIGIN from FREEZE *verb* + -ING[1].]
The action of FREEZE *verb*. Also, freezing point (see below).

V. CRONIN It was so cold—well below freezing—that Sophie's feet swelled.

– COMB.: **freezing mixture** a mixture of substances, such as salt and ice, which is used to produce temperatures below the freezing point of water; **freezing point** the temperature at which a liquid freezes; *spec.* that of water, 0°C, 32°F; **freezing tool** = FREEZER 3; **freezing works** *Austral.* & *NZ* a place where animals are slaughtered and the carcasses frozen for export.

freezing /ˈfriːzɪŋ/ *adjective & adverb*. M16.
[ORIGIN formed as FREEZING *noun*: see -ING[2].]
▸A *adjective*. That freezes (*lit.* & *fig.*); *esp.* (of a person's manner, speech, etc.) coldly repressive, chilling; (of weather) bitterly cold. M16.

LD MACAULAY Many . . had been repelled by his freezing looks. G. VIDAL In freezing weather we went up to Susa.

freezing rain rain composed of drops which freeze on impact with the ground or other solid surface.
▸B *adverb*. ***freezing cold***, bitterly cold. *colloq.* E20.
■ **freezingly** *adverb* LME.

freibergite /ˈfrʌɪbəːgʌɪt/ *noun*. M19.
[ORIGIN from *Freiberg*, a city in Saxony + -ITE[1].]
MINERALOGY. An argentiferous variety of tetrahedrite.

freieslebenite /frʌɪəzˈleɪbənʌɪt/ *noun*. M19.
[ORIGIN from Johann K. *Freiesleben* (1774–1846), German mining official + -ITE[1].]
MINERALOGY. A monoclinic sulphide of lead, silver, and antimony, usu. occurring as grey prisms with a metallic lustre.

freight /freɪt/ *noun*. LME.
[ORIGIN Middle Low German, Middle Dutch *vrecht*, var. of *vracht*: see FRAUGHT *noun*.]
1 Hire of a ship or aircraft for transporting goods; the service of transporting goods in containers or by water, air, or (chiefly *US*) land, *esp.* as distinguished from express by being slower and cheaper; the charge for this. LME.

G. MAXWELL The box would have to travel freight and not in the passenger portion of the aircraft. S. BELLOW It'll cost two hundred bucks in freight.

2 The cargo of a ship; a ship load; goods carried by freight (see sense 1). LME. ▸**b** A load, a burden. E17.

E. LINKLATER One boat had already arrived and discharged its freight.

pull one's freight: see PULL *verb*.

3 More fully ***freight train***. A goods train; (chiefly *US*) a container train. M19.

M. B. HOUSTON There were four trains a day . . not counting the freights.

– COMB.: **Freightliner** (proprietary name for) a container train; ***freight ton***: see TON *noun*[1] 2; ***freight train***: see sense 3 above.

†**freight** *ppl adjective*. LME.
[ORIGIN Contr. of *freighted* pa. pple of FREIGHT *noun*: cf. FRAUGHT *ppl adjective*.]
1 = FRAUGHT *ppl adjective* 1. LME–E18.
2 = FRAUGHT *ppl adjective* 2. M16–E17.

freight /freɪt/ *verb*. LME.
[ORIGIN from the noun. Cf. FRAUGHT *verb*.]
1 *verb trans.* Load (a ship) with cargo; hire or let out (a ship) for the transport of goods and passengers. LME. ▸**b** *fig.* Load, burden. E19.

E. BOWEN Having freighted a small vessel with their household effects, [they] themselves set sail for London. **b** G. VIDAL Dr. Ashok's voice was freighted with emotion. L. HUDSON People and places, apparently trivial, are heavily freighted . . with unspoken significance.

2 *verb trans. & intrans.* Carry or transport (goods) as freight. M16.

Listener Mown down on a turnpike by a container-lorry freighting lavatory-pans to the Midwest.

freightage /ˈfreɪtɪdʒ/ *noun*. L17.
[ORIGIN from FREIGHT *verb* + -AGE.]
1 The freighting or hiring of a ship; the charge made for this; *gen.* the cost of transporting goods. L17.
2 = FREIGHT *noun* 2. E19.
3 Transport of goods. L19.

freighter /ˈfreɪtə/ *noun*. L16.
[ORIGIN from FREIGHT *verb* + -ER[1]. Cf. earlier FRAUGHTER.]
1 A person who loads a ship, or who charters and loads a ship. L16.
2 A person who receives and forwards freight as a business; *US HISTORY* a person who transported freight by wagon across the plains. E18.
3 A ship or aircraft for transporting freight; *US* a freight wagon. M19.

†**freightment** *noun*. M16–M18.
[ORIGIN from FREIGHT *verb* + -MENT, after French *frètement*.]
(The document recording) the hiring of a ship.

Frelimo /frɛˈliːməʊ/ *noun*. M20.
[ORIGIN Portuguese acronym, from *Frente de Libertação de Moçambique* Mozambique Liberation Front.]
The nationalist liberation party of Mozambique, founded in 1962.

fremd /frɛmd/ *adjective*. *obsolete* exc. *Scot. & N. English*. Also (*Scot.*) **fremmit** /ˈfrɛmɪt/.
[ORIGIN Old English *frem(e)de* = Old Frisian *fremethe*, Old Saxon *fremiþi* (Dutch *vreemd*), Old High German *fremidi* (German *fremd*), Gothic *framaþeis* strange, from Germanic base of FROM.]
1 Foreign, not native. OE.
2 Strange, unknown. OE.
3 Estranged, hostile, unfriendly. OE.
4 Not related, not one's kin, of another family. ME.
■ **fremdly** *adverb* LME. **fremdness** *noun* strangeness, coldness L15.

fremescent /frɪˈmɛs(ə)nt/ *adjective*. *rare*. M19.
[ORIGIN from Latin *fremere* to roar + -ESCENT.]
Growing noisy.

fremitus /ˈfrɛmɪtəs/ *noun*. E19.
[ORIGIN Latin, from *fremere* to roar.]
A dull roaring noise; *spec.* (MEDICINE) a palpable vibration.

fremmit *adjective* see FREMD.

French /frɛn(t)ʃ/ *adjective & noun*.
[ORIGIN Old English *frenċisċ* from Germanic, from base of FRANK *noun*[1]: see -ISH[1].]
▸ **A** *adjective*. **1** Of or pertaining to the country of France in western Europe, its Romance language, or its people. OE. ▸**b** French Canadian. L17.
2 Having a quality or qualities attributed to French things or people, esp. (*a*) refinement, (*b*) impropriety. LME.

A. RADCLIFFE Their sprightly melodies, debonnaire steps . . gave a character to the scene entirely French. J. GALSWORTHY I don't advise you to read it; it's very French.

– SPECIAL COLLOCATIONS & COMB.: ***French artichoke***: see ARTICHOKE 1. **French bean** a kidney or haricot bean used as a vegetable, both as unripe sliced pods, and as ripe seeds; the plant (*Phaseolus vulgaris*) bearing such beans. **French bed**, **French bedstead** a bedstead with no bedposts and with the headboard and footboard turned outwards. **French blue** *colloq.* a combination of amphetamine and barbiturate. **French brace** (*a*) a type of breast drill; (*b*) THEATRICAL a hinged brace. **French bread** orig., a kind of fancy bread; now also = ***French loaf*** below. **French Canadian** *noun & adjective* (*a*) *noun* a Canadian of French ancestry, a mainly French-speaking Canadian; the language spoken by such a person; (*b*) *adjective* of or pertaining to French Canada, French Canadians, or their language. **French chalk** a kind of steatite, used for marking cloth, removing grease and, in powder form, as a dry lubricant. **French clock** a clock made in France, *esp.* an elaborately decorated 18th-cent. clock. ***French cotton***: see COTTON *noun*[1]. **French cricket** an informal type of cricket without stumps in which the batsman is out if the ball hits his or her legs. †**French crown** an écu. **French cuff** a double cuff formed by turning back a long cuff and securing it with buttons or links. ***French curve***: see CURVE *noun* 3. **French-cut** *adjective* (*N. Amer.*) (of women's knickers) cut high in the leg. **French defence** CHESS a defence beginning with the black king's pawn moving one square in reply to a two-square move of the white king's pawn. **French disease** (now *rare*) syphilis. **French door** = ***French window*** below. **French drain** a drain consisting of rubble through which water soaks away. **French dressing** a salad dressing consisting of vinegar and oil, usu. seasoned. ***French endive***: see ENDIVE 3. **French flu** = FRANCOPHILIA. **French fried potato** a (fried) potato chip. ***French fry***: see FRY *noun*[2] 1c. **French grey** a shade of grey with a lavender tint. ***French* HONEYSUCKLE. *French horn***: see HORN *noun*. **French kiss** = ***deep kiss*** s.v. DEEP *adjective*. **French kissing** the practice of giving French kisses. **French knickers** wide-legged knickers. **French knot** EMBROIDERY a stitch in which the thread is wound around the needle, which is then passed back through the fabric at almost the same point to form a small dot. **French lavender** a kind of lavender, *Lavandula stoechas*, with large purple bracts at the tops of the flower spikes. **French leave** unannounced or unauthorized departure (or other action): chiefly in ***take French leave***. ***French letter***: see LETTER *noun*[1] 7. **French loaf** a long crisp loaf of bread. ***French lungwort***: see LUNGWORT 1. **French maid** a lady's maid of French origin, to employ whom was freq. regarded as a status symbol in Victorian and Edwardian Britain. ***French marigold***: see MARIGOLD *noun* 1. **French morocco** an inferior quality of Levant morocco. ***French mustard***: see MUSTARD *noun*. **French oak** †(*a*) the ilex; (*b*) *W. Indian* a W. Indian tree, *Catalpa longissima*, of the bignonia family. **French partridge** the red-legged partridge, *Alectoris rufa*. **French pink** *US* (*a*) a cornflower, *Centaurea cyanus*, naturalized in the US; (*b*) a sea pink. **French plait** a woman's hairstyle in which all the hair is gathered tightly into a large plait down the back of the head. **French pleat** (*a*) a pleat at the top of a curtain consisting of three smaller pleats; (*b*) = ***French roll*** below. **French polish** a shellac solution used to produce a high gloss on wood; the smooth finish so produced. **French-polish** *verb trans.* make smooth and glossy with French polish. **French-polisher** a person whose business is the French-polishing of woodwork. **French pox** (now *rare*) syphilis. **French Revolution** the revolution of 1789–99, in which the Bourbon monarchy in France was overthrown. **French roll** a hairstyle in which the hair is tucked into a vertical roll down the back of the head. **French roof** a mansard roof. **French seam**: in which the raw edges are enclosed. **French sixth** MUSIC a chord consisting of a major third, augmented fourth, and augmented sixth. ***French sorrel***: see SORREL *noun*[1] 2. **French stick** = ***French loaf*** above. **French tickler** *colloq.* a condom with stimulant protrusions. **French toast** (*a*) bread buttered on one side and toasted on the other; (*b*) bread coated in beaten egg and milk and fried. **French turnip** (the spindle-shaped root of) a navew, *Brassica napus* subsp. *rapifera*. **French twist** *N. Amer.* = ***French roll*** above. ***French ultramarine***: see ULTRAMARINE *noun* 1. **French vermouth** dry vermouth. ***French whisk***: see WHISK *noun*[1] 2c. **French window** a glazed door in an outside wall, serving both as a window and as a door.

▸ **B** *noun*. **1** The Romance language of France, spoken as a native language also in neighbouring countries (e.g. Belgium where it is one of the two official languages) and in parts of Canada, and the official language of a number of African countries. ME. ▸**b** *euphem.* Bad language. Esp. in ***excuse my French***, ***pardon my French***. L19.
Norman French: see NORMAN *adjective* 1. ***Old French***: see OLD *adjective*. ***pedlar's French***: see PEDLAR *noun*.
2 *collect. pl.* The people of France. Also (*rare*) without article, French people. M16.
3 Dry vermouth; a drink of this. M20.

M. GILBERT He was drinking double gins with single Frenches in them.

4 Fellatio, cunnilingus. *slang*. M20.

B. TURNER You can be whipped or caned . . or you can have French for another pound.

■ **Frencher** *noun* (*derog.*, *rare*) a Frenchman E19. **Frenchery** *noun* (*collect.*, *rare*) French goods, characteristics, etc. L16. **Frenchism** *noun* (*rare*) a French custom, idiom, or characteristic M18. **Frenchlike** *adverb & adjective* like or after the manner of the French, in French fashion M16. **Frenchly** *adverb* (now *rare*) in a (supposedly) French manner E16. **Frenchness** *noun* E19.

French /frɛn(t)ʃ/ *verb*. Also **f-**. M17.
[ORIGIN from the adjective.]
†**1** ***French it***: speak French. *rare*. Only in M17.
2 *verb trans.* Give a French form or style to; make French, translate into French. M18.
3 *verb trans.* Teach (a person) French. *rare*. M19.
4 *verb intrans.* Of tobacco, cotton, or another plant: become diseased and distorted. *US*. M19.
5 *verb trans. & intrans.* Practise fellatio or cunnilingus (with). *slang*. M20.

Frenchie *adjective & noun* var. of FRENCHY.

Frenchify /ˈfrɛn(t)ʃɪfʌɪ/ *verb*. Also **f-**. L16.
[ORIGIN from FRENCH *adjective* + -I- + -FY.]
1 *verb trans.* Make French in form, character, or manners. L16. ▸†**b** As ***Frenchified*** *ppl adjective*: afflicted with the French disease, i.e. syphilis. *slang*. M17–E18.

A. BURGESS The hotel cuisine was good, though a bit Frenchified. J. JONES His Socialism was sadly frenchified and utopian, but his heart was sound.

2 *verb intrans.* Become French in ideas, manners, etc. *rare*. L18.
■ **Frenchifiˈcation** *noun* M19.

Frenchman /ˈfrɛn(t)ʃmən/ *noun*. Orig. two words. Pl. **-men**. OE.
[ORIGIN from FRENCH *adjective* + MAN *noun*.]
1 A man of French birth or nationality. OE. ▸†**b** An ancient Gaul. LME–E17.
2 A French ship. L15.
3 A scholar of the French language. *rare*. *colloq.* L17.
4 A tobacco plant affected by a deformity which causes the leaves to thicken and become narrow and distorted. *US*. L17.
5 A knife or straight-sided trowel used in pointing brickwork. L19.
6 The French or red-legged partridge, *Alectoris rufa*. L19.
■ **Frenchwoman** *noun*, pl. **-women**, (*a*) a woman of French birth or nationality; †(*b*) a woman of ancient Gaul: L16.

Frenchy /ˈfrɛn(t)ʃi/ *adjective & noun*. Also **Frenchie**. E19.
[ORIGIN from FRENCH *adjective* + -Y[6], -IE.]
▸ **A** *adjective*. Characteristic of what is French; Frenchlike. E19.

H. N. COLERIDGE St. Pierre is a pretty . . town . . it is neat and Frenchy. C. O. SKINNER Word had gotten about that the plays in her repertoire were 'Frenchy', meaning naughty.

▸ **B** *noun*. A Frenchman, a Frenchwoman. Also, a French Canadian. *derog.* L19.
■ **Frenchily** *adverb* L19. **Frenchiness** *noun* L19.

frenetic /frəˈnɛtɪk/ *adjective & noun*. Also (now *rare*) **phrenetic**. LME.
[ORIGIN Old French & mod. French *frénétique* from Latin *phreneticus* from late Greek *phrenētikos*, for *phrenitikos*, from *phrenitis* delirium, from *phren-*, *phrēn* heart, mind: see -ITIS, -IC. Cf. FRANTIC.]
▸ **A** *adjective*. **1** Of a person. ▸†**a** Mentally deranged, insane. LME–L18. ▸**b** Wildly excited, (over-)enthusiastic, fanatical. M16.

b N. INGELO He esteems Prophetick Visions only as Dreams of phrenetick men.

†**2** Of a disease: accompanied by delirium or temporary madness. LME–M18.
3 Of an action, quality, etc.: frenzied, erratic, uncontrolled. E16.

D. M. DAVIN The demands she made on herself . . grew greater, more frenetic . . every year.

▸ †**B** *noun*. An insane or delirious person. E16–L19.
– NOTE: Formerly stressed on 1st syll.
■ †**frenetical** *adjective* LME–L17. **frenetically** *adverb* M19.

†**frentic** *adjective & noun* var. of FRANTIC.

frenulum /ˈfriːnjʊləm/ *noun*. Also **fraen-**. Pl. **-la** /-lə/. E18.
[ORIGIN mod. Latin dim. of FRENUM.]
1 ANATOMY. A small frenum. E18.
2 ENTOMOLOGY. A bristle or group of bristles attached to the base of the hindwing in some butterflies and moths, serving to interlock with the forewing in flight. L19.

frenum /ˈfriːnəm/ *noun*. Also **fraenum**. Pl. **-na** /-nə/. M18.
[ORIGIN Latin = bridle.]
ANATOMY. A ligament or membranous fold serving to check the motion of the part to which it is attached, *esp.* any of those underneath the tongue.
ovigerous frenum in some cirripedes, a fold of the mantle to which the fertilized egg masses are attached.

†**frenzical** *adjective*. Also **ph-**. L16–M18.
[ORIGIN from FRENZY *noun & adjective* + -IC + -AL[1].]
Crazy, insane; wildly enthusiastic.
■ Also †**frenzic** *adjective* M–L16.

frenzy /ˈfrɛnzi/ *noun & adjective*. Also (now *rare*) **phrenzy**. ME.
[ORIGIN Old French & mod. French *frénésie* from medieval Latin *phrenesia* for Latin *phrenesis*, from Greek *phren-*, *phrēn* mind: see FRENETIC, -Y[3].]
▸ **A** *noun*. **1** Mental derangement, temporary insanity; the uncontrollable excitement of a paroxysm of mania. ME.

C. THIRLWALL Subject to temporary fits of frenzy. K. LINES In a frenzy they disarranged their hair, tore their garments and rushed screaming out of the city.

2 Mental agitation likened to insanity; a state of delirious fury, rage, enthusiasm, etc. Also, wild folly, craziness. LME. ▸**b** A crazy notion or idea; a craze, a mania. M17.

H. INNES Smoking cigarette after cigarette in a frenzy of frustration. CONAN DOYLE Not . . the reasoned courting of an elderly man, but . . the passionate frenzy of youth. *fig.*: R. HUGHES An impudent leather cap; a frenzy of curls.

– COMB.: **frenzy-fever** *arch.* a delirious fever.
▸ **B** *adjective*. †**1** Mad, insane, crazy. L16–M17.
2 Angry. *dial.* M19.

frenzy /ˈfrɛnzi/ *verb*. L18.
[ORIGIN from the noun.]
1 *verb trans.* Drive (a person, an animal, etc.) mad; infuriate, put into a frenzy. Chiefly as ***frenzied*** *ppl adjective*. L18.

D. ACHESON The Department seemed like a pack of beagles in frenzied pursuit. J. G. FARRELL The frenzied crowd of maddened natives. *New Yorker* For all the hour . . that one of his pieces sometimes lasts . . he frenzies the keyboard.

2 *verb intrans.* Be in or go into a frenzy. *rare*. M20.
■ **frenziedly** *adverb* M19.

F

Freon /ˈfriːɒn/ *noun*. Also **f-**. M20.
[ORIGIN Unknown.]
(Proprietary name for) any of a series of halogenated hydrocarbons (containing fluorine and usu. chlorine or bromine) used esp. as refrigerants and aerosol propellants.

frequence /ˈfriːkw(ə)ns/ *noun*. Now *rare*. LME.
[ORIGIN Old French & mod. French *fréquence* from Latin *frequentia*: see FREQUENCY, -ENCE.]
1 A gathering of people in large numbers; a crowded condition; a crowd, a multitude. *arch*. LME.
†2 Constant use of something; familiarity. Only in E17.
3 Frequent occurrence or repetition, frequency. E17.

frequency /ˈfriːkw(ə)nsi/ *noun*. M16.
[ORIGIN Latin *frequentia*, from *frequent-*: see FREQUENT *adjective & adverb*, -ENCY.]
†1 = FREQUENCE 1. M16–E18.
†2 Constant use or repetition *of*. E17–L18. ▸**b** Familiarity *with*, constant attendance *at*. M–L17.
3 *gen*. The fact of occurring often or of being repeated at short intervals; commonness of occurrence; rate of recurrence. M17.

HOR. SMITH The diminished frequency of wars. C. MCCULLOUGH He wasn't calling her *herzchen* any more; of late she had noticed its frequency declining.

4 *spec*.: ▸**a** MEDICINE. The rate of recurrence *of* the pulse, respiration, or other periodic bodily function. M18. ▸**b** PHYSICS etc. The number of times in a second or other specified time interval that any regular oscillation or vibration is repeated, such as that associated with mechanical vibration, sound, electromagnetic radiation, alternating current, etc.; *esp*. the number of cycles per second of a carrier wave used for radio transmission, (*loosely*) a waveband, a channel. Also, a sound etc. having a definite frequency. M19. ▸**c** STATISTICS. The (relative) number of times something occurs in a given sample. M19. ▸**d** ECOLOGY. A measurement of the way in which the members of a species are distributed in a community. E20.

b L. DEIGHTON Jimmy . . was tuning his radio to the frequencies between 7050 and 7100 kilocycles. H. M. ROSENBERG A wave is usually characterized by its frequency and wavelength. A. BURGESS Bartlett had taken a stick microphone . . and intoned a frequency. **d** K. A. KERSHAW If a species has a frequency of 10 per cent then it should occur once in every ten quadrats examined.

b *audio frequency*, *high frequency*, *intermediate frequency*, *low frequency*, *medium frequency*, *natural frequency*, *video frequency*, etc.

– COMB.: **frequency changer**, **frequency converter** a device for changing the frequency of an alternating current; *spec*. in a superheterodyne receiver, for combining the incoming signal with that from the local oscillator to produce the intermediate frequency; **frequency curve** a frequency diagram in the form of a continuous curve; **frequency diagram**: in which frequency of occurrence is plotted against the value of the variable; **frequency distortion** distortion of a signal due to unequal amplification or attenuation of components of different frequency; **frequency distribution** (a mathematical expression giving) a classification of the members of a population according to the value assumed for each member by some variable; a measurement of how often a variable takes each of its possible values; **frequency modulation** variation of the frequency of a radio or other wave as a means of carrying information such as an audio signal; **frequency polygon** a frequency diagram containing a (small) finite number of data points, each point being joined to the next by a straight line; **frequency response** the way in which the output-input ratio of an amplifier or other device depends on the signal frequency.

frequent /ˈfriːkw(ə)nt/ *adjective & adverb*. LME.
[ORIGIN Old French & mod. French *fréquent* or Latin *frequent-*, *-ens*, crowded, frequent, of unknown origin: see -ENT.]
▸**A** *adjective* **1** †**a** Profuse, ample. Only in LME. ▸**b** Numerous, abundant; found at short distances apart. M16.

b M. B. KEATINGE Walls . . flanked and crowned by frequent square towers.

†2 Crowded, full. M16–E19.

DRYDEN 'Tis fit in frequent senate we confer. SHELLEY Halls, Frequent with crystal column.

3 Commonly used or practised; well or widely known. Now *rare*. M16.

A. STAFFORD I have not . . used any one word not frequent and familiar.

4 (The prevailing sense.) Happening or occurring often or at short intervals; rapidly recurring. M16.

J. B. PRIESTLEY Jobs at which you have to be sustained by frequent cups of tea. J. D. SALINGER They gave me frequent warning to start applying myself.

5 Addicted *to*; accustomed *to do*; inclined to indulge *in* or be repetitive *in*. Now *rare*. M16.

SHAKES. *Wint. T.* He . . is less frequent to his princely exercises than formerly. JOSEPH HALL How frequent the Scripture is in the prohibition of this practice.

6 †**a** Often in company *with* (a person); conversant *in* (a subject). L16–M17. ▸**b** Constant, habitual, regular. E17.

b DAY LEWIS A farmer . . is the only frequent visitor.

▸**B** *adverb*. Frequently, often. *colloq*. & *poet*. E17.
■ **frequentist** *noun* a person who believes that the probability of an event is the limit of its relative frequency in a large number of trials M20. **frequently** *adverb* (**a**) at frequent intervals, often, repeatedly; †(**b**) numerously: M16. **frequentness** *noun* (long *rare*) M17.

frequent /frɪˈkwɛnt/ *verb*. L15.
[ORIGIN Old French & mod. French *fréquenter* or Latin *frequentare*, from *frequent-*: see FREQUENT *adjective & adverb*.]
▸**I** *verb trans*. **1** Visit or make use of (a place) often; go often or habitually to (a place, a house, meetings, etc.). L15.

A. J. TOYNBEE This University City, which is frequented . . by thousands of students. G. GREENE Castle . . entered a bookshop he had frequented for several years now.

2 Visit or associate with (a person); be with (a person) often. Now *rare*. L15.

R. NORTH His Lordship had one friend that used to frequent him much.

†3 Use habitually or repeatedly; practise. L15–M17.
4 Familiarize *with*. Long *obsolete* exc. *Scot*. L16.
†5 Crowd, fill; pack together; supply abundantly. L16–L17.
▸**II 6** *verb intrans*. Resort (*to* a place); associate *with* (a person); be often *in*, *about* (a place). *obsolete* exc. *Scot*. L16.

POPE Far from all the ways Where men frequent.

■ **frequentable** *adjective* (*rare*) that may be frequented, easily accessible L16. **frequenter** *noun* a person who frequents (a place, meetings, etc.) E17.

frequentation /friːkwənˈteɪʃ(ə)n/ *noun*. LME.
[ORIGIN French *fréquentation* from Latin *frequentatio(n-)*, from *frequent-*: see FREQUENT *adjective*, -ATION.]
1 The action or habit of visiting or frequenting; habitual attendance or association. LME.
2 †**a** The act of making use *of* regularly or often. Also, a custom, practice. E16–L17. ▸**b** Frequent celebration of the sacraments. *rare*. E17.

frequentative /frɪˈkwɛntətɪv/ *adjective & noun*. M16.
[ORIGIN French *fréquentatif*, *-ive* or Latin *frequentativus*, from *frequent-*: see FREQUENT *adjective*, -ATIVE.]
GRAMMAR. ▸**A** *adjective*. Of a verb, verbal form, or conjugation: expressing frequent repetition or intensity of action, as English *chatter*, *dribble*, *twinkle*, etc. M16.
▸**B** *noun*. A frequentative verb, verbal form, or conjugation. M16.

frere *noun* see FRIAR.

frescade /frɛsˈkɑːd/ *noun*. M17.
[ORIGIN French from Italian *frescata*, from *fresco* cool, fresh: see -ADE.]
A cool, shady alley or walk.

fresco /ˈfrɛskəʊ/ *noun & verb*. L16.
[ORIGIN Italian = cool, fresh. Earliest in *in fresco* repr. Italian *affresco*, *al fresco* on the fresh (plaster). Cf. AL FRESCO.]
▸**A** *noun*. Pl. **-o(e)s**.
1 A method of painting in which watercolour is applied to wet, freshly laid plaster, so that the colours penetrate and become fixed as it dries. L16. ▸**b** A painting produced by this method. L17.

R. W. EMERSON The grand sibyls . . painted in fresco by Michel Angelo. **b** E. M. FORSTER On the ceiling was a fresco of the battle of Solferino.

†2 Cool fresh air. E17–E19.
– PHRASES: *fresco buono* /ˌfresko ˈbwɔːno/ [= good] = sense A.1 above. *fresco secco* /ˌfresko ˈsekko/ = SECCO *noun* 1. **in fresco** in the fresh air.
▸**B** *verb trans*. Paint in fresco. E19.

L. M. MONTGOMERY Anne gazed at the ceiling as if it were frescoed with angels.

fresh /frɛʃ/ *adjective, adverb, & noun*.
[ORIGIN Old English *fersc* = Old Frisian, Middle Dutch *fersc* (Dutch *vers*), Old High German *frisc* (German *frisch*), Old Norse *ferskr*, from Germanic; replaced in Middle English by forms from Old French *freis* from Proto-Romance from same Germanic base.]
▸**A** *adjective* **I 1** (Of water) not salt; fit for drinking. Also, (now *rare*) of butter: unsalted. OE. ▸**b** Of or pertaining to such water. Formerly also, of fish: freshwater. ME.

R. BOYLE He always found the ice fresh that floated upon the sea-water. **b** SHAKES. *Tit. A.* Till the fresh taste be taken from that clearness, And made a brine-pit with our bitter tears.

2 Of food: new as distinct from being preserved (by salting, pickling, smoking, drying, tinning, freezing, etc.). OE.

W. MARCH He liked them made from fresh coconut, not from that tasteless, shrivelled-up stuff that came in boxes.

3 Retaining its original qualities, not deteriorated or changed by lapse of time; (of food) not stale or musty; (of a flower, memory, etc.) not faded; bright (in colour); clear; (of the complexion etc.) unsullied, looking young or healthy; (of clothing) clean. ME. ▸†**b** Colourfully or finely dressed. LME–L16.

I. M. BEETON It is particularly necessary that they should be quite fresh, as nothing is worse than stale eggs. R. P. WARREN Her clothes had looked perfectly fresh and unwrinkled. D. CUSACK Girls' voices, very fresh and young, sing the hymn. HARPER LEE See if you can tell us what happened, while it's still fresh in your mind.

4 Not tired; full of energy; active, vigorous; refreshed. ME. ▸†**b** Ready, eager, having an inclination (*to*, *to do*). ME–L17. ▸**c** Of a cow: yielding a renewed or increased supply of milk, coming into milk. *US*. L19.

J. HIGGINS Now . . I would like to sleep. I must be fresh for tonight's concert.

5 Esp. of air or water: pure, untainted, cool, refreshing, invigorating. LME. ▸**b** Of the wind: having considerable force, quite strong; formerly also, springing up again. M16. ▸**c** Of the weather: not frosty; rainy. *Scot. & N. English*. L18.

MILTON They among fresh dews and flowers Flie to and fro. W. BOYD Inhaling the . . fresher air on the first floor.

6 **a** Sober; *esp*. sobered up. *obsolete* exc. *Scot*. LME. ▸**b** Slightly intoxicated, tipsy. *arch*. E19.
7 [Perh. infl. by German *frech* impudent.] Forward, impertinent, free in behaviour. Orig. *US*. M19.

BETTY SMITH How fresh she must look—running after a feller like that. *Philadelphia Inquirer* That young, single dentist got fresh with me.

▸**II 8** New, novel; not previously known, used, met with, etc. ME. ▸**b** Additional, other, different. LME.

CONAN DOYLE If the lady will not accept what is already known, why should any fresh discovery . . turn her from her purpose? I. MURDOCH Dorina was to have been a fresh start, a stepping-stone into some sort of elegant life. **b** G. ORWELL It appeared that they had engaged in fresh conspiracies from the very moment of their release. R. WEST Her face was contorted by a fresh spasm of weeping.

9 Recent, newly made; recently arrived, received, etc. ME. ▸**b** Newly come *from* or *out of*. L17.

SWIFT The Author was then young . . and his reading fresh in his head. P. V. WHITE A Tannenbaum, smelling as such trees will when they bleed from fresh wounds. **b** E. BUSHEN A first-year form, thirty boys fresh from their junior schools. *City Limits* Fresh from winning the best director prize at Cannes.

10 Raw, inexperienced; unsophisticated. L16.

DISRAELI Did you ever fight a duel? No! . . Well! you are fresh indeed!

– PHRASES & SPECIAL COLLOCATIONS: *breath of fresh air*. **fresh as a daisy**, **fresh as paint** bright, cheerful, active. *fresh blood*: see BLOOD *noun*. **fresh breeze** a strong breeze, *spec*. a wind of force 5 (19–24 mph) on the Beaufort scale. *fresh off the irons*: see IRON *noun*.
▸**B** *adverb*. In a fresh manner; *esp*. newly. ME.

D. LESSING Picked fresh this morning, morning-picked country strawberries.

fresh-baked, *fresh-caught*, etc. **fresh out of** just sold or run out of (goods, supplies, etc.).
– COMB.: **fresh-find** *verb trans*. find (a deer) after the scent has been lost; **fresh-run** *adjective* (of a fish, esp. a salmon) recently come up from the sea.
▸**C** *noun*. **1** A rush of water in a stream; a flash flood; an ebb tide increased by heavy rain. M16. ▸**b** A gust or squall (of wind). L17.
2 A pool, spring, or stream of fresh water. L16.
3 A freshwater stream running out into a tideway of salt water; (the land adjoining) the part of a tidal river above the salt water. Freq. in *pl*. *N. Amer*. M17.
4 The fresh or early part *of* a day, year, etc. E18.
■ **freshish** *adjective* somewhat fresh M18. **freshness** *noun* the quality or condition of being fresh LME.

fresh /frɛʃ/ *verb*. ME.
[ORIGIN from the adjective.]
1 *verb trans*. Refresh; cheer; renew. (Foll. by *up*.) *arch*. ME.
2 *verb intrans*. Of the sea: roughen. Formerly also, of the wind: increase in strength. L16.

freshen /ˈfrɛʃ(ə)n/ *verb*. L17.
[ORIGIN from FRESH *adjective* + -EN[5].]
1 *verb intrans*. Of the wind: increase in strength, begin to blow fresh. Also foll. by *up*. L17.

D. PAE The wind was again freshening into a gale. J. MASEFIELD It freshened up till it blew like thunder.

2 **a** *verb trans*. Renew, revive, give freshness to. Also foll. by *up*. M18. ▸**b** *verb intrans*. Become (more) fresh; become bright or vivid. E19. ▸**c** *verb intrans*. Wash one's hands and face, tidy one's hair and clothes, etc. Foll. by *up*. Chiefly *N. Amer*. M20. ▸**d** *verb trans*. Add fresh wine, spirits, etc., to (a drink which has been standing for some time); top up. M20.

a H. E. BATES A magical sweetness of dusty earth freshened by rain. J. GLASSCO The hundred yards in the cold night air freshened me up. **b** C. BRONTË A greenness grew over those brown beds, . . freshening daily. S. NAIPAUL The air freshened as I approached the sea. **c** D. ADAMS Assuming you had landed by now and freshened up with a quick dip and shower.

a freshen the nip NAUTICAL alter the position of a rope etc. under strain, so as to expose a different part to friction.

3 *verb trans. & intrans.* (Cause to) lose salt or saltness. **L18.**

New Yorker The Great Salt Lake . . has been freshening in recent years.

4 *verb intrans.* Of a cow: give birth; come into milk. *US.* **E20.**

■ **freshener** *noun* a thing which freshens something **M19.**

fresher /ˈfrɛʃə/ *noun. colloq.* **L19.**
[ORIGIN from FRESH *adjective* + -ER¹.]
A first-year student at university or polytechnic. Cf. FRESHMAN.

freshet /ˈfrɛʃɪt/ *noun & verb.* **L16.**
[ORIGIN Prob. from Old French *freschete* dim. of *freis* FRESH *adjective*: see -ET¹.]
▸ **A** *noun.* **1** A stream or rush of fresh water flowing into the sea; (now only *poet.*) a small freshwater stream. **L16.**

W. McIlvanney The river . . broke into a thousand freshets on the rocks.

2 A flood of a river caused by heavy rain or melted snow. **M17.**

S. N. Cleghorn Wide and shallow in the cowslip marshes Floods the freshet of the April snow.

▸ **B** *verb trans. & intrans.* Flood (as) with a freshet. *rare.* **M19.**

freshly /ˈfrɛʃli/ *adverb.* **ME.**
[ORIGIN from FRESH *adjective* + -LY².]
1 Newly, recently. Now only with ppl adjectives. **ME.** ▸**b** Anew, afresh. Now *rare.* **LME.**

S. Bedford Outside the potting shed stood a large box of freshly dug garden earth. **b** J. Steinbeck The tears started freshly in Rose of Sharon's eyes.

2 With renewed vigour; (of the wind) briskly. Formerly also, fiercely, eagerly. **ME.**

Tennyson [A breeze] gathering freshlier overhead.

3 Clearly, brightly; distinctly; sharply. Formerly also, gaily, magnificently. **LME.**

Shakes. *A.Y.L.* Looks he as freshly as he did the day he wrestled? J. W. Burgon The man lives freshly in the memory of his fellows.

freshman /ˈfrɛʃmən/ *noun.* Pl. **-men. M16.**
[ORIGIN from FRESH *adjective* + MAN *noun.*]
1 A newcomer, a novice. Formerly also, a proselyte. **M16.**

attrib.: D. Acheson The attitude of the leader of the Senate to a freshman senator.

2 A student during his or her first year (and esp. first term) at a university, college, polytechnic, or (*N. Amer.*) high school. **L16.**

R. Jarrell The first thing I do with a freshman . . is to shake her out of her ignorant complacency.

■ **freshmanship** *noun* the condition or state of being a freshman **E17.** **freshwoman** *noun* (*rare*), pl. **-women**, a female freshman **E17.**

freshwater /ˈfrɛʃwɔːtə/ *adjective.* **LME.**
[ORIGIN from FRESH *adjective* + WATER *noun.*]
1 Of, pertaining to, or living in water that is not salt. **LME.** ***freshwater soldier***: see SOLDIER *noun* 4.
2 Unskilled, untrained, raw; now only, unaccustomed or new to the sea. **L16.**
3 Of an institution, college, etc.: insignificant; rustic, provincial. *US.* **M19.**

Fresison /frɪˈsʌɪs(ə)n/ *noun.* **E19.**
[ORIGIN A mnemonic of scholastic philosophers, E indicating a universal negative major, I a particular affirmative minor, and O a particular negative conclusion.]
LOGIC. The fifth mood of the fourth syllogistic figure, in which a particular negative conclusion is drawn from a universal negative major premiss and a particular affirmative minor.

Fresnel /freɪˈnɛl/ *noun.* **M19.**
[ORIGIN A. J. *Fresnel* (1788–1827), French physicist.]
PHYSICS **I 1** Used *attrib.* and in *possess.* to designate devices, phenomena, or concepts related to Fresnel's work in optics. **M19.**
Fresnel biprism = BIPRISM. **Fresnel diffraction** diffraction in which the pattern is a non-linear function of the phase variation across the diffracting aperture or object (cf. ***Fraunhofer diffraction*** s.v. FRAUNHOFER 2). **Fresnel lens** a lens consisting of a number of concentric annular sections, designed to produce a parallel beam free from spherical aberration. **Fresnel rhomb**, **Fresnel's rhomb** a glass parallelepiped in which, by total internal reflection, a beam of plane-polarized light can be converted into a beam of circularly or elliptically polarized light travelling in the same direction. **Fresnel unit** = sense 2 below.
▸ **II 2** (**f-.**) A unit of frequency equal to 10^{12} Hz. **M20.**

fret /frɛt/ *noun*¹. **LME.**
[ORIGIN from FRET *verb*¹.]
1 The action or an act (as) of gnawing or wearing away; an eroded or decayed spot. Now *rare.* **LME.** ▸**b** *sing.* & in *pl.* Colic. Now *dial.* **E17.**

Tennyson Before . . the busy fret Of that sharpheaded worm begins.

2 (An) agitation or torment of the mind; (a state of) irritation, vexation, or peevishness; a cause of worry or irritation; a peevish utterance. **LME.**

C. Lamb The fret and fever of speculation. E. Gaskell He heard his wife's plaintive fret. J. Hilton Repose from which all the fret of existence had ebbed away.

on the fret [perh. infl. by other senses] in a state of irritation or impatience.

†**3** A sudden disturbance of weather; a gust or squall (of wind). **M16–M18.**
4 Secondary fermentation of liquor. **M17.**

fret /frɛt/ *noun*². **LME.**
[ORIGIN Prob. from Old French *frete* trellis, interlaced work (mod. *frette*), of unknown origin: see FRET *verb*².]
1 Ornamental interlaced work; *esp.* a decorative network of jewels or flowers for the hair. **LME.**
2 *HERALDRY.* Orig., a figure formed by alternate interlacing bendlets and bendlets sinister. Later, a device consisting of two narrow bands in saltire interlaced with a mascle. **LME.**
3 An ornamental pattern composed of continuous combinations of straight lines, usu. joined at right angles. Also ***Greek fret***. **E17.**
■ †**fretwise** *adverb* in the form of a fret, interlaced **LME–E18.**

fret /frɛt/ *noun*³. **E16.**
[ORIGIN Unknown.]
Any of various bars or ridges on the fingerboard of some stringed instruments (usu. those played by plucking) used for fixing the position of the fingers to produce the required notes.
– COMB.: **fretboard** a fingerboard provided with frets.

fret /frɛt/ *noun*⁴. *obsolete* exc. *dial.* **L17.**
[ORIGIN Old French *frete* (mod. *frette*) ferrule, ring.]
An iron hoop circling the nave of a cartwheel.

fret /frɛt/ *noun*⁵. *N. English.* **M19.**
[ORIGIN Unknown.]
More fully ***sea fret***. Mist or drizzle coming in off the sea; a sea fog.

fret /frɛt/ *verb*¹. Infl. **-tt-**.
[ORIGIN Old English *fretan* = Middle Low German, Middle Dutch *vrēten* (Dutch *vreten*), Old High German *frezzan* (German *fressen*), Gothic *fraītan*, from Germanic bases of FOR-¹, EAT *verb*. In sense 4 perh. orig. a separate word: cf. Provençal *fretar*, Italian *frettare*, mod. French dial. *fretter*, ult. from Latin *fricare* rub.]
†**1** *verb trans.* Chiefly of animals: eat, devour, consume. **OE–L16.**
2 a *verb trans. & intrans.* Gnaw; consume, torment, or wear away by gnawing; destroy gradually or insidiously by corrosion, erosion, disease, etc. **ME.** ▸**b** Of emotion: consume, torment. *obsolete* exc. as passing into sense 3 in ***fret the heart***. **ME.** ▸†**c** *verb intrans.* Become eaten or corroded; wear away, decay. (Foll. by *off*, *out*.) **L15–E19.**

C. Lamb We cannot bear to have our thin wardrobe eaten and fretted into by moths. B. Mason The surface of these rock shelves is jagged, . . fretted away by the corrosive sea. **b** L. Edel The nagging guilt, fretting at his heart.

3 a *verb trans.* Chafe, irritate; annoy, distress, worry (a person, oneself); bring (*in*)*to* or into a specified condition by worrying. **ME.** ▸**b** *verb intrans.* Worry, distress oneself with regret, discontent, or anxiety; express worry or peevish discontent. (Foll. by *about*, *at*, *over*, *that*, etc.) **M16.** ▸**c** *verb trans.* Spend or pass (time, one's life, etc.) in fretting. (Foll. by *away*, *out*.) **E17.**

a R. Lardner Mother had nearly fretted herself sick for fear I would be left. A. Waugh The innumerable small annoyances that fret and harass us. **b** M. E. Braddon Knows his own interest too well to fret and fume about trifles. R. C. Hutchinson Men do fret over trifles when there are larger things to crowd the mind. J. Barth Jeannine . . began to fret in her crib. P. Ackroyd I fretted that I had no books to read in my cell. **c** Shakes. *Macb.* Life's but a walking shadow, a poor player, That struts and frets his hour upon the stage.

4 a *verb trans.* Rub (*away*), chafe; cause to move against something with friction. **ME.** ▸**b** *verb intrans.* Rub (*on*, *against*); fray *out*. **M17.**

a F. Raphael Fretting the carving knife between the roundels of the sharpener. **b** P. V. White The old woman's head was barely fretting against the pillow.

a fretting corrosion abrasion accompanied by chemical corrosion occurring where metal surfaces are held in contact, with some freedom of relative movement.

5 *verb trans.* & †*intrans.* (with *into*, *through*, *to*). Make (a way, hole, etc.) by gnawing or corrosion. **LME.**

J. Wain What . . shape the sea has fretted into the land.

6 a *verb intrans.* Of a stream, the sea, etc.: flow or rise in little waves, move in agitation. **M16.** ▸**b** *verb trans.* Ruffle (water). **L18.**
7 *verb trans. & intrans.* (Cause to) undergo secondary fermentation. Now chiefly *dial.* **M17.**
■ **fretter** *noun* (**a**) a thing which gnaws or eats away something, *esp.* a caterpillar which eats vines; (**b**) a person who or thing which irritates, chafes, or rubs something; (**c**) a person inclined to fret: **E16.** **frettingly** *adverb* in a fretting manner **M17.**

fret /frɛt/ *verb*² *trans.* Infl. **-tt-**. Pa. pple **fretted**, †**fret**. **LME.**
[ORIGIN Prob. from Old French *freté* (= Anglo-Latin *frectatus*, *frictatus*) pa. pple of *freter* rel. to *frete* trellis: see FRET *noun*².]
1 Chiefly as ***fretted ppl adjective***. Decorate, *esp.* embroider, with interlaced work; ornament with gold, silver, or jewels. Long only *fig.* **LME.**

Longfellow White clouds sail aloft; and vapours fret the blue sky with silver threads.

2 *HERALDRY.* Interlace; decorate with an interlaced pattern. **LME.**
3 Decorate (esp. a ceiling) with fretwork; carve into frets. **M16.**

H. Read He stood against the fretted hedge, which was like white lace.

■ **fretting** *noun* (**a**) the action of the verb; (**b**) a pattern or ornamentation so produced: **LME.**

fret /frɛt/ *verb*³ *trans.* Infl. **-tt-**. **E17.**
[ORIGIN from FRET *noun*³.]
Provide (a guitar etc.) with frets. Chiefly as ***fretted ppl adjective.***

fretful /ˈfrɛtfʊl, -f(ə)l/ *adjective.* **L16.**
[ORIGIN from FRET *verb*¹ + -FUL.]
†**1** Corrosive, irritating. Only in **L16.**
2 Inclined to fret; worried, irritable, peevish; impatient, restless. **E17.** ▸**b** Characterized by or apt to cause irritation. **M18.**

K. Lawrence Rina had always been fretful, needy, unsure of herself.

3 Of water etc.: agitated, troubled, broken into waves. **E17.**
■ **fretfully** *adverb* **L18.** **fretfulness** *noun* **E17.**

fretish /ˈfrɛtɪʃ/ *verb trans.* Long *obsolete* exc. *dial.* Also **-tt-**. **E16.**
[ORIGIN Old French *frediss-* lengthened stem of *fredir*, *freidir* (mod. *froidir*), from *freid* (mod. *froid*) from Proto-Romance alt. of Latin *frigidus* FRIGID: see -ISH².]
Benumb, freeze. Now only as ***fretished ppl adjective***, numb with cold.

†**fretize** *verb trans.* **L16–E18.**
[ORIGIN Rel. to Old French *fraitis* decorated with fretwork.]
= FRET *verb*² 3.

fretless /ˈfrɛtlɪs/ *adjective*¹. *rare.* **L19.**
[ORIGIN from FRET *noun*¹, *verb*¹ + -LESS.]
1 Free from irritation or worry. **L19.**
2 Of water: calm, unruffled. **L19.**

fretless /ˈfrɛtlɪs/ *adjective*². **M20.**
[ORIGIN from FRET *noun*³ + -LESS.]
Of a musical instrument: having no frets on the fingerboard.

fretsaw /ˈfrɛtsɔː/ *noun.* **M19.**
[ORIGIN from FRET *noun*² + SAW *noun*¹.]
A saw with a narrow vertical blade stretched on a frame, used for cutting thin wood to form ornamental designs.

frettish *verb* var. of FRETISH.

fretty /ˈfrɛti/ *adjective*¹. **M16.**
[ORIGIN Old French *freté*, from *frete*: see FRET *noun*², -Y⁵.]
HERALDRY. Covered with alternate interlacing bendlets and bendlets sinister.

fretty /ˈfrɛti/ *adjective*². **M19.**
[ORIGIN from FRET *verb*¹ + -Y¹.]
Inclined to fret; irritable.

fretwork /ˈfrɛtwəːk/ *noun.* **E17.**
[ORIGIN from FRET *noun*² + WORK *noun.*]
1 *ARCHITECTURE.* Carved work in decorative patterns esp. of intersecting straight lines. **E17.**
2 The cutting of wood with a fretsaw to form ornamental designs; wood so cut. **L19.**
■ **fretworked** *adjective* ornamented with or by fretwork **L19.**

Freudian /ˈfrɔɪdɪən/ *adjective & noun.* **E20.**
[ORIGIN from Sigmund *Freud* (1856–1939), Austrian neurologist and founder of psychoanalysis: see -IAN.]
▸ **A** *adjective.* Of or pertaining to Freud or his methods or theories of psychoanalysis; *loosely* relating to (supposed) unconscious feelings. **E20.**

S. Spender A Freudian argument which told me that I only troubled about these things out of a sense of guilt. J. I. M. Stewart There was something Freudian about my forgetfulness.

Freudian slip an unintentional (esp. spoken) error that seems to reveal subconscious feelings.

▸ **B** *noun.* A follower of Freud or his methods. **E20.**
■ **Freudianism** *noun* the theory, system, or methods of Freudian psychoanalysis **E20.** **Freudianly** *adverb* **M20.**

FRG *abbreviation.*
Federal Republic of Germany.

Fri. *abbreviation.*
Friday.

friable /ˈfrʌɪəb(ə)l/ *adjective.* **M16.**
[ORIGIN French, or Latin *friabilis*, from *friare* crumble into small pieces: see -ABLE.]
Able to be easily crumbled or reduced to powder; crumbly.
■ **friaˈbility** *noun* the quality of being friable **E17.** **friableness** *noun* **M17.**

†**friand** *adjective.* **L16–E19.**
[ORIGIN Old French & mod. French, = dainty, in Old French vivacious, for *friant* pres. pple of *frire* FRY *verb.*]
Delicious to the palate; fond of delicate food, epicurean.

F

friandise /fri(j)ɑ̃diːz/ *noun. rare.* Pl. pronounced same. L15.
[ORIGIN French, from *friand*: see FRIAND, -ISE[1].]
1 A delicacy; dainty fare. L15.
†**2** Fondness for delicate fare. Only in E17.

friar /ˈfrʌɪə/ *noun.* Also (earlier, long *arch.*) **frere** /frɛː/. ME.
[ORIGIN Old French & mod. French *frère* from Latin *frater*, *fratr-* brother.]
1 Brother (chiefly *fig.*); comrade. Long *arch. rare.* ME.
2 A member of any of certain religious orders of men, *esp.* the four mendicant orders: the Franciscans (***Grey Friars***, ***Friars Minor***), Augustinians (***Austin Friars***), Dominicans (***Black Friars***, ***Friars Major***), and Carmelites (***White Friars***). ME. ▸**b** In *pl.* The quarters of an order of friars; a name for the part of a town where such a friary once stood. ME.
Pied Friars, ***preaching friars***, etc.
3 Any of various fishes. *local.* E17.
4 PRINTING. A light patch amongst printed matter on a page, due to insufficient inking. (Cf. MONK *noun*[1] 2.) L17.
5 In full *friarbird*. Any of various honeyeaters of the largely Australasian genus *Philemon*, members of which have black, partly naked heads. L18.
– COMB.: *friarbird*: see sense 5 above; **friar's balsam** tincture of benzoin used as an application for ulcers and wounds, or as an expectorant.
■ **friarly** *adjective & adverb* (*a*) *adjective* of or pertaining to friars, resembling or characteristic of a friar; (*b*) *adverb* after the manner of the friars: M16.

friary /ˈfrʌɪəri/ *noun.* ME.
[ORIGIN from FRIAR + -Y[3].]
1 A fraternity or brotherhood of friars. ME.
2 A convent of friars. LME.

†**friation** *noun.* M17–M18.
[ORIGIN from Latin *friat-* pa. ppl stem of *friare*: see FRIABLE, -ATION.]
The action of rubbing or crumbling into small pieces.

frib /frɪb/ *noun. Austral. & NZ.* E19.
[ORIGIN Unknown.]
A small short lock of wool from a sheep. Usu. in *pl.*
■ **fribby** *adjective & noun* (*a*) *adjective* of the nature of a frib, consisting of fribs; (*b*) *noun* a frib: E20.

fribble /ˈfrɪb(ə)l/ *noun & adjective.* In sense A.3 also redupl. **fribble-frabble** /-frab(ə)l/. M17.
[ORIGIN from the verb.]
▸**A** *noun.* **1** A frivolous person, a trifler, a person not engaged in serious work. M17.
2 A trifling thing; a frivolous notion or characteristic. M19.
3 Frivolity, nonsense. M19.
▸**B** *adjective.* Trifling, frivolous, ridiculous. L18.
■ **fribblish** *adjective* characteristic of or suited to a fribble; frivolous, trifling: M18.

fribble /ˈfrɪb(ə)l/ *verb.* E17.
[ORIGIN Symbolic.]
†**1 a** *verb trans. & intrans.* Stammer, mumble. Only in 17. ▸**b** *verb intrans.* Falter; totter in walking. E18–M19.
2 *verb intrans.* Act aimlessly, behave frivolously, mess about. M17. ▸**b** *verb trans.* Foll. by *away*: part with lightly and wastefully, fritter. M17.
3 *verb trans.* Frizzle (a wig). *Scot.* M18.
■ **fribbler** *noun* a trifler E18.

fricandeau /ˈfrɪkandəʊ/ *noun & verb.* Also (earlier) †**-do**. E18.
[ORIGIN French.]
▸**A** *noun.* Pl. **-eaux** /-əʊz/, †**-oes**. (A slice of) veal or other meat fried or stewed and served with sauce; an escalope; a fricassee of veal. E18.
▸**B** *verb trans.* Make into fricandeaux. M18.

fricassee /ˈfrɪkəsiː, frɪkəˈsiː/ *noun & verb.* M16.
[ORIGIN French *fricassée* fem. pa. pple of *fricasser* cut up and stew in sauce.]
▸**A** *noun.* Meat sliced and fried or stewed and served with sauce; *esp.* a ragout of birds or small animals. M16.
▸**B** *verb trans.* Pa. t. & pple **-sseed**. Make a fricassee of; dress as a fricassee. M17.

†**frication** *noun.* LME.
[ORIGIN Latin *fricatio(n-)*, from *fricat-* pa. ppl stem of *fricare* rub: see -ATION.]
1 The action or process of chafing or rubbing the body with the hands. LME–L17.
2 The action of rubbing the surface of one body against that of another; friction. M17–E18.

fricative /ˈfrɪkətɪv/ *adjective & noun.* M19.
[ORIGIN mod. Latin *fricativus*, from Latin *fricare* rub: see -ATIVE.]
PHONETICS. ▸**A** *adjective.* Of a consonant sound: produced by the friction of the airstream through a narrow opening in the mouth (as *v*, *s*). M19.
▸**B** *noun.* A fricative consonant. M19.

fricatrice /ˈfrɪkətrɪs/ *noun.* Now *rare.* E17.
[ORIGIN from Latin *fricare* rub + -TRICE.]
A promiscuous or immoral woman.

fricking /ˈfrɪkɪŋ/ *adjective & adverb. slang* (chiefly *US*). M20.
[ORIGIN Prob. an alt. of **frigging** s.v. FRIG *verb & noun*[2].]
Expr. amazement, anger, exasperation, etc. (used as a euphemism for *fucking*).

friction /ˈfrɪkʃ(ə)n/ *noun & verb.* M16.
[ORIGIN French from Latin *frictio(n-)*, from *frict-* pa. ppl stem of *fricare* rub: see -ION.]
▸**A** *noun.* **1** The action of chafing or rubbing the body or limbs, formerly much used in medical treatment. M16. ▸**b** HAIRDRESSING. A massage of the scalp. M20.
2 The rubbing of one body against another; attrition. E18. ▸**b** MEDICINE. More fully ***friction-murmur***, ***friction-sound***, etc. A scratching sound heard in auscultation when the pleura or pericardium is roughened by inflammation. L19.

> J. MORSE The rocks below . . are worn many feet deep by the constant friction of the water.

3 PHYSICS. The resistance which a body encounters in moving over another body. E18.

> A. S. EDDINGTON Friction which has to be overcome when a train . . is kept moving uniformly. F. HOYLE There is very little friction indeed between one icy surface and another.

angle of friction the maximum angle of slope at which one body will remain on another without sliding down. **coefficient of friction** the ratio between the force necessary to move one surface horizontally over another and the normal force each surface exerts on the other. STATIC ***friction***.
4 *fig.* The jarring or conflict of wills, opinions, temperaments, etc. M18.

> T. C. WOLFE The friction between Helen and Eliza was often acute. A. KOESTLER Constant friction, flaring into heated quarrels.

– ATTRIB. & COMB.: Esp. in the sense 'working, esp. transmitting motion, by frictional contact', as ***friction-brake***, ***friction-clutch***, ***friction-cone***, ***friction-coupling***, ***friction-disc***, ***friction-gear***, ***friction-gearing***, etc. Special combs., as **friction-ball**: used in bearings to lessen friction; **friction match**: that ignites by friction; ***friction-murmur***, ***friction-sound***: see sense 2b above; **friction welding**: in which the heat is produced by rotating one component against the other under compression.
▸**B** *verb.* **1** *verb intrans.* Move with friction; sustain friction. *rare.* M19.
2 *verb trans.* Subject to friction; rub. *rare.* M19.
3 *verb trans.* Impregnate (fabric) with rubber by rolling in a calender. M19.
■ **frictionize** *verb trans.* = FRICTION *verb* 2 M19. **frictionless** *adjective* free from or without friction M19. **frictionlessly** *adverb* L19.

frictional /ˈfrɪkʃ(ə)n(ə)l/ *adjective.* M19.
[ORIGIN from FRICTION + -AL[1].]
Of or pertaining to friction; moved, produced, or operating by friction.
– SPECIAL COLLOCATIONS: **frictional electricity** = STATIC ***electricity***. **frictional unemployment** ECONOMICS the unemployment which exists in any economy through people being in the process of moving between jobs.
■ **frictionally** *adverb* L19.

Friday /ˈfrʌɪdeɪ, -di/ *noun, adverb, & adjective.*
[ORIGIN Old English *Frīgedæg*, corresp. to Old Frisian *frī(g)endei*, Middle Low German, Middle Dutch *vrīdach* (Dutch *vrijdag*), Old High German *frīatag* (German *Freitag*), = day of *Frīg* = Old Norse *Frigg*, the wife of Odin, use as noun of fem. of Germanic base of FREE *adjective*: West Germanic translating late Latin *Veneris dies* day of the planet Venus (whence French *vendredi*), based on Greek *Aphroditēs hēmera* day of Aphrodite.]
▸**A** *noun.* **1** The sixth day of the week, following Thursday. OE.
girl Friday, **Man Friday** [from *Man Friday* in Defoe's novel *Robinson Crusoe*] a helper, *esp.* an assistant who performs general duties in an office. **Golden Friday** the Friday in each of the Ember weeks. ***Good Friday***: see GOOD *adjective*. ***Man Friday***: see ***girl Friday*** above.
2 A reception or entertainment given on a Friday. M19.
▸**B** *adverb.* On Friday. Now chiefly *N. Amer.* ME.

> H. KEMELMAN Friday the Rabbi slept late.

▸**C** *attrib.* or as *adjective.* Of Friday; characteristic of Friday, esp. (formerly) as a day of fasting; taking place on Friday(s). L16.
■ **Fridays** *adverb* (*colloq.*) on Fridays, each Friday ME.

fridge /frɪdʒ/ *noun. colloq.* Also **frig**. E20.
[ORIGIN Abbreviation.]
= REFRIGERATOR.
– COMB.: **fridge-freezer** an upright unit combining a refrigerator and a freezer, each self-contained.

fridge /frɪdʒ/ *verb.* M16.
[ORIGIN App. imit.: cf. FRIG *verb*, FIG *verb*[2], FIDGE *verb*.]
†**1** *verb intrans.* Move restlessly, fidget. M16–L17.
2 *verb trans.* & †*intrans.* Rub, fray, chafe; wear away by rubbing. Now chiefly *dial.* E17.

fried /frʌɪd/ *ppl adjective.* LME.
[ORIGIN pa. pple of FRY *verb*: see -ED[1].]
1 Cooked by frying. LME.
2 Drunk. *slang.* E20.

fried *verb pa. t. & pple* of FRY *verb.*

Friedel–Crafts reaction /friːd(ə)lˈkrafts rɪˌakʃ(ə)n/ *noun phr.* L19.
[ORIGIN from Charles *Friedel* (1832–99), French chemist + James M. *Crafts* (1839–1917), US chemist.]
CHEMISTRY. The catalytic alkylation or acylation of an aromatic compound in the presence of a Lewis acid such as aluminium chloride.

Friedreich /ˈfriːdrʌɪk, -x/ *noun.* L19.
[ORIGIN Nikolaus *Friedreich* (1825–82), German neurologist.]
MEDICINE. **1** ***Friedreich ataxia***, ***Friedreich disease***, ***Friedreich's ataxia***, ***Friedreich's disease***, a hereditary progressive ataxia with onset usu. in adolescence. L19.
2 ***Friedreich's paramyoclonus***, = ***paramyoclonus multiplex*** s.v. PARA-[1]. L19.

friend /frɛnd/ *noun & adjective.*
[ORIGIN Old English *frēond* = Old Frisian, Old Saxon *friund* (Dutch *vriend*), Old High German *friunt* (German *Freund*), Old Norse *frændi*, Gothic *frijonds*, from Germanic pres. pple of verb = 'to love', from base of FREE *adjective*.]
▸**A** *noun.* **1** A person joined by affection and intimacy to another, independently of sexual or family love. OE.

> R. G. COLLINGWOOD An intimate and beloved friend of my own. *Proverb:* A friend in need is a friend indeed.

2 A near relation. Usu. in *pl.*, those responsible for one. OE.

> OED Handed over to the care of his friends.

3 A person who is not hostile or an enemy to another; one who is on the same side. OE.

> J. MASTERS They'd said 'Friend', instead of giving the countersign.

4 A person who wishes another, a cause, etc., well; a sympathizer, helper, patron, (*of*, *to*); (usu. in *pl.*) a supporter *of* an institution etc., who regularly contributes money or other help. ME. ▸**b** A helpful thing. LME. ▸**c** A person who acts for another, *esp.* (*hist.*) as a second in a duel. E19.

> J. PRIESTLEY The Gnostics . . were no friends to marriage. *Guardian* The twenty . . Friends of the Tate Gallery. **b** SHAKES. *Wint. T.* Good expedition be my friend.

5 An acquaintance, an associate; a stranger whom one comes across or has occasion to mention again. Freq. as *voc.* as a polite form or in irony, and (*hist.*) used by members of the Society of Friends as the ordinary form of address. ME.

> R. KIPLING You mustn't bang about as though Delhi station belonged to you, my friend. JONATHAN ROSS The local inspector's calling out friend Twite [a pathologist].

6 A romantic or sexual partner, a lover. Now a euphemism exc. where qualified as ***boyfriend***, ***girlfriend***, ***lady-friend***, ***man-friend***, etc. LME.

> *Guardian* The boy's mother . . was joined . . by a man described as her 'friend'.

7 (**F-**.) A member of the Society of Friends. M17.
– PHRASES: **be friends (with)**, **keep friends (with)** be on good or intimate terms (with). ***best friend(s)***: see BEST *adjective* etc. ***curate's friend***: see CURATE *noun*. ***feathered friend***: see FEATHERED 1. **friend at court** a person in a position to use his or her influence on one's behalf. **friends in high places** highly placed people able or ready to use their influence on one's behalf. ***keep friends (with)***: see ***be friends (with)*** above. **make friends (with)** get on good or intimate terms (with). ***man's best friend***: see MAN *noun*. **my learned friend** (a form of address used of) a fellow lawyer in court. **my noble friend** (a form of address used of) a fellow member of the House of Lords. **my honourable friend**, **my right honourable friend** (a form of address used of) a fellow member of the House of Commons. NEXT ***friend***. PLUMBER'S ***friend***. PRISONER'S ***friend***. ***Society of Friends***: see SOCIETY 6a.
▸†**B** *adjective.* Well-disposed, friendly, not hostile. (Cf. ENEMY *adjective*.) LME–L17.

friend /frɛnd/ *verb trans.* ME.
[ORIGIN from the noun.]
†**1** Gain friends for. *rare.* Only in ME.
2 Make (a person) a friend or friendly; join in friendship. Usu. in *pass. obsolete* exc. *dial.* LME.
3 Act as a friend to, befriend (a person or cause); help. Now *arch. & poet.* M16.
■ **friended** *adjective* having a friend or friends (of a specified kind); *rare* befriended: LME. **friending** *verbal noun* (now *arch., dial., & poet.*) †(*a*) friendliness; (*b*) the action of the verb: E17.

friendless /ˈfrɛndlɪs/ *adjective.* OE.
[ORIGIN from FRIEND *noun* + -LESS.]
Lacking friends.
■ **friendlessness** *noun* E19.

friendlike /ˈfrɛndlʌɪk/ *adjective.* M16.
[ORIGIN from FRIEND *noun* + -LIKE.]
Like a friend or friends, friendly.

friendly /ˈfrɛn(d)li/ *adjective & noun.* OE.
[ORIGIN from FRIEND *noun* + -LY[1].]
▸**A** *adjective.* **1** Having the qualities or disposition of a friend, disposed to act as a friend, kind. OE.

> J. M. COETZEE This morning when I tried to be friendly he shook me off.

2 Characteristic of or befitting a friend or friends; showing friendship. LME.

> M. E. BRADDON Jernam acknowledged their courtesy with a friendly nod.

3 Of a thing: disposed or likely to be helpful; kindly, propitious, favourable, salutary. Foll. by *to*. LME. ▸**b** Suitable to one's comfort, convenient. L17.

J. BUCHAN This time they had not the friendly night to shield them. **b** ADDISON On the first friendly Bank he throws him down.

4 Favourably disposed; inclined to approve or help. LME.

J. C. MORISON The side of his history from which a friendly biographer would most readily turn away.

5 Not hostile or in opposition; on amicable terms. (Foll. by *to*, *with*.) L16. ▸**b** Not proceeding from or carried out with hostility; (of a football match or other game) outside any official competition. L19. ▸**c** *MILITARY*. Of troops or equipment: of, belonging to, or in alliance with one's own forces. E20.

I. MCEWAN Our families must become friendly for reasons of diplomacy and business. A. CHAUDHURI The stray dogs of the lane were friendly with the children. **c** J. WEDGE Friendly aircraft in the distance.

†**6** Of things: not jarring or conflicting. Only in 18.
7 (**F-**.) Of or pertaining to the Society of Friends. L19.
8 *COMPUTING* etc. Easy and convenient to use; designed with the needs of users in mind. L20.
9 Appended to nouns or adverbs to form adjectives with the senses 'adapted to', 'suitable for', 'not harmful to'. L20.

USA Today The most overtly yuppie-friendly show on air. *Financial Times* An environmentally friendly packaging material which breaks down in sunlight.

– SPECIAL COLLOCATIONS: **friendly fire** *MILITARY* gunfire from one's own side, *spec.* when causing accidental injury or damage to that side. **Friendly Society** any of various associations providing mutual insurance schemes.

▸ **B** *noun*. **1** A member of an indigenous people or tribe which is not hostile to invaders. Usu. in *pl.* M19.
2 A friendly football match or other game (see sense A.5b above). L19.
▪ **friendlily** *adverb* in a friendly manner or spirit, like a friend L17. **friendliness** *noun* L15.

friendly /ˈfrɛn(d)li/ *adverb*. OE.
[ORIGIN from FRIEND *noun* + -LY². Later sometimes from the adjective.]
In a friendly manner or spirit, friendlily.

friendship /ˈfrɛn(d)ʃɪp/ *noun*. OE.
[ORIGIN from FRIEND *noun* + -SHIP.]
1 The state or relation of being a friend; association as friends. OE. ▸**b** A relationship of friendliness or intimacy. OE.

BACON Without friendship, society is but meeting. **b** J. MORLEY His friendship with two of the chief actors may have biassed his judgment.

2 Friendly feeling or disposition; friendliness. ME.

A. J. P. TAYLOR Germany and Soviet Russia . . made a pact of mutual friendship at Rapallo.

†**3** A friendly act; a favour; friendly aid. ME–E17.
– COMB.: **friendship bracelet** a brightly coloured bracelet of woven wool, cotton, etc., worn by young people as a token of friendship.

frier *noun* var. of FRYER.

Friesian /ˈfriːzjən, -ʒ(ə)n/ *adjective & noun*. E20.
[ORIGIN Alt. of FRISIAN.]
(An animal of, of or pertaining to) a breed of usu. black and white large dairy cattle orig. bred in Friesland.

Friesic /ˈfriːzɪk/ *adjective*. M19.
[ORIGIN from German *Friese* (see FRISIAN) + -IC. Cf. FRISIC.]
= FRISIAN *adjective*.

frieze /friːz/ *noun*¹. LME.
[ORIGIN French *frise*, from medieval Latin = Frisian (wool). Cf. FRIEZE *verb*¹.]
1 A kind of coarse woollen cloth with a nap, usually on one side only, orig. of Welsh, now esp. of Irish manufacture. LME.

J. DYER Frize of Cambria. F. O'BRIEN Your heavy great-coat of Galway frieze.

2 Bruising or abrasion of the grain in leather. Orig. in †***frieze-leather***, frizzed leather. L16.
†**3** Down on a plant; a tuft of this. M–L17.
▪ **friezy** *adjective* (*a*) dressed in frieze; (*b*) resembling frieze: M19.

frieze /friːz/ *noun*². M16.
[ORIGIN French *frise* from medieval Latin *frisium*, var. of *frigium*, for Latin *Phrygium* (sc. *opus*) Phrygian work.]
1 *ARCHITECTURE*. In the entablature of an order, the member between the architrave and the cornice; a band of sculpture filling this. M16. ▸**b** = HYPOTRACHELIUM. L16.
2 Any broad horizontal band of sculptured, painted, or other decoration, esp. on a wall near the ceiling; a horizontal paper strip bearing pictures or decoration, for mounting on a wall. M17.

R. MACAULAY A long frieze running right across under the windows, with carved flowers and trees. *fig.*: R. COBB The ever-rising frieze of evergreens composed of holly, yew and cypress.

▪ **friezeless** *adjective* M19.

frieze /friːz/ *verb*¹ *trans. obsolete* exc. *hist.* LME.
[ORIGIN French *friser* or Spanish *frisar*: see FRIZZ *verb*¹. Cf. FRIEZE *noun*¹.]
Cover with a nap. Freq. as ***friezed*** *ppl adjective*.
▪ **friezer** *noun* a person who friezes cloth LME.

frieze /friːz/ *verb*² *trans.* M16.
[ORIGIN French *friser* rel. to *frise* FRIEZE *noun*².]
Chiefly as ***friezed*** *ppl adjective*.
1 Embroider with gold; work (gold) into decorative patterns. Now *rare*. M16.
2 Cover (silver) with chased patterns. L17.
3 *NAUTICAL*. Decorate by painting (the bows, stern, and quarters of sailing ships). M18.

frig *noun*¹ var. of FRIDGE *noun*.

frig /frɪɡ/ *verb & noun*². Now *coarse slang*. LME.
[ORIGIN Perh. imit.: cf. FIDGE *verb*, FRIDGE *verb*, FYKE *verb*.]
▸ **A** *verb*. Infl. **-gg-**.
1 *verb intrans.* Move about restlessly; wriggle. *obsolete* exc. *dial.* or passing into sense 3c. LME.

I. MURDOCH Sit down, Sarah, stop frigging about.

†**2** *verb trans.* Rub, chafe. E16–L17.
3 *verb trans. & intrans.* Masturbate. Also = FUCK *verb* 1, 2. L17. ▸**b** *verb trans.* = FUCK *verb* 3. E20. ▸**c** *verb intrans.* [cf. FUCK *verb* 2b, etc.] Muck or mess *about*, fool *around* (*with*); make *off*. M20.

fig.: BYRON Such writing is sort of mental masturbation—he is always f—gg—g his *Imagination*. **b** R. FRAME It was the last straw . . 'Frig this tree. Just *frig* it!' **c** X. HERBERT Don't frig about. Give's my money or there'll be trouble.

▸ **B** *noun*. An act of frigging (sense 3). Also = FUCK *noun* 3. L19.

M. MCCARTHY I don't give a frig about Sinnott's heredity.

▪ **frigging** *adjective & adverb* = FUCKING E20.

frigate /ˈfrɪɡət/ *noun*. L16.
[ORIGIN French *frégate* from Italian *fregata*, †*fragata* (whence Spanish *fragata*), ult. origin unknown.]
1 A light, swift vessel, powered by oar or sail. Now only *poet.* L16.
2 A fast-sailing merchantman. *obsolete* exc. *hist.* E17.
3 a *hist.* A sailing warship; *spec.* one next in size to a ship of the line and carrying 28–60 guns. M17. ▸**b** A general-purpose warship with mixed armament, usu. lighter than, or, in the US and some other navies, heavier than a destroyer; orig., any of a kind designed for convoy escort work. M20.
4 In full ***frigate bird***. Any of several large swift predatory seabirds constituting the genus *Fregata* and family Fregatidae, which have long wings, a long deeply forked tail, and a long hooked bill, and inhabit tropical oceans. M18.
– COMB.: ***frigate bird***: see sense 4 above; **frigate-built** *adjective* (*hist.*) (of a sailing ship) having a descent of some steps from the forecastle or quarterdeck to the waist; **frigate mackerel** a small tropical tuna of the genus *Auxis*, esp. *A. thazard*.

frigger /ˈfrɪɡə/ *noun*¹. Now *coarse slang*. L16.
[ORIGIN from FRIG *verb* + -ER¹.]
A person who masturbates or copulates.

frigger /ˈfrɪɡə/ *noun*². E20.
[ORIGIN Unknown.]
A small glass ornament or glass-maker's test sample.

friggle /ˈfrɪɡ(ə)l/ *verb intrans. obsolete* exc. *Scot. & dial.* E17.
[ORIGIN Frequentative of FRIG *verb*.]
Wriggle. Also, fuss.

fright /frʌɪt/ *noun*.
[ORIGIN Old English *fryhto* metath. (Northumbrian) alt. of *fyrhto*, *-u* = Gothic *faurhtei*, from Germanic, from base = afraid, repr. also by Old English *forht*, Old Saxon *foroht*, *-aht*, Old High German *foraht*, Gothic *faurhts*.]
1 (Sudden) fear, violent terror; alarm; an instance of this. OE.

E. O'NEILL He . . sinks back, too numbed by fright to move. R. MAUGHAM Oh, what a fright you gave me! . . I thought it was burglars.

in a fright in a state of terror. ***stage fright***: see STAGE *noun*. **take fright** become frightened.
2 Anything that inspires terror; *esp.* (*colloq.*) a person or thing of a grotesque or ridiculous appearance. M17.

J. M. SYNGE The fright of seven townlands for my biting tongue. B. BAINBRIDGE Brenda looked such a fright—she had toothache . . and her jaw was swollen.

– COMB.: **fright wig**: with the hair standing on end.
▪ **frighty** *adjective* (*rare*) †(*a*) causing fright; (*b*) suffering from fright, fearful: ME.

fright /frʌɪt/ *verb*. Now only *poet. & dial.* See also FRIT *adjective*.
[ORIGIN Old English (Northumbrian) *fryhta* var. of *fyrhtan* = Old Frisian *fruchtia*, Old Saxon *forahtian*, Old High German *furihten*, *for(a)htan* (German *fürchten*), Gothic *faurhtjan* from Germanic base of FRIGHT *noun*. Cf. FRIGHTEN.]
1 *verb intrans.* Take fright; be afraid. Long *obsolete* exc. *dial.* OE.
2 Frighten (*away*, *off*, etc.). OE.
▪ **frighted** *adjective* frightened, scared; *poet.* pervaded with fear: L16.

frighten /ˈfrʌɪt(ə)n/ *verb trans.* M17.
[ORIGIN from FRIGHT *noun* + -EN⁵, superseding FRIGHT *verb*.]
Throw into a fright; terrify; alarm; scare *away*, *off*; drive *out of* a place etc., *into* submission etc., by fear or menace.

GEO. ELIOT If you can't . . frighten her off touching things, you must . . keep 'em out of her way. W. S. CHURCHILL The activities of the early trade unions frightened the Government into oppressive measures.

frighten the horses: see HORSE *noun*. ***frighten the life out of***: see LIFE *noun*.
▪ **frightenable** *adjective* E19. **frightened** *adjective* thrown into a fright, afraid, (foll. by *at*, *of*, *by*, etc.) E18. **frightenedly** *adverb* L19. **frighteningly** *adverb* in a manner or to an extent that frightens M19.

frightener /ˈfrʌɪt(ə)nə/ *noun*. M19.
[ORIGIN from FRIGHTEN *verb* + -ER¹.]
A person who or thing which frightens; *spec.* (*slang*) a member of a criminal gang who intimidates its victims.
put the frighteners on *slang* intimidate, threaten.

frightful /ˈfrʌɪtfʊl, -f(ə)l/ *adjective*. ME.
[ORIGIN from FRIGHT *noun* + -FUL.]
1 Frightened, alarmed; timid. *obsolete* exc. *dial.* ME.
2 Frightening, alarming; shocking, dreadful; appalling, hideous. Freq. *hyperbol.* (*slang*), notable of its kind, esp. in badness; very unpleasant, ugly, boring, etc. E17.

M. KEANE A hideous and wicked little hat, frightful to wear and frightful to behold. C. S. FORESTER Every man had turned tail and fled from that frightful musketry. W. S. CHURCHILL The casualties in this battle were frightful. I. MURDOCH Shut the window, there's a frightful draught.

▪ **frightfully** *adverb* in a frightful manner; to a frightful extent or degree; (*slang*) extremely, excessively: E17. **frightfulness** *noun* the quality or state of being frightful; *spec.* [after German *Schrecklichkeit*] a deliberate military policy of terrorizing the enemy (esp. civilians): E17.

frightment /ˈfrʌɪtm(ə)nt/ *noun*. *rare*. E17.
[ORIGIN from FRIGHT *verb* + -MENT.]
The state of being in fear; something that causes fear.

frigid /ˈfrɪdʒɪd/ *adjective*. LME.
[ORIGIN Latin *frigidus*, from *frigere* be cold, from *frigus* cold: see -ID¹.]
1 Intensely cold, devoid of warmth. LME.

C. P. SNOW The contrast between the warmth in bed and the frigid air one breathed.

frigid zone each of two areas of the earth's surface, lying north of the Arctic Circle and south of the Antarctic Circle.
2 Usu. of a woman: unable to achieve orgasm, sexually unresponsive. Formerly also, lacking in sexual vigour, impotent. M17.
3 Lacking ardour, apathetic; cold, indifferent, formal; (of a thing) chilling, depressing. M17. ▸**b** Dull, insipid, flat. Now *rare*. M17.

C. MERIVALE The nobles . . let matters take their course with frigid indifference. T. HARDY Anne went home . . bidding Loveday a frigid adieu. E. M. FORSTER 'Pardon me', said a frigid voice. '. . We will incommode you no longer.' **b** LD MACAULAY A hundred and sixty lines of frigid bombast.

▪ **frigidly** *adverb* M17. **frigidness** *noun* (*rare*) E18.

Frigidaire /frɪdʒɪˈdɛː/ *noun*. E20.
[ORIGIN French, formed as FRIGIDARIUM.]
(Proprietary name for) a refrigerator.

frigidarium /frɪdʒɪˈdɛːrɪəm/ *noun*. Pl. **-iums**, **-ia** /-ɪə/. E18.
[ORIGIN Latin, formed as FRIGID: see -ARIUM.]
The room in ancient Roman baths containing the final, cold, bath.

frigidity /frɪˈdʒɪdɪti/ *noun*. LME.
[ORIGIN French *frigidité* from late Latin *frigiditas*, formed as FRIGID: see -ITY.]
1 Intense coldness. LME. ▸†**b** The quality of producing coldness. L16–M18.
2 Inability (usu. in a woman) to achieve orgasm; lack of sexual response. Formerly also, impotence. L16.
3 Lack of ardour or enthusiasm; apathy, coldness, indifference; formality. M17. ▸**b** Lack of imagination; dullness, insipidity. Now *rare*. M17.

frigorific /frɪɡəˈrɪfɪk/ *adjective*. M17.
[ORIGIN Latin *frigorificus*, from *frigor-*, *frigus* cold: see -FIC.]
Producing cold, cooling, freezing.

frijoles /friˈxoles, frɪˈhəʊlɛs/ *noun pl.* L16.
[ORIGIN Spanish, pl. of *frijol* bean, ult. from Latin *phaseolus*.]
Esp. in Mexican cookery: (a dish of) beans.

frikkadel /frɪkəˈdɛl/ *noun*. *S. Afr.* L19.
[ORIGIN Afrikaans, from French *fricadelle*.]
A fried or baked meatball; a rissole.

frill /frɪl/ *noun & verb*. L16.
[ORIGIN from or rel. to Flemish *frul*.]
▸ **A** *noun*. **1** An ornamental edging of woven material, of which one edge is gathered or pleated and the other left loose so as to have a wavy or fluted appearance. L16. ▸**b** A decorative strip of paper etc. for garnishing a hambone, cake, etc. M19.

fig.: A. CARTER The sea remained calm, there was scarcely the frill of a wave to be seen.

2 A fringe of hair, feathers, etc., resembling this; *esp.* a fringe of feathers round the neck of a pigeon. Hence, a frilled pigeon. M18.

F

3 a An affectation of dress or manner, an air. Usu. in *pl. colloq.* M19. **▸b** Something merely ornamental; a useless embellishment; an optional extra; a showy accomplishment. Usu. in *pl. colloq.* (freq. *derog.*). L19.

a M. TWAIN He cussed me for putting on frills, and trying to be better than him. **b** M. McCARTHY She had gone to a sound boarding-school . . with a well-rounded curriculum but no frills. J. C. OATES Jasper drove a smart, practical Ford, with few frills.

4 The mesentery of an animal. L19.
5 *PALAEONTOLOGY.* An upward-curving bony plate extending behind the skull of many ceratopsian dinosaurs. L19.
– COMB.: **frill-lizard** an Australian agamid lizard, *Chlamydosaurus kingii*, with an erectile membrane around its neck.
▸ B *verb.* **1** *verb trans.* Equip or decorate with a frill; be or become a frill for. Also, form into a frill. L16.
2 *verb trans. & intrans. PHOTOGRAPHY.* Cause (the film on a photographic plate) to rise in flutes at the edge; (of the film) rise thus. L19.
■ **frilled** *adjective* provided or decorated with a frill or frills; naturally possessing a frill or frills; ***frilled lizard*** = ***frill-lizard*** s.v. FRILL *noun*: E19. **frillery** *noun* (a mass of) frills L19. **frilling** *noun* (*a*) the action of the verb; (*b*) frills collectively: E19.

F

frilly /ˈfrɪli/ *adjective & noun.* M19.
[ORIGIN from FRILL *noun* + -Y¹.]
▸ A *adjective.* Having or resembling a frill or frills; full of frills; *colloq.* showy, decorative rather than functional. M19.

H. S. HARRISON I am a clerk . . My official title, of course, is a little more frilly. *Financial Times* A red cassock with a large frilly white collar.

▸ B *noun.* **1** In *pl.* (Frilled) underwear. *colloq.* E20.
2 = ***frill-lizard*** s.v. FRILL *noun. Austral. colloq.* M20.
■ **frilliness** *noun* E20.

frim /frɪm/ *adjective. obsolete* exc. *dial.* Compar. & superl. **-mm-**.
[ORIGIN Old English *freme* from Germanic.]
Vigorous, flourishing, luxuriant, rich; succulent, juicy; soluble, fusible.

Frimaire /frɪˈmɛː; *foreign* frimɛːr (*pl. same*)/ *noun.* E19.
[ORIGIN French, from *frimas* hoar frost.]
The third month of the French Republican calendar (introduced 1793), extending from 21 November to 20 December.

fringe /frɪn(d)ʒ/ *noun & adjective.* ME.
[ORIGIN Old French *frenge*, *fringe* (mod. *frange*) from Proto-Romance metath. alt. of late Latin FIMBRIA, earlier only pl., fibres, shreds, fringe.]
▸ A *noun.* **1** An ornamental bordering of threads left loose or made into tassels or twists, sometimes attached to a narrow band of fabric; *collect.* a piece of material forming this. ME.
2 Anything resembling this; a border or edging, *esp.* one that is broken or serrated; an edging of hair or fibres in an animal or plant. E17. **▸b** A portion of front hair cut short and arranged so as to hang over the forehead. L19.

W. B. CARPENTER In Fishes the gills are composed of fringes. K. MANSFIELD On the edge of the sea a white silky fringe just stirred. W. CATHER A fringe of cedars grew along the edge of the cavern.

3 An outer edge or margin; an outer limit of an area, population, sphere of activity, etc. Formerly also, an appendage, a sequel. M17. **▸b** A peripheral or secondary group, *esp.* an unofficial or unconventional one. E20.

H. BELLOC An Inn . . that stood on the fringe of a larch wood. *Cornishman* Frank Gibson was left . . stuck out on the fringe of things. P. D. JAMES They were mostly theatrical people, on the fringe anyway. **b** *Sight & Sound* There is a fringe who bomb places.

4 *OPTICS.* A band or strip of contrasting brightness or darkness (usu. one of a series), produced by diffraction or interference of light. Also, a strip of false colour in an optical image. E18.
5 *ellipt.* = ***fringe benefit*** below. M20.

J. GRISHAM We offer the highest salary and fringes in the country.

– PHRASES: ***Celtic fringe***: see CELTIC *adjective*. **lunatic fringe** a fanatical, eccentric, or visionary minority of a political party etc.
▸ B *attrib.* or as *adjective*. Existing on the edge or margin of anything; of secondary or minor importance; unofficial, unconventional. Formerly also, fringed. L16.

G. CHARLES Fringe characters, not big enough for the central roles. S. BRETT An actor friend . . was setting up a new fringe theatre company.

– SPECIAL COLLOCATIONS & COMB.: **fringe benefit** a perquisite or benefit provided by an employer to supplement a money wage or salary. **fringe medicine** the systems of health care that are not regarded as orthodox by the medical profession. **fringe net**: intended to confine a fringe of hair. **fringe tree** a deciduous N. American shrub or small tree, *Chionanthus virginicus*, of the olive family, bearing white flowers in panicles.
■ **fringer** *noun* a person who occupies or belongs to a fringe (FRINGE *noun* 3) M20. **fringy** *adjective* of the nature of or resembling a fringe; provided, decorated, or covered with fringes: M18.

fringe /frɪn(d)ʒ/ *verb.* ME.
[ORIGIN from the noun.]
1 *verb trans.* Provide, decorate, or encircle with or as with a fringe. Chiefly as ***fringed*** *ppl adjective.* ME.

I. MURDOCH The open fields . . were fringed with ragged lines of elm and hawthorn. W. GOLDING The velvet cloth on the table was fringed with bobbles.

fringing reef a coral reef forming a ring around an island.
2 *verb trans.* Act as a fringe to; appear as a fringe on. L18.

E. B. TYLOR The Esquimaux who fringe the northern coast. G. L. HARDING The pink oleander fringes the banks of every stream.

3 *verb intrans.* Spread like a fringe *away*, *off*, *out*, *over*, etc. Now *rare.* M19.
■ **fringing** *verbal noun* (*a*) the action of the verb; (*b*) the formation or appearance of optical fringes; (*c*) the spreading of electric or magnetic lines of force at the edges of a region, so as to depart from the regular pattern within the region: LME.

fringilline /frɪnˈdʒɪlʌɪn/ *adjective.* L19.
[ORIGIN from Latin *fringilla* finch + -INE¹.]
ORNITHOLOGY. Finchlike, of or pertaining to the finches; *spec.* designating or pertaining to members of the subfamily Fringillinae or the genus *Fringilla*, which includes the chaffinch and the brambling.

†**friponnerie** *noun.* E18–E19.
[ORIGIN French, from *fripon* rogue: cf. -ERY.]
Deception or cheating.

†**fripper** *noun.* L16–L17.
[ORIGIN French *fripier*, alt. of Old French *frepier*, from *frepe* rag, old clothes, ult. origin unknown: see -ER² 2.]
= FRIPPERER.

fripperer /ˈfrɪp(ə)rə/ *noun.* L16.
[ORIGIN Extended form of FRIPPER: see -ER¹ 2.]
A dealer in second-hand clothing.

frippery /ˈfrɪp(ə)ri/ *noun & adjective.* M16.
[ORIGIN French *friperie*, Old French *freperie*, from *frepe*: see FRIPPER, -ERY.]
▸ A *noun.* †**1** Old or second-hand clothes; cast-offs. M16–E19.
†**2** A second-hand clothing shop. Also, trade in cast-offs. L16–M19.
3 Finery; *esp.* unnecessary or tawdry adornment in dress; an item of this. M17. **▸b** A knick-knack, a trifle. Also *collect.* E19.

ARNOLD BENNETT Mrs Hamps followed, the fripperies of her elegant bonnet trembling. S. T. WARNER All the state and frippery of a court. **b** *Sunday Times* When France did win the championship . . they didn't bother with such fripperies as backs.

4 Empty display; showy talk or writing; ostentation. E18.

E. A. FREEMAN All the fopperies and fripperies of chivalry. M. O. W. OLIPHANT A noble young gentleman amid all his frippery of courtier and virtuoso.

▸ B *adjective.* Trifling, frivolous; contemptible. E17.

frippet /ˈfrɪpɪt/ *noun. slang.* E20.
[ORIGIN Unknown.]
A frivolous or showy young woman; such women collectively.

frisado *noun* var. of FRIZADO.

Frisbee /ˈfrɪzbi/ *noun.* Also **f-**. M20.
[ORIGIN Perh. from the *Frisbie* bakery in Bridgeport, Connecticut, USA, whose pie-tins could be used similarly.]
(US proprietary name for) a concave plastic disc which spins when thrown in the air and is used in a throwing and catching game; the game itself.

Punch I . . watched the hippies playing Frisbee with our hubcaps.

ultimate Frisbee: see ULTIMATE *adjective*.

frisé /ˈfriːzeɪ/ *adjective.* L19.
[ORIGIN French, pa. pple of *friser*: see FRIEZE *verb*¹, FRIZZ *verb*¹.]
Of, pertaining to, or designating a pile fabric with cut and uncut loops forming a pattern, chiefly used in upholstery.

Frisesomorum /ˌfrʌɪsɛsəˈmɔːrəm/ *noun.* Also **Frisesmo** /frʌɪˈsɛsməʊ/. L16.
[ORIGIN A mnemonic of scholastic philosophers, I indicating a particular affirmative major proposition, E a universal negative minor proposition, and O a particular negative conclusion.]
The supposed indirect mood of the first syllogistic figure, in which a particular negative conclusion is drawn from a particular affirmative major premiss and a universal negative minor premiss. (Later sometimes taken to be the fourth-figure mood, FRESISON.)

frisette /frɪˈzɛt/ *noun.* E19.
[ORIGIN French, from *friser* to curl, frizz: see -ETTE.]
A cluster of usu. artificial curls attached to a band and worn on the forehead.

friseur /frizœːr/ *noun.* Now *rare.* Pl. pronounced same. M18.
[ORIGIN French, from *friser* (see FRISETTE) + *-eur* -OR.]
A hairdresser.

Frisian /ˈfrɪzɪən/ *adjective & noun.* L16.
[ORIGIN from Latin *Frisii* Frisians, from Old Frisian *Frīsa*, *Frēsa*, whence Old English *Frīsa*, *Frēsa*, Middle Dutch *Vriese* (Dutch *Vries*), Old High German *Friaso* (German *Friese*), Old Norse *Frísir*: see -IAN.]
▸ A *adjective.* Of, pertaining to, or characteristic of Friesland, a region including a northern province of the Netherlands and part of NW Germany, its language, or its inhabitants. L16.
▸ B *noun.* **1** A native or inhabitant of Friesland. L16.
2 The West Germanic language of Friesland (now restricted in use to a small area of the NW Netherlands), the closest relative of English. M19.
■ **Frisic** *adjective* (now *rare* or *obsolete*) = FRISIAN *adjective* L17.

frisk /frɪsk/ *adjective, verb, & noun.* LME.
[ORIGIN Old French *frisque* vigorous, alert, lively, merry, var. of *fri(s)che*, earlier *frique*, perh. ult. rel. to Old High German *frisc* fresh, lively.]
▸ †**A** *adjective.* Full of life; spirited, lively, frisky. LME–M19.
▸ B *verb.* **1** *verb intrans.* Skip, leap, dance, in a lively playful manner; gambol, frolic. E16.

V. WOOLF She came frisking into the room; but her mind is a sedate, literal mind. F. TUOHY Ponies . . were frisking in the sunshine.

2 *verb trans.* Move or wave in a lively playful manner. M17.

R. H. PATTERSON The tail is frisked up into the air in the liveliest manner possible.

3 *verb trans.* Search (a person or place); *esp.* feel quickly over (a person) in search of a concealed weapon etc. Orig. *slang.* L18.

F. FORSYTH The guards checked him at the gate, frisking him from ankles to armpits.

▸ C *noun.* **1** Orig. in *HORSEMANSHIP*, a caracole, a caper. Now *gen.*, a playful leap or skip, (*rare*) a whim. Also, friskiness. E16.
2 An act of frisking, a search (see sense B.3 above). Orig. *slang.* L18.
■ **frisker** *noun* a person who or thing which frisks M16.

frisket /ˈfrɪskɪt/ *noun.* L17.
[ORIGIN French *frisquette* from mod. Provençal *frisqueto*, from Spanish *frasqueta*.]
PRINTING. A thin iron frame hinged to the tympan of a hand press, having tapes or paper stretched across it, for keeping the sheet in position and clean.

frisky /ˈfrɪski/ *adjective.* E16.
[ORIGIN from FRISK + -Y¹.]
Given to frisking; lively, playful.

J. BARTH I . . found my old master a frisky new tubmate fresh from the desert to appease his temper. J. TORRINGTON My hands were free to frolic like frisky salamanders in the brief flame of her dress.

■ **friskily** *adverb* M19. **friskiness** *noun* E18.

frisson /ˈfriːsɔ̃, ˈfrɪsɒn; *foreign* frisɔ̃ (*pl. same*)/ *noun.* L18.
[ORIGIN French = shiver, thrill.]
An emotional thrill; a shiver of excitement.

D. L. SAYERS It absolutely thrilled me. I got shudders all the way down my spine. A genuine frisson. W. BOYD The car . . seemed to trail a frisson of sexuality, like smoke.

frist /frɪst/ *noun & verb. arch.*
[ORIGIN Old English *first*, *frist* = Old Frisian *ferst*, *first*, Old Saxon, Old High German *frist* (German *Frist*), Old Norse *frest*.]
▸ A *noun.* †**1** A period of time; a certain time. OE–ME.
2 A delay, a respite. Formerly also, a truce. ME.
▸ †**B** *verb.* **1** *verb trans. & intrans.* Grant respite to (a person); delay or postpone (a thing). ME–M17.
2 *verb trans.* Lend (money etc.) on credit; give (a debtor) time for payment. LME–E19.

frisure /frɪˈzjʊə/ *noun.* M18.
[ORIGIN French, from *friser*: see FRIZZ *verb*¹.]
A style of curling or frizzing the hair.

frit /frɪt/ *noun & verb.* Also **-tt**. M17.
[ORIGIN Italian *fritta* (perh. through French *fritte*) use as noun of fem. pa. pple of *friggere* FRY *verb*.]
▸ A *noun.* **1** A calcined mixture of silica and fluxes, which can be melted to make glass. M17.
2 A vitreous composition from which soft porcelain, enamel, etc., are made. L18.
▸ B *verb trans.* Infl. **-tt-**. Make into frit; fuse partially, calcine. E19.

frit /frɪt/ *adjective. dial. & colloq.* E19.
[ORIGIN pa. pple of FRIGHT *verb*.]
Frightened.

B. BEHAN I wasn't frit of the farmer's boy, a big lump of a lad.

frit fly /ˈfrɪtflʌɪ/ *noun.* L19.
[ORIGIN from Latin *frit* tiny particle on ear of corn + FLY *noun*¹.]
A small black fly, *Oscinella frit*, which is a destructive pest of cereals.

frith /frɪθ/ *noun*¹. Long *obsolete* exc. *hist.*
[ORIGIN Old English *friþu* (also strong neut. *friþ*) = Old Frisian *frethu*, Old Saxon *friþu* (Dutch *vrede*), Old High German *fridu* (German *Friede*), Old Norse *friðr*, from Germanic.]
1 Peace; protection; safety, security. OE.

†**2** A place where game or fish are preserved for hunting. ME–L16.

— COMB.: **frithborh** [Old English *friþborh*: see BORROW *noun*] = FRANK-PLEDGE; **frith-stool** †(*a*) a refuge, a sanctuary; (*b*) a seat (usu. of stone) formerly placed near the altar of some churches, providing sanctuary.

frith /frɪθ/ *noun*². [ORIGIN Old English (*ge*)*fyrhþe*, *fyrhþ*, from Germanic, perh. ult. from base of FIR.]
1 A wood; (sparsely) wooded country. Now chiefly *poet.* OE.
2 Land grown sparsely with trees or scrub; unused pastureland; a clearing in a wood. Now *dial.* LME.
3 A hedge, esp. made of wattled brushwood; a hurdle for fencing. Now *dial.* LME.
4 Brushwood, undergrowth. Now *dial.* L16.

frith /frɪθ/ *noun*³. ME. [ORIGIN formed as FIRTH *noun*²: perh. infl. by Latin *fretum* arm of the sea.]
= FIRTH *noun*².

frith /frɪθ/ *verb*. *obsolete* exc. *dial.* LME. [ORIGIN from FRITH *noun*².]
1 *verb trans.* Fence in or surround with a hedge. LME.
2 *verb intrans.* Form a hedge of wattled brushwood; cut underwood. E19.
■ **frithing** *verbal noun* (*a*) the action of the verb; (*b*) material cut for hedging, brushwood: LME.

fritillaria /frɪtɪˈlɛːrɪə/ *noun*. L16. [ORIGIN mod. Latin (see below), from Latin *fritillus* dice-box (prob. with ref. to the chequered corolla of *Fritillaria meleagris*) + *-aria* -ARY¹.]
A plant of the genus *Fritillaria*, a fritillary, *esp.* any of the cultivated kinds.

fritillary /frɪˈtɪl(ə)ri/ *noun*. M17. [ORIGIN formed as FRITILLARIA: see -ARY¹.]
1 Any plant of the large genus *Fritillaria* of the lily family; *esp.* (*a*) wild snake's head, *F. meleagris*, which bears drooping purple or white bell-like flowers and grows in damp meadows; (*b*) crown imperial, *F. imperialis*. M17.
2 Any of numerous butterflies, chiefly nymphalids of the genera *Argynnis*, *Boloria*, *Speyeria*, etc., which are characteristically brown with dark brown or black spots. L17.

fritiniency /frɪˈtɪnɪənsi/ *noun*. *rare*. M17. [ORIGIN from Latin *fritinnire* twitter: see -ENCY.]
Twittering.

fritt *noun & verb* var. of FRIT *noun & verb*.

frittata /frɪˈtɑːtə/ *noun*. E20. [ORIGIN Italian = fried.]
An Italian omelette, thick, well-cooked, and usu. containing meat, cheese, potatoes, and/or other vegetables.

fritter /ˈfrɪtə/ *noun*¹. LME. [ORIGIN Old French & mod. French *friture* from Proto-Romance, from Latin *frict-* pa. ppl stem of *frigere* FRY *verb*: see -ER².]
1 A piece of (usu. specified) meat, fruit, etc., coated in batter and deep-fried. LME.
2 WHALING. In *pl.* = FENKS. M17.

fritter /ˈfrɪtə/ *noun*². L17. [ORIGIN Alt. of FLITTERS: perh. rel. to Middle High German *vetze* (German *Fetzen*) rag, scrap.]
1 In *pl.* & (rarely) *sing.* Minute pieces, fragments, shreds; small or unimportant items. L17.
2 Frittering; excessive subdivision or complexity. E19.

T. RICKMAN This window is a series of small panels . . and these . . throw the building into fritter. V. WOOLF People have been staying here . . . such a fritter & agitation.

fritter /ˈfrɪtə/ *verb*. E18. [ORIGIN from FRITTER *noun*².]
1 *verb trans.* Usu. with *away*: do away with piecemeal, wear down, attenuate; *esp.* waste (time, money, energy, etc.) on trifling matters. E18.

Sunday Post (Glasgow) You won't fritter the company profits on taxi fares. J. BARNES She had watched her mother's intelligence being frittered away on calculations about the price of tinned food.

2 *verb trans. & intrans.* Break or separate into minute pieces. Now *rare*. L18.
■ **fritterer** *noun* M19.

fritto misto /fritto ˈmisto/ *noun phr.* E20. [ORIGIN Italian = mixed fry.]
An Italian dish of various foods, usu. types of seafood, deep-fried in batter.

Fritz /frɪts/ *noun*¹. E20. [ORIGIN German, abbreviation of *Friedrich*, male forename.]
A German; *esp.* a German soldier fighting in the First World War. Also, Germans, esp. German soldiers, collectively. Cf. JERRY *noun*³.

fritz /frɪts/ *noun*². *slang* (orig. & chiefly *N. Amer.*). E20. [ORIGIN Unknown.]
on the fritz, out of order, broken, defective.

Friulian /frɪˈuːlɪən/ *adjective & noun*. L19. [ORIGIN from *Friuli*, a district in NE Italy + -AN.]
▸ **A** *adjective*. Of or pertaining to Friuli, its inhabitants, or the dialect spoken there. L19.
▸ **B** *noun*. **1** A native or inhabitant of Friuli. M20.
2 The Rhaeto-Romance dialect spoken in Friuli. M20.

frivel *verb* var. of FRIVOL *verb*.

frivol /ˈfrɪv(ə)l/ *adjective & noun*. Chiefly *Scot.* L15. [ORIGIN Old French & mod. French *frivole*, formed as FRIVOLOUS. As noun, reintroduced 19 from the verb or from mod. French.]
▸ †**A** *adjective*. Frivolous; paltry; absurd. Also, fickle. L15–E17.
▸ **B** *noun*. A frivolous thing or person; *esp.* a frivolous act. L15.

frivol /ˈfrɪv(ə)l/ *verb*. Also **-el**. Infl. **-ll-**, ***-l-**. M19. [ORIGIN Back-form. from FRIVOLOUS.]
1 *verb intrans.* Behave frivolously. M19.
2 *verb trans.* Fritter (*away*). L19.
■ **frivoller** *noun* L19.

frivolity /frɪˈvɒlɪti/ *noun*. L18. [ORIGIN French *frivolité*, from *frivole*, formed as FRIVOLOUS: see -ITY.]
1 The quality of being frivolous; frivolous behaviour. L18.
2 A piece of frivolous behaviour; a frivolous thing. M19.

frivolous /ˈfrɪv(ə)ləs/ *adjective*. LME. [ORIGIN from Latin *frivolus* silly, trifling + -OUS.]
1 Of little or no value or importance, paltry; (of a claim, charge, etc.) having no reasonable grounds. LME.

B. PYM I always try to switch my thoughts to something frivolous like clothes. R. C. A. WHITE Unless the application is clearly frivolous, it will usually be granted.

2 Lacking seriousness or sense; silly. L15.

A. ALVAREZ He thought it frivolous and unbecoming to the serious figure he cut in the world.

■ **frivolously** *adverb* L16. **frivolousness** *noun* L16.

friz *noun*, *verb* vars. of FRIZZ *noun*, *verb*¹.

frizado /frɪˈzɑːdəʊ/ *noun*. *obsolete* exc. *hist.* Also **-s-** /-s-/. Pl. **-o(e)s**. M16. [ORIGIN Spanish *frisado* napped (cloth), from *frisar* = French *friser* raise a nap on (cloth), curl (hair): see FRIZZ *verb*¹, FRIEZE *verb*¹.]
A fine worsted cloth with a nap, similar to baize.

†**frize** *verb* see FRIZZ *verb*¹.

frizz /frɪz/ *noun*. Also **friz**. M17. [ORIGIN from FRIZZ *verb*¹.]
The state of being frizzed or curled. Also, frizzed hair, a row of curls.

frizz /frɪz/ *verb*¹. Also **friz** (infl. **-zz-**); orig. †**frize**. LME. [ORIGIN Old French & mod. French *friser*, perh. from *fris-* stem of *frire* FRY *verb*; the vowel appears to have been shortened under the infl. of FRIZZLE *verb*¹.]
1 *verb trans.* Rub (wash leather etc.) with a pumice stone or blunt knife so as to remove the grain, soften the surface, and give a uniform thickness. LME.
2 *verb trans.* Form (the hair, the nap of a cloth, etc.) into a mass of small crisp curls or tufts. L16.

A. CARTER A huge man . . with black hair frizzed out in a cloud down to his shoulders.

3 *verb intrans.* Of the hair: form small crisp curls. L17.

frizz /frɪz/ *verb*² *intrans.* Chiefly *dial.* M19. [ORIGIN formed as FRIZZLE *verb*².]
Of food: make a sputtering or sizzling noise when frying; burn or dry up in cooking.

frizzante /frɪtˈzanteɪ, -ti/ *adjective*. M20. [ORIGIN Italian, lit 'sparkling'.]
Of (Italian) wine: semi-sparkling.

frizzle /ˈfrɪz(ə)l/ *verb*¹ & *noun*¹. M16. [ORIGIN from FRIZZ *verb*¹: see -LE³.]
▸ **A** *verb*. **1** *verb trans.* Form (hair) into small crisp curls. M16.

A. TYLER The damp weather had frizzled her hair into little corkscrews.

2 *verb intrans.* Of hair: frizz, curl (*up*). E17.
▸ **B** *noun*. A small crisp curl; frizzled hair. E17.
■ **frizzly** *adjective* consisting of frizzles or curls E18.

frizzle /ˈfrɪz(ə)l/ *verb*² & *noun*². M18. [ORIGIN from FRY *verb* with imit. ending: see -LE³. Cf. FIZZLE, SIZZLE.]
▸ **A** *verb*. **1** *verb trans.* Burn or dry up (food) in cooking. M18.
2 *verb trans. & intrans.* Fry, grill, or burn with a sputtering or sizzling noise. M19.

W. S. MAUGHAM He had four little fish cheerfully frizzling in a pan.

▸ **B** *noun*. The action, an act, or the noise of frizzling. L19.

frizzy /ˈfrɪzi/ *adjective*. L19. [ORIGIN from FRIZZ *noun* + -Y¹.]
Consisting of frizzles or small crisp curls; resembling a frizz.
■ **frizziness** *noun* E19.

Frl. *abbreviation*.
Fräulein.

fro /frəʊ/ *preposition*, *adverb*, & *conjunction*. Also (*Scot. & N. English*) **frae** /freɪ/, †**fra**. ME. [ORIGIN Old Norse *frá*, corresp. to Old English *fram* FROM.]
▸ **A** *preposition*. **1** *gen.* = FROM *preposition*. Now only *Scot. & dial.* ME.

DONNE Cal vow'd men fro cloysters, dead from tombs. SIR W. SCOTT Well could he hit a fallow-deer Five hundred feet him fro. JAS. HOGG Up there rase ane wee wee man Franethe the moss-gray stane.

†**2** Of, concerning. *rare*. Only in ME.
▸ **B** *adverb*. In a direction or position that is remote or apart, away. Formerly also, contrary, against. Now only in TO AND FRO. ME.

R. HOLLAND Sum said to and sum fra. A. FLEMING Passage to, fro, and through without danger.

▸ †**C** *conjunction*. **1** From the time that, from the moment when, as soon as, when. LME–E16.
2 Since, seeing that. M16–E17.

Fröbel *noun* var. of FROEBEL.

frock /frɒk/ *noun & verb*. LME. [ORIGIN Old French & mod. French *froc* from Frankish, corresp. to Old High German *hroc*.]
▸ **A** *noun*. **1** A priest's or monk's long gown with loose sleeves; occas., a cassock. Also, priestly status or character. LME.

SIR W. SCOTT The Hermit by it stood, Barefooted, in his frock and hood. W. GLADDEN Such words as these . . cost the great Carmelite preacher . . his frock.

2 A man's upper garment; a long coat, tunic, or mantle. Now *rare* or *obsolete*. LME.

W. K. KELLY Kings at arms covered with long frocks of cloth of gold.

frock of mail a coat of mail, armour.
3 A woman's or girl's garment, consisting of a skirt and bodice; a dress. Formerly also, a skirted garment worn by young children of either sex. M16.

A. TROLLOPE I don't think I've ever been in London since I wore short frocks. J. ARCHER She was dressed in a bright yellow frock.

4 *hist.* = SMOCK 2. Formerly also = SMOCK-FROCK 1. E17. ▸**b** A sailor's woollen jersey. E19.

C. WALFORD Dealers in haubergs, or waggoners' frocks. **b** L. DEIGHTON I know it's a roll-neck pullover but you sign for a Frock. I'm not responsible for Naval Nomenclature.

5 †**a** A man's informal coat. E18–E19. ▸**b** In full ***frock coat***. A man's double-breasted long-skirted coat not cut away in front and now worn chiefly on formal occasions. E19. ▸**c** A person wearing such a coat; *esp.* (*derog.*) a politician, as opp. to a military man, concerned with the administration of the First World War. E20.

J. HANWAY His regimentals . . are a blue cloth frock with silver brandenburgs. **b** *Observer* Contemptible as a soldier, Lord George was impossible as a 'frock'.

— COMB.: ***frock coat***: see sense 5b above; **frock-coated** *adjective* wearing a frock coat.
▸ **B** *verb trans.* Provide with or dress in a frock; *fig.* invest with priestly office. Chiefly as ***frocked*** *ppl adjective*. L16.

froe /frəʊ/ *noun*. Now chiefly *US*. Also **frow**, (orig.) †**frower**. L16. [ORIGIN Use as noun of FROWARD *adjective* in sense 'turned away'.]
A wedge-shaped cleaving tool having a handle set at right angles to the blade.

Froebel /ˈfrəʊb(ə)l, ˈfrɔːb(ə)l/ *noun*. Also **Fröbel**. L19. [ORIGIN F. W. A. *Fröbel* (see below).]
Used *attrib.* to designate (a school organized according to) the system of child education by the use of kindergartens introduced by Friedrich W. A. Fröbel (1782–1852), German teacher and educationalist.
■ **Froeˈbelian** *adjective & noun* (*a*) *adjective* of or pertaining to the Froebel system; (*b*) *noun* an adherent of the Froebel system: L19.

frog /frɒg/ *noun*¹. [ORIGIN Old English *frogga*, a pet form rel. to Old English *forsc*, *frosc*, *frox*, = Middle Low German, Dutch *vorsch*, Old High German *frosc* (German *Frosch*), Old Norse *froskr*, from Germanic. Cf. FROSK.]
1 Any of numerous amphibians of the order Anura (formerly Salientia), which develop from tadpoles and are tailless as adults; *esp.* (as distinct from *toad*) any of those which have a smooth skin and leap rather than walk. Freq. *spec.* (more fully ***common frog***) one of the widespread Eurasian species *Rana temporaria*. OE. ▸**b** With specifying word: any of various animals held to resemble the frog in appearance or habits. L18.
bullfrog, ***edible frog***, ***tree frog***, ***wood-frog***, etc. LEAPFROG *noun & adjective*, *verb*. **b** ***fishing frog***: see FISHING *ppl adjective* 1. ***HORNED frog***.
2 A contemptible or repulsive person. *slang*. *derog*. Long *rare* or *obsolete* exc. as below. ME. ▸**b** A native or inhabitant of the Netherlands, a Dutchman. *derog*. Long *obsolete* exc. *hist.* M17. ▸**c** (Also **F-**.) A Frenchman, a Frenchwoman (cf. ***frog-eater*** below). Also, the French language. *slang*. *derog*. L18.

L. OWEN These infernall frogs [Jesuits] are crept into the West and East Indyes. **c** W. FAULKNER Ask him . . . You can speak Frog. *attrib.*: S. TOWNSEND Another sex book . . by a Frog writer.

3 Any of various diseases of the throat or mouth; a swelling beneath the tongue. Now *rare* or *obsolete* exc. in ***frog in the throat*** below. LME.
frog in the throat an irritation or apparent impediment in the throat, hoarseness.

F

F

4 More fully ***frog-stool***. A toadstool. Long *obsolete* exc. *dial.* LME.
5 A hollow in the face of a brick. L19.
6 *MUSIC.* = NUT *noun* 9c. Orig. & chiefly *US*. E20.
– COMB.: **frogbit** a floating monocotyledonous plant of stagnant water, *Hydrocharis morsus-ranae* (family Hydrocharitaceae), with white flowers and cordate leaves; also, an allied N. American plant, *Limnobium spongia*; **frog-eater** *slang, derog.* a Frenchman, a Frenchwoman, (cf. sense 2c above); **frog-eye** a fungal disease of plants (esp. tobacco and apple) marked by ring-shaped spots on leaves; **frog-face** (a person or animal having) a face thought to resemble that of a frog, with broad brow and nostrils and bulging eyes; *MEDICINE* a type of facial deformity usu. caused by a tumour in the region of the nose; **frog-faced** *adjective* having a frog-face; **frogfish** (*a*) an anglerfish (cf. ***fishing frog*** s.v. FISHING *ppl adjective* 1); (*b*) any of numerous fishes of the families Antennariidae and Brachionichthyidae, resembling anglerfishes esp. in attracting prey by means of a lure; (*c*) *S. Afr.* = TOADFISH 3; **froghopper** any of numerous jumping homopteran insects of the family Cercopidae, the larvae of which surround themselves with protective froth ('cuckoo spit'); **frogland** (*a*) marshy land abounding with frogs; †(*b*) (**F-**) *derog.* the Netherlands; (*c*) (**F-**) *joc. derog.* France; **frog-lily** *US* a yellow water lily, *Nuphar advena*; **frogman** a person wearing a close-fitting suit of rubber or the like, with goggles and flippers, and equipped with self-contained breathing apparatus, for underwater operations (orig. attacking enemy ships); **frogmarch** *noun & verb* (*a*) *noun* (also **frog's march**) the action or an act of carrying a prisoner face downwards with each of four people holding a limb; (*b*) *verb trans.* carry in this way; hustle forward (a refractory or reluctant person) after seizing from behind and pinioning the arms; **frogmouth** any of various Asian and Australasian birds resembling nightjars, of the families Podargidae and (more fully ***owlet-frogmouth***) Aegothelidae (genus *Aegotheles*); **frog orchid** a small green-flowered orchid of short turf, *Coeloglossum viride*; ***frog's march***: see ***frogmarch*** (*a*) above; **frogspawn** (*a*) the spawn of a frog or frogs; (*b*) *colloq.* pond-slime; (*c*) *colloq.* tapioca or sago pudding; **frog spit**, **frog spittle** = ***cuckoo spit*** s.v. CUCKOO *noun*; ***frog-stool***: see sense 4 above.
■ **froggery** *noun* (*a*) a place where frogs are kept or where they are found in great numbers; (*b*) a colony of frogs: M18. **froggish** *adjective* froglike M19. **froglet** *noun* a young or small frog E20. **froglike** *adjective* resembling (that of) a frog M16. **frogling** *noun* a little frog; a tadpole: E17.

frog /frɒg/ *noun*². E17.
[ORIGIN Uncertain: perh. from FROG *noun*¹, and also infl. by synon. Italian *forchetta* dim. of *forca* and French *fourchette* dim. of *fourche*: see FORK *noun*. Cf. also FRUSH *noun*².]
A piece of elastic horny substance growing in the middle of the sole of a horse's hoof.

frog /frɒg/ *noun*³. E18.
[ORIGIN Unknown.]
1 An attachment to a waist belt to support a sword, bayonet, or similar weapon. E18.
2 An ornamental coat-fastening, originally forming part of military dress, consisting of a spindle-shaped button covered with silk or similar material and a loop through which it is passed. M18.
■ **frogged** *adjective* (of a coat or other garment) fastened or ornamented with frogs L18.

frog /frɒg/ *noun*⁴. M19.
[ORIGIN Unknown.]
A grooved piece of metal placed at the junction of the rails where one railway track crosses another.

frogging /ˈfrɒgɪŋ/ *noun*¹. M17.
[ORIGIN from FROG *noun*¹ + -ING¹.]
Catching frogs, fishing for frogs.

frogging /ˈfrɒgɪŋ/ *noun*². L19.
[ORIGIN from FROG *noun*³ + -ING¹.]
The attachments or ornamental fastenings on a frogged garment.

froggy /ˈfrɒgi/ *noun*. M19.
[ORIGIN from FROG *noun*¹ + -Y⁶.]
1 A frog. *joc.* M19.
2 (Also **F-**.) A Frenchman or Frenchwoman. *slang. derog.* L19.

froggy /ˈfrɒgi/ *adjective*. E17.
[ORIGIN from FROG *noun*¹ + -Y¹.]
1 Having (many) frogs. E17.
2 Of or like a frog or frogs. M19.
3 (Also **F-**.) French. *slang. derog.* M20.

Fröhlich's syndrome /ˈfrəːlɪks ˌsɪndrəʊm/ *noun phr.* E20.
[ORIGIN from Alfred *Fröhlich* (1871–1953), Austrian neurologist.]
MEDICINE. A syndrome including obesity and lack of sexual development, which affects young males and is caused by a hypothalamic tumour.

froise /frɔɪz/ *noun*. Also **fraise** /freɪz/. ME.
[ORIGIN Uncertain: perh. from Old French from popular Latin var. of *frixum*, *frixa* neut. and fem. pa. pple of *frigere* FRY *verb*.]
A kind of pancake or omelette, often containing slices of bacon.

†**frokin** *noun*. E17–M18.
[ORIGIN from obsolete Dutch dim. of *vrouw*: see FROW *noun*¹, -KIN; cf. VROU.]
A Dutch girl or woman.

frolic /ˈfrɒlɪk/ *adjective, verb, & noun*. E16.
[ORIGIN Dutch *vrolijk* adjective, from Middle Dutch & mod. Dutch *vro* glad, joyous + *-lijk* -LY¹.]
► **A** *adjective*. **1** Joyous, merry, cheerful; playful. *arch.* E16.

G. ETHEREGE Then sparkling champagne . . Makes us frolic and gay. E. DARWIN Galantha . . prints with frolic step the melting snows.

†**2** Free, liberal. Foll. by *of*. Only in L16.
► **B** *verb*. Infl. **-ck-**.
1 *verb intrans.* Play pranks, gambol, caper about (*with*). Formerly also, make merry. L16.

BYRON Its bounding crystal frolick'd in the ray. J. RUSKIN Horses . . frolicking with each other.

2 *verb trans.* Make joyous or merry. Also, entertain by giving parties to. Now *rare* or *obsolete*. L16.

O. FELTHAM Virtue . . gives such Cordials, as frolick the heart. W. IRVING By dint of dinners, of feeding and frolicking the town.

► **C** *noun*. †**1** In *pl.* Humorous verses circulated at a feast. E–M17.
2 An outburst of fun, gaiety, or merriment; a prank. M17. ▸**b** Fun, merriment, gaiety. L17. ▸**c** A whim. *rare*. E18.

B. FRANKLIN I spent no time in taverns, games, or frolics of any kind. J. R. LOWELL He . . often filled whole pages . . with the gay frolics of his pencil. **b** B. JOWETT All young creatures are full of motion and frolic.

frolic of his own *LAW* an action by an employee that is performed outside the scope of his or her employment, and for which the employer has no liability.
3 A scene or occasion of gaiety or mirth; a merrymaking, a merry party. M17.

H. MARTINEAU They meant to have a reaping frolic when the corn should be ripe.

■ **frolicker** *noun* E19. **frolicky** *adjective* = FROLICSOME M18. †**frolicly** *adverb* mirthfully, gaily L16–L17. †**frolicness** *noun*: only in 17.

frolicsome /ˈfrɒlɪks(ə)m/ *adjective*. L17.
[ORIGIN from FROLIC + -SOME¹.]
Full of playful mirth; inclined to frolic.
■ **frolicsomely** *adverb* L19. **frolicsomeness** *noun* E18.

from /frɒm, *unstressed* frəm/ *preposition, adverb, & conjunction*.
[ORIGIN Old English *fram*, *from* = Old Saxon, Old High German, Gothic *fram*, Old Norse *frá* FRO, from Germanic base = forward (= PRO-¹) + *-m* suffix.]
► **A** *preposition*. Often used in association with *to* (a finishing point).
1 Denoting departure or moving away: expr. relation with a person who or thing which is the starting point or site of motion. OE.

AV *Gen.* 4:16 And Cain went out from the presence of the Lord. H. JAMES She passed from room to room. E. BOWEN The funeral could not . . be expected to take place 'from' Wisteria Lodge.

2 Indicating the starting point or the first of two boundaries of an extent in space. OE. ▸**b** Indicating the starting point in a series, esp. the lower limit in a series or range. OE.

M. PATTISON Neustria . . extended from the Meuse almost to the present southern limits of France. **b** G. WHITE The swallow lays from four to six white eggs.

3 Indicating the starting point of an extent in time. Freq. foll. by *to*, denoting the passage of time or regular recurrence. OE.

SHAKES. *A.Y.L.* And so, from hour to hour, we ripe and ripe. C. BRONTË I knew him from a boy. P. KAVANAGH From half-past five that morning they had been up.

4 Indicating someone or something left behind or at a distance by a person who or thing which withdraws or goes away. OE. ▸**b** Indicating a place or object left on one side by a person who or thing which deflects or turns away. L16.

SHAKES. *3 Hen. VI* We will not from the helm to sit and weep. V. S. PRITCHETT When he came home from his London office. **b** W. S. MAUGHAM To divert him from his chosen path.

5 Indicating the (degree of) distance, remoteness, absence, etc., of a person or thing in a fixed position. OE. ▸**b** Indicating absence: not with (a person), not at (a place). *arch.* ME.

T. ARNOLD Veii lay about ten miles from Rome. **b** J. MOSER He was continually from home. E. PARSONS Georgina she could not bear a moment from her sight.

6 Denoting removal, separation, exclusion, freedom, deliverance, privation, abstention, or similar negation of contact with a concrete or abstract object. OE.

M. ELPHINSTONE The narrow tract . . separated from Mékrán . . by the range of hills. J. BUCHAN The smug suburban life from which he had revolted. G. GREENE Shaded from the sun.

7 Orig., denoting a qualitative remoteness, unlikeness, or incongruity. Now, indicating the unlikeness, distinction, or difference of the person or thing distinguished. OE.

P. MASSINGER But this is from the purpose. L. CARROLL You can't tell one flower from another. W. GOLDING The novelists who stand out from the rest.

8 Indicating a person as a source of action at some degree of distance, esp. as a giver or sender. OE.

LD MACAULAY Independence, veracity, self-respect, were things not required by the world from him. R. KIPLING I got one really exciting letter from you.

9 Denoting the ground of a judgement or belief. Also, denoting a reason, cause, or motive. OE.

DISRAELI Remarkable from the neatness . . of its architecture. T. RALEIGH A person suffering from senile dementia. V. WOOLF No one kills from hatred. G. GREENE 'It's good of you,' she said, and I could tell from her voice that she meant it.

10 With another preposition following: indicating initial position or state. OE.

MILTON The sacred well That from beneath the seat of Jove doth spring. H. MACKENZIE My grandmother . . looking at me from under her spectacles.

11 Indicating a state or condition which is or may be abandoned or changed for another. ME.

GOLDSMITH From being attacked, the French . . became the aggressors. BROWNING Temples . . which tremblingly grew blank From bright.

12 Denoting derivation, source, descent, or the like (*lit.* & *fig.*). ME.

R. HENRY The greatest rivers sometimes flow from the smallest fountains. LD MACAULAY His chief pleasures were commonly derived from field sports. I. MURDOCH Harriet had acquired Ajax . . from the Battersea Dogs Home.

13 Denoting the fixed place or position of origin of an action or motion the range of which extends beyond that point. L16.

DRYDEN They mined it near, they battered from afar. L. CARROLL From their point of view they are perfectly right. R. HARDY Ceilings from the beams of which hung leaves of palm and sisal. I. MCEWAN Mary admired . . the view from the balcony.

14 Indicating a model, rule, or copy, or (now *rare*) a person or thing after whom or which another is named. L16.

SHAKES. *Tam. Shr.* For, sure, Æacides Was Ajax, call'd so from his grandfather. L. M. HAWKINS She sketched objects; she colored from nature.

15 Indicating the place etc. of origin of a person or thing. Also, indicating the range, field, etc., out of which a selection is or may be made. E17.

F. HALL This list I could amplify from my own verbal stores. R. HARDY Pus from the infected wound ran against his fingers. D. ABSE The man on his right was from Manchester.

– PHRASES: (A selection of cross-refs. only is included: see esp. other nouns.) ***as from***: see AS *adverb* etc. ***far from***: see FAR *adverb*. ***from a child***: see CHILD *noun*. ***from hand to mouth***: see HAND *noun*. **from now on** now and in the future. †**from oneself** beside oneself, out of one's wits. **from out of** *arch.* out of, from within, from among. ***from*** PILLAR ***to post***. ***from the way***: see WAY *noun*. **from time to time** occasionally, intermittently.
► †**B** *adverb*. Away. Cf. FRO *adverb*. LME–E17.

E. TOPSELL A sliding snake . . Gliding along the altar, from and back.

► †**C** *conjunction*. From the time when. LME–E17.

G. BABINGTON From wee rise till we goe to bed.

fromage blanc /frɒmɑːʒ ˈblɒ̃/ *noun phr.* M20.
[ORIGIN French = white cheese.]
A type of soft French cheese made from cow's milk and having a creamy, slightly sour taste.

fromage frais /frɒmɑːʒ ˈfreɪ/ *noun phr.* L20.
[ORIGIN French = fresh cheese.]
Soft fresh cheese used esp. as a dessert, with or without added flavouring.

fromward /ˈfrɒmwəd/ *adjective, adverb, & preposition*. *obsolete* exc. *dial.*
[ORIGIN Old English *fromweard*, from FROM + -WARD.]
► †**A** *adjective*. **1** Departing, about to depart. Only in OE.
2 Froward. ME–L16.
► **B** *adverb*. **1** In a direction which leads from or is turned from a given place or object; *fig.* in a different or diverse way, contrarily. OE.
†**2** Of time: onward from a given date. Only in LME.
► **C** *preposition*. In a direction which leads or is turned from (an object etc.); away from. ME.
■ Also **fromwards** *adverb & preposition* (*obsolete* exc. *dial.*) OE.

frond /frɒnd/ *noun*. L18.
[ORIGIN Latin *frond-*, *frons* leaf.]
1 *BOTANY.* A leaflike organ formed by the union of stem and foliage in certain flowerless plants, esp. ferns, and differing from the leaf in usu. bearing a fructification. Also *loosely*, any large compound leaf, e.g. of the palm, banana, etc. L18.
2 *ZOOLOGY.* A leaflike structure. M19.
■ **frondage** *noun* fronds collectively; *loosely* foliage: M19. **frondlet** *noun* a little frond M19.

fronde /frɔ̃d/ *noun*. Pl. pronounced same. L18.
[ORIGIN French, lit. 'sling'.]
1 *FRENCH HISTORY.* (Usu. **F-**.) A political party in mid-17th-cent. France which rose in rebellion against Mazarin and the Court during the minority of Louis XIV. L18.

2 *transf.* A malcontent or disaffected party; violent political opposition. **E19.**

fronded /ˈfrɒndɪd/ *adjective*. **M17.**
[**ORIGIN** from (the same root as) **FROND** + **-ED**².]
†**1** Having leaves or foliage (*lit. & fig.*). Only in **M17.**
2 Having fronds. **L19.**

frondent /ˈfrɒnd(ə)nt/ *adjective*. **L17.**
[**ORIGIN** Latin *frondent-* pres. ppl stem of *frondere* send out leaves, formed as **FROND**: see **-ENT**.]
Having leaves or fronds, leafy.

frondesce /frɒnˈdɛs/ *verb intrans.* **E19.**
[**ORIGIN** Latin *frondescere* frequentative of *frondere*: see **FRONDENT**, **-ESCE**.]
Send out leaves.
■ **frondescent** *adjective* breaking into leaf **E19.** **frondescently** *adverb* in a frondescent manner **M19.**

frondescence /frɒnˈdɛs(ə)ns/ *noun*. **M19.**
[**ORIGIN** mod. Latin *frondescentia*, formed as **FRONDESCE**: see **-ENCE**.]
1 The process or period of sending out leaves. **M19.**
2 Fronds or leaves collectively. **L19.**

frondeur /frɔ̃dœːr/ *noun*. Pl. pronounced same. **L18.**
[**ORIGIN** French, from **FRONDE** + *-eur* **-OR**.]
1 In *FRENCH HISTORY* (usu. **F-**), a member of the *Fronde*. **L18.**
2 *transf.* A malcontent, a political rebel. **M19.**

frondiferous /frɒnˈdɪf(ə)rəs/ *adjective*. **L16.**
[**ORIGIN** from Latin *frondifer*, formed as **FROND**: see **-OUS**, **-FEROUS**.]
Bearing leaves or fronds.

frondose /frɒnˈdəʊs/ *adjective*. **E18.**
[**ORIGIN** Latin *frondosus*, formed as **FROND**: see **-OSE**¹.]
Orig., leafy, leaflike. Now, covered with fronds; having the appearance of a frond.
■ **frondosely** *adverb* **L19.** **frondoseness** *noun* leafiness **E18.** †**frondosity** *noun* (*a*) leafiness; (*b*) a representation of leaves: **M17–L18.**

frondous /ˈfrɒndəs/ *adjective*. **E19.**
[**ORIGIN** from Latin *frondosus*: see **FRONDOSE**, **-OUS**.]
Leafy; *BOTANY* bearing leaves and flowers on the same stem.

frons /frɒnz/ *noun*. **M19.**
[**ORIGIN** Latin: see **FRONT** *noun*.]
ENTOMOLOGY. The middle part of the face of an insect, between the eyes.

front /frʌnt/ *noun, adjective, & adverb*. **ME.**
[**ORIGIN** Old French & mod. French from Latin *front-*, *frons* forehead, front.]
► **A** *noun* **I 1** The forehead. Now only *poet. & rhet.* **ME.** ▸**b** = **FRONS.** *rare.* **E19.**
2 The face. Now *rare* or *obsolete* exc. in ***front to front*** below. **LME.**

W. JONES Till thrice the sun his rising front has shown.

front to front = *face to face* s.v. **FACE** *noun*.

3 Orig., the face as expressing emotion or character. Now, bearing, demeanour; degree of composure or confidence while under threat or in danger. **LME.** ▸**b** *fig.* Outward appearance or aspect; a bluff; a pretext. Cf. sense 6d below. **E20.**

SIR W. SCOTT The . . unclouded front of an accomplished courtier. W. S. MAUGHAM She was putting on a bold front to conceal her wounded feelings. **b** A. BARON It was only a front He was scared stiff. P. BARKER The need to bluster, to keep up a front at all costs.

4 Effrontery, impudence. **M17.**

LD MACAULAY None of the commissioners had the front to pronounce that such a man could properly be made the head of a great college.

► **II** Foremost part.
5 a The foremost line or part of an army, battalion, etc.; line of battle; the foremost part of the ground occupied or of the whole field of operations, the part next to the enemy. Also, the foremost part of a position, as opp. to the *rear*, the scene of actual fighting. **LME.** ▸**b** The direction towards which a line of troops faces when formed. **M19.** ▸**c** *transf. & fig.* A sector of activity regarded as resembling a military front (freq. with specifying word). **E20.** ▸**d** A political group organized to pursue a particular objective or set of objectives. **E20.**

a MILTON Front to Front Presented stood in terrible array. E. HEATH The forces of the Republican government had been pushed back . . and the main front was along the River Ebro. **c** *Times* The industry is fighting back on the marketing as well as the political front. H. KISSINGER Progress in superpower relations . . has to be made on a broad front. J. DIDION He . . is still Top Pineapple on the hospitality front.

a ***action front!***: see **ACTION** *noun*. **go to the front** join troops on campaign. ***Western Front***: see **WESTERN** *adjective*. **b change of front** a radical alteration of one's attitude or position on a particular subject. **change front** (of a line) face in another direction; *fig.* radically alter one's attitude or position on a particular subject. ***second front***: see **SECOND** *adjective*. **d *National Front***, ***patriotic front***, ***popular front***, etc.

6 The side or part of an object which appears to look out or to present itself to the view; the forepart of something, as a vehicle or a building. Also, the side or part of an object (esp. opp. to the *back*) which is less remote from a spectator or which is naturally reached first, as the face in a mine or the like. **LME.** ▸†**b** A frontier. Only in **L16.** ▸**c** Land facing a road, a river, the sea, etc.; frontage; spec. *the* promenade of a seaside resort, often with adjoining gardens. **M18.** ▸**d** A person or organization serving as a cover for subversive or illegal activities. Cf. sense 3b above. **E20.**

F. W. MAITLAND The skin being thin, the writing on the front could be seen upon the back. N. SHAVE For curved blades, the hollow side is the front. *transf.*: SHAKES. *Sonn.* Philomel in summer's front doth sing. **c** G. GREENE A blow along the front'll do you good. **d** M. MILLER It's a front; the Commies control it. M. ERSKINE He was . . respectable-looking and meek, . . just the type to make an excellent front for Madame Rosario.

front of house, **front of the house** *THEATRICAL* the parts of the theatre in front of the proscenium arch; the staff of the theatre or their activities. **c** *seafront*, *waterfront*.

7 *ARCHITECTURE.* Any of the sides or faces of a building; *esp.* the one in which the main entrance is sited. **LME.**

W. P. COURTNEY The fronts of the mansion were decorated with statues. P. PEARCE Along the fronts of the tall, narrow terrace houses she goes.

8 †**a** = **FRONTAL** *noun* 2. **LME–M16.** ▸**b** More fully ***false front***. A half-wig covering the front of the head, worn with a cap or bonnet by women. *obsolete* exc. *hist.* **L17.** ▸**c** The part of a garment, esp. of a dress or shirt, which covers (the upper part) of the front of the body. Also, a false shirt front. **E19.**

b A. TROLLOPE The graces of her own hair had given way to a front.

c ***shirt front***: see **SHIRT** *noun*. ***Y-fronts***: see **Y**, **Y** 2.

†**9** The first part or line of something written or printed. Also, a frontispiece. **L16–E18.**
10 A position or place situated before something or towards an observer; a forward position, a leading position in a race or contest. Only in phrs. with preceding preposition, as ***to the front*** (***of***), ***at the front*** (***of***), ***come to the front***, ***in front of***, etc. **E17.**

W. K. KELLY In the very front of danger.

come to the front take up or move to a forward position; become conspicuous. **in front** advanced or facing an observer; in the lead. **in front of** (*a*) ahead of, in advance of; (*b*) confronting, in the presence of.

11 a *gen.* An advancing boundary at which physical properties alter markedly. **M19.** ▸**b** *METEOROLOGY.* A narrow transition zone at the boundary of an advancing mass of air of distinct properties; the line of intersection of such a boundary with the earth's surface; *esp.* the leading edge (***warm front***) or trailing edge (***cold front***) of the warm sector of a cyclonic weather system. **E20.**

a *Scientific American* A flame front burns back through the vapour.

a ***wavefront***: see **WAVE** *noun*. **b** ***occluded front***: see **OCCLUDE** 5.

► **B** *attrib. adjective*. **1** Of or pertaining to the front, situated in front. **E17.**
2 *PHONETICS.* Of a sound: formed by raising the front part of the tongue, excluding the blade and tip, towards the hard palate. **M19.**
► **C** *adverb*. At the front; in front. **M17.**

E. HICKERINGILL The Enemy . . had beset them Front and Rear.

eyes front: see **EYE** *noun*. **front of** *US* in front of. **out front** (chiefly *N. Amer.*) (*a*) at or to the front, in front, in the forefront, to the fore; (*b*) *THEATRICAL* in the front of the stage; in the auditorium.

– **COMB. & SPECIAL COLLOCATIONS**: **front bench** a bench at the front of an assembly; *spec.* any of such in the House of Commons, occupied by members of the Cabinet or Shadow Cabinet; **frontbencher** an occupant of a front bench; **front bottom** *colloq.* (a child's word for) the female genitals; ***front burner***: see **BURNER** 3; **front door** the principal entrance door of a house or other building (*lit. & fig.*); **front end** (*a*) *colloq.* the forward part of a motor vehicle, train, etc.; (*b*) *ELECTRONICS* the tuner, local oscillator, and mixer of a superheterodyne receiver; (*c*) that part of a computer system that a user deals with directly, esp. a device providing input or access to a central computer or other parts of a network; freq. *attrib.* (with hyphen); (*d*) *attrib.* (with hyphen) designating money paid or charged at the beginning of a transaction; ***front-end loading***, the recovering of fees and service charges at the beginning of a loan repayment period; **front-fanged** *adjective* (*ZOOLOGY*) having venomous fangs at the front of the upper jaw; proteroglyphous, solenoglyphous; **front line** (*a*) = sense A.5a above (***front-line states***, a group of countries adjacent to South Africa and hostile to its former policy of apartheid); (*b*) the players in a jazz band other than the rhythm section; **front-load** distribute or allocate (costs, effort, etc.) unevenly, with the greater proportion at the beginning of the enterprise or process; **front-loader** a machine, esp. a washing machine, which is loaded from the front (rather than from the top); **frontman** (*a*) (orig. *US*) a man acting as a front (see sense A.6d above); (*b*) the leader or most prominent member of a group of musicians; **front matter** (in a book or similar publication) the title page, preface, introduction, and any other matter preceding the text; **front money** (orig. *US*) money paid in advance or at the beginning of a business transaction; **front office** (orig. & chiefly *US*) a main or head office, *esp.* police headquarters; **front page** the first page of a newspaper, esp. as containing important or remarkable news; **front-pager** a famous or notorious person likely to figure as the subject of a story or article on a front page; **front room** a room, esp. a sitting room, situated at the front of a house; **front row** *RUGBY* the forwards who make up the first row in a scrum; **front runner** (orig. *US*) (*a*) an athlete, horse, or other contestant who runs best when in the lead or who can set a fast pace; (*b*) a leading contestant (*lit. & fig.*), the contestant most likely to succeed; **frontsman** *hist.* a salesman who stands on the pavement in front of a shop; **frontstead** (now *dial.*) a piece of ground between the front of a house and the road or street; a forecourt, a front garden; **front yard** *N. Amer.* a piece of ground in front of a house, a front garden.
■ **frontways** *adverb* = **FRONTWISE M19.** **frontwise** *adverb* in a position or direction facing to the front **L18.**

front /frʌnt/ *verb*. **E16.**
[**ORIGIN** Partly from Old French *fronter*, from *front* **FRONT** *noun*, partly directly from **FRONT** *noun*.]
1 *verb intrans.* Have one's or its front facing in a specified direction. **E16.** ▸†**b** *verb trans.* Set the front of (a building) in a specified direction. **M17–E19.**

H. MAUNDRELL Having a few small Rooms fronting outward. W. GOLDING The balcony fronted on the swollen river.

2 *verb trans.* Stand or be face to face with; meet, face boldly; confront; oppose. *arch.* **L16.**

SHAKES. *Ant. & Cl.* Those wars which fronted mine own peace. F. NORRIS Singlehanded, Annixter fronted the monster. V. WOOLF Here she was fronting her audience.

3 *verb trans.* Be or stand in front of; serve as a front to. **L16.** ▸**b** *verb intrans.* Act as a front (**FRONT** *noun* 6d) *for* a person or organization. Orig. *US.* **M20.** ▸**c** *verb trans. & intrans.* Lead or be the most prominent member of (a group of musicians). Orig. *US.* **M20.** ▸**d** *verb trans.* Present (a television show etc.); appear as the major promoter of (a product). **L20.**

W. GOLDING The iron railings that fronted Bounce's house. **d** *Listener* Drug firms are able to employ well-known media people to front their promotions. M. KINGTON A . . TV series . . . I think I'll get Frank Muir to front it.

†**4** *verb trans.* Introduce (a story) *with* a reference or topic; preface. **L16–M18.**

T. BOSTON Solomon . . fronts his writings . . with most express gospel.

5 *verb trans.* **a** Have the front towards; stand opposite to, face. **E17.** ▸**b** Of a building: have its front on the side of (a street etc.). **L17.**

a F. CLISSOLD Fronting us, rose the summit of Mont Blanc. **b** A. M. GILLIAM The church . . was to have fronted the Plaza.

6 *verb trans.* Set face to face *with*, confront *with*. **E17.**

F. W. ROBERTSON Fronting his patron . . with the stern unpalatable truth of God.

7 Chiefly *MILITARY.* ▸†**a** *verb intrans.* March in the front or first rank. *rare.* Only in **E17.** ▸**b** *verb intrans.* Turn the front or face in a specified direction. **M17.** ▸**c** *verb trans. & intrans.* (Cause to) form a front or line. **L18.**

b J. HAYWARD The third fronting to their flanckward spurr'd towards him.

8 *verb trans.* Adorn in front; provide with a front; face (*with* a specified material). **M17.**

T. DWIGHT The Presbyterian church . . is fronted with two towers.

9 *verb intrans.* Become or feel distended or swollen, esp. through the absorption of fluid. *Scot. & dial.* **E19.**
10 *verb trans. PHONETICS.* Articulate (a sound) with the tongue further forward. **L19.** ▸**b** *verb intrans.* Of a sound: be or become formed with the tongue further forward. **M20.**
■ **fronted** *ppl adjective* having or formed with a front (of a specified kind) **E17.**

frontage /ˈfrʌntɪdʒ/ *noun*. **E17.**
[**ORIGIN** from **FRONT** *noun* + **-AGE**.]
1 Land which abuts on a river or other stretch of water, or on a road. Also, the land between the front of a building and a road or the like. **E17.**

A. C. BOULT Devonshire House . . enjoyed a frontage on the Green Park.

2 Extent of front. **M19.**

T. W. HINCHLIFF Shopkeepers . . get very little frontage to display their goods.

3 The front face or part of a building. **M19.**

C. ISHERWOOD Dirty plaster frontages embossed with scroll-work.

4 The action of fronting in a certain direction; the fact of facing a certain way; exposure, outlook. **M19.**

D. G. MITCHELL It has no wide and open frontage to the sun.

– **COMB.**: **frontage road** *N. Amer.* a service road.
■ **frontager** *noun* the owner of land or property adjoining the seashore or a roadway: **E17.**

frontage /ˈfrʌntɪdʒ/ *verb trans. rare.* **E20.**
[**ORIGIN** from the noun.]
Face; have the front towards.

frontal /ˈfrʌnt(ə)l/ *noun*. **ME.**
[**ORIGIN** Old French *frontel* (mod. *frontal*) from Latin *frontale* (pl. *frontalia*), from *frons* **FRONT** *noun*: see **-AL**¹.]
†**1 a** A band or ornament worn on the forehead. **ME–M17.** ▸**b** = **FRONTLET** 1c. **E17–M18.**

2 A movable covering for the front of an altar, an altar cloth. LME. ▸**b** A decorated front for a tomb. L19.
3 The facade of a building. LME.
†**4** *ARCHITECTURE*. A pediment placed over a small door or window. L16–M18.
5 The frontal bone. M19.

frontal /ˈfrʌnt(ə)l/ *adjective*. M17.
[ORIGIN mod. Latin *frontalis*, from *frons*: see FRONT *noun*, -AL¹.]
1 Of or pertaining to the forehead. M17.
frontal bone the cranial bone forming the forehead and the upper parts of the orbits. **frontal lobe** the lobe of the cerebrum lying behind the frontal bone.
2 Of or pertaining to the forepart or foremost edge; of or on the front. M19.
frontal assault, **frontal attack**: delivered directly on the front, not on the flank or rear.
3 Of, pertaining to, or depicting the front of a person, object, etc., or the facade of a building; (of sculpture) displaying frontality. L19.

H. WILLIAMSON Something . . apprehended in the retina of the eye, and not by a frontal stare.

full-frontal *adjective* (*a*) displaying the human body completely naked, seen from the front; (*b*) *fig.* holding nothing back, revealing all.
■ **fronˈtality** *noun* [translating Danish *frontalitet*] a principle in sculpture etc. according to which the figure is represented as seen from the full front E20. **frontally** *adverb* in a frontal manner; *esp.* by a frontal attack (*lit. & fig.*): E20.

frontier /ˈfrʌntɪə, frʌnˈtɪə/ *noun*, *adjective*, & *verb*. LME.
[ORIGIN Anglo-Norman *frounter*, Old French & mod. French *frontière* from Proto-Romance deriv. of Latin *frons*, *front-* FRONT *noun*.]
▸ **A** *noun*. †**1** The front side, the forepart. Also (*rare*), the side that faces in a specified direction. LME–E17.
†**2** = FRONTLET 2. Only in LME.
†**3** The front line or foremost part of an army. LME–E16.
4 *sing.* & in *pl.* The part of a country that borders on another country; the marches; the border or extremity coterminous with that of another. LME. ▸**b** The part of a country held to form the border or furthest limit of its settled or inhabited regions; *esp.* the western edge of settlement of the US before the Pacific settlement. L17.

G. F. KENNAN Establishing an agreed frontier between Poland and Russia. *fig.*: A. PRICE The frontiers of treason are rarely so clearly defined.

†**5** A border fortress, a frontier town. LME–L18. ▸**b** A barrier against attack. L16–E18.
†**6** A settler on the frontier; a frontiersman. L17–E18.
– COMB.: **frontiersman** a man living on a frontier, or on or beyond the borders of civilization.
▸ **B** *adjective*. **1** Of or belonging to the frontier of a country; situated on the frontier; bordering. E16. ▸**b** Characteristic of life on a frontier; remote from the comforts of civilization; pioneering. M19.

C. M. YONGE A few of the frontier castles had fallen into his hands. **b** H. D. THOREAU To live a primitive and frontier life. LADY BIRD JOHNSON An area that's called the American Alps and is still very much frontier.

†**2** Fronting; opposite. *rare*. Only in E17.
▸ **C** *verb*. †**1** *verb intrans.* Act as a frontier; border *on* or *upon*. L16–M17.
2 *verb trans.* Stand on or form the boundary of; face; delimit. Formerly also, bar, oppose. Long *rare*. L16.
■ **frontierism** *noun* a mode of expression characteristic of the (US) frontier L19. **frontierless** *adjective* E20.

frontignac /frɒntɪˈnjak/ *noun*. Also **frontignan** /frɒntɪˈnjɑ̃/. E17.
[ORIGIN Spurious form of *Frontignan* (see below), after many southern French names in *-ignac*.]
1 A muscat wine originally made at Frontignan in the department of Hérault, France. E17.
2 The grape from which this wine is made. M17.

frontispiece /ˈfrʌntɪspiːs/ *noun* & *verb*. L16.
[ORIGIN French *frontispice* or late Latin *frontispicium* facade of a building, from Latin *frons*, *front-* FRONT *noun* + *-spicium* as in *auspicium* AUSPICE, assim. in spelling to PIECE *noun*.]
▸ **A** *noun*. **1** The principal face or front of a building; *esp.* the decorated entrance of a building. L16.
2 The pediment over a door or gate. Also, a sculptured or engraved panel. E17.
3 *gen.* The front part of something; *spec.* (chiefly *joc.*) the face or forehead. E17.
†**4** The first page of a book or pamphlet or what was printed on it; the title page including illustrations and table of contents; an introduction or preface. E17–E18.
5 (Now the usual sense.) An illustration facing the title page of a book. L17.
▸ **B** *verb trans.* Provide with a frontispiece; represent on a frontispiece; put as a frontispiece. Now *rare*. E18.

frontless /ˈfrʌntlɪs/ *adjective*. E17.
[ORIGIN from FRONT *noun* + -LESS.]
1 Shameless, audacious, daring, brazen. Now *rare*. E17.

JONSON The . . most frontlesse piece Of solid impudence.

2 Not having a front. L19.

Daily Express She wore this startling backless—and nearly frontless—dress.

■ **frontlessly** *adverb* E17. **frontlessness** *noun* L17.

frontlet /ˈfrʌntlɪt/ *noun*. L15.
[ORIGIN Old French *frontelet* dim. of *frontel*: see FRONTAL *noun*, -LET.]
1 An ornament or band worn on the forehead. L15. ▸**b** = PHYLACTERY 1b. L16. ▸†**c** (A cloth or bandage containing) a medicament applied to the forehead. E17–E18. ▸**d** A piece of armour or harness for the forehead of an animal. E19.

b AV *Exod.* 13:16 It shall be for a token vpon thine hand, and for frontlets betweene thine eyes.

2 A cloth hanging over the upper part of an altar frontal. Also, an ornamental border to an altar cloth. M16.
3 The forehead: now only of an animal. M17.
4 The front or face of a building, mountain, etc. *rare*. E19.

fronto- /ˈfrɒntəʊ/ *combining form*. M19.
[ORIGIN Irreg. from Latin *frons*, *frontis* FRONT *noun*: see -O-.]
Used (chiefly *ANATOMY*) to form adjectives with the sense 'of or pertaining to the forehead and —', as ***fronto-nasal***, ***fronto-occipital***, ***fronto-parietal***, etc.

frontogenesis /frʌntə(ʊ)ˈdʒɛnɪsɪs/ *noun*. M20.
[ORIGIN formed as FRONT *noun* + -O- + -GENESIS.]
METEOROLOGY. The formation or development of a front or fronts.
■ **frontogeˈnetic** *adjective* M20.

frontolysis /frʌnˈtɒlɪsɪs/ *noun*. M20.
[ORIGIN formed as FRONTOGENESIS + -LYSIS.]
METEOROLOGY. The decay or disappearance of a front or fronts.
■ **frontoˈlytic** *adjective* M20.

fronton /ˈfrʌnt(ə)n/ *noun*. L17.
[ORIGIN French from Italian *frontone*, augm. of *fronte* forehead: see FRONT *noun*, -OON. In sense 3 translating Spanish *frontón*.]
1 A pediment. L17.
2 An altar frontal. *rare*. M18.
3 A building in which pelota is played. L19.

frontward /ˈfrʌntwəd/ *noun*, *adverb*, & *adjective*. Also **-wards** /-wədz/. M16.
[ORIGIN from FRONT *noun* + -WARD.]
▸ †**A** *noun*. The direction towards the front. Only in M16.
▸ **B** *adverb*. **1** Towards or in the direction of the front; to the front *of*. M19.
2 With the front or face in a specified direction. Foll. by *to*. *rare*. M19.
▸ **C** *adjective*. Of or pertaining to the front. M19.

froom *adjective* var. of FRUM.

†**froppish** *adjective*. M17–L18.
[ORIGIN Perh. from var. of FRAP *verb* + -ISH¹.]
Froward, fretful, peevish.
■ †**froppishness** *noun* L17–M18.

frore /frɔː/ *pa. pple* & *adjective*. Also **frorn** /frɔːn/, †**froren**. ME.
[ORIGIN Orig. pa. pple of FREEZE *verb*.]
1 *pa. pple* & *ppl adjective*. Frozen. *obsolete* exc. *dial.* ME.
2 *adjective*. Intensely cold, frosty, frostlike. Now only *poet.* L15.
■ **frory** *adjective* (now *rare* or *obsolete*) frozen, frosty, intensely cold M16.

frosh /frɒʃ/ *noun*¹. *N. Amer. slang*. Pl. same. E20.
[ORIGIN Alt. of FRESHMAN, perh. infl. by German *Frosch* frog, (dial.) grammar school pupil.]
A college freshman; *collect.* freshmen.

†**frosh** *noun*²: see FROSK *noun*.

frosk /ˈfrɒsk/ *noun*. Long *obsolete* exc. *dial.* Also †**frosh**.
[ORIGIN Old English *forsc*, *frosc*, *frox*: see FROG *noun*¹.]
A frog.

frost /frɒst/ *noun*.
[ORIGIN Old English *frost*, usu. *forst* = Old Frisian *frost*, *forst*, Old Saxon, Old & mod. High German *frost* (Dutch *vorst*), Old Norse *frost*, from Germanic, from weak grade of base of FREEZE *verb*: see -T¹.]
1 The action, state, or effect of freezing; the prevalence of a temperature below the freezing point of water; extreme cold; a frozen consistency. OE.

SHAKES. *Rom. & Jul.* Death lies on her like an untimely frost Upon the sweetest flower. J. UPDIKE By night the frost cracks rocks with a typewriter staccato.

black frost frost not accompanied by hoar frost. **degrees of frost** degrees below freezing point. **Jack Frost** frost personified. **white frost** frost accompanied by hoar frost.
2 Frozen dew or vapour forming a white deposit. Also ***hoar frost***. OE. ▸†**b** Ice. LME–L16.

POPE Groves that shine with silver frost.

3 *fig.* An influence that chills or depresses; *esp.* coldness of behaviour or temperament, frigidity; (*slang*) a coolness. ME.

W. H. MALLOCK He could not . . keep a slight frost from his manner.

4 A failure. *slang* (orig. *THEATRICAL*). L19.

R. LINDNER Look, Doc. This analysis is a frost, isn't it?

– COMB.: **frostbound** *adjective* affected by severe frost; **frost crack** a vertical split in a tree trunk caused by freezing; **frost-fish** (*a*) (chiefly *NZ*) the scabbardfish, *Lepidopus caudatus*; (*b*) *N. Amer.* a tomcod, *Microgadus tomcod*; **frost flower** an ice crystal resembling a flower; **frost grape** (the fruit of) any of several N. American wild vines, esp. *Vitis vulpina*, whose fruit turns sweet with the first frosts; **frost heave**, **frost heaving** the uplift of soil or other surface deposits due to expansion of groundwater on freezing; **frost-nail** *hist.* a nail driven into a horse's shoe to prevent slipping in icy weather; **frost-nip** *noun & verb trans.* (affect with) frostbite, usu. slight; **frost pocket** a small low-lying area affected by frost; **frost shattering** the disintegration or fracture of rock due to expansion of water freezing in cracks or pores; **frost-work** (decoration in imitation of) the tracery formed on the surface of glass etc. by frost (freq. *attrib.*).
■ **frostless** *adjective* E18. **frostlike** *adjective* resembling (that of) frost E19.

frost /frɒst/ *verb*. E16.
[ORIGIN from the noun.]
1 *verb trans.* Make (a horse's shoe) rough by inserting frost-nails, to prevent slipping; shoe (a horse) in this way. *obsolete* exc. *hist.* E16.
2 *verb trans.* Cover (as) with hoar frost or rime; *spec.* give a frostlike surface or appearance to (glass etc.), make (glass) opaque. Chiefly as ***frosted*** *ppl adjective*. M17. ▸**b** Turn (hair) white. M17. ▸**c** Ice (a cake). Chiefly as ***frosted*** *ppl adjective*. Now *US*. M18.

D. WELCH Home-made lemonade stood in already frosted glasses. I. MURDOCH The door has an oval panel of opaque frosted glass. A. LURIE Eighteen wigs, one frosted with diamonds.

3 *verb trans.* Freeze; *esp.* injure (a plant etc.) by frost. E19.

C. SAGAN High mountainous regions that remain frosted after the snows of the valleys have melted.

4 *verb intrans.* Become covered (*over*, *up*) with frost. (*lit. & fig.*) L20.

T. HOOPER The honey will 'frost', . . showing a white cloudy area . . often mistakenly thought to be deterioration.

■ **frosting** *noun* (*a*) the action of the verb; (*b*) a frosted surface; icing on a cake etc.: E16.

frostbite /ˈfrɒs(t)bʌɪt/ *noun*. E19.
[ORIGIN from FROST *noun* + BITE *noun*.]
Necrosis produced by exposure to severe cold, usually affecting the superficial tissues of fingers and toes.

frostbite /ˈfrɒs(t)bʌɪt/ *verb trans.* Pa. pple **-bitten** /-bɪt(ə)n/, (*rare*) **-bit** /-bɪt/. L16.
[ORIGIN from FROST *noun* + BITE *verb*.]
Injure with intense cold, expose to frost; affect with frostbite; sustain frostbite in (oneself, one's limbs). Usu. as ***frostbitten*** *ppl adjective*.

National Post The seamen were frostbitten and hypothermic by the time the rescuers reached them.

frosty /ˈfrɒsti/ *adjective*. LME.
[ORIGIN from FROST *noun* + -Y¹. Cf. Old English *fyrstig*.]
1 Affected or characterized by frost, ice-cold. LME.

J. TYNDALL The winter set in with clear frosty weather.

2 *transf.* & *fig.* Cold as frost, chilling; lacking ardour or warmth, frigid. LME.

Sunday Sun (Brisbane) An interview . . was preceded by a gruelling examination from Mr Swan. The atmosphere was decidedly frosty.

3 (Appearing to be) covered with hoar frost; (of the hair) white. LME.

transf.: SHAKES. *Tit. A.* My frosty signs and chaps of age.

■ **frostily** *adverb* E17. **frostiness** *noun* E18.

frot /frɒt/ *verb trans.* Long chiefly *dial.* Infl. **-tt-**. ME.
[ORIGIN Old French *froter* (mod. *frotter*), ult. origin unknown.]
Rub; polish; stroke, caress.

fig.: B. LEVIN Grudges and vendettas, regularly frotted into life. *absol.*: J. SCOTT The dog . . seemed a very friendly creature, standing tall . . to frot against the sergeant's leg.

froth /frɒθ/ *noun*. LME.
[ORIGIN Old Norse *froða* or *frauð*, from a Germanic base repr. also by Old English *āfrēoþan* to froth.]
1 The aggregation of tiny bubbles in a liquid, caused by agitation, fermentation, effervescence, etc.; foam, spume. Also, a state of frothing. LME. ▸**b** Foaming saliva. Now *rare*. LME. ▸**c** Matter rising to the surface of a liquid during boiling etc.; scum. M16.

O. WILDE Collecting contemporaneous things is like trying to hold froth in a sieve. D. L. SAYERS They walked . . slowly, so as not to set the beer all of a froth. *transf.*: D. HEWETT The pink nylon dress in a froth over her arm.

2 Something insubstantial or of little value. Formerly also, something immature or tender. LME.

A. HORNECK Thou hast delighted in froth, and idle talk.

3 A worthless person or persons; 'scum'. *derog.* Now *rare* or *obsolete*. L16.

SHAKES. *Merry W.* Froth and scum, thou liest!

– COMB.: **froth-blower** *joc.* a beer-drinker; formerly esp. (*Froth-Blower*) as a member of a charitable organization; ***froth flotation***: see FLOTATION 3.

froth /frɒθ/ *verb*. LME.
[ORIGIN from the noun. Cf. Old Norse mutated form *freyða*.]
1 *verb intrans.* Emit froth; foam at the mouth; (of a liquid) gather froth, run foaming (*away*, *over*). LME.

T. HARDY His lips frothing like a mug of hot ale. K. MANSFIELD The water frothed up in the big soapy bowl with pink and blue bubbles.

2 *verb trans.* Emit as or like froth. *rare.* **LME.**

TENNYSON Is your spleen froth'd out, or have ye more?

3 *verb trans.* Cause to foam, make frothy. **E17.**

S. JOHNSON She . . made his coffee, and frothed his chocolate.

4 *verb trans.* Cover (as) with froth. **E17.**

SMOLLETT His face frothed up to the eyes with soap lather.

frothy /ˈfrɒθi/ *adjective.* **L15.**
[ORIGIN from FROTH *noun* + -Y¹.]
1 Full of, covered with, or accompanied by froth; foamy. **L15.**

W. SOMERVILLE Wanton Joy . . had spilt the Cyder's frothy Flood.

2 Consisting of or resembling froth. Also *fig.*, insubstantial, trifling, vain; (of a person) shallow. **L16.**

E. LYALL A mere ranter, a frothy mob orator. A. BURGESS A frothy evening frock.

■ **frothily** *adverb* **E18.** **frothiness** *noun* **E17.**

frottage /ˈfrɒtɑːʒ, *foreign* frɔtaːʒ/ *noun.* **M20.**
[ORIGIN French = rubbing, friction, from *frotter*: see FROT.]
1 The practice of touching or rubbing against the (clothed) body of another person (usu. in a crowd), as a means of obtaining sexual gratification. **M20.** **2** ART. The technique or process of taking a rubbing from an uneven surface, such as grained wood, as a basis for an artistic work. **M20.**
■ **frotteur** /frɒˈtəː, *foreign* frɔtœːr (*pl. same*)/ *noun* [French] a person who indulges in frottage (sense 1) **L19.** **frotteurism** /frɒˈtəːrɪz(ə)m/ *noun* = FROTTAGE 1 **M20.**

frottola /ˈfrɒtələ, *foreign* ˈfrɔttola/ *noun.* Pl. **-le** /-leɪ, *foreign* -le/. **M19.**
[ORIGIN Italian, lit. 'fib, tall story'.]
MUSIC. A form of Italian comic or amorous song, esp. from the 15th and 16th cents.

Froude /ˈfraʊd/ *noun.* **M19.**
[ORIGIN William *Froude* (1810–79), English civil engineer.]
PHYSICS. ***Froude number***, a dimensionless number representing the drag on a body moving through a liquid with a free surface, used when modelling the behaviour of surface vessels and evaluated as V^2/Lg (where V is a characteristic speed, L is a characteristic length, and g is the acceleration due to gravity).

frou-frou /ˈfruːfruː/ *noun & verb.* **L19.**
[ORIGIN French, imit.]
▸ **A** *noun.* A rustling, esp. of skirts. Hence, frills, frippery. **L19.**
▸ **B** *verb intrans.* Move with a rustle (of skirts etc.). **E20.**

frough /fraʊ/ *adjective.* Long *dial.* Also **frow.** **ME.**
[ORIGIN Unknown. Cf. FRUSH *adjective.*]
Frail, brittle; not to be depended on.

froughy /ˈfraʊɪ/ *adjective.* Long *dial.* Also **frowy.** **L16.**
[ORIGIN Perh. from FROUGH + -Y¹.]
1 Musty, sour, stale. **L16.**
2 Of wood: spongy, brittle. **M17.**

frounce /fraʊns/ *noun*¹. **LME.**
[ORIGIN Old French & mod. French *fronce*, from Frankish, rel. to Old Norse *hrukka* wrinkle. Cf. FLOUNCE *noun*².]
†**1** A wrinkle. Also, a crease or pleat; *fig.* deceit. **LME–E18.**
†**2** A flounce. Only in **17.**
3 [Infl. by FROUNCE *verb.*] (A piece of) vain display; elaboration. *rare.* **L19.**

frounce /fraʊns/ *noun*². **LME.**
[ORIGIN Unknown.]
FALCONRY. A sore in the mouth of a hawk.

frounce /fraʊns/ *verb.* **ME.**
[ORIGIN Old French & mod. French *froncer*, also Old French *froncir* to wrinkle, fold, formed as FROUNCE *noun*¹.]
1 †**a** *verb trans.* Fold or wrinkle; knit, purse (the brow, lips). **ME–M17.** ▸**b** *verb intrans.* Knit the brow; (of the face) become wrinkled. Now *rare* or *obsolete.* **LME.**
†**2** *verb trans. & intrans.* Make or become creased or pleated. **LME–E19.**
3 *verb trans.* Frizz, curl (hair, a wig). **E16.**

froust *noun & verb* var. of FROWST.

frousty *adjective* var. of FROWSTY.

frow /fraʊ/ *noun*¹. *arch.* **LME.**
[ORIGIN Dutch *vrouw* woman: cf. FRAU, VROU.]
1 A Dutchwoman. **LME.**
2 A woman or wife; a housewife. **L16.**
3 A disreputable or untidy woman. *dial.* **L18.**

frow *noun*² var. of FROE.

frow *adjective* var. of FROUGH.

froward /ˈfrəʊəd/ *adverb, adjective, preposition, & noun. arch.* As preposition also **-wards** /-wədz/.
[ORIGIN Late Old English *frāward*, formed as FRO + -WARD. Cf. FROMWARD.]
▸ †**A** *adverb.* **1** In a direction leading away from a given person, place, or thing. **LOE–L16.**
2 Perversely; untowardly. **ME–L16.**
▸ **B** *adjective.* Perverse, hard to please; refractory, ungovernable; untoward, unfavourable. **ME.**
▸ **C** *preposition.* (In a direction) away from. Long *rare.* **ME.**
▸ †**D** *noun.* A froward person or thing. **LME–L16.**
■ **frowardly** *adverb* **LME.** **frowardness** *noun* **ME.**

†**frower** *noun* see FROE.

frown /fraʊn/ *noun.* **L16.**
[ORIGIN from the verb.]
1 A manifestation or sign of displeasure or disapproval. Now only as passing into sense 2. **L16.**

DEFOE The father's frowns are a part of correction.

2 A furrowed or wrinkled state of the brow; a look expressing severity, disapproval, perplexity, or thought. Formerly also, the habit of frowning. **E17.**

A. J. CRONIN His open and agreeable expression marred by the frown of a man harassed and overworked. A. LURIE A sharp W-shaped frown between his neat dark eyebrows.

frown /fraʊn/ *verb.* **LME.**
[ORIGIN Old French *frognier*, *froignier* (surviving in *re(n)frogner*), from *froigne* surly look, of Celtic origin (cf. Welsh *ffroen* nostril).]
1 *verb intrans.* Knit or furrow the brow in displeasure or thought; express disapproval or anger by a stern look (*at*, *on*, *upon*). **LME.** ▸**b** Of a thing: present a gloomy or threatening aspect. **E17.**

E. BUSHEN I would frown impatiently at the dispute. O. SACKS He thought again deeply, frowning in concentration. A. BLOND Others have been frowned upon for indulging in an unmanly . . occupation. **b** H. MARRYAT A deep ravine of frowning rocks.

2 *verb trans.* **a** Drive or force *into*, (now *rare*) *away*, *down*, *off*, by a frown or frowns. **L17.** ▸**b** Enforce, express, or produce by a frown or frowns. **L18.**

a N. WEBSTER I will be neither frowned nor ridiculed into error. **b** L. STEPHEN In 1861 the Schreckhorn . . still frowned defiance upon all comers.

■ **frowner** *noun* a person who frowns **M17.** **frowningly** *adverb* with a frown; in a frowning manner: **M16.**

frowst /fraʊst/ *noun & verb.* Also **froust.** **L19.**
[ORIGIN Back-form. from FROWSTY.]
▸ **A** *noun.* **1** Extra time in bed in the morning. Also, an armchair. *school slang.* **L19.**
2 (A laze or idle in) the stuffy or fusty warmth of a crowded or unventilated room. *colloq.* **E20.**

J. BETJEMAN Tea and a frowst with crumpets. J. R. ACKERLEY Ask for the window to be opened? Better not . . They preferred their frowst.

▸ **B** *verb intrans.* Stay in a stuffy, warm, or fusty atmosphere, esp. lazily or idly; take pleasure in doing this. **L19.**

K. AMIS No use sitting about . . or frowsting by the fire with a book.

■ **frowster** *noun* **E20.**

frowsty /ˈfraʊsti/ *adjective.* Orig. *dial.* Also **frousty.** **M19.**
[ORIGIN Uncertain: cf. Old French *frouste* ruinous, decayed, FROUGHY, FROWZY.]
Fusty, stuffy; warm and ill-ventilated; frowzy.

C. LASSALLE Their rooms had a frowsty, subterranean atmosphere.

■ **frowstiness** *noun* **E20.**

frowsy *adjective* var. of FROWZY.

frowy *adjective* var. of FROUGHY.

†**frowze** *noun.* **M16–E18.**
[ORIGIN Uncertain; perh. alt. of FROUNCE *noun*¹ with assim. to FRIZZ *noun*, FUZZ *noun*¹.]
A woman's wig of frizzed hair.

frowzy /ˈfraʊzi/ *adjective.* Also (perh. infl. by FROWSTY) **frowsy.** **L17.**
[ORIGIN Prob. rel. to earlier FROUGHY and later FROWSTY; ult. origin unknown.]
1 Smelling fusty, stuffy, or stale from being dirty, unwashed, or unventilated. **L17.**

N. COWARD Some frowsy little hotel.

2 Dirty, untidy, or neglected in appearance; unkempt. **E18.**

K. A. PORTER Badly buttoned and frowsy-haired.

■ **frowzily** *adverb* **L17.** **frowziness** *noun* **E18.**

froze *verb pa. t. & pple*: see FREEZE *verb.*

frozen /ˈfrəʊz(ə)n/ *ppl adjective.* **ME.**
[ORIGIN pa. pple of FREEZE *verb.*]
1 Solidified by exposure to cold; exposed to extreme cold; *spec.* (of food) preserved by refrigeration to below freezing point. **ME.** ▸**b** *fig.* Frigid, unfriendly, unresponsive. **L16.**

R. C. HUTCHINSON The road was still narrowed by a ridge of frozen snow. A. HIGGINS My hands were frozen . . , my feet chilled to the bone. M. PYKE Frozen chickens . . have become industrial products manufactured for a world market.

b *the frozen* MITT.
2 Hard, rigid; fixed, immobile. **L19.** ▸**b** BILLIARDS etc. Of a ball: at rest in close contact with another ball or a cushion. *rare.* **E20.** ▸**c** Of a credit or asset: impossible to liquidate or realize at maturity or some other given time. Cf. LIQUID *adjective* 6. **E20.**
the frozen limit *colloq.* the absolute limit; the ultimate of what is objectionable or unendurable.
■ **frozenly** *adverb* **E18.** **frozenness** /-n-n-/ *noun* **M17.**

frozen *verb pa. pple* of FREEZE *verb.*

FRS *abbreviation.*
Fellow of the Royal Society.

FRSE *abbreviation.*
Fellow of the Royal Society of Edinburgh.

fructan /ˈfrʌktan/ *noun.* **M20.**
[ORIGIN from FRUCTOSE + -AN.]
BIOCHEMISTRY. A polysaccharide whose constituent monosaccharides are fructoses; = FRUCTOSAN.

fructed /ˈfrʌktɪd/ *adjective.* **E17.**
[ORIGIN from Latin *fructus* fruit + -ED².]
HERALDRY. Of a tree or plant: bearing fruit (usu. when of a different colour from the rest).

Fructidor /ˈfrʊktɪdɔː, *foreign* fryktidɔːr (*pl. same*)/ *noun.* **L18.**
[ORIGIN French, from Latin *fructus* fruit + Greek *dōron* gift.]
The twelfth month of the French Republican calendar (introduced 1793), extending from 18 August to 16 September. Also, the purge of conservative deputies that took place on the eighteenth day of that month (4 September) in 1797.

fructiferous /frʌkˈtɪf(ə)rəs/ *adjective.* **M17.**
[ORIGIN from Latin *fructifer* (from *fructus* fruit) + -OUS: see -FEROUS.]
Bearing or producing fruit.
■ **fructiferously** *adverb* **M17.**

fructification /ˌfrʌktɪfɪˈkeɪʃ(ə)n/ *noun.* **L15.**
[ORIGIN Late Latin *fructificatio(n-)*, from Latin *fructificat-* pa. ppl stem of *fructificare*: see FRUCTIFY, -ATION.]
1 The process of bearing fruit (now chiefly BOTANY). Formerly also, fertilization. **L15.**
2 The fruit(s) of a flowering plant; the spore-bearing structures in a fern or other cryptogam. **M18.**

fructify /ˈfrʌktɪfʌɪ/ *verb.* **ME.**
[ORIGIN Old French & mod. French *fructifier* from Latin *fructificare*, from *fructus* fruit: see -FY.]
1 *verb intrans.* Bear fruit, become fruitful. **ME.**

fig.: S. SMILES The good deed . . will live, even though we may not see it fructify.

2 *verb trans.* Cause to bear fruit; make fertile or productive. **L15.**

J. A. MICHENER Without the aid of some god to fructify the earth the farmer was powerless. *fig.*: F. L. WRIGHT Cultural sterility . . might be saved and fructified by this ideal of an organic architecture.

fructivorous /frʌkˈtɪv(ə)rəs/ *adjective.* **L17.**
[ORIGIN from Latin *fructus* fruit + -VOROUS.]
= FRUGIVOROUS.

fructosan /ˈfrʌktəsan/ *noun.* **E20.**
[ORIGIN from FRUCTOSE + -AN.]
BIOCHEMISTRY. = FRUCTAN.

fructose /ˈfrʌktəʊz, -s/ *noun.* **M19.**
[ORIGIN from Latin *fructus* fruit + -OSE².]
CHEMISTRY. A hexose sugar which occurs widely (esp. combined in sucrose) in fruit juices, syrups, and honey.

fructuous /ˈfrʌktjʊəs/ *adjective.* **LME.**
[ORIGIN (Old French from) Latin *fructuosus*, from *fructus* fruit: see -OUS.]
1 (Of a plant) bearing much fruit, prolific; (of soil) fertile. **LME.**
2 *fig.* Beneficial, advantageous. **LME.**
■ **fructuously** *adverb* **LME.** **fructuousness** *noun* **M19.**

frug /frʌg/ *noun & verb.* **M20.**
[ORIGIN Unknown.]
▸ **A** *noun.* A vigorous dance performed to pop music, popularized in the 1960s. **M20.**
▸ **B** *verb intrans.* Infl. **-gg-**. Dance the frug. **M20.**

frugal /ˈfruːg(ə)l/ *adjective.* **M16.**
[ORIGIN Latin *frugalis*, from *frugi* indecl. adjective (orig. dat. of *frux* fruit) = economical, useful: see -AL¹.]
1 Careful or sparing in the use or supply of food, goods, etc.; economical. (Formerly foll. by *of*.) **M16.**

SHAKES. *Merry W.* I was then frugal of my mirth. R. LEHMANN A frugal wage-earner, managing on a few hundreds.

2 Of things, esp. food: provided in small quantity and with avoidance of excess; plain, simple. **E17.**

GOLDSMITH A frugal meal, which consisted of roots and tea.

■ **fru'gality** *noun* frugal character **E16.** **frugally** *adverb* **L16.** **frugalness** *noun* **E18.**

†**frugiferous** *adjective.* **M17–M18.**
[ORIGIN from Latin *frugifer* (from *frux*, *frug-* fruit) + -OUS: see -FEROUS.]
Bearing fruit; fruitful.

F

F

frugivore /ˈfruːdʒɪvɔː/ *noun*. M20.
[ORIGIN formed as FRUGIVOROUS + -VORE.]
An animal that feeds on fruit.

frugivorous /frʊˈdʒɪv(ə)rəs/ *adjective*. E18.
[ORIGIN from Latin *frug-*, *frux* fruit + -VOROUS.]
Esp. of an animal: living on fruit; = FRUCTIVOROUS.

fruit /fruːt/ *noun*. ME.
[ORIGIN Old French & mod. French from Latin *fructus* (enjoyment of) the produce of the soil, harvest, fruit, revenue, from *frui* enjoy from base of *fruges* fruits of the earth.]
▸ **I 1** *sing.* & (now chiefly) in *pl.* Vegetable produce in general. Also ***fruits of the earth***, ***fruits of the ground***. ME.

AV *Exod.* 23:10 Sixe yeres thou shalt sow thy land, and shalt gather in the fruites thereof.

first-fruit: see FIRST.

2 *sing.* & *collect. pl.* The edible product of a tree, shrub, or other plant, consisting of the seed and its envelope, esp. when sweet, juicy, and pulpy. Also *loosely*, another sweet juicy part of a plant, as the stalks of rhubarb, eaten similarly. Cf. VEGETABLE *noun* 2. ME. ▸†**b** A fruit course of a meal; dessert. L16–E17.

M. HENRY The choicest fruits ripen slowly. E. O'NEILL Pompeia . . takes a peach from the bowl of fruit. *Proverb*: He that would eat the fruit must climb the tree. **b** SHAKES. *Haml.* My news shall be the fruit to that great feast.

breadfruit, ***kiwi fruit***, ***miracle fruit***, ***passion fruit***, etc. ***bear fruit***: see BEAR *verb*[1]. ***DEAD SEA fruit***. ***FORBIDDEN fruit***. ***in fruit*** bearing fully formed fruit. ***soft fruit***: see SOFT *adjective*. ***stone fruit***: see STONE *noun, adjective, & adverb*.

†**3** A fruit tree. Also, a food plant. ME–M18.

4 BOTANY. The seed-bearing structure (the matured ovary) of a plant, as a means of reproduction etc. M18.

C. DARWIN Winged seeds are never found in fruits which do not open.

▸ **II** *transf.* & *fig.* **5** Offspring, progeny. More fully ***fruit of the body***, ***fruit of the loins***, ***fruit of the womb***. (Orig. a Hebraism.) *arch.* ME.

SHAKES. *3 Hen. VI* King Edward's fruit, true heir to th' English crown.

6 *sing.* & in *pl.* Anything (concrete or abstract) produced by an activity, process, etc.; product, outcome. ME.

G. GISSING Kindly, intimate talk, the fruit of a lifetime of domestic happiness. *Scouting* Get out that . . type-writer, unleash that tape-recorder . . and send us the fruits.

7 Advantage, profit. *arch.* ME.

J. HOWE I read thy lines with fruit and delight.

8 a A person easily imposed on; a dupe. *slang* (orig. *US*). L19. ▸**b** In familiar greetings: fellow, chap. Only in ***old fruit***. E20. ▸**c** A (passive) male homosexual. *slang* (orig. *US*). E20.

– COMB.: ***fruit acid*** = ALPHA-*hydroxy acid*; **fruit bar** a piece of dried and pressed fruit; **fruit bat** any of numerous fruit-eating bats of the suborder Megachiroptera, which includes the flying foxes; **fruit body** = ***fruiting body*** s.v. FRUIT *verb* 1; **fruit cake** (*a*) a cake made with dried fruit, nuts, spice, etc.; (*b*) *slang* (from phr. ***nutty as a fruit cake***) an eccentric or crazy person; **fruit cocktail** finely chopped fruit salad; **fruit dove** any of numerous Australasian and Indonesian fruit-eating doves of the genera *Ptilinopus* and *Phapitreron*, many of which have brightly coloured plumage; WOMPOO ***fruit dove***; **fruit farm**: on which fruit trees are grown; **fruit fly** (*a*) any of various dipteran flies of the families Tephritidae, whose larvae infest cultivated fruit (also ***large fruit fly***); (*b*) any of various dipteran flies of the family Drosophilidae, which feed on rotting or fermenting fruit (also ***small fruit fly***); **fruit gum** a fruit-flavoured piece of gelatin sucked as a sweet; **fruit juice** (a drink of) the juice of (esp. citrus) fruit; **fruit knife**: for cutting fruit, with a silver etc. blade to withstand the acid; **fruit loaf** a kind of sweet bread or cake containing dried fruit and usu. baked in a rectangular tin; **fruit loop** *N. Amer. slang*[after *Froot Loops*, a brand of breakfast cereal] a crazy person; **fruit machine** a coin- or token-operated gaming machine, in which a player is successful when certain combinations of symbols, usu. representing various kinds of fruit, appear; **fruit salad** an assortment of fruits cut up and served in syrup etc.; *slang* an array of campaign ribbons etc. worn on the chest; **fruit salts** effervescent health salts; ***fruit set***: see SET *noun*[1] 8c; **fruit sugar** sugar obtained from fruit, *esp.* fructose; **fruit tree**: grown for its fruit; **fruitwood** the wood of a fruit tree, esp. as used to make furniture.

fruit /fruːt/ *verb*. LME.
[ORIGIN from the noun.]
1 *verb intrans.* Bear fruit. LME.
fruiting body the spore-producing organ in a fungus.
2 *verb trans.* Induce (a plant) to bear fruit. M17.
■ **fruited** *adjective* bearing (much) fruit E17.

fruitage /ˈfruːtɪdʒ/ *noun*. LME.
[ORIGIN Old French, from *fruit* FRUIT *noun*.]
1 Fruit collectively. LME.
2 The process, season, or state of bearing fruit. L16.
†**3** A decorative arrangement of fruits; a picture, carving, embroidery, etc., representing this. E17–E18.

fruitarian /fruːˈtɛːrɪən/ *noun & adjective*. L19.
[ORIGIN from FRUIT *noun* + -ARIAN, after *vegetarian*.]
▸ **A** *noun*. A person who lives exclusively on fruit. L19.
▸ **B** *adjective*. Of or pertaining to fruitarians or their diet. E20.
■ **fruitarianism** *noun* E20.

fruiter /ˈfruːtə/ *noun*. ME.
[ORIGIN Old French & mod. French *fruitier*, from *fruit* FRUIT *noun*: see -ER[2]. Later prob. from FRUIT *noun*, *verb* + -ER[1].]
1 A fruit-grower. Formerly, a dealer in fruit; a household official in charge of fruit. ME.
2 A vessel engaged in the fruit trade. M19.
3 A tree that fruits in a specified way. L19.

fruiterer /ˈfruːt(ə)rə/ *noun*. LME.
[ORIGIN Extension of FRUITER with -ER[1].]
A dealer in, or (formerly) grower of, fruit.
■ †**fruiteress** *noun* a female fruiterer E18–E19.

fruitery /ˈfruːtəri/ *noun*. Now *rare*. E17.
[ORIGIN Old French & mod. French *fruiterie*, from *fruit* FRUIT *noun*: see -ERY.]
†**1** A place where fruit is grown or stored. E17–E19.
2 Fruit collectively. E17.

fruitful /ˈfruːtfʊl, -f(ə)l/ *adjective*. LME.
[ORIGIN from FRUIT *noun* + -FUL.]
1 Of a tree etc.: bearing abundant fruit. Of soil, weather, etc.: inducing fertility in plants. LME.
2 Bearing many offspring; prolific. LME.

AV *Gen.* 1:22 God blessed them, saying, Be fruitfull, and multiply.

3 *gen.* Abundantly productive of ideas or some other abstract thing. (Foll. by *of*, *in*.) LME.

W. H. PRESCOTT His fruitful genius suggested an expedient. J. BUCHAN He was fruitful of notions . . he could suggest magnificent schemes.

4 Productive of good results; beneficial, rewarding. LME.

H. J. LASKI Problems . . required the absence of passionate debate if they were in any fruitful fashion to be solved.

†**5** Of a crop, reward, etc.: abundant, copious. Only in 17.

DRYDEN Harvests heavy with their fruitful weight, Adorn our fields.

■ **fruitfully** *adverb* LME. **fruitfulness** *noun* LME.

fruition /frʊˈɪʃ(ə)n/ *noun*. LME.
[ORIGIN Old French & mod. French from late Latin *fruitio(n-)*, from Latin *fruit-* pa. ppl stem of *frui* enjoy: see FRUIT *noun*, -ION.]
1 Enjoyment; the pleasure arising from possession. Now *rare* or *obsolete*. LME.

Book of Common Prayer That we . . may after this lyfe have the fruicion of thy glorious Godhead. C. MARLOWE That perfect bliss . . . The sweet fruition of an earthly crown.

2 [By association with FRUIT *noun*.] ▸**a** The state of being in fruit; fructification. L19. ▸**b** *fig.* Successful outcome of a hope, plan, etc.; fulfilment, realization. L19.

a H. JAMES The apples in the . . orchards . . gave a suggestion of sour fruition here and there. **b** E. R. PIKE Trade unions . . were fed . . and brought to fruition by . . toilers in the British industrial scene. C. HILL Cromwell's design . . came to fruition only in 1657.

fruitist /ˈfruːtɪst/ *noun*. E19.
[ORIGIN from FRUIT *noun* + -IST.]
A person who cultivates fruit.

fruitive /ˈfruːɪtɪv/ *adjective*. M17.
[ORIGIN medieval Latin *fruitivus*, from Latin *frui*: see FRUIT *noun*, -IVE.]
Consisting of or based on enjoyment; having the faculty of enjoyment.

fruitless /ˈfruːtlɪs/ *adjective & adverb*. LME.
[ORIGIN from FRUIT *noun* + -LESS.]
▸ **A** *adjective*. **1** Producing no fruit; barren, sterile. Formerly, producing no offspring. LME.
2 Producing no results; vain, unsuccessful, futile, unprofitable. LME.

C. BAX I have no money, and so it is fruitless to talk about a fine. I. MURDOCH What a lot of his . . strength he had wasted on fruitless controversies.

▸ **B** *adverb*. Fruitlessly, without avail. *poet.* M18.

T. GRAY I fruitless mourn to him that cannot hear.

■ **fruitlessly** *adverb* L16. **fruitlessness** *noun* E17.

fruitlet /ˈfruːtlɪt/ *noun*. L19.
[ORIGIN from FRUIT *noun* + -LET.]
A small fruit; (BOTANY) a single member of an aggregate fruit.

fruity /ˈfruːti/ *adjective*. M17.
[ORIGIN from FRUIT *noun* + -Y[1].]
1 Of, relating to, or resembling fruit. M17.
2 Of wine: tasting of the fresh grape. M19.
3 *fig.* Full of rich quality; *esp.*: (of language) unduly strong; (of a story etc.) full of (usu. scandalous) interest or suggestion; (of the voice) mellow and deep, plummy. *colloq.* E20.
■ **fruitily** *adverb* E20. **fruitiness** *noun* M19.

frum /fruːm/ *adjective*. Also **froom**. L19.
[ORIGIN Yiddish from Middle High German *vrum* zealous (German *fromm* pious).]
Esp. of a Jew: pious, religious, orthodox.

frumentaceous /fruːm(ə)nˈteɪʃəs/ *adjective*. *rare*. M17.
[ORIGIN from late Latin *frumentaceus*, from Latin *frumentum*: see FRUMENTARIOUS, -ACEOUS.]
Of the nature of or resembling wheat or other cereal plants.

frumentarious /fruːm(ə)nˈtɛːrɪəs/ *adjective*. *rare*. L17.
[ORIGIN from Latin *frumentarius*, from Latin *frumentum* corn: see -ARIOUS.]
Of or pertaining to corn.

frumentation /fruːm(ə)nˈteɪʃ(ə)n/ *noun*. E17.
[ORIGIN Latin *frumentatio(n-)*, from *frumentat-* pa. ppl stem of *frumentari* provide with corn, from *frumentum*: see FRUMENTY, -ATION.]
ROMAN HISTORY. A general charitable distribution of corn.

frumenty /ˈfruːm(ə)nti/ *noun*. Also **furmety** /ˈfəːmɪti/. LME.
[ORIGIN Old French *frumentee*, *four-*, from *frument*, *fourment* (mod. *froment* wheat) from Latin *frumentum* corn: see -Y[5].]
A dish made of hulled wheat boiled in milk and seasoned with cinnamon, sugar, etc.

frumious /ˈfruːmɪəs/ *adjective*. *joc. colloq.* L19.
[ORIGIN Nonsense word invented by Lewis Carroll.]
Angrily ferocious. Cf. BANDERSNATCH.

†**frummagemed** *pa. pple & ppl adjective*. *slang*. L17–M19.
[ORIGIN Unknown.]
Choked, strangled, hanged.

frump /frʌmp/ *noun*. M16.
[ORIGIN Prob. shortening of FRUMPLE.]
1 A mocking speech or action; a snort, a sneer. *obsolete* exc. *dial.* M16.
2 A derisive deception, a hoax. *obsolete* exc. *dial.* L16.
3 In *pl.* Sulks, ill humour. *obsolete* exc. *dial.* M17.
4 An old-fashioned, dowdily dressed, (originally) bad-tempered woman or (rarely) man. E19.

M. FORSTER She looked like a middle-aged frump, even when she was young.

frump /frʌmp/ *verb*. M16.
[ORIGIN formed as FRUMP *noun*.]
†**1** *verb intrans.* Scoff, mock (*at*). M16–M19.
2 *verb trans.* Mock, taunt, insult, snub. *obsolete* exc. *dial.* L16.
3 *verb trans.* Annoy, irritate. M19.
■ **frumper** *noun* L16.

frumpish /ˈfrʌmpɪʃ/ *adjective*. M17.
[ORIGIN from FRUMP *noun* + -ISH[1].]
1 Disposed to sneer, mocking; bad-tempered, cross. Now *rare*. M17.
2 Like a frump; characteristic of a frump; dowdy and old-fashioned. M19.
■ **frumpishly** *adverb* E20. **frumpishness** *noun* L19.

frumple /ˈfrʌmp(ə)l/ *verb & noun*. LME.
[ORIGIN from Middle Dutch *verrompelen*, from *ver-* FOR-[1] + *rompelen* RUMPLE *verb*.]
▸ **A** *verb trans.* Wrinkle, crumple. Long *obsolete* exc. *dial.* LME.
▸ †**B** *noun*. A wrinkle. LME–L15.

frumpy /ˈfrʌmpi/ *adjective*. M18.
[ORIGIN from FRUMP *noun* + -Y[1].]
1 Bad-tempered, irritable. Now *rare*. M18.
2 Dowdy and old-fashioned. M19.
■ **frumpily** *adverb* M20. **frumpiness** *noun* E20.

frusemide /ˈfruːsəmʌɪd/ *noun*. Also (chiefly *US*) **furosemide** /fjʊəˈrɒsəmʌɪd/. M20.
[ORIGIN from *fru-* alt. of FUR(YL + *sem-* of unknown origin + -IDE.]
PHARMACOLOGY. A strong diuretic, $C_{12}H_{11}ClN_2O_5S$, used esp. in the treatment of oedema.

frush /frʌʃ/ *noun*[1]. Now only *Scot. rare*. LME.
[ORIGIN Old French *fruis*, *frois*, from *fruissier*, *froissier*: see FRUSH *verb*.]
†**1** A charge, a collision. LME–M16.
2 The noise of a crash, crashing. LME.
3 *collect.* Fragments, splinters. LME.
■ **frushy** *adjective* brittle, fragile E17.

frush /frʌʃ/ *noun*[2]. *obsolete* exc. *dial.* M16.
[ORIGIN Perh. from French *fourchette* (see FROG *noun*[2]), but cf. Norwegian, West Frisian *frosk* in same sense.]
The frog of a horse's foot. Also (***running frush***), the disease thrush which affects this.

frush /frʌʃ/ *adjective*. *Scot. & N. English*. E18.
[ORIGIN Perh. from the verb, but cf. FROUGH.]
1 Not firm in substance; soft; crumbly. E18.
2 Brittle, fragile. L18.

frush /frʌʃ/ *verb*. ME.
[ORIGIN Old French *fruissier*, *froissier* (mod. *froisser*) from popular Latin, from Latin FRUSTUM.]
1 *verb trans.* Strike violently so as to injure or damage. *obsolete* exc. *dial.* ME.
2 *verb intrans.* Rush violently (*in*, *out*, *together*). *obsolete* exc. *dial.* LME.
3 *verb trans.* Rub vigorously, scratch. *obsolete* exc. *dial.* LME.
†**4** *verb trans.* Carve (a chicken); dress (a chub). LME–L18.
†**5** *verb intrans.* Break, snap; become crushed. L15–M17.
6 *verb trans.* Straighten, set upright (the feathers of an arrow). *obsolete* exc. *hist.* M16.

†**frust** *noun*. M18–E19.
[ORIGIN Latin FRUSTUM.]
A fragment.

frusta *noun pl.* see FRUSTUM.

frustrable /ˈfrʌstrəb(ə)l/ *adjective. rare.* L16.
[ORIGIN Late Latin *frustrabilis*, from Latin *frustrari*: see FRUSTRATE *verb*, -ABLE.]
Able to be frustrated or foiled.

†**frustraneous** *adjective*. M17–L18.
[ORIGIN from mod. Latin *frustraneus* (from *frustra* in vain, after Latin *extraneus*) + -OUS.]
Vain, ineffectual, unprofitable.

frustrate /ˈfrʌstreɪt/ *ppl adjective & noun*. L15.
[ORIGIN Latin *frustratus* pa. pple of *frustrari*: see FRUSTRATE *verb*, -ATE[2].]
▸ **A** *ppl adjective. arch.*
1 †**a** LAW. Null, invalid. L15–M17. ▸**b** *gen.* Ineffectual, fruitless, unavailing. E16.
†**2** Idle, pointless. E–M16.
3 †**a** Baulked (*of*). M16–E18. ▸**b** Deprived or destitute *of*. L16.
4 Of a hope, purpose, etc.: disappointed, defeated, futile. L16.
▸ **B** *noun*. A frustrated, disappointed, or ineffective person. M20.

frustrate /frʌˈstreɪt, ˈfrʌ-/ *verb trans.* Pa. pple **frustrated**, †**frustrate**. LME.
[ORIGIN Latin *frustrat-* pa. ppl stem of *frustrari*, from *frustra* in vain: see -ATE[3].]
1 Baulk, disappoint (a person). Now also, make discontented through inability to achieve one's desires (material, spiritual, or sexual) (esp. as ***frustrated*** *pa. pple & ppl adjective*). Now *occas.* foll. by *of* (a desired object). LME.

W. DAMPIER Being frustrated of getting over the River. D. ATHILL On the threshold of anything promising he is always frustrated by disaster apparently beyond his control. R. F. HOBSON Feeling frustrated by this apparently insoluble problem.

2 Make ineffectual; counteract; disappoint (a hope, an expectation); foil (a plan). LME. ▸**b** LAW. Annul, invalidate. Now *esp.*, cause (a contract) to be terminated prematurely (see FRUSTRATION). E16.

L. STRACHEY The French intrigue must be frustrated at all hazards. W. S. CHURCHILL His hopes of invading England . . with French assistance were frustrated. E. MUIR These things we know and . . Either frustrate or . . endure. H. CARPENTER Her hopes of frustrating Meg's romance.

■ **frustratedly** *adverb* in a frustrated manner, through frustration L20. **frustrater** *noun* L17. **frustratingly** *adverb* in a frustrating manner, so as to cause frustration M20. ˈ**frustrative** *adjective* tending to frustrate L15. †**frustratory** *adjective* tending to frustrate L15–E18.

frustration /frʌˈstreɪʃ(ə)n/ *noun*. M16.
[ORIGIN Latin *frustratio(n-)*, formed as FRUSTRATE *verb*: see -ATION.]
The action or an instance of frustrating; the state of being frustrated; discontent arising from inability to achieve one's aims; *spec.* in LAW, the premature termination of a contract by supervening circumstances that make performance as envisaged by the terms of the contract impossible or illegal.

G. GROTE Aristeides ascribes the frustration of this attack to the valour of two . . generals. R. LINDNER The total frustration of his deepest affectional needs produced an emotionally starved individual. L. VAN DER POST When once more . . we found our way blocked . . , the sense of frustration was more than some of us could bear. S. HILL Almost in tears at the frustration of finding nothing he desired to buy.

frustrum *noun* var. of FRUSTUM.

†**frustula** *noun* pl. of FRUSTULUM.

frustule /ˈfrʌstjuːl/ *noun*. M19.
[ORIGIN Latin *frustulum* dim. of FRUSTUM: see -ULE.]
BOTANY. The silicified cell wall of a diatom (with or without its contents), which consists of two valves or overlapping halves.

†**frustulum** *noun*. Pl. **-la**. Only in 18.
[ORIGIN Latin: see FRUSTULE.]
A small frustum.

frustum /ˈfrʌstəm/ *noun*. Pl. **-stums**, **-sta** /-stə/. Also **frustrum** /ˈfrʌstrəm/. M17.
[ORIGIN Latin = piece cut off.]
1 MATH. The portion of a solid figure which remains after the upper part has been cut off by a plane parallel to the base, or which is intercepted between two planes. M17.
2 *gen.* A fragment or portion. *rare.* E18.

frutescent /fruːˈtɛs(ə)nt/ *adjective*. E18.
[ORIGIN Irreg. formed as FRUTEX + -ESCENT. Cf. medieval Latin *frutescere* become shrubby.]
BOTANY. Becoming shrubby; having the appearance or habit of a shrub.
■ **frutescence** *noun* shrubbiness L19.

frutex /ˈfruːtɛks/ *noun*. Pl. **frutices** /ˈfruːtɪsiːz/. M17.
[ORIGIN Latin.]
BOTANY. A woody plant smaller than a tree; a shrub.

fruticetum /fruːtɪˈsiːtəm/ *noun*. M19.
[ORIGIN Latin = a place full of shrubs or bushes, formed as FRUTEX.]
A collection of shrubs. Cf. ARBORETUM.

fruticose /ˈfruːtɪkəʊs/ *adjective*. M17.
[ORIGIN Latin *fruticosus*, from *frutic-* FRUTEX: see -OSE[1].]
1 BOTANY. Of the nature of a shrub; woody-stemmed. M17.
2 Resembling a shrub in appearance or manner of growth; *spec.* (of a lichen) having upright or pendulous branching thalli. E19.

fruz /frʌz/ *verb trans. obsolete* exc. *dial.* Infl. **-zz-**. E18.
[ORIGIN Symbolic.]
Spread out (hair) in a frizzy mass; ruffle.

fry /frʌɪ/ *noun*[1]. ME.
[ORIGIN Old Norse *frjó* = Gothic *fraiw*, of unknown origin.]
1 *collect.* Young fish just produced from the spawn; *spec.* (more fully ***salmon fry***) the young of salmon in their first year. ME. ▸**b** The young of other creatures produced in very large numbers. L16.

Coarse Fishing Nearly all fry perish before growing beyond about . . 5 in.

2 Offspring, seed, young (of human beings); a man's children or family. (Cf. sense 4 below.) *obsolete* exc. *dial.* LME.
3 The roe of a fish. LME.
4 Chiefly as ***small fry***. The smaller kinds of fish or other animals; young or insignificant people (collectively or in a body); small or insignificant objects. L16.

N. COX We bring out not onely Pike and Carp, but lesser Fry. HOR. WALPOLE We have burned two frigates, and a hundred and twenty small fry. M. HUNTER My sister was still the oldest child there—which made the rest of us pretty small fry.

fry /frʌɪ/ *noun*[2]. M17.
[ORIGIN from the verb.]
1 (A dish of) food cooked by frying. M17. ▸**b** Any of various internal parts of animals usu. eaten fried, esp. ***lamb's fry*** (see LAMB *noun*). L18. ▸**c** More fully ***French fry***. A (fried) potato chip. Usu. in *pl.* Chiefly *N. Amer.* E20.
2 †**a** Excessive heat. Only in M17. ▸**b** The frying of a meal, a fry-up; *esp.* (*US*) a social gathering at which fried food is eaten. E19.

fry /frʌɪ/ *verb*. Pa. t. & pple **fried** /frʌɪd/. ME.
[ORIGIN Old French & mod. French *frire* from Latin *frigere*, cogn. with Greek *phrugein*, Sanskrit *bhrjjati* grill.]
1 *verb trans. & intrans.* Cook or undergo cooking in hot fat, usu. in a shallow pan. ME.

V. S. PRITCHETT He . . cracked eggs, got breadcrumbs and soon fried one of his wonderful fish suppers.

deep-fried, *deep-frying*: see DEEP *adverb*. †**fry in one's own grease** be burnt alive; be tormented by one's own passions; suffer the consequences of one's own folly. **fry up** heat or reheat in a frying pan. ***have other fish to fry***: see FISH *noun*[1].

2 *verb trans. & intrans. transf. & fig.* Burn, overheat, or destroy, esp. with effects analogous to those of frying food; frizzle, scorch (freq. *hyperbol.*, of the sun). Also, torture or be tortured by fire. LME. ▸**b** Execute or be executed in the electric chair. *US slang.* E20.

JONSON Earth and seas in fire and flame shall fry. SMOLLETT My uncle, frying with vexation.

†**3** *verb intrans.* Boil, seethe, ferment, simmer. L16–L17.

SPENSER Ye might have seene the frothy billowes fry Vnder the ship.

– COMB.: **fry bread** *N. Amer.* a traditional N. American Indian bread cooked by deep-frying; **frying pan** a shallow pan in which food is fried (***out of the frying pan into the fire***: see PAN *noun*[1]); **fry pan** = ***frying pan*** above; **fry-up** a dish of fried food, *esp.* of cold food heated up in a frying pan.

fryer /ˈfrʌɪə/ *noun*. Also **frier**. M19.
[ORIGIN from FRY *verb* + -ER[1].]
1 A person who fries food, esp. fish; a vessel used in frying. M19.
2 A fish, chicken, etc., for frying. M19.

FS *abbreviation*.
Flight Sergeant.

FSA *abbreviation*.
1 Fellow of the Society of Antiquaries.
2 Financial Services Act (or Authority).

FSAVC *abbreviation*.
Free-standing additional voluntary contribution (to a pension scheme).

FSH *abbreviation*.
1 BIOCHEMISTRY. Follicle-stimulating hormone.
2 Full service history (of a motor vehicle).

FSSU *abbreviation*.
Federated Superannuation Scheme for Universities.

FST *abbreviation*.
Flat-screen television.

FT *abbreviation*[1].
Financial Times.
FT index any of a number of stock indices published daily by the *Financial Times*.

Ft *abbreviation*[2].
Fort.

ft *abbreviation*[3].
1 Feet.
2 Foot.

FTAA *abbreviation*.
Free Trade Area of the Americas.

FTC *abbreviation*. *US*.
Federal Trade Commission.

FTP *abbreviation & verb*.
COMPUTING. ▸**A** *abbreviation*. File transfer protocol, a standard for the exchange of program and data files across a network.
▸ **B** *verb trans.* Pa. t. & pple **FTP'd**, **FTPed**. Transfer (a file) from one computer or system to another, esp. on the Internet.

FT-SE *abbreviation*.
(STOCK EXCHANGE) *Financial Times*-Stock Exchange index (of 100, 250, or 350 shares on the London Stock Exchange); cf. FOOTSIE *noun*[2].

†**fuants** *noun pl.* var. of FIANTS.

F

fub /fʌb/ *noun. obsolete* exc. *dial.* Also **fubb**, **fubs** /-z/. E17.
[ORIGIN Perh. blend of *fat* and *chub*: cf. FUBSY.]
1 A small chubby person. E17.
2 Refuse wool. Also, long withered grass. E19.
■ **fubby** *adjective* (*rare*) = FUBSY L18.

fubar /ˈfuːbɑː/ *adjective*. *US slang* (orig. MILITARY). M20.
[ORIGIN Acronym, from *fouled* (or *fucked*) *up beyond all recognition*.]
Ruined, spoiled, disastrously bungled.

fubsy /ˈfʌbzi/ *adjective*. *colloq.* L18.
[ORIGIN from FUB: see -SY.]
Fat and squat. Also *fig.*, stuffy, old-fashioned.

Times Lit. Suppl. A fubsy disinclination to contemplate any kind of change.

fucate /ˈfjuːkeɪt/ *adjective*. Long *rare*. M16.
[ORIGIN Latin *fucatus* pa. pple of *fucare* to colour, paint, dye, from FUCUS: see -ATE[2].]
Artificially coloured or painted; *fig.* falsified, disguised.
■ **fuˈcated** *adjective* = FUCATE M16. †**fucation** *noun* (*rare*) (**a**) the action of painting the face; (**b**) counterfeiting: E17–E18.

fuchsia /ˈfjuːʃə/ *noun*. L18.
[ORIGIN mod. Latin, from Leonhard *Fuchs* (1501–66), German botanist: see -IA[1].]
1 Any of various ornamental shrubs of the chiefly S. American genus *Fuchsia*, of the willowherb family, having drooping flowers freq. with purple-red sepals and perigynous tube. L18.
native fuchsia *Austral.* any of various shrubs, esp. of the genus *Correa* (of the rue family), with flowers resembling the fuchsia; *NZ* any of various endemic species of fuchsia, e.g. the konini.
2 A shade of red like that of the fuchsia flower. E20.

fuchsine /ˈfuːksiːn/ *noun*. Also **-in** /-ɪn/. M19.
[ORIGIN from German *Fuchs* fox translating French *Renard*, name of the chemical company by which this product was first produced commercially + -INE[5].]
An aniline dye, a hydrochloride of rosaniline or pararosaniline, which forms green crystals but dissolves in water to form a deep-red solution and is used esp. as a biological stain; = MAGENTA *noun*.

fuchsinophil /fʊkˈsɪnəfɪl/ *adjective*. Also **-phile** /-fʌɪl/. E20.
[ORIGIN from FUCHSINE + -O- + -PHIL.]
BIOLOGY. Readily stained with fuchsine; produced by staining with fuchsine.
■ **fuchsinoˈphilia** *noun* affinity for fuchsine M20. **fuchsinoˈphilic** *adjective* = FUCHSINOPHIL M20.

fuchsite /ˈfʊksʌɪt/ *noun*. M19.
[ORIGIN from J. N. von *Fuchs* (1774–1856), German mineralogist + -ITE[1].]
MINERALOGY. A green chromium-containing variety of muscovite.

fuci *noun* pl. of FUCUS.

fuck /fʌk/ *noun*. *coarse slang*. L17.
[ORIGIN from the verb.]
1 An act of copulation. L17.

E. J. HOWARD Eat well, don't smoke, and a fuck was equal to a five-mile walk.

2 A person, esp. a woman, considered in sexual terms or as a sexual partner. Also = FUCKER (b). L19.

D. MAMET Don't get smart with me, you young fuck.

3 The slightest amount (esp. in ***not care a fuck***, ***not give a fuck***). Also in other phrs. as a meaningless intensifier. E20.

D. HOLBROOK Driver speed up. Come on, for fuck's sake. J. KELMAN What the fuck's going on!

fuck /fʌk/ *verb*. *coarse slang*. E16.
[ORIGIN Unknown.]
1 *verb intrans.* Copulate. E16.

S. CONRAN Serge . . moved . . into the next-door room where he lived, ate and fucked.

2 *verb trans.* Copulate with. L17. ▸**b** Ruin, spoil; exhaust, wear out. M20.

b A. BEATTIE 'Everything's fucked . . . What does it matter the way things *should* be?'

3 *verb trans. & intrans.* In imprecations and exclamations, freq. in imperative or optative form, expr. anger, hatred, irritation, etc.; damn, curse. Cf. DAMN *verb* 3, 3b. **E20.**

J. DIDION 'Oh fuck it,' she says then, and tears run down her cheeks. A. FUGARD Fuck legends. Me? . . I live my life here!

– PHRASES, & WITH ADVERBS IN SPECIALIZED SENSES: **fuck about**, **fuck around** fool about, mess about. **fuck off** go away, make off. (usu. in *imper.*). **fuck up** (*a*) ruin, spoil, mess up; disturb emotionally; (*b*) blunder, fail, make a serious error.

– COMB.: **fuck-me** *adjective* (of clothing, esp. shoes) inviting or perceived as inviting sexual interest; **fuck-up** a mess, a disastrously bungled matter; **fuckwit** a stupid or contemptible person.

– NOTE: For centuries one of the most taboo words in English. It was not included in the original *Oxford English Dictionary*, and until relatively recently rarely appeared in print; even today, there are a number of euphemistic ways of referring to it, e.g. *the F-word*, *f****, or *f—*.

■ **fucker** *noun* (*a*) a person who copulates; (*b*) used as a general term of abuse: **L16. fucking** *adjective & adverb* (*a*) *adjective* (*lit.*) that copulates; (*b*) *adjective & adverb* (*fig.*) used as an intensifier: **M16.**

fucoid /ˈfjuːkɔɪd/ *adjective & noun.* **M19.**
[ORIGIN from FUCUS + -OID.]

▸ **A** *adjective.* Of the nature of or resembling a seaweed, *spec.* any of the brown seaweeds of the order Fucales, exemplified by bladderwrack (genus *Fucus*); of or relating to such seaweeds. **M19.**

▸ **B** *noun.* A seaweed of the order Fucales; a similar fossil marine plant. **M19.**

■ **fuˈcoidal** *adjective* **M19.**

fucoxanthin /fjuːkəˈzanθɪn/ *noun.* **L19.**
[ORIGIN from FUCUS + -O- + XANTHIN.]
CHEMISTRY. A brown carotenoid pigment occurring in and generally characteristic of the brown algae.

fucus /ˈfjuːkəs/ *noun.* Pl. **fuci** /ˈfjuːsʌɪ/. **E17.**
[ORIGIN Latin *fucus* rock-lichen, red dye or cosmetic from Greek *phukos* seaweed.]

†**1** Paint or make-up for beautifying the skin; a wash or colouring for the face. **E17–M18.**

2 A seaweed with leathery fronds: now *spec.* a member of the genus *Fucus*, e.g. bladderwrack, *F. vesiculosus*. **E18.**

■ **fucused** *adjective* (long *rare*) beautified with paint, made-up **L17.**

fud /fʌd/ *noun*[1]. *Scot. & N. English.* **E18.**
[ORIGIN Unknown.]

1 The buttocks. **E18.**

2 The tail or scut of a rabbit, hare, or other animal. **E18.**

fud /fʌd/ *noun*[2]. *slang* (chiefly *US*). **M20.**
[ORIGIN Abbreviation.]
= FUDDY-DUDDY *noun.*

fuddle /ˈfʌd(ə)l/ *noun. slang.* **L17.**
[ORIGIN from the verb.]

†**1** Drink, liquor, booze. **L17–E18.**

2 Intoxication, drunkenness. **M18.**

3 Confusion, muddled state. **E19.**

T. E. WEBB He rushed about—Vain was his frenzied fuddle.

4 A drinking bout. **E19.**

on the fuddle out on a prolonged spell of drinking.

fuddle /ˈfʌd(ə)l/ *verb.* **L16.**
[ORIGIN Unknown.]

1 *verb intrans.* Have a drinking bout; tipple, booze. **L16.**

2 *verb trans.* Intoxicate; confuse with drink or a drug. **E17.**

E. WAUGH I went to luncheon . . . and drank enough wine to fuddle me slightly. P. LIVELY She had lain fuddled still from the sleeping pills.

fuddle one's cap, **fuddle one's nose** get drunk.

3 *verb trans.* Stupefy, muddle, confuse. **E17.**

S. COWPER He was quite fuddled with joy.

■ **fuddler** *noun* (now *rare*) a person who fuddles, a tippler **L17.**

fuddy-duddy /ˈfʌdɪdʌdi/ *noun & adjective. slang.* Also **fuddydud**. **E20.**
[ORIGIN Unknown.]

▸ **A** *noun.* An old-fashioned person; an ineffectual old fogey. **E20.**

Woman's Realm I work with fashionable young women, . . so I don't want to appear an old fuddy-duddy.

▸ **B** *adjective.* Old-fashioned, ineffectual, stuffy. **E20.**

Q. CRISP We must chart a course between the fuddy-duddy strictures of yesterday and the hapless chaos of today.

fudge /fʌdʒ/ *noun.* **L18.**
[ORIGIN from the verb or interjection.]

1 Nonsense. *arch.* **L18.**

2 A made-up story, a deception. Now *esp.* an instance of presenting information in a vague or inadequate way, or so as to mislead; evasive or imprecise language or reasoning. **L18.**

Listener A new way of settling disputes . . with the arbitrator resisting the usual fudge.

3 An item inserted in a newspaper page, *esp.* a piece of late news. **L19.**

4 A soft crumbly or chewy kind of confectionery made from sugar, butter, and milk or cream; (chiefly *N. Amer.*) rich chocolate used as a sauce or a filling for cakes. **L19.**

attrib.: V. NABOKOV Gooey fudge sundaes, musicals, movie magazines . . were . . on her list of beloved things.

fudge /fʌdʒ/ *verb.* **E17.**
[ORIGIN Perh. alt. of earlier FADGE *verb.*]

1 *verb intrans.* Fit in with what is anticipated; turn out, result. Also, merge together. **E17.**

SIR W. SCOTT We will see how the matter fudges. P. D. JAMES She saw the drab blacks and grays of the marching army fudge, dissolve.

2 *verb trans.* Present or deal with in a vague or inadequate way, esp. so as to conceal the truth or mislead; deal with incompetently. **L17.** ▸**b** *verb trans.* Thrust or force *in* awkwardly or irrelevantly; put or get *in* underhandedly. **L18.** ▸**c** *verb intrans.* Gloss over discrepancies or difficulties; prevaricate, temporize. **L20.**

H. WILSON Without fudging an issue on which a clear decision has to be reached. L. KENNEDY He had been caught fudging the books. **b** T. HEALD The public schools can fudge their pupils into Oxford and Cambridge. **c** S. FALUDI The data supporting the infertility epidemic were nonexistent, so the magazines had to fudge.

3 *verb intrans.* Talk nonsense. *rare.* **M19.**

■ **fudgy** *adjective* (*a*) irritable, uneasy; (*b*) *US* botched, bungling: **E19.**

fudge /fʌdʒ/ *interjection.* **M18.**
[ORIGIN from the verb.]
Nonsense! Rubbish!

Fuegian /fʊˈɪdʒɪən, ˈfweɪdʒɪən, -g-/ *adjective & noun.* **E19.**
[ORIGIN from (Spanish) Tierra del *Fuego* (see below), lit. 'land of fire' + -IAN.]

▸ **A** *adjective.* Of or pertaining to Tierra del Fuego, (the largest island in) an archipelago at the southernmost tip of S. America, or its inhabitants. **E19.**

▸ **B** *noun.* A member of a S. American Indian people inhabiting Tierra del Fuego. **E19.**

fuehrer *noun* var. of FÜHRER.

fuel /fjʊəl, ˈfjuːəl/ *noun.* **ME.**
[ORIGIN Anglo-Norman *fuaille*, *fewaile*, Old French *fouaille* from Proto-Romance, from Latin *focus* hearth, (in late Latin) fire.]

1 Material for burning; combustible matter as used for fire, or as a source of heat or power. **ME.** ▸**b** A kind of fuel, as wood, coal, oil, etc. **E17.**

SWIFT Dry grass and sea-weed, which I intended for feuel.

b *white fuel*: see WHITE *adjective.*

2 *fig.* Anything that sustains or inflames passion, excitement, etc. **L16.**

A. BAIN Difficulty adds fuel to the flame.

3 Food, or the constituents of food, as a source of energy. **L19.**

L. J. BOGERT Calorie values are especially useful in thinking . . of food as body fuel.

4 *spec.* ▸**a** A liquid or other material which provides the power in an internal-combustion engine. **L19.** ▸**b** A material which reacts with an oxidizer to produce thrust in a rocket engine. **E20.** ▸**c** A material which reacts with an oxidizer to produce electricity in a fuel cell. **E20.** ▸**d** A radioactive material used as a source of nuclear energy. **M20.**

– COMB.: **fuel cell** a primary cell producing electric current direct from a chemical reaction between continuously supplied materials; **fuel element** an assemblage of nuclear fuel and other materials for use in a reactor; *esp.* = *fuel rod* below; **fuel food**: that is rich in fats or carbohydrates and provides the body with energy; **fuel gauge** a meter indicating the quantity of fuel in a tank; *fuel-injected*; *fuel injection*; *fuel injector*; *fuel rod*: see ROD *noun* 8b; **fuel-value** (*a*) the value of a combustible article as fuel; (*b*) the amount of energy available from (a quantity of) food.

■ **fuelless** /-l-l-/ *adjective* **L19.**

fuel /fjʊəl, ˈfjuːəl/ *verb.* Infl. **-ll-**, *-**l-**. **L16.**
[ORIGIN from the noun.]

1 *verb trans.* Provide or supply with fuel. **L16.**

City Limits Fuelled by a rather transparent cynicism, the story speeds on to a finale. P. D. JAMES The craft would be fuelled and ready for sea.

2 *verb intrans.* Get or take in fuel. **L19.**

Successful Slimming They have fuelled up with a couple of Mars Bars.

■ **fueller** *noun* (*a*) a person or thing which supplies fuel; †(*b*) a domestic responsible for making the fires: **LME.**

fuff /fʌf/ *verb, noun, & interjection.* Chiefly *Scot. & dial.* **E16.**
[ORIGIN Imit. Cf. FAFFLE *verb.*]

▸ **A** *verb.* **1** *verb intrans.* Puff. **E16.**

2 *verb intrans.* Of an animal, esp. a cat: spit. **L17.**

3 *verb trans.* Puff (a tobacco pipe). **L18.**

▸ **B** *noun.* **1** A puff of wind; the spit of a cat; a whiff. **M16.**

2 A burst of ill temper. **E19.**

▸ **C** *interjection.* An exclamation in imitation of a sound, or expr. contempt. **L18.**

fuffle /ˈfʌf(ə)l/ *verb trans. Scot. rare.* **M16.**
[ORIGIN Imit.]
Throw into disorder; jerk about; hustle.

fufu /ˈfuːfuː/ *noun.* Also **foo-foo**. **M18.**
[ORIGIN Twi *fufuu.*]
Dough made from boiled plantain.

fug /fʌg/ *noun & verb. colloq.* Orig. *school slang.* **L19.**
[ORIGIN Unknown.]

▸ **A** *noun.* A thick, stuffy, smelly atmosphere, *esp.* that of a crowded poorly ventilated room. **L19.**

K. HULME In this fug of smoke and turpentine, who could sleep? *New Yorker* The warm, beery fug of the restaurant.

▸ **B** *verb intrans.* Infl. **-gg-**. Stay in a stuffy atmosphere. Also foll. by *up.* **L19.**

■ **fugged** *ppl adjective* (of a room or atmosphere) stuffy, thick **L20. fuggy** *adjective* (of a room or atmosphere) warm, stuffy, and smelly, through lack of ventilation; (of a person) that lives in or enjoys such an atmosphere: **L19.**

fugacious /fjʊˈgeɪʃəs/ *adjective.* **M17.**
[ORIGIN from Latin *fugax*, *fugac-*, from *fugere* flee: see -ACIOUS.]

1 Apt to flee away or flit; fleeting, transient, evanescent. **M17.** ▸**b** Of a substance: volatile. **L17.**

H. MARTINEAU The fugacious nature of life and time.

2 BOTANY & ZOOLOGY. Falling or fading early; soon cast off. **M18.**

G. WHITE A single rose-like fugacious flower.

■ **fugaciously** *adverb* **E19. fugaciousness** *noun* **M17.**

fugacity /fjʊˈgasɪti/ *noun.* **E17.**
[ORIGIN formed as FUGACIOUS + -ITY.]

1 The quality of being fugacious; instability; transitoriness; volatility. **E17.**

2 PHYSICS. A thermodynamic property of a (real) gas which if substituted for the pressure or partial pressure in the equations for an ideal gas gives equations applicable to the real gas; an analogous property of a solid or liquid derived using equations of the same form. **E20.**

fugal /ˈfjuːg(ə)l/ *adjective.* **M19.**
[ORIGIN from FUGUE + -AL[1].]

1 MUSIC. Of the nature of or characteristic of a fugue or fugues. **M19.**

A. HOPKINS A skilful alternation of fugal sections with more openly dramatic chordal writing.

2 PSYCHIATRY. Of the nature of a fugue; marked by fugues. **M20.**

O. SACKS An element of hysterical or fugal amnesia.

■ **fugally** *adverb* **L19.**

fugato /fjuːˈgɑːtəʊ, fuː-/ *adverb, adjective, & noun.* **M19.**
[ORIGIN Italian = fugued, from *fuga* FUGUE.]
MUSIC. ▸**A** *adverb & adjective.* In the fugue style, but not in strict or complete fugue form. **M19.**

▸ **B** *noun.* Pl. **-os**. A passage in this style. **L19.**

-fuge /fjuːdʒ/ *suffix.*
[ORIGIN from or after mod. Latin *-fugus*, from Latin *fugare* put to flight.]
Forming nouns and adjectives with the sense '(an agent) that dispels or expels', as ***febrifuge***, ***vermifuge***.

fuggle /ˈfʌg(ə)l/ *noun.* Also **fuggles** /-z/. **L19.**
[ORIGIN Unknown.]
A variety of hops used in in making beer.

fughetta /fjuːˈgɛtə/ *noun.* **L19.**
[ORIGIN Italian, dim. of *fuga* FUGUE.]
MUSIC. A short condensed fugue.

fugie /ˈf(j)uːdʒi/ *noun. Scot. obsolete* exc. *hist.* **L18.**
[ORIGIN Perh. from Latin *fugae* in the law Latin phr. *in meditatione fugae* contemplating flight.]
A cock that refuses to fight; a runaway; a coward.

– COMB.: **fugie-warrant**: granted against a debtor, on sworn information that he or she intends to flee.

fugitate /ˈfjuːdʒɪteɪt/ *verb.* **M17.**
[ORIGIN Sense 1 from FUGITIVE; sense 2 from Latin *fugitat-* stem of *fugitare*, from *fugere* flee: see -ATE[3].]

1 *verb trans.* SCOTS LAW. Declare fugitive, outlaw. **M17.**

2 *verb intrans.* Run away. *rare.* **M19.**

■ **fugiˈtation** *noun* (*a*) SCOTS LAW a judicial declaration of outlawry and its associated penalties; (*b*) the action of fleeing: **M18.**

fugitive /ˈfjuːdʒɪtɪv/ *adjective & noun.* **LME.**
[ORIGIN Old French & mod. French *fugitif*, *-ive* from Latin *fugitivus*, from *fugit-* pa. ppl stem of *fugere* flee: see -IVE.]

▸ **A** *adjective.* **1** That has taken flight, esp. from duty, justice, an enemy, or a master. **LME.** ▸**b** Apt or tending to flee; running away. **E17.**

E. KIRKE A Union officer refused to return a fugitive slave. W. DE LA MARE Betrayed and fugitive, I still must roam.

†**2** Driven out, banished, exiled. **LME–L16.**

3 Moving from place to place; flitting, vagrant. Also *fig.*, fickle. **LME.**

4 Evanescent, fleeting, of short duration; (of an impression, colour, etc.) quickly fading. **LME.** ▸**b** Of a substance: volatile. *rare.* **M17.** ▸**c** = FUGACIOUS 2. *rare.* **M19.**

L. DURRELL Their appearances were fugitive and had the air of being illusory.

5 Of literature: of passing interest, ephemeral, occasional. M18.

J. I. M. STEWART A pile of.. fugitive magazines concerned with theatrical affairs.

▸ **B** *noun*. **1** A person who flees or tries to escape from danger, an enemy, justice, a master, etc. LME. ▸†**b** A deserter. M16–M17. ▸**c** An exile, an outlaw. L16.

N. MONSARRAT These people were craven fugitives from war. **c** W. IRVING Fugitives from the Spanish and American frontiers.

2 A person who or animal which shifts about or moves from place to place; a vagrant. L16.

J. CONRAD My other self, now gone from the ship.. to be a fugitive and a vagabond on the earth.

3 Something transient, fleeting, or elusive. L17.

■ **fugitively** *adverb* (*rare*) M19. **fugitiveness** *noun* M17.

fugle /ˈfjuːɡ(ə)l/ *verb*¹ *trans. dial. & slang*. E18.
[ORIGIN Unknown. See also HONEY-FUGGLE.]
Cheat, trick.

fugle /ˈfjuːɡ(ə)l/ *verb*². M19.
[ORIGIN Back-form. from FUGLEMAN.]
1 *verb intrans*. Do the duty of a fugleman (*lit. & fig.*); act as guide or director, signal. M19.
2 *verb trans*. Exemplify, demonstrate. *rare*. M19.

fugleman /ˈfjuːɡ(ə)lmən/ *noun*. Pl. **-men**. E19.
[ORIGIN German *Flügelmann* flank-man, from *Flügel* wing + *Mann* man.]
1 *hist*. A well-drilled soldier placed in front of a regiment or company to demonstrate expert drilling etc. to the others. E19.
2 *transf. & fig*. A leader, organizer, or spokesman. E19.

fugu /ˈfuːɡuː/ *noun*. M20.
[ORIGIN Japanese.]
A puffer fish of the family Tetraodontidae, esp. as a Japanese delicacy.

fugue /fjuːɡ/ *noun & verb*. L16.
[ORIGIN French, or its source, Italian *fuga* from Latin *fuga* flight, rel. to *fugere* flee.]
▸ **A** *noun*. **1** MUSIC. A polyphonic composition in which a short melodic theme, the subject, is introduced by one part or voice, and successively taken up by the others and developed by their interweaving. L16.
double fugue: having two subjects each similarly treated. MIRROR *fugue*.
2 PSYCHIATRY. A flight from or loss of the awareness of one's own identity, sometimes involving wandering away from home, and often occurring as a reaction to shock or emotional stress. E20.

C. P. SNOW He was having fugues.. in which the bad news hadn't happened. *attrib.*: C. PRIEST The fugue state,.. like being in a continuous dream.

▸ **B** *verb intrans*. MUSIC. Pres. pple & verbal noun **fuguing**, **fuging**. Compose or perform a fugue. L17.
■ **fugued**, **fuguing** *ppl adjectives* (MUSIC) in the form of a fugue M19. **fuguist** *noun* (MUSIC) a composer of fugues L18.

führer /ˈfjʊərə/ *noun*. Also **fuehrer**. M20.
[ORIGIN German *Führer* leader. Hitler's full title was *Führer und Reichskanzler*.]
A (ruthless or tyrannical) leader; spec. ***the Führer***, a title assumed by Hitler as leader of the German Reich.
– COMB.: **führer principle** the principle that a führer has the right to command and the people the duty to obey.

Fuji /ˈfuːdʒi/ *noun*. L20.
[ORIGIN Prob. named after Mt. *Fuji* in Japan.]
A Japanese dessert apple of a variety with crisp sweet flesh and an orange flush to the skin.

-ful /fʊl, f(ə)l/ *suffix*.
[ORIGIN from FULL *adjective*.]
1 Forming adjectives. Orig. used in composition with a preceding noun to form adjectives with the sense 'full of or having,' as ***beautiful***, ***graceful***, or, in the 14th cent., with the sense 'having the qualities of' as ***masterful***, ***powerful***. Later, in the 16th and 17th cents., forming adjectives from adjectives or Latin adjective stems with little change of meaning, as ***direful***, ***grateful*** (perh. by analogy with older synonyms in *-ful*). In mod. English forming adjectives from verb stems with the sense 'apt to, able to, accustomed to,' as ***forgetful***, ***mournful***, or occas. with passive force, as ***bashful***.
2 Forming nouns (pl. **-fuls**, occas. **-sful**) with the sense 'the amount that fills or would fill (a receptacle),' as ***handful***, ***mouthful***, ***spoonful***.

Fulah /ˈfuːlə/ *noun & adjective*. Also **Foulah**, **Fula**. L18.
[ORIGIN Cf. Fulfulde *pulo* Fulah person. Cf. FULBE, PEULH.]
▸ **A** *noun*. Pl. **-s**, same.
1 A member of an African people who have tended to migrate eastwards over the centuries and who currently inhabit numerous African countries from Senegal to Sudan. L18.
2 The language of this people, Fulfulde. M19.
▸ **B** *attrib*. or as *adjective*. Of or pertaining to the Fulahs or their language. M19.

Fulani /fʊˈlɑːni/ *noun & adjective*. Pl. **-s**, same. M19.
[ORIGIN Hausa.]
= FULAH *noun & adjective*; *spec*. of or pertaining to, a member of, the Fulahs of northern Nigeria and adjacent territories.

Fulbe /ˈfʊlbeɪ/ *noun*. Pl. **-s**, same. E20.
[ORIGIN Fulfulde = Fulah people.]
= FULAH *noun* 1.

Fulbright /ˈfʊlbrʌɪt/ *noun*. M20.
[ORIGIN William *Fulbright* (1905–95), US Senator.]
1 In full ***Fulbright award***. An award, scholarship, etc., granted under the terms of the Fulbright Act of 1946, by which it was agreed with foreign countries that the money gained from the sale by the US government of surplus war properties should be used to finance higher learning. M20.
2 In full ***Fulbright professor***, ***Fulbright scholar***, etc. A person in receipt of such an award. M20.

†**fulciment** *noun*. M17–L18.
[ORIGIN Latin *fulcimentum*, from *fulcire*: see FULCRUM, -MENT.]
A prop, a support; *spec*. a fulcrum.

fulcrate /ˈfʌlkreɪt/ *adjective*. Now *rare* or *obsolete*. M18.
[ORIGIN from FULCRUM + -ATE².]
BOTANY. Supported by or having fulcra.

fulcrum /ˈfʊlkrəm, ˈfʌl-/ *noun*. Pl. **-cra** /-krə/, **-crums**. L17.
[ORIGIN Latin = post or foot of a couch, from base of *fulcire* prop up, support.]
1 A prop or support; now *spec*. the point against which a lever is placed to get purchase or on which it turns or is supported. L17.

J. S. FOSTER If the projecting arm were.. extended over a support or fulcrum.. counter movement could be obtained.

2 *fig*. The means by which or central source from which influence etc. is brought to bear. L17.

C. MERIVALE The consulship was the fulcrum from which the whole Roman world was to be moved. O. SACKS The fulcrum of her family, giving it balance and power.

3 **a** BOTANY. In *pl*. The accessory organs or appendages of a plant. Now *rare* or *obsolete*. L18. ▸**b** ZOOLOGY. Any of certain anatomical structures having a central position or supporting function, *spec*.: (***a***) a chitinous framework enclosing the pharynx in dipteran flies; (***b***) in rotifers, the stem of the incus of the mastax. E19.
■ **fulcral** *adjective* (*rare*) relating to or of the nature of a fulcrum or fulcra L19.

fulfil /fʊlˈfɪl/ *verb trans*. Also ***fulfill**. Infl. **-ll-**.
[ORIGIN Late Old English *fullfyllan*, from FULL *adjective* + *fyllan* FILL *verb*.]
1 Fill up, make full. *arch*. LOE. ▸†**b** Spread through the whole extent of, pervade. LME–L16.

SIR W. SCOTT I have never known knight more fulfilled of nobleness.

†**2** Provide fully with what is wished for; satisfy the appetite or desire of. ME–E17.
3 Make complete, supply with what is lacking; replace (something); compensate for (a defect). *arch*. ME.
†**4** Hold or occupy (a vacant position); take (the place of something). ME–M16.
5 Bring to consummation, carry out (a prophecy, promise, etc.); satisfy (a desire, prayer). ME. ▸**b** *refl*. Work out one's destiny; develop one's gifts or character to the full. M19.

T. HARDY He had promised silence and absence, and had fulfilled his promise literally. E. BOWEN The weather.. was once more fulfilling the expectations of visitors. **b** F. WELDON Liffey.. did temporary work in offices.. but felt that such work could hardly.. fulfil her.

6 Carry out, perform, do (something prescribed); obey or follow (a command, the law, etc.). ME. ▸†**b** Perform, accomplish (a deed). ME–L16. ▸**c** Meet the requirements of, answer (a purpose); comply with (conditions). L18.

J. H. NEWMAN In what sense do we fulfil the words of Christ? G. VIDAL He fulfilled his historic function with wit and dignity. **c** M. GORDON People who fulfill minimum standards of home care. ANTHONY SMITH Two patients.. had survived after fulfilling the British criteria for brain death.

7 Bring to an end, finish, complete (a period of time, piece of work, etc.). ME.

AV *2 Sam*. 7:12 And when thy dayes be fulfilled, and thou shalt sleepe with thy fathers.

■ **fulfiller** *noun* a person who fulfils LME. **fulfilling** *noun* the action of the verb; an instance of this; *rare* something that fulfils: ME. **fulfilment** *noun* the action or an act or process of fulfilling; accomplishment, performance, completion: L18.

Fulfulde /fʊlˈfʊldeɪ/ *noun & adjective*. M20.
[ORIGIN Fulfulde.]
(Of) the Niger-Congo language of the Fulahs.

fulgent /ˈfʌldʒ(ə)nt/ *adjective*. Now *poet. & rhet*. LME.
[ORIGIN Latin *fulgent-* pres. ppl stem of *fulgere* shine: see -ENT.]
Shining, brilliant, glittering, resplendent.
■ †**fulgence** *noun* = FULGENCY LME–M17. †**fulgency** *noun* brightness, splendour M17–L18. **fulgently** *adverb* (*rare*) L19. **fulgentness** *noun* (*rare*) E18.

fulgid /ˈfʌldʒɪd/ *adjective*. M17.
[ORIGIN Latin *fulgidus*, from *fulgere* shine: see -ID¹.]
Flashing, glittering, shining.

fulgor /ˈfʌlɡɔː, -ɡə/ *noun*. *arch*. Also **fulgour**. M16.
[ORIGIN Latin, from *fulgere*: see FULGID, -OR.]
A brilliant or flashing light; dazzling brightness, splendour.
■ **fulgorous** *adjective* (*rare*) flashing, brilliant L18.

fulgorid /ˈfʌlɡərɪd/ *noun & adjective*. L19.
[ORIGIN mod. Latin *Fulgoridae* (see below), from *Fulgora* genus name from Latin = the goddess of lightning, from *fulgur* lightning: see -ID³.]
ENTOMOLOGY. ▸**A** *noun*. A homopteran insect of the family Fulgoridae, which includes the lantern flies. L19.
▸ **B** *adjective*. Of, pertaining to, or designating this family. E20.

fulgural /ˈfʌlɡjʊr(ə)l/ *adjective*. *rare*. M17.
[ORIGIN French from Latin *fulguralis*, from *fulgur* lightning: see -AL¹.]
Of or pertaining to lightning.

fulgurant /ˈfʌlɡjʊr(ə)nt/ *adjective*. M17.
[ORIGIN Latin *fulgurant-* pres. ppl stem of *fulgurare* lighten, flash, from *fulgur* lightning: see -ANT¹.]
Flashing like lightning.
■ **fulgurantly** *adverb* (*rare*) L19.

fulgurate /ˈfʌlɡjʊreɪt/ *verb intrans*. L17.
[ORIGIN Latin *fulgurat-* pa. ppl stem of *fulgurare*: see FULGURANT, -ATE³.]
Emit flashes like lightning.
■ **fulgurating** *ppl adjective* flashing like lightning; (of pain) darting through the body: L17.

fulguration /fʌlɡjʊˈreɪʃ(ə)n/ *noun*. M17.
[ORIGIN Latin *fulguratio(n-)* lightning, esp. sheet-lightning, from *fulgurat-*: see FULGURATE, -ATION.]
1 The action of lightening or flashing like lightning; usu. in *pl*., flashes of lightning. Now *rare*. M17.

fig.: E. CAIRD The continual fulgurations of deity.

2 In assaying, a brightening in the appearance of a molten metal when only a thin film of lead remains on its surface. *obsolete* exc. *hist*. L17.
3 MEDICINE. The destruction of tissue by means of diathermy. E20.

fulgurite /ˈfʌlɡjʊrʌɪt/ *noun*. M19.
[ORIGIN from Latin *fulgur* lightning + -ITE¹.]
GEOLOGY. (A piece of) sand or other substance fused or vitrified by lightning.

fulgurous /ˈfʌlɡjʊrəs/ *adjective*. E17.
[ORIGIN from Latin *fulgur* lightning + -OUS.]
Resembling, full of, or charged with lightning.

Fulham /ˈfʊləm/ *noun*. *arch. slang*. Also **f-**. E16.
[ORIGIN Perh. from *Fulham* in London, once a haunt of gamesters.]
A die loaded to ensure either a high throw (***high Fulham***) or a low throw (***low Fulham***).

†**fuliginated** *adjective*. *rare*. M17–L18.
[ORIGIN from Latin *fuliginatus*, from *fuligo* soot: see -ATE², -ED¹.]
Of a sooty colour or appearance.

fuliginous /fjuːˈlɪdʒɪnəs/ *adjective*. L16.
[ORIGIN Late Latin *fuliginosus*, from *fuligo*, *fuligin-* soot: see -OUS.]
†**1** Of a vapour or exhalation: thick and noxious, and said to be formed by organic combustion. L16–E18.
2 Of, containing, or resembling soot; sooty. E17. ▸**b** Covered or blackened with soot. Chiefly *joc*. M18.

R. C. HUTCHINSON The fuliginous interior of a one-roomed timber house. *fig.*: CARLYLE A very fuliginous set of doctrines.

3 Sooty-coloured, dusky. E19.
■ **fuligiˈnosity** *noun* the condition or quality of being fuliginous or sooty; (in *pl*.) sooty matter: M18. **fuliginously** *adverb* M18. **fuliginousness** *noun* (*long rare*) L16.

fuligo /fjuːˈlʌɪɡəʊ/ *noun*. Now *rare*. M17.
[ORIGIN Latin.]
Soot.

full /fʊl/ *adjective, adverb, & noun*.
[ORIGIN Old English *full* = Old Frisian *foll*, *full*, Old Saxon *ful* (Dutch *vol*), Old High German *foll* (German *voll*), Old Norse *fullr*, Gothic *fulls*, from Germanic, from Indo-European: cogn. with Greek *polus*, Latin *plenus*.]
▸ **A** *adjective*. **1** Containing all (*of* a substance) that its limits will allow; having no space empty, replete. OE. ▸**b** *postpositive*. = -FUL 2. Now *rare*. OE. ▸**c** Of the heart etc.: overcharged with emotion, ready to overflow. ME. ▸†**d** Of an office: occupied, not vacant. Foll. by *of*. L16–M18. ▸†**e** Having the outline filled in; solid. L16–E18. ▸**f** Of an animal: pregnant. Of a fish: containing roe. E17.

I. MURDOCH The sink had been blocked for several days and was full of.. water. S. BECKETT The hotels were full or would not let me in. **b** W. FULKE An egges shell full of dew. **c** DEFOE His heart was so full, he could say no more.

2 Foll. by *of*: holding or having plenty of; crowded with; containing many or much, characterized by. OE. ▸**b** Having sufficient or ample for one's needs; wealthy. Long *obsolete* exc. *dial*. L16.

J. CONRAD It.. seemed a living thing full of fury. A. MCCOWEN His.. house which was always full of interesting people.

F

3 Having eaten or drunk to repletion. *arch.* or *colloq.* **OE.** ▸**b** Having had plenty *of*. Now only in biblical phrs. ***full of years, full of honours, full of children***, etc. **ME.** ▸**c** Sated, weary *of*. Freq. foll. by *up*. Now *Austral. & NZ slang*. **ME.** ▸**d** Drunk. *slang* (chiefly *Scot., US, Austral., & NZ*). **M16.**

G. W. DASENT They ate and drank . . and when they were all full, they made a raft. **c** M. FRANKLIN He averred he was 'full up of life under the old man's rule'.

4 Abundant, sufficient, copious, satisfying. **OE.** ▸**b** Of a report etc.: complete, detailed. **M17.**

R. W. CHURCH He turned his studies to full account. Z. N. HURSTON Those full, hot meals he had left back in Alabama. **b** E. E. KAY The audience are quite at liberty to take the fullest notes they like.

5 Complete, entire, perfect. **OE.** ▸**b** Answering in every respect to a description; having all the qualifications or privileges of a designation. **OE.** ▸†**c** Of a friend or enemy: avowed, wholehearted. **OE–LME.**

G. GREENE I've got a full set now of these Irish coins. W. TREVOR He was offering a full removal service. **b** T. PARKER I'd like to stay in and perhaps get as high as full corporal.

6 Reaching the specified or usual limit; whole. **OE.** ▸**b** At or to the greatest degree or extent. **LME.** ▸**c** Of an assembly: having all or most of its members present. **M16.**

S. HEANEY Given heavy rain and sun For a full week, the blackberries would ripen. **b** M. MCCARTHY The trees were in full leaf. **c** WILLIAM WALLACE He . . kept the academic senate waiting for him in full conclave.

7 Having a rounded outline; large, swelling, plump. **OE.** ▸**b** Of a garment: amply cut; containing much material arranged in gathers or folds. **L18.**

F. WELDON Her breasts were full and round beneath the old sweater. **b** J. BRAINE However full her skirt, Elspeth always gave the impression that it was inadequate.

8 Having or exerting great force; strong, vigorous. **ME.** ▸**b** Of light: intense. Of colour: deep, rich, intense. Of sound: strong, resonant. Of flavour: rich, mellow. **M17.**

F. MANN The pulse feels full and forceful.

9 *NAUTICAL.* Of a sail: filled with wind. Of a ship: having the sails filled with wind. **LME.**

10 Engrossed with, absorbed in; unable to stop thinking or talking *of*. **E17.**

H. BRACKEN So full of themselves, that they reject all wise Counsel. J. CONRAD The biggest thing in the town, and everybody I met was full of it.

– SPECIAL COLLOCATIONS, PHRASES, & COMB.: ***at full blast***: see BLAST *noun*[1]. **at full length** (*a*) lying stretched out; (*b*) without abridgement. ***at full throttle***: see THROTTLE *noun*. ***at full tilt***: see TILT *noun*[2]. ***come full circle***: see CIRCLE *noun*. **full age** an age at which a person is considered to have the status of an adult. ***full and by***: see BY *adverb*. **full as a bull**, **full as a goog** *Austral. & NZ slang* extremely drunk. ***full as a tick***: see TICK *noun*[1]. **full back** (the position of) a defending player placed near the goal in various ball games. ***full blast***: see BLAST *noun*[1]. **full blood** (a person or animal of) pure breeding. **full-blooded** *adjective* (*a*) pure-bred, not hybrid; (*b*) vigorous, forceful, hearty, sensual. **full-bloodedly** *adverb* in a full-blooded manner, forcefully. **full-bloodedness** the fact or quality of being full-blooded. **full board** (*a*) the provision of a bed and all meals at a hotel etc.; (*b*) *Austral. & NZ* a full complement of shearers on the board. **full-bodied** *adjective* rich in quality, tone, etc. **full-bottom** a full-bottomed wig. **full-bottomed** *adjective* (of a wig) long at the back. **full brother**, **full sister**: born of the same father and mother. ***full chisel***: see CHISEL *noun*[1] 1. **full-colour** *adjective* all in colour; having the full range of colours. **full-court press** *BASKETBALL* an aggressive tactic in which members of a team cover their opponents throughout the court and not just in the region near their own basket. **full-cream** *adjective* unskimmed, made from unskimmed milk. **full dress**: worn on ceremonial or formal occasions (***full-dress debate***, a formal debate in which important speeches are made; ***full dress uniform***, military uniform worn for ceremonial parades etc.). ***full EMPLOYMENT***. **full English breakfast** a fried breakfast usu. consisting of bacon, eggs, sausages, etc. ***full growth***: see GROWTH *noun*. **full hand** *POKER* a hand containing three of a kind plus a pair. **full-hearted** *adjective* (*a*) zealous, confident, courageous; (*b*) full of feeling, emotional. **full-heartedly** *adverb* in a full-hearted manner. **full-heartedness** the quality of being full-hearted. **full house** (*a*) = ***full hand*** above; (*b*) the maximum or a large attendance in a theatre, in Parliament, etc. **full-length** *adjective* not shortened or abbreviated; (of a mirror, portrait, etc.) showing the whole height of the human figure. ***full lock***: see LOCK *noun*[2] 13. **full marks** the maximum award in an examination or assessment. **full measure** not less than the amount stated. **full moon** the moon with the whole disc illuminated; the time when this occurs. **full-motion video** digital video data that is transmitted or stored on video discs for real-time reproduction on a computer (or other multimedia system) at a rate of not less than 25 frames per second (abbreviation *FMV*). **full-mouthed** *adjective* (*a*) (of cattle etc.) having a full set of adult teeth; (*b*) (of a dog) baying loudly; (*c*) (of oratory etc.) sonorous, vigorous; †(*d*) having the mouth full of food. ***full nelson***: see NELSON *noun*[2]. ***full of beans***: see BEAN *noun*. **full-page** *adjective* taking up the entire page of a newspaper etc. **full pay** the amount allowed while on active service or actively employed. ***full pelt***: see PELT *noun*[2] 3. **full pitch** *CRICKET* (*a*) a ball pitched right up to the batsman; (*b*) *adverb* without the ball having touched the ground. **full point** = *full stop* (a) below. **full professor** (orig. *US*) a professor of the highest grade in a university etc. **full-scale** *adjective* not reduced in size; complete. **full score** (*MUSIC*) a score giving the parts for all performers on separate staves. ***full sister***: see *full brother* above. **full speed ahead**, **full steam ahead**: an order to proceed at maximum speed or to pursue a course of action energetically. **full stop** (*a*) a punctuation mark (.) to show the end of a sentence or abbreviation; (*b*) a complete cessation; (as *interjection*) that's all, without qualification (cf. *period*). ***full term***: see TERM *noun*. ***full throttle***: see THROTTLE *noun*. ***full tilt***: see TILT *noun*[2]. **full time** (*a*) the total normal working hours; (*b*) the end of a football or other match. **full-time** *adjective* occupying or using all one's working time. **full-timer** a worker or student attending for the whole working day. **full toss** = ***full pitch*** (a) above. **full up** filled to capacity; replete. ***full vent***: see VENT *noun*[2]. **full word** *LINGUISTICS* having a meaning in itself. ***give full weight to***: see WEIGHT *noun*. ***have one's hands full***: see HAND *noun*. ***in full cry***: see CRY *noun*. ***in full feather***: see FEATHER *noun*. ***in full swing***: see SWING *noun*[1]. **in full view** entirely visible. ***on a full stomach***: see STOMACH *noun*. ***the full monty***: see MONTY *noun*[1]. ***the full treatment***: see TREATMENT *noun* 6.

▸ **B** *adverb*. **1** Very, exceedingly. *arch.* or *poet.* exc. in ***know full well***, be very well aware (of). **OE.**

MILTON The imperial ensign . . full high advanced, Shone like a meteor. T. GRAY Full many a gem of purest ray serene.

2 Completely, entirely, fully; quite (*as*). Now usu. in *comb.* **OE.**

C. KINGSLEY He weighed full fifteen stone. G. M. TREVELYAN Small children were sometimes set to work . . at an age full as early as the factory children of later times.

full out thoroughly, completely; *esp.* at full power or speed.

3 a With ref. to points of the compass: due. Now *rare* or *obsolete*. **LME.** ▸**b** Of position and direction: exactly, directly, straight. **L16.**

b M. ROBERTS She turns right round and looks him full in the face.

– COMB.: **full-blown** *adjective* (*a*) of a flower: in full bloom; (*b*) full of wind, puffed out; *fig.* fully developed, complete; **full-fashioned** *adjective* = ***fully fashioned*** s.v. FULLY *adverb*; **full-fledged** *adjective* = ***fully fledged*** s.v. FULLY *adverb*; ***full-frontal***: see FRONTAL *adjective* 3; **full-grown** *adjective* having attained full size or maturity, fully grown; **full-rigged** *adjective* (of a ship having three or more masts) carrying square sails on all masts; **full-rigger** a full-rigged ship; ***full-summed***: see SUMMED *adjective* 1.

▸ **C** *noun*. **1** With *of*: the whole; the complete scope, entire range, sum total. *arch.* **ME.**

J. H. NEWMAN With my opinions, to the full of which I dare not confess.

2 A sufficient amount; enough to fill a receptacle; one's fill. Now chiefly *dial.* **ME.**

G. W. DASENT They had all stared their full.

3 The period, point, or state of the greatest fullness or strength; the height or middle of a month, season, etc. **ME.** ▸**b** *The* period or state of complete illumination of the moon's disc. **LME.**

BROWNING June was not over Though past the full.

†**4** A set (of pans or kettles). **LME–M17.**

5 In Kent: a ridge of shingle or sand pushed or cast up by the tide. **M19.**

6 A herring full of milt or roe; ***crown full***, one of the best quality. **L19.**

– PHRASES: **at full**, **at the full** †(*a*) completely, at full length, to the full extent; (*b*) at the position or in the state of fullness. ***crown full***: see sense 6 above. **in full**, †**in the full** at full length, unabridged; to the full amount or sum due. **to the full** completely, fully, quite.

full /fʊl/ *verb*[1] *trans.* **ME.**

[ORIGIN Prob. back-form. from FULLER *noun*[1] infl. by Old French & mod. French *fouler* or medieval Latin *fullare*. Cf. FOIL *verb*[1].]

†**1** Beat, trample down; destroy. **ME–M17.**

2 Orig., clean or thicken (cloth) by treading or beating. Now, clean, shrink, and felt (woollen) cloth by heat, pressure, and moisture. **LME.**

fulling mill a mill in which cloth is fulled; a machine for fulling cloth.

full /fʊl/ *verb*[2]. **LME.**

[ORIGIN from FULL *adjective*.]

1 *verb trans.* Make full. Long *obsolete* exc. *dial. & US black English*. **LME.** ▸**b** *verb intrans.* Be or become full. Now chiefly *dial. & US*, of the moon or tide. **LME.**

†**2** *verb trans.* Fulfil, complete. **LME–M17.**

3 *DRESSMAKING.* Gather up fullness, fold, pleat. **M18.**

†**fullage** *noun*. **L17–L18.**

[ORIGIN Perh. from FULYIE.]

Refuse, street-sweepings, filth.

fuller /ˈfʊlə/ *noun*[1]. **OE.**

[ORIGIN from Latin *fullo* (of unknown origin) + -ER[1].]

A person whose occupation is to full cloth.

fuller's earth, **fuller's clay** a fine-grained clay used in fulling cloth and as an adsorbent. ***fuller's teasel***: see TEASEL *noun* 1.

■ **fullery** *noun* (*rare*) = ***fulling-mill*** s.v. FULL *verb*[1] **M18.**

fuller /ˈfʊlə/ *verb & noun*[2]. **E19.**

[ORIGIN Unknown.]

▸ **A** *verb trans.* Stamp (iron etc.) with a fuller (see sense B. below); form a groove or channel in. **E19.**

▸ **B** *noun*. A grooved or rounded tool on which iron etc. is shaped; a groove made by this. **M19.**

fullerene /ˈfʊləriːn/ *noun*. **L20.**

[ORIGIN Abbreviation of BUCKMINSTERFULLERENE.]

CHEMISTRY. Any of several forms of carbon consisting of atoms joined together as a hollow structure.

full face /fʊl ˈfeɪs/ *noun, adjectival, & adverbial phr.* Also **full-face**. **E18.**

[ORIGIN from FULL *adjective* + FACE *noun*. Cf. FULL-FACED.]

▸ **A** *noun phr.* **1** The face seen from the front and entirely visible to the observer; a full-face view. **E18.**

2 *TYPOGRAPHY.* A full-faced character; a font of such characters. **L19.**

▸ **B** *adjectival & adverbial phr.* As seen from the front; with the front or face entirely visible to the observer. **L19.**

full-faced /fʊlˈfeɪst/ *adjective*. **E17.**

[ORIGIN from FULL *adjective* + FACE *noun* + -ED[2]. Cf. FULL FACE.]

1 Having a full or plump face. **E17.**

2 Having the face turned fully towards the observer or in some specified direction. **E17.**

3 *TYPOGRAPHY.* Of a character: having a face occupying the whole depth of type. **E19.**

fullness /ˈfʊlnɪs/ *noun*. Also **fulness**. **ME.**

[ORIGIN from FULL *adjective* + -NESS.]

1 The condition of containing something in abundance. **ME.** ▸**b** In biblical language, all that is contained in the world. **ME.** ▸†**c** Abundance, plenty. **LME–E18.**

b J. WESLEY The Earth and all her Fullness owns Jehovah for her sovereign Lord! **c** DEFOE Before I revelled in fullness, and here I struggled with hard fare.

2 Completeness, perfection. **ME.** ▸**b** Copiousness or exhaustiveness (of knowledge, statement, etc.). **M19.**

G. PRIESTLAND Christianity . . hasn't yet been tried . . What right have we to expect its fullness in *our* time? **b** J. BARZUN He is replying . . with his customary fullness of illustration.

3 The condition of being filled to capacity. **LME.**

4 Satiety; (the effects of) overindulgence. Now only, a feeling of having eaten (more than) enough. **LME.**

5 The quality (of sound, colour, etc.) of being full; richness. **LME.**

6 Roundness (of the body), plumpness. **E17.**

J. FERRIAR A certain degree of fullness improves the figure.

7 The condition (of a garment) of being full; the material gathered or folded to produce this. **E19.**

J. AUSTEN No fullness appears . . the back is quite plain.

– PHRASES: **fullness of the heart**, **fullness of one's heart** strong feelings or emotions. **in the fullness of time** at the destined time; eventually.

fully /ˈfʊli/ *verb trans. slang*. **M19.**

[ORIGIN from the adverb, in phr. 'fully committed for trial'.]

Commit (a person) for trial.

fully /ˈfʊli/ *adverb*. **OE.**

[ORIGIN from FULL *adjective* + -LY[2].]

In a full manner or degree; completely, entirely, thoroughly, exactly, quite.

– COMB.: **fully fashioned** *adjective* (of a garment, esp. a stocking) shaped to fit closely; **fully fledged** *adjective* (*a*) (of a young bird) having a full set of true feathers; (*b*) completely developed or established; of full status.

fulmar /ˈfʊlmə/ *noun*. **L17.**

[ORIGIN Hebridean Norn (Gaelic *fulmair*), from Old Norse *fúll* FOUL *adjective* (with ref. to the bird's habit of regurgitating oily stomach contents when disturbed) + *már* gull (cf. MEW *noun*[1]).]

A gull-sized grey and white northern petrel, *Fulmarus glacialis*.

fulmen /ˈfʌlmən, ˈfʊl-/ *noun*. Pl. ***-mina*** /-mɪnə/. **L17.**

[ORIGIN Latin.]

A thunderbolt; thunder and lightning, *esp.* as an attribute of Jupiter.

fulminant /ˈfʌlmɪnənt, ˈfʊl-/ *adjective & noun*. **E17.**

[ORIGIN French, or Latin *fulminant-* pres. ppl stem of *fulminare*: see FULMINATE *verb*, -ANT[1].]

▸ **A** *adjective*. **1** = FULMINATING. **E17.**

2 *MEDICINE.* Developing suddenly and rapidly. **L19.**

Lancet A fulminant disease which ends in death within 24 h.

▸ **B** *noun*. Something that fulminates; a thunderbolt; an explosive. *rare*. **E19.**

fulminate /ˈfʌlmɪneɪt, ˈfʊl-/ *noun*. **E19.**

[ORIGIN from FULMINIC + -ATE[1].]

CHEMISTRY. A salt or ester of fulminic acid; *esp.* any of a number of unstable explosive salts of metals (e.g. that of mercury, used in detonators).

fulminate /ˈfʌlmɪneɪt, ˈfʊl-/ *verb*. **LME.**

[ORIGIN Latin *fulminat-* pa. ppl stem of *fulminare* lighten, strike with lightning (in sense 1 from medieval Latin *fulminare* issue ecclesiastical censures), from *fulmin-*, *fulmen* lightning: see -ATE[3].]

1 *verb trans.* Utter or publish (a formal denunciation). **LME.** ▸**b** *verb intrans.* (Orig. of the Pope) issue formal censures (*against*); rail or speak violently (*against*). **M17.** ▸**c** *verb trans.* Censure, condemn; denounce vehemently or in scathing terms. **L17.**

G. H. NAPHEYS Kings have fulminated their decrees against it. **b** BOSWELL The holy father used . . to fulminate with serious effect against the greatest powers in Europe. J. ADDAMS Tore his hair, and loudly fulminated in weird Italian oaths. **c** BURKE I would have the Laws rise . . to fulminate such vain and impious wretches.

2 *verb intrans.* Emit thunder and lightning. *rare.* E17. ▸**b** *verb trans.* Cause to flash out like lightning. *rare.* M17. ▸**c** *verb intrans.* Issue as a thunderbolt. M19.
3 *verb trans. & intrans.* (Cause to) explode violently, detonate. M17.

W. GREGORY A dark powder is formed, which fulminates violently when heated.

†**4** *verb intrans.* METALLURGY. Of gold: suddenly become bright and uniform in colour. Cf. FULMINATION 3. Only in E18.
5 *verb intrans.* MEDICINE. Of a disease: come on or develop suddenly and severely. E20.
■ **fulminator** *noun* a person who or thing which fulminates L19.

fulminating /ˈfʌlmɪneɪtɪŋ, ˈfʊl-/ *ppl adjective.* E17.
[ORIGIN from FULMINATE *verb* + -ING².]
1 Sending out violent denunciations etc.; railing. E17.
2 Exploding with a loud noise or bright flash; highly explosive. M17.
fulminating gold, **fulminating mercury**, **fulminating silver**, etc., the explosive fulminate of gold, mercury, silver, etc. (see FULMINATE *noun*).
3 MEDICINE. Of disease: coming on suddenly and progressing rapidly. E20.

fulmination /fʌlmɪˈneɪʃ(ə)n, fʊl-/ *noun.* E16.
[ORIGIN Latin *fulminatio(n-)*, from *fulminat-*: see FULMINATE *verb*, -ATION.]
1 The formal issuing of an ecclesiastical condemnation or censure; *gen.* violent denunciation or threatening; an outburst of indignation. E16.

T. MO I am made uneasy by the tone of your recent fulminations. R. PERLE The way to deal with angry fulmination was to stay calm.

2 Thunder and lightning; a thunderbolt. *arch.* E17.
3 The action of detonating; violent explosion. *arch.* M17.

fulminatory /ˈfʌlmɪnət(ə)ri, ˈfʊl-/ *adjective.* E17.
[ORIGIN French *fulminatoire*, formed as FULMINATE *verb*: see -ORY².]
Sending out fulminations, thundering.

fulmine /ˈfʌlmɪn, ˈfʊl-/ *verb.* L16.
[ORIGIN Old French & mod. French *fulminer* or Latin *fulminare*: see FULMINATE *verb*.]
1 *verb trans.* Emit (thunder or lightning); *fig.* flash *out*. *arch.* or *poet.* L16.

SPENSER As it had beene a flake Of lightning through bright heven fulmined.

2 *verb intrans.* Speak out fiercely or energetically. (Now chiefly after Milton.) E17.

MILTON Whose resistless eloquence . . Shook the Arsenal and fulmined over Greece.

fulmineous /fʌlˈmɪnɪəs, fʊl-/ *adjective. arch.* or *poet.* E18.
[ORIGIN from Latin *fulmineus*, from *fulmen*, *fulmin-* lightning + -OUS: see -EOUS.]
Of or pertaining to thunder or lightning.

fulminic /fʌlˈmɪnɪk, fʊl-/ *adjective.* E19.
[ORIGIN from Latin *fulmin-*, FULMEN + -IC. Cf. FULMINATE *verb* 3.]
CHEMISTRY. ***fulminic acid***, a very unstable acid, CNOH, known only in ethereal solutions in which it polymerizes rapidly. Cf. FULMINATE *noun*.

fulminous /ˈfʌlmɪnəs, ˈfʊl-/ *adjective.* M17.
[ORIGIN from Latin *fulmen*, *fulmin-* lightning + -OUS.]
Of or pertaining to thunder or lightning; fulminating.

fulminuric /fʌlmɪˈnjʊərɪk, fʊl-/ *adjective.* M19.
[ORIGIN from FULMINIC + URIC.]
CHEMISTRY. ***fulminuric acid***, any of a number of isomeric acidic compounds of formula $C_3H_3N_3O_3$; *esp.* nitrocyanoacetamide, $NO_2{\cdot}CH(CN){\cdot}CONH_2$.
■ **fulminurate** *noun* a salt or ester of fulminuric acid M19.

fulness *noun* var. of FULLNESS.

fulsome /ˈfʊls(ə)m/ *adjective.* ME.
[ORIGIN from FULL *adjective* + -SOME¹.]
1 Abundant, plentiful; full, copious, rich. *obsolete* exc. as passing into sense 6. ME.
2 Full and plump, well-grown; *derog.* overgrown. LME. ▸†**b** Overfed, surfeited. M17–E19.

fig.: U. BENTLEY Fulsome white clouds . . billowed over the moors.

3 (Of food) coarse, heavy, filling, cloying; *gen.* satiating, wearisome, tedious. LME. ▸**b** Having a sickly or nauseating taste. *obsolete* exc. *Scot.* E17.

JOSEPH HALL A little honie is sweet; much, fulsome.

4 Physically disgusting; dirty, foul, loathsome. *obsolete* exc. *Scot.* LME. ▸†**b** Foul- or strong-smelling; rank. L16–E18.

ROBERT BURTON She vomited some 24 pounds of fulsome stuffe of all colours.

†**5** Offending against accepted standards of morals or taste; repulsive, odious, obscene. LME–E19. ▸**b** Lustful, wanton. *rare* (Shakes.). Only in E17.

N. AMHURST What followed was too fulsome for the eyes of my chaste readers.

6 (Esp. excessively) complimentary or flattering; (too) effusive, (too) lavish, overdone. E17.

M. EDGEWORTH The fulsome strains of courtly adulation. C. PAGLIA Fulsome praise of prominent academics.

– NOTE: Although the earliest use was 'abundant', many insist that this meaning is incorrect in modern use, and that the correct meaning is 'excessively complimentary or flattering'. Nevertheless the word is often used to mean simply 'abundant' in reference to praise.
■ **fulsomely** *adverb* LME. **fulsomeness** *noun* LME.

fulth /fʊlθ/ *noun.* Long *obsolete* exc. *dial.* See also FOUTH. ME.
[ORIGIN from FULL *adjective* + -TH¹.]
Fullness, one's fill.

fulvid /ˈfʌlvɪd, ˈfʊl-/ *adjective.* Long *rare.* L16.
[ORIGIN Late Latin *fulvidus*, from Latin *fulvus* FULVOUS: see -ID¹.]
= FULVOUS.

fulvous /ˈfʌlvəs, ˈfʊl-/ *adjective.* M17.
[ORIGIN from Latin *fulvus* reddish-yellow + -OUS.]
Reddish-yellow; dull yellowish brown, tawny.
fulvous whistling duck, **fulvous tree duck**, a long-legged tawny-plumaged duck, *Dendrocygna bicolor*, native to E. Africa, the Indian subcontinent, and the New World tropics and subtropics.

fulyie /ˈfuli, ˈfulji/ *verb & noun. Scot.* Also **-zie**. LME.
[ORIGIN Perh. from Old French & mod. French *fouler* trample underfoot: cf. FULL *verb*¹, FOIL *verb*¹.]
▸ **A** *verb trans.* †**1** Trample, overcome, destroy. LME–E18.
2 Defile, pollute. E16.
▸ **B** *noun.* Street-sweepings, refuse; filth; dung, manure. L15.

fum /fʌm/ *verb.* Infl. **-mm-**. E17.
[ORIGIN Imit.]
†**1** *verb intrans.* Strum (on a guitar). Only in 17.
2 *verb trans.* Thump, beat. *W. Indian.* L18.

fumadiddle *noun* var. of FLUMMADIDDLE.

fumado /fjuːˈmɑːdəʊ/ *noun.* Now *dial.* Pl. **-o(e)s**. L16.
[ORIGIN Spanish, pa. pple of *fumar* to smoke from Latin *fumare*: see FUME *verb*, -ADO. See also ***fair maid*** s.v. FAIR *adjective & adverb*.]
A pilchard, orig. smoked, later salted and pressed.

fumage /ˈfjuːmɪdʒ/ *noun.* M18.
[ORIGIN medieval Latin *fumagium*, from Latin *fumus* smoke: see -AGE. Cf. FEUAGE.]
hist. A tax on hearths or chimneys.

fumaric /fjuːˈmarɪk/ *adjective.* M19.
[ORIGIN from mod. Latin *Fumaria* fumitory + -IC.]
CHEMISTRY. ***fumaric acid***, a crystalline unsaturated dibasic acid, *trans*-HOOC·CH=CH·COOH, which is isomeric with maleic acid and occurs in fumitory and many other plants; *trans*-butenedioic acid.
■ ˈ**fumarate** *noun* a salt or ester of fumaric acid M19.

fumarole /ˈfjuːmərəʊl/ *noun.* Also **-mer-**. E19.
[ORIGIN Italian †*fumaruolo* from late Latin *fumariolum* vent, hole for smoke, dim. ult. of Latin *fumus* smoke + *-arium* -ARY¹: see -OLE¹.]
A vent in or near a volcano, from which hot vapour is emitted.
■ **fumarolic** /-ˈrɒlɪk/ *adjective* of, pertaining to, or formed by a fumarole E20.

fumaroyl /ˈfjuːmərəʊʌɪl, -rəʊɪl/ *noun.* M20.
[ORIGIN from FUMARIC + -OYL.]
A divalent radical, *trans*-·OC·CH=CH·CO·, derived from fumaric acid. Usu. in *comb.*
■ Also **fumaryl** *noun* M19.

fumble /ˈfʌmb(ə)l/ *verb & noun.* LME.
[ORIGIN Low German *fummeln*, *fommeln*, Dutch *fommelen*, whence Swedish *fumla*: cf. FAMBLE *verb*.]
▸ **A** *verb.* **1** *verb intrans.* Use one's hands or fingers clumsily or ineffectually; grope (*about*, *at*, *for*, *with*); act hesitantly. LME. ▸**b** *verb trans.* Handle awkwardly or clumsily; *esp.* mishandle (a ball). E17.

I. MURDOCH I fumbled with the catch of the front door, my hands trembling with nervousness. E. FIGES I fumbled in my shopping bag . . for our supper. L. AUCHINCLOSS Mark would not fumble . . he would move with absolute assurance. *fig.*: V. WOOLF Fumbling in his mind for something to say. **b** P. V. WHITE Fumbling the letter out of its envelope.

b fumble one's way find one's way by groping.
2 *verb intrans. & trans.* Copulate impotently or ineffectually (with). *slang.* E16.

fig.: GOLDSMITH Impotent posterity would in vain fumble to produce his fellow. H. REED The early bees are assaulting and fumbling the flowers.

3 *verb intrans. & trans.* Speak (words) hesitantly or indistinctly; mumble, mutter. M16.

SIR W. SCOTT Never lose time fumbling and prating about it. *Company* Bill fumbled through his final goodbyes.

4 *verb trans.* Wrap up clumsily, huddle together. Long *rare* or *obsolete.* L16.
▸ **B** *noun.* An act of fumbling; *esp.* a clumsy attempt; a mishandling of a ball. M17.
■ **fumbler** *noun* a person who fumbles E16. **fumblingly** *adverb* in a fumbling manner L16.

fume /fjuːm/ *noun.* LME.
[ORIGIN Old French *fum* from Latin *fumus* smoke, and Old French *fume*, from *fumer* from Latin *fumare*: see FUME *verb*.]
▸ **I** Now usu. in *pl.*
1 The volatile matter produced by combustion; smoke. Now usu., odorous or fragrant smoke from burning tobacco, incense, diesel fuel, etc. LME. ▸†**b** Something producing aromatic vapour. M16–E18.

DICKENS The fumes of choice tobacco scent the air. L. T. C. ROLT Reeking with the fumes of spent gunpowder.

2 An odour emitted from or by a substance or object. LME.

A. C. SWINBURNE The fume of the flowers of the night.

3 A vapour or gas (esp. a harmful or irritant one) given off by an acid or volatile substance. Formerly also, vapour given off by a substance when heated. LME. ▸**b** A watery vapour, steam, or mist rising from the earth or sea. Now *rare.* M16.

JONATHAN MILLER A patient who developed a spectacular tremor . . as the result of breathing in mercury fumes.

4 A vapour or exhalation produced by the body; *esp.* (now only) a noxious vapour imagined to rise from the stomach to the brain as a result of (excess) food or alcohol. LME.

C. THIRLWALL The fumes of the wine . . thawed their reserve.

▸ **II** *fig.* **5** (A fit of) anger, an irritable mood. Freq. in ***in a fume***. LME.

N. COWARD You're all fuss and fume.

6 Something unsubstantial, transient, or imaginary. Now *rare.* M16.
7 Something which clouds or confuses the faculties or reason. L16.

M. ARNOLD His head gets a little hot with the fumes of patriotism.

– COMB.: **fume chamber**, **fume cupboard** (in a laboratory) a glazed enclosure in which to perform experiments involving harmful gases and vapours, which are removed by means of a ventilator; **fume hood**: for extracting harmful vapours in a laboratory etc.

fume /fjuːm/ *verb.* LME.
[ORIGIN Old French & mod. French *fumer* or Latin *fumare* to smoke.]
1 *verb trans.* Apply fumes to; expose to fumes; fumigate. LME. ▸**b** Perfume (now only with incense); offer incense to. L15. ▸†**c** Preserve by smoking. E–M17.
fumed oak: darkened by exposure to ammonia fumes.
†**2** *verb trans.* Emit as vapour; disperse in vapour. L15–M19.
3 *verb intrans.* Be angry or irritated. E16. ▸**b** *verb trans.* Say or think angrily or irritably. Also, spend (time) in an angry state. L19.

P. G. WODEHOUSE These formalities irked Judson . . . He wrote his name on the form . . fuming. **b** P. LIVELY I haven't time to be ill, she fumed.

4 *verb intrans.* Emit fumes, smoke, or vapour. M16.

C. D. WARNER The fire sputters and fumes.

fuming nitric acid concentrated nitric acid containing excess dissolved nitrogen dioxide. ***fuming sulphuric acid***: see SULPHURIC *adjective* 1.
5 *verb intrans.* (Of fumes etc.) issue, rise, be emitted; pass *away* or *off* as fumes. L16. ▸†**b** Of alcohol or food: rise as fumes (*to* or *into* the brain). L16–E18.

S. PLATH A faint chickeny aroma fumed up to my nostrils.

†**6** *verb intrans.* Become clouded or confused by alcohol, sleep, etc. *rare* (Shakes.). Only in E17.
■ **fumer** *noun* (*rare*) E17. **fumingly** *adverb* in a fuming manner; angrily: L16.

fumerole *noun* var. of FUMAROLE.

fumet /fjuːˈmɛt/ *noun*¹. Also **-ette**. E18.
[ORIGIN French, from *fumer* FUME *verb*.]
1 The smell of game when high; game flavour. E18.
2 A concentrated stock, usu. of game or fish, used as flavouring. E20.

fumet *noun*² var. of FEWMET.

fumette *noun* var. of FUMET *noun*¹.

†**fumid** *adjective.* M17–L18.
[ORIGIN Latin *fumidus*, from *fumus* smoke: see -ID¹.]
Fuming, vaporous.

†**fumiferous** *adjective. rare.* M17–M19.
[ORIGIN from Latin *fumifer*, from *fumus* smoke + -OUS: see -FEROUS.]
Bearing or producing smoke.

fumigant /ˈfjuːmɪg(ə)nt/ *noun.* L19.
[ORIGIN Latin *fumigant-* pres. ppl stem of *fumigare*: see FUMIGATE, -ANT¹.]
Something that fumigates; a substance used in fumigation.

fumigate /ˈfjuːmɪgeɪt/ *verb trans.* M16.
[ORIGIN Latin *fumigat-* pa. ppl stem of *fumigare*, from *fumus* FUME *noun*: see -ATE³.]
1 Scent with fumes; perfume. Now *rare* or *obsolete*. M16.

F

2 Apply fumes to; *esp.* disinfect or disinfest by the application of (chemical) smoke or fumes. L18.

■ **fumigator** *noun* (*a*) a person who fumigates; (*b*) an apparatus used for fumigating: L17. **fumigatory** *adjective* (*rare*) of or pertaining to fumigation L18.

fumigation /fjuːmɪˈɡeɪʃ(ə)n/ *noun*. LME.
[ORIGIN Old French & mod. French, or late Latin *fumigatio(n-)*, formed as FUMIGATE: see -ATION.]
1 The production of aromatic fumes; the action of perfuming with a preparation of herbs, perfumes, etc. Also, the preparation so used or the fumes produced. LME. **2** The action or process of applying (chemical) fumes or smoke, *esp.* as a disinfectant or disinfesting agent. LME. **3** (Exposure of a part of the body to) therapeutic fumes. Now *rare* or *obsolete*. LME.

fumish /ˈfjuːmɪʃ/ *adjective*. Long *arch. rare*. E16.
[ORIGIN from FUME *noun* + -ISH[1].]
†**1** Of the nature of fumes, esp. as rising in the body (cf. FUME *noun* 4); emitting fumes. E16–L17. **2** *fig.* Irascible, bad-tempered; exhibiting anger. E16.
■ **fumishly** *adverb* L16. **fumishness** *noun* E16.

F

fumitory /ˈfjuːmɪt(ə)ri/ *noun*[1]. Also †**fumiter**. LME.
[ORIGIN Old French & mod. French *fumeterre* from medieval Latin *fumus terrae* 'smoke of the earth'.]
Any of various weeds of the genus *Fumaria* (family Fumariaceae), with spikes of pink or white tubular flowers and finely divided greyish leaves; esp. *F. officinalis*. Also, any plant of the related genus *Corydalis*.

fumitory /ˈfjuːmɪt(ə)ri/ *noun*[2]. *rare*. M16.
[ORIGIN Erron. from medieval Latin *fumatorium* chimney, louvre, from Latin *fumat-* pa. ppl stem of *fumare* FUME *verb*: see -ORY[1].]
†**1** A censer. Only in M16. **2** A place set apart for smoking or fumigation. E18.

fummadiddle *noun* var. of FLUMMADIDDLE.

fumose /fjuːˈməʊs/ *adjective*. Now *rare*. LME.
[ORIGIN Latin *fumosus*, from *fumus* smoke: see -OSE[1].]
1 Full of or giving off fumes. Formerly also = FUMOUS 1. LME. **2** Consisting of fumes or smoke, vaporous, smoky. LME.

†**fumosity** *noun*. LME.
[ORIGIN Old French *fumosité* or medieval Latin *fumositas*, formed as FUMOSE: see -ITY.]
1 The state of fuming or being full of fumes; a fume or fumes. LME–M18. **2** The flatulent quality of some foods; the heady quality of alcohol; a fume supposed to rise to the brain from the stomach. LME–L17.

fumous /ˈfjuːməs/ *adjective*. Now *rare*. LME.
[ORIGIN formed as FUMOSE: see -OUS.]
†**1** Causing flatulence or (supposedly) a fume to rise to the brain from the stomach. LME–E18. †**2** Consisting of fumes, vaporous; fumy. LME–L18. †**3** Angry, furious. LME–L17. **4** Pertaining to smoke or (*joc.*) smoking. M17.

fumy /ˈfjuːmi/ *adjective*. E16.
[ORIGIN from FUME *noun* + -Y[1].]
Composed of or full of fumes; of the nature of fumes; giving off or smelling of fumes; vaporous, smoky.

fun /fʌn/ *noun & adjective*. L17.
[ORIGIN from the verb.]
▸ **A** *noun*. **1** A trick, a cheat, a hoax. *obsolete* exc. *dial.* L17. **2** Amusement, light-hearted pleasure; jocularity, drollery. Also, something which provides this, a source of amusement. E18.

M. SHEARMAN Most footballers play for the fun and the fun alone. W. FEATHER Setting a good example for your children takes all the fun out of middle-age. J. WAIN You've had your fun, and now I'm going to have a baby. *Listener* The clothes were . . fun to wear.

– PHRASES: ***figure of fun***: see FIGURE *noun*. **for fun**, **for the fun of it** for amusement or excitement. **fun and games** *colloq.* exciting or amusing goings-on; *esp.* flirtation, carrying-on. **in fun** as a joke; not seriously. **like fun** (now *rare*) vigorously, quickly, much; *iron.* not at all. **make fun of**, **poke fun at** tease, ridicule.
– COMB.: **funfair** (a part of) a fair devoted to amusements and sideshows; **funfest** (*N. Amer.*) a gathering for the purposes of amusement; **fun fur** an artificial fabric with a texture resembling fur, typically in bright colours; **funhouse** *N. Amer.* (in an amusement park) a building equipped with trick mirrors, shifting floors, etc., designed to scare or amuse people as they walk through; **fun run** an organized, largely uncompetitive, long-distance run involving mass participation of occasional (often sponsored) runners.
▸ **B** *attrib.* or as *adjective*. Amusing, entertaining, enjoyable; not serious. M19.

Uncut It seemed like he would be a fun guy to party with. *Time Out* A fun night of nostalgia.

fun /fʌn/ *verb*. Infl. **-nn-**. L17.
[ORIGIN Prob. orig. dial. var. of FON *verb*; later from the noun.]
1 *verb trans.* Cheat, hoax, cajole *of*, *out of*. *obsolete* exc. *dial.* L17. **2** *verb intrans.* Have fun; fool, joke. M19.

funambulator /fjuːˈnambjʊleɪtə/ *noun*. *rare*. L17.
[ORIGIN formed as FUNAMBULIST + -ATOR.]
= FUNAMBULIST.
■ **funambuˈlation** *noun* tightrope walking, rope-dancing E18. **funambulatory** *adjective* of or pertaining to rope-dancing; that walks on a tightrope: L17.

funambulist /fjuːˈnambjʊlɪst/ *noun*. L18.
[ORIGIN from French *funambule* or its source Latin *funambulus* (from *funis* rope + *ambulare* walk) + -IST.]
A rope-walker, a rope-dancer.
■ **funambulism** *noun* E19.

funambulo /fjuːˈnambjʊləʊ/ *noun*. Long *arch.* Pl. **-o(e)s**. E17.
[ORIGIN Spanish or Italian, from Latin *funambulus*: see FUNAMBULIST.]
= FUNAMBULIST.

funckia *noun* var. of FUNKIA.

functi officio *pred. adjectival phr.* see FUNCTUS OFFICIO.

function /ˈfʌŋ(k)ʃ(ə)n/ *noun*. M16.
[ORIGIN Old French & mod. French *fonction* from Latin *functio(n-)*, from *funct-* pa. ppl stem of *fungi* perform: see -ION.]
1 The activity proper or natural to a person or thing; the purpose or intended role of a person or thing; an office, duty, employment, or calling. Also, a particular activity or operation (among several); an organizational unit performing this. M16. ▸**b** An official duty. Orig. usu. in *pl.* M16. ▸†**c** An order or class (of people). L16–M18. ▸**d** CHEMISTRY. (The characteristic mode of reaction of) a functional group. M19. ▸**e** COMPUTING. Any of the basic operations in a computer; *esp.* one that corresponds to a single instruction. Freq. *attrib.* M20.

G. MURRAY The chief function of poetry is the criticism of life. J. G. COZZENS The function of ice was to melt. A. STORR The obsessional's habitual disgust with bodily functions, especially with those of excretion. *Times* The smooth . . running of our centralised cashier function. *Marketing* Finance is shaking off its grey, dowdy image. It is becoming a creative, dynamic function. **b** J. MARQUAND The door was opened . . by the door keeper, . . ready to perform that function at any hour of the day.

2 The action of functioning; performance (*of*). L16.

P. PARISH The function of the liver, kidneys and brain may all be impaired. *Belle (Australia)* Opening up paths of communication so essential to effective office function.

†**3** Activity, action. L16–E17.

SHAKES. *Macb.* Function is smother'd in surmise.

4 a Orig. ROMAN CATHOLIC CHURCH. A religious ceremony. Now *rare*. M17. ▸**b** A public ceremony or occasion; a formal or important social gathering. M19.

b L. WHISTLER Selfconscious and unconfident, I . . made few interesting friends, and went to few functions.

5 MATH. A variable quantity regarded in relation to one or more other variables in terms of which it may be expressed or on which its value depends; a mathematical expression containing one or more variables. Also *transf.*, (with *of*) something dependent on (another factor or factors). L18.

R. M. PIRSIG The time spans of scientific truths are an inverse function of the intensity of scientific effort. *Nature* Functions are considered . . as mappings between sets. W. GOLDING What men believe is a function of what they are.

complementary function: see COMPLEMENTARY *adjective* 2. ***wave function***: see WAVE *noun*. ***ZETA function***.
– COMB.: **function space** MATH. a topological space the elements of which are functions; **function word** LINGUISTICS a word expressing a formal or grammatical purpose.
■ **functionate** *verb intrans.* (*rare*) = FUNCTION *verb* M19. **functionless** *adjective* M19.

function /fʌŋ(k)ʃ(ə)n/ *verb intrans*. M19.
[ORIGIN from the noun, after French *fonctionner*.]
Fulfil a function; perform a duty or role; act, operate.

A. KOESTLER The wash-basin . . had no plug, but the tap functioned. N. O. BROWN Criticism . . functioning as a mask for moral prejudice.

function on all cylinders: see CYLINDER 3.

functional /ˈfʌŋ(k)ʃ(ə)n(ə)l/ *adjective & noun*. M17.
[ORIGIN from FUNCTION *noun* + -AL[1].]
▸ **A** *adjective*. **1** Of, pertaining to, or serving a function, office, or purpose; relating to activity rather than to structure or form. M17. ▸**b** MEDICINE. Of a disorder (esp. mental): not caused by discernible organic disease. M19. ▸**c** *spec.* Of architecture etc.: designed only or primarily with a view to its purpose; practical, utilitarian. M20.

Times Lit. Suppl. In a good poem imagery and rhythm are functional, not merely decorative. R. F. CHAPMAN Even if there is no anatomical differentiation of the midgut there may be functional differentiation. **c** *Illustrated London News* The outside of this building is functional and severe.

functional food a food containing health-giving additives. **functional group** CHEMISTRY an atom or group of atoms present in a molecule of an organic compound which confers characteristic chemical properties on the compound.
2 MATH. Of or pertaining to a function (FUNCTION *noun* 5). E19.

functional calculus LOGIC = ***predicate calculus*** s.v. PREDICATE *noun*.
▸ **B** *noun*. MATH. A function the value of which is a scalar depending on the whole form of another function. E20.
■ **functioˈnality** *noun* L19. **functionally** *adverb* E19.

functionalise *verb* var. of FUNCTIONALIZE.

functionalism /ˈfʌŋ(k)ʃ(ə)n(ə)lɪz(ə)m/ *noun*. E20.
[ORIGIN from FUNCTIONAL + -ISM.]
1 SOCIAL SCIENCES. The study or interpretation of phenomena in terms of the functions which they fulfil (esp. within an overall system). E20. **2** Consideration for the function and purpose of a building etc. as regulating its design. M20.
■ **functionalist** *noun & adjective* (*a*) *noun* an adherent or student of functionalism; (*b*) *adjective* exhibiting or pertaining to functionalism: E20. **functionaˈlistic** *adjective* E20.

functionalize /ˈfʌŋ(k)ʃ(ə)n(ə)lʌɪz/ *verb trans*. Chiefly *US*. Also **-ise**. M19.
[ORIGIN formed as FUNCTIONALISM + -IZE.]
Assign to or place in some function or position; organize according to function.
■ **functionaliˈzation** *noun* E20.

functionary /ˈfʌŋ(k)ʃ(ə)n(ə)ri/ *noun*. L18.
[ORIGIN from FUNCTION *noun* + -ARY[1], after French *fonctionnaire*.]
A person having a duty or function to perform; an official.
■ **functionarism** *noun* (now *rare*) administration by functionaries; officialism: M19.

functionary /ˈfʌn(k)ʃ(ə)n(ə)ri/ *adjective*. E19.
[ORIGIN from FUNCTION *noun* + -ARY[2].]
Of or pertaining to a function, functional; *esp.* official.

functor /ˈfʌŋktə/ *noun*. M20.
[ORIGIN from FUNCTION *noun* + -OR, after *factor* etc.]
1 LOGIC. A function, an operator. M20. **2** LINGUISTICS. = ***function word*** s.v. FUNCTION *noun*. M20.
■ **funcˈtorial** *adjective* M20.

functus officio /ˌfʌŋktəs əˈfɪʃɪəʊ/ *pred. adjectival phr*. Pl. ***functi officio*** /ˈfʌŋktʌɪ/. M19.
[ORIGIN Latin = having discharged an office.]
LAW. Free from further obligations, having discharged its (or their) duty.

fund /fʌnd/ *noun*. M17.
[ORIGIN Latin *fundus* bottom. Partly refashioned from FOND *noun* after this.]
†**1** The bottom, the lowest part. M17–M18. †**2** Basis, foundation. L17–M18. **3** A source of supply, a permanent stock ready to be drawn upon. (Now chiefly of abstract things.) L17.

A. UTTLEY He had . . a fund of good humour and laughter. DAY LEWIS A certain fund of calm within myself.

4 a A stock or sum of money, esp. as set apart for a particular purpose. L17. ▸**b** In *pl.* The money at a person's disposal; financial resources. E18.

a A. C. BOULT He . . organized a fund to give concerts in hospitals. **b** R. CAMPBELL All my funds ran out but I got a job. A. EDEN My mother's effort to raise funds to build a cottage hospital.

5 *spec.* ▸†**a** A portion of revenue set apart as security for specified payments. L17–E19. ▸**b** In *pl.* (exc. in *comb.*). *The* stock of the national debt as a mode of investment; government securities. *arch.* E18.

b C. S. LEWIS He wore the expression of a nineteenth-century gentleman with something in the Funds.

6 = FOUNT *noun*[2]. L17.
– PHRASES: ***Consolidated Fund***: see CONSOLIDATE *verb* 1. **in funds** having money to spend. †**in the fund** at bottom. ***sinking fund***: see SINKING *verbal noun*. ***trust fund***: see TRUST *noun*.
– COMB.: **fundholder** (*a*) *arch.* a person who has money invested in the stock of the national debt; (*b*) a general practitioner controlling a budget provided to his or her practice by the National Health Service. **fund-raiser**, **fund-raising** (a person engaged in) persuading individuals or organizations to provide financial support for a cause, enterprise, etc.

fund /fʌnd/ *verb trans*. L18.
[ORIGIN from the noun.]
1 Orig., provide a fund (FUND *noun* 5b) for the regular payment of the interest on (a national debt). Now, convert (a floating debt) into a more or less permanent debt at a fixed rate of interest. Freq. as ***funded*** *pa. ppl adjective*. L18. ▸**b** Invest money in the stock of the national debt. *arch.* M19. **2** Put into a fund or store; collect or store (something abstract). E19.

R. FORD Every day . . we are unconsciously funding a stock of treasures . . of memory.

3 Supply with funds, finance (a person, position, or project). E20.

Science Journal A system in which research projects are funded by grants.

■ **fundable** *adjective* able to be funded L19. **funder** *noun* L19. **funding** *noun* (*a*) the action of the verb; (*b*) financial support: L18.

fundal /ˈfʌnd(ə)l/ *adjective*. L19.
[ORIGIN from FUNDUS + -AL[1].]
MEDICINE. Of or relating to the fundus of an organ, esp. the uterus or the eyeball.

fundament /ˈfʌndəm(ə)nt/ *noun*. ME.
[ORIGIN Old French & mod. French *fondement* from Latin *fundamentum*, from *fundare* FOUND *verb*[1]: see -MENT.]
†**1** The foundation or base of a wall, building, etc. Also, the action of founding a building, institution, etc.; the building itself. ME–L17.
†**2** The ground, basis, or principle on which anything is founded. ME–L17.
3 The buttocks, the anus. ME.
4 GEOGRAPHY. The landscape as it appeared before humans began to modify it by their activities. E20.

fundamenta divisionis, ***fundamenta relationis*** *noun phrs.* pls. of FUNDAMENTUM DIVISIONIS, FUNDAMENTUM RELATIONIS.

fundamental /fʌndəˈmɛnt(ə)l/ *adjective & noun*. LME.
[ORIGIN French *fondamental* or late Latin *fundamentalis*: see FUNDAMENT, -AL[1].]
▸ **A** *adjective*. **1** Of or pertaining to the basis or groundwork; going to the root of the matter. LME.

M. PATTISON The fundamental question of what is a University. J. MICHIE Is it that you simply aren't willing, Or have you a fundamental moral objection to killing?

2 Serving as the base or foundation; essential or indispensable. Also, primary, original; from which others are derived. LME.

GEO. ELIOT The ideas of strict law and order were fundamental to all his political teaching. S. WEINBERG The hadrons are .. composites of more fundamental particles, known as 'quarks'.

†**3** Of or pertaining to the foundation(s) of a building. E17–M18.
4 Of or pertaining to the fundament (sense 3). *joc.* M18.
5 Of a stratum: lowest, lying at the bottom. L18.
– SPECIAL COLLOCATIONS: **fundamental bass** a supposed bass line consisting of the roots of a series of chords. **fundamental note** (*a*) MUSIC the lowest note of a chord in its original (uninverted) form; (*b*) = ***fundamental tone*** below. **fundamental particle** = ***elementary particle*** s.v. ELEMENTARY *adjective* 4. **fundamental tone**: produced by vibration of a sonorous body acting as a whole (opp. ***harmonic***).
▸ **B** *noun*. **1** A basic or primary principle, rule, or article, which serves as the groundwork of a system; an essential part. Usu. in *pl.* M17.
2 A fundamental note or tone. E18.
■ **fundamenˈtality** *noun* (*rare*) E18. **fundamentally** *adverb* LME.

fundamentalism /fʌndəˈmɛnt(ə)lɪz(ə)m/ *noun*. E20.
[ORIGIN from FUNDAMENTAL + -ISM.]
The strict maintenance of traditional orthodox religious beliefs or doctrines; *esp.* belief in the inerrancy of Scripture and literal acceptance of the creeds as fundamentals of Protestant Christianity.
■ **fundamentalist** *noun & adjective* (*a*) *noun* an adherent of fundamentalism; (*b*) *adjective* of or pertaining to fundamentalism or fundamentalists: E20.

fundamentum divisionis /fʌndəˌmɛntəm dɪvɪʒɪˈəʊnɪs, dɪvɪz-/ *noun phr.* Pl. ***fundamenta divisionis*** /fʌndəˌmɛntə/. M19.
[ORIGIN Latin = foundation or basis of division.]
LOGIC. The principle or basis of logical division of a genus into its constituent species.

fundamentum relationis /fʌndəˌmɛntəm rɪˌleɪʃɪˈəʊnɪs/ *noun phr.* Pl. ***fundamenta relationis*** /fʌndəˌmɛntə/. M19.
[ORIGIN Latin = foundation of the relation.]
LOGIC. Those elements of the objective world that constitute the terms of a relation.

fundatrix /fʌnˈdeɪtrɪks/ *noun*. Pl. **-trices** /-trɪsiːz/. M16.
[ORIGIN mod. Latin, fem. of Latin *fundator*, from *fundat-*: see FOUNDATION, -TRIX.]
†**1** A foundress. Only in M16.
2 ENTOMOLOGY. The founding female of a colony of aphids, producing young parthenogenetically. E20.

fundi /ˈfʌndi/ *noun*[1]. M19.
[ORIGIN W. African name.]
= HUNGRY ***rice***.

fundi *noun*[2] pl. of FUNDUS.

fundie /ˈfʌndi/ *noun*. Sense 2 usu. **fundi**, pl. **-is**. L20.
[ORIGIN from FUNDAMENTALIST + -IE. Sense 2 is via German.]
1 A religious fundamentalist, *esp.* a Christian or Muslim fundamentalist. L20.
2 A radical member of the Green movement. Cf. REALO. L20.

fundiform /ˈfʌndɪfɔːm/ *adjective*. Now *rare*. M19.
[ORIGIN mod. Latin *fundiformis*, from Latin *funda* sling: see -FORM.]
ANATOMY. Sling-shaped; *spec.* designating ligaments (*a*) on the front of the ankle enclosing tendons of the extensor muscles of the leg, and (*b*) forming a loop enclosing the root of the penis.

fundus /ˈfʌndəs/ *noun*. Pl. **fundi** /-dʌɪ/. M18.
[ORIGIN Latin = bottom.]
ANATOMY. The more broadly rounded extremity of a hollow organ, usu. that part opposite to the external aperture; *spec.* (*a*) the upper extremity of the uterus; (*b*) the part of the interior of the eyeball opposite to the pupil.
■ **funduˈscopic** *adjective* of, pertaining to, or involving funduscopy M20. **funˈduscopy** *noun* ophthalmoscopy of the fundus of the eye M20.

funebrial /fjuːˈniːbrɪəl/ *adjective*. Now *rare*. L16.
[ORIGIN from Latin *funebris*, from *funus* funeral: see -IAL.]
= FUNEREAL.
■ Also **funebrious** *adjective* M17.

funeral /ˈfjuːn(ə)r(ə)l/ *noun*. LME.
[ORIGIN Old French *funeraille* collect. fem. sing., from medieval Latin *funeralia* neut. pl. of late Latin *funeralis*: see FUNERAL *adjective*.]
1 *sing.* & †in *pl.* (treated as *sing.*). The ceremonies connected with the burial or cremation of a dead body; a burial or cremation with its attendant ritual; obsequies. LME.
walking funeral: see WALKING *ppl adjective*.
†**2** In *pl.* Funeral expenses. L15–E17.
†**3** Death; a grave or monument. *poet.* L16–E18.
4 *sing.* & †in *pl.* A funeral sermon or service. Now *US*. E17.
5 A procession of mourners accompanying the corpse to the place of burial or cremation. L17.
6 *fig.* With *possess.*: one's own (unpleasant) concern, of which one must accept the consequences. *slang* (orig. *US*). M19.

M. GORDON It's your funeral I mean .. it's up to you.

funeral /ˈfjuːn(ə)r(ə)l/ *adjective* (now usu. regarded as *attrib.* use of the noun). LME.
[ORIGIN Old French from late Latin *funeralis*, from Latin *funer-*, *funus* funeral, death, corpse: see -AL[1].]
1 Of or pertaining to the ceremonial burial or cremation of the dead; concerned with a funeral or funerals. LME.
funeral expenses, ***funeral oration***, ***funeral procession***, ***funeral service***, etc. **funeral director** an undertaker. ***funeral escutcheon***: see ESCUTCHEON 1b. **funeral home** = ***funeral parlour*** below. ***funeral honours***: see HONOUR *noun*. **funeral parlour** an undertaker's establishment. **funeral pile**, **funeral pyre** a pile of wood etc. on which a corpse is burnt. **funeral urn**: holding the ashes of a cremated body.
2 = FUNEREAL. Now *rare*. LME.

BYRON The raven flaps her funeral wing.

funeralize /ˈfjuːn(ə)r(ə)lʌɪz/ *verb*. Also **-ise**. M17.
[ORIGIN from FUNERAL *adjective*, *noun* + -IZE.]
†**1** *verb trans.* Make sad or melancholy. Only in M17.
2 *verb trans.* & *intrans.* Hold a funeral for (a dead person or animal). Chiefly *US*. M19.

funerary /ˈfjuːn(ə)r(ə)ri/ *adjective*. L17.
[ORIGIN Late Latin *funerarius*, from Latin *funus*, *funer-*: see FUNERAL *adjective*, -ARY[1].]
Esp. ARCHAEOLOGY: of or pertaining to a funeral or burial; connected with a funeral or funerals.

funereal /fjuːˈnɪərɪəl/ *adjective*. E18.
[ORIGIN from Latin *funereus* from *funus*, *funer-* see FUNERAL *adjective*.]
Of, pertaining to, or appropriate to a funeral; gloomy, dark, dismal, mournful.

R. CHANDLER Along the empty halls through the big silent .. funereal living-room. O. MANNING The voice rose into a funereal wail.

■ **funereally** *adverb* M19.

funest /fjuːˈnɛst/ *adjective*. M17.
[ORIGIN Old French & mod. French *funeste* from Latin *funestus*, from *funus*: see FUNERAL *adjective*.]
Causing or portending death or evil; fatal, disastrous; dreadful.
■ Also †**funestal** *adjective*: only in M16.

fungaceous /fʌŋˈgeɪʃəs/ *adjective*. L19.
[ORIGIN from Latin FUNGUS + -ACEOUS.]
Of the nature of a fungus or fungi.

fungal /ˈfʌŋg(ə)l/ *adjective & noun*. M19.
[ORIGIN from FUNGUS + -AL[1].]
▸ **A** *adjective*. Of or pertaining to a fungus; of the nature of or resembling a fungus. M19.
▸ **B** *noun*. A fungus. Now *rare* or *obsolete*. M19.

fungate /ˈfʌŋgeɪt/ *verb intrans*. M19.
[ORIGIN from FUNGUS + -ATE[3].]
MEDICINE. Esp. of a tumour: grow outwards from a surface, with a fungoid appearance.
■ **funˈgation** *noun* E20.

†**funge** *noun*. LME.
[ORIGIN Old French *fonge* from Latin FUNGUS.]
1 A fungus. Only in LME.
2 [After Latin *fungus*.] A soft-headed person; a fool. M16–E17.

fungi *noun pl.* see FUNGUS

fungi- /ˈfʌndʒi, ˈfʌŋgi/ *combining form* of FUNGUS: see -I-.
■ **fungiform** *adjective* (chiefly ANATOMY, of papillae on the tongue) having the form of or resembling a fungus or mushroom E19. **fungiˈstasis** *noun* inhibition of the growth of fungi M20. **fungiˈstatic** *adjective* inhibiting the growth of fungi E20. **fungiˈstatically** *adverb* in a fungistatic manner, so as to inhibit the growth of fungi M20. **fungiˈtoxic** *adjective* poisonous to fungi M20. **fungitoˈxicity** *noun* toxicity to fungi M20. **fungivorous** /fʌnˈdʒɪv(ə)rəs/ *adjective* feeding on fungi or mushrooms E19.

fungible /ˈfʌndʒɪb(ə)l/ *noun & adjective*. L17.
[ORIGIN medieval Latin *fungibilis*, from *fungi* 'perform, enjoy' with sense as in *fungi vice* 'take the place of': see -IBLE.]
▸ **A** *noun*. LAW (chiefly *Scot.*). A thing which precisely or acceptably replaces or is replaceable by another. L17.
▸ **B** *adjective*. Chiefly LAW. Precisely or acceptably replacing or replaceable by another item, mutually interchangeable: esp. of goods etc. contracted for, when a particular item is not specified. E19.
■ **fungiˈbility** *noun* E20. **fungibly** *adverb* M20.

fungic /ˈfʌndʒɪk/ *adjective*. Now *rare*. E19.
[ORIGIN from FUNGUS + -IC.]
Of or pertaining to fungi, fungal.

fungicide /ˈfʌndʒɪsʌɪd, ˈfʌŋgɪ-/ *noun*. L19.
[ORIGIN from FUNGI- + -CIDE.]
An application or chemical for destroying fungi.
■ **fungiˈcidal** *adjective* of the nature of, acting as, or characteristic of a fungicide E20.

†**fungite** *noun*. L17–M18.
[ORIGIN from FUNGUS + -ITE[1].]
PALAEONTOLOGY. = ***mushroom coral*** s.v. MUSHROOM *noun* & *adjective*.

fungo /ˈfʌŋgəʊ/ *noun*. *US*. Pl. **-oes**. M19.
[ORIGIN Unknown.]
BASEBALL. A fly ball hit in the air for practice. Also (in full ***fungo bat***), a lightweight practice bat.

fungoid /ˈfʌŋgɔɪd/ *adjective & noun*. M19.
[ORIGIN from FUNGUS + -OID.]
▸ **A** *adjective*. Of, pertaining to, resembling, or of the nature of a fungus. M19.
▸ **B** *noun*. A fungus; a growth resembling a fungus. L19.

fungology /fʌŋˈgɒlədʒi/ *noun*. Now *rare*. M19.
[ORIGIN from FUNGUS + -OLOGY.]
The branch of science that deals with fungi; mycology.
■ **fungoˈlogical** *adjective* L19. **fungologist** *noun* M19.

fungous /ˈfʌŋgəs/ *adjective*. Also (now *rare*) **fungose** /-əʊs/. LME.
[ORIGIN from Latin *fungosus*, from FUNGUS: see -OUS, -OSE[1].]
1 Of or pertaining to a fungus or fungi; resembling or of the nature of a fungus. Also, affected by fungal growth. LME. ▸**b** MEDICINE. Of a tumour etc.: like a fungus in form or growth. M17.
2 Growing or springing up suddenly like a mushroom or toadstool; not durable or substantial. M18.
■ **funˈgosity** *noun* the quality or condition of being fungous; a fungous growth: E18.

fungus /ˈfʌŋgəs/ *noun*. Pl. **fungi** /ˈfʌŋgi, -gʌɪ, ˈfʌndʒi, -dʒʌɪ/, **funguses**. LME.
[ORIGIN Latin, prob. from Greek *sphoggos*, *spoggos* SPONGE *noun*[1]: cf. FUNGE.]
1 Any of a large division of organisms, including mushrooms, toadstools, moulds, rusts, yeasts, and constituents of lichens, which lack chlorophyll, reproduce as cryptogams, and grow on and obtain nutriment from organic matter; *esp.* a mushroom, toadstool, or similar kind. Also *collect.*, a growth formed by such organisms. LME. ▸**b** *fig.* Something growing rapidly or extensively. M18.

S. SPENDER A tree .. rotted by kidney-shaped fungus on the bark. **b** T. PAINE Aristocracy .. a kind of fungus growing out of the corruption of society.

bracket fungus: see BRACKET *noun*.
2 MEDICINE. A growth of soft or spongy diseased tissue on a surface, as a tumour etc. L17. ▸**b** A skin disease in fish. L19.
†**3** An excrescence of lampblack etc. on a wick. L18–E19.
4 A growth of facial hair, a beard. *slang*. E20.

H. HOBSON In addition to the chin-fungus he'd put on a little weight.

– COMB.: **fungus garden** a growth of a fungus cultivated by ants or termites as a source of food; **fungus gnat**, **fungus midge** a small fly of the family Mycetophilidae, the larvae of most of which feed on fungi.
– NOTE: Fungi have usu. been classified as plants but are sometimes regarded as constituting a distinct kingdom.

funicle /ˈfjuːnɪk(ə)l/ *noun*. M17.
[ORIGIN Anglicized from FUNICULUS.]
†**1** = FUNICULUS 1. Only in M17.
2 Any of certain filamentary anatomical structures; *spec.*: (*a*) ENTOMOLOGY a section of an insect's antenna, supporting the club; (*b*) BOTANY the stalk attaching a seed or ovule to the placenta. M19.

funicular /fjʊˈnɪkjʊlə, fəˈnɪk-/ *adjective & noun*. M17.
[ORIGIN formed as FUNICULUS + -AR[1].]
▸ **A** *adjective*. **1** Of or pertaining to a funiculus or funicle; of the nature of a funiculus; filamentary, cordlike. M17.
2 Of or pertaining to a rope or its tension; depending on or worked by a rope. E19.
– SPECIAL COLLOCATIONS: **funicular polygon** a figure assumed by a cord supported at its extremities and having weights attached at various points. **funicular railway**: a cable railway with ascending and descending cars counterbalanced.
▸ **B** *noun*. A funicular railway. E20.

F

funiculus /fjʊˈnɪkjʊləs/ *noun*. Pl. **-li** /-lʌɪ, -liː/. M17.
[ORIGIN Latin, dim. of *funis* rope: see -CULE.]
1 A thin rope or filament; *spec.* a hypothetical filament of matter postulated to support the column of mercury in Torricelli's experiment (which actually demonstrated atmospheric pressure). *obsolete* exc. *hist.* M17.
2 = FUNICLE 2. E19.

funiform /ˈfjuːnɪfɔːm/ *adjective*. M19.
[ORIGIN from Latin *funis* rope + -FORM.]
Shaped like a rope or cord.

funipendulous /fjuːnɪˈpɛndjʊləs/ *adjective*. E18.
[ORIGIN from Latin *funis* rope + PENDULOUS.]
Hanging from a rope; connected with a hanging rope. Chiefly *joc.*

†**funis** *noun*. LME.
[ORIGIN Latin = rope.]
ANATOMY. **1** One of the veins of the arm. Only in LME.
2 The umbilical cord. M18–M19.

†**funk** *noun*[1]. ME–L19.
[ORIGIN Middle Dutch *vonke* (Dutch *vonk*); cf. PUNK *noun*[2], SPUNK *noun*.]
A spark; something used as tinder, touchwood. Latterly only *dial.*

funk /fʌŋk/ *noun*[2] & *verb*[1]. E17.
[ORIGIN Uncertain; perh. French dial. *funkier* verb = Old French *funkier*, *fungier*, from popular Latin word repr. also by Italian *fumicare*, from late Latin *fumigare*, from Latin *fumus* smoke.]
▸ **A** *noun*. **1** A strong smell or stink, *esp.* of tobacco smoke. Now chiefly *US*. E17.
2 Funky music. *slang*. M20.
attrib.: A. J. AUGARDE Very popular with their loony, disjointed brand of funk rock.
▸ **B** *verb*. Now *rare* or *obsolete*.
1 *verb trans.* Blow smoke on (a person); annoy with smoke. L17. ▸**b** Smoke (a pipe, tobacco). E18.
2 *verb intrans.* Smoke. Also, cause a smell. L17.

funk /fʌŋk/ *noun*[3] & *verb*[2]. *slang*. M18.
[ORIGIN Uncertain; perh. = FUNK *noun*[2].]
▸ **A** *noun*. **1** Cowering fear; a state of panic or terror. M18.
W. BOYD A blind funk seized him and he felt . . he wouldn't be able to go through with it.
blue funk: see BLUE *adjective*.
2 A person who funks; a coward. M19.
– COMB.: **funk-hole** a place of safety, *esp.* in wartime, a dugout; *fig.* an employment used as a pretext for avoiding military service; **funkstick(s)** a coward.
▸ **B** *verb*. **1** *verb intrans.* Flinch or shrink through fear; show cowardice. Now *rare*. M18.
2 *verb trans.* Frighten. Now *rare*. E19.
3 *verb trans.* Fight shy of, wish or try to avoid through fear; be afraid of. M19.
E. NESBIT Now it was Albert's turn . . but he funked it. E. WAUGH Had arranged to go to Pixton. Funked train and took taxi.
■ **funker** *noun* M19.

funkia /ˈfʌŋkɪə/ *noun*. Also **funckia**. M19.
[ORIGIN mod. Latin *Funkia* former genus name (obsolete synonym of *Hosta*), from H. C. *Funck* (1771–1839), Prussian botanist: see -IA[1].]
= HOSTA.

funkster /ˈfʌŋkstə/ *noun*. *slang* (chiefly *US*). M20.
[ORIGIN from FUNK *noun*[2] + -STER.]
A performer or fan of funky music.

funky /ˈfʌŋki/ *adjective*[1]. *slang*. L18.
[ORIGIN from FUNK *noun*[2] + -Y[1].]
1 Smelling strong or bad; musty, mouldy. Chiefly *US*. L18.
2 Of jazz or other popular music: down-to-earth and uncomplicated; soulful and bluesy, with a strong rhythm that usu. accentuates the first beat in the bar. Also, fashionable, trendy. M20.
■ **funkily** *adverb* L20. **funkiness** *noun*[1] M20.

funky /ˈfʌŋki/ *adjective*[2]. *slang*. M19.
[ORIGIN from FUNK *noun*[3] + -Y[1].]
In a funk; frightened, nervous, timid.
■ **funkiness** *noun*[2] L19.

funnel /ˈfʌn(ə)l/ *noun* & *verb*. LME.
[ORIGIN App. from Old French (repr. also in Breton *founilh*), from Provençal *fonilh*, *enfonilh*, from Latin *infundibulum*, (late) *fundibulum*, from *(in)fundere* pour (in).]
▸ **A** *noun*. **1** A cone with a small hole or tube at the apex for guiding liquid (orig. esp. wine), powder, etc., through a narrow opening. LME.
2 A tube or shaft for lighting or ventilating; *esp.* the chimney of a steam engine or ship. M16. ▸**b** The flue of a chimney. L17.
3 NAUTICAL. A cylindrical band of metal; *esp.* as fitted to the head of a mast, to which the rigging is attached. L17.
4 Any funnel-shaped thing; ZOOLOGY a funnel-shaped organ; a funnel-shaped opening or shaft in rocks etc. E18.
– COMB.: **funnel beaker** ARCHAEOLOGY a pottery vessel with a flaring neck (***Funnel Beaker Culture***, a prehistoric culture of northern Europe characterized by the use of funnel beakers); **funnel cake** *US* a cake made of batter that is poured through a funnel into hot fat or oil, deep-fried until crisp, and served sprinkled with sugar; **funnel cap** a common edible European mushroom, *Clitocybe infundibuliformis*, with a cream-coloured funnel-shaped cap; **funnel cloud** a rotating funnel-shaped cloud forming the core of a tornado or waterspout; **funnel neck** a high, wide neck on a garment, esp. a sweater; **funnel-web** (***a***) a spider's web with a funnel shape; (***b***) *Austral. colloq.* = ***funnel-web spider*** (a) below; **funnel-web spider** a spider which builds a funnel-shaped web; *esp.* (***a***) one of the family Dipluridae, *spec.* the highly venomous *Atrax robustus* of eastern Australia; (***b***) *US* one of the family Agelenidae. **funnel-web tarantula** = ***funnel-web spider*** (a) above.
▸ **B** *verb*. Infl. **-ll-**, ***-l-**.
1 *verb intrans.* Issue (*out*) or rise (*up*) (as) from a funnel or in a funnel-shaped cloud; move (as) through a funnel. L16.
S. PLATH From between two hills a sudden wind funnels at me. I. BANKS The children were entering the forest, funnelling into the path between the pines.
2 *verb trans.* Cause to move (as) through a funnel; direct, channel. E20.
Scientific American Three magnetic spectrometers, which funnel the electrons into a system of detectors. D. ARKELL Could he funnel those bursting energies down narrow scholastic paths?
■ **funnelled** *ppl adjective* (***a***) provided with a funnel or funnels; funnel-shaped; (***b***) directed (as) through a funnel: L18.

funny /ˈfʌni/ *noun*[1]. *arch.* L18.
[ORIGIN Uncertain: perh. from the adjective.]
A light narrow rowing boat.

funny /ˈfʌni/ *adjective*, *noun*[2], & *adverb*. M18.
[ORIGIN from FUN *noun* + -Y[1].]
▸ **A** *adjective*. **1** Producing fun; comical, amusing. M18.
CONAN DOYLE Excuse my amusement . . but it is really funny to see you trying to play a hand with no cards in it. HENRY MILLER A comedienne of the first water, the only really funny woman I ever met.
2 Not quite in good health or good order; slightly unwell, nauseous, deranged, disordered, etc. Formerly also, tipsy. *colloq.* M18.
J. GRENFELL You let him in . . . I feel funny. B. BAINBRIDGE Bernard probably needed exercise on account of his funny hip.
3 Curious, queer, odd. *colloq.* E19. ▸**b** Underhand, tricky, deceitful; unorthodox. L19.
V. S. REID Funny thing, but when Father is vexed he looks more like white man than brown. B. EMECHETA There was something funny with that ear, it was definitely bigger than the other. **b** P. G. WODEHOUSE He is far too scared of our hostess to try any funny stuff on her.
– SPECIAL COLLOCATIONS & COMB.: **funny bone** the part of the elbow over which the ulnar nerve passes, a blow on which can produce a tingling sensation. **funny business** *slang* jesting, comic behaviour; messing about; deception, underhand behaviour. **funny column**: (in a newspaper etc.) containing humorous matter. **funny farm** *slang* a psychiatric hospital. **funny ha-ha** *colloq.* = sense 1 above. **funny man** a clown or jester. **funny money** *colloq.* (***a***) money reduced in value by rapid inflation; (***b***) counterfeit currency; (***c***) finances amassed by dubious methods. **funny paper** a newspaper etc. containing humorous matter. **funny-peculiar** *colloq.* = sense 3 above.
▸ **B** *noun*. A joke; (usu. in *pl.*) the comic strip(s) in a newspaper etc. M19.
▸ **C** *adverb*. Funnily. *colloq.* M19.
C. M. YONGE They speak so funny, I can't hardly make them out.
■ **funnily** *adverb* in a funny manner; amusingly; oddly: E19. **funniment** *noun* (*joc.*, now *rare* or *obsolete*) comicality; something comical: M19. **funniness** *noun* M19. **funniˈosity** *noun* (*joc.*) [-OSITY] comicality; something or someone comic: L19.

funster /ˈfʌnstə/ *noun*. *colloq.* L18.
[ORIGIN from FUN *noun* + -STER.]
A person who makes fun, a joker.

fur /fəː/ *noun*[1] & *adjective*. ME.
[ORIGIN from FUR *verb*.]
▸ **A** *noun*. **1** The dressed coat of any of various animals, or fabric imitating this (now freq. in *pl.*); a trimming, lining, or garment made of this; *esp.* a piece of fur worn around the neck. ME. ▸**b** Fur worn as a mark of office or state, or as a badge of certain degrees. M17.
W. HOLTBY Muffled in furs to the nose, she did not feel cold.
2 The short, fine, soft hair of certain animals as distinct from the longer coarser hair. LME. ▸**b** In *pl.* Animal skins with the fur on them. M16. ▸**c** *collect.* Furred animals. E19.
LONGFELLOW Cold would the winter be, for thick was the fur of the foxes. P. H. JOHNSON The cat . . jumped down, leaving . . clouds of fur upon her skirt. **b** W. IRVING Mr. Clarke . . packed all his furs on twenty-eight horses.
make the fur fly (orig. *US slang*) make a disturbance, stir up trouble. **c fur and feather** game animals and birds.
3 HERALDRY. A tincture representing animal skins or portions of skins as if sewn together. M16.
4 Something resembling fur or adhering to a surface like fur; *esp.* (***a***) a coating formed on the tongue in ill health; (***b***) the deposit formed by hard water in a kettle, pipe, etc. L17.
DICKENS Empty wine bottles with fur and fungus choking up their throats. S. O'FAOLÁIN The fur of mildew and green damp.
– COMB.: **furball** (***a***) = ***hairball*** s.v. HAIR *noun*; (***b***) *colloq.* a furry pet animal; **fur seal** any of several eared seals constituting the genera *Arctocephalus* and *Callorhinus*, with thick fur on the underside (the source of sealskin for garments).
▸ **B** *attrib.* or as *adjective*. Made of fur. ME.
A. SILLITOE Her brown coat with its fur collar.
be all fur coat and no knickers *colloq.* have an impressive or sophisticated appearance which belies the fact that there is nothing to substantiate it.
■ **furless** *adjective* M19.

fur *noun*[2] see FURROW *noun*.

fur /fəː/ *verb*. Infl. **-rr-**. ME.
[ORIGIN Anglo-Norman, var. of Old French *forrer* (mod. *fourrer*) line, encase, sheathe, from *forre*, *fuerre* sheath from Germanic.]
1 *verb trans.* Line, trim, or cover (a garment etc.) with fur. ME. ▸**b** Serve as a lining or trimming for. L16.
H. AINSWORTH A robe of violet-coloured velvet, furred with . . ermine. **b** T. POWELL As many fox-skins as will fur his . . gowne.
2 *verb trans.* Clothe or adorn (a person) with fur or furs. LME. ▸**b** In *pass.* Be covered with fur. M17.
SIR W. SCOTT Miss Mannering was furred and mantled up to the throat.
3 *verb trans.* Cover or coat with a deposit of fur (cf. FUR *noun*[1] 4). M16.
N. GORDIMER The bath . . was furred with putty-coloured lime like an old kettle. *fig.*: W. GOLDING We are so furred up with the growth of . . laborious knowledge.
4 *verb intrans.* Become covered or coated (as) with fur. M16.
OED This kettle soon furs.
5 *verb trans.* CARPENTRY. Fix a timber strip to (uneven joists etc.) to make a plane surface. L17.

fur. *abbreviation*.
furlong(s).

†**furacan** *noun* see HURRICANE.

furacious /fjʊ(ə)ˈreɪʃəs/ *adjective*. Now *rare*. L17.
[ORIGIN from Latin *furax*, *furac-* (from *furari* steal) + -IOUS: see -ACIOUS.]
Given to thieving, thievish.
■ **furacity** *noun* the inclination or tendency to steal E17.

furaldehyde /fjʊəˈraldɪhʌɪd/ *noun*. E20.
[ORIGIN from FURFURALDEHYDE.]
CHEMISTRY. Either of two isomeric aldehydes, $C_4H_3(CHO)O$, derived from furan; *esp.* (more fully *2-furaldehyde*) = FURFURALDEHYDE.

furan /ˈfjʊəran/ *noun*. L19.
[ORIGIN from FURFURAN.]
CHEMISTRY. An unsaturated heterocyclic compound, $(CH)_4O$, which has a planar five-membered ring in its molecule and is a colourless volatile liquid; any substituted derivative of this.
■ **furanose** *noun* a sugar with a molecular structure containing the five-membered (C_4O) ring present in furan E20. **fuˈranoside** *noun* a glycoside of a sugar in the furanose form M20.

furbelow /ˈfəːbɪləʊ/ *noun*, *adjective*, & *verb*. L17.
[ORIGIN Alt. of FALBALA.]
▸ **A** *noun*. **1** A gathered or pleated strip or border on a skirt or petticoat; a flounce, a ruffle; (in *pl.*, *derog.*) showy ornamentation or trimming on a garment (usu. a woman's). L17.
L. M. MONTGOMERY Those dresses are good, sensible, serviceable dresses, without any frills or furbelows about them.
2 In *pl.* (treated as *sing.*). A seaweed, *Saccorhiza polyschides*, with large frilly fronds divided into ribbons at the ends. M19.
▸ **B** *attrib.* or as *adjective*. Having or suggestive of a furbelow or furbelows. L17.
▸ **C** *verb trans.* Ornament with (something resembling) a furbelow or furbelows. Chiefly as ***furbelowed*** *ppl adjective*. E18.
A. UTTLEY Cold chickens and galantines, all white-frilled and furbelowed.

furbery *noun* var. of FOURBERY.

furbish /ˈfəːbɪʃ/ *verb* & *noun*. LME.
[ORIGIN Old French *forbiss-* lengthened stem of *forbir* (mod. *fourbir*) from Germanic (repr. by Old High German *furben*): see -ISH[2].]
▸ **A** *verb trans.* **1** Remove the rust from, burnish, polish *up* (a sword, armour, etc.). *arch.* LME.
GEO. ELIOT Old arms duly furbished.
2 Clean *up*, renovate, give a new look to; refurbish. L16.
E. BOWEN Artificial forget-me-nots . . to furbish up country summer hats.
▸ **B** *noun*. An act of furbishing. E19.
■ **furbisher** *noun* LME.

furca /ˈfəːkə/ *noun*. Pl. **-cae** /-siː, -kiː/. E17.
[ORIGIN Latin = FORK *noun*.]
1 ROMAN ANTIQUITIES. A gallows. Now *rare* or *obsolete*. E17.
2 ENTOMOLOGY etc. ▸**a** An apodeme or process in the thorax of many insects. L19. ▸**b** A pair of diverging processes at the end of the abdomen in certain crustaceans. Also = FURCULA 3. E20.
■ **furcal** *adjective* furcate; of or pertaining to a furca: M19.

5 A characteristic or peculiarity of one person or thing. L19.

6 *BIOLOGY.* Symbiosis in which the product of the association appears to be a distinct organism, as in lichen. L19.

■ **individualist** *noun & adjective* (*a*) *noun* a person who takes an independent or egoistic course in thought or action; an adherent of individualism; (*b*) *adjective* = INDIVIDUALISTIC: M19. **individua'listic** *adjective* of or pertaining to individualism or individualists; characterized by individualism: L19. **individua'listically** *adverb* L19.

individuality /ˌɪndɪvɪdjʊˈalɪti/ *noun.* E17.
[ORIGIN from INDIVIDUAL + -ITY. In early use from medieval Latin *individualitas*.]

1 The sum of the attributes which distinguish one person or thing from others of the same kind; strongly marked individual character; in *pl.*, individual characteristics. E17.

> J. McDOUGALL It is parents who give their children a sense of self, enjoyment in their individuality.

2 Indivisibility, inseparability; an indivisible or inseparable thing. Now *rare* or *obsolete*. M17.

3 The fact or condition of existing as an individual; separate and continuous existence; the action or position of individual members of a society. M17.

> BURKE Individuality is left out of their scheme of government. The state is all in all. W. PALEY Consciousness carries identity and individuality along with it.

4 An individual thing or personality. L18.

individualize /ɪndɪˈvɪdjʊ(ə)lʌɪz/ *verb trans.* Also **-ise**. M17.
[ORIGIN from INDIVIDUAL + -IZE.]

1 Make individual or give an individual character to; characterize, distinguish by distinctive qualities, esp. from other persons or things. M17.

2 Point out or notice individually; specify, particularize. Now *rare*. M17.

■ **individualizer** *noun* M19. **individuali'zation** *noun* the action of individualizing; the fact or condition of being individualized: M18.

individually /ɪndɪˈvɪdjʊ(ə)li/ *adverb.* L16.
[ORIGIN from INDIVIDUAL + -LY[2].]

†1 Indivisibly; inseparably. L16–E17.

2 Personally; in an individual capacity. M17.

> M. R. MITFORD To me individually it would be a great release to be quit . . of the garden.

3 In an individual or distinctive manner; as individuals; singly, one by one. M17.

> D. ROWE Individually we are very weak, but as part of a group we can be . . strong.

– PHRASES: †**individually the same** identically the same. **individually different** different as individuals though perhaps identical in species.

†**individuate** *adjective.* E17.
[ORIGIN medieval Latin *individuatus* pa. pple, formed as INDIVIDUATE *verb*: see -ATE[2].]

1 Undivided, indivisible, inseparable. E17–M18.

2 = INDIVIDUATED 2. Only in 17.

individuate /ɪndɪˈvɪdjʊeɪt/ *verb trans.* E17.
[ORIGIN medieval Latin *individuat-* pa. ppl stem of *individuare*, from Latin *individuus*: see INDIVIDUAL, -ATE[3].]

1 Give an individual character to; distinguish from others of the same kind; individualize; single out. E17.

> P. L. COURTIER The heart, that loves its object to select, To individuate.

2 Form into an individual or distinct entity; give individual organization or form to. M17.

> J. SCOTT That which individuates any Society, or makes it a distinct Body . . , is the Charter or Law.

■ **individuative** *adjective* (*rare*) individualizing M19.

individuated /ɪndɪˈvɪdjʊeɪtɪd/ *ppl adjective.* M17.
[ORIGIN from INDIVIDUATE *verb* + -ED[1].]

†1 Undivided, indivisible, inseparable. M–L17.

2 Made individual; individualized. L17. ▸**b** *PSYCHOLOGY.* Of a person: that has been through the process of individuation. M20.

individuation /ˌɪndɪvɪdjʊˈeɪʃ(ə)n/ *noun.* E17.
[ORIGIN medieval Latin *individuatio(n-)*, formed as INDIVIDUATE *verb*: see -ATION.]

1 The action or process of individuating, or of distinguishing as individual; *SCHOLASTIC PHILOSOPHY* the means to individual existence, as distinct from that of the species. E17. ▸**b** *JUNGIAN PSYCHOLOGY.* The process of establishing the wholeness and autonomy of the individual self by the integration of consciousness and the collective unconscious. E20.

2 The condition of being an individual; individuality, personal identity. M17.

3 *BIOLOGY.* The development or maintenance of a functional organic unity; in colonial organisms, the development of separate but interdependent units. M19.

†**individuity** *noun.* E17–E19.
[ORIGIN medieval Latin *individuitas*, from Latin *individuus*: see INDIVIDUAL, -ITY.]
Individuality.

individuum /ɪndɪˈvɪdjʊəm/ *noun.* Now *rare*. Pl. **-dua** /-djʊə/ (chiefly in senses 1, 2), **-duums** (chiefly in sense 3). M16.
[ORIGIN Latin = indivisible particle, atom, (in late Latin) an individual, use as noun of neut. of *individuus*: see INDIVIDUAL.]

1 Esp. in *SCHOLASTIC LOGIC.* A member of a species; = INDIVIDUAL *noun* 1b. M16.

2 Something which cannot be divided; an indivisible entity. L16.

3 An individual person or thing. L16.

indivisible /ɪndɪˈvɪzɪb(ə)l/ *adjective & noun.* LME.
[ORIGIN Late Latin *indivisibilis*, formed as IN-[3] + *divisibilis* DIVISIBLE.]

▸ **A** *adjective.* Not divisible; that cannot be divided; incapable of being distributed among a number. LME.

> C. THUBRON So flat and brown were both land and water they seemed indivisible.

▸ **B** *noun.* Something which cannot be divided; an indivisible entity. M17.

■ **indivisi'bility** *noun* M17. **indivisibleness** *noun* (now *rare*) M17. **indivisibly** *adverb* M16.

indivision /ɪndɪˈvɪʒ(ə)n/ *noun.* Now *rare*. E17.
[ORIGIN Late Latin *indivisio(n-)*, from Latin IN-[3] + *divisio(n-)* DIVISION.]
Lack of division; undivided condition.

Indo- /ˈɪndəʊ/ *combining form*[1].
[ORIGIN from Latin *Indus*, Greek *Indos* Indian: see -O-.]
Forming nouns and adjectives with the sense 'Indian and —', chiefly denoting the combination of Indian with some other (ethnological or linguistic) characteristic.

■ **Indo-Aby'ssinian** *adjective* of or pertaining to both the Dravidians of India and the Hamites of NE Africa L19. **Indo-'African** *adjective* (*a*) of or pertaining to both India and Africa; (*b*) pertaining to Indians and Africans in South Africa: M19. **Indo-'Anglian** *adjective & noun* (*a*) *adjective* of or pertaining to literature in English written by Indian authors; (*b*) *noun* a writer of such literature: L19. **Indo-'British** *adjective* of or pertaining to both India and Great Britain, or Indo-Britons, or British rule in India; Anglo-Indian: E20. **Indo-'Briton** *noun* = ANGLO-INDIAN *noun* M19. **Indo-Chi'nese** *adjective & noun* (*a*) *adjective* of or pertaining to Indo-China, the SE Asian peninsula containing Myanmar (Burma), Thailand, Malaya, Laos, Cambodia, and Vietnam, or (*hist.*) French Indo-China, the French colonies of Laos, Cambodia, and Vietnam; (*b*) *noun* (pl. same) a native or inhabitant of (French) Indo-China: E19. **Indo-Ger'manic** *noun & adjective* = INDO-EUROPEAN *noun* 1 & *adjective* E19. **Indo-'Germanist** *noun* = INDO-EUROPEANIST L19. **Indo-'Hittite** *noun* a hypothetical language believed to be the common ancestor of Indo-European and Hittite E20. **Indo-Ma'layan** *adjective* of or pertaining to both India and Malaya; *spec.* designating an ethnological region comprising Sri Lanka, the Malay peninsula, and the Malayan islands: M19. **Indo-Pa'cific** *adjective & noun* (*a*) *adjective* of or pertaining to the Indian Ocean and the adjacent parts of the Pacific; of or pertaining to the group of languages (usu. called ***Austronesian***) spoken in the islands of this region; (*b*) *noun* the Indo-Pacific seas or ocean: L19. **Indo-Pak** *adjective* (*colloq.*) = INDO-PAKISTANI *adjective* M20. **Indo-Paki'stan, Indo-Paki'stani** *adjectives* pertaining to both India and Pakistan, or their inhabitants M20. **Indo-Portu'guese** *noun & adjective* (of or pertaining to) modified Portuguese as used in parts of India L19. **Indo-Sara'cenic** *adjective* designating or pertaining to an architectural style combining Indian and Muslim features L19. **Indo-'Scythian** *noun & adjective* (*a*) *noun* a member of an ancient central Asian people of Scythian origin, dominant in northern India and Bactria *c* 128 BC–*c* AD 450; (*b*) *adjective* of or pertaining to the Indo-Scythians: L18.

indo- /ˈɪndəʊ/ *combining form*[2].
[ORIGIN from IND(IGO + -O-.]
CHEMISTRY. Used in names of compounds related to or derived from indigo, esp. derivatives of indole.

■ **indo'aniline** *noun* a violet aniline dye, $O{=}C_6H_4{=}N{\cdot}C_6H_4NH_2$; any derivative of this: L19.

Indo- /ˈɪndəʊ/ *combining form*[3].
[ORIGIN from *Indus* (see below) + -O-.]
Of or pertaining to the River Indus in the northern part of the Indian subcontinent.

■ **Indo-Gan'getic** *adjective* of the Rivers Indus and Ganges; *spec.* designating the plain through which they flow, occupying much of the northern part of the Indian subcontinent: L19.

Indo-Aryan /ɪndəʊˈɛːrɪən/ *adjective & noun.* M19.
[ORIGIN from INDO-[1] + ARYAN.]
(Designating or pertaining to) the Indian branch of the Indo-Iranian language family, including Sanskrit, Prakrit, and Pali, and the modern languages Hindi, Bengali, Marathi, Nepalese, Sinhalese, etc., and often also including the Dard languages (in this wider sense also called ***Indic***).

indochinite /ɪndəʊˈtʃʌɪnʌɪt/ *noun.* M20.
[ORIGIN from *Indo-China* (see INDO-CHINESE + -ITE[1].]
GEOLOGY. A tektite from the strewn field of Indo-China.

†**indocible** *adjective.* M16–L18.
[ORIGIN French, or late Latin *indocibilis* from *docibilis* DOCIBLE, or from IN-[3] + DOCIBLE.]
Incapable of being taught or instructed; unteachable.

■ †**indocibility** *noun* E17–M19.

indocile /ɪnˈdəʊsʌɪl/ *adjective.* E17.
[ORIGIN French, or Latin *indocilis* from *docilis* DOCILE, or from IN-[3] + DOCILE.]
Not docile; not teachable or submissive, intractable.

■ **indo'cility** *noun* M17.

indoctrinate /ɪnˈdɒktrɪneɪt/ *verb trans.* Also (*rare*) †**en-**. E17.
[ORIGIN from INDOCTRINE + -ATE[3], or from IN-[2], EN-[1] + DOCTRINATE.]

1 Teach (a person); instruct *in* a subject, bring *into* the knowledge of something. E17. ▸**b** Teach (a subject etc.) *rare*. E19.

> D. LIVINGSTONE No pains whatever are taken to indoctrinate the adults of the tribe. C. GEIKIE He rather trained their spiritual character than indoctrinated them in systematic theology.

2 Imbue with an idea or doctrine; *spec.* teach systematically to accept (esp. partisan or tendentious) ideas uncritically; brainwash. M19.

> W. LIPPMANN With the instruments of the terror, censorship and propaganda, the fascist leaders indoctrinated the mass. D. LODGE They had been indoctrinated since adolescence with the idea . . that contraception was a grave sin.

■ **indoctri'nation** *noun* the action or process of indoctrinating; formal instruction; (an instance of) brainwashing: M17. **indoctrinator** *noun* L19. **indoctrinatory** *adjective* that indoctrinates; relating or pertaining to indoctrination: M20.

†**indoctrine** *verb trans.* Also (earlier) **en-**. LME–E19.
[ORIGIN Old French *endoctriner*, formed as EN-[1], IN-[2] + DOCTRINE.]
Teach, instruct.

Indo-European /ˌɪndəʊjʊərəˈpiːən/ *noun & adjective.* E19.
[ORIGIN from INDO-[1] + EUROPEAN.]

▸ **A** *noun* **1 a** The group of cognate languages which includes most European and many Asian ones; the hypothetical parent language of this group (also called ***primitive Indo-European***, ***Proto-Indo-European***). E19. ▸**b** A speaker of an Indo-European language; *spec.* a speaker of Proto-Indo-European. M19.

2 †**a** An Indianized European. *rare*. Only in E19. ▸**b** A native or inhabitant of SE Asia who is wholly or partly of European descent. M20.

▸ **B** *adjective.* Of, pertaining to, or characteristic of Indo-European or Indo-Europeans. E19.

■ **Indo-Europeanist** *noun* an expert in or student of the Indo-European languages E20.

Indo-Iranian /ˌɪndəʊɪˈreɪnɪən, -ˈrɑː-/ *adjective & noun.* L19.
[ORIGIN from INDO-[1] + IRANIAN.]

▸ **A** *adjective.* Of or pertaining to both India and Iran; *spec.* designating a branch of Indo-European comprising the Indo-Aryan (Indic) and Iranian languages. L19.

▸ **B** *noun.* The Indo-Iranian languages collectively; a speaker of (any of) these. L19.

indole /ˈɪndəʊl/ *noun.* Also (now *rare*) **-ol** /-ɒl/. M19.
[ORIGIN from INDO-[2] + -OLE[2].]
CHEMISTRY. A crystalline heteroaromatic compound, C_8H_7N, which has a molecule consisting of fused benzene and pyrrole rings, has an unpleasant odour, and occurs in coal tar, in faeces, and (as derivatives) in plants.

– COMB.: **indoleacetic** *adjective*: ***indoleacetic acid***, each of seven isomeric acetic acid derivatives of indole; *esp.* one of these (***indole-3-acetic acid***), which is an important plant growth hormone.

■ **in'dolic** *adjective* containing, derived from, characteristic of, or characterized by indole E20. **'indolyl** *noun* the radical $\cdot C_8H_6N$, of which seven isomers exist, derived from indole (***indolylacetic acid*** = ***indoleacetic acid*** above) E20.

indolence /ˈɪnd(ə)l(ə)ns/ *noun.* E17.
[ORIGIN French, or Latin *indolentia* freedom from pain, formed as IN-[3] + *dolent-* pres. ppl stem of *dolere* suffer or give pain: see -ENCE.]

†1 Insensibility or indifference to pain. E17–E18.

†2 Freedom from pain; a neutral state in which neither pain nor pleasure is felt. M17–M18.

3 The inclination to avoid exertion or trouble; love of ease, laziness; idleness. E18.

> A. MUNRO Tahiti to her means palm trees . . and the sort of . . indolence that has never interested her. C. PETERS Her indolence—she habitually stayed in bed all morning.

■ Also †**indolency** *noun* E17–M18.

indolent /ˈɪnd(ə)l(ə)nt/ *adjective.* M17.
[ORIGIN Late Latin *indolent-*, *-ens*, formed as IN-[3] + *dolent-*: see INDOLENCE, -ENT.]

1 *MEDICINE.* Of an ulcer, tumour, etc.: causing no pain, painless. Also, slow to heal, (of a disease or condition) slow to develop. M17.

2 Averse to work or exertion; self-indulgent, lazy, idle. E18.

> HOR. WALPOLE I am naturally indolent and without application to any kind of business. R. P. WARREN An appearance of swiftness and great competence despite the indolent posture. E. TEMPLETON She wandered from one dusky room into the other, too indolent to put the light on.

■ **indolently** *adverb* E18.

indoles /ˈɪndɒliːz/ *noun. rare.* L17.
[ORIGIN Latin, from *indu-* in, within, + root of *alescere* grow up: see ADOLESCENT.]
Innate quality or character.

Indology /ɪnˈdɒlədʒi/ *noun.* L19.
[ORIGIN from INDO-[1] + -LOGY.]
The branch of knowledge that deals with the history, literature, philosophy, etc., of India.

■ **Indo'logical** *adjective* M20. **Indologist** *noun* E20.

inexplorable /ɪnɪk'splɔːrəb(ə)l, ɪnɛk-/ *adjective*. M17.
[ORIGIN from IN-[3] + EXPLORE + -ABLE.]
Unable to be explored.

inexplosive /ɪnɪk'spləʊsɪv, ɪnɛk-/ *adjective*. M19.
[ORIGIN from IN-[3] + EXPLOSIVE *adjective*.]
Not explosive; not liable to or capable of explosion.

inexpressible /ɪnɪk'sprɛsɪb(ə)l, ɪnɛk-/ *adjective & noun*. E17.
[ORIGIN from IN-[3] + EXPRESSIBLE.]
▸ **A** *adjective*. Unable to be expressed in words; unutterable, indescribable. E17.
▸ **B** *noun*. **1** An inexpressible thing. M17.
2 *spec*. In *pl*. Trousers. *arch. colloq.* L18.
■ **inexpressibly** *adverb* M17.

inexpressive /ɪnɪk'sprɛsɪv, ɪnɛk-/ *adjective*. M17.
[ORIGIN from IN-[3] + EXPRESSIVE.]
1 = INEXPRESSIBLE *adjective*. *arch.* M17.
2 Not expressive; not expressing (a) meaning, feeling, character, etc. M18.
■ **inexpressively** *adverb* E19. **inexpressiveness** *noun* E19.

inexpugnable /ɪnɪk'spʌgnəb(ə)l, ɪnɛk-/ *adjective*. LME.
[ORIGIN Old French & mod. French from Latin *inexpugnabilis*, formed as IN-[3] + *expugnabilis* EXPUGNABLE.]
(Of a fortress, army, country, etc.) unable to be taken by assault or overthrown by force; impregnable; invincible.

> *fig.*: MRS H. WARD A certain inexpugnable dignity surrounded him.

■ **inexpugnably** *adverb* M17. **inexpugnableness** *noun* E18.

inexpungible /ɪnɪk'spʌndʒɪb(ə)l, ɪnɛk-/ *adjective*. Also **-geable** /-dʒəb(ə)l/. L19.
[ORIGIN from IN-[3] + EXPUNGE + -IBLE.]
Unable to be expunged or obliterated.

inextended /ɪnɪk'stɛndɪd, ɪnɛk-/ *adjective*. *rare*. M18.
[ORIGIN from IN-[3] + EXTENDED.]
Unextended; without extension.

inextensible /ɪnɪk'stɛnsɪb(ə)l, ɪnɛk-/ *adjective*. M19.
[ORIGIN from IN-[3] + EXTENSIBLE.]
Not extensible; unable to be stretched or drawn out in length.
■ **inextensi'bility** *noun* (*rare*) E19.

in extenso /ɪn ɪk'stɛnsəʊ, ɛk-/ *adverbial phr*. E19.
[ORIGIN Latin, from *in* in + *extenso* ablative of *extensus*: see EXTENSE.]
In full, at length.

> M. MEYER A wonderfully mature assessment which repays quoting *in extenso*.

inextinct /ɪnɪk'stɪŋkt, ɪnɛk-/ *adjective*. *rare*. E17.
[ORIGIN Latin *inex(s)tinctus*, or from IN-[3] + EXTINCT *adjective*.]
Unextinguished. Chiefly *fig*.

> J. WILSON He had not supposed such a capacity of love had yet remained inextinct.

inextinguishable /ɪnɪk'stɪŋgwɪʃəb(ə)l, ɪnɛk-/ *adjective*. L15.
[ORIGIN from IN-[3] + EXTINGUISH + -ABLE.]
Unable to be extinguished; unquenchable; indestructible.
■ **inextinguishably** *adverb* E19.

inextinguished /ɪnɪk'stɪŋgwɪʃt, ɪnɛk-/ *adjective*. Now *rare*. M18.
[ORIGIN from IN-[3] + EXTINGUISH + -ED[1].]
Not extinguished; still burning.

inextirpable /ɪnɪk'stəːpəb(ə)l, ɪnɛk-/ *adjective*. E17.
[ORIGIN Latin *inex(s)tirpabilis*, formed as IN-[3] + *ex(s)tirpare* EXTIRPATE: see -ABLE.]
Unable to be extirpated or rooted out.

in extremis /ɪn ɛk'striːmɪs, ɪk-/ *adverbial phr*. M16.
[ORIGIN Latin, from *in* in + *extremis* ablative pl. of *extremus*: see EXTREME.]
At the point of death; in great difficulty.

inextricable /ɪn'ɛkstrɪkəb(ə)l, ɪnɪk'strɪk-/ *adjective*. M16.
[ORIGIN Latin *inextricabilis*, formed as IN-[3] + *extricare* EXTRICATE: see -ABLE.]
1 (Of a circumstance) unable to be escaped from; (of a place, esp. a maze) so complicated or confusing that no means of exit can be found (now *rare*). M16.

> E. COOKE That he should run himself into inextricable Danger by going on.

2 (Of a knot, coil, etc.) unable to be disentangled or untied; (of a problem, difficulty, argument, etc.) unable to be solved or resolved, intricately involved or confused. E17. ▸**b** Of a grasp: unable to be loosened or detached. M19.

> S. SPENDER They know inextricable knots which bind each to himself. L. DURRELL For those of us . . who are at all conscious of the inextricable tangle of human thoughts.

3 Intricate, elaborate, exquisitely wrought. *rare*. L17.

> HANNAH MORE A net of such exquisite art and inextricable workmanship.

■ **inextrica'bility** *noun* M19. **inextricably** *adverb* L16.

†**ineye** *verb trans*. *rare*. LME–E18.
[ORIGIN from IN-[2] + EYE *noun*, after Latin *inoculare*.]
HORTICULTURE. Engraft.

INF *abbreviation*.
Intermediate-range nuclear force(s).

inf /ɪnf/ *noun*. M20.
[ORIGIN Abbreviation.]
MATH. Infimum (of).

inface /'ɪnfeɪs/ *noun*. L19.
[ORIGIN Contr. of *inward facing escarpment*.]
PHYSICAL GEOGRAPHY. The steep scarp face of a cuesta.

infall /'ɪnfɔːl/ *noun*. M17.
[ORIGIN from IN-[1] + FALL *noun*[2], after Dutch *inval*.]
1 An attack, inroad, or incursion *upon* an army, town, etc., or *into* a country. Now *rare*. M17.
2 The place where water enters a reservoir, canal, etc. M17.
3 Chiefly ASTRONOMY. (An instance of) falling into or upon a body (esp. a planet) from an outside source; material which falls or has fallen (e.g. cosmic dust). L19.

infallibility /ɪn,falɪ'bɪlɪti/ *noun*. E17.
[ORIGIN French †*infallibilité* or medieval Latin *infallibilitas*, formed as IN-[3] + FALLIBLE: see -ITY.]
The quality or fact of being infallible.

> N. MOSLEY Goering . . likened what he saw as Hitler's infallibility to that of the Pope.

infallible /ɪn'falɪb(ə)l/ *adjective*. L15.
[ORIGIN French *infaillible* or late Latin *infallibilis*, formed as IN-[3] + Latin *fallere* deceive: see -IBLE.]
1 Of a person, judgement, etc.: not liable to err or be deceived; *spec*. (ROMAN CATHOLIC CHURCH) (of the Pope) incapable of erring in pronouncing dogma as doctrinally defined. L15.

> P. HOWARD It would be nice to pretend that *The Times* is infallible.

2 Of a thing: not liable to prove false or erroneous; not liable to fail in action or operation; *rare* that cannot fail to be or come, certain. L15.

> W. SOYINKA And it barely managed to be sweet, thus failing the infallible test of a real fruit. P. FERGUSON There's always an infallible way to be popular with nurses.

■ **infallibilism** *noun* the principle of the infallibility of a person or thing, esp. of the Pope L19. **infallibilist** *noun* a person who believes in or upholds the infallibility of a person or thing, esp. of the Pope L19. **infallibleness** *noun* (*rare*) infallibility L16. **infallibly** *adverb* L15.

infalling /'ɪnfɔːlɪŋ/ *noun*. Now *rare* or *obsolete*. M16.
[ORIGIN from IN-[1] + FALLING *noun*.]
A falling in. Formerly also, an invasion.

infalling /'ɪnfɔːlɪŋ/ *adjective*. M20.
[ORIGIN from IN-[1] + FALLING *ppl adjective*.]
Falling into or towards something.

infamatory /ɪn'famət(ə)ri/ *adjective*. *rare*. E17.
[ORIGIN medieval Latin *infamatorius*, from *infamat-* pa. ppl stem of *infamare* INFAME *verb*: see -ORY[2].]
Bringing infamy. Formerly also, defamatory.

infame /ɪn'feɪm/ *noun*. Long *arch. rare*. LME.
[ORIGIN Old French (also *en-*) from late Latin *infamium* for classical Latin *infamia* INFAMY.]
= INFAMY.

†**infame** *adjective*. E16–M18.
[ORIGIN French *infâme* from Latin *infamis*: see INFAMY.]
= INFAMOUS.

infame /ɪn'feɪm/ *verb trans*. Now *arch.* or *joc*. LME.
[ORIGIN Old French *enfamer* from Latin *infamare*, from *infamis*: see INFAMY.]
1 Make infamous; hold up to infamy. LME.

> W. PENN This inhuman Practice will infame your Government.

†**2** Defame, speak ill of; accuse of something infamous. L15–L18.

infamize /'ɪnfəmʌɪz/ *verb trans*. Now *rare* or *obsolete*. Also **-ise**. L16.
[ORIGIN from Latin *infamis* (see INFAMY) + -IZE.]
= INFAME *verb*.

†**infamonize** *verb trans*. *rare* (Shakes.). Only in L16.
[ORIGIN Alt.]
= INFAMIZE.

infamous /'ɪnfəməs/ *adjective*. LME.
[ORIGIN medieval Latin *infamosus* for Latin *infamis*: see INFAMY, -OUS.]
1 Of ill fame or repute; notorious, esp. for wickedness, evil, etc. LME.

> C. THIRLWALL He appears to have been more infamous for sacrilege than for bloodshed. C. FRANCIS The vessels packed with Irish emigrants were infamous for overcrowding, disease and frequency of shipwrecks.

2 Deserving of infamy, shamefully wicked or vile; abominable. L15.

> H. MAUNDRELL Detest the very ground on which was acted such an infamous Treachery.

3 LAW (now *hist.*). (Of a person) deprived of all or certain citizen's rights as a consequence of conviction for a serious crime such as forgery, perjury, etc.; (of a crime or punishment) involving or entailing such loss of rights. M16.
– SPECIAL COLLOCATIONS: **infamous crime** *spec*. (LAW, now *hist.*) buggery.
■ **infamously** *adverb* E17. **infamousness** *noun* (*rare*) M17.

infamy /'ɪnfəmi/ *noun*. L15.
[ORIGIN Old French & mod. French *infamie* from Latin *infamia*, from *infamis*, formed as IN-[3] + *fama* FAME *noun*: see -Y[3].]
1 Bad reputation; scandalous repute; public shame or disgrace; an instance of this. L15.

> R. GRENEWEY Now was the time to blot out the infamies of their former conspiracies. E. A. FREEMAN Two caitiffs . . whose names are handed down to infamy.

2 The quality of being shamefully vile; a disgraceful act. L15.

> Q. BELL He . . realised the infamy of slavery when he saw how monstrously a Negro might be treated. P. ACKROYD At the time of my greatest success, I was suspected of the greatest infamies.

3 LAW (now *hist.*). The loss of all or certain citizen's rights resulting from conviction for a serious crime such as forgery, perjury, etc. E17.

infancy /'ɪnf(ə)nsi/ *noun*. LME.
[ORIGIN Latin *infantia* inability to speak, childhood, from *infant-*, *infans*: see INFANT *noun*[1], -ANCY.]
1 The condition of being an infant; the earliest period of human life, early childhood, babyhood. Also (chiefly *literary*), infants collectively. LME.

> P. THOMPSON When tender infancy evinces needless terror at cow, or dog, or shaggy goat. N. MOSLEY This move from prep school to public school was traditionally held to be a release from infancy. M. SCAMMELL There had been twins, but they had been born prematurely and had died in infancy.

2 The earliest period in the history of a thing capable of development; the initial and rudimentary stage in any process of growth. M16.

> R. HUNTFORD The science of nutrition was then in its infancy.

3 LAW (now *hist.*). The condition of not yet being of full age, minority. M17.

†**infand** *adjective*. E17–L19.
[ORIGIN Latin *infandus*, formed as IN-[3] + *fandus* gerundive of *fari* speak: see -AND.]
Unspeakable; nefarious.
■ Also †**infandous** *adjective* M17–L19.

†**infang** *noun*. *Scot. rare*. M16–E19.
[ORIGIN Abbreviation.]
= INFANGTHIEF.

infangthief /'ɪnfaŋθiːf/ *noun*. OE.
[ORIGIN from IN *adverb* + pa. pple of FANG *verb*[1] + THIEF.]
LAW (now *hist.*). The right of the lord of a manor to try and to punish a thief caught within the limits of his demesne.

infant /'ɪnf(ə)nt/ *noun*[1] & *adjective*. LME.
[ORIGIN Old French & mod. French *enfant* from Latin *infant-*, *infans* use as noun of *infans* unable to speak, formed as IN-[3] + pres. pple of *fari* speak: see -ANT[1].]
▸ **A** *noun*. **1** A child during the earliest period of life after birth or (now *rare*) in the womb; a baby, a young child. LME. ▸**b** A beginner in or newcomer to an activity etc.; something in an early stage of development. E16.

> D. W. GOODWIN If the mother is intoxicated while breast feeding, the infant will be intoxicated. J. CRACE I slept, glad to be free of squalling infants and the attentions of the Professor. **b** *New Brunswick Daily Mail* As every political infant cannot fail to recognise, the . . question was . . unconnected with party politics.

TERRIBLE *infant*.
2 a LAW (now *hist.*). A person not yet of full age, a minor. E16. ▸**b** A ruler who has not yet attained the age at which he or she is constitutionally capable of exercising sovereignty. L18.
†**3** A youth of noble birth. *rare*. L16–E17.
4 A thing of exceptional size, strength, etc. *joc*. M19.
▸ **B** *attrib*. or as *adjective*. **1** That is or is like an infant; in the earliest stage of development; undeveloped, nascent, incipient. L16.

> K. AMIS The sheep clustered by the infant oak-tree looked up suddenly and turned their heads. T. MO A girl of seven carries her infant brother in a gay cloth sling.

2 Of, belonging to, or suitable for an infant or infants; childlike; childish, infantile. L16.

> D. WALCOTT Like the sound Of infant voices from the Mission School.

– SPECIAL COLLOCATIONS & COMB.: **infant mistress** a female infant teacher. **infant mortality** the death of infants, *spec*. of those less than a year old. **infant prodigy** a very precocious or talented child. **infant school** (chiefly *hist.*) a primary school intended for children between the ages of 5 and 7. **infant teacher** a teacher of young children; *spec*. a teacher in an infant school.
■ **infanthood** *noun* infancy M19. †**infantical** *adjective* (*rare*) of or pertaining to infants E17–M18. **infantize** *verb trans*. (*rare*) †(**a**) give birth to; (**b**) make childlike: E17.

C. G. WOLFF Edith Wharton began to collect background information for an historical novel. W. WHARTON Can you give me any information about the patient? You were close to him. B. EMECHETA Missy screamed in excitement at this piece of information. *c* *Nature* The precise sequence of the bases is the code which carries the genetical information.

inside information: see INSIDE *adjective*. *white information*: see WHITE *adjective*.

4 *LAW*. **a** A formal (written) statement or accusation presented to a court or magistrate in order to institute criminal proceedings. LME. ▸**b** A statement of the facts of a civil claim presented by the Attorney General or other officer on behalf of the Crown. E17. ▸**c** *SCOTS LAW* (now *hist.*). A written argument on a criminal case ordered by the High Court of Justiciary if the case raises difficult points of law or (formerly) by a Lord Ordinary in the Court of Session when reporting to the Inner House. Now *rare*. L17.
5 The action of informing against, charging, or accusing a person. *obsolete* exc. as a transf. use of sense 4a. L15.
▸†**II 6** The giving of a form or essential character to something; inspiration (as of the body by the soul). M17–L19.

– COMB.: **information booth**, **information bureau**, **information centre**, **information desk**: where information is given and questions answered; **information officer** a person engaged in the provision of specialized information; **information processing** the processing of information so as to yield new or more useful information; **information retrieval** the tracing of information stored in books, computers, etc.; **information revolution** (the economic and industrial impact of) the increase in the availability of information and the changes in its storage and dissemination owing to the use of computers; **information room** a communications centre within a police station where information is collected and disseminated; **information science** (the branch of knowledge that deals with) the storage, retrieval, and dissemination of (esp. scientific or technical) information; **information scientist** a person employed to provide an information service; a person who studies the methods used to do so; an expert in or student of information science; *information superhighway*: see SUPERHIGHWAY 2; **information technologist** an expert in or student of information technology; **information technology** technology that deals with the storage, processing, and dissemination of information esp. using computers; **information theory** the quantitative theory, based on a precise definition of information and the theory of probability, of the coding and transmission of signals and information.
▪ **informational** *adjective* of or pertaining to information; conveying information: E19. **informationally** *adverb* M20.

informative /ɪnˈfɔːmətɪv/ *adjective*. LME.
[ORIGIN medieval Latin *informativus*, from Latin *informat-*: see INFORMATION, -IVE.]
1 Formative; giving life, shape, or an essential quality. LME.
2 Of the nature of or pertaining to legal information. E17.
3 Giving information; instructive. M17.

T. FULLER The most informative Histories to Posterity . . are such as were written by the Eye-witnesses thereof. P. LIVELY One of those busy informative paintings full of detail.

informative double = *INFORMATORY double*.
▪ **informatively** *adverb* M16. **informativeness** *noun* E20.

informator /ɪnˈfɔːmeɪtə/ *noun*. *obsolete* exc. *hist.* M16.
[ORIGIN Late Latin, from Latin *informat-*: see INFORMATION, -OR.]
An instructor, a teacher.

informatory /ɪnˈfɔːmət(ə)ri/ *adjective*. LME.
[ORIGIN from Latin *informat-* (see INFORMATION) + -ORY[2].]
Instructive, informative.
informatory double *BRIDGE* a double intended to give information to one's partner rather than to score a penalty.
▪ **informatorily** *adverb* (*BRIDGE*) informatively, in order to inform E20.

informed /ɪnˈfɔːmd/ *adjective*. LME.
[ORIGIN from INFORM *verb* + -ED[1].]
Knowing or acquainted with the facts; educated, knowledgeable. Now freq. in ***well-informed***, ***ill-informed***.

Daily Express Lights . . to keep the driver informed when anything goes wrong with the lubrication. W. K. HANCOCK Informed opinion was ready to welcome the report. M. SEYMOUR-SMITH It is essential to view his beliefs from an anthropologically informed point of view. R. C. A. WHITE In such cases the consent is illusory because it is not informed.

informed consent permission granted in the knowledge of the possible consequences, esp. that given by a patient to a doctor for treatment with full knowledge of the possible risks and benefits.
▪ **informedly** /-mɪdli/ *adverb* M17. **informedness** /-mɪdnɪs/ *noun* M20.

informer /ɪnˈfɔːmə/ *noun*. LME.
[ORIGIN from INFORM *verb* + -ER[1].]
▸**I** †**1** An instructor, a teacher. LME–M17.

R. MATHEWS Experience which is the truest informer, speaks aloud in this matter also.

2 A person who gives information or intelligence, an informant. LME.

SIR W. SCOTT He talks no Gaelic, nor had his informer much English.

3 A person who informs against another, *spec.* for reward. E16.

R. MACAULAY She's an informer. She set the police on us. C. HOPE Their campus spy, usually an overworked informer.

common informer: see COMMON *adjective*.
▸**II 4** A person or thing which gives form, life, or inspiration. *poet.* LME.

POPE Nature! informer of the Poet's art, Whose force alone can raise or melt the heart.

informercial *noun* var. of INFOMERCIAL.

informidable /ɪnˈfɔːmɪdəb(ə)l, ɪnfɔːˈmɪd-/ *adjective*. *rare*. L17.
[ORIGIN from IN-[3] + FORMIDABLE.]
Not formidable, not to be feared.

informity /ɪnˈfɔːmɪti/ *noun*. Long *rare*. L16.
[ORIGIN Late Latin *informitas*, from Latin *informis*: see INFORM *adjective*, -ITY.]
The condition of being unformed, shapeless, or misshapen.

informosome /ɪnˈfɔːməsəʊm/ *noun*. M20.
[ORIGIN from INFORM(ATION + -O- + -SOME[3].]
CYTOLOGY. A type of ribonucleoprotein in which the messenger RNA may be undetectable until later in development, found in the eggs of certain fishes and echinoderms.

†**infortunate** *verb trans.* L16–L18.
[ORIGIN medieval Latin *infortunat-* pa. ppl stem of *infortunare*, formed as IN-[3] + FORTUNATE *verb*.]
Subject to evil or unlucky influence; make unfortunate.

infortune /ɪnˈfɔːtʃuːn, -tʃ(ə)n/ *noun*. LME.
[ORIGIN Old French & mod. French, formed as IN-[3] + FORTUNE *noun*.]
†**1** Lack of good fortune, ill luck; a misfortune, a mishap. LME–M17.
2 *ASTROLOGY*. An inauspicious or malevolent planet or aspect, *esp.* Saturn or Mars. LME.

†**infortunity** *noun*. LME–E18.
[ORIGIN Old French *infortunité*, formed as INFORTUNE: see -ITY.]
Unfortunate condition, ill luck, adversity; an instance of this, a misfortune.

infotainment /ɪnfəˈteɪnm(ə)nt/ *noun*. L20.
[ORIGIN from INFO(RMATION + ENTER)TAINMENT.]
Broadcast matter that seeks both to inform and to entertain.

infra /ˈɪnfrə/ *adverb*. L19.
[ORIGIN Latin.]
Later, further on (in a book or article); = BELOW *adverb* 1c.

infra- /ˈɪnfrə/ *prefix*.
[ORIGIN Latin *infra* below, underneath, beneath, (in medieval Latin also) within.]
Forming mainly adjectives with the senses 'below, beneath' (in situation or position), 'lower, inferior' (in status or quality).
– NOTE: Opp. SUPRA-. Freq. also treated as opp. SUPER- (cf. SUB-).
▪ **infraclass** *noun* (*TAXONOMY*) a taxonomic grouping ranking next below a subclass M20. **infraˈcostal** *adjective* (*ANATOMY*) situated beneath the ribs L19. **infraˈhuman** *adjective* that is below the human level L19. **infraˈlittoral** *adjective* (*ECOLOGY*) (*a*) = SUBLITTORAL *adjective*; (*b*) designating or pertaining to the region of a lake containing rooted vegetation: M19. **infraˈmarginal** *adjective* & *noun* (a structure, organ, etc.) situated below the margin or border M19. **inframaˈxillary** *adjective* (*a*) = SUBMANDIBULAR; (*b*) of or pertaining to the lower jawbone: M19. **infra-ˈorbital** *adjective* (*ANATOMY*) situated below the orbit of the eye E19. **infraorder** *noun* (*TAXONOMY*) a taxonomic grouping ranking next below a suborder M20. **infraˈrenal** *adjective* (*ANATOMY*) situated below the kidneys L19. **infraspeˈcific** *adjective* (*TAXONOMY*) at a level lower than that of the species M20.

infract /ɪnˈfrakt/ *adjective*. Long *rare*. M16.
[ORIGIN Latin *infractus*, formed as IN-[3] + *fractus* broken.]
Unbroken, unimpaired; sound, whole.

infract /ɪnˈfrakt/ *verb trans.* Chiefly *US*. L18.
[ORIGIN Latin *infract-* pa. ppl stem of *infringere* INFRINGE.]
Break (a rule, an agreement, etc.); violate, infringe.
▪ **infractor** *noun* E16.

infraction /ɪnˈfrakʃ(ə)n/ *noun*. LME.
[ORIGIN Latin *infractio(n-)*, formed as INFRACT *verb*: see -ION.]
1 The action or an act of breaking an agreement; (a) violation, (an) infringement. LME.

A. S. NEILL These and other infractions of rules carry automatic fines. A. BROOKNER Any infraction of the liberty of such simple people would be a form of assault.

2 The action of breaking or fracturing; a fracture. E17.

infradian /ɪnˈfreɪdɪən/ *adjective*. M20.
[ORIGIN from INFRA- + *-dian*, after CIRCADIAN.]
PHYSIOLOGY. Of a rhythm or cycle: having a frequency lower than circadian, i.e. a period longer than a day. Cf. ULTRADIAN.

infra dig /ɪnfrə ˈdɪɡ/ *adjectival phr. colloq.* E19.
[ORIGIN Abbreviation of Latin *infra dignitatem* beneath (one's) dignity.]
Beneath the dignity of one's position; undignified.

Scouting A bit infra dig, . . touting for reader-support like this? S. BELLOW Doing the floors on his knees, didn't bother him . . . It never occurred to him that it was infra dig.

infragrant /ɪnˈfreɪɡr(ə)nt/ *adjective*. E19.
[ORIGIN from IN-[3] + FRAGRANT.]
Lacking fragrance; malodorous.

SYD. SMITH We shall both be a brown infragrant powder in thirty or forty years. M. WEBB Sparsely in the hedges grew the pale, infragrant flowers of early autumn.

infralapsarian /ɪnfrəlapˈsɛːrɪən/ *noun* & *adjective*. Also **I-**. M18.
[ORIGIN formed as INFRA- + Latin *lapsus* fall, LAPSE *noun* + -ARIAN. Cf. SUPRALAPSARIAN.]
THEOLOGY. ▸**A** *noun*. A Calvinist holding the view that God's election of only some to everlasting life was not originally part of the divine plan, but a consequence of the Fall of Man. M18.
▸**B** *adjective*. Of or pertaining to the infralapsarians or their doctrine. L18.
▪ **infralapsarianism** *noun* the doctrine of the infralapsarians M19.

inframe *verb* var. of ENFRAME.

†**infranchise** *verb* var. of ENFRANCHISE.

infrangible /ɪnˈfrandʒɪb(ə)l/ *adjective*. L16.
[ORIGIN French, or medieval Latin *infrangibilis*, formed as IN-[3] + *frangibilis* FRANGIBLE.]
1 Unbreakable. L16.

F. W. ROBERTSON No iron bar is absolutely infrangible. *fig.*: J. UPDIKE That heaping measure of maternal love which makes for an infrangible soundness of spirit.

2 Unable to be infringed; inviolable. M19.
▪ **infrangiˈbility** *noun* E19. **infrangibly** *adverb* E19.

infrared /ɪnfrəˈrɛd/ *adjective* & *noun*. L19.
[ORIGIN from INFRA- + RED *adjective*, *noun*.]
▸**A** *adjective*. **1** Of electromagnetic radiation: lying beyond the red end of the visible spectrum, having a wavelength between that of red light and that of microwaves (about 800 nm to 1 mm). L19.
2 Involving, producing, or pertaining to (the use of) infrared radiation, esp. as emitted by heated bodies; sensitive to infrared radiation. E20.
▸**B** *noun*. (Usu. with *the*.) The infrared part of the spectrum. L19.
the far infrared, **the near infrared** the part of the infrared far from, close to, the visible spectrum.

infrasonic /ɪnfrəˈsɒnɪk/ *adjective*. E20.
[ORIGIN from INFRA- + SONIC.]
Of, pertaining to, or designating sound waves or vibrations having a frequency below the audible range (i.e. less than 15–30 Hz).

infrasound /ˈɪnfrəsaʊnd/ *noun*. M20.
[ORIGIN from INFRA- + SOUND *noun*[2].]
(A) sound of infrasonic frequency.

infrastructure /ˈɪnfrəstrʌktʃə/ *noun*. E20.
[ORIGIN French, formed as INFRA- + STRUCTURE *noun*.]
The foundation or basic structure of an undertaking; *spec.* (*a*) the collective permanent installations (airfields, naval bases, etc.) forming a basis for military activity; (*b*) the installations and services (power stations, sewers, roads, housing, etc.) regarded as the economic foundation of a country.

Broadcast The best laid plans . . come to nothing unless there is a sound and properly considered infrastructure. *Guardian* Britain needs to invest an extra £3.5 billion . . in its basic infrastructure of housing, roads, and sewers.

▪ **infrastructural** *adjective* M20.

infrequency /ɪnˈfriːkw(ə)nsi/ *noun*. E17.
[ORIGIN Latin *infrequentia*, formed as INFREQUENT: see -ENCY.]
†**1** The fact or condition of being deserted or seldom visited. Also, fewness. Only in 17.

P. HOLLAND It was the solitude and infrequency of the place that brought the dragon thither.

2 The fact or condition of being infrequent or occasional; rarity. L17.

C. LAMB The relish of such exhibitions must be in proportion to the infrequency of going. A. FLINT The infrequency of gangrene is shown by its having occurred in but one of 133 cases.

▪ Also **infrequence** *noun* (*rare*) M17.

infrequent /ɪnˈfriːkwənt/ *adjective*. M16.
[ORIGIN Latin *infrequent-*, formed as IN-[3] + *frequent-* FREQUENT *adjective*.]
†**1** Little used or practised; unaccustomed, uncommon. Only in M16.
2 Not occurring often; happening rarely; (qualifying an agent noun) seldom doing the action indicated. E17.

W. WOLLASTON A sparing and infrequent worshiper of the Deity. H. JACOBSON Our meetings became more and more infrequent and then stopped altogether.

3 Seldom met with, not plentiful, uncommon. L17.
▪ **infrequently** *adverb* L17.

infrigidate /ɪnˈfrɪdʒɪdeɪt/ *verb trans.* Long *rare*. M16.
[ORIGIN Late Latin *infrigidat-* pa. ppl stem of *infrigidare*, formed as IN-[2] + *frigidus* cold, FRIGID: see -ATE[3].]
Make cold; chill, cool.

inherit /ɪnˈhɛrɪt/ *verb*. Orig. †**en-**. ME.
[ORIGIN Old French *enheriter* make heir from late Latin *inhereditare* appoint as heir, formed as IN-[2] + *hered-*, *heres* heir.]
1 *verb trans.* Come into possession of, as a right; receive or hold as one's portion. Chiefly in biblical translations and allusions. ME.

AV *Luke* 18:18 Good master, what shall I doe to inherit eternall life?

2 *verb trans.* Take or receive (property, a privilege, title, etc.) as an heir at the death of a former possessor; get or come into possession of by legal descent or succession. LME. ▸**b** Derive or possess (a quality or character, physical or mental) by transmission from a progenitor or progenitors. L16. ▸**c** Receive or have from a predecessor or predecessors in office etc. M19.

b JO GRIMOND His children . . inherited the exemplary character and looks of their parents. **c** G. K. CHESTERTON It is the rule, inherited from the old régime. *Southern Rag* The musical culture which we inherit in this country is frequently . . sexist.

†**3** *verb trans.* Make heir, put in possession. LME–L16.
4 *verb trans.* Be heir to (a person); succeed as heir. LME.
5 *verb intrans.* Come into or take possession of an inheritance. M16. ▸**b** Derive being or a quality *from*. L19.

E. H. JONES He has presumably inherited, his parents being dead.

inheritable /ɪnˈhɛrɪtəb(ə)l/ *adjective*. Also †**en-**. LME.
[ORIGIN Anglo-Norman *enheritable* able to be made heir, formed as INHERIT: see -ABLE.]
1 Capable of inheriting; entitled to succeed (to property etc.) by legal right. LME.
2 Able to be inherited; that may or can descend by law to an heir. L15.
■ **inheritaˈbility** *noun* L18. **inheritableness** *noun* L18. **inheritably** *adverb* M16.

inheritage /ɪnˈhɛrɪtɪdʒ/ *noun*. *rare*. M16.
[ORIGIN from INHERIT + -AGE.]
That which is inherited; an inheritance, a heritage.

inheritance /ɪnˈhɛrɪt(ə)ns/ *noun*. Also †**en-**. LME.
[ORIGIN Anglo-Norman *enheritaunce* being admitted as heir, formed as INHERIT: see -ANCE.]
▸ **I 1** Hereditary succession to a property, title, office, etc.; a continual right to an estate invested in a person and his or her heirs. LME.

C. G. SELIGMAN The eldest son is the chief heir; women have no right of inheritance.

2 The fact or property of inheriting or having inherited something. LME.

H. CARE English Liberties, or the free-born Subject's Inheritance. R. DAWKINS Inheritance of many genetic characters such as human height.

▸ **II 3** Property, or an estate, which passes by law to an heir or heirs on the death of the possessor. LME. ▸**b** A property, quality, characteristic, etc., inherited from a progenitor or progenitors. E17.

R. HOLMES His maternal grandmother died, leaving him a considerable inheritance of . . thirty thousand francs. **b** L. M. MONTGOMERY The merry expression which was her inheritance from her father.

4 A thing that one obtains or comes into possession of by right or divine grant; *esp.* (in biblical use) the blessings received by God's chosen people. M16.
– COMB.: **inheritance tax** a tax on inherited property levied on individual beneficiaries, *spec.* one varying according to their degrees of relationship to the testator.

inheritor /ɪnˈhɛrɪtə/ *noun*. LME.
[ORIGIN from INHERIT + -OR.]
A person who inherits something; an heir. (Foll. by *of*.)

inheritress /ɪnˈhɛrɪtrɪs/ *noun*. E16.
[ORIGIN from INHERITOR: see -ESS[1].]
= INHERITRIX.

inheritrix /ɪnˈhɛrɪtrɪks/ *noun*. Pl. **-trices** /-trɪsiːz/, **-trixes**. M16.
[ORIGIN formed as INHERITRESS: see -TRIX.]
A female inheritor, an heiress.
■ Also †**inheritrice** *noun* E16–L17.

inhesion /ɪnˈhiːʒ(ə)n/ *noun*. M17.
[ORIGIN Late Latin *inhaesio(n-)*, from Latin *inhaes-* pa. ppl stem of *inhaerere*: see INHERE, -ION.]
The action or fact of inhering, esp. as a quality or attribute; inherence.

inhiate /ˈɪnhʌɪeɪt/ *verb intrans*. Now *rare*. M16.
[ORIGIN Latin *inhiat-* pa. ppl stem of *inhiare* gape at, formed as IN-[2] + *hiare* gape: see -ATE[3].]
Open the mouth wide, gape.

inhibin /ɪnˈhɪbɪn/ *noun*[1]. M20.
[ORIGIN from Latin *inhibere* INHIBIT: see -IN[1].]
PHYSIOLOGY. A gonadal hormone which inhibits the secretion of follicle-stimulating hormone.

inhibin *noun*[2] var. of next.

inhibine /ˈɪnhɪbiːn/ *noun*. Also **-in** /-ɪn/. M20.
[ORIGIN from INHIBIT + -INE[5].]
Any of a group of natural antibacterial substances found mainly in honey and saliva.

inhibit /ɪnˈhɪbɪt/ *verb trans*. LME.
[ORIGIN Latin *inhibit-* pa. ppl stem of *inhibere* hold in, hinder, formed as IN-[2] + *habere* hold.]
1 Forbid (a person) to do something, prohibit from doing something; *spec.* forbid (an ecclesiastic) to exercise clerical functions. (Foll. by *from doing*, †*from* a thing, †*to do*.) LME.

LD MACAULAY A clause was . . inserted which inhibited the Bank from advancing money.

†**2** Forbid or prohibit the doing of or engaging in (a thing, action, or practice). L15–E19.

C. LAMB At school all play-going was inhibited.

3 Restrain, prevent. M16.

DAY LEWIS A kind of near-neurotic inertia or negativism which inhibited me from pressing my love upon her. P. GOODMAN Certain aims are forbidden and punishable . . ; so we inhibit them and put them out of our mind. B. PYM Her presence inhibited any attempt at that kind of conversation. I. MURDOCH I had the satisfaction of seeing her inhibit her impulse to ask me where I was going. *Flex* The zinc ion has been shown to inhibit viral duplication.

■ **inhibited** *adjective* (*a*) that has been inhibited; forbidden, restrained; (*b*) subject to inhibition, unable to express feelings or impulses: E17. **inhibitedness** *noun* M20. **inhibiter** *noun* = INHIBITOR 1 E17. **inhibiting** *adjective* (*a*) forbidding, prohibitive; (*b*) causing restraint or inhibition: E17. **inhibitingly** *adverb* M20. **inhibitive** *adjective* serving or tending to inhibit someone or something M19.

inhibition /ɪn(h)ɪˈbɪʃ(ə)n/ *noun*. LME.
[ORIGIN Old French & mod. French, or Latin *inhibitio(n-)*, formed as INHIBIT: see -ION.]
1 Chiefly ECCLESIASTICAL & LAW. The action or an act of forbidding; a (formal) prohibition. LME. ▸**b** *spec.* Formerly in ENGLISH LAW, an order prohibiting dealing with a specified piece of land for a given period or until further notice; also, a writ forbidding a court to proceed in a suit on the grounds that it is beyond the cognizance of that court, a prohibition. In ECCLESIASTICAL LAW, an order suspending the jurisdiction of an inferior court during an episcopal visitation; an order suspending a member of the clergy from ministerial duty. In SCOTS LAW, a writ prohibiting a person from contracting a possible charge on or selling heritable property; formerly also, a writ obtained by a husband to prevent his wife from obtaining credit. M16.
2 The action or an act of preventing, hindering, or checking. E17. ▸**b** PHYSIOLOGY. The checking or repression of an organ or function, esp. in the nervous system, by the action of another or of a drug. L19. ▸**c** CHEMISTRY & BIOCHEMISTRY. The slowing or prevention of a reaction or process by a specific substance. E20.

S. JOHNSON It is said that no torture is equal to the inhibition of sleep, long continued. E. P. THOMPSON A 'religion of the heart' . . notorious for the inhibition of all spontaneity.

3 (A) scrupulous or emotional resistance to thought, action, etc. In PSYCHOLOGY, (a) voluntary or involuntary restraint on the direct expression of a natural impulse; the process whereby a learned response is weakened in the absence of reinforcement. L19.

C. HILL Cromwell . . had no inhibitions about using the loyalty and enthusiasm of the lower-class radicals. E. H. JONES She tried out her half-formed ideas in her circle without inhibition. *Hairdo Ideas* Answers all your questions and helps free you of inhibitions.

reactive inhibition: see REACTIVE *adjective* 3. ***retroactive inhibition***: see RETROACTIVE 3.

inhibitor /ɪnˈhɪbɪtə/ *noun*. M19.
[ORIGIN from INHIBIT + -OR. Cf. earlier INHIBITER.]
1 A person who inhibits something; *spec.* in SCOTS LAW, a person who takes out an inhibition. M19.
2 A thing which inhibits someone or something. E20. ▸**b** GENETICS. A gene whose presence prevents the expression of some other gene at a different locus. E20. ▸**c** CHEMISTRY & BIOCHEMISTRY. A substance which slows down or prevents a particular reaction or process, or diminishes the activity of some reactant or catalyst. E20.

W. JAMES Danger is for most men the great inhibitor of action.

inhibitory /ɪnˈhɪbɪt(ə)ri/ *adjective*. L15.
[ORIGIN medieval Latin *inhibitorius*, formed as INHIBIT + -ORY[2].]
1 Prohibitory. L15.

J. LINGARD An inhibitory breve, forbidding all archbishops . . to give judgment in the . . cause of Henry against Catharine.

2 That restrains or prevents something; causing inhibition. M19.

P. GROSSKURTH Anxiety, if excessive, can be inhibitory to development.

†**inhold** *verb trans*. Infl. as HOLD *verb*; pa. t. & pple usu. **inheld**. L15.
[ORIGIN from IN-[1] + HOLD *verb*.]
1 Keep in, retain, withhold. L15–E18.
2 Contain, enclose. Only in E17.
■ †**inholder** *noun* (*a*) a tenant; (*b*) a thing which holds or contains something: L16–L17.

inhomogeneity /ɪnˌhɒmə(ʊ)dʒɪˈniːɪti, -ˈneɪɪti; ɪnˌhəʊm-/ *noun*. L19.
[ORIGIN from IN-[3] + HOMOGENEITY.]
1 A thing which is not homogeneous with its surroundings; a local irregularity. L19.
2 The property of being inhomogeneous; lack of homogeneity. E20.

inhomogeneous /ˌɪnhɒmə(ʊ)ˈdʒiːnɪəs, -ˈdʒɛn-; ˌɪnhəʊm-/ *adjective*. E20.
[ORIGIN from IN-[3] + HOMOGENEOUS.]
1 Not uniform throughout; composed of diverse constituents; heterogeneous. E20.
2 MATH. Consisting of terms that are not all of the same degree or dimensions. M20.
■ **inhomogeneously** *adverb* E20.

†**inhoop** *verb trans*. *rare* (Shakes.). Only in E17.
[ORIGIN from IN-[1] + HOOP *noun*[1] or *verb*[1].]
Place in a hoop; surround by a hoop.

inhospitable /ɪnhɒˈspɪtəb(ə)l, ɪnˈhɒspɪt-/ *adjective*. L16.
[ORIGIN French, formed as IN-[3] + HOSPITABLE.]
1 Not welcoming to strangers; not showing hospitality to guests. L16.

G. B. SHAW Hector: I'm sorry to be inhospitable; but will you kindly leave the house?

2 Of a region: not offering shelter or sustenance; bleak, hostile. E17.

B. LOPEZ The tree line, where one first encounters the inhospitable soils of the tundra.

■ **inˌhospitaˈbility**, **inhospitableness** *nouns* M17. **inhospitably** *adverb* M17.

†**inhospital** *adjective*. L16–E18.
[ORIGIN Latin *inhospitalis*, formed as IN-[3] + *hospitalis* hospitable: see HOSPITAL *adjective*.]
= INHOSPITABLE.

inhospitality /ˌɪnhɒspɪˈtalɪti/ *noun*. L16.
[ORIGIN Latin *inhospitalitas*, formed as INHOSPITAL: see -ITY.]
The quality or practice of being inhospitable; lack of hospitality.

in-house /*as adjective* ˈɪnhaʊs, *as adverb* ɪnˈhaʊs/ *adjective & adverb*. M20.
[ORIGIN from IN-[1] + HOUSE *noun*[1].]
▸ **A** *adjective*. Of or pertaining to the internal affairs of an institution or organization; existing within an institution or organization. M20.

Lebende Sprachen Microcircuits . . made by outside suppliers or by . . in-house facilities. S. I. LANDAU Will it be written entirely by an in-house staff of dictionary editors?

▸ **B** *adverb*. Internally; without outside assistance. M20.

Flight International Avoid carrying out tasks in-house which can be executed by subcontractors. *Bookcase* Gary felt it was time to keep a good idea and develop it in-house.

inhuman /ɪnˈhjuːmən/ *adjective & noun*. Also (earlier) †**-ane**. LME.
[ORIGIN Latin *inhumanus*, formed as IN-[3] + *humanus* HUMAN *adjective*.]
▸ **A** *adjective*. **1** Of a person: callous, unfeeling, merciless. Of conduct, an action, etc.: brutal, barbarous, cruel. Cf. INHUMANE 2. LME.

SHAKES. *Tit. A.* Her spotless chastity, Inhuman traitors, you constrain'd and forc'd. C. G. WOLFF Having been dehumanized, they act with inhuman indifference to the feelings of others.

2 Not human; not of the normal human type. M16.

J. B. CABELL Planet-stricken folk, who had spied . . upon an inhuman loveliness, and so, must pine away.

▸ †**B** *noun*. A brutal or subhuman person. M17–M18.
■ **inhumanly** *adverb* L15. **inhumanness** /-n-n-/ *noun* (*rare*) M17.

inhumane /ɪnhjʊˈmeɪn/ *adjective*. LME.
[ORIGIN Orig. var. of INHUMAN *adjective*; later from IN-[3] + HUMANE.]
†**1** See INHUMAN *adjective*. LME.
2 Not humane; without compassion for misery or suffering. Cf. INHUMAN *adjective* 1. E19.

inhumanely /ɪnhjʊˈmeɪnli/ *adverb*. L16.
[ORIGIN from INHUMANE + -LY[2].]
Orig., inhumanly, cruelly. Now, not humanely; without compassion (though not with intentional cruelty).

D. ROWE The 'mentally ill' . . are often treated inhumanely and sometimes very cruelly.

inhumanism /ɪnˈhjuːmənɪz(ə)m/ *noun*. E20.
[ORIGIN from IN-[3] + HUMANISM.]
Lack of humanism; inhumanity.

inhumanitarian /ˌɪnhjʊmanɪˈtɛːrɪən/ *noun & adjective*. M20.
[ORIGIN from IN-[3] + HUMANITARIAN.]
▸ **A** *noun*. A person who does not accept the views and practices of humanitarianism. M20.
▸ **B** *adjective*. Rejecting or disregarding humanitarian views or practices. M20.

inhumanity /ɪnhjʊˈmanɪti/ *noun*. L15.
[ORIGIN Old French & mod. French *inhumanité*, or Latin *inhumanitas*, from *inhumanus* INHUMAN *adjective*: see -ITY.]
1 The quality of being inhuman or inhumane; lack of compassion, cruelty. L15. ▸**b** An instance of this; a cruel act. M17.
†**2** Lack of politeness; incivility. M16–M17.

inhumate /ɪnˈhjuːmeɪt, ˈɪnhjʊmeɪt/ *verb trans. rare*. E17.
[ORIGIN Latin *inhumat-* pa. ppl stem of *inhumare* INHUME: see -ATE[3].]
Bury, inter; = INHUME 1.

inhumation /ɪnhjʊˈmeɪʃ(ə)n/ *noun*. L16.
[ORIGIN from INHUMATE or INHUME: see -ATION.]
†**1** A method of distillation in which vessels were buried in earth within a circular fire. L16–M17.
2 The action or practice of burying the dead; the fact of being buried; interment. M17.

F. SMYTH Any corpse dug up after a period of inhumation in the area . . would contain . . arsenic. *Scientific American* Inhumation of the bones . . was the last stage in the treatment of the deceased.

3 The burying of something in or under the ground. M17.

inhume /ɪnˈhjuːm/ *verb trans*. E17.
[ORIGIN Latin *inhumare*, formed as IN-[2] + *humus* ground.]
1 Bury (a corpse); place in the grave, inter. E17. ▸†**b** Of the earth or a tomb: cover (the dead). E17–L18.
2 *gen*. Bury in the ground; cover with soil. Now *rare* or *obsolete*. E17.

inhumorous /ɪnˈhjuːm(ə)rəs/ *adjective*. E20.
[ORIGIN from IN-[3] + HUMOROUS.]
Not humorous; without humour.
■ **inhumorously** *adverb* L19.

iniencephalus /ˌɪnɪɛnˈkɛf(ə)ləs, -ˈsɛf-/ *noun*. M19.
[ORIGIN from INION + Greek *egkephalos* brain.]
MEDICINE. (A deformed fetus exhibiting) iniencephaly.
■ **inience'phalic** *adjective* L19. **iniencephaly** *noun* a developmental abnormality of the skull and upper spine, in which the brain and spinal cord protrude through an opening in the occiput and upper spinal canal E20.

inimic /ɪˈnɪmɪk/ *adjective*. *arch*. *rare*. L17.
[ORIGIN Latin *inimicus*: see ENEMY.]
Adverse, hostile.

inimicable /ɪˈnɪmɪkəb(ə)l/ *adjective*. *rare*. E19.
[ORIGIN from IN-[3] + AMICABLE, after *inimical*.]
= INIMICAL.

inimical /ɪˈnɪmɪk(ə)l/ *adjective*. E16.
[ORIGIN Late Latin *inimicalis*, from *inimicus*: see ENEMY, -AL[1].]
1 Unfriendly, hostile, (*to*). E16.

H. A. L. FISHER The only organized and educated body of men, . . instead of being inimical, was an ally. H. CARPENTER He was firmly convinced . . that the female psychology was . . different from—and largely inimical to—that of the male.

2 Adverse, detrimental, harmful, (*to*). M17.

P. F. BOLLER A dangerous monopoly inimical to the interests of the majority.

■ **inimi'cality** *noun* L18. **inimically** *adverb* M19. **inimicalness** *noun* M17.

†**inimicitious** *adjective*. M17–M18.
[ORIGIN from Latin *inimicitia* enmity, from *inimicus* ENEMY, + -OUS.]
= INIMICAL.

†**inimicous** *adjective*. L16–E18.
[ORIGIN from Latin *inimicus* ENEMY + -OUS.]
= INIMICAL.

inimitable /ɪˈnɪmɪtəb(ə)l/ *adjective & noun*. L15.
[ORIGIN French, or Latin *inimitabilis*, formed as IN-[3] + *imitabilis* IMITABLE.]
▸ **A** *adjective*. Surpassing or defying imitation; without compare, peerless. L15.

Sunday Express In his own inimitable way he tells us what to drink.

▸ **B** *noun*. An inimitable person or thing. M18.

Times A creditable and exuberant expression of one of the great inimitables of jazz.

■ **inimita'bility** *noun* E18. **inimitableness** *noun* M17. **inimitably** *adverb* M17.

in infinitum /ɪn ɪnfɪˈnʌɪtəm/ *adverbial phr*. M16.
[ORIGIN Latin.]
To infinity, without end. Cf. AD INFINITUM.

inion /ˈɪnɪɒn/ *noun*. E19.
[ORIGIN Greek = nape of the neck.]
ANATOMY. The projecting part of the occipital bone at the base of the skull.

†**inique** *adjective*. E16–M18.
[ORIGIN Latin *iniquus*, formed as IN-[3] + *aequus* equal, just.]
Unjust, iniquitous.

iniquitous /ɪˈnɪkwɪtəs/ *adjective*. E18.
[ORIGIN from INIQUITY + -OUS.]
Characterized by or full of iniquity; grossly unjust, wicked.
■ **iniquitously** *adverb* L18. **iniquitousness** *noun* L19.

iniquity /ɪˈnɪkwɪti/ *noun*. ME.
[ORIGIN Old French *iniquité* from Latin *iniquitas*, from *iniquus*: see INIQUE, -ITY.]
▸ **I 1** Immoral, unrighteous, or harmful action or conduct; gross injustice, wickedness, sin. Also, the quality of being wicked or sinful. ME. ▸**b** In *pl*. Wrongful acts; sins, injuries, injustices. L15.

ROBERT WATSON The iniquity and unrelenting cruelty exercised. A. J. P. TAYLOR My father regarded Oxford as a sink of iniquity. **b** A. BRINK To . . expose the iniquities of the Security Police. M. SCAMMELL A feudal system whose iniquities were to provide much of the fuel for the Revolution.

2 (**I-**.) A (comic) character in morality plays, representing a particular vice or vice in general. L16.
3 Inequality, inequity, unfairness. *obsolete* exc. as passing into sense 1. L16.
▸ †**II 4** Unfavourable or adverse influence or operation. M16–E17.

†**iniquous** *adjective*. M17–L18.
[ORIGIN from Latin *iniquus* (see INIQUE) + -OUS.]
Unjust, wicked, iniquitous.

inirritable /ɪnˈɪrɪtəb(ə)l/ *adjective*. Now *rare* or *obsolete*. L18.
[ORIGIN from IN-[3] + IRRITABLE.]
Chiefly *PHYSIOLOGY*. Not irritable, unresponsive to stimulus.
■ **inirrita'bility** *noun* L18.

inisle *verb* var. of ENISLE.

initial /ɪˈnɪʃ(ə)l/ *noun*. E17.
[ORIGIN from the adjective.]
1 An initial letter; *esp*. (in *pl*.) the initial letters of two or more names of a person, or of words forming any name or phrase. E17.

A. UTTLEY A big blue handkerchief with his initials embroidered in the corner. J. HUTCHINSON The earliest books left spaces for initials . . which were completed by illuminators. *New Scientist* The commands are based on initials such as CV for 'centre vertically'.

2 An initial stage or element *of* something; a beginning. Now *rare*. M17.
3 *MUSIC*. More fully ***absolute initial***. Each of the prescribed notes on which a plainsong melody may begin in any given mode. L19.
4 *BOTANY*. An initial cell. E20.

initial /ɪˈnɪʃ(ə)l/ *adjective*. E16.
[ORIGIN Latin *initialis*, from *initium* beginning: see -AL[1].]
1 Of or pertaining to the beginning; existing at, constituting, or occurring at the beginning; first, primary. E16. ▸**b** *BOTANY*. Of a plant cell: dividing into two daughter cells, one of which develops into the tissues and organs of the plant while the other remains within the meristem. L19.

J. GALSWORTHY From this initial mistake of hers all the subsequent trouble, sorrow and tragedy have come. *Gentleman (Mumbai)* The trade protocol . . was valid for an initial period of five years. C. PETERS After a while the initial euphoria of having a place of his own wore off.

initial line *MATH*. (in a system of polar coordinates) the line from which an angle is measured. **initial public offering** (chiefly *US*) a company's flotation on the stock exchange (abbreviation ***IPO***). **initial teaching alphabet** a 44-letter phonetic alphabet used to help those beginning to read and write English, esp. in British primary schools in the 1960s.
2 Standing at the beginning of a word, of a division in a book or piece of writing, or of the alphabet. E17.

G. BURNET The initial letters of his name . . , as W. E . . . for Will. Exon.

■ **initially** *adverb* E17.

initial /ɪˈnɪʃ(ə)l/ *verb trans*. Infl. **-ll-**, ***-l-**. M19.
[ORIGIN from the noun.]
Mark or sign with initials; put one's initials to or on; *spec*. signify thus the intention of later formal ratification.

Time The signing of a Panama Canal treaty that was initialed last month.

initialese /ɪˌnɪʃəˈliːz/ *noun*. M20.
[ORIGIN from INITIAL *noun* + -ESE.]
The use of abbreviations formed by using the initial letters of the words to be shortened.

initialise *verb* var. of INITIALIZE.

initialism /ɪˈnɪʃ(ə)lɪz(ə)m/ *noun*. L19.
[ORIGIN from INITIAL *noun* + -ISM.]
A group of initial letters used as an abbreviation, *esp*. one in which each letter is pronounced separately (cf. ACRONYM); the use of such initials.

initialize /ɪˈnɪʃ(ə)lʌɪz/ *verb trans. & intrans*. Also **-ise**. M19.
[ORIGIN from INITIAL *noun* + -IZE.]
1 Designate by or use an initial or initials instead of the full name. *rare*. M19.
2 *COMPUTING*. Set or become set to a value or in a state suitable for the start of an operation. M20.

Personal Software There is a substantial amount of code to be entered to initialise the program. *Television* The ROM and the CPU were . . faulty, but the machine still wouldn't initialise when these had been replaced.

■ **initiali'zation** *noun* (*COMPUTING*) the action or process of initializing; the computer operations involved in this: M20.

initiand /ɪˈnɪʃɪand/ *noun*. M20.
[ORIGIN Latin *initiandus* gerundive of *initiare* INITIATE *verb*: see -AND.]
A person about to be initiated.

initiate /ɪˈnɪʃɪət/ *adjective & noun*. E17.
[ORIGIN Latin *initiatus* pa. pple, formed as INITIATE *verb*: see -ATE[2].]
▸ **A** *adjective*. **1** Admitted into some society or position; instructed in some (secret) knowledge. E17. ▸†**b** Of or belonging to a newly initiated person. *rare* (Shakes.). Only in E17.

M. AYRTON Lycus was deeply religious and initiate in the mysteries of the Mother . . Demeter.

2 Begun, commenced, introduced. M18.
▸ **B** *noun*. †**1** Something initiated or newly introduced. *rare*. Only in E17.
2 A person who has been initiated; a beginner, a novice. E19.

J. BAYLEY It is hinted that only initiates, those really in the know, can understand. W. STYRON For the initiate ours is a cruel language.

initiate /ɪˈnɪʃɪeɪt/ *verb*. M16.
[ORIGIN Latin *initiat-* pa. ppl stem of *initiare* begin, from *initium* beginning: see -ATE[3].]
1 *verb trans*. Introduce (a person) with due ceremonies or rites into a society or position, or into the knowledge of some (esp. secret or occult) principle or practice; *gen*. acquaint with or instruct in the elements of anything. (Foll. by *in*, *into*.) M16. ▸**b** *verb intrans*. Perform or undergo an initiation. E18.

I. MCEWAN It was Raymond who initiated me into the secrets of adult life.

2 *verb trans*. Begin, introduce, set going, originate. E17. ▸**b** *verb intrans*. Have its beginning; commence. E17.

E. F. BENSON Whether it was customary for unmarried ladies to initiate a call on an unmarried man. J. K. TOOLE I have succeeded in initiating several work-saving methods. **b** S. TOLANSKY If pure deuterium gas can be raised to a temperature . . of 500 million degrees C., then a thermo-nuclear reaction should initiate.

initiated /ɪˈnɪʃɪeɪtɪd/ *ppl adjective & noun*. L16.
[ORIGIN from INITIATE *verb* + -ED[1].]
▸ **A** *ppl adjective*. That has been initiated. L16.
▸ **B** *noun*. **1** An initiate. M18.
2 *collect. pl*. *The* people who have been initiated. M19.

A. EDEN A catch was concealed which the initiated could press to open a door.

initiation /ɪˌnɪʃɪˈeɪʃ(ə)n/ *noun*. L16.
[ORIGIN Latin *initiatio(n-)* (in sense 2 in medieval Latin), formed as INITIATE *verb*: see -ATION.]
1 Formal introduction with due ceremonies or rites into a society, position, or (secret) knowledge; instruction in the elements of a subject or practice; an instance of this. L16.

L. VAN DER POST The long night of the initiation of the Esquire into Knighthood. J. VIORST The recognition that others have . . claims upon her love is our initiation into jealousy.

initiation ceremony, ***initiation rite***, etc.
2 The action or an act of beginning or originating something; the fact of being begun; commencement, origination. M17.

initiative /ɪˈnɪʃɪətɪv, -ʃə-/ *noun*. L18.
[ORIGIN French, formed as INITIATE *verb* + -IVE.]
1 The action of initiating something or of taking the first step or the lead; an act setting a process or chain of events in motion; an independent or enterprising act. L18. ▸**b** *spec*. A proposal made by one nation or group of nations to another, with a view to improving relations between them. M20.

W. SOYINKA Did he contact you or did the initiative come from you? H. KISSINGER The most important diplomatic initiative . . was toward Hanoi. *Dance Theatre Journal* These companies were set up as purely regional initiatives.

2 The power or right to begin something. L18. ▸**b** *spec*. The right of (a specified number of) citizens outside the legislature to propose legislation (as in Switzerland and parts of the US). L19.

C. G. WOLFF The outside world and all that went with it: autonomy and initiative.

3 Mental power to initiate things; enterprise, self-motivation to action. E20.

S. LEACOCK The peculiar quality that is called initiative—the ability to act promptly on one's own judgment.

— PHRASES: **have the initiative** have the first choice of action; *esp*. (*MILITARY*) be able to influence or control the enemy's movements. **on one's own initiative** without being prompted by others. ***Strategic Defense Initiative***: see STRATEGIC *adjective*. **take the initiative** be the first to take action.

M. AMSTERDAM The warden, . . at the asylum, noticed one of the inmates sitting on a small stool.

3 A person not native to the place where he or she lives; a stranger, a foreigner. Now *rare* or *obsolete*. **L16.**
▸ †**B** *attrib.* or as *adjective*. That is an inmate. **E17–E19.**

inmeat /ˈɪnmiːt/ *noun*. *obsolete* exc. *dial.* **LME.**
[**ORIGIN** from **IN-**[1] + **MEAT** *noun*.]
sing. & (usu.) in *pl.* The edible viscera of an animal; entrails.

in medias res /ɪn ˌmɛdɪɑːs ˈreɪz, ˌmiːdɪɑːs ˈriːz/ *adverbial phr.* **L18.**
[**ORIGIN** Latin.]
Into the midst of things; *esp.* into the middle of a narrative, without preamble.

in medio /ɪn ˈmiːdɪəʊ/ *adverbial phr.* **E17.**
[**ORIGIN** Latin.]
In the middle; in an undecided state.

in memoriam /ɪn mɪˈmɔːrɪam/ *prepositional & noun phr.* **M19.**
[**ORIGIN** Latin.]
▸ **A** *prepositional phr.* To the memory of, in memory of. **M19.**
▸ **B** *noun phr.* A poem, notice, etc., in memory of a dead person. **L19.**

in-migrant /ˈɪnmʌɪgr(ə)nt/ *noun & adjective*. Orig. *US*. **M20.**
[**ORIGIN** from **IN-**[1] + **MIGRANT**.]
(Designating) a person who has migrated from one place to another in the same country.

in-migration /ˈɪnmʌɪgreɪʃ(ə)n/ *noun*. Orig. *US*. **M20.**
[**ORIGIN** from **IN-**[1] + **MIGRATION**.]
The action of migrating from one place to another within the same country.

inmix /ɪnˈmɪks/ *verb trans. & intrans.* **L19.**
[**ORIGIN** from **IN-**[1] + **MIX** *verb*.]
Mix in, blend.

inmost /ˈɪnməʊst/ *adjective, noun, & adverb*. **OE.**
[**ORIGIN** from **IN** *adverb* + **-MOST**.]
▸ **A** *adjective*. Situated furthest within, most inward; *spec.* (of thoughts, feelings etc.) most intimate, deepest, closest. **OE.**

SHELLEY From the inmost depths of its green glen. O. SACKS To know about a man, we ask 'What is his story—his real, inmost story?' W. RAEPER It was to Helen that he confided many of his inmost thoughts.

▸ **B** *noun*. The inmost part. **OE.**

J. FORD Be sure To lodge it in the inmost of thy bosom.

▸ **C** *adverb*. Most inwardly. *rare*. **OE.**
■ **inmostly** *adverb* (*rare*) **M19.**

inn /ɪn/ *noun*.
[**ORIGIN** Old English *inn* (corresp. to Old Norse *inni*) from Germanic, from base of **IN** *adverb*.]
1 *sing.* & in *pl.* A dwelling place, an abode, a lodging; a house. Long *obsolete* exc. *Scot.* **OE.**

fig.: COVERDALE *Isa.* 32:18 The soule is the Inne of God.

2 [translating Latin *hospitium*.] A house of residence for students. *obsolete* exc. as preserved in names of buildings (orig.) so used, esp. ***Inns of Chancery***, ***Inn of Court*** below. **ME.**
3 A public house providing accommodation, refreshments, etc., for payment, esp. for travellers. Now also, a public house serving alcoholic liquor for consumption on the premises, whether providing accommodation or not. **LME.**

E. H. JONES The inns where the family stayed on . . the journey. *fig.*: SIR W. SCOTT That dark inn, the grave!

– **PHRASES**: **Inns of Chancery** *hist.* buildings in London formerly used as hostels for law students. **Inn of Court** (*a*) any of the sets of buildings in London belonging to the four legal societies having the exclusive right of admitting people to the English bar; any of these societies; (*b*) a similar society in Ireland. ***motor inn***: see **MOTOR** *noun & adjective*.
– **COMB.**: **innholder** (now *rare* or *obsolete*), **innkeeper** a person who manages or owns an inn. **innkeeping** *noun & adjective* (*a*) *noun* the owning or managing of an inn; (*b*) *adjective* that owns or manages an inn.

inn /ɪn/ *verb*[1]. Now *rare*. **OE.**
[**ORIGIN** from the noun.]
1 *verb trans.* Lodge, house, find accommodation for. **OE.**
2 *verb intrans.* Lodge, find accommodation, stay. **LME.** ▸**b** Of a coach etc.: stop at an inn. **M18.**

†**inn** *verb*[2] var. of **IN** *verb*.

innards /ˈɪnədz/ *noun pl. colloq.* **E19.**
[**ORIGIN** Repr. a pronunc. of *inwards* pl. of **INWARD** *noun*.]
Entrails; bowels; *fig.* the inside or internal parts.

R. KIPLING 'E feels 'is innards 'eavin', 'is bowels givin' way. R. H. MORRIESON I saw her . . curious and scornful expression that wrung out my innards. E. BLISHEN He . . stared into the piano, as if making an inventory of its innards.

innascibility /ɪ(n)ˌnasɪˈbɪlɪti/ *noun*. Now *rare*. **E17.**
[**ORIGIN** ecclesiastical Latin *innascibilitas*, from *innascibilis* incapable of being born, formed as **IN-**[3] + *nascibilis* who can be born, from *nasci* be born: see **-IBLE**, **-ITY**.]
CHRISTIAN THEOLOGY. The attribute of being independent of birth.

R. CUDWORTH God is the only . . Unmade Being . . his very essence is Ingenerability or Innascibility.

innate /ɪˈneɪt, ˈɪneɪt/ *adjective*. **LME.**
[**ORIGIN** Latin *innatus* pa. pple of *innasci*, formed as **IN-**[2] + *nasci* be born.]
1 Inborn, natural, inherent. **LME.**

T. COLLINS The horse has not half the innate sagacity of the ox. J. F. KENNEDY As believers in a democratic system, we have always had faith in its innate powers of resistance. A. STORR The disagreement between biologists as to what is learned and what is innate.

2 *BOTANY*. Of a part or organ: attached at the apex of another, not adnate. **M19.**
■ **innately** *adverb* **M17.** **innateness** *noun* **E18.** **innatism** *noun* (belief in) the innateness of a quality, aptitude, etc. **E20.** †**innative** *adjective* [after **NATIVE** *adjective*] innate; native: **E16–M19.**

innavigable /ɪˈnavɪgəb(ə)l, ɪnˈna-/ *adjective*. **E16.**
[**ORIGIN** French, or Latin *innavigabilis*, formed as **IN-**[3] + **NAVIGABLE**.]
Not navigable; impassable by boat or ship.

inner /ˈɪnə/ *adjective & noun*.
[**ORIGIN** Old English *inner(r)a*, *in(n)ra* (compar. of **IN** *adverb*) = Old Frisian *inra*, Old High German *innaro*, *-ero* (German *innere*), Old Norse *innri*, *iðri*: see **-ER**[3].]
▸ **A** *adjective*. **1** Situated (more) within or inside; (more or further) inward; internal; *fig.* more secret, central, or essential. Opp. ***outer***. **OE.**

U. BENTLEY From the entrance hall . . , glassy corridors led away into the inner reaches of the school. M. PIERCY He was a widely social man with inner and outer circles of pals.

2 Designating the mind or soul; mental; spiritual. **OE.**

A. STORR Dreams are dramatizations of situations existing in the patient's inner world. C. G. WOLFF The difficulties . . of her life—the sense of inner desolation and loneliness.

– **SPECIAL COLLOCATIONS & COMB.**: **inner Bar** *LAW*. King's or Queen's Counsel collectively. **inner Cabinet** a group of decision-makers within a ministerial Cabinet etc. **inner child** a person's supposed original or authentic self, esp. when regarded as damaged or repressed by childhood traumas; that part of one's personality which manifests itself in childish activities. **inner circle** an exclusive group of friends or associates within a larger group. **inner city** the central area of a city, esp. if dilapidated or characterized by overcrowding, poverty, etc. **inner-directed** *adjective* (*PSYCHOLOGY*) governed by one's own standards formed in childhood and not by external pressures. ***inner ear***: see **EAR** *noun*[1]. **inner forme** *PRINTING* the printing surface (orig. type) containing the pages from which the inner side of a sheet is printed, including matter for the second page of the printed sheet. **inner light** in the Society of Friends, direct spiritual contact with God. **inner man**, **inner woman** (*a*) the soul or mind (of a man or woman); (*b*) *joc.* the stomach (of a man or woman). **inner planet**: with an orbit inside the asteroid belt. **inner reserve** *FINANCE* a secret reserve not disclosed in a balance sheet and due to an understatement of certain capital assets. **inner space** (*a*) the region between the earth and outer space, or below the surface of the sea; (*b*) the part of the mind not normally accessible to consciousness. **inner speech** the mental or internal system or structure which lies behind language. **inner-spring** *adjective & noun* (*N. Amer.*) (*a*) *adjective* = ***INTERIOR-sprung***; (*b*) *noun* an interior-sprung mattress. ***Inner Temple***: see **TEMPLE** *noun*[1] 6. **inner tube** a separate inflatable tube inside the cover of a pneumatic tyre. ***inner woman***: see ***inner man*** above.
▸ **B** *noun*. The inner part of something; an inner position; *spec.* (a shot which hits) the division of a target next outside the bull's-eye. **L19.**
■ **innermore** *adverb & adjective* (*obsolete* exc. *dial.*) †(*a*) more inward or within; (*b*) situated more within, inner: **ME.** **innerness** *noun* **L19.**

innerly /ˈɪnəli/ *adjective*. Long *obsolete* exc. *Scot.* **LME.**
[**ORIGIN** from **INNER** *adjective* + **-LY**[1].]
1 Inner, interior. **LME.**
2 Kindly, affectionate. *Scot.* **E19.**

innerly /ˈɪnəli/ *adverb*. Now *literary*. **ME.**
[**ORIGIN** from **INNER** *adjective* + **-LY**[2].]
Inwardly, internally. Formerly also, more within.

innermost /ˈɪnəməʊst/ *adjective & noun*. **LME.**
[**ORIGIN** from **INNER** *adjective* + **-MOST**.]
▸ **A** *adjective*. Most or furthest within; inmost, deepest, most secret. **LME.**

B. BETTELHEIM Asking a child to reveal his . . innermost thoughts to us is a questionable procedure.

▸ **B** *noun*. The or an innermost part. Now *rare*. **L17.**

innervate /ˈɪnəveɪt, ɪˈnəːveɪt/ *verb trans.* **L19.**
[**ORIGIN** from **IN-**[2] + **NERVE** *noun* + **-ATE**[3].]
ANATOMY & PHYSIOLOGY. Supply (an organ or part) with nerves, or with nervous stimulation. Chiefly as ***innervated*** *ppl adjective*.

innervation /ɪnəˈveɪʃ(ə)n, ɪnəː-/ *noun*. **M19.**
[**ORIGIN** formed as **INNERVATE** + **-ATION**.]
1 *ANATOMY & PHYSIOLOGY*. The action or process of innervating; nervous stimulation. Also, the condition of being innervated; the supply of nerve fibres to, or disposition of nerve fibres within, an organ or part. **M19.**
2 *PSYCHOLOGY*. = **KINAESTHESIS**. **L19.**

innerve /ɪˈnəːv/ *verb trans.* **E19.**
[**ORIGIN** from **IN-**[2] + **NERVE** *verb* or *noun*.]
Animate, invigorate.

inness /ˈɪn-nɪs/ *noun*. **M19.**
[**ORIGIN** from **IN** *adverb* or *attrib. adjective* + **-NESS**.]
The quality or state of being in.

†**innew** *verb* var. of **ENNEW**.

inning /ˈɪnɪŋ/ *noun*[1]. **OE.**
[**ORIGIN** from **IN** *verb* + **-ING**[1]. See also **INNINGS**.]
†**1** A putting or getting in; contents; income. Only in **OE.**
2 The action of getting in, esp. of crops; harvesting. Now *rare* or *obsolete*. **LME.**
3 The action of taking in, inclosing, etc.; *esp.* the reclaiming of marsh or flooded land. **M16.** ▸**b** In *pl.* Land taken in or reclaimed (from the sea etc.). **E18.**
4 *BASEBALL*. Each division of a game during which both sides have a turn at batting. **M19.**

inning /ˈɪnɪŋ/ *noun*[2]. Now *rare* or *obsolete*. **OE.**
[**ORIGIN** from **INN** *verb*[1] + **-ING**[1].]
The action of **INN** *verb*[1]; lodging, housing; a lodging.

innings /ˈɪnɪŋz/ *noun*. Pl. same, (*colloq.*) **-es**. **M18.**
[**ORIGIN** from **INNING** *noun*[1] + **-S**[1].]
1 In cricket and similar games: a portion of a game during which a side or a player is in, e.g. batting, hitting, etc.; the play or score of one player during one spell of being in. **M18.**

M. COX Mr. White-Thomson's side owed their victory to the splendid innings of A. C. Benson, Esq.

2 The time during which a person, party, principle, etc., is in power or possession; a term of or opportunity for an activity; a turn. **M19.**

W. R. GREG The new ideas . . got their innings, and . . have ruled the national policy from 1830 till 1875.

a good innings, **a long innings** *colloq.* a long life.

Inniskilling /ɪnɪˈskɪlɪŋ/ *noun*. **E18.**
[**ORIGIN** The county town of Fermanagh, N. Ireland (now *Enniskillen*).]
hist. A soldier of a regiment originally raised for the defence of Enniskillen in 1689, later the 5th Royal Inniskilling Dragoon Guards (cf. ***the Skins*** s.v. **SKIN** *noun*).
■ **Inniskilliner** *noun* **L18.**

innit /ˈɪnɪt/ *interjection*. *colloq.* **M20.**
[**ORIGIN** Repr. a pronunc.]
Isn't it. Cf. **ENNIT**.

†**innoble** *verb* var. of **ENNOBLE**.

innocence /ˈɪnəs(ə)ns/ *noun*. **ME.**
[**ORIGIN** Old French & mod. French from Latin *innocentia*, from *innocent-*: see **INNOCENT**, **-ENCE**. Cf. **INNOCENCY**.]
1 a Freedom from sin or guilt in general; the state of being untouched by evil; moral purity. **ME.** ▸**b** Freedom from specific guilt; the fact of not being guilty of a charge; guiltlessness. **M16.**

a R. SOUTH How came our first Parents to sin, and to lose their Primitive Innocence?

2 Freedom from cunning or artifice; guilelessness, artlessness, simplicity, lack of suspicion; lack of knowledge or sense, naivety. **LME.**

ADDISON My little Daughter . . asked me with a great deal of innocence, why I never told them. B. EMECHETA None of them wished to display their innocence . . by asking any more questions.

3 An innocent person or thing. Now *rare*. **LME.**
4 Harmlessness, innocuousness. *rare*. **E19.**
5 *BOTANY*. = **BLUET** (b). *US*. **E19.**
– **PHRASES**: ***INJURED innocence***.

innocency /ˈɪnəs(ə)nsi/ *noun*. **LME.**
[**ORIGIN** Latin *innocentia*: see **INNOCENCE**, **-ENCY**.]
1 a = **INNOCENCE** 1a. **LME.** ▸**b** = **INNOCENCE** 1b. **E16.**
2 = **INNOCENCE** 2. **L15.**
3 = **INNOCENCE** 4. **M17.**
4 = **INNOCENCE** 3. **E18.**

innocent /ˈɪnəs(ə)nt/ *adjective & noun*. **ME.**
[**ORIGIN** Old French & mod. French, or Latin *innocent-*, formed as **IN-**[3] + *nocent-* pres. ppl stem of *nocere* hurt, injure: see **-ENT**.]
▸ **A** *adjective*. **1** Free from sin or guilt in general; morally pure; untouched by evil. **ME.**

M. LEITCH Changing from the innocent slip of a young thing . . to the ugly old whore.

2 Free from specific guilt; that has not committed the offence in question; not deserving the punishment etc. inflicted; not guilty. (Foll. by *of*.) **LME.** ▸**b** Foll. by *of*: Free or devoid of; without. *colloq.* **E18.** ▸**c** Entirely free of responsibility for or involvement in an event, while suffering circumstantially from it. **E19.**

H. ARENDT Trying to save an innocent man they employed the . . methods . . adopted in the case of a guilty one. P. H. JOHNSON He was innocent of the particular badness with which F. had charged him. Z. MEDVEDEV Grishin was possibly not entirely innocent of corruption. **b** J. COLBORNE The windows are small apertures . . innocent of glass. G. DURRELL His skull-cap was innocent of decoration.

furcate /ˈfəːkeɪt, -kət/ *adjective*. **E19**.
[ORIGIN Late Latin *furcatus* cloven, from Latin FURCA: see -ATE².]
Forked, branched.

furcate /ˈfəːkeɪt, fəːˈkeɪt/ *verb intrans*. **M19**.
[ORIGIN from FURCATE *adjective*: see -ATE³.]
Fork, divide.
■ **furˈcated** *adjective* = FURCATE *adjective*: **E19**.

furcation /fəːˈkeɪʃ(ə)n/ *noun*. **M17**.
[ORIGIN from Latin FURCA + -ATION, prob. extracted from BIFURCATION.]
The action or an act of forking or branching; a forklike division or branch.

furciferous /fəːˈsɪf(ə)rəs/ *adjective*. *rare* (*joc*.). **E19**.
[ORIGIN from Latin *furcifer* fork-bearer, (with ref. to the 'fork' or yoke used to restrain criminals) rascal, jailbird: see -FEROUS.]
Base, despicable.

furcraea /fəːˈkriːə/ *noun*. Also **-croea**. **E19**.
[ORIGIN mod. Latin, from A. F. de *Fourcroy* (1755–1809), French chemist.]
Any of various tropical American plants of the genus *Furcraea*, allied to the agaves.

furcula /ˈfəːkjʊlə/ *noun*. Pl. **-lae** /-liː/. **M19**.
[ORIGIN Latin, dim. of FURCA: see -CULE.]
1 ORNITHOLOGY. The wishbone of a bird, consisting of the united clavicles. **M19**.
2 EMBRYOLOGY. A process from which the epiglottis is developed. **L19**.
3 ENTOMOLOGY. The forked appendage at the end of the abdomen in springtails, by which the insect jumps. **E20**.

furcular /ˈfəːkjʊlə/ *adjective*. **M16**.
[ORIGIN Old French *furculaire* from Latin FURCULA; later from FURCULA: see -AR¹.]
†**1** Of or pertaining to the collarbone. Only in **M16**.
2 Of or pertaining to the furcula of a bird. **M19**.

furculum /ˈfəːkjʊləm/ *noun*. **M19**.
[ORIGIN mod. Latin, incorrectly formed dim. of FURCA.]
= FURCULA 1.

furfur /ˈfəːfə/ *noun*. *arch*. Pl. **-res** /-riːz/. **LME**.
[ORIGIN Latin = bran.]
(A particle of) dandruff or scurf.

furfuraceous /fəːf(j)əˈreɪʃəs/ *adjective*. **M17**.
[ORIGIN from late Latin *furfuraceus*, from Latin FURFUR: see -ACEOUS.]
Scurfy, scaly, flaky; BOTANY covered with scales resembling bran.

furfural /ˈfəːf(j)ərəl/ *noun*. **L19**.
[ORIGIN from FURFUROL + -AL².]
CHEMISTRY. = FURFURALDEHYDE.

furfuraldehyde /fəːf(j)əˈraldɪhʌɪd/ *noun*. **L19**.
[ORIGIN formed as FURFURAL + ALDEHYDE.]
CHEMISTRY. 2-Furaldehyde, $C_4H_3O{\cdot}CHO$, a colourless liquid used in synthetic resin manufacture, orig. obtained by distilling bran.

furfuran /ˈfəːf(j)ərən/ *noun*. **L19**.
[ORIGIN formed as FURFURAL + -AN.]
CHEMISTRY. = FURAN.

furfurol /ˈfəːf(j)ərɒl/ *noun*. Now *rare* or *obsolete*. **M19**.
[ORIGIN from Latin FURFUR + -OL.]
CHEMISTRY. = FURFURALDEHYDE.

furfurous /ˈfəːf(j)ərəs/ *adjective*. Now *rare*. **LME**.
[ORIGIN from Latin FURFUR + -OUS.]
Branlike; containing bran or particles resembling bran.

furfuryl /ˈfəːf(j)ərʌɪl, -rɪl/ *noun*. **L19**.
[ORIGIN from FURFUROL + -YL.]
CHEMISTRY. = FURYL.

furiant /ˈf(j)ʊərɪənt/ *noun*. **L19**.
[ORIGIN Czech.]
MUSIC. A type of Bohemian dance in alternating duple and triple time; a piece of music for this dance.

furibund /ˈfjʊərɪbʌnd/ *adjective*. **L15**.
[ORIGIN Orig. from Old French & mod. French *furibond*; later from Latin *furibundus*, from *furere* to rage.]
Furious, raging.

†**furicano** *noun* see HURRICANE.

furied /ˈfjʊərɪd/ *adjective*. *rare*. **E17**.
[ORIGIN from FURY + -ED².]
Furious.

furiosity /fjʊərɪˈɒsɪti/ *noun*. **LME**.
[ORIGIN Old French *furiosité* or late Latin *furiositas* fury, (in medieval Latin) fury, madness, from Latin *furiosus*: see FURIOUS, -ITY.]
1 Fury, rage; agony. Now *rare*. **LME**.
2 Insanity, madness. Long only SCOTS LAW (now *hist*.). **LME**.

furioso /fjʊərɪˈəʊzəʊ, *foreign* furiˈoːso/ *noun*, *adjective*, & *adverb*. **M17**.
[ORIGIN Italian from Latin *furiosus* FURIOUS.]
▸ **A** *noun*. Pl. **-os**. A furious person. Now *rare*. **M17**.
▸ **B** *adjective* & *adverb*. MUSIC. (A direction:) furious(ly), wild(ly). **E19**.

furious /ˈfjʊərɪəs/ *adjective*. **LME**.
[ORIGIN Old French *furieus* (mod. *-eux*) from Latin *furiosus*, from *furia* FURY: see -OUS.]
1 Full of fury, very angry, raging; resulting from or showing fury; violent, frantic. Formerly also, (of pain etc.) agonizing. **LME**.

> R. GRAVES Caligula was furious with the knight . . and gave him a good beating. O. MANNING He swung away from them and ran at a furious speed down the stairs.

2 (Violently) mad or insane. Long only SCOTS LAW (now *hist*.). **LME**. ▸†**b** Foolish, absurd. *rare*. **E16–E17**.
3 Excessive; extravagant. *rare*. **M17**.

> DE QUINCEY Without a suspicion of his own furious romancing.

— PHRASES: **fast and furious** rapid(ly), hectic(ally), uproarious(ly).
■ **furiously** *adverb* **LME**. **furiousness** *noun* **E16**.

furison /ˈfjʊərɪz(ə)n/ *noun*. *obsolete* exc. HERALDRY. **M16**.
[ORIGIN Middle Dutch *vuurijzen*, *-ijzer*, from *vuur* FIRE *noun* + *ijzen*, *ijzer* IRON *noun*.]
The steel used to strike fire from a flint.

furl /fəːl/ *verb* & *noun*. **L16**.
[ORIGIN Old French & mod. French *ferler*, earlier *ferlier*, *fermlier*, from *fer(m)* FIRM *adjective* + *lier* bind (from Latin *ligare*).]
▸ **A** *verb*. **1** *verb trans*. Roll up and secure neatly (a sail, flag, umbrella, etc.). Also foll. by *up*. **L16**. ▸†**b** Make undulations on (a surface); ruffle, wrinkle. **L17–M18**. ▸**c** Swathe or envelop *in* or *with* something folded or twisted. Now *rare*. **E18**.

> *fig*.: R. LOVELACE All the hopes of your reward you furl.

2 *verb intrans*. Be rolled or gathered up or *up* in a twisted form. **L17**.
3 *verb intrans*. Roll away, vanish. Foll. by *off*, *from*. Now *rare*. **E19**.
▸ **B** *noun*. **1** A roll or fold of something furled. **M17**.
2 The action of furling; the state or manner of being furled. **M19**.

furlong /ˈfəːlɒŋ/ *noun*.
[ORIGIN Old English *furlang*, from *furh* FURROW *noun* + *lang* LONG *adjective*¹.]
1 Orig., the length of the furrow in a common field (regarded as a square of 10 acres), usu. understood to be equal to 40 poles; also, (equal to the Roman *stadium*), the eighth part of a Roman mile. Now, the eighth part of an English mile, 220 yards (201.168 m). **OE**. ▸†**b** A running track. **LME–E16**.
2 An area of land equal to one square furlong; *gen*. an indefinite area of land, a field; the boundary of such an area. Now *dial*. **OE**.

furlough /ˈfəːləʊ/ *noun* & *verb*. Also †**-low**, (earlier as noun) †**forloff**. **E17**.
[ORIGIN Dutch *verlof*, modelled on German *Verlaub*, from *ver-* FOR-¹ + West Germanic base of LEAVE *noun*¹. The stress on the first syll. seems to show infl. of synon. Dutch *oorlof* = German *Urlaub* (military or civilian) leave.]
▸ **A** *noun*. **1** (A permit for) leave of absence, esp. as granted to a soldier, missionary, etc. **E17**.

> WELLINGTON Officers not on furlough . . are to join their corps without delay. M. J. BRUCCOLI To arrange . . for Zelda to have three or four months of furlough a year in the company of a nurse.

†**2** A passport; a permit. **M17–E19**.
▸ **B** *verb*. Chiefly *US*.
1 *verb trans*. Grant (a person) a furlough; give leave of absence to. **L18**.
2 *verb intrans*. Spend a furlough. **L19**.

furmety *noun* var. of FRUMENTY.

furnace /ˈfəːnɪs/ *noun* & *verb*. **ME**.
[ORIGIN Old French *fornais(e)* (mod. *fournaise*), from Latin *fornax*, *fornac-*, from *fornus*, *furnus* oven.]
▸ **A** *noun*. **1** An apparatus or structure consisting of a combustion chamber in which minerals, metals, etc., may be subjected to continuous intense heat. Formerly also, an oven or chamber for producing a low continuous heat (as for incubation). **ME**. ▸**b** *fig*. A place of intense heat; a severe test or trial. **ME**. ▸**c** (The fires of) a volcano. *rhet*. or *poet*. **M17**.

> A. KOESTLER The sky was like a furnace and the sun its open door. **b** AV *Isa*. 48:10 I haue chosen thee in the fornace of affliction.

blast furnace, ***electric arc furnace***, ***open-hearth furnace***, etc.
2 A boiler, a cauldron. *obsolete* exc. *dial*. **ME**.
3 A closed fireplace for heating a building by means of hot-water pipes etc. **L17**.
4 (Usu. **F-**.) *The* constellation Fornax. Orig. ***the Chemist's Furnace***. **M19**.
▸ **B** *verb*. **1** *verb trans*. & *intrans*. *fig*. Exhale or issue as from a smoking furnace. Long *rare* or *obsolete*. **L16**.
2 *verb trans*. Subject to the heat of a furnace. **E17**.

furnage /ˈfəːnɪdʒ/ *noun*. **L15**.
[ORIGIN Old French *fornage* (mod. *fournage*), from *forn* (mod. *four*), from Latin *furnus* oven; in medieval Latin *furn-*, *fornagium*: see -AGE.]
hist. The price paid for baking; in FEUDAL LAW, the fee paid to the lord by tenants bound to bake in the lord's oven, for permission to use their own.

furner /ˈfəːnə/ *noun*. Long *obsolete* exc. *dial*. **LME**.
[ORIGIN Old French *fornier* from late Latin *furnarius*, from Latin *furnus* oven: see -ER².]
A baker.

†**furniment** *noun*. **M–L16**.
[ORIGIN Old French *fornement* (mod. *fourniment* from Italian *fornimento*), from *fornir* (mod. *fournir*) FURNISH *verb*: see -MENT.]
Decoration, fitting out; in *pl*., fittings, furnishings.

furnish /ˈfəːnɪʃ/ *noun*. **E16**.
[ORIGIN from the verb.]
Orig., a provision or supply of anything. Now only *spec*., the materials from which paper is manufactured.

furnish /ˈfəːnɪʃ/ *verb trans*. **LME**.
[ORIGIN Old French *furniss-* lengthened stem of *furnir* (mod. *fournir*) from Proto-Romance from West Germanic verb = promote, accommodate, from base of FRAME *verb*, FROM: see -ISH².]
1 Provide or supply *with* something necessary, useful, or desirable; also foll. by †*in*, †*of*. Formerly also, (foll. by *of*, *with*) fill, occupy (a place) with people. **LME**. ▸†**b** Provide for (a need or occasion). **LME–M17**.

> W. S. CHURCHILL A system which . . had for long furnished mankind with its brightest dreams. G. HEYER I could furnish you with the names of at least three of Stavely's mistresses.

2 Provide, supply, yield (something). **LME**.

> J. W. KRUTCH To furnish reliable evidence of his desires, tastes, . . and even prejudices. P. F. BOLLER Virginia, New York, Massachusetts, and Ohio have furnished most of the nation's Chief Executives.

3 Orig., supply with what is necessary, as prepare or equip (a person, ship, etc.) for work or service. Now only, fit up (a house, room, etc.) with (all) the necessary (*esp*. movable) furniture and accessories; equip *with* furniture of a specified kind. **LME**. ▸†**b** Accomplish, complete, fulfil, (a task). **L15–M16**. ▸†**c** Decorate, adorn. **L16–L17**.

> A. J. CRONIN It had only one room and was . . sparsely furnished. L. DURRELL The interior was . . furnished with chairs of wicker. **c** SHAKES. *Much Ado* I'll show thee some attires, and have thy counsel Which is the best to furnish me to-morrow.

furnished house, **furnished rooms**, etc., premises let with furniture.
— WITH ADVERBS IN SPECIALIZED SENSES: **furnish forth** *arch*. (**a**) supply or equip with or *with* what is necessary; (**b**) provide (something). **furnish out** (now *rare*) (**a**) supply what is lacking, complete; (**b**) provide adequately for.
■ **furnisher** *noun* (**a**) a provider or supplier; *spec*. a furniture supplier; (**b**) a brush or roller supplying colour in fabric printing: **E16**. **furnishment** *noun* (**a**) the action of furnishing; the state of being furnished; (**b**) (in *pl*., now *rare*) supplies, munitions: **M16**.

furnishing /ˈfəːnɪʃɪŋ/ *noun*. **LME**.
[ORIGIN from FURNISH *verb* + -ING¹.]
1 Material or equipment necessary for some purpose. Now only *spec*. (usu. in *pl*.) furniture and other (decorative) accessories (as curtains, carpets, etc.) for a room, house, etc. **LME**. ▸**b** (A) decoration; a clothing accessory. **L16**. ▸†**c** In *pl*. Unimportant appendages; mere externals. *rare* (Shakes.). Only in **E17**.
soft furnishing(s): see SOFT *adjective*.
2 The action of FURNISH *verb*; *arch*. an instance of this. **L15**.

furniture /ˈfəːnɪtʃə/ *noun*. **E16**.
[ORIGIN French *fourniture* (Old French *forneture*, Anglo-Latin *furnitura*), from *fournir* FURNISH *verb*.]
†**1** The action of furnishing; (a) decoration. **E16–L17**.

> SHAKES. *1 Hen. IV* There shalt thou know thy charge, and there receive Money and order for their furniture. ROBERT JOHNSON They adorne themselves with plumes and feathers . . and such like furnitures.

2 The condition of being equipped or prepared in body or mind (*esp*. for military action etc.); mental cultivation or culture. *arch*. **M16**.

> J. MASON A Thing that hath been often attempted by Men of mean Furniture.

3 †**a** *sing*. & in *pl*. Personal belongings; dress, apparel; armour. **M16–M18**. ▸**b** *sing*. & (*rare*) in *pl*. The harness, housings, trappings, etc., of a horse or other animal. **M16**. ▸**c** *sing*. & †in *pl*. Apparatus, tools, military equipment and weaponry; *fig*. mental equipment or apparatus. Now chiefly NAUTICAL, the movable equipment of a ship, as the rigging, sails, tackle, etc. **M16**.
4 *sing*. & †in *pl*. Accessory equipment. Now *spec*. the fingerplate, handle, and lock of a door; the plate, handle, etc., of a coffin; the mountings of a rifle. **M16**. ▸**b** PRINTING. The pieces of wood, metal, etc. placed round or between the type to make blank spaces and fasten the matter in the chase. **L17**.
5 Something to fill or occupy a space, vessel, etc.; contents. Formerly also, a stock or supply of anything; stores, provisions. Now *rare*. **M16**.

> J. RAY The Earth remaining without any Furniture or Inhabitants. T. BEST Fishes . . make a considerable addition to the furniture of the table.

6 (The predominant sense.) The movable (functional) articles in a room, house, etc.; such articles in general. Also (now *rare*), ornamental hangings or drapery, bedlinen. **L16**. ▸**b** *fig*. Something or someone regarded merely as filling a vacant space in a room etc. (cf. ***part of the***

F

furniture below); *esp.* well-bound books intended to fill and adorn bookshelves. E20.

G. B. SHAW The trade in sham antique furniture. J. G. COZZENS The living-room . . had almost no furniture—two chairs, a card-table. **b** B. FRIEDAN The need . . that makes husbands 'furniture' in their own homes.

part of the furniture *colloq.* a person or thing taken for granted.
7 *MUSIC.* A powerful mixture stop in an organ. L17.
– COMB.: **furniture beetle** a small wood-boring beetle of the family Anobiidae (cf. WOODWORM); esp. *Anobium punctatum*; **furniture polish**: for the woodwork of furniture; **furniture van** a large van used to move furniture from one house to another; a removal van.
■ **furnitureless** *adjective* L19.

furor /ˈfjʊərɔː/ *noun*. LME.
[ORIGIN Latin, from *furere* to rage: see -OR.]
1 Fury, rage; madness. Now *rare* or *obsolete*. LME.

T. WYATT What rage is this? What furor?

2 The inspired frenzy of artists and prophets; an excited mood. L16.

GEO. ELIOT They were written in a furor. S. FOOTE I am afraid the poetic Furor may have betray'd me into some Indecency.

With defining adjective in Latin, as **furor academicus**, **furor poeticus**, **furor scribendi**, etc.
3 = FURORE. Now chiefly *N. Amer.* E18.

R. MAY What a furor is made over kissing a girl.

furore /fjʊ(ə)ˈrɔːri, fjʊ(ə)ˈrɔː/ *noun*. L18.
[ORIGIN Italian, formed as FUROR.]
1 Enthusiastic admiration; a craze or rage. L18.
2 (An) uproar, (a) disturbance, (a) fuss M20.

H. CARPENTER Chester's critiques were causing a furore because of their outspokenness.

furosemide *noun* see FRUSEMIDE.

furphy /ˈfəːfi/ *noun*. *Austral. slang*. E20.
[ORIGIN from *Furphy* water and sanitary carts, manufactured by the Furphy family in Victoria during the First World War.]
A false report or rumour; an absurd story.

D. CUSACK Don't tell me you boys believe *that* old furphy?

furred /fəːd/ *adjective*. ME.
[ORIGIN from FUR *noun*[1], *verb*: see -ED[1].]
1 Made of, lined or trimmed with fur. ME.
2 Covered or coated with a deposit of fur (cf. FUR *noun*[1] 4). E16.
3 Of an animal: having fur. M16.
4 Wearing fur; wrapped or clothed in furs. L16.

furrier /ˈfʌrɪə/ *noun*[1]. ME.
[ORIGIN Old French *forreor* (mod. *fourreur*), from *forrer* FUR *verb*; later alt. after CLOTHIER.]
A dealer in or dresser of fur or furs.
■ **furriery** *noun* †(*a*) (*collect.*) furs; (*b*) the process of dressing and making up furs; the business of a furrier: L18.

†**furrier** *noun*[2] var. of FOURRIER.

furrin /ˈfʌrɪn/ *adjective*. *dial.* or *joc.* L19.
[ORIGIN Repr. a pronunc.]
= FOREIGN *adjective*.
■ **furriner** *noun* = FOREIGNER M19.

furring /ˈfəːrɪŋ/ *noun*. LME.
[ORIGIN from FUR *noun*[1], *verb* + -ING[1].]
1 The action of clothing or adorning with fur; a lining or trimming of fur; fur or furs collectively. LME.
2 The state of being or process of becoming furred or crusted; a coating of fur (FUR *noun*[1] 4). E17.
3 a *SHIPBUILDING.* (A piece of timber used in) the action or process of double planking a ship's side. E17. ▸**b** *CARPENTRY.* The fixing of timber strips to uneven joists etc. to make a plane surface. L17.
4 The business of trading in furs or hunting furred animals. L18.

furrow /ˈfʌrəʊ/ *noun*. Also (*obsolete* exc. *Scot.* or *dial.*) **fur**.
[ORIGIN Old English *furh* = Old Frisian *furch*, Middle Low German, Middle Dutch *vore* (Dutch *voor*), Old High German *furuh* (German *Furche*), Old Norse *for* trench, drain, from Germanic from Indo-European base repr. also by Latin *porca* ridge between furrows.]
1 A narrow trench made in the earth by a plough, esp. for seed. OE. ▸**b** Arable land; ploughed land; cornfields. *poet.* LME. ▸**c** A ploughing. Now only *Scot.* E17.

b SHAKES. *Temp.* Sun-burnt sicklemen, of August weary, Come hither from the furrow and be merry.

plough a lonely furrow: see PLOUGH *verb*.
2 A trench, a drain. ME.

N. GORDIMER Make some more furrows, then the water runs away.

†**3** A piece of land having the length and breadth of a furrow. ME–L15.
4 Something resembling a furrow; a rut or track, a groove, a long narrow depression or indentation. LME. ▸**b** A deep wrinkle on the face (esp. on the brow). L16. ▸**c** Any of the grooves in the face of a millstone. E19.

R. HOOKE Great and deep scratches, or furrows. **b** S. O'FAOLÁIN The little angry furrow between her eyebrows.

– COMB.: **furrow slice** the slice of earth turned up by the mould board of a plough.
■ **furrowless** *adjective* M19. **furrow-like** *adjective* M19. **furrowy** *adjective* full of furrows or wrinkles E17.

furrow /ˈfʌrəʊ/ *verb*. LME.
[ORIGIN from the noun.]
1 *verb trans.* Make furrows in (the earth) with a plough; plough. LME.
2 *verb trans.* Make grooves, tracks, or indentations in. LME. ▸**b** Make a track through (water). LME. ▸**c** Make wrinkles in (the face, the brow); (of tears) make a path or mark across. E16. ▸**d** Of a river: excavate (a channel), force (its way) along a channel. E17.

J. FORBES A hard . . surface, furrowed by linear marks. **b** E. BOWEN A swan furrowed the water. **c** BYRON Fair cheeks were furrowed with hot tears. J. L. WATEN A frown furrowing his swarthy face.

3 *verb intrans.* Make furrows with a plough; make a track through water. L16.
4 *verb intrans.* Become furrowed; wrinkle. M20.

C. RAYNER Charles's brow furrowed as he . . politely obeyed his host.

■ **furrowed** *ppl adjective* having furrows, ploughed; wrinkled, grooved: L16.

furry /ˈfʌri/ *noun*. *dial.* L18.
[ORIGIN Uncertain: perh. connected with FAIR *noun*[1], Latin *feria*.]
A festival held annually at Helston, Cornwall on the eighth of May; (more fully ***furry dance***) a distinctive communal dance performed at this (also called ***floral dance***).

furry /ˈfəːri/ *adjective*. L17.
[ORIGIN from FUR *noun*[1] + -Y[1].]
1 Of or consisting of fur; made of, lined or trimmed with fur. L17.
2 Covered with or wearing fur. L17.

G. C. DAVIES A furry little water-rat swimming along.

3 Resembling fur; coated (as) with fur (cf. FUR *noun*[1] 4). M18.

T. HARDY Cushions of furry moss. W. GOLDING The rock was furry with coloured growths.

■ **furriness** *noun* E20.

furthcoming *verbal noun* see FORTHCOMING *verbal noun*.

further /ˈfəːðə/ *noun*. *obsolete* exc. *Scot.* E16.
[ORIGIN from the verb.]
= FURTHERANCE.

further /ˈfəːðə/ *adjective*. See also FARTHER *adjective*.
[ORIGIN Old English *furþra* = Old Frisian *fordera*, Old Saxon *furþ(i)ro*, *forþro*, Old High German *fordaro*, from Germanic base of FORTH: see -ER[3]. Cf. FURTHER *adverb*.]
†**1** That is before another in position, order, or rank. OE–E19.
2 More extended, going beyond what exists or has been dealt with, additional. ME.

T. HARDY She refrained from further speech. J. CONRAD He shuffled uneasily, but took no further notice. E. BOWEN He wrote for booklets containing further particulars.

further education formal education, but not usu. university education, provided for people who have left school. **until further notice**, **until further orders** until explicitly changed.
3 More distant or advanced, remoter; *esp.* the remoter of two. Cf. earlier FARTHER *adjective* 3. L16.

J. CONRAD The passage leading beyond was dark at the further end.

Further India the regions between the Indian subcontinent and China, i.e. the south-east peninsula of Asia.
– NOTE: See note s.v. FARTHER *adverb & adjective*.

further /ˈfəːðə/ *verb*. See also FARTHER *verb*.
[ORIGIN Old English *fyrþr(i)an* from *furþor*, *-þra* FURTHER *adverb*, *adjective*.]
1 *verb trans.* Help on, assist; promote, favour (an undertaking, movement, cause, etc.). OE.

C. CHAPLIN We went to a school for the week . . which did little to further my education. A. BLOND By furthering and enhancing his author's causes, he became highly successful.

2 *verb intrans.* Go on, continue; make progress. *obsolete* exc. *Scot.* ME.
†**3** *verb trans.* Honour. *rare.* Only in LME.
■ **furtherer** *noun* a person who or thing which helps something forward; a promoter, a supporter: LME.

further /ˈfəːðə/ *adverb*. See also FARTHER *adverb*.
[ORIGIN Old English *furþor*, *-ur*, corresp. to Old Frisian *further*, Old Saxon *furþor* (early mod. Dutch *voorder*), Old High German *furdar*, *-ir*, from Germanic base of FORTH: see -ER[3]. Cf. FURTHER *adjective*.]
1 To or at a more advanced point in space or time; = FARTHER *adverb* 1. OE.

T. HARDY Instead of coming further she slowly retraced her steps.

2 Beyond the point reached, to a greater extent, more. OE.

J. MITCHELL His influence was spread even further than his name. M. KEANE He knew she was right so he didn't take the matter further.

3 In addition, additionally; moreover (esp. used when introducing a fresh consideration in an argument). ME.

K. GRAHAME And further, in addition thereto, you shall give me . . breakfast.

further to following on from (esp. an earlier letter etc.).
4 To or at a greater distance; by a greater interval. LME.

B. JOWETT There is nothing further from his thoughts than scepticism.

I'll see you further first used as a strong refusal of a request.
– NOTE: See note s.v. FARTHER *adverb & adjective*.

furtherance /ˈfəːð(ə)r(ə)ns/ *noun*. LME.
[ORIGIN from FURTHER *adverb* + -ANCE.]
The fact of being helped forward; the action of helping forward; advancement, aid, assistance.

H. H. WILSON In furtherance of this project, she kept her son in a state of ignorance.

furtherly /ˈfəːðəli/ *adverb & adjective*. ME.
[ORIGIN from FURTHER *adverb*, *adjective*: see -LY[1].]
▸ **A** *adverb*. = FURTHER *adverb*. ME.
▸ **B** *adjective*. Favourable, advanced, flourishing. E16.

furthermore /fəːðəˈmɔː/ *adverb*. ME.
[ORIGIN from FURTHER *adverb* + MORE *adverb*.]
†**1** = FURTHER *adverb* 1, 2. ME–M16.
2 = FURTHER *adverb* 3. ME.

furthermost /ˈfəːðəməʊst/ *adjective*. See also FARTHERMOST. LME.
[ORIGIN from FURTHER *adjective* + -MOST.]
†**1** Foremost, first. Only in LME.
2 Most distant or remote, furthest. L15.

E. B. PUSEY He . . sets himself to flee to the then furthermost West.

furthersome /ˈfəːðəs(ə)m/ *adjective*. E17.
[ORIGIN from FURTHER *verb*, *adverb* + -SOME[1].]
1 Adapted to further or help forward; advantageous, helpful. E17.

CARLYLE Two little pieces of advice which may prove furthersome to him.

2 Rash, inclined to go forward. M18.

furthest /ˈfəːðɪst/ *adjective & adverb*. See also FARTHEST. LME.
[ORIGIN Formed as superl. to FURTHER *adjective*, *adverb*: see -EST[1].]
▸ **A** *adjective*. **1** Most advanced in any direction; (as superl. of FAR *adjective*) most remote, farthest. LME.

SWIFT The furthest corner of Naboth's vineyard.

2 Most remote in time. *obsolete* exc. as below. M16.
at furthest, **at the furthest** at the greatest distance, at the latest, at most.
▸ **B** *adverb*. To or at the greatest distance, farthest. LME.

D. C. MURRAY Even when his thoughts wandered furthest, he was mechanically accurate.

furtive /ˈfəːtɪv/ *adjective*. E17.
[ORIGIN Old French & mod. French *furtif*, *-ive* or Latin *furtivus*, *-iva*, from *furt-* in *furtum* theft: see -IVE.]
1 Done by stealth; secret, clandestine, surreptitious. E17. ▸**b** Stealthy, sly. M19.

T. C. WOLFE The students made furtive drawings, or passed notes. D. HAMMETT There was nothing furtive about his going in: he entered boldly and directly. **b** CONAN DOYLE A serious change came over the Professor. He became furtive and sly.

2 Stolen; taken by stealth. Now *rare* exc. as passing into sense 1. E18.

M. PRIOR Do they [planets] . . Dart furtive beams, and glory not their own?

3 Thievish. E19.

R. F. BURTON The Highlander could not be . . trusted to withhold his furtive hand from the flocks.

■ **furtively** *adverb* L15. **furtiveness** *noun* L19.

furuncle /ˈfjʊərʌŋk(ə)l/ *noun*. LME.
[ORIGIN Latin *furunculus* lit. 'petty thief', dim. of *fur* thief: see -UNCLE.]
MEDICINE. A boil.
■ **fuˈruncular**, **fuˈrunculous** *adjectives* of, pertaining to, or characterized by boils; of the nature of a boil: M19.

furunculosis /fjʊˌrʌŋkjəˈləʊsɪs/ *noun*. Pl. **-loses** /-ˈləʊsiːz/. L19.
[ORIGIN formed as FURUNCLE + -OSIS.]
1 *MEDICINE.* A condition marked by the occurrence of multiple and often recurrent boils. L19.
2 A bacterial disease of salmonid fishes, marked by ulcers resembling boils. E20.

fury /ˈfjʊəri/ *noun*. LME.
[ORIGIN Old French & mod. French *furie* from Latin *furia*, from *furiosus* FURIOUS, from *furere* to rage: see -Y[3].]
▸ **I 1** (A fit of) fierce passion, madness, wild anger, or frenzied rage. LME.

F. NORRIS One of those furies of impotent grief and wrath . . suddenly took possession of him. S. RUSHDIE In cold fury my uncle hurled his son from the room.

2 Impetuosity or violence, esp. in battle. M16.

R. W. EMERSON To hunt with fury . . all the game that is in nature.

3 Inspired frenzy; (artistic) inspiration. Now *rare* or *obsolete*. **M16.**

POPE A sacred fury fires My ravish'd breast, and all the Muse inspires.

4 Violence of weather, disease, or other agency. **L16.**

E. STILLINGFLEET These waters falling down with so much fury and violence.

▸**II 5** An avenging or tormenting infernal spirit; *spec.* (freq. **F-**) each of the three Greek or Roman goddesses of vengeance and punishment. Freq. in *pl.* **LME.**

T. ARNOLD All prayed that the furies of her father's blood might visit her with vengeance.

6 A person resembling an avenging fury; *esp.* an angry or malignant woman, a virago. **LME.**

DRYDEN Remember, sir, your fury of a wife.

furyl /ˈfjʊərʌɪl, -rɪl/ *noun.* **E20.**
[ORIGIN from FURFURYL.]
CHEMISTRY. A radical, ·C_4H_3O (of which two isomers exist), derived from furan. Usu. in *comb.*

furze /fəːz/ *noun.*
[ORIGIN Old English *fyrs*: ult. origin unknown.]
1 = GORSE. **OE.**
needle furze: see NEEDLE *noun*.
2 *fig.* A beard; a bushy growth of hair. **E17.**
■ **furzy** *adjective* of or like furze; overgrown with furze; bushy; fuzzy: **E17.**

fusain /ˈfjuːzeɪn, *in sense 1 also foreign* fyzɛ̃ (*pl. same*)/ *noun.* **L19.**
[ORIGIN French = spindle tree, charcoal.]
1 Artists' charcoal (from the wood of the spindle tree); a charcoal drawing. **L19.**
2 *GEOLOGY.* Coal resembling wood charcoal. Now *spec.* one of the lithotypes of coal, a dull, friable, porous material. **L19.**

fusarium /fjʊˈzɛːrɪəm/ *noun.* **E20.**
[ORIGIN mod. Latin (see below), from Latin *fusus* spindle.]
A mould of the large genus *Fusarium*, members of which are responsible for various wilting diseases of plants; infestation with any of these or related moulds.

fusarole /ˈfjuːzərəʊl/ *noun.* **M17.**
[ORIGIN French *fusarolle* from Italian *fusaruola*, ult. from Latin *fusus* spindle: see -OLE¹.]
ARCHITECTURE. A semicircular beaded moulding usu. placed under the echinus in the Doric, Ionic, and Corinthian orders.

†**fusby** *noun. slang. derog.* **E18–L19.**
[ORIGIN Prob. alt. of FUBSY.]
A (fat) woman.

fusc *adjective* var. of FUSK.

fuscous /ˈfʌskəs/ *adjective.* **M17.**
[ORIGIN from Latin *fuscus* dusky + -OUS.]
Of a dark or sombre colour; dusky.

fuse /fjuːz/ *noun*¹. Also ***fuze**. **M17.**
[ORIGIN Italian *fuso* spindle, from Latin *fusus*.]
1 Orig., a tube, casing, cord, etc., filled or saturated with combustible matter for igniting a bomb, blasting charge, etc. Now also more widely, any device or component designed to detonate the explosive charge in a bomb, mine, warhead, etc., after an interval of time, or under set circumstances such as impact. **M17.**

I. MURDOCH He felt like someone who had lit a long fuse to a barrel of gun powder. *Guardian* Bombs equipped with photo cells, magnetic and proximity fuses, and vibration detectors that would set off the charge if you so much as looked at it.

short fuse: see SHORT *adjective*.
2 Prepared material of which fuses may be made by cutting it into lengths. **M18.**

fuse /fjuːz/ *noun*². **L19.**
[ORIGIN from FUSE *verb*¹.]
(A safety device containing) a strip or wire of easily melted metal which, when incorporated in an electric circuit, will melt and so interrupt the circuit if the current increases beyond a set magnitude.
blow a fuse (cf. BLOW *verb*¹ 16) cause or undergo the failure of a fuse; *fig.* react with sudden anger or consternation, be incapacitated by exertion or shock.
– COMB.: **fuse box** a small cupboard or box containing the fuses for the circuits in a house etc.; **fuse wire** (a length of) wire suitable for use as a fuse (of given current rating).

fuse /fjuːz/ *verb*¹. **L16.**
[ORIGIN Latin *fus-* pa. ppl stem of *fundere* pour, melt; cf. FOUND *verb*².]
1 a *verb trans.* & (later) *intrans.* Melt or undergo melting by means of intense heat. **L16.** ▸**b** *verb trans.* Liquefy, thin (the blood). *arch.* **E18.**

B. TAYLOR As by fierce heat, the chains be fused apart.

2 *verb trans.* & (later) *intrans.* Blend, unite, or bond (together) as one whole (as) by melting; be blended etc. thus. **M17.** ▸**b** *verb intrans.* Of anatomical structures, groups of atoms, etc.: coalesce, join. Chiefly as ***fused ppl adjective***, congenitally joined, forming one structure. **L19.**

E. TEMPLETON All the other evenings . . had fused together in her memory into one indistinguishable whole. E. JOHNSON No writer so intimately fuses the familiar and the strange as he does. **b** ST G. J. MIVART In Tortoises all the trunk vertebræ are fused.

fused participle *GRAMMAR* a participle grammatically analysed as being joined with a preceding noun or pronoun where there is no clear indication of the nominal or verbal use of the participle (as *we heard them playing*), rather than as a gerund requiring the possessive (as *we heard their playing*).

fuse /fjuːz/ *verb*² *trans.* Also ***fuze**. **E19.**
[ORIGIN from FUSE *noun*¹.]
Provide (a bomb etc.) with a fuse; set by means of a fuse. Chiefly as ***fused*** pa. pple.

L. DURRELL The bomb, placed in a cinema and fused to go off during a charity performance.

fuse /fjuːz/ *verb*³. **E20.**
[ORIGIN from FUSE *noun*²: sense 2 partly use of FUSE *verb*¹.]
1 *verb trans.* Equip with a fuse. Chiefly as ***fused*** pa. pple. **E20.**
2 a *verb intrans.* Of an electric light, appliance, etc.: fail or cease to function owing to the melting of a fuse. **M20.** ▸**b** *verb trans.* Cause (an appliance etc.) to fail or cease to function thus. **M20.**

fusee /fjuːˈziː/ *noun*¹. Also **fuzee**. **L16.**
[ORIGIN French *fusée* spindleful, ult. from Latin *fusus* spindle.]
†**1** A spindle-shaped figure. Only in **L16.**
2 A conical pulley or wheel; *esp.* the wheel of a clock or watch on which the chain is wound and which equalizes the power of the mainspring. **E17.**
3 = FUSE *noun*¹ 1. **L17.**
4 A large-headed match for lighting a cigar or pipe in the wind. **M19.**

fusee /fjuːˈziː/ *noun*². *obsolete* exc. *hist.* Also **fuzee**. **M17.**
[ORIGIN French *fusil*: see FUSIL *noun*².]
= FUSIL *noun*² 2.

fuselage /ˈfjuːzəlɑːʒ, -lɪdʒ/ *noun.* **E20.**
[ORIGIN French, from *fuseler* shape like a spindle, from *fuseau* spindle: see FUSIL *noun*¹, -AGE.]
The elongated body section of an aeroplane, containing the crew and passengers or cargo.

fusel oil /ˈfjuːz(ə)l ɔɪl/ *noun phr.* **M19.**
[ORIGIN German *Fusel* bad brandy etc.; cf. *fuseln* FOOZLE *verb*.]
A mixture of several alcohols, esp. amyl alcohol, which is a by-product of alcoholic fermentation and can sometimes make alcoholic liquors harmful or poisonous.

†**fusht** *interjection. Scot. & dial.* **L18–E19.**
[ORIGIN Repr. Scot. dial. pronunc. of WHISHT.]
Hush!

fusible /ˈfjuːzɪb(ə)l/ *adjective.* **LME.**
[ORIGIN Old French & mod. French, or medieval Latin *fusibilis*, from *fus-* (see FUSE *verb*¹) + *-ibilis* -IBLE.]
Able to be melted.
fusible plug a metal plug in the skin of a boiler, designed to melt and allow escape of pressure if the contents reach too high a temperature.
■ **fusiˈbility** *noun* **E17.**

fusidic /fjʊˈsɪdɪk/ *adjective.* **M20.**
[ORIGIN from mod. Latin *Fusidium* (see below), from Latin *fusus* spindle: see -IC.]
BIOCHEMISTRY. ***fusidic acid***, an antibiotic steroid obtained from a strain of the fungus *Fusidium coccineum* and used esp. to treat staphylococcus infection.

fusiform /ˈfjuːzɪfɔːm/ *adjective.* **M18.**
[ORIGIN from Latin *fusus* spindle + -I- + -FORM. Cf. French *fusiforme*.]
Chiefly *BOTANY & ZOOLOGY.* Tapering at both ends, spindle-shaped.

fusil /ˈfjuːzɪl/ *noun*¹. **LME.**
[ORIGIN Old French *fu(i)sil*, *fusel* (mod. *fuseau*), from Proto-Romance dim. of Latin *fusus* spindle.]
HERALDRY. A charge in the form of an elongated lozenge.

fusil /ˈfjuːzɪl/ *noun*². **L16.**
[ORIGIN French, ult. from Latin FOCUS *noun* hearth (in popular Latin fire).]
†**1** A flint in a tinderbox. Only in **L16.**
2 *hist.* A light musket. **L17.**

fusile /ˈfjuːsʌɪl, -zʌɪl, -zɪl/ *adjective.* Also **fusil** /ˈfjuːzɪl/. **LME.**
[ORIGIN Latin *fusilis* molten, from *fus-*: see FUSE *verb*¹, -ILE.]
1 Formed by melting or casting, cast. **LME.**
2 Able to be melted; molten. Now *rare*. **E17.**

fusilier /fjuːzɪˈlɪə/ *noun.* Also ***-eer**. **L17.**
[ORIGIN French, from *fusil* FUSIL *noun*²: see -IER.]
Orig. (now *hist.*), a soldier armed with a fusil. Now, a member of any of several British regiments orig. armed with fusils (usu. in *pl.*, in regimental titles).

fusillade /fjuːzɪˈleɪd, -ˈlɑːd/ *noun & verb.* **E19.**
[ORIGIN French, from *fusiller* shoot: see -ADE.]
▸**A** *noun.* (Wholesale slaughter by) a simultaneous or successive discharge of firearms; *fig.* a sustained outburst or barrage of criticism etc. **E19.**
▸**B** *verb trans.* Shoot down or assault by a fusillade. **E19.**

fusilli /f(j)ʊˈziːli/ *noun pl.* **M20.**
[ORIGIN Italian, lit., 'little spindles', dim. of *fuso* spindle.]
Spiral-shaped pasta, usu. in short pieces.

fusilly /ˈfjuːzɪli/ *adjective.* **LME.**
[ORIGIN Old French *fuselé*, from *fusel* FUSIL *noun*¹.]
HERALDRY. Of a field: covered with a pattern of fusils.

fusimotor /ˈfjuːzɪməʊtə/ *adjective.* **M20.**
[ORIGIN from Latin *fusus* spindle + MOTOR *adjective*.]
ANATOMY. Of, pertaining to, or designating the motor neurons with slender fibres which innervate muscle spindles.

fusion /ˈfjuːʒ(ə)n/ *noun.* **M16.**
[ORIGIN French, or Latin *fusio(n-)*, from *fus-* pa. ppl stem of *fundere* pour: see FUSE *verb*¹, -ION.]
1 The action or process of melting by means of intense heat; the state of fluidity as a result of being heated. **M16.** ▸**b** A fused mass. **E19.**
2 The union, blending, or bonding together as one whole of different things (as) by melting. **L18.** ▸**b** The coalition of political parties or factions. **M19.** ▸**c** *PHYSIOLOGY & PSYCHOLOGY.* [translating German *Verschmelzung*.] A blending of separate stimuli (e.g. on each eye) into a unitary experience; the process whereby a succession of similar stimuli produces a continuous effect. **L19.**

J. ROSENBERG As in all his greatest works, one feels here a fusion of the real with the visionary. F. HOYLE There were widespread fusions which eventually formed the pieces into a single continent.

3 *PHYSICS.* The union of atomic nuclei to form a heavier nucleus, usu. with release of energy; this process as a source of energy. **M20.**
4 Music in which elements of more than one popular style are combined. **L20.**

attrib.: M. SYAL It was Martin who brought home the latest fusion CDs.

5 *attrib.* Designating food or cooking which incorporates elements of both eastern and western cuisine. **L20.**
– COMB.: **fusion bomb** a bomb deriving its energy from nuclear fusion; *spec.* a hydrogen bomb; **fusion weld**: made by melting and joining the metal without the application of pressure.
■ **fusional** *adjective* of or pertaining to fusion; *spec.* in *LINGUISTICS* (of a language) inflecting: **E20.** **fusionist** *noun & adjective* (**a**) *noun* a person who strives for coalition between political parties, factions, etc.; (**b**) *adjective* of or pertaining to fusionists; supporting political fusion: **M19.**

fusk /fʌsk/ *adjective.* Now *rare*. Also **fusc**. **LME.**
[ORIGIN Latin *fuscus*.]
Dark brown, dusky.
■ Also **fusky** *adjective* **E17.**

fusogenic /fjuːzəˈdʒɛnɪk/ *adjective.* **L20.**
[ORIGIN from FUS(ION + -GENIC.]
BIOCHEMISTRY. Causing or promoting the fusion of membranes.
■ ˈ**fusogen** *noun* a fusogenic agent **L20.**

fusoid /ˈfjuːzɔɪd/ *adjective.* **L19.**
[ORIGIN from Latin *fusus* spindle + -OID.]
= FUSIFORM.

†**fuss** *noun*¹. **M17–E18.**
[ORIGIN Abbreviation.]
= FUSSOCK 1.

fuss /fʌs/ *noun*² *& verb.* **E18.**
[ORIGIN Uncertain: perh. Anglo-Ir.]
▸**A** *noun.* **1** A (disproportionate or excessive) commotion or display of concern (*about* something); ostentatious or officious activity; the treatment of trifling matters as important; abundance of petty detail. Also (*colloq.*), a sustained protest or dispute. **E18.**

MALCOLM X I would cry out and make a fuss until I got what I wanted. B. BAINBRIDGE The brain specialist had kicked up an almighty fuss about it, to no avail.

make a fuss of, **make a fuss over**, †**make a fuss with** pamper, treat with an excessive display of affection or attention.
2 A state of (usu. excessive) concern or anxiety. **E18.**

J. VANBRUGH Why, here's your Master in a most violent fuss.

3 A person who is continually making a fuss. *colloq.* **M19.**
▸**B** *verb.* **1** *verb intrans.* Make a fuss (*about*, *over*); busy oneself excessively with trivial matters etc., bustle (*about*). **L18.**

A. F. LOEWENSTEIN She fussed around, showing how the door locked itself and how to set the alarm clock. K. MOORE Roberta had fussed over her and adored her as a rare little creature.

2 *verb trans.* Agitate, worry, bother (a person). **E19.**
– COMB.: **fussbudget**, **fusspot** = sense A.3 above.
■ **fuˈssation** *noun* the action or practice of fussing; a fuss: **L18.** **fusser** *noun* a person who fusses **L19.** **fussifiˈcation** *noun* = FUSSATION: **M19.** **fussify** *verb intrans.* bustle (*about*), make a fuss **M19.**

fussock /ˈfʌsək/ *noun.* **L17.**
[ORIGIN Unknown.]
1 A fat unwieldy woman. *dial.* (orig. *slang*). **L17.**
2 An untidy mass or bundle. *Scot.* **M19.**
■ **fussocking** *adjective* (now *dial.*) unwieldy, fat **L18.**

F

fussy /ˈfʌsi/ *adjective.* M19.
[ORIGIN from FUSS *noun*[2] + -Y[1]. Earlier in UNFUSSY.]
1 Inclined to fuss; fastidious. M19. ▸**b** Of a place: bustling. *dial. & US.* M19.

B. PYM He's fussy, so I had to pick out all the least greasy of the fried potatoes for him.

2 Of a dress etc.: having excessive detail or ornamentation. M19.
■ **fussily** *adverb* E19. **fussiness** *noun* M19.

fust /fʌst/ *noun*[1]. L15.
[ORIGIN Old French (mod. *fût*) from Latin *fustis* cudgel: cf. FOIST *noun*[1].]
1 A wine cask. *obsolete* exc. *hist.* L15.
2 A musty smell. M18.

fust /fʌst/ *noun*[2]. *arch.* M17.
[ORIGIN Italian *fusto* shaft, trunk, from Latin *fustis* cudgel.]
ARCHITECTURE. The shaft of a column or pilaster.

fust /fʌst/ *verb intrans.* L16.
[ORIGIN from FUST *noun*[1]. Cf. FOIST *verb*[2].]
Become mouldy or stale-smelling. Now chiefly *fig.*

A. S. BYATT Frederica's determination to . . not sit in a house and let her talents . . fust in her unused.

fustanella /fʌstəˈnɛlə/ *noun.* M19.
[ORIGIN Italian, from mod. Greek *phoustani*, *phoustanela*, Albanian *fustan*, prob. from Italian *fustagno* FUSTIAN.]
A full stiff white kilt worn by men in Greece and Albania.

fustet /ˈfʌstɪt/ *noun.* E19.
[ORIGIN Old French & mod. French from Provençal = Spanish *fustete*, an etymologizing corruption (as if dim. of Provençal *fust*, Spanish *fuste* stick) of the Arabic source of FUSTIC.]
= ***young*** FUSTIC.

fustian /ˈfʌstɪən/ *noun & adjective.* ME.
[ORIGIN Old French *fustaigne* (mod. *futaine*) repr. medieval Latin *fustaneum*, (*tela*) *fustanea*, (*pannus*) *fustaneus* = cloth of *Fostat* suburb of Cairo, city in Egypt.]
▸ **A** *noun.* **1** Orig., a napped fabric of a mixture of linen and cotton or wool. Now also, any of various coarse twilled cotton fabrics with a short nap. Formerly also, a blanket made of such material. ME.
2 Pompous or inflated speech or writing; bombast; drivel. Formerly also, gibberish, jargon. L16.

J. JONES Karamazov's powerful fustian about the whole God business.

▸ **B** *adjective.* **1** (Of language) pompous, inflated, (formerly) jargonistic; (of a person etc.) worthless, pretentious. E16.

SHAKES. *2 Hen. IV* For God's sake thrust him down stairs; I cannot endure such a fustian rascal. V. NABOKOV A dismal exchange of . . fustian jokes.

2 Made of fustian. M16.
■ **fustianed** *adjective* dressed in fustian M19.

fustic /ˈfʌstɪk/ *noun.* LME.
[ORIGIN French *fustoc* from Spanish from Arabic *fustuq* from Greek *pistakē* pistachio tree.]
Any of several kinds of wood yielding a yellow dye; *esp.* (more fully ***old fustic***) that of the tropical American tree *Chlorophora tinctoria*, of the mulberry family, or (more fully ***young fustic***) that of the Venetian sumac, *Cotinus coggygria*. Also, the dye obtained from any of these woods.

fustigate /ˈfʌstɪgeɪt/ *verb trans.* Now *joc.* M17.
[ORIGIN Late Latin *fustigat-* pa. ppl stem of *fustigare* cudgel to death, from *fustis* cudgel: see -ATE[3].]
Cudgel, beat.

fustigation /fʌstɪˈgeɪʃ(ə)n/ *noun.* Now *joc.* L16.
[ORIGIN Late Latin *fustigatio(n-)*, from *fustigat-*: see FUSTIGATE, -ATION.]
The action of cudgelling or beating; a beating.

†**fustilarian** *noun. rare* (Shakes.). Only in L16.
[ORIGIN Uncertain: perh. a comic formation on FUSTILUGS (see -ARIAN).]
= FUSTILUGS.

fustilugs /ˈfʌstɪlʌgz/ *noun. obsolete* exc. *dial.* M16.
[ORIGIN App. from FUSTY + LUG *noun*[3].]
A fat, unkempt person, esp. a woman.

fusty /ˈfʌsti/ *adjective.* L15.
[ORIGIN Old French *fusté*, formed as FUST *noun*[1] + -Y[5].]
1 Of bread, corn, (now *dial.*) liquor, etc.: stale-smelling, musty. Of a room etc.: close, stuffy, smelling of dust, damp, etc. L15.

C. P. SNOW The smell of the chapel—earthy, odorous from wood, wax, fusty books.

2 Marked by age or neglect; old-fashioned or antiquated in appearance or behaviour. E17.

City Limits One of the most venerable British companies has managed to shake off its fusty image.

■ **fustily** *adverb* L19. **fustiness** *noun* E16.

futah /ˈfuːtaː/ *noun.* E17.
[ORIGIN Arabic *fūṭa*.]
In Arabic-speaking countries: a long piece of cloth used as a garment, esp. a loincloth, made from fabric of a kind orig. from India.

futchel /ˈfʌtʃ(ə)l/ *noun.* Also **-ll.** L18.
[ORIGIN Unknown.]
Each of the pieces of timber carrying or supporting the shafts, pole, or splinter bar of a carriage.

futhark /ˈfuːθaːk/ *noun.* Also **-orc** /-ɔːk/. M19.
[ORIGIN from the first six letters, *f*, *u*, *þ*, *o* or *a*, *r*, *k*.]
The runic alphabet.

futile /ˈfjuːtʌɪl/ *adjective.* M16.
[ORIGIN Latin *futilis*, *futtilis* that easily pours out, leaky, from *fut-*, app. from *fundere* pour: see -ILE.]
1 Incapable of producing any result; useless, vain. M16. ▸**b** Occupied with worthless or trivial matters; frivolous, lacking in purpose. M18.

CONAN DOYLE Our speculations are futile until we have all the facts. A. STORR His whole life has been a futile striving after the impossible.

2 Talkative, unable to keep silent. Long *rare.* M16.
■ **futilely** *adverb* L19. **futileness** *noun* (now *rare*) E18. **futilize** *verb trans.* make futile M18.

futilitarian /ˌfjuːtɪlɪˈtɛːrɪən/ *noun & adjective. joc.* E19.
[ORIGIN from FUTILITY after UTILITARIAN.]
(A person) devoted to futile pursuits.
■ **futilitarianism** *noun* E20.

futility /fjʊˈtɪlɪti/ *noun.* E17.
[ORIGIN French *futilité* or Latin *futilitas*, from *futilis*: see FUTILE, -ITY.]
1 The quality of being futile; uselessness, pointlessness, ineffectiveness. E17. ▸**b** Tendency to be occupied with worthless or trivial matters; frivolity. L17.

New York Times For us to be instructing people in Central America in . . terrorism is an exercise in futility.

2 A futile person or thing. M17.

E. F. BENSON The futilities in which Aunt Elizabeth's days were passed.

†**3** Talkativeness, inability to keep silent. M–L17.

†**futilous** *adjective.* E17–E18.
[ORIGIN from FUTILE + -OUS.]
Futile.

futon /ˈfuːtɒn/ *noun.* Also **futong.** L19.
[ORIGIN Japanese, from *fu* cloth + *ton* body, group.]
Orig. in Japan, a cotton-stuffed mattress laid out on the floor for use as a bed; more widely, such a mattress (with or without a frame) that can be used as a seat when folded up.

futtah *noun* var. of WHATA.

futtock /ˈfʌtək/ *noun.* ME.
[ORIGIN Uncertain: perh. from FOOT *noun* + HOOK *noun* or from Middle Low German, but cf. PUTTOCK *noun*[2].]
NAUTICAL. Any of the timber pieces forming a ship's frames or ribs.
– COMB.: **futtock plate** each of the metal plates by which the upper ends of the futtock shrouds are secured to the lower mast top; **futtock shroud** each of the small ropes or metal rods supporting the top on a lower mast and running from the futtock plates downwards and inwards towards the lower mast.

futural /ˈfjuːtʃ(ə)r(ə)l/ *adjective.* E20.
[ORIGIN from FUTURE + -AL[1].]
Of or pertaining to the future; *spec.* (GRAMMAR) having a future sense.

future /ˈfjuːtʃə/ *adjective & noun.* LME.
[ORIGIN Old French & mod. French *futur(e)*, from Latin *futurus*, *-ura*, future pple of *esse*, from *fu-*: see BE.]
▸ **A** *adjective.* **1** That is to be, become, or happen; intended, prospective. LME.

LYTTON I wish I were the future Lady Vargrave. I. MURDOCH Plans for future work.

2 Of or pertaining to time to come; *spec.* in GRAMMAR (of a participle or tense) expressing an action yet to happen. LME.
3 Subsequent. E17.

W. L. SARGANT This rhapsody will not be intelligible to those unacquainted with St. Simon's future history.

▸ **B** *noun.* **1** *The* time to come. LME.

E. M. FORSTER She could look into the future and plan for her child. *personified*: T. S. ELIOT And what is spoken remains in the room, waiting for the future to hear it.

for the future, **in future** from now onwards. ***the wave of the future***: see WAVE *noun*.
2 What will happen in time to come. Orig. in *pl.*, future events. LME.

W. R. INGE To predict the future . . is . . the most important part of the work of an historian.

3 The prospective condition (*spec.* a successful, prosperous one) of a person, country, etc. M19.

G. SANTAYANA She saw before her a desolate future. H. CARMICHAEL There's no future in being an accessory after the fact in a murder case.

4 COMMERCE. In *pl.* Goods and stocks bought and sold for future delivery; contracts to sell or buy on these terms. M19.
5 GRAMMAR. (A word or form in) the future tense. L19.
– COMB. & SPECIAL COLLOCATIONS: **future contingent** PHILOSOPHY a proposition which concerns the future and is therefore neither verifiable nor falsifiable in the present; **future life** existence after death, esp. as an object of belief; ***future perfect***: see PERFECT *adjective* 9, *noun* 3; **future-proof** *adjective* (of a product) unlikely to become obsolete; **future shock** a state of distress or disorientation due to rapid social or technological change; **future state** = ***future life*** above.
■ **futureless** *adjective* M19. †**futurely** *adverb* in future, hereafter; later: E17–L18. **futureness** *noun* E19. **futurize** *verb* (*rare*) (***a***) *verb intrans.* (GRAMMAR) form the future tense; (***b***) *verb trans.* make future: M19.

futurism /ˈfjuːtʃərɪz(ə)m/ *noun.* E20.
[ORIGIN from FUTURE + -ISM, after Italian *futurismo*, French *futurisme*.]
A movement in art, literature, music, etc., originating in Italy, characterized by violent departure from traditional forms so as to express movement and growth. Also more widely, futuristic tendencies in any sphere; belief or interest in human progress.

futurist /ˈfjuːtʃərɪst/ *noun & adjective.* M19.
[ORIGIN from FUTURE + -IST.]
▸ **A** *noun.* **1** A person who is concerned with or studies the future; a believer in human progress. M19.
2 THEOLOGY. A person who believes that eschatological prophecies are still to be fulfilled. M19.
3 [Cf. Italian *futuristo*, French *futuriste*.] An adherent of futurism in art etc. E20.
▸ **B** *adjective.* Of futurists or futurism; futuristic. L19.

futuristic /fjuːtʃəˈrɪstɪk/ *adjective.* E20.
[ORIGIN from FUTURIST + -IC.]
Having the characteristics of futurism; ultra-modern; of, pertaining to, or predicted for the future.

S. NAIPAUL H. G. Wells' futuristic fantasy . . in which the hero transports himself to the year 802,700. R. FRAME We had lunch at a round futuristic building beside the autobahn called the Sputnik-Sporthotel.

futurition /fjuːtʃəˈrɪʃ(ə)n/ *noun.* Now *rare.* M17.
[ORIGIN medieval Latin *futuritio(n-)*, irreg. from Latin *futurus*: see FUTURE, -ION. Cf. French *futurition*.]
PHILOSOPHY. **1** Existence or occurrence in the future; a future event or existence. M17.
2 The fact of something having a future existence. M17.

futurity /fjʊˈtjʊərɪti, -tʃ-/ *noun.* E17.
[ORIGIN from FUTURE + -ITY.]
1 Future time. E17.
2 *sing.* & in *pl.* Future events. M17. ▸**b** (A) future condition or state; (an) existence after death. M18.
3 = FUTURITION 2. *rare.* M17.
– COMB.: **futurity stakes** a horse race etc. held long after entries or nominations are made.

futurology /fjuːtʃəˈrɒlədʒi/ *noun.* M20.
[ORIGIN from FUTURE + -OLOGY.]
The systematic forecasting of the future esp. by the study of present trends in society etc.
■ **futuroˈlogical** *adjective* L20. **futurologist** *noun* M20.

futz /fʌts/ *verb intrans. N. Amer. slang.* M20.
[ORIGIN Uncertain: perh. alt. of Yiddish *arumfartzen* fart about.]
Waste time, loaf or mess *around* (*with*).

fu yung *noun phr.* var. of FOO YONG.

fuze *noun, verb* see FUSE *noun*[1], *verb*[2].

fuzee *noun*[1], *noun*[2] vars. of FUSEE *noun*[1], *noun*[2].

fuzz /fʌz/ *noun*[1]. L16.
[ORIGIN Prob. of Low Dutch origin: cf. Dutch *voos*, Low German *fussig* spongy.]
1 In full & now only ***fuzz-ball***. A puffball fungus. L16.
2 A light fluffy mass of particles or fibres; fluffy or frizzy hair; a blur on a photograph etc. L17.

fig.: B. PLAIN There was a fuzz of confusion in his mind right now.

– COMB.: **fuzzbox** a device which imparts a buzzing quality to the sound of an electric guitar etc.; **fuzzword** a deliberately confusing or imprecise term; a piece of jargon.

fuzz /fʌz/ *noun*[2]. *slang* (orig. *US*). E20.
[ORIGIN Unknown.]
collect. The police; police officers. Less commonly as *sing.*, a police officer.

fuzz /fʌz/ *verb*[1] *intrans.* Long *obsolete* exc. *dial.* L17.
[ORIGIN Imit.]
Make a fizzing or popping noise.

fuzz /fʌz/ *verb*[2]. E18.
[ORIGIN from FUZZ *noun*[1].]
1 *verb trans. & intrans.* Make or become fluffy, blurred, or indistinct. E18.

R. COOVER When he tried to picture it in his mind, it fuzzed into a big blur.

2 *verb trans.* Cover with fuzz. M19.

T. O'BRIEN His chest was fuzzed with black hair.

fuzzle /ˈfʌz(ə)l/ *verb trans.* E17.
[ORIGIN Uncertain: cf. FUZZ *noun*[1], FUDDLE *verb*.]
Intoxicate, confuse.

fuzzy /ˈfʌzi/ *adjective & noun*. E17.
[ORIGIN from FUZZ *noun*[1] + -Y[1].]
▸ **A** *adjective*. **1** Not firm, spongy. *obsolete* exc. *dial*. E17.
2 Frayed into loose light fibres; covered with fuzz; fluffy; (of hair) frizzy. E18.
3 Blurred, indistinct; imprecise, vague. L18. ▸**b** *COMPUTING & LOGIC*. Defined so as to allow for imprecise criteria of set-membership. M20.

Philosophical Transactions Venus appeared very dim and fuzzy. H. ROBBINS Rocco answered the phone; his voice was fuzzy with sleep. A. LURIE Escapism and fuzzy thinking; absorbing bogus ideas.

b fuzzy logic: dealing with fuzzy sets and concepts.
▸ **B** *noun*. = FUZZY-WUZZY. *slang (offensive)*. L19.
■ **fuzzily** *adverb* M19. **fuzziness** *noun* E17.

fuzzy-wuzzy /ˈfʌzɪwʌzi/ *noun*. *slang (offensive)*. L19.
[ORIGIN Redupl. of FUZZY.]
A black person, *esp*. one with tightly curled hair; *spec*. †(***a***) a Sudanese soldier; (***b***) *Austral*. a native of New Guinea.

fwd *abbreviation*.
Forward.

f.w.d. *abbreviation*.
1 Four-wheel drive.
2 Front-wheel drive.

FX *abbreviation*.
[ORIGIN from the pronunc. of the two letters forming the syllables of *effects*.]
(Special) effects.

f.y. *abbreviation*. *US*.
Fiscal year.

-fy /fʌɪ/ *suffix*. Also (see below) **-ify**.
[ORIGIN from or after F *-fier* from Latin *-ficare* (cf. -FICATION) and *-facere* (cf. -FACTION).]
Used, usu. with intermediate -I-, to form verbs: (i) from nouns with the senses ‘make, produce’ (***pacify***, ***satisfy***, ***speechify***), ‘make into’ (***deify***, ***petrify***), ‘make like’ (***countrify***); (ii) from adjectives with the sense ‘bring or come into a certain state’ (***Frenchify***, ***sanctify***, ***solidify***); (iii) from Latin verbs with causative sense (***horrify***, ***stupefy***).

FYI *abbreviation*.
For your information.

fyke /fʌɪk/ *noun*[1]. *Scot*. E17.
[ORIGIN from the verb.]
1 A restless movement, a twitch or fidget. Formerly also, something causing this, *esp*. an itch. Now *rare*. E17.
2 (A) fuss; commotion, excitement. Formerly also, (a) flirtation. E18.

fyke /fʌɪk/ *noun*[2]. *US*. M19.
[ORIGIN Dutch *fuik* fish trap.]
A bag net for catching fish. Also ***fyke net***.

fyke /fʌɪk/ *verb*. Also **fike**. Chiefly *Scot. & N. English*. ME.
[ORIGIN Old Norse (Middle Swedish) *fikja* move briskly, be restless or eager.]
1 *verb intrans*. Move restlessly, bustle, fidget. ME.
†**2** *verb trans*. Vex, trouble. L16–M19.

fylfot /ˈfɪlfɒt/ *noun*. L15.
[ORIGIN Uncertain: perh. from *fill-foot* a pattern for filling the foot of a painted window.]
A swastika.

fyrd /fɔːd, fɪəd/ *noun*.
[ORIGIN Old English *ferd*, *fierd*, *fyrd* = Old Frisian *ferd*, Old Saxon *fard*, Old High German *fart* (German *Fahrt*) Old Norse *ferð*, from Germanic base of FARE *verb*.]
The English militia before the Norman Conquest; the duty to serve in this.

FYROM *abbreviation*.
Former Yugoslav Republic of Macedonia.

fytte *noun* var. of FIT *noun*[1].

Gg

G, g /dʒiː/.
The seventh letter of the modern English alphabet and of the ancient Roman one, orig. corresp. to a differentiated form of C. In early Latin the letter represented the voiced velar plosive consonant /g/; subsequently before front vowels it was pronounced as a palatal or palato-alveolar affricate /dʒ/, its representation in the Romance languages being the same as the Latin consonant I, which developed into the same sound. G in mod. English has the following values. (i) G has the 'hard' sound /g/ before *a, o, u*, in a number of words before *e, i, y*, before a consonant, and when final. (ii) G has the 'soft' sound /dʒ/ before *e, i, y*. (iii) *gh* is silent in many words but in a few represents /f/. (iv) G is silent in *gn* at the beginning or end of a word and in some words medially. (v) In *ng* finally, and in many words medially, the g is silent, serving to give the *n* the value of velar /ŋ/. Pl. **gees**, **G's**, **Gs**.
▸ **I 1** The letter and its sound.
2 The shape of the letter.
▸ **II** Symbolical uses.
3 Used to denote serial order; applied e.g. to the seventh group or section, sheet of a book, etc.
4 *MUSIC*. (Cap. G.) The fifth note in the diatonic scale of C major. Also, the scale of a composition with G as its keynote.
G clef the treble clef.
5 The seventh hypothetical person or example.
6 Designating the seventh-highest class (of academic marks etc.).
7 (Italic g.) The acceleration due to gravity (about 9.81 metre/second²). Also (cap. G), a force resulting from this amount of acceleration; *ASTRONOMY* the gravitational constant.
zero G: see ZERO *noun & adjective*.
8 *PHYSICS*. [German *gerade* even.] (Usu. italic g.) Designating functions, esp. wave functions, which do not change sign on inversion through the origin, and atomic states etc. represented by such functions. Cf. **U**, **U** 6.
▸ **III 9** Abbrevs.: **G** = general (*US* denoting films suitable for unrestricted viewing); (*PHYSICS*) (as *prefix*) giga-; (*N. Amer. colloq.*) grand (a thousand dollars); (*BIOLOGY*) guanine (in DNA sequences).

GA *abbreviation*. Also **Ga**.
Georgia (in the US).

Ga *symbol*.
CHEMISTRY. Gallium.

Ga /gɑː/ *noun & adjective*. Pl. of noun same, **-s**. **M19**.
[ORIGIN African name.]
Of or pertaining to, a member of, a people of Ghana; (of) the language of this people.

GAA *abbreviation*.
Gaelic Athletic Association.

gab /gab/ *noun*¹. **ME**.
[ORIGIN Old French = mockery, idle vaunt, from Old Norse *gabb*.]
†**1** Mockery, derisive deception; a lie, deceit. Only in **ME**.
2 A piece of bravado; a boast. **M18**.

gab /gab/ *noun*². **E18**.
[ORIGIN Var. of GOB *noun*².]
1 The mouth. *Scot.* **E18**.
2 The action of gabbing or talking; talk, prattle, twaddle. *colloq.* **E18**.
– PHRASES: **gift of the gab** a talent for speaking; fluency of speech. **stop your gab** be silent.

gab /gab/ *noun*³. **L18**.
[ORIGIN Uncertain: cf. Flemish *gabbe* notch, gash.]
MECHANICS. A hook or notch in a rod or lever which engages with a pin or spindle.

gab /gab/ *verb*¹. *arch.* Infl. **-bb-**. **ME**.
[ORIGIN Old French & mod. French *gaber* mock, deride, vaunt oneself, from *gab* GAB *noun*¹.]
†**1** *verb trans.* Reproach, accuse. Only in **ME**.
†**2** *verb intrans.* Speak mockingly, scoff. (Foll. by *on*, *upon*.) **ME–L16**.
†**3** *verb intrans. & trans.* Lie (to), tell lies (to). **ME–L15**.
4 *verb intrans.* Boast, brag. **E19**.

gab /gab/ *verb*² *intrans. colloq.* Chiefly *Scot.* Infl. **-bb-**. **E18**.
[ORIGIN Perh. abbreviation of GABBLE *verb*.]
Talk glibly; chatter, prattle.

> W. MARCH I'm not like you who's gabbing all the time and won't let nobody get a word in edgeways.

GABA *abbreviation*.
Gamma-aminobutyric acid.

gabardine *noun* var. of GABERDINE.

gabbart /ˈgabət/ *noun*. **L15**.
[ORIGIN French *gabarre* (now *gabare*), from Provençal *gabarra* perh. (with metathesis) from late Latin *carabus* coracle.]
1 A sailing vessel for inland navigation; a sailing barge, a lighter. **L15**.
2 A support used in erecting a scaffold. **L19**.

gabber /ˈgabə/ *noun*. **L18**.
[ORIGIN from GAB *verb*² + -ER¹.]
A chatterer, prattler.

gabber /ˈgabə/ *verb trans.* **E18**.
[ORIGIN from GAB *verb*² + -ER⁵. Cf. JABBER *verb*, GIBBER *verb*.]
Talk volubly, jabber.

gabble /ˈgab(ə)l/ *noun*. **E17**.
[ORIGIN from the verb.]
1 Voluble confused unintelligible talk; an instance of this. **E17**.

> H. E. BATES Forrester heard him shouting, the words simply a gabble of incoherent horror.

2 The inarticulate noises made by some animals. **E17**.

gabble /ˈgab(ə)l/ *verb*. **L16**.
[ORIGIN Middle Dutch *gabbelen*, of imit. origin.]
1 *verb intrans.* Speak incoherently; chatter, jabber, prattle. **L16**.
2 *verb intrans.* Of a goose: gaggle. **L17**.
3 *verb trans.* Utter rapidly and unintelligibly. **M18**.

> E. M. FORSTER Freddy gabbled a grace, and they drew up their heavy chairs and fell to.

■ **gabblement** *noun* gabbling, rapid unintelligible noise **M19**. **gabbler** *noun* **E17**.

gabbro /ˈgabrəʊ/ *noun*. Pl. **-os**. **M19**.
[ORIGIN Italian (Tuscan) from Latin *glaber*, *glabr-* smooth.]
A dark coarse-grained igneous rock of crystalline texture resembling dolerite and granite, and consisting largely of pyroxene (often as diallage), plagioclase feldspar, and often olivine.
■ **gaˈbbroic**, **gabbroˈitic** *adjectives* **L19**.

gabbroid /ˈgabrɔɪd/ *adjective & noun*. **E20**.
[ORIGIN from GABBRO + -OID.]
PETROGRAPHY. ▸ **A** *adjective*. Resembling gabbro; *spec.* belonging to the group of rocks including dolerites and gabbros, which contain a high proportion of ferromagnesian minerals. **E20**.
▸ **B** *noun*. A gabbroid rock. **E20**.
■ **gaˈbbroidal** *adjective* **M20**.

gabby /ˈgabi/ *adjective*. Orig. *Scot.* **E18**.
[ORIGIN from GAB *noun*² + -Y¹.]
Garrulous, talkative.

> A. HIGGINS The two gabby jackeens had strolled away, still talking.

■ **gabbiness** *noun* **M20**.

gabelle /gaˈbɛl/ *noun*. **LME**.
[ORIGIN French from Italian *gabella* corresp. to Spanish ALCAVALA.]
Chiefly *hist.* A tax, *esp.* a foreign tax; *spec.* the salt tax imposed in France before the Revolution.

gaberdine /gabəˈdiːn, ˈgabədiːn/ *noun & adjective*. Also (the usual form in senses A.3, B.) **gabardine**. **E16**.
[ORIGIN Old French *gauvardine*, *gallevardine*, perh. from Middle High German *wallevart* pilgrimage.]
▸ **A** *noun*. **1** *hist.* A loose long upper garment, such as formerly worn by Jews, almsmen, beggars, and others. **E16**.
2 *transf. & fig.* Dress, covering, protection. *arch.* **L16**.
3 A twill-woven cloth, of fine worsted or cotton, freq. waterproofed. **E20**.
▸ **B** *adjective*. Made of gaberdine. **M20**.

gaberlunzie /gabəˈlʌnzi, -nji/ *noun*. *Scot.* **E16**.
[ORIGIN Unknown.]
A beggar, a mendicant.

gabfest /ˈgabfɛst/ *noun*. *slang* (chiefly *N. Amer.*). **L19**.
[ORIGIN from GAB *noun*² + FEST.]
A gathering for talk; a spell of talking; a prolonged conference or conversation.

> A. RADAKOVICH Breaking from our gabfest, we dirty-danced to Tom Jones songs.

gabion /ˈgeɪbɪən/ *noun*. **M16**.
[ORIGIN French from Italian *gabbione* augm. of *gabbia* CAGE *noun*.]
A cylinder of wicker or woven metal bands to be filled with earth or stones for use in engineering or (*hist.*) fortification.
■ **gabioˈnade** *noun* a line of gabions **E18**. **gabionage** *noun* gabions collectively **M19**.

gable /ˈgeɪb(ə)l/ *noun & verb*. **LME**.
[ORIGIN (Old French from) Old Norse *gafl*: corresp. words in the other Germanic langs. mean 'fork'.]
▸ **A** *noun*. **1** The vertical triangular piece of wall at the end of a ridged roof, from the level of the eaves to the summit. **LME**. ▸**b** Any architectural member having the form of a gable, as a gable-shaped canopy over a window or door. **M19**.
2 The triangular-topped end wall of a building; a gable end. **LME**.
– COMB.: **gable end** a gable-topped wall; **gable-topped** *adjective* topped by a gable; having a gable-shaped top; **gable-window** a window in the gable or gable end of a building.
▸ **B** *verb*. **1** *verb intrans.* Form a gable. **M19**.
2 *verb trans.* End (a roof) in a gable. **L19**.
■ **gabled** *adjective* having a gable or gables **M19**.

gablet /ˈgeɪblɪt/ *noun*. **LME**.
[ORIGIN Anglo-Norman.: see GABLE *noun*, -ET¹.]
A small gable, *esp.* one constructed as an ornament.

gablock /ˈgablɒk/ *noun*. **L17**.
[ORIGIN Var. of GAVELOCK.]
1 *hist.* A metal spur for a fighting cock. **L17**.
2 An iron crowbar. *dial.* **M18**.

Gaboon /gəˈbuːn/ *noun*. Also **g-**. **E20**.
[ORIGIN An area (now the state of Gabon) and river in W. Africa.]
1 In full ***Gaboon mahogany***. A hardwood from the W. African tree *Aucoumea klaineana* (family Burseraceae). **E20**.
2 ***Gaboon adder***, ***Gaboon viper***, a venomous African snake, *Bitis gabonica*, largest member of the viper family. **E20**.

gaby /ˈgeɪbi, *dial.* ˈgɔːbi/ *noun*. *colloq. & dial.* **L18**.
[ORIGIN Unknown.]
A simpleton.

gad /gad/ *noun*¹. **ME**.
[ORIGIN Old Norse *gaddr* goad, spike, sting = Old High German *gart*, Gothic *gazds* from Germanic: rel. to YARD *noun*².]
1 A sharp spike of metal. *obsolete* exc. *hist.* **ME**. ▸†**b** A small rod for writing, a stylus. Only in **L16**.
2 A bar of metal; an ingot. Now *rare*. **ME**. ▸**b** *MINING*. A steel wedge; an iron punch. **L17**.
3 A pointed rod or stick used for driving oxen etc.; a goad. **ME**.
†**upon the gad** *rare* (Shakes.) as if pricked with a gad, suddenly.
†**4** A measuring rod for land; a measure of length differing in various districts; a division of open pasture. **LME–L18**.
5 A spear. Long *obsolete* exc. *hist.* **M16**.
6 A rod, a wand, *esp.* a fishing rod; a stake, a stout stick. *dial.* **M16**.

gad /gad/ *noun*². Also **G-**. **L15**.
[ORIGIN Alt. of GOD *noun*: cf. AGAD, BEGAD, EGAD.]
= GOD *noun*: chiefly as interjection & in exclamatory phrs. corresp. to those s.v. GOD *noun* 5.
by gad!, ***gad!***, ***gadsbodikins***, GADZOOKS.

gad /gad/ *noun*³. **E17**.
[ORIGIN from GAD *verb*¹.]
The action of gadding or rambling about. Only in ***on the gad***, ***upon the gad***, on the move, going about.

gad /gad/ *noun*⁴. *Irish & MILITARY*. **E18**.
[ORIGIN Irish & Gaelic.]
A band or rope made of twisted fibres of tough twigs.

gad /gad/ *verb*¹ *intrans.* Infl. **-dd-**. **LME**.
[ORIGIN Back-form. from GADLING *noun*¹.]
1 Wander from place to place; rove about idly or in search of pleasure. (Foll. by *about*, *abroad*, *out*.) **LME**. ▸**b** Esp. of cattle: rush madly about. *obsolete* exc. *dial.* **M16**.

> L. M. MONTGOMERY You're not going to begin gadding about to concerts and staying out all hours of the night.

2 *fig.* Wander or go astray in thought or desire. Now *rare*. **L16**.
†**3** Of an inanimate object: move about. **L16–E17**.
4 Of a plant: grow in a spreading or wayward manner, straggle. **M17**.
■ **gadder** *noun* **M16**.

gad /gad/ *verb*² *intrans.* Infl. **-dd-**. **M18**.
[ORIGIN from GAD *noun*¹.]
MINING. Use a gad.

gadabout /ˈgadəbaʊt/ *adjective & noun*. **E19**.
[ORIGIN from GAD *verb*¹ + ABOUT *adverb*.]
▸ **A** *adjective*. Gadding, roving. **E19**.
▸ **B** *noun*. A person who gads about. **M19**.

> D. MORGAN Walter was a restless charmer and a gadabout.

Gadarene /ˈɡadəriːn/ *adjective.* E19.
[ORIGIN Late Latin *Gadarenus*, from Greek *Gadarēnos*, inhabitant of Gadara (see below).]
Of or pertaining to Gadara, a town of ancient Palestine, near the Sea of Galilee; *esp.* (with ref. to *Matthew* 8:28) involving or engaged in a headlong or suicidal rush or flight.

gadbee /ˈɡadbiː/ *noun.* M16.
[ORIGIN from GAD *noun*[1] + BEE *noun*[1].]
A gadfly.

gaddi /ˈɡʌdiː/ *noun.* Also ***gadi*** /ˈɡɑːdiː/. M19.
[ORIGIN Punjabi *gaddī*, Marathi *gādī*, Bengali *gādi*, lit. 'cushion'.]
A throne, *esp.* the cushioned throne of an Indian ruler. Also *transf.*, the position of ruler, ruling power.

gade /ɡeɪd/ *noun.* M19.
[ORIGIN mod. Latin *gadus* cod from Greek *gados*. Cf. French *gade*.]
A fish of the genus *Gadus*; a codfish.

gadfly /ˈɡadflʌɪ/ *noun.* L16.
[ORIGIN from GAD *noun*[1] or (esp. sense 2) *verb*[1] + FLY *noun*[1].]
1 A horsefly, botfly, or other fly which bites and irritates cattle. L16.

D. L. SAYERS Kirk shook his massive head, like a bull teased by gadflies.

†**2** A person who gads about. E17–M18.
3 *fig.* A person who irritates or harasses another. Also, an irresistible impulse. M17.

gadget /ˈɡadʒɪt/ *noun.* L19.
[ORIGIN Unknown.]
1 Orig. NAUTICAL. A small device, mechanism, or fitting in a piece of machinery etc.; *local* (a vessel equipped with) a winch or small crane. L19.
2 *gen.* An accessory, an adjunct; a knick-knack. E20.
■ **gadgeˈteer** *noun* a person who uses or invents gadgets M20. **gadgetry** *noun* gadgets collectively; the use of gadgets: E20. **gadgety** *adjective* M20.

Gadhelic /ɡəˈdɛlɪk, ɡa-/ *adjective & noun.* Also (earlier) †**Gath-**. E16.
[ORIGIN (medieval Latin *gathelicus*, from *gathelus* from) Irish *Gaedheal*, pl. *Gaedhil* (Old Irish *Goídel* GOIDEL): see -IC. *Gadhelic* is a literary formation dating from L18.]
(The language) of the Scottish, Irish, and Manx Celts.

gadi *noun* var. of GADDI.

gadid /ˈɡeɪdɪd, ˈɡa-/ *noun & adjective.* L19.
[ORIGIN mod. Latin *Gadidae* (see below), from *gadus*: see GADE, -ID[3].]
▸ **A** *noun.* Any fish of the teleost family Gadidae, which includes cod, haddock, and pollack. L19.
▸ **B** *adjective.* Of, pertaining to, or designating this family. E20.

Gaditan /ˈɡadɪt(ə)n/ *adjective & noun.* Also **-tane** /-teɪn/. Pl. same, **-s**. E17.
[ORIGIN Latin *Gaditanus* (Spanish *Gaditano*) from *Gades* Cadiz (see below): see -AN, -ANE.]
(A native or inhabitant) of Cadiz, a port in SW Spain.
■ **Gaditanian** /ɡadɪˈteɪnɪən/ *adjective & noun* M19.

†**gadling** *noun*[1] *& adjective.*
[ORIGIN Old English *gædeling* = Old Saxon *gaduling*, Old High German *gateling*, Gothic *gadiliggs* cousin, from Germanic base repr. also by Old English *gæd* fellowship, *gegada* companion, rel. to GATHER *verb*.]
▸ **A** *noun.* **1** A companion, a fellow. OE–LME.
2 A low-born person. Also, a wanderer, a vagrant. ME–M16.
▸ **B** *adjective.* Wandering, straggling. Formerly also, base, low-born. LME–E18.

gadling /ˈɡadlɪŋ/ *noun*[2]. L16.
[ORIGIN from GAD *noun*[1] + -LING[1].]
hist. Any of the metal spikes on the knuckles of a gauntlet.

gadman /ˈɡadmən/ *noun.* Chiefly *Scot.* Pl. **-men**. LME.
[ORIGIN from GAD *noun*[1] + MAN *noun*.]
hist. A man or boy using a gad or goad to direct a team of animals, esp. in ploughing.

gadoid /ˈɡeɪdɔɪd, ˈɡa-/ *adjective & noun.* M19.
[ORIGIN from mod. Latin *gadus* (see GADE) + -OID.]
▸ **A** *adjective.* Of or pertaining to the order Anacanthini, which includes marine soft-finned fish such as the gadids and hake. M19.
▸ **B** *noun.* A gadoid fish. M19.

gadolinite /ˈɡad(ə)lɪnʌɪt, ɡəˈdəʊlɪnʌɪt/ *noun.* E19.
[ORIGIN from Johan *Gadolin* (1760–1852), Finnish mineralogist + -ITE[1].]
MINERALOGY. A monoclinic silicate of iron, beryllium, yttrium, and other rare earth elements, occurring as black or brown crystals.

gadolinium /ɡadəˈlɪnɪəm/ *noun.* L19.
[ORIGIN from GADOLINITE + -IUM.]
A metallic chemical element of the lanthanide series, atomic no. 64, which is strongly magnetic below room temperature (symbol Gd).

gadroon /ɡəˈdruːn/ *noun.* L17.
[ORIGIN French *godron*, prob. rel. to *goder* pucker, crease: see -OON.]
Any of a series of convex curves or arcs joined at their extremities and forming a decorative edge, like the inverted fluting on silverware etc. Usu. in *pl.*
■ **gadrooned** *adjective* ornamented with gadroons M18.

gadso /ˈɡadsəʊ/ *interjection. arch.* L17.
[ORIGIN Var. of CATSO, infl. by GAD *noun*[2].]
= GADZOOKS.

gadwall /ˈɡadwɔːl/ *noun.* M17.
[ORIGIN Uncertain: perh. imit.]
A greyish-brown freshwater duck, *Anas strepera*, widespread in the northern hemisphere.

gadzooks /ɡadˈzuːks/ *interjection. arch.* L17.
[ORIGIN from GAD *noun*[2] + *zooks* of unknown origin.]
Expr. annoyance, surprise, etc.

SMOLLETT 'Gadszooks!' said he, 'What business had you with that?'

■ **gadzookery** *noun* the exaggeratedly exclamatory dialogue used in some historical novels M20.

gaed *verb* see GO *verb*.

Gaekwar /ˈɡʌɪkwɑː/ *noun.* Also †**Guickwar**. E19.
[ORIGIN Marathi *gāekwāḍ* lit. 'cowherd'.]
hist. (The title of) the native ruler of Baroda, a state in India until 1960, when it became part of Gujarat.

Gael /ɡeɪl/ *noun.* M18.
[ORIGIN Gaelic *Gael*, *Gàidheal*, corresp. to Irish *Gael*, *Gaedheal* from Old Irish *Goídel* GOIDEL.]
A Scottish Celt; a Gaelic-speaking person.
■ **Gaeldom** *noun* the land of the Gaels; Gaelic culture or civilization; the Gaelic people: M19.

Gaelic /ˈɡeɪlɪk, ˈɡalɪk/ *adjective & noun.* M18.
[ORIGIN from GAEL + -IC.]
▸ **A** *adjective.* Of or pertaining to the Gaels or Celtic inhabitants of Scotland. Also more widely, of or pertaining to the Scottish, Irish, and Manx Celts. M18.
Gaelic coffee: see COFFEE *noun.* **Gaelic football** an Irish game involving two teams of 15 players who can kick, punch, or bounce the ball in order to try and get it into the net or over the bar of the goal. **Gaelic League** a movement founded in 1893 to revive Irish language and culture.
▸ **B** *noun.* The Gaelic language, a member of the Celtic branch of the Indo-European language family consisting *spec.* of Scots Gaelic or, more widely, of Scots and Irish Gaelic and Manx. M18.
■ **Gaelicize** *verb trans.* make or treat as Gaelic E19.

Gaeltacht /ˈɡeɪltəxt/ *noun.* E20.
[ORIGIN Irish.]
Any or all of the areas of Ireland where Irish is commonly spoken.

Gaetulian *adjective & noun* var. of GETULIAN.

gaff /ɡaf/ *noun*[1]. ME.
[ORIGIN Provençal *gaf*, whence also French *gaffe* boat-hook.]
1 A hook; a stick etc. with a hook. Now usu. a barbed fishing spear, a stick with a hook for landing large fish. ME. ▸**b** *hist.* A metal spur for a fighting cock. L17.
2 NAUTICAL. A spar situated on the after side of a mast and supporting the head of a fore-and-aft sail. M18.
– COMB.: **gaff-rigged** *adjective* having a gaff on the mainsail; **gaff topsail** small sail having its foot on a gaff.

gaff /ɡaf/ *noun*[2]. *slang.* M18.
[ORIGIN Unknown.]
1 A fair. Now *rare* or *obsolete*. M18.
2 Any public place of amusement, *esp.* (also ***penny gaff***) a popular theatre, a music hall. Now *rare*. E19.
3 A house, flat, shop, or other building. M20.

I. WELSH I sat in my gaff, unable for a while to look at the purchases. J. KING [He was] more friendly once he realized they weren't going to wreck the gaff.

gaff /ɡaf/ *noun*[3]. *slang.* E19.
[ORIGIN Unknown.]
1 Noise; humbug, pretence. E19.

R. SCRUTON I don't want you coming in here with that phoney crap.. I don't need all this gaff.

2 ***blow the gaff***, reveal or let out a plot or secret. E19.
3 ***the gaff***, rough treatment, criticism. Chiefly in ***give the gaff***, ***stand the gaff***, ***take the gaff***. *US.* L19.

W. M. RAINE Neil has got to stand the gaff for what he's done.

gaff *noun*[4] var. of GAFFE.

gaff /ɡaf/ *verb*[1]. L18.
[ORIGIN from GAFF *noun*[1].]
Seize or strike (a fish) with a gaff; draw *out* or *up* with a gaff.

gaff /ɡaf/ *verb*[2]. *slang.* E19.
[ORIGIN Unknown.]
1 *verb intrans.* Gamble; *esp.* toss up. E19.
2 *verb trans.* Deceive, trick; make (a game or device) crooked or dishonest. Orig. *US.* M20.

gaffe /ɡaf/ *noun.* Also **gaff**. E20.
[ORIGIN French.]
A blunder, a clumsy or indiscreet act or remark.

Blackwood's Magazine I had obviously said the wrong thing, committed a gaffe. C. P. SNOW He gave her a piece of jewellery, and by a clerical gaffe the bill went to his wife.

gaffer /ˈɡafə/ *noun.* L16.
[ORIGIN Prob. contr. of GODFATHER, with *ga-* by assoc. with *grandfather*. Cf. GAMMER.]
1 Used as an honourable title usu. preceding a name or as a simple form of address: master, sir; good fellow, old fellow. L16.

SIR W. SCOTT You have marred my ramble, Gaffer Glover. J. H. NEWMAN My good old gaffer, you're one of the old world.

2 An elderly rustic; an old fellow. L16.

P. L. FERMOR Peasant girls, bewildered gaffers with tangled beards.

3 A master, a boss; *esp.* the leader or foreman of a group of workmen. M17. ▸**b** *spec.* The chief electrician of a film crew. M20.

b T. BARR As the crew chief, the gaffer is responsible for.. the.. equipment.

– COMB.: **gaffer tape** strong cloth-backed waterproof adhesive tape.

G

gaffle /ˈɡaf(ə)l/ *noun. obsolete* exc. *hist.* L15.
[ORIGIN Uncertain: in sense 1 perh. from Dutch *gaffel* fork.]
1 A steel lever for bending a crossbow. L15.
2 A metal spur for a fighting cock. L17.
■ **gaffled** *adjective* (*rare*) equipped with gaffles or spurs L18. †**gafflet** *noun* = GAFFLE 2 E–M18.

gag /ɡaɡ/ *noun*[1]. M16.
[ORIGIN from GAG *verb*[1].]
1 Something thrust into or held over the mouth to prevent speech or outcry, or to hold it open for an operation. M16. ▸**b** Closure of a debate in a legislative assembly, guillotine. Orig. *US.* M19.

J. STEINBECK She put her thumb in her mouth for a gag and she cried silently. A. CLARE A gag is inserted in the patient's mouth to prevent him biting his tongue.

2 An actor's interpolations in a dramatic dialogue, an ad lib; a carefully prepared comic effect or business introduced into a music hall sketch, a stage play, etc. Also (*gen.*) a joke; a humorous situation, action, etc. M19.

P. G. WODEHOUSE Some rotten little.. play.. without one good laugh or.. gag in it.

– COMB.: **gag bit** a powerful bit used to control a restive horse; **gag man** a writer of gags; a comedian; **gag-rein**: used to make a bit more powerful; **gag rule** *US* POLITICS (*colloq.*) (***a***) *hist.* a rule of the House of Representatives providing that petitions relating to slavery should be laid on the table without being referred to committee or printed; (***b***) a regulation preventing the staff of federally funded family planning clinics from discussing abortion with patients.
■ **gagster** *noun* [-STER after *punster*] a writer of gags, a comedian M20.

gag /ɡaɡ/ *noun*[2]. E19.
[ORIGIN from GAG *verb*[3].]
An invented story; a deception, an imposture, a lie.

gag /ɡaɡ/ *noun*[3]. L19.
[ORIGIN Unknown.]
Any of various large edible groupers found off the coasts of the southern US, esp. *Mycteroperca microlepis*.

gag /ɡaɡ/ *verb*[1]. Infl. **-gg-**. ME.
[ORIGIN Uncertain; perh. imit. of choking sound, or rel. to Old Norse *gaghāls* with the neck thrown back.]
1 †**a** *verb trans.* Strangle, suffocate. Only in ME. ▸**b** *verb intrans. & trans.* Choke; (cause to) retch. E18.

b T. KENEALLY A dozen people were gagging or comatose from swallowing cyanide. G. KEILLOR A repulsive gelatinous fishlike dish that.. gave off an odor that would gag a goat. *fig.*: CLIVE JAMES Even Mozart.. would gag at so much worship.

2 *verb trans.* Stop the mouth of (a person) to prevent speech or outcry; put a gag into or over (a person's mouth). E16. ▸**b** Keep the mouth of (a patient, an animal) open with a gag. L16. ▸**c** Deprive of the power or freedom of speech; stop the mouth of. E17.

JONSON Gag him, we may have his silence. **c** LD MACAULAY The time was not yet come when eloquence was to be gagged and reason hoodwinked.

gagging order *colloq.* a document signed by a government minister or senior civil servant which prevents specified information from being used in a trial (officially called ***public interest immunity certificate***).
3 *verb trans.* Apply a gag bit to the mouth of (a horse); confine unduly the mouth of (a horse). M19.
4 *verb intrans.* Orig. THEATRICAL. Make gags or jokes. Also, ad-lib. M19.
5 *verb intrans.* ***be gagging for***, be desperately eager for; *esp.* (with *it*) be eager for sex. *slang.* L20.

A. MCNAB Joseph.. was gagging for a cigarette and he was always asking for them. JIM WHITE Floor to ceiling totty, gagging for it. Can't remember mine's name.

■ **gagger** *noun*[1] E17.

†**gag** *verb*². Infl. **-gg-**. L16.
[ORIGIN Unknown.]
1 *verb trans.* Jerk; strike sharply; prick. L16–E17.
2 *verb intrans.* Project, stick out. L16–L19.

gag /gag/ *verb*³ *trans. & intrans. slang.* Now *rare* or *obsolete*. Infl. **-gg-**. L18.
[ORIGIN Perh. fig. use of GAG *verb*¹ in sense of thrusting something down the throat of a credulous person.]
Hoax, trick, deceive (a person).
■ **gagger** *noun*² L18. **gaggery** *noun* hoaxing, the practice of deceiving people E19.

gaga /ˈgɑːgɑː, ˈgagə/ *adjective & noun. slang.* Also **ga-ga**. E20.
[ORIGIN French.]
▸ **A** *adjective.* Senile; mad, crazy; foolish, fatuous. E20.
C. P. SNOW Hiding behind his smoke-screen of platitudes like an amiable old man already a bit ga-ga. D. LODGE This Dempsey character is gaga about computers.
▸ **B** *noun.* A senile or foolish person. M20.

gagaku /ˈgagakuː/ *noun.* M20.
[ORIGIN Japanese, from *ga* refined, graceful, noble + *gaku* music.]
A traditional type of (chiefly ceremonial) Japanese music.

†**gagate** *noun.* OE–E18.
[ORIGIN Latin *Gagates* from Greek *Gagatēs*, from *Gagai* a town in Lycia in Asia Minor.]
= JET *noun*¹.

gage /geɪdʒ/ *noun*¹. ME.
[ORIGIN Old French & mod. French from Proto-Romance, from Germanic base of WED *noun*: see WAGE *noun*.]
1 A valued thing or person deposited as a guarantee of good faith; a pledge, surety, security. Formerly also, payment, ransom. ME.
W. RALEIGH He also left Philip . . for the gage of his promises to Pelopidas.
in gage as a pledge or deposit.
2 A pledge, esp. a glove, thrown down as a symbol of a challenge to do battle; a challenge. Esp. in ***gage of battle***. ME.
LD BERNERS Caste downe your gage in that quarell, and ye shall fynde him that shall take it vp.

gage /geɪdʒ/ *noun*². LME.
[ORIGIN Var. of GAUGE *noun*.]
▸ **I 1** A quart pot. Long *rare* or *obsolete*. LME.
2 A pipe; a pipeful (orig. of tobacco, now chiefly of marijuana). Hence, marijuana. *slang*. L17.
▸ **II** See GAUGE *noun*.

gage /geɪdʒ/ *noun*³. M19.
[ORIGIN Abbreviation.]
= GREENGAGE.

gage /geɪdʒ/ *verb*. LME.
[ORIGIN Old French & mod. French *gager* or aphet. of ENGAGE *verb*.]
†**1** *verb trans.* Pledge, pawn; mortgage the revenues of; pledge oneself to (battle). LME–E17.
†**2** *verb trans.* Bind (as) by a formal promise. L15–E17. ▸**b** Bind or entangle *in*. *rare* (Shakes.). Only in L16.
3 *verb trans.* Stake, wager; risk; offer as a guarantee or forfeit. *arch.* E16.
4 *verb intrans.* Assert or guarantee *that*. *arch.* E19.

gage d'amour /gaːʒ damuːr/ *noun phr.* Pl. ***gages d'amour*** (pronounced same). M18.
[ORIGIN French.]
A pledge of love; a love token.

gaggie *noun* var. of GEGGIE.

gaggle /ˈgag(ə)l/ *verb & noun.* ME.
[ORIGIN Imit.: cf. Middle High German *gāgen*, *gāgern* cry like a goose; Dutch *gaggelen* gabble; Old Norse *gagl* gosling; Old High German *gackizōn*, *gackazzen* (German *gacksen*, also *gackeln*, *gackern*). Cf. GABBLE *verb* 2, CACKLE *verb*.]
▸ **A** *verb.* **1** *verb intrans.* Of a goose etc.: cackle. ME. ▸**b** Make a noise like a goose; chatter. Now chiefly as ***gaggling*** *ppl adjective & verbal noun.* LME.
C. S. LEWIS Crowing cocks and gaggling ducks.
†**2** *verb trans.* Utter or express with noisy chatter like a goose. L16–M17.
▸ **B** *noun.* **1** A flock (of geese); *derog.* a group (of women). LME. ▸**b** A (usu. disorderly or untidy) group of people or things; *slang* a group of aircraft. M20.
b *Listener* There is hardly a modern skyscraper . . that does not have its gaggle of sightseers.
2 Noisy chatter; gabble. LME.
P. QUENNELL Shouting in unison with a gaggle of harsh sound.

gag-toothed /ˈgagtuːθt/ *adjective.* L16.
[ORIGIN from GAG *verb*² + TOOTHED.]
Having a projecting or prominent tooth or teeth.

gah /gɑː/ *interjection.* E20.
[ORIGIN Natural exclam.]
Expr. impatience or exasperation.

gahnite /ˈgɑːnʌɪt/ *noun.* E19.
[ORIGIN from J. G. *Gahn* (1745–1818), Swedish chemist + -ITE¹.]
MINERALOGY. An oxide of zinc and aluminium, which crystallizes in the cubic system, and usu. occurs as dark green octahedra.

Gaia /ˈgʌɪə/ *noun.* L20.
[ORIGIN Greek *gaia* (the) earth.]
The earth regarded as a self-regulating system in which living matter collectively defines and maintains the conditions for the continuance of life; (more fully ***Gaia hypothesis***) the hypothesis that the earth is such a system.
■ **Gaian** *adjective & noun* (***a***) *adjective* of or pertaining to Gaia or the Gaia hypothesis; (***b***) *noun* an advocate of this hypothesis: L20.

gaieté de coeur /gete də kœːr/ *noun phr.* E18.
[ORIGIN French.]
Light-heartedness, playfulness.

gaiety /ˈgeɪəti/ *noun.* Also ***gayety**. M17.
[ORIGIN Old French & mod. French *gaieté* (mod. also *gaîté*), from *gai* GAY *adjective*: see -TY¹, -ITY.]
1 Cheerfulness, mirth; frivolity. M17.
D. M. DAVIN He was full of gaiety, laughing, eyes shining, waving to my wife.
the gaiety of nations (freq. *iron.* or *hyperbol.*) general gaiety or amusement.
2 Merrymaking, festivity; (now *rare*) a festive occasion, an entertainment. M17.
A. RADCLIFFE He was allured by the gaieties of Paris.
3 Cheerful or bright appearance or decoration; showiness. M17.
J. G. MURPHY They . . lay aside all gaiety in dress.
— COMB.: **Gaiety Girl** a chorus girl or performer in a musical show, orig. and esp. at the Gaiety, a former London theatre famous for its musicals.

gaijin /gʌɪˈdʒɪn/ *noun & adjective.* M20.
[ORIGIN Japanese, contr. of *gaikoku-jin*, from *gaikoku* foreign country + *jin* person.]
▸ **A** *noun.* Pl. same. In Japan: a foreigner, an alien. M20.
▸ **B** *attrib.* or as *adjective.* Foreign, alien, (to the Japanese). M20.

gaillardia /geɪˈlɑːdɪə/ *noun.* L19.
[ORIGIN mod. Latin (see below), from *Gaillard* de Marentonneau, 18th-cent. French amateur botanist: see -IA¹.]
Any of various plants of the American genus *Gaillardia*, of the composite family, several of which are cultivated for their showy flowers. Also called ***blanket flower***.

gaily /ˈgeɪli/ *adverb.* Also (now *rare*) **gayly**. ME.
[ORIGIN from GAY *adjective* + -LY².]
1 In a gay manner; brightly, cheerfully, jauntily. Now also, without thinking of the consequences. ME.
M. A. VON ARNIM A sinner should always, I think, sin gaily or not at all. D. WELCH 'Don't forget my party to-night' she called out . . gaily. E. BOWEN Her dear little table lamp, gaily painted with spots.
2 Fairly; pretty well. Chiefly *Scot. & dial.* M16.
DE QUINCEY It's gaily nigh to four mile.

gain /geɪn/ *noun*¹. Long *obsolete* exc. *N. English.* ME.
[ORIGIN Old Norse *gagn*, *gegn* adjective used as noun: see GAIN *adjective*.]
Advantage, use, benefit; help.

gain /geɪn/ *noun*². L15.
[ORIGIN Old French *ga(a)in* (mod. *gain*) masc., *ga(a)igne* (mod. *gagne*) fem., from *ga(a)ignier* (mod. *gagner*): see GAIN *verb*².]
†**1** Booty, spoil. L15–M16.
2 Increase of possessions, resources, or advantages; an instance of this; profit, improvement; *spec.* the acquisition of wealth. (Opp. ***loss***.) L15. ▸**b** In *pl.* Sums acquired by trade etc.; emoluments, winnings. M16. ▸**c** An increase in amount, magnitude, or degree. M19. ▸**d** ELECTRONICS. An increase in power, voltage, or current, produced esp. in an amplifier, expressed as the ratio of the increased quantity to the original quantity or (more commonly) as the logarithm of this. E20.
JOSEPH HALL (After long fightyng) bothe parties departed without either greate gain or losse. LD MACAULAY Greedy as they were of gain, they seldom became rich. **b** H. CECIL A thief, about to put his illgotten gains on a horse. **c** J. CARLYLE I was weighed yesterday and found a gain of five pounds.
capital gain: see CAPITAL *adjective & noun*². **d** ***ride the gain***: see RIDE *verb*.
3 The action of acquiring a possession, winning a battle, etc. *rare*. L16.
— COMB.: **gainsharing** *US* an incentive scheme in which employees or customers receive benefits directly as a result of cost-saving measures that they initiate or participate in.
■ **gainless** *adjective* (now *rare*) M17.

gain /geɪn/ *noun*³. *techn.* M19.
[ORIGIN Unknown.]
A mortise or notch esp. for a timber or connecting piece.

gain /geɪn/ *adjective. obsolete* exc. *dial.* LOE.
[ORIGIN Old Norse *gagn*, *gegn* straight, direct, favourable, helpful, from Germanic.]
1 Of a road or direction: near, straight. Esp. in superl., as ***the gainest way***. LOE.
2 (Of a person) willing, kindly; (of a thing) available, useful, convenient. ME.

gain /geɪn/ *verb*¹ *intrans.* Long *obsolete* exc. *Scot.* ME.
[ORIGIN Old Norse *gegna* meet, encounter, (hence) be meet, fit, or suitable, from *gegn* (adjective & adverb) against, opposite (to): cf. GAIN *adjective*.]
Be suitable, useful, or advantageous; help; suffice.

gain /geɪn/ *verb*². E16.
[ORIGIN Old French *ga(a)ignier* (mod. *gagner*) from Proto-Romance, from Germanic verb repr. also in Old High German *weidenen* graze, pasture, forage, hunt, fish, from noun repr. also in Old High German *weida* fodder, pasture, hunting, Old English *wāþ*, Old Norse *veiðr* hunting.]
1 *verb trans.* Obtain, secure, or acquire (esp. something desired or advantageous). E16. ▸**b** Get *to be*, *to do*. *rare*. M17.
I. FLEMING The dull, flat voice gained a trace of animation. W. GOLDING His ideas on Church Reform . . gained him a good deal of respect. E. GELLNER Psychoanalysis . . can gain access to the contents of the Unconscious.
2 *verb trans.* Obtain or receive (a sum of money) as profit or personal benefit; earn or obtain (a living). M16. ▸**b** Obtain (a quantity or amount of anything) as an addition or increment. E17.
OED He gains a hundred a year by his change of employment. **b** B. SPOCK If he loses weight during an illness, he gains it back promptly.
3 *verb trans.* Acquire or win (land, a victory, a legal judgement, etc.) as the result of a contest or battle; be victorious in (a battle etc.). M16. ▸**b** *verb trans.* Acquire or reclaim (land) from the sea etc. M17.
W. COWPER A meaner than himself shall gain the prize. I. WATTS Either I shall gain the cause or lose it.
4 *verb intrans.* Make a gain or profit; advance; receive a personal benefit. L16. ▸**b** Foll. by *on*, *upon*: win favour with (now *rare*); get closer to (a person or thing pursued); (esp. of the sea) encroach upon. M17. ▸**c** Improve or advance *in* some respect. M19. ▸**d** Be enhanced *by* comparison or contrast. M19.
SHAKES. *Com. Err.* He gains by death that hath such means to die. R. C. HUTCHINSON My mind began to gain in its struggle against the weight of torpor. **c** R. W. EMERSON Popular theology has gained in decorum and not in principle. **d** LD MACAULAY The English Liturgy . . gains by being compared . . with those . . Liturgies from which it is taken.
5 *verb trans.* Win over or *over* to one's own opinion or interests; persuade, bribe. L16.
J. H. NEWMAN He did not try to gain him over by smooth representations. E. BOWEN Ralph's charm so gained his father-in-law . . that he left Mount Bruis to Ralph and Mary.
6 *verb trans.* Arrive at, reach (a desired place); *rare* accomplish (a certain distance). E17.
E. WAUGH She . . led him across the yard . . . They gained the verandah.
7 Of a clock etc.: ▸**a** *verb intrans.* become fast, so as to indicate a time ahead of the correct time. M19. ▸**b** *verb trans.* run fast by (a specified period). M19.
a M. TWAIN My beautiful new watch had run eighteen months without losing or gaining.
— PHRASES: ***gain a march on***: see MARCH *noun*³. **gain ground** (orig. MILITARY), conquer territory belonging to an adversary; *fig.* make progress, advance, acquire ascendancy. **gain ground on**, **gain ground upon** make progress at the expense of; get closer to (someone or something pursued). ***gain the ear of***: see EAR *noun*¹. ***gain one's colours***: see COLOUR *noun*. **gain the wind of** NAUTICAL arrive on the windward side of (another vessel). **gain time** obtain a delay by pretexts, deliberate slowness, etc.
■ **gainable** *adjective* (now *rare*) E17. **gainer** *noun* M16.

gain- /geɪn/ *prefix* (not productive). LOE.
[ORIGIN from GAIN *adjective*.]
Chiefly in verbs & verbal derivs. (now all *obsolete*, *arch.*, or *literary*) with the sense 'against, in opposition to', as ***gainsay***; formerly also 'reciprocal, in return' as ***gain-giving***.

gainful /ˈgeɪnfʊl, -f(ə)l/ *adjective.* M16.
[ORIGIN from GAIN *noun*² + -FUL.]
1 Productive of (esp. financial) gain or profit; (of employment) paid, useful. M16.
M. R. MITFORD She . . speedily established a regular and gainful trade in milk.
2 Bent on making gain or profit. *rare*. M17.
■ **gainfully** *adverb* M16. **gainfulness** *noun* M17.

gain-giving /ˈgeɪngɪvɪŋ/ *noun.* Long *arch.* LME.
[ORIGIN from GAIN- + GIVING *verbal noun*.]
†**1** A giving in return. Only in LME.
2 A misgiving. E17.

gaining /ˈgeɪnɪŋ/ *noun.* M16.
[ORIGIN from GAIN *verb*² + -ING¹.]
1 The action of GAIN *verb*². M16.
2 A thing gained; profit. Usu. in *pl.* M16.

gainly /ˈgeɪnli/ *adjective.* ME.
[ORIGIN from GAIN *adjective* + -LY¹.]
1 Suitable, fitting. *obsolete* exc. *Scot. dial.* ME.
2 Graceful, shapely; tactful. M19.

gainly /ˈgeɪnli/ *adverb. obsolete* exc. *dial.* ME.
[ORIGIN from GAIN *adjective* + -LY².]
1 Suitably, fittingly, readily. ME.
†**2** Thoroughly, very. LME–M17.

gainsay /geɪnˈseɪ/ *verb & noun.* Now chiefly *literary.* ME.
[ORIGIN from GAIN- + SAY *verb*¹: prob. modelled on Old Norse *gagnmæli* gainsaying.]
▸ **A** *verb trans.* Pa. t. & pple **-said**, (*rare*) **-sayed**, /-ˈsɛd, -ˈseɪd/.
1 Deny, contradict, (a statement etc.). ME.

J. LOCKE And that certainly you may think safely . . without fear of being gain-said. E. A. FREEMAN Facts which cannot be gainsaid.

2 Refuse (a thing). *rare.* ME.
3 Speak or act against; oppose; hinder. LME.

P. LIVELY He had insisted on providing hospitality and would not be gainsaid.

▸ **B** *noun.* Contradiction. Now *rare.* M16.
■ ˈ**gainsayer** *noun* LME.

Gainsborough hat /geɪnzb(ə)rə ˈhat/ *noun phr.* L19.
[ORIGIN Thomas *Gainsborough* (1727–88), English painter.]
A large broad-brimmed hat such as is worn by women in certain of Gainsborough's portraits.

gainst /geɪnst/ *preposition. poet.* Also **'gainst**. L16.
[ORIGIN Aphet.]
= AGAINST.

gainstand /geɪnˈstand/ *verb trans.* Long *arch.* Pa. t. & pple **-stood** /-ˈstʊd/. ME.
[ORIGIN from GAIN- + STAND *verb.*]
Withstand, resist.
■ **gainstander** *noun* an opposer, an opponent L15.

†**gainstrive** *verb.* M16.
[ORIGIN from GAIN- + STRIVE *verb.*]
1 *verb trans.* Strive against, oppose. M–L16.
2 *verb intrans.* Make resistance. L16–E17.

†**gairfowl** *noun* var. of GAREFOWL.

gaishen /ˈgeɪʃ(ə)n/ *noun. dial.* E19.
[ORIGIN Unknown.]
A skeleton; a silly-looking person; an obstacle.

gait /geɪt/ *noun.* Also †**gate**. See also GATE *noun*². LME.
[ORIGIN A spec. use of GATE *noun*². The spelling *gait* was orig. Scot.]
▸ **I** **1** Manner of walking or stepping, carriage. Also *transf.* manner of forward movement of a vehicle etc. LME. ▸**b** In *pl.* Esp. of a horse: paces. L17.

SPENSER Scarse thy legs uphold thy feeble gate. D. M. THOMAS She walked with an awkward gait, bending forward from the waist.

go one's own gait pursue one's own course.
2 Chiefly *US.* Rate of movement, pace. M20.
▸ **II** See GATE *noun*².
■ **gaited** *adjective* having a (specified) gait or number of gaits L16.

gait /geɪt/ *verb trans. dial.* or *techn.* M19.
[ORIGIN App. from GATE *noun*².]
Put in working order; fix up.

gaita /ˈgaɪta/ *noun.* M19.
[ORIGIN Spanish & Portuguese.]
A kind of bagpipe played in northern Spain and Portugal.

gaiter /ˈgeɪtə/ *noun*¹. *obsolete* exc. *dial.* Also **gatten** /ˈgat(ə)n/, **gatter** /ˈgatə/. OE.
[ORIGIN Based on Old English *gāte trēow* goat's tree.]
In full ***gaiter-tree***. Dogwood, *Cornus sanguinea*.

gaiter /ˈgeɪtə/ *noun*² *& verb.* E18.
[ORIGIN French *guêtre*, †*guietre*, †*guestre*, perh. repr. metath. alt. of Germanic base of WRIST.]
▸ **A** *noun.* **1** A covering of cloth, leather, etc., for the ankle, or ankle and lower leg. Also, a covering for a part of a machine etc. E18.

F. O'CONNOR He wore a small cloth hat and big gaiters over his long pants. *Mail on Sunday* The rubber gaiter on the gear lever slipped down into the box.

all gas and gaiters, ***gas and gaiters***: see GAS *noun*¹.
2 In full ***gaiter boot***, ***gaiter shoe***. A shoe or overshoe which extends to the ankle or above. Chiefly *US.* L18.
▸ **B** *verb trans.* Dress or provide with gaiters. M18.

gal /gal/ *noun*¹. *slang & dial.* Now chiefly *N. Amer.* L18.
[ORIGIN Repr. a pronunc.]
= GIRL *noun.*

gal /gal/ *noun*². E20.
[ORIGIN Abbreviation of *Galileo*: see GALILEAN *adjective*².]
A unit of gravitational acceleration equal to one centimetre per second per second.

Gal. *abbreviation*¹.
Galatians (New Testament).

gal. *abbreviation*².
Gallon(s).

gala /ˈgɑːlə, ˈgeɪlə/ *noun.* E17.
[ORIGIN French or its source in Italian from Spanish from Old French *gale* merrymaking: see GALLANT *adjective & noun.*]
1 Fine or showy dress. Now only in ***in gala*** E17.
†**2** Festivity, rejoicing. E18–E19.
3 A festive occasion; a festival characterized by finery and show. M18.
– COMB.: **gala day** a day of festivity, finery, and show; **gala dress** a dress for a gala; festal attire; **gala night** a night or evening of festivity, finery, and show.

galabiya /gəˈlɑːbɪjə, galəˈbiːjə/ *noun.* Also **galabieh**, **gallabiya**, & other vars. E18.
[ORIGIN Egyptian var. of Arabic *jallābiyya*: see DJELLABA.]
A long loose garment worn in Arabic-speaking Mediterranean countries, esp. in Egypt.

galactagogue /gəˈlaktəgɒg/ *adjective & noun.* M19.
[ORIGIN from GALACTO- + Greek *agōgos* leading, eliciting.]
▸ **A** *adjective.* Inducing a flow of milk. M19.
▸ **B** *noun.* A galactagogue agent. L19.

galactan /gəˈlaktan/ *noun.* L19.
[ORIGIN from GALACTOSE + -AN.]
BIOCHEMISTRY. A polysaccharide whose constituent monosaccharides are galactoses.

galactase /gəˈlakteɪz/ *noun.* L19.
[ORIGIN from GALACTO- + -ASE.]
BIOCHEMISTRY. A proteolytic enzyme present in the milk of many animals.

galactic /gəˈlaktɪk/ *adjective.* M19.
[ORIGIN from Greek *galaktias* var. of *galaxias* GALAXY + -IC.]
Of or pertaining to the Galaxy or the Milky Way; of or pertaining to another galaxy or galaxies in general.
galactic equator a great circle passing as nearly as possible through the middle of the Milky Way. **galactic latitude**, **galactic longitude**, **galactic pole**, etc.: measured or fixed relative to the galactic equator (and some reference point on it).
■ **galactically** *adverb* M20.

galactico /gəˈlaktɪkəʊ/ *noun. colloq.* Pl. **-os**. E21.
[ORIGIN Spanish *galáctico*, lit. 'galactic person' (because bigger than a 'star').]
An exceptionally skilled and celebrated soccer player.

galacto- /gəˈlaktəʊ/ *combining form.* Before a vowel **galact-**.
[ORIGIN from Greek *gala, galakt-* milk + -O-.]
1 With the sense 'of milk'.
2 With the sense 'of galactose'.
3 With the sense 'of the Galaxy or of a galaxy'.
■ **galactocele** *noun* (MEDICINE) a milk-filled swelling in the breast due to a blocked milk duct M19. **galactoˈcentric** *adjective* with respect to the centre of the Galaxy M20. **galacˈtophorous** *adjective* conveying milk M18. **galactopoiˈesis** *noun* [Greek *poiesis* production] production of milk M19. **galactopoiˈetic** *adjective* [Greek *poietikos* capable of producing] tending to produce milk M17. **galactoˈrrhoea** *noun* excessive or inappropriate production of milk M19. **galactuˈronic** *adjective*: ***galacturonic acid***, the uronic acid derived from galactose, present esp. in pectins E20.

galactonic /galakˈtɒnɪk/ *adjective.* L19.
[ORIGIN from GALACTOSE + -ONIC.]
CHEMISTRY. ***galactonic acid***, an acid, $CH_2OH(CHOH)_4COOH$, derived from galactose by oxidation of the latter's aldehyde group.

galactosaemia /gəlaktə(ʊ)ˈsiːmɪə/ *noun.* Also ***-semia**. M20.
[ORIGIN from GALACTOS(E + Greek *haima* blood: see -IA¹.]
MEDICINE. The presence of galactose in the blood; an inherited metabolic disorder of which this is a sign.

galactosamine /galakˈtəʊsəmiːn/ *noun.* E20.
[ORIGIN from GALACTOSE + AMINE.]
BIOCHEMISTRY. A crystalline amino sugar, $C_6H_{13}NO_5$, of which chondroitin is a derivative.

galactose /gəˈlaktəʊz, -s/ *noun.* M19.
[ORIGIN from GALACTO- + -OSE².]
A hexose sugar which is a common component of natural polysaccharides, notably lactose.
■ **galactoˈsidase** *noun* any enzyme that hydrolyses a galactoside to galactose and an aglycone E20. **galactoside** *noun* any glycoside containing galactose M19.

galactosemia *noun* see GALACTOSAEMIA.

galago /gəˈleɪgəʊ/ *noun.* Pl. **-os**. M19.
[ORIGIN mod. Latin.]
A bushbaby; *spec.* one of the genus *Galago*.

galah /gəˈlɑː/ *noun.* M19.
[ORIGIN Yuwaalaraay (an Australian Aboriginal language of New South Wales) *gilaa*.]
1 A very common small Australian cockatoo, *Eolophus roseicapillus*, with a pink breast and grey back. Also called ***rose-breasted cockatoo***. M19.
2 A fool, a simpleton. *Austral. slang.* M20.

Galahad /ˈgaləhad/ *noun.* L19.
[ORIGIN The noblest knight of the Round Table in Arthurian legend.]
A person characterized by nobility, courtesy, integrity, etc.

galanga /gəˈlaŋgə/ *noun.* LME.
[ORIGIN medieval Latin: see GALINGALE.]
= GALINGALE.

galangal *noun* var. of GALINGALE.

galant /galɑ̃, gəˈlɑːnt/ *adjective.* L19.
[ORIGIN French & German: see GALLANT *noun & adjective.*]
MUSIC. Designating or pertaining to a light and elegant style of 18th-cent. music.

galanterie /galɑ̃tri, (in sense 2 also) gal(ə)ntəˈriː/ *noun.* Pl. ***-ries*** (pronounced same), (in sense 2 also with German pl.) ***-rien*** /-ˈriːn/. E17.
[ORIGIN French or (sense 2) German: see GALLANTRY.]
†**1** = GALLANTRY 1. Only in E17.
2 MUSIC. A light non-essential movement in an early 18th-cent. classical suite. E20.
3 Courtesy, politeness, esp. to women. E20.

galantine /ˈgal(ə)ntiːn/ *noun.* ME.
[ORIGIN Old French & mod. French, alt. of *galatine* from medieval Latin *galatina*.]
†**1** A kind of sauce for fish or fowl. ME–M17.
2 A dish of white meat boned, cooked, pressed, and served cold with aspic, etc. E18.

galanty show /gəˈlantɪ ʃəʊ/ *noun phr.* Now *hist.* E19.
[ORIGIN Perh. from Italian *galanti* pl. of *galante* GALLANT *noun.*]
A shadow pantomime produced by throwing shadows of puppets on to a wall or screen.

galatea /galəˈtiːə/ *noun.* L19.
[ORIGIN HMS *Galatea*, a vessel commanded in 1867 by the Duke of Edinburgh.]
A strong cotton material, usu. with blue and white stripes, orig. used for making children's sailor suits.

G

Galatian /gəˈleɪʃ(ə)n/ *noun & adjective.* M16.
[ORIGIN from *Galatia* (see below) + -AN.]
▸ **A** *noun.* A native or inhabitant of Galatia, an ancient country of central Asia Minor. In *pl.* (treated as *sing.*), St Paul's Epistle to the Galatians, a book of the New Testament. M16.
▸ **B** *adjective.* Of or pertaining to Galatia or its people. M19.

galax /ˈgalaks/ *noun.* E19.
[ORIGIN mod. Latin: cf. Greek *galaxias* GALAXY.]
An evergreen plant, *Galax urceolata* of the family Diapensiaceae, native to the US and having white flowers and shiny leaves.

galaxy /ˈgaləksi/ *noun.* LME.
[ORIGIN Old French & mod. French *galaxie* from medieval Latin *galaxia*, late Latin *galaxias* from Greek *galaxias* (sc. *kuklos* circle), from *gala, galakt-* milk: see -Y³.]
1 The Milky Way. LME. ▸**b** ASTRONOMY. Any of the numerous vast systems of stars, gas, and dust that exist separately in the universe and together contain nearly all of its visible matter; *spec.* (often **G-**) that spiral system to which the earth belongs and whose disc of maximum star density is visible as the Milky Way. M19.

H. MOSELEY The Galaxy, or Milky-way, passes through the heavens like an irregular zone.

2 *transf. & fig.* A brilliant assembly esp. of beautiful or talented people. L16.

C. CHAPLIN The fruit-shop was a galaxy of colour. S. MORLEY A galaxy of stars from Herbert Marshall . . to Charles Laughton.

galbanum /ˈgalbənəm/ *noun.* ME.
[ORIGIN Latin from Greek *khalbanē*, of Semitic origin (cf. Hebrew *helbĕnāh* Exod. 30:34).]
1 A gum resin obtained in the Middle East from a ferula, esp. *Ferula galbaniflua*, and having medicinal uses. ME.
2 *fig.* Bosh, humbug. Now *rare* or *obsolete.* M18.

galbe /galb/ *noun.* L19.
[ORIGIN French.]
A contour, an outline, a profile.

Galbraithian /galˈbreɪθɪən/ *adjective & noun.* M20.
[ORIGIN from *Galbraith* (see below) + -IAN.]
▸ **A** *adjective.* Of, pertaining to, or characteristic of the opinions or writings of the N. American economist and diplomat John Kenneth Galbraith (1908–2006). M20.
▸ **B** *noun.* A person who supports or is influenced by the writings of J. K. Galbraith. M20.

gale /geɪl/ *noun*¹.
[ORIGIN Old English *gagel*, *gagelle* = Middle Dutch *gaghel*, Dutch & German *gagel*: the present form is unexpl.]
Bog myrtle, *Myrica gale*. Also ***sweet gale***.

gale /geɪl/ *noun*². M16.
[ORIGIN Uncertain: perh. orig. an adjective in *gale wind* and, in spite of the late date, of Scandinavian origin and to be connected with Middle Swedish, Norwegian *galen* bad (of weather), Old Norse *galenn* mad, frantic.]
1 A strong wind; *spec.* (on the Beaufort scale) one of force 8 and 9, or with a speed of between 34 and 47 knots; NAUTICAL a storm. M16. ▸**b** A gentle breeze. *poet. & rhet.* L17.

F. CHICHESTER The seas were very rough . . with a gale south-west by west. E. ARDIZZONE By this time it was blowing a gale.

near gale: with a speed of between 34 and 40 knots (8 on the Beaufort scale). **strong gale**: with a speed of between 41 and 47 knots (9 on the Beaufort scale).
2 *transf. & fig.* **a** An outpouring, an outburst, esp. of laughter. Now usu. in *pl.* E17. ▸**b** A state of excitement. *US.* M19.

a W. MARCH She went into gales of merriment, her laughter resounding through the department.

gale /geɪl/ *noun*³. M17.
[ORIGIN Contr. of GAVEL *noun*¹.]
1 A periodical payment of rent; the amount of rent so paid. M17.

2 In the Forest of Dean, a royalty paid for a plot of land and for the right to mine on this land; land granted for this purpose. L18.

gale /geɪl/ *verb*[1] *intrans.* Now *rare.* L17.
[ORIGIN from GALE *noun*[2].]
NAUTICAL. Sail *away* as if before a gale.

gale /geɪl/ *verb*[2] *trans.* M19.
[ORIGIN from GALE *noun*[3].]
Grant or take the gale of (a mine).

galea /ˈgeɪlɪə/ *noun.* M19.
[ORIGIN Latin = helmet.]
BOTANY, ZOOLOGY, & ANATOMY. Any of various structures resembling a helmet in shape, function, or position.

galeate /ˈgalɪeɪt, -ɪət/ *adjective.* E18.
[ORIGIN Latin *galeatus*, from *galea* helmet: see -ATE[2].]
= GALEATED 1.

galeated /ˈgalɪeɪtɪd/ *adjective.* E17.
[ORIGIN formed as GALEATE + -ED[1].]
1 Wearing a helmet, helmeted. E17.

H. PHILLIPS The galeated head of Minerva.

G

2 Chiefly BOTANY & ZOOLOGY. Shaped like a helmet; covered with a galea or similar structure. L17.

†**galeche** *noun* see CALASH.

galeeny /gəˈliːni/ *noun.* Now *dial.* L18.
[ORIGIN Spanish *gallina (morisca)* '(Moorish) hen' (so in Portuguese & Italian) from Latin *gallina*: see -Y[6].]
A guinea fowl.

galega /gəˈliːgə/ *noun.* L15.
[ORIGIN mod. Latin, of unknown origin.]
A Eurasian leguminous plant, *Galega officinalis*, sometimes grown in gardens, with pinnate leaves and racemes of mauve or white flowers; goat's rue. Also, a medicinal preparation of this plant.

Galen /ˈgeɪlən/ *noun. joc.* L16.
[ORIGIN Anglicized from Latin *Galenus* from Greek *Galēnos* Galen: see below.]
With allusion to Galen, a Pergamene physician and writer at the court of Marcus Aurelius in the 2nd cent. AD: a physician.

galena /gəˈliːnə/ *noun.* L17.
[ORIGIN Latin = lead at a certain stage of smelting.]
Lead sulphide, PbS, the principal ore of lead, found as grey, usu. cubic crystals with a metallic lustre.

galenic /gəˈlɛnɪk/ *adjective.* M17.
[ORIGIN from GALEN + -IC.]
Of or pertaining to Galen, his followers, or his principles and practice; *esp.* (of a medicine) being a vegetable as distinct from a synthetic preparation.
■ **Galenian** *adjective* L17.

galenical /gəˈlɛnɪk(ə)l/ *adjective & noun.* M17.
[ORIGIN formed as GALENIC: see -ICAL.]
▸ **A** *adjective.* = GALENIC M17.
▸ **B** *noun.* A galenic or vegetable remedy; a simple. M18.
■ **galenically** *adverb* (now *rare*) with galenical or vegetable remedies L17.

Galenist /ˈgeɪlənɪst/ *noun.* L16.
[ORIGIN from GALEN + -IST.]
A follower of Galen.
■ **Galenism** *noun* the medical principles or system of Galen E18.

galère /galɛːr/ *noun.* Pl. pronounced same. M18.
[ORIGIN French = galley, used fig. in Molière's *Scapin*.]
A coterie; a (usu. undesirable) group of people; an unpleasant situation.

galette /gəˈlɛt/ *noun.* L18.
[ORIGIN French.]
A broad thin cake usu. of pastry.

Galgenhumor /ˈgalgənhuːmɔːr/ *noun.* Also **g-**. E20.
[ORIGIN German, from *Galgen* gallows + *Humor* humour.]
Grim, ironical humour. Cf. ***gallows humour*** s.v. GALLOWS *noun.*

Galibi /gəˈliːbi/ *noun & adjective.* Pl. of noun same, **-s**. L19.
[ORIGIN Carib, lit. 'strong man'.]
Of or pertaining to, a member of, a S. American Indian people of French Guiana; (of) the Carib language of this people.

Galician /gəˈlɪsjən/ *noun*[1] *& adjective*[1]. LME.
[ORIGIN from *Galicia* in the NW corner of the Iberian peninsula + -AN.]
▸ **A** *noun.* A native or inhabitant of Galicia, a medieval Castilian kingdom, subsequently a Spanish province. Also, the language of Galicia, closely related to Portuguese. LME.
▸ **B** *adjective.* Of or pertaining to Galicia or its inhabitants. E19.

Galician /gəˈlɪsjən/ *adjective*[2] *& noun*[2]. M19.
[ORIGIN from *Galicia* in east central Europe + -AN.]
▸ **A** *adjective.* Of or pertaining to Galicia, a former province of the Austro-Hungarian empire now divided between Poland and Ukraine, or its inhabitants. M19.
▸ **B** *noun.* A native or inhabitant of Galicia. Also (*Canad.*, now *rare*) an immigrant from central Europe. E20.

Galilean /galɪˈliːən/ *noun & adjective*[1]. M16.
[ORIGIN from Latin *Galil(a)ea* (Greek *Galilaia*) Galilee (see below) + -AN.]
▸ **A** *noun.* A native or inhabitant of Galilee; *derog.* Jesus Christ. Also, a Christian. M16.

AV *Acts* 2:7 Are not all these which speake, Galileans?

▸ **B** *adjective.* Of or pertaining to Galilee, in Palestine. Also, Christian. M17.

MILTON The pilot of the Galilean lake.

Galilean /galɪˈliːən/ *adjective*[2]. E18.
[ORIGIN from *Galileo* Galilei (1564–1642), Italian astronomer + -AN.]
1 Discovered, developed by, or characteristic of Galileo. E18.
2 PHYSICS. Pertaining to an inertial frame of reference; designating a transformation between such frames. E20.
– SPECIAL COLLOCATIONS: **Galilean moon**, **Galilean satellite** each of the four largest moons of Jupiter (Io, Europa, Ganymede, and Callisto). **Galilean telescope** a simple refracting telescope with convergent objective and divergent eyepiece.

galilee /ˈgalɪliː/ *noun.* LME.
[ORIGIN Old French *galilée* from medieval Latin *galilea*, a use of the place name *Galilee*: see GALILEAN *adjective*[1] *& noun*.]
A porch or chapel at the entrance of a church.

galimatias /galɪˈmatɪəs, -ˈmeɪʃəs/ *noun.* M17.
[ORIGIN French, of unknown origin.]
Confused language, meaningless talk, gibberish.

W. H. AUDEN A tongue With . . no resemblance To the galimatias of nursery and bedroom.

galingale /ˈgalɪŋgeɪl/ *noun.* Also **galangal** /ˈgal(ə)ŋgal/. LOE.
[ORIGIN Old French *galingal* from Arabic *ḵalanjān* (Persian *ḵūlinjān*, Sanskrit *kulañjana*) perh. from Chinese *gāoliángjiāng*, from *gāoliáng* a district in Guangdong Province, China + *jiāng* ginger. Cf. medieval Latin, medieval Greek, Italian *galanga* (French *galangue*), GALANGA.]
1 The aromatic rhizome of certain East Asian plants of the genera *Alpinia* and *Kaempferia*, of the ginger family, used as a spice. LOE.
2 A sedge, *Cyperus longus*, having an aromatic root. Also more fully ***English galingale***, ***sweet galingale***. L16.

†**galion** *noun* var. of GALIUM.

galiot *noun* var. of GALLIOT.

galipot /ˈgalɪpɒt/ *noun.* L18.
[ORIGIN French *galipot*, †*garipot*: cf. Provençal *garapot* pine-tree resin.]
A kind of hardened turpentine formed on the stem of the cluster pine.

galium /ˈgeɪlɪəm/. *noun.* Also (earlier) †**galion**. M16.
[ORIGIN mod. Latin, or Greek *galion* bedstraw.]
= BEDSTRAW 2.

galjoen /xalˈjʊn/ *noun. S. Afr.* M19.
[ORIGIN Afrikaans & Dutch = galleon.]
Either of two deep-bodied marine fishes belonging to the genus *Coracinus*, esp. *C. capensis.*

gall /gɔːl/ *noun*[1].
[ORIGIN Old English *ġealla*, Old Saxon *galla* (Dutch *gal*), Old High German *galla* (German *Galle*), Old Norse *gall*, from Germanic. Cogn. with Greek *kholē*, *kholos*, Latin *fel* bile.]
1 The secretion of the liver, bile (exc. in certain combs. now only of the lower animals). Also, the type of an intensely bitter substance. OE. ▸**b** *fig.* Bitterness; anything bitter. ME.

E. MANNIN The taste in his mouth was as bitter as gall. **b** W. IRVING The gall of disappointment.

2 The gall bladder and its contents. ME.
3 Bitterness of spirit, asperity, rancour (supposed to have its seat in the gall bladder). ME. ▸†**b** Spirit to resent injury or insult. LME–E18.

GIBBON The bitterness of religious gall.

4 Assurance, impudence. *slang.* Orig. *US.* L19.

J. UPDIKE She had the gall to grin right in my face.

– PHRASES ETC.: †**break someone's gall** break the spirit of, cow. **dip one's pen in gall** write with virulence and rancour. **gall of the earth** any of various bitter plants, esp. centaury or (*US*) a rattlesnake root, *Prenanthes trifoliata*. ***glass gall***: see GLASS *noun.*
– COMB.: **gall bladder** the organ which stores bile after its secretion by the liver; **gall-sickness** *S. Afr.* any of several diseases affecting the livers of livestock.
■ **gall-less** /-l-l-/ *adjective* without gall or bitterness LME.

gall /gɔːl/ *noun*[2].
[ORIGIN Old English *ġealle*, Middle Low German, Middle Dutch *galle* (Dutch *gal*), Middle & mod. High German *galle*, Old Norse *galli* (Middle Swedish *galle*) fault, flaw; perh. identical with GALL *noun*[1]. Later forms from Middle Low German, Middle Dutch.]
1 Orig., a painful swelling, pustule, or blister, esp. in a horse (cf. ***windgall*** s.v. WIND *noun*[1]). Later, a sore produced by rubbing or chafing. OE.

P. V. WHITE The old horse . . with girth galls, and saddle sores.

2 A bare or barren spot in a field, coppice, etc. ME. ▸**b** A place rubbed bare; an unsound spot, a fault or flaw. Now only *techn.* M16.
3 *fig.* A person who or thing which irritates, vexes, or harasses. L15.

SPENSER They . . have left a perpetuall gall in the myndes of that people.

– NOTE: The sense has been influenced by GALL *verb*[1] (see note).

gall /gɔːl/ *noun*[3]. LME.
[ORIGIN Old French & mod. French *galle* from Latin *galla* oak apple, gall.]
An excrescence produced on a tree (esp. the oak) or other plant by the action of a fungus, bacterium, an insect, etc.
– COMB.: **gall apple** = GALL *noun*[3]; **gallberry** *US* either of two hollies, *Ilex glabra* and *I. coriacea* (the large or sweet gallberry); **gall fly** any of various insects which cause galls by laying their eggs in plant tissues; *spec.* any fly of the dipteran family Tephritidae; **gall gnat**, **gall midge** any gall-forming insect of the dipteran family Cecidomyidae; **gall nut** = GALL *noun*[3]; **gall wasp** any gall-forming insect of the hymenopteran superfamily Cynipoidea.

gall /gɔːl/ *verb*[1]. ME.
[ORIGIN Back-form. from GALLED *ppl adjective.*]
1 *verb trans.* Make (an animal, a person) sore by rubbing or chafing. ME. ▸**b** Injure or damage (something) by rubbing or contact. E17.

W. COWPER The snorting beast began to trot, Which gall'd him in his seat. *fig.*: J. MORSE Long and heavily did the Tartar yoke gall the neck of Russia. **b** C. MARSHALL Tie the tree . . with a firm hay band that it may not easily get galled.

2 *verb trans.* Harass in warfare, esp. with arrows or shot. L15.

M. ARNOLD The surrounding multitudes galled them . . with a cloud of arrows.

3 *verb trans. fig.* Irritate, annoy; vex, humiliate. L16.

E. JONES It galled him that only very seldom could he give her even a meagre present.

4 *verb intrans.* Become sore or chafed. Now *rare.* E17.
– NOTE: The sense appears to have been infl. by assoc. with Old French *galler* scratch, rub.
■ **gallingly** *adverb* in a galling manner E19.

gall /gɑːl/ *verb*[2] *trans.* L16.
[ORIGIN from GALL *noun*[3].]
DYEING. Impregnate with a decoction of galls.

gall- *combining form* see GALLO-[2].

Galla /ˈgalə/ *noun & adjective.* L19.
[ORIGIN Unknown.]
▸ **A** *noun.* Pl. same, **-s**. A member of a Hamitic people inhabiting mainly parts of Ethiopia and Kenya; the Cushitic language of this people. L19.
▸ **B** *adjective.* Of or pertaining to the Galla or their language. L19.

gallabiya *noun* var. of GALABIYA.

gallack /ˈgalək/ *adjective. dial.* E18.
[ORIGIN Unknown.]
Left. Chiefly in ***gallack-handed***, left-handed, clumsy.

gallamine /ˈgaləmiːn/ *noun.* L19.
[ORIGIN from GALLO-[2] + AMINE.]
1 CHEMISTRY. ***gallamine blue***, a blue gallocyanine dye. L19.
2 PHARMACOLOGY. In full ***gallamine triethiodide***. A quaternary ammonium salt, $C_6H_3{\cdot}[O{\cdot}(CH_2)_2{\cdot}N(C_2H_5)_3]_3I_3$, used as a muscle relaxant, esp. in anaesthesia. M20.

gallanilide /gaˈlanɪlʌɪd/ *noun.* L19.
[ORIGIN from GALLO-[2] + ANILIDE.]
CHEMISTRY. An anilide of gallic acid, $C_6H_2(OH)_3CONH{\cdot}C_6H_5$, used in dye manufacture.

gallant /ˈgal(ə)nt, (*esp. in senses A.4 & B.2*) gəˈlant/ *adjective & noun.* LME.
[ORIGIN Old French & mod. French *galant* pres. pple of *galer* make merry, make a show, from *gale* merrymaking, rejoicing: see -ANT[1].]
▸ **A** *adjective.* **1** Finely or splendidly dressed; smart, showy. Formerly also, (of a woman) attractive, fine-looking; (of language) ornate. *arch.* LME. ▸†**b** Suited to fashionable society and its customs; courtly; polished in manners or behaviour. E16–M17.
2 Brave, heroic; chivalrous. LME. ▸**b** Of a Member of Parliament: having served in the Armed Forces. L19.

E. WAUGH The gallant stand he was making for the decencies of family life. A. GUINNESS She was an old lady by then, suffering acutely from arthritis but remarkably gallant and cheerful.

3 Excellent, fine, (with mixture of senses 1 and 2) splendid, noble. Now *rare* exc. of a ship or horse. M16.

J. FRENCH A few drops . . put into any Wine giveth it a gallant relish. W. H. PRESCOTT A more gallant and beautiful armada never before quitted the shores of Spain.

4 Markedly polite and attentive to women; (now *rare*) concerned with (sexual) love, amatory. L17.

E. WELTY Major Bullock shot his umbrella open and held it over Laurel in gallant fashion.

▸ **B** *noun.* **1** A (usu. dashing) man of fashion and pleasure (formerly also, a woman of this type); a (fine) gentleman. LME.

SHAKES. *1 Hen. VI* Good morrow, gallants! Want ye corn for bread?

2 A man who pays court to women, a ladies' man; a suitor; a lover. LME.

S. SPENDER He had ideas of himself as a gallant, so all through dinner he was markedly attentive to her.

■ **gallantly** *adverb* M16. **gallantness** *noun* (now *rare*) LME.

gallant /gəˈlant, ˈgal(ə)nt/ *verb*. E17.
[ORIGIN from the adjective.]
1 *verb intrans.* & †*trans.* with *it*. Cut a dash, make a show. *rare*. E17.
2 *verb trans.* Pay court to or flirt with (a woman); *esp.* attend or act as an escort to (a woman); escort or conduct (a person). L17. ▸†**b** Use (a fan) flirtatiously. L17–M18.

GEO. ELIOT Ladislaw gallants her about sometimes.

3 *verb intrans.* & †*trans.* with *it*. Flirt (*with*). M18.

G. A. SALA The macaroni-cynic of Strawberry Hill is gallanting in the Mall with Lady Caroline Petersham.

gallantize /ˈgaləntʌɪz/ *verb*. Now *rare*. Also **-ise**. E17.
[ORIGIN from GALLANT *adjective* & *noun* + -IZE. Cf. French *galantiser* treat with gallantry.]
1 *verb intrans.* & *trans.* (with *it*). = GALLANT *verb* 1. E17.
2 *verb trans.* Court, flirt with (a woman). E18.

gallantry /ˈgaləntri/ *noun*. L16.
[ORIGIN French *galanterie*, from *galant*: see GALLANT *adjective* & *noun*, -ERY.]
†**1** Splendour, magnificence; (an) ornamentation; (a) display (of elegance etc.). L16–E19. ▸**b** A knick-knack, a trinket. L17–E18.

R. WELTON In whatever gallantry a man appears upon the stage, he must retire, and be undress'd.

†**2** Fashionable people, gentry. Only in 17.

SHAKES. *Tr. & Cr.* Hector . . and all the gallantry of Troy.

3 Bravery, nobility, dashing courage. Formerly also, a brave or noble deed. M17.

M. LOWRY And for it, or gallantry connected with it, he had received the British Distinguished Service Order.

4 The behaviour of a gallant. M17.

POPE The men of pleasure, dress, and gallantry.

5 Marked politeness or courteousness towards women; an instance of this. L17.

P. H. GIBBS He took Patricia's hand and raised it to his lips with old-fashioned gallantry.

6 Sexual intrigue or flirtation. Formerly also, an instance of this. L17.

BYRON What men call gallantry, and gods adultery.

gallate /ˈgaleɪt/ *noun*[1]. L18.
[ORIGIN from GALLIC *adjective*[2] + -ATE[1].]
CHEMISTRY. A salt or ester of gallic acid.

gallate /ˈgaleɪt/ *noun*[2]. M20.
[ORIGIN from GALLIUM + -ATE[1].]
CHEMISTRY. A salt containing oxyanions of gallium.

gall bladder /ˈgɔːl bladə/ *noun phr.* L17.
[ORIGIN from GALL *noun*[1] + BLADDER.]
A muscular sac, attached to the right lobe of the liver, in which bile is stored after secretion by the liver.

Galle *noun* see GAUL.

galleas *noun* var. of GALLIASS.

galled /gɔːld/ *adjective*. OE.
[ORIGIN Orig. from GALL *noun*[2] + -ED[2], but later as if from GALL *verb*[1] + -ED[1].]
1 Suffering from galls; sore from chafing (freq. with instrument specified as ***saddle-galled***). OE.
2 *fig.* Irritated, distressed. E17.
3 Of land: eroded; sterile through exhaustion. Chiefly *US*. E19.

Gallegan /galˈjeɪg(ə)n/ *adjective* & *noun*. M19.
[ORIGIN from GALLEGO + -AN.]
= GALICIAN *adjective*[1] & *noun*[1].

Gallego /galˈjeɪgəʊ/ *noun*. Also **g-**. Pl. **-os**. E17.
[ORIGIN Spanish.]
Orig. a ship from Galicia in Spain. Now = GALICIAN *noun*[1].

galleon /ˈgalɪən/ *noun*. E16.
[ORIGIN Either from Middle Dutch *galjoen*, from Old French & mod. French *galion* augm. of *galie* GALLEY, or from Spanish *galeón*: see -OON.]
hist. A type of ship, shorter than a galley but usu. with 3 or more decks and masts, mainly square-rigged and having a high forecastle and poop (in (chiefly Spanish) use from 15th to 18th cent., orig. as a warship, later for trading between Spain and America).

galleria /galəˈriːə/ *noun*. L19.
[ORIGIN Italian: see GALLERY.]
A shopping arcade in an Italian city or designed in imitation of one of these.

gallerian /gəˈlɪərɪən/ *noun*. M17.
[ORIGIN French *galérien*, from *galère* slave galley.]
hist. A galley slave.

gallery /ˈgal(ə)ri/ *noun* & *verb*. LME.
[ORIGIN Old French & mod. French *galerie*, from Italian *galleria* gallery, †church porch, from medieval Latin *galeria*, perh. alt. of *galilea* GALILEE by dissimilation of *l* to *r*.]
▸ **A** *noun*. **1** A covered passageway, partly open at the side or having the roof supported by pillars; *US* a porch, a veranda. LME.

H. HUNTER There is in the gallery of the Tuilleries, on the right as you enter the gardens, an Ionic column. W. A. PERCY Well-wishers . . drove him home, and deposited him . . in the swing on his own front gallery.

2 A long narrow balcony constructed on the outside of a building, at some elevation from the ground and open at the front apart from a railing, balustrade, etc. LME. ▸**b** NAUTICAL. A balcony built outside the body of a ship, at the stern or the quarters. E17. ▸**c** ARCHITECTURE. A long narrow passage built into the thickness of a wall or supported on corbels, open towards the interior of a building. M18. ▸†**d** A passenger car like a basket attached to a hot-air balloon. L18–E20.
3 A long narrow room, sometimes one providing access to other parts of a house; a room or building devoted to the exhibition (and sale) of paintings, sculptures, etc. E16. ▸**b** A more or less horizontal underground passage (MILITARY & MINING); a passage made by an animal, now only underground or through a rock. M17. ▸**c** = ***shooting gallery*** s.v. SHOOTING *verbal noun*. M19.

I. MCEWAN She was picking her way slowly through a long gallery of treasures, heirlooms. *fig.*: P. USTINOV His war tales of the provinces, of a gallery of powerful women and indeterminate men. **b** J. G. FARRELL The distance between the ends of the branch galleries should be such that the enemy cannot burrow between them unheard.

4 A platform or balcony projecting from the inner wall of a church, courtroom, hall, etc. serving e.g. to provide extra room for an audience or reserved for musicians etc.; *spec.* in a theatre, the highest of such balconies, containing the cheapest seats. L16. ▸**b** The part of a meeting house of the Society of Friends occupied by the elders. E19. ▸**c** The control room of a television studio. M20.

T. HARDY Her sight Swept the west gallery, and caught its row Of music-men. F. RAPHAEL When I was a girl there wasn't a gallery for the women at the synagogue. H. ROSENTHAL I could have got into the back of the gallery for 6d.

5 *sing.* & †in *pl.* The people occupying the gallery in a theatre etc.; *fig.* the least refined part of an audience. M17. ▸**b** A group of spectators at a golf match etc. L19.

H. IRVING That same gallery which at first roared itself hoarse, while the play went on. **b** *Golf Monthly* Sandy Lyle acknowledges the cheers of the huge gallery on the last green.

play to the gallery, **play for the gallery** appeal to unrefined tastes.
6 REAL TENNIS. Each of eight openings beneath the side penthouses of the court, backed by netting to catch balls and protect spectators. L17.
7 An ornamental rim or railing edging a table, shelf, etc. M19.
– COMB.: **gallery forest** a forest restricted to the banks of a river or stream; **gallery grave** ARCHAEOLOGY an underground megalithic burial chamber which may be divided into sections but has no separate entrance passage; **gallery play** showy or ostentatious play designed to gain applause; **gallery tray** a silver tray with a raised rim, used to carry glasses etc.
▸ **B** *verb trans.* Provide with a balcony or gallery. E17.
■ **galleried** *adjective* provided with a gallery M16. **galleryite** *noun* a member of the audience in the gallery of a theatre L19.

gallet /ˈgalɪt/ *noun* & *verb*. E18.
[ORIGIN French *galet* rounded pebble on the beach, stone chip, from Old French *gal* pebble, stone.]
BUILDING. ▸**A** *noun*. A chip or splinter of stone inserted into wet mortar. E18.
▸ **B** *verb trans.* Insert gallets into the mortar or joints of (a wall etc.). M19.

galley /ˈgali/ *noun*. ME.
[ORIGIN Old French *galie* (mod. *galée*), from medieval Latin *galea*, medieval Greek *galea*, of unknown origin, but rel. to French *galère*, Old Norse *galeið*, medieval Latin *galera*, *galeda*, *-ida*.]
▸ **I** **1** *hist.* A low flat single-decked ship with sails and oars, usu. rowed by slaves or criminals and used chiefly in the Mediterranean; *esp.* such a ship with one or more banks of oars used by the ancient Greeks and Romans in war. ME.
2 *hist.* A large open rowing boat esp. as used by the captain of a man-of-war, or on the Thames by customs officers or the press gang. L16.
3 The kitchen of a ship, aircraft, etc. M18.
▸ **II** **4** PRINTING. [French *galée*.] ▸**a** A usu. metal oblong tray open at one end for holding set type. Now chiefly *hist.* M17. ▸**b** A proof in the form of long single-column strips (as orig. from type on a galley), not in sheets or pages; *loosely* a proof from a phototypesetter. L19.
– PHRASES: **in this galley** [after Molière: see GALÈRE] in this (usu. unpleasant) situation or group of people.
– COMB.: **galley-packet** a made-up story, a lie; **galley proof** = sense 4b above; **galley slave** a person condemned to row in a galley; (*fig.*) a drudge; **galleyworm** a millipede, esp. of the genus *Julus*. **galley-yarn** = *galley-packet* above.

†**galley-tile** *noun*. E17–M18.
[ORIGIN from GALLEY + TILE *noun*: see GALLIPOT.]
A glazed tile used for wall decoration.

galley-west /galɪˈwɛst/ *adverb*. *colloq.* (orig. & chiefly *US*). L19.
[ORIGIN Alt. of COLLY-WEST.]
knock galley-west, knock sideways or askew; confuse; defeat, dispose of completely.

galliambic /galɪˈambɪk/ *noun* & *adjective*. M19.
[ORIGIN from Latin *galliambus* a song of the *Galli* or priests of Cybele (from *Gallus* + IAMBUS) + -IC.]
PROSODY. ▸**A** *noun*. A metre consisting of two catalectic iambic dimeters; (a) verse written in this metre. M19.
▸ **B** *adjective*. Pertaining to or composed of galliambics. L19.

galliard /ˈgalɪɑːd, -ɪəd/ *adjective* & *noun*. *arch.* LME.
[ORIGIN Old French & mod. French *gaillard*, perh. from Proto-Romance = strength, power, of Celtic origin (cf. Irish *gal* valour, Welsh *gallu* (have) power): see -ARD. Earlier as a surname.]
▸ **A** *adjective*. **1** Valiant; sturdy. LME.
2 Lively, brisk, full of high spirits; bright or colourful in appearance. LME.
▸ **B** *noun*. **1** Orig. a valiant man. Now only, a lively man of fashion and pleasure. LME.
2 *hist.* A quick and lively dance for couples in triple time; a piece of music for this dance. M16.

galliardize /ˈgalɪədʌɪz/ *noun*. *arch.* Also **-ise**. L16.
[ORIGIN French *gaillardise*, from *gaillard*: see GALLIARD *adjective* & *noun*.]
Gaiety, mirth, revelry; (an) entertainment.

galliass /ˈgalɪəs/ *noun*. Also **galleas**. M16.
[ORIGIN Old French *gal(l)easse* (mod. *galéace*) from Italian *galeaza* augm. of *galea* GALLEY.]
hist. A large type of galley, chiefly used as a warship during the 16th and 17th cents.

Gallic /ˈgalɪk/ *adjective*[1]. L17.
[ORIGIN Latin *Gallicus*, from *Gallus*, *Gallia* Gaul: see -IC.]
1 (Typically) French. Freq. *joc.* L17.

P. D. JAMES He spread his hands in a Gallic gesture of resignation.

2 Of or pertaining to Gaul or the Gauls. L18.

gallic /ˈgalɪk/ *adjective*[2]. L18.
[ORIGIN from Latin *galla* oak gall + -IC.]
CHEMISTRY. ***gallic acid***, a crystalline acid, $C_6H_2(OH)_3COOH$, prepared from the oak gall and other vegetable products, and used as a tanning agent and in dyes and inks; 3, 4, 5-trihydroxybenzoic acid.

gallic /ˈgalɪk/ *adjective*[3]. M20.
[ORIGIN from GALLIUM + -IC.]
CHEMISTRY. Of or containing gallium in the trivalent state.

gallica /ˈgalɪkə/ *noun*. M19.
[ORIGIN from Latin *Gallicus*: see GALLIC *adjective*[1].]
A rose, *Rosa gallica*, ancestral to many cultivated varieties and native to southern Europe and western Asia.

Gallican /ˈgalɪk(ə)n/ *adjective* & *noun*. LME.
[ORIGIN Either from French = †French, pertaining to the Church of France, or from Latin *Gallicanus*, from *Gallicus*: see GALLIC *adjective*[1], -AN.]
▸ **A** *adjective*. = GALLIC *adjective*[1] (now *rare* in *gen.* sense); ECCLESIASTICAL of or characteristic of the ancient Church of Gaul or France; of or pertaining to Gallicanism. LME.
▸ **B** *noun*. An advocate or supporter of Gallicanism. L19.
■ **Gallicanism** *noun* (ECCLESIASTICAL) the doctrine that asserts the right of the Roman Catholic Church esp. in France to be in certain respects free from papal control M19. **Gallicanist** *noun* = GALLICAN *noun* E18.

gallice /ˈgalɪsi/ *adverb*. *rare*. L19.
[ORIGIN Latin, from *Gallicus*: see GALLIC *adjective*[1], -ICE[1].]
In French.

gallicise *verb* var. of GALLICIZE.

Gallicism /ˈgalɪsɪz(ə)m/ *noun*. M17.
[ORIGIN French *gallicisme*, from Latin *Gallicus*: see GALLIC *adjective*[1], -ISM.]
1 A French word, idiom, or grammatical feature, esp. one which is used in another language but which remains distinctively French in construction or meaning. M17.
2 A (typically) French characteristic, custom, or outlook. E18.

gallicize /ˈgalɪsʌɪz/ *verb trans.* & *intrans.* Also **-ise**. L18.
[ORIGIN from Latin *Gallicus* (see GALLIC *adjective*[1]) + -IZE.]
Make or become French in speech, customs, characteristics, etc.
■ **gallicizer** *noun* M19.

galligaskins /galɪˈgaskɪnz/ *noun pl.* L16.
[ORIGIN Prob. ult. from French †*garguesque* var. of †*greguesque*, from Italian *grechesca* use as noun of fem. of *grechesco*, from *greco* Greek; but the origin of *galli-* remains unkn.]
1 A kind of wide loose hose or breeches worn in the 16th and 17th cents.; later (*joc.*), loose breeches or trousers in general. L16.
2 Leggings, gaiters. Chiefly *dial.* M19.

G

gallimaufry /galɪˈmɔːfri/ *noun*. **M16**.
[ORIGIN French *galimafrée* (Old French *calimafrée*), of unknown origin.]
1 A varied miscellaneous jumble or medley; (chiefly *dial.*) a dish made up of minced (esp. leftover) meat etc., a hash, a ragout. **M16**.

J. I. M. STEWART The canvas is an amazing gallimaufry of allegorical references. H. MANTEL It is Anne's fancy . . to paint a gallimaufry of Cupids on the panels of their bedroom wall.

2 A person of many accomplishments or qualities. Freq. *derog.* Now *rare*. **E17**.

gallimimus /galɪˈmʌɪməs/ *noun*. **L20**.
[ORIGIN mod. Latin (see below), from Latin *galli* (genit. of *gallus* cock) + Greek *mimos* mimic.]
A dinosaur of the genus *Gallimimus*, of the late Cretaceous period, which had toothless jaws and the general proportions of an ostrich.

gallinaceous /galɪˈneɪʃəs/ *adjective*. **L18**.
[ORIGIN from Latin *gallinaceus* (from *gallina* hen from *gallus* cock) + -OUS: see -ACEOUS.]
Of or pertaining to the order Galliformes, which comprises domestic fowls, turkeys, grouse, pheasants, partridges, etc.
■ **gallinacean** *adjective & noun* (*a*) *adjective* = GALLINACEOUS; (*b*) *noun* a gallinaceous bird: **M19**.

gallinazo /galɪˈneɪzəʊ/ *noun*. Pl. **-os**. **M18**.
[ORIGIN Spanish, from Latin *gallina* hen.]
In Latin America: a turkey buzzard or other vulture.

gallinipper /ˈgalɪnɪpə/ *noun*. Chiefly *US*. Also (earlier) †**gurnipper**. **M17**.
[ORIGIN Unknown.]
Any biting or stinging insect; *spec.* a very large American mosquito, *Psorophora ciliata*, whose bite results in a painful swelling.

gallinule /ˈgalɪnjuːl/ *noun*. **L18**.
[ORIGIN mod. Latin *Gallinula* genus name, dim. of Latin *gallina* hen: see -ULE.]
Any of various aquatic birds of the rail family, esp. of the genera *Porphyrio* and *Porphyrula*.
common gallinule *N. Amer.* the moorhen, *Gallinula chloropus*. ***purple gallinule***: see PURPLE *adjective*.

Gallio /ˈgalɪəʊ/ *noun*. Pl. **-os**. **M19**.
[ORIGIN A Roman proconsul of Achaia (*Acts* 18:17).]
An indifferent easy-going person.
■ **Galliˈonic** *adjective* having the characteristics of a Gallio **E20**.

galliot /ˈgalɪət/ *noun*. Also **galiot**. **ME**.
[ORIGIN Old French & mod. French *galiote* (in sense 2 through Dutch *galjoot*), from Italian *galeotta* (Spanish & Portuguese *galeota*) dim. of medieval Latin *galea* GALLEY: see -OT[1].]
1 *hist.* A small fast (esp. Spanish or Mediterranean) single-masted galley. **ME**.
2 A Dutch single-masted cargo boat or fishing boat. Also (more fully ***galliot yacht***, †***galliot hoy***) any of various small vessels resembling this boat. **M17**.

Gallipoli /gaˈlɪp(ə)li/ *noun*. **E19**.
[ORIGIN A town in Apulia, Italy.]
1 ***Gallipoli soap***, soap made from Gallipoli oil. **E19**.
2 ***Gallipoli oil***, a type of olive oil produced in Gallipoli. **M19**.

gallipot /ˈgalɪpɒt/ *noun*. **LME**.
[ORIGIN Prob. from GALLEY (as being brought in galleys from the Mediterranean) + POT *noun*[1].]
1 A small pot of glazed earthenware or metal, esp. as used by apothecaries or pharmacists for ointments and medicines. **LME**.
2 An apothecary. *joc.* or *derog. arch.* **L18**.

Gallithumpian /galɪˈθʌmpɪən/ *noun*. *dial.* **L18**.
[ORIGIN Unknown.]
†**1** A heckler or troublemaker at parliamentary elections. Only in **L18**.
2 *hist.* A member of a society of social reformers. **L18**.

gallium /ˈgalɪəm/ *noun*. **L19**.
[ORIGIN from Latin *Gallia* France + -IUM.]
A soft bluish-white metallic chemical element, atomic no. 31, which melts just above room temperature (symbol Ga).

gallivant /ˈgalɪvant, galɪˈvant/ *verb intrans. colloq.* **E19**.
[ORIGIN Uncertain: perh. alt. of GALLANT *verb*.]
Go out or *off* in search of pleasure or entertainment; gad about; flirt.

M. SHADBOLT Since Ned didn't drink or gallivant, he saved money. D. STOREY Your mother ill and me at work, and you go gallivanting off.

gallivat /ˈgalɪvat/ *noun*. **M18**.
[ORIGIN Portuguese *galeota*: see GALLIOT.]
hist. A large boat with oars and a triangular sail, used in the Indian subcontinent.

galliwasp /ˈgalɪwɒsp/ *noun*. **L17**.
[ORIGIN Unknown.]
Any of various lizards of the Central American genus *Diploglossus*; esp. *D. monotropis* of the W. Indies.

G

Gallo- /ˈgaləʊ/ *combining form*[1].
[ORIGIN from Latin *Gallus*, *Gallia* Gaul: see GAUL, -O-.]
Forming adjective and noun combs. with the sense 'of Gaul or France; Gallic or French and —', as ***Gallo-Celtic***, ***Gallo-German***. Cf. FRANCO-.
■ **Galloˈmaniac** *noun & adjective* (a person) excessively devoted to France or things French **E19**. **Gallophil(e)** *noun* a lover of France or things French **L19**. **Gallophobe** *noun & adjective* (a person) who is affected with Gallophobia **L19**. **Galloˈphobia** *noun* intense fear or hatred of France or what is French **E19**. **Gallo-ˈRoman** *adjective & noun* (an inhabitant or the language) of Gaul when under Roman rule **M19**. **Gallo-Roˈmance** *noun & adjective* (of or pertaining to) the hypothetical Romance language presumed to represent the Latin spoken in Gaul; (of or pertaining to) the group of chiefly northern and Provençal French dialects presumed to represent this: **M20**.

gallo- /ˈgaləʊ/ *combining form*[2]. Before a vowel also **gall-**.
[ORIGIN from GALLIC *adjective*[2] + -O-.]
Used in CHEMISTRY to form names of substances derived from or related to gallic acid.
■ **galloˈcyanine** *noun* any of a group of bluish-violet oxazine dyes derived from gallic acid **L19**. **galloˈtannin** *noun* any of a class of naturally occurring tannins which yield gallic acid on hydrolysis **L19**.

galloglass /ˈgalə(ʊ)glaːs/ *noun*. Also **gallowglass**. **L15**.
[ORIGIN Irish *gallóglach*, from *gall* foreigner + *óglach* youth, servant, warrior, from *óg* young + *-lach* abstract suffix.]
IRISH HISTORY. A member of a special class of soldiers or retainers maintained by Irish chiefs.

gallon /ˈgalən/ *noun*. **ME**.
[ORIGIN Anglo-Norman *galon*, var. of Old French *jalon*, from Proto-Romance, from base of medieval Latin *galleta* (whence Old French *jaloie* liquid measure), *galletum* (whence Old English *ġellet* dish, basin, Old High German *gellita*, German *Gelte* bucket), perh. of Celtic origin.]
1 A measure of liquid or (in Britain) dry capacity, containing 4 quarts or 8 pints: in Britain (more fully ***imperial gallon***) equivalent to 277.42 cu. in. (4.55 litres), in the US (more fully ***US gallon***) equivalent to 231 cu. in. (3.79 litres). **ME**.
Winchester gallon: see WINCHESTER 1.
2 *sing.* & (usu.) in *pl. hyperbol.* A vast amount of a liquid etc. *colloq.* **L16**.

F. CLUNE The terrific heat made me sweat gallons.

■ **gallonage** *noun* the quantity in gallons of a liquid produced or sold **E20**.

galloon /gəˈluːn/ *noun*. Also **galon** /gəˈlɒn/. **E17**.
[ORIGIN French *galon*, from *galonner* trim with braid (of unknown origin): see -OON.]
(A piece of) narrow ornamental fabric, esp. close-woven silk braid or a strip of lace, used to trim or finish costume or upholstery.
■ **gallooned** *adjective* trimmed with galloon **M19**.

gallop /ˈgaləp/ *noun*. **E16**.
[ORIGIN Old French *galop*, from *galoper*: see GALLOP *verb*. Cf. WALLOP *noun*.]
1 The fastest pace of a horse or other quadruped, in which all four feet are off the ground together in each stride. **E16**. ▸**b** A ride at this pace. **E17**.
at a full gallop, **full gallop** as fast as possible. **at a gallop** (of a horse etc.) at its fastest pace, galloping. †**false gallop** a canter. ***snail's gallop***: see SNAIL *noun* 1.
2 A track or ground where horses are exercised at a gallop. **M19**.

gallop /ˈgaləp/ *verb*. **E16**.
[ORIGIN Old French *galoper*: see WALLOP *verb*.]
▸ **I 1** *verb intrans.* Of a horse or its rider: move at a gallop. **E16**. ▸**b** Move or progress rapidly (*lit.* & *fig.*). **L16**. ▸**c** *fig.* Foll. by *through*, (rare) *over*: read, recite, execute, etc., at great speed. *colloq.* **L18**.

c J. W. CROKER Do not gallop through my letter . . but read it over and over again.

b galloping consumption a consumptive disease that progresses at a rapid pace.
2 *verb trans.* Make (a horse etc.) go at a gallop. **M16**.
3 *verb trans.* Traverse (a space) at a gallop. Long *rare*. **L16**.

SHAKES. *Tit. A.* The golden sun . . Gallops the zodiac in his glistering coach.

4 *verb trans.* Transport at a gallop or at great speed. **L19**.
▸ **II 5** *verb intrans.* Dance the galop. Now *rare*. **E19**.

gallopade /galəˈpeɪd/ *noun & verb*. Also **galop-**. **M18**.
[ORIGIN French *galopade*, from *galoper* to gallop: see GALLOP *verb*, -ADE. Cf. GALOP.]
▸ **A** *noun*. **1** A short sidelong or curveting kind of gallop. **M18**.
2 A lively ballroom dance in 2/4 time; a piece of music for this dance. Cf. GALOP *noun*. **M19**.
▸ **B** *verb intrans.* Dance a gallopade. **M19**.

galloper /ˈgaləpə/ *noun*. **L16**.
[ORIGIN from GALLOP *verb* + -ER[1].]
1 A rider, esp. a huntsman, who gallops. **L16**.
2 A horse with special powers of galloping. **M17**. ▸**b** A wooden etc. horse on a roundabout; a roundabout with such horses. **M20**.
3 *transf.* & *fig.* A person who proceeds at speed. Also, a gad-about. **L17**.
4 Chiefly *hist.* A light field gun. Also ***galloper-gun***. **M18**.
5 Chiefly *hist.* A military orderly. **L19**.

gallous *adjective & adverb* var. of GALLUS *adjective & adverb*.

Gallovidian /galəˈvɪdɪən/ *adjective & noun*. **M17**.
[ORIGIN from medieval Latin *Gallovidia* Galloway (see GALLOWAY) + -AN.]
(A native or inhabitant) of Galloway in SW Scotland.

†**gallow** *noun* see GALLOWS *noun*.

†**gallow** *verb* var. of GALLY *verb*.

Galloway /ˈgaləweɪ/ *noun*. **L16**.
[ORIGIN An area of SW Scotland, comprising the former counties of Kircudbrightshire and Wigtownshire.]
1 A small strong horse of a breed originating in Galloway; any small-sized horse, *esp.* one suitable for riding. Also ***Galloway mare***, ***Galloway nag***, etc. **L16**.
2 (An animal of) a breed of sturdy hornless cattle originating in Galloway, black or (***belted Galloway***) black with a broad white stripe. **M18**.

Gallowegian *noun & adjective* var. of GALWEGIAN.

gallowglass *noun* var. of GALLOGLASS.

gallows /ˈgaləʊz/ *noun sing.* & (orig.) †*pl.* Pl. **-es** /-ɪz/. Orig. sing. †**gallow**. See also GALLUS *noun*.
[ORIGIN Old English *ġ(e)alga* = Old Frisian *galga*, Old Saxon, Old High German *galgo* (Dutch *galg*, German *Galgen*), reinforced by Old Norse *gálgi*, also *gálgatré* gallows tree, all from Germanic.]
1 A structure, usu. consisting of two upright posts and a crosspiece, for the hanging of criminals. Formerly also ***pair of gallows***. **OE**. ▸**b** Execution by hanging. **L15**.

ANTHONY WOOD A gallowes being erected before Temple gate. JAMES SULLIVAN That all our liberty-poles will soon be converted into gallowses. **b** *Proverb*: Save a thief from the gallows and he will cut your throat.

b have the gallows in one's face & vars., look like a person destined for, or deserving of, hanging. ***pit and gallows***, ***gallows and pit***: see PIT *noun*[1].
2 Any of various frameworks consisting of two or more supports and a crosspiece as one for athletic exercises or (*Austral.* & *NZ*) for hanging the carcasses of slaughtered animals. **LME**.
3 A person who deserves hanging. **L16**.

DICKENS 'Now, young gallows!' This was an invitation for Oliver to enter.

4 *sing.* & (usu.) in *pl.* = GALLUS *noun*. *Scot.*, *dial.*, & *US*. **M18**.
– COMB.: **gallows bird** a person who deserves to be, or (less usu.) has been, hanged; **gallows humour**= GALGENHUMOR; **gallows tree**, †**gallow tree** = sense 1 above.

gallows *adjective & adverb* see GALLUS *adjective & adverb*.

gallstone /ˈgɔːlstəʊn/ *noun*. **M18**.
[ORIGIN from GALL *noun*[1] + STONE *noun*.]
A calculus or hard mass of bile pigments, cholesterol, and calcium salts, formed in the gall bladder or bile ducts.

Gallup poll /ˈgaləp pəʊl/ *noun phr.* **M20**.
[ORIGIN G. H. *Gallup* (1901–84), US statistician.]
(Proprietary name for) an assessment of public opinion by the questioning of a representative sample, esp. as a basis for forecasting votes.

gallus /ˈgaləs/ *noun*. *Scot.*, *dial.*, & *US*. **M19**.
[ORIGIN Var. of GALLOWS *noun*.]
sing. & (usu.) in *pl.* A pair of braces to support the trousers. Also *sing.*, a single trouser brace.

gallus /ˈgaləs/ *adjective & adverb*. Also **gallous**, (now less usu.) **gallows** /ˈgaləʊz/. **LME**.
[ORIGIN (Var. of) attrib. use of GALLOWS *noun*.]
▸ **A** *adjective*. **1** Fit only to be hanged; wicked, atrocious. Now usu. in milder sense, high-spirited, dashing; full of mischief, cheeky, impish. Now *Scot.*, *dial.*, & *Irish*. **LME**.

R. BURNS An' plunder'd o' her hindmost groat By gallows knaves. KEATS An Irishman likes to be thought a gallous fellow. A. CALDER Mel had settled for modern Strathclyde, and had a nice gallus wee grin to go with it.

2 Extremely great, fine, or handsome. *dial.* (formerly also *slang*). **L18**.

A. L. KENNEDY It's gonny be a gallus night.

▸ **B** *adverb*. Extremely, very. *dial.* (formerly also *slang*). **E19**.

H. KINGSLEY The pleece come in, and got gallus well kicked about the head.

■ **gallusness** *noun* **M19**.

gally /ˈgɔːli/ *adjective*[1]. Now *rare* or *obsolete*. **LME**.
[ORIGIN from GALL *noun*[1] + -Y[1].]
Bitter as gall.

gally /ˈgɔːli/ *adjective*[2]. *obsolete* exc. *dial.* **LME**.
[ORIGIN from GALL *noun*[2] + -Y[1].]
†**1** Having galls or sores. Only in **LME**.
2 Full of bare or wet places. **E17**.

gally /ˈgali/ *verb trans.* Chiefly *dial.* & WHALING. Also †**gallow**. **E17**.
[ORIGIN Uncertain: perh. repr. Old English *āgǣlwan* terrify, of unknown origin.]
Frighten, scare.

SHAKES. *Lear* The wrathful skies Gallow the very wanderers of the dark And make them keep their caves.

– COMB.: **gally-beggar**, **gally-crow** *dial.* a scarecrow.

Galois /ˈgalwɑː/ *noun*. L19.
[ORIGIN Évariste *Galois* (1811–32), French mathematician.]
MATH. Used *attrib.* to designate various concepts arising from Galois's work.
Galois field a field with a finite number of elements. **Galois theory** a method of applying group theory to the solution of algebraic equations.
■ **Galoisian** /gaˈlwɑːzɪən/ *adjective* L19.

galon *noun* var. of GALLOON.

galoot /gəˈluːt/ *noun*. *slang* (chiefly *N. Amer.* & *derog.*). E19.
[ORIGIN Unknown.]
Orig. (*NAUTICAL*), an inexperienced marine. Later *gen.*, a clumsy or stupid person.

M. TWAIN He could lam any galoot of his inches in America. D. HEWETT Why doncha look where you're goin', y' great galoot.

galop /ˈgaləp, gəˈlɒp/ *noun* & *verb*. M19.
[ORIGIN French: see GALLOP *noun*.]
▸ **A** *noun*. A lively ballroom dance in 2/4 time; a piece of music for this dance. Cf. GALLOPADE *noun* 2. M19.
▸ **B** *verb intrans.* Infl. **-p(p)-**. Dance a galop. M19.

galopade *noun* var. of GALLOPADE *noun*.

galopin /ˈgaləpɪn/ *noun*. *Scot.* Now *rare* or *obsolete*. M16.
[ORIGIN French, from *galoper* GALLOP *verb*.]
†**1** A scullion or page in a great house. M16–E19.
2 A street urchin. M19.

galore /gəˈlɔː/ *adverb*, *postpositive adjective*, & *noun*. E17.
[ORIGIN Irish *go leor* (Gaelic *gu leòr*) to sufficiency.]
▸ **A** *adverb* & *postpositive adjective*. In plenty, abundant(ly). E17.

Sport He has scored goals galore with the Essex side.

▸ **B** *noun*. A plentiful supply (*of*). Chiefly *dial.* M19.

W. CARLETON The best of aiting and dhrinking is provided . . . and indeed there was galore of both there.

galosh /gəˈlɒʃ/ *noun* & *verb*. Also **gol-**. LME.
[ORIGIN Old French & mod. French *galoche* repr. (with abnormal phonet. development) late Latin *gallicula* dim. of Latin *gallica* use as noun (sc. *solea* shoe) of *Gallicus* GALLIC *adjective*.]
▸ **A** *noun*. **1** Orig., a clog or wooden sole attached by a strap to a shoe of more delicate material. Now, an overshoe of rubber or other waterproof material. Usu. in *pl.* LME.
2 An edging of leather or other material attached to a boot or shoe for protection or decoration. Now *rare*. M19.
▸ **B** *verb trans.* Provide (a boot or shoe) with a galosh. Chiefly as ***galoshed*** *ppl adjective*. E19.

†**galp** *verb*. ME.
[ORIGIN Perh. alt. of GAPE *verb*. Cf. GAWP.]
1 *verb intrans.* Yawn, gape. ME–L16.
2 *verb trans.* Vomit *forth*. E–M16.

galpon /galˈpəʊn/ *noun*. L19.
[ORIGIN Amer. Spanish *galpón* from Nahuatl *calpulli* large hall.]
A large building like a barn on a S. American farm.

Galsworthian /gɔːlzˈwəːðɪən/ *adjective*. E20.
[ORIGIN from *Galsworthy* (see below) + -AN.]
Relating to or characteristic of the English novelist and dramatist John Galsworthy (1867–1933) or his work.

galt /gɔːlt/ *noun*[1]. *obsolete* exc. *dial.* LME.
[ORIGIN Old Norse *galtr*, *galti* boar: cf. Old High German *galza*, *gelza* a sow (Middle High German *galze*, *gelze*, German *Gelze*). Rel. to GILT *noun*[1].]
A boar, a male pig.

galt *noun*[2] var. of GAULT.

Galton /ˈgɔːltən/ *noun*. L19.
[ORIGIN Sir Francis *Galton* (1822–1911), English scientist.]
1 *BIOLOGY* (now *hist.*). ***Galton's law***, either of two laws propounded by Galton: (***a***) the theory that parents contribute on average half the genes of their offspring, grandparents together a quarter, etc.; (***b***) the theory that offspring of outstanding parents tend to regress to, or below, the average for the species. L19.
2 ***Galton whistle***, ***Galton's whistle***, a whistle producing a variable note of high frequency, used to test the upper limit of hearing. L19.
■ **Galˈtonian** *adjective* of or relating to Galton or his work L19.

galumph /gəˈlʌmf/ *verb intrans.* L19.
[ORIGIN Portmanteau word combining *gallop* and *triumph*, coined by Lewis Carroll in *Through the Looking Glass*.]
Orig., advance exultantly with irregular bounds. Now chiefly, move in a noisy, ponderous, or clumsy way. Freq. as ***galumphing*** *ppl adjective*.

D. LODGE Shrieking and gasping . . . they galumphed across the yard. *transf.*: D. WILKINSON The statement . . may . . give the impression that atoms are large, ungainly galumphing things.

galvanic /galˈvanɪk/ *adjective*. L18.
[ORIGIN French *galvanique*, from *Galvani*: see GALVANISM, -IC.]
1 Of, pertaining to, or resulting from galvanism or (more widely) direct-current electricity; voltaic (as opp. to faradaic). L18.
2 *fig.* **a** Resembling the effects of galvanism; convulsive, spasmodic. M19. ▸**b** Having an effect like that of galvanism; dynamic, electrifying, stimulating. E20.

a H. STURGIS She embraced the whole party with a last galvanic effort at cheerful enthusiasm. **b** P. ROTH So galvanic is the word 'panties' that the trajectory of my ejaculation reaches . . new heights.

– SPECIAL COLLOCATIONS: **galvanic battery**, **galvanic cell** an early form of electrical cell in which plates of alternate dissimilar metals are separated by pads moistened with an electrolyte. **galvanic electricity**: produced by chemical action. **galvanic pile** a galvanic battery with many plates. **galvanic skin response** a change in the electrical resistance of the skin caused by strong emotion, measurable with a sensitive galvanometer, e.g. in lie-detector tests.
■ **galvanical** *adjective* M19. **galvanically** *adverb* M19.

galvanise *verb* var. of GALVANIZE.

galvanism /ˈgalvənɪz(ə)m/ *noun*. Now *arch.* or *hist.* L18.
[ORIGIN French *galvanisme*, from Luigi *Galvani* (1737–98), Italian physiologist: see -ISM.]
1 Electricity produced by chemical action. L18.
2 The therapeutic use of galvanic or other direct-current electricity (cf. FARADISM). E19.
■ **galvanist** *noun* an expert in galvanism E19.

galvanize /ˈgalvənʌɪz/ *verb trans.* Also **-ise**. E19.
[ORIGIN French *galvaniser*, from *Galvani*: see GALVANISM, -IZE.]
1 Apply galvanism to; stimulate (a muscle or nerve) by a galvanic current. Now chiefly *fig.*, stir into violent activity etc. by shock or excitement. (Foll. by *into*, *to*.) E19.

P. KURTH A report from Dr Eitel . . galvanized Zahle into further action. H. CARPENTER What Macdonald found in that library galvanized his imagination.

2 Coat with metal, orig. by means of electrolysis; *esp.* coat (iron) with zinc as a protection against rust, usu. without the use of electricity. M19.
■ **galvaniˈzation** *noun* M19. **galvanizer** *noun* M19.

galvano- /ˈgalv(ə)nəʊ/ *combining form* of GALVANIC, GALVANISM: see -O-.
■ **galvanoˈcautery** *noun* electrocautery (see ELECTRO-) L19.

galvanometer /galvəˈnɒmɪtə/ *noun*. E19.
[ORIGIN from GALVANO- + -METER.]
An instrument for detecting and measuring small electric currents, usu. by the deflection of a magnetic needle by the current in a magnetic field.
BALLISTIC ***galvanometer***.
■ **galvanoˈmetric**, **galvanoˈmetrical** *adjectives* of or pertaining to galvanometers or galvanometry M19. **galvanometry** *noun* the detection and measurement of small electric currents (by means of galvanometers) L19.

galvanoplasty /ˈgalv(ə)nə(ʊ)plasti/ *noun*. L19.
[ORIGIN formed as GALVANOMETER + -PLASTY.]
The process of electroplating a substance with metal; *esp.* the making of an electrotype.
■ **galvanoplastic** *adjective* M19. **galvanoplastically** *adverb* M19.

galvanoscope /ˈgalv(ə)nəskəʊp/ *noun*. M19.
[ORIGIN formed as GALVANOMETER + -SCOPE.]
A galvanometer; *spec.* one acting by the deflection of a magnetic needle in the magnetic field produced by the current to be detected.
■ **galvanoˈscopic** *adjective* of, pertaining to or acting as a galvanoscope M19.

galvanotaxis /galv(ə)nə(ʊ)ˈtaksɪs/ *noun*. L19.
[ORIGIN formed as GALVANOMETER + -TAXIS.]
BIOLOGY. Movement of an organism in response to the direction of an electric current or field.
■ **galvanotactic** *adjective* of or pertaining to galvanotaxis E20.

galvanotropism /galv(ə)nə(ʊ)ˈtrəʊpɪz(ə)m/ *noun*. L19.
[ORIGIN formed as GALVANOMETER + -TROPISM.]
BIOLOGY. Growth or orientation of an organism or part of one in response to the direction of an electric current or field.
■ **galvanotropic** /-ˈtrəʊpɪk, -ˈtrɒpɪk/ *adjective* L19.

galvo /ˈgalvəʊ/ *noun*. Pl. **-os**. M20.
[ORIGIN Abbreviation of GALVANOMETER, GALVANIZE: see -O.]
1 A galvanometer. *colloq.* M20.
2 Galvanized iron. *Austral. slang.* M20.

Galwegian /galˈwiːdʒ(ə)n/ *noun* & *adjective*. Also **Gallowegian** /galəˈwiːdʒ(ə)n/ L18.
[ORIGIN from *Galloway*, after *Norroway*, *Norway*, *Norwegian*.]
= GALLOVIDIAN.

gam /gam/ *noun*[1]. *slang.* L18.
[ORIGIN Prob. var. of GAMB.]
A leg. Now *esp.* a woman's shapely leg.

E. BIRNEY Daphne . . . Delectable child. Blonde . . . Lovely gams, adequate income.

gam /gam/ *noun*[2] & *verb*. M19.
[ORIGIN Unknown.]
NAUTICAL. ▸**A** *noun*. **1** A school of whales, porpoises, or dolphins. M19.
2 A social meeting, orig. *spec.* of whalers at sea; a chat. M19.
▸ **B** *verb*. Infl. **-mm-**.
1 *verb trans.* & *intrans.* Meet (with) socially, exchange gossip (with): orig. of whalers at sea. M19.
2 *verb intrans.* Of whales etc.: gather together, form a school. L19.
3 *verb intrans.* Boast, brag. *slang.* M20.

gama grass /ˈgamə grɑːs/ *noun phr.* Also **-mm-**. M19.
[ORIGIN Perh. alt. of GRAMA *noun*[1].]
A tall strong fodder grass, *Tripsacum dactyloides*, grown in the southern and western US.

gamahuche /ˈgaməhuːʃ/ *verb* & *noun*. *slang.* Also **gamaruche** /ˈgaməruːʃ/. M19.
[ORIGIN French *gamahucher*: perh. imit.]
▸ **A** *verb intrans.* & *trans.* Perform fellatio or cunnilingus (with). M19.
▸ **B** *noun*. An act of fellatio or cunnilingus. M19.

gamash /gəˈmaʃ/ *noun*. Now chiefly *dial.* L16.
[ORIGIN French *gamache* from mod. Provençal *gamacho*, *garamacho*, from Spanish *guadamací* a kind of ornamental leather, from Arabic *ġadāmasī*, from *Gadāmas* (now *Ghadames* or *Ghudāmis*) a town in Libya where such leather was made.]
In *pl.* & †*sing.* Leggings or gaiters, worn to protect the legs from mud and wet.

Gamay /ˈgameɪ/ *noun*. M19.
[ORIGIN A hamlet in Burgundy in eastern France.]
A variety of black wine grape native to the Beaujolais district of France; a fruity red wine made from this grape; *US* (also ***Gamay-Beaujolais***) any of several red wines with a similar flavour.

G

gamb /gamb/ *noun*. Also **gambe**. M17.
[ORIGIN Old Northern French *gambe* var. of *jambe* JAMB.]
HERALDRY. A charge representing the leg of an animal. Cf. JAMB 3b.

gamba /ˈgambə/ *noun*[1]. Also †**gambo**, pl. **-os**. L16.
[ORIGIN Short for VIOLA DA GAMBA.]
1 = VIOLA DA GAMBA 1. L16.
2 An organ stop resembling a violin or cello in tone. Also ***gamba stop***. M19.

gamba /ˈgambə/ *noun*[2]. M20.
[ORIGIN Spanish.]
A kind of prawn, *Palaemon serratus*, as an article of food.

gambade /gamˈbeɪd/ *noun* & *verb*. E16.
[ORIGIN French, from Italian *gambata*, from *gamba* leg: see -ADE. Cf. GAMBADO *noun*[2], GAMBOL *noun* & *adjective*.]
▸ **A** *noun*. A leap or bound (of a horse); a caper, a frisk; a prank. E16.
▸ †**B** *verb intrans.* = GAMBOL *verb*. E–M16.
– NOTE: Supplanted by variant GAMBOL during 16; readopted by Sir Walter Scott in E19.

gambado /gamˈbeɪdəʊ/ *noun*[1]. Pl. **-o(e)s**. M17.
[ORIGIN from Italian *gamba* leg + -ADO.]
A leather boot or gaiter, orig. one attached to a saddle to protect the rider's legs from the weather. Usu. in *pl.*

gambado /gamˈbeɪdəʊ, -ˈbɑːd-/ *noun*[2] & *verb*. E19.
[ORIGIN Spanish *gambada*, from *gamba* leg: see -ADO.]
▸ **A** *noun*. Pl. **-o(e)s**.
1 A leap or bound of a horse. Usu. in *pl.* E19.

SIR W. SCOTT The gambadoes of Sir Piercie and his prancing warhorse.

2 A fantastic movement, a caper; any sudden or fantastic action. Usu. in *pl.* M19.

C. BRONTË Sending him a challenge or performing other gambadoes of the sort.

▸ **B** *verb intrans.* Prance, caper. E19.

†**gambaugium** *noun* see GAMBOGE.

gambe *noun* var. of GAMB.

gambeson /ˈgambɪs(ə)n/ *noun*. ME.
[ORIGIN Old French, from *gambais*, prob. from Old Frankish *wamba* belly (see WOMB *noun*).]
hist. A (padded) tunic of leather or thick cloth, worn orig. under the habergeon to prevent chafing, later as an outer (protective) garment.

†**gambett** *noun* see GAMBIT.

Gambia kino /ˈgambɪə ˈkiːnəʊ/ *noun phr.* L19.
[ORIGIN from *Gambia* (see GAMBIAN) + KINO.]
Kino from W. Africa.

Gambian /ˈgambɪən/ *adjective* & *noun*. E20.
[ORIGIN from *Gambia* (see below) + -AN.]
▸ **A** *adjective*. Of or pertaining to (The) Gambia, a country in W. Africa, or its inhabitants. E20.
▸ **B** *noun*. A native or inhabitant of (The) Gambia. M20.

gambier /ˈgambɪə/ *noun*. Also **-ir**. E19.
[ORIGIN Malay *gambir*, name of the plant.]
An astringent extract used in tanning, obtained from a tropical Asiatic climbing shrub, *Uncaria gambir*, of the madder family. Also, the plant itself.

gambist /ˈgambɪst/ *noun*. E19.
[ORIGIN from GAMBA *noun*[1] + -IST.]
A performer on the viola da gamba.

gambit /ˈgambɪt/ *noun*. Orig. †**gambett**. M17.
[ORIGIN Italian *gambetto* lit. 'tripping up', from *gamba* leg; *-it* from French *gambit* from Spanish *gambito*.]
1 *CHESS*. An attack (usu. an opening) in which a chessman is sacrificed to gain an advantage; a (specified) play of this kind. M17.
King's gambit, ***Queen's gambit***, etc.
2 An opening move in a discussion etc.; a trick, a ruse, a device. M19.

J. R. ACKERLEY Taking Megan apart . . was one of her favourite opening gambits. P. LIVELY She searched for another gambit by which to escape.

– NOTE: The spelling *gambit* is not recorded before M18.

gamble /ˈgamb(ə)l/ *noun*[1]. *obsolete* exc. *dial.* E18.
[ORIGIN Alt. of GAMBREL.]
1 = CAMBREL 2. E18.
2 = CAMBREL 3. L19.

gamble /ˈgamb(ə)l/ *noun*[2]. E19.
[ORIGIN from the verb.]
An act of gambling; a risky undertaking or attempt.

G. SAINTSBURY The real point is the chance, the uncertainty, the gamble.

gamble /ˈgamb(ə)l/ *verb*. E18.
[ORIGIN from GAMEL or GAME *verb*: see -LE[3].]
1 *verb intrans.* Play games of chance for (a lot of) money; indulge in betting, esp. habitually; risk money, fortune, success, etc., on the outcome of an event. (Foll. by *on* an event or outcome, *that* a specified outcome will ensue.) E18.

D. H. LAWRENCE When they played cards, they always gambled. A. J. P. TAYLOR The British government had . . decided to gamble that Japan would remain neutral. F. RAPHAEL He gambled on the horses.

2 *verb trans.* Lose (money etc.) by gaming or betting. Freq. foll. by *away*. E19. ▸**b** Bet (money etc.). L19.

F. HUME He gambled away large sums at his club. **b** JOYCE Gambling every penny they have and losing it on horses.

■ **gambler** *noun* †(***a***) a gamester, a sharper; (***b***) a person who gambles, esp. habitually: M18. **gambling** *verbal noun* the action of the verb; *esp.* the risking of money on games of chance as a pastime or a sphere of human activity: L18.

gambo /ˈgambəʊ/ *noun*[1]. *dial.* Pl. **-oes**. M19.
[ORIGIN Unknown.]
A simple farm cart, trolley, or sledge.

†**gambo** *noun*[2] var. of GAMBA *noun*[1].

gamboge /gamˈbəʊʒ, -ˈbuːʒ/ *noun*. Also (earlier) in Latin form †**gambaugium** M17.
[ORIGIN mod. Latin *gambaugium* var. of *cambugium* etc., from *Cambodia* a country in SE Asia.]
A gum resin used as a bright yellow pigment and as a purgative, obtained from various eastern Asian trees of the genus *Garcinia* (family Guttiferae).

gambol /ˈgamb(ə)l/ *noun & adjective*. Also (earlier) †**-old**. M16.
[ORIGIN Alt. of GAMBADE.]
▸**A** *noun*. **1** A caper, frisk, or frolic, esp. of a child or an animal; a playful action. Usu. in *pl.* M16.

SHAKES. *Wint. T.* A dance which the wenches say is a gallimaufry of gambols. S. RICHARDSON A silly poor girl, set up by the gambol of fortune for a May-game.

†**2** A toy, a plaything. L16–M17.
▸†**B** *attrib.* or as *adjective*. Playful, sportive. L16–M17.

gambol /ˈgamb(ə)l/ *verb intrans.* Infl. **-ll-**, ***-l-**. Also (earlier) †**-old**. E16.
[ORIGIN formed as GAMBOL *noun & adjective*, after French *gambader*.]
Leap or spring in dance or play; frolic.

W. GOLDING The rats . . jumped and gambolled and played on the mud beach.

†**gambold** *noun, verb* see GAMBOL *noun & adjective, verb*.

gambrel /ˈgambr(ə)l/ *noun*. Now chiefly *US* & *dial.* M16.
[ORIGIN Old Northern French *gamberel*, from *gambier* forked stick, from *gambe* var. of *jambe* leg: see JAMB, -REL. Cf. GAMBLE *noun*[1], CAMBREL.]
1 = CAMBREL 3. M16.
2 The joint in the upper part of a horse's hind leg, the hock; = CAMBREL 2. E17. ▸**b** (The underside of) a person's thigh. M18.
3 In full ***gambrel roof***. A curb roof; a hip roof with a small gable forming the upper part of each end. M18.

gambroon /gamˈbruːn/ *noun*. E19.
[ORIGIN *Gambroon* (now *Bandar Abbas*), a seaport in Iran.]
A twilled linen cloth used for linings; a cotton and worsted fabric used for men's coats etc.

game /geɪm/ *noun*.
[ORIGIN Old English *gamen*, *gomen* = Old Frisian *game*, *gome*, Old Saxon, Old High German, Old Norse *gaman*; prob. identical with Gothic *gaman* fellowship (translating Greek *koinōnia*), from Germanic bases of Y-, MAN *noun*.]
▸**I** Amusement, fun, play.
1 Amusement, fun, mirth, pleasure. Now chiefly *dial.* OE.

SHAKES. *L.L.L.* We have had pastimes here, and pleasant game.

†**2** Jest, as opp. to ***earnest***. Also, a jest, a joke. ME–E17. ▸**b** An object of ridicule, a laughing stock. Also ***laughing game***. M16–L17.

SPENSER They . . crowned her twixt earnest and twixt game.

3 An amusement, a diversion, a pastime. ME.

J. SULLY In their games children are actors, architects, and poets.

4 An amusing incident, a bit of fun, a lark. M19.

DICKENS I can't bear it; it is such a jolly game . . Oh, my eye, what a game!

▸**II 5** Sport derived from the hunting, shooting, or catching of animals. *arch.* ME.

DEFOE This [lion] was Game indeed to us, but this was no Food.

6 The object of a hunt; the quarry, the creature hunted. ME.

P. MATTHIESSEN A hill fox . . makes six pounces . . , four of them successful, though its game is small.

7 *collect.* Kinds of wild animals, birds, or fish now or formerly hunted for food or sport. ME. ▸**b** The flesh of such animals and birds used as food. L18.

R. F. BURTON The country round is full of large game, especially elephants, giraffe, and zebras. **b** E. SHERIDAN Dick not yet arrived and what was worse some fish and game he had promised to bring was expected for dinner.

8 A flock or herd of animals kept for pleasure. Now only as *collect. noun* for swans. L15.

P. L. FERMOR An ornamental lake where a . . game of swans were reflected.

9 The spirit of a fighting cock; fighting spirit, pluck; a person or animal with this. Cf. GAME *adjective*[1]. M18.

DICKENS They were thorough game and didn't make the least complaint.

▸**III** Competitive sport or pastimes.
10 A (form of) contest played according to rules and decided by skill, strength, or luck (as opp. ***sport*** esp. one in which opponents actively engage to defeat each other). ME.

M. PUZO He wandered through . . the huge gambling casino . . wondering what game to try next. A. PRICE Women's hockey is a tough game, I'm told.

board game, ***card game***, ***computer game***, ***panel game***, ***paper game***, ***video game***, etc.

11 A complete episode or period of play, usu. terminating in a definite result; in some contests, a single period of play forming a scoring unit. ME.

DAY LEWIS My father was talking . . in the club house after a game of golf.

12 In *pl.* (occas. treated as *sing.*). ▸**a** *CLASSICAL HISTORY*. (An event or entertainment made up of) various athletic, dramatic, or musical contests, gladiatorial displays, and other shows. LME. ▸**b** (Also **G-**.) A (periodic) meeting consisting of various athletic and occas. other sporting contests. E19. ▸**c** Athletics and sports as organized in a school or college. L19.

a L. WALLACE A Roman's love of games and bloody spectacles. M. TIPPETT The games were held in honour of Olympian Zeus. **c** J. BETJEMAN Greatest dread of all, the dread of games!

13 †**a** The winning position in a contest. Also, the prize. LME–E17. ▸**b** The course or outcome of a game. E19.

b *fig.*: C. D. YONGE Napoleon . . said that in war the game is with him who commits the fewest faults.

14 Now chiefly *CHESS*. The position (of one side) in play. L17.

BURKE The advantageous game which we have obtained.

15 Esp. *CHESS*. A method of play; a recognized sequence of moves. Also, a stage in play. M18.

H. GOLOMBEK He was quite outplayed in the early middle game.

16 A person's performance in a game; a person's normal standard or method of play. M19.

F. GALE We had played . . together, and knew each other's game.

17 The score; *esp.* the number of points required to win; *BRIDGE* (a contract providing) a total of one hundred or more points below the line. M19.

OED The game is four all.

18 The apparatus necessary to play a particular game, esp. a board game or computer game. L19.
▸**IV** *transf.* & *fig.* **19** An object of pursuit or attack. ME.

C. GIBBON She is game much too high for him.

20 A proceeding, scheme, or intrigue carried out like a game. ME. ▸**b** A simulation of a contest, battle, operation, etc., in order to test a strategy. E20.

W. H. PRESCOTT While this game of diplomacy was going on. J. LENNON It's the same game, nothing's really changed. **b** *attrib.*: M. LEAPMAN The best chance for Nato, according to the game planners, is to counterattack quickly.

21 Lovemaking (*spec.* sexual intercourse) viewed as a game or pastime. ME.

G. GREENE What mattered was the game. The two main characters made their stately progress towards the bed sheets.

22 A person's policy, behaviour, or plan of action. LME. ▸**b** A ruse, a dodge, a trick. Freq. in *pl.* M17.

E. CALDWELL Whatever his game is, it's a little bit more than just driving around . . looking at the sights. T. GUNN I was at my usual game of stealing what could be of use to me.

23 A (specified) business or occupation. M20.

C. ODETS You're in the fighting game . . . what would you rather do than fight.

– PHRASES: ***anybody's game***: see ANYBODY. **beat a person at his or her own game** outdo a person in his or her chosen procedure. **be in the game** have a chance of succeeding. ***big game***: see BIG *adjective*. ***blow that for a game of soldiers***: see SOLDIER *noun*. ***compendium of games***: see COMPENDIUM 5a. ***endgame***: see END *noun*. **fair game** legitimately to be pursued or attacked. ***fly at higher game***: see FLY *verb*. ***force the game***: see FORCE *verb*[1]. ***fun and games***: see FUN *noun*. **game all** one game won by each side. ***game is not worth the candle***: see CANDLE *noun*. ***game of chance***: see CHANCE *noun*. **game, set, and match** final victory in a lawn tennis match; *fig.* complete and decisive victory. **give the game away** inadvertently reveal one's own or another's intentions. ***Great Game***: see GREAT *adjective*. ***guessing game***: see GUESS *verb*. ***Highland games***: see HIGHLAND. ***laughing game***: see sense 2b above. ***losing game***: see LOSING *ppl adjective*. **make game of** make fun of, ridicule. ***mug's game***: see MUG *noun*[6] 1. **off one's game** playing badly. ***Olympic games***: see OLYMPIC *adjective*. **one's game**, **one's little game** what one hopes to do undetected. **on one's game** playing well. **on the game** *slang* (***a***) engaged in thieving or robbery; (***b***) engaged in prostitution. **play a good game of**, **play a poor game of** be skilful (or not) at a (specified) game. **play games (with)** act dishonestly (towards), pretend. **play a person's game** advance a person's schemes unintentionally. **play the game** observe the rules or conventions; act correctly or honourably. ***run a game (on)***: see RUN *verb*. **the game** †(***a***) cockfighting; (***b***) a form of charades. **the game is up** the scheme is revealed or foiled; success is now impossible. ***waiting game***: see WAITING *verbal noun*. **what's the game?**, **what's your game?** what's going on?, what are you up to?

– COMB.: **game act**, **game law** (usu. in *pl.*): regulating the hunting and preservation of game; **gamebag**: for holding game killed by a sportsman or sportswoman; **game ball** (***a***) the state of the game in fives etc. when one point may win; (***b***) *pred. adjective* (*Irish colloq.*) excellent, fine; **game bird** a (kind of) bird now or formerly shot for sport *esp.* one of the order Galliformes, which includes the pheasants, grouse, etc.; **game-board** = BOARD *noun* 2b; **gamebook**: for recording a sportsman's or sportswoman's kill; **game chips** thin round potato chips served with game; **gamecock** a cock (of a kind) bred for fighting; **game engine** the basic software of a computer game or video game; **game face** *N. Amer.* a neutral or serious facial expression manifesting determination and concentration, as worn esp. by a sports player; **game farm** (esp. in Africa) a farm stocked with a variety of wild animals for visitors to observe or hunt; **game fish** a (kind of) fish caught for sport; **gamefowl** (a bird of) a kind bred for cockfighting; **gamekeeper** a person employed to breed and manage game, prevent poaching, etc.; ***game law***: see ***game act*** above; **game licence** a licence to hunt, or to deal in, game; **game pad** a hand-held controller for video games; **game park** an area set aside for the conservation of game species; **game-piece** (***a***) a piece or man used in a game; (***b***) a still-life painting including game; **game plan** a winning strategy worked out in advance for a particular game; *fig.* a plan of campaign, esp. in politics; **game-playing** the playing of games or sports; *fig.* insincere behaviour; **game point** a state of a game when one side needs only one point to win it; **game-preserver** a landowner etc. who breeds game and applies game laws strictly; **game reserve** = ***game park*** above; **game rhyme** a rhyme accompanying a (children's) game; **games console** a small machine for playing computerized video games, normally requiring connection to a television set; **game show** a television light-entertainment programme in which people compete in a game or quiz, often for prizes; **games theory**, **game theory** mathematical analysis of conflicts in war, economics, games of skill, etc.; **game-tenant**: who rents the hunting, shooting, or fishing rights on an estate etc.; ***game theory***: see ***games theory*** above; **game warden** a person locally supervising game and hunting.

game /geɪm/ *adjective*[1]. E18
[ORIGIN from the noun (sense 9).]
1 Like a gamecock; full of fight; spirited, plucky. E18.

G. STEIN So game, nothing ever scared him.

die game meet death resolutely; keep one's courage to the end. **game as Ned Kelly** *Austral. & NZ colloq.* very brave.

2 Having the necessary spirit or will *for*, *to do*; ready and willing. M19.

P. KURTH An avid tourist, tireless, inquisitive, and game for adventure. A. BROOKNER Mrs Pusey, although still game, suddenly looked rather old.

■ **gamely** *adverb* M19. **gameness** *noun* E19.

game /geɪm/ *adjective*[2]. L18.
[ORIGIN Unknown. Cf. GAMMY.]
Of a limb: permanently injured, lame.

M. SHADBOLT He had a game leg from the war.

game /geɪm/ *verb*.
[ORIGIN Old English *gam(e)nian*, from (the same root as) GAME *noun*.]
1 *verb intrans.* Play, sport, jest; amuse oneself. *obsolete* exc. *dial.* OE. ▸†**b** *verb trans.* Amuse, please, give pleasure to. Only in ME.
2 *verb intrans.* Play at games of chance for money etc.; gamble. E16. ▸**b** *verb trans.* Throw *away* (money etc.), or while *away* time, by gambling. M17.

■ **gamer** *noun* (**a**) a person who plays a game; a gambler; (**b**) *rare* a person who hunts game: ME.

†**gameful** *adjective*. ME.
[ORIGIN from GAME *noun* + -FUL.]
1 Joyful, playful, sportive. ME–E18.
2 Having much game or wildlife that can be hunted. E17–E18.

gamel /ˈgam(ə)l/ *verb intrans*. Long *obsolete* exc. *dial*. L16.
[ORIGIN Frequentative of GAME *verb* or alt. of reflex of Old English *gam(e)nian* GAME *verb*: see -LE³. Cf. GAMBLE *verb*.]
Play games; romp, frolic. Chiefly as ***gameling*** *verbal noun*.

gamelan /ˈgamәlan/ *noun*. E19.
[ORIGIN Javanese.]
An Indonesian, esp. Javanese or Balinese, orchestra consisting mainly of percussion instruments.

gameless /ˈgeɪmlɪs/ *adjective*. M16.
[ORIGIN from GAME *noun* + -LESS.]
†**1** Yielding no fun or pleasure. Only in M16.
2 Containing no game (birds or animals). M19.

gamesman /ˈgeɪmzmən/ *noun*. Pl. **-men**. M20.
[ORIGIN from GAME *noun* + -S¹ + MAN *noun*. Cf. GAMESMANSHIP.]
1 A piece used in a game such as chess. *rare*. M20.
2 A person who takes part in games or sports; *spec*. one skilled in gamesmanship. M20.

gamesmanship /ˈgeɪmzmənʃɪp/ *noun*. M20.
[ORIGIN from GAME *noun* + -S¹ + -MANSHIP.]
The art or practice of defeating an opponent by psychological or other questionable means; unsportsmanlike tactics.

S. POTTER The theory and practice of gamesmanship or the art of winning games without actually cheating.

gamesmen *noun* pl. of GAMESMAN.

gamesome /ˈgeɪms(ə)m/ *adjective*. LME.
[ORIGIN from GAME *noun* + -SOME¹.]
Playful, merry, sportive.
■ **gamesomely** *adverb* LME. **gamesomeness** *noun* E18.

gamester /ˈgeɪmstə/ *noun*. M16.
[ORIGIN from GAME *noun* + -STER.]
1 A gambler. *arch*. M16.
2 A player at any game. Also, an athlete. *arch*. L16. ▸**b** A player at single stick or backsword; a wrestler. *dial*. M19.
†**3** A merry, playful person. L16–E17.
†**4** A promiscuous person. E–M17.
5 A keeper or owner of a game of swans. *obsolete* exc. *hist*. L19.
■ **gamestress** *noun* (now *rare* or *obsolete*) a female gamester M17.

gametangium /gamɪˈtan(d)ʒɪəm/ *noun*. Pl. **-ia** /-ɪə/. L19.
[ORIGIN formed as GAMETE + Greek *aggeion* vessel + -IUM.]
BOTANY. A specialized organ in which gametes are formed, esp. in algae and fungi.

gamete /ˈgamiːt/ *noun*. L19.
[ORIGIN mod. Latin *gameta* from Greek *gametē* wife, *gametēs* husband, from *gamos* marriage.]
BIOLOGY. A mature haploid germ cell (male or female) which unites with another of the opposite sex in sexual reproduction to form a zygote.
– COMB.: **gamete intrafallopian transfer** = *GIFT* s.v. G, G III.

gametic /gəˈmɛtɪk, -ˈmiː-/ *adjective*. E20.
[ORIGIN from GAMETE + -IC.]
BIOLOGY. Of or pertaining to a gamete or gametes; of the nature of a gamete.
■ **gametically** *adverb* E20.

gameto- /gəˈmiːtəʊ/ *combining form* of GAMETE: see -O-.
■ **gametocyst** *noun* a cyst containing gametes E20. **gametocyte** *noun* a cell that gives rise to gametes L19. **gametoˈgenesis** *noun* the formation of gametes E20. **gametoˈgenic** *adjective* of or relating to gametogenesis; giving rise to gametes: E20. **gameˈtogeny**, **gameˈtogony** *nouns* = GAMETOGENESIS E20. **gametophore** *noun* (BOTANY) a specialized filament or branch bearing sexual organs L19. **gametoˈphoric** *adjective* (BOTANY) of, pertaining to, or of the nature of a gametophore L19.

gametophyte /gəˈmiːtə(ʊ)fʌɪt/ *noun*. L19.
[ORIGIN from GAMETO- + -PHYTE.]
BOTANY. In the alternation of generations, the gamete-producing (usu. haploid) phase in the life cycle of a plant (the dominant form in bryophytes) which forms the zygote from which the sporophyte arises. Cf. SPOROPHYTE.
■ **gametophytic** /-ˈfɪtɪk/ *adjective* of, pertaining to, or of the nature of a gametophyte E20.

gamey *adjective* var. of GAMY.

gamgee /ˈgamdʒi/ *noun*. L19.
[ORIGIN Joseph Sampson *Gamgee* (1828–86), English surgeon.]
A wound-dressing devised by Gamgee, consisting of a thickness of cotton wool between two layers of gauze. Also ***Gamgee tissue***, ***Gamgee pad***, etc.

gamic /ˈgamɪk/ *adjective*. M19.
[ORIGIN Greek *gamikos*, from *gamos* marriage: see -IC.]
BIOLOGY. Of an organism: having a sexual nature; reproducing sexually, esp. as distinct from parthenogenetically.

gamin /ˈgamɪn, -mã; *foreign* gamɛ̃ (*pl. same*)/ *noun & adjective*. M19.
[ORIGIN French.]
▸ **A** *noun*. A street urchin, a waif; a streetwise or impudent child. M19.
▸ **B** *adjective*. Of, pertaining to, resembling, or characteristic of a gamin. M19.

gamine /gaˈmiːn; *foreign* gamin (*pl. same*)/ *noun & adjective*. L19.
[ORIGIN French.]
▸ **A** *noun*. A female gamin; a girl with a mischievous, boyish charm. L19.
▸ **B** *adjective*. Of, pertaining to, or characteristic of a gamine; having mischievous, boyish charm. E20.

D. H. LAWRENCE He was fascinated by Lou's quaint aplomb . . her *gamine* knowingness. C. PAGLIA Madonna is raffish, gamine, still full of . . street-urchin mischief.

gaminerie /gaminri/ *noun*. E20.
[ORIGIN French.]
The behaviour or characteristics of a gamin or gamine.

gaminesque /gamɪˈnɛsk, -miː-/ *adjective*. E20.
[ORIGIN from GAMIN, GAMINE + -ESQUE.]
Resembling or characteristic of a gamin or gamine.

gaming /ˈgeɪmɪŋ/ *verbal noun*. LME.
[ORIGIN from GAME *verb* + -ING¹.]
†**1** Playing games; sport; merrymaking. *Scot*. LME–E17.
2 The action or habit of playing at games of chance for money; gambling. E16.
†**3** CLASSICAL HISTORY. In *pl*. Athletic or musical contests. L16–E17.
– COMB.: **gaming table** a table at which games of chance are played for money.

gamma /ˈgamə/ *noun*. LME.
[ORIGIN Latin from Greek.]
1 The third letter (Γ, γ) of the Greek alphabet. LME.
†**2** MUSIC. Gamut. E17–E19.
3 Denoting the third in a numerical sequence: ▸**a** *attrib*. SCIENCE. Freq. written γ. (**a**) ASTRONOMY (preceding the genitive of the Latin name of the constellation) denoting the third brightest star in a constellation; (**b**) CHEMISTRY denoting the third of a number of isomeric forms of a compound, or of allotropes of an element, etc.; (**c**) designating high-energy electromagnetic radiation which consists of photons of wavelengths shorter than those of X-rays and is one of the three main types of decay product emitted by radioactive substances; also designating decay, emission, particles, etc., associated with such radiation. L17. ▸**b** A third-class mark in an examination etc. M20.
a gamma-aˌminobuˈtyric acid BIOCHEMISTRY an amino acid, $H_2NCH_2CH_2CH_2COOH$, which acts to inhibit the transmission of nerve impulses in the central nervous system. ***gamma globulin***: see GLOBULIN. **gamma-linolenic acid** BIOCHEMISTRY a polyunsaturated fatty acid occurring in evening primrose oil and other oils, which the body converts into prostaglandins. **b gamma plus**, **gamma minus** rather better, worse, than the average third class.
4 More fully ***gamma moth***. The silver Y, *Plusia gamma*. M19.
5 a A unit of magnetic field strength equal to 10^{-5} oersted. E20. ▸**b** A unit of mass equal to 10^{-6} gram. M20.
6 PHOTOGRAPHY & TELEVISION. A measure of the contrast of an image compared with that of the scene represented. E20.

gammadion /gaˈmeɪdɪən/ *noun*. M19.
[ORIGIN Late Greek, from GAMMA.]
An arrangement of shapes of capital gamma (Γ), esp. of four, as a swastika or a hollow Greek cross.

gamma grass *noun phr*. var. of GAMA GRASS.

gammarid /ˈgamərɪd/ *noun & adjective*. M19.
[ORIGIN from mod. Latin *Gammarus* (see below), from Latin *g-*, *cammarus* from Greek *kammaros* crab or lobster: see -ID³.]
ZOOLOGY. ▸**A** *noun*. Any member of a large group of amphipod crustaceans typified by freshwater shrimps of the genus *Gammarus*. M19.
▸ **B** *adjective*. Of or relating to this group. E20.

gammer /ˈgamə/ *noun*. *arch*. L16.
[ORIGIN Prob. contr. of GODMOTHER, with *ga-* by assoc. with *grandmother*. Cf GAFFER.]
(A rustic title for) an old woman, corresp. to GAFFER.

R. D. BLACKMORE The rector having learned every gammer's alloverishness and every gaffer's rheumatics.

Gammexane /gamɛkseɪn, gaˈmɛkseɪn/ *noun*. M20.
[ORIGIN from alternative chemical name *gamma*-hexachloro-cyclo*hexane*.]
(Proprietary name for) the insecticide lindane.

gammon /ˈgamən/ *noun*¹. L15.
[ORIGIN Old Northern French *gambon* (mod. French *jambon*) ham, from *gambe* leg: cf. JAMB.]
†**1** The ham or haunch of a pig. L15–E17.
2 The bottom piece of a flitch of bacon, including the leg. Also, ham cured like bacon. E16.
gammon and spinach: see GAMMON *noun*³.

gammon /ˈgamən/ *noun*². L17.
[ORIGIN Perh. identical with GAMMON *noun*¹, with ref. to the tying up of a ham: cf. French *gambes (de hune)* futtock shrouds.]
NAUTICAL. = GAMMONING (b).

gammon /ˈgamən/ *noun*³. *slang*. E18.
[ORIGIN Perh. formed as GAMMON *noun*⁴.]
1 ***give gammon (to)*** give cover to or *to* a pickpocket etc.; ***keep in gammon*** distract (a victim) while a confederate carries out a robbery. *criminals' slang*. E18.
2 Talk, chatter. L18.
gammon and patter talk, chatter, esp. between members of the same trade or profession; shop talk.
3 Nonsense, humbug; deceit. Also as *interjection*, rubbish! poppycock! E19.
gammon and spinach nonsense, humbug (with a pun on GAMMON *noun*¹).

gammon /ˈgamən/ *noun*⁴. M18.
[ORIGIN Perh. repr. reflexes of Old English *gam(e)nian* GAME *verb* or *gamen* GAME *noun*.]
1 The game of backgammon. Now *rare*. M18.
2 A victory in backgammon (carrying a double score) in which the winner removes all his or her pieces before the loser has removed any. M18.

gammon /ˈgamən/ *verb*¹ *trans*. L17.
[ORIGIN from GAMMON *noun*⁴.]
Beat at backgammon by a gammon; *fig*. beat decisively.

gammon /ˈgamən/ *verb*² *trans*. L17.
[ORIGIN from GAMMON *noun*².]
NAUTICAL. Lash (the bowsprit) with ropes to the stem of a ship.
■ **gammoning** *noun* (**a**) the action of the verb; (**b**) the rope or ropes used to lash the bowsprit to the stem: M19.

gammon /ˈgamən/ *verb*³. *slang*. L18.
[ORIGIN from GAMMON *noun*³.]
1 *verb intrans*. Talk plausibly or persuasively. L18.
2 *verb intrans. & trans*. Feign, pretend (*to do* or *to be*). E19.

T. COLLINS He gammoned dead till we poured a pint of beer down his throat.

3 *verb trans*. Flatter, deceive, hoax. E19.

W. BLACK Gammon old Mackenzie into the belief that he can read poetry.

■ **gammoner** *noun* E19.

gammon /ˈgamən/ *verb*⁴ *trans*. M19.
[ORIGIN from GAMMON *noun*¹.]
Cure (ham) by salting or smoking.

gammy /ˈgami/ *adjective*. M19.
[ORIGIN Dial. var. of GAME *adjective*².]
1 Bad; not good or genuine. *slang*. Now *rare* or *obsolete*. M19.
2 Disabled through injury or pain. Cf. GAME *adjective*². L19.

M. KEANE He couldn't dance because of his gammy leg.

gamo- /ˈgaməʊ/ *combining form*.
[ORIGIN Greek, from *gamos* marriage: see -O-.]
Chiefly used in BIOLOGY with the sense 'of sexual reproduction' or in BOTANY with the sense 'of union of parts'.
■ **gamoˈgenesis** *noun* reproduction by union of gametes, sexual reproduction M19. **gamogeˈnetic** *adjective* of, relating to, involving, or produced by gamogenesis M19. **gamoˈpetalous** *adjective* (BOTANY) having petals united along their margins to form a tubular corolla (opp. ***polypetalous***) M19. **gaˈmophyllous** *adjective* (BOTANY) having the perianth segments fused L19. **gamoˈsepalous** *adjective* (BOTANY) having sepals united along their margins to form a tubular calyx (opp. ***polysepalous***) M19.

gamont /ˈgamɒnt/ *noun*. E20.
[ORIGIN from GAMETE + Greek *ont-*, *ōn* pres. pple of *einai* be, exist.]
ZOOLOGY. The sexual form of a protozoan displaying alternation of generations. Cf. SCHIZONT.

gamp /gamp/ *noun*. M19.
[ORIGIN Mrs *Gamp* (see below).]
1 A woman resembling Mrs Sarah Gamp, a monthly nurse in Dickens's *Martin Chuzzlewit*; *spec*. a drunken or disreputable sick nurse. Now *rare*. M19.
2 An umbrella, *esp*. a large untidy one such as that carried by Mrs Gamp. M19.

gamut /ˈgamət/ *noun*. LME.
[ORIGIN Contr. of medieval Latin *gamma ut*, from GAMMA name of the symbol Γ (repr. in the Middle Ages a note one tone lower than A) + UT first of the six notes forming a hexachord.]
▸ **I** MUSIC. **1** *hist*. The lowest note on the medieval sequence of hexachords, equal to modern G on the lowest line of the bass stave. LME.
2 *hist*. A large scale (ascribed to Guido d'Arezzo), formed of seven hexachords or partial scales, and containing all the recognized notes used in medieval music. L15.
3 The full range of notes which a voice or instrument can produce. M17.
4 The major diatonic scale; the scale recognized by any particular people or in any period. E18.
▸ **II 5** *transf. & fig*. The whole range or scope of something. E17.

C. BEATON Her resonant voice covers the gamut from an emphatic whisper to an . . almost Rabelaisian roar.

G

G

gamy /ˈgeɪmi/ *adjective*. Also **gamey**. M19.
[ORIGIN from GAME *noun* + -Y¹.]
1 Having much game or wildlife that can be hunted; intent on game. M19.
2 Spirited, plucky. M19.

J. M. SYNGE A fine, gamy . . lad the like of you.

3 Having the flavour or smell of game, esp. when it is high; strong-tasting or smelling. M19.

P. ROTH Underwear athletically gamy.

4 Racy, spicy; scandalous, sensational; sexy. Chiefly *N. Amer.* M20.

D. ABSE Underweight women in the gamiest of skirts.

■ **gaminess** *noun* L19.

-gamy /gəmi/ *suffix*.
[ORIGIN from Greek *gamos* marriage + -Y³]
Appended to Greek stems to form nouns with the senses 'marriage' or (BIOLOGY) 'reproduction, fertilization' (***cleistogamy***, ***endogamy***, ***polygamy***, etc.).

Gamza /ˈgamzə, ˈgʌm-/ *noun*. Also **Gum-**. M20.
[ORIGIN Bulgarian.]
A dark red Bulgarian grape; the wine made from this.

Gan /gan/ *noun & adjective*. Also **Kan** /kan/. M20.
[ORIGIN Chinese *Gàn*.]
▸ **A** *noun*. A Chinese dialect spoken in Jiangxi province. M20.
▸ **B** *adjective*. Of or pertaining to this dialect. M20.

Ganay /ˈgʊnʌɪ/ *noun & adjective*. Also **Kurnai** /ˈkʊənʌɪ/. L19.
[ORIGIN Aboriginal.]
▸ **A** *noun*. Pl. same. A member of an Aboriginal people of SE Australia; the language of this people. L19.
▸ **B** *attrib.* or as *adjective*. Of or pertaining to the Ganay or their language. E20.

ganbei /ganˈbeɪ/ *interjection*. Also **kan-pei**. M20.
[ORIGIN Chinese *gānbēi*, from *gān* empty, dry + *bēi* glass, cup.]
A Chinese toast, a call to drain one's glass.

ganbu /ˈganbuː/ *noun*. Also ***kanpu*** /ˈkanpuː/. Pl. **-s**, same. M20.
[ORIGIN Chinese *gànbù*.]
= CADRE *noun* 3b.

†**ganch** *noun*. Also **gaunch**. E17.
[ORIGIN French †*ganche* from mod. Provençal *ganche* hook, boathook, from Spanish *gancho* or Italian *gancio* hook.]
1 The apparatus used in execution by ganching; the punishment itself. E17–L18.
2 A gash or wound made by a wild boar's tusk. Only in E19.

ganch /gan(t)ʃ/ *verb trans*. Also †**gaunch**. E17.
[ORIGIN French †*ganché* pa. pple of verb from †*ganche*: see GANCH *noun*.]
1 Impale on sharp hooks or stakes as a means of execution. Now *rare*. E17.
†**2** Of a boar: tear or gash with the tusk. Usu. in *pass.* E17–L18.

gander /ˈgandə/ *noun*.
[ORIGIN Late Old English *ganra*, *gandra*, corresp. to Middle Low German *ganre* (Low German, Dutch *gander*), from Germanic base also of GANNET.]
1 A male goose. LOE.

Proverb: What is sauce for the goose is sauce for the gander.

2 A dull or stupid person; a fool, a simpleton. M16.
3 A look, a glance. Esp. in ***have a gander at***, ***take a gander at***. *slang*. E20.

J. TORRINGTON A wee gander at the London *Times* now, the grown-ups' 'comic'. S. TUROW Wash scowled again and took a gander over his shoulder.

– COMB.: **gander-month**, **gander-moon** (long *rare*) the month after a woman's confinement.

gander /ˈgandə/ *verb intrans*. *dial.* & *US*. L17.
[ORIGIN from the noun.]
1 Wander about aimlessly or foolishly. L17. ▸**b** Stare, look inquisitively at or for something. L19.
2 Ramble in talk. M19.

gandharva /ganˈdɑːvə/ *noun*. Also **-ba** /-bə/. L18.
[ORIGIN Sanskrit *gandharvás*. Perh. connected with Greek *kentauros* CENTAUR.]
HINDU MYTHOLOGY. Any of a class of minor deities or genii of the sky, often represented as celestial musicians, and depicted in a variety of presiding or attendant roles.

Gandhian /ˈgandɪən/ *adjective*. E20.
[ORIGIN from *Gandhi* (see below) + -AN.]
Of, pertaining to, or characteristic of Mohandas Karamchand (known as Mahatma) Gandhi (1869–1948), Indian political leader and social reformer, or his principles, esp. those of non-violent social reform.
■ **Gandhiˈesque** *adjective* M20. **Gandhi-ism**, **Gandhism** *nouns* Gandhian principles or actions E20. **Gandhist** *noun* a follower of Gandhi E20.

Gandhi cap /ˈgandi kap/ *noun phr.* E20.
[ORIGIN from *Gandhi* (see GANDHIAN) + CAP *noun*¹.]
A close-fitting white cap with a wide band encircling the head.

gandoura /ganˈdʊərə/ *noun*. Also **-dourah**, **-dura(h)**. M19.
[ORIGIN Algerian Arab. *gandūra*, classical Arab. *qandūra*.]
A long loose gown worn in the Middle East and N. Africa.

G and T *abbreviation*. Also **G & T**.
A drink of gin and tonic.

gandy dancer /ˈgandɪ ˌdɑːnsə/ *noun phr. slang*. Chiefly *US*. E20.
[ORIGIN Unknown.]
A railroad maintenance worker. Also, a seasonal or itinerant worker.

ganef /ˈganɛf/ *noun. colloq.* E20.
[ORIGIN Yiddish from Hebrew, lit. 'thief'.]
A dishonest or unscrupulous person; a thief.

gang /gaŋ/ *noun*. OE.
[ORIGIN Old Norse *gangr* (masc.), *ganga* (fem.) walking motion, course (Swedish *gång*, Danish *gang* walk, pace, time) = Old Saxon, Old High German (Dutch, German) *gang*, Gothic *gagg*, from Germanic noun of action rel. to base of GO *verb*.]
▸ **I** Action or manner of going.
1 A journey; a travelling, a journeying. *obsolete* exc. *Scot.* OE.
2 †**a** The power of going; the ability to go. OE–ME. ▸**b** Manner of going; gait, carriage. *obsolete* exc. *dial.* ME.
3 A way, a road, a passage. *obsolete* exc. *dial.* OE. ▸†**b** The course of a stream. OE–E19. ▸**c** A pasture for cattle; the right of pasturing. *Scot.* & *N. English*. M16.
4 A turn or spell at any work or exercise. *rare*. *Scot.* & *dial.* M16.
5 A quantity (esp. of a liquid) that can be carried at one time. *Scot.* M16.
▸ **II** A set of things or persons.
6 A set of articles that are usu. taken together. ME. ▸**b** *spec.* A set of tools or instruments arranged to work in coordination. L18.

G. SHELVOCKE I had fitted her with a gang of oars. **b** *Scientific American* The . . machine had a gang of cutter chains mounted . . on a swiveling head.

7 A band or group of people acting or going about together, esp. in a shared cause, or for disreputable or criminal purposes. LME.

A. GIBBS Tomorrow's vote will surprise the old gang of professional politicians. A. PATON A gang of these youths attacked one of our own African girls.

gang of three, **gang of four**, etc., a political group or faction who are outspoken on a particular issue or who hold a minority view on something (orig. of the left-wing faction in the Chinese Communist Party accused of conspiracy after the death of Mao Zedong in 1976 and later discredited).

8 A company of labourers. E17. ▸**b** A company of slaves or prisoners. E18.

C. THUBRON A gang of labourers was shovelling rubble into a cart. **b** OUIDA A gang of . . captives would go by on foot and chained.

9 A herd of animals of the same species. *US*. M17.
– ATTRIB. & COMB.: Designating various implements or pieces of equipment having a set of coordinating tools or instruments, as ***gang drill***, ***gang mower***, ***gang plough***, ***gang press***, etc. Special combs., as **gang-bang** *noun & verb* (*slang*) (*a*) *noun* an occasion on which several people copulate in turn with one other person; (*b*) *verb trans.* & *intrans.* (of several people) copulate in turn with (one other person); **gangboard** (*a*) = GANGWAY 2; (*b*) = ***gangplank*** below; **gangbuster** a person who takes part in the aggressive breaking up of criminal gangs; *transf.* an outstandingly successful person or thing; ***go gangbusters*** (US colloq.), do very well; do something energetically, enthusiastically, or extravagantly; **gang-cask** NAUTICAL a water cask for carrying water to, or storing water on, a boat; **gangland** the domain of gangs or gangsters; gangs or gangsters collectively; **gang-man** a member of a gang; **gangmaster** a person who organizes and oversees the work of casual manual labourers; **gangplank** a movable plank usu. with cleats nailed on to it, for walking into or out of a boat etc.; **gang rape** the successive rape of one person by a group of other people; **gang-shag** *slang* = ***gang-bang*** (a) above; **gang war**, **gang warfare** (an) armed conflict between rival groups of criminals, youths, etc.
■ **gangdom** *noun* the domain of gangs or gangsters, gangland E20.

gang /gaŋ/ *verb*¹ *intrans.* (*inf.* & *pres. trans.*). Now only *Scot.* & *dial.*
[ORIGIN Old English *gangan*, *gongan* = Old Frisian *ganga*, *gunga*, Old Saxon, Old High German *gangan*, Old Norse *ganga*, Gothic *gaggan* from Germanic.]
Walk, go, proceed.

R. BURNS The best laid schemes o' mice an' men Gang aft a-gley. L. G. GIBBON Gang to your bed, lass, I'll tend to the rest.

gang one's gate be on one's way, leave.
■ **ganging** *verbal noun* (*a*) the action or power of going or walking; (*b*) walking in procession (on gang-days): ME.

gang /gaŋ/ *verb*². M19.
[ORIGIN from GANG *noun* II.]
1 *verb trans.* Arrange in a gang or band. M19. ▸**b** Arrange (implements or instruments) in gangs. E20.
2 *verb intrans.* (Of a group) go together or as a company; (of an individual or a group) go in company *with*, act in conjunction *with*, join *up with*. L19.

R. PRICE The little knot of people that had ganged to listen.

3 *verb intrans.* Foll. by *up against*, *up on*: combine or form a gang against; torment, intimidate. E20.

J. BARZUN The . . resentment which makes the majority at school gang up on the bookish boy.

– COMB.: **gang-up** *colloq.* an act of ganging up; a meeting of a gang.

ganga *noun* var. of GANJA.

gangan *noun* see GANG-GANG.

gang-days /ˈgaŋdeɪz/ *noun pl. obsolete* exc. *hist.* OE.
[ORIGIN from GANG *noun* + DAY *noun*; so called from the processions held on these days.]
ECCLESIASTICAL. The three days preceding Ascension Day, the Rogation days.

gange /gan(d)ʒ/ *verb trans.* M19.
[ORIGIN Unknown.]
ANGLING. Protect (a fish hook or part of a fishing line) with fine wire.

ganger /ˈgaŋə/ *noun*¹. *obsolete* exc. *Scot.* & *dial.* LME.
[ORIGIN from GANG *verb*¹ + -ER¹.]
1 A person who goes on foot. LME.
2 A fast horse. E19.

ganger /ˈgaŋə/ *noun*². M19.
[ORIGIN from GANG *noun* or *verb*² + -ER¹.]
A foreman or overseer in charge of a gang of labourers.

ganger /ˈgaŋə/ *noun*³. M19.
[ORIGIN Perh. abbreviation of FOREGANGER.]
NAUTICAL. One or more lengths of cable shackled to a sheet anchor.

Gangetic /ganˈdʒɛtɪk/ *noun & adjective*. L17.
[ORIGIN Latin *Gangeticus*, from *Ganges* (see below), from Greek *Gaggēs*: see -IC.]
▸ †**A** *noun*. In *pl.* Those who live on the banks of the Ganges. Only in L17.
▸ **B** *adjective*. Belonging to the Ganges, a great river in the north of the Indian subcontinent, flowing from the Himalayas to the Bay of Bengal. M19.

gang-gang /ˈgaŋgaŋ/ *noun*. Also (earlier) **gangan** /-gan/. M19.
[ORIGIN Wiradhuri, imit.]
A small grey cockatoo, *Callocephalon fimbriatum*, native to SE Australia, the male of which has a scarlet head and crest.

gangle /ˈgaŋg(ə)l/ *verb intrans.* M20.
[ORIGIN Back-form. from GANGLING.]
Of a person: move the limbs loosely, appear awkward or gangling.

ganglia *noun pl.* see GANGLION.

gangliar /ˈgaŋglɪə/ *adjective*. L19.
[ORIGIN formed as GANGLIFORM + -AR¹.]
Of, pertaining to, or of the nature of a ganglion or ganglia.
■ Also **ganglial** *adjective* M19.

gangliated /ˈgaŋglɪeɪtɪd/ *adjective*. E19.
[ORIGIN formed as GANGLIFORM + -ATE³ + -ED¹.]
Having ganglia.

gangliectomy /gaŋglɪˈɛktəmi/ *noun*. E20.
[ORIGIN formed as GANGLIFORM + -ECTOMY.]
Surgical removal of a ganglion; an instance of this.

gangliform /ˈgaŋglɪfɔːm/ *adjective*. Also (earlier) **-ioform** /-ɪəfɔːm/. L17.
[ORIGIN from GANGLION + -FORM.]
Having the form of a ganglion or ganglia.

gangling /ˈgaŋglɪŋ/ *adjective*. E19.
[ORIGIN from GANG *verb*¹ + -LE³ + -ING². Cf. GANGLY, GANGREL.]
(Of a plant) tall, straggling; (of a person) disproportionately tall and thin, lanky, loose-jointed.

C. P. SNOW He was tall . . slim, probably a trifle gangling.

ganglion /ˈgaŋglɪən/ *noun*. Pl. **-lions**, **-lia** /-lɪə/. L17.
[ORIGIN Greek *gagglion* tumour under the skin, on or near tendons or sinews, (Galen) complex nerve centre.]
1 MEDICINE. A cystic swelling of unknown cause arising from the sheath of a tendon. L17.
2 ANATOMY. A structure containing several nerve cells forming a swelling or knot on a nerve, or, within the central and automatic nervous systems, forming a well-defined mass. L17.
basal ganglion: see BASAL *adjective* 1.
3 *fig.* A centre of force, activity, or interest. E19.
– COMB.: **ganglion-blocking** *adjective* that prevents the transmission of nerve impulses across the synapse in a ganglion.
■ **ganglionated** *adjective* = GANGLIATED M19. **ganglioˈnectomy** *noun* (MEDICINE) = GANGLIECTOMY E20. **gangliˈonic** *adjective* relating to, composed of, or having ganglia E19.

ganglioside /ˈgaŋglɪəsʌɪd/ *noun*. M20.
[ORIGIN from GANGLION + -OSIDE.]
BIOCHEMISTRY. Any of a group of glycolipids which are present in the grey matter of humans and some animals and yield neuraminic acid on hydrolysis (cf. CEREBROSIDE).

gangly /ˈgaŋgli/ *adjective*. L19.
[ORIGIN Alt. of GANGLING: see -Y¹.]
= GANGLING.

G. GREENE His long gangly legs.

gangrel /ˈɡaŋɡr(ə)l/ *noun & adjective*. *arch.* & *dial.* ME.
[ORIGIN App. from GANG *noun* or *verb*[1]. Cf. *haverel*, *wastrel*, etc.]
▸ **A** *noun*. **1** A wandering beggar, a vagrant. ME.
2 A toad. *Scot.* & *N. English*. L15.
3 A lanky loose-jointed person. L16.
4 A child just beginning to walk. *Scot.* M18.
▸ **B** *adjective*. Vagrant, wandering. M16.

gangrene /ˈɡaŋɡriːn/ *noun & verb*. M16.
[ORIGIN French *gangrène* from Latin *gangraena* from Greek *gaggraina* (cf. *goggros* growth on trees).]
▸ **A** *noun*. **1** Localized death of body tissue, accompanied by putrefaction and usu. caused by obstructed circulation. M16.
dry gangrene: caused simply by lack of blood circulation. **gas gangrene**: see GAS *noun*[1]. **moist gangrene**: caused by bacterial infection.
2 *fig.* Moral corruption. E17.
T. FULLER The Gangrene of that Heresy began to spread it self into this Island.
▸ **B** *verb intrans.* & *trans.* Become affected, affect, with gangrene. E17.
■ †**gangrenate** *verb intrans.* & *trans.* = GANGRENE *verb* L16–M18. **gangrenous** *adjective* of the nature of or affected by gangrene M17.

gangsman /ˈɡaŋzmən/ *noun*. Pl. **-men**. L18.
[ORIGIN from GANG *noun* + -S[1] + MAN *noun*.]
1 A dock porter. Now *rare*. L18.
2 A person in charge of a gang of labourers. M19.
3 = GANGSTER. E20.

gangsta /ˈɡaŋstə/ *noun*. *US slang*. L20.
[ORIGIN Alt. of GANGSTER, prob. to reflect African-American pronunc.]
A gang member. Also, gangsta rap; a gangsta rapper.
– COMB.: **gangsta rap** a style of rap music, originating in south-central Los Angeles, featuring aggressive, often misogynistic lyrics and typically centring on the violence of gang culture; **gangsta rapper** a performer of gangsta rap.

gangster /ˈɡaŋstə/ *noun*. L19.
[ORIGIN from GANG *noun* + -STER.]
A member of a gang of violent criminals.
■ **gangsterdom** *noun* the domain of gangsters; gangsters collectively: E20. **gangsterish** *adjective* resembling or characteristic of a gangster or gangsters M20. **gangsterism** *noun* the actions or methods of gangsters E20.

gangue /ɡaŋ/ *noun*. E19.
[ORIGIN French from German *Gang* way, course, vein or lode of metal: cf. GANG *noun*.]
The valueless or unwanted components of an ore deposit.

gangway /ˈɡaŋweɪ/ *noun*.
[ORIGIN Old English *gangweg*; later from GANG *noun* + WAY *noun*.]
1 A road, thoroughfare, or passage of any kind. *obsolete* exc. *dial.* OE.
2 NAUTICAL. **a** A passage or platform on a ship, *esp.* one connecting the quarterdeck and the forecastle. L17. ▸**b** The opening in the bulwarks by which a ship is entered or left. Also (and now usu.), a movable bridge linking a vessel to the shore, or one vessel to another. L18.
3 A passage inside a building, *esp.* one that runs between rows of seats. E18. ▸**b** *spec.* A cross-passage halfway down the British House of Commons which gives access to the back benches. M19.
b above the gangway, **below the gangway** (of a member of the House of Commons, according to which side of the gangway he or she sits on) more, less, closely associated with the policies of his or her party.
4 MINING. A connecting passage or main level in a mine. L18.
5 BUILDING. A temporary arrangement of planks or steps for crossing muddy or difficult ground in a building site. E19.
6 As *interjection*. Make way! Stand back! E20.
– COMB.: **gangway seat** a seat at the end of a row, next to the gangway.

ganister /ˈɡanɪstə/ *noun*. Also **-nn-**. E19.
[ORIGIN Unknown.]
A close-grained hard siliceous stone found in the lower coal measures of South Yorkshire, and used for furnace linings etc.

ganja /ˈɡandʒə, ˈɡɑː-/ *noun*. Also **ganga**. E19.
[ORIGIN Hindi *gãjā*.]
A strong preparation of marijuana, used chiefly for smoking.
J. HEARNE The rest of them smoke ganja, the way you and I smoke tobacco.

gannet /ˈɡanɪt/ *noun*.
[ORIGIN Old English *ganot* corresp. to Middle Low German *gante*, Dutch *gent*, Middle High German *ganiz*, *genz*, Old High German *ganazzo*, Middle High German *ganze* gander from Germanic base also of GANDER *noun*.]
1 Each of three large gregarious seabirds of the genus *Morus* which capture fish by plunging, *M. bassanus* of the N. Atlantic, *M. serrator* of Australasia, and (more fully ***Cape gannet***) *M. capensis* of southern African waters. OE.
2 A greedy person. *colloq.* E20.
■ **gannetry** *noun* a place where gannets breed; a colony of gannets: E20.

gannister *noun* var. of GANISTER.

ganoid /ˈɡanɔɪd/ *adjective & noun*. M19.
[ORIGIN French *ganoïde*, from Greek *ganos* brightness: see -OID.]
▸ **A** *adjective*. **1** Of a fish scale: having a smooth shining surface, from being covered with a layer of enamel (esp. ganoin). M19.
2 Of a fish: having ganoid scales. Orig. designating an order of primitive bony fishes ('Ganoidei') possessing ganoid scales, mostly extinct but including the living garfishes, sturgeon, and bowfin, now classified as either chondrostean or holostean. M19.
▸ **B** *noun*. A ganoid fish. M19.
■ **ganoidal** *adjective* = GANOID *adjective* 2 M19.

ganoin /ˈɡanəʊɪn/ *noun*. Also **-ine** /-ɪn, -iːn/. M19.
[ORIGIN from Greek *ganos* brightness + -IN[1].]
The hard shiny substance resembling enamel which forms the outer layer of ganoid fish scales.

ganomalite /ɡəˈnɒməlʌɪt/ *noun*. L19.
[ORIGIN from Greek *ganōma* brightness + -LITE.]
MINERALOGY. A lustrous silicate of lead and calcium, crystallizing in the hexagonal system and occurring massive or as colourless or grey tetragonal crystals.

ganophyllite /ɡəˈnɒfɪlʌɪt, ɡanəʊˈfɪlʌɪt/ *noun*. L19.
[ORIGIN from Greek *ganos* brightness + *phullon* leaf: see -ITE[1].]
MINERALOGY. A monoclinic aluminosilicate of manganese, occurring foliated or as brown crystals.

ganosis /ɡəˈnəʊsɪs/ *noun*. E20.
[ORIGIN Greek *ganōsis*, from *ganos* brightness, from *ganoun* to polish.]
The process of applying a wax polish to the white marble surface of a statue or occas. to some other surface in order to give warmth to its appearance.

gansel /ˈɡans(ə)l/ *noun*. *obsolete* exc. *dial.* LME.
[ORIGIN Old French *ganse aillie* garlic sauce.]
A garlic sauce, used esp. with goose.

gansey /ˈɡanzi/ *noun*. Chiefly *dial.* Also **gansie**, **ganzy**, & other vars. L19.
[ORIGIN Repr. a pronunc. of GUERNSEY.]
A jersey.

gant /ɡɑːnt/ *noun & verb*. *Scot.* Also **gaunt** /ɡɔːnt/. L15.
[ORIGIN Uncertain: perh. from Old English *ganian* yawn.]
▸ **A** *noun*. A yawn, a gape. L15.
▸ **B** *verb intrans*. Yawn, gape. E16.

gantlet *noun* see GAUNTLET *noun*[2].

gantline /ˈɡantlʌɪn/ *noun*. Orig. **girtline** /ˈɡəːtlʌɪn/. M18.
[ORIGIN from unkn. 1st elem. + LINE *noun*[2].]
NAUTICAL. A line rove through a block near the masthead and used to hoist sails, rigging, etc.

gantlope /ˈɡantləʊp/ *noun*. Now *rare*. M17.
[ORIGIN Swedish *gatlopp*, from *gata* lane, GATE *noun*[2] + *lopp* course.]
run the gantlope, †***pass the gantlope***, = ***run the gauntlet*** s.v. GAUNTLET *noun*[2].

gantry /ˈɡantri/ *noun*. Also **gauntry** /ˈɡɔːntri/. LME.
[ORIGIN Prob. from GAWN + TREE *noun*.]
1 A wooden stand for barrels. LME.
2 A supportive structure used esp. for a travelling crane, railway or road signals, or for equipment to prepare a rocket for launching. E19.
Daily Telegraph The train crashed into an overhead power gantry.

Gantt chart /ˈɡant tʃɑːt/ *noun phr.* Also **g-**. E20.
[ORIGIN from Henry Lawrence *Gantt* (1861–1919), Amer. management consultant + CHART *noun*.]
A chart in which a series of horizontal lines shows the amount of work done or production completed in certain periods of time in relation to the amount planned for those periods.

Ganymede /ˈɡanɪmiːd/ *noun*. L16.
[ORIGIN Latin *Ganymedes* from Greek *Ganumēdēs* Zeus's cupbearer.]
1 A catamite. L16.
2 A cupbearer; *arch. joc.* a pot-boy. E17.

ganzfeld /ˈɡanzfɛld/ *noun*. M20.
[ORIGIN German, lit. 'entire field'.]
PSYCHOLOGY. An empty field of vision; *spec.* in parapsychology, an experimental technique in which subjects are exposed to neutral visual and aural stimuli in order to improve results in tests of telepathy and other paranormal phenomena.

ganzy *noun* var. of GANSEY.

GAO *abbreviation*.
General Accounting Office, a body that undertakes investigations for the US Congress.

gaol *noun & verb* var. of JAIL.

gaoler *noun* var. of JAILER.

gaon /ˈɡɑːəʊn/ *noun*. Pl. **gaons**, **geonim** /ɡeɪˈəʊnɪm/. L18.
[ORIGIN Hebrew *gā'ōn* excellence, pride.]
(An honorific for) a head of a Jewish academy in Babylonia, Palestine, Syria, or Egypt, from the 6th to the 11th cents. Later, esp. in Spain, France, Italy, and Lithuania, an outstanding Talmudic scholar. Also *gen.*, a genius, a prodigy.

gap /ɡap/ *noun*. ME.
[ORIGIN Old Norse = 'chasm' (Swedish *gap*, Danish *gab* open mouth, opening), rel. to Old Norse *gapa* GAPE *verb*.]
1 A breach in a wall, fence, hedge, etc., caused by violence or natural decay. ME. ▸†**b** *fig.* An opening or breach by which an entry, attack, or escape may be effected. M16–M18.
M. MITCHELL There were wide gaps between the buildings . . where dwellings had been shelled or burned. J. T. STORY The path led me . . through a gap in a high elder hedge.
2 A notch; a small break or opening in an edge or surface. Now *rare*. LME.
3 A break or opening in a range of mountains; a gorge, a pass. LME. ▸**b** A hole or chasm in the ground. *rare*. L17.
R. BOLDREWOOD One of those narrow rocky gaps . . over the line of ranges.
†**4** A gash or wound in the body. L16–E17.
5 An unfilled space or interval; a blank; a break in continuity. E17.
A. SILLITOE Through gaps in over-arching branches he could see the stars. B. EMECHETA The door opened a little, and someone peered at them through the small gap. *fig.*: V. WOOLF What vast gaps there were, what blank spaces . . in her knowledge.
6 A disparity, an inequality, an imbalance; a (usu. undesirable) divergence in sympathies, understanding, development, etc. M19.
D. H. LAWRENCE They always kept a gap, a distance between them. J. BARZUN The gap between words and experience in the . . world of professional educators. *Times Lit. Suppl.* The gap that has opened up . . between men of science and students of the humanities.
credibility gap, ***generation gap***.
7 AERONAUTICS. The vertical distance between the upper and lower wings of a biplane. E20.
– PHRASES: **bridge a gap**, **close a gap**, **fill a gap**, **stop a gap** make up a deficiency, supply a want, fill a space.
– COMB.: **gap-toothed** *adjective* having gaps between the teeth; **gap year** a period, typically an academic year, taken by a student as a break between school and university or college education.
■ **gapper** *noun* (**a**) a plant suitable for filling a gap in a flower bed; (**b**) BASEBALL a ball which is hit into the space between outfielders; (**c**) a student who is on a gap year: E20. **gappy** *adjective* full of gaps; full of deficiencies: M19.

gap /ɡap/ *verb*. Infl. **-pp-**. M19.
[ORIGIN from the noun.]
1 *verb trans.* & *intrans.* Make or become notched, break at the edge. M19.
2 *verb trans.* Make a gap or breach in or between. L19.
B. CABLE Eager hands tore down the sandbags to gap a passage for them.
3 *verb intrans.* Have gaps; gape open. M20.

gape /ɡeɪp/ *noun*. E16.
[ORIGIN from the verb.]
1 An act of opening the mouth, a yawn. E16.
2 An open-mouthed stare; a gaze of wonder or curiosity. M17.
E. BLISHEN Sometimes evoking no response at all, sometimes an astonished gape.
3 A rent or opening of any kind. M17.
4 The expanse of an open mouth or beak. M18. ▸**b** The part of a beak which opens. M19. ▸**c** A space between the edges of the closed valves of a bivalve mollusc. M19.
5 ***the gapes***: ▸**a** A disease of birds due to infestation with gapeworms (see below), in which frequent gaping is the symptom. L18. ▸**b** *joc.* A fit of yawning. E19.
– COMB.: **gapeworm** a parasitic nematode worm of the family Syngamidae which infests the respiratory tract of birds, causing the gapes.

gape /ɡeɪp/ *verb*. ME.
[ORIGIN Old Norse *gapa* (Swedish *gapa*, Danish *gabe*) = Middle Dutch & mod. Dutch *gapen*, Middle & mod. High German *gaffen*.]
1 **a** *verb intrans.* Open the mouth wide, esp. in order to bite or swallow something. Also, (of the mouth) open wide. ME. ▸**b** *verb trans.* Open (the mouth) wide. *rare*. M17.
a R. HOLME Such Fellows . . are fed . . as long as they can gape.
2 *verb intrans.* Stare open-mouthed; gaze at in wonder or admiration. (Foll. by *at*, *on*, *upon*.) ME.
A. J. CRONIN She left the local inhabitants gaping by a display of trick riding. R. DAVIES They gaped at the curiosities of the World of Wonders.
3 *verb trans.* & *intrans.* Be eager to obtain, have a longing for (something). (Foll. by *after*, *for*, †*at*, †*upon*.) Now *rare*. ME. ▸**b** *verb intrans.* Desire eagerly *to do*. Now *rare*. ME.
4 *verb intrans.* Of earth, hell, etc.: be or become wide open; yawn. Also, of a wound, an oyster, etc.: split, part, open. LME.
B. GOOGE The ground gapes with the heate of the Sunne. TENNYSON A gulf that ever shuts and gapes. J. K. JEROME A clean-cut wound that gapes wide. *fig.*: R. MACAULAY When the years have all passed, there will gape the . . dark void of death.

G

5 *verb intrans.* Of a person: yawn, esp. from weariness. LME. ▸†**b** Of a dead body: have the mouth open. LME–M16.
†**6** *verb intrans.* Gasp from pain, heat, etc. LME–L16.
7 *verb intrans.* Bawl, shout. *obsolete* exc. *dial.* L16.
■ **gaping** *noun* (*a*) the action of the verb; †(*b*) a deep opening or chasm in the earth: LME. **gapingly** *adverb* with open mouth, eagerly, amazedly L16.

gaper /ˈɡeɪpə/ *noun.* LME.
[ORIGIN from GAPE *verb* + -ER¹.]
1 †**a** A person who longs or gapes for something. LME–E17. ▸**b** A person who stares or gazes in wonder or curiosity. L15.

b *Times Lit. Suppl.* Learned understanders and ignorant gapers.

2 A soft-shelled clam of the genus *Mya*, with a permanent opening between the valves through which the siphon protrudes. L18.
3 The comber fish, *Serranus cabrilla*, which gapes when dead. E19.

gape-seed /ˈɡeɪpsiːd/ *noun.* L16.
[ORIGIN from GAPE *noun* or *verb* + SEED *noun.*]
Something stared at by a gaping crowd. Also, the act of staring.
buy gape-seed, **seek gape-seed**, **sow gape-seed** (*obsolete* exc. *dial.*) stare gapingly at a fair or market instead of doing useful business.

G

gapped /ɡapt/ *adjective.* M16.
[ORIGIN from GAP *noun*, *verb*: see -ED², -ED¹.]
1 Having a notched or serrated edge. M16.
2 Broken through at intervals; full of holes or spaces. M19.

CARLYLE Closing his gapped ranks.

3 MUSIC. Of a scale or mode: having less than seven notes, *esp.* pentatonic. E20.

gar /ɡɑː/ *noun.* M18.
[ORIGIN Abbreviation.]
= GARFISH.
alligator gar: see ALLIGATOR.

gar /ɡɑː/ *verb trans.* Chiefly *Scot.* & *N. English.* Infl. **-rr-**. Pa. t. & pple **garred**, **gart** /ɡɑːt/. ME.
[ORIGIN Old Norse *ger(v)a*, *gør(v)a* make, do = Old English *ġierwan* prepare, Old Saxon *garwian*, *gerwian*, Old High German *garawen* (German *gerben* tan, curry, polish) from Germanic: rel. to GEAR *noun*, YARE.]
†**1** Do, perform; make. *rare.* ME–M17.
2 Make, cause; *esp.* cause (*to*) *do* or *be.* ME.

R. BURNS He screw'd the pipes and gart them skirl.

Gar /ɡɑː/ *interjection.* L16.
[ORIGIN Alt. of GOD *noun.*]
Expr. annoyance, surprise, impatience, etc. Cf. GAD *noun*².

garage /ˈɡarɑː(d)ʒ, -ɪdʒ, ɡəˈrɑːʒ/ *noun* & *verb.* E20.
[ORIGIN French, from *garer* to shelter.]
▸ **A** *noun.* **1** A building or part of a building for keeping one or more motor vehicles when not in use. E20.

Oxford Times Detached freehold House . . . Separate access to brick garage.

2 A commercial establishment which sells petrol, oil, etc., and freq. also repairs and services motor vehicles. M20.

Financial Times Unleaded petrol has gone on sale at about 200 garages.

3 A form of dance music incorporating elements of drum and bass, house music, and soul, characterized by a rhythm in which the second and fourth beats of the bar are omitted. Also *UK garage.* L20.
– COMB.: **garage band** a rock band which rehearses in a garage; any band whose performance is characteristically loud, energetic, and somewhat unpolished; **garage sale** (chiefly *N. Amer.*, *Austral.*, & *NZ*) a sale of miscellaneous second-hand items, usu. held in the garage of a private house.
▸ **B** *verb trans.* Place or accommodate (a motor vehicle) in or at a garage. E20.
■ **garaging** *noun* (*a*) the action of the verb; (*b*) garage accommodation: E20.

garagist /ˈɡarɑːʒɪst/ *noun.* Also *garagiste* /ɡaraʒist (*pl. same*)/. E20.
[ORIGIN French *garagiste*, formed as GARAGE + *-iste*: see -IST.]
The proprietor or an employee of a commercial garage.

garam masala /ɡʌrəm məˈsɑːlə/ *noun phr.* M20.
[ORIGIN Urdu *garam maṣālah.*]
A spice mixture used in Indian cookery.

Garamond /ˈɡarəmɒnd/ *noun.* M19.
[ORIGIN Claude *Garamond* (1499–1561), French type founder.]
TYPOGRAPHY. A typeface modelled on those designed by or attributed to Garamond.

garancin /ˈɡar(ə)nsɪn/ *noun.* Also **-ine**. M19.
[ORIGIN French, from *garance* madder, of Germanic origin: see -IN¹, -INE⁵.]
A dye made by treating madder with dilute sulphuric acid, formerly much used in calico printing and to produce the scarlet cotton known as Turkey red.
■ Also *garance* /ɡarɑ̃ːs/ *noun* L19.

Garand /ˈɡar(ə)nd/ *noun.* Also **g-**. M20.
[ORIGIN John C. *Garand* (1888–1974), US gun designer.]
In full *Garand rifle*. A type of semi-automatic rifle.

garb /ɡɑːb/ *noun*¹. *obsolete* exc. HERALDRY. E16.
[ORIGIN Old Northern French *garbe* (Old French *jarbe*, mod. *gerbe*) from Frankish: see GERBE.]
A wheatsheaf.

garb /ɡɑːb/ *noun*². L16.
[ORIGIN French †*garbe* (now *galbe*) from Italian *garbo* ult. from Germanic (cf. Old High German *garawī* adornment) from base of GAR *verb.*]
†**1** Grace, elegance, esp. of manners or appearance. L16–L17.
†**2** Style, manner, fashion; a prevailing custom, the current fashion. L16–L17.
†**3** A person's outward bearing. E17–E18.
4 Dress, costume, esp. of a distinctive kind. Also, manner of dress. E17.

J. MAY Most of the people were dressed in buckskin or homespun peasant garb. *fig.*: MILTON Words cloath'd in reasons garb.

■ **garbless** *adjective* (*rare*) without clothing M19.

garb /ɡɑːb/ *verb trans.* L16.
[ORIGIN from GARB *noun*².]
Clothe, dress.

L. M. MONTGOMERY A child . . garbed in a . . very ugly dress. *fig.*: S. DOBELL To garb with joy The naked soul of Grief.

garba /ˈɡɑːbə/ *noun.* M20.
[ORIGIN from Sanskrit *Garbadeep*, lit. 'lamp inside a pot'.]
A traditional Gujarati folk dance and song, orig. performed as a fertility ritual.

garbage /ˈɡɑːbɪdʒ/ *noun.* LME.
[ORIGIN Anglo-Norman, of unknown origin.]
†**1** The offal of an animal used as food. LME–M19.
†**2** A mixture of straw etc. used as horse-feed. E16–E17.
3 Rubbish, filth; domestic waste, household refuse. Now chiefly *N. Amer.* L16.

N. PEVSNER Antediluvian dust-carts scattering more garbage than they collect.

4 *fig.* Anything worthless; *spec.* worthless literary matter. L16. ▸**b** COMPUTING. Incorrect or inappropriate input; data that is useless or no longer required. M20.

P. CAREY A lot of sentimental garbage was spoken on the subject.

b garbage in, garbage out COMPUTING incorrect or poor quality input will always produce faulty output (cf. *GIGO* s.v. G, G).
– COMB.: **garbage can** *N. Amer.* a dustbin; **garbage collection** (*a*) *N. Amer.* the removal of household refuse; (*b*) COMPUTING the removal from a memory of useless or unnecessary information; **garbage disposal unit**, **garbage disposer** a waste-disposal unit.

garbanzo /ɡɑːˈbanzəʊ/ *noun.* Pl. **-os**. M18.
[ORIGIN Spanish = chickpea: cf. CALAVANCE.]
A chickpea.

garberator *noun* var. of GARBURATOR.

garble /ˈɡɑːb(ə)l/ *noun.* E16.
[ORIGIN Prob. from Italian *garbello*, from *garbellare*: see GARBLE *verb.*]
†**1** Extraneous matter, *esp.* refuse of spices. E16–E19.
†**2** Merchandise containing an element of waste. E–M17. ▸**b** A mixture of base and precious metal; = ALLOY *noun* 3. Only in M19.
3 The process of garbling; selection, mutilation. Also, something garbled, distorted or mutilated information. E19.

G. KENDALL The screen . . was still filled with a garble of codes.

■ **garbler** *noun* (*a*) (*obsolete* exc. *hist.*) an official who garbled spices etc., a sifter; (*b*) a person who distorts or mutilates statements, stories, facts, etc.: LME.

garble /ˈɡɑːb(ə)l/ *verb trans.* LME.
[ORIGIN Anglo-Latin & Italian *garbellare* sift, sort, from Arabic *ġarbala* sift, select, rel. to *ġirbāl* sieve, perh. from late Latin *cribellare*, from *cribellum*, dim. of Latin *cribrum* sieve.]
†**1** Remove the extraneous matter or refuse from (spice etc.); sift (*out*), cleanse (*of*). LME–E19.
2 Select or sort out the best in (any thing or set of things). (Foll. by *out.*) Now *rare.* L15. ▸†**b** *spec.* Select undesirable or unfit members for expulsion from (a body of people). M17–E19.
3 Make (usu. unfair or malicious) selections from (statements, facts, etc.); distort (a statement, story, theory, etc.) unintentionally; mutilate in order to misrepresent. Esp. as *garbled ppl adjective.* L17.

J. CLAVELL It was much better to hear the truth than a garbled version.

garbo /ˈɡɑːbəʊ/ *noun. Austral. slang.* Pl. **-os**. M20.
[ORIGIN from GARBAGE + -O.]
A dustman, a collector of rubbish.

garboard /ˈɡɑːbɔːd/ *noun.* E17.
[ORIGIN Dutch †*gaarboord*, perh. from *garen* contr. of *gaderen* GATHER *verb* + *boord* BOARD *noun.*]
NAUTICAL. In full *garboard strake*. The first range of wooden planks or metal plates on the outer hull of a vessel next to the keel.

garboil /ˈɡɑːbɔɪl/ *noun. arch.* M16.
[ORIGIN Old French *garbouil(le)* from Italian *garbuglio.*]
Confusion, tumult; a brawl, a disturbance.

garbologist /ɡɑːˈbɒlədʒɪst/ *noun.* M20.
[ORIGIN from GARB(AGE + -OLOGIST.]
1 A dustman, a collector of rubbish. M20.
2 A person who studies and analyses the discarded rubbish of modern society. L20.

garbology /ɡɑːˈbɒlədʒi/ *noun.* L20.
[ORIGIN from GARB(AGE + -OLOGY.]
The study or investigation of the discarded rubbish of modern society, esp. regarded as an aspect of social science.

garburator /ˈɡɑːbəreɪtə/ *noun.* Also **garberator**. Chiefly *Canad.* M20.
[ORIGIN Perh. blend of GARBAGE and INCINERATOR.]
A kitchen waste-disposal unit.
– NOTE: Proprietary name in Canada.

garcinia /ɡɑːˈsɪnɪə/ *noun.* L19.
[ORIGIN mod. Latin (see below), from Laurent *Garcin* (1683–1751), French botanist + -IA¹.]
Any of various evergreen trees of the genus *Garcinia* (family Guttiferae), which are native to the tropics of Asia, Africa, and Polynesia, and include the mangosteen, *G. mangostana*.

garçon /ɡarsɔ̃/ *noun.* Pl. pronounced same. E17.
[ORIGIN French, lit. 'boy'.]
A waiter in a French hotel or restaurant.

garçonnière /ɡarsɔnjɛːr/ *noun.* Pl. pronounced same. E20.
[ORIGIN French.]
A bachelor's set of rooms or flat.

Garda /ˈɡɑːdə/ *noun.* Pl. **-dai** /-diː/, **-s**. E20.
[ORIGIN Irish *Garda Síochána* Civic Guard.]
1 The state police force of the Republic of Ireland. E20.
2 A member of the Garda; an Irish police officer. M20.

garde champêtre /ɡard ʃɑ̃pɛːtr/ *noun phr.* Pl. **-s -s** (pronounced same). E19.
[ORIGIN French, lit. 'rural guard'.]
In France: a rural police officer; a gamekeeper.

garde-du-corps /ɡardədykɔːr/ *noun.* Pl. ***gardes-*** (pronounced same). M17.
[ORIGIN French.]
A bodyguard; a member of a bodyguard.

Garde Mobile /ɡard mɔbil/ *noun phr.* Pl. **-s -s** (pronounced same). M19.
[ORIGIN French, lit. 'mobile guard'.]
A French military force, now chiefly engaged in police activity; a member of this force.

garden /ˈɡɑːd(ə)n/ *noun.* ME.
[ORIGIN Old Northern French *gardin* var. of Old French & mod. French *jardin*, from Proto-Romance, from Germanic: cf. YARD *noun*¹.]
1 A piece of ground (often enclosed) where fruits, flowers, herbs, or vegetables are cultivated; without specification *esp.* one adjoining a house or other residential building. With specifying noun *esp.* an area of this kind where the specified plants are grown, with the specified function or central feature, or in the specified place. ME. ▸**b** *transf.* A region of great fertility. L16.

V. BRITTAIN A gracious little garden where lilac and laburnum and pink hawthorn were already in flower.

flower garden, *herb garden*, *kitchen garden*, *market garden*, *rock garden*, *roof garden*, *rose garden*, *water garden*, etc.
2 An enclosed piece of ground or (now, chiefly *US*) a large building where public entertainment is provided or where refreshments are served; *sing.* & in *pl.*, a park or grounds ornamented with plants and trees or with other displays or exhibits for public recreation. Usu. with specification of the type of entertainment, refreshment, or display provided. L16.
bear garden, *beer garden*, *botanic garden(s)*, *tea garden*, *zoological garden(s)*, etc.
3 (**G-**.) *sing.* & (usu.) in *pl.* A street, square, etc., with or near gardens, *esp.* one in which the buildings overlook private communal gardens. Freq. in proper names. M18.
Crown Gardens, *Spring Gardens*, etc.
– PHRASES ETC.: *common or garden*: see COMMON *adjective*. *cultivate one's garden*. **everything in the garden is lovely** all is well. *garden of Eden*. *lead up the garden*: see LEAD *verb*¹. **the Garden** (*a*) the area of Covent Garden in London; (*b*) the philosophy or school of Epicurus (Greek philosopher who taught in a garden). **the garden of England**: *spec.* (*a*) Kent; (*b*) the Vale of Evesham. *garden of* REMEMBRANCE. *winter garden*: see WINTER *noun*.
– ATTRIB. & COMB.: Designating a plant, vegetable, etc. that is grown in the garden or cultivated (often opp. to 'wild') as *garden lettuce*, *garden rocket*, *garden thyme*, etc. Special combs., as *garden balsam*: see BALSAM *noun* 6; **garden carpet** (*a*) a grey and brown geometrid moth, *Xanthorhoe fluctuata*; (*b*) a Persian carpet with a formal design of plants and animals; **garden centre** a (usu. specialist) establishment where gardening tools, plants, etc., are sold; **garden chafer** a small brown and metallic-green chafer, *Phyllopertha horticola*, which sometimes swarms in sunshine and may damage pasture and fruit crops; **garden chair**: for use in a garden; **garden city** a town or part of a town of limited size, located in or laid out systematically with spacious rural or landscaped surroundings; **garden cress** the cruciferous

plant *Lepidium sativum*, grown for its pungent seedlings, which form one of the two components of mustard and cress; **garden flat** a flat which opens on to a garden, usu. a basement flat with access to a garden at the back; **garden gnome** a figure of a gnome used as a garden ornament; **garden-house** (*a*) a house situated in or having a garden; a suburban house; (*b*) a small building in a garden; a summer house; **garden party** a party or society event held on a lawn or in a garden; **garden path** a path in a garden; ***lead up the garden-path***: see LEAD *verb*[1]; **garden pea** (*a*) any variety of pea cultivated for human consumption; (*b*) a pea canned or frozen when freshly picked; **garden-pot** †(*a*) a watering can; (*b*) a plant pot; ***garden privet***: see PRIVET 1; **garden produce** vegetables etc. from a garden; **garden roller**: for use in a garden; **garden seat**: for use in a garden; **garden snail** *Helix aspersa*, commonly found in gardens; **Garden State** *US* the state of New Jersey; **garden stuff** garden produce; **garden suburb**: laid out like a garden city; **garden valerian** a valerian, *Valeriana phu*, grown for its medicinal root; also = ***red valerian*** s.v. VALERIAN 1; cf. SETWALL 2; **garden-variety** *adjective* (*N. Amer.*) of the usual or ordinary type; commonplace; **garden village**: laid out like a garden city; **garden warbler** a small greyish-brown Eurasian warbler, *Sylvia borin*.

▪ **gardenage** *noun* horticulture; garden produce: E17. **garde'nesque** *adjective* resembling a garden or what belongs to a garden M19. **gardenful** *noun* as many or much as a garden can contain M19. **gardenist** *noun* a planner of gardens; an enthusiast for gardens: L18. **gardenless** *adjective* M19.

garden /ˈɡɑːd(ə)n/ *verb*. L16.
[ORIGIN from the noun.]
1 *verb intrans.* Cultivate a garden; work in a garden as a gardener. L16.

> E. FITZGERALD I . . read scraps of books, garden a little, and am on good terms with my neighbours.

2 *verb trans.* Cultivate as a garden. E17.
3 *verb trans.* Provide with a garden or gardens. Now *rare*. E19.
4 *verb intrans.* CRICKET. Of a batsman: smooth the pitch by cleaning away loose fragments, patting the ground flat, etc. L19.
▪ **gardening** *noun* the action of the verb; horticulture; (freq. *attrib.*): L16.

gardener /ˈɡɑːdnə/ *noun*. ME.
[ORIGIN Anglo-Norman var. of Old French *gardinier* (mod. *jardinier*), Anglo-Latin *gardinarius*: cf. GARDEN *noun* see -ER[2].]
A person who tends, cultivates, or lays out a garden; a person employed to tend and cultivate a garden. Also (more fully ***jobbing gardener***), an employee who works periodically in a garden.

> DAY LEWIS Keyes, the gardener, was digging potatoes or stooping amongst raspberry canes.

– COMB.: **gardener-bird** any of a number of bowerbirds of the genus *Amblyornis*, which make 'gardens' of moss etc. in front of their bowers; **gardener's garters** ribbon grass, *Phalaris arundinacea* var. *picta*.
▪ **gardenership** *noun* (*rare*) the position or office of a gardener M16. **gardenery** *noun* (long *rare*) gardenership M16.

gardenia /ɡɑːˈdiːnɪə/ *noun*. M18.
[ORIGIN mod. Latin (see below), from Alexander *Garden* (*c* 1730–91), Scottish-American naturalist + -IA[1].]
Any of various evergreen trees and shrubs of the tropical and subtropical African and Asiatic genus *Gardenia*, of the madder family, bearing large fragrant tubular white or yellow flowers; a flowering spray of such a shrub.

garderobe /ˈɡɑːdrəʊb/ *noun*. *obsolete* exc. *hist*. LME.
[ORIGIN French, from *garder* keep + *robe* ROBE *noun*[1]. Cf. WARDROBE.]
A storeroom, esp. for clothing or armour; a wardrobe or its contents. Also, a private room, a bedroom; a privy, a lavatory.

gardes champêtres, ***gardes-du-corps***, ***Gardes Mobiles*** *nouns* pls. of GARDE CHAMPÊTRE etc.

gardie *noun* var. of GARDY.

gardy /ˈɡɑːdi/ *noun*. *Scot.* Also **gardie**. E16.
[ORIGIN Unknown.]
An arm.

gardyloo /ɡɑːdɪˈluː/ *interjection & noun*. L18.
[ORIGIN App. from *gare de l'eau*, pseudo-Fr. for *gare l'eau* beware of the water. Cf. GARE *verb*.]
hist. Beware of the water: a warning formerly shouted in Edinburgh before dirty water or slops were thrown from a window into the street; the act of throwing out such water or slops.

gare /ɡɛː/ *noun*[1]. *rare*. M16.
[ORIGIN Anglo-Norman from Old French *gard*, *jort*.]
Coarse wool that grows on the legs of sheep.

gare /ɡaːr/ *noun*[2]. Pl. pronounced same. M19.
[ORIGIN French.]
1 A dock-basin on a river or canal. Also, a pier, a wharf. M19.
2 A railway station in France and French-speaking countries. L19.

gare /ɡaːr/ *verb intrans.* (*imper.*). M17.
[ORIGIN French, imper. of *garer*: see GARAGE *noun*.]
Look out! Beware! Take care.

garefowl /ˈɡɛːfaʊl/ *noun*. Also †**gairfowl**. L17.
[ORIGIN Old Norse *geirfugl* (Faroese *gorfuglur*, Swedish *garfogl*), perh. from *geirr* spear + *fugl* bird, FOWL *noun*. Cf. GYRFALCON.]
The great auk, *Pinguinus impennis*.

garfish /ˈɡɑːfɪʃ/ *noun*. Pl. **-es** /-ɪz/, (usu.) same. Cf. GAR *noun*, GARPIKE. LME.
[ORIGIN App. from Old English *gār* spear + FISH *noun*[1].]
Any of various fishes of the family Belonidae, with slender bodies and long spearlike snouts (also called ***needlefish***); esp. *Belone belone*, of the N. Atlantic Ocean and Mediterranean and Black Seas. Also, any of certain other fishes of similar form: (*a*) any of various mainly freshwater fishes of the genus *Lepisosteus* and family Lepisosteidae, found in Central and North America; (*b*) a halfbeak.

garganey /ˈɡɑːɡ(ə)ni/ *noun*. M17.
[ORIGIN Italian dial. *garganei*, imit.]
A migratory Palaearctic duck, *Anas querquedula*, similar to the teal, the male of which has a broad white stripe above the eye.

gargantuan /ɡɑːˈɡantjʊən/ *adjective*. L16.
[ORIGIN from *Gargantua* the large-mouthed voracious giant in Rabelais's book of the same name + -AN.]
Enormous, gigantic.

> A. STORR These frugal periods alternated with gargantuan feasts.

gargarism /ˈɡɑːɡərɪz(ə)m/ *noun*. Long *rare* or *obsolete*. LME.
[ORIGIN Late Latin *gargarisma*, *-mum* from Greek *gargarismos* gargle from *gargarizein*: see GARGOYLE.]
1 A gargle. LME.
†**2** A disease of the throat which attacks swine. Only in 17.

garget /ˈɡɑːɡɪt/ *noun*. ME.
[ORIGIN Old French *gargate*, *garguete* throat from Provençal *gargata* rel. to Latin *gargarizare*: see GARGOYLE.]
†**1** The throat. Only in ME.
2 An inflammation of the head or throat in cattle, pigs, or poultry. *arch.* L16.
3 An inflammation of the udder (mastitis) in domestic animals; *esp.* persistent bovine mastitis with gross changes in the form and texture of the udder. E18.
4 In full ***garget plant***, ***garget root***. Pokeweed, *Phytolacca americana*. *US*. L18.

†**gargil** *noun*. M16.
[ORIGIN Old French *gargouille* throat: see GARGOYLE.]
1 The gullet. M16–E18.
2 = GARGET 2. E17–M18.
3 = GARGET 3. M18–L19.

gargle /ˈɡɑːɡ(ə)l/ *noun*. M17.
[ORIGIN from the verb.]
1 A liquid used for gargling. M17.
2 A sound (as) of gargling. M19.

> *Guardian* With a throaty gargle of a laugh.

3 An act of gargling; *slang* an act of drinking, a drink. L19.

gargle /ˈɡɑːɡ(ə)l/ *verb*. E16.
[ORIGIN French *gargouiller* gurgle, bubble, from *gargouille* throat: see GARGOYLE.]
1 *verb trans. & intrans.* Keep (a liquid) suspended and in motion in the throat by means of the breath, esp. for medicinal purposes. Also, wash (the throat or mouth) in this way. E16.

> W. COLES The decoction of mint gargled in the mouth, cureth the Gums. A. BURGESS She made me gargle with chloride of lime.

2 *verb trans. & intrans.* Utter with or make a gargle or gargling sound. M17. ▸**b** *verb intrans.* Drink. *slang*. L19.

> W. OWEN If you could hear . . the blood Come gargling from the froth-corrupted lungs.

gargouillade /ɡarɡujad/ *noun*. Pl. pronounced same. M20.
[ORIGIN French, from *gargouiller*: see GARGLE *verb*.]
BALLET. A series of steps in which the left leg describes two circular movements in the air, before the left foot is drawn up to the right knee.

gargoyle /ˈɡɑːɡɔɪl/ *noun*. ME.
[ORIGIN Old French *gargouille* throat, in a spec. sense from the water passing through the mouth of the figure, rel. to Latin *gargarizare* gargle, from Greek *gargarizein*, of imit. origin.]
A grotesque carving usu. in the form of a human or animal mouth, head, or body, projecting from the gutter of a building, esp. in Gothic architecture, and usu. acting as a spout to drain off rainwater.

> *Daily Telegraph* Police talked him down from the roof of Amiens Cathedral . . . He had been balancing . . near a gargoyle. *transf.*: LONGFELLOW A tall brass candlestick with gruesome gargoyles carved on the base. C. RAINE An old tormented master . . screaming like a gargoyle.

gargoylism /ˈɡɑːɡɔɪlɪz(ə)m/ *noun*. E20.
[ORIGIN from GARGOYLE + -ISM.]
1 Grotesqueness. *rare*. E20.
2 MEDICINE. Hurler's disease (see HURLER *noun*[2]). *arch.* E20.

gari *noun* var. of GARRI.

garibaldi /ɡarɪˈbɔːldi, -ˈbaldi/ *noun*. Also **G-**. M19.
[ORIGIN *Garibaldi*, Italian patriot, general, and statesman (1807–82).]
1 A kind of loose blouse formerly worn by women and children, orig. of a bright red colour like the shirts worn by Garibaldi and his followers. M19.
2 A bright orange-red damselfish, *Hypsypops rubicundus*, of the Californian coast. L19.
3 More fully ***garibaldi biscuit***. A thin biscuit containing a compressed layer of currants. L19.

Garibaldian /ɡarɪˈbɔːldɪən, -ˈbaldɪən/ *adjective & noun*. M19.
[ORIGIN from *Garibaldi* (see GARIBALDI) + -AN.]
▸ **A** *adjective*. Of, pertaining to, or supporting Garibaldi (1807–82). M19.
▸ **B** *noun*. A supporter of Garibaldi. M19.

garigue /ɡariɡ/ *noun*. Also **-rr-**. Pl. pronounced same. L19.
[ORIGIN French.]
In the south of France: uncultivated land of a calcareous soil overgrown with low scrub; the vegetation found on such land.

garimpeiro /ɡarĩˈpeiru/ *noun*. Pl. **-os** /-uʃ/. M19.
[ORIGIN Portuguese.]
In Brazil: an independent prospector for diamonds, gold, etc.

garish /ˈɡɛːrɪʃ/ *adjective*. M16.
[ORIGIN Unknown.]
1 Of dress, ornament, ceremonial, etc.: gaudy, bright, showy. M16.

> DICKENS All sorts of garish triumphal arches were put up.

2 Of colour or light: excessively bright, glaring. M16.

> *Successful Slimming* I tend to go for muted colours rather than anything garish.

▪ **garishly** *adverb* L16. **garishness** *noun* L16.

garland /ˈɡɑːlənd/ *noun*. ME.
[ORIGIN Old French *gerlande*, *garlande* of unknown origin.]
1 A wreath of flowers, leaves, etc., worn on the head or around the neck, or hung about an object for decoration. ME. ▸**b** A naturally growing loop or wreath of vegetation. M19. ▸**c** Chiefly NAUTICAL. A wreath of ribbons. M19.

> W. MORRIS Round about her shapely head A garland of dog-violet . . meetly had she set. M. CONEY Cat-girls had hung garlands of flowers around the captains' necks. *fig.*: TENNYSON Where Past and Present, wound in one, Do make a garland for the heart. **b** F. A. KEMBLE An ivy . . growing in profuse garlands from branch to branch.

virgin's garland: see VIRGIN *noun*.
2 A wreath or coronet of gold, silver, or some other costly material. *obsolete* exc. *hist.* ME.
3 †**a** A royal crown or diadem. ME–E17. ▸**b** Orig., a wreath or crown conferred on a victor or hero, esp. in the games of ancient Greece or Rome. Now also more widely, a prize, a distinction. LME. ▸†**c** *fig.* A person, thing, quality, etc., regarded as the glory or most prized part of something. L16–M17.
b gain the garland, **win the garland**, etc., gain the victory.
4 A circular object, *esp.* one which surrounds another object; *spec.* (ARCHITECTURE) an ornamental band around a spire. L15.
5 a NAUTICAL. A band of rope or iron used as a securing device on a mast or spar. L15. ▸**b** NAUTICAL & MILITARY. A container for storing shot. L17.
6 A representation of a garland in metal, stone, etc. E16. ▸**b** HERALDRY. A charge representing a ring of flowers, leaves, etc.; a chaplet. E19.

> H. PHILLIPS On the reverse a garland of olives encloses the words.

7 *fig.* A collection of short literary pieces, usu. poems and ballads; an anthology, a miscellany. *arch.* E17.
▪ **garlandry** *noun* (*rare*) garlands collectively; decoration composed of or resembling garlands: M19.

garland /ˈɡɑːlənd/ *verb trans.* LME.
[ORIGIN from the noun.]
1 Form (flowers) into a garland. *rare*. LME.
2 Crown with a garland, deck with garlands. LME.

> JONSON Their hair loose, and flowing, gyrlanded with sea grass. P. V. WHITE Green was garlanding the windows, the . . balconies, the . . gateways, in celebration. *transf.*: J. HERRIOT Spareribs, onions, liver and pork . . garlanded with those divine farm sausages.

▪ **garlanding** *noun* (*a*) the action of the verb; (*b*) something which forms a garland: M19.

garled /ɡɑːld/ *adjective*. *obsolete* exc. *dial.* E16.
[ORIGIN App. from Old French *garre*, *garré* of similar meaning.]
Chiefly of cattle: spotted, speckled.

garlic /ˈɡɑːlɪk/ *noun*.
[ORIGIN Old English *gārlēac*, from *gār* spear (with ref. to the cloves of the plant) + *lēac* LEEK.]
A bulbous plant of the lily family, *Allium sativum*, grown as a herb; the strong-smelling pungent-tasting bulb of this plant (divisible into cloves or smaller bulbs) much used as a flavouring. Also (with specifying word), any of various wild plants of the genus *Allium*.
bear's garlic, ***crow garlic***, ***field garlic***, ***hedge garlic***, ***Spanish garlic***, etc. **wild garlic** any of various wild alliums, *esp.* ramsons, *Allium ursinum*.
– ATTRIB. & COMB.: In the sense 'made with or containing garlic', as ***garlic butter***, ***garlic sausage***, etc. Special combs., as **garlic bread**: spread with garlic butter and heated; **garlic mustard** a cruciferous plant, *Alliaria petiolata*, with white flowers and cordate leaves, common in shady places; also called ***hedge***

G

garlic, *Jack-by-the-hedge*; **garlic pear** any of several tropical shrubs or trees of the genus *Crateva*, of the caper family, with a smell of garlic and pear-shaped fruit; **garlic press** a device for crushing a clove or cloves of garlic.
■ **garlicky** *adjective* smelling or tasting of garlic L18.

garlits /ˈɡɑːlɪts/ *noun.* Now *rare* or *obsolete*. L17.
[ORIGIN Alt. of *Görlitz* a city in Germany and former centre of the textile industry.]
A kind of linen cloth first imported from Germany.

garment /ˈɡɑːm(ə)nt/ *noun & verb.* ME.
[ORIGIN Old French & mod. French *garnement* equipment, from *garnir* GARNISH *verb*: see -MENT.]
▸ **A** *noun.* **1** An article of dress; in *pl.*, clothes. ME.
J. A. MICHENER He wore the plain sheepskin garment of a countryman.
2 *fig.* The outward and visible covering of anything. M16.
M. L. KING Their rationalizations clothed obvious wrongs in the beautiful garments of righteousness.
▸ **B** *verb trans.* Dress, clothe. Chiefly as **garmented** *ppl adjective.* Usu. *rhet.* M16.
fig.: D. M. MOIR When the snow-mantle garments the land.
■ **garmentless** *adjective* M19.

G

garms /ɡɑːmz/ *noun pl. slang.* L20.
[ORIGIN Shortened from *garments*, pl. of GARMENT.]
Clothes, garments.

garn /ɡɑːn/ *noun. N. English.* L15.
[ORIGIN Old Norse = Old English *gearn* YARN *noun*.]
Yarn.

garn /ɡɑːn/ *interjection. colloq.* L19.
[ORIGIN Cockney alt. of *go on*.]
'Go on!': expr. disbelief, ridicule, etc.

garnacha /ɡɑːˈnatʃə/ *noun.* M19.
[ORIGIN Spanish, from Italian *vernaccia* (see VERNACCIA).]
A variety of dark wine grape grown in Spain; a sweet red or rosé wine made from this grape.

garner /ˈɡɑːnə/ *noun & verb.* ME.
[ORIGIN Anglo-Norman *gerner*, Old French *gernier* (mod. *grenier*) from Latin *granarium* GRANARY: see -ER².]
▸ **A** *noun.* A storehouse, a granary. Now *rare*. ME.
R. LLOYD Their garners bursting with their golden grain.
▸ **B** *verb.* **1** *verb trans.* Store (corn etc.) in a garner. Now chiefly *literary*. LME.
CARLYLE The harvest is reaped and garnered. TENNYSON The little pitted speck in garner'd fruit.
2 *verb trans.* Collect or deposit as in a garner; make a store of; harvest, gather. M16.
H. JAMES Any place where ancient prejudices are garnered up. B. PLAIN As for enemies, you could hardly get through life . . without garnering some. N. GORDIMER When her hands were full, she dropped what she had garnered.
3 *verb intrans.* Accumulate, be stored up. *rare*. M19.
TENNYSON On Death I wreak The wrath that garners in my heart.

garnet /ˈɡɑːnɪt/ *noun*¹. ME.
[ORIGIN Prob. from Middle Dutch *gernate*, *garnate* from Old French & mod. French *grenat* from medieval Latin *granatus*, perh. a transf. use of *granatum* POMEGRANATE. Cf. GRANATE *noun*¹.]
Any of a large group of usu. red, yellow, or green silicate minerals which occur widely as components of rocks, crystallize in the cubic system, and have the general formula $A_3B_2(SiO_4)_3$, where A and B are respectively di- and trivalent metals; *esp.* a deep-red glassy form of this occurring as large crystals; a gem consisting of this.
■ **garneˈtiferous** *adjective* (of a rock) containing or yielding garnets M19.

garnet /ˈɡɑːnɪt/ *noun*². Now *rare* or *obsolete* exc. in CROSS-GARNET. ME.
[ORIGIN Uncertain: perh. from dim. of Old Northern French *carne* hinge from Latin *cardinem*.]
= CROSS-GARNET.

garnet /ˈɡɑːnɪt/ *noun*³. L15.
[ORIGIN Prob. from Dutch *garnaat*: ult. origin unknown.]
NAUTICAL. A tackle used in a square-rigged ship for hoisting provisions and light cargo on board.

Garnet *noun*⁴ var. of GARNETT.

Garnett /ˈɡɑːnɪt/ *noun & verb.* Also **-et** (as verb infl. **-tt-**). L19.
[ORIGIN The surname *Garnett*.]
▸ **A** *noun.* A carding machine for the preparation of woollen waste. L19.
▸ **B** *verb trans.* Prepare (woollen waste) by means of a Garnett. L19.

garnierite /ˈɡɑːnɪərʌɪt, ɡɑːˈnɪərʌɪt/ *noun.* L19.
[ORIGIN from Jules *Garnier* (?1839–1904), French geologist + -ITE¹.]
MINERALOGY. A green amorphous mineral of the serpentine series, consisting of hydrated nickel magnesium silicate and constituting an important ore of nickel.

garnish /ˈɡɑːnɪʃ/ *noun.* LME.
[ORIGIN from the verb.]
†**1** A set of vessels for use at table. LME–L17.
2 †**a** Trimming for articles of dress; material used for this. E–M16. ▸**b** *gen.* Embellishment, decoration; a decoration, an ornament. Now usu. regarded as *fig.* use of sense 5 below. E17.
†**3** Outfit, dress. *rare* (Shakes.). Only in L16.
4 Money extorted from a new prisoner as a jailer's fee or a drink allowance for other prisoners. *slang. obsolete* exc. *hist.* L16. ▸**b** Money extorted from a (new) labourer to pay for drink for other labourers. M18.
5 COOKERY. A decorative or savoury addition to a prepared dish of food. Formerly also, a side dish. E17.

garnish /ˈɡɑːnɪʃ/ *verb trans.* LME.
[ORIGIN Old French & mod. French *garniss-* lengthened stem of *garnir*, *guarnir* from Germanic verb prob. rel. to base of WARN *verb*¹: see -ISH².]
▸ **I** Supply, equip.
†**1** Equip (a place) with means of defence; garrison. LME–M19.
†**2** Equip or arm (oneself). LME–M18. ▸**b** In *pass.* Be provided *with* a retinue; be accompanied. L15–E17.
3 Fit out, esp. with something that beautifies; decorate, ornament, embellish. (Foll. by *with*.) Now usu. regarded as *fig.* use of sense 5 below. LME. ▸†**b** Dress, clothe, esp. elegantly. E–M16.
SIR W. SCOTT An under tunic of dark purple silk, garnished with furs. D. L. SAYERS Uncle Delagardie made a speech, garnished with flowers of French eloquence.
†**4** Adorn with a commendable or excellent quality. LME–L16.
5 COOKERY. Decorate (a dish of food) for presentation at table. L17.
H. GLASSE Garnish the dish with lemon, and send it to table.
▸ **II** LAW. **6** Serve notice on (a person) for the purpose of legally seizing money belonging to a debtor or defendant; legally seize (money owed by a debtor) from the keeping of a third party. LME.
■ **garnished** *ppl adjective* †(**a**) garrisoned; (**b**) equipped, decorated, ornamented; (**c**) HERALDRY (of a charge) provided with decorations etc. of a different (specified) tincture: LME. **garnisher** *noun* (*rare*) a person who garnishes E16. **garnishing** *noun* (**a**) the action of the verb; (**b**) a furnishing, a decoration; a garnish: LME.

garnishee /ɡɑːnɪˈʃiː/ *noun & verb.* E17.
[ORIGIN from GARNISH *verb* II + -EE¹.]
LAW. ▸**A** *noun.* **1** A third party required to surrender money belonging to a debtor or defendant in compliance with a court order obtained by the creditor or plaintiff. E17.
2 The legal process of recovering a debt by serving a garnishee order; an instance of this. E20.
– COMB.: **garnishee order**, **garnishee proceedings**: requiring a garnishee to surrender money that he or she holds on behalf of or owes to a debtor.
▸ **B** *verb trans.* Pa. t. & pple **-sheed**. Recover a debt from (a person, his or her wages, etc.) by garnishee proceedings. L19.

garnishment /ˈɡɑːnɪʃm(ə)nt/ *noun.* E16.
[ORIGIN from GARNISH *verb* + -MENT.]
1 LAW. A legal notice, *esp.* one seizing the money owed by a debtor and in the keeping of a third party. E16.
2 Ornament, decoration. M16.

garniture /ˈɡɑːnɪtʃə/ *noun.* L15.
[ORIGIN French, from *garnir* GARNISH *verb*.]
1 Embellishment, decoration; *esp.* ornament or trimming of dress. L15.
F. NORRIS Minna's silk dress, with its garniture of lace, its edging of velvet.
2 Apparel, equipment, appurtenances. M16. ▸**b** Trappings or harness of a horse etc. *rare*. L17. ▸**c** Costume, dress. *rare*. E19.
3 COOKERY. A garnish, a trimming for a prepared dish of food. E18.

garnwindle /ˈɡɑːnwɪnd(ə)l/ *noun. obsolete* exc. *dial.* LME.
[ORIGIN from GARN *noun* + as WINDLE *noun*¹.]
An appliance for winding yarn or thread.

Garo /ˈɡɑːrəʊ/ *noun & adjective.* L19.
[ORIGIN from the *Garo* Hills, Assam.]
▸ **A** *noun.* Pl. **-os**, same.
1 A member of one of a group of people of the Garo Hills, Assam. L19.
2 The Sino-Tibetan language of this people. L19.
▸ **B** *attrib.* or as *adjective*. Of or pertaining to the Garos or their language. L19.

garotte *noun, verb* vars. of GARROTTE *noun, verb*.

garpike /ˈɡɑːpʌɪk/ *noun.* L18.
[ORIGIN from GAR *noun* + PIKE *noun*³.]
= GARFISH.

garret /ˈɡarət, -ɪt/ *noun.* ME.
[ORIGIN Old French *garite* watchtower (mod. *guérite*), from *garir*: see GARRISON.]
†**1** A turret projecting from the top of a tower or from the parapet of a fortification; a watchtower. ME–L16.
2 A (wretched) room or apartment on the top floor of a house, *esp.* one partly or wholly within the roof; an attic. ME.
G. GISSING We . . lost everything, and we had to go and live in a garret. *attrib.*: R. COTGRAVE A garret window, or window in the roofe of a house.
3 The head. *slang*. Now *rare*. L18.
■ **garreˈteer** *noun* a person who lives in a garret; *esp.* an impecunious author or literary hack: E18. **garreted** *adjective* having a garret or garrets M16.

garret /ˈɡarət, -ɪt/ *verb trans.* Infl. **-t(t)-**. M19.
[ORIGIN Prob. alt. of GALLET *verb*.]
BUILDING. = GALLET *verb*.
■ **garreting** *noun* (**a**) the action of the verb; (**b**) = GALLET *noun*: M19.

garri /ˈɡari/ *noun.* Also **gari**. E20.
[ORIGIN from a W. African lang.]
In W. Africa, = CASSAVA 2.

garrigue *noun* var. of GARIGUE.

garrison /ˈɡarɪs(ə)n/ *noun & verb.* ME.
[ORIGIN Old French *garison* defence, safety, provision, store, from *garir* defend, furnish, from Germanic.]
▸ **A** *noun.* †**1** Store, treasure; a gift. Only in ME.
†**2** Defence; safety; a means of protection. ME–E17.
3 A body of troops stationed in a fortress, town, etc., esp. for defensive purposes. LME.
S. RUSHDIE A string of border posts, each with its lonely garrison of six men.
in garrison serving as (a member of) a garrison.
4 A place or building in which troops are quartered in a fortress, town, etc., esp. for defensive purposes; a garrison town. Formerly also, a fortress. LME.
W. ROBERTSON Werk Castle, a garrison of the English.
– COMB.: **garrison cap** *US* a peakless cap, esp. one worn as part of a military uniform; **garrison town**: having a permanent garrison.
▸ **B** *verb trans.* **1** Provide with or occupy as a garrison. M16.
C. THIRLWALL He fortified the citadel and garrisoned the port. W. S. CHURCHILL Visiting the townships and posts garrisoned by the Spaniards.
2 Station (a body of troops) as a garrison; place on duty as a garrison. L16.
SPENSER I would wish the chief power of the armye to be garrisoned in one countrey.

Garrisonian /ɡarɪˈsəʊnɪən/ *adjective & noun.* M19.
[ORIGIN from W. L. *Garrison* (see below) + -IAN.]
▸ **A** *adjective.* Of or pertaining to W. L. Garrison (1805–79) a leader in the American anti-slavery movement, or his views; abolitionist. M19.
▸ **B** *noun.* A supporter of Garrison; an abolitionist. L19.

garrocha /ɡaˈrɒtʃa/ *noun.* M19.
[ORIGIN Spanish.]
A goad, *esp.* (in bullfighting) a short-pointed spear.

garron /ˈɡarən/ *noun.* M16.
[ORIGIN Gaelic *gearran*, Irish *gearrán*.]
(An animal of) a breed of small, sturdy workhorse originating in Ireland and Scotland.

garrotte /ɡəˈrɒt/ *noun.* Also **garotte**, ***garrote**. E17.
[ORIGIN Spanish *garrote* (orig.) cudgel, from a base perh. of Celtic origin, repr. also in Provençal *garra* kneecap, Spanish *garra* claw.]
†**1** A stick used to twist and tighten a cord securing a load. *rare*. Only in E17.
2 A method of execution by strangulation, of Spanish origin, in which an iron or wire collar is tightened around the neck; strangulation by means of a wire, cord, etc.; the apparatus, a piece of wire, etc., used for this. E17.
3 *hist.* Highway robbery in which the victim is throttled. M19.

garrotte /ɡəˈrɒt/ *verb trans.* Also **garotte**, ***garrote**. M19.
[ORIGIN French *garrotter*, from *garrot* stick, lever or Spanish *garrotear*, formed as GARROTTE *noun*.]
1 Execute by means of the garrotte. M19.
2 Throttle in order to rob. M19.
3 Strangle, choke. L19.
■ **garrotter** *noun* a person who garrottes someone M19. **garrotting** *noun* execution or robbery by garrotte M19.

garrulity /ɡaˈruːlɪti/ *noun.* L16.
[ORIGIN French †*garrulité* from Latin *garrulitas*, formed as GARRULOUS: see -ITY.]
The quality of being garrulous or wordy; loquaciousness.

garrulous /ˈɡarʊləs, -rjʊl-/ *adjective.* E17.
[ORIGIN from Latin *garrulus*, from *garrire* chatter, prattle: see -ULOUS.]
Talkative, esp. on trivial matters; loquacious; wordy, verbose.
W. BLACK The . . keeper might have kept up his garrulous talk for hours. P. G. WODEHOUSE A matter which called for silent meditation, not for chit-chat with a garrulous butler. *fig.*: TENNYSON Hear the magpie gossip Garrulous under a roof of pine.
■ **garrulously** *adverb* M19. **garrulousness** *noun* E18.

garrya /ˈɡarɪə/ *noun.* M19.
[ORIGIN mod. Latin (see below), from Nicholas *Garry* (see GARRY OAK) + -A¹.]
Any of various N. American evergreen shrubs of the genus *Garrya* (family Garryaceae), allied to the cornels, with flowers in drooping clusters resembling catkins;

esp. *G. elliptica*, native to California and Oregon. Also called ***silk-tassel* (*bush*)**, ***tassel-bush***.

Garry oak /ˈɡari əʊk/ *noun phr.* **E20.**
[ORIGIN Nicholas *Garry* (1781–1856), officer of the Hudson's Bay Company.]
An oak, *Quercus garryana*, native to the Pacific coast of N. America. Also called ***Oregon oak***.

garryowen /ɡarɪˈəʊɪn/ *noun.* **M20.**
[ORIGIN An Irish rugby club in Limerick.]
RUGBY. An up-and-under.

†garse *noun, verb*, **†garsh**, *noun, verb* see GASH *noun*[1], *verb*.

Garshuni /ɡɑːˈʃuːni/ *noun.* Also **C-**, **K-**. **M19.**
[ORIGIN (Arabic *karšūnī*) from Syriac *garšūnī*.]
Arabic written in Syriac characters.

garter /ˈɡɑːtə/ *noun.* Also (*Scot.*) **-ten** /-t(ə)n/. **ME.**
[ORIGIN Old French *gartier* var. of *jartier* (also *jartière*, mod. *jarretière*), from *garet*, *jaret* bend of the knee, calf of the leg, prob. of Celtic origin: cf. GARROTTE *noun*.]
1 A band worn round the leg to keep a sock or stocking up; *US* a suspender. **ME.** ▸**b** In *pl.* Fetters, irons. *nautical slang.* **L18.**

E. LINKLATER Rosy, with shoes and garters already gone, was pulling off a stocking.

cast one's garter *Scot.* (now *rare*) secure a husband. ***have a person's guts for garters***: see GUT *noun*.
2 *The Garter*: the badge of the highest order of British knighthood, the Order of the Garter, consisting of a dark blue velvet ribbon trimmed with gold, worn below the left knee by men and on the left arm by women; also, membership of this order; the order itself. **LME.**

N. MITFORD His long thin legs in silk stockings and knee breeches, the Garter round one . . its ribbon across his shirt front.

3 *HERALDRY.* In full ***Garter King of Arms***. (The title of) the principal King of Arms of the College of Arms. **LME.**
4 A band resembling a garter in shape or function. **M16.** ▸**b** *spec.* The belt or band used in the cheating game of prick (in) the garter (see below); the game itself; a person who plays this game. **M18.**
fly-the-garter: see FLY *verb*. **b prick in the garter**, **prick the garter** (*a*) the old cheating game fast and loose; (*b*) a confidence trick.
5 *HERALDRY.* A bendlet; a charge representing a garter. **M17.**
6 = ***garter snake*** below. **L19.**
– COMB.: **garter belt** *N. Amer.* a suspender belt; **garter blue** *noun & adjective* (of) the colour (orig. pale, now dark blue) of the ribbon worn by Knights of the Garter; **garter snake** (*a*) any of several harmless, viviparous, largely semi-aquatic colubrid snakes of the genus *Thamnophis*, often with more or less distinct longitudinal stripes on the back, widespread in N. America; (*b*) any of various banded venomous elapid snakes of southern and tropical Africa; **garter stitch** the simplest knitting stitch, forming ridges in alternate rows, and orig. used in making garters; plain stitch; **garter-webbing** narrow elastic webbing used for garters.

garter /ˈɡɑːtə/ *verb trans.* Also (*Scot.*) **-ten** /-t(ə)n/. **LME.**
[ORIGIN from the noun.]
1 Tie (*on*, *up*) with a garter; encircle with a garter. **LME.**
†2 Bandage tightly. **L16–L17.**
3 Fetter. Long *rare*. **E17.**

gartered /ˈɡɑːtəd/ *adjective.* **E17.**
[ORIGIN from GARTER *noun*, *verb*: see -ED[2], -ED[1] and cf. earlier UNGARTERED.]
1 Wearing a garter; *esp.* wearing the badge of the Order of the Garter. **E17.**

POPE In this hall . . have dined gartered knights and courtly dames.

2 That has been gartered; tied with a garter. **M18.**
3 *HERALDRY.* Surrounded by a garter. **E19.**

gartering /ˈɡɑːt(ə)rɪŋ/ *noun.* **E16.**
[ORIGIN from GARTER *verb* + -ING[1].]
1 The action of GARTER *verb*; an instance of this. **E16.**
2 The material of which garters are made; in *pl.*, garters. **L16.**

garth /ɡɑːθ/ *noun*[1]. Now *arch.* & *N. English*. **ME.**
[ORIGIN Old Norse *garðr* = Old English *geard* YARD *noun*[1].]
1 A small area of enclosed ground, esp. beside a house or other building, used as a yard, garden, or paddock. **ME.** ▸**b** A cloister-garth. **L19.**
2 A fence, a hedge. Now chiefly *hist.* **ME.**
3 A fishgarth. **E17.**

garth /ɡɑːθ/ *noun*[2]. *N. English*. **LME.**
[ORIGIN Alt. of GIRTH *noun*[1].]
1 A saddle-girth. **LME.**
2 A (wooden) hoop, esp. for a barrel. **LME.**
3 Girth or measurement, esp. of a fighting cock. Now *rare* or *obsolete*. **L17.**

Gartner /ˈɡɑːtnə/ *noun.* **L19.**
[ORIGIN Herman T. *Gartner* (1785–1827), Danish anatomist.]
ANATOMY. ***Gartner's duct***, ***duct of Gartner***, a vestigial part of the mesonephric duct present in some female mammals.
■ **Gartnerian** /ɡɑːtˈnɪərɪən/ *adjective* (of a cyst) originating in Gartner's duct **E20.**

garuda /ˈɡarʊdə/ *noun.* **L19.**
[ORIGIN Sanskrit *garuḍa*.]
INDIAN MYTHOLOGY. A fabulous bird, half-eagle, half-man, ridden by the god Vishnu.

garum /ˈɡɛːrəm/ *noun.* **L16.**
[ORIGIN Latin from Greek *garon* earlier *garos*.]
hist. A sauce made from fermented fish, popular in ancient Rome; this sauce used as a medicine for horses.

gas /ɡas/ *noun*[1]. Pl. **gases** /ˈɡasɪz/. **M17.**
[ORIGIN Invented by J. B. van Helmont (1577–1644), Belgian chemist, after Greek *khaos* chaos, Dutch *g* representing Greek *kh*.]
1 An occult principle supposed to be contained in all bodies, and to represent an ultra-rarefied condition of water. Long *obsolete* exc. *hist.* **M17.**
2 Any airlike fluid that can change its volume indefinitely, *esp.* one that does not become liquid or solid at ordinary temperatures (cf. ***vapour***); any substance normally existing in this state. **E18.**
bottled gas, ***coal gas***, ***exhaust gas***, ***harassing gas***, ***ideal gas***, ***inert gas***, ***marsh gas***, ***mustard gas***, ***natural gas***, ***nerve gas***, ***noble gas***, ***producer gas***, ***rare gas***, ***tear gas***, ***town gas***, ***water gas***, etc.
3 *spec.* ▸**a** Such a substance, usu. a hydrocarbon or hydrocarbon mixture, suitable for burning in order to provide heat, light, or power. **L18.** ▸**b** Hydrogen, helium, or other substance used to fill a balloon or airship. **L18.** ▸**c** *MINING.* An explosive mixture of firedamp (methane) and air. **M19.** ▸**d** = ***laughing gas*** s.v. LAUGHING *noun*. **L19.** ▸**e** Vapour generated in the alimentary canal; wind. Chiefly *N. Amer.* **L19.** ▸**f** Any of various gases or vapours used in warfare to disable the enemy by poisoning, asphyxiation, irritation, etc. Also ***poison gas***. **E20.**

e P. BARRY Baby better. It was only gas.

4 A jet or jets of flammable gas, used for lighting, cooking, etc.; the supply of gas to a house etc. **M19.**
5 a Pointless idle talk; a chat; boasting, humbug, nonsense. *slang.* **M19.** ▸**b** Fun; a joke. *Irish colloq.*. **E20.** ▸**c** A person who or thing which is very attractive, exciting, impressive, etc. *slang.* **M20.**

R. W. EMERSON Lord Shaftesbury . . reads sermons to them, and they call it 'gas'. DAY LEWIS The sisters would sit . . shelling peas and having a great old gas. **b** B. BEHAN Someone was imitating my accent, and getting great gas out of it. **c** E. JONG Isn't that interesting? . . Isn't that a gas?

all gas and gaiters, **gas and gaiters** *slang* (*a*) a satisfactory state of affairs; (*b*) pomposity, verbosity.
– ATTRIB. & COMB.: In the sense 'using gas as a fuel', as ***gas cooker***, ***gas engine***, ***gas fire***, ***gas lamp***, ***gas motor***, ***gas range*** (*N. Amer.*), ***gas stove***, ***gas welding***, etc.; ***gas-fired*** *adjective*. Special combs., as **gas alarm** an alarm device: (*a*) giving warning of the presence of esp. poisonous gas; (*b*) operated by gas; **gas black** a pigment made of carbon produced by the burning of gas; **gas bracket** a (usu. decorative) projecting metal pipe supporting and supplying a gas lamp or burner; **gas centrifuge** a centrifuge for partially separating gases (esp. gaseous compounds of different isotopes of the same element); **gas chamber** an airtight chamber used for killing people or animals by gas poisoning; **gas chromatography** a method of chromatography in which the moving phase is a carrier gas (cf. ***gas-liquid chromatography*** below); **gas coal** bituminous coal used in the manufacture of coal gas; **gas constant** (*PHYSICAL CHEMISTRY*) the constant of proportionality, R (= 8.314 joule kelvin^{-1} mole^{-1}), in the gas equation (see below); **gas-cooled** *adjective* (of an engine, nuclear reactor, etc.) cooled by a current of gas; **gas engine** an internal-combustion engine using gas as fuel; **gas equation** (*PHYSICAL CHEMISTRY*) the equation of state of an ideal gas, $PV = nRT$, where P = pressure, V = volume, T = absolute temperature, R = the gas constant (see above), and n = the number of moles of gas; **gas-fitter** a person who installs and services gas fittings; **gas fittings** the apparatus used for heating etc. with gas; **gas gangrene**: resulting from infection by *Clostridium welchii* or a similar bacterium and characterized by the generation of gas; **gas giant** *ASTRONOMY* a large planet composed mostly of gaseous material (usu. surrounding a solid core); *spec.* any of the four largest planets in the Solar System, Jupiter, Saturn, Uranus, or Neptune; **gas gland**: secreting gas; **gas gun**: using gas as a propellant or as fuel; **gas helmet**: worn as protection against (poison) gas; **gasholder** a large structure for storing gas, a gasometer; **gas-house** (chiefly *US*) (a building forming part of) a gasworks; ***gas kinetics***: see KINETICS 2; **gas laws** *PHYSICAL CHEMISTRY* a set of laws (e.g. Boyle's, Charles', Graham's laws) that describe the physical properties of gases; **gaslight** light given off by burning (esp. coal) gas; a jet of burning gas; a gas lamp; **gas lighter** (*a*) a device for igniting gas; (*b*) a cigarette lighter with gaseous fuel; **gas-liquid chromatography** gas chromatography in which the stationary phase is liquid; **gas main** a main pipe supplying gas to a building or buildings; ***gas mantle***: see MANTLE *noun* 6; **gas mask** an appliance including a respirator worn over the face as a defence against poisonous gas; **gas meter** an apparatus recording the amount of gas consumed; **gas oil** petroleum distillate intermediate in viscosity and boiling point between paraffin (kerosene) and lubricating oils; **gas oven** (*a*) an oven heated by gas; (*b*) = ***gas chamber*** above; **gas-permeable** *adjective* (of a contact lens) allowing the diffusion of gases into and out of the cornea; **gas plant** = FRAXINELLA; **gas poker** a perforated hollow poker through which gas flows to be ignited and so provide heat to kindle a fire; ***gas producer***: see PRODUCER 3; **gas ring** a perforated hollow ring supplied with gas and on which a pan etc. can be heated; **gas thread** a standard form of screw thread of relatively fine pitch, used on metal tubes; ***gas trap***: see TRAP *noun*[1] 6c; **gas turbine**: driven by a flow of gas or by gas produced from combustion; **gasworks** a building or buildings where gas is manufactured.
■ **gasless** *adjective* without gas; not lighted by gas: **M19.**

gas /ɡas/ *noun*[2]. *N. Amer.* **E20.**
[ORIGIN Abbreviation.]
= GASOLINE.
give it the gas, **give her the gas**, **step on the gas** accelerate a car etc. by pressing down on the accelerator; *fig.* hurry.
– COMB.: **gas boat**: driven by a petrol engine; **gas guzzler** *N. Amer. slang* a motor vehicle, esp. a large car, that uses fuel extravagantly; **gas pedal** the accelerator in a car etc.; **gas station** a filling station.

gas /ɡas/ *verb*[1]. Infl. **-ss-**. **M19.**
[ORIGIN from GAS *noun*[1].]
1 *verb trans.* Pass (a fabric) through a gas flame to remove superfluous fibres. **M19.**
2 a *verb trans.* Deceive by idle or boastful talk. *colloq.* **M19.** ▸**b** *verb intrans.* Talk idly or boastfully. *colloq.* **M19.** ▸**c** *verb trans.* Excite, thrill, impress. *slang* (orig. *US*). **M20.**

b M. GORDON All those others gassing on about volume and the picture plane. S. KING Sometimes he couldn't tell when Mary was serious and when she was just gassing. **c** L. ARMSTRONG Just the same the game gassed me.

3 *verb trans.* Supply with gas; *spec.* inflate (an airship) with gas. **L19.**
4 *verb trans.* Expose to gas, esp. deliberately so as to cause death, injury, or unconsciousness. (Earlier as GASSED *ppl adjective* 1.) **E20.**

H. WILLIAMSON Phillip wondered if he had been gassed, for his face was the colour of rotten eggs.

5 *verb intrans.* Of a storage battery or dry cell: give off gas. **E20.**

gas /ɡas/ *verb*[2] *trans. & intrans. colloq.* (chiefly *N. Amer.*). Infl. **-ss-**. **M20.**
[ORIGIN from GAS *noun*[2].]
Fill (*up*) the tank of (a car etc.) with petrol.

gasbag /ˈɡasbaɡ/ *noun.* **E19.**
[ORIGIN from GAS *noun*[1] + BAG *noun*.]
1 A bag for holding gas; *esp.* (the gas container of) an airship or balloon. **E19.**
2 An empty or idle talker. *colloq.* **L19.**

S. BELLOW It's just as Thompson says. He's a big gasbag, but this time it's true.

Gascon /ˈɡask(ə)n/ *noun & adjective.* **ME.**
[ORIGIN Old French & mod. French from Latin *Vasco*, *-on-*, whence also BASQUE.]
▸ **A** *noun.* **1** A native of Gascony, a former province in SW France. **ME.** ▸**b** A braggart, a boaster. **L18.**
†2 Wine from Gascony. **LME–M17.**
3 The dialect of Gascony. **E19.**
▸ **B** *attrib.* or as *adjective*. Of or pertaining to Gascony. **LME.**

gasconade /ɡaskəˈneɪd/ *noun & verb.* **M17.**
[ORIGIN French *gasconnade*, from *gasconner* talk like a Gascon, brag, formed as GASCON: see -ADE.]
▸ **A** *noun.* (An instance of) extravagant boasting. **M17.**

O. HENRY Whosoever entered it must sit . . and listen to the imp's interminable gasconade concerning his scandalous career.

▸ **B** *verb intrans.* [Cf. French *gasconner*.] Boast extravagantly. **E18.**

Listener Boyish, gasconading, gaily sincere, he talked easily.

■ **gasconader** *noun* a braggart **M18.**

gaseity /ɡaˈsiːɪti, -ˈseɪɪti, ˈɡas-/ *noun.* **M19.**
[ORIGIN from GASE(OUS + -ITY.]
The state of being a gas.

gaselier /ɡasəˈlɪə/ *noun.* Also **gasolier**. **M19.**
[ORIGIN from GAS *noun*[1] after CHANDELIER.]
An ornamental frame to hold gas burners, usu. hung from the ceiling of a room.

gaseosa /ɡaseˈosa, ɡasɪˈəʊsə/ *noun.* **E20.**
[ORIGIN Spanish.]
A fizzy drink; (a drink of) carbonated (mineral) water.

gaseous /ˈɡasɪəs, ˈɡeɪsɪəs/ *adjective.* **L18.**
[ORIGIN from GAS *noun*[1] after AQUEOUS: see -EOUS.]
Of the nature or form of a gas; involving or relating to a gas or gases.
■ **gaseousness** *noun* **M20.**

gash /ɡaʃ/ *noun*[1]. Also (earlier) **†garse**, **†garsh**. **ME.**
[ORIGIN Old French noun from *garcer*, *jarcer* (mod. *gercer* chap, crack). For loss of *r* cf. BASS *noun*[1], DACE. The mod. form is recorded from **M16.**]
1 A long deep cut or slash, esp. in the flesh; a cleft resembling this in any object. **ME.** ▸**b** An act of making a gash. **E19.**

R. DAHL He touched the gash that the axe had made in the wood. *fig.*: R. FRAME Under an early moon the water against the fields was like a gash of silver.

2 The mouth. *US slang.* **M19.** ▸**b** The vulva. Also, a woman. *derog. slang.* **L19.**

gash /ɡaʃ/ *noun*[2]. *slang* (orig. *NAUTICAL*). Also **gashion** /ˈɡaʃɪən/. **E20.**
[ORIGIN Uncertain: cf. GAISHEN.]
Something superfluous or extra; waste, rubbish.

gash /ɡaʃ/ *adjective*[1]. **L16.**
[ORIGIN Prob. rel. to GASHFUL and GASHLY.]
Pale or dismal in appearance.

G

gash /gaʃ/ *adjective*[2]. *Scot.* E18.
[ORIGIN Perh. from Scot. pronunc. of *sagacious* with short vowel.]
1 Sagacious, wise; dignified. E18.
2 Well-dressed, trim. L18.

gash /gaʃ/ *adjective*[3]. *slang.* M20.
[ORIGIN from GASH *noun*[2].]
Superfluous, extra, spare; free.

gash /gaʃ/ *verb trans.* Also (earlier) †**garse**, †**garsh**. LME.
[ORIGIN Old French *garcer*: see GASH *noun*[1].]
Make a deep cut or slash in (flesh, a garment, etc.); cut (a hole).

V. WOOLF Any weapon that would have gashed a hole in his father's breast and killed him. J. L. WATEN The lofty walls of their bare rooms were gashed and punctured with . . cracks and holes.

■ **gashed** *ppl adjective* (**a**) slashed, cut; †(**b**) produced by gashing: L16.

gashful /ˈgaʃfʊl, -f(ə)l/ *adjective. obsolete* exc. *dial.* E17.
[ORIGIN Perh. alt. of GHASTFUL; cf. GASH *adjective*[1], GASHLY.]
Ghastly.

gashion *noun* see GASH *noun*[2].

G

gashly /ˈgaʃli/ *adjective & adverb. obsolete* exc. *dial.* M17.
[ORIGIN Perh. alt. of GHASTLY; cf. GASHFUL, GASH *adjective*[1].]
Ghastly.

gasification /ˌgasɪfɪˈkeɪʃ(ə)n/ *noun.* E19.
[ORIGIN from GAS *noun*[1] + -I- + -FICATION.]
The process of converting into a gas. Also, treatment of a substance to yield a gaseous product; *esp.* distillation of coal to yield coal gas.

gasiform /ˈgasɪfɔːm/ *adjective.* E19.
[ORIGIN from GAS *noun*[1] + -I- + -FORM.]
In a gaseous state.

gasify /ˈgasɪfʌɪ/ *verb trans. & intrans.* E19.
[ORIGIN from GAS *noun*[1] + -I- + -FY.]
Make or become gaseous. Also, subject (coal etc.) to gasification.
■ **gasifiable** *adjective* L19. **gasifier** *noun* an apparatus for manufacturing gas L19.

gasket /ˈgaskɪt/ *noun & verb.* As noun also **-kin** /-kɪn/, †**gassit**. E17.
[ORIGIN Perh. alt. of French *garcette* little girl, thin rope, dim. of *garce* fem. of *gars* boy.]
▸ **A** *noun.* **1** *NAUTICAL.* A rope, plaited cord, or strip of canvas used to secure a sail when furled to a yard or boom. E17.
2 A strip of tow, plaited hemp, etc., for packing a piston or caulking a joint. E19.
3 A flat sheet or ring of rubber, asbestos, etc., inserted between two adjoining metal surfaces, esp. between the cylinder head and the cylinder block in an internal-combustion engine, in order to seal the joint against the pressure of gas or liquid. E20.
blow a gasket (**a**) cause or undergo the failure of a gasket; (**b**) *slang* lose one's temper.
▸ **B** *verb trans. NAUTICAL.* Fasten (a sail) with gaskets. L19.

gaskin /ˈgaskɪn/ *noun*[1]. L16.
[ORIGIN Perh. from GALLIGASKINS or from GASCON.]
†**1** *sing.* & (usu.) in *pl.* = GALLIGASKINS 1. L16–M18.
2 The muscular part of the hind leg of a horse between the stifle and the hock. M17.

gaskin *noun*[2] see GASKET.

gasman /ˈgasman/ *noun.* Pl. **-men**. E19.
[ORIGIN from GAS *noun*[1] + MAN *noun.*]
1 A man employed in the manufacture or supply of gas; *esp.* a man who installs or repairs equipment for supplying household gas, reads gas meters, etc. E19.
†**2** A man who lights gas lamps in the street; a man in charge of the gaslights in a theatre. M–L19.

gasohol /ˈgasəhɒl/ *noun.* L20.
[ORIGIN from GAS *noun*[2] + ALC)OHOL.]
A mixture of petrol and ethyl alcohol used as fuel.

gasolene *noun* var. of GASOLINE.

gasolier *noun* var. of GASELIER.

gasoline /ˈgasəliːn/ *noun.* Chiefly *N. Amer.* Also **-lene**. M19.
[ORIGIN from GAS *noun*[1] + -OL + -INE[5], -ENE.]
Orig., a petroleum distillate used for heating and lighting; gas oil. Now usu. = PETROL.

gasometer /gaˈsɒmɪtə/ *noun.* L18.
[ORIGIN French *gazomètre*, from *gaz* gas + *-mètre* -METER.]
1 *CHEMISTRY.* A vessel for holding and measuring gas. Now *rare* or *obsolete.* L18.
2 A large tank or reservoir in which gas is stored for distribution by pipes; a gasholder. E19.

gasometry /gaˈsɒmɪtri/ *noun.* L18.
[ORIGIN French *gazométrie*, formed as GASOMETER: see -METRY.]
The science of measuring gases.
■ **gasoˈmetric** *adjective* pertaining to gasometry M19.

gasp /gɑːsp/ *noun.* L16.
[ORIGIN from the verb.]
A convulsive catching of the breath from distress, exertion, surprise, etc.
last gasp the final attempt to draw breath before dying (***at the last gasp***, ***at one's last gasp***, at the point of death; *fig.* exhausted).

gasp /gɑːsp/ *verb.* LME.
[ORIGIN Old Norse *geispa* yawn, (with metathesis) from base of *geip* idle talk, *geipa* talk idly.]
1 *verb intrans.* Catch the breath with open mouth, as from exhaustion or astonishment. LME.

G. SWIFT She was gasping, her chest heaving, long jagged breaths came from her throat.

2 *verb trans.* Utter with gasps. (Foll. by *out.*) L16.
3 *verb intrans.* Pant or strain *for* air; *fig.* crave or long *for.* L16.

H. E. BATES Alex was quivering terribly all over as he gasped for his catarrh-choked breath.

– PHRASES: **gasp one's breath away**, **gasp one's breath out**, **gasp one's last**, **gasp one's life away**, **gasp one's life out** die.
■ **gasper** *noun* (**a**) a person who gasps; (**b**) *slang* a (cheap) cigarette: M19. **gaspingly** *adverb* in a gasping manner E19.

gaspacho *noun* var. of GAZPACHO.

gaspereau /ˈgaspərəʊ/ *noun. Canad.* Pl. **-eaux** /-əʊ, -əʊz/, **-eaus**. E18.
[ORIGIN Canad. French *gaspareau*, *gasparot*.]
= ALEWIFE 2.

gassed /gast/ *ppl adjective.* L19.
[ORIGIN from GAS *verb*[1] + -ED[1].]
1 Affected by poisonous gas. L19.
2 Drunk, intoxicated. *slang.* E20.

Gassendist /gaˈsɛndɪst/ *noun.* L17.
[ORIGIN from *Gassendi* (see below) + -IST.]
A follower of the French metaphysician Pierre Gassendi (1592–1655).

gasser /ˈgasə/ *noun.* L19.
[ORIGIN from GAS *verb*[1] + -ER[1].]
1 A person who is employed in gassing fabric etc. L19.
2 An outstanding or highly successful person or thing. *slang.* M20.
3 A talkative or boastful person; an idle talker. *slang.* M20.

†**gassit** *noun* see GASKET.

gassy /ˈgasi/ *adjective.* M18.
[ORIGIN from GAS *noun*[1] + -Y[1].]
1 Full of or of the nature of gas. M18.
2 (Of a person) inclined to talk idly or boastfully; (of talk) pointless, verbose. *colloq.* M19.
■ **gassiness** *noun* L19.

†**gast** *noun.* Long only *Scot.* LME–E20.
[ORIGIN from the verb.]
A fright.

†**gast** *verb & adjective.*
[ORIGIN Old English *gǣstan*, from Germanic base of GHOST *noun.*]
▸ **A** *verb trans.* Frighten, terrify. OE–E17.

SHAKES. *Lear* Or whether gasted by the noise I made, Full suddenly he fled.

▸ **B** *adjective.* Frightened, terrified. LME–L16.

Gastarbeiter /ˈgastɑːrbaɪtər/ *noun.* Pl. **-s**, same. M20.
[ORIGIN German, from *Gast* guest + *Arbeiter* worker.]
A person with temporary permission to work in another (esp. western European) country.

gaster /ˈgastə/ *verb trans. & intrans. obsolete* exc. *dial.* L16.
[ORIGIN Frequentative of GAST *verb*: see -ER[5].]
(Cause to) have fear.

gasteral *adjective* var. of GASTRAL.

gasteromycete /ˌgast(ə)rəʊˈmʌɪsiːt/ *noun.* Orig. only in pl. **-mycetes** /-ˈmʌɪsiːts, -mʌɪˈsiːtiːz/. L19.
[ORIGIN Anglicized sing. of mod. Latin *Gasteromycetes* (see below), from Greek *gastēr*, *gaster-* stomach + *mukētes* pl. of *mukēs* fungus.]
MYCOLOGY. A fungus of the class Gasteromycetes of basidiomycetes, characterized by bearing spores in cavities in the fruiting body and not discharging them violently.
■ **gasteromyˈcetous** *adjective* M19.

†**gastful** *adjective* see GHASTFUL.

Gasthaus /ˈgasthaʊs/ *noun.* Pl. ***-häuser*** /-hɔyzər/. M19.
[ORIGIN German, from *Gast* GUEST *noun* + *Haus* HOUSE *noun*[1].]
A small inn or hotel in a German-speaking country.

Gasthof /ˈgasthoːf/ *noun.* Pl. ***-hofs***, ***-höfe*** /-høːfə/. M19.
[ORIGIN German, from *Gast* GUEST *noun* + *Hof* hotel, large house.]
A German hotel, usu. larger than a ***Gasthaus***.

†**gastly** *adjective & adverb* see GHASTLY.

†**gastness** *noun.* LME–E17.
[ORIGIN from GAST *adjective* + -NESS.]
A threat; (a cause of) terror; terrified state or appearance.

SHAKES. *Oth.* Look you pale, mistress?—Do you perceive the gastness of her eye.

Gastornis /gaˈstɔːnɪs/ *noun.* L19.
[ORIGIN mod. Latin, from the name of the French scientist *Gaston* Planté (1834–89) + Greek *ornis* bird.]
A very large flightless bird of the Eocene epoch.

gastraea /gaˈstriːə/ *noun.* Also ***gastrea**. L19.
[ORIGIN mod. Latin, from Greek *gastēr*, *gaster-* stomach + Latin *-aeus*, Greek *-aios* adjectival suffix.]
ZOOLOGY. A hypothetical ancestral form of metazoan (multicellular animal) having two layers of cells, corresponding in organization to the gastrula in the embryonic development of living metazoans.

gastral /ˈgastr(ə)l/ *adjective.* Also **gasteral** /ˈgast(ə)r(ə)l/. E19.
[ORIGIN formed as GASTRO- + -AL[1].]
Chiefly *ZOOLOGY.* = GASTRIC.

gastralgia /gaˈstraldʒə/ *noun.* Now *rare.* M19.
[ORIGIN formed as GASTRO- + -ALGIA.]
MEDICINE. Pain in the stomach.
■ **gastralgic** *adjective* L19.

gastrectomy /gaˈstrɛktəmi/ *noun.* L19.
[ORIGIN from GASTRO- + -ECTOMY.]
Surgical removal of all or part of the stomach; an instance of this.

gastric /ˈgastrɪk/ *adjective.* M17.
[ORIGIN mod. Latin *gastricus*, from Greek *gastēr*, *gastr-* stomach: see -IC.]
Of, pertaining to, or affecting the stomach.
gastric fever fever involving the stomach; now usu., an enteric fever or typhoid. **gastric flu**, **gastric influenza** *colloq.* any intestinal disorder of unknown or supposedly viral cause. **gastric juice** the thin, clear fluid secreted by glands in the stomach wall, containing hydrochloric acid and enzymes such as pepsin, and important in digestion. **gastric mill** *ZOOLOGY* a masticatory apparatus in the gut; *esp.* (**a**) in malacostracan crustaceans, a framework of movable calcareous or chitinous pieces; (**b**) in birds and reptiles, the gizzard together with the small stones swallowed to aid its action.

gastrin /ˈgastrɪn/ *noun.* E20.
[ORIGIN from GASTRIC + -IN[1].]
PHYSIOLOGY. A polypeptide hormone which stimulates secretion of gastric juice, and is secreted into the bloodstream by the stomach wall in response to the presence of food.

gastritis /gaˈstrʌɪtɪs/ *noun.* E19.
[ORIGIN from GASTRO- + -ITIS.]
MEDICINE. Inflammation of the mucosa of the stomach.

gastro- /ˈgastrəʊ/ *combining form* of Greek *gastēr*, *gaster-*, *gastr-* stomach, used esp. in *MEDICINE*: see -O-. Before a vowel also **gastr-**.
■ **gastrocele** *noun* a hernia of the stomach E19. **gastroduodeˈnostomy** *noun* (an instance of) surgical connection of the stomach and the duodenum L19. **gastro-enˈteric** *adjective* = GASTROINTESTINAL. **gastro-enteˈrostomy** *noun* (an instance of) surgical connection of the stomach and the intestine L19. **gastrointeˈstinal** *adjective* of or involving the stomach and intestines M19. **gastrojejuˈnostomy** *noun* (an instance of) surgical connection of the stomach and the jejunum L19. **gastrolith** *noun* a hard concretion in the stomach, usu. formed around foreign material which has been swallowed M19. **gaˈstropathy** *noun* any disease of the stomach M19. **gastropexy** *noun* (an instance of) the surgical attachment of the stomach to the abdominal wall L19. **gastroplasty** *noun* (an instance of) surgical correction of deformity of the stomach; *spec.* reduction by stapling as a treatment for obesity: M20. **gastroˈvascular** *adjective* (*ZOOLOGY*) (of the body cavity of certain coelenterates) fulfilling both digestive and circulatory functions L19. **gastroˈzooid** *noun* (*ZOOLOGY*) in colonial hydrozoans and some colonial tunicates, a nutritive zooid L19.

gastrocnemius /gastrəʊˈkniːmɪəs/ *noun.* Pl. **-mii** /-mɪʌɪ/. L17.
[ORIGIN mod. Latin from Greek *gastroknēmia* the calf of the leg, from *gaster* stomach, belly + *knēmē* leg: so called from its 'bellying' or bulging form.]
ANATOMY. The chief muscle of the calf of the leg. Also ***gastrocnemius muscle***.
■ **gastrocnemial** *adjective* L19. **gastrocnemian** *adjective* M19.

gastrocolic /gastrəʊˈkɒlɪk/ *adjective.* M19.
[ORIGIN from GASTRO- + COLIC *noun & adjective.*]
MEDICINE. Pertaining to the stomach and colon.
gastrocolic fistula an abnormal passage between the stomach and the colon, resulting from disease. **gastrocolic reflex** a wave of peristalsis produced in the colon by introducing food into a fasting stomach.

gastroenteritis /ˌgastrəʊɛntəˈrʌɪtɪs/ *noun.* E19.
[ORIGIN from GASTRO- + ENTERITIS.]
MEDICINE. Inflammation of the stomach and intestines, causing vomiting and diarrhoea.

gastroenterology /ˌgastrəʊɛntəˈrɒlədʒi/ *noun.* E20.
[ORIGIN from GASTRO- + ENTERO- + -LOGY.]
The branch of medicine that deals with the diseases and abnormalities of the stomach and intestines.
■ **gastroenteroˈlogical** *adjective* E20. **gastroenterologist** *noun* M20.

gastrology /gaˈstrɒlədʒi/ *noun.* E19.
[ORIGIN Greek *gastrologia*: see GASTRO-, -LOGY.]
= GASTRONOMY.
■ **gastrologer** *noun* = GASTRONOME E19.

gastromancy /ˈgastrəmansi/ *noun. obsolete* exc. *hist.* E17.
[ORIGIN from GASTRO- + -MANCY.]
Divination by the belly; *spec.* divination by figures etc. seen in bellied glass vessels full of water or by sounds from, or signs on, the stomach.

gastronome /ˈgastrənəʊm/ *noun.* E19.
[ORIGIN French, back-form. from *gastronomie* GASTRONOMY.]
A connoisseur of good eating and drinking; a gourmet.

gastronomic /gastrəˈnɒmɪk/ *adjective*. E19.
[ORIGIN French *gastronomique*, formed as GASTRONOMY: see -IC.]
Of or pertaining to gastronomy.
■ **gastronomical** *adjective* E19. **gastronomically** *adverb* M19.

gastronomy /gaˈstrɒnəmi/ *noun*. E19.
[ORIGIN French *gastronomie*, from Greek *gastronomia* alt. of *gastrologia* GASTROLOGY: see -NOMY.]
The art and science of good eating and drinking.
■ **gastronomer** *noun* [after *astronomer*] = GASTRONOME E19. **gastronomist** *noun* = GASTRONOME E19.

gastropod /ˈgastrəpɒd/ *noun & adjective*. Also **gastero-** /ˈgast(ə)rə(ʊ)-/. E19.
[ORIGIN French *gastéropode* from mod. Latin *Gasteropoda* (see below), formed as GASTRO-: see -POD.]
► **A** *noun*. Any mollusc of the class Gastropoda (including snails, slugs, whelks, and limpets), typically having a flattened ventral foot for locomotion and a univalve shell. E19.
► **B** *adjective*. Gastropodous. M19.
■ **gaˈstropodan** *adjective & noun* = GASTROPOD L19. **gaˈstropodous** *adjective* of, belonging to, pertaining to, or characteristic of the class Gastropoda E19.

gastroscope /ˈgastrəskəʊp/ *noun*. L19.
[ORIGIN from GASTRO- + -SCOPE.]
MEDICINE. An instrument for inspecting the interior of the stomach when passed into it via the mouth and oesophagus.

gastroscopy /gaˈstrɒskəpi/ *noun*. M19.
[ORIGIN from GASTRO- + -SCOPY.]
MEDICINE. **1** An examination of the abdomen. Now *rare*. M19.
2 (An) examination of the stomach by means of a gastroscope; the practice and technique of using a gastroscope. L19.
■ **gastroˈscopic** *adjective* of or pertaining to the gastroscope or gastroscopy L19. **gastroˈscopically** *adverb* L19.

gastrostomy /gaˈstrɒstəmi/ *noun*. M19.
[ORIGIN from GASTRO- + -STOMY.]
A surgical operation involving the opening of the stomach for the introduction of food.

gastrotomy /gaˈstrɒtəmi/ *noun*. M17.
[ORIGIN from GASTRO- + -TOMY.]
Surgical cutting open of the abdomen, or (now usu.) of the stomach through the abdominal walls; an instance of this.
■ **gastroˈtomic** *adjective* M19.

gastrotrich /ˈgastrətrɪk/ *noun*. M20.
[ORIGIN from GASTRO- + -TRICH.]
Any minute aquatic multicellular animal of the phylum Gastrotricha, having a short wormlike body covered with cilia and bristles, thought to be related to the rotifers and nematodes.

gastrula /ˈgastrʊlə/ *noun*. Pl. **-lae** /-liː/, **-las**. L19.
[ORIGIN mod. Latin, from Greek *gastēr*, *gastr-* stomach: see -ULE.]
An embryo at the stage following inward migration of the cells of the blastula, typically consisting of a hollow cup-shaped structure having three layers of cells enclosing the archenteron. Cf. BLASTULA, MORULA *noun*[1].
■ **gastrular** *adjective* M20. **gastruˈlation** *noun* the process of formation of a gastrula L19.

gat /gat/ *noun*[1]. E16.
[ORIGIN App. from Old Norse *gat* (Swedish, Danish *gat*) hole, opening, passage: see GATE *noun*[1].]
1 A hole in the ground. E16.
2 An opening between sandbanks; a channel, a strait. L16.

gat /gat/ *noun*[2]. *slang*. Also **gatt**. E20.
[ORIGIN Abbreviation of GATLING.]
A revolver or other firearm.

gatch /gatʃ/ *noun*. L19.
[ORIGIN Persian *gač*.]
A type of plaster used in Iran for architectural decoration.

gate /geɪt/ *noun*[1]. Also (*Scot. & N. English*) **yett** /jɛt/.
[ORIGIN Old English *ġæt*, *ġeat*, pl. *gatu*, corresp. to Old Frisian *gat* hole, opening, Old Saxon *gat* eye of a needle (Low German, Dutch gap, hole, breach), Old Norse *gat* hole, opening, passage (cf. GAT *noun*[1]) from Germanic. Forms with *y-* remain in north. but *gate* has been standard since 16.]
1 An opening in the wall of a city, an enclosure, or a large building, made for entrance and exit, and able to be closed by a movable barrier. Also, the gateway over or around such an opening. OE.

> B. GOOGE I made a square wall . . with a great gate, for the bringing in of my cariages. SHAKES. *Jul. Caes.* Brutus and Cassius Are rid like madmen through the gates of Rome.

2 A barrier which closes the opening across a wall, road, or passage; a wooden or iron framework either solid or consisting of bars or gratings, turning on pivots or hinges, or sliding, and used either singly or in pairs. OE. ▸**b** A contrivance for stopping or regulating the passage of water in a lock etc. L15. ▸**c** *spec.* A starting gate. E20.

> E. F. BENSON Six . . steps led up from a small clanging gate to the front door. J. UPDIKE The gates were swung open, the mob laughingly pushed through. **c** T. FITZGEORGE-PARKER She spoilt three starts and then, when the gate went up, ran right out.

floodgate, *lychgate*, *sluice gate*, *starting gate*, *tailgate*, *tide gate*, *toll gate*, *watergate*, etc. *bull-at-a-gate*: see BULL *noun*[1].
3 In biblical translations and allusions, a place of judicial assembly. OE.
4 *fig.* A means of entrance or exit. ME.

> SHAKES. *Much Ado* For thee I'll lock up all the gates of love.

5 A mountain pass, *esp.* one providing entry to a country. LME.
6 A frame in which a saw or set of saws is stretched to prevent buckling. E19.
7 *CRICKET*. The space between the bat and the batsman's body. Formerly also, the wicket. M19.
8 The total number of people entering through the gates to see a football match etc. L19. ▸**b** The amount of admission money paid to see a football match etc. L19.

> E. HEATH There was an enormous gate and the crowd was forthright in its advice.

9 A device in a cine camera or projector which holds each frame of a film momentarily in position. E20.
10 An arrangement of slots through which the lever of a motor vehicle gearbox is moved to engage different gears. E20.
11 *ELECTRONICS*. **a** An electrical signal that causes or controls the passage of other signals in a circuit. M20. ▸**b** A digital circuit producing one output signal that is determined by a combination of two or more input signals; *esp.* (in full ***logic gate***) a logic circuit of this kind. M20. ▸**c** The material in a unipolar transistor forming the electrodes to which the input signal is applied. M20.
12 A numbered place of access to an aircraft at an airport. M20.
13 The mouth. *slang*. M20.
14 [Perh. from sense 4, or perh. abbreviation of *alligator*.] A person, *esp.* a jazz musician. *US slang*. M20.
– PHRASES: ***creaking gate***: see CREAK *verb* 3. DECUMAN ***gate***. ***gate of horn***: see ***ivory gate*** below. **get the gate** *slang* be dismissed, rejected, or jilted. **give the gate to** *slang* dismiss, reject, jilt, (a person). **ivory gate**, **gate of horn** in Greek legend, those gates through which false and true dreams respectively pass. **open a gate for**, **open a gate to** provide an opportunity for, make possible. ***Pearly Gates***: see PEARLY *adjective*. ***swing the gate***: see SWING *verb*. **the gate of death**, **the gates of death** the near approach of death.
– COMB.: **gate array** (an electronic chip consisting of) a regular arrangement of logic gates; **gate-bill** formerly, at Oxford and Cambridge Universities, a record of the times at which a student returns to college after hours; a weekly account of the fines charged for this; **gate city** *US* a city located at the entrance to an administrative district; **gatecrash** *verb intrans. & trans.* enter (a party etc.) as a gatecrasher; **gatecrasher** a person who enters a sports ground, private party, entertainment, etc., without an invitation or ticket; **gatefold** a folded oversize page or insert in a magazine etc.; **gatehouse** (**a**) a house at the gates or entrance of a park or other enclosure, a lodge; (**b**) *hist.* a room over a city or palace gate, often used as a prison; **gatekeeper** (**a**) an attendant at a gate; (**b**) any of several Eurasian satyrid butterflies, esp. *Pyronia tithonus* (also called ***hedge brown***), brownish orange with a black spot on the forewing; **gatekeeping** the work or action of a gatekeeper; *transf.* the control of general access to something; **gateleg table**, **gatelegged table**: with a leg or legs in a frame resembling a gate, which may be swung round to allow the leaves to drop down; **gate-lodge** a lodge at the gate of the grounds of a country house etc.; **gateman** a man in charge of a gate, a gatekeeper; **gate-money** (**a**) = sense 8b above; (**b**) money charged on a gate-bill; **gate-net** a net hung loosely across a gateway in order to catch hares driven at night; **gatepost** a post on which a gate is hung or against which it shuts (***between you and me and the gatepost***: see BETWEEN *preposition* 3); **gate pulse** = sense 11a above; **gate receipts** = ***gate-money*** (a) above; **gatestead** *rare* a gateway; **gate-table** a gateleg table; **gate valve**: in which a sliding part controls the extent of the aperture; **gateward** *arch.* = ***gatekeeper*** (a) above.
■ **gateless** *adjective* E17.

gate /geɪt/ *noun*[2]. Now only *Scot. & N. English*. Also †**gait**. See also GAIT *noun*. ME.
[ORIGIN Old Norse *gata* = Old High German *gazza* (German *Gasse* street, lane), Gothic *gatwō* from Germanic.]
► **I 1 a** A way, a road, a path. ME. ▸**b** A street. Freq. in street names in Scotland and N. England, as Gallowgate, Kirkgate, etc. LME. ▸**c** Length of way, distance. *obsolete* exc. *Scot.* E16. ▸**d** *MINING*. An underground passage. M18.
2 A going, a journey, a course. ME. ▸†**b** The flight of a bird, esp. a hawk. ME–L17. ▸†**c** *fig.* Proceeding. *rare* (Shakes.). Only in E17.
3 A way, manner, or method of doing or behaving; a peculiar habit. ME.
4 A right to a run or pasturage for a cow, horse, etc. *N. English*. L16.
► **II** See GAIT *noun*
– PHRASES: ***gang one's gate***: see GANG *verb*[1]. **take gate**, **take the gate** take the road, leave; follow a path or course. **that gate** that way; in that direction. **this gate** this way; in this direction.
■ **gateward(s)** *adverb* on the road or way towards; by the direct road: E16.

gate /geɪt/ *noun*[3]. L17.
[ORIGIN Perh. same as GATE *noun*[1]: cf. synon. Dutch *gietgat*, from *gieten* pour, cast + *gat* opening = GATE *noun*[1].]
FOUNDING. **1** The opening or channel through which molten metal flows into a mould. L17.
2 The waste piece of metal cast in the gate. M19.

gate /geɪt/ *verb*[1] *trans.* M19.
[ORIGIN from GATE *noun*[1].]
1 Confine (a student) to the precincts of a college or school either entirely or after certain hours. M19.

> G. SAINTSBURY He was . . gated for a fortnight for disobedience and contumacy.

2 *ELECTRONICS*. Subject to the action of a gate; select parts of (a signal) that occur within a given time interval or range of amplitude; switch by means of a gate circuit. Chiefly as ***gated*** *ppl adjective*, ***gating*** *verbal noun & ppl adjective*. Cf. GATE *noun*[1] 11. M20.

gate /geɪt/ *verb*[2] *trans. & intrans.* E20.
[ORIGIN from GATE *noun*[3].]
FOUNDING. Provide (a mould etc.) with a gate or gates.
■ **gating** *noun* the action of providing gates; the arrangement of gates, runners, etc., provided: E20.

-gate /geɪt/ *suffix*.
[ORIGIN Extracted from WATER)GATE.]
Forming nouns denoting an actual or alleged scandal (and usu. an attempted cover-up) comparable in some way to the Watergate scandal of 1972, esp. with the name of the place associated with the scandal, as ***Dallasgate***, ***Irangate***.

G

gateau /ˈgatəʊ/ *noun*. Also **gâ-**. Pl. **-eaux** /-əʊ(z)/, **-eaus**. M19.
[ORIGIN French *gâteau* cake.]
1 A large rich cake, *esp.* one with layers of cream or fruit. M19. ▸**b** In full ***gâteau de riz*** /də riːz/ [= of rice]. A rich rice dessert in the shape of a cake. Now *rare*. M19.
2 Meat or fish baked and served in the form of a cake. Now *rare*. L19.

gated /ˈgeɪtɪd/ *adjective*. M17.
[ORIGIN from GATE *noun*[1] + -ED[2].]
Provided with a gate or gates.
gated community a residential development in which access is allowed only through a secured gate, often protected by other security measures.

gateway /ˈgeɪtweɪ/ *noun*. M17.
[ORIGIN from GATE *noun*[1] + WAY *noun*.]
1 An opening or passage that is or may be closed by a gate. Now *rare*. M17.
2 A frame or arch in which a gate is hung; a structure built at or over a gate. L18.

> M. PATTISON A lofty massive front with three fortified and portcullised gateways.

3 *transf. & fig.* A means of entrance or exit. M19. ▸**b** = GATE *noun*[1] 5. L19.

> *City Limits* Sutton, gateway to the Downs.

4 *COMPUTING*. A device used to connect two different networks. L20.
– COMB.: **gateway drug** a drug which supposedly leads the user on to more addictive or dangerous drugs.

Gatha /ˈgɑːθɑː/ *noun*. Also **g-**. M19.
[ORIGIN Avestan *gāθā*.]
Any of the seventeen poems which are the most ancient texts of the Avesta and are attributed to Zoroaster.

gather /ˈgaðə/ *noun*[1]. M16.
[ORIGIN from the verb.]
1 An amount gathered. Long *rare* or *obsolete*. M16.
2 In *pl.* & (occas.) *sing.* Part of a garment or fabric which is gathered or drawn in. L16.
3 The action of gathering; a drawing together. L19.
4 *GLASS-MAKING*. A mass of molten glass on the end of a blowing iron. M20.

†**gather** *noun*[2]. LME–L18.
[ORIGIN Prob. a spec. sense of GATHER *noun*[1].]
The pluck (heart, liver, and lungs) of an animal.

gather /ˈgaðə/ *verb*.
[ORIGIN Old English *gaderian* = Old Frisian *gaderia*, Middle Low German *gadern*, Middle Dutch & mod. Dutch *gaderen*, Middle High German *gatern* from West Germanic base of TOGETHER.]
► **I** *verb trans.* †**1** Join, unite; put together. OE–ME.
2 Bring together, collect, assemble. Also foll. by *together*, *up*. OE.

> R. LYND He would in time gather a great crowd round him. G. GREENE He had gathered up in his novels the two divided strands of Restoration fiction.

be gathered to one's fathers, **be gathered to one's people** be buried with one's ancestors; die.
†**3** Collect or compile (literary matter) from various written or printed sources. OE–L17.
4 Collect or pick (flowers, fruit) from the place of growth. OE. ▸**b** Collect (grain etc.) as harvest. Also foll. by *in*. OE. ▸**c** Pick or pluck individually (a flower or fruit). L16.

> W. CATHER She had . . gone into the meadow to gather wild flowers.

5 Pick up, collect from the ground. Usu. foll. by *up*. ME. ▸**b** *spec.* Catch (a ball) in rugby football or baseball as it moves through the air; pick up (a rolling ball) in cricket etc. when fielding. M19.

H. KELLER I gathered up the fruit in my pinafore. N. SHUTE She gathered up her gloves and her bag.

gather up one's crumbs: see CRUMB *noun*.

6 Of a material object: receive addition of, accumulate (something). **OE.**

Proverb: A rolling stone gathers no moss.

7 Collect as a contribution (money etc.). *obsolete* exc. *dial.* **LME.**

8 Make or scrape together (a living). *rare*. **LME.**

9 Bring into activity, summon up (strength, energy, one's thoughts, oneself) esp. for an effort. Also foll. by *together*, *up*. **LME.** ▸**b** Gain or recover (breath). **L15.**

LEIGH HUNT It only made him gather up his determination. R. L. STEVENSON It was some time before either I or the captain seemed to gather our senses. D. H. LAWRENCE Ursula thought a moment, gathering her straying wits together.

10 Acquire (knowledge) by observation and reasoning; infer, deduce. **M16.**

T. HARDY Jim gathered from inquiries he made that he had come the wrong way. D. CUSACK She'd had a row with Rex . . something about Portia, I gathered.

11 Draw together (a garment, the sails of a ship, etc.) in folds; bring into smaller compass. Also foll. by *up*. **M16.** ▸**b** Draw up (a fabric, a garment, esp. a dress) along a thread which has been run through it. Also foll. by *up*. **L16.** ▸**c** *ARCHITECTURE*. Contract, make narrower (a chimney, drain, etc.). **E18.** ▸**d** Wrinkle, contract (one's brow). *rare*. **L18.**

M. SINCLAIR She would look down at her shawl and gather it about her. **b** C. BRONTË A dress . . as full in the skirt as it could be gathered.

12 Acquire by way of increase (a specified quality, condition, etc.), develop a higher degree of. **L16.**

P. G. WODEHOUSE Horace . . pressed his foot on the accelerator and the Bingley gathered speed.

†**gather ground** gain ground, make progress. **gather head** come to a head; grow stronger. **gather way** *NAUTICAL* (of a ship) begin to move.

13 Of a ship: gain on or draw nearer to, in following. Also foll. by *on*. **E17.**

14 *techn.* **a** *BOOKBINDING*. Collect and put in order (the leaves or sheets of a book). **L17.** ▸**b** *GLASS-MAKING*. Collect (molten glass) on the end of a blowing iron. **M19.**

▸ **II** *verb intrans.* **15** Of people: come together, congregate, assemble. **OE.**

G. VIDAL A crowd was beginning to gather.

16 Accumulate and come to a head; develop a purulent swelling. **OE.**

E. NESBIT He had hurt his foot with a nail in his boot that gathered. *fig.*: SHAKES. *Temp.* Now does my project gather to a head.

17 †**a** Accumulate wealth. Only in **ME.** ▸**b** Make a collection of money or other contributions. *obsolete* exc. *dial.* **M16.**

18 Of things: collect, come together in a mass; form or increase by coming together. **LME.**

SIR W. SCOTT It seemed as if a tear . . were gathering in his . . eye. T. COLLINS Dusk was gathering by this time.

19 Contract; form folds or wrinkles. *rare*. **M16.**

J. L. WATEN Slowly a frown gathered on Mother's face.

20 *NAUTICAL*. Of a ship: make its way (towards something). **L16.**

– WITH ADVERBS IN SPECIALIZED SENSES: **gather out** select, pick out. **gather up** (*a*) draw up (one's limbs or person); (*b*) sum up, summarize, (something); (*c*) plough (land, a ridge) so that the earth is turned over towards the highest part of the ridge; (*d*) compose (one's features) *into* an expression; (see also senses 2, 5, 9, 11 above).

■ **gatherable** *adjective* that may be gathered or inferred **M16.**

gatherer /ˈɡað(ə)rə/ *noun*. **ME.**
[ORIGIN from GATHER *verb* + -ER[1].]

1 A person who gathers or collects something. Also foll. by *together*, *up*. **ME.** ▸**b** *spec.* A collector of money. Now *rare*. **LME.** ▸†**c** An accumulator of wealth, a miser. Only in **16.**

2 *techn.* **a** *BOOKBINDING*. A person who or machine which collects and orders the leaves or sheets of a book. **L17.** ▸**b** *GLASS-MAKING*. A person who accumulates molten glass or metal on the end of a blowing iron. **M19.**

3 Each of the front teeth of a horse. **L17.**

gathering /ˈɡað(ə)rɪŋ/ *noun*. **OE.**
[ORIGIN formed as GATHERER + -ING[1].]

1 *gen.* The action of GATHER *verb* I; collecting something. Also foll. by *together*, *up*, etc. **OE.** ▸†**b** The action or practice of collecting wealth. **ME–M16.** ▸**c** The action of drawing up the fabric in a garment; the gathers so formed. **L16.**

2 The action of GATHER *verb* II; coming together, uniting; a union, an accumulation. **OE.**

3 A bringing together or coming together of people; an assembly, meeting; *spec.* an (annual) assembly of dancing, piping, or sporting contests held in various parts of the Scottish Highlands. **OE.** ▸**b** A signal to assemble, sounded on drums or pipes. Chiefly *Scot.* **M17.**

QUEEN VICTORIA We . . went . . to the Gathering at the *Castle of Braemar*. V. SACKVILLE-WEST They all thoroughly enjoyed their gatherings over the tea-table.

4 An accumulation of purulent matter; a suppurated swelling. **OE.**

5 That which is gathered or brought together. Now *rare* or *obsolete*. **LME.**

R. PALTOCK Some few new sorts of berries and greens were the gathering of that day.

6 *techn.* **a** *BOOKBINDING*. The arrangement of the leaves or sheets of a book in proper order; a group of leaves or sheets brought together to form part of a book. **L17.** ▸**b** *GLASS-MAKING*. = GATHER *noun*[1] 4. **E20.**

a E. DIEHL The book sections, or gatherings, were marked . . in order.

7 *ARCHITECTURE*. The narrowing or contracting of (esp. the wings of) a chimney. **E18.**

J. S. FOSTER The gathering over of the flue above the fire-place opening . . should be steep.

– COMB.: **gathering coal** (chiefly *Scot.*) a large piece of coal put on the fire to keep it burning through the night; **gathering cry** (chiefly *Scot.*, *hist.*) a summons to assemble for war; **gathering ground** a region from which the feeding waters of a river or reservoir are collected; **gathering peat** (chiefly *Scot.*) a peat laid on the fire to keep it burning through the night; **gathering sound** *hist.* = *gathering cry* above.

Gathic /ˈɡɑːθɪk/ *adjective & noun*. **E20.**
[ORIGIN from GATHA + -IC.]

▸ **A** *adjective*. Of or pertaining to the Gathas or the language in which they are written. **E20.**

▸ **B** *noun*. The Gathic language, a more archaic form of the Avestan language. **M20.**

■ **Gathaic** /ɡɑːˈθeɪɪk/ *adjective* (*rare*) = GATHIC *adjective* **L19.**

Gatling /ˈɡatlɪŋ/ *noun*. **M19.**
[ORIGIN R. J. *Gatling* (1818–1903), US inventor.]

In full ***Gatling gun***. An early type of machine gun with clustered barrels into which cartridges were automatically loaded.

gator /ˈɡeɪtə/ *noun*. *colloq.* Chiefly *US*. Also **'gator**. **M19.**
[ORIGIN Abbreviation.]

= ALLIGATOR.

Gatso /ˈɡatsəʊ/ *noun*. Pl. **-os**. **L20.**
[ORIGIN from Maurice *Gatso*nides, 20th-cent. Dutch racing driver.]

A camera which automatically takes a photograph of vehicles travelling over a certain speed (as measured by radar). Also ***Gatso camera***.

GATT /ɡat/ *abbreviation*.

hist. General Agreement on Tariffs and Trade, an international treaty (1948–94) to promote trade and economic development, superseded by the establishment of the World Trade Organization.

gatt *noun* var. of GAT *noun*[2].

gatten *noun* see GAITER *noun*[1].

gatter /ˈɡatə/ *noun*[1]. *slang*. **E19.**
[ORIGIN Unknown.]

Beer; liquor in general.

gatter *noun*[2] var. of GAITER *noun*[1].

gattine /ɡaˈtiːn/ *noun*. **E19.**
[ORIGIN French.]

A disease of the silkworm; = PÉBRINE.

gauche /ɡəʊʃ/ *adjective*. **M18.**
[ORIGIN French, lit. 'left(-handed)'.]

1 Lacking in tact or ease of manner, awkward, blundering; lacking in subtlety or skill, crude, unsophisticated. **M18.**

C. CHAPLIN He was gauche in his attempt at conversation, asking inconsequential questions about my films. *Times* His illustrator scarcely ever achieves anything that is not gauche and lifeless.

2 *MATH.* Skew, not plane. *arch.* **L19.** ▸**b** *CHEMISTRY*. Of a molecular conformation: skew, having two groups staggered along a central axis by (about) 60 degrees. **M20.**

■ **gauchely** *adverb* **L19.** **gaucheness** *noun* **L19.**

gaucherie /ˈɡəʊʃ(ə)riː/ *noun*. **L18.**
[ORIGIN French, from *gauche*: see GAUCHE, -ERY.]

Gauche or awkward manner; a gauche action.

DISRAELI An elegant . . lad, with just enough of dandyism to preserve him from committing *gaucheries*. C. BAX Whitman uses rhyme . . with some awkwardness or, as he would have put it, gaucherie.

Gaucher's disease /ˈɡəʊʃeɪz dɪˌziːz, ɡəʊˈʃeɪz/ *noun phr.* **M20.**
[ORIGIN P. C. E. *Gaucher* (1854–1918), French physician.]

MEDICINE. An inherited lipid storage disorder, characterized by bone fragility, neurological disturbance, anaemia, and enlargement of the liver and spleen.

gaucho /ˈɡaʊtʃəʊ, ˈɡɔː-/ *noun*. Pl. **-os**. **E19.**
[ORIGIN Amer. Spanish, prob. from Mapuche *kauču*.]

A mounted herdsman of the S. American pampas, usu. of mixed European and American Indian descent.

gaud /ɡɔːd/ *noun*[1]. **ME.**
[ORIGIN Perh. from Anglo-Norman deriv. of Old French *gaudir* from Latin *gaudere* rejoice. In later senses infl. by GAUD *noun*[2].]

1 A trick; *esp.* a deceitful trick or pretence. Long only *Scot.* & *N. English*. Now *rare* or *obsolete*. **ME.** ▸†**b** A piece of mockery, a jest. Also, an object of mockery. **LME–M17.**

2 A showy ornament, a piece of finery; a gewgaw. Now *rhet.* **LME.**

H. L. MENCKEN Their . . inclination to dress up, to strike the public eye with arresting gauds.

3 In *pl.*, showy ceremonies; *sing.* idle display. Now *rhet.* **M17.**

LYTTON The pomp, the gaud . . strongly contrasted the patriarchal simplicity which marked his justice court. C. C. FELTON Its bishops . . surrounded themselves with the pomps and gauds of this world.

gaud /ɡɔːd/ *noun*[2]. *obsolete* exc. *hist.* **LME.**
[ORIGIN Anglo-Latin *gaudium*, prob. based on medieval Latin *quinque gaudia* the five 'joyful mysteries' of the rosary. Cf. Anglo-Norman *gaudes* in same sense.]

Each of the large ornamental beads in a rosary, placed between the decades of aves.

†**gaud** *verb trans.* **LME.**
[ORIGIN from GAUD *noun*[1] or *noun*[2].]

1 Equip (a rosary) with gauds. **LME–M16.**

2 Adorn, make showy. **M16–E17.**

SHAKES. *Coriol.* Their nicely gawded cheeks.

gaudeamus /ɡaʊdɪˈɑːməs, ɡɔːdɪˈeɪməs/ *noun*. Chiefly *Scot.* Now *rare* or *obsolete*. **E18.**
[ORIGIN First word of the mod. Latin students' song *Gaudeamus igitur, juvenes dum sumus* 'Then let us be merry while we are still young'.]

A convivial gathering, esp. of college or university students.

gaudery /ˈɡɔːd(ə)ri/ *noun*. **E16.**
[ORIGIN from GAUD *noun*[1] + -ERY.]

†**1** Trickery. Only in **E16.**

2 Gaudy decoration or show; a piece of finery. **L16.**

DRYDEN A plain suit . . Is better than to be by tarnished gawdry known.

gaudy /ˈɡɔːdi/ *noun*. **LME.**
[ORIGIN Latin *gaudium* joy, from *gaudere* rejoice, or *gaude* imper. of this verb.]

†**1** = GAUD *noun*[2]. **LME–M16.**

2 (An instance of) rejoicing or making merry. Now *rare* or *obsolete*. **M16.**

3 A grand feast. Now usu., an annual celebratory dinner held by a college for old members. **M17.**

– COMB.: **gaudy-day**, **gaudy-night** a gala day or night, *esp.* one on which a college gaudy is held.

gaudy /ˈɡɔːdi/ *adjective*. Also †**gawdy**. **L15.**
[ORIGIN In sense 3 perh. from GAUDY *noun*. In other senses from GAUD *noun*[1]: see -Y[1].]

1 Brilliantly or (now chiefly) glaringly or vulgarly colourful or ornate; (excessively) showy, garish. **L15.**

C. MCCULLERS The show was gaudy with coloured lights. E. CRISPIN Nice figure, and dressed well—plain . . clothes, nothing gaudy. *fig.*: *New Yorker* By pressuring [Nicaragua] . . to hold off from some of its more gaudy outrages.

†**2** Full of trickery. Only in **E16.**

†**3** Of food: luxurious. **M16–E17.**

4 Very good, splendid. Usu. in neg. contexts. *slang*. Now *rare* or *obsolete*. **L19.**

M. TWAIN We played it to a hundred guests . . and had a perfectly gaudy time.

■ **gaudily** *adverb* **E17.** **gaudiness** *noun* **E17.**

gaudy-green /ɡɔːdɪˈɡriːn/ *adjective & noun*. Long *arch.* **LME.**
[ORIGIN from Old French & mod. French *gaude* weld (assim. to -Y[1]) + GREEN *noun*, *adjective*.]

(Of) a green dyed with the plant weld; (of) a yellowish green.

gauge /ɡeɪdʒ/ *noun*. Also (esp. *US* & in sense 2) **gage**. **ME.**
[ORIGIN Old Northern French var. of (also mod.) *jauge*: ult. origin unknown. For the pronunc. cf. *safe* /seɪf/ from Old French & mod. French *sauf*.]

▸ **I** A measure.

1 A standard measure or scale of measurement; *esp.* a measure of the capacity or contents of a barrel, of the diameter of a bullet, of the thickness of sheet metal, or of the fineness of a textile. **ME.** ▸**b** *transf.* & *fig.* Extent, capacity, scope. **E17.** ▸**c** *PHYSICS*. In full ***gauge function***. A function introduced as an additional term into a field equation, often for symmetry purposes, without altering the derived equations of observable physical quantities. Freq. in *comb.* (see below). **E20.**

b A. W. KINGLAKE His intellect . . was much above the low gauge which people used to assign to it.

b take the gauge of estimate, assess.

2 *NAUTICAL*. (Usu. **gage**.) The position of one vessel relative to another and to the wind. **L16.**

have the weather gauge of, **keep the weather gauge of** be windward of; *fig.* get the better of. **have the lee gauge of** be leeward of.

3 BUILDING. The length of projection of a tile or slate beyond that which overlaps it. **E18.**
4 The distance between the rails of a railway track, tramline, etc. Also, the distance between the wheels at each end of the same axle of a railway vehicle. **M19.**
broad gauge: see BROAD *adjective*. ***narrow gauge***: see NARROW *adjective*.
▸ **II** An instrument for measuring.
†**5** = ***gauging-rod*** s.v. GAUGE *verb*. Also (*dial.*), a pair of connected rods dropped into a furnace to test whether it needs more fuel. **M16–L18.**
6 A graduated instrument for measuring a fluctuating quantity or force, as rainfall, tide, wind, a stream. **L17.**

S. HAUGHTON The sea-waves were recorded on the self-registering tide gauges.

7 An instrument for testing whether a tool, a machine part, wire, etc., conforms to standard dimensions. **L17.**

JAMES SMITH It is much easier to file correctly with the assistance of a gauge than a pair of callipers.

8 *fig.* A means of judging or assessing; a standard, a criterion. **L17.**

M. HUNTER Duration of an emotion is no gauge of its intensity.

9 A carpenter's adjustable tool for making parallel lines. **L17.**
10 PRINTING. A strip of metal or other material used for measuring and controlling the depth of a margin, the length of a page, etc. Now chiefly *hist.* **L17.**
11 A device attached or linked to a receptacle in order to indicate the extent, depth, condition, etc., of its contents. **L18.**
fuel gauge, ***oil gauge***, ***pressure gauge***, ***tyre gauge***, etc.
– COMB. (all PHYSICS): **gauge boson** a boson that is invariant under a gauge transformation, such as a photon or a gluon; ***gauge function***: see sense 1c above; **gauge invariance** the property of remaining unaltered under a gauge transformation; **gauge theory** a quantum field theory of subatomic particles and their interactions which makes use of gauge functions; **gauge transformation** the introduction of a gauge function into an equation.

gauge /geɪdʒ/ *verb trans.* Also ***gage**. **LME.**
[ORIGIN Old Northern French *gauger*, var. of (also mod.) *jauger*: cf. GAUGE *noun*.]
1 Measure or determine the exact dimensions, proportions, or amount of (esp. an object of standard size, as wire, a bolt, or a fluctuating force, as rainfall or wind); ascertain the exact depth of (a liquid). **LME.**

LD BERNERS He gauged yᵉ depnesse of the dyche with a speare. JOHN PHILLIPS I have gauged . . the river . . and obtained . . the quantity of water in cubic feet per day. P. WARNER The copper-tin alloy was not always accurately gauged. *Industry Week* Productivity is gaged by output per manhour.

2 Find the capacity or content of (a cask or similar vessel) by measurement and calculation, esp. by means of a gauging rod. **LME.**
3 Mark or measure off (a specified distance). **LME.**
4 *fig.* Evaluate, appraise; estimate, take the measure of; *esp.* assess the character, temperament, etc., of (a person). **L16.**

G. ORWELL With no clocks and no daylight it was hard to gauge the time. G. GREENE Money was never the standard by which values were gauged. E. L. DOCTOROW Everyone talked around Freud, glancing at him . . to gauge his mood.

5 Cause to conform to standard dimensions; *spec.* cut (bricks or stones) to a uniform size. **E17.**
6 BUILDING. Mix (plaster) in the proper proportions for quick drying. **L17.**
7 DRESSMAKING. Draw up (part of a garment) in a series of parallel gathers. **L19.**
– COMB.: **gauging rod** an instrument for measuring the capacity or contents of casks.
■ **gaugeable** *adjective* (*a*) *hist.* (of a cask of liquor etc.) liable to be gauged for excise duty; (*b*) able to be measured or gauged: **LME.** **gauger** *noun* (*a*) a person who or an instrument which gauges; (*b*) *spec.* an official who measures the quantity of liquor in a cask; *esp.* (now *hist.* & *Scot.*) an exciseman: **ME.**

gauk *adjective* var. of GAWK *adjective*.

Gaul /gɔːl/ *noun*. Also (earlier) †**Galle**. **LME.**
[ORIGIN from Latin *Gallus*, prob. from Celtic. Cf. GALLIC *adjective*¹.]
1 A native or inhabitant of ancient Gaul, a region roughly corresponding to modern France and Belgium with parts of Germany and the Netherlands, and formerly including the northern part of Italy. **LME.**
2 A Frenchman, a Frenchwoman. *poet.* & *joc.* **M17.**
■ **Gaulic** *adjective* (now *rare*) = GALLIC *adjective*¹ 2 **E17.**

†**gaulding** *noun* var. of GAULIN.

Gauleiter /ˈgaʊlʌɪtə/ *noun*. **M20.**
[ORIGIN German, from *Gau* administrative district + *Leiter* leader.]
A political official controlling a Nazi district; *transf.* an overbearing (local) official.

M. MCLUHAN Exclusive playgrounds for the *gauleiters* of big business.

gaulin /ˈgɔːlɪn/ *noun*. *W. Indian.* Also (earlier) †**gaulding**. **E18.**
[ORIGIN Unknown.]
Any of various kinds of heron and egret.

Gaulish /ˈgɔːlɪʃ/ *adjective* & *noun*. **M17.**
[ORIGIN from GAUL + -ISH¹.]
▸ **A** *adjective*. Of or pertaining to the ancient Gauls or their language. Also (chiefly *poet.* or *joc.*) French. **M17.**
▸ **B** *noun*. The language of the ancient Gauls. **M17.**

Gaullism /ˈgəʊlɪz(ə)m/ *noun*. Also **de Gaull-** /də ˈgəʊl-/. **M20.**
[ORIGIN French *Gaullisme*, from de *Gaulle* (see below): see -ISM.]
(Adherence to) the nationalist principles of General Charles de Gaulle (1890–1970), French military and political leader.

Gaullist /ˈgəʊlɪst/ *adjective* & *noun*. Also **de Gaull-** /də ˈgəʊl-/. **M20.**
[ORIGIN French *Gaulliste*, formed as GAULLISM: see -IST.]
▸ **A** *adjective*. Supporting or pertaining to Gaullism. **M20.**
▸ **B** *noun*. An adherent of Gaullism. **M20.**

gault /gɔːlt/ *noun*. **L16.**
[ORIGIN Unknown.]
A thick heavy clay; *spec.* (GEOLOGY, usu. **G-**) a series of clays and marls between the upper and lower greensand in S. England. Also ***gault clay***.
■ **gaulty** *adjective* boggy and clayey **L18.**

gaultheria /gɔːlˈθɪərɪə/ *noun*. **M19.**
[ORIGIN mod. Latin, from J.-F. *Gaultier* (*c* 1708–56), Canad. botanist: see -IA¹.]
Any of various evergreen shrubs constituting the genus *Gaultheria*, of the heath family; *esp.* the checkerberry, *G. procumbens*, of N. America.

gaum /gɔːm/ *noun*¹. *obsolete* exc. *dial.* Orig. †**gome**. **ME.**
[ORIGIN Old Norse *gaumr* care, heed = Old Saxon *gōma* Old High German *gouma*, from Gothic base repr. by *gaumjan* take notice of.]
Heed, attention, notice; wit, understanding.

gaum *noun*² see GORM *noun*.

gaum /gɔːm/ *verb*¹ *trans. obsolete* exc. *dial.* **M17.**
[ORIGIN Unknown.]
Pull about with the hands; handle improperly.

gaum /gɔːm/ *verb*² *intrans.* Chiefly *dial.* Also **gorm**. **L17.**
[ORIGIN Unknown.]
Stare vacantly or stupidly.

gaum /gɔːm/ *verb*³ *trans.* Also **gorm**. **L18.**
[ORIGIN Cf. COOM *noun* 3.]
Smear with a sticky substance; daub (something sticky) on a surface.

gaumless *adjective* see GORMLESS.

gaumy /ˈgɔːmi/ *adjective*. Also **gormy**. **L19.**
[ORIGIN from GAUM *verb*³ + -Y¹.]
Of painting: coarsely executed, daubed. Also (*dial.*), sticky.

†**gaunch** *noun*, *verb* vars. of GANCH *noun*, *verb*.

gaunt *noun* & *verb*¹ var. of GANT *noun* & *verb*.

gaunt /gɔːnt/ *adjective* & *verb*². **LME.**
[ORIGIN Unknown.]
▸ **A** *adjective*. †**1** Not fat; slender, slim. **LME–M18.**
2 Abnormally lean, esp. from exhaustion or lack of nourishment; thin and angular in appearance. **LME.**

J. WAINWRIGHT He was a tall man and gaunt to the point of emaciation.

3 *transf.* Of an inanimate thing: desolate and forbidding in appearance or character. Formerly, of a sound: hollow. **E19.**

T. HARDY I am . . surrounded by gaunt realities. T. C. WOLFE The trees rose gaunt and stark.

▸ **B** *verb trans.* Make (excessively) lean or thin. Chiefly as ***gaunted*** *ppl adjective*. Now chiefly *US*. **L16.**
■ **gauntly** *adverb* **M18.** **gauntness** *noun* **E17.**

gauntlet /ˈgɔːntlɪt/ *noun*¹. **LME.**
[ORIGIN Old French & mod. French *gantelet* dim. of *gant* glove, from Germanic base extant only in Old Norse *vǫttr* glove (Swedish, Danish *vante*): see -LET.]
1 A usu. leather-lined glove of mail worn as part of medieval armour. Also = CESTUS *noun*². **LME.**
2 A stout glove, reaching to the lower part of the arm, used in riding, fencing, falconry, wicketkeeping, etc. **M19.** ▸**b** The part of a glove designed to cover the wrist. **L19.**
– PHRASES: **fling down the gauntlet**, **throw down the gauntlet**, **throw the gauntlet** [from the medieval custom of throwing down a gauntlet when challenging someone to combat] *fig.* issue a challenge; show defiance. **pick up the gauntlet**, **take up the gauntlet** *fig.* accept a challenge; undertake the defence of a person or opinion.
■ **gauntleted** *adjective* armed or equipped with a gauntlet **E19.**

gauntlet /ˈgɔːntlɪt/ *noun*². Also ***gant-** /ˈgɑːnt-/. **M17.**
[ORIGIN Alt. of GANTLOPE, by assim. to GAUNTLET *noun*¹.]
run the gauntlet, †***pass the gauntlet***, run between two rows of people and be struck by them with sticks, knotted cords, etc., as a form of (orig. military or naval) punishment; *transf.* & *fig.* pass through a series of dangerous or unpleasant experiences.

gauntry *noun* var. of GANTRY.

gaup *verb* see GAWP.

gaupus *noun* var. of GAWPUS.

gaur /ˈgaʊə/ *noun*. Also **gour**. **E19.**
[ORIGIN Sanskrit *gaura* from base also of COW *noun*¹.]
A large wild ox, *Bos gaurus*, found in forests from India to Malaysia. Also called ***Indian bison***.

gauss /gaʊs/ *noun*. **L19.**
[ORIGIN K. F. *Gauss* (1777–1855) German mathematician.]
PHYSICS. Orig., a unit of magnetic field strength: = OERSTED. Later, a cgs unit of magnetic induction (equivalent to 10^{-4} tesla) equal to the flux density which exerts a force of one dyne per centimetre on a wire carrying one electromagnetic unit of current (ten amperes) perpendicular to the field.

Gaussian /ˈgaʊsɪən/ *adjective*. **L19.**
[ORIGIN formed as GAUSS + -IAN.]
Discovered or formulated by Gauss; *esp.* (STATISTICS) designating a curve, function, statistical process, etc., that is described mathematically by a function of the form (exp $[-(x-\mu)^2/2\sigma^2])/\sigma\sqrt{(2\pi)}$, where x is the variable, μ the mean, and σ^2 the variance. Cf. NORMAL *adjective* 7.
Gaussian distribution a normal distribution.

gauze /gɔːz/ *noun* & *adjective*. **M16.**
[ORIGIN French *gaze*, perh. from *Gaza* a town in Palestine.]
▸ **A** *noun*. **1** A thin transparent fabric of silk, linen, cotton, etc. Also MEDICINE, thin loosely woven material used for dressings and swabs. **M16.**
2 In full ***wire gauze***. A very fine wire mesh. **E19.**
3 A thin transparent haze. **M19.**

T. HARDY A blue gauze of smoke.

▸ **B** *adjective*. Made of gauze. **M18.**
■ **gauzelike** *adjective* resembling gauze, gauzy **L18.**

gauze /gɔːz/ *verb*. **L18.**
[ORIGIN from the noun.]
1 *verb trans.* Cover (as) with gauze; give a gauzy appearance to. Chiefly as ***gauzed*** *ppl adjective*. **L18.**

E. BOWEN Midges gauzed the air.

2 *verb intrans.* Melt hazily *into*. **E20.**

gauzy /ˈgɔːzi/ *adjective*. **L18.**
[ORIGIN from GAUZE *noun* + -Y¹.]
Of the nature of or resembling gauze; thin and transparent.

J. UPDIKE Isabel carried a gauzy beach dress . . but chose to leave the beach not wearing it.

■ **gauzily** *adverb* **E20.** **gauziness** *noun* **E19.**

gavage /gaˈvɑːʒ/ *noun*. **L19.**
[ORIGIN French.]
A method of forcible feeding by means of a force pump and a stomach tube.

gavel /ˈgav(ə)l/ *noun*¹ & *adjective*. Long *obsolete* exc. *hist.*
[ORIGIN Old English *gafol* from Germanic, rel. to base of GIVE *verb*.]
▸ **A** *noun* **1** †**a** Payment to a superior; tribute. **OE–L15.** ▸**b** Rent. **OE.**
†**2** Interest on money lent; usury. **OE–L15.**
▸ **B** *attrib.* or as *adjective*. Chiefly LAW. Of or relating to payments or services exacted from a tenant. **OE.**

gavel /ˈgav(ə)l/ *noun*². *obsolete* exc. *dial.* **LME.**
[ORIGIN Old Northern French *gavel* masc., *gavelle* fem. (mod. *javelle*).]
A quantity of corn cut and ready to be made into a sheaf.
lie on the gavel (of corn) lie unbound.

gavel /ˈgav(ə)l/ *noun*³. **E19.**
[ORIGIN from GAVEL(KIND.]
hist. A partition of land made among a whole tribe or sept on the death of the holder. Cf. GAVELKIND 3b.
– COMB.: **Gavel Act**, **Gavel Law** a statute (1704) enforcing the practice of English gavelkind on Irish Catholics, but allowing the eldest son to inherit the whole estate if he conformed to the Church of Ireland.

gavel /ˈgav(ə)l/ *noun*⁴. Orig. *US*. **E19.**
[ORIGIN Unknown.]
1 A stonemason's mallet. **E19.**
2 An auctioneer's hammer; a small hammer used by a chairman, judge, etc., to call for order. **M19.**

R. P. WARREN Somebody snickered in the courtroom and the judge rapped with his gavel.

gavel-to-gavel *US* designating television coverage of a conference, debate, etc., which shows the event from beginning to end.

gavel /ˈgav(ə)l/ *verb*¹ *trans. obsolete* exc. *dial.* Infl. **-ll-**. **LME.**
[ORIGIN from GAVEL *noun*². Cf. Old French & mod. French *javeler*, medieval Latin *gavellare*.]
Gather (mown corn) into heaps for loading.

gavel /ˈgav(ə)l/ *verb*² *trans.* Infl. **-ll-**. **E19.**
[ORIGIN from GAVEL *noun*³.]
hist. Divide and distribute (land) according to the practice of gavelkind.

gavel /ˈgav(ə)l/ *verb*³. Chiefly *US*. Infl. **-ll-**, ***-l-**. **E20.**
[ORIGIN from GAVEL *noun*⁴.]
1 *verb intrans.* Use a gavel. **E20.**

T. DREISER Gaveling for order and ordering the arrest of the offender.

2 *verb trans.* Bring (an assembly) to order or dismiss (a speaker) by use of a gavel. **M20.**

G

Time He gaveled his Senate . . committee into session.

†**gavelet** *noun.* ME–M18.
[ORIGIN from GAVEL *noun*[1]. Cf. medieval Latin *gavelettum*.]
LAW. A legal process against a tenant for non-payment of rent, esp. for lands held in gavelkind.

gavelkind /ˈgav(ə)lkʌɪnd, -kɪnd/ *noun.* ME.
[ORIGIN from GAVEL *noun*[1] + KIND *noun*.]
hist. **1** A kind of (chiefly Kentish) land tenure (abolished in 1925) similar to socage but distinguished by the custom of dividing a deceased tenant's land equally among his sons. ME.
2 *gen.* The custom of dividing a deceased person's property equally among all (male) heirs. M16.

fig.: DONNE For God shall impart to us all a mysterious Gavel-kind, a mysterious Equality of fulness of Glory to us all.

3 *transf.* **a** A Welsh system of property inheritance similar to the Kentish (see sense 1 above). M16. ▸**b** More fully ***Irish gavelkind***. A system of adding a deceased person's land to the common stock and redividing the whole area among all members of the tribe or sept. E17.
– COMB.: **Gavelkind Act** = *Gavel Act* s.v. GAVEL *noun*[3].
■ **gavelkinder** *noun* (*rare*) a person holding land in gavelkind L16.

G

gaveller /ˈgav(ə)lə/ *noun.* *obsolete* exc. *hist.* ME.
[ORIGIN from GAVEL *noun*[1] + -ER[1].]
†**1** A usurer. Only in ME.
2 In the Forest of Dean: an officer of the Crown who grants mining rights and collects dues. L17.
3 A person who pays gavel (GAVEL *noun*[1] 1b) for rented land. M19.

gavelock /ˈgav(ə)lɒk/ *noun.*
[ORIGIN Old English *gafeluc* dim. of *gafol*, *geafel* fork: cf. GABLE *noun*.]
1 A javelin, a dart. Long *obsolete* exc. *hist.* OE.
2 An iron crowbar or lever. Now *dial.* L15.
†**3** A metal spur for a fighting cock. Only in L17.

gavial *noun* var. of GHARIAL.

gavotte /gəˈvɒt/ *noun & verb.* L17.
[ORIGIN French from mod. Provençal *gavoto*, from *Gavot* an inhabitant of the Alps.]
▸ **A** *noun.* **1** A medium-paced dance popular in the 18th cent. L17.
2 A piece of music for this dance, composed in common time with each phrase beginning on the third beat of the bar; a piece of music in this rhythm, *esp.* one which forms a movement of a suite. E18.
▸ **B** *verb intrans.* Dance a gavotte. E19.

gavroche /gavrɔʃ/ *noun.* Pl. pronounced same. L19.
[ORIGIN French, a gamin in Victor Hugo's novel *Les misérables*.]
A gamin, gamine, or street urchin, esp. in Paris.

†**gaw** *verb intrans.* ME–E19.
[ORIGIN Old Norse *gá* heed.]
Gape, stare; look intently.

Gawd /gɔːd/ *noun.* *slang.* Also **g-**. L19.
[ORIGIN Alt.]
= GOD *noun*: chiefly as interjection & in exclamatory phrs. corresp. to those s.v. GOD *noun* 5.
for Gawd's sake, ***Gawd knows***.
– COMB.: **Gawdelpus**, **Gawd-help-us** a helpless or exasperating person.

†**gawdy** *adjective* var. of GAUDY *adjective*.

gawk /gɔːk/ *noun.* L17.
[ORIGIN In sense 1 perh. from GAWK *adjective*; in sense 2 from GAWK *verb*.]
1 An awkward, stupid, or bashful person. L17.

A. CARTER Great gawk of an ignorant black girl.

2 A look, a glance. M20.

E. O'BRIEN I had a gawk at the letter she got.

■ **gawkish** *adjective* awkward, bashful L19.

gawk /gɔːk/ *adjective.* *dial.* Also **gauk**. E18.
[ORIGIN App. contr. of GALLACK.]
Left. Chiefly in ***gawk-handed***, left-handed.

gawk /gɔːk/ *verb intrans.* *colloq.* L18.
[ORIGIN Perh. from GAWK *noun* 1, but perh. an iterative from GAW *verb* (with suffix as in *tal-k*, *wal-k*, *lur-k*).]
Stare stupidly, gape.

K. KESEY I want you workin', not gawkin' around like some big useless cow! C. D. EBY Gawking in wonder at the falling bombs.

■ **gawker** *noun* M20.

gawky /ˈgɔːki/ *noun & adjective.* E18.
[ORIGIN from GAWK *noun* or *verb* + -Y[1].]
▸ **A** *noun.* An awkward or stupid person; a lout. E18.

GEO. ELIOT Nothing makes a woman more of a gawky than . . showing tempers in public.

▸ **B** *adjective.* Of a person, occas. a thing: awkward, ungainly. M18.

G. GREENE The big boyish lover with his sulks . . and his gawky abandonment to joy and grief. *Sport* Are you fat and flabby? Or skinny and gawky?

■ **gawkily** *adverb* E19. **gawkiness** *noun* L19.

gawn /gɔːn/ *noun.* Now *dial.* L15.
[ORIGIN Contr. of GALLON.]
1 A gallon, a gallon measure. L15.
2 A bucket, *spec.* with one long stave serving as a handle. Also, a ladle. L17.

gawp /gɔːp/ *verb intrans.* Also (*arch.* & *dial.*) **gaup**, (*dial.*) **gorp**. L17.
[ORIGIN Perh. alt. of GAPE *verb*: cf. GALP.]
Yawn, gape; stare stupidly or in astonishment.

R. CAMPBELL Roaring mouths that gawp like cod. B. BAINBRIDGE It was raining heavily, but they stood there, gawping up at the windows.

■ **gawper** *noun* M20.

gawpus /ˈgɔːpəs/ *noun.* *dial.* Also **gaupus**. L18.
[ORIGIN from GAWP.]
A fool, a clumsy stupid lout.
– NOTE: Earliest in comb. *gilly-gawpus*, with 1st elem. of unkn. origin.

gay /geɪ/ *adjective, adverb, & noun.* ME.
[ORIGIN Old French & mod. French *gai*, of unknown origin.]
▸ **A** *adjective.* **1** Full of, disposed to, or indicating joy and mirth; light-hearted, carefree. ME. ▸**b** Airy, offhand, casual. L18.

J. RHYS The music was gay but the words were sad. M. MOORCOCK This event lifted my spirits and I became quite gay. **b** O. SITWELL A gay, insouciant race of extroverts.

2 Given to pleasure; freq. *euphem.*, dissolute, immoral. LME. ▸**b** Leading an immoral life; *spec.* engaging in prostitution. *slang.* E19.

W. COWPER Silent and chaste she steals along, far from the world's gay busy throng.

3 Good, excellent, fine. Now chiefly *dial.* LME. ▸**b** Of a woman: beautiful, charming, debonair. Long *arch.* & *poet.* LME. ▸**c** In good health, well. *dial.* M19.

M. TWAIN My business and your Law practice ought to make a pretty gay team.

4 Showy, brilliant, brightly coloured. Also, brightly decorated *with*. LME. ▸**b** Finely or showily dressed. Now *rare.* LME. ▸†**c** Superficially attractive; (of reasoning etc.) specious, plausible. LME–L18.

E. PEACOCK Their costumes were gay with ribbons. **b** SHAKES. *Oth.* Never lack'd gold, and yet went never gay.

5 Of a quantity or amount: considerable, reasonable, fair. (Cf. GEY *adjective*.) Chiefly *Scot.* L18.
6 Of an animal: lively, spirited, alert. E19. ▸**b** Of a (dog's) tail: carried high or erect. E20.

B. VESEY-FITZGERALD This terrier should impress with his fearless and gay disposition.

7 (Of a person, esp. a man) homosexual; of or pertaining to homosexuals; (of a place etc.) intended for or frequented by homosexuals. M20.

D. LODGE They thought Philip was gay because he had taken Charles Boon into his apartment. JONATHON GREEN The emergence of gay discos like Heaven.

– SPECIAL COLLOCATIONS & PHRASES: **gay cat** *US slang* (**a**) a hobo who accepts occasional work; (**b**) a young tramp, *esp.* one in company with an older man. **gay dog** a man given to revelling or self-indulgence. **gay deceiver** (**a**) a deceitful seducer; (**b**) in *pl.* (*slang*), shaped pads for increasing the apparent size of the female breasts. ***gay Greek***: see GREEK *noun* 5. **gay liberation**, **gay lib** (the advocacy of) the liberation of homosexuals from social stigma and discrimination. **gay plague** *colloq.* (*offensive*) Aids (so called because first identified amongst homosexuals). **get gay** *US slang* act in an impertinent or overfamiliar way. **gay pride** a sense of strong self-esteem associated with a person's public acknowledgement of his or her homosexuality. **the gay science** [Provençal *gai saber*] the art of poetry.
▸ **B** *adverb.* **1** Merrily, joyously; brightly, showily. Now chiefly with pres. and pa. pples, as ***gay-chirping***, ***gay-painted***, etc. *arch.* & *poet.* LME.

J. THOMSON Those gay-spent, festive nights.

2 Very, considerably, somewhat. (Cf. GEY *adverb*.) *Scot.* & *dial.* L17.

SIR W. SCOTT I ken I'm gay thick in the head.

▸ **C** *noun.* **1** Anything bright or showy; an ornament, a child's toy. Now *dial.* LME. ▸†**b** *fig.* A trifle, a childish amusement. L16–L17.
2 A picture, esp. in a book. Also, a picture book. Now *dial.* M17.
3 A homosexual, esp. a man. M20.
– NOTE: *Gay* meaning 'homosexual' became established in the 1960s as the term preferred by homosexual men to describe themselves. It is now the standard accepted term throughout the English-speaking world, and has overshadowed the other senses.
■ **gaydom** *noun* (chiefly *colloq.*) the realm or world of homosexuals L20.

gay /geɪ/ *verb.* L16.
[ORIGIN from the adjective.]
1 *verb trans.* Make gay or pleasant, embellish, brighten *up*. L16.

News Chronicle The charming effect of houses gayed up with these flower-filled boxes.

2 *verb intrans.* Be gay; play. *obsolete* exc. *dial.* M17.

gayal /gʌɪˈjɑːl/ *noun.* L18.
[ORIGIN Bengali.]
A semi-domesticated ox, *Bos frontalis*, of India and SE Asia, which is black or brown with white legs, and possibly a variety of the gaur.

gayatri /ˈgɑːjətriː/ *noun.* L18.
[ORIGIN Sanskrit, from *ga* sing.]
A Vedic metre comprising three octosyllabic lines; a hymn, verse, etc., composed in this metre, *esp.* the verse of the Rig Veda repeated daily as a prayer by brahmins.

gaydar /ˈgeɪdɑː/ *noun.* *slang.* L20.
[ORIGIN Blend of GAY and RADAR.]
A homosexual person's supposed ability to discern another by interpreting subtle signals conveyed by his or her appearance, interests, etc.

gayety *noun* see GAIETY.

Gay-Lussac's law /geɪˈluːsaks lɔː/ *noun phr.* E19.
[ORIGIN *Gay-Lussac* (see GAYLUSSITE).]
CHEMISTRY. A law stating that the volumes of gases undergoing a reaction at constant pressure and temperature are in a simple ratio to each other and to that of the product.

gaylussite /geɪˈlʌsʌɪt/ *noun.* E19.
[ORIGIN from J. L. *Gay-Lussac* (1778–1850), French physicist + -ITE[1].]
MINERALOGY. A rare monoclinic hydrated carbonate of calcium and sodium occurring as white or yellowish crystals.

gayly *adverb* see GAILY.

gayness /ˈgeɪnɪs/ *noun.* LME.
[ORIGIN from GAY *adjective* + -NESS.]
†**1** (A) delight, (a) pleasure; merriment. LME–E17.
2 Brilliant or showy appearance, brightness. Long *rare* or *obsolete*. LME.
3 Cheerfulness, mirth. L19.
4 Homosexuality. L20.

gaysome /ˈgeɪs(ə)m/ *adjective.* *arch.* & *poet.* E17.
[ORIGIN from GAY *adjective* + -SOME[1].]
Full of or giving rise to gaiety; merry, cheery, pleasant.

gazabo /gəˈzeɪbəʊ/ *noun.* *slang* (freq. *derog.*). Chiefly *US.* Also **gazebo**. Pl. **-os**. L19.
[ORIGIN Perh. from Spanish *gazapo* a sly fellow.]
A fellow, a guy.

B. PENTON Aw, leave the old gazabo He's drunk.

gazania /gəˈzeɪnɪə/ *noun.* E19.
[ORIGIN mod. Latin (see below), from Theodorus *Gaza* (1398–1478), Greek scholar.]
Any of various mostly southern African plants of the genus *Gazania*, of the composite family, with conspicuous orange, yellow, scarlet, etc., ray florets; esp. *G. rigens* (also called ***treasure-flower***), grown as an ornamental flower.

gaze /geɪz/ *noun.* M16.
[ORIGIN from the verb.]
1 That which is gazed at; a spectacle, a sight. *obsolete* exc. *dial.* M16.

A. M. BENNETT His father lolled in his coach, and was the gaze of the village.

2 The act of staring; a steady or intent look. M16.

F. TUOHY Witek watched her, with hurt love in his gaze.

at gaze, †**at a gaze**, †**at the gaze** gazing in wonder etc.; *spec.* in HERALDRY (of a stag etc.) looking out of the shield, full-face. ***meet a person's gaze***: see MEET *verb*.
– COMB.: **gazehound** a hound that hunts by sight.
■ †**gazeful** *adjective* (*rare*, Spenser) gazing intently: only in L16. **gazement** *noun* (*rare*) a stare, a look; observation: L16.

gaze /geɪz/ *verb.* LME.
[ORIGIN Uncertain: perh. rel. to GAW.]
1 *verb intrans.* Orig., stare vacantly or curiously. Now usu., look intently or fixedly (*at*, *on*, *upon*, etc.). LME.

J. STEINBECK He gazed about with mild, half-blind eyes. DAY LEWIS I would tag around . . content to gaze upon him idolatrously.

gaze at one's navel: see NAVEL 1.
2 *verb trans.* Look fixedly at, stare at. *poet.* L16.

P. J. BAILEY Who dare gaze the sun.

– COMB.: **gazing stock** (now *rare*) a person on whom others gaze or stare.
■ **gazer** *noun* M16.

gazebo /gəˈziːbəʊ/ *noun*[1]. Pl. **-o(e)s**. M18.
[ORIGIN Perh. joc. from GAZE *verb*, in imitation of Latin futures in *-ebo*.]
1 A building or structure (as a turret, lantern, summer house, etc.) which commands a view. M18.
2 A projecting window or balcony. M19.

gazebo *noun*[2] var. of GAZABO.

gazelle /gəˈzɛl/ *noun.* Also **-el**. Pl. same, **-s**. E17.
[ORIGIN Old French *gazel*, prob. from Spanish *gacel* from Arabic *ghazāl*.]
Any of various small, graceful, usu. fawn and white antelopes of Africa and Asia, of the subfamily

Antilopinae, *esp.* any of those of the genera *Gazella* and *Procapra*.

gazette /gəˈzɛt/ *noun*. Also **G-**. **E17.**
[ORIGIN French, or its source Italian *gazzetta*, orig. Venetian Italian *gazeta de la novità* i.e. a 'halfpennyworth of news', so called because sold for a *gazeta*, a Venetian coin of small value: see -ETTE.]
1 Orig., a news-sheet; a periodical publication giving an account of current events. Now, a newspaper, *esp.* (the title of) the official newspaper of an organization or institution. **E17.**

R. KIPLING Far-off Calcutta papers, such as the *Indigo Planters' Gazette*

2 *spec.* (The title of) an official journal in Britain containing lists of government appointments, bankruptcies, and other public notices; an official journal of any government. **M17.**
be in the gazette have one's bankruptcy published. ***The Belfast Gazette***, ***The Edinburgh Gazette***, ***The London Gazette***, etc.

gazette /gəˈzɛt/ *verb trans.* **L17.**
[ORIGIN from the noun.]
Publish in a gazette. Usu. in *pass.*, be the subject of an announcement in an official gazette, *esp.* be named as appointed *to* a post, command, etc.

W. S. CHURCHILL In March 1895 I was gazetted to the 4th Hussars. P. PORTER Though the crime is not gazetted Punishment is palpable and that's the same As Law.

gazetteer /gazɪˈtɪə/ *noun & verb*. **E17.**
[ORIGIN French *gazettier* (now *gazetier*) from Italian *gazzettiere*, formed as GAZETTE *noun*: see -EER.]
▸ **A** *noun*. **1** A journalist; *spec.* one appointed and paid by the Government. Now *hist.* **E17.**
2 A geographical index or dictionary. **E18.**
†**3** A newspaper. Only in **M18.**
▸ **B** *verb*. **1** *verb intrans.* Write for a gazette or gazetteer. Now *rare*. **L18.**
2 *verb trans.* Describe geographically in a gazetteer. *rare*. **L19.**

gazillion /gəˈzɪljən/ *noun*. *colloq.* (orig. *US*). Also **kazillion** /kəˈzɪljən/. **L20.**
[ORIGIN Arbitrarily after *million*, *billion*, etc., prob. influenced by ZILLION.]
A very large number or quantity; (in *pl.*) a very large amount of money.

S. KING *The Firm* sold roughly nine gazillion copies.

gazob /gəˈzɒb/ *noun*. *Austral. slang*. **E20.**
[ORIGIN Uncertain: perh. from GAZABO.]
A fool, a blunderer.

†**gazon** *noun*. **E–M18.**
[ORIGIN French = grass, a piece of turf.]
A wedge-shaped piece of turf used in fortification to line parapets etc. Usu. in *pl.*

gazoo *noun* var. of KAZOO.

gazook /gəˈzuːk/ *noun*. *slang*. **E20.**
[ORIGIN Unknown. Cf. GAZABO, GAZOB.]
A fool, a stupid or unpleasant person.

gazoomph *verb & noun* see GAZUMP.

gazpacho /gəsˈpɑːtʃəʊ, *foreign* gaθˈpatʃo/ *noun*. Also **gas-**. Pl. **-os**, /-əʊz, *foreign* -ɔs/. **E19.**
[ORIGIN Spanish.]
A Spanish soup made from tomatoes, peppers, cucumber, garlic, etc., and served cold.

gazump /gəˈzʌmp/ *verb & noun*. *colloq.* Also **-zoomph** /-zʊmf/, **-zumph** /-zʌmf/. **E20.**
[ORIGIN Unknown.]
▸ **A** *verb trans.* Swindle; *spec.* raise the price of a house etc. after accepting an offer from (an intending buyer). **E20.**
▸ **B** *noun*. A swindle. **M20.**

gazunder /gəˈzʌndə/ *verb trans.* *colloq.* **L20.**
[ORIGIN from GAZUMP + UNDER *adverb*.]
Of a house-buyer: reduce the value of an offer already accepted by (a seller) while threatening otherwise to withdraw.
■ **gazunderer** *noun* **L20.**

GB *abbreviation*.
Great Britain.

GBE *abbreviation*.
Knight (or Dame) Grand Cross (of the Order) of the British Empire.

GBH *abbreviation*.
Grievous bodily harm.

GC *abbreviation*.
George Cross.

GCB *abbreviation*.
Knight (or Dame) Grand Cross (of the Order) of the Bath.

GCE *abbreviation*. *hist.*
General Certificate of Education.

GCHQ *abbreviation*.
Government Communications Headquarters.

GCIE *abbreviation*.
Knight Grand Commander (of the Order) of the Indian Empire.

GCMG *abbreviation*.
Knight (or Dame) Grand Cross (of the Order) of St Michael and St George.

GCSE *abbreviation*.
General Certificate of Secondary Education.

GCSI *abbreviation*.
Knight Grand Commander (of the Order) of the Star of India.

GCVO *abbreviation*.
Knight (or Dame) Grand Cross of the Royal Victorian Order.

Gd *symbol*.
CHEMISTRY. Gadolinium.

gdn *abbreviation*.
Garden.

Gdns *abbreviation*.
Gardens.

GDP *abbreviation*.
Gross domestic product.

GDR *abbreviation*.
hist. German Democratic Republic.

Ge *symbol*.
CHEMISTRY. Germanium.

Ge'ez /ˈgiːɛz, gəˈɛz/ *noun & adjective*. Also **Geez**. **L18.**
[ORIGIN Ethiopic.]
(Of or pertaining to) the ancient Semitic language of Ethiopia, now used only as a liturgical language. Cf. ETHIOPIC.

†**geal** *verb trans. & intrans.* **LME–E19.**
[ORIGIN Old French & mod. French *geler* from Latin *gelare* freeze.]
Congeal.

gean /giːn/ *noun*. **M16.**
[ORIGIN Old French *guine* (mod. *guigne*): ult. origin unknown.]
The wild sweet cherry, *Prunus avium*. Also, the fruit of this tree.

geanticlinal /ˌdʒiːantɪˈklʌɪn(ə)l/ *noun & adjective*. **L19.**
[ORIGIN from Greek *gē* earth + ANTICLINAL.]
GEOLOGY. ▸ **A** *noun*. = GEANTICLINE. Now *rare*. **L19.**
▸ **B** *adjective*. Of, pertaining to, or of the nature of a geanticline. **L19.**

geanticline /dʒiːˈantɪklʌɪn/ *noun*. **L19.**
[ORIGIN Back-form. from GEANTICLINAL.]
GEOLOGY. A large-scale upward flexure of the earth's crust; a broad anticline.

gear /gɪə/ *noun & verb*. Also †**geer**. **ME.**
[ORIGIN Old Norse *gervi*, *gorvi* corresp. to Old Saxon *garawī*, *gar(e)wī* from Germanic: rel. to GAR *verb*, YARE.]
▸ **A** *noun*. **I** Equipment.
1 *collect. sing.* Items of personal wear; apparel, attire, esp. (*colloq.*) for young people. **ME.** ▸†**b** In *pl.* Habits, manners. Only in **ME.**

WORDSWORTH Peasants in their homely gear. *Daily Mail* Prince William . . starts new fashions in toddler gear.

2 Armour, arms, equipment for battle. *arch.* **ME.**

CARLYLE Of serviceable fighting-gear small stock.

3 **a** Harness for draught animals. Formerly usu. in *pl.* **ME.** ▸**b** Accoutrements of a riding horse, or of the rider. Freq. with specifying word. **LME.**

a S. JOHNSON She rises before the sun to order the horses to their geers. **b** J. YEATS The Egyptians were skilful manufacturers of riding gear.

▸ **II** Apparatus.
4 Apparatus for a specified activity; appliances, implements, tackle, tools. **ME.** ▸†**b** A set of heddles. **E16–M19.**
5 A combination of wheels, levers, and other mechanical appliances usu. for a given purpose; *esp.* the appliances or furnishings connected with the acting portions of any piece of mechanism. Freq. preceded by defining word. **E16.** ▸**b** Wheels working upon one another by means of teeth etc. **E19.** ▸**c** In full ***landing gear***. The undercarriage of an aircraft. **E20.**

A. S. NEILL Another tried to put my lathe in screw-cutting gear when it was running.

6 NAUTICAL. Rigging. **M17.**
7 The arrangements connecting a motor or engine with its work. **E19.** ▸**b** Any of the several sets of gearwheels in a motor vehicle, bicycle, etc., which can be used to alter the relation between the speed of the driving mechanism and of the driven part. Also, the particular state of adjustment of this relation. **L19.**

b J. GARDNER The grind of gears came, meaning he was halfway up the hill. *fig.*: *New Statesman* If Labour is to win the next election . . there now has to be a shift into a different gear.

in gear connected with the motor, working (*lit.* & *fig.*). **out of gear** with the connection with the motor interrupted or not working; *fig.* out of order. ***b bottom gear***: see BOTTOM *adjective*. **change gear** engage a different gear in a vehicle. ***differential gear***: see DIFFERENTIAL *adjective* 4. *FIRST* ***gear***. ***high gear***: see HIGH *adjective*. ***low gear***: see LOW *adjective*. ***reverse gear***: see REVERSE *adjective*. ***top gear***: see TOP *adjective*.
▸ **III** Stuff.
8 Goods, movable property, household utensils. **LME.** ▸†**b** Objects of a specified kind. **LME–E19.** ▸**c** Possessions in general, wealth, money. *Scot. & N. English*. **M16.**

K. HULME The gear he spoke of is three suitcases and a forlorn carton of books. **c** A. S. SWAN That foolish, misguided sister of yours has married an old man for his gear!

9 **a** Discourse, doctrine, talk; *derog.* 'stuff', nonsense. Long *arch. & dial.* **LME.** ▸**b** Doings, 'goings on'. Now *arch. & dial.* **LME.** ▸**c** A matter, an affair, a business. *obsolete* exc. *dial.* **M16.**

a DRYDEN Priests with prayers and other godly gear. **b** E. L. LINTON We shall have such fun! . . It will be good gear, I can tell you! **c** SIR W. SCOTT I understand this gear better than you do.

10 A material substance or stuff; *derog.* rubbish. *obsolete* exc. *dial.* **L15.** ▸**b** Corrupt matter, pus. **M16–M17.**

C. HEYDON That out of wheat there should spring vp darnell . . and smuttie geare. **b** HENRY MORE The wound of his throat gaping, but no gear or corruption in it.

– COMB.: **gearbox**, **gearcase** (a box, case enclosing) the gearing of a motor vehicle etc.; **gear change** (*a*) the action or an act of engaging a different gear in a vehicle; (*b*) *US* a gear lever; **gearhead** *N. Amer. colloq.* an enthusiast for cars or motor vehicles; **gear lever** a lever employed to engage or change gear; **gear shift** *N. Amer.* a gear lever; **gearwheel** a cogwheel, *esp.* one such in a bicycle which is driven directly by the pedals.
▸ **B** *verb*. †**1** *verb trans.* Adorn; array; dress. **ME–L17.**
2 *verb trans.* Equip. *arch.* **LME.**
3 *verb trans.* Harness (a draught animal). Also foll. by *up*. **M17.**
4 **a** *verb intrans.* Be in gear, work smoothly *with*. **M18.** ▸**b** *verb trans.* Put (machinery) into gear; connect, link (as if) by gearing. **M19.**

b *fig.*: *Spectator* An entire [ballet] production geared to the Bolshoi interpretation.

– WITH ADVERBS IN SPECIALIZED SENSES: **gear down** provide with a low gear, put into a lower gear. **gear up** (*a*) provide with a high gear, put into a higher gear; (*b*) set in readiness, prepare (usu. in *pass.*); (*c*) equip oneself, get ready.
■ **geared** *adjective* †(*a*) equipped, armed; (*b*) having or provided with gears; (*c*) FINANCE having (high, low) gearing (GEARING *noun* 4): **L15.** **gearless** *adjective* **L19.**

gearing /ˈgɪərɪŋ/ *noun*. **E19.**
[ORIGIN from GEAR *noun & verb* + -ING[1].]
1 Equipment, working implements. *rare*. **E19.**
2 Harness. *dial.* **M19.**
3 The process of fitting with gears. Also, the set or arrangement of gears in a machine. **M19.**

Footloose Incredibly low gearing allowing the pedals to be turned quickly.

4 FINANCE. The ratio of a company's total capital to its equity capital; the proportion of capital existing in the form of debt. **M20.**

Fortune [Rupert] Murdoch operates with a phenomenal amount of debt, or gearing.

geas /gɛʃ, geɪʃ, gɑːʃ/ *noun*. Also **geis** /gɛʃ/. Pl. **geasa**, **geisa**. **L19.**
[ORIGIN Irish.]
In Irish folklore: an obligation or prohibition magically imposed on a person.

geason /ˈgiːz(ə)n/ *adjective*.
[ORIGIN Old English *gǣsne*, *gēsne* barren. Cf. Old High German *keisinī* barrenness.]
†**1** Producing scantily, barren, unproductive. **OE–LME.**
2 Scantily produced; rare, scarce, uncommon. Long *obsolete* exc. *dial.* **LME.**
†**3** Seldom encountered, extraordinary, amazing. Only in **L16.**

gebang /dʒɪˈbaŋ/ *noun*. **E19.**
[ORIGIN Malay.]
More fully ***gebang palm***. A fan palm, *Corypha elata*, of tropical Asia, the fibre of whose leaf petioles is used to make hats and ropes.

Gebrauchsmusik /gəˈbraʊksmuziːk/ *noun*. **M20.**
[ORIGIN German, from *Gebrauch* use + *Musik* music.]
Music intended primarily for practical use and performance; *esp.* music considered suitable for amateur groups and domestic playing.

gebur /gəˈbʊə/ *noun*.
[ORIGIN Old English *gebūr* = Old Saxon *gibūr*, Old High German *gibūr(o)*: cf. BOOR, NEIGHBOUR *noun & adjective*.]
hist. A tenant farmer in the pre-Conquest English community.

geck /gɛk/ *noun*[1]. *obsolete* exc. *dial.* **E16.**
[ORIGIN Of Low Dutch origin: cf. Middle Low German *geck*, Middle Dutch *g(h)ec(k)*, Dutch *gek* adjective & noun: rel. to *gecken* GECK *verb*.]
A fool, a simpleton; a butt, a dupe.

geck /gɛk/ *noun*[2]. Chiefly *Scot.* E16.
[ORIGIN Dutch (= German) *geck* noun corresp. to *gecken*: see GECK *verb*.]
A gesture of derision; an expression of scorn or contempt.

geck /gɛk/ *verb*. *Scot. & N. English*. L16.
[ORIGIN App. from Low German *gecken* = Middle Dutch *ghecken*, Dutch *gekken*, German *gecken*: see GECK *noun*[1].]
†**1** *verb trans.* Mock, deceive, cheat. Only in L16.
2 *verb intrans.* Scoff *at*, use mocking language or gestures. E17.
3 *verb intrans. & trans.* Toss (the head) scornfully; look proudly (at). E18.

gecko /ˈgɛkəʊ/ *noun*. Also **gekko**. Pl. **-o(e)s**. L18.
[ORIGIN Malay dial. *geko*, *gekok*, ult. imit. Cf. TOKAY *noun*[2].]
Any of various small insectivorous usu. nocturnal lizards of the family Gekkonidae, widespread in warm regions, many being notable for adhesive pads on the feet enabling them to climb smooth or overhanging surfaces, and for their vocalizations.
Moorish gecko: see MOORISH *adjective*[2] 1.

GED *abbreviation*. *N. Amer.*
General Educational Development, a certificate attesting that the holder has passed examinations considered by the Department of Education as equivalent to completion of high school.

G

ged /gɛd/ *noun*. *Scot. & N. English*. ME.
[ORIGIN Old Norse *gedda* rel. to *gaddr* GAD *noun*[1].]
The pike (fish).

gedact /gəˈdakt/ *noun*. M19.
[ORIGIN German *gedackt*, obsolete pa. pple of *decken* cover.]
MUSIC. An organ flue-stop having its pipes closed at the top.

Gedankenexperiment /gəˈdaŋk(ə)nɛˌkspɛrɪm(ə)nt/ *noun*. M20.
[ORIGIN German, from *Gedanken* thought + *Experiment* experiment.]
= ***thought experiment*** s.v. THOUGHT *noun*[1].

geddit /ˈgɛdɪt/ *interjection*. *slang*. L20.
[ORIGIN Alt. of (*do you*) *get it*? Cf. INNIT.]
Do you understand?, do you see what I mean?

gee /dʒiː/ *noun*[1]. *Scot. & N. English*. E17.
[ORIGIN Unknown.]
A fit of bad temper or sullenness.

gee /dʒiː/ *noun*[2]. *colloq*. M19.
[ORIGIN Orig. a child's word, from GEE *interjection*[1]. Cf. GEE-GEE.]
A horse.

gee /dʒiː/ *noun*[3]. *slang*. L19.
[ORIGIN Unknown: cf. GEE *noun*[4], GEE *verb*[2].]
More fully ***gee-man***. The assistant to a cheapjack or showman.

gee /dʒiː/ *noun*[4]. *US slang*. E20.
[ORIGIN from the first letter of GUY *noun*[2].]
A person, a fellow.

gee /dʒiː/ *noun*[5]. *US slang*. M20.
[ORIGIN from the first letter of GRAND *noun*.]
A thousand dollars.

gee /giː, dʒiː/ *noun*[6]. *slang* (orig. *US*). M20.
[ORIGIN Uncertain, perh. rel. to GHEE.]
Any of various narcotic drugs; *esp.* opium.
■ **geed-up** *adjective* drugged. M20.

Gee /dʒiː/ *noun*[7]. M20.
[ORIGIN from the first letter of GRID.]
hist. A British navigational radar designed to guide bombers to their targets, developed in the Second World War.

gee /dʒiː/ *verb*[1] *intrans. slang*. Pa. t. & pple **geed**. L17.
[ORIGIN Uncertain: perh. from GEE *interjection*[1].]
'Go', fit, suit, accord; (of people) behave as is desired, agree, get on well (together). Only in neg. phrases.

gee /dʒiː/ *verb*[2]. Pa. t. & pple **geed**. E19.
[ORIGIN from GEE *interjection*[1].]
1 *verb trans.* **a** = JEE *verb* 2. E19. ▸**b** Direct (a horse etc.) by the command 'gee'. M19. ▸**c** *fig.* Incite or encourage (a person); cause (a person or animal) to move more quickly. Freq. foll. by *up*. L19.
2 *verb intrans.* = JEE *verb* 1. M19.

gee /dʒiː/ *interjection*[1]. E17.
[ORIGIN Unknown.]
A word of command used to a horse etc.: go on, go faster; occas., turn to the right.

gee /dʒiː/ *interjection*[2]. *slang* (orig. *US*). M19.
[ORIGIN Perh. alt. of JESUS.]
Expr. discovery, enthusiasm, surprise, or emphasis.
– NOTE: Earliest in phrs. as GEE WHILLIKINS etc.

geebung /ˈdʒiːbʌŋ/ *noun*. L18.
[ORIGIN Dharuk *jibung*.]
(The edible fruit of) any of several chiefly Australian trees or shrubs of the genus *Persoonia* (family Proteaceae).

Geechee /ˈgiːtʃiː/ *noun*. *US dial.* E20.
[ORIGIN The *Ogeechee* River, Georgia, USA.]
A dialect, comprising words of English and African origin, spoken originally by black slaves in the region of the Ogeechee River, Georgia. Also *derog.*, a black person from the southern US.

geed *verb*[1], *verb*[2] *pa. t. & pple* of GEE *verb*[1], *verb*[2].

gee-gee /ˈdʒiːdʒiː/ *noun*. *nursery & colloq.* M19.
[ORIGIN Redupl. of GEE *interjection*[1]. Cf. GEE *noun*[2].]
A horse.

gee-ho /dʒiːˈhəʊ/ *interjection & verb*. M17.
[ORIGIN from GEE *interjection*[1] + HO *interjection*[2].]
▸ **A** *interjection*. = GEE *interjection*[1]. M17.
▸ **B** *verb intrans.* = GEE *verb*[2] 1b. M17.

gee-hup *interjection* see GEE-UP *interjection*.

geek /giːk/ *noun*. *slang*. L19.
[ORIGIN Var. of GECK *noun*[1].]
1 A foolish person, a simpleton, a dupe. Orig. *N. English*. L19.
R. A. HEINLEIN Want me to wake the dumb geek?
2 An assistant at a sideshow whose purpose is to appear as an object of disgust or derision. *US*. E20.
R. DAVIES I was compelled to exhibit Willard as a geek.
3 A person who is socially inept, boringly conventional, or overly studious. Orig. *US*. M20 ▸**b** A person who is knowledgeable and obsessive about computers and related technology. L20.
JACQUELINE WILSON He's OK if you don't mind him looking and acting like a total geek. **b** D. COUPLAND The geeks are swarming like bees around the latest gizmo. *Vanity Fair* A 16-year-old geek can hack into any computer system.
■ **geekdom** *noun* L20. **geeky** *adjective* socially inept, boringly conventional or studious; strange, odd: L20.

geelbek /ˈxɪəlbɛk/ *noun*. *S. Afr.* Also **-bec(k)**. Pl. **-s**, same. M19.
[ORIGIN Afrikaans, from Dutch *geel* YELLOW *adjective* + *bek* BEAK *noun*[1].]
1 A large edible sciaenid fish, *Atractoscion aequidens*, which has bright yellow edges to the jaws and gill covers and is found off the coasts of southern Africa and NE Australia. Also called ***Cape salmon***, (*Austral.*) ***teraglin***. M19.
2 = ***yellowbill*** (a) s.v. YELLOW *adjective*. M19.

geelhout /ˈxɪəl(h)əʊt/ *noun*. *S. Afr.* L18.
[ORIGIN Afrikaans, from Dutch *geel* YELLOW *adjective* + *hout* wood: see HOLT *noun*[1].]
Any of several southern African trees of the genus *Podocarpus* (family Podocarpaceae), yielding yellow timber; the timber of such trees, used for furniture and in carpentry.

geelum *noun* see GUILLAUME.

†**geer** *noun & verb* var. of GEAR.

geese *noun* pl. of GOOSE *noun*.

gee string *noun phr.* see G STRING.

gee-up /dʒiːˈʌp/ *interjection & verb*. Also **-hup** /-ˈhʌp/. M18.
[ORIGIN from GEE *interjection*[1] + HUP *interjection* (confused with UP *adverb*[1]).]
▸ **A** *interjection*. = GEE *interjection*[1]. M18.
▸ **B** *verb*. Infl. **-pp-**.
1 *verb trans.* Say 'gee-up' to; cause (a horse etc.) to move faster in this way. M18.
2 *verb intrans.* Say 'gee-up'; (of a horse etc.) move faster in response to such encouragement. E19.

gee whillikins /dʒiː ˈwɪlɪkɪnz/ *interjection*. Orig. *US*. M19.
[ORIGIN Uncertain: rel. to GEE *interjection*[2].]
= GEE *interjection*[2].

gee whiz /dʒiː ˈwɪz/ *interjection*. Orig. *US*. Also **-zz**. L19.
[ORIGIN Rel. to GEE WHILLIKINS.]
= GEE *interjection*[2].

geez(e), **Geez(e)** *interjection* var. of JEEZ.

geezer /ˈgiːzə/ *noun*. *colloq.* L19.
[ORIGIN Repr. dial. pronunc. of GUISER.]
A person, now usu. a man; an old fellow.
N. DEMILLE I watched some old geezers playing a card game.

GEF *abbreviation*.
Global Environment Facility.

gefilte fish /gəˈfɪltə fɪʃ/ *noun phr.* Also **gefüllte fish**. L19.
[ORIGIN Yiddish =stuffed fish, from *gefilte* infl. pa. pple of *filn* FILL *verb*: see FISH *noun*[1].]
A dish either of stewed or baked stuffed fish or of fishcakes boiled in a fish or vegetable broth.

Geg *noun & adjective* var. of GHEG.

gegenschein /ˈgeɪgənʃʌɪn/ *noun*. Also **G-**. L19.
[ORIGIN German, from *gegen* opposite + *Schein* shine, glow.]
ASTRONOMY. A patch of very faint nebulous light occurring in the ecliptic opposite the sun, thought to be the image of the sun reflected from gas and dust outside the atmosphere; = COUNTERGLOW.

geggie /ˈgɛgi/ *noun*. *Scot.* Also **gaggie** /ˈgagi/. L19.
[ORIGIN from GAG *noun*[1].]
A travelling theatrical show, *esp.* one held in a tent.

Geheimrat /gəˈhaɪmraːt/ *noun*. Pl. ***-räte*** /-rɛːtə/. M19.
[ORIGIN German.]
hist. In Germany, a privy counsellor (often as an honorific title).

Gehenna /gəˈhɛnə/ *noun*. Also (earlier) in French form **Gehenne**. L15.
[ORIGIN French *gehenne* or its source, ecclesiastical Latin, from Hellenistic Greek *geenna* from Hebrew *gē' hinnōm* hell, orig. the valley of Hinnom near Jerusalem where children were sacrificed (2 *Kings* 23:10).]
1 Hell; a place of burning, torment, and misery. L15.
2 A prison, esp. one where captives are tortured. Long *rare*. L16.

Geiger counter /ˈgʌɪgə kaʊntə/ *noun phr.* Also **g-**, **Geiger-Müller counter** /ˈmʊːlə/. E20.
[ORIGIN Hans *Geiger* (1882–1945), German physicist; var. also from W. *Müller*, 20th-cent. German physicist.]
An instrument for detecting and measuring ionizing radiation (e.g. from a radioactive substance or from cosmic rays) by means of the electrical discharges produced by the radiation in a gas-filled tube.

geiger tree /ˈgʌɪgə triː/ *noun phr.* L19.
[ORIGIN John *Geiger*, 19th-cent. Amer. naturalist.]
A Caribbean sebesten tree, *Cordia sebestena*, with orange or red flowers.

G8 *abbreviation*.
Group of Eight, the eight leading industrial nations (the US, Japan, Germany, France, the UK, Italy, Canada, and Russia), whose heads of government meet regularly.

geikielite /ˈgiːkɪlʌɪt/ *noun*. L19.
[ORIGIN from Archibald *Geikie* (1835–1924), Scot. geologist + -LITE.]
MINERALOGY. A trigonal magnesium titanate, which also contains ferrous iron and forms a series with ilmenite.

†**geir** *noun*. M16–M19.
[ORIGIN Dutch *gier*.]
A vulture. Also ***geir-eagle***.

geis *noun* var. of GEAS.

geisha /ˈgeɪʃə/ *noun*. Pl. **-s**, same. L19.
[ORIGIN Japanese *geisha* entertainer, from *gei* (performing) arts + *sha* person.]
A trained Japanese hostess who entertains men with conversation, dance and song, etc.; *loosely* a Japanese prostitute. Also ***geisha girl***.

Geissler tube /ˈgʌɪslə tjuːb/ *noun phr.* Also **Geissler's tube**. M19.
[ORIGIN from Heinrich *Geissler* (1814–79), German glass-blower.]
A sealed glass or quartz tube with a narrow central section, filled with gas at low pressure, for the production of visible or ultraviolet light by electrical discharge (esp. for spectral analysis).

Geist /gaɪst/ *noun*. L19.
[ORIGIN German: see GHOST *noun*.]
The spirit of an individual or a group; intellectuality; intelligence.

Geisteswissenschaft /ˈgaɪstəsˌvɪsənʃaft/ *noun*. Pl. ***-en*** /-ən/. E20.
[ORIGIN German, formed as GEIST + *Wissenschaft* learning (from *wissen* know).]
Usu. in *pl.* The arts or humanities as opp. to the sciences.

geitonogamy /gʌɪtəˈnɒgəmi/ *noun*. L19.
[ORIGIN from Greek *geitōn*, *geitono-* neighbour + -GAMY.]
BOTANY. Fertilization of a flower by pollen from another flower on the same plant.

gekko *noun* var. of GECKO.

gel /dʒɛl/ *noun*[1] *& verb*. L19.
[ORIGIN Abbreviation of GELATIN.]
▸ **A** *noun*. **1** A semi-solid colloidal solution of a solid dispersed in a liquid, more or less elastic, and formed by the coagulation of a sol (colloidal liquid). L19.
2 A substance for setting or styling the hair, sold as a jelly. M20.
3 BIOCHEMISTRY. A semi-rigid slab or cylinder of an organic polymer (e.g. starch, polyacrylamide) used as a medium for the separation of macromolecules. M20.
▸ **B** *verb intrans.* Infl. **-ll-**. Form a gel; *fig.* (of an idea etc.) take a definite form, achieve a sense of coherence, jell. L19.

gel /gɛl/ *noun*[2]. *colloq.* E20.
[ORIGIN Repr. a pronunc.]
An upper-class or well-bred girl or young woman.
J. BURCHILL The great English models of the Sixties . . were all fastidiously-reared upper-middle Home Counties gels.

gelada /dʒəˈlɑːdə/ *noun*. M19.
[ORIGIN Amharic *č'ällada*.]
A gregarious, chiefly herbivorous baboon, *Theropithecus gelada*, of the Ethiopian mountains, having a long brownish coat and characterized by a bare red patch on the chest and (in the adult male) a heavy mane. Also ***gelada baboon***.

Gelalaean /dʒɛlə'liːən/ *adjective*. Also **Jel-**. L18.
[ORIGIN from Persian (Arabic) *Jalālī* pertaining to *Jalāl ad-Din* (formerly written *Gelal ed-din*) 'Glory of the Faith' or *Jalāl ad-Dawla* 'Glory of the Dynasty', titles of Malik-Shah, Seljuk Sultan of Khorasan and reformer of the Persian calendar.]
Of or pertaining to (the calendar instituted by) Jalal ad-Din in 1079.

Gelasian /gə'leɪzɪən/ *adjective*. L18.
[ORIGIN from *Gelasius* (see below) + -IAN.]
Of or pertaining to Pope Gelasius I (492–6), or the liturgical books etc. attributed to him.

gelastic /dʒə'lastɪk/ *adjective*. E18.
[ORIGIN Greek *gelastikos*, from *gelan* laugh: see -IC.]
Of or pertaining to laughter. Also (*rare*), risible.

gelate /dʒə'leɪt/ *verb intrans*. E20.
[ORIGIN Back-form. from GELATION *noun*².]
Form a gel.

gelati *noun* pl. of GELATO.

gelatification /dʒə,latɪfɪ'keɪʃ(ə)n/ *noun*. M19.
[ORIGIN from GELATIN + -FICATION.]
Production of, or conversion into, gelatin or jelly.

gelatigenous /,dʒɛlə'tɪdʒɪnəs/ *adjective*. M19.
[ORIGIN formed as GELATIFICATION + -GENOUS.]
Producing or developing gelatin.

gelatin /'dʒɛlətɪn/ *noun*. Also **-ine** /-iːn/. E19.
[ORIGIN French *gélatine* from Italian *gelatina*, from *gelata* JELLY *noun*¹: see -IN¹, -INE⁵.]
1 An amorphous yellowish or colourless transparent tasteless substance, brittle when dry, which is derived from collagen and obtained by prolonged boiling of animal skin, tendons, ligaments, etc., and is used in food preparation as the basis of jellies, in various photographic processes, and in glue; also, any of various substances containing or resembling gelatin. E19.
vegetable gelatin a constituent of gluten, identical with gelatin from animal sources.
2 Any of various gelatinous explosives; *esp.* (more fully ***blasting gelatin***) a high explosive chiefly consisting of a gel of nitroglycerine with added cellulose nitrate, used esp. under water. L19.
– COMB.: **gelatin dynamite** a powerful explosive containing blasting gelatin absorbed on to an inert base (cf. GELIGNITE); **gelatin paper**: coated with sensitized gelatin for photography.
■ **ge'latinase** *noun* (BIOCHEMISTRY) an enzyme which liquefies gelatin, produced by certain bacteria, yeasts, etc.: E20. **ge'latinoid** *adjective & noun* (*a*) *adjective* gelatinous; (*b*) *noun* a substance resembling gelatin: M19.

gelatinate /dʒə'latɪneɪt/ *verb*. Long *rare* or *obsolete*. L18.
[ORIGIN from GELATIN + -ATE³.]
1 *verb intrans*. = GELATINIZE 1. L18.
2 *verb trans*. = GELATINIZE 2. E19.
■ **gelati'nation** *noun* = GELATINIZATION *noun* L18.

gelatine *noun* var. of GELATIN.

gelatiniform /dʒɛlə'tɪnɪfɔːm/ *adjective*. M19.
[ORIGIN from GELATIN + -I- + -FORM.]
Having the form, consistency, or appearance of gelatin.

gelatinize /dʒə'latɪnʌɪz/ *verb*. Also **-ise**. E19.
[ORIGIN formed as GELATINIFORM + -IZE.]
1 *verb intrans*. Take the form of a jelly; become gelatinous. E19.
2 *verb trans*. Make gelatinous or jelly-like. M19.
3 *verb trans*. Coat with gelatin, apply gelatin to. L19.
■ **ge'latinizable** *adjective* (*rare*) E19. **gelatini'zation** *noun* conversion into a gelatinous state M19.

gelatinous /dʒə'latɪnəs/ *adjective*. E18.
[ORIGIN French *gélatineux*, formed as GELATIN + *-eux* -OUS.]
1 Having the character or consistency of a jelly; jelly-like. E18.
2 Of, pertaining to, or consisting of gelatin. L18.
■ **gelatinously** *adverb* L19. **gelatinousness** *noun* E20.

gelation /dʒə'leɪʃ(ə)n/ *noun*¹. M19.
[ORIGIN Latin *gelatio(n-)*, from *gelat-* pa. ppl stem of *gelare* freeze: see -ATION.]
Solidification by freezing.

gelation /dʒə'leɪʃ(ə)n/ *noun*². E20.
[ORIGIN from GEL *noun*¹ + -ATION.]
Formation of or conversion into a gel.

gelato /dʒɛ'lɑːtəʊ/ *noun*. Pl. **-ati** /-ɑːti/. M19.
[ORIGIN Italian.]
An Italian or Italian-style ice cream, usu. with a rich, creamy flavour.

geld /gɛld/ *noun*. Also **†gelt**. L15.
[ORIGIN medieval Latin *geldum* from Old English. *ġ(i)eld* (see YIELD *noun*). Cf. GILD *noun*¹, GUILD *noun*².]
hist. A tax paid to the Crown by English landholders before the Norman Conquest, and continued under the Norman kings.

geld /gɛld/ *adjective*. *obsolete* exc. *dial*. ME.
[ORIGIN Old Norse *gelda* = Old Swedish *galder* (Swedish dial. *gall*, *gäll*, Danish *gold*), Old High German *galt* (German *gelt*), from Germanic. Cf. YELD.]
Of a female animal, esp. a cow: barren.

geld /gɛld/ *verb*¹ *trans*. Pa. t. & pple **gelded**, **gelt** /gɛlt/. ME.
[ORIGIN Old Norse *gelda*, from *geldr* GELD *adjective*.]
1 Deprive (usu. a male animal) of the ability to reproduce; excise the testicles of; castrate. ME. ▸**b** Excise the ovaries of; spay. M16.

W. HOLTBY Treating his gelded toms with specially tender indulgence.

2 *transf*. & *fig*. Deprive *of* some essential part; cut down the resources of; impair the strength or force of; weaken, enfeeble. Long *rare*. E16. ▸**†b** Mutilate (a book etc.) by abridgement; expurgate. Also, (*rare*), edit *out*. M16–E18.

SHAKES. *Rich. II* Bereft and gelded of his patrimony. A. COOKE To geld a lively memory in the interests of good form.

3 a Cut (a plant); *esp*. prune or remove superfluous shoots from (a plant or tree). E16. ▸**†b** Cut out the old comb from (a beehive); take out (the comb). L16–M17.
■ **gelder** *noun* (long *rare*) LME.

geld /gɛld/ *verb*². Also **†gelt**. See also GILD *verb*². M19.
[ORIGIN from GELD *noun*. Cf. medieval Latin *geldare* pay geld, tax.]
hist. **1** *verb trans*. Levy geld on. M19.
2 *verb intrans*. Pay geld. M19.
■ **geldable** *adjective* liable to pay geld E17.

gelding /'gɛldɪŋ/ *noun*. LME.
[ORIGIN Old Norse *geldingr*, formed as GELD *adjective*: see -ING³.]
1 A gelded person, a eunuch. Long *rare* or *obsolete*. LME.
2 A gelded animal; *esp*. a gelded male horse. LME.

Gelehrte /gə'leːrtə, gə'lɛːtə/ *noun*. Also **-ter** /-tə(r)/. Pl. **-ten** /-tən, -t(ə)n/. M19.
[ORIGIN German, from *gelehrt* learned, *lehren* instruct.]
A learned (German) person; a scholar; a savant.

gelid /'dʒɛlɪd/ *adjective*. E17.
[ORIGIN Latin *gelidus*, from *gelu* frost, intense cold: see -ID¹.]
1 Extremely cold, cold as ice, frosty. E17.

W. SCORESBY As the air passes over the gelid surface of the ice. S. SCHAMA Standing on the gelid green spikes of one of Mont Blanc's glaciers. *fig*.: W. STYRON Emmi had her father's voice, utterly gelid and remote.

2 Cold, chill; cool. M17.

J. THOMSON By gelid founts and careless rills to muse.

■ **ge'lidity** *noun* extreme cold, frigidity M17. **gelidly** *adverb* M19. **gelidness** *noun* E18.

gelignite /'dʒɛlɪgnʌɪt/ *noun*. L19.
[ORIGIN Prob. from GEL(ATIN + Latin *l)ign-* wood + -ITE¹.]
A powerful explosive containing nitroglycerine and cellulose nitrate in a base of potassium or sodium nitrate and (orig. & usu.) wood pulp.

gelly /'dʒɛli/ *noun*. *slang*. Also **j-**. M20.
[ORIGIN Abbreviation.]
= GELIGNITE.

gelsemium /dʒɛl'siːmɪəm/ *noun*. L19.
[ORIGIN mod. Latin (see below), from Italian *gelsomino* JASMINE.]
The rhizome of a twining shrub, *Gelsemium sempervirens* (family Loganiaceae) of southern N. America (also called ***Carolina jasmine***); a preparation of this used medicinally, esp. in the treatment of neuralgia.
■ **'gelsemine** *noun* (CHEMISTRY) an indole-based alkaloid with depressant properties, present in gelsemium root L19.

gelt /gɛlt/ *noun*¹. Now only *slang*. E16.
[ORIGIN German *Geld*.]
Money.

J. GASH When he popped off in 1753 . . Parliament enacted a lottery to raise the gelt.

gelt /gɛlt/ *noun*². Long *arch*. *rare*. L16.
[ORIGIN Irish *geilt* a frenzied person.]
A mad person.

†gelt *noun*³ var. of GELD *noun*.

gelt *verb*¹ *pa. pple*: see GELD *verb*¹.

†gelt *verb*² var. of GELD *verb*².

gem /dʒɛm/ *noun*.
[ORIGIN Old English *ġim(m)* from Latin *gemma* bud, jewel; re-adopted or refashioned in late Middle English after Old French & mod. French *gemme*.]
1 A precious stone of any kind, *esp*. when cut and polished for ornament; a jewel. Also ***gemstone***. OE. ▸**b** A precious or semi-precious stone, bearing an engraved design either in relief or intaglio. M17.

K. CLARK A lot of gems—hyacinths, sapphires, rubies, topazes, emeralds.

2 *fig*. A person or thing highly valued or of rare quality. ME.

MAX-MÜLLER Among the Hottentots . . we find the following gem of a fable.

†3 A bud; *esp*. a leaf bud. Cf. GEMMA 1. LME–E19.
4 A common geometrid moth, *Orthonama obstipata*, found in Eurasia, Africa and America. M19.
5 A former size of type equal to about 4 points. L19.
– COMB.: **gemfish** *Austral*. & *NZ* an edible marine fish, *Rexea solandri*; also called ***hake***.
■ **gemlike** *adjective* resembling (that of) a gem E19.

gem /dʒɛm/ *verb*. Infl. **-mm-**. ME.
[ORIGIN from the noun.]
†1 a *verb intrans*. Bud. Only in ME. ▸**b** *verb trans*. Put forth (a blossom, a fruit). M17–M18.
2 *verb trans*. Adorn (as) with gems (*lit*. & *fig*.). Freq. as ***gemmed*** *ppl adjective*. ME.

J. M. FAULKNER The lawns are gemmed with dew.

3 *verb trans*. Extract gems from; excavate to obtain gems. M19.
■ **gemmer** *noun* a person who seeks or digs for gems L19.

Gemara /gə'mɑːrə/ *noun*. E17.
[ORIGIN Aramaic *gĕmārā* completion.]
The later of the two parts of the Palestinian or the Babylonian Talmud, consisting of a rabbinical commentary on the first part (the Mishnah).
■ **Gemaric** *adjective* of, pertaining to, or concerned with the Gemara E18.

gematria /gɪ'meɪtrɪə/ *noun*. Also (earlier) anglicized as **†gematry**. M17.
[ORIGIN Aramaic *gimatrēyā* from Greek *geōmetria* GEOMETRY.]
A Kabbalistic method of interpreting the Hebrew Scriptures by computing the numerical values of words, based on those of their constituent letters.

Gemeinschaft /gə'maɪnʃaft/ *noun*. M20.
[ORIGIN German, from *gemein* common, general + *-schaft* -SHIP.]
SOCIOLOGY. A form of social integration based on personal ties; community. Cf. GESELLSCHAFT.

gemel /'dʒɛm(ə)l/ *noun & adjective*. Also **†gemew**, **†gemow**. LME.
[ORIGIN Old French from Latin *gemellus*, dim. of *geminus* twin. See also GIMMAL.]
▸ **A** *noun*. **†1** In *pl*. Twins; things associated in pairs. LME–E17.
†2 HERALDRY. In *pl*. Bars or barrulets placed together as a couple. LME–M18.
3 A hinge. Now only in ***gemel-hinge***, a hinge consisting of an eye or loop and a hook. LME.
4 A kind of ring, much worn in the 16th cent., which can be divided into two (rarely, three) rings. Also ***gemel-ring***. Cf. GIMMAL. L15.
▸ **B** *attrib*. or as *adjective*. Twin; double. Now only in HERALDRY. L15.

gemellion /dʒɪ'mɛlɪən/ *noun*. L19.
[ORIGIN medieval Latin *gemellio(n-)*, from Latin *gemellus* a twin.]
Either of a pair of basins used for washing the hands, esp. for liturgical use; any decorative basin.

†gemew *noun & adjective* var. of GEMEL.

geminal /'dʒɛmɪn(ə)l/ *adjective*. M20.
[ORIGIN from Latin *geminus* twin + -AL¹.]
CHEMISTRY. Of, pertaining to, or containing like atoms or groups attached to the same atom in a molecule. Cf. VICINAL.

geminate /'dʒɛmɪneɪt, -nət/ *adjective & noun*. LME.
[ORIGIN Latin *geminatus* pa. pple of *geminare*: see GEMINATE *verb*, -ATE².]
▸ **A** *adjective*. Duplicated, combined in pairs, twin, binate. LME.
geminate leaves BOTANY leaves springing in pairs from the same node, one leaf beside the other.
▸ **B** *noun*. A doubled consonant. L19.

geminate /'dʒɛmɪneɪt/ *verb trans*. M17.
[ORIGIN Latin *geminat-* pa. ppl stem of *geminare*, from *geminus* twin: see -ATE³.]
Double, duplicate; combine as a pair.
■ **geminated** *ppl adjective* doubled, occurring in pairs E19.

gemination /dʒɛmɪ'neɪʃ(ə)n/ *noun*. L16.
[ORIGIN Latin *geminatio(n-)*, formed as GEMINATE *verb*: see -ATION.]
1 A doubling, duplication, repetition. L16.
2 DENTISTRY. The union of contiguous teeth. M19.
3 LINGUISTICS. **a** The doubling of an originally single consonantal sound. L19. ▸**b** The doubling of a letter in the orthography of a word. L19.
■ **'geminative** *adjective & noun* (*a*) *adjective* characterized by gemination; (*b*) *noun* a geminated letter: L19.

Gemini /'dʒɛmɪnʌɪ, -ni/ *noun & interjection*. Exc. in sense A.1 also **g-**. OE.
[ORIGIN Latin *gemini* pl. of *geminus* twin.]
▸ **A** *noun*. **1** (The name of) a conspicuous constellation on the ecliptic between Auriga and Cancer, on the edge of the Milky Way; ASTROLOGY (the name of) the third zodiacal sign, usu. associated with the period 21 May to 21 June (see note s.v. ZODIAC); the Twins (Castor and Pollux). OE. ▸**b** = GEMINIAN. E20.

TENNYSON When . . the starry Gemini hang like glorious crowns Over Orion's grave. *attrib*.: L. MACNEICE All astrologers agree that the Gemini type enjoys argument.

†2 A couple, a pair (*of*); *esp*. in *pl*., a pair of eyes. Now *rare*. L16.

SHAKES. *Merry W.* Like a geminy of baboons.

▸ **B** *interjection*. A mild oath or exclamation. Cf. JIMINY. M17.
■ **Gemi'nian** *noun* a person born under the sign Gemini E20. **Geminid** *noun* any of an annual shower of meteors which appear to radiate from the constellation Gemini in December L19.

G

geminous /ˈdʒɛmɪnəs/ *adjective. rare.* **M17.**
[**ORIGIN** from Latin *geminus* twin + **-OUS**.]
Double; occurring in pairs.

gemma /ˈdʒɛmə/ *noun.* Pl. **gemmae** /ˈdʒɛmiː/. **L18.**
[**ORIGIN** Latin = bud, jewel.]
1 *BOTANY.* A leaf bud, as distinct from a flower bud. Cf. **GEM** *noun* 3. Now *rare.* **L18.**
2 *BOTANY & ZOOLOGY.* A small, usu. cellular, asexual reproductive body which becomes detached from the parent organism and develops into a new individual, esp. in mosses, liverworts, some fungi, etc. **M19.**

gemman /ˈdʒɛmən/ *noun. slang.* Now *rare.* Pl. **gemmen**. **M16.**
[**ORIGIN** Contr.]
= **GENTLEMAN**.

gemmary *noun*[1] var. of **GEMMERY**.

†**gemmary** *adjective & noun*[2]. **LME.**
[**ORIGIN** Late Latin *gemmarius*, from *gemma*: see **GEM** *noun*, **-ARY**[1].]
▸ **A** *adjective.* Of or pertaining to gems; concerned with or skilled with gems. **LME–L17.**
▸ **B** *noun.* A jeweller. Only in **LME.**

gemmate /ˈdʒɛmeɪt, -mət/ *adjective.* **M19.**
[**ORIGIN** Latin *gemmatus* pa. pple of *gemmare*: see **GEMMATE** *verb*, **-ATE**[2].]
BIOLOGY. Possessing gemmae; gemmiparous.

gemmate /ˈdʒɛmeɪt/ *verb intrans.* **E17.**
[**ORIGIN** Latin *gemmat-* pa. ppl stem of *gemmare* put forth buds, from *gemma* bud, jewel: see **-ATE**[3].]
BIOLOGY. Produce gemmae; reproduce by gemmation.

gemmation /dʒɛˈmeɪʃ(ə)n/ *noun.* **M18.**
[**ORIGIN** French, from *gemmer* form buds, from *gemme* bud: see **-ATION**.]
1 *BOTANY.* The action of putting out buds. Also, the arrangement of buds on the stem, or of leaves within the bud. **M18.**
2 *ZOOLOGY.* The production of gemmae; the mode of asexual reproduction in which a small growth from the parent organism (detaches and) develops into a new individual; budding. **M19.**

gemmen *noun* pl. of **GEMMAN**.

gemmeous /ˈdʒɛmɪəs/ *adjective.* **E17.**
[**ORIGIN** from Latin *gemmeus* (from *gemma* **GEM** *noun*) + **-OUS**.]
Of, pertaining to, of the nature of, or resembling a gem.

gemmery /ˈdʒɛməri/ *noun.* Also **-ary**. **M17.**
[**ORIGIN** from **GEM** *noun* + **-ARY**[1].]
†**1** A jewel house. **M17–E18.**
2 Gems as an object of connoisseurship. *rare.* **M19.**

gemmiferous /dʒɛˈmɪf(ə)rəs/ *adjective.* **M17.**
[**ORIGIN** from Latin *gemmifer* (from *gemma* **GEM** *noun*) + **-OUS**: see **-FEROUS**.]
1 Yielding or containing precious stones. **M17.**
2 *BIOLOGY.* = **GEMMATE** *adjective.* **E19.**

gemmiparous /dʒɛˈmɪp(ə)rəs/ *adjective.* **L18.**
[**ORIGIN** from mod. Latin *gemmiparus* (from *gemma* **GEM** *noun*) + **-OUS**.]
BIOLOGY. **1** Producing offspring by gemmation. **L18.**
2 Of, pertaining to, or resulting from the process of gemmation. **M19.**
■ **gemmiˈparity** *noun* the condition or character of being gemmiparous **M19.** **gemmiparously** *adverb* **M19.**

gemmology /dʒɛˈmɒlədʒi/ *noun.* **E19.**
[**ORIGIN** from Latin *gemma* **GEM** *noun* + **-OLOGY**.]
The branch of geology or crystallography that deals with gems.
■ **gemmoˈlogical** *adjective* **M20.** **gemmologist** *noun* **M20.**

gemmule /ˈdʒɛmjuːl/ *noun.* **M19.**
[**ORIGIN** French from Latin *gemmula* dim. of **GEMMA** bud, jewel: see **-ULE**.]
1 *BOTANY.* †**a** = **PLUMULE** *noun* 1. Only in **M19.** ▸**b** A small gemma. **L19.**
2 *ZOOLOGY.* A gemma; *spec.* a tough-coated cluster of cells produced in sponges for development in more favourable conditions. **M19.**
3 *BIOLOGY* (now *hist.*). In the theory of pangenesis, a hypothetical minute hereditary particle transferred from the various cells in the body to the germ cells, to effect production of those cell types in the offspring. **L19.**
■ **gemmuˈliferous** *adjective* bearing gemmules **M19.**

gemmy /ˈdʒɛmi/ *adjective.* **LME.**
[**ORIGIN** from **GEM** *noun* + **-Y**[1].]
1 Having many gems; covered or set with gems or something resembling gems. **LME.**
2 Resembling a gem; brilliant; glittering. **L17.**

gemot /gɪˈməʊt/ *noun.* Also **gemote**.
[**ORIGIN** Old English *gemōt*, from *ge-* **Y-** + *mōt* **MOOT** *noun*[1].]
ENGLISH HISTORY. A meeting; an assembly (in England before the Norman Conquest) for judicial or legislative purposes. See also **WITENAGEMOT**.

†**gemow** *noun & adjective* var. of **GEMEL**.

gemsbok /ˈgɛmzbɒk/ *noun.* Also **-bock**, **-buck** /-bʌk/. Pl. same, **-s**. **L18.**
[**ORIGIN** Afrikaans, from Dutch = chamois, from *gems* chamois + *bok* buck.]
A large antelope, *Oryx gazella*, of SW and E. Africa, having long straight horns and black markings on the face and flanks; *esp.* the southern form of this. Cf. **BEISA**, **ORYX**.

gemshorn /ˈgɛmzhɔːn/ *noun.* **E19.**
[**ORIGIN** German, lit. 'chamois horn'.]
MUSIC. A light-toned organ stop.

gemütlich /gəˈmyːtlɪç, -ˈmuːtlɪʃ/ *adjective.* **M19.**
[**ORIGIN** German.]
Pleasant, cheerful; cosy, snug, homely; genial, good-natured.

T. CAPOTE Their five-room apartment, with its *gemütlich* mélange of plump hassocks and squashy chairs.

Gemütlichkeit /gəˈmyːtlɪçkaɪt, -ˈmuːtlɪkʌɪt/ *noun.* **M19.**
[**ORIGIN** German: cf. **GEMÜTLICH**.]
The quality of being ***gemütlich***; geniality; cosiness; cheerfulness.

gen /dʒɛn/ *noun & verb. slang* (orig. *MILITARY*). **M20.**
[**ORIGIN** Perh. from first syll. of *general information*.]
▸ **A** *noun.* Information; facts. **M20.**

J. RABAN The good navigator has to make the most of whatever gen he has to hand.

▸ **B** *verb* (foll. by *up*). Infl. **-nn-**.
1 *verb intrans.* Provide oneself with information; learn about something (hurriedly). **M20.**

HELEN FIELDING I grabbed a couple of newspapers to gen up and ran for a taxi.

2 *verb trans.* Provide with information, 'put in the picture'. **M20.**

Gen. *abbreviation.*
1 General.
2 Genesis (in the Bible).

-gen /dʒ(ə)n/ *suffix.*
[**ORIGIN** French *-gène* from Greek *-genēs* -born, of a specified kind, from *gen-* base of *gignesthai* be born, become, *genos* kind (noun), etc.]
1 *SCIENCE* (orig. *CHEMISTRY*). A substance that produces, as ***hydrogen***, ***oxygen*** (the earliest words so formed); ***cyanogen***, ***halogen***; ***phellogen***; ***allergen***, ***androgen***.
2 *BOTANY.* A substance or plant that grows or is produced, as ***acrogen***, ***cultigen***.

gena /ˈdʒiːnə/ *noun.* Pl. **-nae** /-niː/. **E19.**
[**ORIGIN** Latin = cheek.]
In an invertebrate, esp. an insect: either lateral part of the head below the level of the eyes.
■ **genal** *adjective* **L19.**

genappe /dʒɪˈnap/ *noun.* **M19.**
[**ORIGIN** from *Genappe* a town in Belgium, the orig. place of manufacture.]
A smooth lustrous yarn used in the manufacture of braids, fringes, etc. Also ***genappe yarn***.

gendarme /ˈʒɒndɑːm; *foreign* ʒɑ̃darm (*pl. same*)/ *noun.* Pl. **gendarmes**, (now *hist.*) ***gens d'armes*** /ʒɑ̃ darm/. **M16.**
[**ORIGIN** French, a sing. from the pl. (now *hist.*) *gens d'armes* men of arms.]
1 In the older French army, a horseman in full armour, having several others under his command; later, a mounted trooper, esp. of the royal companies. Usu. in *pl. obsolete* exc. *hist.* **M16.**
2 In France and French-speaking countries: a police officer; orig. a member of a military force employed in policing. **L18.** ▸**b** *gen.* A police officer. *slang.* **E20.**

gendarmerie /ʒɒnˈdɑːməri; *foreign* ʒɑ̃darməri (*pl. same*)/ *noun.* Also **-ery**. **M16.**
[**ORIGIN** French, from *gendarme*: see **GENDARME**.]
1 *hist.* A body of cavalry, esp. in the older French army (cf. **GENDARME** 1). **M16.**
2 In France and French-speaking countries: a body of police officers, a police force; orig. a military force employed as police. **L18.** ▸**b** A headquarters or station of gendarmes; a police station. **M20.**

gender /ˈdʒɛndə/ *noun.* **LME.**
[**ORIGIN** Old French *gendre* (mod. *genre*) from Proto-Romance from Latin *genus*, *gener-*: see **GENUS**.]
†**1** Kind, sort, class, genus. **LME–L18.**
2 *GRAMMAR.* Any of the classes (***masculine***, ***feminine***, ***neuter***, ***common***) of nouns and pronouns distinguished by the modification which they require in words syntactically associated with them and roughly corresponding to the sex or sexlessness of the objects which they denote; the property of belonging to such a class; (of adjectives) the appropriate form for accompanying a noun of one such class; the classification of nouns and other words in this way, as a grammatical principle. **LME.**

C. ISHERWOOD Das Glueck, le bonheur, la felicidad—they have given it all three genders.

grammatical gender: see **GRAMMATICAL** *adjective.*
3 The state of being male, female, or neuter; sex; the members of one or other sex. Now chiefly *colloq.* or *euphem.* **LME.** ▸**b** Sex as expressed by social or cultural distinctions. **M20.**

M. W. MONTAGU My only consolation for being of that gender has been the assurance . . of never being married to any one among them. **b** *attrib.*: A. OAKLEY Sex differences may be 'natural', but gender differences have their source in culture.

– **COMB.**: **gender bender** *colloq.* a person who dresses and behaves in a way characteristic of the opposite sex.
■ **gendered** *adjective* specific to or biased towards one particular sex **L20.** **genderless** *adjective* (*GRAMMAR*) without distinction of gender **L19.**

gender /ˈdʒɛndə/ *verb.* **ME.**
[**ORIGIN** Old French *gendrer* from Latin *generare* **GENERATE** *verb.*]
1 *verb trans. & intrans.* Of a parent or parents: beget, engender, produce (offspring). *arch.* **ME.**
2 *verb trans.* †**a** Produce by natural processes, generate. **LME–M17.** ▸**b** Give rise to, engender. *arch.* **LME.**
3 *verb intrans.* Esp. of animals: copulate. *arch.* **LME.**

gene /dʒiːn/ *noun.* **E20.**
[**ORIGIN** German *Gen*, from *Pangen* **PANGENE**.]
Each of the units of heredity which are transmitted from parent to offspring in gametes, usually as part of a chromosome, and control or determine a single characteristic in the offspring.
– **COMB.**: **gene bank** a collection of living organisms maintained as a repository of genetic material, esp. for developing new breeds etc. or safeguarding the survival of existing ones; **gene flow** the movement of genes from one population to another as a result of interbreeding, hybridization, etc.; **gene pool** the stock of different genes in an interbreeding population; **gene splicing** the process of removing a chosen gene or sequence of genes from one organism and causing it to be integrated into the genetic material of another (usu. a bacterium), in order that it may produce the protein for which the gene codes; **gene therapy** the practice of introducing normal genes into cells in place of defective or missing ones in order to correct hereditary disorders.
– **NOTE**: Orig. defined as the ultimate units of mutation and recombination, genes are now regarded as sequences of nucleotides in a nucleic acid molecule each of which determines a single polypeptide.

-gene /dʒiːn/ *suffix.*
[**ORIGIN** from (the same root as) **-GEN**.]
(A substance, structure, etc.) that is produced or formed, as ***epigene***; ***palaeogene***, ***phosgene***.

gêne /ʒɛn, ʒɛːn/ *noun.* **E19.**
[**ORIGIN** French.]
Constraint, embarrassment, discomfort.

gêné /ʒɛne/ *adjective.* Fem. **-née**. **E19.**
[**ORIGIN** French, pa. ppl adjective of *gêner* embarrass: rel. to **GÊNE**.]
Constrained, embarrassed, discomforted.

genealogic /dʒiːnɪəˈlɒdʒɪk, dʒɛn-/ *adjective.* **M18.**
[**ORIGIN** French *généalogique* from Greek *genealogikos*, from *genealogos* genealogist: see **GENEALOGY**, **-IC**.]
= **GENEALOGICAL**.

genealogical /dʒiːnɪəˈlɒdʒɪk(ə)l, dʒɛn-/ *adjective.* **L16.**
[**ORIGIN** formed as **GENEALOGIC** + **-AL**[1].]
Pertaining to genealogy, or the tracing of family descent.

A. EDEN An elaborate genealogical table tracing my descent to a saintly early Swedish king.

genealogical tree a diagram, esp. one in the form of a tree with branches, which shows the different generations of a family and their members.
■ **genealogically** *adverb* **M17.**

genealogy /dʒiːnɪˈalədʒi, dʒɛn-/ *noun.* **ME.**
[**ORIGIN** Old French & mod. French *généalogie* from late Latin *genealogia*, from Greek *genealogia*, from *genealogos* genealogist, from *genea* race, generation: see **-LOGY**.]
1 An account of a person's descent from an ancestor or ancestors, by enumeration of the intermediate people; a pedigree. **ME.**

C. H. PEARSON The early mention of genealogies in the Welsh laws is proof of the importance attached to noble birth.

†**2** Lineage, pedigree, family stock. **ME–M16.**
†**3** Progeny, offspring. **E16–M18.**
4 (The branch of knowledge that deals with) the investigation of the details of ancestry. **E19.**

A. TUCKER Genealogy and chronology can scarcely be called sciences.

5 The line of development of a plant or animal from earlier forms. **L19.**
■ **genealogist** *noun* a person who researches or studies genealogies **E17.** **genealogize** *verb trans. & intrans.* (**a**) *verb trans.* draw up a genealogy of; (**b**) *verb intrans.* trace the descent of people or families; make out genealogies: **E17.**

geneat /gɪˈniːt, jɛˈneɪat/ *noun.*
[**ORIGIN** Old English *genēat*, from *nēotan* enjoy, use.]
hist. A retainer, a vassal; a person who held lands in return for service or rent.

genecology /dʒɛnɪˈkɒlədʒi, dʒiːn-/ *noun.* **E20.**
[**ORIGIN** from Greek *genos* kind, race + **ECOLOGY**.]
The branch of science that deals with genetic differences between related species and populations in relation to their environment.
■ **genecoˈlogic** *adjective* **M20.** **genecoˈlogical** *adjective* **E20.**

genera *noun* pl. of GENUS.

generable /ˈdʒɛn(ə)rəb(ə)l/ *adjective*. L15.
[ORIGIN Latin *generabilis*, from *generare*: see GENERATE *verb*, -ABLE.]
1 Able to be generated or produced. L15.
†**2** Capable of generating. *rare*. L16–M17.
■ **genera'bility** *noun* (*rare*) E18.

general /ˈdʒɛn(ə)r(ə)l/ *adjective*, *noun*, & *verb*. ME.
[ORIGIN Old French & mod. French *général*, from Latin *generalis*, from *genus*, *gener-* class, race, kind: see GENUS, -AL[1].]
▸ **A** *adjective*. **1** Including, involving, or affecting all or nearly all the parts of a (specified or implied) whole, as a territory, community, organization, etc.; completely or nearly universal; not partial, particular, local, or sectional. ME. ▸†**b** Belonging or pertaining in common *to*. LME–M17. ▸**c** With collect. or pl. noun: all, collective, whole. *obsolete* exc. in ***general body***. L16.

G. ORWELL If it once became general, wealth would confer no distinction. W. PLOMER To the general agitation a particular one of my own was added.

2 Chief, head; having unrestricted authority. LME. ▸**b** *MILITARY*. Having superior rank and extended command; *spec.* (of an officer) above the rank of a colonel. L16.
3 Pertaining to or current among the majority; prevalent, widespread, usual, common. LME.

C. IVES A matter nowadays of common impression or general opinion.

4 Not specifically limited in application; relating to a whole class of objects, cases, occasions, etc.; (of a rule, law, etc.) true for all or nearly all cases coming under its terms. LME. ▸**b** Indefinite, imprecise; vague. E17.

J. HERSEY On his first visit, he kept the conversation general, formal. ISAIAH BERLIN We must always avoid applying general principles but examine each case in its full individual detail. A. THWAITE He seemed to have a general grudge against writers. **b** H. JAMES A general conviction that it was horribly late and a particular objection to looking at my watch. F. FORSYTH He too was planning his campaign; not in detail like Shannon, but in general terms.

5 Including the main features, elements, etc., and neglecting or ignoring unimportant details or exceptions. M16. ▸**b** Of a name, term, concept, etc.: intended to include or cover those features common to the individuals of a class and neglect the differences. M16.

T. HARDY Their general likeness to each other . . suggested that . . they were brothers. G. VIDAL Each story varies a bit from the other but the general sense is as follows. **b** C. D. E. FORTNUM The general term . . Majolica, has long been . . applied to all varieties of glazed earthenware of Italian origin.

6 Not restricted to one field, class or area; not specialized; concerned with or skilled in all the branches of a particular business or activity (freq. used preceding an agent noun esp. of employment). Formerly also, widely accomplished. M16.

J. TYNDALL Never . . has this longing been more liberally responded to, both among men of science and the general public. R. HOGGART He has little call to move if he is a general labourer, . . hardly more if he is skilled.

– SPECIAL COLLOCATIONS & PHRASES: **as a general rule** in most cases. ***Attorney general***, ***Attorney General***: see ATTORNEY *noun*. ***consul general***: see CONSUL 5. ***cook-general***: see COOK *noun*. ***General American***: see AMERICAN *noun* 3. ***general*** ANAESTHESIA. ***general anaesthetic***: see ANAESTHETIC *noun*. **General Assembly** (***a***) the highest ecclesiastical court of various national churches, esp. the Church of Scotland; (***b***) the legislature of some states of the US. ***general average***: see AVERAGE *noun*[2] 3. ***General Certificate of Education***, ***General Certificate of Secondary Education***: see CERTIFICATE *noun* 2. **general confession** *ECCLESIASTICAL* (***a***) a confession to be made by the whole congregation; (***b***) a private confession of all past sins, including those previously confessed. **general counsel** (in the US) the main lawyer who gives legal advice to a company. ***general court***: see COURT *noun*[1]. **general dealer** a trader in many kinds of goods. **general delivery** *N. Amer.* poste restante. ***general*** ELECTION. **general headquarters** *MILITARY*: of a commander-in-chief. **general hospital** (***a***) a hospital not specializing in any particular field or restricted to patients of a particular age or sex; (***b***) a military hospital receiving sick and wounded from field hospitals. **general knowledge**: of miscellaneous facts, information, etc. **general meeting**: open to all members of a society. ***general paralysis*** (***of the insane***): see PARALYSIS 1. **general post** (***a***) the first morning delivery; (***b***) an indoor game in which players are each given a place name and exchange seats to evade the blindfolded 'postman'; *fig.* a general and rapid exchange of positions etc. **General Post Office** orig., the central office established in London with responsibility for the collection and dispatch of mail and later for the telephone system; now chiefly, the main post office in a town or city. **general practice** *MEDICINE* the work of general practitioners. **general practitioner** *MEDICINE* a doctor based in the community rather than a hospital and dealing with cases of all kinds in the first instance, as opp. to a consultant or specialist. ***general*** PUBLIC. **general reader**: of miscellaneous literature. ***general relativity***: see RELATIVITY 2. **general staff**: assisting a military commander in planning and administration. **general store**: in which many kinds of goods are sold. **general strike** (***a***) a strike by all the workers of one industry; (***b***) a strike by the workers in all or most of the important trades; *spec.* that in Britain in 1926. ***General Synod***: see SYNOD. ***general theory of relativity***: see RELATIVITY 2. ***general warrant***: see WARRANT *noun*[1]. **in a general way** ordinarily, usually. ***Inquisitor General***: see INQUISITOR *noun* 2. ***Justice General***, ***Lord Justice General***: see JUSTICE *noun*. ***minister general***: see MINISTER *noun* 2c. ***Postmaster General***: see POSTMASTER *noun*[1] 1b. ***Secretary General***: see SECRETARY *noun*. ***Solicitor General***: see SOLICITOR. ***Surgeon General***: see SURGEON *noun*.
▸ **B** *noun*. **I** A general thing or things collectively.
1 A general fact, truth, rule, etc. (usu. in *pl.*). Formerly also (esp. in *LOGIC*), a genus. Now *rare* exc. as opp. to ***particulars***. LME. ▸†**b** A quality or characteristic common to all. *rare* (Shakes.). Only in E17.

I. MURDOCH We should start by considering art in general, and then move from the general to the particular. **b** SHAKES. *Tr. & Cr.* And in this fashion All our abilities, gifts, natures, shapes, Severals and generals of grace exact.

†**2** A neutral colour. LME–L17.
3 The public, the multitude. Formerly also *gen.*, the total or whole; the majority. *arch.* E17.

F. BURNEY The general of people at his time of life are confined by infirmities. DISRAELI He . . understood all about . . sleepers and branch lines, which were then cabalistic terms to the general.

4 *MILITARY HISTORY*. The first beat of the drum for the assembly of all the troops. E18.
▸ **II** A person of authority.
5 *ECCLESIASTICAL*. The chief or head of a religious order. M16.
6 *MILITARY*. Orig., the commander of the whole army; later, the commander of a division. Now, an officer ranking next below a field marshal; *US* a general of the army or air force. Also, by courtesy, a lieutenant general, a major-general. L16. ▸†**b** *NAUTICAL*. An admiral. L16–E18. ▸**c** The head of the Salvation Army; *spec.* (***the General***) its founder, General William Booth (1829–1912). L19.
7 A general servant. *arch. colloq.* L19.
– PHRASES: *CAVIAR* ***to the general***. †**for the general** for the most part. **in general** †(***a***) in a body; universally, without exception; †(***b***) in all respects; (***c***) in general terms, generally; (***d***) as a rule, usually. **in the general** in general terms, generally.
▸ **C** *verb trans.* Infl. **-ll-**, *-**l**-. Lead or command like a general. M19.

D. L. EDWARDS This campaign, generalled by the inflexible Anselm.

generalate /ˈdʒɛn(ə)rəleɪt/ *noun*. M17.
[ORIGIN from GENERAL *noun* + -ATE[1]. Cf. French *généralat*.]
The (period of) office of a military or ecclesiastical general.

generaless /dʒɛn(ə)rəˈlɛs/ *noun*. *rare*. M17.
[ORIGIN from GENERAL *noun* + -ESS[1].]
1 The wife of a general. Chiefly *joc.* M17.
2 A female general. M19.

generalia /dʒɛn(ə)ˈreɪlɪə/ *noun pl.* M19.
[ORIGIN Neut. pl. of Latin *generalis* GENERAL *adjective*.]
General principles.

generalisation *noun* var. of GENERALIZATION.

generalise *verb* var. of GENERALIZE.

generalism /ˈdʒɛn(ə)rəlɪz(ə)m/ *noun*. E19.
[ORIGIN from GENERAL *noun* + -ISM.]
1 A general statement or conclusion. E19.
2 The fact, quality, or action of generalizing; an instance of this. E20.

generalissimo /dʒɛn(ə)rəˈlɪsɪməʊ/ *noun*. Pl. **-os**. E17.
[ORIGIN Italian, superl. of *generale* GENERAL.]
The commander of a combined military, naval, and air force, or of several armies.

fig.: *Times* Cricket does not lend itself, in the way that football may, to a generalissimo.

■ **generalissima** *noun* a female generalissimo M17.

generalist /ˈdʒɛn(ə)rəlɪst/ *noun*. E17.
[ORIGIN from GENERAL *adjective* + -IST.]
A person trained or competent in several different fields or subjects. Opp. SPECIALIST *noun* 2.

Business Education Today These staff need to see themselves as generalists as well as bringing their areas of expertise to the team.

generality /dʒɛnəˈralɪti/ *noun*. LME.
[ORIGIN Old French & mod. French *généralité* from late Latin *generalitas*, from *generalis* GENERAL: see -ITY.]
1 The quality or fact of being general; now *esp.* applicability to a whole class of instances; vagueness, lack of detail (in a statement etc.). Formerly also, prevalence, commonness. LME.

BURKE When an epitaph is very short, it is in danger of getting into a cold generality. E. E. KAY The subsequent words . . did not restrain the generality of the former words.

2 Something that is general; a general principle, law, point, or statement. Formerly also, a general class or category. Usu. in *pl.* LME.

H. JAMES Mrs Vivian ventured upon nothing special; she contented herself with soft generalities. R. MACAULAY All generalities about human beings are nonsense.

glittering generality: see GLITTER *verb*.
3 The bulk, the greater part, the majority, (*of*). Formerly also, people in general. Now with *noun pl.* or *collect.* LME.

L. VAN DER POST Once more he would have to isolate himself from the generality of men. D. LESSING I am talking of the generality, not of the rare individual.

4 *FRENCH HISTORY*. A fiscal and administrative division of the French kingdom. M17.

generalization /dʒɛn(ə)rəlʌɪˈzeɪʃ(ə)n/ *noun*. Also **-isation**. M18.
[ORIGIN French *généralisation*, from *généraliser*: see GENERALIZE, -ATION.]
1 The action, the process, or an act of forming a general concept or proposition on the basis of induction; the result of this process. M18.

J. HUTTON Here then is a generalization of many facts respecting light and heat. J. GATHORNE-HARDY What I am about to write . . are only generalisations; I could supply a mass of exceptions.

hasty generalization: based on too few instances.
2 The process of becoming more general or widespread. L19.

generalize /ˈdʒɛn(ə)rəlʌɪz/ *verb*. Also **-ise**. LME.
[ORIGIN from GENERAL *adjective* + -IZE. Cf. French *généraliser*.]
1 *verb trans.* Reduce to general laws; express in a general form; give a general character to; extend the application of. LME.
2 a *verb trans.* Infer (a conclusion, law, etc.) by induction; base a general law or conclusion on. L18. ▸**b** *verb intrans.* Make general inferences or conclusions by induction; be inclined to make or express such inferences. L18.
3 a *verb trans.* Erode, soften, or blur the particulars or details of. L18. ▸**b** *verb trans. & intrans.* *PAINTING*. Portray only the typical or salient characteristics of (an object). E19.
4 *verb trans.* Bring into general use; make common, familiar, or generally known; spread or extend. E19.
5 *verb intrans.* Of a law, theory, etc.: apply more generally; become extended in application *to*. L20.
■ **generaliza'bility** *noun* M20. **generalizable** *adjective* M19. **generalized** *ppl adjective* that has been generalized; *spec.* (*MEDICINE*) (of a disease) that has extended to other parts of the body: M19. **generalizer** *noun* L18.

Général Jacqueminot /ʒeneral zakmino (*pl. same*), ˈdʒɛnər(ə)l ˈʒakmɪnəʊ/ *noun phr.* M19.
[ORIGIN See JACQUEMINOT.]
= JACQUEMINOT.

generally /ˈdʒɛn(ə)rəli/ *adverb*. ME.
[ORIGIN from GENERAL *adjective* + -LY[2].]
1 As a whole, collectively; universally, without exception. Now only in weaker sense, for the most part, on the whole; extensively. ME.
2 In a general sense or way, without reference to particulars or individuals. ME.
3 As a general rule; usually. LME.

generalness /ˈdʒɛn(ə)rəlnɪs/ *noun*. Now *rare*. M16.
[ORIGIN from GENERAL *adjective* + -NESS.]
The state, quality, or fact of being general.

generalship /ˈdʒɛn(ə)rəlʃɪp/ *noun*. L16.
[ORIGIN from GENERAL *noun* + -SHIP.]
1 (The discharge of) the office of general. Formerly also, the tenure of such an office. L16.
2 (Military) skill in command, strategy; tact, diplomacy. M18.

B. BEAUMONT His generalship and steadying influence were a great comfort to his team.

generant /ˈdʒɛn(ə)r(ə)nt/ *noun*. M17.
[ORIGIN Latin *generant-* pres. ppl stem of *generare*: see GENERATE *verb*, -ANT[1].]
A thing which generates; *spec.* in *MATH.* = GENERATRIX 2.

generate /ˈdʒɛn(ə)rət/ *ppl adjective*. LME.
[ORIGIN Latin *generatus* pa. pple of *generare*: see GENERATE *verb*, -ATE[2].]
Generated.

generate /ˈdʒɛnəreɪt/ *verb*. E16.
[ORIGIN Latin *generat-* pa. ppl stem of *generare* beget, from *genus*, *gener-* stock, race: see -ATE[3].]
1 *verb trans. & intrans.* Beget or reproduce (offspring). Now *rare*. E16.

H. L. MENCKEN Man tries to protect himself against change even beyond the grave: he acquires property; he generates children.

2 *verb trans.* Bring into existence, produce; cause to arise, give rise to; *MATH.* (of a point, line, or surface) move and so notionally form (a line, surface, or solid). M16. ▸**b** Produce (electricity, esp. electric current). L19. ▸**c** *MATH. & LINGUISTICS*. Produce (a set, sequence, or string of items) by performing specified operations on or applying specified rules to an initial set. L19.

T. H. HUXLEY Steam is generated from the water in the boiler. N. MOSLEY After he had gone the local enthusiasm he generated seemed to wane. *Times* The practice . . has the primary objective of generating commission income. J. KRANTZ The vast amount of publicity they generated was immediately reflected in sales.

b generating station a building and site for generating electric current.

generation /dʒɛnəˈreɪʃ(ə)n/ *noun.* ME.
[ORIGIN Old French & mod. French *génération* from Latin *generatio(n-)*, formed as GENERATE verb: see -ATION.]
▸ **I** That which is generated.
1 The offspring of the same parent or parents regarded as a single step or stage in descent; such a step or stage. ME. ▸†**b** Offspring, progeny; descendants. LME–E18. ▸†**c** Family, race, stock; a class or kind of people or animals. LME–E18. ▸**d** A kind or type, esp. of a computer, that is seen as representing a distinct advance on earlier kinds, or a recognized further stage of development. M20.

L. HELLMAN Nobody in his family had earned a living for three generations. **d** *Natural World* The M54. . . the first of a new generation of motorways.

clogs to clogs in three generations: see CLOG noun 3. **d *first-generation, second-generation***, etc.
2 The whole body of people born and living at about the same time; later also, the average length of time in which children become ready to take the place of their parents, usu. reckoned at about thirty years. ME.

R. MACAULAY The last generation, the elderly people, were . . responsible for the unfortunate state. E. H. GOMBRICH Some two hundred years, scarcely more than six generations. B. PYM Like most girls of her generation and upbringing she had expected to marry.

lost generation: see LOST adjective.
▸ **II** The action of generating.
3 The act or process of reproducing or being reproduced; procreation; propagation; *spec.* in THEOLOGY, the origin of Christ from God the Father. LME. ▸**b** Genealogy, lineage, pedigree. *rare.* LME.
4 The process of producing a substance, animal, plant, force, etc., by natural or artificial means; *spec.* the production of electricity. LME. ▸**b** LINGUISTICS. The process of deriving a sentence by the application of a rule or a series of rules which constitute the grammar. M20.
– COMB.: **generation gap** differences in opinions, tastes, behaviour, etc. between those of different generations; **Generation X** a generation of young people about whose future there is uncertainty; *spec.* a generation of young Americans reaching adulthood in the 1980s and 1990s and perceived to be disaffected, directionless, or irresponsible, and reluctant to participate in society.
■ **generational** *adjective* L19. **generationism** *noun* (THEOLOGY) the doctrine or belief that the soul as well as the body of a child is reproduced by the parents; traducianism: M19.

generative /ˈdʒɛn(ə)rətɪv/ *adjective.* LME.
[ORIGIN Old French & mod. French *génératif* or late Latin *generativus*, from Latin *generat-*: see GENERATE verb, -IVE.]
1 Pertaining to generation or reproduction; able to produce offspring or reproduce. LME.

S. PEPYS We . . had very good discourse concerning the insects and their having a generative faculty as well as other Creatures.

2 Able to produce, productive. LME. ▸**b** LINGUISTICS. Able to generate; involving the application of a finite set of rules to linguistic input in order to produce all and only the well-formed items of a language. M20.

Medical Journal This agent is known to be the generative cause of several diseases of the bones. **b** R. G. COLLINGWOOD The generative act which produces that utterance is an act of consciousness.

b generative grammar a type of grammar which describes a language in terms of a set of logical rules formulated so as to be capable of generating the infinite number of possible sentences of that language and providing them with the correct structural description. TRANSFORMATIONAL-*generative*.
■ **generatively** *adverb* M17. **generativeness** *noun* E18. **generativism** *noun* (LINGUISTICS) the theory of the study of language on the basis of a generative grammar L20. **generativist** *noun* (LINGUISTICS) an adherent or practitioner of generativism M20. **generaˈtivity** *noun* M20.

generator /ˈdʒɛnəreɪtə/ *noun.* M17.
[ORIGIN Latin *generator*, from *generat-*: see GENERATE verb, -OR. Later techn. uses directly from GENERATE verb.]
1 *gen.* A person who or thing which generates or reproduces. Now *rare.* M17.
2 A thing which generates or produces something; *spec.* (***a***) an apparatus for producing gases, steam, etc.; (***b***) a machine for converting mechanical into electrical energy, as a dynamo. L18.
3 MUSIC. The fundamental tone of a series of harmonics or of a chord. M19.
4 MATH. A point, line, or surface regarded as moving and so notionally forming a line, surface, or solid respectively. Also called ***generatrix***. M19.
5 MATH. Each of a subset of elements in forms of which the other elements of the set can be represented. L19.
6 COMPUTING. A routine that constructs other routines or subroutines using given parameters, for specific applications. M20.

generatrix /dʒɛnəˈreɪtrɪks/ *noun.* Pl. **-trices** /-trɪsiːz/. M17.
[ORIGIN Latin, fem. of *generator*: see GENERATOR, -TRIX.]
†**1** A female parent. Only *fig.* M17–E19.
2 MATH. = GENERATOR 4. M19.

generic /dʒɪˈnɛrɪk/ *adjective & noun.* L17.
[ORIGIN French *générique*, from Latin *genus*, *gener-* GENUS: see -IC.]
▸ **A** *adjective.* **1** Characteristic of or belonging to a genus or class; applicable to (any individual of) a large group or class, general, non-specific. L17.

ALDOUS HUXLEY The derisive individual in her . . repelled him, but the attraction of what was generic, . . the entire sex, was stronger. B. COTTLE Primitive languages have words for various trees but no generic term for 'tree'.

2 Of the name of a commercial product: not protected by legislation from general use; of a product, esp. a drug: not protected by a registered trademark. Orig. *US.* L20.
▸ **B** *noun.* Something generic; *spec.* (***a***) a general word as an element of a compound proper name; (***b***) (orig. *US*) a generic product. E19.
■ **generical** *adjective* = GENERIC *adjective* M17. **generically** *adverb* with reference to genus M17. **genericalness** *noun* (*rare*) E18. **genericize** *verb trans.* make generic L20. **genericness** *noun* generic quality or characteristics M20.

generification /dʒɪˌnɛrɪfɪˈkeɪʃ(ə)n/ *noun.* M19.
[ORIGIN from Latin *genus*, *gener-* GENUS + -FICATION.]
LOGIC. = GENERALIZATION 1.

generosity /dʒɛnəˈrɒsɪti/ *noun.* LME.
[ORIGIN Latin *generositas*, from *generosus*: see GENEROUS, -ITY.]
1 Excellence or nobility of birth. *arch.* LME.
2 Orig., courage, nobility of conduct. Now only, magnanimity, willingness to forgive. Also (*rare*), an instance of this. E17.

R. BENTLEY His Judgment, like other mens Valour, has commonly the generosity to favour the weaker side.

3 Liberality in giving, munificence; *rare* an instance of this. L17.

R. DAVIES He gave away . . all sorts of stuff at every performance . . . What was all that generosity meant to conceal?

generous /ˈdʒɛn(ə)rəs/ *adjective.* L16.
[ORIGIN Old French & mod. French *généreux* from Latin *generosus* noble, magnanimous, from *genus*, *gener-*: see GENUS, -OUS.]
1 Of noble birth, high-born. Formerly also, (of an animal) of good stock. *arch.* L16.
2 Orig., characteristic of noble birth, gallant, courageous. Now only, noble-minded, magnanimous, free from meanness or prejudice. L16.

G. GREENE She had to be satisfied with that; one did not expect any generous response from an employer. H. KISSINGER He urged us to make concessions because great powers could afford a generous attitude.

3 Ample, large; abundant, copious. E17. ▸**b** Of wine etc.: rich and full. E17.

A. EDEN Everything about Potter was of generous proportions, including his weight. *House & Garden* Curtains with swags and tails to match the splendour of the generous windows.

4 Free in giving, liberal, munificent. L17.

A. GUINNESS Ralph Richardson, always generous to a fault, gave me a number of presents.

■ **generously** *adverb* L16. **generousness** *noun* (now *rare*) E17.

genesis /ˈdʒɛnɪsɪs/ *noun.* LOE.
[ORIGIN Latin from Greek = generation, creation, nativity, horoscope, name of the Old Testament book in Septuagint, hence in Vulgate, from base of *gignesthai* be born or produced.]
1 (**G-**.) (The name of) the first book of the Bible, containing an account of the creation of the world. LOE.

T. H. HUXLEY The reconcilers of Genesis with science.

†**2** ASTROLOGY. Nativity, horoscope. LME–M17.
†**3** Synthesis. Only in 17.
4 Origin, mode of formation or generation. E17.

E. CLODD The theory of evolution must embrace the genesis and development of mind.

■ **Geneˈsiacal** *adjective* (*rare*) = GENESITIC L19. **Geneˈsitic** *adjective* (*rare*) of or belonging to Genesis M19.

-genesis /ˈdʒɛnɪsɪs/ *suffix.*
[ORIGIN Repr. Greek GENESIS.]
In compounds denoting modes of generation, as ABIOGENESIS, BIOGENESIS, PARTHENOGENESIS, etc.

genet /ˈdʒɛnɪt/ *noun*[1]. Also **gentte** /dʒɪˈnɛt/. LME.
[ORIGIN Old French *genete* (mod. *-ette*); cf. Arabic *jarnaiṭ*.]
1 †**a** In *pl.* Skins of the genet used as fur. LME–L17. ▸**b** Fur obtained from genets; fur sold in imitation of this. L19.
2 Any of several small carnivorous catlike mammals constituting the genus *Genetta*, native to Africa and southern Europe and having spotted fur and long ringed bushy tails. L15.

genet /ˈdʒɛnət/ *noun*[2]. L20.
[ORIGIN from GENET(IC after ORTET, RAMET.]
BIOLOGY. A genetically distinct entity, such as may be produced by asexual reproduction from a single zygote. Cf. RAMET.

genet *noun*[3] var. of JENNET.

genethliac /dʒɛˈnɛθlɪak/ *noun & adjective.* Long *arch. rare.* L16.
[ORIGIN Ult. from Greek *genethliakos* belonging to one's birth or birthday (= *genethlios*, from *genethlē*, from base of *gignesthai*: see GENESIS).]
▸ **A** *noun.* A person who calculates nativities or horoscopes, an astrologer. L16.
▸ **B** *adjective.* = GENETHLIACAL. E17.

genethliacal /dʒɛnɪˈθlʌɪək(ə)l/ *adjective.* E17.
[ORIGIN formed as GENETHLIAC + -AL[1].]
Relating to the calculation of nativities; relating to a birthday.
■ **genethliacally** *adverb* M17.

genethliacon /dʒɛnɪˈθlʌɪəkɒn/ *noun.* Pl. **-ca** /-kə/. L16.
[ORIGIN Latin from Greek neut. sing. of *genethliakos* GENETHLIAC.]
A birthday ode.

genethlialogy /dʒɛˌnɛθlɪˈalədʒi/ *noun.* M17.
[ORIGIN Greek *genethlialogia* from *genethlialogein* cast nativities: see -LOGY.]
The calculating or casting of nativities.

genetic /dʒɪˈnɛtɪk/ *adjective.* M19.
[ORIGIN from GENESIS after *antithesis*, *antithetic*, etc.]
1 Of, pertaining to, or involving origin; arising from a common origin. M19. ▸**b** Of or pertaining to genetics or genes; hereditary. E20.

MAX-MÜLLER The only scientific and truly genetic classification of religions. **b** J. UPDIKE You shouldn't be drinking and smoking pot . . , you'll cause genetic damage. J. BRONOWSKI By some genetic accident, the wild wheat crossed with a natural goat grass and formed a fertile hybrid.

2 Generative; productive. *rare.* M19.
– SPECIAL COLLOCATIONS: **genetic code** the basis on which genetic information is stored as sequences of nucleotides in chromosomal DNA or RNA, different groups of three consecutive nucleotides corresponding to different amino acids. **genetic counselling**: given to prospective parents concerning the chances of genetic disorders in a future child. **genetic drift** variation over time in the relative frequency of different genotypes in a small population owing to the chance disappearance of particular genes as individuals die or do not reproduce. **genetic engineering** the manipulation of genetic material in order to alter genes and hence the characteristics of the organism concerned. **genetic fingerprint** a set of genetic characteristics derived from the tissues or secretions of an individual and used to identify him or her. **genetic imprinting** the differential expression of genetic traits depending on the parent from which they were inherited. **genetic information** the genetic potential of an organism carried in the base sequence of its DNA (or, in some viruses, RNA) according to the genetic code. **genetic load** the presence of unfavourable genetic material in the genes of a population. **genetic pollution** the spread of altered genes from genetically engineered organisms to other, non-engineered organisms. **genetic profile** a description listing the significant genetic characteristics of an individual and used for identification, the prediction of inherited disorders, etc. **genetic screening** the study of a person's DNA in order to identify susceptibility to particular diseases or abnormalities.

-genetic /dʒɪˈnɛtɪk/ *suffix.*
[ORIGIN from GENETIC.]
Forming adjectives corresp. to nouns in *-genesis* or *-geny*, as ***biogenetic***, ***phylogenetic***: = -GENIC 1, 2.

genetical /dʒɪˈnɛtɪk(ə)l/ *adjective.* M17.
[ORIGIN formed as -GENETIC: see -AL[1].]
†**1** Synthetic, as opp. to analytic. Cf. GENESIS 3. Only in M17.
2 = GENETIC. M19.

genetically /dʒɪˈnɛtɪk(ə)li/ *adverb.* M19.
[ORIGIN from GENETIC or GENETICAL: see -ICALLY.]
1 As regards origin. M19.
2 As regards genetics; by the agency of genes. E20.
genetically modified (of genetic material) modified by natural processes of mutation, selection, and recombination, or (now usu.) artificially manipulated in order to produce a desired characteristic.

geneticism /dʒɪˈnɛtɪsɪz(ə)m/ *noun.* M20.
[ORIGIN from GENETIC + -ISM.]
Orig., the theory that an individual's form and behaviour can be explained in terms of the history of both the individual and the race. Now (usu. *derog.*), the belief that human characteristics are genetically determined.

genetics /dʒɪˈnɛtɪks/ *noun.* L19.
[ORIGIN from GENETIC + -S[1].]
1 The principles or laws of origination. Now *rare* or *obsolete.* L19.
2 a The branch of science that deals with heredity and the variation of inherited characteristics in living organisms. E20. ▸**b** The genetic characteristics of an organism or condition. M20.

b *Nature* A world authority on the taxonomy and genetics of the cottons.

■ **geneticist** /-sɪst/ *noun* an expert in or student of genetics E20.

genetrix /ˈdʒɛnɪtrɪks/ *noun.* Now *rare.* Also (earlier) †**-ice**. Pl. **-ices** /-ɪsiːz/. LME.
[ORIGIN Old French *genitris* or Latin *genetrix*, *-itrix* fem. of GENITOR *noun*[2]: see -TRIX.]
A female parent, a mother.

genette *noun*[1] var. of GENET *noun*[1].

genette *noun*[2] var. of JENNET.

Geneva /dʒɪˈniːvə/ *noun*[1]. L16.
[ORIGIN A city in Switzerland.]
1 Used ***attrib.*** to designate things found in, originating in, or associated with Geneva. L16.

Geneva bands clerical bands resembling those worn by the Swiss Calvinist clergy. **Geneva Bible**: the English translation first printed at Geneva in 1560; also called ***Breeches Bible***. **Geneva Convention** an international agreement first made at Geneva in 1864 and later revised, governing the status and treatment of captured and wounded military personnel in wartime. **Geneva cross** a red cross (distinguishing hospitals, ambulances, etc., in war). **Geneva gown** a long loose black gown worn by (esp. Calvinist) clergy and academics. **Geneva Protocol**: any of various protocols drawn up in Geneva, *esp.* that of 1925 limiting chemical and bacteriological warfare. **Geneva watch** a Swiss-made watch.

2 Designating (a mechanism employing) a driving wheel with a pin that engages with a radial slot or slots in a driven wheel for part of each revolution, so converting continuous motion into intermittent motion. L19.
Geneva stop: consisting of a pair of gears in which the driven wheel lacks cogs or slots on part of its circumference.
■ ˈ**Genevize** *verb intrans.* (now *rare*) imitate or introduce the practice or doctrines of the Genevan (Calvinist) church L17.

geneva *noun*² see GENEVER.

Genevan /dʒɪˈniːv(ə)n/ *noun & adjective*. Also (earlier) †**-vian**. M16.
[ORIGIN from GENEVA *noun*¹ + -AN.]
▸ **A** *noun*. A native or inhabitant of the city of Geneva in Switzerland. Also (now *rare*), a person who follows the Calvinist doctrine associated with Geneva. M16.
▸ **B** *adjective*. Of or pertaining to Geneva (orig. esp. to its ecclesiastical organization); (now *rare*) Calvinistic. L16.

genever /dʒɪˈniːvə, jəˈneɪvə/ *noun*. Also **jenever** /jəˈneɪvə/, (now *literary*) **geneva**. E18.
[ORIGIN Dutch (now *jenever*) from Old French *genevre* (mod. *genièvre*) from alt. of Latin *juniperus* JUNIPER. Var. assim. to GENEVA *noun*¹. See also GIN *noun*².]
Dutch gin.

Genevese /dʒɛnəˈviːz/ *noun & adjective*. M17.
[ORIGIN from GENEVA *noun*¹ + -ESE.]
▸ **A** *noun*. Pl. same. A native or inhabitant of the city of Geneva in Switzerland. M17.
▸ **B** *adjective*. Of or pertaining to Geneva. E19.

†**Genevian** *noun & adjective* see GENEVAN.

Genevois /ʒən(ə)vwa, ʒnɛv-/ *noun & adjective*. Pl. same. M16.
[ORIGIN French *genévois*.]
= GENEVESE.

genial /ˈdʒiːnɪəl/ *adjective*¹. M16.
[ORIGIN Latin *genialis* nuptial, productive, joyous, from GENIUS: see -AL¹.]
1 Of or pertaining to marriage, nuptial; of or pertaining to reproduction or procreation. Now *rare*. M16.

SPENSER The bridal bowre and geniall bed.

†**2** Festive. E17–M18.

DRYDEN In Winter shall the Genial Feast be made Before the Fire.

3 Conducive to growth. Now chiefly of air, climate, sunshine, etc.: pleasantly warm, mild. M17.

COLERIDGE Applause scarcely less genial to a poet, than the vernal warmth to the feathered songsters during their nest-building.

†**4** Of or pertaining to natural disposition; natural. M17–M19.

MILTON So much I feel my genial spirits droop.

5 Jovial, kindly, sociable; sympathetically cheerful. M18.

V. S. PRITCHETT To find oneself among affectionate, genial and cultivated families . . must be heaven. O. SACKS He was a genial soul, very ready to talk and to answer any questions.

6 [Infl. by German *genial*, *-isch*.] Of, pertaining to, or characterized by genius (GENIUS 6). Now *rare* or *obsolete*. E19.
■ **geniˈality** *noun* E17. **genialize** *verb trans.* (*rare*) make genial or agreeable M19. **genially** *adverb* M17. **genialness** *noun* (*rare*) geniality E18.

genial /dʒɪˈniːəl/ *adjective*². M19.
[ORIGIN from Greek *geneion* chin, from *genus* jaw: see -AL¹.]
ANATOMY. Of, pertaining to, or situated on the chin.

genic /ˈdʒiːnɪk, ˈdʒɛn-/ *adjective*. E20.
[ORIGIN from GENE + -IC.]
Of or pertaining to a gene or genes.
■ **genically** *adverb* M20.

-genic /ˈdʒɛnɪk/ *suffix*.
[ORIGIN from -GEN + -IC.]
Forming adjectives, mostly corresp. to nouns in *-gen*, *-genesis*, or *-geny*.
1 Producing, causing, as ***carcinogenic***, ***pathogenic***.
2 Caused by, originating in, as ***iatrogenic***.
3 [After *photogenic*.] Well suited to: in adjectives referring to modes of dissemination or reproduction of information etc.

genicular /dʒɪˈnɪkjʊlə/ *adjective*. E19.
[ORIGIN from Latin *geniculum*: see GENICULATE, -AR¹.]
1 = GENICULATE. *rare*. E19.
2 ANATOMY. Of or pertaining to the knee or a genu. E20.

geniculate /dʒɪˈnɪkjʊlət/ *adjective*. M17.
[ORIGIN Latin *geniculatus*, from *geniculum* joint in a plant stem, small knee, dim. of *genu* knee: see -CULE, -ATE².]
Bent at a sharp angle; ANATOMY situated at a sharp bend. Also, resembling a knee.
geniculate body ANATOMY either of two protuberances on each side of the inferior surface of the thalamus which relay auditory and visual impulses respectively to the cerebral cortex. **geniculate ganglion** ANATOMY a sensory ganglion at a bend of the facial nerve. **geniculate nucleus** ANATOMY = ***geniculate body*** above.
■ Also **geniculated** *adjective* M17.

geniculation /dʒɪˌnɪkjʊˈleɪʃ(ə)n/ *noun*. E17.
[ORIGIN Late Latin *geniculatio(n-)*, from *geniculare* bend the knee, from Latin *geniculum*: see GENICULATE, -ATION.]
†**1** (A) genuflection. E–M17.
2 The state of being geniculate. L19.

geniculum /dʒɪˈnɪkjʊləm/ *noun*. Pl. **-lums**, **-la** /-lə/. E19.
[ORIGIN Latin: see GENICULATE.]
ANATOMY. A small kneelike structure; a sharp bend; BOTANY (*rare*) a joint in the stalk of a plant.

genie /ˈdʒiːni/ *noun*. Pl. **genii** /ˈdʒiːnɪʌɪ/, **-s**. M17.
[ORIGIN French *génie* from Latin GENIUS.]
†**1** = GENIUS 1. M17–E18.
2 A spirit or jinn (in Arabian stories), esp. one trapped in or inhabiting a bottle, lamp, etc., and capable of granting wishes. Cf. GENIUS 2. M18.

S. RUSHDIE I just rub my jolly old lamp and out pops the genie bringing fame and fortune.

— NOTE: See note s.v. GENIUS. *Genie* was adopted in sense 2 by the French translators of the *Arabian Nights' Entertainments* on account of its resemblance in both sound and sense to Arab. *jinnī*.

genii *noun* pl. of GENIE, GENIUS.

genin /ˈdʒɛnɪn/ *noun*. E20.
[ORIGIN Ending of SALIGENIN, SAPOGENIN.]
CHEMISTRY. Any of various steroids that occur as the non-sugar part of glycosides in some plants and toad venoms.

†**genio** *noun*. Pl. **-o(e)s**. E17–E18.
[ORIGIN Italian from Latin GENIUS.]
= GENIUS.

genio- /dʒɪˈnʌɪəʊ/ *combining form* of Greek *geneion* chin: see GENIAL *adjective*², -O-.
■ **genioˈglossus**, (orig.) †**-glosse** *noun*, pl. **-ssi**, a muscle which is inserted in the undersurface of the tongue and the hyoid and protrudes and retracts the tongue; also ***genioglossus muscle***: M17. **genioˈhyoid** *noun* a muscle inserted in the hyoid which elevates the bone and draws it forward; also ***geniohyoid muscle***: M19.

genip *noun* var. of GUINEP.

genipapo /dʒɛnɪˈpapəʊ/ *noun*. Also **genipap** /ˈdʒɛnɪpap/. E17.
[ORIGIN Portuguese *jenipapo* from Tupi *ianipaba*.]
A tropical American tree, *Genipa americana*, which yields a dye used in tattooing; its fruit, resembling an orange in appearance.

Genist /ˈdʒiːnɪst/ *noun*. E17.
[ORIGIN Late Latin *Genistae* pl. from Greek *Genistai*, prob. from base of *gignesthai* be born.]
A member of a sect of ancient Jews who claimed pure-blooded descent from Abraham.

genista /dʒɪˈnɪstə, dʒɛ-/ *noun*. E17.
[ORIGIN Latin = the plant broom.]
Any of several yellow-flowered leguminous heathland shrubs belonging to or formerly included in the genus *Genista*; *esp.* dyer's greenweed, *G. tinctoria*, and petty whin, *G. anglica*.

genistein /dʒɪˈnɪstiːn/ *noun*. E20.
[ORIGIN from GENISTA + -EIN.]
CHEMISTRY. A yellow isoflavone derivative, $C_{15}H_{10}O_5$, that occurs in subterranean clover and as an aglycone in dyer's greenweed, and is weakly oestrogenic.

genital /ˈdʒɛnɪt(ə)l/ *adjective & noun*. LME.
[ORIGIN Old French & mod. French *génital* or Latin *genitalis* (neut. sing. and pl. as noun), from *genitus* pa. pple of *gignere* beget: see -AL¹.]
▸ **A** *adjective*. Of or pertaining to the organs of reproduction; (now *rare*) pertaining to reproduction. LME.
▸ **B** *noun*. The external organ or organs of reproduction, esp. of the male. Usu. in *pl.* LME.
■ **genitally** *adverb* M20.

genitalia /dʒɛnɪˈteɪlɪə/ *noun pl.* L19.
[ORIGIN Latin, use as noun of neut. pl. of *genitalis*: see GENITAL.]
The interior or exterior reproductive organs (of male or female); the genitals.

genitival /dʒɛnɪˈtʌɪv(ə)l/ *adjective*. E17.
[ORIGIN from GENITIVE + -AL¹.]
†**1** Of birth or reproduction. *rare*. Only in E17.
2 = GENITIVE *adjective* 1. E19.
■ **genitivally** *adverb* L19.

genitive /ˈdʒɛnɪtɪv/ *adjective & noun*. LME.
[ORIGIN Old French & mod. French *génitif*, *-ive* or Latin *genitivus*, *-iva* (*gene-*), (sc. *casus* case), from *genit-* pa. ppl stem of *gignere* beget, produce: see -IVE.]
▸ **A** *adjective*. **1** Designating, being in, or pertaining to a case in inflected languages indicating relationship between nouns (in English corresponding to *of*, *from*, and other prepositions with a noun representing the source, possessor, etc.). LME.
†**2** Pertaining to reproduction. M16–M17.
▸ **B** *noun*. *The* genitive case; a word, form, etc., in the genitive case. LME.
genitive absolute a construction in Greek similar to the Latin ablative absolute.

genitor /ˈdʒɛnɪtə/ *noun*¹. LME.
[ORIGIN Old French & mod. French *géniteur* or Latin *genitor*, from base of *gignere* beget: see -OR.]
1 A male parent, father; (in *pl.*) parents. *arch.* LME.
2 ANTHROPOLOGY. A person's biological as opp. to legal father. Cf. PATER 3b. M20.

†**genitor** *noun*² var. of GENITORY.

genitory /ˈdʒɛnɪt(ə)ri/ *noun*. Now *rare*. Also †**-or**. LME.
[ORIGIN Old French & mod. French *génitoires* pl., suffix-variant (-ORY¹) of synon. †*genitaire(s*, †*genitailles*, *génitures*.]
A testicle. Usu. in *pl.*: testicles, (in later use) genitals.

genito-urinary /ˌdʒɛnɪtəʊˈjʊərɪn(ə)ri/ *adjective*. M19.
[ORIGIN from Latin *genitalis* GENITAL + -O- + URINARY.]
Chiefly MEDICINE. = URINOGENITAL.

Daily Telegraph VD clinics, now designated genito-urinary clinics.

geniture /ˈdʒɛnɪtʃə/ *noun*. LME.
[ORIGIN Old French & mod. French *géniture* or Latin *genitura*, from base of *gignere* beget: see -URE.]
1 Begetting; birth. LME.

QUILLER-COUCH A man's lineage and geniture being reckoned . . among the things he cannot reasonably be asked to amend.

†**2** Offspring; product. LME–L17.
†**3** ASTROLOGY. Nativity, horoscope. E17–E19.
†**4** Animal semen. Only in 17.

genius /ˈdʒiːnɪəs/ *noun*. Pl. **-ii** /-ɪʌɪ/, **-iuses**. LME.
[ORIGIN Latin, from base of *gignere* beget, Greek *gignesthai* be born, come into being.]
1 The tutelary or attendant spirit in classical pagan belief allotted to every person at birth, or to a place, institution, etc. Formerly also, an allegorical figure representing the moral instincts keeping passion within bounds. LME. ▸**b** Esp. in ***good genius***, ***evil genius***. Either of the two mutually opposed spirits or angels supposed to attend each person. Hence, a person or thing that powerfully influences another. L16. ▸**c** The personification or embodied type of something abstract. *rare*. L16. ▸**d** ASTROLOGY. The combination of sidereal influences represented in a person's horoscope. M17.

K. WHITE Kind genii of my native fields benign. **c** SHAKES. *2 Hen. IV* His dimensions . . were invisible. 'A was the very genius of famine.

2 A demon or spirit; *esp.* = GENIE 2. L16.

G. BUCK Another kind of Genius, or *ignis fatuus*.

3 †**a** Characteristic disposition, bent, or inclination; natural character or constitution. L16–E19. ▸**b** Prevalent feeling, opinion, taste, or character (of a nation, age, etc.). M17. ▸**c** The prevailing character or spirit, or characteristic method (of a law, language, etc.). M17. ▸**d** The body of associations connected with or inspirations derived from a place. Cf. sense 5 below. E19.

a EVELYN Suitable to my rural genius, born as I was at Wotton, among the woods. **b** D. HUME The barbarous and violent genius of the age. **c** J. C. CALHOUN The genius of our constitution is opposed to the assumption of power. **d** C. LAMB Is the being shown over a place the same as . . detecting the genius of it.

4 Natural ability or tendency; attributes which fit a person for a particular activity. Passing into sense 6. E17. ▸**b** Natural aptitude, talent, or inclination *for*, †*to* (something). M17.

B. FRANKLIN Different men have geniuses adapted to a variety of different arts and manufactures. **b** M. KEANE He had a genius for prolonging a visit if a house suited him.

5 ***genius loci*** /ˈləʊsʌɪ, ˈlɒkiː/ [Latin, of the place], the presiding god or spirit of a place. Also = sense 3d above. E17.

N. PEVSNER The *genius loci*, . . in modern planning terms, is the character of the site.

6 Inborn exalted intellectual power; instinctive and extraordinary imaginative, creative, or inventive capacity, freq. opp. to ***talent***; a person having this. M17.

H. SIDDONS Isaac was a good-dispositioned, industrious boy, but no genius. J. A. FROUDE A man of genius . . is a spring in which there is always more behind than flows from it.

— NOTE: The pl. *genii* is not usu. distinguishable from a pl. of GENIE. Ambiguous early examples have been regarded as belonging here.

genizah /gɛˈniːzə/ *noun*. Also **-za**. L19.
[ORIGIN Hebrew, lit. 'a hiding, hiding place', from *gānaz* set aside, hide.]
(The contents of) a storeroom for damaged, discarded, or heretical manuscripts and sacred relics, usu. attached to a synagogue.

genlock /ˈdʒɛnlɒk/ *noun & verb.* M20.
[ORIGIN from GEN(ERATOR + LOCK *verb*[1].]
ELECTRONICS & COMPUTING. ▸**A** *noun.* A device for maintaining synchronization between two different video signals or between a video signal and a computer or audio signal, esp. so as to enable video images and computer graphics to be mixed. Also, this technique or process. M20.
▸**B** *verb.* **1** *verb intrans.* Maintain synchronization between two signals using this technique. M20.
2 *verb trans.* Lock (one signal or signal source) *to* or *onto* another in this way. L20.

gennel *noun* var. of GINNEL.

gennemic /dʒəˈnɛmɪk/ *adjective.* M20.
[ORIGIN from Greek *gennēma* product + -IC.]
PHONETICS. Of or pertaining to speech sounds after they have been uttered.
■ **geˈnnemically** *adverb* M20.

gennet *noun* var. of JENNET.

geno- /ˈdʒɛnəʊ, ˈdʒiːnəʊ/ *combining form.*
[ORIGIN from Greek *genos* offspring, race: see -O-.]
Forming nouns and adjectives with the senses 'gene' or 'genus'.
■ **genophore** *noun* (BIOLOGY) a structure carrying genetic information in prokaryotes, viruses, and some organelles M20. **genoˈtoxic** *adjective* (BIOLOGY & MEDICINE) designating a substance, esp. a carcinogen, that has a direct toxic effect on genetic material L20. **genotoxicity** /-tɒkˈsɪsɪti/ *noun* (BIOLOGY & MEDICINE) the property or degree of being genotoxic L20.

Genoa /ˈdʒɛnəʊə, dʒɛˈnəʊə/ *noun.* L16.
[ORIGIN A city and seaport of NW Italy.]
†**1** ***paste of Genoa***, a baked sweet made of quince, spices, and sugar. L16–E17.
2 Used *attrib.* to designate things originating in or associated with Genoa. M17. ▸**b** In full ***Genoa velvet***. Velvet woven on a twilled ground. M18. ▸**c** In full ***Genoa cake***. A rich fruit cake topped with almonds. L19. ▸**d** In full ***Genoa jib***. A large jib with a low foot used on a racing yacht. M20.
■ **Genoan** *adjective & noun* (now *rare* or *obsolete*) = GENOESE E17.

genocide /ˈdʒɛnəsʌɪd/ *noun.* M20.
[ORIGIN from GENO- + -CIDE.]
The (attempted) deliberate and systematic extermination of an ethnic or national group.
■ **genoˈcidal** *adjective* M20.

Genoese /dʒɛnəʊˈiːz/ *noun & adjective.* M16.
[ORIGIN from GENOA + -ESE after Italian GENOVESE. Cf. GENOWAY.]
▸**A** *noun.* Pl. same, †-**s**. A native or inhabitant of Genoa; the dialect of Genoa. M16.
▸**B** *adjective.* Of or pertaining to Genoa. M18.
Genoese sponge a sponge cake made of eggs, butter, and sugar beaten into a light, even batter.

genoise /dʒɛnˈwɑːz/ *noun.* Chiefly *N. Amer.* Also **G-**. M20.
[ORIGIN French, fem. of *genois* of GENOA.]
= *GENOESE sponge*.

genome /ˈdʒiːnəʊm/ *noun.* M20.
[ORIGIN from GENO- + CHROMOSOME.]
BIOLOGY. The complete set of genes or genetic material present in a cell, organelle, virus, etc., or in each cell of an organism. Also, (the genes in) a complete haploid set of chromosomes of a particular organism.
■ **geˈnomic** *adjective* M20.

genomics /dʒɪˈnəʊmɪks, -ˈnɒmɪks/ *noun pl.* (treated as *sing.*). L20.
[ORIGIN from GENOME + -ICS.]
The scientific study of nucleotide sequencing, gene mapping, and the analysis of genomes; the branch of molecular biology concerned with this.

genotype /ˈdʒɛnətʌɪp, ˈdʒiːn-/ *noun*[1]. Now *rare.* L19.
[ORIGIN from GENO- + -TYPE.]
TAXONOMY. The type species of a genus.

genotype /ˈdʒɛnətʌɪp, ˈdʒiːn-/ *noun*[2] *& verb.* E20.
[ORIGIN German *Genotypus*, formed as GENO-: see TYPE *noun*.]
▸**A** *noun.* BIOLOGY. The genetic constitution of an individual, esp. as distinguished from the phenotype; the whole of the genes in an individual or group. E20.
▸**B** *verb trans.* MEDICINE. Investigate the genotype of. M20.
■ **genotypic** /-ˈtɪp-/ *adjective* M20. **genotypical** /-ˈtɪp-/ *adjective* E20. **genotypically** /-ˈtɪp-/ *adverb* E20.

-genous /dʒɪnəs/ *suffix.*
[ORIGIN from -GEN + -OUS.]
Forming adjectives.
1 = -GENIC 1, as ***erogenous***.
2 = -GENIC 2, as ***endogenous***.

Genovese /ˈdʒɛnəviːz/ *noun & adjective.* Now *rare.* E17.
[ORIGIN Italian, from *Genova* GENOA.]
▸**A** *noun.* Pl. same, †-**s**. = GENOESE *noun.* E17.
▸**B** *adjective.* = GENOESE *adjective.* M17.

†**Genoway** *noun & adjective.* Also (earlier) **Jenoway**. LME–M17.
[ORIGIN Old French *Genoueis* from Italian *Genovese*: see GENOVESE.]
= GENOESE.

genre /ˈʒɒ̃rə, ˈʒɒnrə/ *noun.* E19.
[ORIGIN French = kind: see GENDER *noun*.]
Kind, type; *esp.* a style or category of painting, novel, film, etc., characterized by a particular form or purpose; *spec.* a style of painting depicting scenes of ordinary life.

T. MOORE Two very remarkable men . . but of entirely different genres. V. CRONIN Catherine particularly liked satirical comedies and encouraged two playwrights in this genre. *attrib.*: E. H. GOMBRICH Pictures in which the painters . . cultivated a certain . . kind of subject, particularly scenes from daily life . . became known as 'genre pictures'.

Genro /ˈgɛnrəʊ/ *noun.* Pl. same. L19.
[ORIGIN Japanese = principal elders, from *gen* origin + *rō* old.]
hist. (A member of) a body of personal counsellors to the Japanese throne, who dominated the government from 1889 to the 1930s.

gens /dʒɛnz/ *noun.* Pl. **gentes** /ˈdʒɛntiːz, -teɪz/. M19.
[ORIGIN Latin, from base of *gignere* beget.]
1 In ancient Rome: a group of families with a supposed common origin, a common name, and common religious rites. Also, a similar group of families in other cultures, e.g. in ancient Greece [translating Greek *genos*]. M19.
2 ANTHROPOLOGY. A kinship group composed of people related through their male ancestors. L19.

gens d'armes *noun phr. pl.* see GENDARME.

gens de la robe /ʒɑ̃ də la rɔb/ *noun phr.* Also ***gens de robe***. L17.
[ORIGIN French, lit. 'folk of the long robe'.]
Lawyers.

gent /dʒɛnt/ *noun.* M16.
[ORIGIN Abbreviation.]
1 A gentleman. Now *colloq.* M16.

S. LEWIS George's missus went into the gent's wear department . . to buy him some collars. I. MURDOCH 'He'll murder you.' 'Not he,' said Norman . . . 'He's a gent'.

2 In *pl.* (treated as *sing.* & *pl.*). A public convenience for males, = GENTLEMAN 4d. M20.

†**gent** *adjective.* ME.
[ORIGIN Old French from popular Latin contr. of classical Latin *genitus* born, hence well-born, noble. Cf. GENTLE *adjective*.]
1 Noble, high-born. Of a knight or warrior: brave and chivalrous. In later use, graceful in manners, polite. ME–L17.

SPENSER The prowest and most gent, That ever brandished . . steele on hye!

2 Of the body or limbs, of a woman, child, etc.: slender, shapely; freq. ***gent and small***, ***fair and gent***. Also, tasteful, refined. ME–E19.

R. GREENE Her middle was both small and gent. R. HOLME A Shooe of the Gentest fashion.

gentamicin /dʒɛntəˈmʌɪsɪn/ *noun.* M20.
[ORIGIN from *genta-* perh. aphet. from *magenta* + alt. of -MYCIN.]
A broad-spectrum antibiotic composed of sulphates of substances produced by the actinomycete *Micromonospora purpurea* and used esp. for severe systemic infections.

†**gentee** *adjective* var. of GENTY.

genteel /dʒɛnˈtiːl/ *adjective, noun, & adverb.* Orig. †-**tile**. L16.
[ORIGIN Re-adoption of French *gentil*, which had become GENTLE *adjective*.]
▸**A** *adjective.* **1** Fashionably elegant or sumptuous; stylish. *arch.* L16. ▸**b** Of a person: suggestive of a gentleman or lady in appearance; stylishly dressed. Now *slang.* E17.

V. KNOX The entertainment was sumptuous and genteel. A. TROLLOPE He was possessed of a genteel villa and ornamental garden. **b** GOLDSMITH Did I not work that waistcoat, to make you genteel?

2 Of behaviour, manners, etc.: appropriate to or characteristic of a person of good social position. E17.

W. TENNANT A genteel business, such as jewellery . . or perfumery. JOCELYN BROOKE He seemed, though not . . wealthy, to have more than a genteel sufficiency. J. FOWLES In those days a genteel accent was not the great social requisite it later became.

3 Of a person, family, etc.: of good social position. Cf. GENTLE *adjective* 1. *arch.* E17.

J. RAY All the Knights are of noble or gentile extraction.

4 Qualified by manners or style of life to form part of good society. Formerly, polished, well-bred. E17. ▸†**b** Liberal in money matters. Of a present etc.: handsome. E17–L18. ▸†**c** Of behaviour: courteous, obliging. M17–E19.

L. RITCHIE A man . . might be rich without being genteel, and poor without being vulgar. T. HARDY The accomplishment was one which she did not care to profess in genteel company.

5 Elegant or graceful in shape or appearance. Now *obsolete* exc. with mixture of sense 1. L17. ▸†**b** Of an abstract thing: refined, delicate. L17–M18.

D. HUME His countenance beautiful; his limbs genteel and slender.

6 In derog. use: cultivating the (supposed) manners or conventions of good society; marked by affected or excessive refinement, politeness, respectability, etc. L19.

R. L. STEVENSON The parlour—a very genteel room, with Bible prints . . and a selection of dried grasses. G. B. SHAW We are much too pious and genteel to allow such things to be mentioned. J. B. PRIESTLEY She turned to Miss Trant and . . became very stiff and genteel 'I'm sure it's very kind of you.'

▸**B** *noun.* A genteel person. L17.

T. D'URFEY Ye lofties, Genteels, who above us all sit.

▸**C** *adverb.* In a genteel manner. Now *slang.* L18.
■ **genteelish** *adjective* somewhat genteel M18. **genteelism** *noun* (a) genteel practice; *esp.* the substitution, for an everyday word or expression, of one considered socially more acceptable, e.g. ***perspiration*** for ***sweat***; also, a word or expression so substituted: E20. **genteelly** *adverb* E17. **genteelness** *noun* genteel quality; an instance of this: M17.

genteelity *noun* see GENTILITY.

gentes *noun* pl. of GENS.

gentian /ˈdʒɛnʃ(ə)n/ *noun & adjective.* LME.
[ORIGIN Latin *gentiana* (sc. *herba*), named, according to Pliny, after *Gentius*, king of Illyria: see -IAN.]
▸**A** *noun.* **1** Any of numerous plants of the genus *Gentiana* (family Gentianaceae), with four- or five-lobed corollas freq. of a brilliant deep blue, chiefly growing in damp alpine places; a flower or flowering stem of such a plant. Also, (a flower or stem of) any of a number of similar plants (esp. of the related genus *Gentianella*). LME.
autumn gentian, ***willow gentian***, etc.
2 A bitter tonic or (more fully ***gentian brandy***, ***gentian spirit***) liqueur made from gentian root (see below). M19.
– COMB.: ***gentian brandy***: see sense 2 above; **gentian root** the rhizome and root of the yellow-flowered *Gentiana lutea* of the Alps etc., used in pharmacy; ***gentian spirit***: see sense 2 above; **gentian violet** a dye used as an antiseptic, esp. in the treatment of burns.
▸**B** *adjective.* Having the blue colour of the gentian. E20.

gentianella /dʒɛnʃəˈnɛlə/ *noun.* M17.
[ORIGIN mod. Latin, dim. of *gentiana* GENTIAN.]
Any of several dwarf plants belonging to the genus *Gentiana* or related genera; *esp.* the blue-flowered *G. acaulis* of the Alps.
– NOTE: In botanical Latin *Gentianella* is now recognized as a genus distinct from *Gentiana*, containing various species formerly included in the latter.

gentil *noun, adjective* see GENTLE *noun, adjective & adverb*.

gentile /ˈdʒɛntʌɪl/ *noun.* LME.
[ORIGIN from the adjective.]
▸**I** (Usu. **G-**.) In senses from Vulgate.
1 Among Jews: a person not belonging to the Jewish people or faith. LME. ▸**b** *transf.* A person not belonging to one's Church; *esp.* a non-Mormon. M17.
2 A pagan, a heathen. Now *rare.* LME. ▸†**b** *spec.* A Hindu (opp. a Muslim). M16–E18.
▸**II** In senses from classical Latin.
3 A word denoting nationality. E17.
†**4** ROMAN LAW. A member of the same gens. Only in L19.
■ **gentiledom** *noun* the Gentile world; the state of being a Gentile in practice or belief: M17.

gentile /ˈdʒɛntʌɪl/ *adjective.* LME.
[ORIGIN Latin *gentilis*, from *gens*, *gent-* clan, race, from base of *gignere* beget.]
▸**I** (Freq. **G-**.) In senses from Vulgate.
1 Pagan, heathen. LME.

J. BRAND The basilicae of gentile Rome . . were converted into churches.

2 From a Jewish standpoint: non-Jewish. L17.

F. RAPHAEL Her friends were both Gentile and Jewish.

3 *transf.* (Pertaining to a person) that does not belong to one's Church; *esp.* non-Mormon. M19.

W. H. DIXON The Shakers . . smile at our Gentile ailments.

▸**II** In senses derived from classical Latin.
4 Pertaining to a nation or tribe. Now *rare.* E16.
5 GRAMMAR. Of a word: indicating nationality. E19.
6 Pertaining to a gens or clan. M19.

gentilesse /dʒɛntɪˈlɛs/ *noun.* Long *arch.* LME.
[ORIGIN Old French & mod. French *gentillesse*, from *gentil*: see GENTLE *adjective*, -ESS[2].]
Courtesy, good breeding; an instance of this.

gentilic /dʒɛnˈtɪlɪk/ *adjective.* E17.
[ORIGIN from Latin *gentilis* GENTILE *noun, adjective* + -IC.]
†**1** Pagan. Only in E17.
2 Belonging to a tribe or nation. L19.

gentilician *adjective* var. of GENTILITIAN.

gentilise *verb*[1], *verb*[2] vars. of GENTILIZE *verb*[1], *verb*[2].

gentilism /ˈdʒɛntɪlɪz(ə)m/ *noun.* L16.
[ORIGIN Old French or medieval Latin *gentilismus*, from ecclesiastical Latin *gentilis* GENTILE *noun, adjective*: see -ISM.]
(A) heathen belief or practice.

gentilitial /dʒɛntɪˈlɪʃ(ə)l/ *adjective*. E17.
[ORIGIN from Latin *gentilicius* + -AL¹. In sense 3, perh. from medieval Latin *gentilitia* GENTILESSE.]
1 Peculiar to a gens or clan. E17.
2 Peculiar to a nation or people; national. M17.
3 Gently born. E19.
■ **gentilitian**, **-lician** *adjective* = GENTILITIAL 1 M17.

gentilitious /dʒɛntɪˈlɪʃəs/ *adjective*. E17.
[ORIGIN formed as GENTILITIAL + -OUS.]
†1 Characteristic of a Gentile or non-Christian; pagan. Only in E17.
2 = GENTILITIAL *adjective* 1. M17.
3 = GENTILITIAL *adjective* 2. M17.

gentility /dʒɛnˈtɪlɪti/ *noun*. Also (*Scot.*) **genteelity** /-ˈtiːl-/. ME.
[ORIGIN In branch I from Old French & mod. French *gentilité*, from *gentil*: see GENTLE *adjective*, -ITY. In branch II, eccl. & medieval Latin *gentilitas* paganism has at least been contributory.]
▸ **I** In senses rel. to GENTLE *adjective*, GENTEEL *adjective*.
1 Gentle birth, honourable extraction. *arch.* ME. ▸**b** People of gentle birth; *the* gentry. *obsolete* exc. *Scot.* L16. ▸**c** The rank or heraldic status of a gentleman. M17.

J. COLLIER An ancient Gentility does not . . convey to us any Advantage . . of Body or Mind. **b** THOMAS SMITH The Nobility, the rest of the gentilitie, & the yeomanrie.

†2 Polite manners, courtesy. Only in L16.

SPENSER Such wilde woodes should far expell All civile usage and gentility.

3 Social superiority as shown by manners, behaviour, appearances, etc.; (an instance of) manners, behaviour, etc., displaying such superiority. Now chiefly *derog.*, genteel behaviour: see GENTEEL *adjective* 6. M17.

J. RUSKIN Once get the wealthy classes to imagine that the possession of pictures . . adds to their gentility. GEO. ELIOT Let him forsake a decent craft that he may pursue the gentilities of a profession. J. GROSS No more staid men with sound views, no more suffocating gentility.

†4 Elegance, refinement. M–L18.
▸ **II** In senses rel. to GENTILE *adjective*.
†5 Heathen belief or practice; paganism. Also, the pagan world. E16–M17.
6 Relationship between members of a gens. Formerly, the gens itself. L16.

gentilize /ˈdʒɛntɪlʌɪz/ *verb*¹ *trans. arch.* Also **-ise**. L16.
[ORIGIN from French *gentil* GENTLE *adjective* + -IZE.]
Turn into a person of breeding; make genteel.

gentilize /ˈdʒɛntɪlʌɪz, -tʌɪl-/ *verb*². Also **-ise**. L16.
[ORIGIN from GENTILE *noun* or *adjective* + -IZE.]
1 *verb intrans.* Of a Jew: live like a Gentile. L16.
2 *verb trans.* Make Gentile, i.e. non-Jewish or pagan. E19.

gentle /ˈdʒɛnt(ə)l/ *noun*. Also (*obsolete* exc. as in sense 3) **gentil**. LME.
[ORIGIN from the adjective.]
1 A person of gentle birth or good social position. Usu. in *pl.* (formerly sometimes in polite address). Now mostly *arch.* LME.
2 A maggot, the larva of the flesh fly or bluebottle, used by anglers. L16.
3 = ***falcon-gentle*** s.v. GENTLE *adjective* 1b. L18.

gentle /ˈdʒɛnt(ə)l/ *adjective & adverb*. Also (*obsolete* exc. FALCONRY) **gentil**. ME.
[ORIGIN Old French & mod. French *gentil* high-born (in mod. French = pleasant, agreeable) from Latin *gentilis* of the same clan, (Proto-Romance) belonging to a good family: see also GENTEEL, GENTILE *adjective*, JAUNTY *adjective*.]
▸ **A** *adjective*. **1** Of a person: well (orig. nobly) born; *spec.* entitled to bear a coat of arms. Formerly freq. as a vague epithet of commendation. *obsolete* exc. in arch. phr. ***gentle and simple***, and in comb. GENTLEFOLK, GENTLEMAN, etc. ME. ▸**b** Of an animal: of excellent breed or spirit. Now only in ***falcon-gentle***, ***gentle falcon***, (the female of) the peregrine falcon, and ***TIERCEL-gentle***. ME. ▸†**c** Of a thing: noble, excellent. ME.

J. FLETCHER I am as gentle as your self, as free born. **b** J. SKELTON A ientyll hownde shulde neuer play the kur. **c** J. MANDEVILLE Wyn . . that is fulle myghty and gentylle in drynkynge.

2 Of birth, family, etc.: distinguished, honourable. ME. ▸**b** Of an activity or pursuit: suitable to a person of good social position; honourable, gentlemanly. L15.

SIR W. SCOTT His birth being admitted as gentle, gave him access to the best society. **b** R. ADAMS Peasant girls, ignorant of gentle ways.

3 Of a person: having the character appropriate to one of gentle birth; noble, courteous, chivalrous. *arch.* ME. ▸**b** In complimentary address. Now only as a playful archaism, in ***gentle reader***. LME. ▸†**c** Of language, an action, etc.: courteous, polite. LME–M17.

SIR T. MORE Sithe I am so gentle to graunt you so many things, I trust ye wyl grant me this one. **b** SHAKES. *Haml.* Thanks, Rosencrantz and gentle Guildenstern. A. THWAITE Such questions exercise the gentle reader Snug in his study. **c** B. YOUNG She gave him . . thankes for the gentle entertainment she had in his Castle.

†4 Graceful, slender, handsome. ME–E16.

5 Of a plant, fruit, etc.: having mild properties; cultivated. *arch.* LME. ▸**b** Of an animal: quiet, tractable. M16.

B. JOWETT Tending the gentle shoots, and preventing the wild ones from growing. **b** W. FAULKNER To buy a good gentle horse.

†6 Not harsh to the touch; soft, pliant. M16–M18.
7 Moderate in action, effect, or degree; not violent, severe, or boisterous. M16. ▸**b** Of a sound: low, soft. E17. ▸**c** Of a slope etc.: gradual, not abrupt. L17.

A. REID Liquors . . evaporated by a gentle heat. E. O'NEILL She gives him a gentle shake. J. STEINBECK The brown algae waved in the gentle currents. **b** J. GRAHAME The murmuring So gentle of the brook. **c** P. PORTER I will not roll down this gentle bank.

8 Of a person, action, etc.: mild or benign in disposition; free from sternness or aggression. (Foll. by *to*, *with*.) M16.

H. JAMES A gentle pedagogue, prompting her with small caresses. H. ROBBINS Life had not been gentle with either of them. They had to fight for everything they got. *New York Times* Gentle persuasion is not going to make the Argentine Government give up what it has seized by force.

9 Sacred to or haunted by fairies. See also ***gentle people*** below. *dial.* (chiefly *Irish*). E19.
– SPECIAL COLLOCATIONS: ***falcon-gentle***: see sense 1b above. **gentle art** *the* sport of angling. **gentle craft** = ***gentle art*** above; formerly, *the* trade of shoemaking. ***gentle falcon***: see sense 1b above. **gentle people** (*Irish*) *the* fairies. **gentle-people** gentlefolk. NAVEW ***gentle***. TIERCEL-***gentle***. ***the gentler sex***, ***the gentle sex***: see SEX *noun*.
▸ **B** *adverb*. In a gentle manner. E17.

DYLAN THOMAS Do not go gentle into that good night.

gentle /ˈdʒɛnt(ə)l/ *verb*. LME.
[ORIGIN from the adjective.]
†1 *verb trans.* Raise to a high social position; ennoble. LME–M17.

SHAKES. *Hen. V* Be he ne'er so vile, This day shall gentle his condition.

2 *verb trans.* Make mild or gentle in character, manner, etc. M17. ▸**b** *spec.* Make (an animal) docile or tractable. Also, stroke or massage gently. M18. ▸**c** Soothe the feelings of, pacify (a person). L18.

R. BROUGHTON A smile . . sweetening and gentling the . . sullenness of her face. *absol.*: E. HYAMS The gentling influence of the Atlantic allows . . trees to grow farther north. **b** W. HOLTBY He . . knelt by the kicking animal, . . gentling her head. E. FERBER A nice gentled riding pony. *fig.*: R. BRADBURY When you lay . . in your . . bed and were gentled to sleep by the sound. **c** J. LE CARRÉ He didn't get angry . . . He gentled him and smiled.

3 *verb intrans.* Become mild or gentle. E20.

V. BUCHANAN-GOULD The African world gentled to soft femineity. P. BARKER Gradually . . the red gentles through purple and gold to rose.

gentlefolk /ˈdʒɛnt(ə)lfəʊk/ *noun pl.* Earlier **-folks** /-fəʊks/. L16.
[ORIGIN from GENTLE *adjective* + FOLK.]
People of gentle birth or good social position.

gentlehood /ˈdʒɛnt(ə)lhʊd/ *noun*. M19.
[ORIGIN from GENTLE *adjective* + -HOOD.]
Position or character attaching to gentle birth.

gentleman /ˈdʒɛnt(ə)lmən/ *noun*. Pl. **-men**. ME.
[ORIGIN from GENTLE *adjective* + MAN *noun*, after Old French *gentilz homme* (mod. *gentilhomme*).]
1 A man of gentle (orig. noble) birth. In later use, a man of good birth (according to heraldic interpretations, one entitled to bear arms) who is not a nobleman; (formerly sometimes placed as a title after a man's name). Now chiefly *hist.* ME.

A. RADCLIFFE Pierre de la Motte was a gentleman descended from an ancient house of France.

2 A man who demonstrates his gentle birth by appropriate behaviour or moral qualities, e.g. chivalrous conduct, consideration for others, sense of honour, etc.; *gen.* a man (of whatever rank) who displays such qualities. ME.

P. G. WODEHOUSE Clarence is a gentleman He is incapable of insulting a woman. E. O'NEILL I give you my word as an officer and a gentleman.

3 A man of gentle birth attached to the household of a monarch or other person of high rank. Freq. in titles, as ***Gentleman of the Bedchamber***, ***Gentleman of the Chapel Royal***, etc. See also ***gentleman-at-arms***, ***gentleman pensioner*** below. LME. ▸**b** A man (orig. of gentle birth) acting as personal attendant to a man of rank or quality. See also ***gentleman's gentleman*** below. LME.

C. V. WEDGWOOD The King was still accompanied by . . Thomas Herbert, the gentleman in attendance, and three or four lower servants. **b** SMOLLETT I took the name from his gentleman, Mr. O'Frizzle.

4 Used as a courteous designation for a member of certain societies and professions, a fellow member of the House of Commons or the House of Representatives, etc.; esp. ***the gentleman from*** (a specified constituency). M16. ▸**b** In *pl.*, as a polite form of address to a group (esp. an audience) of men of whatever rank (corresp. to 'sir' in *sing.*). Formerly also *sing.*, as a polite form of address to one man. L16. ▸**c** As a genteelism: a man, of whatever rank. E19. ▸**d** ***the gentlemen('s)*** (treated as *sing.*), a public convenience for males. E20.

W. S. CHURCHILL The hon. Gentleman opposite . . tries to suggest it is all some fake propaganda. **c** A. LOOS Gentlemen always seem to remember blondes. J. ORTON Miss Barclay, a gentleman wishes to see you.

5 A man of superior social standing; a man with the refinement of manners, breeding, etc., that qualify him to mix in the best society. L16. ▸**b** As a status: a man whose wealth frees him from the need to follow a trade or profession. Also (*dial.* & *joc.*), a man without employment. L18. ▸**c** CRICKET (now *hist.*). A non-professional player (opp. PLAYER 2c). E19.

R. L. STEVENSON In the steerage there are males and females; in the second cabin ladies and gentlemen. J. WAIN He was dressed in a quiet grey suit and looked . . every inch a gentleman. **c** *fig.*: H. GREENE Broadcasting is no longer a profession for gentlemen: the players have taken over.

6 *euphem.* (**a**) = ***gentleman of the road*** below; (**b**) a smuggler. L18.
– PHRASES ETC.: COUNTRY ***gentleman***. ***fine gentleman***: see FINE *adjective*. **gentleman-at-arms** any of the forty gentlemen acting as bodyguard to the British monarch on ceremonial occasions. **gentleman of fortune** an adventurer. **gentleman of the road** (**a**) a highwayman; (**b**) a commercial traveller; (**c**) a Gypsy. ***gentleman of virtu***: see VIRTU *noun* 1. **gentleman's agreement** (orig. *US*): binding in honour, but not enforceable at law. **gentleman's gentleman** a valet. **Gentleman's Relish** (proprietary name for) a highly seasoned anchovy paste. **gentlemen of the press** journalists. **gentlemen's agreement** = ***gentleman's agreement*** above. ***ladies and gentlemen***: see LADY *noun & adjective*. **Old Gentleman** *the* Devil. ***walking gentleman***: see WALKING *ppl adjective*.
– ATTRIB. & COMB.: Esp. in the sense 'practising a specified occupation as an amateur rather than for profit or pay', as ***gentleman adventurer***, ***gentleman farmer***, etc. Special combs., as **gentleman-commoner** *hist.* (at Oxford and Cambridge) a member of a class of undergraduates enjoying special privileges; **gentleman friend** *arch. colloq.* a boyfriend, a beau; †**gentleman-pensioner** = ***gentleman-at-arms*** above; **gentleman-usher** a gentleman acting as usher to a person of superior rank.
■ **gentlemanhood** *noun* the position or character of a gentleman M18. **gentlemanlike** *adjective & adverb* (**a**) *adjective* = GENTLEMANLY (a); †(**b**) *adverb* in the manner of a gentleman: M16. **gentlemanliness** *noun* gentlemanly quality L16. **gentlemanly** *adjective & adverb* (**a**) *adjective* natural or appropriate to a gentleman; resembling a gentleman in appearance or conduct; (**b**) *adverb* (now *rare*) as befits a gentleman: LME.

gentleness /ˈdʒɛnt(ə)lnɪs/ *noun*. ME.
[ORIGIN from GENTLE *adjective* + -NESS.]
†1 Gentle or noble birth. ME–L17.
†2 Courteous or chivalrous nature. Only in LME.
3 Mildness of temper; freedom from sternness or aggression. M16.
4 Freedom from intensity, suddenness, steepness, etc.; moderateness. E17.

gentlewoman /ˈdʒɛnt(ə)lwʊmən/ *noun*. Pl. **-women** /-wɪmɪn/. ME.
[ORIGIN from GENTLE *adjective* + WOMAN *noun*.]
1 A woman of good birth or breeding; a lady. Now *arch.* or *joc.* ME.
2 A woman (orig. of gentle birth) acting as attendant to a lady of rank. *obsolete* exc. *hist.* LME.
■ **gentlewomanhood** *noun* the character appropriate to a gentlewoman M19. **gentlewomanlike** *adjective* having the manners or appearance of a gentlewoman; appropriate to a gentlewoman: L16. **gentlewomanliness** *noun* gentlewomanly quality E19. **gentlewomanly** *adjective* = GENTLEWOMANLIKE E19.

gently /ˈdʒɛntli/ *adverb*. ME.
[ORIGIN from GENTLE *adjective* + -LY².]
1 With gentleness of birth; only in ***gently born***. Formerly, as befits a person of gentle birth; graciously, generously, etc. ME.
2 With moderate or subdued action; slowly, quietly, by easy stages. M16.

J. BUCHAN A valley . . tilted up gently towards the west. J. STEINBECK Tom laid his hammer gently on the floor.

3 Without sternness or severity; mildly, benignly. M16.

M. W. MONTAGU I can bear being told that I am in the wrong, but tell me gently.

Gentoo /dʒɛnˈtuː/ *noun*¹ & *adjective*. *Indian* (*obsolete* exc. *hist.*). M17.
[ORIGIN Portuguese *gentio* GENTILE *noun*, *adjective*.]
▸ **A** *noun*. **1** A non-Muslim inhabitant of Hindustan; a Hindu. Also *spec.*, a Telugu-speaking Hindu of southern India. M17.
2 The language spoken by Gentoos. L17.
▸ **B** *attrib.* or as *adjective*. Of or pertaining to the Gentoos. L17.

gentoo /dʒɛnˈtuː/ *noun*². M19.
[ORIGIN Perh. a use of GENTOO *noun*¹ & *adjective*.]
A penguin, *Pygoscelis papua*, of the Falklands and other Antarctic islands. Also ***gentoo penguin***.

G

gentrice /ˈdʒɛntrɪs/ *noun*. *obsolete* exc. *Scot*. ME.
[ORIGIN Old French *genterise* var. of *gentelise*, from *gentil* GENTLE *adjective* + *-ise* -ICE[1].]
1 Superiority of birth or rank. ME.
2 Good breeding. Formerly, graciousness, magnanimity, etc. ME.
3 People of good birth or rank. LME.

gentrify /ˈdʒɛntrɪfʌɪ/ *verb trans*. L20.
[ORIGIN from GENTRY + -FY.]
Make genteel in character; *esp*. convert (a working-class or inner-city district) into an area of middle-class residence.

> M. BLONSKY We can . . feel gentrified as we glance through *Gourmet* magazine. C. BATEMAN Marcus Savant lived in a gentrified apartment block off Morningside in Harlem.

■ **gentrifiˈcation** *noun* L20.

gentry /ˈdʒɛntri/ *noun*. LME.
[ORIGIN Old French *genterie*.]
1 Superiority of birth or rank; gentility. Formerly also occas. in neutral sense, quality of birth or rank. *obsolete* exc. *Scot*. LME.

> JONSON We haue raised Seianus from obscure, and almost vnknowne Gentry. ALAN ROSS 'Tis madness to presume too much upon our birth and Gentry.

2 Conduct characteristic of a person of gentle birth; politeness of manners, good breeding. Formerly also, graciousness, magnanimity, etc. *obsolete* exc. *Scot*. LME.
3 People of gentle birth or good breeding; *the* class composed of such people, *spec*. that below the nobility. L16.

> G. B. SHAW The horrible condition of the working classes that underlies . . the prestige of the landed gentry and peerage. H. ARENDT The English gentry . . had assimilated the higher ranks of the bourgeoisie.

4 People of a specified kind. *joc*. or *derog*. E18.

> THACKERAY The light-fingered gentry pick pockets furiously. *transf*.: GEO. ELIOT The broken discourse of poultry and other lazy gentry in the afternoon sunshine.

5 *The* fairies. *Irish*. L19.

genty /ˈdʒɛnti/ *adjective*. Also †**gentee**. M17.
[ORIGIN Var. of GENTEEL, with attempt to render the sound of French *gentil* more closely: see also JAUNTY *adjective*.]
1 Well-bred, genteel, courteous. Formerly, fashionably dressed. *obsolete* exc. *Scot*. M17.
2 Dainty, graceful. *Scot*. E18.
■ **gentiness** *noun* L17.

genu /ˈdʒɛnjuː/ *noun*. M19.
[ORIGIN Latin.]
1 The knee. Chiefly MEDICINE, in mod. Latin phrs. (see below). Also, a kneelike joint in invertebrates. M19.
genu valgum [Latin VALGUS] knock-knee. **genu varum** [Latin VARUS *noun*[2]] bow legs.
2 A kneelike angle or bend. L19.
■ **genual** *adjective* pertaining to the knee (or kneelike joint) M19.

genuant /ˈdʒɛnjʊənt/ *adjective*. L17.
[ORIGIN from Latin *genu* knee + -ANT[1].]
HERALDRY. Kneeling.

genuflect /ˈdʒɛnjʊflɛkt/ *verb*. M17.
[ORIGIN ecclesiastical Latin *genuflectere*, from *genu* knee + *flectere* to bend.]
†**1** *verb trans*. Bend (the knee). Only in M17.
2 *verb intrans*. Chiefly in Catholic or Anglo-Catholic ritual: lower one knee (or both knees simultaneously) momentarily to the ground, as an act of worship. (Foll. by *before*, *to*.) M19. ▸**b** *fig*. Display servile obedience or deference *to*. L19.

> **b** JANET MORGAN The lower servants genuflected to those in higher authority.

■ **genuflector** *noun* a person who genuflects M19. **genuflectory** *adjective* relating to genuflection M19.

genuflection /dʒɛnjʊˈflɛkʃ(ə)n/ *noun*. Also **-flexion**. LME.
[ORIGIN ecclesiastical Latin *genuflexio(n-)*, from *genuflex-* pa. ppl stem of *genuflectere*: see GENUFLECT, -ION.]
An act of genuflecting.

genuine /ˈdʒɛnjʊɪn/ *adjective*. L16.
[ORIGIN Latin *genuinus*, perh. from *genu* knee, with ref. to the Roman custom of a father acknowledging paternity of a newly born child by placing him or her on his knee.]
†**1** Natural or proper to a person or thing. L16–E18.

> WOODES ROGERS I . . keep to the Language of the Sea, which is more genuine, and natural for a mariner.

2 Having the character claimed for it; real, true, not counterfeit. M17. ▸**b** Esp. of a literary or artistic work: really originating from its reputed author; authentic. M17. ▸**c** Properly so called. L17.

> L. P. HARTLEY She didn't know if the delay was genuine, for sometimes her employer deliberately kept his clients waiting. LD BRAIN A psychological illness . . may be the result of very genuine worries. **b** R. W. EMERSON The . . question concerning his reputed works—what are genuine, what spurious. **c** JAS. HARRIS The genuine pronoun always stands by itself.

genuine article: see ARTICLE *noun* 10.
3 Belonging to the original stock; pure-bred. E18.

> E. A. FREEMAN The founder of a great name, whose genuine bearers soon passed away.

4 Of a person: free from affectation or hypocrisy. M19.

> J. B. HILTON She used to . . tell her how grateful she was. Not smarmy, like; genuine.

5 Of a horse or greyhound: that always does its best in races etc. L20.
■ **genuinely** *adverb* M17. **genuineness** *noun* M17.

genus /ˈdʒɛnəs, ˈdʒiːnəs/ *noun*. Pl. **genera** /ˈdʒɛn(ə)rə/, **genuses**. M16.
[ORIGIN Latin = birth, family, nation.]
1 LOGIC. A class of things containing a number of subordinate classes (called species) with certain common attributes; the first of the five predicables (PREDICABLE *noun*). M16.

> K. DIGBY Rarity and Density . . can not change the common nature of Quantity, that is, their Genus.

middle genus: see MIDDLE *adjective*.
2 BIOLOGY. A basic taxonomic grouping ranking below family and subfamily, which contains a number of related and morphologically similar species (or sometimes a single species). Formerly also used in the classification of minerals, chemical substances, etc. E17. ▸**b** *gen*. A category, a kind. M17.

> T. THOMSON The genus sulphates contains several salts of . . importance. P. THEROUX There were spurges, plants of the genus euphorbia. **b** N. MITFORD I had never seen a slut before but recognized the genus . . as soon as I set eyes on this one.

the genus Homo: see HOMO *noun*[1] 2. ***type genus***: see TYPE *noun* & *adjective*.
3 In ancient Greek music, each of the three kinds of tetrachord. M18.

-geny /dʒəni/ *suffix*.
[ORIGIN Corresp. to French *-génie*, both repr. Greek *-geneia*, forming nouns from adjectives in *-genēs*.]
Forming nouns denoting '(mode of) generation', as in ***biogeny***, ***ontogeny***; = -GENESIS (which has tended to supersede it).

geo /gjəʊ, ˈdʒiːəʊ/ *noun*. Orig. *Orkney & Shetland*. Also **gio**. Pl. **-os**. E17.
[ORIGIN Old Norse *gjá*.]
A rocky gully or inlet in the coast (in Orkney and Shetland); PHYSICAL GEOGRAPHY a long, narrow steep-sided cleft formed by erosion in coastal cliffs.

geo- /ˈdʒiːəʊ/ *combining form* repr. Greek *geō-* from *gē* earth: see -O-.
■ **geocacher** *noun* a person who participates in geocaching E21. **geocaching** *noun* a form of treasure hunt in which an item is hidden somewhere in the world and its coordinates posted on the Internet, so that GPS users can locate it E21. **geocode** *noun & verb* (*US*) (***a***) *noun* the characterization of an area based on statistics such as the average age or income of its inhabitants, used esp. for marketing purposes; (***b***) *verb trans*. characterize (an area) in this way: M20. **geocoˈrona** *noun* an envelope of gas (chiefly ionized hydrogen) forming the outermost layer of the earth's atmosphere and extending to the limit of the magnetosphere (also called ***protonosphere***) M20. **geocoˈronal** *adjective* of or pertaining to the geocorona M20. **geodyˈnamic**, **geodyˈnamical** *adjectives* of, pertaining to, or designating the (latent) forces of the earth L19. **geodyˈnamics** *noun* the branch of science that deals with geodynamic forces L19. **geoˈmembrane** *noun* a non-woven geotextile L20. **geophone** *noun* an instrument for detecting vibrations in the ground E20. **geophyte** *noun* (BOTANY) a perennial plant which propagates by means of underground buds L19. **geoplaˈnarian** *noun* [Latin *planus* flat] a person who believes the earth to be flat M20. **geopoˈtential** *noun* the work that must be done against gravity to raise unit mass to a given point from sea level E20. **geoˈspatial** *adjective* of, relating to, or designating data that is associated with a geographical location L20. **geosphere** *noun* (***a***) any of the more or less spherical concentric regions of the earth and its atmosphere; (***b***) the lithosphere: L19. **geoˈstrategy** *noun* strategy as applied to the problems of geopolitics; global strategy: M20. **geoˈtechnic** *adjective* of or pertaining to geotechnics E20. **geoˈtechnical** *adjective* geotechnic M20. **geoˈtechnics** *noun* the art of modifying and adapting the physical nature of the earth to the needs of man E20. **geotechˈnology** *noun* the application of technology to the utilization of the natural resources of the earth M20. **geotecˈtonic** *adjective* = TECTONIC *adjective* 2 L19. **geoˈtextile** *noun* an artificial material in the form of a woven or continuous sheet, used in combination with soil or rock in civil engineering, landscaping, etc. L20. **geotherˈmometer** *noun* (***a***) an instrument for measuring temperature within the earth; (***b***) a petrological phenomenon or property from which temperatures within the earth's crust can be inferred: M19.

Geo. *abbreviation*.
George.

geobotany /dʒiːəʊˈbɒtəni/ *noun*. E20.
[ORIGIN from GEO- + BOTANY.]
= PHYTOGEOGRAPHY.
■ **geoboˈtanic** *adjective* E20. **geoboˈtanical** *adjective* L19. **geoˈbotanist** *noun* E20.

geocentric /dʒiːə(ʊ)ˈsɛntrɪk/ *noun & adjective*. M17.
[ORIGIN from GEO- + -CENTRIC.]
▸**A** *noun*. Chiefly *hist*. A person who believes that the earth is the centre of the universe. M17.
▸**B** *adjective*. **1** Considered as viewed from the earth's centre; referred to the earth as centre. L17.
geocentric latitude, **geocentric longitude**: at which a planet etc. would appear if observed from the position of the earth's centre.
2 Having or representing the earth as the centre. Freq. opp. ***heliocentric***. L17.

> *fig*.: T. HARDY The geocentric view . . a zenithal paradise, a nadiral hell.

■ **geocentrically** *adverb* E18. **geocenˈtricity** *noun* the state of having the earth as centre or of being determined with reference to the centre of the earth M20. **geocentrism** *noun* (*hist*.) the theory or belief that the earth is the centre of the universe L19.

geochemistry /dʒiːəʊˈkɛmɪstri/ *noun*. E20.
[ORIGIN from GEO- + CHEMISTRY.]
The chemistry of the earth; the science of the chemical composition of the earth.
■ **geochemical** *adjective* L19. **geochemically** *adverb* M20. **geochemist** *noun* E20.

geochronology /dʒiːəʊkrəˈnɒlədʒi/ *noun*. L19.
[ORIGIN from GEO- + CHRONOLOGY.]
The chronology of the earth; the measurement of geological time and the ordering of geological events.
■ **geochronoˈlogical** *adjective* M20. **geochronoˈlogically** *adverb* M20. **geochroˈnologist** *noun* M20.

geochronometry /dʒiːəʊkrəˈnɒmɪtri/ *noun*. E20.
[ORIGIN from GEO- + CHRONOMETRY.]
1 Geometry extended to include time as the fourth dimension; a system of this. E20.
2 The measurement of geological time; absolute geochronology. M20.
■ **geochronoˈmetric** *adjective* M20.

geocronite /dʒɪˈɒkrənʌɪt, dʒiːəʊˈkrəʊnʌɪt/ *noun*. M19.
[ORIGIN from GEO- + Greek *Kronos* Saturn (in alchemy assoc. with lead) + -ITE[1].]
MINERALOGY. A grey to grey-blue orthorhombic sulphide of lead, antimony, and arsenic, usu. found as massive, granular, or earthy deposits.

geode /ˈdʒiːəʊd/ *noun*. L17.
[ORIGIN Latin *geodes* from Greek *geōdēs* earthy, from *gē* earth: see -ODE[1].]
1 A rock formation or a stone containing a cavity lined with crystals or other mineral matter. L17.

> O. W. HOLMES An aphorism . . has been forming itself in one of the blank interior spaces of my intelligence, like a crystal in the cavity of a geode.

2 The cavity itself; the crystals within it. M19.
■ **geˈodic** *adjective* of, pertaining to, or resembling a geode M19.

geodesic /dʒiːə(ʊ)ˈdɛsɪk, -ˈdiːsɪk/ *adjective & noun*. E19.
[ORIGIN from GEODESY + -IC.]
▸**A** *adjective*. Of or pertaining to geodesy; relating to the geometry of the earth's surface or, more generally, to curved surfaces; *spec*. designating, or built according to, constructional principles involving the use of spheres and geodesic lines (see below). Cf. GEODETIC. E19.
geodesic curve a geodesic line on a curved surface. **geodesic line** the shortest possible line on a surface between two points on that surface.
▸**B** *ellipt*. as *noun*. A geodesic curve or line; a geodesic structure. L19.
■ **geodesical** *adjective* = GEODESIC *adjective* E19.

geodesy /dʒɪˈɒdɪsi/ *noun*. L16.
[ORIGIN mod. Latin *geodaesia* from Greek *geōdaisia*, from *daiein* divide: see GEO-, -Y[3].]
Orig., land surveying. Now, the branch of mathematics that deals with the shape and area of the earth or of large parts of it.
■ **geodesist** *noun* M19.

geodetic /dʒiːə(ʊ)ˈdɛtɪk/ *noun & adjective*. L17.
[ORIGIN from Greek *geōdaitēs* land surveyor, from *daiein* divide: see GEODESY, -IC.]
▸**A** *noun*. †**1** In *pl*. A cardinal number regarded as expressing an attribute, or as counting, rather than as an abstract quantity. Only in L17.
2 A geodesic line. L19.
▸**B** *adjective*. = GEODESIC. M19.

geodetical /dʒiːə(ʊ)ˈdɛtɪk(ə)l/ *adjective*. E17.
[ORIGIN formed as GEODETIC + -AL[1].]
1 Of or pertaining to geodesy; geodesic. E17.
†**2** MATH. ***geodetical number***, = GEODETIC *noun* 1. L17–E18.
■ **geodetically** *adverb* L17.

geogeny /dʒɪˈɒdʒəni/ *noun*. Now *rare*. M19.
[ORIGIN from GEO- + -GENY.]
= GEOGONY.
■ **geoˈgenic** *adjective* M19.

geognost /ˈdʒiːəgnɒst/ *noun*. Now chiefly *hist*. E19.
[ORIGIN French *géognoste*, from Greek *gēo-* GEO- + *gnōtēs* a person who knows.]
An expert in or student of geognosy.
■ **geogˈnostic**, **geogˈnostical** *adjectives* of or pertaining to geognosy L18. **geogˈnostically** *adverb* M19.

geognosy /dʒɪˈɒgnəsi/ *noun*. Now chiefly *hist*. L18.
[ORIGIN French *géognosie*, from Greek *gēo-* GEO- + *gnōsis* knowledge.]
1 The branch of science that deals with the structure and composition of the earth; *loosely* geology. L18.

2 The mineralogy of particular rocks (esp. in a region), together with the grouping, distribution and relations of those rocks. **E19.**

geogony /dʒɪˈɒɡəni/ *noun.* **E19.**
[ORIGIN from GEO- + -GONY.]
The science or a theory of the formation of the earth.
■ **geoˈgonic** *adjective* **L19.**

geographer /dʒɪˈɒɡrəfə/ *noun.* **M16.**
[ORIGIN from late Latin *geographus* (from Greek *geōgraphos*: see GEO-, -GRAPH) + -ER[1]: see -GRAPHER.]
An expert in or student of geography.

geographic /dʒɪəˈɡrafɪk/ *noun & adjective.* **E17.**
[ORIGIN French *géographique* or late Latin *geographicus*, from Greek *geōgraphikos*, from *geōgraphos*: see GEOGRAPHER, -IC.]
▸ **A** *noun.* †**1** A treatise on geography. Only in **E17.**
2 In *pl.* = GEOGRAPHY 1. *rare.* **M19.**
▸ **B** *adjective.* = GEOGRAPHICAL. **M17.**

geographical /dʒɪəˈɡrafɪk(ə)l/ *adjective.* **M16.**
[ORIGIN formed as GEOGRAPHIC: see -ICAL.]
Of, pertaining to, or of the nature of, geography.
geographical latitude the angle made with the plane of the equator by a perpendicular to the earth's surface at any point. **geographical mile** (**a**) a unit of length equal to one minute of longitude on the equator, or of latitude; = approx. 1850 metres; (**b**) the nautical mile of 1852 m. ***geographical pole***: see POLE *noun*[2] 2.
■ **geographically** *adverb* **E17.**

geography /dʒɪˈɒɡrəfi/ *noun.* **L15.**
[ORIGIN Latin *geographia* (partly through French) from Greek *geōgraphia*: see GEO-, -GRAPHY.]
1 The branch of knowledge that deals with the earth's surface, its form and physical features, natural and political divisions, climate, products, population, etc. **L15.**
DIALECT ***geography***. **economic geography** the branch of geography that deals with the geographical distribution of economic resources. **human geography** the branch of geography that deals with the activities of humankind as they affect or are influenced by the earth's surface. *LINGUISTIC* ***geography***. **mathematical geography**: studied using mathematical methods. ***physical geography***: see PHYSICAL *adjective*. ***plant geography***: see PLANT *noun*. ***social geography***: see SOCIAL *adjective*.
2 A treatise on this. **M16.**
3 The subject matter of geography; (knowledge of) the features or arrangement of a region or (*colloq.*) a place, building, etc. **M18.**

> *transf.*: OED The geography of Mars. R. W. EMERSON We have seen the railroad and the telegraph subdue our enormous geography.

the geography (of the house) *euphem.* the whereabouts of the lavatory.
4 Chiefly *BUSINESS*. A geographical area, a region. Usu. in *pl.* **L20.**

geoid /ˈdʒiːɔɪd/ *noun.* **L19.**
[ORIGIN Greek *geoeidēs* adjective, earthlike, from GEO-: see -OID.]
The earth's figure; a hypothetical solid figure the surface of which corresponds to mean sea level (and its imagined extension under land) and is perpendicular to the direction of gravity at all points.
■ **geˈoidal** *adjective* **L19.**

geologic /dʒɪəˈlɒdʒɪk/ *adjective.* Now chiefly *US.* **L18.**
[ORIGIN from GEOLOGY + -IC.]
= GEOLOGICAL.

geological /dʒɪəˈlɒdʒɪk(ə)l/ *adjective.* **L18.**
[ORIGIN formed as GEOLOGIC + -AL[1].]
Of, pertaining to, or derived from geology.
geological map: showing the rock formations exposed at or underlying the surface of a region. **geological survey** detailed investigation of the geological features and resources of a region; an official body responsible for conducting such surveys. **geological time** the time which has elapsed since the earth's formation (up to the beginning of the historical period); time measured with reference to geological events.
■ **geologically** *adverb* **E19.**

geologize /dʒɪˈɒlədʒʌɪz/ *verb.* Also **-ise**. **E19.**
[ORIGIN from GEOLOGY + -IZE.]
1 *verb trans.* Examine (a place) geologically. **E19.**
2 *verb intrans.* Carry out geological investigations. **M19.**

geology /dʒɪˈɒlədʒi/ *noun.* **M18.**
[ORIGIN mod. Latin *geologia*, formed as GEO- + -LOGY.]
†**1** The branch of science that deals with the earth in general. Only in **M18.**
2 The branch of science that deals with the physical structure and substance of the earth (or *transf.* of another planet etc.), the processes which act on these, and the earth's development since its formation. **L18.**
3 The geological features of a particular region. **E19.**
■ **geologer** *noun* (*rare*) = GEOLOGIST **E19.** †**geoˈlogian** *noun* = GEOLOGIST **M–L19.** **geologist** *noun* an expert in or student of geology **L18.**

geomagnetism /dʒiːə(ʊ)ˈmaɡnɪtɪz(ə)m/ *noun.* **M20.**
[ORIGIN from GEO- + MAGNETISM.]
The branch of science that deals with the magnetic properties of the earth and related phenomena; terrestrial magnetism.
■ **geomagˈnetic** *adjective* of or pertaining to geomagnetism **E20.** **geomagˈnetically** *adverb* **M20.** **geomagneˈtician** *noun* an expert in or student of geomagnetism **M20.** **geomagnetist** *noun* = GEOMAGNETICIAN **E20.**

geomancy /ˈdʒiːəmansi/ *noun.* **LME.**
[ORIGIN medieval Latin *geomantia*, formed as GEO- + -MANCY.]
(The art of) divination from the configuration of a handful of thrown earth or a number of random dots. Also, the art of siting cities, buildings, tombs, etc., auspiciously.
■ **geomancer** *noun* a person who practises geomancy **LME.**

geomantic /dʒiːə(ʊ)ˈmantɪk/ *adjective & noun.* **L16.**
[ORIGIN formed as GEOMANCY + -IC: as noun from medieval Latin *geomanticus*.]
▸ **A** *adjective.* Of or pertaining to geomancy. **L16.**
▸ †**B** *noun.* A geomancer. Only in **M17.**
■ **geoˈmantical** *adjective* = GEOMANTIC *adjective* **M16.**

geomatics /dʒiːə(ʊ)ˈmatɪks/ *noun pl.* Treated as *sing.* **L20.**
[ORIGIN Blend of GEOGRAPHY and INFORMATICS.]
The application of computerization to information in the fields of geography, hydrography, surveying, etc.
■ **geomatic** *adjective* **L20.**

geometer /dʒɪˈɒmɪtə/ *noun.* **LME.**
[ORIGIN Late Latin *geometra* for classical Latin *geometres* from Greek = land-measurer, formed as GEO- + *metrēs* measurer.]
1 An expert in or student of geometry. **LME.**
†**2** A surveyor. *US.* **L18–E19.**
3 **a** A moth caterpillar which moves by alternately hunching and stretching its body, as if measuring the ground; an inchworm, measuring worm, or looper. **E19.** ▸**b** = GEOMETRID *noun.* **M19.**

geometric /dʒɪəˈmɛtrɪk/ *adjective.* **M17.**
[ORIGIN Old French & mod. French *géometrique* from Latin *geometricus* from Greek *geōmetrikos*, from *geōmetrēs*: see GEOMETER, -IC.]
1 = GEOMETRICAL. **M17.**
geometric mean (of *n* numbers) obtained by multiplying the numbers together and finding the *n*th root of their product. **geometric progression**, **geometric series**: in which there is a constant ratio between successive quantities, as 2, 4, 8, 16.
2 *ARCHAEOLOGY* (**G-**.) Designating or pertaining to a period of ancient Greek culture (*c* 900–*c* 700 BC) characterized by the use of geometrical decoration esp. for pottery. **E20.**

geometrical /dʒɪəˈmɛtrɪk(ə)l/ *adjective.* **LME.**
[ORIGIN formed as GEOMETRIC + -AL[1].]
1 Of or pertaining to geometry; determined or constructed according to the methods of geometry. **LME.** ▸**b** That works by the methods of geometry. **L17.** ▸**c** *ARCHITECTURE* (**G-**.) Designating or pertaining to an early style of English Decorated tracery, marked by the use of simple geometrical figures. **E19.**
2 Designating measures of length defined by geographical computation. *obsolete* exc. *hist.* **M16.**
– SPECIAL COLLOCATIONS: ***geometrical isomerism***: see ISOMERISM 1. **geometrical progression**, **geometrical series**: in which there is a constant ratio between successive quantities, as 1, 3, 9, 27, 81. **geometrical proportion** a proportion which involves an equality of ratio between its two parts, as 1 : 3 :: 4 : 12. ***geometrical ratio***: see RATIO *noun* 2a. ***geometrical series***: see ***geometrical progression*** above. **geometrical spider**: that constructs a web of geometrical pattern.
■ **geometrically** *adverb* in geometrical manner; according to geometry; by geometrical progression: **M16.**

geometrician /dʒɪəmɪˈtrɪʃ(ə)n/ *noun.* **L15.**
[ORIGIN Old French *geometricien*, from *geometrique*, Latin *geometricus*: see GEOMETRIC, -ICIAN.]
1 An expert in or student of geometry. **L15.**
†**2** A person who measures the land; a surveyor. **L16–L17.**

geometrid /dʒɪˈɒmɪtrɪd/ *noun & adjective.* **L19.**
[ORIGIN mod. Latin *Geometridae* (see below), from *Geometra* genus name: see -ID[3].]
▸ **A** *noun.* Any of various moths of the large family Geometridae, the caterpillars of which move by alternately hunching and stretching the body. Cf. GEOMETER 3. **L19.**
▸ **B** *adjective.* Of, pertaining to, or designating this family. **L19.**
■ **geomeˈtrideous** *adjective* (now *rare* or *obsolete*) = GEOMETRID *adjective* **M19.**

geometrize /dʒɪˈɒmɪtrʌɪz/ *verb.* Also **-ise**. **E17.**
[ORIGIN from GEOMETRY + -IZE.]
1 *verb trans.* Form geometrically; represent in geometric form. **E17.**
2 *verb intrans.* Work by geometrical methods. **M17.**
■ **geometriˈzation** *noun* **E20.**

geometry /dʒɪˈɒmɪtri/ *noun.* **ME.**
[ORIGIN Old French & mod. French *géométrie* from Latin *geometria* from Greek, formed as GEO- + -METRY.]
1 The branch of mathematics that deals with the properties and relations of magnitudes (as lines, surfaces, solids) in space; a particular system describing these properties etc. **ME.** ▸**b** The spatial arrangement of objects or constituent parts. **M19.**

> D. R. HOFSTADTER The sum of the angles in a triangle is 180 degrees only in Euclidean geometry; it is greater in elliptic geometry. *fig.*: R. S. THOMAS You are old now; time's geometry Upon your face. **b** B. LOVELL The epicyclic geometry of the Ptolemaic Universe. *Bicycle* The geometry of the Savoy gives reasonable manoeuvrability at low speed.

†**hang by geometry** (of clothes) hang in a stiff, angular fashion.
†**2** The art of measuring land; surveying. **LME–E17.**

geomorphic /dʒiːə(ʊ)ˈmɔːfɪk/ *adjective.* **L19.**
[ORIGIN from Greek GEO- + *morphē* form + -IC.]
Of or pertaining to the natural features of the earth's surface; geomorphological.
■ **geomorphically** *adverb* **M20.**

geomorphogeny /ˌdʒiːə(ʊ)mɔːˈfɒdʒəni/ *noun.* **L19.**
[ORIGIN from GEO- + MORPHOGENY.]
(The branch of geomorphology that deals with) the genesis of the physical features of the earth's surface.
■ **geomorphoˈgenic** *adjective* **L19.**

geomorphology /ˌdʒiːə(ʊ)mɔːˈfɒlədʒi/ *noun.* **L19.**
[ORIGIN from GEO- + MORPHOLOGY.]
The branch of science that deals with the physical features of the earth's surface and their relation to the underlying geological structure. Also, the geomorphological features of a particular region.
■ **geomorphoˈlogical** *adjective* of or pertaining to geomorphology **L19.** **geomorphoˈlogically** *adverb* **M20.** **geomorphologist** *noun* an expert in or student of geomorphology **E20.**

geomorphy /ˈdʒiːəmɔːfi/ *noun.* **L19.**
[ORIGIN from Greek GEO- + *morphē* form.]
= GEOMORPHOLOGY.

geonim *noun pl.* see GAON.

geophagy /dʒɪˈɒfədʒi/ *noun.* **M19.**
[ORIGIN from GEO- + -PHAGY.]
The practice of eating earth.
■ **geophagist** *noun* a person who eats earth **L19.**

geophysics /dʒiːə(ʊ)ˈfɪzɪks/ *noun.* **L19.**
[ORIGIN from GEO- + PHYSICS.]
The physics of the earth; geological investigation using the methods of physics.
■ **geophysical** *adjective* **L19.** **geophysically** *adverb* **E20.** **geophysicist** *noun* **E20.**

geopolitics /dʒiːə(ʊ)ˈpɒlɪtɪks/ *noun.* **E20.**
[ORIGIN from GEO(GRAPHY + POLITICS.]
1 Politics (esp. relations between states) as influenced by geographical factors; the branch of knowledge that deals with this. **E20.**
2 *hist.* A theory developed in Nazi Germany which regarded the state as an organism with powers independent of and superior to those of its constituent groups or individuals. **M20.**
■ **geopoˈlitical** *adjective* of or pertaining to geopolitics **E20.** **geopoˈlitically** *adverb* **M20.** **geopolitician** /-ˈtɪʃ(ə)n/ *noun* an expert in or student of geopolitics; *hist.* an exponent or supporter of the theory of geopolitics: **M20.**

geoponic /dʒiːə(ʊ)ˈpɒnɪk/ *adjective.* Now *rare* or *obsolete.* **M17.**
[ORIGIN Greek *geōponikos*, from *geōponos* farmer: see -IC.]
Of or pertaining to cultivation; agricultural.
■ **geoponical** *adjective* = GEOPONIC **M17.** **geoponics** *noun* the science of agriculture; a treatise on this: **E17.**

Geordie /ˈdʒɔːdi/ *noun & adjective.* **L18.**
[ORIGIN Dim. of GEORGE.]
▸ **A** *noun.* **1** A guinea. Also ***yellow Geordie***. Cf. GEORGE 3(b). *Scot. & N. English* (now *hist.*). **L18.**
2 A native or inhabitant of Tyneside in NE England; the dialect spoken on Tyneside. *colloq.* **M19.** ▸**b** A coalminer; a miner's safety lamp; a coal ship. Chiefly *N. English.* **L19.**
3 A Scotsman. *Austral. & NZ colloq.* **L19.**
▸ **B** *attrib.* or as *adjective.* Of or pertaining to Tyneside, its natives or inhabitants, or their dialect. *colloq.* **M20.**

George /dʒɔːdʒ/ *noun.* **E16.**
[ORIGIN Male forename.]
▸ **I** **1** A jewel bearing the image of St George, forming part of the insignia of the Order of the Garter. **E16.**
2 In interjectional phrs.: a mild oath, expr. surprise or assertion; chiefly as ***by George!*** **L16.**
3 A British coin bearing the image of St George; *spec.* (*hist.*) (**a**) a half-crown; (**b**) *slang* (also ***yellow George***) a guinea (cf. GEORDIE *noun* 1). **M17.**
4 *military slang.* **a** (A name for) an airman. *arch.* **E20.** ▸**b** (A name for) an aeroplane's automatic pilot. **M20.**
▸ **II** In sense 5 chiefly, in senses 6 & 7 only, as ***brown George***.
5 A loaf of coarse brown bread; a hard biscuit. *obsolete* exc. *dial.* **L16.**
6 A kind of wig, as worn by George III, king of Great Britain 1760–1820. *obsolete* exc. *hist.* **M19.**
7 A brown earthenware vessel. Now *dial.* **M19.**
– PHRASES & COMB.: ***brown George***: see branch II above. ***by George!***: see sense 2 above. **George Cross**, **George Medal** decorations for gallantry in civilian life instituted by George VI, King of Great Britain 1936–52. **George-noble** *hist.* an English gold coin worth one-third of a pound. **let George do it** (orig. *US*) let someone else do the work or take the responsibility. ***yellow George***: see sense 3 above. See also ***St George's cross***, ***St George's day***, ***St George's mushroom*** s.v. SAINT *noun & adjective*.

georgette /dʒɔːˈdʒɛt/ *noun & adjective.* **E20.**
[ORIGIN from Mme *Georgette* de la Plante (fl. *c* 1900), French modiste.]
(Made of) a thin plain-woven crêpe dress material, usu. of silk.

G

Georgian /ˈdʒɔːdʒ(ə)n/ *noun*[1] & *adjective*[1]. LME.
[ORIGIN from *Georgia* (see below) + -AN.]
▸ **A** *noun*. **1** A native or inhabitant of Georgia in the Caucasus (formerly a constituent republic of the USSR); the Caucasian language of this region. LME.
2 A native or inhabitant of the state of Georgia, USA. M18.
▸ **B** *adjective*. **1** Of or pertaining to Georgia in the Caucasus, its inhabitants, or their language. E17.
2 Of or pertaining to the state of Georgia, USA. M18.

Georgian /ˈdʒɔːdʒ(ə)n/ *adjective*[2] & *noun*[2]. L18.
[ORIGIN from *George*, name of several kings of Great Britain + -IAN.]
▸ **A** *adjective*. **1** ***Georgian Planet***, = GEORGIUM SIDUS. *obsolete* exc. *hist*. L18.
2 Of, belonging to, or characteristic of the reigns of any of the first four Kings of Great Britain called George (1714–1830). M19. ▸**b** *spec*. Designating, of or resembling the style of (esp. domestic) architecture characteristic of this period. L19.
Georgian green a slightly yellowish green popular in the 18th and early 19th cents.
3 Belonging to or characteristic of the reign of George V (1910–36) or George VI (1936–52), Kings of Great Britain; *spec*. designating the writers or literature of the early years of George V's reign. E20.
▸ **B** *noun*. **1** A person of the time of any of the Kings of Great Britain called George. E20.
2 *spec*. A writer of the early part of the reign of George V. E20.
■ **Georgiˈana** *noun pl*. articles or buildings of the Georgian period M20.

G

georgic /ˈdʒɔːdʒɪk/ *noun & adjective*. E16.
[ORIGIN Latin *georgicus* from Greek *geōrgikos*, from *geōrgos* farmer: see -IC.]
▸ **A** *noun*. A book or poem dealing with husbandry or other rural matters. Orig. & usu. in *pl*. (**G-**) as the title of a poetical treatise by Virgil. E16.
▸ **B** *adjective*. Relating to agriculture. *obsolete* exc. *joc*., rustic, bucolic. E18.

georgical /ˈdʒɔːdʒɪk(ə)l/ *adjective*. Now *rare*. M17.
[ORIGIN formed as GEORGIC + -AL[1].]
Rustic, agricultural.

Georgium Sidus /ˌdʒɔːdʒɪəm ˈsʌɪdəs/ *noun phr*. L18.
[ORIGIN mod. Latin, lit. 'planet of George'.]
hist. The name given to the planet Uranus by its discoverer, William Herschel, in honour of King George III of Great Britain.

geostationary /dʒiːə(ʊ)ˈsteɪʃ(ə)n(ə)ri/ *adjective*. M20.
[ORIGIN from GEO- + STATIONARY.]
Of an artificial satellite: that orbits the earth in exactly one day and hence always remains above the same point on the earth's surface. Of an orbit: (able to be) occupied by such a satellite.

geostrophic /dʒiːə(ʊ)ˈstrɒfɪk/ *adjective*. E20.
[ORIGIN from GEO- + Greek *strophē* a turning (from *strephein* to turn) + -IC.]
METEOROLOGY & OCEANOGRAPHY. Of or pertaining to the Coriolis force; *esp*. (of a wind or ocean current) in which there is a balance between the Coriolis force and the horizontal pressure gradient. Cf. AGEOSTROPHIC.

geosynclinal /dʒiːəsɪŋˈklʌɪn(ə)l/ *noun & adjective*. L19.
[ORIGIN from GEO- + SYNCLINAL.]
GEOLOGY. ▸**A** *noun*. = GEOSYNCLINE. Now *rare*. L19.
▸ **B** *adjective*. Of, pertaining to, or of the nature of a geosyncline. L19.

geosyncline /dʒiːə(ʊ)ˈsɪŋklʌɪn/ *noun*. L19.
[ORIGIN Back-form. from GEOSYNCLINAL.]
GEOLOGY. A large-scale downward flexure of the earth's crust containing sedimentary and volcanic deposits of great thickness.

geotaxis /dʒiːə(ʊ)ˈtaksɪs/ *noun*. L19.
[ORIGIN from GEO- + -TAXIS.]
BIOLOGY. Movement related to the direction of the earth's gravity.
negative geotaxis: in which movement is upwards. **positive geotaxis**: in which movement is downwards.
■ **geotactic** *adjective* of, pertaining to, or of the nature of geotaxis L19.

geothermal /dʒiːə(ʊ)ˈθəːm(ə)l/ *adjective*. L19.
[ORIGIN from GEO- + THERMAL.]
Of, pertaining to, or derived from the internal heat of the earth.
■ Also **geothermic** *adjective* L19.

geotropic /dʒiːə(ʊ)ˈtrəʊpɪk, -ˈtrɒpɪk/ *adjective*. L19.
[ORIGIN from GEOTROPISM + -IC.]
BOTANY. Pertaining to, marked by, or of the nature of geotropism.
■ **geotropically** *adverb* L19.

geotropism /dʒiːə(ʊ)ˈtrəʊpɪz(ə)m/ *noun*. L19.
[ORIGIN from GEO- + Greek *tropē* turning + -ISM.]
BOTANY. The growth of part of a plant in response to gravity.
negative geotropism tendency (of stems etc.) to grow upwards. **positive geotropism** tendency (of roots etc.) to grow downwards.

gephyrocercal /ˌdʒɛfɪrəʊˈsəːk(ə)l/ *adjective*. L19.
[ORIGIN from Greek *gephura* bridge + *kerkos* tail + -AL[1].]
Of a fish: having the caudal tail formed by the meeting of dorsal and anal fins.

Ger. *abbreviation*.
German.

gerah /ˈɡɪərə/ *noun*. M16.
[ORIGIN Hebrew *gērāh*.]
An ancient Hebrew coin and weight, the twentieth part of a shekel.

Geraldton wax /ˈdʒɛr(ə)l(d)tən waks/ *noun phr*. *Austral*. E20.
[ORIGIN *Geraldton*, a town in W. Australia.]
A western Australian evergreen shrub, *Chamaelaucium uncinatum*, of the myrtle family, with pink or white waxy flowers.

geranial /dʒɪˈreɪnɪəl/ *noun*. L19.
[ORIGIN formed as GERANIOL + -AL[2].]
CHEMISTRY. The *trans* isomer of citral, a fragrant oil present in lemon grass oil and used in perfumery.

geraniol /dʒɪˈreɪnɪɒl/ *noun*. L19.
[ORIGIN from GERANIUM + -OL.]
CHEMISTRY. A colourless oily unsaturated alcohol, $C_{10}H_{18}O$, with a fragrant odour, present in geranium oil and rose oil and used in perfumery.

geranium /dʒɪˈreɪnɪəm/ *noun*. M16.
[ORIGIN Latin from Greek *geranion*, from *geranos* crane: see -IUM.]
1 Any plant of the genus *Geranium* (family Geraniaceae); = ***cranesbill*** (a) s.v. CRANE *noun*[1]. M16.
2 In popular use: any of various plants of the mostly southern African genus *Pelargonium*, which are related to true geraniums but with zygomorphic flowers and include many kinds grown as house or bedding plants for their showy scarlet, pink, etc., flowers or scented leaves. M18.
ivy geranium, ***lemon geranium***, ***peppermint geranium***, etc.
3 The colour of the scarlet pelargonium. M19.

gerardia /dʒɪˈrɑːdɪə/ *noun*. E19.
[ORIGIN mod. Latin (see below), from John *Gerard* (1545–1612), English herbalist + -IA[1].]
Any of various purple- or yellow-flowered parasitic N. American plants of the figwort family, formerly referred to a genus *Gerardia* and now to the genera *Agalinis* and *Aureolaria* respectively.

†**gerate** *verb trans*. L15–M19.
[ORIGIN Unknown.]
HERALDRY. Powder or strew with minor charges.

geratology /dʒɛrəˈtɒlədʒi/ *noun*. L19.
[ORIGIN from Greek *gērat-*, *geras* old age + -OLOGY.]
†**1** The branch of biology that deals with the extinction of plant and animal species. Only in L19.
2 = GERONTOLOGY. M20.

gerbe /ˈdʒəːb/ *noun*. L16.
[ORIGIN French = wheatsheaf from Frankish *garbe* = Old High German *garba* (German *Garbe*).]
1 Something resembling a wheatsheaf in form or appearance; *esp*. a kind of firework. L16.
†**2** A wheatsheaf. Only in E19.

gerbera /ˈdʒəːb(ə)rə, ˈɡəː-/ *noun*. L19.
[ORIGIN mod. Latin (see below), from T. *Gerber* (d. 1743), German naturalist.]
BOTANY. Any of several African and Asian plants of the genus *Gerbera*, of the composite family; *esp*. the Transvaal daisy, *G. jamesonii*, grown for its large daisy-like flowers in many shades.

gerbil /ˈdʒəːbɪl/ *noun*. Also **gerbille**, **jerbil**. M19.
[ORIGIN French *gerbille* from mod. Latin *gerbillus*, dim. of *gerboa* JERBOA.]
Any of various mouselike burrowing rodents of African and Asian deserts, of the subfamily Gerbillinae (family Muridae); esp. *Meriones unguiculatus* of Mongolia, commonly kept elsewhere as a pet (cf. JIRD).

gerent /ˈdʒɪər(ə)nt, ˈdʒɛ-/ *noun*. *rare*. L16.
[ORIGIN Latin *gerent-* pres. ppl stem of *gerere* carry on, manage: see -ENT.]
A manager, a ruler.

gerenuk /ˈɡɛrənʊk/ *noun*. L19.
[ORIGIN Somali.]
A long-necked antelope, *Litocranius walleri*, of E. Africa that is similar to the gazelles.

gerfalcon *noun* var. of GYRFALCON.

geriatric /dʒɛrɪˈatrɪk/ *adjective & noun*. E20.
[ORIGIN from Greek *gēras* old age + *iatrikos* (see IATRIC *adjective*), after *paediatric*.]
▸ **A** *adjective*. **1** Relating to geriatrics or to old people; designed for use by old people. E20.
2 Of a person: old; senile. *derog*. M20.

> *Times* Geriatric judges with 19th century . . prejudices only bring the rule of law into disrepute.

▸ **B** *noun*. **1** In *pl*. (treated as *sing*.). The branch of medical or social science that deals with the health and welfare of old people. E20.
2 An old person receiving geriatric care. Also *derog*., an old or senile person. L20. ▸**b** Anything old or outdated. *colloq*. L20.
■ **geriatrician** /-ˈtrɪʃ(ə)n/, **geriˈatrist** *nouns* a doctor who specializes in geriatrics M20.

germ /dʒəːm/ *noun & verb*. LME.
[ORIGIN Old French & mod. French *germe* from Latin *germen* seed, sprout.]
▸ **A** *noun*. **1** A part of a living organism which is capable of developing into a similar organism or part of one. LME.

> J. R. LOWELL A strong oak, doth from its boughs shed down The ripe germs of a forest. P. GALLICO The ageless germ of a patriarchal race ran in his blood-stream.

2 *fig*. A thing from which something may spring or develop; an elementary principle; a rudiment. Usu. foll. by *of*. M16.

> F. W. FARRAR His keen eye marked the germs of coming danger. C. S. LEWIS There is not even the germ of a feeling for design.

in germ in a rudimentary form, not yet developed.
3 †**a** The ovary of a plant. M18–E19. ▸**b** A plant seed. E19. ▸**c** The embryo and scutellum of a plant seed, esp. of a grain of cereal. L19.

> **c** *Health Guardian* Natural sources are egg yolks, . . wheat germ and lecithin.

4 A micro-organism; *esp*. one which is supposed to cause disease. L19.

> P. H. JOHNSON I picked up this wretched germ somehow—it's a virus pneumonia. E. O'BRIEN There's probably germs floating everywhere.

– COMB.: **germ bomb**: containing germs, for use in germ warfare; **germ cell** a cell of a living organism that is specialized for reproductive purposes and ultimately gives rise to sperm cells and egg cells or (in plants) to spores; a sperm cell, an egg cell; cf. *SOMATIC cell*; **germ layer** BIOLOGY each of the three layers of cells (ectoderm, mesoderm, and endoderm) that arise in the early stages of embryonic development; **germ line** a series of germ cells each descended or developed from earlier cells in the series, regarded as continuing through successive generations of an organism; **germ plasm** (*a*) *hist*. the part of a germ cell which carries hereditary factors and is itself transmitted unchanged from generation to generation; (*b*) germ cells collectively; their genetic material; **germ theory** *hist*.: that infectious diseases are caused by micro-organisms; **germ warfare** the spreading of disease germs among an enemy as a weapon of war.
▸ **B** *verb intrans*. Germinate, sprout. Now only *fig*. L15.
■ **germless** *adjective* L19. **germy** *adjective* full of germs; unclean, polluted: E20.

†**germaine** *noun* see GERMEN.

German /ˈdʒəːmən/ *noun*[1] & *adjective*[1]. LME.
[ORIGIN Latin *Germanus* used as noun and adjective to designate a group of related peoples of north and central Europe.]
▸ **A** *noun*. **1** A native or inhabitant of Germany, a country in central Europe orig. consisting of a series of small states only fully united as one country in the mid 19th cent., and from 1945 divided into East Germany (the German Democratic Republic) and West Germany (the Federal Republic of Germany) until unified in 1990. Formerly also, a member of any of the Germanic peoples of north and central Europe. LME. ▸**b** A scholar of the German language. E19.
2 The principal language of Germany, spoken also in Austria and Switzerland and belonging to the West Germanic division. M17.
3 = ***German cotillion*** s.v. COTILLION *noun* 1. M19.
▸ **B** *adjective*. **1** Of or pertaining to Germany or its inhabitants; native to or originating in Germany; characteristic of or attributed to Germans or Germany. M16.
2 Belonging to, written in, or spoken in the German language. E17.
– PHRASES (of adjective & noun): **East German** *hist*. (*a*) of or pertaining to the German Democratic Republic; (*b*) a native or inhabitant of this state. **High German** (of or pertaining to) the variety of German orig. confined to 'high' or southern Germany, but now in literary or cultured use throughout Germany. **Low German** (*a*) (of or pertaining to) the dialects of Germany which are not High German, Plattdeutsch; (*b*) (of or pertaining to) all forms of West Germanic, including English and Dutch, except High German. ***Old High German***: see OLD *adjective*. **West German** *hist*. (*a*) of or pertaining to the Federal Republic of Germany; (*b*) a native or inhabitant of this state.
– SPECIAL COLLOCATIONS & COMB.: **German-American** *noun & adjective* (*a*) *noun* an American of German extraction; (*b*) *adjective* of or pertaining to Americans of German extraction. **German band** a band of street musicians, properly of German extraction. ***German CATHOLIC***. **German clock** an elaborately constructed clock, often with moving figures etc., of a type popular in the 16th and 17th cents. **German cockroach** a common indoor cockroach, *Blatella germanica*, found worldwide; also called ***Croton bug***, ***steam fly***. ***German cotillion***: see COTILLION *noun* 1. **German ivy** a twining southern African plant, *Delairea odorata*, of the composite family, grown for its fragrant yellow flowers which appear in winter. ***German MADWORT***. **German measles** a contagious virus disease that resembles a mild form of measles but can cause fetal malformations if caught by a woman early in a pregnancy, rubella. **German ocean** *arch*. the North Sea. **German sausage** a large sausage stuffed with partially cooked spiced meat. **German shepherd (dog)** a strong dog of a breed frequently used as guard dogs or for police work; an Alsatian. **German silver** = ***nickel silver*** s.v. NICKEL *noun*. **German sixth** MUSIC a chord consisting of a major third, a perfect fifth, and an

augmented sixth. **German Swiss** *adjective & noun* (*a*) *adjective* of or pertaining to the part of Switzerland where Schweizerdeutsch is spoken; (*b*) *noun* a native or inhabitant of the part of Switzerland where Schweizerdeutsch is spoken (cf. ***Swiss German***). ***German*** TAMARISK. **German wool** = ***BERLIN*** ***wool***.

■ **Germanify** *verb trans.* = GERMANIZE 2 M19. **Germanish** *adjective* having German characteristics L18. **Germanist** *noun* (*a*) a person who has a knowledge of Germany and the German language; (*b*) an expert in Germanic philology; (*c*) a person influenced by Germanic thought: M19. **Ger'manity** *noun* (*a*) the characteristic qualities of Germany and the Germans; (*b*) devotion to German interests: M19. **Germanly** *adverb* L18.

german /'dʒəːmən/ *adjective*² & *noun*². Also (now the only form in sense A.4) **germane** /dʒəː'meɪn/. ME.

[ORIGIN Old French & mod. French *germain* (in Old French also 'brother') from Latin *germanus* having the same parents, genuine (as nouns *germanus* brother, *germana* sister).]

► **A** *adjective*. **I** Closely akin.

1 Having the same parents. *obsolete* exc. in ***brother german***, ***sister german*** (see BROTHER *noun*, SISTER *noun*). ME.

2 That is the child of one's uncle or aunt; that is one's first cousin. *obsolete* exc. in COUSIN-GERMAN. ME.

†**3** Closely related, akin. L15–M17.

4 Relevant, pertinent, (*to* a matter or subject). E17.

J. STEINBECK Any sound that was not germane to the night would make them alert. E. JONES Four considerations would appear to be germane here.

► **II 5** Genuine; true; thorough. *arch.* LME.

► †**B** *noun*. A close relative, *esp.* a sibling. L15–E18.

■ **ger'manely** *adverb* in a germane manner, pertinently M19. **ger'maneness** *noun* M20.

germander /dʒə'mandə/ *noun*. LME.

[ORIGIN medieval Latin *germandra*, *-drea* (cf. Old French *gemandree*, French *germandrée*), alt. of *gamandrea* (cf. German *Gamander*) ult. from Greek *khamaidrus* lit. 'ground-oak', from *khamai* on the ground + *drus* oak.]

Any of certain plants with leaves thought to resemble the oak; *spec.* (more fully ***wall germander***) a labiate plant, *Teucrium chamaedrys*, sometimes naturalized on old walls; also (with specifying word), any of several other plants of this genus.

water germander a rare marsh plant, *Teucrium scordium*. ***wood germander***: see WOOD *noun*¹ & *adjective*¹.

– COMB.: **germander speedwell** a common hedge speedwell, *Veronica chamaedrys*, with bright blue flowers.

germane *adjective & noun* see GERMAN *adjective*² & *noun*².

Germanic /dʒəː'manɪk/ *adjective*¹ & *noun*. M17.

[ORIGIN Latin *Germanicus* from *Germanus* GERMAN *adjective*¹: see -IC.]

► **A** *adjective*. **1** German; now *esp.* characteristic of or attributed to Germans or Germany. M17.

J. UPDIKE Germanic thoroughness characterized . . the bibliographical rigor.

2 Of, pertaining to, or designating the former peoples of the Germanic-speaking areas of north and central Europe, *spec.* the Scandinavians, Anglo-Saxons, or Germans. L18. ►**b** Of, pertaining to, or designating the language of the Germanic peoples or any of its forms. E19.

► **B** *noun*. A branch of the Indo-European language family including English, German, Dutch, Flemish, Frisian, the Scandinavian languages, and the earlier languages from which they have developed; *spec.* (and in this dictionary) Proto-Germanic. E19.

East Germanic (of or pertaining to) the now extinct division of Germanic represented chiefly by Gothic. **North Germanic** (of or pertaining to) the division of Germanic represented by the modern and ancient Scandinavian languages. **primitive Germanic** Proto-Germanic. **West Germanic** (of or pertaining to) the division of Germanic including English, German, Dutch, Flemish, Frisian, and the languages from which they have developed.

– NOTE: Cf. DUTCH *noun*¹, *adjective & adverb*, TEUTONIC. See also PROTO-GERMANIC.

■ **Germanical** *adjective* (*rare*) = GERMAN *adjective*¹ 1 M16. **Germanically** *adverb* M19. **Germanicism** /-sɪz(ə)m/ *noun* a German characteristic, idiom, etc.; Germanic quality: E20.

germanic /dʒəː'manɪk/ *adjective*². L19.

[ORIGIN from GERMAN(IUM + -IC.]

CHEMISTRY. Of, pertaining to, or containing germanium in the tetravalent state.

Germanise *verb* var. of GERMANIZE.

Germanism /'dʒəːmənɪz(ə)m/ *noun*. E17.

[ORIGIN from GERMAN *adjective*¹ + -ISM.]

1 A German idiom, *esp.* one used in some other language. E17.

American Speech Germanisms are most numerous in eastern Pennsylvania.

2 Affectation of what is German. E19.

3 German ideas or attitudes; attachment to these. M19.

germanium /dʒəː'meɪnɪəm/ *noun*. L19.

[ORIGIN from Latin *Germanus* GERMAN *adjective*¹ + -IUM.]

A brittle metalloid chemical element, atomic no. 32, used as a semiconductor in solid-state electronic devices and as a constituent of alloys, phosphors, and infrared glasses (symbol Ge).

Germanize /'dʒəːmənʌɪz/ *verb*. Also **-ise**. L16.

[ORIGIN from GERMAN *adjective*¹ + -IZE.]

1 *verb trans.* Translate into the German language. L16.

2 *verb trans.* Make German in character, appearance, etc. E17.

3 *verb intrans.* Adopt German manners or customs; become German in style, attitude, habits, etc. M17.

■ **Germani'zation** *noun* the action or process of Germanizing M19. **Germanizer** *noun* M19.

Germano- /dʒəː'manəʊ, 'dʒəːmənəʊ/ *combining form*.

[ORIGIN from GERMAN *noun*¹ & *adjective*¹ + -O-.]

Forming adjectives and nouns with the sense 'German, of Germany'.

■ ˌ**Germano-Cole'ridgean** *adjective* (*rare*) (of opinions) derived from German writers through Coleridge or from the Germans and Coleridge jointly M19. ˌ**Germano'mania** *noun* a craze or excessive liking for Germany and things German L19. **Ger'manophil(e)** *adjective & noun* (a person who is) friendly towards Germany or fond of Germany and things German L19. ˌ**Germa'nophilist** *noun* = GERMANOPHILE *noun* M19. **Ger'manophobe** *adjective & noun* (a person who is) affected with Germanophobia E20. ˌ**Germano'phobia** *noun* dread or dislike of Germany and things German L19.

germanous /dʒəː'meɪnəs/ *adjective*. L19.

[ORIGIN from GERMAN(IUM + -OUS.]

CHEMISTRY. Of, pertaining to, or containing germanium in the divalent state.

Germantown /'dʒəːmәntaʊn/ *noun*. *US*. Also **g-**. M19.

[ORIGIN A suburb of Philadelphia.]

Chiefly *hist.* A one-horse covered vehicle used by farmers and other country people in the US.

germarium /dʒəː'mɛːrɪəm/ *noun*. Pl. **-ria** /-rɪə/. L19.

[ORIGIN from Latin *germen* seed, sprout, GERM *noun* + -ARIUM.]

ZOOLOGY. In certain invertebrates, the part of an ovary or testis where eggs and sperm are produced by germ cells.

germen /'dʒəːmən/ *noun*. Also (earlier) †**germaine**. E17.

[ORIGIN Latin *germen* seed, sprout, GERM *noun*.]

1 The rudiment of an organism. Now only *fig.* (= GERM *noun* 2). E17.

†**2** A shoot, a sprout. E17–L18.

3 *BOTANY*. The rudiment of a seed vessel. M18.

germicide /'dʒəːmɪsʌɪd/ *noun & adjective*. L19.

[ORIGIN from GERM *noun* + -I- + -CIDE.]

► **A** *noun*. A substance that kills germs, esp. ones which cause disease. L19.

► **B** *adjective*. Germicidal. Now *rare*. L19.

■ **germi'cidal** *adjective* that has the effect of a germicide L19.

germin /'dʒəːmɪn/ *verb intrans. arch.* LME.

[ORIGIN Latin *germinare*: see GERMINATE *verb*.]

Send out shoots; sprout, bud; begin to produce vegetation.

germinable /'dʒəːmɪnəb(ə)l/ *adjective*. L19.

[ORIGIN from GERMIN(ATE + -ABLE.]

Capable of germinating.

■ **germina'bility** *noun* M20.

Germinal /'dʒəːmɪn(ə)l; *foreign* ʒɛrminal (*pl. same*)/ *noun*. E19.

[ORIGIN French, formed as GERMINAL *adjective*.]

The seventh month of the French Republican calendar (introduced 1793) extending from 21 March to 19 April.

germinal /'dʒəːmɪn(ə)l/ *adjective*. E19.

[ORIGIN from Latin *germin-*, *germen* seed, sprout, GERM *noun* + -AL¹.]

1 *ANATOMY, ZOOLOGY, & BOTANY*. Of or belonging to a germ or germs; of the nature of a germ (GERM *noun* 1). E19.

germinal cell = ***germ cell*** s.v. GERM *noun*. **germinal vesicle** the enlarged nucleus of a maturing oocyte.

2 *transf.* In the earliest stage of development; *joc.* rudimentary, undeveloped. E19.

G. H. LEWES A forecasting tendency, germinal in animals and . . conspicuous in the civilized man.

3 Capable of development; productive of new ideas, influences, etc.; seminal. M20.

Music Teacher Seven varied and contrasted pieces (chiefly constructed around germinal motives).

■ **germinally** *adverb* M19.

germinant /'dʒəːmɪnənt/ *adjective*. LME.

[ORIGIN Latin *germinant-* pres. ppl stem of *germinare*: see GERMINATE, -ANT¹.]

Germinating, sprouting; capable of developing or producing life.

germinate /'dʒəːmɪneɪt/ *verb*. L16.

[ORIGIN Latin *germinat-* pa. ppl stem of *germinare*, from *germin-*, *germen* seed, sprout, GERM *noun*: see -ATE³.]

1 a *verb trans.* Cause (a seed, bud, etc.) to send out shoots or begin development; *fig.* cause to arise or develop. L16. ►**b** *verb intrans.* Send out shoots; sprout, bud; begin to develop. M17.

a *Nature* Doku stated that he had germinated yam seeds. H. CAINE A crowd of people gathered in the street and germinated alarming rumours. **b** HARTLEY COLERIDGE From the first, or initiative idea . . successive ideas germinate. ANTHONY HUXLEY In the tropics seeds are apt to germinate immediately.

2 *verb intrans.* Of a salt etc.: effloresce. Now *rare* or *obsolete*. E17.

■ **germinative** *adjective* (*a*) of or belong to germination; (*b*) capable of germinating: E18. **germinator** *noun* a thing which causes or promotes germination L19.

germination /dʒəːmɪ'neɪʃ(ə)n/ *noun*. LME.

[ORIGIN Latin *germinatio(n-)*, formed as GERMINATE: see -ATION.]

1 The action or process, or an instance, of germinating; sprouting. LME.

ANTHONY HUXLEY Pebble-like seeds which can float for . . years without losing their powers of germination.

2 Efflorescence. Now *rare* or *obsolete*. M17.

germon /'dʒəːmən/ *noun*. M19.

[ORIGIN French.]

A tunny, *esp.* the albacore, *Thunnus alalonga*.

gerocomy /dʒə'rɒkəmi/ *noun*. *rare*. E19.

[ORIGIN Greek *gērokomia* care of the aged, from *gēro-*, *gēras* old age + *komia* tending: see -Y³.]

= GERONTOLOGY.

■ †**gerocomical** *adjective*: only in M17.

Geronimo /dʒə'rɒnɪməʊ/ *interjection*. *US*. M20.

[ORIGIN Name of an Apache Indian chief (1829–1909), adopted as a slogan in the Second World War by US paratroops.]

Expr. exhilaration on performing a daring leap etc.

Geronomite /dʒə'rɒnəmʌɪt/ *noun*. M18.

[ORIGIN Spanish or Italian *geronomita*.]

= HIERONYMITE *noun*.

geront- *combining form* see GERONTO-.

gerontic /dʒə'rɒntɪk/ *adjective*. L19.

[ORIGIN from GERONT- + -IC.]

Of or pertaining to old age; senile.

geronto- /dʒə'rɒntəʊ, dʒɛrɒn'tɒ/ *combining form*. Before a vowel **geront-**.

[ORIGIN from Greek *geront-*, *gerōn* old man + -O-.]

Old age.

■ **geronto'morphic** *adjective* of, pertaining to, or designating anatomical specialization most fully represented in the mature male of a species M20. **ge'rontophil(e)** *noun & adjective* (a person) favouring old people, esp. old men; (a person) desiring sexual relations with old people: M20. **geronto'philia** *noun* desire for sexual relations with old people E20. **geronto'philic** *adjective* = GERONTOPHIL(E) *adjective* M20. **geron'tophily** *noun* = GERONTOPHILIA M20.

gerontocracy /dʒɛrɒn'tɒkrəsi/ *noun*. M19.

[ORIGIN from GERONT-: see -CRACY.]

Government by old people; a governing body consisting of old people.

■ **ge'rontocrat** *noun* a member of a gerontocracy M20. **geˌronto'cratic** *adjective* of, pertaining to, or characteristic of (a) gerontocracy E20.

gerontology /dʒɛrɒn'tɒlədʒi/ *noun*. E20.

[ORIGIN from GERONT- + -OLOGY.]

The branch of science that deals with old age, the ageing process, and the problems faced by old people.

■ **geˌronto'logical** *adjective* M20. **gerontologist** *noun* M20.

geropiga /dʒɛrə'piːgə/ *noun*. Also **jeru-**. M19.

[ORIGIN Portuguese *jeropiga*.]

A grape juice mixture added in the making of port.

-gerous /dʒ(ə)rəs/ *suffix*.

[ORIGIN from Latin *-ger* bearing (from base of *gerere* bear, carry) + -OUS.]

Forming adjectives, usu. with intermediate **-i-**, with the sense 'bearing', as ***cornigerous***, ***frondigerous***, etc.

gerrymander /'dʒɛrɪmandə/ *noun & verb*. E19.

[ORIGIN from Elbridge *Gerry* (1744–1814), US governor + SALA)MANDER *noun*, from the supposed resemblance to a salamander of the outline of an electoral district in Massachusetts formed by Gerry in 1812 for party purposes.]

► **A** *noun*. **1** The action of manipulating the boundaries of a constituency etc. so as to give an unfair advantage at an election to a particular party or class. E19.

H. EVANS His . . government . . retained power by a gerrymander giving two out of every three seats to the minority country voters.

2 A person elected by gerrymandering. E19.

► **B** *verb trans.* Subject (a constituency, voting area, etc.) to a gerrymander; *gen.* manipulate in order to gain an unfair advantage. E19.

■ **gerrymanderer** *noun* L19.

gersum /'gəːsəm/ *noun*. Also (chiefly *Scot.*) **grassum**.

[ORIGIN Late Old English *gærsum*, *gersum* = Old Norse *gersimi*, Middle Swedish *görsam*.]

1 A treasure, a precious possession; a costly gift. *obsolete* exc. *hist.* LOE.

2 A sum paid to a feudal superior by a feuar on taking up a holding. Also, a sum paid or pledged to a landlord by a tenant on the receipt or renewal of a lease. Chiefly *Scot.* ME.

gertcha /'gəːtʃə/ *interjection*. *slang*. M20.

[ORIGIN Repr. a joc. pronunc. of *get away* or *along with you*.]

Expr. derisive disbelief.

G

gerund /ˈdʒɛrʌnd/ *noun*. E16.
[ORIGIN Late Latin *gerundium* from *gerundum* var. of *gerendum* gerund of Latin *gerere* carry on.]
A form of the Latin verb which is used as a noun but retains the syntactic relationships of the verb; a similar verbal form in other languages, *spec.* the English verbal noun, ending in *-ing*, esp. when used distinctly as part of the verb.
– COMB.: **gerund-grinder** *arch.* a teacher of Latin, a pedantic teacher.
■ **geˈrundial** *adjective* M19. **geˈrundially** *adverb* L16.

gerundive /dʒəˈrʌndɪv/ *noun & adjective*. LME.
[ORIGIN Late Latin *gerundivus* (sc. *modus* mood), from *gerundium* GERUND: see -IVE.]
▸ **A** *noun*. **1** = GERUND. LME.
2 In Latin, the verbal adjective formed from the gerund stem and having the sense 'that can or must be done'; a similar grammatical form in other languages. E18.
▸ **B** *adjective*. Of or like a gerund. E17.
■ **gerundival** *adjective* L19. **gerundively** *adverb* M19.

gerusia /gɛˈruːzɪə/ *noun*. M19.
[ORIGIN Latin from Greek *gerousia*, from *gerōn* old man: see -IA¹.]
hist. An assembly of elders, *spec.* the senate in Sparta and other Dorian cities of ancient Greece.

Gervais /ʒɛrvɛ/ *noun & adjective*. Pl. same. L19.
[ORIGIN Charles *Gervais* (1830–92), French cheesemaker.]
(Proprietary name designating) a soft creamy cheese.

Gerzean /gəːˈziːən/ *adjective*. E20.
[ORIGIN from el-*Gerza* a district in Egypt + -AN.]
ARCHAEOLOGY. Designating or pertaining to the later period (or middle period if the Semainean period is reckoned separately) of the ancient predynastic culture of upper Egypt.

Gesamtkunstwerk /gəˈzamtkʊnst,vɛrk/ *noun*. Pl. ***-e*** /-ə/. M20.
[ORIGIN German, from *gesamt* total + *Kunstwerk* work of art.]
An ideal work of art in which drama, music, and other performing arts are integrated and each is subservient to the whole.

Gesellschaft /gəˈzɛlʃaft/ *noun*. Also ***g-***. M20.
[ORIGIN German, from *Gesell(e)* companion + *-schaft* -SHIP.]
SOCIOLOGY. A form of social integration based on impersonal ties; association. Cf. GEMEINSCHAFT.

†**gesine** *noun*. ME–L18.
[ORIGIN Old French, from *gesir* to lie, from Latin *jacere*.]
Childbirth.

gesnera /ˈgɛsnərə, ˈdʒɛs-/ *noun*. Also **gesneria** /-ˈnɪərɪə/. M19.
[ORIGIN mod. Latin (see below), from Conrad von *Gesner* (1516–65), Swiss naturalist + -IA¹.]
Any of various tropical American plants of the genus *Gesneria* (family Gesneriaceae), grown elsewhere for their showy flowers.

Gesolreut /ˌdʒiːsɒlreɪˈʊt/ *noun*. *obsolete* exc. *hist.* Also **G sol re ut**. ME.
[ORIGIN from *G* as a pitch letter + *sol*, *re*, *ut* designating tones in the solmization of Guido d'Arezzo (*c* 990–1050).]
MEDIEVAL MUSIC. The note G in Guido d'Arezzo's 2nd, 3rd, and 4th hexachords, where it was sung to the syllables *sol*, *re*, and *ut* respectively. Cf. ALAMIRE, CEFAUT, etc.

gesso /ˈdʒɛsəʊ/ *noun*. Pl. **-oes**. L16.
[ORIGIN Italian from Latin GYPSUM. Cf. YESO.]
Gypsum, plaster of Paris, now only as prepared for use in painting and sculpture; any white substance that can be mixed with water to make a ground.
■ **gessoed** *adjective* made of or covered with gesso M20.

gest /dʒɛst/ *noun*¹. Also †**jest**. See also JEST *noun*. ME.
[ORIGIN Old French *geste*, *jeste* from Latin *gesta* actions, exploits, use as noun of neut. pl. of pa. pple of *gerere* bear, carry, carry on, perform.]
▸ **I 1** A (heroic) deed or exploit, esp. as narrated or recorded; in *pl.*, actions, conduct. *arch.* ME.
2 Orig., a story, esp. a romance, in verse. Later also, a prose romance or tale. *obsolete* exc. *hist.* ME.
▸ †**II** See JEST *noun* II.

gest /dʒɛst/ *noun*². *arch.* Also **geste**. LME.
[ORIGIN Old French & mod. French *geste* from Latin *gestus*, from *gerere* bear, carry, carry on, perform.]
1 A gesture, a movement, an action. LME.
2 Bearing, carriage. E16.
■ †**gested** *adjective* accompanied by gestures L16–M18.

†**gest** *noun*³. M16.
[ORIGIN Later form of GIST *noun*¹.]
1 In *pl.* The stages of a (royal) journey; the route followed or planned. M16–M18.
2 The time allotted for a halt or stay. *rare* (Shakes.). Only in E17.

†**gest** *verb*. See also JEST *verb*. LME.
[ORIGIN from GEST *noun*¹.]
1 *verb intrans.* Recite a romance or tale. Only in LME.
2 See JEST *verb*.

gestagen /ˈdʒɛstədʒ(ə)n/ *noun*. Also **gesto-**. M20.
[ORIGIN from GESTATION (+ -O-) + -GEN.]
= PROGESTOGEN.

gestalt /gəˈʃtɑːlt, -ˈʃtalt/ *noun*. Also **G-**. E20.
[ORIGIN German = form, shape.]
Chiefly PSYCHOLOGY. An integrated perceptual structure or unity conceived as functionally more than the sum of its parts.
– COMB.: **gestalt psychology** a school of psychology maintaining that perceptions, reactions, etc., are gestalts; **gestalt therapy** a psychotherapeutic approach that focuses on insight into gestalts in patients and their relations to the world, and often uses role playing to aid the resolution of past conflicts.
■ **gestaltism** *noun* gestalt psychology M20. **gestaltist** *noun* an adherent or practitioner of the principles of gestalt psychology M20.

Gestapo /gəˈstɑːpəʊ/ *noun*. Pl. **-os**. M20.
[ORIGIN German acronym, from *Geheime Staatspolizei* Secret State Police.]
(An officer of) the secret police of the Nazi regime in Germany.

gestate /dʒɛˈsteɪt/ *verb*. M19.
[ORIGIN Latin *gestat-*: see GESTATION, -ATE³.]
1 *verb trans. & intrans.* Carry and develop (offspring) in the womb. M19.
2 *verb intrans.* Develop in the womb; *fig.* undergo elaboration and refinement before being made public. M20.

Times The proposals . . have been gestating in the Department of Education and Science for the past year.

■ **ˈgestative** *adjective* = GESTATIONAL E19.

gestation /dʒɛˈsteɪʃ(ə)n/ *noun*. M16.
[ORIGIN Latin *gestatio(n-)*, from *gestat-* pa. ppl stem of *gestare* carry, carry in the womb, frequentative of *gerere* bear, carry: see -ATION.]
1 The action or an act of carrying or being carried (on horseback, in a carriage, etc.) as a form of exercise. Now *rare*. M16.
2 The action or process of carrying or being carried in the womb between conception and birth; the length of time for which an embryo or fetus has been developing in the womb. E17.
3 *fig.* The development of an idea, plan, etc., in the mind. L17.
■ **gestational** *adjective* of or pertaining to gestation L19.

gestatorial /dʒɛstəˈtɔːrɪəl/ *adjective*. M19.
[ORIGIN formed as GESTATORY + -AL¹.]
Designating a chair in which the Pope is carried on certain occasions.

gestatory /dʒɛˈsteɪt(ə)ri/ *adjective*. L17.
[ORIGIN Latin *gestatorius*, from *gestator* a person who carries, from *gestare*: see GESTATION, -ORY².]
†**1** Adapted for carrying or wearing. *rare*. L17–L19.
2 = GESTATIONAL. L19.

geste *noun* var. of GEST *noun*².

†**gesten** *verb* see GUESTEN *verb*.

†**gestening** *noun*. Also **gestning**. ME–L16.
[ORIGIN Prob. from Old Norse: cf. Old Swedish *gestning*, *gist-*, *gäst-*, from *gästa* lodge as a guest, from *gäster* (mod. *gäst*) = Old Norse *gestr* GUEST *noun*.]
Entertainment or lodging given to a guest; hospitality. Also, a feast, a banquet.

†**gester** *noun* var. of JESTER.

gestic /ˈdʒɛstɪk/ *adjective*. M18.
[ORIGIN from GEST *noun*² + -IC.]
Of or pertaining to gestures; consisting or full of gestures.

gesticulant /dʒɛˈstɪkjʊl(ə)nt/ *adjective*. *rare*. L19.
[ORIGIN Latin *gesticulant-* pres. ppl stem of *gesticulari* GESTICULATE: see -ANT¹.]
Gesticulating.

gesticular /dʒɛˈstɪkjʊlə/ *adjective*. M19.
[ORIGIN from Latin *gesticulus* (see GESTICULATE) + -AR¹.]
Of or pertaining to gesticulation.

gesticulate /dʒɛˈstɪkjʊleɪt/ *verb*. E17.
[ORIGIN Latin *gesticulat-* pa. ppl stem of *gesticulari*, from *gesticulus* dim. of *gestus* action, gesture: see -ATE³.]
1 *verb intrans.* Use lively and expressive movements of the limbs or body with or instead of speech. E17.

C. S. FORESTER It was natural when one spoke French to gesticulate, to indicate his men with a wave of the hand. M. ROBERTS A man . . gesticulating and coughing to catch her attention.

2 *verb trans.* Convey or express by such movements. E17.
■ **gesticulatingly** *adverb* in a gesticulating manner; with gesticulations: L19. **gesticulative** *adjective* given to or characterized by gesticulation L18. **gesticulator** *noun* L17. **gesticulatory** *adjective* consisting or full of gesticulation L18.

gesticulation /dʒɛˌstɪkjʊˈleɪʃ(ə)n/ *noun*. LME.
[ORIGIN Latin *gesticulatio(n-)*, formed as GESTICULATE: see -ATION.]
The action or an act of gesticulating.

gestion /ˈdʒɛstjən, -tʃ(ə)n/ *noun*. L16.
[ORIGIN Latin *gestio(n-)*, from *gest-* pa. ppl stem of *gerere* carry, carry on: see -ION.]
Performance, conduct, management. Formerly also, working order.

†**gestning** *noun* var. of GESTENING.

gestogen *noun* var. of GESTAGEN.

gesture /ˈdʒɛstʃə/ *noun & verb*. LME.
[ORIGIN medieval Latin *gestura*, from Latin *gerere* bear, carry, carry on, perform: see -URE.]
▸ **A** *noun*. †**1** Manner of carrying the body; carriage, deportment. LME–E19. ▸**b** (A) position, posture, or attitude of the body, esp. in prayer or worship. M16–E18.

BURKE The fashion of the countenance and the gesture of the body . . is so correspondent to this state of mind.

2 (A) movement of the body or limbs, now only as an expression of thought or feeling; the use of such movements as an expression of feeling or a rhetorical device. LME.

A. MILLER With a gesture of his head he indicates the open country. D. M. DAVIN A first-rate raconteur who was able to act out his stories with gesture and mimicry. M. AMIS She crinkled her nose—a gesture which in her indicated uncertainty.

3 An action performed as a courtesy, formality, or symbol to indicate an intention or evoke a response. E20.

J. RABAN He had offered me a room to stay in; a characteristically kind and open-handed gesture. A. STORR This was clearly a gesture rather than a seriously intended attempt at suicide.

▸ **B** *verb*. †**1** *verb trans.* Order the position or carriage of (the body, oneself). M16–M17.
2 *verb intrans.* Make or use a gesture or gestures. M16.

C. HAMPTON Carlos gestures and one of the others lays his gun down . . and gags her.

3 *verb trans.* Express or indicate (a thought or feeling) by a gesture or gestures. L16.
4 *verb trans.* Direct (a person) by a gesture or gestures. L19.

F. RAPHAEL Alma gestured Julia to her place.

■ **gestural** *adjective* E17. **gestureless** *adjective* M19. **gesturer** *noun* L19.

gesundheit /gɛˈzʌndhʌɪt, *foreign* gəˈzʊnthaɪt/ *interjection*. E20.
[ORIGIN German = health.]
Wishing good health, esp. to a person who has sneezed.

get /gɛt/ *noun*¹. See also GIT *noun*¹. ME.
[ORIGIN from GET *verb*.]
1 a Offspring; descendants; a child. Now only of animals. ME. ▸**b** A brat, a bastard (*Scot. & N. English*); a contemptible person, a fool, an idiot, (*dial. & slang*). E16.
2 Begetting, procreation. Now only of animals. ME.
3 Gain, booty, earnings. Long *obsolete* exc. *dial.* LME.
4 A getaway, a hasty retreat. Chiefly in ***do a get***, ***make a get***. *Austral. & NZ slang*. L19.
5 GAMES. An act of returning or retrieving a difficult ball; an act of making a difficult catch. E20.

get /dʒɛt/ *noun*². In senses 1 & 2 also †**jet**. ME.
[ORIGIN Old French *get* (mod. *jet*): see JESS *noun*.]
†**1** Fashion, style, mode, manner. ME–E16.
†**2** A device, a contrivance. Only in LME.
3 A jess for a hawk. *rare*. E17.

get *noun*³ var. of GETT.

get /gɛt/ *verb*. Also (now chiefly *US dial.* exc. in sense 36) **git** /gɪt/. Pres. pple **getting**. Pa. t. **got** /gɒt/, (*arch.*) **gat** /gat/; perf. also (*colloq.*) **got** (= has or have got). Pa. pple **got**, (now *N. Amer. & dial.* exc. *arch.* & in comb., *rare* in branch IV) **gotten** /ˈgɒt(ə)n/. ME.
[ORIGIN Old Norse *geta* obtain, beget, guess = base of Old English *begietan* BEGET, *forgietan* FORGET *verb*, from Germanic from Indo-European base also of Latin *praeda* booty, PREY *noun*, *praedium* estate, *praehendere* lay hold of, Greek *khandanein* (aorist *ekhadon*) hold, contain, be able.]
▸ **I 1** *verb trans.* Obtain as the result of effort or contrivance; procure, acquire for oneself or another; seek out and take, cause to come or be provided, fetch; prepare (a meal). (Foll. by indirect obj. or *for* a recipient or beneficiary.) ME. ▸**b** *verb trans.* Obtain in marriage, marry. Now *Scot. & N. English*. LME. ▸**c** *verb intrans.* Acquire wealth or property. Now *rare*. L16.

R. W. EMERSON Men are not born rich; and in getting wealth the man is generally sacrificed. E. A. FREEMAN It was all honourably gotten and was designed to be honourably spent. B. T. WASHINGTON The news was usually gotten from the . . man who was sent to the post-office for the mail. J. CONRAD I ran back to the verandah to get my hat. D. H. LAWRENCE Mellors went into the country and got work on a farm. W. S. MAUGHAM I could have got all the women I wanted in London. J. C. POWYS He . . got his own breakfast. J. KEROUAC Dean got a table, bought drinks. I. MURDOCH I got myself a reasonably sound education. P. ROTH An Army friend . . had gotten us tickets for a Tchaikovsky extravaganza.

2 *verb trans.* Come into possession of; be the recipient of. ME.

J. RHYS It's a great thrill getting your letters—so write again soon.

3 *verb trans.* Obtain as the proceeds of business or employment; earn; receive in payment. ME. ▸**b** *verb intrans.* Earn money, make a living. Now *rare*. M16.

ADDISON Methods for getting a livelihood in this strange country. H. JAMES He got about two dollars a sitting.
b WORDSWORTH Getting and spending, we lay waste our powers.

4 *verb trans.* Win or earn (something abstract, as love, credit, fame, etc.) by one's actions or character; obtain as a concession or favour; extract by insistence, entreaty, or inquiry. **ME.**

> STEELE I knocked and called, but could get no answer. V. WOOLF Required and got in the end an effort of attention. N. MOSLEY You committed suicide for love; but you did not get love because you were dead.

5 *verb trans.* Achieve, attain, gain, come to have, (a position of superiority (in ***get the better of***, ***get the upper hand of***, etc.); a desired state or quality; a feeling, an impression, etc.); (with noun of action) succeed in having (*a glance, a glimpse, (a) hold of*, etc.). **ME.** ▸**b** Win (a victory). Now *rare*. **LME.**

> T. SHADWELL It's nothing but a way of speaking, which young amorous fellows have gotten. D. HUME Their enemies . . had gotten possession of their sovereign's confidence. G. K. CHESTERTON For Rome was given to rule the world, And gat of it little joy. J. RHYS Get all the sleep you can my dear. G. VIDAL Occasionally they would come out . . to get a glimpse of me. A. BEATTIE I got the feeling he didn't like my prices.

get a grip on, ***get a kick out of***, ***get a shot at***, etc.

6 *verb trans.* Capture, get hold of, (a person, †a castle etc.). **ME.** ▸†**b** Take hold of in one's hands. **LME–L16.**

> SHAKES. *Coriol.* The plebeians have got your fellow tribune And hale him up and down. HOBBES And when the city Troy we shall have got.

7 *verb trans.* Procure by hunting or fishing, catch; (orig. *US*) (deliberately) kill or injure, shoot. **ME.**

> E. GLYN She did not hit any rabbits, but she got a gardener in the leg. S. BELLOW The person who charges me with this cruelty is not without prejudice toward me, he is out to get me.

8 *verb trans.* (Now usu. of an animal, esp. a stallion) beget, procreate, sire. **ME.**

> A. E. HOUSMAN Get you the sons your fathers got. T. FITZGEORGE-PARKER At stud, Hurry On . . got three Derby winners.

9 *verb trans.* Acquire by study or experience; learn (a lesson, †a language); commit to memory (esp. in ***get by heart***, ***get by rote***). **LME.**

> CHARLES CHURCHILL Without the least finesse of art He gets applause!—I wish he'd get his part. A. C. SWINBURNE In such wise I gat knowledge of the Gods. H. H. RICHARDSON The Getting of Wisdom.

10 *verb trans.* Arrive at, reach. Now *rare* or *obsolete*. **LME.**

11 *verb trans.* Have inflicted on one, suffer, (a fall, blow, defeat, etc.); receive by way of punishment or penalty. **LME.**

> V. WOOLF One got only a glare in the eye from looking at the line of the wall. R. K. NARAYAN Seven years . . is what one gets for murder only half-proved.

get the boot, ***get the chop***, ***get the sack***, etc.

12 *verb trans.* Obtain by way of profit; be benefited or advantaged to the extent of. **L15.** ▸†**b** *verb intrans.* Derive profit, be a gainer (*by*). **L16–M18.**

> G. GREENE One never got anything for nothing.

13 *verb trans.* Bring in as harvest; gather, carry home, (a crop). **E16.**

14 *verb trans.* SPORTS & GAMES. Gain and be credited with, score, (a goal, points, runs, etc.); make as a score; take (a wicket in cricket). **M16.**

15 *verb trans.* Obtain or ascertain as a result of calculation, logic, or experiment. **M16.**

> L. CARROLL By taking *x* as subject, we get 'all *x* are *y* prime'.

16 *verb trans.* Succeed in finding, locate; obtain an audible signal from, pick up (a broadcast signal); communicate with (a person or place) by telephone. **E17.**

> M. LOWRY Hugh . . turned the radio dial back and forth, trying to get San Antonio. P. G. WODEHOUSE He took up the receiver . . . 'I hear you've been trying to get me.'

17 *verb trans.* Contract, catch, (an illness etc.). **E17.**

> S. SONTAG He sickens . . . gets TB, and dies. J. MORTIMER Simeon Simcox got a dose of flu.

18 *verb trans.* Obtain by mining, extract (coal etc.). **M17.**

19 *verb trans.* **a** Puzzle, perplex, mystify, catch in argument. Chiefly in pa. t. or *pass. colloq.* **M19.** ▸**b** Worry, annoy, exercise. *colloq.* **M19.** ▸**c** Enthral, attract, appeal to; touch emotionally. *colloq.* **E20.**

> **a** W. DE LA MARE 'Why was it mistaken?' He shook his head . . . 'That's got me, miss.' **b** *Scouting* It's the 'not knowing' that gets them. **c** *People* As soon as you enter any jazz club the atmosphere gets you.

20 *verb trans.* Eat (a meal etc.). *colloq.* **L19.**

21 *verb trans.* Understand (a person or thing). *colloq.* **E20.** ▸**b** *verb intrans.* Grasp the point, understand. *colloq.* **M20.**

> T. DREISER Just what do you mean by that? . . I don't get you. J. HELLER You're doing a better job in your position than I'm doing in mine. Do you get what I mean? T. MALLON He got the jokes. **b** M. INNES Okay, okay. I get.

22 *verb trans.* Take as transport, catch (a train, bus, etc.). **M20.**

> M. FORSTER She went to get the last train home and missed it.

23 *verb trans.* Respond to, answer, (a telephone, doorbell, etc.). **M20.**

24 *verb trans.* Notice or look at (a person), esp. to criticize or ridicule. Usu. in *imper. colloq.* **M20.**

> *News Chronicle* If he is conceited, the girls mutter *get yew!*

▸**II** *verb trans.* with compl. (see also specialized senses below).

25 With preposition or adverb (phr.). Succeed in bringing, sending, placing, or putting (another person, (*arch.*) oneself, a thing) *to, from, into, out of* a place, etc., *through, over* a space, etc.; succeed in bringing (another person, oneself, a thing) into or out of a specified position or state; incur or suffer the coming or bringing of (a person or thing) into a specified position or state. **ME.**

> HENRY FIELDING Get you both about your business. B. JOWETT A difficulty into which I have got myself. SCOTT FITZGERALD We . . got her into a cold bath. DAY LEWIS Knos . . was always getting bees in her hair.

26 With inf. Induce or prevail on (a person) *to do* (†*do*); cause (a person) *to do*. **LME.** ▸†**b** With pass. inf. Cause to undergo the specified action. *rare*. **L16–M18.**

> P. ROTH Lifting his voice so as to get Andrea to hear him. S. CHITTY Only by speaking to them like 'an angel' could Gwen John get them to go away.

27 With pa. pple. Cause or succeed in causing a specified action to be done to (a person or thing) or a specified result to happen to (a person or thing). **E16.**

> T. JEFFERSON I got my right wrist dislocated. W. GOLDING Have you time to get your hair cut?

28 With adjective. Succeed in bringing (a person or thing) to be in the specified state. **L16.**

> B. EMECHETA She was very slow in getting herself pregnant again. W. WHARTON Annastina's getting a bed ready for me.

29 With pres. pple. Cause (a person or thing) to be *doing*. **E20.**

▸**III** *verb intrans.* (chiefly with compl.: see also specialized senses below).

30 With preposition or adverb (phr.). Succeed in coming, going, or bringing oneself *to, from, into, out of* a place, etc., *through, over* a space, etc.; attain or come *to* an end aimed at or condition towards which progress has been made. **ME.**

> T. JEFFERSON The scene has not yet got to its height. T. HARDY The cow had got out of the paddock. E. HEMINGWAY You have to get there on time. P. MORTIMER I got clumsily to my feet.

31 With inf. Come or happen *to be, to do*; have or secure an opportunity *to do*; be allowed *to do*. **L16.** ▸**b** With impers. *it* & *to be (so) that*: reach the point or stage where, be or become such that. Cf. sense 35 below. *N. Amer. colloq.* **L19.**

> M. LAVIN It gets to be a habit with us fellows. L. KAUFMAN It isn't every day that an old man gets to meet his daughter's beau. *Wall Street Journal* If his salary doubles to $48,000, he gets to keep $18,074. K. VONNEGUT That is how you get to be a writer. A. BROOKNER One gets to fear one's own boredom.

32 With adjective or equivalent. Become, succeed in becoming, make oneself; (with compar. & superl.) grow. **L16.**

> SCOTT FITZGERALD The sun's getting colder every year. S. BRILL We're finished until we or some local prosecutor gets lucky. J. KEROUAC Terry and I . . got ready to hit the sack. J. GATHORNE-HARDY It got too much for them as they got older.

get clear of, ***get rid of***, ***get shot of***, etc.

33 With pa. pple. ▸**a** With pple of trans. verb. Cause a specified action or result to be done to oneself; have a specified action or result happen to oneself; come to be the object of a specified action. Freq. as pass.-forming aux. where a continuous state is not intended. **M17.** ▸**b** With pple of intrans. verb. Accomplish or complete the specified action. Now *colloq.* **E18.**

> C. P. SNOW He had just got engaged. ISAIAH BERLIN Nothing ever gets articulated save enormous, sonorous generalisations.

34 With pres. pple. Come to be *doing*; *Scot.* find an opportunity for *doing*. **E18.**

> J. RUSKIN I got thinking about the dry bed of the stream.

35 With adverbial clause introduced by *so, so as (so's), so that, that, where*: reach the point or stage where, be or become such that. Cf. sense 31b above. *colloq.* (chiefly *N. Amer.*). **M19.**

> R. LARDNER I got so as I could beat him. SCOTT FITZGERALD My ambition is to get where I need write no more but only novels. J. STEINBECK Fella can get so he misses the noise of a saw mill. *Daily Telegraph* It is getting that you can't wear a badge . . for fear of being beaten up.

36 Leave, go away. Freq. in *imper. colloq.* (orig. *US*). **M19.**

> D. BUCKINGHAM I want you out of the way—so git. K. GILES Anybody in a room either gets or pays for another twenty-four hours.

37 Manage to go, make it. Chiefly *Scot.* **L19.**

▸**IV** Special perfect uses.

38 ***has got***, ***have got*** (colloq. simply ***got***), has or have, possess(es). **E17.** ▸**b** ***has got to***, ***have got to*** (also simply ***got to***), has or have to, must (*be*). Cf. GOTTA. *colloq.* **M19.**

> V. WOOLF Why be always trying to bring up some feeling she had not got? E. BAGNOLD Got any boy friends? G. GREENE He hadn't got that courage. G. PALEY They got it in for men. **b** A. CHRISTIE Got to go up to Scotland to-night. J. P. DONLEAVY I've got to go and see my tutor.

– PHRASES: (A selection of cross-refs. only is included: see esp. other nouns.) ***get a person's goat***: see GOAT *noun*. ***get a person's gruel***: see GRUEL *noun*. **get better** recover from illness. ***get cracking***: see CRACK *verb*. **get done (with)** have done (with), finish. **get going** (*a*) *verb phr. intrans.* begin; become talkative or animated; begin working or proceeding steadily, settle into a steady course; (*b*) *verb phr. trans.* start; get (a person or thing) into a steady course; get (a person) excited. †**get ground** make progress, advance. **get hers**, **get his** *slang* (of an individual) be killed (cf. ***get theirs*** below). ***get hold of***: see HOLD *noun*[1]. **get it** *spec.* (*a*) be successful, get what one wants, (freq. iron. in ***I wish you may get it***, ***don't you wish you may get it***); (*b*) understand a joke, grasp a point made; ***get it in one***: see ONE *adjective, noun, & pronoun*; (*c*) be killed or injured; ***get it in the neck***: see NECK *noun*[1]; (*d*) get into trouble; also **get it hot (and strong)**; (*e*) answer a telephone, doorbell, etc. ***get knotted***: see KNOTTED. ***get lost***: see LOST *adjective*. ***get NOWHERE***. **get oneself gone** *arch.* go away, leave. ***get religion***: see RELIGION. ***get STUFFED***. **get theirs** *slang* (of two or more people) be killed. **get to know** become personally acquainted with (a person, place, etc.). **get well** recover from illness. **get with child** make pregnant. ***give as good as one gets***: see GIVE *verb*. **have got it bad(ly)** *slang* be infatuated, be in love. ***have got something***: see SOMETHING *pronoun & noun*. ***play hard to get***: see HARD *adverb*.

– WITH ADVERBS IN SPECIALIZED SENSES: **get about** (*a*) go from place to place; visit many places; move about; begin to walk after an illness etc.; (*b*) (of a rumour, news, etc.) be circulated, esp. orally. **get abroad** *arch.* = ***get about*** (b) above. ***get across***: see ACROSS *adverb* 2. **get ahead** make progress, meet with success. **get along** (*a*) proceed, progress, advance, meet with success; manage, cope, fare, (*well* etc., *without*); (*b*) coexist or communicate in a specified manner (*together, with*); live harmoniously, be or remain on good terms (*together, with*); (*c*) ***get along with you!***, go away!, be off! nonsense! **get around** (*a*) get about, go round; (*b*) get round to. **get away** (*a*) escape, succeed in departing; manage to go away (*from, into, to* a place), esp. for rest or recreation; ***get away from***, disregard, avoid the fact of, (usu. in neg. contexts); ***get away from it all***, escape all demands and responsibilities, go away from one's everyday environment, tasks, and worries; (*b*) ***get away (with you)!*** (*colloq.*), expr. incredulity or astonishment; (*c*) ***get away with***, succeed in winning or stealing; succeed in (an act) without detection, criticism, or punishment, accomplish with impunity; ***get away with murder***, get away with anything, be able to do anything one wants; (*d*) CRICKET hit (the ball) so as to make a run or runs; (*e*) begin; (of a plant) begin to grow vigorously or well. **get back** (*a*) return, arrive home; (of a statement etc.) come to the notice of an interested party etc. (foll. by *to* the person(s) concerned); (*b*) recover (something lost); ***get one's own back (on)*** (*colloq.*), ***get some of one's own back (on)*** (*colloq.*), get revenge (on), get even (with); (*c*) ***get back at*** (*colloq.*), retaliate against; (*d*) ***get back to*** (*colloq.*), contact (a person) again later. **get by** *colloq.* (just) manage or cope, be adequate, do enough; pass or be acceptable *as*; get away *with*. **get down** (*a*) succeed in coming or going down; alight; (esp. of a child) leave the table; (*b*) succeed in bringing or lifting down; swallow (food etc.); (*c*) record (something) in writing; (*d*) ***get down to***, begin work on, turn one's attention seriously to, settle down to; consider the essentials or fundamentals of; (*e*) *colloq.* depress, weary; (*f*) *US slang* be successful, fulfil one's potential, participate fully, achieve mental harmony. **get in** (*a*) make one's way in; arrive at a destination, arrive home; gain entrance or admission; *slang* (of a man) have sexual intercourse; ***get in there*** (slang), take positive action, get to work; (*b*) succeed in bringing or placing (something) in; bring home, gather in, (a crop); collect (money owed); buy in, acquire a stock of; call in (a person, firm, etc.) to perform a specific function; gain admission or membership for; plant, sow; ***get one's hand in***: see HAND *noun*; (*c*) ***get in with***, become friendly with, gain intimacy or favour with, cultivate the acquaintance of; NAUTICAL come close up to; (*d*) be elected to an office, parliament etc.; obtain membership of an institution; obtain a place at a college, university; (*e*) enter a vehicle; (*f*) succeed in doing, have time for (an activity); fit (work etc.) into a given time; succeed in delivering (a blow etc.); succeed in interposing (a comment etc.); *colloq.* allow or experience the lapse of (a period of time); ***get a word in (edgeways)***: see WORD *noun*; (*g*) ***get in bad***, ***get in wrong*** (*slang*), incur dislike, get or bring into disfavour or trouble (*with*); ***get in good***, inspire liking, come or bring into favour (*with*). **get off** (*a*) escape, start (on a journey, in a race, etc.), succeed in leaving or setting off; *slang* stop having to use drugs etc.; ***get off on the right foot***, ***get off on the wrong foot***: see FOOT *noun*; ***get off to a good start***, ***get off to a poor start***, etc., begin well, poorly, etc.; (*b*) be acquitted or pardoned; be let off *lightly* etc., *with* or *for* a specified loss or penalty; procure acquittal, pardon, or a slight penalty for (a person); (*c*) get (a ship) under way; send off (on a journey, in a race, etc.); *arch. colloq.* marry off (a female dependant); dispatch, post, (a letter etc.); (*d*) remove, take off; (*e*) commit to memory, learn; (*f*) dismount from a horse, bicycle, etc.; alight or disembark from a bus, train, aeroplane, etc.; ***tell a person where to get off***, ***tell a person where he or she gets off*** (*colloq.*), rebuke a person for interference or presumption; (*g*) succeed in uttering (esp. a joke); (*h*) (cause to) go to sleep; (*i*) *colloq.* become on friendly or amorous terms *with*, establish a romantic or sexual relationship *with*; (*j*) *Jazz slang* improvise skilfully; (*k*) *imper.* (*colloq.*) expr. incredulity or astonishment; (*l*) *slang* become intoxicated on drugs; achieve sexual satisfaction, experience an orgasm; ***get off on***, be excited or aroused by, enjoy. **get on** (*a*) put on (clothes), don; ***get one's skates on***: see SKATE *noun*[2]; (*b*) advance, make progress, prosper, succeed, (*with*); fare (*with*); pursue one's course, continue with or *with* one's activities; manage *without*; (*c*) be able to conduct relations (*together, with*) in a specified manner or to a specified degree; agree or live sociably (*together, with*); (*d*) acquire, display, (pace);

G

get a move on: see MOVE *noun*; (*e*) *getting on for*, *getting on to*, approaching, coming close to, (a specified age, time, number, etc.); *getting on*, becoming old (more fully *getting on in years*, *getting on in life*, etc.), (of time) becoming late; (*f*) mount on to a bus, train, etc.; (*g*) *get on to* (*colloq.*), succeed in understanding, become aware of (a fact); get into communication with, get in touch with; begin or bring round to discussing (a subject); (*h*) *colloq.* take or bring oneself *off*, *up*, etc. (usu. in *imper.*); (*i*) **get it on** (*US slang*), give oneself up to an activity, enjoy oneself; become elated or intoxicated (*with*); have sexual intercourse (*with*). **get out** (*a*) leave a place of confinement, escape, leave one's house; become known; alight from a vehicle etc.; in *imper.* (*colloq.*) go away!, be off!, nonsense!; *get out from under*: see UNDER *adverb*; (*b*) take from a place of confinement or storage, take out, bring out; elicit (information); publish (a book etc.); succeed in uttering; succeed in solving or finishing (a puzzle etc.); *get one's finger out*: see FINGER *noun*; (*c*) dismiss or be dismissed at cricket; (*d*) *get out of*, issue or escape from, leave; alight from; go beyond (reach, sight, etc.); evade, avoid, (an act, *doing*); abandon (a habit) gradually; elicit, obtain, or extract from; *get a rise out of*: see RISE *noun*; *get out of bed on the wrong side*: see BED *noun*; *get out of hand*: see HAND *noun*. **get outside of** = *get outside* below. **get over** (*a*) succeed in reaching or bringing to the other side; cross over; move over; (*b*) finish; bring (esp. a troublesome task) to an end; *get it over with*, perform a troublesome or unwelcome task, endure an unwelcome experience; (*c*) communicate successfully, get across; *US slang* be successful. **get round** (*a*) get about, go round; (*b*) *arch.* recover from illness, get well; (*c*) *get round to*, find the time or occasion for (an act, *doing*). **get through** (*a*) reach or bring to a destination; (of legislation) be passed by a legislative body; ensure the passage of (legislation etc.); (*b*) succeed in an examination or course; (*c*) make contact by radio or telephone; (*d*) *get through with*, succeed in accomplishing or enduring, finish with; (*e*) *get through to*, reach the attention or understanding of (a person). **get together** (*a*) collect (persons or things); gather together; meet, esp. to confer; (*b*) *slang* put in order, organize, harmonize; *get it together*, *get one's act together*, bring some order or purpose into one's life, start performing well; *get one's head together*, overcome emotional difficulties or inhibitions. **get up** (*a*) rise; raise oneself, esp. to a standing posture; rise from bed; climb up; mount, esp. on horseback; (of fire, wind, the sea) begin to be violent, increase in force; (of game) rise from cover; (of a cricket ball) rise sharply from the pitch; *imper.* (as a command to a horse) go! go ahead! move more quickly! (see also GIDDY-UP); *get up and go*, (*US*) *get up and get*, start moving quickly or acting energetically; (*b*) come close (*arch.*); come close *to*, come up *to*; (*c*) organize, set on foot; make ready; make presentable, arrange the appearance of (hair, oneself), produce (a play, a book, etc.) in a specified manner; (*d*) *arch.* make good, recover, (arrears etc.); (*e*) raise, lift up; produce or build up (speed etc.); work up, create in oneself, (a factitious emotion); acquire knowledge of (a subject) for a special purpose or by a special effort; *get a person's back up*: see BACK *noun*[1]; *get it up* (*slang*), get an erection of the penis, have sexual intercourse (*with* a woman); *get the wind up*: see WIND *noun*[1]; *get up steam*: see STEAM *noun*.

– WITH PREPOSITIONS IN SPECIALIZED SENSES: **get across** — *colloq.* annoy, get on the wrong side of. **get around** — circumvent, get round. **get at** — (*a*) reach, gain access to, get hold of; (*b*) find out, ascertain, learn; (*c*) *colloq.* attack, taunt, try to upset (a person); (*d*) *slang* tamper with, bribe, try to influence; (*e*) start work on, turn one's attention to; (*f*) *colloq.* imply, mean, try to say, (usu. with *what* as obj.). **get by** — *colloq.* succeed in getting past. **get from** — †(*a*) escape from; (*b*) inherit (esp. a characteristic or habit) from, derive or develop in imitation of. **get inside** — penetrate, investigate closely; achieve a deep or intimate understanding of. **get into** — (*a*) come to be in, result in being in, (a specified state or condition); *get into one's stride*: see STRIDE *noun*; *get into the act*: see ACT *noun* 7c; *get into trouble*: see TROUBLE *noun*; (*b*) make one's way into, gain admittance to; (*c*) *colloq.* put on (boots, clothes); (*d*) become occupied, interested, absorbed, or involved in; (*e*) get knowledge of; (*f*) take possession of, cause to behave in an extraordinary way; (*g*) (of alcoholic drink) affect, confuse (one's head etc.); (*h*) have sexual intercourse with (a woman); (*i*) *get it into one's head that*, come to think, be convinced that. **get off** — (*a*) dismount from (a horse, bicycle, etc.); alight or disembark from (a bus, train, aeroplane, etc.); (*b*) obtain release from (an engagement etc.); (*c*) stop having to use (drugs etc.); (*d*) not remain on, remove oneself from on top of; leave, deviate from (a subject etc.); *get off a person's back*: see BACK *noun*[1]; *get off it* (colloq.), stop saying or doing such things, come off it; *get off the ground*: see GROUND *noun*; (*e*) remove or detach from; *get off one's chest*: see CHEST *noun*. **get on** — (*a*) place oneself on, mount on to (a horse, bicycle, train, etc.); *get on a person's nerves*: see NERVE *noun*, *get on a person's wick*: see WICK *noun*[1]; *get on the telephone*, *get on the phone*, make a telephone call; (*b*) rise on (one's feet or legs) to speak in public; (*c*) begin or bring round to discussing (a subject); get (a person) on to (a subject); (*d*) find out to the disadvantage or detriment of (a person); (*e*) lay or place (something) on; have or develop (something) on; *get one's hands on*: see HAND *noun*; *get on the brain*: see BRAIN *noun*; *get the jump on*: see JUMP *noun*[1]. **get onto** *colloq.* = *get on to* above. **get outside** — *slang* eat, consume. **get over** — (*a*) overcome, surmount (a difficulty); cease to be troubled or surprised by; recover from (an illness, shock, loss, etc.); (*b*) travel over, cover, (a distance); (*c*) accomplish (a task); (*d*) *slang* take advantage of, circumvent. **get round** — (*a*) cajole, win round; (*b*) evade. **get through** — (*a*) bring to an end, reach the end of; spend (money); (*b*) (of a legislative bill etc.) be passed by (a legislative body); (*c*) while away (time etc.); (*d*) be successful in, pass, (an examination or course). **get to** — (*a*) reach, arrive at; *get to a point where*, *get to a place where*, *get to the point where*, *get to the place where*, *get where* (*US colloq.*) = sense 35 above; *get to the bottom of*: see BOTTOM *noun*; *where a person has got to*, where an expected person is, what has happened to a person who should be present; (*b*) begin (an activity, *doing*), settle down to; (*c*) affect emotionally, upset; worry, depress; (*d*) *slang* tamper with, bribe, try to influence. **get upon** — = *get on* above. **get with** — *slang* become involved or absorbed in; become in tune with, reach harmony with. †**get within** — succeed in coming within the defences of (an adversary).

– COMB.: **get-at-able** *adjective* accessible, reachable, able to be got at; **get-rich-quick** *adjective* concerned (esp. exclusively) with the rapid accumulation of wealth; **get-well** *adjective* designating a card or message wishing a full recovery to a sick person.

geta /ˈgeɪtə/ *noun pl.* L19.
[ORIGIN Japanese.]
Japanese wooden shoes with a thong to pass between the first (big) toe and the second toe.

Getae /ˈdʒɛtʌɪ, ˈgɛtʌɪ/ *noun pl.* E19.
[ORIGIN Latin from Greek *Getai*.]
An ancient people inhabiting a region corresponding to parts of Bulgaria and Romania.

Getan /ˈdʒɛt(ə)n, ˈgɛt(ə)n/ *adjective & noun.* L16.
[ORIGIN formed as GETAWAY + -AN.]
▸ **A** *adjective.* = GETIC *adjective.* L16.
▸ **B** *noun.* A member of the Getae. E20.

getaway /ˈgɛtəweɪ/ *noun & adjective.* M19.
[ORIGIN from *get away* s.v. GET *verb*.]
▸ **A** *noun.* An act of getting away; an escape, esp. after a crime. Freq. in *make a getaway*, *make one's getaway*. M19.
▸ **B** *adjective.* Designating a vehicle, boat, etc., in which to get away or make a getaway. M20.

get-go /ˈgɛtgəʊ/ *noun. colloq.* (chiefly *N. Amer.*). M20.
[ORIGIN from *get going* s.v. GET *verb*.]
The very beginning.

M. NORMAN I told her from the get-go that I meant it.

Gethsemane /gɛθˈsɛməni/ *noun.* E20.
[ORIGIN A garden on the Mount of Olives, scene of the agony of Christ (*Matthew* 26:36–46), late Latin (Vulgate) *Gethsemani*, Greek *Gethsēmanē*, from Aramaic *gaṯ šamnē* oil press.]
A scene or occasion of spiritual or mental anguish.

Getic /ˈdʒɛtɪk, ˈgɛtɪk/ *adjective & noun.* M17.
[ORIGIN Latin *Geticus* from GETAE: see -IC.]
▸ **A** *adjective.* Of or pertaining to the Getae or their language; *loosely.* Thracian. M17.
▸ **B** *noun.* The language of the Getae. M20.

get-off /ˈgɛtɒf/ *noun.* M19.
[ORIGIN from *get off* s.v. GET *verb*.]
1 An evasion, a subterfuge. M19.
2 A take-off by an aeroplane etc. *rare.* E20.
3 A skilful improvisation or break in jazz. *slang.* M20.

get-out /ˈgɛtaʊt/ *noun.* M19.
[ORIGIN from *get out* s.v. GET *verb*.]
1 *as get-out*, *like get-out*, *as all get-out*, *like all get-out*, to the highest degree, with the utmost vigour. *slang.* M19.
2 A means of evasion; a withdrawal. *colloq.* L19.
3 *THEATRICAL.* Orig., the ability of a touring company to pay all expenses and move on. Now usu., the total weekly cost of a production. M20.

gett /gɛt/ *noun.* Also **get**. L19.
[ORIGIN Hebrew.]
A Jewish bill of divorce, in prescribed form; a divorce by such a bill.

gettable /ˈgɛtəb(ə)l/ *adjective.* M16.
[ORIGIN from GET *verb* + -ABLE.]
That can be got.

getter /ˈgɛtə/ *noun & verb.* LME.
[ORIGIN from GET *verb* + -ER[1].]
▸ **A** *noun.* **1** A person who gets or obtains something, esp. wealth; a person who or (now only) an animal which begets offspring. Also with adverbs, *getter-in*, *getter-up*, etc., a person who gets in, up, etc. See also GO-GETTER. LME.
2 *spec.* A coalminer who extracts the coal after a seam has been undercut. M19.
3 A substance used to remove residual gas from an evacuated vessel. E20.
▸ **B** *verb trans.* Remove (gas) by means of a getter; evacuate (a vessel) by means of a getter. E20.

getting /ˈgɛtɪŋ/ *verbal noun.* ME.
[ORIGIN from GET *verb* + -ING[1].]
1 The action of GET *verb*. Also with adverbs, as *getting-in*, *getting-out*, *getting-up*, etc. ME.
2 *sing.* & (usu.) in *pl.* Acquisitions, gains, earnings. *arch.* LME.

get-together /ˈgɛt-təgɛðə/ *noun. colloq.* E20.
[ORIGIN from *get together* s.v. GET *verb*.]
An informal social gathering, a sociable meeting.
■ **get-togetherness** *noun* tendency to get together, sociability M20.

Getulian /gɪˈtjuːlɪən/ *adjective & noun.* Also **Gaet-**. L16.
[ORIGIN from Latin *Gaetuli*, *Getuli* from Greek *Gaitouloi* perh. from a Berber base.]
▸ **A** *adjective.* Designating or pertaining to an ancient nomadic Berber people inhabiting the desert region south and east of Numidia. L16.
▸ **B** *noun.* A member of this people. E17.

get-up /ˈgɛtʌp/ *noun.* M19.
[ORIGIN from *get up* s.v. GET *verb*.]
1 A style of equipment or costume; an outfit. M19.
2 A style of production or finish, esp. of a book. M19.
3 Energy, enterprise, determination. Also *get-up-and-go*, (*US*) *get-up-and-get*. M19.

geum /ˈdʒiːəm/ *noun.* M16.
[ORIGIN mod. Latin (see below), var. of Latin *gaeum*.]
Any of various plants of the genus *Geum*, of the rose family, which includes herb bennet, *G. urbanum*, and water avens, *G. rivale*.

GeV *abbreviation.*
Gigaelectronvolt.

gewgaw /ˈgjuːgɔː/ *noun & adjective.* ME.
[ORIGIN Uncertain: perh. redupl. of Old French *gogue* game, joke or from GAW *verb*.]
▸ **A** *noun.* A (gaudy) plaything or ornament; *fig.* a (showy) worthless thing or person. ME.

J. P. HENNESSY A boutique, to sell gewgaws, bric-à-brac and imitation jewellery.

▸ **B** *attrib.* or as *adjective.* Resembling a gewgaw; *fig.* showy, worthless. M17.
■ **gewgawed** *adjective* ornamented with gewgaws L19.

Gewürztraminer /gəˈvʊətstrə,miːnə/ *noun.* M20.
[ORIGIN German, from *Gewürz* spice + TRAMINER.]
A variety of Traminer grape grown esp. in the Rhine valley, Alsace, and Austria; the mildly spicy white wine made from this grape.

gey /geɪ, gʌɪ/ *adverb & adjective. Scot.* E18.
[ORIGIN Var. of GAY *adjective & adverb*. Cf. similar use of JOLLY *adverb*.]
▸ **A** *adverb.* Very; considerably. Also *gey and*. E18.

J. BUCHAN They'll be gey sick o' Antrobus by then.

▸ **B** *adjective.* (Of quantity) good, considerable; (of quality etc.) fine, excellent. E19.

L. G. GIBBON A gey man in Kinraddie, and maybe one of the gentry. A. RANSOME It's brought a gey lot down for me to clear.

geyser /ˈgiːzə, *in sense 1 also* ˈgʌɪ-/ *noun.* L18.
[ORIGIN Icelandic *Geysir*, name of a particular hot spring in Iceland, rel. to *geysa* (Old Norse *geysa*) gush.]
1 A hot spring (usu. in a volcanic area) which intermittently spouts steam and water; *fig.* a jet or stream of liquid etc. L18.

T. WILLIAMS The bottle cap pops off and a geyser of foam shoots up.

2 An apparatus connected to a bath, sink, etc., for rapidly heating water for washing. L19.
■ **geyseric** *adjective* pertaining to or of the nature of a geyser L19.

geyserite /ˈgiːz(ə)rʌɪt, ˈgʌɪ-/ *noun.* E19.
[ORIGIN from GEYSER + -ITE[1].]
MINERALOGY. A siliceous usu. opaline sinter occurring in thermal springs and geysers.

G5 *abbreviation.* Also (*US*) **G-5**.
Group of Five.

GG *abbreviation.*
Governor General.

ghaffir /ˈgɑːfɪə/ *noun.* E19.
[ORIGIN Arabic dial. *gafir*.]
In the Middle East: an Egyptian police officer; a guard, a watchman.

ghaghra /ˈgagrə, ˈgɑːgrɑː/ *noun.* Also **ghagra**. M19.
[ORIGIN Hindi *ghāghrā*, from Sanskrit *gharghara* gurgle, rattle.]
In the Indian subcontinent: a long full skirt, often decorated with embroidery, mirrors, or bells.

ghan /gan/ *noun. Austral. slang.* E20.
[ORIGIN from AF)GHAN.]
1 An Afghan or Muslim immigrant to Australia, *esp.* one who drives or breeds camels. E20.
2 *the Ghan*, a train that runs between Adelaide and Alice Springs. M20.

Ghanaian /gɑːˈneɪən/ *noun & adjective.* M20.
[ORIGIN from *Ghana* (see below) + -IAN.]
▸ **A** *noun.* A native or inhabitant of Ghana, a country on the coast of W. Africa known until 1957 as the Gold Coast. M20.
▸ **B** *adjective.* Of, pertaining to, or characteristic of Ghana. M20.

ghap /gɑːp/ *noun.* Also **guaap**. E19.
[ORIGIN Nama.]
Any of several succulent southern African plants of the genus *Trichocaulon* (family Asclepiadaceae), formerly used by the Nama as a thirst-quencher.

gharana /gəˈrɑːnə/ *noun.* M20.
[ORIGIN Hindi *gharānā* family.]
INDIAN MUSIC. A school of players who practise a particular style of interpretation.

gharial /ˈgarɪɑːl, gʌrɪˈɑːl, ˈgɛːrɪəl/ *noun.* Also **gavial** /ˈgeɪvɪəl/. E19.
[ORIGIN Hindi *ghariyāl*; form with *-v-* from French, prob. alt. by scribal error.]
A slender-snouted fish-eating crocodilian of the Indus and Ganges basins, *Gavialis gangeticus* (more fully ***Indian gharial***); any slender-snouted crocodilian related to or resembling this, esp. *Tomistoma schlegeli* of SE Asia (more fully ***false gharial***, ***Malayan gharial***).

gharry /ˈgɑːri, ˈgari/ *noun*. *Indian*. E19.
[ORIGIN Hindi *gāṛī*.]
A horse-drawn carriage available for hire.

Ghassulian /gaˈsuːlɪən/ *adjective & noun*. M20.
[ORIGIN French *Ghassoulien*, from Teleilat el-*Ghassul* (see below): see -IAN.]
ARCHAEOLOGY. ▸**A** *adjective*. Designating or pertaining to a Chalcolithic culture of which remains have been found at Teleilat el-Ghassul, near Jericho in the Jordan valley. M20.
▸**B** *noun*. A person who belonged to this culture. M20.

ghast /gɑːst/ *adjective*. *arch.* or *poet.* E17.
[ORIGIN Back-form. from GHASTFUL or GHASTLY.]
= GHASTLY *adjective*.

ghastful /ˈgɑːstfʊl, -f(ə)l/ *adjective*. *arch.* Orig. †**gastful**. LME.
[ORIGIN from GAST *verb* + -FUL. Cf. GHASTLY.]
1 Full of fear, scared. LME.
2 Dreadful, terrible. LME.
■ †**ghastfully** *adverb* LME–E18. †**ghastfulness** *noun* LME–L16.

ghastly /ˈgɑːs(t)li/ *adjective & adverb*. Orig. †**gastly**. ME.
[ORIGIN from GAST *verb* + -LY[1]. The spelling with *gh-* (after GHOST *noun*) became current after Spenser.]
▸**A** *adjective*. **1** Orig., causing real terror. Now, horrible, frightful; very unpleasant. ME. ▸**b** Objectionable, shocking, tasteless. *colloq.* M19.

J. WILSON The ghastly dreams, That haunt the parting soul. A. J. P. TAYLOR I had made a ghastly mistake. K. CROSSLEY-HOLLAND The ghastly rotting smell rose towards him. **b** A. BURGESS A ghastly metal model of Blackpool Tower. A. N. WILSON The ghastly little trade unionist.. whingeing and whining.. for more money.

2 Like a ghost or corpse; deathly pale, wan; very ill; (of a smile, laugh, etc.) painfully forced. L16.

J. M. COETZEE His face is ghastly.. his wounds plainly still cause him pain. A. THWAITE Feeling worn and ghastly after the steamer voyage.

†**3** Full of fear. L16–M17.

SHAKES. *Temp.* Why are you drawn? Wherefore this ghastly looking?

▸**B** *adverb*. **1** Frightfully, horribly. Formerly also, in a frightened manner. L16.

SHAKES. *2 Hen. VI* His eye-balls.. Staring full ghastly like a strangled man.

2 Deathly, deathlike. M17.

W. IRVING Her face was ghastly pale.

■ **ghastlily** *adverb* E19. **ghastliness** *noun* L16.

ghat /gɑːt, gɔːt/ *noun*. *Indian*. Also **ghaut**. E17.
[ORIGIN Hindi *ghāṭ*.]
1 In *pl.* & †*sing.* Either of two mountain chains running parallel to the east and west coasts of southern India. E17.
2 A mountain pass. L17.
3 A flight of steps leading to a riverbank; a landing place. L18.

J. G. FARRELL The devout.. stood on the steps of the bathing ghat.

4 In full ***burning ghat***. A level place at the top of a river ghat where Hindus cremate their dead. L19.

J. LAHIRI In Calcutta the burning ghats are the most forbidden of places.

ghawazee *noun* pl. of GHAZEEYEH.

ghazal /ˈgazal/ *noun*. Also **-el**. L18.
[ORIGIN Persian from Arabic *ġazal*.]
A usu. amatory Arabic, Turkish, Urdu, or (esp.) Persian lyric poem or song characterized by a limited number of stanzas and the recurrence of the same rhyme.

ghazeeyeh /gəˈziːjeɪ/ *noun*. Pl. **ghawazee** /gəˈwɑːzi/. L18.
[ORIGIN Arabic *ġāziya*, pl. *ġawāzī*.]
In Egypt, a dancing girl. Usu. in *pl.*

ghazi /ˈgɑːzi/ *noun*. Also (as a title) **G-**. Pl. **-is**. M18.
[ORIGIN Arabic *al-ġāzī* active pple of *ġazā* raid, invade, foray.]
In the Middle East: a champion, esp. of Muslims against non-Muslims; a dedicated Muslim fighter. Freq. as an honorific title.

GHB *abbreviation*.
PHARMACOLOGY. (Sodium) gamma-hydroxybutyrate, CH_2OH-$(CH_2)_2COONa$, a designer drug with anaesthetic properties.

ghee /giː/ *noun*. Also **ghi**. M17.
[ORIGIN Hindi *ghī*, from Sanskrit *ghṛta* pa. pple of *ghṛ-* sprinkle.]
Indian clarified butter made from the milk of a buffalo or cow.

Gheg /gɛg/ *noun & adjective*. Also **Geg**. E19.
[ORIGIN Albanian *Geg*.]
▸**A** *noun*. Pl. **-s**, same. A member of a people of northern Albania; the language spoken by this people. E19.
▸**B** *attrib.* or as *adjective*. Of or pertaining to the Ghegs or their language. M19.

Ghent /gɛnt/ *adjective*. M19.
[ORIGIN A city in Belgium (= Flemish *Gent*, French *Gand*).]
Designating any of a number of hybrid azaleas first raised at Ghent between 1804 and 1834.

†**ghenting** *noun*. L17–M18.
[ORIGIN from GHENT + -ING[1].]
A kind of linen originally made in Ghent.

gherao /gɛˈraʊ/ *noun & verb*. M20.
[ORIGIN from Hindi *gherna* surround, besiege.]
▸**A** *noun*. Pl. **-os**. In the Indian subcontinent: a form of protest or harassment in labour disputes whereby employers etc. are prevented by workers from leaving the place of work until their claims have been granted. M20.
▸**B** *verb trans.* Detain (a person) in this manner. M20.

gherkin /ˈgəːkɪn/ *noun*. E17.
[ORIGIN Dutch (*au*)*gurkje* dim. of *a*(*u*)*gurk*, *gurk*, ult. from Slavonic word repr. also by Polish *ogórek*, Russian *ogurets* cucumber, derivs. with dim. suffix of late Greek *aggourion* (mod. *aggouri*).]
A small variety of cucumber, or a young green cucumber, used for pickling.

ghetto /ˈgɛtəʊ/ *noun & verb*. E17.
[ORIGIN from Italian: perh. abbreviation of *borghetto* dim. of *borgo* BOROUGH, or from *getto* foundry, where the first ghetto established in Venice, in 1516, was sited.]
▸**A** *noun*. Pl. **-o(e)s**.
1 *hist.* The quarter in a city, chiefly in Italy, to which Jews were restricted. E17.
2 A densely populated slum area occupied by a minority group or groups, usu. as a result of social or economic pressures; an isolated or segregated social group or area. L19.

M. L. KING In the ghettos of Chicago.. the problems of poverty and despair are graphically illustrated. *Nursery World* Our negotiators are pushing.. to break up the traditional 'women's work' ghettos.

– COMB.: **ghetto blaster** *colloq.* a large and powerful stereo radio-cassette player; **ghetto fabulous** *colloq.* pertaining to or favouring an ostentatious style of dress associated with the hip-hop subculture.
▸**B** *verb trans.* Put or keep (people) in a ghetto. M20.

fig.: *Listener* The narrow financial aspects ghettoed conveniently towards the back of newspapers or on late-night programmes.

■ **ghettoize** *verb trans.* = GHETTO *verb* M20. **ghettoiˈzation** *noun* the action of ghettoing; the state of being in a ghetto: M20.

ghi *noun* var. of GHEE.

Ghibelline /ˈgɪbɪlʌɪn/ *noun & adjective*. L16.
[ORIGIN Italian *Ghibellino*, supposedly from German *Waiblingen*, an estate belonging to the Hohenstaufen family, said to have been used as a war cry by partisans of the Hohenstaufen emperor Conrad III at the battle of Weinsberg in 1140.]
▸**A** *noun*. A member of the emperor's faction in the medieval Italian states. Opp. GUELPH. L16.
▸**B** *adjective*. Of or adhering to the Ghibellines. E19.
■ **Ghibellinism** /-lɪn-/ *noun* (adherence to) the principles of the Ghibelline faction E19.

ghibli /ˈgɪbli/ *noun*. Also **gi-**, **qi-**. E19.
[ORIGIN Arabic *qiblī* southern.]
A hot dry southerly wind of N. Africa.

ghilgai *noun* var. of GILGAI.

Ghilji *noun* see GHILZAI.

ghillie *noun* var. of GILLIE *noun*[1].

Ghilzai /ˈgɪlzʌɪ/ *noun*. Also (earlier) **Ghilji**. E19.
[ORIGIN Afghan name.]
A member of a Pathan people of Afghanistan.

Ghiordes /gɪˈɔːdəz/ *adjective*. E20.
[ORIGIN *Gördes*, a town in western Turkey.]
1 Designating a fine type of Turkish rug. E20.
2 Designating a kind of double knot used in weaving some oriental rugs, made by twisting the knot around two warp threads and bringing both ends of the yarn on to the surface between them. E20.

gholam /gəʊˈlɑːm/ *noun*. E19.
[ORIGIN Arabic *ġulām* boy, servant.]
In the Middle East: a courier or messenger.

ghoont /guːnt/ *noun*. Pl. **-s**, same. E17.
[ORIGIN Hindi.]
A Himalayan pony.

ghoor *noun* var. of GUR.

Ghoorkha *noun & adjective* see GURKHA.

ghost /gəʊst/ *noun*.
[ORIGIN Old English *gāst* = Old Frisian *gāst*, Old Saxon *gēst* (Dutch *geest*) Old & mod. High German *geist*, from West Germanic. The spelling with *gh-* (established in L16) is prob. from Flemish *gheest*.]
▸**I 1** The soul or spirit as the source of life. *obsolete* exc. in ***give up the ghost***, ***yield the ghost***, ***yield up the ghost*** below. OE. ▸†**b** Breath; a blast of wind. OE–E17.
2 The spiritual or abstract part of a person, as distinct from the physical part; a person's emotional, mental, and moral nature. Now *rare* or *obsolete*. OE. ▸**b** A person; *esp.* a wicked-looking person, a villain. OE–L16.
3 The Spirit or active essence of God; the Holy Spirit. *obsolete* exc. in HOLY GHOST. OE.
†**4** An incorporeal being; a (good or evil) spirit. OE–E17.
5 †**a** The soul of a dead person (later esp. of an ancestor), regarded as inhabiting the unseen world and freq. deified or revered. OE–L17. ▸**b** The soul of a dead person which manifests itself to the living visibly (as a shadowy nebulous image), audibly, etc.; any apparition of a person or thing, a spectre. LME.
†**6** A corpse. ME–L16.
7 *fig.* An emaciated person. Long *rare*. L16.
▸**II** With ref. to the pale nebulous appearance attributed to ghosts.
8 A faint or unsubstantial mark; a slight trace or vestige. E17.

S. SASSOON He hadn't the ghost of an idea whether we could get through the Boche wire. D. LODGE A ghost of a smile hovered on Mrs Swallow's lips.

9 A spurious image in a photograph, a television or radar picture, or a spectrogram, caused usually by a defect in the image-forming system. M19.
10 A person who does creative or artistic work on behalf of another person who takes the credit; *spec.* = ***ghostwriter*** below. L19.
11 BIOLOGY. A wall or membrane of a cell that has lost its contents; *spec.* a red blood cell that has lost its cytoplasm. Also, a phage whose head end has lost its contents. L19.
12 A faint band on the surface of steel owing to the segregation of certain of its constituents. E20.
– PHRASES: **give up the ghost** die; *fig.* give up hope. **lay a ghost** cause a ghost to cease appearing. **not the ghost of a chance** no chance at all. **raise a ghost** cause a ghost to appear. **the ghost in the machine** PHILOSOPHY the mind viewed as distinct from the body. **yield the ghost**, **yield up the ghost** *arch.* = ***give up the ghost*** above.
– COMB.: **ghostbuster** *colloq.* (**a**) a person who professes to banish ghosts, poltergeists, etc.; (**b**) *US* a person who investigates tax fraud; **ghost crab** a pale sand crab, *Ocypode albicans*, of W. Atlantic coasts; **Ghost Dance** US HISTORY a 19th-cent. N. American Indian religious cult based on the performance of a dance to bring the dead to life and drive away white people; **ghost gum** *Austral.* a pallid smooth-trunked inland gum tree, *Eucalyptus papuana*; **ghost moth** a large moth, *Hepialus humuli* (family Hepialidae, the swifts), some of the males of which have pale wings; **ghost story** a story about ghosts or the supernatural; *fig.* an untrue statement or report; **ghost town** (orig. *US*) a town partially or completely devoid of inhabitants; **ghost train** (**a**) a train of cars at a funfair that travels through dark tunnels in which there are ghostlike effects; (**b**) a train run during the night to keep the track clear in periods of heavy snowfall or severe frost; **ghost word** a word originating in a writer's or printer's error or by popular etymology; **ghostwrite** *verb trans. & intrans.* write as a ghostwriter; **ghostwriter** a person who writes something on behalf of another person who takes the credit (cf. sense 10 above).
■ **ghosˈtess** *noun* a female ghost M19. **ghosthood** *noun* the state of being a ghost L19. **ghostish** *adjective* (*rare*) L19. = GHOSTLY *adjective* 3 E20. †**ghostishly** *adverb* in the manner of a ghost: only in L16. **ghostless** *adjective* OE. **ghostlike** *adjective & adverb* (**a**) *adjective* resembling a ghost or a place haunted by ghosts; (**b**) *adverb* in the manner of a ghost: E17. **ghoˈstology** *noun* the lore of ghosts E19. **ghostship** *noun* ghosthood; *joc.* (with possess. adjective, as ***his ghostship*** etc.) a mock title of respect given to a ghost: E19.

ghost /gəʊst/ *verb*. L16.
[ORIGIN from the noun.]
†**1** *verb intrans.* Give up the ghost, die. L16–L17.
2 *verb trans.* Haunt as a ghost. E17.
3 *verb intrans.* & (now *rare*) *trans.* (with *it*). Move like a ghost; *esp.* (of a boat) make good progress in very little wind. M19.

G. GREEN Clarke.. ghosted his way past three tackles across midfield. I. MURDOCH His empty boat.. was found later ghosting along by itself.

4 *verb trans.* & *intrans.* Write as a ghostwriter. E20.

A. KOESTLER I enjoyed fussing over her, ghosting her dispatches.

■ **ghoster** *noun* (**a**) a person who or thing which ghosts; NAUTICAL a lightweight sail for use in very light winds; (**b**) a person who does night work as well as a daytime job: M20. **ghosting** *verbal noun* (**a**) the action of the verb; (**b**) the appearance of 'ghosts' or spurious images in a television picture: E19.

ghostly /ˈgəʊs(t)li/ *adjective*. OE.
[ORIGIN from GHOST *noun* + -LY[1].]
1 Pertaining to the soul or spirit; spiritual. *arch.* OE. ▸†**b** Of a being: incorporeal, insubstantial. ME–L17.

SIR W. SCOTT Qualified to administer both worldly and ghostly comfort.

2 Concerned with spiritual, sacred, or ecclesiastical matters. *arch.* OE. ▸†**b** Devout. ME–L15.

TENNYSON Father.. bid call the ghostly man Hither, and let me shrive me clean.

3 Of, pertaining to, or resembling, a ghost; spectral, shadowy; (of a place) haunted by a ghost. OE.

A. P. HERBERT The two quiet boats seemed to glide through the mist by some ghostly power.

■ **ghostlily** *adverb* M19. **ghostliness** *noun* ME.

ghostly /ˈɡəʊs(t)li/ *adverb*. Now *rare*. OE.
[ORIGIN from GHOST *noun* + -LY².]
As a ghost. Formerly, in a spiritual manner or sense; in spirit.

ghosty /ˈɡəʊsti/ *adjective*. M19.
[ORIGIN from GHOST *noun* + -Y¹.]
Of or resembling a ghost or ghosts.
▪ **ghostily** *adverb* M19. **ghostiness** *noun* L19.

ghoul /ɡuːl/ *noun*. L18.
[ORIGIN Arabic *ġūl*.]
In Arabic mythology: a desert demon preying on travellers; *gen.* an evil spirit or demon supposed to rob graves and devour corpses; a person unnaturally interested in death.
▪ **ghoulish** *adjective* resembling or characteristic of a ghoul M19. **ghoulishly** *adverb* M19. **ghoulishness** *noun* E20.

GHQ *abbreviation*.
General Headquarters.

ghurry /ˈɡʌri/ *noun*. Also **ghuree**. M17.
[ORIGIN Hindi *ghaṛī* water clock with a cycle of typically 24 minutes.]
1 In the Indian subcontinent: 24 minutes (a 60th of a day); among Anglo-Indians, an hour. M17.
2 The metal plate of a clock on which the hours are struck; a timepiece E19.

G

ghusl /ˈɡuːs(ə)l/ *noun*. M19.
[ORIGIN Arabic *ġusl* washing, from *ġasala* to wash.]
Ritual washing of the whole body, as prescribed by Islamic law to be performed in preparation for prayer and worship, and after sexual activity, childbirth, menstruation, etc. Cf. WUDU.

Ghuzz /ɡuːz/ *noun & adjective*. M19.
[ORIGIN Persian *ġuz* from Turkic OGHUZ.]
▸ **A** *noun*. Pl. same. = OGHUZ *noun*. M19.
▸ **B** *attrib.* or as *adjective*. Of, pertaining to, or designating the Oghuz. M20.

ghyll *noun* see GILL *noun*².

GHz *abbreviation*.
Gigahertz.

GI *abbreviation*
Glycaemic index.

GI /dʒiːˈʌɪ, dʒiːˈʌɪ/ *noun & adjective*. M20.
[ORIGIN Abbreviation of *government* or *general issue*.]
▸ **A** *noun*. A US private soldier. M20.
▸ **B** *adjective*. For or pertaining to the US armed forces or servicemen. M20.
GI bride a foreign woman married to a US serviceman on duty abroad. **GI Joe** *colloq.* a US private soldier.

Giacobinid /dʒakəˈbɪnɪd/ *noun & adjective*. M20.
[ORIGIN from Comet *Giacobini–Zinner*, (M. *Giacobini* (fl. 1900), Italian astronomer): see -ID³.]
ASTRONOMY. = DRACONID.

giallo antico /ˌdʒallo anˈtiːko, ˌdʒaləʊ anˈtiːkəʊ/ *noun & adjectival phr.* M18.
[ORIGIN Italian, lit. 'ancient yellow'.]
(Made of) a rich yellow marble found among ruins in Italy, and used as a decoration.

giallolino /dʒialloˈliːno/ *noun*. *rare*. E18.
[ORIGIN Italian, now *giallorino*, dim. of *giallo* yellow.]
The pigment Naples yellow.

giant /ˈdʒʌɪənt/ *noun & adjective*. ME.
[ORIGIN Old French & mod. French *géant*, †*jaiant* from Proto-Romance var. of Latin *gigantem*, (nom.) *gigas*, from Greek *gigas*, *gigant-*.]
▸ **A** *noun*. **1** A mythical, pseudo-historical, or fictional being in human form but of superhuman size; GREEK MYTHOLOGY a member of a race of such beings who fought against the gods. ME. ▸**b** *fig.* An influence or agency of enormous power. M17. ▸**c** ECONOMICS. A large or powerful industrial company; a business that dominates its market. M20.

R. EDEN The Gyaunte Atlas beareth the worlde on hys shoulders. **c** *Spectator* One of the soap giants, Unilever.

2 An exceptionally large human being (freq. *hyperbol.*); any abnormally large creature or thing. M16. ▸**b** ASTRONOMY. Any of a class of large stars of high intrinsic luminosity and low mean density, as distinguished from the more common (dwarf) stars of the main sequence. Cf. SUPERGIANT. E20.

R. DAHL Their . . father, an amiable giant nearly seven foot tall.

3 A person who has some notable quality to an extraordinary degree. M16.

J. H. BLUNT The schoolmen were mental giants.

4 MINING. A discharge pipe used in washing ore. *US*. L19.
– PHRASES: **battle of the giants** a contest between two pre-eminent parties. ***sleeping giant***: see SLEEPING *ppl adjective*.
▸ **B** *adjective*. Of extraordinary size or force, gigantic, monstrous; (of species or varieties of plants or animals) much larger than the average of their kind; *colloq.* (of a packet, carton, etc.) extra large. LME.

POPE His giant voice the echoing region fills. E. AMADI Port Harcourt . . was a clean little town, cleaner by far than giant Kano.

– SPECIAL COLLOCATIONS & COMB.: **giant brain** *colloq.* an electronic computer. **giant cell** BIOLOGY any unusually large cell; *esp.* (**a**) a platelet-forming cell in the bone marrow; (**b**) a multinuclear cell formed by fusion of macrophages. ***giant clam***: see CLAM *noun*² 1(b). **giant fibre** ZOOLOGY an enlarged or fused nerve fibre modified for rapid conduction of impulses, esp. in various invertebrates. **giant kangaroo** = FORESTER 3a(b). **giant-killer** a person who defeats a seemingly much more powerful opponent. **giant order** ARCHITECTURE an order whose columns extend through more than one storey. ***giant panda***: see PANDA *noun*¹ 2. **giant petrel** either of two large petrels of the genus *Macronectes*, of southern oceans, which occur in dark and white morphs. **giant-powder** a kind of dynamite. **giant racer** a large switchback at a funfair. ***giant sequoia***. ***giant slalom***. **giant's stride**, **giant stride** a gymnastic apparatus consisting of a pole with a revolving head and hanging ropes enabling the user to take huge strides round the pole. **giant toad** = ***cane toad*** s.v. CANE *noun*¹.
▪ **giantess** *noun* a female giant LME. **gianthood** *noun* the nature or characteristics of a giant; the race of giants: M19. **giantish** *adjective* (*rare*) approaching the size of a giant; giantlike: M17. **giantize** *verb trans.* (*rare*) give the appearance of a giant to E17. **giantlike** *adjective* resembling a giant; like that of a giant; gigantic: L16. **giantly** *adjective* (now *rare*) giantlike M16. **giantry** *noun* (*rare*) the race of giants; giants collectively: E17. **giantship** *noun* (**a**) the state of being a giant; (**b**) (with possess. adjective, as ***your giantship*** etc.) a mock title of respect given to a giant: L17.

giantism /ˈdʒʌɪəntɪz(ə)m/ *noun*. M17.
[ORIGIN from GIANT *noun* + -ISM.]
1 The quality of a giant; the state of being a giant. M17.
2 BIOLOGY. (Tendency to) abnormally large size; gigantism. L19.

giaour /ˈdʒaʊə/ *noun*. *arch. derog.* M16.
[ORIGIN Turkish *gâvur* from Persian *gaur* var. of *gabr*, prob. from Arabic *kāfir* KAFFIR.]
A non-Muslim, *esp.* a Christian.

giardia /dʒɪˈaːdɪə/ *noun*. Also **G-**. E20.
[ORIGIN mod. Latin (see below), from A. *Giard* (1846–1908), French biologist: see -IA¹.]
BACTERIOLOGY. A flagellate protozoan, *Giardia lamblia*, sometimes found in the mammalian gut; any member of the genus *Giardia*.
▪ **giardiasis** /-ˈdʌɪəsɪs/ *noun* (MEDICINE) infection of the gut with giardias E20.

gib /ɡɪb/ *noun*¹. Now *arch. & dial.* LME.
[ORIGIN Abbreviation of the name *Gilbert*.]
1 (Orig. used as a familiar name for) a cat, *esp.* a male cat; *dial.* a cat that has been castrated. Now usu. more fully ***gib-cat***. LME.
†**2** A woman, *esp.* an old woman. *derog.* E16–L17.

gib /ɡɪb/ *noun*². M16.
[ORIGIN Unknown.]
1 Orig., an iron hook. Later, a hooked stick. Long *obsolete* exc. *dial.* M16.
2 = KYPE. E19.
– COMB.: **gib-staff** a quarterstaff; a hooked stick.

gib /dʒɪb, ɡɪb/ *noun*³. L18.
[ORIGIN Unknown.]
1 A piece of wood or metal used to keep some part of a machine etc. in place; a bolt, a pin, a wedge. L18.
2 MINING. A piece of wood used to support the roof of a coalmine. M19.

gib *verb*¹ var. of GIP.

gib *verb*² var. of JIB *verb*².

Gib. *abbreviation*.
Gibraltar.

gibbed cat /ɡɪbd ˈkat/ *noun phr.* Long *rare* or *obsolete*. M17.
[ORIGIN Orig. var. of *gib-cat* (GIB *noun*¹), later taken as pa. pple of an assumed verb = geld + CAT *noun*¹.]
A (male) cat; a castrated cat.

gibber /ˈɡɪbə/ *noun*¹. *Austral.* L18.
[ORIGIN Dharuk *giba* stone.]
A boulder, a (large) stone.
– ATTRIB. & COMB.: In the sense 'characterized by boulders and stones', as ***gibber country*** etc. Special combs., as **gibber gunyah** an Aboriginal cave-dwelling; **gibber-plain** (chiefly *Austral.*) a level area of desert covered with siliceous gravel or broken pebbles.

gibber /ˈdʒɪbə, ˈɡɪbə/ *noun*². M19.
[ORIGIN from GIBBER *verb*.]
Rapid and inarticulate utterance.

ARNOLD BENNETT The mumbling toothless gibber of his shrill protesting.

gibber /ˈɡɪbə/ *noun*³ *& adjective*. M19.
[ORIGIN Latin = hump.]
BOTANY. ▸**A** *noun*. A hump, a bulge. M19.
▸ **B** *adjective*. = GIBBOUS. E20.

gibber /ˈdʒɪbə, ˈɡɪbə/ *verb intrans.* E17.
[ORIGIN Imit. Cf. GIBBERISH.]
Speak rapidly and inarticulately; chatter, talk nonsense; (of an ape or monkey) utter a quick series of vocal noises.

H. MARTINEAU Monkeys . . hung by one arm from the boughs overhead, gibbering and chattering. A. HALEY To stare . . at the other naked men, most of them gibbering in their terror. I. BANKS I . . listened to the studio pundits gibber about surgical strikes and pinpoint accuracy.

gibberellic /dʒɪbəˈrɛlɪk/ *adjective*. M20.
[ORIGIN from mod. Latin *Gibberella* (see below), dim. of *Gibbera* genus name, from Latin *gibber* hump: see -IC.]
gibberellic acid, one of the gibberellins, a tetracyclic lactonic acid first isolated from the fungus *Gibberella fujikuroi*, a parasite of cereals.

gibberellin /dʒɪbəˈrɛlɪn/ *noun*. M20.
[ORIGIN formed as GIBBERELLIC + -IN¹.]
Any of various tetracyclic compounds, e.g. gibberellic acid, present in many higher plants as growth hormones, promoting stem elongation, germination, flowering, etc.

gibberish /ˈdʒɪb(ə)rɪʃ, ˈɡɪb-/ *noun & adjective*. E16.
[ORIGIN Perh. rel. to GIBBER *verb* (but found earlier) + -ISH¹ as used in *Spanish*, *Swedish*, etc.]
▸ **A** *noun*. Unintelligible speech belonging to no known language, a series of meaningless sounds; blundering or ungrammatical talk; nonsense. E16.

J. L. WATEN Martin and Benny were whispering together in some strange gibberish. E. H. GOMBRICH A language consisting only of new words and a new syntax would be indistinguishable from gibberish.

▸ †**B** *adjective*. Of or pertaining to gibberish, expressed in gibberish; unintelligible, unmeaning. L16–E19.

gibberose /ˈɡɪbərəʊs/ *adjective*. E18.
[ORIGIN from Latin *gibberosus*, from *gibber* hump: see -OSE¹.]
BOTANY. = GIBBOUS.

gibbet /ˈdʒɪbɪt/ *noun*¹. ME.
[ORIGIN Old French *gibet* staff, cudgel, gallows, dim. of *gibe* staff, club, prob. ult. from Germanic.]
1 *hist.* Orig., a gallows. Later, an upright post with a projecting arm from which the bodies of criminals were hung after execution. ME.

GOLDSMITH There, the black gibbet glooms beside the way.

2 The punishment of death by hanging. LME.
3 a A frame for hanging a pot over the fire. *Scot. rare*. L15. ▸†**b** A short beam projecting from a wall, having a pulley fixed at the end. Only in 16. ▸**c** The projecting arm of a crane; a jib. E18.
†**4** A cudgel. Only in 17.

†**gibbet** *noun*². L16–M18.
[ORIGIN Uncertain: cf. Old French *juppet* the distance to which one can shout, from *jupper*, *juper* whoop, cry out.]
A note on a horn, a call or whistle as a signal to a dog or hawk.

gibbet /ˈdʒɪbɪt/ *verb*. L16.
[ORIGIN from GIBBET *noun*¹.]
†**1** *verb intrans.* Hang as on a gibbet. Only in L16.
2 *verb trans. fig.* Hold up to infamy or contempt. M17.
3 *verb trans.* Put to death by hanging. E18. ▸**b** Expose on a gibbet; hang up as on a gibbet. M18.

gibble-gabble /ˈɡɪb(ə)lɡab(ə)l/ *noun*. E17.
[ORIGIN Redupl. of GABBLE *noun*. Cf. FIDDLE-FADDLE.]
Senseless chatter.

gibbon /ˈɡɪb(ə)n/ *noun*. L18.
[ORIGIN French, of unknown origin.]
Any of various small long-armed tailless arboreal apes of the SE Asian genus *Hylobates*.

Gibbonian /ɡɪˈbəʊnɪən/ *adjective*. L18.
[ORIGIN from Edward *Gibbon* (see below) + -IAN.]
Relating to or resembling the style or opinions of the historian Edward Gibbon (1737–94).

gibbose /ˈɡɪbəʊs/ *adjective*. L17.
[ORIGIN Late Latin *gibbosus*, from Latin *gibbus* hump: see -OSE¹.]
= GIBBOUS.

gibbosity /ɡɪˈbɒsɪti/ *noun*. LME.
[ORIGIN Old French & mod. French *gibbosité* hump or medieval Latin *gibbositas* gibbosity, tumour, from late Latin *gibbosus*: see GIBBOUS, -ITY.]
1 A swelling; a protuberance. LME.
2 The state, quality, or condition of being gibbose or gibbous. M16.

gibbous /ˈɡɪbəs/ *adjective*. LME.
[ORIGIN Late Latin *gibbosus*, from Latin *gibbus* hump: see -OUS.]
1 Convex, rounded, protuberant. LME. ▸**b** ASTRONOMY. Of the moon or a planet: having the visible disc more than half but less than fully illuminated. L17. ▸**c** BOTANY. Very convex or bulging, esp. of solid convexities. M19.

b A. S. BYATT He . . through the window saw the irregular lump of a gibbous moon.

2 Of a person or an animal: hunch-backed; having a hump. Of a part of the body: hump-shaped. LME.
▪ **gibbously** *adverb* M19. **gibbousness** *noun* (*rare*) L17.

gibbsite /ˈɡɪbzʌɪt/ *noun*. E19.
[ORIGIN from G. *Gibbs* (1776–1833), Amer. mineralogist + -ITE¹.]
MINERALOGY. A monoclinic hydrated aluminium oxide occurring as stalactitic encrustations, or more commonly as a major constituent of bauxite.

gibby /ˈɡɪbi/ *noun*. Chiefly *dial.* L18.
[ORIGIN from GIB *noun*² + -Y⁶.]
In full ***gibby-stick***. A hooked stick; a stick with a bent handle.

gibe *noun* var. of JIBE *noun*[1].

gibe *verb*[1] var. of JIBE *verb*[1].

gibe *verb*[2] var. of JIBE *verb*[2].

†**gibecrack** *noun* see GIMCRACK.

gibel /ˈgiːb(ə)l/ *noun*. *rare*. **M19.**
[ORIGIN German *Giebel*, earlier *Gibel*.]
More fully ***gibel carp***. = CRUCIAN ***carp***.

Gibeonite /ˈgɪbɪənʌɪt/ *noun*. **LME.**
[ORIGIN from *Gibeon* (see below) + -ITE[1].]
A native or inhabitant of Gibeon (mod. Al-Jīb), a city in ancient Palestine north-west of Jerusalem which made a league with Joshua to avoid the fate of Jericho. Also *fig.* (with ref. to *Joshua* 9:27), a menial, a drudge (long *rare*).

gibier /ˈdʒɪbɪə, *foreign* ʒibje/ *noun*. Now *rare*. **E16.**
[ORIGIN French.]
Game; wildfowl.

giblet /ˈdʒɪblɪt/ *noun*. **ME.**
[ORIGIN Old French *gibelet* game stew, perh. formed as GIBIER Cf. mod. French *gibelotte* rabbit stew, (Walloon) *giblè d'awe* goose giblets.]
†**1** An inessential appendage. Only in **ME.**
†**2** A piece of offal, garbage. Only in **LME.**
3 In *pl.* & (now *rare* exc. *attrib.*) *sing.* The edible parts of a goose or other fowl, as the liver, gizzard, etc., that are removed before cooking. **M16.**

D. BARTHELME Inside the Game Hens were the giblets in a plastic bag.

4 *fig.* In *pl.* Things of little value, odds and ends. Now chiefly *dial.* **M17.**
– COMB.: **giblet pie**, **giblet soup**: made with giblets.

gibli *noun* var. of GHIBLI.

Gibraltar /dʒɪˈbrɔːltə/ *noun*. **L16.**
[ORIGIN A fortified town and rocky headland at the southern tip of Spain, since 1704 a Brit. colony.]
†**1** A monkey. **L16–E17.**
2 More fully ***Gibraltar rock***. A kind of hard sweet; a piece of this. **M19.**
3 *fig.* Something impregnable. *rare*. **M19.**
■ **Gibraltarian** /dʒɪbrɔːlˈtɛːrɪən/ *noun* & *adjective* (*a*) *noun* a native or inhabitant of Gibraltar; (*b*) *adjective* of or pertaining to Gibraltar or the Gibraltarians: **L19.**

Gibson /ˈgɪbs(ə)n/ *noun*. **E20.**
[ORIGIN A surname.]
In full ***Gibson cocktail***. A cocktail consisting of gin and vermouth garnished with pearl onions.

Gibson girl /ˈgɪbs(ə)n gəːl/ *noun phr*. **L19.**
[ORIGIN Charles Dana *Gibson* (see below).]
A girl typifying the fashionable ideal of the late 19th and early 20th cents., as represented in the work of Charles Dana Gibson (1867–1944), American artist and illustrator.

gibus /ˈdʒʌɪbəs/ *noun*. **M19.**
[ORIGIN *Gibus*, its 19th-cent. French inventor.]
In full ***gibus hat***. A collapsible opera hat.

gid /gɪd/ *noun*. **E17.**
[ORIGIN Back-form. from GIDDY *adjective*.]
(Usu. with *the*.) A fatal disease of sheep and goats, caused by larvae of the dog tapeworm *Taenia coenurus* encysted in the brain, and characterized by unsteady gait and loss of balance. Also called ***staggers***, ***sturdy***, & other names.

giddap *interjection* & *verb* var. of GIDDY-UP.

giddify /ˈgɪdɪfʌɪ/ *verb trans*. **E17.**
[ORIGIN from GIDDY *adjective* + -FY.]
Make giddy, daze (*lit.* & *fig.*).

giddily /ˈgɪdɪli/ *adverb*. **ME.**
[ORIGIN from GIDDY *adjective* + -LY[2].]
In a giddy manner.

OUIDA It all swam giddily before my sight. J. GALSWORTHY He wondered giddily how old she was—she seemed so much more . . experienced than himself.

giddiness /ˈgɪdɪnəs/ *noun*. **ME.**
[ORIGIN from GIDDY *adjective* + -NESS.]
1 Thoughtless folly, flightiness; inconstancy, instability. Also (*rare*), an instance of this. **ME.**

DICKENS The mincing vanities and giddinesses of empty-headed girls. W. PHILLIPS A few mere giddiness hurries to ruin.

2 The state of having a sensation of whirling and a tendency to fall, stagger, or spin round; dizziness. **LME.**

J. WAIN An attack of giddiness and a black-out.

giddup *interjection* & *verb* var. of GIDDY-UP.

giddy /ˈgɪdi/ *noun*. **E17.**
[ORIGIN from the adjective.]
= GID.

giddy /ˈgɪdi/ *adjective*.
[ORIGIN Old English *gidig* from Germanic, from base of GOD *noun* (the primary sense being 'possessed by a god'): see -Y[1].]
1 †**a** Insane, mad, foolish, stupid. **OE–ME.** ▸**b** Mad with anger, furious. *dial.* **L17.**
2 Having a sensation of whirling and a tendency to fall, stagger, or spin round (with sickness, pleasure, etc.); dizzy. **LME.** ▸**b** Causing or apt to produce dizziness. **L16.** ▸**c** Circling with bewildering speed. **L16.** ▸**d** Of sheep: affected by the gid. **M19.**

G. BERKELEY They seem to me drunk and giddy with a false notion of liberty. I. MURDOCH His head ached and when he sat up he felt giddy. **b** M. PRIOR The giddy precipice, and the dangerous flood. **c** POPE So whirls a wheel, in giddy circle toss'd.

3 Mentally intoxicated; incapable of attention; excitable; frivolous, flighty, inconstant. Also (*colloq.*), used as an (esp. iron.) intensive. Cf. earlier GIDDINESS 1. **M16.**

J. BUCHAN A giddy lot Scudder's friends cared for peace and reform. K. TYNAN This Rosalind was a gay and giddy creature—loads of fun, game for any jape.

my giddy AUNT. *play the giddy* GOAT. *play the giddy* OX.

giddy /ˈgɪdi/ *verb*. **E17.**
[ORIGIN from GIDDY *adjective*.]
1 *verb trans.* Make giddy. **E17.**
2 *verb intrans.* Become giddy. **M19.**

giddy-up /ˈgɪdɪʌp, gɪdɪˈʌp/. Also **giddap** /ˈgɪdap, gɪˈdap/, **giddup** /ˈgɪdʌp, gɪˈdʌp/. *interjection* & *verb*. **E20.**
[ORIGIN Repr. a pronunc. of *get up*.]
▸**A** *interjection*. A command to a horse: go on!, go faster! **E20.**
▸**B** *verb*. **1** *verb intrans.* Of a horse: go on, go faster. **M20.**
2 *verb trans.* Urge (a horse) to go on or to go faster. **M20.**

Gideon /ˈgɪdɪən/ *noun*. **E20.**
[ORIGIN An Israelite leader: see *Judges* 6:11 ff.]
A member of a Christian organization of American business people, founded in 1899.
– COMB.: **Gideon Bible** a bible purchased by this organization and placed in a hotel bedroom etc. for the occupant's use.

gidgee /ˈgɪdʒiː/ *noun*[1]. *Austral.* Also **gidgie**. **M19.**
[ORIGIN Yuwaalaraay (an Australian Aboriginal language of New South Wales) *gijirr*.]
An Aboriginal spear.

gidgee /ˈgɪdʒiː/ *noun*[2]. Also **gidya**, **gidyea** /ˈgɪdɪə/, & other vars. **M19.**
[ORIGIN Aboriginal *gijir*.]
An Australian wattle tree, *Acacia cambagei*, the leaflike phyllodes of which give off a foul smell at the approach of rain.

†**gierfalcon** *noun* var. of GYRFALCON.

GIF *abbreviation*.
COMPUTING. Graphic interchange format, a popular format for image files, with built-in data compression.

gif /gɪf/ *conjunction*. *Scot.* & *N. English*. **LME.**
[ORIGIN Alt. of IF, prob. infl. by GIVE *verb*. Cf. GIN *conjunction*[2].]
If (*that*).

giff-gaff /ˈgɪfgaf/ *noun*. *Scot.* & *N. English*. **M16.**
[ORIGIN Redupl. of GIVE *verb*. Cf. Middle Dutch *ghivegave*.]
1 Mutual giving, mutual help; give and take. **M16.**
2 Interchange of remarks; casual conversation. **L18.**

GIFT /gɪft/ *abbreviation*.
Gamete intrafallopian transfer (the transfer of sperm and ova directly into the Fallopian tubes of a woman to facilitate conception).

gift /gɪft/ *noun*. **ME.**
[ORIGIN Old Norse *gipt* corresp. to Old English *ġift* payment for a wife, (in pl.) wedding, Old Frisian *jeft*, Old Saxon *sundargift* privilege, Middle Dutch *gift(e)* (Dutch *gift* gift), Old High German *gift* gift, (German *Gift* gift), Gothic *fragifts* espousal, from Germanic base of GIVE *verb*.]
▸**I** Giving.
1 The action or an act of giving. **ME.**

H. REED Language always makes gift of its best wealth to a great poet.

in the gift of (of a church living or other appointment) within the power or right of a specified person or institution to bestow.
2 LAW. The voluntary transference of property without anything in return. **L15.**
deed of gift a deed by which property is conveyed from the donor to the donee without anything being given in return.
▸**II** Something given.
3 A thing given; a present, a donation. Also *fig.*, an accidental or unexpected opportunity or benefit. **ME.**

G. SWIFT My pet hamster, Sammy, a gift for my tenth birthday. JANET MORGAN To the press, the story of Agatha's disappearance was a gift.

as a gift, (*arch.*) **at a gift** even gratis (freq. in ***would not have it as a gift*** etc.). ***free gift***: see FREE *adjective*. ***Grecian gift***: see GRECIAN *adjective*. ***Greek gift***: see GREEK *adjective*.
4 An offering to God or to a god. **ME.**

AV *Matt.* 5:24 Leaue there thy gift before the altar.

5 A faculty, power, or quality miraculously bestowed; a virtue or endowment looked on as an emanation from heaven. **ME.** ▸**b** A natural endowment, faculty, ability, or talent. **ME.**

J. H. NEWMAN To obtain the gift of holiness is the work of a life. **b** D. ATHILL I knew in my bones that I had no gift for nursing.

the gift of tongues: see TONGUE *noun*. **b** ***gift of the gab***: see GAB *noun*[2].

†**6** Something given with the intent to corrupt, a bribe. **LME–E17.**

AV *2 Chron.* 19:7 There is no iniquitie with the Lord our God . . nor taking of gifts.

7 A white speck on the fingernail, supposed to portend a gift. Now *dial.* **E18.**
8 An easy task etc. *colloq.* **M19.**
– COMB.: **gift book**: given or suitable for giving as a present; **gift coupon**: issued with certain commodities and entitling the holder of a specified number of such coupons to a free gift; **gift-horse**: given as a present (chiefly in ***look a gift-horse in the mouth***, find fault with a gift); **gift shop**: dealing in articles suitable for gifts; **gift token**, **gift voucher**: used as a gift and exchangeable for goods esp. at a specified shop etc.; **gift-wrap** *verb trans.* wrap (a purchase etc.) attractively as a gift.
■ **giftless** *adjective* **LME.**

gift /gɪft/ *verb trans*. **L16.**
[ORIGIN from the noun.]
1 Endow or provide with a gift or gifts; endow or present *with* as a gift. **L16.**

P. G. WODEHOUSE She was gifted with a sort of second sight. *Daily Telegraph* You can . . be gifted up to £90,000 before you become liable to tax.

2 Bestow as a gift (foll. by *to*); give *away*. **E17.**

J. C. LEES The Regent Murray gifted all the Church Property to Lord Sempill.

gifted /ˈgɪftɪd/ *adjective*. **M17.**
[ORIGIN from GIFT *noun*, *verb*: see -ED[2], -ED[1].]
1 Endowed with a gift or gifts; *spec.* exceptionally talented or intelligent. **M17.**

C. CONNOLLY There can have been few young writers as gifted. R. HOLMES Dr Labrunie regarded him as a brilliant and gifted child.

†**2** Given, bestowed. Only in **L17.**
■ **giftedly** *adverb* **M20.** **giftedness** *noun* **M17.**

giftie /ˈgɪfti/ *noun*. *Scot.* **L18.**
[ORIGIN from GIFT *noun* + -IE.]
= GIFT *noun* 5b.

R. BURNS O wad some Pow'r the giftie gie us To see oursels as others see us!

gig /gɪg/ *noun*[1]. **ME.**
[ORIGIN Prob. imit.]
▸**I** †**1** A flighty girl. **ME–L18.**
2 An awkward, odd-looking, or boorish person; *dial.* a fool. Now *rare*. **LME.**
▸**II** **3** In full ***gig-mill***. Orig., a building which housed rotary machines designed to raise the nap on fabric by the use of teasels, wire-cards, etc. Later, a machine employed in this process. **M16.**
4 A thing that whirls; *spec.* (*a*) (*obsolete* exc. *dial.*) a whipping top; †(*b*) a device consisting of an arrangement of feathers used to attract birds to a net by revolving. (Earlier in WHIRLIGIG.) **L16.**
▸**III** †**5** **a** A fancy, a joke, a whim. **L16–E19.** ▸**b** Fun, merriment, glee. Now *arch.* & *dial.* **L18.**
b in high gig, **on the gig**, **on the high gig** in a state of boisterous hilarity.
■ **giggish** *adjective* †(*a*) wanton; (*b*) *arch.* lively, flighty: **E16.**

gig /gɪg/ *noun*[2]. **E18.**
[ORIGIN Abbreviation of FISHGIG or FIZGIG *noun*[2].]
1 = FIZGIG *noun*[2]. **E18.**
2 An arrangement of hooks set back to back and attached to a handline, used for catching fish by being dragged through a shoal. *US*. **L19.**

gig /gɪg/ *noun*[3]. **L18.**
[ORIGIN App. transf. sense of GIG *noun*[1] II.]
1 Chiefly *hist.* A light two-wheeled one-horse carriage. **L18.**
2 A light narrow clinker-built ship's boat for rowing or sailing; a rowing boat chiefly used for racing. **L18.**
3 = KIBBLE *noun*[1]. Also, a two-storied lift used by miners in ascending or descending a pit shaft. **L19.**
– COMB.: **gig-lamps** *arch. slang* spectacles.

gig /gɪg/ *noun*[4]. *colloq.* **E20.**
[ORIGIN Unknown.]
1 A performance of popular music or jazz, esp. for one night only; the place of such a performance. **E20.**

C. J. STONE He organised a gig to raise money and wanted to throw a party afterwards.

2 A task or assignment. **M20.**

I. PATTISON His was a tough gig but being poor was tougher. K. LETTE My next gig is glamour-posing for amateur photographers in Milton Keynes.

gig /gɪg/ *verb*[1] *trans*. Infl. **-gg-**. **L18.**
[ORIGIN Prob. from GIG *noun*[1] 3.]
Raise the nap of (fabric) with a gig.

gig /gɪg/ *verb*[2] *trans*. Infl. **-gg-**. **E19.**
[ORIGIN from GIG *noun*[2].]
Fish for with a gig.

gig /gɪg/ *verb*[3] *intrans.* & *trans*. (with *it*). Infl. **-gg-**. **E19.**
[ORIGIN from GIG *noun*[3].]
Ride or travel in a gig.

G

G

gig /gɪg/ *verb*[4] *trans.* Chiefly *US*. Infl. **-gg-**. L19.
[ORIGIN Uncertain: perh. imit.]
Move backwards and forwards; move *back* (the carriage of a sawmill) after a cut has been made.

gig /gɪg/ *verb*[5] *intrans. colloq.* Infl. **-gg-**. M20.
[ORIGIN from GIG *noun*[4].]
Of a musician: perform at a gig or gigs.

giga- /ˈgʌɪgə, ˈgɪgə, dʒ-/ *combining form*. M20.
[ORIGIN from Greek *gigas* giant.]
Used in names of units etc. to denote a factor of 10^9 (one thousand million), as ***gigahertz***, ***gigametre***, ***gigawatt***; also in COMPUTING, used to denote a factor of 2^{30}, as ***gigabit***. Abbreviation ***G***.
■ **gigabyte** *noun* (COMPUTING) a unit of information equal to one thousand million (10^9) bytes or (strictly) 2^{30} bytes L20.

gigaflop /ˈgʌɪgəflɒp, ˈgɪgə-, dʒ-/ *noun*. L20.
[ORIGIN from GIGA- + acronym from *floating-point* operations per second (with -s taken as pl. suffix -S[1]).]
COMPUTING. A unit of computing speed equal to one thousand million or 2^{30} floating-point operations per second.

giganotosaurus /dʒʌɪgəˌnəʊtəˈsɔːrəs/ *noun*. Pl. **-ruses**, **-ri** /-rʌɪ/. L20.
[ORIGIN mod. Latin (see below), from Greek *gigas* giant + *nōton* back + -SAUR.]
An enormous carnivorous theropod dinosaur of the genus *Giganotosaurus*, resembling the tyrannosaurs.

gigantean /dʒʌɪganˈtiːən/ *adjective*. E17.
[ORIGIN from Latin *giganteus*, from *gigant-*: see GIANT, -EAN.]
= GIGANTIC *adjective*.

gigantesque /dʒʌɪganˈtɛsk/ *adjective*. E19.
[ORIGIN French from Italian *gigantesco*, from *gigante* GIANT *noun*: see -ESQUE.]
Having the characteristics of a giant; befitting a giant.

gigantic /dʒʌɪˈgantɪk/ *adjective*. E17.
[ORIGIN from Latin *gigant-* (see GIANT) + -IC.]
†**1** Of, pertaining to, or characteristic of a giant or giants. E17–L18.

J. BRYANT He was the son of Uricus, and of the gigantic race.

2 Having the proportions of a giant; giantlike in size, stature, etc.; abnormally large; huge, enormous. M17.

HOR. WALPOLE Jeffery . . had many squabbles with the king's gigantic porter. D. ADAMS Three gigantic doors, maybe sixty feet high. J. M. ROBERTS A gigantic influence on the later development of Christian religion and civilisation.

■ **gigantically** *adverb* in a gigantic manner, to a gigantic degree L17.

giganticide /dʒʌɪˈgantɪsʌɪd/ *noun*. E19.
[ORIGIN formed as GIGANTIC + -I- + -CIDE.]
1 A giant-killer. E19.
2 The action or an act of killing of a giant or giants. M19.

gigantise *verb* var. of GIGANTIZE.

gigantism /ˈdʒʌɪgantɪz(ə)m, dʒʌɪˈgantɪz(ə)m/ *noun*. L19.
[ORIGIN from Latin *gigant-*, *gigas* GIANT + -ISM.]
Abnormally large or excessive size; *spec.* (***a***) MEDICINE excessive size of the entire body due to overproduction of growth hormone by the pituitary gland during childhood (cf. ACROMEGALY); (***b***) BOTANY excessive size due to polyploidy. Also *fig.* Cf. GIANTISM.

gigantize /dʒʌɪˈgantʌɪz/ *verb trans.* Also **-ise**. M17.
[ORIGIN formed as GIGANTISM + -IZE.]
Cause to appear gigantic.

gigantology /dʒʌɪganˈtɒlədʒi/ *noun*. *rare*. L18.
[ORIGIN formed as GIGANTISM + -OLOGY.]
The branch of study that deals with giants.

gigantomachy /dʒʌɪganˈtɒmәki/ *noun*. Also **gigantomachia** /ˌdʒʌɪgantəˈmeɪkɪə/. L16.
[ORIGIN Greek *gigantomakhia*, from *gigas*, *gigant-* GIANT *noun*: see -O-, -MACHY.]
In GREEK MYTHOLOGY, the war waged by the giants against the gods; a contest resembling this.

Gigantopithecus /dʒʌɪgantəˈpɪθɪkəs, -pɪˈθiːkəs/ *noun*. M20.
[ORIGIN mod. Latin, from Greek *giganto-*, *gigas* giant + *pithēkos* ape.]
A large fossil primate of the genus *Gigantopithecus*, sometimes considered hominid.

giggle /ˈgɪg(ə)l/ *verb & noun*. E16.
[ORIGIN Imit.: cf. Dutch *gi(e)chelen*, Low German *giggeln*, Middle High German *gickeln*, Russian *khikhikat'*.]
▸**A** *verb*. **1** *verb intrans.* Laugh in an affected, silly, or nervous manner; titter; give small bursts of half-suppressed laughter. E16.

M. SPARK One or two . . giggled with hands to their helpless mouths.

2 *verb trans.* Utter with a giggle or giggles. M17.
▸**B** *noun*. †**1** A giggling girl. Only in E17.
2 A giggling laugh. Freq. in ***the giggles***, ***a fit of the giggles***. L17. ▸**b** An amusing person or thing; a joke; fun. *colloq.* M20.

K. MANSFIELD Geraldine couldn't help a little giggle of amusement. **b** J. RATHBONE He enjoyed the course, which was mostly rather a giggle.

b for a giggle as a joke, not seriously, for fun.

3 A group (of girls). *colloq.* M20.
– COMB.: **giggle-house** *Austral. & NZ arch. slang* a psychiatric hospital; **giggle-water** *slang* intoxicating liquor.
■ **giggler** *noun* a person who giggles, esp. habitually M17. **giggliness** *noun* the state of being giggly L20. **gigglish** *adjective* disposed to giggle L17. **giggly** *adjective* much given to giggling M19.

giglet /ˈgɪglɪt/ *noun*. Also **-ot** /-ət/. ME.
[ORIGIN Perh. from GIG *noun*[1] and later assoc. with GIGGLE *verb*: see -LET.]
Orig., a wanton woman. Later, a giggling girl.

gigman /ˈgɪgmən/ *noun*. Pl. **-men**. Now *rare*. M19.
[ORIGIN from GIG *noun*[3] + MAN *noun*.]
A person who keeps or uses a gig, esp. as a typical representative of the respectable unimaginative middle classes; a philistine.
■ **gigmanic** /gɪgˈmanɪk/ *adjective* of, pertaining to, or characteristic of a gigman or gigmanity L19. **gigmanity** /gɪgˈmanɪti/ *noun* (*collect.*) respectable unimaginative middle-class people M19.

GIGO /ˈgʌɪgəʊ/ *abbreviation*.
COMPUTING. Garbage in, garbage out.

gigolo /ˈʒɪgələʊ, dʒ-/ *noun*. Pl. **-os**. E20.
[ORIGIN French, formed as masc. of *gigole* dancehall woman.]
A professional male dancing partner or escort; a (usu. young) man supported by a (usu. older) woman in return for his attentions.

M. MOORCOCK Gigolos on the look-out for the wives or widows of self-satisfied merchants.

gigot /ˈdʒɪgət/ *noun*. E16.
[ORIGIN French, dim. of dial. *gigue* leg, from *giguer* hop, jump, of unknown origin.]
1 A leg of mutton etc. E16.
†**2** A dish made from minced meat, a sausage. M16–M17.
3 More fully ***gigot sleeve***. A leg-of-mutton sleeve. E19.

gigster /ˈgɪgstə/ *noun*[1]. E19.
[ORIGIN from GIG *noun*[3] + -STER.]
A horse suitable for drawing a gig.

gigster /ˈgɪgstə/ *noun*[2]. M20.
[ORIGIN from GIG *noun*[4] + -STER.]
A musician who performs at a gig or gigs.

gigue /ʒiːg/ *noun*. L17.
[ORIGIN French, from JIG *noun*[1].]
A lively piece of music in duple or triple time, often forming the last movement of a suite.

Gila /ˈhiːlə/ *noun*. Also **g-**. L19.
[ORIGIN A river in New Mexico and Arizona.]
In full ***Gila monster***. A large carnivorous venomous lizard of Mexico and the south-western US, *Heloderma suspectum*, black with orange or pink markings.

gilbert /ˈgɪlbət/ *noun*. L19.
[ORIGIN William *Gilbert* (1544–1603), English physician and natural philosopher.]
PHYSICS. An electromagnetic unit of magnetomotive force in the cgs system, equal to $^{10}/_{4\pi}$ ampere-turns.

Gilbertese /gɪlbəˈtiːz/ *noun & adjective*. *hist.* E20.
[ORIGIN from the *Gilbert* Islands, from the English adventurer Thomas *Gilbert* who arrived there in 1788 + -ESE.]
▸**A** *noun*. Pl. same. A native or inhabitant of the Gilbert Islands in the mid-Pacific, formerly a British colony and since 1979 part of Kiribati. Also, the Micronesian language of the Gilbert Islands. E20.
▸**B** *adjective*. Of or pertaining to the Gilbert Islands or the Gilbertese. E20.

Gilbertian /gɪlˈbəːtɪən, -bəːʃ(ə)n/ *adjective*. L19.
[ORIGIN from W. S. *Gilbert* (see below) + -IAN.]
Of, pertaining to, or characteristic of W. S. Gilbert (1836–1911), librettist of the Gilbert and Sullivan operas, or his work; *esp.* resembling or reminiscent of a characteristically ludicrous or paradoxical situation in a Gilbert and Sullivan opera.

Daily Chronicle The Gilbertian question whether a Lord Chancellor could bring himself to justice for contempt of his own court.

Gilbertine /ˈgɪlbətiːn, -tʌɪn/ *adjective & noun*. *hist.* M16.
[ORIGIN medieval Latin *Gilbertinus*, from *Gilbertus* Gilbert of Sempringham (see below): see -INE[1].]
▸**A** *adjective*. Of or pertaining to St Gilbert of Sempringham (*c* 1083–1189) or the English religious order for men and women founded by him. M16.
▸**B** *noun*. A member of the Gilbertine order. L17.

gild /gɪld/ *noun*[1]. Also **guild**. E17.
[ORIGIN medieval Latin *gildum*, *geldum*: see GELD *noun*. Cf. GUILD *noun*[1].]
A payment, a tax.

gild *noun*[2] var. of GUILD *noun*[1].

gild /gɪld/ *verb*[1] *trans.* Pa. t. & pple **gilded**, (now chiefly in lit. sense) **gilt** /gɪlt/.
[ORIGIN Old English *gyldan* (in pa. pple *gegyld*) = Old Norse *gylla*, from Germanic base of GOLD *noun*[1].]
1 Cover with a thin layer of gold, esp. as gold leaf. OE. ▸**b** *transf.* Smear (with blood). Now *rare* or *obsolete*. L16.

R. CUMBERLAND Its magnificent owner . . had gilt and furnished the apartments with a profusion of luxury. **b** SHAKES. *Macb.* If he do bleed, I'll gild the faces of the grooms withal, For it must seem their guilt.

2 Esp. of the sun: cover, tinge, or adorn with a golden colour or light. ME.

DRYDEN Stars . . shooting through the darkness, guild the Night With sweeping Glories, and long trails of Light. E. CRISPIN Gilded and warmed by the steady October sunlight.

†**3** ALCHEMY. Impregnate (a liquid) with gold. L15–L17.
4 Supply with gold or money; make reputable or attractive by supplying with money. Now chiefly as passing into sense 5. L16. ▸**b** Of money: make reputable or attractive. E17.

C. MERIVALE The missions of proconsuls . . were gilded . . by gifts from states and potentates.

5 Give a (specious or illusory) brilliance or lustre to, esp. by the use of favourable or complimentary speech. L16.

SHAKES. *1 Hen. IV* If a lie may do thee grace, I'll gild it with the happiest terms I have.

†**6** Impart a brilliant colour or flush to (the face). *rare* (Shakes.). Only in E17.

SHAKES. *Temp.* This grand liquor that hath gilded 'em.

– PHRASES, & WITH ADVERBS IN SPECIALIZED SENSES: **gild over** cover with gilding, esp. to conceal defects (chiefly *fig.*). ***gild the lily***: see LILY *noun*. **gild the pill** make something unpleasant seem more acceptable.

†**gild** *verb*[2] *intrans. rare.* Also **guild**. M17–M18.
[ORIGIN Var. of GELD *verb*[2]. Cf. medieval Latin *geldare*, *gildare* pay geld, tax.]
Pay a tax or taxes.

gildable /ˈgɪldəb(ə)l/ *adjective & noun*. *obsolete* exc. *hist.* Also **guild-**. L15.
[ORIGIN from GILD *verb*[2] + -ABLE.]
(An area) subject to taxation.

†**gildard** *noun* see GILDER *noun*[2].

gilded /ˈgɪldɪd/ *ppl adjective*. OE.
[ORIGIN pa. pple of GILD *verb*[1]: see -ED[1]. Cf. GILT *ppl adjective*.]
1 That has been gilded; *spec.* overlaid wholly or partially with a thin coating of gold. OE.
2 Tinged with a golden colour. L16.
– SPECIAL COLLOCATIONS: **gilded cage** a luxurious but restrictive environment. †**gilded spurs** = ***gilt spurs*** s.v. GILT *ppl adjective*. **gilded youth** = JEUNESSE DORÉE.

†**gilden** *adjective*.
[ORIGIN Old English *gylden* = Old Frisian *gulden*, *gelden*, Old Saxon *guldīn* (Dutch *gulden*), Old High German *guldīn* (arch. German *gülden*), Old Norse *gullenn*, Gothic *gulþeins*, from Germanic base of GOLD *noun*[1]: see -EN[4].]
1 Golden. OE–L16.
2 Gilded, gilt. (*rare* after M17.) M16–L19.

gilder /ˈgɪldə/ *noun*[1]. ME.
[ORIGIN from GILD *verb*[1] + -ER[1].]
A person who gilds something, *esp.* one who practises gilding as an art or a trade.

gilder /ˈgɪldə/ *noun*[2]. *obsolete* exc. *N. English*. In sense 2 also †**gildard**. ME.
[ORIGIN Old Norse *gildra* (fem.) a trap, *gildri* (neut.) the laying of a trap.]
1 A snare of horsehair etc., esp. for catching birds. ME.
2 A piece or section of an angler's line made of twisted horsehair; a tought. L17.

Gilderoy /ˈgɪldərɔɪ/ *noun*. Chiefly *US colloq.* M19.
[ORIGIN A Scot. robber said to have been hanged higher than other criminals on account of the wickedness of his crimes.]
higher than Gilderoy's kite, extremely high, out of sight.

gilding /ˈgɪldɪŋ/ *verbal noun*. LME.
[ORIGIN from GILD *verb*[1] + -ING[1].]
1 The action or process of GILD *verb*[1]. LME.
2 The golden surface produced by gilding; a thin layer (of gold) with which something is gilded. M17.
– COMB.: **gilding metal** a copper-rich alloy formerly used to make objects to be gilded; now *esp.* brass containing 95 per cent copper and 5 per cent zinc.

gilet /ˈʒiːleɪ, *foreign* ʒilɛ (*pl. same*)/ *noun*. L19.
[ORIGIN French.]
A light padded waistcoat, worn esp. by women.

gilgai /ˈgɪlgʌɪ/ *noun*. *Austral.* Also **ghilgai**. M19.
[ORIGIN Wiradhuri and Kamilaroi *gilgaay*.]
A shallow depression between mounds or ridges, in which rainwater collects, probably formed by differential expansion in certain alluvial soils.

gilguy /ˈgɪlgʌɪ/ *noun*. M19.
[ORIGIN Unknown.]
NAUTICAL. **1** A temporary guy for bearing up a boom or a derrick. M19.
2 A gadget, esp. of an unspecified kind. *slang*. L19.

gill /gɪl/ *noun*[1]. ME
[ORIGIN Old Norse (whence Swedish *gäl*, †*gel*, Danish *gjælle*), from a base rel. to Old Norse *gjǫlnar* pl. = gills of a fish (cf. Old Danish *fiskegæln*), from a base cogn. with Greek *khelunē* lip, jaw, *kheilos* lip.]
1 An organ of respiration in fish and some amphibians, in which oxygen is taken up into the blood from a current of

water over vascular tissue within or connected to the wall of the pharynx or gullet. ME. ▸**b** An organ of respiration in many aquatic invertebrates, variously situated and functioning as the gills of fish. E19.
2 *sing.* & (usu.) in *pl.* **a** The wattles on the neck of a fowl. E17. ▸**b** The flesh below a person's jaw and ears. E17.

b C. SMITH 'My dear Sir!' replied Sir Appulby, in visible confusion, his fat gills quivering.

b green about the gills, yellow about the gills, white about the gills, blue about the gills miserable-looking, sickly looking. **rosy about the gills** healthy-looking.
3 Usu. in *pl.* The radiating plates arranged vertically in the underside of the cap of mushrooms and other agaric fungi. E18.
4 In *pl.* The corners of a stand-up collar. *arch. slang.* E19.
– COMB.: **gill arch, gill bar** any of a series of bony or cartilaginous curved bars placed along the pharynx and supporting the gills of fish and amphibians; any of the corresponding rudiments in the embryos of higher vertebrates; **gill cleft** = *gill slit* below; **gill cover**: of skin protecting the gills of fish, usu. stiffened with bony plates; = OPERCULUM; **gill filament, gill lamella, gill leaflet** any of the vascular plates forming the gills of fish, molluscs, etc.; **gill maggot** a copepod of the genus *Salmincola*, the larvae of which are ectoparasitic on the gills of salmon; **gill net**: hung vertically to trap fish by entangling the gills; **gill plate** = *gill filament* above; **gill pouch** (*a*) ZOOLOGY a pouch containing the gills (as in cyclostome fish) or into which they open (as in acorn worms); (*b*) EMBRYOLOGY any of a series of paired indentations in the pharyngeal wall of all vertebrate embryos, which give rise to the gill slits of fish and amphibians; **gill raker** any of the processes on the inner side of a gill arch which prevent solid matter from entering the gill; **gill slit** any of a series of openings between gill arches a net through which water passes from the pharynx to the exterior; any of the corresponding grooves in the embryos of higher vertebrates.

gill /gɪl/ *noun*[2]. Also **ghyll**. ME.
[ORIGIN Old Norse *gil* deep glen, cogn. with *geil*. The spelling *ghyll* was introduced in L18 by Wordsworth.]
1 A deep cleft or ravine, usu. wooded and forming the course of a stream. ME.
2 A narrow mountain torrent. E17.

gill /dʒɪl/ *noun*[3]. ME.
[ORIGIN Old French *gille, gelle*, in medieval Latin *gillo, gillus, gellus*, late Latin *gello, gillo* water pot.]
1 A measure of liquid or (in Britain) dry capacity, containing a quarter of a pint: in Britain (more fully ***imperial gill***) equivalent to 8.67 cu. in. (0.142 litre), in the US (more fully ***US gill***) equivalent to 7.22 cu. in. (0.118 litre). Also *local*, half a pint, esp. of wine, beer, etc. ME.
2 A container having the capacity for such a measure. *rare.* LME.

gill /dʒɪl/ *noun*[4]. Also **j-**. LME.
[ORIGIN Abbreviation of female forename *Gillian* from French *Juliane* from Latin *Juliana*, orig. fem. adjective from *Julius* name of a Roman gens: see -AN, -IAN.]
1 (Also **G-**.) A young woman. Freq. *derog.* LME.
Jack and Jill: see JACK *noun*[1].
2 In full ***gill-creep-by-ground***, ***gill-go-by-ground***. Ground ivy. *dial.* L16.
3 A female ferret. *colloq.* M19.

gill /dʒɪl/ *noun*[5]. Chiefly *dial.* Also **j-**. L18.
[ORIGIN Unknown.]
A two-wheeled machine used for the transport of timber.

gill /gɪl/ *noun*[6]. E19.
[ORIGIN Uncertain: perh. from French *aiguille* needle.]
hist. A device for preparing and combing flax etc., having a series of points used to divide the fibres into filaments.

gill /gɪl/ *verb*[1] *trans.* LME.
[ORIGIN from GILL *noun*[1].]
1 Gut or clean (fish). LME.
2 Cut off the gills of (a mushroom). E18.
3 Catch (fish) in a gill net. L19.
■ **giller** *noun* ME.

gill /gɪl/ *verb*[2] *trans.* L19.
[ORIGIN from GILL *noun*[6].]
hist. Prepare (flax etc.) using a gill.

gillaroo /gɪlə'ruː/ *noun.* L18.
[ORIGIN Irish *giolla ruadh*, from *giolla* lad, fellow + *ruadh* red.]
A trout, *Salmo trutta*, of a variety ('*stomachicus*') found locally in Ireland, having a part of the stomach toughened for crushing the shells of molluscs.

gilled /gɪld/ *adjective.* E19.
[ORIGIN from GILL *noun*[1], *verb*[1]: see -ED[2], -ED[1].]
1 Having gills (of a specified kind). E19.
2 That has been gilled. L20.

gillenia /dʒɪ'liːnɪə, gɪ-/ *noun.* E19.
[ORIGIN mod. Latin (see below), from Arnold Gill or *Gillenius*, 17th-cent. German botanist: see -IA[1].]
Either of two N. American herbaceous plants of the genus *Gillenia*, of the rose family (also called ***Indian physic***); the root of such a plant, used as an emetic.

gillery /'gɪl(ə)ri/ *noun. obsolete* exc. *dial.* Also †**guilery**. ME.
[ORIGIN Old French *g(u)ilerie*, from *guiler*: see GUILE *verb*.]
Deception, deceit, trickery.

gill-flirt /'dʒɪlfləːt/ *noun. arch. derog.* Also **j-**. M17.
[ORIGIN from GILL *noun*[4] + FLIRT *noun* or *verb*. Cf. FLIRT-GILL.]
A wanton; a girl or young woman of giddy character.

gillie /'gɪli/ *noun*[1]. Orig. *Scot.* Also **ghillie**, **gilly**. L17.
[ORIGIN Gaelic *gille* = Irish *giolla* lad, servant.]
1 *hist.* An attendant on a Highland chief. Earliest in ***gillie-wetfoot*** (*derog.*), the servant who carried a chief across a stream. L17.
2 A man or boy attending a person hunting or fishing, esp. in Scotland. M19.

R. MACAULAY Sir Angus . . knew all their names, . . those of the ponies, the gillies, the keepers.

3 (Usu. **ghillie**) A type of shoe with laces along the instep and no tongue, esp. as used for Scottish country dancing. M20.

gillie /'dʒɪli/ *noun*[2]. *Scot. rare.* L18.
[ORIGIN from GILL *noun*[3] + -IE.]
A gill of liquor.

gillion /'gɪljən, 'dʒɪ-/ *noun.* M20.
[ORIGIN from GI(GA- + MI)LLION.]
A thousand million; a large number.

gilly *noun* var. of GILLIE *noun*[1].

gillyflower /'dʒɪlɪflaʊə/ *noun.* Also (now *dial.*) **gilliver** /'dʒɪlɪvə/ & other vars. ME.
[ORIGIN Alt. (by assim. to *flower*) of Old French *gilofre, girofle* from medieval Latin *caryophyllum* clove from Greek *karuophullon*, from *karuon* nut + *phullon* leaf: cf. ***clove gillyflower*** s.v. CLOVE *noun*[2] I.]
†**1** A clove. ME–E16.
2 Any of various cultivated flowers with a scent like that of cloves; *esp.* = CLOVE *noun*[2] 2. Also (*dial.*), the wallflower, *Erysimum cheiri*; (in full ***stock-gillyflower***) the stock, *Matthiola incana*. LME.

gilpy /'gɪlpi/ *noun* & *adjective. Scot.* E18.
[ORIGIN Unknown.]
▸ **A** *noun.* A lively young girl. E18.
▸ **B** *adjective.* Lively, sportive. M19.

gilravage /gɪl'ravɪdʒ/ *verb* & *noun. Scot.* & *N. English.* M18.
[ORIGIN Unknown.]
▸ **A** *verb intrans.* Feast or revel riotously or excessively. M18.
▸ **B** *noun.* Riotous or lively behaviour; (an act of) romping. L18.
■ **gilravager** *noun* E19.

Gilsonite /'gɪlsənʌɪt/ *noun.* Also **g-**. L19.
[ORIGIN from S. H. *Gilson*, 19th-cent. US mineralogist + -ITE[1].]
MINERALOGY. (Proprietary name for) the mineral uintaite.

gilt /gɪlt/ *noun*[1]. ME.
[ORIGIN Old Norse *gyltr.*]
A female pig; *spec.* a young sow.

gilt /gɪlt/ *noun*[2]. LME.
[ORIGIN from GILT *ppl adjective.*]
1 = GILDING 2. LME.
take the gilt off the gingerbread strip something of its attractions.
2 Gold; money. *arch.* L16. ▸**b** A gilt-edged security. Freq. in *pl.* M20.

†**gilt** *noun*[3]. *slang.* E17.
[ORIGIN Unknown.]
1 A thief, a burglar. E17–L18.
2 A skeleton key, a picklock. L17–M19.

gilt /gɪlt/ *ppl adjective.* ME.
[ORIGIN pa. pple of GILD *verb*[1]: cf. GILDED.]
Gilded.
silver gilt: see SILVER *noun* & *adjective*.
– COMB. & SPECIAL COLLOCATIONS: **gilt bronze**: gilded over fire with a gold-mercury amalgam, used for ornamental work (cf. ORMOLU); **gilt-edge** *adjective* & *noun* (*a*) *adjective* = ***gilt-edged*** below; (*b*) *noun* a gilt-edged security; **gilt-edged** *adjective* & *noun* (*a*) *adjective* having a gilt edge or edges; (of a security, esp. British government stock) having a high degree of reliability as an investment; high quality; (*b*) *noun* in *pl.*, gilt-edged securities; **gilthead** any of several fishes having golden markings on the head; *esp.* an edible bream, *Sparus aurata*, of the Mediterranean and eastern Atlantic; **gilt spurs** *arch.* an emblem of knighthood; **gilt-tail** any of various yellowish maggots used for trout-fishing; **giltwood** *adjective* made of wood and gilded; †**gilt youth** = GILDED ***youth***.

gilt /gɪlt/ *verb*[1] *trans.* Now only *Scot.* & *N. English.* LME.
[ORIGIN from GILT *adjective* by extension of the ppl form to the rest of the verb.]
= GILD *verb*[1].

gilt *verb*[2] *pa. t.* & *pple*: see GILD *verb*[1].

Gilyak /'gɪljak/ *noun* & *adjective.* M19.
[ORIGIN Russian *gilyak.*]
▸ **A** *noun.* Pl. **-s**, same. A member of a people of the northern part of Sakhalin Island or the adjacent part of Siberia; the language of this people. M19.
▸ **B** *adjective.* Of or pertaining to this people or their language. L19.

gim /dʒɪm/ *adjective. obsolete* exc. *dial.* E16.
[ORIGIN Uncertain: perh. var. of JIMP *adjective*.]
Smart, spruce.

†**gimar** *noun* var. of JUMART.

gimbal /'gɪmb(ə)l, 'dʒɪm-/ *noun.* L16.
[ORIGIN Var. of GIMMAL. Cf. GIMMER *noun*[2].]
†**1** = GIMMAL 2. L16–M17.
†**2** = GEMEL 4. E17–E18.
3 *sing.* & (usu.) in *pl.* A contrivance (usu. of rings and pivots) for keeping instruments such as a compass and chronometer horizontal at sea, in the air, etc. L18.
– COMB.: **gimbal-ring** = sense 3 above.
■ **gimballed** *adjective* fitted or equipped with gimbals L19.

†**gimblet** *noun* & *verb* see GIMLET.

gimbri /'gɪmbri/ *noun.* Also **gunibri** /'guːnɪbri/. L19.
[ORIGIN Dial. var. of Arabic *qunbura* pomegranate.]
A small Moorish guitar; a player of this instrument.

gimcrack /'dʒɪmkrak/ *noun* & *adjective.* Also (earlier) †**gibe-**. ME.
[ORIGIN Unknown.]
▸ **A** *noun.* †**1** A kind of inlaid work in wood. Only in ME.
2 Orig., a contrivance, a device, a stratagem; a (fanciful) notion. Now, a useless ornament, a knick-knack. LME.

I. WALTON Nut-crackers, . . and Hobbyhorses, and many other gim-cracks . . that make a compleat Country Fair.

†**3** An affected, showy, or worthless person. E17–E19.
4 A person adept at dealing with mechanical contrivances. Now *dial.* M18.
▸ **B** *adjective.* Trivial, worthless, showy and flimsy, trumpery. M18.

C. BEATON The lack of solidity and craftsmanship, the gimcrack way in which things are put together.

■ **gimcrackery** *noun* gimcrack articles collectively L18. **gimcracky** *adjective* of a gimcrack nature E19.

gimlet /'gɪmlɪt/ *noun*, *adjective*, & *verb.* Also (now *rare* or *obsolete* exc. as in sense A.1) **gimblet** /'gɪmblɪt/. ME.
[ORIGIN Old French *guimbelet* dim. of *guimble*, from Germanic base repr. also by WIMBLE *noun*.]
▸ **A** *noun.* **1** A kind of small boring tool, usu. with a cross-piece handle and a screw at the pointed end. ME.
2 A cocktail of one part gin (occas. vodka) to one part lime juice. E20.
▸ **B** *attrib.* or as *adjective.* Of an eye etc.: piercing, penetrating; *dial.* squinting. M18.

N. MITFORD With her gimlet eye nothing escaped her. S. KING The eagle turned its gimlet gaze on him, talons shifting their grip on Ralph.

▸ **C** *verb.* **1** *verb trans.* & *intrans.* NAUTICAL. Turn (an anchor) round by rotating the stock. Chiefly as ***gimleting*** *verbal noun.* M18.
2 *verb trans.* Pierce (as) with a gimlet. M19.

J. T. FARRELL Gimleting Studs with a searching eye-to-eye gaze.

■ **gimlety** *adjective* (of an eye etc.) sharp, piercing L19.

gimmal /'dʒɪm(ə)l, 'gɪ-/ *noun.* M16.
[ORIGIN Alt. of GEMEL. See also GIMBAL, GIMMER *noun*[2].]
†**1** In full ***gimmal song***. A duet. Only in M16.
†**2** In *pl.* & (*rare*) *sing.* Joints, links, or connecting parts in machinery, esp. for transmitting motion, as in clockwork. L16–M17.
3 = GEMEL 4. Now *rare.* L16.
†**4** = GIMBAL 3. E17–L18.
■ †**gimmalled** *adjective* (*rare*) jointed: only in L16.

gimme /'gɪmi/ *verb* & *noun. colloq.* L19.
[ORIGIN Contr.: cf. LEMME.]
▸ **A** *verb trans.* & *intrans.* (*imper.*). Give me; give (it) to me. L19.

R. BOLDREWOOD Gimme some grub. P. G. WODEHOUSE 'Will you have a whisky and soda, Uncle Donald?' . . 'Yes' said his relative, . . 'Gimme.'

▸ **B** *noun.* **1** *sing.* & (usu.) in *pl.* Acquisitiveness, greed. Freq. in ***have the gimmes***, ***get the gimmes***. E20.
2 GOLF. A short easy putt, *esp.* one conceded without being played. E20.

gimmer /'gɪmə/ *noun*[1]. LME.
[ORIGIN Old Norse *gymbr* (Icelandic *gimbur*, Danish *gimmerlam*): ult. origin unknown.]
1 A ewe lamb between its first and second shearing. Orig. *Scot.* & *N. English.* LME.
2 A woman. *derog. Scot.* L18.
– COMB.: **gimmer-hog** a ewe lamb between weaning and first shearing; **gimmer-lamb** a ewe lamb between birth and weaning.

gimmer /'dʒɪmə/ *noun*[2]. *obsolete* exc. *dial.* E16.
[ORIGIN Alt. of GIMMAL. Cf. GIMBAL.]
1 A hinge. E16.
†**2** = GIMMAL 2. L16–M17.

gimmick /'gɪmɪk/ *noun* & *verb.* Orig. *US slang.* E20.
[ORIGIN Unknown.]
▸ **A** *noun.* A tricky or ingenious device (orig. in gambling or conjuring); *esp.* a contrivance, gadget, idea, etc., adopted for the purpose of attracting attention or publicity. E20.

I. BROWN Many comedians have their gimmicks, either as catch-phrase, theme-song, or bit of 'business'. *attrib.*: *Punch* Refuse to buy all goods with attached gimmick offers.

▸ **B** *verb trans.* Provide with a gimmick; alter or tamper with. M20.

G

D. BAGLEY I wasn't stupid enough to search Slade's luggage . . He would have gimmicked it so that he could tell.

■ **gimmickry** *noun* (*a*) the use of a gimmick or gimmicks; (*b*) gimmicks collectively: M20. **gimmicky** *adjective* employing or characterized by a gimmick or gimmicks; designed to attract attention or publicity: M20.

gimp /gɪmp/ *noun*[1]. Also **guimp**, **gymp**. M17.
[ORIGIN Dutch: ult. origin unknown.]
1 A silk, worsted, or cotton twist, with a cord or wire running through it, used esp. as a trimming. M17.
2 A fishing line of silk etc. bound with wire to strengthen it. E19.
3 The coarser thread which forms the outline of the design in some techniques of lace-making. M19.

gimp /gɪmp/ *noun*[2]. *rare*. M18.
[ORIGIN French *guimpe* repr. Old French *guimple* WIMPLE *noun*.]
A neckerchief worn by a nun.

gimp /gɪmp/ *noun*[3]. *slang*. E20.
[ORIGIN Unknown.]
Courage.

J. POTTS She didn't even have the gimp to make the break herself.

G

gimp /gɪmp/ *noun*[4]. *slang* (orig. *US*). E20.
[ORIGIN Uncertain: perh. alt. of GAMMY *adjective*.]
A lame or disabled person or leg. Also, a limp.
■ **gimpy** *noun & adjective* (a person who is) lame or disabled E20.

gimp /gɪmp/ *noun*[5]. *slang*. *derog*. (orig. *US*). E20.
[ORIGIN Unknown: perh. from German *Gimpel* simpleton. Cf. GIMP *noun*[4].]
A stupid or contemptible person.

gimp *adjective & adverb* var. of **JIMP** *adjective & adverb*.

gimp /dʒɪmp/ *verb*[1] *trans*. *colloq*. (now *rare* or *obsolete*). L17.
[ORIGIN Unknown.]
Give a scalloped or indented outline to.

gimp /gɪmp/ *verb*[2] *trans*. *rare*. M18.
[ORIGIN from GIMP *noun*[1].]
Trim or make with gimp.

gimp /gɪmp/ *verb*[3] *intrans*. M20.
[ORIGIN from GIMP *noun*[4].]
Limp, hobble.

gin /dʒɪn/ *noun*[1]. ME.
[ORIGIN Aphet. from Old French *engin* ENGINE *noun*.]
†**1** Skill, ingenuity. Also, cunning, craft, artifice. ME–L15.
†**2** A scheme, a device; a trick. ME–E18.
3 †**a** An instrument, a tool. ME–E17. ▸**b** A mechanical contrivance or device, a machine. *arch*. LME.
4 A contrivance for catching game etc.; a snare, a net, a trap. ME.
†**5** An instrument of torture; *spec*. the rack. ME–L16.
†**6** A military machine for hurling stones or other missiles. ME–M16.
7 A device for fastening a door or window; a bolt, a bar. *obsolete* exc. *dial*. ME.
8 a A hoisting apparatus; *spec*. a three-legged crane or derrick. LME. ▸**b** *MINING*. A windlass for pumping, lifting, etc. L17.
9 A machine for separating cotton from its seeds. M18.
10 *NAUTICAL*. An all-metal tackle block with a skeleton frame. M19.

gin /dʒɪn/ *noun*[2]. E18.
[ORIGIN Abbreviation of *geneva*, GENEVER.]
1 An alcoholic spirit distilled from grain or malt and flavoured with juniper berries; a drink of this. E18.

G. GREENE He only felt his loneliness after his third gin.

gin and orange, ***gin and tonic***, etc. ***gin and it***: see IT *noun*. HOLLANDS ***gin***. ***pink gin***: see PINK *adjective*[2].
2 In full ***gin rummy***. A form of rummy in which a player holding cards totalling ten or less may terminate play. M20.
OKLAHOMA ***gin***.
– COMB.: **gin berry** the juniper berry; ***gin-crawl***: see CRAWL *noun*[2] 1b; **gin mill** *US slang* a bar, a run-down or seedy nightclub; **gin palace** a gaudily decorated public house; **gin pennant** *NAUTICAL* a green and white flag hoisted to invite officers of other ships to come aboard for drinks; ***gin rummy***: see sense 2 above; **gin sling** a sweetened and flavoured drink of gin and water; **gin-soaked**, **gin-sodden** *adjectives* soaked with gin, given to drinking large quantities of gin.
■ **ginny** *adjective* affected by, addicted to, characterized by, or resembling gin L19.

gin /dʒɪn/ *noun*[3]. *Austral*. *slang*. *offensive*. L18.
[ORIGIN Dharuk *diyin*.]
An Aboriginal woman.

gin /gɪn/ *verb*[1]. *arch*. Also **'gin**. Infl. **-nn-**. Pa. t. **gan** /gan/, (as aux. also) †**can**. ME.
[ORIGIN Aphet. from BEGIN or Old English *onginnan*.]
1 *verb intrans*. Begin (*to*) *do*. In pa. t. formerly also in weakened sense as aux.: did *do*. ME.

R. W. DIXON Forth from that evil house gin they proceed.

2 *verb intrans*. Begin, commence; have or make a beginning. Also foll. by *at*. ME.

R. GREENE You shall to Henley . . 'Fore supper gin.

3 *verb trans*. Begin (something). ME.

gin /dʒɪn/ *verb*[2] *trans*. Infl. **-nn-**. E17.
[ORIGIN from GIN *noun*[1].]
1 Catch in a gin or trap; ensnare. E17.

M. E. G. DUFF Men are stationed with lassos to gin you dexterously.

2 Remove the seeds of (cotton) with a gin. L18.

gin /dʒɪn/ *verb*[3] *intrans*. *colloq*. Infl. **-nn-**. L19.
[ORIGIN from GIN *noun*[2].]
Drink gin or other intoxicating liquor; become drunk. Usu. foll. by *up*.
■ **ginned (up)** *adjective* drunk E20.

gin /gɪn/ *preposition & conjunction*[1]. *Scot*. & *N. English*. M18.
[ORIGIN Aphet. from AGAIN *preposition & conjunction*.]
▸**A** *preposition*. By, before (a specified time); in view of a future event. M18.

D. S. MELDRUM He'll tak' me as a 'prentice gin summer.

▸**B** *conjunction*. Before, by the time that, when, until. M18.

gin /gɪn/ *conjunction*[2]. *Scot*. & *dial*. E17.
[ORIGIN App. rel. to GIF.]
If; whether.

R. BURNS Ye shall gang in gay attire . . Gin ye'll leave your Collier Laddie.

ginep *noun* var. of **GUINEP**.

ging /gɪŋ/ *verb trans*. Now *rare* or *obsolete*. M18
[ORIGIN Unknown.]
MINING. Shore or wall up (a shaft). Also foll. by *up*.

gingall /ˈdʒɪŋg(ə)l/ *noun*. Also **-gal**, **j-**. E19.
[ORIGIN Urdu *janjāl*.]
hist. A heavy musket fired from a rest; a light swivel gun.

ginger /ˈdʒɪndʒə/ *noun & adjective*[1].
[ORIGIN Late Old English *gingifer(e)*, *gingiber* conflated in Middle English with Old French *gingi(m)bre* (mod. *gingembre*), both from medieval Latin *gingiber*, *zingeber* from Latin *zingiberi* from Greek *ziggiberis* from Pali *siṅgivera* from Dravidian: cf. Tamil *iñci* ginger, *ver* foot (Sanskrit *śṛṅgavera* infl. by *śṛṅga* horn from its antler-shaped root).]
▸**A** *noun*. **1** The hot spicy rhizome of the plant *Zingiber officinale*, used in cookery and medicine and candied as a sweet or preserved in syrup. LOE.
2 The monocotyledonous plant yielding this rhizome, *Zingiber officinale* (family Zingiberaceae), native to SE Asia. LME.

H. ALLEN Next year he would . . put in indigo, cotton, sugar cane, and ginger.

3 A fighting cock with reddish-brown plumage. L18.
4 A light reddish-yellow colour; the sandy or reddish colour of a person's hair. M19.

J. MASTERS Red hair, a sort of dull ginger.

5 *fig*. Mettle, spirit; stimulation. M19.

G. SANTAYANA This . . boy has no ginger in him, no fire.

6 (Also **G-**.) (A nickname for) a person with red hair. *colloq*. L19.
– PHRASES: **black ginger** unscraped root of ginger. **green ginger** undried root of ginger, usu. in a preserve. ***Jamaica ginger***: see JAMAICA 1. ***root ginger***: see ROOT *noun*[1]. ***stem ginger***: see STEM *noun*[1]. **white ginger** scraped root of ginger. ***wild ginger***: see WILD *adjective, noun, & adverb*.
▸**B** *adjective*. Of a light reddish-yellow colour; (of hair) sandy, reddish; (of a person) having sandy or red hair. E19.
– COMB. & SPECIAL COLLOCATIONS: **ginger ale** an aerated ginger-flavoured drink; **ginger beer** (*a*) ginger ale; *spec*. an aerated drink made by fermenting sugar, water, and bruised or ground ginger; ***ginger-beer plant***, a mixture of yeast and bacteria to ferment sugar solution in making ginger beer; (*b*) *slang* a homosexual man; **gingerbeery** *adjective* frothy, lively; **ginger group** a group within an organization which stimulates or enlivens the main body; **ginger lily** any of various chiefly Indo-Malayan plants of the genus *Hedychium*, of the ginger family, grown for their spikes of showy fragrant flowers; **ginger-nob** *slang* (*a*) a red-haired person; (*b*) a head of ginger hair; **ginger nut** (*a*) = *GINGERBREAD* ***nut***; (*b*) a ginger-flavoured biscuit; **ginger-pop** *colloq*. ginger beer, ginger ale; **ginger-race** a root of ginger; **ginger snap** a thin brittle ginger-flavoured biscuit; **ginger wine** a drink made from fermented sugar, water, and bruised ginger.
■ **gingery** *adjective* (*a*) ginger-coloured, sandy; (*b*) spiced with or as with ginger: M19.

ginger /ˈdʒɪndʒə/ *adjective*[2]. Now chiefly *dial*. E17.
[ORIGIN Back-form. from GINGERLY *adjective*.]
= **GINGERLY** *adjective*.

ginger /ˈdʒɪndʒə/ *verb trans*. E19.
[ORIGIN from GINGER *noun*.]
1 Flavour with ginger. E19.
2 Put ginger into a horse's anus to make it appear lively and spirited. E19.
3 *fig*. Enliven; stimulate, rouse *up*. M19.

M. KINGTON I just put her in to ginger things up.

gingerade /dʒɪndʒəˈreɪd/ *noun*. M19.
[ORIGIN from GINGER *noun* after *lemonade*.]
A sweet fizzy ginger-flavoured drink.

gingerbread /ˈdʒɪndʒəbrɛd/ *noun & adjective*. ME.
[ORIGIN Old French *gingembras*, *-brat* from medieval Latin *gingibratum*, *-etum*, from *gingiber* GINGER *noun & adjective*[1] + *-atum* -ATE[1]; later assim. to *ginger*, *bread*.]
▸**A** *noun*. **1** Orig., ginger, *esp*. preserved ginger. Later, cake made with treacle and flavoured with ginger (formerly made into fancy shapes which were often gilded). ME.
take the gilt off the gingerbread: see GILT *noun*[2].
2 Something showy or insubstantial. Now *esp*. elaborate carving or gaudy decoration on a building. E17.

Caribbean Quarterly Small wooden houses with much architectural gingerbread.

3 Money. *slang*. Now *rare* or *obsolete*. E18.
– COMB.: **gingerbread man** a flat gingerbread cake cut out in a shape resembling the outline of the human figure with a head, arms, and legs; **gingerbread-palm** = DOUM; **gingerbread nut** a small button-like gingerbread cake; **gingerbread-plum** (the fruit of) the gingerbread tree; **gingerbread tree** a W. African tree, *Neocarya macrophylla* (family Chrysobalanaceae), with an edible starchy fruit.
▸**B** *adjective*. Resembling the figures made of (gilded) gingerbread; *esp*. designating the ornate carved and gilded scrollwork on a ship or a building; showy, elaborate, gaudy. M18.

LADY BIRD JOHNSON A gingerbread bandstand decorated with . . bunting.

gingerly /ˈdʒɪndʒəli/ *adjective*. M16.
[ORIGIN formed as or directly from GINGERLY *adverb*: see -LY[1].]
Orig., dainty, fastidious. Later, tentative, wary, reluctant.

MRS H. WOOD Tim treading with gingerly feet past his own door. T. ROETHKE Much too wary, much too gingerly in its approach to experience.

■ **gingerliness** *noun* (*rare*) L16.

gingerly /ˈdʒɪndʒəli/ *adverb*. E16.
[ORIGIN Perh. from Old French *gensor*, *genzor* pretty, delicate, compar. of *gent* graceful from Latin *genitus* (well)-born: see -LY[2].]
†**1** Elegantly, daintily; *derog*. mincingly. E16–E17.
2 Delicately, tentatively, with great caution. M16.

R. V. JONES Gingerly opening the box because it might easily have been a bomb.

gingham /ˈgɪŋəm/ *noun & adjective*. E17.
[ORIGIN Dutch *gingang* from Malay *genggang* (orig. adjective = striped).]
▸**A** *noun*. **1** A plain-woven cotton cloth of dyed yarn, often striped or checked. E17.
2 An umbrella, *esp*. one covered with gingham. *colloq*. (now *rare* or *obsolete*). M19.
▸**B** *adjective*. Of or pertaining to gingham; made of gingham. L18.

gingili /ˈdʒɪndʒɪli/ *noun*. Also **gingelly**. E18.
[ORIGIN Hindi & Marathi *jiñjalī* from Arabic dial. *jonjolīn* from Arabic *juljulān*.]
Sesame, *Sesamum indicum*; oil from sesame seeds.

gingiv- *combining form* see **GINGIVO-**.

gingiva /ˈdʒɪndʒɪvə/ *noun*. Pl. **-vae** /-viː/. L17.
[ORIGIN Latin.]
DENTISTRY. The gum; also *spec*., the mucous membrane and underlying tissue attached to the alveolar process and cementum at the neck of a tooth.

gingival /dʒɪnˈdʒʌɪv(ə)l/ *adjective*. M17.
[ORIGIN mod. Latin *gingivalis*, from Latin *gingiva* (see GINGIVA) + -AL[1].]
Of or pertaining to the gums; (of a consonant) alveolar.

gingivitis /dʒɪndʒɪˈvʌɪtɪs/ *noun*. L19.
[ORIGIN from GINGIVA + -ITIS.]
MEDICINE. Inflammation of the gums.

gingivo- /ˈdʒɪndʒɪvəʊ, dʒɪnˈdʒʌɪvəʊ/ *combining form*. Before a vowel **gingiv-**.
[ORIGIN from GINGIVA: see -O-.]
■ **gingiˈvectomy** *noun* (an instance of) surgical removal of excess gum tissue L20. **gingivostomaˈtitis** *noun* inflammation of the gums and the mucous lining of the mouth M20.

gingko *noun* var. of **GINKGO**.

†**gingle** *verb & noun* var. of **JINGLE**.

ginglymus /ˈgɪŋglɪməs/ *noun*. Pl. **-mi** /-mʌɪ, -miː/. L16.
[ORIGIN mod. Latin from Greek *gigglumos* hinge.]
ANATOMY. A joint in the body resembling a hinge in having movement in only one plane, as the elbow.
■ **ginglyform** *adjective* hinge-shaped M19. **ginglymoid** *adjective* resembling a hinge M17.

gink /gɪŋk/ *noun*. *slang* (orig. *US*). Usu. *derog*. E20.
[ORIGIN Unknown.]
A fellow, a man.

B. BROADFOOT Skinny little ginks, but men all the same.

ginkgo /ˈgɪŋkgəʊ, ˈgɪŋkəʊ/ *noun*. Also **gingko** /ˈgɪŋkəʊ/. Pl. **-o(e)s**. L18.
[ORIGIN Japanese *ginkyō* from *gin* silver + *kyō* apricot, ult. from Chinese *yínxìng*.]
A freq. cultivated Chinese gymnospermous tree, *Ginkgo biloba*, with fan-shaped leaves and fleshy yellow fruit, the only living member of an order which flourished in Mesozoic times. Also called ***maidenhair tree***.

ginnel /ˈɡɪn(ə)l/ *noun*. Chiefly *dial*. Also **gennel** /ˈdʒɛn(ə)l/. E17.
[ORIGIN Perh. from French *chenel* CHANNEL *noun*[1].]
†1 A channel, a gutter. E–M17.
2 A long narrow (roofed) passage between buildings; an alley. M17.

D. STOREY A figure came out of the ginnel at the end of the terrace.

ginormous /dʒʌɪˈnɔːməs/ *adjective*. *slang*. M20.
[ORIGIN from GI(GANTIC + E(NORMOUS.]
Very large; impressively or shockingly big.

ginseng /ˈdʒɪnsɛŋ/ *noun*. M17.
[ORIGIN Chinese *rénshēn* (Wade–Giles *jên shên*), from *rén* man + *shēn* kind of herb.]
1 A tuberous root credited, esp. in east Asia, with valuable tonic properties. M17.
2 The source of this root, any of several plants of the genus *Panax* (family Araliaceae), with palmate leaves and umbels of small greenish flowers; esp. *P. pseudoginseng*, of Korea and Manchuria, and *P. quinquefolius*, of eastern N. America. L17.

ginzo /ˈɡɪnzəʊ/ *noun* & *adjective*. *US slang* (usu. *derog.*). Also **guinzo**. Pl. of noun **-os**. M20.
[ORIGIN Perh. from GUINEA 2b.]
(Designating) an Italian or a person of Italian descent.

gio *noun* var. of GEO.

Gioconda /dʒɪəˈkɒndə/ *adjective*. E20.
[ORIGIN *La Gioconda*, a portrait (also known as *Mona Lisa*) by Leonardo da Vinci of the wife of Francesco del Giocondo, noted for the sitter's enigmatic smile.]
Of a smile etc.: enigmatic, reminiscent of the woman in the painting *La Gioconda*. Cf. MONA LISA.

giocoso /dʒəʊˈkəʊsəʊ/ *adverb* & *adjective*. E19.
[ORIGIN Italian = merry.]
MUSIC. A direction: merrily, joyous(ly).

Giorgionesque /ˌdʒɔːdʒɪəˈnɛsk/ *adjective*. E20.
[ORIGIN from *Giorgione* (see below) + -ESQUE.]
Resembling the style of the Italian painter Giorgione Barbarelli (1478–1510).

Giorgi system /ˈdʒɔːdʒɪ ˌsɪstəm/ *noun phr*. E20.
[ORIGIN Giovanni *Giorgi* (1871–1950), Italian physicist.]
A system of units based on the metre, kilogram, second, and (usu.) ampere, which was expanded to form the SI system.

Giottesque /dʒɒˈtɛsk/ *adjective* & *noun*. M19.
[ORIGIN from *Giotto* (see below) + -ESQUE.]
▸ **A** *adjective*. Resembling the style of the Italian painter Giotto di Bondone (*c* 1267–1337). M19.
▸ **B** *noun*. The style developed by Giotto; an artist of the school, or imitating the style, of Giotto. M19.

gip /ɡɪp/ *verb trans*. Infl. **-pp-**. Also **gib** /ɡɪb/, infl. **-bb-**. E17.
[ORIGIN Unknown.]
Gut and clean (fish).

gipon /ˈdʒɪpɒn, dʒɪˈpɒn/ *noun*. LME.
[ORIGIN Old French *gip(p)on* var. of *jup(p)on*: see JUPON. Cf. GIPPO *noun*[1].]
hist. A close-fitting, padded tunic, usu. worn under a hauberk.

†**gippo** *noun*[1]. Pl. **-o(e)s**. Only in 17.
[ORIGIN French †*jup(p)eau*, earlier *jupel*: cf. GIPON, JUPON.]
A short tunic; *fig.* a scullion.

gippo *noun*[2] var. of GYPPO *noun*.

gippy /ˈdʒɪpi/ *noun* & *adjective*. *colloq*. (*offensive*). Also **gy-**, **G-**. L19.
[ORIGIN from GYPSY *noun* & *adjective* infl. by EGYPTIAN: see -Y[6]. Cf. GYPPO *noun*[2].]
▸ **A** *noun*. **1** An Egyptian, *esp*. an Egyptian soldier. L19. ▸**b** An Egyptian cigarette. E20.
2 A Gypsy. E20.
▸ **B** *attrib*. or as *adjective*. **1** Egyptian. E20.
gippy tummy diarrhoea suffered by visitors to hot countries.
2 Of or pertaining to a Gypsy or Gypsies. *rare*. E20.

†**gips** *noun pl*. var. of GIPSIES.

gipser /ˈdʒɪpsə/ *noun*. *arch*. Also **-sire** /-sʌɪə/. LME.
[ORIGIN Old French *gibecier(e*, *gibessiere* purse, pouch, gamebag (mod. *gibecière*): ult. origin unknown.]
A purse or small bag hung from a belt.

gipsies /ˈdʒɪpsɪz/ *noun pl*. Also †**gips**, †**yipseys**. ME.
[ORIGIN Prob. from or connected with the *Gypsey* Race, a river in Humberside, England.]
Springs which flow only seasonally or intermittently.

Gipsify *verb* var. of GYPSYFY.

gipsire *noun* var. of GIPSER.

gipsy *noun* & *adjective*, *verb* vars. of GYPSY *noun* & *adjective*, *verb*.

Gipsyfy *verb* var. of GYPSYFY.

giraffe /dʒɪˈrɑːf, -ˈraf/ *noun*. Also †**giraffa**. L16.
[ORIGIN Ult. from Arabic *zarāfa* through French *girafe*, Italian *giraffa*, etc.]
1 A ruminant mammal, *Giraffa camelopardalis*, of the African savannah, the tallest living animal, beige with red-brown patches, having a very long neck and forelegs. L16.
2 (Usu. **G-**.) *The* constellation Camelopardalis. M19.
3 A tall upright piano of Viennese origin, ascending in height as the strings increase in length, popular in the early 19th cent. L19.
– NOTE: The animal was earlier called CAMELOPARD.
■ **giraffid** *adjective* & *noun* of or pertaining to, any animal of, the artiodactyl family Giraffidae, comprising the giraffe, okapi, and related extinct forms L19. **giraffine** *adjective* & *noun* = GIRAFFID E20. **giraffoid** *adjective* = GIRAFFID *adjective* L19.

girandola /dʒɪˈrandola, dʒɪːr(ə)nˈdəʊlə/ *noun*. M17.
[ORIGIN Italian: see GIRANDOLE.]
1 = GIRANDOLE 2. M17.
2 = GIRANDOLE 1. L17.

girandole /ˈdʒɪr(ə)ndəʊl/ *noun*. M17.
[ORIGIN French from Italian *girandola*, from *girare* from late Latin *gyrare* gyrate.]
▸ **I 1** A kind of revolving firework; a discharge of rockets etc. from a revolving wheel. M17.
2 A revolving jet of water; a series of jets in an ornamental fountain. E19.
▸ **II 3** A branched support for candles or other lights which either stands on a surface or projects from a wall. M18.
4 An earring, a pendant, *esp*. one which has a large central stone surrounded by smaller ones. E19.

girasol /ˈdʒɪrəsɒl, -səʊl/ *noun*. Also **-sole** /-səʊl/. L16.
[ORIGIN French *girasol* or Italian *girasole*, from *girare* (see GIRANDOLE) + *sole* sun.]
†1 A sunflower. *rare*. Only in L16.
2 A variety of opal which reflects a reddish glow, a fire opal. L16.

girba /ˈɡəːbə/ *noun*. L18.
[ORIGIN Dial. var. of Arabic *qirba* waterskin.]
A leather water vessel used in N. Africa etc.

gird /ɡəːd/ *noun*[1]. *obsolete* exc. *Scot*. & *N. English*. ME.
[ORIGIN Var. of GIRTH *noun*[1], perh. infl. by GIRD *verb*[1].]
1 †**a** A girdle; a strap or band of any kind. ME–M17. ▸**b** *spec*. A saddle-girth. L16.
2 A hoop for a barrel; a hoop used as a child's plaything. M16.

gird /ɡəːd/ *noun*[2]. LME.
[ORIGIN from GIRD *verb*[2].]
1 A sharp stroke or blow. *obsolete* exc. *Scot*. & *dial*. LME.
2 A sudden movement or jerk; a spurt of action. *obsolete* exc. *dial*. M16.
3 A sharp or biting remark, a jibe, a dig. M16.
4 A spasm of pain, a sudden pang. *obsolete* exc. *Scot*. & *dial*. E17.

gird /ɡəːd/ *verb*[1] *trans*. Pa. t. & pple **girded**, **girt** /ɡəːt/. See also GIRT *ppl adjective*.
[ORIGIN Old English *gyrdan* = Old Saxon *gurdian* (Dutch *gorden*), Old High German *gurten* (German *gürten*), Old Norse *gyrða* from Germanic. Cf. GIRDLE *noun*[1], GIRTH *noun*[1].]
1 Surround, encircle (the waist), encircle the waist of (a person) with a belt or girdle, esp. in order to confine the clothes. Also foll. by *about*, *up*. OE. ▸†**b** Bind (a horse) with a saddle-girth. ME–L17. ▸**c** *fig*. Prepare (oneself) for action; brace (oneself) *for*, *to*, *to do*; summon up (one's courage). Freq. foll. by *up*. LME.

DICKENS She girded herself with a white apron. G. K. CHESTERTON Girt round the waist with a red sash. M. M. KAYE A lean, bearded tribesman . . girt about with a bandolier. **c** S. LEACOCK A great nation . . was girding itself to join in the fight for . . democracy. D. M. FRAME Man's bleak condition obliges the noble humanist to . . gird up his soul to meet the ills of life. J. A. MICHENER Let every person . . gird his courage for the days ahead.

2 *fig*. Invest *with* strength, power, or other attributes. *arch*. OE.
3 **a** Equip (oneself or another) *with* a sword suspended from a belt; invest *with* the sword of knighthood. OE. ▸**b** Fasten or fasten *on* (a sword etc.) to one's person with a belt. (Foll. by *on* one's person, *to* one's side, etc.) OE.

a S. BUTLER Was I for this entitled Sir, And girt with trusty sword and spur. **b** DICKENS Girt to his side was the steel hilt of an old sword. T. H. WHITE Sir Ector girds on the sword.

4 Secure (clothing etc.) on one's body by means of a girdle, belt, etc. Also, secure (a belt etc.) firmly or tightly. ME.

W. IRVING His blanket being girt round his waist. W. GOLDING The women . . in their long robes of linen girt above the breast.

5 Surround, encircle, enclose. ME. ▸**b** Encircle (a town etc.) with or *with* an armed force or siege works; besiege, blockade. M16.

R. L. STEVENSON Girt about on every side by clocks and chimes. JOYCE A big hall girded at half its height by a gallery. S. HEANEY His silver watch chain girds him like a hoop.

†6 Surround as with a belt; tie firmly, confine. Usu. foll. by *up*, *in*, *about*, *together*. L16–L17.
– PHRASES: **gird one's loins**, **gird up one's loins** surround one's loins with a belt, girdle, or other clothing; put on one's clothes, esp. for action; *fig*. gather or summon up one's courage.
■ **girding** *noun* (*a*) the action of the verb; (*b*) (now *rare*) that which girds; *spec*. a girdle, a saddle-girth: ME.

gird /ɡəːd/ *verb*[2]. ME.
[ORIGIN Unknown. Cf. GRIDE *verb*.]
1 *verb trans*. Strike, smite, push. *obsolete* exc. *Scot*. & *dial*. ME.
†2 *verb trans*. Move or thrust hastily or roughly; pierce, stab. ME–M17.
3 *verb intrans*. Move suddenly or rapidly; rush, start, spring. *obsolete* exc. *Scot*. & *dial*. LME.
4 *fig*. **a** *verb intrans*. Jeer or jibe *at*. M16. ▸**b** *verb trans*. Sneer or scoff at. Now *rare*. L16.

girder /ˈɡəːdə/ *noun* & *verb*. E17.
[ORIGIN from GIRD *verb*[1] + -ER[1].]
▸ **A** *noun*. **1** A main beam, orig. of wood but now often of steel or iron, used to support the joists of a floor. E17.

ANTHONY HUXLEY Strong steel girders in a ferro-concrete building.

2 A latticed or other compound structure of esp. steel or iron used to form the span of a bridge, a roof, etc. M19.
– COMB.: **girder bridge**: with a superstructure of longitudinal girders.
▸ **B** *verb trans*. Support or strengthen with or as with a girder M20.

girdle /ˈɡəːd(ə)l/ *noun*[1].
[ORIGIN Old English *gyrdel* = Middle Dutch *gurdel* (Dutch *gordel*), Old High German *gurtil*, *-ila* (German *Gürtel*), Old Norse *gyrðill*, from Germanic base of GIRD *verb*[1]: see -LE[1].]
1 A belt or cord worn around the waist to secure the clothing or as a means of carrying a purse or weapon. OE. ▸**b** A corset, *esp*. one which is elasticated and extends from the waist to the thighs. E20.

E. LINKLATER A green dress and a girdle of twisted gold. J. HAWKES The gun and the gun's girdle—the holster, straps, strings—were visible. **b** J. MASTERS She stood in the tiny bathroom . . struggling into her brassiere and girdle.

girdle of chastity a chastity belt. *VENUS'S girdle*. †**put a girdle about** go round, make a circuit of (the earth). †**turn one's girdle** (*rare*, Shakes.) make a challenge. **under one's girdle** in subjection, under one's control.
2 Something which surrounds like a girdle. OE. ▸**b** Something which confines or binds in. E17.

W. MACGILLIVRAY The horizon was bounded by a girdle of forest.

†3 That part of the body round which a girdle is worn. ME–E18.
4 *spec*. ▸**a** ANATOMY & ZOOLOGY. The bony structure supporting (*a*) the arms, forelimbs, or pectoral fins (more fully ***shoulder girdle***, ***pectoral girdle***); (*b*) the legs, hind limbs, or ventral fins (more fully ***hip girdle***, ***pelvic girdle***). E17. ▸**b** ARCHITECTURE. A small circular band around a column. E18. ▸**c** The part of a cut gem dividing the crown from the base and embraced by the setting. E19. ▸**d** A ring round the trunk of a tree made by removing the bark. E19.
– COMB.: **girdlestead** (long *arch*. *rare*) the part of the body round which a girdle is worn; the waist; **girdle-tailed lizard** any of various lizards of the family Cordylidae, esp. the genus *Cordylus*, which have the tail ringed with spiny scales and are found in southern Africa and Madagascar (also called ***zonure***).

girdle /ˈɡəːd(ə)l/ *noun*[2]. *Scot*. & *N. English*. LME.
[ORIGIN Metath. alt. of GRIDDLE.]
= GRIDDLE *noun* 2.
like a hen on a hot girdle in considerable unease or discomfort.
– COMB.: **girdle cake**: made on a griddle.

girdle /ˈɡəːd(ə)l/ *verb trans*. L16.
[ORIGIN from GIRDLE *noun*[1].]
1 Surround with or as with a girdle. (Foll. by *about*, *in*, *round*.) L16.

P. L. FERMOR Fragmentary walls . . girdled most of the little towns. K. CROSSLEY-HOLLAND A massive stronghold, girdled by flame and guarded by a giant.

2 Remove a ring of bark from (a tree, a branch) esp. as a means of killing, or from (a branch) as a means of increasing a tree's fruitfulness. M17.

girdler /ˈɡəːdlə/ *noun*. LME.
[ORIGIN from GIRDLE *noun*[1], *verb* + -ER[1].]
1 A maker of girdles. *arch*. exc. as a guild-name. LME.
2 A person who or animal which girdles something. Cf. ***twig-girdler*** s.v. TWIG *noun*[1]. L19.

giri *noun* pl. of GIRO *noun*[1].

girl /ɡəːl/ *noun*. See also GAL *noun*[1]. ME.
[ORIGIN Perh. cogn. with Low German *gör* boy, girl.]
†1 A child or young person of either sex. Usu. in *pl*. Only in ME.
†2 A roebuck in its second year. L15–E18.
3 A female child; a young or relatively young woman. Also *gen*., a woman; in *pl*., women who mix socially. M16. ▸**b** A female servant; a female employee, *esp*. a secretary or other assistant in an office, shop, factory, etc. M17.

▸c One's girlfriend or wife. M17. ▸d A black woman. *S. Afr.* & †*US* (now *offensive*). M19.

L. STRACHEY The child grew into the girl, the girl into the young woman. C. ODETS I like how you dress. The girls look nice in the summer time. *Guardian* A pretty, personable, and articulate 28-year-old girl. **b** *Times Literary Supplement* Office girls in thick scarves push heedlessly past each other. J. DORAN The shop girls had to be on their toes. **c** U. SINCLAIR Each man would bring his 'girl' with him.

– PHRASES ETC.: ***be a big girl (now)***: see BIG *adjective*. ***big girl's blouse***: see ***girl's blouse*** below. ***best girl***: see BEST *adjective* etc. ***boy-meets-girl***: see BOY *noun*. †**girl about town** a prostitute. ***girl band***: see BOY *noun*. †**girl of ease**, †**girl of the town** a prostitute. **girl's blouse** *colloq.* a weak, cowardly, or oversensitive man. ***girls together***: see ***all girls together*** above. ***hired girl***: see HIRED *ppl adjective*. **les girls** /leɪ/ [French *les* (pl.) the] girls collectively; *spec.* chorus girls. ***old girl***: see OLD *adjective*. ***sporting girl***: see SPORTING *adjective*. ***the girl next door***: see NEXT *adjective*. ***working girl***. ***Ziegfeld girl***.

– COMB.: ***girl Friday***: see FRIDAY *noun* 1; **girlfriend** a female friend, *esp.* a person's (esp. a young man's) usual or preferred female companion or sexual partner; ***Girl Guide***: see GUIDE *noun*; ***Girl Scout***: see SCOUT *noun*[3].

■ **girldom** *noun* the domain or world of girls; girls collectively: M19. **girleen** *noun* (*Irish*) a young girl M19. **girlhood** *noun* the state of being a girl; the time during which one is a girl; girls collectively: L18. **girl-less** /-l-l-/ *adjective* (*rare*) without a girl or girls E20.

girl /gəːl/ *verb*. M17.
[ORIGIN from the noun.]
1 *verb trans.* Provide with girls; *spec.* provide (a ship etc.) with girls as crew, workers, etc. *rare. joc.* M17.
2 *verb intrans.* Keep company or consort with women. L18.

girlie /ˈgəːli/ *noun & adjective*. Also **girly**. M19.
[ORIGIN from GIRL *noun* + -IE, -Y[6].]
▸ **A** *noun*. (A term of endearment for) a girl, *esp.* a little girl. M19.

S. CONRAN Kate's father . . was delighted that his girlie was featuring so prominently in local life.

▸ **B** *adjective*. **1** Girlish; characteristic of or appropriate for a girl. L19.
2 Of a publication, entertainment, etc.: featuring young women, usu. naked or semi-naked, in erotic contexts. M20.

P. ROTH The girlie magazines piled up in his barbershop.

girlish /ˈgəːlɪʃ/ *adjective*. M16.
[ORIGIN from GIRL *noun* + -ISH[1].]
Of or pertaining to a girl or girlhood; characteristic of or like a girl.

R. GITTINGS Looking more girlish than her twenty years.

■ **girlishly** *adverb* E18. **girlishness** *noun* E17.

girly *noun & adjective* var. of GIRLIE.

girly-girly /gəːlɪˈgəːli/ *adjective & noun*. L19.
[ORIGIN Redupl. of GIRLISH.]
▸ **A** *adjective*. Exaggeratedly or affectedly girlish; effeminate. L19.
▸ **B** *noun*. A girl; a little girl. L19.

girn /gəːn/ *noun*. Chiefly *Scot. & N. English*. Also **gurn**. E16.
[ORIGIN Metath. alt. of GRIN *noun*[2].]
1 The act of snarling or showing the teeth in rage, pain, disappointment, etc. E16.
2 The act of laughing or grinning. M17.

girn /gəːn/ *verb intrans*. Chiefly *Scot. & N. English*. Also (the usual form in sense 4) **gurn**. LME.
[ORIGIN Metath. alt. of GRIN *verb*[2].]
1 Show the teeth in rage, pain, disappointment, etc.; snarl. LME.
2 Show the teeth in laughing; grin. M16.
3 Whine, complain; be fretful or peevish. E18.

L. G. GIBBON Of a morning John Guthrie grumbled and girned at him.

4 Distort the features; pull a hideous face. L18.

Sunday Times Gordon Mattison . . won the world gurning championship . . by pulling the most hideous face.

girnel /ˈgəːn(ə)l/ *noun & verb*. *Scot.* Also †**garnel**. LME.
[ORIGIN Var. of GARNER *noun*.]
▸ **A** *noun*. A granary. Also, a large chest for meal. LME.
▸ †**B** *verb trans.* Infl. **-ll-**. Store up in a girnel. L15–E18.

giro /ˈdʒiːro, -əʊ/ *noun*[1]. Pl. ***-ri*** /-ri/ L17.
[ORIGIN Italian = round, circuit.]
A tour, a circuit; a turn.

giro /ˈdʒʌɪrəʊ/ *noun*[2] *& verb*. L19.
[ORIGIN German from Italian = circulation (of money).]
▸ **A** *noun*. Pl. **-os**.
1 A system of credit transfer between banks, post offices, etc.; *spec.* (freq. **G-**) a system run by the British Post Office for the banking and transfer of money. Also ***giro system***. L19.
2 In full ***giro cheque***, ***giro order***. A cheque or money order issued through the giro system; *spec.* in Britain, such a cheque used for unemployment benefit or social security payments. L20.

J. KELMAN All I'm fucking asking is regular giros and punctual counter clerks.

▸ **B** *verb trans.* Pay by giro. L20.

Gironde /dʒɪˈrɒnd, *foreign* ʒirɔ̃ːd/ *noun*. L18.
[ORIGIN A department of SW France.]
FRENCH HISTORY. The Girondist party.

Girondin /dʒɪˈrɒndɪn/ *noun & adjective*. M19.
[ORIGIN French, from GIRONDE + *-in* -INE[4].]
FRENCH HISTORY. = GIRONDIST.

Girondism /dʒɪˈrɒndɪz(ə)m/ *noun*. M19.
[ORIGIN French *Girondisme*, from GIRONDE + *-isme* -ISM.]
FRENCH HISTORY. The doctrine or practice of the Girondists.

Girondist /dʒɪˈrɒndɪst/ *noun & adjective*. L18.
[ORIGIN French *Girondiste*, from GIRONDE + *-iste* -IST.]
FRENCH HISTORY. ▸ **A** *noun*. A member of the French moderate Republican Party, in power in France during the Revolution from 1791 to 1793, and so called because the party leaders came from Gironde. L18.
▸ **B** *adjective*. Of or pertaining to the Girondists or their principles. E19.

girouette /ʒirwɛt/ *noun*. Pl. pronounced same. E19.
[ORIGIN French.]
A weathercock.

girr /gəː/ *noun*. *Scot.* M16.
[ORIGIN Var. of GIRTH *noun*[1].]
A hoop for a barrel; a hoop used as a child's plaything.

girran /ˈgɪrən/ *noun*. *Scot.* (now *dial.*). Also **gurrag** /ˈgʌrəg/, **gurry** /ˈgʌri/. E19.
[ORIGIN Gaelic *guirean* dim. of *gur* pimple.]
A small boil, a pustule.

girse /gəːs/ *noun*. *obsolete* exc. *dial.* L16.
[ORIGIN Var. of GIRTH *noun*[1], prob. from pl. *girths*.]
1 A saddle-girth; = GIRTH *noun*[1] 1. L16.
†**2** A band, a hoop; = GIRTH *noun*[1] 2. Only in L16.

girsh *noun* var. of QURSH.

girt /gəːt/ *noun*. Now *rare*. M16.
[ORIGIN Var. of GIRTH *noun*[1] surviving in techn. uses, infl. by *girt* pa. pple of GIRD *verb*[1].]
1 A saddle-girth; = GIRTH *noun*[1] 1. *obsolete* exc. *dial.* M16.
2 A girder. Latterly *US*. L16.
3 = GIRTH *noun*[1] 3. Also (*techn.*), measurement across or around a surface which is not flat, as a moulded cornice, taking into account all elevations and depressions. M17.
†**4** = GIRTH *noun*[1] 5. Only in L17.

girt /gəːt/ *ppl adjective*. E17.
[ORIGIN pa. pple of GIRD *verb*[1].]
1 *NAUTICAL*. Of a ship: moored so tightly by its cables that it cannot swing about when the tide turns. E17.
2 That has been girt. Also ***girt-up*** etc. L18.

girt /gəːt/ *verb*[1]. Now *rare*. Pa. t. & pple **girt**. LME.
[ORIGIN from GIRT *noun*.]
1 *verb trans.* = GIRD *verb*[1]. LME.
2 *verb trans.* Secure with a girth. M17.
3 a *verb trans.* Surround with a measuring line in order to ascertain the girth of. M17. ▸**b** *verb intrans.* Take a measurement by leading a line round or across the object to be measured. E19.
4 *verb intrans.* Of a tree etc.: measure (so much) in girth. M18.

– COMB.: **girting place** (*a*) that part of a horse's body where the girth is worn; (*b*) that part of a tree trunk which is girthed or measured.

girt *verb*[2] *pa. t. & pple*: see GIRD *verb*[1].

girth /gəːθ/ *noun*[1]. ME.
[ORIGIN Old Norse *gjǫrð* girdle, girth, hoop, Gothic *gairda* girdle from Germanic. See also GARTH *noun*[2], GIRD *noun*[1], GIRR, GIRSE, GIRT *noun*, and cf. GIRD *verb*[1], GIRDLE *noun*[1].]
1 A belt or band of leather or cloth tightened round the body of a horse or other beast of burden, so as to secure a saddle, pack, etc., on its back. Also ***saddle-girth***. ME. ▸**b** The part of a horse's body where the girth is fastened. M19.

W. HOLTBY Loosened her girth, pulled aside the saddle.

2 A hoop of wood or iron, esp. for a barrel. *obsolete* exc. *dial.* LME.
3 Measurement round the circumference of any more or less cylindrical object, as the trunk of a tree, the human body, etc. M17.

J. RUSKIN Walnuts, with trunks eight or ten feet in girth. V. NABOKOV Hip girth, twenty-nine inches; thigh girth . . seventeen. R. LOWELL He'd admire father's trim girth.

4 A horizontal beam or girder. *US*. E19.
5 *PRINTING*. Either of the two leather thongs or bands of webbing on the carriage of a hand printing press by which it is moved back and forth. E19.
6 *transf.* Something that encircles; the area etc. encircled. E19.

A. C. SWINBURNE That is girdled about with the round sea's girth As a town with its wall.

– COMB.: **girth-web** woven material of which girths are made; a strong broad tape or band of this material.

girth *noun*[2] see GRITH.

girth /gəːθ/ *verb*. LME.
[ORIGIN from the noun.]
1 *verb trans.* Gird, surround, encompass. LME.

SIR W. SCOTT The four seas that girth Britain.

2 *verb trans.* Fit or bind (a horse etc.) with a girth. L16.
3 *verb trans.* Secure (a saddle etc.) by means of a girth. Also foll. by *on*, *up*. E19.
4 *verb trans. & intrans.* Draw (a string or measuring line) close round or across a surface being measured. E19.
5 *verb intrans.* Measure (so much) in girth. M19.
■ **girthing** *noun* (*a*) the action of the verb; (*b*) material for making girths: LME.

girtline *noun* see GANTLINE.

Girtonian /gəːˈtəʊnɪən/ *noun*. L19.
[ORIGIN from *Girton* (see below) + -IAN.]
A student or former student of Girton College in Cambridge, orig. a women's college, but mixed since 1977.

GIS *abbreviation*.
Geographic information system, a system for storing and manipulating geographical information on computer.

gisarme /gɪˈzɑːm/ *noun*. *obsolete* exc. *hist.* ME.
[ORIGIN Old French *g(u)isarme*, *wisarme* from Frankish *wis-arm* lit. 'guide-arm': cf. Old Saxon *wisian* (= Old English *wisan*, Old High German *wisen*) show, teach.]
A kind of battleaxe, bill, or halberd, having a long blade in line with the shaft, sharpened on both sides and ending in a point.

gise /dʒʌɪz/ *verb*. *dial.* L17.
[ORIGIN Var. of or back-form. from GIST *verb*[2].]
1 *verb trans.* Pasture (land) with cattle other than one's own. L17.
2 *verb trans. & intrans.* Put (cattle) out to feed at a certain rate of payment. M19.

gisement /ˈdʒʌɪzm(ə)nt/ *noun*[1]. Also (earlier) †**gistment**. E16
[ORIGIN Aphet. from AGISTMENT. Current form recorded from L17.]
Cattle taken on to one's land to remain and feed at a certain rate per head; the payment received for this.

gisement /ʒizmɑ̃/ *noun*[2]. *rare*. M19.
[ORIGIN French.]
The way in which something lies, position.

gism *noun* var. of JISM.

gismo *noun* var. of GIZMO.

gismondine /ˈgɪzm(ə)ndiːn/ *noun*. E19.
[ORIGIN from C. G. *Gismondi* (1762–1824), Italian mineralogist + -INE[5].]
MINERALOGY. A hydrated calcium aluminosilicate of the zeolite group occurring as whitish or purple crystals, esp. in Italian volcanic rocks.
■ Also **gismondite** *noun* L19.

†**gist** *noun*[1]. ME–E18.
[ORIGIN Old French *giste* (mod. *gîte*) resting place etc.; rel. to *gésir*, *gis-* lie. See GEST *noun*[3], GIST *noun*[3].]
A stopping place, a lodging.

gist /dʒɪst/ *noun*[2]. *obsolete* exc. *dial.* LME.
[ORIGIN from GIST *verb*[2].]
The right of pasture for cattle at a certain rate of payment etc.; the payment made for this; agistment.

gist /dʒɪst/ *noun*[3]. Also (earlier, & in sense 1 only) †**git**. E18.
[ORIGIN Old French (mod. *gît*), 3rd person sing. pres. indic. of *gésir* lie (from Latin *jacere*), as in the French legal phr. *cest action gist* this action lies.]
1 *LAW*. The real ground or point of an action etc. E18.
2 The substance, essence, or main part of a matter. E19.

R. L. STEVENSON Making believe is the gist of his whole life. R. HUGHES Even though the words were unintelligible, their gist . . was not. E. BOWEN She had joined the sermon late and just got the gist of it.

†**gist** *noun*[4] *& verb*[1] see JOIST *noun & verb*.

gist /dʒɪst/ *verb*[2]. *obsolete* exc. *dial.* L15.
[ORIGIN Aphet. from AGIST. Cf. GISE.]
1 *verb trans.* = AGIST 2. L15.
†**2** *verb intrans.* = AGIST 3. E16–E17.

†**gistment** *noun* see GISEMENT *noun*[1].

git /gɪt/ *noun*[1]. *slang*. *derog.* M20.
[ORIGIN Var. of GET *noun*[1].]
A worthless person.

Listener That bald-headed, moon-faced, four-eyed git.

†**git** *noun*[2] see GIST *noun*[3].

git *verb* see GET *verb*.

gitana /dʒɪˈtɑːnə, *foreign* xiˈtana/ *noun*. M19.
[ORIGIN Spanish, fem. of GITANO.]
A female (Spanish) Gypsy.

gitano /dʒɪˈtɑːnəʊ, *foreign* xiˈtano/ *noun*. Pl. **-os** /-əʊz, *foreign* -ɔs/. M19.
[ORIGIN Spanish repr. of popular Latin = Egyptian, from Latin *Aegyptus* Egypt + *-anus* -AN.]
A male (Spanish) Gypsy.

gîte /ʒiːt, *foreign* ʒit/ *noun*. Pl. pronounced same. **L18.**
[ORIGIN French: see GIST *noun*[1].]
1 A stopping place, a lodging. Now *rare*. **L18.**
2 In France and French-speaking countries: a furnished holiday home usu. in a rural district. **M20.**

gith /gɪθ/ *noun*. Now *rare* or *obsolete*. **LME.**
[ORIGIN Latin *gith*, *git*, *gicti*, from Semitic.]
Any of various plants of the genus *Nigella*, of the buttercup family; *esp.* the fennel flower, *N. sativa*.

gittern /ˈgɪtəːn/ *noun*. **LME.**
[ORIGIN Old French *guiterne* (perh. through Middle Dutch *giterne*), obscurely rel. to CITTERN and GUITAR.]
An early plucked gut-stringed musical instrument of the guitar kind.
■ **gitterner** *noun* (long *rare*) a player on the gittern **LME.**

Giunta /ˈdʒʊntə/ *noun*. **L17.**
[ORIGIN Italian (= Spanish, Portuguese JUNTA), from *giungere* join.]
hist. In the Venetian republic: a number of patricians chosen to act as advisers in special emergencies; later, the co-opted members of the council which ran the affairs of the state.

Giuoco Piano /dʒʊˌəʊkəʊ ˈpjɑːnəʊ, pɪˈɑːnəʊ/ *noun phr.* **E19.**
[ORIGIN Italian = quiet game.]
CHESS. An initially quiet opening, formerly popular esp. among Italian players; *spec.* = ***Italian opening*** s.v. ITALIAN *adjective*.

†**giust** *noun* see JOUST *noun*.

give /gɪv/ *noun*. **M19.**
[ORIGIN from the verb.]
Giving; *spec.* the quality of yielding to pressure, elasticity, flexibility.

> *Times* If the weather stays fine we should have a fair surface with some give in it. P. ANGADI It was a one-way thing, this concern for one's children; all give and no take. *New Yorker* He's terribly conservative in things that matter. He has absolutely no give about them at all.

give /gɪv/ *verb*. Pa. t. **gave** /geɪv/; pa. pple **given** /ˈgɪv(ə)n/.
[ORIGIN Old English *ġiefan*, *ġefan* = Old Frisian *jeva*, Old Saxon *gean* (Dutch *geven*), Old High German *geban* (German *geben*), Old Norse *gefa*, Gothic *giban*, from Germanic, with no certain Indo-European cognates. Initial /g/ from Scandinavian in Middle English. See also GIMME.]
(As *verb trans.* where appropriate foll. by indirect obj. or *to*, (arch.) *unto* a recipient.)
▸ **I 1** *verb trans.* Hand over as a present; transfer the possession of gratuitously; confer ownership on with or without actual delivery. **OE.** ▸**b** *verb intrans.* Bestow alms or donations (*to*), give presents. **ME.** ▸**c** *verb trans.* LAW. Bequeath, devise. Chiefly in ***give and bequeath***, ***give and devise***. **LME.** ▸**d** *verb trans.* Render (a benefit or service) without payment. **E18.**

> J. STEINBECK The little brown pennies he gave sparingly for alms. **b** C. M. YONGE She gave largely to hospitals. **d** OED He has charged only for the material; he has given his labour.

2 *verb trans.* Confer, grant, bestow, (favour, honour, etc., (of a higher power, esp. God) a physical or mental quality, a blessing, an advantage, etc.); grant *to be*, *to do*; accord to another (one's affection, confidence, etc.). **OE.** ▸**b** ***give me*** — (*imper.*), I prefer or admire, I am in favour of. **L16.**

> F. W. ROBERTSON It was given to the Apostle Paul to discern that this was the ground of unity. J. BRYCE Under such a charter the mayor is given power and opportunity to accomplish something. TENNYSON Sweet is true love tho' given in vain. **b** S. J. PERELMAN Give me home cooking every time.

3 *verb trans.* Sanction the marriage of (a daughter or female ward). Now chiefly in ***give in marriage***. **OE.**

> V. WOOLF Prue Ramsay, leaning on her father's arm, was given in marriage.

4 *verb trans.* Deliver, hand over, (with no reference to ownership); put (food, drink) for a person to consume (also with ellipsis of obj. (now *literary*) ***give to eat***, ***give to drink***); administer as a medicine or drug. **OE.** ▸**b** Communicate or impart (a message, one's love, compliments, etc.) to a person. **E17.** ▸**c** Connect telephonically with (a specified person or place). Usu. in *imper.* **L19.**

> H. T. LANE Often a child is simply given a rubber ring to bite. E. J. HOWARD He gave her the water, and stood beside her while she drank.

give the boot, ***give the sack***, etc.

5 *verb trans.* Commit, consign, entrust, (usu. *into the care, custody, hands*, etc., *of*); hand over as a pledge, assign as a guarantee. **OE.**
6 Make over in exchange or payment; exchange, buy, or sell *for* a price; pay (a price); (now *rare* exc. in biblical allusions) pay as due or demanded. **ME.** ▸**b** *verb intrans.* In neg. contexts: care *a curse*, *a damn*, etc. *colloq.* **L17.**

> J. LOCKE He would give his Nuts for a piece of Metal. W. GOLDING It was just my size and I should have it for no more than he had given for it. **b** A. LURIE In his present mood he doesn't give a shit.

7 *verb trans.* Sacrifice, submit to the loss of for some object; dedicate, devote; apply or devote (oneself) exclusively *to*, †*to do*; *refl.* (esp. of a woman) yield (*to*) in sexual intercourse. **ME.**

> E. A. FREEMAN The Abbots . . had given their lives in the cause of England. M. J. GUEST He made a resolution to give to God the half of his services. R. MACAULAY Barbara . . gives herself to a young fisherman. O. MANNING She tried to give her attention to the menu.

8 *verb trans.* Perform (an action), exert (an effort), esp. to affect another person or as a reaction or response; emit (a cry etc.). **ME.** ▸**b** *verb intrans.* Deal a blow, make an attack or charge (*at*, *on*, *upon*). *obsolete* exc. BOXING. **LME.** ▸**c** *verb trans.* Punish a person for (esp. an idea just expressed or words just uttered). *colloq.* **E20.** ▸**d** *verb intrans.* JAZZ. Play music excitingly or enthusiastically. Also foll. by *out*. **M20.**

> E. WAUGH Lady Circumference gave a resounding snort of disapproval. A. SILLITOE He gave her a vicious clout across the face. E. WELTY He gave another imploring look. H. BASCOM The first mate . . gives a blast on the steamer's siren. *New Yorker* A novel I would need to give a final reading to. **c** M. ALLINGHAM 'The bear, perhaps,' he suggested . . . 'I'll give you bear,' the woman said.

9 *verb trans.* Address (words) *to*; issue (a command etc.); pronounce (a blessing etc.); provide (information, evidence, etc.) verbally; [prob. from ellipsis of *God* etc. in complimentary wishes] wish *good day* etc.; *colloq.* tell, offer, (esp. something unacceptable). **ME.** ▸**b** *verb intrans.* Tell what one knows. *colloq.* **M20.**

> DICKENS He heard them give each other Merry Christmas. R. TRAVERS He enlisted as a private . . , giving his name as John McKnight. *Daily Telegraph* The Ulster Defence Association gave warning yesterday that it will take 'appropriate' action against police officers. S. BELLOW He gave his okay. **b** P. LIVELY Come on then, give! Where did you find him?

10 *verb trans.* Deliver (a judgement etc.) authoritatively; decide (a case, *it*) *for* or *against* a litigant; (of an umpire in cricket) declare a batsman etc. *out* or *not out*. **ME.**
11 *verb trans.* As **given** pa. pple: (of a document) dated. **LME.**
12 *verb trans.* Provide (a party, meal, etc.) as a host or benefactor or for the gratification of others; provide or conduct (a tour etc.) as a guide or helper. **E16.**

> GOLDSMITH Intended that night giving the young ladies a ball. J. GALSWORTHY No Forsyte has given a dinner without providing a saddle of mutton.

▸ **II 13** *verb trans.* Present, offer; hold out to be taken; expose to view or observation; show, indicate; state to be *at*; mention, include in a list. **OE.** ▸†**b** Display as an armorial bearing, bear. **M16–M17.** ▸**c** Represent, describe, report to be. Now *rare*. **E17.** ▸**d** Propose as a sentiment or toast. **E18.**

> DRYDEN All . . Give to the wanton Winds their flowing Hair. N. HAWTHORNE He holds out his hand; she gives her own. OED Such words ought not to be given in a dictionary. *Times* The conclusions, details of which are given today. E. CRISPIN Radio Three gave rain. **c** TENNYSON What practice howso'er expert . . Hath power to give thee as thou wert? **d** R. DAVIES 'I give you the Devil!' He raised his glass.

†**14** *verb trans.* Of one's mind, conscience, etc.: suggest to one *that*; misgive; prompt one *to do*. **ME–E19.**
15 *verb trans.* Read, recite, sing, or act in the presence of auditors or spectators; perform, produce, (a play etc.); deliver (a lecture etc.). **LME.**

> THACKERAY Who will give us a song? A. S. NEILL I gave a lecture in the village hall. S. BRETT We worked together on a pantomime . . . *Cinderella*. You gave your Baron Hardup.

▸ **III 16** *verb trans.* Allot, apportion, cause to have as one's share; assign, impose. **OE.** ▸†**b** Appoint to an office or function. **M16–E17.** ▸**c** Allow or predict (a period of time) for completion or accomplishment. **M19.**

> H. JAMES The amount of thought they give to their clothing. E. WAUGH She gave us the best room. **c** *Observer* The wiseacres . . gave Charles Chaplin and Oona O'Neill's marriage six months. It's lasted decades. A. F. LOEWENSTEIN She'll last a month . . . I give her till Thanksgiving.

17 *verb trans.* Cause to have or receive; induce (a state etc.); impart, communicate, be the source or origin of. **ME.** ▸**b** Cause *to do*. **M16.**

> M. PATTISON The Loire, its banks still clad with the broom which gives their title to the Plantagenets. W. S. MAUGHAM He gave her life an interest and excitement. J. FOWLES It gave . . the lovely illusion that one was the . . first man that had ever stood on it. *Daily Telegraph* He had accused her of . . having given him VD.

18 *verb trans.* Supply, yield, provide as a product; yield as the result of calculation or measurement. **ME.** ▸†**b** Yield the conclusion *that*; signify. **LME–L17.** ▸†**c** Be worth, fetch (a price). **L16–L18.**

> D. CARNEGIE A cow has to give milk. J. BARNES Orange on red gives dark brown.

19 *verb trans.* Ascribe, attribute. **L15.** ▸†**b** Consider to be, account as. Also ***give for***. **E17–M18.**

> M. J. GUEST Henry . . gave all the glory to God.

20 *verb trans.* Allow to have or take; concede. **M16.**

> DRYDEN They give their Bodies due Repose at Night. J. PUDNEY He was a trier/I'll give him that, the Hun. *New Yorker* Winning . . by slightly more than a length from Sharp Gary, to whom he gave five pounds.

21 *verb trans.* As **given** pa. pple: assigned or posited as a basis for calculation or reasoning; assuming as a fact. **L16.**

> H. CARPENTER Childlike resilience was a distinct asset, given her domestic situation.

▸ **IV 22** *verb intrans.* Be affected, esp. detrimentally, by physical conditions; fade; deteriorate; become damp; shrink. **M16.**
23 *verb intrans.* Yield to pressure or strain; collapse, lose firmness (*lit.* & *fig.*); become relaxed; accommodate oneself or itself *to*; make concessions. **L16.** ▸**b** Of weather: relax in severity, become milder, thaw. **L17.**

> V. WOOLF It was her odious, weak, vacillating character again, always giving at the critical moment. I. MURDOCH Some stretched cord seemed to twang far away, something gave and broke. *Time Out* Thames have given and given over this but received no concessions from the other side. M. AMIS The heavy door at the top didn't give until the fifth push.

24 *verb intrans.* Afford a view or passage; look, lead, *into*, *on to*, *(up)on*, etc. **M19.**

> C. JACKSON The windows that gave on Seneca Street, six floors below. D. ADAMS Other corridors gave off it to the left and right.

25 *verb intrans.* Be happening. Chiefly in ***what gives?*** *colloq.* **M20.**

G

– PHRASES: (A selection of cross-refs. only is included: see esp. other nouns.) ***give a back***: see BACK *noun*[1]. ***give a free hand***: see FREE *adjective*. ***give a good account of***: see ACCOUNT *noun*. ***give a hand***: see HAND *noun*. ***give (a horse) its head***: see HEAD *noun*. ***give a miss***: see MISS *noun*[1]. **give and take** exchange words, blows, or concessions. ***give a person a hand***: see HAND *noun*. ***give a person beans***: see BEAN *noun*. ***give a person fits***: see FIT *noun*[2]. **give a person furiously to think** [translating French *donner furieusement à penser*] set a person thinking hard; give a person cause for thought, puzzle. ***give a person his or her colours***: see COLOUR *noun*. ***give a person his or her due***: see DUE *noun* 2. ***give a person ideas***: see IDEA *noun*. ***give a person the air***: see AIR *noun*[1] 3. ***give a person the gate***: see GATE *noun*[1]. ***give a person the hump***: see HUMP *noun*. ***give a person the push***: see PUSH *noun*[1]. ***give a person the slip***: see SLIP *noun*[3] 6. ***give a person the wall***: see WALL *noun*[1]. ***give a piece of one's mind***: see MIND *noun*[1]. **give as good as one gets** retort adequately in words or blows. ***give a wide berth to***: see BERTH *noun* 1a. ***give battle***: see BATTLE *noun*. ***give best***: see BEST *adjective* etc. ***give birth to***: see BIRTH *noun*[1] 1. ***give chase (to)***: see CHASE *noun*[1] 1. ***give colour to***: see COLOUR *noun*. ***give credence to***: see CREDENCE 1. ***give ground***: see GROUND *noun*. ***give guard***: see GUARD *noun*. ***give hell***: see HELL *noun*. ***give in charge***: see CHARGE *noun* 9. †**give into** yield to, give in to. **give it to**, **give it hot to**, **give it hot and strong to** administer punishment to. ***give mouth***: see MOUTH *noun*. ***give occasion to***: see OCCASION *noun*. **give of oneself** act unselfishly, devote oneself to a specified person or thing. ***give oneself airs***: see AIR *noun*[1] 10. ***give one's hand***: see HAND *noun*. ***give one's heart to***: see HEART *noun*. ***give one's love to***: see LOVE *noun*. ***give one's mind to***: see MIND *noun*[1]. ***give one's word***: see WORD *noun*. **give or take** *colloq.* add or subtract (a quantity etc.) in estimating. ***give pause to***: see PAUSE *noun*. ***give place to***: see PLACE *noun*[1]. ***give rein (to)***: see REIN *noun*[1]. ***give rise to***: see RISE *noun*. **give something to cry about**, **give something to cry for** chastise (esp. a child) for causeless crying. ***give suck***: see SUCK *verb*. ***give thanks***: see THANK *noun*. ***give the devil his due***: see DUE *noun* 2. ***give the finger to***: see FINGER *noun*. ***give the gun***: see GUN *noun*. ***give the guy to***: see GUY *noun*[2]. ***give the lie to***: see LIE *noun*[1]. ***give the long handle***: see HANDLE *noun*[1]. ***give thought to***: see THOUGHT *noun*[1]. **give to know** inform, assure. ***give tongue***: see TONGUE *noun*. **give to understand** inform, assure. ***give vent to***: see VENT *noun*[2] 3. ***give way***: see WAY *noun*. **give what for** *slang* punish or scold (a person) severely. ***not give a hang***: see HANG *noun*. **would give anything**, **would give one's ears**, **would give one's eye teeth**, **would give the world**, etc., would make any sacrifice *for*, *if*, *to do*.

– WITH ADVERBS IN SPECIALIZED SENSES: **give about** *arch.* circulate (writings etc.), spread (a rumour etc.). **give again** (*obsolete* exc. *dial.*) soften, yield. **give away** (*a*) transfer by gift, dispose of as a present; hand over (a bride) ceremonially to a bridegroom; ***give away with a pound of tea***, ***give away with a packet of tea***, part with cheaply, regard as worthless; †(*b*) sacrifice (another's interest or rights); (*c*) betray or expose to ridicule or detection, let slip inadvertently; ***give the game away***: see GAME *noun*; ***give the show away***, ***give the whole show away***: see SHOW *noun*[1]; (*d*) distribute, present, (prizes etc.); (*e*) *Austral.* & *NZ slang* abandon, give up, stop, (chiefly in ***give it away***); (*f*) (now *US*) give way. **give back** (*a*) return (a thing) to a previous owner or in exchange, return, restore; reflect, echo; †(*b*) retreat, fall back. **give down** (of a cow) let flow (milk), give milk. **give forth** (*a*) emit; (*b*) publish, report. **give in** (*a*) yield (*to*), concede defeat (*to*); stop fighting or arguing; (*b*) hand in (a document etc.) to a proper official. **give off** †(*a*) relinquish, leave off (something); cease, quit the field; (*b*) emit (a smell, vapour, etc., light, noise); (*c*) send out as a branch or other outgrowth. **give out** (*a*) announce, proclaim, profess, (*that*, *to be*); publish; (*b*) emit; (*c*) issue, distribute; (*d*) desist, now esp. through exhaustion or lack of patience; break down; run short, come to an end. **give over** (*a*) cease from (an action, *doing*); abandon (a habit etc.); cease, desist; (*b*) devote, surrender, hand over, (*to*); *arch.* = ***give up*** (*h*) below. **give up** (*a*) hand over, part with, resign, surrender; deliver (a fugitive etc.) into the hands of pursuers; abandon (oneself) *to* a feeling or influence; (*b*) relinquish the prospect of, cease to have to do with, cease from (an action, *doing*); (*c*) cease from effort, stop trying; succumb; (*d*) devote entirely *to* (chiefly *refl.* or in *pass.*); †(*e*) deliver (an account etc.); present (a petition etc.); (*f*) emit, breathe forth, (now only in ***give up the ghost*** s.v. GHOST *noun*); (*g*) divulge, reveal; (*h*) pronounce incurable or insoluble, abandon hope for

or of; (foll. by *for*) abandon hope for as (dead, lost, etc.); (foll. by *on*) lose one's belief or trust in, forsake, abandon.
■ **giveable** *adjective* (*rare*) capable of giving or yielding **L19.**

give and take /gɪv (ə)n(d) ˈteɪk/ *adjective & noun.* Also (esp. as adjective) **give-and-take**. **M18.**
[ORIGIN from *give and take* s.v. GIVE *verb*.]
▸ **A** *adjective* (usu. *attrib.*).
1 *hist.* Designating a horse race in which horses above a standard height carried more weight and those below the standard carried less. **M18.**
2 Involving give and take. **E19.**
▸ **B** *noun.* **1** Mutual yielding, compromise. **L18.**
2 Exchange of words, repartee. **M19.**

giveaway /ˈɡɪvəweɪ/ *noun & adjective. colloq.* Also **give-away**. **L19.**
[ORIGIN from *give away* s.v. GIVE *verb*.]
▸ **A** *noun.* **1** The action or an act of giving a present etc. away; a free gift; a low price; a game in which the object is to make an opponent lose points, (in chess etc.) capture pieces, etc. **L19.**

Listener A host of special offers and giveaways. *Bird Watching* The land giveaway may continue.

2 The action or an act of giving a secret etc. away; an inadvertent betrayal; a person who or thing which betrays inadvertently. **L19.**

J. DIDION It was the giveaway, the proof of how she felt.

dead giveaway something that makes an inadvertent revelation.
▸ **B** *attrib.* or as *adjective.* **1** Involving giving something away; given away, distributed free. **L19.**

Times Giveaway newspapers and free local directories are now Britain's fastest-growing media.

2 That betrays someone or something inadvertently; revealing. **M20.**

G. SWIFT It is impossible to climb those .. steps without a give-away medley of creaks.

giveback /ˈɡɪvbak/ *noun.* Chiefly *US.* **L20.**
[ORIGIN from *give back* s.v. GIVE *verb*.]
A refund; a concession; *spec.* a giving up by workers in industry of benefits and conditions previously agreed or accepted.

given /ˈɡɪv(ə)n/ *ppl adjective & noun.* **LME.**
[ORIGIN pa. pple of GIVE *verb*.]
▸ **A** *ppl adjective.* **1** Usu. *attrib.* That has been given; handed over, conferred, or bestowed as a gift; assigned or posited as a basis for calculation or reasoning, fixed, specified. Also foll. by adverb. **LME.** ▸**b** Of a personal name: chosen for the particular individual and conferred at birth, baptism, etc. **E19.**

DICKENS The second hand took the risk out of the given-out work. *Daily News* Given goods never prosper. B. MOORE How many there were on any given weekend. **b** P. ROTH One of the few remaining professors who address students .. as 'Mr.' and 'Miss', rather than by their given names.

2 *pred.* Inclined, disposed, prone, *to* (or †*absol.*). **LME.**

E. WHARTON He .. was given to telling anecdotes about his children. J. RATHBONE Something of a blue-stocking, given to books. A. BROOKNER A type of emotional gangster, given to hijackings and other acts of terrorism.

▸ **B** *noun.* What is given; a known fact or situation. **L19.**

J. CARROLL He had no need to establish his standing ... His standing was a given. E. JONG I feel .. as if I've been set adrift, as if all the givens of my life have suddenly changed.

■ **givenness** /-n-n-/ *noun* **M19.**

giver /ˈɡɪvə/ *noun.* **ME.**
[ORIGIN from GIVE *verb* + -ER¹.]
A person who gives. Freq. as 2nd elem. of comb. Also foll. by adverb.
Indian giver: see INDIAN *adjective.*

give-up /ˈɡɪvʌp/ *noun. US.* **L19.**
[ORIGIN from *give up* s.v. GIVE *verb*.]
1 The action or an act of giving up; relinquishment; a concession. **L19.**
2 STOCK EXCHANGE. A broker's revealing of the name of the principal in a transaction, who is obliged to complete the transaction. **M20.**

givey /ˈɡɪvi/ *adjective. dial. & colloq.* Also **givy**. **E19.**
[ORIGIN from GIVE *verb* + -Y¹.]
Inclined to give or yield; pliable, springy, soft.

giving /ˈɡɪvɪŋ/ *verbal noun.* **LME.**
[ORIGIN from GIVE *verb* + -ING¹.]
1 The action of GIVE *verb*; an instance of this. Also foll. by adverb. **LME.**

ADDISON Upon the first Giving of the Weather. W. ROBERTSON When the spirit of giving was substituted for the spirit of mere rivalry. *Daily News* The cruiser .. having broken down through the giving out of her cylinders.

2 A thing given, a gift. **LME.**
– COMB.: **giving set** an apparatus for giving blood transfusions, drips, etc.

givy *adjective* var. of GIVEY.

gizmo /ˈɡɪzməʊ/ *noun. colloq.* (orig. *US*). Also **gismo**. Pl. **-os**. **M20.**
[ORIGIN Unknown.]
A gadget, a gimmick.

Listener Electronic gismos for demagnetizing the heads of an audio tape-recorder.

gizz /dʒɪz/ *noun. Scot.* Now *rare* or *obsolete.* Also (earlier) †**jeezy**. **L17.**
[ORIGIN Unknown.]
A wig. Also, the face.

gizzard /ˈɡɪzəd/ *noun.* **LME.**
[ORIGIN Old French *giser, gesier, juisier* (mod. *gésier*) from Proto-Romance alt. of Latin *gigeria* noun the cooked entrails of a fowl.]
1 The thick-walled second region of a bird's stomach, in which food is ground, often together with small stones or grit. **LME.** ▸**b** The muscular grinding stomach of some fishes, insects, molluscs, etc. **L18.**
2 *gen.* The stomach, the entrails; the throat. Freq. *joc.* **M17.**

K. S. MACQUOID Pick a quarrel and .. run him through the gizzard.

stick in one's gizzard be distasteful, remain as something distasteful.
– COMB.: **gizzard trout** = GILLAROO.

gjetost /ˈjɛtɒst/ *noun.* **E20.**
[ORIGIN Norwegian, from *gjet, geit* goat + *ost* cheese.]
A Norwegian cheese made from goat's milk.

GLA *abbreviation.*
1 Gamma-linolenic acid.
2 Greater London Authority.

glabella /ɡləˈbɛlə/ *noun.* Pl. **-llae** /-liː/. **E19.**
[ORIGIN mod. Latin use as noun of Latin adjective, dim. of *glaber*: see GLABROUS.]
1 ANATOMY. The smooth area of the forehead between the eyebrows; the underlying smooth projection of the frontal bone (used as a reference point in skull measurements). **E19.**
2 ZOOLOGY. The smooth median portion of the cephalic shield of a trilobite. **M19.**
■ **glabellar** *adjective* of or pertaining to the glabella **E19.**

glabrate /ˈɡleɪbrət, ˈɡlabreɪt/ *adjective.* **M19.**
[ORIGIN Latin *glabratus* pa. pple of *glabrare* make bald, from *glaber*: see GLABROUS, -ATE².]
BOTANY & ZOOLOGY. Glabrous; glabrescent.

glabrescent /ɡleɪˈbrɛs(ə)nt, ɡla-/ *adjective.* **M19.**
[ORIGIN from Latin *glabrescere* become smooth, formed as GLABROUS: see -ESCENT.]
BOTANY. Of a surface: hairy when young but smooth when mature.

glabrous /ˈɡleɪbrəs, ˈɡla-/ *adjective.* **M17.**
[ORIGIN from Latin *glabr-*, *glaber* hairless, smooth + -OUS.]
Esp. of the skin or a leaf: free from hair or down, smooth.

D. OLIVER Foliage-leaves .. may be hairy, or nearly glabrous, that is, destitute of hairs. J. BARNES He was in his early forties, balding with a pinky glabrous complexion.

†**glace** *verb* see GLEASE.

glacé /ˈɡlaseɪ/ *adjective & noun.* **M19.**
[ORIGIN French, pa. pple of *glacer* ice, give a gloss to, from *glace* ice.]
▸ **A** *adjective.* **1** Of cloth, leather, etc.: smooth, highly polished, glossy. **M19.**
2 Of fruit: covered with icing or sugar. Of icing: made with icing sugar and water. **L19.**
▸ **B** *noun.* Glacé silk, glacé leather. **M19.**

glacial /ˈɡleɪʃ(ə)l, -sɪəl/ *adjective & noun.* **M17.**
[ORIGIN French, or Latin *glacialis* icy, from *glacies* ice: see -AL¹.]
▸ **A** *adjective.* **1** Of the nature of ice; (partly) consisting of ice; cold, icy, freezing (*lit.* & *fig.*). **M17.**

W. GOLDING We were too angry .. for anything but the stiffest and most glacial farewell. C. THUBRON Central Siberia, bounded by the glacial waters of the Arctic Ocean.

2 CHEMISTRY. Crystalline (*arch.*); (esp. of pure acids) tending to form crystals resembling ice. Now chiefly in ***glacial acetic acid***. **M17.**
3 GEOLOGY. Characterized or produced by the presence or agency of ice in the form of glaciers; pertaining to glaciers. **M19.**

J. MONTAGUE The only beauty nearby is a small glacial lake sheltering between drumlin moons of mountains.

glacial epoch, **glacial period**: during which glaciers covered a large part of the earth's surface, esp. the Pleistocene epoch.
4 Of movement, progress: resembling that of a glacier, very slow. **E20.**

D. ACHESON Negotiations with the Swiss moved at their glacial rate.

▸ **B** *noun.* A glacial epoch or period. **M20.**
■ **glacialist** *noun* a person who studies ice and esp. its action as a cause of certain geological phenomena **M19.** **glacially** *adverb* **M19.**

glaciarium /ɡleɪʃɪˈɛːrɪəm/ *noun. rare* exc. *hist.* **M19.**
[ORIGIN from Latin *glacies* ice + -ARIUM.]
A skating rink with artificially produced ice.

glaciate /ˈɡleɪsɪeɪt/ *verb.* **E17.**
[ORIGIN Latin *glaciat-* pa. ppl stem of *glaciare* freeze, from *glacies* ice: see -ATE³.]
1 *verb trans. & intrans.* Freeze. Long *rare* or *obsolete* (chiefly in Dicts.). **E17.**
2 *verb trans.* GEOLOGY. Mark or polish by the action of ice; cover with glaciers or ice sheets. Chiefly as ***glaciated*** *ppl adjective.* **M19.**

F. HOYLE Ice ages are not all-or-nothing affairs that glaciate the entire earth.

■ **glaciˈation** *noun* †(*a*) (a result of) the process of freezing; (*b*) GEOLOGY the action, condition, or result of being covered by glaciers or ice sheets: **M17.**

glacier /ˈɡlasɪə, ˈɡleɪs-/ *noun.* **M18.**
[ORIGIN French (earlier *glacière*), from *glace* ice, from Proto-Romance alt. of Latin *glacies* ice: see -IER.]
A slowly moving mass or river of ice formed by accumulation and compaction of snow on higher ground.
hanging glacier: see HANGING *adjective.*
– COMB.: **glacier burst** the sudden release of water impounded by a glacier; **glacier mill** = MOULIN; **glacier snow**: at the upper end of a glacier, not yet compacted into ice.
■ **glaciered** *adjective* covered with glaciers **E19.** **glacieˈret** *noun* a small alpine glacier **L19.** **glacieriˈzation** *noun* (*a*) *rare* conversion into a glacier; (*b*) the covering of land by an ice sheet; the state of being so covered: **M19.**

glacio- /ˈɡleɪsɪəʊ, ˈɡleɪʃɪəʊ/ *combining form* of GLACIER: see -O-.
■ **glacio-ˈeustasy** *noun* = GLACIO-EUSTATISM **M20.** **glacio-euˈstatic** *adjective* of or pertaining to glacio-eustatism **M20.** **glacio-ˈeustatism** *noun* changes in sea level caused by the waxing and waning of ice sheets **M20.** **glacioˈfluvial** *adjective* = FLUVIOGLACIAL **E20**; **glaciolaˈcustrine** *adjective* of or pertaining to a lake or lakes deriving water from the melting of ice **E20.**

glaciology /ɡleɪsɪˈɒlədʒi/ *noun.* **L19.**
[ORIGIN from GLACIO- + -LOGY.]
The science of the geological action of ice.
■ **glacioˈlogical** *adjective* **L19.** **glaciologist** *noun* **L19.**

glacis /ˈɡlasɪs, -si/ *noun.* Pl. same /-sɪz, -siːz/. **L17.**
[ORIGIN French, from Old French *glacier* to slip, slide, from *glace*: see GLACIER.]
1 A gently sloping bank; *spec.* in FORTIFICATION, a natural or artificial bank sloping down from the covered way of a fort so as to expose attackers to the defenders' missiles etc. **L17.** ▸**b** *fig.* A zone or area, *esp.* a small country, acting as a protective barrier or buffer between two (potentially) enemy countries. **M20.**
2 In full ***glacis plate***. A sloping sheet of armour plate protecting an opening in a ship. **L19.**

glad /ɡlad/ *noun*¹. **OE.**
[ORIGIN from the adjective.]
†**1** Gladness, joy (surviving as a first element in ***gladful***, ***gladless***, etc.). **OE–E17.**
2 = ***the glad eye*** s.v. GLAD *adjective.* **E20.**

glad /ɡlad/ *noun*². *colloq.* **E20.**
[ORIGIN Abbreviation.]
= GLADIOLUS.

glad /ɡlad/ *adjective & adverb.*
[ORIGIN Old English *glæd* = Old Saxon *glad* (only in *gladmōd*), Old Norse *glaðr* bright, joyous, Old High German *glat* (German *glatt*) smooth, from Germanic base rel. to Latin *glaber* smooth, GLABROUS.]
▸ **A** *adjective.* Compar. & superl. **-dd-**.
†**1** Bright, shining, beautiful. (Cf. sense 6 below.) **OE–L15.**
2 Of a person: having a naturally cheerful or happy disposition; joyful, happy. *arch.* **OE.**

WORDSWORTH Often, glad no more, We wear a face of joy, because We have been glad of yore.

3 Orig., delighted, filled with joy by something particular. Now only (*pred.*) in weakened sense, made happy or pleased. (Foll. by *about*, (arch.) *at*, *for*, *of*, *that*, *to do*.) **OE.**

H. JAMES It was a happy chance—he was uncommonly glad to see him. E. WAUGH Come in, come in. I'm very glad you've come. S. HILL I don't need them yet but when the weather gets colder .. I shall be pretty glad of them. R. CARVER He turned off the radio and was glad for the privacy. A. MUNRO He stopped saying such things and she was glad.

4 (Of a feeling, a look, an action, etc.) filled with, marked by, or expressing joy; (of news) causing joy. **OE.** ▸†**b** Welcome, acceptable. **L16–L17.**

AV *Luke* 8:1 He went throughout euery citie and village preaching, and shewing the glad tidings of the kingdome of God. R. KIPLING He bought sweetmeats .. from a Hindu trader, and ate them with glad rapture.

5 Of a door, bolt, etc.: working smoothly and easily. *dial.* **M16.**
6 Esp. of a natural object: full of brightness or beauty; cheering. **M17.**

LYTTON The glad sun rising gorgeously from the hills revived his wearied spirit. C. BRONTË What a living spring! What a warm, glad summer!

– PHRASES ETC.: **glad-hand** *verb trans. & intrans.* greet or welcome (someone) cordially (freq. *iron.*). **glad rags** *colloq.* best clothes, evening dress. **the glad eye** *colloq.* an amorous glance. **the glad hand** (freq. *iron.*) a cordial handshake, greeting, or welcome (freq. in *give the glad hand*).

▸ **B** *adverb*. Compar. & superl. **-dd-**. Gladly. *poet.* ME.

glad /glad/ *verb*. Infl. **-dd-**.
[ORIGIN Old English *gladian* = Old Norse *glaða*, from Germanic base of GLAD *adjective*.]
†**1** *verb intrans.* Be or become glad; rejoice. Foll. by *on, in, of, for*. OE–E17.
2 *verb trans.* Make glad; cause to rejoice. *arch.* or *poet.* OE.

gladden *noun* var. of GLADDON.

gladden /ˈglad(ə)n/ *verb*. LME.
[ORIGIN from GLAD *adjective* + -EN⁵.]
1 *verb intrans.* Be or become glad, rejoice. Long *rare* before E19. LME.
WORDSWORTH That all the Alps may gladden in thy might.
2 *verb trans.* Make glad. M16.
J. RUSKIN [An orchard] which was gladdened . . by flushes of almond and . . peach blossom.
■ **gladdener** *noun* L19.

gladdie /ˈgladi/ *noun*. *Austral. colloq.* M20.
[ORIGIN from GLAD *noun*² + -IE.]
= GLADIOLUS.

gladdon /ˈglad(ə)n/ *noun*. Now chiefly *dial.* Also **gladden**, **gladwin**, **-wyn**.
[ORIGIN Old English *glædene* from popular Latin alt. of Latin GLADIOLUS.]
A plant of the iris family, *Iris foetidissima*, of western Europe and N. Africa, having purplish flowers and an unpleasant odour when bruised (also called ***stinking gladdon***, ***stinking iris***). Formerly also, any of various plants with long, sword-shaped leaves, *esp.* yellow flag, sweet flag, or reed mace.

†**glade** *noun*¹. ME–L18.
[ORIGIN Perh. of Scandinavian origin: cf. Swedish dial. *gladas*, *glad(d)na* (of the sun) to set, Norwegian dial. *gla* (of the sun and moon) to set.]
go to glade, (of the sun) set.

glade /gleɪd/ *noun*². LME.
[ORIGIN Uncertain: cf. GLAD *adjective* 1.]
1 A clear open space or passage between the trees in a wood, either naturally or artificially produced. LME.
†**2** A clear or bright space between clouds in the sky; a flash or gleam of light. LME–M18.
3 A marshy area of low-lying grass-covered land. *US.* M17.
4 An unfrozen part or a break or opening in the ice of a stretch of water. *local (US).* L17.
– SPECIAL COLLOCATIONS: **glade mallow** *US* a tall plant of the mallow family, *Napaea dioica*, of the eastern US, having small white flowers.

gladful /ˈgladfʊl, -f(ə)l/ *adjective*. *arch.* ME.
[ORIGIN from GLAD *noun*¹ + -FUL.]
Full of gladness, joyful.
– NOTE: Rare after L16.
■ **gladfully** *adverb* LME. **gladfulness** *noun* L16.

gladiate /ˈgleɪdɪət/ *adjective*. L18.
[ORIGIN from Latin *gladius* sword + -ATE².]
BOTANY. Sword-shaped.

gladiator /ˈgladɪeɪtə/ *noun*. LME.
[ORIGIN Latin *gladiator*, from *gladius* sword: see -ATOR.]
1 ROMAN HISTORY. A man, usu. a slave or captive criminal, trained to fight with a sword or other weapon against other men similarly trained or wild animals, in combats freq. to the death, staged for public entertainment. LME. ▸†**b** A professional swordsman or fencer. E17–M18.
2 A person who disputes with another esp. publicly in support of a political etc. cause. M17.
H. H. ASQUITH Huxley, the young gladiator of Evolution.
■ **gladiaˈtorial** *adjective* (*a*) of or pertaining to a gladiator; (*b*) (of debate) contentious: M18. †**gladiatorian** *adjective* of, pertaining to, or resembling a gladiator L17–M18. **gladiatorism** *noun* (now *rare*) gladiatorial fighting or arguing M19. **gladiatorship** *noun* the occupation or skill of a gladiator E19. †**gladiatory** *adjective* = GLADIATORIAL E17–M18.

gladiolus /gladɪˈəʊləs/ *noun*. Pl. **-li** /-lʌɪ, -liː/, **-luses**. Also **gladiole** /ˈgladɪəʊl/. OE.
[ORIGIN Latin, dim. of *gladius* sword.]
1 Any of numerous plants constituting the genus *Gladiolus*, of the iris family, native to Eurasia and (chiefly) Africa, having erect sword-shaped leaves and spikes of (often brilliantly coloured) flowers, including many cultivars of mainly southern African origin; a flowering stem of such a plant. Formerly also, the gladdon. Cf. ***corn-flag*** s.v. CORN *noun*¹. OE.
2 ANATOMY. The large middle section of the sternum. L19.

gladius /ˈgleɪdɪəs/ *noun*. E16.
[ORIGIN Latin = sword.]
†**1** A swordfish. Only in E16.
2 The horny, feather-shaped internal shell of a squid. Also called ***pen***. L19.

gladless /ˈgladlɪs/ *adjective*. *rare*. E16.
[ORIGIN from GLAD *noun*¹ + -LESS.]
Joyless.

gladly /ˈgladli/ *adjective*. *arch.* OE.
[ORIGIN formed as GLADLESS + -LY¹.]
†**1** Bright, beautiful, splendid. Only in OE.
2 Glad, joyful. OE.

gladly /ˈgladli/ *adverb*. OE.
[ORIGIN from GLAD *adjective* + -LY².]
1 With joy or pleasure. Freq. also in weakened sense, willingly, with alacrity. OE.
SCOTT FITZGERALD I would gladly welcome any alienist you might suggest. P. LIVELY She could gladly hit him, lolling there complacent on the sofa.
†**2** Readily, easily; usually, regularly; habitually and with enjoyment. LME–L15.
CHAUCER Thise olde wommen, that been gladly wyse As is hir maistresse. CAXTON Where as ben corners there is gladly filth.

gladness /ˈgladnɪs/ *noun*. OE.
[ORIGIN from GLAD *adjective* + -NESS.]
The state of being glad; (a) joy. Formerly also, alacrity.

gladsome /ˈglads(ə)m/ *adjective*. Now *poet.* or *arch.* LME.
[ORIGIN Orig. from GLAD *noun*¹; later regarded as from GLAD *adjective*: see -SOME¹.]
1 = GLAD *adjective* 2, 3. LME.
2 = GLAD *adjective* 4. LME.
3 = GLAD *adjective* 6. E16.
■ **gladsomely** *adverb* LME. **gladsomeness** *noun* LME.

Gladstone /ˈgladstən/ *noun*. M19.
[ORIGIN William Ewart *Gladstone* (1809–98), Brit. statesman.]
1 *hist.* Cheap French wine, imports of which greatly increased as a result of Gladstone's reduction in Customs duty. Also ***Gladstone claret***. M19.
2 In full ***Gladstone bag***. A light portmanteau opening into two equal compartments. L19.

Gladstonian /gladˈstəʊnɪən/ *adjective* & *noun*. M19.
[ORIGIN from GLADSTONE + -IAN.]
▸ **A** *adjective*. Of, pertaining to, or characteristic of Gladstone or his policies. M19.
C. R. ATTLEE My father was a Gladstonian Liberal but the rest of the family was Conservative. A. J. P. TAYLOR Arthur Rowntree had a Gladstonian air and a Gladstonian way of speaking.
▸ **B** *noun*. *hist.* A supporter of Gladstone or his policies. M19.
■ **Gladstonianism** *noun* the principles or policies of Gladstone, esp. as relating to the establishment of Home Rule in Ireland M19.

Gladstonism /ˈgladstənɪz(ə)m/ *noun*. L19.
[ORIGIN formed as GLADSTONIAN + -ISM.]
= GLADSTONIANISM *noun*.
■ **Gladstonite** *noun* = GLADSTONIAN *noun* L19.

gladwin, **gladwyn** *nouns* vars. of GLADDON.

glady /ˈgleɪdi/ *adjective*. L18.
[ORIGIN from GLADE *noun*² + -Y¹.]
Full of glades; of, pertaining to, or resembling a glade.

Glagolitic /glagəˈlɪtɪk/ *adjective*. E19.
[ORIGIN mod. Latin *glagoliticus*, from Croatian *glagòljica* the Glagolitic alphabet from Old Church Slavonic *glagolŭ* word.]
Of, pertaining to, or designating an ancient Slavonic alphabet (ascribed to St Cyril and long superseded by Cyrillic), retained in the liturgy of some Roman Catholic Churches in Dalmatia, Montenegro, etc.

glaik /gleɪk/ *noun*. *Scot.* E16.
[ORIGIN Uncertain: cf. GLEEK *noun*².]
†**1** In *pl.* Tricks, pranks; mocking deceptions. E16–L19.
2 A foolish person. *derog.* M16.
†**3** In *pl.* Interlocking pieces of wood, linked rings, etc., forming a puzzle or toy. L16–L19.
†**4** A dazzling flash of light. L18–E20.

glaikit /ˈgleɪkɪt/ *adjective*. *Scot. & N. English.* LME.
[ORIGIN Rel. to GLAIK.]
Slow-witted, stupid. Also, thoughtless, flighty.
I. WELSH His glaikit, open-moothed expression inspired ma instant contempt. K. ATKINSON One of the lenses in his . . spectacles had acquired a crack, giving him an oddly glaikit look.
■ **glaikitly** *adverb* (*rare*) M19. **glaikitness** *noun* LME.

glair /glɛː/ *noun* & *verb*. As noun also (earlier) **glaire**. ME.
[ORIGIN Old French & mod. French *glaire* from medieval Latin *glarea* from var. of medieval Latin use as noun of Latin *clarus* clear.]
▸ **A** *noun*. **1** The white of an egg, esp. as used in various preparations; *spec.* in BOOKBINDING, an adhesive made from this applied before blocking or tooling in gold leaf. ME.
2 Any slimy viscous substance resembling egg white. E16.
▸ **B** *verb trans.* Orig., paint, daub. Later, smear with glair. M16.
■ **glaireous** *adjective* of the nature of glair; slimy, viscous: M17. **glairy** *adjective* (freq. in MEDICINE) = GLAIREOUS M17.

glaistig /ˈglastɪk/ *noun*. Also **glastick**. E20.
[ORIGIN Gaelic.]
In (esp. Scottish) folklore: a fairy with a variety of forms and characters, freq. appearing in the shape of a goat or as half-woman, half-goat, but also as a beautiful water sprite.

glaive /gleɪv/ *noun*. ME.
[ORIGIN Old French & mod. French (also †*glavie*) †lance, sword, app. from Latin *gladius* sword.]
†**1** A weapon consisting of a blade or sharp point fixed to a long handle; a lance; a halberd. ME–L17. ▸**b** A lance set up as the winning post in a race and freq. given as a prize to the winner; *gen.* a prize. LME–M16.
2 A sword; *esp.* a broadsword. *arch.* or *poet.* L15.
C. BOWEN [He] girds on the Achæan's glittering glaive.
3 A fish spear. Chiefly *dial.* M17.

glam /glam/ *noun*¹. *obsolete* exc. *dial.* LME.
[ORIGIN Old Norse *glam(m)* noise, din (Swedish *glam* merriment, loud mirth, Danish *glam* barking of dogs etc.), prob. of imit. origin.]
A loud noise esp. of talking or merrymaking; a din, a clamour.

glam /glam/ *noun*². In sense 1 also **glaum**. L16.
[ORIGIN Var. of CLAM *noun*¹. Cf. GLAND *noun*³.]
1 In *pl.* The iron jaws of a vice; a clamp. *Scot.* L16.
2 The hand. *N. English.* M19.

glam /glam/ *noun*³ & *adjective*. *colloq.* M20.
[ORIGIN Abbreviation.]
▸ **A** *adjective*. **1** Glamorous. M20.
K. LETTE If only you were one of those glam girls in restaurants who pick at lettuce leaves. *New Scientist* It may not be glam but it's true: it was probably a worm that invented sex.
2 Of or pertaining to glam rock (see below). L20.
C. BATEMAN Someone had found an old glam compilation in the depths of our record collection.
▸ **B** *noun*. Glamour. M20.
– COMB.: **glam rock** a style of rock music characterized by male performers wearing exaggeratedly flamboyant clothes and make-up.

glam /glam/ *verb*¹ *trans. colloq.* Infl. **-mm-**. M20.
[ORIGIN Abbreviation.]
Make glamorous; glamorize. (Foll. by *up*.)
Cosmopolitan You should be able to glam up your hair, or wear it in a natural style without much effort.

glam *verb*² see GLAUM *verb*.

Glam. *abbreviation*.
Glamorgan(shire).

glamazon /ˈglaməz(ə)n/ *noun*. *slang*. M20.
[ORIGIN from GLAM *adjective* + AMAZON.]
A glamorous, powerfully assertive woman.

glamorize /ˈglaməraɪz/ *verb trans.* Orig. *US.* Also **-ise**, **-our-**. M20.
[ORIGIN from GLAMOUR *noun* + -IZE.]
Make glamorous or attractive.
■ **glamoriˈzation** *noun* M20.

glamorous /ˈglamərəs/ *adjective*. Also **-our-**. L19.
[ORIGIN from GLAMOUR *noun* + -OUS.]
Full of glamour.
■ **glamorously** *adverb* L19.

glamour /ˈglamə/ *noun* & *verb*. Orig. *Scot.* Also ***-or**. E18.
[ORIGIN Alt. of GRAMMAR with the sense of GRAMARYE. For the form with *gl-* cf. medieval Latin *glomeria* grammar, *glomerellus* a school-boy learning grammar.]
▸ **A** *noun*. **1** Magic, enchantment. *arch.* E18.
TENNYSON That maiden in the tale, Whom Gwydion made by glamour out of flowers.
cast the glamour over enchant, bewitch.
2 (A) deceptive or bewitching beauty or charm; (a) mysteriously exciting or alluring physical attractiveness, esp. when artificially contrived. M19.
F. RAPHAEL But Isidore's offences were sordid and commercial, quite without glamour. M. AYRTON He has an animal magnetism, or a glamour at once insupportable but compelling.
– COMB.: **glamour boy**, **glamour girl**: possessing glamour; **glamour puss** *slang* a glamorous person.
▸ **B** *verb trans.* **1** Enchant, bewitch. *arch.* E18.
R. GRAVES Woman and tree prove of a stuff Wholly to glamour his wild heart?
2 Glamorize. Foll. by *up*. *colloq.* M20.
L. HOBSON It's lost some of the subtlety of the book . . and they've glamoured it up a little too much.
▸ **C** *attrib.* or *as adj.* Designating or pertaining to sexually suggestive or mildly pornographic photography or publications. L20.
JONATHON GREEN There are different qualities for a glamour model and a fashion model.

glamourise, **glamourize** *verbs*, **glamourous** *adjective* vars. of GLAMORIZE, GLAMOROUS.

glamoury /ˈglaməri/ *noun*. Chiefly *Scot.* Also **-rie**. M18.
[ORIGIN Var. of GLAMOUR *noun*; for ending cf. GRAMARYE.]
= GLAMOUR *noun* 1.

glance /glɑːns/ *noun*¹. E16.
[ORIGIN from GLANCE *verb*.]
1 A sudden movement producing a flash or gleam (of light); a flash, a gleam. E16.

G

SIR W. SCOTT The silver light, with quivering glance, Played on the water's still expanse.

2 A swift oblique movement or impact. Now *rare*. L16. ▸**b** *CRICKET*. More fully ***leg glance***. A stroke made with the bat's face turned slantwise to deflect the ball. L19.

H. L'ESTRANGE Though these speeches did not take their aime directly at his Majesty, yet did they by glance and obliquely deeply wound him.

3 A brief or hurried look (*at, into, over*, etc.). Also, a gaze. L16.

R. MACAULAY Sir Gulliver's experienced eyes, in one glance, summed his daughter up. J. THURBER We exchanged a brief, knowing masculine glance of private understanding. R. INGALLS Flora's glance flickered lightly over the other people.

at a glance immediately upon looking. ***throw a glance***: see THROW *verb*.

†**4** An allusion or reference, *esp.* a satirical or jesting one. E17–E18.

BACON Not knowing where to carp at him . . he gave a glance at his patience towards his wife.

G

glance /glɑːns/ *noun*[2]. LME.
[ORIGIN German *Glanz* (Dutch *glans*) lustre: cf. Dutch *glanserts* glance ore.]
Orig. †***glance ore***. Any of various metallic ores, chiefly sulphides, with a grey or black lustre.
antimony glance, bismuth glance, copper glance, iron glance, lead glance, silver glance.
– COMB.: **glance coal**: of high lustre (esp. anthracite); ***glance ore***: see above; **glance pitch** a brilliant black variety of bitumen.

glance /glɑːns/ *verb*. LME.
[ORIGIN Prob. alt. of †*glace* verb (see GLEASE), infl. by GLENT *verb*, LANCE *verb*.]
1 *verb intrans.* Of a weapon, tool, etc.: glide or slip *off* an object instead of striking it squarely. LME.

SIR W. SCOTT The blow only glanced on the bone, and scarce drew blood. E. BIRNEY His axe glanced from a frosted branch and sank in his boot.

2 *verb intrans.* Move, usu. rapidly, in an oblique direction; go off at a tangent; spring *aside*. LME.

T. BLACKBURN Strange it is, since there's no fences, I do not take the path which glances Aside from this.

3 *verb intrans.* Orig., shine. Later, cause a flash of light by rapid movement; (of a bright object or light) flash, dart, gleam. M16.

E. BOWEN The light glanced on Hilary's waved and burnished hair.

4 *verb intrans.* Of a discussion, a speaker, etc.: pass quickly *over*, glide *off* or *from* a subject. L16. ▸**b** Foll. by *at, (up)on*, †*against*: allude or refer to in passing, esp. sarcastically. L16.

O. W. HOLMES I glanced off, as one often does in talk. **b** SWIFT Verses . . wherein he glanced at a certain reverend doctor.

5 *verb intrans.* Of the eye, a person looking: cast a swift brief look (*at*); look quickly or read hurriedly or cursorily *over* or *through*. L16.

J. CONRAD He sniffed from time to time, glancing out of the corners of his . . eyes. A. GUINNESS Down the Grand Canal in a gondola . . never once so much as glancing at the Venetian palaces.

6 *verb trans.* Orig., allude to. Later, graze, barely touch. L16.
7 *verb trans.* **a** Orig., turn (one's gaze) aside as when dazzled. Later, direct (one's eye) quickly *over* or *at* an object. Chiefly in ***glance one's eye***. L16. ▸**b** Survey with a glance or glances; catch a glimpse of. Now *rare* or *obsolete*. M17. ▸**c** Convey with a glance or glances (of the eye). Now *rare*. E18.
8 *verb trans.* Direct obliquely. Also, emit with a flash or gleam; reflect *back*. Now *rare*. M17. ▸**b** *verb trans. & intrans. CRICKET.* Deflect (the ball) with the bat's face turned slantwise. Also, strike the ball in this way off (the bowler). L19.

W. DAMPIER Strike their Harpoons . . aside, or so glance them as to kill nothing.

■ **glancer** *noun* M16. **glancingly** *adverb* in a glancing manner M16.

gland /gland/ *noun*[1]. Now *rare* or *obsolete*. LME.
[ORIGIN French, or directly from Latin *glans, gland-* acorn.]
1 An acorn or similar nut. Cf. GLANS 2. LME.
2 = GLANS 1. M19.
3 *hist.* An acorn-shaped ball of lead used as a missile. M19.

gland /gland/ *noun*[2]. L17.
[ORIGIN French *glande*, alt. of Old French *glandre*: see GLANDER.]
1 *ANATOMY & ZOOLOGY.* Any cell or organ which synthesizes and secretes some particular chemical substance or substances for use by the body or for excretion. Also (now *loosely*), an organ resembling a gland; *esp.* a lymph node. Cf. ENDOCRINE, EXOCRINE. L17.
mammary gland, monkey gland, scent gland, thyroid gland, Tyson's gland, etc.
2 *BOTANY.* Any of various (groups of) cells on or within a plant structure which secrete some particular substance or substances (e.g. oils, nectar, etc.). Also, any small protuberance like a gland. L18.
– NOTE: The glands were orig. characterized as extracting substances from the blood, a wider definition which included the lymph nodes. Cf. GLANDULE.
■ **glandiform** *adjective* resembling a gland E19. **glandlike** *adjective* = GLANDIFORM M19.

gland /gland/ *noun*[3]. E19.
[ORIGIN Prob. var. of GLAM *noun*[2].]
A sleeve which fits around a piston rod or other shaft to form a seal, esp. by compressing a packing around the rod.

glander /ˈglandə/ *noun*. L15.
[ORIGIN Old French *glandre* from Latin *glandulae* pl., throat glands, swollen glands in the neck: see GLANDULE.]
†**1** A glandular swelling about the neck. L15–E16.
2 In *pl.* (treated as *sing.*; often with *the*). An infectious fatal disease of horses, donkeys, etc. (also transmissible to humans), caused by the bacterium *Pseudomonas mallei*, and characterized by inflammation or ulceration of the nasal mucous membranes and lymph nodes, and nodule formation in the lungs, spleen, etc. E16.
■ **glandered** *adjective* affected with glanders M17. **glanderous** *adjective* affected with, or of the nature of, glanders E18.

glandes *noun* pl. of GLANS.

glandiferous /glanˈdɪf(ə)rəs/ *adjective*. M17.
[ORIGIN from Latin *glandifer* (from *glans, gland-* acorn) + -OUS: see -FEROUS.]
Bearing acorns or similar fruit.

glandular /ˈglandjʊlə, ˈglan(d)ʒʊlə/ *adjective*. M18.
[ORIGIN French *glandulaire*, from *glandule* GLANDULE: see -AR[1].]
Of or pertaining to a gland; containing, bearing, or functioning as, a gland or glands.
glandular fever an infectious viral disease characterized by fever, inflammation of the lymph nodes, and abnormal lymphocytes; also called ***infectious mononucleosis***.

glandulation /glandjʊˈleɪʃ(ə)n, glan(d)ʒʊ-/ *noun*. M18.
[ORIGIN formed as GLANDULE: see -ATION.]
BOTANY. The disposition of glandular cells or tissues in a plant.

glandule /ˈglandjuːl/ *noun*. LME.
[ORIGIN French, or directly from Latin *glandula* (usu. in pl.) glands in the neck, tonsils (dim. of *glans, gland-* acorn): see -ULE.]
†**1** *MEDICINE & VETERINARY MEDICINE.* A gland; *esp.* a lymph node (usu. in *pl.*). LME–M18.
†**2** *MEDICINE & VETERINARY MEDICINE.* A swelling of the lymph nodes in the neck. Usu. in *pl.* Cf. GLANDER. LME–E17. ▸†**b** *MEDICINE.* Any rounded swelling in the body. *rare*. LME–M19.
3 *ZOOLOGY & BOTANY.* A small gland, esp. in certain fungi and orchids. M18.
■ **glanduˈliferous** *adjective* bearing glands or glandules E18.

glandulose /ˈglandjʊləʊs, ˈglan(d)ʒʊ-/ *adjective*. M19.
[ORIGIN Latin *glandulosus*: see GLANDULOUS.]
BOTANY. Bearing glands or formations like glands.

glandulous /ˈglandjʊləs, ˈglan(d)ʒʊ-/ *adjective*. LME.
[ORIGIN Old French & mod. French *glanduleux*, or directly from Latin *glandulosus*, from *glandula* GLANDULE: see -ULOUS.]
1 Of or pertaining to a gland or glandule; containing, bearing, or functioning as a gland or glands. LME.
2 *BOTANY.* Glandulose. L18.

glans /glanz/ *noun*. Pl. **glandes** /ˈglandiːz/. M17.
[ORIGIN Latin.]
1 *ANATOMY.* A small conical or acorn-shaped structure, *esp.* that at the end of the mammalian penis (more fully ***glans penis***) or clitoris (more fully ***glans clitoridis***). M17.
2 *BOTANY.* A unicellular nut having the base enclosed in a cupule, as the acorn, beech mast, etc. E18.

glare /glɛː/ *noun*[1]. LME.
[ORIGIN from the verb.]
1 Dazzling brilliance (of a light, the sun, etc.); a strong fierce light; *spec.* oppressive unrelieved sunshine. LME. ▸**b** The glistening or shining of some surface. M17.

A. B. EDWARDS A little before midday, when the heat and glare were becoming intolerable. S. LEACOCK I turned up the lights and the bright glare revealed . . the tattered figure. *fig.*: *Blitz* The 74-year-old GP scrupulously keeps himself away from the glare of publicity.

2 A fierce, esp. fixed, look or stare. M17.

CONAN DOYLE His face turned upon us with a glare of baffled rage. R. HOLMES Eyes . . staring straight out at the onlooker with a glare of absolute defiance.

3 Showy appearance; gaudiness; tawdry brilliance. E18.

BYRON Maidens, like moths, are ever caught by glare.

■ **glareless** *adjective* E19.

glare /glɛː/ *noun*[2]. *obsolete* exc. *N. Amer.* M16.
[ORIGIN Uncertain: perh. rel. to GLARE *noun*[1] 1.]
Orig., frost, icy condition. Later, a sheet of ice.

glare /glɛː/ *adjective*. *N. Amer.* M19.
[ORIGIN Prob. attrib. use of GLARE *noun*[2].]
Esp. of ice: smooth and bright or translucent, glassy.

glare /glɛː/ *verb*. ME.
[ORIGIN Middle Low German, Middle Dutch *glaren* gleam, glare.]
1 *verb intrans.* Shine (esp. too) brilliantly or dazzlingly. ME. ▸**b** Display oneself ostentatiously (now *rare*); be obtrusively evident or conspicuous. E18.

CHAUCER Hyt is not al golde that glareth. J. T. STORY In the kitchen the bulb glared naked from its holder. **b** BOSWELL A writer . . whose ungenerous prejudice against the house of Stuart glares in misrepresentation.

2 *verb intrans.* Look or stare fixedly and fiercely (*at, (up)on*). Cf. earlier GLARING *ppl adjective* 1. E17.

H. A. VACHELL You needn't glare at me as if I'd left the old lady to burn on purpose.

3 *verb trans.* Express or convey by staring fixedly and fiercely. M17.

H. H. MILMAN Two popes glaring defiance at each other.

4 *verb trans.* Reflect dazzlingly. Also foll. by *back*. *rare*. L17.

T. SOUTHERNE The images Of a long mis-spent life were rising . . To glare a sad reflection of my crimes.

glareal /ˈglɛːrɪəl/ *adjective*. M19.
[ORIGIN from Latin *glarea* gravel + -AL[1].]
BOTANY. Growing on dry, exposed soils. Cf. GLAREOUS 2.

glareose /glɛːrɪˈəʊs/ *adjective*. M19.
[ORIGIN Latin *glareosus*: see GLAREOUS, -OSE[1].]
BOTANY. = GLAREOUS 2.

glareous /ˈglɛːrɪəs/ *adjective*. LME.
[ORIGIN from Latin *glareosus*, from *glarea* gravel: see -OUS.]
†**1** Of soil: gravelly. LME–L17.
2 *BOTANY.* Growing on gravel. L19.

glaring /ˈglɛːrɪŋ/ *ppl adjective*. LME.
[ORIGIN from GLARE *verb* + -ING[2].]
1 Of the eyes: staring fiercely or wildly. LME.

DRYDEN And hissing, rowls his glaring Eyes around.

2 That gives out or reflects a dazzling light; (of light, colour, etc.) vivid, dazzling, excessively bright. E16.

H. MARTINEAU Reflected in gleams upon the glaring white fronts of the houses.

3 That displays itself openly; that is obtrusively evident and conspicuous. Freq. *derog.* E18.

A. N. WILSON Some of the mistranscriptions were so glaring that she thought they must have been mere typing errors.

■ **glaringly** *adverb* L16. **glaringness** *noun* M17.

glarney /ˈglɑːni/ *noun*. M20.
[ORIGIN Prob. alt. of GLASSY *noun*[1].]
A glass marble.

glary /ˈglɛːri/ *adjective*[1]. Now *US*. L16.
[ORIGIN from GLARE *noun*[2] + -Y[1].]
Smooth and slippery; icy.

glary /ˈglɛːri/ *adjective*[2]. M17.
[ORIGIN from GLARE *noun*[1] + -Y[1].]
Full of glare; dazzling, glaring.
■ **glariness** *noun* M17.

glasnost /ˈglaznɒst, ˈglɑːs-/ *noun*. L20.
[ORIGIN Russian *glasnost'* the fact of being public.]
In the former USSR: the policy or practice of more open consultative government and wider dissemination of information.

glass /glɑːs/ *noun & adjective*.
[ORIGIN Old English *glæs* = Old Saxon *glas, gles*, Old & mod. High German *glas*, from West Germanic var. of Germanic word repr. by Old Norse *gler* glass, prob. rel. to Old English *glǣr*, Middle Low German *glār* amber.]
▸**A** *noun* **I 1** A substance, usu. transparent, lustrous, hard, and brittle, made by fusing soda or potash or both with other ingredients. OE.

H. M. ROSENBERG Many materials . . such as glass and cast iron, exhibit brittle fracture.

2 Any of various other substances of similar properties or composition; any more or less rigid substance which has solidified from a molten state without adopting a regular internal (crystalline) structure. L16.

J. PINKERTON The volcanic glass called obsidian, appears in such quantities as to constitute rocks.

3 The substance thus obtained considered as the material from which articles for use or ornament are made; *collect. sing.* such articles. E17. ▸**b** *spec.* in *HORTICULTURE*. The main constituent of a greenhouse, frame, etc.; *collect.* greenhouses. M19.

W. HOLTBY The array of glass and silver on the sideboard. **b** ANTHONY HUXLEY This plant prefers a very moist atmosphere under glass.

▸**II 4** A glass vessel or receptacle. Also, the contents of such a vessel or receptacle. ME.

SWIFT Miss, will you reach me that Glass of Jelly?

5 *spec.* A drinking vessel made of glass; a drink (esp. an alcoholic one) contained in such a vessel. LME.

J. FOWLES She had another glass, and drank it off in a minute. W. TREVOR Tippling away at glasses of sherry wasn't going to help the boy.

beer glass, liqueur glass, wine glass, etc.

6 A double-chambered glass receptacle containing sand etc. for the measurement of a specified unit of time. (Earlier in HOURGLASS.) M16. ▸**b** Chiefly *NAUTICAL*. The time taken by the sand etc. of such a glass to run completely from the upper to the lower chamber; *esp.* a half-hour. L16. ▸**c** *fig.* An allotted period of existence. *arch.* M17.

JONATHAN MILLER I will wait . . until Time he shall break his glass. **c** G. GROTE The glass of this worthless dynasty is run out.

▸ **III 7** A single sheet of glass made to form a transparent protective covering; *esp.* (**a**) *arch.* a window in a coach; (**b**) a plate of glass covering a picture; (**c**) a glazed frame for plants. LME.

T. HOOK Bang went the door, up went the glass.

8 A glass mirror. Formerly also, a mirror made of some other material. LME. ▸**b** A mirror, crystal, etc., used in fortune-telling. Long *rare*. M16.

D. LESSING She had put the dress on and was looking at herself in the long glass. **b** SHAKES. *Macb.* The eighth appears, who bears a glass which shows me many more.

9 A piece of glass shaped for a special purpose, as a lens in a pair of spectacles, a convex glass disc covering the face of a watch, etc. (Earliest in ***burning glass*** below.) E16. ▸†**b** (The lens of) an eye. *poet.* L16–E17.

SIR W. SCOTT Pleydell wiped the glasses of his spectacles. R. HUGHES I wiped the misty glass of my watch. **b** SHAKES. *Rich. II* Even in the glasses of thine eyes I see thy grieved heart.

10 An optical instrument with a lens or lenses, used to aid sight esp. by magnifying; a telescope; (freq. in *pl.*) binoculars; *arch.* a microscope. E17. ▸**b** A lens for correcting or assisting defective sight, an eyeglass; in *pl.*, spectacles. M17.

H. B. TRISTRAM Even without a glass we could distinctly make out Jerusalem. R. MACAULAY I was on deck looking through glasses for the first sight of Trebizond. **b** W. COWPER With glass at eye, and catalogue in hand. J. WESLEY My eyes were so dim, that no glasses would help me.

field glass(es), ***opera glass(es)***, ***sunglasses***, etc.

11 A barometer. Formerly also, a thermometer. M17.

H. ALLEN The fourth day of calm, with the glass still low but no change.

– PHRASES ETC.: **burning glass** a lens or concave mirror by which the rays of the sun may be concentrated on an object to burn it if combustible. ***cut glass***: see CUT *ppl adjective*. ***dark glasses***: see DARK *adjective*. **glass of antimony** a vitreous mixed oxide and sulphide of antimony formed in antimony refining. ***ground glass***: see GROUND *ppl adjective*. ***musical glasses***: see MUSICAL *adjective*. ***soap of glass***: see SOAP *noun*[1]. STAINED ***glass***. ***Venetian glass***: see VENETIAN *adjective*. ***vernal glass***: see VERNAL *adjective* 1b. ***volcanic glass***: see VOLCANIC *adjective*. ***Wood's glass***: see WOOD *noun*[3] 1.

▸ **B** *attrib.* or as *adjective*. **1** Made of glass. OE.

2 Glazed, having pieces or panes of glass set in a frame. L16.

– COMB. & SPECIAL COLLOCATIONS: **glass ball** a ball made of glass, used esp. as an ornament; **glass-blower** a person who blows and shapes semi-molten glass; **glass-blowing** the action or an act of blowing and shaping semi-molten glass; **glass case** a case made chiefly of glass, for the exhibition and protection of its contents; **glass ceiling** *fig.* a barrier to personal advancement, esp. of a woman or members of ethnic minorities; **glass cloth** (**a**) a linen cloth used for drying glassware etc.; (**b**) cloth covered with powdered glass, used for smoothing and polishing; (**c**) a woven fabric of fine-spun glass thread; **glass coach** (*obsolete* exc. *hist.*) a coach with glass windows as opp. to an unglazed one; **glass crab** the larva of any of various shrimps; **glass cutter** a person who or thing which shapes or decorates glass by cutting; **glass dust** powdered glass; **glass eye** †(**a**) = sense 10b above; (**b**) an artificial eye, *esp.* one made of glass; **glass-faced** *adjective* (*rare*) having a face that reflects the looks of another; **glass fibre** (**a**) a filament of glass; (**b**) glass in the form of such filaments, as made into fabric or embedded as a reinforcement in plastic; **glass furnace**: in which the constituents of glass are fused; **glass gall** sandiver; **glass-gazing** *adjective* (long *rare* or *obsolete*) given to contemplating oneself in a mirror, self-regarding, vain; **glass-green** *adjective & noun* (*poet.*) (of) a clear green colour; ***glass harmonica***: see HARMONICA 1(b). **glasshouse** (**a**) a building where glass is made; (**b**) a building made chiefly of glass; *esp.* a greenhouse, a conservatory; (**c**) *slang* a military prison or guard room; †**glass humour** the vitreous humour; **glass lizard** = ***glass snake*** below; **glass-making** the manufacture of glass; **glass-man** (now *rare*) a dealer in or maker of glass; **glass paper**: covered with powdered glass and used for polishing; **glass-rope sponge** a sponge of the genus *Hyalonema*, which roots itself to the seabed by a stem of twisted siliceous threads; **glass slipper** [mistranslating French *pantoufle en vair* fur slipper through confusion with *verre* glass] a slipper made of glass; *esp.* the one worn and lost by Cinderella in the fairy tale; **glass snail** a snail with a thin translucent shell; spec. *Retinella pura*; **glass snake** any of various snakelike lizards of the genus *Ophisaurus*, of the southern US; **glass sponge** ZOOLOGY (**a**) any of various deep-water sponges of the class Hexactinellida, which often have a skeleton composed of fused six-pointed siliceous spicules; (**b**) = ***glass-rope sponge above***; **glassware** articles made of glass; **glass wool** glass in the form of fine fibres for packing and insulation; **glass work** (**a**) (usu. in *pl.*) the works or factory where glass is manufactured; (**b**) the manufacture of glass and glassware, glazing; (**c**) glassware; **glasswort** a maritime plant of the goosefoot family rich in alkali and formerly used in the manufacture of glass: (**a**) any of various succulent jointed apparently leafless plants of the genus *Salicornia*, freq. dominant in salt marshes; (**b**) (more fully ***prickly glasswort***) prickly saltwort, *Salsola kali*.

■ **glassful** *noun* as much as a glass will hold E17. **glassless** *adjective* E19. **glasslike** *adjective & adverb* (**a**) *adjective* resembling glass, glassy, vitreous; (**b**) *adverb* (*rare*) in the manner of glass: E17.

glass /glɑːs/ *verb*. LME.
[ORIGIN from the noun: cf. GLAZE *verb*[1].]
1 *verb trans.* Fit or fill in with glass, glaze. Freq. in *pass.* LME.

JONATHAN ROSS Above the main doors a glassed-in bulb pushed out a sickly . . light.

2 *verb trans.* Protect by a covering of glass; cover with a vitreous or glassy surface; encase in glass. Long *rare* or *obsolete*. L16.

WORDSWORTH A flower Glassed in a green-house.

3 *verb trans.* Set (a person, freq. oneself, or thing) before a mirror or other reflecting surface so as to cause an image to be reflected; view the reflection of; see as in a mirror. L16. ▸**b** Of a mirror or other reflecting surface: reflect, give back an image of. E17.

BYRON Thou glorious mirror, where the Almighty's form glasses itself in tempests. **b** T. HARDY Both looked attractive as glassed back by the faithful reflector.

4 *verb trans.* View or scan with field glasses or other optical instrument. L18.
5 *verb trans.* Dress leather with a device for smoothing and polishing. Also foll. by *out*. L19.
6 *verb intrans.* *esp.* in SURFING. Of water: become smooth and glassy in appearance. (Foll. by *off*.) L19.

glassen /ˈglɑːs(ə)n/ *adjective*. Now *arch.* & *dial.* Also **glazen** /ˈgleɪz(ə)n/.
[ORIGIN Old English *glæsen*, formed as GLASS *noun* + -EN[4].]
1 Made of glass. OE.
2 Resembling glass; (of the eyes) glassy, glazed. LME.

glassen /ˈglɑːs(ə)n/ *verb trans.* Long *obsolete* exc. *dial.* Also **glazen** /ˈgleɪz(ə)n/. M16.
[ORIGIN from GLASS *verb* + -EN[5]. Cf. GLAZE *verb*[1].]
1 = GLAZE *verb*[1] 1. M16.
2 = GLAZE *verb*[1] 2. M17.
■ **glassener** *noun* a glazier L16.

glassichord /ˈglɑːsɪkɔːd/ *noun*. *US. obsolete* exc. *hist.* M19.
[ORIGIN from GLASS *noun* after *harpsichord*.]
= HARMONICA 1(b).

glassify /ˈglɑːsɪfʌɪ/ *verb trans.* L20.
[ORIGIN from GLASS *noun* + -I- + -FY.]
Vitrify (nuclear waste) for convenience of handling and storage.
■ **glassifiˈcation** *noun* L20.

glassine /ˈglɑːsiːn/ *noun & adjective*. E20.
[ORIGIN from GLASS *noun* + -INE[5].]
(Designating or made of) a kind of glossy transparent paper.

Glassite /ˈglɑːsʌɪt/ *noun & adjective*. *hist.* L18.
[ORIGIN from John *Glass* (see below) + -ITE[1].]
▸**A** *noun*. A member of the religious sect founded by Revd John Glass, a minister of the Established Church of Scotland (deposed in 1728). L18.
▸ **B** *adjective*. Of or pertaining to this sect. M19.

glassy /ˈglɑːsi/ *noun*[1]. L19.
[ORIGIN from GLASS *noun* + -Y[6].]
A glass marble.

glassy /ˈglɑːsi/ *noun*[2]. M20.
[ORIGIN from the adjective.]
SURFING. (A stretch of) smooth water.

glassy /ˈglɑːsi/ *adjective*. LME.
[ORIGIN from GLASS *noun* + -Y[1].]
1 Having the properties of glass, vitreous; resembling or characteristic of glass; appearing to be made of glass. LME. ▸†**b** Brittle or fragile like glass. L16–L18.

J. PINKERTON The glassy quartz retains its natural consistency. P. H. GOSSE The shell is glassy and colourless. B. HARTE The glassy tinkle of water. G. GREENE This unhappy man in all his curious glassy transparency. **b** W. COWPER The glassy threads with which the Fancy weaves her brittle toils.

†**glassy humour** = VITREOUS ***humour***; cf. GLAZY 1.

2 Of the eye etc.: having a fixed unintelligent look; lacking fire or life; dull. LME.

T. HEALD To approach . . with outstretched hand and glassy smile. H. BASCOM He stares glassy eyed and weeps.

†**3** Made or consisting of glass. LME–E19.

G. CRABBE A glassy globe, in frame of ivory, prest.

4 Of water etc.: lustrous and transparent as glass; having a smooth unruffled surface like glass. M16.

C. MACKENZIE The strait was glassy calm. E. BOWEN The harbour . . lay glassy under the close sky.

■ **glassily** *adverb* E19. **glassiness** *noun* E17.

glastick *noun* var. of GLAISTIC.

Glastonbury /ˈglast(ə)nb(ə)ri/ *noun*. L17.
[ORIGIN A town in Somerset.]
1 ***Glastonbury thorn***, a winter-flowering form of hawthorn, *Crataegus monogyna*, said to have originally sprung up at Glastonbury from the staff of Joseph of Arimathea. L17.
2 ***Glastonbury chair***, a kind of folding armchair, supposedly designed after a chair owned by the last Abbot of Glastonbury (executed 1539). M19.

Glaswegian /glazˈwiːdʒ(ə)n, glas-, glɑːz-, glɑːs-/ *noun & adjective*. E19.
[ORIGIN from *Glasgow* (see below) after *Norwegian* etc.: see -IAN.]
▸ **A** *noun*. A native or inhabitant of Glasgow, a city in Scotland. E19.
▸ **B** *adjective*. Of or pertaining to (a native or inhabitant of) Glasgow. L19.

glatt /glat/ Also **glatt kosher**. *adjective*. L20.
[ORIGIN Yiddish from German, lit. 'smooth'.]
JUDAISM. Of food: prepared according to a strict interpretation of Jewish dietary law, completely kosher.

Glauber /ˈglɔːbə, ˈglaʊbə/ *noun*. M18.
[ORIGIN Johann Rudolf *Glauber*, German chemist (1604–1668).]
Glauber salt(s), ***Glauber's salt(s)***, crystalline (hydrated) sodium sulphate, used esp. as a laxative.

glauberite /ˈglaʊb(ə)rʌɪt/ *noun*. E19.
[ORIGIN formed as GLAUBER + -ITE[1].]
MINERALOGY. A monoclinic sulphate of sodium and calcium occurring usu. as glassy white or faintly coloured dipyramidal crystals, esp. in salt lake deposits.

glaucescent /glɔːˈsɛs(ə)nt/ *adjective*. E19.
[ORIGIN formed as GLAUCOUS: see -ESCENT.]
Chiefly BOTANY. Somewhat glaucous.
■ **glaucescence** *noun* L19.

G

glaucodot /ˈglɔːkədɒt/ *noun*. M19.
[ORIGIN German *Glaukodot*, formed as Greek *glaukos* GLAUCOUS + *dotēr* giver.]
MINERALOGY. An orthorhombic arsenide and sulphide of cobalt and iron, occurring as greyish or reddish-white crystals with a metallic lustre.

glaucoma /glɔːˈkəʊmə/ *noun*. M17.
[ORIGIN Greek *glaukōma*, from *glaukos*: see GLAUCOUS, -OMA.]
MEDICINE. An eye condition characterized by increased pressure within the eyeball and a gradual impairment or loss of sight.
■ **glaucoˈmatic** *adjective* of or pertaining to glaucoma M19. **glauˈcomatous** *adjective* of, pertaining to, or affected with glaucoma E19.

glauconite /ˈglɔːkənʌɪt/ *noun*. M19.
[ORIGIN German *Glaukonit*, formed as Greek *glaukon* neut. of *glaukos*: see GLAUCOUS, -ITE[1].]
MINERALOGY. A ferromagnesian clay mineral of the illite group. Also, a greenish earthy material consisting of pellets of this or similar minerals (also called ***green earth***).
■ **glaucoˈnitic** *adjective* M19.

glaucophane /ˈglɔːkəfeɪn/ *noun*. M19.
[ORIGIN German *Glaukophan*, from Greek *glaukos* (see GLAUCOUS) + *-phanēs* shining.]
MINERALOGY. Any of a group of sodium-containing monoclinic amphiboles occurring esp. in schists and other metamorphic rocks.

glaucose /ˈglɔːkəʊs/ *adjective*. *rare*. E18.
[ORIGIN formed as GLAUCOUS: see -OSE[1].]
= GLAUCOUS.

glaucous /ˈglɔːkəs/ *adjective*. L17.
[ORIGIN Latin *glaucus* from Greek *glaukos* bluish-green, bluish-grey: see -OUS.]
Of a dull greyish green or greyish blue; *esp.* in BOTANY, covered with a powdery bloom as of grapes.
glaucous gull a large grey and white gull, *Larus hyperboreus*, of Arctic coasts.

glaucus /ˈglɔːkəs/ *noun*. E16.
[ORIGIN (mod. Latin from) Latin: see GLAUCOUS.]
†**1** A marine fish of uncertain identity. E16–E18.
2 = GLAUCOUS ***gull***. Now *rare* or *obsolete*. L18.
3 A sea slug (mollusc) of the genus *Glaucus*, usu. blue in colour and freq. floating in the open sea. M19.

glaum *noun* var. of GLAM *noun*[2].

glaum /glɔːm/ *verb intrans.* *Scot.* Also **glam** (infl. **-mm-**). L18.
[ORIGIN Origin unkn: cf. GLOM.]
Snatch *at*; make threatening gestures.

glaver /ˈgleɪvə/ *noun & verb*. Long *obsolete* exc. *Scot. & N. English*. LME.
[ORIGIN Unknown.]
▸ **A** *noun*. Chatter; loud noise. LME.
▸ **B** *verb*. **1** *verb trans.* Flatter, deceive with flattery. LME.
2 *verb intrans.* Talk plausibly and deceitfully, flatter. LME.

glaze /gleɪz/ *noun*. L17.
[ORIGIN from GLAZE *verb*[1].]
1 A window. *arch. slang*. L17.
2 A coating or covering of ice; a stretch of ice. *US*. M18.

E. K. KANE Old seasoned hummock, covered with a slippery glaze.

3 A smooth, lustrous, usu. transparent coating; *esp.* an edible coating of gelatin, sugar, egg, etc., on food; a smooth glossy surface. L18.

W. GREENER Dense hard powder will take a higher glaze than the softer kinds.

4 The vitreous substance fixed by fusion to the surface of pottery etc. and forming an impervious decorative coating. E19.

J. CLAVELL The . . glaze had run just short, leaving an uneven rim of bare porcelain.

5 A thin top coat of transparent paint used to modify the tone of an underlying colour. **M19.**

JONATHAN MILLER With newly discovered glazes, painters take delight in showing the play of light on . . flesh.

glaze /gleɪz/ *verb*[1]. **LME.**

[**ORIGIN** from **GLASS** *noun* as *graze* from *grass*: cf. Middle High German *glasen* and **GLASS** *verb*.]

1 *verb trans.* Fit or fill in (a window etc.) with glass; cover (a painting etc.) with glass; provide (a building) with glass windows. **LME.**

BROWNING Somebody saw a portrait framed and glazed At Croisic. M. FRAYN The upper half of the door was glazed with dusty panes.

2 *verb trans.* Cover (pottery etc.) with glaze; fix (glaze, paint) *on* pottery etc. by fusion. **LME.**

T. THOMSON The vessel now being baked, the paint is glazed on.

3 *verb trans.* Cause to shine like glass; give a smooth glassy surface to, esp. by rubbing; polish. **LME.**

G

R. BOYLE Like polish'd Silver, or well glaz'd Arms.

4 *verb trans.* Overlay or cover with a smooth lustrous coating. Also, cover (the eyes) with a film (as of moisture etc.), dull. **L16.**

SHAKES. *Rich. II* Sorrow's eye, glazed with blinding tears. V. WOOLF Little red and green vegetables glazed in sauce.

5 *verb trans.* Cover (a painted surface) with glaze. Also, lay (a transparent colour) *over* another. **E17.**

J. RUSKIN Red . . mixed with the pure blue, or glazed over it.

6 *verb intrans.* Be or become glazed; *esp.* (of the eyes) take on a glassy or fixed appearance. **M18.**

T. KENEALLY Harry tried to understand the point. His eyes glazed with the import of it.

■ **glazed** *ppl adjective* (*a*) that has been subject to the action or an act of glazing; (*b*) METALLURGY having a smooth shining surface or fracture; (*c*) ***glazed frost*** = ***silver thaw*** s.v. **SILVER** *adjective*: **M16.** **glazer** *noun* †(*a*) = **GLAZIER** 2; (*b*) a person who applies the glaze to pottery; (*c*) an implement for glazing; *esp.* a wheel used in polishing knives etc.: **LME.**

glaze /gleɪz/ *verb*[2] *intrans. obsolete* exc. *dial.* **E17.**

[**ORIGIN** Perh. blend of **GAZE** *verb* and **GLARE** *verb*.]

Stare.

glazen *adjective* var. of **GLASSEN** *adjective*.

glazen *verb* var. of **GLASSEN** *verb*.

glazier /ˈgleɪzɪə/ *noun*. **ME.**

[**ORIGIN** from **GLAZE** *verb*[1] + **-IER**.]

1 A person whose trade is to glaze windows etc. **ME.**

†**2** A person engaged in the manufacture of glass, a glass-maker. **LME–L15.**

†**3** In *pl.* The eyes. *slang.* **M16–L18.**

†**4** A thief, *esp.* one who broke a window etc. to steal. *slang.* **L17–L18.**

■ **glaziery** *noun* the work of a glazier **M19.**

glazing /ˈgleɪzɪŋ/ *noun*. **LME.**

[**ORIGIN** from **GLAZE** *verb*[1] + **-ING**[1].]

1 The action of providing a building with windows or filling windows with glass; the trade or business of a glazier. **LME.** ▸**b** Glass fixed in windows or frames. **LME.**
b double glazing: see **DOUBLE** *adjective & adverb*.

2 The action of polishing or burnishing. **LME.**

3 The operation of coating with a glaze, or of giving a smooth shiny surface. **L17.** ▸**b** The substance used for producing a glaze or glossy surface; a glossy surface. **E18.**

4 The application of a thin top coat of transparent paint to modify the tone of the underlying colour; this paint. **E18.**

glazy /ˈgleɪzi/ *adjective*. **E17.**

[**ORIGIN** from **GLAZE** *noun* or *verb*[1] + **-Y**[1].]

†**1** ***glazy humour***, the vitreous humour. *rare.* Only in **E17.**

2 Glassy, shining like glass; resembling or characteristic of a glaze or glazed surface. **E18.**

3 = **GLASSY** *adjective* 2. **M19.**

■ **glazily** *adverb* **M19.** **glaziness** *noun* **E18.**

GLB *abbreviation*.

Gay, lesbian, or bisexual.

GLBT *abbreviation*.

Gay, lesbian, bisexual, or transgendered.

GLC *abbreviation*.

1 Gas–liquid chromatography.

2 *hist.* Greater London Council.

gleam /gliːm/ *noun*[1] & *verb*[1].

[**ORIGIN** Old English *glǣm* corresp. to Low German *glēm*, Old High German *gleimo* glow-worm, and rel. to Old Saxon *glīmo* brightness, Old High German *glīmo*, Middle High German *glimen* shine, glow. Cf. **GLIMMER** *verb*.]

▸ **A** *noun*. **1** Orig., a brilliant light. Now only, a subdued or transient light, *esp.* one that is reflected. **OE.** ▸**b** *fig.* A bright or vivid manifestation of some quality. Now chiefly, a faint, transient, or intermittent appearance of this quality. **ME.** ▸**c** A warm ray of sun; a bright warm interval between rain showers. Long *dial.* **E17.**

F. M. FORD In the sunlight gleams come from . . the glass of windows; from the gilt signs. J. T. STORY Distantly, far beyond the sound, I saw the gleam of a torch. **b** T. KEN When first my Heart, thou Lord, didst melt, And of thy Love one Gleam I felt. N. MITFORD A gleam of amusement crossed Lady Patricia's sad face.

b a gleam in one's eye: see **EYE** *noun*.

2 Brilliance; radiant beauty. Long *dial.* **OE.** ▸**b** A bright or joyous look. Long *rare.* **M18.**

SPENSER Then was the faire Dodonian tree far seene . . to spred his gladsome gleame.

▸ **B** *verb*. **1** *verb intrans.* Emit a gleam or gleams; shine with esp. a reflected, subdued, or intermittent brightness; (of a quality) be indicated. **ME.**

V. BRITTAIN A hundred lights gleamed like jewels against the deep cobalt of sky and water. R. WARNER I . . saw most vividly the candlelight gleaming on the mahogany table. G. VIDAL Eusebia's eyes gleamed with mischief.

2 *verb trans.* Shine or reflect (a subdued or intermittent light). **L16.**

SHAKES. *Lucr.* And dying eyes gleam'd forth their ashy lights.

■ **gleaming** *noun* the action of the verb; an instance of this, a gleam: **LME.** **gleamingly** *adverb* in a gleaming manner **M19.** **gleamless** *adjective* **L19.**

gleam /gliːm/ *verb*[2] & *noun*[2]. **L16.**

[**ORIGIN** Var. of **GLEIM** *verb*.]

▸ **A** *verb intrans.* Of a hawk: regurgitate gleam. Long *rare* or *obsolete*. **L16.**

▸ **B** *noun*. The meat etc. regurgitated from the crop by a hawk. **L19.**

gleamy /ˈgliːmi/ *adjective*. **L16.**

[**ORIGIN** from **GLEAM** *noun*[1] + **-Y**[1].]

1 That gleams. **L16.**

DISRAELI Fish, gleamy with prismatic hues.

2 That is lighted by a gleam or gleams; *esp.* (of weather) marked by intermittent sunshine. Now chiefly *dial.* **L17.**

WORDSWORTH And antique castles seen through gleamy showers.

3 Of light or colour: of the nature of a gleam; subdued, hazy. **E18.**

J. INGELOW Stands by his fire, and dulls its gleamy light.

■ **gleaminess** *noun* **M19.**

glean /gliːn/ *noun*. *obsolete* exc. *dial.* **LME.**

[**ORIGIN** Old French *glene*, *glane*, from *glener*: see **GLEAN** *verb*.]

1 Something that has been gleaned; *esp.* a head of corn or other cereal. **LME.**

2 A bundle or sheaf of corn, hemp, etc. **M17.**

glean /gliːn/ *verb*. **ME.**

[**ORIGIN** Old French *glener* (mod. *glaner*) from late Latin *glen(n)are*, ult. from Celtic base repr. by Old Irish *do-glenn* (he) gathers.]

1 *verb trans.* Gather or collect in small quantities, scrape together, (news, facts, etc.); find out or discover (something). **ME.** ▸†**b** Gather or collect *into* a receptacle or mass. **LME–M17.**

E. F. BENSON She would not . . read letters that were left about, but she constantly . . tried to glean their contents. R. H. MOTTRAM She was gleaning every scrap of information she could.

2 ▸**a** *verb trans. & intrans.* Gather or pick up (ears of corn or other produce) left by reapers or harvesters. **LME.** ▸**b** *verb trans.* Strip (a field etc.) thus. **M16.**

a J. CARY The field where we had been gleaning for our chickens. A. R. AMMONS The women glean remnant peas. **b** AV *Lev.* 19:10 Thou shalt not gleane thy vineyard.

■ **gleaner** *noun* **LME.** **gleaning** *noun* (*a*) the action or an act of the verb; (*b*) something that is gleaned (usu. in *pl.*): **LME.**

glease /gliːz/ *verb*. Orig. †**glace**. **ME.**

[**ORIGIN** Old French *glacer*, *glacier* glide, slip, ult. from Latin *glacies* ice.]

†**1** *verb intrans.* Of a weapon: glance off, strike with a glancing blow. **ME–L15.**

†**2** *verb trans.* Glide, glance. Only in **LME.**

3 *verb trans.* Glide or skim past, pass very close to. *dial.* **L19.**

gleba /ˈgliːbə/ *noun*. Pl. **-bae** /-biː/. **M19.**

[**ORIGIN** formed as **GLEBE**.]

MYCOLOGY. The fleshy, spore-bearing tissue of certain fungi (Gasteromycetales and Tuberales), e.g. puffballs and stinkhorns.

glebe /gliːb/ *noun*. **LME.**

[**ORIGIN** Latin *gleba*, *glaeba* clod, land, soil.]

1 The soil of the earth; earth, land. Now *poet.* **LME.**

T. CAMPBELL The glebe of fifty kingdoms shall be till'd To feed his . . train.

2 A piece of cultivated land, a field. Now *poet.* **LME.** ▸**b** *spec.* A piece of land assigned as part of a parish clergyman's living. **LME.**

TENNYSON Many an . . upland glebe wealthy in oil and wine. **b** W. COBBETT This parish . . has a glebe, and a good solid house.

†**3** A clod or mass of earth, ore, etc.; an earthy mineral. **E16–M18.**

T. AMORY The glittering glebes of a gold colour found here.

– COMB.: **glebe-house** (now *rare* or *obsolete*) a parsonage; **glebe-land** = sense 2b above.

■ **gleby** *adjective* (now *rare* or *obsolete*) (of soil) rich, fertile, full of clods **M16.**

glebous /ˈgliːbəs/ *adjective*. *rare.* **L17.**

[**ORIGIN** Latin *glebosus*, from *gleba* **GLEBE**: see **-OUS**.]

Earthy; full of clods.

gled /glɛd/ *noun*. Now chiefly *Scot. & N. English*. Also **glede** /gliːd/.

[**ORIGIN** Old English *glida* corresp. to Middle Low German *glede*, Old Norse *gleða*, from Germanic base of **GLIDE** *verb*.]

A bird of prey, *esp.* the kite.

gledge /glɛdʒ/ *verb & noun*. *Scot.* **E19.**

[**ORIGIN** Uncertain: cf. **GLEG** *noun & verb*, **GLEY** *verb*.]

▸ **A** *verb intrans.* Squint; look sideways, esp. cunningly or slyly. **E19.**

▸ **B** *noun*. A side glance, a (sly) look. **E19.**

gleditsia /gləˈdɪtsɪə/ *noun*. Also **gleditschia** /-tʃɪə/. **L18.**

[**ORIGIN** mod. Latin (see below), from J. G. *Gleditsch* (1714–86), German botanist + **-IA**[1].]

Any of various usu. spiny Asian or American leguminous trees of the genus *Gleditsia* (e.g. the N. American honey locust, *G. triacanthos*), of which some species are cultivated as ornamentals, for the pods, or as hedges or timber.

glee /gliː/ *noun*.

[**ORIGIN** Old English *glēo*, *glēow*, *glīw* = Old Norse *glý*, from Germanic.]

†**1** Entertainment, play, fun; occas., mockery. **OE–E17.**

2 Musical entertainment; music, melody. Now *Scot.* (*arch.*) exc. in ***gleeman*** below. **OE.** ▸**b** A part-song, *spec.* an unaccompanied one, for three or more (usu. adult male) voices and freq. consisting of contrasted movements. **M17.**

3 Mirth, joy. Now *esp.* triumphant or exuberantly displayed delight. **ME.**

J. HELLER Wintergreen crowed with malicious glee. J. G. FARRELL They shouted with laughter, held their sides, and even rolled in the dust in undignified glee.

†**4** Bright colour, beauty. **LME–L16.**

– COMB.: **glee club** a society for singing glees and other part-songs; **gleeman** *hist.* a professional esp. musical entertainer; a minstrel.

■ **gleeful** *adjective* **L16.** **gleefully** *adverb* **M19.** **gleefulness** *noun* **M20.** **gleesome** *adjective* = **GLEEFUL** **E17.** **gleesomely** *adverb* **M19.** **gleesomeness** *noun* **M19.**

glee *verb* var. of **GLEY** *verb*.

gleed /gliːd/ *noun*.

[**ORIGIN** Old English *glēd* = Old Frisian *glēd*, Old Saxon *glōd-* (Dutch *gloed*), Old High German *gluot* (German *Glut*), Old Norse *glóð*, ult. from Germanic base of **GLOW** *verb*[1].]

1 An ember, a live coal; a (glowing) fire. Now *dial.* or *arch.* **OE.**

2 A spark or glimmer (of fire); a beam (of light). Now *dial.* **M16.**

3 In *pl.* Cinders; coke used as fuel. *dial.* **M19.**

gleek /gliːk/ *noun*[1]. **E16.**

[**ORIGIN** Old French *glic*, *ghelicque*, perh. from Middle Dutch *ghelic* (mod. *gelijk*) **LIKE** *adjective*.]

1 *hist.* A card game for three people using forty-four cards, twelve being dealt to each player and eight forming a common stock. **E16.**

†**2** A set of three court cards of the same rank in one hand in the game of gleek; *transf.* a set of three, a trio. **E17–E18.**

gleek /gliːk/ *noun*[2] & *verb*. **M16.**

[**ORIGIN** Perh. dim. of **GLEE** *noun*. Cf. **GLAIK**.]

▸ **A** *noun*. †**1** A jibe, a jest; a joke, a trick. **M16–E19.**

2 A glance, *esp.* a coquettish one. *rare.* **L16.**

▸ **B** *verb*. **1** *verb trans.* Trick, outwit. *arch.* **M16.**

2 *verb intrans.* Make a jest, jibe (*at* a person). Now *arch. rare.* **L16.**

3 *verb intrans.* Look sideways, glance. *rare.* **E17.**

gleet /gliːt/ *noun & verb*. Also (earlier, chiefly *Scot. & N. English*) **glit** /glɪt/, **glet** /glɛt/, (infl. **-tt-**). **ME.**

[**ORIGIN** Old French & mod. French *glette* slime, filth, secretion, (now) litharge, of unknown origin.]

▸ **A** *noun*. **1** Mucus formed in the stomach, esp. of a hawk. *obsolete* exc. *Scot.* **ME.**

2 Slimy, sticky, or greasy matter. *obsolete* exc. *Scot. & N. English.* **LME.**

3 (A) watery discharge, now only *spec.* from the urethra, usu. as a result of chronic gonorrhoea. **M16.**

▸ **B** *verb*. †**1** *verb intrans.* Esp. of a watery discharge: ooze, flow slowly. **E16–E18.**

2 *verb intrans.* & †*trans.* Of a wound, the nose, etc.: discharge (a thin purulent matter). **L17.**

■ **gleety** *adjective* (*a*) (*obsolete* exc. *Scot. & N. English*) slimy; (*b*) watery, purulent: **LME.**

gleg /glɛg/ *noun & verb*. M17.
[ORIGIN Uncertain: cf. GLEDGE, GLEY *verb*.]
▸ **A** *noun*. = GLEDGE *noun*. *obsolete* exc. *N. English*. M17.
▸ **B** *verb intrans*. Infl. **-gg-**. = GLEDGE *verb*. *dial*. L18.

gleg /glɛg/ *adjective & adverb*. *Scot*. & *N. English*. ME.
[ORIGIN Old Norse *gleggr*, *gloggr* clear, clear-sighted, corresp. to Old English *glēaw* wise, clever, Old Saxon, Old High German *glau* clever, from Germanic base of Gothic *glaggwuba* (adverb) accurately.]
▸ **A** *adjective*. **1** Quick or sharp in perception by any of the senses, esp. by sight. Chiefly in ***gleg of the eye***, sharp-eyed. ME. ▸**b** Of the eye, a blade, etc.: sharp, keen. E18.
2 Quick or clever *at* (doing) something; nimble; alert. M18.
3 Lively, cheery, happy. E19.
▸ **B** *adverb*. = GLEGLY. E18.
■ **glegly** *adverb* quickly, cleverly, readily; brightly, clearly: M18. **glegness** *noun* M19.

glei *noun* see GLEY *noun*.

Gleichschaltung /ˈglaɪçʃaltʊŋ/ *noun*. Also **g-**. M20.
[ORIGIN German.]
The standardization of political, economic, and cultural institutions in authoritarian states.

gleification /ˌgleɪɪfɪˈkeɪʃ(ə)n/ *noun*. M20.
[ORIGIN from GLEY *noun* + -FICATION.]
SOIL SCIENCE. = GLEIZATION.

†**gleim** *verb & noun*. LME.
[ORIGIN Uncertain: cf. Old Norse *kleima* daub corresp. to Old English *clǣman* CLEAM *verb*, also GLEAM *verb*[2] & *noun*[2].]
▸ **A** *verb trans*. Smear with a sticky substance; *fig*. in *pass*., be attached *to* something. Only in LME.
▸ **B** *noun*. A sticky or slimy substance; *spec*. rheum; *fig*. attachment, affection. LME–E16.

†**gleimy** *adjective*. LME–E18.
[ORIGIN from GLEIM *noun* + -Y[1].]
Sticky, slimy.

gleization /gleɪˈzeɪʃ(ə)n, gleɪʌɪ-/ *noun*. Also **gley-** /gleɪ-/. M20.
[ORIGIN from GLEY *noun* + -IZATION.]
SOIL SCIENCE. The process of formation of a gley soil by waterlogging and chemical reduction of iron.

glen /glɛn/ *noun & adjective*. LME.
[ORIGIN Gaelic, Irish *gleann*, earlier *glenn* = Welsh *glyn*.]
▸ **A** *noun*. A mountain valley, esp. narrow and steep-sided and forming the course of a stream or river. LME.

L. MACNEICE Three glens, each leading up to a loch in the mountains.

▸ **B** *attrib*. or as *adjective*. Designating any of various check fabrics, esp. the Glenurquhart check. LME.

glendoveer /glɛndəˈvɪə/ *noun*. E19.
[ORIGIN formed as GANDHARVA.]
(In the artificial quasi-Hindu mythology of the poet Robert Southey) a member of a race of beautiful sprites.

glengarry /glɛnˈgari/ *noun*. Also **G-**. M19.
[ORIGIN from *Glengarry* in the Highlands of Scotland.]
A man's flat-sided cap, pointed at the front and back and usu. with a pair of ribbons hanging behind; chiefly worn as part of Highland dress.

gleno- /ˈgliːnəʊ/ *combining form* of GLENOID, used in *ANATOMY*: see -O-.
■ **glenoˈhumeral** *adjective* of or relating to the shoulder joint M19.

glenoid /ˈgliːnɔɪd/ *adjective*. E18.
[ORIGIN French *glénoïde* from Greek *glēnoeidēs*, from *glēnē* ball or pupil of the eye: see -OID.]
ANATOMY. ***glenoid cavity***, ***glenoid fossa***, a socket or cavity on a bone into which another bone fits to form a joint; *esp*. that on the scapula articulating with the humerus.
■ **glenoidal** *adjective* M19.

glent /glɛnt/ *verb & noun*. Long *dial*. ME.
[ORIGIN Prob. of Scandinavian origin: cf. Swedish dial. *glänta*, *glinta* slip, slide; shine, gleam. See also GLINT *verb*, *noun*[1].]
▸ **A** *verb intrans*. **1** Move quickly esp. in an oblique direction. ME. ▸**b** Of a weapon, missile, blow, etc.: glance, strike obliquely. LME.
2 Look sideways, glance. ME.
3 Flash, gleam, shine; be reflected. LME.
▸ **B** *noun*. **1** A look, a glance; a glimpse. ME.
2 A gleam, a flash. LME.
3 A sudden movement, a jump, a leap; a slip, a stumble. E16.

Glenurquhart /glɛnˈɜːkət/ *noun & adjective*. E20.
[ORIGIN *Glenurquhart* in the Highlands of Scotland.]
(Designating) a kind of Scottish plaid or check.

glet *noun & verb* see GLEET.

gletcher /ˈglɛtʃə/ *noun*. Orig. (now *rare*) **Gletscher**. M18.
[ORIGIN German *Gletscher* from Swiss dial. = French *glacier*.]
A glacier.

glew /gluː/ *verb*. Now *rare*.
[ORIGIN Old English *glēowian*, *glīwian*, from *glēow*, *glīw* GLEE *noun*.]
1 *verb intrans*. Make merry, jest, play music. OE.
†**2** *verb trans*. Entertain, make happy. ME–E16.

gley /gleɪ/ *noun*. Also **glei**. E20.
[ORIGIN Ukrainian *gleĭ* sticky bluish clay, cogn. with CLAY *noun*.]
SOIL SCIENCE. A sticky blue-grey waterlogged soil or soil layer in which iron is reduced to the ferrous form; such a soil having brownish mottling due to oxidation during intermittent dry periods. Also ***gley soil***.
■ **gleyed** *adjective* turned into a gley M20. **gleying** *noun* = GLEIZATION M20.

gley /glʌɪ/ *verb intrans*. Also **glee** /gliː/. *obsolete* exc. *Scot*. & *N. English*. ME.
[ORIGIN Unknown. Cf. GLEDGE *verb & noun*, GLEG *noun & verb*.]
Squint, look sideways; have a cast in one or both eyes.
■ **gleyd** *adjective* (**a**) having a cast in one or both eyes; squint-eyed; (**b**) crooked, twisted; wrong, awry: L15.

gleyde *noun* var. of GLYDE.

gleyzation *noun* var. of GLEIZATION.

glia /ˈglʌɪə, ˈgliːə/ *noun*. L19.
[ORIGIN Greek = glue.]
ANATOMY. The connective tissue of the nervous system, consisting of several different types of cell associated with neurons; = NEUROGLIA. Also ***glia cell***, ***glia tissue***.
■ **glial** *adjective* of or pertaining to glia L19.

gliadin /ˈglʌɪədɪn/ *noun*. Also **-ine** /-iːn, -ɪn/. M19.
[ORIGIN French *gliadine*, from Greek *glia* glue: see -IN[1], -INE[2].]
BIOCHEMISTRY. Orig., any prolamine (plant protein soluble in aqueous alcohol). Now *spec*. a proline-rich protein, one of the components of cereal gluten.

glib /glɪb/ *noun*. M16.
[ORIGIN Irish.]
IRISH HISTORY. A thick mass of matted hair worn hanging over the forehead and eyes.

glib /glɪb/ *adjective & adverb*. Compar. & superl. **-bb-**. L16.
[ORIGIN Rel. to GLIBBERY.]
▸ **A** *adjective*. **1** Smooth and slippery; offering no resistance to motion; moving easily; (of movement) unimpeded, easy. Now *arch*. & *dial*. L16.

BROWNING The snow lies glib as glass and hard as steel.

2 Of an action etc.: casual, offhand. L16.

B. RUBENS She hated herself for her glib and ready cruelty.

3 Of a speaker, speech, etc.: fluent, ready, more voluble than sincere or thoughtful. L16.

G. ALLEN The ordinary glib commonplaces of obituary notices. O. NASH Oh to be glib! Oh to be ever prepared with a plausible fib!

▸ **B** *adverb*. **1** Smoothly; easily. Now *rare*. L16.
2 Volubly; fluently. E17.

E. S. BARRETT You talked so glib of your great estates.

■ **glibly** *adverb* E17. **glibness** *noun* E17.

glib /glɪb/ *verb*[1]. Infl. **-bb-**. L16.
[ORIGIN from the adjective.]
†**1** *verb trans*. Make smooth or slippery. L16–E19.
2 *verb trans*. Make fluent or plausible. *arch*. E17.
3 *verb intrans*. Talk glibly. *obsolete* exc. *dial*. E17.

†**glib** *verb*[2] *trans*. *rare*. Infl. **-bb-**. E–M17.
[ORIGIN App. alt. of LIB *verb*[1].]
Castrate, geld.

†**glibbery** *adjective*. E–M17.
[ORIGIN Corresp. to Dutch *glibberig*, Middle Low German *glibberich*, Low German *glibbrig*, from Germanic base (cf. Old High German *gleif* sloping): perh. ult. imit.]
Slippery.

glidder /ˈglɪdə/ *noun*. *Scot*. & *N. English*. L18.
[ORIGIN Rel. to GLIDDER *adjective & verb*.]
A loose stone on a hillside.

glidder /ˈglɪdə/ *adjective & verb*. *obsolete* exc. *dial*.
[ORIGIN Old English *glid(d)er*, from weak grade of the base of GLIDE *verb*: see -ER[5].]
▸ **A** *adjective*. Slippery. Long *rare*. OE.
▸ **B** *verb trans*. Glaze over; cover with ice. E17.
■ **gliddery** *adjective* slippery; *fig*. treacherous: M19.

glide /glʌɪd/ *noun*. LME.
[ORIGIN from GLIDE *verb*.]
1 The action or an act of gliding. LME. ▸**b** = GLANCE *noun*[1] 2b. L19. ▸**c** A gliding dance step or dance. L19. ▸**d** *AERONAUTICS*. The act of gliding; a flight in a glider. E20.

J. WILSON With a winged glide this maiden would rove. J. G. WHITTIER The dip of Indian oars, The glide of birch canoes.

2 A shallow section of a stream. Formerly also, a stream. L16.
3 *PHONETICS*. A smoothly changing sound produced in passing from one position of the speech organs to another; a semivowel. M19.
4 *CRYSTALLOGRAPHY*. Plastic deformation of a crystal lattice by lateral displacement along an atomic plane. M20.
– COMB.: **glide bomb** a bomb fitted with aerofoils that enable it to glide towards its target when released from an aircraft; **glide path**, **glide slope** an aircraft's line of descent to land, esp. as indicated by ground radar.
■ **glideless** *adjective* (*PHONETICS*) unaccompanied by a glide E20.

glide /glʌɪd/ *verb*. Pa. t. & pple **glided**, (*arch*.) **glode** /gləʊd/.
[ORIGIN Old English *glīdan* = Old Frisian *glīda*, Old Saxon *glīdan* (Dutch *glijden*), Old High German *glītan* (German *gleiten*), from West Germanic.]
1 *verb intrans*. Pass from one place to another or change position by a smooth continuous movement, esp. without effort or difficulty or perceptible means of locomotion. OE. ▸**b** Of an aircraft: fly without engine power. E20.

DRYDEN [The Snake] in some secret Cranny slowly glides. J. WILSON She glides away like a lambent flame. W. H. BARTLETT The little stream glided and rippled by.

2 *verb intrans*. Move quietly or stealthily; steal *into*, *out of*, a place. ME.

D. G. MITCHELL He . . glides out stealthful as a cat. C. KINGSLEY A great dog-fox as red as the fir-stems through which he glides.

†**3** *verb intrans*. Pass from one place to another, go, come. *poet*. ME–L16.

SPENSER Like sparke of fire that from the andvile glode.

4 *verb intrans*. Slide; (now *dial*.) slide on ice as a sport. Formerly also, slip. ME. ▸**b** Slip *away*, elude one's grasp. E16.

J. SCHEFFER The Laplanders gliding upon the ice. **b** ADDISON It glided through the Fingers like a smooth Piece of Ice.

5 Of time, life, etc.: pass gently and imperceptibly *along*, *away*, etc. ME.

DISRAELI Two serene and innocent years had glided away.

6 *verb trans*. Cause to glide. M17. ▸**b** Traverse in a glider. M20.

A. C. GUNTER Ferdie glides the graceful Louise through the room in poetic motion.

7 *verb intrans*. Pass lightly and without interruption *along* or *over* a surface. E19.

GEO. ELIOT His hand glided from the face and rested on the young man's shoulder. *transf*.: C. LAMB Books of quick interest . . are for the eye to glide over only.

glide into pass gradually into (a condition or state), pass unconsciously into (doing something).
8 *verb intrans*. *CRYSTALLOGRAPHY*. Of units in a crystal: be displaced, esp. along an atomic plane. Also, of a crystal: undergo glide. Cf. GLIDE *noun* 4. L19.
gliding plane = ***glide plane*** below.
9 *verb intrans*. & *trans*. = GLANCE *verb* 8b. L19.
– COMB.: **glide plane** *CRYSTALLOGRAPHY* (**a**) a plane in a crystal along which lateral deformation (slip) may occur; (**b**) a plane of symmetry such that reflection in the plane and translation parallel to it produce a lattice congruent with the original; **glide twin** *CRYSTALLOGRAPHY* a twin crystal produced by the gliding of adjacent layers of a crystal lattice over one another; **glide-twinning** the formation of glide twins.
■ **gliding** *ppl adjective* (**a**) that glides; ***gliding possum*** = ***flying phalanger*** s.v. FLYING *ppl adjective*; (**b**) = GLISSANT: LME. **glidingly** *adverb* L18.

glider /ˈglʌɪdə/ *noun*. LME.
[ORIGIN from GLIDE *verb* + -ER[1].]
1 A person or thing which glides. Also, something that aids in gliding, a fitment that facilitates smooth continuous movement. LME.
2 A light aircraft designed to fly without using an engine. Also, a (skilled) user of such an aircraft. L19.
3 A long swing seat suspended from a vertical frame. *US*. M20.
4 Any of various small Australasian marsupials that glide from tree to tree; *spec*. a flying phalanger, a flying mouse. M20.
– COMB.: **glider bomb** = ***glide bomb*** s.v. GLIDE *noun*.

gliff /glɪf/ *verb & noun*. Now only *Scot*. & *N. English*. ME.
[ORIGIN Unknown.]
▸ **A** *verb*. †**1** *verb intrans*. Slip, glance aside; *fig*. make a slip in reading. Only in ME.
†**2** **a** *verb intrans*. & (*rare*) *trans*. Direct (the eyes) in a glance. Only in ME. ▸**b** *verb intrans*. Shine suddenly, flash. LME–L16.
3 *verb trans*. Frighten. E19.
▸ **B** *noun*. **1** A passing view; a glance, a glimpse. ME.
2 A sudden fright; a scare. M18.
3 A short period of time. L18.
■ **gliffing** *noun* (**a**) the time required to give a glance, an instant; (**b**) a surprise, a fright: E19.

glim /glɪm/ *noun*. LME.
[ORIGIN Perh. abbreviation of GLIMMER *noun*[1] or GLIMPSE *noun*.]
†**1** Brightness. *rare*. Only in LME.
2 Orig., a passing look, a glimpse. Later, as much as is seen at a glance; a scrap. *Scot*. E17.
3 **a** A candle, a lantern, (*arch*. *slang*). Also, a faint light. L17. ▸**b** An eye. *slang*. Now *rare* or *obsolete*. E19.

†**glimflashy** *adjective*. *slang*. L17–M19.
[ORIGIN from GLIM *noun* + FLASHY *adjective*.]
Angry.

glimmer /ˈɡlɪmə/ *noun*¹. **M16.**
[**ORIGIN** from the verb.]
†**1** Fire. **M16–M17.**
2 A faint or wavering light, a shimmer, a sheen. **L16.**
TENNYSON In gloss of satin and glimmer of pearls. R. L. STEVENSON The men bustling to their places in the glimmer of the ship's lanterns.
3 a Showiness of manner. Now *rare* or *obsolete*. **E19.** ▸**b** A faint gleam (*of* hope, understanding, etc.); a glimpse, a half-view. **M19.**
b E. A. FREEMAN Here we get the first glimmer of Austin canons. C. HAMPTON The man hasn't a glimmer of talent.
■ **glimmerless** *adjective* **L19.** **glimmery** *adjective* full of glimmer **E20.**

glimmer /ˈɡlɪmə/ *noun*². **L17.**
[**ORIGIN** German, from *glimmen* to glow.]
MINERALOGY. Mica.

glimmer /ˈɡlɪmə/ *verb intrans.* **LME.**
[**ORIGIN** Prob. of Scandinavian origin (cf. Swedish *glimra*, Danish *glimre*, corresp. to Middle & mod. High German, Dutch *glimmern*), from Germanic. Cf. **GLEAM** *noun*¹ & *verb*¹.]
†**1** Shine brightly, glitter; (of the eyes) flash. **LME–M16.**
2 Shine faintly or intermittently. **LME.**
T. GRAY Now fades the glimmering landscape on the sight. W. CATHER The light of a lamp glimmered through the cracks. *fig.*: GEO. ELIOT The idea of ever recovering happiness never glimmered in her mind for a moment.
go glimmering *US slang* die away, die out, vanish.
3 Look with half-closed eyes; see indistinctly. *rare*. **L16.**
■ **glimmeringly** *adverb* in a glimmering manner **M16.**

glimmering /ˈɡlɪm(ə)rɪŋ/ *noun*. **LME.**
[**ORIGIN** from **GLIMMER** *verb* + **-ING**¹.]
1 The action of **GLIMMER** *verb*; an instance of this; the shining of a faint or intermittent light. **LME.**
R. ADAMS He could just perceive a glimmering of water.
2 A half-view; a glimpse, an inkling; a faint notion. **LME.**
G. B. AIRY It is only possible to give a glimmering of what I desire to convey.

glimpse /ɡlɪm(p)s/ *noun*. **M16.**
[**ORIGIN** from the verb.]
1 A faint and transient appearance. Formerly also, an occasionally perceptible resemblance; a trace (of a quality). **M16.**
MILTON In his face The glimpses of his Father's glory shine.
2 A brief glance, a momentary and imperfect view (*of*). **L16.**
V. WOOLF A glimpse of the church through the trees. C. PRIEST Glimpses into other people's lives.
catch a glimpse of: see **CATCH** *verb*.
3 A momentary shining, a flash. Freq. in ***the glimpses of the moon*** below. Now *arch.* or passing into sense 2. **E17.**
SIR W. SCOTT A glimpse of the moon showed the dark and huge tower.
the glimpses of the moon [after Shakes. *Haml.*] the earth by night; sublunary scenes.

glimpse /ɡlɪm(p)s/ *verb*. **ME.**
[**ORIGIN** from the base of **GLIMMER** *verb*, perh. repr. Old English = Middle High German *glimsen*, ult. from West Germanic.]
1 *verb intrans.* Shine faintly or intermittently; glimmer, glitter. **ME.** ▸**b** Appear faintly; dawn. Now *poet.* or *arch.* **E17.**
A. MUNDAY Little glow-worms glimpsing in the dark. *fig.*: E. PAGITT The Law of God, which glimpsed in their hearts. **b** P. FLETCHER Then glimpst the hopefull morrow.
†**2** *verb intrans.* Have imperfect vision. **LME–E16.**
3 *verb intrans.* Glance briefly. (Foll. by *at*, *upon*, etc.) **LME.**
C. LAMB I read your letter, and glimpsed at your beautiful sonnet.
4 *verb trans.* Give a glimpse of. *rare*. **M17.**
G. MACKENZIE The twilight of darkned reason glimpsing to man, that impressa of the divine Image.
5 *verb trans.* Catch a glimpse of; see faintly or partly. **L18.**
I. MURDOCH He glimpsed her ahead, hurrying, and then she was gone. P. BROOK For a few rare flashes she glimpses her condition.

glint /ɡlɪnt/ *noun*¹. **M16.**
[**ORIGIN** from the verb.]
1 A gleam; a faint appearance of light or of some lustrous object; a flash, a glitter, a sparkle. **M16.** ▸**b** Shining appearance; shine. **M19.**
H. WILLIAMSON She saw the glint of scales as the fish sped in zigzag course.
a glint in one's eye: see **EYE** *noun*.
2 A passing look, a glance; a momentary view, a glimpse. Chiefly *Scot. & N. English*. **E19.**
W. BLACK I . . was having a glint at the newspaper.

glint /ɡlɪnt/ *noun*². **E20.**
[**ORIGIN** Danish, Swedish *klint* cliff, rel. to Icelandic *klettur* (Old Norse *klettr*) rock, crag: cf. **CLINT** *noun*.]
PHYSICAL GEOGRAPHY. A steep cliff or escarpment of almost horizontal strata, produced by erosion of adjacent rock.
– **COMB.**: **glint lake**: formed along a glint line; **glint line** an extensive glint or escarpment, *spec.* that at the boundary between an ancient shield (as the Baltic shield) and younger rocks.

glint /ɡlɪnt/ *verb*. **LME.**
[**ORIGIN** Alt. of **GLENT**.]
1 *verb intrans.* = **GLENT** *verb* 1, 1b. Now *rare*. **LME.**
LYTTON From the mirth of sunny Leofwine sorrow glints aside.
2 *verb intrans.* Shine with a flashing light; gleam, glitter. **LME.** ▸**b** *verb trans.* Make (something) shine with a flashing light. **M19.**
G. MACDONALD A few silvery threads glinted in his hair. J. BUCHAN The sun glinted on the metals of the line and the wet stones in the stream.
3 *verb intrans.* Peep, take a glance. **L17.**

glioblastoma /ˌɡlʌɪə(ʊ)blaˈstəʊmə/ *noun*. Pl. **-mas**, **-mata** /-mətə/. **E20.**
[**ORIGIN** from **GLIA** + **-O-** + **-BLAST** + **-OMA**.]
MEDICINE. A fast-growing brain glioma.

glioma /ɡlʌɪˈəʊmə/ *noun*. Pl. **-mas**, **-mata** /-mətə/. **L19.**
[**ORIGIN** from Greek *glia* glue + **-OMA**. Cf. **GLIA**.]
MEDICINE. Any malignant tumour of non-nervous cells (glia) in the nervous system.
■ **gliomatous** *adjective* of the nature of a glioma **L19.**

gliosis /ɡlʌɪˈəʊsɪs/ *noun*. Pl. **-oses** /-ˈəʊsiːz/. **L19.**
[**ORIGIN** from **GLIA**: see **-OSIS**.]
MEDICINE. Reparative or pathological proliferation of glial cells.

glirine /ˈɡlʌɪrʌɪn, ˈɡlɪ-/ *adjective*. **M19.**
[**ORIGIN** from Latin *glis*, *glir-* dormouse + **-INE**¹.]
ZOOLOGY. Orig., pertaining to rodents or lagomorphs (formerly grouped together in the order Glires). Now, pertaining to the family Gliridae of Palaearctic dormice.

glisk /ɡlɪsk/ *noun & verb*. **L17.**
[**ORIGIN** Uncertain: perh. rel. to **GLITTER**.]
▸ **A** *noun*. A glimpse; a glance; a gleam. *Scot.* **L17.**
▸ **B** *verb intrans.* **1** Glance *over*. *obsolete* exc. *dial.* **E18.**
2 Glitter, shine. *dial.* **M19.**

gliss /ɡlɪs/ *noun*. **E20.**
[**ORIGIN** Abbreviation.]
= **GLISSANDO**.

glissade /ɡlɪˈsɑːd, -ˈseɪd/ *noun & verb*. **M19.**
[**ORIGIN** French, from *glisser* slip, slide: see **-ADE**.]
▸ **A** *noun*. **1** *DANCING.* A step consisting of a glide or slide in any direction, usu. a joining step. **M19.**
2 *MOUNTAINEERING.* The action or an act of sliding down a steep slope esp. of snow, usu. on the feet with the support of an ice axe etc. **M19.**
▸ **B** *verb*. **1** *verb intrans. & trans.* (with *it*). *DANCING.* Perform a glissade; progress by glissades. **M19.**
2 *MOUNTAINEERING.* Slide down a steep slope esp. of snow by means of a glissade. **M19.**
■ **glissader** *noun* **M19.**

glissando /ɡlɪˈsandəʊ/ *noun*. Pl. **-di** /-di/, **-dos**. **L19.**
[**ORIGIN** Italian from French *glissant* pres. pple of *glisser* slip, slide.]
MUSIC. A continuous slide of adjacent notes upwards or downwards.

glissant /ˈɡlɪs(ə)nt/ *adjective*. **M19.**
[**ORIGIN** French, pres. pple of *glisser* slip, slide: see **-ANT**¹.]
HERALDRY. Of a serpent: shown moving forward in fess.

glissé /ɡlise/ *noun*. Pl. pronounced same. **E20.**
[**ORIGIN** French, pa. pple of *glisser* slip, slide.]
BALLET. More fully ***pas glissé*** /pɑ/. A sliding step in which the flat of the foot is often used.

glist /ɡlɪst/ *verb & noun*. **ME.**
[**ORIGIN** App. abbreviation of **GLISTEN** *verb*.]
▸ **A** *verb intrans.* Glisten. Now only *Scot.* **ME.**
▸ **B** *noun*. †**1** Mica. Only in **18.**
2 A gleam, glistening. *rare*. **M19.**

glisten /ˈɡlɪs(ə)n/ *verb & noun*.
[**ORIGIN** Old English *glisnian*, from base of *glisian* (= Old Frisian *glisa*, Middle Low German *glisen*), from Germanic: see **-EN**⁵. Cf. **GLISTER**.]
▸ **A** *verb intrans.* Gleam, shine fitfully, glitter, sparkle (*lit.* & *fig.*). **OE.**
R. P. WARREN The pavements glistened in the quick sunlight that had followed a flurry of rain. T. WILLIAMS Her eyes are glistening with tears.
▸ **B** *noun*. Glitter; sparkle. **M19.**
D. H. LAWRENCE A glisten like sunshine refracted through crystals of ice.
■ **glisteningly** *adverb* in a glistening manner **E17.**

glister /ˈɡlɪstə/ *verb & noun*. **LME.**
[**ORIGIN** Corresp. to and prob. from Middle Low German *glistern*, Middle Dutch & mod. Dutch *glisteren*, from Germanic: see **-ER**⁵. Cf. **GLISTEN**.]
▸ **A** *verb intrans.* Shine, sparkle, glitter. Now *arch.* & *dial.* **LME.**
▸ **B** *noun*. A bright light; sparkle, glitter. **M16.**
C. E. CRADDOCK She caught a glimpse of . . the glister of a great lucent, tremulous star.
■ **glisteringly** *adverb* in a glistering manner **L16.** **glistery** *adjective* full of glister **E19.**

glit *noun & verb* see **GLEET**.

glitch /ɡlɪtʃ/ *noun & verb*. *slang*. **M20.**
[**ORIGIN** Unknown: cf. *hitch* and Yiddish *glitsh* slippery place, *glitshik* elusive.]
▸ **A** *noun*. A sudden irregularity or malfunction of equipment etc. **M20.**
W. GARNER We have a minor glitch. I'd appreciate your help.
▸ **B** *verb intrans.* Suffer a glitch. **L20.**
■ **glitchy** *adjective* prone to malfunction **L20.**

glitter /ˈɡlɪtə/ *verb & noun*. **LME.**
[**ORIGIN** Old Norse *glitra* = Middle High German, German *glitzern* sparkle, frequentative from Germanic, in Old Saxon *glītan*, Old High German *glīʒan* (German *gleissen*) shine, Old Norse *glita* glitter, Gothic *glitmunjan* (of clothes) shine bright: see **-ER**⁵.]
▸ **A** *verb intrans.* **1** Shine with a brilliant tremulous light; gleam, sparkle. **LME.**
W. CATHER A diamond necklace glittered about her . . throat. G. ORWELL A high-ceilinged windowless cell with walls of glittering white porcelain.
2 Esp. of a person: make a brilliant appearance or display; be showy or splendid. **LME.**
BURKE I saw her [the Queen of France] . . glittering like the morning star. JAN MORRIS The social brilliance of Oxford . . when this was the most glittering university in Europe.
glittering generality a platitude, a cliché, a superficially convincing but empty phrase, (usu. in *pl.*).
▸ **B** *noun*. **1** Brilliant tremulous light, (a) sparkle; brightness, brilliance; splendour, showiness. **E17.**
M. MCCARTHY There was a glitter in his hollow, dark eyes. G. BORDMAN She is intrigued by the glitter of the big city.
2 A powder consisting of tiny pieces of sparkling material used as a cosmetic or for decoration. **M20.**
– **COMB.**: **glitter dust** = sense B.2 above; **glitter rock** rock music played by performers dressed in glittering costumes.
■ **glitterer** *noun* a person who or thing which glitters **E19.** **glitteringly** *adverb* in a glittering manner **E17.** **glitterless** *adjective* **L19.** **glittery** *adjective* full of glitter **M18.**

glitterati /ɡlɪtəˈrɑːti/ *noun pl.* *slang* (orig. *US*). **M20.**
[**ORIGIN** Punningly from **GLITTER** *verb & noun* + **LITERATI** *noun pl.*]
The fashionable and prominent people in the literary or show-business worlds.
R. PERLE Waterman's much-anticipated weekend with the Paris glitterati turned out to be pedestrian in all respects.

glitz /ɡlɪts/ *noun*. *slang* (orig. *N. Amer.*). **L20.**
[**ORIGIN** Back-form. from **GLITZY**.]
Extravagant but superficial display; ostentation; show-business glamour.
C. BATEMAN I like New York away from the glitz.

glitzy /ˈɡlɪtsi/ *adjective*. *slang* (orig. *N. Amer.*). **M20.**
[**ORIGIN** Prob. from **GLITTER** *noun* after **RITZY** *adjective*: cf. German *glitzerig* glittering.]
Characterized by glitter or extravagant show; tawdry, gaudy; glitteringly spectacular but in poor taste.
Listener The Oscars are . . a glitzy, vulgar affirmation that they're getting things right.
■ **glitzily** *adverb* **L20.** **glitziness** *noun* **L20.**

†**gloak** *noun*. *slang*. **L18–M19.**
[**ORIGIN** Unknown.]
A man, a fellow.

gloam /ɡləʊm/ *noun*. *poet.* **E19.**
[**ORIGIN** Back-form. from **GLOAMING**.]
Twilight, gloaming.

gloam /ɡləʊm/ *verb intrans.* Chiefly *Scot.* **E18.**
[**ORIGIN** formed as **GLOAM** *noun*.]
Darken, become dusk.

gloaming /ˈɡləʊmɪŋ/ *noun*. *literary*.
[**ORIGIN** Old English *glōmung* from *glōm* twilight, prob. from Germanic base of **GLOW** *verb*¹.]
1 Evening twilight. **OE.**
S. DONALDSON Before the gloaming had thickened into darkness. *fig.*: J. M. BARRIE The help . . needed in the gloaming of their lives.
2 Morning twilight. *rare*. **M19.**
– **COMB.**: **gloaming shot** (***a***) a shot made in the twilight; (***b***) the beginning of twilight; **gloaming sight** (***a***) an indistinct view; (***b***) a front gunsight for use in twilight.
– **NOTE**: From **LME**, chiefly *Scot.* In general literary use from **E19.**

gloat /ɡləʊt/ *noun*¹. **M17.**
[**ORIGIN** from **GLOAT** *verb*.]
†**1** A side glance; a furtive or sullen look. Only in **M17.**
2 An act of gloating; a look, feeling, or expression of triumphant satisfaction. **L19.**
A. HUNTER He was having a gloat over his gold.

gloat /ɡləʊt/ *noun*². *obsolete* exc. *dial.* **M18.**
[**ORIGIN** Unknown.]
An eel.

gloat /gləʊt/ *verb intrans.* L16.
[ORIGIN Uncertain: perh. of Scandinavian origin (cf. Old Norse *glotta* grin, Swedish dial. *glotta* peep, corresp. to Middle & mod. High German *glotzen* stare).]
1 Look with a furtive or sidelong glance. Also, appear sulky. *obsolete* exc. *dial.* L16.
T. CREECH I . . with a squinting Eye glote o'er the Pit.
2 Shine, gleam; (of light) fall obliquely. *rare.* M17.
G. W. THORNBURY The light gloated on some strange-shaped glasses.
†**3** Cast amorous or admiring glances (*on, upon*). L17–E18.
N. ROWE Teach . . her deluding Eyes to gloat for you.
4 Dwell on one's success or another's misfortune with smugness or malignant pleasure. Usu. foll. by *on, upon, over.* M18.
P. H. GIBBS Our enemies are gloating over our ruin. A. TYLER She seemed to be gloating. She was . . so sure of her place.
■ **gloatingly** *adverb* in a gloating manner L17.

glob /glɒb/ *noun.* E20.
[ORIGIN Perh. blend of BLOB *noun* and GOB *noun*[1].]
A mass or lump of some liquid or semi-liquid substance; a dollop.
H. LAWSON A glob of mud on the sand. T. O'BRIEN Bullets struck . . exploding globs of flesh.

global /ˈgləʊb(ə)l/ *adjective.* L17.
[ORIGIN from GLOBE *noun* + -AL[1].]
1 Spherical, globular. *rare.* L17.
H. BASCOM The gate with frosted global lights on the concrete pillars.
2 Pertaining to or embracing the whole of a group of items etc.; comprehensive, total; *spec.* pertaining to or involving the whole world, worldwide. L19.
A. E. STEVENSON Global plans for solving all the world's problems by some master stroke.
global distillation a process whereby certain volatile substances vaporize in warm climates and condense in cooler areas, causing the accumulation of pollutants. **global search** COMPUTING a search through the whole of a computer file; a search for every occurrence of an item. **global variable** COMPUTING: whose value is the same in all parts of a program. **global village** (orig. *N. Amer.*) the whole world considered as a single community brought together by high technology and international communications. **global warming** an increase in temperature at the surface of the earth supposedly caused by the greenhouse effect.
■ **globalism** *noun* internationalism M20. **globalist** *noun & adjective* (a person) advocating a global approach to economic etc. issues M20. **globaliˈzation** *noun* the action or an act of globalizing; *spec.* the process by which businesses etc. develop international influence or start operating on an international scale M20. **globalize** *verb trans.* make global M20. **globally** *adverb* M20.

globate /ˈgləʊbeɪt/ *adjective. rare.* M19.
[ORIGIN from GLOBE *noun* + -ATE[2].]
Having the form of a globe; spherical.
■ **globated** *adjective* given the form of a globe; made spherical: M18.

globe /gləʊb/ *noun & verb.* LME.
[ORIGIN Old French, or Latin *globus* spherical body.]
▸ **A** *noun* **I 1** A spherical body. LME.
B. JOWETT In the form of a globe, round as from a lathe.
2 a A planet, a star. Chiefly *poet.* M16. ▸**b** *The* earth. L16.
a J. H. NEWMAN Some unknown globe in the heavens. **b** V. NABOKOV The gloom of yet another World War had settled upon the globe.
3 A spherical representation of the earth (more fully ***terrestrial globe***) or the constellations (more fully ***celestial globe***). M16.
use of the globes *arch.* the learning or teaching of geography and astronomy by using terrestrial and celestial globes.
4 A golden orb as an emblem of sovereignty. E17.
SIR W. SCOTT With crown, with sceptre, and with globe, Emblems of empery.
5 An approximately spherical glass vessel, esp. a lampshade, fishbowl, electric light bulb, etc. M17.
G. JONES An oil-lamp, the flame turned low in the frosted globe.
6 More fully ***globe of the eye***. The eyeball. L18.
▸ **II 7** A compact body (of people etc.). *rare.* E17.
MILTON Him round A Globe of fierie Seraphim inclos'd.
– COMB.: ***globe amaranth***: see AMARANTH 1; ***globe artichoke***: see ARTICHOKE 1; **globe daisy** any plant of the genus *Globularia* (family Globulariaceae), *esp.* the European *G. trichosantha* and *G. vulgaris*; **globefish** any of various chiefly tropical fishes with more or less rounded bodies; *esp.* = PUFFER 1b; **globeflower** any of various plants of the genus *Trollius*, of the buttercup family, with large globular flowers composed of many overlapping yellow petaloid sepals; esp. *T. europaeus*, native to upland meadows; **globe lightning** = ***ball lightning*** s.v. BALL *noun*[1]; **globe thistle** any of several thistles of the genus *Echinops*, esp. *E. sphaerocephalus*, grown in gardens for their globular heads of pale blue flowers; **globetrot** *verb intrans.* go globetrotting; **globetrotter** a person who travels (orig., hurriedly, now usu., extensively) through countries, esp. for sightseeing; **globetrotting** hurried or extensive travelling through countries, esp. for sightseeing; **globe tulip** any of certain mariposa lilies with nodding globular flowers.
▸ **B** *verb.* **1** *verb trans.* Form into a globe; make globular. Usu. in *pass.* LME.
refl.: TENNYSON The great stars that globed themselves in heaven.
2 *verb intrans.* Be or become globular. M19.
■ **globed** *adjective* (*a*) having the form of a globe, spherical; (*b*) having a globe, enclosed in a globe: E19.

globi *noun* pl. of GLOBUS.

globical /ˈglɒbɪk(ə)l, ˈgləʊb-/ *adjective.* E17.
[ORIGIN from GLOBE *noun* + -ICAL.]
†**1** Globular, spherical. Only in 17.
2 HERALDRY. Having the general outline circular. L17.

globigerina /ˌgləʊbɪdʒəˈrʌɪnə/ *noun.* Pl. **-nae** /-niː/, **-nas**. M19.
[ORIGIN mod. Latin (see below), from Latin *globus, globi-* GLOBE + *-ger* carrying + -INA[2].]
ZOOLOGY. Any marine planktonic foraminiferan of the genus *Globigerina*, having a calcareous shell with globular chambers and spiny processes.
– COMB.: **globigerina ooze** a deposit of soft pale mud over wide areas of the ocean floor, consisting largely of the shells of globigerinae.
■ **gloˈbigerine** *adjective* pertaining to or derived from globigerinae M19.

globin /ˈgləʊbɪn/ *noun.* L19.
[ORIGIN Abbreviation of HAEMOGLOBIN.]
BIOCHEMISTRY. Any of various polypeptides forming the protein component of haemoglobin and related compound proteins.

globoid /ˈgləʊbɔɪd/ *adjective & noun.* L19.
[ORIGIN from GLOBE *noun* + -OID.]
▸ **A** *adjective.* Approximately globe-shaped. L19.
▸ **B** *noun.* BOTANY. A rounded mineral aggregate in the aleurone granules of plant seeds, consisting of amorphous phytin. L19.

globose /ˈgləʊbəʊs, gləʊˈbəʊs/ *adjective.* LME.
[ORIGIN Latin *globosus*, from *globus* GLOBE *noun*: see -OSE[1].]
Globe-shaped; (approximately) spherical.
■ **globosely** *adverb* M19. **globoseness** *noun* (*rare*) E18. **gloˈbosity** *noun* the condition of being globose; a rounded part: M17.

globoside /ˈgləʊbəsʌɪd/ *noun.* M20.
[ORIGIN from GLOB(ULE + -OSIDE.]
BIOCHEMISTRY. A sphingolipid forming spherical globules, found in human erythrocytes.

globous /ˈgləʊbəs/ *adjective.* Now *rare.* E17.
[ORIGIN French †*globeux* or Latin *globosus*, from *globus* GLOBE *noun*: see -OUS.]
= GLOBOSE.

globular /ˈglɒbjʊlə/ *adjective.* M17.
[ORIGIN from Latin *globulus* (see GLOBULE) + -AR[1].]
1 Globe-shaped, spherical. M17. ▸**b** Of a protein: having a relatively compact molecular structure with considerable folding. M20.
2 Composed of globules. M18.
– SPECIAL COLLOCATIONS: **globular cluster** ASTRONOMY a large compact star cluster of spherical form, numbers of which surround the Milky Way and other galaxies. **globular lightning** = ***ball lightning*** s.v. BALL *noun*[1].
■ **globuˈlarity** *noun* the property of being globular E19. **globularly** *adverb* M19. **globularness** *noun* (*rare*) E18.

globule /ˈglɒbjuːl/ *noun.* M17.
[ORIGIN French, or Latin *globulus* dim. of *globus* GLOBE *noun*: see -ULE.]
1 A small spherical body or globe; a round drop (of liquid); BIOLOGY (*arch.*) a blood corpuscle. M17. ▸**b** BOTANY. The male reproductive structure of a charophyte (stonewort). Cf. NUCULE 2. M19.
2 A small pill. M19.
3 ASTRONOMY. More fully ***Bok globule*** [Bart J. *Bok* (1906–83), Dutch-born US astronomer]. A small dark cloud of gas and dust seen against a brighter background such as a luminous nebula. M20.

globulin /ˈglɒbjʊlɪn/ *noun.* M19.
[ORIGIN from GLOBULE (= blood corpuscle) + -IN[1].]
BIOCHEMISTRY. Any of a class of simple proteins with little or no solubility in water but soluble in salt solutions; *esp.* any of those forming the second largest electrophoretic fraction of blood plasma protein.
alpha globulin, **beta globulin**, **gamma globulin** (any protein belonging to) each of the three fractions of blood plasma globulin distinguished by decreasing electrophoretic mobility from alpha to gamma. IMMUNOGLOBULIN, LACTOGLOBULIN.

globulite /ˈglɒbjʊlʌɪt/ *noun.* L17.
[ORIGIN from GLOBULE + -ITE[1].]
1 *gen.* A small globule. *rare.* L17.
2 PETROGRAPHY. A small spherical crystallite (in volcanic glass). L19.

globulous /ˈglɒbjʊləs/ *adjective.* Now *rare.* M17.
[ORIGIN French *globuleux*, formed as GLOBULE: see -ULOUS.]
Globular in form; consisting of globules.

globus /ˈgləʊbəs/ *noun.* Pl. **globi** /ˈgləʊbʌɪ/. L18.
[ORIGIN Latin = globe.]
1 MEDICINE. In full ***globus hystericus*** /hɪˈstɛrɪkəs/. A subjective sensation of a rounded object, esp. of a lump in the throat. L18.
2 ANATOMY. Any of various spherical or rounded structures. Usu. with specifying word. M19.
globus pallidus /ˈpalɪdəs/ [= pale] the median part of the lentiform nucleus in the brain.

globy /ˈgləʊbi/ *adjective.* L16.
[ORIGIN from GLOBE *noun* + -Y[1].]
Globular, spherical.

glocalize /ˈgləʊk(ə)lʌɪz/ *verb intrans.* Also **-ise**. L20.
[ORIGIN Blend of GLOBAL *adjective* and LOCALIZE *verb*.]
COMMERCE. Conduct business globally with adaptation to local conditions.
■ **glocaliˈzation** *noun* L20.

glochid /ˈgləʊkɪd/ *noun.* L19.
[ORIGIN Greek *glōkhis, glōkhid* arrowhead.]
BOTANY. A glochidium or other barbed hair; *spec.* a barbed bristle on the areole of some cacti.

glochidia *noun* pl. of GLOCHIDIUM.

glochidiate /gləʊˈkɪdɪət/ *adjective.* E19.
[ORIGIN formed as GLOCHIDIUM + -ATE[2].]
BOTANY. (Of a hair) barbed at the tip; (of a plant structure) bearing barbed hairs.

glochidium /gləʊˈkɪdɪəm/ *noun.* Pl. **-dia** /-dɪə/. L19.
[ORIGIN mod. Latin from Greek, dim. of *glōkhis* arrowhead.]
1 ZOOLOGY. The parasitic larva of certain freshwater mussels, which attaches to the fins or gills of fish by suckers or hooks. L19.
2 BOTANY. A barbed hair or bristle; *spec.* a barbed organ of attachment on the surface of a spore mass, as in the aquatic fern *Azolla*. L19.

glockenspiel /ˈglɒk(ə)nspiːl, -ʃpiːl/ *noun.* E19.
[ORIGIN German = bell-play.]
MUSIC. **1** An organ stop imitating the sound of bells. E19.
2 Any of several percussion instruments, *esp.* (*a*) a series of tuned metal bars mounted on a horizontal frame; (*b*) a series of bells or metal bars in a lyre-shaped frame carried in marching bands (also ***lyra glockenspiel***). M19.

glode *verb pa. t. & pple*: see GLIDE *verb*.

Gloger's rule /ˈgləʊgəz ruːl/ *noun phr.* M20.
[ORIGIN from C. L. *Gloger* (1803–63), German zoologist.]
ZOOLOGY. The observation that races of an animal inhabiting warmer or more humid regions tend to be more heavily pigmented than those of cooler or drier regions.

glögg /glœg, glɒg/ *noun.* Also **glugg** /glʌg/. E20.
[ORIGIN Swedish.]
A Scandinavian winter drink, consisting of hot sweetened red wine with brandy, almonds, raisins, and spices.

gloire /glwaːr/ *noun.* M19.
[ORIGIN French.]
In full ***la gloire*** /la/. Glory; *spec.* the national glory and prestige of France.
R. HOLMES The Napoleonic dreams of *La gloire*.

Gloire de Dijon /glwaːr də diʒɔ̃/ *noun phr.* M19.
[ORIGIN French = glory of Dijon.]
A yellow hybrid tea rose.

glom /glɒm/ *verb trans. & intrans.* with *on to. slang* (chiefly *US*). Infl. **-mm-**. E20.
[ORIGIN Var. of GLAUM *verb*.]
Steal; grab.
Sunday Mail (Brisbane) She glommed . . cash and jewellery from the good doctor. W. SAFIRE Glomming on to a technical phrase and stretching its meaning.

glome /gləʊm/ *noun.* M17.
[ORIGIN Latin *glomus*: see GLOMERATE *verb*.]
†**1** A skein or ball of yarn or thread. Only in M17.
2 BOTANY. A flower head, a glomerule. *rare.* L18.

glomera *noun* pl. of GLOMUS.

glomerate /ˈglɒm(ə)rət/ *adjective.* Now *rare.* L18.
[ORIGIN Latin *glomeratus* pa. pple of *glomerare*: see GLOMERATE *verb*, -ATE[2].]
Chiefly BOTANY. Compactly clustered; having the form of a rounded mass or cluster.

glomerate /ˈglɒməreɪt/ *verb intrans. & trans.* Now *rare* or *obsolete.* M17.
[ORIGIN Latin *glomerat-* pa. ppl stem of *glomerare*, from *glomus, glomer-* ball or clue of yarn etc.: see -ATE[3].]
Wind or twist about; wind into a ball, gather into a rounded mass.
■ **glomeˈration** *noun* (*a*) the action or process of glomerating; (*b*) a compact cluster: E17.

glomerular /glɒˈmɛr(j)ʊlə/ *adjective.* L19.
[ORIGIN from GLOMERULUS + -AR[1].]
Of or pertaining to glomeruli, esp. those of the kidney.

glomerule /ˈglɒməruːl/ *noun.* L18.
[ORIGIN French *glomérule* from mod. Latin GLOMERULUS.]
1 BOTANY. A condensed cymose flower head. Now *rare.* L18.
2 MICROBIOLOGY. A small clump or cluster of cells or spores, esp. of algal cells in lichens. M19.
3 ANATOMY. = GLOMERULUS 1. *rare.* M19.
■ **gloˈmerulose** *adjective* (chiefly BOTANY) bearing or occurring as glomerules L19.

glomeruli *noun* pl. of GLOMERULUS.

G

glomerulitis /glɒˌmɛr(j)ʊˈlʌɪtɪs/ *noun*. **L19**.
[ORIGIN from GLOMERULUS + -ITIS.]
MEDICINE. An inflammation of the renal glomeruli.

glomerulo- /glɒˈmɛr(j)ʊləʊ/ *combining form*.
[ORIGIN from GLOMERULUS + -O-.]
MEDICINE. Of the glomeruli of the kidney.
■ **glomerulone'phritis** *noun* a disease of the kidneys, usually allergic in origin, resulting in acute inflammation **L19**.

glomerulus /glɒˈmɛr(j)ʊləs/ *noun*. Pl. **-li** /-lʌɪ, -liː/. **M19**.
[ORIGIN mod. Latin dim. of Latin *glomer-*, *glomus* ball of thread: cf. -ULE.]
1 *ANATOMY & ZOOLOGY*. A tuft or plexus of capillaries, nerve endings, etc.; *esp.* the network of capillaries in the end capsule of each tubule in the vertebrate kidney, where waste products are filtered from the blood. **M19**.
2 *MICROBIOLOGY*. = GLOMERULE 2. **M19**.

glomus /ˈgləʊməs/ *noun*. Pl. **glomera** /ˈgləʊm(ə)rə/, (not after Latin) **glomi** /ˈgləʊmʌɪ/. **M19**.
[ORIGIN Latin = ball of thread.]
ANATOMY & ZOOLOGY. A small body consisting of blood vessels and associated tissue; *esp.* any of numerous small structures in the skin of the hands and feet involving a connection between a vein and an artery, and functioning in temperature regulation. Freq. with specifying word.

gloom /gluːm/ *noun*[1]. **L16**.
[ORIGIN In sense 1 from GLOOM *verb*; in senses 2, 3 perh. back-form. from GLOOMY.]
1 A sullen look; a frown, a scowl. *Scot.* **L16**.
2 Partial or total darkness; sombreness, obscurity. **E17**. ▸**b** A dark place. *poet.* **E18**.

N. MAILER In the gloom of the jungle each minute seemed more ominous.

3 Melancholy, despondency. Also ***the glooms***, ***a fit of the glooms***. **M18**.

Daily Mirror Got the glooms? . . How about an evening out? Just us two.

gloom and doom pessimism, despondency.
■ **gloomful** *adjective* (*rare*) melancholy, dark **M19**.

gloom /gluːm/ *noun*[2]. Now *rare* or *obsolete*. **L16**.
[ORIGIN Perh. repr. 1st elem. of GLOAMING.]
†**1** ***hot gloom***, excessive heat (of the sun). **L16–M18**.
2 In full ***gloom stove***. A drying oven used in making gunpowder. **M19**.

gloom /gluːm/ *verb*. **LME**.
[ORIGIN Unknown.]
1 *verb intrans.* Look sullen or displeased, frown, scowl; be or appear dejected or depressed. **LME**. ▸**b** *verb trans.* Express with gloom. **M19**.

Century Magazine I hate myself for glooming about the house in secret. E. BOWEN Marcelle . . who had lately quarrelled with her best friend . . gloomed at Sir Robert's right hand. **b** CARLYLE 'What interloping fellow is this?' gloomed Valori.

2 *verb intrans.* Of the weather, sky, etc.: lour; be or become dull or threatening. **LME**. ▸**b** Darken, become dusk. **L16**.

C. IVES It rains and darkens, and the sky glooms. **b** G. MACDONALD In the midst of the forest it gloomed earlier than in the open country.

3 *verb trans.* Make dark or sombre; cover with gloom. **L16**. ▸**b** Make dismal or melancholy. **M18**.

G. MACBETH Then smoke . . gloomed the whole sky.

4 *verb intrans.* Look dark or sombre; appear darkly or obscurely. **L18**.

A. CARTER The shop gloomed behind its blinds.

■ **glooming** *noun* (**a**) the action or an instance of being or looking gloomy; (**b**) *poet.* = GLOAMING: **LME**.

gloomth /gluːmθ/ *noun*. *rare*. **M18**.
[ORIGIN from GLOOM *noun*[1] or *verb* + -TH[1].]
= GLOOM *noun*[1] 2.

gloomy /ˈgluːmi/ *adjective*. **L16**.
[ORIGIN from GLOOM *noun*[1] 1 + -Y[1].]
1 Dark, unlighted, shadowy. **L16**.

G. SWIFT He passed into the bedroom, gloomy behind the drawn curtains.

2 Sullen, depressed, despondent. **L16**.

T. WRIGHT People of that gloomy character who never laugh.

3 Causing gloom; dismal, disheartening. **E18**.

W. K. KELLY A gloomy and forbidding spectacle.

■ **gloomily** *adverb* **E18**. **gloominess** *noun* **E17**.

gloop /gluːp/ *noun*. *colloq.* **L20**.
[ORIGIN Imit.: cf. GLOP *noun*.]
Unpleasantly viscid matter; slime.

A. ASHWORTH I was trying not to get my socks splashed by the filthy gloop underfoot.

■ **gloopy** *adjective* **L20**.

glop /glɒp/ *noun*. *slang* (orig. *US*). **E20**.
[ORIGIN Imit.]
A liquid or viscous substance or mixture; *spec.* inferior or unappetizing food or drink.

fig.: *Newsweek* Metaphysical glop and heavy-breathing symbolism.

■ **gloppy** *adjective* **L20**.

glop /glɒp/ *verb intrans.* *obsolete* exc. *dial.* Infl. **-pp-**. **LME**.
[ORIGIN Perh. abbreviation of GLOPPEN.]
Stare, gaze in wonder or alarm.

gloppen /ˈglɒp(ə)n/ *verb*. Long *obsolete* exc. *dial.* **ME**.
[ORIGIN Old Norse *glúpna* be downcast.]
1 *verb trans.* Startle, frighten, astound. Freq. as ***gloppened*** *ppl adjective*. **ME**.
2 *verb intrans.* Be distressed, downcast, or startled; stare in amazement. **LME**.

glore /glɔː/ *verb intrans.* Long *obsolete* exc. *dial.* **LME**.
[ORIGIN Low German *glōren* or Scandinavian (cf. Icelandic *glóra* gleam, stare) rel. to GLOW *verb*[1]: see GLOWER.]
1 Shine, glitter, glisten. **LME**.
2 Gaze intently, stare, glower. **LME**.

gloria /ˈglɔːrɪə/ *noun & adjective*. In sense 1 **G-**. **ME**.
[ORIGIN Latin *gloria* GLORY *noun*.]
▸ **A** *noun*. **1** Any of several Christian liturgical formulae, as ***Gloria*** (***Patri***) the doxology 'Glory be to the Father', ***Gloria*** (***tibi***) the response 'Glory be to thee', ***Gloria*** (***in excelsis***) the hymn 'Glory be to God on high', forming part of the Mass etc. **ME**. ▸**b** The music to which any of these is set. **L16**.
2 An aureole, a nimbus. **L18**.
3 In France: (a drink of) coffee mixed with brandy or rum. **M19**.
4 A closely woven fabric of silk and wool or cotton etc.; a garment made of this. **L19**.
▸ **B** *adjective*. Made of the fabric gloria. **E20**.

gloriation /glɔːrɪˈeɪʃ(ə)n/ *noun*. Now *rare* or *obsolete*. **LME**.
[ORIGIN Latin *gloriatio(n-)*, from *gloriat-* pa. ppl stem of *gloriari*: see GLORY *verb*, -ATION.]
The action of glorying; boasting, triumphing.

gloriette /glɔːrɪˈɛt/ *noun*. **M19**.
[ORIGIN French.]
A highly decorated chamber in a castle or other building.

glorification /ˌglɔːrɪfɪˈkeɪʃ(ə)n/ *noun*. **LME**.
[ORIGIN ecclesiastical Latin *glorificatio(n-)*, from *glorificat-* pa. ppl stem of *glorificare*: see GLORIFIED, -ATION.]
1 The action or an act of glorifying a person or thing, the condition of being glorified. **LME**. ▸**b** *spec.* The exaltation of Christ or a human soul to heaven. **LME**. ▸**c** Transformation to a more magnificent form; that which is transformed. **L19**.

JER. TAYLOR They whose sins accidentally thus serv'd the glorification of God. **b** R. BAXTER His Ascension they beheld, and his Glorification they believed. **c** *Century Magazine* These houses . . are . . glorifications of the humble, early . . New England farm-house.

2 A set form of worship; a doxology. **M17**.

W. D. WHITNEY The songs are . . simple invocations and glorifications of the divinity.

3 The attribution of glory or praise to a person or thing; enthusiastic or extravagant praise. **M19**.

H. J. LASKI His glorification of reason as the great key which is to unlock all doors.

glorified /ˈglɔːrɪfʌɪd/ *adjective*. **ME**.
[ORIGIN from GLORIFICATION + -ED[1].]
1 *gen.* That has been glorified. **ME**.

W. SPALDING Angels and glorified saints adore the Mother and her Son.

2 Esp. of a common or inferior thing: that has been transformed into something more splendid. *colloq.* (freq. *iron.*). **E19**.

A. BURGESS A professional man, not a glorified foreman.

glorify /ˈglɔːrɪfʌɪ/ *verb*. **ME**.
[ORIGIN Old French & mod. French *glorifier* from ecclesiastical Latin *glorificare*, from late Latin *glorificus*, from Latin *gloria*: see GLORY *noun*, -FY.]
1 *verb trans.* Make glorious; *spec.* exalt (Christ, a human soul) to the glory of heaven. **ME**. ▸**b** Invest with radiance. Formerly also, adorn, embellish. **LME**. ▸**c** Transform into something more splendid; (try to) make (a common or inferior thing) seem unrealistically splendid. **M19**.

S. DANIEL Those righteous issues, which shall glorifie And comfort many Nations with their worth. **b** SHAKES. *Ven. & Ad.* The bright sun glorifies the sky. **c** J. F. CLARKE Burns, Wordsworth, Whittier . . have known how to glorify common life and every-day people.

2 *verb trans.* Advance the glory of (God, His name) by one's actions, suffering, etc.; ascribe glory or praise in adoration to (God). **ME**.

G. PRIESTLAND Being religiously inclined, she or he is anxious to serve God and glorify him.

3 *verb refl.* & †*intrans.* Think oneself exceedingly fortunate, pride oneself, boast of one's good fortune. (Foll. by *in*, *to do*, *that*.) Now *rare*. **ME**.

EDWARD HOWARD For the which he glorified himself exceedingly.

4 *verb trans.* Describe or represent as glorious; praise enthusiastically or extravagantly; extol. **M16**.

J. A. FROUDE Cæsar, who was being so much praised and glorified.

■ **glorifier** *noun* **LME**.

gloriole /ˈglɔːrɪəʊl/ *noun*. **E19**.
[ORIGIN French from Latin *gloriola* dim. of *gloria* GLORY *noun*: see -OLE[1].]
†**1** A small measure of renown. Only in **E19**.
2 An aureole, a halo. **M19**.

glorious /ˈglɔːrɪəs/ *adjective*. **ME**.
[ORIGIN Anglo-Norman *glorious*, Old French *glorios*, *-eus* from Latin *gloriosus*, from *gloria* GLORY *noun*: see -OUS.]
1 **a** Having glory; renowned; illustrious; *spec.* designating a date or event considered particularly notable. **ME**. ▸**b** Conferring glory; honourable. **M16**.

a M. ARNOLD By nothing is England so glorious as by her poetry. **b** W. S. CHURCHILL The Indian Army, revived and reorganised, was to play a glorious part . . in two world wars.

a ***Glorious Fourth***: see FOURTH *noun*. **Glorious Revolution** the expulsion of James II from England in 1688. ***Glorious Twelfth***: see TWELFTH *noun* 1.

2 Magnificently beautiful, splendidly adorned. Formerly also, shining, lustrous. **LME**. ▸**b** Splendid, magnificent, intensely delightful. Also (*joc.*) *hyperbol.* or *iron.* **E17**.

H. POWER The Iris . . as . . glorious as a Cat's eye. G. MACDONALD The heavens were glorious with stars. **b** M. HOWITT What glorious afternoons and evenings have I spent at Phalerus! OED The glorious uncertainty of cricket.

3 Boastful; proud, haughty, ostentatious. *obsolete* exc. in VAINGLORIOUS. **LME**.

R. NORTH After he was possessed of the Great Seal, he was in Appearance the gloriousest Man alive.

†**4** Eager for glory. **E17–E18**.

T. HEARNE He always left such to Heroes as were purely Glorious.

5 Ecstatically happy with drink, (happily) drunk. *colloq.* **L18**.

EDWARD HOWARD As fast as one man could be . . flogged into sobriety, another would become glorious.

■ **gloriously** *adverb* **ME**. **gloriousness** *noun* **LME**.

glory /ˈglɔːri/ *noun*. **ME**.
[ORIGIN Anglo-Norman, Old French *glorie* from Latin *gloria* fame, praise, renown.]
1 Exalted (now esp. merited) renown; honourable fame. **ME**.

DEFOE You are to live here to the glory of Him that made you. P. SCOTT If . . not covered in warlike glory he was not covered in shame.

2 Adoring praise and thanksgiving, esp. offered to God. **ME**.

COLERIDGE Glory to Thee, Father of Earth and Heaven!

3 The splendour and bliss of heaven. **ME**.

MILTON Thou, bright Saint, high sitt'st in glory.

4 Resplendent majesty, beauty, or magnificence; a feature of resplendent beauty or magnificence, a splendour (freq. in *pl.*). Also, an effulgence of light; *fig.* an imagined unearthly beauty. **LME**.

WORDSWORTH There hath past away a glory from the earth. DISRAELI The scarlet glories of the *pyrus japonica*.

5 Something which brings renown; a special distinction, a splendid ornament. **LME**.

J. BUCHAN The little valleys which are the glory of the Oxford countryside.

6 Extreme vanity, boastfulness. *obsolete* exc. in VAINGLORY. **LME**.

P. MASSINGER A little glory in a soldier's mouth Is not uncomely.

7 A state of exaltation, splendour, or prosperity. **E17**.

W. IRVING They thought that the days of their ancient glory were about to return.

8 A circle of light, esp. as depicted around the head or whole figure of Jesus or a saint; a circle or ring of light; a halo. **M17**. ▸**b** *spec.* A luminous halo projected on to a cloud or fog bank by the sun; an anthelion. **E19**.

H. KINGSLEY Her own glorious golden hair, which hung round her lovely face like a glory.

9 A representation of the heavens opening and revealing celestial beings. Now *rare* or *obsolete*. **E18**.

R. CUMBERLAND The Holy Virgin is displayed in the center of the piece, above is a glory of Angels.

– PHRASES ETC.: ***crowning glory***: see CROWNING *ppl adjective* 2. ***death-or-glory***: see DEATH. **Glory Be** (esp. in Roman Catholic use) the *Gloria Patri*. **glory be** (**to God**)**!** *expr.* enthusiastic piety or (*colloq.*) surprise or delight. **glory-of-the-snow** = CHIONODOXA. **go to glory** go to heaven, die. ***GREENWELL's glory***. **in one's glory** in one's highest state; *colloq.* in a state of unbounded gratification or enjoyment. *KENTISH glory. MORNING glory. Old Glory*: see OLD *adjective. reflected glory*: see REFLECT *verb*.

– COMB.: **glory box** *Austral. & NZ* a box for a woman's store of clothes and household linen in preparation for marriage; **glory pea** = CLIANTHUS; **glory-tree** any of several trees or shrubs of the genus *Clerodendrum*, of the verbena family; esp. *C. thomsoniae* of tropical W. Africa, with clusters of crimson flowers.

glory /ˈglɔːri/ *verb*. LME.

[ORIGIN Latin *gloriari*, from *gloria* GLORY *noun*.]

1 *verb intrans.* Rejoice, exult, pride oneself. Freq. foll. by *in*, *to do*. LME.

H. MARTINEAU Cries.. which Archie always gloried in provoking. E. F. BENSON She gloried in it; she laughed with exultation at the thought of its success.

†**2** *verb intrans. & trans.* Boast (of). LME–L17.

E. SYMMONS We have seen a glimpse of that perspicuity and modesty which is gloried to be in these annotations.

†**3** *verb trans.* Honour; make glorious, adorn. LME–L17.

H. WOTTON Be ever gloried here Thy Soveraign Name.

glory hole /ˈglɔːrɪhəʊl/ *noun & verb*. E19.

[ORIGIN Unknown.]

▸ **A** *noun*. **1** An untidy small room, cupboard, drawer, etc., in which odds and ends are kept. E19. ▸**b** Any of various small compartments on a ship, *esp.* one used for storage or as sleeping quarters. *nautical slang*. M19. ▸**c** A small billet or dugout. *military slang*. E20.

M. WILMOT A sort of play room or glory-hole for poor Wilmot to keep his rubbish. **b** R. BEDFORD I.. sneak out on the boat deck to sleep, the glory hole being so hot.

2 GLASS-MAKING. **a** A small furnace used in hand-working to keep the glass malleable. M19. ▸**b** An opening in the wall of a furnace exposing the hot interior. L19.

3 A large cavernous opening into a mine; an open quarry. *N. Amer.* E20.

▸ **B** *verb intrans.* Carry on surface mining. *N. Amer.* E20.

Glos. *abbreviation*.

Gloucestershire.

†**glose** *noun, verb* see GLOZE *noun, verb*[1].

gloss /glɒs/ *noun*[1]. M16.

[ORIGIN Refashioning of GLOZE *noun* after medieval Latin *glossa* explanation of difficult word from Greek *glōssa* word needing explanation (also tongue, language: cf. GLOSSO-).]

1 A word inserted between the lines or in the margin in order to explain a foreign or otherwise difficult word in a text; a similar explanation of a word in a glossary or dictionary. Also (more widely), a comment, an explanation, an interpretation, a paraphrase. M16.

J. BARZUN Dewey.. should be read in the original, not in his followers' gloss.

2 A collection of such words, a glossary. Also, an interlinear translation or series of annotations. L16.

3 A sophistical or disingenuous explanation; a misrepresentation of another's words. E17.

V. GLENDINNING Some of the stories.. are.. untrue, fantastic glosses on a genuinely appalling situation.

■ **glossist** *noun* a writer of glosses, a commentator M17.

gloss /glɒs/ *noun*[2]. M16.

[ORIGIN Unknown.]

1 (A) superficial lustre. M16.

F. RAPHAEL There was a gloss of tears in her large eyes. C. HAYES Some colours dry matt, others dry to a gloss. *fig.*: SHAKES. *Tr. & Cr.* Yet all his virtues.. Do in our eyes begin to lose their gloss.

2 (A) deceptive external appearance, (a) plausible pretext. (Sometimes confused with or merging into GLOSS *noun*[1] 3.) M16.

J. WAINWRIGHT That which is difficult to describe still lurks beneath the gloss. G. S. FRASER An ambassador's business is not to lie but to set a polite gloss on the most awkward truth.

3 A layer of glowing matter, esp. in a fire. *rare*. M18.

4 = GLAZE *noun* 4. *rare*. E19.

5 In full ***gloss enamel***, ***gloss paint***. An enamel or paint which contains varnish and dries to a bright glossy finish. E20.

Which? A coat of primer, followed by two finishing coats of gloss.

gloss /glɒs/ *verb*[1]. L16.

[ORIGIN from GLOSS *noun*[1].]

1 *verb intrans.* Write glosses; make (esp. unfavourable) comments or remarks. (Foll. by *on*, *upon*.) L16.

SWIFT Those laws, which they assumed the liberty of interpreting and glossing upon. G. S. FRASER The poets are much less in need of illustration by.. quotation and glossing.

2 *verb trans.* Insert glosses or comments in (a text etc.); comment on, explain (a word, a passage, etc.). L16.

A. BURGESS Cornwall, which could be glossed as not really England.

3 *verb trans.* Veil with glosses; read a different sense into. (Foll. by *away*, *over*.) M17.

■ **glosser** *noun*[1] a person who glosses a text; a glossator: E17.

gloss /glɒs/ *verb*[2] *trans.* L16.

[ORIGIN from GLOSS *noun*[2], perh. infl. (esp. in sense 1b) by GLOSS *noun*[1].]

1 Give a deceptively fair appearance to. L16. ▸**b** Veil or conceal (something), esp. with specious language or under a fair appearance; explain away. (Foll. by *over*.) M17.

b A. CARTER She tried to gloss over the humiliation of it. L. DEIGHTON The girl.. had been killed, but the inquiry had glossed over it.

2 Make bright and glossy, glaze; *spec.* coat with gloss paint. M18.

SOUTHEY The moonlight fell, glossing the sable tide. *Options* Brickwork walls were painstakingly glossed in brilliant white.

■ **glosser** *noun*[2] a person who puts on a gloss M19.

glossal /ˈglɒs(ə)l/ *adjective*. E19.

[ORIGIN from Greek *glōssa* (see GLOSSO-) + -AL[1].]

Of or pertaining to the tongue, lingual.

glossalalia *noun* var. of GLOSSOLALIA.

glossary /ˈglɒs(ə)ri/ *noun*. LME.

[ORIGIN Latin *glossarium*, from *glossa*: see GLOSS *noun*[1], -ARY[1].]

A collection of glosses; a list with explanations, often accompanying a text, of abstruse, obsolete, dialectal, or technical terms.

C. WILSON He... began making a glossary of basic alchemical terms.

■ **gloˈssarial** *adjective* of, pertaining to, or of the nature of a glossary E19. **glossarist** *noun* a person who writes a gloss or compiles a glossary L18.

glossator /glɒˈseɪtə/ *noun*. LME.

[ORIGIN medieval Latin, from *glossare*, from Latin *glossa*: see GLOSS *noun*[1].]

A writer of glosses; a commentator, esp. on the texts of civil and canon law.

■ **glossaˈtorial** *adjective* of the nature of glosses L19.

glossematic /glɒsəˈmatɪk/ *noun & adjective*. M20.

[ORIGIN from GLOSSEM(E after Greek words like *phōnēma*, *phōnēmatik-* and *thema*, *thematik-* and the names of sciences like *mathematics*: see -IC.]

LINGUISTICS. ▸**A** *noun*. In *pl.* (treated as *sing.*). A theory of language introduced by the Danish scholar Louis Hjelmslev (1899–1965), and concerned esp. with the reduction of language to minimal units (glossemes) and the distribution and mutual relationships of these units. M20.

▸ **B** *adjective*. Of, relating to, or characteristic of glossematics. M20.

■ **glossematician** /-ˈtɪʃ(ə)n/, **gloˈssematist** *nouns* an expert in or student of glossematics M20.

glosseme /ˈglɒsiːm/ *noun*. E20.

[ORIGIN Greek *glōssēma* word requiring explanation, from *glōssa*: see GLOSSO-, -EME.]

LINGUISTICS. In glossematics, a linguistic feature which carries meaning and cannot be broken down into smaller meaningful units.

glossic /ˈglɒsɪk/ *adjective & noun*. L19.

[ORIGIN from Greek *glōssa* (see GLOSSO-) + -IC.]

(Designating) a phonetic alphabet or spelling system invented by A. J. Ellis (1814–90), in which each letter or digraph represents the sound it most commonly expresses in English.

glossitis /glɒˈsʌɪtɪs/ *noun*. E19.

[ORIGIN from Greek *glōssa* (see GLOSSO-) + -ITIS.]

MEDICINE. Inflammation of the tongue.

glosso- /ˈglɒsəʊ/ *combining form*.

[ORIGIN Greek *glōsso-* combining form of *glōssa* tongue, language, word requiring an explanation (cf. GLOSS *noun*[1]): see -O-. Cf. GLOTTO-.]

Forming adjectives and nouns with the senses '(of) the tongue', '(of) glosses or glossaries.'

■ **glosso-epiˈglottic** *adjective* pertaining to the tongue and to the epiglottis M19. **gloˈssographer** *noun* a writer of glosses or commentaries E17. **gloˈssography** *noun* the writing of glosses or commentaries; the compiling of glossaries: E17. **glossolaˈryngeal** *adjective* pertaining to the tongue and the larynx L19. **glossophaˈryngeal** *adjective & noun* (**a**) *adjective* of or pertaining to the tongue and the pharynx or gullet; (**b**) *noun* either of the glossopharyngeal or ninth pair of cranial nerves, which supply these organs: E19. **glossoˈplegia** *noun* (MEDICINE) paralysis of the tongue M19.

glossolalia /glɒsəˈleɪlɪə/ *noun*. Also **glossa-**. L19.

[ORIGIN from GLOSSO- + -LALIA, with allus. to *Acts* 10:46, *1 Corinthians* 14:6, 23.]

The gift of speaking with tongues (see TONGUE *noun* 6c).

■ **glossolalic** /-ˈlalɪk/ *adjective & noun* (**a**) *adjective* of or pertaining to speaking with tongues; (**b**) *noun* a glossolalist: E20. **glossolalist** /-ˈleɪlɪst, -ˈlalɪst/ *noun* a person who speaks with tongues L19.

glossology /glɒˈsɒlədʒi/ *noun*. Now *rare*. E18.

[ORIGIN from GLOSSO- + -LOGY.]

1 Orig., the study of a particular language or languages. Later, (comparative) philology. E18.

2 (The explanation of) the terminology used in any science. M19.

■ **glossoˈlogical** *adjective* of or pertaining to glossology E18. **glossologist** *noun* (**a**) a person who defines and explains terms; (**b**) an expert in or student of language or languages: E19.

glossopetra /glɒsəˈpɛtrə/ *noun*. *obsolete* exc. *hist.* Pl. **-trae** /-triː/. L17.

[ORIGIN mod. Latin from Latin, a stone supposedly shaped like the human tongue from Greek *glōssopetra*, from *glōssa* (see GLOSSO-) + *petra* rock.]

A kind of fossil tooth.

glossophagine /glɒˈsɒfədʒʌɪn/ *adjective & noun*. L19.

[ORIGIN from mod. Latin *Glossophaga* genus name, from Greek *glōssa* (see GLOSSO-) + *phagein* eat: see -INE[1].]

▸ **A** *adjective*. Of or pertaining to the subfamily Glossophaginae (family Phyllostomidae) of S. American bats, which feed on nectar by means of an extensible tongue. L19.

▸ **B** *noun*. A glossophagine bat. L19.

glossopteris /glɒˈsɒpt(ə)rɪs/ *noun*. L19.

[ORIGIN French from Greek *glōssa* (see GLOSSO-) + *pteris* fern.]

Any of various primitive angiosperms (orig. regarded as ferns) of the extinct genus *Glossopteris*, widespread as fossils.

G

glossy /ˈglɒsi/ *adjective & noun*. M16.

[ORIGIN from GLOSS *noun*[2] + -Y[1].]

▸ **A** *adjective*. **1** Having a gloss; smooth and shining; highly polished. M16.

W. GOLDING They had washed the pillars.. and painted the balcony glossy white.

glossy ibis a cosmopolitan ibis, *Plegadis falcinellus*, with glossy wings.

2 *fig.* Having a deceptively smooth and attractive external appearance. L17.

H. S. RANDALL The smooth, glossy pretences of diplomacy. *Pan Am Clipper* The elegant shops and other glossy pleasures of Palm Beach.

3 Of a type of paper: smooth and shiny; (of a magazine etc.) printed on such paper, expensive and attractive in appearance but sometimes lacking in depth or substance. L19.

A. S. BYATT The other woman... leafed through.. a heap of glossy magazines.

▸ **B** *noun*. A photograph with a glossy surface; a glossy magazine etc. M20.

A. WILSON The slightly too smart appearance, which the world of women's glossies had imposed upon her.

■ **glossily** *adverb* E18. **glossiness** *noun* L17.

glost /glɒst/ *noun*. L19.

[ORIGIN App. dial. alt. of GLOSS *noun*[2] 4.]

CERAMICS. A lead glaze used for pottery.

– COMB.: **glost-fire** *verb trans. & intrans.* fire (pottery etc.) after glazing; **glost oven** an oven in which glazed ware is fired.

glottal /ˈglɒt(ə)l/ *adjective*. M19.

[ORIGIN from GLOTT(IS + -AL[1].]

Pertaining to or produced by the glottis.

J. HELLER The same splintered syllable, the same glottal stutter, kept coming out.

glottal catch, **glottal stop** a sound produced by the sudden opening or shutting of the glottis before or after an emission of breath or voice.

■ **gloˈttalic** *adjective* relating to the glottis and its total or partial closure M20.

glottalize /ˈglɒt(ə)lʌɪz/ *verb trans.* Also **-ise**. E20.

[ORIGIN from GLOTTAL + -IZE.]

Articulate with total or partial closure of the glottis.

■ **glottaliˈzation** *noun* M20.

glottic /ˈglɒtɪk/ *adjective*[1] *& noun*. *rare*. E19.

[ORIGIN Greek *glōttikos* of the tongue from *glōtta*: see GLOTTO-, -IC.]

▸ **A** *adjective*. Of or pertaining to language. E19.

▸ **B** *noun*. *sing.* & (usu.) in *pl.* (treated as *sing.*). The branch of knowledge that deals with language. M20.

■ †**glottical** *adjective*: only in M17.

glottic /ˈglɒtɪk/ *adjective*[2]. M19.

[ORIGIN from GLOTT(IS + -IC.]

Of or pertaining to the glottis.

glottis /ˈglɒtɪs/ *noun*. L16.

[ORIGIN mod. Latin from Greek *glōttis*, from *glōtta*: see GLOTTO-.]

ANATOMY & ZOOLOGY. The upper aperture of the vertebrate larynx between the vocal cords, open during breathing but closed by the epiglottis during swallowing.

glotto- /ˈglɒtəʊ/ *combining form*. M19.

[ORIGIN Greek *glōtto-* combining form of *glōtta* Attic form of *glōssa*: see GLOSSO-.]

Forming adjectives and nouns with the sense '(of) language or languages.'

glottochronology /ˌglɒtəʊkrəˈnɒlədʒi/ *noun*. M20.

[ORIGIN from GLOTTO- + CHRONOLOGY.]

LINGUISTICS. The use of statistics to determine the degree of relationship between two or more languages and the chronology of their divergence from a common source.

■ **glottochronoˈlogic**, **glottochronoˈlogical** *adjectives* M20.

glottogonic /glɒtə(ʊ)ˈgɒnɪk/ *adjective*. L19.
[ORIGIN from GLOTTO- + Greek *gonikos* pertaining to production.]
Relating to the origin of language or languages.

glottology /glɒˈtɒlədʒi/ *noun*. Now *rare* or *obsolete*. M19.
[ORIGIN from GLOTTO- + -LOGY.]
Philology, linguistics; *spec.* comparative philology.
■ **glottoˈlogical** *adjective* M19.

Gloucester /ˈglɒstə/ *noun*. L18.
[ORIGIN A city in SW England.]
A kind of cheese orig. made in Gloucestershire. Also ***Gloucester cheese***.
double Gloucester (***cheese***): see DOUBLE *adjective & adverb*. ***single Gloucester*** (***cheese***): see SINGLE *adjective & adverb*.

Glou-morceau /gluːmɔːˈsəʊ/ *noun*. Pl. **-ceaux** /-ˈsəʊ/. M19.
[ORIGIN French dial. = titbit.]
A late-ripening variety of pear, producing fruit of high quality.

glout /glaʊt/ *verb & noun*. Chiefly *dial.* LME.
[ORIGIN Perh. var. of GLOAT *verb*.]
► **A** *verb intrans.* Look sullen, frown, scowl. LME.
► **B** *noun*. A frown, a sullen look. M17.

G

glove /glʌv/ *noun*.
[ORIGIN Old English *glōf* corresp. to Old Norse *glófi*, from Germanic, perh. from base of Y- + base of Old Norse *lófi*, Gothic *lofa* hand.]
1 A covering for the hand to protect it or keep it warm, clean, or cool, usu. with separated fingers. OE. ▸**b** A token of a pledge or of a challenge to battle. ME.

B. PYM She was wearing old black cotton gloves . . to protect her hands.

fit like a glove fit or suit exactly. **go for the gloves** bet recklessly. ***hand and glove*** (***with***), ***hand in glove*** (***with***): see HAND *noun*. ***iron hand in a velvet glove***: see IRON *adjective*. ***kid glove***: see KID *noun*[1]. ***oven glove***: see OVEN *noun*. ***velvet glove***: see VELVET *adjective*. **b** †**cast the glove** = ***throw down the glove*** below. **take up the glove** accept a challenge. **throw down the glove** issue a challenge.
2 = ***boxing glove*** s.v. BOXING *verbal noun*[2]. E18.

ALBERT SMITH I . . put on the gloves . . and knocked him about.

take the gloves off show no mercy, set to in earnest. **without gloves**, **with the gloves off**, etc., severely, without mercy.
– COMB.: **glovebox** (*a*) a box for holding gloves; (*b*) = ***glove compartment*** below; (*c*) a closed chamber with sealed-in gloves for handling radioactive or other material; **glove compartment** a recess in the dashboard of a motor vehicle for small articles like gloves etc.; **glove-fit** something that fits like a glove; **glove money** *hist.* (*a*) a gratuity given to servants ostensibly to buy them gloves; (*b*) LAW extraordinary rewards formerly given to officers of English Courts etc.; *spec.* money given by a sheriff to other officers in a county in which there were no offenders left for execution; **glove puppet** a puppet made to fit on the hand like a glove and operated by the fingers.
■ **gloveless** *adjective* E19.

glove /glʌv/ *verb trans.* LME.
[ORIGIN from the noun.]
Cover with or as with a glove; provide with gloves.

DAY LEWIS Her gloved hand holds a parasol.

glover /ˈglʌvə/ *noun*[1]. ME.
[ORIGIN from GLOVE *noun* + -ER[1].]
A person who makes or sells gloves.
■ **gloveress** *noun* (*rare*) a female glover ME.

glow /gləʊ/ *noun*. LME.
[ORIGIN from the verb.]
1 The state or condition of glowing, esp. with heat or light. LME.

R. W. EMERSON Summer's scorching glow. A. MACLEAN On a dark night the glow from a torch can be seen from a considerable distance.

in a glow hot, flushed.
2 Brightness and warmth of colour; *esp.* a warm redness of the cheeks indicating youth or health. L16.

G. STEIN The heat gave a pretty pink glow to her . . attractive face.

3 Warmth of feeling; ardour, passion. M18.

M. DRABBLE I went upstairs . . in a glow of contentment.

– COMB. (partly from the verb): **glow discharge** a sparkless electrical discharge, esp. in a low-pressure gas, producing a diffuse luminous glow; **glow-fly** a firefly; **glow-lamp** an electric lamp containing a high-resistance filament, esp. one in which most of the light is produced by the incandescence of an enclosed gas (usu. neon or argon); **glow-light** a glowing light; *spec.* a glow-lamp; **glow plug** an electrically heated plug used to ignite the gas in a gas turbine or diesel engine; **glow-worm** a beetle, *Lampyris noctiluca*, the wingless female and other stages of which emit light from the abdomen; any of numerous similar beetles constituting the family Lampyridae.

glow /gləʊ/ *verb*[1].
[ORIGIN Old English *glōwan* strong verb corresp. to the weak verbs Old Saxon *glōjan* (Dutch *gloeien*), Old High German *gluoen* (German *glühen*), Old Norse *glóa*, from Germanic. Cf. GLEED *noun*.]
1 *verb intrans.* Be heated to incandescence; emit bright light and heat without flame. OE.

S. JOHNSON I . . found it in ruins, with the fire yet glowing.

2 *verb intrans.* Shine, emit light, (as if) owing to intense heat. LME.

P. BOWLES The court glowed with reflected moonlight. D. LESSING There was a single . . electric-light bulb glowing down from the rafters. S. KING It had been treated with fluorescent paint so it would glow in the dark.

3 *verb intrans.* Be warm and bright in colouring. LME. ▸**b** Pass *to* or *into* a glowing colour. L19.

E. O. M. DEUTSCH Pictures teeming with life, glowing with colour.

4 *verb intrans.* Be excessively hot; be on fire, burn. LME.

fig.: EDMUND SMITH Yawning Gulphs with flaming Vengeance glow.

5 *verb intrans.* Burn with or be indicative of bodily heat, esp. when accompanied by heightened colour. LME.

W. C. SMITH Girls, all glowing with the flush of life. B. PYM Their skins glowed from the fresh air.

6 *verb intrans.* Burn with the fervour of emotion or passion. LME.

M. IGNATIEFF Not knowing whether to burn with shame or glow with pride.

†**7** *verb trans.* Make hot; heat. L16–L17.
■ **glowing** *ppl adjective* that glows; *spec.* (of an account etc.) ardent, impassioned, expressing great pride or praise: OE. **glowingly** *adverb* E17.

glow /gləʊ/ *verb*[2] *intrans. obsolete* exc. *dial.* LME.
[ORIGIN Perh. a use of GLOW *verb*[1]; but cf. Swedish, Danish *glo* stare, look sullen.]
Stare.

glower /ˈglaʊə/ *verb & noun*. L15.
[ORIGIN Perh. Scot. var. of synon. GLORE or from GLOW *verb*[2] + -ER[5].]
► **A** *verb intrans.* **1** Stare with wide open eyes; gaze, look. (Foll. by *at*.) Chiefly *Scot.* L15.
2 Look angrily or crossly; scowl. (Foll. by *at*.) E18.

R. F. HOBSON Sam sat rigidly . . and glowered at me—a picture of dumb insolence.

► **B** *noun*. The action of glowering; an intense look, a stare. Chiefly *Scot.* E17.

gloxinia /glɒkˈsɪnɪə/ *noun*. E19.
[ORIGIN mod. Latin (see below), from P. B. *Gloxin*, 18th-cent. German botanist.]
Any of various tropical American plants of or formerly included in the genus *Gloxinia* (family Gesneriaceae); *esp.* any of the forms or hybrids of the Brazilian *Sinningia speciosa*, with large velvety trumpet-shaped corollas, grown as hothouse plants.

gloze /gləʊz/ *noun*. Now *rare*. Also (earlier) †**glose**. ME.
[ORIGIN Old French & mod. French *glose* from medieval Latin *glosa*, *gloza*, for Latin *glossa*: see GLOSS *noun*[1].]
1 A marginal note, a comment. = GLOSS *noun*[1] 1. *arch.* ME.
2 Flattery, deceit; a flattering speech or comment. ME.
3 A pretence, a specious appearance. Also, a disguise. ME.

gloze /gləʊz/ *verb*[1]. Also (earlier) †**glose**. ME.
[ORIGIN Old French & mod. French *gloser*, formed as GLOZE *noun*; in medieval Latin *glossare*.]
1 *verb trans.* Flatter, deceive with smooth talk or specious words. *arch.* ME.
2 *verb intrans.* Talk smoothly and speciously; use flattering language; fawn. *arch.* ME.
3 *verb trans.* Veil with specious language; explain away, extenuate. (Foll. by *over*, †*out*.) LME.

R. GLOVER It is not charity to gloze over the sins and sorrows of men.

4 a *verb trans.* Make glosses on; expound, interpret; comment on or about. LME. ▸**b** *verb intrans.* Insert a gloss or explanation; comment. (Foll. by *on*, *upon*). Now *rare*. LME.

a E. CRISPIN Policemen whose activities he glozed and expounded.

■ †**glozer** *noun* (*a*) a person who writes glosses, a commentator; (*b*) a flatterer, a sycophant: LME–L18. **glozing** *noun* (*a*) the action of the verb; (*b*) (*a*) flattery, specious talk: ME. **glozingly** *adverb* in a glozing manner LME.

gloze /gləʊz/ *verb*[2] *trans. & intrans. rare*. E19.
[ORIGIN Unknown: cf. GLOSS *noun*[2].]
(Cause to) shine, gleam, blaze.

gluc- *combining form* see GLUCO-.

glucagon /ˈgluːkəg(ə)n, -gɒn/ *noun*. E20.
[ORIGIN from GLUCO- + Greek *agōn* pres. pple of *agein* lead, bring.]
A polypeptide hormone formed in the pancreas which promotes the breakdown of glycogen in the liver and thereby increases blood sugar.

glucan /ˈgluːkan/ *noun*. M20.
[ORIGIN from GLUCO- + -AN.]
Any polysaccharide composed chiefly of glucose residues, e.g. cellulose and starch.

glucaric /gluːˈkarɪk/ *adjective*. M20.
[ORIGIN from GLUCO- after SACCHARIC.]
CHEMISTRY. ***glucaric acid***, a dibasic acid, $C_6H_{10}O_8$, formed by the oxidation of various sugars.

†**glucina** *noun*. Also **-ine**. Only in 19.
[ORIGIN mod. Latin (after *magnesia*, *soda*, etc.) from French *glucine*, formed as GLUCO-: see GLYCO-, -INE[5].]
Beryllium oxide.

glucinum /gluːˈsʌɪnəm/ *noun*. *obsolete* exc. *hist.* E19.
[ORIGIN formed as GLUCINA: cf. -IUM.]
= BERYLLIUM.

gluck /glʌk/ *verb & noun*. M19.
[ORIGIN Imit.: cf. GLUG.]
(Make) a light usu. repetitive gurgling sound as of liquid being poured from a bottle.

gluco- /ˈgluːkəʊ/ *combining form*. Before a vowel also **gluc-** /gluːk/.
[ORIGIN French, from GLUCOSE and (later) Greek *glukus* sweet: see -O-. Cf. GLYCO-.]
CHEMISTRY. **1** Glucose; containing, related to, or yielding glucose; affecting the metabolism of glucose.
2 = GLYCO-.
■ **glucoˈcorticoid** *noun* any of a group of corticosteroids (e.g. hydrocortisone) which are involved in the metabolism of carbohydrates, proteins, and fats and have anti-inflammatory activity M20. **gluconeoˈgenesis** *noun* the formation of glucose in the body from non-carbohydrate precursors, esp. from proteins E20. **gluconeogeˈnetic**, **gluconeoˈgenic** *adjectives* of or pertaining to gluconeogenesis M20. **glucoˈprotein** *noun* †(*a*) any of various amino acids or mixtures of amino acids to which were ascribed the empirical formula $C_nH_{2n}N_2O_4$, where *n* is between 6 and 12; (*b*) = GLYCOPROTEIN: L19. **glucoˈstatic** *adjective* (*PHYSIOLOGY*) pertaining to or designating a mechanism for maintaining a constant level of glucose in the blood, or a theory of metabolism that postulates such a mechanism M20.

†**glucogen** *noun* var. of GLYCOGEN.

gluconic /gluːˈkɒnɪk/ *adjective*. L19.
[ORIGIN from GLUCO- + -ONIC.]
CHEMISTRY. ***gluconic acid***, an acid, $CH_2OH\,(CHOH)_4COOH$, derived from glucose by oxidation of the latter's aldehyde group.
■ **ˈgluconate** *noun* a salt or ester of gluconic acid L19.

glucosamine /gluːˈkəʊsəmiːn, -ˈkəʊz-/ *noun*. L19.
[ORIGIN from GLUCO- after *glycosamine*.]
CHEMISTRY. A crystalline amino sugar, $CH_2OH(CHOH)_3CHNH_2CHO$, that is derived from glucose and is the principal constituent of chitin.

glucosan /ˈgluːkəsan/ *noun*. M19.
[ORIGIN French *glucosane*, formed as GLUCOSE.]
CHEMISTRY. **1** Any of several isomeric anhydrides, $C_6H_{10}O_5$, of glucose. M19.
2 = GLUCAN. E20.

glucose /ˈgluːkəʊs, -z/ *noun*. M19.
[ORIGIN French from Greek *gleukos* sweet wine, rel. to *glukus* sweet: see -OSE[2].]
1 One of the hexose sugars, obtainable in dextrorotatory and laevorotatory forms and as a racemic mixture; *spec.* the dextrorotatory form (also called **D-*glucose***, ***dextrose***, ***grape sugar***), a white or colourless sweet-tasting solid which is an important energy source in living organisms and which occurs free in fruit juices and the blood and combined in glucosides, some oligosaccharides (e.g. sucrose), and some polysaccharides (e.g. cellulose and starch). M19.
†**2** Any of the hexoses, $C_6H_{12}O_6$; any monosaccharide. M19–E20.
3 A syrup containing D-glucose, maltose, dextrin, and water, obtained by the incomplete hydrolysis of starch and used in the food industry as a sweetener and thickener. Also ***glucose syrup***. M19.
– COMB.: **glucose phosphate** any phosphoric acid ester of glucose, esp. a monophosphate (***glucose-1-phosphate***, a phosphate formed in the body from glucose-6-phosphate in the synthesis of polysaccharides; ***glucose-6-phosphate***, a phosphate formed in the body by the reaction of glucose with ATP in the initial step of glucose metabolism); **glucose tolerance test** a test for abnormal carbohydrate metabolism, esp. diabetes, in which glucose is given orally after a period of fasting and the blood sugar measured at intervals afterwards.
■ **gluˈcosic** *adjective* M19. **glucoˈsinolate** *noun* [from Latin *sinapis* mustard + *oleum* oil] any of a group of toxic glucosides produced by some brassicas and yielding mustard oil on ingestion M20.

glucosidase /gluːˈkɒsɪdeɪz, gluːkəˈsʌɪdeɪz/ *noun*. E20.
[ORIGIN from GLUCOSIDE + -ASE.]
BIOCHEMISTRY. An enzyme, such as maltase, which hydrolyses a glucoside to form glucose.

glucoside /ˈgluːkəsʌɪd/ *noun*. Also †**glyco-**. See also GLYCOSIDE. M19.
[ORIGIN from GLUCOSE + -IDE.]
CHEMISTRY. A glycoside in which the sugar is glucose.
■ **glucoˈsidal**, **glucoˈsidic** *adjectives* characteristic of a glucoside E20. **glucoˈsidically** *adverb* M20.

glucuronic /gluːkjʊˈrɒnɪk/ *adjective*. E20.
[ORIGIN from GLUCO- after GLYCURONIC.]
CHEMISTRY & BIOCHEMISTRY. ***glucuronic acid***, the uronic acid, $HOOC(CHOH)_4CHO$, derived from glucose, which occurs naturally as a constituent of hyaluronic acid and other mucopolysaccharides, and in glucuronides.
■ **gluˈcuronate** *noun* a salt or ester of glucuronic acid E20. **glucuˈronidase** *noun* an enzyme which hydrolyses a glucuronide M20. **gluˈcuronide** *noun* any glycosidic compound

formed by glucuronic acid; *esp.* one of those formed in the body by conjugation with another compound as part of the metabolic process by which the latter is excreted: M20. **glucuronyl** /gluːˈkjuːrənʌɪl, -nɪl/ *noun* the monovalent radical $\cdot OC(CHOH)_4\cdot CHO$ derived from glucuronic acid M20.

glue /gluː/ *noun*. ME.
[ORIGIN Old French & mod. French *glu* from late Latin *glus*, *glut-*, from Latin *gluten*.]
1 A sticky or viscous substance used for sticking things together (orig. a brownish gelatin made by boiling hides and bones and used in solution). ME.
†**2** A plant gum. LME–E19.
†**3** Birdlime. LME–E18.
†**4** Bitumen, pitch. Only in LME.
– COMB.: **glueball** *PARTICLE PHYSICS* a bound state of two or more gluons; **glue ear** a condition in which a viscous fluid blocks the Eustachian tube and impairs hearing, occurring chiefly in children as a result of infection of the middle ear; **glue pot** (**a**) a pot in which glue is heated, having an outer vessel which holds hot water; (**b**) *colloq.* an area of ground sticky because of wet or mud; **glue-sniffing** the inhalation of the fumes of plastic cement for their stimulating effects.
■ **gluish** *adjective* (now *rare*) somewhat gluey LME. **gluelike** *adjective* resembling glue E19.

glue /gluː/ *verb*. Pres. pple & verbal noun **glu(e)ing**. LME.
[ORIGIN Old French & mod. French *gluer*, formed as GLUE *noun*.]
1 *verb trans.* Join or fasten (*to* something, *together*) with glue. Also foll. by *on*, *up*. LME. ▸†**b** Involve or entangle in some sticky substance so as to impede free motion (*lit.* & *fig.*). LME–L17. ▸**c** Seal (as) with glue; shut up tightly. Now only foll. by *up*. M17.

P. ROTH The saucer . . had broken neatly in two . . . 'She can glue it.'

2 *verb trans. fig.* Cause to adhere closely or firmly; apply or attach tightly or firmly; *esp.* apply (one's eyes or ears) closely *to* something in rapt attention (usu. in *pass.*). LME.

SMOLLETT She now began to glue herself to his favour with the grossest adulation. C. BRONTË Her ear having been glued to the key-hole. N. MAILER They were all glued to the TV set. S. BRETT The . . chat-show . . kept millions glued to their armchairs every Saturday night.

3 *verb intrans.* Admit of being fastened by glue. Formerly also, stick *together*, adhere (*lit.* & *fig.*). Long *rare*. LME.

EVELYN Oak will not easily glue to other Wood.

4 *verb trans.* Daub or smear with glue or some similar viscous substance. Now *rare* or *obsolete*. LME.
■ **gluer** *noun* L15.

gluey /ˈgluːi/ *adjective*. LME.
[ORIGIN from GLUE *noun* + -Y[1].]
Resembling or of the nature of glue; viscous, glutinous; sticky.
■ **gluily**, **glueily** *adverb* E20. **glueyness** *noun* E17.

glug /glʌg/ *noun* & *verb*. L17.
[ORIGIN Imit.: cf. GLUCK.]
▸ **A** *noun*. A hollow usu. repetitive gurgling sound as of liquid being poured from a bottle. L17.
▸ **B** *verb*. Infl. **-gg-**.
1 *verb intrans.* Make a glug or glugs. Chiefly as ***glugging*** *verbal noun* & *ppl adjective*. L19.
2 *verb trans.* Pour (liquid) so that it glugs. L20.

glugg *noun* var. of GLÖGG.

Glühwein /ˈglyːvaɪn, ˈgluːvʌɪn/ *noun*. Also ***Gluh-***. L19.
[ORIGIN German, from *glühen* mull, GLOW *verb*[1] + *wein* WINE *noun*.]
Mulled wine.

gluino /glʊˈiːnəʊ/ *noun*. Pl. **-os**. L20.
[ORIGIN from GLUON + -INO.]
PARTICLE PHYSICS. The supersymmetric counterpart of a gluon, with spin ½ instead of 1.

glulam /ˈgluːlam/ *noun*. M20.
[ORIGIN from GLU(E *noun* + LAM(INATION.]
A building material consisting of laminations of timber glued together.

glum /glʌm/ *noun*. Long *obsolete* exc. *dial.* E16.
[ORIGIN from GLUM *verb* or *adjective*. Cf. GLOOM *noun*[1].]
A sullen look, a frown. Also, a glum person.

glum /glʌm/ *adjective*. Compar. & superl. **-mm-**. M16.
[ORIGIN Rel. to GLUM *verb*.]
1 Of a person or a person's expression: sullen, frowning; silent and morose; looking or feeling dejected or displeased. M16.
2 Of a thing: conducive to glumness; gloomy, dismal, depressing. Now only *fig.* from sense 1. M16.

THACKERAY We walked in the park . . surveying . . the glum old bridge.

■ **glumly** *adverb* E19. **glummy** *adjective* (*rare*) †(**a**) gloomy; (**b**) glum: L16. **glumness** *noun* E18.

glum /glʌm/ *verb intrans. obsolete* exc. *dial.* Infl. **-mm-**. LME.
[ORIGIN Var. of GLOOM *verb*.]
Look sullen; frown, scowl.

glume /gluːm/ *noun*. L18.
[ORIGIN Latin *gluma* hull, husk rel. to *glubere* to shell, to peel.]
BOTANY. Any of certain chaffy or membranous scales in the inflorescence of grasses or related plants: (**a**) (in grasses) either of the two empty bracts subtending the spikelet (more fully ***empty glume***, ***sterile glume***); also (now *rare*) = LEMMA *noun*[2] 2 (more fully ***flowering glume***); (**b**) (in sedges and other plants of the Cyperaceae) the bract enclosing the flower.
■ **gluˈmaceous** *adjective* resembling or having glumes; characterized by bearing glumes, as the grasses and sedges: E19. **ˈglumose** *adjective* (now *rare*) having a glume or husk L18.

glump /glʌmp/ *verb* & *noun*. *dial.* or (*rare*) *colloq.* M18.
[ORIGIN Unknown: cf. *glum*, *dump*, etc.]
▸ **A** *verb intrans.* Sulk; be glum or sullen. M18.
▸ **B** *noun*. A sulky person. Also, in *pl.*, the sulks. M18.
■ **glumpish** *adjective* = GLUMPY E19.

glumpy /ˈglʌmpi/ *adjective*. L18.
[ORIGIN from GLUMP + -Y[1]. Cf. GRUMPY.]
Glum, sullen, sulky.
■ **glumpily** *adverb* M19.

glunch /glʌn(t)ʃ/ *verb*, *noun*, & *adjective*. *Scot.* E18.
[ORIGIN Unknown: cf. GLUM *adjective*, CLUNCH *adjective*.]
▸ **A** *verb intrans.* Look sour or glum. E18.
▸ **B** *noun*. A sour look. L18.
▸ **C** *adjective*. Glum, sulky. E19.

†**glunimie** *noun*. *Scot. derog.* M18–E19.
[ORIGIN Perh. alt. of Gaelic *glùineanach* (a person) wearing garters.]
A Highlander.

gluon /ˈgluːɒn/ *noun*. L20.
[ORIGIN from GLUE *noun*, *verb* + -ON.]
PARTICLE PHYSICS. Any of a hypothetical group of massless bosons that are thought to be the carriers of the colour force that binds quarks together in hadrons.
■ **gluˈonic** *adjective* L20.

glut /glʌt/ *noun*[1]. Long *obsolete* exc. *dial.* LME.
[ORIGIN from Old French *gl(o)ut* greedy, gluttonous.]
A glutton.

glut /glʌt/ *noun*[2]. *obsolete* exc. *dial.* M16.
[ORIGIN Old French *glout* gulp, rel. to *gloutir* GLUT *verb*[1].]
A full draught; the amount of liquid swallowed at a gulp.

glut /glʌt/ *noun*[3]. L16.
[ORIGIN from GLUT *verb*[1].]
1 The action of glutting or the condition of being glutted with food etc.; full indulgence in a pleasure to the point of satiety or disgust; a surfeit. L16. ▸†**b** In *pl.* Excesses. L16–L17.

J. MARSTON Even I have glut of blood. J. LONDON I knew what it was to sleep my full and to awake naturally from very glut of sleep.

2 A supply of some commodity which greatly exceeds demand. L16.

W. LIPPMANN There is a scarcity of some goods and a glut of others.

3 †**a** An excessive flow of saliva, bile, etc. L16–E18. ▸†**b** An excessive influx of water, rain, etc. Now *rare*. M17.
4 An excessive quantity or number. Foll. by *of*. Now *rare*. M17.
†**5** Something which chokes a channel. L17–E18.

glut /glʌt/ *noun*[4]. M18.
[ORIGIN Perh. alt. of dial. var. of CLEAT.]
1 A wedge. M18.
2 *NAUTICAL.* A piece of strengthening canvas sewn into the centre of a square sail at the bunt. M19.
3 A small brick or block, *esp.* one such placed in a building course to complete it. L19.

glut /glʌt/ *verb*[1]. Infl. **-tt-**. ME.
[ORIGIN Prob. from Old French *gloutir* swallow (with causative sense perh. developed in Anglo-Norman) from Latin *gluttire* swallow: see GLUTTON *noun*.]
1 a *verb trans.* Feed to repletion; indulge (appetite) to the utmost. ME. ▸**b** *verb intrans.* Feed (*on*) to repletion. M17.

a N. HAWTHORNE Destined to glut the ravenous maw of that detestable man-brute. P. V. WHITE The beasts were glutting themselves on dew and grass.

2 *verb trans.* Overload with food (*lit.* & *fig.*); surfeit, cloy, or sicken with excess of something. LME.

GOLDSMITH Swallowing their blood at large draughts, and seeming rather glutted than satiated. HAZLITT The ear is cloyed and glutted with warbled ecstasies.

3 *verb trans.* Fill (a receptacle, channel, etc.) to excess, choke; saturate, impregnate thoroughly *with* some substance. Now *rare*. L15.

E. L. DOCTOROW The sidewalks were glutted with shoppers.

4 *verb trans.* Gratify (esp. a ferocious or lustful desire) to the full. M16. ▸**b** *verb intrans.* Take one's fill of thinking, gazing, etc., *on* something; long greedily *for*. *rare*. M17.

J. R. GREEN His ambition was glutted . . with the rank of Cardinal. **b** T. CAREW Love doth with an hungry eye Glut on Beauty.

5 *verb trans.* Overstock (a market) with goods. E17.

glut /glʌt/ *verb*[2] *trans.* Now *rare*. Infl. **-tt-**. M16.
[ORIGIN Old French *gloutir* swallow: see GLUT *verb*[1] Cf. ENGLUT.]
Swallow greedily; gulp down.

glutaei *noun pl.* see GLUTEUS.

glutaeo- *combining form* var. of GLUTEO-.

glutaeus *noun* var. of GLUTEUS.

glutamate /ˈgluːtəmeɪt/ *noun*. L19.
[ORIGIN from GLUTAMIC + -ATE[1].]
BIOCHEMISTRY. A salt or ester of glutamic acid, *esp.* a sodium salt used as a food additive to enhance flavour; the ion of glutamic acid, which is involved in nitrogen metabolism in humans and other organisms.
MONOSODIUM ***glutamate***.

glutamic /gluːˈtamɪk/ *adjective*. L19.
[ORIGIN from GLUT(EN + AM(INE + -IC.]
BIOCHEMISTRY. ***glutamic acid***, an acidic amino acid, $HOOCCH_2CH_2CH(NH_2)COOH$, which occurs in proteins and is the source of the glutamate ion.

glutamine /ˈgluːtəmiːn/ *noun*. L19.
[ORIGIN from GLUT(AMIC + AMINE.]
BIOCHEMISTRY. A hydrophilic amino acid, $H_2N{\cdot}COCH_2{\cdot}CH_2(NH_2)COOH$, which occurs in proteins and is an amide of glutamic acid, from which it is formed metabolically.

glutaric /gluːˈtarɪk/ *adjective*. L19.
[ORIGIN from GLUT(EN + TAR)TARIC.]
glutaric acid, the crystalline acid $HOOC(CH_2)_3COOH$; pentanedioic acid.

G

glutathione /gluːtəˈθʌɪəʊn/ *noun*. E20.
[ORIGIN from GLUTA(MIC + THIO- + -ONE.]
BIOCHEMISTRY. A tripeptide composed of glutamate, cysteine, and glycine which is important in metabolism, esp. as a coenzyme.

glutch /glʌtʃ/ *verb trans.* & *intrans.* *dial.* E19.
[ORIGIN Imit. or from GULCH *verb* with metathesis.]
Swallow, gulp. Also foll. by *down*.

glute /gluːt/ *noun*. *slang*. M20.
[ORIGIN Abbreviation.]
= GLUTEUS. Usu. in *pl.*

glutei *noun pl.* see GLUTEUS.

gluten /ˈgluːt(ə)n/ *noun*. L16.
[ORIGIN French from Latin *gluten* glue.]
†**1** = FIBRIN. L16–E19.
2 A sticky substance; a gum, a glue; a viscid secretion. *rare*. M17.
3 A substance containing a large number of proteins that is present in cereal grains, esp. wheat, and is responsible for the elastic texture of dough. E19.
– COMB.: **gluten bread** bread with a high gluten content.

glutenin /ˈgluːtɪnɪn/ *noun*. L19.
[ORIGIN from GLUTEN + -IN[1].]
BIOCHEMISTRY. The chief protein present in wheat flour.

gluteo- /ˈgluːtɪəʊ/ *combining form*. Also **-taeo-**.
[ORIGIN from GLUTEUS + -O-.]
Pertaining to or designating the gluteus and —, as ***gluteofemoral***.

glutethimide /gluːˈtɛθɪmʌɪd/ *noun*. M20.
[ORIGIN from GLUT(ARIC + ETH(YL + IMIDE.]
PHARMACOLOGY. A bicyclic compound with hypnotic properties, formerly used as an alternative to barbiturates.

gluteus /gluːˈtiːəs/ *noun*. Also **-taeus**. Pl. **-t(a)ei**, /-ˈtiːʌɪ/. L17.
[ORIGIN mod. Latin from Greek *gloutos* buttock.]
Each of three paired muscles of the buttocks (in full ***gluteus maximus*** /ˈmaksɪməs/ [Latin = largest], ***gluteus medius*** /ˈmiːdɪəs/ [Latin = middle], ***gluteus minimus*** /ˈmɪnɪməs/ [Latin = smallest]) which extend the thigh at the hip joint. Also ***gluteus muscle***.
■ **gluteal** *adjective* L18. **glutean** *adjective* (*rare*) E19.

†**glutinate** *verb trans.* LME.
[ORIGIN Latin *glutinat-* pa. ppl stem of *glutinare* glue together, close up (a wound), from *glutin-*, *gluten*: see GLUTEN, -ATE[3].]
1 *MEDICINE.* Close or heal (a wound); counter relaxation of (the bowels, veins, etc.). LME–M18.
2 Glue or stick together. Only in 17.

glutinize /ˈgluːtɪnʌɪz/ *verb trans.* Also **-ise**. M18.
[ORIGIN from Latin *glutin-*, *gluten* glue + -IZE.]
Make viscous or sticky.

glutinosity /gluːtɪˈnɒsɪti/ *noun*. LME.
[ORIGIN medieval Latin *glutinositas*, from Latin *glutinosus*: see GLUTINOUS, -OSITY.]
The quality or condition of being glutinous.

glutinous /ˈgluːtɪnəs/ *adjective*. LME.
[ORIGIN Old French & mod. French *glutineux* or Latin *glutinosus*, from *glutin-*, *gluten* glue: see -OUS.]
Gluelike, sticky, viscid.

KEATS A glutinous pine. *fig.*: O. MANNING Priests . . trailed around all day in the glutinous heat.

■ **glutinously** *adverb* E17. **glutinousness** *noun* (long *rare*) M17.

glutton /ˈglʌt(ə)n/ *noun* & *adjective*. ME.
[ORIGIN Old French *gluton*, *gloton* (mod. *glouton*) from Latin *glutto(n-)* rel. to *gluttire* swallow, *gluttus* greedy, *gula* throat.]
▸ **A** *noun*. **1** A person who eats to excess, or who takes pleasure in immoderate eating; a greedy person. ME.

▸**b** *fig.* A person who is inordinately fond (*of* a specified pursuit), or insatiably eager (*for* something). **E18.**

b R. KIPLING He's honest, and a glutton for work.

†**the rich glutton** the rich man of the biblical parable (Luke 16:19) whose fate is contrasted with that of the beggar Lazarus. **b a glutton for punishment** a person who is (apparently) eager to take on an onerous workload or an exacting task.

†**2** A vile wretch. **ME–E16.**

3 The wolverine, *Gulo gulo*. **L17.**

▸**B** *adjective*. Gluttonous. Formerly also, villainous. Now *rare*. **LME.**

■ **gluttoness** *noun* (*rare*) a female glutton **E17. gluttonish** *adjective* (*rare*) (somewhat) like a glutton, voracious **LME. gluttonize** *verb intrans.* (now *rare*) feed gluttonously (*on*) **M17.**

glutton /ˈɡlʌt(ə)n/ *verb*. **E17.**
[ORIGIN from the noun.]

†**1** *verb intrans.* Feed voraciously or to excess (*on*). **E17–E19.**

2 *verb trans.* = GLUT *verb*[1] 1a; swallow or devour greedily. *rare*. **M17.**

gluttonous /ˈɡlʌt(ə)nəs/ *adjective*. **LME.**
[ORIGIN from GLUTTON *noun* + -OUS.]

Given to excess in eating; characterized by or of the nature of gluttony (*lit.* & *fig.*).

J. L. MOTLEY Philip the Prudent, as he grew older . . seemed to become more gluttonous of work. N. MONSARRAT Crumbs and a ring of milky white round his mouth betrayed the gluttonous boy.

■ **gluttonously** *adverb* **LME.**

gluttony /ˈɡlʌt(ə)ni/ *noun*. **ME.**
[ORIGIN Old French *glutonie* etc. (mod. *gloutonnerie*), formed as GLUTTON *noun*: see -Y[3].]

Habitual (and culpable) greed or excess in eating and drinking; inordinate and uncontrolled desire for food. Also (*rare*), an instance of this.

glycaemia /ɡlʌɪˈsiːmɪə/ *noun*. Also ***glycemia**. **E20.**
[ORIGIN from GLYC(O- + -AEMIA.]

The presence of glucose in the blood.

■ **glycaemic** *adjective* pertaining to glycaemia; ***glycaemic index***, a figure representing the relative ability of a carbohydrate food to increase the level of glucose in the blood: **E20.**

glycan /ˈɡlʌɪkan/ *noun*. **M20.**
[ORIGIN from GLYCO- + -AN.]

CHEMISTRY. = POLYSACCHARIDE.

glyceraldehyde /ɡlɪsəˈraldɪhʌɪd/ *noun*. **L19.**
[ORIGIN from GLYCER(IC + ALDEHYDE.]

A sweet-tasting compound, $CHO{\cdot}CHOH{\cdot}CH_2OH$, that is an intermediate in the metabolic breakdown of glucose.

glyceria /ɡlɪˈsɪərɪə/ *noun*. **E19.**
[ORIGIN mod. Latin (see below), from Greek *glukeros* sweet: see -IA[1].]

Any of several aquatic grasses of the genus *Glyceria*, relished by cattle for their succulent foliage. Also called ***sweetgrass***.

glyceric /ɡlɪˈsɛrɪk, ˈɡlɪs(ə)rɪk/ *adjective*. **M19.**
[ORIGIN formed as GLYCERIDE + -IC.]

CHEMISTRY. Of or pertaining to glycerol.

glyceric acid a syrup, $HOOC{\cdot}CH(OH)CH_2OH$, produced by the action of nitric acid on glycerol.

glyceride /ˈɡlɪs(ə)rʌɪd/ *noun*. **M19.**
[ORIGIN from GLYCERINE + -IDE.]

CHEMISTRY. An ester of glycerol, esp. with a fatty acid.

glycerin *noun* see GLYCERINE.

glycerinate /ˈɡlɪs(ə)rɪneɪt/ *verb trans.* **L19.**
[ORIGIN from GLYCERINE: see -ATE[3].]

Preserve in or treat with glycerine or a glycerine-based liquid.

■ **glyceriˈnation** *noun* **L19.**

glycerine /ˈɡlɪs(ə)riːn, -ɪn/ *noun*. Also ***-in** /-ɪn/. **M19.**
[ORIGIN French *glycerin* from Greek *glukeros* sweet: see -INE[5], -IN[1].]

Glycerol.

– COMB.: **glycerine tear** a drop of glycerine used in theatrical make-up to simulate a tear.

glycero- /ˈɡlɪs(ə)rəʊ/ *combining form* of GLYCERINE and GLYCEROL: see -O-.

■ **glyceroˈkinase** *noun* (*BIOCHEMISTRY*) an enzyme in the liver that catalyses the reaction of glycerol and ATP to glycerophosphate and ADP **M20. glyceroˈphosphate** *noun* a salt or ester, or the ion, of glycerophosphoric acid, *esp.* the calcium or magnesium salts, given as tonics and dietary supplements **M19. glycerophosˈphoric** *adjective*: ***glycerophosphoric acid***, an acid, $C_3H_5(OH)_2{\cdot}H_2PO_4$, that is a colourless combustible liquid produced by the action of phosphoric acid on glycerol **M19.**

glycerol /ˈɡlɪs(ə)rɒl/ *noun*. **L19.**
[ORIGIN from GLYCER(INE + -OL.]

A colourless sweet viscous liquid, $CH_2OHCHOH{\cdot}CH_2OH$, that is an alcohol formed as a by-product in the manufacture of soap and used as an emollient and laxative and in the manufacture of many chemicals. Also called (esp. in non-technical use) ***glycerine***.

glycerole /ˈɡlɪs(ə)rəʊl/ *noun*. Now *rare* or *obsolete*. **M19.**
[ORIGIN formed as GLYCEROL + *-ole*.]

A pharmaceutical preparation with glycerine as a vehicle.

glyceryl /ˈɡlɪs(ə)rɪl, -rʌɪl/ *noun*. **M19.**
[ORIGIN from GLYCER(INE + -YL.]

CHEMISTRY. A radical derived from glycerol by the removal of one or more hydroxyl groups; *esp.* the trivalent radical $C_3H_5{\equiv}$.

– COMB.: **glyceryl trinitrate** = NITROGLYCERINE.

glycin /ˈɡlʌɪsɪn/ *noun*. **L19.**
[ORIGIN from GLYCINE.]

BIOCHEMISTRY. A crystalline derivative of glycine used as a photographic developer; *p*-hydroxyphenylglycine, $HO{\cdot}C_6H_4{\cdot}NH{\cdot}CH_2COOH$.

glycine /ˈɡlʌɪsiːn/ *noun*. **M19.**
[ORIGIN from Greek *glukus* sweet + -INE[5].]

BIOCHEMISTRY. The simplest naturally occurring amino acid, $H_2N{\cdot}CH_2COOH$, a sweet-tasting crystalline compound which occurs in proteins and is used in food technology; aminoacetic acid.

glyco- /ˈɡlʌɪkəʊ/ *combining form*.
[ORIGIN from Greek *glukus* sweet + -O-.]

CHEMISTRY & BIOCHEMISTRY. Sugar; containing, related to, or yielding sugar; affecting the metabolism of sugar. Formerly also, glycerol. Cf. GLUCO-.

■ **glycobiˈology** *noun* the branch of science that deals with the role of sugars in biological processes **L20. glycocalyx** *noun* (*BIOLOGY*) a layer on the outer surface of a plasma membrane, composed of carbohydrate chains of proteoglycans or glycoproteins **M20. glycocholic** /-ˈkɒl-/ *adjective* (*BIOCHEMISTRY*) designating one of the principal acids in bile **M19. glycoˈlipid** *noun* (*BIOCHEMISTRY*) any compound in which a sugar or other carbohydrate is combined with a lipid **M20. glycoˈphorin** *noun* (*BIOCHEMISTRY*) a glycoprotein found in erythrocyte membranes **L20. glycophyte** *noun* (*ECOLOGY*) a plant whose growth is inhibited by saline soil **M20. glycophytic** /-ˈfɪtɪk/ *adjective* (*ECOLOGY*) pertaining to or designating a glycophyte **M20.** †**glycoproteid** *noun* a glycoprotein **L19–E20. glycoˈprotein** *noun* a protein that has short side chains of carbohydrate in its molecule **E20. glycotropic** /-ˈtrəʊpɪk, -ˈtrɒpɪk/ *adjective* (*BIOCHEMISTRY*) antagonistic to insulin **M20.**

glycocoll /ˈɡlʌɪkəkɒl/ *noun*. *obsolete* exc. *hist.* **M19.**
[ORIGIN from GLYCO- + Greek *kolla* glue.]

= GLYCINE.

glycogen /ˈɡlʌɪkədʒ(ə)n/ *noun*. Also †**gluc-**. **M19.**
[ORIGIN from GLYCO- + -GEN.]

BIOCHEMISTRY. A polysaccharide composed of glucose residues that is the form in which carbohydrate is stored in animals (corresponding to starch in plants) and is present esp. in liver and muscle.

■ **glycoˈgenesis** *noun* the formation of glycogen from glucose **L19. glycogeˈnetic** *adjective* = GLYCOGENIC **L19. glycoˈgenic** *adjective* of or pertaining to glycogenesis **M19. glycogeˈnolysis** *noun* the breakdown of glycogen to glucose in the body **E20. glycogenoˈlytic** *adjective* of or pertaining to glycogenolysis **E20.**

glycol /ˈɡlʌɪkɒl/ *noun*. **M19.**
[ORIGIN from GLYC(ERINE + -OL.]

= *ETHYLENE* ***glycol***; *CHEMISTRY* any diol.

■ **glyˈcollate**, **-ˈcolate** *noun* (*CHEMISTRY*) a salt or ester of glycollic acid **M19. glyˈcollic**, **-ˈcolic** *adjective* (*CHEMISTRY*): ***glycollic acid***, a crystalline acid, $CH_2OH{\cdot}COOH$ (also called ***hydroxyacetic acid***), which occurs in sugar-cane syrup and has numerous industrial uses **M19.**

glycolyse /ˈɡlʌɪk(ə)lʌɪz/ *verb trans.* Also ***-lyze**. **M20.**
[ORIGIN Back-form. from GLYCOLYSIS.]

BIOCHEMISTRY. Metabolize in glycolysis.

glycolysis /ɡlʌɪˈkɒlɪsɪs/ *noun*. Pl. **-lyses** /-lɪsiːz/. **L19.**
[ORIGIN from GLYCO- + LYSIS.]

BIOCHEMISTRY. The breakdown of sugar; *esp.* the metabolic process in which sugar and other carbohydrates are broken down by enzymes in most living organisms to yield pyruvic acid or lactic acid.

■ **glycoˈlytic** *adjective* **L19. glycoˈlytically** *adverb* **M20.**

Glyconean /ɡlʌɪkəˈniːən/ *adjective*. *rare*. Also **Glyconian** /ɡlʌɪˈkəʊnɪən/. **E18.**
[ORIGIN from late Latin *Glyconius* from Greek *Glukōneios*, from *Glukōn*: see GLYCONIC, -EAN, -IAN.]

= GLYCONIC *adjective*.

Glyconic /ɡlʌɪˈkɒnɪk/ *noun & adjective*. **L17.**
[ORIGIN from Greek *Glukōn* a Greek lyric poet + -IC.]

▸**A** *noun*. A Glyconic verse. **L17.**

▸**B** *adjective*. Of, pertaining to, or characterized by a metre in which there are three trochees and a dactyl in each line. **L17.**

glycosamine /ɡlʌɪˈkəʊsəmiːn, -ˈkəʊz-/ *noun*. **L19.**
[ORIGIN from *glycose*, obsolete var. of GLUCOSE + AMINE.]

CHEMISTRY. **1** = GLUCOSAMINE. **L19.**

2 Any amino sugar in which an amino group replaces a hydroxyl group of a sugar other than the group attached to the first carbon atom. **M20.**

glycosaminoglycan /ɡlʌɪˌkəʊsəmiːnəʊˈɡlʌɪkan/ *noun*. **M20.**
[ORIGIN from GLYCOSAMINE + -O- + GLYCO- + -AN.]

BIOCHEMISTRY. Any of a group of polysaccharides which contain amino-sugar residues, are often found in complexes with protein molecules as proteoglycans, and include heparin, chondroitin, hyaluronic acid, and the blood-group substances.

glycoside /ˈɡlʌɪkəsʌɪd/ *noun*. **L19.**
[ORIGIN from GLYCO- after GLUCOSIDE.]

CHEMISTRY. †**1** See GLUCOSIDE. **L19.**

2 Any of a class of sugar derivatives, many of which occur in plants, in which the hydroxyl group attached to the first carbon atom of a sugar is replaced by some other group, usually an alcohol or phenol. **M20.**

■ **glycosidic** /-ˈsɪd-/ *adjective* of the nature of or characteristic of a glycoside **E20. glycosidically** /-ˈsɪd-/ *adverb* **M20.**

glycosuria /ɡlʌɪkəˈsjʊərɪə/ *noun*. **M19.**
[ORIGIN French *glycosurie*, †*gluco-* formed as GLUCOSE, -URIA.]

MEDICINE. The presence of glucose in the urine.

■ **glycoˈsuric** *adjective* pertaining to or exhibiting glycosuria **L19.**

glycosyl /ˈɡlʌɪkə(ʊ)sɪl, -sʌɪl/ *noun*. **M20.**
[ORIGIN from GLYCO- + -OSE[2] + -YL.]

BIOCHEMISTRY. A monovalent radical derived from a sugar by removing a hydroxyl group from an anomeric carbon atom. Usu. in *comb.*

■ **glyˈcosylate** *verb trans.* introduce a glycosyl group into (a compound) **M20. glycosyˈlation** *noun* **M20.**

glycuronic /ɡlʌɪkjʊˈrɒnɪk/ *adjective*. **L19.**
[ORIGIN Irreg. from GLYCO- + Greek *ouron* urine + -IC.]

CHEMISTRY & BIOCHEMISTRY. = GLUCURONIC.

glycyl /ˈɡlʌɪsʌɪl, -sɪl/ *noun*. **E20.**
[ORIGIN from GLYC(INE + -YL.]

CHEMISTRY. The monovalent radical $H_2N{\cdot}CH_2CO{\cdot}$ derived from glycine.

glycyrrhizin /ɡlɪsɪˈrʌɪzɪn/ *noun*. **M19.**
[ORIGIN from late Latin *glycyrrhiza* from Greek *glukurrhiza* LIQUORICE: see -IN[1].]

CHEMISTRY. A very sweet-tasting glycoside from liquorice root which has a triterpene as the aglycone and is used in the food and drug industries.

glyde /ɡlʌɪd/ *noun*. *Scot. arch.* Also †**gleyde**. **M16.**
[ORIGIN Unknown.]

An old worn-out horse.

glyoxal /ɡlʌɪˈɒksal/ *noun*. **M19.**
[ORIGIN from GLY(COL + OX(ALIC + -AL[2].]

CHEMISTRY. The compound $(CHO{\cdot})_2$, occurring as yellow crystals or a yellow liquid and used industrially.

■ **glyoxylate** *noun* a salt or ester, or the anion, of glyoxylic acid (***glyoxylate cycle***, a variant of the Krebs cycle in some micro-organisms) **M19. glyoxaline** *noun* = IMIDAZOLE **M19. glyoˈxylic** *adjective*: ***glyoxylic acid***, the acid $CHO{\cdot}COOH$, a syrupy liquid, and its hydrated crystalline form $CH(OH)_2{\cdot}COOH$, which is a metabolic intermediate and occurs esp. in unripe fruit **M19.**

glyph /ɡlɪf/ *noun*. **L18.**
[ORIGIN French *glyphe* from Greek *gluphē* carving, rel. to *gluphein* carve.]

1 *ARCHITECTURE*. An ornamental groove or channel, usu. vertical. **L18.**

2 A sculptured character or symbol. **E19.**

■ **glyphic** *noun & adjective* (**a**) *noun* (*rare*) an illustration, a glyph; (**b**) *adjective* carved, sculptured: **E18.**

glyphography /ɡlɪˈfɒɡrəfi/ *noun*. Now *hist.* **M19.**
[ORIGIN from Greek *gluphē* (see GLYPH) + -OGRAPHY.]

A printing process in which a relief electrotype block is made from an image engraved through a coating of wax on a metal plate.

■ **ˈglyphograph** *noun* a plate made by glyphography; an impression taken from such a plate: **M19. glyphographer** *noun* **M19. glyphoˈgraphic** *adjective* pertaining to or produced by glyphography **M19.**

glyphosate /ˈɡlʌɪfəseɪt/ *noun*. **L20.**
[ORIGIN from GLY(CINE + PHOS(PHO- + -ATE[1].]

A non-selective systemic herbicide that is especially effective against perennial weeds.

glyptal /ˈɡlɪpt(ə)l/ *noun*. Also ***G-**. **E20.**
[ORIGIN Perh. from GLY(CEROL + *phthalic*.]

An alkyd resin, *esp.* one made from glycerol and phthalic anhydride or phthalic acid.

– NOTE: Proprietary name in the US.

glyptic /ˈɡlɪptɪk/ *noun & adjective*. **E19.**
[ORIGIN French *glyptique* or Greek *gluptikos*, from *gluptēs* carver, from *gluphein* carve: see -IC.]

▸**A** *noun*. *sing.* & in *pl.* (treated as *sing.*). The art of carving or engraving, esp. on precious stones. **E19.**

▸**B** *adjective*. Of or pertaining to glyptics. **M19.**

■ **glyptical** *adjective* (*rare*) = GLYPTIC *adjective* **L19. glyptically** *adverb* **M20.**

glyptodont /ˈɡlɪptədɒnt/ *noun*. Also **-don** /-dɒn/. **M19.**
[ORIGIN formed as GLYPTOGRAPHY + -ODONT.]

An extinct mammal of Cenozoic times whose few teeth were grooved, related to the armadillos but much larger and with a bony shield round the body and tail.

glyptography /ɡlɪpˈtɒɡrəfi/ *noun*. **L18.**
[ORIGIN from Greek *gluptos* carved + -OGRAPHY. Cf. French *glyptographie*.]

The art of engraving gems; the branch of knowledge that deals with engraved gems.

GM *abbreviation*[1].

1 Genetically modified.

2 George Medal.

3 Grant-maintained.

gm *abbreviation*[2].
Gram(s).

G-man /ˈdʒiːman/ *noun*. Pl. **G-men** /-mɛn/. **E20.**
[**ORIGIN** Prob. from Government + **MAN** *noun*; in sense 1 perh. an arbitrary use of *G*.]
1 In Ireland, a political detective. **E20.**
2 A special agent of the Federal Bureau of Investigation. *US*. **E20.**

GMT *abbreviation*.
Greenwich Mean Time.

GMWU *abbreviation*.
General and Municipal Workers' Union.

gn. *abbreviation*.
guinea(s).

gnädige Frau /ˈgnɛːdɪgə frau/ *noun phr.* **M20.**
[**ORIGIN** German, lit. 'gracious lady': see **FRAU**.]
A polite title or form of address for a German or German-speaking (esp. married) woman, corresp. to English *Madam*.

gnädiger Herr /ˈgnɛːdɪgər hɛː/ *noun phr.* **E20.**
[**ORIGIN** German, lit 'gracious sir': see **HERR**.]
A polite title or form of address for a German or German-speaking man, corresp. to English *Sir*.

gnamma hole /ˈnamə həʊl/ *noun phr. Austral.* Also **namma hole**. **L19.**
[**ORIGIN** Nyungar *ngamar* + **HOLE** *noun*[1].]
A natural hole in a rock, containing water; a waterhole.

gnap /nap/ *verb & noun*. **ME.**
[**ORIGIN** Imit.]
▸ **A** *verb intrans. & trans.* Infl. **-pp-**. Make a snapping bite (at). Now *Scot.* **ME.**
gnap at *fig.* find fault with.
▸ **B** *noun*. A bite, a morsel. *Scot.* **M18.**

gnar *noun* var. of **KNAR**.

gnar /nɑː/ *verb intrans.* Now *arch. & dial.* Infl. **-rr-**. Also **gnarr**, **narr**. **LME.**
[**ORIGIN** Imit.: cf. Middle Low German *gnarren*, German *knarren* creak, *knurren* snarl.]
Snarl, growl.

gnarl /nɑːl/ *noun*. **E19.**
[**ORIGIN** Back-form. from **GNARLED**. Cf. **KNARL**, **KNURL** *noun*.]
A contorted knotty protuberance, esp. on a tree.

†**gnarl** *verb*[1] *intrans.* **L16–M19.**
[**ORIGIN** Frequentative of **GNAR** *verb*.]
Snarl.

gnarl /nɑːl/ *verb*[2] *trans.* **E19.**
[**ORIGIN** Back-form. from **GNARLED**.]
Contort, twist, make knotted and rugged like an old tree. Chiefly as ***gnarled*** pa. pple.

gnarled /nɑːld/ *adjective*. **E17.**
[**ORIGIN** Var. of **KNURLED**.]
Of a tree or a part of the body: covered with knotty protuberances; knobbly and rough, as with age and exposure to the weather.

C. MACKENZIE The old man held out his gnarled fist. M. RENAULT The oldest of the apple trees, too gnarled to bear.

– **NOTE**: Rare (Shakes.) before **E19.**

gnarly /ˈnɑːli/ *adjective*. **M19.**
[**ORIGIN** from **GNARL** *noun*[1] + **-Y**[1]: cf. **KNURLY**. Sense 2 (first used by surfers) perh. referred orig. to the appearance of rough sea.]
1 = **GNARLED**. **M19.**
2 Difficult, dangerous, challenging. Also, unpleasant, unattractive; (of music, sound, etc.) harsh, rough. *colloq.* (orig. and chiefly *US*). **L20.**

gnarr *verb* var. of **GNAR** *verb*.

gnash /naʃ/ *verb & noun*. In sense B.2 also **nash**. **LME.**
[**ORIGIN** Uncertain: perh. imit., or alt. of **GNAST**.]
▸ **A** *verb*. **1** *verb intrans.* (Of a person or animal) strike together or grind the teeth, esp. in rage; (of the teeth) strike together. **LME.**
2 *verb trans.* Strike together or grind (the teeth), esp. in rage. **L16.**
3 *verb trans.* Bite, gnaw. **E18.**
▸ **B** *noun*. **1** A gnashing or snap of the teeth. *rare.* **E19.**
2 Biting remarks; insolent talk. *Scot.* **E19.**
■ **gnasher** *noun* †(**a**) a person who gnashes; (**b**) in *pl.* (*slang*) teeth, *esp.* false teeth: **L15.** **gnashing** *verbal noun* the action of the verb; an instance of this: **L15.** **gnashingly** *adverb* with gnashing teeth; in a way that makes one gnash one's teeth: **E20.**

†**gnast** *verb*. **ME.**
[**ORIGIN** from base of Old Norse *gnast(r)an* gnashing of teeth, *gneista* emit sparks, *gnesta* clatter.]
1 *verb intrans.* = **GNASH** *verb* 1. **ME–M16.**
2 *verb trans.* = **GNASH** *verb* 2. Only in **ME.**

gnat /nat/ *noun*[1].
[**ORIGIN** Old English *gnætt* corresp. to Low German *gnatte*, German dial. *Gnatze* rel. to Middle Low German *gnitte*, German *Gnitze*.]
1 Any of numerous small mostly biting dipteran insects with long thin fragile legs, many of which are in the family Culicidae (cf. **MOSQUITO** *noun*[1]); spec. *Culex pipiens*, found near stagnant water. **OE.**
2 Something small and insignificant. **OE.**
strain at a gnat: see **STRAIN** *verb*[1].
– **COMB.**: **gnatcatcher** any of various tiny Old World warblers of the genus *Polioptila*, found in the warmer parts of N. and S. America; **gnat-eater** any of various small birds of the genus *Conopophaga*, related to the antbirds, which occur in the forests of northern and eastern S. America; **gnat-snap**, **gnat-snapper** a bird that catches gnats; **gnat's piss** *slang* a very weak or poor-quality drink.
■ **gnatlike** *adjective & adverb* (**a**) *adjective* resembling (that of) a gnat; (**b**) *adverb* in the manner of a gnat: **L19.**

gnat /nat/ *noun*[2]. *obsolete* exc. *dial.* **E17.**
[**ORIGIN** Var. of **KNOT** *noun*[2], prob. infl. by *gnat-snap*, *-snapper* (see **GNAT** *noun*[1]).]
= **KNOT** *noun*[2].

gnathic /ˈnaθɪk, ˈneɪ-/ *adjective*. **L19.**
[**ORIGIN** from Greek *gnathos* jaw + **-IC**.]
Of or pertaining to the jaws.
■ Also **gnathal** *adjective* **L19.**

gnathion /ˈneɪθɪɒn/ *noun*. **L19.**
[**ORIGIN** formed as **GNATHIC** + *-ion*, after *inion*.]
ANATOMY. The lowest point in the middle of the lower edge of the lower jaw.

†**gnatho** *noun*. Pl. **-os**. **M16–E18.**
[**ORIGIN** Latin *Gnatho*: see **GNATHONIC**.]
A parasite, a sycophant.

gnatho- /ˈneɪθəʊ/ *combining form* of Greek *gnathos* jaw, forming terms chiefly in *ZOOLOGY*: see **-O-**.
■ **gnathobase** *noun* (*ZOOLOGY*) a process on the proximal part of a segmented limb in some arthropods which is used to bite or crush food **L19.** **gnatho'basic** *adjective* (*ZOOLOGY*) of, pertaining to, or of the nature of a gnathobase **E20.** **gnathochi'larium** *noun* [Greek *kheilos* lip] *ZOOLOGY* a platelike structure in the floor of the mouth of a millipede **L19.** **gnatho'stomatous** *adjective* = **GNATHOSTOME** *adjective* **L19.** **gnathostome** *noun & adjective* (of, pertaining to, or designating) a vertebrate with fully developed upper and lower jaws **E20.**

gnathonic /neɪˈθɒnɪk/ *adjective*. Now *rare*. **M17.**
[**ORIGIN** Latin *Gnathonicus*, from *Gnatho(n-)* sycophantic character in Terence's *Eunuchus*, from Greek *gnathōn* parasite, from *gnathos* jaw: see **-IC**.]
Sycophantic, toadying.
■ †**gnathonical** *adjective* = **GNATHONIC** **M16–M17.** †**gnathonically** *adverb* **L16–E17.**

gnatling /ˈnatlɪŋ/ *noun*. **E17.**
[**ORIGIN** from **GNAT** *noun*[1] + **-LING**[1].]
A small gnat.

gnatoo /nəˈtuː, *foreign* ˈŋatuː/ *noun*. **E19.**
[**ORIGIN** Polynesian (now *gatu*).]
A textile made in Tonga from the bark of the paper mulberry.

gnatter /ˈnatə/ *verb*[1] *trans. & intrans. obsolete* exc. *dial.* **M18.**
[**ORIGIN** Unknown.]
Nibble (at or *at*).

gnatter *verb*[2] *& noun* see **NATTER**.

gnatty /ˈnati/ *adjective*. **M19.**
[**ORIGIN** from **GNAT** *noun*[1] + **-Y**[1].]
Resembling a gnat; infested with gnats.

gnaur *noun* var. of **KNAR**.

gnaw /nɔː/ *verb & noun*. Pa. t. **gnawed**; pa. pple **gnawed**, **gnawn** /nɔːn/.
[**ORIGIN** Old English *gnagan* = Old Saxon *gnagan*, Old High German *(g)nagan* (German *nagen*), Old Norse *gnaga*, of imit. origin.]
▸ **A** *verb*. **1** *verb trans.* (with *away*, *off*, etc.) & *intrans.* (with *at*, *into*, *on*). Bite (something) persistently so as to damage or remove parts of it; wear away by continued biting; make (a hole etc.) by gnawing. **OE.**

J. BUCHAN In the loft the rats had gnawed great holes in the floor. E. BLYTON He . . sat down contentedly to gnaw the fine bone. A. CARTER Philip made a hearty meal and gnawed on the bones like Henry VIII.

2 *verb trans. & intrans.* (with *at*, *into*, †*on*). Of a destructive agent, or a pain or emotion: corrode, eat away, consume; torture, torment. **ME.**

J. LONDON The thought gnawed in his brain, an unceasing torment. A. MILLER She is almost content; she knows she might well be content but something gnaws at her.

▸ **B** *noun*. (A) gnawing. **M18.**
■ **gnawable** *adjective* **L19.** **gnawer** *noun* a person who or thing which gnaws; *spec.* a rodent: **L15.** **gnawing** *verbal noun* the action of the verb; an instance of this: **ME.** **gnawing** *adjective* that gnaws; (of a worry, pain, etc.) persistent; worrying: **M16.** **gnawingly** *adverb* **M19.**

gneeve /gniːv/ *noun*. *Irish*. Now *rare*. **M17.**
[**ORIGIN** Irish *gníomh*.]
The twelfth part of a ploughland.

gneiss /nʌɪs/ *noun*. Also (earlier) †**kneiss**. **M18.**
[**ORIGIN** German from Old High German *gneisto* (= Old English *gnāst*, Old Norse *gneisti*) spark.]
A foliated usu. coarse-grained metamorphic rock in which bands of granular minerals alternate with bands of flaky or prismatic ones, and typically consisting of feldspar, quartz, and mica.
■ **gneissic** *adjective* of the nature of or composed of gneiss; characteristic of gneiss: **M19.** **gneissoid** *adjective* resembling gneiss **M19.** **gneissose** *adjective* = **GNEISSIC** **M19.** **gnei'ssossity** *noun* gneissic character or structure **E20.** **gneissy** *adjective* = **GNEISSIC** **M18.**

gnocchi /ˈn(j)ɒki, ˈgnɒki, *foreign* ˈɲokki/ *noun pl.* **L19.**
[**ORIGIN** Italian, pl. of *gnocco*, from *nocchio* knot in wood.]
Small dumplings made with flour, semolina, or potato.

gnome /nəʊm, ˈnəʊmi/ *noun*[1]. **L16.**
[**ORIGIN** Greek *gnōmē* thought, judgement, opinion, *gnōmai* pl., sayings, maxims, from *gnō-* base of *gignōskein* **KNOW** *verb*.]
A short pithy statement expressing a general truth; a maxim, an aphorism.

gnome /nəʊm/ *noun*[2]. **M17.**
[**ORIGIN** French from mod. Latin *gnomus* used by Paracelsus as a synonym of *Pygmaeus*.]
1 A member of a legendary subterranean race of diminutive beings, typically represented as bearded old men and supposedly guardians of the earth's treasure; a goblin, a dwarf. **M17.**
2 A statue or figure of a gnome, *esp.* one used as a garden ornament. **M20.**
3 An international, esp. Swiss, financier or banker, regarded as having sinister influence. Chiefly in ***gnomes of Zurich***, ***Zurich gnome***. *colloq.* **M20.**

gnomic /ˈnəʊmɪk/ *adjective*[1]. **E19.**
[**ORIGIN** Greek *gnōmikos* (perh. through French *gnomique*), formed as **GNOME** *noun*[1]: see **-IC**.]
1 Of, consisting of, or of the nature of gnomes or aphorisms; (of a writer) given to using gnomes or aphorisms. **E19.**

N. FRYE Blake . . is perhaps the finest gnomic artist in English literature. CLIVE JAMES Auden has for a long time been manufacturing gnomic utterances and quiddities of his own.

2 *GRAMMAR*. Of a tense: used to express a general truth without implication of time. **M19.**
■ **gnomical** *adjective* = **GNOMIC** *adjective*[1] **E17.** **gnomically** *adverb* **E17.**

gnomic /ˈnəʊmɪk/ *adjective*[2]. **M19.**
[**ORIGIN** from **GNOME** *noun*[2] + **-IC**.]
Of or resembling a gnome or dwarf.

gnomish /ˈnəʊmɪʃ/ *adjective*. **E19.**
[**ORIGIN** from **GNOME** *noun*[2] + **-ISH**[1].]
Resembling a gnome or dwarf.

gnomist /ˈnəʊmɪst/ *noun*. *rare*. **E18.**
[**ORIGIN** from **GNOME** *noun*[1] + **-IST**.]
A gnomic poet or writer.

gnomology /nəʊˈmɒlədʒi/ *noun*. **M17.**
[**ORIGIN** Greek *gnōmologia*, formed as **GNOME** *noun*[1]: see **-OLOGY**.]
1 A collection of general maxims or precepts. **M17.**
2 The gnomic element in writing or a work. **E19.**
■ **gnomo'logic** *adjective* (*rare*) = **GNOMIC** *adjective*[1] **M18.** **gnomologist** *noun* (*rare*) = **GNOMIST** **E19.**

gnomon /ˈnəʊmɒn/ *noun*. **M16.**
[**ORIGIN** French or Latin from Greek *gnōmōn* inspector, indicator, carpenter's square, from *gnō-*: see **GNOME** *noun*[1].]
1 A pillar, rod, etc., which shows the time of day by casting its shadow on a marked surface; *esp.* the pin or triangular plate of a sundial. **M16.** ▸**b** A column etc. used in observing the meridian altitude of the sun. **E17.**
†**2** The nose. *joc.* **L16–E19.**
3 **a** *GEOMETRY*. The part of a parallelogram left after a similar parallelogram is taken away from one of its corners. **L16.** ▸†**b** *gen.* Something shaped like a carpenter's square; an L-shaped bar. **M17–L18.**
†**4** A guide, an indicator; an indicating instrument. **L16–M18.**
†**5** A rule, a canon of belief or action. Only in **17.**

gnomonic /nəʊˈmɒnɪk/ *adjective & noun*. **E17.**
[**ORIGIN** Latin *gnomonicus* from Greek *gnōmonikos*, from *gnōmōn*: see **GNOMON**, **-IC**.]
▸ **A** *adjective*. **1** Of or pertaining to a gnomon or sundial or the measuring of time by this. **E17.** ▸**b** Designating a map projection in which the centre of projection is the centre of the sphere being mapped. **E18.**
2 = **GNOMIC** *adjective*[1]. **E18.**
▸ †**B** *noun*. = **GNOMONICS**. Only in **M17.**
■ **gnomonical** *adjective* = **GNOMONIC** *adjective* **L16.** **gnomonically** *adverb* **E18.**

gnomonics /nəʊˈmɒnɪks/ *noun*. **L17.**
[**ORIGIN** Pl. of **GNOMONIC** *noun*: see **-ICS**.]
hist. The art of using or constructing dials.

gnoscopine /ˈnɒskəpiːn/ *noun*. **L19.**
[**ORIGIN** from Greek *gignōskein* know + **OP**(IUM + **-INE**[5].]
Either of two isomeric alkaloids, $C_{22}H_{23}NO_7$, of which one occurs in opium.

gnosiology /nəʊzɪˈɒlədʒi/ *noun*. Also **gnose-**. **L19.**
[**ORIGIN** formed as **GNOSIS** + **-OLOGY**.]
The branch of knowledge that deals with cognition or the cognitive faculties.
■ **gnosio'logical** *adjective* **E20.**

gnosis /ˈnəʊsɪs/ *noun*. Pl. **gnoses** /ˈnəʊsiːz/. **L16.**
[**ORIGIN** Greek *gnōsis* investigation, knowledge, from *gno-*: see **GNOME** *noun*[1].]
A special knowledge of spiritual mysteries; *spec.* in *THEOLOGY*, the redemptive knowledge that the Gnostics

claimed to have of God and of the origin and destiny of humankind.

gnostic /ˈnɒstɪk/ *noun & adjective*. L16.
[ORIGIN ecclesiastical Latin *gnosticus* from Greek *gnōstikos*, from *gnōstos* known, from *gnō-*: see GNOME *noun*[1], -IC.]
▸ **A** *noun*. (**G-**.) A member of a heretical Christian sect of the 1st to the 3rd cents. AD who claimed gnosis. Usu. in *pl.* L16.
▸ **B** *adjective*. **1** Relating to knowledge; cognitive; intellectual. M17. ▸†**b** Clever, knowing. *joc.* or *slang*. E–M19.
2 (**G-**.) Of or pertaining to the Gnostics; mystic, occult. M19.
■ **gnostical** *adjective* = GNOSTIC *adjective* E19. **gnostically** *adverb* E19. **Gnosticism**, **g-** *noun* (the principles of) the religious movement or beliefs of the Gnostics M17. **gnosticize** /-saɪz/ *verb trans. & intrans.* (*a*) *verb intrans.* adopt or expound Gnostic principles; (*b*) *verb trans.* give a Gnostic character to: M17.

gnotobiology /ˌnəʊtəʊbʌɪˈɒlədʒi/ *noun*. M20.
[ORIGIN formed as GNOTOBIOTIC + BIOLOGY.]
= GNOTOBIOTICS.

gnotobiotic /ˌnəʊtəʊbʌɪˈɒtɪk/ *adjective*. M20.
[ORIGIN from Greek *gnōtos* known, from *gnō-*: see GNOME *noun*[1], -O-, BIOTIC.]
Of an animal or an environment: rendered free from the bacteria etc. normally present, or having only a few known organisms of this kind present.
■ **gnotoˈbiote** *noun* a gnotobiotic animal M20.

gnotobiotics /ˌnəʊtəʊbʌɪˈɒtɪks/ *noun*. M20.
[ORIGIN from GNOTOBIOTIC: see -ICS.]
The branch of knowledge that deals with producing and using gnotobiotic organisms.

GNP *abbreviation*.
Gross national product.

Gnr *abbreviation*.
Gunner.

gns *abbreviation*.
Guineas.

gnu /nuː, njuː; gn-/ *noun*. L18.
[ORIGIN from Khoisan, prob. through Dutch *gnoe*.]
= WILDEBEEST.
brindled gnu = *blue* WILDEBEEST. **white-tailed gnu** = *black* WILDEBEEST.

GNVQ *abbreviation*.
General National Vocational Qualification.

go /gəʊ/ *noun*[1]. Pl. **goes**. L17.
[ORIGIN from the verb.]
1 The action or an act of going. L17.
2 An unforeseen turn of affairs, esp. causing embarrassment. *colloq.* L18.
> K. AMIS 'Rum go, that,' said George when she had left.

3 A turn or attempt at something; a spell of something; a period of activity; *spec.* (*a*) a delivery of the ball or bowl at skittles etc.; (*b*) an attack of an illness; (*c*) a fight, an argument. L18.
> R. DAHL It looked like a bad go of malaria. J. JOSEPH You can . . grow more fat And eat three pounds of sausages at a go. W. GOLDING Most of the pyramid collapsed in one go.

4 A quantity of liquor, food, etc., served at one time. Formerly also, a vessel containing this quantity. *colloq.* L18.
> W. COBBETT Plates of beef and goes of gin. K. MOORE After consuming . . chocolate buns and a second go of sandwiches.

5 *The* height of fashion, *the* rage. Now only in ***be all the go, be quite the go***. *colloq.* L18.
6 Mettle, spirit, dash, animation; *colloq.* vigorous activity. E19.
> F. NORRIS There's no go, no life in me at all these days. A. BROOKNER It is all go here, a veritable whirl of activity.

7 A success; a bargain, an agreement. L19.
> U. SINCLAIR It's a go, then. I'm your man. A. WEST How any two people could make a go of a union that began with so much resentment and hostility.

— PHRASES: **give it a go** *colloq.* make an effort to succeed. ***great go***: see GREAT *adjective*. **have a go** (*a*) make an attempt, act resourcefully; *spec.* take independent or single-handed action against a criminal or criminals; (*b*) (foll. by *at*) attack, find fault with. ***little go***: see LITTLE *adjective*. **near go** *colloq.* a narrow escape. ***no go***: see NO *adjective*. **on the go** *colloq.* †(*a*) on the verge of destruction or decline; (*b*) in constant motion, in a restless state. ***open go***: see OPEN *adjective*. ***square go***: see SQUARE *adjective*.
— COMB.: **go-devil** *US* a movable contrivance used to clean the interior of pipes etc.; **go-fever** *colloq.* feverish restlessness or longing for movement.

go /gəʊ/ *noun*[2]. L19.
[ORIGIN Japanese.]
A Japanese board game of territorial possession and capture, played with usu. black and white stones or counters on a board marked with intersecting lines. Cf. WEI CH'I.

go /gəʊ/ *adjective*. E20.
[ORIGIN from the verb.]
1 Designating a gauge which must pass through or be passed through the piece. Cf. NO-GO, NOT-GO. E20.
2 Esp. of a device in a spacecraft: functioning properly; ready and prepared. *colloq.* M20.
3 Fashionable, progressive. *colloq.* M20.

go /gəʊ/ *verb*. Pa. t. **went** /wɛnt/, (*Scot. & N. English*) **gaed** /geɪd/, †**yede**, †**yode**; pa. pple **gone** /gɒn/, (*dial.*) **went**. 2 sing. pres. (*arch.*) **goest** /ˈgəʊɪst/; 3 sing. pres. **goes** /gəʊz/, (*arch.*) **goeth** /ˈgəʊɪθ/.
[ORIGIN Old English *gān* = Old Frisian *gān*, *gēn*, Old Saxon *gān* (Dutch *gaen*), Old High German *gān*, *gēn* (German *gehen*), from Germanic. The original pa. t. (Old English *ēode*) was superseded in southern English by forms from WEND *verb*[1] from 15.]
▸ **I** Of movement, irrespective of point of departure or destination.
†**1** *verb intrans.* Walk; move on foot at an ordinary pace; (esp. of a horse) step in a specified manner. OE–M19.
> BUNYAN I have resolved to run when I can, to go when I cannot run, and to creep when I cannot go. DEFOE My horse went very awkwardly and uneasy.

2 *verb intrans.* Move or pass along, proceed, journey, travel, progress (by any means); HUNTING ride to hounds. OE. ▸**b** *verb trans.* with *adverbial obj.* Travel over (a specified distance) or at (a specified speed); (with cognate obj.) go on (an errand, journey, etc.). Formerly also with direct obj.: go through (a tract of country etc.) or over (a river etc.). ME.
> T. HARDY The four went in one cab to Raye's lodgings. J. PUDNEY Our child now marches through the town, Bearing her own child as she goes. E. WELTY The train . . was going at eighty miles an hour. A. PRICE You'll have to go carefully . . . You'll need professional advice. ISAIAH BERLIN One cannot try and go up a staircase down which an army is trying to march. W. TREVOR High above them an aeroplane goes over. **b** SPENSER I went the wastefull woodes and forest wyde. L. MACNEICE Dials Professing to tell the distance We have gone, the speed we are going.

3 *verb intrans. & trans.* with *adverbial obj.* Take a specified course (of movement or action). OE. ▸**b** *verb intrans.* Be guided or regulated *by*; act in accordance or harmony *with*; judge or act (*up*)*on*; *colloq.* base a conclusion or course of action (*up*)*on*. L15. ▸**c** *verb intrans.* Of a line etc.: lie, point in a specified direction. L19.
> THOMAS HUGHES An exhortation to . . go outside of the barge which was coming up. M. CORELLI She will never go my way,—nor, I fear, shall I ever go hers. **b** V. S. PRITCHETT You mustn't go by faces. P. ACKROYD If the editorials of *The Times* are anything to go by. P. ROTH They had nothing to go on but the most elemental manhood.

go astray, go wrong, etc.
4 *verb intrans.* Be habitually or for a time in a specified state (now esp. of privation or disadvantage). Cf. sense 14 below. OE.
> J. GATHORNE-HARDY I went for years thinking there was something wrong with me. P. ACKROYD At first he went hungry because he did not know how to beg.

5 *verb intrans.* Of a female: be pregnant (more fully ***go with child*** etc.), esp. for a specified time. Now chiefly as ***gone*** *ppl adjective* (see sense 34 below). ME.
6 *verb intrans.* Of time: pass, elapse. ME.
> R. C. HUTCHINSON There was still over half an hour to go before my day's work began. J. RATHBONE The next two hours or so went quickly.

7 *verb intrans.* Be current or accepted; be known *by* or *under the name* etc. *of*. ME.
> DRYDEN Love is the only coin in heaven will go. LD MACAULAY The monk who . . sometimes went by the alias of Johnson. R. TRAVERS Butler in fact went under the name Newman.

8 *verb intrans.* (Of events, a performance, activity, etc.) have a course or outcome of a specified kind, proceed or turn out *well* etc.; (of a contest, election, etc.) issue or result in a specified manner, result *for* or *against*; (of a constituency, voter, etc.) take a specified course or view. ME. ▸**b** Be successful; *colloq.* be acceptable or permitted, be accepted without question. M18.
> SCOTT FITZGERALD Things went from bad to worse, until finally he had to give up his position. E. BOWEN How is your book going? A. TYLER The marriage wasn't going well and I decided to leave my husband. **b** M. ALLINGHAM Anything goes if it's done by someone you're fond of.

9 *verb intrans.* Be moving, acting, or working; (of a clock, watch, etc.) keep time in a specified manner; (of a bell, striking clock, gun, etc.) emit a sound in functioning; make a specified movement; (with imit. interjection or verb stem used adverbially) make a specified sound or (audible) movement. ME. ▸**b** *verb trans.* Of a clock etc.: strike to indicate (a specified hour). Of an hour etc.: be struck (chiefly in *perf. tenses*, has been struck). E18.
> R. C. HUTCHINSON My fire was still going when I finished. D. MAHON The empty freighters . . In a fine rain, their sirens going. N. MAILER Boom! the waves would go against the wall. A. T. ELLIS She didn't go 'Aah' over babies and brides and the Princess of Wales. **b** K. HULME The clock's just gone eleven.

10 *verb intrans.* Have ordinarily in degree or range of value or quality, be on average. LME.
> L. WOOLF As professional journalists go, Sharp was not a bad editor.

11 *verb intrans.* Of a verse, song, etc.: be pleasingly or rhythmically constructed, proceed fluently; admit of being sung, or be usually sung, *to* a specified tune. L16.
> SHAKES. *Wint. T.* This is a passing merry one, and goes to the tune of 'Two maids wooing a man'.

12 *verb intrans.* Of a document, verse, tune, etc.: run, have a specified content, wording, or tenor. E17.
> DICKENS Those who are put in authority over me (as the catechism goes).

▸ **II** With the point of departure prominent.
13 *verb intrans.* Move away, depart, leave; begin to move from a given point or state; begin an action. In *imper.*, used as a starter's word in a race. OE.
> J. CONRAD The last vestiges of youth had gone off his face. G. GREENE His anger went as quickly as it came. C. ODETS Pack up your clothes and go! Go! Who the hell's stopping you? I. MURDOCH At any sign of emotion he quietly went, leaving the room noiselessly like an animal.

14 *verb intrans.* Get away *free*, *unpunished*, etc., (orig. from a court of justice etc.). Passing into sense 4. ME.
> T. TANNER It . . has not gone unnoticed—that her language is marked by a minimum of physical action.

15 *verb intrans.* Be relinquished, dismissed, abolished, or lost; (of money) be spent (*in*, *on* a thing); be sold (*at*, *for* an amount). ME.
> M. J. GUEST Whatever money he got . . it all went in books. W. GOLDING His hair was gone on top except for a tiny black tuft. K. VONNEGUT The money was gone. S. CHITTY A small gouache of a girl in church . . went for £2,000.

16 *verb intrans.* Die. LME.
> D. LESSING You'll get what money I have when I go.

17 *verb intrans.* Fail, give way, break down, crack; succumb to pressure or any deteriorating influence. M18.
> J. RHYS The fuse which lights the whole house has gone. M. DRABBLE She still thought that her brain might go or that her nerve might snap.

▸ **III** With the direction or destination prominent, of self-originated movement.
18 *verb intrans.* Make one's way or proceed to or towards a specified place etc. or in a specified direction (in some contexts with the notion of an activity to be engaged in or way of life to be adopted uppermost); (of a road etc.) lead. (Foll. by *to, towards, into*, etc.) OE. ▸**b** Urinate, defecate. *colloq.* M20.
> J. STEINBECK She lighted a candle and went to the kitchen in her bare feet. P. ROTH Maria thought she'd have to go over to New York to buy the black underwear.

19 *verb intrans.* Make one's way or proceed with a specified purpose (foll. by preposition phr., *to do, and do*, (now *colloq. & N. Amer.*) *do*). Foll. by *doing*, (arch.) *a-doing*: make an expedition to engage in the specified activity, *colloq.* be so foolish as to do the specified thing. OE. ▸**b** (With noun compl.) Be employed as, go to be, become. Now only in ***go bail***, act as bail (*for* a person). M17.
> SHAKES. *Com. Err.* Our dinner done, and he not coming thither, I went to seek him. DONNE Goe and catch a falling starre. GOLDSMITH I was resolved not to go sneaking to the lower professors. R. SUTCLIFF We went for picnics and for days out in the car. J. DAVIS Are you ready to go play golf?

20 *verb intrans.* Proceed to some specified course of action or means of attaining one's object; have recourse, refer, appeal, *to*. ME.
> J. S. BLACKIE You must go to Aristotle for that.

21 *verb intrans. & trans.* with *adverbial obj.* Carry action to a specified point of progress or completeness; raise a bid or offering price to a specified level. L16. ▸**b** *verb intrans.* Put or subject oneself *to* (trouble, expense). M19. ▸**c** *verb trans.* Venture as far as, go to the extent of; like to partake of or engage in (esp. in ***I could go a*** — etc.). M19.
> M. J. GUEST Strafford really went some way towards bringing his scheme to pass. H. JAMES My mother has not gone into details. E. WAUGH Twenty-five pounds . . . Thirty. I can't go higher than that. A. J. AYER He went so far as to quarrel with Gilbert Ryle. **b** A. T. ELLIS You needn't have gone to all this trouble our first night. **c** D. BALLANTYNE I could go a good feed of eels just now.

22 *verb trans.* Stake, wager, risk, adventure; bid, declare; *US* enter into a wager with (a person). E17.
> MARVELL This Gentleman would always go half a Crown with me. D. L. SAYERS He went three no trumps on the ace of spades singleton, five hearts to the king, queen.

▸ **IV** With the direction or destination prominent, of imparted movement.
23 *verb intrans.* Be carried, moved, or impelled; penetrate, sink. Foll. by *to, towards, into*, etc. OE.
> I. MURDOCH The casement windows were open as wide as they could go.

24 *verb intrans.* Be applied or appropriated *to*, *to do*; contribute *to* or *towards* a result, *to do*; conduce or tend *to*, *to do*. ME. ▸**b** Amount together or be equivalent *to*. M19.

W. COWPER There goes more to the composition of a volume than many critics imagine. T. JEFFERSON Those geographical schisms which go immediately to a separation. W. GOLDING Never let her know . . . It would just go to feed her vanity.

25 *verb intrans. & trans.* with **adverbial obj.** Reach, attain, extend, hold out, suffice, or last to a specified point. **LME.** ▸**b** *verb trans.* Yield, produce, (a specified amount). *US*. **E19.**

J. LOCKE No man's knowledge here can go beyond his experience.

26 *verb intrans.* Pass into a specified condition; become, get to be; be transformed or reduced *to*. **L16.**

E. WAUGH And he went to sleep for a little, with his head in her lap. M. PUZO Sandra noticed that her husband's face had gone red with flushing blood. A. BROOKNER She was recognizable, he saw thankfully, not gone to seed.

27 *verb intrans.* Be allotted or awarded *to*; pass by inheritance, succession, or otherwise *to*. **E17.**

R. H. MOTTRAM Two of the sadly depleted companies went to adjacent farms, two remained on the premises. A. MCCOWEN Sometimes I was given a part that should perhaps have gone to another actor.

28 *verb intrans.* Be able to pass *into, through*, etc.; be able to find room or fit *in, into*; (of a number) admit of being contained in another either without remainder or at all. **L17.** ▸**b** Be usually placed or kept, belong, *in, on*, etc. **E18.**

M. J. GUEST All the good we can find about him will go into a very few words. P. ROTH Eight from one doesn't go, so we must borrow one from the preceding digit.

▸ **V** Special uses of ***gone*** pa. pple. See also **GONE** *ppl adjective*.

29 †**a** Ago, formerly. **ME–M17.** ▸**b** Reckoned from the specified past date. **M19.** ▸**c** (Of time) past; over the specified age. **M19.**

c *Temple Bar* A man 'gone ninety years of age'. B. UNSWORTH He glanced at his watch. It was gone twelve.

30 ***be gone***, depart. Cf. **BEGONE** *verb*[1]. **L16.**

31 Dead. Formerly also, unconscious. **L16.**

32 Lost; hopeless, ruined; failed. **L16.**

SCOTT FITZGERALD It possessed the interest of a souvenir by representing a mood that was gone. J. BAYLISS With broken wing they limped across the sky/ . . with their gunner dead, / one engine gone.

33 Infatuated. (Foll. by *on* a person.) **L17.**

F. ASTAIRE Anything and everything about Phyllis was first and foremost with me. I was gone. S. BELLOW I was gone on her and . . gave her a real embrace.

34 Pregnant; having spent the specified period in gestation. (More fully ***gone with child*** etc.) **L17.**

J. CARY The woman was far gone with child. D. JACOBSON She must have been about five months gone. Even her face looked pregnant, somehow.

35 ***gone!***, just sold (an auctioneer's announcement). **L18.**

▸ **VI** Special uses of ***going*** pres. pple (in senses 39, 40 orig. verbal noun after **A** *preposition*[1] 8: see **GOING** *noun* III). See also **GOING** *ppl adjective*.

36 ***going to do, going to be done***: orig., on the way to, preparing to, tending to; now usu., about to, intending or intended to, likely to. See also **GONNA**. **LME.**

J. BUCHAN Listen, Sir Harry . . . You're a good fellow, and I'm going to be frank. *Observer* One man wrote and said he was going to kill me—but he gave his name and address. P. ROTH 'You are going to get yourself in trouble.' 'Not me.'

37 ***going*** —, ***going on (for)*** —, †***going upon*** —, †***going in*** —, †***going of*** —, approaching the specified number (esp. of years of age), time, etc. **E17.**

E. BOWEN At this hour, going on six o'clock. J. RABAN She had been five, going six. A. BURGESS How clever we are when we are seventeen going on eighteen. P. LIVELY The Lisa of today is an anxious busy woman going on for forty.

38 ***going!***, on the point of being sold (an auctioneer's announcement). **L18.**

39 Existing; to be had. **L18.**

S. L. ELLIOTT There's a cup of cocoa going. V. GLENDINNING Ear trouble, eye trouble, bronchial trouble . . and every infection going.

40 In or into action or motion. **E19.**

W. J. KNOX-LITTLE She kept the conversation going. J. GARDNER Lit the new cigarette from the one he had going.

41 ***going for***, favourable or advantageous to, to be said in favour of. **M20.**

W. WHARTON The only thing a bird has going for it is that it can fly away. *Times* I think the plans . . seem excellent. The offer has a lot going for it.

– **PHRASES ETC.**: (A selection of cross-refs. only is included: see esp. other nouns.) ***been and*** —, ***been and gone and*** —: see **BE** *verb*. ***be gone***: see sense 30 above. ***easy come, easy go***: see **EASY** *adverb* 1. ***far gone***: see **FAR** *adverb*. **from the word go** *colloq.* from the very beginning. ***get going***: see **GET** *verb*. ***get oneself gone***: see **GET** *verb*. ***get up and go***: see **GET** *verb*. ***go a long way***: see **WAY** *noun*. **go at it** *slang* copulate. ***go bail***: see sense 19b above. **go big** *slang* be a big success, have a large sale. ***go by the name of***: see sense 7 above. †**go by the worse, go by the worst** be worsted. **go for it** make an all-out attempt at something. ***go gangbusters***: see **GANG** *noun*. **go it** *slang* go at great speed, act rapidly, vigorously, or furiously; engage in reckless dissipation. ***go it alone***: see **ALONE** 1. **go it strong** *slang* go to great lengths, use exaggeration. ***go like hot cakes***: see **CAKE** *noun*. ***go near***: see **NEAR** *adverb*[2]. ***go off the handle***: see **HANDLE** *noun*[1]. ***go one better***: see **BETTER** *adjective* etc. ***go one's way(s)***: see **WAY** *noun*. **go on the stage** *spec.* become an actor. **go on the streets** *spec.* become a prostitute. ***go over big***: see **BIG** *adverb*. ***go* OVERBOARD**. ***go places***: see **PLACE** *noun*[1]. ***go public***: see **PUBLIC** *adjective & noun*. ***go shares with***: see **SHARE** *noun*[2]. ***go short***: see **SHORT** *adverb*. ***go sick***: see **SICK** *adjective*. **go slow** *spec.* work at a deliberately slow pace. ***go soft on***: see **SOFT** *adjective*. **go somewhere** *euphem.* go to the toilet. ***go steady***: see **STEADY** *adverb*. ***go the distance***: see **DISTANCE** *noun*. ***go the pace***: see **PACE** *noun*[1]. ***go the vole***: see **VOLE** *noun*[1]. **go the way of all the earth, go the way of all flesh** [*1 Kings* 2:2, *Joshua* 23:14] die. ***go the whole hog***: see **HOG** *noun*. **go to a better place, go to a better world** die. **go to it** *colloq.* begin work (usu. in *imper.*). ***go to one's account***: see **ACCOUNT** *noun*. **go to sea** (*a*) go on a sea voyage; (*b*) become a sailor. **go to show** serve as evidence or proof (*that*). **go to the Bar** *spec.* become a barrister. ***go under the name of***: see sense 7 above. ***go* WALKABOUT**. ***go west***: see **WEST** *adverb*. ***go with child***: see sense 5 above. ***go without saying***: see **SAYING** *noun* 1. **go with the tide, go with the times** do as others do. ***have* SOMETHING *going***. ***here goes!***: see **HERE** *adverb*. **how goes it?**, **how is it going?**, **how are things going?** what progress is being made? how are things with you? ***leave go***: see **LEAVE** *verb*[1]. ***let go***: see **LET** *verb*[1]. **let it go at that** let that account etc. be accepted, let us say no more about it. **not go far** *esp.* be soon spent or used. ***there you go***: see **THERE** *adverb*. ***the story goes***: see **STORY** *noun*[1]. **to be going on with** to start with, for the time being. **to go** (chiefly *N. Amer.*) (of refreshments etc.) for taking away from the place of supply before consumption. ***to hell and gone***: see **HELL** *noun*. ***touch-and-go***: see **TOUCH** *verb*. **what has gone of —?** *arch.* what has become of —? what is the matter with —? **who goes there?**: a sentry's challenge.

– **WITH ADVERBS IN SPECIALIZED SENSES** (see also Phrases above): **go about** (*a*) move from place to place, circulate; (*b*) endeavour *to do*; be in the habit of *doing*; (*c*) *NAUTICAL* change to the opposite tack. **go ahead** proceed without hesitation (*with*). **go aloft** *slang* die. **go along** (*a*) ***go along with you!***: expr. dismissal, impatience, or derision; (*b*) proceed or travel in company *with*; go *with*. **go around** = ***go round*** below. **go away** depart, leave, esp. from home for a holiday; (of a problem etc.) cease to be an issue. **go back** (*a*) return (*to*); (*b*) turn one's thoughts backward in time (*to*); (*c*) extend backwards (in space or time), have a history going back *to*; (*d*) ***go back on***: change one's mind about honouring (one's word etc.); prove disloyal to, betray; ***go back from***: go back on (one's word etc.); (*e*) (of a clock, watch, etc.) be set to an earlier time representing a changed basis for national time-reckoning. **go by** (*a*) pass, go past; †(*b*) go unregarded. **go down** (*a*) proceed, move, or change to a lower place or condition; (of a ship etc.) sink, (of a person) be *on* a ship etc. that sinks; (of the sun etc.) set; (*b*) be continued *to* a specified point; (*c*) be overthrown, be defeated, be beaten, (foll. by *before* a conquering influence etc., *to* a conqueror); fail, deteriorate, decline in health or prosperity; (of a computer etc.) cease to function; fall ill *with* (a disease); (*d*) be recorded in writing; (*e*) be swallowed; (*f*) find acceptance *with*; be received in a specified manner; (*g*) leave a university or college, esp. permanently; *slang* be sent to prison; (*h*) *BRIDGE* fail to fulfil one's contract; (*i*) *slang* happen; (*j*) ***go down*** (slang), perform fellatio or cunnilingus (*on*). **go far** *fig.* (*a*) achieve much, be successful; (*b*) contribute greatly *towards*; (*c*) (of food, money, etc.) last long, suffice for long or for many, buy much. **go in** (*a*) enter as a competitor (***go in and win!***: expr. encouragement); (*b*) *CRICKET* take or begin an innings; (*c*) (of the sun etc.) become obscured by cloud; (*d*) ***go in for***: adopt as an object, pursuit, interest, style, or principle; enter as a candidate or competitor. **go off** (*a*) leave, depart, esp. suddenly; leave the stage; (*b*) (of a firearm etc.) explode, be discharged; (of an alarm etc.) sound, be activated; (*c*) die; gradually cease to be felt; (*d*) deteriorate; lose brightness, quality, or vigour; decay; (*e*) start *into* a sudden action, break *into* a fit of laughter etc.; pass suddenly *into* a state; (*f*) become unconscious in sleep, a faint, etc. (also ***go off to sleep*** etc.); (*g*) be disposed of by sale or (of a daughter, *arch.*) in marriage; (*h*) be received or accomplished in a specified manner, result in a specified way; (*i*) ***go off at*** (Austral. & NZ slang), reprimand, scold. **go on** (*a*) proceed on a journey or to another place; continue, persevere, persist, (*doing, with, in*); (*b*) proceed *to, to do* as one's next step; in *imper.* (*colloq.*) encouraging the overcoming of reluctance; (*c*) fare, manage, get on, (*arch.*); conduct oneself, behave, (esp. reprehensibly); (*d*) be in progress, happen, take place; (*e*) talk tediously or persistently (*about*) (also ***go on and on***: continually, at tedious length); *colloq.* rail or grumble *at*; (*f*) appear on stage; *CRICKET* begin bowling; (*g*) (of a garment etc.) be large enough for the wearer; (*h*) as *interjection* (*colloq.*) expr. disbelief, ridicule, etc. (cf. **GARN** *interjection*); (see also sense 37 above). **go out** (*a*) leave a room, house, or other building; (*b*) go on a military campaign, take to the field (chiefly *hist.*); fight a duel; (*c*) be extinguished; cease to be lit; *colloq.* fall asleep, lose consciousness, (esp. in ***go out like a light***); (*d*) (of the tide) recede; (*e*) (of a Government etc.) leave office; be defeated in or eliminated from a contest (foll. by *to* a victor); (*f*) (of a year) come to its end; (*g*) cease to be fashionable or popular; (*h*) depart *to* a colony etc.; (*i*) *arch.* (esp. of a girl or woman) find employment away from home; (*j*) mix in society, attend social engagements; keep company (*together, with*), esp. regularly in a romantic or sexual relationship; (*k*) (of workers) abandon work, go on strike; (*l*) be published, be issued, be broadcast; (*m*) (of the heart etc.) expand with love or sympathy *to* (a person); (*n*) play the first 9 holes in a round of golf (comprising 18 holes); (*o*) *CARDS* be the first to dispose of one's hand. **go over** (*a*) change one's allegiance or religion (*to*); (*b*) communicate to an audience in a specified manner; be well received, be successful. **go round** (*a*) revolve, rotate; (of the head) reel, swim; (*b*) circulate, pass from person to person; move about; be regularly in company *with*; be in the habit of *doing*; (*c*) make a detour; pay an informal visit *to*; (*d*) be long enough to encompass the desired thing; (of food etc.) suffice for the whole party, satisfy need or demand. **go through** †(*a*) complete an enterprise or undertaking; (*b*) be approved, accepted, or carried; pass all stages to completion; (*c*) ***go through with***, carry to completion, not leave unfinished; (*d*) *Austral. slang* desert, abscond. **go to** †(*a*) go about one's work; (*b*) in *imper.* (*arch.*) expr. remonstrance, incredulity, impatience, etc. **go together** (*a*) be concomitant or compatible, match; (*b*) go out together on a romantic or sexual basis. **go under** sink, fail, succumb, die. **go up** (*a*) proceed, move, or change to a higher place or condition; (of sound) become audible); (*b*) (*colloq.*, chiefly *US*) go to ruin, go bankrupt, die, be killed; (*c*) be raised, be erected, be reared; (*d*) begin to attend a university or college; (*e*) increase in price, number, or value; (*f*) explode; be consumed *in flames, smoke*. **to go** *US* (of food and drink) to be taken away for consumption, for taking away.

– **WITH PREPOSITIONS IN SPECIALIZED SENSES** (see also Phrases above): **go about —** busy oneself about, set to work at, take in hand. **go against —** (*a*) result unfavourably to; (*b*) run counter to, oppose, militate against. **go at —** attack, take in hand energetically; (see also sense 15 above). **go before —** (*a*) precede in time or serial order; †(*b*) *rare* take precedence of, be superior to. †**go between —** act as mediator or messenger between. **go by —** †(*a*) neglect, pass without notice; (*b*) pass by; *US* call in at or on, visit; (see also sense 3b above). **go for —** †(*a*) set out for; (*b*) go to fetch or reach; go to become; (*c*) pass as or as equivalent to, be accounted or valued as, (now only *nothing, little*, etc.); (*d*) have as one's aim, strive to attain; (*e*) prefer, choose, like; (*f*) *colloq.* attack, assail, (physically or verbally); (*g*) be valid for, be applicable to; (see also senses 15, 41 above). **go into —** (*a*) become a member of, start a career in, (a profession, Parliament, etc.); frequent (society etc.); (*b*) join or take part in, be a part of; (of effort, resources, etc.) be invested in, be devoted to; †(*c*) agree to, accede to; (*d*) pass into (a state or condition), enter into (a process); allow oneself to pass into (hysterics etc.); (*e*) dress oneself in (mourning etc.); (*f*) investigate, examine or discuss minutely; (*g*) go to stay in, be admitted to, (hospital etc.); (see also senses 18, 23, 28 above). **go off —** (*a*) *rare* shirk, fail to fulfil; (*b*) begin to dislike. **go on —** †(*a*) take up (a subject) for discussion; begin, undertake, (an action); (*b*) become chargeable to (the parish, relief funds, etc.); (*c*) *colloq.* care for or concern oneself (*much* etc.) about (usu. in neg. contexts); (see also senses 3b, 15, 28b above). **go over —** (*a*) inspect the various parts or details of; (*b*) review, rehearse, repeat; (*c*) retouch; (*d*) *slang* search and rob. **go through —** (*a*) deal with the successive stages of; (*b*) discuss or examine in detail, scrutinize (successively); (*c*) perform (a ceremony, recitation, etc.), *spec.* at full length; (*d*) undergo, experience, suffer; (*e*) use up, spend (money), make holes in; (*f*) (of a book) be successively published in (so many editions); (*g*) *slang* search and rob, search. **go upon —** †(*a*) attack; †(*b*) (of a judicial authority) consider the case of; (*c*) *arch.* take in hand; (see also sense 3b above). **go with —** (*a*) accompany; *colloq.* go out with on a romantic or sexual basis; (*b*) be associated with, be a concomitant of; (*c*) take the same view as, side with; (*d*) harmonize with, match; (*e*) follow the drift of, understand; (see also sense 3b above). **go without —** not have, put up with the lack of, (something specified or (*absol.*) understood contextually).

– **COMB.**: **go-ashore** *adjective & noun* (*a*) *adjective* designating clothes worn or articles used by sailors when ashore; (*b*) *noun* (*NZ*) an iron cauldron with three feet and attachments for hanging it over a fire; **go-as-you-please** *adjective & noun* (*a*) *adjective* unfettered by regulations; (*b*) *noun* absence of (concern for) regulations; **go-easy** *adjective* easy-going, characterized by going easy; **go-faster stripes** striped stickers on the bodywork of a car, esp. horizontally along the doors, intended to make it look more sporty; **go-in** *arch. colloq.* (foll. by *at*) an attack on, a spell of work on; **go-off** the action or an act of going off, a time of going off, a start, (esp. in ***at the first go-off***); **go-round** *N. Amer.* (*a*) the action or an act of going round; (*b*) a fight, a beating, an argument; a bad experience; **go-slow** an industrial protest in which work is done at a deliberately slow pace; **go-team** *US* a group of investigators who can be dispatched immediately to investigate an accident, attack, etc.; **go-to guy** *US colloq.* a person who can be relied upon for help or support; **go-to-meeting** *adjective* (*US colloq.*) (of clothing) fit or kept for going to church in.

Goa /ˈgəʊə/ *noun*[1]. **L17.**

[**ORIGIN** A district on the west coast of India, or its seaport (now Panaji).]

Used ***attrib.*** to designate things found in or associated with Goa.

Goa ball = ***Goa stone*** below. **Goa bean** (the seed of) a twining leguminous plant of tropical Asia and Africa, *Psophocarpus tetragonolobus*, grown esp. in SE Asia for its edible roots and four-winged seed pods. **Goa butter** = **KOKUM**. **Goa powder** a bitter yellowish powder obtained from cavities in the wood of the Brazilian araroba tree, containing the drug chrysarobin and used to treat skin diseases; also called ***araroba***. **Goa stone** (*obsolete* exc. *hist.*) an amalgam of fever remedies in a hard ball.

goa /ˈgəʊə/ *noun*[2]. **M19.**

[**ORIGIN** Tibetan *dgoba*.]

The Tibetan gazelle, *Procapra picticaudata*, with backward-curving horns.

goad /gəʊd/ *noun*.

[**ORIGIN** Old English *gād* = Lombard *gaida* arrowhead, from Germanic.]

1 A pointed stick for driving cattle. **OE.** ▸**b** *fig.* Anything which torments, excites, or stimulates. **M16.**

b E. P. THOMPSON Poverty was an essential goad to industry.

2 A linear measure, orig. the length of a goad. Also, a square measure of varying quantity. Long *obsolete* exc. *dial.* **LME.**

– **COMB.**: **goadman**, **goadsman** a cattle driver.

goad /gəʊd/ *verb trans.* **L16.**

[**ORIGIN** from the noun.]

Urge on or drive with or as with a goad; spur, incite, torment.

D. H. LAWRENCE The blame was torture, like knives goading him. I. HAMILTON Recriminations simply goaded him into a deeper fury. J. A. MICHENER He galloped to the river's edge and goaded the beast to plunge in. P. USTINOV The inconstancy of a crowd goaded by rhetoric.

G

goaf /ɡəʊf/ *noun*[1]. *obsolete* exc. *dial.* ME.
[ORIGIN Old Norse *gólv* floor, apartment (Swedish *golv*, Danish *gulv* floor, bay of a house or barn). Cf. GOAVE *verb*.]
A grain stack made in one bay of a barn.

goaf /ɡəʊf/ *noun*[2]. Also **goave** /ɡəʊv/. M19.
[ORIGIN Uncertain: cf. GOB *noun*[3].]
MINING. An empty space from which coal has been extracted, and where the roof has been allowed to fall in.

go-ahead /ˈɡəʊəhɛd/ *adjective & noun*. M19.
[ORIGIN from GO *verb* + AHEAD *adverb*.]
▸ **A** *adjective*. Enterprising, having energy and initiative. M19.
▸ **B** *noun*. **1** Enterprise, energy and initiative. *US*. M19. **2** Permission to proceed. Chiefly in ***the go-ahead***. M20.
■ **go-aˈheadative** *adjective* (*US*) characterized by enterprise or energy and initiative M19. **go-aˈheadativeness** *noun* (*US*) M19. **go-aˈheadism** *noun* enterprise, energy and initiative M19.

goal /ɡəʊl/ *noun*. ME.
[ORIGIN Unknown.]
†**1** A boundary, a limit. Only in ME.
2 In various games: the space between two posts, a net, basket, etc., into which a ball or puck is driven in order to score a point or points; a successful attempt to get the ball etc. into this area; the point or points scored. M16.

H. H. TAN The ball arced over the goal. C. NEWLAND The PE team scored a goal in extra time to win.

keep goal: see KEEP *verb*. ***own goal***: see OWN *adjective*.
3 The finishing point of a journey or race; something marking this. M16.

fig.: E. YOUNG Crown'd with Laurels, fairly won, Sits smiling at the goal, while others run.

4 The object of one's ambition or effort; a desired end or result. E17. ▸**b** *spec.* in *PSYCHOLOGY*. An end or result towards which behaviour is consciously or unconsciously directed. E20.

C. STEAD The ultimate goal—to get a rich husband.

5 *ROMAN ANTIQUITIES*. **a** A conical column marking either of two turning points in a chariot race. M17. ▸**b** The starting point of a race. *rare*. L17.
– COMB.: **goal average** the ratio of numbers of goals scored by and against a team in a series of matches; **goal difference** the difference between the number of goals scored and goals conceded by a team in a series of matches; **goalhanger** *SOCCER* (*derog.*) a player who spends much of the game near the opposing team's goal in the hope of scoring easy goals; **goalkeeper** a player whose duty is to prevent a ball etc. from entering a goal; **goal kick** (*a*) *SOCCER* a kick by a defending side after the attackers have sent a ball over the goal line; (*b*) *RUGBY* a kick at goal; **goal line** the line between each pair of goalposts, extended to form the end boundary of the field of play; **goalmouth** the area between goalposts or immediately in front of a goal; **goalminder** = *goaltender* below; **goalpost** either of the two upright posts of a goal; ***move the goalposts***, unfairly alter the conditions or rules of a procedure during its course; **goaltender** *N. Amer.* a goalkeeper in ice hockey.
■ **goalie** *noun* (*colloq.*) a goalkeeper E20. **goalless** /-l-l-/ *adjective* (*a*) having no destination or purpose, aimless; (*b*) without a goal scored by either side: L19. **goalward** *adjective* M19. **goalwards** *adverb* L19.

goal /ɡəʊl/ *verb trans.* E20.
[ORIGIN from the noun.]
RUGBY. Convert (a try) into a goal.

Goan /ˈɡəʊən/ *noun & adjective*. E20.
[ORIGIN from GOA *noun*[1] + -AN.]
= GOANESE.

Goanese /ɡəʊəˈniːz/ *noun & adjective*. M19.
[ORIGIN from GOA *noun*[1] + -*n*- + -ESE.]
▸ **A** *noun*. Pl. same. A native or inhabitant of Goa. M19.
▸ **B** *adjective*. Of or belonging to Goa. M19.

goanna /ɡəʊˈanə/ *noun*. *Austral.* M19.
[ORIGIN Alt. of GUANA.]
Any of various lizards, esp. large monitors of the genus *Varanus*.

go-around /ˈɡəʊəraʊnd/ *noun*. Chiefly *US*. E20.
[ORIGIN from ***go around*** s.v. GO *verb*.]
1 The action of avoiding, evading, or slighting. Chiefly in ***give the go-around to***. *colloq.* E20.
2 *AERONAUTICS*. The action of taking a circular flight path, esp. after an aborted landing. M20.
3 A confrontation or argument. *colloq.* M20.

goat /ɡəʊt/ *noun*.
[ORIGIN Old English *gāt* (pl. *gǣt*) = Old Saxon *gēt* (Dutch *geit*), Old High German *geiz* (German *Geiss*), Old Norse *geit*, Gothic *gaits*, from Germanic base rel. to Latin *haedus* kid.]
▸ **I 1** Any of various agile, coarse-haired, hollow-horned ruminant mammals of the bovid genus *Capra*, native to rocky terrain of N. Africa and Eurasia; *esp.* the domesticated *C. hircus*, descended from the wild bezoar and reared worldwide for milk, wool, and meat. Orig. (in Old English) *spec.* a female animal of this kind (cf. BUCK *noun*[1] 1). OE. ▸**b** The flesh of this as food. ME. ▸**c** Leather made from goatskin. L19.
angora goat, ***Kashmir goat***, etc.
2 Any of various horned bovids resembling *Capra*, esp. any of the same subfamily Caprinae, e.g. the chamois. Cf. ***goat-antelope*** below. ME.
▸ **II 3** The domestic goat as a symbol of a (damned) sinner (usu. in *pl.*, with ref. to *Matthew* 25:32, 33). Cf. SHEEP *noun* 2. OE. ▸**b** A licentious man; a lecher. L16. ▸**c** A scapegoat; a person who (rightly or wrongly) takes the blame. *US*. L19. ▸**d** A fool. *colloq.* E20.
4 (Usu. **G-**.) *The* constellation and zodiacal sign Capricorn. LME.
– PHRASES ETC.: **act the goat** = ***play the giddy goat*** below. ***billy goat***: see BILLY *noun*[2] 3. **get a person's goat** *colloq.* make him or her angry; annoy. **goat and bee jug** a moulded Chelsea porcelain jug with two goats and a small bee in relief. ***JUDAS goat***. NANNY GOAT. **play the giddy goat**, **play the goat** frolic, fool about, act irresponsibly. ***ROCKY MOUNTAIN goat***. **separate the sheep from the goats** (with allus. to *Matthew* 25:32, 33) sort the good persons or things from the bad or inferior.
– COMB.: **goat-antelope** a bovid of the subfamily Caprinae; *spec.* one of the tribe Rupicaprini of goats resembling antelopes, which includes the goral, serow, chamois, and Rocky Mountain goat; **goat-fig** any of various wild figs; **goatfish** orig., any of various fishes usu. having barbels below the mouth; now *spec.* (chiefly *US*), a red mullet; **goat-foot** a faun or satyr, the Greek god Pan; **goat-footed** *adjective* (*a*) having cloven hoofs like a goat; (*b*) sure-footed, nimble; **goat god** the Greek god Pan; **goathair** *adjective & noun* (made of) the skin or hair of a goat; **goatherd** a person who tends goats; **goatherdess** (now *rare*) a female goatherd; **goat moth** any moth of the worldwide family Cossidae, having reduced mouthparts and often wood-boring larvae, *esp.* the large Eurasian *Cossus cossus*, whose caterpillar smells like a goat; **goat nut** = JOJOBA; **goat-rue** = ***goat's rue*** below; **goat's foot** a South African low-growing plant of the wood sorrel family, *Oxalis caprina*; **goat's horns** a South African dwarf succulent plant of the carpetweed family, *Cheiridopsis candidissima*; **goatskin** *adjective & noun* (made of) the skin of a goat; **goat's rue** (*a*) = GALEGA; (*b*) a N. American leguminous plant, *Tephrosia virginiana*, having pink and yellow flowers; **goat's thorn** any of several spiny plants of the mainly north temperate leguminous genus *Astragalus*, of which some are a source of gum tragacanth; **goatsucker** (now chiefly *N. Amer.*) a nightjar; **goat tang** a red seaweed, *Polyides rotundus* (order Gigartinales), which grows around the low-water mark; **goat weed** any of various tropical weeds with a goatlike odour, esp. *Ageratum conyzoides* of the composite family; **goat willow** a pussy willow, *Salix caprea*.
■ **goatish** *adjective* goatlike; *spec.* lecherous: E16. **goatishly** *adverb* M19. **goatishness** *noun* M19. **goatlike** *adjective* resembling or characteristic of a goat L16. **goatling** *noun* a young goat, *spec.* between twelve months and two years old L19. **goaty** *adjective* resembling or characteristic of a goat E17.

goatee /ɡəʊˈtiː/ *noun & adjective*. M19.
[ORIGIN from GOAT + -EE[2].]
(Designating) a beard resembling that of a goat, a narrow chin-tuft.

D. CAUTE A man in a yachting blazer and a goatee beard.

■ **goateed** *adjective* having a goatee M19.

goat's beard /ˈɡəʊtsbɪəd/ *noun*. Also ***goatsbeard**. M16.
[ORIGIN from GOAT + BEARD *noun*, translating Greek *tragopōgon* or Latin *barba capri*.]
1 Any of various plants of the genus *Tragopogon*, of the composite family, native to Eurasia, esp. *T. pratensis*, which has yellow flowers (also called ***Jack-go-to-bed-at-noon***). M16.
†**2** Meadowsweet. L16–E17.
3 Any of several fungi of the genus *Clavaria*. L17.
4 A plant of the rose family of (esp. American) northern temperate and subarctic regions, *Aruncus dioicus*, cultivated for its long spikes of small white flowers. M19.

goave *noun* var. of GOAF *noun*[2].

goave /ɡəʊv/ *verb trans.* Long *obsolete* exc. *dial.* ME.
[ORIGIN Rel. to GOAF *noun*[1].]
Stack (grain) in a goaf.

go-away /ɡəʊəˈweɪ, ˈɡəʊəweɪ/ *noun*. Also **go-way**. L19.
[ORIGIN Imit.]
In full ***go-away bird***. Any of several turacos constituting the genus *Corythaixoides*.

gob /ɡɒb/ *noun*[1]. LME.
[ORIGIN Old French *gobe*, *goube* mouthful, lump (mod. *gobbe* food-ball, pill), from *gober* swallow, gulp, perh. from Celtic Cf. GOB *noun*[2], GOBBET *noun*.]
1 A mass, a lump. Now chiefly *US* & *dial.* LME.

W. A. PERCY English was my favorite course . . because of the huge undigested gobs . . I'd already read.

†**2** A large sum of money. M16–L17.
3 A lump or large mouthful of food, esp. raw meat, fat, or gristle. M16.

H. B. STOWE They . . swallows it as a dog does a gob o' meat.

4 A lump or clot of any slimy or viscous substance. M16.

J. DOS PASSOS Let fly towards the cuspidor with a big gob of phlegm.

5 A lump of molten glass used to make a single bottle, jar, etc. E20.

gob /ɡɒb/ *noun*[2]. *dial.* (chiefly *N. English*) & *slang*. M16.
[ORIGIN Perh. from Gaelic & Irish = beak, mouth. Sense 2 may be a different word. See also GAB *noun*[2] and cf. GOB *noun*[1].]
1 The mouth. M16.
2 = GAB *noun*[2] 2. L17.
– COMB.: **gobsmacked** *adjective* (*slang*) [from the gesture of clapping a hand over the mouth] astounded, flabbergasted; speechless with amazement; **gobstick** (*a*) *dial.* a large spoon; (*b*) a device for freeing a hook from a fish's mouth; (*c*) *slang* a clarinet; **gobstopper** a large hard sweet for sucking; **gobstruck** *adjective* (*slang*) = ***gobsmacked*** above.

gob /ɡɒb/ *noun*[3]. M19.
[ORIGIN Perh. alt. of GOAF *noun*[2], infl. by GOB *noun*[1].]
MINING. An empty space from which coal has been extracted. Also, the rubbish used to pack such a space.

gob /ɡɒb/ *noun*[4]. *slang* (orig. *US*). E20.
[ORIGIN Uncertain: cf. GOBBY.]
An American sailor or ordinary seaman.

gob /ɡɒb/ *verb*[1] *intrans.* Infl. **-bb-**. M19.
[ORIGIN Perh. from GOB *noun*[1].]
Of a furnace: become choked or blocked.

gob /ɡɒb/ *verb*[2] *intrans. & trans.* Infl. **-bb-**. L19.
[ORIGIN from GOB *noun*[1].]
Expectorate, spit, cough *up*.

W. BOYD One particularly irate jaywalker went so far as to gob . . on his windscreen.

gobang /ɡəʊˈbaŋ/ *noun*. L19.
[ORIGIN Japanese *goban*, from *go* GO *noun*[2] + *ban* board.]
A simplified form of the game of go, in which each player seeks to place five counters in a row.

gobar /ˈɡɒbə(r)/ *noun*. *Indian*. E20.
[ORIGIN Hindi.]
Cattle dung.

gobbet /ˈɡɒbɪt/ *noun*. ME.
[ORIGIN Old French *gobet* dim. of *gobe* GOB *noun*[1].]
1 A piece, a portion, a fragment. ME. ▸**b** *spec.* A piece of raw flesh. ME. ▸**c** An extract from a literary or musical work; *spec.* a piece of text set for translation or comment in an examination. E20.

fig.: K. DOUGLAS Snatching little gobbets of glory for the regiment wherever possible. **c** *Daily Telegraph* Embellished with bits of Greek and well-worn gobbets from Milton and Yeats.

2 A lump or mass, now chiefly of viscous, congealed, or (semi-)liquid material. LME.

D. WELCH Rolls . . spread thickly with . . gobbets of rich black cherry jam.

3 A lump or mouthful of food. LME. ▸**b** A lump of half-digested food. M16.

†**gobbet** *verb trans.* LME.
[ORIGIN Partly from Old French *gobeter*, from *gobet* GOBBET *noun*, partly from the noun.]
1 Divide (esp. trout) into portions. LME–E18.
2 Swallow (*down*, *up*) as a gobbet or in gobbets. Only in 17.

gobbing /ˈɡɒbɪŋ/ *noun*. Also (chiefly *dial.*) **-in** /-ɪn/. M19.
[ORIGIN from GOB *noun*[3] + -ING[1].]
MINING. The packing of an excavated space with waste rock; the material used for this.

gobble /ˈɡɒb(ə)l/ *noun*[1]. L18.
[ORIGIN from GOBBLE *verb*[2].]
A characteristic gurgling sound made in the throat by a turkeycock.

gobble /ˈɡɒb(ə)l/ *noun*[2]. Now *hist.* M19.
[ORIGIN Prob. from GOBBLE *verb*[1].]
GOLF. A rapid straight putt into a hole.

gobble /ˈɡɒb(ə)l/ *verb*[1]. E17.
[ORIGIN Prob. from GOB *noun*[1] + -LE[3].]
1 *verb trans.* (foll. by *up*) & *intrans.* Eat hurriedly and noisily; consume greedily. E17.

B. MALAMUD Gobbled it down in three bites. *fig.*: K. AMIS Mrs. Welch's bill would gobble up his bank-balance.

2 *verb trans.* Seize avidly, grab, snatch (*up*). Orig. & chiefly *N. Amer.* E19.

Sunday Times Greig hit his first ball . . for two and the next one was gobbled up at short square.

gobble /ˈɡɒb(ə)l/ *verb*[2] *intrans.* L17.
[ORIGIN Imit., perh. infl. by GOBBLE *verb*[1].]
Of a turkeycock: make a characteristic gurgling sound in the throat. Also (*rare*), of a person: make a similar sound when speaking.
■ **gobbler** *noun* a turkey M18.

gobbledegook /ˈɡɒb(ə)ldɪɡuːk, -ʊk/ *noun*. Orig. *US*. Also **-dy-**. M20.
[ORIGIN Prob. imit., after GOBBLE *noun*[1].]
Official, professional, or pretentious verbiage or jargon.

†**gobbon** *noun*. LME–L16.
[ORIGIN Old French, app. rel. to *gobbe* and *gobet*: see GOB *noun*[1], GOBBET *noun*. Cf. GUBBIN.]
A piece, a slice, a gobbet; a gob of slimy material.

gobby /ˈɡɒbi/ *noun*. *slang*. L19.
[ORIGIN Perh. from GOB *noun*[1] + -Y[2]. Cf. GOB *noun*[4].]
A coastguard. Also (*US*), a sailor.

gobdaw /ˈgɒbdɔː/ *noun*. *slang* (chiefly *Irish*). M20.
[ORIGIN Perh. from GOB *noun*² + DAW *noun*, but cf. Irish *gabhdán* gullible person.]
A fool; a pretentious person.

Gobelin /ˈgəʊb(ə)lɪn, ˈgɒb-, -lɪn/ *adjective & noun*. Also (as noun) **Gobelins**. L18.
[ORIGIN from *Gobelins*, the French state-owned carpet and tapestry factory in Paris, named after its founders, the 15th-cent. Gobelin family, weavers and dyers.]
▸ **A** *adjective*. Designating things obtained from or associated with the Gobelins factory. L18.
Gobelin blue a greenish blue typically used in Gobelin tapestry. **Gobelin stitch** a short upright embroidery stitch, sometimes worked over a padded backing, giving the effect of tapestry. **Gobelin tapestry** (an imitation of) a tapestry made at the Gobelins factory.
▸ **B** *noun*. (A) Gobelin tapestry. E19.
C. WILMOT The apartments were hung over with fine Gobelins.

gobemouche /ˈgɒbmuːʃ/ *noun & adjective*. E19.
[ORIGIN French *gobe-mouches* fly-catcher, from *gober* swallow + *mouche* fly.]
(Designating) a person who credulously accepts all news.
C. MACKENZIE A new swarm of rumours the gobemouche parishioners swallowed . . eagerly.

go-between /ˈgəʊbɪtwiːn/ *noun*. L16.
[ORIGIN from GO *verb* + BETWEEN *adverb*.]
1 An intermediary, a negotiator. L16.
K. LAWRENCE He . . was reduced to being . . a go-between, who kept the machinery of other children's friendships working. J. HERSEY He had hired the notary . . as a go-between to find a suitable bride.
2 A thing that connects two others. M19.

gobiid /ˈgəʊbɪɪd/ *noun & adjective*. L19.
[ORIGIN mod. Latin *Gobiidae* (see below), formed as GOBY + -ID³.]
ZOOLOGY. ▸ **A** *noun*. Any fish of the family Gobiidae of gobies. L19.
▸ **B** *adjective*. Of, pertaining to, or designating this family. E20.

gobioid /ˈgəʊbɪɔɪd/ *noun & adjective*. M19.
[ORIGIN from mod. Latin *Gobioides* (former family name), formed as GOBY + -OID.]
ZOOLOGY. ▸ **A** *noun*. Any spiny-finned teleost fish of the perciform suborder Gobioidea, including the gobies and sleepers. M19.
▸ **B** *adjective*. Of or pertaining to the suborder Gobioidea. E20.

goblet /ˈgɒblɪt/ *noun*¹. LME.
[ORIGIN Old French & mod. French *gobelet* dim. of *gobel* cup: see -ET¹.]
1 A metal or glass drinking vessel, bowl-shaped and without handles, usu. having a foot and sometimes a cover. Also *poet*., any kind of drinking cup. LME. ▸**b** A glass or other vessel with a foot and a stem. L19.
2 A drink contained in such a vessel; a gobletful. LME.
†**3** A conical cup or thimble used by conjurors. E16–L17.
4 A thing resembling a goblet, as a goblet-shaped part of a flower. M19.
5 A goblet-shaped receptacle for food forming part of a food-blender or liquidizer. L20.
– COMB.: **goblet cell** ANATOMY any of numerous column-shaped cells found in the respiratory and intestinal tracts, which secrete the main component of mucus.
■ **gobletful** *noun* as much as a goblet will hold LME.

†**goblet** *noun*². L15–M18.
[ORIGIN Alt. of GOBBET *noun*: see -LET.]
= GOBBET *noun*.

goblin /ˈgɒblɪn/ *noun*¹. ME.
[ORIGIN Prob. Anglo-Norman (cf. Latin *gobelinus* an evil spirit which haunted Évreux, France in 12) and French *gobelin*; prob. dim. of the name *Gobel* (now *Gobeau*), app. rel. to KOBOLD, COBALT.]
A mischievous ugly demon.
■ **gobliˈnesque** *adjective* resembling a goblin E20. **goblinize** *verb trans.* (*rare*) change into a goblin E19. **goblinry** *noun* the practices of a goblin or goblins E19.

goblin /ˈgɒblɪn/ *noun*². *slang* (*obsolete* exc. *hist.*). Also **o'goblin** /əʊˈgɒblɪn/. L19.
[ORIGIN Abbreviation of ***Jimmy O'Goblin*** s.v. JIMMY *noun*² 2.]
A sovereign, twenty shillings.

gobo /ˈgəʊbəʊ/ *noun*. Orig. *US*. Pl. **-os**. M20.
[ORIGIN Unknown.]
CINEMATOGRAPHY & PHOTOGRAPHY. A portable screen used to shield a camera lens from light or a microphone from noise.

†**gobonated** *adjective*. L15–M19.
[ORIGIN from medieval Latin *gobonatus* (formed as GOBONY) + -ED¹.]
= GOBONY.

gobony /gɒˈbəʊni/ *adjective*. LME.
[ORIGIN from Old French base of GOBBON + -Y⁵.]
HERALDRY. Divided into squares of alternate tinctures in a single row; compony.

gobshite /ˈgɒbʃʌɪt/ *noun*. *coarse slang*. E20.
[ORIGIN Prob. from GOB *noun*² + SHITE: perh. two different words.]
1 An enlisted seaman. *US Naval slang*. *rare*. E20.
2 A stupid, incompetent, or contemptible person; *esp.* an ignorant loudmouth. Chiefly *Irish*. M20.

goby /ˈgəʊbi/ *noun*. M18.
[ORIGIN Latin *gobius*, *cobius* from Greek *kōbios* some small fish: cf. GUDGEON *noun*².]
Any of numerous small fishes of the worldwide perciform family Gobiidae, of marine coastal and fresh water, having typically a sucker formed of the united pelvic fins. Also, any other gobioid.

go-by /ˈgəʊbʌɪ/ *noun*. E17.
[ORIGIN from GO *verb* + BY *adverb*.]
1 The action of passing, outstripping, leaving behind, eluding, evading, disregarding, or slighting. Chiefly in ***give the go-by to***. E17.
THACKERAY Becky . . gave Mrs. Washington White the go-by in the Ring. R. L. STEVENSON A French ship . . gave us the go-by in the fog. H. JAMES Paul always gave the pleasantest go-by to any attempt to draw out his views.
2 *gen*. The action of going by. *rare*. L17.

GOC *abbreviation*.
General Officer Commanding.

go-cart /ˈgəʊkɑːt/ *noun*. L17.
[ORIGIN from GO *verb* + CART *noun*. See also GO-KART.]
1 A baby-walker. *arch*. L17.
2 A handcart. M18.
3 *hist*. A kind of light open carriage. E19.
4 A pushchair. M19.

Goclenian /gɒˈkliːnɪən/ *adjective*. E20.
[ORIGIN from Rudolph *Goclenius* (1547–1628), German logician who first formulated it: see -AN.]
LOGIC. Designating a variety of the sorites in which the order of the premisses is reversed, the subject of each proposition being the predicate of the next, the conclusion being formed of the last subject and first predicate.

god /gɒd/ *noun*. In branch II now usu. **G-**.
[ORIGIN Old English *god* (pl. *godu* neut., *godas* masc.) = Old Frisian, Old Saxon (Dutch) *god* masc., Old High German *got* (German *Gott*) masc., Old Norse *goð* neut. (as branch I), *guð* masc. and neut. (as branch II), Gothic *guþ* (pl. *guda* neut.), from Germanic, prob. ult. from Indo-European, repr. by Sanskrit *hū-* invoke the gods.]
▸ **I 1** A superhuman person regarded as having power over nature and human fortunes; a deity. Also, *the* deity *of* a specified area of nature, human activity, etc. OE.
D. CUPITT The gods have set bounds which cannot be overstepped with impunity. *Health Shopper* The Romans dedicated the garlic bulb to Mars, the god of war.
2 An image or object (as a plant or an animal) worshipped as symbolizing or constituting the visible habitation of a divinity or as itself possessing divine power; an idol. OE.
R. GRAVES The Romans trusted to their own visible tutelary gods, the golden Eagles of their legions.
3 *transf.* **a** An adored, admired, or supremely powerful person. OE. ▸**b** An adored or worshipped object; something exercising great or supreme influence. L16.
a SHAKES. *Rom. & Jul.* Swear by thy gracious self, which is the god of my idolatry. F. POLLOCK The ruling gods of the circulating libraries. **b** P. SIDNEY Like a man whose will was his God, and his hand his law.
4 In *pl.* (The occupants of) *the* gallery in a theatre. *colloq.* M18.
H. ROSENTHAL It was a wonderful experience to be downstairs instead of in the gods.
▸ **II 5** In Christianity and other monotheistic religions, the supreme being, regarded as the creator and ruler of the universe and source of all moral authority. Freq. as interjection & in exclamatory phrs. expressive (***a***) of a strong desire for the benefit or injury of a particular person or thing, as in ***God bless (you)***, ***God curse him***, ***God damn her***, ***God preserve you***, etc.); (***b***) of assertion or affirmation, as in ***as God sees me***, ***as God is my judge***, etc.; (***c***) of astonishment or shock, as in ***God bless me***, ***my God***, etc.; (***d***) of imprecation, as in ***God blast (it)*** etc.; (***e***) of outrage, pain, or anger, as in ***good God***, ***my God***, etc.; (***f***) of exasperation, as in ***for God's sake*** etc.; (***g***) of pleasure or relief, as in ***God be thanked***, ***thank God***, etc.; or (***h***) of (urgent) supplication, as in ***God forbid***, ***please God***, etc. Also in phrs. with possessive combinations expressive of an oath or adjuration, as in ***God's blood***, †***God's bodikins***, †***God's lid***, ***God's wounds***, etc., and formerly freq. with altered or fabricated words not otherwise found, as in †***God's sonties*** etc. OE.
HOBBES God, in which is contained Father, King, and Lord. C. V. WEDGWOOD The idea that he could be tried and condemned by the people over whom God had placed him.
– PHRASES ETC. (see also sense 5 above): **act of God** (an instance or the result of) the operation of uncontrollable natural forces. **a feast fit for the gods**, **a feast for the gods**, **a sight fit for the gods**, **a sight for the gods**, etc., something exquisite, a supremely pleasing prospect. ***blind god***: see BLIND *adjective*. ***by guess and by God***: see GUESS *noun*. ***find God***: see FIND *verb*. **God-a-mercy** *interjection & noun* (*arch.*) (***a***) *interjection* may God reward you; (***b***) *noun* an expression of approval or gratitude. ***God bless***: see BLESS *verb*¹. ***God bless the mark***: see MARK *noun*¹. ***God defend***: see DEFEND *verb*. ***God forbid***: see FORBID *verb*. **god from the machine** = DEUS EX MACHINA. ***God help (you)***: see HELP *verb*. ***God is for the big battalions***: see BATTALION *noun* 1. ***God knows***: see KNOW *verb*. **God of the gaps** God as an explanation of the unaccountable. ***God save the mark***: see MARK *noun*¹. **God the Father, God the Son, and God the Holy Spirit**, **God the Father, God the Son, and God the Holy Ghost**: the persons of the Trinity. **God willing** if Providence allows. **God wot** *arch.* God knows. ***Greek god***: see GREEK *adjective*. ***Hottentot god***: see HOTTENTOT *noun & adjective*. HOUSEHOLD ***gods***. ***house of God***: see HOUSE *noun*¹. ***in God's name***: see NAME *noun*. **in the lap of the gods** beyond human control. ***like the wrath of God***: see WRATH *noun*. ***little tin god***: see TIN *noun & adjective*. ***Lord God***: see LORD *noun* 5. ***Lord God of hosts***: see HOST *noun*¹. ***Mother of God***: see MOTHER *noun*¹. **on the knees of the gods** beyond human control. **play God** seek to be or behave as if all-powerful. ***put the fear of God into***: see FEAR *noun*¹. ***so help me God***: see HELP *verb*. ***Son of God***: see SON *noun*¹. ***thank God***: see THANK *verb*. ***the City of God***: see CITY 2. ***the Scourge of God***: see SCOURGE *noun* 2. ***the voice of God***: see VOICE *noun*. ***tin god***: see TIN *noun & adjective*. **under God** excepting the power and agency of God. ***wait on God***: see WAIT *verb*. ***walk with God***: see WALK *verb*¹ 6. **with God** dead and in heaven. **ye gods (and little fishes)** *interjection* (*mock-heroic*) expr. amazement, disbelief, etc.
– COMB.: **God-awful** *adjective* (*slang*, orig. *US*) extremely unpleasant, frightful; **God-botherer** *slang* (orig. MILITARY) (***a***) a chaplain or priest; (***b***) a deeply religious person; **God-bothering** *adjective slang* (orig. MILITARY) deeply religious; **God-box** *slang* a church or other place of worship; **godchild** a person (usu. a child) sponsored at baptism by a godparent or godparents, esp. as considered in relation to his or her godparents; **god-daughter** a female godchild; **God-fearing** *adjective* that fears God; deeply religious; **godmamma** (*nursery & colloq.*, esp. as a form of address) godmother; **godpapa** (*nursery & colloq.*, esp. as a form of address) godfather; **God's acre** [German *Gottesacker* 'God's seed-field' in which the bodies of the dead are 'sown' (*1 Corinthians* 15:36–44)] a churchyard; ***God's blood!***: see BLOOD *noun*; ***God's bodikins***: see sense 5 above; **God's book** the Bible; **God's country** = ***God's own country*** below; **God's earth** the whole earth; **God's gift** (freq. *iron.*) a godsend; **God slot** *colloq.* a period in a broadcasting schedule regularly reserved for religious programmes; **godson** a male godchild; **God's own (country)**, an earthly paradise, esp. (*joc.*) the US, Australia, or New Zealand regarded as such; **God's penny** [translating medieval Latin *denarius Dei* (whence French *denier à dieu*, Du *godspenning*, German *Gottespfennig*)] (now *dial.*) a small sum given as earnest money; **God squad** *slang* (the members of) a religious organization, esp. an evangelical Christian group; ***God's sonties***: see sense 5 above; ***God's wounds***: see WOUND *noun*. **Godzone** *Austral. & NZ colloq.* = ***God's own country*** above;
■ **goddize** *verb trans.* (long *rare*) make into or treat as a god, deify L16. **godkin** *noun* (now *rare*) = GODLING E19. **godlet** *noun* = GODLING L19. **godness** *noun* †(***a***) = GODHEAD; (***b***) *rare* divine element or nature: ME. **godship** *noun* (freq. *joc.*) the position or personality of a god (chiefly with possess. pronoun) M16. **Godward** *adverb* (***a***) in the direction of God, towards God; (***b***) in relation to God, with respect or reference to God: LME. **Godwards** *adverb* = GODWARD M16.

god /gɒd/ *verb trans.* Now *rare*. Infl. **-dd-**. L16.
[ORIGIN from the noun.]
1 Treat as a god; deify, worship. L16.
2 (Usu. **G-**.) Make partaker of the divine nature *with God*. Chiefly as ***Godded*** *ppl adjective*. Long *rare* or *obsolete*. L16.
3 Foll. by *it*: behave as a god. L19.

God Almighty /gɒd ɔːlˈmʌɪti/ *noun & adverbial phr.* OE.
[ORIGIN from GOD *noun* + ALMIGHTY *adjective*.]
▸ **A** *noun phr.* **1** = GOD *noun* 5. OE.
2 A person regarded as omnipotent; a person demanding an unreasonable degree of compliance and deference. Chiefly *joc.* or *derog.* L17.
▸ **B** *adverbial phr.* (Usu. with hyphen.) Extremely, excessively. *colloq.* E20.
D. H. LAWRENCE Why should people . . be so God-Almighty puffed up?

goddam /ˈgɒdam/ *noun, adjective, & adverb*. Also **-damn**, **G-**. M17.
[ORIGIN Abbreviation of *God damn (me)*: see GOD *noun*.]
▸ **A** *noun*. **1** An utterance of 'God damn (me)'; an imprecation, a curse. M17. ▸**b** = DAMN *noun* 2. E20.
M. REID The 'sacre' and the English 'Goddam', were hurled at everything Mexican. **b** B. SCHULBERG I don't give a goddam if you never move your ass off this seat again.
†**2** A person given to swearing. M17–E18.
3 [After French, from Old French *godon*.] An Englishman; *esp.* an English soldier. *arch.* M19.
G. B. SHAW If the goddams . . do not make an end of me, the French will.
▸ **B** *adjective*. Accursed, damnable, wretched; perverse, annoying. *colloq.* E20.
P. ROTH Stop looking for that goddam bus and listen to me. A. T. ELLIS Oh, what a goddam waste of time.
▸ **C** *adverb*. Extremely, to an excessive degree. *colloq.* M20.
L. ALTHER Do you have to be so goddam intense all the time?
■ **goddamned** *adjective* (*colloq.*) = GODDAM *adjective* M20.

goddard /ˈgɒdəd, -ɑːd/ *noun*. *obsolete* exc. *dial.* LME.
[ORIGIN Old French *godart*, app. rel. to GODET.]
A drinking cup, a goblet.

goddess /ˈɡɒdɪs/ *noun*. ME.
[ORIGIN from GOD *noun* + -ESS[1].]
1 A woman who is adored or worshipped, esp. by a particular admirer. ME.

L. GORDON His veneration for his second wife was less discerning. He made of her a goddess.

2 A female god, esp. in any of various polytheistic systems of belief. LME.

J. A. MICHENER Astarte, the tempting, rich-breasted goddess of fertility.

3 A female occupant of a theatre gallery. Now *rare* or *obsolete*. E19.
■ **goddesshood** *noun* the nature, character, or position belonging to a goddess; divine female personality: M18. **goddesslike** *adjective & adverb* (**a**) *adjective* resembling a goddess; (**b**) *adverb* in the manner of a goddess: L16. **goddess-ship** *noun* goddesshood E17.

G

Gödel /ˈɡəːd(ə)l/ *noun*. M20.
[ORIGIN Kurt *Gödel* (1906–78), Austrian-born US mathematician.]
MATH. & PHILOSOPHY. ***Gödel's proof***, ***Gödel's theorem***, the demonstration that in logic and in mathematics there must be true but unprovable statements, and that the consistency of a system such as arithmetic cannot be proved within that system.

godemiche /ˈɡɒd(ə)miːʃ/ *noun*. L19.
[ORIGIN French.]
= DILDO 1.

godet /ɡəʊˈdɛt, ˈɡəʊdeɪ/ *noun*. ME.
[ORIGIN Old French & mod. French Cf. GODDARD.]
†**1** A drinking cup. ME–E17.
2 A triangular piece of material inserted into a dress, glove, or other garment. L19.
3 A driven roller or wheel around which the filaments of any of various man-made fibres are drawn during manufacture. E20.

godetia /ɡə(ʊ)ˈdiːʃə/ *noun*. M19.
[ORIGIN mod. Latin (see below), from C. H. *Godet* (1797–1879), Swiss botanist + -IA[1].]
Any of several N. American plants of the former genus *Godetia* (now included in *Clarkia*), of the willowherb family, much grown as summer annuals.

godfather /ˈɡɒdfɑːðə/ *noun & verb*. OE.
[ORIGIN from GOD *noun* + FATHER *noun*. Cf. GAFFER.]
▸ **A** *noun*. **1** A male godparent. OE. ▸**b** A male sponsor at the consecration of a bell. L15. ▸**c** A male sponsor at a confirmation. Long *rare*. M16.
2 *transf. & fig.* A person who sponsors or provides care or support for a person, project, etc.; a person who or thing which gives a name to another. L16. ▸†**b** In *pl.* Jurors delivering a capital verdict. *joc.* L16–L17.
3 A person directing an illegal and esp. criminal organization; *spec.* any of the leaders of the American Mafia. *slang*. M20.
▸ **B** *verb trans.* Act as a godfather to; take under one's care, make oneself responsible for; give a name to. L18.
■ **godfatherhood** *noun* the position of godfather L19. **godfathership** *noun* the status or position of godfather L17.

godforsaken /ˈɡɒdfəseɪk(ə)n/ *adjective*. M19.
[ORIGIN from GOD *noun* + FORSAKEN.]
Esp. of a place: desolate, grim, dismal, dreary.

C. HIAASEN An immediate transfer to some godforsaken cowtown would be a certainty.

Godfrey /ˈɡɒdfri/ *noun*. *obsolete* exc. *hist.* L18.
[ORIGIN Thomas *Godfrey* of Hunsdon, Hertfordshire, fl. early 18th cent.]
In full ***Godfrey's cordial***. A sweet flavoured tincture of opium, popular as a medicine in the 18th and 19th cents.

Godfrey /ˈɡɒdfri/ *interjection*. *US slang*. M19.
[ORIGIN Alt. and assim. of *God* to the name *Godfrey*.]
Expr. strong feeling, surprise, etc.
by guess and by Godfrey: see GUESS *noun*.

godhead /ˈɡɒdhɛd/ *noun*. ME.
[ORIGIN from GOD *noun* + -HEAD[1].]
1 The character or quality of being God or a god; divine nature or essence. ME. ▸†**b** With possess. pronoun, as a title: divine personality. LME–E18.

COLERIDGE He [Christ] on the thought-benighted sceptic beamed Manifest Godhead. B. JOWETT Do you mean that I do not believe in the godhead of the sun or moon? **b** POPE Supreme he sits: and sees.. Your vassal godheads grudgingly obey.

2 (Usu. **G-**.) *The* supreme being, God. LME. ▸**b** A god, a deity. Now *rare*. L16.

Derby Diocesan News The complex problem of sexuality in the Godhead.

godhood /ˈɡɒdhʊd/ *noun*. ME.
[ORIGIN from GOD *noun* + -HOOD.]
In early use, = GODHEAD 1. Now chiefly, the state or rank of being God or a god.

godless /ˈɡɒdlɪs/ *adjective*. E16.
[ORIGIN from GOD *noun* + -LESS.]
Without a god; not recognizing or worshipping God; irreligious, ungodly. Also, undertaken without regard to God, impious, wicked.

THACKERAY Military men.. rushed thither.. to.. partake of all sorts of godless delights. *absol.*: MILTON Behold Gods indignation on these Godless poured.

godless florin = GRACELESS *florin*.
■ **godlessness** *noun* M16.

godlike /ˈɡɒdlʌɪk/ *adjective & adverb*. LME.
[ORIGIN from GOD *noun* + -LIKE.]
▸ **A** *adjective*. **1** Resembling God or a god in some quality, esp. in nature or disposition; divine. LME.

MILTON Thus the Godlike Angel answerd milde. D. HEWETT Brawny, godlike, brief-trunked young men. *absol.*: CARLYLE Is not a Symbol.. some dimmer or clearer revelation of the Godlike!

2 Fit for, appropriate to, or characteristic of God or a god. LME.

J. MACKINTOSH To forego his work of heroic, or rather godlike benevolence. N. SYMINGTON To tell a patient.. she needs psychoanalysis.. is a very godlike judgement.

▸ **B** *adverb*. In a godlike manner. Long *rare* or *obsolete*. M17.

DRYDEN Praise Him alone, who god-like formed thee free.

■ **godlikeness** *noun* M17.

godling /ˈɡɒdlɪŋ/ *noun*. Freq. *joc.* or *derog.* L16.
[ORIGIN from GOD *noun* + -LING[1].]
A small or minor god; a representation of such a god.

R. KIPLING Till ye become little Gods again—Gods of the jungle—.. Godlings of the tree. *Times* Mark Hateley.. has become the new godling of Italian football.

godly /ˈɡɒdli/ *adjective*. LME.
[ORIGIN from GOD *noun* + -LY[1].]
1 Of, pertaining to, or coming from God or a god; divine; spiritual. Long *arch.* LME.

SHERWOOD ANDERSON Something like a halo of Godly approval hung over him.

2 Of a person or (*arch.*) conduct, speech, etc.: devoutly observant of the laws of God; religious; pious. LME.

J. FRITH That the unfaithful might see the godly and virtuous conversation of his faithful. E. F. BENSON There was a new cook.., a very godly woman. *absol.*: LD MACAULAY Soon the world begins to find out that the godly are not better than other men.

■ **godlily** *adverb* (now *rare*) M16. **godliness** *noun* M16.

godly /ˈɡɒdli/ *adverb*. Now *rare*. E16.
[ORIGIN from GOD *noun* + -LY[2].]
In a godly manner.

God-man /ˈɡɒdman/ *noun*. M16.
[ORIGIN from GOD *noun* + MAN *noun*, translating ecclesiastical Greek *theandros*, *theanthrōpos*, whence ecclesiastical Latin *deus-homo*: cf. French *homme-Dieu* (late Latin *homo-deus*), Dutch *Godmensch*, German *Gottmensch*.]
A person who is both God and man; Christ.

godmother /ˈɡɒdmʌðə/ *noun*. OE.
[ORIGIN from GOD *noun* + MOTHER *noun*[1]. Cf. GAMMER.]
1 A female godparent. OE.
FAIRY ***godmother***.
2 A female sponsor at the consecration of a bell. *rare*. M19.
■ **godmothership** *noun* the status or position of godmother L17.

godown /ˈɡəʊdaʊn, ɡəʊˈdaʊn/ *noun*. L16.
[ORIGIN Portuguese *gudão* from Tamil *kiṭaṅku*, Malayalam *kiṭaṅṅu*, Kannada *gaḍaṅgu* store, godown. Cf. Malay *gedong*, *gadong*, *gudang*.]
In the Indian subcontinent and other parts of eastern Asia: a warehouse or store for goods.

go-down /ˈɡəʊdaʊn/ *noun*. M17.
[ORIGIN from GO *verb* + DOWN *adverb*.]
†**1** A draught or gulp of liquid, a drink; a drinking match. M17–L19.
2 A cutting allowing animals access to a stream etc. *US dial.* L19.

godparent /ˈɡɒdpɛːr(ə)nt/ *noun*. M19.
[ORIGIN from GOD *noun* + PARENT *noun*, after *godfather*, *godmother*.]
A person who, in various Christian Churches, traditionally takes responsibility for the Christian upbringing or education of a person being baptized, and (if the latter is a child) makes the promises on behalf of the child at the baptism ceremony; a godfather, a godmother. Also called ***sponsor***.

godsend /ˈɡɒdsɛnd/ *noun*. E19.
[ORIGIN from *God's send*: see SEND *noun*[1].]
1 A person or thing of great value or usefulness, unexpectedly arriving or present. E19.

E. F. BENSON You are going to be a perfect godsend to us all. W. STYRON The money was a godsend, bailing me out. A. S. BYATT For the sake of information.. Conrad's talkativeness was, in its way, a godsend.

2 A wreck of a ship cast up on a shore. *dial.* E19.

SIR W. SCOTT It's seldom sic rich Godsends come on our coast.

Godspeed /ɡɒdˈspiːd/ *noun*. Also **g-**. ME.
[ORIGIN from *God speed (you)* may God prosper (you): see SPEED *verb*.]
An utterance of 'God speed you' to a departing person; an expression of goodwill at parting.

E. K. KANE Three hearty cheers.. followed us,—a God-speed as we pushed off. P. L. FERMOR With his wishes for Godspeed in my ears.. I set off.

†**in the Godspeed** in the nick of time.

Godwinian /ɡɒdˈwɪnɪən/ *adjective & noun*. E19.
[ORIGIN from *Godwin* (see below) + -IAN.]
▸ **A** *adjective*. Of, pertaining to, or characteristic of the English writer and social reformer William Godwin (1756–1836) or his political and social views. E19.
▸ **B** *noun*. A follower or adherent of Godwin or his views. M20.

Godwinism /ˈɡɒdwɪnɪz(ə)m/ *noun*. L18.
[ORIGIN formed as GODWINIAN + -ISM.]
The doctrine or ideas of William Godwin (see GODWINIAN).

godwit /ˈɡɒdwɪt/ *noun*. M16.
[ORIGIN Unknown.]
Any of several large migratory wading birds constituting the genus *Limosa*, related to the curlews, having long legs and a long, straight or upcurved bill.

Godwottery /ɡɒdˈwɒt(ə)ri/ *noun*. Also **g-**. M20.
[ORIGIN from *God wot* in a line from T. E. Brown's poem *My Garden* (1876): see -ERY.]
An affected, fussily decorative, or overelaborate style of gardening or garden design. Also, archaic and affected language.

A. BURGESS The tiny gates which you could step over; the godwottery in the toy gardens.

Godzilla /ɡɒdˈzɪlə/ *noun*. *colloq.* L20.
[ORIGIN Allusively from *Godzilla*, the name of a huge prehistoric monster featuring in a series of Japanese films from 1954, from Japanese *Gojira*, from *go-* (in *gorira* gorilla) + *-jira* (in *kujira* whale).]
A particularly enormous example of its type; a monster.

New York Review of Books The Construction State has become an all-devouring monster, a Godzilla of development.

goer /ˈɡəʊə/ *noun*. ME.
[ORIGIN from GO *verb* + -ER[1].]
1 A person who or thing which goes. Formerly also foll. by adverb. ME.

SWIFT The intervening officious impertinence of those goers between us. F. E. PAGET My watch is a perfect goer. *Manchester Examiner* All the comers and goers appear to be fairly well pleased.

2 As 2nd elem. of comb.: a person who (regularly) goes to the specified place, event, etc. L17.
churchgoer, ***theatregoer***, etc.
3 A lively or persevering person; a sexually promiscuous or unrestrained person, a profligate; a horse etc. that goes fast; a successful person or thing; *Austral. & NZ* a project, proposal, etc., likely to be accepted or to succeed. *colloq.* E19.

T. C. HALIBURTON He looks.. as if he'd trot a considerable good stick... I guess he is a goer. F. MUIR Lady Caroline had been a bit of a goer in her youth. *Bulletin (Sydney)* Does not think privatisation is a goer in political terms.

goes *verb* see GO *noun*[1], *verb*.

goest *verb* see GO *verb*.

goeth *verb* see GO *verb*.

Goethean /ˈɡəːtɪən/ *adjective*. M19.
[ORIGIN from Johann Wolfgang von *Goethe* (1749–1832), German writer: see -IAN.]
Of, pertaining to, or characteristic of (the writings of) Goethe.
■ Also **Goethian** *adjective* M19.

goethite /ˈɡəːtʌɪt/ *noun*. E19.
[ORIGIN formed as GOETHEAN + -ITE[1].]
MINERALOGY. A reddish or brown hydrated iron oxide occurring as orthorhombic crystals or in massive form.

goety /ˈɡəʊɪti/ *noun*. *arch.* M16.
[ORIGIN Late Latin *goetia* from Greek *goēteia* witchcraft, from *goēs*, *goēt-* sorcerer.]
Witchcraft or magic performed by the invocation and employment of evil spirits; necromancy.
■ **goˈetic** *adjective* of or pertaining to goety E17.

gofer /ˈɡəʊfə/ *noun*[1]. *dial.* M18.
[ORIGIN French *gaufre* honeycomb: see GOFFER *verb*.]
A thin batter cake stamped in a honeycomb pattern by iron plates between which it is baked.

gofer /ˈɡəʊfə/ *noun*[2]. *slang* (chiefly *N. Amer.*). Also **gofor**, (the usual form in sense 2) **gopher**. M20.
[ORIGIN Alt. of *go for* repr. pronunc.: see GO *verb*.]
1 A person who runs errands, esp. as a job on a film set or in an office; a general dogsbody. M20.
2 BASEBALL. In full ***gofer ball***. A pitch that can be hit for a run, esp. a home run. M20.

goff /ɡɒf/ *noun*. *obsolete* exc. *dial.* L16.
[ORIGIN App. from French *goffe* awkward, stupid from Italian *goffo* from medieval Latin *gufus*.]
A dolt, a stupid fellow.

goffer /ˈɡɒfə/ *verb trans.* L16.
[ORIGIN French *gaufrer* stamp with a patterned tool, from *gaufre* honeycomb, Anglo-Norman *walfre* from Middle Low German *wâfel*: see WAFFLE *noun*[1], WAFER *noun*.]
Make wavy, flute, or crimp (a lace edge, a frill, etc.) by the use of a heated iron or similar instrument.
goffering iron an iron tool heated and used to flute or crimp lace, frills, etc.
■ **goffered** *adjective* (**a**) made wavy by goffering, fluted, crimped; (**b**) (of the edges of a book) embossed or stamped with repeated patterns: E18.

gofor *noun* var. of GOFER *noun*[2].

gog /ɡɒɡ/ *noun*[1]. *obsolete* exc. *dial.* ME.
[ORIGIN Unknown.]
A bog, a swamp.

gog /ɡɒɡ/ *noun*[2]. *Scot.* E19.
[ORIGIN Unknown.]
An object forming a mark in a game of quoits, marbles, etc.

go-get /ˈɡəʊɡɛt/ *verb intrans. colloq.* Infl. **-tt-** (no pa.). E20.
[ORIGIN from GO *verb* + GET *verb*.]
Be ambitious and enterprising. Chiefly as ***go-getting*** *ppl adjective & verbal noun*.

go-getter /ˈɡəʊɡɛtə/ *noun. colloq.* E20.
[ORIGIN from (the same root as) GO-GET + -ER[1].]
An ambitious and enterprising person.

goggie /ˈɡɒɡi/ *noun. N. English* & (now only) *Scot. dial.* L18.
[ORIGIN Prob. alt. In Scot. use cf. Gaelic *gogaidh*. Cf. GOOG.]
(A child's name for) an egg.

goggle /ˈɡɒɡ(ə)l/ *verb*[1], *adjective*, & *noun*. LME.
[ORIGIN Prob. frequentative from imit. base *gog* (cf. JOG *verb*, JOGGLE *verb*[1]): see -LE[3].]
▸ **A** *verb*. **1** *verb intrans.* Of a person: (orig.) turn the eyes to one side or the other, squint; (later) look with wide open, bulging, or protruding eyes, esp. in bewilderment or surprise; roll the eyes about. LME. ▸**b** Of the eyes: (orig.) turn to one side or the other, squint; (later) roll about, bulge, or protrude, esp. with an expression of bewilderment or surprise. M16.

S. BUTLER Which made him . . goggle like an Owl. G. GREENE She goggled hopelessly at the boy. **b** THACKERAY The frog's hideous large eyes were goggling out of his head.

2 *verb intrans.* Sway or roll about; move loosely and unsteadily. *obsolete* exc. *dial.* LME.
3 *verb trans.* Turn (the eyes) sideways or from side to side. L16.

T. L. PEACOCK The stranger goggled about his eyes in an attempt to fix them steadily on Taliesin.

▸ **B** *adjective*. Of the eyes: protuberant, full and rolling. Formerly also, squinting. (See also earlier GOGGLE-EYE.) M16.

THACKERAY His goggle eyes were always rolling about wildly.

▸ **C** *noun*. **1** In *pl.* Spectacles for protecting the eyes from glare, dust, etc., (esp. during a specified activity), often having side shields and coloured glass, wire gauze, etc. M16. ▸**b** In *pl.* The eyes. *slang.* E18.
2 A person who goggles or stares. *rare.* E17.
†**3** A goggling look, a squint; a leer; a stare. M–L17.
4 In *pl.* A disease of sheep; = GID. L18.
– COMB.: **goggle-box** *slang* a television set; **goggle dive** an underwater dive by a person wearing goggles.
■ **goggler** *noun* †(**a**) a person with a squint; (**b**) *slang* an eye; (**c**) *US* = GOGGLE-EYE 2(b): LME. **goggly** *adjective* (of the eyes) goggling, having a tendency to goggle L17.

goggle /ˈɡɒɡ(ə)l/ *verb*[2]. Long *rare* or *obsolete*. E17.
[ORIGIN Imit.]
1 *verb trans.* = GOBBLE *verb*[1] 1. E17.
2 *verb intrans.* = GOBBLE *verb*[2]. M19.

goggled /ˈɡɒɡ(ə)ld/ *adjective*[1]. Now *rare*. E16.
[ORIGIN from GOGGLE *verb*[1] + -ED[1].]
= GOGGLE *adjective*.

goggled /ˈɡɒɡ(ə)ld/ *adjective*[2]. E20.
[ORIGIN from GOGGLE *noun* + -ED[2].]
Equipped with or wearing goggles.

goggle-eye /ˈɡɒɡ(ə)lʌɪ/ *noun*. LME.
[ORIGIN from GOGGLE *verb*[1] or *adjective* + EYE *noun*.]
†**1** A person with a squint. Also, the action or an act of squinting. LME–M19.
2 Any of various fishes with particularly large or prominent eyes, *esp.* (**a**) *Priacanthus hamrur*, a common tropical Indo-Pacific fish; (**b**) *US* (more fully ***goggle-eye Jack***) *Selar crumenophthalmus*, a large carangid fish of shallow (sub-)tropical waters worldwide. L19.

goggle-eyed /ɡɒɡ(ə)lˈʌɪd/ *adjective*. LME.
[ORIGIN formed as GOGGLE-EYE + -ED[2].]
Having protruberant, staring, or rolling eyes, esp. fixed in an expression of bewilderment or surprise. Formerly also, squint-eyed.

E. PAUL The way in which the American male seemed to be pushed around by his womenfolk left Parisians goggle-eyed.

goglet /ˈɡɒɡlɪt/ *noun. Indian.* L17.
[ORIGIN Portuguese *gorgoleta*.]
A long-necked usu. porous vessel for keeping water cool.

Gogo /ˈɡəʊɡəʊ/ *noun & adjective*. L19.
[ORIGIN Perh. from Nyamwezi.]
▸ **A** *noun*. Pl. same, **-os**, **WAGOGO** *noun*. A member of a people inhabiting central Tanzania; the Bantu language of this people. L19.
▸ **B** *attrib.* or as *adjective*. Of or pertaining to the Gogo or their language. M20.

go-go /ˈɡəʊɡəʊ/ *adjective. colloq.* M20.
[ORIGIN Redupl. of GO *verb*, perh. infl. by A GOGO, GO *adjective*.]
Unrestrained, energetic; (of music etc.) full of verve, movement, and excitement; (of a dancer) performing rhythmic and usu. erotic dance routines; (of investment) speculative.

Goidel /ˈɡɔɪd(ə)l/ *noun*. L19.
[ORIGIN Old Irish *Goídel*: see GAEL.]
A Gael; a member of the Scottish, Irish, or Manx Celts as opp. to the Welsh, Cornish, or Breton Celts.
■ **Goiˈdelic** *adjective & noun* (**a**) *adjective* of or pertaining to the Goidels; (**b**) *noun* the language group Celtic comprising Irish, Gaelic, and Manx, = ***Q-Celtic*** s.v. CELTIC *noun*: L19.

going /ˈɡəʊɪŋ/ *noun*. ME.
[ORIGIN from GO *verb* + -ING[1].]
▸ **I 1** The action of GO *verb*; an instance of this. Also foll. by adverb (see also branch II). ME. ▸**b** *spec.* Departure; an act or instance of departing. ME. ▸†**c** The ability to walk. LME–M17.

SHAKES. *Macb.* Stand not upon the order of your going, But go at once. P. ACKROYD His hopes of perpetual comfort, of happiness, of 'going steady', were being dismantled. *attrib.*: *Family Circle* And I discovered, reluctantly, that the *real* test of success was the 'going-home' present. **b** A. MACLEAN To monitor the comings and goings of everybody in the hospital.

2 †**a** A path, a road, a passage. ME–E18. ▸**b** The width of a stairway or step. E18.
†**3** Manner or style of going, gait; in *pl.*, paces (of a horse). LME–E19.
4 The condition of the ground for walking, riding, etc., esp. for horse-racing; advance or progress as helped or hindered by the condition of the ground or *fig.* circumstances, subject matter, etc. M19.

T. FITZGEORGE-PARKER The going is not too heavy for my horse. K. AMIS The going was ideal here, short turf, level surface, dry but not baked hard. P. THEROUX The canal was choked with hyacinths, so the going was slow. J. H. CUTLER Joe [Kennedy] made his children stay on their toes . . . He would bear down on them and tell them, 'When the going gets tough, the tough get going'.

heavy going *fig.* something difficult to negotiate, slow or difficult progress. **while the going is good** *fig.* while conditions are favourable.

▸ **II** Special uses with adverbs.
5 ***going down***, ***going-down***, (†***going adown***), setting (of the sun), sunset. ME.
6 ***going away***, departure, freq. *spec.* on one's honeymoon. LME.

attrib.: L. OLIVIER The time had come for the newly-weds to change into their 'going-away' clothes.

7 ***going over***, ***going-over***: ▸†**a** A passage over a stream. *US.* M17–L18. ▸**b** A scolding, a dressing-down. *colloq.* (orig. *US*). L19. ▸**c** An inspection, an examination, an overhaul. *colloq.* (orig. *US*). E20. ▸**d** A beating, a thrashing. *slang* (orig. *US*). M20.

b M. TWAIN I got a good going over in the morning . . on account of my clothes. A. BURGESS I gave him the worst going over in really dirty French that he must ever have had. **c** H. PINTER How do you think the place is looking? I gave it a good going over. J. GATHORNE-HARDY 'Nobody takes this headache seriously.' I said, 'OK. . . let's give you a good going over'. **d** ALAN ROSS 'Got a going over, did you?' 'Not much . . Want to see the bruises?'

†**8** ***goings-out***, expenses, outgoings. E18–E19.
9 ***goings-on***, (esp. questionable or reprehensible) actions or proceedings, frolics. L18.

G. PRIESTLAND There will be all sorts of cloak-and-dagger goings-on. LD DENNING A curtain which conceals the goings on of the directors and managers of a company.

▸ **III** ***a-going*** [A *preposition*[1] 8, verbal noun later interpreted as pres. pple: see GO *verb* 39, 40]. Now *arch.* & *dial.*
10 *gen.* Going. E16.
11 In or into action or motion. L16.
12 Existing, to be had. E18.

going /ˈɡəʊɪŋ/ *ppl adjective*. ME.
[ORIGIN from GO *verb* + -ING[2]. For pred. uses see GO *verb* VI.]
That goes; departing; working, in action or operation; currently valid.

B. I. LANE The classical theological, . . theatre-going, card-playing Reverend Gentleman. M. PUZO The going price was now two thousand dollars.

going concern a business in operation and thriving.

goitre /ˈɡɔɪtə/ *noun*. Also ***goiter**. E17.
[ORIGIN French, either (i) from Old French *goitron* from Provençal from Proto-Romance, from Latin *guttur* throat, or (ii) back-form. from French *goitreux* goitred, from Latin adjective from *guttur*.]
MEDICINE. A swelling of the neck due to enlargement of the thyroid gland, as caused by disease of the gland, iodine deficiency, etc.

exophthalmic goitre goitre accompanied by exophthalmos; Graves' disease.
■ **goitred**, **goitered** *adjective* afflicted with goitre M19. **goiˈtrigenous**, **goitroˈgenic** (also **-ter-**), **goiˈtrogenous** *adjectives* causing goitre E20.

goitrous /ˈɡɔɪtrəs/ *adjective*. L18.
[ORIGIN from French *goitreux*: see GOITRE, -OUS.]
MEDICINE. Of, pertaining to, resembling, or affected with a goitre. Also, of a place: characterized by the prevalence of goitre.

go-kart /ˈɡəʊkɑːt/ *noun*. M20.
[ORIGIN Alt. of GO-CART.]
A low light racing car with a skeleton body.
■ **go-karting** *noun* racing go-karts M20.

goky /ˈɡəʊki/ *noun*. Long *rare* or *obsolete* exc. *Scot.* LME.
[ORIGIN Uncertain: perh. rel. to GOWK.]
A fool, a simpleton.

gola /ˈɡəʊlə/ *noun*[1]. Also (earlier) **gula** /ˈɡjuːlə/. M17.
[ORIGIN Italian = throat from Latin *gula*.]
ARCHITECTURE. = CYMA 1.

Gola /ˈɡəʊlə/ *noun*[2] & *adjective*. Also **Golah**, **Gora** /ˈɡɔːrə/. L17.
[ORIGIN Gola.]
▸ **A** *noun*. Pl. same, **-s**.
1 A member of an agricultural people of Liberia and Sierra Leone. L17.
2 The Niger-Congo language of this people. E20.
▸ **B** *attrib.* or as *adjective*. Of or pertaining to the Gola or their language. L17.

G

gola *noun*[3] var. of GOLAH *noun*[1].

golah /ˈɡəʊlə/ *noun*[1]. Also **gola**. M18.
[ORIGIN Hindi *golā* round storage jar, granary, from *gol* round.]
In the Indian subcontinent: a storehouse or silo for grain, salt, etc.

Golah *noun*[2] var. of GOLA *noun*[2].

Golconda /ɡɒlˈkɒndə/ *noun*. L19.
[ORIGIN A city near Hyderabad, India, famous for its diamonds.]
A mine, a rich source, *lit.* & *fig.*

New Yorker There is a veritable Golconda of guidebooks . . at the traveller's disposal.

gold /ɡəʊld/ *noun*[1] & *adjective*.
[ORIGIN Old English *gold* = Old Frisian, Old Saxon, Old High German *gold* (Dutch *goud*, German *Gold*), Old Norse *goll*, *gull*, Gothic *gulþ*, ult. from Indo-European base of YELLOW *adjective*.]
▸ **A** *noun*. **1** A precious metal which is characterized by its yellowish colour, resistance to tarnishing and corrosion, and great malleability and ductility, and is a chemical element of the transition series, atomic no. 79 (symbol Au). Also (with specifying word), any of various substances containing, resembling, or imitating, this. OE. ▸**b** = ***gold medal*** below. M20.

b *Sunday Express* When British teams could only come second at best, our singular athletes kept on grabbing Golds.

fairy gold, ***fool's gold***, ***mosaic gold***, ***red gold***, ***roman gold***, ***white gold***, etc.
2 Gold as a valuable possession or as a medium of exchange; coin(s) made of gold, money in large sums; *gen.* wealth. OE. ▸**b** *FINANCE.* A share in a gold-mining company. E20. ▸**c** Marijuana. *slang.* L20.

A. HAILEY If I were an Arab I'd refuse paper dollars for my oil and demand gold. **b** *Times* Golds were a few cents down.

3 Gold used to ornament textiles; thread or wire wholly or partly made of gold. Formerly also, fabric embroidered with or partly made of gold. OE. ▸**b** Gold used as a pigment or coating; gilding. LME.

E. WILSON Various companies put out a gold you can sew with.

4 *fig.* Something precious, beautiful, or brilliant. ME.
5 The colour of gold. LME.

G. MACDONALD Gazing at the red and gold and green of the sunset sky.

6 *ARCHERY.* The gilt centre or bull's eye of a target. L19.
▸ **B** *adjective*. **1** Made wholly or chiefly of gold. ME.

A. MASON It was a small gold satyr, set with gems, supporting a sweetmeat tray.

2 Coloured like gold. ME.

ANNE STEVENSON Then the hills fill with gold wheat.

3 *FINANCE.* Of a currency: reckoned at its full undepreciated value according to a gold standard. E20.
– PHRASES: **age of gold** a golden age. ***as good as gold***: see GOOD *adjective*. ***black gold***: see BLACK *adjective*. ***cloth of gold***: see CLOTH *noun* 4. ***coronary gold***: see CORONARY *adjective* 2. **go gold** (of a piece of recorded music) achieve sales meriting a gold disc. ***heart of gold***: see HEART *noun*. **old gold** (of) the dulled yellow colour of old gold. ***pot of gold***: see POT *noun*[1]. ***worth its weight in gold***, ***worth one's weight in gold***: see WEIGHT *noun*.
– COMB. & SPECIAL COLLOCATIONS: **gold amalgam** an easily mouldable combination of gold with mercury; **gold-beater** a person who beats out gold into gold leaf; ***gold-beater's skin***, an animal membrane used to separate the leaves of gold during beating and (formerly) to cover slight wounds; **gold bloc** the bloc of countries having a gold standard; **gold blocking** the stamping of a gold leaf design on a book cover using a block or heated die; **gold brick** (**a**) a brick made or apparently made of gold; *fig.* a

thing with only a surface appearance of value, a sham, a fraud; (*b*) *US slang* a lazy person, a shirker; **goldbrick** *verb* (*a*) *verb trans.* cheat, swindle; (*b*) *verb intrans.* shirk, have an easy time; ***gold bridge***: see BRIDGE *noun*[1]; **gold bug** (chiefly *US*) (*a*) an advocate of a single gold standard; (*b*) a person favouring gold as an investment; **gold card** (proprietary name for) a preferential credit or charge card conferring special benefits on the holder; **gold certificate** *US* a certificate or note issued by the US Treasury to the Federal Reserve Banks and (now rarely) the public certifying that gold to the amount stated on the face of the certificate has been deposited and is redeemable; **goldcrest** a tiny olive-green Eurasian kinglet, *Regulus regulus*, having a bright yellow crown; **gold-dig** *verb trans.* (*slang*) extract money from; **gold-digger** (*a*) a person who digs for gold; (*b*) *slang* a woman who forms relationships with men solely with intent to extract money from them; **gold disc** a framed golden disc awarded to a recording artist or group for sales of a recording exceeding a million in the US or 500,000 in Britain for a single, or 500,000 in the US or 250,000 in Britain for an album; **gold dust** (*a*) gold in very fine particles; (*b*) either of two low-growing garden plants with many small yellow flowers, the alyssum *Alyssum saxatile* and the stonecrop *Sedum acre*; **gold-eye** an edible N. American freshwater fish, *Hiodon alosoides*, silvery-blue in colour with a conspicuous golden iris; **gold fever** the rage for going in search of gold; **goldfinch** any of several finches of the genus *Carduelis* with yellow in the plumage, *esp.* the Eurasian *C. carduelis* and the N. American *C. tristis*; **goldfinny** = *goldsinny* below; **goldfish** a fish with golden coloration or markings; now *spec.* a small reddish-golden Chinese carp, *Carassius auratus*, freq. kept as an ornamental fish or as a pet; ***goldfish bowl***, a usu. globe-shaped glass bowl for keeping goldfish; *fig.* a place or situation with no privacy; **gold foil** gold beaten into a thin sheet, slightly thicker than gold leaf; **gold fringe** a small pink and yellow pyralid moth, *Hypsopygia costalis*; **gold leaf** gold beaten into a fragile wafer-thin sheet, thinner than gold foil, and used esp. in gilding; **gold medal** a gold-coloured medal awarded for a first place in a contest, esp. the modern Olympic Games; **gold mine** a mine from which gold is obtained; *fig.* a source of wealth, income, or profit; **gold of pleasure** a yellow cruciferous European weed, *Camelina sativa*, grown sometimes for its oil-rich seeds; **gold plate** (*a*) vessels made of gold; (*b*) material plated with gold; **gold record** = ***gold disc*** above; **gold reserve**: of gold coin or bullion held by a central authority, bank, etc.; **gold rush**: to goldfields in search of gold; **gold salt** a salt of gold; *esp.* in PHARMACOLOGY, any of several compounds containing gold and sulphur used to treat rheumatoid arthritis and lupus erythematosus; **goldsinny** any of several small European wrasses, esp. *Ctenolabrus rupestris*; **goldsmith** a worker in gold, a manufacturer of gold articles, (formerly acting also as a banker); ***goldsmith beetle***, any of various scarabaeid beetles having wing cases with a metallic golden lustre; *esp.* (*a*) the rose chafer; (*b*) the N. American *Cotalpa lanigera*, a pest of deciduous forests; ***gold standard***: see STANDARD *noun*; **Gold Stick** (the bearer of) the gilt rod borne on state occasions by the colonel of the Life Guards or their successors the Household Cavalry Regiment, or the captain of the gentlemen-at-arms; **gold thread** (*a*) thread of silk etc. with gold wire wound round it; (*b*) (usu. *goldthread*) (the root of) a plant, *Coptis trifolia* of the buttercup family, native to Alaska and NE Asia, with thin yellow rhizomes used in medicines or dyes; **goldwork** gold objects collectively.

■ **goldish** *adjective* somewhat golden LME. **goldless** *adjective* LME.

gold /gəʊld/ *noun*[2]. *obsolete* exc. *dial.*

[ORIGIN Old English *golde* rel. to GOLD *noun*[1] & *adjective*: cf. Dutch *goudbloem*, German *Goldblume*, Swedish *guldblomma* lit. 'gold-flower'.]

Corn marigold, *Chrysanthemum segetum*. Formerly also, the garden marigold.

goldarn /gɒlˈdɑːn/ *adjective, adverb, & verb. N. Amer. slang.* M19.

[ORIGIN Alt. of GODDAM. Cf. GOLLY *noun*[1].]

= DAMN *adjective & adverb, verb.*

■ **goldarned** *adjective* = DAMNED *adjective* M19.

Goldbach /ˈgəʊldbɑːx/ *noun.* E20.

[ORIGIN C. *Goldbach* (1690–1764), German mathematician.]

MATH. ***Goldbach's conjecture***, ***Goldbach's hypothesis***, ***Goldbach's theorem***, the hypothesis that every even number greater than two can be represented as the sum of two primes.

golden /ˈgəʊld(ə)n/ *adjective & verb.* ME.

[ORIGIN from GOLD *noun*[1] + -EN[4], superseding GILDEN.]

▸ **A** *adjective.* **1** Made of gold. ME.

G. VIDAL I prostrated myself at the golden footstool.

kill the goose that lays the golden eggs, ***kill the goose that laid the golden eggs***: see GOOSE *noun*.

2 Yielding or containing much gold. LME.

3 Of the colour of gold; shining like gold. LME.

B. EMECHETA The sun rose, warm and golden. R. WEST Her golden hair was all about her shoulders.

4 Resembling gold in value; precious, important, excellent; (of an opportunity) very favourable or propitious. LME.

H. KELLER The golden words that Dr. Howe uttered . . helped her on the road to usefulness. ARNOLD BENNETT He understood that there was no golden and magic secret of the building.

5 Of a time or epoch: characterized by great prosperity and happiness; flourishing. LME.

U. BENTLEY He had picked on this . . golden future in order to characterize, by contrast, his wretched present.

†**6** Of or pertaining to the search or desire for gold. E17–E18.

– SPECIAL COLLOCATIONS & COMB.: **golden age** (*a*) an idyllic past time of prosperity, happiness, and innocence; (*b*) the period of a nation's greatest prosperity or literary etc. merit. **golden ager** *N. Amer.* an old person. **golden alga**: of the family Chrysophyceae. **golden balls**: a pawnbroker's sign. **golden boy** a popular or successful boy or man. **golden calf** [*Exodus* 32] something, esp. wealth, as an object of excessive or unworthy worship. **golden chain** laburnum, *Laburnum anagyroides*. **golden-crested** *adjective* that has a golden crest; ***golden-crested wren*** = ***goldcrest*** s.v. GOLD *noun*[1] & *adjective*. **Golden Delicious** a variety of eating apple, a form of Delicious with pale yellow skin. **golden disc** = ***gold disc*** s.v. GOLD *noun*[1] & *adjective*. **golden eagle** a large brown eagle, *Aquila chrysaetos*, of northern mountain regions, having golden feathers on the head and neck. **goldeneye** a diving duck of the genus *Bucephala*; spec. *B. clangula*, a migratory holarctic duck with a large dark head and bright yellow eyes. ***Golden Fleece***: see FLEECE *noun* 1. **golden girl** a popular or successful girl or woman. **golden goal** (*a*) a particularly outstanding or notable goal; (*b*) (in some competitions) the first goal scored during extra time in a soccer or hockey match, which ends the match and gives victory to the scoring side. ***golden*** HAMSTER. **golden handcuffs** benefits and esp. deferred payments provided by an employer to discourage an employee from taking employment elsewhere. **golden handshake** a gratuity given as compensation for dismissal or compulsory retirement. **golden hello** a substantial sum of money offered to an individual, esp. a director or senior executive, as an inducement to change employers, and paid in advance on acceptance of the post. ***Golden Horde***: see HORDE 1. **Golden Horn** the harbour of Istanbul. **golden hour** MEDICINE the first hour after the occurrence of a traumatic injury, considered the most critical for successful emergency treatment. ***golden jackal***: see JACKAL *noun* 1. **golden jubilee** the fiftieth anniversary of a monarch's accession, etc. ***Golden Legend***: see LEGEND *noun*. ***golden lion tamarin***: see ***lion tamarin*** s.v. LION *noun*. ***golden maidenhair***: see MAIDENHAIR 3. **golden mean** (*a*) the avoidance of extremes, moderation; (*b*) = ***golden section*** below. ***golden mole***: see MOLE *noun*[2] 1. **golden-mouthed** *adjective* eloquent. **golden number** the number of a year in the Metonic lunar cycle, calculated by adding 1 to the remainder after dividing the number of the year by nineteen, and of importance in fixing the date of Easter. **golden oldie** *colloq.* an old and well-known thing; *esp.* a film or former hit record that is still popular. **golden opinions** high regard. ***golden*** ORFE. ***golden*** ORIOLE. **golden parachute** *colloq.* financial compensation guaranteed to executives of a company dismissed as result of a merger or takeover. **golden perch** a green and gold serranid game fish, *Plectroplites ambiguus*, of Australian rivers; also called ***callop***, ***yellowbelly***. **golden pheasant** a golden-headed pheasant, *Chrysolophus pictus*, native to central China and feral in Britain. **golden plover** either of two plovers, the Eurasian *Pluvialis apricaria* and the N. American *P. dominica*, having golden brown plumage on the head, back, and wings. **golden raisin** *N. Amer.* a sultana. **golden retriever** a retriever dog with a thick golden-coloured coat. **golden rice** a genetically modified variety of rice rich in the orange or red plant pigment beta-carotene. **goldenrod** any of various plants of the genus *Solidago*, of the composite family, with long panicles of small yellow flowers; *esp.* the N. American *S. canadensis* and *S. gigantea*, much grown for their autumn blossom, and the European *S. virgaurea*, of woods and heaths; *collect.* flowering stems of such a plant. ***golden rose***: see ROSE *noun*. **golden rule** (*a*) a basic principle of action; (*b*) [*Matthew* 7:12] the precept of 'do as you would be done by'. **golden samphire** a yellow-flowered plant, *Inula crithmoides*, of western European coasts, related to the fleabanes and having long fleshy leaves enclosing the stem. **golden saxifrage** either of two small plants of the saxifrage family, *Chrysosplenium oppositifolium* and *C. alternifolium*, with inconspicuous flowers surrounded by greenish-yellow bracts, forming mats in wet shady places. **goldenseal** a N. American woodland plant, *Hydrastis canadensis*, of the buttercup family, with a bright yellow medicinal root. **golden section** (the proportion resulting from) the division of a straight line into two parts so that the ratio of the whole to the larger part is the same as that of the larger to the smaller part, equal to $\frac{1}{2}(\sqrt{5} + 1)$ or 1.61803 . . . . **golden share** a residual government share in a privatized company, enabling the holder to veto major changes such as takeovers. **Golden State** *US* the state of California. ***golden syrup***: see SYRUP *noun*. ***golden*** TETTIX. ***golden triangle***: see TRIANGLE *noun* 2. **golden wattle** any of certain wattles with golden flowers; esp. *Acacia pycnantha*, the flowers of which are used as the Australian national emblem, and (more fully ***Sydney golden wattle***) *A. longifolia*. **golden wedding** the fiftieth anniversary of a wedding.

▸ **B** *verb trans. & intrans.* Make or become golden in colour. *rare.* M19.

■ **goldenly** *adverb* (*a*) excellently, splendidly; (*b*) like or as with gold: E17. **goldenness** /-n-n-/ *noun* E19.

goldilocks /ˈgəʊldɪlɒks/ *noun.* M16.

[ORIGIN from GOLDY *adjective* + LOCK *noun*[1] + -S[1].]

1 A person with golden hair. Formerly also, golden hair. M16.

2 Any of several yellow-flowered plants, *esp.* †(*a*) a kind of helichrysum, *Helichrysum stoechas*; (*b*) a buttercup, *Ranunculus auricomus*, found in hedges and woods; (*c*) a rare yellow-flowered plant of the composite family, *Aster linosyris*, of limestone cliffs. L16.

golding /ˈgəʊldɪŋ/ *noun.* L18.

[ORIGIN Said to be from a Mr *Golding*, an early grower.]

A variety of hops used in making beer.

goldwasser /ˈgəʊldvasə, *foreign* ˈgɔldvasər/ *noun.* E20.

[ORIGIN German = gold water.]

A liqueur containing particles of gold leaf, orig. made at Gdańsk in Poland.

Goldwynism /ˈgəʊldwɪnɪz(ə)m/ *noun.* M20.

[ORIGIN from *Goldwyn* (see below) + -ISM.]

A witticism involving contradictory words or statements uttered by or typical of the American film producer Samuel F. Goldwyn (1882–1974).

goldy /ˈgəʊldi/ *adjective.* LME.

[ORIGIN from GOLD *noun*[1] + -Y[1].]

Of the colour or brilliance of gold; made of gold.

†**gole** *adjective.*

[ORIGIN Old English *gāl* = Old Saxon *gēl* (Dutch *geil*), Old High German, German *geil*, cogn. with Gothic *gailjan* cheer, make glad, from Germanic.]

1 Merry; wanton, lustful. OE–ME.

2 Of rank or luxuriant growth. Chiefly *dial.* L16–M19.

golem /ˈgəʊləm, ˈgɔɪl-/ *noun.* L19.

[ORIGIN Yiddish *goylem* from Hebrew *gōlem* shapeless mass.]

A human figure of clay etc. supernaturally brought to life; an automaton, a robot.

goles /gəʊlz/ *noun.* Now *arch. & dial.* M18.

[ORIGIN Alt. Cf. GOLLY *noun*[1].]

God: used in oaths and exclams. Chiefly in ***by goles!***

golf /gɒlf/ *noun & verb.* LME.

[ORIGIN Perh. rel. to Dutch *kolf* club.]

▸ **A** *noun.* An open-air game in which a small hard ball is struck with a club having a wooden or metal head into each of a series of (usu. 18 or 9) holes at varying distances apart and separated by fairways, rough ground, hazards, etc., the aim of the game being to complete the course using the fewest possible strokes. LME.

clock golf, ***miniature golf***, etc.

– COMB.: **golf bag**: for carrying clubs and balls; **golfball** (*a*) a small hard usu. rubber-cored ball used in golf; (*b*) a small spherical ball used to carry the type in certain kinds of electric typewriters; **golf cart** (*a*) a trolley for carrying golf clubs; (*b*) a motorized cart for transporting golfers and their equipment; **golf club** (*a*) a club used in golf; (*b*) (the premises of) an association for playing golf; ***golf course***: see COURSE *noun*[1] 6b; ***golf links***: see LINK *noun*[1] 2; **golf widow** a woman whose husband spends much of his spare time playing golf.

▸ **B** *verb intrans.* Play golf. L17.

■ **golfdom** *noun* the realm of golf E20. **golfer** *noun* (*a*) a person who plays golf; (*b*) a cardigan: M17.

Golgi /ˈgɒldʒi, -gi/ *noun.* L19.

[ORIGIN Camillo *Golgi* (1844–1926), Italian histologist.]

BIOLOGY. Used *attrib.* and in *possess.* to designate structures studied by Golgi and methods which he introduced.

Golgi apparatus, **Golgi body**, **Golgi complex**, a complex of membranous vesicles in the cytoplasm involved in secretion and intracellular transport. **Golgi method** a method of staining cells with silver salts or osmium tetroxide. **Golgi organ**, **Golgi spindle** a sensory apparatus in tendons responsive to tension. **Golgi stain** a metal compound used in the Golgi method of staining (see above).

golgotha /ˈgɒlgəθə/ *noun.* E17.

[ORIGIN Late Latin (Vulgate), from Greek by metathesis from Aramaic *gōgolṯā*, perh. under infl. of Hebrew *gulgōleṯ*: see CALVARY.]

1 A place of interment; a graveyard, a charnel house. E17.

†**2** The meeting place of the heads of university colleges or halls. *slang.* E18–E19.

goliard /ˈgəʊlɪɑːd/ *noun.* L15.

[ORIGIN Old French = glutton, from *gole* (mod. *gueule*) from Latin *gula* gluttony: see -ARD.]

hist. Any of a class of educated jesters or buffoons specializing in the writing of satirical Latin verse, who flourished chiefly in the 12th and 13th cent. in Germany, France, and Britain.

■ **goliardery** *noun* the poetry of the goliards M19. **goliardic** *adjective* of or pertaining to (the poetry of) the goliards L19.

Goliath /gəˈlʌɪəθ/ *noun.* Also **g-**. L16.

[ORIGIN ecclesiastical Latin = Hebrew *golyaṯ* the giant slain by David (*1 Samuel* 17).]

1 A giant. Freq. with allusion to the biblical story of David and Goliath. L16.

2 More fully ***Goliath beetle***. Any of several very large arboreal scarabaeid beetles constituting the tropical genus *Goliathus*, up to 20 cm (8 inches) in length. E19.

3 More fully ***Goliath crane***. A kind of powerful travelling crane. L19.

– COMB.: ***Goliath beetle***: see sense 2 above; ***Goliath crane***: see sense 3 above; **Goliath frog** a giant frog, *Rana goliath*, of west central Africa; **Goliath heron** a very large reddish-brown and grey heron, *Ardea goliath*, of African coastal and inland water margins.

gollan /ˈgɒlən/ *noun. obsolete* exc. *dial.* Also **-and** /-ənd/. LME.

[ORIGIN Perh. rel. to GOLD *noun*[2].]

Any of various (meadow) plants with yellow flowers; *esp.* a corn or marsh marigold, or a crowfoot. Cf. GOWAN.

golliwog /ˈgɒlɪwɒg/ *noun.* L19.

[ORIGIN from *Golliwogg* a doll character in books by B. Upton (d. 1912), US writer. Perh. suggested by GOLLY *noun*[1] and POLLIWOG.]

A black-faced brightly dressed soft doll with fuzzy hair; *offensive* a person resembling such a doll.

gollop /ˈgɒləp/ *verb & noun. dial. & colloq.* E19.

[ORIGIN Perh. extended form of GULP *verb*, infl. by GOBBLE *verb*[1].]

▸ **A** *verb trans.* Swallow greedily or hastily. Freq. foll. by *down* or *up*. E19.

▸ **B** *noun.* A greedy or hasty gulp. M20.

golly /ˈgɒli/ *noun*[1]. L18.

[ORIGIN Alt. Cf. GOLES, GOLDARN, GORRY.]

God: used in oaths and exclams.

by golly!, ***good golly!***

golly /ˈɡɒli/ *noun*[2]. **M20.**
[ORIGIN Abbreviation.]
= GOLLIWOG.

golosh *noun & verb* var. of GALOSH.

golpe /ɡɒlp/ *noun*. **M16.**
[ORIGIN Perh. from Spanish = wound, blow: cf. HURT *noun*[2].]
HERALDRY. A purple roundel.

goluptious /ɡəˈlʌpʃəs/ *adjective*. *joc.* **M19.**
[ORIGIN Perh. from VOLUPTUOUS.]
Luscious, delightful.

GOM *abbreviation*.
Grand Old Man (*spec.* William Ewart Gladstone).

gom *noun* see GORM *noun*.

Gomarist /ˈɡəʊmərɪst/ *noun*. **L17.**
[ORIGIN from *Gomar* (see below) + -IST.]
An advocate of the views of Francis Gomar (1563–1641), a professor of divinity at Leiden University who defended orthodox Calvinism in opposition to the views of Arminius. Cf. ARMINIAN.
■ Also **Gomarian** /ɡəʊˈmɛːrɪən/ *noun* (*rare*) **E17.**

gomashta /ɡɒˈmɑːʃtə/ *noun*. *Indian*. Now *rare* or *obsolete*. **M18.**
[ORIGIN Urdu, from Persian *gumāšta* appointed, delegated.]
A non-European agent or factor; a clerk dealing with vernacular correspondence.

gombeen /ɡɒmˈbiːn/ *noun & adjective*. *Irish*. **M19.**
[ORIGIN Irish *gaimbín*.]
▸ **A** *noun*. Usury. **M19.**
– COMB.: **gombeen-man**, **gombeen-woman** a usurer, a money-lender.
▸ **B** *adjective*. Selfishly materialist. **M20.**

Listener This whirlpool of *gombeen* capitalism.

gombroon /ˈɡɒmbruːn/ *noun*. **L17.**
[ORIGIN from *Gambroon* (now Bandar Abbas), a seaport in Iran.]
A kind of white semi-transparent pottery made in Iran in imitation of Chinese porcelain; similar pottery made in England.

†**gome** *noun* see GAUM *noun*[1].

gomer /ˈɡəʊmə/ *noun*. *US slang*. *derog*. **M20.**
[ORIGIN Origin obscure: sense 1 perh. from the name of *Gomer* Pyle, US television character, portrayed as an ignorant hillbilly; sense 2 may be an acronym from *Get out of my emergency room*.]
1 An inept or stupid colleague, esp. a trainee. *military slang*. **M20.**
2 A difficult or unrewarding patient, esp. an elderly one (used by doctors). **L20.**

gomerel /ˈɡɒm(ə)r(ə)l/ *noun*. *Scot. & N. English*. **E19.**
[ORIGIN Unknown.]
A fool, a simpleton.

gompa /ˈɡɒmpə/ *noun*. **E20.**
[ORIGIN Tibetan *gön-pa*, *gōm-pa* a solitary place, a hermitage.]
A Tibetan temple or monastery.

gomphosis /ɡɒmˈfəʊsɪs/ *noun*. Pl. **-phoses** /-ˈfəʊsiːz/. **L16.**
[ORIGIN Greek, from *gomphoun* bolt together, from *gomphos* bolt: see -OSIS.]
ANATOMY & ZOOLOGY. A form of joint in which one hard part (as a mammalian or crocodilian tooth) is immovably set into a cavity in another.

gomuti /ɡəˈmuːti/ *noun*. Also **-ta** /-tə/. **E19.**
[ORIGIN Malay *gemuti*.]
More fully ***gomuti palm***. A Malaysian feather palm, *Arenga pinnata*, cultivated in the tropics for palm sugar. Also (more fully ***gomuti fibre***), a strong black fibre obtained from the leaf sheaths of this palm and used in rope-making etc.

-gon /ɡ(ə)n, ɡɒn/ *suffix*.
[ORIGIN Greek *-gōnos* angled.]
Forming nouns denoting plane figures with a specified number of angles; also (*rare*) forming adjectives with the sense 'possessing a specified number of angles', as ***septagon***. Usu. with Greek combining forms, as ***hexagon***, ***polygon***; also with algebraic symbols or numerals, as ***n-gon***, ***16-gon***.

gonad /ˈɡəʊnad/ *noun*. **L19.**
[ORIGIN mod. Latin *gonas*, pl. *gonades*, from Greek *gonē*, *gonos* generation, seed: see -AD[1].]
BIOLOGY. An organ in an animal (as a testis or an ovary) that produces gametes.
■ **gonadal** /ɡə(ʊ)ˈneɪd(ə)l/ *adjective* of or pertaining to the gonads **M20.** **gonaˈdectomy** *noun* (an instance of) surgical removal of a gonad **E20.** **gonadial** /ɡə(ʊ)ˈneɪdɪəl/, **gonadic** /ɡə(ʊ)ˈnadɪk/ *adjectives* gonadal **E20.**

gonadotrophic /ˌɡəʊnadə(ʊ)ˈtrəʊfɪk, -ˈtrɒfɪk/ *adjective*. Also **-tropic** /-ˈtrəʊpɪk, -ˈtrɒpɪk/. **M20.**
[ORIGIN from GONAD + -O- + -TROPHIC, -TROPIC.]
PHYSIOLOGY. Regulating the activity of the gonads; of or pertaining to gonadotrophins.
■ **gonadotrophin**, **gonadotropin** *nouns* any of several glycoprotein hormones secreted by the mammalian pituitary or placenta and controlling gonadal activity **M20.**

gonangium /ɡə(ʊ)ˈnandʒɪəm/ *noun*. Pl. **-ia** /-ɪə/. **L19.**
[ORIGIN mod. Latin, from Greek *gonos* offspring + *aggeion* vessel.]
1 ZOOLOGY. = GONOTHECA. **L19.**
2 MYCOLOGY. In lichens, a hyphal organ in which propagative cells develop. **L19.**

Gond /ɡɒnd, ɡəʊnd/ *noun & adjective*. **E19.**
[ORIGIN Sanskrit *goṇḍa*.]
▸ **A** *noun*. **1** A member of a Dravidian people of central India. **E19.**
2 The Dravidian language of this people. **M19.**
▸ **B** *attrib.* or as *adjective*. Of or pertaining to the Gonds or their language. **M19.**
■ **Gondi** /ˈɡɒndi/ *noun & adjective* (of) the Gond language **M19.**

gondola /ˈɡɒndələ/ *noun*. **M16.**
[ORIGIN Venetian Italian, from Rhaeto-Romance *gondolà* to roll or rock.]
1 A light asymmetric flat-bottomed boat used on the Venetian canals, having a high pointed prow and stern and usu. propelled by a single oar at the stern. **M16.**

H. JAMES A gondola passed along the canal with its slow rhythmical plash.

2 A large light flat-bottomed riverboat; a lighter, used also as a gunboat. *US*. **L17.**
3 A car or nacelle attached to the underside of a dirigible or airship; something resembling this. **M19.**

I. ASIMOV Balloons with sealed gondolas reach the stratosphere.

4 More fully ***gondola car***, ***gondola wagon***. An open railway goods wagon with low sides. *US*. **L19.**

Time Hopping aboard slow-moving railroad gondolas to knock off a few chunks of coal.

5 A car attached to a ski lift. **M20.**

Skiing Today Ride a chair or gondola a couple of thousand feet up into the heart of the . . mountains.

6 An island display counter in a self-service shop. **M20.**
■ **gondole** /ɡɒnˈdəʊl/ *verb trans. & intrans.* row or travel in a gondola **L19.** **gondolet** *noun* a small (Venetian) gondola **E17.**

gondolier /ɡɒndəˈlɪə/ *noun & verb*. **E17.**
[ORIGIN French from Italian *gondoliere*, from GONDOLA: see -IER.]
▸ **A** *noun*. A person who rows a Venetian gondola. **E17.**
▸ **B** *verb*. **1** *verb intrans*. Be a gondolier. Chiefly as ***gondoliering*** *verbal noun*. **L19.**
2 *verb trans*. Convey in a gondola. **M20.**

F. CLUNE Albert gondoliered us across the stream.

Gondwana /ɡɒnˈdwɑːnə/ *noun & adjective*. **L19.**
[ORIGIN from *Gondwāna* a region in central north India, from Sanskrit *goṇḍavana*, from *goṇḍa* GOND + *vana* forest.]
GEOLOGY. ▸ **A** *noun*. **1** Orig., any of a series of rocks in India, chiefly fluviatile shales and sandstones, of Upper Carboniferous to Cretaceous age. Later also, any similar rock systems in other countries with the same characteristic fossil flora. Also, the period of their formation. **L19.**
2 = GONDWANALAND. **M20.**
▸ **B** *attrib.* or as *adjective*. **1** Of, pertaining to, or characteristic of the Gondwana systems or their period of formation. **L19.**
2 Of or pertaining to Gondwanaland. **M20.**

Gondwanaland /ɡɒnˈdwɑːnəland/ *noun*. **L19.**
[ORIGIN from GONDWANA + LAND *noun*[1].]
GEOLOGY. A supercontinent thought to have existed in the southern hemisphere in Palaeozoic times, comprising the present Africa, S. America, Australia, Antarctica, and the Indian peninsula. Also, these land masses collectively as they exist today.

gone /ɡɒn/ *adjective*. **L16.**
[ORIGIN pa. pple of GO *verb*. For pred. uses see GO *verb* V.]
1 That has gone (also foll. by adverb); departed; lost, hopeless; dead. **L16.** ▸**b** ***gone by***, bygone, past, long gone. **E19.**

SIR W. SCOTT Up heart, master, or we are but gone men. DICKENS In the chair before the gone-out fire . . was the gentleman whom she sought.

gone coon *US slang*, **gone goose**, **gone gosling** *colloq.* a person or thing beyond hope or help.
2 Excellent, inspired. *US slang*. **M20.**

J. KEROUAC I have found the gonest little girl in the world.

■ **goneness** *noun* faintness, exhaustion **M19.**

gone *verb pa. pple*: see GO *verb*.

goner /ˈɡɒnə/ *noun*. *slang*. **M19.**
[ORIGIN from GONE *adjective* + -ER[1].]
A person or thing which is doomed, ended, or irrevocably lost; a person or thing beyond hope or help.

W. H. AUDEN Rome will be a goner. E. JONG The minute he walked into a room and smiled at me, I was a goner. P. BAILEY I plunged in and swam to his rescue. He was a goner when I reached him.

gonfalon /ˈɡɒnf(ə)lən/ *noun*. **L16.**
[ORIGIN Italian *gonfalone* = French, later form of GONFANON.]
A banner, often with tails or streamers, hung from a crossbar.

MILTON Standards, and Gonfalons . . Stream in the Aire.

gonfalonier /ɡɒnf(ə)ləˈnɪə/ *noun*. **L16.**
[ORIGIN French (Old French *gonfanonier*): see GONFALON, -IER.]
A standard-bearer; *spec.* (**a**) the Pope's standard-bearer; (**b**) *hist.* any of various officials or magistrates in the Italian city states.
■ **gonfaloniership** *noun* the office of a gonfalonier **E18.**

gonfanon /ˈɡɒnfənɒn/ *noun*. *obsolete* exc. *hist.* **ME.**
[ORIGIN Old French from Frankish (= Old English *gūþfana*, Old High German *gundfano*, Old Norse *gunnfani*) from Germanic. Cf. FANON.]
A gonfalon. Also, a small flag or pennant immediately below the head of a knight's lance.

gong /ɡɒŋ/ *noun*. **E17.**
[ORIGIN Malay *gong*, *gung*, of imit. origin.]
1 A metallic disc with an upturned rim which gives a resonant sound when struck, used esp. as a summons to a meal or in an orchestra. **E17.** ▸**b** A saucer-shaped bell struck by a mechanical clapper, used as an alarm. **M19.** ▸**c** A warning bell on a police car. *slang*. **M20.**

D. H. LAWRENCE The gong sounded for the luncheon. **c** P. LAURIE We turn on the light and gong and go.

2 A medal; a decoration, an honour. *slang*. **E20.**

Evening Advertiser (Swindon) Civil servants and military men who get these gongs merely for doing their normal job.

3 A narcotic drug, *spec.* opium. *US slang*. **E20.**
beat the gong, **hit the gong**, **kick the gong (around)** smoke opium.
■ **gonger** *noun* (*US slang*) opium; an opium pipe: **E20.** **gongeˈrine** *noun* (*US slang*) an opium pipe **E20.**

gong /ɡɒŋ/ *verb*. **E20.**
[ORIGIN from the noun.]
1 *verb intrans*. Sound a gong or warning bell; make a sound like that of a gong. **E20.**
2 *verb trans*. Summon (a person) by sounding a gong; *slang* order (a driver) to stop by ringing the warning bell of a police car. **M20.**

gong-gong /ˈɡɒŋɡɒŋ/ *noun*. **L18.**
[ORIGIN Redupl. of Malay *gong*: see GONG *noun*.]
Any of various simple percussion instruments.

gongoozler /ɡɒŋˈɡuːzlə/ *noun*. *dial. & slang*. **E20.**
[ORIGIN Unknown.]
A person who stares for prolonged periods at something unusual. Orig. & chiefly, an idler who watches activity on a canal.

J. GAGG The gongoozlers—the hangers-around that canals often attract. *New Yorker* To watch a game on one of three huge outdoor screens . . supplied for gongoozlers like me.

gongora /ˈɡɒŋɡərə/ *noun*. **E19.**
[ORIGIN mod. Latin (see below), from Don Antonio Caballero y *Góngora* (fl. 1782), Viceroy of New Granada.]
Any of various tropical American epiphytic orchids of the genus *Gongora*, sometimes cultivated as curiosities.

gongorism /ˈɡɒŋɡərɪz(ə)m/ *noun*. **E19.**
[ORIGIN from *Góngora* (see below) + -ISM.]
A Spanish literary style marked by inversion, antithesis, and classical allusion, introduced by the Spanish poet Luis de Góngora y Argote (1561–1627).
■ **gongorist** *noun* a person who writes in this style **M19.** **gongoˈristic** *adjective* **E20.**

goniatite /ˈɡəʊnɪətʌɪt/ *noun*. **M19.**
[ORIGIN from mod. Latin *Goniatites* (see below), from Greek *gōnia* angle: see -ITE[1].]
PALAEONTOLOGY. Any ammonoid fossil of the genus *Goniatites* or a related genus, common in Devonian and Carboniferous rocks, and having simple usu. angular suture lines. Cf. AMMONITE, CERATITE.
■ **goniaˈtitic** /ɡəʊnɪəˈtɪtɪk/ *adjective* **L19.**

gonidium /ɡə(ʊ)ˈnɪdɪəm/ *noun*. Pl. **-ia** /-ɪə/. **M19.**
[ORIGIN mod. Latin, from Greek *gonos* offspring + Latin dim. *-idium*.]
BOTANY. An asexual reproductive cell in certain algae. Also (*arch.*), an algal cell in a lichen.
■ **gonidial** *adjective* **M19.**

gonif(f) *noun* var. of GONOPH.

goniometer /ɡəʊnɪˈɒmɪtə/ *noun*. **M18.**
[ORIGIN French *goniomètre*, from Greek *gōnia* angle: see -METER.]
Any of various instruments used for the measurement of angles, as in surveying, crystallography, radio direction-finding, medicine (e.g. in the study of joints, and of balance), etc.
■ **gonioˈmetric**, **gonioˈmetrical** *adjectives* of or pertaining to goniometry **M19.** **goniometry** *noun* the measurement of angles **E19.**

gonion /ˈɡəʊnɪɒn/ *noun*. **L19.**
[ORIGIN French, from Greek *gōnia* angle + *-ion*, after INION.]
ANATOMY. The outermost point on the angle of the lower jaw on each side.

gonioscopy /ɡəʊnɪˈɒskəpi/ *noun*. **E20.**
[ORIGIN from Greek *gōnia* angle: see -O-, -SCOPE, -Y[3].]
MEDICINE. Examination of the angle of the anterior chamber of the eye.
■ **ˈgonioscope** *noun* an instrument for gonioscopy **E20.** **gonioˈscopic** *adjective* **E20.**

G

G

Gonk /gɒŋk/ *noun*. M20.
[ORIGIN Arbitrary.]
(Proprietary name for) an egg-shaped soft doll with frizzy hair.

gonna /ˈgɒnə/ *verb* (*pres. pple*). *non-standard*. E20.
[ORIGIN Repr. a pronunc.]
Going to (see GO *verb* 36).

M. SHULMAN I'm gonna keep on yelling till you let me out.

gonnoff *noun* var. of GONOPH.

gono- /ˈgɒnəʊ, ˈgəʊnəʊ/ *combining form* of Greek *gonos*, *gonē* generation, offspring, semen, etc.: see -O-. Before a vowel also **gon-**.
■ **gonoduct** *noun* (ZOOLOGY) in various invertebrates, a duct through which gametes are discharged from a gonad L19. **gonophore** *noun* (*a*) BOTANY in certain flowers, an elongate structure bearing the stamens and pistil; (*b*) ZOOLOGY any structure bearing gonads; *esp*. in some colonial hydrozoans, a sessile medusoid polyp bearing gonads: M19. **gonopore** *noun* (ZOOLOGY) a small genital aperture L19. **gonoˈtheca** *noun*, pl. **-thecae**, ZOOLOGY in colonial hydrozoans of the order Thecata, an extension of the perisarc into a capsule surrounding the gonophores M19. **goˈnotocont**, **-kont** *noun* (chiefly MYCOLOGY) any cell or organ in which meiosis occurs E20. **gonoˈzooid** *noun* (ZOOLOGY) in colonial hydrozoans and some colonial tunicates, a zooid which performs a reproductive function L19.

gonococcus /gɒnəˈkɒkəs/ *noun*. Pl. **-cci** /-k(s)ʌɪ, -ˈkɒk(s)iː/. L19.
[ORIGIN from GONO(RRHOEA + COCCUS.]
MEDICINE. A spherical bacterium, *Neisseria gonorrhoeae*, the causative agent of gonorrhoea.
■ **gonococcal** /gɒnəˈkɒk(ə)l/ *adjective* E20.

gonoph /ˈgɒnɒf/ *noun*. *slang*. Also **gonnoff**, **gonif(f)**. M19.
[ORIGIN from Yiddish *ganev* from Hebrew *gannāḇ* thief.]
A pickpocket, a thief; a swindler.

gonorrhoea /gɒnəˈrɪə/ *noun*. Also ***-rrhea**. E16.
[ORIGIN Late Latin from Greek *gonorrhoia*, from *gonos* semen: see -RRHOEA.]
A venereal disease caused by the gonococcus bacterium, characterized by purulent inflammation of the genital mucous membranes, and consequent pain during urination and discharge.
■ **gonorrhoeal** *adjective* of, pertaining to, or affected with gonorrhoea E19.

gony /ˈgəʊni/ *noun*. In sense 2 freq. **goon(e)y** /ˈguːni/. L16.
[ORIGIN Unknown.]
1 A simpleton, a fool. Now *dial*. L16.
2 An albatross; *esp*. (*a*) the black-footed albatross, *Diomedea nigripes*, of the N. Pacific; (*b*) = LAYSAN ***albatross***. *colloq*. (chiefly *US*). M19.

attrib.: R. ARDREY The albatross . . became known to all the American fleet as the gony bird.

-gony /gəni/ *suffix*.
[ORIGIN from Greek *-gonia* generation, production + -Y³.]
Forming nouns denoting '(mode of) generation', as ***cosmogony***, ***heterogony***, ***theogony***.

gonyaulax /gəʊnɪˈɔːlaks/ *noun*. E20
[ORIGIN mod. Latin (see below), from Greek *gonu* knee + *aulax* furrow.]
A dinoflagellate of the genus *Gonyaulax*, toxic to marine life.

gonys /ˈgɒnɪs/ *noun*. M19.
[ORIGIN App. erron. from Greek *genys* underjaw.]
ORNITHOLOGY. The central ridge in the lower part of a bird's beak.

gonzo /ˈgɒnzəʊ/ *adjective* & *noun*. *slang* (orig. & chiefly *US*). L20.
[ORIGIN Perh. from Italian = foolish, or Spanish *ganso* goose, fool.]
▸ **A** *adjective*. Of, pertaining to, or designating a style of subjective journalism characterized by factual distortion and exaggerated rhetoric; *gen*. bizarre, crazy. L20.
▸ **B** *noun*. Pl. **-os**. Gonzo journalism; a journalist writing in this style; *gen*. a crazy or foolish person. L20.

goo /guː/ *noun*. *colloq*. E20.
[ORIGIN Uncertain: perh. abbreviation of BURGOO.]
A viscous or sticky substance; *fig*. sickly sentiment.

W. S. BURROUGHS Cat shit and nameless goo. *Times Lit. Suppl.* Subjects which . . have . . so embarrassingly degenerated into a mess of gush and goo.

goo /guː/ *verb intrans*. M20.
[ORIGIN Imit.]
Make an inarticulate cooing or gurgling sound like that made by a baby; converse affectionately.

goober /ˈguːbə/ *noun*. *N. Amer. colloq*. M19.
[ORIGIN Kikongo (& other west central African langs.) *Nguba*.]
1 The peanut. M19.
2 A person from the south-eastern US, esp. Georgia or Arkansas. Also, an unsophisticated person, a yokel. *derog*. L19.

good /gʊd/ *noun*. Also (*Scot.*) **guid** /gɪd/. OE.
[ORIGIN from the adjective.]
1 What is good or beneficial; well-being; profit or benefit; resulting advantage. OE. ▸**b** The good part or aspect (of anything). L17.

JONSON If he had employ'd Those excellent gifts . . Vnto the good, not ruin, of the State. N. ROWE What is the good of Greatness but the Power. W. S. TYLER A prayer-meeting . . has become a power for good in the College. W. S. JEVONS There could be no good in building docks unless there were ships to load in them. **b** J. B. NORTON The absence of necessity for the measure, its many evils, and its little good.

2 A desirable object or end; something advantageous or worth attaining. OE. ▸†**b** A good quality, virtue, grace. OE–M16. ▸†**c** A good action. OE–E18.

GEO. ELIOT Life . . is a doubtful good to many.

3 Property or possessions; *esp*. movable property. Now only in *pl*. OE. ▸†**b** Money. ME–M16. ▸†**c** In *pl*. Livestock. L15–L18.

R. BAXTER Stay not to save your Goods or Clothes.

4 In *pl*. Saleable commodities; merchandise, wares. Also occas. in *sing*., a type of merchandise. ME. ▸**b** Items for transmission by rail etc. (freq. *attrib*. in ***goods train***, ***goods yard***, etc.). Also *ellipt*., a goods train. M19.

A. BURGESS Indian cotton goods . . competed . . with the products of our own Lancashire mills. *Times* The consumer . . being misled into thinking a good is British.

5 *collect*. Virtuous people; *the* class of good people. Formerly also *sing*., a good person. ME.

M. PRIOR Sought by the good, by the oppressor fear'd.

– PHRASES & COMB.: **a bit of no good** a lot of harm. **all to the good** generally advantageous. ***a nasty bit of goods***, ***a nasty piece of goods***: see NASTY *adjective*. **be any good**, **be much good**, **be some good**, **be no good**, etc., be of any etc. use. **be — to the good** have — as a profit, gain, or advantage. ***bill of goods***: see BILL *noun*³. ***bit of goods***: see BIT *noun*² 6. ***brown goods***: see BROWN *adjective*. ***capital goods***: see CAPITAL *adjective* & *noun*². **come to good** yield a good result. **come to no good** yield no good result; come to a bad end. ***deliver the goods***: see DELIVER *verb* 6. **do any good** effect any good result; make progress, succeed. **do good** act rightly; show kindness *to*; be involved in charitable work; improve the condition of, be beneficial to. ***do more harm than good***: see HARM *noun*. ***do one's heart good***: see HEART *noun*. ***dry goods***: see DRY *adjective*. ***fancy goods***: see FANCY *adjective*. **for good (and all)** finally, permanently. **good-doer** a person who does good, a do-gooder; an animal or plant which thrives; ***goods and chattels***: see CHATTEL 2. **have the goods on** *slang* have (information etc. giving one) a hold over (another). **chief good**, **first good**, **highest good** = SUMMUM BONUM. **in good** *colloq*. in favour *with*. ***no good***: see NO *adjective*. **piece of goods** *joc*. a person. ***soft goods***: see SOFT *adjective*. **the goods** (*a*) what is provided or required; the real thing; the genuine article; (*b*) stolen articles found in a thief's possession; clear evidence, positive proof. ***the great and the good***: see GREAT *noun*. ***the sovereign good***: see SOVEREIGN *adjective* 2. ***the unco guid***: see UNCO *adverb*. **up to no good** up to mischief. ***white goods***: see WHITE *adjective*.

good /gʊd/ *adjective*. Compar. BETTER *adjective*, (*joc.*, *rare*) **gooder**; superl. BEST *adjective*, (*joc.*) **goodest**. Also (*Scot.*) **guid** /gɪd/.
[ORIGIN Old English *gōd* = Old Frisian, Old Saxon *gōd* (Dutch *goed*), Old High German *guot* (German *gut*), Old Norse *góðr*, Gothic *gōþs*, from Germanic, from var. of base 'bring together, unite' repr. also in GATHER *verb*.]
▸ **I 1** Having (enough of) the appropriate qualities; adequate; satisfactory, effective. Occas., excellent. OE. ▸**b** Of food or drink: fit for consumption; fresh. OE. ▸**c** Of soil: fertile. LME. ▸**d** Fine, worthy. Now only as a conventional epithet in ***the good ship —***, ***the good town of —***, etc. LME. ▸**e** Of money: genuine, not counterfeit. Now usu., a proper or considerable amount of (money); (money) which might have been spent usefully elsewhere. L16.

W. BLIGH One half of us slept on shore by a good fire. M. PATTISON A good history of our foreign policy would be very useful. **b** OED In the cold chamber meat will keep good for an indefinite time. **c** G. BERKELEY The seed of the gospel sown in good ground. **e** J. CONRAD Father was earning good money.

2 Adapted to a purpose; useful, suitable. Foll. by *for*, †*to* (a function), *to* with inf. OE.

F. MORYSON Like a Quince, requiring great cost ere it be good to eat. CARLYLE He was not now good for much; alas, it had been but little he was ever good for.

3 Of a person: distinguished in moral worth, (formerly) in rank or valour. Now *rare* exc. in ***as good as***, ***good enough for***, ***too good for***, (arch.) ***good men and true***. OE. ▸**b** As a conventional epithet used preceding titles of high rank; ***good lady***, ***one's good lady***, a patroness, ***good lord***, ***one's good lord***, a patron. Also, in forms of address, as ***good my lord*** etc. Now *arch*. or *hist*. OE. ▸**c** In courteous, patronizing, ironically polite, or indignant address, esp. in ***my good man***, ***my good sir***, etc., ***your good lady***, ***your good self***, etc. Cf. GOODMAN, GOODWIFE. OE.

OED His wife is far too good for him. **c** I. BANKS We were heading for the good doctor's office.

4 Commendable, desirable, right, proper; expedient. OE. ▸**b** As *interjection* expr. approval, pleasure, etc.: excellent, fine. LME.

MAX-MÜLLER It was not good to be without an ancestor.

5 a Of birth, family, rank, etc.: elevated, not humble. OE. ▸**b** (Of condition, health, etc.) satisfactory, unimpaired; (of courage or spirits) not dejected. ME. ▸**c** Of reputation: honourable. L15. ▸**d** Of a quality: commendable, conducive to value or merit. L16. ▸**e** Of appearance, a physical attribute: attractive. E17.

a DEFOE I was born in the Year 1632 . . of a good Family. **b** LD MACAULAY The health of the crews had . . been . . wonderfully good. J. CARLYLE I don't feel in such good heart about the Devonshire visit as I did. **d** OED The author's style is not without some good qualities. **e** A. N. WILSON A good chin, and a long swan-like throat.

6 Having the characteristics or aptitudes necessary or suitable in a certain capacity or relationship. OE. ▸**b** Competent, skilful, efficient, or clever *at*, *in*, *with*. LME.

DRYDEN Good Shepherds after shearing drench their sheep. DICKENS The Doctor, I believe, is a very good shot. **b** A. THWAITE He cared about children and was good with them. I. COLEGATE Few people like doing what they are not very good at.

7 Of a right, claim, contract, etc.: valid, sound, effectual. OE.

F. MORYSON Having the Lawes . . together with a good cause on his side.

8 Sufficient in quantity or degree; ample; considerable. Also as intensifier. OE.

W. H. DIXON The composition of this work kept Penn at home a good part of the year. OED He writes a good bold hand.

9 Not less than and usu. greater than (a specified quantity). OE.

GEO. ELIOT He . . played a good hour on the violoncello.

10 Of an action or activity: adequate to the purpose; sufficient; thorough. ME.

SHELLEY I have taken good care That shall not be. S. WALPOLE Society did not see anything unseemly . . in a man administering a good beating to his wife.

11 Reliable, safe, sure; financially sound; able to meet one's liabilities; *spec*. (of a life) likely to be profitable to an insurer. E16.

T. FULLER He is called . . a Good Man upon the exchange, who hath a responsible estate.

▸ **II 12** Morally excellent or commendable; virtuous. OE.

H. B. STOWE She is as good as she is beautiful. H. SPENCER If we call good every kind of conduct which aids the lives of others.

13 Kind, benevolent; gracious; friendly. (Foll. by *to*.) Formerly also, naively trusting. OE.

H. JAMES The lady with whom you were so good as to make me acquainted. G. GORDON Edward wanted to be thanked for his good intentions.

In exclamations: ***good God!***, ***good gracious*** (***me***)***!***, ***good grief!***, ***good heavens!***, (Austral.) ***good iron!***, ***good Lord!***; arch. also ***good hallow!***, ***good lack!***, ***good me!***

14 Pious, devout; spiritually edifying. OE. ▸**b** Of a day or season: observed as holy. Now only in ***Good Friday*** below. LME.

15 Esp. of a child: well behaved, quiet, obedient. L17.

W. CONGREVE Be a good Girl, don't perplex your poor Uncle.

▸ **III 16** Fortunate; welcome; *spec*. (of a wind) favourable. OE.

H. JAMES Bring the good news from Ghent to Aix.

17 Pleasant to the senses or feelings; tasty, appetizing; agreeable; amusing, entertaining, witty. OE.

W. HAY Wine, and good fare. J. CONRAD The young man laughed as if at a good joke.

18 Beneficial; advantageous; wholesome. (Foll. by *for*, †*to*). OE. ▸**b** Useful as a remedy (*for*, †*against*). LME.

G. GREENE Lime juice is very good for you . . It contains . . vitamins.

19 Of an opinion or account: favourable, approving, laudatory. L16.

SHAKES. *Jul. Caes.* His silver hairs will purchase us a good opinion.

– SPECIAL COLLOCATIONS, PHRASES, & COMB.: In comb. (*Scot. & N. English*) denoting a grandparent (***good-dame***, ***good-sire***), or a relation by marriage (= -IN-LAW; rarely also = STEP-), (***good-brother***, ***good-daughter***, ***good-father***, ***good-mother***, ***good-sister***, ***good-son***). Generally: ***a good cry***: see CRY *noun*. ***a good day's work***: see WORK *noun*. ***a good few***. ***a good field***: see FIELD *noun*. **a good one**, **a good 'un** *colloq*. an incredible lie or exaggeration; an excellent joke. **a good question** a difficult question; a question requiring careful consideration before answering. **a good way**, (*dial.*) **a good ways** a considerable distance. **all in good time** in due course; not immediately. ***as good as***: see AS *adverb* etc. **as good as gold** extremely or angelically good (GOOD *adjective* 15). **be as good as one's word** carry out one's promise fully. **be good** *joc*. (esp. said at parting) behave yourself. **be good enough to (do)** please (do). ***be in the good graces of***: see GRACE *noun*. **be so good as to (do)** please (do). ***get in good***: see GET *verb*. ***give a good account of***: see ACCOUNT *noun*. ***give as good as one gets***: see GIVE *verb*. **good-bad** *adjective* good but of an inferior or second-rate type. ***Good Book***: see BOOK *noun*. **good breeding** courteous or correct manners (resulting from a good education). **good buddy** *slang* (chiefly *N. Amer.*) (among Citizens' Band radio operators) chum, pal. ***good buy***: see BUY *noun*. ***good cause***: see CAUSE *noun*. ***good cheer***: see CHEER *noun*¹ 2, 5. ***good conscience***. ***good creature***: see CREATURE 1C. **good debt**: which is sure to be paid. **good deed** a good or kind action; *esp*. an act of service for another person performed by a Scout, Guide, etc. ***good egg***: see EGG *noun* 3. **good fairy** a benefactor or benefactress; a fairy godmother. ***good faith***: see FAITH *noun*. **good for** (of a person) that may be relied on to pay (a sum); (of a promissory note etc.) drawn for (a sum); *gen.* capable of producing, valid for, able to accomplish (something); likely to live or last for (a period of time); acting as surety for (a person). ***good form***: see FORM *noun*. **good for nothing** worthless (cf. GOOD-FOR-NOTHING). **good for you**, **good for her**, etc. *colloq.* well done. **Good Friday** the Friday before Easter Day, observed as the anniversary of Jesus's Crucifixion. **goodhap** *arch.* good fortune. **good-hearted** *adjective* kindly, well-meaning. ***good job***: see JOB *noun*[1]. **Good King Henry** a herb of the goosefoot family, *Chenopodium bonus-henricus*. **good-liking** (now *rare* or *obsolete*) friendly or kindly feeling towards a person; approval, goodwill. ***good liver***: see LIVER *noun*[2]. ***good living***: see LIVING *noun*[1]. **good-looker** an attractive or handsome person. **good-looking** *adjective* attractive, handsome. **good looks** attractiveness, personal beauty. ***good loser***: see LOSER 2. ***good luck!***, ***good luck to you!*** etc.: see LUCK *noun*. **good man!** *colloq.* well done! ***good name***: see NAME *noun*. ***good now*** *interjection*: see NOW *adverb*. ***good oil***: see OIL *noun*. ***good old***: see OLD *adjective*. **good on** knowledgeable and usu. helpful or informative about (a subject). **good on you**, **good on her**, etc. (chiefly *Austral.* & *NZ*) = ***good for you*** above. **good people** the fairies; occas., witches. ***good Samaritan***: see SAMARITAN *noun* 2. ***good sense***: see SENSE *noun*. ***good show!***: see SHOW *noun*[1]. **good-tempered** *adjective* having a good temper; not easily angered. ***Good Templar***: see TEMPLAR *noun* 1c. ***good thing***: see THING *noun*[1]. **good-time** *adjective* (of a person) recklessly pursuing pleasure; loose-living. **good times** a period of prosperity. ***good turn***: see TURN *noun* 18. ***good value***: see VALUE *noun*. ***good word***: see WORD *noun*. **good works** charitable acts. ***have a good mind***: see MIND *noun*[1]. **have a good time** enjoy oneself. ***have a good war***: see WAR *noun*[1]. ***hold good***: see HOLD *verb*. **in good time** (***a***) with time to spare; punctual, without risk of being late; †(***b***) at the right moment; †(***c***) (as *interjection*) to be sure! indeed! ***in good voice***: see VOICE *noun*. ***in someone's good books***: see BOOK *noun*. **make good** (***a***) *verb phr. trans.* make up for, compensate for; supply (a deficiency), pay (an expense); (***b***) *verb phr. trans.* fulfil, perform (a promise etc.); carry out, effect (a purpose); (***c***) *verb phr. trans.* prove to be true or valid; substantiate; (***d***) *verb phr. trans.* (*arch.*) make sure of; make secure, hold, retain; (***e***) *verb phr. trans.* replace or restore (what is lost or damaged); (***f***) *verb phr. intrans.* & *trans.* make (a surface) even or level; (***g***) *verb phr. intrans.* (orig. *US*) succeed; satisfy expectations; fulfil an obligation; (***h***) *verb phr. intrans.* (POKER) add enough to an ante or bet to make it equal the stake of the other player(s). **not good enough** *colloq.* unsatisfactory; not worth doing, accepting, etc. ***of good family***: see FAMILY *noun*. **one's good lady** one's wife. ***stand good***: see STAND *verb*. ***take in good part***: see PART *noun*. **too good to be true** incredibly good or pleasant. ***very good***: see VERY *adjective*[1] & *adverb*. ***walk good!***: see WALK *verb*[1]. ***well and good***: see WELL *adjective*. ***while the going is good***: see GOING *noun* 4. ***with a good grace***: see GRACE *noun*. **your good self**, **your good selves** (as a polite form of address) you.

good /gʊd/ *verb*. Long *obsolete* exc. *Scot.* Also (*Scot.*) **guid** /gɪd/. OE.
[ORIGIN from the adjective.]
†**1** *verb intrans.* Become better, improve. OE–ME.
†**2** *verb trans.* Enrich, endow (a church etc.). OE–ME.
3 *verb trans.* †**a** Make good; improve. ME–M17. ▸**b** Improve (land) by manuring it. M16.
†**4** *verb trans.* Do good to, benefit (a person). ME–E17.

good /gʊd/ *adverb*. Also (*Scot.*) **guid** /gɪd/. *colloq.* ME.
[ORIGIN from the adjective.]
Well, properly, thoroughly.

D. CROCKETT I . . shot him the third time, which killed him good. J. P. DONLEAVY My mother could never cook this good.

as good as well. **good and —** *colloq.* (orig. *US*) thoroughly —, extremely —.

good afternoon /gʊd ˌɑːftəˈnuːn/ *interjection & noun*. E20.
[ORIGIN from GOOD *adjective* + AFTERNOON *noun*.]
(A conventional utterance) expr. good wishes on meeting or parting during the afternoon.

goodbye /gʊdˈbʌɪ/ *interjection & noun*. Also ***-by**. Pl. **-byes**, ***-bys**. L16.
[ORIGIN Contr. of *God be with you*, with later substitution of GOOD *noun* for GOD *noun*, after GOOD DAY, GOODNIGHT.]
▸ **A** *interjection*. Farewell. Cf. BYE *interjection*, BYE-BYE *interjection*. L16.
▸ **B** *noun*. A farewell, an act of saying goodbye. L16.

attrib.: T. W. HIGGINSON Her father would seize Annie for a goodbye kiss.

good day /gʊdˈdeɪ/ *noun & interjection*. OE.
[ORIGIN from GOOD *adjective* + DAY *noun*.]
(A conventional utterance) expr. good wishes on meeting or parting during the daytime. Orig. in phrs. ***God give you good day***, ***have good day***, etc.

good-den *interjection & noun* see GOOD-EVEN.

gooder, **goodest** *adjectives* see GOOD *adjective*.

good-even /gʊdˈiːv(ə)n/ *interjection & noun*. Now *dial.* or *arch.* Also (*dial.*) **good-den** /gʊˈdɛn/. LME.
[ORIGIN from GOOD *adjective* + EVEN *noun*[1].]
= GOOD EVENING. Formerly also = GOOD AFTERNOON. Orig. in ***God give you good even***, etc.

good evening /gʊdˈiːvnɪŋ/ *interjection & noun*. M19.
[ORIGIN from GOOD *adjective* + EVENING *noun*.]
(A conventional utterance) expr. good wishes on meeting or parting in the evening.

goodfella /gʊdˈfɛlə/ *noun*. *colloq.* L20.
[ORIGIN Var. of GOOD FELLOW: cf. FELLA.]
A mobster; *spec.* a member of a Mafia family.
– NOTE: Popularized by the 1990 film *GoodFellas*.

good fellow /gʊd ˈfɛləʊ/ *noun phr.* ME.
[ORIGIN from GOOD *adjective* + FELLOW *noun*.]
1 An agreeable or jovial companion, a convivial person; a reliable or true friend. ME.
†**2** A thief. E–M17.
– NOTE: See also ROBIN GOODFELLOW.
■ **good-fellowship** *noun* conviviality; true friendship or companionship: LME.

good-for-nothing /ˈgʊdfənʌθɪŋ/ *adjective & noun*. E18.
[ORIGIN The phr. *good for nothing* (see GOOD *adjective*) used attrib. or as noun.]
▸ **A** *attrib. adjective*. Useless; worthless. E18.

BYRON A little curly-headed, good-for-nothing, And mischief-making monkey.

▸ **B** *noun*. A useless or worthless person or (formerly) thing. M18.

A. BIRRELL His brother was a good-for-nothing, with a dilapidated reputation.

■ **good-for-nothingness** *noun* M18. **good-for-nought** *adjective & noun* = GOOD-FOR-NOTHING E19.

good humour /gʊd ˈhjuːmə/ *noun phr.* E17.
[ORIGIN from GOOD *adjective* + HUMOUR *noun*.]
The state or disposition of amiable cheerfulness.
■ **good-ˈhumoured** *adjective* characterized by good humour; in a good humour: M17. **good-ˈhumouredly** *adverb* M18.

goodie *noun* var. of GOODY *noun*[2].

gooding /ˈgʊdɪŋ/ *verbal noun*. L15.
[ORIGIN from GOOD *verb* + -ING[1]. Sense 2 prob. from GOOD *noun*.]
1 The action of improving something (esp. land by manuring); manure. *obsolete* exc. *Scot.* L15.
2 Orig., the practice of begging. Now only *local*, the custom of collecting alms on St Thomas's Day (21 December). M16.

goodish /ˈgʊdɪʃ/ *adjective*. M18.
[ORIGIN from GOOD *adjective* + -ISH[1].]
Somewhat good, fairly good.

DICKENS A goodish bit ago.

†**goodlike** *adjective*. M16–M19.
[ORIGIN from GOOD *adjective* + -LIKE.]
Goodly; good-looking.

goodly /ˈgʊdli/ *adjective*.
[ORIGIN Old English *gōdlīc*: see GOOD *adjective*, -LY[1].]
1 Good-looking, comely, attractive, handsome; well-proportioned. *arch.* OE.
2 Considerable in size or quantity. ME.
3 Of good quality, admirable, excellent. Also, convenient, suitable. *arch.* LME.

iron.: SHAKES. *Oth.* Here's a goodly watch indeed!

†**4** Gracious, kindly. Only in LME.
■ †**goodlihead** *noun* comeliness, beauty; good character or personality: LME–M19. **goodliness** *noun* comeliness, beauty; goodness: LME.

goodly /ˈgʊdli/ *adverb*. Now *rare* or *obsolete*. ME.
[ORIGIN from GOOD *adjective* + -LY[2].]
†**1** Beautifully, elegantly. ME–M16.
†**2** Favourably, graciously; courteously, becomingly. ME–L17.
3 Excellently. ME.
4 Conveniently; with propriety. LME.
†**5** In neg. contexts: easily, readily. LME–M17.

goodman /ˈgʊdmən/ *noun*. Pl. **-men**. ME.
[ORIGIN from GOOD *adjective* + MAN *noun*.]
1 The master or male head of a household or other establishment; *esp.* a husband (in relation to his wife). Now chiefly *Scot. arch.* ME.
2 As a prefix to the surname (or occupation) of a man of humble birth or low rank: Mr. *obsolete* exc. *hist.* LME.
3 A man of substance, not of gentle birth, a guildsman, burgess; a yeoman; a Scottish laird. *obsolete* exc. *hist.* LME.

good morning /gʊdˈmɔːnɪŋ/ *interjection & noun*. LME.
[ORIGIN from GOOD *adjective* + MORNING *noun*.]
(A conventional utterance) expr. good wishes on meeting or parting in the morning.

good-morrow /gʊdˈmɒrəʊ/ *interjection & noun*. *arch.* LME.
[ORIGIN from GOOD *adjective* + MORROW *noun*.]
▸ **A** *interjection*. Hello, goodbye (said during the morning). LME.
▸ **B** *noun*. A hello or farewell (said during the morning). Formerly also, an idle or trivial saying, a trifling matter. M16.

good nature /gʊd ˈneɪtʃə/ *noun phr.* LME.
[ORIGIN from GOOD *adjective* + NATURE *noun*.]
Friendly or kindly disposition; *esp.* (unselfish) readiness to be imposed upon.

good-natured /gʊdˈneɪtʃəd/ *adjective*. L16.
[ORIGIN from GOOD NATURE + -ED[2].]
Having a good nature.
■ **good-naturedly** *adverb* M18.

good neighbour /gʊd ˈneɪbə/ *noun phr.* Also ***-or**. LME.
[ORIGIN from GOOD *adjective* + NEIGHBOUR *noun*.]
1 A friendly and helpful neighbour. Also, a good Samaritan. LME.
†**the good neighbours** fairies; witches.
2 A country which has good relations with neighbouring countries. Chiefly *N. Amer.* E20.

attrib.: *Listener* The shelving of a good neighbour policy in favour of the Dulles mania.

■ **good-neighbourhood** *noun* friendly or helpful disposition or behaviour L16. **good-neighbourliness** *noun* = GOOD-NEIGHBOURHOOD: L19.

goodness /ˈgʊdnɪs/ *noun*.
[ORIGIN Old English *gōdnes*: see GOOD *adjective*, -NESS.]
1 The quality or condition of being good; excellence in respect of some quality; moral virtue. OE.

W. TEMPLE Goodness . . makes men prefer their Duty . . before their Passions. T. JEFFERSON Our superiority in the goodness, though not in the number of our cavalry.

2 Benevolence, beneficence (freq. that of God); kindness, generosity; clemency. OE.

G. BURNET Goodness is an inclination to promote the Happiness of others. J. WESLEY I sing the goodness of the Lord, the goodness I experience. L. STERNE Have the goodness, madam . . to step in.

In various exclamatory phrases: ***for goodness' sake!***, ***goodness!***, ***goodness gracious!***, ***goodness knows***, ***goodness only knows***, ***I wish to goodness!***, ***surely to goodness!***, ***thank goodness!***, etc.

3 †**a** Advantage, profit. ME–L16. ▸**b** A good act or deed. Long *rare* or *obsolete*. ME.
4 (Freq. with *the*.) That which is good in anything; the strength or essence of something. L16.

Times The liquor in which canned vegetables are packed . . contains flavour and goodness from the vegetables.

goodnight /gʊdˈnʌɪt/ *interjection & noun*. LME.
[ORIGIN from GOOD *adjective* + NIGHT *noun*.]
(A conventional utterance) expr. good wishes on parting or going to bed at night. Orig. in phrs. ***have good night***, ***give you good night***, ***God give you good night***, etc.

attrib.: HARPER LEE Give me a good night kiss.

goodo /ˈgʊdəʊ, gʊdˈəʊ/ *interjection, adverb, & adjective*. Also **good-oh**. E20.
[ORIGIN from GOOD *adjective* + O, OH *interjections*.]
▸ **A** *interjection*. Good! Excellent! E20.
▸ **B** *adverb & adjective*. Excellent(ly); well; good. *Austral.* & *NZ*. E20.

goodwife /ˈgʊdwʌɪf/ *noun*. Pl. **-wives** /-wʌɪvz/. ME.
[ORIGIN from GOOD *adjective* + WIFE *noun*.]
1 The female head of a household, a housewife; *esp.* a wife (in relation to her husband). Now chiefly *Scot. arch.* ME.
2 As a prefix to the surname of a woman (usu. of low rank): Mrs. *obsolete* exc. *hist.* E16.

goodwill /gʊdˈwɪl/ *noun*. Also **good will**. OE.
[ORIGIN from GOOD *adjective* + WILL *noun*[1].]
†**1** Virtuous, pious, or honest disposition or intention. OE–E17.
2 Kindly feeling towards a person, cause, etc.; favour; benevolence. Freq. *attrib.*, as ***goodwill mission***, ***goodwill visit***, etc. OE.

LD MACAULAY Some pious men . . spoke of him, not indeed with esteem, yet with goodwill. E. WAUGH Every man of goodwill should devote all his powers to preserving the few good things remaining to us.

3 Cheerful acquiescence or consent; heartiness, zeal. ME.

WORDSWORTH Horses have worked with right good-will. T. BENN Capital can't do without the goodwill of labour.

†**of one's goodwill**, †**with one's goodwill**, †**by one's goodwill** voluntarily, freely.
4 The established custom or popularity of a business etc.; (a sum paid for) the privilege, granted to the purchaser by the seller of a business, of trading as the recognized successor of the seller. L16.

T. LUNDBERG Goodwill is normally measured by reference to a percentage of . . turnover or by a multiple of . . pre-tax profit.

goodwives *noun pl.* of GOODWIFE.

goody /ˈgʊdi/ *noun*[1]. M16.
[ORIGIN Hypocoristic from GOODWIFE; cf. HUSSY from HOUSEWIFE *noun*.]
1 = GOODWIFE. *arch.* M16.
2 At Harvard University: a female servant, *esp.* a bedmaker. E19.

goody /ˈgʊdi/ *noun*[2]. *colloq.* Also **-die**. M18.
[ORIGIN from GOOD *adjective* + -Y[6].]
A good, attractive, or desirable thing, esp. to eat; a sweet confection. Usu. in *pl.*

G

– COMB.: **goody bag** a bag containing a selection of desirable items, esp. one given away as a promotional offer.

goody /ˈgʊdi/ *noun*[3]. *colloq.* Also **-die**. M19.
[ORIGIN from GOOD *adjective* + -Y[6].]
A good person (*esp.* in a film, play, etc., as opp. BADDY); a goody-goody.

goody /ˈgʊdi/ *adjective*. *colloq.* E19.
[ORIGIN from GOOD *adjective* + -Y[6].]
Goody-goody. Formerly also, pleasant.
goody two-shoes: see TWO.
▪ **goodiness**, **goodyness** nouns E19.

goody /ˈgʊdi/ *interjection*. L18.
[ORIGIN from GOOD *adjective* + -Y[6].]
Expr. childish delight or surprise. Freq. redupl.

N. FREELING Buttered toast, and cherry cake, as well as Marmite. Goody, goody gumdrops.

goodyear /ˈgʊdjɪə/ *noun*. *obsolete* exc. *dial.* M16.
[ORIGIN GOOD *adjective* + YEAR *noun*[1], perh. ellipt. from 'I hope for a good year.']
A more or less meaningless expletive, chiefly used in interrog. phr. ***what the goodyear?***, ***what a goodyear?***; [through equivalence with *devil*] a malevolent power, an evil spirit.

goodyera /gʊdˈjɪərə, ˈgʊdjərə/ *noun*. E19.
[ORIGIN mod. Latin (see below), from John *Goodyer* (1592–1664), English botanist.]
Any of various orchids of the genus *Goodyera*, with creeping rhizomes and small chiefly whitish flowers; *esp.* (in full ***creeping goodyera***) *G. repens*, native to moist pinewoods in northern temperate regions. Also called ***creeping lady's tresses***.

goody-goody /ˈgʊdɪgʊdi/ *adjective* & *noun*. M19.
[ORIGIN Redupl. of GOODY *adjective* or *noun*[3].]
(A person who is) sentimentally, primly, affectedly, or obtrusively virtuous.

E. J. WORBOISE I abominate your goody-goody, circumspect, infallibly-proper young lady. P. LEACH Four year olds often sound goody-goody as well as bossy.

▪ Also **goody-good** *adjective* & *noun* M19.

gooey /ˈguːi/ *adjective*. *colloq.* (orig. *US*). E20.
[ORIGIN from GOO *noun* + *-ey* (-Y[1]).]
Soft and viscous; *fig.* mawkishly sentimental.

News of the World Gooey chocolate gateau. *Daily Express* Her once tough father has gone positively gooey over Fawn.

▪ **gooily** *adjective* M20.

goof /guːf/ *noun*. *slang*. E20.
[ORIGIN Unknown.]
1 A person who is always making stupid blunders. E20.
2 A stupid blunder or gaffe, esp. by an entertainer. M20.
– COMB.: **goof-proof** *adjective* (*colloq.*) simple enough for anyone to use, foolproof.

goof /guːf/ *verb*. *slang* (chiefly *N. Amer.*). M20.
[ORIGIN from the noun.]
1 *verb intrans.* Spend time idly or irresponsibly; *esp.* fool *about*, *around*, skive *off*. Also, watch in wide-eyed amazement. M20.

M. PUZO He never . . goofed off into restaurants when he was on foot patrol. J. LENNON It was just ad libbing and goofing about.

2 *verb intrans.* Make a stupid blunder. Also foll. by *off*, *up*. M20.

M. AMSTERDAM The laundry sure goofed; they must have sent me the wrong shirt.

3 *verb trans.* In *pass.* Be under the influence of drugs. Foll. by *up*. M20.
4 *verb trans.* Foll. by *up*: bungle, mess up. M20.
– COMB.: **goofball** (*a*) a pill containing a narcotic drug, esp. a barbiturate; (*b*) a blundering or eccentric person; **goof-up** a stupid blunder; a cock-up, a goof.

goofer /ˈguːfə/ *noun*[1]. *US*. Also **goopher**. L19.
[ORIGIN Of African origin: cf. Mende *ngafa* spirit, devil.]
A (magic) spell; a practitioner of magic.
– COMB.: **goofer dust** a powder (esp. dust from a grave) used in casting spells.

goofer /ˈguːfə/ *noun*[2]. E20.
[ORIGIN from GOOF *verb* + -ER[1].]
A person who goofs.

go-off /ˈgəʊɒf/ *noun*. *colloq.* M19.
[ORIGIN from *go off* s.v. GO *verb*.]
A commencement, a start. Chiefly in ***first go-off***, ***at first go-off***, at one's first attempt; ***at one go-off***, at one go.

goofus /ˈguːfəs/ *noun*. E20.
[ORIGIN from GOOF *noun*; cf. DOOFUS. Sense 2 may be a different word.]
1 A foolish or stupid person; an idiot. *US slang.* E20.
2 A variety of harmonica made in the form of a miniature saxophone. *obsolete* exc. *hist.* E20.

goofy /ˈguːfi/ *adjective*. *slang*. E20.
[ORIGIN from GOOF *noun* + -Y[1].]
1 Stupid, fatuous, inane. E20.

P. G. WODEHOUSE He was lying back . . with his mouth open and a . . goofy expression in his eyes.

2 Of teeth: protruding. M20.
– SPECIAL COLLOCATIONS: **goofy foot** *SURFING* (the position of) a person who rides a surfboard with the right (instead of the left) foot forward.
▪ **goofily** *adverb* E20. **goofiness** *noun* E20.

goog /gʊg/ *noun*. *Austral. slang*. Also **googie** /ˈgʊgi/. E20.
[ORIGIN Uncertain: cf. GOGGIE.]
An egg.
full as a goog: see FULL *adjective*.

google /ˈguːg(ə)l/ *verb trans.* & *intrans.* Also **G-**. L20.
[ORIGIN from *Google*, the proprietary name of a popular Internet search engine.]
Use the Internet, esp. the Google search engine, to find information about someone or something.

Mojo I've Googled my name and there are a couple of other Yanuls.

googly /ˈguːgli/ *noun*. E20.
[ORIGIN Unknown.]
CRICKET. An off-break ball bowled with apparent leg-break action; *fig.* a disconcertingly awkward question etc.

googly /ˈguːgli/ *adjective*. E20.
[ORIGIN Cf. GOO-GOO *adjective*.]
Of the eyes: round and staring. Also, of a person: casting amorous looks.

googol /ˈguːgɒl/ *noun*. M20.
[ORIGIN Arbitrary.]
Ten raised to the hundredth power (10^{100}).
– NOTE: This word and its deriv. are not in formal mathematical use.
▪ **googolplex** *noun* [cf. *-plex* in *multiplex*] ten raised to the power of a googol M20.

goo-goo /ˈguːguː/ *adjective* & *noun*. *slang*. E20.
[ORIGIN Perh. rel. to GOGGLE *adjective* & *verb*[1].]
▸ **A** *adjective*. Of the gaze: amorously adoring. Usu. in ***goo-goo eyes***. E20.
▸ **B** *noun*. An amorous look. E20.

gook /guːk, gʊk/ *noun*[1] & *adjective*. *slang* (orig. & chiefly *US*). *derog.* & *offensive*. E20.
[ORIGIN Unknown.]
▸ **A** *noun*. A foreigner, *esp.* a member of an Asian or Pacific people. E20.
▸ **B** *adjective*. Foreign, *esp.* Asian; made in a foreign country. M20.

gook /guːk, gʊk/ *noun*[2]. *colloq.* M20.
[ORIGIN var. of GUCK.]
A sloppy wet or viscous substance.

gool /guːl/ *noun*. ME.
[ORIGIN Anglo-Norman *gole*, *goule*, spec. use of Old French *gole*, *goule* throat: cf. GULL *noun*[3].]
1 A small channel, a ditch; an outlet for water. Chiefly *dial.* ME.
2 Chiefly *LAW*. A breach in a sea wall or embankment. M17.

goolie /ˈguːli/ *noun*. *slang*. Also **gool(e)y**. E20.
[ORIGIN Sense 1 perh. from an Aboriginal language of New South Wales. Sense 2 app. of Indian origin; cf. Hindi *golī* bullet, ball, pill.]
1 A stone or pebble. *Austral.* & *NZ*. E20.
2 A testicle. Usu. in *pl.* M20.

goombah /ˈguːmbɑː/ *noun*[1]. *W. Indian*. Also **-bay** /-beɪ/. L18.
[ORIGIN W. Indian creole: cf. Kikongo *ŋkumbi* a kind of drum, Twi *gumbe* drum music.]
Any of various types of drum played with the fingers (rather than with sticks).

goombah /guːmˈbɑː/ *noun*[2]. *US slang*. M20.
[ORIGIN Prob. from Italian dial. alt. of *compàre* godfather, friend, accomplice.]
A close friend or associate, a crony; a patron; occas. *spec.*, a godfather.

goon /guːn/ *noun*. *slang*. M19.
[ORIGIN Perh. from *goon(e)y* var. of GONY, but in part infl. by name of Alice the *Goon*, a subhuman creature invented by US cartoonist E. C. Segar (1894–1938).]
†**1** A simple affectionate person. *rare*. Only in M19.
2 A foolish or stupid person; a simpleton, a dolt. Orig. & chiefly *N. Amer.* E20.
3 A bully boy, a thug; orig., one hired to terrorize workers. Orig. & chiefly *N. Amer.* M20.
4 Among prisoners of war in the Second World War: a German guard. *derog.* M20.
5 (**G-**.) Any of the members of the cast of a British radio show of the 1950s and 1960s, the Goon Show, noted for its zany and surrealist humour; *transf.* a person who exhibits similar humour. M20.
▪ **goonery** *noun* zany humour typical of the Goons M20. **goonish** *adjective* typical of or resembling a goon E20.

goonda /ˈguːndə/ *noun*. Also **-ah**. E20.
[ORIGIN Hindi *guṇḍā* rascal.]
In the Indian subcontinent: a hired bully.

goondie *noun* var. of GUNDY.

goon(e)y *noun* see GONY.

goop /guːp/ *noun*. *slang* (orig. *US*). E20.
[ORIGIN Arbitrary formation: cf. GOOF *noun*.]
A fatuous or stupid person.
▪ **goopy** *adjective* fatuous, silly; *esp.* amorous in a silly way: E20.

goopher *noun* var. of GOOFER *noun*[1].

goor *noun* var. of GUR.

Goorkha *noun* & *adjective* see GURKHA.

gooroo *noun* var. of GURU.

goosander /guːˈsandə/ *noun*. E17.
[ORIGIN Prob. from GOOSE *noun* + 2nd elem. of BERGANDER.]
A Eurasian saw-billed duck, *Mergus merganser*.

goose /guːs/ *noun*. Pl. **geese** /giːs/, (sense 5) **gooses**.
[ORIGIN Old English *gōs* = Old Frisian, Middle Low German *gōs*, Middle Dutch & mod. Dutch, Old High German (mod. German) *gans*, Old Norse *gás*, from Germanic, from Indo-European base also of Latin *anser*, Greek *khēn*, Sanskrit *haṃsá* masc., *haṃsī* fem.]
1 Any of various large web-footed birds, intermediate between ducks and swans in size, belonging to the genera *Anser*, *Branta*, or related genera of the family Anatidae; *spec.* the domesticated form of the greylag goose, *Anser anser*. See also SOLAN ***goose***. OE. ▸**b** *spec.* The female bird (the male being the *gander*). ME. ▸**c** The flesh of the (usu. domestic) goose. M16.
barnacle goose, ***brent goose***, ***Canada goose***, ***Hawaiian goose***, ***pink-footed goose***, ***snow goose***, etc. ***green goose***: see GREEN *adjective*. **c *colonial goose***: see COLONIAL *adjective* 1.
2 A foolish person, a simpleton. LME.
†**3** In full ***game of goose***, ***royal game of goose***. A game played with counters on a board divided into sections, some of which had a goose depicted on them. L16–E19.
†**4** In full ***Winchester goose***. A venereal infection. L16–E18.
5 A tailor's smoothing iron (so called from the resemblance of the handle to a goose's neck). E17.
6 A hissing sound like that of a goose; *spec.* (*theatrical slang*) one expressing disapproval of an actor's performance. E19.
– PHRASES: ***can't say boo to a goose***: see BOO *noun*[1] & *interjection*. ***cook someone's goose***: see COOK *verb*. ***fox and geese***: see FOX *noun* 1. ***game of goose***: see sense 3 above. ***gone goose***: see GONE *adjective* 1. **kill the goose that lays the golden eggs**, **kill the goose that laid the golden eggs** sacrifice long-term advantage to short-term gain. **turn geese into swans** exaggerate the merits of people. ***Winchester goose***: see sense 4 above.
– COMB.: **goose barnacle** [see note s.v. BARNACLE *noun*[1]] any of various stalked barnacles of the genus *Lepas*; **goosebumps** (chiefly *N. Amer.*) = GOOSEFLESH; **goose-cap** *arch.* a simpleton, a fool; **goose egg** (*a*) the egg of a goose; (*b*) *transf.* (*N. Amer.*) a zero score in an athletic contest etc.; **goose-fair**: held at certain English towns (still at Nottingham) about Michaelmas, when geese are in season; **goosefish** *N. Amer.* a bottom-dwelling anglerfish, esp. *Lophius americanus*; **goose-girl**: employed to tend geese; **goosegrass** any of several plants, *esp.* (*a*) silverweed, *Potentilla anserina*; (*b*) cleavers, *Galium aparine*; **gooseneck** (*a*) *NAUTICAL* a metal fitting at the end of a boom, connecting it to a metal ring round the base of the mast; also, a davit; (*b*) a pipe or piece of iron etc. curved like a goose's neck; **goose pimples** = GOOSEFLESH; **goose quill** a quill pen made from a goose's feather; **gooseskin** = GOOSEFLESH; **goose-step** a marching step, esp. associated with Nazi Germany, in which the legs are advanced alternately without bending the knees; also, a form of drill in which the soldier balances alternately on either leg and swings the other leg; **goose-step** *verb intrans.* do the goose-step; **goose-winged** *adjective* (*NAUTICAL*) (of a sail in a square-rigged ship) with only the goose-wings spread; (of a fore-and-aft rig) with two working sails boomed out, one on either side; **goose-wings** *adjective* (*NAUTICAL*) in a square-rigged ship, the clews of a course or topsail spread for scudding under when the wind is strong, the bunt of the sail being hauled up to the yard; in a fore-and-aft rigged ship, having the sails goose-winged.
▪ **gooselike** *adjective* resembling (that of) a goose M16.

goose /guːs/ *verb trans.* M17.
[ORIGIN from the noun.]
1 Press (clothes) with a tailor's smoothing iron. M17.
2 Express disapproval of (a play, an actor, etc.) by hissing. M19.
3 Poke or tickle in a sensitive part of the body; *esp.* poke between the buttocks. *slang* (chiefly *US*). L19.
4 In *pass.* Be ruined or done for. *slang*. E20.
5 Give a boost to, invigorate; spur into action. Freq. foll. by *up*. *N. Amer. colloq.* M20.

gooseberry /ˈgʊzb(ə)ri, ˈguːs-/ *noun*. M16.
[ORIGIN 1st elem. perh. alt. (by unexpl. assim. to GOOSE *noun*) of forms such as French dial. *groser*, *gozell*, repr. remotely Old French & mod. French *groseille*, †*grozelle*; but perh. from GOOSE *noun* + BERRY *noun*[1].]
1 An acid green or red-tinged freq. hairy edible berry, the fruit of the European thorny shrub *Ribes uva-crispa* and related species or hybrids; the shrub producing this berry. M16. ▸†**b** The berry of other species of *Ribes*; a (red, black, etc.) currant. L16–M17. ▸**c** With specifying word: (the fruit of) any of various shrubs resembling the gooseberry. M19.
c Barbados gooseberry (the edible fruit of) *Pereskia aculeata*, a West Indian vine of the cactus family. ***Cape gooseberry***: see CAPE *noun*[1]. ***Chinese gooseberry***: see CHINESE *adjective*. OTAHEITE ***gooseberry***.
2 Gooseberry wine. Also (*joc.*), inferior champagne. M18.
3 ***old gooseberry***, the Devil; esp. in ***play old gooseberry***, create havoc. *slang*. L18.
4 A chaperone; an unwanted third party. Freq. in ***play gooseberry***. *slang*. M19.

G. SWIFT Her husband . . a clumsy gooseberry to this scene of painful intimacy.

– COMB.: **gooseberry bush** a shrub producing gooseberries, *esp.* as a supposed place where (in coy explanations of the human reproduction) newly born babies are found; **gooseberry eyes** dull grey eyes; ***gooseberry fool***: see FOOL *noun*[2]; **gooseberry season** the time when gooseberries are ripe (***big gooseberry season*** (*arch.*) = ***SILLY season***).

gooseflesh /ˈguːsflɛʃ/ *noun*. LME.
[ORIGIN from GOOSE *noun* + FLESH *noun*.]
1 The flesh of a goose. LME.
2 A rough pimply state of the skin produced by cold, fear, etc. E19.
■ **goosefleshy** *adjective* exhibiting gooseflesh L19.

goosefoot /ˈguːsfʊt/ *noun*. Pl. (in sense 1) **-feet**, (in sense 2) **-foots**. E16.
[ORIGIN from GOOSE *noun* + FOOT *noun*.]
1 Something made or arranged in the shape of a goose's foot; *esp.* (***a***) a three-branched hinge; (***b***) a number of roads radiating from a common point. E16.
2 [from the shape of the leaf in some species] Any of various plants of the genus *Chenopodium* (family Chenopodiaceae), chiefly mealy weeds with spikes of inconspicuous greenish flowers. E16.

goosegog /ˈgʊzgɒg, ˈguːsgɒg/ *noun*. *dial. & colloq.* E19.
[ORIGIN Alt. of GOOSEBERRY; the 2nd elem. is alt. of GOB *noun*[1].]
A gooseberry.

gooseherd /ˈguːshəːd/ *noun*. Also **gozzard** /ˈgɒzəd/. ME.
[ORIGIN from GOOSE *noun* + HERD *noun*[2].]
A person who tends a flock of geese.

goosery /ˈguːsəri/ *noun*. M17.
[ORIGIN from GOOSE *noun* + -ERY.]
1 Silliness such as is attributed to geese. *rare*. M17.
2 A place where geese are kept; a collection of geese. E19.

goosey /ˈguːsi/ *noun*. Also redupl. **goosey-goosey**. Also **goosie**, **goosy**. E19.
[ORIGIN from GOOSE *noun* + -Y[6].]
1 ***goosey gander***, ***goosey-goosey gander***, (a pet name for) a gander. E19.
2 A silly person. Also ***goosey-gander***. M19.

goosey *adjective* var. of GOOSY *adjective*.

goosish /ˈguːsɪʃ/ *adjective*. LME.
[ORIGIN from GOOSE *noun* + -ISH[1].]
Resembling a goose, silly.
■ **goosishness** *noun* M19.

goosy *noun* var. of GOOSEY *noun*.

goosy /ˈguːsi/ *adjective*. Also **goosey**. E19.
[ORIGIN from GOOSE *noun* + -Y[1]. In sense 3, cf. GOOSE *verb* 3.]
1 Resembling a goose; *fig.* foolish, silly. E19.
2 Exhibiting gooseflesh (GOOSEFLESH *noun* 2). M19.
3 Sensitive to being goosed, ticklish, nervous. *US slang*. E20.
■ **goosiness** *noun* L19.

GOP *abbreviation*. *US*.
Grand Old Party (the Republican Party).

gopak /ˈgəʊpak/ *noun*. E20.
[ORIGIN Russian from Ukrainian *hopak*.]
A lively Ukrainian dance in 2/4 time.

gopher /ˈgəʊfə/ *noun*[1]. E17.
[ORIGIN Hebrew *gōper*.]
The (unidentified) tree from whose wood Noah's ark was said to be made. Chiefly in ***gopher wood*** below.
– COMB.: **gopher wood** (***a***) the wood of the gopher; (***b***) *US* (the wood of) the yellow-wood, *Cladrastis lutea*.

gopher /ˈgəʊfə/ *noun*[2]. L18.
[ORIGIN Uncertain: perh. from Canad. French *gaufre* lit. 'honeycomb', with ref. to the animals' burrowing habits.]
1 In full ***gopher tortoise***. Any of several N. American burrowing land tortoises of the genus *Gopherus*, esp. *G. polyphemus* of the south-eastern US. L18.
2 In full ***pocket gopher***. Any of various burrowing rodents belonging to the family Geomyidae, which are native to N. and Central America, and have external food pouches on the cheeks. E19.
3 A chipmunk, ground squirrel, or prairie dog. *N. Amer.* M19.
4 [W. allus. to sense 2 or 3 above.] (A nickname for) a native or inhabitant of Minnesota or (formerly) Arkansas. M19.
5 COMPUTING. Also **G-**. [from the gopher mascot of the University of Minnesota, US, where the system was invented.] A menu-based system which allows users of the Internet to search for and retrieve documents on topics of interest. L20.
– COMB.: **gopher hole** the opening of a gopher's burrow; a hole dug in small-scale or haphazard mining; **gopher snake** (***a***) = ***bull snake*** s.v. BULL *noun*[1]; (***b***) = ***indigo snake*** s.v. INDIGO *noun*; **Gopher State** *US* the state of Minnesota.

gopher *noun*[3] var. of GOFER *noun*[2].

gopher /ˈgəʊfə/ *verb intrans.* *N. Amer.* L19.
[ORIGIN from GOPHER *noun*[2].]
Burrow like a gopher; *spec.* carry out small-scale or haphazard mining operations.

gopi /ˈgəʊpiː/ *noun*. Also **G-**. L18.
[ORIGIN Sanskrit.]
HINDU MYTHOLOGY. Any of the milkmaids of Brindavan, companions of Krishna.

gopik /ˈgəʊpɪk/ *noun*. Pl. same, **-s**. L20.
[ORIGIN Azerbaijani = kopek.]
A monetary unit of Azerbaijan, equal to one-hundredth of a manat.

gopura /ˈgəʊpʊrə/ *noun*. Also **-ram** /-rəm/. M19.
[ORIGIN Sanskrit *gopura* city gate, from *go* cow, cattle + *pura* city, quarter.]
In southern India: the great pyramidal tower over the entrance gate to a temple precinct.

gora /ˈgɔːrə/ *adjective & noun*. M19.
[ORIGIN Hindi *gorā* fair, white.]
▸ **A** *adjective*. In the Indian subcontinent: of or designating a white person. M19.
▸ **B** *noun*. In the Indian subcontinent, and among British Asians: a white person. L20.

gorah /ˈgɔːrə/ *noun*. Also **goura** /ˈgʊərə/. L18.
[ORIGIN Prob. from Nama or San.]
A musical instrument of indigenous southern African peoples, consisting of a string stretched along a stick, and played by blowing on a piece of quill attached to these.

goral /ˈgɔːr(ə)l/ *noun*. Also **gur-** /ˈgʊə-/. M19.
[ORIGIN Local (Himalayan) name.]
A goat-antelope, *Nemorhaedus goral*, which inhabits montane forest from Myanmar (Burma) and northern India to Siberia.

Gorbachevian /gɔːbəˈtʃɛvɪən/ *adjective*. Also **Gorbachovian** /gɔːbəˈtʃəʊvɪən/. L20.
[ORIGIN from *Gorbachev* (see below) + -IAN.]
Of, pertaining to, or characteristic of Mikhail Sergeyevich Gorbachev (b. 1931), General Secretary of the Communist Party of the Soviet Union (1985-90) and later its President, or his policies.

gorbelly /ˈgɔːbɛli/ *noun*. E16.
[ORIGIN Uncertain: perh. from GORE *noun*[1] + BELLY *noun*; cf. Swedish dial. *går-bälg*.]
†**1** A protuberant stomach. E16–L18.
2 A person with a protuberant stomach. *obsolete* exc. *dial.* M16.
■ **gorbellied** *adjective* (long chiefly *dial.*) corpulent E16.

gorblimey /gɔːˈblʌɪmi/ *interjection, noun, & adjective*. *slang*. L19.
[ORIGIN Alt. of *God blind me*: cf. BLIMEY.]
▸ **A** *interjection*. Expr. surprise, amazement, etc. L19.
▸ **B** *noun*. A soft unwired service cap. Chiefly MILITARY. E20.
▸ **C** *attrib.* or as *adjective*. **1** Designating such a cap, or any ostentatious clothing. E20.
2 Of a person or thing: common, ordinary; vulgar. M20.
> *ellipt.*: *Daily Telegraph* Descending from the sublime to the gorblimey.

gorbuscha /gɔːˈbʊʃə/ *noun*. L18.
[ORIGIN Russian *gorbusha*, from *gorb* hump.]
= ***humpback salmon*** s.v. HUMPBACK *adjective*.

†**gorce** *noun*. Also **gort** & other vars. L15.
[ORIGIN Anglo-Norman *gortz* pl. of *gort* (Old French *gord*, *gourt*) from Latin *gurges*, *gurgit-* whirlpool.]
1 A whirlpool. L15–E17.
2 Any form of obstruction in a river, as a weir, dam, etc. E18–L19.

gorcock /ˈgɔːkɒk/ *noun*. *Scot. & N. English*. E17.
[ORIGIN Unknown.]
The male of the red grouse.

gorcrow /ˈgɔːkrəʊ/ *noun*. Now chiefly *dial.* E17.
[ORIGIN from GORE *noun*[1] + CROW *noun*[1].]
The carrion crow.

Gordian /ˈgɔːdɪən/ *noun & adjective*. M16.
[ORIGIN from Latin *Gordius* or *Gordium* (see sense B.1) + -AN.]
▸ **A** *noun*. †**1** = ***Gordian knot*** below. M16–E18.
2 A native or inhabitant of Gordium in Phrygia. *rare*. E17.
▸ **B** *adjective*. **1** ***Gordian knot***, an intricate knot tied by Gordius, king of Gordium, Phrygia, and cut through by Alexander the Great in response to the prophecy that only the future ruler of Asia could loosen it; *fig.* or *allus.*, an extremely difficult problem or task, an indissoluble bond. L16.
cut the Gordian knot solve a problem by force or by evading the conditions.
2 Resembling the Gordian knot; intricate, convoluted, involved. E17.

Gordon /ˈgɔːd(ə)n/ *noun*. M19.
[ORIGIN from Alexander *Gordon*, 4th Duke of Gordon (1743–1827), who promoted the breed.]
In full ***Gordon setter***. A breed of black and tan setter, used as a gun dog; an animal of this breed.

Gordon Bennett /gɔːd(ə)n ˈbɛnɪt/ *interjection*. L20.
[ORIGIN Prob. alt. of GORBLIMEY *interjection* after James *Gordon Bennett* (1841–1918), US publisher and sponsor of sporting events.]
Expr. surprise, incredulity, or exasperation.

gore /gɔː/ *noun*[1].
[ORIGIN Old English *gor* = Middle Dutch & mod. Dutch *goor* mud, filth, Old High German, Old Norse *gor* cud, slimy matter, rel. to Old Irish *gor*, Welsh *gôr* matter, pus.]
1 Dung, faeces; dirt of any kind; slime, mucus. *obsolete* exc. *dial.* OE.
2 Blood shed and thickened or clotted; (chiefly *poet.*) blood shed in carnage. M16.
> V. NABOKOV Hands . . black and bloody . . anointed with his thick gore.

†**in a gore of blood** bathed in or besmeared with blood.

gore /gɔː/ *noun*[2].
[ORIGIN Old English *gāra* = Old Frisian *gāra*, Middle Dutch *ghēre* (Dutch *geer*), Old High German *gēro* (German *Gehre*), Old Norse *geiri* prob. rel. to Old English *gār* spear.]
1 Orig., a promontory, a corner of land. Now, (long *dial.*) a wedge-shaped piece of land on the side of an asymmetric field; (chiefly *US*) a small strip or tract of land lying between larger divisions such as parishes, townships, etc. OE.
2 A wedge-shaped or triangular piece of cloth used to adjust the width of a garment where required, esp. to narrow a dress or skirt at the waist. Formerly also, *gen.* a skirt or the lower part of a gown or robe. ME. ▸**b** Any of several triangular or lune-shaped pieces used to form the surface of a hot-air balloon, umbrella, dome, globe, etc. L18. ▸**c** NAUTICAL. A piece of canvas cut at an angle to increase the breadth or depth of a sail; an angular piece of plank used to fill up the planking of a wooden vessel where necessary. L18.
3 HERALDRY. A charge formed by two concave curved lines meeting in the fesse point, the one drawn from the sinister or dexter chief corner of the shield and the other from the base point. M16.

gore /gɔː/ *verb*[1] *trans.* LME.
[ORIGIN Unknown.]
1 Cut, pierce, or stab deeply with a sharp weapon, spur, etc. Now *rare* exc. as sense 2. LME.
> J. DICKEY I wondered if I should tell whatever doctor dressed it that I had gored myself on my own arrow.

2 Of an animal: pierce or stab with the horns or (rarely) tusks. E16.
> W. S. MAUGHAM His hired man had been gored by a bull and was in hospital. *absol.*: ADAM SMITH The dog that bites, the ox that gores.

†**gore** *verb*[2]. LME.
[ORIGIN from GORE *noun*[1].]
1 *verb intrans.* Of a wound: fester. Only in LME.
2 As ***gored*** pa. pple: covered (as) *with* or *in* gore or blood. M16–M17.

gore /gɔː/ *verb*[3]. M16.
[ORIGIN from GORE *noun*[2].]
1 *verb trans.* Cut or shape into a gore; shape using a gore or gores. M16.
2 *verb intrans.* Plough a gore. Chiefly as GORING *noun*[2]. *obsolete* exc. *dial.* L18.

goree /gɒˈriː/ *noun*. Also **gori**. M19.
[ORIGIN Nyanja *goli*.]
hist. A forked stick used by Arabs to fasten slaves together by the neck. Also ***goree-stick***.

Gore-Tex /ˈgɔːtɛks/ *noun*. L20.
[ORIGIN from W. L. *Gore* & Associates, Inc., the manufacturers + TEX(TILE).]
(Proprietary name for) a breathable waterproof fabric used mainly in outdoor clothing.

gorge /gɔːdʒ/ *noun*[1]. LME.
[ORIGIN Old French & mod. French = throat from Proto-Romance alt. of Latin *gurges* whirlpool.]
▸ **I 1** The external throat; the front of the neck. *arch.* LME.
2 The internal throat. Now only *rhet.* LME.
3 Orig. in FALCONRY, (the contents of) the crop of a hawk. Now *gen.*, the contents of the stomach (chiefly in phrs. below). LME.
4 A meal, *esp.* (in FALCONRY) for a hawk. Long *rare*. LME.
▸ **II** *transf.* **5** FORTIFICATION. The neck of a bastion or other outwork; the rear entrance to the platform or body of a work. M17.
6 ARCHITECTURE. A hollow or concave moulding. E18.
7 A narrow opening between hills or mountains, *esp.* one with rocky walls and a stream. M18.
8 The groove of a pulley. E19.
9 A mass of ice obstructing a narrow passage, esp. a river. M19.
10 ANGLING. A bait intended to ensure capture of the fish when swallowed. Also ***gorge-bait***, ***gorge-hook***. M19.
– PHRASES: **cast gorge**, **cast the gorge** FALCONRY = GLEAM *verb*[2]. **cast the gorge at** reject with loathing. **cast up gorge**, **cast up the gorge**, FALCONRY = ***cast gorge*** above. ***heave the gorge***: see HEAVE *verb*. **one's gorge rises at** one is sickened or disgusted by.

gorge /gɔːdʒ/ *noun*[2]. M19.
[ORIGIN from GORGE *verb*.]
An act of gorging oneself; a glut (of food, wine, etc.).

gorge /gɔːdʒ/ *verb*. ME.
[ORIGIN Old French & mod. French *gorger*, formed as GORGE *noun*[1].]
1 a *verb intrans.* Orig. *spec.* of a bird of prey: fill the gorge. Now *gen.* of a person or animal: feed greedily (*on*, *upon*). ME. ▸**b** *verb trans.* (freq. *refl.*) Stuff with food (also foll. by

G

with, (*up*)*on*); satiate (the appetite); (now *rare*) fill the gorge of (a hawk). L15.

> **a** J. WAIN Robert gorged like a man driven insane by hunger. D. M. FRAME Some men gorged while others . . . starved. **b** R. LINDNER She would be seized by an overwhelming compulsion to gorge herself, to eat almost continuously. *fig.*: P. DE VRIES She would gorge herself on the outrage a moment or two.

2 a *verb trans.* Fill full, distend; choke up. Chiefly as ***gorged*** pa. pple. Cf. ENGORGE 1b. LME. ▸**b** *verb intrans.* Of ice: become fixed so as to form an obstruction. *US*. M19.

> **a** C. DARWIN During excessive laughter . . the head and face become gorged with blood.

3 *verb trans.* Gobble up, devour greedily. E17.

> P. G. WODEHOUSE Half a century of gorging food and swilling wine. *Times* The deal with CCF is better than being gorged by one of the financial giants.

■ **gorger** *noun* a person or animal that gorges E19.

gorgeaunt /ˈgɔːdʒ(ə)nt/ *noun*. Long *obsolete* exc. *hist*. LME.
[ORIGIN French, pres. pple of *gorger* GORGE *verb*.]
A boar in its second year.

gorged /gɔːdʒd/ *adjective*. E17.
[ORIGIN from GORGE *noun*[1] + -ED[2].]
HERALDRY. Having the gorge or neck encircled with a coronet, collar, etc.

gorgeous /ˈgɔːdʒəs/ *adjective*. L15.
[ORIGIN Old French *gorgias* fine, stylish, elegant, of unknown origin; assim. in ending to words in -EOUS.]
1 Richly or brilliantly coloured, sumptuous, magnificent, (esp. in attire); dazzling. L15.

> H. L. MENCKEN The gorgeous tricolor baldrics, sashes and festoons of the Légion d'Honneur. J. I. M. STEWART The college organist (in the most gorgeous of all Oxford's robes).

2 Wonderful, splendid, delightful. *colloq*. L19.
■ **gorgeously** *adverb* E16. **gorgeousness** *noun* M16.

gorgeret /ˈgɔːdʒərɪt/ *noun*. Now *rare* or *obsolete*. M18.
[ORIGIN French, formed as GORGE *noun*[1]: see -ET[1].]
SURGERY. = GORGET *noun*[2].

gorgerin /ˈgɔːdʒərɪn/ *noun*. M17.
[ORIGIN French = gorget, frieze of a Doric capital, formed as GORGE *noun*[1].]
1 ARCHITECTURE. = HYPOTRACHELIUM. M17.
2 = GORGET *noun*[1] 1. M19.

gorget /ˈgɔːdʒɪt/ *noun*[1]. LME.
[ORIGIN Old French *gorgete*, formed as GORGE *noun*[1]: see -ET[1].]
1 A piece of armour for the throat. *obsolete* exc. *hist*. LME. ▸**b** A woman's wimple, covering the head, neck, and shoulders. *obsolete* exc. *hist*. M16. ▸**c** A collar. E17.
2 An ornament for the neck; a necklace, a decorative collar, etc.; MILITARY HISTORY a gilt crescent-shaped badge worn on a chain round the neck by officers on duty. L15.
3 In *pl*. A type of pillory consisting of a hinged iron collar worn about the neck. *Scot*. *obsolete* exc. *hist*. M17.
4 ZOOLOGY. A patch of colour on the throat or breast of an animal, esp. a bird. E19.

gorget /ˈgɔːdʒɪt/ *noun*[2]. M18.
[ORIGIN Alt. of GORGERET.]
SURGERY. An instrument with a wide longitudinal groove or channel used in the removal of stones from the bladder.

gorgio /ˈgɔːdʒɪəʊ/ *noun*. Pl. **-os**. M19.
[ORIGIN Romany *gorjo*.]
Among Gypsies: (a name for) a non-Gypsy.

gorgon /ˈgɔːg(ə)n/ *noun & adjective*. Also **G-**. LME.
[ORIGIN Latin *Gorgo*, *Gorgon-* from Greek *Gorgō*, from *gorgos* terrible.]
▸ **A** *noun*. **1** GREEK MYTHOLOGY. Each of three sisters, Stheno, Euryale, and Medusa (the only mortal one), who had snakes for hair and whose gaze turned the beholder to stone. LME. ▸†**b** = DEMOGORGON. *rare* (Spenser). Only in L16.
2 A person resembling a gorgon in manner or appearance; *esp*. an ugly or terrifying woman. E16.
▸ **B** *attrib*. or as *adjective*. Petrifying, terrible. L16.

> J. FOWLES Other passengers . . were rebuffed by that Gorgon stare . . the English have so easily at command.

gorgoneion /gɔːgəˈnʌɪən/ *noun*. Pl. **-neia** /-ˈnʌɪə/. M19.
[ORIGIN Greek *gorgoneion* neut. of *gorgoneios* of or pertaining to a GORGON.]
A representation of a gorgon's head.

gorgonia /gɔːˈgəʊnɪə/ *noun*. Pl. **-ias**, **-iae** /-iiː/. M18.
[ORIGIN mod. Latin *Gorgonia* (see below), fem. of *gorgonius*, from Latin *Gorgo* GORGON: so named from its petrifaction.]
= GORGONIAN *noun*; *esp*. a member of the genus *Gorgonia*.

gorgonian /gɔːˈgəʊnɪən/ *noun & adjective*[1]. M19.
[ORIGIN formed as GORGONIA + -IAN.]
▸ **A** *noun*. Any of various horny corals of the order Gorgonacea, with upright, plantlike forms. M19.
▸ **B** *adjective*. Belonging to or characteristic of this order. L19.

gorgonian /gɔːˈgəʊnɪən/ *adjective*[2]. L16.
[ORIGIN from GORGON + -IAN.]
Of or pertaining to a gorgon; resembling a gorgon in effect or appearance.

gorgonize /ˈgɔːg(ə)nʌɪz/ *verb trans*. Also **-ise**. E17.
[ORIGIN from GORGON + -IZE.]
Petrify as by the gaze of a gorgon; stare at like a gorgon.

Gorgonzola /gɔːg(ə)nˈzəʊlə/ *noun*. L19.
[ORIGIN from *Gorgonzola* a village near Milan, Italy, where originally made.]
A type of Italian blue cheese usu. made from cow's milk.

gorgy /ˈgɔːdʒi/ *adjective*. L19.
[ORIGIN from GORGE *noun*[1] + -Y[1].]
Full of gorges or ravines.

gorilla /gəˈrɪlə/ *noun*. M19.
[ORIGIN mod. Latin (see below), from an alleged African word (= wild or hairy man) found in accus. pl. fem. *gorillas* in the Greek account of the voyage of the Carthaginian Hanno.]
1 A large powerful anthropoid ape, *Gorilla gorilla*, inhabiting forest in parts of central Africa. M19.
2 A person resembling a gorilla in appearance; *colloq*. a heavily built thug. L19.

> S. BELLOW The union guy called off his gorillas and they came to position round him.

gorily /ˈgɔːrɪli/ *adverb*. M19.
[ORIGIN from GORY *adjective* + -LY[2].]
In a gory manner.

goring /ˈgɔːrɪŋ/ *noun*[1]. L15.
[ORIGIN from GORE *verb*[1] + -ING[1].]
The action of GORE *verb*[1]; an instance of this; (a) stabbing, (a) piercing.

goring /ˈgɔːrɪŋ/ *noun*[2]. E17.
[ORIGIN from GORE *verb*[3] or *noun*[2] + -ING[1].]
1 The cutting out or fitting of gores. E17. ▸**b** NAUTICAL. A piece of cloth used as a gore. M18.
2 The action of ploughing a gore. Also = GORE *noun*[2] 1. Chiefly *dial*. M19.

gorm /gɔːm/ *noun*. Also (earlier) **gaum**, (*Irish*) **gom** /gɒm/. M19.
[ORIGIN Cf. GAUM *verb*[2], GORMLESS: Anglo-Ir. use may represent an independent word (cf. Irish *gamal* stupid-looking person).]
A fool; a stupid lout.

gorm /gɔːm/ *verb*[1] *trans*. M19.
[ORIGIN Alt. of (*God*) *damn*.]
= DAMN *verb* 3.

gorm *verb*[2], *verb*[3] see GAUM *verb*[2], *verb*[3].

gormandise, **gormandize** *noun*, *verb* vars. of GOURMANDIZE *noun*, *verb*.

gormless /ˈgɔːmlɪs/ *adjective*. *colloq*. (orig. *dial*.). Also (earlier) **gaumless**. M18.
[ORIGIN from GAUM *noun*[1] + -LESS.]
Slow-witted, stupid, lacking sense.

> A. ASHWORTH Kids read the first line out loud in gormless voices, crossing their eyes.

■ **gormlessly** *adverb* M20. **gormlessness** *noun* M19.

gormy *adjective* var. of GAUMY.

gorp /gɔːp/ *noun*. *N. Amer. colloq*. L20.
[ORIGIN Perh. an acronym from good old raisins and peanuts.]
= TRAIL MIX.

gorp *verb* see GAWP.

gorry /ˈgɒri/ *interjection & noun*. M19.
[ORIGIN Alt. of GOD *noun*. Cf. GOLLY *noun*[1].]
God. Chiefly in ***by gorry***.

gorse /gɔːs/ *noun*.
[ORIGIN Old English *gors*, *gorst*, from Indo-European base meaning 'rough, prickly', repr. in Latin *hordeum* barley, rel. to Old High German *gersta* (German *Gerste*) barley.]
Any of several spiny yellow-flowered leguminous shrubs of the genus *Ulex* (esp. *U. europaeus*), characteristic of heathy places. Also called ***furze***, ***whin***.
■ **gorsy** *adjective* overgrown with gorse; characteristic of gorse: E16.

Gorsedd /ˈgɔːseð/ *noun*. L18.
[ORIGIN Welsh = mound, throne, assembly, Gorsedd.]
A meeting of Welsh bards and Druids; *esp*. the assembly that meets to announce the next Royal National Eisteddfod and at certain times during this festival.

†**gort** *noun* var. of GORCE.

gory /ˈgɔːri/ *adjective*. LME.
[ORIGIN from GORE *noun*[1] + -Y[1].]
1 Covered with gore, stained with blood, bloody. LME. ▸†**b** Of blood: clotted. M–L16. ▸**c** Resembling blood in colour. *rare*. E19.

> SIR W. SCOTT Away the gory axe he threw.

2 = BLOODY *adjective* 3. L16.

> A. GHOSH It is a gory history in parts; a story of greed and destruction.

gos /gɒs/ *noun*. *colloq*. L18.
[ORIGIN Abbreviation.]
= GOSHAWK.

gosain /gə(ʊ)ˈsʌɪn/ *noun*. L18.
[ORIGIN Hindi *gosāī̃* from Sanskrit *gosvāmin* 'lord of cows', from *go* COW *noun*[1].]
A Hindu who professes a life of religious mendicancy.

gosh /gɒʃ/ *noun & interjection*. M18.
[ORIGIN Alt.]
(In mild exclamations and other expressions substituted for) God.

> *New Yorker* My gosh, we're so up to here in church activities.

– COMB.: **gosh-awful** *adjective* (*colloq*.) = ***God-awful*** s.v. GOD *noun*; **gosh-darned** *adjective* = GODDAM *adjective*.

goshawk /ˈgɒshɔːk/ *noun*.
[ORIGIN Old English *gōshafoc*, from *gōs* GOOSE *noun* + *hafoc* HAWK *noun*[1]: cf. Old Norse *gáshaukr*.]
Any of various large short-winged hawks; spec. *Accipiter gentilis*, occurring widely throughout the northern hemisphere.
chanting goshawk any of a number of grey hawks of the genus *Melierax*, native to Africa, notable for the melodious calls of the male in the breeding season.

Goshen /ˈgəʊʃ(ə)n/ *noun*. E17.
[ORIGIN Hebrew, the fertile land allotted to the Israelites in Egypt, in which (*Exodus* 10:23 implies) there was light during the plague of darkness.]
A place of plenty or of light.

gosling /ˈgɒzlɪŋ/ *noun*. ME.
[ORIGIN Old Norse *gæslingr* (Swedish *gäsling*, Danish *gæsling*), from *gás* GOOSE *noun*; assim. to English *goose*: see -LING[1].]
1 A young goose. ME.
2 *fig*. A foolish, inexperienced person. Now *rare*. E17.
3 A catkin or blossom on a tree. E18.
– COMB.: **gosling green** *noun & adjective* (of) a pale yellowish green.

go-slow /gəʊˈsləʊ, ˈgəʊsləʊ/ *noun*. E20.
[ORIGIN from GO *verb* + SLOW *adverb*.]
A form of industrial protest in which employees work at a deliberately slow pace. Cf. CA'CANNY.

gospel /ˈgɒsp(ə)l/ *noun*.
[ORIGIN Old English *gōdspel*, i.e. *gōd* GOOD *adjective*, *spel* news, tidings (see SPELL *noun*[1]), rendering of ecclesiastical Latin *bona annuntiatio*, *bonus nuntius*, used as literal renderings of ecclesiastical Latin *evangelium*, Greek *euaggelion* EVANGEL *noun*[1]. Later assoc. with *God*, as in all the forms adopted in the Germanic langs. of peoples evangelized from England, viz. Old Saxon *godspell*, Old High German *gotspell*, Old Norse *guð-*, *goðspjall*.]
1 The 'good news' preached by Jesus; the religious doctrine of Christ and his apostles; the Christian revelation, religion, or dispensation. OE. ▸**b** *gen*. Any revelation from heaven. L15. ▸**c** (A term used by Protestants for) the doctrines of Protestantism; the doctrine of salvation according to Puritans or Evangelicals. M16.

> W. IRVING To spread the light of the gospel in that far wilderness. **c** OED 'Why don't you go to church?' 'Because the Gospel is not preached there'.

c ***social gospel***: see SOCIAL *adjective*.
2 (**G-**.) The record of Jesus's life and teaching, contained in the first four books of the New Testament. OE. ▸**b** One of these books (of the Four Evangelists: Matthew, Mark, Luke, and John), or of some other texts of doubtful authenticity. ME. ▸†**c** The Holy Scriptures generally. LME–L15.
3 ***the Gospel***, ***the Gospel for the day***, ***the Gospel of the day***: the portion from one of the four Gospels read at the Eucharist in various Christian denominations. (Cf. EPISTLE *noun* 2b.) OE.
4 A thing regarded as undoubtedly true. ME.

> M. WEBB He'll take it for gospel that Gideon writes the letters.

5 A principle that one acts upon, believes in, or preaches. M17.

> P. G. WODEHOUSE Physical fitness was her gospel.

6 In full ***gospel music***. A type of fervent or evangelical singing performed typically by black Americans. M20.
– COMB.: ***gospel music***: see sense 6 above; **gospel oath**: sworn on the Gospels; **gospel-sharp** *US colloq*. a Christian minister of religion; **Gospel side** CHRISTIAN CHURCH the north end of an altar, from which the Gospel is traditionally read; **gospel singer**: of gospel music; **gospel song** (one performed in the style of) gospel music; **gospel truth** (*a*) the truth or truths contained in the Gospel; (*b*) something completely true.

gospel /ˈgɒsp(ə)l/ *verb*. Infl. **-ll-**, ***-l-**.
[ORIGIN Old English *gōdspellian*, from the noun, repr. ecclesiastical Latin *benenuntiare*, Greek *euaggelizesthai*.]
1 *verb intrans*. Preach the gospel. *rare*. OE.
†**2** *verb trans*. Preach the gospel to; evangelize. M16–M17.

gospeler *noun* see GOSPELLER.

gospelize /ˈgɒspəlʌɪz/ *verb trans*. Also **-ise**. E17.
[ORIGIN from GOSPEL *noun* + -IZE.]
1 = EVANGELIZE 3. E17.
†**2** Impart the spirit of the gospel to. Only in M17.

gospeller /ˈɡɒsp(ə)lə/ *noun.* Also ***-eler.** OE.
[ORIGIN from GOSPEL *noun* or *verb* + -ER[1].]
1 Each of the four evangelists. OE.
2 A book containing the Gospels. Now *rare.* LME.
3 A person who reads the Gospel at a Eucharist. E16.
4 A person who professes the faith of the gospel, or who claims personally or for a sect the exclusive possession of gospel truth. M16.
5 A preacher of the gospel; a missionary. *rare.* L16.
– PHRASES: **hot gospeller** a fervent gospel preacher; a zealous puritan, a rabid propagandist.

goss /ɡɒs/ *noun*[1]. *slang.* M19.
[ORIGIN Unknown.]
Punishment. Only in ***give goss***, ***get goss***.

Goss /ɡɒs/ *noun*[2]. E20.
[ORIGIN from W. H. *Goss* (1833–1906), English china manufacturer.]
In full ***Goss china***. A kind of china orig. manufactured by Goss, and later made esp. as mementoes of places, events, etc.

gossamer /ˈɡɒsəmə/ *noun, adjective, & verb.* ME.
[ORIGIN App. from GOOSE *noun* + SUMMER *noun*[1]; perh. from the time of year (around 'St Martin's Summer') when geese were eaten, which is when gossamer tends to be most seen. Cf. German *Mädchensommer, Altweibersommer.*]
▸ **A** *noun.* **1** A fine filmy substance, consisting of cobwebs spun by small spiders, which is seen esp. in autumn, floating in the air or spread over a grassy surface. Also, a thread or web of this. ME. ▸**b** *transf. & fig.* Something light and flimsy. LME.

H. WILLIAMSON Gossamers glinted across the stubbles.

2 **a** A light make of silk hat; *joc.* a hat generally. *arch.* M19. ▸**b** A very light kind of waterproof. *US.* L19.
3 A rich silk gauze used for veils and dresses. L19.
▸ **B** *adjective.* **1** Made of gossamer. E19.
2 *fig.* Light and flimsy as gossamer; frivolous, volatile. E19.

A. LEWIS The rain . . a gossamer stream Too light to stir the acorns.

▸ **C** *verb trans.* Coat (as) with gossamer. Chiefly as ***gossamered*** *ppl adjective.* M19.
■ **gossamery** *adjective* made of or like gossamer; flimsy, unsubstantial: L18.

gossan /ˈɡɒz(ə)n/ *noun.* L18.
[ORIGIN Unknown.]
GEOLOGY & MINING (orig. *Cornish*). A ferruginous secondary deposit, largely consisting of oxides, occurring at an outcrop of a metallic ore.

gossip /ˈɡɒsɪp/ *noun.*
[ORIGIN Late Old English *godsibb*, corresp. to Old Norse *guðsifi* godfather, *guðsifja* godmother, formed as GOD *noun* + SIB *adjective*, denoting the spiritual affinity of the baptized and their sponsors.]
1 A godfather or godmother; a sponsor. *obsolete* exc. *hist.* or *dial.* LOE.
2 A familiar acquaintance, a friend, esp. a female one. *arch.* ME. ▸**b** *spec.* A female friend invited to be present at a birth. *arch.* L16.

C. BRONTË The old duenna—my mother's gossip.

3 A person who habitually indulges in idle talk, esp. the spreading of rumours and discussion of the private concerns of others. M16.

E. F. BENSON Edgar is a dreadful gossip . . I recommend you never tell him anything private.

4 Idle talk; groundless rumour; tittle-tattle; informal, unrestrained talk or writing, esp. about people or social incidents. E19.

G. SANTAYANA Talk . . was chiefly gossip, and gossip encouraged a morbid interest in matters that didn't concern one.

– COMB.: **gossip column** a section of a newspaper devoted to social news; **gossip columnist** a person who regularly writes a gossip column; **gossip-monger** a person who habitually passes on confidential information, or spreads rumours.
■ **gossipdom** *noun* gossips as a class; the realm of gossip: L19. **gossiphood** *noun* (now *rare*) †(*a*) spiritual relationship; (*b*) a body of gossips: E16. **gossipy** *adjective* inclined to gossip; characterized by or full of gossip: E19.

gossip /ˈɡɒsɪp/ *verb.* L16.
[ORIGIN from the noun.]
†**1** *verb intrans.* Act as a familiar acquaintance; take part (in a feast); make oneself at home. L16–M17.
†**2** *verb trans.* Be a sponsor to; give a name to. E17–E18.
3 *verb intrans.* Indulge in gossip; talk idly or lightly; write in a gossipy style. E17.

O. MANNING He imagined they were gossiping about him.

4 *verb trans.* Tell or discuss like a gossip; communicate by gossip. E17.
■ **gossiper** *noun* a person who gossips M16. **gossiping** *noun* †(*a*) a meeting of gossips; orig. a christening feast, or a meeting of friends at a birth; (*b*) the action of the verb; idle talking, tattling: M16. **gossipingly** *adverb* in a gossiping manner E19.

gossipred /ˈɡɒsɪprɛd/ *noun. obsolete* exc. *hist.* ME.
[ORIGIN from GOSSIP *noun* + -RED.]
1 The relationship of gossips (see GOSSIP *noun* 1, 2); spiritual affinity. ME.
†**2** = GOSSIP *noun* 4. Only in 19.

gossipry /ˈɡɒsɪpri/ *noun.* E16.
[ORIGIN from GOSSIP *noun* + -RY.]
1 Spiritual relationship: = GOSSIPRED 1. *obsolete* exc. *hist.* E16.
2 The practice of gossiping; small talk, gossip. E19. ▸**b** A body of gossips. M19.

gossoon /ɡɒˈsuːn/ *noun.* Chiefly *Irish.* L17.
[ORIGIN Old French & mod. French *garçon* boy.]
A youth, a boy; a servant boy.

gossypol /ˈɡɒsɪpɒl/ *noun.* L19.
[ORIGIN from mod. Latin *Gossypium* genus name of the cotton plant, from Latin *gossypinum, -pion* cotton plant (ult. origin unknown): see -OL.]
BIOCHEMISTRY. A toxic crystalline phenolic compound, $C_{30}H_{30}O_8$, present in cotton-seed oil.

got /ɡɒt/ *ppl adjective.* L16.
[ORIGIN pa. pple of GET *verb.* Cf. GOTTEN *ppl adjective.*]
1 = GOTTEN *ppl adjective* 1. Now *rare.* L16.
2 ***got up***, artificially produced or adorned to impress or deceive. E19.

got *verb pa. t. & pple*: see GET *verb.*

gotcha /ˈɡɒtʃə/ *interjection non-standard.* Also **gotcher.** M20.
[ORIGIN Repr. a pronunc.]
(I) have got you (see GET *verb* 37).

gote /ɡəʊt/ *noun.* Chiefly *N. English.* LME.
[ORIGIN from *got-* weak base of Old English *gēotan* pour; cf. Middle Low German, Middle Dutch *gote* (Dutch *goot*) of similar meaning. See GOUT *noun*[3].]
1 A watercourse; a channel for water; a stream. LME.
2 A sluice. LME.

Goth /ɡɒθ/ *noun.*
[ORIGIN Old English *Gota*, usu. in pl. *Gotan*, superseded in Middle English by adoption of late Latin *Gothi* pl. = Greek *Gothoi, Gotthoi* pl. from base of Gothic *Gutþiuda* the Gothic people.]
1 A member of a Germanic tribe which invaded the Eastern and Western Empires between the 3rd and the 5th cents. and founded kingdoms in Italy, France, and Spain. OE.
2 A person who behaves like a barbarian, esp. in the destruction or neglect of works of art; a rude, uncivilized, or ignorant person. Cf. VANDAL. M17. ▸**b** = GOTHICIST. M19.
3 (A performer or fan of a) style of rock music derived from punk, characterized by mystical lyrics and associated with black clothing and dramatic make-up; a person dressed in this style. L20.
■ **Gothish** *adjective* resembling something Gothic, looking like a Goth; barbarous: E17. **Gothism** *noun* barbarism, bad taste E18.

Gotham /ˈɡɒθəm, ˈɡəʊθəm, -t-/ *noun.* LME.
[ORIGIN English place name.]
1 The name of a village proverbial for the folly of its inhabitants. LME.
wise man of Gotham a fool.
2 New York City. *US colloq.* E19.
– NOTE: Allusion to Gotham in Nottinghamshire is not certain.
■ **Gothamite** *noun* (*a*) a simpleton; (*b*) *US colloq.* a New Yorker: L16.

Gothic /ˈɡɒθɪk/ *adjective & noun.* Also **g-**, (*pseudo-arch.*) **-ck.** L16.
[ORIGIN French *gothique* or late Latin *Gothicus*, from *Gothi*; see GOTH, -IC.]
▸ **A** *adjective.* **1** Of or pertaining to the Goths or their language. L16. ▸**b** = MOZARABIC. M19.
2 †**a** = GERMANIC *adjective*[1] 2. M17–M19. ▸**b** Designating the style of handwriting used in Western Europe from the 13th cent. and the typefaces derived from it, such as Fraktur and, formerly, black letter. M17.
3 Designating the style of architecture prevalent in western Europe from the 12th to the 16th cent., of which familiar features include the pointed arch and the flying buttress; (of a building, an architectural detail, ornamentation, etc.) in this style. Also, of the Gothic revival (see below). M17.

M. ROBERTS The attic floor of a decaying Gothic mansion in North Oxford.

4 Belonging to or (supposedly) characteristic of the Middle Ages; medieval, romantic. Orig. & freq. *derog.*, redolent of the Dark Ages, portentously gloomy or horrifying. L17.

W. COWPER Tedious years of Gothic darkness. R. BARBER The ideals of chivalry . . flourish best in a Gothic and romantic climate. *Nature* A large sunken arena, with gothick grottos around the edges.

5 Barbarous, crude, uncouth. *arch.* E18.

J. T. HEWLETT Dinner . . at the Gothic hour of one o'clock.

6 Of or pertaining to the rock music of Goths. L20.
– SPECIAL COLLOCATIONS: **Gothic novel**: of a style popular in the 18th and 19th cents., with a complex plot characterized by supernatural or horrifying events. ***Gothic revival***: see REVIVAL 1C.
▸ **B** *noun.* **1** Gothic architecture, or ornamentation; Gothic style in literature etc. Also (*rare*), a Gothic building. M17.
collegiate Gothic: see COLLEGIATE *adjective.* ***Victorian Gothic***: see VICTORIAN *adjective*[2].
2 *TYPOGRAPHY.* Gothic type. Also (*US*), grotesque. L17.
3 The East Germanic language of the Goths. M18.
CRIMEAN ***Gothic.***
■ **gothically** *adverb* M19. †**gothicly** *adverb*: only in L18. **gothicness** *noun* M19.

Gothicise *verb* var. of GOTHICIZE.

Gothicism /ˈɡɒθɪsɪz(ə)m/ *noun.* E18.
[ORIGIN from GOTHIC + -ISM.]
1 Barbarism, crudity; absence of polish or taste; an instance of this. *arch.* E18.
2 Conformity or devotion to the Gothic style, esp. of architecture. M18.
■ **Gothicist** *noun* a person who uses or is familiar with the Gothic style, esp. in architecture M19.

Gothicize /ˈɡɒθɪsʌɪz/ *verb.* Also **-ise** M18.
[ORIGIN from GOTHIC + -IZE.]
†**1** *verb intrans.* Indulge one's taste for something Gothic. *rare.* Only in M18.
2 *verb trans.* **a** Give an architecturally Gothic character to. L18. ▸**b** Give a medieval look or character to; make Gothic (GOTHIC *adjective* 4). E19.

Gothick *adjective & noun* see GOTHIC.

Gothonic /ɡɒˈθɒnɪk/ *adjective & noun.* Now *rare.* E20.
[ORIGIN from Latin *Gothones* Goths + -IC.]
▸ **A** *adjective.* Of or belonging to the primitive Germanic stock. E20.
▸ **B** *noun.* The common language of this stock. E20.

gotra /ˈɡəʊtrə/ *noun.* L19.
[ORIGIN Sanskrit *gotra.*]
Amongst Hindus of brahmin caste, any of the group of families supposedly descended from the seven mythical sages.

gotta /ˈɡɒtə/ *verb perf. colloq.* E20.
[ORIGIN Repr. a pronunc.]
= ***has got to***, ***have got to*** s.v. GET *verb* 38b.

gotten /ˈɡɒt(ə)n/ *ppl adjective.* LME.
[ORIGIN pa. pple of GET *verb*: see -EN[6]. Cf. GOT *ppl adjective.*]
1 Acquired, obtained, won, esp. in a specified manner. Now *rare* exc. in ***ill-gotten***. LME.
†**2** Begotten. LME–M17.

gotten *verb pa. pple*: see GET *verb.*

Götterdämmerung /ˈɡœtərˌdɛmərʊŋ; ɡɒtəˈdamərʊŋ, ɡəːt-, -ˈdɛm-/ *noun.* E20.
[ORIGIN German, lit. 'twilight of the gods', (esp. as title of opera by Wagner).]
In *GERMANIC MYTHOLOGY*, the twilight of the gods; *gen.* a cataclysmic downfall of a regime, institution, etc. Cf. RAGNAROK.

gouache /ɡuːˈɑːʃ, ɡwaʃ/ *noun.* L19.
[ORIGIN French from Italian *guazzo.*]
A method of opaque watercolour painting, in which the pigments are bound by a glue to form a sort of paste; a painting executed in this way; the pigments thus used.

Gouda /ˈɡaʊdə/ *noun.* M19.
[ORIGIN A town in the Netherlands.]
In full ***Gouda cheese***. A flat round cheese orig. made at Gouda.

Goudy /ˈɡaʊdi/ *noun & adjective.* M20.
[ORIGIN F. W. *Goudy* (1865–1947), US typographer.]
(Designating) any of a number of typefaces introduced by Goudy.

gouge /ɡaʊdʒ, ɡuːdʒ/ *noun.* LME.
[ORIGIN Old French & mod. French from late Latin *gubia, gulbia*, perh. of Celtic origin (cf. Old Irish *gulba* beak, Welsh *gylf* sharp-pointed instrument, beak).]
1 A chisel with a concave blade for cutting rounded grooves or holes. Also, a surgical chisel for removing portions of bone. LME. ▸**b** *BOOKBINDING.* A tool for impressing a curved line or segment of a circle on the leather; such a marking itself. L19.
2 An act of gouging; a groove or mark made by gouging. M19.
3 A swindle. *US colloq.* L19.
– COMB.: **gouge-bit** a bit shaped at the end like a gouge.

gouge /ɡaʊdʒ, ɡuːdʒ/ *verb.* L16.
[ORIGIN from the noun.]
1 *verb trans.* Cut or make holes in with or as with a gouge. L16. ▸**b** *verb intrans.* Work with a gouge. M19.
2 *verb trans.* Cut, hollow, scoop, or force (*out*) with or as with a gouge. E17.

P. P. READ The torrent . . had gouged out the earth from the bank.

3 *verb trans. & intrans.* Force out the eye of (a person); force out (a person's eye). L18.
4 *verb trans. & intrans.* Cheat, steal, impose upon. *N. Amer. colloq.* M19.
5 *verb intrans.* In opal-mining, make an exploratory search to locate worthless material; dig for opal generally. *Austral.* E20.
■ **gouger** *noun* L18.

goujon /ˈɡuːdʒ(ə)n; *in sense* 2 ˈɡuː(d)ʒɒn, *foreign* ɡuʒɔ̃ (*pl. same*)/ *noun*. L19.
[ORIGIN French, formed as GUDGEON *noun*[2].]
1 The flathead catfish, *Pylodictis olivaris*. *US*. L19.
2 *COOKERY*. In *pl*. Narrow, deep-fried, strips of fish or chicken. M20.

Goulard /ɡuˈlɑːd/ *noun*. *obsolete* exc. *hist*. E19.
[ORIGIN Thomas *Goulard* (1720–90), French surgeon.]
A solution of lead acetate used as a lotion in cases of inflammation. Also ***Goulard lotion***, ***Goulard water***, etc.

goulash /ˈɡuːlaʃ/ *noun*. M19.
[ORIGIN Hungarian *gulyás(hús)*, from *gulyás* herdsman + *hús* meat.]
1 A stew or ragout of meat and vegetables highly seasoned. M19.
2 *BRIDGE*. A fresh deal of unshuffled cards, usu. three or more at a time, after the hands have been thrown in without bidding. E20.

goum /ɡuːm/ *noun*. Also **G-**. M19.
[ORIGIN French from Arabic *gūm* dial. var. of *qawm* tribe, troop.]
1 A group of N. African people; a contingent of N. African soldiers (in French service). M19.
2 A member of such a group. M19.

G

†gound *noun*. OE–L17.
[ORIGIN Old English *gund* = Gothic *gund*, Old High German *gunt*.]
Foul matter, pus, *esp*. that secreted in the eye.
– NOTE: Survived in BARNGUN.

gour *noun* var. of GAUR.

goura /ˈɡʊərə/ *noun*[1]. M19.
[ORIGIN Name in New Guinea.]
= ***crowned pigeon*** s.v. CROWNED 5.

goura *noun*[2] var. of GORAH.

gourami /ɡʊ(ə)ˈrɑːmi, ˈɡʊərəmi/ *noun*. L19.
[ORIGIN Malay *gurami*.]
A large perciform freshwater food fish, *Osphronemus goramy* (family Osphronemidae), native to SE Asia. Also, any of various fishes belonging to the related families Belontiidae and Helostomatidae, often kept as aquarium fish.
kissing gourami: see KISSING *ppl adjective*.

gourbi /ˈɡʊəbi/ *noun*. M18.
[ORIGIN Algerian Arab. *gurbi* (straw) hut.]
In N. Africa: a hovel or hut.

gourd /ɡʊəd, ɡɔːd/ *noun*. ME.
[ORIGIN Anglo-Norman *gurde*, Old French & mod. French *gourde*, repr. ult. Latin *cucurbita*.]
1 The fleshy, often large fruit of any of various trailing or climbing plants of the family Cucurbitaceae; *spec*. (also ***bottle gourd***) that of *Lagenaria siceraria*, native to the Old World tropics. Also, any of certain similar fruit from unrelated plants. ME. ▸**b** The plant producing such a fruit. LME.
2 The dried, empty rind of such a fruit, used as a bottle, float, etc. Formerly also, a bottle or vessel of any kind. ME. ▸**b** A gourdful. M18.
3 *HERALDRY*. A charge representing such a fruit. E16.
4 The head. Freq. in ***out of one's gourd***, crazy. *US slang*. M19.
– PHRASES ETC.: ***bitter-gourd***: see BITTER *adjective & adverb*. ***bottle gourd***: see sense 1 above ***out of one's gourd***: see sense 4 above. ***snake gourd***: see SNAKE *noun*. ***sour gourd***: see SOUR *adjective*.
■ **gourdful** *noun* as much as a gourd will hold M19.

gourde /ɡʊəd/ *noun*. M19.
[ORIGIN French, fem. of *gourd* lit. 'stupid, dull, heavy', from Latin *gurdus* a dolt.]
1 In the former French and Spanish-American colonies: a local name for the dollar. *obsolete* exc. *dial*. M19.
2 The principal monetary unit of Haiti, equal to 100 centimes. M19.

†gourdy *adjective*. M16.
[ORIGIN Old French *gourdi* swollen, pa. pple of *gourdir* swell (mod. *s'engourdir* grow numb).]
1 Swollen with stuffing. Only in M16.
2 *VETERINARY MEDICINE*. (Of a horse's legs) swollen; (of a horse) with swollen legs. E18–E19.
■ **†gourdiness** *noun* E18–E19.

gourmand /ˈɡʊəmənd, ˈɡɔː-; *foreign* ɡurmɑ̃ (*pl. same*)/ *noun & adjective*. Occas. fem. **-mande** /-mɑːnd; *foreign* ɡurmɑ̃ːd (*pl. same*)/. LME.
[ORIGIN Old French & mod. French, of unknown origin.]
▸ **A** *noun*. **1** A person who is overfond of eating; a glutton. LME.
2 A lover or connoisseur of good food; a gourmet. M18.
▸ **B** *adjective*. Gluttonous, greedy; fond of eating. M16.
■ **gourmandism** *noun* E19.

gourmandize /ˈɡɔːm(ə)ndʌɪz, ɡʊəmɒ̃ˈdiːz/ *noun*. Also **-ise**, **gor-**. LME.
[ORIGIN French *gourmandise*, from GOURMAND.]
Orig., gluttony. Now chiefly, the appreciation or consumption of good food, indulgence in good eating.

gourmandize /ˈɡɔːm(ə)ndʌɪz, ˈɡʊəmɒ̃dʌɪz/ *verb*. Also **-ise**, **gor-**. M16.
[ORIGIN from the noun.]
1 *verb intrans*. Eat greedily; indulge in good eating. M16.

Y. MENUHIN One of my clearest memories . . is of gormandizing at a luncheon given in the park.

2 *verb trans*. Devour greedily. E17.
†**3** *verb trans*. Satiate. E17–L18.
■ **gourmandizer** *noun* a glutton L16.

gourmet /ˈɡʊəmeɪ, ˈɡɔː-, *foreign* ɡurmɛ (*pl. same*)/ *noun & adjective*. E19.
[ORIGIN French, formerly = wine-merchant's assistant, wine taster, infl. in sense by GOURMAND.]
▸ **A** *noun*. A connoisseur in eating and drinking; a judge of good food. E19.
▸ **B** *attrib*. or as *adjective*. Of the nature of a gourmet; of a kind or standard suitable for gourmets. E20.

gousty /ˈɡaʊsti/ *adjective*. *Scot. & N. English*. E16.
[ORIGIN Unknown.]
Large and empty or hollow; dreary, desolate; (of a sound) hollow.

gout /ɡaʊt/ *noun*[1]. ME.
[ORIGIN Old French *gote*, *goute* (mod. *goutte*) or medieval Latin *gutta* lit. 'drop' (with ref. to the medieval theory of a flowing down of bodily humours).]
1 A disease in which defective metabolism of uric acid characteristically causes arthritis, esp. in the smaller bones of the feet, deposition of chalk-stones, and episodes of acute pain. Also (*arch*.), a painful attack of this disease. ME.

SPENSER Eke in foote and hand A grievous gout tormented him full sore. H. ALLEN A round of high living at Paris . . was not calculated to help the gout. G. HEYER Thin fingers . . twisted by gout.

†**2** A disease of hawks or other birds, *esp*. a swelling on the feet. L15–E17.
3 Infestation and destruction of wheat etc. by the larva of a dipteran fly, *Chlorops pumilionis*, which causes swollen stems. E19.
– COMB.: **gout fly** the fly whose larva causes gout in wheat (see sense 3 above); **goutweed** ground elder, *Aegopodium podagraria* (formerly used to treat gout).

gout /ɡaʊt/ *noun*[2]. LME.
[ORIGIN Old French *gote* (mod. *goutte*) from Latin *gutta*.]
Orig., a drop, esp. of blood or (*Scot*.) medicine. Now usu. a splash, streak (of blood or other fluid, smoke, flame, etc.).

DAY LEWIS Fuchsia bushes which splash its white wall with blood-red gouts. CLIVE JAMES The huge machine . . belching gouts of flame from the exhausts.

gout /ɡaʊt/ *noun*[3]. *obsolete* exc. *dial*. L16.
[ORIGIN Prob. aphet. from French *égout* sewer.]
A water channel; a sluice; a covered drain or culvert. Cf. GOTE.

gout *noun*[4] var. of GOÛT.

gout /ɡaʊt/ *verb intrans. & trans*. L19.
[ORIGIN from GOUT *noun*[2].]
Spurt, pour.

S. HASSEL The hail of bullets throws him backwards . . . Gouting blood he slides down from the tank. *fig*.: M. AYRTON My fears returned, first gouting in my belly and then dribbling . . to my brain.

goût /ɡuː/ *noun*. Also ***gout***. L16.
[ORIGIN French, earlier *goust* from Latin *gustus* taste. Cf. GUST *noun*[1], GUSTO.]
1 Liking, relish, fondness (*for*). L16.

A. BURN Relished a dish of fine-flavoured tea with as high a goût as . . any man ever did.

2 The ability to perceive and discriminate between flavours, smells, etc.; the faculty of aesthetic appreciation or judgement; (good) taste. E18.

HENRY FIELDING This last opera . . is too light for my goût.

3 Style or manner; *esp*. a prevailing or fashionable style. E18.

Times Dubious furniture in the goût *Rothschild*.

4 Flavour, savour, taste. M18.
goût de terroir: see TERROIR 2.

goûter /ɡuːte/ *noun*. Pl. pronounced same. L18.
[ORIGIN French, from *goûter* to taste.]
A light afternoon meal; five-o'clock tea.

†goutify *verb trans*. M18–M19.
[ORIGIN from GOUT *noun*[1] + -I- + -FY.]
Make gouty; afflict with gout.

goutish /ˈɡaʊtɪʃ/ *adjective*. LME.
[ORIGIN from GOUT *noun*[1] + -ISH[1].]
1 Of a person: somewhat gouty, predisposed to gout. LME.
2 Of, pertaining to, or of the nature of gout. E18.

goutte /ɡuːt/ *noun*. LME.
[ORIGIN French Cf. GUTTÉ.]
HERALDRY. A charge shaped like a drop of liquid.

gouty /ˈɡaʊti/ *adjective*. LME.
[ORIGIN from GOUT *noun*[1] + -Y[1].]
1 Affected by or subject to gout. LME.

M. IGNATIEFF Nursing a gouty foot.

2 Swollen or bulging; out of shape, ill-proportioned; distorted, esp. with swellings. L16. ▸**b** Full of knots or knobs. *obsolete* exc. *dial*. L16.
gouty-stem *Austral*. an Australian tree, *Adansonia gregorii*, related to the baobab.
3 Of, pertaining to, or resembling, gout. E17. ▸**b** Used during an attack of gout. *obsolete* exc. *hist*. M18. ▸**c** (Supposedly) predisposing to gout. E19.

S. RICHARDSON The torture of a gouty paroxysm. **b** HOR. WALPOLE Wheeled into the room in gouty chairs. **c** T. BEDDOES The weaker wines of France are reputed more gouty than those in common use among the English.

4 Of land: boggy. *obsolete* exc. *Scot. & dial*. L17.
■ **goutily** *adverb* M19. **goutiness** *noun* M17.

gouvernante /ɡuːvəˈnɒnt, *foreign* ɡuvɛrnɑ̃t/ *noun*. Now *rare* or *obsolete*. Pl. pronounced same. Also (earlier) anglicized as **†governante**. L16.
[ORIGIN French, use as noun of fem. pres. ppl adjective of *gouverner* GOVERN.]
1 A female governor or ruler. L16.
2 A chaperone; a governess, a female teacher. M17.
3 A housekeeper (usu. to a single man). M17.

Gov. *abbreviation*.
1 Government.
2 Governor.

gove /ɡəʊv/ *verb intrans*. *Scot*. ME.
[ORIGIN Unknown.]
Gaze, stare (esp. stupidly).

govern /ˈɡʌv(ə)n/ *verb*. ME.
[ORIGIN Old French *governer* (mod. *gouverner*) from Latin *gubernare* steer, direct, rule from Greek *kubernan* steer.]
1 *verb trans. & intrans*. Rule with authority, conduct the policy, actions, and affairs of (a state, subjects), constitutionally or despotically; regulate the proceedings of (a corporation etc.); be in military command of (a fort, town). ME. ▸**b** Direct and control, have under protective guardianship. Now *rare* or *obsolete*. ME.

J. A. FROUDE The country had been governed by a succession of ecclesiastical ministers. C. KINGSLEY When God has to govern a nation because it cannot govern itself. M. PATTISON The throne was occupied by a minor . . whose mother . . governed as regent.

governing body the body of managers of a hospital, school, etc.
2 *verb trans*. Control, influence, regulate, or determine (a person, another's action, the course or issue of events). ME. ▸†**b** Guide, direct, lead (*in* some course, *to* or *towards* an object). LME–M18. ▸†**c** Master, prevail over. *rare* (Shakes.). Only in L16.

STEELE Ordinary Minds are wholly governed by their Eyes and Ears. R. NIEBUHR He is governed far more by imagination than by reason. G. VIDAL We . . govern our days by clocks and watches. **b** R. CORBET A straying starr . . governd those wisemen to Christ. **c** SHAKES. *Ven. & Ad*. She . . govern'd him in strength, though not in lust.

3 *verb trans*. Conduct (oneself) in a particular way; restrain, curb, bridle (oneself, one's feelings). ME.

BURKE I have no doubt of the principles on which you govern yourself. DICKENS I appeal to you to govern your temper.

4 *verb intrans*. Hold sway; have or be the predominating or decisive influence. LME.

E. POUND The same laws govern, and you are bound by no others.

†**5** *verb trans*. Administer, manage (an undertaking, an establishment, etc.). LME–M18.

EVELYN My Lord Sandwich . . always govern'd his affaires with successe.

†**6** *verb trans*. Attend to, look after (a person), esp. with reference to health; tend (a plant). LME–L17.

I. WALTON His pensions . . were given to a woman that governed him.

†**7** Work or manage (a ship, the sails, the helm). LME–L17.
8 *verb trans*. Regulate the working of, manage, manipulate, operate, control (an implement, machine, etc.). LME.

Which Micro? If you have two joysticks . . you can set them both to govern different controls.

9 *verb trans*. *GRAMMAR*. Esp. of a verb or preposition: have (a noun, pronoun, etc., or a case) depending on it; require a dependent word to be in (a certain case). LME.
10 *verb trans*. Constitute a law, rule, standard, or principle for; serve to decide (a legal case). E19.

W. CRUISE The case of Peacock v. Spooner having been decided by the House of Lords, must govern this case. Y. WINTERS We assume that constant principles govern the poetic experience.

governable /ˈɡʌv(ə)nəb(ə)l/ *adjective*. M17.
[ORIGIN from GOVERN + -ABLE.]
Able to be governed, amenable to being governed.
■ **governaˈbility** *noun* L19. **governableness** *noun* L18. **governably** *adverb* M19.

†governail *noun*. ME.
[ORIGIN Old French (mod. *gouvernail*) from Latin *gubernaculum*, pl. *-la* rudder, from *gubernare* GOVERN.]
1 A ship's rudder. Also, steering. ME–M16.
2 Government, authority. Also, a person who governs; the community governed. LME–L16. ▸**b** Behaviour, self-control. LME–L16. ▸**c** Management; treatment. L15–L16.

governance /ˈgʌv(ə)nəns/ *noun*. ME.
[ORIGIN Old French (mod. *gouvernance*) from *governer* GOVERN: see -ANCE.]
1 The action, manner, or fact of governing; government. ME. ▸**b** Controlling or regulating influence; control, mastery. LME. ▸†**c** The state of being governed; good order. LME–L16.

BROWNING I have submitted wholly.. to your rule and governance. **b** P. GAY Bentham saw man as an animal under the governance of the pleasure principle. **c** SPENSER Whose countries he.. shortly brought to civile governaunce.

2 The function or power of governing; authority to govern. LME. ▸†**b** A governing person or body. M16–M17.

J. PAYNE The king invested him with the governance of one of the provinces.

†**3** Conduct of life or business; behaviour. LME–M17.

W. LAMBARDE Men.. learned in the Lawe and of good gouernance.

†governante *noun* see GOUVERNANTE.

governess /ˈgʌv(ə)nɪs/ *noun*. Also †**governeress**. LME.
[ORIGIN Old French *governeresse* fem. of *governëo(u)r*: see GOVERNOR, -ESS[1].]
1 A female governor or ruler. Formerly also, a presiding goddess or tutelary. Now *rare* or *obsolete*. LME.
2 A female teacher, usu. of children in a private household. Formerly also, a woman in charge of a (young) person. LME.
3 The wife of a governor. Now only *joc.* L17.
– COMB.: **governess cart** *hist.* a light two-wheeled tub-shaped cart with a rear entrance and side seats face-to-face.
■ **governessy** *adjective* having the characteristics of a governess; *esp.* prim: L19.

governess /ˈgʌv(ə)nɪs/ *verb*. E19.
[ORIGIN from the noun.]
1 *verb intrans.* Work as a governess (GOVERNESS *noun* 2). E19.

M. R. MITFORD Sixteen years of governessing.. tamed that romantic imagination.

2 *verb trans.* Act as governess to; teach. M19.

C. M. YONGE She has been governessed and crammed till she is half sick of all reading.

government /ˈgʌv(ə)nm(ə)nt, -vəm(ə)nt/ *noun & adjective*. LME.
[ORIGIN Old French *governement* (mod. *gouvernement*), formed as GOVERN: see -MENT.]
▸ **A** *noun*. **1** The action of governing; continuous exercise of authority over subjects; authoritative direction or regulation; control; chiefly *spec.* the action of governing the affairs of a state; political rule and administration. LME. ▸**b** Guidance (in action). *arch.* E18.

J. BENTHAM The business of government is to promote the happiness of the society by punishing and rewarding. TENNYSON They [horses].. felt Her low firm voice and tender government. **b** L. MURRAY Examples.. which may serve as some government to the scholar.

†**2** The manner in which a person's action is governed; demeanour; conduct. LME–M17.
3 The function of governing; authority to govern. LME. ▸†**b** An appointment as governor. E17–E19.

SPENSER The first.. Of all the house had charge and governement, As Guardian and Steward.

4 The (freq. specified) system by which a nation, community, etc., is governed. LME.

T. GRAY Three sorts of government, Despotism, the limited Monarchy, and the Republican. G. BANCROFT Government, in early times, was very imperfectly organized.

civil government, ***coalition government***, ***constitutional government***, ***local government***, ***military government***, ***republican government***, etc.
5 The fact that a particular person governs. M16. ▸**b** (Freq. **G-**.) Period of governing, tenure of office. E17.

W. ROBERTSON The government of a Queen was unknown in Scotland. **b** MARVELL God.. bless your Majesty with a long and happy Government.

6 *hist.* The area ruled over by a governor; a subdivision of a kingdom or empire (esp. in France or Russia). E17.

C. WHITWORTH In 1710, the Czar.. divided the Empire into eight governments.

7 (Freq. **G-**.) The governing power in a state; the body or successive bodies of people governing a state; the state as an agent; an administration, a ministry. E18. ▸**b** In *pl.* government securities. L19.

SOUTHEY Government are acting like themselves. W. S. CHURCHILL The Government advise the House, and the House decides.

form a government (of a Prime Minister etc.) establish an administration esp. after a general election.
8 GRAMMAR. The influence of one word over another in determining the case of a noun, the mood of a verb, etc. M18.
– COMB.: **Government House** the official residence of a governor; **government man** (*a*) AUSTRAL. HISTORY a convict; (*b*) a government official; **government paper**, **government securities** bonds or other promissory certificates issued by a government; **government stroke** *Austral. & NZ* (*a*) *hist.* a convict's work rate; (*b*) *slang* lazy or leisurely work rate; **government surplus** unwanted equipment sold by the government through retailers (freq. ***government-surplus*** attrib.).
▸ **B** *attrib.* or as *adjective*. Of or pertaining to government esp. of a state. L18.
■ **govern'mental** *adjective* of or pertaining to a government, esp. of a state: M18. **govern'mentally** *adverb* L19.

governmentese /gʌv(ə)nmənˈtiːz/ *noun*. M20.
[ORIGIN from GOVERNMENT + -ESE.]
Long-winded or obscure language held to be characteristic of government departments.

governor /ˈgʌv(ə)nə/ *noun*. ME.
[ORIGIN Anglo-Norman *governour*, Old French *governëo(u)r* (mod. *gouverneur*) from Latin *gubernator*, from *gubernare*: see GOVERN, -OR.]
†**1** A steersman, pilot, or captain of a ship. ME–E17.
2 A person who governs or exercises authoritative control over subjects etc.; a ruler. ME.

SHAKES. *Merch. V.* Her gentle spirit Commits itself to yours to be directed, As from her lord, her governor, her king. R. CUDWORTH The Deity.. which is the supreme Governour of all things.

3 (Freq. **G-**.) An official appointed to govern a province, country, town, etc.; a representative of the Crown in a Commonwealth country or colony that regards the British monarch as head of state; the executive head of each state of the US. ME. ▸**b** The officer commanding a fortress or garrison. M17.
†**4** The commander of a company, esp. an armed force. ME–E17.
5 The head, or one of the governing body, of an institution, establishment, etc.; *spec.* the official in charge of a prison. LME.

W. HOLTBY Carne alone among the governors had opposed her appointment to the High School.

†**6** A person in charge of a young man's education; a tutor. M16–L18.

J. LOCKE The great Work of a Governour is to.. form the Mind.

7 *colloq.* Cf. GUV, GUVNER. ▸**a** An employer. E19. ▸**b** One's father. E19. ▸**c** As *voc.*: Sir; Mister. M19.

a DICKENS Tell your governor that Blathers.. is here. **b** C. BEDE The bills will come in some day.. but the governor will see to them. **c** DICKENS 'My youngest died last week'. 'I'm sorry for it, governor, with all my heart.'

8 An automatic regulator of the supply of fuel, steam, water, etc., to a machine, ensuring uniform motion or limiting speed. E19.

Which? Nearly all diesel engines have a 'governor' which prevents the engine being revved too fast.

9 ANGLING. A type of fly. M19.
■ **governorate** *noun* the residence or office of a governor; the area ruled by a governor: L19. **governorship** *noun* (the exercise or tenure of) the office of governor M17.

governor general /gʌv(ə)nəˈdʒɛn(ə)r(ə)l/ *noun*. L16.
[ORIGIN from GOVERNOR + GENERAL *adjective*.]
A governor having authority over deputy or lieutenant governors.
■ **governor generalship** *noun* the (term of) office of a governor general M19.

Govr *abbreviation*.
Governor.

govt *abbreviation*.
Government.

gowan /ˈgaʊən/ *noun*. *Scot. & N. English*. M16.
[ORIGIN Prob. alt. of GOLLAN.]
A yellow or white field flower; *spec.* a daisy.
■ **gowany** *adjective* covered with gowans E18.

gowk /gaʊk/ *noun & verb*. Orig. & chiefly *Scot. & N. English*. ME.
[ORIGIN Old Norse *gaukr* = Old English *ġēac*, Old Frisian, Old Saxon *gāk*, Old High German *gouh* (German *Gauch* cuckoo, fool) from Germanic, of imit. origin.]
▸ **A** *noun*. **1** A cuckoo. ME.
2 A fool; a half-witted or awkward person. L16.

L. G. GIBBON He would stand staring like a gowk for minutes on end.

▸ **B** *verb intrans.* Stare foolishly. L15.

gowl /gaʊl/ *verb & noun*. Chiefly *Scot. & N. English*. ME.
[ORIGIN Old Norse *gaula*, perh. from a base meaning 'to bark', but cf. YOWL *verb*.]
▸ **A** *verb intrans.* Of a person, animal, the wind: howl, yell, cry. ME.
▸ **B** *noun*. A howl or yell. E16.

gown /gaʊn/ *noun & verb*. ME.
[ORIGIN Old French *goune*, *gon(n)e* from late Latin *gunna* fur garment (cf. Byzantine Greek *gouna* fur, fur-lined garment).]
▸ **A** *noun*. **1** A loose flowing outer robe indicating the wearer's office, profession, or status, esp. as worn by a lawyer, alderman, or judge, or by a member of the clergy or of a university, college, or school. ME. ▸**b** The office, profession, or status denoted by the wearing of a gown; *collect.* the members or holders of this. E17. ▸**c** *spec.* (*collect.*) The resident members of a university. Now chiefly in ***town and gown***, non-members and members of a university in a particular place. M17.

SHAKES. *Twel. N.* Put on this gown and this beard; make him believe thou art.. the curate. W. M. PRAED A scholar, in my cap and gown. **b** DRYDEN The Cut-throat Sword and clamorous Gown. J. POTTER I have now taken the gown [holy orders]. **c** C. BEDE When Gown was absent, Town was miserable.

2 Orig., a long loose upper garment for everyday wear by men or women. Now, a woman's (long, formal, or elegant) dress. LME. ▸**b** *ellipt.* A nightgown; a dressing gown. L16.

A. LURIE No mini-dresses.. it was all long gowns of chiffon, lace and watered satin. **b** DEFOE I came down.. in my gown and slippers.

blue gown: see BLUE *adjective*. ***dressing gown***, ***nightgown***, etc.
3 A Roman toga, or similar garment. LME.

R. GRAVES His patrician's gown was disgracefully stained.

4 A protective garment worn in a hospital by a staff member during surgery, or (more fully ***hospital gown***) by a patient. E20.
– COMB.: **gownsman**, †**gownman** a person who wears a gown, esp. as an indication of status, office, or profession; a member of the legal profession, a clergyman, a member of a university.
▸ **B** *verb*. **1** *verb trans.* Attire in a gown. Freq. as ***gowned*** *pa. pple or ppl adjective*. LME.

A. LEVY Gorgeously gowned and bejewelled women.

2 *verb intrans.* Put on a gown. Chiefly in ***gown up***, put on a protective overall, esp. in an operating theatre. L19.

gowpen /ˈgaʊp(ə)n/ *noun*. *Scot. & N. English*. ME.
[ORIGIN Old Norse *gaupn* (Norwegian dial. *gaupn*, Swedish *göpen*, etc.) = Old High German *coufana* (Middle High German *goufen*). Cf. YEPSEN.]
1 The two hands held together to form a bowl; as much as they can hold, a double handful. ME.
2 LAW. A perquisite of grain or flour allowed to a miller's servant. *obsolete* exc. *hist.* M18.
■ **gowpenful** *noun* as much as can be held in both hands cupped together L17.

goy /gɔɪ/ *noun*. Pl. **goyim** /ˈgɔɪɪm/, **goys**. M19.
[ORIGIN Hebrew *gōy* people, nation, pl. *gōyim*.]
Among Jews: a non-Jew, a Gentile.
■ **goy'ish** *adjective* M20.

Goyaesque /gɔɪəˈɛsk/ *adjective*. Also **Goyesque** /gɔɪˈɛsk/. M20.
[ORIGIN from *Goya* (see below) + -ESQUE.]
Of, pertaining to, or characteristic of the Spanish painter Francisco de Goya y Lucientes (1746–1828) or his work.

goyal /ˈgɔɪəl/ *noun*. *dial.* Also (earlier) **goyle**. E17.
[ORIGIN Unknown.]
A deep gully, a ravine.

Goyesque *adjective* var. of GOYAESQUE.

goyim *noun pl.* see GOY.

goyle *noun* var. of GOYAL.

gozzard *noun* var. of GOOSEHERD.

GP *abbreviation*.
1 General practitioner.
2 Grand Prix.

GPA *abbreviation*. *N. Amer.*
Grade point average.

Gp Capt. *abbreviation*.
Group Captain.

gph *abbreviation*.
Gallons per hour.

GPI *abbreviation*.
General paralysis (of the insane).

gpm *abbreviation*.
Gallons per minute.

GPMU *abbreviation*.
Graphical, Paper, and Media Union (formed by the merger of the NGA and SOGAT).

GPO *abbreviation*.
1 General Post Office.
2 Government Printing Office. *US*.

GPRS *abbreviation*.
General packet radio services, a technology for radio transmission of small packets of data, esp. between mobile phones and the Internet.

G

GPS *abbreviation.*
Global Positioning System, a navigational and surveying facility based on the reception of signals from orbiting satellites.

GR *abbreviation.*
Latin *Georgius Rex* King George.

gr. *abbreviation.*
1 Grain(s).
2 Gram(s).
3 Grey.
4 Gross.

gra /grɑː/ *noun. Irish.* Long *rare.* **E18.**
[ORIGIN Irish *a ghráidh* my dear.]
Freq. as form of address: dear. Also, affection, love.

Graafian /ˈgrɑːfɪən/ *adjective.* **M19.**
[ORIGIN from R. de *Graaf* (1641–73), Dutch anatomist + -IAN.]
ANATOMY. ***Graafian follicle, Graafian vesicle***, any of the small sacs in the mammalian ovary in which ova are matured.

G

†**graal** *noun* var. of GRAIL *noun*[2].

grab /grab/ *noun*[1]. **L17.**
[ORIGIN Arabic *ḡurāb* light galley.]
A large coasting vessel, built with a prow and usually two-masted, formerly in use in the waters around the Indian subcontinent.

grab /grab/ *noun*[2]. **L18.**
[ORIGIN from GRAB *verb.*]
1 Something which is grabbed. *Scot.* **L18.**
2 A quick sudden clutch or grasp; an attempt to seize. **E19.** ▸**b** The action or practice of grabbing; *esp.* rapacious proceedings in business or commerce. **L19.**

DE QUINCEY The chairman . . made a grab at it.

b up for grabs *colloq.* open to offer; easily obtainable; inviting capture.
3 A person who grabs; *spec.* a body-snatcher, a bailiff, a police officer. Now *rare* or *obsolete.* **E19.**
4 A mechanical device or implement for clutching or gripping (and usu. also lifting) objects. **M19.**
PETERSEN GRAB.
5 A children's card game resembling snap in which cards of equal value may be snatched from the table. **L19.**
6 A frame of video or television footage that is digitized and stored as a still image in a computer memory for subsequent display, printing, or editing. **L20.**
– COMB.: **grab bag** *N. Amer.* a lucky dip; **grab handle**, **grab rail**: to steady passengers in a moving vehicle; **grab-hook** a hook used for gripping or clutching; ***grab rail***: see ***grab handle*** above.

grab /grab/ *verb.* Infl. **-bb-**. **L16.**
[ORIGIN Middle Low German, Middle Dutch *grabben*, perh. from modification of the base of GRIP *verb*[1], GRIPE *verb*[1], GROPE *verb.*]
1 *verb trans.* Grasp or seize suddenly and eagerly; snatch up; appropriate rapaciously or unscrupulously; *colloq.* obtain. **L16.**

W. WHARTON He grabs my shovel and pushes me aside. G. BOYCOTT A situation where batsmen . . must grab every opportunity to score a run. D. LODGE I'll grab another sherry while there's still time.

grab hold of seize. ***smash-and-grab***: see SMASH *verb*[1].
2 *verb trans.* Capture or arrest (a person). **E19.** ▸**b** Attract the attention of, make an impression on. *slang.* **M20.**

H. NISBET A very dangerous young criminal . . whom I reckon we won't be able to grab in a hurry. **b** *Grimsby Evening Telegraph* Hoping that the book will grab so many people that something will eventually be done.

3 *verb intrans.* Make a sudden snatch *at*, *for*. **M19.**
4 *verb intrans.* Of the brakes of a motor vehicle: act harshly or jerkily. **E20.**
■ **grabbable** *adjective* **E19.**

grabber /ˈgrabə/ *noun.* **M19.**
[ORIGIN from GRAB *verb* + -ER[1].]
A person who or thing which grabs.
land-grabber: see LAND *noun*[1].

grabble /ˈgrab(ə)l/ *verb & noun.* **L16.**
[ORIGIN Prob. from Dutch, Low German *grabbeln* scramble for a thing, frequentative of *grabben*: see GRAB *verb*, -LE[3].]
▸**A** *verb.* **1** *verb intrans.* Feel or search with the hands, grope about. **L16.** ▸**b** *verb trans.* Feel (one's way). **E17.**
†**2** *verb trans.* Handle rudely or roughly. **L17–L18.**
3 *verb intrans.* Sprawl or tumble about; scramble (for money etc.). **M18.**
4 *verb trans.* Seize, appropriate. **L18.** ▸**b** *verb intrans.* Grab *at* (something). **M19.**
5 *verb intrans.* Grapple *with*. *rare.* **M19.**
▸**B** *noun.* **1** A grapple or struggle. *rare.* **L16.**
2 A device to catch or grab. Chiefly in ***fish on the grabble***, fish with a line held down by a plummet so that the hook-link is in the water. **E18.**

grabby /ˈgrabi/ *noun. slang.* **M19.**
[ORIGIN Unknown.]
A foot soldier.

grabby /ˈgrabi/ *adjective. colloq.* **E20.**
[ORIGIN from GRAB *verb* + -Y[1].]
Having a tendency to grab; greedy, grasping; arresting.

J. H. VANCE Nice when they don't steal my copra. Some people are pretty grabby. *Oxford Mail* A grabby front page headline.

graben /ˈgrɑːb(ə)n/ *noun.* Pl. **-s**, same. **L19.**
[ORIGIN German, orig. = ditch.]
GEOLOGY. A depression in the earth's surface between faults, a rift valley.

grace /greɪs/ *noun.* **ME.**
[ORIGIN Old French (mod. *grâce*) from Latin *gratia*, from *gratus* pleasing: cf. GRATEFUL.]
▸**I 1** The quality of pleasing, attractiveness, charm, *esp.* that associated with elegant proportions or ease and refinement of movement, action, expression, or manner. **ME.** ▸**b** Seemliness, becomingness; favourable or creditable aspect. Freq. with specifying word, as in ***with a bad grace, with an ill grace, with a good grace*** below. **L16.**

STEELE It gives new Grace to the most eminent Accomplishments. G. ORWELL In spite of the bulkiness of his body there was a remarkable grace in his movements. **b** H. MARTINEAU As soon as she could with any grace leave the company.

2 An attractive or pleasing quality or feature; an agreeable accomplishment. Freq. in *pl.* **ME.** ▸**b** Something that imparts beauty; an ornament; the part in which the beauty of a thing consists. Long *rare.* **L16.** ▸**c** A mode of behaviour, attitude, etc., adopted with a view to elegance or refinement. *obsolete* exc. in ***airs and graces*** below. **E17.**

SMOLLETT Possess'd of ev'ry manly grace. JOHN BROOKE George I lacked the graces and never became an English gentleman. P. G. WODEHOUSE A fellow lacking in the softer social graces. **b** DRYDEN A spreading laurel stood, The grace and ornament of all the wood.

3 CLASSICAL MYTHOLOGY (**G-**.) Each of the three beautiful sister goddesses, Aglaia, Thalia, and Euphrosyne, regarded as the bestowers of beauty and charm. **L16.**

TENNYSON The Muses and the Graces, group'd in threes. *transf.*: A. S. BYATT Attendant nymphs and graces.

4 MUSIC. In full ***grace note***. An additional note (often printed smaller than the others) introduced as an embellishment not essential to the harmony or the melody of a piece. **M17.**

transf.: J. BRAINE The extra refinement, the grace-note, was Jack's waving away of my offer to buy the drinks.

5 In *pl.* with *the* (treated as *sing.*). A game in which a player holds a hoop on a pair of slender rods and by drawing one rod rapidly across the other impels the hoop into the air. Long *rare.* **M19.**
▸**II 6** Favour; favourable or kindly regard or its manifestation (now only on the part of a superior); unconstrained good will as a ground of concession. **ME.**

SIR W. SCOTT The marks of grace which Elizabeth . . shewed to young Raleigh. B. EMECHETA But for God's grace he would have been a dead person by now.

7 An instance or manifestation of favour; a favour conferred on or offered to another. Also (*obsolete* exc. *hist.*), an exceptional favour granted by someone in authority, a privilege, a dispensation. **ME.** ▸†**b** Permission to do something, leave. Only in **ME.**

DRYDEN But, to return and view the chearful skies, . . To few great Jupiter imparts this Grace. TENNYSON Do me this grace my child, to have my shield In keeping.

†**8** The share of favour allotted to one by Providence; fate, destiny; luck, fortune. Freq. with specifying word. **ME–L16.**

SIR T. MORE Elizabeth, whose fortune and grace was after to bee Quene.

9 THEOLOGY. **a** The free and unmerited favour of God as manifested in the salvation of sinners and the bestowing of blessings. **ME.** ▸**b** The divine regenerating, inspiriting, and strengthening influence. Freq. with specifying word. **ME.** ▸**c** An individual virtue or excellence, divine in origin; a divinely given talent etc. **ME.** ▸**d** The condition of a person under such divine influence. **LME.**

a S. PURCHAS Holding that they are saved by Merit, without Law or Grace. **b** SHAKES. *1 Hen. VI* Chosen from above By inspiration of celestial grace. WORDSWORTH Blest Is he who can, by help of grace, enthrone The peace of God within his single breast! **c** EDWARD WHITE A general acknowledgement of worldly virtues as Christian graces. **d** W. LITHGOW The flying from evil, is a flying to grace.

10 †**a** In a thing: beneficent virtue or efficacy. **ME–E17.** ▸**b** In a person: virtue; an individual virtue; a sense of duty and propriety. **M16.**

a SHAKES. *Rom. & Jul.* Mickle is the powerful grace that lies In plants. **b** SIR W. SCOTT He blushes again, which is a sign of grace.

11 Mercy, clemency; pardon, forgiveness. *arch.* **ME.**

MILTON To bow and sue for grace With suppliant knee.

12 a A royal or noble personage, designated in the complimentary periphrasis ***his grace, her grace, my lord's grace, the king's grace***, etc. *arch.* **ME.** ▸**b** Now usu. **G-**. The designation of a duke, duchess, or archbishop, used as a form of address. Formerly also, the designation of a king or queen. **E16.**
13 The condition or fact of being favoured. Now only in ***be in the good graces of*** below. **LME.**
14 Orig., a dispensation from some of the statutory conditions required by a university for a degree. Now, permission to take a university degree; a dispensation from the University statutes; at Cambridge University, a decree of the Senate or Regent House. **LME.**
15 Favour shown by granting a delay in the performance of an action, or the discharge of a duty, or immunity from penalty during a specified period. **E18.**

J. P. HOPPS Your long day of grace is gone. M. CORELLI I give you a day's grace to decide.

▸**III** †**16** In *pl.* Thanks, thanksgiving. **ME–M16.**

LD BERNERS I . . gyue great graces to my goddes of my good happe.

17 (Orig. chiefly *pl.*, treated as *sing.*, now only *sing.*) A short prayer uttered as a thanksgiving before or after eating. **ME.**

TINDALE *Matt.* 26:30 When they had sayd grace they went out. DAY LEWIS Family prayers and grace before meals were taken for granted.

– PHRASES: **act of grace** (**a**) a privilege or concession that cannot be claimed as a right; (**b**) (***Act of Grace***) a formal pardon, esp. a free and general pardon, granted by Act of Parliament. ***actual grace***: see ACTUAL *adjective* 1. **airs and graces** behaviour displaying an affected elegance of manner designed to attract or impress. **be in the good graces of** have the favour, liking, and sympathy of. **by the grace of God** through God's favour, *esp.* [translating Latin *Dei gratia*] appended to the formal statement of a monarch's title, and formerly to that of some ecclesiastical dignitaries. ***Covenant of Grace***: see COVENANT *noun.* **days of grace** the period of time allowed by law for the payment of a bill of exchange or an insurance premium after it falls due. †**do grace to** reflect credit on (a person), embellish, do honour to. ***effectual grace***: see EFFECTUAL *adjective.* **efficacious grace** ROMAN CATHOLIC CHURCH a divine influence which inspires its recipient to effect some good act. ***expectative grace***: see EXPECTATIVE *adjective.* **fall from grace** lapse from a state of grace into sin; *loosely* lapse from good behaviour into disgrace. ***free grace***: see FREE *adjective.* **grace and favour** *adjective* designating a house or other residence occupied by permission of the British monarch, the British Government, or other owner. ***grace expectative***: see EXPECTATIVE *adjective.* ***herb-grace, herb of grace***: see HERB *noun.* **have the grace to** be sufficiently conscious of duty or decency to. ***means of grace***: see MEAN *noun*[1]. ***prevenient grace***: see PREVENIENT *adjective* 1. ***saving grace***: see SAVING *ppl adjective.* **state of grace** the condition of a person who is generally subject to the divine regenerating, inspiriting, and strengthening influence. **sufficient grace** ROMAN CATHOLIC CHURCH a divine influence which renders its recipient capable of some good act. ***take heart of grace***: see HEART *noun.* ***Throne of Grace***: see THRONE *noun.* **with a bad grace, with an ill grace** with a display of unwillingness, reluctantly and ungraciously. **with a good grace** with a show of willingness, pleasantly and readily. **year of grace** *arch.* a year as reckoned from the birth of Jesus.
– COMB.: **grace-cup** a cup of wine etc. passed round after grace has been said; the last drink before going to bed, a parting drink; ***grace note***: see sense 4 above; **grace-wife** (long *obsolete* exc. *dial.*) a midwife.
■ **gracy** *adjective* (long *obsolete* exc. *Scot.*, *rare*) full of grace, devout **M17.**

grace /greɪs/ *verb trans.* **ME.**
[ORIGIN Partly (in sense 1) from Old French *gracier* thank, partly from GRACE *noun.*]
†**1** Thank. Usu. in *pass.* Only in **ME.**
†**2** Show favour or be gracious to; countenance. **L15–E17.**
3 Lend or add grace to; adorn, embellish, set off; enhance *with*; bring honour or credit to, esp., by one's attendance or participation. **L16.** ▸†**b** W. compl.: name or designate honourably. *rare* (Milton). Only in **M17.**

M. ATWOOD A nonstop talker graced with no narrative skill or sense of timing. *Toronto Life* A meeting graced by the presence of Ken Thomson himself.

†**4** Give pleasure to, gratify, delight. **L16–E18.**
5 MUSIC. Embellish with grace notes or similar detail. **E17.**
6 Address by the courtesy title of 'your grace'. Long *rare* or *obsolete.* **E17.**
7 Endow with divine grace. Long *rare.* **M17.**

graced /greɪst/ *ppl adjective.* **L16.**
[ORIGIN from GRACE *noun* or *verb*: see -ED[1], -ED[2].]
Endowed with grace; favoured; having a grace or graces; embellished.

SHAKES. *Rich. II* After a well-grac'd actor leaves the stage.

graceful /ˈgreɪsfʊl, -f(ə)l/ *adjective.* **LME.**
[ORIGIN from GRACE *noun* + -FUL.]
†**1** Full of divine grace; (of a person) holy. **LME–E17.**

SHAKES. *Wint. T.* You have a holy father, A graceful gentleman.

2 Orig. pleasant, possessed of pleasing and attractive qualities. Now chiefly (of form, movement, expression, or action) elegant; (of actions, esp. acts of courtesy, etc.) aptly timed, well chosen, happy. **LME.**

P. GAY His gift for graceful exposition. H. BASCOM The plane glides and sails . . in a graceful descent.

†**3** Conferring grace or honour. Only in L16.
†**4** Of a person: possessed of graces of character, virtuous. E17–E18.
5 Favourable, friendly. *rare* (Shakes.). Only in E17.
■ **gracefully** *adverb* L16. **gracefulness** *noun* L16.

graceless /ˈɡreɪslɪs/ *adjective*. LME.
[ORIGIN from GRACE *noun* + -LESS.]
1 Not in a state of grace, unregenerate; depraved, wicked, ungodly, impious. Also, unseemly, uncouth, improper. Now chiefly *arch.* or *joc.* LME.
†**2** Lacking favour. LME–L16.
†**3** Merciless, unfeeling, cruel, pitiless. LME–M17.
4 Lacking charm or elegance. M17.

C. P. SNOW A big, broad-shouldered woman, . . physically graceless apart from her smile. J. LE CARRÉ The graceless tower . . posturing against the racing clouds.

– SPECIAL COLLOCATIONS: **graceless florin** a florin, minted in 1849, from which the words 'Dei gratia' were omitted.
■ **gracelessly** *adverb* LME. **gracelessness** *noun* L16.

gracile /ˈɡrasɪl, ˈɡrasʌɪl/ *adjective*. E17.
[ORIGIN Latin *gracilis*.]
Slender, thin, lean. Now also, gracefully slender.

G. GOODLAND I take each gracile finger and one by one interlock them into my hands.

■ **graˈcility** *noun* (*a*) slenderness; (*b*) unornamented simplicity of literary style: E17.

gracilis /ˈɡrasɪlɪs/ *noun*. E17.
[ORIGIN Latin: see GRACILE.]
ANATOMY. A superficial muscle on the medial side of the thigh, passing from the hip bone to the tibia. Also ***gracilis muscle***.

graciosity /ɡreɪʃɪˈɒsɪti, ɡreɪs-/ *noun*. L15.
[ORIGIN French *gracieuseté* or late Latin *gratiositas*, from *gratiosus*: see GRACIOUS, -ITY.]
The quality or state of being gracious; graciousness.

gracioso /ɡreɪʃɪˈəʊzəʊ/ *noun*. Pl. **-os**. M17.
[ORIGIN Spanish = GRACIOUS *adjective*.]
†**1** A court favourite. M–L17.
2 In Spanish comedy, a buffoon. M18.

gracious /ˈɡreɪʃəs/ *adjective & interjection*. ME.
[ORIGIN Old French (mod. *gracieux*) from Latin *gratiosus*, from *gratia*: see GRACE *noun*, -OUS.]
▸ **A** *adjective*. **1** Of a character likely to find favour; agreeable, pleasing. *arch.* or *poet.* ME. ▸†**b** Endowed with grace or charm of appearance; graceful, elegant. LME–M17.

HOR. WALPOLE The body . . was found almost entire, and emitted a gracious perfume. M. ARNOLD How gracious is the mountain at this hour! **b** EVELYN His person is not very gracious, the small-pox having put out one of his eyes.

2 Characterized by or exhibiting kindness or courtesy; kindly, courteous. *poet.* ME.

TENNYSON Sir Lancelot . . Was gracious to all ladies.

3 Of exalted people: kind, indulgent, and beneficent to inferiors (freq. also *joc.* or *iron.*); *esp.* and orig., as a polite epithet of royal persons, their actions, etc. ME.

SWIFT When I am fixed anywhere . . I may be so gracious to let you know. G. B. SHAW Your most gracious majesty's desire To see some further triumphs. P. ROTH A warm and gracious letter from the famous writer.

4 Of God etc.: disposed to show or dispense grace, merciful, benignant. ME.
5 Characterized by or inspired by divine grace; godly, righteous, regenerate. Long *arch. rare*. ME.

BUNYAN All the holy and truly gracious Souls that are with him on the Mount Zion.

†**6** Enjoying favour; in good standing, acceptable, popular. Also (of an action), winning favour or goodwill. LME–E19.

J. RAY Which renders persons gracious and acceptable in the eyes of others.

7 Happy, fortunate, prosperous. Long *obsolete* exc. *Scot.* LME.

SHAKES. *Wint. T.* Go; fresh horses. And gracious be the issue!

†**8** Given as an indulgence or a mercy. Only in E18.
– SPECIAL COLLOCATIONS: **gracious living** an elegant style of life distinguished by a particular observance of standards of propriety and comfort.
▸ **B** *interjection*. (Orig. *ellipt.* for ***gracious God!***). Expr. surprise, dismay, or indignation. Freq. in ***good gracious!***, ***gracious me!*** E18.
■ **graciously** *adverb* ME. **graciousness** *noun* LME.

grackle /ˈɡrak(ə)l/ *noun*. L18.
[ORIGIN mod. Latin *Gracula* (see below) from Latin *graculus* jackdaw.]
Any of various New World orioles belonging to the genus *Quiscalus* and related genera, esp. *Q. quiscula* with glossy purplish-black plumage. Also, any of various Asian mynahs of the genus *Gracula*.

grad /ɡrad/ *noun*[1]. L19.
[ORIGIN Abbreviation.]
A graduate. Also, an undergraduate. Cf. UNDERGRAD, POSTGRAD.

grad /ɡrad/ *noun*[2]. E20.
[ORIGIN from GRADE *noun*.]
= GRADE *noun* 1b.

grad /ɡrad/ *noun*[3]. E20.
[ORIGIN Abbreviation.]
MATH. = GRADIENT *noun* 2b.

gradable /ˈɡreɪdəb(ə)l/ *adjective*. M20.
[ORIGIN from GRADE *verb* + -ABLE.]
LINGUISTICS. (Of an adjective) that can be used in the comparative and superlative and take a submodifier.
■ **gradaˈbility** *noun* (cf. GRADEABILITY) L20.

gradal /ˈɡreɪd(ə)l/ *adjective*. *rare*. L19.
[ORIGIN from Latin *gradus* degree + -AL[1].]
Of or pertaining to degree.

gradate /ɡrəˈdeɪt/ *verb*. M18.
[ORIGIN Back-form. from GRADATION.]
1 *verb trans.* & *intrans.* (Cause to) pass by imperceptible degrees from one shade of colour to another. M18.

J. RUSKIN Take the two extreme tints and carefully gradate the one into the other.

2 *verb trans.* Arrange in steps or grades. Usu. in *pass.* M19.

gradatim /ɡrəˈdeɪtɪm/ *adverb*. Now *rare* or *obsolete*. L16.
[ORIGIN Latin, from *gradus* step.]
Step by step, gradually.

gradation /ɡrəˈdeɪʃ(ə)n/ *noun*. M16.
[ORIGIN Latin *gradatio(n-)*, from *gradus* step: see GRADE *verb*, -ATION.]
1 A series of successive conditions, qualities, events, or (formerly) locations, forming stages in a process or course. M16. ▸**b** RHETORIC. = CLIMAX *noun* 1. M16.

C. CIBBER One continual gradation of political errors.

2 In *pl.* Stages of transition, advance, development, or (formerly) gradual movement. L16.
†**3** ALCHEMY. = EXALTATION 4. E17–E18.
4 In *pl.* Degrees of rank, merit, intensity, etc., constituting a series between two extremes. E17. ▸†**b** *sing.* Position in a scale, relative rank. E17–E19.

L. MACNEICE Gradations of puddles and pools for the young seals, who do not take easily to swimming.

5 A scale or series of degrees of rank, merit, intensity, or divergence from a standard; arrangement in such a scale. L17.
†**6** In *pl.* Steps, tiers; anything resembling these. L17–E19.
7 *spec.* A gradual passing from one colour, shade, or tone, to another. E18.

QUILLER-COUCH Their leaves . . knew no gradations of red and yellow, but turned at a stroke to brown.

8 The action of arranging in a series of grades. M19.
9 PHILOLOGY. = ABLAUT. Also ***vowel gradation***. L19.
■ **gradational** *adjective* pertaining to or characterized by gradation M19. **gradationally** *adverb* M19.

gradatory /ˈɡreɪdət(ə)ri/ *noun*. L17.
[ORIGIN medieval Latin *gradatorium* flight of steps, from *gradatio(n-)*: see GRADATION, -ORY[1].]
A flight of steps, *esp.* those leading from the cloisters to the choir of a church.

gradatory /ˈɡreɪdət(ə)ri, ɡrəˈdeɪt(ə)ri/ *adjective*. *rare*. L18.
[ORIGIN from GRADATION + -ORY[2].]
Proceeding by steps or gradations.

grade /ɡreɪd/ *noun*. E16.
[ORIGIN French, or Latin *gradus* step.]
1 MATH. †**a** A unit of angular measurement, the ninetieth part of a right angle; a degree. Only in 16. ▸**b** In the centesimal system: a hundredth part of a right angle. E19.
2 A crossbred animal; *spec.* (one of) a variety produced by crossing native stock with a superior breed. Freq. *attrib.* L18.

attrib.: C. WILSON Grade animals . . can be made . . as productive as thorough-breds.

3 A step or stage in a process. L18.
4 A degree in rank, proficiency, quality, intensity, or value. E19. ▸**b** PHILOLOGY. The position in an ablaut series occupied by a particular form. L19. ▸**c** A mark (usu. alphabetical) indicating an assessment of the year's work, examination papers, etc., of a student. L19.

F. C. SELOUS The ore was of such low grade that it would not pay to work it. R. V. JONES A promotion of only one grade, to Principal Scientific Officer. **c** S. BRILL His grades were not terribly good, but he managed to get into . . Law School.

b ***low grade***, ***strong grade***, ***weak grade***, ***zero grade***, etc.

5 A class of persons or things of a similar degree of ability, rank, or quality. E19. ▸**b** A class or form in a school, usu. numbered from first up to twelfth according to age. *N. Amer.* M19. ▸**c** ZOOLOGY. A group of species held to represent a similar level of development or organization. L19.

J. GATHORNE-HARDY There seem to have been five grades of patient in the class-conscious thirties. **b** *Scientific American* The study . . involved 4,500 schoolgirls between the fifth and the 12th grade.

6 The rate of ascent or descent of a slope; the gradient. Chiefly *N. Amer.* E19. ▸**b** A slope, an ascent or descent on a railway, road, etc. E19. ▸**c** A length of (made or improved) road, esp. in a hilly district. *US*. M19.

G. A. SHEEHAN A . . long hill with a fairly steep grade. **b** J. DOS PASSOS The train began going fast down long grades.

7 Of a surface: a degree of altitude, a level. M19.
8 PHYSICAL GEOGRAPHY. The condition or profile of a river in which there is a state of equilibrium between riverbed erosion and sedimentation. E20.
– PHRASES: **at grade** (*a*) *US* on the same level; (*b*) PHYSICAL GEOGRAPHY (of a river) at equilibrium between erosion and sedimentation. **grade A**, **Grade A** of the highest grade or quality; *colloq.* excellent, first-rate; **grade B**, **grade C**, etc.: lower grades. ***grade of comparison***: see COMPARISON 4. **make the grade** *colloq.* reach the proper standard, be successful. **on the down grade** descending; *fig.* getting worse. **on the up grade** ascending; *fig.* getting better.
– COMB.: **grade cricket** *Austral.* club cricket with teams competing in various grades; **grade crossing** *US* a place where a road and a railway, or two railways, cross each other at the same level; **grade line** a prescribed or notional line to which a road or railway is built; **grade school** *US* = ***elementary school*** (b) s.v. ELEMENTARY *adjective*.

grade /ɡreɪd/ *verb*. M16.
[ORIGIN from (the same root as) the noun.]
†**1** *verb trans.* Admit to a (specified) university degree. Only in M16.
†**2** *verb trans.* Lay out (a map etc.) by degrees of latitude and longitude. Only in E17.
3 *verb trans.* Arrange or categorize according to quality, merit, rank, intensity, etc. M17.

S. BELLOW Neuroses might be graded by the inability to tolerate ambiguous situations.

4 *verb trans.* Reduce (the line of a road, railway, etc.) to levels or practicable gradients. E19.
5 *verb trans.* Erode the surface of so as to produce or alter a slope. M19.
6 *verb intrans.* Be of good or specified quality; reach a required or expected standard. L19.
grade up with *US* be equal or comparable to, measure up to.
7 *verb trans.* Blend with other things so as to affect the grade or quality. L19.
8 *verb trans.* Cross (cattle, etc.) with some better breed. Foll. by *up*: improve (stock) by so doing. L19.

F. FRANCIS Turning in a good bull and grading up your stock.

9 *verb trans.* & *intrans.* (Cause to) shade or pass gradually (*up*, *down*) from one grade into another. L19.

V. NABOKOV That silky shimmer above her temple grading into bright brown hair.

10 *verb trans.* PHILOLOGY. In *pass.*: be altered by gradation or ablaut. L19.
11 *verb trans.* Give a grade to (a student, his or her work). M20.

American Poetry Review If anyone will tell me how to grade creative writing, I'll be grateful.

■ **grader** *noun* a person who or a machine which grades; *spec.* a wheeled machine for levelling the ground in road-making: M19.

gradeability /ɡreɪdəˈbɪlɪti/ *noun*. M20.
[ORIGIN from GRADE *noun* + -ABILITY.]
The ability of a vehicle to climb a gradient at an efficient speed.

graded /ˈɡreɪdɪd/ *ppl adjective*. M19.
[ORIGIN from GRADE *noun*, *verb*: see -ED[1].]
1 Formed like a flight of steps. Now chiefly *fig.*, proceeding by degrees, graduated. M19.
2 Divided or arranged according to grades of rank or quality. M19.
graded school = ***grade school*** s.v. GRADE *noun*.
3 Of a road etc.: levelled or reduced to easy gradients. M19.
4 Of livestock: improved by crossing with superior stock. L19.
5 PHYSICAL GEOGRAPHY. Of a river: that has attained grade (GRADE *noun* 8). L19.

gradely /ˈɡreɪdli/ *adjective & adverb*. Now *N. English*. ME.
[ORIGIN Old Norse *greiðligr*, from *greiðr* GRAITH *adjective & adverb*: see -LY[1].]
▸ **A** *adjective*. **1** Excellent, noble; fine, suitable; real, proper. ME.

W. WOODRUFF 'Real gradely', father said, smacking his lips.

2 Decent, respectable, worthy; healthy, well. M18.
▸ **B** *adverb*. †**1** Promptly, readily, willingly. ME–L15.
2 Exactly, carefully, properly; quite, really, well. ME.

Gradgrind /ˈɡradɡrʌɪnd/ *noun*. M19.
[ORIGIN Thomas *Gradgrind*, character in Charles Dickens's novel *Hard Times*.]
A person resembling Gradgrind; a person lacking warm feelings and interested only in facts.
■ **Gradgrindery** *noun* E20.

gradience /ˈɡreɪdɪəns/ *noun*. M20.
[ORIGIN from GRADIENT *noun*: see -ENCE.]
LINGUISTICS. (An instance of) the property of being continuously variable between two values or categories.

gradient /ˈgreɪdɪənt, -djənt/ *noun*. **M19**.
[ORIGIN Prob. from GRADE *noun* after *salient*.]
1 The degree of slope of a road, railway, etc.; amount of inclination to the horizontal. **M19**. ▸**b** An inclined part of a road etc.; a slope. **M19**.

F. HOYLE Slopes with gradients up to about 18°. **b** D. M. THOMAS They were soon crawling up the steep gradient—their train pushed by two engines.

2 An increase or decrease in the magnitude of a property, e.g. temperature, pressure, concentration, etc., observed in passing from one point to another; the rate of such a change. **L19**. ▸**b** *MATH*. The vector formed by the operator ∇ (see DEL) acting on a scalar function at a given point in a scalar field. **E20**.

R. F. CHAPMAN Water passes directly from the midgut to the hindgut along an osmotic gradient. T. PYNCHON A gradient of . . 50° between the wind at their backs and the warmth in front.

3 *MATH*. The degree of steepness of a graph at any point. Hence, the first derivative of a function (cf. DERIVATIVE *noun* 3). **L19**.

A. BARTON A line whose gradient is zero is parallel to the *x*-axis.

G

– COMB.: **gradient post**: beside a railway line, indicating a change of gradient; **gradient wind** *METEOROLOGY* a (hypothetical) wind having the direction of the geostrophic wind but with calculated speed allowing for centrifugal effects arising from the curved path of the wind.

gradient /ˈgreɪdɪənt, -djənt/ *adjective*. **M17**.
[ORIGIN Latin *gradientem* pres. pple of *gradi* proceed, walk, from *gradus* step: see -ENT.]
Of an animal: adapted for walking, ambulant; *HERALDRY* in a walking attitude.

gradine /grəˈdiːn/ *noun*. Also **gradin** /ˈgreɪdɪn/. **M19**.
[ORIGIN Italian *gradino* dim. of *grado* step.]
1 Each of a series of low steps or seats raised one above the other. **M19**.
2 A shelf or ledge at the back of an altar. **L19**.

gradiometer /greɪdɪˈɒmɪtə/ *noun*. **L19**.
[ORIGIN from GRADIENT *noun* + -OMETER.]
1 Any of various surveying instruments used for setting out or measuring the gradient of a slope. **L19**.
2 An instrument for measuring the gradient of a field, esp. the horizontal gradient of the earth's gravitational or magnetic field. **E20**.

gradual /ˈgradʒʊəl/ *noun*. **LME**.
[ORIGIN medieval Latin *graduale* use as noun of neut. of *gradualis*: see GRADUAL *adjective & adverb*, and cf. GRAIL[1].]
1 A service book containing various sung parts of the Mass. **LME**.
2 An antiphon sung between the Epistle and the Gospel at the Eucharist. **M16**.

gradual /ˈgradʒʊəl/ *adjective & adverb*. **LME**.
[ORIGIN medieval Latin *gradualis*, from *gradus* step: see -AL[1].]
▸ **A** *adjective*. †**1** Having or arranged in degrees; graduated. **LME–M18**.
†**2** Of or pertaining to degree. **M17–E18**.
3 Taking place by degrees, slowly progressive; (of a slope) gentle, not steep or abrupt. **M17**. ▸**b** Tapering, gently sloping; moving or changing slowly. *poet*. **M18**.

KEATS Isabel By gradual decay from beauty fell. **b** E. B. BROWNING Back to the gradual banks and vernal bowers.

– SPECIAL COLLOCATIONS: **gradual psalms** Psalms 120–34 (from the title of each, rendered *Song of Degrees* (AV), *Song of Ascents* (RV)).
▸ **B** *adverb*. Little by little, by degrees. *poet*. **M18**.

G. WHITE The distant view, That gradual fades till sunk in misty blue.

■ **graduˈality** *noun* the quality or condition of being gradual **M17**. **gradually** *adverb* **M17**. **gradualness** *noun* **M19**.

gradualism /ˈgradʒʊəlɪz(ə)m/ *noun*. **M19**.
[ORIGIN from GRADUAL *adjective & adverb* + -ISM.]
The principle or method of gradual as opp. to immediate or abrupt change, esp. in politics; belief in gradual change.
■ **gradualist** (*a*) *noun* a person who believes in or advocates gradualism; *BIOLOGY* a person who views evolution as a process of continuous gradual change; (*b*) *adjective* of or pertaining to gradualists or gradualism: **M19**. **graduaˈlistic** *adjective* **E20**.

graduand /ˈgradʒʊand, -dj-, -ənd/ *noun*. Chiefly *Scot. & Canad.* **L19**.
[ORIGIN medieval Latin *graduandus* gerundive of *graduare* GRADUATE *verb*: see -AND.]
A person about to receive a degree or other academic qualification.

graduate /ˈgradʒʊət, -djʊət/ *noun & adjective*. **LME**.
[ORIGIN medieval Latin *graduatus* pa. pple (used as noun) of *graduari* GRADUATE *verb*: see -ATE[1], -ATE[2].]
▸ **A** *noun*. **1** A person holding a degree or other academic qualification; *N. Amer.* a person who has completed a course at high school; a former student *of* a place of learning; *loosely*, one who has successfully completed any course of education or training. **LME**.

P. NORMAN She was no recent learner, no stumbling graduate from beginners' bars, but someone to whom movement on skates was inborn.

2 An experienced or proficient person in any art or occupation. Now *rare*. **L16**.

T. WALL A graduate in ungraciousness.

3 A graduated vessel, *esp.* a chemist's measuring glass. **L19**.
▸ **B** *adjective*. **1** That has graduated; having a university degree. Now only *attrib*. **LME**.
2 Arranged by steps or degrees. Now *rare*. **E17**.
– COMB. & SPECIAL COLLOCATIONS: **graduate nurse** *US* a trained nurse; **graduate school** *N. Amer.* a department of a university for advanced work by graduate students.
■ **graduateship** *noun* (*a*) the condition of being a graduate; †(*b*) the period during which one is a graduate: **M17**.

graduate /ˈgradʒʊeɪt, -djʊeɪt/ *verb*. **LME**.
[ORIGIN medieval Latin *graduat-* pa. ppl stem of *graduare* take a degree, from Latin *gradus* degree, step: see -ATE[3].]
▸ **I** **1** *verb trans*. Confer a degree, diploma, or other academic qualification on; send (a person) *from* a place of learning with an academic qualification. Usu. in *pass*. Now *US*. **LME**.

D. ACHESON Our daughter-in-law was being graduated with honors from Bryn Mawr College.

†**2** *verb trans*. Be sufficient to qualify (a person) for a degree or other distinction. **E17–E19**.
3 *verb intrans*. Take a university degree or (*N. Amer.*) high school diploma; successfully complete a course of education or training. **E19**. ▸**b** *verb intrans*. Qualify (as); train in order to qualify. **E19**.

J. CHEEVER Russell had graduated from the local high school and gone off to college.

4 *verb intrans*. Progress to a more advanced or more extreme activity or position. **E20**.

G. GREENE I had already graduated into the position of the old friend.

▸ **II** **5** *verb intrans*. Change gradually or step by step. **LME**.

D. CECIL Eight long-tailed ponies whose colour graduated from dark to pale brown.

6 *verb trans*. Arrange in a series or according to a scale. **LME**. ▸**b** Mark out in degrees or portions. **L16**.
†**7** *verb trans*. Improve the grade or quality of; *spec.* in *ALCHEMY*, transmute to a higher grade. Only in **M17**.
■ **graduator** *noun* a person who or thing which graduates **E19**.

graduated /ˈgradʒʊeɪtɪd, -djʊ-/ *ppl adjective*. **M17**.
[ORIGIN from GRADUATE *verb* + -ED[1].]
1 Having successfully completed a course of education or training; qualified. **M17**.
2 Arranged in grades or gradations; advancing or proceeding by degrees. **L17**.

G. GORER The respondents . . choose one of a graduated series of answers—always, often, occasionally, never.

3 Marked with lines to indicate degrees, grades, or quantities. **M18**.

L. DURRELL A huge register graduated and squared.

– SPECIAL COLLOCATIONS: **graduated filter** *PHOTOGRAPHY* a lens filter that increases in colour density from one edge to the opposite edge; **graduated pension**: paid on a scale related to one's previous earnings. **graduated response** = *flexible response* s.v. FLEXIBLE *adjective* 4.

graduation /gradʒʊˈeɪʃ(ə)n, -djʊ-/ *noun*. **LME**.
[ORIGIN from GRADUATE *verb* + -ATION.]
▸ **I** **1** The receiving or (*US*) conferring of an academic degree, diploma, etc. Also, the ceremony of conferring degrees. **LME**.
▸ **II** **2** The action or process of dividing into degrees or other proportionate divisions on a graduated scale. (*rare* before **M19**.) **LME**. ▸**b** Each or all of the marks on a vessel, instrument, etc., which indicate degrees of a quantity; a gradation on a scale; a line of latitude or longitude on a map. Usu. in *pl.* **L16**. ▸**c** The manner in which something is graduated. **M17**.
3 Arrangement by degrees or gradations; a gradation. **L15**. ▸**b** Progression or elevation by degrees; a step in the process. **M17**.
†**4** *ALCHEMY*. The process of tempering or refining a substance. **L15–L17**.
†**5** The process of grading a railway etc.; a gradient. *US*. Only in **M19**.

gradus /ˈgreɪdəs/ *noun*. **M18**.
[ORIGIN Latin = step(s) in *Gradus ad Parnassum* 'Step(s) to Parnassus', the title of a manual of Latin prosody. Cf. VULGUS *noun*[2].]
hist. A manual of classical prosody used in schools to help in writing Greek and Latin verse.

Graecise *verb* var. of GRAECIZE.

Graecism /ˈgriːsɪz(ə)m, ˈgrʌɪ-/ *noun*. Also **Grecism** /ˈgriːsɪz(ə)m/. **L15**.
[ORIGIN French *grécisme* or medieval Latin *Graecismus*, from *Graecus* Greek: see -ISM.]
†**1** The *Graecismus*, a grammatical treatise in Latin, of the early 13th cent. Only in **L15**.
2 A Greek idiom, grammatical feature, etc., *esp.* one as used in some other language. **L16**.

ADDISON Milton . . has infused a great many . . Graecisms . . into the Language of his Poem.

3 Greek spirit, style, mode of expression, etc.; adoption or imitation of any of these. **E17**.

Graecize /ˈgriːsʌɪz, ˈgrʌɪ-/ *verb*. Also **Grecize** /ˈgriːsʌɪz/, **-ise**. **L17**.
[ORIGIN Latin *Graecizare* imitate the Greeks, from *Graecus* Greek: see -IZE.]
1 *verb trans*. Give a Greek cast, character, or form to. **L17**.
2 *verb intrans*. **a** Favour the cause of the Greeks. *rare*. **M19**. ▸**b** Become like the Greeks; adopt Greek expressions, idioms, modes of life, etc. **L19**.

Graeco- /ˈgriːkəʊ, ˈgrʌɪ-/ *combining form*. Also **Greco-** /ˈgriːkəʊ, ˈgrɛ-/.
[ORIGIN from Latin *Graecus* GREEK *noun* + -O-.]
Forming: (*a*) adjectives with the senses 'relating to Greek settlements or states established abroad' as ***Graeco-Asiatic*** or 'Greek and —' as ***Graeco-Latin***; (*b*) adjectives and nouns with the sense 'Greek, of Greece'.
■ **Graecoˈmania** *noun* a craze or excessive liking for Greece and things Greek **E19**. **Graecophil(e)** *noun & adjective* (a person who is) friendly towards Greece or fond of Greece and things Greek **L19**. **Graeco-Roman** *adjective* Greek and Roman; *spec.* (of a style of wrestling) like that of the Greeks and Romans, attacking only the upper part of the body: **L19**. **Graecotrojan** *adjective* relating to the Greeks and the Trojans **M17**.

Graf /grɑːf/ *noun*. **M17**.
[ORIGIN German: see GRAVE *noun*[2].]
A German nobleman corresponding in rank to a European count or British earl. (Chiefly in titles.)

graff /grɑːf/ *noun*[1]. *arch*. **LME**.
[ORIGIN Old French *grafe*, *grefe*, (also mod.) *greffe* from Latin *graphium* from Greek *graphion*, *grapheion* stylus, from *graphein* write.]
= GRAFT *noun*[2] 1, 2.

graff /grɑːf/ *noun*[2]. Long *dial*. **E16**.
[ORIGIN Perh. var. of GRAFT *noun*[1].]
1 = GRAFT *noun*[1] 2. Usu. more fully ***spade graff***, ***spade's graff***. **E16**.
2 = GRAFT *noun*[1] 3. **L19**.

graff /grɑːf/ *noun*[3]. *obsolete* exc. *hist*. **M17**.
[ORIGIN Prob. from Middle Dutch *grave* = GRAVE *noun*[1]. Cf. GRAFT *noun*[1].]
A trench serving as a fortification; a ditch; a moat.

graff /grɑːf/ *verb*. *arch*. **LME**.
[ORIGIN from GRAFF *noun*[1].]
1 *verb trans*. = GRAFT *verb*[1] 1. **LME**. ▸†**b** = GRAFT *verb*[1] 1b, 4. **LME–M17**.
2 *verb intrans*. = GRAFT *verb*[1] 4. **L15**.
3 *verb trans*. = GRAFT *verb*[1] 3. **M16**.
■ †**graffer** *noun* = GRAFTER *noun*[1] **LME–L17**.

graffiti *noun* see GRAFFITO.

graffiti /grəˈfiːti/ *verb trans*. **L20**.
[ORIGIN from pl. of GRAFFITO.]
Apply graffiti to; write as graffiti.

graffito /grəˈfiːtəʊ/ *noun*. Pl. (freq. used as *sing.*) **-ti** /-ti/. **M19**.
[ORIGIN Italian, from *graffio* scratching.]
1 A drawing, writing, or scribbling on a wall etc., orig. *spec.* on an ancient wall, as at Rome and Pompeii. Usu. in *pl.* **M19**.

J. BARNES The concrete bus-shelters were still unstained by damp or graffiti.

2 A method of decoration or design produced by scratching through a plaster layer to reveal a different colour below. **L19**.
– NOTE: In Italian *graffiti* is a pl. noun and its sing. form is *graffito*. Traditionally, the same distinction has been maintained in English, so that *graffiti* would require a plural verb, but exc. in archaeology and in sense 2 above, *graffiti* is now usu. treated as if it were a mass noun, with a sing. verb.
■ **graffitist** *noun* a person who writes graffiti **M20**.

graft /grɑːft/ *noun*[1]. Now *dial*. **ME**.
[ORIGIN Old Norse *groftr* action of digging, from Germanic: cf. GRAVE *verb*[1], GRAFF *noun*[2]. Perh. reinforced from Middle Dutch *graft*, from *graven* dig. Cf. GRAFF *noun*[3].]
1 A ditch, a moat. **ME**.
2 The depth of earth that may be thrown up at once with a spade. Also more fully ***spade graft***, ***spade's graft***. **E17**.
3 A kind of spade for digging drains **L19**.

graft /grɑːft/ *noun*[2]. **L15**.
[ORIGIN Alt. of GRAFF *noun*[1], perh. due to confusion of *-ff* and *-ft* at the end of words.]
1 A shoot or scion inserted into a slit made in another plant or stock, from which the shoot receives sap and on which it grows. **L15**.
†**2** A twig, shoot, or scion for use in grafting; *gen.* a branch, plant. **L16–E17**.
3 The place in a stock where a scion is inserted. **E19**.
4 The process of grafting; an instance of grafting. **M19**.
5 A piece of living tissue surgically transplanted to another place on the same organism, or to another organism, so that it might adhere and grow; the process of transplanting tissue for this purpose. **L19**.

graft /grɑːft/ *noun*³. *colloq.* M19.
[ORIGIN Uncertain: perh. dial. extension of GRAFT *noun*¹ with the sense 'digging'.]
1 Work, *esp.* hard work. M19.

F. S. ANTHONY Twenty-six bob for a day's graft. M. DUFFY When it comes to the hard graft they're not so keen.

2 A trade, a craft. *rare.* L19.

graft /grɑːft/ *noun*⁴. *colloq.* M19.
[ORIGIN Perh. a use of GRAFT *noun*³ or perh. rel. to GRAFT *noun*² with the additional notion of 'excrescence'.]
Illicit gain, esp. in connection with politics or business; the practices used to secure this, *esp.* bribery, blackmail, or the abuse of one's power or influence.

C. ACHEBE The excesses of the last regime, . . its graft, oppression and corrupt government. S. BELLOW A business agent who takes graft from him.

graft /grɑːft/ *verb*¹. L15.
[ORIGIN Alt. of GRAFF *verb*.]
1 *verb trans.* Insert (a shoot or scion from one plant) as a graft into another plant. (Foll. by *in, into, on, upon, together.*) L15. ▸**b** *gen.* Plant, implant. Now *rare.* M16.

P. V. PRICE The Spaniards in Mexico actually grafted European vines on to native vine stocks, as a protection against phylloxera.

grafting clay, **grafting wax** a composition for covering the united parts of graft and stock.
2 *verb trans. fig.* ▸**a** Insert or fix in or on so as to produce a vital or indissoluble union. Foll. by *in, into, on, upon.* M16. ▸**b** *verb trans. spec.* Join together (two unfinished or broken pieces of knitting) by weaving an extra row of stitches between the pieces. M19.

a R. G. COLLINGWOOD That kind of collaboration in which one artist grafts his own work upon that of another. R. V. JONES The Germans seemed simply to have grafted their radar stations on to their existing Observer Corps network.

3 *verb trans.* Fix a graft or grafts on (a stock). Also, produce (fruit) by grafting. E17.
4 *verb intrans.* Insert a graft or grafts; use grafts as a method of propagation. E17.
5 *verb trans.* NAUTICAL. Cover (the end of a rope, a block-strop etc.) with a weaving of small yarns to form a decorative finish. E19.
6 *verb trans.* Transplant (a piece of living tissue) surgically to another place on the same organism, or to another organism. M19.

G. GREENE Dr Gogol grafted the hands of a guillotined murderer on to the smashed stumps of . . the great pianist.

■ **grafter** *noun*¹ †(*a*) a tree from which a shoot is taken for grafting; (*b*) a person who grafts trees etc.; (*c*) a tool for grafting: L16.

graft /grɑːft/ *verb*² *intrans. colloq.* M19.
[ORIGIN from GRAFT *noun*³.]
Work, *esp.* work hard.

Radio Times My father was a miner, hard-working . . . He grafted.

■ **grafter** *noun*² a person who works (hard); a steady worker: E20.

graft /grɑːft/ *verb*³ *intrans. colloq.* M19.
[ORIGIN from GRAFT *noun*⁴.]
Practise graft; obtain profit or make money by shady or dishonest means.

J. FLYNT They make their living, such as it is, by grafting. U. SINCLAIR The bosses grafted off the men, and they grafted off each other.

■ **grafter** *noun*³ a person who makes gains by shady or dishonest means; *spec.* a politician or other public figure who abuses his or her position to make dishonest gains: L19.

Graham /ˈgreɪəm/ *adjective.* Chiefly *N. Amer.* Also **g-**. M19.
[ORIGIN Sylvester *Graham* (1794–1851), US advocate of dietary reform.]
Designating wholewheat flour; (of bread, biscuits, etc.) made from wholewheat flour in accordance with the vegetarian principles of Graham.
■ **Grahamism** *noun* the vegetarian principles advocated by Graham M19. **Grahamite** *noun* a follower of Graham M19.

Graham's law /ˈgreɪəmz lɔː/ *noun phr.* M19.
[ORIGIN Thomas *Graham* (1805–69), Scot. chemist.]
CHEMISTRY. A law stating that the rates of diffusion and effusion of a gas are inversely proportional to the square root of the density of the gas.

grail /greɪl/ *noun*¹. *arch.* ME.
[ORIGIN Old French *grael* from medieval Latin *gradale* for *graduale* GRADUAL *noun*.]
= GRADUAL *noun* 1, 2.

Grail /greɪl/ *noun*². Also **g-**, (earlier) †**greal**, †**graal**. ME.
[ORIGIN Old French *graal, grael, greel, greil* from medieval Latin *gradalis* dish, of unknown origin.]
More fully ***Holy Grail***. In medieval legend, the cup or platter used by Christ at the Last Supper, and in which Joseph of Arimathea received Christ's blood at the Cross; this cup or platter as the object of long quests by many knights; *fig.* the (elusive) object of a long and difficult quest.

J. A. BAKER For ten years I followed the peregrine . . . It was a Grail to me. *Sunday Times* The holy Grail for the ceramics industry is the ceramic engine.

grail /greɪl/ *noun*³. *poet.* L16.
[ORIGIN Perh. contr. of GRAVEL *noun*.]
Gravel.

grail /greɪl/ *noun*⁴. L17.
[ORIGIN French *grêle*, from *grêler* make slender, taper and smooth (the teeth of a comb).]
A comb-maker's file.

grain /greɪn/ *noun*¹. ME.
[ORIGIN Old French *grain, grein* (mod. *grain*) from Latin *granum* grain, seed, exc. Branch III from Old French *graine* from Proto-Romance base of pl. of Latin *granum*.]
▸ **I** Seed; corn.
1 †**a** A single seed of a plant, *esp.* one which is small, hard and roundish. Later, the stone or pip of a fruit. ME–E19. ▸**b** The fruit or seed of a cereal. LME.
2 *collect.* Wheat or the other cereal grasses; the fruit or seeds of these plants; corn. ME. ▸**b** A particular kind of corn; a cereal. LME.

R. GRAVES Nor could he starve Naples out, since it was plentifully supplied with grain. *attrib.*: J. STEINBECK Fruit trees took the place of grain fields.

3 In *pl.* ▸**a** In full ***grains of Paradise***. The capsules of *Aframomum melegueta*, a W. African plant of the ginger family, used as a spice and in medicine. ME. ▸**b** Refuse malt after brewing or distilling. E16.
4 †**a** A berry, a grape. ME–L17. ▸**b** Any of the parts of a collective fruit. *rare.* L17.
▸ **II** *transf.* from sense 1.
†**5** A bead; *esp.* any of the beads on a rosary. Also, a pearl. ME–M17.
6 A small, hard, usu. roundish particle of sand, gold, salt, incense, etc. ME. ▸**b** A particle of gunpowder, or of solid fuel for rockets, of a definite size. M17. ▸**c** Any of the usu. small discrete particles or crystals in a rock or metal. E19.

DEFOE Gold-dust, Guinea grains. V. WOOLF He ground the grains of sugar against the wall of his cup.

7 The smallest unit of weight in the avoirdupois, troy, and apothecaries' systems (orig. the average weight of a grain of wheat) being 1/7000 pound avoirdupois or (equivalently) 1/5760 pound troy or apothecaries' (approx. 0.0648 gram). LME.

J. G. FARRELL Every half hour he gave pills of calomel (half a grain), opium and capsicum (of each one-eighth of a grain).

8 *fig.* The smallest possible quantity. Freq. in neg. contexts. LME.

H. JAMES She has treated me without a grain of spite. P. G. WODEHOUSE I have ceased to expect intelligence in a man, and I am grateful for the smallest grain.

▸ **III** With ref. to dyeing.
9 *hist.* Kermes, cochineal; the dye made from either of these. ME.
10 Dye; *esp.* a fast dye; colour, hue. Now only *poet.* ME.

fig.: J. TRUMBULL Crimes of blackest grain.

▸ **IV** Texture.
11 Roughness of surface, giving an appearance of small grains or roundish particles side by side; granular appearance or texture. LME. ▸**b** PHOTOGRAPHY. A granular appearance in a photograph or negative. L19.

b *Listener* Faster films . . suffer more from grain.

12 a The longitudinal arrangement of fibres or particles in wood, flesh, paper, etc., which often form a pattern and along which such substances can more easily be cut. M16. ▸**b** The lamination or plane of cleavage in coal, stone, etc. M16.

a BETTY SMITH She brought her eyes close to the . . desk and examined the patterned grain of the wood.

13 The rough or wrinkled surface of leather or any similar artificially produced material. M16. ▸**b** In full ***grain side***. The side of a skin on which the hair originally grew. M19. ▸**c** In full ***grain leather***. Leather dressed with the grain side outwards. M19.
14 a A textured internal substance, usu. visible in a cross-section or fracture. Now *rare.* L16. ▸**b** Texture; the arrangement and size of the constituent particles of any substance, esp. of flesh, wood, stone, or metal. E17.

a R. HAKLUYT The graine of the bone is somewhat more yellow than the Ivorie. **b** J. SMEATON A large flat stone, of a close grain. DICKENS His hands . . were of a rough coarse grain.

15 *fig.* Nature, temper, quality; tendency. M17.

GEO. ELIOT Hatred of innocent human obstacles was a form of moral stupidity not in Deronda's grain. G. S. HAIGHT Her mind was of much finer grain than her husband's.

– PHRASES ETC.: **against the grain** contrary to one's inclination. ***dyed-in-the-grain***, ***dyed-in-grain***: see DYE *verb* 1. ***fine grain***: see FINE *adjective*. ***grains of Paradise***: see sense 3 above. **in grain** fast-dyed; *fig.* thorough, genuine, by nature, downright; indelible, ingrained. ***take with a grain of salt***: see SALT *noun*¹.
– COMB.: **grain colour** (*a*) scarlet dye; (*b*) a fast colour; a cloth dyed with this; **grain-cradle** = CRADLE *noun* 7; **grain elevator** = ELEVATOR 2, 2b; **grain-gold** †(*a*) gold dust; (*b*) gold formed into grains by heat; ***grain leather***: see sense 13c above; ***grain side***: see sense 13b above; **grain whisky**: made mainly from unmalted barley and maize or rye; cf. ***malt whisky*** s.v. MALT *noun*¹ *& adjective*.
■ **grainless** *adjective* without a grain or grains L19.

grain /greɪn/ *noun*². In sense 4b also **grane**. ME.
[ORIGIN Old Norse *grein* division, distinction, branch (Swedish, Danish *gren*), of unknown origin.]
1 In *pl.* The fork of the body, the lower limbs. *obsolete* exc. *dial.* ME.
2 a A fork in a river valley; a valley branching out from another. *obsolete* exc. *Scot. & dial.* ME. ▸**b** An arm of the sea; a branch of a stream. *obsolete* exc. *Scot.* LME.
†**3** An edge, a blade. Only in ME.
4 Each of the prongs of a fork. *obsolete* exc. *Scot. & dial.* L15. ▸**b** Freq. in *pl.* (treated as *sing.*). A fish spear or harpoon with more than one prong. L18.
5 A tree branch or bough; the fork between two boughs. *obsolete* exc. *Scot. & dial.* E16.

grain *noun*³ see GRAINE.

grain /greɪn/ *verb*¹. LME.
[ORIGIN from GRAIN *noun*¹.]
1 *verb intrans.* Yield grain; (of corn) form grains. Long *rare.* LME. ▸**b** *verb trans.* Feed with grain. *US.* M19.
2 *verb trans.* Dye in grain. M16.
3 *verb trans.* TANNING. Remove the hair from (a skin); soften and raise the grain of (leather etc.). M16.
4 *verb trans. & intrans.* (Cause to) deposit or form grains of any substance. L17.
5 *verb trans.* Paint in imitation of the grain of wood or marble. L18.
6 *verb trans.* Give a granular surface to. L19.
■ **grainer** *noun* a person who or thing which grains; *spec.* a vat or device for graining leather: E19. **grainering** *noun* the preparation of hides with a grainer M19.

G

grain /greɪn/ *verb*² *trans. rare.* M17.
[ORIGIN from GRAIN *noun*².]
†**1** *refl.* Branch, divide. Only in M17.
2 Spear (fish) with a grain. L19.

grainage *noun* var. of GRANAGE.

graine /greɪn/ *noun.* Also **grain**. M19.
[ORIGIN French.]
The eggs (formerly, an egg) of the silkworm.

grained /greɪnd/ *adjective*¹. LME.
[ORIGIN from GRAIN *verb*¹ + -ED¹]
1 Dyed in grain. LME.
2 Of leather: without hair; softened, raised. E18.
3 Painted to imitate the grain of wood or marble. L18.
4 Of sugar etc.: formed into grains. E19.

grained /greɪnd/ *adjective*². LME.
[ORIGIN from GRAIN *noun*¹ + -ED².]
1 Of wood, stone, leather, flesh, etc.: having a grain, or a granular structure or texture. LME.

R. C. HUTCHINSON Features which testified to his actual age—the grained skin, the crevices about the eyes.

coarse-grained, ***fine-grained***, etc.
2 Having grains, seeds, or particles. *obsolete* exc. in ***large-grained***, ***small-grained***, etc. E17.

grained /greɪnd/ *ppl adjective*³. *obsolete* exc. *dial.* E16.
[ORIGIN from GRAIN *noun*² + -ED².]
Having prongs or grains. Also ***two-grained***, ***three-grained***.

graining /ˈgreɪnɪŋ/ *noun.* LME.
[ORIGIN from GRAIN *verb*¹ + -ING¹.]
1 The action of GRAIN *verb*¹; the result of this action. LME.
2 A ring of grooves round the edge of a coin, or (formerly) of other similar marks in relief; milling. M17.

grainy /ˈgreɪni/ *adjective.* LME.
[ORIGIN from GRAIN *noun*¹ + -Y¹.]
1 Resembling grain in composition, texture, appearance, etc.; granular. LME. ▸**b** Of a voice or other sound: rough, gritty. M20. ▸**c** Of a photograph: showing visible grains of emulsion. M20.

R. CARVER He smoothed his fingers over the grainy wood. M. DRABBLE Lady Henrietta's grey, diminutive, pinched, grainy features. **c** A. TYLER Little old grainy newspaper picture, heap of grey dots nobody'll recognize.

2 Full of grain or corn. M18.
■ **graininess** *noun* E20.

graip /greɪp/ *noun. Scot. & N. English.* LME.
[ORIGIN Old Norse *greip* corresp. to Old English *grāp* grasp.]
A three- or four-pronged fork used as a dung fork or for digging.

graith /greɪθ/ *noun.* Now only *Scot. & dial.* ME.
[ORIGIN Old Norse *greiði* weak masc., cogn. with Old English *gerǣde* strong neut., = trappings, equipage, from Germanic bases of Y-, READY *adjective*. Cf. GEAR.]
†**1** A state of preparation, readiness. Only in ME.
2 Personal equipment; attire, apparel. ME. ▸**b** Armour. LME. ▸**c** Harness; the harness and tackle of a plough. M16.
3 Possessions; wealth. ME.
4 Apparatus, gear, tackle; a structure, a contrivance. LME.
5 Material, stuff (for a particular purpose); *spec.* (*Scot.*) soapy water. LME.

G

†graith *adjective & adverb.* ME.
[ORIGIN Old Norse *greiðr* = Old English *gerǣde* ready, formed as GRAITH *noun* Cf. GRADELY.]
▸ **A** *adjective.* **1** Ready. ME–L15.
2 (Of a road) direct; (of a measure) exact; (of a sign, truth, etc.) clear, plain. Only in ME.
▸ **B** *adverb.* Readily; clearly, plainly. Only in ME.

graith /greɪθ/ *verb. obsolete* exc. *Scot. & dial.* ME.
[ORIGIN Old Norse *greiða*, from *greiðr* ready: see GRAITH *adjective & adverb.*]
1 *verb trans.* Make ready, prepare. Also, procure. ME. ▸†**b** *refl.* Prepare oneself, get ready. ME–M17.
2 *verb trans.* Equip, supply; array; fit out. ME.
†**3** *verb trans.* Make up, compose; constitute; set *up*. Only in ME.
■ **graithing** *noun* (*a*) the action of the verb; (*b*) furniture, attire: ME.

grallatorial /graləˈtɔːrɪəl/ *adjective.* M19.
[ORIGIN from mod. Latin *grallatorius*, from Latin *grallator* walker on stilts, from Latin *grallae* stilts: see -ATOR, -IAL.]
ORNITHOLOGY. Belonging or pertaining to the group of long-legged wading birds (formerly comprising the order Grallatores).

gralloch /ˈgraləx/ *noun & verb.* Also **-ck**. M19.
[ORIGIN Gaelic *grealach* entrails.]
▸ **A** *noun.* **1** The viscera of a dead deer. M19.
2 An act of gralloching. L19.
▸ **B** *verb trans.* Disembowel (a deer etc.). M19.

gram /gram/ *noun*[1]. E18.
[ORIGIN Portuguese *grão*, †*gram* from Latin *granum* GRAIN *noun*[1].]
(The seed or fruit of) any of several kinds of pulse grown esp. in the Indian subcontinent and other parts of Asia, *spec.*: (*a*) (in full ***Bengal gram***) the chickpea, *Cicer arietinum*; (*b*) (in full ***black gram***) *Vigna mungo*, which has small black or green seeds; (*c*) (in full ***green gram***) *Vigna radiata*, which has small green or golden seeds. Cf. MUNG *noun*[1].

gram /gram/ *noun*[2]. Also **gramme**. L18.
[ORIGIN French *gramme* from late Latin *gramma* small weight from Greek.]
A unit of mass or (*loosely*) weight in the metric system, orig. defined as the mass of a cubic centimetre of pure water at the maximum density, now defined as a thousandth part of a kilogram.
fluid gram: see FLUID *adjective*.
– COMB.: **gram-atom** the quantity of a chemical element whose mass in grams numerically equals its atomic weight; **gram-force** a unit of force (or weight) equal to the weight of a mass of one gram under standard gravity; **gram-equivalent** *CHEMISTRY* the equivalent of an element expressed in grams (see EQUIVALENT *noun* 3); **gram-molecular weight**, **gram-molecule** the quantity of a chemical compound whose mass in grams numerically equals its molecular or formula weight; **gram-weight** = ***gram-force*** above.

gram /gram/ *noun*[3]. *colloq.* L19.
[ORIGIN Abbreviation.]
1 = TELEGRAM. L19.
2 = GRAMOPHONE. M20.

Gram /gram/ *noun*[4]. L19.
[ORIGIN H. C. J. *Gram* (1853–1938), Danish physician.]
1 Used *attrib.* and in *possess.* to designate a method of staining bacteria first employed by Gram, and the iodine solution used in this method. L19.
2 ***Gram-positive***, ***Gram-negative***, adjectives, (of bacteria) stained, not stained, by Gram's method (a test used as a broad initial classification of bacteria). E20.

-gram /gram/ *suffix.*
[ORIGIN Repr. Greek *gramma*, *-atos* thing written, letter of the alphabet, from *graphein* write.]
Forming nouns with the sense 'a thing written', as ***chronogram***, ***ideogram***; *esp.* with the sense 'a (written) message', as ***telegram***, ***cablegram***, whence in recent use in the names of special types of humorous greetings message sent through commercial agencies and delivered by their representatives, as ***kissogram***.

grama /ˈgramə/ *noun*[1]. Also **gramma**. E19.
[ORIGIN Spanish = grass.]
Any of various low grasses of the genus *Bouteloua* of the western US. Also ***grama grass***.

grama /ˈgrɑːmə/ *noun*[2]. E19.
[ORIGIN Sanskrit *grāma*.]
Either of two octave scales in Indian music consisting of an ascending series of seven notes.

gramarye /ˈgraməri/ *noun.* Long *arch.* ME.
[ORIGIN Anglo-Norman *gramarie* = Old French *gramaire* GRAMMAR: cf. French *grimoire* book of magic, earlier †*gramoire* (dial. var. of *gramaire*) †Latin grammar.]
†**1** Grammar; learning. ME–L15.
2 Occult learning; magic, necromancy. L15.

gramash /grəˈmaʃ/ *noun. Scot.* Now *rare* or *obsolete.* L17.
[ORIGIN Var. of GAMASH.]
= GAMASH.

gramdan /ˈgrɑːmdɑːn/ *noun.* M20.
[ORIGIN from Sanskrit *grāma* village + *dāna* gift.]
In India: the pooling by villagers of their land for the collective good, esp. as advocated by Vinoba Bhave (1895–1982). Cf. BHOODAN.

grame /greɪm/ *noun.* Long *arch.*
[ORIGIN Old English *grama*.]
†**1** Anger. OE–E17.
2 Grief, sorrow; harm. OE.

gramercy /grəˈmɜːsi/ *interjection & noun. arch.* ME.
[ORIGIN Old French *grant merci* (God give you) great reward: see GRAND *adjective*[1], MERCY.]
▸ **A** *interjection.* **1** Thank you kindly. Formerly also ***gramercies***. ME. ▸†**b** Foll. by *dat.* of agent or instrument, later *to*: by the instrumentality of, thanks to. LME–M18.

> R. H. BARHAM Gramercy for thy benison!

2 As an exclam. of surprise: mercy on us! E17.

> COLERIDGE Gramercy! They for joy did grin.

▸ **B** *noun.* An expression of thanks. Now *rare* or *obsolete.* L15.

gramicidin /gramɪˈsʌɪdɪn/ *noun.* M20.
[ORIGIN from GRAM *noun*[4] + -I- + -CIDE + -IN[1].]
PHARMACOLOGY. Any of various polypeptide antibiotics obtained from the bacterium *Bacillus brevis* and active esp. against Gram-positive bacteria. Cf. TYROTHRICIN.

graminaceous /gramɪˈneɪʃəs/ *adjective.* M19.
[ORIGIN from Latin *gramen*, *-min-* grass + -ACEOUS.]
= GRAMINEOUS.

gramineous /grəˈmɪnɪəs/ *adjective.* M17.
[ORIGIN from Latin *gramen*, *-min-* grass: see -EOUS.]
Of, pertaining to, or resembling grass; *spec.* belonging to the Gramineae or grass family.

graminivorous /gramɪˈnɪv(ə)rəs/ *adjective.* M18.
[ORIGIN from Latin *gramin-*, *-men* grass + -VOROUS.]
Feeding on grass, cereals, etc.

graminology /gramɪˈnɒlədʒi/ *noun. rare.* L19.
[ORIGIN formed as GRAMINIVOROUS + -OLOGY.]
The branch of botany that deals with grasses.

graminous /ˈgramɪnəs/ *adjective.* Now *rare* or *obsolete.* M17.
[ORIGIN Latin *graminosus*, formed as GRAMINIVOROUS: see -OUS.]
= GRAMINEOUS. Also, covered with grass.

gramma *noun* var. of GRAMA *noun*[1].

grammalogue /ˈgraməlɒg/ *noun.* M19.
[ORIGIN Irreg. from Greek *gramma* written character + *logos* word, on the analogy of *catalogue* etc.: see -LOGUE.]
A word represented in shorthand by a single sign. Also, a letter or character representing a word; a logogram.

grammar /ˈgramə/ *noun.* LME.
[ORIGIN Anglo-Norman *gramere*, Old French *gramaire* (mod. *grammaire*) ult. from Latin *grammatica* from Greek *grammatikē* use as noun (sc. *tekhnē* art) of fem. of *grammatikos* relating to letters, from *grammat-*, *gramma* letter, written character.]
1 The branch of language study or linguistics which deals with the means of showing the relationship between words in use, traditionally divided into the study of inflections (or morphology) and of the structure of sentences (syntax) accidence, and often including also phonology. LME.
case grammar, ***comparative grammar***, ***generative grammar***, ***historical grammar***, ***philosophical grammar***, ***prescriptive grammar***, ***transformational grammar***, ***universal grammar***, etc.
†**2** Latin. Cf. ***grammar school*** below. LME–L16.
3 A treatise or book on grammar. M16.
4 A person's manner of using grammatical forms; speech or writing judged as good or bad according as it conforms to or violates the rules of grammar. Also, what is correct according to these rules. L16.

> DRYDEN *Varium et mutabile semper Femina*... the adjectives are neuter, and *animal* must be understood to make them grammar. J. BRODSKY If her sayings were dark, it wasn't due to her grammar.

5 (Usu. **G-**.) (The name of) a class in a Roman Catholic school, college, or seminary, now only *spec.* the fourth class, immediately above Rudiments and below Syntax, in certain Jesuit schools. E17.
6 *transf.* The basic rules or principles of an art or science; a book embodying these. E17.

> J. H. NEWMAN An Essay in aid of a Grammar of Assent. *Daily Telegraph* The fact is that the grammar of television demands movement.

7 The system of inflections and syntactical forms characteristic of a language. M19.
have little grammar, **have no grammar** (of a language) be sparingly inflected.
8 = ***grammar school*** below. *colloq.* M20.
9 *COMPUTING.* A set of rules governing what strings are valid or allowable in a language or text. M20.
– COMB.: **grammar school** (*a*) any of a class of (usu. endowed) English schools founded in or before the 16th cent. orig. for teaching Latin, later secondary schools with a 'liberal' curriculum which included languages, literature, history, and the sciences; after the Education Act of 1944, any of the secondary schools offering a similar curriculum and taking only pupils selected for their ability; (*b*) *US* = ***elementary school*** (b) s.v. ELEMENTARY *adjective*; formerly, a school intermediate between a primary school and a high school.
■ **grammarless** *adjective* ignorant of grammar; (of a language) not having a highly inflected structure: E19.

grammarian /grəˈmɛːrɪən/ *noun.* LME.
[ORIGIN Old French *gramarien* (mod. *grammairien*), from *gramaire* GRAMMAR: see -IAN.]
1 A person expert in grammar or linguistics; *spec.* the author of a grammar (GRAMMAR *noun* 3). LME.
†**2** A pupil at a grammar school. L16–L18.
3 A member of the class called Grammar in a Roman Catholic school, college, or seminary, now only *spec.* in certain Jesuit schools. L17.

grammatic /grəˈmatɪk/ *adjective.* L16.
[ORIGIN (Old French *gramatique* from) Latin *grammaticus* from Greek *grammatikos*: see GRAMMAR, -IC.]
= GRAMMATICAL *adjective*.

grammatical /grəˈmatɪk(ə)l/ *adjective & noun.* E16.
[ORIGIN French, or late Latin *grammaticalis*, formed as GRAMMATIC: see -AL[1], -ICAL.]
▸ **A** *adjective.* **1** Of, relating to, or based on grammar. E16. ▸**b** *LOGIC.* Relating to the mere arrangement of words in a proposition, as opp. to its logical structure. L19.
2 Conforming to the rules of grammar or (*transf.*) of an art or science. M18.
3 Of a language: relying more on diversity of inflections than on richness of vocabulary. M20.
– SPECIAL COLLOCATIONS: **grammatical change** *PHILOLOGY* (in Germanic languages) the system of contrasting consonants found in the strong verb, exemplifying Verner's law. **grammatical gender**: determined by the form of a word, not by the real or attributed sex. **grammatical meaning** the meaning of a word or inflection as judged by its function in a sentence; opp. ***lexical meaning***.
▸ †**B** *noun.* In *pl.* The subjects taught in a grammar school. L17–E19.
■ **grammatiˈcality** *noun* (*LINGUISTICS*) conformity with grammatical rules M20. **grammatically** *adverb* LME. **grammaticalness** *noun* M17.

grammaticalize /grəˈmatɪk(ə)lʌɪz/ *verb trans.* Also **-ise**. M20.
[ORIGIN from GRAMMATICAL + -IZE.]
Express by or adopt in grammar; *spec.* (*LINGUISTICS*) change (an element) from being one having lexical meaning into one having a largely grammatical function.
■ **grammaticaliˈzation** *noun* M20.

grammaticaster /grəmatɪˈkastə/ *noun. derog.* E17.
[ORIGIN medieval Latin, from Latin *grammaticus*: see GRAMMATIC, -ASTER.]
A petty grammarian.

grammaticise *verb* var. of GRAMMATICIZE.

grammaticism /grəˈmatɪsɪz(ə)m/ *noun.* Now *rare.* E17.
[ORIGIN from GRAMMATIC + -ISM.]
A point or principle of grammar.

grammaticize /grəˈmatɪsʌɪz/ *verb.* Also **-ise**. L17.
[ORIGIN formed as GRAMMATICISM + -IZE: cf. medieval Latin *grammatizare*.]
1 *verb intrans.* Discuss grammatical points. *rare.* L17.
2 *verb trans.* Reduce to grammatical rules; make grammatical. Also = GRAMMATICALIZE. L17.

grammatist /ˈgramətɪst/ *noun.* L16.
[ORIGIN (French *grammatiste* from) Latin *grammatista* from Greek *grammatistēs*, from *gramma*, *grammat-* letter: see -IST.]
A student of grammar (usu. *derog.*). Also, in Greek sense, a teacher of reading and writing.

grammatolatry /graməˈtɒlətri/ *noun.* M19.
[ORIGIN from Greek *gramma grammat-* letter + -O- + -LATRY.]
The worship of letters; *spec.* rigid adherence to the letter of Scripture.

gramme *noun* var. of GRAM *noun*[2].

Grammy /ˈgrami/ *noun.* Orig. *US.* M20.
[ORIGIN from GRAM *noun*[3] after EMMY.]
(Proprietary name for) any of several annual awards given by the American National Academy of Recording Arts and Sciences for outstanding achievements in the record industry.

gramophile /ˈgraməfʌɪl/ *noun. arch.* E20.
[ORIGIN from GRAMOPHONE *noun* + -PHILE.]
= DISCOPHILE.

gramophone /ˈgraməfəʊn/ *noun & verb.* L19.
[ORIGIN Inversion of elems. of PHONOGRAM.]
▸ **A** *noun.* An instrument (orig. driven by clockwork, later by electricity) for reproducing recorded sound by the vibrations of a stylus travelling in an irregular spiral groove in a disc rotating on a turntable. Now *arch.* or *hist.* (the later electrically driven model being usu. called a ***record player***). L19.
– COMB.: ***gramophone record***: see RECORD *noun* 5a.
▸ **B** *verb trans.* Play on or record for the gramophone. Now *arch. rare.* E20.

■ **gramophonic** /-ˈfɒnɪk/ *adjective* of, relating to, or of the nature of a gramophone or gramophone record **E20**. **gramoˈphonically** *adverb* **E20**.

gramp /gramp/ *noun*. *dial.* & *colloq.* Also **grampy** /-pi/. **L19**.
[ORIGIN Contr. of GRANDPAPA.]
= GRANDFATHER.

grampus /ˈgrampəs/ *noun*. **E16**.
[ORIGIN Alt. (through assim. to GRAND *adjective*[1]) of GRAPEYS.]
1 Any of various blowing, spouting, blunt-nosed cetaceans of the family Delphinidae; *esp.* (**a**) Risso's dolphin, *Grampus griseus*; (**b**) the killer whale, *Orcinus orca*. **E16**.
2 A person given to puffing and blowing. **M19**.

grampy *noun* var. of GRAMP.

gran /gran/ *noun*. *colloq.* **M19**.
[ORIGIN Abbreviation.]
= GRANDMOTHER.

grana *noun* pl. of GRANUM.

granadilla /granəˈdɪlə/ *noun*. Also **gren-** /grɛn-/. **L16**.
[ORIGIN Spanish, dim. of *granada* pomegranate.]
1 (A fruit of) any of various tropical kinds of passion flower. **L16**.
purple granadilla = *passion fruit* s.v. PASSION *noun*.
2 A W. Indian leguminous tree, *Brya ebenus*, yielding cocus wood; the timber itself. Usu. more fully ***granadilla tree***. **M17**.

Granadine /ˈgranədiːn/ *adjective*. **M19**.
[ORIGIN Spanish *Granadino*, from *Granada* (see below) + *-ino* -INE[1].]
Of or pertaining to Granada, a province of southern Spain.

granage /ˈgranɪdʒ/ *noun*. Long *obsolete* exc. *hist.* Also **grain-** /ˈgreɪn-/. **L16**.
[ORIGIN Anglo-Norman, formally corresp. to Old French *grenage* duty on grain, from *grain* GRAIN *noun*[1] + -AGE. The Anglo-Norman sense is unaccounted for.]
A duty formerly levied by the City of London on salt imported by foreigners.

granary /ˈgran(ə)ri/ *noun*. **L16**.
[ORIGIN Latin *granarium* (usu. pl. *-ia*), from *granum* GRAIN *noun*[1]: see -ARY[1].]
1 A storehouse for threshed grain. **L16**.

F. FITZGERALD The French and Japanese administrations had neglected to fill the emergency rice granaries.

2 *fig.* A country or region producing a large amount of grain; esp. such a region considered as the supplier of another region. **L16**.

BOSW. SMITH Palestine was the granary of Tyre, supplying it with corn and oil. J. RABAN The rest of Arabia had looked to the fertile soil of the plateau to provide a granary for the subcontinent.

– COMB.: **Granary bread** (proprietary name for) a type of brown bread containing whole grains of wheat.

†**granate** *noun*[1]. **LME–E19**.
[ORIGIN medieval Latin *granatus*: see GARNET *noun*[1].]
= GARNET *noun*[1]. Also, a deep red colour.

granate /ˈgranɪt/ *noun*[2]. Long *rare* or *obsolete*. **LME**.
[ORIGIN medieval Latin (*pomum*) *granatum*, Old French (*pome*) *grenate* (mod. *grenade*): see POMEGRANATE.]
A pomegranate.

grand /grand/ *adjective*[1] & *noun*. **LME**.
[ORIGIN Anglo-Norman *graunt*, Old French *grand*, *grant* masc. and fem. (mod. *grand(e)*), from Latin *grandis* fully grown, big, great, which in Proto-Romance superseded Latin *magnus* in all its uses.]
▸ **A** *adjective*. †**1** — ***the Grand***: designating a famous country, city, or person. Cf. GREAT. **LME–E16**.

CAXTON He was . . borne in grece not ferre fro Troye the graunt.

2 Of a personal designation: pre-eminent, chief, leading. Formerly also, eminent, great. Cf. ARCH- 2. Now *rare* or *obsolete*. **E16**. ▸**b** Designating a (now only foreign) monarch or an official who is senior to others of the same general rank. Now chiefly *hist.* **L16**.

MILTON To conquer Sin and Death, the two grand Foes.

3 Great, large; main or principal by virtue of greatest size. Now only, (of a specified part of a large building) main or principal by virtue of size and magnificence. **E16**. ▸**b** Comprehensive, complete. *obsolete* exc. in ***grand total*** below. **L16**.

LD MACAULAY The Swedish minister alighted at the grand entrance.

4 LAW. (Of a tribunal etc.) of great importance, chief, principal; (of a crime) serious, on a large scale. Cf. PETTY *adjective*. Now chiefly *hist.* **E16**.
5 Of most or great importance, value, or scope; great, vital. **L16**.

H. JAMES She rose . . with an indescribable grand melancholy of indifference and detachment. G. SAINTSBURY Defoe had done a great deal; but nothing in the direction of his two grand achievements.

6 (Esp. of architecture, a natural object, etc.) imposing, impressive, magnificent; (of an idea, style, design, etc.) lofty and dignified in conception or expression. **E18**.

E. H. GOMBRICH The grand classical manner of narrative painting died a natural death in the eighteenth century. G. GORDON Realizing that he'd outlined his entire grand plan. A. N. WILSON The dome of the Oratory, . . grand and black against the pale English sky.

7 (Of a person) stately, dignified; now *esp.* imposing, superior, haughty; (of appearance) rich, splendid. **M18**.

E. FEINSTEIN She is very grand in such matters, and has always believed herself far above domestic work.

8 Of a ceremony, occasion, etc.: conducted with great solemnity and splendour esp. on a large scale. **M18**.

JANET MORGAN Five-course dinners were prepared daily by Jane . . with a professional cook and butler hired for grand occasions. M. DRABBLE He thought a grand finale would be her kind of thing, better wrap it up in style, he said.

9 Splendid, excellent; (of a person) in good health, well. *colloq.* **E19**.

E. COXHEAD You don't look too grand . . Are you sure you're all right? J. O'FAOLAIN It'll mean you'll be with all blood relatives. Isn't that grand? M. BINCHY He's in Africa, he's grand, he's got a lovely English friend.

– SPECIAL COLLOCATIONS & PHRASES: **grand air** a distinguished appearance or bearing; an affected dignity. ***grand*** CLIMACTERIC. ***Grand Cross***: see CROSS *noun* 12. **Grand Fleet** *hist.* (**a**) in the 18th cent., the British fleet based at Spithead; (**b**) the British battle fleet operating in the North Sea 1914–16. ***grand horizontal***: see HORIZONTAL *noun* 4. ***grand inquest***: see INQUEST 2. ***Grand Inquisitor***: see INQUISITOR *noun* 2. **grand jury** (now *US* LAW) a jury selected to examine the validity of an accusation prior to trial. **grand lama** = DALAI LAMA. ***grand*** LARCENY. ***Grand Lodge***: see LODGE *noun* 7. **grand manner** a style suited to noble or stately matters. ***Grand Mufti***: see MUFTI *noun*[1]. ***Grand National***: see NATIONAL *noun* 4. **grand old man** a venerated person esp. in a specified field or profession. **Grand Old Party** *US* the Republican Party (now usu. abbreviated *GOP*). **grand opera** serious opera without spoken dialogue. **grand passion** an intensely passionate and overwhelming love or love affair. **grand piano** a usu. large, harp-shaped, full-toned piano with horizontal strings. **grand scale** a very large or magnificent scale (of activity etc.). **Grand Seignior** *hist.* the Sultan of Turkey. ***grand slam***: see SLAM *noun*[1]. ***grand Sophy***: see SOPHY 1. **grand style** = ***grand manner*** above. **grand total** the sum or final amount after the adding together of all other totals. **grand tour** a tour of major cities and places of interest esp. in Europe, formerly undertaken as part of a person's education; any extensive tour or journey. ***grand unified field theory***, ***grand unified theory***: see UNIFIED. ***grand*** VIZIER.

▸ **B** *noun*. †**1** = GRANDEE. **E–M17**.
2 With *the*: that which is grand, impressive, or magnificent. **M18**.
3 A Freemason official whose title is qualified by 'grand'. **M18**.
4 A grand piano. **M19**.

Y. MENUHIN The piano was a small grand of blond wood.

baby grand: see BABY *adjective*.
5 *sing.* & (occas.) in *pl.* A thousand pounds or dollars. *slang.* **E20**.

M. GEE Bozo's getting over two hundred grand as an advance.

grand /grɑ̃, grɒ̃; *before a vowel* grɑ̃d, grɒnd/ *adjective*[2]. **E17**.
[ORIGIN French: see GRAND *adjective*[1] & *noun* Cf. GRANDE.]
The French (masc.) for 'great', occurring in various phrases used in English
■ ***grand battement*** /batmɑ̃, ˈbatmɒ̃/, pl. **-s -s** (pronounced same), BALLET a battement executed with the moving leg stretched **M19**. ***grand coup*** /ku, kuː/, pl. **-s -s** (pronounced same), (**a**) a bold or important stroke or effort; (**b**) WHIST & BRIDGE the deliberate disposal of a superfluous trump by ruffing a winning card from the opposite hand: **E19**. ***grand*** CRU. ***grand*** JETÉ. ***Grand Marnier*** /marnje, ˈmɑːnɪeɪ/ [*Marnier*-Lapostolle, manufacturer's name] an orange-flavoured cognac-based liqueur; a drink of this: **E20**. ***grand monarque*** /mɔnark, mɒˈnɑːk/, pl. **-s -s** (pronounced same), a supreme and absolute ruler; *spec.* an epithet of Louis XIV of France: **L17**. ***grand monde*** /mɔ̃ːd, mɒnd/ = BEAU MONDE **E18**. ***grand seigneur*** /sɛɲœːr, seɪnˈjəː/, pl. **-s -s** (pronounced same), a great nobleman (see also EN GRAND SEIGNEUR) **E17**. ***grand siècle*** /sjɛkl, sɪˈɛk(ə)l/ [lit. 'great century or age'] a classical or golden age; *esp.* the reign of Louis XIV in France: **M19**.

grand- /grand/ *combining form*. **ME**.
[ORIGIN French, use of GRAND *adjective*[2].]
With the names of family relationships denoting the second degree of ascent or descent from the relationship specified.
grand-aunt great-aunt. **grand-baby** N.AMER. a grandchild who is still a baby. **grandkid** N.AMER. *colloq.* a grandchild. **grand-nephew** the son of a person's nephew or niece. **grand-niece** the daughter of a person's nephew or niece. **grand-uncle** a great-uncle. See also GRANDCHILD, GRANDDAUGHTER, GRANDFATHER, etc.

grandad /ˈgrandad/ *noun*. *colloq.* Also (earlier) **grand-dad**. **L18**.
[ORIGIN from GRAND- + DAD *noun*[1].]
Grandfather.

grandaddy /ˈgrandadi/ *noun*. *colloq.* Also (earlier) **grand-daddy**. **M18**.
[ORIGIN formed as GRANDAD + DADDY.]
1 Grandfather. **M18**.
2 A superlative or the largest example *of*. **M20**.

M. BEADLE The grandaddy of all electrical storms dumped a cloudburst.

– COMB.: **grandaddy-long-legs** *US* a daddy-long-legs.

■ Earlier **grandada** *noun* **L17**.

grandam /ˈgrandam/ *noun*. Also (exc. in sense 1b) **-dame** /-deɪm/. **ME**.
[ORIGIN from GRAND- + DAM *noun*[2].]
1 Grandmother; an old woman. *arch.* **ME**. ▸**b** The dam of an animal's dam. **M19**.
†**2** Great-grandmother. *Scot.* **LME–M17**.

grandchild /ˈgran(d)tʃʌɪld/ *noun*. Pl. **-children** /-tʃɪldrən/. **L16**.
[ORIGIN from GRAND- + CHILD *noun*.]
A child of one's son or daughter.

grand-dad(dy) *nouns* vars. of GRANDAD(DY).

granddaughter /ˈgrandɔːtə/ *noun*. **E17**.
[ORIGIN from GRAND- + DAUGHTER.]
A daughter of one's son or daughter.
– COMB.: **granddaughter clock** a small grandfather clock.

grand-ducal /gran(d)ˈdjuːk(ə)l/ *adjective*. **M18**.
[ORIGIN from GRAND *adjective*[1] + DUCAL.]
Of, pertaining to, or characteristic of a grand duke or grand duchess.

grand duchess /gran(d) ˈdʌtʃɪs/ *noun phr.* **M18**.
[ORIGIN from GRAND *adjective*[1] + DUCHESS.]
A female ruler of a grand duchy; the wife or widow of a grand duke. Also (*hist.*), a daughter of a Russian tsar.

grand duchy /gran(d) ˈdʌtʃi/ *noun phr.* **M19**.
[ORIGIN from GRAND *adjective*[1] + DUCHY.]
A territory ruled over by a grand duke or grand duchess.

grand duke /gran(d) ˈdjuːk/ *noun phr.* **L17**.
[ORIGIN from GRAND *adjective*[1] + DUKE *noun*, after French *grand duc*.]
1 A male ruler of any of various territories whose monarch is or was considered to have royal or noble status one degree below that of king or queen. Also (*hist.*), a son of a Russian tsar. **L17**.
2 [translating French *grand duc*.] The eagle owl, *Bubo bubo*. **M19**.

grande /grɑ̃d/ *adjective*. **M18**.
[ORIGIN French: see GRAND *adjective*[1]. Cf. GRAND *adjective*[2].]
The French (fem.) for 'great', occurring in various phrases used in English
■ ***grande amoureuse*** /amurøːz/, pl. **-s -s** /grɑ̃dz amurøːz/, a passionate or amorous woman **E20**. ***grande dame*** /dam/, pl. **-s -s** (pronounced same), a woman of high rank or eminence and dignified bearing **M18**. ***grande*** HORIZONTALE. ***grande passion*** /pasjɔ̃/, pl. **-s -s** (pronounced same), = ***grand passion*** s.v. GRAND *adjective*[1] **E19**. ***grande sonnerie*** /sɔnri, ˈsɒnəri/ a system of clock chiming in which the hour and the quarter is struck each quarter **M20**. ***grande tenue*** /təny/ full dress; *esp.* full military costume: **M19**.

grandee /granˈdiː/ *noun*. **L16**.
[ORIGIN Spanish, Portuguese *grande*, use as noun of *grande* (adjective) grand, the ending assim. to -EE[1].]
A Spanish or Portuguese nobleman of the highest rank; *gen.* a person of high rank, position, or eminence.

A. WEST Sir Hugh Rigby was the titled medical grandee called in to give the second opinion. M. IGNATIEFF He made the rounds . . . dispensing rewards and punishments like an Asiatic grandee.

■ **grandeeship** *noun* the office or rank of a grandee **L18**.

grandeur /ˈgrandjə, -(d)ʒə/ *noun*. **E16**.
[ORIGIN Old French & mod. French, from *grand* great, GRAND *adjective*[1] + *-eur* -OR.]
†**1** Height; tall stature. *rare.* **E16–M17**.
2 Great power, rank, or eminence. Now *rare*. **E17**.
3 Greatness or nobility of character; dignity or stateliness in conduct, attitude, etc. Formerly also, haughtiness, arrogance. **M17**.

CLIVE JAMES His grandeur really *was* grandeur, not grandiloquence.

delusions of grandeur: see DELUSION 2.
4 The quality of being grand; magnificence, splendour, majesty of appearance, style, composition, etc.; an instance or example of this. **M17**.

LONGFELLOW Switzerland . . outbids the imagination by its grandeurs and surprises. H. A. L. FISHER Many of these buildings . . impress the traveller with a sense of grandeur and force. J. RABAN Ordinary courtesies in Arabic take on a quality of Miltonic grandeur when translated directly into English.

grandeval /granˈdiːv(ə)l/ *adjective*. *rare*. **M17**.
[ORIGIN from Latin *grandaevus* aged, from *grandis* great + *aevum* age: see -AL[1].]
Old, ancient.

grandezza /granˈdɛddza/ *noun*. Long *rare*. Also ***grandeza*** /granˈdeθa/. **E17**.
[ORIGIN Italian, also Spanish *grandeza*, from *grande* grand: see -ESS[2].]
Grandeur, greatness, magnificence; stateliness. Formerly also, an instance of this.

grandfather /ˈgran(d)fɑːðə/ *noun* & *verb*. **LME**.
[ORIGIN from GRAND- + FATHER *noun*, after Old French & mod. French *grandpère*.]
▸ **A** *noun*. **1** The father of one's mother or father. **LME**.
2 = GRANDSIRE 2. Long *rare*. **E17**.
3 The founder or originator *of*; a superlative example *of*. *colloq.* **E17**.

P. BARRY There's been the grandfather of a mix-up somewhere.

G

4 [After the title of a popular song by H. C. Work (1876).] In full ***grandfather clock***, (now rare) ***grandfather's clock***. A weight-and-pendulum clock in a tall wooden case, a long-case clock. **L19.**
5 *COMPUTING.* A tape of data two versions earlier than the one currently being processed. Cf. **FATHER** *noun* 7. **M20.**
– **COMB.:** **grandfather clause** *US colloq.* a legislative clause exempting certain pre-existing classes of people or things from the requirements of a regulation; ***grandfather clock***, ***grandfather's clock***: see sense A.4 above.
▸ **B** *verb trans.* **1** Be excessively deferential or flattering to. Foll. by *up. rare.* **M18.**
2 Fix the status of grandfather or (*fig.*) originator of (a person or thing) *on. rare.* **L19.**
3 Exempt by means of a grandfather clause. *US colloq.* **M20.**
▪ **grandfatherhood** *noun* the condition of being a grandfather **M19. grandfatherless** *adjective* **LME. grandfatherly** *adjective* of, pertaining to, resembling, or characteristic of a grandfather **E19.**

grandfer *noun* var. of **GRANFER.**

grandfilial /gran(d)ˈfɪlɪəl/ *adjective.* **E20.**
[**ORIGIN** from **GRAND-** + **FILIAL.**]
Of or due from a grandchild.

G

Grand Guignol /grɒn giːˈnjɒl, *foreign* grɑ̃ giɲɔl/ *noun phr.* **E20.**
[**ORIGIN** French (= Great Punch), the name of a theatre in Paris.]
A dramatic entertainment in which short horrific or sensational pieces are played successively. Cf. **GUIGNOL.**
▪ **Grand Guignolesque** *adjective* pertaining to, characteristic of, or of the nature of Grand Guignol **E20.**

grandiflora /grandɪˈflɔːrə/ *adjective.* **E20.**
[**ORIGIN** mod. Latin (freq. used in the specific names of large-flowered plants), from Latin *grandis* great + *flos flor-* flower + fem. adjectival suffix *-a.*]
Bearing large flowers.

grandiloquent /granˈdɪləkwənt/ *adjective.* **L16.**
[**ORIGIN** from Latin *grandiloquus*, from *grandis* great + *loquus* speaking, from *loqui* speak; ending assim. to that of **ELOQUENT.**]
Characterized by a pompous or boastful manner or quality, esp. in speech or writing.

> K. VONNEGUT A grandiloquent coda not entirely in keeping with the facts.

▪ **grandiloquence** *noun* the quality of being grandiloquent; the use of pompous or boastful language: **L16. grandiloquently** *adverb* **M19. grandiloquous** *adjective* = **GRANDILOQUENT L16.**

grandiose /ˈgrandɪəʊs/ *adjective.* **M19.**
[**ORIGIN** French from Italian *grandioso*, from *grande* grand: see **-OSE**[1].]
1 Impressive or imposing on account of grandeur or extravagance of appearance, manner, design, etc. **M19.**

> D. MORRIS Despite our grandiose ideas and our lofty self-conceits, we are still humble animals. E. REVELEY The whole . . was built on an absurdly grandiose scale, avenues wide as air strips, colossal white monuments.

2 Of speech, manner, etc.: characterized by (esp. affected) grandeur or stateliness; pompous, arrogant. **M19.**

> E. JOHNSON Forster was so grandiose that Fitzgerald half complained to Dickens about his intolerable condescension.

▪ **grandiosely** *adverb* **M19. grandiˈosity** *noun* the quality of being grandiose; an instance or example of this: **M19.**

grandioso /grandiˈoːso/ *adverb, adjective, & noun.* **L19.**
[**ORIGIN** Italian: see **GRANDIOSE.**]
MUSIC. ▸**A** *adverb & adjective.* A direction: in a grand or imposing manner. **L19.**
▸ **B** *noun.* Pl. ***-si*** /-si/. A movement or passage played in this way. **L20.**

grandisonant /granˈdɪs(ə)nənt/ *adjective. rare.* **L17.**
[**ORIGIN** from late Latin *grandisonus*, from *grandis* **GRAND** *adjective*[1] + *sonus* sounding: see **-ANT**[1].]
Stately-sounding.
▪ Also **grandisonous** *adjective* **L17.**

Grandisonian /grandɪˈsəʊnɪən/ *adjective. literary.* **E19.**
[**ORIGIN** from Sir Charles *Grandison*, the eponymous hero of Samuel Richardson's novel (1754) + **-IAN.**]
Of manner, bearing, etc.: resembling that of Sir Charles Grandison; stately, courteous, magnanimous.

†**grandity** *noun.* **L16–M19.**
[**ORIGIN** Latin *granditas*, from *grandis*: see **GRAND** *adjective*[1], **-ITY.**]
Grandeur, stateliness.

grandly /ˈgrandli/ *adverb.* **M17.**
[**ORIGIN** from **GRAND** *adjective*[1] + **-LY**[2].]
In a grand manner; magnificently, splendidly, grandiosely.

grandma /ˈgran(d)mɑː/ *noun. colloq.* Also **granma** /ˈgranmɑː/. **L18.**
[**ORIGIN** from **GRAND-** + **MA.**]
Grandmother.

grand mal /grɒn ˈmal, *foreign* grɑ̃ mal/ *noun phr.* **L19.**
[**ORIGIN** French, lit. 'great sickness'.]
General convulsive epilepsy, with loss of consciousness. Cf. **PETIT MAL.**

grandmamma /ˈgran(d)məmɑː/ *noun. colloq.* (now *arch.*). Also **-mama. M18.**
[**ORIGIN** from **GRAND-** + **MAMMA** *noun*[2].]
Grandmother.

grand master /grand ˈmɑːstə/ *noun phr.* In sense 3 usu. **grandmaster. M16.**
[**ORIGIN** from **GRAND** *adjective*[1] + **MASTER** *noun*[1].]
†**1** The chief officer of a royal household. **M16–M18.**
2 (**G- M-.**) The head of a military order of knighthood (as the Templars), or of the Freemasons or other similar society. **M16.**
3 (A title accorded to) a chess player of the highest class; usu. one who has achieved a stipulated level of performance in international tournaments. **M19.**
▪ **grandmasterly** *adjective* (*CHESS*) **M20. grandmastership** *noun* the office or position of grand master **M18.**

grandmaternal /gran(d)məˈtəːn(ə)l/ *adjective.* **L18.**
[**ORIGIN** from **GRAND-** + **MATERNAL.**]
Of, pertaining to, or characteristic of a grandmother; grandmotherly.

grandmother /ˈgran(d)mʌðə/ *noun & verb.* **LME.**
[**ORIGIN** **GRAND-** + **MOTHER** *noun*[1], after Old French & mod. French *grandmère.*]
▸ **A** *noun.* **1** The mother of one's mother or father. **LME.**
2 An ancestress, *spec.* as a designation of Eve. Long *rare.* **E16.**
3 = **GRANDFATHER** *noun* 3. **E17.**
4 In full ***grandmother clock***. A clock resembling a grandfather clock but with a smaller case. **E20.**
– **PHRASES:** **grandmother's footsteps**, **grandmother's steps** a children's game in which one player turns around often and without warning with the aim of catching (and sending back) the other players stealthily creeping up to touch him or her on the back. **my grandmother!**, **your grandmother!** *interjections* expr. disagreement with a preceding word or phrase. **teach one's grandmother to suck eggs** presume to advise someone who is more experienced.
▸ **B** *verb trans.* Take care of or behave towards (a person) as a grandmother. **E20.**
▪ **grandmotherhood** *noun* the condition or state of being a grandmother **M19. grandmotherless** *adjective* **LME. grandmotherly** *adjective* of, pertaining to, resembling, or characteristic of a grandmother **M19.**

grandness /ˈgran(d)nɪs/ *noun.* **E18.**
[**ORIGIN** from **GRAND** *adjective*[1] + **-NESS.**]
The state or quality of being grand. Also, a grand action.

grandpa /ˈgran(d)pɑː/ *noun. colloq.* **L19.**
[**ORIGIN** from **GRAND-** + **PA** *noun*[2].]
Grandfather.

grandpapa /ˈgran(d)pəpɑː/ *noun. colloq.* (now *arch.*). Also **-pappy** /-papi/. **M18.**
[**ORIGIN** from **GRAND-** + **PAPA** *noun*[2].]
Grandfather.
▪ Also **grandpop** *noun* **L19.**

grandparent /ˈgran(d)pɛːr(ə)nt/ *noun.* **M19.**
[**ORIGIN** from **GRAND-** + **PARENT** *noun.*]
A parent of either of one's parents.
▪ **ˈgrandparentage** *noun* the state or condition of being a grandparent; descent from grandparents: **L19. grandpaˈrental** *adjective* of, pertaining to, or characteristic of a grandparent **E20.**

grandpaternal /gran(d)pəˈtəːn(ə)l/ *adjective.* **M19.**
[**ORIGIN** from **GRAND-** + **PATERNAL.**]
Of, pertaining to, or characteristic of a grandfather; grandfatherly.

Grand Prix /grɒnˈ priː, *foreign* grɑ̃ ˈpriː/ *noun phr.* Pl. **Grands Prix** (pronounced same). **M19.**
[**ORIGIN** French = great prize.]
1 In full ***Grand Prix de Paris*** /də paˈriː/. An international horse race for three-year-olds run annually in June at Longchamps, Paris. **M19.**
2 The highest prize awarded in a competition or exhibition. **L19.**
3 Any of a series of motor or motorcycle races forming the World Championship, held in various countries under international rules. Also, a very important competitive event in various other sports. **E20.**

grandsire /ˈgran(d)sʌɪə/ *noun.* **ME.**
[**ORIGIN** from **GRAND-** + **SIRE** *noun.*]
1 Grandfather; an old man. Now *arch. & dial.* **ME.** ▸**b** The sire of an animal's sire. **L19.**
2 A forefather, a male ancestor. *arch.* **ME.**
†**3** A great-grandfather. *Scot.* **E16–E20.**
4 *BELL-RINGING.* A basic method of change-ringing using an odd number of bells. **L17.**

grandson /ˈgran(d)sʌn/ *noun.* **L16.**
[**ORIGIN** from **GRAND-** + **SON** *noun*[1].]
A son of one's son or daughter.

grandstand /ˈgran(d)stand/ *noun & verb.* **M19.**
[**ORIGIN** from **GRAND** *adjective*[1] + **STAND** *noun*[1].]
▸ **A** *noun.* The principal stand for spectators at a racecourse or other sporting venue. **M19.**
▸ **B** *verb intrans.* Perform with a view to getting applause from spectators in the grandstand; seek to attract favourable public or media attention. Chiefly as ***grandstanding*** *verbal noun.* **E20.**

> R. WRIGHT A prime minister who had tried to build an international reputation by grandstanding on the evils of apartheid. R. BENNETT She embarrasses you when she's doing her revolutionary grandstanding bit.

– **COMB.:** **grandstand finish** a close or exciting finish in a race or competition; **grandstand play** *US* a way of performing with a view to getting applause. **grandstand view** a very good view of events such as is afforded by a seat in a grandstand.
▪ **grandstander** *noun* (**a**) a spectator in a grandstand; (**b**) a person who grandstands: **L19.**

grane *noun* see **GRAIN** *noun*[2].

granfer /ˈgranfə/ *noun. dial.* Also **grandfer. L19.**
[**ORIGIN** Contr.]
= **GRANDFATHER.**

grange /greɪn(d)ʒ/ *noun.* **ME.**
[**ORIGIN** Old French & mod. French, or Anglo-Norman *graunge*, from medieval Latin *granica* (fem.) pertaining to grain, used as noun (sc. *villa*), from Latin *granum* **GRAIN** *noun*[1].]
1 A granary, a barn. *arch.* **ME.**
2 A farm; *esp.* a country house with farm buildings attached. **ME.** ▸**b** *hist.* An outlying farmstead with tithe barns etc. belonging to a monastery or feudal lord. **LME.**
3 A country house (for recreation). Now only in house names. **M16.**
4 *US HISTORY.* (Also **G-.**) (A local branch of) the 'Patrons of Husbandry', a national association of agriculturists. **L19.**

granger /ˈgreɪn(d)ʒə/ *noun.* **ME.**
[**ORIGIN** Anglo-Norman *graunger* = Old French *grangier*, from **GRANGE**: see **-ER**[2].]
1 *hist.* The steward of a grange. **ME.**
2 *US HISTORY.* (Also **G-.**) A member of a grange (see **GRANGE** 4). **L19.** ▸**b** In *pl.* = ***granger shares*** below. *US.* **L19.**
3 A farmer. Chiefly *joc.* or *derog. N. Amer.* **L19.**
– **COMB.:** **granger railroad**, **granger road** *US HISTORY* a railway carrying grain etc. from the western states; **granger shares** *US HISTORY* shares in a granger road.

grangerize /ˈgreɪn(d)ʒərʌɪz/ *verb trans.* Also **-ise. L19.**
[**ORIGIN** from James *Granger* (1723–76), English biographer + **-IZE.**]
Illustrate (a book) by later insertion of material, esp. prints cut from other works (Granger's *Biographical History of England* had blank pages to allow for this).
▪ **grangerism** *noun* the practice of grangerizing **L19. grangerite** *noun* = **GRANGERIZER L19. grangeriˈzation** *noun* **L19. grangerizer** *noun* a person who grangerizes **L19.**

graniferous /grəˈnɪf(ə)rəs/ *adjective.* **M17.**
[**ORIGIN** from Latin *granum* **GRAIN** *noun*[1] + **-FEROUS.**]
Producing grain or seed resembling grain.

graniform /ˈgranɪfɔːm/ *adjective.* **L18.**
[**ORIGIN** formed as **GRANIFEROUS** + **-I-** + **-FORM.**]
Formed like a grain or as if made of grains.

granita /grəˈniːtə, *foreign* graˈniːta/ *noun.* Pl. **-ite** /-ti, *foreign* -te/. **M19.**
[**ORIGIN** Italian.]
A coarse water ice or sherbet; a drink made with crushed ice.

granite /ˈgranɪt/ *noun & adjective.* **M17.**
[**ORIGIN** Italian *granito* lit. 'grained, granular', pa. ppl formation on *grano* **GRAIN** *noun*[1].]
▸ **A** *noun.* **1** Any of a broad class of granular crystalline plutonic rocks, consisting essentially of quartz, orthoclase, feldspar, and mica or hornblende, often used for building. **M17.**
bite on granite *fig.* waste pains, persist in vain. ***graphic granite***: see **GRAPHIC** *adjective.*
2 *fig.* This as the type of something solid, hard, or unyielding; unyielding quality. **M19.**
3 = **GRANITA.** *US.* **L19.**
▸ **B** *attrib.* or as *adjective.* **1** Consisting or made of granite. **E18.**
Granite City the city of Aberdeen, Scotland. **Granite State** *US* the state of New Hampshire.
2 *fig.* Like granite; hard, stern, unfeeling. **E20.**

> *Daily Chronicle* His countenance expressed neither the . . tenderness of the saint nor the granite severity of the prophet.

– **COMB. & SPECIAL COLLOCATIONS:** **granite-porphyry** any porphyritic hypabyssal rock of granitic composition; **graniteware** (**a**) speckled pottery imitating the appearance of granite; (**b**) a kind of enamelled ironware.

†**granitell** *noun.* **L18–L19.**
[**ORIGIN** French *granitelle* from Italian *granitello*, dim. of *granito* **GRANITE.**]
GEOLOGY. Any granular crystalline rock having two principal components.

granitic /grəˈnɪtɪk/ *adjective.* **L18.**
[**ORIGIN** from **GRANITE** + **-IC.**]
1 Of, pertaining to, or of the nature of granite; composed of or containing granite. **L18.**
2 *fig.* Hard, rigid, unimpressionable. **M19.**

> F. C. L. WRAXALL The granitic solidity of certain celebrated prose.

▪ Also **granitical** *adjective* (now *rare*) **L18.**

granitize /ˈgranɪtʌɪz/ *verb trans.* Also **-ise. L19.**
[**ORIGIN** formed as **GRANITIC** + **-IZE.**]
GEOLOGY. Alter so as to give a granitic character to. Chiefly as ***granitized*** *ppl adjective.*
▪ **granitiˈzation** *noun* **L19.**

granitoid /ˈgranɪtɔɪd/ *noun & adjective.* **L18.**
[**ORIGIN** formed as **GRANITIC** + **-OID.**]
GEOLOGY. (A rock) resembling granite in having a granular crystalline texture.

granivorous /ɡraˈnɪv(ə)rəs/ *adjective*. M17.
[ORIGIN from Latin *granus* GRAIN *noun*[1] + -VOROUS.]
Feeding on grain.

granma *noun* var. of GRANDMA.

grannam /ˈɡranəm/ *noun*. *obsolete* exc. *dial*. Also **-um**. L16.
[ORIGIN Repr. colloq. pronunc. of GRANDAM.]
A grandmother, an old woman.

grannie *noun* var. of GRANNY.

grannom /ˈɡranəm/ *noun*. L18.
[ORIGIN Unknown.]
A caddis fly (spec. *Brachycentrus subnubilus*), or an imitation of this, used in fly-fishing.

grannum *noun* var. of GRANNAM.

granny /ˈɡrani/ *noun*. Also **grannie**. M17.
[ORIGIN from GRANNAM + -Y[6], -IE.]
1 Grandmother. Also, any elderly woman. *colloq*. M17.
MAX-MÜLLER Stories . . for which we are indebted to the old grannies in every village.
your granny! *interjection* expr. disagreement with a preceding word or phr.
2 More fully ***granny woman***. A nurse, a midwife. *US colloq*. & *Canad. dial*. L18.
3 More fully ***granny knot***, ***granny's knot***. A reef knot incorrectly tied and therefore insecure or easily jammed. M19.
A. RANSOME Oh gosh! He's tied my legs with a granny and it's stuck.
4 A stupid or fussy person (of either sex). *colloq*. & *dial*. L19.
– ATTRIB. & COMB.: Designating garments etc. resembling those (formerly) typical of old women, worn by young people, as ***granny bonnet***, ***granny dress***, ***granny shoe***. Special combs., as **granny annexe** a detached part of a property designed as self-contained accommodation for an elderly relative; **granny bashing**, **granny battering** violence towards an elderly person, esp. a member of one's family; **granny bond** *colloq*. an index-linked National Savings certificate originally available only to those of pensionable age; **granny's bonnet** *colloq*. columbine, aquilegia; **granny flat** part of a house made into self-contained accommodation for an elderly relative; **granny glasses** round steel-rimmed spectacles; ***granny knot***: see sense 3 above; **granny-sit** *verb intrans*. look after or stay with an elderly person while the usual carer is out; **granny-sitter** a person engaged to granny-sit; ***granny's knot***: see sense 3 above; ***granny woman***: see sense 2 above.

Granny Smith /ɡranɪ ˈsmɪθ/ *noun phr*. L19.
[ORIGIN Maria Ann *Smith* (c 1801–70): see below.]
An (orig. Australian) variety of bright green eating and cooking apple, first propagated in Australia by Maria 'Granny' Smith.

granodiorite /ɡranə(ʊ)ˈdʌɪərʌɪt/ *noun*. L19.
[ORIGIN from GRANITE + -O- + DIORITE.]
GEOLOGY. Any of a class of coarse-grained quartz-containing plutonic rocks intermediate between granite and diorite in composition, with plagioclase forming at least two-thirds of the total feldspar content.

granola /ɡraˈnəʊlə/ *noun* & *adjective*. *N. Amer*. E20.
[ORIGIN from *gran-* repr. GRAIN *noun*[1] or GRANULAR + -OLA.]
▸ **A** *noun*. Orig., a proprietary name for a breakfast cereal. Now, a kind of breakfast cereal resembling muesli. E20.
▸ **B** *attrib*. or as *adjective*. Denoting people with liberal or Green political views, typified as eating health foods. *derog*. L20.

granolithic /ɡranəˈlɪθɪk/ *adjective* & *noun*. L19.
[ORIGIN from Latin *grano-* (irreg. combining form of *granum* GRAIN *noun*[1]) + Greek *lithos* stone + -IC.]
(Designating or made of) a kind of concrete containing crushed granite.

granophyre /ˈɡranə(ʊ)fʌɪə/ *noun*. L19.
[ORIGIN German *Granophyr*, from *Granit* GRANITE + -O- + *Porphyr* PORPHYRY.]
GEOLOGY. Any of a class of porphyritic plutonic rocks of granitic composition characterized by a medium- to fine-grained groundmass of intergrown feldspar and quartz.
■ **granoˈphyric** *adjective* L19.

grant /ɡrɑːnt/ *noun*. ME.
[ORIGIN from the verb.]
†**1** Consent, permission. ME–M17. ▸**b** A promise. LME–L16. ▸**c** Admission, acknowledgement. E16–L17.
2 The action of granting (a request etc.). LME.
Law Times The grant or refusal of an injunction upon a matter of law is appealable.
3 A formal gift or legal assignment of money, privilege, etc. LME. ▸**b** The thing granted; *esp*. a sum of money given for a specific purpose. E19.
R. STUART Fifty years after the grant of the patent. LD MACAULAY He obtained a grant of all the lands . . belonging to Jesuits. **b** A. HAILEY Our company does give grants for academic research. J. WAIN Till I go to college and my student grant comes through.
b *direct grant*: see DIRECT *adjective*.
4 *LAW*. A transfer of (real) property by deed or other written instrument. L16.
5 A piece of land occupied by a specified person. Chiefly *US*, in place names; *spec*. (***the Grants***, ***the New Hampshire Grants*** (*hist*.), the area now forming the state of Vermont. E18.
– COMB.: **grant-aid** *verb* & *noun* (**a**) *verb trans*. give financial assistance to (a school etc.); (**b**) *noun*= ***grant-in-aid*** below; **grant-aided** *ppl adjective* (of a school etc.) assisted by an allowance from government or official funds; **grant-in-aid** a sum given as a grant, *esp*. by an authority or institution to support research or education; **grant-maintained** *ppl adjective* (*hist*.) (of a school) funded by central rather than local government, and self-governing.

grant /ɡrɑːnt/ *verb*. ME.
[ORIGIN Old French *gra(a)nter*, *greanter* alt. of *creanter* guarantee, assure from Proto-Romance, from Latin *credent-* pres. ppl stem of *credere* believe, trust.]
†**1** *verb intrans*. Consent to a request; agree *to* (*do*). ME–E18.
SHAKES. *3 Hen. VI* The soldiers should have toss'd me . . Before I would have granted to that act.
2 *verb trans*. Agree to, promise, undertake; consent *to do*, *that*. *obsolete* exc. *LAW*. ME.
W. CRUISE A. covenanted, granted, and agreed that B. should have the land.
3 *verb trans*. Accede to, consent to fulfil (a request etc.). ME.
T. HARDY This entreaty he granted; but on her asking for yet another, he was inexorable.
4 *verb trans*. Concede as an indulgence, bestow as a favour; allow (a person) to have. ME. ▸**b** In pa. pple ***granted***, as a polite rejoinder to an apology. E20.
N. EZEKIEL God grant me privacy. P. ROTH He . . granted no public interviews. **b** H. CALVIN She yawned a great yawn and said, 'Sorry.' 'Granted,' I said.
take for granted regard as necessarily true or certain to happen; cease to appreciate through familiarity.
5 *verb trans*. Give or confer (a possession, a right, etc.) formally; transfer (property) legally. ME.
L. STEFFENS The charters were granted on June 5. *Soldier* He was granted the BEM for his services.
†**6** *verb trans*. Yield, give up. ME–E17.
7 *verb trans*. Admit, acknowledge. Now usu., concede (a proposition) as a basis for argument. Freq. as ***granted*** pa. pple. ME. ▸**b** With compl.: admit (a person) to be. *rare*. LME.
A. WHITE And, granted the initial assumptions . . I think it stands the test. E. BOWEN I do grant . . it's a good deal to ask. **b** SIR W. SCOTT I grant him brave, But wild.
■ **grantable** *adjective* possible to grant M16. **granˈtee** *noun* the person to whom a grant or conveyance is made LME. **granter** *noun* a person who grants LME. **grantor** *noun* (*LAW*) a person who makes a grant or conveyance E17.

Granth /ɡrʌnt/ *noun*. Also **Grunth**. L18.
[ORIGIN from Sanskrit *grantha* tying, literary composition, from *granth* tie.]
Any of the sacred scriptures of the Sikhs. Also (more fully ***Adi Granth*** /ˈɑːdi/ [*ādigrantha* lit. 'first book']), these collectively. See also GUM GRANTH SAHIB.

Grantha /ˈɡrʌntə/ *noun*. Also **-am** /-(ə)m/. L19.
[ORIGIN Sanskrit: see GRANTH.]
A southern Indian alphabet used by the Tamil brahmins for the Sanskrit transcripts of their sacred books.

Granthi /ˈɡrʌntiː/ *noun*. L19.
[ORIGIN Punjabi *granthī*; see GRANTH.]
A custodian of the Adi Granth; a person who reads from this.

gran turismo /ɡran tuˈrizmo, tʊəˈrɪzməʊ/ *noun* & *adjectival phr*. M20.
[ORIGIN Italian, lit. 'great touring'.]
(Designating) a comfortable high-performance model of car. Abbreviation ***GT***.
I. FLEMING He had . . a white convertible Lancia Gran Turismo.

†**granula** *noun*. Pl. **-lae**. M17–M19.
[ORIGIN mod. Latin, irreg. dim. of *granum*, = late Latin *granulum* GRANULE.]
= GRANULE.

granular /ˈɡranjʊlə/ *adjective*. L18.
[ORIGIN formed as GRANULE + -AR[1].]
1 Consisting of grains or granules. L18.
2 Having a granulated surface or structure. M19.
3 Of the nature of a granule or granules. M19.
■ **granuˈlarity** *noun* L19. **granularly** *adverb* E20.

granulate /ˈɡranjʊlət, -leɪt/ *adjective*. L18.
[ORIGIN formed as GRANULE + -ATE[2].]
Chiefly *BOTANY* & *ZOOLOGY*. = GRANULATED 2.

granulate /ˈɡranjʊleɪt/ *verb*. M17.
[ORIGIN formed as GRANULE + -ATE[3].]
1 *verb trans*. & *intrans*. Form into or take the form of granules or grains; make or become granular. M17.
2 *verb trans*. Raise in granules; roughen the surface of. L17.
3 *verb intrans*. *MEDICINE*. Of a wound, tissue, etc.: form multiple small prominences, as the beginning of the process of healing or joining. M18.
■ **granulator** *noun* an apparatus for making granules of a substance M19.

granulated /ˈɡranjʊleɪtɪd/ *ppl adjective*. L17.
[ORIGIN from GRANULATE *verb* + -ED[1].]
1 Of a solid material: formed into or consisting of granules. L17.
ellipt. *as noun*: D. FRANCIS 'Sugar?' He had a two-pound bag of granulated, and a . . spoon.
2 (Of a surface) raised in small projections; having a surface roughened in this manner. Also, mottled so as to appear granular. L17.
Times A granulated gold pendant.
3 *MEDICINE*. Displaying granulation. M19.

granulation /ɡranjʊˈleɪʃ(ə)n/ *noun*. E17.
[ORIGIN formed as GRANULE + -ATION.]
1 The action or process of forming into granules or grains; the condition of being granulated. Also (in *pl*.), granules. E17.
2 *MEDICINE*. (The process of healing by) the formation of multiple small prominences on the surface of injured tissue, as part of the growth of new connective tissue. Also (in *pl*.), the prominences so formed. M18.
3 *gen*. The formation or existence of small granular projections or bodies on the surface or in the substance of an object. Also, the structure, or (in *pl*.) the granules, so formed. L18.
– COMB.: **granulation tissue** connective tissue newly grown at the site of a wound etc.

G

granule /ˈɡranjuːl/ *noun*. M17.
[ORIGIN Late Latin *granulum* dim. of Latin *granum* GRAIN *noun*[1]: see -ULE.]
A small grain or compact particle, usu. larger than a particle of a powder; a prominence resembling a grain on a surface.
G. F. CHAMBERS Granule is the best word to describe the luminous particles on the Sun's surface. M. DRABBLE Nescafé . . in those days came not in granules in jars but in powder in tins.

granuliform /ɡranˈjuːlɪfɔːm/ *adjective*. M19.
[ORIGIN formed as GRANULE + -I- + -FORM.]
Having a granular structure.

granulite /ˈɡranjʊlʌɪt/ *noun*. M19.
[ORIGIN from GRANULE + -ITE[1].]
GEOLOGY. Any of a class of fine-grained granulose metamorphic rocks in which the main component minerals are usu. feldspars and quartz.
■ **granulitic** /-ˈlɪtɪk/ *adjective* L19.

granulo- /ˈɡranjʊləʊ/ *combining form*. M19.
[ORIGIN formed as GRANULE + -O-.]
Forming nouns and adjectives with the sense 'of granules, having granules' or (*rare*) adjectives with the sense 'granular and —'.

granulocyte /ˈɡranjʊləsʌɪt/ *noun*. E20.
[ORIGIN from GRANULO- + -CYTE.]
PHYSIOLOGY. A cell containing or developing conspicuously granular cytoplasm; *spec*. any of a class of leucocytes which show a granular appearance of the cytoplasm when stained.
■ **granulocytic** /-ˈsɪtɪk/ *adjective* E20. **granulocytoˈpenia** *noun* [Greek *penia* poverty] the presence of abnormally small numbers of granulocytes in the blood M20. **granulocyˈtosis** *noun* the presence of abnormally large numbers of granulocytes in the blood M20.

granuloma /ɡranjʊˈləʊmə/ *noun*. Pl. **-mas**, **-mata** /-mətə/. M19.
[ORIGIN formed as GRANULE + -OMA.]
MEDICINE. A mass of granulation tissue produced in any of various disease states, usu. in response to infection, inflammation, or the presence of a foreign substance.
granuloma inguinale /ɪŋɡwɪˈnɑːli/ [mod. Latin = inguinal granuloma] (the granulomatous formation characteristic of) donovanosis.
■ ˌ**granulomaˈtosis** *noun*, pl. **-toses** /-ˈtəʊsiːz/, any condition marked by the growth of granulomas E20. **granulomatous** *adjective* of, pertaining to or of the nature of a granuloma L19.

granulometric /ˌɡranjʊlə(ʊ)ˈmɛtrɪk/ *adjective*. E20.
[ORIGIN French *granulométrique*, formed as GRANULO- + -METRIC.]
Relating to the size distribution of grains of sand or other materials; relating to or involving the measurement of grain sizes.

granulose /ˈɡranjʊləʊs/ *adjective*. M19.
[ORIGIN from GRANULE + -OSE[1].]
Granular; *spec*. (*PETROGRAPHY*) (of a rock structure) marked by the presence of granular minerals, usu. in streaks and bands.

granulous /ˈɡranjʊləs/ *adjective*. LME.
[ORIGIN from medieval Latin *granulosus* (see -ULOUS); later directly from GRANULE + -OUS.]
Granular.

granum /ˈgrɑːnəm, ˈgreɪnəm/ *noun*. Pl. **grana** /ˈgrɑːnə, ˈgreɪnə/. L19.
[ORIGIN German from Latin *granum* grain.]
BOTANY. Any of the stacks of thylakoids in a chloroplast.

grape /greɪp/ *noun*. ME.
[ORIGIN Old French (mod. *grappe* bunch of grapes), prob. verbal noun from *graper* gather (grapes), from *grap(p)e* hook, from Proto-Romance from Germanic (Old High German *krāpfo*) hook, rel. to CRAMP *noun*[1].]
†**1** A bunch of grapes. Chiefly ***wine-grape***. ME–L15.
2 Each of the small oval berries, usu. green, purple, or black, growing in clusters on a vine and eaten fresh or dried as fruit or used for making wine. With specifying word: a variety of this. ME. ▸**b** The (fermented) juice of the grape; wine. M17.
black grape, ***muscat grape***, ***seedless grape***, ***white grape***, etc. **sour grapes** [alluding to Aesop's fable of 'The Fox and the Grapes'] an expression or attitude of deliberate disparagement of a desired but unattainable object.
3 The berry or fruit of any of various other plants. Now only with specifying word as in sense 4. LME.
4 A climbing plant of the genus *Vitis* (family Vitaceae), on which grapes grow; a vine. Also (with specifying word), any of various other fruit-bearing plants resembling the vine. LME.
5 In *pl.* A diseased growth resembling a bunch of grapes on the pastern of a horse etc., or on the pleura in cattle. E17.
†**6** More fully ***grape-paper***. A size of paper. E17–L19.
7 *hist.* Small cast-iron balls grouped several together to make a scattering charge for cannon. Orig. in *pl.*; now only *collect.* or as ***grapeshot***. L17.
– COMB.: **grape brandy** brandy distilled solely from grapes or from wine; ***grape HYACINTH***; **Grape-Nuts** (proprietary name for) a breakfast cereal, a preparation of maize or wheat in a crisp granular form; ***grape-paper***: see sense 6 above; ***grape PHYLLOXERA***; **grape scissors** (***a***) clippers used for thinning grapes on the vine; (***b***) scissors used for dividing a bunch of grapes at table; ***grapeshot***: see sense 7 above; **grape stone** (***a***) the seed of a grape; (***b***) *GEOLOGY* a cemented cluster of calcareous or other particles in a sedimentary deposit; **grape sugar** dextrose; **grape tree** (***a***) = ***SEASIDE grape*** (***tree***); (***b***) a grapevine.
■ **grapelet** *noun* a small grape E17. **grapelike** *adjective* resembling (that of) a grape or grapes E17. **grapery** *noun* a greenhouse etc. in which grapes are grown; a plantation of vines; a vinery: E19.

grapefruit /ˈgreɪpfruːt/ *noun*. Pl. same. E19.
[ORIGIN from GRAPE *noun* + FRUIT *noun*: prob. from the fruits being borne in clusters.]
A large round yellow-skinned citrus fruit having pale yellow, occas. pink, juicy acid pulp. Also (usu. ***grapefruit tree***), the tree bearing this fruit, *Citrus paradisi*, a hybrid or mutation of the shaddock, *C. maxima*, of W. Indian origin.

grapevine /ˈgreɪpvʌɪn/ *noun*. M18.
[ORIGIN from GRAPE *noun* + VINE.]
1 A vine which bears grapes. M18.
2 An unofficial means of transmission of information (often of a secret or private nature) or rumour. Orig. (*US colloq.*) as ***grapevine telegraph***. M19.

> T. HEALD Contacts who had heard, on the grapevine, that he was looking for work. J. HELLER The grapevine says I'm finished. *Bird Watching* The 'grapevine' is a loose association of active birders who keep in touch by passing on news of rare and interesting birds.

3 A skating figure in which both feet are on the ice together and form interlacing lines. M19.
4 A hold in wrestling. L19.

grapey /ˈgreɪpi/ *adjective*. Also **grapy**. LME.
[ORIGIN from GRAPE *noun* + -Y[1].]
†**1** Designating the choroid coat of the eye. LME–L17.
2 Of or pertaining to grapes or the vine; composed or savouring of grapes. L16.

†**grapeys** *noun*. Only in ME.
[ORIGIN Old French *grapois*, *graspeis* (also *craspois*) from medieval Latin *craspiscis*, from Latin *crassus* thick + *piscis* fish.]
The flesh of the grampus.
– NOTE: Later history unrecorded, but the source of GRAMPUS (E16).

graph /grɑːf, graf/ *noun*[1] & *verb*. L19.
[ORIGIN Abbreviation of *graphic formula*: see GRAPHIC *adjective*.]
▸ **A** *noun*. **1** A diagram showing the relation between two variable quantities each measured along one of a pair of axes usu. at right angles. L19.

> *fig.*: A. COOKE Somewhere along the falling graph of our allegiance to authority.

2 *MATH.* A symbolic diagram in which connections between items are represented by lines. Now also in abstract terms, a finite non-empty set of elements together with a set of unordered pairs of these elements. L19.
▸ **B** *verb trans.* Plot or trace on a graph; represent by means of a graph. L19.

> I. JEFFRIES Anybody graph the survival rates against the day of admission? *fig.*: *Listener* The book graphs . . the hostility between generations.

– COMB.: **graph paper**: printed with a network of lines to assist the drawing of graphs; **graph theory** the mathematical theory of the properties and applications of graphs (sense 2).

graph /grɑːf, graf/ *noun*[2]. M20.
[ORIGIN Greek *graphē* writing.]
LINGUISTICS. A visual symbol representing a phoneme or cluster of phonemes or some other feature of speech; *esp.* a letter or a combination of letters.

-graph /grɑːf, graf/ *suffix*.
[ORIGIN from or after French *-graphe* from Latin *-graphus* from Greek *-graphos* written, writing.]
Forming nouns with the sense 'something written, drawn, recorded, etc., in a specified way,' as ***autograph***, ***photograph***, ***pictograph***, etc., or with the sense 'an instrument that records something or by some means,' as ***heliograph***, ***seismograph***, ***telegraph***, etc.

grapheme /ˈgrafiːm/ *noun*. M20.
[ORIGIN from GRAPH *noun*[2] + -EME.]
LINGUISTICS. The class of letters and other visual symbols that represent a phoneme or a cluster of phonemes; a feature of written expression that constitutes a minimal distinctive unit.
■ **grapheˈmatic**, **graˈphemic** *adjectives* of or relating to graphemes or graphemics M20. **graˈphemically** *adverb* M20. **graˈphemics** *noun* the branch of knowledge that deals with systems of written symbols in relation to spoken language: M20.

-grapher /grəfə/ *suffix*.
[ORIGIN from or after Greek *graphos* writer + -ER[1].]
Forming nouns (usu. corresp. to nouns in -GRAPH, -GRAPHY) with the sense 'a person skilled in a style or method of writing, drawing, recording, etc.', as ***calligrapher***, ***stenographer***, etc.; with the sense 'a person who writes (about) (something denoted by the first element)', as ***hagiographer***, ***historiographer***; with the sense 'a person skilled in a particular descriptive science or the use of a recording instrument' as ***bibliographer***, ***geographer***, ***radiographer***, etc.

graphic /ˈgrafɪk/ *noun*. L19.
[ORIGIN from the adjective.]
▸ **I** In *pl.*, usu. treated as *sing.*
1 The technical use of diagrams and figures as an aid to mathematical calculation or to engineering or architectural design. L19. ▸**b** The use of computers linked to VDUs to generate and manipulate visual images. More fully ***computer graphics***. M20.
2 Design and decoration involving or accompanying typographic work; the production of pictures, diagrams, etc., in association with text. M20.
▸ **II** *sing.* (with *pl.*).
3 A product of the graphic arts or of graphic design. M20.
4 A diagram, picture, or other visual image produced by means of a computer. In *pl.* also ***computer graphics***. M20.

graphic /ˈgrafɪk/ *adjective*. M17.
[ORIGIN Latin *graphicus* from Greek *graphikos*, from *graphē* drawing, writing: see -IC.]
†**1** Drawn with a pencil or a pen. Only in M17.
2 Producing by words the effect of a clear pictorial representation; vividly descriptive; conveying all (esp. unpleasant or unwelcome) details, clear, unequivocal. M17.

> H. B. STOWE Expressions, which not even the desire to be graphic in our account shall induce us to transcribe. C. DARWIN A graphic description of the face of a young Hindoo at the sight of castor-oil.

3 Relating to or producing pictorial representations; of or pertaining to drawing, painting, engraving, etching, etc. M18.

> G. STEINER Brilliant, instantaneous graphic devices—the photograph, the poster, the moving picture.

4 Of or pertaining to handwriting etc.; *occas.* suitable for writing on. L18. ▸**b** Of a mineral: showing marks like writing on the surface or in fracture. E19.

> E. R. CONDER Letters, hieroglyphics, or any kind of graphic symbol.

5 Pertaining to or involving diagrams, graphs, or similar figures; graphical. M19.
– SPECIAL COLLOCATIONS: ***graphic arts***: see ART *noun*[1]. **graphic design** the art or skill of combining text and pictures in advertisements, magazines, or books. **graphic equalizer** a device enabling the quality of an audio signal to be varied by adjusting its strength in each of a series of frequency bands independently, usu. by means of slides. **graphic granite** *PETROGRAPHY* a pegmatite with intergrown crystals of feldspar and quartz producing a pattern resembling cuneiform script. **graphic novel** a full-length story in the form of a comic strip, published as a book.
■ **graphicness** *noun* M19.

-graphic /ˈgrafɪk/ *suffix*.
[ORIGIN Partly from or after Greek *graphikos*, (see GRAPHIC *adjective*), partly from nouns in -GRAPH(Y) + -IC.]
Forming adjectives (usu. corresp. to nouns in -GRAPH, -GRAPHY) with the sense 'of or pertaining to or by a style or method of writing, drawing, recording, etc.', as ***calligraphic***, ***photographic***, etc.; with the sense 'of or pertaining to the writing of or about (something denoted by the first element)', as ***hagiographic***, ***historiographic***; with the sense 'of or pertaining to a descriptive science or method of instrumental recording', as ***geographic***, ***bibliographic***, ***radiographic***, etc.

graphicacy /ˈgrafɪkəsi/ *noun*. M20.
[ORIGIN from GRAPHIC *adjective* after *literacy*, *numeracy*.]
The ability to understand maps, graphs, etc., or to present information by means of diagrams.
■ **graphicate** *adjective* [after *numerate*] possessing or displaying graphicacy M20.

graphical /ˈgrafɪk(ə)l/ *adjective*. E17.
[ORIGIN formed as GRAPHIC *adjective*: see -ICAL.]
†**1** Clearly drawn or traced. Only in E17.
2 = GRAPHIC *adjective* 3. Formerly also, skilled in drawing. E17.
3 = GRAPHIC *adjective* 2. Now *rare*. M17.
4 Of or pertaining to writing; consisting of letters. M17.
5 = GRAPHIC *adjective* 5. L18.
– SPECIAL COLLOCATIONS: **graphical user interface** a visual way of interacting with a computer using items such as windows, icons, and menus, used by most modern operating systems (abbreviation ***GUI***).
■ **graphicalness** *noun* L19.

-graphical /ˈgrafɪk(ə)l/ *suffix*.
[ORIGIN formed as *-graphic* + -ICAL.]
= -GRAPHIC.

graphically /ˈgrafɪk(ə)li/ *adverb*. L16.
[ORIGIN from GRAPHIC *adjective* or -GRAPHICAL: see -ICALLY.]
1 As in a clear pictorial representation; in a vividly descriptive manner; so as to convey all (esp. unpleasant or unwelcome) details; clearly, unequivocally. L16.

> D. W. GOODWIN The . . study makes this point graphically clear . . . Those who came back for booster sessions did better.

2 Orig., in the manner of writing. Now, by means of or in respect of written signs. E17.

> OED The verbs *read* and *rede* differ only graphically; in etymology and pronunciation they are the same word.

†**3** By means of drawing, painting, etc. *rare*. Only in M17.
4 By the use of diagrams, linear figures, or symbolic curves; by the construction of diagrams or graphs. L18.

> *Which Micro?* You can . . display figures graphically.

graphite /ˈgrafʌɪt/ *noun*. L18.
[ORIGIN German *Graphit*, from Greek *graphein* write (from its use as pencil 'lead'): see -ITE[1].]
A grey electrically conducting allotropic form of carbon, with a crystalline structure containing layers of carbon atoms.
■ **graphited** *adjective* lubricated with graphite; containing added graphite: E20. **graphitoid** *adjective* = GRAPHITOIDAL L19. **graphiˈtoidal** *adjective* having the appearance or structure of graphite M19.

graphitic /grəˈfɪtɪk/ *adjective*. M19.
[ORIGIN from GRAPHITE + -IC.]
Of, pertaining to, or of the nature of graphite.

graphitization /ˌgrafɪtʌɪˈzeɪʃ(ə)n/ *noun*. Also **-isation**. L19.
[ORIGIN formed as GRAPHITIC + -IZATION.]
1 Conversion of carbon (wholly or partially) into the form of graphite. Also, graphitic character. L19.
2 *METALLURGY*. **a** The formation of graphite from combined carbon in a ferrous alloy. E20. ▸**b** Corrosion of grey cast iron in which the metallic iron constituents are lost leaving a soft porous residue largely of graphite. E20.

graphitize /ˈgrafɪtʌɪz/ *verb trans.* & *intrans.* Also **-ise**. L19.
[ORIGIN formed as GRAPHITIC + -IZE.]
(Cause to) undergo graphitization.

graphology /grəˈfɒlədʒi/ *noun*. M19.
[ORIGIN from Greek *grapho-* combining form from *graphē* writing + -LOGY.]
1 *LINGUISTICS*. The branch of knowledge that deals with written and printed symbols and of writing systems. M19.
2 The branch of knowledge that deals with handwriting, esp. as used to infer a person's character etc. from his or her handwriting. L19.
■ **graphoˈlogical** *adjective* L19. **graphoˈlogically** *adverb* M20. **graphologist** *noun* L19.

graphomania /grafəˈmeɪnɪə/ *noun*. Now *rare*. M19.
[ORIGIN formed as GRAPHOLOGY + -MANIA.]
A mania for writing.
■ **graphomaniac** *noun* E19.

graphometer /grəˈfɒmɪtə/ *noun*. L17.
[ORIGIN French *graphomètre*, formed as GRAPHOLOGY + -METER.]
A semicircle used in measuring angles in surveying.

graphotype /ˈgrafə(ʊ)tʌɪp/ *noun*. Now *hist.* M19.
[ORIGIN formed as GRAPHOLOGY + -TYPE.]
A printing process in which a stereotype or electrotype copy is made from a drawing which has been put in relief; the block or plate produced by this means.

graphy /ˈgrafi/ *noun*. M20.
[ORIGIN French *graphie* system of writing.]
= GRAPH *noun*[2].

-graphy /grəfi/ *suffix.*
[ORIGIN French, German *-graphie* from Latin from Greek *-graphia* writing.]
Forming nouns (freq. with **-O-**: see **-OGRAPHY**) with the sense 'a style or method of writing, drawing, etc.,' as ***calligraphy***, ***lithography***, ***stenography***; with the sense 'the writing of or about (something denoted by the first element)', as ***hagiography***, ***historiography***; with the sense 'the branch of knowledge relating to a particular descriptive science or instrumental recording technique,' as ***bibliography***, ***geography***, ***radiography***.

grapnel /ˈgrapn(ə)l/ *noun.* LME.
[ORIGIN Anglo-Norman, from Old French *grapon* (mod. *grappin*) from Germanic base of GRAPE *noun*: see -EL[2].]
1 A grappling iron. Also, a small anchor with several flukes. LME.
2 = GRAPPLE *noun* 2. L19.

grappa /ˈgrapə/ *noun.* L19.
[ORIGIN Italian.]
A brandy distilled from the refuse of grapes after wine-making.

grappier /ˈgrapɪə, *foreign* grapje (*pl. same*)/ *noun.* L19.
[ORIGIN French, from *grappe (de la chaux)* cluster (of lime).]
A hard lump of unslaked material left in hydraulic lime after slaking.
– COMB.: **grappier cement**: made by pulverizing grappiers.

grapple /ˈgrap(ə)l/ *noun.* ME.
[ORIGIN Branch I from Old French *grapil* from Provençal from *grapa* hook from Germanic base of GRAPE *noun*; branch II from the verb.]
▸ **I 1** A grappling iron. ME.
2 Any of various contrivances or implements for clutching and grasping. L16.
3 A small anchor with several flukes. *obsolete* exc. *dial.* E17.
▸ **II 4** The action or an act of grappling (*with*); the state of being grappled. Also, the grip or close hold (as) of a wrestler; a contest at close quarters. E17.

grapple /ˈgrap(ə)l/ *verb.* M16.
[ORIGIN from the noun.]
1 *verb trans.* Seize or hold with a grappling iron (*lit. & fig.*); fasten *to* something by this means. M16.

P. WARNER The English . . grappled their own boats to the French with hooks and chains. *Daily Telegraph* To locate the wreck, grapple it and fix its position. *fig.*: BURKE Never to be torn from thence, but with those holds that grapple it to life.

2 *verb intrans.* **a** Fasten oneself firmly (*to* an object) by means of a grapple (*lit. & fig.*). Now *rare.* M16. ▸**b** Foll. by *for*: seek to locate or retrieve by means of a grapnel. L18.

F. SMITH The Piece of Ice we grappled to had a Pond upon it.

3 *verb trans.* Take hold of with the hands; seize; grip firmly; come to close quarters with. L16.

T. PRINGLE Grappling its antagonist by the throat with its fore-paws. R. L. STEVENSON I've seen him grapple four, and knock their heads together.

4 *verb intrans.* Take a firm grip, esp. in wrestling; get a tight grip of another person or thing; contend in close fighting. L16.

P. PEARCE The two boys were grappling in real fight.

5 *verb intrans.* Make movements with the hands as if to grasp something; grope. Also foll. by *after*, *at*, *for*, *to*. Long *rare* exc. *Scot.* L16.

SIR W. SCOTT Their hands oft grappled to their swords.

– WITH PREPOSITIONS IN SPECIALIZED SENSES: **grapple with** (**a**) contend or struggle with, esp. at close quarters; (**b**) grip as in wrestling; seize with the hands and arms, close with bodily; (**c**) NAUTICAL make one's ship fast to (an enemy) with grappling irons; come to close quarters with; (**d**) *fig.* try to overcome, accomplish, or deal with.
■ **†grapplement** *noun* (*rare*) a grappling, a close grasp in fighting: only in L16. **grappler** *noun* (**a**) a person who or thing which grapples; *spec.* a grappling iron, a grapnel; (**b**) *slang* (*rare*) a hand: E17.

grappling /ˈgraplɪŋ/ *noun.* L16.
[ORIGIN from GRAPPLE *verb* + -ING[1].]
1 Orig. *collect.*, instruments for grappling. Now, a grappling iron (see below). Also = GRAPPLE *noun* 3. L16.
2 The action of GRAPPLE *verb.* E17.
†**3** A place where a vessel could be grappled. Only in 18.
– COMB.: **grappling hook**, **grappling iron** an iron-clawed instrument intended to be thrown with a rope attached in order to get a firm hold on an object such as a wall or an enemy ship, or to be used when dragging a river.

grapsoid /ˈgrapsɔɪd/ *adjective.* M19.
[ORIGIN from mod. Latin *Grapsus* (see below: cf. Greek *grapsaios* crab) + -OID.]
Of or pertaining to a large cosmopolitan family of crabs, Grapsidae, typified by the genus *Grapsus*, with a quadrilateral carapace.

graptolite /ˈgraptəlʌɪt/ *noun.* M19.
[ORIGIN from Greek *graptos* painted or marked with letters + -LITE; in sense 1 from mod. Latin *graptolithus*.]
†**1** A stone showing a resemblance to a drawing. Only in M19.
2 Any member of a group of fossil hemichordates, remains of which (esp. of their tubular skeletons) are widely distributed in rocks of Lower Palaeozoic age. M19.
■ **grapto'litic** *adjective* of or pertaining to graptolites (sense 2); rich in graptolite fossils: M19.

grapy *adjective* var. of GRAPEY.

grasp /grɑːsp/ *verb & noun.* LME.
[ORIGIN Uncertain: perh. ult. from Germanic base parallel to that of GROPE *verb*, or of Low German origin (cf. Low German, East Frisian *grapsen*).]
▸ **A** *verb* **1 a** *verb intrans.* Make clutches with the hand, grope, try (usu. successfully) to seize. Now only foll. by *at*: also *fig.*, accept eagerly or greedily. LME. ▸†**b** *verb intrans.* Grapple *with.* L16–M18. ▸**c** *verb trans.* Seize or clutch at greedily. M17.

a LD MACAULAY By grasping at too much, the government would lose all. **c** *absol.*: DRYDEN Like a miser 'midst his store, Who grasps and grasps 'till he can hold no more.

a grasp at a straw, ***grasp a straw***, ***grasp at straws***, ***grasp straws***: see STRAW *noun.*

2 *verb trans.* Seize and hold firmly (as) with the hand or fingers, grip. L16. ▸†**b** Clasp or hold firmly in or *in* the arms, embrace. E17–M18.

G. GREENE His small steely hand grasped hers, like one half of a handcuff. E. CALDWELL She was grasped by her arm and pulled into the hall.

grasp the nettle *fig.* tackle a difficulty or danger with courage or boldness.

3 *verb trans.* Get a mental hold of, comprehend fully. L17.

W. TREVOR He frowned, . . unable to grasp immediately what was being implied. P. ROTH I cannot grasp it—I don't understand what has happened *at all*.

▸ **B** *noun.* **1** Something that is fitted or designed to grasp or be grasped. Now only NAUTICAL, the handle of an oar. M16.
2 The action of grasping; a grip or firm hold; *fig.* control, mastery. Formerly also, an embrace. L16.

W. OWEN The burying-party, picks and shovels in their shaking grasp, Pause over half-known faces.

3 Mental hold; *esp.* comprehension, mastery (of a subject). L17.

J. ARCHER How well the French speak our language compared with our grasp of theirs.

– PHRASES: **beyond one's grasp** (**a**) out of one's reach or control; (**b**) beyond one's mental hold or comprehension. **within one's grasp** (**a**) close enough to be grasped; (**b**) within one's mental hold or comprehension.
■ **graspable** *adjective* (earlier in UNGRASPABLE) E19. **grasper** *noun* †(**a**) a grappling iron; (**b**) a person who or thing which grasps: M16. **grasping** *adjective* that grasps; *fig.* avaricious, greedy: LME. **graspingly** *adverb* M19. **graspingness** *noun* M18. **graspless** *adjective* (**a**) without grasp or grip; loose, relaxed; (**b**) unable to be grasped: L18.

grass /grɑːs/ *noun.*
[ORIGIN Old English *græs*, *gærs* = Old Frisian *gres*, *gers*, Old Saxon (Dutch), Old High German, German, Old Norse, Gothic *gras*, ult. from Germanic base of GREEN *adjective*, GROW *verb.*]
1 Herbage of which the blades or leaves and stalks are eaten by cattle, sheep, horses, etc.; low-growing plants (chiefly as in sense 4b below) blanketing the ground. OE. ▸**b** The blade stage of growth (formerly esp. of corn); young shoots esp. of the carnation. OE.

JONSON Her treading would not bend a blade of grasse! R. S. THOMAS The ewes starve Milkless, for want of the new grass.

cut the grass from under a person's feet foil or thwart a person. **not let the grass grow under one's feet** be quick to act or seize an opportunity.

2 Pasture or grazing, esp. as sufficient for the animal(s) specified; land on which grass is the permanent crop, pastureland. OE. ▸**b** The time or season when grass grows, spring and early summer; grazing time. Now *arch.* & *dial.* L15.

JAS. ROBERTSON They have not only a house, but . . a cow's grass to afford milk to their families. **b** M. R. MITFORD She is five years old this grass.

at grass at pasture. **out to grass**, **to grass**: to pasture; *fig.* redundant, in retirement, on holiday.

3 Grass-covered ground; a lawn in a public or private garden. ME. ▸**b** The ground (*slang*); MINING the earth's surface, the pithead. E17. ▸**c** A fuzzy appearance along the time baseline of a cathode-ray tube display due to random fluctuating deflections caused by electrical noise. M20.

DICKENS Two men . . seated in easy attitudes upon the grass.

keep off the grass *fig.* do not take liberties, interfere, encroach. **b go to grass** be knocked down. **send to grass** knock down.

4 †**a** A small herbaceous plant; a (medicinal) herb. ME–L16. ▸**b** Any of the plants which form grass (sense 1); *gen.* any plant of the large cosmopolitan family Gramineae (including cereals, reeds, and bamboos besides the characteristic plants of pastureland), members of which typically have erect jointed stems (culms) bearing narrow bladelike leaves and insignificant flowers. Also, any of various plants resembling the members of Gramineae in appearance. M16.
b ***arrowgrass***, ***bluegrass***, ***cotton grass***, ***couch grass***, ***crabgrass***, ***goose-grass***, ***hair grass***, ***knot-grass***, ***lemon grass***, ***meadow-grass***, ***pampas grass***, ***quaking grass***, ***ryegrass***, ***scurvy grass***, ***tore grass***, ***velvet grass***, etc. ***grass of Parnassus***: see PARNASSUS 2.
5 An individual plant of grass (formerly also, of corn). Long only in *pl.* LME.

B. EMECHETA They gave the . . white women long grasses tied together for sweeping.

6 = SPARROW GRASS. Now *arch.* & *dial.* M18.
7 Marijuana, esp. as smoked. *slang* (orig. *US*). M20.
8 A police informer. Cf. GRASSER. *slang.* M20.

G. F. NEWMAN All the while the grass offered him information he'd get whatever immunity Pyle could give him.

– COMB.: **grassbird** any of various birds associated with grass; *spec.* (**a**) a southern African warbler, *Sphenoeacus afer* (more fully ***Cape grassbird***); (**b**) any of a number of Australasian warblers of the genus *Megalurus*; **grass box** the receptacle on a lawnmower for collecting the cut grass; **grass carp** a Far Eastern river fish, *Ctenopharyngodon idella*, sometimes introduced to control aquatic vegetation, on which it feeds; **grasscloth** a cloth resembling linen, woven from ramie etc.; **grass-comber** NAUTICAL (*arch.*, *derog.*) a landlubber, esp. a farmworker; **grass court** a grass-covered tennis court; **grass-finch** any of various finches associated with grassland, *esp.* of the Australian genus *Poephila*; **grass frog** the common frog, *Rana temporaria*, esp. as found in Continental Europe and Asia; **grass hockey** *Canad.* hockey played on grass, as opp. to ***ice hockey***; **grass hook** a sickle for cutting grass; **grassland** (an area of) land covered with grass, esp. as used for grazing; **grass moth** any of numerous small pyralid moths of the subfamily Crambinae, whose larvae feed on grasses; **grass parakeet**, **grass parrot** *Austral.* any of various small parrots frequenting grassland, esp. of the genus *Neophema*; **grass pea** (the edible seed of) a leguminous plant, *Lathyrus sativus*, cultivated esp. as a fodder crop in the Middle East and Indian subcontinent; **grass-plat**, **grass-plot** a piece of ground covered with turf, sometimes ornamented with flower beds; ***grass poly***: see POLY *noun*[1] 2; **grassquit** any of various neotropical finches of the genera *Tiaris*, *Volatinia*, and *Loxipasser*; **grass roots** *fig.* (**a**) the fundamental level or source; (**b**) the ordinary people as representative of a basic viewpoint etc.; *esp.* in POLITICS, the voters themselves; **grass sickness** an equine disease which can occur when a horse is put on to certain pastures and is usu. fatal; **grass ski** a short ski mounted on wheels or rollers used for skiing down grass- or straw-covered slopes; **grass skiing** skiing with grass skis; **grass skirt**: made of long grass and leaves fastened to a waistband, orig. worn by the hula dancers of some Pacific islands; **grass snake** any of various colubrid snakes; *esp.* (**a**) a common Eurasian snake, *Natrix natrix*, generally greenish brown or greenish grey with a yellow collar; (**b**) *N. Amer.* the smooth green snake, *Opheodrys vernalis*; (**c**) *S. Afr.* either of two spotted or striped mildly venomous snakes of the genus *Psammophylax*; **grass staggers**, **grass tetany** VETERINARY MEDICINE a disease of livestock caused by magnesium deficiency, occurring esp. when there is a change from indoor feeding to outdoor grazing; **grass tree** any of various Australasian woody plants with grasslike leaves in tufts at the top of the trunk; *esp.* (**a**) *Austral.* = ***blackboy*** (b) s.v. BLACK *adjective*; (**b**) *NZ* the cabbage tree, *Cordyline australis*; **grass warbler** *Austral.* the gold-capped fantail warbler, *Cisticola exilis*; **grass-wrack** eelgrass, zostera; **grass-wren** any of several Australian wrens of the genus *Amytornis* (family Maluridae).
■ **grasslike** *adjective* resembling (that of) grass L17.

grass /grɑːs/ *verb.* LME.
[ORIGIN from the noun Cf. GRAZE *verb*[1].]
1 *verb trans.* & (now *rare*) *intrans.* Cover or become covered with grass. LME.

T. HARDY The gardeners were beginning to grass down the front. C. THUBRON The vegetable plots . . . were grassed in years ago.

2 *verb trans.* Provide with pasture; (of land) yield enough grass for. Formerly also, graze (cattle etc.). L15.
3 *verb trans.* Spread out (flax etc.) on the grass or ground for bleaching. M18.
4 *verb trans.* Put down on the grass; *esp.* knock or bring down, fell (an opponent). E19. ▸**b** Bring (a fish) to bank; bring down (game) by a shot. M19.

Times In Rugby football . . players were not tackled but grassed.

5 *verb intrans.* PRINTING. Of a compositor: do casual work. L19.
6 *verb trans.* & *intrans.* (with *on*). Betray (someone); inform the police about (someone). *slang.* M20.

J. R. ACKERLEY So it looked bad for me, like as if I'd grassed 'im. F. DHONDY The Kray brothers hired a tank to attack a lad that grassed on them.

■ **grassed** *adjective* (**a**) covered with grass; †(**b**) GOLF (of a club or driver) with a slightly filed-back face: LME. **grasser** *noun* (*slang*) = GRASS *noun* 6 M20. **grassing** *noun* (**a**) the action of the verb; an instance of such action; (**b**) *Scot.* the privilege of grazing in a particular place; the place for grazing or cutting turfs: E16.

†**grassant** *adjective.* M17–M18.
[ORIGIN Latin *grassant-* pres. ppl stem of *grassari* lie in wait: see -ANT[1].]
Roaming about or lurking with evil intent.

grasserie /ˈgras(ə)riː/ *noun.* M19.
[ORIGIN French, from *gras* fat.]
A virus disease of silkworms, characterized by yellowing of the skin and liquefaction of the internal tissues.

grass-green /grɑːsˈgriːn, ˈgrɑːsgriːn/ *adjective & noun.* OE.
[ORIGIN from GRASS *noun* + GREEN *adjective.*]
▸ **A** *adjective.* **1** Green as grass; of the colour of grass. OE.
2 Green with grass. E17.

TENNYSON Two graves grass-green beside a gray church-tower.

▸ **B** *noun.* The colour of grass. M17.

G

G

†**grasshop** *noun.* OE–E17.
[ORIGIN Old English *gærshoppa*, *-e*, Orm *gresshoppe* (from *gærs* GRASS *noun* + *hoppa*, agent noun of *hoppian* HOP *verb*¹), perh. after Old Swedish *gräshoppare* or Low German *grashüpper* (German *Grashüpfer*); cf. synon. Old Saxon *feldhoppo*.]
A grasshopper, a locust.

grasshopper /ˈɡrɑːshɒpə/ *noun & verb.* LME.
[ORIGIN Extended form of GRASSHOP.]
▸ **A** *noun.* **1** Any orthopterous insect of the families Acrididae (locusts) and Tettigoniidae (bush crickets), characterized by having legs adapted for jumping and the ability of the males to make chirping sounds. LME. **knee-high to a grasshopper** *colloq.* very small or very young.
2 *fig.* A person held to resemble a grasshopper in character or behaviour; an inconstant, flighty, or frivolous person. L16.
3 MUSIC. = HOPPER *noun*¹ 8. E19.
4 An artificial bait for fish. M19.
5 = COPPER *noun*². *rhyming slang.* L19.

B. BEHAN Put the paper inside your shirt, so . . that old bastard of a grass-'opper won't tumble it.

6 WATCHMAKING. More fully ***grasshopper escapement***. A type of recoil escapement equipped with springs and requiring no lubrication. L19.
7 A small light aircraft for observation or liaison. *US slang.* M20.
– COMB.: **grasshopper escapement**: see sense 6 above; **grasshopper mouse** any of a number of mice of the genus *Onychomys*, native to N. America and Mexico; **grasshopper sparrow** a N. and Central American sparrow, *Ammodramus savannarum*; **grasshopper warbler** any of various warblers of the genus *Locustella*, spec. *L. naevia*, characterized by prolonged buzzing calls.
▸ **B** *verb intrans.* **1** Live in a frivolous, improvident manner. E19.

A. GILBERT [We] enjoy ourselves . . by working. We shouldn't get any fun out of grasshoppering.

2 Of a riverboat: move *over* sandbars or shallow waters with the aid of poles. *US.* L19.
3 Jump like a grasshopper. Chiefly *fig.* M20.

J. FOWLES My mind travelled up to the Bonnards, and grasshoppered from them to Alison.

■ **grasshoppery** *adjective* like a grasshopper E20.

grassless /ˈɡrɑːslɪs/ *adjective.* LME.
[ORIGIN from GRASS *noun* + -LESS.]
Without grass, bare of grass.

Grassmann's law /ˈɡrɑːsmənz lɔː/ *noun phr.* L19.
[ORIGIN Hermann *Grassmann* (1809–77), German mathematician and polymath.]
A phonetic law stating that where two aspirated plosives occurred in neighbouring syllables in Indo-European, dissimilation took place and the first of the two lost its aspiration in Greek and Sanskrit.

grassum *noun* see GERSUM.

grass widow /ɡrɑːs ˈwɪdəʊ/ *noun phr.* E16.
[ORIGIN from GRASS *noun* + WIDOW *noun*¹. Cf. Middle Low German *graswedewe*, Dutch *grasweduwe*, Swedish *gräsenka*, Danish *graesenke*; also German *Strohwitwe* 'straw widow'.]
1 An unmarried woman who has cohabited with one or more men, or has had an illegitimate child. *obsolete* exc. *dial.* E16.
2 A woman living apart from her husband (temporarily or permanently). M19.
■ **grass widower** *noun phr.* a man living apart from his wife (temporarily or permanently) M19. **grass-widowhood** *noun* L19.

grassy /ˈɡrɑːsi/ *adjective.* LME.
[ORIGIN from GRASS *noun* + -Y¹.]
1 Covered with grass, having much grass. LME.

D. H. LAWRENCE The upper road is all grassy, fallen into long disuse.

the grassy knoll [with ref. to the supposed location of a second gunman in conspiracy theories of the assassination of US President John F. Kennedy (1963)] a location for a clandestine criminal act or conspiracy.
2 Resembling grass in colour, form, or smell. M16.

H. CRANE A marvelous stillness and grassy perfume pervade the district.

3 Of or pertaining to grass; consisting of or containing grass. E17.
■ **grassiness** *noun* E18.

grate /ɡreɪt/ *noun.* ME.
[ORIGIN Old French, or Spanish *grada* hurdle, corresp. to Italian *grata* grate, gridiron, hurdle (cf. medieval Latin *grata* hurdle), perh from Proto-Romance from Latin *cratis*.]
1 = GRATING *noun*² 1. Now chiefly *N. Amer.* ME.

K. KESEY And got his finger stuck . . in the grate . . over the drain at the bottom of the pool.

2 The railing round a monument, building, etc. *obsolete* exc. *hist.* LME.
†**3** A (barred) prison or cage (for people or animals). M16–L18.

J. HOWARD Every debtor that lies in the common grate.

4 A frame of metal bars for holding the fuel in the recess of a fireplace or furnace; the fireplace itself. E17.

G. CHARLES Whoever sees a fire these days; real living flames? You hardly see a grate any more!

5 MINING. = GRATING *noun*² 2. L18.

†**grate** *adjective.* E16.
[ORIGIN Latin *gratus*. Cf. earlier INGRATE.]
1 Pleasing, agreeable. E16–M17.
2 Thankful, grateful. M–L16.

grate /ɡreɪt/ *verb*¹. LME.
[ORIGIN Old French *grater* (mod. *gratter*) from Proto-Romance, from Germanic (rel. to Old High German *krazzōn*, German *kratzen* scratch).]
1 *verb trans.* Scrape, file, abrade; wear *away*, *down*, *to nothing*, etc., by abrasion. Now *rare.* LME.

T. NASHE Some of them have grated . . theyr smooth tender skinnes, with hayre shirts.

2 *verb trans.* Reduce (esp. food) to small particles by rubbing against a grater. LME.

G. H. NAPHEYS A little nutmeg grated over the surface. J. AIKEN They were all on a low diet of lemon-juice, olives, grated carrot and tomatoes.

†**3 a** *verb trans.* Cause (a weapon) to strike *on*. Only in LME. ▸**b** *verb intrans.* Of a weapon: strike. E16–L17.
†**4** *verb intrans.* Dwell querulously or harp (*up*)*on* a subject. M16–L17.
5 *verb trans.* Affect painfully, as if by abrasion; irritate, annoy. Now *rare.* M16.

W. BLACKSTONE With sounds uncouth, and accents dry, That grate the soul of harmony.

6 *verb intrans.* Have an irritating effect (*on*, *upon*). Formerly also, oppress with exactions (*up*)*on*. M16.

L. DURRELL The falseness of his gestures . . grated disagreeably. A. CARTER The voices that grated daily on her nerves.

7 *verb trans.* Make a harsh grinding noise by rubbing against (something) roughly; grind (the teeth). Also, utter in a harsh voice. M16.

SPENSER Thereat the feend his gnashing teeth did grate. KEATS His galley now Grated the quay-stones. G. GREENE She . . grated a greeting in a voice full of discords.

8 *verb intrans.* Rub *against*, *upon*, etc., with a harsh, grinding noise; move creakingly; make a harsh noise. L16.

A. RADCLIFFE A Key grated in the lock. TENNYSON Lest the harsh shingle should grate underfoot.

■ **gratingly** *adverb* in a grating manner L17.

grate /ɡreɪt/ *verb*². Now *rare* or *obsolete.* LME.
[ORIGIN from GRATE *noun*.]
Provide with a grate or grating. Formerly also, confine behind bars.

EVELYN A well . . grated over with iron.

grateful /ˈɡreɪtfʊl, -f(ə)l/ *adjective.* M16.
[ORIGIN from GRATE *adjective* + -FUL.]
1 Feeling gratitude; actuated by or showing gratitude; thankful. M16.

LYNDON B. JOHNSON I told him how grateful I was for his counsel and his support.

2 Pleasing, agreeable, *arch.* welcome. M16.

E. DARK Two trees gave a sparse but grateful shade.

■ **gratefully** *adverb* M16. **gratefulness** *noun* L16.

grater /ˈɡreɪtə/ *noun.* LME.
[ORIGIN Partly from Old French *grateor*, *-our*, partly from GRATE *verb*¹: see -ER¹, -ER².]
1 An instrument with a rough surface for grating or scraping; *spec.* a kitchen utensil with a rasping surface formed by sharp protuberances, used for grating cheese, carrot, nutmeg, etc. LME.
†**2** A person who or thing which grates. Chiefly *fig.* LME–E17.

†**gratia dei** *noun phr.* LME.
[ORIGIN medieval Latin = grace of God.]
1 Any of various medicinal herbs; *esp.* hedge hyssop, *Gratiola officinalis.* LME–M19.
2 A salve or plaster. LME–M17.

graticulation /ɡrətɪkjʊˈleɪʃ(ə)n/ *noun.* E18.
[ORIGIN French, from *graticuler* divide into squares, formed as GRATICULE: see -ATION.]
The drawing or provision of a network of lines or graticule on a surface; such a network, a graticule.

graticule /ˈɡratɪkjuːl/ *noun.* L19.
[ORIGIN French from medieval Latin *graticula* for (also classical Latin) *craticula* small gridiron, dim. of Latin *cratis* hurdle.]
1 A network of lines representing meridians and parallels, on which a map or plan can be represented. L19.
2 A series of fine lines or fibres incorporated in a telescope or other optical instrument as a measuring scale or an aid in locating objects; a plate etc. bearing this. E20.

gratification /ˌɡratɪfɪˈkeɪʃ(ə)n/ *noun.* L16.
[ORIGIN Old French & mod. French, or Latin *gratificatio(n-)*, from *gratificat-* pa. ppl stem of *gratificari*: see GRATIFY, -ATION.]
1 The action of gratifying, satisfaction; the giving of pleasure or doing of a favour. L16. ▸**b** The satisfaction or indulgence of, or compliance with a feeling, desire, etc. E17.

H. T. BUCKLE Men, in the pursuit of wealth, consider their own gratification oftener than the gratification of others. **b** E. STILLINGFLEET The pleasure of humane life lies in the gratifications of the senses.

2 Something given to gain favour; a reward, recompense, gratuity; a bribe. Now *rare.* L16.

LD MACAULAY Six thousand guineas was the smallest gratification that could be offered.

3 The state of being gratified or pleased; enjoyment, satisfaction. E18. ▸**b** An instance of being gratified; a thing that gratifies; a source of pleasure or gratification. Usu. in *pl.* E18.

A. STORR He obtains gratification from having a number of patients who turn to him. **b** S. JOHNSON That insatiable demand of new gratifications, which seems . . to characterize the nature of man.

gratify /ˈɡratɪfʌɪ/ *verb trans.* LME.
[ORIGIN French *gratifier*, or its source Latin *gratificari* do a favour to, make a present of, from *gratus* GRATE *adjective* + -I- + -FY.]
†**1** Make pleasing or acceptable; grace. LME–L17.
2 Reward, esp. financially, (a person, a service, etc.); recompense, remunerate; bribe. Formerly also, show gratitude to or for. *arch.* M16.

W. S. CHURCHILL His rewards were princely; . . and the chief personalities were gratified with rich presents.

†**3** Express pleasure at, welcome. M16–E17.
4 Please, satisfy; oblige; *esp.* please by compliance; give free rein to, indulge, satisfy (a feeling, desire, etc.). M16.

W. CATHER It gratified him to hear these gentlemen admire his fine stock. E. TEMPLETON It is always gratifying to have one's suspicions confirmed by others. D. CECIL It is clear that Jane Austen enjoyed . . a chance to gratify her taste and talent for nonsense and comic fantasy.

■ **gratifier** *noun* M16. **gratifyingly** *adverb* in a gratifying manner E19.

†**gratility** *noun. rare. joc.* E17–E19.
[ORIGIN Alt. of GRATUITY.]
= GRATUITY.

gratin /ˈɡratã, *foreign* ɡratɛ̃ (*pl. same*)/ *noun.* M17.
[ORIGIN French, from *gratter*, earlier *grater* GRATE *verb*¹.]
1 A method of cooking, or a dish cooked, with a crisp brown crust, usu. of grated cheese or breadcrumbs. Cf. AU GRATIN. M17.
2 The highest class of society. M20.

S. PAKENHAM One of the most famous Paris salons, where all but the very highest gratin of the French nobility congregates.

gratiné /ɡratine (*pl. same*), ˈɡratɪneɪ/ *noun & adjective.* Also ***-ée***. E20.
[ORIGIN French, pa. ppl adjective of *gratiner* cook *au gratin*.]
COOKERY. (A dish) cooked with a crisp topping or stuffing of breadcrumbs or grated cheese.
■ ***gratinéed*** *adjective* = GRATINÉ *adjective* L20.

grating /ˈɡreɪtɪŋ/ *noun*¹. LME.
[ORIGIN from GRATE *verb*¹ + -ING¹.]
1 The action of breaking something into small particles by rasping or rubbing; the product of this. LME.
2 The action of rasping against something; a harsh grinding noise so produced; *fig.* irritation. E17.

grating /ˈɡreɪtɪŋ/ *noun*². E17.
[ORIGIN from GRATE *noun* + -ING¹.]
1 A framework of parallel or crossed bars, usu. preventing access through an opening while permitting communication, ventilation, the draining away of liquid, etc. Formerly esp. NAUTICAL, an open woodwork cover for the hatchway. E17.

F. RAPHAEL The only fresh air came from a window which opened up to a pavement grating. B. BAINBRIDGE The first time I saw him through a grating in the door.

2 MINING. A perforated plate used for separating large from small ore. M19.
3 OPTICS. A set of equally spaced parallel wires, or a surface ruled with equally spaced parallel lines, used to produce spectra by diffraction. Also ***diffraction grating***. L19.

gratiola /ɡrəˈtʌɪələ/ *noun.* L16.
[ORIGIN mod. Latin, from *gratia* grace. Cf. GRATIA DEI.]
Hedge hyssop, *Gratiola officinalis*; a medicinal preparation of this. Now only as mod. Latin genus name.

gratis /ˈɡratɪs, ˈɡrɑː-, ˈɡreɪ-/ *adverb & adjective.* LME.
[ORIGIN Latin *gratis* contr. of *gratiis* out of favour or kindness, abl. pl. of *gratia* grace, favour.]
▸ **A** *adverb.* **1** Freely, for nothing, without return made or expected; without charge, cost, or pay. LME.

E. JONES Take low fees, treat a good many people gratis. A. BEATTIE On Fridays a second drink [was] provided gratis with the last one you ordered.

free, gratis, and for nothing: see FREE *adverb*.
†2 Without a reason; gratuitously, unjustifiably. L16–E19.
▸ **B** *adjective*. Given or done for nothing; free; gratuitous. M17.

E. TEMPLETON I once saw him . . squeeze out a gratis consultation.

gratitude /ˈgratɪtjuːd/ *noun*. LME.
[ORIGIN French, or Latin *gratitudo*, formed as GRATE *adjective*: see -TUDE. Cf. earlier INGRATITUDE.]
1 The quality or condition of being grateful or thankful; the appreciation of and inclination to return kindness; gratefulness. LME. ▸**b** An instance or expression of gratefulness. Long *rare*. LME.

N. EZEKIEL Express your gratitude By giving what you have to give. B. EMECHETA Every living being had to be able to contribute something, . . in gratitude for being alive.

2 A gift, gratuity, or reward; *esp.* (*Scot.*) a grant of money made to the monarch. Long *rare*. L15.
†**3** Grace; a favour. Chiefly *Scot*. E–M16.

grattage /grəˈtɑːʒ/ *noun*. L19.
[ORIGIN French = scraping.]
SURGERY. The scraping or rubbing of a surface to remove excessive granulation tissue and promote healing.

grattoir /ˈgratwɑː/ *noun*. L19.
[ORIGIN French = stratcher, scraper.]
ARCHAEOLOGY. = ***end-scraper*** s.v. END *noun*.

gratuitous /grəˈtjuːɪtəs/ *adjective*. M17.
[ORIGIN (Old French *gratuiteus*, French †-*eux*) from Latin *gratuitus* freely given, spontaneous: see -OUS.]
1 Given or obtained for nothing; not earned or paid for; free. M17.

R. L'ESTRANGE We are given to Mistake the Gratuitous Blessings of Heaven, for the Fruits of our Own Industry. G. S. HAIGHT Except for her teaching, which was gratuitous, Marian had not found the literary work she was hoping for.

2 Uncalled for, unwarranted, unjustifiable; done or acting without a good or assignable reason; motiveless. L17.

Daily Telegraph I should be held up to execration as . . a gratuitous liar. P. GAY Killing animals for sport . . came to seem gratuitous, coarse, indecent, inhuman.

■ **gratuitously** *adverb* L17. **gratuitousness** *noun* E18.

gratuity /grəˈtjuːɪti/ *noun*. L15.
[ORIGIN Old French *gratuité* or medieval Latin *gratuitas* gift, formed as GRATE *adjective*: see -ITY.]
†**1** Graciousness, favour; *esp.* God's grace or favour; a favour, a kindness. L15–M17.
2 A gift (usu. of money) of an amount decided by the giver. Now usu. = TIP *noun*[5]. M16. ▸†**b** Payment, wages. M17–M19.

OED The attendants . . are forbidden to receive gratuities.

3 A bounty given to service personnel on discharge etc. E19.

W. S. CHURCHILL The subject of gratuities and other release benefits for members of the Forces.

4 Gratuitousness. *rare*. M19.

gratulant /ˈgratjʊl(ə)nt/ *adjective*. *rare*. L15.
[ORIGIN Latin *gratulant-* pres. ppl stem of *gratulari*: see GRATULATE *verb*, -ANT[1].]
Pleased, joyful, satisfied; congratulatory.

†**gratulate** *adjective*. *rare*. L15–E17.
[ORIGIN Latin *gratulatus* pa. pple of *gratulari*: see GRATULATE *verb*, -ATE[2].]
Pleasing, to be rejoiced at.

gratulate /ˈgratjʊleɪt/ *verb trans*. Now *arch.* or *poet.* M16.
[ORIGIN Latin *gratulat-* pa. ppl stem of *gratulari*, formed as GRATE *adjective*: see -ATE[3].]
1 Welcome, hail; greet joyfully, salute. M16.
2 = CONGRATULATE *verb* 1, 2a. L16.
†**3** Be grateful or show gratitude for or to. L16–L17.
†**4** Gratify, please. L16–E19.

gratulation /gratjʊˈleɪʃ(ə)n/ *noun*. Now *arch.* or *poet.* L15.
[ORIGIN Old French, or Latin *gratulatio(n-)*, formed as GRATULATE *verb*: see -ATION.]
1 A feeling of gratification or joy, inward rejoicing. Now with mixture of sense 4 below, self-congratulation. L15.
†**2** (An) expression of gratitude. L15–L17.
3 Expression of delight; an instance of expressing delight. M16.
4 (A) compliment, felicitation, or congratulation. M16.
†**5** A welcome; a joyful greeting. L16–M17.

gratulatory /ˈgratjʊlət(ə)ri/ *adjective*. M16.
[ORIGIN Late Latin *gratulatorius*, formed as GRATULATE *verb*: see -ORY[2].]
†**1** Expressing gratitude; thankful. M16–M18.
2 Congratulatory, complimentary. L16.
■ **gratulatorily** *adverb* E17.

graunch /grɔːn(t)ʃ/ *verb & noun*. *colloq.* (orig. *dial.* & *NZ*). L19.
[ORIGIN Imit.]
▸ **A** *verb trans. & intrans.* (Cause to) make a crunching or grinding noise, esp. with resulting damage; damage (a mechanism) thus. L19.

Observer Many people graunch their gears.

▸ **B** *noun*. A crunching or grinding sound, esp. one associated with damage. M20.

Autosport An ominous graunch came from the rear wheel.

graupel /ˈgraʊp(ə)l/ *noun*. L19.
[ORIGIN German.]
METEOROLOGY. Soft hail, small snow pellets with a fragile ice crust.

Grauwacke *noun* see GREYWACKE.

gravadlax *noun* var. of GRAVLAX.

gravamen /grəˈveɪmɛn/ *noun*. Pl. **-mens**, **-mina** /-mɪnə/. E17.
[ORIGIN Late Latin *gravamen* physical inconvenience, (in medieval Latin) grievance, from Latin *gravare* weigh on, oppress, from *gravis* GRAVE *adjective*[1].]
1 a In the Anglican Church, a memorial from the Lower House of Convocation to the Upper House representing the existence of disorders and grievances within the Church. E17. ▸†**b** A formal complaint or accusation. M17–L19.
2 A grievance. M17.
3 The essential or most serious part of an accusation; the part that bears most heavily on the accused. M19.

†**gravaminous** *adjective*. M17–E19.
[ORIGIN from Latin *gravamen*, *-min-* (see GRAVAMEN) + -OUS.]
Grievous, annoying, distressing.

†**gravative** *adjective*. L16–E18.
[ORIGIN from Latin *gravare*: see GRAVAMEN, -ATIVE.]
MEDICINE. Designating a sensation of pain accompanied by that of pressure.

grave /greɪv/ *noun*[1].
[ORIGIN Old English *græf* = Old Frisian *gref*, Old Saxon *graf*, Old High German *grap* (German *Grab*), from West Germanic, parallel to North Germanic & East Germanic base repr. by Old Norse *grǫf*, Gothic *graba*; ult. from base of GRAVE *verb*[1].]
1 A place of burial; an excavation made to receive a corpse; the monument etc. raised over it. Formerly also, a mausoleum or the like. OE. ▸**b** A grave mound. M19.

H. ASQUITH A skull, torn out of the graves nearby. M. MITCHELL The new grave lying by the three short mounds of her little brothers.

bloody grave: see BLOODY *adjective & adverb*. **dig the grave of** *fig.* cause the downfall of. ***have one foot in the grave***: see FOOT *noun*. **secret as the grave** kept as a close secret. **someone walking on my grave** an explanation of an otherwise unaccountable shivering. **turn in one's grave** (of a deceased person) supposedly react thus through extreme outrage at an action or an event. ***watery grave***: see WATERY 7.

2 The condition or state of being buried; the state of being dead; death. LME.

SWIFT I shall carry the Mark to my Grave. A. MASON Those who put their faith in Joshua's return from the grave would themselves survive death.

on this side of the grave, ***on this side the grave***: see SIDE *noun*.

3 An excavation of any kind; a pit, a trench. Now chiefly *Scot.* E16.
4 Anything that is, or may become, a receptacle for what is dead. Freq. with specifying word. M16.

C. KINGSLEY They had only just escaped a watery grave.

grave of reputations a place where many reputations have been lost. ***White man's grave***: see WHITE *adjective*.
– COMB.: **grave-cloth** a pall; **grave-clothes** the clothes or wrappings in which a corpse is buried; **gravedigger** (**a**) a person who digs graves, esp. as a form of employment (*lit.* & *fig.*); (**b**) *colloq.* an insect that buries prey or carrion in the ground as food for its larvae; *esp.* a burying beetle; **grave goods** (esp. valuable) objects deposited with corpses in ancient graves; **grave mound** a hillock constructed over the site of an interment; **graveside** the edge of a grave; the ground immediately adjacent to a grave; **gravestone** a stone placed at the mouth of a tomb or over a grave; *esp.* an inscribed headstone; **grave-trap** THEATRICAL a trap-door sited approximately in the centre of the stage.
■ **graveless** *adjective* E17. **graveward** *adjective & adverb* (leading) towards the grave M19. **gravewards** *adverb* graveward L19.

grave /greɪv/ *noun*[2]. ME.
[ORIGIN Sense 1 from Old Norse *greifi* from Old Low German *grēve*; sense 2 from Old Low German *grēve* rel. to Middle High German *grâve* (German GRAF).]
1 Orig., a steward. Later, each of a number of elected administrative officials in townships in certain parts of Yorkshire and Lincolnshire. *obsolete* exc. *hist.* ME.
2 A foreign nobleman, a count; *spec.* a Count of Nassau. Earlier and now only as 2nd elem. in ***burgrave***, ***landgrave***, ***margrave***, etc. E17.

grave /greɪv/; *in sense 5 and as noun* grɑːv/ *adjective*[1] *& noun*[3]. L15.
[ORIGIN Old French & mod. French, or Latin *gravis* heavy, important.]
▸ **A** *adjective*. †**1** Of a wound: serious, severe. (Cf. sense 6b below.) Only in L15.
2 Physically ponderous, heavy. Long *arch.* or *poet. rare*. E16.

WORDSWORTH The mountains against the heaven's grave weight Rise up.

3 Dignified in behaviour or delivery; solemn; serious as opp. to mirthful or jocular. E16. ▸**b** Expressive of or befitting serious feelings; solemn, serious; slow-moving. L16.

G. BERKELEY The nation ought to be too grave for such trifles. I. MURDOCH His grave frowning gaze betrayed weighty thoughts. **b** DICKENS The children had ancient faces and grave voices.

†**4** Of people, their writings, etc.: having weight or importance; influential; respected; authoritative. M16–M18.

SHAKES. *Coriol.* Most reverend and grave elders.

5 Of a sound: low-pitched, deep (PHONETICS a classificatory feature opp. ***acute***). M16.

A. BEDFORD The Verse was also mixt with acute and grave Sounds.

grave accent the mark ` placed over letters in some languages to show quality, vowel length, pronunciation, etc.

6 Of a matter: weighty, significant; requiring serious consideration. M16. ▸**b** Of a fault, difficulty, responsibility: highly serious, formidable. Of a symptom: threatening a serious or fatal outcome. E19.

SIR W. SCOTT When our council is assembled, we will treat of graver matters. **b** OED Grave news from the front.

7 Of dress, colour, etc.: sombre, plain; not striking or showy. L16.

GEO. ELIOT The folds of his . . garment . . hang in grave unbroken lines from neck to ankle.

▸ **B** *noun*. A grave accent. Formerly also, a grave note. E17.
■ **gravely** *adverb* in a grave manner M16. **graveness** *noun* the quality or state of being grave, sobriety, gravity: L16.

grave /greɪv/ *verb*[1]. Pa. t. **graved**; pa. pple **graven** /ˈgreɪv(ə)n/, **graved**.
[ORIGIN Old English *grafan* strong verb (also in *begrafan* bury) = Old Low Frankish *gravan* (Dutch *graven*) dig, Old High German *graban* dig, carve (German *graben* dig, *begraben* bury), Old Norse *grafa* dig, bury, Gothic *graban* dig, from Germanic: cf. GRAVE *noun*[1], GROOVE *noun*.]
▸ **I 1** *verb intrans.* Dig. *obsolete* exc. *dial.* OE.
2 *verb trans.* Dig (out), excavate; form by digging. Also foll. by *out*, *up*, †*away*. Long *rare* exc. *dial.* OE.

COVERDALE *Jer.* 18:14 Maye the springes off waters be grauen awaye.

▸ **II 3** *verb trans.* Form by carving; carve; sculpt. *obsolete* exc. *poet.* OE.

MILTON Affirming it thy Star new graven in Heaven. H. PHILLIPS I graved for thee a silver god.

†**4** *verb trans.* Cut into (a hard material) (*lit.* & *fig.*). Also, mark by incisions; ornament by incised marks; engrave. ME–L17.

SHAKES. *Ven. & Ad.* Being steel'd, soft sighs can never grave it [thy heart].

5 *verb trans.* Engrave (an inscription, figure, etc.) on a surface; engrave (a surface) *with* letters etc. Also, record by engraved or incised letters. *arch.* ME. ▸**b** *fig.* Impress deeply, fix indelibly (*on*, *in* the mind etc.). LME.

R. D. BLACKMORE My name . . graven on that very form. C. BOWEN Graved on the doors is the death of Androgeos.

†**6** *verb trans.* Portray or copy in an engraving. M17–E19.
▸ **III 7** *verb trans.* Deposit (a corpse) in the ground or in a tomb; bury; inter. Long *arch.* ME. ▸†**b** Deposit or hide underground. Only in ME. ▸†**c** Swallow up (as) in a grave. ME–E17.

J. GRANT Dead too and graved in yonder kirk. **c** SHAKES. *Timon* Ditches grave you all!

grave /greɪv/ *verb*[2] *trans.* LME.
[ORIGIN Prob. from dial. French *grave* (Old French = GRAVEL *noun*), var. of Old French & mod. French *grève* shore from Celtic base = gravel, pebbles, repr. by Breton *grouan* GROWAN.]
Clean (a ship's bottom) by burning off accretions and tarring while aground or in dry dock. Now *hist.* exc. in ***graving dock*** s.v. DOCK *noun*[3].

grave /grɑːv, ˈgrɑːveɪ/ *adverb & adjective*[2]. L16.
[ORIGIN French or Italian, = GRAVE *adjective*[1].]
MUSIC. A direction: with slow and solemn movement.

†**gravedo** *noun*. E18–L19.
[ORIGIN Latin = heaviness (in the limbs or head), from *gravis* heavy.]
MEDICINE. A cold in the head; coryza.

gravel /ˈgrav(ə)l/ *noun*. ME.
[ORIGIN Old French *gravel* masc., *gravel(l)e* fem., dim. of Old French *grave* gravel, coarse sand: see GRAVE *verb*[2], -EL[2].]
†**1** Sand. ME–E18.
2 Coarse sand and small water-worn or pounded stones, sometimes with an intermixture of clay, used for laying paths and roads. ME. ▸**b** A stratum of this; formerly *esp.* one containing gold. M19.
3 MEDICINE. Aggregations of visible calculi in the urinary tract; a disease marked by these. LME.

G

– COMB.: **gravel-blind** *adjective* almost completely blind (orig. *joc.* 'more than sand-blind', with reference to Shakes. *Merch. V.*); **gravel court** a tennis court with a surface of gravel; **gravel culture** a hydroponic method of plant cultivation, using beds of gravel supplied with nutrient solutions; **gravel pit** an excavation from which gravel is or has been obtained; **gravel-rash** abrasions caused by a fall on a gravelly or rough surface; **gravel voice** a deep rough-sounding voice; **gravel-voiced** *adjective* having a gravel voice; **gravel-walk** an alley or path laid with gravel.
■ **gravelish** *adjective* M16.

gravel /ˈgrav(ə)l/ *verb trans.* Infl. **-ll-**, *-**l-**. LME.
[ORIGIN from the noun.]
1 Lay or cover (a path etc.) with gravel or sand. Freq. (earlier) as ***gravelled*** *ppl adjective.* LME. ▸†**b** Choke or block (*up*) with gravel or sand. Only in 17.
2 *fig.* Bring to a standstill, confound, embarrass, nonplus, perplex, puzzle. Also (chiefly *US & dial.*), irritate, be uncongenial to. M16.

R. BURNS These English songs gravel me to death. E. P. WHIPPLE We might hear . . Sophocles gravel a sophist with his interrogative logic.

†**3** Bury in gravel or sand; overwhelm with gravel; *fig.* suppress, stifle. L16–L17.
†**4** Run (a ship) aground. Usu. in *pass.* L16–L17.

fig.: J. HEALEY Graueled in the quick-sands of erroneous ignorance.

5 Cause (a horse) to suffer from gravelling (see below). Usu. in *pass.* L16.
6 ***gravelled voice***, = ***gravel voice*** s.v. GRAVEL *noun.* M20.
■ **graveller** *noun* (*rare*) something which perplexes or puzzles, a 'poser' L17.

gravelling /ˈgrav(ə)lɪŋ/ *noun*[1]. Also **graveling**. E16.
[ORIGIN from GRAVEL *verb* + -ING[1].]
1 Injury to a horse caused by particles of gravel forced between the shoe and the hoof. E16.
2 The action of GRAVEL *verb.* L16.

gravelling /ˈgrav(ə)lɪŋ/ *noun*[2]. Also **graveling**. L16.
[ORIGIN Unknown.]
A parr; a young salmon or trout.

gravelly /ˈgrav(ə)li/ *adjective.* LME.
[ORIGIN from GRAVEL *noun* + -Y[1].]
1 Full of gravel; consisting of or containing gravel; strewn with gravel; resembling gravel. Formerly also, containing much sand, sandy. LME.
2 MEDICINE. Of the nature of gravel (GRAVEL *noun* 3); characterized by or arising from the presence of gravel. LME.
†**3** Containing gritty particles. M17–E18.
4 Of a voice: deep and rough-sounding. M20.

†**gravelous** *adjective.* LME–M18.
[ORIGIN Old French & mod. French *graveleux*, formed as GRAVEL *noun*: see -OUS.]
Gravelly; granular.

graven /ˈgreɪv(ə)n/ *ppl adjective.* LME.
[ORIGIN pa. pple of GRAVE *verb*[1].]
1 Sculptured, hewn. LME.
graven image an idol (esp. in allusion to *Exodus* 20:4).
2 Carved on a surface; engraved. E19.

L. DURRELL The mason's signature upon the graven iron plaque.

graven *verb pa. pple*: see GRAVE *verb*[1].

Gravenstein /ˈgrɑːv(ə)nstʌɪn/ *noun.* E19.
[ORIGIN German form of *Graasten*, a village in Denmark formerly in Schleswig-Holstein, Germany.]
A variety of eating apple, which has large fruit with yellow, red-streaked skin.

graveolent /grəˈvɪəl(ə)nt/ *adjective.* M17.
[ORIGIN Latin *graveolent-*, from *grave* use as adverb of neut. of *gravis* heavy (see GRAVE *adjective*[1]) + *olent-*, *-ens* pres. pple of *olere* have a smell: see -ENT.]
Having a rank offensive smell; fetid.
■ †**graveolency** *noun* (*rare*) E17–E18.

graver /ˈgreɪvə/ *noun.* OE.
[ORIGIN from GRAVE *verb*[1] + -ER[1].]
1 Orig., a sculptor. Later, a carver, an engraver. Now *rare.* OE.
2 A person who digs, or digs up turf. Long *obsolete* exc. *dial.* ME.
3 Any of various tools for cutting and shaving; now *esp.* an engraver's tool, a burin. LME.

Graves /grɑːv/ *noun*[1]. Pl. same /grɑːvz/. E17.
[ORIGIN French (see below).]
A white or red wine produced in the Graves district of SW France.

graves *noun*[2] *pl.* var. of GREAVES.

Graves' disease /ˈgreɪvz dɪˌziːz/ *noun phr.* M19.
[ORIGIN from Robert J. *Graves* (1796–1853), Irish physician.]
MEDICINE. A disease caused by excessive thyroid secretion, characterized by weight loss, a nervous tremor, staring eyes, and a swollen neck; exophthalmic goitre.

Gravette /grəˈvɛt/ *noun.* Also **g-**. E20.
[ORIGIN La *Gravette*, a site in SW France.]
ARCHAEOLOGY. Used (usu. *attrib.*) to designate a type of long narrow knifelike flint characteristic of the Gravettian culture (see below).
■ **Gravettian** *adjective & noun* (*a*) *adjective* designating or pertaining to an upper Palaeolithic culture represented by remains found at La Gravette; (*b*) *noun* (a person of) *the* Gravettian culture: M20.

graveyard /ˈgreɪvjɑːd/ *noun.* L18.
[ORIGIN from GRAVE *noun*[1] + YARD *noun*[1].]
A burial ground.

fig.: D. W. GOODWIN The history of medicine is a graveyard of treatments that were worthless but flourished.

– COMB.: **graveyard cough** = ***churchyard cough*** s.v. CHURCH *noun*; **graveyard shift** (chiefly *N. Amer.*) (the relay of workers on duty during) the work period between midnight and 8 a.m.; **graveyard watch** NAUTICAL the middle watch between midnight and 4 a.m.

gravid /ˈgravɪd/ *adjective.* L16.
[ORIGIN Latin *gravidus* laden, pregnant, from *gravis* heavy: see GRAVE *adjective*[1], -ID[1].]
Of an animal or (now *literary*) a woman: pregnant, heavy with young.
■ †**gravidation** *noun* the condition or fact of being pregnant L15–E18. **graˈvidity** *noun* the state of being gravid, pregnancy M17.

gravida /ˈgravɪdə/ *noun.* M20.
[ORIGIN Latin, use as noun of fem. of *gravidus* GRAVID.]
MEDICINE. A woman who is pregnant; (with preceding or following numeral) a woman who had had the specified number of pregnancies, including a present one. Cf. MULTIGRAVIDA, PRIMIGRAVIDA, SECUNDIGRAVIDA, PARA *noun*[4].

Lancet Born to a 36-year-old gravida 7, para 5 mother by vaginal delivery.

gravific /grəˈvɪfɪk/ *adjective.* E19.
[ORIGIN French *gravifique* from Latin *gravis* heavy + *-fique* -FIC.]
That makes heavy or produces weight.

gravimeter /grəˈvɪmɪtə/ *noun.* L18.
[ORIGIN French *gravimètre*, from Latin *gravis* heavy: see -METER.]
1 A kind of hydrometer for measuring the relative density of solid or liquid bodies. L18.
2 (Now the usual sense.) Any instrument designed to measure the variation in the force of gravity from one place to another. M20.

gravimetric /gravɪˈmɛtrɪk/ *adjective.* L19.
[ORIGIN from GRAVIMETER + -METRIC.]
Of or pertaining to gravimeters or gravimetry.
gravimetric analysis quantitative chemical analysis based on the weighing of reagents and products.
■ **gravimetrical** *adjective* = GRAVIMETRIC L19. **gravimetrically** *adverb* M19.

gravimetry /grəˈvɪmɪtri/ *noun.* M19.
[ORIGIN formed as GRAVIMETRIC + -METRY.]
The measurement of weight; *esp.* the use of a gravimeter to measure gravitational force.

graving /ˈgreɪvɪŋ/ *noun.* ME.
[ORIGIN from GRAVE *verb*[1] + -ING[1].]
1 Digging. *obsolete* exc. *dial.* ME.
†**2** Burial. Only in ME.
3 †**a** Carving, sculpturing; incision of ornamental lines etc. in stone, metal, or other material. LME–E18. ▸**b** Something cut or carved; a carving, a sculpture; an inscription. *arch.* LME.
4 The engraving of a design, picture, etc., on metal or wood. *arch.* M17.
– COMB.: **graving tool** (*a*) = GRAVER 3; (*b*) (*dial.*, *rare*) a spade used in making drains etc.

gravitas /ˈgravɪtɑːs, -tas/ *noun.* E20.
[ORIGIN Latin.]
Solemn demeanour; seriousness.

gravitate /ˈgravɪteɪt/ *verb.* M17.
[ORIGIN mod. Latin *gravitat-* pa. ppl stem of *gravitare*, from Latin *gravitas* gravity: see -ATE[3].]
†**1** *verb intrans.* Exert weight or pressure, press *on.* Of a heavy body: (tend to) move downward by its own weight. M17–E19.
2 *verb intrans.* Be affected by gravitation; move or tend to move by the force of gravity (*towards* etc.). L17. ▸**b** Sink or fall (as) by gravitation; tend to reach a low level; settle down. E19. ▸**c** *verb trans.* Cause to descend or sink by gravitation. *rare.* L19.

J. N. LOCKYER Systems of bodies which gravitate round a central body. T. HARDY That natural law of physics which causes lesser bodies to gravitate towards the greater. **b** F. W. ROBERTSON The soul gravitates downward beneath its burden.

3 *verb intrans.* Move or tend to move towards a certain point or object as a natural goal or destination; be strongly attracted to some centre of influence. Freq. foll. by *to*, *towards*. L17.

G. F. KENNAN Governmental power in Russia gravitated increasingly to the left. D. M. DAVIN I gravitated of an evening to the Wheatsheaf. J. LE CARRÉ Gravitating by instinct towards Cambridge Circus.

gravitation /gravɪˈteɪʃ(ə)n/ *noun.* M17.
[ORIGIN mod. Latin *gravitatio(n-)*, formed as GRAVITATE: see -ATION.]
1 The action or process of gravitating; the falling of bodies to earth; movement, or tendency to move, towards a centre of attractive force. M17.

D. BREWSTER The moon . . kept in her orbit by gravitation to the earth.

2 The attractive force exerted by each particle of matter on every other particle. M17.

S. WEINBERG Galaxies . . slowing down under the influence of their mutual gravitation.

law of gravitation the law according to which the force of gravity acting between two bodies is directly proportional to the product of their masses and inversely proportional to the square of the distance between them.
3 *transf.* & *fig.* Attraction or tendency to move towards a centre of influence; natural tendency (*to*, *towards*). M17.

W. COWPER That low And sordid gravitation of his pow'rs To a vile clod.

gravitational /gravɪˈteɪʃ(ə)n(ə)l/ *adjective.* M19.
[ORIGIN from GRAVITATION + -AL[1].]
Of, pertaining to, or caused by gravitation.
gravitational constant the constant of proportionality in the equation relating the strength of the gravitational attraction between two bodies to their masses and their separation, equal to 6.67×10^{-11} N m^2 kg^{-2} approx. (symbol *G*). **gravitational lens** ASTRONOMY a region of space containing a massive body whose gravitational field acts like a lens on electromagnetic radiation. **gravitational mass** the mass of a body as measured by the force exerted on the body by a gravitational field. **gravitational radiation** gravitational waves (sense a below). **gravitational system (of units)** a system of units based on a fundamental unit of weight rather than a unit of mass. **gravitational wave** (*a*) a periodic variation in gravitational field strength which is propagated through space; (*b*) = ***gravity wave*** s.v. GRAVITY.
■ **gravitationally** *adverb* L19.

gravitative /ˈgravɪteɪtɪv/ *adjective.* L18.
[ORIGIN from GRAVITATE + -IVE.]
= GRAVITATIONAL.

gravitino /gravɪˈtiːnəʊ/ *noun.* Pl. **-os**. L20.
[ORIGIN from GRAVITON + -INO.]
PARTICLE PHYSICS. The supersymmetric counterpart of a graviton, with spin 3/2 instead of 2.

graviton /ˈgravɪtɒn/ *noun.* M20.
[ORIGIN from GRAVIT(ATION + -ON.]
PARTICLE PHYSICS. A hypothetical subatomic particle supposed to propagate the gravitational force.

gravity /ˈgravɪti/ *noun.* L15.
[ORIGIN Old French & mod. French *gravité* or Latin *gravitas*, from *gravis* GRAVE *adjective*[1]: see -ITY.]
▸ **I 1** Grave or serious character or nature; importance; seriousness. L15.

JOSEPH PARKER Great questions should be considered in a spirit worthy of their gravity.

2 Dignity, solemnity, serious and dignified formality; solemn conduct or demeanour, staidness. Now *esp.* seriousness as opp. to levity or gaiety. E16.

LD MACAULAY The gravity and pomp of the whole proceeding. H. CAINE She grew uneasy at the settled gravity of his face.

3 †**a** Weight, influence, authority. M16–M18. ▸**b** Something grave; a grave or serious subject, speech, or remark. Formerly also as a respectful title. *arch.* E17.

b GIBBON Your Gravity, Your Excellency, Your Eminence. GEO. ELIOT Books of German science, and other gravities.

▸ **II 4** †**a** The quality of having weight; tendency to downward motion. Only in 17. ▸**b** Weight, heaviness. Now chiefly in ***centre of gravity*** s.v. CENTRE *noun*, ***specific gravity*** s.v. SPECIFIC *adjective.* M17.
5 Lowness of pitch of sound. M17.
6 The attractive force by which bodies are drawn towards the centre of the earth or of another celestial object; the degree of intensity of this measured by the acceleration produced; gravitational force. L17.

BURKE If I were to explain the motion of a body falling to the ground, I would say it was caused by gravity. P. DAVIES Stars so massive that their gravity even traps their own light.

zero gravity: see ZERO *noun & adjective*.
– COMB.: **gravity-fed** *adjective* supplied with material by gravity feed; **gravity feed** a supply system that makes use of gravity to maintain the flow of material; the supply of material in this way; **gravity wave** (*a*) a wave on a liquid surface in which the dominant force is gravity; (*b*) = ***GRAVITATIONAL wave*** (a).

gravlax /ˈgravlaks/ *noun.* Also **gravadlax** /ˈgravədlaks/. M20.
[ORIGIN Swedish, from *grav* grave, trench + *lax* salmon; so called because the salmon was orig. marinated and fermented in a hole in the ground.]
A Scandinavian dish of dry-cured salmon marinated in a mixture containing salt, spices, and dill.

gravure /grəˈvjʊə/ *noun.* L19.
[ORIGIN Abbreviation.]
= PHOTOGRAVURE.

gravy /ˈgreɪvi/ *noun*. ME.
[ORIGIN Perh. from misreading as *gravé* of Old French *grané*, prob. from *grain* spice (cf. Old French *grenon* stew): see GRAIN *noun*[1], -Y[5].]
1 A kind of dressing used for white meats, fish, and vegetables, comprising broth, milk of almonds, spices, and (usu.) wine or ale; a sauce. Long *obsolete* exc. *Scot.* ME.
2 The fat and juices that exude from meat during and after cooking; a dressing for food made from these and other ingredients. L16. ▸**b** Laughter readily obtained from an audience; good comic lines. *theatrical slang.* M19. ▸**c** Money easily acquired; an unearned or unexpected bonus; a tip. *slang* (orig. *US*). E20.
– COMB.: **gravy boat** a boat-shaped vessel for serving gravy; **gravy train** *slang* a source of easy financial benefit; freq. in ***board the gravy train***, ***ride the gravy train***, etc.

Gray /greɪ/ *noun*[1]. M20.
[ORIGIN F. *Gray* (1887–1969), US physicist.]
Used *attrib.* with ref. to a code in which consecutive integers are represented by binary numbers differing in only one digit.

gray /greɪ/ *noun*[2]. L20.
[ORIGIN L. H. *Gray* (1905–65), English radiobiologist.]
PHYSICS. The SI unit of absorbed dose of ionizing radiation, corresponding to the absorption of one joule of energy per kilogram of irradiated material. (Symbol Gy.)

gray *noun*[3], *adjective*, *verb* see GREY *noun*, *adjective*, *verb*.

grayling /ˈgreɪlɪŋ/ *noun*. ME.
[ORIGIN from *gray* var. of GREY *adjective* + -LING[1].]
1 A European freshwater salmonid fish, *Thymallus thymallus*, with a long, high dorsal fin. Also (in full ***Arctic grayling***), a related holarctic fish, *T. arcticus*. ME. ▸**b** A silvery freshwater fish of the genus *Prototroctes*, superficially resembling a trout, native to Australia and New Zealand. L19.
2 A brown Eurasian satyrid butterfly, *Hipparchia semele*, with grey undersides to its wings. Also, a similar, related N. American butterfly, *Cercyonis pegala*. E19.

†**graymill** *noun*. M16–M18.
[ORIGIN Alt. of French *grémil* GROMWELL after GRAY *adjective*.]
= GROMWELL.

graywacke *noun* see GREYWACKE.

grazable *adjective* var. of GRAZEABLE.

graze /greɪz/ *noun*. L17.
[ORIGIN from GRAZE *verb*[2].]
1 An act or instance of (esp. shot) grazing or touching lightly. L17.
2 A superficial wound or abrasion. M19.

graze /greɪz/ *verb*[1].
[ORIGIN Old English *grasian*, from GRASS *noun*; cf. Middle Dutch, Middle High German *grasen* and GRASS *verb*.]
1 *verb intrans.* Of an animal: feed on growing grass or other herbage. OE. ▸**b** Of a person: eat small quantities of food at frequent intervals in the course of other activities. Chiefly *US*. L20.

J. A. MICHENER A few goats grazed among the scattered boulders. *fig.*: *Times* Anyone who grazes . . off the front page of *The Times*.

2 *verb trans.* & *intrans.* Put (an animal) to feed on growing grass; tend (an animal) while so feeding. M16.

J. R. MCCULLOCH Great numbers of cattle . . are grazed in the fens.

3 *verb trans.* (Of an animal) feed on (grass etc.); (of a person) put cattle to feed on (grass, land). E17.

S. JOHNSON You may graze the ground when the trees are grown up. *Sunday Express* Cattle grazed meadows which flooded regularly in the spring.

4 *verb intrans.* Of land: produce grass; be suitable for grazing. *obsolete* exc. *dial.* E17.
■ **grazer** *noun* an animal or person that grazes E18. **grazing** *noun* (*a*) the action of the verb; (*b*) pastureland, pasture: LME.

graze /greɪz/ *verb*[2]. L16.
[ORIGIN Perh. a spec. use of GRAZE *verb*[1], as if 'take off the grass close to the ground'; cf. German *grasen* browse, pasture, scythe, glance off, Swedish *gräsa* (of a shot) graze, Danish *græsse* pasture, (of a bullet) ricochet.]
1 *verb intrans.* Touch lightly in passing, esp. so as to produce a slight abrasion. Formerly also, (of a bullet) ricochet. Usu. foll. by *against*, *along*, *by*, *past*, etc. L16.

H. BASCOM Wharf timbers creak . . as a tethered steamer grazes and pounds against them.

2 *verb trans.* Touch (a surface) lightly in passing; abrade (skin etc.) in rubbing past; suffer a slight abrasion of (a part of the body). E17.

M. STOTT I was always falling over and grazing my knee. M. IGNATIEFF She leans over him, her hand grazing the back of his head.

grazeable /ˈgreɪzəb(ə)l/ *adjective*. Also **grazable**. M17.
[ORIGIN from GRAZE *verb*[1] + -ABLE.]
Of land: that may be grazed, suitable for grazing.

grazet /grəˈzɛt/ *noun*. *obsolete* exc. *hist.* or *poet.* L17.
[ORIGIN Perh. from French *grisette* a cheap grey woollen fabric.]
A silk and worsted dress material.

grazier /ˈgreɪzɪə/ *noun*. ME.
[ORIGIN from GRASS *noun*: see -IER. Formerly assoc. with French *graissier* fattener.]
A person who grazes or feeds cattle for the market; *Austral.* & *NZ* a sheep-farmer.
■ **graziery** *noun* the occupation or business of a grazier M18.

grazioso /gratsiˈoːzo/ *adjective* & *adverb*. E19.
[ORIGIN Italian = gracious, graceful.]
MUSIC. A direction: graceful(ly).

†**greal** *noun* var. of GRAIL *noun*[2].

grease /griːs/ *noun*. ME.
[ORIGIN Anglo-Norman *grece*, *gresse*, Old French & mod. French *graisse* from Proto-Romance from Latin *crassus*: see CRASS.]
1 †**a** *gen.* The fat part of the body of an animal; fatness. ME–L17. ▸**b** HUNTING. The fat of a game animal. ME.
b in grease, **in pride of grease**, **in prime of grease** fat and fit for killing.
2 Melted fat of a (usu. specified) dead animal; *gen.* oily or fatty matter, esp. in semi-solid state as a lubricant. ME. ▸**b** Butter. *dial.* & *slang.* L18. ▸**c** The oily matter in wool; uncleansed wool. M19.

J. MORTIMER A pole's covered with grease and you have to try and climb it but of course you can't. B. LOPEZ The husband wiped seal grease from his fingers with a ptarmigan wing.

c in the grease that has not been cleansed after shearing.
3 = *GREASY* ***heels***. L17.
4 Money given as a bribe, or as protection money. (Cf. GREASE *verb* 3). *slang*. L18.
– COMB.: **greaseball** *N. Amer. slang, offensive* (*a*) a foreigner, esp. of Mediterranean or Latin American origin; (*b*) = GREASER 3c; **grease band** *noun* & *verb* (*a*) *noun* a band of sticky material applied to a tree trunk, as a barrier against insects; (*b*) *verb trans.* apply such a band to (a tree); **grease cup**: from which machinery is supplied with grease; ***grease gun***: see GUN *noun* 5; **grease monkey** *slang* a mechanic; **greasepaint** a waxy substance used as make-up by a stage performer; **greaseproof** *adjective* (esp. of paper) impervious to the penetration of grease; **grease-trap** an appliance for catching grease in drains; **greasewood** any of various dwarf resinous shrubs of the goosefoot family, esp. *Sarcobatus vermiculatus*, which grow in dry alkaline valleys in the western US.

grease /griːs, -z/ *verb*. LME.
[ORIGIN from the noun. Cf. French *graisser*.]
1 *verb trans.* Smear or anoint with grease. LME. ▸**b** *verb trans.* & *intrans.* Apply a salve of tallow and tar to (sheep). Now *rare*. LME. ▸**c** *verb trans.* Make greasy; soil with grease or fat. E17.
like greased lightning: see LIGHTNING *noun* 1.
2 *verb trans.* Lubricate with grease. LME.

D. W. JERROLD Silently went the window up . . as though greased by some witch.

grease the wheels *fig.* make things run smoothly; provide the entertainment, pay the expenses.
3 *verb trans.* Ply with money, bribe. Chiefly in ***grease a person's hand***, ***grease a person's palm***. E16.
grease the fat pig, **grease the fat sow** give to a person needing nothing.
4 *verb trans.* Cause (a horse) to contract the disease greasy heels. E18.

greaser /ˈgriːsə, -z-/ *noun*. M17.
[ORIGIN from GREASE *verb* + -ER[1].]
†**1** A person who greases sheep. Only in M17.
2 A person who cleans and lubricates machinery with grease; *spec.* an engineer on a ship. M19.
3 A Latin American; *spec.* a Mexican. *US slang* (*derog.* & *offensive*). M19. ▸**b** An objectionable person; a sycophant. *slang*. E20. ▸**c** A member of a gang of (typically long-haired) motorcyclists. *slang*. M20.
4 A machine used to separate diamonds from the material in which they are found. E20.
5 A smooth or gentle aircraft landing. *slang*. L20.

greasy /ˈgriːsi, -zi/ *adjective*. E16.
[ORIGIN from GREASE *noun* + -Y[1].]
1 Smeared, covered, or soiled with grease. E16. ▸†**b** Esp. of language: obscene. L16–E19.

V. WOOLF I hate your greasy handkerchiefs—you will stain your copy of *Don Juan*. O. MANNING A waiter . . producing from an inner pocket a greasy, food-splashed card. *Practical Hairstyling & Beauty* If your hair tends to get greasy after a week without washing—that's normal.

2 Composed of or containing grease; of the nature of grease; *spec.* (of food or diet) containing too much grease. L16. ▸**b** *spec.* Of wool: containing natural grease, uncleansed. L16.

T. HOOD When a German dish is not sour it is sure to be greasy.

3 Having the appearance or feel of containing or being covered with grease. E18. ▸**b** Of a road, path, etc.: slippery with moisture or mud. E19. ▸**c** Of the weather or the sky: threatening, stormy. E19.

T. SHARPE Their foreheads greasy with perspiration. **b** DICKENS Just enough damp gently stealing down to make the pavement greasy.

4 Of a horse: suffering from greasy heels (see below). E18.
5 Of manner or expression: disagreeably unctuous. M19.

THACKERAY With a . . greasy simper—he fawns on everybody.

– SPECIAL COLLOCATIONS: **greasy heels** a chronic inflammation of the skin and sebaceous glands of a horse's heels. **greasy pole**: greased for difficult climbing or walking on in sports. **greasy spoon (restaurant)** *slang* a cheap inferior cafe or restaurant.
■ **greasily** *adverb* L16. **greasiness** *noun* M16.

great /greɪt/ *adjective*, *noun*, & *adverb*.
[ORIGIN Old English *grēat* = Old Frisian *grāt*, Old Saxon *grōt* (Dutch *groot*), Old High German *grōz* (German *gross*), from West Germanic, of unknown origin.]
▸ **A** *adjective*. **I** Thick, coarse, massive, big.
1 Composed of large particles; coarse of grain or texture. Formerly also, (of diet) coarse, not delicate. *obsolete* exc. *Scot.* OE.
2 Thick; massive, big, bulky; stout, corpulent. *obsolete* exc. *Scot.* OE.
3 Pregnant; far advanced in pregnancy. Foll. by *with*. Now *arch.* & *dial.* ME.

fig.: SHAKES. *Per.* I am great with woe, and shall deliver weeping.

4 Esp. of the heart: full of emotion, esp. grief; angry, grieved, proud. *obsolete* exc. *Scot.* ME.
5 (Of the sea) high, stormy; (of a river) swollen, in flood. *dial.* LME.
▸ **II** Highly placed in a scale of measurement or quantity.
6 Of relatively large or above average size, extent, duration, quantity, number, degree, or intensity. OE. ▸†**b** A great number or quantity of; many, much. LME–L17. ▸**c** *attrib.* in compar. ***Greater***. (Of a city etc.) including adjacent urban areas; (of a country) including dependencies. E17.

LD MACAULAY To raise a great army had always been the King's first object. T. HARDY I feel it a great relief, Farfrae, to tell some friend o' this. E. WAUGH Soon everyone was eating and drinking at a great pace. I. MURDOCH These matters had occupied Christopher for a greater part of the night. G. GORDON What he had in mind would cost a great deal. *Southern Rag* They played a great variety of songs and tunes. A. THWAITE He had no great hopes of immortality and his reputation certainly suffered . . after his death. E. AMADI Right now my greatest desire is to patch up this quarrel. **c** *Listener* Apart from Greater London and Greater Birmingham all the conurbations were . . increasing their population.

7 a Of an object: big, large, (now usu. with implied surprise, admiration, contempt, indignation, etc.). Freq. preceding a partly synon. adjective with intensive force. ME. ▸**b** *attrib.* Designating the larger or largest of things of the class specified; forming names of animals (esp. birds), towns, rivers, streets, districts, etc., that are larger or more important, earlier established, etc., than another or others of that name. Opp. LITTLE *adjective* 1b. LME. ▸**c** Of a letter: capital. *arch.* M16. ▸**d** Of a specified part of a building or a particular building etc.: main, principal. L16. ▸**e** *attrib.* in compar. *greater*. Designating the larger of two similar or related plants, animals, anatomical parts, or places. Opp. LESSER *adjective* 2a. L18.

a S. RICHARDSON A great over grown, lank-haired, chubby boy. J. STEINBECK There it lay, the great pearl, perfect as the moon. L. P. HARTLEY It was a great big thing, the size of a small haystack. E. ARDIZZONE A gale was blowing and the great waves were crashing on the beach. **c** *Church Times* Canon Gore will lecture . . in the Great Hall of the Church House.

b *great mullein*, *great reed warbler*, *great tit*, *great willowherb*, etc.; ***Great Malvern***, ***Great Ouse***, ***Great Portland Street***, etc. **e** *greater celandine*, *greater horseshoe bat*, etc.
†**8** Of an animal, esp. above a particular age: full-grown, mature. L15–L18.
▸ **III** Important, elevated, distinguished.
9 Of more than ordinary importance; weighty; distinguished; pre-eminent; famous. ME. ▸**b** Of a time, day, etc.: having important results; critical. LME. ▸†**c** Distinguished or impressive in appearance. L16–L17.

J. BUCHAN I felt that great things, tremendous things, were happening. DAY LEWIS In youth, I thought it great and glorious to be a poet. P. V. PRICE When the Cabernet Sauvignon makes a good wine, it is so good that it verges on great. I. MURDOCH Would he be called upon to make great choices, world-altering decisions? R. HUNTFORD Dulwich was not exactly one of the great public schools with aristocratic connections. **b** LD MACAULAY The great day of the Exclusion Bill.

10 (Of a person) eminent by reason of birth, rank, wealth, or power; (of a thing) of or pertaining to such a person. ME. ▸**b** — ***the Great***: designating a person, esp. a monarch, as pre-eminent amongst those of that name. LME. ▸**c** Designating an official who is senior to others of the same general rank. *obsolete* exc. in ***Lord Great Chamberlain***. M16.

LD MACAULAY The great man, at whose frown, a few days before, the whole kingdom had trembled. R. H. TAWNEY None are too mean to be beneath or too great to be above it [religion]. R. GRAVES Aren't you someone greater than Jove? **b** J. H. BURTON Napoleon was little, so was Frederic the Great.

11 Of a person: extraordinary or remarkable in ability, genius, or achievement in some specific or specified activity. ME. ▸**b** *gen.* Eminent in (esp. mental) achievement or moral worth; having integrity or nobility of

G

character. E18. ▸**c** Of the soul, ideas, etc.: lofty, magnanimous, noble. E18.

Law Times If he was great as an advocate, he was still greater as a judge. M. LOWRY She might under other conditions have become a really first-rate, even a great artist. T. S. ELIOT He was a great financier—And I am merely a successful one. **b** SCOTT FITZGERALD He had been told Lincoln was a great man whom he should admire. M. KLINE Pascal was great in many fields. **c** A. THWAITE I tried to open up so many eyes To the great minds of all humanity.

12 *attrib.* Being or having the quality of the noun indicated to a high degree; (of an agent) that does the action indicated habitually or extensively. ME. ▸**b** *pred.* Having considerable knowledge of a specified subject; skilled in doing something specified. Foll. by *at*, *on*. *colloq.* E17.

SHAKES. *Twel. N.* I am a great eater of beef. J. FORBES Epicures esteem the black pomfret a great dainty. H. JAMES Are you and he such great friends? SCOTT FITZGERALD I was just as beautiful as the great beauties. T. WOGAN My beloved cockatiel . . was in his day a great pecker of . . fingers. **b** THACKERAY He was great at cooking many of his Virginian dishes.

13 Intimate, familiar, friendly, *with* (now only *Scot. & dial.*); much in use, high in favour *with* (now *rare*). LME.
14 Excellent, very good, fine, admirable. *colloq.* E19.

P. KAVANAGH It was such nice sweet land, . . great for growing potatoes and oats. G. SWIFT Great! I'm glad you've got it all so worked out! A. TYLER I play a great guitar. P. ROTH 'I want you to work with me.' 'Oh, great.'

— SPECIAL COLLOCATIONS & PHRASES: **a great one for** a habitual doer of, an enthusiast for. ***go great guns***: see GUN *noun*. ***great argus***: see ARGUS 3. **great attractor** ASTRONOMY a large aggregation of galaxies several hundred million light years away that is thought to be the cause of the deviation of nearer galaxies from uniform recession. ***great AUK***. ***Great Bear***: see BEAR *noun*[1] 2. **Great Bible** the English version of the Bible by Coverdale (1539). **great blue heron** a large grey-blue heron, *Ardea herodias*, which is found in N. and Central America. ***Great Britain***: see BRITAIN *noun*[1]. **Great British Public** (*joc.* or *iron.*) the British people. ***great CALORIE***. ***great CASSINO***. ***Great Charter***: see CHARTER *noun*. ***great circle***: see CIRCLE *noun*. ***Great Council***: see COUNCIL *noun*. ***great cry and little wool***: see CRY *noun*. ***Great Dane***: see DANE 2. **great day** *arch.* (*a*) the Day of Judgement; (*b*) an important feast or fast day. ***great deal***: see DEAL *noun*[1]. **Great Deliverer**: William III of Great Britain (1650–1702). ***Great Dipper***: see DIPPER 5a. ***great divide***: see DIVIDE *noun*. ***Great Dog***: see DOG *noun* 5. ***great egret***: see *great white egret* below. ***Great Entrance***: see ENTRANCE *noun*. ***Greater BAIRAM***. ***greater diesis***: see DIESIS 1. ***Greater Doxology***: see DOXOLOGY 2. ***greater PANATHENAEA***. **Great Fire**: which destroyed much of London in September 1666. **Great Game** (*a*) golf; (*b*) spying; (*c*) the rivalry between Britain and Russia in central Asia during the 19th cent. **great go** *arch. slang* the final examination for the degree of BA at the Universities of Oxford and Cambridge. ***great grief!***: see GRIEF *noun*. **great gross** twelve gross, 1,728. ***great gun***: see GUN *noun*. **great horse** *hist.* a warhorse, *spec.* that of a knight in armour. **great house** the large house belonging to the person of highest social standing of a locality. ***great hundred***: see HUNDRED *noun* 5. ***great inquest***: see INQUEST 2. **great insertion** the section of St Luke's Gospel, 9:51–18:14, which is independent of St Mark. **great kangaroo** = FORESTER 3a(b). **Great Lakes** a group of large lakes along the boundary of US and Canada, comprising Superior, Huron, Michigan, Erie, and Ontario. **great laurel** an evergreen shrub of the heath family, *Rhododendron maximum*, of the eastern US. **Great Leap (Forward)** an unsuccessful attempt, begun in 1958, to modernize China rapidly by introducing advanced techniques into industry. **great-line** a long line used in deep-sea fishing for cod, ling, etc. ***great northern diver***: see DIVER 1. **great omission** the section of St Mark's Gospel, 6:45–8:26, which is omitted in St Luke's. **great organ** the chief manual in a large organ, with its related pipes and mechanism. **Great Power** a nation of considerable economic or military strength and so playing an important part in international relations. †**great pox** syphilis. ***great primer***: see PRIMER *noun*[1] 3. **Great Russian** *noun & adjective* (*a*) *noun* a member of one of the principal ethnic groups in central Asia; the language of this group; (*b*) *adjective* of or pertaining to the Great Russians or Great Russian. **Great Satan** (*a*) the ultimate source of evil; (*b*) *derog.* the United States regarded as an imperialistic and malevolent power, esp. in the context of its policies in the Middle East; **Great Scott!** *interjection* expr. surprise, exasperation, etc. ***Great Seal***: see SEAL *noun*[2]. †**great ship** a man-of-war, a warship. **Great Spirit** [translating Ojibwa *kitchi manitou*] the supreme god in the traditional religion of many N. American Indians. **great thought** (freq. *iron.*) a maxim, an apophthegm. **great toe** big toe. ***great vassal***: see VASSAL *noun* 1. ***Great Vowel Shift***: see VOWEL *noun*. **Great War** (*a*) the French Revolutionary and Napoleonic wars (1792–1815), jointly; (*b*) the First World War. **Great Week** = ***Holy Week*** s.v. HOLY *adjective*. ***great white chief***: see CHIEF *noun*. **great white egret**, **great egret** a large white egret, *Egretta alba*, which has a yellow bill and black legs and occurs worldwide. **great white heron** (*a*) = ***great white egret*** above; (*b*) *US* a white variety of the great blue heron, *Ardea herodias*, found in Florida. **great white shark** = ***white shark*** s.v. WHITE *adjective*. **Great White Way** [with ref. to the brilliant street illumination] Broadway in New York City. **great year** *hist.* = ***Platonic year*** s.v. PLATONIC *adjective* 1. ***Lord Great Chamberlain***: see sense 10c above. ***the great — in the sky***: see SKY *noun*. ***the great assize(s)***: see ASSIZE *noun* 3. †***the great Author***: see AUTHOR *noun* 1. **the great majority** (*a*) by far the most; (*b*) the dead; ***join the great majority***, die. **the great outdoors** the open air; outdoor life. ***the Great Rebellion***: see REBELLION. ***the great unwashed***: see UNWASHED *noun*. **to a great extent** largely.

▸ **B** *noun*. †**1** Thickness. *rare*. OE–ME.
2 Great, eminent, or distinguished people. (Now usu. with *the*.) ME. ▸**b** Something great. Now only (*US colloq.*), a great part or amount, a great deal. ME. ▸**c** That which is great; great things collectively. Formerly also, great quantity. M16.

LD MACAULAY The masques which were exhibited at the mansions of the great.

3 A great, eminent, or distinguished person. ME.

J. WALSH Statues and paintings of the greats of French science and literature. L. ARMSTRONG I had hit the big time. I was up North with the greats.

4 (**G-**.) In *pl.* The final examination for the degree of BA at Oxford University. Now *spec.* (the final examinations for) an honours course in classics and philosophy. *colloq.* M19.
— PHRASES: **by the great** (*a*) (now *dial.*) (of work done) at a fixed price for the whole amount; by the piece; †(*b*) in large quantities, wholesale. ***modern Greats***: see MODERN *adjective*. †**in great** for the whole amount; wholesale; on a large scale. **the great and the good** (freq. *iron.*) worthy people. **the greatest** *colloq.* the best, the most wonderful, (person or thing).

▸ **C** *adverb*. **1** In a great degree; to a great extent; much; very. *obsolete* exc. *dial.* ME.
†**2** In a distinguished manner; imposingly. L17–M18.
3 Well, successfully. *colloq.* M20.

New Yorker 'How is Charlotte?' Vivian and I asked. 'Doing great,' Barry said.

■ **greaterness** *noun* (now *rare*) the condition or quality of being greater M16. **greatish** *adjective* somewhat great M19.

great- /ɡreɪt/ *combining form*. M16.
[ORIGIN Use of GREAT.]
With the names of family relationship denoting one degree further removed in ascent or descent: repeatable according to the number of degrees to be expressed, as ***great-great-great-grandmother*** etc.
great-aunt a father's or mother's aunt. **great-grandchild** a grandchild's child. **great-granddaughter** a grandson's or granddaughter's daughter. **great-grandfather** a grandfather's or grandmother's father. **great-grandmother** a grandfather's or grandmother's mother. **great-grandson** a grandson's or granddaughter's son. **great-nephew** a nephew's or niece's son. **great-niece** a nephew's or niece's daughter. **great-uncle** a father's or mother's uncle.

greatcoat /ˈɡreɪtkəʊt/ *noun*. L17.
[ORIGIN from GREAT *adjective* + COAT *noun*.]
A large heavy overcoat; a topcoat.
■ **greatcoated** *adjective* wearing a greatcoat M18. **greatcoatless** *adjective* L19.

greaten /ˈɡreɪt(ə)n/ *verb*. *arch.* LME.
[ORIGIN from GREAT *adjective* + -EN[5].]
†**1** *verb intrans.* Become pregnant. Only in LME.
2 *verb trans.* Make great or greater in size or amount. E17.
3 Make eminent, prominent, distinguished, or important. E17. ▸**b** Exalt mentally or spiritually; elevate (the mind). M17.
4 *verb intrans.* Become great or greater in size or extent. E18.

great-hearted /ɡreɪtˈhɑːtɪd, ˈɡreɪthɑːtɪd/ *adjective*. LME.
[ORIGIN from GREAT *adjective* + HEARTED.]
Magnanimous; having a noble or generous spirit.
■ **great-ˈheartedness** *noun* E19.

greatly /ˈɡreɪtli/ *adverb*. ME.
[ORIGIN from GREAT *adjective* + -LY[2].]
1 To a great extent; in a great degree; much; very. ME.

R. KIPLING Careless and lazy is he, Greatly inferior to Me. J. CONRAD 'It looks queer to me,' burst out Jukes, greatly exasperated. J. KOSINSKI Yours is the spirit which this country so greatly needs.

2 In a great manner; grandly. *arch.* LME.
3 On a large scale; in large numbers. Now *rare* or *obsolete*. L17. ▸**b** For the most part; mainly. *rare*. M18.
4 In or to a high rank or position. *rare*. E19.

J. AUSTEN You encourage her to expect to marry greatly.

greatness /ˈɡreɪtnɪs/ *noun*. OE.
[ORIGIN from GREAT *adjective* + -NESS.]
†**1** Thickness, coarseness; stoutness. OE–M16. ▸**b** Pregnancy. LME–M17.
2 The quality of being great in size, extent, or degree. ME. ▸†**b** Magnitude, size. LME–M18.
3 Great or high rank; eminence, distinction, importance. ME. ▸†**b** With possess. adjective (as ***your greatness*** etc.): an honorific title given to a person of high rank or importance. L16–M18.

LD MACAULAY Nothing in the early existence of Britain indicated the greatness which she was destined to attain.

4 Inherent nobility or dignity (of mind, character, action, or expression). L16.
†**5** Intimacy, familiarity. E17–L19.

greave /ɡriːv/ *noun*[1]. *obsolete* exc. *dial.*
[ORIGIN Old English *grǣfa*, *grǣfe*, from Germanic. Cf. GROVE.]
†**1 a** Brushwood. Only in OE. ▸**b** A branch, a twig. LME–E17.
2 A thicket; a grove. OE.

greave /ɡriːv/ *noun*[2]. ME.
[ORIGIN Old French *greve* calf of the leg, shin, armour (mod. French dial. *grève*, *graive* upper part of the leg) = Spanish *greba*, of unknown origin.]
A piece of armour for the leg below the knee, esp. the shin. Usu. in *pl.*
■ **greaved** *adjective* equipped with greaves M19.

greaves /ɡriːvz/ *noun pl.* Also **graves** /ɡreɪvz/. E17.
[ORIGIN Low German *greven* pl. (whence also Danish *grever*) corresp. to Old High German *griubo*, *griobo* (German *Griebe* refuse of lard or tallow), of unknown origin: orig. a whaler's term.]
The fibrous refuse of tallow, used as dog food, fish bait, etc.

grebe /ɡriːb/ *noun*. M18.
[ORIGIN French *grèbe*, of unknown origin.]
1 Any of various long-necked aquatic birds constituting the family Podicipedidae (and order Podicipediformes), having unwebbed lobate toes and able to dive and swim under water. Cf. ***sungrebe*** s.v. SUN *noun*[1]. M18.
great crested grebe, ***little grebe***, ***Slavonian grebe***, etc.
2 The plumage of a grebe. Now *rare*. M19.

grebo /ˈɡriːbəʊ/ *noun*. Pl. **-os**. L20.
[ORIGIN Perh. from GREASER + *-bo* after *dumbo* etc.]
(A member of) an urban youth cult favouring heavy metal and punk rock music and freq. characterized by long hair and antisocial attitudes.

grece /ɡriːs/ *noun*. *obsolete* exc. *dial.* & HERALDRY. Also **grice**, (HERALDRY) **griece**. ME.
[ORIGIN Old French *gres*, *grez*, *greis* pl. of *gré* GREE *noun*[1].]
A set or flight of stairs; a step, a stair; in *pl.*, steps, stairs, a stairway.

Grecian /ˈɡriːʃ(ə)n/ *adjective & noun*. LME.
[ORIGIN Old French *grecien* or medieval Latin, from Latin *Graecia* Greece: see -IAN.]
▸ **A** *adjective*. Of or pertaining to Greece or its inhabitants; Greek. Now *rare* exc. with ref. to architecture or facial outline. LME.

TENNYSON A Gothic ruin and a Grecian house.

Grecian bend an affected way of walking in which the body is bent forward from the hips, prevalent in the late 19th cent. **Grecian gift** = ***Greek gift*** s.v. GREEK *adjective*. **Grecian knot** a way of dressing the hair at the back of the head in imitation of the ancient Greeks. **Grecian nose** a straight nose which continues the line of the forehead. **Grecian plait** an elaborate plait of hair made from about 13 strands. **Grecian slipper** a soft slipper with low-cut sides.

▸ **B** *noun*. **1** A native or inhabitant of Greece; a Greek. Long *arch.* LME. ▸**b** [translating Greek *Hellēnistēs*.] A Greek Jew, a Hellenist. *hist.* E17.

SHAKES. *All's Well* Was this fair face the cause . . Why the Grecians sacked Troy?

2 A person skilled in Greek; a Greek scholar. M16.
†**3** A member of the Greek Orthodox Church. M16–M18.
4 An Irish person; = GREEK *noun* 6. *slang*. M19.
■ **Grecianize** *verb trans.* make Grecian or Greek E17.

grecing /ˈɡriːsɪŋ/ *noun*. *obsolete* exc. *dial.* LME.
[ORIGIN from GRECE *noun* + -ING[1].]
In *pl.*, the stairs in a flight; flights of stairs. In *sing.* (*rare*), a step.

Grecism *noun*, **Grecize** *verb*, **Greco-** *combining form* vars. of GRAECISM etc.

grecque /ɡrɛk/ *noun*. M19.
[ORIGIN French, fem. of *grec* GREEK *noun*.]
ARCHITECTURE. A Greek fret.

gree /ɡriː/ *noun*[1]. *obsolete* exc. *Scot. & dial.* ME.
[ORIGIN Old French *gré* from Latin *gradus* step: cf. GRECE.]
1 = DEGREE *noun* 1a. ME.
†**2** *fig.* = DEGREE *noun* 5. ME–L16.
†**3** = DEGREE *noun* 2. ME–E17.
4 Pre-eminence; mastery; victory in battle. Also, the prize for a victory. ME.
5 = DEGREE *noun* 3. LME.
†**6** = DEGREE *noun* 6. LME–M16.

gree /ɡriː/ *noun*[2]. *arch.* ME.
[ORIGIN Old French & mod. French *gré* pleasure, goodwill, will from Latin *gratum* use as noun of neut. of *gratus* pleasing. Cf. MAUGRE.]
1 Favour, goodwill. Long *rare* exc. *Scot.* ME.
in gree with goodwill or favour, in good part.
2 Satisfaction. Chiefly in phrs. ME.
do gree, **make gree** give satisfaction for an injury. **make one's gree** make one's peace *with*, give satisfaction *to*.
†**3** (One's) good pleasure; will, desire; consent. ME–M18.

gree /ɡriː/ *verb*. *obsolete* exc. *Scot. & dial.* Pa. t. & pple **greed**. LME.
[ORIGIN Aphet. from AGREE *verb* or from GREE *noun*[2]. Cf. Old French *gréer*, which may be the direct source.]
1 *verb trans.* Please, make pleased; reconcile (people); settle (a matter). LME.
2 *verb intrans.* Consent, accede, agree. LME.
3 *verb intrans.* Come into or be in accord or harmony; agree. LME.
■ **greement** *noun* agreement, consent, accord LME.

greed /ɡriːd/ *noun*. L16.
[ORIGIN Back-form. from GREEDY.]
Intense or inordinate longing, esp. for wealth or food; avarice, covetous desire.

P. GALLICO He saw the naked greed and possessive desire come into her eyes.

greed /griːd/ *verb*[1]. *rare*. L17.
[ORIGIN from the noun.]
1 *verb intrans.* Indulge one's greed; be avaricious. L17.
2 *verb trans.* Long for. M19.

greed *verb*[2] *pa. t. & pple* of GREE *verb*.

greedily /ˈgriːdɪli/ *adverb*. OE.
[ORIGIN Partly Old English *grǣdelīce*, from base also of Old Norse *gráðr*, partly Old English *grǣdi(g)līce*, formed as GREEDY: see -LY[2].]
1 With keen appetite; hungrily, ravenously, voraciously. OE.

J. MITCHELL Shrieve found Jumbo there, munching greedily from a plate.

2 Avariciously, covetously, rapaciously. OE.

J. R. GREEN The eyes of the feudal baronage turned greedily on the riches of the Church.

3 Keenly, eagerly. Formerly also, zealously, fervently. ME.

greediness /ˈgriːdɪnɪs/ *noun*.
[ORIGIN Old English *grǣdignes*, formed as GREEDY: see -NESS.]
1 Excessive longing for wealth or gain; avarice, greed. OE.
2 *gen.* Eagerness, keenness. ME.

R. BOYLE A Greediness of Knowledge, that is impatient of being confin'd.

3 Excessive longing for food or drink; gluttony, voracity. LME.

greedy /ˈgriːdi/ *adjective*.
[ORIGIN Old English *grēdiġ*, *grǣdiġ* = Old Saxon *grādag*, Old High German *grātac*, Old Norse *gráðugr*, Gothic *grēdags*, from Germanic, from base meaning 'hunger, greed', of unknown origin.]
1 Having an intense desire or inordinate appetite for food or drink; voracious, gluttonous. Formerly also, hungry. (Foll. by *of*.) OE.

W. BOYD Three sausages! You greedy thing!

2 Eager for gain, wealth, etc.; avaricious, covetous, rapacious. (Foll. by *of*, *for*.) OE.

P. LIVELY Jasper is greedy; he has to have money for its own sake.

3 Keen, eager; intensely desirous *of*, †*to do*. ME.
– COMB.: **greedy-gut(s)** *colloq.* a voracious eater, a glutton.

Greek /griːk/ *noun & adjective*.
[ORIGIN Old English *Grēcas* pl. (so for the most part until 16) corresp. to Middle Low German *Grēke*, Middle Dutch *Grieke*, German *Grieche*, Old Norse *Grikkir* pl., of which the earliest forms are Old English *Crēcas*, Old High German *Chrēch*, Gothic *Krēks*, from Germanic from Latin *Graecus* (applied by the Romans to the people who called themselves *Hellēnes* (see HELLENE)) from Greek *Graikos* adjective (according to Aristotle a prehistoric name of the Hellenes).]
▸ **A** *noun*. **I** A person.
1 A native or inhabitant of Greece, a country in SE Europe occupied by Greek-speaking peoples since about 2000 BC; a person of Greek descent. OE.
2 A member or adherent of the Greek Orthodox Church. LME.
†**3** = GRECIAN *noun* 1b. LME–L17.
4 A cunning or wily person; a cheat, a card sharper. *arch.* E16.

THACKERAY He was an adventurer, a pauper, a blackleg, a regular Greek.

5 In full ***merry Greek***, ***mad Greek***, ***gay Greek***. A boisterous or dissolute person. Long *rare*. M16.
6 An Irish person. *slang*. E19.
▸ **II** [absol. use of the adjective.] Language.
7 The language of Greece or the Greeks, a member of the Hellenic branch of the Indo-European language family; *spec.* Ancient Greek (see ***ancient Greek*** (a) below). OE.

L. DURRELL I asked in Greek and was answered in English.

8 Unintelligible speech or language, gibberish. E17.

DICKENS I am a stranger and this is Greek to me.

▸ **B** *adjective*. [Infl. by Latin *Graecus*, French *grec* adjectives.]
1 Of or pertaining to Greece or its inhabitants; native to or originating in Greece; characteristic of or attributed to Greece or the Greeks; *spec.* ancient Greek (see ***ancient Greek*** (b) below). LME.
2 Belonging to, written in, or spoken in the language of Greece. M16.

MILTON Wretched barbarizing against the Latin and Greek idiom, with their untutored Anglicisms.

3 Designating or pertaining to the national church of Greece, the Greek Orthodox Church. M16.
– SPECIAL COLLOCATIONS & PHRASES: **ancient Greek** (*a*) (also **A-**) (of or pertaining to) the earliest form of Greek, consisting of the Aeolic, Arcadic, Doric, and Ionic (including Attic) dialects, and surviving until about 300 BC; (*b*) of or pertaining to, a native or inhabitant of, Greece from about 2000 to 300 BC. ***at the Greek Calends***: see CALENDS 3. **Greek chorus** (*a*) the chorus in Greek drama; (*b*) *transf.* conduct imitative of this chorus, consisting of open wailing or wise sympathetic comments. **Greek cross** an upright cross with limbs of equal length. ***Greek Cypriot***: **Greek Fathers** the Fathers of the Church who wrote in Greek. ***Greek fire***: see FIRE *noun* 2C. ***Greek fret***: see FRET *noun*[2] 3. **Greek gift** a gift given with intent to harm (with allus. to Virgil's *Aeneid* ii. 49). **Greek god** (*a*) *fig.* a paragon of male beauty; (*b*) a hairstyle with short curls all over the head. ***Greek key***: see KEY *noun*[1]. ***on the Greek Calends***: see CALENDS 3. **Greek salad**: typically containing olives, feta cheese, tomatoes, cucumber, and onion, dressed with olive oil and often lemon juice or vinegar. **Greek valerian** the plant Jacob's ladder, *Polemonium caeruleum*. ***till the Greek Calends***: see CALENDS 3.
■ **Greekdom** *noun* (*a*) the Greek world; (*b*) *arch.* the fraternity of card sharpers: M19. **Greekery** *noun* (*rare*) the practices of or attributed to Greeks; *spec.* (*arch.*) cheating at cards: L17. **Greekess** *noun* (*rare*) a female Greek M19. **Greekless** *adjective* (*rare*) without knowledge of Greek L19. **Greekly** *adverb* (*arch.*) in a Greek fashion, in the Greek language LME. **Greekness** *noun* M19.

Greek /griːk/ *verb*. E17.
[ORIGIN from the noun Cf. Latin *Graecari*.]
†**1** *verb trans.* (with *it*). Follow the practice of the Greeks; play the Greek scholar. E17–L18.
†**2** *verb intrans.* Cheat at cards. *slang*. Only in E19.
3 *verb trans.* COMPUTING. (Usu. **g-**.) Print or reproduce with random or arbitrary characters in place of the actual ones, so as to give an impression of the appearance of a page etc. L20.

Greekish /ˈgriːkɪʃ/ *adjective*. OE.
[ORIGIN In branch I repr. Old English *Crēcisċ*, *Grēcisċ*, from *Crēcas*, *Grēcas* (see GREEK *noun & adjective*); in branch II from GREEK *noun or adjective*: see -ISH[1].]
▸ **I** †**1** = GREEK *adjective* 2. OE–M17.
2 Of or pertaining to Greece or the Greeks. *arch.* ME.

R. CUDWORTH The very Names of many of the Greekish Gods were originally Egyptian.

†**3** = GREEK *adjective* 3. E–M17.
▸ **II 4** Somewhat Greek; resembling Greek persons or things; characteristic of a Greek or Greeks. M16.

R. BURNS There, Learning, with his Greekish face, Grunts out some Latin ditty.

Greekling /ˈgriːklɪŋ/ *noun*. *rare*. M17.
[ORIGIN from GREEK *noun* + -LING[1], after Latin *Graeculus* (Juvenal) dim. of *Graecus* Greek.]
A little Greek; a degenerate contemptible Greek.

green /griːn/ *noun*. In sense 9 also **G-**. OE.
[ORIGIN The adjective used ellipt. or absol.]
1 That which is green; the green part of something; *spec.* a thing distinguished by green colour, as green tea, the green ball in snooker, a green signal, a green bird, etc. OE.

Cue World Chambers wrapped up the first frame . . after missing a straightforward green.

2 Green colour; a shade of this (freq. with specifying word). ME. ▸**b** A pigment of a green colour. Freq. with defining word. E17. ▸**c** The emblematic colour of Ireland. L18.

E. M. FORSTER The main colour was an agricultural green. G. HEYER In a dressing-gown . . of . . material dyed every shade of green.

b ***Brunswick green***, ***Paris green***, ***Scheele's green***, etc.
3 Green clothing or dress; green fabric; in *pl.*, green clothes esp. as uniform. ME.

T. O'BRIEN Harvey wore his dress greens.

4 Verdure, vegetation. Formerly also, a tree, a herb, a plant (usu. in *pl.*). ME. ▸**b** *fig.* Vigour, youthfulness, vitality. LME.

H. BASCOM A vast clearing of felled trees . . in an immeasurably vaster carpet of green.

5 Grassy ground; a grassy area. Now chiefly, a piece of public or common grassy land in the centre of a village or town; a grass plot used for some specified purpose. ME. ▸**b** GOLF. A putting green; a fairway. Also, a golf course. M18.

J. WYNDHAM A small village . . disposed neatly about a triangular green.

bleaching green, ***bowling green***, ***putting green***, etc.
6 In *pl.* †**a** The green parts of a plant or flower. Only in E17. ▸**b** Freshly cut branches or leaves for decoration. Now *US*. L17. ▸**c** The (boiled etc.) leaves and stems of various plants, esp. certain vegetables, for eating; *slang* sexual intercourse. E18.

c L. MACNEICE Fruits and greens are insufficient for health. G. GREENE Why not go after the girl? . . She's not getting . . what is vulgarly called her greens.

c ***collard greens***, ***spring greens***, etc.
7 *sing.* & in *pl.* Money. Cf. GREENBACK *noun* 2. *slang* (orig. *US*). E20.
8 Marijuana of poor quality. *slang* (orig. *US*). M20.
9 A supporter of environmentalism; a conservationist; a member or supporter of an ecological political party. Cf. GREENIE 3. L20.
– PHRASES & COMB.: **green fee** the charge for playing one round on a golf course. **green in one's eye** signs of gullibility or inexperience. **greenkeeper** the keeper of a golf course. **green spot** the spot on which the green ball is placed in snooker. **in the green** in the period of youthful growth or vigour. **on the green** on the stage (cf. GREENGAGE). **the long green** *slang* money. **through the green** GOLF between the tee and the putting green. ***VERDIGRIS green***. ***wigs on the green***: see WIG *noun*[3].

green /griːn/ *adjective & adverb*.
[ORIGIN Old English *grēne* = Old Frisian *grēne*, Old Saxon *grōni* (Dutch *groen*, Old High German *gruoni* (German *grün*), Old Norse *grœnn*, from Germanic, from base of GRASS *noun*, GROW *verb*.]
▸ **A** *adjective*. In sense 2d also **G-**.
▸ **I 1** Of the colour of grass, foliage, an emerald, etc., between blue and yellow in the spectrum. OE. ▸**b** Designating the green-coloured light in a set of lights which when illuminated gives permission to proceed in railway or road traffic signals. L19.
apple green, ***bottle green***, ***grass green***, ***olive green***, ***sea green***, etc.
2 Covered with herbage or foliage; (of a tree) in leaf. OE. ▸**b** (Of a season of the year) characterized by much verdure; (of a winter, Christmas, etc.) mild, without snow. LME. ▸**c** Consisting of green plants or vegetables. LME. ▸**d** Of, pertaining to, or supporting environmentalism, esp. as a political issue; belonging to or supporting an ecological political party. Also, (of a product etc.) not harmful to the environment. L20. ▸**e** ECONOMICS. Designating a currency unit of account or the exchange rate according to which national currencies are translated, used for the payment of agricultural produce in the European Union. L20.

J. RABAN In a green country it is almost impossible to communicate the . . price . . put on vegetation in the desert. A. MASON They were green hills, not the bare stony highlands of the south. **d** *Scientific American* Non-polluting 'green chemicals', detergents, and . . bio-degradable plastics. **e** *Times* The effect . . will be qualified . . by a 4 per cent devaluation of the green pound.

3 Of fruit, a plant, etc.: unripe; young and tender; flourishing; retaining the natural moisture, not dried. OE.

R. BRAUTIGAN Take green walnuts before the shell is formed. P. V. PRICE The berries develop quite rapidly, passing from green to ripe. C. CONRAN Fresh or green pepper is soft and subtle.

4 Having or designating a pale sickly complexion; *fig.* full of jealousy or envy. ME.

B. PLAIN He looked sallow and faintly green. M. ROBERTS She stops, hearing her voice green with jealousy and envy.

▸ **II** *transf.* & *fig.* of sense 3.
5 Not prepared or treated; (of wood etc.) undried, unseasoned; (of meat or fish) uncured, undried, raw; (of hide) untanned; (of pottery, bricks, etc.) unfired. OE. ▸**b** Fresh, new; (of a fire) recently kindled (now chiefly *Scot.*); (of a wound) recent, unhealed, *arch.* ME.
6 Full of vitality; vivid, not faded or worn out; (now only *Scot.*) youthful. OE.

R. L. STEVENSON To lead an adventurous and honourable youth, and to settle . . into a green and smiling age. G. GREENE My memory was green and retentive.

7 (Of a thought, plan, etc.) not fully developed or elaborated; (of a person) immature, inexperienced, naive, gullible; (of an animal) untrained. ME.

H. ROBBINS I might be green in the picture business, but I'm not so dumb as you think. SLOAN WILSON They had been green troops, . . boys who had never been on a combat jump before. M. GEE Her green hopes sprouting in darkness.

– SPECIAL COLLOCATIONS, PHRASES, & COMB.: **be not so green as one is cabbage-looking** *colloq.* be less of a fool than might be assumed. ***green about the gills***: see GILL *noun*[1] 2. **green alga** an alga of the division Chlorophyta, members of which typically have two types of chlorophyll, cellulose cell walls, and starch grains, as in land plants. ***green alkanet***: see ALKANET 2. ***green amaranth***: see AMARANTH 1. **green audit** an assessment of a business as regards its observance of practices which seek to minimize harm to the environment. **green baize** baize of a green colour, used for covering esp. office or card tables; such a table. **green bean** any bean plant, *esp.* the French bean, *Phaseolus vulgaris*, grown for its edible young pods rather than for its seeds; the pod of such a plant (usu. in *pl.*). **green belt** an area of countryside usu. enclosing a built-up area and officially designated as not to be built on. **Green Beret** *colloq.* a British or American commando. **green-blind** *adjective* affected with green-blindness. **green-blindness** = DEUTERANOPIA. **greenbottle** any of various green-bodied dipteran flies of the genus *Lucilia*, esp. *L. caesar*. ***green briar***: see BRIAR *noun*[1]. **green card** (*a*) a card to be filled in by a person seeking an interview with an MP at the Houses of Parliament; (*b*) an international insurance document for motorists taking their cars abroad; (*c*) *US* a permit enabling a foreign national to live and work permanently in the US. **green carder** a holder of a US green card. **green channel** at a port, airport, etc., the channel through which passengers should pass who have no goods to declare. **green cheese** (*a*) whey cheese; (*b*) cheese coloured green with sage; (*c*) unripened or unmatured cheese. ***green COPPERAS***. **green crop**: used for fodder while in a green or unripe state rather than as hay etc. **Green Cross code** a kerb drill esp. taught to children. ***green dragon***: see DRAGON *noun* 9. ***green drake***: see DRAKE *noun*[1] 4. **green earth** = GLAUCONITE. **green eye** (*a*) an eye with a green iris; (*b*) *fig.* jealousy. **green-eyed** *adjective* with green eyes; *fig.* jealous (***green-eyed monster***, jealousy). ***green fallow***: see FALLOW *noun*. **green fat**: of a turtle, esteemed by gourmets. **greenfeed** (chiefly *Austral. & NZ*) forage grown to be fed fresh to livestock. **greenfield** *adjective* designating a site with no previous (similar) building development, or (*fig.*) a business with only the prospect rather than the record of profitability. **greenfinch** any of a number of green-plumaged

G

Old World finches of the genus *Carduelis*; *spec.* a common Eurasian and N. African finch, *Carduelis chloris*, with green and yellow plumage. **green fingers** *colloq.* skill in making plants grow. **greenfly** a green aphid; *collect.* green aphids. ***green ginger***: see GINGER *noun*. **green goose** (now chiefly *dial.*) a young goose, *esp.* one killed under four months old. **greenhead** (*a*) (now *rare*) an inexperienced or ignorant person; (*b*) *N. Amer.* a green-eyed biting tabanid fly, esp. *Tabanus nigrovittatus*; (*c*) an Australian ant, *Ectatomma metallicum*, with a painful sting. **greenheart** a tall evergreen tree of northern S. America, *Ocotea rodiaei*, of the laurel family (also called ***bebeeru***, ***sipeera***); its strong dark green wood, used for shipbuilding etc. ***green*** HELLEBORE. **green heron** either of two small herons with greenish upperparts, the pantropical *Butorides striatus* and the N. American *B. virescens* (often considered conspecific). **greenhorn** an inexperienced person, a novice, a raw recruit; an ignoramus, a simpleton. **greenhouse** (*a*) a transparent glass or plastic building for rearing or hastening the growth of plants; ***greenhouse effect***, the heating of the surface and lower atmosphere of a planet due to the greater transparency of the atmosphere to visible radiation from the sun than to infrared radiation from the planet; ***greenhouse gas***, carbon dioxide or another gas contributing to the greenhouse effect; (*b*) *slang* the cockpit of a plane. **green lane** a permanent untarred lane giving access to woodland, fields, etc. ***green leek***: see LEEK 3. **green light** *fig.* permission to proceed on a project. **green-light** *verb trans. & intrans.* give (a person) permission to proceed on a project etc. **green linnet** *arch.* the common greenfinch, *Carduelis chloris*. **green man** (*a*) (chiefly *hist.*) a man dressed up in greenery to represent a wild man of the woods or seasonal fertility; †(*b*) an inexperienced sailor on a whaling vessel; (*c*) *colloq.* a symbol of a walking figure illuminated green on some types of pedestrian crossing to indicate a time to cross. **green manure** growing plants ploughed into the soil as fertilizer. ***green*** MEALIE. ***green meat***: see MEAT *noun*. **green monkey** the common African savannah monkey, *Cercopithecus aethiops*; *spec.* one of a dark-faced W. African race, often tamed (cf. VERVET). **Green Mountain State** *US* Vermont. **green onion** *N. Amer.* a spring onion. **Green Paper** a tentative report of British government proposals without any commitment to action. **Green Party** (in the UK) an ecological political party. ***green plant***: see PLANT *noun* 2. **green plover** the lapwing, *Vanellus vanellus*. **green porphyry** PETROGRAPHY = *greenstone* (a) below. **green pound** the exchange rate for the pound for payments for agricultural produce in the European Union. **green revolution** greatly increased crop production in developing countries through the introduction of modern farming methods and higher-yielding seeds. **green road** a permanent untarred road, esp. a farm road, giving access to fields etc. **green room**: in a theatre for actors and actresses who are not onstage. **green salad**: chiefly composed of green ingredients such as lettuce, chicory, cucumber, watercress, etc. **greensand** (*a*) = GLAUCONITE; (*b*) a kind of sandstone consisting largely of grains of quartz and glauconite; *esp.* (**G-**) as forming strata in the Cretaceous System in southern England. **green sandpiper** a migratory Eurasian sandpiper, *Tringa ochropus*, with dark greenish-brown upperparts. **green sauce** a savoury sauce with a sharp taste made with sorrel or with herbs and vinegar. **greenshank** an elegant green-legged Eurasian sandpiper, *Tringa nebularia*. **greensick** *adjective* (now *rare*) affected with greensickness. **greensickness** = CHLOROSIS *noun* 1. **greenstick** *adjective* designating a type of bone fracture, esp. in children, in which one side of the bone is broken and one only bent. **greenstone** (*a*) any igneous rock of dark-green appearance, esp. containing chlorite, epidote, hornblende, etc.; (*b*) nephrite, esp. of New Zealand origin. **greenstuff** (*a*) vegetation; (*b*) in *pl.*, green vegetables. **greensward** *arch.* grassy turf; an expanse of this. **green tea**: made from steam-dried rather than fermented leaves (cf. ***black tea*** s.v. BLACK *adjective*). **green thumb** *colloq.* = ***green fingers*** above. **green tobacco**: see TOBACCO 2. **green turtle** a turtle, *Chelonia mydas*, with a brown or olive carapace, found in warm seas worldwide. ***green*** VITRIOL. **greenwash** [after WHITEWASH] misleading publicity or propaganda designed to present an image of environmental responsibility. **greenweed** a low-growing yellow-flowered leguminous shrub of rough pastures, *Genista tinctoria*, formerly used to make a green dye (more fully ***dyer's greenweed***); also, any of several other shrubs of this genus. **greenwood** a wood or forest in leaf, esp. as the typical scene of medieval outlaw life. **green woodpecker** a large European woodpecker, *Picus viridis*, with largely green and yellow plumage and a red crown. **greenyard** (chiefly *dial.*) an enclosure for stray animals, a pound. ***little green man***: see LITTLE *adjective*. ***wear the green willow***: see WILLOW *noun*.

▸ **B** *adverb*. ***run green***, (of a racehorse etc.) be easily upset or distracted during a race through lack of experience. L19.

Sporting Life She ran very green and didn't seem to know what racing was about until the final two furlongs.

green /griːn/ *verb*[1].

[ORIGIN Old English *grēnian*, from *grēne*: see GREEN *adjective & adverb*.]

1 *verb intrans.* Become green; *esp.* become covered (*over*) with verdure. OE.

M. SARTON Slowly the grass has been greening over. D. DUNN The first leaves are greening.

2 a *verb trans.* Colour or stain green; cover (*over*) with verdure. Also foll. by *up*. L16. ▸**b** *verb trans.* & (*rare*) *intrans.* Turn (oysters) green in the gills by putting them in pits. M17.

a T. HARDY The .. white frock .. which she had so carelessly greened .. on the damping grass. S. NAIPAUL Elephantine limbs, greened with moss, spread .. high above their heads.

3 *verb trans.* Hoax, take in. *slang.* L19.

4 *verb trans.* **a** Make (an urban area) more verdant by tree-planting etc.; reclaim (desert); *fig.* rejuvenate. M20. ▸**b** Cause to adopt policies or behaviour beneficial to the environment. L20.

green /griːn/ *verb*[2] *intrans. Scot.* LME.

[ORIGIN Perh. (with metathesis) from Old Norse *girna* = Old English *giernan*, (Northumbrian) *giorna*: see YEARN *verb*[1].]

Desire earnestly; yearn *after*, *for*.

greenback /ˈgriːnbak/ *noun*. L18.

[ORIGIN from GREEN *adjective* + BACK *noun*[1].]

1 An animal, bird, fish, or other creature with a green back. L18.

2 A monetary note issued by the US Government; *gen.* the US dollar; in *pl.*, money. Cf. GREEN *noun* 7. M19.

S. BELLOW A check? Hell with a check. Get me the greenbacks. *Times* Every currency heaved in the wake of the mighty greenback.

3 A book with a green cover. L19.

4 A disease of tomatoes, often due to potassium deficiency, shown by hard green patches on the calyx side of the fruit. E20.

green cloth /griːn ˈklɒθ/ *noun phr.* In sense 1 also **G- C-**. LME.

[ORIGIN from GREEN *adjective* + CLOTH *noun*, with ref. to the green-covered table at which business was orig. transacted.]

1 A board or department of the royal household, consisting of the Lord Steward and his staff and controlling various financial, legal, and judicial matters within the sovereign's household. LME.

2 (The green woollen material covering) a billiard, pool, etc., table. L19.

Greeneian /ˈgriːnɪən/ *adjective*. Also **Greenian**. M20.

[ORIGIN from Graham *Greene* (1904–91), English writer + -IAN.]

Typical or characteristic of the style or matter of the works of Graham Greene. Cf. GREENELAND.

Greeneland /ˈgriːnlənd/ *noun*. M20.

[ORIGIN formed as GREENEIAN + LAND *noun*[1].]

The seedy politically unstable and dangerous world said to be the typical setting for the characters in the novels of Graham Greene.

greener /ˈgriːnə/ *noun*[1]. *slang.* L19.

[ORIGIN from GREEN *adjective* + -ER[1]. Cf. Yiddish *griner* greenhorn.]

An inexperienced or naive person.

N. ALGREN He's over there shakin' down the greenhorns 'n the biggest greener on his beat is his own brother.

Greener /ˈgriːnə/ *noun*[2] & *adjective*. L19.

[ORIGIN W. *Greener* (1806–69) or his son, W. W. *Greener*, gunsmiths and authors.]

▸ **A** *noun*. A gun made by or according to the designs of W. or W. W. Greener. L19.

▸ **B** *adjective*. Designating guns, rifles, cartridges, etc., made by or according to the designs of W. or W. W. Greener. L19.

greenery /ˈgriːn(ə)ri/ *noun*. L18.

[ORIGIN from GREEN *adjective* or *noun* + -ERY.]

1 Green foliage or vegetation; this used for decoration. L18.

A. MASON The dense greenery which clothed the banks on either side was rank and tangled jungle. A. MUNRO There is a hot tub surrounded by windows and greenery.

2 A place where plants are reared, kept, or exhibited. Now *rare*. M19.

greenery-yallery /ˌgriːn(ə)rɪˈjal(ə)ri/ *adjective*. *colloq.* L19.

[ORIGIN from GREEN *adjective* + *yaller* var. of YELLOW *adjective* + -Y[1], with redupl. suffix.]

Of, pertaining to, or affecting the colours green and yellow, after the style of the late 19th-cent. Aesthetic Movement; *transf.* affected.

B. PYM The advance copy has a springlike or greenery-yallery cover. CLIVE JAMES Greenery-yallery fin de siècle lyricism.

greeney *noun* see GREENIE.

greengage /ˈgriːngeɪdʒ/ *noun*. E18.

[ORIGIN from GREEN *adjective* + Sir William *Gage* (1657–1727), who introduced it to England.]

1 Any of several round green-fleshed fine-flavoured kinds of plum; the tree bearing this fruit. E18.

2 The stage; in *pl.*, wages. *rhyming slang.* M20.

greengrocer /ˈgriːngrəʊsə/ *noun*. E18.

[ORIGIN from GREEN *noun* or *adjective* + GROCER.]

A retail dealer in fruit and vegetables.

■ **greengrocery** *noun* the business of or the goods sold by a greengrocer E19.

Greenian *adjective* var. of GREENEIAN.

greenie /ˈgriːni/ *noun*. Also (exc. in sense 3) **green(e)y**. E19.

[ORIGIN from GREEN *adjective* + -IE.]

1 A green-coloured bird; *spec.* (*dial.*) a greenfinch. E19.

2 A greenhorn. *colloq.* M19.

3 A conservationist. Cf. GREEN *noun* 9. *colloq.* (chiefly *Austral. & NZ*). L20.

greening /ˈgriːnɪŋ/ *noun*. E17.

[ORIGIN Prob. from Middle Dutch *groeninc* (Dutch *groening*) kind of apple: see GREEN *adjective*, -ING[3].]

Orig., a kind of pear. Now, a kind of apple which is green when ripe (also ***Rhode Island greening***).

greenish /ˈgriːnɪʃ/ *adjective*. LME.

[ORIGIN from GREEN *adjective* + -ISH[1].]

Somewhat green.

Greenland /ˈgriːnlənd/ *noun*. L17.

[ORIGIN A large island in the Arctic Ocean.]

Used ***attrib.*** to designate animals, plants, etc., native to or associated with Greenland.

Greenland dove: see DOVE *noun* 1b. **Greenland right whale**, **Greenland whale** a large right whale, *Balaena mysticetus*, of Arctic seas; also called ***bowhead***. **Greenland shark** a shark of the northern N. Atlantic, *Somniosus microcephalus*; also called ***gurry-shark***, ***sleeper shark***. ***Greenland whale***: see ***Greenland right whale*** above.

■ **Greenlander** *noun* (*a*) a native or inhabitant of Greenland; †(*b*) a type of small sailing ship used in war: L17. **Green'landic** *adjective & noun* (*a*) *adjective* of or pertaining to Greenland, its inhabitants, or its language, a dialect of Inupiaq; (*b*) *noun* the language or dialect of Greenland: E19. **Greenlandish** *adjective & noun* (*a*) *adjective* characteristic of Greenland; (*b*) *noun* = GREENLANDIC *noun*: L18.

greenless /ˈgriːnlɪs/ *adjective*. E17.

[ORIGIN from GREEN *noun* + -LESS.]

Without greenness or verdure.

greenlet /ˈgriːnlɪt/ *noun*. M19.

[ORIGIN from GREEN *adjective* + -LET: app. formed to render the etym. sense of Latin *vireo*.]

= VIREO; *spec.* a member of the S. and Central American genus *Hylophilus*.

greenling /ˈgriːnlɪŋ/ *noun*. ME.

[ORIGIN from GREEN *adjective* + -LING[1].]

1 A fish of the family Gadidae, *esp.* a pollack. *local.* ME.

2 A food fish, *Hexagrammos duagrammus*, of the N. Pacific. E20.

greenly /ˈgriːnli/ *adverb*. L16.

[ORIGIN from GREEN *adjective* + -LY[2].]

1 With a green colour; with green vegetation. L16.

J. MITCHELL Primrose Hill rose greenly above the surrounding roofs.

2 In an inexperienced or untrained manner; unskilfully. *arch.* exc. in ***run greenly*** below. L16.

run greenly = ***run green*** s.v. GREEN *adverb*.

3 Freshly, vigorously; vividly. M17.

greenmail /ˈgriːnmeɪl/ *noun*. L20.

[ORIGIN from GREEN *adjective* + BLACK)MAIL *noun*: cf. GREEN *noun* 7.]

STOCK EXCHANGE. The practice of purchasing enough shares in a company to threaten a takeover, thereby forcing the owners to buy them back at a higher price in order to retain control of the business.

■ **greenmailer** *noun* L20.

greenness /ˈgriːnnɪs/ *noun*. OE.

[ORIGIN from GREEN *adjective* + -NESS.]

1 Green colour; green vegetation. OE.

2 Vigour; vitality; youth. ME. ▸**b** Freshness, newness. Long only *Scot.* M16.

3 Unripeness of fruit etc. Now *rare*. LME. ▸**b** *fig.* Immaturity; inexperience; gullibility, naivety. LME.

4 Awareness of ecological issues; commitment to environmental conservation. L20.

greenockite /ˈgriːnəkʌɪt/ *noun*. M19.

[ORIGIN from Charles Murray Cathcart, Lord *Greenock*, later Earl Cathcart, (1783–1859), Scot. general + -ITE[1].]

MINERALOGY. Native cadmium sulphide, which crystallizes in the hexagonal system and usu. occurs as a yellow crust on zinc ores.

greenth /griːnθ/ *noun*. *literary.* M18.

[ORIGIN from GREEN *adjective* + -TH[1].]

Verdure.

Greenwell /ˈgriːnwɛl/ *noun*. L19.

[ORIGIN The Revd William *Greenwell* (1820–1918), English archaeologist and angler.]

In full ***Greenwell's glory***. A fishing fly designed by Greenwell.

Greenwich /ˈgrɛnɪtʃ, -ɪdʒ/ *noun*. M19.

[ORIGIN Former site of the Royal Observatory, in London.]

1 ***Greenwich Mean Time***, ***Greenwich time***, the mean solar time on the meridian of Greenwich, used as an international basis of time reckoning. M19.

2 ***Greenwich meridian***, the prime meridian, passing through Greenwich. L19.

greeny *noun* see GREENIE.

greeny /ˈgriːni/ *adjective*. L16.

[ORIGIN from GREEN *adjective* + -Y[1].]

†**1** Green, verdant; vigorous. L16–L17.

2 = GREENISH. E19.

greeshoch /ˈgriːʃɔx/ *noun*. *Scot.* E19.

[ORIGIN Gaelic *griosach* embers, from *grios*, *gris* heat.]

(A fire of) hot embers.

greet /griːt/ *noun*. *obsolete* exc. *Scot.* ME.

[ORIGIN from GREET *verb*[2].]

Weeping, lamentation; a cry of sorrow.

greet /griːt/ *verb*¹.
[ORIGIN Old English *grētan* = Old Frisian *grēta* salute, complain, Old Saxon *grōtian* call upon (Dutch *groeten* salute), Old High German *gruozzen* address, attack (German *grüssen* salute, greet), from West Germanic.]
†**1** *verb trans.* Approach; begin on, begin to treat or handle. Only in OE.
†**2** *verb trans.* Assail, attack. OE–LME.
3 *verb trans.* Accost or address with a salutation customary on meeting; send one's own or another's regards to (a person) (now chiefly *literary*). OE. ▸**b** Salute *with* words or gestures; receive on meeting or arrival *with* some speech or action (friendly or otherwise). OE. ▸†**c** Offer congratulations on (an achievement etc.). *rare* (Spenser). Only in L16. ▸†**d** Gratify, please. L16–E17.
P. BOWLES She . . rose . . to greet him. 'Mr. Tunner! How delightful!' J. HELLER He greeted Milo jovially each time they met. *absol.*: DRYDEN None greets, for none the greeting will return. **b** V. SACKVILLE-WEST They greeted her arrival always with beaming smiles. M. L. KING He forgot to greet me with the usual 'hello.' G. GREENE He greeted his mother with an exaggerated hug. KARL MILLER When the doctor arrived to deliver Frost, the father greeted him with a revolver. **d** SHAKES. *Per.* It greets me as an enterprise of kindness Perform'd to your sole daughter.
4 †**a** *verb intrans.* Meet *with*. *rare*. Only in L16. ▸**b** *verb trans.* Receive or meet with demonstrations of welcome. E17.
b LD MACAULAY The cavalcade . . was greeted two miles from the city by the bishop and clergy.
5 *verb trans.* Orig., of a thing: present itself to. Now only, of sights or sounds: meet, become apparent to or noticed by. L17.
J. FRYER The Sea on one side greets its Marble Walls. H. I. JENKINSON A wide extent of sea greets the eye.
6 Of a response: be addressed to (a person) or evoked by (an action etc.); hail. L19.
J. R. GREEN Shouts of assent greeted the resolution. A. S. NEILL The contemptuous glance that usually greets the man who blows his own horn. B. EMECHETA The laughter that greeted this remark was unreal.
■ **greeter** *noun*¹ LME.

greet /griːt/ *verb*². Now *Scot.* & *N. English*. OE.
[ORIGIN Partly Old English (Anglian) *grētan* = Old Saxon *grātan*, Middle High German *grāzen* cry out, rage, storm, Old Norse *gráta*, Gothic *grētan* from Germanic, orig. redupl. strong verb rel. to GREET *verb*¹; partly Old English *grēotan* (= Old Saxon *griotan*) perh. from Germanic base of Y- + verb repr. by synon. Old English *rēotan*.]
1 *verb intrans.* Weep, cry, lament, grieve. OE. ▸†**b** *verb trans.* Shed (tears). ME–E18.
†**2** *verb trans.* Weep for, lament, bewail. OE–ME.
†**3** *verb intrans.* Cry or call out in supplication or anger. ME–E16.
■ **greeter** *noun*² (*rare*) E19. **greety** *adjective* (*rare*) inclined to shed tears, tearful LME.

greeting /ˈgriːtɪŋ/ *noun*. OE.
[ORIGIN from GREET *verb*¹ + -ING¹.]
The action of GREET *verb*¹. Also, an instance of this, a salutation, (freq. in *pl.*).
H. JAMES They had exchanged greetings. J. BARTH I met Col. Morton . . and tipped my hat in greeting.
– COMB.: **greetings card** a (usu. folded) card having a decorated outer cover and inside a message of goodwill etc. for a particular anniversary etc.

greffier /ˈgrɛfɪə/ *noun*. L16.
[ORIGIN French from medieval Latin *graphiarius* registrar, from *graphium* register: see GRAFF *noun*¹.]
A registrar or notary, esp. in the Channel Islands.

gregal /ˈgriːg(ə)l/ *adjective*. M16.
[ORIGIN Latin *gregalis*, from *grex, greg-*: see -AL¹.]
1 Pertaining to a flock or to the common people. *rare*. M16.
†**2** = GREGARIOUS 1. E–M17.

gregale /greɪˈgɑːleɪ/ *noun*. E19.
[ORIGIN from Italian *grecale*, app. repr. late Latin noun from Latin *Graecus* Greek.]
A strong north-east wind blowing in the Mediterranean.

gregarian /grɪˈgɛːrɪən/ *adjective*. Long *rare* or *obsolete*. M17.
[ORIGIN from Latin *gregarius* (see GREGARIOUS) + -AN.]
Of or pertaining to flocks or crowds, common.

gregarine /ˈgrɛgərʌɪn/ *noun* & *adjective*. M19.
[ORIGIN from mod. Latin *Gregarina* genus name, from Latin *gregarius*: see GREGARIOUS, -INE¹.]
▸ **A** *noun*. Any of numerous vermiform protozoans of the sporozoan subclass Gregarinidia (or Gregarina), internal parasites chiefly of insects, annelids, and other invertebrates. M19.
▸ **B** *adjective*. Of or relating to this subclass. L19.

gregarious /grɪˈgɛːrɪəs/ *adjective*. M17.
[ORIGIN from Latin *gregarius*, from *grex, greg-* flock, herd + -OUS: see -ARIOUS.]
1 Of kinds of animal: tending to live in flocks or loosely organized communities. M17. ▸**b** Of a person: inclined to associate with others, fond of company. L18.
b R. COBB Edward was naturally gregarious, always in need of a wide audience of friends. M. MEYER Strindberg in his gregarious way was to enjoy many . . contacts.
2 *BOTANY*. Growing in open clusters or (*ECOLOGY*) in pure associations. E19.
3 Of or pertaining to a flock or community; characteristic of or affecting people gathered together in a crowd. M19.
DICKENS An instance of the gregarious effect of an excitement.
■ **gregariously** *adverb* L17. **gregariousness** *noun* E19.

gregarization /grɛgərʌɪˈzeɪʃ(ə)n/ *noun*. Also **-isation**. M20.
[ORIGIN from mod. Latin *gregaria* swarming form of locust + -IZATION.]
ENTOMOLOGY. The development of swarming behaviour and morphology in locusts.

grège *noun* var. of GREIGE.

grego /ˈgreɪgəʊ/ *noun*. Pl. **-os**. M18.
[ORIGIN from some Proto-Romance alt. of Latin *Graecus* GREEK *adjective*.]
A coarse jacket with a hood, worn in the eastern Mediterranean region. Also (*arch. slang*) a rough greatcoat.

Gregorian /grɪˈgɔːrɪən/ *adjective* & *noun*. L16.
[ORIGIN Partly from medieval Latin *Gregorianus* (in sense 2 *cantus Gregorianus*) from late Latin *Gregorius* from Greek *Grēgorios*; partly from the English name *Gregory*: see -IAN.]
▸ **A** *adjective*. **1** Of, pertaining to, or established by Pope Gregory XIII (1502–85). L16.
Gregorian calendar the modified form of the Julian calendar, established by Pope Gregory XIII in 1582 and adopted in Britain in 1752.
2 Of or pertaining to Pope Gregory I (*c* 560–604); *esp.* designating or according to the plainsong ritual music or chant founded on the Antiphoner attributed to him. L16.
Gregorian tones in the RC Ch., the eight plainsong melodies prescribed for the psalms.
†**3** ***Gregorian tree***, the gallows. (Cf. GREGORY 2.) M17–L18.
4 Designating a kind of reflecting telescope, invented by J. Gregory (1638–75), Scottish mathematician, in which light reflected from a secondary mirror passes through a hole in the primary mirror. M18.
▸ **B** *noun*. †**1** A variety of wig worn in the 16th and 17th cents. and supposedly named after its inventor, a Strand barber. L16–M17.
2 A member of a society (often classed with the Freemasons) which existed in England in the 18th cent. *obsolete* exc. *hist.* M18.
3 A Gregorian chant. L19.

gregory /ˈgrɛg(ə)ri/ *noun*¹. Also **G-**. L16.
[ORIGIN The English name *Gregory* in various applications.]
†**1** A gentleman of fashion. *rare*. Only in L16.
†**2** A hangman. (Cf. GREGORIAN *adjective* 3.) Only in M17.
3 A feast, a party; *esp.* one held on St Gregory's day (12 March). *Irish*. E19.

Gregory /ˈgrɛg(ə)ri/ *noun*². L19.
[ORIGIN James *Gregory* (1758–1822), Scot. physician.]
In full ***Gregory powder***, ***Gregory's powder***. A laxative powder containing rhubarb, ginger, and magnesium carbonate.

greige /greɪʒ/ *adjective* & *noun*. Also **grège** /greʒ/. E20.
[ORIGIN French, in *soie grège* raw silk, from Italian *greggio* raw, crude, unprocessed.]
(Of) a colour between beige and grey.

greisen /ˈgrʌɪz(ə)n/ *noun*. L19.
[ORIGIN German, prob. dial. from *greis* grey with age.]
PETROGRAPHY. A light-coloured rock containing quartz, mica, and fluorine-rich minerals, produced by the pneumatolysis of granite.
■ **greisening**, **greiseniˈzation** *nouns* the pneumatolytic alteration of granite by fluorine-rich vapour E20.

greking /ˈgriːkɪŋ/ *noun*. Long *obsolete* exc. *Scot.* ME.
[ORIGIN Corresp. to Middle Dutch *griekinge*, prob. from base of Old Norse *grýja* to dawn.]
Daybreak, dawn.

Grelling /ˈgrɛlɪŋ/ *noun*. M20.
[ORIGIN Kurt *Grelling* (1886–1942), German logician.]
PHILOSOPHY. ***Grelling's paradox***, ***Grelling's antinomy***, a semantic paradox concerning the applicability of the word 'heterological' to itself.

gremial /ˈgriːmɪəl/ *noun* & *adjective*. M16.
[ORIGIN medieval Latin *gremialis* alumnus, *gremiale* bishop's apron, from Latin *gremium* lap, bosom: see -IAL.]
▸ **A** *noun*. **1** A resident member (of a university or society). *obsolete* exc. *hist.* M16.
2 A silk apron placed on a bishop's lap when celebrating Mass or conferring orders. E19.
▸ **B** *adjective*. **1** Of or pertaining to the bosom or lap; *fig.* (of a friend etc.) intimate. *obsolete* exc. in ***gremial veil*** = sense A.2 above. M17.
2 Living within a university or society, resident. Also, designating ordinary or full members of a society as opp. to honorary members. *obsolete* exc. *hist.* M18.

gremlin /ˈgrɛmlɪn/ *noun*. E20.
[ORIGIN Prob. after *goblin*.]
1 Orig., a menial, a dogsbody. Now, a mischievous sprite alleged to cause mechanical or other faults, esp. in aircraft. *colloq.* E20.
2 A young surfer. Also, a troublemaker who frequents the beaches but does not surf. *Surfing slang*. M20.

gremmie /ˈgrɛmi/ *noun*. *Surfing slang*. Also **gremmy**. M20.
[ORIGIN from GREM(LIN: see -IE, -Y⁶.]
= GREMLIN 2.

Grenache /grəˈnaʃ/ *noun*. M19.
[ORIGIN French.]
(The black grape producing) a sweet dessert wine from the Languedoc-Roussillon region of France.

Grenadan /grɪˈneɪdən/ *noun* & *adjective*. M20.
[ORIGIN formed as GRENADIAN + -AN.]
= GRENADIAN.

grenade /grəˈneɪd/ *noun*¹. M16.
[ORIGIN French, alt. of Old French & mod. French (*pome*) *grenate* POMEGRANATE after Spanish *granada*.]
†**1** A pomegranate. M16–M17.
2 A small explosive shell designed to be thrown by hand or launched mechanically. L16.
hand grenade, ***rifle grenade***.
3 A glass receptacle thrown to break and disperse chemicals etc. for testing drains, extinguishing fires, etc. L19.
– COMB.: **grenade launcher** a device for launching grenades.

G

grenade /grəˈneɪd/ *noun*². Long *rare*. E18.
[ORIGIN Perh. from French *grain* GRAIN *noun*¹ with the sense 'something spiced' (cf. Old French *grané* mentioned s.v. GRAVY). Cf. GRENADINE *noun*¹.]
A dish consisting of pieces of larded veal braised with pigeons.

grenade /grəˈneɪd/ *verb trans.* M19.
[ORIGIN from GRENADE *noun*¹.]
Attack with a grenade or grenades.

Grenadian /grɪˈneɪdɪən/ *noun* & *adjective*. E20.
[ORIGIN from *Grenada* (see below) + -IAN.]
▸ **A** *noun*. A native or inhabitant of Grenada, an island in the W. Indies. E20.
▸ **B** *adjective*. Of or pertaining to Grenada or its inhabitants. M20.

grenadier /grɛnəˈdɪə/ *noun*. L17.
[ORIGIN French, formed as GRENADE *noun*¹: see -IER.]
1 Orig., a soldier who threw grenades. Later, each of a company formed from the tallest men in a regiment. Now, a member of the Grenadier Guards (see below). L17.
Grenadier Guards (in the British army) the first regiment of household infantry.
2 Any of several African weaver birds or waxbills, usu. with red in the plumage; *esp.* (more fully ***common grenadier***) *Uraeginthus granatina*, and the red bishop, *Euplectes orix*. M18. ▸**b** A notably tall person. E19. ▸**c** A rat-tail (fish). L19.

grenadilla *noun* var. of GRANADILLA.

grenadine /ˈgrɛnədiːn/ *noun*¹. E18.
[ORIGIN French *grenadin*: cf. GRENADE *noun*².]
A dish of veal or of poultry fillets, trimmed, larded, and glazed.

grenadine /ˈgrɛnədiːn/ *noun*² & *adjective*. M19.
[ORIGIN French (formerly *grenade*) silk of a grained texture, from *grenu* grained, from *grain* GRAIN *noun*¹: see -INE⁴.]
(Of) a fabric of loosely woven silk or silk and wool.

grenadine /ˈgrɛnədiːn/ *noun*³. L19.
[ORIGIN French (*sirop de*) *grenadine* from *grenade* GRENADE *noun*¹.]
A cordial syrup made from pomegranates; a drink of this.

grenado /grɪˈneɪdəʊ/ *noun*. *arch.* Pl. **-o(e)s**. E17.
[ORIGIN Spanish *granada*: see GRENADE *noun*¹, -ADO.]
= GRENADE *noun*¹ 2.

grenat /grənа/ *noun* & *adjective*. M19.
[ORIGIN French: see GARNET *noun*¹.]
(Of) a deep red colour, like that of a garnet.

Grenfell /ˈgrɛnfɛl/ *noun*. E20.
[ORIGIN Sir Wilfred Thomason *Grenfell* (1865–1940), English medical missionary who founded the Labrador Medical Mission in 1893.]
(Proprietary name for) a type of tough closely woven windproofed cotton fabric.

Grenzbegriff /ˈgrɛntsbəgrɪf/ *noun*. L19.
[ORIGIN German, from *Grenze* limit, boundary + *Begriff* concept.]
In Kantian philosophy, a concept showing the limitation of sense experience, a limiting concept; *gen.* a conception of an unattained ideal.

grep /grɛp/ *noun* & *verb*. L20.
[ORIGIN Acronym from *get* (or *global*) *regular expression print*.]
COMPUTING. ▸**A** *noun*. A utility in the Unix operating system used to search files for the occurrence of a chosen string of characters.
▸ **B** *verb trans.* Search (a file or files) for a string of characters by means of this utility.

Grepo /ˈgrɛpəʊ/ *noun*. Pl. **-os**. M20.
[ORIGIN German *Gre(nz)po(lizei* frontier police.]
hist. An East Berlin border guard.

grès /grɛ/ *noun*. **L19**.
[**ORIGIN** French.]
Stoneware. Chiefly in ***grès de Flandres*** /də flɑ̃:dr/, Flemish ware.

Gresham's law /ˈgrɛʃ(ə)mz lɔː/ *noun phr.* **M19**.
[**ORIGIN** Sir Thomas *Gresham* (d. 1579), English financier and founder of the Royal Exchange.]
ECONOMICS. The tendency for money of lower intrinsic value to circulate more freely than money of higher intrinsic and equal nominal value.

gressible /ˈgrɛsɪb(ə)l/ *adjective*. Long *rare* or *obsolete*. **E17**.
[**ORIGIN** Late Latin *gressibilis* from Latin *gress-* pa. ppl stem of *gradi* proceed, walk: see **-IBLE**.]
Able to walk.

gressorial /grɛˈsɔːrɪəl/ *adjective*. **M19**.
[**ORIGIN** from mod. Latin *gressorius*, from *gress-* (see **GRESSIBLE**) + **-AL**[1].]
ZOOLOGY. Walking; adapted for walking.

Gretchen /ˈgrɛtʃ(ə)n/ *noun*. **L19**.
[**ORIGIN** See below.]
A girl held to resemble Gretchen, the heroine seduced by Faust in Goethe's play; a typically German girl or woman. Freq. *attrib.*

Gretna Green /grɛtnə ˈgriːn/ *adjectival phr.* **E19**.
[**ORIGIN** A village in Scotland, close to the border with England.]
hist. Designating or pertaining to a marriage contracted by an eloping couple from England immediately after entering Scotland, where parental consent was not necessary.

†**greund** *noun*. **LME–M19**.
[**ORIGIN** App. contr.]
A greyhound.

grevillea /grɪˈvɪlɪə/ *noun*. **M19**.
[**ORIGIN** mod. Latin (see below), from Charles Francis *Greville* (1749–1809), Scot. horticulturist.]
Any of various chiefly Australian trees and shrubs of the genus *Grevillea* (family Proteaceae), bearing conspicuous but petalless flowers with prominent styles.

Grevy's zebra /ˌgrɛvɪz ˈziːbrə, ˈzɛbrə/ *noun phr.* Also **Grévy's zebra** /ˌgreɪviːz/. **L19**.
[**ORIGIN** from F. P. Jules *Grévy* (1807–91), French president.]
An endangered zebra, *Equus grevyi*, which has narrow stripes, a white belly, and prominent broad ears, and is found on arid steppe from Ethiopia to Kenya.

grew /gruː/ *noun & adjective*. **ME**.
[**ORIGIN** Old French *griu* from Latin *Graecus* **GREEK** *noun & adjective*. In sense A.2 abbreviation of *grew-hound*.]
▸ **A** *noun*. †**1** The Greek language; a Greek. **ME–M16**.
2 A greyhound. *Scot. & N. English*. **M16**.
▸ **B** *adjective*. Greek. Long *obsolete* exc. *Scot.* in ***grew-hound*** [alt. of **GREUND**], a greyhound. **LME**.

grew *verb pa. t.*: see **GROW** *verb*.

grex /grɛks/ *noun*. **M20**.
[**ORIGIN** Latin = flock.]
MYCOLOGY. A cohesive, often mobile clump of amoeboid cells formed during the migratory phase of the life cycle of some cellular slime moulds. Also called ***slug***.

grey /greɪ/ *noun*. Also ***gray**. **ME**.
[**ORIGIN** The adjective used ellipt. or absol.]
1 Grey clothing or fabric. **ME**. ▸**b** The uniform of the Confederate troops in the American Civil War. *US*. **M19**. ▸**c** Unbleached fabric. **L19**. ▸**d** In *pl.* Grey flannel trousers. *colloq.* **M20**.

G. DOWNES A blind old man, dressed in grey.

†**2** (The fur or dressed skin of) a badger; *gen.* grey fur. **ME–L19**.
3 An animal distinguished by grey colour, as a grey whale, a grey squirrel, etc.; *spec.* a grey or white horse. (Earliest in **DAPPLE GREY** *noun*) **LME**.

R. GRAVES Pituazes's men, all mounted on greys, came at him.

4 †**a** A grey-haired person, an old man. **LME–E16**. ▸**b** A white-skinned person. *black slang*. **M20**. ▸**c** A dull, anonymous, or nondescript person. **M20**.
5 A grey or subdued light; the cold sunless light of the morning or evening twilight. **L16**.

W. PIKE The first grey of dawn being the favourite time of attack.

6 In *pl.* In full ***the Scots Greys***. A regiment in the British army raised in 1681 as the Royal Regiment of Dragoons and now the 2nd Dragoons, orig. wearing a grey uniform. **M18**.
7 Grey colour; a shade of this; greyness. **E19**. ▸**b** A pigment of a grey colour. Freq. with specifying word. **L19**.

J. A. SYMONDS The colour of the olive tree is delicate. Its pearly greys . . in no wise interfere with the lustre. *fig.*: D. BAGLEY A world in which black and white merged into an indeterminate grey, where bad actions were done for good reasons and good actions were suspect.

ash-grey, ***dapple grey***, ***iron-grey***, ***pearl-grey***, ***silver-grey***, etc. ***French grey***: see **FRENCH** *adjective*.

8 A coin with two heads or two tails. *arch. slang*. **E19**.
■ **greyers** *noun pl.* (*arch. colloq.*) = **GREY** *noun* 1d **E20**.

grey /greɪ/ *adjective*. Also ***gray**.
[**ORIGIN** Old English *grǣg* = Old Frisian *grē*, Middle Dutch *grau*, *gra* (Dutch *grauw*), Old High German *grāo* (German *grau*), Old Norse *grár*, from Germanic.]
1 Of the colour intermediate between black and white; of the colour of the sunless sky, ash, lead, etc.; *spec.* (of a horse) of this or a white colour. Freq. prefixed with specifying word denoting some particular shade of grey. **OE**. ▸**b** Of fabric: unbleached, untreated. **M19**. ▸**c** Of a person: white-skinned. *black slang*. **M20**.

BROWNING Down the grass path grey with dew. G. GREENE He dusted the ashes from his white trousers, leaving one more grey smear.

ash-grey, ***dapple grey***, ***iron-grey***, ***pearl-grey***, ***silver-grey***, etc.
2 Of hair: turning white with age, grief, etc. Of a person: having grey hair. **OE**. ▸**b** *fig.* Ancient, immemorial; belonging to old age; experienced, wise. **E17**. ▸**c** *colloq.* Pertaining to old people collectively. **L20**.

W. H. PRESCOTT He had grown grey in the service of the court. J. GALSWORTHY Her hair . . was going grey. **b** W. SHENSTONE Herbs for use, and physic, not a few Of grey renown. L. MORRIS Gray wisdom comes with time and age. **c** *Independent* The ageing of the British population means that 'grey power' will increasingly dominate leisure and consumer spending.

3 Of weather etc.: dull, sunless; clouded, overcast. **ME**. ▸**b** *fig.* Not bright or hopeful; dismal, gloomy, sad, depressing. **E18**. ▸**c** Esp. of a person: dull, anonymous, nondescript, without distinction. **M20**. ▸**d** Less extreme than 'black'; indeterminate, not clearly defined. **M20**.

J. TYNDALL In the gray light of the evening. B. EMECHETA The bright night gradually gave way to a grey, damp morning. **b** E. F. BENSON Without seeing anything that broke the endless grey monotony of my days. J. GROSS He represented everything . . most at enmity with joy, everything grey, ponderous, drearily rationalistic. **c** *Times* The identity of these grey men of politics should be revealed. G. PRIESTLAND The grey fellowship of the depressed is wider than it knows. **d** *Guardian* As for the over-prescribing doctors, it was not just the black sheep we had to worry about. It was the grey sheep too.

4 [from the colour of the habit.] Designating a Cistercian monk, a Franciscan friar, or a sister of the third order of St Francis. **ME**.
– **SPECIAL COLLOCATIONS & COMB.**: ***grey ANTIMONY***. **grey area** (*a*) a situation or subject not clearly or easily defined or categorized, or not clearly covered by existing rules etc.; (*b*) *S. Afr.* a residential area where black people formerly lived illegally alongside white people by tacit consent. **grey-back** (*a*) *hist.* (*US colloq.*) a Confederate soldier in the American Civil War; (*b*) *dial. & US colloq.* a louse; (*c*) (chiefly *local*) any of various grey-backed birds or animals, as the hooded crow, the scaup, etc. **greybeard** (*a*) a man with a grey beard; (freq. *derog.*) an old man; (*b*) a large earthenware or stoneware jug or jar for spirits; (*c*) *dial.* traveller's joy, *Clematis vitalba*, in seed. **greybearded** *adjective* having a grey beard. **grey birch** a small birch, *Betula populifolia*, with light-coloured bark, found in eastern N. America; also called ***old-field birch*** (*US*), ***wire birch*** (*Canad.*). **grey box** any of various Australian eucalypts, esp. *Eucalyptus moluccana*. **grey cells** *colloq.* = ***grey matter*** below. **grey-coat** a person wearing grey clothing; *spec.* (*hist.*) a Cumberland yeoman. **grey crow** = ***HOODED crow***. ***grey drake***: see **DRAKE** *noun*[1] 4. **grey duck** an Australasian duck, *Anas superciliosa*, with mainly grey-brown plumage and a striped head. **grey economy** the part of the economy that is not accounted for in official statistics. **grey eminence** = **ÉMINENCE GRISE**. **grey eye** an eye with a grey iris. **grey-eyed** *adjective* having grey eyes; *poet.* designating the early morning. **grey fowl** (*a*) grouse in winter plumage. **grey fox** a greyish American fox, *Urocyon cinereoargenteus*, noted for an ability to climb trees. **Grey Friar** [from the colour of the order's habit] a Franciscan friar. **grey goods** (*a*) woven or knitted fabrics as they leave the loom, before being dyed, bleached, or finished; (*b*) computers and computing equipment (cf. ***BROWN goods***, ***WHITE goods***). **grey goose** any goose of the genus *Anser* with predominantly grey plumage; *esp.* the greylag. **grey groat** *arch.* a groat; *fig.* something of little value. **grey gurnard** a small gurnard, *Trigla gurnardus*. **greyhen** the female black grouse. **grey jay** a fluffy long-tailed jay, *Perisoreus canadensis*, which has dark grey upperparts and a whitish face, and is found in Canada and the north-western US (also called ***Canada jay***). **grey kangaroo** either of two large woodland kangaroos, the eastern *Macropus giganteus* and the western *M. fuliginosus*. **grey knight** *STOCK EXCHANGE* a person or company making a possibly hostile counter-offer for a company already facing a hostile takeover bid. **greymail** *colloq.* (*US*) [after *blackmail*] (a ploy involving) the threat by the defence, esp. in a spy trial, to expose government secrets unless charges are dropped. **grey mare** (*a*) a mare with a grey coat; (*b*) *fig.* a wife who dominates her husband. **grey market** [after *black market*] (a place of) traffic of questionable status in officially controlled goods or in commodities in short supply; *spec.* trading in a security not yet quoted on the Stock Exchange. **grey marketeer** one engaged in dealing in the grey market. **grey marketeering** dealing in the grey market. **grey matter** (*a*) the greyish unmyelinated tissue in the vertebrate central nervous system containing nerve cell bodies, dendrites, and glial cells, and forming the cortex of the cerebrum and cerebellum and the core of the spinal cord (cf. ***white matter*** s.v. **WHITE** *adjective*); (*b*) *colloq.* intelligence, brains. **grey mullet** any of various thick-bodied detritus-feeding fish of the worldwide family Mugilidae, esp. of inshore and estuarine waters, many of which are important food fish. **grey nurse** a large Australasian shark, *Odontaspis arenarius*. **grey oak** any of several N. American oaks, esp. *Quercus coccinea* and *Q. borealis*. **grey-out** *noun & verb intrans.* (*AERONAUTICS*) (suffer from) a dimming of the vision, less severe than a blackout. **grey parrot** a parrot, *Psittacus erithacus*, of western equatorial Africa, which has red tail feathers and is often kept as a pet for its mimicking abilities. ***grey partridge***: see **PARTRIDGE** *noun* 1. ***grey pea***: see **PEA** *noun*[1] 2. **grey phalarope** a northern holarctic phalarope, *Phalaropus fulicarius*, which has grey upperparts in winter and chestnut red underparts in its breeding plumage. **grey pine** any of several N. American pines, esp. the jack pine, *Pinus banksiana*. **greyscale** a range of tones from white to black. **grey seal** a common seal, *Halichoerus grypus*, of the N. Atlantic and Baltic. **grey snapper** an edible Atlantic snapper fish, *Lutjanus griseus*; also called ***mangrove snapper***, ***sea lawyer***. **grey squirrel** a common squirrel of eastern N. America, *Sciurus carolinensis*, introduced into the British Isles in the late 19th cent. **grey tin** the alpha allotrope of tin, which is a brittle form to which white tin slowly changes at temperatures below 18 degrees C. **grey trout** (*a*) the sea trout; (*b*) *US* the lake trout, *Salvelinus namaycush*; (*c*) *US* the weakfish, *Cynoscion regalis*. ***grey wethers***: see **WETHER**. **grey whale** a baleen whale, *Eschrichtius robustus*, of N. Pacific coastal waters. **grey willow** any of several kinds of willow with leaves hoary beneath, esp. *Salix cinerea* and (*N. Amer.*) *S. sericea*. ***grey wolf***: see **WOLF** *noun* 1.
■ **greyish** *adjective* somewhat grey **M16**. **greyly** *adverb* **E19**. **greyness** *noun* **L15**.

grey /greɪ/ *verb*. Also ***gray**. **LME**.
[**ORIGIN** from the adjective.]
1 *verb intrans.* Become or grow grey. **LME**. ▸**b** Of a population: increase in average age, tend to include more old people. **L20**.

S. R. CROCKETT It was already greying for the dawn. E. FEINSTEIN Tsvetayev was forty-five, a greying, slightly stooped figure.

2 *verb trans.* Make grey. **M19**.

F. MACLEOD He is a man whose hair has been greyed by years and sorrow. P. PEARCE The green of the garden was greyed over with dew.

greyhound /ˈgreɪhaʊnd/ *noun*.
[**ORIGIN** Old English *grīghund* (= Old Norse *greyhundr*) from Germanic base also of Old Norse *grey* bitch (ult. origin unknown) + *hund* **HOUND** *noun*[1].]
1 (An animal of) a tall slender long-legged and keen-sighted breed of dog capable of high speed and used in racing and hare-coursing. **OE**.
2 The figure or representation of this, esp. used as a badge of office. **LME**.
3 *hist.* More fully ***ocean greyhound***. An ocean steamship specially designed for great speed. **L19**.
– **COMB.**: **greyhound racing** a sport in which a mechanical hare is coursed by greyhounds on a track.

greylag /ˈgreɪlag/ *noun*. Also (earlier) **grey lag**. **E18**.
[**ORIGIN** Prob. from **GREY** *adjective* + **LAG** *noun*[3].]
A large, grey-brown and white Eurasian goose, *Anser anser*, ancestor of the farmyard goose. Also ***greylag goose***.

greywacke /ˈgreɪwakə/ *noun*. Also ***gray-**; earlier in German form ***Grauwacke*** /ˈgraʊvakə/, pl. ***-wacken*** /-vakən/. **L18**.
[**ORIGIN** German *Grauwacke*, from *grau* grey + **WACKE**.]
PETROGRAPHY. Any coarse-grained, usu. dark sandstone containing angular mineral and rock fragments in a fine-grained clayey matrix.

gribble /ˈgrɪb(ə)l/ *noun*[1]. *obsolete* exc. *dial.* **L16**.
[**ORIGIN** Perh. rel. to dial. var. of **CRAB** *noun*[2].]
A young crab tree or blackthorn; a stick made from it. Also, the stock of a crab tree used for grafting on.

gribble /ˈgrɪb(ə)l/ *noun*[2]. **L18**.
[**ORIGIN** Perh. cogn. with **GRUB** *verb*.]
A wood-boring marine isopod crustacean, *Limnoria lignorum*.

grice /grʌɪs/ *noun*[1]. Now *arch. & Scot.* Pl. **-s**, (long *rare* or *obsolete*) same. **ME**.
[**ORIGIN** Old Norse *griss* (Swedish, Danish *gris*) young pig, pig.]
A pig; *esp.* a young pig.

grice *noun*[2] var. of **GRECE**.

gricer /ˈgrʌɪsə/ *noun*. *colloq.* **M20**.
[**ORIGIN** Unknown.]
A railway enthusiast; *esp.* a person who seeks out and photographs unusual trains.
■ **gricing** *noun* the activity of a gricer **M20**.

grid /grɪd/ *noun*. **M19**.
[**ORIGIN** Back-form. from **GRIDIRON** *noun*.]
1 An arrangement of parallel bars with openings between them; a grating. Formerly also = **GRIDIRON** *noun* 1. **M19**. ▸**b** *NAUTICAL*. = **GRIDIRON** *noun* 2c. **M19**. ▸**c** *THEATRICAL*. = **GRIDIRON** *noun* 2d. **L19**. ▸**d** An electrode (orig. a wire mesh) placed between the cathode and anode of a thermionic valve or cathode-ray tube, and serving to control or modulate the flow of electrons. Also ***control grid***. **E20**.
2 A network of lines, esp. of two series of regularly spaced lines crossing one another at right angles; *spec.* such a network on a map, numbered to enable the precise location of a place, feature, etc. **E20**. ▸**b** = **GRIDIRON** *noun* 2f. **E20**. ▸**c** Esp. in *MOTOR RACING*. A pattern of lines painted on a race-track at the starting point to indicate the starting positions. **M20**. ▸**d** The layout of a town divided into roughly equal blocks by streets at right angles to each other. Usu. *attrib.* in ***grid plan***, ***grid system***, etc. **M20**.
3 A bicycle. *slang*. **E20**.
4 A network of high-voltage transmission lines by which electrical power from a number of generating stations is

distributed throughout a country or region; a similar distribution network for gas or water supply. E20.
– COMB.: **grid reference** a map reference indicating a location in terms of vertical and horizontal grid lines.

gridded /ˈɡrɪdɪd/ *adjective*. E20.
[ORIGIN from GRID + -ED².]
Covered with, forming, or containing a grid.

griddle /ˈɡrɪd(ə)l/ *noun & verb*. ME.
[ORIGIN Old French *gredil*, *gridil* gridiron (mod. *gril*) from Proto-Romance dim. of Latin *cratis*: see CRATE *noun*, GRATE *noun*. Cf. GRILLE.]
▸ **A** *noun*. **1** A gridiron for cooking food. ME.
2 A flat metal (esp. iron) plate that is heated and used for cooking food. LME.
3 MINING. A sieve for separating ore. L18.
– COMB.: **griddle cake**: cooked on a griddle.
▸ **B** *verb trans*. **1** Cook on a griddle. LME.
2 Sieve *out* with a griddle. L18.

gride /ɡrʌɪd/ *verb*. Chiefly *poet*. LME.
[ORIGIN Metath. alt. of GIRD *verb*²: adopted by Spenser from Lydgate.]
1 *verb trans*. Pierce with a weapon; wound. Now *rare*. LME.
2 *verb intrans*. Pierce *through*; cut, scrape, or graze *along*, *through*, etc., with a grating sound or a rasping pain. L16.
3 *verb trans*. (Cause to) clash or grate against. E19.

gridelin /ˈɡrɪdəlɪn/ *noun & adjective*. Now *rare*. E17.
[ORIGIN French *gridelin*, *gris-de-lin* lit. 'grey of flax'.]
(Of) a pale purple or greyish-violet colour.

gridiron /ˈɡrɪdʌɪən/ *noun*. Also (earlier) †**gridire**. ME.
[ORIGIN Alt. of GRIDDLE *noun*, with assim. of 2nd syll. to IRON *noun*. Cf. ANDIRON.]
1 A cooking utensil of parallel metal bars for boiling or grilling; a grill; *hist*. a similar but larger structure used as an instrument of torture. ME.
on the gridiron *arch*. in a state of anguish or uneasiness.
2 An object resembling a gridiron; *esp*. the flag of the US. ME. ▸**b** *hist*. In full ***gridiron pendulum***. A compensation pendulum made of parallel rods of different metals. M18. ▸**c** NAUTICAL. An open framework of parallel beams for supporting a ship in dock. M19. ▸**d** THEATRICAL. An open framework of beams above a stage from which scenery or lights can be hung. L19. ▸**e** = GRID 2d. L19. ▸**f** An American football field, with parallel lines marking out the area of play; the game of American football. L19.

gridiron /ˈɡrɪdʌɪən/ *verb trans*. M19.
[ORIGIN from the noun.]
Mark with parallel lines or in a gridiron pattern.

gridlock /ˈɡrɪdlɒk/ *noun*. Orig. *US*. L20.
[ORIGIN from GRID + LOCK *noun*².]
1 A state of congestion bringing road traffic to a standstill; a traffic jam affecting several intersecting roads. L20.

> J. WILCOX A gridlock on the corner of North Gladiola held her up.

2 A state of deadlock; an impasse. L20.

> P. THEROUX I tell you, Charlie, it's an imperfect world. America's in gridlock.

■ **gridlocked** *adjective* L20.

griece *noun* see GRECE.

grief /ɡriːf/ *noun*. ME.
[ORIGIN Anglo-Norman *gref*, Old French *grief* (mod. *grief* grievance, injury, complaint), from *grever* GRIEVE *verb*.]
1 Orig. *gen*., mental anguish or sorrow. Now *spec*. deep sorrow caused esp. by bereavement, or bitter regret or remorse. Also, *colloq*. trouble, annoyance. ME. ▸**b** The cause or subject of grief. E16.

> A. BRINK The woman lost her husband. She was shattered with grief. QUILLER-COUCH I got some grief on that because it took three days to do Maxwell's Silver Hammer. **b** COVERDALE *Prov*. 17:25 An indiscrete sonne is a grefe unto his father.

†**2** (A kind or cause of) hardship or suffering. ME–E18.
†**3** Hurt, harm, damage, or injury, done or caused by another. ME–L16. ▸**b** = GRIEVANCE 3. LME–M19.
†**4** Anger, displeasure; offence. ME–L16.
†**5** Physical pain or discomfort; a physical injury or illness. ME–E18.
– PHRASES & COMB.: **bring to grief** bring to disaster. **come to grief** meet with disaster, fail. **good grief!**, **great grief!** *interjections* expr. surprise, alarm, etc. **grief-stricken** *adjective* overcome by grief.
■ **griefful** *adjective* painful; full of grief, sorrowful: LME. **griefless** *adjective* M16. **grieflessness** *noun* (now *rare*) L16.

grievance /ˈɡriːv(ə)ns/ *noun*. ME.
[ORIGIN Old French *grevance*, *grievance*, from *grever*: see GRIEVE *verb*, -ANCE.]
†**1** The infliction of wrong or hardship; (a cause of) injury or oppression. ME–M18.
†**2** The state or fact of being oppressed, injured, or distressed; trouble, distress, pain. ME–L16.
3 A (real or imagined) wrong or ground of complaint. ME.

> G. A. BIRMINGHAM A letter to *The Times*, the usual resort of an Englishman with a grievance. V. CRONIN He listened personally to any grievances and when justified put them right.

†**4** Displeasure, indignation, offence. ME–E16.
†**5** A disease, an ailment. LME–M18.

grieve /ɡriːv/ *noun*.
[ORIGIN Old English (Northumbrian) *grǣfa* = West Saxon *ġerēfa*: see REEVE *noun*¹.]
1 A governor of a province, town, etc. Now only *hist*., a sheriff. OE.
2 The manager, overseer, or bailiff on a farm. *Scot*. & *N. English*. L15.
■ **grieveship** *noun* a district under the charge of a grieve LME.

grieve /ɡriːv/ *verb*. ME.
[ORIGIN Old French *grever* burden, encumber from Proto-Romance alt. of Latin *gravare*, from *gravis* GRAVE *adjective*¹.]
†**1** *verb trans*. Harass, trouble, oppress; do wrong or harm to (a person). ME–M19. ▸**b** Cause harm or damage to (a thing). ME–L16.
†**2** *verb trans*. & *intrans*. Do bodily or material injury (to). ME–E19.
†**3** *verb trans*. Affect with pain or disease. (Cf. GRIEVED *adjective* 2.) ME–L16.
4 *verb trans*. Affect with grief or deep sorrow. Also, trouble, annoy, cause pain or anxiety to. ME.

> H. B. STOWE It really grieves me to have you be so naughty. I. MURDOCH I . . was grieved to see his tools so idle.

†**5** *verb trans*. Make angry; offend. ME–M16.
6 *verb intrans*. Feel grief or distress; sorrow deeply *at*, *for*, *about*, *over*, *to do*. ME. ▸**b** *verb trans*. Feel or show grief or regret at or for. Chiefly *poet*. L16.

> A. ALVAREZ She began to sob, weeping for her father as she had never grieved before.

■ **grievingly** *adverb* with grief E17.

grieved /ɡriːvd/ *adjective*. LME.
[ORIGIN from GRIEVE *verb* + -ED¹.]
†**1** Annoyed, made angry. Only in LME.
†**2** Afflicted with pain or disease. L16–E18.
3 Affected with grief; distressed, troubled. L16.
†**4** Harassed, oppressed, harmed; having a grievance. E17–E19.

griever /ˈɡriːvə/ *noun*. LME.
[ORIGIN from GRIEVE *verb* + -ER¹.]
†**1** A person who harms or wrongs another or is the cause of a grievance. LME–M17.
2 A person who feels or shows grief. E19.

grievous /ˈɡriːvəs/ *adjective & adverb*. ME.
[ORIGIN French *grevos*, *-eus*, from *grever*: see GRIEVE *verb*, -OUS.]
▸ **A** *adjective*. **1** Burdensome, oppressive; heavy, severe. *obsolete* exc. as passing into sense 4. ME. ▸†**b** Arduous, difficult; troublesome, annoying. LME–E17.

> LD MACAULAY The High Commission . . the most grievous of the many grievances under which the nation laboured.

2 Bringing serious trouble; harmful. ME.

> G. VIDAL It had been a grievous mistake for Sparta to join the enemies of our family.

3 Serious, grave; (of a wound, pain, etc.) severe; (of a fault, crime, etc.) atrocious, heinous. ME.

> SHAKES. *1 Hen. IV* The complaints I hear of thee are grievous. R. L. STEVENSON His wounds were grievous indeed, but not dangerous.

4 Causing mental pain or distress, exciting grief; *rare* full of grief, sorrowful. LME.
– SPECIAL COLLOCATIONS: **grievous bodily harm** (orig. LAW) (the act of causing) serious physical injury.
▸ †**B** *adverb*. Grievously. *rare* (Shakes.). Only in L16.
■ **grievously** *adverb* ME. **grievousness** *noun* ME.

griff /ɡrɪf/ *noun*¹. *Indian*. E19.
[ORIGIN Abbreviation.]
= GRIFFIN *noun*².

griff /ɡrɪf/ *noun*². *slang*. L19.
[ORIGIN Abbreviation.]
= GRIFFIN *noun*³; a tip (in betting etc.); a hint, a signal; news, reliable information.

griff *noun*³ var. of GRIFFE *noun*¹.

griffaun /ɡrɪˈfɔːn/ *noun*. *Irish*. L18.
[ORIGIN Irish *grafán*, from *grafaim* scrape, grub.]
A sturdy hoe for cutting turf.

griffe /ɡrɪf/ *noun*¹. Also **griff**. LME.
[ORIGIN Old French *grif* (mod. *griffe*), from *griffer* seize as with a claw, or from Frankish.]
A claw; *esp*. in ARCHITECTURE a claw-shaped decoration at the base of a column.
– NOTE: Rare before E19.

griffe /ɡrɪf/ *noun*². *US* (*obsolete* exc. *hist*.). M19.
[ORIGIN French, from Spanish *grifo* curly, frizzy.]
A person of mixed race; *spec*. a person having one black and one mixed-race parent.

griffin /ˈɡrɪfɪn/ *noun*¹. Also †**griffon**, **gryphon**. See also GRIFFON. ME.
[ORIGIN Old French *grifoun* (mod. *griffon*) from Proto-Romance augm. of late Latin *gryphus*, from *gryps*, *gryph-* from Greek *grups*, *grup-*.]
1 A mythical creature usu. represented as having the head and wings of an eagle and the body of a lion; a representation of this. ME.
2 See GRIFFON.
■ **griffiˈnesque** *adjective* in the style of a griffin M19. **griffiness** *noun* (*rare*) a female griffin M19.

griffin /ˈɡrɪfɪn/ *noun*². *Indian*. L18.
[ORIGIN Perh. fig. use of GRIFFIN *noun*¹. Cf. GRIFF *noun*¹.]
A European newly arrived in India; a novice, a newcomer, a greenhorn.
■ **griffinage** *noun* the state of being a griffin E19. **griffinhood** *noun* = GRIFFINAGE M19. **griffinish** *adjective* M19.

griffin /ˈɡrɪfɪn/ *noun*³. *slang*. L19.
[ORIGIN Unknown: cf. GRIFF *noun*².]
A tip (in betting etc.); a hint, a signal; news, reliable information. Freq. abbreviated to GRIFF *noun*².

> A. N. LYONS 'This is the Straight Griffin, Fred,' . . 'the absolute straight Tip'.

griffon /ˈɡrɪfən/ *noun*. In sense 2 also †**-in**. ME.
[ORIGIN formed as GRIFFIN *noun*¹. In sense 3 from mod. French.]
▸ **I 1** See GRIFFIN *noun*¹. ME.
▸ **II 2** A vulture; now (also ***griffon vulture***) any of several vultures of the chiefly Eurasian genus *Gyps*, esp. *G. fulvus*. LME.
3 (An animal of) any of various European breeds of coarse-haired dog similar to terriers. L18.
Brussels griffon a small (variety of) griffon with a flat face and reddish-brown hair.

griffonage /ɡrɪfəˈnɑːʒ/ *noun*. Now *rare*. E19.
[ORIGIN French, from *griffonner* to scrawl.]
Scrawl, scribble.

grift /ɡrɪft/ *noun & verb*. *US slang*. E20.
[ORIGIN Perh. alt.]
▸ **A** *noun*. = GRAFT *noun*⁴. E20.
▸ **B** *verb intrans*. = GRAFT *verb*³. E20.
■ **grifter** *noun* = GRAFTER *noun*³. E20.

grig /ɡrɪɡ/ *noun*¹. LME.
[ORIGIN Unknown.]
†**1** A small person; a dwarf. LME–E17.
2 A young or small eel in fresh water. E17.
3 A merry, lively, etc., person. Freq. in ***as merry as a grig*** or with pleonastic adjective M17. ▸**b** A grasshopper, a cricket. *dial*. M19.
4 A farthing; in *pl*., money, cash. *slang*. Now *rare* or *obsolete*. M17.
■ **griggish** *adjective* (*rare*) merry, happy L19.

grig /ɡrɪɡ/ *noun*². Chiefly *dial*. L17.
[ORIGIN Welsh *grug*.]
Heather, *Calluna vulgaris*.

grig /ɡrɪɡ/ *verb trans*. Now *Irish* & *US*. Infl. **-gg-**. M16.
[ORIGIN Unknown.]
Irritate, annoy.

griggle /ˈɡrɪɡ(ə)l/ *noun*¹. *dial*. E19.
[ORIGIN Uncertain: perh. from GRIG *noun*¹.]
A small apple left on the tree by a gatherer. Usu. in *pl*.

Grignard /ˈɡriːnjɑː, -jɑːd, *foreign* ɡriɲaːr/ *noun*. E20.
[ORIGIN from Victor *Grignard* (1871–1934), French chemist.]
CHEMISTRY. ***Grignard compound***, ***Grignard reagent***, ***Grignard's compound***, ***Grignard's reagent***, any of a class of organometallic magnesium compounds of formula RMgX (R = alkyl, X = halogen), widely used in organic syntheses.

Grignolino /ɡrɪnjəˈliːnəʊ/ *noun*. L19.
[ORIGIN Italian.]
An Italian wine grape grown in Piedmont; red wine made from this.

gri-gri *noun* var. of GRUGRU.

grihastha /ɡrɪˈhʌstə/ *noun*. L19.
[ORIGIN Sanskrit *gṛhastha* a married Hindu householder.]
A brahmin in the second stage of life, which entails social obligations such as marriage and parenthood.

grike /ɡrʌɪk/ *noun*. Orig. *N. English*. Also **gryke**. L18.
[ORIGIN Unknown.]
A crack in rock, or between flagstones; a ravine in a hillside; now chiefly *spec*. in GEOLOGY, a fissure enlarged by rainwater dissolution between limestone clints.

grill /ɡrɪl/ *noun*¹. L17.
[ORIGIN Old French & mod. French *gril*, earlier *grail*, *greil* masc. form (cf. GRIDDLE *noun*) based on fem. *grille*: see GRILLE.]
Orig., a gridiron. Now, a device on a cooker for the downward emission of heat, used for cooking food on one side at a time.

> *Successful Slimming* All the meals can be cooked under the grill.

grill /ɡrɪl/ *noun*². M18.
[ORIGIN from GRILL *verb*.]
1 (A dish of) grilled food. M18.
MIXED ***grill***.
2 A period of grilling. M19.
3 In full ***grill room***. A restaurant or eating place specializing in grilled food. L19.

grill *noun*³ see GRILLE.

grill /grɪl/ *verb*. **M17**.
[ORIGIN French *griller*, from *gril* (*grille*) GRILL *noun*[1].]
1 *verb trans.* Cook under a grill or on a gridiron. **M17**. ▸**b** Subject to severe questioning or interrogation. **L19**.
fig.: J. HILTON Midday sunlight, blazing on the roof of the cabin, grilled the air inside. **b** *New Yorker* He is grilled by a police detective.
2 *verb intrans.* Be cooked under a grill or on a gridiron. **M19**.
fig.: R. CURZON Malta . . was cool in comparison to the fiery furnace in which we were at present grilling.
■ **griller** *noun* a person or thing which grills **M19**.

grillade /grɪˈleɪd, -ˈjɑːd, ˈgriːɑːd/ *noun*. **M17**.
[ORIGIN French, formed as GRILL *verb*: see -ADE.]
(A dish of) grilled food; a grill.

grillage /ˈgrɪlɪdʒ/ *noun*. **L18**.
[ORIGIN French, formed as GRILLE: see -AGE.]
ENGINEERING. A heavy framework of cross-timbering, sometimes resting on piles, providing a foundation for building on unstable soil.

grille /grɪl/ *noun & verb*. As noun also (earlier) **grill**. **M17**.
[ORIGIN Old French & mod. French, earlier *graille* from medieval Latin *graticula*, *crat-* = Latin *craticula* dim. of *cratis*: see CRATE *noun*, GRATE *noun*. Cf. GRIDDLE.]
▸ **A** *noun*. †**1** Each of the bars in the visor of a helmet. Only in **M17**.
2 A framework of parallel or crossed bars or a structure of open metalwork dividing one area from another, esp. to allow discreet communication or vision etc., but not entry or exit; a grating. **L17**. ▸**b** A similar structure positioned in front of the radiator in a motor vehicle, providing protection without preventing the flow of air over it. Also ***radiator grille***. **M20**.
D. F. CHESHIRE A private supper-room in the gallery, looking down on the hall through a grille. A. TYLER All the shops were locked behind iron grilles.
3 REAL TENNIS. A square opening in the end wall adjacent to the hazard side, backed by a wooden board or grating. **E18**.
4 A rectangular pattern of small dots impressed on some issues of postage stamps. **L19**.
– COMB.: **grille-work** open or lattice work.
▸ **B** *verb trans.* Equip with a grille; fence *off* with a grille. **M19**.
L. NKOSI I sit at a small wooden table by the grilled window of my cell.

grillo /ˈgrɪləʊ/ *noun*. Pl. **-os**. **M19**.
[ORIGIN Italian & Spanish from Latin *gryllus* from Greek *grullos*.]
A cricket.

grilse /grɪls/ *noun*. **LME**.
[ORIGIN Unknown.]
A young salmon that has returned to fresh water after one year in the sea.

grim /grɪm/ *adjective & adverb*. Compar. & superl. **-mm-**.
[ORIGIN Old English *grim* = Old Frisian, Old Saxon (Dutch), Old High German *grim* (German *grimm*), Old Norse *grimmr*, from Germanic.]
▸ **A** *adjective*. **1** Orig., fierce, cruel, savage. Later, formidable, of fierce, frightening, or forbidding appearance or aspect. Formerly also, fiercely angry. **OE**. ▸**b** Of a situation, scene, etc.: repellent, uninviting. **ME**.
J. THOMSON Bony, and gaunt, and grim, Assembling wolves in raging troops descend. DICKENS With a grim and ghastly stare. **b** J. BUCHAN Grey Yorkshire moors, grim at first sight.
the Grim Reaper: see REAPER 1.
2 Stern, unrelenting, merciless; resolute, uncompromising. **OE**.
I. MURDOCH Together, like a grim tribunal, they looked disapprovingly down upon their stepfather.
like grim DEATH.
3 Extremely painful or unpleasant; severe, unremitting. Now passing into senses 1 and 2. **OE**.
W. HOLTBY The grim hand of poverty lay upon them. C. CHAPLIN The war was now grim Ruthless slaughter and destruction were rife over Europe.
4 Of a smile or laughter: mirthless. Of humour: dealing with a ghastly or painful subject. **M17**.
SIR W. SCOTT One of those grim smiles, of which it was impossible to say, whether it meant good or harm.
5 Dreadful, ominous, sinister. **L19**.
J. BRODSKY The financial situation in our family was grim. B. LOPEZ The grim news—three ships . . were lost, crushed in the ice.
▸ **B** *adverb*. In a grim manner or mood. Now *rare* and only in *comb.*, as ***grim-frowning***, ***grim-set***, etc. **OE**.
■ **grimful** *adjective* (long *rare*) full of grimness, fierce, terrible **ME**. **grimness** *noun* **OE**.

grim /grɪm/ *verb*. Infl. **-mm-**. **LME**.
[ORIGIN Sense 1 from Dutch *grimmen*, from *grim* GRIM *adjective*; sense 2 from GRIM *adjective*.]
1 *verb intrans.* Be angry; have or take on a fierce appearance. Long *rare*. **LME**.
2 *verb trans.* Make grim or fierce; give a grim look to. **E18**.
J. BARLOW Grimm'd by the horrors of the dreadful night.

grimace /grɪˈmeɪs, ˈgrɪməs/ *noun & verb*. **M17**.
[ORIGIN French, earlier †*grimache* from Spanish *grimazo* caricature, from *grima* fright.]
▸ **A** *noun*. **1** A distortion of the face expressing annoyance, pain, etc. or intending to cause laughter; a wry face. **M17**.
D. JACOBSON His lips twist into a crabbed, enigmatic grimace. I. MURDOCH His face was distorted in a grimace of mingled fear and annoyance.
2 Affectation, pretence, sham. Now *rare*. **M17**.
LD MACAULAY It was natural for them to consider all piety as grimace.
3 An affected look or (formerly) gesture; the use of this. **L17**.
GEO. ELIOT Too well-bred to have . . the grimaces and affected tones that belong to pretentious vulgarity.
▸ **B** *verb intrans.* [Perh. from French *grimacer*.] Make a grimace; pull a face. **M18**.
P. ACKROYD He . . stood up, grimacing at a pain in his back.
■ **grimacer**, **grimacier** *nouns* a person who grimaces **E19**.

Grimaldi /grɪˈmaldi/ *noun*. **E20**.
[ORIGIN See below.]
ARCHAEOLOGY. Used *attrib.* to designate (remains of) a group of upper Palaeolithic hominids known from discoveries in the Grimaldi caves in Liguria, Italy.
■ **Grimaldian** *adjective* of, pertaining to, or characteristic of Grimaldi man **M20**.

grimalkin /grɪˈmalkɪn, -ˈmɔːl-/ *noun*. *arch.* **L16**.
[ORIGIN from GREY *adjective* + MALKIN.]
(A name for) a cat, esp. an old she-cat; *transf.* an unpleasant old woman.

Grimbarian /grɪmˈbɛːrɪən/ *noun*. **L19**.
[ORIGIN from *Grimsby* + -ARIAN with unexpl. loss of -*s*-.]
A native or inhabitant of the town of Grimsby in NE England.

grime /grʌɪm/ *noun*. **ME**.
[ORIGIN formed as GRIME *verb*.]
1 Soot, coal dust, etc., on or ingrained in a surface; dirt, filth. **ME**.
U. LE GUIN The ends of the sleeves were black with grime. *Glaswegian* Glasgow has cast off the grime of its industrial past.
2 A form of dance music influenced by UK garage, characterized by machine-like sounds and hip-hop vocals. **E21**.

grime /grʌɪm/ *verb trans.* **LME**.
[ORIGIN Middle Low German, Middle Dutch (cf. Flemish *grijmen*, Low German *gremen*). Cf. BEGRIME.]
Blacken with grime; dirty.
TED HUGHES Comes home dull with coal-dust deliberately To grime the sink and foul towels.

grimgribber /ˈgrɪmgrɪbə/ *noun*. **L18**.
[ORIGIN from *Grimgribber*, an imaginary estate invented by a sham lawyer in Richard Steele's play *The Conscious Lovers* (1722).]
Legal jargon; learned gibberish.
J. H. TOOKE The grimgribber of Westminster-Hall is a more fertile source of imposture.

grimly /ˈgrɪmli/ *adjective*. Now *rare* or *obsolete*. **OE**.
[ORIGIN from GRIM *adjective* + -LY[1].]
Grim-looking; grim in appearance or nature.
■ **grimliness** *noun* (*rare*) **LME**.

grimly /ˈgrɪmli/ *adverb*. **OE**.
[ORIGIN from GRIM *adjective* + -LY[2].]
1 With stern or cruel action, intention, or feelings. Also, rigidly, doggedly. **OE**.
J. CONRAD 'I haven't any half-crowns to spare for tips', he remarked grimly. E. ARDIZZONE It was a long, long row . . but he kept grimly on.
†**2** Dreadfully, terribly, hideously. Only in **ME**.
3 With a grim look or air. **ME**. ▸**b** So as to produce a grim appearance. *rare*. **LME**.
POPE Grimly frowning with a dreadful look. F. SWINNERTON She sat grimly still, shoulders contracted, and brain busy. **b** S. LEWIS His face was as grimly creased as the mask of tragedy.

Grimm's law /ˈgrɪmz lɔː/ *noun phr.* **M19**.
[ORIGIN Jacob *Grimm* (1785–1863), German philologist.]
A set of rules specifying regular differences in the consonants of related words in different Indo-European languages, primarily accounting for the separation of the Germanic languages from other Indo-European languages.

grimoire /grɪmˈwɑː/ *noun*. **M19**.
[ORIGIN French, alt. of *grammaire* GRAMMAR.]
A manual of black magic supposedly used to cast spells, invoke demons, etc.
H. AINSWORTH A witch with a Bible! It should be a grimoire.

grimpen /ˈgrɪmpən/ *noun*. **M20**.
[ORIGIN from the *Grimpen* Mire in Conan Doyle's *The Hound of the Baskervilles*.]
A marshy area.
T. S. ELIOT On the edge of a grimpen, where is no secure foothold.

Grim the Collier /grɪm ðə ˈkɒlɪə/ *noun phr.* **E17**.
[ORIGIN A character in *Grim the Collier of Croyden*, a comedy by William Haughton (*c* 1575–1605).]
A kind of hawkweed, *Hieracium aurantiacum*, grown in gardens, with orange or red flowers and calyces covered with black hairs.

grimthorpe /ˈgrɪmθɔːp/ *verb trans.* **L19**.
[ORIGIN Sir Edmund Becket, first Lord *Grimthorpe* (1816–1905), restorer of St Albans Cathedral.]
Restore (an ancient building) with lavish expenditure rather than skill and taste.
Daily Chronicle The parish church, which despite of vigorous 'grimthorping' still shows . . its old Norman architecture.

grimy /ˈgrʌɪmi/ *adjective*. **E17**.
[ORIGIN from GRIME *noun* + -Y[1].]
1 Covered with grime, begrimed, dirty. **E17**.
2 *fig.* Unpleasant, mean. **L19**.
■ **grimily** *adverb* **L19**. **griminess** *noun* **M17**.

grin /grɪn/ *noun*[1]. *obsolete* exc. *dial.* **OE**.
[ORIGIN Unknown.]
1 A snare made of cord, wire, etc. with a running noose; *transf.* & *fig.* a trap, a pitfall. **OE**.
2 A noose; a halter. **OE**.

grin /grɪn/ *noun*[2]. **M17**.
[ORIGIN from GRIN *verb*[2].]
An act of grinning. Now usu., a broad smile.
H. ROBBINS Her smile broadened to a mischievous grin. A. S. BYATT He had a nice, frank grin, friendly, not cheeky.

grin /grɪn/ *verb*[1] *trans.* *obsolete* exc. *dial.* Infl. **-nn-**. **OE**.
[ORIGIN from GRIN *noun*[1].]
Catch in a noose, ensnare; choke, strangle.

grin /grɪn/ *verb*[2]. Infl. **-nn-**.
[ORIGIN Old English *grennian* rel. to Old High German *grennan* mutter (Middle High German *grennen* wail, grin), *granōn* grunt, Old Norse *grenja* howl, Old Swedish *grānia* roar, gnash the teeth, from Germanic. Cf. GROAN *verb*, GIRN *verb*.]
1 *verb intrans.* Draw back the lips and reveal the teeth in pain or (formerly) anger. **OE**.
SIR W. SCOTT Here grins the wolf as when he died.
2 *verb intrans.* Smile broadly usu. showing the teeth. (Now the usual sense.) **L15**. ▸**b** *verb trans.* Form the mouth into, give, (a grin, a broad smile). **M17**.
W. SOYINKA They were grinning, laughing at me. **b** T. HEGGEN He just stood and grinned the widest and most foolish grin Billings had ever seen.
3 *verb trans.* Express by grinning. **L17**.
G. GRANVILLE He grins defiance at the gaping crowd. SMOLLETT The surgeon grinned approbation.
4 *verb intrans.* Of a surface: show gaps, gape; show through a covering. **M19**.
R. A. FREEMAN When you have drilled the holes, . . put a drop of walnut stain in each, or else they 'grin'. *Times* Cheaper ones have a tendency to 'grin' . . . that is, to show the backing through the all-too-sparse pile.
– PHRASES: **grin and bear it** take pain, adversity, etc., stoically. ***grin like a Cheshire cat***: see CHESHIRE 2. **grin through a horse collar** (chiefly *hist.*) put one's head through a horse collar and grimace in a contest or entertainment (cf. GIRN *verb*).
■ **grinner** *noun* **LME**.

grinagog /ˈgrɪnəgɒg/ *noun*. Chiefly *dial.* **M16**.
[ORIGIN Fanciful formation from GRIN *verb*[2].]
A person who is always grinning, esp. foolishly and without cause.

Grinch /grɪn(t)ʃ/ *noun*. *N. Amer. colloq.* Also **g-**. **L20**.
[ORIGIN Name of a character in the children's story *How the Grinch Stole Christmas* (1957) by Dr Seuss.]
A spoilsport or killjoy.
Entertainment Weekly I'm no grinch, but as stocking stuffers go, this calendar is barely better than a lump of coal.

†**grincome** *noun* var. of CRINKUM.

grind /grʌɪnd/ *noun*. **ME**.
[ORIGIN from the verb.]
1 *gen.* The action or an act of grinding. **ME**.
D. DU MAURIER The grind of the gate itself, as it scraped the stone beneath and was opened. T. GUNN Dry rough / substance encountered the grind / of my teeth.
2 Hard monotonous work or study; a dull and laborious task. *colloq.* **M19**.
CONAN DOYLE He . . settled down to rest after a life of ceaseless grind.
the daily grind *colloq.* one's usual day's work.

3 A walk taken for exercise; a steeplechase. *Univ. slang*. M19.

N. ANNAN The pair of them pounded the last ten miles of the grind back to Cambridge.

4 Intensive study or tuition for an examination etc.; an instance of this. *slang*. M19.

A. HIGGINS He was giving grinds in mathematics to the clergyman's two . . sons.

5 A hard-working student; a swot. *US slang*. L19.

E. JONG Just because you were a grub and a grind and did well in school.

6 A ferry. *Cambridge Univ. slang*. L19.
7 (An act of) sexual intercourse. *slang*. L19. ▸**b** The action of rotating the hips or pelvis in a dance etc. Also in ***bump and grind***. *slang*. M20.

J. WAINWRIGHT A grind with a cheap scrubber?

8 The size of the particles of a powder or other ground substance, *spec.* of ground coffee. E20.

W. H. UKERS A mixture of a very fine with a coarse grind gives the best results in the cup.

– COMB.: **grind house**, **grind movie house** *US slang* a cinema showing a continuous programme with no intermissions.

grind /grʌɪnd/ *verb*. Pa. t. & pple **ground** /graʊnd/, †**grinded**.
[ORIGIN Old English *grindan*, of which there are no Germanic cognates. Cf. Latin *frendere* rub away, gnash.]
1 *verb trans. & intrans.* Reduce to small particles or powder by crushing between millstones, the teeth, etc. Also foll. by *down*, & with other adverbs or adverbial phrs. OE. ▸**b** *verb trans.* Produce by grinding. LME.

LONGFELLOW Though the mills of God grind slowly, yet they grind exceeding small. N. MAILER What we did not . . devour we could grind away in the electric Disposall beneath the sink. W. WHARTON A bird needs sharp gravel to grind food in its crop.

2 *verb intrans.* Scrape or rub on or against something; make a harsh or grating sound. Also, proceed noisily and laboriously, with or by means of friction. OE. ▸**b** *verb trans.* Rub (one thing) roughly or gratingly against or upon another (foll. by *against*, *into*, *upon*, etc.). Also make (one's way) laboriously. M17.

J. BETJEMAN No lorries grind in bottom gear Up steep and narrow lanes. R. WEST The voices of my father and mother grinding quietly against each other in an interminable argument. **b** W. GOLDING I ground the cigarette out in the ashtray.

grind to a halt (freq. *fig.*) be brought to a standstill by pressure or friction.

3 †**a** *verb intrans.* Gnash with the teeth. OE–L16. ▸**b** *verb trans.* Rub (the teeth) together with a grating sound. ME.

b E. O'BRIEN He was in a . . temper and I could see him grind his false teeth.

4 *verb trans.* Sharpen (a tool, weapon, etc.) by friction. ME. ▸**b** Make smooth or reduce to the required size or shape by friction. M17. ▸**c** *spec.* Make (a machine part, esp. a valve) fit its seat or housing by moving it to and fro in place with a suitable abrasive. Foll. by *in* (adverb & preposition), *into*, *on to*. L19.

SHAKES. *Per.* I have ground the axe myself: Do you but strike the blow. **b** I. NEWTON Good Workmen who can grind and polish Glasses truly spherical. **c** *Boy's Own Paper* To make the valves fit tight you should grind them . . with . . fine emery and oil.

grind an axe, ***have an axe to grind***: see AXE *noun*[1].

5 *verb trans. fig.* ▸**a** Afflict, torment. Now chiefly *US*, annoy. LME. ▸**b** Crush, oppress, exploit. Also foll. by *down*. E17.

b *New Yorker* I see the economic system grinding people down . . the poor are getting poorer.

b grind the faces of = sense 5b above.

6 *verb intrans. & trans.* Copulate (with). *slang*. M17. ▸**b** *verb intrans.* Rotate the hips or pelvis in a suggestive manner, esp. in a dance. *slang*. M20.

H. R. BROWN Her breath smells bad, but she sure can grind.

7 *verb intrans. & trans.* Produce (music) on a barrel organ; *esp.* produce or bring *out* laboriously or monotonously. L18.

A. JESSOPP A half-starved organ grinder comes and delights my heart by grinding for half an hour. L. GORDON All through Virginia's childhood . . her father was grinding out immense numbers of biographies.

8 *verb trans.* Teach (a subject, a pupil) in a steady laborious manner. E19.
9 *verb intrans.* Work (*away*, *on*) doggedly *at*; *spec.* study hard. M19. ▸**b** Study hard with a tutor or grinder. *arch.* M19.

A. BURGESS I ground away at Pliny's Letters and Virgil Book Six.

– COMB.: **grinding stone** a grindstone; **grinding wheel** (**a**) a wheel adapted for grinding or polishing; (**b**) a building in which cutlery or tools are ground.
■ **grinda'bility** *noun* the extent to which a material is easily ground or pulverized M20. **grindable** *adjective* able to be ground M17.

grinder /ˈgrʌɪndə/ *noun*. OE.
[ORIGIN from GRIND *verb* + -ER[1].]
1 A person who grinds corn etc. in a mill; a miller. OE. ▸**b** A person who grinds cutlery, tools, glass, etc. LME. ▸**c** A person who works a barrel organ, a winch on a yacht, etc. E19.

b *New York Times* Jewellery. Grinders and Polishers. Experienced only.

2 A molar tooth. In *pl.* also (*colloq.*), the teeth. LME.

W. GOLDING They were the grinders of old age. Worn away. M. GEE He spluttered with irritation as one of his treacle toffees stuck to his grinders.

3 A machine or implement for grinding. L17.
4 A person who prepares students for examinations; a crammer. *slang*. E19. ▸**b** A diligent student. *US slang*. M19.

M. EDGEWORTH A clever grinder . . would soon cram the necessary portion of Latin and Greek into him.

5 †**a** A person who works for another. *rare*. Only in E19. ▸**b** An employer of sweated labour. M19.
6 More fully ***scissor-grinder***, ***scissors-grinder***. The restless flycatcher, *Myiagra inquieta*. *Austral.* M19.
7 A derisive gesture made by putting the thumb to the nose and working the little finger like the handle of a coffee mill. *slang*. M19.
8 A large sandwich or filled roll usu. with several fillings. *US slang*. M20.

grindery /ˈgrʌɪnd(ə)ri/ *noun*. E19.
[ORIGIN from GRIND *verb* + -ERY.]
1 Materials, tools, etc. (orig. only the whetstone) used by shoemakers and other leather-workers. E19.
2 A place for grinding tools, weapons, etc. L19.

grinding /ˈgrʌɪndɪŋ/ *ppl adjective*. OE.
[ORIGIN from GRIND *verb* + -ING[2].]
1 That grinds. OE. ▸**b** Of a sound: grating, strident. E19.

b E. K. KANE You become conscious of a sharp, humming, grinding murmur.

come to a grinding halt = ***grind to a halt*** s.v. GRIND *verb* 2.
2 Crushing, exacting, oppressive. L16.

Times Civil strife fuelled by grinding poverty has continued to flare.

3 Of pain etc.: excruciating, racking, wearing. L16.
grinding pains: in the first stage of childbirth.
■ **grindingly** *adverb* E19.

grindle /ˈgrɪnd(ə)l/ *noun*[1]. Long *obsolete* exc. *dial.* LME.
[ORIGIN Unknown.]
A narrow ditch or drain.

grindle /ˈgrɪnd(ə)l/ *noun*[2]. *US*. E18.
[ORIGIN German *Gründel*, from *Grund* GROUND *noun*, bottom.]
= ***bowfin*** s.v. BOW *noun*[1].

grindle stone /ˈgrɪnd(ə)l stəʊn/ *noun phr. obsolete* exc. *dial.* ME.
[ORIGIN Prob. from instrumental noun from GRIND *verb* + STONE *noun*, & already in Old English.]
1 A grindstone. ME.
†**2** A piece, or kind, of stone suitable for making grindstones. E16–E18.

grindstone /ˈgrʌɪn(d)stəʊn/ *noun*. ME.
[ORIGIN from GRIND *verb* + STONE *noun*.]
1 A millstone. Long *rare*. ME.
2 A thick revolving stone disc used for grinding, sharpening, or polishing. ME.
hold a person's nose to the grindstone, **keep a person's nose to the grindstone** †(**a**) oppress, grind down; (**b**) cause to work hard and incessantly.
3 A kind of stone suitable for making grindstones. Also ***grindstone grit***. E18.

gringo /ˈgrɪŋgəʊ/ *noun & adjective*. Usu. *derog.* M19.
[ORIGIN Spanish = foreign, foreigner, gibberish.]
▸ **A** *noun*. Pl. **-os**. A (male) foreigner, esp. British or American, in a Spanish-speaking country. M19.
▸ **B** *adjective*. Of or pertaining to a gringo or gringos; foreign. L19.

High Times From Belize to Bolivia flows a growing trickle of gringo tourists in pursuit of the primitive.

■ **gringa** /-gə/ *noun & adjective* (of or pertaining to) a female gringo M20.

griot /ˈgriːəʊ/ *noun*. E19.
[ORIGIN French.]
A member of a class of travelling poets, musicians, and folk-historians, in N. and W. Africa; a praise singer.

grip /grɪp/ *noun*[1]. OE.
[ORIGIN Partly Old English *gripe* grasp, clutch, corresp. to Old High German *grif-* in comb., Middle High German *grif* (mod. *Griff*) grasp, handle, claw, Old Norse *grip* grasp, clutch, and partly Old English *gripa* handful, sheath, both from weak base of *gripan* GRIPE *verb*[1].]
1 A firm hold or grasp; the action of gripping, grasping, or clutching, esp. with the hand or claw; grasping power; ability to maintain contact, esp. by friction. Cf. HANDGRIP. OE. ▸**b** A way of grasping or clasping hands, esp. as a means of recognition by members of a secret society such as the Freemasons. M18. ▸**c** A way or style of grasping or holding something, as a racket, club, bat, etc. L19.

D. LODGE Melanie smiled . . and attempted to disengage her arms from his grip. K. LAING His teeth had a sharper grip of it than his hands. M. IGNATIEFF He held on to his blanket with a grip no one could loosen. *What Car?* We were impressed by the excellent grip of the tyres. **b** F. O'BRIEN Hands were extended till they met, the generous grip of friendship.

2 As much as can be seized in the hand; a handful. *obsolete* exc. *dial.* OE.
3 A seizure or spasm of pain. *obsolete* exc. *Scot.* LME.
4 *fig.* A firm or tenacious hold, grasp, or control; power, mastery; *spec.* oppressive power, irresistible force. L15. ▸**b** An intellectual hold; power to understand or master a subject. M19. ▸**c** The quality in a drink which gives it a lasting taste or other sensation on the palate. L19.

S. KING His mother was in the grip of a religious mania. J. M. ROBERTS The grip of the emperors at Constantinople and Ctesiphon was already loosened. **b** J. I. M. STEWART I kept a grip on the facts as they came together.

5 Something which grips or clips; *spec.* (**a**) *Scot.* in *pl.*, bonds, fetters; (**b**) *techn.* a device or machine part which grips, clips, or secures; (**c**) a hairgrip. M18.
hairgrip, ***kirby grip***, etc.
6 That which is gripped or grasped; *esp.* the part of a weapon or handle of an implement etc. by which it is held; the cover of such a part, enabling it to be held more firmly. M19.

W. VAN T. CLARK It was a long, blue-barrelled Colt six-shooter with an ivory grip.

7 THEATRICAL & CINEMATOGRAPHY. A stagehand; a member of a camera crew responsible for moving and setting up equipment. L19.
8 In full ***grip car***. A tramcar linked to a cable by a grip; a cable car. *US*. L19.
9 A travelling bag; a piece of hand luggage. Orig. *US*. L19.
10 A job, an occupation. *Austral. slang*. E20.

– PHRASES: **at grips** in close combat. **come to grips with** come into close quarters or into combat with. **get a grip on oneself** keep or recover one's self-control. **get to grips with** approach with determination, get control of. **lengthen one's grip** hold one's bat, club, etc., further from the point of impact. **lose one's grip** *fig.* lose control. **shorten one's grip** hold one's bat, club, etc., nearer to the point of impact. **take a grip on oneself** = ***get a grip on oneself*** above.
– COMB.: ***grip car***: see sense 8 above; **gripman** *US* a cable car operator; **gripsack** = sense 9 above.
■ **gripless** *adjective* having no grip or hold E17.

grip /grɪp/ *noun*[2]. Now chiefly *dial.* or HUNTING. Also (*dial.*) **gripe** /grʌɪp/.
[ORIGIN Old English *grypa*, *-e* rel. to *grēop* burrow, Middle Low German *grüppe*, Middle Dutch *grippe*, *greppe*, from Germanic base meaning 'hollow out'.]
A small open furrow or ditch, esp. for carrying off water; a trench, a drain, a channel.

grip /grɪp/ *verb*[1]. Infl. **-pp-**.
[ORIGIN Old English (late Northumbrian) *grippa* corresp. to Middle High German *gripfen*.]
1 *verb trans.* Grasp, seize, or hold firmly or tightly, esp. with the hand, claw, etc. OE. ▸**b** Of a disease: afflict strongly. E19.

S. R. CROCKETT He . . held it [his weapon] gripped between his knees as he rowed. J. BUCHAN I . . gripped his arm, for I thought he was going to faint.

2 *verb trans. gen.* Seize, catch; obtain hold or possession of. *obsolete* exc. *Scot.* LME. ▸**b** *spec.* Seize or encroach on (land). *Scot.* E17.
3 *verb intrans.* Take firm hold, maintain contact, esp. by friction; grasp something, get a grip. LME.

T. BOSTON Like a bird on the side of a wall gripping with its claws.

4 *verb trans.* Join firmly *to*. L19.
5 *verb trans. fig.* Compel the attention or interest of; take hold of (the mind, the emotions, etc.). L19.

P. G. WODEHOUSE It gripped him from the first page. F. HERBERT Deathly stillness gripped the arena. T. SHARPE A sense of righteous anger gripped him.

■ **gripper** *noun* a person who or thing which grips; *spec.* any contrivance or implement used to hold or secure an object: L16. **gripping** *adjective* that grips, clutches, or clips tightly; *fig.* that compels the attention: E16. **grippingly** *adverb* M20. **grippy** *adjective* (**a**) that grips or holds; *spec.* that holds the attention; (**b**) *Scot.* grasping, avaricious: E19.

grip /grɪp/ *verb*[2] *trans.* Now *dial.* Infl. **-pp-**. Also (*dial.*) **gripe** /grʌɪp/. L16.
[ORIGIN from GRIP *noun*[2].]
Make furrows or grips in; ditch, trench.

†**gripe** *noun*[1]. ME.
[ORIGIN Old French *grip* griffin, corresp. to medieval Latin *grypus*, *-is*, *gripes*, *grippis*, *gripa* griffin, vulture, vars. of *gryphus* from Latin *gryps*, *gryph-* (*gryphus*) from Greek *grups*, *grup-*: see GRIFFIN *noun*[1].]
1 A griffin. ME–M17.
2 A vulture. ME–M18.
– COMB.: **gripe's egg** a large egg, supposedly that of a gripe; *transf.* an oval-shaped vessel or cup.

G

gripe /grʌɪp/ *noun*². LME.
[ORIGIN from GRIPE *verb*¹.]
1 The action of gripping, clutching, or grasping, esp. with the hand, arm, claw, etc. LME. ▸**b** *fig.* Grasp, hold, control, grip. LME. ▸**c** SURGERY. An act of compressing an artery etc. with the fingers. Now *rare.* L17.

SIR W. SCOTT Rescue me from the gripe of this iron-fisted . . clown.

2 *transf.* & *fig.* **a** The clutch or pinch of something painful. Formerly also (in *pl.*), spasms of pain, pangs of grief. Now *rare* or *obsolete.* M16. ▸**b** An intermittent spasmodic pain in the bowels. Usu. in *pl.*, colic pains. E17.

b JOHN BAXTER Excess of green food, sudden exposure to cold, are . . occasional causes of gripes.

†**3** The hand held in a grasping or clutching position. M16–L18.
4 A handful or other specified quantity. *local.* L16.
†**5** **a** A shrewd gambler who places or leads bets. *slang.* L16–E17. ▸**b** A grasping covetous person, a usurer. *slang.* Only in 17.
6 Something which grasps or clutches; *spec.* something which restrains, a brake. L16.
7 Something which is held or grasped; the handle of an implement, the hilt of a sword. E17.
8 NAUTICAL. In *pl.* Lashings securing a boat on a deck or hanging in davits. M18.
9 A complaint, a grumble. Freq. in *pl. slang.* M20.

Observer It is a perpetual gripe from spectators that the toilet facilities are inadequate.

– COMB.: **Gripe Water** (proprietary name for) a solution given to babies to relieve colic, wind, and indigestion.

gripe /grʌɪp/ *noun*³. L16.
[ORIGIN Dutch *greep*, later assim. to GRIPE *noun*².]
NAUTICAL. The piece of timber etc. terminating the forward part of the keel. Also *gen.*, = FOREFOOT 2.

gripe *noun*⁴ see GRIP *noun*².

gripe /grʌɪp/ *verb*¹.
[ORIGIN Old English *grīpan* = Old Frisian *grīpa*, Old Saxon *grīpan* (Dutch *grijpen*), Old High German *grīfan* (German *greifen*), Old Norse *grípa*, Gothic *greipan*, from Germanic. Cf. GRIP *noun*¹, GROPE *noun, verb.*]
1 *verb intrans.* Grasp or clutch something; seek to get a hold. Long *rare.* OE.
2 *verb trans.* Lay hold of, seize; get into one's power or possession. *arch.* OE.
3 *verb trans.* & *intrans.* Clutch or grip with the hand, claw, etc. *arch.* ME. ▸†**b** *verb trans.* Embrace, encircle tightly. LME–M18.

MILTON Let each . . gripe fast his orbed Shield.

†**4** *verb trans. fig.* Apprehend; comprehend. ME–M18.
5 *verb trans.* Grieve, distress, annoy. Now chiefly *Scot.* & *N. Amer.* M16.
6 *verb trans.* Produce spasmodic pain in (the bowels); affect with gripes or colic. Now chiefly as **griped** pa. pple. E17. ▸**b** *verb intrans.* Produce pain in the bowels as if by constriction or contraction; cause gripes. E18.
7 NAUTICAL. **a** *verb intrans.* Of a ship: turn to face the wind in spite of the helm. E17. ▸**b** *verb trans.* Secure (a boat) with gripes. M19.
†**8** *verb trans.* Close (the fingers) tightly; clench (the fist). *rare.* M17–E18.
9 *verb trans.* & *intrans.* Oppress (someone) by miserly or penurious treatment; pinch, squeeze. *arch.* M17.

DICKENS He feeds the poor baby when he himself is griped with want.

10 *verb intrans.* Complain, grumble, grouse. *colloq.* M20.

W. WHARTON Lotte's griping because I'm dividing her place.

■ **griper** *noun* (*a*) a thing which gripes; (*b*) a person who oppresses others by extortionate or miserly means; (*c*) *colloq.* a person who complains or grumbles: L16. **griping** *ppl adjective* that gripes, that clutches tightly; grasping; painful, distressing: M16. **gripingly** *adverb* E17. **gripingness** *noun* L17.

gripe *verb*² see GRIP *verb*².

†**griph** *noun.* M17–L19.
[ORIGIN Latin *griphus* from Greek *griphos* creel, (fig.) riddle.]
A puzzling question; a riddle; an enigma.

griphite /ˈgrɪfʌɪt/ *noun.* L19.
[ORIGIN from Greek *griphos* riddle (on account of its complex composition) + -ITE¹.]
MINERALOGY. A basic phosphate of manganese and other elements, which crystallizes in the cubic system and usu. occurs as brown or black masses.

grippe /grɪp, *foreign* grip/ *noun.* L18.
[ORIGIN French.]
Influenza.
■ **grippé** /gripe/ *adjective* affected with grippe L19.

†**gripple** *noun. rare.* M16.
[ORIGIN from GRIP *noun*¹, GRIPE *verb*¹: see -LE¹. Cf. GRAPPLE *noun.*]
1 A hook to seize things with. Only in M16.
2 Grasp. *rare* (Spenser). Only in L16.

gripple /ˈgrɪp(ə)l/ *adjective. obsolete* exc. *dial.*
[ORIGIN Old English *gripul*, from *grip-* weak base of *grīpan* GRIPE *verb*¹: see -LE¹.]
1 Miserly, niggardly, usurious. OE.
2 Gripping, tenacious. E16.
■ **grippleness** *noun* avarice, greed, niggardliness L16.

Griqua /ˈgriːkwə/ *noun* & *adjective.* M18.
[ORIGIN Nama.]
▸**A** *noun.* A member of a people of mixed European and Khoikhoi origin, living mainly in the Eastern and Western Cape provinces of South Africa. M18.
▸**B** *adjective.* Of or pertaining to this people. E19.

grisaille /grɪˈzeɪl, -ˈlɪ; *foreign* grizaːj (*pl. same*)/ *noun* & *adjective.* M19.
[ORIGIN French, from *gris* grey + *-aille* -AL¹.]
▸**A** *noun.* A method of painting in grey monochrome, used to represent objects in relief or to decorate stained glass; a stained-glass window or other work of this kind. M19.
▸**B** *adjective.* Executed in grisaille. M19.

grisard /ˈgrɪzɑːd/ *adjective* & *noun. rare.* E17.
[ORIGIN Old French & mod. French, from *gris* grey: see -ARD.]
▸†**A** *adjective.* Greyish. Only in E17.
▸**B** *noun.* A grey-haired man. L19.

Griselda /grɪˈzɛldə/ *noun.* Also (*arch.*) **Grizel** /ˈgrɪz(ə)l/. LME.
[ORIGIN *Grisilde*, the heroine in Chaucer's *Clerk's Tale*, typifying a meek, patient wife.]
A meek patient woman or wife.

griseofulvin /ˌgrɪzɪə(ʊ)ˈfʊlvɪn/ *noun.* M20.
[ORIGIN from mod. Latin (*Penicillium*) *griseofulvum* (species name), from medieval Latin *griseus* grey + Latin *fulvus* reddish-yellow.]
PHARMACOLOGY. An antifungal antibiotic produced by moulds of the genus *Penicillium* and used to treat ringworm and other fungal infections.

griseous /ˈgrɪzɪəs/ *adjective.* E19.
[ORIGIN from medieval Latin *griseus* + -OUS.]
Chiefly BOTANY & ZOOLOGY. Grey; pearl-grey; greyish; mottled with grey.

grisette /grɪˈzɛt/ *noun* & *adjective.* E18.
[ORIGIN French, from *gris* grey: see -ETTE.]
▸**A** *noun.* **1** A cheap grey dress fabric, formerly worn by working girls in France. E18.
2 A young working-class Frenchwoman. E18.
▸**B** *adjective.* Made of grisette. E18.

gris-gris /ˈgriːgriː/ *noun.* Also **greegree**. L17.
[ORIGIN French *grigri*, *grisgris*, of W. African origin.]
An African charm, amulet, or fetish.

griskin /ˈgrɪskɪn/ *noun.* L17.
[ORIGIN Obscurely from GRICE *noun*¹ + -KIN.]
The lean part of a loin of pork.

grisly /ˈgrɪzli/ *adjective.*
[ORIGIN Late Old English *grislic*, from weak base of *-grīsan* (in *āgrīsan* terrify) = Middle Low German, Middle Dutch *grīsen*: see -LY¹.]
1 Causing horror, terror, or superstitious fear; causing unpleasant feelings; grim, ghastly. LOE.

A. JESSOPP The tangible memories of grisly conflict. J. GATHORNE-HARDY Hare suddenly thought of . . selling the body . . . the grisly tale is well known but still grips.

†**2** Full of fear, inspired by fear. LOE–L17.
3 Ugly. *dial.* L17.
■ **grisliness** *noun* ME.

grisly /ˈgrɪzli/ *adverb. arch.* ME.
[ORIGIN from weak base of Old English *-grīsan* (see GRISLY *adjective*) + -LY².]
Horribly, terribly; grimly.

grison /ˈgrɪz(ə)n, ˈgrʌɪs(ə)n/ *noun.* L18.
[ORIGIN French, use as noun of adjective from *gris* grey: see -OON.]
Each of three carnivorous mustelid mammals of the genus *Galictis*, of Central and S. America, which are grey with black legs, face, and underparts.

grissino /grisˈsiːno, grɪˈsiːnəʊ/ *noun.* Pl. ***-ni*** /-ni/. M19.
[ORIGIN Italian.]
A long thin stick of crisp bread. Usu. in *pl.*

grist /grɪst/ *noun*¹ & *verb.*
[ORIGIN Old English from Germanic, formed as GRIND *verb.*]
▸**A** *noun.* **1** The action or an act of grinding. OE.
2 Corn to be ground. Also, a batch of such corn. ME.

fig.: E. BAYNARD This grinds life's grist, yet takes small tole.

grist for the mill, **grist to the mill** useful experience, knowledge, material, etc.

3 Corn that has been ground. L15.
4 Malt crushed or ground for brewing. E19.
5 A lot, a large number or quantity. *US.* M19.
▸**B** *verb trans.* Grind (corn). E19.
– COMB.: **gristmill** a mill for grinding corn.

grist /grɪst/ *noun*². Now chiefly *Scot.* E18.
[ORIGIN Perh. rel. to GIRD *verb*¹.]
The size or thickness of a yarn or rope.

gristle /ˈgrɪs(ə)l/ *noun.*
[ORIGIN Old English *gristle* = Old Frisian, Middle Low German *gristel*, *gerstel*, Old High German *chrustila*, Middle High German *krustel* rel. to Old English *grost* gristle: ult. origin unknown.]
1 Cartilage, or a cartilaginous structure: now chiefly when occurring in meat. OE. ▸**b** *fig.* The unformed or initiatory stage of anything (with ref. to the cartilaginous nature of the bones in infancy). Now *rare.* L18.
†**2** *fig.* A tender or delicate person. M16–M17.

gristly /ˈgrɪsli/ *adjective.* LME.
[ORIGIN from GRISTLE *noun* + -Y¹.]
1 Pertaining to or of the nature of gristle; consisting or full of gristle; cartilaginous. LME.

M. MACKENZIE A piece of gristly meat one inch in length.

2 Having a texture like gristle, tough. E17.

†**grisy** *adjective*¹. L16–M19.
[ORIGIN formed as GRISLY *adjective* + -Y¹.]
Horrible, grim, grisly.

†**grisy** *adjective*². *rare.* L16–E17.
[ORIGIN from French *gris* grey + -Y¹.]
Grey, grizzled.

grit /grɪt/ *noun*¹.
[ORIGIN Old English *grēot* = Old Saxon *griot*, Old High German *grioz* (German *Griess*), Old Norse *grjót*, from Germanic base also of GRIT *noun*².]
1 *collect.* Formerly, sand, gravel, small stones. Now, minute particles of stone or sand, *spec.* as causing discomfort, clogging machinery, etc. OE. ▸**b** A grain of sand. *rare.* E17.

Soldier The road . . is unmetalled and covered in grit.

2 Coarse sandstone. ME.
3 Earth, soil, mould; the ground. *obsolete* exc. *dial.* ME.
4 The grain or texture of a stone; the fineness, coarseness, etc., of a stone. E16.
5 Strength of character; pluck, endurance, stamina. Also ***clear grit***, ***true grit***. *colloq.* E19. ▸**b** CANAD. HISTORY. More fully ***clear grit***. Orig., a supporter of the Clear Grit party, a 19th cent. liberal reform group which ultimately merged with the Liberal Party. Later, a liberal, a radical. M19.

G. STEIN She had grit and endurance and a vital courage.

– PHRASES & COMB.: ***clear grit***: see senses 5, 5b above. **grit-blast** *verb trans.* & *intrans.* clean and roughen (a surface) by using a directed stream of abrasive particles; sandblast. **gritstone** = sense 2 above. MILLSTONE ***grit***. **the clear grit** *slang* the real thing, the genuine article. ***true grit***: see sense 5 above.
■ **gritless** *adjective* (*rare*) L19.

grit /grɪt/ *noun*². Now *dial.* & *US.*
[ORIGIN Old English *grytt(e)* = Middle Low German, Dutch *grutte*, Old High German *gruzzi* (German *Grütze*) from West Germanic, from Germanic base also of GRIT *noun*¹, GROATS, GROUT *noun*¹.]
†**1** Bran, chaff, mill-dust. OE–ME.
2 In *pl.* (treated as *sing.* or *pl.*). Coarse oatmeal. Also (*US*), any coarsely ground grain, esp. when made into a kind of porridge. L16.

Orlando (Florida) Sentinel Eat Real Jail Food, such as cold grits and fried bologna.

grit /grɪt/ *verb.* Infl. **-tt-**. LME.
[ORIGIN from GRIT *noun*¹.]
1 *verb intrans.* Produce or move with a grating sound, such as is caused by the crushing of grit. LME. ▸**b** *verb trans.* Cause to make such a sound. M19.

E. GASKELL A slate-pencil gritting against a slate.

2 *verb trans.* Grind or clench (the teeth). L18. ▸**b** *verb trans.* Utter through gritted teeth. E20.

A. HALEY Gritting her teeth to keep from crying out.

3 *verb trans.* Cover with grit or sand; spread grit on (an icy road etc.). M19.
■ **gritter** *noun* a machine or vehicle for spreading grit on roads etc. M20.

grith /grɪθ/ *noun. obsolete* exc. *hist.* Also (esp. in sense 1b) **girth** /gəːθ/. LOE.
[ORIGIN Old Norse *grið* domicile, home, (pl.) truce, peace, pardon, quarter.]
1 †**a** Guaranteed security; protection, defence; safe conduct. LOE–M17. ▸**b** A place of protection; a sanctuary, an asylum. ME.
2 LAW (now *hist.*). In Anglo-Saxon England, security, peace, or protection guaranteed under specific limits of time or place; (more fully ***church-grith***) sanctuary, security within the precincts of a church. LOE.
†**3** Peace. LOE–LME.
†**4** Mercy, quarter, esp. in battle. ME–L15.
– COMB.: **grithbreach** breach of the peace; the penalty for this; **grith-man** a man, esp. a criminal, who has taken sanctuary.

gritty /ˈgrɪti/ *adjective*¹. L16.
[ORIGIN from GRIT *noun*¹ + -Y¹.]
1 Of the nature of or resembling grit; containing, consisting of, or covered with grit; sandy. Also, (of sound) low and rough, gravelly. L16.

R. SHAW He saw that their . . bodies were gritty from the ashes of the fires. O. MANNING A hot and gritty wind blew through the streets. A. TYLER The gritty click of heels on the sidewalk.

2 *spec.* Containing minute hard particles which impair or make unpleasant the substance harbouring them. E17.

▸**b** *fig.* Of literary style: difficult to read through, tedious. L19.

W. S. LANDOR These young bakers make their bread very gritty.

3 Having strength of character; plucky, courageous. *colloq.* M19.

USA Today The kind of people who made it from nothing—gritty and gutsy people.

■ **grittily** *adverb* E20. **grittiness** *noun* E17.

gritty /ˈɡrɪti/ *adjective*². Long *rare*. L15.
[ORIGIN Unknown.]
HERALDRY. Of a field: composed equally of a metal and a colour.

grivet /ˈɡrɪvɪt/ *noun*. M19.
[ORIGIN French, of unknown origin.]
The common African savannah monkey, *Cercopithecus aethiops*; *spec.* one of a race with long white facial hairs found in Ethiopia and Sudan. Cf. ***green monkey*** s.v. GREEN *adjective*, VERVET.

Grizel *noun* see GRISELDA.

grizzle /ˈɡrɪz(ə)l/ *adjective* & *noun*¹. ME.
[ORIGIN Old French *grisel*, from *gris* grey: see -EL¹.]
▸ **A** *adjective*. Of grey colour; grey, grizzled. Formerly also, (of a horse) roan. ME.
▸ **B** *noun*. †**1** (A nickname for) a grey-haired old man. ME–L17.
2 A grey animal; *esp.* a grey or (formerly) roan horse. ME.
3 Grey hair; a sprinkling of grey hair. E17. ▸**b** A grey wig. M18.
4 Grey colour; the colour grey. E17.
5 A second-class stock brick, so called from its grey colour. M19.

grizzle /ˈɡrɪz(ə)l/ *verb*¹ *trans.* & *intrans.* M18.
[ORIGIN from GRIZZLE *adjective*, or back-form. from GRIZZLED.]
Make or become grey or grey-haired.

A. T. ELLIS The old wolf-coloured woods, grizzled with snow.

grizzle /ˈɡrɪz(ə)l/ *verb*² & *noun*². M18.
[ORIGIN Unknown.]
▸ **A** *verb intrans.* **1** Show the teeth; grin, laugh. *dial.* M18.
2 Fret, sulk, grumble; (esp. of a child) whine or cry fretfully. *colloq.* M19.

M. DUFFY The baby beside her . . had grizzled hungrily. *Times Lit. Suppl.* Fat and fractious babies strapped in their high-chairs and grizzling for attention.

▸ **B** *noun*. **1** A person who grizzles or frets. Chiefly *dial.* L19.
2 A bout of grumbling or sulking; a bout of whining or fretfulness. *colloq.* E20.
■ **grizzler** *noun* (*dial.* & *colloq.*) a person who grumbles or frets E20.

grizzled /ˈɡrɪz(ə)ld/ *adjective*. LME.
[ORIGIN from GRIZZLE *adjective* + -ED².]
1 Grey; *spec.* (of hair) greyish, sprinkled with grey. LME.

A. J. P. TAYLOR He was a fine figure of a man . . with a grizzled beard.

2 Having grey or greying hair. E17.

W. C. WILLIAMS A wonderful man, a tough grizzled old primitive.

grizzly /ˈɡrɪzli/ *noun*¹. E19.
[ORIGIN from GRIZZLY *adjective*¹.]
A grizzly bear.

grizzly /ˈɡrɪzli/ *noun*². *US* & *S. Afr.* L19.
[ORIGIN Unknown.]
MINING. A grating of parallel iron bars for screening off larger stones from finer material.

grizzly /ˈɡrɪzli/ *adjective*¹. M16.
[ORIGIN from GRIZZLE *adjective* + -Y¹.]
1 Grey; greyish; grey-haired; grizzled. M16.

DICKENS He had a grizzly jagged beard of some three weeks' date.

2 *grizzly bear*: A large brown bear (*Ursus arctos*) of a race found in western N. America, distinguished by having brown fur with white-tipped hairs. E19. ▸**b** A jazz dance in which the hug and walk of the grizzly bear are imitated. E20.

grizzly /ˈɡrɪzli/ *adjective*². *colloq.* E20.
[ORIGIN from GRIZZLE *verb*² + -Y¹.]
Inclined to grizzle, grumble, or whine fretfully.

groan /ɡrəʊn/ *noun*. ME.
[ORIGIN from the verb.]
An act of groaning. Also, a deep inarticulate vocal sound expressing esp. pain, distress, complaint, or disapproval.

SIR W. SCOTT A low groan went through the assembly. D. WELCH We gave mock groans to show what a dreary old joke we thought it was. T. MO A groan escapes from Gideon's lips. *transf.*: N. ROWE In hollow Groans the falling Winds complain.

■ **groanful** *adjective* (*rare*) full of groans or groaning; lugubrious: L16.

groan /ɡrəʊn/ *verb*.
[ORIGIN Old English *grānian* from Germanic, whence also Old High German *grīnan* grin with laughing or weeping (German *greinen*), Middle High German *grinnen* gnash the teeth (German *grinsen* laugh, weep); cf. Middle Dutch *grinsen* (Dutch *grijnsen*) grin. Cf. GRIN *verb*².]
1 *verb intrans.* Breathe with a deep-toned murmur; make a deep inarticulate sound expressing esp. pain, distress, complaint, or disapproval. OE. ▸**b** *verb trans.* Breathe (one's life, soul, etc.) *out*, *away*, with a groan or groans. M17.

G. STEIN The pain came hard . . . and he groaned. **b** J. EATON Christ groaned out his blood and life upon the Crosse.

groan inwardly feel but not express or display misgiving, dismay, distress, etc.

†**2** *verb intrans.* Of a buck: utter a characteristic call in the rutting season. L15–L17.
3 *verb intrans.* Make a deep harsh sound resembling a groan. E16.

W. COWPER He heard the wheels . . Groan heavily along the distant road. KEATS The key turns, and the door upon its hinges groans.

4 *verb intrans.* Express earnest longing (as if) by groans; yearn or long *for*, *to do*. Now *rare*. M16.

SHAKES. *Jul. Caes.* This foul deed shall smell above the earth With carrion men, groaning for burial.

5 *verb trans.* Utter with groans; say miserably or despairingly. E17.

J. CONRAD He groaned, 'Oh, my leg!' R. GRAVES My father whispered, 'She read my letter?' 'Before I did myself,' groaned my uncle Tiberius.

6 *verb intrans.* Be oppressed or overloaded (as) to the point of groaning. Foll. by *beneath*, *under*, *with*. E17.

JAS. MILL The injustice under which he appeared to himself to groan. D. M. THOMAS At the dinner table which groaned with flowers, silver and cut glass.

7 *verb trans.* Express disapproval of by groans. *rare*. L18.

A. SEWARD They would be hissed, groaned, and cat-called.

■ **groaner** *noun* (*a*) a person who groans or complains; (*b*) *US local* a whistling buoy: LME. **groaning** *noun* (*a*) the action of the verb; (*b*) (long *obsolete* exc. *dial.*) a lying-in: OE. **groaningly** *adverb* in a groaning manner M16.

groat /ɡrəʊt/ *noun*. LME.
[ORIGIN Middle Dutch *groot*, Middle Low German *grōte*, use as noun of the adjective (= GREAT) in the sense 'thick' (cf. Middle High German *grōze* (later *grosse*) *pfennige* 'thick pennies', GROSCHEN).]
1 A denomination of coin issued from the 13th cent. in any of various European countries, having from the 14th cent. a theoretical value equal to that of ⅛ oz of silver but varying in actual intrinsic value. Long *obsolete* exc. *hist.* LME.
2 *hist.* An English silver coin issued 1351–1662, in value equal to four pennies. Later also, a fourpenny piece. LME. ▸†**b** A denarius; a drachma. Only in 16.
3 A small sum or amount. *arch.* E16.

CHESTERFIELD I do not care a groat what it is.

– PHRASES: ***grey groat***: see GREY *adjective*. ***Harry groat***: see HARRY *adjective* & *noun*².

groats /ɡrəʊts/ *noun pl.*
[ORIGIN Late Old English *grotan* (pl.) rel. to GROT *noun*¹, GRIT *noun*¹, *noun*², GROUT *noun*¹.]
Hulled (sometimes also crushed) grain, esp. oats.

Grobian /ˈɡrəʊbɪən/ *noun*. E17.
[ORIGIN German, or its source medieval Latin *Grobianus* an imaginary typical German boor (15–16), from German *grob* coarse, rude, GRUFF *adjective*.]
A coarse slovenly person.

grocer /ˈɡrəʊsə/ *noun*. ME.
[ORIGIN Anglo-Norman *grosser*, Old French *grossier* from medieval Latin *grossarius*, from *grossus* GROSS *adjective*.]
†**1** A person buying and selling in large quantities; a wholesale dealer or merchant. ME–L17.
2 A dealer in esp. dried and preserved foods and other miscellaneous household provisions. LME.
grocer's itch eczema caused by prolonged contact with material, e.g. flour or animal feeds, contaminated by acarid mites. **grocer's port**, **grocer's sherry**, **grocer's wine** cheap port etc. of low quality (supposedly) bought from a grocer's shop.
■ **grocerdom** *noun* (*rare*) the realm or world of grocers E19. **grocering** *noun* the trade or occupation of a grocer L19.

grocery /ˈɡrəʊs(ə)ri/ *noun*. LME.
[ORIGIN from GROCER + -Y³: see -ERY.]
1 In *pl.* & (now *rare*) *collect. sing.* Goods sold by or bought from a grocer. LME.

attrib.: A. TOFFLER In a grocery store . . milk turns over more rapidly than, say, canned asparagus.

2 The trade of a grocer. L17.
†**3** Small change. *slang*. E18–E19.
4 A grocer's shop; *dial.* a bar, a public house. *US*. E19.

groceteria /ɡrəʊsɪˈtɪərɪə/ *noun*. *N. Amer.* E20.
[ORIGIN from GROCERY after *cafeteria*.]
A self-service grocer's shop.

grockle /ˈɡrɒk(ə)l/ *noun*. *dial.* & *slang* (freq. *derog.*). M20.
[ORIGIN Unknown.]
A holidaymaker or summer visitor, esp. in Devon.

grody /ˈɡrəʊdi/ *adjective*. *US slang*. Also **groaty**. M20.
[ORIGIN from GROT(ESQUE + -Y¹ with regular US change of intervocalic *t* to *d*. Cf. GROTTY.]
Disgusting, revolting; slovenly, squalid.
grody to the max unspeakably awful.

Groenendael /ˈɡrəːnəndeɪl, ˈɡruːn-, -dɑːl/ *noun*. E20.
[ORIGIN A town in Belgium where the breed was developed.]
(An animal of) a breed of black smooth-coated Belgian sheepdog.

grog /ɡrɒɡ/ *noun*. M18.
[ORIGIN App. abbreviation of GROGRAM: first as a nickname of Admiral Vernon (1684–1757), who wore a grogram cloak, afterwards applied to the mixture he ordered to be served out to sailors instead of neat rum.]
1 A drink consisting of spirits (orig. rum) and water. M18. ▸**b** (An) alcoholic drink of any kind, *esp.* (a) beer. *Austral.* & *NZ colloq.* M19.
2 Pulverized burnt clay or pottery mixed with ordinary clay to increase its heat resistance. L19.
– COMB.: **grog-shanty** (*hist.*, chiefly *Austral.* & *NZ*) a shanty serving as a public house; **grog-shop** *arch.* a public house.
■ **groggery** *noun* (*arch.*) a public house E19.

grog /ɡrɒɡ/ *verb*. Infl. **-gg-**. M19.
[ORIGIN from the noun.]
1 *verb intrans.* Drink grog. M19.
2 *verb trans.* Extract spirit from (an empty cask) by pouring hot water into it and letting it stand. L19.

groggy /ˈɡrɒɡi/ *adjective*. L18.
[ORIGIN from GROG *noun* + -Y¹.]
1 Intoxicated, drunk. *arch.* L18.
2 Dazed, muzzy, weak, unsteady; (of a horse) unsteady or tottering due to weakness in the forelegs. E19.

B. BETTELHEIM A heavy blow on the head . . led to a loss of blood that left me groggy. E. AMADI He felt groggy from loss of sleep.

■ **groggified** *adjective* (*colloq.*, now *rare* or *obsolete*) affected by grog, tipsy L18. **groggily** *adverb* L19. **grogginess** *noun* E19.

grognard /ɡrɔɲaːr/ *noun*. Pl. pronounced same. E20.
[ORIGIN French, lit. 'grumbler'.]
A member of Napoleon's Old Guard; *transf.* a veteran soldier.

grogram /ˈɡrɒɡrəm/ *noun* & *adjective*. M16.
[ORIGIN French *gros grain* lit. 'coarse grain': see GROSS *adjective*, GRAIN *noun*¹ & cf. GROSGRAIN. For the change of final *n* to *m* cf. *buckram*, *vellum*.]
▸ **A** *noun*. **1** A coarse fabric of silk, or of mohair and wool, or of a mixture of all these, often stiffened with gum. M16.
2 A garment made of grogram. M17.
▸ **B** *adjective*. Made or consisting of grogram. L16.

groin /ɡrɔɪn/ *noun*¹. *obsolete* exc. *dial.* ME.
[ORIGIN Old French *groign* (= medieval Latin *grugnum*) mod. *groin* from late Latin *grunium*, *grunia*, medieval Latin *grunnium* snout, from Latin *grunnire* grunt like a pig (cf. GROIN *verb*¹). In sense 2 alt. of Spanish *La Coruña*.]
1 The snout of an animal, esp. a pig. ME.
†**2** (**G-**.) *The* port of Corunna in NW Spain. *nautical slang*. LME–E19.

groin /ɡrɔɪn/ *noun*². Orig. †**grynde**. LME.
[ORIGIN Uncertain: perh. repr. Old English *grynde* depression.]
1 The fold or depression on either side of the body between the abdomen and the upper thigh; *colloq.* the (esp. male) genitals. LME.
2 ARCHITECTURE. The edge formed by the intersection of two vaults; the rib or fillet of stone or wood covering this; the arch supporting a vault. Cf. earlier GROINING. E18.
3 A ring. *slang*. E20.

groin *noun*³ see GROYNE.

groin /ɡrɔɪn/ *verb*¹ *intrans.* ME.
[ORIGIN Old French *grognir*, (also mod.) *grogner* from Latin *grunnire*: see GROIN *noun*¹.]
1 Of an animal: grunt, growl. Long *obsolete* exc. *Scot.* ME. ▸†**b** Of a buck: utter a characteristic call in the rutting season. L15–E18.
†**2** Of a person: grumble, murmur. ME–L16.

groin /ɡrɔɪn/ *verb*² *trans.* E19.
[ORIGIN from GROIN *noun*². Cf. earlier GROINING.]
ARCHITECTURE. Form into or provide with groins; build with groins.

groin *verb*³ see GROYNE.

groined /ɡrɔɪnd/ *adjective*. L18.
[ORIGIN from GROIN *noun*², *verb*²: see -ED², -ED¹.]
ARCHITECTURE. Built or provided with groins.

groining /ˈɡrɔɪnɪŋ/ *noun*. M17.
[ORIGIN from GROIN *noun*² or *verb*²: see -ING¹.]
ARCHITECTURE. A groin or an arrangement of groins; groined work.

grok /ɡrɒk/ *verb*. *US slang*. Infl. **-kk-**. M20.
[ORIGIN Invented by Robert Heinlein (1907–88), US author.]
1 *verb trans.* Understand intuitively or by empathy; establish rapport with. M20.

R. A. HEINLEIN Smith had been aware of the doctors but had grokked that their intentions were benign.

G

2 *verb intrans.* Empathize or communicate sympathetically (*with*). Also, experience enjoyment. M20.

New Yorker We ought to get together somewhere . . and grok about our problems.

Grolier /ˈgrɒljeɪ, ˈgrəʊlɪə/ *adjective & noun*. E19.
[ORIGIN Jean *Grolier* de Servin (see below).]
▸ **A** *adjective*. Designating (a book decorated with) the interlacing geometrical designs adorning the bindings of books bound for the French book collector Jean Grolier de Servin, Vicomte d'Aiguisy (1479–1565). E19.
▸ **B** *noun*. (A book in) a Grolier binding. L19.

gromel(l) *noun* see GROMWELL.

grommet /ˈgrɒmɪt/ *noun*[1]. Also **grummet** /ˈgrʌmɪt/. E17.
[ORIGIN French †*grom(m)ette*, *gourmette* curb chain, from *gourmer* to curb, to bridle, of unknown origin.]
1 NAUTICAL. A ring or wreath of rope, usu. consisting of a single strand laid three times round, and used as a fastening, a wad in a gun, or a substitute for a rowlock. Also, an eyelet of metal. E17.
2 A washer used to insulate electric conductors passing through a hole in a conducting material. M20.
3 A stiffener used inside a cap worn by a member of the Armed Forces. M20.
4 MEDICINE. A small tube passed through the eardrum in surgery to make a communication with the middle ear. M20.

grommet /ˈgrɒmɪt/ *noun*[2]. *slang* (chiefly *Austral.* & *NZ*). Also **-it**. L20.
[ORIGIN Unknown. Cf. GRUMMET *noun*[1].]
A young surfer or skateboarder.

gromwell /ˈgrɒmw(ə)l/ *noun*. Also (earlier) **gromel(l)** /ˈgrɒm(ə)l/. ME.
[ORIGIN Old French *gromil*, *grumil* (mod. *grémil*), prob. from medieval Latin collocation meaning 'crane's millet'.]
Any of several related plants of the borage family with polished stony nutlets and white or blue flowers in bracteate cymes; *esp.* (more fully ***common gromwell***) *Lithospermum officinale*, of bushy places, and (more fully ***corn gromwell***, ***field gromwell***) *L. arvense*, a weed of arable land.

groof /gruːf/ *noun & adverb*. *obsolete* exc. *Scot.* & *N. English*. Also **grufe**. LME.
[ORIGIN Old Norse *grúfa*, in *á grúfu* face downwards. Cf. GROVELLING.]
▸ **A** *noun*. The face, the front. Chiefly in ***on one's groof***, ***on groof***, ***a-groof***, face downwards, in a prone position. LME.
▸ †**B** *adverb*. On the face, prone. LME–E18.

groo-groo *noun* var. of GRUGRU.

groom /gruːm/ *noun*[1]. ME.
[ORIGIN Uncertain: cf. Anglo-Norman *gromet*, Anglo-Latin *gromus*, *grometus* in sense 3.]
†1 A male child, a boy. ME–L17.

C. COTTON To bring him Plums and Mackaroons Which welcome are to such small Grooms.

2 A male adult, a man. *arch.* ME.

WORDSWORTH What sprinklings of blithe company! Of lasses and of shepherd grooms.

3 A man of low position or birth, a male servant or attendant (*arch.*); in later use *spec.* a person employed to take care of horses. ME.

SHAKES. *Rich. II* I was a poor groom of thy stable. C. KINGSLEY Your nephew's lands are parted between grooms and scullions. A. HIGGINS She saw . . a groom in hobnail boots leading out a docile roan mare.

4 *spec.* (Also G-.) Any of various officers of the royal household. Freq. with defining preposition phr. LME.

Pall Mall Gazette Sir Henry was a Groom-in-Waiting to Her Majesty.

groom of the ladder: see LADDER *noun*. ***groom of the stool***: see STOOL *noun*. ***groom of the stole***: see STOLE *noun*[2].

5 = BRIDEGROOM. E17.

R. HOGGART A bride must not see her groom before the ceremony on her wedding-day.

– COMB.: **groom-porter** (*obsolete* exc. *hist.*) in the royal household, the holder of an office (abolished under George III) whose principal function was to regulate gaming; **groomsman** a male friend officially attending the bridegroom at a wedding; *esp.* the best man.

■ **groomish** *adjective* (*rare*) characteristic of a groom M19. **groomless** *adjective* (*rare*) L19. **groomship** *noun* (*rare*) the office or condition of a groom L17. **groomy** *adjective* (now *rare*) of, pertaining to, or characteristic of a groom M19.

groom /gruːm/ *noun*[2]. *dial.* L18.
[ORIGIN Uncertain: perh. rel. to CROME.]
A forked stick used in thatching.

groom /gruːm/ *verb trans.* E19.
[ORIGIN from GROOM *noun*[1].]
1 Clean or brush the coat of and generally attend to (esp. a horse); (of an ape or monkey) clean and comb the fur of (its fellow) with the fingers. E19.
2 Attend to carefully; give a neat, tidy, or smart appearance to. M19.

N. GORDIMER A white woman lawyer so perfectly groomed she appeared to be under glaze. J. LE CARRÉ His grey hair was groomed with military correctness.

3 *fig.* Prepare (a person) as a political candidate; prepare or coach (a person) for a particular career, activity, etc. Orig. *US*. L19. ▸**b** Prepare (a child) for a meeting, esp. via an Internet chat room, with the intention of committing a sexual offence. L20.

P. G. WODEHOUSE A man whom the committee were grooming for the amateur championship. C. MCCULLOUGH They could simply have earmarked Senator Hillier for the job and begun to groom him.

■ **groomer** *noun* L19.

groop /gruːp/ *noun*. Now *dial.* ME.
[ORIGIN Middle Dutch *groepe* (Dutch *groep*) = Old Frisian, Low German *gröpe*; cf. also Icelandic *gróp* groove, Norwegian, Swedish *grop* hollow, cavity, Danish dial. *grob* ditch.]
1 A small trench, a ditch, an open drain; *spec.* the drain or gutter in a stable or cow-house. ME.
2 A groove, a mortice. Long *obsolete* exc. *Scot.* LME.

groop /gruːp/ *verb trans.* Long *obsolete* exc. *dial.* ME.
[ORIGIN Cf. Icelandic *grópa* make a groove; Faroese *grópa* dig (a hole).]
†1 Dig (a trench). Only in ME.
2 Make a groove in, hollow out, incise. Long *obsolete* exc. *Scot.* LME.

groose /gruːz/ *verb intrans.* *Scot.* & *N. English*. L17.
[ORIGIN App. from GRUE *verb*.]
Shiver, shudder.

groot /gruːt/ *noun*. *obsolete* exc. *dial.* LME.
[ORIGIN Uncertain: rel. to GRIT *noun*[1], GROUT *noun*[1].]
Mud, soil, earth; sediment, refuse.

groot /gruːt/ *verb intrans. & trans.* *obsolete* exc. *Scot.* E19.
[ORIGIN App. from GROOT *noun*. Cf. earlier GROUT *verb*[1].]
= GROUT *verb*[1].

groove /gruːv/ *noun*. ME.
[ORIGIN Dutch †*groeve* furrow, ditch (now *groef*) = Old High German *gruoba* (German *Grube* pit, ditch), Old Norse *gróf*, Gothic *grōba*, from Germanic, rel. to base of GRAVE *noun*[1], *verb*[1].]
1 A mining shaft; a mine, a pit. Now *dial.* ME.
2 A channel or furrow cut by artificial means in metal, wood, etc.; *esp.* one made to direct motion or to receive a corresponding ridge. M17. ▸**b** THEATRICAL, *hist.* A wooden channel permitting a piece of scenery to be moved easily onstage and offstage. M19. ▸**c** The spiral cut in a gramophone record (or a phonographic cylinder) to form a path for the stylus or needle. E20.

W. GREENER He formed a number of circular grooves on the cylindrical part of the bullet. *Practical Woodworking* A drawer side needs a groove for the runner.

3 A channel or furrow of natural formation, as in a plant or animal structure, a rock, etc. L18.

A. GEIKIE Its rocks covered with ruts and grooves. W. VAN T. CLARK Heavy lines under the eyes . . and heavy, unhappy grooves down from her mouth.

4 *fig.* A fixed routine; a narrow limited unchanging course; a rut. M19.

A. HELPS His ideas were wont to travel rather in a groove. R. LEHMANN But folk are apt to get in a groove as they grow older.

5 A style of playing pop or jazz music, esp. particularly well; a style of doing anything well or in a favoured way. *slang* (orig. *US*). M20.

Melody Maker The rhythm team . . developed a very propulsive rhythmic groove.

– PHRASES & COMB.: **groove cast** GEOLOGY a ridge on the lower surface of a layer of sandstone corresponding to a groove on underlying mudstone. **in the groove** *slang* = GROOVY 3.

■ **grooveless** *adjective* M19.

groove /gruːv/ *verb*. L15.
[ORIGIN from the noun.]
1 *verb intrans.* Sink a mining shaft, mine. *dial. rare*. L15.
2 *verb trans.* Cut a groove or grooves in, provide with grooves. L17.

R. HOLME In these holes are threads of Screws grooved inwards. S. BELLOW What a face he saw, how grooved with woe and age.

3 *verb trans.* Cut in the form of a groove or channel; excavate (a channel). M19.
4 *verb trans. & intrans.* (Cause to) settle *in(to)* a groove (chiefly *fig.*). M19.

J. A. FROUDE Morality . . grooved into habits of action creates strength.

5 *verb intrans.* Play pop, rock, or jazz music with ease and skill; dance or listen *to* such music with enjoyment; please; get on well *with*. M20. ▸**b** *verb trans.* Play (pop, rock, etc.) well; please (someone). M20.

Melody Maker. The rhythm section . . grooves along in true Basie manner. A. HOLLINGHURST Most of the group started grooving around at once . . with happy, determined expressions.

■ **groover** *noun* (**a**) (now *dial.*) a miner; (**b**) a tool for making grooves, a gouge; (**c**) *slang* a fashionable person: E17.

grooved /gruːvd/ *adjective*. L18.
[ORIGIN from GROOVE *noun*, *verb*: see -ED[2], -ED[1].]
Provided with or having a groove or grooves.
grooved ware ARCHAEOLOGY a late Neolithic pottery ware characterized by a flat base, vertical or outward sloping walls, and decoration including grooves made in the clay before firing.

groovy /ˈgruːvi/ *adjective*. M19.
[ORIGIN from GROOVE *noun* + -Y[1].]
1 Resembling a groove. M19.
2 Of a person: having a tendency to adhere to a narrow limited unchanging course; in a rut. *colloq.* (now *rare*). L19.
3 (Capable of) playing pop or jazz music with ease and brilliance; *gen.* fashionable, sophisticated; very good, excellent. *slang* (orig. *US*). M20.

Sunday Express Thinking back, I must have looked like hell. But I thought I looked ever so groovy.

■ **groovily** *adverb* L20. **grooviness** *noun* M19.

grope /grəʊp/ *noun*.
[ORIGIN Old English *grāp* = Old High German *greifa* fork, from Germanic ablaut var. of base of GRIP *noun*[1]. In sense 2 from GROPE *verb*.]
†1 A hold, a grasp. OE–ME.
2 The action or an act of groping. E16.

grope /grəʊp/ *verb*.
[ORIGIN Old English *grāpian* = Old High German *greifōn* from West Germanic, from Germanic base of GRIPE *verb*[1].]
†1 *verb intrans.* Use the hands in feeling, touching, or grasping; handle or feel something. OE–M16.
2 *verb intrans.* Attempt to find something by feeling about esp. with the hand as if blind or in the dark (also foll. by *for*, *after*); feel about in order to find one's way; move *along* etc. in this manner. OE. ▸**b** *fig.* Search for mentally with hesitation or uncertainty; have difficulty in finding. (Foll. by *for*, *after*.) ME. ▸**c** Try to catch fish by feeling in the water. Foll. by *for*. E17.

S. SASSOON We were groping and stumbling along a deep ditch. R. C. HUTCHINSON His hand groped in the deep pocket of his coat for the coin. **b** F. HERBERT Paul groped for words, could find nothing to say. D. W. WINNICOTT The scientist . . gropes towards a facet of the truth.

3 *verb trans.* Touch or examine with the hands or fingers; handle, feel; grasp, seize. Now chiefly *spec.* (*colloq.*), feel or fondle (a person) clumsily for sexual pleasure. OE.

C. PHILLIPS Michael pushed the key into the door, opened it and groped the wall. T. WOGAN The girlish giggles of typists being groped in the safe.

†4 *verb trans.* *fig.* Examine or sound out (a person, the conscience, etc.); investigate (a matter). ME–M17. ▸**b** Perceive, understand, (something, *that*). LME–M17.

D. CALDERWOOD Davie gropped their mindes, how they were affected to the banished lords. **b** D. ROGERS When you might have felt and groped the Lord in his manifest providence.

– PHRASES: **grope one's way** find one's way by groping; proceed in this manner. **grope out** find by groping, search out, (chiefly *fig.*).

■ **gropingly** *adverb* in a groping manner, blindly M16.

groper /ˈgrəʊpə/ *noun*[1]. M16.
[ORIGIN from GROPE *verb* + -ER[1].]
1 A person who gropes. M16.
2 A West Australian. Also more fully ***sandgroper***. *Austral.* (*joc.*). L19.

groper /ˈgrəʊpə/ *noun*[2]. *Austral.* & *NZ*. M19.
[ORIGIN Var. of GROUPER.]
1 Any of several serranid fishes; esp. (**a**) (more fully ***Queensland groper***) a large voracious Indo-Pacific grouper, *Promicrops lanceolatus*; (**b**) the hapuku. M19.
2 More fully ***blue groper***. Any of various large Australasian wrasses, esp. *Achoerodus gouldii*. L19.

gros /grəʊ/ *noun*. Pl. same. M18.
[ORIGIN French, use as noun of *gros* GROSS *adjective*.]
†1 ***gros du soie***, a heavy silk fabric. Only in M18.
2 A silk fabric orig. from or associated with a specified city etc., as ***gros de Londres*** /də lɔ̃dr/, ***gros de Lyons*** /də ljɔ̃/, ***gros de Naples*** /də napl/, etc. L18.

grosbeak /ˈgrəʊsbiːk/ *noun*. L17.
[ORIGIN French *grosbec*, from *gros* GROSS *adjective* + *bec* BEAK *noun*[1].]
Any of various finches or finchlike birds with heavy bills, *esp.* (**a**) a finch of the genus *Coccothraustes* or *Pinicola*; (**b**) a cardinal (CARDINAL *noun* 2).
evening grosbeak, ***pine grosbeak***, ***sociable grosbeak***, ***song grosbeak***, etc.

gros bleu /gro blø/ *noun & adjectival phr.* L19.
[ORIGIN French = dark blue.]
(Of) a deep blue used to paint china.

groschen /ˈgrəʊʃ(ə)n/ *noun*. Pl. same. E17.
[ORIGIN German (Bohemian) alt. of late Middle High German *gros(se)*, from medieval Latin *denarius grossus* thick penny: see GROSS *adjective*, GROAT.]
1 *hist.* A small German silver coin of low denomination; the sum represented by this. E17.
2 *hist.* A German ten-pfennig piece. *colloq.* E20.
3 A monetary unit of Austria (until the introduction of the euro in 2002), equal to one-hundredth of a schilling. E20.

groser /ˈɡrəʊzə/ *noun*. *obsolete* exc. *Scot. & N. English*. **E16**.
[ORIGIN French *groseille*.]
= GROSET.

groset /ˈɡrəʊzɪt/ *noun*. *Scot.* **L18**.
[ORIGIN Alt. of GROSER.]
A gooseberry.

grosgrain /ˈɡrəʊɡreɪn; *foreign* ɡroɡrɛ̃ (*pl. same*)/ *noun & adjective*. **M19**.
[ORIGIN French: see GROGRAM.]
(Made of) any of various heavy ribbed fabrics, esp. silk or rayon.

Gros Michel /ɡrəʊ mɪˈʃɛl/ *noun phr.* **L19**.
[ORIGIN French.]
A variety of banana originating in the W. Indies.

gros point /ɡro pwɛ̃/ *noun phr.* **M19**.
[ORIGIN French = large stitch.]
1 More fully ***gros point de Venise*** /də vəniːz/. A type of lace, originally from Venice, worked in bold relief. **M19**.
2 Any of various embroidery stitches worked over two or more horizontal and vertical threads of the canvas. **M20**.

gross /ɡrəʊs/ *noun*[1]. Pl. same. **LME**.
[ORIGIN French *grosse* use as noun (sc. *douzaine* dozen) of fem. of *gros* great: see GROSS *noun*[2] and cf. Spanish *gruesa*, Portuguese, Italian *grossa*.]
A quantity of twelve dozen.
by the gross in large quantities, wholesale. ***great gross***: see GREAT *adjective*.

gross /ɡrəʊs/ *noun*[2]. **LME**.
[ORIGIN from the adjective.]
1 The gross or coarse part of something; the dregs, dross; sediment. *obsolete* exc. *dial.* **LME**.
2 The greater part, the majority, the bulk; *esp.* the main body of a military force. *arch.* **LME**. ▸†**b** A large body, a mass. Chiefly MILITARY. Only in **17**.

BURKE This denial of landed property to the gross of the people has further evil effect.

3 The sum, sum total; now *esp.*, the whole amount earned. **L16**.

G. BORDMAN Disappointing grosses on the road . . warned that show would not prove . . long-lasting.

– PHRASES: †**by gross** in large quantities, wholesale. **in gross, in the gross** (*a*) (now *rare*) generally, without going into particulars; on the whole; †(*b*) in a body; †(*c*) in bulk, wholesale; †(*d*) in full; (*e*) LAW (*in gross*) absolute and independent.

†**gross** *noun*[3]. **M16–E18**.
[ORIGIN Repr. French *gros*, Italian *grosso*.]
Any of various coins of low denomination in various currencies, as the German groschen.

gross /ɡrəʊs/ *adjective*. **ME**.
[ORIGIN Old French & mod. French *gros*, fem. *grosse* from late Latin *grossus* (freq. in late Latin (Vulgate)), of similar formation to *bassus* BASE *adjective*, *crassus* CRASS.]
▸ **I 1** †**a** Thick, stout, massive, bulky. Also (of printed or written letters), large. **ME–L18**. ▸**b** Of a shoot or stalk: bulky, esp. as a result of abnormal growth; luxuriant, rank. **L16**.

DRYDEN Your finger is more gross than the great monarch's loins.

†**2** Of conspicuous magnitude; plain, evident, obvious, easy to understand. **LME–L18**.

DEFOE We should . . give him up for a Magician in the grossest acceptation of the word.

3 Overfed, bloated, repulsively fat; (now *dial.*) big-bodied, burly. **M16**.

LONGFELLOW He was a gross, corpulent fellow. M. GEE She knew he looked heavy. Now she realised he must have looked gross. S. MORLEY I was so gross . . that I actually sent off for . . a fat dissolvent.

4 As an intensive: flagrant, glaring, complete. **L16**.

A. TROLLOPE [He] had in his opinion made a gross fool of himself. A. TREW There must be gross inefficiency on board.

▸ **II 5** Concerned with a large area or mass; general, not particular or in detail. **LME**. ▸**b** MEDICINE. Visible to the naked eye, not microscopic. **L19**.

G. WINOKUR There is no gross or microscopic abnormality of the brain.

6 Entire, total, whole. Now *spec.* (of an amount, value, weight, etc.), without deductions, not net. **E16**. ▸†**b** Main; the great majority of. **L16–L18**.

LD MACAULAY The gross receipt was about seventy thousand pounds. J. UPDIKE Gross sales are down about eleven per cent over last year. **b** N. LUTTRELL Admirall Russell with the grosse fleet arrived at Torbay.

gross domestic product the annual total value of goods produced and services provided in a country excluding transactions with other countries. **gross national product** the annual total value of goods produced and services provided in a country.

†**7** Of a denomination of value or weight: relatively large; containing lower denominations. Of a method of calculation: using large units. **M16–E19**.

▸ **III 8 a** Dense, thick, (now only of air, vapour, darkness, etc.). Now *arch. & poet.* **LME**. ▸**b** Material, perceptible to the senses; not spiritual or ethereal. **E16**.

a LONGFELLOW Through the gross vapours, Mars grows fiery red. **b** M. ELPHINSTONE Each soul is invested with a subtile body, which again is clad in a grosser body.

†**9** Of a body of armed men: compact, solid. **L16–L17**.

F. VERE The enemy, seeing no grosse troop to follow them, began to take heart.

▸ **IV** †**10** Consisting of comparatively large parts or particles; lacking in fineness or delicacy of texture, etc. **LME–L18**. ▸**b** Of a file, whetstone, etc.: coarse, rough. Only in **17**.
11 Orig. (chiefly of food), plain, not delicate; coarse; inferior. Now (of food or diet), coarse, greasy, unwholesome. *arch.* **LME**.

DEFOE Dealing only in fish and oil, and such gross commodities. E. W. LANE Their diet is extremely gross.

12 †**a** Of workmanship, a method of work etc.: rough, improvised, clumsy. **L15–M17**. ▸†**b** Not clear or definite; approximate, general. **L15–E19**. ▸**c** Of a sense or faculty or (formerly) a person: dull, stupid, lacking in perception. (Now chiefly after *Matthew* 13:15.) *arch.* **E16**.

a J. WILKINS But this would have been too grosse a way for so excellent an artificer. **b** DRYDEN The crowd cannot be presumed to have more than a gross instinct, of what pleases . . them. **c** J. RAY Our Eyes and Senses . . are too gross to discern the Curiosity of the Workmanship of Nature.

13 Of a person: uneducated, ignorant. Formerly also (of a dialect, word, etc.), uncultivated, barbarous. Now *rare*. **E16**.

S. PURCHAS The Inhabitants were so grosse . . , that they knew not the use of fire. GIBBON The vulgar dialect of the city was gross and barbarous.

14 Of a person, behaviour, language, etc.: extremely coarse; brutally lacking in refinement or decency; *slang* repulsive, disgusting. **M16**.

J. HYAMS 'She really thinks he's gross, huh?' . . 'The pits,' said Freda. D. M. THOMAS The gross expressions which her illness has dredged up from this normally shy and prudish girl. P. THEROUX I don't want to be gross, but sometimes they eat their prisoners.

■ **grossen** *verb trans.* (*rare*) make coarse or gross **L19**. **grossy** *adjective* (long *obsolete* exc. *dial.*) somewhat gross **M17**.

gross /ɡrəʊs/ *verb*. **LME**.
[ORIGIN from the adjective.]
†**1** *verb trans.* Foll. by *up*: = ENGROSS 1. **LME–E16**.
2 †**a** *verb trans.* Foll. by *up*: = ENGROSS 3, 4. **LME–M16**. ▸†**b** *verb intrans.* Save, amass wealth. *dial.* **L18**.
†**3 a** *verb intrans.* Become gross, increase. Only in **M16**. ▸**b** *verb trans.* Make gross or coarse. Only in **M17**.
4 *verb trans.* Make a gross profit of; earn a total of. **L19**. ▸**b** Foll. by *up*: count or add as part of the total; increase (a net amount) to its value before deductions. **M20**.

H. ROBBINS This picture looks like it will gross a quarter of a million dollars. *Bookseller* Ghostbusters, currently the biggest grossing movie in the States.

5 *verb trans.* Foll. by *out*: Disgust or shock, esp. by repulsive or obscene behaviour. *N. Amer. slang.* **M20**.

A. LURIE Some of the jokes told by grownups . . really gross Vinnie out. T. O'BRIEN Let us discuss obesity. You porkers gross me out.

– COMB.: **gross-out** *adjective & noun* (*N. Amer. slang*) (designating) something repulsive or obscene.
■ **grosser** *noun* (*a*) (*obsolete* exc. *dial.*) a person who amasses wealth (orig. by buying up land etc.); (*b*) a film etc. that brings in a (*big* etc.) sum of money: **M16**.

grossly /ˈɡrəʊsli/ *adverb*. **L15**.
[ORIGIN from GROSS *adjective* + -LY[2].]
†**1** Plainly, obviously; in plain or understandable terms. **L15–L18**.
2 Indelicately, coarsely, indecently. **L15**.
†**3** Stupidly, clumsily, unskilfully. **E16–E18**.
4 Roughly, generally, without regard to detail (*arch.*); MEDICINE by visual inspection. **M16**.

Nature The bones were examined grossly, by radiography, and histologically.

†**5** Densely, thickly. **M16–E18**.
†**6** Of grinding, milling, etc.: coarsely, as opp. to finely. **L16–E19**.
†**7** Materially, as opp. to spiritually. **L16–E17**.
8 Excessively; glaringly, flagrantly; to a shocking degree. **L16**.

J. MITCHELL The official inquiry . . found them grossly exaggerated. I. MURDOCH The eyelids of both eyes were so grossly red and swollen with weeping.

grossness /ˈɡrəʊsnɪs/ *noun*. **LME**.
[ORIGIN from GROSS *adjective* + -NESS.]
†**1** Bigness, bulkiness. **LME–M17**.
2 Thickness, denseness, materiality. Now *rare*. **LME**.
3 Lack of education, ignorance; dullness, stupidity. **M16**.
4 Coarseness, lack of delicacy, decency, or refinement. **M16**.
5 Exaggerated or flagrant character, excessiveness. **L16**.

grosso modo /ɡrosso ˈmɔːdo, ɡrɒsəʊ ˈməʊdəʊ/ *adverbial phr.* **M20**.
[ORIGIN Italian.]
Roughly, approximately.

grossular /ˈɡrɒsjʊlə/ *noun*. **E19**.
[ORIGIN mod. Latin *grossularia* (former specific epithet of) gooseberry.]
A garnet containing calcium and aluminium, occurring in grey, pinkish, or yellow-green crystals and used as a gemstone. Also (when green) called ***gooseberry garnet***.
■ **grossularite** *noun* = GROSSULAR **M19**.

Gros Ventre /ɡrəʊ ˈvɒntrə/ *noun & adjectival phr.* Pl. **Gros Ventres** (pronounced same). **E19**.
[ORIGIN French, lit. 'big belly'.]
1 = HIDATSA. **E19**.
2 = ATSINA. **M19**.

grosz /ɡrɒʃ/ *noun*. Pl. **-szy** /-ʃi/, **-sze** /-ʃə/. **L19**.
[ORIGIN Polish.]
A monetary unit in Poland, equal to one-hundredth of a zloty.

†**grot** *noun*[1]. **OE–M18**.
[ORIGIN Rel. to GROATS, GROUT *noun*[1].]
A fragment, a particle.

grot /ɡrɒt/ *noun*[2]. Now chiefly *poet.* **E16**.
[ORIGIN French *grotte* from Italian *grotta* from Proto-Romance vars. of Latin *crypta* from Greek *kruptē* vault, CRYPT.]
1 = GROTTO 1. **E16**.
2 = GROTTO 2. **M17**.

grot /ɡrɒt/ *adjective & noun*[3]. *slang.* **M20**.
[ORIGIN Abbreviation.]
▸ **A** *adjective*. = GROTTY. **M20**.

Listener What with grot hotels . . and general anxiety, I had not had what I would call a meal since leaving Khartoum.

▸ **B** *noun*. Something or someone grotty; *esp.* rubbish, dirt. **M20**.

Civil Service Motoring Old cars . . may be coated with a couple of decades worth of grot.

grotesque /ɡrə(ʊ)ˈtɛsk/ *noun & adjective*. **M16**.
[ORIGIN French *crotesque* from (with assim. to Old French *crote* (mod. *grotte*) GROT *noun*[2]) Italian *grottesca* ellipt. use (for *opera* or *pittura grottesca* work or painting resembling a grotto) of fem. of *grottesco*, from *grotta*; finally assim. to French *grotesque*: see -ESQUE.]
▸ **A** *noun*. Also (esp. in sense 1b) in Italian form ***grottesco*** /ɡrotˈtesko, ɡrəʊˈtɛskəʊ/, pl. ***-schi*** /-ski/.
1 A style of decorative painting or sculpture consisting of a fantastic interweaving of human and animal forms with flowers and foliage. **M16**. ▸**b** A work of art, a figure or design in this style (usu. in *pl.*); *loosely* a comically distorted figure or design. **M17**.

EVELYN The foliage and grotesque about some of the compartments are admirable. **b** C. G. LELAND Adorned with fifteenth century grotesques.

2 A grotesque person or thing. **M17**. ▸**b** That which is grotesque. **E19**.

M. AYRTON The sting-ray, that flat, long-tailed sea grotesque. **b** C. PETERS The grotesque is rare in his mature work.

3 TYPOGRAPHY. A sans serif type. **L19**.
▸ **B** *adjective*. **1** ARCHITECTURE. In the style of a grotesque. **E17**.

R. W. EMERSON Let there be grotesque sculpture about the gates and offices of temples.

2 Comically or repulsively distorted; unnatural, bizarre. **M17**. ▸†**b** Of landscape: romantic, picturesquely irregular. **M17–M18**.

H. BASCOM The hammock, distorted by his body, casts a grotesque shadow. **b** R. DODSLEY The more pleasing parts of this grotesque and hilly country.

3 Ludicrous from incongruity; fantastically absurd. **M18**.

LYTTON O'Carroll gave a grotesque sort of signal between a wink and a beckon. M. IGNATIEFF Cabinet discussions which took on an increasingly grotesque and surreal character.

■ **grotesquely** *adverb* **M18**. **grotesqueness** *noun* **L18**. **grotesquerie** /ɡrəʊˈtɛskəri/ *noun* grotesque objects collectively; grotesque quality; an example of grotesqueness: **L17**.

Grotian /ˈɡrəʊʃɪən/ *adjective & noun*. **M19**.
[ORIGIN from *Grotius* (see below) + -AN.]
▸ **A** *adjective*. Of or pertaining to the Dutch lawyer, statesman, and theologian Hugo Grotius (1583–1645), esp. as the founder of the modern science of international law. **M19**.
▸ **B** *noun*. An adherent of the tenets or policies of Grotius. **M20**.
■ **Grotianism** *noun* the views or policies of Grotius **E20**.

grotteschi *noun pl.*, ***grottesco*** *noun* see GROTESQUE *noun*.

grotto /ˈɡrɒtəʊ/ *noun*. Pl. **-o(e)s**. **E17**.
[ORIGIN Italian *grotta*: see GROT *noun*[2].]
1 A cave or cavern, *esp.* one which is picturesque or forms a pleasant retreat. **E17**.

2 An ornamental room, structure, etc., adorned with shells etc. in imitation of a cave and serving as a pleasant retreat. E17.

3 *hist.* A structure of oyster shells in the form of a grotto, erected and exhibited by London street boys on the 5th of August, the feast of St James of Compostella. M19.

■ **grottoed** *adjective* ensconced in a grotto; formed into a grotto: M18. **grotto'esque** *adjective* resembling a grotto M19.

grotty /ˈgrɒti/ *adjective. slang.* M20.
[ORIGIN from GROT(ESQUE + -Y[1].]
Unpleasant, dirty, nasty, ugly; generally displeasing or disagreeable.

J. GASH I went into platform nine's grotty nosh bar for a pasty. N. WHITTAKER Wormwood is a bluey-green herb that sprouts up in any old grotty patch.

■ **grottiness** *noun* L20.

grouch /graʊtʃ/ *noun*[1]. *colloq.* L19.
[ORIGIN Var. of GRUTCH *noun*.]
1 A fit of grumbling, bad temper, or the sulks; (a cause for) a complaint. L19.
2 A (habitual) grumbler. E20.

Listener I am probably a humourless old grouch.

– COMB.: **grouch bag** a hidden pocket or purse for concealing money or valuables; hidden money.

†**grouch** *noun*[2] var. of KURUS.

grouch /graʊtʃ/ *verb intrans. & trans. colloq.* E20.
[ORIGIN Var. of GRUTCH *verb*.]
Grumble, complain.

H. L. FOSTER The tourists . . all came back to the train at a painfully slow walk . . and grouched all the way home.

grouchy /ˈgraʊtʃi/ *adjective.* L19.
[ORIGIN from GROUCH *noun*[1] or *verb* + -Y[1].]
Grumbling; sulky, irritable, bad-tempered.

H. ROBBINS You've been grouchy as a bear the last month.

■ **grouchily** *adverb* E20. **grouchiness** *noun* E20.

ground /graʊnd/ *noun.*
[ORIGIN Old English *grund* = Old Frisian, Old Saxon *grund* (Dutch *grond*), Old High German *grunt* (German *Grund*), from Germanic. No cognates outside Germanic are known.]

▸ **I** The lowest or deepest part.

1 The bottom or the depths of a hole, a well, or a container of any kind. Long *obsolete* exc. *Scot.* OE. ▸**b** THEOLOGY. The Godhead as the source of all being. Also, the divine essence of the soul. LME.

fig.: J. WESLEY We praised God from the ground of the heart.

2 The seabed. Now only NAUTICAL. OE. ▸**b** The bottom of shallow water; the point where a vessel may run aground. Now chiefly in phrs. below. L16.

SHAKES. *1 Hen. IV* Or dive into the bottom of the deep, Where fathom-line could never touch the ground.

3 In *pl.* ▸**a** Solid particles, now esp. of coffee, forming a residue; dregs, lees, sediment. ME. ▸**b** Refuse; refuse particles or scraps (of meal, wool, etc.). *rare.* E17.

▸ **II** Base, foundation.

†**4** The base or (in *pl.*) foundations of a building or other structure. OE–E18. ▸**b** The basic constituent or essential part of a substance or object. L16–E18.

5 The basis or foundation of a system, institution, or state of affairs. Now *rare.* ME. ▸†**b** A fundamental principle; in *pl.*, the elements of a branch of knowledge. M16–M18.

6 The basis of an opinion or argument, the reason or motive for an action, (now freq. in *pl.*). In *pl.* also, sufficient reason or reasons *for*, *that.* ME.

K. CLARK Have we grounds for thinking that landscape painting will continue to be a dominant form of art? S. UNWIN An action was brought on the ground that the name and occupation were the same. A. J. AYER Russell's family disapproved of the engagement, partly on social grounds. T. BENN They operate in secrecy on the grounds that secrecy is inseparable from security.

7 a A piece of cloth on which embroidery etc. is worked. In LACE-MAKING, the mesh on which the pattern is constructed. LME. ▸**b** A first coat of paint or colouring serving as a base for further colouring or as background for a design; a part left undecorated; the prevailing colour or tone. LME. ▸**c** MUSIC. The melody on which a descant is raised. L16. ▸**d** ART. An acid-resistant coating applied to a plate, through which the design is traced with a fine point. E18. ▸**e** A piece of wood embedded in the surface of a wall, to which a skirting board etc. may be attached. Usu. in *pl.* E19.

b B. JOWETT Dyers first prepare the white ground and then lay on the dye of purple. V. WOOLF White letters upon a blue ground.

▸ **III** The earth, land.

8 The earth as distinguished from heaven. Chiefly in ***on ground, on the ground***. Now *rare* exc. as passing into sense 10. OE.

†**9** The earth as distinguished from the sea; dry land. OE–L17.

10 The earth's surface, on which human, animal, and plant life exists; a part of this. In AERONAUTICS, the earth as distinguished from the air. OE. ▸†**b** The pit of a theatre. (Cf. GROUNDLING 2.) L16–E17. ▸**c** The floor. M19.

E. CRANKSHAW When the shooting stopped some 200 lay dead on the ground. **c** A. CHRISTIE We . . forced the door open. Mrs. Allen was lying in a heap on the ground.

11 (The) soil; earth, mould. OE. ▸†**b** A kind or variety of soil. LME–L18. ▸**c** = EARTH *noun*[1] 7. Chiefly *N. Amer.* L19.

S. HEANEY When the spade sinks into gravelly ground.

†**12** A region, a land, a country. *rare.* OE–E17.

13 In *pl.*, a large enclosed area of land surrounding or attached to a house or other building. Also ***sing.***, a piece of (cultivated) land (*obsolete* exc. *dial.*). LME.

W. H. PRESCOTT Extensive grounds were also laid out around the palace.

14 Area or distance (usu. of a specified extent) on the face of the earth; land. LME. ▸**b** *fig.* Subject matter; object(s) of study or discourse. L18.

S. PEPYS I have a mind to buy enough ground to build a coach-house and stable.

15 The area or piece of land owned or occupied by a particular person. LME.

SHAKES. *Merry W.* Like a fair house built on another man's ground.

16 An area of (specified) extent or character. Now *spec.* a piece of land or other area or expanse used for a specific or specified purpose; the place of action of a sporting or other contest. LME. ▸**b** CRICKET. The space within which a player is allowed to stand while taking a particular part in the game; *esp.* that of the batsman behind the popping crease. L18.

E. BLISHEN We played on a ground lent to us by a local club. *New Yorker* They fish in deep water, and stay out on the grounds several days at a time.

cricket ground, fishing ground, football ground, parade ground, etc.

– PHRASES: **above ground** (*a*) alive; (*b*) dead but not yet buried. **below ground** dead and buried. ***bite the ground***: see BITE *verb*. ***blue ground***: see BLUE *adjective*. ***break ground, break the ground***: see BREAK *verb*. **cover much ground** (of an inquiry, report, etc.) be wide-ranging. **cover the ground** deal adequately with the subject. **cut the ground from under a person's feet** anticipate and defeat his or her arguments or plans. **down to the ground** *colloq.* completely. ***fall to the ground***: see FALL *verb*. **forbidden ground** a subject which should be avoided. **from the ground up** *colloq.* completely. ***fruits of the ground***: see FRUIT *noun* 1. ***gain ground***: see GAIN *verb*[2]. ***get ground***: see GET *verb*. **get in on the ground floor** be admitted to a project, company, etc., as one of the initiators or in the early stages. **get off the ground** start successfully. **give ground** recede, retire, retreat. **go to ground** (of an animal) go into a burrow; (of a person) withdraw from public notice. ***happy hunting ground***: see HAPPY *adjective*. ***have one's ear to the ground***: see EAR *noun*[1]. ***have one's feet on the ground***: see FOOT *noun*. **hold one's ground** hold one's own. **into the ground** to exhaustion, to a standstill. **lose ground** fall back, fall behind, decline. ***middle ground***: see MIDDLE *adjective*. **on firm ground, on solid ground** using soundly based reasoning. **on one's own ground** on one's own territory or subject, on one's own terms; freq. in ***meet on one's own ground***. **on the ground** on the spot, in practical conditions; (see also sense 8 above). ***run into the ground***: see RUN *verb*. **run to ground** = ***run to earth*** s.v. EARTH *noun*[1]. **shift one's ground** change one's line of argument. **smell the ground** (of a ship) steer erratically as a result of being in shallow water. ***stand one's ground***: see STAND *verb*. **take the ground** run aground. ***thick on the ground***: see THICK *adjective*. ***thin on the ground***: see THIN *adjective*.

– COMB.: **ground-ash** (a stick made from) an ash sapling; **groundbait** *noun & verb* (ANGLING) (*a*) *noun* bait thrown into the water to attract fish; (*b*) *verb trans.* prepare (a fishing ground) with groundbait; **ground ball** SPORTS & GAMES a ball hit along the ground; **ground bass** MUSIC a short passage usu. in the bass, constantly repeated with varying melody and harmony; *fig.* a constant background or undertone; **groundbreaking** *adjective* pioneering, innovative; **ground cedar** = ***ground pine*** (*b*) below; **ground cherry** (chiefly *US*) = PHYSALIS; **ground cloth** (*US*) = ***groundsheet*** below; **ground-colour** (*a*) the first coat of paint; (*b*) the prevailing colour of any object; **ground control** (*a*) the directing of an aircraft's landing from the ground; (*b*) the personnel and equipment for monitoring and controlling an aircraft or spacecraft from the ground; **ground cover** plants covering the surface of the earth; *spec.* (HORTICULTURE) low, rapidly spreading plants grown to suppress weeds; **ground dove** a pigeon of terrestrial habits, *spec.* (in full ***scaly-breasted ground dove***) *Columbina passerina* of the southern US, Central America, and parts of S. America; **ground effect** the aerodynamic effect of the ground on a vehicle, aircraft, etc., travelling close to it; **ground elder** an umbelliferous plant, *Aegopodium podagraria*, troublesome as a garden weed; also called ***goutweed***; **ground-fielding** CRICKET fielding or stopping a cricket ball near the ground; **groundfish**: that lives at the bottom of the water; **ground floor** the storey of a building approximately level with the ground; **ground frost**: which forms on the surface of the ground or in the top layer of the soil; **ground game** ground-dwelling game animals, as rabbits and hares; **ground hemlock** a N. American yew, *Taxus canadensis*, growing as a low straggling shrub; **ground ice**: formed below the surface of the water and esp. adhering to the bed of a river, lake, etc.; **ground itch** the presence of small blisters which itch intensely, usu. on the feet or legs, as a result of the penetration of the skin by hookworm larvae; **ground ivy** a common early-flowering hedge plant, *Glechoma hederacea*, with blue-purple flowers in the axils of kidney-shaped leaves; **groundkeeper** *US* = ***groundsman*** below; **ground-landlord** the owner of land which is leased for building on; **ground laurel** = ARBUTUS 2; **ground level** (*a*) the level of the ground, *spec.* that outside a building; (*b*) PHYSICS (the energy level of) a ground state; **ground loop** a violent uncontrolled movement of an aircraft while landing, taking off, or taxiing; **groundmass** PETROGRAPHY the compact basic material of a porphyritic rock, in which larger grains (phenocrysts) are embedded; **ground moraine**: situated underneath a glacier; **groundnut** (*a*) (the edible tuber of) a N. American wild bean, *Apios americana*; (*b*) (the fruit of) the peanut, *Arachis hypogaea*; **ground parrot** a parrot of terrestrial habits; *spec.* (*a*) *Pezoporus wallicus* of the Australian coasts; (*b*) = KAKAPO; **ground pine** (*a*) a rare yellow-flowered labiate weed, *Ajuga chamaepitys*, reputedly so called from its resinous smell; (*b*) *N. Amer.* any of several clubmosses resembling miniature conifers, esp. *Lycopodium obscurum* and *L. tristachyum*; **ground plan** a plan of the ground floor of a building; the outline or general plan of anything; **ground plate** the lowest horizontal timber in a framing; **ground rent**: payable to the owner of the land on which a building stands; **ground robin** *US* = TOWHEE; ***ground roller***: see ROLLER *noun*[2]; **ground rule** a fundamental precept, a basic principle; **groundsheet** a waterproof sheet spread on the ground to give protection from moisture; ***ground-sill***: see GROUNDSEL *noun*[2]; **ground sloth** any of various extinct terrestrial edentates from the Tertiary and Pleistocene of S. America, esp. of the genera *Megatherium* and *Mylodon*, and often of very large size; **groundsman** a person employed to maintain a sports ground; ***ground* SPEARING**; **ground speed** an aircraft's speed relative to the ground; **ground squirrel** any of several rodents resembling squirrels in build but of terrestrial habits, *esp.* a spermophile; **ground staff** (*a*) the non-flying members of an airline or airport staff; (*b*) a paid staff of (now esp. promising young) players kept by a cricket club; **ground state** PHYSICS the state of lowest energy of an electron, atom, molecule, etc.; **groundstroke** TENNIS a stroke played near the ground after the ball has bounced; **groundswell** (*a*) a large or extensive swell of the sea; (*b*) an apparently spontaneous movement or build-up of or *of* feeling, opinion, etc., in a group of people, esp. the public; **ground tackle** the equipment (cable, anchor, etc.) used to anchor or moor a boat or ship; **ground thrush** any of various Old World thrushes of the genus *Zoothera*, most of which are ground-feeders in forests; **groundwater** water held in the soil or in pores, crevices, etc., in rock, *esp.* that below the water table; any underground water; **ground wave** a radio wave reaching a receiver directly from the transmitter or by some other means that does not involve reflection by the ionosphere; **ground zero** (*a*) the point at or directly above which a devastating event occurred (orig. *spec.* a nuclear explosion); (*b*) *US colloq.* the (very) beginning, the starting point; (*c*) the site of the World Trade Center in New York, destroyed by terrorists on 11 September 2001.

ground /graʊnd/ *ppl adjective.* LME.
[ORIGIN pa. pple of GRIND *verb*.]
1 Reduced to fine particles by grinding or crushing. Also foll. by *down.* LME. ▸**b** *fig.* Foll. by *down*: exhausted, worn out. E20. ▸**c** Of meat: minced. Chiefly *N. Amer.* E20.
2 Shaped or sharpened by grinding; having the surface abraded or polished by grinding. L16.

– SPECIAL COLLOCATIONS & COMB.: **ground-down** a short thick pointed sewing needle. **ground glass** (*a*) powdered glass; (*b*) glass made semi-opaque by having its surface roughened. **ground wood** wood pulp.

ground /graʊnd/ *verb*[1]. ME.
[ORIGIN from the noun.]

▸ **I** †**1** *verb trans.* Lay the foundations of (a house etc.); found, establish firmly. ME–E17.

2 *verb trans.* Establish, base (an institution, principle, or belief) *on*, *upon*, or *in* some fact or authority. Now usu. in ***pass.*** LME. ▸**b** In *pass.* Of a conjecture, fear, etc.: be (*well* or *ill*) founded. M18.

H. L. MENCKEN A large part of altruism, . . is grounded upon the fact that it is uncomfortable to have unhappy people about. P. FULLER Culture itself is grounded in man's highly specific psycho-biological nature.

3 *verb trans.* Establish or settle (a person) in respect of his or her position, beliefs, etc. Foll. by *in*, *of*. Long *obsolete* exc. *dial.* LME.

†**4** *verb refl. & intrans.* Rest or rely *upon*, esp. in argument. LME–E19.

5 *verb trans.* Foll. by *in*: instruct (a person) thoroughly in the rudiments of a subject; in ***pass.***, be (*well* or *ill*) acquainted with a subject. LME.

C. RYCROFT My father grounded his sons in the first principles of mathematics.

6 *verb trans.* Provide with a ground or basis for painting, embroidery, etc. LME.

7 *verb trans.* Form or supply grounds or a reason for. *rare.* M17.

▸ **II 8** *verb trans.* Bring to the ground, knock down. ME.

fig.: J. N. ISBISTER His theories had well and truly grounded the old enemy, religion.

9 *verb trans. & intrans.* NAUTICAL. (Cause to) run aground; in *pass.* be beached or stranded. LME.

Lifeboat Launched to help a Grimsby steam trawler, . . which had grounded on a reef.

10 *verb trans. & intrans.* NAUTICAL. (Cause to) sink to the bottom. M17.

J. SMEATON We proceeded lowering till our anchor was grounded.

11 *verb trans.* Place or set (esp. a weapon) on the ground; put down. M17. ▸**b** *verb intrans.* Come to or strike the ground; land. M18. ▸**c** *verb intrans.* BASEBALL. Hit a ground ball to the infield; be thrown *out* at first base as a result of this. E20.

R. ADAMS Each man grounded his spear and laid it beside his belt.

ground arms lay down one's weapons, esp. in surrender.
12 *verb trans.* ELECTRICITY. Connect with the soil as a conductor; earth. Chiefly *N. Amer.* L19.
13 *verb trans.* Prevent or prohibit (an aircraft, pilot, etc.) from flying. Also *transf.* curtail the actions or activities of (a person), esp. as a punishment. M20.

Daily Telegraph Three . . jets were grounded by mechanical faults and an accident. T. K. WOLFE Slayton's problem was that the Air Force had decided to ground him altogether.

– COMB.: **groundout** BASEBALL a play in which a batter grounds out.

ground *verb*[2] *pa. t.* & *pple* of GRIND *verb*.

groundage /ˈɡraʊndɪdʒ/ *noun*. LME.
[ORIGIN from GROUND *noun* + -AGE.]
A toll, a tax; *spec.* a duty levied on vessels lying in harbour. Cf. TERRAGE.

grounded /ˈɡraʊndɪd/ *adjective*. LME.
[ORIGIN from GROUND *noun*, *verb*[1]: see -ED[2], -ED[1].]
†**1** Thoroughly instructed or proficient in a branch of knowledge. Also, deeply imbued with certain principles. LME–E19.
2 Firmly fixed or established; on a sound basis. Also with adverbs: *well*, *ill*, etc., founded. L15.

J. KRANTZ I wish I didn't have so much common sense. I get so tired of being grounded in reality.

3 a Of lace: having the spaces in the pattern filled with plain stitches. Now *rare*. L17. ▸**b** Having a ground of a specified colour. M18.
4 Placed on or brought to the ground; run aground, stranded. L18.
5 Having an electrical connection with the soil; earthed. Chiefly *N. Amer.* L19.
6 Of an aircraft, pilot, etc.: prevented or prohibited from flying. Also *transf.* having one's actions or activities curtailed, esp. as a punishment. M20.

S. BELLOW My flight is grounded. *New Yorker* Can I go out? Am I still grounded?

7 Of a person: having his or her feet on the ground; realistic, sensible, well-balanced. L20.
■ **groundedly** *adverb* (now *rare*) fundamentally, deeply, thoroughly; with good reason: M16. **groundedness** *noun* (*rare*) the quality or condition of being well grounded or firmly established E17.

grounder /ˈɡraʊndə/ *noun*. LME.
[ORIGIN from GROUND *verb*[1] + -ER[1].]
1 A person who or thing which founds, establishes, or causes something. Long *spec.* a foundation stone of a wall. *obsolete* exc. *dial.* & ARCHAEOLOGY. LME.

Antiquity The walls consist of huge 'grounders', whose triangular interstices are filled with smaller stones.

2 SPORTS & GAMES. A ball passed or hit along the ground. M19.

R. COOVER I never wanted to be just an ordinary ballplayer, stooping for grounders.

3 A person who applies background colour, *spec.* to wallpaper. L19.

groundhog /ˈɡraʊndhɒɡ/ *noun*. L18.
[ORIGIN from GROUND *noun* + HOG *noun*.]
1 A woodchuck. *N. Amer.* L18.
2 A caisson worker. Also, the brakeman of a train. *US slang*. E20.
– COMB.: **groundhog case** *US* a desperate or urgent affair; **Groundhog Day** *N. Amer.* a day (in most areas 2 February) which, if sunny, is believed to indicate wintry weather to come.

grounding /ˈɡraʊndɪŋ/ *verbal noun*. LME.
[ORIGIN from GROUND *verb*[1] + -ING[1].]
1 The action or an act of founding or establishing something; the basis or foundation of something. Now *rare*. LME.
2 The preparation or laying of a ground on which a design is to be worked. LME.
3 Instruction in or knowledge of the rudiments or fundamental principles of a subject. M17.

A. N. WILSON He was indebted to his teachers for giving him a thorough grounding in the classics.

4 The beaching of a ship for inspection or repair; (accidental) running aground. L17.

Independent As the general standard of those ships declines, so the prospect of collisions and groundings increases.

groundless /ˈɡraʊndlɪs/ *adjective*. OE.
[ORIGIN from GROUND *noun* + -LESS.]
†**1** Bottomless, unfathomable. OE–E17.
2 Without basis, authority, or support; unfounded. E17.

R. BAXTER A groundless fiction that cannot be proved.

■ **groundlessly** *adverb* M17. **groundlessness** *noun* M17.

ground-line /ˈɡraʊndlʌɪn/ *noun*. LME.
[ORIGIN from GROUND *noun* + LINE *noun*[2]. Cf. Dutch *grondlijn*, German & Swedish *grundlinie* (in senses 2 and 3).]
1 A line used for bottom-fishing. Long *rare* or *obsolete*. LME.
2 †**a** GEOMETRY. A line to which a perpendicular is drawn. M16–M17. ▸**b** A line in a drawing, diagram, etc., that represents the ground or the horizon. M19.
3 In *pl.* Outlines, bases, foundations. E17.
4 The (actual or notional) line at the base of a jump from which a horse judges its take-off point. M20.

groundling /ˈɡraʊndlɪŋ/ *noun*. E17.
[ORIGIN from GROUND *noun* + -LING[1]. Cf. Middle Dutch *grundelinck* (Dutch *grondeling*), Middle High German *grundelinc* (German *Gründling*) gudgeon.]
1 Any of various small bottom-dwelling freshwater fishes, *esp.* a gudgeon or a loach. E17.
2 A frequenter of the pit of a theatre (see GROUND *noun* 10b); an ignorant or undiscerning spectator or reader. Chiefly *literary*. E17.

J. A. SYMONDS The soliloquies of Hamlet . . must have been lost upon the groundlings of Elizabeth's days.

3 A creeping or low-growing plant. E19.
4 A person on the ground, as opp. to one in an aircraft or spacecraft. M20.

Guardian Of the R.A.F.'s courage and skill it would be almost presumptuous for any mere groundling to speak.

groundsel /ˈɡraʊn(d)s(ə)l/ *noun*[1].
[ORIGIN Old English *grundeswylige*, earlier *gundæswelg(i)æ*, prob. from *gund* pus + base of SWALLOW *verb*, with ref. to its use in poultices.]
A common weed, *Senecio vulgaris*, of the composite family, with small rayless heads and lobed leaves. Also (with qualifying adjectives), any of several related plants.
– COMB.: **groundsel tree** a N. American coastal shrub, *Baccharis halimifolia*, of the composite family, with axillary panicles of rayless flowers.

groundsel /ˈɡraʊn(d)s(ə)l/ *noun*[2]. Also **ground-sill** /ˈɡraʊn(d)sɪl/. LME.
[ORIGIN App. from GROUND *noun* + SILL *noun*[1], but the 2nd elem. early became a mere termination.]
1 The lowest horizontal timber in a (wooden) building; the foundation or lowest part of any structure. LME. ▸**b** *fig.* An underlying principle. Now *rare* or *obsolete*. E17.
2 The bottom timber of a door frame; a door sill, a threshold. E16.

ground truth /ˈɡraʊnd truːθ/ *noun phr.* M19.
[ORIGIN from GROUND *noun* + TRUTH *noun*. In sense 1 prob. after German *Grundwahrheit*.]
1 A fundamental truth. Also, information that has been checked or facts that have been collected at source. M19.
2 a In remote sensing: information obtained by direct measurement at ground level, rather than by interpretation of remotely obtained data, esp. as used to verify or calibrate remotely obtained data. M20. ▸**b** Information obtained by direct observation of a real system, as opp. to a model or simulation; a set of data considered to be accurate and reliable and used to calibrate a model, algorithm, etc. L20.

groundward /ˈɡraʊndwəd/ *adverb*. M16.
[ORIGIN from GROUND *noun* + -WARD.]
Towards the ground.
■ Also **groundwards** *adverb* L19.

groundwork /ˈɡraʊndwəːk/ *noun*. LME.
[ORIGIN from GROUND *noun* + WORK *noun*. Cf. Middle Dutch *grontwerck* (mod. *grondwerk*), German *Grundwerk*.]
1 The basis or foundation of a (now chiefly abstract) thing; preliminary work, preparation. LME.

K. ISHIGURO A case of laying the groundwork for the real negotiations.

2 The base on which a design is worked in various crafts; the background of a painting etc. M17.
3 Exercises or movements performed on the ground. E20.

group /ɡruːp/ *noun*. Also (earlier) †**groupe**. L17.
[ORIGIN French *groupe* from Italian *gruppo* from Germanic: rel. to CROP *noun*. The etymological sense is app. 'lump' or 'mass'.]
1 Two or more people, animals, or things standing or positioned close together so as to form a collective unity; a knot or cluster (of people, animals, or things); *spec.* in ART, two or more figures or objects forming (a part of) a design. L17. ▸**b** MUSIC. = GRUPPETTO. Cf. earlier GRUPPO. E18. ▸**c** A set of letters, figures, etc., used in coding. E20. ▸**d** A cluster or set of hits made by a series of shots fired at a target. Also ***shot-group***. E20.

CONAN DOYLE I found that a little group of wondering folk had gathered round it. A. J. CRONIN Men were standing in groups around the cafes. N. MITFORD The great steep Gothic double staircase . . meeting at a marble group.

2 A number of people or things regarded as forming a unity or whole on the grounds of some mutual or common relation or purpose, or classed together because of a degree of similarity. E18. ▸**b** CHEMISTRY. Any combination of atoms bound together within a molecule, which behaves as a unit and is regarded as a distinct entity; a radical. M19. ▸**c** (Also **G-**.) Any of the constituent bodies of the Oxford Group Movement (see OXFORD *adjective*). E20. ▸**d** A division of an air force, esp. the Royal Air Force, comprising a number of wings. E20. ▸**e** A number of commercial companies together with the holding company controlling them. M20. ▸**f** A number of musicians or singers performing esp. popular music together. M20. ▸**g** POLITICS. A unit smaller than a party. L20.

A. STORR When men form groups, . . it may be on a basis of common interest or shared background. F. WELDON Phillip belonged to a reform group who were trying to legalise . . cannabis. C. PRIEST We were the same age group—she was thirty-one, two years older than myself. *Times* The Group of five finance ministers of the biggest industrial market economies . . have been meeting at No 11. ***attrib.***: J. M. ROBERTS For almost the whole of history . . clothes have been signs of group membership. **g** *Times* Svecia Antique is a recently formed company, backed by a large multi-national group.

primary group: see PRIMARY *adjective*. ***e pop group***, ***rock group***, etc.

3 BIOLOGY. An assemblage of organisms or classificatory division of unspecified rank; *esp.* a set of closely related species not formally recognized as a subgenus. E19. ▸**b** GEOLOGY. Formerly, any of various categories into which rocks were classified, corresponding to modern geological time units. Now, a stratigraphic unit consisting of two or more formations. M19. ▸**c** CHEMISTRY. (***a***) In qualitative analysis, a set of ions or radicals which are characterized by common behaviour during specific tests; (***b***) any of several sets of elements having (similar electronic structure and hence) similar chemical and physical properties, commonly represented as the columns of the periodic table. M19. ▸**d** = ***blood group*** s.v. BLOOD *noun*. E20.

G

4 MATH. Orig., a set of elements, together with a binary operation, which is closed with respect to the operation. Now *spec.* such a set in which the operation is associative, and which contains an inverse for each element and an identity element. M19.

M. BÔCHER The positive and negative integers with zero form a group if the rule of combination is addition.

– COMB.: **group assurance** = ***group life assurance*** below; **group captain** a rank in the Royal Air Force next below air commodore and equivalent to colonel in the army; **group dialect** (a) distinctive language used by members of a group identified as such by a common occupation or interest; **group dynamics** a branch of social psychology that deals with the interactions of people in groups; **group genitive** the construction in English whereby the genitive ending is added to the last element in a noun phrase; **group insurance** = ***group life insurance*** below; **group language** = ***group dialect*** above; **group life assurance**, **group life insurance** (chiefly *N. Amer.*) the assurance or insurance of a group of lives at reduced premiums; ***group marriage***: see MARRIAGE; **group practice** a medical practice consisting of several doctors; **group rate** a reduced rate (of the charge for entry, travel, shipment, etc.) for a group of people or things; **Group Settlement** AUSTRAL. HISTORY (a settlement under) a scheme to settle British immigrants in SW Australia; **Group Settler** AUSTRAL. HISTORY a member of a Group Settlement; **group sex** sexual activity in which more than two people take part; **group theory** the branch of algebra that deals with the properties of groups and their applications, esp. in physics; **group therapy**: in which patients having a similar problem meet together to help each other psychologically; **group velocity** PHYSICS the speed at which the energy of a wave travels; **groupware** COMPUTING software designed to facilitate collaborative working by a number of different users; **group work**: done by a group working in close association.
■ **groupist** *noun* an adherent of a group, esp. (**G-**) of the Oxford Group Movement L19. **grouplet** *noun* a small group M19.

group /ɡruːp/ *verb*. E18.
[ORIGIN from the noun, or from French *grouper*.]
1 *verb trans.* Esp. in ART & PHOTOGRAPHY. Arrange (figures, colours, etc.) into a well-proportioned and harmonious whole. E18.

Studio Week The central panels are grouped within easy reach.

2 *verb trans.* Form into a group; place in a group *with*. Also foll. by *together*. M18. ▸**b** *verb intrans.* Form a group; gather into a group or groups. E19. ▸**c** *verb intrans.* (Of shots from a firearm) cluster about a point (on a target); (of a firearm or marksman) fire shots which do this. E20.

A. SCHLEE Unconsciously they had grouped themselves in a semi-circle facing the door. **b** W. GOLDING Tourists walk through. Conducted parties group to listen.

3 *verb intrans.* Belong to a group; harmonize *with*. E19.
4 *verb trans.* Arrange in groups according to some common feature or property; classify. M19. ▸**b** MEDICINE. Assign to a particular blood group; determine the blood group of. M20.
■ **groupage** *noun* the arrangement of objects in a group or groups M19. **grouping** *verbal noun* (***a***) the action of the verb; (***b***) a formation resulting from this action: M18. **groupment** *noun* (***a***) a group; (***b***) the action of placing in groups: L19.

†**groupe** *noun* see GROUP *noun*.

grouper /ˈɡruːpə/ *noun*. See also GROPER *noun*². E17.
[ORIGIN Portuguese *garoupa*, prob. from a S. Amer. name. For the alt. of form cf. BREAKER *noun*².]
1 Any of numerous large marine serranid fishes of warm and tropical seas; *esp.* any of those of the genera *Epinephelus* and *Mycteroperca*. Cf. GROPER *noun*² 1. E17.
2 Locally, any of various large marine fishes; *esp.* (**a**) the Californian rockfish, *Sebastes paucispinis*; (**b**) the tripletail, *Lobotes surinamensis*. L19.

groupie /ˈɡruːpi/ *noun*. In sense 3 also **-py**. E20.
[ORIGIN from GROUP *noun* + -IE.]
1 AUSTRAL. HISTORY. = ***Group Settler*** s.v. GROUP *noun*. E20.
2 = ***group captain*** s.v. GROUP *noun*. *RAF slang*. M20.
3 A fan of a pop group or groups; *esp.* a (female) fan following a group on tour and providing sexual favours; *gen.* a fan, a follower. M20.
J. LENNON If we couldn't get groupies, we would have whores. G. KAUFMAN I do not mean . . I have become a cinema groupie, attaching myself to film-makers.

groupism /ˈɡruːpɪz(ə)m/ *noun*. M20.
[ORIGIN from GROUP *noun* + -ISM.]
1 (**G-**.) The principles of the Oxford Group Movement. M20.
2 The principle of arranging or dividing into groups, or thinking as or conforming to the social behaviour of a group. M20.

groupuscule /ˈɡruːpəskjuːl, *foreign* ɡrupyskyl (*pl. same*)/ *noun*. M20.
[ORIGIN French, dim. of *groupe*: see -CULE.]
A small political group; an extremist splinter group.

grouse /ɡraʊs/ *noun*¹. Pl. same. E16.
[ORIGIN Uncertain: perh. orig. pl. of form rel. to medieval Latin *gruta*, or Old French *grue*, Latin *grus* crane.]
1 Any of various stocky feather-footed birds of the gallinaceous family Tetraonidae, of which several are valued as game birds; *esp.* in Britain (more fully ***red grouse***), a moorland game bird conspecific with the willow grouse, *Lagopus lagopus*, but lacking white plumage in winter. E16.
black grouse, ***hazel grouse***, ***pinnated grouse***, ***willow grouse***, etc.
2 The flesh of one of these birds, eaten as food. L18.
■ **grousey** *adjective* (**a**) having many grouse; (**b**) having the flavour of grouse: M19.

grouse /ɡraʊs/ *noun*². *colloq*. E20.
[ORIGIN from GROUSE *verb*².]
A grumble, a complaint; a reason for grumbling.
G. BOYCOTT Our team meeting for general discussion . . , the grouses and grumbles as well as the good points.

grouse /ɡraʊs/ *adjective*. *Austral. & NZ slang*. E20.
[ORIGIN Unknown.]
Very good, excellent.
L. GLASSOP You know them two grouse sheilas we've got the meet on with tomorrer night?

grouse /ɡraʊs/ *verb*¹ *intrans*. L18.
[ORIGIN from GROUSE *noun*¹.]
Shoot grouse. Chiefly as ***grousing*** *verbal noun*.
■ **grouser** *noun*¹ M19.

grouse /ɡraʊs/ *verb*² *intrans. colloq*. E19.
[ORIGIN Unknown. Cf. GROUCH *verb*, *noun*¹.]
Grumble, complain.
H. T. LANE It's no good grousing about things you don't like.
■ **grouser** *noun*² L19.

grout /ɡraʊt/ *noun*¹.
[ORIGIN Old English *grūt* corresp. to Middle Dutch *grūte*, *gruut* coarse meal, peeled grain, malt, yeast, (Dutch *gruit* dregs), Middle High German *grūz* (German *Grauss*) grain, small beer, from Germanic var. of base of GRIT *noun*¹, *noun*², GROATS. Cf. GROOT *noun*.]
1 Coarse meal, peeled grain. In *pl.*, = GROATS. Now *rare*. OE. ▸**b** A kind of coarse wholemeal porridge. Now *rare* or *obsolete*. L16.
2 The infusion of malt before and during fermentation. Also, small beer. OE.
3 Orig., slime, mud. Now, sediment; in *pl.*, dregs, lees, grounds. LME.
DICKENS Old women might have told fortunes in them, better than in grouts of tea. A. E. COPPARD When he coughed . . his insides come up out of him like coffee grouts.

grout /ɡraʊt/ *noun*². M17.
[ORIGIN Perh. a use of GROUT *noun*¹, but cf. French dial. *grouter* grout a wall.]
Orig., a fluid mortar used to fill gaps or interstices, esp. in stonework. Now also, a waterproof cement-based paste used to fill gaps between wall or floor tiles.

grout /ɡraʊt/ *verb*¹. E18.
[ORIGIN from GROUT *noun*¹ or var. of GROOT *verb*.]
1 *verb intrans*. Of a pig: turn up the ground with the snout; root. E18.
fig.: N. ANNAN Jowett . . encouraged his undergraduates to grout among the pearls that he cast before them.
2 *verb trans*. Turn *up* with the snout. L19.

grout /ɡraʊt/ *verb*² *trans*. M19.
[ORIGIN from GROUT *noun*².]
Fill up or finish with grout; cement.
■ **grouting** *noun* (**a**) the action of the verb; (**b**) = GROUT *noun*²: L18.

grout /ɡraʊt/ *verb*³ *intrans*. *US*. M19.
[ORIGIN Unknown.]
Grumble, sulk.
■ **groutiness** *noun* crossness, sulkiness L19. **grouty** *adjective* cross, sulky M19.

grouter /ˈɡraʊtə/ *noun*¹. *Austral. slang*. E20.
[ORIGIN Unknown.]
An unfair advantage. Esp. in ***come in on the grouter***.

grouter /ˈɡraʊtə/ *noun*². M20.
[ORIGIN from GROUT *verb*² + -ER¹.]
1 An instrument or tool for grouting a wall etc. M20.
2 A person who grouts a wall etc. M20.

grove /ɡrəʊv/ *noun*.
[ORIGIN Old English *grāf* rel. to *grǣfa* brushwood, thicket, from Germanic. Cf. GREAVE *noun*¹.]
A (small) wood; a group of trees, often deliberately planted as an avenue, walk, etc.; an orchard, esp. of olives, citrus fruit, etc.
J. THURBER The avenue dwindled to a wood road that led into a thick grove of oak and walnut trees. *fig.*: N. GORDIMER The baby . . making its way through a grove of legs.
– NOTE: Used in biblical translations to render Hebrew *'ăšērāh* (see ASHERAH) and *'ēšel*, now understood to mean 'sacred tree' and 'tamarisk' respectively.
■ **groved** *adjective* having or planted with a grove or groves; encircled by a grove: E19. **groveless** *adjective* M19. **grovet** *noun* (*obsolete* exc. *dial.*) [-ET¹] a little grove E16. **grovy** *adjective* (now *rare*) of, pertaining to, or resembling a grove; situated in a grove, provided with groves: L16.

grovel /ˈɡrɒv(ə)l, ˈɡrʌv-/ *noun*. *colloq*. L19.
[ORIGIN from the verb.]
The action or an act of grovelling.
Daily Telegraph A telephone call . . advises that a grovel is owed to the M.P.

grovel /ˈɡrɒv(ə)l, ˈɡrʌv-/ *verb intrans*. Infl. **-ll-**, ***-l-**. LME.
[ORIGIN Back-form. from GROVELLING.]
Lie or move in a prone position or with the face downwards, esp. in abject humility; *fig.* humble oneself, behave obsequiously, esp. in seeking favour or forgiveness.
G. ORWELL He saw himself grovelling on the floor, screaming for mercy. P. LIVELY Sylvia . . drops the packet, grovels for it on the floor.
■ **groveller** *noun* L18.

grovelling /ˈɡrɒv(ə)lɪŋ, ˈɡrʌv-/ *adverb* (now regarded as *pres. pple*) & *adjective*. Also ***groveling**. ME.
[ORIGIN from GROOF: see -LING², -LIN(G)S.]
▸ **A** *adverb*. Also †**grovellings**. Face downward; in or to a prone or prostrate position. ME.
E. A. FREEMAN The Earl . . bowed himself to the ground, and lay grovelling.
▸ **B** *adjective*. **1** Having the face or front of the body on or towards the ground; prone. LME.
S. BUTLER Nature gave Man an erect Figure, to raise him above the groveling Condition of . . the Beasts.
2 Abject, base; low, mean. E17.
H. T. BUCKLE Some of the most powerful minds were still corrupted by . . grovelling superstition.
■ **grovellingly** *adverb* M16.

grow /ɡrəʊ/ *noun*. *obsolete* exc. *Scot*. M16.
[ORIGIN from the verb.]
The process or result of growing; growth.

grow /ɡrəʊ/ *verb*. Pa. t. **grew** /ɡruː/, (*dial. & colloq.*) **growed** /ɡrəʊd/. Pa. pple **grown** /ɡrəʊn/, (*dial. & colloq.*) **growed** /ɡrəʊd/.
[ORIGIN Old English *grōwan* = Old Frisian *grōwa*, *grōia*, Middle Dutch *groeyen* (Dutch *groeien*), Old High German *gruoan*, Old Norse *gróa*, from Germanic strong verb from base also of GRASS *noun*, GREEN *adjective*.]
▸ **I** *verb intrans*. **1** Orig. (of a plant), show vigorous life, put out foliage, flourish. Now only (of land), produce vegetation. *rare*. OE.
I. MURDOCH The garden could be begun . . , and grow with the membership of the community.
2 Develop or exist as a living plant (in a specified habitat or with a specified characteristic). OE. ▸**b** Orig. (of a mineral), be native to a certain place. Now (*gen., joc.*), be found or available in a certain place. LME.
DRYDEN Green Beds of Parsley near the River grow. J. FOWLES Trees . . grew more thickly there than anywhere else. **b** HOR. WALPOLE All the tables and chairs and conveniences . . which he seems to think don't grow out of England.
3 Germinate, sprout, spring up; be produced. OE.
SHAKES. *Oth.* Men whose heads Do grow beneath their shoulders. F. BROOKE Sugar-canes grow without planting. A. URE There grew upon the oak in Africa . . a small excrescence like a bird.
4 Of an abstract thing: come naturally into existence; arise, originate, develop (as from a seed). (Foll. by *from*, *out of*.) OE.
TENNYSON As months ran on and rumour of battle grew.
5 Of (the hair, nails, etc. of) a living thing: increase gradually in size, length, or height by natural development. (Orig. only of plants: cf. WAX *verb*¹.) OE.
J. CONRAD His red-gold pair of horizontal moustaches had grown to really noble proportions. T. S. ELIOT You were always getting yourself measured To prove how you had grown since the last holidays.
6 With compl. (esp. adjective): become by degrees; *esp.* become increasingly. ME. ▸**b** Come or pass by degrees (*in*)*to* some state or condition; develop gradually (*in*)*to*. LME. ▸†**c** Arrive at, come to, (an agreement, conclusion, etc.). Foll. by *to*, *upon*. L16–M17.
G. K. CHESTERTON Evening was closing in, and the room had grown darker. G. GREENE Married people grow like each other. D. ABSE He grew older, fatter, greyer, balder. B. PYM Tom was beginning to grow tired of her. H. CRANE I have grown accustomed to an 'ivory tower' sort of existence. **b** G. GREENE I had grown to love the place. *Grimsby Gazette* She watches her own chosen dress grow from just a drawing . . into a beautiful gown.
7 Of a thing: increase gradually in magnitude, power, quantity, or degree. LME.
C. S. FORESTER A yellow light grew until the ship there was wrapped in flame. C. P. SNOW He felt that niggle of disquiet growing.
8 Increase *in* some specified quality or property. *arch*. LME.
MILTON They . . In mean estate live moderate, till grown In wealth and multitude, factious they grow.
9 **a** ***grow up***. Esp. of a person: develop to maturity. Freq. as GROWN-UP *ppl adjective*. M16. ▸**b** Of a custom, condition, etc.: arise gradually, come into existence. L16. ▸**c** Be sensible or mature. Freq. in *imper*. M20.
a B. JOWETT His children, one of whom is growing up. **b** LD BRAIN A strong friendship grew up between the two men. **c** A. WESKER Oh, grow up, Ronnie. You should know that by now.
10 Become gradually fixed *in*(*to*) or united *to* something. Esp. in ***grow into one***, ***grow together***, coalesce, become united. Now *arch.* or *poet*. L16.
SHELLEY Clasp me till our hearts be grown Like two lovers into one.
▸ **II** *verb trans*. **11** Produce (plants, fruit, wool, etc.) by cultivation; (of land, plants, etc.) bring forth. (*rare* before **19**.) LME. ▸**b** Develop, enlarge; now *spec.* cause (a business) to expand or increase. (*rare* before **20**.) L15. ▸**c** Let (beard etc.) develop or increase in length etc. E19. ▸**d** CRYSTALLOGRAPHY. Bring about formation of (a crystal); cause (a crystal) to increase in size. E20.
W. S. MAUGHAM. On the plantation . . we'd have grown rice and rye and corn and kept pigs. B. PATTEN The trees outside her window have grown leaves. **b** *Observer* We've grown our sterling turnover to 18 per cent. **c** G. GREENE With the years he had grown a small pot-belly under a double-breasted waistcoat.
12 In *pass.* Be covered (*up* or *over*) with growth. LME.
J. DICKEY We came out among some fields grown up six or seven feet high in grass.
– PHRASES: ***grow on trees***: see TREE *noun*. ***grow whiskers***, ***have grown whiskers***: see WHISKER *noun*. ***not let the grass grow under one's feet***: see GRASS *noun* 1.
– WITH ADVERBS & PREPOSITIONS IN SPECIALIZED SENSES: **grow away** develop (well). **grow down**, **grow downwards** (**a**) extend downwards; (**b**) diminish. ***grow into one***: see sense 10 above. **grow on** keep (seedling plants) in situations or conditions conducive to development. **grow on** — become more appealing to or acquire gradually more influence over (a person). **grow out** become obliterated by growth. **grow out of** — (**a**) be the result or development of; (**b**) become too large to wear (a garment etc.); (**c**) become too mature to retain (a childish habit etc.). **grow to** — †(**a**) come into existence to the benefit or injury of (a person etc.); †(**b**) be an integral part of; (**c**) see sense 10 above. ***grow together***: see sense 10 above. ***grow up***: see sense 9 above.
■ **growable** *adjective* L19. **growingly** *adverb* increasingly M18.

growan /ˈɡrəʊən/ *noun*. *Cornish dial*. Also **grouan**. M18.
[ORIGIN from base of Middle Cornish *grow* sand, cogn. with Welsh *graean*, Breton *grouan*: see GRAVE *verb*².]
The soft gravelly decomposed granite overlying a tin vein. Also ***soft growan***.
hard growan solid granite.

grower /ˈɡrəʊə/ *noun*. LME.
[ORIGIN from GROW *verb* + -ER¹.]
1 A person who or commercial company which grows esp. a specified type of produce. LME.
fruit-grower, ***rose-grower***, etc.
2 A plant that grows in a specified way. M16.
free grower, ***slow grower***, etc.

growing /ˈɡrəʊɪŋ/ *noun*. LME.
[ORIGIN from GROW *verb* + -ING¹.]
1 The action of GROW *verb*. LME.
†**2** (A) growth. LME–E18.
†**3** Advance, progress. *rare* (Shakes.). Only in E17.
– COMB.: **growing bag**: containing peat-based potting compost in which plants may be grown; **growing pains** neuralgic pains

popularly attributed to growth; *fig.* early difficulties in the development of a project etc.; **growing point** the point at which growth originates; *spec.* (BOTANY) the primary meristematic region at the apex of a plant shoot at which continuous cell division and differentiation occur; **growing season**: when rainfall and temperature allow plants to grow; **growing stock** FORESTRY the total quantity of trees in an area; **growing zone** the region in an annelid or tapeworm in which growth of new parts occurs.

growl /graʊl/ *verb & noun.* M17.
[ORIGIN Prob. imit. Perh. continuous with GURL *verb*, but more likely an independent formation.]
▸ **A** *verb.* **1** *verb intrans.* Of an animal: make a low guttural sound, expressive of (rising) hostility. M17. ▸**b** Of a person: speak in a low and angry voice. E18. ▸**c** Of thunder, a storm, etc.: rumble. M18.

W. IRVING The bear . . turned, reared, showed his teeth, and growled. **b** F. BURNEY Though he pretended to growl, he was evidently delighted. **c** *Observer* The big jets of . . BOAC growl in and out daily on their way round the world.

2 *verb trans.* Of a person: utter with a growl or in a growling manner. Freq. foll. by *out.* M18.

S. JOHNSON She growls out her discontent.

3 *verb intrans.* Esp. JAZZ. (Of a wind instrument) make a low rasping sound; (of a musician) make such a sound on an instrument. M20.
▸ **B** *noun.* **1** A low hostile guttural sound made by an animal. E18. ▸**b** A low angry expression of complaint etc. uttered by a person or group of persons. E19. ▸**c** A rumble (of thunder, gunfire, etc.). M19.

LD MACAULAY The growl of a fierce watch-dog but half-aroused from sleep. **b** M. MCCARTHY 'Shut up,' came a furious growl from her other side.

2 Esp. JAZZ. A deep rasping sound made on a wind instrument. M20.
■ **growlingly** *adverb* in a growling manner E19. **growly** *adjective* like a growl; in a growling mood or manner: L19.

growler /ˈgraʊlə/ *noun.* M18.
[ORIGIN from GROWL *verb* + -ER[1].]
1 A person who or an animal or thing which growls. M18.
2 A four-wheeled cab. *colloq. obsolete* exc. *hist.* M19.
3 A small iceberg showing very little above the water. M19.
4 A container for fetching beer. *US slang.* L19.
5 ELECTRICITY. An electromagnet with two poles designed to test for short circuits in the windings of an armature. E20.

growlery /ˈgraʊləri/ *noun.* M19.
[ORIGIN from GROWL *verb* + -ERY.]
1 Growling. Now *rare.* M19.
2 [After Dickens's use in *Bleak House.*] A place to growl or be grumpy in; a private sitting room or study. M19.

Growmore /ˈgrəʊmɔː/ *noun.* M20.
[ORIGIN from GROW *verb* + MORE *adverb.*]
Orig. ***National Growmore***. Vegetable fertilizer of a standard kind.

grown /grəʊn/ *ppl adjective.* LME.
[ORIGIN pa. pple of GROW *verb.*]
1 Advanced in growth; increased in size, quantity, etc. Now *rare.* LME. ▸**b** Of a crystal: artificially produced by growing. E20.
2 Adult, grown-up. LME.

J. CHEEVER Theresa had been too young . . for her to have, as a grown person, any clear memories.

3 Of the sea: running high. E17.
4 Of corn: that has sprouted in the ear after reaching maturity. L17.
■ **grownness** /-n-n-/ *noun* (now *rare*) the state or condition of being (esp. excessively) increased in size etc. L16.

grown-up /ˈgrəʊnʌp, grəʊnˈʌp/ *ppl adjective & noun.* Also **grown up**. LME.
[ORIGIN from GROWN + UP *adverb*[1].]
▸ **A** *ppl adjective.* **1** Having reached the age of maturity; adult. LME.

A. KOESTLER People who have learnt the alphabet late, when already grown-up.

2 Suitable for or characteristic of an adult; sensible, worthwhile. M19.

C. M. YONGE As to books, all the real good grown-up ones are down in Mr. Lyddell's library.

▸ **B** *noun.* A grown-up person; an adult. E19.

J. WAIN I have absolutely no need to talk *down* to you, as a grown-up to a kid.

■ **grown-upness** *noun* the state of being grown-up M19.

growth /grəʊθ/ *noun & adjective.* LME.
[ORIGIN from GROW *verb* + -TH[1].]
▸ **A** *noun.* **1** The action, process, or manner of growing; development; increase in size or value. LME. ▸**b** A crop or yield of grapes, esp. as used in the classification of quality; a wine of a specified (*first, second,* etc.) crop or classification of quality. Cf. CRU. E18. ▸**c** More fully ***economic growth***. The increase per head in the production of goods and services over a stated period of time; the rate of expansion of national income. M20.

J. YEATS Barley, oats, and rye may be measured in their daily growth.

2 Something which grows or has grown; produce, product; *spec.* (MEDICINE) a tumour. LME.

H. BELLOC A thick growth of low chestnuts with here and there a tall silver birch. G. ORWELL The half-conscious belief that language is a natural growth. D. M. THOMAS She had recently had a breast removed because of a growth.

3 A stage in the growing process; size or stature attained by growing. Now *rare* exc. *Scot.* and in ***full growth*** below. M16.

W. COWPER Pride has attained its most luxuriant growth, And poisoned every virtue in them both.

4 Production and development by cultivation. M17.

R. BOLDREWOOD A yeoman class . . could use these great levels for the growth of certain semi-tropical crops.

– PHRASES: ***classed growth***: see CLASS *verb* 3. **full growth** the size ultimately attained. **of foreign growth** etc., grown or originating abroad etc.
▸ **B** *attrib.* or as *adjective.* Of or pertaining to growth. M17.
– SPECIAL COLLOCATIONS & COMB.: **growth area** an area of or designated for economic growth. **growth curve** a line representing growth by showing how some quantity varies with time. **growth factor** BIOLOGY any substance required by an organism in minute amounts to maintain its growth. **growth industry**: developing faster than most other industries. **growth point** (*a*) = ***growth area*** above; (*b*) = ***GROWING point***. **growth regulator** BIOLOGY any natural or synthetic substance, such as a hormone or auxin, which regulates growth. **growth ring** BIOLOGY a layer (of wood, shell, etc.) developed during a single period of growth, esp. an annual ring in wood. **growth stock**: tending to increase in capital value rather than yield a high income. **growth zone** (*a*) = ***growth area*** above; (*b*) = ***GROWING zone***.

groyne /grɔɪn/ *noun & verb.* Also ***groin**. L16.
[ORIGIN Transf. use of GROIN *noun*[1].]
▸ **A** *noun.* A (timber) framework or low broad wall run out into the sea to check the drifting of sand etc. and so stop encroachment of the sea; a breakwater. L16.
▸ **B** *verb trans.* Provide (a beach) with groynes. L19.
■ **groyning** *noun* the erection of groynes; a system of groynes: M19.

grozing iron /ˈgrəʊzɪŋʌɪən/ *noun.* LME.
[ORIGIN formed as Middle Dutch *gruis-* stem of *gruizen* trim glass, crush, from Middle Dutch *gruus, gruis* fragments + IRON *noun.*]
hist. **1** Nippers used for cutting glass. LME.
2 A tool heated to smooth solder joints on pipes. E19.

grrrl /grrl/ *noun.* Also **grrl**. L20.
[ORIGIN Blend of *grrr*, repr. the sound of an animal growling, and GIRL.]
A young woman perceived as independent and strong or aggressive, esp. in her attitude to men or in her sexuality. Freq. in ***riot grrrl, riot girl***, an aggressive young feminist expressing herself esp. through punk-style rock music.

grt *abbreviation.*
Gross registered tonnage, a measure of a ship's size found by dividing the volume of the space enclosed by its hull (measured in cubic feet) by one hundred.

grub /grʌb/ *noun.* LME.
[ORIGIN Prob. from the verb.]
1 The larva of an insect, esp. of a beetle; a caterpillar, a maggot; (now *dial.*) a worm. LME.

Sunday Express He was talking about some grubs he'd dug up in a crocodile swamp.

bardi grub, white grub, witchetty grub, etc.
2 *derog.* †**a** A short person. LME–E18. ▸**b** A person of low ability; a drudge; *US* an industrious student. Now *rare* or *obsolete.* M17.
3 Food. *colloq.* M17.

A. MOOREHEAD We were not long in getting out the grub . . , and we made a good supper.

grub up! *colloq.* the food is ready.
4 An acne pimple. Now *rare* or *obsolete.* M18.
5 A root left in the ground after clearing; a stump. *US.* L18.
6 CRICKET. A ball bowled underarm along the ground. L19.
– COMB.: **grub-kick** RUGBY = GRUBBER 6; **grub screw** a small headless screw with a recess at one end to receive a screwdriver or key; **grubstake** *noun & verb* (*N. Amer. colloq.*) (*a*) *noun* rations etc. granted to a prospecting miner in return for a share in any find or profits; (*b*) *verb trans.* supply with grubstake; **grubstaker** a prospector supplied with a grubstake; the supplier of a grubstake; **grub-worm** = sense 1 above; *fig.* (*derog.*) an unpleasant person.
■ **grubhood** *noun* (now *rare*) the condition of being a grub or larva M19.

grub /grʌb/ *verb.* Infl. **-bb-**. ME.
[ORIGIN Uncertain: cf. Old High German *grubilōn* dig, search closely, Middle Dutch *grobben* scrape together, Dutch *grobbelen* root out, from Germanic base rel. to base of GRAVE *noun*[1], *verb*[1].]
1 *verb trans.* (foll. by *up*) & *intrans.* Dig superficially, break up the surface of, (the ground); clear (ground) of roots and stumps. ME. ▸†**b** *verb trans.* Dig round the roots of (a plant). LME–E16. ▸**c** *verb intrans.* Of an animal: root, search for something in the earth etc. Now *esp.* (of a person) search in an undignified or grovelling manner; rummage. M17. ▸**d** *verb intrans.* Plod, toil, (*along, away, on*). M18.

J. RABAN Children dressed in cast-offs grubbed in the dirt. A. S. BYATT The bulldozers were grubbing up pastureland to make the new university. **c** R. CAMPBELL We used to grub about for arrowheads, ancient beads, and other things. R. ADAMS Along the foot of a tilted, red rock a porcupine came nosing and grubbing. **d** A. MILLER If I have to grub for money all day long at least at evening I want it beautiful. S. MIDDLETON Like your inspector grubbing away until the truth's revealed.

2 *verb trans.* Extract by digging; uproot. Foll. by *up, out.* LME.

A. CARTER He was crouching on the ground grubbing up plants with a small spade.

3 [Prob. from the noun.] ▸**a** *verb intrans.* Feed, eat. *slang.* E18. ▸**b** *verb trans.* Provide with food. *slang.* E19.

grubber /ˈgrʌbə/ *noun.* ME.
[ORIGIN from GRUB *verb* + -ER[1].]
1 A person who digs; a searcher; a laborious worker. ME.
2 An implement for digging etc. L16.
3 Now usu. more fully ***money-grubber***. A person who is sordidly intent on amassing money. L16.
4 An eater, a feeder. *arch. colloq.* M19.
5 CRICKET. = GRUB *noun* 6. M19.
6 RUGBY. In full ***grubber kick***. A forward kick of the ball along the ground. M20.

grubbery /ˈgrʌbəri/ *noun.* L18.
[ORIGIN from GRUB *noun* or *verb* + -ERY.]
†**1** A room for hard work or study. *rare.* Only in L18.
2 Food; a dinner; a place where one eats. *slang.* E19.
3 Sordid or sleazy way of life. *rare.* M19.

grubble /ˈgrʌb(ə)l/ *verb.* L17.
[ORIGIN Var. of GRABBLE *verb*, infl. by GRUB *verb.*]
†**1** *verb intrans. & trans.* Grope; gather up or *up.* L17–E18.
2 *verb intrans.* = GRUB *verb* 1C. *rare.* M19.

grubby /ˈgrʌbi/ *adjective.* E17.
[ORIGIN from GRUB *noun* + -Y[1].]
1 Stunted, dwarfish. Now *dial.* E17.
2 Infested with grubs. E18. ▸**b** Of the nature of a grub or larva. M19.
3 Dirty, grimy, slovenly. (The usual sense.) M19.

T. E. LAWRENCE I then washed my very grubby hands.

■ **grubbily** *adverb* M20. **grubbiness** *noun* M19.

Grubean /ˈgrʌbɪən/ *adjective. joc.* E18.
[ORIGIN from GRUB (STREET) + -EAN.]
= GRUB STREET *adjectival phr.*

Grübelsucht /ˈgryːbəlzʊxt/ *noun.* L19.
[ORIGIN German, from *grübeln* to brood + *Sucht* mania.]
A form of obsession in which even the simplest facts are compulsively queried.

Grub Street /ˈgrʌb striːt/ *noun & adjectival phr.* Also **Grubstreet**. M17.
[ORIGIN A street in London (later Milton Street, Moorgate) where many needy and struggling authors lived.]
(Pertaining to or typical of) the world or class of needy authors or literary hacks.

SWIFT Till of late Years, a Grubstreet Book was always bound in Sheepskin. V. S. PRITCHETT If we have one foot in Grub Street we write to be readable.

grudge /grʌdʒ/ *noun.* LME.
[ORIGIN from GRUDGE *verb* or var. of GRUTCH *noun.*]
†**1** Discontent, complaint, grumbling, reluctance. LME–E17.
2 Uneasiness of the conscience or mind; doubt, misgiving; an instance of this. Long *obsolete* exc. *Scot.* L15.
3 Orig., ill will or resentment due to some special cause. Now only, a particular, esp. enduring, instance of such resentment. (Foll. by *against.*) L15.

P. BOWLES Adelkader was very sorry to hear of his death. He bore him no grudge, you know. A. S. NEILL If . . a man succeeds in sending a reluctant wife to be analysed, she quite naturally goes with a grudge. D. JACOBSON Say it was a grudge I had against all David's children for having so many advantages over me. D. NOBBS She wasn't one to hold a grudge just because you had called her mother a hippopotamus.

†**4** Injury, harmful influence or effect. *rare.* L15–M17.
– COMB.: **grudge fight** a fight based on personal antipathy.
■ **grudgeful** *adjective* (*rare*) resentful L16.

grudge /grʌdʒ/ *verb.* LME.
[ORIGIN Var. of GRUTCH *verb.*]
1 *verb intrans.* Murmur; grumble, complain; be discontented. (Foll. by *against, with, at, of, that.*) *obsolete* exc. *Scot.* LME.
†**2** *verb trans.* (in *pass.*) & *intrans.* Be seized or suffer *with* a disease or disability; have the first symptoms of a fever. LME–M16.
†**3** *verb trans. & intrans.* Trouble or vex (a person, the conscience); (of the conscience) be troubled. LME–E17.
4 *verb trans.* Be unwilling to give, grant, or allow, (a thing, *to do*); begrudge. Usu. with person as indirect obj. L15.

H. A. VACHELL He never grudged the time spent in showing his wares to non-buyers. D. H. LAWRENCE The women made way for them, but barely sufficient, as if grudging to yield ground. E. AMADI He did not grudge the expatriate engineers their fatter pay-packets.

■ **grudgement**, **-dgm-** *noun* (*rare*) envy, resentment **M19**. **grudger** *noun* **M16**. **grudgingly** *adverb* in a grudging manner; with reluctance: **M16**. **grudgingness** *noun* the quality of being grudging **E19**.

†**grue** *noun*[1]. **LME–L19**.
[ORIGIN Unknown.]
A particle, a whit. Usu. in neg. contexts.

grue /gruː/ *noun*[2]. *Chiefly Scot. & N. English*. **L18**.
[ORIGIN Unknown.]
Ice, esp. in pieces, on the surface of a body of water.

grue /gruː/ *noun*[3]. *Chiefly Scot. & N. English*. **E19**.
[ORIGIN from GRUE *verb*.]
Shivering, shuddering; a shiver, a shudder.

grue /gruː/ *verb intrans.* *Chiefly Scot. & N. English*. Pres. pple & verbal noun **gru(e)ing**. **ME**.
[ORIGIN from Scandinavian word repr. by Old Swedish *grua*, Old Danish *grue* (= Old High German *ingrûēn* shudder, German *grauen* be awed, Dutch *gruwen* abhor).]
Feel terror or horror; be troubled; shrink from something; shiver, shudder.

gruel /ˈgrʊəl/ *noun*. **ME**.
[ORIGIN Old French (mod. *gruau*) from Proto-Gallo-Romance dim. (repr. by medieval Latin *grutellum*), from Frankish: see -EL[2].]
1 Flour, meal, or other farinaceous substance. *obsolete* exc. *dial.* **ME**.
2 Oatmeal or similar food boiled in water or milk (sometimes with the addition of other ingredients), esp. as part of an invalid's diet. **LME**.
3 Punishment, defeat. *arch.* **L18**.
■ **gruelly** *adjective* resembling gruel **M19**.

gruel /ˈgrʊəl/ *verb trans.* Infl. **-ll-**, ***-l-**. **E19**.
[ORIGIN from the noun.]
1 Feed with gruel. *rare*. **E19**.
2 Exhaust, punish, tax severely. Chiefly as GRUELLING *adjective*. **M19**.
■ **grueller** *noun* †(*a*) a person who feeds on gruel; (*b*) (chiefly *dial.*) a difficult problem; an ordeal: **L17**.

gruelling /ˈgrʊəlɪŋ/ *noun*. Also ***grueling**. **L19**.
[ORIGIN from GRUEL *verb* + -ING[1].]
A harsh or exhausting experience; (a) punishment or defeat.

gruelling /ˈgrʊəlɪŋ/ *adjective*. Also ***grueling**. **M19**.
[ORIGIN from GRUEL *verb* + -ING[2].]
Exhausting, extremely demanding, severe.

Tennis Lendl's training programme is so gruelling that few people can keep up with it.

■ **gruellingly** *adverb* **L20**.

gruesome /ˈgruːs(ə)m/ *adjective*. **L16**.
[ORIGIN from GRUE *verb* + -SOME[1].]
1 Inspiring fear or horror; horrific, grisly; repulsive, disgusting. **L16**.

F. SMYTH It was a particularly gruesome killing, for . . he had been shot twice more through each eye.

2 Full of or inspired by fear. *rare*. **M19**.
■ **gruesomely** *adverb* **L19**. **gruesomeness** *noun* **L19**.

gruff /grʌf/ *adjective & verb*. **L15**.
[ORIGIN Flemish, Dutch *grof* coarse, rude = Middle Low German *grof*, Old High German, German *grob*, from West Germanic.]
▸ **A** *adjective*. **1** Coarse-grained; containing coarse particles. *obsolete* exc. *Scot.* **L15**. ▸**b** Of an abstract thing: rough, rude, unrefined. *Scot.* **L17**.
2 Rough, surly, or sour in manner or aspect; curt, awkwardly taciturn; (of speech or the voice) characterized by hoarse or guttural sounds. **L17**.

H. READ A gruff country man, not conscious of, and therefore not ashamed of, his provinciality. V. WOOLF Speaking in the gruff voice of deep emotion. S. RAVEN Then a hearty handshake, a resumption of the usual gruff manner.

▸ **B** *verb*. †**1** *verb trans.* Treat gruffly. Only in **E18**.
2 *verb intrans.* Grunt, snore. *dial.* **M18**.
3 *verb trans.* Say or utter gruffly. **E20**.

J. T. FARRELL Young Horn said hello to him. He gruffed a reply.

■ **gruffish** *adjective* somewhat gruff **E19**. **gruffly** *adverb* in a gruff manner, with a gruff voice **E18**. **gruffness** *noun* **L17**. **gruffy** *adjective* (*obsolete* exc. *Scot.*) gruff **L18**.

gruft /grʌft/ *noun*. *dial.* **E19**.
[ORIGIN Unknown.]
Particles of soil which are washed up by rain among the grass.
■ **grufted** *adjective* dirty **L19**.

grugru /ˈgruːgruː/ *noun*. Also **groo-groo**, **gri-gri**. **L18**.
[ORIGIN Amer. Spanish (Puerto Rican) *grugrú* from Carib.]
1 More fully ***grugru palm***. Any of various spiny tropical American palms of the genus *Acrocomia*; esp. *A. totai* of northern Argentina and Paraguay, an important source of palm kernel oil. **L18**.
2 More fully ***grugru grub***, ***grugru worm***. The edible larva of any of various S. American insects, esp. weevils of the genus *Rhyncophorus*, which feeds on the pith of palms and sugar cane. **L18**.

gruiform /ˈgruːɪfɔːm/ *adjective*. **L19**.
[ORIGIN mod. Latin *Gruiformes*, from Latin *grus*, *grui-* crane + -FORM.]
ORNITHOLOGY. Belonging or pertaining to the order Gruiformes, which includes the cranes and rails.

grum /grʌm/ *adjective*. Now *rare*. **E17**.
[ORIGIN Prob. blend of GRIM *adjective* and GLUM *adjective*. Cf. Danish *grum* cruel.]
Gloomy, surly, glum.
■ **grumly** *adverb* **E18**. **grumness** *noun* **L17**.

grumble /ˈgrʌmb(ə)l/ *verb & noun*. **L16**.
[ORIGIN Frequentative of GRUMME + *-b-* -LE[1]. Cf. Middle Dutch & mod. Dutch *grommen*, Middle Low German *grommelen*; from imit. Germanic.]
▸ **A** *verb*. **1** *verb intrans.* Of a person or animal: utter low inarticulate sounds; growl faintly; mutter, murmur. **L16**. ▸**b** Of thunder etc.: rumble, esp. faintly or as from a distance. **E17**.

D. ABSE Bluebottles grumbling up and down the window-pane. **b** J. I. M. STEWART Thunder had been grumbling in the distance.

2 *verb intrans.* Utter murmurs of discontent; complain, esp. in a repetitive ineffectual way. (Foll. by *about*, *at*, *over*, *that*.) **L16**.

D. H. LAWRENCE They grumble a lot, but they're not going to alter anything. A. S. BYATT Her ghosts only grumbled, they did not threaten.

grumbling appendix *colloq.* an appendix that causes intermittent discomfort without developing appendicitis.

3 *verb trans.* Express or utter complainingly. (Foll. by *out*.) **E19**.

B. EMECHETA There were murmurs and grumbled protests.

▸ **B** *noun*. **1** An act of grumbling; a complaint; a rumble (of thunder etc.). **L16**. ▸**b** In *pl.* *The* sulks. *colloq.* **M19**.

B. PYM The dull routine, the petty grumbles and the shared irritation of the men. *Blackwood's Magazine* The thunder . . fading at last to a distant grumble.

2 In full ***grumble and grunt*** [rhyming slang] = CUNT. Esp. in ***a bit of grumble***, a sexually desirable woman. *slang*. **M20**.
■ **grumbler** *noun* a person who habitually grumbles **M17**. **grumblesome** *adjective* grumbling, complaining **E20**. **grumbling** *verbal noun* the action of the verb; an instance of this: **E17**. **grumblingly** *adverb* (*a*) in a grumbling manner; †(*b*) mumblingly: **L17**. **grumbly** *adjective* (*colloq.*) (*a*) resembling a grumble; (*b*) inclined to grumble: **M19**.

Grumbletonian /grʌmb(ə)lˈtəʊnɪən/ *noun & adjective*. **L17**.
[ORIGIN from GRUMBLE *verb* after *Muggletonian* etc.]
▸ **A** *noun*. †**1** Orig., a member of the Country Party in 17th-cent. English politics, allegedly motivated by dissatisfied personal ambition. Later, a supporter of the Opposition. *derog.* **L17–M19**.
2 A grumbler. **L18**.
▸ †**B** *attrib.* or as *adjective*. Of, pertaining to, or characteristic of a Grumbletonian or Grumbletonians. **L17–M18**.

grume /gruːm/ *noun*. Now *rare* or *obsolete*. **M16**.
[ORIGIN Latin *grumus* little heap. Cf. French †*grume* (now *grumeau*) clot.]
†**1** A lump. Only in **M16**.
2 *MEDICINE*. A blood clot; a clotted fluid, esp. blood. **E17**.

†**grumme** *verb intrans.* **LME–L16**.
[ORIGIN Uncertain: cf. Dutch *grommen*.]
Grumble.

grummel /ˈgrʌm(ə)l/ *noun*. *obsolete* exc. *dial.* **M16**.
[ORIGIN Unknown: cf. Swedish *grummel*.]
Mud, sediment; in *pl.*, dregs, coffee grounds.

grummet /ˈgrʌmɪt/ *noun*[1]. *obsolete* exc. *hist.* **L16**.
[ORIGIN Old French *gro(u)met* servant, valet, shop boy, wine-merchant's assistant (see GOURMET) = Spanish *grumete* ship's boy.]
A ship's boy; a cabin boy.

grummet *noun*[2] var. of GROMMET *noun*[1].

grumose /ˈgruːməʊs/ *adjective*. *rare*. **M18**.
[ORIGIN from GRUME + -OSE[1].]
Chiefly *MEDICINE & BOTANY*. Formed of clustered grains or clots. Cf. GRUMOUS.

grumous /ˈgruːməs/ *adjective*. **M17**.
[ORIGIN from GRUME + -OUS.]
1 Of a fluid, esp. blood: clotted, viscid. **M17**.
2 *BOTANY*. Of a root etc.: granular, knotty. **L17**.
3 *GEOLOGY*. Of a rock: formed of clustered or aggregated granules or grains. **L20**.

grump /grʌmp/ *noun*. **E18**.
[ORIGIN Imit. of a sound expr. displeasure.]
†**1** A slight, a snub. Chiefly in ***humps and grumps***. **E–M18**.
2 A bad mood; in *pl.*, the sulks. **M19**.

L. M. ALCOTT Hannah had the grumps, for being up late. Never did suit her. *Expression!* I knew that sitting in the crowd could put her in a real grump.

3 A gruff or grumpy person. *colloq.* **E20**.

A. TYLER You always were a grump when you weren't feeling well.

grump /grʌmp/ *verb intrans.* **L19**.
[ORIGIN from the noun: cf. GLUMP *verb*.]
Sulk, be grumpy.

grumph /grʌmf/ *noun & verb*. *Chiefly Scot.* **M18**.
[ORIGIN Imit.: cf. GRUNT *verb*, GRUMP *noun*.]
▸ **A** *noun*. A grunt. **M18**.
▸ **B** *verb intrans. & trans.* Grunt or utter with a grunt. **E19**.
■ **grumphie** *noun* (a name for) a pig **L18**. **grumphy** *adjective* grumpy **M19**.

grumpish /ˈgrʌmpɪʃ/ *adjective*. **L18**.
[ORIGIN from GRUMP *noun* + -ISH[1].]
Grumpy.
■ **grumpishly** *adverb* **L20**.

grumpy /ˈgrʌmpi/ *adjective*. **L18**.
[ORIGIN from GRUMP *noun* + -Y[1].]
Surly, bad-tempered.

F. BURNEY You were so grumpy you would not let me.

■ **grumpily** *adverb* **L19**. **grumpiness** *noun* **M19**.

Grundy /ˈgrʌndi/ *noun*. **L18**.
[ORIGIN The surname of a character in T. Morton's play *Speed the Plough* (1798).]
Mrs Grundy, a person embodying conventional propriety and prudery.

H. JAMES It was anything but Bohemia—it was the very temple of Mrs. Grundy.

■ **Grundyish** *adjective* prudish **L19**. **Grundyism** *noun* the principles of Mrs Grundy, conventionalism **M19**. **Grundyite** *noun* a stickler for propriety **M19**.

grunerite /ˈgruːnərʌɪt/ *noun*. Also **grü-**. **M19**.
[ORIGIN German *Grünerit*, from E. L. *Gruner* (1809–83), French geologist + -ITE[1].]
MINERALOGY. A monoclinic iron silicate of the amphibole group, also containing magnesium.

grunge /grʌn(d)ʒ/ *noun*. **M20**.
[ORIGIN Rel. to GRUNGY.]
1 A repugnant, unpleasant, or dull person or thing. *slang* (chiefly *N. Amer.*). **M20**.
2 A style of rock music characterized by a raucous guitar sound and lazy delivery. **L20**.

grungy /ˈgrʌn(d)ʒi/ *adjective*. *slang* (chiefly *N. Amer.*). **M20**.
[ORIGIN App. arbitrary formation after GRUBBY *adjective*, DINGY *adjective*, etc.: cf. GRUNGE and GUNGY *adjective*.]
1 Grimy, dirty; of poor quality, unappealing; unpleasant, repugnant. **M20**.
2 Of music: of the nature of or resembling grunge. **L20**.
■ **grunginess** *noun* **L20**.

grunion /ˈgrʌnjən/ *noun*. **E20**.
[ORIGIN Prob. from Spanish *gruñón* grunter.]
A small silverside fish of Californian coasts, *Leuresthes tenuis*, which comes ashore to spawn.

grunt /grʌnt/ *noun & adjective*. **M16**.
[ORIGIN from the verb.]
▸ **A** *noun*. **1** A low guttural sound made esp. by pigs; a similar sound made by humans to indicate approval or disapproval. Formerly also, a groan. **M16**.

DICKENS With a deprecatory grunt, the jackal again complied. B. EMECHETA He . . answered their questions with grunts.

2 Any of numerous tropical marine fishes of the family Haemulidae, which produce a grunting sound by grinding together the pharyngeal teeth; *esp.* (***a***) (more fully ***blue-striped grunt***) *Haemulon sciurus*, (***b***) (more fully ***French grunt***) *H. flavolineatus*. Cf. GRUNTER 2. **L17**.
3 a A junior assistant to a worker on electricity or telephone lines; *gen.* an unskilled or low-ranking assistant, a dogsbody. *US slang*. **E20**. ▸**b** An infantry soldier. *slang* (orig. *US*). **M20**.

b *Times Lit. Suppl.* The first Vietnamese film to try and tell the story like it was for the ordinary American grunt.

4 Mechanical power, esp. of (part of) a motor vehicle. *colloq.* **L20**.
— PHRASES: ***grumble and grunt***: see GRUMBLE *noun* 2.
▸ **B** *attrib.* or as *adjective*. Of an occupation or task: suitable for a low-ranking worker, menial, tedious. *colloq.* **L20**.

grunt /grʌnt/ *verb*.
[ORIGIN Old English *grunnettan* = Old High German *grunnizōn* (German *grunzen*), intensive formation on imit. Germanic base (whence also Old English *grunian* grunt, which has an analogue in Latin *grunnire* grunt).]
1 *verb intrans.* Of an animal, esp. a pig, or a person: utter a grunt or grunts. **OE**. ▸**b** Utter a grunt or grunts expressing discontent, dissent, effort, etc.; grumble. **ME**. ▸†**c** Groan. **ME–E17**.

W. IRVING Sleek unwieldy porkers were grunting in the repose and abundance of their pens. **b** A. MACLEAN An ill-advised move that made him grunt with pain.

2 *verb trans.* Utter or express with a grunt; breathe or speak *out* with a grunt. **E17**.

W. SOYINKA He grunted a response to the greeting of a passer-by.

■ **grunting** *verbal noun* the action of the verb; an instance of this: **ME**. **gruntingly** *adverb* in a grunting manner **E17**.

grunter /ˈgrʌntə/ *noun*. LME.
[ORIGIN from GRUNT *verb* + -ER[1].]
1 An animal or person that grunts; *esp.* a pig. LME.
2 Any of various marine or freshwater fishes which emit a grunting noise when caught. Cf. CROAKER, GRUNT *noun* 2. E18.

Grunth *noun* var. of GRANTH.

gruntle /ˈgrʌnt(ə)l/ *noun*. *Scot.* E16.
[ORIGIN from the verb.]
1 The snout of a pig or other animal; *transf.* a person's face. E16.
2 A little or subdued grunt. L17.

gruntle /ˈgrʌnt(ə)l/ *verb*[1] *intrans.* Now chiefly *dial.* LME.
[ORIGIN from GRUNT *verb* + -LE[3]. Cf. DISGRUNTLE.]
1 Chiefly of a pig: utter a little or subdued grunt. LME.
2 Grumble, murmur, complain. L16.

gruntle /ˈgrʌnt(ə)l/ *verb*[2] *trans. colloq.* E20.
[ORIGIN Back-form. from DISGRUNTLE *verb*.]
Please, satisfy, make content. Chiefly as ***gruntled*** *ppl adjective*.

gruntling /ˈgrʌntlɪŋ/ *noun*. L17.
[ORIGIN from GRUNT *verb* + -LING[1].]
A young pig.

gruppetto /grupˈpetto, grʊˈpɛtəʊ/ *noun*. Pl. **-tti** /-t(t)i/, **-ttos** /-təʊz/. M19.
[ORIGIN Italian, dim. of *gruppo*.]
MUSIC. A melodic ornament consisting of a group of three, four, or five notes, comprising the principal note and the notes one degree above and below it; a turn.

gruppo /ˈgruppo/ *noun*. Long *rare*. Pl. **-ppi** /-ppi/. L17.
[ORIGIN Italian.]
= GRUPPETTO.

Grus /grʊs/ *noun*. M17.
[ORIGIN Latin *grus* crane (bird).]
(The name of) a small constellation of the southern hemisphere, south of Piscis Austrinus; the Crane.

grush /grʌʃ/ *verb trans. obsolete* exc. *Scot.* LME.
[ORIGIN Var. of CRUSH *verb*.]
Crush. Formerly also, make a deep wound in, gash.

grushie /ˈgrʌʃi/ *adjective*. *Scot.* L18.
[ORIGIN Unknown.]
Healthy, thriving.

grutch /grʌtʃ/ *noun*. Now *Scot.* & *US*. LME.
[ORIGIN from the verb. Cf. GROUCH *noun*[1], GRUDGE *noun*.]
†**1** = GRUDGE *noun* 1. LME–M16.
2 = GRUDGE *noun* 3. M16.

grutch /grʌtʃ/ *verb*. Long *arch.* & *dial.* ME.
[ORIGIN Old French *groucier*, *grouchier* grumble, murmur, of unknown origin. Cf. GROUCH *verb*, GRUDGE *verb*.]
1 *verb intrans.* = GRUDGE *verb* 1. ME.
2 *verb trans.* = GRUDGE *verb* 4. LME.
†**3** *verb intrans.* Make a jarring or grating sound; gnash one's teeth. LME–E16.
■ †**grutchingly** *adverb*: only in ME.

Gruyère /ˈgruːjɛː, *foreign* gryjɛːr/ *noun & adjective*. E19.
[ORIGIN A town in Switzerland.]
(Designating) a firm pale cow's milk cheese with many cavities.

gryke *noun* var. of GRIKE.

gryllotalpa /grɪləˈtalpə/ *noun*. L18.
[ORIGIN from Latin *gryllo-* comb. from *gryllus* cricket + *talpa* mole.]
A mole-cricket, of the orthopteran family Gryllotalpidae. Now only as mod. Latin genus name.

gryphite /ˈgrɪfʌɪt/ *noun*. L18.
[ORIGIN mod. Latin *gryphites*, from late Latin *gryphus*: see GRIFFIN *noun*[1].]
PALAEONTOLOGY. A kind of fossil oyster.

gryphon *noun* see GRIFFIN *noun*[1].

grysbok /ˈgrʌɪsbɒk, ˈxreɪs-/ *noun*. Also **-buck** /-bʌk/. Pl. same, **-s**. L18.
[ORIGIN Afrikaans, from Dutch *grijs* grey + *bok* BUCK *noun*[1].]
Either of two small reddish-brown straight-horned antelopes, *Raphicerus melanotis* and *R. sharpei*, of central and southern Africa.

gs *abbreviation*.
Guineas.

G7 *abbreviation*. Also (*US*) **G-7**.
Group of Seven.

GSM *abbreviation*[1].
Global System (or Standard) for Mobile, a standardized international system for digital mobile telecommunication.

gsm *abbreviation*[2].
Grams per square metre.

GSOH *abbreviation*.
Good sense of humour (used in personal advertisements).

G-spot /ˈdʒiːspɒt/ *noun*. L20.
[ORIGIN from *G*, from Ernst *Gräfenberg* (1881–1957), US gynaecologist + SPOT *noun*.]
A sensitive area of the anterior wall of a woman's vagina, believed by some to be highly erogenous and capable of ejaculation.

GST *abbreviation*. *Austral.*, *NZ*, & *Canad.*
Goods and Services Tax.

G string /ˈdʒiː strɪŋ/ *noun phr.* In sense 2 usu. **G-string**. M19.
[ORIGIN from G, G + STRING *noun*.]
1 MUSIC. The string on a violin etc. tuned to the note G. M19.
2 A strip of cloth covering the pubic area, attached to a narrow waistband or string; *esp.* a similar garment of minimal extent worn e.g. by striptease artists. L19.

G-suit /ˈdʒiːsuːt/ *noun*. Also **g-**. M20.
[ORIGIN from G, G + SUIT *noun*.]
A garment equipped with inflatable areas, designed to enable the wearer to withstand high acceleration.

GT *abbreviation*[1].
Italian *Gran turismo* (of a high-performance car designed for touring).

Gt *abbreviation*[2].
Great.

G10 *abbreviation*. Also (*US*) **G-10**.
Group of Ten.

guaap *noun* var. of GHAP.

guaca *noun* see HUACA.

guacamole /gwɑːkəˈməʊli/ *noun*. Also **guaco-**. E20.
[ORIGIN Amer. Spanish from Nahuatl *ahuacamolli*, from *ahuacatl* avocado + *molli* sauce.]
A Mexican dish made from mashed avocados, onions, tomatoes, chillies, and seasoning.

guacharo /ˈgwɑːtʃərəʊ/ *noun*. Pl. **-os**. E19.
[ORIGIN Spanish *guáchero*, of S. Amer. origin.]
= ***oilbird*** s.v. OIL *noun*.

guaco /ˈgwɑːkəʊ/ *noun*[1]. Pl. **-os**. M19.
[ORIGIN Amer. Spanish.]
1 Any of several tropical American plants used as antidotes to snakebites; esp. *Mikania guaco*, of the composite family, and *Aristolochia maxima* (family Aristolochiaceae). Also, the medicinal substance obtained from the plant. M19.
2 = ***Rocky Mountain bee plant*** s.v. BEE *noun*[1]; a black pigment obtained from this, used by Pueblo Indians to decorate pottery. M19.

guaco *noun*[2] var. of HUACO.

guacomole *noun* var. of GUACAMOLE.

Guadalupe /ˈgwɑːdəluːp, -pi/ *noun*. L19.
[ORIGIN A Mexican island situated off the coast of California.]
Used **attrib.** in the names of plants and animals found there.
– COMB.: **Guadalupe palm** an ornamental palm, *Brahea edulis*, bearing edible pulpy fruit.

Guadeloupian /gwɑːdəˈluːpɪən/ *noun & adjective*. M20.
[ORIGIN from *Guadeloupe* (see below) + -IAN.]
▸ **A** *noun*. A native or inhabitant of Guadeloupe, a group of islands in the Lesser Antilles. M20.
▸ **B** *adjective*. Of or pertaining to Guadeloupe or its inhabitants. M20.
■ Also **Guadeloupean** *adjective & noun* M20. **Guadeloupan** *adjective & noun* L20.

guaiac /ˈgwʌɪək/ *noun*. M16.
[ORIGIN Anglicized from GUAIACUM. Cf. French *gaïac*.]
Guaiacum; *esp.* = GUAIACUM 2, 3.
– COMB.: **guaiac test** = *GUAIACUM* ***test***.

guaiacol /ˈgwʌɪəkɒl/ *noun*. M19.
[ORIGIN from GUAIACUM + -OL.]
A liquid with a penetrating aromatic odour obtained by the fractional distillation of wood tar and the dry distillation of guaiacum resin; *o*-methoxyphenol, $OH{\cdot}C_6H_4{\cdot}OCH_3$, the principal constituent of this, a yellow crystalline solid or oily liquid used as a synthetic flavouring.

guaiacum /ˈgwʌɪəkəm/ *noun*. M16.
[ORIGIN mod. Latin from Spanish *guayaco*, *guayacan*, from Taino *guayacan*.]
1 Any of various trees and shrubs of the genus *Guaiacum* (family Zygophyllaceae), native to the W. Indies and tropical America, esp. *G. officinale* and *G. sanctum*. M16.
2 The hard very heavy wood of such a tree; lignum vitae. M16.
3 A resin obtained from such a tree, formerly used to treat gout and rheumatism, now as a flavouring; a drug prepared from it. Also ***gum guaiacum***. M16.
– COMB.: **guaiacum test** MEDICINE: for the absence of blood from urine or faeces, involving guaiacum.

Guaicuru *noun & adjective* var. of GUAYCURU.

guajira /gwaˈxira/ *noun*. E20.
[ORIGIN Cuban Spanish, fem. of GUAJIRO.]
A Cuban song and dance tune whose rhythm shifts from 6/8 to 3/4 time.

guajiro /gwaˈxiro/ *noun*. Pl. **-os** /-ɔs/. M19.
[ORIGIN Cuban Spanish = rustic, rural.]
A Cuban agricultural worker.

guan /gwɑːn/ *noun*. L17.
[ORIGIN from Amer. Spanish from Miskito *kwamu*.]
Any of various game birds of tropical America of the genus *Penelope* or other genus of the family Cracidae (which also contains the curassows).

guana /ˈgwɑːnə/ *noun*. E17.
[ORIGIN Aphet. from IGUANA.]
1 An iguana. E17.
2 A goanna. Latterly *Austral.* Now *rare* or *obsolete*. L17.

guanaco /gwəˈnɑːkəʊ/ *noun*. Pl. **-os**. E17.
[ORIGIN Spanish from Quechua *huanacu*.]
A mammal of the Andean foothills, *Lama guanicoe*, which belongs to the same family as the llama, vicuña, and camels and has a coat of soft pale brown hair used for wool.

guanay /ˈgwɑːneɪ/ *noun*. M19.
[ORIGIN Amer. Spanish *guanae*.]
A cormorant, *Phalacrocorax bougainvillei*, of the coasts of Chile and Peru. Also ***guanay cormorant***.

Guanche /ˈgwɑːntʃi/ *noun*. L16.
[ORIGIN Spanish.]
Any of the aboriginal inhabitants of the Canary Islands who were absorbed by the Spanish on their conquest of the islands in the 15th cent.

guanethidine /gwəˈnɛθɪdiːn/ *noun*. M20.
[ORIGIN from GUANIDINE by insertion of ETH(YL).]
PHARMACOLOGY. A derivative of guanidine that is used esp. to treat moderate to severe hypertension.

guango /ˈgwaŋgəʊ/ *noun*. *W. Indian*. Pl. **-os**. L19.
[ORIGIN Amer. Spanish, of unknown origin.]
= ***rain tree*** (b) s.v. RAIN *noun*[1].

guanidine /ˈgwɑːnɪdiːn/ *noun*. M19.
[ORIGIN from GUANO + -IDE + -INE[5].]
CHEMISTRY. A strongly basic compound, $NH_2{\cdot}C(NH){\cdot}NH_2$, used in organic synthesis.

guanidino /gwɑːnɪˈdiːnəʊ/ *adjective*. M20.
[ORIGIN from GUANIDINE + -O-.]
CHEMISTRY. Containing or designating the group $H_2N{\cdot}C(NH){\cdot}NH{\cdot}$ derived from guanidine. Used before a noun.
■ Also ˈ**guanido** *adjective* M20.

guanine /ˈgwɑːniːn/ *noun*. M19.
[ORIGIN from GUANO + -INE[5].]
BIOCHEMISTRY. A derivative of purine that occurs in guano and fish scales and is one of the four bases of nucleic acids, paired with cytosine in double-stranded DNA; 6-oxy-2-aminopurine, $C_5H_5N_5O$.

guano /ˈgwɑːnəʊ/ *noun & verb*. E17.
[ORIGIN Spanish, or S. Amer. Spanish *huano*, from Quechua *huanu* dung.]
▸ **A** *noun*. Pl. **-os**.
1 The excrement of seabirds as found esp. on the islands off Peru and Chile and used as fertilizer. E17. ▸**b** A seabird which produces guano. Now *rare* or *obsolete*. L17.
2 More fully ***fish guano***. An artificial fertilizer resembling natural guano, *esp.* one made from fish. M19.
▸ **B** *verb trans.* Fertilize with guano. M19.

guanophore /ˈgwɑːnəfɔː/ *noun*. E20.
[ORIGIN from GUAN(INE + -O- + -PHORE.]
ZOOLOGY. A chromatophore containing crystals of guanine, found in the skin of fishes and reptiles.

guanosine /ˈgwɑːnəsiːn/ *noun*. E20.
[ORIGIN from GUANINE by insertion of -OSE[2].]
BIOCHEMISTRY. A nucleoside composed of guanine linked to ribose, a constituent of RNA and coenzymes.

guanxi /gwanˈʃiː/ *noun*. L20.
[ORIGIN Mandarin, lit. 'connection'.]
In China: the system of social networks and influential relationships which facilitate business and other dealings.

guanylic /gwɑːˈnɪlɪk/ *adjective*. L19.
[ORIGIN formed as GUANOSINE + -YL + -IC.]
BIOCHEMISTRY. ***guanylic acid***, a nucleotide composed of a phosphoric acid ester of guanosine, present in most DNA and RNA.

guar /gwɑː/ *noun*. L19.
[ORIGIN Hindi *guār*.]
1 A drought-resistant leguminous plant, *Cyamopsis tetragonoloba*, grown esp. in the Indian subcontinent as a vegetable and fodder crop and as a source of guar gum. L19.
2 More fully ***guar flour***, ***guar gum***. A fine powder obtained by grinding the endosperm of guar seeds and used in the food, paper, and other industries. M20.

G

G

guara /ˈgwɑːrə/ *noun*. Now *rare*. **E17**.
[**ORIGIN** (Portuguese *guerá* from) Tupi *agwa'rá*.]
The scarlet ibis, *Eudocimus ruber*.

guaracha /gwaˈratʃa/ *noun*. **M19**.
[**ORIGIN** Spanish.]
A lively Cuban song and dance in 3/4 and 6/8, or 2/4, time; a ballroom dance resembling this.

guarache *noun* var. of **HUARACHE**.

guarana /gwəˈrɑːnə, ˈgwɑːrənə/ *noun*. **M19**.
[**ORIGIN** Portuguese from Tupi *guaraná*.]
A Brazilian liana, *Paullinia cupana*, of the soapberry family; a paste prepared from the seeds of this shrub, used as a food or medicine and esp. to make a drink resembling coffee.

†**guarand** *noun*. **L17–E18**.
[**ORIGIN** Prob. from French *garant*: see **GUARANTEE**.]
= **GUARANTEE** *noun* 1.

Guarani /gwɑːrəˈniː; *in sense 3* ˈgwɑːrəni/ *noun*. In sense 3 **g-**. **L18**.
[**ORIGIN** Spanish, from *Guarini*.]
▸ **A** *noun*. Pl. same, **-s**.
1 A member of a S. American Indian people of Paraguay and adjacent regions. **L18**.
2 The language of this people, one of the main divisions of the Tupi-Guarani language family. **E20**.
3 (**g-**.) A monetary unit of Paraguay, equal to 100 céntimos. **M20**.
▸ **B** *attrib.* or as *adjective*. Of or pertaining to the Guarani or their language. **L19**.

guarantee /gar(ə)nˈtiː/ *noun & verb*. Also (earlier, as noun) **garanté**. **L17**.
[**ORIGIN** Prob. orig. from Spanish *garante* = French *garant* **WARRANT** *noun*[1]; later infl. by French *garantie* **GUARANTY**.]
▸ **A** *noun*. **1** = **GUARANTOR**. **L17**.
2 = **GUARANTY** *noun* 1. **L18**.
3 A thing, esp. a document from a manufacturer etc., given or existing as security for the fulfilment (esp. by a product, service, etc.) of certain conditions. **M19**.

C. FRANCIS The proximity of the shore is no guarantee of safety.

4 A person to whom a guaranty is given. **M19**.
– **COMB.**: **guarantee fund** a sum pledged as a contingent indemnity for future loss.
▸ **B** *verb trans*. **1** Be a guarantee for; undertake to be responsible for the fulfilment of (a contract), the nature of (a product), etc.; secure the persistence or existence of; ensure *that*; engage *to do*. **L18**.

N. SHUTE If I didn't stop drinking . . he couldn't guarantee my life for longer than a year. P. GOODMAN A ten-foot drop to a concrete pavement, guaranteed to break both ankles. D. CAUTE You will personally guarantee our safety?

2 Secure (a person or thing) *against* or *from* risk, injury, etc., or *in* the possession of something. **E19**.
3 Secure the possession of (something) *to*. **M19**.

guarantor /gar(ə)nˈtɔː/ *noun*. **M19**.
[**ORIGIN** from **GUARANT**(**EE** *verb* + **-OR**, after **WARRANTOR**.]
A person who makes or gives a guarantee.

guaranty /ˈgar(ə)nti/ *noun & verb*. **E16**.
[**ORIGIN** Anglo-Norman *guarantie*, Old French & mod. French *garantie* use as noun of fem. pa. pple of *g(u)arantir* to guarantee, from Proto-Romance (whence *guarant*: see **WARRANT** *noun*[1]). Cf. **WARRANTY**.]
▸ **A** *noun*. **1** The action of securing, warranting, or guaranteeing; *spec.* a written undertaking to answer for the payment of a debt or the performance of an obligation by another person liable in the first instance to such payment or obligation. **E16**.
2 Something which secures or guarantees the existence or permanence of a thing. **L17**.
▸ **B** *verb*. = **GUARANTEE** *verb*. Now *rare*. **M18**.

guard /gɑːd/ *noun*. **LME**.
[**ORIGIN** Old French & mod. French *garde* from Proto-Romance from West Germanic, whence also **WARD** *noun*.]
†**1** Care; keeping, guardianship, custody. **LME–E18**. ▸**b** A precaution. Formerly also, caution. Now *rare*. **L16**.
2 A keeper, a protector, a defender; a sentry; *N. Amer.* a prison warder. Freq. also with defining word, as ***coastguard***. **LME**. ▸**b** *ASTRONOMY*. Either of two stars in Ursa Minor that are the next brightest in it after the Pole Star; either of the two stars in the Plough which form a line indicating the direction of the Pole Star. Chiefly as ***the Guards***. **L16**. ▸**c** An official in general charge of a train or (*hist.*) a stagecoach. **L18**. ▸**d** Either of two players in basketball or American football responsible for offensive play and defensive marking. **L19**. ▸**e** = **GARDA** 2. **M20**.

P. BOWLES The main gate . . was locked at night so that no guard was necessary. R. ELLISON Armoured cars with alert guards went by. E. ARDIZZONE Sail it alone to the coastguard station and tell the guards to come and help us.

3 A body of soldiers etc. appointed to protect a person or position or to act as a sentry or escort; a separately designated section of an army. **LME**. ▸**b** (**G-**.) In *pl. The* household troops of the British army, consisting of the Foot Guards, the Horse Guards, the Life Guards, and by extension some (orig. seven) regiments of the Dragoon Guards. (These, with the exception of the Foot Guards, are now merged in the Household Cavalry Regiment.) **L17**.
home guard, ***Swiss guards***, ***Varangian Guard***, etc. **b *Grenadier Guards***, etc. *attrib.*: ***Guards battalion***, ***Guards officer***, ***Guards tie***, etc.
4 Something which protects or defends; a protection, a defence; *esp.* a device to prevent injury, damage, or an accident; *spec.* (**a**) the part of a sword hilt that protects the user's hand; (**b**) a metal device protecting the trigger of a gun; (**c**) a reinforcing slip of paper inserted between the pages of a book for the attachment of additional leaves; (**d**) a piece of protective sports equipment. **LME**. ▸**b** An ornamental binding or trimming on a garment. *obsolete* exc. *hist.* **E16**.

SHAKES. *Tr. & Cr.* There is between my will and all offences A guard of patience.

fireguard, ***leg guard***, ***mudguard***, etc.
5 A defensive posture or motion in fencing, boxing, etc.; the position in which a cricket bat is held to defend the wicket. **M16**.

C. S. LEWIS After being knocked down sufficiently often I began to know a few guards and blows. H. WILLIAMSON Blows, which wove . . through the almost static guard of his right arm. C. FRANCIS Night is the time when your guard is down and your reactions slow.

6 Protection, defence. *arch.* **L16**.

GIBBON The rivals . . . had withdrawn the greatest part of their forces from the guard of the general frontier.

7 The condition or fact of protecting or defending; watch, vigilance; sentry duty. Freq. in phrs. (see below). **L16**.

T. HARDY It was characteristic of Ethelberta's jealous motherly guard over her young sisters. E. AMADI The crunch crunch of the boots of the soldier on guard outside.

†**8** A guardroom or guardhouse. **E17–L18**.
9 *CURLING*. A stone delivered so as to lie directly in front of another so that it protects it from an opponent's play. **E19**.
– **PHRASES**: **give guard** *CRICKET* (of an umpire) indicate to a batsman the position of the bat with respect to the wicket. **guard of honour** a body of usu. uniformed people appointed to receive a person of distinction or perform a special ceremonial duty. ***hanging guard***: see **HANGING** *adjective*. **keep guard** act as a sentry, keep watch. **off guard**, **off one's guard** unprepared against attack, surprise, etc. **on guard**, **on one's guard** prepared for attack, surprise, etc.; cautious. **mount guard** take up sentry duty. **relieve guard** take another's place on sentry duty. **take guard** *CRICKET* (of a batsman) take up position before the wicket, esp. by requesting the umpire to give guard. **stand guard** = ***keep guard*** above. ***Yeoman of the Guard***: see **YEOMAN**.
– **COMB.**: **guard band** (**a**) a narrow frequency band left vacant in order to prevent interference between communication bands on either side of it; (**b**) an unrecorded strip separating neighbouring recording tracks on magnetic tape; **guard-boat** (**a**) a boat detailed to ensure that a good watch is kept by officers of a fleet in harbour; (**b**) an official harbour boat enforcing quarantine or customs regulations; **guard book**: arranged for the reception of additional leaves, cuttings, etc.; **guard cell** *BOTANY* each of the pair of cells bordering a stoma, which becomes larger or smaller according to the turgor of the cells; **guard chain**: for securing a watch, brooch, etc.; **guard dog** a watchdog; **guard hair** any of the hairs forming the coarse outer fur of an animal; **guardhouse**: accommodating a military guard or securing prisoners; **guard rail**: preventing a fall, derailment, etc.; **guard ring** (**a**) a ring preventing another ring from slipping off a finger etc.; (**b**) *PHYSICS* a plate placed round and close to a disc electrode so that the field of the latter is not made irregular by edge effects; **guardroom**: for accommodating a military guard or securing prisoners; **guardsman** a soldier belonging to a guard or the Guards.

guard /gɑːd/ *verb*. **L15**.
[**ORIGIN** from the noun or Old French & mod. French *garder*, †*guarder* from Proto-Romance from West Germanic whence also **WARD** *verb*.]
1 *verb trans.* Trim or ornament (a garment) with braid, lace, etc. *arch.* **L15**.
2 *verb trans.* Keep safe; protect, defend, (*against*, *from*); stand guard over, esp. to control entry or exit through (a door, passage, etc.). **L15**. ▸**b** Accompany or escort as a guard *to* a place. *arch.* **L16**. ▸**c** *CHESS & CARDS*. Protect or support (a piece, a card) with another. **E17**. ▸**d** *CRICKET*. Defend or protect (the wicket). **M18**. ▸**e** *CURLING & BOWLS*. Defend (a stone, a bowl) by placing another between it and another player. **L18**.

L. DURRELL The talisman which . . guards a house against the evil eye. P. S. BUCK To his uncle's wife he said nothing, guarding his purpose from her. A. MACLEAN The entrance . . was sealed off by a . . gate guarded by heavily armed soldiers.

3 *verb intrans.* Stand on guard; take up a defensive position, esp. in fencing; *esp.* be on one's guard, take precautions *against*. **L15**.

J. BARNES Her mother was always telling her to guard against over-excitement.

4 *verb trans.* Keep watch over, keep in check, control, (thoughts, speech). **L16**.

W. COWPER Guard what you say.

5 *verb trans.* Provide with a guard (chiefly *techn.*); *fig.* protect against misunderstanding by stipulation or explanation. **L19**.
6 *verb trans.* Supply (a guard book) with guards; insert into a guard book. **L19**.
■ **guardable** *adjective* **L16**. †**guardage** *noun* (*rare*) keeping, guardianship: only in **E17**. **guarder** *noun* a keeper, a protector; a guard: **M16**. **guarding** *noun* (**a**) the action of the verb; (**b**) a binding or trimming (*hist.*); *Scot.* a border on a herring net: **M16**. **guardingly** *adverb* in a guarding manner **E19**.

guarda-costa /gwardaˈkosta, gɑːdəˈkɒstə/ *noun*. **M18**.
[**ORIGIN** Spanish, from *guarda-* stem of *guardar* to guard + *costa* coast.]
hist. A Spanish ship used for protecting the coast.

guardant /ˈgɑːd(ə)nt/ *adjective & noun*. **L16**.
[**ORIGIN** French *gardant* pres. pple of *garder*: see **GUARD** *verb*, **-ANT**[1].]
▸ **A** *adjective*. **1** *HERALDRY*. Of an animal: depicted in profile or with the face turned towards the spectator. **L16**.
2 Guarding, protecting. *arch.* **E17**.
▸ **B** *noun*. A guardian, a protector. Long *rare* or *obsolete*. **L16**.

guarda-roba /gwardaˈrɔːba, gwɑːdəˈrəʊbə/ *noun*. *arch.* **E17**.
[**ORIGIN** Italian, from *guarda-* stem of *guardare* to guard + *roba* clothes.]
A wardrobe.

guarded /ˈgɑːdɪd/ *adjective*. **E16**.
[**ORIGIN** from **GUARD** *verb*, *noun*: see **-ED**[1], **-ED**[2].]
1 Trimmed, ornamented. *arch.* **E16**.
2 Defended, protected; having a guard or sentry. **L16**.

E. JOHNSON Dickens's friends knew about Ellen, although he kept her as closely guarded a secret as possible.

3 On one's guard; *esp.* (of speech, behaviour, etc.) careful, cautious, unrevealing, non-committal. **E18**.

M. RENAULT A suitable smile which, without being exactly guarded, revealed nothing whatever. P. ACKROYD He sounded guarded—whether out of suspicion or embarrassment, it was impossible . . . to tell.

4 *techn.* Provided with a guard or guards. **L19**.
■ **guardedly** *adverb* cautiously (earlier in **UNGUARDEDLY**) **L18**. **guardedness** *noun* cautiousness **E19**.

guardee /gɑːˈdiː/ *noun*. *colloq.* **E20**.
[**ORIGIN** from **GUARD** *noun* + **-EE**[2].]
A guardsman, esp. as representing smartness or elegance.

guardful /ˈgɑːdfʊl, -f(ə)l/ *adjective*. Now *rare* or *obsolete* exc. *dial.* **E17**.
[**ORIGIN** from **GUARD** *noun* + **-FUL**.]
Watchful; careful.
■ **guardfully** *adverb* **E17**.

guardia civil /gwarˌdia θiˈbil/ *noun phr.* Pl. ***guardias civiles*** /gwarˌdias θiˈbiles/. **M19**.
[**ORIGIN** Spanish = civil guard.]
(A member of) a police force in Spain organized on military lines.

guardian /ˈgɑːdɪən/ *noun*. **LME**.
[**ORIGIN** Anglo-Norman *gardein*, Old French *garden*, earlier *gardenc* (mod. *gardien*, with assim. of suffix to *-ien* **-IAN**, which was followed in English), from Frankish, from Germanic base of **WARD** *noun*. Cf. **WARDEN** *noun*[1].]
1 A keeper, a defender, a protector; *hist.* (in full ***Guardian of the Poor***) a member of a board elected to administer the poor laws in a parish or district. **LME**.

F. WARNER So we, the guardians of Mosaic Law, . . Have killed the prophets?

2 *spec.* in *LAW*. A person who has legal custody of the person or property of a minor or other person deemed incapable of managing his or her own affairs; *esp.* one who has been given this by legal appointment. **LME**.

V. NABOKOV Alabama prohibits a guardian from changing the ward's residence without an order of the court.

3 In various official titles, now superseded by **WARDEN** *noun*[1]. *obsolete* exc. *hist.* **LME**.
4 The superior of a Franciscan convent. **LME**.
5 *ASTRONOMY*. = **GUARD** *noun* 2b. Chiefly as ***the Guardians (of the Pole)***. **M16**.
– **COMB.**: **guardian angel** an angel conceived as watching over or protecting a particular person or place.
■ **guardiaˈness** *noun* a female guardian **E17**. **guardianless** *adjective* **E17**.

guardianship /ˈgɑːdɪənʃɪp/ *noun*. **M16**.
[**ORIGIN** from **GUARDIAN** + **-SHIP**.]
1 The condition or fact of being a guardian. **M16**.
2 Keeping, protection. **M17**.

guardias civiles *noun phr.* pl. of **GUARDIA CIVIL**.

guardless /ˈgɑːdlɪs/ *adjective*. **E17**.
[**ORIGIN** from **GUARD** *noun* + **-LESS**.]
1 Undefended, unprotected. **E17**.
2 Off one's guard; careless. **M17**.
3 Esp. of a sword: having no guard. **L19**.

guardo /ˈgɑːdəʊ/ *noun*. Pl. **-os**. **M19**.
[**ORIGIN** from **GUARD** *noun* + *-o*, in imitation of Spanish words.]
US HISTORY. A receiving ship for enlisted men who are to be drafted to seagoing vessels.

guardship /ˈɡɑːdʃɪp/ *noun. rare.* **E17.**
[ORIGIN from GUARD *noun* + -SHIP.]
= GUARDIANSHIP.

guardy /ˈɡɑːdi/ *noun. colloq.* **M19.**
[ORIGIN from GUARD *noun* + -Y[6].]
= GUARDIAN 2.

guarea /ˈɡwɑːrɪə/ *noun.* **M20.**
[ORIGIN mod. Latin (see below) from Cuban Spanish *guara*.]
Any of various tropical hardwood trees of the genus *Guarea*, esp. the mainly W. African *G. cedrata* and *G. thompsonii*, which yield a pale timber like mahogany; this timber.

guariba /ɡwəˈriːbə/ *noun.* **M18.**
[ORIGIN (Portuguese & Spanish from) Tupi *waˀriwa*.]
A howler monkey.

†**guarish** *verb trans.* **L15–L16.**
[ORIGIN Old French *g(u)ariss-* lengthened stem of *g(u)arir* (mod. *guérir*) from Frankish verb cogn. with WERE *verb*[1]: see -ISH[2]. Cf. GARRISON *noun*.]
Cure, heal.

Guarnerius /ɡwɑːˈnɪərɪəs/ *noun.* **M19.**
[ORIGIN Latinized form of Joseph *Guarnieri* del Gesù. Cf. JOSEPH 3.]
A violin or cello made by a member of the Guarnerius family of Cremona, Italy, during the 17th and 18th cents.

guarri /ˈɡwari/ *noun. S. Afr.* **L18.**
[ORIGIN Nama *um-gwali*.]
(The small succulent fruit of) any of various trees and shrubs of the genus *Euclea*, of the ebony family, esp. *E. undulata* and *E. crispa* var. *crispa*.

Guatemalan /ɡwɑːtəˈmɑːl(ə)n, ɡwa-/ *noun & adjective.* **E19.**
[ORIGIN from *Guatemala*: see below, -AN.]
▸ **A** *noun.* A native or inhabitant of Guatemala, the northernmost country of Central America, bordering Mexico. **E19.**
▸ **B** *adjective.* Of or pertaining to Guatemala. **L19.**

guava /ˈɡwɑːvə/ *noun.* **M16.**
[ORIGIN Spanish *guayaba*, *-abo*, of S. Amer. origin.]
1 Any of various tropical American evergreen trees and shrubs of the genus *Psidium*, of the myrtle family; esp. *P. guajava*, widely cultivated in tropical and subtropical regions for its edible fruit and freq. naturalized. **M16.**
2 The yellow pink-fleshed fruit of the guava, used to make jams, jellies, etc. **M16.**

guayabera /ɡwʌɪəˈbeɪrə/ *noun.* **M20.**
[ORIGIN Cuban Spanish: appar. orig. from the name of the *Yayabo* river, infl. by Spanish *guayaba* guava.]
A lightweight open-necked Cuban or Mexican shirt with two breast pockets and two pockets over the hips, typically having short sleeves and worn untucked.

Guaycuru /ɡwʌɪkʊˈruː/ *noun & adjective.* Also **Guai-**. **E19.**
[ORIGIN Spanish from Tupi, lit. 'fast runners'.]
▸ **A** *noun.* Pl. **-s**, same.
1 A member of a S. American Indian people inhabiting the Gran Chaco in Paraguay. **E19.**
2 The language of the Guaycurus or the language group of which their language is the principal member. **M20.**
▸ **B** *attrib.* or as *adjective.* Of or pertaining to the Guaycurus or their language. **L19.**
■ **Guaycuruan** *noun & adjective* (of or pertaining to) the language or language group Guaycuru **E20.**

guayule /ɡwʌɪˈuːli/ *noun.* **E20.**
[ORIGIN Amer. Spanish from Nahuatl *cuauhuli*.]
A silvery-leaved shrub of Mexico and Texas, *Parthenium argentatum*, of the composite family, formerly used as a source of rubber.

gubbin /ˈɡʌbɪn/ *noun.* **M16.**
[ORIGIN Var. of GOBBON.]
1 a A fragment. Usu. in *pl.*, shavings, fragments, esp. (formerly) of fish. *obsolete* exc. *dial.* **M16.** ▸**b** In *pl.* Unspecified articles; equipment, gear. Also (treated as *sing.*), a piece of equipment, a gadget. *slang.* **E20.**
2 In *pl.* (A *derog.* nickname for) the people living near Brent Tor, Dartmoor, formerly reputed to be like savages. *obsolete* exc. *hist.* **M17.**
3 In *pl.* (treated as *sing.*). A fool. *slang.* **E20.**

Gubbio /ˈɡʊbɪəʊ/ *adjective.* **M19.**
[ORIGIN A town in Umbria, Italy.]
Designating the majolica (esp. a ruby-lustred type) made in the 16th cent. at Gubbio.

gubble /ˈɡʌb(ə)l/ *verb intrans.* **E20.**
[ORIGIN Imit.]
Make an inarticulate gurgling or murmuring sound like 'gub'.

gubernaculum /ɡjuːbəˈnakjʊləm/ *noun.* Pl. **-la** /-lə/. **M17.**
[ORIGIN Latin = steering oar, from *gubernare* steer, govern: see GOVERN, -CULUM.]
†**1** Some part of an insect. Only in **M17.**
2 ANATOMY. Each of a pair of fibrous strands in the male fetus that connect the testes to the scrotum and guide their descent into it. **L18.**
3 ANATOMY. A band of fibrous tissue joining a permanent tooth follicle to the gum during the early development of the tooth. **M19.**
■ **gubernacular** *adjective* **L19.**

gubernation /ɡjuːbəˈneɪʃ(ə)n/ *noun.* Now *rare.* **LME.**
[ORIGIN Old French, or Latin *gubernatio(n-)*, from *gubernat-* pa. ppl stem of *gubernare* steer, govern: see GUBERNACULUM, -ATION.]
The action of controlling; government.

gubernative /ˈɡjuːbənətɪv/ *adjective.* Now *rare.* **LME.**
[ORIGIN (Old French *gubernatif*, *-ive* from) late Latin *gubernativus*, from Latin *gubernat-*: see GUBERNATION, -IVE.]
Concerned with government.

gubernator /ˈɡjuːbəneɪtə/ *noun. rare.* **E16.**
[ORIGIN Latin, from *gubernat-*: see GUBERNATION, -ATOR.]
A ruler, a governor.

gubernatorial /ɡjuːbənəˈtɔːrɪəl/ *adjective.* Chiefly *US.* **M18.**
[ORIGIN formed as GUBERNATOR + -AL[1].]
Belonging to a governor (esp. the Governor of an American state) or the office of governor.

guck /ɡʌk/ *noun. N. Amer. colloq.* **M20.**
[ORIGIN Perh. from GOO + MUCK: cf. GOOK *noun*[2].]
A slimy, dirty, or otherwise unpleasant substance.

guddle /ˈɡʌd(ə)l/ *verb.* Chiefly *Scot.* **M17.**
[ORIGIN Unknown.]
1 *verb intrans.* Grope in the water for fish, as under the stones or banks of a stream. **M17.**
2 *verb trans.* Catch (a fish) by groping in the water. **E19.**
■ **guddler** *noun* **L19.**

gudgeon /ˈɡʌdʒ(ə)n/ *noun*[1]. **ME.**
[ORIGIN Old French *goujon* dim. of *gouge* GOUGE *noun*.]
1 A device attached to a gate etc. incorporating a ring or socket into which the pin or hook on the post fits so as to form a hinge. **ME.**
2 A metallic pin or other device for screwing together slabs of stone. **ME.**
3 A pivot, usu. of metal, fixed on or let into the end of a beam, spindle, axle, etc., and on which a wheel turns, a bell swings, or the like. **LME.**
4 NAUTICAL. The socket in which the pintle of a rudder turns. **M16.**

gudgeon /ˈɡʌdʒ(ə)n/ *noun*[2]. **LME.**
[ORIGIN Old French *goujon* from Latin *gobio(n-)*, from *gobius* GOBY.]
1 A small European freshwater fish, *Gobio gobio*, used as bait. **LME.** ▸†**b** = GOBY *noun.* **L16–M19.**
2 *fig.* A person easily imposed on; a dupe. **L16.**
3 A thing that is swallowed greedily or credulously; a bait. Chiefly *fig.*, esp. in ***gape for gudgeons***, ***swallow a gudgeon***. **L16.**

gudgeon /ˈɡʌdʒ(ə)n/ *verb.* **L18.**
[ORIGIN from GUDGEON *noun*[2].]
†**1** *verb intrans.* Become a dupe. *slang.* Only in **L18.**
2 *verb trans.* Defraud *of*; delude *into*. **L18.**

Guebre /ˈɡiːbə, ˈɡeɪbə/ *noun.* **L17.**
[ORIGIN French *guèbre* from Persian *gabr*: see GIAOUR.]
A Zoroastrian, a Parsee.

guelder rose /ˈɡɛldə rəʊz/ *noun phr.* **L16.**
[ORIGIN Dutch *geldersche roos*, from *Gelderland* Dutch province, or its capital *Gelders*.]
(The flower of) a deciduous shrub, *Viburnum opulus*, of the honeysuckle family, with leaves like those of the maple and cymes of creamy-white flowers, the outer of which are larger and sterile. Orig. *spec.*, the snowball tree, *V. opulus* var. *roseum*.

Guelph /ɡwɛlf/ *noun & adjective.* Also **Guelf**. **L16.**
[ORIGIN Italian *Guelfo* from Middle High German *Welf*, (the founder of) one of the two great rival dynasties in the Holy Roman Empire.]
▸ **A** *noun.* A member of the papal faction in the medieval Italian states. Opp. GHIBELLINE. **L16.**
▸ **B** *adjective.* Of or adhering to the Guelph faction. **M19.**
■ **Guelphic** *adjective* of the family or faction of the Guelphs **E19.**

guemal /ˈɡweɪm(ə)l/ *noun.* Also **huemal** /ˈhweɪ-/. **E19.**
[ORIGIN Spanish from Mapuche *güemul*, *hüemul*.]
Either of two small S. American deer, *Hippocamelus bisulcus* and *H. antisiensis*, with simply forked antlers.

guenon /ɡəˈnɒn/ *noun.* **M19.**
[ORIGIN French, of unknown origin.]
Any of a group of African monkeys with characteristic long tails and hind limbs, mostly belonging to the genus *Cercopithecus* and including the vervet.

guerdon /ˈɡəːd(ə)n/ *noun & verb.* Now *literary.* **LME.**
[ORIGIN Old French *guer(e)don* from Proto-Romance (medieval Latin) *widerdonum* from West Germanic (= Old High German *widarlōn*, Old English *wiþerlēan*, from *wiþer* again + *lēan* payment), with 2nd elem. assim. to Latin *donum* gift.]
▸ **A** *noun.* A reward, a recompense. **LME.**

> M. BEERBOHM The true conjurer finds his guerdon in the consciousness of work done perfectly.

▸ **B** *verb trans.* Reward; make compensation for. **LME.**

> TENNYSON Him we gave a costly bribe To guerdon silence.

■ **guerdonless** *adjective* **LME.**

guereza /ˈɡɛrɪzə/ *noun.* **M19.**
[ORIGIN Prob. from an African lang.]
The eastern black and white colobus, *Colobus guereza*, a black monkey with a white patch on each side and at the tip of the tail that is found in parts of central Africa.

guéridon /ˈɡɛrɪd(ə)n; *foreign* ɡerɪdɔ̃ (*pl. same*)/ *noun.* **M19.**
[ORIGIN French.]
A small ornamental table or stand, usu. round, with a single central pedestal and ornately carved.

guerilla *noun* var. of GUERRILLA.

guérite /ɡerit/ *noun.* Pl. pronounced same. **E18.**
[ORIGIN French: see GARRET *noun*.]
hist. A wooden or stone turret or box for a sentry.

Guernsey /ˈɡəːnzi/ *noun.* **L16.**
[ORIGIN The second largest of the Channel Islands. Cf. GANSEY.]
▸ **I** *attrib.* **1** Used *attrib.* to designate things found in or associated with Guernsey. **L16.**
†**Guernsey coat** = *Guernsey frock* below. **Guernsey cow** an animal of a breed of usu. brown and white dairy cattle that originated in Guernsey. †**Guernsey frock** a type of knitted tunic worn esp. by sailors. **Guernsey lily** a southern African amaryllis, *Nerine sarniensis*, with umbels of red lily-like flowers, once believed to be naturalized in Guernsey. †**Guernsey shirt** a type of knitted shirt worn esp. by men doing physical work.
▸ **II** *ellipt.* **2 a** (Also **g-**.) Orig., = ***Guernsey frock***, ***Guernsey shirt*** above. Now, a close-fitting woollen sweater, *esp.* a navy blue one worn by sailors. **E19.** ▸**b** (**g-**.) A usu. sleeveless shirt worn by an Australian Rules player. **E20.**
b get a Guernsey, **draw a Guernsey** *Austral.* be selected for a team; *fig.* be successful; gain recognition; get mentioned, included, etc.
3 A Guernsey cow. **M19.**

guerrilla /ɡəˈrɪlə/ *noun & adjective.* Also **guerilla**. **E19.**
[ORIGIN Spanish dim. of *guerra* war: introduced into France and England during the Peninsular War (1808–14).]
▸ **A** *noun.* **1** A person taking part in an irregular war waged by small bands operating independently (freq. against a stronger more organized force) with surprise attacks etc. **E19.**
urban guerrilla: see URBAN *adjective.*
2 A war waged by guerrillas. Now *rare.* **E19.**
▸ **B** *attrib.* or as *adjective.* Of fighting: carried on by small irregular bands. Of a person: taking part in such fighting. **E19.**

guerrillero /ɡɛrɪˈlɛːrəʊ/ *noun.* Also **gueri-**. Pl. **-os**. **E19.**
[ORIGIN Spanish, from GUERRILLA.]
= GUERRILLA *noun* 1.

Guesdist /ˈɡeɪdɪst/ *noun.* **L19.**
[ORIGIN from *Guesde* (see below) + -IST.]
A follower of the principles of revolutionary Marxism advocated by the French political leader Jules Guesde (1845–1922).
■ **Guesdism** *noun* the policy or principles of the Guesdists **M20.**

guess /ɡɛs/ *noun.* Also †**ghess**. **ME.**
[ORIGIN from GUESS *verb*: cf. Middle Dutch *gisse* (Dutch *gis*).]
The action or an act of guessing; an opinion not based on certain knowledge or exact calculation; a conjecture.

> J. BUTLER Mere guess, supposition and possibility, when opposed to historical evidence, prove nothing. M. SHADBOLT I don't need three guesses to know what you're talking about.

– PHRASES: ***anybody's guess***: see ANYBODY. **at a guess**, **by guess**, **by one's guess** at a rough estimate. **by guess and by God**, **by guess and by Godfrey** *slang* (orig. NAUTICAL) (to steer) blind, without the guidance of landmarks. ***by one's guess***: see ***at a guess*** above. **have another guess coming**, **have got another guess coming** *colloq.* be destined to have one's expectations disappointed. **miss one's guess** *US* be mistaken in one's assumption. **my guess is** I am tolerably sure (*that*).

guess /ɡɛs/ *adjective* (*attrib.*). *arch.* & *dial.* **E19.**
[ORIGIN Use as independent word of *-guess* in ***anotherguess*** s.v. ANOTHER, OTHERGUESS.]
Kind or sort of.

> *Blackwood's Magazine* He had no guess-idea of what bemused his vision.

guess /ɡɛs/ *verb.* Also †**ghess**. **ME.**
[ORIGIN Perh. orig. nautical and from vars. with *-e-* of Middle Low German, Middle Dutch (Dutch, Frisian) *gissen*, or Old Swedish *gissa*, Old Danish *gitse*, all ult. from base of GET *verb* (cf. Old Norse *geta* guess). The spellings with *gu-* and *gh-* date from 16: cf. GUEST *noun*.]
1 *verb trans.* Form a rough estimate of (an amount, size, distance, etc.) without actual measurement or calculation. **ME.**

> J. TYNDALL The eye being liable to be grossly deceived in guessing the direction of a perpendicular. T. HARDY Guess my surprise when . . I received a mysterious note.

†**2** *verb intrans.* Take aim (foll. by *to*); purpose *to do*. **ME–M16.**
†**3** *verb trans.* (with compl.). Consider to be; regard *as*. Only in **ME.**
4 *verb trans.* Suppose, think; think it likely, believe. Foll. by clause as obj. Long *obsolete* exc. in *N. Amer. colloq.* in 1st person sing. ***(I) guess.*** **LME.**

> R. MACDONALD 'May I come in for a minute?' 'I guess so.' W. WHARTON Joe knows everybody, everywhere. I guess that's part of being a cop. M. CALLAGHAN There's no harm in you talking to Mother if you want to, I guess.

5 *verb trans.* & *intrans.* Form an opinion (about), or form the opinion *that*, on the basis of uncertain indications or none; hazard an opinion as to *why*, *who*, *whether*, etc.; estimate *to be*; conjecture. Also foll. by subord. clause, & †with. obj. & compl. **LME.**

G

SHAKES. 1 *Hen. VI* Discover . . what cause that was, For I am ignorant and cannot guess. G. A. BIRMINGHAM I should guess the island to be about two miles around. E. O'NEILL Guess which one of Mamie's charmers I picked. J. UPDIKE Nelson guesses she's three or four years younger than he is. J. RATHBONE I did not need to listen, for already I had guessed her tale. I. WALLACE Dilman guessed that there must be more than three thousand persons present.

6 *verb intrans.* Indulge in conjecture or speculation. Foll. by *at*: (attempt to) solve or discover by conjecture. LME.

J. RABAN People could only guess at the total amounts involved. V. WOOLF Lye seemed to hold infinite possibilities she had never guessed at. A. BURGESS Laurence had a great capacity to see into things, to guess and be proved right.

7 *verb trans. & intrans.* Conjecture rightly; solve (a riddle etc.), divine the nature of (a thing), by guesswork. M16.

H. BUSHNELL But which is worse . . it is not difficult, I think, to guess. DICKENS Sure enough it's Barnaby—how did you guess? G. GREENE The others had to guess his wish by asking questions.

– PHRASES: **guessing game** a game in which much of the playing consists of guessing; *fig.* a situation in which one is kept constantly in the dark. **keep a person guessing** *colloq.* (orig. *US*) keep a person in a state of uncertainty about one's feelings, future intentions, etc.

■ **guessable** *adjective* E19. **guesser** *noun* LME. **guessingly** *adverb* by guesswork E17.

G

guess rope *noun* var. of GUEST ROPE.

guesstimate /*as noun* ˈɡɛstɪmət, *as verb* ˈɡɛstɪmeɪt/ *noun & verb.* Orig. *US.* Also **guest-**. M20.
[ORIGIN from GUESS *noun, verb* + ESTIMATE *noun, verb*.]
▸ **A** *noun.* An estimate based more on guesswork than calculation. M20.
▸ **B** *verb trans. & intrans.* Form a guesstimate (of). M20.

guess-warp /ˈɡɛswɔːp/ *noun.* L15.
[ORIGIN from unkn. 1st elem. + WARP *noun*: cf. GUEST ROPE.]
1 A rope carried to a distant object in order to warp a vessel towards it, or make fast a boat. L15.
2 = GUEST ROPE 2. M19.

guesswork /ˈɡɛswəːk/ *noun.* E18.
[ORIGIN from GUESS *noun* + WORK *noun*.]
(Procedure based on) guessing, as opp. to knowledge or reasoning.

guest /ɡɛst/ *noun.* ME.
[ORIGIN Old Norse *gestr*, superseding Old English *ġiest*, *ġest* = Old Saxon, Old High German (Dutch, German) *gast*, Gothic *gasts*, from Germanic, from an Indo-European base repr. also by Latin *hostis* enemy, (orig.) stranger. The spelling *gu-* (L16) marks the hard *g*, like the earlier var. with *gh*: cf. GUESS *verb*.]
1 A person staying in another's house etc. at his or her invitation; a person having a meal at the expense of another. ME.

E. WAUGH Father Aelred Watkin came to stay. A very agreeable guest. P. H. JOHNSON She took out her purse to pay the bill, forgetting she was my guest.

be my guest! *colloq.* you are welcome (to take the action indicated)! **guest of honour** the chief guest at a dinner or other function. **paying guest** a lodger.

†**2** A stranger. ME–L16.
3 A person having (temporary) accommodation in a hotel, inn, or boarding house. ME.
4 A person (of a specified kind), a fellow. Long *obsolete* exc. *dial.* ME.
5 An object regarded as an omen of an approaching stranger. *local.* E18.
6 A parasitic organism. M19.
7 An occasional performer appearing by special invitation with a company other than his or her regular one. E20.

– ATTRIB. & COMB.: In the sense 'reserved or suitable for the use of guests in a house', as ***guest room***, ***guest towel***, etc.; in the sense 'performing or appearing as a guest (sense 7)', as ***guest artist***, ***guest conductor***, ***guest star***; 'involving such a performer', as ***guest appearance***. Special combs., as **guest beer** (*a*) (in a free house) a beer which is available only temporarily; (*b*) (in a tied public house) a beer (usu. an independent real ale) offered in addition to those produced by the brewery; **guestbook** COMPUTING a facility on a website on which visitors to the site may record their comments; **guest house** a house where strangers are accommodated; now usu., a (superior) boarding house, *esp.* one catering for holidaymakers; **guest list** a list of the people invited to a function; **guest-master** a member of a monastery or other religious establishment who looks after guests; **guest night**: on which members of a club, college, mess, etc., bring guests to dinner; **guest speaker** a public speaker entertained to a dinner at which he or she gives an address; **guest worker** [translating German *Gastarbeiter*] a person with temporary permission to work in another country, esp. Germany.

■ **guestless** *adjective* having no guests; [translating Greek *axenos*] inhospitable: L16. **guestship** *noun* the status of a guest M19.

guest /ɡɛst/ *verb.* ME.
[ORIGIN from the noun.]
1 *verb trans.* Receive as a guest. ME.
2 *verb intrans.* Lodge or enjoy hospitality as a guest. *rare.* LME.
3 *verb intrans.* Appear in a show or programme as a guest performer or star. M20.

Melody Maker Ian Carr guested with the Roy Budd Trio . . on Saturday.

guesten /ˈɡɛst(ə)n/ *adjective. arch.* L15.
[ORIGIN Perh. repr. Middle English genit. pl. of GUEST *noun*.]
Reserved for guests. Only in ***guesten chamber***, ***guesten hall***.

guesten /ˈɡɛst(ə)n, ˈɡɛs(ə)n/ *verb trans. & intrans.* Long *arch. rare.* Orig. †**gesten**. ME.
[ORIGIN from GUEST *noun* + -EN[5] or back-form. from GESTENING.]
= GUEST *verb* 1, 2.

guestimate *noun & verb* var. of GUESSTIMATE.

guest rope /ˈɡɛstrəʊp/ *noun.* Also **guess rope**. E17.
[ORIGIN The first elem. may be a var. of *guess-* in GUESS-WARP, to which *guest rope* may be a later parallel formation.]
1 A second rope, fastened to a boat in tow, to keep it steady. E17.
2 A stout rope slung outside a vessel fore and aft (formerly also fastened to the end of a boom) to give a hold for boats coming alongside. L18.

guestwise /ˈɡɛstwʌɪz/ *noun & adverb.* Now *rare* or *obsolete.* LME.
[ORIGIN from GUEST *noun* + -WISE.]
▸ †**A** *noun.* ***in guestwise***, ***on guestwise*** = sense B. below. LME–M17.
▸ **B** *adverb.* As a guest. L16.

gueux /ɡø/ *noun pl.* E17.
[ORIGIN French, pl. of *gueux* ragamuffin, beggar.]
hist. The Dutch nobles who in 1566 petitioned Margaret, Governess of the Netherlands, on behalf of Protestants; the Dutch and Flemish Protestant partisans who subsequently fought against Spain in the wars of the 16th cent.

gueuze /ɡəːz/ *noun.* E20.
[ORIGIN Flemish.]
A sour, strong, sparkling Belgian beer, made by blending new and aged Lambic beers before a secondary fermentation.

Guevarist /ɡɪˈvɑːrɪst/ *adjective & noun.* M20.
[ORIGIN from *Guevara* (see below) + -IST.]
▸ **A** *adjective.* Of, pertaining to, or characteristic of the S. American revolutionary and guerilla leader Ernesto ('Che') Guevara (1928–67) or his beliefs. M20.
▸ **B** *noun.* A follower of Guevara. M20.
■ **Guevarism** *noun* the political principles or actions of Guevara or his followers M20.

gufa /ˈɡʊfə/ *noun.* Also †**kuphar**. E19.
[ORIGIN Arabic, dial. var. of *quffa* large basket.]
A Mesopotamian round boat made of straw and palm branches.

guff /ɡʌf/ *noun.* E19.
[ORIGIN Imit.: cf. Norwegian dial. *gufs* puff of wind, *guffa* blow softly.]
1 A whiff, esp. of a bad smell; a puff of wind, vapour, etc. *Scot.* E19.

J. KESSON The foosty guff of an ancient wood drifted over and past in great imprisoning waves.

2 Empty or meaningless verbiage. *colloq.* (orig. *US*). L19.

G. SWIFT The craven guff into which we slide in order to settle the most intimate facts of our lives.

guffaw /ɡəˈfɔː/ *noun & verb.* Orig. *Scot.* E18.
[ORIGIN Imit.]
▸ **A** *noun.* A coarse or boisterous laugh. E18.
▸ **B** *verb.* **1** *verb intrans.* Laugh coarsely or boisterously. E18.
2 *verb trans.* Say with a guffaw. M19.

guffer /ˈɡʌfə/ *noun. Scot.* E19.
[ORIGIN Unknown.]
The viviparous blenny, *Zoarces viviparus*.

guga /ˈɡuːɡə/ *noun. Scot.* M19.
[ORIGIN Gaelic.]
A young gannet.

Gugelhupf /ˈɡuːɡəlhʊpf/ *noun.* Also ***Gugl-***, ***Kugel-*** /ˈkuːɡəl-/. Pl. **-e** /-ə/. L19.
[ORIGIN German; the form with *k* is from dial.]
A light Austrian cake baked in a ring-shaped mould.

Guggenheim /ˈɡʊɡ(ə)nhʌɪm/ *adjective & noun.* M20.
[ORIGIN John Simon *Guggenheim*, in whose memory his father Simon Guggenheim (1867–1941), US Senator and industrialist, established the Guggenheim Foundation in 1925.]
▸ **A** *adjective.* Designating any of the fellowships awarded annually by the John Simon Guggenheim Memorial Foundation for creative work in the arts and for advanced study and research. M20.
▸ **B** *noun.* A Guggenheim fellowship or award. M20.

guggle /ˈɡʌɡ(ə)l/ *noun.* L17.
[ORIGIN from the verb.]
1 The windpipe. *obsolete* exc. *dial.* L17.
2 A guggling sound. E19.

guggle /ˈɡʌɡ(ə)l/ *verb.* E17.
[ORIGIN Imit.]
1 *verb intrans.* Make a sound like that of liquid pouring from a small-necked bottle; flow with such a sound. E17.
2 Bring *up* or pour *forth* with a guggling sound. M18.

Guglhupf *noun* var. of GUGELHUPF.

guglia /ˈɡuːljə/ *noun.* Also **-glio** /-ljəʊ/, pl. **-os**. M17.
[ORIGIN Italian, aphet. var. of *agugliа* lit. 'needle'. Cf. medieval Latin *aculea*.]
An obelisk, esp. in Italy.

Guhr /ɡuːr, ɡʊə/ *noun.* L18.
[ORIGIN German dial., lit. 'ferment'.]
A loose earthy deposit from water found in the cavities of rocks.

GUI /ˈɡuːi/ *abbreviation.*
COMPUTING. Graphical user interface.

Guianese /ɡʌɪəˈniːz, ɡɪə-/ *noun & adjective.* M19.
[ORIGIN from *Guiana* (see below) + -ESE. Cf. GUYANESE.]
▸ **A** *noun.* Pl. same. A native or inhabitant of Guiana, a tropical region in north-eastern S. America. M19.
▸ **B** *adjective.* Of or pertaining to Guiana. L19.
■ **Guianan** /ɡʌɪˈanən, ɡɪˈɑːnən/ *noun & adjective* (*a*) *noun* a Guianese; (*b*) *adjective* = GUIANESE *adjective*: M19. **Guianian** /ɡɪˈɑːnɪən/ *noun & adjective* = GUIANAN E17.

guib /ɡwɪb/ *noun.* L18.
[ORIGIN Wolof.]
= ***bushbuck*** s.v. BUSH *noun*[1].

guichet /ˈɡiːʃeɪ/ *noun.* M19.
[ORIGIN French.]
A wicket, a hatch; *esp.* one through which tickets are sold.

guid *noun, adjective, verb, adverb* see GOOD *noun, adjective*, etc.

guidance /ˈɡʌɪd(ə)ns/ *noun.* M16.
[ORIGIN from GUIDE *verb* + -ANCE.]
1 The action of guiding; leadership, direction; *spec.* counselling or advice about marriage problems, career decisions, etc. M16. ▸**b** The control of a missile or spacecraft in its course. M20.

R. ELLMANN He looked to Ruskin for spiritual guidance. N. SYMINGTON With guidance from Winnicott the family was able to cope with his need. **b** *attrib.*: *Listener* The shuttle had been given four separate guidance computers.

2 Something which guides. E18.

guide /ɡʌɪd/ *noun.* LME.
[ORIGIN Old French & mod. French, alt. of Old French †*guie* (whence GUY *noun*[1]), from *guider* GUIDE *verb*.]
▸ **I 1** A person who or thing which shows the way; *spec.* (*a*) a person who conducts less experienced mountaineers; (*b*) a person (usu. hired) who indicates and gives information on objects of interest in a city, building, etc., to a tourist. LME. ▸**b** MILITARY. A person employed to give information to an invading army about the enemy's country; a member of a reconnaissance group; a soldier, vehicle, or ship whose movements are taken as a guide for the movement and formation of others. M16. ▸**c** (Usu. **G-**.) A member of an organization of girls similar to the Scouts, known as the Guides Association. Orig. ***Girl Guide***. E20.

R. KIPLING He was an agreeable guide, ever keen to point out the beauties of his royal master's domain. E. BAKER A pretty, uninformed guide . . told him the tours didn't begin until ten o'clock.

c King's Guide, **Queen's Guide** a Guide who has reached the highest rank of proficiency. ***Ranger Guide***: see RANGER *noun* 4. ***Queen's Guide***: see ***King's Guide*** above.

2 An adviser, a director; a directing principle or standard. Formerly also, a ruler, a leader. LME. ▸**b** SPIRITUALISM. = CONTROL *noun* 4b. M19.

A. MASON He was looking for a guide, a teacher.

3 a A manual or book of instruction on a specified subject. E17. ▸**b** A book of information on a city, building, etc., for the use of tourists. Also ***guidebook***. M18.
4 a An object which steadies or guides by physical contact the motion of a tool or machine part. L17. ▸**b** SCIENCE. A linear structure or a surface along or over which an electromagnetic wave is propagated and to which it is confined; *spec.* a waveguide. L19.

R. CARVER He threaded the line through the guides of his rod.

5 Something which marks a position or guides the eye. L19.
▸ **II 6** The action of GUIDE *verb*; direction, guidance. Now *rare.* E16.

SHAKES. *Timon* Pray entertain them; give them guide to us.

– COMB.: **guide-board** a sign in a road indicating the way; **guidebook**: see sense 3b above; **guide dog**: trained to lead a blind person; **guide fossil** = ***index fossil*** s.v. INDEX *noun*; **Guide Law** a code of conduct enjoined on a Guide to which a member must promise obedience; **guideline** a line for guiding; *fig.* a directing or standardizing principle laid down as a guide to procedure, policy, etc.; **guidepost** a signpost; **guide rope** (*a*) a small rope attached to the load of a crane, by which its movement may be guided; (*b*) a rope trailed by a balloon or small airship to assist in maintaining a constant altitude by the drag of part of the rope on the ground; (*c*) any of several ropes used to steady an airship before flight; **Guide's honour** the oath taken by a Guide, used as a protestation of honour and sincerity; **guideway** a groove, a track.

■ **guideless** *adjective* L15.

guide /gʌɪd/ *verb trans.* LME.
[ORIGIN Old French & mod. French *guider* alt. of †*guier* (whence GUY *verb*[1]), from Proto-Romance from Germanic, from alt. of base of WIT *verb*.]
1 Act or serve as a guide to; go with or before to lead the way. LME.

R. H. MOTTRAM She dropped her things, and, guided by George's voice, found the bedroom. N. SHUTE He took her arm to guide her through the Saturday evening crowds.

guided tour: led by or having a guide in charge.
2 †**a** Lead, command, (an army, soldiers). LME–M16. ▸**b** Manage, control, (money, property, a process). Now *Scot.* LME. ▸**c** Manage the affairs of (a household, a state). Long *rare*. LME.

b SIR W. SCOTT Them that sells the goods guide the purse—them that guide the purse rule the house.

3 Lead or direct in a course of action, the formation of opinions, etc.; influence; advise; be the principle, motive, or ground of (an action, judgement, etc.). LME.

O. SITWELL Policy is guided by feeling, not by cold reason. M. MCCARTHY She wanted to guide Dottie to discover her own real feelings.

4 Direct the motion or course of (something inanimate). LME.

J. B. PRIESTLEY Long rows of sewing machines worked by electric power but guided by hand. R. V. JONES Bosch was to design the radio beam system that guided some of the V-2 rockets.

guided imagery a method of relaxation which concentrates the mind on positive images in an attempt to reduce pain, stress, etc. **guided missile**: operating by remote control or as directed automatically by equipment inside it. **guiding telescope** a visual telescope fixed to a photographic telescope so that the latter can be manually made to follow a star etc. kept in position in the field of view of the former during an exposure.
5 Treat or handle (a person) in a specified way. *Scot. & N. English*. E18.
■ **guidable** *adjective* L17.

guider /ˈgʌɪdə/ *noun*. LME.
[ORIGIN In sense 1 from GUIDE *verb*, in sense 2 from GUIDE *noun*: see -ER[1].]
1 A person who or thing which guides someone or something. LME.
2 (**G-**.) An adult leader of the Guides (GUIDE *noun* 1c). Orig. *Girl Guider*. E20.

guidguid *noun* var. of HUET-HUET.

guiding /ˈgʌɪdɪŋ/ *noun*. LME.
[ORIGIN In sense 1 from GUIDE *verb*, in sense 2 from GUIDE *noun*: see -ING[1].]
1 The action or practice of GUIDE *verb*. LME.
2 The characteristic activity and occupation of a Guide (GUIDE *noun* 1c). Also, the Guide movement. E20.

guidon /ˈgʌɪd(ə)n/ *noun*. M16.
[ORIGIN French from Italian *guidone*, from *guida* guide: see -OON.]
1 A pennant narrowing to a point or fork at the free end, esp. as used as the standard of a regiment or (*US*) a troop of cavalry. M16.
2 An officer who carries a guidon. L16.

Guidonian /gwɪˈdəʊnɪən/ *adjective*. E18.
[ORIGIN from *Guidon-* taken as stem of *Guido* (see below) + -IAN.]
MUSIC. Of or pertaining to the 11th-cent. Italian musician Guido d'Arezzo, the reputed inventor of the system of hexachords. Chiefly in ***Guidonian hand***, a drawing of the left hand marked with the degrees of the scale and the solmization according to the system devised by Guido.

guige /giːʒ/ *noun*. LME.
[ORIGIN Old French & mod. French.]
hist. A strap passing over the neck or shoulder and serving as an additional support for a medieval soldier's shield.

Guignet's green /ˈgiːnjeɪz ˈgriːn/ *noun phr.* M19.
[ORIGIN C. E. *Guignet*, 19th-cent. French chemist.]
= VIRIDIAN *noun*.

Guignol /giːˈnjɒl/ *noun*. L19.
[ORIGIN French = Punch.]
In France, (a) marionette drama resembling Punch and Judy. Also = GRAND GUIGNOL.
■ **guignoˈlesque** *adjective* resembling or characteristic of (Grand) Guignol M20.

guild /gɪld/ *noun*[1]. Also (in sense 1) **gild**. LOE.
[ORIGIN Prob. from Middle Low German, Middle Dutch *gilde* (Dutch *gild*) from Germanic; rel. to Old English *gi(e)ld* payment, offering, sacrifice, idol, (also) guild (continued in Middle English as *ȝild*, *yeld*), Old Frisian *geld*, *ield* money, Old Saxon *geld* payment, sacrifice, reward, Old High German *gelt* payment, tribute (Dutch, German *Geld* money), Old Norse *gjald* payment and *gildi* guild, payment, Gothic *gild* tribute, from Germanic.]
1 An organization formed for the mutual aid and protection of its members, or for the furtherance of some common purpose; *esp.* (occas. **gild**) a medieval association of craftsmen or merchants. LOE. ▸**b** *gen.* A company, a fellowship. M17.
†**2** The meeting place of a guild; the home of a religious guild. LOE–M17.
3 ECOLOGY. A group of species which have similar roles in the same community. E20.
– COMB.: **guild-brother** a man who belongs to a guild; **guildhall** a hall in which a medieval guild met; a town hall; (*Guildhall*) the building in the City of London used by the Corporation of the City for meetings, banquets, etc.; **guild socialism** an economic system in which the resources, methods, and profits of each industry are controlled by a council of its members.
■ **guildry** *noun* (*Scot.*) (*a*) the municipal corporation of a Scottish royal burgh; †(*b*) = GUILDSHIP 2: E16.

guild *noun*[2] var. of GILD *noun*[1].

†**guild** *verb* see GILD *verb*[2].

guildable *adjective & noun* see GILDABLE.

guilder /ˈgɪldə/ *noun*. LME.
[ORIGIN Alt. of Dutch GULDEN.]
Orig., a gold coin of the Netherlands and parts of Germany; now, the basic monetary unit of the Netherlands and Suriname, equal to 100 cents (replaced in the Netherlands by the euro in 2002).

guildship /ˈgɪldʃɪp/ *noun*.
[ORIGIN Old English *gieldscipe*, formed as GUILD *noun*[1], -SHIP.]
1 = GUILD *noun*[1] 1. OE.
2 Membership of a guild. M16.

guile /gʌɪl/ *noun*. ME.
[ORIGIN Old French from Old Norse: see WILE *noun*.]
1 Insidious cunning, deceit, treachery. ME.

B. PYM Was he being sarcastic? . . he was too nice a man for that, too lacking in guile.

†**2** An instance of this, a trick, a stratagem. ME–M18.

guile /gʌɪl/ *verb trans. arch.* ME.
[ORIGIN Old French & mod. French *guiler*, formed as GUILE *noun*. Cf. WILE *verb*.]
Beguile, deceive.

guileful /ˈgʌɪlfʊl, -f(ə)l/ *adjective*. Now *literary*. ME.
[ORIGIN from GUILE *noun* + -FUL.]
Full of guile; deceitful.
■ **guilefully** *adverb* LME. **guilefulness** *noun* LME.

guileless /ˈgʌɪllɪs/ *adjective*. E18.
[ORIGIN from GUILE *noun* + -LESS.]
Devoid of guile; artless, innocent.
■ **guilelessly** *adverb* E18. **guilelessness** *noun* E18.

†**guiler** *noun*. ME–L16.
[ORIGIN Old French *guileor*, *gyllour*, formed as GUILE *verb*: see -OUR, -ER[2].]
A beguiler, a deceiver.

†**guilery** *noun* var. of GILLERY.

Guillain–Barré syndrome /gijanˈbareɪ ˈsɪndrəʊm/ *noun phr.* M20.
[ORIGIN G. *Guillain* (1876–1961) and J. *Barré* (1880–1967), French physicians, two of those who first described the disease.]
MEDICINE. An acute inflammatory polyneuropathy usu. causing temporary paralysis.

guillaume /ˈgiːləm, *foreign* gijoːm/ *noun*. Also (*Scot.*) **geelum** /ˈgiːləm/. E19.
[ORIGIN French = William.]
A rabbet plane.

guillem /ˈgɪləm, ˈgwɪ-/ *noun*. E17.
[ORIGIN Welsh *Gwilym* William, (as common noun) guillemot. Cf. GUILLEMOT.]
= GUILLEMOT.

guillemet /ˈgiːmeɪ, *foreign* gijmɛ/ *noun*. E20.
[ORIGIN French, of uncertain origin; prob. derived from the male forename *Guillaume* or the surname *Guillemet*.]
Each of a pair of punctuation marks (« ») used as quotation marks in French and other European languages.

guillemot /ˈgɪlɪmɒt/ *noun*. L17.
[ORIGIN French, dim. of *Guillaume* William.]
Any of several diving seabirds of northern latitudes constituting the genera *Uria* and *Cepphus*, of the auk family, with black (or brown) and white plumage and pointed bills; *spec.* (also ***common guillemot***) *Uria aalge*. Cf. MURRE.
black guillemot *Cepphus grylle*, with less white than the common guillemot. **BRÜNNICH'S GUILLEMOT**.

guilloche /gɪˈləʊʃ, -ˈlɒʃ/ *noun*. M19.
[ORIGIN French *guillochis* guilloche, or *guilloche* the tool used in making it.]
An architectural or metalwork ornament imitating braided or twisted ribbons.

guillotine /ˈgɪlətiːn, gɪləˈtiːn/ *noun*. L18.
[ORIGIN French, from Joseph-Ignace *Guillotin* (1738–1814), French physician, who suggested its use for executions in 1789.]
1 An instrument for beheading consisting of a weighted blade with a diagonal edge which is allowed to drop between two tall grooved uprights, used in France esp. during the Revolution. L18. ▸**b** ***the guillotine***, execution by means of a guillotine. M19.
2 A surgical instrument with a blade that slides in a long groove, suitable for excising tonsils etc. M19.
3 A machine with a long blade for cutting paper; a machine for cutting other material. L19.
4 A method used in a legislative assembly for preventing obstruction or delays by fixing the times at which different parts of a bill must be voted on. L19.

guillotine /ˈgɪlətiːn, gɪləˈtiːn/ *verb trans.* L18.
[ORIGIN French *guillotiner*, formed as GUILLOTINE *noun*.]
1 Behead by means of a guillotine. L18.
2 Cut with a guillotine; *fig.* cut short. L19.

guilt /gɪlt/ *noun & verb*.
[ORIGIN Old English *gylt*; ult. origin unknown.]
▸ **A** *noun*. †**1** A failure of duty, an offence, a sin. OE–LME.
†**2** Responsibility for an action or event; the fault *of*. OE–L17.
†**3** Desert (*of* a penalty). OE–E17.
4 The fact or state of having (wilfully) committed, or of being guilty of, a crime or moral offence; guiltiness, culpability. OE. ▸**b** An instance, kind, or degree of guilt. *rare*. LME. ▸**c** A feeling or sense of being guilty. L17. ▸**d** Conduct involving guilt; sin; crime. E18.

H. H. WILSON Positive proof of his guilt could not be adduced. **c** C. G. WOLFF The guilt Wharton felt in fighting free of Lucretia . . cannot easily be dismissed.

guilt by association guilt ascribed to a person not because of any evidence but because of his or her association with an offender.
– COMB.: **guilt culture** ANTHROPOLOGY a culture in which conformity of behaviour is maintained through the individual's internalization of a moral code (cf. ***shame culture***). **guilt-trip** *noun & verb* (*colloq.*) (*a*) *noun* an experience of feeling guilty about something, esp. when such guilt is excessive, self-indulgent, or unfounded; (*b*) *verb intrans. & trans.* experience a guilt-trip; try to induce (someone) to feel guilty about something.
▸ **B** *verb trans.* Try to induce (a person) to feel guilty about something. *colloq.* L20.

guiltless /ˈgɪltlɪs/ *adjective & noun*. ME.
[ORIGIN from GUILT + -LESS.]
▸ **A** *adjective*. **1** Free from guilt; innocent. (Foll. by *of*.) ME.

T. GRAY Some Cromwell, guiltless of his country's blood.

2 Having no knowledge or experience *of* something. M17.

L. CARR Distinguishing it from other farm-houses, which were guiltless of that special ornamentation.

▸ **B** *absol.* as *noun*. Guiltless people as a class. Now only with *the*. ME.
■ **guiltlessly** *adverb* LME. **guiltlessness** *noun* L16.

guilty /gɪlti/ *adjective & noun*.
[ORIGIN Old English *gyltig*, formed as GUILT: see -Y[1].]
▸ **A** *adjective*. **1** That has incurred guilt; deserving punishment; criminal, culpable. Formerly also, that has offended or been at fault. OE.

WOODES ROGERS We put ten of the Mutineers in Irons. . . Others less guilty I punish'd and discharg'd. *transf.*: BYRON He hangs his guilty head.

2 That has committed a particular offence or crime, or is justly chargeable with a particular fault. (Foll. by *of*.) ME.

H. JAMES I indignantly protest that I am never guilty of *that* clumsiness. *Sunday Express* An Old Bailey jury found Patrick Reilly . . not guilty.

†**3** Foll. by *of*: culpably responsible for, to blame for. ME–E18.
†**4** Deserving *of*, liable *to*, (a penalty). LME–M17.
5 Of an action or condition: involving guilt, culpable, criminal. L16.
6 Conscious of or prompted by guilt. L16.

P. H. GIBBS 'I feel a little guilty in eating cream buns,' said Maria Theresa.

guilty CONSCIENCE.
†**7** Conscious, cognizant, (*of*, *to*). L16–L17.
▸ **B** *absol.* as *noun*. **1** Guilty people as a class. Now only with *the*. LME.
†**2** A guilty person. Usu. with *the*. M16–E18.
■ **guiltily** *adverb* L16. **guiltiness** *noun* the condition, quality, or state of being or feeling guilty; an instance of this: LME.

guimauve /gɪˈməʊv, *foreign* gimoːv/ *noun*. E19.
[ORIGIN French.]
The marsh mallow, *Althaea officinalis*; a medicinal preparation made from the root of this.

guimp *noun* var. of GIMP *noun*[1], GUIMPE.

guimpe /gɪmp, *foreign* gɛ̃ːp/ *noun*. Also **guimp**. M19.
[ORIGIN French: cf. GIMP *noun*[2], WIMPLE *noun*.]
A high-necked chemisette; a blouse designed for wearing under a low-necked dress.

Guinea /ˈgɪni/ *noun*. M16.
[ORIGIN Orig. a region bordering part of the west coast of Africa; now a state on that coast.]
▸ **I** Also **g-** in certain combs.
1 Used *attrib.* to designate persons or things from Guinea or W. Africa. M16.
Guinea corn any of several varieties of sorghum, ***Sorghum bicolor***, esp. durra. **guinea fowl** any of numerous gallinaceous birds of sub-Saharan Africa of the subfamily Numidinae (family Phasianidae), with wattles and a head and neck largely bare of feathers; *spec.* (also ***helmeted guinea***) *Numida meleagris*, a species domesticated throughout the world. **Guinea grass** a tall African grass, *Panicum maximum*, grown as fodder, esp. in tropical America. **guinea hen** †(*a*) a turkey, *esp.* a female; (*b*) a guinea fowl, *esp.* a female; †(*c*) *slang* a prostitute. ***Guinea*** LINSANG. **Guineaman** (*a*) *hist.* a ship trading to the Guinea coast; a slave ship; (*b*) (a man descended from) a black man from Guinea. **Guinea Negro** = sense 2a. ***Guinea peach***: see PEACH *noun*[1] 2(a).

G

Guinea pepper: see PEPPER *noun*. **Guinea worm** a nematode worm, *Dracunculus medinensis*, up to several feet long, which lives under the skin (usu. of the legs) of infected people in rural parts of tropical Africa and Asia.

2 a A black person, *esp.* one recently arrived from Africa. *US* (now *hist.*). E19. ▸**b** An immigrant of Italian or Spanish origin. *US slang. derog.* L19.

▸ **II g-**.

3 *hist.* A British gold coin with a nominal value of a pound first struck in 1663 for the African trade, and from 1717 legal tender in Britain with a value fixed at 21 shillings. M16.

4 A sum of money equal to 21 shillings or £1.05. Now only used in stating professional fees, auction prices, etc. L17.

– COMB.: **Guinea flower** any of various Australian shrubs of the genus *Hibbertia* (family Dilleniaceae), with flat golden or white flowers.

Guinean /ˈɡɪnɪən/ *noun & adjective*. L16.
[ORIGIN from GUINEA + -AN.]
▸ **A** *noun*. A native or inhabitant of Guinea or a country whose name contains 'Guinea'. L16.
▸ **B** *adjective*. Of or pertaining to such a region or country. E17.

G

guinea pig /ˈɡɪnɪpɪɡ/ *noun*. M17.
[ORIGIN from GUINEA + PIG *noun*[1].]
1 A dumpy tailless rodent, *Cavia porcellus*, now found only in captivity as a pet or a subject for biological research, but related to the wild cavies of S. America. M17. ▸**b** A person who or thing which is used as a subject for experiment or to test something. E20.

> **b** *Radio Times* He coerces the criminal into agreeing to be a guinea pig in experiments in exchange for his freedom.

2 A midshipman on board an East Indiaman; a young or inefficient seaman. *colloq.* (now *hist.*). M18.
3 A recipient of a fee of a guinea; *spec.* a director of a company appointed chiefly because of the prestige of his or her name or title. *colloq.* (now *hist.*). E19.
4 A person evacuated or billeted in the Second World War. *colloq.* (now *hist.*). M20.

guinep /ɡɪˈnɛp/ *noun*. Also **genip** /ɡɛˈnɪp/, **ginep**, **kinep** /kɪˈnɛp/. M18.
[ORIGIN Amer. Spanish *quenepo* guinep tree, *quenepa* its fruit, both from Arawak.]
(The fruit of) the W. Indian tree *Melicoccus bijugatus* (family Sapindaceae). Also called ***Spanish lime***.

guinguette /ɡɛ̃ɡɛt/ *noun*. Pl. pronounced same. M18.
[ORIGIN French.]
Chiefly *hist.* A garden where public entertainment, esp. drinking and dancing, is provided.

†**guiniad** *noun* var. of GWYNIAD.

Guinness /ˈɡɪnɪs/ *noun*. M19.
[ORIGIN Family name.]
(Proprietary name for) a brand of stout manufactured by the firm of Guinness; a bottle or glass of this.

guinzo *noun* var. of GINZO.

guipure /ɡɪˈpjʊə/ *noun*. M19.
[ORIGIN French, from *guiper* cover with silk, wool, etc., from Germanic base meaning 'wind round'.]
A kind of openwork lace in which the motifs are connected by brides.

guira /ˈɡwʌɪrə/ *noun*. M19.
[ORIGIN Amer. Spanish from Tupi *wiˀra* bird.]
In full ***guira cuckoo***. A non-parasitic cuckoo, *Guira guira*, of eastern S. America.

guiro /ˈɡwʌɪrəʊ/ *noun*. Pl. **-os**. L19.
[ORIGIN Spanish = gourd.]
A gourd with an artificially serrated surface which gives a rasping sound when scraped with a stick, used (orig. in Latin America) as a musical instrument.

guisard /ˈɡʌɪzəd/ *noun & verb*. E17.
[ORIGIN from GUISE *verb* + -ARD.]
= GUISER.

guise /ɡʌɪz/ *noun & verb*. ME.
[ORIGIN Old French & mod. French from Proto-Romance from Frankish (= Old Saxon *wīsa*) from Germanic base repr. also by WISE *noun*[1].]
▸ **A** *noun*. †**1** Manner, method; style. ME–L18.

> W. COWPER And thus unto the Calender In merry guise he spoke.

†**2** Custom, habit, practice. ME–E18.
3 Behaviour, conduct. ME.
4 Style or fashion of dress or personal appearance; costume, garb. *arch.* ME.

> BYRON Thou know me? in this guise Thou canst not know me.

5 External appearance, aspect; assumed appearance, pretence. ME.

> W. S. CHURCHILL This was a peace proposal in martial guise. W. C. WILLIAMS The witch . . . made these weird visits to the sufferer, in the guise of a cat. A. BURGESS Sex and violence under the guise of a lesson in morality.

6 A disguise, a mask. Hence, a masquerade, a show. *Scot.* E16.

▸ **B** *verb*. Also **guize**.
1 *verb trans.* Dress, esp. fantastically; dress up. LME.
2 *verb trans.* Disguise. *Scot. & N. English.* E16.
3 *verb intrans.* Go about in disguise or fantastic dress. Chiefly *Scot. & N. English.* M19.
■ **guising** *noun* the action of the verb; a masquerade, a mummery: M16.

guiser /ˈɡʌɪzə/ *noun & verb*. Also **guizer**. L15.
[ORIGIN from GUISE *verb* + -ER[1].]
▸ **A** *noun*. A masquerader, a mummer. Cf. GUISARD. L15.

> G. PRIESTLAND The guisers would come round performing the play of St. George and the Dragon.

▸ **B** *verb intrans.* Masquerade; go mumming. E20.

Guisian /ˈɡiːzɪən/ *noun & adjective*. *hist.* M16.
[ORIGIN from French (*duc de*) *Guise* + -IAN.]
▸ **A** *noun*. A supporter of the faction led by the Catholic Ducs de Guise in 16th-cent. France. M16.
▸ **B** *adjective*. Of or pertaining to the Guisians. L16.

guitar /ɡɪˈtɑː/ *noun & verb*. Also (earlier) †**guitarra**. E17.
[ORIGIN Orig. from Spanish *guitarra*, later from French *guitare* (superseding Old French *guiterne* GITTERN) from Spanish *guitarra* from Greek *kithara* (adopted in Latin as *cithara*, whence Provençal *cedra*, Italian *cetera*, Old High German *cithara* (German *Zither*)): cf. CITHERN, CITOLE, ZITHER.]
▸ **A** *noun*. A stringed musical instrument with a fretted fingerboard, incurved sides, and six or twelve strings, played by plucking or strumming with the fingers or a plectrum. E17.
bass guitar, ***classical guitar***, ***folk guitar***, etc. ***electric guitar***: see ELECTRIC *adjective*. ***Hawaiian guitar***: see HAWAIIAN *adjective*. ***Spanish guitar***: see SPANISH *adjective*.
– COMB.: **guitarfish** any fish of the family Rhinobatidae, comprising bottom-dwelling cartilaginous fishes of tropical and subtropical oceans, like rays with fiddle-shaped bodies.
▸ **B** *verb intrans.* Play the guitar. E19.
■ **guitarist** *noun* a person who plays the guitar L18.

guiver *noun* var. of GUYVER.

guize *verb*, **guizer** *noun* vars. of GUISE *verb* etc.

Gujarat /ɡuːdʒəˈrɑːt, ɡʊ-/ *noun*. Also **-jer-**. L16.
[ORIGIN Hindi *Gujarāt*: see GUJARATI.]
= GUJARATI *noun* 1.

Gujarati /ɡuːdʒəˈrɑːti, ɡʊ-/ *adjective & noun*. Also **-jer-**. E19.
[ORIGIN Hindi from *Gujarāt* (Sanskrit *Gurjara*): see -I[2].]
▸ **A** *adjective*. Of or pertaining to Gujarat, a state in western India, its people, or their language. E19.
▸ **B** *noun*. Pl. same, **-s**.
1 A native or inhabitant of Gujarat. M19.
2 The Indo-Aryan language of Gujarat. M19.

Gujerat *noun*, **Gujerati** *adjective & noun* vars. of GUJARAT, GUJARATI.

gul /ɡʊl/ *noun*. E19.
[ORIGIN Persian.]
1 A flower; *esp.* a rose. Freq. in ***gardens of gul***. *poet.* E19.
2 A large geometrical motif derived from the shape of the rose that forms part of the design of a Turkoman rug. E20.

gula /ˈɡjuːlə/ *noun*[1]. LME.
[ORIGIN Latin = throat, appetite. Cf. GULE *noun*[1].]
†**1 a** The external throat; the gullet. Only in LME. ▸**b** An animal's gullet. *rare.* Only in M17.
†**2** Gluttony. Only in LME.
3 A sclerite on the lower middle part of an insect's head, between the two genae. E19.

gula *noun*[2] see GOLA *noun*[1].

Gulag /ˈɡuːlaɡ, *foreign* ɡuˈlak/ *noun*. Also **g-**. M20.
[ORIGIN Russian acronym, from *Glavnoe upravlenie ispravitel'no-trudovykh lagereĭ* Chief Administration for Corrective Labour Camps.]
1 A department of the Soviet secret police that administered corrective labour camps and prisons between 1934 and 1955. *rare.* M20.
2 The Soviet network of labour camps; a camp or prison within it; *fig.* an oppressive environment. L20.

gular /ˈɡjuːlə/ *adjective & noun*. E19.
[ORIGIN from GULA *noun*[1] + -AR[1].]
▸ **A** *adjective*. Of, pertaining to, or situated on the throat of an animal, esp. a reptile, fish, or bird. E19.
▸ **B** *noun*. A plate, scale, etc., on the throat of a reptile or fish. L19.

gulch /ɡʌltʃ/ *noun*[1]. Long *obsolete* exc. *Scot. & dial.* L16.
[ORIGIN from GULCH *verb*.]
A glutton, a drunkard.
■ **gulchin** *noun* a (little) glutton; a fat or greedy person: L17.

gulch /ɡʌltʃ/ *noun*[2]. Long *obsolete* exc. *dial.* L17.
[ORIGIN Perh. imit.]
A heavy fall.

gulch /ɡʌltʃ/ *noun*[3]. Chiefly *N. Amer.* M19.
[ORIGIN Perh. from GULCH *verb*.]
A narrow deep steep-sided ravine, often forming the course of a torrent; *esp.* one containing gold.

gulch /ɡʌltʃ/ *verb trans.* Long *obsolete* exc. *Scot. & dial.* ME.
[ORIGIN Imit.: cf. Norwegian *gulka*, Swedish dial. *gölka*.]
1 Swallow or devour greedily. Also foll. by *down*, *in*, *up*. ME.
2 Foll. by *out*: expel (as) by vomiting. ME.

gulden /ˈɡʊld(ə)n/ *noun*. Pl. **-s**, same. L15.
[ORIGIN Dutch & German, use as noun of adjective corresp. to GILDEN. Cf. GUILDER.]
Orig., any gold coin, esp. of Germany or the Netherlands. Later, a guilder.

†**gule** *noun*[1]. ME.
[ORIGIN Latin GULA *noun*[1].]
1 Gluttony. ME–M16.
2 The gullet. M17–M18.

gule /ɡjuːl/ *noun*[2]. *arch.* Also **G-**. M16.
[ORIGIN Old French *g(o)ule*, medieval Latin *gula Augusti*, of unknown origin.]
the gule of August, 1 August, Lammas Day.

gules /ɡjuːlz/ *noun & adjective*. ME.
[ORIGIN Old French *go(u)les* (mod. *gueules*) pl. of *gole* throat (mod. *gueule* mouth), used like medieval Latin pl. *gulae* for pieces of red-dyed fur used as a neck ornament.]
(Of) the heraldic tincture red; *poet. & rhet.* red.

gulet /ˈɡuːlɛt/ *noun*. L20.
[ORIGIN Turkish, from French *goëlette* schooner, prob. via Italian *goletta*.]
A traditional Turkish wooden sailing boat, now used esp. for holiday cruises.

gulf /ɡʌlf/ *noun & verb*. Also †**-ph**. LME.
[ORIGIN Old French & mod. French *golfe* from Italian *golfo* from Proto-Romance from Greek *kolpos*, (late) *kolfos* bosom, fold, gulf.]
▸ **A** *noun* **I 1** A portion of the sea, proportionally narrower at the mouth than a bay, partly surrounded by the coast. LME.
the Gulf of Mexico, ***the Persian Gulf***, etc.
2 A profound depth (in a river, the sea); the deep. *poet.* LME.

> *transf.*: LONGFELLOW The headlong plunge through eddying gulfs of air.

3 A yawning chasm or abyss, esp. one produced by an earthquake; a wide ravine or gorge. LME. ▸**b** [After *Luke* 16:26.] An impassable gap; a wide difference of feelings, opinions, etc. M16.

> MILTON The Gulf of Tartarus, which . . opens wide His fiery Chaos. **b** M. DRABBLE The gulf between them had widened with the years.

4 An eddy that sucks things from the surface; a whirlpool; *fig.* something which devours or swallows up anything. *arch.* L15. ▸**b** A voracious appetite. Also, the stomach. *arch.* M16.
5 A large deposit of ore in a lode. *obsolete* exc. *dial.* L18.
▸ **II** [from the verb.]
†**6** = GULP *noun*. M17–L18.
– COMB.: **Gulf Country** *Austral.* the hinterland of the Gulf of Carpentaria, in the northern part of Queensland and the Northern Territory; **Gulf State** a state bordering the Persian Gulf or the Gulf of Mexico; **Gulf Stream** (*a*) a warm ocean current flowing north along the N. American coast from the Florida Straits (or Cape Hatteras) to the Grand Banks of Newfoundland; (*b*) *colloq.* the warm North Atlantic Drift, flowing from where the Gulf Stream proper ends north-eastwards to (esp. northern) Europe; **Gulf War** either of two wars waged against Iraq, the one by Iran from 1980 to 1988 and the other by a multinational force in 1991; ***Gulf War syndrome***, a medical condition affecting many veterans of the 1991 Gulf War, characterized by fatigue, chronic headaches, and skin and respiratory disorders; **gulfweed** any brown alga of the genus *Sargassum*, members of which form dense floating masses in the Gulf Stream.
▸ **B** *verb*. **1** *verb intrans.* Move swiftly and strongly like a whirlpool; eddy, swirl. Long *rare.* M16.
2 *verb trans.* Engulf, swallow up (*lit. & fig.*). Also foll. by *down*, *in*, *up*. E19.
■ **gulfy** *adjective* (*a*) full of eddies or whirlpools, like a whirlpool; †(*b*) deep as an abyss; (*c*) full of hollows or depths: L16.

gulix /ˈɡjuːlɪks/ *noun*. L17.
[ORIGIN Dutch *Gulik* = Jülich in Germany.]
A kind of fine linen. Also ***gulix Holland***.

gull /ɡʌl/ *noun*[1]. LME.
[ORIGIN British: cf. Old Cornish *guilan*, Welsh *gwylan*, Breton *gouelan*, *gwelan* (whence French *goéland*).]
Any of numerous birds of the family Laridae, related to the terns, comprising long-winged gregarious mainly coastal birds that occur worldwide and are usually white with a grey or black mantle and a bright bill; *colloq.* a tern or skua.
herring gull, ***ivory gull***, ***Ross's gull***, ***wagel gull***, etc.
– COMB.: **gull-billed tern** a tern, *Gelochelidon nilotica*, found near water in temperate and subtropical parts of the western Palaearctic; **gull-wing** *noun & adjective* (*a*) *noun* an aeroplane wing composed of a shorter part sloping upwards from the fuselage and a longer part more nearly horizontal; (*b*) *adjective* designating a car door that opens upwards.
■ **gull-like** /-l-l-/ *adjective* resembling (that of) a gull L19.

gull /ɡʌl/ *noun*[2]. Now *dial.* LME.
[ORIGIN Prob. use as noun of GULL *adjective*.]
An unfledged bird; *esp.* a gosling.

gull /gʌl/ *noun*³. LME.
[ORIGIN Anglo-Norman *gule*, *gole*, Old French *gola*, *gole* (mod. *gueule* mouth) from Latin GULA *noun*¹. Cf. GOOL.]
†**1** The throat, the gullet. LME–M17.
2 A breach or channel made by a stream or torrent, a gully, (now *dial.*); a chasm, a fissure, (now *dial.*); GEOLOGY a fissure in rock produced by tension and filled with rock fragments. M16.

gull /gʌl/ *noun*⁴. L16.
[ORIGIN Perh. from GULL *adjective*. In sense 2 also infl. by GULL *verb*¹.]
1 A credulous person; a dupe, a fool. L16.
2 A trick, a deception, a fraud. Long *obsolete* exc. *Scot.* L16.
3 A trickster, a cheat; an impostor. *arch. slang.* E17.

†**gull** *adjective*. ME–L16.
[ORIGIN Old Norse *gulr* (Danish, Swedish *gul*) ult. from Indo-European base of YELLOW *adjective*.]
Yellow, pale.

gull /gʌl/ *verb*¹ *trans.* M16.
[ORIGIN Rel. to GULL *noun*⁴.]
1 Dupe; trick (*into*); deceive. M16.
†**2** Deprive *of* by trickery or deception; cheat *out of*. E17–L18.
■ **gullable** *adjective* = GULLIBLE E19.

gull /gʌl/ *verb*² *trans.* & *intrans.* Long *rare* exc. *dial.* L16.
[ORIGIN from GULL *noun*³.]
(Of water) make channels (in); wear by friction; wear *down*; sweep *away*.

Gullah /ˈgʌlə/ *adjective* & *noun*. US. M18.
[ORIGIN Uncertain: perh. abbreviation of *Angola*, or from GOLA *noun*².]
▸ **A** *adjective*. Pertaining to or designating black people living on the sea-islands and tidewater coastline of South Carolina. M18.
▸ **B** *noun*. **1** The dialect spoken by such people. L19.
2 A person from this region. M20.

gullery /ˈgʌləri/ *noun*¹. Now *rare* or *obsolete*. L16.
[ORIGIN from GULL *verb*¹ + -ERY.]
Deception, trickery, a deception, a trick.

gullery /ˈgʌləri/ *noun*². M19.
[ORIGIN from GULL *noun*¹ + -ERY.]
A place where gulls breed; a colony or roost of gulls.

gullet /ˈgʌlɪt/ *noun* & *verb*. LME.
[ORIGIN Old French *goulet* dim. of *go(u)le*: see GULES, -ET¹.]
▸ **A** *noun*. **1** The passage in the neck by which food passes from the mouth to the stomach. LME. ▸**b** The throat; the neck. M17.
†**2** A piece of armour or part of a hood covering the neck. LME–L15.
3 A water channel; a narrow, deep passage through which a stream flows; a strait; an estuary. Now *local*. LME.
4 a A long narrow piece of land. *dial.* M16. ▸**b** A gorge, a pass; a gully, a ravine; a narrow passage. Now chiefly *dial.* E17.
5 A hollow in front of each tooth of a saw, on alternate sides. M19.
▸ **B** *verb trans.* Make gullets in (a saw). L19.
■ **gulleting** *noun* †(*a*) swallowing, guzzling; (*b*) the action of the verb; (*c*) a groove in a rudder post to receive the rudder: M17.

gulley *noun* & *verb* var. of GULLY *noun*¹ & *verb*.

gullible /ˈgʌlɪb(ə)l/ *adjective*. E19.
[ORIGIN from GULL *verb*¹ + -IBLE.]
Easily cheated or duped; credulous.
■ **gulli'bility** *noun* L18. **gullibly** *adverb* L19.

gulli-gulli *noun* var. of GULLY-GULLY.

gullish /ˈgʌlɪʃ/ *adjective*. L16.
[ORIGIN from GULL *noun*⁴ + -ISH¹.]
Of the nature of a gull; foolish, credulous.

gully /ˈgʌli/ *noun*¹ & *verb*. Also **-ey**. M16.
[ORIGIN French *goulet*: see GULLET.]
▸ **A** *noun*. †**1** The gullet. Only in M16.
2 A channel or ravine worn in the earth by water, esp. on a mountain or hillside. M17.
3 A deep narrow artificial watercourse; a deep gutter, drain, or sink. M18.
4 A river valley. *Austral.* & *NZ*. M19.
5 CRICKET. (The position of) a fieldsman between point and the slips. E20.
– COMB.: **gully-hole** an opening from a street into a drain or sewer.
▸ **B** *verb trans.* Make gullies in. M18.
■ **gullied** *adjective* L18.

gully /ˈgʌli/ *noun*². *Scot.* & *N. English*. M16.
[ORIGIN Unknown.]
A large knife. Also ***gully-knife***.

gully-gully /ˈgʌlɪˌgʌli/ *interjection*. Also **gulli-gulli**. M20.
[ORIGIN Unknown.]
A conjuror's catch word.

gulose /ˈgjuːləʊz, -s/ *noun*. L19.
[ORIGIN Alt. of GLUCOSE.]
CHEMISTRY. An artificial hexose that is a stereoisomer of glucose.

gulosity /gjʊˈlɒsɪti/ *noun*. Now *rare*. L15.
[ORIGIN Late Latin *gulositas*, from *gulosus* gluttonous, formed as GULA *noun*¹: see -ITY.]
Gluttony, greediness, voracity.

gulp /gʌlp/ *noun*. L15.
[ORIGIN from the verb.]
1 The action or an act of gulping. L15. ▸**b** An effort to swallow; the noise caused by this; a choke. L19.
2 As much as is swallowed at a gulp; a mouthful. E17.

gulp /gʌlp/ *verb*. LME.
[ORIGIN Prob. from Middle Dutch *gulpen* swallow, guzzle: ult. origin imit.]
1 *verb trans.* & *intrans.* Swallow hastily or greedily, esp. in large draughts or pieces. Freq. foll. by *down*. LME. ▸**b** *verb trans.* Keep in or suppress as if by swallowing. Freq. foll. by *back*. M17.

> S. LEWIS He gulped a cup of coffee in the hope of pacifying his stomach. E. BOWEN The girl answered . . by making a bee line for the spring-water crock . . and thirstily gulping straight from the dipper. *fig.*: SIR W. SCOTT The worthy knight fairly gulped down the oaths.

2 *verb intrans.* Swallow only with difficulty; gasp, choke. M16.

> C. MACKENZIE The sergeant-major gulped in embarrassment.

■ **gulpin** *noun* [prob. from GULP *verb* + IN *adverb*] (*a*) a credulous person, a simpleton; (*b*) *nautical slang* a marine: E19. **gulpingly** *adverb* in a gulping manner, with a gulp E18. **gulpy** *adjective* marked by gulps or choking M19.

gulper /ˈgʌlpə/ *noun*. M17.
[ORIGIN from GULP *verb* + -ER¹.]
1 A person or thing that gulps. M17.
2 Any of various deep-sea eels of the order Saccopharyngiformes with very large jaws that open to give an enormous gape and with tiny eyes near the tip of the snout, esp. *Eupharynx pelecanoides*. Also ***gulper eel***. M20.

GUM *abbreviation*.
Genito-urinary medicine.

gum /gʌm/ *noun*¹.
[ORIGIN Old English *gōma*, corresp. to Old High German *guomo* gum, Old Norse *gómr* roof or floor of the mouth, fingertip, rel. to Old High German *goumo* (German *Gaumen* roof of the mouth).]
†**1** *sing.* & in *pl.* The inside of the mouth or throat. OE–M18.
2 In *pl.*, the firm flesh at the base of the teeth; *sing.* the part of this next to any one tooth. ME.
3 Impertinent talk, chatter. *obsolete* exc. *dial.* M18.
– COMB.: **gumboil** a small abscess on the gums; **gumshield** a pad worn to protect the teeth and gums, esp. by boxers.

gum /gʌm/ *noun*². ME.
[ORIGIN Old French *gomme* from Proto-Romance alt. of Latin *gummi* var. of *cummi* from Greek *kommi* from Egyptian *kemai*.]
▸ **I** A substance.
1 A viscous secretion of some trees and shrubs that hardens on drying but unlike a resin is soluble in water; a kind of this. Now also, any of various natural or synthetic polymers which dissolve or swell in water. ME. ▸**b** Such a substance used as a glue for paper etc., to stiffen textiles, and in food products, detergents, etc. LME. ▸†**c** A product of gum employed as a drug or perfume, or for burning as incense. Freq. in *pl.* LME–L18.
KAURI ***gum***. XANTHAN ***gum***.
2 The sticky secretion that collects in the inner corner of the eye. L16.
3 The viscous or waxy substance surrounding the filaments of raw silk. L18.
4 A mixture containing gelatin used for making sweets; a hard translucent sweet made from this (also ***gumdrop***). E19.
fruit gum, ***wine gum***, etc.
5 Chewing gum. M19.
6 A solid or semi-solid substance deposited by some petroleum products when stored for long periods or heated, formed by the oxidation of some constituents. E20.
▸ **II 7** In full ***gum tree***. A tree that exudes gum; *esp.* = EUCALYPTUS 1. Freq. preceded by specifying word. L17. ▸**b** A hollowed-out or otherwise adapted log, esp. from a gum tree, used as a beehive, water trough, etc. *US*. E19.
bluegum, ***flooded gum***, etc. ***black gum***: see BLACK *adjective*.
8 = GUMMOSIS. E18.
9 A gumboot; a galosh. *US*. M19.
– COMB.: ***gum acacia***: see ACACIA 1C; ***gum*** ADRAGANT; ***gum ammoniac***: see AMMONIAC *adjective* 2; ***gum*** ANIMÉ; ***gum arabic***: see ARABIC *adjective* 1; **gumball** *N. Amer.* a ball of chewing gum, usu. with a coloured sugar coating; ***gum benzoin***: see BENZOIN 1; **gumboot** a long rubber boot; ***gum*** COPAL; ***gumdrop***: see sense 4 above; ***gum*** ELEMI; **gum ivy** the congealed juice of the stem of the ivy; **gum juniper** sandarac; **gum lac** an inferior grade of lac from Madagascar; ***gum mastic***: see MASTIC *noun* 1; ***gum*** OLIBANUM; **gum resin** a vegetable secretion of resin mixed with gum, e.g. gamboge; ***gum sandarac***: see SANDARAC 3; ***gum storax***: see STORAX 1; ***gum succory***: see SUCCORY 2; **gumsucker** *Austral.* [from sense 1] (a nickname for) a native-born Australian, esp. a Victorian; ***gum thus***: see THUS *noun*; ***gum*** TRAGACANTH; **gum tree** (*a*) see sense 7 above; (*b*) ***up a gum tree*** (*colloq.*), unable to escape, in a predicament, in great difficulties (cf. ***up a tree*** s.v. TREE *noun*). **gum-water** a solution of gum arabic in water; **gum-wood** (the wood of) a gum tree.

gum /gʌm/ *noun*³. Orig. *Scot.* L18.
[ORIGIN Uncertain: perh. rel. to CULM *noun*¹, COOM.]
MINING. Coal dust, fine coal; now *esp.* that produced by a coal-cutting machine.
■ **gumming** *noun* (*a*) the clearing away of gum during the operation of a coal-cutting machine; (*b*) in *pl.*, fine particles of gum: M20.

gum /gʌm/ *noun*⁴. E19.
[ORIGIN Alt.]
God: used in oaths and exclams.
by gum!, ***my gum!***, etc.

gum /gʌm/ *verb*¹. Infl. **-mm-**. LME.
[ORIGIN from GUM *noun*².]
†**1** *verb trans.* Treat with aromatic gums. LME–L15.
2 *verb trans.* Fasten or fix in position with gum or other sticky substance. Also foll. by *down*, *together*, *up*. L16.
3 *verb trans.* Stiffen with gum; coat or smear with gum. E17.
4 *verb intrans.* **a** Of a fruit tree: exude gum as a result of disease. L18. ▸**b** Of a petroleum product: turn into or deposit gum. Chiefly as ***gumming verbal noun***. L19.
5 *verb trans.* Cheat, delude, humbug. *US slang*. M19.
6 a *verb intrans.* Foll. by *up*: (of a machine) become clogged or obstructed with a viscous substance, such as dried oil. E20. ▸**b** *verb trans. fig.* Interfere with the smooth running of; spoil, wreck. Usu. foll. by *up*, esp. in ***gum up the works***. Orig. *US*. E20.

G

gum /gʌm/ *verb*² *trans.* Infl. **-mm-**. L18.
[ORIGIN from GUM *noun*¹.]
Deepen and enlarge the spaces between the teeth of (a worn saw).

Gumban /ˈgʌmb(ə)n/ *adjective* & *noun*. M20.
[ORIGIN from Kikuyu *Gumba*, a diminutive people believed to have been former inhabitants of Kikuyu country: see -AN.]
ARCHAEOLOGY. (Designating or pertaining to) a late Stone Age culture of E. Africa.

gumbo /ˈgʌmbəʊ/ *noun*. *N. Amer.* Pl. **-os**. E19.
[ORIGIN Of African origin: cf. Bantu (Angolan) *kingombo* (with prefix *ki-*) okra.]
1 Okra. Also, a spicy chicken or seafood soup thickened with okra pods, rice, filé, etc. E19.
chicken gumbo, ***shrimp gumbo***.
2 A fine clayey soil that becomes sticky and impervious when wet. Also, thick clinging mud. M19.
3 (**G-**.) A French-based creole language spoken in Louisiana. M19.
– COMB.: **gumbo filé** (*a*) gumbo soup thickened with filé; (*b*) filé as used to thicken gumbo soup.

gumbo-limbo /gʌmbəʊˈlɪmbəʊ/ *noun*. Pl. **-os**. M19.
[ORIGIN from GUMBO *noun* + 2nd elem. of unknown origin. Perh. alt. of *gum elemi*.]
A deciduous tree of Florida, Central America, and the W. Indies, *Bursera simaruba* (family Burseraceae), a source of gum elemi.

gumbotil /ˈgʌmbətɪl/ *noun*. E20.
[ORIGIN from GUMBO + TILL *noun*³.]
A leached grey clay, very sticky when wet and very hard when dry, formed in regions of poor drainage by the weathering of clay-rich till.

gum-gum /ˈgʌmgʌm/ *noun*. Now *rare*. E18.
[ORIGIN Prob. from Malay. Cf. GONG-GONG.]
A musical instrument consisting of an iron bowl which is struck with an iron or wooden stick; a series of these of different sizes and pitches.

gumlah /ˈgʌmlə/ *noun*. M19.
[ORIGIN Hindi *gamlā*.]
In the Indian subcontinent, an earthenware water jar.

gumly /ˈgʌmli/ *adjective*. *Scot.* & *dial.* Now *rare* or *obsolete*. L18.
[ORIGIN Unknown.]
Muddy, turbid; gloomy.

gumma /ˈgʌmə/ *noun*. Pl. **-as**, **-ata** /-ətə/. E18.
[ORIGIN mod. Latin from Latin *gummi* GUM *noun*².]
MEDICINE. A granulomatous lesion characteristic of tertiary syphilis, with a firm rubbery core of dead tissue.
■ **gummatous** *adjective* of the nature of or resembling a gumma; characterized by gummas: L17.

gummed /gʌmd/ *adjective*¹. ME.
[ORIGIN from GUM *noun*² or *verb*¹: see -ED², -ED¹.]
Mixed with gum; coated, smeared, or stiffened with gum.

gummed /gʌmd/ *adjective*². E16.
[ORIGIN from GUM *noun*¹ + -ED².]
That has gums (of a specified kind).

gummer /ˈgʌmə/ *noun*¹. *N. Amer.* M19.
[ORIGIN from GUM *verb*² + -ER¹.]
A person who or machine which gums saws.

gummer /ˈgʌmə/ *noun*². L19.
[ORIGIN from GUM *verb*¹ + -ER¹.]
A person who applies gum.

gummer /ˈgʌmə/ *noun*³. E20.
[ORIGIN from GUM *noun*³ + -ER¹.]
A person who or machine which removes the gum from under a coal-cutting machine.

G

Gummidge /ˈɡʌmɪdʒ/ *noun & verb*. **L19**.
[**ORIGIN** Mrs *Gummidge*, a character in Dickens's *David Copperfield*.]
▸ **A** *noun*. Peevish, self-pitying, and pessimistic complaining; a person who indulges in this. **L19**.
▸ **B** *verb intrans*. Complain in this manner. **L19**.

gummite /ˈɡʌmʌɪt/ *noun*. **M19**.
[**ORIGIN** from **GUM** *noun*[2] + **-ITE**[1].]
MINERALOGY. A reddish-yellow hydrated uranium oxide that resembles gum.

gummosis /ɡəˈməʊsɪs/ *noun*. **L19**.
[**ORIGIN** from **GUM** *noun*[2] + **-OSIS**.]
The production and exudation of gum by a diseased tree; a disease of fruit trees marked by this.

†**gummosity** *noun*. **LME**.
[**ORIGIN** medieval Latin *gummositas*, formed as **GUMMOUS** *adjective*[2]: see **-OSITY**.]
1 A gummy substance, deposit, or concretion. **LME–L17**.
2 The quality of being gummy or resembling gum; *ALCHEMY* a supposed attribute of metals. **M17–E18**.

gummous /ˈɡʌməs/ *adjective*[1]. **L16**.
[**ORIGIN** from **GUMMA** + **-OUS**.]
= **GUMMATOUS**.

gummous /ˈɡʌməs/ *adjective*[2]. **M17**.
[**ORIGIN** Latin *gummosus*, from *gummi* **GUM** *noun*[2]: see **-OUS**.]
Of the nature of gum, resembling gum.

gummy /ˈɡʌmi/ *noun & adjective*[1]. **L19**.
[**ORIGIN** from **GUM** *noun*[1] + **-Y**[6].]
▸ **A** *noun*. **1** A small shark, *Mustelus antarcticus*, with rounded teeth that is found off the south coasts of Australia and New Zealand, where it is fished commercially for food. Also ***gummy shark***. **L19**.
2 A sheep that has lost or is losing some teeth. *Austral. & NZ*. **L19**.
3 A toothless person; an old person. *Austral. slang*. **E20**.
▸ **B** *adjective*. Toothless. **E20**.
▪ **gummily** *adverb* **M20**.

gummy /ˈɡʌmi/ *adjective*[2]. **LME**.
[**ORIGIN** from **GUM** *noun*[2] + **-Y**[1].]
1 Of the nature of gum, resembling gum; sticky, viscid. **LME**.
2 Suffused with or exuding gum. **LME**.

> TENNYSON I came and lay Beneath those gummy chestnutbuds. P. D. JAMES She looked . . at the eyes, still gummy with sleep.

3 Of an ankle or leg: puffy, swollen. **M18**.
▪ **gumminess** *noun* (*a*) the quality or condition of being gummy; (*b*) something gummy: **E17**.

gummy /ˈɡʌmi/ *adjective*[3]. **M19**.
[**ORIGIN** from **GUMMA** + **-Y**[1].]
MEDICINE. Gummatous.

gump /ɡʌmp/ *noun*[1]. *dial. & US*. Also **gumph** /ɡʌmf/. **E19**.
[**ORIGIN** Unknown.]
A foolish person, a dolt.

gump /ɡʌmp/ *noun*[2]. *US slang*. **E20**.
[**ORIGIN** Perh. same word as **GUMP** *noun*[1].]
A chicken.

gump /ɡʌmp/ *noun*[3]. Also **gumph** /ɡʌmf/. **E20**.
[**ORIGIN** Abbreviation.]
= **GUMPTION** 1.

gumph *noun*[1] var. of **GUMP** *noun*[1].

gumph *noun*[2] var. of **GUMP** *noun*[3].

gumpheon /ˈɡʌmfɪən/ *noun*. *Scot*. Long *rare* or *obsolete*. **E18**.
[**ORIGIN** Alt. of **GONFANON** or **GONFALON**.]
A funeral banner.

gumption /ˈɡʌm(p)ʃ(ə)n/ *noun*. Orig. *Scot*. **E18**.
[**ORIGIN** Unknown.]
1 Common sense; ready practical sense; initiative, enterprising spirit, courage. *colloq*. **E18**.

> J. WAINWRIGHT If he'd any gumption he'd give himself up.

2 *PAINTING*. The art of preparing colours. Also, a vehicle for colours. Now *rare*. **E19**.
▪ **gumptionless** *adjective* **E19**.

gumptious /ˈɡʌm(p)ʃəs/ *adjective*. Now *rare*. **M19**.
[**ORIGIN** from **GUMPTION** by assoc. with *bumptious*.]
Clever; vain, self-important.

gumshoe /ˈɡʌmʃuː/ *noun & verb*. **M19**.
[**ORIGIN** from **GUM** *noun*[2] + **SHOE** *noun*.]
▸ **A** *noun*. **1** A galosh. **M19**.
2 A stealthy action. *colloq*. **E20**.
3 A detective; a police officer. *N. Amer. colloq*. **E20**.
▸ **B** *verb intrans*. Pres. pple & verbal noun **-shoeing**. Move or act stealthily; act as a police officer or a detective. *colloq*. (orig. *US*). **E20**.

Gumza *noun* var. of **GAMZA**.

gun /ɡʌn/ *noun*. **ME**.
[**ORIGIN** Prob. from application to ballistae etc. of pet form (in Swedish dial. *Gunne*) of Scandinavian female name *Gunnhildr*, from *gunnr* + *hildr* both meaning 'war'.]
▸ **I** †**1** Any large piece of equipment used in medieval warfare. **ME–M16**.
2 A weapon consisting of a large metal tube mounted on a carriage or fixed substructure from which missiles are expelled by the force of an explosion; a cannon. **ME**. ▸**b** The firing of such a weapon as a salute or signal; the time of such a signal. **E17**.

> J. G. FARRELL They had two camel guns, small cannons which could be . . fired from the backs of camels. **b** A. WEST Sleeping till the morning gun.

3 Any portable firearm (formerly, excluding the pistol). **LME**. ▸**b** *spec*. in *ATHLETICS*. The starting pistol; the start of a race. **E20**.

> **b** *Swimming Times* Andrew Jameson was going all out for gold as he led from the gun.

4 A member of a shooting party; a gunner; *N. Amer*. a gunman. **E19**.
5 A hand-held device from which a substance can be discharged at will by means of compressed air etc. (freq. with defining word); *US slang* a hypodermic syringe used by drug addicts. **L19**.
grease gun, ***popgun***, etc. ***airgun***: see **AIR** *noun*[1].
6 = ***electron gun*** s.v. **ELECTRON** *noun*[2]. **E20**.
▸ **II** *transf*. **7** [Cf. **GAWN**.] A flagon of ale. *slang & dial*. (now *rare* or *obsolete*). **M17**.
8 A tobacco pipe. *slang* or *joc*. Now only *Scot*. **E18**.
9 A thief or villain. *slang*. **M19**.
10 [Cf. ***big gun*** s.v. **BIG** *adjective*.] A person expert at an activity, esp. sheep-shearing. *Austral. & NZ*. **L19**.
11 In *pl*. A gunnery officer. *nautical slang*. **E20**.
12 A large heavy surfboard used for riding big waves. **M20**.
– **PHRASES**: **(as) sure as a gun** beyond all question. **at gunpoint** under threat of injury from a gun. **beat the gun** = ***jump the gun*** below. ***big gun***: see **BIG** *adjective*. ***blow great guns***: see **BLOW** *verb*[1]. **give her the gun**, **give it the gun**, etc. *colloq*. = **GUN** *verb* 5b. **go great guns** *colloq*. have a run of success; proceed rapidly or vigorously towards success. **great gun** †(*a*) a piece of ordnance, a cannon; (*b*) = ***big gun*** s.v. **BIG** *adjective*. **have the guns for** have the ability or strength for. **jump the gun** start before the signal is given; *fig*. act before the proper time. **son of a gun** *colloq*. a chap, a fellow. **stick to one's guns** maintain one's position under attack (*lit. & fig*.). ***sure as a gun***: see **(as) *sure as a gun*** above.
– **COMB**.: **gun carriage** a wheeled support of a gun; **gun cotton** nitrocellulose, made by steeping cotton or wood pulp in a mixture of nitric and sulphuric acids; *esp*. a highly nitrated form used as an explosive and a smokeless powder for guns; **gun deck** a deck of a ship on which guns are placed; *spec*. (*hist*.) the lowest such deck on a ship of the line; **gun dog** a dog trained to retrieve etc. for a gamekeeper or the members of a shoot; a dog of a breed suited to such training; **gunfight** *colloq*. a fight with revolvers; **gunfighter** *colloq*. a person who frequently participates in gunfights; **gun-harpoon**: fired from a gun instead of being thrown by hand; **gun-layer** a person, esp. a soldier, whose task is to aim a large gun; ***gunlock***: see **LOCK** *noun*[2] 3; ***gun-lascar***: see **LASCAR** 2; **gunman** a man armed with a gun; an assassin who uses a gun; **gunmetal** (*a*) orig., a bronze used for guns; now, an alloy of copper, tin, and a small amount of zinc; (*b*) a dull bluish-grey colour (freq. *attrib*. or as *adjective*); **gun microphone**: with a number of parallel tubes of different length in front of the diaphragm to increase its directional property; **gun moll** *slang* (*a*) a gangster's mistress; (*b*) an armed woman criminal; **gun-pit** an excavation to protect guns and gun crews from enemy fire; **gunplay** (skill in) the use of firearms; a fight with firearms; **gunpower** the number and strength of guns available; **gun-range** (*a*) the range of a gun's fire; (*b*) a place where the firing of guns is practised; **gunroom** (*a*) a room in a house for keeping sporting guns etc.; (*b*) a compartment in a warship orig. occupied by the gun crew, but now fitted up for junior officers or as a lieutenants' mess room; **gunrunner** a person engaged in gunrunning; **gunrunning** the smuggling or illegal transportation of firearms and ammunition into a country; ***gun shearer***: see sense 10 above; **gunship** a heavily armed helicopter; **gunshot** (*a*) (*a*) shot fired from a gun; (*b*) the range of a gun (chiefly in ***out of gunshot***, ***within gunshot***); **gun-shy** *adjective* (esp. of a sporting dog) frightened by the report of a gun; *fig*. nervous and apprehensive. **gun-site** an emplacement, usu. fortified, for guns; **gunslinger** *colloq*. (*a*) = ***gunman*** above; (*b*) *US* a forceful and adventurous participant in a particular sphere; ***gun slip***: see **SLIP** *noun*[3] 4d; **gunsmith** a maker and repairer of small firearms; **gunstock** (*a*) the wooden mounting of a gun barrel; †(*b*) the support of a cannon on board ship; **gunstone** †(*a*) a cannonball; a bullet; (*b*) *HERALDRY* an ogress, a pellet.

gun /ɡʌn/ *verb*. Infl. **-nn-**. **E17**.
[**ORIGIN** from **GUN** *noun*.]
1 *verb intrans*. Shoot with a gun; go shooting. **E17**.
2 *verb trans*. Shoot at; *esp*. shoot *down*. **L17**.

> *Times* Police 'gunned down innocent man by mistake.'

3 *verb trans*. Look at closely, examine. *colloq*. **E19**.
4 *verb intrans*. Foll. by *for*: go in search of with a gun; seek to attack, harm, or destroy; go determinedly or energetically after. **L19**.

> B. FRIEDAN She doesn't realise how lucky she is—her own boss, . . no junior executive gunning for her job.

5 a *verb trans*. Accelerate (a vehicle); open the throttle of (an engine). **M20**. ▸**b** *verb intrans*. Accelerate; drive or move *off* quickly. **M20**.

> **a** S. BELLOW He gunned his motor at the stoplight. S. KING He left the store and gunned the Harley into life. **b** N. ALLEY We gunned into an easy takeoff.

guna /ˈɡuːnə/ *noun*. **E19**.
[**ORIGIN** Sanskrit *guṇa*.]
1 *SANSKRIT GRAMMAR*. The middle grade of an ablaut series of vowels; the process of raising a vowel to the middle grade (considered to be produced by the prefixing of *a*). **E19**.
2 *HINDUISM*. In Sankhya philosophy, each of the three dominating principles of nature. **M19**.
▪ ***gunate*** *verb trans*. (*SANSKRIT GRAMMAR*) subject to the process of guna **M19**.

gunboat /ˈɡʌnbəʊt/ *noun*. **L18**.
[**ORIGIN** from **GUN** *noun* + **BOAT** *noun*.]
1 A small vessel of shallow draught (fitted for) carrying relatively heavy guns. **L18**.
2 Large shoes; large feet. Usu. in *pl*. *US slang*. **L19**.
– **COMB**.: **gunboat diplomacy**: supported by the use or threatened use of military force.

gundi /ˈɡʌndi/ *noun*. **L18**.
[**ORIGIN** N. African Arabic]
Any rodent of the family Ctenodactylidae, the members of which resemble guinea pigs and live on rock outcrops in the deserts of N. and E. Africa.

gundy /ˈɡʌndi, ˈɡʊndi/ *noun*. *Austral*. Also **goondie** /ˈɡuːndi/. **L19**.
[**ORIGIN** Either from Yuwaaliyaay (an Australian Aboriginal language of northern New South Wales) and Kamilaroi *gundhi*, or from Wiradhuri *gunday* stringy bark.]
An Aboriginal hut; = **GUNYAH**.

†**gundy-gut** *noun*. **L18–E20**.
[**ORIGIN** from *gundy* of unknown origin + **GUT** *noun* (cf. *greedy-guts*).]
A fat paunch; in *pl*., a greedy person.

gunfire /ˈɡʌnfʌɪə/ *noun*. **E19**.
[**ORIGIN** from **GUN** *noun* + **FIRE** *noun*.]
1 The firing of a gun or guns, esp. rapidly and repeatedly; *NAUTICAL & MILITARY* the time of the morning or evening gun. **E19**.
2 An early morning cup of tea served to troops before going on first parade. *military slang*. **E20**.

gunge /ɡʌn(d)ʒ/ *noun*[1]. **L18**.
[**ORIGIN** Persian & Urdu *ganj* store, store-house, market.]
An Indian market.

gunge /ɡʌn(d)ʒ/ *noun*[2]. *colloq*. **M20**.
[**ORIGIN** Uncertain: cf. **GOO** *noun*, **GUNK**.]
A sticky or viscid mass; any messy clogging substance, esp. one considered otherwise unidentifiable.
▪ **gungy** *adjective* **L20**.

gung-ho /ɡʌŋˈhəʊ/ *adjective*. **M20**.
[**ORIGIN** Chinese *gōnghé*, taken as 'work together', adopted as a slogan in the Second World War by the US Marines.]
Enthusiastic, eager.

> A. TAN I can just see her now, wowing the angels with her Chinese cooking and gung-ho attitude. B. ELTON Public interest in the army was unprecedented, with gung-ho movies like *Rambo* and *Top Gun* filling the cinemas.

gunibri *noun* var. of **GIMBRI**.

gunite /ˈɡʌnʌɪt/ *noun*. **E20**.
[**ORIGIN** from **GUN** *noun* + **-ITE**[1].]
BUILDING. A mixture of cement, sand, and water applied through a hose.

gunk /ɡʌŋk/ *noun*. Orig. *US*. **M20**.
[**ORIGIN** Uncertain: cf. **GUNK HOLE**.]
1 Also **G-**. (Proprietary name for) a detergent used for heavy-duty cleaning. **M20**.
2 Any viscous or liquid substance. *colloq*. **M20**.

> D. DELILLO He had jellified gunk all over his mouth and tongue.

3 A person. *slang. derog*. **M20**.

gunkhole /ɡʌŋkhəʊl/ *noun*. *colloq*. (chiefly *N. Amer*.). **E20**.
[**ORIGIN** Unknown.]
NAUTICAL. A shallow inlet or cove difficult or dangerous to navigate because of mud, rocks, etc.
▪ **gunkholing** *noun* cruising around gunkholes **L20**.

gunless /ˈɡʌnlɪs/ *adjective*. **M19**.
[**ORIGIN** from **GUN** *noun* + **-LESS**.]
Having no gun.

Gunn /ɡʌn/ *noun*. **M20**.
[**ORIGIN** J. B. *Gunn* (b. 1928), physicist.]
ELECTRONICS. ***Gunn effect***, an effect in some semiconductors in which a constant electric field greater than a threshold value, applied between opposite faces of a thin piece of the material, results in an oscillatory current with a frequency in the microwave region. Hence ***Gunn diode***, a semiconductor diode in which the Gunn effect occurs.

gunned /ɡʌnd/ *adjective*. **M17**.
[**ORIGIN** from **GUN** *noun* + **-ED**[2].]
Provided with guns. Chiefly with qualifying adverb.

gunnel /ˈɡʌn(ə)l/ *noun*[1]. **L17**.
[**ORIGIN** Unknown.]
Any of various small slender fishes of the family Pholidae, found along the Atlantic and Pacific coasts; *spec*. the butterfish, *Pholis gunnellus*, of Atlantic coastal and intertidal waters.

gunnel *noun*² var. of GUNWALE.

gunner /ˈɡʌnə/ *noun*. ME.
[ORIGIN from GUN *noun* after Anglo-Norman analogies: see -ER². Cf. Anglo-Latin *gunnarius*.]
1 A person who operates a gun, esp. a large one. Now chiefly, an artillery soldier, *esp.* (in official use) a private. ME. ▸**b** *hist.* A warrant officer in the navy in charge of the battery, ordnance stores, etc. L15. ▸**c** A member of an aircraft crew who operates a gun. E20.
Master Gunner (*a*) orig., the chief gunner in charge of ordnance and ammunition; now only as an honorary title conferred on a distinguished soldier; (*b*) a Royal Artillery warrant officer in charge of the stores and equipment in a fort or other armed place.
2 A gunsmith. *obsolete* exc. *dial.* LME.
3 A person who shoots game. M18.
4 With number prefixed: a vessel carrying a specified number of guns. E19.
– COMB.: **gunner's daughter** *joc.* the gun to which a sailor, esp. a boy serving on warship, was lashed for flogging.

gunnera /ˈɡʌn(ə)rə, ɡʌˈnɪərə/ *noun*. L18.
[ORIGIN mod. Latin (see below), from J. E. *Gunnerus* (1718–73), Norwegian botanist.]
Any of various plants of the genus *Gunnera* (family Gunneraceae); esp. *G. tinctoria* and *G. manicata*, gigantic S. American plants with palmate leaves, often grown as waterside ornamentals.

gunnery /ˈɡʌnəri/ *noun*. L15.
[ORIGIN from GUN *noun* + -ERY.]
1 Guns collectively. *rare*. L15.
2 The construction and management of guns, esp. large ones. E17.
3 The firing of guns; the use of guns in hunting. E19.

gunnis /ˈɡʌnɪs/ *noun*. Also **-ies**. L18.
[ORIGIN Prob. from Cornish *gonys* working.]
MINING. A crevice; a space left by the working of a lode.

gunny /ˈɡʌni/ *noun & adjective*. E18.
[ORIGIN Marathi *gōṇī* from Sanskrit *goṇī* sack.]
▸**A** *noun*. A coarse material made from jute or sunn fibre, used chiefly for sacking; a sack made of this. E18.
▸**B** *adjective*. Made of gunny. E19.
– COMB.: **gunny bag**, **gunnysack**: made of gunny or similar material.

gunpowder /ˈɡʌnpaʊdə/ *noun & adjective*. LME.
[ORIGIN from GUN *noun* + POWDER *noun*¹.]
▸**A** *noun*. **1** A low-explosive powder consisting of a mixture of potassium nitrate, ground charcoal, and sulphur, used for fuses, fireworks, and blasting and in muzzle-loading guns. LME.
2 In full *gunpowder tea*. A fine kind of green tea, each leaf of which is rolled up into a pellet. L18.
– COMB.: **Gunpowder Plot** *hist.* the conspiracy to blow up James I and Parliament at Westminster on 5 November 1605; *gunpowder tea*: see sense 2 above.
▸**B** *adjective*. Easily angered, fiery. L16.
■ †**gunpowdered** *adjective* (*a*) charged with gunpowder; (*b*) = GUNPOWDER *adjective*; (*c*) begrimed with gunpowder: M16–E18. **gunpowdery** *adjective* of, pertaining to, or characteristic of gunpowder; *fig.* fiery, easily angered: M19.

gunsel /ˈɡʌns(ə)l/ *noun*. *US slang*. E20.
[ORIGIN Yiddish *gendzel* = German *Gänslein* gosling, little goose; in sense 2 infl. by GUN *noun*.]
1 A naive youth; a homosexual youth, *esp.* a passive one kept by a tramp. E20.
2 An informer; a criminal, a gunman. M20.

Gunter /ˈɡʌntə/ *noun*. L17.
[ORIGIN Edmund *Gunter* (1581–1626), English mathematician.]
1 *Gunter's chain*, a surveyor's chain 66 feet long, the use of which gave rise to this distance as a unit of length (cf. CHAIN *noun* 6b). L17.
2 (Also **g-**.) A long ruler graduated on one side with trigonometrical and other functions and on the other side with the logarithms of these, formerly used in surveying and navigation. Also more fully *Gunter's scale*. E18.
3 NAUTICAL. Orig., a type of rig in which the topmast slides up and down the lower mast on rings. Now, a fore-and-aft sail whose spar is nearly vertical, so that the sail is nearly triangular. Also *Gunter rig*. L18.

gunwale /ˈɡʌn(ə)l/ *noun*. Also **gunnel**, **gunwhale**. LME.
[ORIGIN from GUN *noun* + WALE *noun*¹, having formerly been used to support guns.]
The upper edge of a ship's side; in large wooden vessels, the uppermost planking covering the timber heads.

> M. RULE I held on to my mask, sat on the gunwale and fell backwards into the sea. P. SCOTT She has ridden . . low, laden heavily to the gunwales.

gunwale to, **gunwale under** level with, below, the surface of the water.

gunyah /ˈɡʌnjə/ *noun*. *Austral.* E19.
[ORIGIN Dharuk *ganyi*.]
An Aboriginal hut; a bush hut.

gunyang /ˈɡʌnjaŋ/ *noun*. M19.
[ORIGIN Ganay.]
Any of several Australian shrubby nightshades of the genus *Solanum*, esp. *S. vescum*, with edible greenish berries.

Günz /ɡʊnts, *foreign* ɡynts/ *adjective & noun*. E20.
[ORIGIN A river near the Alps in southern Germany.]
GEOLOGY. (Designating or pertaining to) a middle Pleistocene glaciation in the Alps, preceding the Mindel and possibly corresponding to the Menapian of northern Europe.

Guomindang *noun* var. of KUOMINTANG.

gup /ɡʌp/ *noun*. *colloq.* (orig. *Indian*). E19.
[ORIGIN Urdu from Persian *gap*.]
Gossip, chatter; silly talk, nonsense.

guppie /ˈɡʌpi/ *noun*¹. *colloq.* Also **-y**. L20.
[ORIGIN Blend of GAY *adjective* and YUPPIE *noun*.]
A homosexual yuppie.

guppie /ˈɡʌpi/ *noun*². *colloq.* Also **-y**. L20.
[ORIGIN Blend of GREEN *adjective* and YUPPIE *noun*.]
A yuppie who professes concern about the environment and ecological issues.

guppy /ˈɡʌpi/ *noun*¹. E20.
[ORIGIN R. J. L. *Guppy* (1836–1916), who sent the first specimen to the British Museum.]
A small topminnow, *Poecilia reticulata*, of the W. Indies and S. America, popular as an aquarium fish. Also called ***millions (fish)***.

guppy *noun*², *noun*³ vars. of GUPPIE *noun*¹, *noun*².

Gupta /ˈɡʊptə/ *adjective & noun*. L19.
[ORIGIN from *Candragupta*, the founder of the dynasty.]
(A member) of a dynasty which ruled in northern India from the 4th to the 6th cents.

gur /ˈɡʊə/ *noun*. Also **ghoor**, **goor**. L17.
[ORIGIN Hindi *gur*, Marathi *gūr* from Sanskrit *guḍa*.]
In the Indian subcontinent: unrefined sugar, molasses.

gurdwara /ɡʊəˈdwɑːrə, ɡəːˈdwɑːrə/ *noun*. E20.
[ORIGIN Punjabi *gurduārā*, from Sanskrit GURU + *dvāra* door.]
A Sikh temple.

gurge /ɡəːdʒ/ *noun*. M17.
[ORIGIN Latin *gurges*.]
1 A swirling mass of liquid; a whirlpool. Chiefly *poet.* M17.
2 HERALDRY. A charge representing a whirlpool, consisting of a spiral of two narrow bands, usu. blazoned argent and azure. M19.

gurge /ɡəːdʒ/ *verb intrans.* E16.
[ORIGIN formed as GURGE *noun*.]
Esp. of water: rise or swell turbulently.

gurgeons /ˈɡəːdʒ(ə)nz/ *noun pl.* Now *dial.* Also **grudgeons**. L15.
[ORIGIN Uncertain: cf. French †*grugeons* lumps of crystalline sugar in brown sugar, rel. to *gruger* to crunch.]
Coarse meal; the coarse refuse from flour.

gurgeon stopper /ˈɡəːdʒ(ə)n ˈstɒpə/ *noun phr.* L19.
[ORIGIN Origin of 1st elem. uncertain: cf. GURJUN. See STOPPER *noun* 5.]
A hardwood tree, *Eugenia foetida*, of the myrtle family, occurring in Florida and the W. Indies.

gurges /ˈɡəːdʒiːz/ *noun*. LME.
[ORIGIN Latin.]
1 = GURGE *noun* 1. Also (*dial.*) a lake, a fish pond. LME.
2 HERALDRY. = GURGE *noun* 2. LME.

gurgitate /ˈɡəːdʒɪteɪt/ *verb*. M17.
[ORIGIN Late Latin *gurgitat-* pa. ppl stem of *gurgitare*: see GURGITATION, -ATE³.]
†**1** *verb trans.* Swallow, devour. *rare*. Only in M17.
2 *verb trans. & intrans.* Discharge or be discharged with a swirling motion. E20.

gurgitation /ɡəːdʒɪˈteɪʃ(ə)n/ *noun*. M16.
[ORIGIN from late Latin *gurgitat-*, pa. ppl stem of *gurgitare* engulf, formed as GURGES: see -ATION.]
1 The action of swallowing or absorbing. *rare*. M16.
2 Surging or swirling motion of a liquid etc. L19.

gurgle /ˈɡəːɡ(ə)l/ *noun*. M16.
[ORIGIN from the verb.]
†**1** A gargle. Only in M16.
2 A gurgling sound or cry. M18.

gurgle /ˈɡəːɡ(ə)l/ *verb*. LME.
[ORIGIN Prob. imit., if not directly from similarly formed words such as Middle Low German, Dutch *gorgelen*, German *gurgeln*, medieval Latin *gurgulare*, all ult. from Latin *gurgulio* gullet.]
▸**I 1** *verb intrans.* Make a bubbling sound as of liquid escaping intermittently from a bottle or of water flowing among stones; flow with such a sound. LME.

> T. SHARPE The radiators gurgled gently. E. FIGES He could hear fresh water gurgling through the sluice.

2 *verb intrans.* Utter broken guttural cries. M18.

> D. MORRIS A baby may gurgle and burble, but it does not laugh.

3 *verb trans.* Utter with gurgling cries. E19.
▸†**II 4** *verb intrans.* Gargle. M16–E17.
■ **gurgler** *noun* a person who or thing which gurgles; *spec.* (*Austral. & NZ colloq.*) a plughole (***down the gurgler***, = ***down the drain*** s.v. DOWN *preposition*): L20. **gurglingly** *adverb* in a gurgling way L19. **gurgly** *adjective* characterized by gurgling L19.

gurjun /ˈɡəːdʒ(ə)n/ *noun*. Also **-jan**, **-jon**. M19.
[ORIGIN Bengali *garjan*.]
Any of various large Indian trees of the genus *Dipterocarpus* (family Dipterocarpaceae) which are sources of gurjun oil.
– COMB.: **gurjun balsam**, **gurjun oil** a viscid resin obtained from trees of the genus *Dipterocarpus* and formerly used as a varnish and medicinally.

gurk /ɡəːk/ *verb & noun*. *colloq.* E20.
[ORIGIN Imit.]
▸**A** *verb intrans.* Emit a belch. E20.
▸**B** *noun*. A belch. M20.

Gurkha /ˈɡəːkə, ˈɡʊəkə/ *noun & adjective*. Also (*arch.*) **G(h)oorkha**. E19.
[ORIGIN Name of locality from Sanskrit *gorakṣa* cowherd (from *go* cow + *rakṣ-* protect) as epithet of patron deity.]
▸**A** *noun*. A member of the principal Hindu community in Nepal, renowned for its military prowess and forming special regiments in the British army. E19.
▸**B** *attrib.* or as *adjective*. Of or pertaining to the Gurkhas. E19.

Gurkhali /ɡəːˈkɑːli/ *noun*. L19.
[ORIGIN formed as GURKHA.]
1 A Gurkha. Only in *pl.* L19.
2 The Indo-Aryan language of the Gurkhas. E20.

gurl /ɡəːl/ *adjective & noun*. E16.
[ORIGIN Rel. to GURL *verb*.]
▸**A** *adjective*. = GURLY 1. *Scot.* E16.
▸**B** *noun*. A growl; rough weather. Now *Scot.* M18.

gurl /ɡəːl/ *verb intrans.* Now *Scot.* LME.
[ORIGIN Imit.: cf. GURL *adjective & noun*, *growl*.]
Of a dog etc.: growl. Of the stomach: rumble. Of the wind: roar, howl.

gurly /ˈɡəːli/ *adjective*. *Scot.* E18.
[ORIGIN from GURL *verb* + -Y¹.]
1 Of weather, the wind, etc.: rough, stormy. E18.
2 Surly, bad-tempered. E18.

Gurmukhi /ˈɡʊəmʊki/ *noun & adjective*. M19.
[ORIGIN Punjabi, from Sanskrit GURU + *mukha* mouth.]
▸**A** *noun*. The script used by Sikhs; the Punjabi language as written in this script. M19.
▸**B** *adjective*. Of or designating this script or language. M19.

gurnard /ˈɡəːnəd/ *noun*. Also **-net** /-nɪt/. Pl. **-s**, same. ME.
[ORIGIN Old French *gornart*, from *gronir* by-form of *grondir* from Latin *grundire*, *grunnire* GRUNT *verb*: see -ARD. Cf. Anglo-Latin *gurnardus*.]
Any of various marine fishes of the genus *Trigla* or the family Triglidae, characterized by a large spiny head with mailed cheeks and by three free pectoral fins. Also, any of various related fishes.

> *fig.*: SHAKES. *1 Hen. IV* If I be not ashamed of my soldiers, I am a sous'd gurnet.

red gurnard: see RED *adjective*.

gurney /ˈɡəːni/ *noun*. *US*. L19.
[ORIGIN App. from J. T. *Gurney* of Boston, Massachusetts, who patented a new cab design in 1883.]
1 *hist.* In full ***Gurney cab***. A two-wheeled horse-drawn cab with a rear door and lengthwise seating. Also, a similar vehicle used as a police wagon or ambulance. L19.
2 A wheeled stretcher used for transporting hospital patients. M20.

Gurneyite /ˈɡəːnɪʌɪt/ *noun & adjective*. M19.
[ORIGIN from *Gurney* (see below) + -ITE¹. Cf. WILBURITE.]
▸**A** *noun*. A follower of Joseph John Gurney (1788–1847), leader of an evangelical movement among English Quakers. M19.
▸**B** *adjective*. Of or pertaining to Gurney or his followers. M19.

†**gurnipper** *noun* see GALLINIPPER.

gurrag *noun* var. of GIRRAN.

gurrah /ˈɡʌrə/ *noun*. E19.
[ORIGIN Hindi *gharā* from Sanskrit *ghaṭa*.]
In the Indian subcontinent, an earthen jar.

gurry /ˈɡʌri/ *noun*¹. Chiefly *US*. L18.
[ORIGIN Unknown.]
The mixture of blood, slime, etc., obtained in cutting up a whale and melting down its blubber for oil; fish offal; any mixture of dirt and grease.
– COMB.: **gurry-shark** = *GREENLAND shark*.

gurry *noun*² var. of GIRRAN.

gurry sore /ˈɡʌri sɔː/ *noun phr.* L19.
[ORIGIN from *gurry* (prob. = GURRY *noun*²) + SORE *noun*¹.]
A sore or boil caused by repeated exposure to salt water.

guru /ˈɡʊruː, ˈɡuːruː/ *noun*. Also **gooroo**. E17.
[ORIGIN Sanskrit *guru* elder, teacher.]
1 A (Hindu) spiritual teacher. E17.
2 Anyone looked up to as a source of wisdom or knowledge; an influential leader or pundit. M20.

> C. WILSON Jung suddenly became the guru of the Western World, a universal oracle. *Times* Wall Street guru Mr. Joe Granville predicted world stock markets were going to enter a bear market.

■ **guruship** *noun* the position of a guru M19.

Guru Granth Sahib /ˈɡʊruː ɡrʌnt sɑː(h)ɪb/ *noun.* E20.
[ORIGIN Punjabi. Cf. GRANTH.]
The sacred scriptures of the Sikhs, the Adi Granth.

Gurung /ˈɡʊrʊŋ/ *noun & adjective.* E19.
[ORIGIN Nepali *gurung*, perh. from Gurung.]
▸ **A** *noun.* Pl. **-s**, same.
1 A member of a people of western Nepal. E19.
2 The Tibeto-Burman language of the Gurungs. L20.
▸ **B** *attrib.* or as *adjective.* Of or pertaining to the Gurungs or their language. L19.

gush /ɡʌʃ/ *noun.* L17.
[ORIGIN from the verb.]
1 A sudden copious emission of liquid; a torrent or flood *of* liquid so emitted. L17.

M. REID A red gush spurted over the garments of the Indian.

2 A gust *of* wind (now *dial.*); a burst *of* light, heat, sound, etc. E18. ▸**b** An outburst of feeling or of expressive speech, gestures, etc. E18. ▸**c** A strong smell, a whiff. *colloq.* M19.

DICKENS The host of that tavern approached in a gush of cheerful light to help them to dismount. **b** M. HOLROYD She had always been swept upward by gushes of enthusiasm.

3 Overeffusive or sentimental display of feeling, esp. in language. *colloq.* M19.

N. ANNAN The man who hated sentimentality and gush.

gush /ɡʌʃ/ *verb.* LME.
[ORIGIN Prob. of northern, imit. origin.]
1 *verb intrans.* Rush in a sudden copious stream, as water released from confinement, blood from a wound, etc. Freq. with *down*, *out*, *up*, etc. LME.

K. MANSFIELD The noise of water gushing out of a pump into a big pail. J. HELLER Statements gush from her in a high shriek.

2 *verb intrans.* Of a person, a part of the body, etc.: have a copious flow of blood, tears, etc. M16.

S. RICHARDSON Father, not able to contain himself, . . gushed out into a flood of tears.

3 *verb trans.* Emit in a copious stream. M16.

D. C. PEATTIE Spurge . . that gushes a spurt of milky juice upon the hands.

4 *verb intrans.* & *trans.* Act, speak, or utter in an overeffusive manner. *colloq.* M19.

J. RUSKIN Few things he hated more than hearing people gush about particular drawings. C. MACKENZIE 'Oh, I'd love a cup of tea,' she gushed gratefully.

■ **gusher** *noun* (*a*) a person who speaks or behaves effusively; (*b*) a well from which oil flows profusely without being pumped: M19.

gushing /ˈɡʌʃɪŋ/ *ppl adjective.* L16.
[ORIGIN from GUSH *verb* + -ING².]
That gushes; *esp.* given to effusive outbursts of feeling.
■ **gushingly** *adverb* E19. **gushingness** *noun* M19.

gushy /ˈɡʌʃi/ *adjective.* M19.
[ORIGIN from GUSH *noun* + -Y¹.]
Gushing, overeffusive.
■ **gushily** *adverb* E20. **gushiness** *noun* M19.

gusle /ˈɡʊslə/ *noun.* Also **-la**. E19.
[ORIGIN Serbian.]
A simple usu. one-stringed fiddle used in the Balkans, esp. to accompany the chanting of Slavonic epics.
■ **guslar** /ˈɡʊslɑː/ *noun*, pl. **-ri** /-ri/, a person who plays the gusle or accompanies epic ballads on it M19.

gusset /ˈɡʌsɪt/ *noun.* LME.
[ORIGIN Old French & mod. French *gousset* dim. of *gousse* pod, shell, of unknown origin.]
1 A (triangular) piece of material let into a garment to strengthen or enlarge some part. LME.
2 *hist.* A piece of flexible material introduced in a coat of mail to fill up a space at the joints between two adjoining pieces of mail. LME.
3 HERALDRY. A charge formed by a line drawn from the dexter or sinister chief to a central point, from where the line is continued perpendicularly to the base of the escutcheon. Cf. GORE *noun*² 3. M16.
4 A triangular piece or corner of land. Chiefly, & now only, *Scot.* L16.
5 A flat bracket or angular piece fixed at an angle of a structure to give strength or firmness. M19.
■ **gusseted** *adjective* having a gusset or gussets L19.

gussy /ˈɡʌsi/ *verb trans. slang.* E20.
[ORIGIN Perh. from *Gussie* pet form of male first name *Augustus*: see -Y⁶.]
Smarten *up*. Usu. in *pass.*

gust /ɡʌst/ *noun*¹. *arch.* LME.
[ORIGIN Latin *gustus* taste: cf. GOÛT, GUSTO.]
1 The sense of taste. Formerly also, an act of tasting. LME.

T. HERBERT The fruit is somewhat unpleasant at first gust.

2 Flavour, taste (of food). LME. ▸**b** Pleasing taste. M17.

C. LAMB The whole vegetable tribe have lost their gust with me.

†**3** Individual taste or preference. L16–M18.

4 Keen enjoyment; relish, zest. M17.

W. COWPER He drinks his simple beverage with a gust.

have a gust for, **have a gust of** appreciate, have a taste for.
†**5** An experience or taste *of* something. M–L17.

SIR T. BROWNE In seventy or eighty years, a man may have a deep gust of the world.

gust /ɡʌst/ *noun*². L16.
[ORIGIN Old Norse *gustr*, from weak grade of base of Old Norse *gjósa* gush.]
1 A sudden violent rush of or *of* wind. Formerly also, a whirlwind. L16.
2 A sudden burst of rain, fire, sound, etc. E17.

P. H. GIBBS The inn door opened and there came out a gust of laughter.

3 An outburst or sudden fit of feeling. E18.

H. JAMES Strether had . . been subject to sudden gusts of fancy . . . odd starts of the historic sense.

gust /ɡʌst/ *verb*¹ *trans.* LME.
[ORIGIN from GUST *noun*¹ or Latin *gustare*, from *gustus* GUST *noun*¹.]
†**1** Taste (food); taste with pleasure, relish. LME–M17.
2 Give pleasure to. Only in ***gust the mouth***, ***gust the gab***, please the palate. *Scot.* LME.

gust /ɡʌst/ *verb*². L18.
[ORIGIN from GUST *noun*².]
1 *verb trans.* Blast with sea spray. *Scot.* L18.
2 *verb intrans.* Of wind etc.: blow or rise in gusts. E19.

D. BAGLEY The wind was now fifty miles an hour, gusting to sixty. P. THEROUX The dust whirled out of the corridor and gusted around the light-bulbs.

gustable /ˈɡʌstəb(ə)l/ *adjective & noun.* Now *rare.* L15.
[ORIGIN Late Latin *gustabilis*, from *gustare* to taste: see GUST *verb*¹, -ABLE.]
▸ **A** *adjective.* **1** Able to be tasted; having a pleasant taste, appetizing. L15.
2 Of a quality: perceptible to the taste. M17.
▸ **B** *noun.* A thing that can be tasted; *esp.* an article of food. Usu. in *pl.* M17.

gustation /ɡʌˈsteɪʃ(ə)n/ *noun.* L16.
[ORIGIN French, or Latin *gustatio(n-)*, from *gustat-* pa. ppl stem of *gustare* to taste: see GUST *verb*¹, -ATION.]
The action or faculty of tasting.

gustative /ˈɡʌstətɪv/ *adjective.* E17.
[ORIGIN medieval Latin *gustativus*, from Latin *gustat-*: see GUSTATION, -IVE.]
= GUSTATORY.

gustatory /ɡʌˈsteɪt(ə)ri, ˈɡʌstət(ə)ri/ *adjective.* L17.
[ORIGIN from Latin *gustat-*: see GUSTATION, -ORY².]
Concerned with tasting or the sense of taste.
■ Also **gustaˈtorial** *adjective* M20.

gustful /ˈɡʌstfʊl, -f(ə)l/ *adjective.* M17.
[ORIGIN from GUST *noun*¹ + -FUL.]
1 Tasty, appetizing; *fig.* delightful to the mind or feeling. M17.
2 Marked by relish or zest. *arch.* L17.
■ **gustfully** *adverb* M17. **gustfulness** *noun* L17.

gusto /ˈɡʌstəʊ/ *noun.* Pl. **-o(e)s**. E17.
[ORIGIN Italian from Latin *gustus* GUST *noun*¹.]
1 An individual fondness or preference. *arch.* E17.
2 Keen enjoyment displayed in action or speech, esp. in eating or drinking; relish, zest. Freq. in ***with gusto***, ***with great gusto***, etc. E17.

J. M. COETZEE Though it was no more than fish . . served with lettuce, I ate with gusto. H. WOUK His gusto for the work was evident.

3 Style in which a work of art etc. is executed; esp. ***great gusto***, ***grand gusto*** (= Italian *gran gusto*). *arch.* M17.

J. JAMES The Designs . . are of very mean Gusto.

gusty /ˈɡʌsti/ *adjective*¹. E17.
[ORIGIN from GUST *noun*² + -Y¹.]
1 Blowing in gusts; marked or accompanied by gusts of wind. E17. ▸**b** Disturbed or blown by gusts of wind. E18.

E. WAUGH A gusty night always brought down a litter of dead timber. **b** KEATS The long carpets rose along the gusty floor.

2 Marked by sudden bursts of feeling or action. L17.

New Yorker Energetic, sociable, gusty of temperament.

■ **gustily** *adverb*¹ E19. **gustiness** *noun* E20.

gusty /ˈɡʌsti/ *adjective*². Chiefly *Scot.* E18.
[ORIGIN from GUST *noun*¹ + -Y¹.]
Tasty, appetizing.
■ **gustily** *adverb*² with taste or gusto E19.

GUT *abbreviation.*
PHYSICS. Grand unified theory.

gut /ɡʌt/ *noun & adjective.*
[ORIGIN Old English *guttas* pl., prob. from base of Old English *gēotan*, Gothic *giutan* pour.]
▸ **A** *noun.* **1** In *pl.* The contents of the abdominal cavity (of a human now *colloq.*); bowels, entrails. OE. ▸**b** In *pl.* The entrails of animals as food; offal. E17.

P. MACGILL A cramp in my guts! . . It isn't 'arf giving me gyp!

2 **a** *sing.* & †in *pl.* The intestine; intestinal tissue. LME. ▸**b** The alimentary canal as a whole (of a human now *colloq.*); the enteron of an embryo or coelenterate. LME.
3 *sing.* & in *pl.* The stomach, esp. as the seat of appetite or gluttony. Now *dial.* & *slang.* LME. ▸**b** In *pl.* A corpulent or gluttonous person. L16.
4 A narrow passage; a lane; a channel of water, a strait. M16.
5 A material made from the intestines of animals for use in violin or racket strings, and in surgery. Formerly also, in *pl.*, strings made from this material. Cf. CATGUT. E17. ▸**b** A silky fibrous material obtained from inside a silkworm about to spin, formerly used for fishing lines. M19.

C. FORD Pass a loop of gut over the fingerboard from bass to treble.

6 In *pl.* The physical contents of something; substance, substantial meaning or impact; the essential part, the heart, *of* something. M17.

R. L. STEVENSON It's got life to it and guts. K. AMIS Cliff . . peered for a moment into the guts of the ruined set. *New Yorker* To me, that's really the guts of it.

7 In *pl.* Courage, force of character; energy, verve, staying power. *colloq.* L19.

A. GIBBS Someone . . who's had the guts to appeal to the electorate on what he really thinks.

8 In machine sheep-shearing, a flexible shaft which conveys the power from an overhead source to the hand-held shearing device. *Austral.* & *NZ.* M20.
– PHRASES: ***blind gut***: see BLIND *adjective*. **bust a gut**, **rupture a gut** *slang* exert oneself, make a great effort. ***greedy-gut(s)***: see GREEDY *adjective*. ***hate a person's guts***: see HATE *verb*. **have a person's guts for garters** *slang*: a hyperbolical threat. **have no guts in it** *slang* be of no real value or force. ***misery guts***: see MISERY. ***rupture a gut***: see ***bust a gut*** above. **slog one's guts out**, **sweat one's guts out**, **work one's guts out** *slang* work extremely hard; make a great effort. ***small gut(s)***: see SMALL *adjective*.
– COMB.: **gutbucket** *noun & adjective* (*slang*) (designating) a primitive, unsophisticated style of jazz; **gut-level** *adjective & noun* (of or pertaining to) basic principles or a basic level; **gut-rot** *colloq.* unwholesome or unpalatable liquor or food; **guts-ache** *colloq.* stomach ache; **gut-shoot** *verb trans.* (*slang*) shoot in the stomach; **gut-tie** a condition in which a length of a bullock's bowel has become entangled with the spermatic cord. **gut-wrenching** *adjective* (*colloq.*) extremely unpleasant or upsetting.
▸ **B** *attrib.* or as *adjective.* (Of an issue) basic, fundamental; (of a feeling or reaction) instinctive and emotional rather than rational. M20.

Marxism Today This is a real gut issue. J. BRODSKY It wasn't so much a conscious choice as a gut reaction.

gut instinct a compellingly intuitive feeling.
■ **gutful**, **gutsful** *noun* (*slang*) = BELLYFUL E20. **gutling** *noun* (long *obsolete* exc. *dial.*) a great eater, a glutton L16.

gut /ɡʌt/ *verb.* Infl. **-tt-**. ME.
[ORIGIN from the noun.]
1 *verb trans.* Take out the guts of (a fish); eviscerate. ME.
2 *verb intrans.* Eat voraciously or greedily. *slang.* E17.
3 *verb trans.* **a** Clear out the contents or inside of; empty thoroughly; *esp.* remove or destroy the internal fittings of (a building etc.). (Foll. by *of*.) Now freq. in *pass.* L17. ▸**b** Extract the essential contents or the important passages of (a book etc.) in reading or in a review or abridgement. E18.

a R. HUGHES All nautical instruments gone, cabin stores—the saloon in fact gutted of everything. U. LE GUIN The shopfronts . . were all covered up . . , except for one which had been gutted by fire.

4 Disappoint bitterly, make desolate, exasperate, disgust. Only as ***gutted*** *ppl adjective. slang.* L20.

Sun I've heard nothing for four months. I'm gutted because I still love him.

Guthrie test /ˈɡʌθri tɛst/ *noun phr.* M20.
[ORIGIN Robert *Guthrie* (1916–95), US microbiologist.]
MEDICINE. A routine blood test carried out on babies a few days after birth to detect the condition phenylketonuria.

Gutian /ˈɡuːtɪən/ *noun & adjective.* E20.
[ORIGIN from *Guti*, the tribe or *Gutium*, their country + -AN.]
ARCHAEOLOGY. ▸**A** *noun.* A member of a people from the Zagros Mountains in western Iran who overthrew the Dynasty of Akkad in Mesopotamia in the late 3rd millennium BC. E20.
▸ **B** *adjective.* Of or pertaining to this people. E20.

gutkha /ˈɡuːtˌkə/ *noun.* L20.
[ORIGIN from Hindi *gutkhā* shred, small piece.]
A sweetened mixture of chewing tobacco, betel nut, and palm nut, originating in India as a breath freshener.

gutless /ˈɡʌtlɪs/ *adjective. colloq.* E17.
[ORIGIN from GUT *noun* + -LESS.]
†**1** Having no guts; disembowelled. Only in E17.
2 Lacking in energy, courage, or determination. E20.
■ **gutlessly** *adverb* L20. **gutlessness** *noun* M20.

Gutnish /ˈgʊtnɪʃ/ *noun & adjective*. L19.
[ORIGIN German *Gutnisch*, from Old Norse *gotneskr* adjective, of Gotland.]
▸ **A** *noun*. An East Norse dialect spoken on the island of Gotland, off SE Sweden in the Baltic Sea. L19.
▸ **B** *adjective*. Of or pertaining to Gotland or its inhabitants. E20.

guts /gʌts/ *verb intrans. & trans. colloq.* E20.
[ORIGIN from GUT *verb*.]
Eat greedily.

gutser /ˈgʌtsə/ *noun*. Chiefly *Austral. & NZ colloq.* Also **gutzer**. E20.
[ORIGIN from GUT *noun* + -S[1] + -ER[1].]
A heavy fall.
come a gutser come a cropper, make a mistake; *Air Force slang* crash.

gutsy /ˈgʌtsi/ *adjective*. In sense 1 also **-sie**. E19.
[ORIGIN from GUT *noun* + -SY.]
1 Greedy, voracious. Chiefly *Scot.* E19.
2 Tough, spirited, courageous. *colloq.* L19.
■ **gutsily** *adverb* E19. **gutsiness** *noun* E19.

gutta /ˈgʌtə/ *noun*[1]. Pl. **-ttae** /-tiː/. LME.
[ORIGIN Latin = drop. Cf. GOUT *noun*[1].]
†**1** Gum; gum resin, *esp.* gamboge. LME–E18.
2 ARCHITECTURE. Each of a row of usu. conical projections resembling drops underneath the triglyph (and sometimes the mutule) of a Doric capital. M16.
3 PHARMACOLOGY & MEDICINE. A drop of liquid. Now *rare* or *obsolete*. M16.
4 A roundish coloured dot on an insect's wing, *esp.* one of a light colour. E19.
– COMB.: †**gutta rosacea**, †**gutta rosea** acne rosacea; †**gutta serena** = AMAUROSIS.

gutta /ˈgʌtə/ *noun*[2]. M19.
[ORIGIN Malay *getah*: see GUTTA-PERCHA.]
1 = GUTTA-PERCHA. M19.
2 A gutta-percha golf ball. Cf. GUTTY *noun*. M19.

gutta-percha /gʌtəˈpəːtʃə/ *noun*. M19.
[ORIGIN Malay *getah perca*, from *getah* gum + *perca* strips of cloth (which it resembles); assim. to GUTTA *noun*[2].]
1 The coagulated latex of certain Malaysian trees, a hard tough thermoplastic substance consisting chiefly of a hydrocarbon isomeric with rubber and now used esp. in dentistry and for electrical insulation. M19.
2 Any of the trees, of the family Sapotaceae, which yield gutta-percha, esp. *Palaquium gutta*, a tall evergreen. M19.

guttate /ˈgʌteɪt/ *adjective*. E19.
[ORIGIN Latin *guttatus*, formed as GUTTA *noun*[1]: see -ATE[2].]
Having drops or marks resembling drops; in the form of or resembling drops.
■ **guˈttated** *adjective* guttate; characterized by marks resembling drops E18.

guttatim /gʌˈteɪtɪm/ *adverb*. Now *rare*. L17.
[ORIGIN Latin, formed as GUTTA *noun*[1].]
Drop by drop.

guttation /gʌˈteɪʃ(ə)n/ *noun*. L19.
[ORIGIN from GUTTA *noun*[1] + -ATION.]
BOTANY. The secretion of droplets of water from the hydathodes.

gutté /gyte/ *adjective*. Also **gutty**. L16.
[ORIGIN Anglo-Norman = Old French *gouté* spotted, from *goute* (mod. *goutte*) drop (formed as GUTTA *noun*[1]) + -é -ATE[2].]
HERALDRY. Powdered or spotted with drops of liquid.

gutter /ˈgʌtə/ *noun*[1] *& adjective*. ME.
[ORIGIN Anglo-Norman *gotere*, Old French *gotiere* (mod. *gouttière*) from Proto-Romance formed as GUTTA *noun*[1]: see -ER[2].]
▸ **A** *noun*. †**1** A watercourse. Orig. also, a downpour. ME–M19. ▸**b** A furrow or track made by running water. L16–M19.
2 A shallow trough fixed below the eaves of a roof, or a channel at the side of a road, to carry off rainwater. ME. ▸**b** A channel forming a receptacle for refuse or foul matter (*lit. & fig.*), a sink. Now *dial.* LME. ▸**c** *sing.* & (usu.) in *pl.* Mud, filth. Chiefly *Scot.* E18. ▸**d** *fig.* The milieu of very poor people or people without breeding. M19.

> **d** *Times* Middle-class courtesans . . were always the toast of society when lower-class street walkers were considered the gutter.

†**3** A groove or elongated hollow in a living organism. LME–E18.
4 An artificial groove. Now only *techn.* M16.
5 A trough or pipe for the removal of fluid in an industrial process. M17.
6 PRINTING & TYPOGRAPHY. A piece of furniture separating adjacent pages in a forme (also ***gutter-stick***); the space between facing pages of an open book etc. or (*loosely*) between columns on a page; the space between adjacent (rows and columns of) stamps on a sheet. M19.
▸ **B** *adjective*. Brought up in or appropriate to the gutter (sense 2d above); of a low or disreputable character. M19.

> A. BURGESS Her beauty was marred by a gutter accent and vocabulary.

– COMB. & SPECIAL COLLOCATIONS: **gutter-blood** *Scot.* a person of low breeding; **gutter-crawling** kerb-crawling; **gutter journalism**, **gutter press**: (considered as) fit only for the gutter; marked by sensationalism and vulgarity; **gutter-splint** a splint moulded to the shape of the limb; ***gutter-stick***: see sense A.6 above; **gutter-tile** a tile used in the construction of gutters, or to line the valleys of a roof.
■ **gutterling** *noun* a person of low breeding M19.

gutter /ˈgʌtə/ *noun*[2]. L16.
[ORIGIN from GUT *verb* + -ER[1].]
1 A person employed in gutting animals, esp. fish. L16.
2 A person who guts buildings. M18.

gutter /ˈgʌtə/ *verb*. LME.
[ORIGIN from GUTTER *noun*[1].]
1 *verb trans.* Make gutters or channels in; channel, furrow; cut grooves in. LME.
2 *verb intrans.* Flow in streams, stream *down*. L16.
3 *verb intrans.* Of water: form gutters or gullies. M17.
4 *verb intrans.* Of a candle: melt away rapidly by becoming channelled on one side. (Foll. by *down*, *out*.) E18.

> JOYCE The porter halted on the stairs to settle his guttering candle.

■ **guttering** *noun* (*a*) the action of the verb; (*b*) material used for making gutters, gutters collectively; (*c*) the melted tallow or wax which runs down a candle: LME.

guttered /ˈgʌtəd/ *adjective*. M16.
[ORIGIN from GUTTER *noun*[1], *verb*: see -ED[2], -ED[1].]
1 Furrowed, gullied. M16.
2 Having gutters. L18.
3 Esp. of a candle: that has guttered. M19.

guttersnipe /ˈgʌtəsnʌɪp/ *noun & adjective*. M19.
[ORIGIN from GUTTER *noun*[1] + SNIPE *noun*.]
▸ **A** *noun*. **1** A street urchin; a person of low breeding. M19.
2 A gatherer of refuse from street gutters. M19.
3 A person who deals in shares on the street. *US slang*. Now *rare* or *obsolete*. M19.
▸ **B** *attrib.* or as *adjective*. Typical of a guttersnipe. E20.

> L. OLIVIER Here was I, with guttersnipe rashness, chalking some rudeness upon Sir Barry Jackson's fine escutcheon.

guttery /ˈgʌtəri/ *noun*. M19.
[ORIGIN from GUT *verb* + -ERY.]
A place where fish are gutted or the offal of slaughtered animals is disposed of.

guttery /ˈgʌtəri/ *adjective*. M18.
[ORIGIN from GUTTER *noun*[1] + -Y[1].]
1 Of corn: grooved, channelled. Now *rare*. M18.
2 Miry, muddy. *Scot.* L18.

Gut-tide /ˈgʊttʌɪd/ *noun*. Long *dial.* E17.
[ORIGIN Alt. of *good tide*. Perh. also assoc. with GUT *noun*.]
Shrove Tuesday; *gen.* a time of feasting.

guttiform /ˈgʌtɪfɔːm/ *adjective*. L19.
[ORIGIN from Latin GUTTA *noun*[1] + -I- + -FORM.]
= GUTTATE, GUTTATED.

gutting /ˈgʌtɪŋ/ *noun*. M17.
[ORIGIN Unknown.]
A kind of canvas.

guttle /ˈgʌt(ə)l/ *verb*. M17.
[ORIGIN from GUT *noun* after *guzzle*.]
1 *verb intrans.* Eat voraciously. M17.
2 *verb trans.* Devour or swallow greedily. (Foll. by *up*, *down*.) L17.
■ **guttler** *noun* E18.

guttur /ˈgʌtə/ *noun*. Now *rare*. M16.
[ORIGIN Latin: see GUTTURAL.]
The throat of a person or an animal.

guttural /ˈgʌt(ə)r(ə)l/ *adjective & noun*. L16.
[ORIGIN French, or medieval Latin *gutturalis*, from Latin *guttur* throat: see -AL[1].]
▸ **A** *adjective*. **1** Of a sound: produced in the throat, or by the back of the tongue and the (soft) palate; of articulation: throaty, harsh-sounding. L16.

> C. S. FORESTER A portly, kindly gentleman with . . a deep guttural voice.

2 Chiefly ANATOMY. Of or pertaining to the throat. E17.
▸ **B** *noun*. A guttural sound. L16.
■ **gutturalism** *noun* guttural quality or characteristics L19. **gutturˈrality** *noun* guttural nature, gutturalism L18. **gutturalize** *verb trans.* pronounce or utter gutturally; make (a sound) guttural in character: E19. **gutturally** *adverb* †(*a*) indistinctly; (*b*) in a guttural manner; with a guttural sound: M17.

gutturo- /ˈgʌt(ə)rəʊ/ *combining form*. L18.
[ORIGIN from Latin GUTTUR + -O-.]
ANATOMY. Pertaining to the throat and —, as ***gutturo-maxillary***; PHONETICS guttural and —, as ***gutturo-labial***.

guttus /ˈgʌtəs/ *noun*. M19.
[ORIGIN Latin.]
ARCHAEOLOGY. A narrow-necked cruet or oil flask of ancient Roman times.

gutty /ˈgʌti/ *noun*. *slang*. L19.
[ORIGIN from GUTTA *noun*[2] + -Y[6].]
In full ***gutty ball***. A gutta-percha golf ball. Cf. GUTTA *noun*[2] 2.

gutty /ˈgʌti/ *adjective*[1]. L18.
[ORIGIN from GUT *noun* + -Y[1].]
1 Corpulent, pot-bellied. Chiefly *Scot.* L18.
2 Earthy, primitive. *Jazz slang*. M20.
3 = GUTSY *adjective* 2. *slang*. M20.

gutty *adjective*[2] var. of GUTTÉ *adjective*.

gutzer *noun* var. of GUTSER.

guv /gʌv/ *noun*. *slang*. L19.
[ORIGIN Abbreviation.]
= GOVERNOR 7c. Cf. GUVNER.

guvner /ˈgʌvnə/ *noun*. Also **guv'ner**, **guvnor**, **guv'nor**. M19.
[ORIGIN Repr. non-standard or colloq. pronunc.]
= GOVERNOR 7c. Cf. GUV.

guy /gʌɪ/ *noun*[1]. LME.
[ORIGIN Sense 1 from Old French *guie* guide, from *guier* GUY *verb*[1]. Sense 2 prob. of Low German origin, as are Dutch *gei* brail, *geitouw* clew-garnet, *geiblok* pulley, German *Geitau* clew-line, (pl.) brails.]
†**1** A guide; a conductor, a leader. *rare*. LME–E16.
2 In full ***guy rope***. A rope, chain, etc., used to guide, secure, or steady something, esp. on a ship; a line helping to hold a tent in place. LME.

G

guy /gʌɪ/ *noun*[2]. E19.
[ORIGIN *Guy* Fawkes (1570–1606), English Catholic, who was hanged for his part in the Gunpowder Plot.]
1 An effigy of a man, usu. a crude one in ragged clothes, which is burnt on a bonfire on or near 5 November, the anniversary of the Gunpowder Plot. Cf. GUY FAWKES. E19. PENNY ***for the guy***.
2 A person of grotesque appearance, esp. in dress. M19.
3 A man, a fellow; in *pl.* also (chiefly *N. Amer.*), people (of either sex). *colloq.* (orig. *N. Amer.*). L19.

> B. SCHULBERG I never saw a guy work so hard for twelve bucks a week.

regular guy: see REGULAR *adjective*. ***tough guy***: see TOUGH *adjective*. ***wise guy***: see WISE *adjective* & *noun*[2].
4 An act of running off secretly. *slang*. L19.
do a guy run away. **give the guy to** give the slip to.

guy /gʌɪ/ *verb*[1] *trans.* *obsolete* exc. *Scot.* ME.
[ORIGIN Old French *guier*: see GUIDE *verb*.]
†**1** Control, direct, (a person, his or her action). ME–E16.
†**2** Command (an army); govern (a country); manage (affairs). Cf. GUIDE *verb* 2. ME–E17.
3 = GUIDE *verb* 1. LME.

guy /gʌɪ/ *verb*[2] *trans.* E18.
[ORIGIN from GUY *noun*[1].]
Fasten or secure with a guy or guys. (Foll. by *down*, *out*, *up*, etc.)

> *Scientific American* Hemp was woven into rigging and line that would guy the masts.

guy /gʌɪ/ *verb*[3]. M19.
[ORIGIN from GUY *noun*[2].]
1 a *verb intrans.* Carry or exhibit a guy in the streets around 5 November. M19. ▸**b** *verb trans.* Exhibit (a person) in effigy. L19.
2 a *verb trans.* Make fun of, ridicule by innuendo; trifle with (a theatrical part). M19. ▸**b** *verb intrans.* Mock (*at*); play the fool. L19.

> **a** G. GREER Vociferous women are guyed in the press.

3 *verb intrans.* Run away or *off*; go away. *slang*. L19.

Guyanese /gʌɪəˈniːz/ *adjective & noun*. M20.
[ORIGIN from *Guyana* (see below) + -ESE. Cf. GUIANESE.]
▸ **A** *noun*. Pl. same. A native or inhabitant of Guyana (until 1966 British Guiana), a country in north-eastern S. America. M20.
▸ **B** *adjective*. Of or pertaining to Guyana. M20.
■ Also **Guyanan** /gʌɪˈanən/ *noun & adjective* M20.

Guy Fawkes /gʌɪ ˈfɔːks/ *noun*. E19.
[ORIGIN See GUY *noun*[2].]
= GUY *noun*[2] 1. Chiefly as below.
– COMB.: **Guy Fawkes Day**, **Guy Fawkes Night** 5 November, the anniversary of the Gunpowder Plot (cf. ***Bonfire Night*** s.v. BONFIRE *noun*).

guyot /ˈgiːəʊ/ *noun*. M20.
[ORIGIN A. H. *Guyot* (1807–84), Swiss geographer.]
A seamount with a flat top.

guyver /ˈgʌɪvə/ *noun*. *Austral. & NZ slang*. Also **gui-**, **gy-**. M19.
[ORIGIN Unknown.]
Talk intended to impress or deceive; affectation of behaviour. Freq. in ***put on the guyver***

guz /gʌz/ *noun*. Pl. same. L17.
[ORIGIN Urdu & Persian *gaz*.]
In the Indian subcontinent and Iran, a measure of length varying between approximately 67 and 102 cm (or 27 and 41 inches).

guze /gjuːz/ *noun*. M16.
[ORIGIN Uncertain: cf. Turkish *göz* eye.]
HERALDRY. A roundel of a sanguine tincture.

guzzle /ˈɡʌz(ə)l/ *noun*. L16.
[ORIGIN App. from the verb.]
1 A gutter, a drain. *obsolete* exc. *dial.* L16.
2 The throat. *dial.* M17.
3 Drink, liquor. L17.
4 A bout of excessive eating and drinking. M19.
– COMB.: **guzzle-guts** *slang* a glutton.

guzzle /ˈɡʌz(ə)l/ *verb*. L16.
[ORIGIN Perh. from Old French *gosillier* chatter, vomit, from Old French & mod. French *gosier* throat from late Latin *geusiae* cheeks.]
1 *verb trans.* Swallow (esp. drink) greedily or to excess. (Foll. by *down*, *up*.) L16.
A. SILLITOE They were guzzling tea in the common room.
2 *verb intrans.* Drink a large amount, drink greedily. L16.
L. DEIGHTON Tequila.. or imported whisky, it's all the same to him once he starts guzzling.
3 *verb trans.* Consume (time, money) in guzzling. Usu. foll. by *away*, *down*. M17.
4 *verb trans.* Seize by the throat; choke, strangle. *slang & dial.* L19.
■ **guzzler** *noun* E18. **guzzling** *ppl adjective* that guzzles; drunken; gluttonous, greedy: M17.

G

GVW *abbreviation*. *US*.
Gross vehicle weight.

GW *abbreviation*[1]. *hist.*
Great Western (Railway).

Gw *abbreviation*[2].
Gigawatt(s).

gwan /ɡwɑːn/ *verb intrans.* (usu. *imper.*). *non-standard* (chiefly *Irish* & *US*). E20.
[ORIGIN Repr. a pronunc.]
Go on: esp. in expressions of impatience or encouragement.

gweilo /ˈɡweɪləʊ/ *noun*. Pl. same, **-s**. L20.
[ORIGIN Chinese (Cantonese), lit. 'ghost man'.]
In SE Asia: a foreigner.

gwely /ˈɡwɛli/ *noun*. L19.
[ORIGIN Welsh.]
hist. A social unit formerly traditional in Wales, comprising four generations of one family in which the great-grandfather as head of the group had proprietary rights over landed property; the land held by the members of such a group.

Gwentian /ˈɡwɛntɪən/ *noun & adjective*. M19.
[ORIGIN from *Gwent* (see below) + -IAN.]
▸ **A** *noun*. A native or inhabitant of Gwent, formerly a Welsh principality and since 1974 a Welsh county formed from parts of the former counties of Monmouthshire (England) and Breconshire (Wales); the dialect of this region. M19.
▸ **B** *adjective*. Of or pertaining to Gwent. M19.

gwine /ɡwʌɪn/ *verb* (*pres. pple*). *dial.* & *non-standard* (esp. *US*). M19.
[ORIGIN Repr. a pronunc.]
Going.

GWR *abbreviation*. *hist.*
Great Western Railway.

gwyniad /ˈɡwɪnɪad/ *noun*. Also †**guin-**. E17.
[ORIGIN Welsh, from *gwyn* white.]
The houting, *Coregonus lavaretus*, of a race occurring in Bala Lake, N. Wales. Cf. POWAN, SKELLY *noun* 1.

Gy *abbreviation*.
PHYSICS. Gray (the unit).

†**gybe** *noun*[1]. *slang*. M16–E19.
[ORIGIN Unknown.]
A counterfeit pass or licence.

gybe /dʒʌɪb/ *noun*[2]. Also ***jibe**. L19.
[ORIGIN from the verb.]
NAUTICAL. The action or an act of gybing.

gybe /dʒʌɪb/ *verb*. Also ***jibe**. L17.
[ORIGIN Dutch †*gijben* (now *gijpen*, whence German *geipen*). Cf. JIB *verb*[1].]
NAUTICAL **1** **a** *verb intrans.* Of a fore-and-aft sail or its boom: swing from one side of a vessel to the other (now, when the vessel is running before the wind). L17. ▸**b** *verb trans.* Cause (a fore-and-aft sail or its boom) to gybe. L19.
2 **a** *verb intrans.* Of a vessel or its crew: change course in such a way that the mainsail gybes. Cf. TACK *verb*[1] 7. L17. ▸**b** *verb trans.* Cause (a vessel) to gybe. L19.

gyle /ɡʌɪl/ *noun*. ME.
[ORIGIN Middle Dutch *ghijl* (Dutch *gijl*) rel. to *gijlen* ferment; ult. origin unknown.]
BREWING. **1** Wort in the process of fermentation. (Earliest in ***gyle-fat*** below.) ME.
2 A brewing; the quantity of beer or ale brewed at one time. L16.
– COMB.: **gyle-fat** (*obsolete* exc. *Scot.* & *dial.*) = ***gyle-tun*** below; **gylekier** (*obsolete* exc. *dial.*) a tub or other vessel for holding wort; the wort itself; **gyle-tun** a vat in which the wort is left to ferment.

gym /dʒɪm/ *noun*. *colloq.* L19.
[ORIGIN Abbreviation.]
A gymnasium; gymnastics. Freq. *attrib.*
– COMB.: **gym rat** *N. Amer. colloq.* a person who frequents a gym; **gymslip**, **gym tunic** a schoolgirl's sleeveless usu. belted garment reaching from shoulder to knee.

gymkhana /dʒɪmˈkɑːnə/ *noun*. Orig. *Indian*. M19.
[ORIGIN Alt. by assim. to GYM, GYMNASTIC of Urdu *gendkānah* racket-court, from Hindi *gēd* ball + Persian *kānah* house.]
Orig., a public place in India with facilities for athletics; later, an athletics display. Now *spec.* a meeting for competition between horse-riders or car-drivers.

gymnadenia /dʒɪmnəˈdiːnɪə/ *noun*. E19.
[ORIGIN mod. Latin (see below), from Greek *gumnos* naked + *adēn*, *aden-* gland: see -IA[1].]
Any of various orchids of the genus *Gymnadenia*; *esp.* the fragrant orchid, *G. conopsea*.

gymnasiarch /dʒɪmˈneɪzɪɑːk/ *noun*. M17.
[ORIGIN Latin *gymnasiarchus*, *-archa* from Greek *gumnasiarkhos*, *-arkhēs*, from *gumnasion* GYMNASIUM: see -ARCH.]
1 *GREEK HISTORY*. An Athenian official whose duty was to superintend athletic schools and games. M17. ▸**b** A leader among athletes, an expert athlete. E19.
2 A governor of a school, college, or academy, esp. a Continental gymnasium; a head instructor. L17.
■ **gymnasiarchy** *noun* the position or function of a gymnasiarch M19.

gymnasiast /dʒɪmˈneɪzɪast/ *noun*. E19.
[ORIGIN from Greek *gumnasion* GYMNASIUM after German *Gymnasiast*.]
1 A student in a Continental gymnasium. E19.
2 A gymnast. M19.

gymnasium /dʒɪmˈneɪzɪəm/; *in sense 2 also foreign* ɡʏmˈnaːzɪʊm/ *noun*. Pl. **-iums**, **-ia** /-ɪə/, (in sense 2 also) **-ien** /-ɪən/. L16.
[ORIGIN Latin from Greek *gumnasion*, from *gumnazein* exercise naked, from *gumnos* naked. In sense 2 partly from German.]
1 A place, room, or building equipped for gymnastics, indoor sports, and other physical exercise. L16.
2 Formerly, a high school, college, or academy in Continental Europe. Now *spec.* in Germany and some other Continental countries, a school of the highest grade, preparing pupils for universities. L17.
■ **gymnasial** *adjective* of or pertaining to a gymnasium in Continental Europe M19.

gymnast /ˈdʒɪmnast/ *noun*. L16.
[ORIGIN French *gymnaste* or Greek *gumnastēs* trainer of athletes, from *gumnazein*: see GYMNASIUM.]
A person skilled or trained in gymnastics.

gymnastic /dʒɪmˈnastɪk/ *adjective & noun*. L16.
[ORIGIN Latin *gymnasticus* from Greek *gumnastikos*, from *gumnazein*: see GYMNASIUM, -IC.]
▸ **A** *adjective*. **1** Pertaining to or concerned with gymnastics. L16.
2 *fig.* Pertaining to mental exercise, discipline, effort, or activity. E18.
3 Of an initial letter in an illuminated manuscript: decorated with human figures etc. which are represented climbing like gymnasts round the letter. M20.
▸ **B** *noun*. **1** In *pl.* (now usu. treated as *sing.*) or (now *rare*) *sing.* The performance of athletic exercises and feats of physical agility, esp. in a place equipped for the purpose. L16.
fig.: R. BROUGHTON It seemed an impossible feat in mental gymnastics to.. wrench his thoughts away.
†**2** An authority on gymnastics. *rare*. L16–E17.
3 A gymnastic feat. *rare*. M19.
■ **gymnastical** *adjective* = GYMNASTIC *adjective* L16. **gymnastically** *adverb* in a gymnastic manner; pertaining to gymnastics: M17.

gymnic /ˈdʒɪmnɪk/ *adjective & noun*. Now *rare*. E17.
[ORIGIN Latin *gymnicus* from Greek *gumnikos* pertaining to bodily exercises from *gumnos* naked: see -IC.]
▸ **A** *adjective*. = GYMNASTIC *adjective* 1. E17.
▸ **B** *noun*. In *pl.* Gymnastics; gymnastic exercises. E17.
■ †**gymnical** *adjective* = GYMNIC *adjective* L16–M18.

gymno- /ˈdʒɪmnəʊ/ *combining form*.
[ORIGIN Greek *gumnos* naked: see -O-.]
Bare, uncovered, naked.

gymnosophist /dʒɪmˈnɒsəfɪst/ *noun*. Now *rare*. LME.
[ORIGIN French *gymnosophiste* from Latin *gymnosophistae* pl. from Greek *gumnosophistai* pl., formed as GYMNO- + *sophistēs* SOPHIST.]
A member of a reputed Hindu sect, reported in ancient history, who wore very little clothing and were given to asceticism and contemplation; *transf.* an ascetic, a mystic.
■ **gymnosophy** *noun* (*rare*) the doctrine or system of gymnosophists E19.

gymnosperm /ˈdʒɪmnəspəːm/ *noun*. M19.
[ORIGIN mod. Latin *gymnospermus* from Greek *gumnospermos*, formed as GYMNO- + *sperma* seed.]
A woody plant belonging to the Gymnospermae, one of the two main divisions of seed plants, lacking flowers and with seeds unprotected by an ovary or fruit, and including conifers, cycads, and ginkgos.
■ **gymnoˈspermous** *adjective* characteristic of or designating a gymnosperm E18.

gymnotus /dʒɪmˈnəʊtəs/ *noun*. Pl. **-ti** /-tʌɪ/. L18.
[ORIGIN mod. Latin *Gymnotus* (see below), formed as GYMNO- + Greek *nōton* back, with ref. to the absence of dorsal fins.]
An electric eel (formerly placed in the genus *Gymnotus*).

gymnure /ˈɡɪmnjʊə/ *noun*. L19.
[ORIGIN mod. Latin *Gymnura* former genus name, from Greek *gumnos* naked + *oura* tail.]
ZOOLOGY. Any of several ratlike nocturnal insectivores constituting the subfamily Galericinae of the hedgehog family, native to SE Asia. Also called ***moon rat***.

gymp *noun* var. of GIMP *noun*[1].

gympie /ˈɡɪmpi/ *noun*. L19.
[ORIGIN Gabi-Gabi (an Australian Aboriginal language of SE Queensland) *gimbi*.]
An Australian evergreen shrub, *Dendrocnide moroides*, of the nettle family, with leaves covered with stinging hairs.

gyn- *combining form* see GYNO-.

gynae /ˈɡʌɪni/ *noun*. *colloq.* Also **gynie**. M20.
[ORIGIN from GYNAE(COLOGY etc.: see -IE.]
Gynaecology; the gynaecology department of a hospital; a gynaecologist.

gynaeceum /dʒʌɪnɪˈsiːəm, ɡ-/ *noun*. Also **-cium**, †**-caeum**, ***-nec-**. Pl. **-cea**, **-cia**, /-sɪə/. E17.
[ORIGIN Latin from Greek *gunaikeion*, formed as GYNAECO-.]
1 *hist.* The women's apartments in a household; any room or building set aside for women, esp. in ancient Greece or Rome. E17.
†**2** A textile factory under the Roman Empire. E17–L18.
3 *BOTANY*. See GYNOECIUM. E17.

gynaeco- /ɡʌɪˈniːkəʊ, dʒ-/ *combining form*. Also ***-nec-**.
[ORIGIN Greek *gunaiko-*, from *gunaik-*, *gunē* woman, female: see -O-.]
Woman, women; female(s).
■ **gynaecoˈmastia**, †**-masty** *noun* the state in a man of having breasts like those of a woman, owing to hormone imbalance or hormone therapy M19. **gynaecoˈmazia** *noun* (now *rare* or *obsolete*) = GYNAECOMASTIA M19.

gynaecocracy /ɡʌɪnɪˈkɒkrəsi, dʒ-/ *noun*. Also ***-nec-**. E17.
[ORIGIN French *gynécocratie* or mod. Latin *gynaecocratia* from Greek *gunaikokratia*, formed as GYNAECO-: see -CRACY.]
Government by a woman or women; female dominance; *derog.* petticoat government; an instance of this. Cf. GYNARCHY.
■ **gynaecoˈcratic** *adjective* L19. **gynaecoˈcratical** *adjective* M19.

gynaecoid /ˈɡʌɪnɪkɔɪd, ˈdʒʌɪ-/ *adjective*. Also ***-nec-**. E20.
[ORIGIN from GYNAECO- + -OID.]
1 *ENTOMOLOGY*. Designating a worker ant that lays eggs. E20.
2 Resembling or characteristic of (that of) a female. M20.
R. GORDON Petunia appeared, in an evening gown nicely displaying her gynaecoid pelvis.

gynaecology /ɡʌɪnɪˈkɒlədʒi, dʒ-/ *noun*. Also ***-nec-**. M19.
[ORIGIN from GYNAECO- + -OLOGY.]
The branch of medicine that deals with the physiology and diseases of women and girls, esp. of their reproductive organs.
■ **gynaecoˈlogic** *adjective* (*US*) M20. **gynaecoˈlogical** *adjective* L19. **gynaecoˈlogically** *adverb* in accordance with gynaecology L19. **gynaecologist** *noun* L19.

gynander /dʒɪˈnandə, ɡʌɪ-/ *noun*. E19.
[ORIGIN formed as GYNANDROUS.]
†**1** *BOTANY*. A gynandrous plant. *rare*. Only in E19.
2 = GYNANDROMORPH. M20.

gynandromorph /dʒɪˈnandrəmɔːf, ɡʌɪ-/ *noun*. L19.
[ORIGIN formed as GYNANDROUS + -O- + Greek *morphē* form.]
An individual, esp. an insect, with some male and some female characteristics.
■ **gynandroˈmorphic** *adjective* = GYNANDROMORPHOUS L19. **gynandroˈmorphism** *noun* the state of being a gynandromorph M19. **gynandroˈmorphous** *adjective* pertaining to or designating a gynandromorph M19.

gynandrous /dʒɪˈnandrəs, ɡʌɪ-/ *adjective*. E19.
[ORIGIN from Greek *gunandros* of doubtful sex, from *gunē* woman, female: see -ANDROUS.]
1 *BOTANY*. Having the stamens and pistils united in a column, as in orchids. E19.
2 Of people or animals: hermaphrodite. M20.

gynarchy /ˈɡʌɪnɑːki, ˈdʒʌɪ-/ *noun*. Now *rare*. Orig. †**gun-**. L16.
[ORIGIN from GYNO- + -ARCHY.]
Government by a woman or women. Cf. GYNAECOCRACY.

gyne /dʒʌɪn/ *noun*. E20.
[ORIGIN Greek *gunē* woman, female.]
A queen ant.

gyneco- *combining form*, **gynecocracy** *noun*, etc.: see GYNAECO-, GYNAECOCRACY, etc.

gyneocracy /ɡʌɪnɪˈɒkrəsi/ *noun*. *rare*. E17.
[ORIGIN from GYNO- + -CRACY.]
= GYNAECOCRACY.

gynie *noun* var. of GYNAE.

gyno- /ˈɡʌɪnəʊ, ˈdʒʌɪ-/ *combining form*. Before a vowel **gyn-**.
[ORIGIN from Greek *gunē* woman, female + -O-.]
Used in senses (***a***) woman, women; (***b***) female reproductive organ, esp. (*BOTANY*) of a plant.

■ **gynobase** *noun* (BOTANY) an enlargement of the receptacle that supports the gynoecium in some plants M19. **gyno'basic** *adjective* (BOTANY) pertaining to or having a gynobase M19. **gyno'centric** *adjective* centred on or concerned exclusively with women; taking a female (*spec.* feminist) point of view: L20. **gynodioecious** /-dʌɪ'iːʃəs/ *adjective* (BOTANY) having female and hermaphrodite flowers on separate individuals L19. **gynodioecism** /-dʌɪ'iːsɪz(ə)m/ *noun* = GYNODIOECY L19. **gyno-dioecy** /-dʌɪ'iːsi/ *noun* (BOTANY) the condition of being gynodioecious M20. **gyno'genesis** *noun* (ZOOLOGY) reproduction in which a sperm penetrates an ovum but their nuclei do not fuse, and the embryo develops with maternal chromosomes only E20. **gynoge'netic** *adjective* (ZOOLOGY) of the nature of, arising by, or involving gynogenesis E20. **gynomonoecious** /-mə'niːʃəs/ *adjective* (BOTANY) having female and hermaphrodite flowers on the same individual L19. **gynomonoecism** /-mə'niːsɪz(ə)m/ *noun* (BOTANY) = GYNOMONOECY L19. **gynomonoecy** /-mə'niːsi/ *noun* (BOTANY) the condition of being gynomonoecious M20. **gyno'phobia** *noun* fear of women L19. **gyno'phobic** *adjective* pertaining to or affected with gynophobia L20. **gynophore** *noun* (BOTANY) a stalk which in some plants supports the ovary etc. above the level of other parts of the flower E19. **gynostegium** /-'stiːdʒɪəm/ *noun*, pl. **-gia** /-dʒɪə/, BOTANY a united anther and stigma in certain plants L19.

gynocracy /gʌɪ'nɒkrəsi, dʒ-/ *noun*. E18.
[ORIGIN from GYNO- + -CRACY.]
= GYNAECOCRACY; a government of women; women as the ruling class.
■ **gyno'cratic** *adjective* M19.

gynoecium /gʌɪ'niːsɪəm, dʒ-/ *noun*. Also ***-nec-**, †**gynaeceum**. Pl. **-ia** /-ɪə/. M19.
[ORIGIN mod. Latin, from GYNO- + Greek *oikos* house; *gynaecium* by alt., after Latin GYNAECEUM.]
BOTANY. The female part of an angiosperm flower, which may consist of a single carpel, a number of unfused carpels (apocarpous), or a number of fused carpels (syncarpous).

-gynous /'dʒʌɪnəs/ *suffix*.
[ORIGIN from mod. Latin *-gynus* from Greek *-gunos*, formed as GYNO-: see -OUS.]
1 BOTANY. Having female reproductive organs of an indicated kind or number, as ***androgynous***, ***monogynous***.
2 Of or pertaining to women, as ***androgynous***.

gyoza /gɪ'əʊzə/ *noun*. Pl. same, **-s**. L20.
[ORIGIN Japanese, from Chinese *jiaozi*.]
In Japanese cookery: a crescent-shaped dumpling, usu. stuffed with minced meat and vegetables then fried, steamed, or boiled.

gyp /dʒɪp/ *noun*[1]. M18.
[ORIGIN Perh. abbreviation of GYPPO *noun*.]
A college servant, esp. at the Universities of Cambridge and Durham.

gyp /dʒɪp/ *noun*[2]. *colloq.* L19.
[ORIGIN App. contr. of GEE-UP.]
Only in ***give a person gyp***, (*a*) (of a person) scold or punish a person severely; (*b*) (of a pain etc.) hurt a person very much.

gyp /dʒɪp/ *noun*[3] & *verb*. *colloq.* L19.
[ORIGIN Unknown.]
▸ **A** *noun*. **1** A thief, a swindler. L19.
2 A fraudulent action, a swindle. E20.
▸ **B** *verb trans.* Infl. **-pp-**. Cheat, swindle. (Foll. by *of*.) L19.

gyp /dʒɪp/ *noun*[4]. *US*. L19.
[ORIGIN Perh. abbreviation of GYPSY *noun* used as a proper name.]
A bitch.

gyppo /'dʒɪpəʊ/ *noun*. *colloq.* (*offensive*). Also **gip(p)o**, **G-**. E20.
[ORIGIN Alt. of GIPPY: see -O.]
▸ **A** *noun*. Pl. **-os**.
1 An Egyptian. E20.
2 A Gypsy. E20.

gyppy *noun & adjective* var. of GIPPY.

gyps /dʒɪps/ *noun*. LME.
[ORIGIN Anglicization.]
Gypsum.

gypseous /'dʒɪpsɪəs/ *adjective*. LME.
[ORIGIN from late Latin *gypseus*, from Latin GYPSUM: see -OUS.]
1 Resembling gypsum; hardened, calcified. LME.
2 Containing gypsum, composed chiefly of gypsum. L18.

gypsiferous /dʒɪp'sɪf(ə)rəs/ *adjective*. M19.
[ORIGIN from GYPSUM + -I- + -FEROUS.]
Containing or yielding gypsum.

Gypsologist *noun* var. of GYPSYOLOGIST.

gypsophila /dʒɪp'sɒfɪlə/ *noun*. L18.
[ORIGIN mod. Latin (see below), from Greek *gupsos* chalk, gypsum + *-philos* -loving.]
Any of several plants constituting the genus *Gypsophila*, of the pink family; esp. *G. elegans* and *G. paniculata*, grown for their profusion of delicate white flowers.

gypsophilous /dʒɪp'sɒfɪləs/ *adjective*. E20.
[ORIGIN from Greek *gupsos* chalk + -OUS.]
ECOLOGY. Growing on soils rich in gypsum or, formerly, on limestone.
■ **'gypsophile** *noun* a gypsophilous plant M20.

gypsous /'dʒɪpsəs/ *adjective*. M17.
[ORIGIN from GYPSUM + -OUS.]
= GYPSEOUS.

gypsum /'dʒɪpsəm/ *noun & verb*. LME.
[ORIGIN Latin from Greek *gupsos* chalk, gypsum.]
▸ **A** *noun*. Hydrated calcium sulphate, a soft mineral that occurs as colourless, white, or grey monoclinic prismatic crystals in many sedimentary rocks and is used for making plaster of Paris and as a fertilizer. LME.
▸ **B** *verb trans.* AGRICULTURE. Dress with gypsum. E19.

gypsy /'dʒɪpsi/ *noun & adjective*. Also **gi-**, (orig.) †**gipcyan**, †**gipsen**. M16.
[ORIGIN Aphet. from EGYPTIAN, Gypsies having been orig. thought to have come from Egypt. Later form *gypsy* perh. from Latin *Aegyptius*.]
▸ **A** *noun*. **1** (**G-**.) A member of a travelling people in Europe and N. America who have dark skin and hair and came originally from India, their language (Romany) being related to Hindi; (usu. **g-**) a nomadic or free-spirited person. M16.
†**2** An Egyptian. Only in E17.
3 A cunning, deceitful, or fickle woman (*derog.*); (a playful name for) a woman or girl. E17.
4 In full ***gypsy moth***. A kind of tussock moth, *Lymantria dispar*, which has become a serious pest of trees in parts of N. America since it was introduced there from Europe. E19.
5 (In full ***gypsy winch***) a small winch used on board ship; a toothed or recessed drum on the shaft of a windlass for taking an anchor chain; *US* a smooth drum used similarly to take a rope. L19.
6 An independent truck-driver. *US*. M20.
– COMB.: **gypsy cab** *US* a taxi that is licensed only to respond to telephone calls to the company, *esp.* one that nevertheless cruises for prospective fares; ***gypsy moth***: see sense 4 above; **gypsy rose** *dial.* the field scabious, *Knautia arvensis*; **Gypsy's warning** a cryptic or sinister warning. ***gypsy winch***: see sense 5 above; **gypsywort** [from its reputed use by Gypsies to stain the skin] a labiate plant of watersides, *Lycopus europaeus*, with deeply cut leaves and whorls of small white flowers.
▸ **B** *attrib.* or as *adjective*. (Usu. **G-**.) Of, pertaining to, or characteristic of a Gypsy or Gypsies; characteristic of Gypsies. M17.
■ **Gypsydom** *noun* (*a*) Gypsies collectively; (*b*) *rare* the state of being a Gypsy or living like a Gypsy: M19. **Gypsyhood** *noun* = GYPSYDOM M19. **Gypsyish** *adjective* L19. **Gypsyism** *noun* the life and customs of Gypsies E17.

gypsy /'dʒɪpsi/ *verb intrans.* Also **gi-**. E17.
[ORIGIN from GYPSY *noun*.]
Live or behave like a Gypsy. Chiefly as ***gypsying*** *verbal noun & ppl adjective*.

Gypsyfy /'dʒɪpsɪfʌɪ/ *verb trans.* Usu. **Gipsify**, **Gipsyfy**. E17.
[ORIGIN from GYPSY *noun & adjective* + -FY.]
Make like a Gypsy.

Gypsyologist /dʒɪpsɪ'ɒlədʒɪst/ *noun*. Also **Gypsol-** /dʒɪp'sɒl-/. M19.
[ORIGIN from GYPSY *noun* + -OLOGIST.]
A person who studies Gypsies and their ways.

gyral /'dʒʌɪr(ə)l/ *adjective*. E19.
[ORIGIN from GYRE *noun* + -AL[1].]
Moving in a circle or spiral; of or pertaining to a gyre or gyrus.
■ **gyrally** *adverb* M18.

gyrase /'dʒʌɪreɪz/ *noun*. L20.
[ORIGIN from GYRE *noun* + -ASE.]
BIOCHEMISTRY. An enzyme which removes supercoils from double-helix DNA.

gyrate /'dʒʌɪrət/ *adjective*. M19.
[ORIGIN Latin *gyratus*, formed as GYRUS: see -ATE[2].]
Chiefly BOTANY. Arranged in rings or convolutions; circinate.

gyrate /dʒʌɪ'reɪt/ *verb intrans.* E19.
[ORIGIN Late Latin *gyrat-* pa. ppl stem of *gyrare*, from Latin *gyrus*: see GYRUS, -ATE[3].]
Move in a circle or spiral; revolve round a fixed point or axis; rotate, whirl.

> V. WOOLF Twisting couples gyrating in time to the tune of the gramophone.

gyration /dʒʌɪ'reɪʃ(ə)n/ *noun*. E17.
[ORIGIN Late Latin *gyratio(n-)*, formed as GYRATE *verb*: see -ATION.]
The action or process, or an act, of gyrating; rotation, whirling.

> *fig.*: S. WADDINGTON The vortex of religious excitement . . kept him idly moving in its ceaseless gyrations.

gyrator /dʒʌɪ'reɪtə/ *noun*. M19.
[ORIGIN from GYRATE *verb* + -OR.]
1 A person or thing which gyrates. M19.
2 ELECTRICITY. A passive circuit element with two pairs of terminals which introduces a 180-degree phase shift in one direction of propagation but none in the other. M20.

gyratory /dʒʌɪ'reɪt(ə)ri, 'dʒʌɪrət(ə)ri/ *adjective & noun*. E19.
[ORIGIN from GYRATE *verb* + -ORY[2].]
▸ **A** *adjective*. Moving in a circle or spiral; rotating, whirling; (esp. of a road junction or road system) involving such movement. E19.
▸ **B** *noun*. A road junction or traffic system requiring the circular movement of traffic, larger or more complex than an ordinary roundabout. L20.

gyre /'dʒʌɪə, 'gʌɪə/ *noun*. M16.
[ORIGIN Latin *gyrus* from Greek *guros*.]
▸ **I** Chiefly *literary*.
1 A circular movement or turn; a revolution, a gyration. M16.

> S. O'FAOLÁIN I . . felt the new day come up . . and life begin once more its ancient, ceaseless gyre.

2 A circle, a spiral; a vortex. L16.

> J. A. BAKER Seven hundred lapwings . . dwindled up in spiral tiers and widening gyres.

▸ **II 3** SCIENCE. A circular pattern of surface currents round an ocean basin. M20.

gyre /'dʒʌɪə, 'gʌɪə/ *verb*. LME.
[ORIGIN Late Latin *gyrare*: see GYRATE *verb*.]
1 *verb trans.* Turn or whirl round. *rare*. LME.
2 *verb intrans.* Turn round, rotate, gyrate, whirl. L16.

G

gyre-carline /gʌɪə'kɑːlɪn/ *noun*. *Scot.* (now *rare* or *obsolete*). M16.
[ORIGIN from Old Norse *gýgr* ogress, witch + CARLINE *noun*[1].]
A witch, a hag.

gyrectomy /dʒʌɪ'rɛktəmi/ *noun*. M20.
[ORIGIN from GYRUS + -ECTOMY.]
Surgical removal of a gyrus of the brain; an instance of this.

gyrene /dʒʌɪ'riːn, 'dʒʌɪriːn/ *noun*. *US slang*. Also **-ine**, **ji-**, **jy-**. L19.
[ORIGIN Uncertain: *-rene* from alt. of MA)RINE.]
A US marine.

gyrfalcon /'dʒəːfɔː(l)k(ə)n, -fɒlk(ə)n/ *noun*. Also **ger-**, †**jer-**, †**gier-**, etc. ME.
[ORIGIN Old French *gerfaucon* (mod. *gerfaut*) from Frankish (German *Gerfalke*) = Old Norse *geirfálki*, prob. from Old High German *gêr* spear: see FALCON. Spelling *gyr-* by false etym. from Latin *gyrare* GYRATE *verb*.]
Orig., any large falcon, *esp.* one used to fly at herons. Now, a heavy, powerful falcon, *Falco rusticolus*, of cold northerly regions, occurring in a wide range of colour forms from almost pure white to dark brown.

gyrine *noun* var. of GYRENE.

gyrinid /dʒɪ'rɪnɪd/ *adjective & noun*. E20.
[ORIGIN mod. Latin *Gyrinidae* (see below), from *Gyrinus* genus name from Greek *gurinos* tadpole, from *guros*: see GYRO-, -ID[3].]
(Of, pertaining to, or designating) a beetle of the family Gyrinidae, comprising the whirligig beetles.

gyro /'dʒʌɪrəʊ/ *noun*[1]. Pl. **-os**. E20.
[ORIGIN Abbreviation.]
1 = GYROSCOPE. *colloq.* E20.
2 = GYROCOMPASS. *colloq.* E20.
– COMB.: **gyro-horizon** = ARTIFICIAL ***horizon***; **gyropilot** a gyrocompass used to provide automatic steering for an aircraft or ship; **gyrostabilizer** a gyroscope kept continuously spinning and mounted so as to counter any tendency to roll on the part of a ship, aircraft, platform, etc.

gyro /'jɪərəʊ, 'dʒɪə-, 'dʒʌɪ-; *foreign* 'jiro/ *noun*[2]. *US*. Pl. **-os** /-əʊz, *foreign* -ɔs/. L20.
[ORIGIN mod. Greek *guros* turning: see GYRO-.]
A sandwich of pitta bread filled with slices of spiced meat cooked on a spit, tomatoes, onions, etc.

gyro- /'dʒʌɪrəʊ/ *combining form* of Greek *guros* ring, circle, used also with the sense 'rotation': see -O-.
■ **gyrocopter** *noun* a kind of autogiro, now *spec.* a small light single-seater one E20. **gyrofrequency** *noun* (PHYSICS) the frequency with which a charged particle spirals about the lines of force of a magnetic field M20. **gyroplane** *noun* an aircraft in which lift is provided by aerofoils rotating in an approximately horizontal plane; *esp.* one in which these are not driven by an engine but rotate as a result of the aircraft's forward motion E20. **gyrostat** *noun* any of various forms of gyroscope L19. **gyro'static** *adjective* of or pertaining to a gyrostat or the principle of the gyroscope L19. **gyro'statically** *adverb* = GYROSCOPICALLY L19. **gyro-the'odolite** *noun* a type of theodolite that incorporates a gyroscope as an aid to orientation M20. **gyrotiller** *noun* (AGRICULTURE) a cultivator in which tines rotate about an axis M20.

gyrocompass /'dʒʌɪrə(ʊ)kʌmpəs/ *noun*. E20.
[ORIGIN from GYRO(SCOPE + COMPASS *noun*.]
A non-magnetic compass in which a continuously driven gyroscope is so mounted that its axis remains parallel to the earth's axis of rotation.

gyromagnetic /ˌdʒʌɪrəʊmag'nɛtɪk/ *adjective*. E20.
[ORIGIN from GYRO- + MAGNETIC.]
1 PHYSICS. Of or pertaining to the interaction between the spin of a charged particle and the magnetic moment that it causes. E20.

gyromagnetic ratio: of the magnetic moment of a spinning charged particle to its angular momentum.
2 Designating a compass in which the reading is provided by a directional gyroscope whose gradual deviations are automatically corrected by a magnetic compass. **M20.**

gyromancy /ˈdʒʌɪrəmansi/ *noun.* **M16.**
[**ORIGIN** Old French & mod. French *gyromancie*, formed as **GYRO-**: see **-MANCY.**]
hist. Divination by inference from the point at which a person walking round and round a marked circle fell down from dizziness.

gyron /ˈdʒʌɪərən/ *noun.* **L16.**
[**ORIGIN** Old French & mod. French *giron*, †*geron* gusset from Old Frankish equiv. of Old High German *gēro*: see **GORE** *noun*².]
HERALDRY. A triangular ordinary made by two lines drawn from the edge of the shield to meet in the fess point and occupying half of the quarter.

gyronny /dʒʌɪˈrɒni/ *adjective.* **LME.**
[**ORIGIN** French *gironné*, formed as **GYRON**: see **-Y**⁵.]
HERALDRY. Of a shield: divided into gyrons by lines crossing at the fess point.

G

gyroscope /ˈdʒʌɪrəskəʊp/ *noun.* **M19.**
[**ORIGIN** French, formed as **GYRO-**, **-SCOPE.**]
A wheel or disc mounted so that it can spin rapidly about an axis which itself can rotate about either of two other axes perpendicular to it and to each other; because the spin axis tends to maintain the same direction in space, gyroscopes are used in different devices to provide stabilization or a reference direction, and to measure angular velocity and acceleration.
■ **gyroˈscopic** *adjective* of, pertaining to, or employing a gyroscope **L19.** **gyroˈscopically** *adverb* by or with a gyroscope; in a gyroscopic manner: **E20.**

gyrose /ˈdʒʌɪrəʊs/ *adjective.* **M19.**
[**ORIGIN** from Latin *gyrus*: see **GYRUS**, **-OSE**¹.]
BOTANY. Wavy; marked with wavy lines.

gyrous /ˈdʒʌɪrəs/ *adjective. rare.* **L17.**
[**ORIGIN** from Latin *gyrus*: see **GYRUS**, **-OUS.**]
Circular; spiral.

gyrus /ˈdʒʌɪrəs/ *noun.* Pl. **-ri** /-rʌɪ/. **M19.**
[**ORIGIN** Latin from Greek *guros* ring, circle.]
ANATOMY. A ridge or convolution of the brain; (now *rare*) a convolution or turn of another organ.
FASCIOLAR ***gyrus***. ***uncinate gyrus***: see **UNCINATE** *adjective* 1.

gyte /gʌɪt/ *noun. Scot. derog.* **L19.**
[**ORIGIN** Perh. alt. of **GET** *noun*¹. Cf. **GIT** *noun*¹.]
A child; a brat.

gyte /gʌɪt/ *adjective. Scot.* **E18.**
[**ORIGIN** Unknown.]
Mad.

gytrash /ˈgʌɪtraʃ/ *noun.* Chiefly *N. English.* **M19.**
[**ORIGIN** Unknown.]
An apparition, usu. in the form of a large dog or other animal.

gyttja /ˈjɪtʃə/ *noun.* **L19.**
[**ORIGIN** Swedish = mud, ooze.]
A usu. black sediment, rich in organic matter, deposited in productive lakes.

gyve /dʒʌɪv, gʌɪv/ *noun & verb.* Now *arch.* or *poet.* **ME.**
[**ORIGIN** Unknown.]
▸ **A** *noun.* A shackle, orig. esp. one for the leg. Usu. in *pl.* **ME.**
▸ **B** *verb trans.* Fasten (as) with gyves; fetter. **ME.**

gyver *noun* var. of **GUYVER.**

H, h /eɪtʃ/.
The eighth letter of the modern English alphabet and of the ancient Roman one, repr. a Semitic letter adopted by Greek as eta, orig. the eighth and later, after the omission of Ϝ (see **F, F**), the seventh letter of the alphabet. In Semitic the letter represented a voiceless laryngeal fricative; in early Greek and subsequently in Latin the letter represented the voiceless glottal fricative /h/ (in later Greek H represented a long vowel). In the Germanic languages the letter represented /h/ initially, and a voiceless velar or palatal fricative medially and finally. In Old English the letter occurred before vowels and before the consonants *l, n, r, w*, as in *hlāf* loaf, *hræfn* raven, *hwā* who. H in mod. English has the following values. (i) H has the sound /h/ before *a, e, i, o, u, y*. (ii) H following the consonants *c, p, s, t*, forms the digraphs *ch* /tʃ/; *occas.* x, ç/, *ph* /f/, *sh* /ʃ/, *th* /θ, ð/. Pl. **H's, Hs**. See also **AITCH**.
▸ **I 1** The letter and its sound.
2 The shape of the letter.
H-block an H-shaped building in the former Maze prison in Northern Ireland. **H-iron** a girder of H-shaped section. **H-shaped** *adjective* having a shape or a cross-section like the capital letter H; having two long side pieces with a right-angled crosspiece joining them at or near the middle.
▸ **II** Symbolical uses.
3 Used to denote serial order; applied e.g. to the eighth group or section, sheet of a book, etc.
4 The eighth hypothetical person or example.
5 *PHYSICS* etc. ▸**a** (Cap. H.) Magnetic field strength. ▸**b** (Cap. H.) The Hamiltonian function of classical mechanics; the Hamiltonian operator of quantum mechanics. ▸**c** (Italic *h*) Planck's constant. Also $\hbar = h/2\pi$. ▸**d** (Cap. H.) Enthalpy.
▸ **III 6** Abbrevs.: **H** = hardness; hard (pencil lead); (*ELECTRICITY*) henry(s); heroin; hydrogen. **h** = (as *prefix*) hecto-; hour(s).

Ha *symbol.*
CHEMISTRY. Hahnium.

ha /hɑː/ *verb intrans.* Also **hah**. **E17.**
[**ORIGIN** from **HA** *interjection.*]
Utter 'ha' in hesitation. Esp. in ***hum and ha***: see **HUM** *verb*[1] 1.

ha /hɑː/ *interjection & noun.* Also **hah**. **ME.**
[**ORIGIN** Natural exclam. Cf. **AH** *interjection*, **AHA** *interjection*, **HE** *interjection*, **HO** *interjection*[1].]
▸ **A** *interjection.* **1** Expr. surprise, joy, suspicion, indignation, etc. (Earlier in **HA HA** *interjection*) **ME.**
2 Used as an interjectional interrogative, *esp.* one which follows a question; = **EH** 2. **L16.**
3 Expr. hesitation or interruption in speech. Cf. **HAW** *interjection*[1], **HUM** *interjection.* **E17.**
▸ **B** *noun.* This interjection, esp. as an expression of hesitation. Freq. in ***hums and ha's***: see **HUM** *noun*[1] 1. **E17.**

ha' *noun* see **HALL** *noun.*

ha. *abbreviation.*
Hectare(s).

haaf /hɑːf, haf/ *noun.* **L18.**
[**ORIGIN** Old Norse *haf* (Swedish *haf*, Danish *hav*) sea, high sea, ocean.]
In Orkney and Shetland, the deep or main sea, esp. as used for deep-sea fishing.

haar /hɑː/ *noun.* Chiefly *Scot. & N. English.* **L17.**
[**ORIGIN** Perh. from Old Norse *hárr* hoar, hoary.]
A wet mist or fog; *esp.* a cold sea fog.

haarder *noun* var. of **HARDER**.

HAART *abbreviation.*
MEDICINE. Highly active antiretroviral therapy.

haat /hɑːt/ *noun. Indian.* **L20.**
[**ORIGIN** Hindi.]
A market.

hab /hab/ *adverb & noun. obsolete* exc. *dial.* **M16.**
[**ORIGIN** Repr. Old English *hæbbe* pres. subjunct. of **HAVE** *verb*, with corresp. neg. form *næbbe*. Cf. **HOB** *adverb & noun*[3], **HOB-NOB** *adverb*.]
by hab or nab, hab or nab, by habs and nabs, = **HOB-NOB** *adverb*.

Hab. *abbreviation.*
Habakkuk (in the Bible).

habanera /(h)abəˈnɛːrə/ *noun.* **L19.**
[**ORIGIN** Spanish, short for *danza habanera* Havanan dance, fem. of *habanero*: see **HABANERO**.]
A slow Cuban dance and song in duple time.

habanero /(h)abəˈnɛːrəʊ/ *noun.* Pl. **-os**. **L19.**
[**ORIGIN** Spanish = of *Havana* the capital of Cuba.]
1 = **HABANERA**. *rare.* **L19.**
2 A small chilli pepper of an extremely hot variety. *N. Amer.* **L20.**

habara /ˈhab(ə)rə/ *noun.* Also **-ah**, **habra**. **E19.**
[**ORIGIN** Arabic *ḥabara*.]
In N. Africa, a woman's silk outdoor garment.

habdabs *noun pl.* var. of **ABDABS**.

Habdalah /havˈdɑːlə/ *noun.* Also **Hav-**. **M18.**
[**ORIGIN** Hebrew *habdālāh* separation, division.]
A Jewish religious ceremony marking the end of the Sabbath; a prayer said at this ceremony.

habeas corpora /ˌheɪbɪəs ˈkɔːpərə/ *noun phr.* **LME.**
[**ORIGIN** Latin = thou (shalt) have the bodies (*sc.* in court).]
LAW (now *hist.*). A process formerly issued from the Court of Common Pleas, directing the sheriff to compel the attendance of reluctant jurors.

habeas corpus /ˌheɪbɪəs ˈkɔːpəs/ *noun phr.* **LME.**
[**ORIGIN** Latin = thou (shalt) have the body (*sc.* in court).]
LAW. A writ requiring a person to be brought before a judge or into a court; *spec.* such a writ requiring the investigation of the legality of a person's detention, by which his or her release may be secured.
– **COMB.**: **Habeas Corpus Act** an Act of Charles II in 1679 which greatly facilitated the use of such writs.

habendum /həˈbɛndəm/ *noun.* **E17.**
[**ORIGIN** Latin, lit. 'to be had, to be possessed', gerundive of *habere* have.]
LAW (now *hist.*). The part of a deed determining the estate or quantity of interest granted by the deed.

haberdash /ˈhabədaʃ/ *noun.* Long *rare.* **LME.**
[**ORIGIN** Back-form. from **HABERDASHER** or formed as **HABERDASHER**.]
Small wares or merchandise.

haberdasher /ˈhabədaʃə/ *noun.* **ME.**
[**ORIGIN** Prob. from unrecorded Anglo-Norman (cf. Anglo-Latin *habardasshator*) presumably from recorded *hapertas*, of unknown origin, perh. the name of a fabric: see **-ER**[2].]
†**1** A dealer in a variety of household articles; *esp.* from the 16th cent., a dealer in hats and caps, a hatter. **ME–E18.**
2 A dealer in small articles related to dress, as thread, tape, ribbon, etc. Also (*N. Amer.*), a dealer in men's clothing and accessories. **E17.**
3 A drink-seller. *slang.* Now *rare.* **E19.**

haberdashery /ˈhabədaʃ(ə)ri/ *noun.* **LME.**
[**ORIGIN** formed as **HABERDASHER**: see **-ERY**.]
1 The goods and wares sold by a haberdasher. **LME.**

> R. BROUGHTON A whirlwind of haberdashery, Brussels lace, diamonds.

2 The shop or establishment of a haberdasher, esp. as a department in a store. **E19.**

habergeon /ˈhabədʒ(ə)n, həˈbəːdʒ(ə)n/ *noun.* **ME.**
[**ORIGIN** Old French & mod. French *haubergeon* from Old French *hauberc* (mod. *haubert*): see **HAUBERK**, **-OON**.]
hist. A sleeveless coat or jacket of mail or scale armour; a small hauberk.

habile /ˈhabɪl/ *adjective.* **LME.**
[**ORIGIN** Var. of **ABLE** *adjective*, conformed to mod. French *habile* or Latin *habilis*.]
1 a Suited; suitable; competent; = **ABLE** *adjective* 2. *obsolete* exc. *Scot.* **LME.** ▸†**b** Manageable, easy to use; = **ABLE** *adjective* 1. Only in **M18.**
2 Having the capacity or power (*to do*); = **ABLE** *adjective* 4. Now *literary.* **LME.**
3 Handy, ready; skilful, adroit, dexterous. Now *literary.* **L15.**

habiliment /həˈbɪlɪm(ə)nt/ *noun.* Also †**a-**. **LME.**
[**ORIGIN** Old French *abillement* (later & mod. *hab-*), from *habiller* make fit, fit out, (hence, by assoc. with *habit*) clothe, dress, formed as **HABILE**: see **-MENT**.]
1 Outfit, equipment, attire, dress. **LME.**

> S. ROGERS In rich habiliment Two Strangers at the Convent-gate.

†**2** In *pl.* Munitions, weapons, apparatus of war. **LME–L17.** ▸**b** In *pl.* Pieces of armour, apparel of war. Also, the trappings of a horse. **L15–E19.**
3 In *pl.* The garments or apparel appropriate to any office or occasion. Also (*joc.*), ordinary clothes or dress. **L15.**

> A. B. JAMESON The Saviour is seen in the habiliments of a gardener.

†**4** Anything worn as an ornament; = **BILIMENT**. **L15–E17.**
†**5** *fig.* Mental equipment or capacity; in *pl.*, abilities, faculties, powers. **L16–M17.**

■ **habilimented** *adjective* (*arch.*) equipped, apparelled, dressed **E17.**

habilitate /həˈbɪlɪteɪt/ *verb.* **E17.**
[**ORIGIN** medieval Latin *habilitat-* pa. ppl stem of *habilitare*, from *habilitas* **ABILITY**: see **-ATE**[3].]
1 *verb trans.* **a** Make capable, qualify. Now *rare.* **E17.** ▸**b** Fit out (esp. the workings of a mine). *US.* **E19.**
2 *verb intrans.* [German *habilitieren*.] Qualify as a teacher in a German university. **L19.**
3 *verb trans.* Clothe, dress. **L19.**
■ **habiliˈtation** *noun* the action of enabling; capacitation, qualification: **E17.**

hability /həˈbɪlɪti/ *noun.* **LME.**
[**ORIGIN** Var. of **ABILITY**. In sense 2 after French *habileté*.]
†**1** See **ABILITY**. **LME.**
2 The quality of being habile; readiness; adroitness. *rare.* **M19.**

habit /ˈhabɪt/ *noun.* **ME.**
[**ORIGIN** Old French *abit* (later & mod. *habit*) from Latin *habitus*, from *habit-* pa. ppl stem of *habere* have, hold, (refl.) be constituted, be.]
▸ **I** Dress.
1 Bodily apparel or attire; clothing, dress. *arch.* **ME.** ▸**b** A set or suit of clothes; a dress (of a specified kind). *arch.* **LME.** ▸**c** A garment; a gown, a robe. Usu. in *pl. arch.* **L15.** ▸**d** *transf. & fig.* Outward form or appearance; guise. **M16.**

> H. J. LASKI Bolingbroke's Patriot King, dressed up in the habit of the elder Pitt.

2 *spec.* The dress or attire characteristic of a particular rank, profession, function, etc.; *esp.* the dress of a religious order. **ME.**

> L. DURRELL Her body lay shrouded in the habit of St Francis.

riding habit etc.
3 A costume designed to be worn by a woman on horseback, a riding habit. **L18.**

> *Pony* Ready made side-saddle habits.

▸ **II** Physical appearance or constitution.
†**4** Bearing, demeanour, deportment; posture. **LME–L17.**
5 Bodily condition or constitution. **LME.** ▸†**b** The bodily system. **L16–M18.** ▸†**c** The surface or outward appearance of the body. **M17–E18.**

> J. PRIESTLEY A being . . of a delicate tender habit.

6 *BIOLOGY & CRYSTALLOGRAPHY.* The characteristic mode of growth and general external form of an organism (esp. a plant), mineral, etc. **L17.**

> *Scientific American* The pepper plant usually has a very leafy habit. *Photography* Controlling crystal habit (its shape) is closely determined by the sort of chemicals added to improve sensitivity.

▸ **III** Mental disposition or constitution.
7 A person's mental or moral qualities; mental constitution, disposition, character. **LME.**

> E. YOUNG You . . suit the gloomy habit of my soul.

8 A settled disposition or tendency to act in a certain way, *esp.* one acquired by frequent repetition of the same act until it is almost involuntary; a customary practice or way of acting; (usu. in *pl.*) a characteristic action or mode of behaviour of an animal. **LME.** ▸**b** Custom, usage. **E17.** ▸**c** *spec.* A craving for or dependency on an addictive drug or drugs; the practice of taking such a drug or drugs. *colloq.* **E19.** ▸**d** *PSYCHOLOGY.* An automatic reaction to a specific situation, acquired by learning or repetition. **M19.**

> J. THURBER Her habit of starting sentences in the middle bewildered him. T. A. COWARD The Red-footed Falcon . . shares with the Hobby one habit, that of hawking for crepuscular moths. **c** L. D. ESTLEMAN As innocent as a hooker with a heroin habit.

†**9** The condition of being accustomed to something; familiarity. **L16–M19.**
▸ **IV** †**10** *LOGIC.* The eighth of the ten categories or predicaments postulated by Aristotle: having, possession. **M16–M19.**
– **PHRASES**: **break the habit** stop doing a habitual thing, *esp.* give up an addictive or otherwise damaging practice. ***creature of habit***: see **CREATURE** 5. **fall into the habit of** begin to do regularly. **from force of habit**, **from habit** because it is one's usual or customary behaviour. **get into the habit of** = ***fall into the habit of*** above. **get out of the habit of** cease to do regularly. **in the habit of**, †**in habits of** having the custom or regular practice of. **kick the habit** = ***break the habit*** above. **make a habit of** do regularly. **out of habit** = ***from force of habit*** above.
– **COMB.**: **habit-forming** *adjective* addictive; **habit-shirt** *hist.* a kind of chemisette with a collar, formerly worn by women under an outer bodice; **habit-training** the training of a child in regular patterns of behaviour.

habit /ˈhabɪt/ *verb*. LME.
[ORIGIN Old French & mod. French *habiter* from Latin *habitare* have possession of, inhabit, from *habit-*: see HABIT *noun*.]
1 †**a** *verb intrans.* Dwell, reside. LME–M17. ▸**b** *verb trans.* Dwell in, inhabit. *arch.* L16.
2 *verb trans.* Dress, clothe, attire. LME.
M. INNES Two elderly women, habited in old-fashioned . . mourning.
3 *verb trans.* Accustom, familiarize, habituate. *obsolete* exc. *Scot. & dial.* E17.

habitable /ˈhabɪtəb(ə)l/ *adjective*. LME.
[ORIGIN Old French *abitable* (later & mod. *hab-*) from Latin *habitabilis*, from *habitare*: see HABIT *verb*, -ABLE.]
Fit or suitable for habitation; that can be inhabited.
E. F. BENSON The house . . was habitable again after a period of prolonged neglect.
■ **habitaˈbility** *noun* E19. **habitableness** *noun* M17. **habitably** *adverb* E19.

habitacle /ˈhabɪtək(ə)l/ *noun*. Now *rare*. LME.
[ORIGIN Old French & mod. French from Latin *habitaculum* dwelling place, from *habitare*: see HABIT *verb*, -CULE.]
1 A dwelling place, a habitation. LME.
2 A niche in the wall of a building. LME.

†**habitance** *noun*. *rare* (Spenser). Only in L16.
[ORIGIN Old French, formed as HABIT *verb*: see -ANCE.]
A dwelling place, a habitation.

H

habitancy /ˈhabɪt(ə)nsi/ *noun*. L18.
[ORIGIN from HABITANT: see -ANCY.]
1 Residence as an inhabitant. L18.
2 Inhabitants collectively. E19.

habitant /ˈhabɪt(ə)nt; *in sense A.2 & corresp. adjective foreign* abitɑ̃ (*pl. same*)/ *noun & adjective*. LME.
[ORIGIN Old French & mod. French, pres. pple of *habiter*: see HABIT *verb*, -ANT[1].]
▸ **A** *noun*. **1** A person who dwells or resides in a place; a resident, an inhabitant. LME.
2 (A descendant of) a French settler in Canada, *esp.* one who works the land. Also, a native of Louisiana of French descent. L18.
▸ **B** *adjective*. Inhabiting, residing; of or pertaining to a habitant; used for habitation. M19.

habitat /ˈhabɪtat/ *noun*. L18.
[ORIGIN Latin, lit. 'it inhabits', 3rd person sing. pres. of *habitare*: see HABIT *verb*.]
1 The natural environment characteristically occupied by a particular organism; an area distinguished by the set of organisms which occupy it. Also, such areas collectively. L18.
E. NEWMAN The Black Spleenwort . . occurs on rocks as a native habitat. ANTHONY HUXLEY Desert and mountain habitats. B. LOPEZ Bailey Point . . the best muskox habitat in the high Arctic. *Photography* The wood . . has a lot of varied habitat.
2 *gen.* One's dwelling place; a habitation; usual surroundings. M19.
K. WATERHOUSE A transport café in the Huddersfield Road, her natural habitat.

habitate /ˈhabɪteɪt/ *verb*. Long *rare*. E17.
[ORIGIN Latin *habitat-* pa. ppl stem of *habitare*: see HABIT *verb*, -ATE[3].]
1 *verb trans.* Accustom, habituate. E17.
2 *verb intrans.* Dwell. M19.

habitation /habɪˈteɪʃ(ə)n/ *noun*. LME.
[ORIGIN Old French & mod. French from Latin *habitatio(n-)*, formed as HABITATE: see -ATION.]
1 The action of dwelling in or inhabiting; occupancy by inhabitants. LME.
Daily Chronicle The premises to be closed . . until they were made fit for human habitation.
2 A place of abode, a dwelling place; *spec.* a house, a home. LME.
I. MURDOCH The only habitation near it was a farmhouse. W. SOYINKA If monster snakes had a choice, the bamboo clumps would be their ideal habitation.
3 A settlement. M16.
– COMB.: **habitation site** ARCHAEOLOGY a site where there has been a settlement.

habitative /ˈhabɪteɪtɪv, -tət-/ *adjective*. L16.
[ORIGIN formed as HABITATE: see -IVE.]
Of or pertaining to habitation.

habitual /həˈbɪtʃʊəl, -tjʊəl/ *adjective & noun*. LME.
[ORIGIN medieval Latin *habitualis*, from *habitus*: see HABIT *noun*, -AL[1].]
▸ **A** *adjective*. †**1** Belonging to the inward disposition; inherent or latent in the mental constitution. See HABIT *noun* 7. LME–M19.
2 Of the nature of a habit; fixed by habit; constantly repeated or continued; customary. E17. ▸**b** Given to a specified habit; that habitually does or is what is denoted by the noun. E19.
K. AMIS He turned with his habitual abruptness and went into the room. **b** P. G. HAMERTON Almost all English people are habitual tea-drinkers.
3 Usual, constant, continual. M17.
O. SACKS Her migraines turned from habitual to occasional.
▸ **B** *noun*. †**1** A latent disposition of the soul. *rare*. Only in M17.
2 A person who does something habitually; *esp.* a habitual criminal or drunkard. L19.
■ **habituˈality** *noun* E19. **habitualize** *verb trans.* make habitual L18. **habitually** *adverb* †(**a**) with respect to habit; inherently; potentially; (**b**) in the way of habit or settled practice; usually, customarily: LME. **habitualness** *noun* M17.

habituate /həˈbɪtʃʊeɪt, -tjʊeɪt/ *verb trans.* L15.
[ORIGIN Latin *habituat-* pa. ppl stem of late Latin *habituare*, from Latin *habitus*: see HABIT *noun*, -ATE[3].]
1 Settle (a person) in a habit; accustom *to*, familiarize *with*. L15.
R. DAVIES School had habituated Francis to shabbiness and discomfort and stinks.
†**2** Make (something) habitual; form into a habit. E–M17.
†**3** Settle as an inhabitant *in*. Only in 17.
4 Be in or visit frequently; frequent. *N. Amer.* L19.

habituation /həbɪtʃʊˈeɪʃ(ə)n, -tjʊ-/ *noun*. LME.
[ORIGIN French, or medieval Latin *habituatio(n-)*, formed as HABITUATE; in mod. use from HABITUATE: see -ATION.]
1 The action of making or becoming habitual; formation of habit; *spec.* the formation of a damaging or addictive habit, as a dependency on a drug or drugs. LME.
2 The action of habituating or the condition of being habituated; *spec.* in PSYCHOLOGY, the diminishing of an innate response to a frequently repeated stimulus. E19.

habitude /ˈhabɪtjuːd/ *noun*. LME.
[ORIGIN Old French & mod. French from Latin *habitudo*, from *habit-*: see HABIT *noun*, -TUDE.]
1 Manner of being or existing; mental or bodily constitution; disposition; = HABIT *noun* 5, 7. LME.
2 A disposition to act in a certain way; a custom, a tendency; = HABIT *noun* 8. LME. ▸**b** Custom, usage; = HABIT *noun* 8b. L16.
J. BUTLER Many habitudes of life, not given by nature, but which nature directs us to acquire. **b** H. ALLEN The orphan out of habitude from old times came close to the Virgin.
†**3** Familiar relation or acquaintance; familiarity. L15–L18.
†**4** Manner of being with relation to something else; relation, respect. M16–M18.
†**5** CHEMISTRY. Chemical behaviour; reactions. L18–M19.
■ **habiˈtudinal** *adjective* †(**a**) habitual, customary; (**b**) of or pertaining to habit: LME.

habitué /həˈbɪtjʊeɪ, *foreign* abitɥe (*pl. same*)/ *noun*. E19.
[ORIGIN French, pa. pple of *habituer* from Latin *habituare*: see HABITUATE *verb*.]
A habitual visitor or resident (*of* a place).
E. WAUGH I stayed at the Cavendish once . . but I was never an habitué.

habitus /ˈhabɪtəs/ *noun*. L19.
[ORIGIN Latin.]
Bodily constitution.

hab-nab *adverb* see HOB-NOB *adverb*.

haboob /həˈbuːb/ *noun*. L19.
[ORIGIN Arabic *habūb* blowing furiously.]
A violent and oppressive seasonal wind blowing in Sudan and bringing sand from the desert.

habra *noun* var. of HABARA.

habs-nabs *adverb* see HOB-NOB *adverb*.

habutai /ˈhɑːbʊtʌɪ/ *noun*. L19.
[ORIGIN Japanese *habutae*, from *ha* wing + *futa* two + *e* fold.]
Fine soft silk of a type orig. made in Japan. Also called ***Japanese silk***, ***Jap silk***.

HAC *abbreviation*.
Honourable Artillery Company.

háček /ˈhɑːtʃɛk, ˈha-/ *noun*. M20.
[ORIGIN Czech, dim. of *hák* hook.]
A diacritic mark (ˇ) used chiefly in Baltic and Slavonic languages, esp. to indicate various types of palatalization.

hacendado /ɑːsɛnˈdɑːdəʊ, *foreign* aθenˈdaðo/ *noun*. Also **hacien-** /ˌɑːsɪɛn-, *foreign* aθien-/. Pl. **-os** /-əʊz, *foreign* -os/. M19.
[ORIGIN Spanish.]
The owner of a hacienda.

hachis /haˈʃiː, *foreign* aʃi/ *noun*. Pl. same. M18.
[ORIGIN French.]
A hash, a mess.

hachure /haˈʃjʊə/ *noun & verb*. M19.
[ORIGIN French, from *hacher* HATCH *verb*[2]: see -URE.]
CARTOGRAPHY. ▸**A** *noun*. Any of a number of short lines of shading on a map running in the direction of a slope and indicating steepness by their closeness and thickness. Also ***hachure line***. Usu. in *pl.* M19.
▸ **B** *verb trans.* Shade (a map) with hachures. M19.

†**hachy** *noun*. ME–M17.
[ORIGIN Old French & mod. French *haché* pa. pple of *hacher* to hash; later infl. by *hachis*. Cf. HASH *noun*[1], HACHIS.]
= HASH *noun*[1].

hacienda /hasɪˈɛndə, *foreign* aθiˈenda/ *noun*. M18.
[ORIGIN Spanish from Latin *facienda* things to be done, from *facere* do.]
In Spain and Spanish-speaking countries, an estate including a house; a large farm, a plantation; a rural factory.
O. HENRY Ranch supplies, bound on the morrow for some outlying hacienda.

hack /hak/ *noun*[1]. ME.
[ORIGIN Partly from Middle Low German *hakke*, from *hacken* HACK *verb*[1]; partly from HACK *verb*[1].]
1 An implement for breaking or chopping up, esp. used in agriculture and mining; *spec.* a two-pronged tool resembling a mattock. ME.
2 A cut, a notch; a gash, a wound, (esp. caused by a kick with the toe of a boot); a chap in the skin. LME. ▸**b** CURLING. A notch made in the ice, or a metal or wooden insert into the ice, used to steady the foot when delivering a stone. E19.
3 A hesitation in speech. Now *rare*. M17.
4 An act of hacking or chopping, a hacking blow; *fig.* (*N. Amer.*) a try, an attempt. M19.
5 A short dry hard cough. L19.
6 A spell of, or the action of, hacking on a computer. *colloq.* L20.

hack /hak/ *noun*[2] *& adjective*. Chiefly *colloq.* ME.
[ORIGIN Abbreviation of HACKNEY *noun & adjective*.]
▸ **A** *noun*. **1** A horse for ordinary riding. ME. ▸**b** A horse let out for hire; *derog.* a worn-out horse, a jade. E18.
Illustrated London News Sir Charles Knightley . . stuck to his road hack long after his neighbours had taken to post-horses.
†**2** The driver of a hackney carriage. L17–M19.
3 A person hired to do esp. dull or routine work, a drudge; *esp.* a writer of poor or average quality literary or (esp.) journalistic work; a writer or journalist who will take on any available work. L17. ▸**b** A prostitute. M18.
C. CONNOLLY There are no pensions for literary hacks. J. CRITCHLEY The cluster of hacks . . notebooks in hand . . ready to transmit their ramblings to the nation.
4 A vehicle plying for hire; a taxi. Now *N. Amer.* E18.
†**5** Anything that is hackneyed or made commonplace by frequent indiscriminate use. Cf. sense B.2. E18–E19.
6 NAUTICAL. In full ***hack watch***. A chronometer watch used on deck to take an astronomical sight for navigational purposes. M19.
▸ **B** *attrib.* or as *adjective*. **1** Of a person: employed as a hack; for hire. Of writing etc.: like that undertaken by a hack. M18.
B. CASTLE The hack journalists of the right-wing press must be desperate . . to discredit Harold.
2 Commonplace; hackneyed; trite. L18.
BYRON When the old world grows dull And we are sick of its hack sounds and sights.
3 Of or pertaining to a hack or taxi. E19.
– COMB.: **hackwork** work, esp. literary work, (of a kind) which a person is hired to do; menial work.
■ **hackˈette** *noun* (*colloq.*, somewhat *derog.*) a female journalist L20.

hack /hak/ *noun*[3]. In senses 2, 3 also **hake** /heɪk/. LME.
[ORIGIN Var. (from inflected forms) of HATCH *noun*[1]. Cf. HECK *noun*[1].]
†**1** = HATCH *noun*[1] 1. Only in LME.
2 = HECK *noun*[1] 2. *Scot. & N. English*. M16.
3 FALCONRY. A board on which a hawk's meat is laid (also ***hack board***). Hence, the state of partial liberty of a young hawk. L16.
at hack (of a young hawk) given partial liberty.
4 A wooden frame for drying cheeses, fish, bricks, etc. Also, a row of bricks laid out to dry. L17.

hack /hak/ *verb*[1].
[ORIGIN Old English (*tō*)*haccian* cut in pieces = Old Frisian (*tō*)*hakia*, Middle Low German, Middle Dutch, Middle & mod. High German *hacken* (Dutch *hakken*), ult. from West Germanic deriv. of imit. base: cf. synon. Old English *hæććan*, Old High German *hecken*. Cf. HECK *verb*.]
▸ **I** *verb trans.* **1** Cut or chop with heavy blows in a rough or random fashion; mangle or mutilate by jagged cuts. (Foll. by *at*, *away*, *down*, *off*, etc.) OE. ▸**b** *spec.* in AGRICULTURE. Break or plough up the surface of (the ground); hoe *in* (seed); reap (a crop). Now *dial.* E17. ▸**c** Of cold or frost: chap or crack the skin. *dial.* L17.
J. M. BARRIE Crichton and Treherne . . hacking and hewing the bamboo . . making a clearing. A. J. TOYNBEE To hack one's way with a machete through hundreds of miles of jungle. B. VINE He hacked off a slice from the new brown loaf and ate it dry.
†**2** *fig.* Mangle (words) in utterance. L16–L17.
3 SPORT, esp. FOOTBALL. Kick the shin of (an opponent) intentionally with the toe of the boot. (Foll. by *over*, *up*.) M19.
M. SHEARMAN No hacking, or hacking over, or tripping up shall be allowed.
4 *slang*. **a** Annoy; embarrass, disconcert, confuse. Also with *off*. Freq. as **hacked(-off)** *ppl adjective*. *N. Amer.* L19. ▸**b** Cope with, manage; tolerate, accept; comprehend. Freq. with *it*. M20.

a *Rolling Stone* I wouldn't be so hacked off about it if I didn't love country music. b *Newsweek* I had proved to the world during my four years in the Senate . . that I can hack it. T. PARKER If you're going to be an officer, it's no use saying you can't hack something.

5 Gain unauthorized access to (a computer file or system or the data held in one). Also, program quickly and roughly. *colloq.* L20.
▸ **II** *verb intrans.* **6** Make rough or random cutting or chopping blows. Freq. foll. by *at*. OE. ▸**b** Massage by striking with the edge of the hand. Chiefly as ***hacking*** *verbal noun*. L19.

H. INNES Engles and Keramikos were hacking away at the concrete flooring with pick and hammer.

7 Of the teeth: chatter. *obsolete* exc. *dial.* OE.
8 Hesitate in speech; stammer. Cf. HACKER *verb*. *obsolete* exc. *dial.* M16. ▸†**b** Hesitate, haggle. L16–L17.
9 Cough repeatedly with a short dry cough. Cf. HECK *verb*. E19.
hacking cough a short, dry, frequently repeated cough.
10 Use a computer purely for one's own satisfaction; gain unauthorized access *into* (a computer file, system, etc.). Freq. as ***hacking*** *verbal noun*. *colloq.* L20.
– COMB.: **hack-and-slash** *adjective* designating a game, film, etc., characterized by combat and violence; **hack-hammer** a tool resembling an adze but with a short handle, used in dressing stone; **hacksaw** a saw with a narrow blade set in a frame, used for cutting metal.
▪ **hacking** *noun* (*a*) the action of the verb; (*b*) *dial.* a large Christmas pudding of sausage or mincemeat: LME. **hackster** *noun* (*obsolete* exc. *dial.*) a cutthroat, a murderer L16.

hack /hak/ *verb*[2]. M18.
[ORIGIN from HACK *noun*[2].]
1 *verb trans.* Make trite or commonplace by overuse; = HACKNEY *verb* 2. M18.
2 *verb trans.* Employ as a literary hack. E19.
3 *verb intrans.* & *trans.* Use (a horse) for ordinary riding. Now *esp.* ride (a horse) in the country for pleasure. Cf. HACKNEY *verb* 1. M19.
hacking coat, **hacking jacket**: for use when riding, with slits at the sides or back and freq. tailored in tweed.
4 *verb intrans.* Ride in a hack or taxi. *US.* L19.

hack /hak/ *verb*[3] *trans.* L19.
[ORIGIN from HACK *noun*[3].]
1 Place (bricks) in rows on a hack or drying frame. L19.
2 FALCONRY. Keep (a young hawk) at hack or in a state of partial liberty. L19.

hackamore /ˈhakəmɔː/ *noun*. *US.* M19.
[ORIGIN Perh. from Spanish *jaquima*, formerly *xaquima* halter.]
A type of bitless bridle with a hard oval noseband which allows pressure to be exerted on the nose by means of the reins attached just in front of a heavy counterbalancing knot. Also, a bitless bridle with a single rein.

hackberry /ˈhakb(ə)ri/ *noun*. M18.
[ORIGIN Var. of HAGBERRY.]
1 = HAGBERRY. *N. English*. M18.
2 Any of several N. American kinds of nettle tree (genus *Celtis*), esp. *C. occidentalis*; the edible purplish-black fruit of such a tree, resembling that of the hagberry or bird cherry. M18.

hackbut /ˈhakbət/ *noun*. Also **hag-** /ˈhag-/, (earliest) †**-bush**. L15.
[ORIGIN (French *haquebut(e* alt. of) *haquebusche* from Middle Dutch *hakebus*, *hagebus* (Dutch *haakbus*), Middle Low German *hakebusse*, from *hake(n* HOOK *noun* + *bus(se* gun, firearm (cf. BLUNDERBUSS). Cf. HARQUEBUS.]
= HARQUEBUS 1.
▪ **hackbuˈteer** *noun* (*hist.*) = HACKBUTTER E17. **hackbutter** *noun* (*hist.*) a soldier armed with a hackbut E16.

hackee /ˈhaki/ *noun*. *N. Amer.* M19.
[ORIGIN Prob. imit.]
A chipmunk.

hacker /ˈhakə/ *noun*. ME.
[ORIGIN from HACK *verb*[1] + -ER[1].]
1 A person who or thing which hacks (something). ME.
2 *spec.* An enthusiastic computer programmer or user; a person who tries to gain unauthorized access to a computer or to data held in one. *colloq.* L20.
▪ **hackerdom** *noun* the realm or world of computer hackers L20.

hacker /ˈhakə/ *verb intrans.* *dial.* L18.
[ORIGIN Frequentative of HACK *verb*[1].]
Stammer, stutter.

hackery /ˈhak(ə)ri/ *noun*. *Indian.* L17.
[ORIGIN Hindi *chakṛā* two-wheeled cart.]
A bullock cart; a carriage.

hackia /ˈhakɪə/ *noun*. M19.
[ORIGIN Guyanese name.]
= GUAIACUM 1, 2.

hackie /ˈhaki/ *noun*. *US colloq.* Also **-ky**. M20.
[ORIGIN from HACK *noun*[2] + -IE.]
A taxi-driver.

hackle /ˈhak(ə)l/ *noun*[1].
[ORIGIN Old English *hacele*, *hæcile*, corresp. (exc. in formative suffix) to Old High German *hachul*, Middle High German *hachel*, Old Norse *hǫkull*, Gothic *hakuls*.]
†**1** A cloak, a mantle, an outer garment; a chasuble. OE–ME.
2 A covering of any kind, as a bird's plumage, a snake's skin, etc. *obsolete* exc. *dial.* LME.
3 A conical straw roof on a beehive. E17.

hackle /ˈhak(ə)l/ *noun*[2]. LME.
[ORIGIN Var. of HATCHEL *noun*. Cf. HECKLE *noun*.]
▸ **I 1** A long shining feather or a series of feathers on the neck or saddle of a domestic cock, peacock, pigeon, etc., which is erected in anger. LME. ▸**b** A stickleback. *dial.* M17.
2 ANGLING. An artificial fly dressed wholly or chiefly with a hackle. Also ***hackle fly***. L17.
3 A cockade of hackles in a Highland soldier's bonnet. L18.
4 *transf.* In *pl.* The erectile hairs along the back of a dog, which rise when it is angry or alarmed. L19.
make a person's hackles rise, **raise a person's hackles** anger or annoy a person.
▸ **II 5** An instrument with parallel steel pins for splitting and combing the fibres of flax or hemp; a flax comb. (Earlier as HECKLE *noun* 1.) L15. ▸**b** A tool with spikes used in wig-making for combing or carding skeins of hair. E20.

hackle /ˈhak(ə)l/ *verb*[1] *trans.* L16.
[ORIGIN Dim. or frequentative of HACK *verb*[1]: see -LE[3], cf. HAGGLE *verb*.]
= HACK *verb*[1] 1.

hackle /ˈhak(ə)l/ *verb*[2] *trans.* *obsolete* exc. *dial.* E17.
[ORIGIN from HACKLE *noun*[1].]
Cover (a beehive) with a hackle.

hackle /ˈhak(ə)l/ *verb*[3] *trans.* L17.
[ORIGIN from HACKLE *noun*[2]. Cf. HECKLE *verb*.]
1 Dress or comb (flax or hemp) with a hackle, in preparation for spinning. L17.
2 ANGLING. Dress (a fly) with a hackle. Chiefly as ***hackled*** *ppl adjective*. M19.
3 Dress (hair) in wig-making. M20.
▪ **hackler** *noun* a flax-dresser M18.

hacklet /ˈhaklɪt/ *noun*. *dial.* M19.
[ORIGIN Unknown.]
= KITTIWAKE.

hackly /ˈhakli/ *adjective*. L18.
[ORIGIN from HACKLE *verb*[1] + -Y[1].]
Rough, jagged; *esp.* (of a metal or mineral surface) having short sharp points.

hackman /ˈhakmən/ *noun*. *US.* Pl. **-men**. L18.
[ORIGIN from HACK *noun*[2] + MAN *noun*.]
A driver of a hack; a cabman.

hackmatack /ˈhakmətak/ *noun*. L18.
[ORIGIN Perh. from Western Abnaki.]
Any of several N. American coniferous trees; *esp.* the American larch or tamarack, *Larix laricina*.

hackney /ˈhakni/ *noun* & *adjective*. ME.
[ORIGIN Anglo-Norman *hakeney*, Anglo-Latin *hakeneius*, prob. from *Hackney* (formerly *Hakenei*) in London where horses were pastured.]
▸ **A** *noun*. **1** Orig., a horse of medium size and quality, used for ordinary riding and frequently kept for hire. Now *spec.* (an animal of) a breed of light harness-horse with a compact body and a characteristic high-stepping striding trot. Also ***hackney horse***. ME.

SIR W. SCOTT He rode . . a strong hackney for the road, to save his gallant warhorse.

†**2** A person hired to do menial or servile work. M16–M19. ▸**b** A prostitute. L16–L17.

S. PEPYS I should . . become the hackney of this office, in perpetual trouble and vexation.

3 A vehicle plying for hire. Now only in ***hackney carriage***, the official British term for a taxi. M17.

W. CONGREVE If you won't lend me your Coach, I'll take a Hackney, or a Chair.

▸ **B** *attrib.* or as *adjective*. **1** Of, pertaining to, or designating a hackney. LME.
†**2** Trite, commonplace; hackneyed. L16–L18.
– SPECIAL COLLOCATIONS & COMB.: ***hackney carriage***: see sense A.3 above. **hackney cab** a taxi. †**hackney chair** a sedan chair, a bath chair for public hire. **hackney chairman** the bearer, drawer, or keeper of a hackney chair. **hackney coach** *hist.* a two-horse four-wheeled coach kept for hire. **hackney coachman** the driver of a hackney coach. ***hackney horse***: see sense A.1 above.

hackney /ˈhakni/ *verb*. Now *rare* exc. as HACKNEYED *ppl adjective*. L16.
[ORIGIN from HACKNEY *noun*.]
1 *verb trans.* Use (a horse) for ordinary riding. Cf. HACK *verb*[2] 3. Long *dial.* L16.
2 *verb trans.* Make trite or commonplace by overuse. (Foll. by *out*, *about*.) L16. ▸**b** *verb intrans.* Make experienced *in* or (esp. excessively) familiar with. M18. ▸†**c** Make vulgar or indelicate. L18–E19.
†**3** *verb trans.* & *intrans.* Hasten, hurry. E17–L18.
†**4** *verb trans.* Let *out* for hire. E17–M18.

hackneyed /ˈhaknɪd/ *ppl adjective*. M18.
[ORIGIN from HACKNEY *verb* + -ED[1].]
1 Trite, uninteresting, or commonplace through familiarity or indiscriminate and frequent use. M18.

D. PIPER Two of the most insistently reproduced, not to say hackneyed, images.

2 Experienced, habituated (sometimes with the idea of disgust or weariness). M18.
†**3** Hired; kept for hire. M18–E19.
▪ **hackneydom** *noun* a state of commonplaceness L19.

hacky *noun* var. of HACKIE.

had *verb pa. t.* & *pple* of HAVE *verb*.

hadada /ˈhɑːdədɑː/ *noun*. Orig. *S. Afr.* Also **-ah**, (esp. *S. Afr.*) **hadeda(h)** /ˈhɑːdɪdɑː/. L18.
[ORIGIN Imit.]
A greenish-brown ibis, *Hagedashia hagedash*, of sub-Saharan Africa, with a characteristic raucous cry. Also ***hadada ibis***.

hadal /ˈheɪd(ə)l/ *adjective*. M20.
[ORIGIN from HADES + -AL[1].]
Of, pertaining to, or designating the zone of the sea greater than 6000 metres in depth (chiefly oceanic trenches). Cf. ABYSSAL.

Hadassah /həˈdasə/ *noun*. E20.
[ORIGIN Hebrew *hădassāh* myrtle, the name of the biblical character Esther (*Esther* 2:7).]
An American Zionist women's organization, founded in 1912, which contributes to welfare work in Israel.

hadda /ˈhadə/ *verb pa. trans.* *non-standard*. M20.
[ORIGIN Repr. a pronunc.]
Had to.

haddie /ˈhadi/ *noun*. *Scot.* M17.
[ORIGIN Dim. of HADDOCK: see -IE.]
A haddock.

haddock /ˈhadək/ *noun*. Pl. same. ME.
[ORIGIN Anglo-Norman *hadoc* from Old French (*h*)*adot*, pl. *hadoz*, *haddos*, of unknown origin.]
A gadoid food fish, *Melanogrammus aeglefinus*, of the N. Atlantic; (with specifying word) any of various other (edible) marine fishes. Also, the flesh of these fishes as food.
NORWAY ***haddock***.

hade /heɪd/ *noun*[1]. *obsolete* exc. *dial.* E16.
[ORIGIN Unknown.]
A strip of land left unploughed as a boundary line and means of access between two ploughed portions of a field.

hade /heɪd/ *noun*[2]. L18.
[ORIGIN from the verb.]
MINING & GEOLOGY. The inclination of a mineral vein, fault, etc., from the vertical; the complement of the **dip**.

hade /heɪd/ *verb intrans.* L17.
[ORIGIN Perh. a dial. form of HEAD *verb*, retaining the older pronunc. of that word.]
MINING & GEOLOGY. Of a shaft, vein, fault, etc.: incline or slope from the vertical.

Hadean /ˈheɪdɪən, heɪˈdiːən/ *adjective*. M19.
[ORIGIN from HADES + -AN.]
Of or pertaining to Hades.

Hades /ˈheɪdiːz/ *noun*. L16.
[ORIGIN Greek *haidēs* (orig. *aidēs*), of unknown origin; in biblical Greek used as translating Hebrew *šᵉʼōl*, the abode of departed spirits.]
1 GREEK MYTHOLOGY. The god of the dead, also called Pluto; *transf.* the kingdom of Hades, the underworld, the abode of the spirits of the dead. L16. ▸**b** Used as a substitute for *hell* in imprecations etc. *colloq.* E20.

SIR T. BROWNE The dead seem all alive in the humane Hades of Homer.

2 In biblical use (esp. in the New Testament), the state or abode of the spirits of the dead, esp. as a place of waiting before judgement. L16.

Hadith /haˈdiːθ/ *noun*. E18.
[ORIGIN Arabic *ḥadīṯ* statement, tradition.]
The body of traditions concerning the sayings and doings of the Prophet Muhammad, now considered to be second in authority to the Koran and to embody the Sunna. Also, one of these sayings.

hadj *noun* var. of HAJJ.

hadji *noun* var. of HAJJI.

Hadley cell /ˈhadlɪ sɛl/ *noun*. M20.
[ORIGIN from G. *Hadley* (1685–1768), English lawyer and scientific writer + CELL *noun*[1].]
METEOROLOGY. An atmospheric convection cell on a global scale, *spec.* each of two in which air rises at the equator and sinks at latitude 30° N. or S.

hadn't *verb* see HAVE *verb*.

Hadrianic /heɪdrɪˈanɪk/ *adjective*. L19.
[ORIGIN from Latin *Hadrian*(*us*) (of) the Emperor Hadrian + -IC.]
Of or pertaining to the Roman Emperor Hadrian (76–138).

hadrome /ˈhadrəʊm/ *noun*. Now *rare*. L19.
[ORIGIN German *Hadrom*, from Greek *hadros* thick, bulky: see -OME.]
BOTANY. The conducting tissue of the xylem, excluding fibres. Cf. LEPTOME.

hadron /ˈhadrɒn/ *noun*. M20.
[ORIGIN from Greek *hadros* bulky + -ON.]
PARTICLE PHYSICS. Any of a class of subatomic particle, including baryons and mesons, which can take part in the strong interaction. Cf. LEPTON *noun*[2].
■ **haˈdronic** *adjective* of or pertaining to hadrons M20.

hadrosaur /ˈhadrəsɔː/ *noun*. L19.
[ORIGIN mod. Latin *Hadrosaurus* genus name, from Greek *hadros* thick, stout: see -SAUR.]
Any of a family of bipedal herbivorous ornithischian dinosaurs of the Upper Cretaceous, which have beaked and often elaborately crested skulls.
■ **hadroˈsaurian** *adjective* L20. **hadroˈsaurid** *noun & adjective* (*a*) *noun* an animal of the family Hadrosauridae; (*b*) *adjective* of, pertaining to, or designating this family: L20. **hadroˈsaurine** *noun & adjective* of or pertaining to, or an animal of, a group of largely crestless hadrosaurs L20.

hadst *verb* see HAVE *verb*.

hae *verb* see HAVE *verb*.

haecceity /hɛkˈsiːɪti, hiːk-/ *noun*. M17.
[ORIGIN medieval Latin *haecceitas*, from Latin *haec* fem. of *hic* this + *-itas* -ITY. Cf. QUIDDITY, SEITY.]
PHILOSOPHY. The quality that makes a thing describable as 'this'; particular character, individuality.

Haeckelian /hɛˈkiːlɪən/ *adjective*. L19.
[ORIGIN from *Haeckel* (see below) + -IAN.]
Of, pertaining to, or in accordance with the theories of the German biologist E. H. Haeckel (1834–1919), esp. relating to recapitulation of evolutionary development in embryos.

haem /hiːm/ *noun*. Also **heme**. E20.
[ORIGIN Back-form. from HAEMOGLOBIN.]
CHEMISTRY & BIOCHEMISTRY. A coordination compound in which an iron atom is chelated within a porphyrin molecule; *esp.* (the original sense) that complex of ferrous iron and protoporphyrin forming the red non-protein constituent of haemoglobin.

haem- *combining form* see HAEMO-.

haemagglutinate /hiːməˈgluːtɪneɪt/ *verb trans.* Also ***hem-** /hiːm-, hɛm-/. E20.
[ORIGIN from HAEMO- + AGGLUTINATE *verb*.]
Cause (red blood cells) to coagulate.
■ **haemaggluti'nation** *noun* the action or process of haemagglutinating cells E20.

haemagglutinin /hiːməˈgluːtɪnɪn/ *noun*. Also ***hem-** /hiːm-, hɛm-/. E20.
[ORIGIN formed as HAEMAGGLUTINATE + AGGLUTININ.]
Any substance that causes agglutination of red blood cells.

haemal /ˈhiːm(ə)l/ *adjective*. Also ***hem-**. M19.
[ORIGIN from Greek *haima* blood + -AL[1].]
ANATOMY. Of the blood or circulatory system; *esp.* belonging to, situated on, or towards that side of the body containing the heart and major blood vessels, ventral. (Chiefly with ref. to animals.)

haemangioma /ˌhiːmandʒɪˈəʊmə/ *noun*. Also ***hem-** /hiːm-, hɛm-/. Pl. **-mas**, **-mata** /-mətə/. L19.
[ORIGIN from HAEMO- + ANGIOMA.]
MEDICINE. A benign angioma, esp. forming a birthmark.

haemanthus /hiːˈmanθəs/ *noun*. L18.
[ORIGIN mod. Latin (see below), from Greek *haima* blood + *anthos* flower.]
Any of various bulbous plants of the genus *Haemanthus*, of the amaryllis family, of central and southern Africa, grown for their umbels of red, pink, or white flowers.

haemarthrosis /hiːmɑːˈθrəʊsɪs/ *noun*. Also ***hem-** /hiːm-, hɛm-/. Pl. **-throses** /-ˈθrəʊsiːz/. L19.
[ORIGIN from HAEMO- + ARTHROSIS.]
MEDICINE. Haemorrhage into a joint.

haemat- *combining form* see HAEMATO-.

haematemesis /hiːməˈtɛmɪsɪs/ *noun*. Also ***hem-** /hiːm-, hɛm-/. E19.
[ORIGIN from HAEMATO- + Greek *emesis* vomiting.]
MEDICINE. Vomiting of blood.

haematic /hiːˈmatɪk/ *adjective*. Also ***hem-** /hiːm-, hɛm-/. M19.
[ORIGIN Greek *haimatikos*, from *haima*, *haimat-* blood: see -IC and cf. HAEMIC.]
Of or containing blood. Also, acting on the blood.

haematin /ˈhiːmətɪn/ *noun*. Also ***hem-** /ˈhiːm-, ˈhɛm-/. E19.
[ORIGIN from Greek *haima*, *haimat-* blood +-IN[1].]
CHEMISTRY. †**1** = HAEMATOXYLIN. E–M19.
2 A bluish-black oxidized derivative of haem, containing ferric iron. M19.
■ **haemaˈtinic** *noun & adjective* (*a*) *noun* a medicine used to treat anaemia; (*b*) *adjective* of or relating to haematin: M19.

haematite /ˈhiːmətʌɪt/ *noun*. Also ***hem-** /ˈhiːm-, ˈhɛm-/. Also in Latin form †**haematites**. LME.
[ORIGIN Latin *haematites* from Greek *haimatitēs* (*lithos*) lit. 'bloodlike (stone)', from *haima*, *haimat-* blood: see -ITE[1].]
Ferric oxide, Fe_2O_3, occurring as a dark-red, reddish-brown, or reddish-black mineral which crystallizes in the hexagonal system and constitutes an important ore of iron.
brown haematite = LIMONITE.
■ **haemaˈtitic** *adjective* L18.

haemato- /ˈhiːmətəʊ/ *combining form*. Before a vowel **haemat-**. Also ***hem-** /ˈhiːm-, ˈhɛm-/.
[ORIGIN from Greek *haima*, *haimat-* blood: see -O-.]
Forming nouns etc. esp. in MEDICINE, with the sense 'of blood, containing blood'. Cf. HAEMO-.
■ **haematiˈdrosis** *noun* [Greek *hidrōsis* sweating] the secretion of sweat containing blood M19. †**haematoblast** *noun* a blood platelet: only in L19. **haematocele** *noun* [Greek *kēlē* tumour] a swelling containing extravasated blood M18. **haematocyst** *noun* a cyst containing blood M19. †**haematoglobulin** *noun* = HAEMOGLOBIN: only in M19. **haematomyˈelia** *noun* [Greek *muelos* marrow] haemorrhage into the tissue of the spinal cord L19. **haematopoiˈesis** *noun* = HAEMOPOIESIS M19. **haematopoiˈetic** *adjective* = HAEMOPOIETIC M19. **haematoˈporphyrin** *noun* [Greek *porphuros* purple: see -IN[1]] a dark violet porphyrin obtained from haem by hydration in strong acid L19. **haematoˈsalpinx** *noun*, pl. **-pinges** /-pɪn(d)ʒiːz/, [Greek SALPINX: cf. SALPINGO-] (an) accumulation of menstrual blood in the Fallopian tubes L19. **haematoˈthorax** *noun* = HAEMOTHORAX M19.

haematocrit /ˈhiːmətə(ʊ)krɪt/ *noun*. Also ***hem-** /ˈhiːm-, ˈhɛm-/. Also †**-krit**. L19.
[ORIGIN from HAEMATO- + Greek *kritēs* judge.]
An instrument for determining the ratio of the volume of red cells to the total volume of a blood sample. Also, the measured ratio, usu. expressed as a percentage.

haematogenous /hiːməˈtɒdʒɪnəs/ *adjective*. Also ***hem-** /hiːm-, hɛm-/. M19.
[ORIGIN formed as HAEMATOCRIT + -GENOUS.]
Having its origin in or carried by the blood.

haematoid /ˈhiːmətɔɪd/ *adjective*. Also ***hem-** /ˈhiːm-, ˈhɛm-/. M19.
[ORIGIN Greek *haimatoeidēs*, formed as HAEMATO- + -OID.]
Resembling blood; characterized by the presence of blood.

haematoidin /hiːməˈtɔɪdɪn/ *noun*. Also ***hem-** /hiːm-, hɛm-/. M19.
[ORIGIN formed as HAEMATOID + -IN[1].]
MEDICINE. Bilirubin, esp. as formed from the breakdown of haemoglobin in extravasated blood.

†**haematokrit** *noun* var. of HAEMATOCRIT.

haematology /hiːməˈtɒlədʒi/ *noun*. Also ***hem-** /hiːm-, hɛm-/. L17.
[ORIGIN from HAEMATO- + -LOGY.]
The branch of medicine that deals with the blood, esp. its disorders.
■ **haematoˈlogic** *adjective* M20. **haematoˈlogical** *adjective* M19. **haematoˈlogically** *adverb* M20. **haematologist** *noun* E20.

haematoma /hiːməˈtəʊmə/ *noun*. Also ***hem-** /hiːm-, hɛm-/. Pl. **-mas**, **-mata** /-mətə/. M19.
[ORIGIN formed as HAEMATOLOGY + -OMA.]
MEDICINE. A swelling containing (coagulated) extravasated blood.

haematophagous /hiːməˈtɒfəgəs/ *adjective*. Also ***hem-** /hiːm-, hɛm-/. M19.
[ORIGIN formed as HAEMATOLOGY + -PHAGOUS.]
Feeding or subsisting on blood.

haematosis /hiːməˈtəʊsɪs/ *noun*. Now *rare* or *obsolete*. Also ***hem-** /hiːm-, hɛm-/. L17.
[ORIGIN medieval or mod. Latin from Greek *haimatōsis*, from *haimatoun* make into blood, formed as HAEMATO-: see -OSIS.]
1 = SANGUIFICATION. L17.
2 Oxygenation of the blood. M19.

haematoxylin /hiːməˈtɒksɪlɪn/ *noun*. Also ***hem-** /hiːm-, hɛm-/. M19.
[ORIGIN from mod. Latin *Haematoxylum* genus name of logwood, formed as HAEMATO- + Greek *xulon* wood: see -IN[1].]
CHEMISTRY. A colourless crystalline polycyclic phenol, $C_{16}H_{14}O_6$, which is present in logwood, can be easily converted into a number of red, blue, or purple dyes, and is used as a biological stain.

haematuria /hiːməˈtjʊərɪə/ *noun*. Also ***hem-** /hiːm-, hɛm-/. E19.
[ORIGIN from HAEMATO- + -URIA.]
MEDICINE. The presence of blood in the urine.
■ **haematuric** *adjective* pertaining to, characterized by, or affected with haematuria M19.

haemerythrin /hiːməˈrɪθrɪn/ *noun*. Also ***hem-** /hiːm-, hɛm-/. E20.
[ORIGIN from HAEMO- + ERYTHRO- + -IN[1].]
BIOCHEMISTRY. A rare red respiratory pigment present in the blood of some invertebrates.

haemic /ˈhiːmɪk/ *adjective*. Also ***hemic**. M19.
[ORIGIN from Greek *haima* blood + -IC. Cf. HAEMATIC.]
Of or pertaining to the blood.

haemin /ˈhiːmɪn/ *noun*. Also ***hem-**. M19.
[ORIGIN formed as HAEMIC + -IN[1].]
BIOCHEMISTRY. The red, crystalline salt of haematin with hydrochloric acid.

haemo- /ˈhiːməʊ/ *combining form*. Also ***hemo-** /ˈhiːməʊ, ˈhɛməʊ/. Before a vowel **h(a)em-**.
[ORIGIN from Greek *haima* blood + -O-.]
Forming nouns etc., esp. in MEDICINE, with the sense 'of blood'. Cf. HAEMATO-.
■ **haeˌmangioblaˈstoma** *noun*, pl. **-mas**, **-mata** /-mətə/, a tumour of the blood vessels E20. **haemochromaˈtosis** *noun* a hereditary disorder of iron metabolism in which excessive haemosiderin is deposited in the tissues, leading to bronze skin coloration, liver damage, and diabetes mellitus (also called ***bronze diabetes***) L19. **haemocoel(e)** *noun* [Greek *koilos* hollow, cavity] ZOOLOGY the primary body cavity of metazoan invertebrates, containing circulatory fluid L19. **haemoconcenˈtration** *noun* an increase in the relative proportion of red cells in the blood M20. **haemocyte** *noun* a blood cell; orig., an erythrocyte; now, a blood cell of the haemolymph of various invertebrates, esp. arthropods, typically involved in clotting mechanisms and the immune response: L19. **haemoˈdialyser** *noun* a kidney dialysis machine M20. **haemodiˈalysis** *noun* purification of a patient's blood by dialysis (DIALYSIS 3) M20. **haemogram** *noun* the set of results of a number of tests on a blood sample E20. **haemolymph** *noun* the fluid analogous to blood or lymph which circulates in the body cavity of invertebrates L19. **haemoˈsiderin** *noun* [Greek *sidēros* iron] a brownish-yellow substance consisting of protein and iron salts, deposited in the body as a means of storing iron L19. **haemosideˈrosis** *noun* excessive deposition of iron (chiefly as haemosiderin) in the tissues E20. **haemoˈthorax** *noun* haemorrhage into or an accumulation of blood in the pleural cavities L19.

haemocyanin /hiːmə(ʊ)ˈsʌɪənɪn/ *noun*. Also ***hem-** /hiːm-, hɛm-/. M19.
[ORIGIN formed as HAEMO- + CYAN- + -IN[1].]
BIOCHEMISTRY. A blue pigment present in blood. Now only *spec.*, a copper-containing respiratory protein (blue when oxygenated, colourless when deoxygenated), present in the blood of some crustaceans, molluscs, and arachnids.

haemocytometer /ˌhiːmə(ʊ)sʌɪˈtɒmɪtə/ *noun*. Also ***hem-** /ˌhiːm-, ˌhɛm-/. L19.
[ORIGIN from HAEMO- + CYTO- + -METER.]
BIOLOGY. A device for visual counting of the numbers of cells in a specimen of blood or other fluid under a microscope.

haemodynamic /ˌhiːmə(ʊ)dʌɪˈnamɪk/ *adjective*. Also ***hem-** /ˌhiːm-, ˌhɛm-/. E20.
[ORIGIN from HAEMO- + DYNAMIC.]
Of or relating to the motion of the blood.
■ **haemodynamically** *adverb* L20. **haemodynamics** *noun* the science of the motion of the blood M19.

haemoglobin /hiːməˈgləʊbɪn/ *noun*. Also ***hem-** /hiːm-, hɛm-/. M19.
[ORIGIN Abbreviation of HAEMATOGLOBULIN.]
The iron-containing pigment, resolvable into four subunits consisting of haem and a globulin, which is the oxygen-carrying substance present in the red blood cells of vertebrates, and is red when oxygenated and purple when deoxygenated.
■ **haemogloˈbinaemia** *noun* the presence of free haemoglobin in blood plasma L19. **haemogloˈbinometer** *noun* an instrument for measuring the concentration of haemoglobin in a blood sample L19. **haemogloˈbinometry** *noun* the measurement of the concentration of haemoglobin in a blood sample L19. **haemogloˈbinopathy** *noun* any of a group of hereditary conditions in which there is an abnormality in the production of haemoglobin M20. **haemogloˈbinuria** *noun* the presence of free haemoglobin in the urine M19.

haemolysis /hiːˈmɒlɪsɪs/ *noun*. Also ***hem-**. L19.
[ORIGIN from HAEMO- + -LYSIS.]
The dissolution or lysis of red blood cells with the consequent liberation of their haemoglobin.
■ **ˈhaemolyse**, ***ˈhemolyze** *verb trans. & intrans.* (cause to) undergo haemolysis E20. **haemolysin** /hiːˈmɒlɪsɪn, hiːməˈlʌɪsɪn/ *noun* any substance which causes haemolysis E20.

haemolytic /hiːməˈlɪtɪk/ *adjective*. Also ***hem-** /hiːm-, hɛm-/. L19.
[ORIGIN from HAEMO- + -LYTIC.]
Of, pertaining to, characterized by, or producing haemolysis.
haemolytic disease of the newborn a severe anaemia that results when the mother develops antibodies against the blood of the fetus; also called ***erythroblastosis*** (***fetalis***).
■ **haemolytically** *adverb* E20.

†**haemony** *noun*. *rare* (Milton). Only in M17.
[ORIGIN from Greek *haima* blood, after *agrimony*.]
An imaginary plant having supernatural virtues.

haemophilia /hiːməˈfɪlɪə/ *noun*. Also ***hem-** /hiːm-, hɛm-/. Also (earlier) anglicized as †**haemophily**. M19.
[ORIGIN from HAEMO- + -PHILIA.]
A hereditary disease in which the ability of the blood to coagulate is severely reduced owing to a deficiency of the coagulation factor VIII, the person concerned having a tendency to prolonged bleeding from even minor injuries.
haemophilia B a hereditary disease clinically identical to ordinary haemophilia but due to the absence of a different coagulation factor; also called ***Christmas disease***.
■ **haemophiliac** *noun & adjective* (*a*) *noun* a person with haemophilia; (*b*) *adjective* = HAEMOPHILIC *adjective*: L19. **haemophilic** *adjective & noun* (*a*) *adjective* of or pertaining to haemophilia; affected with haemophilia; (*b*) *noun* = HAEMOPHILIAC *noun*: M19.

haemopoiesis /ˌhiːməʊpɔɪˈiːsɪs/ *noun*. Also ***hem-** /ˌhiːm-, ˌhɛm-/. E20.
[ORIGIN from HAEMO- + Greek *poiēsis* making. Cf. earlier HAEMATOPOIESIS.]
The production of blood cells and platelets, which occurs in the bone marrow.
■ **haemopoietic** /-pɔɪˈɛtɪk/ *adjective* of, pertaining to, or concerned with haemopoiesis L19.

haemoptysis /hiːˈmɒptɪsɪs/ *noun*. Also ***hem-**. M17.
[ORIGIN mod. Latin *hemoptysis*, formed as HAEMO- + Greek *ptusis* spitting.]
MEDICINE. Expectoration of blood or bloody mucus.

haemorrhage /ˈhɛmərɪdʒ/ *noun & verb*. Also ***hem-**. L17.
[ORIGIN Alt. of HAEMORRHAGY.]
▸ **A** *noun*. **1** An escape of blood from the blood vessels; bleeding, esp. when profuse. L17.
2 *fig.* A damaging or uncontrolled outflow of something. M19.
D. H. LAWRENCE This haemorrhage of self-esteem tortured him to the end. *Washington Post* An economic hemorrhage threatening Israel's stability.
▸ **B** *verb*. **1** *verb intrans.* Undergo a haemorrhage. E20.
2 *verb trans.* Dissipate or expend in large amounts. L20.
D. ADAMS He had been simply haemorrhaging money.

†**haemorrhagia** *noun* var. of HAEMORRHAGY.

haemorrhagic /hɛməˈradʒɪk/ *adjective*. Also ***hem-**. E19.
[ORIGIN Greek *haimorrhagikos*, from *haimorrhagia*: see HAEMORRHAGY, -IC.]
Pertaining to or of the nature of haemorrhage; accompanied by or produced by haemorrhage.

†**haemorrhagy** *noun*. Also ***hem-**, & in Latin form **haemorrhagia**. LME–M19.
[ORIGIN from Old French *emorogie* (mod. *hémorr(h)agie*), or its source Latin *haemorrhagia* from Greek *haimorrhagia*, formed as HAEMO- + base of *rhēgnunai* break, burst.]
= HAEMORRHAGE *noun*.

haemorrhoid /ˈhɛmərɔɪd/ *noun*. Also ***hem-**. LME.
[ORIGIN Old French *emeroyde*, later *hémorrhoïdes* from Latin *haemorrhoida* from Greek *haimorrhois*, *-oid-* discharging blood, pl. *-oides* (sc. *phlebes* veins) bleeding piles, from *haimorrhoos*, formed as HAEMO- + *-roos* flowing. Cf. EMERODS.]
In *pl.*, abnormally distended groups of veins in the region of the rectum and anus; piles. Also occas. *sing.* (usu. *attrib.*).
E. BAKER Norma . . could tell . . that his haemorrhoids were bothering him again. *attrib.*: M. PIERCY He had not taken his hemorrhoid medicine.
■ **haemorrhoiˈdectomy** *noun* (an instance of) surgical removal of haemorrhoids E20.

haemorrhoidal /hɛməˈrɔɪd(ə)l/ *adjective*. LME.
[ORIGIN from HAEMORRHOID + -AL[1].]
1 ANATOMY. Of veins, nerves, etc.: distributed to the region of the rectum and anus. LME.
2 Of or pertaining to haemorrhoids. M17.

†**haemorrhois** *noun*. LME–L18.
[ORIGIN Latin from Greek *haimorrhois*: see HAEMORRHOID.]
A snake whose bite was fabled to cause unstaunchable bleeding.

haemostasis /hiːmə(ʊ)ˈsteɪsɪs/ *noun*. Also ***hem-** /hiːm-, hɛm-/. M19.
[ORIGIN from HAEMO- + STASIS.]
MEDICINE. Stoppage of bleeding; stoppage or esp. prevention of the flow of blood.

haemostatic /hiːmə(ʊ)ˈstatɪk/ *noun & adjective*. Also ***hem-** /hiːm-, hɛm-/. E18.
[ORIGIN from HAEMO- + -STATIC.]
▸ **A** *noun*. **1** A substance that arrests bleeding, a styptic. E18.
†**2** In *pl.* (treated as *sing.*). The hydrostatics of the blood. M18–M19.
▸ **B** *adjective*. Having the property of arresting bleeding, styptic; serving to prevent the flow of blood. M19.
■ ˈ**haemostat** *noun* an instrument for preventing blood flow by compression of a blood vessel E20.

haere mai /ˈhʌɪrə ˈmʌɪ/ *interjection & noun phr. NZ*. M18.
[ORIGIN Maori, lit. 'come hither'.]
(A Maori term expr.) welcome.

haet /heɪt/ *noun*. *Scot.* Also **hate**. L16.
[ORIGIN Contr. of *hae* (= *have*) *it*.]
1 ***deil a haet***, ***deil haet***, ***fiend a haet***, ***fiend haet***, & vars. (in emphatic negatives) not a bit, nothing at all. L16.
2 A bit, a small quantity. Usu. in neg. contexts. E19.

haff /haf/ *noun*. M19.
[ORIGIN German, from Middle & mod. Low German *haf* sea, corresp. to Old Norse *haf*, Old English *hæf* sea.]
A shallow freshwater lagoon found at a river mouth, esp. on the Baltic coast.

haffet /ˈhafɪt/ *noun*. *Scot. & N. English*. E16.
[ORIGIN Prob. from Old English *healfhēafod* the front part of the head, formed as HALF- + HEAD *noun*.]
The side of the head above and in front of the ear; the temple; the cheek.

Hafflinger *noun* see HAFLINGER.

hafiz /ˈhɑːfɪz/ *noun*. M17.
[ORIGIN Persian from Arabic *ḥāfiẓ* pres. pple of *ḥafiẓa* guard, know by heart.]
A Muslim who knows the Koran by heart.

Haflinger /ˈhaflɪŋə/ *noun*. Also (earlier) **Haff-**. L19.
[ORIGIN German, from *Hafling*, a village in the Tyrol where the breed originated.]
(An animal of) a breed of sturdy chestnut draught horse.

hafnium /ˈhafnɪəm/ *noun*. E20.
[ORIGIN from *Hafnia* Latinized form of Danish *Havn* (= harbour), orig. name of Copenhagen, Dan. capital city: see -IUM.]
A chemical element, atomic no. 72, which is one of the transition metals and occurs naturally in association with zirconium, which it resembles (symbol Hf).

haft /hɑːft/ *noun*[1]. Also (now chiefly *Scot. & dial.*) **heft** /hɛft/.
[ORIGIN Old English *hæft(e)* corresp. to Middle Low German *hechte* (Dutch *hecht*, *heft*), Old High German *hefti* (German *Heft*), Old Norse *hepti*, from Germanic base of HEAVE *verb*: see -T[1].]
The handle of a cutting or piercing instrument, as a knife, spear, etc.; the hilt of a sword, dagger, etc.

haft *noun*[2] var. of HEFT *noun*[2].

haft /hɑːft/ *verb*[1] *trans.* Also (chiefly *Scot. & N. English*) **heft** /hɛft/. LME.
[ORIGIN from HAFT *noun*[1].]
Provide (a knife etc.) with a haft or handle.
■ **hafter** *noun* ME.

haft *verb*[2] var. of HEFT *verb*[1].

hag /hag/ *noun*[1]. ME.
[ORIGIN Perh. abbreviation of Old English *hægtesse*, *hegtes* fury, witch = Middle Dutch *haghetisse* (Dutch *hecse*), Old High German *hagazissa* (German *Hexe*), of unknown origin. Cf. HEX *noun*[1].]
1 A woman supposed to have dealings with the Devil; a witch; an evil woman; (now *arch. & dial.*) an evil spirit or demon in female form, a malicious fairy or goblin, a nightmare conceived of as caused by this. ME.
SHAKES. *Macb.* How now, you secret, black, and midnight hags!
2 An ugly repulsive old woman, *esp.* a vicious or malicious one. Formerly also, an ugly repulsive man. LME.
P. THEROUX The zone which turned lovely little girls into bad-tempered and rapacious hags.
3 Orig., a kind of hazy light or mist supposedly appearing about a horse's mane or a human head at night. Now only (*dial.*), a mist usually accompanying a frost. M16.
4 *ellipt.* A hagfish. E19.

hag /hag/ *noun*[2]. *Scot. & N. English*. ME.
[ORIGIN from Old Norse *hǫgg* gap, breach, cutting blow, from *hǫggva*: see HAG *verb*[1] and cf. HEDGE *noun*.]
▸ **I** †**1** A break, gap, or chasm in a crag or cliff. Only in ME.
2 A soft marshy break in a moor resulting from peat-cutting or the flow of water; a firm turfy or heathery clump in a peatbog. M17.
SIR W. SCOTT A small and shaggy nag, That through a bog, from hag to hag, Could bound.
3 An overhang of peat or turf. E19.
▸ **II 4** A hack, a cut; a cutting or felling of a certain quantity of wood; a portion of a wood marked off for cutting. Earliest in place names. ME.
5 The stump of a tree left after felling; an amount of firewood. E17.

hag /hag/ *noun*[3]. *N. English*. L15.
[ORIGIN Old Norse *hagi* enclosed field, pasture, rel. to Old English *haga*: see HAW *noun*[1].]
†**1** A hedge. Only in L15.
2 A wooded enclosure; a copse. E17.

hag *noun*[4] var. of HAKE *noun*[2].

hag /hag/ *verb*[1] *trans. & intrans. Scot. & N. English*. Infl. **-gg-**. ME.
[ORIGIN from Old Norse *hǫggva* strike with a sharp weapon, hack, hew = Old English *heawan* HEW *verb*.]
Hack, cut, or hew (something).
R. L. STEVENSON That he should have a hand in hagging and hashing at Christ's Kirk.

hag /hag/ *verb*[2] *trans.* Now *dial.* Infl. **-gg-**. M16.
[ORIGIN Uncertain: sense 3 prob. from HAG *noun*[1].]
1 Fatigue, tire out. M16.
2 Incite, urge. L16.
3 Torment, terrify; trouble. L16.

Hag. *abbreviation*.
Haggai (in the Bible).

Haganah /hagaˈnɑː/ *noun*. E20.
[ORIGIN Hebrew *hāgannāh* defence.]
hist. An underground defence force comprising a group of Jewish settlers in Palestine and playing a leading part in the creation of the state of Israel in 1948.

Hagarene /hagəˈriːn/ *noun*. M16.
[ORIGIN medieval Latin *Agarenus*, *Hagarenus* from *Agar* Hagar.]
A reputed descendant of Hagar the concubine of Abraham and the mother of Ishmael (*Genesis* 16:3); a Saracen.

hagberry /ˈhagb(ə)ri/ *noun*. *N. English*. Also **heck-** /ˈhɛk-/, **heg-** /ˈhɛg-/. See also HACKBERRY. L16.
[ORIGIN Of Norse origin: cf. Danish *hæg(g)ebær*, Norwegian *heggebær*, etc.]
(The fruit of) the bird cherry, *Prunus padus*.

hag-boat /ˈhagbəʊt/ *noun*. Now *rare* or *obsolete*. L17.
[ORIGIN Unknown.]
A large type of ship with a very narrow stern, used as a man-of-war and in the timber and coal trade.

hagfish /ˈhagfɪʃ/ *noun*. Pl. same, **-es**. E17.
[ORIGIN from HAG *noun*[1] + FISH *noun*[1].]
Any of various scavenging or predatory cyclostome fishes of the family Myxinidae, having an eel-like body without paired fins, slime glands, and a jawless mouth with movable toothed plates, found chiefly in oxygen-poor mud in deep cold seas and estuaries.

Haggadah /həˈgɑːdə, hagaˈdɑː/ *noun*. Also **Agga-** /əˈgɑː-, agə-/. Pl. **-doth**, **-dot**, /-dəʊt/. M18.
[ORIGIN Hebrew *Haggāḏāh* tale, esp. an edifying one, from biblical Hebrew *higgīḏ* declare, tell, expound.]
1 (A book containing) the text recited at the Seder, on the first two nights of the Passover. M18.
2 An illustrative legend or parable in the Talmud; the non-legal element of the Talmud. M19.
■ **Haˈggadic**, **Haˈggadical** *adjectives* of, pertaining to, or of the nature of the Haggadah M19. **Haˈggadist** *noun* a writer or user of Haggadoth L19. **Haggaˈdistic** *adjective* of, pertaining to, or characteristic of a Haggadist M19.

H

haggard /ˈhagəd/ *noun*[1]. Chiefly *Irish & dial.* ME.
[ORIGIN Repr. Old Norse *heygarðr*, from *hey* hay + *garðr* GARTH *noun*[1].]
A rickyard.
P. KAVANAGH The corn was gathered, and in one or two haggards the threshing mills were set up.

haggard /ˈhagəd/ *noun*[2]. M16.
[ORIGIN Absol. use of HAGGARD *adjective*.]
A wild (usu. female) hawk caught in its adult plumage; *fig.* a wild intractable person.
M. FRENCH The oppressive, demanding wife . . , the grim-faced haggard who did not understand.

†**haggard** *noun*[3]. M17–E18.
[ORIGIN from HAG *noun*[1] + -ARD.]
A hag, a witch.

haggard /ˈhagəd/ *adjective*. M16.
[ORIGIN Old French & mod. French *hagard*, perh. from Germanic word meaning 'hedge, bush'. Cf. HAG *noun*[3], HAW *noun*[1], HEDGE *noun*, & see -ARD. Later infl. in sense by HAG *noun*[1] (cf. HAGGARD *noun*[3]); cf. also HAGGED.]
1 Of a hawk: caught after having assumed its adult plumage; wild, untamed. Formerly also, of a person: wild, perverse. M16. ▸†**b** Of plumage: ragged. *rare*. E17–L18.
2 Of a person: half-starved, emaciated, gaunt. *obsolete* exc. as in sense 3. M17.
3 Of a person: wild-looking; *esp.* having a worn or gaunt appearance as a result of fatigue, privation, worry, old age, etc. Formerly, of the eyes: having a wild expression. L17.
H. JAMES His face was haggard, his whole aspect was that of grim and hopeless misery. R. HOGGART Her face . . was well-lined but not haggard.
■ **haggardly** *adverb* L17. **haggardness** *noun* L16.

hagged /hagd, ˈhagɪd/ *adjective*. Now *dial.* L17.
[ORIGIN from HAG *verb*[2]; in sense 1 cf. HAGGARD *noun*[3] and HAGGARD *adjective*.]
1 Gaunt, haggard, worn-out. L17.
2 Resembling a hag; (*rare*) bewitched. Long *rare* or *obsolete*. L17.

haggis /ˈhagɪs/ *noun*. LME.
[ORIGIN Prob. from HAG *verb*[1].]
1 A dish consisting of the heart, lungs, and liver of a sheep etc. minced with suet, oatmeal, and onions, stuffed into the maw of the animal or into an artificial bag like a large sausage and usu. boiled. LME.
2 *fig.* A mixture, a hotchpotch; a mess. L19.

haggish /ˈhagɪʃ/ *adjective*. L16.
[ORIGIN from HAG *noun*[1] + -ISH[1].]
Resembling or of the nature of a hag.
■ **haggishly** *adverb* M19. **haggishness** *noun* L19.

haggle /ˈhag(ə)l/ *verb & noun*. L16.
[ORIGIN formed as HAG *verb*[1] + -LE[3]. Cf. HACKLE *verb*[1].]
▸ **A** *verb*. **1** *verb trans. & intrans.* Hack or mangle (something) with repeated irregular or clumsy cuts. Now chiefly *Scot. & dial.* L16.
SHAKES. *Hen. V* Suffolk first died; and York, all haggled over, comes to him.
2 *verb intrans.* Advance with difficulty, struggle forward. Now chiefly *Scot.* L16.
3 *verb intrans.* Dispute or wrangle over a price, deal, etc. (Foll. by *about*, *over*.) E17. ▸**b** *verb trans.* Harass or weary (as) with haggling. Now *dial.* M17.
E. AMADI The wives of rich politicians . . hardly bothered to haggle over prices.
▸ **B** *noun*. A dispute, a wrangle. M19.

B. CHATWIN No one could be fiercer in a haggle over stock-prices.

haggler /ˈhaglə/ *noun*. L16.
[ORIGIN from HAGGLE *verb* + -ER¹.]
1 A clumsy awkward worker. *obsolete* exc. *dial.* L16.
2 A person who haggles over a price etc. E17.
3 An itinerant dealer, a pedlar. *obsolete* exc. *dial.* E17.

haggy /ˈhagi/ *adjective*¹. M17.
[ORIGIN from HAG *noun*¹ + -Y¹.]
Of, pertaining to, or resembling a hag.

haggy /ˈhagi/ *adjective*². Chiefly *Scot.* L18.
[ORIGIN from HAG *noun*² + -Y¹.]
Boggy and full of holes.

hagi- *combining form* see HAGIO-.

hagigah /haˈgiːgɑː, x-/ *noun pl.* Also **ch-**. M19.
[ORIGIN Hebrew *ḥăgīgāh*.]
JUDAISM. The peace offering brought by pilgrims to the Temple at the three great feasts of Passover, Pentecost, and Tabernacles.

hagio- /ˈhagɪəʊ/ *combining form*. Before a vowel also **hagi-**.
[ORIGIN from Greek *hagios* holy, saintly: see -O-.]
Of or pertaining to saints; saintly.
■ **hagiarchy** *noun* the hierarchy of saints E19. **hagiˈocracy** *noun* (a) government by people regarded as holy M19. **hagiˈolatrous** *adjective* tending to hagiolatry M19. **hagiˈolatry** *noun* the worship of saints E19. **hagioscope** *noun* an opening in a chancel wall enabling worshippers in an aisle or side chapel to see the altar M19.

H

Hagiographa /hagɪˈɒgrəfə/ *noun pl.* LME.
[ORIGIN Late Latin from Greek: see HAGIO-, -GRAPH.]
One of the three canonical divisions of the Hebrew Scriptures, comprising Psalms, Proverbs, Job, Canticles, Ruth, Lamentations, Ecclesiastes, Esther, Daniel, Ezra, Nehemiah, and Chronicles, the other two divisions being the Law and the Prophets. Also called *Writings*, *Kethubim*.
■ **hagiographal** *adjective* of or pertaining to the Hagiographa M17.

hagiographer /hagɪˈɒgrəfə/ *noun*. M17.
[ORIGIN from late Latin *hagiographus* + -ER¹: see HAGIO-, -GRAPHER.]
1 An author of sacred writings; *spec.* any of the writers of the Hagiographa. M17.
2 A writer of saints' lives. M19.

hagiographic /hagɪəˈgrafɪk/ *adjective*. E19.
[ORIGIN formed as HAGIOGRAPHER + -IC.]
1 Of or pertaining to hagiography. E19.
2 Of or pertaining to the Hagiographa. L19.

hagiographical /hagɪəˈgrafɪk(ə)l/ *adjective*. L16.
[ORIGIN formed as HAGIOGRAPHER + -AL¹.]
1 Of or pertaining to the Hagiographa or (formerly) other sacred writings. L16.
2 = HAGIOGRAPHIC 1. M19.

J. N. ISBISTER One-sided pictures of Freud abound—from the hagiographical to the derogatory.

hagiography /hagɪˈɒgrəfi/ *noun*. E19.
[ORIGIN from HAGIO- + -GRAPHY.]
†**1** Holy Scripture; the Hagiographa. *rare*. Only in E19.
2 The writing of saints' biographies; saints' biographies as a branch of literature or legend; *transf.* the writing of an idealized biography of any person. E19.

J. UPDIKE Busch avoids hagiography as well as criticism.

hagiology /hagɪˈɒlədʒi/ *noun*. E19.
[ORIGIN from HAGIO- + -LOGY.]
1 The literature dealing with the lives and legends of saints; a work on this subject; a catalogue of saints. E19.
2 The history of sacred writings. M20.
■ **hagioˈlogic** *adjective* of or pertaining to hagiology E19. **hagioˈlogical** *adjective* = HAGIOLOGIC L19. **hagiologist** *noun* a writer or student of hagiology E19.

hag-ridden /ˈhagrɪd(ə)n/ *adjective*. L17.
[ORIGIN from HAG *noun*¹ + RIDDEN *adjective*.]
1 Ridden by a hag (see RIDE *verb* 12), afflicted by a nightmare. L17.
2 Oppressed in mind, harassed. E18.

T. BANKHEAD As long as I can remember, I've been absolutely hagridden with ambition.

hag-ride /ˈhagrʌɪd/ *verb trans.* Infl. as RIDE *verb*; pa. t. usu. **-rode** /-rəʊd/, pa. pple usu. **-ridden** /-rɪd(ə)n/. M17.
[ORIGIN from HAG *noun*¹ + RIDE *verb*.]
Afflict by nightmares; *esp.* harass or oppress mentally. Now chiefly as HAG-RIDDEN *adjective*.

hagship /ˈhagʃɪp/ *noun*. E17.
[ORIGIN from HAG *noun*¹ + -SHIP.]
(A humorous title for) a hag.

hag-taper /ˈhagteɪpə/ *noun*. Now *dial.* Also **hag's taper** /ˈhagz teɪpə/. M16.
[ORIGIN 2nd elem. TAPER *noun*¹; 1st elem. unexpl.: cf. German *Kerzenkraut* lit. 'taperwort', Middle Dutch *tortsecruyt* lit. 'torchwort'.]
The great mullein, *Verbascum thapsus*, a plant of the figwort family.

hah *interjection, verb, & noun* vars. of HA *interjection, verb, & noun*.

ha-ha /ˈhɑːhɑː/ *noun*. Also **haw-haw** /ˈhɔːhɔː/. E18.
[ORIGIN French, perh. from the cry of surprise on discovering the obstacle: cf. HA *interjection*.]
A ditch with a wall on its inner side below ground level, forming a boundary to a garden or park without interrupting the view from within, being visible only from a close proximity.

ha ha /hɑː ˈhɑː/ *interjection, verb, & noun*. Also **ha ha ha**, **ha-ha(-ha)**, **hah hah**, etc. OE.
[ORIGIN Natural exclam.: see HA *interjection*.]
▸**A** *interjection*. Expr. hearty or open amusement or repr. laughter. ***funny ha-ha***: see FUNNY *adjective*. OE.

New Yorker I thought I might want to be a teacher, ha, ha, ha.

▸**B** *verb intrans.* Laugh aloud. E17.
▸**C** *noun*. A loud or open laugh; a joke. E19.

Times Lit. Suppl. Death-bed confessions from the forger's family who thought it a great 'Ha-ha' as it, sadly, was.

haham /ˈhɑːhəm/ *noun*. Also **chacham** /ˈxɑːxəm/ & other vars. L17.
[ORIGIN Hebrew *ḥāḵām* wise.]
A person learned in Jewish law; a wise man; *spec.* among Sephardic Jews, a rabbi; the spiritual head of a Sephardic community.

hahnium /ˈhɑːnɪəm/ *noun*. L20.
[ORIGIN from Otto *Hahn* (1879–1968), German physicist + -IUM.]
(A name proposed for) the artificially produced transuranic chemical element of atomic no. 105 (symbol Ha).

haick *noun* var. of HAIK.

Haida /ˈhʌɪdə/ *noun & adjective*. Also **Haidah**, **Hydah**. M19.
[ORIGIN Haida = people.]
▸**A** *noun*. **1** Pl. **-s**, same. A member of a N. American Indian people living on the Queen Charlotte Islands in British Columbia, and on Prince of Wales Island, Alaska. M19.
2 The language of this people. E20.
▸**B** *attrib.* or as *adjective*. Of or pertaining to the Haidas or their language. M19.

haidingerite /ˈhʌɪdɪŋərʌɪt/ *noun*. E19.
[ORIGIN from W. K. von *Haidinger* (1795–1871), Austrian mineralogist + -ITE¹.]
MINERALOGY. An orthorhombic hydrated arsenate of calcium, occurring as minute white crystals.

haik /heɪk, ˈhɑːɪk/ *noun*. Also **haick**. E18.
[ORIGIN Arabic *ḥā'ik*.]
In N. Africa, a large outer wrap, usu. white, worn by both sexes.

haikal /ˈhʌɪk(ə)l/ *noun*. L19.
[ORIGIN Arabic = temple.]
The central chapel of three forming the sanctuary of a Coptic Church.
– COMB.: **haikal screen** a screen, often carved or decorated, which separates the haikal from the body of the church.

haiku /ˈhʌɪkuː/ *noun*. Pl. same, **-s**. L19.
[ORIGIN Japanese, from *hai* amusement + *ku* phrase.]
A short Japanese poem in three parts and usu. having 17 syllables; an English imitation of such a poem.

hail /heɪl/ *noun*¹.
[ORIGIN Old English *hagol*, *hægl*, corresp. to Old Frisian *heil*, Old Saxon, Old High German *hagal* (Dutch, German *Hagel*), Old Norse *hagl*, from Germanic, rel. to Greek *kakhlēx* pebble.]
1 Frozen rain falling in a shower or storm of pellets. OE.

J. C. OATES A harsh percussive rain hardened suddenly into hail.

2 A shower or storm of hail. Now usu. ***hail shower***, ***hailstorm***. OE.
3 *transf.* & *fig.* A storm or shower of something falling like hail, as bullets, curses, questions, etc. LME.

M. LOWRY A continuous hail of golf balls flying out of bounds bombarded the roof. E. BAKER This hail of hissing accusations and threats.

– COMB.: **hailstone** a pellet of hail; †**hail-shot** small shot which scatters like hail when fired; ***hail shower***: see sense 2 above; ***hailstorm***: see sense 2 above.
■ **haily** *adjective* (now *rare*) consisting of or characterized by hail or hailstorms M16.

hail /heɪl/ *noun*². E16.
[ORIGIN from HAIL *interjection* or *verb*².]
1 An exclamation of 'hail!'; a greeting, a salutation. E16.
2 An act of hailing someone or something; a shout of welcome; a call to attract attention. L17.

R. L. STEVENSON I could hear hails coming and going between the old buccaneer and his comrades.

– PHRASES: **within hail** within call, close enough to be hailed.

†**hail** *noun*³ see HALE *noun*¹.

hail /heɪl/ *adjective*¹. *obsolete* exc. *hist.* in *drink hail* (see DRINK *verb*). ME.
[ORIGIN Old Norse *heill* = Old English *hāl* HALE *adjective*, WHOLE *adjective*. See also WASSAIL *noun*.]
Sound, healthy, wholesome; = HALE *adjective*.

hail *adjective*² see HALE *adjective*.

hail /heɪl/ *verb*¹.
[ORIGIN Old English *hagalian* = Old Norse *hagla*. Repl. in Middle English by forms from HAIL *noun*¹.]
1 *verb intrans. impers.* in ***it hails***, ***it is hailing***, etc., hail falls, hail is falling, etc. OE.
2 a *verb intrans.* Pour or send down hail. *rare*. LME. ▸**b** *verb trans.* Pour down as hail; throw or send *down* or *upon* violently like hail in a storm. LME.

b TENNYSON Walter hail'd a score of names upon her.

3 *verb intrans.* Fall as or like hail. M19.

www.fictionpress.com Burning segments of roof hailed down around them.

hail /heɪl/ *verb*². ME.
[ORIGIN from *hail* var. of HALE *noun*¹.]
1 *verb trans.* Salute with 'hail!'; salute, greet; welcome. ME.

V. WOOLF Friends hailed each other in passing. I. WALLACE Her father had hailed her prestigious government job as the inevitable triumph of her upbringing.

2 *verb trans.* Call, shout, or wave to (a person, a ship, etc.) from a distance, in order to attract attention; signal to (a taxi, a bus, etc.) to stop and take one as a passenger. L15.

J. CONRAD Being hailed across the street he looked up. W. STYRON We hailed a taxi and headed back to the McAlpin.

within hailing distance: see DISTANCE *noun*.
3 *verb intrans.* Call out in order to attract attention. L16.
4 *verb intrans.* Of a ship, a person: have come originally *from* a place. M19.

Golf Illustrated Simpson is 31 and hails from San Diego.

■ **hailer** *noun* (*a*) a person who hails or calls to attract attention; (*b*) ***loudhailer***: see LOUD *adjective*: L19.

hail /heɪl/ *interjection*. Now *arch.* or *rhet.* exc. in comb. ME.
[ORIGIN from HAIL *adjective*¹ in expressions of good wishes as †*hail be thou* (cf. WASSAIL *noun*).]
Used as an exclamation of greeting or salutation or of acclamation. Also foll. by *to*.
all hail: see ALL *adjective, pronoun, noun, & adverb*.
– COMB.: **hail-fellow(-well-met)** *adjective & adverb* on most intimate terms (*with*), *esp.* overfamiliar(ly); **Hail Mary** = AVE MARIA 1.

hain /heɪn/ *verb trans.* Now *Scot.* & *dial.* ME.
[ORIGIN Old Norse *hegna* to hedge, fence, protect, from Germanic.]
1 Enclose or protect with a fence or hedge; *esp.* preserve (grass) from cattle. ME.
2 Spare, save; refrain from using or spending. E16.

hair /hɛː/ *noun*.
[ORIGIN Old English *hǣr*, *hēr* = Old Frisian *hēr*, Old Saxon, Old High German *hār* (Dutch, German *Haar*), Old Norse *hár*, from Germanic. In branch II orig. Old English *hǣre*, *hēre* reinforced in Middle English by Old French *haire*, from Frankish, identified with this.]
▸**I 1** Any of the numerous fine flexible keratinized filaments that grow from beneath the skin of a mammal, esp. from the head of a person; any fine filament growing from the integument of an animal. OE.

J. WILSON And would not hurt a hair upon his head.

2 (*collect.* & (*arch.*) in *pl.*) All such filaments growing on an animal; *spec.* those growing on the head of a person. Also, hairs in a mass, as used in manufacture etc. OE. ▸**b** *fig.* Something radiating, spreading, or trailing in the manner of hair, as the rays of the sun, the foliage of a tree, etc. L16.

T. MORRISON His eyes were so wild, his hair so long and matted.

3 A very small degree or quantity; the slightest thing; a jot, an iota. ME.

T. KENEALLY Anyone who has loaded weapons is only a hair away from savagery.

†**4** The distinctive type of something; sort, kind; stamp, character. LME–E17.
5 *transf.* Something resembling (a) hair in shape, appearance, or consistency. LME.
6 A fine elongated or filamentous plant structure, as a stamen or leaf fibre; *spec.* in BOTANY, any elongated outgrowth from the epidermis, as a root hair. L16.
▸**II 7** Cloth made of hair, haircloth; *esp.* a hair shirt worn next to the skin by ascetics and penitents. OE.
– PHRASES: **against the hair** contrary to the natural lie of an animal's hair; *fig.* contrary to inclination. **a hair in one's neck** *rare* a cause of trouble or annoyance. ***curl a person's hair***: see CURL *verb*. ***get by the short hairs***: see SHORT *adjective*. **hair of the dog (that bit one)** an alcoholic drink taken to cure a hangover, so called because it is a cure consisting of a small amount of the cause. ***hang by a hair***: see HANG *verb*. ***have by the short hairs***: see SHORT *adjective*. ***head of hair***: see HEAD *noun*. **in one's hair** (*a*) (now *rare*) with the hair down; bareheaded; (*b*) *fig.* encumbering, persistently annoying, in one's way. **keep one's hair on** *slang* remain calm. **let one's hair down** (*a*) release one's hair from a style where it is secured against the head or tied back; (*b*) *fig.* (*colloq.*) cease to be formal, behave unconventionally or unrestrainedly. **lose one's hair** lose one's temper. ***make a person's hair curl***: see CURL *verb*. ***neither hide nor hair***: see HIDE *noun*¹. **not turn a hair** show no sign of discomposure or exhaustion. **out of one's hair** out of difficulty, out of one's way. **put up one's hair** arrange one's hair in a style where it is secured against the head, formerly a sign of the transition from girlhood to womanhood. **split hairs** make overfine distinctions. ***tear one's hair***: see TEAR *verb*¹. **to a hair** exactly.

– **COMB.**: **hair bag** (*a*) a bag made of hair; (*b*) a bag for keeping hair in; **hairball** a ball of hair which collects esp. in the stomach of various animals; **hairband** a band for securing the hair; **hairbreadth** *noun & adjective* = ***hair's breadth***, ***hair's-breadth*** below; **hairbrush** (*a*) a brush for smoothing and styling the hair; (*b*) a kind of hand grenade; **hair cell** ANATOMY any of the ciliated vibration-sensitive cells of the inner ear and (in fish etc.) the lateral-line system; **hair clip** a clip, often ornamental, for securing the hair; **haircloth** (*a*) a cloth or fabric of hair used for making tents, towels, shirts, etc., or in drying malt, hops, etc.; (*b*) an article made of this fabric; **hair-cord** (*a*) a finely striped fabric resembling hair in appearance; (*b*) a cord made of human hair; **hair crack** a hairline crack; **haircut** an act of cutting the hair; the shape or style into which the hair is cut; **hairdo** *colloq.* the process of styling the hair; a particular way in which the hair is styled; **hairdress** (*a*) a way of dressing the hair; (*b*) a headdress; **hairdresser** a person whose occupation is the cutting or styling of hair; **hairdressing** (*a*) the action, process, or occupation of cutting or styling the hair; (*b*) a liquid preparation for the hair; **hairdryer** an electrical device for drying the hair by blowing warm air over it; ***hair follicle***: see FOLLICLE *noun* 1; **hair grass** (*a*) any of various slender grasses, esp. of the northern temperate genera *Aira* and *Deschampsia*; (*b*) any of several thin-leaved aquatic plants used in aquaria, esp. of the genus *Eleocharis* (family Cyperaceae); **hairgrip** a grip for securing the hair, *esp.* one similar to a hairpin but with the ends close together; **hair lace** (now *rare*) a tie or net for securing the hair; **hair lacquer**: for holding the hair in place; **hair-lock** a lock of hair on or from the head; **hair mattress**: stuffed with hair; **hair moss**: of the genus *Polytrichum*; esp. *P. commune*, a large moss of damp or acid soils, with a hairy calyptra; **hairnet** a fine net for keeping the hair in place; **hair oil** cosmetic oil for dressing the hair; **hairpiece** a piece of false hair used to augment a person's natural hair; **hair-point** the fine tip of some moss leaves; **hair powder** *hist.* a scented powder for sprinkling on the hair or a wig; **hair-raising** *adjective* fearsome, horrifying, exciting, esp. so as to make the hair stand on end; **hair-restorer** a substance used to promote the growth of esp. receding or thinning hair; **hair's breadth** the breadth of a hair; a minute distance; **hair's-breadth** *adjective* extremely narrow or close; **hair seal** a seal without a thick fur undercoat; (cf. ***fur seal*** s.v. FUR *noun*[1]); **hair shirt** a shirt made of haircloth, worn by penitents or ascetics; **hair-shirt** *adjective* austere, harsh, self-sacrificing; **hair-sieve** (now *rare*) a sieve which has a base made of finely woven hair; ***hairslide***: see SLIDE *noun* 6; **hair-space** TYPOGRAPHY a very thin space between letters or words; **hair-splitter** a person who splits hairs; **hair-splitting** *verbal noun & ppl adjective* making overfine distinctions; **hairspray** spray-on hair lacquer; **hairspring** a fine spring which regulates the balance wheel in a watch; **hairstreak** any of various lycaenid butterflies belonging to the genus *Thecla* and related genera, having fringed wings often with pale markings like streaks (***white-letter hairstreak***: see WHITE *adjective*); **hair-stroke** a very fine stroke made in writing or drawing; **hairstyle** a particular way of dressing the hair; **hairstylist** a person who advises on and creates hairstyles for individual people; **hair trigger** a secondary trigger in a firearm which releases the main trigger by very slight pressure; **hair-triggered** *adjective* having a hair trigger; **hair worm** any of various long slender worms, *esp.* one whose larva is parasitic; *spec.* an aquatic worm of the class (or phylum) Nematomorpha (also called ***horsehair worm***), whose larvae are parasites of arthropods, *esp.* one of the common freshwater species *Gordius aquaticus*.
■ **hairlike** *adjective* resembling hair; finely drawn-out like hair: M17.

hair /hɛː/ *verb*. M16.
[ORIGIN from the noun.]
†**1** *verb trans.* Edge with hair or fur. *Scot.* M–L16.
2 *verb trans.* Free from hair; depilate. E19.
3 *verb intrans.* Produce or grow hair or a hairlike substance. L19.

haired /hɛːd/ *adjective*. LME.
[ORIGIN from HAIR *noun* + -ED[2].]
Having hair; covered with hair or hairs. Freq. with qualifying adjective, as ***black-haired***, ***long-haired***, etc.

hairen /ˈhɛːrən/ *adjective*. Long *obsolete* exc. *Scot. & dial.*
[ORIGIN Old English *hǣren* = Old High German *hārīn*, from Germanic base of HAIR *noun*: see -EN[4].]
Made or consisting of hair.

hairif /ˈhɛːrɪf/ *noun*. Chiefly *dial.* Also **harif** /ˈharɪf/, **hayrif**.
[ORIGIN Old English *hegerīfe*, app. from *hege* HAY *noun*[2] + *rīfe*, of unknown origin.]
The plant cleavers, *Galium aparine*.

hairless /ˈhɛːlɪs/ *adjective*. M16.
[ORIGIN from HAIR *noun* + -LESS.]
Without hair; bald.
■ **hairlessness** *noun* L19.

hairline /ˈhɛːlʌɪn/ *noun*. L16.
[ORIGIN from HAIR *noun* + LINE *noun*[2].]
1 A line or rope made of hair. L16.
2 A fine line; *spec.* the upstroke in a written or printed letter. M19.
3 = ***hair-cord*** (a) s.v. HAIR *noun*. M19.
4 The natural line on the head at which the hair stops growing. E20.

L. C. DOUGLAS The forward curve of the hair-line on the temples.

5 In full ***hairline crack***. A very fine crack, *esp.* one which occurs in steel or other metals. E20.
6 A fine line on glass, plastic, paper, etc., often used as a measuring guide or a dividing line. M20. ▸**b** *fig.* A very fine dividing line. M20.

b *attrib.*: *Times* It looked a hairline decision indeed.

– **COMB.**: ***hairline crack***: see sense 5 above; **hairline fracture** MEDICINE a very fine crack in a bone.

hairpin /ˈhɛːpɪn/ *noun*. L18.
[ORIGIN from HAIR *noun* + PIN *noun*[1].]
1 A kind of pin used to secure the hair, *esp.* a long-legged U-shaped pin. L18.
2 A person, *esp.* a thin person. *joc. slang.* L19.

J. O'FAOLAIN Maybe someone should give the old hairpin a bit of a fright.

3 In full ***hairpin bend***, ***hairpin corner***. A sharp U-shaped bend in a road or track. E20.

P. M. M. KEMP Its sudden ascents and declivities, its blind curves and hairpin bends.

hairy /ˈhɛːri/ *adjective & noun*. ME.
[ORIGIN from HAIR *noun* + -Y[1].]
▸ **A** *adjective*. **1** Having much hair; covered in hair. Also, having a rough appearance suggestive of hair(s). ME.

D. W. GOODWIN Maybe men can't see their bruises because of those hairy legs.

2 a Hairlike. Now *rare*. LME. ▸**b** Made of hair. M16.
3 BOTANY. Pubescent, esp. with separately distinguishable hairs. L16.
4 *fig.* Difficult; unpleasant, frightening; crude, clumsy. *slang*. M19.

D. LODGE Landing at Genoa is a pretty hairy experience at the best of times.

5 Uncouth, ill-mannered. *slang*. L19.
– **PHRASES ETC.**: **give someone the hairy eyeball** *N. Amer. colloq.* stare at someone in a disapproving or angry way. ***great hairy willowherb***: see WILLOW. **hairy about the heels**, **hairy at the heels** *slang* = sense 5 above. **hairy-heeled** *adjective* (*slang*) = sense 5 above. **hairy frog** a W. African frog, *Trichobatrachus robustus*, the males having hairlike filaments on the sides and thighs. **hairy in the heels** *slang* = sense 5 above. **hairy woodpecker** a black and white N. American woodpecker, *Dendrocopos villosus*. ***hairy woubit***.
▸ **B** *noun*. A draught horse (from its hairy fetlocks). Also, a hairy person; an aggressive or unpleasant person. M19.
■ **hairily** *adverb* M19. **hairiness** *noun* LME.

hait /heɪt/ *interjection*. *obsolete* exc. *dial.* Also **heit**. LME.
[ORIGIN Cf. German *hott* go right.]
Used to urge a horse forward.

haith /heɪθ/ *interjection*. *Scot.* L17.
[ORIGIN Alt. of FAITH.]
Used as an oath.

Haitian /ˈheɪʃ(ə)n, hɑːˈiːʃ-, hʌɪˈiːʃ-, -tɪən/ *adjective & noun*. Also (now *rare*) **Haytian**. E19.
[ORIGIN from *Haiti* (see below) + -IAN.]
▸ **A** *adjective*. Of or pertaining to Haiti, the French-speaking western portion of the Caribbean island of Hispaniola. E19.
Haitian creole the creolized French spoken in Haiti.
▸ **B** *noun*. A native or inhabitant of Haiti. Also, Haitian creole. E19.

hajeen *noun* var. of HYGEEN.

hajj /hadʒ/ *noun*. Also **hadj**, **haj**. E18.
[ORIGIN Arabic (*al-*) *ḥajj* (the Great) Pilgrimage.]
The greater Muslim pilgrimage to the Sacred Mosque at Mecca, which takes place in the twelfth month of the year and which all Muslims are expected to make at least once during their lifetime if they can afford to do so (one of the Five Pillars of Islam). Cf. UMRAH.

hajji /ˈhadʒiː/ *noun*. Also (fem.) **hajja** /ˈhadʒə/, **-dj-**. L16.
[ORIGIN Persian, Turkish *ḥājjī*, *ḥājī* pilgrim, formed as HAJJ.]
(The title given to) a person who has undertaken the hajj. Cf. AL-HAJJ.

haka /ˈhɑːkə/ *noun*. M19.
[ORIGIN Maori.]
A ceremonial Maori dance accompanied by chanting.

hakama /ˈhakəmə, ˈhɑː-/ *noun*. M19.
[ORIGIN Japanese, from *haku* put on, wear + *mo* ancient skirt.]
Japanese loose trousers with many pleats in the front.

hake /heɪk/ *noun*[1]. ME.
[ORIGIN Perh. from Old English *haca* hook: cf. Old English *hacod* pike.]
1 Any of various blue-grey and silver gadoid fishes of shallow temperate seas, of the genus *Merluccius* or the family Merlucciidae, having a rather elongate body with two dorsal fins, most species being commercially fished; *spec.* the European *M. merluccius*. Also, the flesh of these as food. ME.
2 a Either of two reddish-brown gadid food fishes, *Urophycis chuss* and *U. tenuis*, of the NW Atlantic (both also more fully ***red hake***, ***squirrel hake***, ***white hake***). *US*. L19. ▸**b** = ***gemfish*** s.v. GEM *noun*. *Austral. & NZ*. M20.

hake /heɪk/ *noun*[2]. *obsolete* exc. *hist.* Also **hag** /hag/. M16.
[ORIGIN App. abbreviation of *haquebut*: see HACKBUT.]
A short firearm used in the 16th cent.

hake *noun*[3] see HACK *noun*[3].

hakea /ˈhɑːkɪə, ˈheɪ-/ *noun*. E19.
[ORIGIN mod. Latin (see below), from C. L. von *Hake* (1745–1818), German patron of botany: see -IA[1].]
Any of numerous xerophytic shrubs and small trees of the genus *Hakea*, of the protea family, endemic to Australia.

hakeem *noun* var. of HAKIM *noun*[2].

Hakenkreuz /ˈhɑːkənkrɔyts/ *noun*. Also **h-**. Pl. **-e** /-ə/. M20.
[ORIGIN German, from *Haken* hook + *Kreuz* cross.]
A swastika, esp. as a Nazi symbol.

hakim /ˈhɑːkɪm/ *noun*[1]. E17.
[ORIGIN Arabic *ḥākim* ruler, governor, judge from *ḥakama* pass judgement.]
A judge, ruler, or governor in a Muslim country.

hakim /haˈkiːm/ *noun*[2]. Also **hakeem**. M17.
[ORIGIN Arabic *ḥakīm* wise man, philosopher, physician, formed as HAKIM *noun*[1].]
A physician in a Muslim country.

Hakka /ˈhakə/ *noun & adjective*. M19.
[ORIGIN Chinese (Cantonese) *haak ka* lit. 'guest, stranger'.]
▸ **A** *noun*. A member of a people of SE China, esp. Canton, Taiwan, and Hong Kong; the form of Chinese, comprising a group of dialects, spoken by this people. M19.
▸ **B** *attrib.* or as *adjective*. Of or pertaining to this people or this group of dialects. L19.

H

Halacha /halɑːˈxɑː, həˈlɑːkə/ *noun*. Also **-chah**, **-kah**. M19.
[ORIGIN Hebrew *hălākāh* law.]
The body of Jewish law contained in the Mishnah and in later Jewish literature; the legal element of the Talmud; a legal ruling included as a binding part of this law.
■ **Halachic** *adjective* M19.

Halafian /həˈlɑːfɪən/ *adjective*. M20.
[ORIGIN from Tell *Halaf* in NE Syria + -IAN.]
ARCHAEOLOGY. Designating or pertaining to a culture (*c* 6000–5400 BC) which extended from northern Syria to eastern Iraq and the neighbouring parts of Iran and Turkey and was characterized by polychrome pottery first discovered at Tell Halaf.

Halakah *noun* var. of HALACHA.

halal /həˈlɑːl/ *adjective, verb, & noun*. Also **hallal**. M19.
[ORIGIN Arabic *ḥalāl* according to religious law.]
▸ **A** *adjective*. Killed or prepared in the manner prescribed by Islamic law. M19.
▸ **B** *verb trans.* Kill (an animal) in this manner. M19.
▸ **C** *noun*. An animal killed, or meat prepared, in this manner. M20.

halala /həˈlɑːlə/ *noun*. Pl. **-s**, same. M20.
[ORIGIN Arabic]
A monetary unit of Saudi Arabia, equal to one-hundredth of a rial.

Halalcor /həˈlɑːlkɔː/ *noun*. M17.
[ORIGIN Urdu *halāl-ḵōr*, from Arabic HALAL + base of Persian *ḵordan* eat.]
A person of the lowest and poorest class in India, Iran, etc., to whom everything is lawful food.

halation /həˈleɪʃ(ə)n/ *noun*. M19.
[ORIGIN Irreg. from HALO *noun* + -ATION.]
The spreading of light beyond its proper boundaries to form a fog round the edges of a bright image in a photograph or on a television screen.

halawi /həˈlɑːwi/ *noun*. M19.
[ORIGIN Arabic *ḥalāwī*, pl. of *ḥalwā* HALVA.]
= HALVA.

halberd /ˈhalbəːd/ *noun*. Also **-ert** /-əːt/. L15.
[ORIGIN French *hallebarde*, †*alabarde* from Italian *alabarda* from Middle High German *helmbarde* (German *Hellebarde*), from *helm* handle, HELM *noun*[2] + *barde*, *barte* hatchet, rel. to *bart* beard (cf. Old Norse *skeggja* halberd, lit. 'the bearded', from *skegg* beard).]
hist. **1** A weapon, in use esp. during the 15th and 16th cents., consisting of a long handle ending in a combined spearhead and battleaxe. L15.
2 The rank of sergeant (from the right of a sergeant to carry a halberd). M18.
– **COMB.**: **halberdman** a halberdier.
■ **halberded** *adjective* armed with a halberd L18.

halberdier /halbəˈdɪə/ *noun*. E16.
[ORIGIN French *hallebardier*, formed as HALBERD: see -IER.]
A soldier armed with a halberd; a guardsman carrying a halberd as a badge of office.

halch /hal(t)ʃ/ *verb trans.* *obsolete* exc. *dial.* LME.
[ORIGIN Var. of HALSE *verb*[1].]
†**1** Embrace, greet, salute. LME–M17.
2 Fasten, tie, knot. LME.

halcyon /ˈhalsɪən, ˈhalʃ(ə)n/ *noun & adjective*. LME.
[ORIGIN Latin (*h*)*alcyon* from Greek *alkuōn* kingfisher (also *halkuōn* by assoc. with *hals* sea and *kuōn* conceiving), rel. to Latin *alcedo* kingfisher.]
▸ **A** *noun*. **1** A bird said by the ancients to breed in a nest floating on the sea around the time of the winter solstice, and to charm the wind and waves so that the sea was calm for this purpose; *poet.* a kingfisher. LME. ▸**b** Any of various brightly coloured tropical kingfishers of the genus *Halcyon*. L18.

†**2** Calm, quietude. **M17–L18.**

▸**B** *adjective.* **1** Calm, peaceful; happy, prosperous, idyllic. **L16.**

2 Of or pertaining to the halcyon or kingfisher. **E17.**

halcyon days orig., fourteen days of calm weather supposed to occur when the halcyon was breeding; now, days of idyllic happiness or prosperity.

haldi /ˈhʌldi/ *noun.* Also **huldee**. **M19.**

[**ORIGIN** Hindi from Sanskrit *haridrā*.]

The plant *Curcuma longa*, of the ginger family, whose powdered tubers yield turmeric. Also, turmeric itself.

haldu /ˈhaldu:/ *noun.* **E20.**

[**ORIGIN** Hindi.]

A tree, *Adina cordifolia*, of the madder family, found in the Indian subcontinent, Myanmar (Burma), and Thailand; the yellowish hardwood obtained from it.

hale /heɪl/ *noun*¹. Long *rare*. Also †**hail**. **ME.**

[**ORIGIN** Old Norse *heill* health, prosperity, good luck, rel. to **HEAL** *noun*; assim. to **HALE** *adjective*.]

1 Health, safety, welfare. **ME.**

†**2** Luck, fortune: in ***evil hale***, ***ill hale***, etc. **ME–E16.**

hale /heɪl/ *noun*². Long *rare* or *obsolete*. **ME.**

[**ORIGIN** Old French & mod. French *halle* covered marketplace, from Frankish = Old Saxon, Old High German *halla*: see **HALL** *noun*.]

A place roofed over, but usu. open at the sides; a tent, a pavilion; a temporary shelter.

hale /heɪl/ *noun*³. Now *rare* or *obsolete*. **L15.**

[**ORIGIN** from **HALE** *verb*¹.]

1 ***hale and how***: an exclam. of sailors in hauling. **L15.**

2 An act of hauling. **L17.**

3 A haul of fish. Chiefly *Scot.* **M18.**

hale /heɪl/ *noun*⁴. **E17.**

[**ORIGIN** App. from Old Norse *hali*, Danish *hale* tail.]

Either of the two handles of a plough or wheelbarrow. Usu. in *pl.*

hale /heɪl/ *adjective.* Also (*Scot.*) **hail**. **OE.**

[**ORIGIN** North. dial. repr. of Old English *hāl* **WHOLE** *adjective*. Cf. **HAIL** *adjective*¹.]

▸**I** Sound, healthy.

1 Free from injury; safe, unhurt. Now only *Scot. & N. English.* **OE.**

2 Free from disease, healthy; recovered from disease, healed. Now only *Scot. & N. English.* **OE.**

3 Esp. of an old person: free from infirmity; sound, robust, vigorous. Freq. in ***hale and hearty***. **E18.**

▸**II** **4** Whole, entire, complete; unbroken, undecayed. Now only *Scot. & N. English.* **ME.**

the hale ware: see **WARE** *noun*².

– **NOTE**: In Scottish *hail* the *i* indicated a long vowel not a diphthong as in **HAIL** *adjective*¹.

■ **halely** *adverb* **ME.** **haleness** *noun* **ME.**

hale /heɪl/ *verb*¹. **ME.**

[**ORIGIN** Old French & mod. French *haler* from Old Norse *hala* = Old Saxon *halon*, Old High German *halōn*, *holōn* (Dutch *halen*, German *holen* fetch): cf. Old English *ġeholian* acquire & **HAUL** *verb*.]

1 *verb trans.* Draw, pull; *spec.* drag, tug, or haul forcibly. **ME.**

R. ELLMANN He was haled before the Vice-Chancellor's court in November 1877.

2 *verb trans. fig.* Draw forcibly to, into, out of, a course of action, feeling, condition, etc. (Foll. by *to*, *into*, *out of*.) **LME.**

J. H. FRISWELL Garrick haled on one hand by Tragedy and on the other by Comedy.

3 *verb intrans.* Pull, tug. **LME.**

4 *verb intrans.* †**a** Move along as if drawn or pulled; hasten, rush; *spec.* (of a ship) proceed before the wind with the sails set. **LME–E18.** ▸**b** Flow, run, pour. *obsolete* exc. *Scot. & N. English.* **LME.**

hale /heɪl/ *verb*². *obsolete* exc. *Scot.* **ME.**

[**ORIGIN** from **HALE** *adjective*, or var. of **HEAL** *verb*¹ assim. to **HALE** *adjective*.]

Make hale or whole; heal.

haler /ˈhɑːlə/ *noun.* Pl. **haleru** /ˈhɑːləruː/, **halers**, or same. **M20.**

[**ORIGIN** Czech *haléř* (genit. pl. *haléřů*) from Middle High German *haller*: see **HELLER** *noun*¹.]

A monetary unit of the Czech Republic, equal to one-hundredth of a koruna.

halesia /həˈliːzɪə/ *noun.* **M18.**

[**ORIGIN** mod. Latin (see below), from Stephen *Hales* (1677–1761), English plant physiologist: see **-IA**¹.]

Any of several trees of the southern US constituting the genus *Halesia*, of the styrax family, with pendulous white flowers; esp. *H. tetraptera*, freq. grown for ornament. Also called ***silver-bell tree***, ***snowdrop tree***.

halesome /ˈheɪls(ə)m/ *adjective.* Chiefly *Scot.* **ME.**

[**ORIGIN** from **HALE** *adjective* + **-SOME**¹. Cf. **HEALSOME**.]

Wholesome.

half /hɑːf/ *noun.* Pl. **halves** /hɑːvz/, †**halfs**.

[**ORIGIN** Old English *healf* fem. = Old Frisian *halve*, Old Saxon *halа*, Old High German *halba*, Old Norse *hálfa*, Gothic *halba* side (earliest sense), half; in sense 6 from the adjective.]

†**1** Side; either of the (two) sides of an object etc. as a specification of position or direction; the *right* or *left* side. **OE–M16.**

SIR T. MORE Then thou shalte see me on the backe halfe.

†**2** *fig.* Either of two opposing sides identified contextually, as two parties in a conflict, the representatives of male and female lines of descent, etc. **OE–M16.** ▸**b** Side, part (as of each of the parties to a transaction). Freq. in ***on my half***, ***on this half***, etc. **OE–E16.**

J. DOLMAN On princes halves the myghty god doth fyght.

3 Either of two opposite, corresponding, or equal parts into which a thing is or may be divided; either of two equal parts into which a number or quantity is or may be divided. **OE.** ▸**b** *spec.* Either of two equal periods of play, usu. separated by an interval, into which a game of football etc. is divided. **L19.**

AV *1 Kings* 3:25 Diuide the liuing childe in two, and giue halfe to the one, and halfe to the other. J. MCLEOD One of his attendants . . received . . about a dozen and a half blows with a flat bamboo. W. SCORESBY Of this number of whales, considerably above half have been taken by five ships. A. J. P. TAYLOR He had lost the return half of his ticket. D. PRATER Clara joined him . . for the first half of August. *Gentleman (Mumbai)* The two halves of east and west . . joined by a common heritage. J. VIORST More than half of those with children under the age of six now go to work. **b** *Sporting Mirror* For most of the first half . . it seemed that only one end of the field was in use.

4 Either of two divisions more or less approaching equality (freq. with preceding compar. adjective). Formerly also, each of three or more divisions. **ME.**

H. SPENCER The larger half of the phenomena. R. KIPLING Half of them were thin-legged, gray-bearded Ooryas from down country.

†**5** Either of two partners or sharers. Only in **16.**

SHAKES. *Tam. Shr.* Son, I'll be your half.

6 [Absol. use of the adjective.] *colloq.* ▸**a** A half-sized thing; a half quantity or division according to some specific measure. **M17.** ▸**b** A school term (the school year formerly being divided into two portions). **E19.** ▸**c** A half-pint of beer, lager, etc.; *Scot.* a half-gill of spirits (esp. of whisky). **L19.** ▸**d** A halfback. Usu. with specifying word, as ***fly half***, ***left-half***, etc. **L19.** ▸**e** A fare or ticket at a reduced (usu. half) rate, esp. for a child. Also, a person entitled to travel at such a rate. **M20.** ▸**f** *AMER. FOOTBALL.* Half-time. Freq. with *the*. **M20.**

a N. ALGREN He found three halves, wrapped in a ten-dollar bill, in her apron. **b** A. POWELL I went to Eton in the summer half of 1919. **c** A. BURGESS Our men sat gloomily over their halves of washy bitter. **e** *New Statesman* Two adults and three halves, please.

7 *GOLF.* A halved hole. **L19.**

Daily Telegraph He . . secured the necessary 5 for the half and the match.

– **PHRASES**: **and a half** *fig.* (*colloq.*) of an exceptional kind; and more. **by halves** imperfectly or incompletely (usu. in neg. contexts). **cry halves** claim an equal share. **go halves**, **go half and half** share equally (foll. by *in*, *on* a thing, *with* a person). ***one's better half***: see **BETTER** *adjective* etc. ***one's worse half***: see **WORSE** *adjective, noun, & adverb*. **other half** (**a**) the people having a different (esp. superior) social, cultural, or economic standing (chiefly in ***how the other half lives***); (**b**) *colloq.* (freq. *joc.*) a person's spouse or boyfriend or girlfriend; (**c**) *slang* the second drink (esp. when bought in return for the first). **the half of it** the more significant or important part (usu. in neg. contexts). **too clever by half** far more clever than is satisfactory or desirable.

half /hɑːf/ *adjective* (in mod. usage also classed as a *determiner*) *& adverb.*

[**ORIGIN** Old English *half* (*healf*) = Old Frisian, Old Saxon (Dutch) *half*, Old & mod. High German *halb*, Old Norse *hálfr*, Gothic *halbs*, from Germanic.]

▸**A** *adjective.* **1** Forming either of two equal parts or corresponding groups into which something is or may be divided; of an amount or quantity equal to a half. Following or (passing into **HALF** *noun* 3) preceding a determiner (article, demonstrative, or possessive adjective). **OE.**

LD MACAULAY His victory . . had deprived him of half his influence. J. M. MURRY Keats spent half the year at his side. G. GREENE Sickness benefit; half wages; incapacity; the management regrets. W. BOYD The Norfolk was half a mile further on. *fig.*: A. TROLLOPE If you are half the woman I take you to be, you will understand this.

†**2** Designating a half-unit less than the cardinal numeral that corresponds to the preceding or following ordinal numeral. **OE–ME.**

3 Falling short of the full or perfect amount, degree, type, etc.; partial, incomplete, imperfect. **ME.**

M. B. KEATINGE Contented with half views of things and truths. *UnixWorld* You can instruct the processor to run at half speed.

4 Half the length or breadth of. Now *rare* or *obsolete*. **L15.**

J. DAVIES Their hair . . hangs down over their shoulders to half their backs.

– **PHRASES**: **half a crown** = *half-crown* s.v. **HALF-**. **half a dozen** a half of a dozen, six; ***six and half a dozen***, ***six of one and half a dozen of the other***: see **SIX** *noun* 1. **half a minute** a half of a minute, thirty seconds. ***half an eye***: see **EYE** *noun*. **half an hour** a half of an hour, thirty minutes. ***half the battle***: see **BATTLE** *noun*. ***half the time***: see **TIME** *noun*. ***with half a heart***: see **HEART** *noun*.

▸**B** *adverb.* **1** To the extent or amount of half; *loosely* in part, partially, to a certain extent, in some degree, nearly. **OE.**

J. CONRAD They would . . address him half seriously as Rajah Laut. D. H. LAWRENCE His talk was fragmentary, he was only half articulate. J. BUCHAN They were only foolish people scared half out of their minds. B. PYM 'These men see . . His wonders in the deep', Julian said half to himself. O. MANNING Hugh found Simon prone, eyes half closed. H. SECOMBE Miss Thomas gave a little shriek which she half stifled with a gloved hand. L. GORDON Lying half asleep, half awake in her warm bed. J. ARCHER She only hoped that Raymond's remarks would be half as flattering.

2 ***not half***: not, not sufficiently (now *rare* exc. with *enough* following adjective); *slang* not at all, rather the reverse of; also (*slang*) (as a mere intensive), in no small measure, certainly, undoubtedly, etc. **L16.**

V. WOOLF I could live on fifteen shillings a week . . It wouldn't be half bad. L. P. HARTLEY 'You don't half like getting your own way, do you?' grumbled Harold. A. WESKER He didn't half upset them. *Beano* Coo! Smashing film, eh, lads? . . Not half! P. BARKER They aren't half a price.

3 *NAUTICAL.* **a** By the amount of half a point beyond a (preceding) specified compass point towards a (following) specified compass point. **E18.** ▸**b** By the amount of half a unit more than the following specified number of fathoms in a sounding. **E19.**

a G. SHELVOCKE Bearing South East half East, distant six leagues. **b** F. MARRYAT We shall have *half four* directly, and after that the water will deepen.

4 By the amount of half an hour past (or *past*) the (following) specified hour. **M18.**

M. AMSTERDAM This morning at half past three.

half /hɑːf/ *verb intrans. & trans.* Chiefly *dial.* **L19.**

[**ORIGIN** from **HALVE** *verb*.]

Halve; go halves in (something).

half- /hɑːf/ *combining form.* **OE.**

[**ORIGIN** Repr. **HALF** *adjective & adverb*.]

Forming combs. with nouns, adjectives, verbs, and adverbs in various relations and senses, as 'forming a half' (***half-belt***, ***half-share***); 'of an amount or quantity equal to a half' (***half-dozen***, ***half-pound***); 'incomplete(ly), imperfect(ly), partial(ly)' (***half-thought-out***, ***half-done***, ***half-kill***). Can be written with or without a hyphen.

half adder *COMPUTING* a logic device which has two inputs (addend and augend) and generates two outputs (sum and carry digits). **half-and-half** *noun, adjective, & adverb* (**a**) *noun* something that is half one thing and half another; *spec.* (*arch.*) a mixture of ale and porter in equal quantities, (*US*) a mixture of milk and cream; (**b**) *adjective* that is half one thing and half another; (**c**) *adverb* in equal parts; half — and half not. **half-arse**, **half-arsed**, **half-ass**, **half-assed** *adjectives* (*slang*) incompetent, inadequate. **halfback** *FOOTBALL & HOCKEY* etc. (the position of) a player playing between the forwards and the backs; *AMER. FOOTBALL* (now *rare*) a flanker. **half-baked** *adjective* (*fig.*) (**a**) not thorough, not thoroughly planned, not serious, incomplete; (**b**) stupid, half-witted. **half-ball** *BILLIARDS & SNOOKER* etc. a stroke in which the cue is aimed through the cue ball at the edge of the object ball, and so covers half of it. **half-bapˈtize** *verb trans.* baptize privately or without full rites. **halfbeak** any of various small, slender, mostly marine surface-skimming tropical fishes of the family Hemiramphidae, related to flying fish and typically having the lower jaw much longer than the upper. **half-ˈbelt** a belt extending only halfway around the body, *esp.* one worn at the back of a garment. **half binding** a style of bookbinding in which the back and corners are covered in one material and the sides in another, usu. less durable. **half blood** (**a**) the relation between people having only one parent in common; (**b**) a person or group of persons related in this way; (**c**) *offensive* a person of mixed descent. **half-blooded** *adjective* of mixed descent. **half-blue** (the holder of) the colours awarded to the player who is second choice to represent his or her university (esp. Oxford or Cambridge) in inter-university contests or who plays a minor sport in such contests. **half board** accommodation at a hotel etc. providing bed, breakfast, and one main meal (usu. dinner) a day. **half-boot** a boot which reaches up to the calf. **half-bound** *adjective* (of a book) bound with leather back and corners and cloth or paper sides. **half-bred** *adjective & noun* (an animal, esp. (*Austral. & NZ*) a sheep) of mixed breed. **half-breed** (*derog. & offensive*) a person with parents from different races, esp. (*N. Amer.*) with white and black parents or with white and American Indian parents. **half-brother** a male related to one or more other persons (male or female) by having one biological parent in common. **half-butt** *BILLIARDS* a cue of a length between an ordinary cue and a long butt. **half-cap** †(**a**) a half-courteous salute given by a slight movement of the cap; (**b**) *hist.* a kind of woman's headdress. **half-caste** *adjective & noun* (*offensive*) (designating or pertaining to) a person with parents of different races, *spec.* with a European father and an Indian mother. †**half-cheek** a face in profile. **half-circle** a semicircle. **half cock** the position of the cock of a gun when partly raised; freq. in ***at half cock*** (see **COCK** *noun*¹ 12). **half-cocked** *adjective* (**a**) at half cock (*lit. & fig.*); (**b**) *dial.* partly drunk, tipsy; (**c**) incompletely prepared or realized. **half-court** *TENNIS & BADMINTON* etc. a section of the court demarcated by a line parallel with the sidelines, a service court. **half-crown** *hist.* a British silver (orig. gold) coin worth two shillings and sixpence; the amount represented by this. **half-crowner** *arch. colloq.* a person who paid a half-crown for admission etc. **half-cut** *adjective* (*colloq.*) partly drunk, tipsy. **half-day** half a working day, esp. taken as holiday. **half-dead** *adjective* in a state in which death seems as likely as recovery; in a state of extreme exhaustion or weakness. **half-deck** (**a**) a deck covering half the length of a ship or boat, fore and aft; *spec.* (*hist.*) in a ship of war, a deck extending aft from the mainmast between the upper deck and the quarterdeck; (*b*) the quarters of cadets and apprentices on a merchant vessel. **half-dime** US HISTORY a (silver) coin worth five cents; the amount represented by this. **half-dollar** in the US and other countries, a coin worth fifty cents; the amount represented by this. **half-door** a door of half the normal size, usu. with a space above it. **half-dozen** a half of a dozen, six. **half-dress** *hist.* costume worn at day and informal evening functions during the late 18th and 19th cents. **half-eagle** US HISTORY a gold coin worth five dollars; the amount represented by this. **half-ebb** the state or time of the tide halfway to its ebb. **half-face** (*a*) a half of a face; a face as seen in profile; a profile on a coin etc.; (*b*) MILITARY an act or a position of facing halfway to the right or left. **half-ˈfaced** *adjective* (*a*) presenting a half-face or profile; (of a coin) stamped with a profile; (of a person) having a thin, pinched face; (*b*) with only half the face visible; (*c*) imperfect, incomplete, half-and-half; (*d*) *US* (of a camp or shelter) left open on one side. **half-flood** the state or time of the tide halfway to its flood. **half-frame** *adjective* (*a*) designating reading spectacles consisting of only the lower half of the frames and lenses; (*b*) PHOTOGRAPHY (taking) half the standard 35 mm picture size. **half-frames** half-frame spectacles. **half-galley** a galley of about half the full size. **half-god** a demigod. **half-groat** (*obsolete* exc. *hist.*) a British silver coin worth two old pence; the amount represented by this. **half-guinea** *hist.* a British gold coin worth ten shillings and sixpence; the amount represented by this. **half-hardy** *noun & adjective* (a plant) able to grow in the open air at all times except in severe frost. **half-headed** *adjective* (*arch.*) deficient in intellect, stupid. **half-hearted** *adjective* not having one's whole heart in a matter; lacking in courage, enthusiasm, or determination; feeble. **half-heartedly** *adverb* in a half-hearted manner. **half-heartedness** the state or condition of being half-hearted. ***half hitch***: see HITCH *noun*. **half holiday** †(*a*) a day considered only half a holy day; a saint's day or holy day other than Sunday; (*b*) the (usu. latter) half of a working day used for recreation or esp. taken as holiday. **half-hose** socks. **half-hour** a half of an hour, thirty minutes. **half-hourly** *adjective & adverb* (occurring) at intervals of half an hour. ***half-*HUNTER**. **half-inch** *noun & verb* (*a*) *noun* a unit of length half as long as an inch; (*b*) *verb trans.* [rhyming slang for *pinch*] steal. **half integer** any member of the set of numbers obtained by dividing the odd integers by two. **half-integral** *adjective* equal to half an odd integer. **half-jack** *hist.* a counter made to resemble a half sovereign. ***half-James***: see JAMES 1b. **half-joe** *hist.* a Portuguese gold coin, formerly current in N. America, worth 3,200 reis; the amount represented by this. **half landing** a landing halfway up a flight of stairs. ***half lap***: see LAP *noun*[3]. **half-leg** *US* half the height of a person's leg (chiefly in ***half-leg high***). **half-length** a portrait of the upper half of a person. **half-life** (*a*) a life of half the full length; an unsatisfactory way of life; (*b*) the length of time in which a quantity (esp. of a substance) is reduced by half; *spec.* (i) the time in which half of any number of atoms of a given radioactive isotope will decay; (ii) the time required for half of a quantity of a given substance to be broken down chemically or otherwise lost in the body, the environment, etc. **half-lift** PROSODY a half or secondary stress. **half-light** a dim imperfect light. **half-line** PROSODY half of a line of verse, esp. as a structural unit in Old English and related poetry. **half-man** (*a*) a being who is only half human, or deficient in humanity; (*b*) an effeminate man; a eunuch. **half-mark** (*obsolete* exc. *hist.*) an English money of account worth six shillings and eightpence. **half mast** *noun & verb* (*a*) *noun* the half of a mast, half the height of a mast; ***at half mast***, ***half-mast high***, (of a flag) lowered towards the middle of the mast as a mark of respect for the dead; (*b*) *verb trans.* hang at or lower to half mast. **half measure** an inadequate or unsatisfactory compromise, policy, etc. (usu. in *pl.*). **half-mile** *noun & adjective* (a race) extending to or covering half a mile. **half-miler** a runner who competes in a half-mile or whose preferred distance is half a mile. **half-minute** a half of a minute, thirty seconds. †**half-mourner** the marbled white butterfly, *Melanargia galathea*. **half-mourning** (*a*) the second stage or period of mourning after the expiry of full mourning; (*b*) (dress of) black relieved or replaced by grey, mauve, etc., in token of this. **half-move** COMPUTING either of a pair of moves (one by each side) investigated by a chess-playing program during the course of a game. **half-naked** *adjective* nearly naked. ***half nelson***: see NELSON *noun*[2]. **half-noble** (*obsolete* exc. *hist.*) an English or British gold coin equal to half a noble; the amount represented by this. **half note** MUSIC †(*a*) a semitone; (*b*) *N. Amer.* a minim. **half-part** (*long rare* or *obsolete*) a half. **half-pass** a dressage movement in which the legs on the side to which the horse is moving pass and cross behind the outside legs. **half pay** (*a*) half of the full or usual wages or salary, *esp.* a reduced allowance made to an army etc. officer when retired or not in actual service; (*b*) (now *rare*) an officer on half pay. **half-pie** *adjective* (*NZ slang*) [perh. Maori *pai* good] halfway towards, imperfect, mediocre. **half-pike** *hist.* a small pike with a shaft about half the length of a full-sized one. **half-pint** (*a*) an amount of liquid equal to half a pint; (*b*) *fig.* a small, insignificant, or ineffectual person. **half-pipe** a channel made of concrete or cut into the snow with a U-shaped cross-section, used by skateboarders, snowboarders, etc. to perform jumps and other manoeuvres. **half-plane** MATH. that part of a plane which lies to one side of a line in the plane. **half plate** (a photograph reproduced from) a photographic plate measuring 4¾ by 6½ inches. **half-price** *adjective & noun* (at) half of the full or usual price. ***half relief***: see RELIEF *noun*[2] 1. **half-rhyme** an imperfect or near rhyme; *esp.* the rhyming of one word or syllable with another in consonants but not in vowels. **half-round** *adjective & noun* (*a*) *adjective* semicircular, semi-cylindrical; (*b*) *noun* (now *rare*) a semicircle, a hemispherical figure. **half seas over** *adverb & adjective* (*a*) *adverb* (*arch.*) halfway across the sea; *transf.* & *fig.* halfway towards a goal or destination or between one state and another; (*b*) *adjective* (*slang*) half-drunk. ***half-*SHAVED**. **half-sheet** (*a*) a size of paper equal to half a sheet; (*b*) a kind of printing in which all the pages of a signature are in one forme. **half-shell** half of the shell of an oyster etc., esp. as used for serving food (chiefly in ***on the half-shell***). **half-shot** GOLF a shot played with about half the full swing. **half-sibling** a half-brother or half-sister. **half-sister** a female related to one or more other persons (male or female) by having one biological parent in common. **half-slip** the lower half of a slip, a waist petticoat. **half-sole** *noun & verb* (*a*) *noun* the part of the sole of a boot or shoe extending from the shank to the toe; (*b*) *verb trans.* provide (a boot or shoe) with a half-sole. **half-sovereign** *hist.* a British gold coin worth ten shillings; the amount represented by this. **half-standard** a tree or shrub that grows on an erect stem of half height and stands alone without support. **half-starved** *adjective* having insufficient food; poorly fed; suffering from malnourishment. **half step** MUSIC a semitone. **half-stress** PROSODY a secondary stress. **half-stuff** PAPER-MAKING partly prepared pulp. **half-term** a period about halfway through a school term, esp. taken as a short holiday. **half-tester** a canopy extending over half the length of a bed. **half-tide** the state or time of the tide halfway between flood and ebb. **half-timber** *adjective* (*a*) = *half-timbered*; (*b*) made of timber split in half. **half-timbered** *adjective* (of a building) having walls with a timber frame and brick or plaster filling. **half-time** (*a*) half the usual or full time during which work is carried on; (*b*) the time at which half of a game or contest is completed; the interval then occurring. **half-title** (*a*) the title or short title of a book, printed on the recto of the leaf preceding the title leaf or at the head of the first page; (*b*) the title of the section of a book printed on the recto of the leaf preceding it. **halftone** (*a*) MUSIC (*US*) a semitone; (*b*) an image, produced by photographic or electronic means, in which an effect of continuous tone is simulated by dots of various sizes or lines of various thicknesses; the process which produces such an image; (*c*) ART an intermediate tone between the extreme lights and the extreme shades. **half-topped** *adjective* (GOLF) designating a stroke in which the ball is partly topped. **half-track** (a vehicle having) a propulsion system with the wheels at the front and endless driven bands at the back. **half-truth** a proposition or statement that (esp. deliberately) conveys only half the truth. **half-uncial** *adjective & noun* (designating) writing which shares some of the features of both uncial and cursive; semi-uncial. **half-value** a value of a physical property, esp. intensity of radioactivity, that is half of an earlier value. **half-verse** = *half-line* above. **half-volley** *noun & verb* TENNIS & FOOTBALL etc. (*a*) *noun* a stroke or shot in which a ball is hit or kicked immediately after it bounces on the ground; such a ball; (*b*) *verb trans.* hit or kick (a ball) immediately after it bounces. **half-wave** *noun & adjective* (*a*) *noun* one half of a complete (electromagnetic) wave; (*b*) *adjective* using or involving half a wave or wavelength. **halfwit** a stupid or foolish person; an imbecile. **half-witted** *adjective* stupid, foolish; imbecile. **half-wittedness** the state or condition of being half-witted. **half-word** a word that hints at or suggests something. **half-world** †(*a*) a hemisphere; (*b*) the demi-monde. **half-year** (*a*) a half of a year, six months; (*b*) (now *rare*) = HALF *noun* 6b. **half-yearly** *adjective & adverb* (happening) every half-year or six months.

halfa *noun* var. of ALFA.

†**halfen** *adjective*. *pseudo-arch. rare* (Spenser). Only in L16.
[ORIGIN Perh. from HALFENDEAL or irreg. from HALF *adjective*.]
Half.

halfendeal /ˈhɑːf(ə)ndiːl/ *noun & adverb*. *obsolete* exc. *dial.*
[ORIGIN Old English *þone healfan dǣl*, accus. case of *se healfa dǣl* the half part: see DEAL *noun*[1].]
▸ **A** *noun*. A half; a half share. OE.
▸ †**B** *adverb*. Half, by half. ME–L16.

halfling /ˈhɑːflɪŋ/ *noun & adjective*. L18.
[ORIGIN Orig. Scot. & north, from HALF *noun* + -LING[1].]
▸ **A** *noun*. A person who is not fully grown; a stripling. In the stories of J. R. R. Tolkien (1892–1973), a hobbit. L18.
▸ **B** *adjective*. Not fully grown; that is a halfling. E19.

half moon /hɑːf muːn/ *noun phr. & adjective*. As adjective usu. **half-moon**. LME.
[ORIGIN from HALF- + MOON *noun*.]
▸ **A** *noun*. **1** The moon when only half its disc is illuminated; the time when this occurs; *loosely* a crescent. LME.
2 Something shaped like a half moon or crescent; a semicircular object; *spec.* the white crescent-shaped mark at the base of a fingernail. L16.
3 FORTIFICATION. A demilune. M17.
▸ **B** *adjective*. Shaped like a half moon or crescent; *spec.* designating spectacles with lenses shaped like half moons. L16.
■ **half-mooned** *adjective* (long *rare*) shaped like a half moon, semilunate E17.

halfness /ˈhɑːfnɪs/ *noun*. Now *rare*. M16.
[ORIGIN from HALF *adjective* + -NESS.]
The condition or quality of being half; incompleteness; irresoluteness.

half-pace /ˈhɑːfpeɪs/ *noun*. M16.
[ORIGIN Alt. of HALPACE after HALF *adjective*.]
1 A step or platform on which a throne, dais, etc. stands; *spec.* the platform at the top of steps on which an altar stands. M16.
2 A broad step or small landing between two half flights in a staircase. E17.

halfpenny /ˈheɪpni/ *noun & adjective*. Also **ha'penny**. Pl. **halfpennies** /ˈheɪpnɪz/, (see sense 1 below) **halfpence** /ˈheɪp(ə)ns/. ME.
[ORIGIN from HALF- + PENNY.]
▸ **A** *noun*. **1** *hist.* A British bronze (orig. copper) coin worth half a penny; (pl. **-pence**) the amount represented by this, *loosely* a very small amount of money. (Earlier in HALFPENNYWORTH.) ME. ▸**b** A stamp costing a halfpenny. L19.

> *Lancashire Evening Telegraph* Any judge . . would have . . awarded these sharks a halfpenny as their share of the compensation.

three halfpence a penny and a halfpenny. ***twopenny-halfpenny***: see TWOPENNY *adjective* 1.
†**2** A small fragment or piece. *rare* (Shakes.). Only in L16.
3 A form of earmark on cattle and horses. *US*. M17.
▸ **B** *attrib.* or as *adjective*. That costs a halfpenny; *fig.* worth no more than a halfpenny, of contemptible value, trumpery. LME.

> W. S. CHURCHILL Writing, dictating & sifting papers like the Editor of a ha'penny paper.

halfpennyworth /ˈheɪpəθ, ˈheɪpnɪwəθ/ *noun*. Also **ha'p'orth** /ˈheɪpəθ/.
[ORIGIN Old English *healfpenigwurþ*, formed as HALFPENNY, WORTH *noun*[1].]
As much as might be bought for a halfpenny; a very small amount.

> *Proverb*: Do not spoil the ship for a ha'p'orth of tar.

halfway /hɑːfˈweɪ, ˈhɑːfweɪ/ *adverb, preposition, noun, & adjective*. Also **half-way**. ME.
[ORIGIN from HALF- + WAY *noun*.]
▸ **A** *adverb*. At or to half the way or distance; *loosely* partially. ME.

> *Times Higher Educ. Suppl.* In science, there are fields which are a gift for any half-way decent PR Officer. A. GHOSH Bahram stopped only when he was halfway to his own house.

meet halfway: see MEET *verb*.
▸ †**B** *preposition*. Halfway up, down, along, etc. E17–E18.

> I. WATTS Faint devotion panting lies, Half way th' ethereal hill.

▸ **C** *noun*. A point or position midway between two extreme points; a halfway place. Now *rare*. M17.

> L. HUTCHINSON In the half-way between Owthorpe and Nottingham.

▸ **D** *adjective*. Midway or equidistant between two points; *fig.* midway between two states or conditions, half one thing and half another. L17.

> HANNAH MORE Some half-way state, something between paganism and christianity. E. K. KANE My aim was to reach the half-way tent.

halfway house (*a*) a house or esp. an inn midway between two towns or stages of a journey; (*b*) *fig.* a compromise; (*c*) the halfway point in a progression; (*d*) a centre for rehabilitating ex-prisoners, mental patients, or others unused to normal life. **halfway line** FOOTBALL, HOCKEY, etc. a line midway between the two goals.

H

halgh *noun* var. of HAUGH.

halibut /ˈhalɪbət/ *noun*. Also **hol-** /ˈhɒl-/. Pl. same, **-s**. LME.
[ORIGIN Alt. of HOLY + BUTT *noun*[1] (from its commonly being eaten on holy days).]
A very large flatfish of the N. Atlantic, *Hippoglossus hippoglossus*, fished intensively for food; any of several closely related fishes, *esp.* (more fully ***Pacific halibut***) *Hippoglossus stenolepis* and (more fully ***Greenland halibut***) *Reinhardtius hippoglossoides*. Also, the flesh of any of these as food.

halide /ˈheɪlʌɪd/ *noun*. L19.
[ORIGIN from HAL(OGEN + -IDE.]
CHEMISTRY. A binary compound formed from a halogen and another element or a radical.

halidom /ˈhalɪdəm/ *noun*. Long *rare* or *obsolete*.
[ORIGIN Old English *hāligdōm* = Middle Dutch *heilichdoem*, Old High German *heilagtuom* (cf. Old Norse *helgidómr*): see HOLY, -DOM.]
†**1** Holiness, sanctity. OE–E17.
2 A holy place; a sanctuary. OE.
3 A holy thing, *esp.* a relic. Freq. in interjection ***by my halidom***, expr. surprise, assertion, etc. OE.

halier /ˈhaljɛː/ *noun*[1]. Pl. same, **haliers**. L20.
[ORIGIN Slovak; cf. HALER.]
A monetary unit of Slovakia, equal to one-hundredth of a koruna.

†**halier** *noun*[2] see HALYARD.

halieutic /halɪˈjuːtɪk/ *noun & adjective*. Now *rare*. M17.
[ORIGIN Latin *halieuticus* from Greek *halieutikos*, from *halieutēs* fisher: see -IC.]
▸ **A** *noun*. In *pl.* (treated as *sing.*), the art or practice of fishing; *sing.* a treatise on fishing. M17.
▸ **B** *adjective*. Of or pertaining to fishing. M19.

Halifax /ˈhalɪfaks/ *noun*. *euphem.* M17.
[ORIGIN The name of towns in W. Yorkshire, England, and Nova Scotia, Canada.]
Hell. Chiefly in ***go to Halifax***.

haliotis /halɪˈəʊtɪs/ *noun*. Pl. same. M18.
[ORIGIN from Greek *hals*, *hali-* sea + *ous*, *ōt-* ear.]
A marine gastropod of the genus *Haliotis*, with an ear-shaped shell lined with mother-of-pearl; the shell of this.

halite /ˈhalʌɪt/ *noun*. M19.
[ORIGIN from Greek *hals* salt + -ITE[1].]
Rock salt; sodium chloride, NaCl, as a mineral, crystallizing in the cubic system.

halitosis /halɪˈtəʊsɪs/ *noun*. L19.
[ORIGIN from Latin HALITUS + -OSIS.]
Foul-smelling breath.
■ **halitotic** *adjective* having halitosis M20.

halituous /həˈlɪtjʊəs/ *adjective*. E17.
[ORIGIN formed as HALITOSIS + -OUS.]
Resembling or characterized by breath or vapour.

halitus /ˈhalɪtəs/ *noun. rare.* **M17.**
[ORIGIN Latin, lit. 'breath', from *halare* breathe.]
A vapour, an exhalation.

hall /hɔːl/ *noun.* Also (*Scot.*) **ha'** /hɔː/.
[ORIGIN Old English *hall*, *heall* = Old Saxon, Old High German *halla* (Dutch *hal*, German *Halle*), Old Norse *hǫll*, from a Germanic base meaning 'cover, conceal': cf. HELL *noun*.]
1 A place, orig. *spec.* a large place, covered by a roof; in early use, any spacious roofed place; a temple, a palace, a court. *obsolete* exc. as passing into specific senses below and with specifying word. **OE.**
banqueting hall, ***city hall***, ***dancehall***, ***dining hall***, ***entrance hall***, ***guildhall***, ***music hall***, ***town hall***, ***village hall***, etc.
2 A large residence, esp. of a landed proprietor; a mansion. Now chiefly in names or with *the* (referring to a specific local hall). **OE.**

A. TROLLOPE He would certainly sell Vavasor Hall in spite of all family associations.

3 A large public room in a mansion, palace, etc., used for receptions and banquets. **ME.**

T. HARDY Maryann . . show them in to me in the hall.

4 A house or building belonging to a guild or fraternity. **ME.**
5 A large room or building for public gatherings. **ME.** ▸†**b** A formal assembly called by the monarch, or by the principal officer of a town. **M16–L17.** ▸**c** A music hall. Usu. in *pl.* **M19.**

H

Dumfries & Galloway Standard The church would provide an elegant hall capable of seating approximately 250. **c** S. BRETT And then you toured the halls as a double-act?

6 At Oxford and Cambridge Universities: orig., any of the educational institutions including the colleges (now *arch.* or *hist.*); later *spec.*, an educational institution which is not a corporate body and whose property is held in trust, as opp. to a college. **LME.** ▸**b** A building, administered by a university, polytechnic, etc., in which students live (also ***hall of residence***); an establishment of higher education in certain university towns, sometimes with (usu. restricted) affiliation to the university. **L19.**
7 In a college, university, polytechnic, etc.: the dining room for all members of the institution. Hence, dinner in a hall. **L16.**

THOMAS HUGHES You ought to dine in hall perhaps four days a week. Hall is at five o'clock.

8 The entrance passage or entrance room of a house; a vestibule; (chiefly *N. Amer.*) a corridor, a passage. **M17.**

S. SPENDER There was a stone-tiled hall . . out of which doors led.

– PHRASES: †**a hall! a hall!** *interjection* clear the way! make room! (esp. for dancing). ***bachelor's hall***: see BACHELOR. ***Exeter hall***: see EXETER *noun* 2. **Hall of Fame** (chiefly *N. Amer.*) a building containing memorials etc. of famous people; *fig.* the class of those who are most celebrated (in a particular sphere). ***hall of residence***: see sense 6b above. ***liberty hall***: see LIBERTY *noun*[2]. ***medical hall***: see MEDICAL *adjective*. **servants' hall** a common room or dining room for servants in a house. ***Tammany Hall***: see TAMMANY. †**the Hall** *spec.* Westminster Hall, formerly the seat of the High Court of Justice.
– COMB.: **hall bedroom** *US* a small bedroom partitioned off the end of a hall; **hall boy** a pageboy, a call boy in a hotel; **hall door** the door of a hall; the front door of a house; **hall house** a manor house; a house (esp. a medieval one) with a hall as a distinguishing feature; **hall porter** the porter in charge of the hall of a hotel and esp. responsible for the care of guests' luggage; **hallstand** a piece of furniture for hanging coats etc. on, kept in an entrance hall; **hall table** *(a)* a large table for a dining hall; *(b)* a small table for an entrance hall; **hall tree** *US* a hallstand; **hallway** an entrance hall or corridor.

†**hall** *verb* see HAUL *verb*.

hallabaloo *noun, interjection, & verb* var. of HULLABALOO.

†**hallage** *noun.* **E17–E18.**
[ORIGIN Old French & mod. French, from *halle* covered market: see -AGE.]
A fee or toll paid for goods sold in a covered market.

hallal *adjective, verb, & noun* var. of HALAL.

Hall effect /ˈhɔːl ɪfɛkt/ *noun phr.* **E20.**
[ORIGIN Edwin H. *Hall* (1855–1938), US physicist.]
PHYSICS. The production of a potential difference across an electrical conductor when a magnetic field is applied in a direction perpendicular to that of the flow of current.

Hallel /haˈleɪl, ˈhalɛl/ *noun.* **E18.**
[ORIGIN Hebrew *hallēl* praise.]
A portion of the service for certain Jewish festivals consisting of Psalms 113 to 118 inclusive.

hallelujah /halɪˈluːjə/ *interjection & noun.* Also **-luia**, **-luja**, **-luya(h)**. **M16.**
[ORIGIN Hebrew *hallĕlūyāh* praise Jah (God), from imper. pl. of *hallēl* to praise: cf. HALLEL.]
▸ **A** *interjection.* = ALLELUIA *interjection.* **M16.**
▸ **B** *noun.* = ALLELUIA *noun.* **M17.**
– COMB.: **Hallelujah Chorus** a musical composition based on the word hallelujah, *esp.* that in the oratorio 'Messiah' by G. F. Handel (1685–1759); ***hallelujah lass***: see LASS 3.

†**haller** *noun* see HELLER *noun*[1].

†**hallier** *noun*[1], *noun*[2] see HALYARD, HAULIER.

halling /ˈhalɪŋ/ *noun.* **M19.**
[ORIGIN Norwegian, from *Hallingdal* a valley in S. Norway.]
A Norwegian country dance in duple rhythm; a piece of music for this dance.

hallion /ˈhaljən/ *noun. Scot. & N. English derog.* **L18.**
[ORIGIN Perh. rel. to French *haillon* rag.]
An idle or worthless person.

hallmark /ˈhɔːlmɑːk/ *noun & verb.* **E18.**
[ORIGIN from HALL *noun* + MARK *noun*[1].]
▸ **A** *noun.* **1** Any of various official marks used at Goldsmiths' Hall and by the other British assay offices for marking the standard of gold, silver, and platinum. **E18.**
2 *fig.* A mark or indication, esp. of excellence; a distinctive or striking feature. **M19.**

D. ADAMS And . . gives it that poignant twist which is the hallmark of the really great documentary. N. MOSLEY The . . image of ruthlessness that was the hallmark of Mussolini.

▸ **B** *verb trans.* Stamp with a hallmark. **M19.**

hallmote /ˈhɔːlməʊt/ *noun.* Also **-moot** /-muːt/. **OE.**
[ORIGIN from HALL *noun* + *mote* var. of MOOT *noun*[1].]
hist. The court of the lord of a manor; later also, the court of a trade guild.

hallo /həˈləʊ, ha-/ *verb, interjection, & noun.* Also **halloa**. **L18.**
[ORIGIN Prob. var. of HOLLO *verb, interjection, & noun* with shifted stress. See also HELLO, HULLO.]
▸ **A** *verb intrans.* Say or shout 'hallo!'; call out to attract attention or in greeting. **L18.**
▸ **B** *interjection.* Commanding or attempting to attract attention. Also = HELLO *interjection.* **M19.**

A. CHRISTIE Hallo, 'allo, 'allo, what's this?

▸ **C** *noun.* Pl. **-o(e)s**. A shout of 'hallo!' **L19.**

hallock /ˈhalək/ *noun. Scot.* **E16.**
[ORIGIN Unknown.]
A thoughtless or foolish person; *esp.* a flighty young woman.

hallockit /ˈhaləkɪt/ *adjective & noun. Scot.* Also (after Sir W. Scott) **hellicat** /ˈhɛlɪkət/. **L17.**
[ORIGIN from HALLOCK + Scot. adjectival suffix *-it* -ED[2].]
▸ **A** *adjective.* Esp. of a young woman: foolish, light-headed, flighty, reckless. **L17.**
▸ **B** *noun.* = HALLOCK. Also, a mischievous person, a good-for-nothing. **L17.**

halloo /həˈluː, ha-/ *verb.* **M16.**
[ORIGIN Prob. var. of HALLOW *verb*[2], HOLLO *verb* with shifted stress.]
1 *verb intrans.* Shout 'halloo!'; cry out or yell to attract attention, give encouragement, etc. **M16.**
2 *verb trans.* Encourage (esp. dogs to the chase) by shouting. **E17.**
3 *verb trans.* Shout out. **E17.**

halloo /həˈluː, ha-/ *interjection & noun.* Also **hulloo** /həˈluː, hʌ-/. **L17.**
[ORIGIN Prob. var. of HOLLO *interjection & noun* with shifted stress.]
▸ **A** *interjection.* Inciting dogs to the chase; calling attention, esp. at a distance; expr. surprise. **L17.**
▸ **B** *noun.* A shout of 'halloo!' Cf. ***view-halloo*** s.v. VIEW *noun.* **E18.**

halloumi /həˈluːmi/ *noun.* **L20.**
[ORIGIN Egyptian Arab. *ḥalūm*, prob. from Arabic *ḥaluma* be mild.]
A mild, firm, white Cypriot cheese made from goats' or ewes' milk and used esp. in cooked dishes. Also ***halloumi cheese***.

hallow /ˈhaləʊ/ *noun*[1].
[ORIGIN Old English *halga* use as noun of definite form of *hālig* HOLY.]
1 A holy person, a saint. Usu. in *pl.* *obsolete* exc. in ALL HALLOWS & in *comb.* below. **OE.**
†**2** In *pl.* The shrines or relics of saints; (the shrines of) heathen gods. **ME–M16.**
– COMB.: **Hallow day** *Scot. & dial.* All Hallows' Day; a saint's day, a holiday; **Hallowmass** (now chiefly *Scot.*) Allhallowmass; **Hallowtide** Allhallowtide.

hallow /ˈhaləʊ/ *noun*[2]. Now *rare.* **LME.**
[ORIGIN from HALLOW *verb*[2].]
A loud shout or cry to encourage, esp. dogs in the chase, or to attract attention.

hallow /ˈhaləʊ/ *verb*[1] *trans.*
[ORIGIN Old English *hālgian* = Old Saxon *hēlagon*, Old High German *heilagōn* (German *heiligen*), Old Norse *helga*, from Germanic verb from base of HOLY.]
1 Make holy; sanctify, purify. **OE.**

J. P. HENNESSY Her death was tranquil and . . hallowed by a kind of beauty. H. WILSON This is a question hallowed by tradition.

2 Consecrate or set apart as sacred; dedicate to a sacred or religious purpose; bless. **OE.** ▸**b** Consecrate (a king, bishop, etc.) to an office. Long *obsolete* exc. *hist.* **OE.**
3 Honour as holy; regard and treat with reverence; observe (a day, festival, etc.) solemnly. **OE.**
■ **hallowedness** *noun* sanctity, blessedness **E19.**

hallow /ˈhaləʊ/ *verb*[2]. Now *rare.* **LME.**
[ORIGIN Prob. from Old French *halloer*, of imit. origin. See also HALLOO *verb*, HOLLO *verb*.]
1 *verb trans.* Pursue with shouting; urge on by shouting; call *in*, *back*, etc., by shouting. **LME.**
2 *verb intrans. & trans.* Shout in encouragement, esp. of dogs in the chase; shout to attract attention. **LME.**

Halloween /haləʊˈiːn/ *noun.* Also **-e'en**. **L18.**
[ORIGIN Contr. of *All Hallow Even*: see ALL HALLOWS, EVEN *noun*[1].]
The eve of All Saints, 31 October (the last night of the year in the early Celtic calendar).

halloysite /haˈlɔɪzʌɪt/ *noun.* **E19.**
[ORIGIN from J. B. J. d'Omalius-d'*Halloy* (1783–1875), Belgian geologist + *-s-* + -ITE[1].]
MINERALOGY. Any of a number of clay minerals chemically resembling kaolinite but with a greater (although variable) water content.

Hallstatt /ˈhalʃtat/ *adjective.* **M19.**
[ORIGIN A village in Upper Austria, site of a prehistoric burial ground.]
Designating (the culture and products of) a phase of the early Iron Age in Europe.

hallucal /ˈhaljʊk(ə)l/ *adjective.* **L19.**
[ORIGIN from HALLUX + -AL[1].]
ANATOMY. Of or pertaining to the hallux or big toe.

hallucinant /həˈluːsɪnənt, -ˈljuː-/ *adjective & noun.* **L19.**
[ORIGIN from HALLUCIN(ATE + -ANT[1].]
▸ **A** *adjective.* Producing or experiencing hallucinations. **L19.**
▸ **B** *noun.* A person who experiences hallucinations; a drug which produces hallucinations. **E20.**

hallucinate /həˈluːsɪneɪt, -ˈljuː-/ *verb.* **E17.**
[ORIGIN Latin *hallucinat-* pa. ppl stem of *hallucinari* late form of *alucinari* wander in thought or speech, from Greek *alussein* be distraught or ill at ease: see -ATE[3].]
1 †**a** *verb trans.* Deceive. Only in **E17.** ▸**b** *verb trans. & intrans.* Affect with hallucinations; produce false impressions in the mind (of). **E19.**

b J. DIDION But Durango. The very name hallucinates.

2 *verb intrans.* Orig., be deceived, suffer illusions. Now, have a hallucination or hallucinations. **M17.**

D. W. GOODWIN After a day or two without drinking, the alcoholic coming off a bender may start hallucinating.

3 *verb trans.* Experience a hallucination of. **L20.**

J. WAIN I'm imagining things, hallucinating a conversation with my . . sister, who's no longer alive.

■ **hallucinative** *adjective* causing hallucinations **L19.** **hallucinator** *noun* **M19.** **hallucinatorily** *adverb* in a hallucinatory manner **L19.** **hallucinatory** *adjective* characterized by, pertaining to, or resembling (a) hallucination **M19.**

hallucination /həluːsɪˈneɪʃ(ə)n, -ljuː-/ *noun.* **E17.**
[ORIGIN Latin *hallucinatio(n-)*, formed as HALLUCINATE: see -ATION.]
1 Esp. MEDICINE & PSYCHOLOGY. The apparent perception of an external object or sense datum when no such object or stimulus is present; an instance of this. **E17.**

F. KING Had her distracted mind produced an hallucination?

2 The mental state of being deceived, mistaken, or deluded; an unfounded idea or belief, an illusion. **M17.**

hallucinè /həˈluːsɪneɪ, -ljuː-/ *noun. rare.* **L19.**
[ORIGIN French.]
A person who (regularly) has hallucinations.

hallucinogen /həˈluːsɪnədʒ(ə)n, -ˈljuː-/ *noun.* **M20.**
[ORIGIN from HALLUCIN(ATION + -O- + -GEN.]
Any substance which induces hallucinations when ingested.
■ **hallucinoˈgenic** *adjective* **M20.**

hallucinosis /həˌluːsɪˈnəʊsɪs, -ˌljuː-/ *noun.* Pl. **-noses** /-ˈnəʊsiːz/. **E20.**
[ORIGIN from HALLUCINATION + -OSIS.]
PSYCHIATRY. A mental condition, associated esp. with alcoholism, marked by persistent hallucination, often auditory.

hallux /ˈhaləks/ *noun.* Pl. **halluces** /ˈhaljʊsiːz/. **M19.**
[ORIGIN mod. Latin alt. of medieval Latin *allex*, Latin *(h)allus*.]
ANATOMY & ZOOLOGY. The big toe; the first or innermost digit on the hind foot of a tetrapod vertebrate, in birds (if present) often directed backwards.

halm *noun & verb* var. of HAULM.

halma /ˈhalmə/ *noun.* **L19.**
[ORIGIN Greek = leap.]
A game played by two or four people on a chequerboard of 256 squares, with pieces advancing from one corner to the opposite corner by being moved over other pieces into vacant squares.

halo /ˈheɪləʊ/ *noun.* Pl. **-o(e)s**. **M16.**
[ORIGIN medieval Latin *halo* for Latin *halos* from Greek = threshing floor, disc of the sun, moon, or a shield.]
1 A circle of light, either white or prismatically coloured, seen round a luminous body and caused by the refraction of light through vapour; *spec.* that seen round the sun or moon, usu. of 22° or 46° radius, with the red end

of the spectrum inside the circle. Cf. CORONA *noun*[1] 3a. **M16.** ▸**b** A coloured ring surrounding a pustule etc. Also, the areola of a nipple. **E18.** ▸**c** Any circle of light or other substance that serves to frame a thing. **E19.**

> **c** E. M. FORSTER The light of a candle-lamp, which threw a quivering halo round her hands. J. UPDIKE His hair, . . stood far out from his head in wiry rays, a halo of wool.

2 A disc of light shown surrounding or hovering over the head in representations of Jesus and the saints; *fig.* an aura of glory, sanctity, etc., with which a person or thing is surrounded. **M17.**

> H. T. BUCKLE That halo which time had thrown round the oldest monarchy in Europe.

– COMB.: **halo-brimmed** *adjective* [cf. *halo-hat* below] (of a woman's hat) worn so that the brim frames the face; **halo effect** the tendency of a favourable (or unfavourable) impression created by an individual in one area to influence one's judgement of him or her in other areas; **halo hat** a woman's hat worn at the back of the head so that the brim frames the face.

halo /ˈheɪləʊ/ *verb trans.* **L18.**
[ORIGIN from the noun.]
Surround or invest (as) with a halo.

> V. WOOLF The windows were blurred, the lamps haloed with fog.

halo- /ˈhaləʊ/ *combining form* of Greek *hals*, *halos* salt, sea, and of HALOGEN: see -O-.
■ **ha'lobiont** *noun* [-BIONT] ECOLOGY an organism that lives in a saline environment **E20.** **halobi'ontic**, **halobi'otic** *adjectives* (ECOLOGY) living in a saline environment **E20.** **halo'carbon** *noun* (CHEMISTRY) a compound in which the hydrogen of a hydrocarbon is replaced by halogens **M20.** **haloform** *noun* [after *chloroform*] CHEMISTRY = TRIHALOMETHANE **M20.** **halo'methane** *noun* (CHEMISTRY) a halogenated derivative of methane, with the general formula CH_nX_{4-n}, where X is a halogen **M20.** **halo'morphic** *adjective* (SOIL SCIENCE) (of a soil) containing, or developed in the presence of, large quantities of salts other than calcium carbonate **M20.** **halo'peridol** *noun* [PI)PERID(INE] PHARMACOLOGY a tricyclic compound used to treat psychotic disorders, esp. mania **M20.** **halo'phosphate** *noun* (CHEMISTRY) any of various compounds containing both halide and phosphate ions, some of which are used as phosphors **M20.** **halophyte** *noun* (ECOLOGY) a plant adapted to growing in saline conditions, e.g. salt marshes **L19.** **halophytic** /-ˈfɪtɪk/ *adjective* of the nature of a halophyte **L19.**

halogen /ˈhalədʒ(ə)n, ˈheɪl-/ *noun.* **M19.**
[ORIGIN from Greek *hals*, *halo-* salt + -GEN.]
CHEMISTRY. Any of the group of elements fluorine, chlorine, bromine, iodine, and astatine (together forming group VIIA of the periodic table), which are typically gaseous or volatile, strongly electronegative non-metals readily forming binary compounds with metals.
quartz-halogen: see QUARTZ.

halogenate /həˈlɒdʒ(ə)neɪt, ˈhalədʒ(ə)neɪt/ *verb trans.* **L19.**
[ORIGIN from HALOGEN + -ATE[3].]
CHEMISTRY. Introduce one or more atoms of a halogen into (a compound or molecule), usu. in place of hydrogen. Freq. as ***halogenated*** *ppl adjective*.
■ **haloge'nation** *noun* **E20.**

halon /ˈheɪlɒn/ *noun.* **M20.**
[ORIGIN from HALO- + -ON, after *neon*, *argon*, etc.]
Any of the compounds of carbon, bromine, and another halogen, many of which are gases noted for their lack of reactivity.

halophile /ˈhaləfʌɪl/ *noun & adjective.* **E20.**
[ORIGIN from HALO- + -PHILE.]
ECOLOGY. ▸**A** *noun.* An organism that grows in or can tolerate saline conditions. **E20.**
▸**B** *adjective.* = HALOPHILIC. **E20.**
■ **ha'lophilous** *adjective* **L19.**

halophilic /haləˈfɪlɪk/ *adjective.* **E20.**
[ORIGIN formed as HALOPHILE: see -IC.]
ECOLOGY. Growing in or tolerating saline conditions.

halothane /ˈhaləθeɪn/ *noun.* **M20.**
[ORIGIN from HALO- + E)THANE.]
CHEMISTRY. A halogenated derivative of ethane, $CF_3CHBrCl$, which is a volatile liquid used as a general anaesthetic.

halotrichite /haləˈtrɪkʌɪt/ *noun.* **M19.**
[ORIGIN from HALO- + -TRICH, after German *Haarsalz* 'hair salt': see -ITE[1].]
MINERALOGY. A monoclinic alum (hydrated double sulphate) containing aluminium and ferrous iron, usu. occurring as greenish- or yellowish-white fibrous masses.

halpace /ˈhalpəs/ *noun.* Long *arch. rare.* Also **halpas.** **E16.**
[ORIGIN Alt. of HAUT-PAS from French *haut pas* lit. 'high step'. Cf. HALF-PACE.]
= HAUT-PAS, HALF-PACE 1.

†**halse** *noun* see HAWSE *noun*[1].

†**halse** *verb*[1] *trans.*
[ORIGIN Old English *halsian*, *healsian* = Old High German *heilisōn* augur, expiate, Old Norse *heilsa* hail, greet (with good wishes), from Germanic base also of HEAL *verb*[1]. Cf. HAUSE *verb*.]
1 Call on in the name of something holy; adjure, implore. **OE–M16.**
2 Hail, greet. **LME–L16.**

†**halse** *verb*[2] see HAUSE *verb*.

halt /hɔːlt/ *noun*[1]. *arch.* **L15.**
[ORIGIN from HALT *verb*[1] or *adjective*.]
A lameness, a limp.

halt /hɔːlt/ *noun*[2]. Also †**alt**, (earlier) †**alto**, pl. **-oes.** **L16.**
[ORIGIN Orig. in phr. *make halt* (or †*alto*) from German *halt machen* (or its Spanish version *alto hacer*): in the German phr. *halt* is prob. orig. based on the imper. ('stop', 'stand still') of *halten* HOLD *verb*.]
1 Orig. MILITARY. A temporary stop on a march or journey; *gen.* a sudden suspension of movement or activity. **L16.**

> TOLKIEN At last they could go no further without a halt. K. WILLIAMS The radio series came to a temporary halt in June.

call a halt (***to***): see CALL *verb*. ***grind to a halt***: see GRIND *verb* 2.
2 A place where a halt is made; *spec.* a railway stopping place, usu. on a local line, without the normal station buildings, staff, etc. **E20.**

> P. LEVI A lorry-drivers' halt . . that served bacon sandwiches until midnight.

halt /hɔːlt/ *adjective.* Now *arch. & literary.*
[ORIGIN Old English *halt*, *healt* = Old Frisian, Old Saxon *halt*, Old High German *halz*, Old Norse *haltr*, Gothic *halts*, from Germanic base of unknown origin.]
Lame, limping; disabled. Now usu. *absol.*

> P. PORTER I'll never know with what halt steps You mounted to this plain eclipse. *absol.*: N. BARBER The halt and the maimed . . joined in as best they could.

halt /hɔːlt/ *verb*[1] *intrans. arch.*
[ORIGIN Old English *healtian* (corresp. to Old Saxon *halton*, Old High German *halzēn*), from the adjective.]
1 Walk lamely; limp. **OE.**
†**2** Play false; deviate *from* the proper course. **OE–E17.**
3 Hesitate or waver (*between* alternatives). **LME.**

> AV 1 *Kings* 18:21 How long halt ye between two opinions?

4 Of reasoning, verse, etc.: lack smooth progress; proceed awkwardly or defectively. **LME.**

> T. GRAY Where the verse seems to halt, it is very probably occasioned by the transcriber's neglect.

halt /hɔːlt/ *verb*[2]. **M17.**
[ORIGIN from HALT *noun*[2].]
1 *verb intrans.* Stop momentarily on a march or journey; make a halt. Freq. in *imper.* as a military command. **M17.**

> G. B. SHAW A sentry's voice westward: Halt! Who goes there? H. FAST He raced down the deck, halting to caress the rusty winches.

2 *verb trans.* Bring to a halt or abrupt stop; stop the advance or continuation of. **L18.**

> A. J. P. TAYLOR The German pursuit was halted. *Studio Week* Capitol Magnetics . . has halted production at its US factory.

– COMB.: **halt sign** a former traffic sign requiring a driver or rider to halt before entering a major road; *fig.* a warning to desist from speech or action.

halter /ˈhɔːltə/ *noun*[1].
[ORIGIN Old English *hælfter*, *hælftre*, corresp. to Old Low German *heliftra* (Middle Low German *helchter*, Middle Dutch *halfter*, *halter*), from West Germanic (with instr. suffix), from base repr. also by HELVE.]
1 A cord or strap with a headstall or noose, for leading or fastening a horse or other animal. **OE.**
2 A rope with a noose for hanging a criminal; execution by this means. **LME.**
3 A strap by which the top of a dress etc. is fastened or held behind at the neck, leaving the back and shoulders bare. **M20.** ▸**b** *ellipt.* = ***halter top*** below. **M20.**
– COMB.: **halter-break** *verb trans.* (orig. *US*) accustom (an animal) to the halter; **halter neck**, **halter neckline** a type or style of neckline incorporating a halter (sense 3 above); **halter top** a blouse or top with a halter neck.

halter /ˈhɔːltə/ *noun*[2]. *arch.* **LME.**
[ORIGIN from HALT *verb*[1] + -ER[1].]
A person who is lame; *fig.* a waverer.

halter /ˈhɔːltə/ *verb trans.* **ME.**
[ORIGIN from HALTER *noun*[1].]
1 Put a halter on (a horse or other animal); *fig.* hamper, restrain. **ME.**
2 Catch (a bird etc.) with a noose or lasso. **L16.**
3 Execute (a person) by hanging. **L16.**

haltere /halˈtɪə/ *noun.* Pl. **halteres** /halˈtɪəriːz/. **M16.**
[ORIGIN Greek *haltēres* pl. (sense 1), from *hallesthai* to jump.]
1 In *pl.* Weights, like dumb-bells, held in the hand to give an impetus in jumping. **M16.**
2 ENTOMOLOGY. Either of the two knobbed filaments which in dipteran insects take the place of posterior wings. Also called ***balancer***, ***poiser***. Usu. in *pl.* **E19.**

haltered /ˈhɔːltəd/ *adjective.* **E16.**
[ORIGIN from HALTER *noun*[1] or *verb*: see -ED[2], -ED[1].]
Having a halter on; fastened (as) with a halter.

halting /ˈhɔːltɪŋ/ *ppl adjective.* **LME.**
[ORIGIN from HALT *verb*[1] + -ING[2].]
That halts; *esp.* lacking in smoothness of progress, fluency, or ease; stumbling, faltering.

> F. TUOHY On the little dance-floor their progress was halting. W. M. SPACKMAN They all had to converse in halting Italian for some minutes.

■ **haltingly** *adverb* **L16.** **haltingness** *noun* **L19.**

halutzim /hɑːˈluːtsɪm, x-/ *noun pl.* Also **-luz-**, **ch-**. **E20.**
[ORIGIN Hebrew *ḥălūṣīm*.]
hist. Jewish pioneers who entered Palestine from 1917 onwards to build it up as a Jewish state.

halva /ˈhalvɑː, -və/ *noun.* Also **halvah**, (earlier) †**hulwa.** **M17.**
[ORIGIN Yiddish *hal(a)va*, mod. Hebrew *ḥalḇāh*, mod. Greek *khalbas*, Turkish *helva*, etc., from Arabic (& Persian) *ḥalwā* sweetmeat.]
A Middle Eastern sweet confection made of sesame flour and honey.

halve /hɑːv/ *verb.* **ME.**
[ORIGIN from HALF *noun*.]
1 *verb trans.* Divide in two, share in two equal parts; reduce by a half. Formerly also, break in two. **ME.**

> *Proverb*: A trouble shared is a trouble halved.

†**2** *verb intrans.* Show divided loyalty. (Foll. by *with*.) Chiefly as ***halving*** *verbal noun.* **M16–L17.**

> T. BROOKS God neither loves halting nor halving; he will be served truly and totally.

3 *verb trans.* GOLF. Play (a hole) in the same number of strokes as another player; win the same number of holes as another player in (a match etc.). **E19.**
4 *verb trans.* CARPENTRY. Join (timbers) together by cutting out half the thickness of each, so that one can be let into the other. Chiefly as ***halving*** *verbal noun.* **E19.**

H

halver /ˈhɑːvə/ *noun.* Now chiefly *Scot.*, *N. English*, & *US.* **E16.**
[ORIGIN from HALVE + -ER[1].]
1 A half-share. Usu. in *pl.*; esp. in ***go halvers*** (***with***). Also ***halvers!***, an exclam. by a child claiming half of something found. **E16.**
†**2** A person who has a half-share in something; a partner. **E17–L18.**

halyard /ˈhaljəd/ *noun.* Orig. †**hal(l)ier.** Also **halliard**, **haul-** /ˈhɔːl-/. **LME.**
[ORIGIN from HALE *verb*[1] + -IER, alt. in 18 by assoc. with YARD *noun*[2]: cf. LANYARD.]
NAUTICAL. A rope or tackle for raising or lowering a sail, yard, etc.

ham /ham/ *noun*[1] & *adjective.*
[ORIGIN Old English *ham*, *hom* = Middle Low German *hamme*, Old High German *hamma* (German dial. *Hamm*) rel. to synon. Middle Low German *hame*, Old High German *hama*, Old Norse *ham*, from Germanic verb meaning 'be crooked'.]
▸**A** *noun.* **I 1** The hollow or bend of the knee. *arch.* **OE.**
2 The back of the thigh; the thigh and buttock collectively. Usu. in *pl.* **L15.**

> T. MO I believe I can sit again up on my bruised hams.

3 The thigh of an animal (now usu. a pig) used as food; *esp.* (the meat from) a cured pig's thigh. Also, the hock of an animal. **L15.**

> J. CARY Hams, and often whole sides of bacon, dangled from the blackened ceiling.

▸**II** [Cf. HAMFATTER.]
4 An inexpert performer; an inferior, amateurish, or excessively theatrical actor, actress, or performance. *slang* (orig. *US*). **L19.**
5 An amateur telegraph operator. Now *esp.* (more fully ***radio ham***), an amateur radio operator. *slang* (orig. *US*). **E20.**
– COMB.: **hambone** (**a**) the bone from a ham joint; such a bone with the meat still attached; (**b**) *N. Amer. slang* an inferior actor or performer, *esp.* one who uses a spurious black accent.
▸**B** *attrib.* or as *adjective.* **1** Esp. of an actor, actress, or a performance: inexpert; amateurish; excessively theatrical. *slang.* **M20.**

> D. M. DAVIN The actor in him, too often ham, made him long to play God.

2 Clumsy, incompetent. Cf. HAM-FISTED, HAM-HANDED. *slang.* **M20.**

> W. WHARTON Sasha punches me again, tough, thick, ham hands.

ham /ham/ *noun*[2]. Long *dial.*
[ORIGIN Old English *ham(m)*, *hom(m)* = Old Frisian *ham* a meadow enclosed with a ditch, Low German *hamm* piece of enclosed ground.]
A plot of (esp. enclosed) pasture or meadowland.

ham /ham/ *verb trans. & intrans. slang.* Infl. **-mm-.** **M20.**
[ORIGIN from HAM *noun*[1] II.]
Overact (a part, a scene, etc.). Freq. foll. by *up*.

> M. DICKENS She had hammed her scene with the seducer at the final run through. S. MIDDLETON I have to act . . And the temptation to ham it up is constant.

hamachi /haˈmatʃi/ *noun.* **L20.**
[ORIGIN Japanese.]
The young of the Japanese amberjack or yellowtail; this fish as food.

hamada *noun* var. of HAMMADA.

Hamadan /ˈhamədan/ *noun & adjective*. **E20.**
[ORIGIN A town in NW Iran.]
(Designating) a heavy hard-wearing long-pile carpet or rug, often having brightly coloured animal designs.

hamadryad /haməˈdrʌɪəd, -ad/ *noun*. Also (the usual form in sense 3) **-as** /-əs/, pl. **-ases**, †**-ades**. **LME.**
[ORIGIN Latin *Hamadryas*, *-ad*, from Greek *Hamadruas*, *-ad*, from *hama* together + *drus* tree.]
1 *CLASSICAL MYTHOLOGY*. A wood nymph supposed to live and die with the tree she inhabited. **LME.**
2 The king cobra, *Ophiophagus hannah*. **M19.**
3 A large baboon, *Papio hamadryas*, of Ethiopia, Somalia, and southern Arabia, held sacred in ancient Egypt. Also ***hamadryad baboon***. **L19.**

hamamelis /haməˈmiːlɪs/ *noun*. Pl. same. **M18.**
[ORIGIN mod. Latin (see below), from Greek *hamamēlis* medlar.]
Any of various ornamental N. American and eastern Asian shrubs of the genus *Hamamelis* (family Hamamelidaceae), with yellow flowers which appear in winter before the leaves; a witch hazel. Also, the medicinal lotion prepared from the leaves and bark of *H. virginiana*.

Haman /ˈheɪmən/ *noun*. **M17.**
[ORIGIN The chief minister of Ahasuerus, who was hanged on the gallows he prepared for the Jew Mordecai (*Esther* 7:10).]
A person resembling Haman in behaviour or circumstance. Chiefly in ***hang as high as Haman***, be well and truly hanged; be hoist with one's own petard.
Haman's ears fritters or cakes eaten at the Jewish festival of Purim.

H

hamartia /həˈmɑːtɪə/ *noun*. **L18.**
[ORIGIN Greek = fault, failure, guilt.]
The fault or error leading to the destruction of the tragic hero or heroine of a play, novel, etc.

hamartiology /həmɑːtɪˈɒlədʒi/ *noun*. **L19.**
[ORIGIN formed as HAMARTIA + -OLOGY.]
THEOLOGY. The doctrine of sin.

hamartoma /hamɑːˈtəʊmə/ *noun*. Pl. **-mas**, **-mata** /-mətə/. **E20.**
[ORIGIN from Greek *hamartanō* go wrong + -OMA.]
MEDICINE. A tumour-like mass resulting from the faulty growth or development of normal tissue.

hamate /ˈheɪmət/ *adjective*. **E18.**
[ORIGIN Latin *hamatus* hooked, from *hamus* hook: see -ATE².]
Having hooks; hook-shaped; *spec*. (*ANATOMY*) designating one of the bones of the wrist, having an anterior hooked process.
■ Also **hamated** *adjective* (now *rare* or *obsolete*) **L17.**

Hamathite /ˈheɪməθʌɪt/ *noun & adjective*. **E17.**
[ORIGIN from *Hamath* the biblical name for Hama, a city in western Syria + -ITE¹.]
► **A** *noun*. A native or inhabitant of the ancient Syrian city of Hamath. **E17.**
► **B** *adjective*. Of or pertaining to Hamath; *spec*. designating an ancient script found in the Taurus Mountains (now usu. called ***Hittite***). **E17.**

hamber-line *noun* see HAMBRO-LINE.

hamble /ˈhamb(ə)l/ *verb*. Also **hammle** /ˈham(ə)l/.
[ORIGIN Old English *hamelian* = Old High German *hamalōn*, Old Norse *hamla*, from Germanic adjective appearing as Old High German *hamal* maimed, whence German *Hammel* castrated sheep. Cf. HAMEL *noun*².]
1 *verb trans*. Mutilate, maim; dock; dehorn; *spec*. cut off the balls of the feet of (a dog) to prevent it from hunting. Also, hamstring. Now *dial*. or *hist*. **OE.**
2 *verb intrans*. Walk lame, hobble. *dial*. **E19.**

hambro-line /ˈhambrəʊlʌɪn/ *noun*. Also (now *rare*) **hamber-** /ˈhambə-/. **L18.**
[ORIGIN from alt. of HAMBURG + LINE *noun*².]
NAUTICAL. A three-stranded small-sized rope (esp. of tarred hemp) used for lashings, lacing sails, etc.

Hamburg /ˈhambəːg/ *adjective & noun*. **LME.**
[ORIGIN A city in northern Germany.]
► **A** *adjective* (*attrib*.). †**1** Designating a type of barrel, chiefly used as a measure of salmon. *Scot*. **LME–E16.**
2 Designating a variety of parsley grown for its thick edible root like a turnip. **L18.**
3 ***Hamburg grape*** = sense B.1 below. **L19.**
4 ***Hamburg steak***, a dish composed of flat cakes of chopped lean beef, mixed with beaten eggs, chopped onions, and seasoning, and fried. *US*. **L19.**
► **B** *noun*. **1** More fully ***Black Hamburg***. A black variety of grape of German origin, specially adapted to hothouse cultivation. **M18.**
2 A small variety of domestic fowl. **M19.**

hamburger /ˈhambəːgə/ *noun*. **E17.**
[ORIGIN German, formed as HAMBURG.]
1 (**H-**.) A native or inhabitant of Hamburg, a city in northern Germany. **E17.**
2 (A bread bun containing) seasoned minced beef formed into a round flat cake or patty, fried or grilled and usu. served with onion, relish, etc. Also (now *rare*), ***hamburger steak***. Orig. *US*. **L19.**

> *attrib*.: S. BELLOW She had kept the hamburger stand on Route 158.

hame /heɪm/ *noun*¹. **ME.**
[ORIGIN Middle Dutch (Dutch *haam*), corresp. to Middle High German *ham(e)* fishing rod, of unknown origin.]
Either of two curved pieces of iron or wood forming (part of) the collar of a draught horse. Usu. in *pl*.
make a hames of *Irish* do (a thing) very badly or ineptly; make a mess of.

hamel /ˈham(ə)l/ *noun*¹. *obsolete* exc. *dial*. **LME.**
[ORIGIN Old French (mod. *hameau*), dim. of *ham* village, from Middle Low German *hamm*: see -EL².]
= HAMLET *noun*¹.

hamel /ˈhɑːm(ə)l/ *noun*². *S. Afr*. **M19.**
[ORIGIN Afrikaans = Dutch *hamel*, German *Hammel*. Cf. HAMBLE *verb*.]
A castrated ram, a wether.

hamerkop /ˈhɑːməkɒp/ *noun*. Also (earlier) **hammer-** /ˈhamə-/. **M19.**
[ORIGIN Afrikaans, from *hamer* HAMMER *noun* + *kop* head.]
= HAMMERHEAD 4.

hamesucken /ˈheɪmsʌk(ə)n/ *noun*. Now *arch. & hist*.
[ORIGIN Old English *hāmsōcn*, from *hām* home, dwelling + *sōcn* seeking, visiting, attack, assault, Old Norse *sókn* attack.]
ANGLO-SAXON & SCOTS LAW. (The crime of committing) an assault on a person in his or her own house or dwelling place. Formerly also, the fine or penalty for this.

hametz /hɑːˈmɛts, ˈxɑː-/ *noun*. Also **cha-**, **cho-**. **M19.**
[ORIGIN Hebrew *ḥāmēṣ*.]
Leaven or food mixed with leaven, prohibited during the Passover.

hamfatter /ˈhamfatə/ *noun*. *US slang*. Also **hamfat**. **L19.**
[ORIGIN Uncertain: perh. alt. of AMATEUR. Cf. HAM *noun*¹ II.]
An inexpert or amateurish performer; *esp*. a mediocre jazz musician.

ham-fisted /hamˈfɪstɪd/ *adjective*. **E20.**
[ORIGIN from HAM *noun*¹ + FISTED *adjective*.]
Having large or clumsy hands; awkward, bungling.

> *Daily Mail* A ham-fisted BBC driver locked the entire film crew out of their van.

■ **ham-fistedly** *adverb* **M20.** **ham-fistedness** *noun* **M20.**

ham-handed /hamˈhandɪd/ *adjective*. **E20.**
[ORIGIN from HAM *noun*¹ + HANDED *adjective*.]
= HAM-FISTED.

> J. GASKELL Old Ginger tailors . . but he's so ham-handed he always breaks his needles.

■ **ham-handedly** *adverb* **M20.** **ham-handedness** *noun* **E20.**

Hamiltonian /ham(ə)lˈtəʊnɪən/ *noun & adjective*. **L18.**
[ORIGIN from *Hamilton* (see below) + -IAN.]
► **A** *noun*. In sense 2 also **h-**.
1 *US POLITICS*. A follower or adherent of the American statesman and Federalist leader Alexander Hamilton (1757–1804) or his doctrines. **L18.**
2 A Hamiltonian operator or function (see sense B.2 below). **M20.**
► **B** *adjective*. **1** Of or pertaining to the British language teacher James Hamilton (1769–1831) or his system of language teaching. **E19.**
2 Of, pertaining to, or invented by the Irish mathematician Sir W. R. Hamilton (1805–65); *esp*. designating certain concepts employed in the wave-mechanical description of particles. **M19.**
Hamiltonian function a function used to describe a system of particles in terms of their positions and momenta. **Hamiltonian operator** an operator that generates a Hamiltonian function when applied e.g. to a wave function.
3 Of or pertaining to Alexander Hamilton or his doctrines. **L19.**

Hamite /ˈhamʌɪt/ *noun & adjective*. **M17.**
[ORIGIN from *Ham* (formerly *Cham*), Greek *Ham*, Latin *Cham*, the second son of Noah (*Genesis* 6:10) + -ITE¹.]
► **A** *noun*. †**1** A follower of Ham. *derog*. *rare*. Only in **M17.**
2 A member of a people supposedly descended from Ham, as an Egyptian or other N. African. **M19.**
► **B** *adjective*. = HAMITIC *adjective*. **M19.**

Hamitic /həˈmɪtɪk/ *adjective & noun*. **M19.**
[ORIGIN from HAMITE + -IC.]
► **A** *adjective*. Of or pertaining to the Hamites; *spec*. of, pertaining to, or designating a group of northern African languages, formerly analysed as one of two branches of the Hamito-Semitic family, but now regarded as forming four separate groups: Egyptian, Berber, Chadic, and Cushitic. **M19.**
► **B** *noun*. The Hamitic group of languages. **L19.**

Hamito-Semitic /ˌhamɪtəʊsəˈmɪtɪk/ *noun & adjective*. **L19.**
[ORIGIN from HAMIT(IC + -O- + SEMITIC.]
(Of, pertaining to, or designating) a language family spoken in the Middle East and northern Africa and divided into five groups: Semitic, Berber, Chadic, Cushitic, and Egyptian.

hamlet /ˈhamlɪt/ *noun*¹. **ME.**
[ORIGIN Anglo-Norman *hamelet(t)e*, Old French *hamelet*, dim. of *hamel*: see HAMEL *noun*¹, -ET¹.]
A group of houses or a small village, *esp*. one without a church; the people living there.

Hamlet /ˈhamlɪt/ *noun*². **E19.**
[ORIGIN A legendary prince of Denmark, the hero of a tragedy by Shakespeare.]
1 Used allusively (now chiefly as ***Hamlet without the Prince (of Denmark)***) to refer to a performance or event taking place without the central figure, actor, etc. **E19.**

> H. GRANVILLE I am not used to be newsmonger and perhaps I leave out Hamlet. L. STRACHEY The Catholic Church without . . the Pope might resemble the play of Hamlet without the Prince of Denmark.

2 An anxious indecisive person. **E20.**
■ **Hamletish** *adjective* resembling or of the nature of Hamlet; anxious, indecisive: **M19.** **Hamletism** *noun* an attitude or attitudes characteristic of Hamlet; anxiety, indecision: **M19.** **Hamletize** *verb intrans*. (*rare*) soliloquize, meditate **M19.**

hammada /həˈmɑːdə/ *noun*. Also **hamada**. **M19.**
[ORIGIN Arabic *ḥammāda*.]
A flat rocky area of desert blown free of sand by the wind, typical of the Sahara.

hammal /həˈmɑːl/ *noun*. **M18.**
[ORIGIN Arabic *ḥammāl*, from *ḥamala* carry.]
A Turkish or Asian porter.

hammam /ˈhamam, həˈmɑːm, ˈhʌmʌm/ *noun*. Also **hummum** /ˈhʌmʌm/. **E17.**
[ORIGIN from Turkish or its source Arabic *ḥammām* bath, from *ḥamma* to heat.]
An establishment where one may take a Turkish bath.

hammed /hamd/ *adjective*. **E18.**
[ORIGIN from HAM *noun*¹ + -ED².]
Having hams (of a specified kind).

> *Farmer & Stockbreeder* The boar in question was sound on his legs, well hammed and extremely robust.

hammer /ˈhamə/ *noun*.
[ORIGIN Old English *hamor*, *hamer*, *homer* = Old Frisian *homer*, Old Saxon *hamur* (Dutch *hamer*), Old High German *hamar* (German *Hammer*), Old Norse *hamarr* hammer, back of an axe, crag.]
1 A tool or instrument with a hard solid (now usu. steel) head set at right angles to the handle, used for beating, breaking, driving nails, etc.; a machine with a metal block serving the same purpose. **OE.**

> J. GARDNER He was one with . . the hammer that sent nails in cleanly at two blows.

†**2** A door knocker. **LME–E17.**
3 In a flintlock gun, a piece of steel covering the flash pan and struck by the flint; in a percussion-lock gun, a spring lever which strikes the percussion cap to ignite the charge; in a modern gun, a part of the firing mechanism which either strikes the firing pin to ignite the cartridge or has the firing pin as an integral part. **LME.**

> W. STYRON A white man standing over him with a musket, hammer cocked, ready to shoot.

4 A lever with a hard head for striking a bell in a clock etc. **M16.**

> W. W. SKEAT Within the gray church-tower The hammer strikes the midnight hour.

5 *ANATOMY*. = MALLEUS 1. **L16.**
6 An auctioneer's mallet, used to indicate by a rap that an article is sold. **E18.**

> W. C. KETCHUM Upon the fall of the Auctioneer's hammer . . the item purchased remains at the purchaser's . . responsibility.

7 *MUSIC*. A small padded mallet forming part of the mechanism for striking the strings of a piano; a small hand-held mallet for playing various percussion instruments, as the xylophone, dulcimer, etc. **L18.**
8 *ATHLETICS*. A heavy metal ball attached to a flexible wire; the contest of throwing this as far as possible. **L19.**
– PHRASES: **be on a person's hammer** pursue, pester, bother, (a person). **come under the hammer**, **go under the hammer** be put up for sale at an auction. **hammer and sickle** an emblem of a crossed hammer and sickle symbolizing the industrial worker and the peasant respectively, used esp. on the national flag of the former USSR and to represent international Communism. **hammer and tongs** with great energy and noise.
– COMB.: **hammer action** (*a*) the action of a hammer, an action like that of a hammer; (*b*) the mechanism of a piano comprising and controlling the hammers; **hammerbeam**: projecting from the wall at the foot of a principal rafter in a roof; **hammer blow** a stroke (as) with a hammer; **hammer-dressed** *adjective* (of stone) roughly faced or smoothed by a hammer; **hammer drill**: having a bit which moves forwards and backwards whilst rotating; **hammer-harden** *verb trans*. harden (a metal) by hammering; **hammerlock** a position in which a wrestler is held with one arm bent behind his or her back; **hammerman** a man who works with a hammer; *spec*. a smith or worker in metal, a blacksmith's assistant; **hammer price** (*a*) the actual price realized by an item sold by auction; (*b*) *STOCK EXCHANGE* the price realized for the shares of a hammered defaulter; **hammer-smith** = *hammerman* above; **hammer toe**: permanently bent downwards; **hammer-work** (*a*) work performed with a hammer; (*b*) something constructed or shaped with a hammer.

■ **hammerless** *adjective* (of a gun) having no hammer; having a concealed hammer: L19.

hammer /ˈhamə/ *verb*. LME.
[ORIGIN from the noun.]
▸ **I** *verb trans.* **1** Strike, drive, beat (*out*), shape, (as) with the repeated blows or the force of a hammer. LME. ▸**b** Fasten (as) with a hammer; nail *up*, *down*, *together*, etc. LME.

D. H. LAWRENCE The man was hammering a piece of metal, with quick, light blows. *Lancashire Evening Telegraph* Mark Loram . . hammered in a stunning 14th minute goal. T. C. WOLFE The pianist began to hammer out a tune on the battered piano. **b** B. MALAMUD You work up a sweat sawing wood apart and hammering it together. TENNYSON All that long morn the lists were hammer'd up.

2 Devise laboriously, shape with effort, work hard or forcefully at (a task, plan, etc.); smooth out (difficulties etc.). Usu. foll. by *out*. L16. ▸**b** Drive (an idea, a fact, etc.) into a person's head by means of repeated or forceful argument. Usu. foll. by *in*, *into*. E17. ▸**c** Inflict heavy defeat(s) on in a war, game, etc.; beat up (a person); squash (a proposal etc.). *colloq.* E20.

M. HUNTER A philosophy has to be hammered out, a mind shaped, a spirit tempered. A. BROOKNER Before they have hammered out the final details it is all arranged. **b** G. B. SHAW All the cognate tribal superstitions which are hammered into us in our childhood. **c** *City Limits* The social ownership strategy . . was hammered by the Campaign Group MPs. *Pot Black* Dennis Taylor . . hammered Cliff Thorburn 5–1 to reach the semi-finals.

b hammer home make fully understood by means of repeated or forceful argument.

3 *STOCK EXCHANGE*. **a** Beat down the price of (a stock); depress (a market). *slang*. M19. ▸**b** Declare (a person or firm) a defaulter with three taps of a hammer on the London Stock Exchange rostrum. L19.

▸ **II** *verb intrans.* **4** Beat, strike, thump, (as) with repeated blows or the force of a hammer. LME. ▸†**b** Debate earnestly *at*, *of*, *(up)on*. L16–L17. ▸**c** Of a thought, an idea, etc.: agitate, be persistently in one's mind. L16. ▸**d** Work hard or toil (*at*); move quickly and forcefully. M18.

S. O'FAOLÁIN We hammered with our rifle butts on the door. J. M. COETZEE His legs were weak, his head hammered. **b** SHAKES. *Two Gent.* Whereon this month I have been hammering. **c** A. F. LOEWENSTEIN It was . . hard to concentrate with all the voices hammering at her. **d** L. STEPHEN He liked . . to hammer away at his poems in a study where chaos reigned supreme. J. HIGGINS He . . ran across the parkland . . he . . hammered along the grass verge of the main road.

5 Stammer. Now *dial.* E17.

■ **hammered** *adjective* (*colloq.*) very drunk L20. **hammerer** *noun* a person who operates or works with a hammer E17.

hammer-cloth /ˈhaməklɒθ/ *noun*. LME.
[ORIGIN from elem. of unknown origin + CLOTH *noun*.]
A cloth covering the driver's seat or box in a coach.

hammerhead /ˈhaməhɛd/ *noun*. M16.
[ORIGIN from HAMMER *noun* + HEAD *noun*.]
1 The head or striking part of a hammer. M16.
2 A person's head (*derog.*); a stupid person, a blockhead. Now chiefly *US* & *dial.* M16.
3 Any of a number of sharks of the genus *Sphyrna*, with a flattened, laterally elongated head bearing the eyes and nostrils at the extremities. Also ***hammerhead shark***. M19.
4 A long-legged African marsh bird, *Scopus umbretta*, with a thick bill and an occipital crest. L19.
■ **hammerheaded** *adjective* having a head shaped like that of a hammer; *fig.* stupid: M16.

Hamming /ˈhamɪŋ/ *noun*. M20.
[ORIGIN R. *Hamming* (1915–98), US scientist.]
Used *attrib.* to designate concepts in information coding.
Hamming code: in which errors are detected by multiple parity bits. **Hamming distance** the number of positions at which two words of equal length are different.

hammle *verb* var. of HAMBLE.

hammochrysos /haməʊˈkrʌɪsɒs/ *noun*. E18.
[ORIGIN Latin from Greek *hammokhrusos*, from *hammos* sand + *khrusos* gold.]
A legendary sparkling stone, usu. identified with a yellow micaceous sand.

hammock /ˈhamək/ *noun*[1]. Orig. †**hamaca**. M16.
[ORIGIN Spanish *hamaca* from Taino *hamaka*; the ending has been assim. to -OCK.]
1 A hanging bed made from a large piece of canvas or netting suspended from supports by cords at each end, formerly used esp. on board ship. M16.
sling one's hammock hang up one's hammock ready for sleeping in; *nautical slang* have a period of time off duty to get used to a new ship.
2 Something resembling a hammock, as a hanging nest, a cocoon, etc. M19.
– COMB.: **hammock chair** a folding reclining chair with canvas support for the body; a deckchair.

hammock /ˈhamək/ *noun*[2]. Also **hu-** /ˈhʌ-/. See also HUMMOCK. M16.
[ORIGIN Orig. form of HUMMOCK.]
†**1** See HUMMOCK. M16.
2 A densely wooded area of ground rising above a plain or swamp. *US.* M16.

Hammond organ /hamənd ˈɔːg(ə)n/ *noun phr.* M20.
[ORIGIN Laurens *Hammond* (1895–1973), Amer. mechanical engineer.]
(Proprietary name for) a type of electric organ. Freq. *ellipt.* as ***Hammond***.

hammy /ˈhami/ *adjective*. M19.
[ORIGIN from HAM *noun*[1] + -Y[1].]
1 Covered with ham. M19.
2 Resembling ham. L19.
3 Of, pertaining to, or characteristic of a ham actor or ham acting. *slang*. E20.

Listener Bela Lugosi's hammy Count Dracula.

■ **hammily** *adverb* M20.

hamous /ˈheɪməs/ *adjective*. Now *rare* or *obsolete*. M17.
[ORIGIN from Latin *hamus* hook + -OUS.]
Having hooks, hooked.
■ Also **hamose** *adjective* E18.

hamper /ˈhampə/ *noun*[1]. ME.
[ORIGIN Reduced form of Anglo-Norman HANAPER.]
1 Orig., any large case or casket for safe keeping. Now usu., a large basket or wickerwork packing case with a cover, used esp. for packing or transporting food, drink, etc.; *transf.* a consignment of food, drink, etc., usu. as a present, in any type of case or box. ME.

P. THEROUX It was like stocking a hamper for a two-day picnic. G. CLARE I can still see and smell in my memory the big hampers which Father sent.

†**2** = HANAPER 2b. LME–E18.

hamper /ˈhampə/ *noun*[2]. E17.
[ORIGIN from HAMPER *verb*[1].]
1 An impediment, a hindrance. Now *rare*. E17.
2 *NAUTICAL*. A necessary but cumbersome part of the equipment of a vessel. Earliest and chiefly in ***top hamper*** s.v. TOP *adjective*. L18.

hamper /ˈhampə/ *verb*[1] *trans.* LME.
[ORIGIN Uncertain: cf. Middle High German, German *hemmen* restrain, hamper, -ER[5].]
1 Obstruct or prevent the movement of (a person or animal) by material obstacles or restraints; fetter, shackle; entangle, catch, (*in*). Now *rare* exc. as passing into sense 2. LME. ▸**b** Restrain by confinement. Long only *Scot.* LME. ▸**c** Interfere with the workings of (a lock, mechanism, etc.). Now *rare*. E19.

DEFOE He caused them to be hampered by ropes, and tied together. F. SMITH At five we engaged with Ice . . and were hampered in it until eleven. **c** R. A. FREEMAN It is useless to wrench at that key, because I have hampered the lock.

2 *fig.* Impede, hinder, burden. LME.

J. SYMONS The Club was hampered by lack of money from holding exhibitions. J. A. MICHENER If he had not been hampered by this irritating calf, he could have beaten back the wolves.

3 Pack together in a bundle, case, etc. Now *rare*. LME.

hamper /ˈhampə/ *verb*[2] *trans.* & *intrans.* *obsolete* exc. *dial.* E16.
[ORIGIN Unknown.]
Beat, strike.

hamper /ˈhampə/ *verb*[3] *trans.* *joc.* E18.
[ORIGIN from HAMPER *noun*[1].]
Load with hampers; present with a hamper.

Hampshire /ˈhampʃə/ *noun*. M17.
[ORIGIN A county in southern England.]
▸ **I** **1** Used *attrib.* to designate things from or associated with Hampshire, *esp.* (***a***) (an animal of) a breed of black pig with a white saddle and prick ears, (***b***) (more fully ***Hampshire Down***) (an animal of) a breed of large hornless sheep with close wool and dark brown face and legs. M17.
Hampshire hog *fig.* (*colloq.* or *derog.*) a native or inhabitant of Hampshire.
▸ **II** **2** In *pl.* (The soldiers of) the Royal Hampshire Regiment. E20.
3 A Hampshire pig. M20.

Hampstead /ˈham(p)stɪd/ *noun*. *rhyming slang*. L19.
[ORIGIN *Hampstead Heath*, a district in north London.]
In *pl.* or ***Hampstead Heath***. Teeth.

hamsin *noun* var. of KHAMSIN.

hamster /ˈhamstə/ *noun*. E17.
[ORIGIN German from Old High German *hamustro* = Old Saxon *hamustra* corn weevil.]
Any of various short-tailed ratlike burrowing rodents of the Eurasian subfamily Cricetinae (family Muridae), with cheek pouches used to carry grain etc. for storage.
golden hamster a largely tawny Asian hamster, *Mesocricetus auratus*, kept as a pet or laboratory animal.

hamstring /ˈhamstrɪŋ/ *noun* & *verb*. M16.
[ORIGIN from HAM *noun*[1] + STRING *noun*.]
▸ **A** *noun*. In humans, apes, etc., each of the five tendons at the back of the knee; in quadrupeds, the great tendon at the back of the hock. M16.
▸ **B** *verb trans.* Pa. t. & pple **-strung** /-strʌŋ/, (now *rare*) **-stringed**. Lame or disable (a person or animal) by cutting the hamstrings; *fig.* destroy the activity or efficiency of. M17.

T. H. WHITE They were crawling along the roads on hands and knees, because they had been hamstrung. A. STORR I know of no creative person who was more hamstrung by his inability to write.

hamular /ˈhamjʊlə/ *adjective*. M19.
[ORIGIN from HAMULUS + -AR[1].]
Chiefly *ANATOMY*. Of the form of a small hook, hooked.

hamulus /ˈhamjʊləs/ *noun*. Pl. **-li** /-lʌɪ, -liː/. E18.
[ORIGIN Latin *hamulus* dim. of *hamus* hook: see -ULE.]
A small hook or hooklike part on a bone etc.
■ **hamular** *adjective* of the form of a small hook, hooked M19.

hamza /ˈhamzə/ *noun*. E19.
[ORIGIN Arabic, lit. 'compression'.]
(A symbol in the Arabic script representing) the glottal stop.

Han /han/ *noun*[1] & *adjective*. M18.
[ORIGIN Chinese *Hàn*.]
(Designating or pertaining to) a dynasty which ruled China from the 3rd cent. BC to the 3rd cent. AD, a period noted for religious and cultural changes and technological developments.

han *noun*[2] var. of KHAN *noun*[2].

H

Hanafi /ˈhanəfi/ *noun* & *adjective*. M18.
[ORIGIN Arabic *ḥanafī*, from *Ḥanīfah* (see below).]
A follower of, of or pertaining to, the school of Islamic law founded by the jurist Abū Ḥanīfa (*c* 699–767).

Hanafite /ˈhanəfʌɪt/ *noun* & *adjective*. M19.
[ORIGIN formed as HANAFI + -ITE[1].]
= HANAFI.

hanap /ˈhanəp/ *noun*. *obsolete* exc. *hist.* L15.
[ORIGIN Old French & mod. French from Frankish, = Old English *hnæp*, Old High German *hnapf* (German *Napf*).]
A drinking vessel, a wine cup. Now *esp.* an ornate medieval goblet.

hanaper /ˈhanəpə/ *noun*. *obsolete* exc. *hist.* ME.
[ORIGIN Anglo-Norman = Old French *hanapier* (Anglo-Latin *hanaperium*), formed as HANAP: see -ER[2].]
†**1** A case or basket for a hanap or hanaps; a repository for plate or treasure. Only in ME.
2 The department of the Chancery into which fees were paid for the sealing and enrolment of charters etc. LME. ▸**b** A (wicker) case or basket for keeping documents. M18.

hanaster /ˈhanəstə/ *noun*. *obsolete* exc. *hist.* Also †**hanster**. ME.
[ORIGIN from HANSE + -ER[1] (= Anglo-Latin *hansterus*, *hanasterius*).]
In the City of Oxford, a person who paid the entrance fee to the merchant guild and was admitted as a freeman.

Hanbali /ˈhanbəli/ *noun* & *adjective*. M19.
[ORIGIN Arabic *ḥanbalī*, from *Ḥanbal* (see below).]
A follower of, of or pertaining to, the school of Islamic law founded by the jurist Ahmad Ibn Ḥanbal (780–855).

Hanbalite /ˈhanbəlʌɪt/ *noun*. M19.
[ORIGIN formed as HANBALI + -ITE[1].]
= HANBALI.

hance /hɑːns/ *noun*. Also **-se**. M16.
[ORIGIN Anglo-Norman, alt. of Old French *hau(l)ce* (mod. *hausse*), from *hau(l)cer* (mod. *hausser*), from Proto-Romance base repr. also by ENHANCE.]
1 A lintel. *obsolete* exc. *dial.* M16.
2 *NAUTICAL*. A curved ascent or descent from one part of a ship to another. M17.
3 *ARCHITECTURE*. The arc at the springing of an elliptical or many-centred arch. Also = HAUNCH 2. E18.

†**hanch** *noun* var. of HAUNCH.

hand /hand/ *noun*.
[ORIGIN Old English *hand*, *hond* = Old Frisian *hānd*, *hōnd*, Old Saxon *hand*, Old High German *hant* (Dutch, German *Hand*), Old Norse *hǫnd*, Gothic *handus*, from Germanic, of unknown origin.]
▸ **I** The member; its use; its position; its symbolic representation.
1 The terminal part of the human arm beyond the wrist, consisting of the palm, fingers, and thumb; a similar (i.e. prehensile) member forming the terminal part of a limb of any animal, e.g. of all four limbs of a monkey; the forefoot of a quadruped. OE. ▸†**b** The whole arm. E17–M18.

V. S. NAIPAUL She started to count off the fingers of her left hand. ALDOUS HUXLEY The hand he gave to Jeremy was disagreeably sweaty. M. AMIS His hands palm-upwards on its grained surface.

2 Possession, care, custody, authority, disposal. Chiefly in ***in a person's hands*** below. Usu. in *pl.* OE.

D. CUSACK The future of social morality is in the hands of women. S. SPENDER It was expected that Madrid would fall into their hands within a matter of hours. V. S. NAIPAUL The farm manager retired . . . The farm passed into new hands.

3 Action performed with the hand; agency, instrumentality; manual assistance. OE. ▸**b** A part or share in an action. L16. ▸**c** A turn in various games, as billiards, rackets, etc.; an innings in cricket. Cf. sense 19c below. L18.

A. HALEY All of this had happened to her at the hands of Massa Waller. G. WINOKUR 15 per cent will die by their own hand. *Times* Listing all the troublespots attributed by the Americans to 'the hand of Moscow'. **b** K. AMIS I'm sorry it's happened, but I had no hand in it. R. RENDELL Wexford felt sure no true architect had had a hand in its building.

4 Side, position, direction. (See also LEFT HAND, RIGHT HAND.) OE.

R. L. STEVENSON The bed of a stream, lined on either hand with sweet-smelling willows. J. MORTIMER At Doughty's right hand sat Grace.

5 A pledge (of agreement or acceptance); *esp.* a promise of marriage. ME.

J. AUSTEN When the dancing recommenced . . and Darcy approached to claim her hand. L. STRACHEY Various candidates for her hand were proposed—among others . . Prince Leopold of Saxe-Coburg. HENRY MILLER All I had to do was to ask her to marry me, ask her hand.

6 A round of applause. *colloq.* L16.

L. ARMSTRONG The kids gave me a big hand when they saw the gleaming bright instrument. F. ASTAIRE At the final exit of our closing dance number we received a sparse, sympathetic kind of hand.

7 In *pl.* = HANDBALL *noun* 5. L19.

▸ **II** Something resembling the hand in size or form.

8 An image of or device shaped like a hand. OE. ▸**b** TYPOGRAPHY. = FIST *noun*[1] 2b. Now *rare*. E17.

H

9 A pointer on a clock for indicating the divisions of the dial. M16.

J. MASTERS The hands were very dim on its blurred white face.

hour hand, minute hand, seconds-hand.

10 A linear measure, now only used of a horse's height, equal to four inches; a hand-breadth. M16. ▸**b** A measure of quantity of various commodities etc., as a cluster of bananas, a handful of tobacco leaves, or a palmate root of ginger. E18.

Horse International He . . already stands 16.3 hands after wintering out. **b** DOUGLAS STUART Two hands of men, ten men, all proper men, had charge of them. H. BASCOM He . . took a hand of green plantains from off a bunch.

11 COOKERY. A shoulder of pork or, formerly, of mutton. L17.

▸ **III** As representing a person.

12 a A performer of some action; *spec.* a performer, writer, etc., of some artistic or literary work. ME. ▸**b** A manual worker; *spec.* a member of a ship's crew. M17.

a W. PALEY Every thing about them indicates that they come from the same hand. *Proverb*: Many hands make light work. **b** W. SCORESBY All hands on board perished. BETTY SMITH The poor do everything with their own hands and the rich hire hands to do things. P. USTINOV The son of a stable hand.

13 A person as a source from which something originates or is obtained. Now only with ordinal numerals, as ***first hand, second hand***, etc. LME.

W. BEDELL You have it but at the third, or fourth hand, perhaps the thirtieth or fortieth. W. COWPER I might . . serve your Honour with cauliflowers and broccoli at the best hand. J. W. CROKER I hear from a good hand that the King is doing much better.

14 A person of a specified skill, ability, or character. *colloq.* L18.

V. WOOLF I was never a great hand at that. M. COX But you know I am no hand at expressing myself.

▸ **IV** Capacity, performance.

15 Capacity for or skill in doing something with the hand; *gen.* skill, ability, knack. ME. ▸**b** HORSEMANSHIP. Skill in handling the reins. LME.

A. RADCLIFFE I had always a hand at carpentry.

16 Style of writing, esp. as belonging to a particular person, historical period, profession, etc. LME. ▸**b** The signature of a person. M16.

F. O'CONNOR It was written in a drunken-looking hand. G. GREENE A message written in his clear slanting American hand. J. GARDNER An old almanac with notes in the margin, written in his father's childish hand. **b** OED As witness the hands of the said A.B. and C.D.

Italian hand, round hand, running hand, etc.

17 Style of artistic execution; touch; handiwork. M17.

HOR. WALPOLE By what I have seen of his hand, . . he was an admirable master. M. ARNOLD The compiler did not put his last hand to the work.

▸ **V** Something held in the hand.

18 A handle. Now only *Scot.* LME.

19 The cards dealt to each player at the beginning of a card game; the cards held at any stage of a game (esp. poker). L16. ▸**b** The person holding the cards. L16. ▸**c** A round of play with these cards. E17.

M. PIERCY You have to find out what kind of hand she's holding. *fig.*: I. MURDOCH She had been dealt a rotten hand by fate. **c** V. SACKVILLE-WEST She played an admirable hand at Bridge.

– PHRASES ETC.: ***a bird in the hand***: see BIRD *noun*. ***as easy as kiss my hand***: see KISS *verb*. **at hand** (*a*) near, close by; (*b*) near in time; †(*c*) at the start. ***at* FIRST HAND**. **at the hands of** from, through the action of. ***bear a hand***: see BEAR *verb*[1]. ***bear in hand***: see BEAR *verb*[1]. **bind hand and foot** bind completely. ***bite the hand that feeds one***: see BITE *verb*. ***bloody hand***: see BLOODY *adjective & adverb*. **by hand** (*a*) with the hand or hands, by manual action or labour; (*b*) (of writing) not typed, printed, etc.; (*c*) (of a delivery etc.) by messenger, not posted. **by my hand, by this hand**: introducing a solemn oath. ***cap in hand***: see CAP *noun*[1]. **change hands** (*a*) pass to a different owner; (*b*) use opposite hands for a task, action, etc. ***clean hands***: see CLEAN *adjective*. ***come in foot and hand***: see FOOT *noun*. **come to hand** turn up, come into one's possession; be received. ***dab hand***: see DAB *noun*[3]. ***dead hand***: see DEAD *adjective* etc. **do a hand's turn** do a stroke of work, make the slightest effort (usu. in neg. contexts). ***easy as kiss my hand***: see KISS *verb*. ***eat out of a person's hand***: see EAT *verb*. ***fine-hand***: see FINE *adjective*. FIRST HAND. ***force a person's hand***: see FORCE *verb*[1]. **for one's own hand** for one's own benefit, on one's own account. ***free hand***: see FREE *adjective*. **from hand to mouth, hand to mouth** improvidently, precariously, with provision for immediate needs only. ***full-hand***: see FULL *adjective*. **get one's hand in** get in practice. **get one's hands on** find, get hold of. ***give a free hand***: see FREE *adjective*. **give a hand** help, lend assistance, (to a person). **give one's hand** present one's hand to be grasped to seal a bargain, make peace, etc. **hand and glove (with), hand in glove (with)** on intimate terms (with), in close association (with). **hand in hand** with hands mutually clasped; *fig.* together, in close association. **hand of glory** [translating French *main de gloire*, alt. of *mandegloire*, orig. *mandragore* mandrake] orig., a French charm made from a mandrake root; later, a charm made from the hand of an executed criminal. **hand of writ** *Scot.* handwriting. **hand over hand, hand over fist** with each hand successively passing the other as in climbing a rope etc.; *fig.* with steady or rapid progress. **hands down** with ease, with little or no effort; esp. in ***win hands down***. **hands off!** do not touch! do not interfere! (cf. ***hands-off*** below). **hands up!**: ordering a person or persons to raise one hand to signify assent or both hands to signify surrender. **hand to hand** (of fighting) at close quarters, man to man. ***hand to mouth***: see ***from hand to mouth*** above. ***have a free hand***: see FREE *adjective*. **have a hand in** have a share in, be involved in. **have one's hand in** be in practice. **have one's hand in the till** *fig.* steal, embezzle. **have one's hands full** be fully occupied. **have one's hands tied** *fig.* be powerless to act. ***heel of the hand***: see HEEL *noun*[1]. ***helping hand***: see HELP *verb*. ***hidden hand***: see HIDDEN *adjective*. **hold a person's hand** *fig.* give close guidance or moral support to a person. **hold hands** be hand in hand. **hold one's hand** refrain from action, esp. punishment. **in a person's hands** to be dealt with by a person, subject to his or her control. **in hand** (*a*) held in the hand; (*b*) in actual possession, at one's disposal; to spare; (*c*) in process or preparation, receiving attention; (*d*) under control; †(*e*) led by the hand, a leash, etc.; †(*f*) in suspense. ***in huckster's hands***: see HUCKSTER *noun*. ***in the hollow of one's hand***: see HOLLOW *noun*[1]. ***iron hand in a velvet glove***: see IRON *adjective*. **join hands** = ***hold hands*** above. **keep one's hand in** keep in practice. ***kiss hands***: see KISS *verb*. ***know like the back of one's hand***: see BACK *noun*[1]. ***lay hands on***: see LAY *verb*[1]. ***lay hands on the ark***: see ARK 2. **lay one's hands on** = ***get one's hands on*** above. **lend a hand** = ***give a hand*** above. ***light hand***: see LIGHT *adjective*[1]. ***lone hand***: see LONE *adjective & adverb*. **make a fine hand, make a good hand**, etc., make a fine, good, etc., success or profit. **man of his hands** a practical or skilful person. **off one's hands** no longer one's responsibility or on one's hands. ***old hand***: see OLD *adjective*. **on hand** (*a*) in one's possession, in one's charge or keeping; (*b*) in attendance. **on all hands, on every hand** on all sides, to or from every quarter. **on one hand** = ***on the one hand*** below. **on one's hands** resting on one as a charge or responsibility. **on the one hand**: introducing a point of view, fact, etc. (often followed by another which contrasts with it, introduced by ***on the other hand***). **on the other hand**: introducing a point of view, fact, etc., contrasting with another previously mentioned (often introduced by ***on one hand, on the one hand***). **out of hand** (*a*) at once, immediately, without thinking; (*b*) out of control; (*c*) done with, dealt with. ***play into the hands of***: see PLAY *verb*. ***put one's hand in one's pocket***: see POCKET *noun*. **put one's hands on** = ***get one's hands on*** above. **put one's hand to** set about, undertake. ***put one's hand to the plough***: see PLOUGH *noun*. SECOND HAND. **serve hand and foot, wait on hand and foot**: assiduously, servilely. ***set in hand***: see SET *verb*[1]. **set one's hand to** (*a*) = ***put one's hand to*** above; (*b*) write one's signature on, authorize by signing. ***set one's hand to the plough***: see PLOUGH *noun*. ***shake a person's hand, shake by the hand, shake hands (with)***: see SHAKE *verb*. ***show one's hand***: see SHOW *verb*. ***sit on one's hands***: see SIT *verb*. ***stay one's hand, stay a person's hand***: see STAY *verb*[1]. ***strike hands***: see STRIKE *verb*. **take hands** join hands, esp. in marriage. **take in hand** take the responsibility of; undertake (a task); *esp.* undertake the charge or care of (a person). ***take one's courage in both hands***: see COURAGE *noun* 4. ***throw in one's hand***: see THROW *verb*. **tie hand and foot** = ***bind hand and foot*** above. ***time on one's hands***: see TIME *noun*. **to hand** (*a*) within reach, accessible; (*b*) (now *rare*) under control. **to one's hand** ready for one to deal with easily. ***try one's hand***: see TRY *verb*. **turn one's hand to** undertake for the first time. **under one's hand, under hand** with one's signature, properly signed. ***upper hand***: see UPPER *adjective*. ***wait on hand and foot***: see ***serve hand and foot*** above. ***wash one's hands***: see WASH *verb*. ***wash one's hands of***: see WASH *verb*. WEAKEN ***the hands of***. ***with a heavy hand***: see HEAVY *adjective*. ***with a high hand***: see HIGH *adjective*. **with both hands** *fig.* with all one's might.

– ATTRIB. & COMB.: In the senses 'held or carried in the hand', as ***hand baggage, hand mirror***, 'operated by hand', as ***handbrake, hand drill, hand press, handpump, hand puppet***, or with ref. to action performed by or with the hand, as opp. to by machine, as ***hand-knitted, hand-painted, hand-sewn, hand-written*** *adjectives*, ***hand-wash*** *verb*. Special combs., as **hand axe** an axe used or wielded with one hand; *spec.* in ARCHAEOLOGY, a large bifacially worked stone cutting tool with no haft, typical of certain lower and Middle Palaeolithic industries. ***hand-barrow***: see BARROW *noun*[3] 1; **handbell** a small bell rung by being swung in the hand; *spec.* each of a set of such bells specially designed for musical performance; **handbill** a printed notice delivered or circulated by hand; **hand-breadth, hand's-breadth** a unit of linear measure (not now in technical use) based on the width of the average adult hand and equal to approx. four inches; **handcar** *N. Amer.* a light railway vehicle propelled by cranks or levers and used by workers for inspecting the track; **handcart**: drawn or pushed by hand; **handclasp** (chiefly *US*) = HANDGRIP 2; **hand cream** an emollient for the hands; **hand gallop** an easy controlled gallop; **hand grenade** a grenade designed to be thrown by hand; **handhold** a hold for the hand; a projection, crack, etc., which one can hold on to in climbing; **hand-holding** the provision of support, reassurance, or assistance to someone; **handhorn** MUSIC a natural horn played by stopping the bell with the hand; **hand-jam** *verb & noun* (MOUNTAINEERING) (*a*) *verb intrans.* wedge a hand in a crack as a handhold; (*b*) *noun* the action of hand-jamming; **handjob** *coarse slang* an act of (usu. male) masturbation; **hand-labour** manual labour; **handline** *noun & verb* (ANGLING) (fish using) a line worked or drawn by hand; **handlist**: of books etc. for easy reference; **handloom** a weaver's loom worked by hand as opp. to by machine; **handmade** *adjective* made by hand as opp. to by machine; **handmaid, handmaiden** (*arch.* exc. *fig.*), a female attendant or servant; **hand mill** a mill consisting of one millstone turned on another by hand; a small mill for grinding coffee etc.; **hand organ** a barrel organ played by means of a crank turned by the hand; **handphone** *SE Asian* a mobile phone; **handpicked** *adjective* carefully chosen; **hand press** a printing press operated by hand; **handprint** the mark left by the impression of a hand; **handrail** a rail or railing used as support for the hand or as a guard along the edge of a platform, stairs, etc.; **handrunning** *adverb* (*dial.* or *colloq.*) consecutively, in a row; **hands-across-the-sea** promoting closer links, friendly. **handsaw** a saw used or worked with one hand; ***know a hawk from a handsaw***: see HAWK *noun*[1]; ***hand's-breadth***: see ***hand-breadth*** above; **handset** a telephone mouthpiece and earpiece as one unit; **hands-free** *adjective* (esp. of a telephone) designed to be operable without the use of the hands; **hand signal** a manual indication by a cyclist or driver of a motor vehicle of his or her intention to stop, turn, etc.; **hands-off** *adjective & adverb* [from *hands off!* above] (*a*) *adjective* (of a policy, attitude, etc.) non-intervening, aloof; (of a flight) automatic; (*b*) *adverb* automatically. **hands-on** *adjective* involving direct participation, practical, not theoretical; (of a person) having or willing to gain practical experience; **handspan** = SPAN *noun*[1]; **handspring** a gymnastic movement in which a performer moves forwards or backwards from a standing position on to the hands and completes a somersault, landing on the feet; **hand-staff** a handle resembling a staff; *esp.* that of a flail; **handstand** a gymnastic movement in which the body is supported vertically in an upside-down position by the hands alone; **hand-to-mouth** *adjective* improvident, precarious, providing for immediate needs only (cf. ***(from) hand to mouth*** above); **hand towel** a small towel for drying the hands after washing; **hand-wringing** an excessive display of concern or distress.

hand /hand/ *verb.* LME.

[ORIGIN from the noun.]

1 *verb trans.* Touch, grasp, seize, with the hand or hands; manipulate, handle. *obsolete* exc. *techn.* LME.

SHAKES. *Temp.* If you can command these elements to silence, . . we will not hand a rope more.

2 *verb trans.* Help or conduct (a person) *up* or *down* a step, *over* an obstacle, *into* or *out of* a carriage, etc. M17.

A. TROLLOPE He handed her into the carriage. E. M. FORSTER Henry . . handed Margaret down the cellar-stairs.

3 *verb trans.* Deliver, pass, or transfer with the hand or hands. Freq. foll. by *back, in, over*. M17. ▸**b** *spec.* Offer, serve, or distribute (food) at a meal. Freq. foll. by *round*. E19.

A. CARNEGIE The five hundred dollars which I handed over to Mr. Scott. P. ACKROYD Monro handed the poem back to him. A. TYLER His waiter . . handed him a menu. M. DRABBLE Charles had raged, stormed, and handed in his resignation. **b** H. JAMES I wonder whether Verena hadn't better hand the cake. V. WOOLF Amelia Whatshername, handing round cups of tea.

hand it to a person *fig. colloq.* congratulate, acknowledge the merit of a person.

4 *verb trans.* Pass on, transfer, transmit. Now only with adverbs (see below). M17. ▸**b** Give, impose; palm off. *N. Amer.* E20.

b T. MORRISON Don't hand me that mess.

5 *verb trans. & intrans.* NAUTICAL. Take in or furl (a sail). M17.

E. LINKLATER Before they rounded the Horn Sam could hand, reef, and steer.

6 *verb trans.* Join hand in hand, *spec.* in marriage. Only in ***handed*** *ppl adjective. rare.* M17.

– WITH ADVERBS IN SPECIALIZED SENSES: **hand down** (*a*) pass on to a later generation or age; *spec.* pass on (an outgrown or unwanted garment) to another (esp. younger) member of one's family; (*b*) deliver or transmit (a verdict) from a superior court etc. **hand off** (*a*) RUGBY push off (a tackling opponent) with the hand; (*b*) AMER. FOOTBALL pass the ball by hand. **hand on** pass to the next in a series or succession (***hand on the torch***: see TORCH *noun*). **hand out** distribute, give out. **hand over** transfer; relinquish.

– COMB.: **hand-in** REAL TENNIS, SQUASH, & BADMINTON the person who or side which is serving the ball (cf. HAND-OUT 1); **hand-me-down** *noun & adjective* (designating) a second-hand garment or (*fig.*) idea; **hand-off** RUGBY the action of pushing off an opponent; **handover** an act or instance of handing something over.

handbag /ˈhan(d)bag/ *noun & verb.* M19.

[ORIGIN from HAND *noun* + BAG *noun*.]

▸ **A** *noun.* **1** A woman's small bag for holding personal items. Formerly also, a light travelling bag. M19.

2 handbags (at ten paces, at dawn, etc.), a minor confrontation or squabble, esp. in sport. *colloq.* L20.

News of the World It was handbags in the dressing room but we were able to sort things out.

▸ **B** *verb trans.* [coined by the Brit. Conservative MP Julian Critchley with reference to Margaret Thatcher's ministerial style in cabinet meetings] Of a woman: verbally attack (a person) ruthlessly and forcefully. L20.

> *Independent* She's on top form—I saw her last week and got handbagged for 15 minutes.

handball /ˈhan(d)bɔːl, *in sense A.5* -ˈbɔːl/ *noun & verb.* LME.
[ORIGIN from HAND *noun* + BALL *noun*¹.]
▸ **A** *noun.* **I 1** A ball for throwing with the hand; *spec.* (*a*) an inflated leather ball used in handball (sense 2 below); (*b*) a small hollow rubber ball used in handball (sense 3 below). LME.
2 A game similar to football in which the ball is thrown rather than kicked in the attempt to get it into the opposing team's goal. L16.
3 A game resembling fives in which a ball is hit with the hand in a walled court. L19.
▸ **II 4** AUSTRAL. RULES FOOTBALL. = HANDPASS *noun.* M19.
5 SOCCER. A foul involving unlawful handling of the ball. E20.
▸ **B** *verb trans. & intrans.* AUSTRAL. RULES FOOTBALL = HANDPASS *verb.* M20.

handbook /ˈhan(d)bʊk/ *noun.* OE.
[ORIGIN from HAND *noun* + BOOK *noun*, translating medieval Latin *manualis liber*, late Latin *manuale* (translating Greek *egkheiridion*) MANUAL *noun*; the word in current use was introduced, after German *Handbuch*, in the 19th cent.]
†**1** The manual of medieval ecclesiastical offices and ritual. OE–L16.
2 A book containing concise information on a particular subject; a guidebook. E19.

> J. P. DONLEAVY Dignity in debt. A handbook for those just starting out.

3 A bookmaker's betting book; a bookmaking establishment. Chiefly *US.* L19.

> S. BELLOW. He went to a handbook on Fifty-third Street to bet on horses.

h. & c. *abbreviation.*
Hot and cold (water).

handclap /ˈhan(d)klap/ *noun.* E19.
[ORIGIN from HAND *noun* + CLAP *noun*¹.]
A clap of the hands; a round of applause; *fig.* an instant.

> K. AMIS Cries of approval as well as handclaps followed the final triumphant chord.

slow handclap: see SLOW *adjective & adverb.*
▪ **handclapping** *noun* M19.

handcraft /ˈhan(d)krɑːft/ *noun & verb.* OE.
[ORIGIN from HAND *noun* + CRAFT *noun.*]
▸ **A** *noun.* = HANDICRAFT 1. OE.
– COMB.: **handcraftsman** a handicraftsman; **handcraftsmanship** skilled craftsmanship with the hands.
▸ **B** *verb trans.* Make by handicraft. M20.

> *Belle (Australia)* Moran features hand-crafted Mountain Ash hardwood frames.

handcuff /ˈhan(d)kʌf/ *noun & verb.* E17.
[ORIGIN from HAND *noun* + CUFF *noun*¹.]
▸ **A** *noun.* †**1** = CUFF *noun*¹ 2a. E–M17.
2 *sing.* & (usu.) in *pl.* A pair of lockable metal rings, joined by a short chain or bar, which can secure both a prisoner's wrists together or one wrist to that of his or her captor. M17.
golden handcuffs: see GOLDEN *adjective.*
▸ **B** *verb trans.* Put handcuffs on, manacle. E18.

handed /ˈhandɪd/ *adjective.* L15.
[ORIGIN from HAND *noun* + -ED². See also earlier LEFT-HANDED, RIGHT-HANDED.]
1 Having a hand or hands; (as 2nd elem. of comb.) having hands of a specified kind or number. L15.
empty-handed, ***free-handed***, ***open-handed***, ***two-handed***, etc.
2 Of a tool or implement: specially designed for either right-handed or left-handed use. L20.

handedness /ˈhandɪdnɪs/ *noun.* E20.
[ORIGIN from HANDED + -NESS. See also earlier LEFT-HANDEDNESS, RIGHT-HANDEDNESS.]
1 The quality or state of being handed; *esp.* the tendency to use or the preference for the use of either the right or the left hand. E20.

> P. LEACH His handedness is controlled by the part of the brain that controls language.

2 That property of the configuration of a molecule, crystal, or other object (defined as ***left-handedness***, ***right-handedness*** by arbitrary convention), which distinguishes it from its mirror image. M20.

> *Listener* Proteins . . contain amino acids (all of one particular handedness) joined together.

Handelian /hanˈdiːlɪən, -ˈdeɪl-/ *noun & adjective.* M18.
[ORIGIN from *Handel* (orig. *Händel*) (see below) + -IAN.]
▸ **A** *noun.* A person who favours or imitates the style of the German musician and composer Georg Friedrich Handel (1685–1759). M18.
▸ **B** *adjective.* Of, pertaining to, or characteristic of Handel or his style of composition. L18.

> H. ROSENTHAL Handel's *Julius Caesar* in a performing edition that understandably upset Handelian experts.

hander /ˈhandə/ *noun*¹. L17.
[ORIGIN from HAND *verb* + -ER¹.]
A person who hands, delivers, or passes. Usu. with *back*, *down*, *on*, *over*, etc.

> LEIGH HUNT The hander down of his likeness to posterity.

hander /ˈhandə/ *noun*². *colloq.* M19.
[ORIGIN from HAND *noun* + -ER¹.]
A blow on the hand.

handfast /ˈhan(d)fɑːst/ *noun.* M16.
[ORIGIN App. from HAND *noun* + FAST *adjective*; sense 2 from HANDFAST *verb.*]
†**1** (A) firm hold or grip with the hands. M16–M17.

> R. HAWKINS Such were the blowes he gave them . . as both left their hand-fast.

2 A contract; *spec.* a betrothal or marriage contract, *esp.* such a contract sealed by a handshake. *obsolete* exc. *hist.* E17.

> SHAKES. *Cymb.* And the remembrancer of her to hold the hand-fast to her lord. *attrib.*: *Daily Telegraph* The 'handfast' marriage by which a couple could marry by clasping hands and swearing their vows before witnesses.

handfast /ˈhan(d)fɑːst/ *adjective.* ME.
[ORIGIN In senses 1, 2, orig. pa. pple of HANDFAST *verb*; in sense 3 from HAND *noun* + FAST *adjective.*]
1 Contracted by the joining of hands; betrothed, espoused. *obsolete* exc. *hist.* ME.
†**2** Bound; manacled. ME–M17.
3 Close-fisted (*lit. & fig.*). Now *rare* or *obsolete.* E17.

handfast /ˈhan(d)fɑːst/ *verb trans.* LOE.
[ORIGIN In sense 1 from Old Norse *handfesta* strike a bargain by joining hands etc.; in senses 2, 3 from HAND *noun* + FAST *adjective.*]
1 Betroth (two people or one person *to* another); *esp.* contract (a person or two people) to cohabit with another or together for a trial period before marriage. *obsolete* exc. *hist.* LOE. ▸**b** Of a man: become betrothed to, cohabit with (a woman). Long *rare.* L16.
†**2** Grasp, seize firmly with the hand. M16–M17.
†**3** Manacle, secure the hands of. L16–E17.
▪ **handfasting** *noun* (*obsolete* exc. *hist.*) betrothal; the ceremony of contracting a trial period of marriage: L15.

handful /ˈhan(d)fʊl, -f(ə)l/ *noun.* OE.
[ORIGIN from HAND *noun* + FULL *adjective* (in early use not inflected as from -FUL).]
1 A quantity that fills the hand; as much or as many as a hand can grasp or contain. OE. ▸**b** A small number or amount. E16.

> R. C. HUTCHINSON He put down the handful of crayons he was holding. D. PRATER He . . stooped now and then to gather great handfuls from the carpet of forget-me-nots. **b** R. SUTCLIFF The valiant handful of cavalry were struggling to keep clear the line of retreat. M. DRABBLE He studied Current Affairs, along with a handful of public schoolboys.

†**2** = HAND *noun* 10. LME–M18.
3 A person, animal, or task that is troublesome or difficult to manage. *colloq.* M18.

> P. G. WODEHOUSE Bailey will find her rather a handful. Does she ever sit still, by the way?

4 A five-year prison sentence. *slang.* M20.

handglass /ˈhan(d)glɑːs/ *noun.* L18.
[ORIGIN from HAND *noun* + GLASS *noun.*]
1 A small portable glass frame for protecting or bringing on plants. L18.
2 A magnifying glass held in the hand. E19.
3 A small mirror with a handle. L19.

handgrip /ˈhan(d)grɪp/ *noun.* Also †**handygrip**. OE.
[ORIGIN from HAND *noun* + GRIP *noun*¹; var. after HANDIWORK.]
1 Firm hold or grasp with the hand. OE.

> J. SYLVESTER Hee, that both Globes in his own hand-gripe holds.

at handgrips, **in handgrips** (now *rare* or *obsolete*) in close combat.
2 *spec.* A grip or clasp of the hand in greeting or leave-taking. L19.

> E. H. YATES With his warmest handgrip.

3 A part of something designed to be held or gripped; a handle, a hilt, etc. L19.

> *Camera Weekly* The other . . change is in the hand-grip cover.

handgun /ˈhan(d)gʌn/ *noun.* ME.
[ORIGIN from HAND *noun* + GUN *noun.*]
Orig., a gun (with or without a rest) held and fired with the hand or hands, as opp. to a cannon. Now, a gun held and fired with one hand only.
▪ **handgunner** *noun* a person who uses a handgun M16.

hand-habend /ˈhandhɑːbənd/ *adjective.* Long *arch. rare.* ME.
[ORIGIN from Old English *æt hæbbendre handa* lit. 'at or with a having hand'.]
LAW. Of a thief: apprehended in the possession of stolen goods.

hand-held /ˈhandhɛld/ *adjective & noun.* E20.
[ORIGIN from HAND *noun* + HELD *adjective.*]
▸ **A** *adjective.* Held in the hand. E20.
▸ **B** *noun.* A small hand-held computer for business or recreational use. L20.

handi /ˈhandi/ *noun.* L19.
[ORIGIN Hindi *hā̃ḍī*, from Sanskrit *bhāṇḍa* pot.]
An earthenware or metal pot used in Indian cooking.

handicap /ˈhandɪkap/ *noun & verb.* M17.
[ORIGIN App. from 'hand i' cap' or 'hand in the cap', referring to the drawing out of full or empty hands: see below.]
▸ **A** *noun.* **1** *hist.* A game in which a challenger laid claim to an article belonging to another person, offering something in exchange for it, the difference in the value of the two items being determined by an umpire who stood to gain the forfeit money deposited by all three contestants if the other two parties both signified (by drawing out full or empty hands from a cap, pocket, etc.) their acceptance or rejection of his award (otherwise the one who accepted it won the forfeit money). M17.
2 A horse race in which an umpire determines, according to the horses' merits, what weights have to be carried by each in order to equalize their chances (also ***handicap race***); any race or competition in which the chances of an inferior competitor are made more equal by some means, as by having a head start etc. L18.
welter handicap: see WELTER *noun*³ 1b.
3 The extra weight or other disadvantageous condition imposed upon a superior in favour of an inferior in a competition; *spec.* in GOLF, the number of strokes by which a golfer normally exceeds the par for the course, used to equalize the chances between players by granting the inferior player or players an advantage based on the difference between handicaps as extra strokes. L19.

> G. SANTAYANA He had intended to race in earnest, having given a generous handicap.

4 An encumbrance, a hindrance; *spec.* a condition that markedly restricts a person's ability to function physically, mentally, or socially, a disability. See note below. L19.

> C. POTOK His sickness is quite a handicap.

▸ **B** *verb trans.* Infl. **-pp-**.
†**1** Draw out or gain (money) in a game of handicap. Only in M17.
2 Impose a handicap on (a competitor, esp. a racehorse). M19.
3 *fig.* Be a handicap to, hamper, disadvantage. M19.

> E. HEMINGWAY He was handicapped by his short stature. *Look Now* Guilt . . handicaps the way we think.

– NOTE: In British English *handicap* and *handicapped* were for much of the 20th cent. the standard forms of reference to mental or physical disabilities, but have been superseded by terms such as *disability* and *disabled*, or, in reference to mental disability, (*having*) *learning difficulties*, *learning disability*, or *learning-disabled*. In American English *handicapped* remains acceptable as an adjective. As with *disabled*, use of *the handicapped* as a collective noun is best avoided.
▪ **handicapper** *noun* (*a*) the official who determines the weights the horses are to carry in a handicap; (*b*) a horse running in a handicap: M18.

handicapped /ˈhandɪkapt/ *adjective & noun.* E20.
[ORIGIN pa. pple of HANDICAP *verb*: see -ED¹.]
▸ **A** *adjective.* Having a disability, disabled. E20.
▸ **B** *noun collect. pl. The* class of disabled people. M20.
– NOTE: See note at HANDICAP.

handicraft /ˈhandɪkrɑːft/ *noun.* ME.
[ORIGIN Alt. of HANDCRAFT after HANDIWORK.]
1 Manual skill. ME.
2 A manual art, trade, or occupation. Formerly also, a handicraftsman. M16.
– COMB.: **handicraftsman** a person employed or skilled in a manual occupation, an artisan.

handicuffs /ˈhandɪkʌfs/ *noun pl. arch.* Also **handy-**. E18.
[ORIGIN from HAND *noun* or HANDY *adjective* + CUFF *noun*², app. after FISTICUFFS *noun.*]
Blows with the hand; fighting hand to hand.

handie-talkie /ˈhandɪˌtɔːki/ *noun.* M20.
[ORIGIN from HAND *noun* after WALKIE-TALKIE.]
A light form of walkie-talkie two-way radio set, easily carried in the hand.

handily /ˈhandɪli/ *adverb.* E17.
[ORIGIN from HANDY *adjective* + -LY².]
In a handy manner; expertly; *N. Amer.* easily. Formerly also, manually.

> T. O'BRIEN With Eddie as captain the Third Squad won handily.

handiness /ˈhandɪnɪs/ *noun.* M17.
[ORIGIN formed as HANDILY + -NESS.]
1 The quality of being handy or expert. M17.
2 Manageableness; convenience. L19.

handiwork /ˈhandɪwəːk/ *noun.* Also (now *rare*) **handywork**.
[ORIGIN Old English *handġeweorc*, from *hand* HAND *noun* + *ġeweorc* collect. formation (see Y-) on *weorc* WORK *noun*; analysed in 16 as from HANDY *adjective* + WORK *noun.*]
1 A thing or things made by the hands. OE.

H

J. B. PRIESTLEY 'Ow's the repairs going, George?' He.. began to inspect the other's handiwork. B. BETTELHEIM Man is afraid of being robbed of his own humanity by his own handiwork the machine.

2 Work done by the hands or by direct personal agency. **OE.**

P. PEARCE He had drawn the creature.., and then was startled by his own handiwork.

3 Working with the hands; practical work. **M16.**

E. H. GOMBRICH Artists had to insist that their real work was not handiwork but brain work. A. S. BYATT She came first in the theoretical paper.., but her handiwork let her down.

4 Work of any kind; doing, performance, achievement. **M19.**

DICKENS That was your handiwork, Giles, I understand.

handkercher /ˈhaŋkətʃə/ *noun. dial. & slang.* **M16.**
[ORIGIN from HAND *noun* + KERCHER.]
= HANDKERCHIEF.

handkerchief /ˈhaŋkətʃɪf/ *noun.* Pl. **-chiefs**, **-chieves** /-tʃiːvz/. **M16.**
[ORIGIN from HAND *noun* + KERCHIEF.]
A small square of cotton, linen, silk, or (now, more fully ***paper handkerchief***) soft absorbent paper, used for wiping the nose, eyes, face, etc., and formerly also worn about the neck.

A. PATON He.. took out a large red handkerchief to wipe his face. J. BARTH He drew a handkerchief from his sweater pocket and blew his nose violently.

pocket handkerchief: see POCKET *noun.*

handle /ˈhand(ə)l/ *noun*¹. **OE.**
[ORIGIN from HAND *noun* + -LE¹.]
1 A part of a thing by which it is to be held in order to use, move, or carry it. **OE.**

D. LESSING He lifted the handles to propel the cart onwards. H. BASCOM Over his other arm a long umbrella.. hangs by an ornate handle.

2 *fig.* A fact or circumstance that may be taken advantage of; an opportunity, a pretext. **M16.**

L. STRACHEY Victoria's retirement gave an unpleasant handle to the argument. *Gainesville Daily Sun* The floodplain.. is vegetated by plants not on the old list, so we don't.. have a good handle on protecting it.

3 A thing resembling a handle; *joc.* the nose. **M17.** ▸**b** (The beer contained in) a glass with a handle. *Austral. & NZ colloq.* **E20.**

4 A title of rank or courtesy. Freq. in ***a handle to one's name***. *colloq.* **M19.** ▸**b** A name; *spec.* a Citizens' Band radio operator's call sign. *slang.* **E20.**

b M. LAURENCE Got this real classy name. Alvin Gerald Cummings—some handle, eh?

– PHRASES: **fly off the handle**, **go off the handle** lose one's temper. **get a handle on** *colloq.* (chiefly *N. Amer.*) gain control over; acquire an understanding of. ***go off the handle***: see ***fly off the handle*** above. ***long handle***: see LONG *adjective*¹. **up to the handle** *US colloq.* thoroughly, completely.

handle /ˈhand(ə)l/ *noun*². **L19.**
[ORIGIN from HANDLE *verb*¹.]
The feel of goods, esp. textiles, when handled.

Belle (Australia) Wool has superior handle and resilience.

handle /ˈhand(ə)l/ *verb*¹.
[ORIGIN Old English *handlian* corresp. to Old Frisian *handelia*, Old Saxon *handlon*, Old High German *hantalōn* (German *handeln*), Old Norse *hǫndla* seize, treat: see -LE³.]
▸**I** Touch, take hold of, etc., with the hand; manage.
1 *verb trans.* Touch or feel with the hand or hands; take hold of in or with the hand or hands; use the hands on. **OE.** ▸**b** *verb intrans.* Have a specified feel when touched. Now *rare.* **E18.** ▸**c** *verb trans.* FOOTBALL & CRICKET. Touch (the ball) in contravention of the rules. **L18.**

G. GREENE I have.. been in the habit of wearing gloves when I handle the notes. B. EMECHETA There was an intrinsic satisfaction in handling and touching natural things.

2 *verb trans.* Use, operate, manipulate, (a tool, machine, car, etc.) in a controlled manner. **ME.** ▸**b** TANNING. Move (hides) up and down in the tannin infusion in which they are immersed. **M19.** ▸**c** *verb intrans.* Of a tool, machine, car, etc.: react or behave in a specified way in response to use, operation, or direction. **L19.**

R. HUNTFORD It was also the fastest and the most dangerous sailing ship to handle. A. BURGESS None of us could be trusted to handle a knife and a fork. **c** *Which?* The car won't handle as well in an emergency. *Shooting Life* The gun handles far too quickly for most people.

3 *verb trans.* Manage, direct, control, cope with, (a thing or person). **E16.** ▸†**b** Conduct *oneself*, behave. **M16–M19.**

J. CARY I'd no idea you could handle a crowd like that. L. GOULD Extraordinary niceness in a man was one of those things she couldn't handle. K. ISHIGURO Women can't handle saké.

▸**II** Deal with, treat.
4 *verb trans.* Deal with in speech or writing, discuss, (a theme, subject, etc.). **OE.**

I. WATTS The very same theme may be handled.. in several different methods.

5 *verb trans.* Deal with; treat; *spec.* act towards in some specified way. **ME.** ▸**b** Portray or represent (an artistic subject) in a specified way. **M16.**

C. ODETS The job is to handle him gently. R. K. NARAYAN I had a small lawyer handling my case in the court. *Dumfries Courier* Complaints about new vehicles are handled by the trade association of the motor manufacturers. **b** C. KINGSLEY Our painting is only good when it handles landscapes and animals.

6 *verb trans.* Trade or deal in (goods). **L16.**

J. UPDIKE We only handle silver in the form of pre-'65 silver dollars.

■ **handleaˈbility** *noun* ease of handling **M20.** **handleable** *adjective* able to be (easily) handled **E17.**

handle /ˈhand(ə)l/ *verb*² *trans.* Now *rare* or *obsolete.* **E17.**
[ORIGIN from HANDLE *noun*¹.]
Provide with a handle.

handlebar /ˈhand(ə)lbɑː/ *noun.* **L19.**
[ORIGIN from HANDLE *noun*¹ + BAR *noun*¹.]
sing. & (usu.) in *pl.* A transverse bar, freq. curved at each end to form handles (usu. fitted with some form of grip) and fixtures for the brake levers, connected to the front wheel of a bicycle, motorcycle, etc., and used to steer the vehicle.
– COMB.: **handlebar moustache** a long heavy moustache with curved ends.

handled /ˈhand(ə)ld/ *adjective.* **L18.**
[ORIGIN from HANDLE *noun*¹, *verb*²: see -ED², -ED¹.]
Having a handle, esp. of a specified type or material, as ***ivory-handled***, ***long-handled***, ***silver-handled***.

handleless /ˈhand(ə)llɪs/ *adjective.* **L19.**
[ORIGIN from HANDLE *noun*¹ + -LESS.]
Without a handle.

W. WHARTON She hands me a big handleless cup of tea whenever I come.

handler /ˈhandlə/ *noun*¹. **LME.**
[ORIGIN from HANDLE *verb*¹ + -ER¹.]
▸**I 1** A person who handles esp. something specified. **LME.**

Times These specially preposed dies.. are brought together.., the handlers wearing gloves.

2 a A person who controls and incites a dog or gamecock in a fight. **E19.** ▸**b** A person who shows the points of a dog at a trial. **L19.** ▸**c** A person, esp. a police officer, who is in charge of a trained dog. **M20.**

b *National Trust Magazine* Thirty-five collie dogs and their handlers.. competed on the hilly terrain. **c** N. GORDIMER Alsatian dogs strapped to their handlers kept passers-by back.

3 BOXING. A person who trains and acts as a second to a boxer. **E20.**
▸**II 4** TANNING. A pit containing a weak tannin infusion in which hides are handled. **L18.**

handler /handlə/ *noun*². **L16.**
[ORIGIN from HANDLE *verb*² + -ER¹.]
A person who fixes a handle to a vessel, tool, etc.

handless /ˈhandlɪs/ *adjective.* **ME.**
[ORIGIN from HAND *noun* + -LESS.]
1 Without hands. **ME.**
2 *fig.* Inept or incompetent, esp. with the hands. Now chiefly *dial.* **LME.**

J. M. BARRIE He is most terribly handless.

hand-off /ˈhandɒf/ *noun.* **E20.**
[ORIGIN from ***hand off*** s.v. HAND *verb.*]
1 RUGBY. The action of pushing off an opponent with the hand. **E20.**
2 AMER. FOOTBALL. The action or an instance of passing the ball by hand to another team member. **M20.**

hand-out /ˈhandaʊt/ *noun.* **L19.**
[ORIGIN from ***hand out*** s.v. HAND *verb.*]
1 REAL TENNIS, SQUASH, & BADMINTON. The person or side to whom the ball is served. **L19.**
2 That which is handed out; *spec.* a gift of food, clothes, or money to a beggar or other person in need. **L19.**

A. T. ELLIS Government hand-outs can never be the same as simple generosity. S. BELLOW Eating your own meal.. is different from a hand-out.

3 A prepared statement given out to the press or some other group of people; *spec.* a circular or pamphlet giving information, guidance, etc. **E20.**

handpass /ˈhan(d)pɑːs/ *noun & verb.* **M20.**
[ORIGIN from HAND *noun* + PASS *noun*² or *verb.*]
AUSTRAL. RULES FOOTBALL. ▸**A** *noun.* An act of handpassing. **M20.**
▸**B** *verb trans.* & *intrans.* Pass (the ball) by punching it with the fist. **M20.**

Hand–Schüller–Christian /handʃʊləˈkrɪstʃ(ə)n/ *noun.* **M20.**
[ORIGIN from Alfred *Hand* (1868–1949), US paediatrician, Artur *Schüller* (1874–1958), Austrian neurologist, and H. A. *Christian* (1876–1951), US physician.]
MEDICINE. ***Hand–Schüller–Christian disease***, a pathological condition, often associated with diabetes insipidus, in which the bones, esp. of the skull, are invaded by lipid-laden histiocytes. Also called ***Schüller-Christian disease***, ***Schüller-Christian syndrome***, ***Schüller-Christian's disease***, ***Schüller-Christian's syndrome***.

handsel *noun & verb* var. of HANSEL *noun & verb.*

handshake /ˈhan(d)ʃeɪk/ *noun.* **L19.**
[ORIGIN from HAND *noun* + SHAKE *noun.*]
An act of handshaking, esp. in greeting or leave-taking; *fig.* an exchange of standardized signals between devices in a computer network regulating the transfer of data.

E. CRANKSHAW He preferred to surround himself with applauding sycophants, turning others away with a chilly handshake.

golden handshake: see GOLDEN *adjective.*

handshake /ˈhan(d)ʃeɪk/ *verb intrans.* **L18.**
[ORIGIN from HAND *noun* + SHAKE *verb.*]
Participate in a handshake (*lit.* & *fig.*). Orig. & chiefly as HANDSHAKING.
■ **handshaker** *noun* **E20.**

handshaking /ˈhan(d)ʃeɪkɪŋ/ *verbal noun.* **L18.**
[ORIGIN from HAND *noun* + SHAKING *verbal noun.*]
The action of shaking hands with a person. Also (COMPUTING), an exchange between a computer system and an external device or another computer, indicating that a process can be started after establishment of communication, is running properly, or is complete.

handsome /ˈhans(ə)m/ *adjective, adverb, & noun.* **LME.**
[ORIGIN from HAND *noun* + -SOME¹.]
▸**A** *adjective* **1** †**a** Easy to handle, deal with, or use in any way. **LME–L16.** ▸**b** Handy, convenient, suitable. Now *rare* exc. *dial.* **M16.**
2 Of an action, speech, agent, etc.: apt, skilled, clever. Now chiefly *US.* **M16.**

HENRY FIELDING He determined to quit her, if he could but find a handsome pretence.

3 Orig. (of conduct, action, dress, etc.), fitting, proper, becoming. Now (only of conduct or action), generous, magnanimous. **L16.**

B. TARKINGTON George.. was doing.. a handsome thing in taking a risky job for.. his aunt.

4 Now chiefly of a sum of money, a fortune, etc.: considerable; generous, ample. **L16.**

C. S. FORESTER He had seen to it that the tip was handsome without being extravagant. J. GROSS They offered serious writers.. handsome rates of pay.

5 Of fine, impressive, or stately appearance; (esp. of a man) good-looking, attractive. **L16.**

A. S. NEILL I saw some handsome lads and some pretty girls on that campus. N. MONSARRAT Her face,.. beautiful when young, markedly handsome in old age, betrayed nothing of her feelings. A. MUNRO The apartment and office are in a handsome old brick house.

▸**B** *adverb.* = HANDSOMELY. Now *rare* exc. as below. **LME.**
handsome is as handsome does one is judged by behaviour not appearance. ***high, wide, and handsome***: see HIGH *adverb.*
▸**C** *noun.* A handsome person. Used chiefly as a form of address. *colloq.* **E20.**

E. WAUGH Be a sport, handsome: no one's seen anything but you.

■ **handsomeish** *adjective* (*rare*) somewhat handsome **M18.** **handsomely** *adverb* (**a**) in a handsome manner; (**b**) (now only NAUTICAL) carefully, gradually, without haste: **M16.** **handsomeness** *noun* **M16.**

handspaik *noun* var. of HANDSPOKE.

handspike /ˈhan(d)spʌɪk/ *noun & verb.* **E16.**
[ORIGIN Dutch †*handspaeke* (now *-spaak*), from *hand* HAND *noun* + Middle Dutch *spāke* pole, rod; assim. to SPIKE *noun*².]
▸**A** *noun.* A wooden lever usu. shod with iron, used chiefly on board ship and in artillery. **E16.**
▸**B** *verb trans.* Move or strike with a handspike. **L18.**

handspoke /ˈhan(d)spəʊk/ *noun.* Chiefly *Scot.* Also **-spaik** /-speɪk/. **E18.**
[ORIGIN from HAND *noun* + SPOKE *noun.*]
A spoke or bar of wood held in the hand and used esp. for carrying the coffin at a funeral.

handwork /ˈhandwəːk/ *noun.* **OE.**
[ORIGIN from HAND *noun* + WORK *noun.*]
†**1** = HANDIWORK 1. **OE–L19.**
2 Working with the hands; work done by the hands, esp. as opp. to work done by or with machinery. **OE.**
■ **handworked** *adjective* worked or made by hand not machine **E19.** **handworker** *noun* a manual worker **M19.**

handwrite /ˈhandrʌɪt/ *noun. Scot., Irish, & US.* Also (earlier) †**-writ**. **ME.**
[ORIGIN from HAND *noun* + WRITE *noun.*]
Handwriting.

handwrite /ˈhandrʌɪt/ *verb trans.* Pa. t. **-wrote** /-rəʊt/, pa. pple **-written** /-rɪt(ə)n/. E19.
[ORIGIN from HAND *noun* + WRITE *verb*.]
Write by hand; write with one's own hand. Chiefly as ***handwritten*** *ppl adjective*.

handwriting /ˈhandrʌɪtɪŋ/ *noun*. LME.
[ORIGIN from HAND *noun* + WRITING *noun*: cf. Latin *manuscriptum*, Greek *kheirographon*.]
1 Writing by hand with a pen or pencil, esp. as done by a particular person or characteristic of a particular country or historical period; *fig.* a distinctive, individually identifiable style of doing something, as painting, designing, etc. LME.

J. MORTIMER Simcox has got such awful handwriting, he's going to copy it out neatly later. J. T. STORY I looked at the page of neat, close-written, feminine handwriting.

2 That which is written by hand; a written document etc. *arch.* M16.

A. RADCLIFFE Adeline took it up, and opening it perceived a hand-writing.

– COMB.: **handwriting expert** a person who studies handwriting in order to detect forgeries etc. or infer aspects of a person's character from his or her style of writing.

handwritten, **handwrote** *verbs* see HANDWRITE *verb*.

handy /ˈhandi/ *adjective*. ME.
[ORIGIN from HAND *noun* + -Y¹; in sense 2 after HANDIWORK.]
1 Clever with the hands; dexterous. ME.

K. GRAHAME I'll teach you to row, and.. swim, and you'll soon be handy on the water. N. PEVSNER The practical, handy, inventive Englishman who rather makes a thing himself than relies on others.

2 Of or done by the hand; manual. *obsolete* exc. *Scot.* M16.
3 Ready to hand, conveniently accessible. Usu. *pred.* M17.

R. C. HUTCHINSON One keeps a coin handy for a cab-fare. A. T. ELLIS If.. I'd had a gun handy, I'd've widowed myself more than once.

4 Convenient to handle or use. L17.

A. CHRISTIE And I remember picking up the Mauser—it was a nice handy little gun.

– PHRASES: **come in handy** be (occasionally) useful. **handy for** *colloq.* conveniently situated for. **handy to** *dial.* & *N. Amer.* = ***handy for*** above.
– COMB.: **handy-billy** NAUTICAL a small tackle with one double and one single block which can multiply the power exerted by four times when required; **handyman** a person able to do various odd jobs esp. in house or building maintenance; **handy-sized** *adjective* of a convenient size.

handycuffs *noun pl.* var. of HANDICUFFS.

handy-dandy /ˈhandɪdandi/ *noun* & *adverb*. LME.
[ORIGIN Redupl. rhyme from HANDY *adjective*.]
▸ **A** *noun*. †**1** A covert bribe or present. Only in LME.
2 A children's game in which one player guesses which of the other players' hands conceals some object. Also as *interjection*, the call offering the choice between the two hands. L16.
▸ **B** *adverb*. †**1** With bribery or other covert payment. Only in LME.
2 With change of places; alternately. Long *rare*. E16.

handygrip *noun* var. of HANDGRIP.

handy-work *noun* see HANDIWORK.

hanepoot /ˈhɑːnəpʊət/ *noun*. *S. Afr.* L18.
[ORIGIN Afrikaans, from Dutch *haan* cock + *poot* foot.]
1 A variety of sweet muscat grape, often used for making wine or raisins. L18.
2 A sweet white wine made from these grapes. E19.

hang /haŋ/ *noun*. L18.
[ORIGIN from the verb.]
1 The way in which a thing (esp. a garment) hangs or is poised. L18. ▸**b** The hanging of pictures, esp. for an exhibition. M20.

A. BROOKNER The minute adjustments to.. the hang of a skirt.

2 The action of hanging, drooping, or bending down. Also, a downward inclination, a droop; a declivity. E19. ▸**b** A slackening or suspension of motion. M19.

LEIGH HUNT Never shall I forget her face.. with that weary hang of the head on one side.

3 Something that hangs or is suspended, esp. a crop of fruit. E19.

A. JOBSON She had.. a nice hang of apples.

4 A negligible amount. Chiefly in ***not care a hang***, ***not give a hang*** below. *colloq.* M19.

V. WOOLF They don't care a hang for the upper classes.

– PHRASES: **get the hang of** *colloq.* become familiar with the use of (a tool etc.); *fig.* come to understand or manage, get the knack of. **hang of a** *adjective* & *adverb* (*Austral.* & *NZ colloq.*); (*a*) *adjective* a great, a big, a terrible; (*b*) *adverb* very, extremely, terribly. **like hang** *Austral.* & *NZ colloq.* exceedingly. **not care a hang**, **not give a hang** *colloq.* not care at all.

hang /haŋ/ *verb*. Pa. t. & pple **hung** /hʌŋ/, (*arch.* exc. in sense 2) **hanged**.
[ORIGIN Old English *hangian* verb intrans. = Old Frisian *hangia*, Old Saxon *hangon*, Old High German *hangēn* (Dutch, German *hangen*), from a West Germanic weak verb; partly from Old Norse *hanga* verb trans. = Old English *hōn*, Old Frisian *hūa*, Old Saxon, Old High German *hāhan*, Gothic *hāhan*, from a Germanic redupl. verb.]
▸ **I** *verb trans.* **1** Support or suspend (a thing) from above, allowing it otherwise to take the position determined by gravity or any external force; fasten or attach to an object above. OE. ▸**b** Suspend (meat) in the air to mature or dry. L16.

P. MORTIMER In the next garden but one, a woman was hanging washing on the line. G. CHARLES Where did we finally decide to hang those two Broidal portraits..? **b** J. GRIGSON Their butchers.. choose good animals, hang them properly and cut and present the meat well.

2 Orig., crucify. Later, kill by suspending by the neck, esp. as a form of capital punishment; *colloq.* in imprecations as ***hang it*** (***all***), ***hang me***, etc., expr. anger, contempt, irritation, etc. (cf. DAMN *verb* 3). OE. ▸**b** *refl.* Commit suicide by suspending oneself by the neck. ME.

J. ARBUTHNOT Part with my country-seat.. I'll see him hanged first. R. S. SURTEES 'Hang the rain!' exclaimed Jawleyford. *Observer* I am hanged if I will ask a woman to offload 30 tons of peat. J. CARY This unsavoury Lothario killed his paramour.. ran away to London, was.. arrested and duly hanged. **b** W. LOWTHER You may regard it as only giving them rope to hang themselves!

3 Cause or allow to droop, bend downward, or lean over. Freq. in ***hang one's head*** below. OE. ▸**b** SURFING. Allow (a specified number of toes) to project beyond the nose of the surfboard. M20.
4 Attach so as to allow free movement about the point of attachment; attach in a well-balanced or poised position. LME.

W. WHARTON I build and hang the door.

5 Decorate or provide *with* (things suspended or fastened on); *esp.* attach (wallpaper) to a wall. Also, furnish (a gallery etc.) with pictures. Freq. in *pass.* LME.

Listener The National Gallery is most beautifully hung now. J. RATHBONE The walls were not hung with painted paper but whitewashed.

6 Reduce to or keep in a state of indecision or inaction. Freq. in ***hang a jury*** below. Chiefly *US*. L18.

Guardian The lone juror who finally hangs the jury will not emerge.. unless.. his view has some support.

7 Catch or fasten in something; *esp.* hitch up (a horse). Chiefly *US*. M19.
▸ **II** *verb intrans.* **8** Be or remain fastened or suspended from above; dangle; swing loose. OE. ▸**b** Be decorated or furnished with things suspended or attached. LME. ▸**c** Of meat: be suspended in the air to mature or dry. M19.

J. BUCHAN A flagstaff from which an enormous Union Jack hung limply in the still air. S. BARSTOW A suit hangs well on him when he lets it. DAY LEWIS A photograph that.. used to hang in dark corners or passages of the houses we occupied.

9 Orig., be crucified. Later, be killed by being suspended by the neck, esp. as a form of capital punishment. OE. ▸**b** In imprecations expr. anger, irritation, displeased surprise, etc. Esp. in ***go hang*** below. *colloq.* E17.

G. GREENE I found Marcel hanging from his own belt from the centre light.

10 Lean or project (*over*); bend forward or downward. OE.

E. A. FREEMAN The later castle, whose picturesque turrets and battlements hang so proudly over the river. *fig.*: S. ROGERS O'er infant innocence to hang and weep.

11 Rely *on* for support or authority; depend *on*, be dependent *on*. Also (now *rare* or *obsolete*), remain or rely in faith or expectation, count confidently *on*. OE. ▸**b** Consider attentively; listen with rapt attention. Freq. in ***hang on a person's lips***, ***hang on a person's words*** below. ME.

T. HARDY Everything now hung upon their mother's assent. J. BUCHAN My neck's safety was to hang on my own wits. **b** *Times Lit. Suppl.* Desdemona.. hung on to every detail in Othello's narrative.

12 Be attached or suspended so as to allow free movement or attachment; be attached in a well-balanced or poised position. ME.

C. PHILLIPS The gate still hung drunkenly from its hinges.

13 Appear to be suspended; rest or float (in air etc.). ME. ▸**b** *fig.* Esp. of something unpleasant: hover *over*, ready to fall; impend, be imminent. M16.

V. BRITTAIN The harvest moon hung like a Chinese lantern in the sky. **b** *fig.*: H. NICOLSON The dread of the ordeal.. had been hanging over me like a sullen cloud. R. INGALLS They ought to get rid of the duties first, so as not to have them hanging over their heads.

14 Attach oneself, esp. for support, cling (*up*)*on*; adhere, stick *on*, *to*, etc.; *arch.* be a hanger-on or dependant. ME. ▸**b** Of the wind: remain persistently in a certain point of the compass. L17.

SHAKES. *Tam. Shr.* She hung about my neck, and kiss on kiss she vied so fast. I. MCEWAN. I hang on to the side of the boat. E. FEINSTEIN She hung on to her job for five and a half months. *fig.*: W. SOMERVILLE The patient Pack Hang on the Scent unweary'd.

15 Cling or adhere as an encumbrance; (esp. of time) be a burden. LME.

SHELLEY Most heavy remorse hangs at my heart. W. PIKE Time did not hang at all heavily.

16 Be or remain in suspense; be doubtful or undecided. LME. ▸†**b** Remain unsettled or unfinished. L15–E18. ▸**c** Of a jury: be unable to reach a verdict because of disagreement. Chiefly *US*. M19.

G. GREENE I hung between life and death.. for exactly five days.

17 Of (a note in) music: be prolonged. L16.
18 Slacken motion perceptibly (esp. in CRICKET & BASEBALL); remain with motion suspended. M17.
19 Stay as unwilling or unable to leave or move on, freq. as a parasitical attachment; loiter, linger, wait, *about*, *around*, etc. M19.

H. JAMES He hung about,.. took up the time of busy people. W. SOYINKA The occasional kind-hearted guard who would.. let him hang outside for a while. R. INGALLS Trouble-maker.. who had the money and the time to hang around getting drunk.

20 Of a horse: veer to one side. M20.

– PHRASES, & WITH ADVERBS & PREPOSITIONS IN SPECIALIZED SENSES: **go hang** *colloq.* go to hell; be dismissed or rejected. **hang about** loiter about, not move away or disperse. **hang a jury** (chiefly *US*) prevent a jury by disagreement from reaching a verdict. **hang a left**, **hang a right**, etc., (orig. *US*) turn left, right, etc. **hang around** = *hang about* above. *hang as high as* HAMAN. **hang back** resist advance esp. by inertia; show reluctance to act or move, keep to the rear. **hang by a hair**, **hang by a thread**, etc., (of a person's life etc.) be in a precarious state; be determinable either way by something still in doubt. **hang fire** (of a firearm) be slow in going off; *fig.* be delayed in action. **hang heavy**, **hang heavily** (of time) pass slowly. **hang in** *colloq.* (chiefly *N. Amer.*) persist in spite of adversity, hold out. ***hang in the balance***: see BALANCE *noun*. ***hang it*** (***all***): see sense 2 above. **hang it up** (*a*) *slang* give credit; (*b*) *US colloq.* resign or retire from a post. **hang loose** *colloq.* be casual or unconcerned. ***hang me*** etc.: see sense 2 above. **hang off** (*a*) *arch.* let go; (*b*) hesitate, hang back. **hang on** (*a*) linger, esp. with reluctance or inability to leave, wait for a short time (freq. as *imper.*, be patient! be reasonable!), *colloq.* (in telephoning) not ring off; (*b*) see sense 11 above; (*c*) attend closely to; (*d*) ***hang on a person's lips***, ***hang on a person's words***, listen attentively to a person; (*e*) stick or hold closely (*to*); (*f*) remain in office, stick to duty etc.; (*g*) ***hang on to*** (colloq.), retain, not let go of. **hang one on** *colloq.* deal (someone) a blow. **hang one's head** show shame, embarrassment, or despondency by letting one's head droop forward. **hang out** (*a*) (cause to) protrude downwards; ***let it all hang out*** (slang), be uninhibited; (*b*) suspend (a sign, colours, etc.) from a window on a projecting pole etc.; (*c*) suspend (washing etc.) from a clothes line etc. outside (*to dry*); ***hang one's bat out to dry*** (CRICKET), play an indecisive defensive stroke at a ball outside off stump, either missing or edging the ball; (*d*) *slang* reside, be often present; associate *with*; (*e*) (chiefly *Austral.* & *NZ*) endure, hold out. ***hang the rap on***: see RAP *noun*¹. **hang together** (*a*) stick or adhere together loosely; (*b*) be coherent or consistent; make a coherent or consistent whole; (*c*) be associated, united, or mutually dependent; (of a person) keep body and soul together, survive. **hang tough** *N. Amer.* be or remain inflexible or firmly resolved. **hang up** (*a*) suspend (a garment, utensil, etc.) from a hook, rail, etc.; freq. in ***hang up one's boots***, give up playing a sport, ***hang up one's fiddle*** (see FIDDLE *noun*), ***hang up one's hat***, make one's home, ***hang up one's sword***, ***hang up one's gun***, etc., lay aside, give up using, one's sword, gun, etc.; (*b*) (of a garment, utensil, etc.) be suspended from a hook, rail, etc.; (*c*) put aside, postpone indefinitely, hinder; (*d*) *Austral.* & *NZ* hitch up (a horse); (*e*) end a telephone conversation with someone (freq. foll. by *on*); (*f*) replace (a telephone receiver); (*g*) cause delay or difficulty or (*slang*, freq. in *pass.*) obsession to. ***let it all hang out***: see ***hang out*** above.
– COMB.: **hang-by** (*obsolete* exc. *dial.*) (*a*) *derog.* a dependant, a hanger-on; (*b*) an appendage, an adjunct; **hang-fire** a delay in the igniting of a firearm or a blasting charge; **hang-glider** a small glider from which the operator is suspended in a frame and which is controlled by movements of the body; **hang-gliding** the operation of a hang-glider, esp. as a sport; **hang-out** *slang* a place of residence or frequent visitation; **hang-up** a difficulty, an obsession, an inhibition.
■ **hangable** *adjective* able or liable to be hanged; *esp.* (of an offence) punishable by hanging: L16. **hangworthy** *adjective* (*rare*) worthy of being hanged L16.

hangar /ˈhaŋə/ *noun*. L17.
[ORIGIN French, of unknown origin.]
A shed, a shelter. Now *spec.*, a large building for housing aircraft etc.
– NOTE: Rare before M19.

hangarage /ˈhaŋərɪdʒ/ *noun*. M20.
[ORIGIN from HANGAR + -AGE.]
Accommodation for aircraft etc. in a hangar.

hangbird /ˈhaŋbəːd/ *noun*. *N. Amer.* L18.
[ORIGIN from HANG *verb* + BIRD *noun*.]
A bird which builds a hanging nest; *esp.* the northern oriole *Icterus galbula*.

hangdog /ˈhaŋdɒg/ *noun* & *adjective*. L17.
[ORIGIN from HANG *verb* + DOG *noun*.]
▸ **A** *noun*. A despicable or degraded fellow. L17.
▸ **B** *adjective*. Having a dejected or guilty appearance; shamefaced. L17.

H

H

S. T. WARNER I am feeling hangdog and apprehensive. E. BLISHEN The headmaster was addressing a hangdog group of boys.

hanger /ˈhaŋə/ *noun*[1].
[ORIGIN Old English *hangra* deriv. of HANG *verb*: now identified with HANGER *noun*[2].]
A wood on the side of a steep hill or bank.

hanger /ˈhaŋə/ *noun*[2]. LME.
[ORIGIN from HANG *verb* + -ER[1].]
1 A person who hangs (someone or something); *spec.*: ▸**a** A person who kills or causes another to be killed by hanging, esp. as a form of capital punishment; one who advocates this. LME. ▸**b** A person who causes a thing to be suspended or fastened on; *spec.* one who selects and hangs pictures for an exhibition. L18.

a I. MCEWAN He decided to speak against the hangers in the annual punishment debate.

2 Something that hangs down or is suspended. LME.
3 A device by or on which something is hung; a support. E16. ▸**b** A loop or strap on a sword belt for hanging the sword from. *obsolete* exc. *hist.* L16. ▸**c** A chain or rod in a fireplace for suspending a pot or kettle from by means of a pot-hook. Also, (a child's name for) a stroke with a double curve made in learning to write (chiefly in ***pot-hooks and hangers***). L16. ▸**d** A loop by which something, esp. a garment, is hung up. L17. ▸**e** A coat hanger. L19.

J. S. FOSTER Floor joists.. should preferably not be supported by metal hangers. **e** P. ROTH Then from a hanger she took down a plaid hooded jacket.

4 Something that overhangs; *MINING* the rock over a lode or vein. M17.
– COMB.: **hanger-back** a person who hangs back; **hanger-on** (freq. *derog.*) a follower, a dependant.

hanger /ˈhaŋə/ *noun*[3]. LME.
[ORIGIN Prob. identical with HANGER *noun*[2]: cf. early mod. Dutch *hangher*, perh. the immediate source.]
hist. A type of short sword, orig. hung from the belt.

hangi /ˈhaŋi, ˈhɑːŋi/ *noun*. Chiefly *NZ*. M19.
[ORIGIN Maori.]
A pit in which food is cooked on heated stones; the food cooked in such a pit.

hangie /ˈhaŋi/ *noun*. *Scot.* (now chiefly *arch.*). E18.
[ORIGIN from HANG *verb* + -IE.]
A hangman; a worthless person. Also, the Devil.

hanging /ˈhaŋɪŋ/ *noun*. ME.
[ORIGIN from HANG *verb* + -ING[1].]
1 The action or an instance of hanging a person (esp. as a form of capital punishment); the fact of being hanged. ME.
2 The action of suspending; the fact of being suspended; suspension. LME.
3 Something that hangs or is suspended, *esp.* (usu. in *pl.*), tapestries etc. with which walls etc. are hung; something attached, an appendage. LME.

J. S. FOSTER Solid wall covered externally with slate, tile or other hanging. A. S. BYATT The room had no character, and dark green silk hangings.

4 A downward slope or curve; *esp.* (now *local*) a steep slope or declivity of a hill. LME.
5 The state of being in suspense, left aside, or waiting for some time. M17.
– COMB.: **hanging committee**: to decide the hanging of pictures in an exhibition; **hanging day**: on which judicial hangings are carried out; **hanging matter** a matter likely to result in severe punishment; a serious matter; **hanging wardrobe**: designed for clothes hanging at full length.

hanging /ˈhaŋɪŋ/ *adjective*. ME.
[ORIGIN from HANG *verb* + -ING[2].]
1 Leaning over; overhanging; steep, declivitous; *esp.* (of a wood, garden, etc.) so situated as to (appear to) hang. ME.
†**2** Remaining in suspense or abeyance; pending. LME–L16.
3 Supported or suspended from above; projecting downward; drooping. L15.
4 Gloomy or depressed-looking. L16.
5 That causes (people) to be hanged. Chiefly in ***hanging judge*** below. M19.
– SPECIAL COLLOCATIONS: **hanging basket** a suspended basket or other container for growing decorative plants. **hanging bird** = HANGBIRD. **hanging bowl** *ARCHAEOLOGY* a metal bowl of the Bronze Age or Anglo-Saxon period designed to be suspended. **hanging drop** a drop of liquid containing living cells or organisms, suspended from a cover glass to allow viewing in a microscope. **hanging glacier** a small glacier on a steep slope, from whose lower end ice may occasionally fall. **hanging guard** *FENCING* (chiefly *hist.*) a type of defence. **hanging indentation**, **hanging indention** *TYPOGRAPHY* the indentation of all lines but the first of a paragraph. **hanging judge** a judge who habitually sentences harshly, *esp.* one who is predisposed towards sentencing to death. **hanging lie** *GOLF* the position of a ball lying on ground sloping downhill in the direction of play. **hanging paragraph** = ***hanging indentation*** above. **hanging pawn** *CHESS* either of two advanced pawns, side by side with no adjacent pawns to support them. **hanging shelf** a suspended shelf. **hanging sleeve** a loose open sleeve hanging down from the arm, formerly worn by children. **hanging valley**: that is cut across by the side of a deeper valley (esp. one enlarged by glaciation) or by a sea cliff. **hanging wall** (**a**) *MINING* the rock which hangs over a lode; (**b**) *GEOLOGY* the fault block which lies above an inclined fault.

hangman /ˈhaŋmən/ *noun*. Pl. **-men**. ME.
[ORIGIN from HANG *verb* + MAN *noun*.]
1 An executioner, *esp.* one who executes by hanging. Also, a worthless person. ME.
2 A word game for two or more players, in which a tally of failed guesses is kept by drawing a gallows one stroke at a time. M20.
■ **hangmanlike** *adjective & adverb* (*rare*) (in the manner) of a hangman L17. **hangmanship** *noun* (*rare*) the office or function of hangman E19.

hangment /ˈhaŋm(ə)nt/ *noun*. *obsolete* exc. *dial.* LME.
[ORIGIN from HANG *verb* + -MENT.]
Hanging; execution.
who the hangment, **what the hangment**, etc.: expr. surprise.

hangnail /ˈhaŋneɪl/ *noun*. L17.
[ORIGIN Alt. of AGNAIL.]
A piece of torn skin at the root of a fingernail or toenail; soreness resulting from this.

hang-nest /ˈhaŋnɛst/ *noun*. *N. Amer.* Now *rare*. L17.
[ORIGIN from HANG *verb* + NEST *noun*.]
A hangbird.

hangover /ˈhaŋəʊvə/ *noun*. L19.
[ORIGIN from HANG *verb* + OVER *adverb*.]
1 A person or thing remaining, left over or behind; a remainder, a survival; an after-effect. L19.

L. DENNY That easily inspired hatred of Germany remained as a hang-over in America.

2 *spec.* A set of unpleasant after-effects of (esp. alcoholic) overindulgence. E20.

P. PARISH Even moderate amounts of alcohol, and even a slight hangover, impair driving ability.

3 *ELECTRICITY.* Delay in the cessation of output, esp. of a loudspeaker. M20.

Hang Seng /haŋ ˈsɛŋ/ *adjective*. M20.
[ORIGIN A bank in Hong Kong.]
Designating an index of selected securities on the Hong Kong Stock Exchange.

hangul /ˈhaŋɡʊl/ *noun*[1]. M19.
[ORIGIN Kashmiri *hāngul*.]
A red deer, *Cervus elaphus*, of the Kashmiri subspecies.

hangul /ˈhaŋɡʊl/ *noun*[2]. M20.
[ORIGIN Korean, from *Han* Korea + *kul* script, alphabet.]
The Korean phonetic alphabet. Also called ***onmun***.

hanif /haˈniːf/ *noun*. Also **haneef**. M18.
[ORIGIN Arabic *ḥanīf*, an epithet applied to Abraham in the Koran.]
Among Muslims, a follower of the original and true (monotheistic) religion.

haniwa /ˈhanɪwə/ *noun*. Pl. same. M20.
[ORIGIN Japanese.]
ARCHAEOLOGY. A clay image based on a cylindrical shape of a type placed outside Japanese tombs of the 5th to 7th cent.

hanjar *noun* var. of KHANJAR.

hanjee *noun* var. of KHANJEE.

hank /haŋk/ *noun*. ME.
[ORIGIN Old Norse *hǫnk*, genit. *hankar* (cf. *hanki* hasp, clasp; Swedish *hank* hank, withy-band, farrier's rowel, Danish *hank* handle, ear of a pot).]
1 A (circular) loop or coil of something flexible. ME. ▸**b** A skein or coil of yarn, thread, etc.; *spec.* a definite length of cotton yarn (840 yards), worsted (560 yards), etc. E16.

D. LODGE The hank of dark hair falling across his eyes. **b** *Embroidery* Crewel wools are obtainable in skeins or the larger hanks.

2 A loop of string, wire, etc., used to fasten things together or hang a thing up; *spec.* a fastening for a gate. Chiefly *dial.* ME. ▸**b** *NAUTICAL.* A hoop or ring of rope, iron, etc., for securing staysails to stays. E18.
3 The handle of a jug or pot. *dial.* M16.
4 A restraining hold, a power of restraint. Freq. in ***have a hank on someone***, ***have a hank over someone***. Now *rare* or *dial.* E17.
5 A propensity, an evil habit. Chiefly *dial.* E18.
†**6** A baiting of an animal. *slang.* L18–L19.

hank /haŋk/ *verb*. ME.
[ORIGIN Old Norse *hanka* to coil, from *hǫnk*: see HANK *noun* Sense 2 perh. formed as HANKER.]
1 *verb trans.* Fasten by a loop; catch by a loop etc. (now *dial.*); *NAUTICAL* fasten (staysails) to stays. ME.
2 *verb intrans.* = HANKER *verb*. Now *dial.* L16.
3 *verb intrans.* Hang or remain fastened; catch. E17.
4 *verb trans.* Make up (yarn etc.) in hanks. E19.
†**5** *verb trans.* Bait (an animal). *slang.* Only in 19.

hanker /ˈhaŋkə/ *verb & noun*. E17.
[ORIGIN Prob. rel. to HANG *verb*: cf. synon. Dutch *hunkeren*, dial. *hankeren*. Cf. HANK *verb* 2.]
▸ **A** *verb intrans.* **1** Linger or loiter *about* in longing or expectation. Now *dial.* E17.

JOYCE He hankered about the coffee-houses and low taverns.

2 Have a longing or craving *after*, *for*, *to do*. E17.

SAKI Instead of the news she was hankering for, she had to listen to trivial gossip. N. MOSLEY The hankering after small boys seldom got beyond.. loitering romantically in passageways.

▸ **B** *noun.* A hankering. *rare.* E19.
■ **hankerer** *noun* M19. **hankering** *noun* (**a**) the action of the verb; (**b**) a craving, a longing: M17.

hanksite /ˈhaŋksʌɪt/ *noun*. L19.
[ORIGIN from H. G. *Hanks* (1826–1907), US mineralogist + -ITE[1].]
MINERALOGY. A hexagonal sulphate and carbonate of sodium, also containing potassium and chloride, occurring as white or yellow prisms.

†**Hankton** *noun & adjective* see YANKTON.

hanky /ˈhaŋki/ *noun*. *colloq.* Also **-kie**. L19.
[ORIGIN Contr.: see -Y[6], -IE.]
A handkerchief.

hanky-panky /haŋkɪˈpaŋki/ *noun*. M19.
[ORIGIN Rel. to HOCUS-POCUS, perh. with a suggestion of 'sleight of hand'.]
Orig., juggling, conjuring. Later, trickery, underhand dealing; questionable behaviour, esp. surreptitious or illicit sexual activity.

E. H. YATES If there was any hanky-panky, any mystery I mean. *New Yorker* They were still 'courting'.. in Dr. Rounds' boarding house.. where.. no hanky-panky was permitted.

Hannibal /ˈhanɪb(ə)l/ *noun*. Long *rare* or *obsolete*. L16.
[ORIGIN *Hannibal* (247–182 BC), Carthaginian general.]
A great general.

Hannibalic /hanɪˈbalɪk/ *adjective*. L17.
[ORIGIN from HANNIBAL + -IC.]
Of, pertaining to, or characteristic of Hannibal.

Hanoverian /hanə(ʊ)ˈvɪərɪən/ *adjective & noun*. E18.
[ORIGIN from *Hanover*, a northern German state, an electorate of the Empire ruled by the Guelph dynasty and subsequently a province of Prussia, or the town of the same name, capital of Lower Saxony and formerly capital of the state of Hanover: see -IAN.]
▸ **A** *adjective*. Of, pertaining to, or characteristic of (the House of) Hanover, the dynasty of British monarchs from George I (Elector of Hanover) to Victoria, reigning in the period 1714–1901. E18.
▸ **B** *noun*. A native or inhabitant of Hanover; a member or an adherent of the House of Hanover. L18.

Hans /hans/ *noun*. M16.
[ORIGIN German & Dutch abbreviation of *Johannes* John.]
(A name for) a German, a Dutchman.

Hansard /ˈhansɑːd, -səd/ *noun*[1]. ME.
[ORIGIN from HANSE + -ARD.]
A merchant or citizen of a Hanseatic town.

Hansard /ˈhansɑːd, -səd/ *noun*[2]. L19.
[ORIGIN Thomas C. *Hansard*, English printer (1776–1833): see below.]
The official (verbatim) report of the proceedings of the British Parliament, (compiled by Messrs Hansard 1774–1892, now published by HMSO). Also, the official report of certain other legislative bodies.
■ **Hansardize** *verb trans.* (now *rare*) confront (a Member of Parliament) with his former statements recorded in Hansard; prove (a person) to have expressed a different opinion previously: M19.

Hanse /hans/ *noun*[1]. Also **h-**. ME.
[ORIGIN Middle Low German *hanshūs* and medieval Latin *hansa* from Old High German *hansa*, Middle & mod. High German *hanse* (whence Middle Low German *hanse*) = Old English *hōs* (instr. only) troop, company, Gothic *hansa* company, crowd, from Germanic, whence also Finnish *kansa* people, company.]
hist. **1** A merchant guild. ME. ▸**b** *spec.* (A merchant, citizen, or town of) the Hanseatic League. LME.
2 A membership fee payable to a merchant guild; a trading fee imposed on non-members of the guild. ME.
– COMB.: **Hanse-house** a guildhall; **Hanse town** a town of the Hanseatic League.

hanse *noun*[2] var. of HANCE.

Hanseatic /hansɪˈatɪk/ *adjective*. E17.
[ORIGIN medieval Latin *Hanseaticus*, formed as HANSE *noun*[1] + -ATIC.]
hist. Designating, of, or pertaining to a political and commercial league of northern German towns, established in the mid 14th cent.

hansel /ˈhans(ə)l/ *noun & verb*. *arch.* or *US*. Also **handsel**. ME.
[ORIGIN Corresp. to late Old English *handselen* delivery into the hand and Old Norse *handsal* giving of the hand, esp. in a promise or bargain (Old Swedish *handsal*, Swedish *handsöl* money handed over, gratuity, Danish *handsel* earnest money); ult. formed as HAND *noun* + base of SELL *verb*.]
▸ **A** *noun*. †**1** Luck, fortune; a token, omen or indication of (good or bad) luck. ME–L17.
2 A gift supposedly bringing good luck, given to mark the beginning of a new year, a new enterprise, etc. LME.

H. T. COCKBURN About the New Year.. every child had got its handsel, and every farthing of every handsel was spent there.

3 A first instalment of a payment; the first money taken by a trader in the morning; *gen.* anything given or taken as a pledge of what is to follow. LME.
4 The first use, experience, trial, etc., of anything; a foretaste. L16.

P. HOLLAND But this Perillus was the first himselfe that gaue the handsell to the engine of his own inuention.

▸ **B** *verb trans.* Infl. **-ll-**.

1 Give hansel to (a person). LME.

2 Inaugurate with some ceremony or gift; *gen.* inaugurate the use of, be the first to use, try, or test. E17.

M. DELANY Send in . . wine to your cellar at Welsbourne, by way of hanselling a new place.

Hansen /ˈhans(ə)n/ *noun.* E20.
[ORIGIN G. H. A. *Hansen* (1841–1912), Norwegian physician.]
MEDICINE. **1** ***Hansen's bacillus***, ***Hansen bacillus***, the causative agent of Hansen's disease, *Mycobacterium leprae*. E20.
2 ***Hansen's disease***, a chronic bacterial disease of low infectivity, confined mainly to the tropics, affecting the skin, nerves, and mucous membranes and causing numbness, discoloration and lumps on the skin, and, in severe cases, disfigurement and deformity (now the most usual condition referred to as ***leprosy***). M20.

hansom /ˈhans(ə)m/ *noun.* M19.
[ORIGIN Joseph Aloysius *Hansom* (1803–82) architect, who registered a Patent Safety Cab in 1834.]
Chiefly *hist.* In full ***hansom cab***. A two-wheeled cabriolet for two inside, with the driver mounted behind and the reins going over the roof.

†**hanster** *noun* var. of HANASTER.

hantavirus /ˈhantəvʌɪrəs/ *noun.* L20.
[ORIGIN mod. Latin, from *Hantaan*, the Korean river where the virus was first isolated + VIRUS.]
Any of a group of viruses carried by rodents and causing various febrile haemorrhagic diseases, often with kidney damage or failure.

hantle /ˈhant(ə)l/ *noun. Scot. & N. English.* L17.
[ORIGIN Unknown.]
A (large) number or quantity.

L. G. GIBBON He ran a hantle more silver into his own pouch than he ran into theirs.

Hants *abbreviation.*
Hampshire.

hantu /ˈhantuː/ *noun.* E19.
[ORIGIN Malay.]
An evil spirit; a ghost etc.

Hanukkah /ˈhanʊkə, x-/ *noun.* Also **Chanuk(k)ah** /ˈxan-/. L19.
[ORIGIN Hebrew *ḥănukkāh* consecration.]
A Jewish festival, commemorating the purification and rededication of the Temple at Jerusalem in 165 BC by Judas Maccabaeus after its pollution by the Syrians. Also called ***festival of lights***.

Hanuman /hʌnʊˈmɑːn/ *noun.* In sense 2 now usu. **h-**. E19.
[ORIGIN Sanskrit *hanumant*, nom. *hanumān* large-jawed.]
1 *HINDU MYTHOLOGY.* (The name of) a semi-divine being represented as resembling a monkey with extraordinary powers. E19.
2 A common grey monkey of India, *Presbytis entellus*, venerated by Hindus. Also ***Hanuman langur***. M19.

hào /haʊ/ *noun.* Pl. same, **-s**. M20.
[ORIGIN Vietnamese.]
A monetary unit of Vietnam, equal to one-tenth of a dong.

haole /ˈhaʊli/ *noun.* E19.
[ORIGIN Hawaiian.]
In Hawaii: a person who is not a native Hawaiian; a white person.

haoma *noun* var. of HOM.

haori /ˈhɑːɒri/ *noun.* L19.
[ORIGIN Japanese.]
In Japan, a short loose coat.

hap /hap/ *noun. arch.* ME.
[ORIGIN Old Norse *happ* rel. to Old English *ġehæp(lić)* fitting, convenient, orderly.]
1 The fortune (good or bad) that falls to a person; one's lot. ME.

W. WARING It has not been my hap to meet with it elsewhere.

2 A fortuitous occurrence, a happening; *esp.* an unfortunate event, a mischance. ME.

GEO. ELIOT All the 'haps' of my life are so indifferent.

†**3** Success, prosperity, good fortune. ME–E19.
4 Chance considered as determining events. ME.

Quiver By curious hap . . [she] was actually located at 'The Beeches'.

by hap, **through hap** casually, by chance.

hap /hap/ *verb*[1] *intrans. arch. & dial.* Infl. **-pp-**. Pa. t. & pple **happed**, **hapt**. ME.
[ORIGIN from the noun: superseded by HAPPEN *verb*.]
1 Of an event etc.: come about by chance. (Freq. with impers. subj.; formerly also with person affected as indirect obj.) ME.

TENNYSON Never had huger slaughter of heroes . . Hapt in this isle.

2 Have the fortune or luck *to do*. LME.

J. GAY A maiden fine bedight he hapt to love.

3 Foll. by *on*, *upon*: meet with or find by chance. LME.

A. B. GROSART [This book] I have not been fortunate enough to hap upon.

†**4** Have luck of a specified kind; fare (*well*, *ill*, etc.). LME–E17.

hap /hap/ *verb*[2] *trans.* Now only *Scot. & dial.* Infl. **-pp-**. ME.
[ORIGIN Prob. of Scandinavian origin]
Cover; *esp.* cover with bedclothes or extra clothing, wrap up warmly, (foll. by *up*).

hapax /ˈhapaks/ *noun.* M20.
[ORIGIN Abbreviation.]
= HAPAX LEGOMENON.

hapaxanthic /hapakˈsanθɪk/ *adjective.* L19.
[ORIGIN from Greek *hapax* once + *anthein* to flower + -IC.]
BOTANY. Of a plant: flowering and fruiting only once in its life; monocarpic.
■ Also **hapaxanthous** *adjective* E20.

hapax legomenon /hapaks lɛˈgɒmənɒn/ *noun phr.* Pl. **hapax legomena** /-mənə/. M17.
[ORIGIN Greek = (a thing) said only once.]
A word, form, etc., of which only one recorded instance is known.
– NOTE: Used in Greek characters until L19.

haphazard /hapˈhazəd/ *noun, adjective, & adverb.* L16.
[ORIGIN from HAP *noun* + HAZARD *noun*, lit. 'hazard of chance'.]
▸ **A** *noun.* **1** Mere chance, fortuitousness. Chiefly in ***at haphazard***, ***by haphazard***. L16.

Spectator The . . hereditary principle, with all its necessary haphazard.

†**2** A matter of chance. L16–L17.
▸ **B** *adjective.* Occurring, put together, etc., casually or without design; random. L17.

S. BELLOW It was a shuffle, all, all accidental and haphazard. K. MOORE The haphazard ways of the household harassed her.

▸ **C** *adverb.* Casually, at random. M19.

F. HARRISON This new social system did not come hap-hazard.

■ **haphazardly** *adverb* L19. **haphazardness** *noun* M19. **haphazardry** *noun* haphazard quality E20.

haphtarah /hɑːftɑːˈrɑː/ *noun.* Also **haf-**, **haphtorah** /hɑːfˈtəʊrə/. Pl. **-rot(h)** /-rəʊt/. E18.
[ORIGIN Hebrew *hapṭārāh* lit. 'dismissal', from *pāṭar* dismiss (because this once marked the end of the service).]
JUDAISM. A lesson from one of the Former or Latter Prophets, read in synagogues after the parashah (the reading from the Law).

hapkido /ˌhapkiːˈdəʊ/ *noun.* L20.
[ORIGIN Korean, lit. 'way of coordinated energy', from *hap* harmony, coordination + *ki* energy, strength, spirit.]
A Korean martial art of self-defence, characterized by the use of kicking and circular movements of the arms and legs.

hapless /ˈhaplɪs/ *adjective.* LME.
[ORIGIN from HAP *noun* + -LESS.]
Ill-starred, luckless.

W. BOYD The Maseru hunt took off after some hapless hyena.

■ **haplessly** *adverb* E17.

haplo- /ˈhapləʊ/ *combining form* of Greek *haploos* single, simple: see -O-. Cf. DIPLO-.
■ **haploˈdiploid** *adjective* (*BIOLOGY*) denoting or possessing a genetic system in which females develop from fertilized (diploid) eggs and males from unfertilized (haploid) ones M20. **haploˈdiploidy** *noun* (*BIOLOGY*) the haplodiploid process of reproduction M20. **haplophase** *noun* (*BIOLOGY*) the phase of an organism's life cycle in which its cells are haploid E20. **haplotype** *noun* (*BIOLOGY*) a set of genetic determinants located on a single chromosome M20.

haplography /hapˈlɒgrəfi/ *noun.* L19.
[ORIGIN from HAPLO- + -GRAPHY.]
PALAEOGRAPHY. The inadvertent writing of a letter, word, etc., once, when it should have been repeated. Opp. ***dittography***.

haploid /ˈhaplɔɪd/ *adjective & noun.* E20.
[ORIGIN from Greek *haploos* single + -OID.]
BIOLOGY. ▸**A** *adjective.* (Of a cell) containing a single set of unpaired chromosomes, as in a gamete; (of an individual) composed of haploid cells; *BOTANY* gametophytic. E20.
▸ **B** *noun.* A haploid organism, a gametophyte. E20.
■ **haploidy** *noun* haploid condition E20.

haplology /hapˈlɒlədʒi/ *noun.* L19.
[ORIGIN from HAPLO- + -LOGY.]
The utterance of one letter, syllable, or word instead of two (as *idolatry* for *idololatry*).

haplont /ˈhaplɒnt/ *noun.* E20.
[ORIGIN from HAPLOID + -ONT.]
Chiefly *BOTANY.* A sexually reproducing organism at a stage in its life cycle when it is haploid; an organism which is haploid throughout its life except as a zygote.
■ **haˈplontic** *adjective* E20.

haply /ˈhapli/ *adverb.* Now *arch. & dial.* LME.
[ORIGIN from HAP *noun* + -LY[2].]
By any chance; perhaps.

AV *Mark* 11:13 Hee came, if haply hee might find any thing thereon.

happen /ˈhap(ə)n/ *verb intrans.* LME.
[ORIGIN from HAP *noun* + -EN[5], superseding HAP *verb*[1].]
1 Of an event, experience, etc.: come about, occur. (Foll. by *to* the person or thing affected; also (*obsolete* exc. *dial.*) with indirect obj.) LME. ▸**b** With impers. subj.: occur, be the situation (*that*). LME. ▸**c** Occur or come into existence by pure chance or spontaneously. M20.

H. NELSON If anything happens to me, recollect that death is a debt we must all pay. E. S. BARRETT No harm shall happen you. G. VIDAL When we crossed into Gael, an interesting thing happened. P. ROTH I'm not someone who makes miracles happen. **b** T. BLOUNT Some of their party . . might quarter at the house (as had often hapned). W. CATHER It happened that none of the Captain's closest friends could come to his funeral. **c** L. MACNEICE As for my supporting symbols, they happened; I did not usually look for them.

2 Have the (good or bad) fortune *to do*. LME.

G. GREENE He happened to be at the airport when they arrived.

do you happen to, **you don't happen to** (in tentative requests), is it possible that you (have, know, etc.).

3 With pred. adjective or phr.: chance to be. *obsolete* exc. *dial.* LME.

SIR W. SCOTT It's the only book thou canst not happen wrong in.

4 Foll. by *on*, *upon*: find or meet with by chance. M16.
5 Foll. by *along*, *around*, *by*, *in*, *into*, *over*, etc.: come or turn up in a place casually or as if by chance. Now chiefly *N. Amer.* M16.

R. FROST I go nowhere on purpose: I happen by. P. MATTHIESSEN I . . set out binoculars in case wild creatures should happen into view.

†**6** Foll. by *to*, *unto*: fall to the lot of. L16–M18.

J. WHITGIFT If temporal dominion or possession happen to the minister of the gospel.

7 Of music, a player, etc.: succeed, come off, be effective, make an impression. *slang.* M20.

Down Beat They were all trying to create . . but it didn't really happen.

happen /ˈhap(ə)n/ *adverb. Scot. & N. English.* L15.
[ORIGIN from the verb.]
It may be that; possibly, perhaps.

happenchance /ˈhap(ə)ntʃɑːns/ *noun.* Chiefly *US.* M20.
[ORIGIN Blend of HAPPENING and CHANCE *noun*.]
= HAPPENSTANCE.

happening /ˈhap(ə)nɪŋ/ *noun & adjective.* LME.
[ORIGIN from HAPPEN *verb* + -ING[1].]
▸ **A** *noun.* **1** Occurrence (*of* an event). Formerly, chance. LME.
2 A (significant or unusual) event or occurrence. L16.
3 An improvised or spontaneous theatrical display, demonstration, etc. M20.
▸ **B** *attrib.* or as *adjective.* Eventful, significant; fashionable. *slang.* L20.

H. KUREISHI He knew the happenin' cinemas, jazz clubs, parties.

happen-so /ˈhap(ə)nsəʊ/ *noun.* Chiefly *US.* E20.
[ORIGIN from HAPPEN *verb* + SO *adverb*.]
A chance event.

happenstance /ˈhap(ə)nstans/ *noun.* Chiefly *N. Amer.* L19.
[ORIGIN Blend of HAPPENING and CIRCUMSTANCE *noun*.]
Chance; a chance event.

happi coat /ˈhapɪkəʊt/ *noun.* L19.
[ORIGIN from Japanese *happi* workman's livery coat + COAT *noun*.]
A Japanese loose outer coat. Also, a fashion garment modelled on this.

happify /ˈhapɪfʌɪ/ *verb trans.* Now chiefly *US.* E17.
[ORIGIN from HAPPY *adjective* + -FY.]
Make happy.

happily /ˈhapɪli/ *adverb.* LME.
[ORIGIN from HAPPY *adjective* + -LY[2].]
1 By chance, possibly. Long *arch.* LME.
2 By or with good fortune; fortunately. Freq. modifying a sentence. LME.

Sunday (Kolkata) Happily for India, potentially profitable sites lie along the east and west coast.

3 Appropriately, felicitously. L16.
4 With mental pleasure or contentment. L16.

happiness /ˈhapɪnɪs/ *noun.* LME.
[ORIGIN from HAPPY *adjective* + -NESS.]
1 Good fortune, success; an instance of this. LME.
2 Pleasant appropriateness, felicity; an instance of this. L16.

3 Deep pleasure in, or contentment with, one's circumstances; an instance of this. **L16.**

happy /ˈhapi/ *adjective*. **LME.**
[**ORIGIN** from **HAP** *noun* + **-Y**¹.]
1 Of a person: favoured by good fortune; fortunate, successful. Formerly also, blessed. Now chiefly *arch. & dial.* **LME.** ▸**b** Of an event or period: marked by good fortune, auspicious; esp. (now largely assoc. with sense 4) in greetings etc., as ***happy birthday!***, ***happy New Year!*** **E18.**

AV *John* 13:17 If yee know these things, happy are ye if ye doe them. C. MIDDLETON The happy seat of liberty, plenty, and letters. *Law Times* A testator in the happy position of having .. realty both in Lancashire and in America.

2 Of a chance, circumstance, etc.: involving, or occurring by, good fortune; lucky, fortunate. **LME.**

LD BERNERS It was happy for them that the wether was so fayre. W. CONGREVE What a happy Discovery. H. L. MENCKEN There is in writing the constant joy of sudden discovery, of happy accident.

3 Of an action, speech, etc.: pleasantly appropriate to the occasion or circumstances; felicitous. Of a person: dexterous in hitting on the action, words, etc., appropriate to the circumstances. **LME.**

R. BENTLEY English Translators have not been very happy in their Version of this Passage. J. S. MILL This happy thought was considered to get rid of the whole difficulty.

H

4 Feeling deep pleasure in, or contentment with, one's circumstances. Also, marked by or expressive of such feeling. **E16.** ▸**b** (In weakened sense.) Pleased, glad (*at, that, to do*); satisfied (*with*). **L18.** ▸**c** *euphem.* Mildly drunk. *colloq.* **L18.**

SCOTT FITZGERALD Happy .. bursts of laughter. S. HILL She would tell the people joyful things, cheer them up, make them happy. A. THWAITE The second marriage .. was a very happy one. *fig.*: S. M. GAULT The .. floribunds are not generally happy on chalk. **b** D. J. ENRIGHT The soldiers were happy to quit Vietnam. *South Oxfordshire Guardian* Chris .. says he's happy with the compensation from the Ministry of Defence.

5 Of an organization etc.: marked by a pleasant spirit of harmony and mutual goodwill. Freq. in ***happy ship*** below. **E20.**

— **SPECIAL COLLOCATIONS & PHRASES**: **happy as a clam**, **happy as a king**, **happy as a sandboy**, & vars., blissfully happy. **happy camper** *colloq.* a person in a good mood (usu. in neg. contexts). **happy-clappy** *adjective & noun* (*colloq., derog.*) (**a**) *adjective* belonging to or characteristic of a Christian group whose worship is marked by enthusiasm and spontaneity; (**b**) *noun* a member of such a Christian group. **happy couple** *the* bridal couple. **happy day** *the* day of a couple's wedding. **happy days!**: used as a drinking toast. **happy dispatch**: see **DISPATCH** *noun*. **happy dust** *slang* cocaine. **happy ending** an ending in a novel, play, etc., in which the leading characters acquire spouses, become rich, etc. **happy event** the birth of a child. **happy families** a game usu. played with special cards in sets of four, each set depicting the various members of a family, in which the object is to collect as many complete sets as possible. **happy family** (**a**) a group of (esp. diverse) people or creatures living together in harmony; (**b**) *Austral.* = **APOSTLE-bird**. **happy hour** (orig. *US*) a period during which a bar etc. sells drinks at reduced prices or offers free hors d'oeuvres. ***happy hunting ground***: see ***hunting ground*** s.v. **HUNTING** *verbal noun*. **happy land** a land of unusual prosperity; *spec.* heaven. **happy landings!**: used as a toast among aviators. **happy medium** = ***golden mean*** (a) s.v. **GOLDEN** *adjective*. **happy pair** = ***happy couple*** above. **happy pill** *slang* a tranquillizer. **happy release** release from misfortune; *esp.* death. **happy ship** a ship in which the crew work harmoniously together; *fig.* an organization marked by team spirit. **happy warrior** a person dauntless in the face of difficulty (esp. as a conventional designation of a good soldier). **many happy returns** (**of the day**): a greeting to a person on his or her birthday.

happy /ˈhapi/ *verb trans.* Now *arch. rare.* **L16.**
[**ORIGIN** from the adjective.]
Make happy.

-happy /ˈhapi/ *suffix*.
[**ORIGIN** from **HAPPY** *adjective*.]
Placed after nouns to form adjectives in senses (**a**) dazed or suffering stress as a result of exposure to something, as ***bomb-happy***; (**b**) preoccupied with or overfree in the use of something, as ***trigger-happy***.

happy-go-lucky /ˌhapɪɡəʊˈlʌki/ *adverb & adjective*. **L17.**
[**ORIGIN** from **HAPPY** *adjective* + **GO** *verb* + **LUCKY** *adjective*.]
▸ **A** *adverb*. Just as it may happen; haphazardly. Now *rare* or *obsolete*. **L17.**
▸ **B** *adjective*. Taking things as they come; easy-going. **M19.**
■ **happy-go-luckiness** *noun* **L19.**

hapten /ˈhapt(ə)n/ *noun*. **E20.**
[**ORIGIN** from Greek *haptein* fasten.]
IMMUNOLOGY. A small molecule which, when combined with a carrier protein, can elicit the production of antibodies.
■ **hapˈtenic** *adjective* **M20.**

hapteron /ˈhaptərɒn/ *noun*. Pl. **-ra** /rə/. **L19.**
[**ORIGIN** mod. Latin, from Greek *haptein* fasten.]
BOTANY. An organ or structure of a cryptogamic plant which serves to anchor it to a support; *esp.* the holdfast of an alga (occas. *spec.*, one of the rootlike branches into which the holdfast may be divided).

haptic /ˈhaptɪk/ *adjective*. **L19.**
[**ORIGIN** Greek *haptikos*, from *haptesthai* to grasp or touch, middle voice of *haptein* fasten: see **-IC**.]
Relating to the sense of touch; dependent on feeling by touch rather than seeing.
■ **haptically** *adverb* **M20.** **haptics** *noun* the branch of psychology or linguistics that deals with touch, esp. as a means of communication **L19.**

haptoglobin /haptəˈɡləʊbɪn/ *noun*. **M20.**
[**ORIGIN** from Greek *haptein* fasten + **-O-** + **GLOBIN**.]
BIOCHEMISTRY. Any of several alpha globulins which form complexes with free haemoglobin which are then removed from the plasma.

haptotropism /haptə(ʊ)ˈtrəʊpɪz(ə)m, -ˈtrɒp-/ *noun*. **L19.**
[**ORIGIN** from Greek *haptein* fasten + **-O-** + **-TROPISM**.]
BOTANY. The tendency of parts of a plant (e.g. tendrils) to move in a particular direction in response to external contact.

hapu /ˈhɑːpuː/ *noun*. *NZ*.
[**ORIGIN** Maori.]
A division of a Maori tribe.

hapuku /ˈhɑːpʊkuː/ *noun*. *NZ*. Also **-ka** /-kə/. **M19.**
[**ORIGIN** Maori.]
A large marine serranid food fish, *Polyprion oxygeneios*.

haqueton /ˈhakt(ə)n/ *noun*. *obsolete* exc. *hist.* **ME.**
[**ORIGIN** Alt. of **ACTON** after Old French *hocqueton* (mod. *hoqueton*).]
= **ACTON**.

harai-goshi /harʌɪˈɡɒʃi/ *noun*. **M20.**
[**ORIGIN** Japanese, from *harai* sweep + *koshi* waist, hips.]
A type of sweeping hip throw in judo.

hara-kiri /harəˈkɪri/ *noun*. Also (corruptly) **hari-** /harɪ-/. **M19.**
[**ORIGIN** Japanese, from *hara* belly + *kiri* cutting.]
In Japan, a ritual form of disembowelling, formerly prescribed by a feudal superior to disgraced members of the samurai class as an alternative to simple execution. Also, suicide by disembowelling practised voluntarily from a sense of shame, as a protest, etc.

haram /hɑːˈrɑːm/ *noun & adjective*. **E17.**
[**ORIGIN** Arabic *ḥarām* forbidden. Cf. **HAREM**.]
▸ **A** *noun*. A Muslim sacred place, forbidden to non-Muslims. **E17.**
▸ **B** *adjective*. Of food: forbidden under Islamic law. Opp. **HALAL** *adjective*. **E17.**

harambee /həˈrambiː/ *noun*. **L20.**
[**ORIGIN** Swahili, lit. 'pulling or working together' (a slogan of the first independent government of Kenya).]
In E. Africa: an event held to raise funds for a charitable purpose.

harangue /həˈraŋ/ *noun*. **LME.**
[**ORIGIN** French, earlier †*arenge* from medieval Latin *harenga*, perh. ult. from Germanic elems.]
A speech addressed to an assembly; a long, loud, or impassioned address or monologue.

T. MALLON The volumes read like a lifelong harangue from Speaker's Corner in Hyde Park.

harangue /həˈraŋ/ *verb trans. & intrans.* **L17.**
[**ORIGIN** French *haranguer*, formed as **HARANGUE** *noun*.]
Deliver a harangue or long address (to).

COLERIDGE There is no subject, which men in general like better to harangue on than politics. P. LIVELY Madame Charlot harangues the cook, in an unbroken monologue that lasts five minutes.

■ **haranguer** *noun* **M17.**

haras /arɑ/ *noun*. Pl. same. **ME.**
[**ORIGIN** Old French & mod. French, of unknown origin.]
An enclosure or establishment in which horses are kept for breeding. Formerly, a herd of such horses.
— **NOTE**: Orig. a naturalized English word, with anglicized pronunc.

harass /ˈharəs/ *noun*. **M17.**
[**ORIGIN** from the verb.]
Harassment.

harass /ˈharəs, həˈras/ *verb trans.* **E17.**
[**ORIGIN** French *harasser* pejorative deriv. of *harer* set a dog on, from *hare* cry used for this purpose.]
1 Trouble by repeated attacks. Now freq., subject to constant molesting or persecution. **E17.**

F. PARKMAN The Indians unceasingly harassed their march. S. NAIPAUL The .. programme organized by the FBI .. to harass, discredit and destroy the radical movements.

harassing agent, **harassing gas** a gas designed to incapacitate enemy troops, rioters, etc., without being lethal.
†**2** Lay waste, devastate. **E17–E18.**
†**3** Tire out, exhaust. **E17–M18.**
4 Overwhelm with cares, misfortunes, etc. Chiefly as ***harassed*** *ppl adjective*. **M17.**

D. M. THOMAS She helped a harassed woman .. who had four children to cope with.

■ **harasser** *noun* **E18.** **harassment** *noun* **M18.**

haratch *noun* see **CARATCH**.

harbinge /ˈhɑːbɪn(d)ʒ/ *verb*. Also (earlier) †**harberge**. **L15.**
[**ORIGIN** Old French *herbergier*: see **HARBINGER** *noun*, and cf. **HARBOUR** *verb*. In sense 2 back-form. from **HARBINGER** *noun*.]
†**1** *verb trans. & intrans.* Provide with or occupy lodgings. **L15–E17.**
2 *verb trans.* Be a harbinger of. *rare.* **M19.**

harbinger /ˈhɑːbɪn(d)ʒə/ *noun*. Also (earlier) †**herberger**, †**herbergeour**. **ME.**
[**ORIGIN** Anglo-Norman, Old French *herbergere* (oblique case *-geour*), from *herbergier* provide lodging for, from *herberge* lodging from Old Saxon (= Old High German) *heriberga* shelter for an army, from *heri*, *hari* host, army (see **HARRY** *verb*) + Germanic base meaning 'protect' (see **BOROUGH**). For the intrusive *n* cf. *messenger*, *passenger*, etc.]
†**1** A person who provides lodging; an entertainer, a host. **ME–E16.**
2 A person sent in advance to procure lodgings for an army, a royal train, etc. Now only *hist.*, and as title of an officer of the gentlemen-at-arms. **LME.**
3 A person sent to announce the approach of someone; a herald, a forerunner. Now chiefly *transf. & fig.*, a sign *of* some coming event or condition. **M16.**

L. GARFIELD The mad daughter of the mad father was come as harbinger of doom. J. UPDIKE The first few pimples, harbingers of messy manhood.

— **COMB.**: **harbinger-of-spring** an early-flowering N. American umbelliferous plant, *Erigenia bulbosa*.

harbinger /ˈhɑːbɪn(d)ʒə/ *verb trans.* **M17.**
[**ORIGIN** from the noun.]
Announce the approach of.

SOUTHEY The star that harbingers a glorious day.

harbor *noun*, *verb* see **HARBOUR** *noun*¹, *verb*.

harborage *noun* see **HARBOURAGE**.

†**harborough** *noun*, *verb* vars. of **HARBOUR** *noun*¹, *verb*.

harbour /ˈhɑːbə/ *noun*¹. Also ***harbor**, †**harb(o)rough**.
[**ORIGIN** Late Old English *herebeorg* corresp. to Old Saxon, Old High German *heriberga* (Dutch *herberg*, German *Herberge*), Old Norse *herbergi*: see **HARBINGER** *noun*, **-OUR**.]
1 (A place of) shelter; (a) refuge, (a) lodging. Now *arch. & dial.* **LOE.**

P. HOLLAND That the legions from out of their winter harboroughs, should there meete together. DRYDEN For harbour at a thousand doors they knocked. W. COWPER Give harbour in thy breast on no account To after-grudge or enmity.

cold harbour a roadside shelter from the weather (esp. as a place name).
2 A piece of sheltered seawater providing anchorage for ships; *esp.* one protected from rough water by piers, jetties, and other artificial structures; *spec.* such a place under statutory control as regards its use. **ME.**

DYLAN THOMAS Its cobble streets and its little fishing harbour.

3 The covert of a deer or other wild animal. **L16.**
4 A halting place for tanks. **M20.**
— **COMB.**: **harbour due(s)** a charge for the use of a harbour; **harbour master** the official in charge of a harbour, responsible for allocating berths and collecting harbour dues; **harbour seal** *N. Amer.* the common seal, *Phoca vitulina* (so called because it often frequents estuaries).

harbour *noun*² see **ARBOUR**.

harbour /ˈhɑːbə/ *verb*. Also ***harbor**, †**harborough**.
[**ORIGIN** Late Old English *hereborgian* corresp. to Middle Dutch & mod. Dutch *herbergen*, Old High German *heribergōn*, Old Norse *herbergja*, cogn. with **HARBOUR** *noun*¹.]
▸ **I** *verb intrans.* **1** Occupy shelter or lodging, latterly esp. for concealment. Now *arch. & dial.* **LOE.**

Z. M. PIKE I was suspicious that possibly some party of Indians might be harboring round.

2 Of an animal, *spec.* a stag: have its lair or covert. **L15.**
3 Of a ship etc.: take shelter in a harbour. **L16.** ▸**b** Of tanks, military forces, etc.: shelter, halt for the night. **M20.**
▸ **II** *verb trans.* **4** †**a** Give lodging or temporary accommodation to; billet (troops). **ME–L17.** ▸**b** *fig.* Cherish (an idea or feeling, freq. a suspicion or grudge) in the mind. **ME.**

a *fig.*: MILTON The anguish of my soul, that suffers not Mine eyes to harbour sleep. **b** LD MACAULAY He believed them to harbour the worst designs. L. ALTHER She still harbored a faint hope Diana would change her mind.

5 Give shelter or refuge to. Now freq., give secret refuge to (a wanted criminal, a noxious animal, etc.). **LME.** ▸†**b** Of a thing: contain, hold within itself. **LME–L17.**

W. S. CHURCHILL Soon Canada was to harbour many refugees from the United States. E. HUXLEY Leeds .. harbours the largest ready-made clothing business in the world. E. BOWEN Crannied giltwork harboured more dust than energy could extract. *Blitz* The rural populace .. allegedly harbour terrorists. **b** R. BOYLE The Aeriall particles, that are wont to be harboured in the Pores of that liquor.

6 Trace (a stag) to its lair or covert. **LME.**
7 Shelter (a ship) in a harbour. **M16.**

harbourage /ˈhɑːb(ə)rɪdʒ/ *noun*. Also ***-bor-**. **L15.**
[**ORIGIN** from **HARBOUR** *noun*¹ + **-AGE**.]
1 *gen.* (A place of) shelter, (a) refuge. **L15.**

SHAKES. *John* Your King . . Craves harbourage within your city walls.

2 Shelter for ships in a harbour. **L17.**

harbourer /ˈhɑːb(ə)rə/ *noun.* Also *-**bor-**. **ME.**
[ORIGIN from HARBOUR *verb* + -ER[1].]
1 A person who provides shelter or (formerly) lodging. **ME.**
2 A person whose office is to trace a stag to its covert. **LME.**

harbourless /ˈhɑːbəlɪs/ *adjective.* **ME.**
[ORIGIN from HARBOUR *noun*[1] + -LESS.]
1 Having no shelter or home. **ME.**
2 Without harbours for ships. **E17.**

†**harbrough** *noun* var. of HARBOUR *noun*[1].

hard /hɑːd/ *adjective, adverb, & noun.*
[ORIGIN Old English *h(e)ard* = Old Frisian *herd*, Old Saxon (Dutch) *hard*, Old & mod. High German *hart*, Old Norse *harðr*, Gothic *hardus*, from Germanic from Indo-European whence Greek *kratus* strong, powerful.]
▸ **A** *adjective* **I 1** That does not yield to pressure; not easily penetrated, cut, or separated into particles; firm; compact in substance and texture. **OE.** ▸**b** Of porcelain: made of hard paste. **E19.** ▸**c** Of a tennis court: surfaced with asphalt or other hard material as opp. to grass. **L19.**

E. WAUGH The infantry: hard, bare feet rhythmically kicking up the dust. E. HARDWICK English muffins which had been toasted in the morning and were as hard as cement.

2 Orig., courageous, bold. Later, not easily worn out or made to give way; capable of great physical endurance and exertion. **OE.** ▸†**b** Firm, steadfast, unyielding, (*lit. & fig.*). **ME–M17.** ▸†**c** Inured, obdurate. *rare* (Shakes.). Only in **E17.**
3 Not easily impressed or moved; unfeeling, callous; hard-hearted. **OE.**

T. HARDY Allenville, cold and hard as he was, had some considerable affection for . . his daughter.

4 Not easily persuaded to part with money; stingy, niggardly. Now chiefly *Scot.* **ME.**

LD MACAULAY Many wondered that a man . . could be so hard and niggardly in all pecuniary dealings.

5 Requiring effort or skill; occasioning trouble; difficult, laborious, fatiguing, troublesome. Foll. by *to do, of.* **ME.** ▸**b** Not easily able or capable, having difficulty in doing something. *obsolete* exc. in ***hard of hearing*** below. **ME.**

N. BAILEY Bread made of spelt is hard of digestion. L. STERNE I was hard to please. H. MARTINEAU It is a hard thing to manage. J. B. MOZLEY Often . . what we must do as simply right . . is just the hardest thing to do. J. LE CARRÉ The snow was blurring his glasses, he found it hard to see. **b** DICKENS I have been very hard to sleep too, . . last night I was all but sleepless.

6 Difficult to understand or explain. **LME.**

J. W. BURGON To ask hard questions. H. HENDERSON Then I understood the meaning of the hard word '*pietas*'.

7 Of the pulse: beating strongly because of high blood pressure. **LME.**
8 Difficult to manage, control, or resist. Now chiefly in ***hard case*** below. **L16.** ▸**b** Of (a) fact: unable to be denied or explained away. **L19.** ▸**c** Of news or information: factual, reliable, substantiated. Cf. SOFT *adjective* 21. **E20.**

b A. H. COMPTON The hard fact is that war, like business, reduces to a question of gain versus cost. **c** D. W. GOODWIN Will treatment . . improve the prognosis? . . There is little hard evidence.

9 Of money: in specie as opp. to paper currency, or in currency as opp. to cheques etc. Cf. SOFT *adjective* 19a. **E18.**

J. BENTHAM Husbandmen, like other labourers, are paid in hard money by the week.

10 Not easily moved by sentiment; of a practical, shrewdly intelligent character. **M18.** ▸**b** Not readily affected by alcohol. **M19.**

LYTTON My books don't tell me . . a good heart gets on in the world: it is a hard head.

▸ **II 11** Difficult to bear, endure, or consent to; involving undue or unfair suffering; severe, oppressive, cruel. **OE.** ▸**b** Of the season or weather: severe, esp. frosty; rigorous, violent. **M16.**

W. HONE It is . . hard . . that I should have these . . compliments and . . reproaches at the same time. G. GREENE An old couple driven by hard times to live on their children. **b** R. BOYLE Very hard frost. Thames frozen. Carts went over.

12 Of a person: harsh or severe in dealing with someone. Freq. foll. by *on, upon.* **OE.** ▸**b** Of a thing, action, etc.: characterized by harshness or severity; cruel. **OE.** ▸**c** Of a bargain etc.: strict, without abatement or concession. **E17.** ▸**d** POLITICS. Designating a strict or extreme faction at the wing of a political party. Esp. in ***hard left, hard right.*** Cf. SOFT *adjective* 8d. **L20.**

A. TROLLOPE Felix began to perceive that he had been too hard upon her. **b** R. GARNETT She almost invariably took a hard view of persons and things. **c** N. WARD They never complain of me for giving them hard measure, or under-weight.

▸ **III** †**13** Intense in force or degree; strong, deep, profound. **OE–E19.**

COVERDALE *Gen.* 2:21 The Lorde God caused an herde slepe to fall vpon man.

14 Acting with, involving, or requiring great exertion, energy, or persistence; strenuous, unremitting. **OE.**

C. KINGSLEY The hardest rider for many a mile round. *Law Times* Every hard worker . . requires sufficient and regular holidays. E. AMADI His neatness and hard work had made him a favourite of the teachers.

▸ **IV 15** Harsh or unpleasant to the eye or ear; aesthetically unpleasing. (Earliest in ***hard-favoured.***) **E16.**

P. CAREY Painted in the colours of railway stations and schools: hard green and dirty cream.

16 a Of wine etc.: harsh or sharp to the taste; acid. **L16.** ▸**b** Of water: having a high proportion of mineral (esp. calcareous) salts which make the use of soap difficult. Cf. SOFT *adjective* 17. **M17.** ▸**c** Strongly alcoholic, intoxicating; (of a drug) potent and addictive. **L18.**

a P. V. PRICE Too high in elements that can make the wine hard, astringent and generally unpalatable. **b** N. G. CLARK Produce insoluble scums with hard water. **c** J. GARDNER You start on pot and . . you're mixing with people who've graduated to the hard stuff. *Dumfries & Galloway Standard* You should aim, therefore, to cut down on: . . soft drinks and hard alcohol.

17 PHONETICS. Of a consonant: velar, guttural; not palatalized; (now *rare*) voiceless, fortis. Cf. SOFT *adjective* 3b. **L18.**

N. WEBSTER When *a* is preceded by the gutturals hard *g* or *c*.

18 Of markets and prices: high, unyielding. **M19.**

Daily Telegraph A widely held view that yields will be harder in a year's time.

19 PHYSICS. **a** Of a vacuum: (almost) complete. Of a vacuum tube or valve: containing a hard vacuum. **L19.** ▸**b** Of radiation: having great penetrating power. **E20.**
20 Of pornography: highly obscene. **L20.**
▸ **B** *adverb.* **1** With effort or violence; strenuously, vigorously; fiercely; (now *US colloq.*) intensely, extremely. **OE.**

M. SINCLAIR It had blown hard all day, and now the wind had dropped. E. WAUGH He had fought long and hard since then and won a DSO. C. PHILLIPS Father Daniels looked hard at them.

2 So as to bring or involve pain, difficulty, or hardship; cruelly, harshly. **ME.** ▸†**b** At an uneven pace. **L16–E19.**

ADDISON I shall be very hard put to it to bring my self off handsomly. L. GORDON Any judgement worth having is hard won. **b** SHAKES. *A.Y.L.* He trots hard with a young maid.

3 Firmly, securely; tightly; fast. Now *rare.* **ME.**

SHAKES. *Haml.* He took me by the wrist, and held me hard.

4 So as to be hard; to the point of hardness. **ME.** ▸**b** On a hard surface, floor, etc. **L16.**

b E. TOPSELL That so he may lie soft and stand hard.

5 With difficulty, hardly; scarcely. **ME.**

SIR W. SCOTT And hard his labouring breath he drew.

6 In close proximity. **LME.** ▸**b** NAUTICAL. To the full extent possible. **M16.**

F. HALL Incongruity which trenches hard on nonsense.

▸ **C** *noun.* **1** That which is hard, something hard (*lit. & fig.*); hardship. **ME.**

Daily Chronicle She . . has given her life to nursing, and has gone through its hards. **b** R. PRICE When evening comes and I lay a-hold of Lois, I'll have up a hard.

†**2** The hard part, the shell. *rare.* Only in **ME.** ▸**b** An erection of the penis. Also ***hard-on.*** (*coarse slang*). **L19.**
3 (A piece of) hard or firm ground. Long *obsolete* exc. *Scot.* **L16.**
4 A firm beach or foreshore; a sloping esp. stone roadway or jetty across a foreshore. **M19.**

DICKENS The Common Hard, a dingy street leading down to the dock-yard. F. CHICHESTER The yacht had looked powerful and tall standing on the hard of the river bank.

5 Tobacco in the form of a cake. **M19.**
6 = ***hard labour*** below. *slang.* **L19.**

H. L. WILSON I would . . be . . left to languish in gaol, perhaps given six months' hard.

– PHRASES: ***a hard act to follow***: see ACT *noun* 7c. ***a hard nut to crack***: see NUT *noun.* ***a hard row to hoe***: see ROW *noun*[1]. ***as hard as nails***: see NAIL *noun.* ***bear hard***: see BEAR *verb*[1]. **be hard put to do** have difficulty in accomplishing. **be hard put to it** be in difficulties. ***die hard***: see DIE *verb*[1] ***drive a hard bargain***: see DRIVE *verb.* **go hard with** turn out to the disadvantage of (a person). **hard and fast** *adjective* (*a*) NAUTICAL (of a ship) on shore; (*b*) *gen.* (of a distinction made, a rule of behaviour, etc.) strict, inflexible. **hard at it** working hard. **hard by** close by, in close (local) proximity (to), very near (to). **hard done by** harshly or unfairly treated. **hard of hearing** somewhat deaf. **hard to get** aloof, unapproachable, uninterested, (freq. in ***play hard to get***). **hard up** (*a*) NAUTICAL (of a tiller) put as far as possible to windward to turn the ship's head away from the wind (usu. as a command); (*b*) in want, esp. of money; at a loss *for.* ***heavens hard***: see HEAVEN *noun.* ***hold hard***: see HOLD *verb.* **put the hard word on (a person)** *Austral. & NZ slang* ask (a person) for a favour or a loan; *esp.* proposition (a woman). **run (a person) hard** pursue (a person) closely. ***school of hard knocks***: see SCHOOL *noun*[1]. **the hard way** by one's own unaided efforts, through bitter experience. ***wink hard***: see WINK *verb*[1].
– SPECIAL COLLOCATIONS & COMB.: **hardbake** almond toffee. **hardball** *N. Amer.* (*a*) baseball; (*b*) rough uncompromising dealings or actions (esp. in a political context); chiefly in ***play hardball.*** †**hardbeam** the hornbeam, *Carpinus betulus.* **hardbitten** *adjective* tough in fight etc.; hardened by experience, hard-headed, sceptical. **hardboard** *noun & adjective* (made of) a stiff board of compressed and processed wood pulp fibre. **hardbody** *slang* a person with very toned or well-developed muscles. **hard-boil** *verb trans.* boil (an egg) so that the white and the yolk solidify. **hard-boiled** *adjective* (*a*) boiled so as to be hard; *spec.* (of an egg) boiled so that the white and the yolk have solidified; (*b*) *fig.* tough, callous, shrewd; shrewdly practical. **hard-bound** *adjective* (*a*) *rare* slow in action; (*b*) (of a book) bound in stiff covers. **hard bread** a kind of hard-baked cake or biscuit. **hard case** (*a*) a difficult or intractable person; (*b*) *Austral. & NZ* an eccentric or incorrigible person, a character; (*c*) an instance of hardship. ***hard cash***: see CASH *noun*[1]. **hard cheese** (*a*) any of various firm-textured cheeses; (*b*) *colloq.* bad luck, too bad. **hard chine** a join of the side and bottom of a ship which is angular as opp. to rounded. ***hard clam***: see CLAM *noun*[2] 1. **hard coal** anthracite. **hard copy** a legible permanent record of material stored on microfilm etc., *esp.* (COMPUTING) a printed record of data intended for output. **hard core** (*a*) heavy material, *spec.* rubble, forming the foundation of a road; (*b*) an irreducible nucleus or residuum; *fig.* a stubborn, reactionary, or highly committed minority, something blatant or intractable; (*c*) (usu. ***hardcore***) hardcore music or pornography. **hardcore** *adjective* (*a*) blatant, uncompromising; stubborn, highly committed; (*b*) (of pornography) highly obscene; (*c*) (of popular music) experimental in nature and usually characterized by high volume and aggressive presentation. **hard cover** the stiff durable binding case of a book. **hard currency** currency that is not likely to depreciate suddenly or fluctuate greatly in value. **hard disk, hard drive** COMPUTING a disk that is rigid and has a large storage capacity. **hard-favoured** *adjective* (*arch.*) having a hard or unpleasing appearance or look; ill-favoured, ugly. **hard-featured** *adjective* having hard, harsh, or unpleasing features. **hard feeling(s)** resentment. **hard fern** a fern of heathy places, *Blechnum spicant*, with leathery simply pinnate fronds. **hard-fisted** *adjective* stingy. **hardgainer** (in bodybuilding) a person who does not find it easy to gain muscle through exercise. **hard-grass** any of several tough-stemmed grasses; *esp.* (more fully ***sea hard-grass***) either of two salt-marsh grasses, *Parapholis strigosa* and *P. incurva.* ***hard*** GROWAN. **hardhack** a low shrub, *Spiraea tomentosa*, of the rose family, common in eastern N. America, with dense panicles of rose-coloured or white flowers. **hard-handed** *adjective* (*a*) having hard hands from manual labour; †(*b*) *rare* = ***hard-fisted*** above; (*c*) ruling with a firm or cruel hand, severe. **hard hat** (*a*) a hat made of hard or stiffened felt, a bowler hat; (*b*) (a person who wears) an article of protective headgear such as is worn on a building site; (*c*) a reactionary or conservative person. **hard-heart** *adjective* (*arch.*) = HARD-HEARTED. **hard hit** *adjective* severely stricken by misfortune, grief, or disaster, or by love. **hard-hitter** *Austral. & NZ colloq.* a bowler hat. **hard-hitting** *adjective* vigorous, not sparing the feelings. **hard labour** compulsory physical labour by prisoners without privileges, formerly (until 1948) in Britain undertaken during the first few weeks of a sentence. **hard-laid** *adjective* (of string, fabric, etc.) tightly twisted or woven. **hard landing** (*a*) an uncontrolled landing in which a spacecraft is destroyed; (*b*) *fig.* the slowing down of economic growth at an unacceptable degree relative to inflation and unemployment. **hard line** an unyielding adherence to a hard or firm policy without abatement or concession. **hardliner** a person who maintains a hard line habitually or on a specified issue. ***hard lines***: see LINE *noun*[2]. ***hard luck***: see LUCK *noun.* **hard-lying money** extra pay made to naval men serving in small craft. **hard-meat** (now *rare* or *obsolete*) corn and hay used as fodder as opp. to grass; ***at hard-meat*** (*fig.*), in close confinement. **hard money** *US* coins. **hard-mouthed** *adjective* (of a horse) not easily controlled by the bit; *fig.* self-willed, obstinate. **hard-nose** *adjective* (*N. Amer. colloq.*) = ***hard-nosed*** (b) below. **hard-nosed** *adjective* (*a*) (of a dog used in hunting etc.) having little or no sense of smell; (*b*) *N. Amer. colloq.* (of a person) obdurate, realistic, uncompromising. **hard-on** (*a*) see sense C.2b above; (*b*) *US slang* an obsession, passion, or fixation (freq. in ***have a hard-on for***). **hard pad** a form of distemper of dogs etc., sometimes causing hardness of the pads of the feet. ***hard palate***: see PALATE *noun* 1. **hardpan** (orig. *US*) a hard, impervious layer of clay, sand, or gravel; hard unbroken ground; *fig.* the lowest level or foundation, bottom, bedrock. **hard paste** the mixture of clay and water, fired at a high temperature, from which porcelain is made. **hard power** a coercive approach to international political relations, esp. one that involves the use of military power. **hard-pressed** *adjective* closely pursued (*lit. & fig.*), hard-pushed. **hard-pushed** *adjective* in difficulties, almost at the end of one's resources. **hard rock** highly amplified rock music with a heavy beat. ***hard roe***: see ROE *noun*[2]. **hard rubber** ebonite. **hard sauce** a sweet relish made with butter and sugar and often with brandy etc. **hardscape, hardscaping** (chiefly *US*) the man-made features used in landscape architecture, e.g. paths or walls, as contrasted with vegetation. **hardscrabble** *adjective & noun* (*N. Amer.*) (*a*) (land) that yields subsistence only with difficulty, barren land; (*b*) (requiring) a vigorous effort made with great difficulty. **hard sell** (an instance of) aggressive salesmanship or advertising. **hard set** *adjective* set so as to be hard; (of an egg) that has been subjected to incubation; (of a person) hungry. **hard shoulder** a strip of land with a hard surface beside a motorway enabling vehicles to leave the road during an emergency. **hard soap** soap made with sodium compounds. ***hard solder***: see SOLDER *noun* 1. **hardstanding** an area of hard material for a vehicle to stand on when not in use. **hardstone** precious or semi-precious stone used for intaglio, mosaic work, etc. **hard stuff** strong alcoholic drink, *esp.* whisky. **hard swearing** unabashed perjury. **hard tack** ship's biscuit; *gen.* hard bread or biscuit (*lit. & fig.*). **hardtail** (*a*) *US* the blue runner, a carangid fish, *Caranx crysos*, of the west Atlantic; (*b*) *slang* a mule. **hard tick** a tick of the family Ixodidae, having a rigid dorsal shield. **hard ticket** *US slang* = ***tough nut*** (a) s.v. NUT *noun.* **hardtop** the metal roof of a car; a car having such a roof. **hard-up** tobacco from cigarette ends. **hardware** (*a*) small ware or goods of metal; ironmongery; (*b*) weapons, machines; (*c*) the physical components of a computer etc. (opp. ***software***). **hard-wearing** *adjective*

H

able to stand a considerable amount of wear. **hard wheat**: with a hard grain rich in gluten. **hard-wired** *adjective* (COMPUTING) using or having permanently connected circuits designed to perform a specific unchangeable function. **hardwood** the wood of any non-coniferous tree (orig. that of the oak or other trees noted for their hardness); *ellipt.* a hardwood tree. **hard word** (*a*) (chiefly *dial.*) important or scandalous information; a hint, a password, a proposal, a refusal; (*b*) in *pl.*, words that are difficult to understand; (*c*) in *pl.*, angry talk. **hard-working** *adjective* diligent.

▪ **hardish** *adjective* somewhat hard L16. **hardness** *noun* (*a*) the quality or condition of being hard; (*b*) an instance of this quality, a hardship: OE.

†**hard** *verb intrans. & trans.* OE–E17.
[ORIGIN Old English *heardian* = Old Saxon *hardon*, Old High German *hartēn*, *hartōn*, from base of HARD *adjective*.]
Make or become hard (*lit. & fig.*).

Hardanger /ˈhɑːdaŋə/ *adjective*. L19.
[ORIGIN A district in W. Norway, the original place of manufacture.]
1 Designating a kind of folk violin strung with four stopped and four sympathetic strings. L19.
2 Designating a form of ornamental needlework characterized by a diamond or square pattern. E20.

hardback /ˈhɑːdbak/ *noun & adjective*. M18.
[ORIGIN from HARD *adjective* + BACK *noun*¹.]
▸ **A** *noun*. **1** A (flying) beetle. *W. Indian*. M18.
2 A book bound in stiff covers. M20.
in hardback in a hardback edition.
▸ **B** *attrib.* or as *adjective*. Of or pertaining to a hardback; *spec.* (of a book) bound in stiff covers. M20.

H

harden /ˈhɑːd(ə)n/ *noun & adjective*. LME.
[ORIGIN from HARD(S + -EN⁴.]
hist. (Of) a coarse fabric made from hards.

harden /ˈhɑːd(ə)n/ *verb*. ME.
[ORIGIN from HARD *adjective* + -EN⁵, after Old Norse *harðna*: repl. HARD *verb*.]
▸ **I** *verb trans.* **1** Render or make hard. ME.

J. R. GREEN The rise of a lawyer class was everywhere hardening customary into written rights. W. WHARTON The statues . . spotted black, green and yellow with clots of hardened moss.

2 Make bold in action; embolden; incite to action. Long *obsolete* exc. *dial.* ME.
†**3** Maintain stiffly, affirm. Only in ME.
4 Make difficult to make an impression on; make callous or unfeeling. ME.

LYTTON I hardened my heart against his voice. D. W. WINNICOTT We may become hardened, because the repeated losses of patients make us wary against getting fond of the newly-ill.

5 Make persistent or obdurate in a course of action or state of mind. LME.

Manchester Examiner It would . . confirm and harden her in a policy of settled hostility.

6 Chiefly NAUTICAL. Make firm and tight. Freq. foll. by *in*. E16.
7 Make hardy, robust, or capable of endurance. L16. ▸**b** Increase the resistance to attack of (a nuclear missile or base). M20.

R. HOLMES A hardened campaigner of forty-three . . limped from the effect of two leg wounds.

harden off inure (plants) to cold by gradually reducing the temperature of a hotbed or forcing house or by increasing the exposure to wind and sunlight.
▸ **II** *verb intrans.* **8** *gen.* Become hard. LME.

TENNYSON That we might . . watch The sandy footprint harden into stone. *fig.*: GEO. ELIOT That cold dislike . . was hardening within him.

9 Become hard in feeling, emotion, constitution, etc. M17.

C. KINGSLEY He hardened into a valiant man. DAY LEWIS Her sadness at certain insensitivities of my father would have hardened into resentment.

10 Of prices, markets, etc.: become higher and less yielding. L17.

Economist The hardening Yen knocked nearly 16% off Nissan's pre-tax profits in 1985.

▪ **hardenaˈbility** *noun* (METALLURGY) the extent to which metal may be hardened M20. **hardener** *noun* E17.

harder /ˈhɑːdə/ *noun*. *S. Afr.* Also **haarder**. M18.
[ORIGIN Afrikaans from Dutch.]
Any of various grey mullets resembling herring, of South African waters, esp. *Mugil cephalus* and *Liza ramada*.

Harderian /hɑːˈdɪərɪən/ *adjective*. M19.
[ORIGIN from J. J. *Harder* (1656–1711), Swiss anatomist + -IAN.]
ZOOLOGY. ***Harderian gland***, in many reptiles, birds, and mammals, a gland in the inner angle of the eye which lubricates the nictitating membrane or third eyelid.

hard-head /ˈhɑːdhɛd/ *noun*. Also (esp. in sense 3) **hardhead**. E16.
[ORIGIN from HARD *adjective* + HEAD *noun*. In branch II alt. of some word of unknown origin.]
▸ **I 1** A hard-headed person, *esp.* someone who is practical and unsentimental. Also, a stupid person. E16. ▸**b** A person not easily affected by alcohol. M19.
†**2** A contest of headbutting. L17–M19.
3 *sing.* & in *pl.* A tough-stemmed kind of knapweed, *Centaurea nigra*, common in grassland, with heads of dense purple florets. L18.
4 Any of various fishes said to have hard heads; *spec.* (*Scot.*) the father-lasher, *Myoxocephalus scorpius*. E19.
▸ **II 5** A Scottish copper coin of Mary and James VI of Scotland worth about three halfpence of English money. Long *obsolete* exc. *hist.* M16.

hard-headed /hɑːdˈhɛdɪd/ *adjective*. L16.
[ORIGIN from (the same root as) HARD-HEAD + -ED².]
†**1** Not easily led (*lit. & fig.*) or persuaded; obstinate; stubborn. L16–M17.
2 Not easily swayed by sophistry or sentiment; matter-of-fact, logical, practical. L18.
▪ **hard-headedly** *adverb* L19. **hard-headedness** *noun* M19.

hard-hearted /hɑːdˈhɑːtɪd/ *adjective*. ME.
[ORIGIN from HARD *adjective* + HEART *noun* + -ED².]
Having a hard heart; incapable of being moved to pity or tenderness; unfeeling; unmerciful.
▪ **hard-heartedly** *adverb* E19. **hard-heartedness** *noun* L16.

hardiesse /hɑːdɪˈɛs/ *noun*. *literary*. ME.
[ORIGIN Old French & mod. French, from *hardi* HARDY *adjective* + *-esse* -ESS².]
Hardihood, boldness.

hardihead /ˈhɑːdɪhɛd/ *noun*. *arch.* L16.
[ORIGIN from HARDY *adjective* + -HEAD¹.]
= HARDIHOOD 1.

hardihood /ˈhɑːdɪhʊd/ *noun*. M17.
[ORIGIN from HARDY *adjective* + -HOOD.]
1 Boldness, hardiness; audacity. M17.
2 Robust physique or constitution. *rare*. L18.

hardily /ˈhɑːdɪli/ *adverb*. In sense 2 also †**hardly**. ME.
[ORIGIN from HARDY *adjective* + -LY².]
1 Boldly; courageously; with audacity. ME.
†**2** It may be asserted; freely, certainly, by all means. ME–E17.
†**3** Robustly, not tenderly. *rare*. L17–L18.

hardiment /ˈhɑːdɪm(ə)nt/ *noun*. *arch.* LME.
[ORIGIN Old French = act of daring, from *hardier* attack, charge, harass + -MENT.]
1 Boldness, courage, daring, hardihood. LME.
†**2** A deed of daring, a bold exploit. LME–E17.

hardly /ˈhɑːdli/ *adverb*¹. ME.
[ORIGIN from HARD *adjective* + -LY².]
†**1** With energy, force, or strenuous exertion; vigorously, forcibly, violently. ME–E19.

E. TOPSELL The Lamprey caught fast hold on his hand, biting hardly.

†**2** Boldly, daringly, hardily. ME–E17.

W. PAINTER Speake hardly thy minde.

†**3** Firmly. ME–L16.
4 With severity or rigour; harshly. E16.

R. KNOLLES The unconstant people . . now began to speak hardly of him. W. STEBBING The honour and loyalty of the hardly-used veteran.

5 With trouble or hardship; uneasily, painfully. Now *rare*. M16.

LD MACAULAY What is made is slowly, hardly, and honestly earned.

6 Not easily, with difficulty. Long *rare* exc. as passing into sense 7. M16.

A. S. BYATT His self-effacement was a little strained, his security too hardly achieved.

7 Barely, only just; almost not; not quite; scarcely. M16.

D. H. LAWRENCE It was hardly to be borne. I. MURDOCH I constantly try and hardly ever succeed! E. FEINSTEIN It is hardly likely that he was still ignorant of the Reiss murder.

8 In close proximity, closely. *rare*. L16.

R. KNOLLES They were so hardly pursued.

†**hardly** *adverb*² see HARDILY *adverb*.

hards /hɑːdz/ *noun pl.* (also treated as *sing.*). Now *local*. Also **hurds** /hɜːdz/.
[ORIGIN Old English *heordan* weak fem. pl. corresp. to Old Frisian, Old Low German *hēde* (Dutch *heede*), ult. origin unknown.]
The coarser parts of flax or hemp; tow.

hardshell /ˈhɑːdʃɛl/ *adjective & noun*. M19.
[ORIGIN from HARD *adjective* + SHELL *noun*.]
▸ **A** *adjective*. Having a hard shell (*lit. & fig.*); (of a person) rigid and uncompromising in religious orthodoxy, *esp.* (*US*) belonging to a strict sect of Baptists of extreme Calvinist views. M19.
▸ **B** *noun*. A hardshell Baptist. M19.
▪ **hardshelled** *adjective* E17.

hardship /ˈhɑːdʃɪp/ *noun*. ME.
[ORIGIN from HARD *adjective* + -SHIP.]
†**1** The quality of being hard to bear; painful difficulty. ME–L17.
2 Hardness of fate or circumstance; severe suffering or privation. Also, an instance of this. ME. ▸†**b** A piece of harsh treatment. M–L18.

K. M. E. MURRAY For many scholars it is no hardship to sit indoors studying on a fine afternoon. N. ANNAN His body learnt to endure hardship. **b** BURKE I do not know that I have ever offered . . a hardship . . to the religious prejudices of any person.

hardy /ˈhɑːdi/ *noun*. L19.
[ORIGIN Prob. from HARD *adjective* or HARDY *adjective*.]
A blacksmith's edged blade of hard iron for shaping metal on.

hardy /ˈhɑːdi/ *adjective*. ME.
[ORIGIN Old French & mod. French *hardi* pa. pple of *hardir* become bold, from Germanic, from base of HARD *adjective*.]
1 Bold, daring; reprehensibly audacious. ME.

HOR. WALPOLE Art thou so hardy, as to dare my vengeance? J. W. KRUTCH Few . . are hardy enough openly to advocate starting a war.

2 Capable of endurance; physically robust, vigorous. M16. ▸**b** Of a plant: able to grow in the open all the year. M17.

A. SCHLEE The sudden cooling of the air had driven . . the less hardy into the cabin.

half-hardy: see HALF-. **hardy annual** an annual plant that may be sown, or sows itself, in the open; *fig.* (*joc.*) a subject that comes up at regular intervals. **hardy perennial** a herbaceous plant with a perennial rootstock; *fig.* (*joc.*) a subject that comes up at regular intervals.

Hardyesque /hɑːdɪˈɛsk/ *adjective*. E20.
[ORIGIN from *Hardy* (see below) + -ESQUE.]
Of, pertaining to, or characteristic of the English novelist and poet Thomas Hardy (1840–1928) or his work.

hare /hɛː/ *noun*¹.
[ORIGIN Old English *hara* = Old Frisian *hasa*, Middle Dutch *haese* (Dutch *haas*), Old High German *haso* (German *Hase*), Old Norse *heri*, from Germanic.]
1 Any of various fast-running plant-eating mammals of the family Leporidae (order Lagomorpha), esp. of the genus *Lepus*, typically larger than rabbits, with longer ears and hind legs and a short tail. Also, the flesh of any of these as food. OE.
Arctic hare, ***blue hare***, ***brown hare***, ***calling hare***, ***mountain hare***, ***snowshoe hare***, ***varying hare***, etc.
2 *fig.* A person likened to a hare in some way, as in swiftness or timidity, or in allusion to various phrasal or proverbial uses. ME. ▸**b** The player in the game of hare and hounds who lays the 'scent' for the hounds to follow. Cf. HOUND *noun*¹ 2b. M19. ▸**c** More fully ***electric hare***. A dummy hare propelled by electricity, used to lead the dogs in greyhound racing. E20.
3 (Usu. **H-**.) *The* southern constellation Lepus. M16.
4 More fully ***sea hare***. Any marine opisthobranch mollusc of the genus *Aplysia*, with tentacles resembling projecting ears. L16.
– PHRASES: BELGIAN ***hare***. **first catch your hare** [an instruction erron. ascribed to Mrs Glasse's *Art of Cookery* (1747)]: as the first step in trying to cook it, or (*fig.*) to do anything. ***give a hare a turn***: see TURN *noun*. **hare and hounds** a paperchase. **hare and tortoise** [with allus. to Aesop's fable] the defeat of ability by persistence. **hold with the hare and hunt with the hounds** = ***run with the hare and hunt with the hounds*** below. ***hunt the hare***: see HUNT *verb*. ***March hare***: see MARCH *noun*¹. **run with the hare and hunt with the hounds** try to remain on good terms with both sides in a quarrel etc.; play a double role. ***steady from hare***: see STEADY *adjective* 6c. **start a hare** raise a topic of discussion.
– COMB.: **harebell** either of two plants with nodding blue bell-shaped flowers: (*a*) orig., the bluebell or wild hyacinth, *Hyacinthoides non-scripta* (now *dial.*); (*b*) now usu. (orig. *N. English*), a slender bellflower, *Campanula rotundifolia*, of dry grassy banks etc.; **hare-finder** (long *rare*) a person employed to find or sight a hare in its form; **harefoot** (*a*) (long *rare* or *obsolete* exc. as an epithet for Harold I of England, d. 1040) a swift-footed person; (*b*) a long narrow foot found in some dogs; **hare-pipe** *hist.* a trap for catching hares; **hare's-ear** (*a*) any of various umbelliferous plants of the genus *Bupleurum*, esp. thorow-wax, *B. rotundifolium*; (*b*) ***hare's-ear mustard***, a cruciferous weed, *Conringia orientalis*, with broadly clasping leaves; **hare's foot** (*a*) the foot of a hare, esp. (THEATRICAL) as used to apply make-up to the face; (*b*) (more fully ***hare's-foot trefoil***) a clover of sandy ground, *Trifolium arvense*, with pink flowers almost hidden by the hairy calyx teeth; (*c*) ***hare's-foot fern***, a Mediterranean fern, *Davallia canariensis*, the rhizome of which is covered in brown hairs; **hare's fur** a brown or black glaze streaked with silvery white or yellow used on some Chinese pottery; **hare's-tail** (*a*) ***hare's-tail grass***, an ornamental grass, *Lagurus ovatus*, with softly hairy spikelike panicles; (*b*) ***hare's tail cotton grass***: see ***cotton grass*** s.v. COTTON *noun*¹.
▪ **harelike** *adjective* resembling (that of) a hare L16.

hare /hɛː/ *noun*². Long *rare* exc. in HAREWOOD. M17.
[ORIGIN German dial. *Ehre* from Proto-Romance from Latin *acer* maple.]
= HAREWOOD.

†**hare** *verb*¹ *trans.* E16.
[ORIGIN Uncertain: perh. partly from HARRY *verb* and partly from HARE *noun*¹.]
1 Harry, worry, harass. E16–L17.
2 Frighten, scare. M17–M18.

hare /hɛː/ *verb*[2]. L19.
[ORIGIN from HARE *noun*[1].]
†1 *verb trans.* (with *it*). Double back like a hare. Only in L19.
2 *verb intrans. & trans.* (with *it*). Run or move with great speed. E20.

S. BARSTOW I'm.. haring down the hill to the bus stop.

hare-brain /ˈhɛːbreɪn/ *noun*. Also **hair-**. M16.
[ORIGIN from HARE *noun*[1] (later app. also assoc. with HAIR *noun*) + BRAIN *noun*.]
▸ †**A** *noun*. A hare-brained person. M16–L17.
▸ **B** *adjective*. = HARE-BRAINED. M16.

hare-brained /ˈhɛːbreɪnd/ *adjective*. Also **hair-**. M16.
[ORIGIN from HARE-BRAIN + -ED[2].]
Having or showing no more sense than a hare; reckless, rash.

G. CLARE This hare-brained scheme went too far.

Haredi /haˈrɛdi/ *noun*. Pl. **-dim** /-dɪm/. L20.
[ORIGIN Hebrew, lit. 'one who trembles (in awe at the word of God)' (*Isaiah* 66:5), from *ḥārēdh* trembling.]
JUDAISM. A member of any of various Orthodox Jewish sects which adhere strictly to the traditional form of Jewish law and reject modern secular culture, and of which some do not recognize the modern state of Israel as a spiritual authority.

Hare Krishna /harɪ ˈkrɪʃnə, hɑːreɪ/ *adjective & noun*. L20.
[ORIGIN The words (= 'O Vishnu Krishna') of a Sanskrit devotional chant: see HARIJAN, KRISHNAISM.]
Designating or pertaining to, a member of, a sect devoted to the worship of the Hindu god Krishna.

hareld /ˈhar(ə)ld/ *noun*. *rare*. M19.
[ORIGIN from mod. Latin *Harelda* former genus name, alt. of *Havelda*, from Icelandic *haferla*, *hávella*.]
The long-tailed duck, *Clangula hyemalis*.

harelip /hɛːˈlɪp/ *noun*. Now regarded as *offensive*. M16.
[ORIGIN from HARE *noun*[1] + LIP *noun*.]
A congenital cleft in the upper lip on one or both sides of the centre, often associated with cleft palate; cleft lip.
■ **harelipped** *adjective* E17.

harem /ˈhɑːriːm, hɑːˈriːm, ˈhɛːrəm/ *noun*. M17.
[ORIGIN Orig. (from Turk *harem*) from Arabic *ḥaram* (that which is) prohibited, (hence) sacred or inviolable place, sanctuary, women's apartments, wives, women, later also from Arabic *ḥarīm* with same meaning, both from *ḥaruma* to be prohibited or unlawful.]
1 Separate women's quarters in a Muslim house, designed for the privacy and seclusion of the occupants. M17.

N. BARBER The old ladies of the harem.. could.. watch, unseen, as the men below listen to the music.

2 The occupants of such quarters collectively; *spec.* a Muslim's wives and concubines. L18. ▸**b** A group of female animals of a single species sharing a mate. L19.

BYRON Were it less toil.. to head an army than to rule a harem? **b** R. DAWKINS Elephant seals win and hold on to their harems.

– COMB.: **harem skirt** a (divided) skirt of a full billowy cut gathered into a narrow hem, supposedly resembling the costume traditionally worn by an inhabitant of a harem.

haremlik /həˈriːmlɪk, ˈhɛːrəm-/ *noun*. E20.
[ORIGIN Turkish *haremlık* from HAREM + *-lık* place.]
= HAREM 1.

harewood /ˈhɛːwʊd/ *noun*. L17.
[ORIGIN from HARE *noun*[2] + WOOD *noun*[1].]
Stained sycamore wood used in cabinetmaking.

Hargrave /ˈhɑːɡreɪv/ *adjective*. E20.
[ORIGIN Lawrence *Hargrave* (see below).]
Designating a kind of cellular box kite invented in 1894 by Lawrence Hargrave (1850–1915), an Australian pioneer in aeronautics.

haricot /ˈharɪkəʊ/ *noun*. M17.
[ORIGIN French, in sense 1 in *febves de haricot* (17), perh. from Nahuatl *ayacotli*, in sense 2 Old French *hericoq*, *hericot* (*de mouton*), prob. rel. to *harigoter* cut up.]
1 More fully ***haricot bean***. A leguminous plant, *Phaseolus vulgaris*, native to tropical America but having numerous widely cultivated varieties; the edible pod or seed of this plant; *esp.* white varieties of the dried seed. Cf. BEAN *noun* 1b. M17.
2 A ragout, esp. of mutton or lamb. M17.

harif *noun* var. of HAIRIF.

Harijan /ˈhʌrɪdʒ(ə)n, ˈharɪdʒan/ *noun & adjective*. M20.
[ORIGIN Sanskrit *harijana* person devoted to the Hindu god Vishnu, from *Hari* Vishnu + *jana* person.]
▸ **A** *noun*. Pl. **-s**, same. In the Indian subcontinent, a Hindu of a hereditary low caste, regarded as defiling by contact members of higher castes. Cf. UNTOUCHABLE *noun*. M20.
▸ **B** *attrib.* or as *adjective*. Of or pertaining to this caste. M20.
– NOTE: The term was adopted and popularized by Gandhi.

hariolate /ˈharɪəleɪt/ *verb intrans. arch.* M17.
[ORIGIN Latin *hariolat-* pa. ppl stem of *hariolari*, from *hariolus* soothsayer: see -ATE[3].]
1 Prophesy, soothsay. M17.
†2 Practise ventriloquism. M–L17.

harissa /ˈarɪsə/ *noun*. E20.
[ORIGIN Arabic *harīsa*, from *harasa* to crush, pound, tenderize by beating.]
1 A Mediterranean, North African, or Middle Eastern dish of ground meat (chiefly lamb) and couscous, served or prepared with a chilli sauce or paste. E20.
2 A hot sauce or paste of chillies, garlic, and various spices, used in cooking or as a condiment. L20.

hark /hɑːk/ *verb & noun*. ME.
[ORIGIN Corresp. to Old Frisian *herkia*, *harkia* rel. to Middle Low German, Middle Dutch, Flemish dial. *horken*, Old High German *hōrechen* (German *horchen*): cf. HEARKEN.]
▸ **A** *verb*. **1** *verb trans.* Listen to; hear with active attention. Now *arch. & poet.* ME.

J. MASEFIELD I've shaked to hark The peewits.. in the dark.

2 *verb intrans.* Listen. (Foll. by *at*, *to*.) ME.

G. MORTIMER 'I can't trust you...' 'Hark at him!' laughed Mrs. Larpenti. S. SASSOON Hark! There's the big bombardment.

3 *verb trans.* Speak in one's ear; whisper, mutter. *Scot. & N. English*. L16.
4 HUNTING. **a** *verb intrans.* Go (*away*, *forward*, *off*, etc.). Chiefly in *imper.* E17. ▸**b** *verb intrans.* Foll. by *back*: (of hounds) retrace the course taken to find a lost scent; *fig.* revert (*to* a subject). E19. ▸**c** *verb trans.* Urge (hounds) *on*, *forward*, with encouraging cries; call (hounds) *back*. E19.

b R. SUTCLIFF He harked back to an earlier point in their discussion.

▸ **B** *noun*. The action or an act of harking (*away*, *back*, etc.); an utterance of 'hark!'. M18.
■ **harker** *noun* (*rare*) E19.

harka /ˈhɑːkə/ *noun*. E20.
[ORIGIN Moroccan Arab. *ḥarka*: cf. classical Arab. *ḥaraka* movement, action, military operation.]
A body of Moroccan irregular troops.

harken *verb* see HEARKEN.

harl /hɑːl/ *noun*[1]. Also **harle**. See also HERL. M17.
[ORIGIN App. = Middle Low German *herle*, *harle*, etc., Low German *harl*, East Frisian *harrel* fibre of flax or hemp.]
1 A filament or fibre (of flax or hemp). M17.
2 A barb or fibre of a feather. L19.

harl /hɑːl/ *noun*[2]. *Scot. & N. English*. E19.
[ORIGIN from HARL *verb*.]
1 The action or an act of harling; something dragged or scraped together. E19.
2 A small quantity, a scraping (of something). (*lit. & fig.*) E19.
3 A composition of lime and gravel or sand; roughcast. M19.

harl /hɑːl/ *verb*. *Scot. & N. English*. ME.
[ORIGIN Unknown.]
1 *verb trans.* Drag, usu. with friction or scraping of the ground. ME.
2 *verb intrans.* Drag or trail oneself, go with dragging feet. E16. ▸**b** Come as if dragged off. *rare*. L18.
3 *verb trans.* Roughcast with lime mingled with small gravel. L16.
4 *verb intrans.* Troll for fish. M19.

harle *noun* var. of HARL *noun*[1].

Harleian /hɑːˈliːən, ˈhɑːlɪən/ *adjective*. M18.
[ORIGIN mod. Latin *Harleianus* from surname *Harley* (see below): see -AN, -IAN.]
Of or belonging to Robert Harley, Earl of Oxford (1661–1724) and his son Edward Harley, and esp. designating or pertaining to their library of books and manuscripts now deposited in the British Library.

Harlem /ˈhɑːləm/ *noun & adjective*. M20.
[ORIGIN A predominantly black area in Manhattan, New York.]
(Designating) a strongly swinging jazz style.

M. T. WILLIAMS The Harlem style of James P. Johnson and Fats Waller.

Harlemese /hɑːləˈmiːz/ *noun & adjective*. E20.
[ORIGIN from HARLEM + -ESE.]
(Designating) a regional type of speech characteristic of the inhabitants of Harlem, New York.

Harlemite /ˈhɑːləmʌɪt/ *noun*. L19.
[ORIGIN formed as HARLEMESE + -ITE[1].]
A person born in or residing in Harlem, New York.

harlequin /ˈhɑːlɪkwɪn/ *noun & adjective*. L16.
[ORIGIN Obsolete French (now *arlequin* after Italian *arlecchino*), later var. of *Herlequin* (also *Hellequin*, as in Old French *maisnie Hellequin*, in medieval Latin *familia Hellequini* or *Herlechini*) leader of a legendary nocturnal troop of demon horsemen, also called in medieval Latin *familia Herlethingi*, perh. ult. rel. to Old English *Herla cyning* king Herla. For the Italian associations cf. COLUMBINE *noun*[2], PUNCH *noun*[4] 3, ZANY *noun*.]
▸ **A** *noun*. **1** (Usu. **H-**.) A stock character of the witty servant in Italian comedy (and subsequently French light comedy). Also, a mute character in English pantomime, and a mischievous buffoon invisible to the clown and the pantaloon and usu. wearing a mask and particoloured tights. L16. ▸**b** A buffoon. L19.
2 A dog of a black and white variety or breed. L18.
3 = ***harlequin duck*** below. M19.
4 An opal (variety) with a mosaic pattern of colours. L19.
▸ **B** *attrib.* or as *adjective*. Of, pertaining to, or characteristic of (esp. the dress of) a harlequin; gaily coloured, *esp.* (of an animal, bird, etc.) having distinctively variegated markings. L18.
– SPECIAL COLLOCATIONS & COMB.: **harlequin beetle** a large S. American longhorn beetle, *Acrocinus longimanus*, having red, white, and black elytra. **harlequin bronzewing** the Australian flock pigeon, *Phaps histrionica*. **harlequin bug** (**a**) = ***harlequin cabbage-bug*** below; (**b**) either of two brightly coloured Australian heteropteran bugs, *Tectocoris diophthalmus*, a cotton pest, or *Dindymus versicolor*, a fruit pest. **harlequin cabbage-bug** a red and black stink bug of southern N. America, *Murgantia histrionica*, a pest of vegetables. **harlequin cup** each of a set of cups in which each cup is a different colour. **harlequin duck** a duck of northern coasts and rivers, *Histrionicus histrionicus*, the breeding males having deep grey-blue plumage with chestnut and white markings. **harlequin fish** (**a**) a small freshwater cyprinid fish of SE Asia, *Rasbora heteromorpha*, popular in aquariums; (**b**) *Austral.* any of several edible red rockfish. **harlequin quail** (**a**) a small nomadic African quail, *Coturnix delagorguei*; (**b**) any of several American quails of the genus *Cyrtonyx*. **harlequin ring**: set round with variously coloured stones. **harlequin smiler** a perciform fish of Australian waters, *Merogymnus eximius* (family Opistognathidae).
■ **harlequiˈnesque** *adjective* having the style of a harlequin L19. **harlequinism** *noun* the performance of a harlequin; an action characteristic of a harlequin: E19.

harlequin /ˈhɑːlɪkwɪn/ *verb*. M18.
[ORIGIN from the noun.]
1 *verb trans.* Conjure *away*, as a harlequin in a pantomime. *rare*. M18.
2 *verb intrans.* Play the harlequin. *rare*. E19.
3 *verb trans.* Colour, decorate, with contrasting colours. Chiefly as ***harlequined*** *ppl adjective*. M20.

D. FRANCIS She wore a black and white harlequined ski-ing jacket.

harlequinade /ˌhɑːlɪkwɪˈneɪd/ *noun & adjective*. L18.
[ORIGIN French *arlequinade*, from *arlequin* HARLEQUIN *noun*: see -ADE.]
▸ **A** *noun*. **1** A kind of pantomime; the part of a pantomime in which a harlequin plays the chief part. L18. ▸**b** A piece of buffoonery. E19.
2 A piece of gaily coloured variegated work. L19.
▸ **B** *attrib.* or as *adjective*. Of, pertaining to, or characteristic of a harlequinade; gaily coloured, variegated. M20.

C. BEATON Bright futuristic scarves of checkered or harlequinade triangles or squares.

harlequinade /ˌhɑːlɪkwɪˈneɪd/ *verb intrans.* L18.
[ORIGIN from the noun.]
Play the harlequin; act fantastically.

Harley Street /ˈhɑːli striːt/ *noun phr.* M19.
[ORIGIN A street in London associated with eminent physicians and surgeons.]
Medical specialists collectively.

attrib.: M. GILBERT Two Harley Street surgeons discussing a difficult case.

harlot /ˈhɑːlət/ *noun, adjective, & verb*. *arch. derog.* ME.
[ORIGIN Old French (*h*)*arlot*, *herlot* young fellow, knave, vagabond = Provençal *arlot*, medieval Latin *harlotus*, *herlotus* vagabond, beggar: cf. also Italian *arlotto*, medieval Latin *arlotus*, *erlotus* glutton, Old Spanish *arlote*, *alrote* lazy, Old Portuguese *alrotar* go about begging.]
▸ **A** *noun*. †**1** A vagrant, beggar, or criminal. Also, a lecher. ME–M17.
†2 An itinerant jester, buffoon, or juggler; a person who tells or does something to raise a laugh. ME–L15.
†3 A male servant or attendant; a menial. Cf. KNAVE. ME–M16.
†4 A fellow; *joc.* a good chap. LME–M17.
†5 A kind of pointed boot or shoe worn in the 14th cent. LME–E17.
6 **a** A promiscuous woman (*derog.*); a prostitute. LME. ▸**b** A woman. Long *rare* or *obsolete*. L15.

a E. AMADI Any woman in trousers is a harlot as far as they are concerned.

▸ **B** *attrib.* or as *adjective*. That is a harlot; of or pertaining to a harlot. ME.
▸ **C** *verb intrans.* Behave as or like a harlot; prostitute oneself. M17.

harlotry /ˈhɑːlətri/ *noun & adjective*. *arch. derog.* ME.
[ORIGIN from HARLOT *noun* + -RY.]
▸ **A** *noun*. †**1** Buffoonery, jesting, ribaldry; obscene talk or behaviour. ME–E19.
2 (An act of) promiscuity; the practice or trade of prostitution. LME.
3 A prostitute, a harlot. Now *rare* or *obsolete*. L16.
4 *fig.* Meretriciousness, showy but false attractiveness. M18.
▸ †**B** *attrib.* or as *adjective*. Base, filthy, worthless, trashy. L16–M17.

harm /hɑːm/ *noun & verb*.
[ORIGIN Old English *hearm* = Old Frisian *herm*, Old Saxon, Old High German, German *harm*, Old Norse *harmr* grief, sorrow, from Germanic.]
▸ **A** *noun*. **1** Hurt, injury, damage, mischief; an instance of this. OE.

H

E. M. FORSTER She had done wrong..; she only hoped that she had not done harm. D. CUSACK Dora, you're too sweet to wish harm even to Hitler!

do more harm than good make matters worse (despite good intentions). **do no harm** do no damage; *colloq.* be beneficial. *GRIEVOUS bodily harm.* **out of harm's way** in safety.

2 (A) sorrow, (an) affliction. Long *obsolete* exc. *Scot.* OE.

▸ **B** *verb.* **1** *verb trans.* Do harm to; injure, damage. OE.

B. EMECHETA The people of Shavi didn't plan to harm them. J. GATHORNE-HARDY Never give them anything likely to harm them.

†**2** *verb intrans.* Do harm or damage. ME–M17.

H

harmala /ˈhɑːmələ/ *noun.* Also **harmal**, **-el**, /-m(ə)l/. OE.
[ORIGIN Late Latin from Greek, prob. of Semitic origin (cf. Syriac *ʾarmēlā*, Arabic *ḥarmal*).]
A Mediterranean plant, *Peganum harmala* (family Zygophyllaceae), having aromatic seeds containing various alkaloids and used locally for medicines, oil, and dye.
■ **harmaline** *noun* an alkaloid found in harmala seeds M19.

harman /ˈhɑːmən/ *noun. arch. slang.* M16.
[ORIGIN 1st syll. unexpl.; 2nd syll. cf. DARKMANS, LIGHTMANS.]
†**1** In *pl.* The stocks. M16–E17.
2 In full ***harman beck*** [cf. BEAK *noun*[2].]. A constable, *esp.* a parish constable; a beadle. M16.

harmattan /hɑːˈmat(ə)n/ *noun.* L17.
[ORIGIN Twi *haramata*.]
A parching dusty land-wind on the W. African coast from December to February. Also ***harmattan wind***.

harmel *noun* var. of HARMALA.

harmful /ˈhɑːmfʊl, -f(ə)l/ *adjective.* ME.
[ORIGIN from HARM *noun* + -FUL.]
Apt to cause harm; detrimental, damaging.

A. J. CRONIN He had.. to *prove* that the dust was harmful, ..destructive to lung tissue.

■ **harmfully** *adverb* LME. **harmfulness** *noun* L16.

harmine /ˈhɑːmiːn/ *noun.* M19.
[ORIGIN from HARMALA + -INE[5].]
CHEMISTRY. An alkaloid drug derived from harmala seeds or by oxidation of harmaline.

harmless /ˈhɑːmlɪs/ *adjective.* ME.
[ORIGIN from HARM *noun* + -LESS.]
1 Free from injury or damage; unharmed. Now *rare.* ME.
2 Free from guilt; innocent. Now *rare* or *obsolete.* ME.

C. CLARKE She bears him harmless of all suspicion.

3 Free from liability to punishment or payment for damages. Now *rare.* LME.
hold harmless, **save harmless** indemnify.
4 Doing or causing no harm; inoffensive, innocuous. M16.

D. W. GOODWIN Everything is either a poison or harmless depending on the dose. A. N. WILSON Chesterton, in reality the most.. harmless of men, loved to fantasise about battle.

■ **harmlessly** *adverb* M16. **harmlessness** *noun* L16.

harmolodics /hɑːməˈlɒdɪks/ *noun pl.* L20.
[ORIGIN Blend of HARMONY, MOVEMENT (or MOTION), and MELODIC, coined by the US saxophonist Ornette Coleman (b. 1930).]
A form of free jazz in which musicians improvise simultaneously on a melodic line at various pitches.
■ **harmolodic** *adjective* L20.

harmonial /hɑːˈməʊnɪəl/ *adjective. rare.* M16.
[ORIGIN from Latin *harmonia* HARMONY + -AL[1].]
= HARMONIOUS.

harmonic /hɑːˈmɒnɪk/ *adjective & noun.* L16.
[ORIGIN Latin *harmonicus* from Greek *harmonikos* (in neut. pl. *harmonika* used as noun = theory of music), from *harmonia* HARMONY: see -IC.]
▸ **A** *adjective.* **1** Relating to music, musical; (of ancient music) relating to melody as distinguished from rhythm. *obsolete* in *gen.* sense. L16.
2 **a** Sounding in harmony, harmonious. M17. ▸**b** Relating to or marked by harmony, agreement, or concord. M18.
3 *MUSIC.* Relating to harmony; belonging to the combination of musical notes in chords. M17.
4 *MATH.* **a** Designating or involving the relation of quantities whose reciprocals are in arithmetical progression, as in the series 1 + ½ + ⅓ + ¼ + . . . E18. ▸**b** Expressible in the form of sine and cosine functions. M19.
5 *PHYSICS & MUSIC.* Designating or relating to tones produced by the vibration of the aliquot parts of strings etc. M19.
– SPECIAL COLLOCATIONS: **harmonic analysis**: of a periodic function into simple trigonometrical components. **harmonic function**: that satisfies any of a class of differential equations including that of simple harmonic motion. **harmonic minor** a scale with the minor sixth and major seventh both ascending and descending. **harmonic motion** symmetrical oscillatory motion under a retarding force proportional to the displacement from the equilibrium position (more fully ***simple harmonic motion***), like the projection of uniform motion in a circle on to a diameter; periodic motion having simple harmonic components. **harmonic progression** (the relation between) a series of quantities whose reciprocals are in arithmetical progression. **harmonic series** (*a*) *MATH.* a series of quantities in harmonic progression; (*b*) *ACOUSTICS & MUSIC* the scale formed by the harmonics of a fundamental note.

▸ **B** *noun.* **1** In *pl.* & (occas.) *sing.* Musical sounds or intervals constituting a theory or system; acoustics as relating to music. *obsolete* exc. *hist.* E18.
2 *PHYSICS & MUSIC.* A secondary tone produced by the vibration of an aliquot part of a string, reed, etc., usu. accompanying the fundamental tone produced by a vibrating body as a whole. L18. ▸**b** *PHYSICS.* A component or subsidiary (electromagnetic) wave or oscillation whose frequency is a multiple of the fundamental. L19.
3 *MATH.* A harmonic function. M19.

harmonica /hɑːˈmɒnɪkə/ *noun.* M18.
[ORIGIN Use as noun of fem. sing. or neut. pl. of Latin *harmonicus*: see HARMONIC.]
1 Any of various musical instruments; *spec.* (***a***) a mouth organ consisting of one or more rows of free reeds arranged in a case and vibrated by blowing and sucking; (***b***) more fully ***glass harmonica***, an instrument consisting of a row of concentric glass bowls kept moist and played by finger pressure or by means of a keyboard. M18.
2 Any of various organ stops. M19.

harmonical /hɑːˈmɒnɪk(ə)l/ *adjective.* L15.
[ORIGIN from HARMONIC + -AL[1].]
†**1** Of sounds: harmonious, sweet-sounding, tuneful. L15–L18.
2 Marked by harmony or agreement. Now *rare.* M16.
3 = HARMONIC *adjective* 4. M16.
†**4** Relating to the collation of parallel texts, esp. of the four Gospels. Only in 17.
†**5** Relating to music; musical. E17–M19.
†**6** Relating to the combination of notes in music. Only in 18.

harmonically /hɑːˈmɒnɪk(ə)li/ *adverb.* L16.
[ORIGIN from HARMONIC or HARMONICAL: see -ICALLY.]
†**1** With harmony or concord (esp. of sounds); harmoniously. L16–L18.
2 *MATH.* In a harmonic relation or proportion; in the manner of harmonic motion. L16.
3 *MUSIC.* In relation to harmony. L18.

harmonicon /hɑːˈmɒnɪk(ə)n/ *noun.* M19.
[ORIGIN Greek *harmonikon* neut. sing. of *harmonikos* HARMONIC.]
hist. = HARMONICA.

harmonious /hɑːˈməʊnɪəs/ *adjective.* M16.
[ORIGIN from HARMONY + -OUS.]
1 Tuneful, sweet-sounding; sounding together in harmony. M16. ▸**b** Of a person: singing, playing, or speaking tunefully or pleasantly. M16.
2 Forming a consistent, orderly, pleasing, or agreeable whole. M17.

F. L. WRIGHT No part of anything is of any great value in itself except as.. part of the harmonious whole.

3 Free from dissent or ill feeling; amicable, cordial. E18.

LD MACAULAY No constitutional question had ever been decided ..with more harmonious consent. J. I. M. STEWART I believe I enjoy harmonious relationships with everybody.

■ **harmoniously** *adverb* E17. **harmoniousness** *noun* L17.

harmonisation *noun* var. of HARMONIZATION.

harmonise *verb* var. of HARMONIZE.

harmonist /ˈhɑːmənɪst/ *noun.* L16.
[ORIGIN from HARMONY + -IST.]
1 **a** *GREEK HISTORY.* A member of a school of musical theorists in ancient Greece who founded the rules of music on the subjective effects of tones as opp. to their mathematical relations. L16. ▸**b** A musician. *arch.* M18. ▸**c** A composer skilled in, or an expert in the theory of, harmony. L18.

b G. HUDDESFORD Ballads I have heard rehears'd By harmonists itinerant. **c** E. GURNEY Modern harmonists are unwilling to acknowledge that the minor triad is less consonant than the major.

2 A collator of parallel or related texts, esp. of the four Gospels. E18.
3 A person who brings things into harmony or agreement. E19.
4 (**H-**.) A member of the Harmony Society, a 19th-cent. communistic Christian religious sect which settled in Pennsylvania. E19.

harmonistic /hɑːməˈnɪstɪk/ *adjective & noun.* M19.
[ORIGIN from HARMONIST + -IC.]
▸ **A** *adjective.* Of or pertaining to the collation and harmonizing of parallel or related texts, esp. of the four Gospels. M19.
▸ **B** *noun sing.* & in *pl.* The branch of biblical criticism which seeks to harmonize parallel or related texts, esp. the four Gospels. L19.
■ **harmonistically** *adverb* L19.

harmonium /hɑːˈməʊnɪəm/ *noun.* M19.
[ORIGIN French, from Latin *harmonia* HARMONY or Greek *harmonios* harmonious.]
A keyboard instrument in which reeds are made to vibrate by air from a pedal-operated bellows.

harmonization /ˌhɑːmənʌɪˈzeɪʃ(ə)n/ *noun.* Also **-isation**. M19.
[ORIGIN from HARMONIZE + -ATION.]
1 The action or process of bringing into harmony or agreement; reconciliation, standardization. M19.
2 Agreement in colour; matching or blending of tones. L19.
3 The adding of harmony to a melody. L19.

harmonize /ˈhɑːmənʌɪz/ *verb.* Also **-ise**. L15.
[ORIGIN Old French & mod. French *harmoniser*, formed as HARMONY: see -IZE.]
1 *verb intrans.* Sing or play in harmony. L15.
2 *verb intrans.* Be in harmony (*with*); accord, be agreeable, in artistic effect. E17.

G. P. R. JAMES It harmonizes well with his general character. J. KRANTZ I.. pick out colors that harmonize with what I planted last year.

3 *verb trans.* **a** Bring into harmony, attune. E18. ▸**b** Reduce to internal harmony; make agreeable in artistic effect. E18. ▸**c** Bring into agreement (*with*), reconcile. M18.

a TENNYSON A music harmonizing our wild cries. **c** E. A. FREEMAN A harmonized narrative of the martyrdom.

4 *verb trans. & intrans.* Add notes to (a melody) to form chords; add harmony (to). L18.
■ **harmonizer** *noun* L17.

Harmon mute /ˈhɑːmən ˈmjuːt/ *noun phr.* M20.
[ORIGIN Perh. from HARMON(ICA + MUTE *noun*[2].]
(Proprietary name for) a type of trumpet or trombone mute. Also called ***wah-wah mute***.

harmonogram /hɑːˈmɒnəgram/ *noun.* E20.
[ORIGIN from French *harmonie* HARMONY: see -O-, -GRAM.]
A figure or curve drawn with a harmonograph.

harmonograph /hɑːˈmɒnəgrɑːf/ *noun.* L19.
[ORIGIN formed as HARMONOGRAM: see -O-, -GRAPH.]
An instrument for tracing curves representing sonorous vibrations.

harmonometer /hɑːməˈnɒmɪtə/ *noun.* E19.
[ORIGIN French *harmonomètre*, irreg. from *harmonie* HARMONY + *-mètre* (see -METER).]
An instrument for measuring the harmonic relations of musical notes.

harmony /ˈhɑːməni/ *noun.* LME.
[ORIGIN Old French & mod. French *harmonie* from Latin *harmonia* agreement, concord from Greek, from *harmos* joint, *harmozein* fit together.]
1 Combination or adaptation of parts, elements, or related things, so as to form a consistent and orderly whole; agreement, accord, congruity. LME.

SOUTHEY To heavenliest harmony Reduce the seeming chaos. H. MACMILLAN We should hold frequent consultations.. that our policies and purposes might be kept in harmony.

vowel harmony: see VOWEL *noun*.
2 The combination of (simultaneous or successive) musical notes to produce a pleasing effect; music; tuneful sound; *gen.* pleasing combination of sounds, as in poetry etc.; sweet or melodious sound. LME.

R. DAHL There is a new exciting music being made, with subtle harmonies and grinding discords.

harmony of the spheres: see SPHERE *noun* 2.
3 *MUSIC.* The combination of (simultaneous) notes to form chords; the structure of a piece of music with regard to its chords; the branch of music that deals with these. Cf. MELODY *noun* 4. LME.

Classical Music An experienced teacher of A level Harmony, to take over all Sixth Form harmony.

close harmony: see CLOSE *adjective & adverb*. ***open harmony***: see OPEN *adjective*.
4 Agreement of feeling or sentiment; accord, peace. E16.

H. H. WILSON The harmony which had thus been re-established with the Court of Baroda.

5 A collation of parallel narratives etc., esp. of the four Gospels. L16.

Church Times A concordance or harmony of the Gospels, produced.. by slicing up similar editions of the Bible.

6 Combination of parts to produce an aesthetically pleasing effect; agreeable effect of apt arrangement of parts. M17.

JAS. HARRIS How pleasing the harmony between hills and woods, between rivers and lawns.

harmost /ˈhɑːmɒst/ *noun.* L18.
[ORIGIN Greek *harmostēs*, from *harmozein* fit, regulate.]
hist. Any of the governors sent out by the Spartans after the Peloponnesian War to control subject cities and islands.

harmotome /ˈhɑːmətəʊm/ *noun.* E19.
[ORIGIN French, from Greek *harmos* joint + *-tomos* cutting (app. in ref. to the way the octohedral crystal divides).]
MINERALOGY. A monoclinic hydrated silicate of aluminium and barium, occurring often in cruciform twin crystals of various colours.

harness /ˈhɑːnɪs/ *noun*. ME.
[ORIGIN Old French *harneis* military equipment (mod. *harnais*) from Old Norse = provisions for an army (with assim. of the termination: cf. Old French *harneschier* equip), from *herr* army (see HARRY *verb*) + *nest* = Old English, Old High German *nest* provisions.]
1 Orig., the equipment of a horse for riding, driving, etc. Now *spec*. the equipment by which a horse or other draught animal may be fastened to a cart etc. and controlled; *fig*. working equipment. ME. ▸**b** Any of various arrangements of straps etc. resembling a horse's harness, as, (**a**) one fitted to a dog in place of a collar, (**b**) one used for fastening a thing to a person, (**c**) one used for holding a person (esp. round a child and held by an adult) for safety or restraint. L19.

Lancashire Evening Telegraph Thieves stole £400 worth of harness, including a horse collar and various straps. **b** C. G. BURGE Safety belts and safety harness have been specially designed for use in aircraft. J. P. PHILIPS She unbuckled the dog's harness. C. RYAN Without removing his harness, and dragging his parachute behind him, Raub rushed the Germans.

double harness: see DOUBLE *adjective & adverb*. **in harness** in the routine of daily work (*die in harness*: see DIE *verb*[1].). ***single harness***: see SINGLE *adjective & adverb*.
2 The armour of a foot soldier or of a mounted soldier and his horse; a suit of mail. Now *arch*. or *hist*. ME.

LONGFELLOW A single warrior, In sombre harness mailed.

†**3** The baggage or portable equipment of an army, a party of travellers, etc. Only in ME.
4 †**a** Household and personal equipment; furniture; clothing. ME–E17. ▸**b** Formal clothing, uniform. *US slang*. L19.
†**5** The genitals. Also ***privy harness***. LME–E16.
6 Tackle, gear, armament; the equipment or mounting of something. Now only *spec*. the mechanism by which a large bell is suspended and hung. LME.
7 The apparatus in a loom for shifting the warp threads. L16.
8 AERONAUTICS. A system of engine ignition leads, esp. when screened to prevent interference with radio signals. M20.
– COMB.: **harness bull** *US slang* a uniformed policeman; **harness cask** NAUTICAL a cask of salt meat for current consumption; **harness cop** *US slang* = ***harness bull*** above; **harness racing**: in which a horse pulls a two-wheeled vehicle and a driver.

harness /ˈhɑːnɪs/ *verb trans*. ME.
[ORIGIN Old French *harneschier* equip, from base of Old French *harneis* (see HARNESS *noun*), or directly from the noun.]
1 Put a harness on (a horse etc.); fasten (a horse etc.) *to* a cart etc. with a harness. ME. ▸**b** *fig*. Utilize (a river, a waterfall, natural forces) for motive power. L19.

J. CARY We harnessed the old sheep-dog to the sledge. *fig*.: V. GLENDINNING Neither sex can achieve much .. without harnessing the complementary attributes of the other. **b** A. E. STEVENSON The powers of the atom are about to be harnessed for ever-greater production.

2 Equip with armour, arm. Now *arch*. or *hist*. LME.
†**3** Dress, clothe, array. LME–M19.
†**4** Equip, adorn, esp. with fittings of precious material. LME–L19.

harnessed /ˈhɑːnɪst/ *adjective*. LME.
[ORIGIN from HARNESS *noun* or *verb*: see -ED[2], -ED[1].]
1 Armed, in armour. Long *arch*. or *hist*. LME.
†**2** Equipped; mounted with (precious) metal. LME–M16.
3 Yoked, in harness. L15.
– SPECIAL COLLOCATIONS: **harnessed antelope**: of the genus *Tragelaphus* with white stripes across the back; *spec*. the bushbuck, *T. scriptus*.

haro *interjection* var. of HARROW *interjection*.

haroseth /həˈrəʊsɛθ/ *noun*. Also **ch-** /x-/; **-set** /-sɛt/. L19.
[ORIGIN Hebrew *ḥărōseṯ*, from *ḥereś* earthware.]
A mixture of apples, nuts, spices, etc., eaten at the Passover Seder service to symbolize the clay mixed by the Israelites during their slavery in Egypt.

harp /hɑːp/ *noun & verb*.
[ORIGIN Old English *hearpe* = Old Saxon *harpa* (Dutch *harp*), Old High German *harfa* (German *Harfe*), Old Norse *harpa*, from Germanic, whence also late Latin *harpa*.]
▸ **A** *noun*. **1** A stringed musical instrument usu. consisting of a (roughly triangular) framework fitted with a series of strings of definite lengths, played by plucking with the fingers (esp. traditionally by those in heaven), now esp. in the form of a large vertical orchestral instrument resting on the floor and equipped with pedals to alter the pitch of the strings. OE. ▸**b** A representation of a harp, esp. as the national device of Ireland. M17. ▸**c** More fully ***mouth harp***. A mouth organ, a harmonica. *US colloq*. L19. ▸**d** A person of Irish origin or descent. *US slang*. E20.

attrib.: DAY LEWIS I .. sang .. to the harp accompaniment of Sidonie Goossens.

Aeolian harp: see AEOLIAN 2. **double harp**: having two sets of strings differently tuned. ***Irish harp***: see IRISH *adjective*. ***Jew's harp***: see JEW *noun*. **triple harp**: having three sets of strings differently tuned. ***Welsh harp***: see WELSH *adjective*.
2 (Usu. **H-**.) *The* constellation Lyra. M16.
†**3** Either of two Irish coins bearing the representation of a harp. Cf. HARPER *noun*[1] 2. M16–E17.
4 Any of various types of sieve. M17.
5 In full ***harp shell***. Any of various marine gastropods of the family Harpidae, having large ornate shells with a widely flared aperture, mainly found in the Indian and Pacific Oceans. M18.
6 More fully ***harp seal***. A light grey-brown seal with distinctive dark markings, *Pagophilus groenlandicus* (or *Phoca groenlandica*), of the north-west Atlantic, and the Barents and White Seas. L18.
▸ **B** *verb*. **1** *verb intrans*. Play (on) a harp. OE. ▸**b** *verb trans*. Play (notes, music, etc.) on a harp. Now *arch. rare*. ME.

F. O'BRIEN A hunchback that harped for his living about the streets.

2 *verb intrans*. Dwell tediously *on* a subject in speech, writing, etc. E16.

CARLYLE Harping mainly on the religious string. E. TAYLOR Still harping on the money she had lent him.

3 *verb trans*. Bring *out of*, *into*, etc., a place or state by playing the harp. E16.
4 *verb trans*. Give voice to; guess. Now *rare* or *obsolete*. E17.
5 *verb intrans*. Make a sound like that of a harp. M17.

harper /ˈhɑːpə/ *noun*[1]. OE.
[ORIGIN from HARP *noun* + -ER[1].]
1 A person who plays (on) the harp. OE.
2 Any of various Irish coins, esp. a shilling, bearing the figure of a harp. Cf. HARP *noun* 3. Long *obsolete* exc. *hist*. L16.

†**harper** *noun*[2]. *rare*. Also **harpier**. L16–E17.
[ORIGIN App. erron. from HARPY.]
A harpy.

harping /ˈhɑːpɪŋ/ *noun*. Also (earlier) †**-pon**. LME.
[ORIGIN Old French *harpon* clamp: see HARPOON.]
NAUTICAL. **1** Any of various pieces of timber for supporting and strengthening, esp. as used to hold the frames of a wooden vessel in place until the outside planking is done. Also, the forward part of the wales which encompass the bow of a ship and are fastened to the stem. Freq. in *pl*. LME.
2 In *pl*. In full ***cat-harpings***. Ropes or cramps used to brace in the shrouds of lower masts behind their yards. E17.

†**harping-iron** *noun*. LME–E19.
[ORIGIN Perh. from French *harpin* boat-hook (from *harper* grasp, grapple) + IRON *noun*. Repl. by HARPOON *noun*.]
A barbed spear used for spearing whales and large fish; a harpoon.

harpist /ˈhɑːpɪst/ *noun*. E17.
[ORIGIN from HARP *noun* + -IST.]
A (professional) harper.

†**harpon** *noun* see HARPING.

harpoon /hɑːˈpuːn/ *noun & verb*. E17.
[ORIGIN French *harpon*, from *harpe* dog's claw, cramp-iron, clamp, from Latin (also *harpa*) from Greek *harpē* sickle.]
▸ **A** *noun*. Orig., a barbed dart or spear. Later, a barbed spearlike missile with a cord attached to the shank, for catching whales and large fish. Cf. earlier HARPING-IRON. E17.
– COMB.: **harpoon gun**: for firing a harpoon.
▸ **B** *verb trans*. Strike or spear with a harpoon. L18.
■ **harpooˈneer** *noun* (now *rare* or *obsolete*) a harpooner E17. **harpooner** *noun* a person who throws or fires a harpoon E18.

†**harpsical** *noun*. E17–L18.
[ORIGIN Alt. of HARPSICHORD, prob. after *virginal*.]
A harpsichord.

harpsichord /ˈhɑːpsɪkɔːd/ *noun*. E17.
[ORIGIN French †*harpechorde* = Italian *arpicordo*, mod. Latin *harpichordium*, from late Latin *harpa* HARP *noun* + *chorda* string (see CORD *noun*[1]), with unexpl. intrusive *s*.]
A keyboard musical instrument shaped like a grand piano, having strings in line with the direction of the keys and plucked by quill or leather points, esp. popular from the 16th to the 18th cent.
■ **harpsichordist** *noun* a person who plays the harpsichord L19.

harpuisbos /hɑːˈpœysbɒs/ *noun*. Also ***-bosje*** /-bɒsi/, (in semi-anglicized form) ***harpuis bush*** /hɑːˈpœys bʊʃ/. E19.
[ORIGIN Afrikaans, from Dutch *harpuis* resin + *bos* BUSH *noun*[1].]
Any of various southern African shrubs of the genus *Euryops*, of the composite family, which bear yellow-rayed flowers and exude resin. Also called ***resin-bush***.

harpy /ˈhɑːpi/ *noun*. LME.
[ORIGIN Old French & mod. French *harpie* or its source Latin *harpyia*, pl. *-iae* from Greek *harpuiai* snatchers, rel. to *harpazein* seize.]
1 CLASSICAL MYTHOLOGY. Also **H-**. A rapacious monster covered in filth, having a woman's face and body and a bird's wings and claws, supposed to be a minister of divine vengeance. LME. ▸**b** A representation of a harpy. L16.
2 A greedy, cruel or grasping person, *esp*. a rapacious woman. L15.

J. DISKI She was, undoubtedly, a witch, a harpy, a filth-minded old baggage.

3 In full ***harpy eagle***. A very large, powerful eagle, *Harpia harpyja*, of Central and S. America. M19.

harquebus /ˈhɑːkwɪbəs/ *noun*. Also **arq-** /ˈɑːk-/. M16.
[ORIGIN French *(h)arquebuse*, ult. from Middle Low German *hakebusse* (mod. *Haakbus*) or Middle High German *hake(n)bühse* (mod. *Hakenbüchse*): see HACKBUT.]
hist. **1** An early type of portable firearm; *spec*. one supported on a tripod by a hook or on a forked rest. M16.
2 Soldiers armed with harquebuses collectively. Long *rare* or *obsolete*. L16.
■ **harquebuˈsier** *noun* a soldier armed with a harquebus M16.

harquebusade /ˈhɑːkwɪbəseɪd/ *noun*. *obsolete* exc. *hist*. Also **arq-** /ˈɑːk-/. M16.
[ORIGIN French *(h)arquebusade*, formed as HARQUEBUS: see -ADE.]
1 A continuous discharge of harquebus shots, a fusillade. Formerly also, a single harquebus shot. M16.
2 Usu. **a-**. In full ***harquebusade water***. A lotion used to treat gunshot and other wounds; a restorative. M18.

harr /hɑː/ *noun*. Now chiefly *dial*. Also **harre**.
[ORIGIN Old English *heorr* corresp. to Middle Dutch *herre*, *harre* (Dutch *har(re)*), and *heorra* corresp. to Old Norse *hjarri*, both from Germanic.]
The hinge of a door or gate; the part of a gate or door to which hinges are fastened.

harr /hɑː/ *verb intrans*. *obsolete* exc. *dial*. LME.
[ORIGIN Imit.]
Make a rough guttural sound; snarl.

harrateen /ˈharətiːn/ *noun & adjective*. *obsolete* exc. *hist*. Also **hara-**. E18.
[ORIGIN Unknown.]
(Of) a linen fabric used for curtains, bed hangings, etc.

H

harre *noun* var. of HARR *noun*.

Harri *noun* var. of HURRI.

Harrian *adjective & noun* var. of HURRIAN.

harridan /ˈharɪd(ə)n/ *noun*. *derog*. (orig. *slang*). L17.
[ORIGIN Perh. alt. of French *haridelle* old horse: ult. origin unknown.]
A haggard or bad-tempered (old) woman.

P. BAILEY I have complained till I'm hoarse. They must not find me an impossible old harridan.

harrier /ˈharɪə/ *noun*[1]. LME.
[ORIGIN from HARE *noun*[1] + -ER[1] after Old French & mod. French *levrier*, repr. medieval Latin *leporarius* greyhound, with assim. to HARRIER *noun*[2].]
1 A kind of hound used for hunting hares. LME. ▸**b** In *pl*. Such hounds as a pack with huntsmen etc. Also, cross-country runners as a group or club. L19.
2 Any of the pursuers in the game of hare and hounds. L19.

harrier /ˈharɪə/ *noun*[2]. E16.
[ORIGIN from HARRY *verb* + -ER[1].]
A person who harries, ravages, or lays waste.

harrier /ˈharɪə/ *noun*[3]. Also (earlier) †**harrower**. M16.
[ORIGIN from HARROW *verb*[1] + -ER[1], assim. in 17 to HARRIER *noun*[2].]
Any of a number of medium-sized, long-winged, slender-bodied hawks of the genus *Circus*.
hen harrier, ***marsh harrier***, ***Montagu's harrier***, etc.
– COMB.: **harrier eagle** a serpent eagle; **harrier hawk** (**a**) = ***forest falcon*** s.v. FOREST *noun*; (**b**) either of two long-tailed, long-legged hawks of the genus *Polyboroides*, of sub-Saharan Africa and Madagascar.

Harriet Lane /harɪət ˈleɪn/ *noun*. *slang* (chiefly NAUTICAL). L19.
[ORIGIN A murder victim: cf. FANNY ADAMS.]
Preserved meat; *esp*. Australian tinned meat.

Harrington /ˈharɪŋt(ə)n/ *noun*. M20.
[ORIGIN from Rodney *Harrington*, a character in the 1960s TV serial *Peyton Place*.]
A man's short lightweight jacket with a collar and a zipped front.

Harris /ˈharɪs/ *noun*. L19.
[ORIGIN The island of Lewis with *Harris* in the Outer Hebrides.]
More fully ***Harris tweed***. (Proprietary name for) the handwoven tweed produced in the Outer Hebrides, esp. on the island of Lewis with Harris.

Harrogate /ˈharəgət/ *noun*. L18.
[ORIGIN A borough in North Yorkshire.]
1 ***Harrogate water***, a mineral water from springs in Harrogate. L18.
2 ***Harrogate toffee***, (proprietary name for) a kind of toffee. L19.

Harrovian /həˈrəʊvɪən/ *noun & adjective*. E19.
[ORIGIN from mod. Latin *Harrovia* Harrow (see below): see -AN, -IAN.]
▸ **A** *noun*. A past or present member of Harrow School, a public school at Harrow-on-the-Hill, Middlesex. E19.
▸ **B** *adjective*. Of, pertaining to, or characteristic of Harrow School. M19.

harrow /ˈharəʊ/ *noun*. ME.
[ORIGIN from Old Norse *herfi*, *hervi* (Swedish *harf*, *härf*, Danish *harv*) obscurely rel. to Middle Low German, Middle Dutch *harke* (Dutch *hark*) rake. Sense 3 from HARROW *verb*[2].]
1 A heavy frame set with esp. iron teeth or tines, drawn over ploughed land to break up clods, root up weeds, cover seed, etc. ME.

fig.: L. STRACHEY The Napoleonic harrow passed over Saxe-Coburg.

under the harrow in distress.
2 *transf.* A similar contrivance used for other purposes. **ME.**
3 The action or an act of harrowing. **L19.**

harrow /ˈharəʊ/ *verb*[1] *trans.* **ME.**
[**ORIGIN** By-form of **HARRY** *verb*.]
Harry, rob, spoil. Now chiefly in ***Harrowing of Hell***, (in medieval Christian theology) the defeat of the powers of evil and the release of its victims by the descent of Christ into hell after his death.

J. CLAPHAM These Picts . . did oft-times harrow the borders.

harrow /ˈharəʊ/ *verb*[2] *trans.* **ME.**
[**ORIGIN** from **HARROW** *noun*.]
1 Draw a harrow over; break up, crush, or pulverize with a harrow. **ME.**

H. E. BATES Parker was harrowing ground for spring seed.

harrow in cover (seed) by harrowing.
2 Lacerate, wound, (the body, the feelings, etc.); cause to suffer, distress. **E16.**

H. ACTON For fear of harrowing them by the spectacle of her agony. D. ADAMS The heavy movement and breath that had first so harrowed the Professor.

harrow /ˈharəʊ/ *interjection.* Now *rare.* Also **haro**. **ME.**
[**ORIGIN** Old French & mod. French *harou*, (also mod.) *haro*, imit.: cf. **HARASS** *verb*.]
Expr. distress or alarm.
cry harrow (on) denounce (a person).

Harrow drive /harəʊ ˈdrʌɪv/ *noun phr.* **M19.**
[**ORIGIN** from *Harrow* (see **HARROVIAN**) + **DRIVE** *noun*.]
CRICKET. Orig., a drive through extra cover. Now, a mishit drive in which the ball deflects off the inside edge of the bat behind the wicket.

harrower /ˈharəʊə/ *noun*[1]. **ME.**
[**ORIGIN** from **HARROW** *verb*[2] + **-ER**[1].]
A person who or thing which harrows land, the body, feelings, etc.

†**harrower** *noun*[2] see **HARRIER** *noun*[3].

harrowing /ˈharəʊɪŋ/ *adjective.* **E19.**
[**ORIGIN** from **HARROW** *verb*[2] + **-ING**[2].]
That harrows the feelings; acutely distressing or painful.

J. A. MICHENER The ordeal he had undergone . . was so much more harrowing.

■ **harrowingly** *adverb* **L18.** **harrowingness** *noun* (*rare*) **L19.**

harrumph /həˈrʌmf/ *noun, interjection, & verb.* **M20.**
[**ORIGIN** Imit.]
▸ **A** *noun & interjection.* (A guttural sound made by clearing the throat) expr. disapproval. **M20.**
▸ **B** *verb.* **1** *verb intrans.* Make a guttural sound, esp. expressing disapproval. **M20.**

J. A. MICHENER The old man harrumphed.

2 *verb trans.* Speak (words) in a guttural way, esp. expressing disapproval. **M20.**

harry /ˈhari/ *noun*[1]. *rare.* **ME.**
[**ORIGIN** from the verb.]
The action or an act of harrying.

Harry /ˈhari/ *adjective & noun*[2]. **L15.**
[**ORIGIN** Familiar by-form of the male name *Henry*.]
▸ **A** *adjective.* Designating any of various coins of Henry VI, Henry VII, or Henry VIII. Long *rare* or *obsolete.* **L15.**
▸ **B** *noun* **1 a** (A name for) a country fellow, a rustic. Now *dial. rare.* **L18.** ▸**b** (A name for) a lower-class young man. Now chiefly in ***Flash Harry*** below. **L19.**
2 In *pl.* Playing cards of the second quality. *rare.* **M19.**
– **PHRASES:** **By the Lord Harry!** *interjection* (*arch.*) expr. surprise or assertion. **Flash Harry** an ostentatious, loudly dressed and extrovert man. **Old Harry** the Devil; esp. in ***play Old Harry with***, play the devil with, work mischief on, ruin.
– **SPECIAL COLLOCATIONS & COMB.:** **Harry groat** a groat of Henry VIII. **Harry-long-legs** (now *dial.*) a crane fly. **Harry noble** a gold coin of Henry VI.

harry /ˈhari/ *verb.*
[**ORIGIN** Old English *hergian*, *herian* corresp. to Old Frisian *-heria*, Old Saxon *herion*, Old High German *heriōn*, Old Norse *herja*, from Germanic, from a base meaning 'host, army'. Prob. conflated with synon. Old French *harier*, *her(r)ier*. Cf. **HARROW** *verb*[1].]
1 *verb intrans.* Make predatory raids. **OE.** ▸**b** *verb trans.* Plunder, carry off (cattle etc.) in a raid. *Scot.* **LME.**

E. A. FREEMAN The Danes spread themselves over the country, harrying.

2 *verb trans.* Overrun (a territory) with an army; lay waste, pillage, spoil. **ME.**

J. R. GREEN Pirate-boats were harrying the western coast of the island.

3 *verb trans.* Harass, persecute; despoil. **ME.** ▸**b** Drive out; deprive of house or possessions. *Scot.* **M16.**

W. S. CHURCHILL American privateers . . continued to harry British shipping.

4 *verb trans.* Worry, goad, harass; ill-treat. **ME.**

A. S. BYATT She had a reputation for driving and harrying her subordinates.

5 *verb trans.* Drag. *obsolete* exc. *dial.* **ME.**

harsh /hɑːʃ/ *adjective.* Also (orig. & *N. English*) **harsk** /hɑːsk/. **ME.**
[**ORIGIN** Middle Low German, German *harsch* rough, lit. 'hairy', from *haer* (German *Haar*): see **-ISH**[1]. Cf. Old Swedish *harsk* (mod. *härsken*) rank, rancid and **HASK**.]
1 a Hard and rough to the touch; coarse-textured. **ME.** ▸**b** Rough to the taste or smell; astringent. **LME.** ▸**c** Rough to the ear; grating, jarring, discordant. **M16.** ▸**d** Physically disagreeable; lacking any comfort; bleak, stark. **E17.** ▸**e** Of a rough or forbidding appearance; inharmonious or unpleasant to the eye. **L18.**

a W. BOORER A few harsh-coated breeds need no trimming. **b** P. V. PRICE Such wines can be harsh rather than truly dry. **c** V. WOOLF It shattered the song of another bird with harsh discord. **d** R. P. JHABVALA There was a white glare in which everything looked very clean and harsh. *Sunday Express* These boots keep you warm in the harshest of conditions. **e** J. MASTERS The lights seemed harsh to me, coming in out of the soft night. C. P. SNOW A harsh red brick village interrupted the flow of fields. P. ROTH The harsh and rugged pioneer with that pistol in his pocket.

2 Of an action, a person, etc.: severe, rigorous, cruel, unfeeling. **L16.**

H. WOUK With difficulty Pug refrained from saying something harsh. J. M. ROBERTS They were so harsh, intransigent, cruel, uncompromising. *Practical Hairstyling & Beauty* Protect hair . . from the harsh drying effects of the sea and sun.

3 Lacking smoothness; jarring or grating to the mind or one's taste. **L16.**

CAPT. J. SMITH Though the beginning may seeme harsh . . a pleasanter Discourse ensues. F. MYERS No harsh transitions Nature knows.

■ **harshen** *verb trans.* make (more) harsh **E19.** **harshly** *adverb* **LME.** **harshness** *noun* **LME.**

harsh /hɑːʃ/ *verb.* **L16.**
[**ORIGIN** from the adjective.]
†**1** *verb intrans.* Make a harsh sound, creak. Only in **L16.**
2 *verb trans.* Rub or crash roughly against. *rare.* **L19.**

harsk *adjective* see **HARSH** *adjective.*

hart /hɑːt/ *noun.*
[**ORIGIN** Old English *heort*, earlier *heorot* = Old Saxon *hirot* (Dutch *hert*), Old High German *hir(u)z* (German *Hirsch*), Old Norse *hjǫrtr*, from Germanic.]
The male of the deer, esp. of the red deer; *spec.* a male deer after its fifth year.

hartal /ˈhɑːtɑːl, ˈhəːtɑːl/ *noun.* **E20.**
[**ORIGIN** Hindi *haṛtāl*, *hartāl* for *haṭṭal* lit. 'locking of shops' (Sanskrit *haṭṭa* shop, *tāla* lock, bolt).]
In the Indian subcontinent: the organized closing of shops and offices as a mark of protest or as an act of mourning.

hartebeest /ˈhɑːtɪbiːst/ *noun.* Also (earlier) †**hartbeest**. Pl. same, **-s**. **L18.**
[**ORIGIN** Afrikaans (now *hartebees*) from Dutch *hert* hart + *beest* beast.]
A large African antelope, *Alcelaphus buselaphus*, with a long head, a sloping back, and hooked horns, of which there are several races, including the kongoni (now extinct), the bubal, and the tora. Also, any of several related antelopes, esp. *Sigmoceros lichtensteinii* and members of the genus *Damaliscus* (as the hirola and the tsessebi).
bastard hartebeest = **TSESSEBI**. ***BUBAL hartebeest***. **Cape hartebeest** a red hartebeest of the southern African race. **northern hartebeest** = **BUBAL**. ***red hartebeest***: see **RED** *adjective*. ***TORA hartebeest***.

Hartleian /ˈhɑːtlɪən, hɑːtˈliːən/ *adjective.* Also **Hartleyan**. **E19.**
[**ORIGIN** from David *Hartley* (see below): see **-AN**, **-IAN**.]
Of or pertaining to the doctrines of the English psychologist David Hartley (1705–57), regarded as the founder of English associationist psychology.

hartshorn /ˈhɑːtshɔːn/ *noun.* **OE.**
[**ORIGIN** from **HART** + **-'S**[1] + **HORN** *noun*.]
1 The horn or antler of a hart; the substance obtained by rasping, slicing, or calcining this, formerly the chief source of ammonia. **OE.**
2 The aqueous solution of ammonia from any source. Also ***spirit of hartshorn***. Now *arch.* or *hist.* **L17.**

hart's tongue /ˈhɑːts tʌŋ/ *noun phr.* **ME.**
[**ORIGIN** translation of medieval Latin *lingua cervi*: so named from the shape of the fronds. Cf. German *Hirschzunge*, Danish *hertstong*, French *langue de cerf*, etc.]
An evergreen fern, *Phyllitis scolopendrium*, of shady places, with long strap-shaped undivided fronds. Also ***hart's tongue fern***.

hartwort /ˈhɑːtwəːt/ *noun.* Also (earlier) †**hert-**. **LME.**
[**ORIGIN** from var. of **HEART** *noun* + **WORT** *noun*[1], from the heart-shaped form of the leaves or seeds.]
†**1** A plant resembling bugle, perhaps self-heal, *Prunella vulgaris*. Only in **LME.**
†**2** The plant birthwort, *Aristolochia clematitis*. **M16–E17.**
3 An umbelliferous plant, *Tordylium maximum*. Formerly, any of various plants of the related genus *Seseli*. **M16.**

harum-scarum /hɛːrəmˈskɛːrəm/ *adverb, adjective, & noun. colloq.* **L17.**
[**ORIGIN** A rhyming comb., app. from **HARE** *verb*[2] + **SCARE** *verb*.]
▸ **A** *adverb.* Recklessly, wildly. Now *rare* or *obsolete.* **L17.**

J. PORTER I should not like a son of mine to run harum-scarum through my property.

▸ **B** *adjective.* Reckless, wild. **M18.**

V. WOOLF The manner of a harum-scarum Irish hostess.

▸ **C** *noun.* A reckless person; reckless action or behaviour. **L18.**

HOLME LEE His reminiscences of Basil as a handsome harum-scarum.

■ **harum-scarumness** *noun* **M19.**

haruspex /həˈrʌspɛks/ *noun.* Orig. †**a-**. Pl. **-spices** /-spɪsiːz/. **L15.**
[**ORIGIN** Latin *(h)aruspex*, *-spicem*, from a base appearing in Sanskrit *hirā* artery + Latin *-spex*, from *specere* look at.]
ROMAN HISTORY. A person who inspected the entrails of sacrificial victims in order to foretell the future.

haruspical /həˈrʌspɪk(ə)l/ *adjective.* **M17.**
[**ORIGIN** Latin *(h)aruspicalis*, formed as **HARUSPEX**: see **-ICAL**.]
Of, pertaining to, or having the function of a haruspex.

haruspication /hərʌspɪˈkeɪʃ(ə)n/ *noun. rare.* **L19.**
[**ORIGIN** Late Latin *haruspicatio(n-)*, formed as **HARUSPEX**: see **-ATION**.]
= **HARUSPICY**.

haruspicy /həˈrʌspɪsi/ *noun.* Orig. †**a-**. **M16.**
[**ORIGIN** Latin *haruspicium*, formed as **HARUSPEX**.]
ROMAN HISTORY. Divination by inspection of the entrails of sacrifices.

Harvardian /hɑːˈvɑːdɪən/ *noun.* **E18.**
[**ORIGIN** from *Harvard* College, Cambridge, Mass., now part of *Harvard* University.]
A student or graduate of Harvard University.

Harveian /ˈhɑːvɪən, hɑːˈviːən/ *adjective.* **M18.**
[**ORIGIN** from William *Harvey* (see below): see **-AN**, **-IAN**.]
Of, pertaining to, or commemorating the English physician William Harvey (1578–1657), who discovered how the blood circulated.

harvest /ˈhɑːvɪst/ *noun & verb.*
[**ORIGIN** Old English *hærfest* = Old Frisian, Middle Dutch & mod. Dutch *herfst*, Old High German *herbist* (German *Herbst* autumn, (dial.) fruit harvest), Old Norse *haust*, from Germanic, from Indo-European base repr. by Latin *carpere* pluck, Greek *karpos* fruit.]
▸ **A** *noun.* **1** The third season of the year, autumn. *obsolete* exc. *dial.* or passing into sense 2. **OE.**

M. MACKENZIE Toward the End of Harvest, when the Days are turning short.

2 (The season for) the cutting and gathering in of ripened grain and other produce. **ME.**

MILTON Seed time and Harvest, Heat and hoary Frost Shall hold thir course. M. IGNATIEFF It was the season of the grape harvest.

3 The crop of ripened grain. **ME.** ▸**b** *gen.* The season's yield of any natural product. **E17.**

A. GHOSH Bhudet Roy . . had a magnificent harvest that year. **b** J. G. FARRELL At one time this orchard alone must have provided a great harvest of fruit.

4 *fig.* The product of any action or effort. **LME.**

SHAKES. *Rich. III* To reap the harvest of perpetual peace. R. S. THOMAS Your eyes betray The heart's rich harvest.

– **COMB.:** **harvest-bug** = ***harvest mite*** below; **harvest festival** a Christian church service giving thanks for the completion of the harvest, for which the church is usu. decorated with grain, fruit, etc.; **harvest field** a field in the process of being harvested; ***harvest maiden***: see **MAIDEN** *noun* 7a; **harvestman** (***a***) a reaper, a harvester; (***b***) any arachnid of the order Opiliones, characteristically with very long legs and a small rounded waistless body; **harvest mite** any of various mites, or their biting larvae, which are common at harvest time; esp. (in Great Britain and Ireland) *Trombicula autumnalis*; **harvest moon**: full within a fortnight of the autumnal equinox (22 or 23 September) and rising at almost the same time for several nights, at points successively further north on the eastern horizon; **harvest mouse** (***a***) a small Eurasian mouse, *Micromys minutus*, which builds a nest above ground in the stems of growing grain or other vegetation; (***b***) any of various small Central and N. American mice of the genus *Reithrodontomys*, that resemble brownish house mice; **harvest queen** a doll made from or decorated with sheaves of corn or a young woman chosen from the reapers, representing the goddess of agriculture and crops and given a place of honour at the harvest home; **harvest-spider** = ***harvestman*** (b) above.
▸ **B** *verb.* **1** *verb trans.* & (later) *intrans.* Reap and gather in (ripe grain or other produce). **LME.** ▸**b** *verb trans.* Remove (cells) from a culture; remove (cells, tissues, organs) from a person or animal for experimental or transplantation purposes. **M20.** ▸**c** *verb trans.* Kill or remove (wild animals) for food, sport, or population control. **M20.**

C. MORGAN All the barley was not yet harvested. E. O'BRIEN Fields that have been mown, others that have been harvested. **b** *Nature* Macrophages were harvested from the peritoneal cavity 10 days after the second immunization. *British Medical Journal* They could harvest skin 24 hours after irreversible asystole and transplant it.

2 *verb trans. fig.* Gather up, collect, (and store); receive as the consequence of previous actions. L19.

> S. NAIPAUL He . . looked forward contentedly to harvesting a decent Second at the end of his three years. *transf.*: B. NEIL She went back to the sitting-room and harvested her scattered clothes.

■ **harvestless** *adjective* devoid of harvests; sterile: M19.

harvester /ˈhɑːvɪstə/ *noun*. L16.
[ORIGIN from HARVEST *verb* + -ER[1].]
1 A person who reaps and gathers in the harvest. L16. **2** A machine for reaping and esp. also for binding up the sheaves. Cf. ***combine harvester*** s.v. COMBINE *noun* 3. M19. **3** A harvestman (arachnid); a harvest mite. L19.

harvest home /hɑːvɪst ˈhəʊm/ *noun phr.* L16.
[ORIGIN from HARVEST *noun* + HOME *adverb*.]
1 The fact, time, or occasion of bringing in the last of the harvest; the festival (now rarely held) celebrating this. L16.

> SHAKES. *1 Hen. IV* His chin new reap'd Show'd like a stubble-land at harvest-home.

2 A song of rejoicing on this occasion. M17.

> SIR W. SCOTT Harvest-home hath hush'd the clanging wain.

Harvey /ˈhɑːvi/ *noun*. M17.
[ORIGIN from surname *Harvey* (see below).]
1 [Prob. from Gabriel *Harvey* (?1545–1630), English writer.] A variety of cooking and cider apple. M17. **2** [Peter *Harvey* (fl. 1760), English publican.] More fully ***Harvey sauce***. ***Harvey's sauce***. (Proprietary name for) a savoury sauce or relish for accompanying meat or fish. E19. **3** ***Harvey Wallbanger***, a cocktail made from vodka or gin and orange juice. Orig. *US*. L20.

harveyize /ˈhɑːvɪʌɪz/ *verb trans.* Also **-ise**. L19.
[ORIGIN from H. A. *Harvey* (1824–93), US manufacturer + -IZE.]
METALLURGY. Case-harden (steel, esp. for armour-plating) by means of a cementation process invented by Harvey.

harzburgite /ˈhɑːtsbəːɡʌɪt/ *noun*. L19.
[ORIGIN from (Bad) *Harzburg*, a town in Germany + -ITE[1].]
GEOLOGY. A rock of the peridotite group consisting largely of orthopyroxene and olivine.

has *verb* see HAVE *verb*.

has-been /ˈhazbiːn/ *noun*. *colloq.* E17.
[ORIGIN from *has* 3 sing. pres. indic. of HAVE *verb* + *been* pa. pple of BE.]
A person who or thing which has lost a quality or proficiency formerly possessed; an out-of-date person or thing.

> I. WALLACE A doddering and reactionary has-been who ought to have been interred long ago.

hasenpfeffer /ˈhɑːz(ə)n(p)fɛfə/ *noun*. L19.
[ORIGIN German, from *Hasen* hare's + *Pfeffer* pepper.]
A highly seasoned hare stew.

hash /haʃ/ *noun*[1]. M17.
[ORIGIN from the verb, replacing earlier HACHY.]
1 Something cut up into small pieces; *spec.* a dish of chopped (esp. previously cooked) meat heated with gravy, potatoes, etc.; *fig.* old matter served up in a new form (now chiefly passing into sense 3). M17. **2** A stupid person, one who is careless or muddled in speech or action. *Scot.* M17. **3** A (spoiled) mixture of jumbled incongruous things; a mess, a muddle. Freq. in ***make a hash of*** below. M18. **4** Noise in a received signal due to imperfect equipment; *gen.* radio noise. M20. **5** COMPUTING. An act or the action of hashing. M20. **6** In full ***hash sign***. The symbol #, esp. used before a numeral that is a number in a series. L20.

– PHRASES: **make a hash of** spoil in attempting to deal with, make a mess of. **settle a person's hash** *colloq.* silence or subdue a person.

– COMB.: **hash browns** (chiefly *N. Amer.*) a dish made of chopped cooked potatoes and onions (sometimes shaped into a patty), fried until brown; **hash house** *colloq.* (chiefly *N. Amer.*) a cheap eating house; ***hash sign***: see sense 6 above.

■ **hashy** *adjective* of the nature of a hash; muddled, careless: L19.

hash /haʃ/ *noun*[2]. *colloq.* M20.
[ORIGIN Abbreviation.]
= HASHISH.

> *attrib.*: *Daily Telegraph* All claimed that they were unaware of any hash smuggling operation.

hash /haʃ/ *verb*. L16.
[ORIGIN Old French & mod. French *hacher*, from *hache* HATCHET *noun*.]
1 *verb trans.* Cut (esp. meat) up or *up* into small pieces; make into a hash, serve up as a hash; hack about, mangle (now only *fig.* exc. *Scot.* & *dial.*). L16.

> *fig.*: SCOTT FITZGERALD The things . . they had hashed and rehashed for many a frugal conversational meal. *New Socialist* People are offered the same view hashed up as 'left' culture.

2 *verb trans.* Talk *over*, discuss exhaustively. *colloq.* M20.

> *New Yorker* Asked him in to hash over a point or two.

3 *verb trans.* & *intrans.* COMPUTING. Apply an algorithm to (a character string, esp. a record key) in order to obtain a number, esp. as an address for a record. M20.

Hashemite /ˈhaʃɪmʌɪt/ *noun* & *adjective*. Also **Hashimite**. L17.
[ORIGIN from *Hāshim*, great-grandfather of Muhammad + -ITE[1].]
▸ **A** *noun*. A member of an Arabian princely family claiming descent from Hashim and ruling Mecca from the 10th cent. until 1924. L17.
▸ **B** *adjective*. Of, pertaining to, or characteristic of the Hashemites; *spec.* designating or pertaining to the Kingdom of Jordan established in 1948. L19.

Hashimoto /haʃɪˈməʊtəʊ/ *noun*. M20.
[ORIGIN Hakaru *Hashimoto* (1881–1934), Japanese surgeon.]
MEDICINE. ***Hashimoto's disease***, ***Hashimoto's goitre***, ***Hashimoto's thyroiditis***, an autoimmune disease causing chronic inflammation and consequential failure of the thyroid gland.

hashish /ˈhaʃiːʃ, -ʃɪʃ, haˈʃiːʃ/ *noun*. L16.
[ORIGIN Arabic *ḥašīš* dry herb, hay, powdered hemp-leaves, intoxicant made from this.]
= CANNABIS 2.

> R. OWEN A drive against the growing use of drugs in Georgia, mainly hashish and opium.

Hasid /ˈhasɪd/ *noun*. Also **Cha(s)sid** /ˈxa-/, **Hassid**. Pl. **-im** /-ɪm/. E19.
[ORIGIN Hebrew *ḥāsīḏ* pious, pietist.]
A member of a Jewish sect founded in the 18th cent. by Israel Baal Shem Tov and emphasizing joy in the service of God. Also = ASSIDEAN.

■ **Haˈsidic** *adjective* of or belonging to the Hasidim E20. **Hasidism** *noun* the tenets of the Hasidim L19.

hask /hɑːsk/ *adjective*. Long *dial.* LME.
[ORIGIN Alt. of *harsk*: see HARSH *adjective*.]
Rough and hard to the touch or taste, esp. from lack of moisture.

■ **hasky** *adjective* dry, rough, coarse M17.

haslet /ˈheɪzlɪt, ˈhazlɪt/. *noun*. Also **harslet** /ˈhɑːslɪt/. LME.
[ORIGIN Old French *hastelet* (mod. *hâtelet(te)*) dim. of *haste* (mod. *hâte*) spit, roast meat (cf. Dutch *harst* sirloin) = Old High German *harst*: see -LET.]
Orig., a piece of meat for roasting; *esp.* a pig's pluck. Now chiefly, a meat loaf made from cooked minced and seasoned pig's pluck, usu. served cold.

Hasmonean /hazməˈniːən/ *noun* & *adjective*. Also **As-** /az-/. E17.
[ORIGIN from mod. Latin *Asmonaeus*, from Greek *Asamonaios* = *hašmonāy*, the reputed grandfather of Mattathias, the head of the Maccabee family of priests: see -AN, -EAN.]
▸ **A** *noun*. A member of a Jewish dynasty established by the Maccabees. E17.
▸ **B** *adjective*. Of, pertaining to, or designating this dynasty. E17.

hasp /hɑːsp/ *noun*.
[ORIGIN Old English *hæpse*, *hæsp* corresp. to Middle Low German *haspe*, *hespe*, Old High German *haspa* (German *Haspe*), Old Norse *hespa*, rel. further to Middle Low German, Dutch *haspel*, Old High German *haspil*.]
1 A contrivance for fastening a door or lid; *esp.* a hinged metal plate with a hole which fits over a staple and is secured by a pin or padlock; in a trunk or case, a similar metal plate with a projecting piece which is secured by the lock. OE. ▸**b** Any of various similar simple devices for fastening a door, window, etc. L18. **2** A clasp or catch for fastening two parts of a garment, the covers of a book, etc. ME. **3** A hank or skein of yarn or thread; a definite quantity of yarn, the fourth part of a spindle. Now *dial.* LME.

hasp /hɑːsp/ *verb trans.* OE.
[ORIGIN from the noun.]
1 Fasten (as) with a hasp. OE. ▸†**b** Confine, imprison; lock *up*. L17–E18. †**2** Clasp, embrace. LME–E17.

Hassid *noun* & *adjective* var. of HASID.

hassium /ˈhasɪəm/ *noun*. L20.
[ORIGIN from Latin *Hassia* Hesse (the German state where the laboratory in which the element was discovered is located) + -IUM.]
A radioactive transuranic chemical element, atomic no. 108, produced artificially by high-energy atomic collisions (symbol Hs).

hassle /ˈhas(ə)l/ *verb* & *noun*. L19.
[ORIGIN Uncertain: perh. blend of HAGGLE *verb* and TUSSLE *verb*.]
▸ **A** *verb*. **1** *verb trans.* Hack or saw at. *dial.* L19. **2** *verb trans.* & *intrans.* Bother, pester, harass (a person); quarrel or wrangle *over* (something). *colloq.* M20.

> W. WHARTON I hassle a guy into moving his truck.

▸ **B** *noun*. A problem, a difficulty; a quarrel, an argument; fuss, bother. *colloq.* M20.

> K. AMIS Since the end of the legal hassle, we had not met more than a couple of times. A. BLOND To write a book without having the hassle of having to sell it too.

hassock /ˈhasək/ *noun*. OE.
[ORIGIN Unknown.]
1 A firm tuft or clump of grass etc., esp. as occurring in boggy ground. OE. ▸**b** A shock of hair. *Scot.* M18. **2** A thick firm cushion, formerly freq. stuffed with straw, used to rest the feet on or, esp. in church, to kneel on. E16. **3** The soft calcareous sandstone separating the beds of ragstone in Kent. E18.

■ **hassocky** *adjective* (***a***) (of a marsh or bog) having many hassocks; (***b***) of the nature of or consisting of calcareous sandstone: M17.

hast *verb* see HAVE *verb*.

hasta la vista /ˈasta la ˈvista/ *interjection*. M20.
[ORIGIN Spanish.]
Goodbye, *au revoir*.

hastate /ˈhasteɪt/ *adjective*. L18.
[ORIGIN Latin *hastatus*, from *hasta* spear: see -ATE[2].]
Shaped like a spearhead, narrowly triangular; BOTANY (of a leaf) triangular with basal corners laterally projecting.

■ Also †**hastated** *adjective* M–L18.

haste /heɪst/ *noun*. ME.
[ORIGIN Old French (mod. *hâte*) from Germanic (whence Old English *hǣst* violence, fury, Old Norse *heifst*, *heipt* hate, revenge, Gothic *haifsts* strife; Old English *hǣste* violent, Old Frisian *hāste*, Old High German *heisti* powerful), of unknown origin.]
1 Quickness or speed of motion or action, esp. as prompted by urgency or pressure. ME.

> A. J. CRONIN His haste was desperate, a frantic race against her ebbing strength. R. C. HUTCHINSON Without haste . . he turned and went away.

2 Quickness of action without due consideration; rashness, precipitancy. ME.

> W. COWPER Friends, not adopted with a schoolboy's haste.

3 Eagerness to do something quickly; impatience, hurry. LME.

> P. V. WHITE Such was his haste, he scarcely paused for his due reward. E. O'BRIEN The men and women . . seemed to be devoid of fret or haste.

– PHRASES: **in haste** (***a***) quickly; (***b***) hurriedly. **make haste** move or act quickly. **more haste, less speed** best results are obtained by proceeding with deliberation.

■ **hasteful** *adjective* (*arch.*) full of haste; hurrying, hurried: E17. **hastefully** *adverb* (*rare*) L19.

haste /heɪst/ *verb*. *arch.* ME.
[ORIGIN Old French *haster* (mod. *hâter*), formed as HASTE *noun*. Superseded by HASTEN.]
1 *verb trans.* = HASTEN 1. ME.

> SHAKES. *Coriol.* Let's hence, And with our fair entreaties haste them on.

2 *verb intrans.* & *refl.* = HASTEN 2. ME.

> C. BRONTË The hour is hasting but too fast.

hasten /ˈheɪs(ə)n/ *verb*. M16.
[ORIGIN from HASTE *verb* + -EN[5].]
1 *verb trans.* Cause to move more quickly; urge on; quicken, hurry. M16. ▸†**b** Send in haste. E17–M18.

> D. L. SAYERS How easy it would be . . to hasten Mrs. Wrayburn's death a trifle.

2 *verb intrans.* Make haste (*to do*); come or go quickly; hurry. M16.

> W. S. CHURCHILL Parliament hastened to send the exiled Charles a large sum of money. J. G. FARRELL The Major hastened along the corridor, up the stairs three at a time.

■ **hastener** *noun* L16.

hastilude /ˈhastɪljuːd/ *noun*. *obsolete* exc. *hist.* L16.
[ORIGIN medieval Latin *hastiludus*, *-dium*, from Latin *hasta* spear + *ludus* play.]
A kind of joust or tournament; spear-play.

hastily /ˈheɪstɪli/ *adverb*. ME.
[ORIGIN from HASTY *adjective* + -LY[2].]
1 Quickly, speedily; now usu., hurriedly. Formerly also, soon; suddenly. ME.

> J. B. PRIESTLEY She withdrew her hand, though not hastily. J. SIMMS I hastily did my utmost to reassure him.

2 Rashly, inconsiderately, precipitately; in sudden anger. Formerly also, violently, fiercely. ME.

> ADDISON That the Reader may not judge too hastily of this Piece of Criticism. M. KEANE She gave in hastily, 'if you must you must'.

hastiness /ˈheɪstɪnɪs/ *noun*. ME.
[ORIGIN formed as HASTILY + -NESS.]
†**1** Quickness; suddenness. ME–L16. **2** Hurriedness; precipitancy, rashness; quickness of temper. ME.

hasting /ˈheɪstɪŋ/ *noun* & *adjective*. M16.
[ORIGIN from HASTE *verb* + -ING[2] (prob. orig. as ppl adjective).]
▸ **A** *noun*. †**1** In *pl.* People making haste or hurrying. M16–L17. **2** An early-ripening fruit or vegetable; *spec.* a variety of early pea. *obsolete* exc. *local*. L16.

H

▸ **B** *adjective*. †**1** Of a fruit or vegetable: ripening early. L16–M18.
2 That hastens or hurries. Now *rare* or *obsolete*. L16.

†**hastive** *adjective*. Also **hastif**. ME.
[ORIGIN Old French *hastif*, *-ive*: see HASTY.]
1 = HASTY 1, 2, 3. ME–L15.
2 = HASTY 1C. Only in E18.

hasty /ˈheɪsti/ *adjective, verb, & adverb*. ME.
[ORIGIN Old French *hasti(f)* (mod. *hâtif*), formed as HASTE *noun*; see -Y[7]. Superseded HASTIVE (cf. TARDY *adjective*).]
▸ **A** *adjective*. **1** Speedy or quick, esp. in movement or action. *arch.* exc. as in sense 1b. ME. ▸**b** Speedy or quick due to pressure of time; hurried; made or done in haste. LME. ▸†**c** Of a fruit or vegetable: that ripens early. Cf. HASTIVE 2. LME–L17.

S. BELLOW Walking quickly there, back and forth in his hasty style. **b** J. KRANTZ She gave them . . a hasty kiss before she was finally free to dash away.

2 Rash, precipitate; quick-tempered; (of speech or action) said or done in anger or without due consideration. ME.

S. O'CASEY You're a bit hasty at times . . an' say things you shouldn't say. A. THWAITE Philip . . cautioned him not to be hasty in committing himself. R. DAVIES I don't like to make hasty judgements.

†**3** Eager or impatient (*to do*). LME–M18.
– SPECIAL COLLOCATIONS: **hasty pudding**: of wheat flour or (*US*) maize flour stirred to a thick batter in boiling milk or water.
▸ **B** *verb trans. & intrans.* = HASTEN. *obsolete* exc. *Scot.* ME.
▸ †**C** *adverb*. Hastily. LME–M16.

H

hat /hat/ *noun*.
[ORIGIN Old English *hætt* corresp. to Old Norse *hǫttr* hood, cowl, from Germanic, from base of HOOD *noun*[1].]
1 A shaped covering for the head worn for warmth, as a fashion item, or as part of a uniform. OE.

DAY LEWIS The . . beautiful face is shadowed by a perfectly enormous hat. E. WELTY A stylish hat with a quill slanting up from the crown.

bowler hat, ***Cossack hat***, ***Gainsborough hat***, ***hard hat***, ***high hat***, ***opera hat***, ***stovepipe hat***, ***straw hat***, ***top hat***, etc.

2 A hat as showing the wearer's rank or office; *spec.* (in full ***red hat***) the hat or dignity of a cardinal. ME.
3 A person's official capacity; one's status. Freq. in ***wear one's — hat***, ***wear two hats***, below. M20.

J. D. WATSON The hat he now displayed was that of the chairman of a committee.

– PHRASES: ***at the drop of a hat***: see DROP *noun* 7. **bad hat** *arch. slang* a ne'er-do-well. **be all hat and no cattle** *US colloq.* tend to talk boastfully without acting on one's words. ***cock one's hat***, ***cocked hat***: see COCK *verb*[1] 6b. ***hang up one's hat***: see HANG *verb*. **hats off to —**: a call to acknowledge the outstanding qualities of a person or thing. **I'll eat my hat if —** *colloq.* I shall be greatly astonished if (a predicted event does not take place). **in a hat**, **in the hat** *slang* in trouble, in a fix. **keep under one's hat** keep secret or confidential. **my hat!** expr. surprise. **old hat** *slang* (something regarded as) old-fashioned or tediously familiar. **pass round the hat** (*lit. & fig.*) solicit donations by personal appeal. **pick out of a hat** *fig.* select completely at random. **pull one out of the hat** bring off an unexpected trick in an apparently desperate situation. **raise one's hat** (of a man) lift the hat a short distance above the head, as a respectful salutation (foll. by *to* the person saluted). **send round the hat** = ***pass round the hat*** above. **take off one's hat** (**a**) (of a man) doff the hat, as a salutation or sign of respect; (**b**) *fig.* (foll. by *to*) acknowledge the outstanding qualities of. ***talk through one's hat***: see TALK *verb*. **throw one's hat into the ring** announce one's intention of entering a contest. **touch one's hat** (of a man) touch the brim of the hat with the hand, as a respectful greeting (*to* a person). **wear one's — hat** operate in one's — capacity. **wear two hats** operate in two capacities simultaneously. **whose hat covers his or her family** (& vars.) who has only himself or herself to provide for. ***Yellow Hat***: see YELLOW *adjective*.
– COMB.: **hatband** (**a**) a narrow ribbon worn round a hat above the brim (***gold hatband*** (*hist.*), a gentleman commoner at a university); (**b**) a band of crape worn round a hat as a sign of mourning; **hatbox** a box to hold a hat, esp. for travelling; **hatcheck boy**, **hatcheck girl** *N. Amer.* a cloakroom attendant; **hat-money** a gratuity paid by a merchant to the master of a ship; primage; **hatpin** a long pin usu. with an ornamental head, used to secure a woman's hat to her hair; **hatstand** *noun & adjective* (**a**) *noun* an upright stand with hooks for hanging hats etc. on; (**b**) *adjective* (*slang*) eccentric, crazy; **hat-tree** *US* = ***hatstand*** (a) above; **hat trick** (in cricket) the feat of taking three wickets with three successive balls; *gen.* the achievement of three (consecutive) successes in any other sport or activity.
■ **hatful** *noun* as much as a hat will hold; a large quantity: M17. **hatless** *adjective* LME. **hatlessness** *noun* L19.

hat /hat/ *verb trans.* Infl. **-tt-**. LME.
[ORIGIN from the noun.]
Provide or equip with a hat.

hatable /ˈheɪtəb(ə)l/ *adjective*. Also **hateable**. LME.
[ORIGIN from HATE *verb* + -ABLE.]
That deserves to be hated; odious.

hatch /hatʃ/ *noun*[1].
[ORIGIN Old English *hæċċ*, *heċċ*, corresp. to Middle Low German *heck*, Middle Dutch *hecke* (Dutch *hek*), from Germanic. Cf. HACK *noun*[3], HECK *noun*[1].]
1 The lower half of a divided door, which may be closed while the upper half is open. Also (now *dial.*), a small gate or wicket. OE. ▸**b** An opening in a wall through which dishes etc. may be passed between a kitchen and a dining area. Also ***serving hatch***. E18.

b M. SCAMMELL His better rations, which he now received from a different hatch in the canteen.

2 *NAUTICAL*. (The trapdoor or grated framework covering) a hatchway. Formerly (usu. in *pl.*), a movable planking forming a kind of deck; the permanent deck. ME. ▸**b** *transf.* (The trapdoor covering) an opening in the floor of a timber shed or other building. L19.

J. HAWKES Midships were three hatches, two battened permanently shut.

†**3** = HACK *noun*[3] 2, 4. Only in ME.
4 A floodgate, a sluice. Also = HECK *noun*[1] 1. LME.
5 An opening or door in an aeroplane or spacecraft. M20.
– PHRASES: **down the hatch** *slang*: a call to drink up. **under hatches** (**a**) below deck; (**b**) *fig.* in a state of servitude or adversity (*arch.*); concealed from knowledge, under wraps.
– COMB.: **hatchback** (a car having) a sloping rear door hinged at the top, usu. giving access to storage space; **hatch-boat** a half-decked fishing boat with hatches through which the fish are passed into the hold; **hatchway** *NAUTICAL* an opening in a ship's deck through which cargo is lowered into the hold; one leading to a lower deck.

hatch /hatʃ/ *noun*[2]. E17.
[ORIGIN from HATCH *verb*[1].]
The action or an act of hatching, (an) incubation. Also, a set of young birds etc. hatched, a brood.

C. DARWIN Two hybrids from the same parent but from different hatches.

hatches, matches, and dispatches *joc.* (the notices in a newspaper etc. of) births, marriages, and deaths.

hatch /hatʃ/ *noun*[3]. M17.
[ORIGIN from HATCH *verb*[2].]
An engraved line or stroke; *esp.* one used to represent shading in an engraving.

†**hatch** *noun*[4]. E18–E19.
[ORIGIN French *hache*.]
A hatchet.

hatch /hatʃ/ *verb*[1]. ME.
[ORIGIN Rel. to Middle High German *hecken*, Swedish *häcka*, Danish *hække*, of unknown origin.]
1 *verb trans. & intrans.* Produce (young birds etc.) from an egg by incubation. Also foll. by *out*. ME. ▸**b** *verb trans. gen.* Bring into existence, generate (an animal, a plant). ME.

T. D'URFEY My Hen has hatched today. J. CONRAD A strange bird is hatched sometimes in a nest in an unaccountable way. **b** W. BARTRAM Serving as a nursery bed to hatch . . the infant plant.

count one's chickens before they are hatched: see CHICKEN *noun*[1].
2 *verb trans.* Cause (an egg) to break open when incubation is complete. LME.
3 *verb trans. fig.* Devise (a plot etc.) by secret scheming. Also foll. by *up*. M16. ▸**b** *verb intrans.* Of a plot etc.: be in the process of being devised. Only in ***be hatching***. M17.

E. O'BRIEN Perhaps it was then I hatched my revenge. **b** C. MIDDLETON The great dangers and plots, that were now hatching against the state.

4 *verb intrans.* (Of a young bird etc.) emerge from an egg after incubation; (of an insect) emerge from a chrysalis. Freq. foll. by *out*. L16.

A. HARDY In about 10 days' time the first little herrings began to hatch. C. MILNE Caterpillars, . . you can keep them until they finally hatch into moths.

5 *verb intrans.* Of an egg: break open when incubation is complete, so as to release the young bird etc. inside. Also foll. by *out*. E18.
■ **hatchaˈbility** *noun* capacity (of an egg) to hatch; ability (of a bird etc.) to produce eggs that will hatch: E20. **hatcher** *noun* (**a**) a person who or thing which hatches; *spec.* an incubator; (**b**) *fig.* a secret deviser *of* plots etc.: L16.

hatch /hatʃ/ *verb*[2] *trans.* L15.
[ORIGIN Old French & mod. French *hacher*, from *hache* axe: see HATCHET *noun*.]
1 Inlay with or *with* gold, silver, or other metal in narrow strips. Formerly, inlay (metal) *on* a surface. L15.
2 Mark (a surface) with (close parallel) lines, esp. to represent shading in engraving. L16.
hatched moulding *ARCHITECTURE*: formed by two series of oblique parallel incisions crossing each other.

†**hatch** *verb*[3]. L16–E17.
[ORIGIN from HATCH *noun*[1].]
Close (a door) with a hatch.

fig.: P. SIDNEY While sleepe begins with heauy wings To hatch mine eyes.

hatchel /ˈhatʃ(ə)l/ *noun & verb*. Also (earlier, now *dial. & US*) **hetchel** /ˈhɛtʃ(ə)l/. Infl. **-ll-**, ***-l-**. ME.
[ORIGIN Ult. from West Germanic base repr. also by HOOK *noun*: cf. HACKLE *noun*[2], HECKLE *noun*, *verb*.]
▸ **A** *noun* = HACKLE *noun*[2] 5. ME.
▸ **B** *verb trans.* **1** = HACKLE *verb*[3] 1. ME.
2 *fig.* Harass, persecute. E19.
■ **hatcheller** *noun* a flax-dresser E17.

hatchery /ˈhatʃəri/ *noun*. L19.
[ORIGIN from HATCH *verb*[1] + -ERY.]
A place for the artificial hatching of eggs, esp. of fish or poultry.

hatchet /ˈhatʃɪt/ *noun*. ME.
[ORIGIN Old French & mod. French *hachette* dim. of *hache* axe from medieval Latin *hapia*, from Germanic (Old High German *happa*, *heppa* sickle-shaped knife) see -ET[1].]
1 A small or light short-handled axe, adapted for use with one hand. ME.
sling the hatchet, **throw the hatchet** *slang* (now *rare* or *obsolete*) spin yarns, talk in an exaggerated way. **throw the helve after the hatchet**, [by confusion] **throw the hatchet after the helve** risk adding fresh loss to that already incurred.
2 A N. American Indian tomahawk, esp. as used as a symbol of war. M17.
bury the hatchet (now chiefly *fig.*) cease hostilities and resume friendly relations. **dig up the hatchet**, **take up the hatchet** (now *hist.*) renew hostilities.
– COMB.: **hatchet-face** a narrow sharp face; **hatchet-faced** *adjective* having a hatchet-face, grim-looking; **hatchet fish** either of two kinds of fish with broad strongly compressed bodies and slender tails: (**a**) any of various deep-sea fishes of the family Sternoptychidae; (**b**) any of various tropical American flying freshwater fishes of the family Gasteropelecidae, often kept in aquariums; **hatchet job** a piece of hatchet work (freq. in ***do a hatchet job on***); **hatchet man** (orig. *US*) (**a**) a hired (orig. Chinese) assassin; (**b**) a person, esp. a journalist, used to destroy another's reputation; (**c**) a person employed to coerce or intimidate others; **hatchet work** (orig. *US*) journalistic or other criticism designed to destroy a person's reputation.

hatchet /ˈhatʃɪt/ *verb trans.* E17.
[ORIGIN from the noun.]
†**1** Cut or destroy with a hatchet. E17–M18.
2 Perform hatchet work on. M20.

hatchettite /ˈhatʃɪtʌɪt/ *noun*. M19.
[ORIGIN from Charles *Hatchett* (1765–1847), English chemist + -ITE[1].]
MINERALOGY. Naturally occurring paraffin wax or mineral tallow.
■ Also **hatchettine** *noun* E19.

hatchety /ˈhatʃɪti/ *adjective*. M19.
[ORIGIN from HATCHET *noun* + -Y[1].]
Esp. of the face: resembling a hatchet blade; thin and sharp.

hatching /ˈhatʃɪŋ/ *noun*. M17.
[ORIGIN from HATCH *verb*[2] + -ING[1].]
The drawing of parallel lines so as to produce the effect of shading; a series of lines so drawn; *HERALDRY* a system for identifying tincture in monochrome by lines and dots.

hatchling /ˈhatʃlɪŋ/ *noun*. L19.
[ORIGIN from HATCH *noun*[2] + -LING[1].]
A fish, bird, etc., just hatched (esp. artificially) and not yet able to take care of itself.

hatchment /ˈhatʃm(ə)nt/ *noun*. E16.
[ORIGIN Prob. from French †*hachement* from Old French *acesmement* adornment.]
An escutcheon or armorial device; *esp.* a square or diamond-shaped panel or canvas with a deceased person's armorial bearings, affixed to his or her house during mourning or placed in a church.

hate /heɪt/ *noun*[1].
[ORIGIN Old English *hete* = Old Saxon *heti*, Old High German *haz* (German *Hass*), Old Norse *hatr*, Gothic *hatis*, superseded in Middle English by Old Norse *hatr* or after HATRED.]
1 Hatred. OE.

M. O. W. OLIPHANT Generations which succeeded each other in the same hates and friendships. QUILLER-COUCH A look of cold hate.

2 An object of hatred. Chiefly *poet.* exc. (*colloq.*) in ***one's chief hate***, ***one's pet hate***, etc. L16.

Nature One of his particular hates is the fallacy that the Church impeded the progress of Science.

3 An artillery bombardment. *arch. slang.* E20.

E. J. THOMPSON He was watching a spasmodic 'hate' of some violence.

– ATTRIB. & COMB.: In the sense 'expressive of hate', as ***hate literature***, ***hate message***; 'designed to stir up hate', as ***hate campaign***. Special combs., as **hate crime** (orig. *US*) a crime (usu. violent) motivated by racial, sexual, or other form of intolerance; **hate mail** letters sent (often anonymously) in which the senders express their hostility towards the recipient.
■ **hateless** *adjective* L16.

hate *noun*[2] var. of HAET.

hate /heɪt/ *verb trans.*
[ORIGIN Old English *hatian* = Old Frisian *hatia*, Old Saxon *haton* (Dutch *haten*), Old High German *hazzōn*, *-ēn* (German *hassen*), Old Norse *hata*, Gothic *hatan*, from Germanic, from base of HATE *noun*[1].]
1 Have feelings of hostility or strong antipathy towards. OE.

G. GREENE I hated him for the very quality which had once helped my love. P. ROTH You hate them and wish they were dead.

hate a person's guts hate a person intensely.

2 In weakened sense: have a (strong) distaste for, be unable to endure. Freq. foll. by *to do, doing*. ME.

> T. HARDY Stephen's wife hated the sea . . and couldn't bear the thought of going into a boat. G. B. SHAW Don't you hate people who have no character . . ? W. S. MAUGHAM You know how I hate to interfere in other people's business. G. VIDAL I hate being called by my first name by strangers.

■ **hater** *noun* LME.

hateable *adjective* var. of HATABLE.

hateful /ˈheɪtfʊl, -f(ə)l/ *adjective*. LME.
[ORIGIN from HATE *noun*[1] + -FUL.]
1 Full of hatred; malignant. *arch.* LME.

> SHAKES. *2 Hen. VI* Ah, Gloucester, hide thee from their hateful looks.

2 Exciting hate; odious, repugnant. LME.

> J. PRIESTLEY No vice is universally so hateful as ingratitude. W. SOYINKA A hateful job this, hardly time for leisure.

■ **hatefully** *adverb* LME. **hatefulness** *noun* M16.

hath *verb* see HAVE *verb*.

hatha yoga /hʌtə ˈjəʊgə, haθə/ *noun phr.* E20.
[ORIGIN Sanskrit, from *haṭha* force + YOGA.]
A system of physical exercises and breathing control used in yoga.

hatha yogi /ˈhʌtə ˈjəʊgi, ˈhaθə/ *noun phr.* M20.
[ORIGIN Sanskrit, formed as HATHA YOGA + YOGI.]
A person who practises hatha yoga.

Hathoric /haˈθɔːrɪk/ *adjective*. E20.
[ORIGIN from *Hathor* (see below) from Greek *Hathōr* from Egyptian *Ḥet-Ḥeru* house of Horus: see -IC.]
Of or pertaining to Hathor, the Egyptian goddess of love, a representation of whose head (depicted with a cow's ears and horns) was used to ornament columns.

hatred /ˈheɪtrɪd/ *noun*. ME.
[ORIGIN from HATE *verb* + -RED.]
A feeling of hostility or strong aversion towards a person or thing; active and violent dislike.

> G. GREENE He had a hatred of undressing before another man. E. FEINSTEIN She disliked the old man's bigoted hatred of all minorities.

hatted /ˈhatɪd/ *adjective*. M16.
[ORIGIN from HAT *noun*, *verb*: see -ED[2], -ED[1].]
Wearing a hat.

> P. LIVELY Women in silk and crêpe-de-chine, gloved and hatted.

hatted kit [KIT *noun*[1]] a preparation of buttermilk and warm milk, which forms a creamy top.

hatter /ˈhatə/ *noun*. ME.
[ORIGIN from HAT *noun* + -ER[1].]
1 A maker of or dealer in hats. ME.
as mad as a hatter wildly eccentric.
2 A person (orig. a miner) working or living alone; a solitary bushman. *Austral. & NZ.* M19.

hatter /ˈhatə/ *verb trans.* Now *Scot. & N. English*. LME.
[ORIGIN Perh. of imit. origin, with frequentative ending: cf. *batter, shatter*, etc.: see -ER[5].]
1 Knock about, batter. LME.
2 Exhaust with fatigue or drudgery. (Foll. by *out*.) L17.

> DRYDEN He's hattered out with penance.

hattery /ˈhatəri/ *noun*. E19.
[ORIGIN from HAT *noun* + -ERY.]
A place where hats are made or sold. Also, hats collectively.

Hatti /ˈhati/ *noun*. Also **Kh-**. L19.
[ORIGIN Assyrian & Hittite.]
1 *collect. pl.* A pre-Hittite people of Anatolia. L19.
2 = HATTIC *noun*. L20.

Hattic /ˈhatɪk/ *adjective & noun*. E20.
[ORIGIN from HATTI + -IC.]
► A *adjective*. Of or pertaining to the Hatti. E20.
► B *noun*. The (non-Indo-European) language spoken by the Hatti. M20.
■ **Hattian** *adjective & noun* (*a*) *adjective* = HATTIC *adjective*; (*b*) *noun* the Hattic language; a member of the Hattic race: E20.

hatti-sherif /ˌhatɪʃəˈriːf/ *noun*. L17.
[ORIGIN Persian *ḵaṭṭ-i-šarīf*, from Arabic *ḵaṭṭ* writing + *i* (Persian) connective + Arabic *šarīf* noble.]
hist. A decree bearing a Sultan's personal mark and so made irrevocable.

hattock /ˈhatək/ *noun*. E16.
[ORIGIN from HAT *noun* + -OCK.]
1 A little (esp. fairy) hat. Chiefly in ***horse and hattock***, orig. a supposed call by witches to be on their way. *Scot.* E16.
2 A shock of standing sheaves of corn, the tops of which are protected by two sheaves laid along them in such a way as to carry off the rain. *dial.* L17.

hau /haʊ/ *noun*. M19.
[ORIGIN Hawaiian & Marquesan.]
A bushy tree of tropical coasts, *Hibiscus tiliaceus*, the bast of which yields a valuable fibre. Also ***hau tree***.

hauberk /ˈhɔːbəːk/ *noun*. ME.
[ORIGIN Old French *hau(s)berc, holberc*, from Frankish (= Old High German *halsberc*, Old English *healsbeorg*, Old Norse *halsbjǫrg*), from base of HAUSE *noun* + Germanic base meaning 'protect'.]
hist. A piece of defensive armour, orig. for the neck and shoulders, but early developed into a long coat of mail or military tunic.

haubitz *noun* var. of HOWITZ.

hauerite /ˈhaʊərʌɪt/ *noun*. M19.
[ORIGIN from Franz von *Hauer* (1822–99), Austrian geologist + -ITE[1].]
MINERALOGY. Native manganese disulphide, a cubic mineral crystallizing in the cubic system and usu. occurring as octahedral or cubo-octahedral reddish-brown crystals.

haugh /hɔː, hɑːx/ *noun*. *Scot. & N. English*. Also (*N. English*) **halgh**. ME.
[ORIGIN Prob. repr. Old English *healh* corner, nook, rel. to *holh* HOLLOW *noun*[1].]
A piece of flat alluvial land by the side of a river, forming part of the floor of the river valley.

haught /hɔːt/ *adjective*. *arch.* Also (earlier) †**haut**. LME.
[ORIGIN French *haut(e)* (Old French *ha(u)lt*) = high, from Latin *altus* high, infl. by Germanic base of HIGH *adjective*.]
1 Haughty. LME.
†2 High-minded. L15–L16.
†3 High-ranking, high-born. L15–E17.

haughtonite /ˈhɔːt(ə)nʌɪt/ *noun*. L19.
[ORIGIN from Samuel *Haughton* (1821–97), Irish scientist + -ITE[1].]
MINERALOGY. An iron-rich variety of biotite.

haughty /ˈhɔːti/ *adjective*. M16.
[ORIGIN Extension of HAUGHT *adjective* with -Y[1].]
1 High in one's own estimation; lofty and disdainful. M16.
▸b *fig.* Imposing, grand, stately, dignified. L16.

> A. BURGESS They were a haughty lot who found Manchester inferior to Hamburg. HENRY MILLER Look at his haughty air of pride and arrogance!

2 Of exalted character, style, or rank. *arch.* M16.
†3 *lit.* High, lofty. L16–E17.
■ **haughtily** *adverb* L16. **haughtiness** *noun* M16.

Hauhau /ˈhaʊhaʊ/ *noun*. *NZ*. Pl. same, **-s**. M19.
[ORIGIN Maori.]
(A follower of) the Pai-Marire religion during the 19th-cent. New Zealand Wars.
■ **Hauhauism** *noun* L19.

haul /hɔːl/ *noun*. L17.
[ORIGIN from the verb.]
1 The act of hauling; a pull; *spec.* the draught of a fishing net. L17. ▸b The distance over which something is hauled; a journey; *fig.* a project, a task. Freq. in ***long haul***, ***short haul***. L19.

> b R. SUTCLIFF An aged ferry steamer whose normal run was only the short haul between Malta and Syracuse.

2 a A quantity of yarn for rope-making. L18. ▸b (The quantity of) a draught of fish. M19.
3 *fig.* The making of a substantial gain; an amount gained, seized, stolen, etc. L18.

> *Cricket World* A career best haul of eight wickets for 107 runs.

haul /hɔːl/ *verb*. Also (earlier) †**hall**. M16.
[ORIGIN Var. of HALE *verb*[1].]
1 *NAUTICAL*. **a** *verb trans.* Trim the sails etc. of (a ship) so as to sail closer to the wind; ***haul one's wind***, ***haul the wind***, sail closer to the wind, change course (*lit.* & *fig.*). M16. ▸b *verb intrans.* Sail closer to the wind; sail in a specified direction; change course (*lit.* & *fig.*). Also ***haul to the wind***, ***haul upon the wind***. L16.
2 *verb trans.* Pull or draw with force; drag, tug. L16. ▸†b *verb trans.* Worry, torment, pester. *colloq.* L17–M18. ▸c *verb trans.* Transport by cart or other conveyance. M18. ▸d *verb trans.* Bring *up* for a reprimand, call to account. *colloq.* L18. ▸e *verb intrans.* Of a bachelor seal: come out of the water to rest on the hauling grounds. M19.

> V. WOOLF She clutched the banisters and hauled herself upstairs. d G. SWIFT In Quinn's office you are the luckless schoolboy hauled before the headmaster.

haul ass: see ASS *noun*[2]. ***haul down one's colours***: see COLOUR *noun*. **d** ***haul over the coals***: see COAL *noun*.
3 *verb intrans.* Pull, tug, (*at* or *on* something). M18.

> J. DICKEY Lew and Bobby pulled the canoes up the bank . . hauling on the bow ropes.

4 *verb intrans.* Of the wind: change direction; *spec.* (more fully ***haul forward***) shift to a direction nearer the bow of a boat. M18.
– WITH ADVERBS IN SPECIALIZED SENSES: **haul off** (*a*) *verb phr. trans.* & *intrans.* (*NAUTICAL*) trim the sails etc. of (a ship) so as to sail closer to the wind; (*b*) *verb phr. intrans.* (chiefly *N. Amer. colloq.*) withdraw a little in preparation; ***haul off and —***, proceed to —. **haul out** *verb phr. intrans.* (*US*) go out, depart.
– COMB.: **haulabout** *US* a vessel like a barge used for coaling ships; **hauling ground** a place where bachelor seals congregate.

haulage /ˈhɔːlɪdʒ/ *noun*. E19.
[ORIGIN from HAUL *verb* + -AGE.]
1 The action or process of hauling; the conveyance of a load in a vehicle; the practice of conveying loads as a business. E19.
2 The expense of or charge for the transport of goods. M19.

hauler /ˈhɔːlə/ *noun*. L17.
[ORIGIN from HAUL *verb* + -ER[1].]
A person who or thing which hauls; a haulier.

haulier /ˈhɔːlɪə/ *noun*. Also (earlier) †**hall-**. LME.
[ORIGIN from HAUL *verb* + -IER.]
1 A person employed in hauling. Formerly *spec.*, a person who transported coal in tubs in a mine. LME.
2 A firm or a person engaged in road transport of goods. E20.

haulm /hɔːm/ *noun & verb*. Also **halm** /hɑːm/.
[ORIGIN Old English *halm* (*healm*) = Old Saxon, Old High German (Dutch, German) *halm*, Old Norse *hálmr*, from Germanic, from Indo-European base repr. also by Latin *culmus*, Greek *kalamos* reed.]
► A *noun*. 1 *collect. sing.* The stems of various cultivated plants, esp. peas, beans, vetches, hops, potatoes, etc., or (now less commonly) corn or grass, esp. as left after gathering the crop and used for litter or thatching; straw. OE.
2 A single stalk or stem (of a bean, potato, grass, etc.). OE.
► B *verb trans.* Lay (straw or haulm) straight for thatching. M17.

haulyard *noun* var. of HALYARD.

haunch /hɔːn(t)ʃ/ *noun*. Also †**hanch**. ME.
[ORIGIN Old French & mod. French *hanche* = Provençal, Spanish, Italian *anca* of Germanic origin (cf. Low German *hanke* hind leg of a horse).]
1 In humans and quadrupeds, the part of the body between the ribs and the thigh; in the horse, the part of the hindquarters between the reins or back to the hock or ham. ME. ▸b The leg and loin of a deer, sheep, or other animal as a joint of meat for cooking and eating. L15. ▸†c The pelvis as containing the womb. L16–M17. ▸†d *fig.* The last part of anything. Only in L16.

> GEO. ELIOT A fine black retriever . . sat on his haunches, and watched him.

2 *ARCHITECTURE*. The underside of an elliptical arch immediately above the springing; the corresponding part of any arched figure. Cf. HANCE 3. E18.
3 The end of a tenon reduced in width. E20.
4 The side of a made-up road. M20.
– COMB.: **haunch-bone** the ilium or the innominate bone of which it forms part.
■ **haunched** *adjective* (of a tenon) having its end reduced in width L19. **haunching** *noun* (*a*) the parts of an arch belonging to the haunch collectively; (*b*) a recess in a style for the end of a tenon: L19. **haunchy** *adjective* having prominent haunches M19.

haunt /hɔːnt/ *noun*. Also (now only in sense 4) **hant**, **ha'nt**. ME.
[ORIGIN from the verb.]
1 Habit, wont, custom. Now *Scot. & dial.* ME. ▸†b Habitual practice or use. LME–L16.
†2 The act or practice of frequenting a place. ME–E18.
3 A frequented place, an abode, (esp. of a specified person); the habitation or feeding place of particular animals. ME.

> G. ORWELL He frequented the Chestnut Tree Café, haunt of painters and musicians.

4 A spirit supposed to haunt a (specified) place. M19.

haunt /hɔːnt/ *verb*. ME.
[ORIGIN Old French & mod. French *hanter* from Germanic verb (repr. by Old English *hāmettan* provide with a home, house, Old Norse *heimta* get home, recover), from base of HOME *noun*.]
► I *verb trans.* †1 Practise or employ habitually or frequently. ME–L16.
2 Frequent (a place); associate habitually with (a person). ME.

> D. CAUTE The despondent Gilson had begun to haunt the bars.

3 *transf.* & *fig.* **a** Of a thought or feeling: occur to or affect frequently, esp. as a cause of trouble. LME. ▸b Of a ghost, a spirit, etc.: visit frequently, with manifestations of its presence. L16.

> a D. WIGODER An awful and unforgettable memory which still haunts me. b G. GREENE The Glowrie ghost, which is condemned to haunt an impoverished castle in the Highlands.

► II *verb intrans.* †4 Be accustomed. ME–M16.
5 Be present habitually (in a specified place); associate (with a specified person). ME.
†6 Go *to*. ME–M17.
■ **haunted** *adjective* much visited by a ghost, a spirit, etc.; much resorted to; (*obsolete* exc. *dial.*) practised, habituated: ME. **hauntedness** *noun* the state of being haunted L19. **haunter** *noun* LME.

haunting /ˈhɔːntɪŋ/ *adjective*. LME.
[ORIGIN from HAUNT *verb* + -ING[2].]
That haunts (esp. the thoughts or memory); evocative.

H

E. WAUGH One of his most haunting impressions. R. HUNTFORD A haunting fear of being left behind. *Studio Week* A single which . . was quite a haunting tune.

■ **hauntingly** *adverb* †(**a**) frequently, customarily; (**b**) so as to haunt (esp. the thoughts or memory): LME.

haurient /ˈhɔːrɪənt/ *adjective*. L16.
[ORIGIN Latin *haurient-* pres. ppl stem of *haurire* draw (water etc.): see -ENT.]
HERALDRY. Of a fish borne as a charge: placed palewise or upright with the head in chief (as if to draw in air).

Hausa /ˈhaʊsə/ *noun & adjective*. E19.
[ORIGIN Hausa.]
▸ **A** *noun*. Pl. **-s**, same. A member of a people of northern Nigeria and adjacent regions; the Chadic language of this people, widely used in W. Africa. E19.
▸ **B** *attrib*. or as *adjective*. Of or pertaining to the Hausas or their language. M19.

hause /hɔːs/ *noun*. *Scot. & N. English*. Also **hawse**.
[ORIGIN Old English *hals*, *heals* = Old Frisian, Old Saxon, Old High German, Old Norse *hals*, from Germanic base rel. to Latin *collum* neck. Cf. HAWSE *noun*[1].]
1 The neck. OE.
2 *transf*. A narrow neck of land or channel of water; a col or narrow ridge joining two summits. ME.
3 The throat, the gullet. LME.

H

hause /hɔːs/ *verb trans*. Now only *Scot. & N. English*. Also **hawse**, (earlier) †**halse**. ME.
[ORIGIN from HAUSE *noun*, or use of HALSE *verb*[1] assoc. with it.]
Clasp, embrace.

hausen /ˈhaʊz(ə)n/ *noun*. Pl. same. M18.
[ORIGIN German from Old High German *hūso*.]
The beluga, *Huso huso*.

hausfrau /ˈhaʊsfraʊ/ *noun*. Pl. **-s**, **-en** /-ən/. L18.
[ORIGIN German, from *Haus* house + *Frau* wife, woman.]
A (German) housewife; a person who embodies housewifely qualities.

S. BELLOW I am not just another suburban hausfrau.

Hausmaler /ˈhaʊsmɑːlə/*noun*. M20.
[ORIGIN German, from *Haus* house + *Maler* painter.]
A person who paints undecorated china at home or in a private workshop.

hausmannite /ˈhaʊsmənʌɪt/ *noun*. M19.
[ORIGIN from J. F. L. *Hausmann* (1782–1859), German mineralogist + -ITE[1].]
MINERALOGY. A mixed-valence oxide of manganese, Mn_3O_4, usu. occurring as brownish-black pseudo-octahedral crystals belonging to the tetragonal system.

hausse /oːs, hɒʊs/ *noun*. Pl. pronounced same. L18.
[ORIGIN French, from *hausser* raise.]
A type of sight for the breech of a cannon.

hausse-col /oskɔl, ˈhəʊskɒl/ *noun*. Pl. pronounced same. E19.
[ORIGIN French, from *hausser* raise + *col* neck.]
hist. A gorget of chainmail, or (later) of plate armour.

Haussmannize /ˈhaʊsmənʌɪz/ *verb trans*. Also **-ise**. M19.
[ORIGIN from Baron Eugène-Georges *Haussmann*, who, when prefect of the Seine (1853–70), remodelled a great part of Paris: see -IZE.]
Widen and straighten (a street); rebuild (a district) to a more open plan.
■ **Haussmaniˈzation** *noun* M19.

haustella *noun* pl. of HAUSTELLUM.

haustellate /ˈhɔːstələt, -leɪt/ *adjective*. M19.
[ORIGIN mod. Latin *haustellatus*, formed as HAUSTELLUM + -ATE[2].]
ZOOLOGY. **1** Esp. of an insect: provided with a mouth adapted for sucking (rather than mastication); provided with a haustellum (rather than mandibles). M19.
2 Of a mouth or mouthparts: adapted for sucking, suctorial. M19.

haustellum /hɔːˈstɛləm/ *noun*. Pl. **-lla** /-lə/. E19.
[ORIGIN mod. Latin, dim. of *haustrum* bucket, scoop, from *haust-* pa. ppl stem of *haurire* draw (water).]
ZOOLOGY. The sucking organ or proboscis of an insect or crustacean.

haustorium /hɔːˈstɔːrɪəm/ *noun*. Pl. **-ia** /-ɪə/. L19.
[ORIGIN from Latin *haustor* agent noun from *haurire* to draw, to drain: see -ORIUM.]
A slender projection from the root of a parasitic plant, such as a dodder, or from the hyphae of a parasitic fungus, enabling the parasite to penetrate the tissues of its host and absorb nutrients from it.
■ **haustorial** *adjective* of or pertaining to a haustorium M20.

haustrum /ˈhɔːstrəm/ *noun*. Pl. **-stra** /-strə/. L19.
[ORIGIN mod. Latin: see HAUSTELLUM.]
ANATOMY. Each of the small sacs enclosed by folds in the colon.
■ **haustral** *adjective* E20.

haut *adjective* see HAUGHT.

hautboy /ˈ(h)əʊbɔɪ/ *noun*. *arch*. Also (now usual in sense 2) **hautbois**, (now *rare*) **hoboy**. M16.
[ORIGIN French *hautbois*, from *haut* high + *bois* wood. Cf. OBOE.]
1 = OBOE 1. *arch*. M16. ▸**b** = OBOE 2. E18.
2 More fully ***hautboy strawberry***. A central European strawberry, *Fragaria muricata*, formerly grown for its fruit. M18.
■ **hautboyist** *noun* M19.

haute /əʊt, *foreign* ot/ *adjective*. L20.
[ORIGIN French: see HAUGHT.]
Fashionably elegant; high-class.

haute Bohème /ot bɔɛm, əʊt bəʊˈɛm/ *noun phr*. E20.
[ORIGIN from French, lit. 'high Bohemia' (coined by M. Baring after HAUTE BOURGEOISIE).]
An upper-class bohemian set of people.

haute bourgeoisie /ot burʒwazi, ˌəʊt bʊəʒwɑːˈziː/ *noun phr*. L19.
[ORIGIN French, lit. 'high bourgeoisie': see BOURGEOISIE.]
The upper middle class.

haute couture /əʊt kʊˈtjʊə, *foreign* ot kutyːr/ *noun phr*. E20.
[ORIGIN French, lit. 'high dressmaking': see COUTURE.]
High fashion; the leading dressmakers and fashion houses or their products collectively.

haute cuisine /əʊt kwɪˈziːn, *foreign* ot kɥizin/ *noun phr*. E20.
[ORIGIN French, lit. 'high cooking': see CUISINE.]
High-class (French) cooking.

haute école /ot ekɔl, əʊt eɪˈkɒl/ *noun & adjectival phr*. M19.
[ORIGIN French, lit. 'high school'.]
(Of or pertaining to) the more difficult feats of horsemanship, or *transf*. of music or other arts.

haute noblesse /ot nɔblɛs, əʊt nəʊˈblɛs/ *noun phr*. L18.
[ORIGIN French, lit. 'high nobility': see NOBLESSE.]
The upper stratum of the aristocracy.

hauteur /əʊˈtəː, *foreign* otœːr/ *noun*. E17.
[ORIGIN French, from *haut* high + *-eur* -OR.]
Haughtiness of manner.

B. TARKINGTON In their hearts they must be humiliated by his languid hauteur.

haute vulgarisation /ot vylgarizasjɔ̃, ˌəʊt vʌlgərʌɪˈzeɪʃ(ə)n/ *noun phr*. M20.
[ORIGIN French, lit. 'high vulgarization': see VULGARIZATION.]
The popularization of abstruse or complex matters.

haut-goût /ogu, ˈəʊguː/ *noun*. M16.
[ORIGIN French, lit. 'high flavour'. See also HOGO.]
1 A strong flavour or relish, seasoning, (*lit. & fig*.). M16.
†**2** A highly flavoured or seasoned dish. M17–E19.
3 A slightly rotten flavour; a taint. L17.

haut monde /o mɔ̃:d, əʊ ˈmɒnd/ *noun phr*. M19.
[ORIGIN French, lit. 'high world'.]
The fashionable world. Cf. BEAU MONDE.

haut-pas /opɑ/ *noun*. Pl. same. LME.
[ORIGIN French, lit. 'high step'.]
A dais raised one or more steps above the level of the rest of the floor.
— NOTE: Formerly fully naturalized.

haut-relief /orəljɛf, əʊrɪˈliːf/ *noun*. M19.
[ORIGIN French, lit. 'high relief'.]
= ALTO-RELIEVO.

haut ton /o tɔ̃/ *noun phr*. Now *rare*. E19.
[ORIGIN French, lit. 'high tone'.]
(People of) high fashion.

haüyne /ˈhaʊiːn/ *noun*. E19.
[ORIGIN from René Just *Haüy* (1743–1822), French crystallographer + -I)NE[5].]
MINERALOGY. A blue feldspathoid mineral of the sodalite group containing calcium and sulphur.
■ Also **haüynite** *noun* M19.

havan /ˈhavən/ *noun*. M20.
[ORIGIN Hindi.]
HINDUISM. A ritual burning of offerings to mark births, marriages, and other special occasions.

Havana /həˈvanə/ *noun*. E19.
[ORIGIN The capital of Cuba.]
1 In full ***Havana cigar***. A cigar made in Cuba, or from Cuban tobacco. E19.
2 In full ***Havana brown***. The shade of brown of a Havana cigar. Freq. *attrib*. E19.
3 In full ***Havana rabbit***. (An animal of) a variety of domestic rabbit, orig. from the Netherlands, bred for meat and its dark brown fur. E20.

Havarti /həˈvɑːti/ *noun*. M20.
[ORIGIN Danish, named after *Havarthigård*, the farm of the cheese-maker Hanne Nielsen.]
A mild, semi-soft Danish cheese with small irregular holes.

have /hav/ *noun & adjective*. ME.
[ORIGIN from the verb.]
▸ **A** *noun*. **1** Possession. Long *rare*. ME.
2 A person, country, etc., that possesses wealth or resources. Usu. in *pl*., contrasted with ***have-nots***. *colloq*. M18.
▸ **B** *attrib*. or as *adjective*. Designating a 'have'. *colloq*. M20.

have /hav, *unstressed* həv/ *verb*. Pres. indic.: 1 **have**, (*Scot*.) **hae** /heɪ, ha/; 2 **have**, (*arch*.) **hast** /hast/; 3 **has** /haz, həz/, (*arch*.) **hath** /haθ, həθ/; *pl*. **have**, (*Scot*.) **hae**. Past indic.: **had** /had, həd/; 2 *sing*. also (*arch*.) **hadst** /hadst/. Pres. subjunct.: **have**. Past subjunct.: **had**. Imper.: **have**. Pa. pple: **had**. Informal abbreviated forms: **'d** = *had*; **'s** = *has*; **'ve** = *have*; **hadn't** /had(ə)nt/ = *had not*; **hasn't** /haz(ə)nt/ = *has not*; **haven't** /hav(ə)nt/ = *have not*; (*joc. & colloq*.) **ain't** = *have not*; (*arch*.) **an't** = *have not*.
[ORIGIN Old English *habban* = Old Frisian *hebba*, Old Saxon *hebbian* (Dutch *hebben*), Old High German *habēn* (German *haben*), Old Norse *hafa*, Gothic *haban*, from Germanic base prob. rel. to HEAVE *verb*. In Middle English the *habb-* forms were reduced by levelling to *hav-*; the *haf-* forms (in Old English in past indic. and 2nd & 3rd person sing. pres. indic.) lost their *f* before the following consonant to give *ha-th*, *ha-s*, etc.]
▸ **I** *verb trans*. Possess.
1 Hold in possession as one's property or as something at one's disposal. OE.

J. STEINBECK You have only ragged overalls and no hat. W. GOLDING They had more toys than they wanted.

2 Possess in a certain relationship. OE.

T. HERBERT They used to have their Wives in common. R. C. HUTCHINSON He had no brothers or sisters.

3 Possess or contain as a part or adjunct. OE.

C. P. SNOW She had a large, blunt, knobbly nose. SCOTT FITZGERALD Every cross has just a date on it, and the word 'Unknown'.

4 Possess as an attribute, function, position, etc.; be characterized by. OE.

H. JAMES If he hadn't a sense of beauty he had after all a sense of justice. J. BUCHAN The air . . had the strangest effect on my spirits. W. GOLDING The universe had a beginning.

5 a Experience, be affected with; enjoy; suffer. OE. ▸**b** Hold, or allow to be present, in the mind; be the subject of (a feeling). OE. ▸**c** Possess with the mind; understand; know. LME.

a R. RENDELL Mr Knightow had a shock. He went white. J. RHYS I am having one devil of a time. B. NEIL Did people like Ben have athlete's foot and piles? **b** B. JOWETT They have the feelings of old men about youth. J. H. SHORTHOUSE I have no doubt the Italian is at the bottom of all this. **c** V. WOOLF I had all Shakespeare by heart before I was in my teens. I. MURDOCH He knew Latin and Greek . . , I had only a little French.

6 Possess as a thing to be done or to happen. Foll. by obj. & inf. OE. ▸**b** Be under an obligation *to do*; be necessitated by circumstances *to do*. L16.

J. H. NEWMAN He had nothing special to say for himself. *Strand Magazine* Her contract . . had two years more to run. **b** R. C. HUTCHINSON I had to make a mental effort to remember where I was going. Q. CRISP I have to go back to work. R. RENDELL She got pregnant and . . Adam had to marry her.

7 Hold or keep *in* some relation to oneself. Now chiefly in certain set phrs. OE.
have in mind, ***have in one's possession***, ***have in safekeeping***, ***have in sight***, etc.
8 Hold in a specified estimation; regard as. (Foll. by *in*, †*at*.) *arch*. OE.
9 Engage in, carry on, (an activity); organize and bring about (a meeting, party, etc.). OE.

P. ROTH Shuki apologized for being unable to have dinner with me. R. HUNTFORD Shackleton and Elspeth Beardmore were having an affair.

have a go, ***have a look***, ***have a try***, etc.
10 Exercise (a personal attribute or quality) or show the presence of (a feeling) by one's action or attitude, esp. towards a person. ME.

I. MURDOCH I'm still a rational being, so have the decency to address me as one.

have a care, ***have mercy***, etc. ***have patience with***, ***have regard to***, ***have the goodness to do***, ***have the impudence to do***, etc.
†**11** *refl*. Behave. LME–M16.
12 Assert, maintain; claim, allege, (*that*). Chiefly with *it*. LME. ▸**b** Foll. by obj. & inf. without *to*. Represent (a person) as doing, esp. in a work of fiction. *colloq*. E20.

W. GOLDING The scurvy politician, as my favourite author would have it. M. MILNER Tradition has it that this is the place where the heathen used to sacrifice their children.

▸ **II** *verb trans*. Obtain, get.
13 Possess by obtaining or receiving; get, obtain; take and imbibe (a drink) or eat (food, a meal); conceive (an idea); have obtained (a qualification). OE. ▸**b** Give birth to. LME. ▸**c** In imper. Cheers! (as a drinking toast). *dial*. & (with *to you*) *arch*. LME.

G. ROSE If Lord Spencer returns he must have the Admiralty. *Times Lit. Suppl*. All these books may be had of any bookseller. G. S. HAIGHT Mary Ann asked to have her letters back. **b** G. ORWELL I'm thirty-nine and I've had four children. I. MURDOCH A spider . . which lives in a burrow and has its young in the late summer.

14 With obj. & compl. ▸**a** With pres. or pa. pple or inf. Experience or suffer the specified action happening to or being done to (a thing or person). ME. ▸**b** With adjective or adverb (phr.). Bring into a specified condition or state. ME. ▸**c** With pa. pple or inf. (now usu. without *to*). Cause or oblige (a person or thing) to be subject to a specified action or to carry out a specified action. LME.

a T. HARDY You would rather have me die than have your equatorial stolen. **b** E. WAUGH She can't print *that*. She'll have us all in prison. **c** J. P. DONLEAVY I can call the police and have you thrown out. B. MOORE She had him bring the car up to the entrance. E. BOWEN I'm going . . to have my hair cut. K. HULME For a moment . . you had me worried.

15 With *will*, *would*. Wish, will, or require (a person) to (arch. *to*) *do* or (a deed) to be *done*; (with *it*) wish or require the doing of (a deed) or the occurrence of (an event, situation, etc.). ME. ▸**b** With *will not*, *would not*: not permit or tolerate. Foll. by obj., or obj. & pple or inf. (without *to*). L16.

SHAKES. *Two Gent.* What would your Grace have me to do in this? G. BERKELEY Those who will have us judge of distance by lines and angles. I. FLEMING As luck would have it, there were no vacancies and I had to turn him down. I. COLEGATE He was a village boy, though his mother would have it he was something better. **b** TENNYSON O my friend, I will not have thee die! V. WOOLF She would have none of it.

16 Cause to come or go; bring; take. *arch.* ME.

R. L. STEVENSON A little later he was had to bed.

17 Have got into one's power or at a disadvantage; *colloq.* get the better of in an argument etc. L16.

New Yorker 'How many other politicians would take a chance on asking this question?' he asked . . —and he had them there.

18 Have sexual intercourse with. *slang.* L16.
19 Outwit; deceive; cheat. *slang.* E19.

M. E. BRADDON If you've advanced money on 'em, you've been had.

▸ **III** *verb intrans.* †**20** Of a person: go; come *over* here. LME–M19.
21 Foll. by *at* (or, *arch.*, other prepositions): go at, esp. aggressively; attack; make an attempt at. Usu. in *imper.* LME.

J. BUCHAN Sit down, sir, and have at that pie.

▸ **IV** Idiomatic uses.
22 *had* (pa. subjunct.), †*have* (pres. indic.), would: in expressions of preference, desirability, or obligation. Foll. by adjectives (or adverbs) in compar., superl., or positive with *as*. Now esp. in ***had better*** below, ***had rather***. ME.

J. B. MOZLEY You must give way; and you had as well do so voluntarily. W. H. MALLOCK I had best not give her any.

23 With subj. duplicated by pers. or refl. pronoun as indirect (dative) obj. Provide or get for oneself; indulge oneself with. *colloq.* (chiefly *N. Amer.*). E20.

O. LA FARGE He had himself two good highballs. *New Yorker* I got to have me one of them.

▸ **V** As aux. verb with pa. pple of another verb, forming past tenses of the latter expressing action already completed at the time indicated.
24 **a** Pres. tense. OE. ▸**b** Pa. tense. OE. ▸**c** Compound tenses. ME. ▸**d** In compound tenses with redundant ***have*** or ***had***. Now *US dial.* LME.

a E. BOWEN You could have run the world. **b** J. C. POWYS Three months had passed. J. CONRAD The carpenter had driven in the last wedge. **c** SHELLEY Before the whirlwind wakes I shall have found My inn of lasting rest. C. M. KIRKLAND I thought I never should have got out. **d** J. F. WILSON 'If the fire hadn't have gone out,' he mused.

– PHRASES: (A selection of cross-refs. only is included: see esp. other nouns.) **had better** *colloq.* would find it wiser to; ought to. **have a nice day** (orig. *US*) (a wish expressed on saying) goodbye. ***have a person's guts for garters***: see GUT *noun*. ***have a wolf by the ears***: see WOLF *noun*. ***have got***: see GET *verb* 38. **have to be**, **have got to be** *colloq.* must be (expr. certainty). **have had —** *colloq.* have had enough of, be tired of or discontented with. **have had it** *colloq.* (*a*) have lost one's chance, have no chance; (*b*) be past one's prime or past its best; (*c*) have been killed, defeated, exhausted, etc. **have it** (*a*) gain a victory or advantage; win (esp. a vote); (*b*) *colloq.* receive a beating, punishment, etc. (chiefly in ***let a person have it***); (*c*) have thought of the answer, a solution, etc.; (*d*) **have it away** (*slang*) = ***have it off***, sense (i) below; (*e*) ***have it both ways***, choose now one, now the other of alternatives or contradictories to suit one's argument etc.; (*f*) ***have it coming to one***: see COME *verb*; (*g*) ***have it in for*** (*colloq.*), intend revenge on; seek to harm; (*h*) ***have it in one***, have the capacity (*to do*); (*i*) ***have it off*** (*slang*), have sexual intercourse (*with*); (*j*) ***have it off*** (*criminals' slang*), commit a robbery; (*k*) ***have it on***, ***have it over***, have the advantage of; be superior to; (*l*) ***have it out***: see ***have out*** below; (*m*) ***have it so good*** (*colloq.*), possess so many advantages, esp. of a material kind; usu. in neg. contexts; (see also sense 12 above). **have nothing on —** (*a*) have no advantage or superiority over; (*b*) know nothing discreditable or incriminating about. ***have sex (with)***: see SEX *noun* 4b. ***have to wife***: see WIFE *noun*. ***have way***: see WAY *noun*. ***have words***: see WORD *noun* 7. **to have and to hold** have or receive and continue to keep. ***WHAT have you***.
– WITH ADVERBS IN SPECIALIZED SENSES: **have on** *colloq.* hoax, deceive jocularly; (see also ON *adverb*). **have out** (*a*) *colloq.* bring (a contentious matter) to a resolution by discussion or argument; (*b*) get (a tooth, appendix, etc.) taken out. **have up** bring before a court of justice; call to account.

haveless /ˈheɪvlɪs/ *adjective*.
[ORIGIN Old English *hafenlēas*, *hæfen-*, from *hæfen* property, from *haf-*, *hæf-* stem of *habban* HAVE *verb*: see -LESS.]
†**1** Destitute. OE–LME.
2 Not resourceful; shiftless. *Scot. & dial.* M19.

havelock /ˈhav(ə)lɒk/ *noun*. Chiefly *US*. M19.
[ORIGIN Sir Henry *Havelock* (1795–1857), major-general of the Brit. army in India.]
A cloth covering for a military cap, with a neck flap to give protection from the sun.

haven /ˈheɪv(ə)n/ *noun*. LOE.
[ORIGIN Old Norse *hǫfn* (genit. *hafnar*) = Middle Low German, Middle Dutch *havene*, Dutch *haven* (whence German *Haven*).]
1 A place providing good sheltered mooring for ships; a port, a harbour. Now chiefly *literary*. LOE.

N. MONSARRAT For wandering sailors a safe haven was bound to be the crucial magnet of their lives.

2 A place of shelter, safety, or retreat; a refuge. ME.

Encounter San Francisco, which 'is already a haven for wandering psychotics'. A. BROOKNER Reaching the haven of her room, closing the door behind her.

■ **havenage** *noun* harbour dues M19. **havener** *noun* a harbour master ME. **havenless** *adjective* LME.

haven /ˈheɪv(ə)n/ *verb*. LME.
[ORIGIN from the noun.]
†**1** *verb intrans.* Go into or shelter in a haven. LME–E17.
2 *verb trans.* Put (a ship etc.) into a haven. Now chiefly *fig.*, give shelter to, protect. E17.

KEATS Blissfully haven'd both from joy and pain.

have-not /havˈnɒt/ *noun & adjective*. *colloq.* M18.
[ORIGIN from *have not* neg. of HAVE *verb*: see NOT *adverb*.]
▸ **A** *noun*. A person, country, etc., that has little wealth or resources. Usu. in *pl.*, contrasted with *haves*. M18.
▸ **B** *attrib.* or as *adjective*. Designating a 'have-not'. M20.

haven't *verb* see HAVE *verb*.

haver /ˈhavə/ *noun*[1]. Chiefly *Scot. & N. English*. ME.
[ORIGIN Old Norse *hafr* = Old Saxon *haero*, Middle Low German, Middle Dutch *haver(e)* (Dutch *haver*), Old High German *habaro* (German dial. *Haber*; *Hafer* from Low German).]
Oats.
– COMB.: **haver-cake** oatcake.

haver /ˈhavə/ *noun*[2]. LME.
[ORIGIN from HAVE *verb* + -ER[1].]
A person who has or possesses; *spec.* in SCOTS LAW, the holder of a document required as evidence in court.

SHAKES. *Coriol.* It is held That valour is the chiefest virtue and Most dignifies the haver.

haver /ˈheɪvə/ *noun*[3]. *Scot. & N. English*. Also **haiver**. L18.
[ORIGIN Unknown. Cf. HAVER *verb*.]
sing. & (usu.) in *pl.* Foolish talk, idle chatter. Also as *interjection*, nonsense!

haver /ˈheɪvə/ *verb intrans.* E18.
[ORIGIN Unknown. Cf. HAVER *noun*[3].]
1 Talk foolishly, babble. *Scot. & N. English*. E18.

W. MCILVANNEY Tom havered on, the certainties growing more empty, the promises wilder.

2 Vacillate, hesitate, dither. Orig. *Scot.* M19.

A. FRASER Still the Scots havered. Their army lurked uncertainly west of Fife.

■ **haverel** *noun & adjective* (*Scot.*) (a person) given to foolish chattering L18.

haversack /ˈhavəsak/ *noun*. M18.
[ORIGIN French *havresac* from German †*Habersack* orig. = bag in which cavalry carried oats for their horses, from *Haber* (see HAVER *noun*[1]) + *sack* SACK *noun*[1].]
A strong bag for provisions carried on the back or over the shoulder by a soldier, traveller, hiker, etc.

M. PATTISON Every private in the French army carries in his haversack the bâton of a marshal.

Haversian /həˈvəːsɪən/ *adjective*. M19.
[ORIGIN from Clopton *Havers* (d. 1702), English anatomist + -IAN.]
ANATOMY. Designating or pertaining to the minute cylindrical passages (***Haversian canals***) in bone, through which blood vessels pass; ***Haversian system***, a Haversian canal together with its associated tissue.

haversine /ˈhavəsʌɪn/ *noun*. Also **-sin**. L19.
[ORIGIN Contr. of *half versed sine*.]
Half of the versed sine of an angle.

havier /ˈheɪvjə/ *noun*. L17.
[ORIGIN Unknown.]
A gelded deer.

havildar /ˈhavɪldɑː/ *noun*. L17.
[ORIGIN Urdu *hawildār* from Persian *ḥawāl(a)dār* charge holder, from *ḥawāl*, from Arabic *ḥawāl(a)* charge, assignment + Persian *-dār* holding, holder.]
An Indian non-commissioned officer equivalent to a sergeant.

having /ˈhavɪŋ/ *noun*. ME.
[ORIGIN from HAVE *verb* + -ING[1].]
1 A possession. Freq. in *pl.*, property, belongings. ME.
2 The action or condition of having; possession. LME.
3 *sing.* & in *pl.* Behaviour, manners, deportment. Chiefly *Scot.* LME.

having /ˈhavɪŋ/ *adjective*. ME.
[ORIGIN from HAVE *verb* + -ING[2].]
1 Possessing property. Long *rare* or *obsolete*. ME.
2 Covetous, grasping. *obsolete* exc. *dial.* L16.

haviour /ˈheɪvjə/ *noun*. Also †**havour**. LME.
[ORIGIN Anglo-Norman *aver* = Old French *aveir*, (also mod.) *avoir* possession, property, use as noun of inf. *aveir*, *avoir* have (infl. by HAVE *verb*) from Latin *habere*: see -OUR. Cf. BEHAVIOUR.]
†**1** The fact of having, possession; a possession, wealth. LME–E17.
2 Bearing, behaviour, manner. Also in *pl.*, manners. *obsolete* exc. *dial.* E16.

havoc /ˈhavək/ *noun*. LME.
[ORIGIN Anglo-Norman *havok* alt. of Old French *havo(t)* pillage: ult. origin unknown.]
1 Used as a signal cry to an army etc. to seize spoil. Only in ***cry havoc***, give this cry. Now *rare* or *obsolete* exc. as *fig.* (usu. after Shakes., and assoc. with sense 2), predict imminent disaster. LME.

SHAKES. *Jul. Caes.* And Caesar's spirit . . Shall . . Cry 'Havoc!' and let slip the dogs of war.

2 Devastation, destruction; (now freq.) confusion, disorder. L15.

B. LOPEZ A place of spiritual havoc, the abode of the Antichrist.

cause havoc, **make havoc**, **wreak havoc** devastate, cause damage (*to*), throw into chaos or confusion. **play havoc (with)** damage, impair; confound. ***wreak havoc***: see ***cause havoc*** above.

havoc /ˈhavək/ *verb trans.* Infl. **-ck-**. L16.
[ORIGIN from the noun.]
Devastate, lay waste; bring into confusion or chaos.

†**havour** *noun* var. of HAVIOUR.

haw /hɔː/ *noun*[1]. *obsolete* exc. *hist.*
[ORIGIN Old English *haga* corresp. to Old Saxon *hago*, Middle Dutch *hage*, *haghe* (Dutch *haag*), Old Norse *hagi*, from Germanic base also of HAG *noun*[3], HAY *noun*[2], HEDGE *noun*.]
A hedge or fence enclosing a dwelling or piece of land; what is enclosed, a yard, a close, an enclosure.

haw /hɔː/ *noun*[2].
[ORIGIN Old English *haga* prob. same word as HAW *noun*[1].]
1 A hawthorn berry. (Formerly used as a symbol of something valueless.) OE.
2 A hawthorn. E19.
– COMB.: **hawfinch** a large Eurasian and N. African finch of deciduous woodland, *Coccothraustes coccothraustes*, with a heavy, strong beak.

haw /hɔː/ *noun*[3]. LME.
[ORIGIN Unknown.]
†**1** A morbid excrescence in the eye. LME–L17.
2 The nictitating membrane of the eye of a horse, dog, or other animal. E16.

haw /hɔː/ *noun*[4] *& interjection*[1]. L17.
[ORIGIN Imit. Cf. HAW-HAW.]
(A slight inarticulate vocal sound) expr. hesitation. Freq. in ***hums and haws***: see HUM *noun*[1] 1.

haw /hɔː/ *noun*[5] *& interjection*[2]. Chiefly *dial. & N. Amer.* L17.
[ORIGIN Unknown. Cf. HAW *verb*[2].]
(A call) directing a draught animal or team to turn to the left.

haw /hɔː/ *verb*[1] *intrans.* M17.
[ORIGIN Imit. Cf. HAW *noun*[4] *& interjection*[1].]
Utter 'haw', esp. as an expression of hesitation. Freq. in ***hum and haw***: see HUM *verb*[1] 1.

HENRY FIELDING Don't stand humming and hawing, but speak out.

haw /hɔː/ *verb*[2]. Chiefly *dial. & N. Amer.* M19.
[ORIGIN Unknown. Cf. HAW *noun*[5] *& interjection*[2].]
1 *verb intrans.* Of a draught animal or team: turn or move left. M19.
2 *verb trans.* Direct (a draught animal or team) to move or turn left. M19.

Hawaiian /həˈwʌɪən/ *adjective & noun*. Also **-waian**. E19.
[ORIGIN from *Hawaii* (see below) + -AN.]
▸ **A** *adjective*. Of or pertaining to the island of Hawaii in the N. Pacific, or the archipelago of which it is part, now the American state of Hawaii. E19.
Hawaiian goose = NENE. **Hawaiian guitar** a steel-stringed instrument, usu. held horizontally, in which a characteristic glissando effect is produced by sliding a metal bar along the strings as they are plucked. **Hawaiian shirt** a highly coloured and gaily patterned shirt.
▸ **B** *noun*. A native or inhabitant of Hawaii; the Austronesian language of Hawaii. M19.

hawala /həˈwɑːlə/ *noun*. M20.
[ORIGIN Arabic *ḥawāla*, lit. 'assignment, bill of exchange'.]
A traditional system of transferring money used in Arab countries and the Indian subcontinent, whereby money is paid via an agent.

H

H

hawbuck /ˈhɔːbʌk/ *noun*. Chiefly *dial.* E19.
[ORIGIN from HAW *noun*[1] or *noun*[2] + BUCK *noun*[1].]
A country bumpkin, an oaf.

Hawcubite /ˈhɔːkəbʌɪt/ *noun*. E18.
[ORIGIN Unknown.]
hist. A member of a band of violent young men frequenting the London streets in the early 18th cent. Cf. MOHOCK.

haw-haw /ˈhɔːhɔː/ *noun*, *adjective*, & *verb*. M19.
[ORIGIN Imit. Cf. HAW *noun*[4] & *interjection*[1], HAW *verb*[1].]
▸ **A** *noun*. (A repeated slight inarticulate vocal sound) expr. hesitation or affected pausing in speech. Also, (repr.) a loud or boisterous laugh. Also as *interjection*. M19.
▸ **B** *adjective*. Resembling or imitating so-called upper-class speech or manner; affected. M19.

Daily News One of those haw-haw officers, who look down on men like me. *Times* Declaring that BBC announcers were 'too haw-haw' in their diction. R. C. HUTCHINSON You think I wanted him for his haw-haw accent or his old school tie.

▸ **C** *verb*. **1** *verb intrans*. Utter 'haw-haw'; laugh loudly and boisterously. M19.
2 *verb trans*. Laugh at. M19.

hawk /hɔːk/ *noun*[1].
[ORIGIN Old English *hafoc*, *heafoc*, earlier *haebuc*, *habuc* = Old Frisian *havek*, Old Saxon *hauk* (Dutch *havik*), Old High German *habuh* (German *Habicht*), Old Norse *haukr*, from Germanic.]
1 A bird of prey used in falconry; any diurnal bird of prey. Now *esp.* any of the smaller or moderate-sized birds of the family Accipitridae with relatively short, rounded wings. Cf. FALCON. OE.
black hawk, *blue hawk*, *Cooper's hawk*, *goshawk*, *sharp-shinned hawk*, *sparrowhawk*, *Swainson's hawk*, etc. *ignoble hawk*: see IGNOBLE *adjective*. **know a hawk from a handsaw**, **know a hawk from a heronshaw** have ordinary discernment (now chiefly in allusion to Shakes. *Haml.*). *noble hawk*: see NOBLE *adjective*.
2 A rapacious, aggressive, or ruthless person. M16. ▸**b** A person who advocates an uncompromising or warlike policy. (Opp. *dove*.) M20.
3 *ellipt*. As 2nd elem. of comb.: = *hawkmoth* below. M19.
oleander hawk, *poplar hawk*, *privet hawk*, etc.
– COMB.: **hawkbill (turtle)** = *hawksbill* below; **hawkbit** [from *hawk(weed* (see below) + *devil's bit* s.v. DEVIL *noun*] any of several plants constituting the genera *Leontodon*, of the composite family, with heads of yellow ligulate florets and leaves in rosettes; *esp.* autumnal hawkbit, *L. autumnalis*, a common late-flowering plant of grassland; **hawk-cuckoo** any of various south and east Asian cuckoos of the genus *Cuculus*, of somewhat hawk-like appearance, esp. the brain-fever bird, *C. varius*; **hawk eagle** any of various tropical or subtropical eagles of the genus *Spizaetus*; **hawk-eye** (*a*) a keen-sighted or perceptive person; (*b*) *US colloq.* a native or inhabitant of Iowa; *Hawkeye State*, the state of Iowa; **hawk-eyed** *adjective* keen-sighted; **hawk-faced** *adjective* sharp-faced, hard-faced; **hawkmoth** any of various large, swift-flying moths constituting the family Sphingidae, with elongated forewings; **hawk-nose** a nose curved like a hawk's bill, an aquiline nose; **hawk-nosed** *adjective* having a hawk-nose; **hawk owl** †(*a*) the short-eared owl, *Asio flammeus*; (*b*) a somewhat long-tailed, partly diurnal owl, *Surnia ulula*, of northern coniferous woodland; **hawksbeard** any of various plants constituting the genus *Crepis*, of the composite family, allied to the hawkweeds; **hawksbill (turtle)** a small sea turtle, *Eretmochelys imbricata*, with hooked jaws, found in tropical seas; **hawkweed** any of the numerous microspecies of the genus *Hieracium* and *Pilosella*, of the composite family, plants of banks, rocks, etc., with heads of usu. yellow ligulate florets.
■ **hawkish** *adjective* (*a*) resembling a hawk in appearance or nature; (*b*) inclined to favour uncompromising or warlike policies: M19. **hawkishness** *noun* M20. **hawklike** *adjective* resembling (that of) a hawk E17.

hawk /hɔːk/ *noun*[2]. LME.
[ORIGIN Unknown.]
A rectangular board with a handle underneath, used by a plasterer or bricklayer to hold wet plaster or mortar.

hawk /hɔːk/ *noun*[3]. E17.
[ORIGIN from HAWK *verb*[3].]
An effort made to clear the throat; the noise thus made.

hawk /hɔːk/ *verb*[1]. ME.
[ORIGIN from HAWK *noun*[1].]
1 *verb intrans*. Hunt game with a trained hawk. ME.
2 *verb intrans*. Hunt on the wing. LME. ▸**b** *verb trans*. Hunt (prey) on the wing. E19.

R. JEFFERIES A dragon fly, hawking to and fro on the sunny side of the hedge.

3 *verb intrans*. Foll. by *at*: attack as a hawk does, fly at; (of a person) fly a hawk at. LME.

SHAKES. *Macb.* A falcon, tow'ring in her pride of place, Was by a mousing owl hawk'd at and kill'd.

†**4** *verb intrans*. Foll. by *after*, *for*: pursue; try to catch or gain. E16–E18.

hawk /hɔːk/ *verb*[2]. L15.
[ORIGIN Back-form. from HAWKER *noun*[2].]
1 *verb trans*. Carry *about* from place to place and offer for sale. L15.

R. W. CLARK The quacks who hawked medicines at fairgrounds. C. FRANCIS He hawked his idea around England, France and Portugal.

hawk one's mutton: see MUTTON.

2 *verb intrans*. Travel around touting or selling one's wares. M16.

J. ARBUTHNOT To go hawking and peddling about the streets, selling knives, scissors, and shoe-buckles.

hawk /hɔːk/ *verb*[3]. L16.
[ORIGIN Prob. imit.]
1 *verb intrans*. Clear the throat noisily or with an effort. L16.

N. BAWDEN My mother coughed. She hawked, with a disgusting liquid noise.

2 *verb trans*. Bring *up* (phlegm etc.) from the throat with an effort. L16.

hawked /hɔːkt/ *adjective*[1]. *Scot.* & *N. English*. Also **hawkit** /ˈhɔːkɪt/. L15.
[ORIGIN Unknown.]
Of cattle: spotted, streaked.

hawked /hɔːkt/ *adjective*[2]. L16.
[ORIGIN from HAWK *noun*[1] + -ED[2].]
Curved like a hawk's beak; aquiline.

hawker /ˈhɔːkə/ *noun*[1]. OE.
[ORIGIN from HAWK *noun*[1] + -ER[1].]
A person who breeds, trains, or hunts with, hawks; a falconer.

hawker /ˈhɔːkə/ *noun*[2]. E16.
[ORIGIN Prob. of Low Dutch origin (cf. Middle Low German *hoker*, Low German *höker*, Dutch *heuker*): see HUCKSTER *noun*.]
A person who travels about selling goods.
– COMB.: **hawker centre** (in SE Asia) a market at which vendors sell ready-to-eat food from booths.

hawker /ˈhɔːkə/ *noun*[3]. M20.
[ORIGIN from HAWK *verb*[1] + -ER[1].]
A dragonfly whose flight behaviour is characterized by patrolling a particular area; *spec.* any of the family Aeschnidae.

Hawking radiation /ˈhɔːkɪŋ reɪdɪˌeɪʃ(ə)n/ *noun phr*. L20.
[ORIGIN Stephen *Hawking* (b. 1942), English physicist.]
PHYSICS. The radiation emitted by a black hole.

hawkit *adjective* var. of HAWKED *adjective*[1].

hawkshaw /ˈhɔːkʃɔː/ *noun*. Also **H-**. E20.
[ORIGIN A detective in *The Ticket-of-Leave Man*, a play by Tom Taylor (1817–80), English dramatist; also in the comic strip *Hawkshaw the Detective* by Augustus Charles ('Gus') Mager (1878–1956), Amer. cartoonist.]
A detective.

hawse /hɔːz/ *noun*[1]. Earlier †**halse**. LME.
[ORIGIN Prob. from Old Norse *hals* neck, ship's bow, tack of a sail, rope's end (= Old English *heals* neck, prow). Cf. HAUSE *noun*.]
NAUTICAL. **1** A ship's bow; now *spec.* the part through which the anchor cables pass. Also in *pl.*, the hawseholes. LME.
†**2** A cable, a hawser. L16–M17.
3 The arrangement of cables when a ship is moored with port and starboard forward anchors; the space between the head of a moored vessel and its anchor(s). L16.
athwart-hawse, **athwart the hawse**, †**thwart the hawse** transversely in front of an anchored ship.
– COMB.: **hawse-full**, †**hawse-fallen** *adverbs* in a rough sea with the water coming into the hawse. **hawsehole** the hole through which the anchor cable passes; **hawsepiece** a plank or plate through which a hawsehole is cut; **hawsepipe** a metal pipe fitted in the hawsehole of a wooden ship to prevent wear by the cable; **hawseplug** a plug fitted into a hawsehole to keep water out.

hawse *noun*[2], *verb* vars. of HAUSE *noun*, *verb*.

hawser /ˈhɔːzə/ *noun*. ME.
[ORIGIN Anglo-Norman *haucer*, *-eour* (in Anglo-Latin *haucerus*, *ausorus*, *aunceris*) from Old French *haucier* (mod. *hausser*) hoist, from Proto-Romance, from Latin *altus* high: see -ER[2]. Assoc. from an early period with HAWSE *noun*[1].]
NAUTICAL. A large rope or small cable used for mooring or anchoring.
– COMB.: **hawser-laid** *adjective* = *cable-laid* s.v. CABLE *noun*.

hawthorn /ˈhɔːθɔːn/ *noun*.
[ORIGIN Old English *hagaþorn*, *hagu-* (= Middle Dutch *hagedorn* (Dutch *haagdoorn*), Middle High German *hage(n)dorn* (German *Hagedorn*), Old Norse *hagþorn*) from *haga* HAW *noun*[1] + THORN *noun*.]
Any of various thorny shrubs or low trees of the genus *Crataegus*, of the rose family, with white or pink blossom (may) and usu. red berries (haws); *esp.* (*a*) (more fully *common hawthorn*) the Eurasian *C. monogyna*, much used for hedging; (*b*) (more fully *midland hawthorn*) the European *C. laevigata*, found in woodlands. Also, any of several related shrubs.
Yeddo hawthorn: see YEDDO *noun*.
– COMB.: **hawthorn china** a kind of oriental porcelain with a pattern of plum blossom on a dark blue ground.

Hawthorne effect /ˈhɔːθɔːn ɪˈfɛkt/ *noun phr*. M20.
[ORIGIN from the *Hawthorne* plant of the Western Electric Company in Chicago, where first observed in the 1920s.]
PSYCHOLOGY. The alteration of behaviour by the subjects of a study due to their awareness of being observed.

hay /heɪ/ *noun*[1].
[ORIGIN Old English *hēg*, *hīeg*, *hīg* = Old Frisian *hā*, *hē*, Old Saxon *hōi*, Old High German *hewi*, *houwi* (Dutch *hooi*, German *Heu*), Old Norse *hey* (whence the native word was reinforced), Gothic *hawi*, from Germanic = cut down, HEW *verb*.]
Grass mown or cut and dried for fodder. Also (now *rare*), grass ready or kept for mowing.

J. GALSWORTHY A machine drawn by a grey horse was turning an early field of hay.

a roll in the hay an act of making love, a sex session. *hit the hay*: see HIT *verb*. *look for a needle in a bottle of hay*: see NEEDLE *noun*. **make hay** mow grass and turn it over for exposure to the sun; *make hay of*, throw into confusion; *make hay (while the sun shines)*, seize opportunities for advantage, pleasure, etc. **not hay** *US colloq.* a large amount of money. **roll in the hay** *colloq.* make love, have sexual intercourse.
– COMB.: **hay asthma** = *hay fever* below; **haybag** *slang*, *derog.* a woman; **hay-band** a rope of twisted hay used to bind up a truss or bundle of hay; **hay-barn** a barn for the storage of hay; **haybox** (*a*) *dial.* a hayloft; (*b*) a box stuffed with hay, in which heated food may be left to continue cooking; **haycock** a conical heap of hay in a field; **hay fever** an allergic reaction to the airborne pollen of grasses or other plants, manifested in early summer and causing sneezing, nasal congestion, conjunctival irritation, and in some cases asthmatic symptoms; **hayfield** a field where hay is being or is to be made; **hay-fork** a long-handled fork for turning over or loading hay; **hay-home supper** *hist.* a meal to celebrate the successful bringing home of the hay (cf. HARVEST HOME); **hayloft** a loft or storing place for hay over a stable or barn; **haymaker** (*a*) a person employed in making hay, *esp.* one who lifts, tosses, and spreads hay after mowing; (*b*) a machine for shaking and drying hay; (*c*) *colloq.* a swinging blow or punch; (*d*) CRICKET a sweeping stroke with the bat; **haymaking** the action or process of making hay (*lit.* & *fig.*); **haymow** a stack etc. of hay; hay stored in a barn; the part of a barn for the storage of hay; **hayrick** a haystack; **hayride** *US* a pleasure ride in a wagon carrying hay; **hay-scales** *US* a public weighing machine for weighing loads of hay or other produce; **hayseed** (*a*) the grass seed from hay; (*b*) *N. Amer., Austral., & NZ colloq.* a rustic; **haystack** a regular pile of hay built in the open air and having a ridged or pointed top; *look for a needle in a haystack*: see NEEDLE *noun*.

hay /heɪ/ *noun*[2]. Now *arch.* & *dial.*
[ORIGIN Old English *hege* from Germanic base of HAG *noun*[3], HAW *noun*[1], HEDGE *noun*.]
1 A hedge, a fence. OE.
2 An enclosed space; an enclosure; a park. ME.
†**3** MILITARY. An extended line of men. L17–M19.
– COMB.: †**hayhove** [Old English *hōfe* with same meaning: cf. ALE-HOOF] ground ivy, *Glechoma hederacea*; **hayward** an officer of a parish etc. in charge of fences and enclosures. Also, a herdsman in charge of cattle etc. grazing on common land.

hay /heɪ/ *noun*[3]. Long *obsolete* exc. *dial.* LME.
[ORIGIN Anglo-Norman *haie*, prob. an extension of HAY *noun*[2] or of the equiv. Old French & mod. French *haie*: cf. Old French *haier*.]
More fully *hay-net*. A net used for catching wild animals, esp. rabbits.

hay /heɪ/ *noun*[4]. Also **hey**. E16.
[ORIGIN French †*haie* a kind of dance.]
(A figure in) a country dance with interweaving steps.
dance the hay(s) *arch.* perform winding movements (around numerous objects); *fig.* go through varied stages of development.

†**hay** *noun*[5]. Only in L16.
[ORIGIN Italian *hai* you (sing.) have (it). Cf. Latin *habet* = he has (it), exclaimed when a gladiator was wounded.]
A home thrust.

hay /heɪ/ *noun*[6]. L19.
[ORIGIN translating French *foin*.]
The choke of an artichoke.

hay /heɪ/ *verb*. M16.
[ORIGIN from HAY *noun*[1].]
1 *verb intrans*. Make hay. M16.
2 *verb trans*. Provide or supply with hay; put (land) under grass for hay. E18.
3 *verb trans*. Make (grass) into hay. L19.

haybote /ˈheɪbəʊt/ *noun*. ME.
[ORIGIN from HAY *noun*[2] + BOTE. Cf. HEDGEBOTE.]
Chiefly LAW. Wood or thorns for the repair of fences; the right of a tenant to take such material from a landlord's estate.

Hay diet /heɪ/ *noun*. E20.
[ORIGIN from the name of the American physician William Howard *Hay* (1866–1940), who devised the diet.]
A diet in which carbohydrates are eaten at separate times from fruit and proteins, in the belief that this aids digestion.

†**haye** *noun*. Also (earlier) **-en**. E17–M19.
[ORIGIN Dutch *haai*, Western Flemish *haaie* rel. to Swedish *haj*, German *Hai*: cf. Old Norse *hár(r)* dogfish, *há-* shark.]
A shark.

haylage /ˈheɪlɪdʒ/ *noun*. M20.
[ORIGIN from HAY *noun*[1] + SI)LAGE *noun*.]
Silage made from grass which has been partially dried.

hayrif *noun* var. of HAIRIF.

Haytian *adjective* & *noun* see HAITIAN.

haywire /ˈheɪwʌɪə/ *noun* & *adjective*. E20.
[ORIGIN from HAY *noun*[1] + WIRE *noun*.]
▸ **A** *noun*. Wire for binding bales of hay, straw, etc. E20.
▸ **B** *adjective*. **1** Poorly or roughly contrived (with ref. to the practice of using wire for baling hay to effect makeshift repairs). E20.

Listener A haywire, unpredictable, one-man business.

2 Of a person: in an emotional state, distracted, crazy. Of circumstances: tangled, in disorder, confused. *colloq.* (orig. *US*). M20.

> J. O'HARA A married man . . and absolutely haywire on the subject of another woman. E. C. R. LORAC The time element's all haywire.

go haywire go wrong, become confused or crazy.

hazan *noun* var. of HAZZAN.

hazard /ˈhazəd/ *noun*. ME.
[ORIGIN Old French & mod. French *hasard* from Spanish *azar* from colloq. Arabic *az-zahr* from *az-* AL-[2] + Persian *zār* gaming die or Turkish *zar* die, dice, chance.]
1 A dice game in which the chances are complicated by arbitrary rules. ME.
2 Risk of loss or harm; (a source of) danger, jeopardy. M16.

> T. O'BRIEN People were asking one another about the hazards of nuclear fallout.

3 *REAL TENNIS*. Each of the various openings or galleries around the court; *spec.* those which are not winning openings. M16.
4 Chance, venture; a chance. L16.

> LYTTON On what hazards turn our fate!

†**5** Something risked or staked. *rare*. Only in L16.
6 *BILLIARDS*. †**a** Any of the holes or pockets in the sides of a billiard table. L16–M18. ▸**b** A stroke by which one of the balls is driven into a pocket. Freq. in ***losing hazard***, ***winning hazard*** below. L18.
7 *GOLF*. An obstruction in playing a shot such as a bunker, water, a road, etc. M18.
– PHRASES: **at all hazards** despite all risks. **at hazard** *arch.* (**a**) at random; (**b**) at risk. **losing hazard** *BILLIARDS* the pocketing of one's own ball off another. *OCCUPATIONAL* ***hazard***. **winning hazard** *BILLIARDS* the striking of the object ball into a pocket.
– COMB.: **hazard light** = *hazard warning light* below; **hazard side** *REAL TENNIS* the side of the court into which the ball is served; **hazard warning light** a flashing light used to warn that a vehicle is stationary or decelerating unexpectedly, usu. each of a vehicle's direction indicators operating simultaneously (usu. in *pl.*).

hazard /ˈhazəd/ *verb*. L15.
[ORIGIN French *hasarder*, formed as HAZARD *noun*.]
1 *verb intrans.* Play at hazard. Chiefly as ***hazarding*** *verbal noun*. *rare*. L15.
2 *verb trans.* Put (a thing) to the risk of being lost in a game of chance etc.; stake; expose to hazard. M16.

> F. FORSYTH The general cargo business is too risky for a rich man . . to hazard money on it.

3 *verb trans.* Run the risk of (a penalty, a misfortune). Also foll. by *to do*. M16.
†**4** *verb trans.* Endanger. L16–L18.
†**5** *verb trans.* Get by chance or luck; chance on. L16–M17.
6 *verb trans.* Take the chance or risk of; venture on (an action, statement, guess, etc.); venture *to do*. L16.

> P. BAILEY If I were ordered to put a date on it, I'd hazard a guess.

†**7** *verb trans. BILLIARDS*. Strike (a ball) into a pocket. *rare*. Only in L17.
■ **hazarder** *noun* (now *rare*) a player at hazard or dice; a person who hazards: ME.

†**hazardize** *noun*. *rare* (Spenser). Only in L16.
[ORIGIN from HAZARD *noun* after *merchandise* etc.]
A hazardous position, a condition of peril or risk.

hazardous /ˈhazədəs/ *adjective*. M16.
[ORIGIN from French *hasardeux*, formed as HAZARD *noun*: see -OUS.]
1 Fraught with hazard, risky. M16.
†**2** Tending to take risks; venturesome. M16–M17.
3 Dependent on chance; casual, fortuitous. Now *rare*. L16.
■ **hazardously** *adverb* E17. **hazardousness** *noun* L17.

hazardry /ˈhazədri/ *noun*. Long *rare* or *obsolete*. ME.
[ORIGIN Old French, formed as HAZARD *noun*: see -ERY. Cf. Anglo-Latin *hasarderia*.]
1 The playing of hazard; dicing; gambling. ME.
†**2** The incurring of risk; venturesomeness. Only in L16.

Hazchem /ˈhazkɛm/ *noun*. L20.
[ORIGIN from HAZ(ARDOUS + CHEM)ICAL *noun*.]
Hazardous chemical or chemicals; *spec.* used **attrib.** to designate a system of codes and symbols for labelling hazardous chemicals.

haze /heɪz/ *noun*. E18.
[ORIGIN Prob. back-form. from HAZY. Cf. HAZE *verb*[2].]
1 Orig., fog, hoar frost. Now, (an) obscuration of the atmosphere near the earth, esp. by fine particles of water, smoke, or dust, tending to make distant objects indistinct. E18.

> E. HARDWICK A steamy haze blurred the lines of the hills.

2 *fig.* Mental obscurity or confusion. L18.

> A. J. P. TAYLOR I moved in a haze and have not the slightest recollection what the examination papers were about.

haze /heɪz/ *verb*[1]. L17.
[ORIGIN Uncertain: cf. French †*haser* tease, anger, insult.]
1 *verb trans.* Frighten; scold; punish by blows. *Scot. & dial.* L17.
2 *verb trans. NAUTICAL*. Harass with overwork. M19.
3 *verb trans.* Bully; try to disconcert; *spec.* force (a new recruit to the military or a university fraternity) to perform strenuous, humiliating, or dangerous tasks. *US*. M19.
4 *verb intrans.* Frolic, lark. *US*. M19.
5 *verb intrans.* Loaf or roam *about*. M19.
6 *verb trans.* Drive (cattle etc.) while on horseback. L19.
■ **hazer** *noun* L19. **hazing** *noun* (**a**) the action of the verb; (**b**) *rare* a sound beating, a thrashing: E19.

haze /heɪz/ *verb*[2]. L17.
[ORIGIN Prob. back-form. from HAZY. Cf. HAZE *noun*.]
1 *verb intrans.* Drizzle. *dial.* L17.
2 *verb trans.* Make hazy. E19.

hazel /ˈheɪz(ə)l/ *noun*[1] & *adjective*[1].
[ORIGIN Old English *hæsel*, corresp. to Middle Dutch *hasel* (Dutch *hazelaar* hazel-tree, *hazelnoot* hazelnut), Old High German *hasal*, *-ala* (German *Hasel*), Old Norse *hasl*, from Germanic, from an Indo-European base repr. also by Latin *corylus*.]
▸ **A** *noun*. **1** Any of various deciduous shrubs and low trees constituting the genus *Corylus*, of the birch family, bearing edible nuts enclosed in leafy involucres; *esp.* the European hazel, *C. avellana*, and its N. American counterpart, *C. americana*. Also ***hazel bush***, ***hazel tree***, etc. OE. ▸**b** With specifying word: any of several trees thought to resemble the hazel in some respect. (Earlier in WITCH HAZEL.) L19.
b Australian hazel either of two Australian trees, *Pomaderris apetala* and *P. lanigera*, of the buckthorn family. **Chile hazel**, **evergreen hazel** a Chilean evergreen tree, *Guevina avellana* (family Proteaceae), the seeds of which taste like hazelnuts.
2 **a** The wood of the hazel. LME. ▸**b** A stick made from a hazel branch. E17.
3 The light (reddish- or greenish-) brown colour of a ripe hazelnut. L18.
– COMB.: **hazel grouse**, **hazel hen** a brown speckled grouse of European woodland, *Bonasa bonasia*; **hazelnut** the fruit of the hazel, a round hard-shelled nut.
▸ **B** *adjective*. Esp. of the eyes: of a hazel colour. L16.

hazel /ˈheɪz(ə)l/ *adjective*[2] & *noun*[2]. Chiefly *dial.* Also **hazle**. E17.
[ORIGIN Unknown. Cf. HAZELLY *adjective*[1].]
▸ **A** *adjective*. Consisting of a mixture of sand, clay, and earth; loamy; easily worked. E17.
▸ **B** *noun*. A kind of freestone. *local*. L18.

hazeled /ˈheɪz(ə)ld/ *adjective*. M17.
[ORIGIN from HAZEL *noun*[1] + -ED[2].]
Covered with hazels. Formerly, hazel-coloured.

hazelly /ˈheɪz(ə)li/ *adjective*[1]. Chiefly *dial.* L16.
[ORIGIN formed as HAZEL *adjective*[2] & *noun*[2] + -Y[1].]
= HAZEL *adjective*[2].

hazelly /ˈheɪz(ə)li/ *adjective*[2]. L18.
[ORIGIN from HAZEL *noun*[1] + -Y[1].]
Full of or covered with hazel bushes.

hazelwort /ˈheɪz(ə)lwəːt/ *noun*. Now *rare* or *obsolete*. L16.
[ORIGIN German *Haselwurz*, from *Hasel* HAZEL *noun*[1] + *Wurz* herb, WORT *noun*[1].]
(A herbalists' name for) the plant asarabacca, *Asarum europaeum*.

hazle *adjective* & *noun* var. of HAZEL *adjective*[2] & *noun*[2].

Hazlittian /hazˈlɪtɪən/ *adjective* & *noun*. Also **-ean**. E20.
[ORIGIN from William *Hazlitt* (see below) + -IAN, -EAN.]
▸ **A** *adjective*. Of, pertaining to, or characteristic of the English critic William Hazlitt (1778–1830) or his work. E20.
▸ **B** *noun*. An admirer or student of Hazlitt or his writing. M20.

hazmat /ˈhazmat/ *noun*. L20.
[ORIGIN from HAZ(ARDOUS + MAT(ERIAL *noun*.]
Hazardous material or materials.

hazy /ˈheɪzi/ *adjective*. E17.
[ORIGIN Unknown.]
1 Orig., foggy. Later, characterized by the presence of haze; misty; not distinctly visible. E17.

> A. S. BYATT The room was hazy with soft smoke.

2 *fig.* Vague, indistinct, uncertain. E19. ▸**b** Slightly drunk. *arch. colloq.* E19.

> R. MACAULAY I was becoming pretty hazy about right and wrong.

■ **hazily** *adverb* M19. **haziness** *noun* E18.

hazzan /xəˈzɑːn, ˈhɑːz(ə)n/ *noun*. Also **chaz(z)an**, **hazan**. Pl. **-im** /-ɪm/. M17.
[ORIGIN Hebrew *ḥazzān* beadle, cantor, prob. from Assyrian *ḫazannu* overseer or governor.]
= CANTOR 1b.

HB *abbreviation*[1].
1 Hardback.
2 Hard black (pencil lead).

Hb *abbreviation*[2].
MEDICINE. Haemoglobin.

HBM *abbreviation*.
Her Britannic Majesty('s), His Britannic Majesty('s).

HC *abbreviation*.
1 Holy Communion.
2 House of Commons.

h.c. *abbreviation*.
= HONORIS CAUSA.

HCF *abbreviation*.
1 Highest common factor.
2 Honorary Chaplain to the Forces.

HCFC *abbreviation*.
Hydrochlorofluorocarbon.

HCG *abbreviation*.
MEDICINE. Human chorionic gonadotropin.

HDD *abbreviation*.
COMPUTING. Hard disk drive.

HDL *abbreviation*.
BIOCHEMISTRY. High-density lipoprotein.

HDTV *abbreviation*.
High-definition television.

HE *abbreviation*.
1 High explosive.
2 His Eminence.
3 Her, His, Excellency.

He *symbol*.
CHEMISTRY. Helium.

he /hiː, *unstressed* ɪ/ *pers. pronoun*, *3 sing. masc. subjective (nom.)*, *noun*, & *adjective*.
[ORIGIN Old English *he*, *hē* = Old Frisian *hi*, *he*, Old Saxon *hi*, *he*, *hie*, from Germanic demonstr. stem repr. also in Old High German (Franconian) *er*, *her*, *hē* he, dat. *himo*, Old Norse *(h)inn* him, Gothic *himma* to him, *hina* (direct objective) him. Cf. HIM, HIS *pronoun*[1] & *adjective*, UN *pronoun*[1].]
▸ **A** *pronoun*. **1** The male person or animal, or the person or animal of unknown or unspecified sex, previously mentioned or implied or easily identified. OE.

> DRYDEN He first, and close behind him followed she. LONGFELLOW The skipper he stood beside the helm. T. HARDY Anne thought, 'Perhaps that's he, and we are missing him.' L. STEFFENS The business man has failed in politics as he has in citizenship. J. STEINBECK When Danny came home from the army he learned that he was an heir. W. S. MAUGHAM When someone . . wants to write the story . . he'll find all the material ready. G. GREENE Perhaps she . . fought his doubts (she was more a fighter than he). I. MURDOCH You and he were appointed her joint guardians. P. ACKROYD Of course he, Sir Frederick, would not stand for their bullying tactics.

2 The thing personified or conventionally treated as male (as a mountain, a river, a tree, the sun) or (in early use) the thing grammatically masculine, previously mentioned or implied or easily identified. ME.

> TENNYSON Tonight I saw the sun set: he set and left behind The good old year. T. HARDY The Bear had swung round it . . he was now at a right angle with the meridian.

3 The or any male person *who* (or *that*); the or any person *who* (or *that*); (with preposition phr., now *arch.* or *literary*) the (male) person *of*, *with*, etc. ME.

> SHAKES. *Merry W.* He in the red face had it. J. CONRAD He who loves the sea loves also the ship's routine.

4 ***he and he***, this and that, the one and the other, both. *arch.* ME.
5 The player who has to catch others in a children's game, 'it'. Cf. sense B.3 below. E19.
▸ **B** *noun*. **1** The male; a male. OE.

> J. MAPLET It is also carefull in laying vp store for Winter, both the Hee and Shee. B. JOWETT Do we divide dogs into hes and shes, and take the masculine gender out to hunt?

2 A person, a man. LME.

> BUNYAN He has shewed as much honesty . . as any he in Mansoul.

3 A children's chasing game in which one player is 'he' (see sense A.5 above). E20.
▸ **C** *adjective*. (Usu. hyphenated with following noun.) Male. Now chiefly of animals. ME.
he-goat etc. **he-man** a particularly strong, masterful, or virile man. **he-oak** *Austral.* any of various trees of the genus *Casuarina* (family Casuarinaceae), esp. *C. stricta*.
– NOTE: Use to refer to a person of unspecified sex is now regarded as old-fashioned or sexist. Since 18 *they* has been used as an alternative after an indefinite pronoun, e.g. *everyone* or *someone*, and is becoming acceptable in standard English.

he /hiː/ *interjection*. OE.
[ORIGIN Natural exclam. Cf. HA *interjection*, HO *interjection*[1], etc.]
Repr. laughter, usu. affected or derisive. Chiefly in conjunction with other similar interjections & redupl. HE HE.

head /hɛd/ *noun* & *adjective*.
[ORIGIN Old English *hēafod* = Old Frisian *hāved*, *hād*, Old Saxon *hōid* (Dutch *hoofd*), Old High German *houbit* (German *Haupt*), Old Norse *haufuð*, *hofuð*, Gothic *haubiþ*, from Germanic, the relation of which with Latin *caput*, Greek *kephalē*, Sanskrit *kapāla* skull is not clear.]
▸ **A** *noun* **I** **1** The foremost part of the body of an animal or the upper part of the human body, separated from the rest of the body by a more or less distinct neck, and containing the mouth, the sense organs, and the brain. OE.

H

▸**b** The length of a head as a measure. **M16.** ▸**c** A headache. Usu. with specifying word. **L18.**

R. INGALLS Kelsoe. . had had his head. . torn from his body. J. MASTERS The only starers were the glass eyes of a pair of buffalo heads. **b** E. LINKLATER He topped Nikitin by half a head. **c** J. WADE I get one of those blinding heads.

2 a A part essential to life; life. **OE.** ▸**b** The seat of intellect and imagination. Also, a natural mental aptitude or talent *for*. **LME.**

a L. MACNEICE Charles Edward lost Culloden, hid near Arnish in Lewis, thirty thousand pounds on his head. **b** *Times Lit. Suppl.* He had a head for figures. M. L. KING Only through the bringing together of head and heart—intelligence and goodness—shall man rise. R. G. COLLINGWOOD The bridge exists only in his mind, or (as we also say) in his head.

3 The hair on the head. Cf. ***head of hair*** below. *obsolete* exc. *dial.* **OE.**

TENNYSON I curl'd and comb'd his comely head.

4 The hair dressed in a particular style. *arch.* **ME.**

ADDISON At my toilette, try'd a new head.

5 a A person with a head of a specified kind; an individual. **ME.** ▸**b** An individual animal of cattle, game, etc. (usu. treated as *pl.* following a numeral); *collect.* cattle, game. Also, an indefinite number *of* animals. **E16.** ▸**c** Freq. with specifying word prefixed: a drug user or addict. Also, a hippy or other unconventional person. *slang.* **E20.**

a *Times Educ. Suppl.* Wise heads. . are counselling against opening up the. . list. W. WHARTON They have a movie at ten cents a head. **b** A. HIGGINS A Kildare farmer. . had lost thirteen head of cattle. *Coarse Fishing* 18 years ago my favourite water contained a very small head of pike. **c** *Q* Pop was for teeny-boppers, usually girls, and rock was for serious 'heads'.

c *acid-head*, ***hophead***, ***pot-head***, etc.

6 A representation of a head, esp. as the image on the obverse of a coin; in *pl.*, this side turned upwards after a toss. **LME.** ▸**b** A postage stamp (bearing the monarch's head). *arch. colloq.* **M19.**

J. FOWLES A penny. . with all but that graceful head worn away. G. PRIESTLAND The penny is still spinning; heads for war, tails for peace.

7 The antlers of a deer. **LME.**

G. MARKHAM Stags yearly cast their Heads in March, April, May or June.

▸ **II 8** A compact mass of leaves, flowers, etc., at the top of a plant's stem; *esp.* = CAPITULUM (b). Also, a compound bulb (of garlic). **OE.** ▸**b** The rounded leafy top of a tree or shrub. **E16.**

V. WOOLF Laying the flowery heads of the grasses together. G. SANTAYANA Plenty of bread and cheese and a nice fresh head of lettuce. **b** T. MORRISON Shadrack stood. . watching the heads of trees tossing.

9 The upper end of something, as: the end of a lake at which a river enters it; the end of a bed, grave, etc., at which a person's head rests; the end of a table at which the host sits. **OE.**

P. LIVELY Mother sits at the head of the table. *National Trust Magazine* This embraces 5,000 acres of mud-flats at the head of the lough.

10 The part of an object which resembles a head in form or position, as: the cutting, striking, etc., end of a weapon, tool, etc.; the knobbed end of a nail, pin, screw, etc.; the rounded part of a musical note; the flat surface of a cask, drum, etc.; the hood of a carriage, roof of a car, etc.; the pommel of a saddle; the closed end of a cylinder of a pump or (esp. an internal-combustion) engine. **ME.**

J. CARY Rake-handles waiting for new heads. O. NASH When you go to strike a match the head dissolves on the box.

11 The top or upper end of something, as of a pile, a mast, a staircase, etc. **ME.**

SHAKES. *Haml.* The skyish head of blue Olympus. F. BURNEY I then accompanied her to the head of the stairs.

12 The fully developed part of a spot, boil, etc., where it tends to break. **ME.**

DRYDEN To lance the Sore, And cut the Head.

13 The foremost part or end of something; *esp.* the front of a procession, army, etc. Also, the front part of a plough holding the share. **ME.**

A. W. KINGLAKE The head of the vast column of troops. E. AMADI The head of the comet-like procession turned right.

14 The source of a river or stream. Also *fig.*, a source, the origin (now chiefly in ***fountainhead***). **ME.**

A. DAY I will go to the head of the matter. I. WATTS Jordan beheld their march and fled with backward Current to his Head.

15 A promontory. Now usu. in place names. **ME.**

LD MACAULAY High on St. Michael's Mount it shone: it shone on Beachy Head.

16 †**a** The beginning of a word, passage, etc. Latterly only ASTROLOGY, the point at which the sun enters a sign of the zodiac. **LME–E19.** ▸**b** PHONETICS. The first accented element or elements in a sequence of sounds before the nucleus. **E20.** ▸**c** LINGUISTICS. An element that has the same functions as the larger structure of which it is part and is therefore regarded as central to that structure. **M20.**

17 The top of a page, passage of text, etc. Also, a title etc. appearing there, a heading. **LME.** ▸**b** The top of a book. **E17.** ▸**c** A headline in a newspaper. **E20.**

ADDISON Without seeing his name at the head of it.

18 An end or extremity of something having greater length than breadth. Now *rare.* **LME.**

LD MACAULAY As that great host. . Rolled slowly towards the bridge's head.

19 A body of water or other liquid kept at a height in order to provide a supply (e.g. for a mill); the height of such a body or the pressure it exerts. **L15.** ▸**b** = BORE *noun*[2] 2. **L16.** ▸**c** The pressure of a confined body of steam etc. **M19.**

W. FAIRBAIRN The head of the water is 132 feet.

20 The bows of a ship. Also *spec.*, (now chiefly *hist.*) any part of the structure forward of the stern, *esp.* a figure-head. **L15.** ▸**b** NAUTICAL. *sing.* & in *pl.* A seamen's latrine (orig. in a ship's bows). Also (*N. Amer.*), a lavatory ashore. **M18.**

G. GROTE They were moored by anchors head and stern.

21 (A layer of) foam on the top of liquor, esp. beer. Also, (a layer of) cream on the top of milk. **M16.**

22 A measure of flax etc. **M16.**

23 = HEADING 7. **M17.**

24 BOWLS & CURLING etc. A playing of one end in a game to its conclusion. **E19.**

25 A component in an audio, video, information, etc., system by which information is transferred from an electrical signal to the recording medium, or vice versa. **M20.**

read/write head, ***record head***, ***recording head***, etc.

▸ **III 26** A person to whom others are subordinate; a ruler, a chief. **OE.** ▸**b** The master etc. of a college; a headmaster, a headmistress. **M16.**

S. KINGSLEY President ain't a good title for the head of the United States. P. CAREY You are the head of this household. *transf.*: AV *Isa.* 7:8 The head of Syria is Damascus. **b** D. CUSACK She'll make a splendid head Such an inspiring influence for the girls.

27 Position of leadership or supreme command. **ME.**

LD MACAULAY He was placed at the head of the administration.

28 Result; culmination, crisis; strength, force. Chiefly in ***come to a head***, ***bring to a head***, ***gather head***, etc. **ME.**

J. WESLEY Vice is risen to such a head, that it is impossible to suppress it. R. F. HORTON But it is time to draw to a head this somewhat lengthened discussion.

†**29** A force gathered esp. in insurrection. **L15–M17.**

S. PEPYS Some talk to-day of a head of Fanatiques that do appear about Barnett.

30 A main division in a discourse, a category. **E16.**

ISAIAH BERLIN The main issues between my serious critics and myself may be reduced to four heads.

31 Advance against opposing force; resistance, insurrection. Chiefly in ***make head***, ***keep head against***. **L16.**

32 A hunted animal's backward change of course to elude pursuit. Now *rare* or *obsolete*. **E17.**

– PHRASES: ***a bone in one's head***: see BONE *noun*. **above one's head** = *over one's head* below. ***a price on one's head***: see PRICE *noun*. **bang one's head against a brick wall**: see WALL *noun*[1]. ***bite a person's head off***: see BITE *verb*. ***break one's head***: see BREAK *verb*. ***by the head***: see BY *preposition*. ***comb a person's head with a three-legged stool***: see COMB *verb* 1. ***come into one's head***: see COME *verb*. **come to a head** (*a*) (of a boil etc.) suppurate; (*b*) *fig.* reach a climax or crisis. **count heads** (merely) determine the number present, voting, etc. ***crowned head***: see CROWNED 1. ***do one's head***: see DO *verb*. **do someone's head in** *colloq.* cause someone to feel annoyed, confused, or frustrated. ***eat its head off***: see EAT *verb*. ***enter one's head***: see ENTER *verb* 1b. **from head to foot**, **from head to heel**, **from head to toe** all over a person. ***get it into one's head that***: see GET *verb*. ***get one's head together***: see GET *verb*. **get one's head round** *colloq.* understand or come to terms with (something). **give (a horse) its head** allow it to go freely; *fig.* allow (a person) to act without restraint or guidance. **give (someone) head** *coarse slang* perform oral sex on (someone). **go to a person's head** (*a*) intoxicate; (*b*) make vain or proud. ***go upside a person's head***: see UPSIDE *preposition*. ***greenhead***: see GREEN *adjective*. ***hang one's head***: see HANG *verb*. ***have one's head screwed on the right way***: see SCREW *verb*. **head and front** (*a*) *rare* (Shakes.) the highest extent; (*b*) *arch.* the essence *of* an offence, the leader *of* an action. ***head first***: see FIRST. **head for heights** the ability to be close to the edge of a high cliff, roof, etc., without giddiness. **head of hair** the hair on a person's head, esp. as a noticeable feature. **head of the river** (the boat, crew, etc. holding) the leading position in a series of boat races; a regatta in which several crews attempt to gain this position. ***head over ears***: see EAR *noun*[1]. **head over heels** topsy-turvy, so as to turn completely over in a somersault etc. **heads I win, tails you lose** I win in any event. **heads will roll** *fig.* there will be some people dismissed or disgraced. **head to head** *colloq.* (orig. *US*) a conflict or contest (between two adversaries) at close quarters; a confrontation. ***hide one's head***: see HIDE *verb*[1]. ***hit the nail on the head***: see HIT *verb*. ***hold one's head high***: see HOLD *verb*. **keep one's head** remain calm. ***keep one's head above water***: see WATER *noun*. **keep one's head down** avoid distraction or danger. ***knock one's head against a brick wall***: see WALL *noun*[1]. ***knock on the head***: see KNOCK *verb*. ***laugh one's head off***: see LAUGH *verb*. **lay their heads together** consult one another. **let (a horse) have its head** = *give (a horse) its head* above. ***like a bear with a sore head***: see BEAR *noun*[1]. **lose one's head** (*a*) be beheaded; (*b*) become agitated or confused. †**make a head** raise a body of troops. **make head** make progress, advance or make resistance *against*. **make head or tail of** understand in any way (usu. in neg. contexts or interrog.). **need one's head examined** *joc. colloq.* be foolish, be crazy. ***need like a hole in the head***: see HOLE *noun*[1]. **off one's head** *colloq.* crazy. **off the top of one's head** *slang* impromptu. **of one's own head** (now *rare* or *obsolete*) by one's own decision, of one's own accord. **of the first head** (of a deer) at the age when the antlers are first developed; *fig.* of the first importance. **on one's head**, **on one's own head** (of vengeance, guilt, responsibility, etc.) falling on one. **out of one's head** (*a*) from one's own invention; (*b*) forgotten by one; (*c*) *N. Amer. colloq.* crazy. ***over head and ears***: see EAR *noun*[1]. **over one's head** (*a*) above one, *esp. fig.* (of impending danger) threatening one; (*b*) beyond one's comprehension; (*c*) (of another's promotion, involvement, etc.) when one has a prior or stronger claim; (*d*) *arch.* (of time) past, over; (*e*) out of one's depth (*lit.* & *fig.*). **put a pistol to one's head** commit suicide by shooting. **put a pistol to someone's head** (chiefly *fig.*) coerce someone. ***put a price on a person's head***: see PRICE *noun*. ***put ideas into a person's head***: see IDEA *noun*. **put into a person's head** suggest to a person. ***put one's head in a noose***: see NOOSE *noun*. **put their heads together** = *lay their heads together* above. ***run one's head against a brick wall***: see WALL *noun*[1]. ***set a price on a person's head***: see PRICE *noun*. ***show one's head***: see SHOW *verb*. ***snap a person's head off***: see SNAP *verb* 3. ***strong head***: see STRONG *adjective*. **take it into one's head** conceive a notion (*that*, *to do*). ***talk a person's head off***: see TALK *verb*. **to one's head** (*obsolete* exc. *dial.*) to one's face, directly. ***turn a person's head***: see TURN *verb*. ***wash a person's head (without soap)***: see WASH *verb*. ***wash one's head***: see WASH *verb*. ***wet the baby's head***: see WET *verb*. **win by a head** RACING win by the length of the horse's head. ***wiping head***: see WIPE *verb*. ***wolf's head***: see WOLF *noun*.

▸ **B** *attrib.* or as *adjective*. **1** In the position of command or superiority; chief, principal, capital. **OE.**

2 Situated at the top or front. Also, coming from the front, meeting one directly in front. **LME.**

– COMB. & SPECIAL COLLOCATIONS: **headband** (*a*) a band worn round the head; (*b*) an ornamental band of silk etc. fastened to the inner back of a bound book at the head and tail; (*c*) (long *rare* or *obsolete*) a band round the top of a pair of trousers etc.; **headbanding** (the action or process of fastening) the headbands of a book; **headbanger** (*a*) a person who practises headbanging; (*b*) *colloq.* an enthusiast for heavy metal music; **headbanging** (*a*) violent rocking of the body and shaking or knocking of the head, associated with mental disorder in adults; (*b*) vigorous head-shaking in time to heavy metal music etc.; **headboard** a board forming the head of a bed etc.; **headborough** *hist.* = BORSHOLDER; **head boy** the senior male pupil in a school; **headbutt** *verb trans.* & *noun* (attack with) a forceful thrust with the top of the head into another's chin or body; **headcase** *colloq.* a crazy person; **head cheese** *N. Amer.* brawn made from a pig's head etc.; **head-chief** the paramount chief of a N. American Indian people; **headcloth** a cloth or covering for the head; **headcount** (*a*) an instance of counting the number of people present; (*b*) a total number of people, esp. the number of people employed in a particular organization; **head-court** *hist.* a chief court (of justice); **headdress** a covering for the head, esp. an ornamental one worn by women; **headdresser** (*a*) a hairdresser; †(*b*) a maker of headdresses; **headend** TELECOMMUNICATIONS a control centre in a cable television system where various signals are brought together and monitored before being introduced into the cable network; **headfast** a rope or chain securing the head of a vessel to the quay etc.; **head gasket** the gasket which fits between the cylinder head and the cylinders or cylinder block in an internal-combustion engine; **headgear** (*a*) something worn on the head, as a hat, cap, headdress, etc.; (*b*) machinery etc. at the top of a mine shaft; **head girl** the senior female pupil in a school; **headhunt** *verb trans.* (seek to) obtain by headhunting; **headhunter** (*a*) a person who headhunts (another); (*b*) *spec.* an employment agent or agency specializing in the recruitment for an organization etc. of skilled personnel already employed elsewhere; **headhunting** (*a*) the practice of collecting the heads of one's enemies as trophies; (*b*) the action or practice of seeking to recruit on behalf of an organization etc. skilled personnel already employed elsewhere; **headkerchief** *arch.* a kerchief for the head; **headlamp** (*a*) a headlight; (*b*) a lamp carried on the front of a bicycle; **headland** (*a*) a strip of land left unploughed at the edge of a field; (*b*) a high point of land projecting into the sea etc., a promontory; **headlight** (the beam from) a powerful lamp carried on the front of a locomotive, motor vehicle, etc.; **headlock** a wrestling hold in which the arm is round an opponent's head; **head louse** a louse of the form infesting the hair of the human head; **headman** (*a*) a chief man, the chief of a tribe, etc.; †(*b*) *rare* = HEADSMAN 2; **headmaster** the principal master of a school; **headmastership** the office or position of a headmaster; **headmistress** the principal mistress of a school; **head-money** a fee paid by or for each person; **headnote** (*a*) LAW a summary giving the principle of the decision and an outline of the facts prefixed to the report of a decided case; (*b*) MUSIC a note produced in a high register of the voice; (*c*) a note or comment inserted at the head of a page, document, etc.; **head noun** the noun which other words in a noun phrase qualify; **head office** the principal office of a business organization constituting the centre for administration, policymaking, etc.; **headphone** a radio, telephone, etc., earphone held by a band fitting over the head; **headpiece** (*a*) a helmet; (*b*) (now *rare*) a cap etc.; (*c*) *arch.* the head, the skull; (*d*) the intellect; (*e*) a person of intellect; (*f*) a halter, a headstall; (*g*) the top part of something; **head race** the part of a mill race bringing water to the wheel; **headrest** a support for the head attached to the seat of a motor vehicle etc.; **head restraint** a headrest that prevents the head from jerking back suddenly; **headroom** overhead space; **head rope** †(*a*) one of the stays of a mast; (*b*) the part of a bolt rope sewn on to the upper edge of a sail; a small rope for hoisting an attached flag to the masthead etc.; (**c**) a rope along the top of a fishing net; (**d**) a rope for leading or tethering a horse etc.; **headsail** a sail on the foremast or bowsprit; **headscarf** a scarf worn instead of a hat; **head sea** waves from a forward direction; **headset** an attachment for fitting earphones and microphone to the head; **head shop** *colloq.* (chiefly *N. Amer.*) a shop selling paraphernalia associated with recreational drug use; **headshot** (**a**) a film sequence that captures a close-up of a person's head; (**b**) a bullet or gunshot aimed at the head; **headshrinker** (**a**) a headhunter who preserves and shrinks the heads of enemies; (**b**) *slang* a psychiatrist; **headspace** (**a**) the volume of air or empty space left at the top of a filled container, between the contents and the lid; (**b**) *colloq.* the space (notionally) occupied by a person's mind; **headspring** a fountainhead, a source (*lit. & fig.*); **headsquare** a (square) scarf for the head; **headstall** the part of a bridle or halter that fits round a horse's head; **headstand** an act of balancing on one's head and hands with the feet in the air; **head start** (**a**) an advantage at the start of a race (*lit. & fig.*); (**b**) *spec.* (with cap. initials) an educational and welfare programme in the US; ***head-stave***: see STAVE *noun* 2; **headstock** (**a**) the bearings or supports of revolving parts in various machines; (**b**) the horizontal end members in the underframe of a railway vehicle; **headstone** (**a**) the chief stone in a foundation, the cornerstone of a building (*lit. & fig.*); (**b**) a gravestone; **headstream** a headwater stream; **heads-up** *noun & adjective* (*N. Amer. colloq.*) (**a**) *noun* an advance warning; (**b**) *adjective* showing alertness or perceptiveness; **head tax** *US* a poll tax; **head teacher** the principal teacher or administrator of a school; a headmaster, a headmistress; **headtie** a headcloth, esp. a strip of colourful fabric worn tied around the head by women in the West Indies; **head-tire** (now *arch. & dial.*) covering for the head; a headdress; **head-trip** (*colloq.*) (**a**) an intellectually stimulating experience; (**b**) an act performed chiefly for self-gratification; **head-turning** *adjective* extremely noticeable or attractive; **head-up** *adjective* (of the instrument readings in an aircraft, vehicle, etc.) shown so as to be visible without lowering one's eyes from the view ahead; **head voice** a high register of the voice in speaking or singing; **headwater(s)** the part of a river or stream closest to the head or source; **headwear** what is worn on the head; hats, scarves, etc.; **headwind** a wind blowing from directly in front; **headword** (**a**) a word forming a heading (of an entry in a dictionary etc.); (**b**) LINGUISTICS a word that is the head (sense 16c above) of a syntactic group; **headwork** mental work; **headwrap** a strip of decorative material worn around the head by women; **head yard** any of the yards on the foremast of a sailing ship.

■ **headage** *noun* the number of animals in question M20. **headlet** *noun* (*obsolete* exc. *dial.*) a little head L16. **headship** *noun* the position or office of a head or principal; leadership; supremacy: L16.

head /hɛd/ *verb*. ME.
[ORIGIN from the noun.]

▸ **I 1** *verb trans.* Cut off or remove the head of; *esp.* (*arch.*) behead (a person). ME.

SHAKES. *Meas. for M.* If you head and hang all that offend that way.

2 *verb trans.* Lop off the upper part or branches of (a plant or tree). Also foll. by *down*. E16.

J. JAMES The willow.. is headed every three or four years.

▸ **II 3** Put a head on; provide with a head. LME. ▸**b** Close *up* (a cask etc.) by fitting the head on; enclose in a cask etc. by this means. E17. ▸**c** Form the head of. M17.

DRYDEN Whet the shining Share.. Or sharpen Stakes, or head the Forks.

4 *verb intrans.* Form a head; come, grow to a head. Also foll. by *out*, *up*. LME.

G. WASHINGTON All my early wheat.. was headed and heading.

5 *verb intrans.* Of a stream: have its source, rise. Chiefly *US*. M18.

H. M. BRACKENRIDGE The Kansas, a very large river.. heads between the Platte and the Arkansas.

6 *verb trans.* Foll. by *up*: collect (water) to form a head (*lit. & fig.*). E19.

ISAAC TAYLOR Religious knowledge long.. accumulated and headed up above the level of the plains of China.

7 *verb trans.* Provide with a heading; place a title, name, etc., at the head of (a chapter, list, etc.). Also, form the heading of. M19.

TENNYSON Heaven heads the count of crimes with that wild oath. M. MEYER Heading his letters with the month but not the date.

▸ **III 8** *verb trans.* Be the head or ruler of; be or put oneself at the head of. Also (chiefly *N. Amer.*) foll. by *up*. LME.

W. S. CHURCHILL Essex soon headed the war party in the Council. B. T. BRADFORD He thinks you're ideally suited to head up a wholesale supply company. A. J. P. TAYLOR I found our house full of Thompson relatives, headed by my grandmother.

9 *verb trans.* Go in front or at the head of; lead, precede; *fig.* surpass. E18.

J. DAVIDSON And he tossed his branching antlers high/As he headed the hunt.

▸ **IV 10** *verb intrans.* Face in a specified direction. E17.

C. C. ADLEY Two strong veins.. heading on in the direction of the main lode.

11 *verb trans.* Go round the head of (a stream or lake). M17.

T. H. HUXLEY It is shorter to cross a stream than to head it.

12 *verb trans.* Move forward so as to meet, advance in opposition to the course of; confront (*lit. & fig.*). *arch.* L17. ▸**b** Get in front of so as to turn back or aside. Freq. foll. by *off*. E18.

M. E. BRADDON He has to cover his face with a muffler, and head the driving snow. **b** R. H. SAVAGE To head my rival off I indulged in a tremendous flirtation.

13 *verb intrans.* Move towards (a particular point); proceed (in a specified direction); make *for*. M19.

P. ROTH Beside me in the taxi heading away from the sea. P. BAILEY A great articulated lorry heading straight in their direction.

▸ **V 14** *verb trans.* Chiefly FOOTBALL. Strike (esp. the ball) with the head; score (a goal) thus. L18.

-head /hɛd/ *suffix*[1].
[ORIGIN Var. of -HOOD.]
Forming nouns of condition or quality or grouping from nouns and adjectives. Now chiefly repl. by ***-hood*** exc. in ***godhead***, ***maidenhead***.

-head /hɛd/ *suffix*[2].
[ORIGIN from HEAD *noun*.]
1 Designating the front, forward, or upper part or end of a specified thing, as ***spearhead***, ***masthead***.
2 Forming informal nouns expressing disparagement of a person, as ***airhead***.
3 Forming informal nouns denoting an addict or habitual user of a specified drug, as ***crackhead***. ▸**b** Forming informal nouns denoting an enthusiast of a particular thing, as ***gearhead***.

headache /ˈhɛdeɪk/ *noun*. OE.
[ORIGIN from HEAD *noun* + ACHE *noun*[1].]
1 A continuous pain (usu. dull and deep-seated) in the head. OE. ▸**b** *fig.* A troublesome or annoying situation etc., a worry. *colloq.* M20.

b *Yachting World* Freak weather conditions are a constant headache for skippers.

sick headache: see SICK *adjective*.
2 A wild poppy (so called from the effect of its odour). *dial.* E19.

■ **headachy** *adjective* (**a**) suffering from or subject to headache; (**b**) accompanied by or causing headache: L18.

head and shoulders /hɛd ən(d) ˈʃəʊldəz/ *noun, adverbial, & adjectival phr.* L16.
[ORIGIN from HEAD *noun* + AND *conjunction*[1] + SHOULDER *noun*.]
▸ **A** *noun phr.* **1** ***by head and shoulders***, by force, violently. Now *rare*. L16.
2 A head and shoulders portrait. L19.
▸ **B** *adverbial phr.* (*Taller* etc.) by the measure of the head and shoulders; *fig.* considerably. M19.
▸ **C** *adjectival phr.* Designating a portrait etc. in which only the head and shoulders are shown. M19.

headed /ˈhɛdɪd/ *adjective*. ME.
[ORIGIN from HEAD *noun*, *verb*: see -ED[2], -ED[1].]
1 Having a head (of a specified kind); having heads (of a specified number). ME.

T. SCOTT All the arrowes they shoote.. are both headed and feathered.

clear-headed, ***light-headed***, ***many-headed***, etc. ***half-headed***: see HALF-.
2 That has come to a head or matured (*lit. & fig.*). *rare*. E17.

SHAKES. *A.Y.L.* All th' embossed sores and headed evils.

3 Having a (written or printed) heading. M19.

Daily News A letter on the headed notepaper of a firm in New Bond-Street.

header /ˈhɛdə/ *noun*. LME.
[ORIGIN from HEAD *verb* or *noun* + -ER[1].]
1 A person or thing which removes the head; *esp.* a reaping machine which cuts off the heads of grain. LME.
2 A brick or stone laid at right angles to the face of a wall. Cf. STRETCHER *noun* 3. L17.
3 A person who puts heads on casks etc. M18.
4 A person who heads a party etc., a leader. *rare*. E19.
5 A dive or plunge head first. *colloq.* M19.
6 FOOTBALL. A ball which is headed; the action or an act of heading the ball. Also, a player who heads the ball. E20.
7 = ***heading dog*** s.v. HEADING *noun*. M20.
8 A line of information appearing at the top of each page of a document, containing the date, chapter heading, etc. L20.
– PHRASES: ***double header***: see DOUBLE *adjective & adverb*. **take a header** *colloq.* fall head first.

heading /ˈhɛdɪŋ/ *noun*. ME.
[ORIGIN from HEAD *verb* + -ING[1].]
▸ **I 1** *gen.* The action of HEAD *verb*. ME.

FRANK ROBERTSON The heading up of the water. *Athenaeum* Plots and rumours of plots, with their consequences of headings and hangings.

2 The action or an act of facing or moving in a particular direction; *spec.* the course of a ship, aircraft, etc. E17.

C. A. LINDBERGH A degree or two change in heading could easily cause a crash. *Scientific American* The Pacific plate.. switched to that course from a more northerly heading about 40 million years ago.

3 FOOTBALL. The action of striking the ball with the head. L19.
▸ **II 4** †**a** A bank, a dam. M17–M19. ▸**b** *gen.* A distinct or separate part forming the head, top, or front of something. L17.
5 Material for making cask heads. L17.
6 A top layer or covering. L18.
7 A horizontal passage driven in preparation for a tunnel; a drift. E19.
8 A title etc. at the head of a page etc.; (the title of) a category. M19.

P. LEVI His business letter heading carried a wonderful rigmarole of which I was very proud. J. O'HARA Joe Montgomery could be classified under many headings.

– COMB.: **heading course** a course of bricks consisting of headers; **heading dog** *Austral. & NZ* a dog trained to round up etc.

headless /ˈhɛdlɪs/ *adjective*. OE.
[ORIGIN from HEAD *noun* + -LESS.]
1 Without a head, beheaded; having no head. OE.
2 Having no chief or leader. ME.
3 Lacking in brains or intellect; senseless, stupid. Long *rare*. M16.

headline /ˈhɛdlʌɪn/ *noun & verb*. LME.
[ORIGIN from HEAD *noun* + LINE *noun*[2].]
▸ **A** *noun*. **1** NAUTICAL. A line making a sail fast to the yard. Also, a strengthening line sewn on the upper edge of a flag. LME.
2 A baseline used in surveying. Long *rare*. M17.
3 TYPOGRAPHY. †**a** The notional upper line that bounds a small letter. Only in L17. ▸**b** The line at the top of a page containing the title etc.; a title or subtitle in large type in a newspaper etc. Also (usu. in *pl.*), a summary of main items given during a broadcast news bulletin. E19.

b G. HUNTINGTON He studied the headlines of the *Corriere della Sera*. *attrib.*: R. OWEN Yalta is again headline-news rather than the stuff of faded documents.

b hit the headlines, **make the headlines** be very important news, come suddenly to public notice. ***running headline***: see RUNNING *adjective*.
4 A fold in the palm of the hand regarded in palmistry as significant of a person's abilities. M19.
5 A line etc. attached to the head of something; *spec.* a line fastening a vessel's head to the shore. L19.
▸ **B** *verb*. **1** *verb trans.* Provide with a headline; display in a headline. L19.

Listener The answer.. faithfully reported and perhaps headlined the next day in the local press.

2 *verb intrans. & trans.* Appear as the chief performer (at). L20.

Sounds Siouxsie and the Banshees.. will be headlining the Ostend Festival.

■ **headliner** *noun* (*US*) a star performer L19. **headliˈnese** *noun* the elliptical style of language characteristic of (esp. popular) newspaper headlines E20.

headlong /ˈhɛdlɒŋ/ *adverb & adjective*. Orig. †**-ling**. LME.
[ORIGIN from HEAD *noun* + -LING[2], assim. in late Middle English to -LONG.]
▸ **A** *adverb*. **1** Head foremost (in falling etc.); head downmost. LME.

J. CONRAD Shaw was thrown headlong against the skylight.

2 With an unrestrained forward motion, precipitately (*lit. & fig.*). LME.

B. JOWETT He amongst us who would be divine.. should not rush headlong into pleasures. J. B. MORTON Hastily collecting his things he runs headlong from the room.

▸ **B** *adjective*. **1** Rushing forward without restraint; impetuous; precipitate (*lit. & fig.*). E16.

LD MACAULAY Wild mountain passes.. torn by headlong torrents. W. STYRON Plunging in panicky headlong flight toward the fields and the woods beyond. R. MACAULAY What a child she was for enthusiasms and ideas and headlong plans.

2 Of a height etc. from which a person might fall headlong; precipitous. Now *rare*. M16.

BYRON Like a tower upon a headlong rock.

3 Plunging downwards head foremost as in falling etc. L16.

M. KINGSLEY Taking a headlong dive into the deep Atlantic.

■ **headlongness** *noun* (*rare*) headlong quality or speed, precipitateness (*lit. & fig.*) E18. **headlongs** *adverb* (*obsolete* exc. *dial.*) = HEADLONG *adverb* LME.

headmost /ˈhɛdməʊst/ *adjective*. E17.
[ORIGIN from HEAD *noun & adjective* + -MOST.]
1 Foremost (esp. of a ship). E17.
2 Topmost. Chiefly *dial.* L18.

H

head-on /*as adverb* hɛdˈɒn, *as adjective* ˈhɛdɒn/ *adverb & adjective*. Orig. *US*. **M19.**
[ORIGIN from HEAD *noun* + ON *adverb*.]
▸ **A** *adverb*. With the head pointed directly towards an object (*lit. & fig.*). **M19.**
▸ **B** *adjective*. Involving the (violent) meeting of two vehicles head to head, or of the head of a vehicle with a stationary object; *fig.* with direct opposition. **E20.**

headquarter /ˈhɛdkwɔːtə/ *verb trans.* **E20.**
[ORIGIN from HEADQUARTERS.]
Provide with headquarters (at a specified location). Usu. in *pass.*

headquarters /hɛdˈkwɔːtəz/ *noun* (treated as *sing.* or *pl.*). **M17.**
[ORIGIN from HEAD *noun* + QUARTER *noun* + -S[1].]
1 MILITARY. The quarters of the officer commanding an army, a corps, a division, etc.; the officers stationed there. **M17.**
2 A central or chief place of business etc.; a centre of operations. **L18.**

headrail /ˈhɛdreɪl/ *noun*[1]. **L18.**
[ORIGIN from HEAD *noun* + RAIL *noun*[2].]
1 In *pl.* The teeth. *slang*. **L18.**
2 A rail at the head of a ship. **L18.**

headrail /ˈhɛdreɪl/ *noun*[2]. **M19.**
[ORIGIN from HEAD *noun* + RAIL *noun*[1].]
A woman's headdress of the Old English period.

headsman /ˈhɛdzmən/ *noun*. Pl. **-men**. **LME.**
[ORIGIN from HEAD *noun* + -'S[1] + MAN *noun*.]
1 A chief, a headman. Now *rare*. **LME.**
2 An executioner who beheads. **E17.**
3 *hist.* The commander of a whaling boat. **M19.**
4 A miner who moves loads of coal etc. from the workings into position for transport to the surface. **M19.**

headstrong /ˈhɛdstrɒŋ/ *adjective*. **LME.**
[ORIGIN from HEAD *noun* + STRONG *adjective*.]
1 Violently self-willed, obstinate. **LME.**

R. W. EMERSON They are testy and headstrong through an excess of will and bias. V. S. PRITCHETT The parentless boy would tend to run wild, to resemble his headstrong father.

2 Proceeding from wilfulness or obstinacy. **L16.**

R. ELLIS Should . . humour headstrong Drive thee wilfully . . to such profaning.

▪ **headstrongly** *adverb* (long *rare* or *obsolete*) **M17.** **headstrongness** *noun* **E17.**

headward /ˈhɛdwəd/ *noun, adjective, & adverb*. **LME.**
[ORIGIN from HEAD *noun* + -WARD.]
▸ †**A** *noun*. ***to the headward***, towards the head; NAUTICAL ahead. **LME–L17.**
▸ **B** *adjective*. That is in the region or direction of the head; *esp.* (of erosion) occurring along the course of a stream etc. in an upstream direction. **M17.**
▸ **C** *adverb*. Towards or in the direction of the head. **L18.**
▪ Also **headwards** *adverb* **M19.**

headway /ˈhɛdweɪ/ *noun*. **E18.**
[ORIGIN from HEAD *noun* + WAY *noun*.]
▸ **I 1** MINING. A narrow passage or gallery connecting broad parallel passages. **E18.**
2 ARCHITECTURE. Headroom; the clear height of a door, tunnel, etc. **L18.**
3 The interval of time between successive buses etc. on a route. **L19.**
▸ **II 4** A ship's movement ahead or forward; rate of progress; *gen.* advance, progress (*lit. & fig.*). **M18.**

M. SCAMMELL Solzhenitsyn was too naïve and inexperienced to make much headway. *Ships Monthly* The ship was losing headway, the engines stopped.

heady /ˈhɛdi/ *adjective*. **LME.**
[ORIGIN from HEAD *noun* + -Y[1].]
1 Headlong, impetuous, violent; passionate; headstrong. **LME.**

SHAKES. *Hen. V* Never came reformation in a flood, With such a heady currance, scouring faults. S. JOHNSON Passions by which the heady and vehement are seduced and betrayed.

2 Apt to intoxicate (*lit. & fig.*). **L16.**

M. HOLROYD The heady cosmopolitan world of Montparnasse intoxicated him. A. S. BYATT The fruit salad had been heady with some dark and potent wine.

3 Headachy. *colloq.* **L19.**

E. HILLARY I felt thick and heady and a sharp cough rasped my sore throat.

▪ **headily** *adverb* **LME.** **headiness** *noun* **LME.**

†**heal** *noun*. Also **hele**.
[ORIGIN Old English *hælu*, *hæl*, corresp. to Old Saxon *hēli*, Old High German *heili*, from *hāl* adjective: see HALE *adjective*, WHOLE *adjective*.]
1 Sound bodily condition; health. In later use *Scot.* **OE–E20.**
▸**b** Healing, recovery. **ME–L17.**
2 Welfare, prosperity. **OE–E17.**
3 Spiritual health or healing. **OE–L16.**

heal /hiːl/ *verb*[1].
[ORIGIN Old English *hǣlan* = Old Frisian *hēla*, Old Saxon *hēlian* (Dutch *heelen*), Old & mod. High German *heilen*, Old Norse *heila*, Gothic *hailjan*, from Germanic, from base repr. also by WHOLE *adjective*.]
1 *verb trans.* Free (a person) from disease or ailment, restore to health (now chiefly by miraculous, spiritual, or psychic means). (Foll. by (*arch.*) *of* a disease.) **OE.** ▸**b** *fig.* Restore to a sound condition; save from sin, danger, etc. **OE.** ▸**c** *spec.* Of a monarch: touch for the 'king's evil'. *obsolete* exc. *hist.* **E16.**
2 *verb trans.* Make whole (a wound); cure (a disease). (Foll. by *over*, *up*.) **OE.** ▸**b** *fig.* Repair, correct (an undesirable condition, esp. a breach of relations). **ME.**

J. KOSINSKI Whatever had been broken by the butt of the Kalmuk's rifle was now healed. **b** G. GREENE I will make you a bet . . that . . relations are healed and the American Ambassador returns.

3 *verb intrans.* Of a wound, a part of the body, etc.: become whole or sound again, esp. by the growth of new tissue; become cured. **LME.**

B. EMECHETA One of his feet had a nasty scar that had healed badly. M. AMIS Father's ankle had healed . . he now claimed to be fleeter of foot.

– COMB.: **heal-all** (**a**) a universal remedy, a panacea; (**b**) any of various plants with reputed healing powers; *esp.* roseroot, *Sedum rosea*, and (chiefly *US*) self-heal, *Prunella vulgaris*.
▪ **healer** *noun* a person or thing which heals; *spec.* a faith healer: **ME.** **healing** *ppl adjective* that heals; *esp.* having therapeutic or curative properties: **LME.** **healingly** *adverb* **M19.**

heal *verb*[2] var. of HELE *verb*.

heald /hiːld/ *noun*.
[ORIGIN Old English *hefel*, *hefeld*, Old Saxon *hevild*, Old Norse *hafald*, from base meaning 'raise': see HEDDLE.]
WEAVING. †**1** The warp and weft. **OE–L15.**
2 = HEDDLE. **M18.**

heald *verb* var. of HIELD.

healsome /ˈhiːls(ə)m/ *adjective*. *obsolete* exc. *Scot.* **LME.**
[ORIGIN from HEAL *noun* + -SOME[1]: cf. HALESOME.]
Wholesome, healthy.

health /hɛlθ/ *noun*.
[ORIGIN Old English *hǣlþ* = Old High German *heilida*, from West Germanic, from Germanic base repr. also by WHOLE *adjective*: see -TH[1].]
1 Sound condition of body; freedom from disease. **OE.**

S. SPENDER This . . period of alternating health and illness. J. GATHORNE-HARDY Dr. Wasing's astonishment . . as M and B swept his pneumonia patients to health. *fig.*: *Community Librarian* The revenue from this source is essential for the continuing health of our journal.

to your health!, **to your good health!** expr. a wish for another's well-being uttered by a person drinking.
†**2** Healing, cure. **OE–M16.**
3 Spiritual or moral soundness. Also, salvation. *arch.* **OE.**

E. LYALL As you value the health of your own souls.

†**4** Welfare, safety; deliverance. **ME–E17.**

G. CHAPMAN There is no mercy in the wars, your healths lie in your hands.

5 Condition of body in respect of its vigour and soundness. Freq. with qualifying adjective, as ***good health***, ***bad health***, ***delicate health***. **M16.**

V. GLENDINNING He was . . nervous about his health and suffered from asthma.

bill of health: see BILL *noun*[3]. **mental health** condition of a person or group in respect of the functioning of the mind. **not for one's health** *colloq.* (orig. *US*) for serious (financial) motives.
6 A toast drunk in a person's honour. **L16.**

T. S. ELIOT Now I'll propose a health. Can you guess whose health I'm going to propose?

– COMB.: **health camp** *NZ* a camp for the improvement of children's physical or mental health; **health care** the maintenance and improvement of personal health; **health centre** a local headquarters of medical facilities; *spec.* one containing the surgery and offices of a group practice; **health club** an establishment providing facilities for gymnastic exercises, massage, etc.; **health farm** (orig. *US*) a place where visitors stay for an intensive course of dieting etc.; **health food** food, usu. produced by non-artificial methods, eaten for its supposed health-giving properties; **health insurance** insurance against loss of earnings through illness or to cover the cost of medical treatment; **Health Maintenance Organization** (chiefly *US*) an organization which administrates a form of comprehensive health care on the free market, paid for by a predetermined fixed insurance fee per customer; **health officer**: charged with the administration of health laws and sanitary inspection; **health physics** the branch of radiology that deals with the health of those working with radioactive materials; **health resort** a place, such as a spa, resorted to by visitors for the benefit of their health; **health salts** magnesium sulphate or other salts taken in effervescent form as a mild laxative; **health service** the aggregate of public medical facilities available to members of a community; **health tourism** the practice of travelling abroad in order to receive medical treatment; **health visitor** a trained person who visits people, esp. expectant mothers and the elderly, in their homes to give them advice on their health.

healthful /ˈhɛlθfʊl, -f(ə)l/ *adjective*. **LME.**
[ORIGIN from HEALTH + -FUL.]
1 Wholesome, salubrious. **LME.**
2 Of a person etc.: full of or marked by moral, intellectual, or (now *rare*) physical health; healthy. **LME.**
▪ **healthfully** *adverb* **LME.** **healthfulness** *noun* **M16.**

healthless /ˈhɛlθlɪs/ *adjective*. Now *rare*. **M16.**
[ORIGIN formed as HEALTHFUL + -LESS.]
1 Lacking physical or spiritual health; unhealthy. **M16.**
2 Not conducive to health; unwholesome. **M17.**

healthsome /ˈhɛlθs(ə)m/ *adjective*. Now *rare*. **M16.**
[ORIGIN formed as HEALTHFUL + -SOME[1].]
1 Wholesome, salutary. **M16.**
†**2** Enjoying good health; healthy. **M16–M17.**

healthy /ˈhɛlθi/ *adjective*. **M16.**
[ORIGIN from HEALTH + -Y[1].]
1 Possessing good health; sound in body, free from disease. **M16.**

P. ROTH Men . . young and healthy enough to make a rapid physical recovery from bypass surgery. *fig.*: J. GROSS The infected areas of his work cannot simply be cordoned off from the healthy.

2 Conducive to health, salubrious; *fig.* salutary in effect. **M16.** ▸**b** In ironical use: safe, prudent. **M19.**

W. S. CHURCHILL London was a healthier place to live in than rural Prussia. J. KRANTZ Raspberries sounded very healthy to both Dolly and Lester. *Oxford Mail* The fall [in the market] is a healthy reminder that the small print in the unit trust advertisements . . is true. **b** G. D. BREWERTON It would not have been 'healthy' . . for Major Clarke to have entered the place.

3 Indicative or characteristic of good health or sound condition (*lit. & fig.*). Opp. ***morbid***. **L16.**

STEELE With a fresh, sanguine, and healthy Look. H. M. STANLEY An interchange of small gifts served as a healthy augury for the future. E. O'NEILL Now I'm going to give an honest healthy yell. K. ISHIGURO People . . need to express their views openly and strongly—now that's a healthy thing.

4 Of a quantity etc.: gratifyingly or impressively large. *colloq.* **L19.**

G. BORDMAN The healthy salaries stars were beginning to draw. *Keyboard Player* Output from the monitor speakers is a healthy 20 watts.

▪ **healthily** *adverb* **M17.** **healthiness** *noun* (earlier in UNHEALTHINESS) **L17.**

heap /hiːp/ *noun*.
[ORIGIN Old English *hēap* = Old Frisian *hāp*, Old Saxon *hōp* (Dutch *hoop*: cf. FORLORN HOPE), Old High German *houf* (rel. to Middle Low German *hūpe*, Old High German *hūfo*, German *Haufen*), from West Germanic.]
1 A collection of objects or material piled up so as to form a high (freq. conical) mass. Cf. PILE *noun*[3]. **OE.**

K. MANSFIELD An old gardener . . was sweeping the path, brushing the leaves into a neat little heap.

compost heap, ***dust heap***, ***scrap heap***, ***slag heap***, etc.
†**2** A large company (esp. of people); a crowd, a host. **OE–L16.**

SHAKES. *Rich. III* Among this princely heap, if any here, By false intelligence or wrong surmise, Hold me a foe.

3 *sing.* & in *pl.* A large number or quantity; a great deal, a lot. Foll. by *of*. *colloq.* **ME.** ▸**b** Without preceding *a*, as *adverb* in representations (now freq. *joc.*) of N. American Indian speech: very (much); esp. ***heap big***. **M19.**

W. BESANT He got into trouble a heap of times. J. B. MORTON There are heaps of candidates. E. WHARTON We'd be heaps hotter up where Miss Mellins is. A. LURIE I've got a heap to tell you.

4 A heaped measure of capacity. **LME.**
5 A slovenly woman. Usu. with qualifying adjective. *colloq.* (orig. *dial.*). **E19.**
6 A battered old car. *colloq.* (orig. *US*). **E20.**
– PHRASES: **a heap sight** *US colloq.* to a considerable degree or extent. **(at the) bottom of the heap** *colloq.* in a losing, inferior, or disadvantaged position. **(at the) top of the heap** *colloq.* in a winning, pre-eminent, or advantageous position. ***bottom of the heap***: see ***at the bottom of the heap*** above. †**by heaps**, †**in heaps** in great numbers, in crowds. ***heap big***: see sense 3b above. **knock all of a heap** = ***strike all of a heap*** below. †**on a heap**, †**on heaps** in a prostrate mass. **strike all of a heap** knock (a person) prostrate, esp. (*hyperbol.*) with surprise or dismay. ***top of the heap***: see ***at the top of the heap*** above.

heap /hiːp/ *verb*.
[ORIGIN Old English *hēapian* (corresp. to Old High German *houfōn*), from HEAP *noun*.]
1 *verb trans.* Form into a heap; pile (*up*). **OE.** ▸**b** *fig.* Bestow in large quantities (*up*)*on*. **L16.**

M. PATTISON Generations of antiquaries have heaped together vast piles of facts. J. TYNDALL The snow had been heaped in oblique ridges across my path. J. WAIN Canvases, dirty crockery, and clothes . . had been heaped on to this [table] in a kind of unsteady mound. **b** L. DEIGHTON The miseries that airline companies heap upon their clients. P. ROTH The ridicule he'd heaped upon them all in that book.

heap coals on a person's head, ***heap coals of fire on a person's head***: see COAL *noun*. **b** ***heap praises on***: see PRAISE *noun*.

2 *verb trans.* Cover or fill with or *with* objects or a substance piled high. **ME.** ▸**b** *fig.* Overwhelm *with* large quantities of something (e.g. praise, blame). **LME.**

> G. MACDONALD A side-table, heaped up with books and papers. *Harper's Magazine* That is stinted measure. I heap my cup, before emptying. **b** C. KINGSLEY We are received with open arms, and heaped with hospitality.

3 *verb intrans.* Become piled up, form a heap. Now *US.* **LME.**

> *Harper's Magazine* Fallen avalanches heap whitely at intervals below.

■ **heaped** *ppl adjective* that has been heaped; *esp.* having its contents piled above the brim instead of being levelled: **LME.** **heaper** *noun* **L15.** **heaping** *ppl adjective* (*N. Amer.*) heaped above the brim **M19.**

heapy /ˈhiːpi/ *adjective. rare.* **M16.**
[ORIGIN from HEAP *noun* + -Y[1].]
Full or consisting of heaps.

hear /hɪə/ *verb.* Pa. t. & pple **heard** /həːd/.
[ORIGIN Old English *hēran*, (West Saxon) *hīeran* = Old Frisian *hēra*, *hōra*, Old Saxon *hōrian* (Dutch *hooren*), Old High German *hōren* (German *hören*), Old Norse *heyra*, Gothic *hausjan*, from Germanic.]
▸ **I 1** *verb trans.* Perceive with the ear (a sound etc., someone or something *do* (pass. *to do*), *doing*, *done*). (See also ***hear say***, ***hear tell*** below.) **OE.** ▸**b** *verb intrans.* Possess or exercise the faculty of perceiving sounds. **OE.**

> T. HARDY He heard at that moment the noise of wheels behind him. SCOTT FITZGERALD I heard the phone taken up inside. A. CHRISTIE In the stillness you could have heard a pin drop. T. FRISBY You could hear that drummer half-way down the street. A. SHAFFER The front door is heard to close. ANNE STEVENSON Listen and you can hear them bustling in my lost rooms. **b** B. JOWETT [He] whispered . . so that Menexenus should not hear.

2 *verb trans. & intrans.* Listen (to) with attention or understanding. **OE.** ▸**b** *verb trans.* Listen to (a play, religious service, etc.) as a member of an audience or congregation. **ME.** ▸**c** *verb trans.* Listen to someone reciting (something learned by heart). Also (*arch.*) with indirect obj. **E19.**

> F. MORYSON There is a Chamber [in the Vatican] . . wherein Ambassadours are heard. D. H. LAWRENCE Madame and Max heard in silence. R. MACAULAY Father Chantry-Pigg was hearing confessions. E. WAUGH They talk entirely for their own pleasure. Nothing they say is designed to be heard. B. ENGLAND I should be interested to hear your reasoning. P. O'BRIAN I hear what you say. I think that you are probably mistaken. **b** H. HALLAM Many persons were sent to prison for hearing Mass. G. B. SHAW He actually took me to hear his performance. **c** R. D. BLACKMORE Three pupils, and not a lesson have I heard them.

3 a *verb trans.* Chiefly in scriptural and liturgical use: listen to with favour; grant (a prayer). **OE.** ▸**b** *verb intrans.* Foll. by *of*, (US) *to*: entertain the notion of. Usu. preceded by *will* (*would*) and neg. **L16.**

> **a** AV *Ps.* 116:1. I loue the LORD: because hee hath heard . . my supplications. **b** O. WILDE Constance's doctor . . won't hear of her going out tonight. E. POOLE When I tried . . to turn our talk . . , at first she would not hear to it.

4 *verb trans.* (orig. with indirect obj.). Be obedient to. Long *arch.* **OE.**

> M. PRIOR The fiery Pegasus disdains To mind the Rider's Voice, or hear the Reins.

5 a *verb trans.* Get to know (a fact etc.) by hearing; learn, be told. (Foll. by subord. clause, adverbial obj.) **OE.** ▸**b** *verb intrans.* Be told *about*; learn *of*. **ME.**

> **a** SCOTT FITZGERALD I've just heard the most amazing thing. E. WAUGH Nina, I hear you're engaged. J. LE CARRÉ 'Mundt . . found it quite easy.' 'So I hear'. E. WELTY So you're the young man we've heard so much about. **b** M. SINCLAIR Roucliffe was coming to dinner. Such a thing had never been heard of. L. HUGHES I heard on the radio about the Freedom Train. E. JOHNSON He was saddened to hear of the death of his old friend.

6 *verb trans.* Listen to in a court of law; consider judicially. **ME.**

> H. H. WILSON Three Judges were appointed to the special duty of hearing appeals from the courts below. J. LE CARRÉ We shall hear evidence as we think fit. D. M. WALKER Only very exceptionally . . can a criminal case be heard 'in camera'.

†**7** *verb intrans.* With adverbs [after Greek *eu, kakōs akouein*, Latin *bene, male audire*]: be spoken (favourably or unfavourably) of. **L16–E18.**

> JOSEPH HALL Aristotle himself is wont to hear ill for his opinion of the soul's mortality.

8 *verb intrans.* Receive a communication *from*; receive a warning or reprimand *from*. **E17.**

> *Fraser's Magazine* You shall hear from my attorney. A. BROOKNER When the telephone rang . . she had not expected to hear from anyone.

▸ **II** Special uses of the imper.
9 ***hear! hear!*** (orig. †***hear him!*** (***hear him!***)), an exclam. calling attention to a speaker's words, e.g. in the House of Commons, and now usu. expressing enthusiastic assent, occas. ironical derision. **L17.**
– PHRASES, & WITH ADVERBS IN SPECIALIZED SENSES: **be unable to hear oneself think** be unable etc. to think clearly for the noise. **do you hear?** *colloq.*: a phr. appended by way of emphasis to an impatient request, a warning, etc. **hear of it** *colloq.* be called to account over a matter. **hear out** listen to (a person, something said) to the end. †**hear rather** prefer to be called. **hear say** *arch.* be informed. **hear tell** (now *colloq. & dial.*) learn, be informed (*of*, *that*). ***hear the last of***: see LAST *noun*[5] 8. **hear things** have auditory hallucinations. **like to hear oneself speak**, **like to hear oneself talk** be fond of talking. **you hear?** *colloq.* = ***do you hear?*** above.
– COMB.: **hear-hear** *noun & verb* (**a**) *noun* a cheer expressed in the words 'hear! hear!'; (**b**) *verb intrans. & trans.* utter or cheer with cries of 'hear! hear!'; †**hear-him** a cry of 'hear him!' (see sense 9 above).

hearable /ˈhɪərəb(ə)l/ *adjective.* **LME.**
[ORIGIN from HEAR + -ABLE.]
Able to be heard; audible.

heard *verb pa. t. & pple* of HEAR.

hearer /ˈhɪərə/ *noun.* **ME.**
[ORIGIN from HEAR *verb* + -ER[1].]
1 A person etc. who hears; a listener. **ME.**
2 A person who receives oral instruction or attends lectures etc.; *Scot.* a member of the congregation *of* a particular minister. **L17.**
3 [translating Latin *audiens*.] ECCLESIASTICAL HISTORY. A person admitted to readings of the Scriptures and to instruction, but not to church worship; a catechumen or a penitent of the second order. **L17.**

hearing /ˈhɪərɪŋ/ *noun.* **ME.**
[ORIGIN from HEAR *verb* + -ING[1].]
1 The action or faculty of perceiving sounds by the ear. **ME.** ▸**b** Earshot. Esp. in ***out of hearing***, ***within hearing***. **LME.**

> *Daily Telegraph* Mr Betts was left with impaired sight and hearing.

come to someone's hearing become known to one through report. ***hard of hearing***: see HARD *adjective*. **in one's hearing** in such a way as to be heard by one.
2 The action or an act of listening; an opportunity to be listened to. **ME.**

> C. IVES When a new . . work is accepted as beautiful on its first hearing. R. P. GRAVES The Liberal speakers were not given a fair hearing.

3 (A piece of) news, (a) report. Now *dial.* **ME.**

> DICKENS This is a pleasant hearing I thank Heaven for it. A. CHRISTIE Miss Marple smiled at him and said that that was a good hearing.

4 The action or process of listening to evidence etc. in a court of law or before an official; *spec.* a trial before a judge without a jury. **L16.**

> P. HOWARD In February 1897 a Select Committee of the House of Commons began its hearings.

5 A scolding. *Scot.* **E19.**
– COMB.: **hearing aid** a small sound amplifier worn by people who are hard of hearing; **hearing dog** a dog trained to alert people who are deaf or hard of hearing to such sounds as the ringing of an alarm, doorbell, or telephone.

hearken /ˈhɑːk(ə)n/ *verb.* Also ***harken**.
[ORIGIN Old English *hercnian*, *heorcnian*: see HARK, -EN[5]. The spelling with *-ea-* is due to assoc. with HEAR.]
1 *verb intrans.* Listen. Freq. foll. by *to* (Old English & Middle English *dat.*). *arch. & literary.* **OE.** ▸**b** Listen with compliance or sympathy *to*. **ME.** ▸**c** Listen as an eavesdropper (*to*). *obsolete* exc. *Scot.* **LME.**

> SHAKES. *Ven. & Ad.* She hearkens for his hounds and for his horn. **b** A. FRASER Their determination not even to be seen to hearken to outside pleadings.

2 *verb trans.* Hear with attention, listen to (a person, words, etc.). Now *Scot., dial., & poet.* **OE.**

> W. DE LA MARE Sadly that music she hearkened.

†**3** *verb intrans.* Enquire *after*; seek news *of*. **ME–M19.**
4 *verb intrans.* Wait, lie in wait. *obsolete* exc. *dial.* **L16.**

> SHAKES. *Tam. Shr.* The youngest daughter, whom you hearken for, Her father keeps from all access of suitors.

†**5** *verb trans.* Usu. foll. by *out*: search out or get to hear of by enquiry. **L16–E18.**
6 *verb trans. & intrans.* Whisper in one's ear. *obsolete* exc. *Scot.* **E17.**
■ **hearkener** *noun* **ME.**

hearsay /ˈhɪəseɪ/ *noun.* **LME.**
[ORIGIN Orig. in phr. *by hear say*, translating Old French *par ouïr dire* (now *ouï-dire*), i.e. *par* by, *ouïr* hear, *dire* say.]
That which one hears or has heard someone say; report, rumour, common talk. Also (*arch.*), an instance of this, a piece of gossip.

> J. I. M. STEWART Not many people knew of the scandal other than by hearsay.

– ATTRIB. & COMB.: In the senses 'of the nature of hearsay', 'founded on hearsay', as ***hearsay account***, ***hearsay knowledge***, ***hearsay report***; 'speaking by hearsay', as ***hearsay witness*** etc. Special combs., as **hearsay evidence** evidence in support of an allegation based not on the witness's direct knowledge but on what he or she has heard others say.

hearse /həːs/ *noun*[1]. Also (in branch I formerly, in branch II usu.) **herse**. **ME.**
[ORIGIN Old French & mod. French *herse* lit. 'harrow' from medieval Latin *erpica* from Latin (*h*)*irpex* kind of harrow, from Samnite (*h*)*irpus* wolf, with ref. to the teeth.]
▸ **I** Applied to things associated with funerals and other religious rites.
1 A structure placed over the bier or coffin of a distinguished person while it rested in church: orig., a lattice-work canopy bearing many lighted tapers; later, a wooden structure resembling a pagoda decorated with banners, heraldic devices, and lighted candles, sometimes bearing complimentary verses attached by friends. *obsolete* exc. *hist.* **ME.** ▸**b** A permanent framework of iron or other metal placed over a tomb to support rich coverings. **M16.** ▸**c** A light wooden framework for supporting the pall over the body at funerals. **M16.**

> A. COWLEY Be this my latest Verse With which I now adorn his Herse.

2 A harrow-shaped triangular frame designed to hold candles and used in Holy Week at the Tenebrae service. Also, a triple candlestick used in the Holy Saturday rite. *obsolete* exc. *hist.* **LME.**
†**3** A funeral pall. **M16–E17.**
†**4** A corpse. **M16–M17.**
5 A bier, a coffin; vaguely, a tomb. *arch.* **L16.**

> LONGFELLOW Decked with flowers a simple hearse To the churchyard forth they bear.

†**6** A funeral obsequy; any solemn religious ceremony. *rare* (Spenser). Only in **L16.**
7 A carriage or car for conveying the coffin at a funeral. (The current use.) **M17.**
▸ **II** In other contexts.
8 A portcullis. *obsolete* exc. *hist.* **LME.**
†**9** A harrow, used in agriculture or to perform the function of chevaux de frise. **L15–M18.**
10 A kind of battle formation. *obsolete* exc. *hist.* **E16.**
– COMB.: **hearse-cloth** a black cloth used to cover a bier or coffin; a funeral pall.

†**hearse** *noun*[2] var. of HEARST.

hearse /həːs/ *verb trans.* **L16.**
[ORIGIN from HEARSE *noun*[1].]
1 Place (a corpse) on a bier or in a coffin; bury with funeral rites. Now usu., convey to the grave in a hearse (HEARSE *noun*[1] 7). **L16.**

> SHAKES. *Haml.* Tell why thy . . bones, hearsed in death, Have burst their cerements.

2 *fig.* Provide with something suggestive of a hearse. **M17.**

> LONGFELLOW The hill-top hearsed with pines.

hearst /həːst/ *noun.* Also †**hearse**. **L17.**
[ORIGIN Unknown.]
HUNTING. A hind of the second or third year.

heart /hɑːt/ *noun.*
[ORIGIN Old English *heorte* = Old Frisian *herte*, Old Saxon *herta* (Dutch *hart*), Old High German *herza* (German *Herz*), Old Norse *hjarta*, Gothic *hairtō*, from Germanic, from Indo-European base repr. also by Greek *kēr*, *kardia*, Latin *cor*, *cord-*.]
▸ **I** The bodily organ.
1 The hollow muscular organ which in vertebrates keeps up the circulation of the blood by rhythmic contraction and dilatation; an organ of analogous function in some invertebrates. **OE.** ▸**b** A diseased condition of this organ. *colloq.* **M19.**

> *attrib.*: A. MUNRO The gray-faced people in his waiting room, the heart cases. **b** W. HAGGARD He's got a heart, by the way, and I'm afraid this might finish him.

2 The heart as the centre of vital bodily functions; (the seat of) life. Long *arch.* **OE.**

> W. RALEIGH That the king . . had granted my heart under the Great Seal.

3 The region of the heart in humans; the chest. **ME.**

> H. S. CUNNINGHAM He pressed her to his heart.

4 The stomach. Orig. in ***next the heart***, on an empty stomach. *obsolete* exc. *dial.* **ME.**
▸ **II** The seat of feeling and thought.
5 The mind, intellect; *esp.* (the seat of) one's inmost thoughts and secret feelings; the soul. **OE.**

> H. CONWAY Capable of any villainy that the heart of man could devise. H. BASCOM Deep down in his heart he wants to go back.

6 (The seat of) perception, understanding, or (rarely) memory. *obsolete* exc. in ***by heart***, by rote, in or from memory. **OE.**
7 (The seat of) the emotions, esp. love, as opp. to reason. Freq. contrasted with ***head***. **OE.** ▸**b** Susceptibility to emotion; feeling, sensitivity. Also, kindliness, cordiality. **M17.**

> A. MASON The religion of his childhood . . retains its hold on his heart. F. WARNER She had my adolescent heart, and I Had her entire devotion. **b** MRS ALEXANDER Which would have been pain and humiliation to a woman of real heart and delicacy.

H

8 Purpose, inclination, desire. *obsolete* exc. in ***after one's own heart***, just such as one likes or desires. **OE.**
9 (The seat of) courage, spirit. **OE.** ▸**b** (The source of) energy, enthusiasm, or ardour. **L18.**

B. STOKER I plucked up what heart I could and said that we had better hasten. W. SOYINKA He had lost heart since the failure of that nation-wide movement. **b** W. VAN T. CLARK He had no heart in his effort.

10 Disposition, temperament, character. **ME.**

A. E. HOUSMAN And many the handsome of face and the handsome of heart. N. MOSLEY It's a poor heart that never rejoices.

11 Conscience. Now only in ***one's heart smote one*** etc. *arch.* **ME.**

▸**III** Substituting for the person.
12 As a term of endearment, usu. qualified with *dear, sweet*, etc.: a loved one. Cf. SWEETHEART. **ME.**

TENNYSON Dear heart, I feel with thee the drowsy spell.

13 A man of courage or spirit. **E16.**

W. COWPER History.. Tells of a few stout hearts that fought and died.

▸**IV** A central part; a vital or essential part.
14 The centre, middle, or innermost part of anything. Often passing into sense 16. **ME.** ▸**b** The part of a time or season when its character is most intense; the height, depths. **L16.**

H

SHAKES. *Merch. V.* A goodly apple rotten at the heart. *Grimsby Gazette* A site for their information office in the heart of the town. **b** DISRAELI It was the heart of the London season.

15 *esp.* A central part of distinct conformation or character, e.g. the white tender centre of a cabbage, lettuce, etc. **LME.** ▸**b** The dense inner wood of a tree, hardened by age and lacking functioning vascular tissue. Also called ***heartwood***. **LME.**

C. CONRAN Cook the artichokes whole, to conserve the full flavour of the hearts.

16 The vital, essential, or working part of something. Also, the best or most important part. Cf. sense 14 above. **M16.**

R. HOGGART The living-room is the warm heart of the family. *fig.*: E. AMADI The heart of the dance was in the flutes and the huge bass drum.

17 Vigour, fertility (of soil etc.). **L16.**

W. RYE The heart of the land was so improved that Coke began to sow wheat.

▸**V** Something heart-shaped.
18 A representation of the human heart, usu. a conventional symmetrical figure with two equal curves meeting in a lower point and an upper cusp; an object of this shape. **LME.**
19 CARDS. In *pl.* (occas. treated as *sing.*), one of the four suits into which a pack of playing cards is divided, distinguished by representations of hearts in red; in *sing.*, a card of this suit. **E16.** ▸**b** (*Hearts.*) A card game of which the object is to avoid taking a trick containing a heart or any other penalty card. **L19.**
20 NAUTICAL. A kind of deadeye with only one hole, for a lanyard. **M18.**

– PHRASES: ***after one's own heart***: see sense 8 above. **at heart** in one's inmost feelings or true character; inwardly, really. ***bless her heart, bless his heart, bless my heart***: see BLESS *verb*[1]. **break someone's heart** overwhelm someone with sorrow. ***by heart***: see sense 6 above. **change of heart** conversion to a different frame of mind. **close one's heart (to)** keep one's feelings or thoughts secret (from); refuse to feel sympathy (for) or consider. **cross my heart (and hope to die)** I promise or guarantee. ***cry from the heart***: see CRY *noun*. ***cry one's heart out***: see CRY *verb* 5d. **dear heart** *interjection* (long *rare*) expr. surprise, dismay, etc. **do one's heart good** cheer one, make one happy. ***eat one's heart (out)***: see EAT *verb*. ***enlarge the heart***: see ENLARGE *verb*. ***find in one's heart, find it in one's heart***: see FIND *verb*. **from one's heart, from the bottom of one's heart** with the sincerest or deepest feeling. **give one's heart (to)** fall in love (with). **go to one's heart, go to the heart** deeply touch or grieve one. **have a heart** *colloq.* be merciful; freq. in *imper.*: be reasonable, have some pity. **have at heart** be deeply interested in; have in mind. **have one's heart in** be deeply involved in or committed to. **have one's heart in one's boots** be afraid or dejected. **have one's heart in one's mouth** be very alarmed or apprehensive. **have one's heart in the right place** have good intentions, mean well. **have the heart** be courageous or strong enough (*to do*); (esp. in neg. contexts) be hard-hearted enough. **heart and dart** a common noctuid moth, *Agrotis exclamationis*, so called from the black markings on the forewing. **heart and soul** (with) all one's energies and affections. **heart of gold** a kind or generous nature. **heart of oak** (a person with) a strong, courageous nature. **hearts and minds** emotional and intellectual support; complete approval. **heart-to-heart** a sincere, frank, and usu. intimate conversation (freq. *attrib.*). ***hole in the heart***: see HOLE *noun*[1]. ***hollow heart***: see HOLLOW *adjective*. **in heart** (*a*) = *at heart* above; (*b*) in (good) spirits; (of soil etc.) in (good) condition. **in good heart** in good spirits; (of soil etc.) in good condition. **in one's heart** = *at heart* above. **lay to heart** (now *rare*) = *take to heart* below. ***LEARN by heart***. ***lift up the heart of***: see LIFT *verb*. **lose heart** be discouraged. **lose one's heart (to)** = *give one's heart (to)* above. **nearest one's heart, nearest the heart** dearest to one, affecting one most deeply. **near one's heart, near the heart** dear to one, affecting one deeply. ***next the heart***: see sense 4 above. **one's heart breaks** one is extremely upset. **one's heart goes out to** one feels strong attraction to or sympathy for. **one's heart of hearts** one's inmost thoughts or feelings. ***one's heart bleeds***: see BLEED *verb* 1. **open one's heart (to)** reveal one's feelings or thoughts (to), confide (in); feel sympathy for; consider. **out of heart** in low spirits, discouraged; (of soil etc.) in poor condition. **put one's heart into** apply oneself to with enthusiasm. ***Sacred Heart***: see SACRED *adjective*. ***searcher of hearts, searcher of men's hearts***: see SEARCHER 1. ***set one's heart on***: see SET *verb*[1]. **shut one's heart (to)** = *close one's heart (to)* above. **take heart, take heart of grace** pluck up courage. **take to heart** take seriously, be much affected or upset by. ***the cockles of one's heart***: see COCKLE *noun*[2]. ***the heart bleeds***: see BLEED *verb* 1. **to one's heart's content** to the full extent of one's desires. **wear one's heart on one's sleeve** allow one's feelings to be obvious. **with all one's heart, with one's whole heart** with sincerity or devotion; with great goodwill. **with half a heart** with divided enthusiasm, half-heartedly.

– COMB.: **heartache** †(*a*) a form of dyspepsia, heartburn; (*b*) distress of mind, esp. from a disappointment in love; **heart attack** a sudden severe failure of the heart to function normally; **heartbeat** a beat of the heart; *transf.* a very brief space of time; **heart block** (a) failure of the parts of the heart to beat synchronously; **heart-blood** = *heart's-blood* below. **heartbreak** overwhelming sorrow or distress; **heartbreaker** a person who or thing which causes emotional turmoil or great distress; **heartbreaking** *adjective* causing (overwhelming) sorrow or distress; **heartbreakingly** *adverb* in a heartbreaking manner; **heartbroken**, (*arch.*) **heart-broke** *adjectives* affected by (overwhelming) sorrow or grief; **heartbrokenly** *adverb* in a heart-broken manner; **heart-cherry** a heart-shaped cultivated sweet cherry; **heart cockle** a bivalve mollusc, *Glossus humanus*, the shell of which is heart-shaped when seen laterally; **heart-disease** (a) disease affecting the heart; **heart failure** severe derangement of the functioning of the heart, esp. as a cause of death; **heartfelt** *adjective* (of emotion etc.) sincere, genuine; **heartland** the central or most important part of an area; **heart-lung** *attrib. adjective* involving the heart and lungs; ***heart-lung machine***: providing the means to bypass these organs in blood circulation during an operation; **heart-moth** a noctuid moth, *Dicycla oo*, with heart-shaped markings on the forewing; **heart-piercing** *adjective* that pierces or is capable of piercing the heart; *fig.* that appeals sharply to the emotions; **heartquake** palpitation of the heart; *fig.* sudden and violent emotion; **heart-rending** *adjective* very distressing; **heart-rendingly** *adverb* very distressingly; **heart-root** *arch.* (*a*) the bottom of the heart, the seat of deepest emotion and most genuine feelings (freq. in *pl.*); (*b*) a sweetheart; **heart rot** any disease causing decay in the heart of a tree, or of a root vegetable; **hearts-and-flowers** extreme sentimentality, cloying sweetness (freq. *attrib.*); **heart's-blood** blood from the heart, lifeblood; life; **heart-searching** *adjective & noun* (*a*) *adjective* that closely examines one's own feelings; (*b*) *noun* close examination of one's own feelings; **heart-shaped** *adjective* shaped like a heart (see sense 18 above); **heartsick** *adjective* depressed, despondent, very miserable; **heartsickness** the condition of being heartsick; **heartsome** *adjective* (chiefly *Scot.*) †(*a*) courageous; (*b*) cheering, heartening; cheerful, merry; **heartsore** *noun & adjective* (*a*) *noun* mental anguish; (*b*) *adjective* grieved; characterized by grief; **heart sounds** sounds of the working of the heart, heard in auscultation; **heart-spoon** (*obsolete* exc. *dial.*) (*a*) the depression at the base of the breastbone; (*b*) the pit of the stomach, the midriff; **heart-stricken** *adjective* = *heart-struck* (a) below; **heartstrings** †(*a*) the tendons or nerves formerly supposed to brace the heart; (*b*) *fig.* one's deepest emotions (often with allusion to stringed musical instruments); **heart-struck** *adjective* (*a*) affected by mental anguish; †(*b*) affecting the heart; **heart-throb** (*a*) a heartbeat; (*b*) *colloq.* an extremely attractive (male) person, esp. an actor or other celebrity; (a male) lover; **heart urchin** a sea urchin of the order Spatangoida, with a heart-shaped body; **heart-warming** *adjective* emotionally moving and encouraging; **heartwater** VETERINARY MEDICINE a rickettsial disease of livestock, occurring esp. in southern Africa, producing an accumulation of fluid in the pericardium of the heart; **heart-whole** *adjective* (*a*) (now *rare*) undismayed, unafraid; (*b*) not emotionally attached, not in love; (*c*) wholehearted, sincere, genuine; **heartwood** (*a*) see sense 15b above; (*b*) *Austral.* (the timber of) Tasmanian ironwood, *Notelaea ligustrina*; **heartworm** (disease caused by) a parasitic nematode worm which infests the hearts of some carnivores.

■ **heartful** *noun & adjective* (*a*) *noun* as much as a heart will hold (chiefly *fig.*); (*b*) *adjective* characterized by deep emotion or sincere affection: **LME. heartfully** *adverb* **LME. heartfulness** *noun* **E17. heartlike** *adjective* resembling (that of) a heart **E17.** †**heartling** *noun* (*rare*, Shakes.) dear heart (only in interjection ***'ods heartlings***): only in **L16. heartwise** *adverb* in the shape of a heart **E18.**

heart /hɑːt/ *verb.*

[ORIGIN Old English *hiertan*, from HEART *noun*: superseded by HEARTEN.]

1 *verb trans.* Give heart to; inspire with confidence, encourage. *obsolete* exc. *poet.* **OE.**
2 *verb trans.* Take to heart. Long *rare* or *obsolete*. **E17.**
3 *verb trans.* Fill up the central space in (a piece of masonry) with rubble etc. **L18.**
4 *verb intrans.* Of cabbage, lettuce, etc.: form a heart (HEART *noun* 15) or close compact globe of leaves. **M19.**

heartburn /ˈhɑːtbəːn/ *noun & verb.* ME.

[ORIGIN from HEART *noun* + BURN *noun*[2].]

▸**A** *noun.* †**1** Fire of passion. *rare*. Only in **ME.**
2 A form of dyspepsia felt as a pain in the chest, caused by acid regurgitation into the oesophagus. **L16.**
3 Rankling jealousy or hatred. Now *rare* or *obsolete*. **E17.**
▸†**B** *verb trans.* Make jealous or full of hatred. **M16–M17.**

heart-burning /ˈhɑːtbəːnɪŋ/ *noun & adjective.* LME.

[ORIGIN from HEART *noun* + *burning* verbal noun & pres. pple of BURN *verb*.]

▸**A** *noun.* **1** Rankling jealousy or hatred; anger, bitterness; in *pl.*, feelings of this kind, grudges. **LME.**
†**2** = HEARTBURN *noun* 2. **LME–M18.**
▸**B** *adjective.* That angers or consumes one; distressing. *poet.* **L16.**

hearted /ˈhɑːtɪd/ *adjective.* ME.

[ORIGIN from HEART *noun, verb*: see -ED[2], -ED[1].]

1 Having a heart, esp. one of a specified kind. **ME.** ***faint-hearted, free-hearted, full-hearted, half-hearted, hard-hearted, heavy-hearted***, etc. (hence ***faint-heartedly, faint-heartedness***, etc.).
2 Fixed or established in the heart. **E17.**
3 Heart-shaped. **M19.**

hearten /ˈhɑːt(ə)n/ *verb.* E16.

[ORIGIN from HEART *verb* + -EN[5]: superseding HEART *verb*.]

1 *verb trans.* Give heart to; inspire with confidence, encourage; rouse to energy or enthusiasm; animate, cheer. (Foll. by *to do, on, up*.) **E16.**

M. STOTT We.. feel heartened and even exhilarated by their enthusiasm. *refl.*: G. STANHOPE Let us hearten our selves with their Assistance against Temptations.

†**2** *verb trans.* Give physical strength or stimulus to. **L16–L18.**
3 *verb refl. & intrans.* Cheer (oneself) *up*. **E18.**

hearth /hɑːθ/ *noun.*

[ORIGIN Old English *heorþ* = Old Frisian *herth, herd*, Old Saxon *herþ* (Dutch *haard*), Old High German *hert* (German *Herd*), from West Germanic.]

1 The floor of a fireplace; the area in front of a fireplace. **OE.**
2 *transf.* The home or household. Freq. in alliterative phr. ***hearth and home***, home and its comforts. **OE.**
3 The floor or bottom of a furnace; the fireplace of a forge. **ME.**
open-hearth furnace, open-hearth process: see OPEN *adjective*.

– COMB.: **hearth-money** *hist.* a tax on hearths, esp. a 17th-cent. tax of two shillings per year on every hearth in England and Wales; **hearth-penny** *hist.* = ***Peter's pence*** s.v. PETER *noun*[1]; **hearthrug** a rug laid in front of a fireplace (to protect the carpet or floor); **hearthside** the area around a hearth or fireplace, a fireside; **hearthstead** a fireplace, hearth; hence, a home, a homestead; **hearthstone** *noun & verb* (*a*) *noun* a flat stone forming a hearth; a material used to whiten hearths, doorsteps, etc.; (*b*) *verb trans.* whiten (a hearth etc.) with hearthstone; **hearth tax** = ***hearth-money*** above.

heartless /ˈhɑːtlɪs/ *adjective.* ME.

[ORIGIN from HEART *noun* + -LESS.]

1 Lacking courage or spirit; disheartened. **ME.** ▸**b** Without warmth or zeal; not heartfelt. **M17.**
†**2** Stupid, foolish. **LME–E17.**
3 *lit.* Having no heart; (of a tree) lacking heartwood; (of a vegetable) not forming a heart. **L16.**
4 Unfeeling, pitiless; callous, unkind. (Now the usual sense.) **L16.**
5 Of land: unfertile. **L16.**
6 Of food etc.: lacking sustaining or stimulating power. **M17.**
■ **heartlessly** *adverb* **E17. heartlessness** *noun* **L16.**

heartsease /ˈhɑːtsiːz/ *noun.* Also **heart's-ease**. LME.

[ORIGIN from HEART *noun* + -'S[1] + EASE *noun*.]

1 Peace of mind, content, freedom from cares or trouble. **LME.**
2 A pansy; *esp.* the wild pansy, *Viola tricolor* and *V. arvensis*. **M16.**

hearty /ˈhɑːti/ *adjective, adverb, & noun.* LME.

[ORIGIN from HEART *noun* + -Y[1].]

▸**A** *adjective.* **1** Orig., courageous, bold. Now, zealous in support of a person, cause, etc.; energetic, enthusiastic. Also, of the nature of a hearty (sense C.2 below). **LME.** ▸**b** Giving unrestrained expression to the feelings; vehement, vigorous. **M17.**

LD MACAULAY Two of the allied powers.. were hearty in the common cause. P. ROTH I knew about Palestine and the hearty Jewish teenagers there reclaiming the desert. **b** K. AMIS Rarely in the past could the theatre have rung with so much happy, hearty laughter.

2 Heartfelt, genuine, sincere. Also, kindly, affectionate; genial. **LME.** ▸**b** Of or pertaining to the inner feelings. *rare*. **M16.**

LYTTON No hearty welcoming smile on his face. B. T. WASHINGTON I received very hearty congratulations.

3 In good health; robust, hale. **M16.** ▸**b** Of soil: fertile. **L16.** ▸**c** Of timber: strong, durable; consisting of heartwood. **E17.**

R. C. SHERRIFF He is a big hearty man: .. full of vigour.

4 Of food: nourishing, invigorating. Of a meal: satisfying to the appetite, ample. **L16.**

SPENSER Ech drunk an harty draught. G. VIDAL It is Rusty's favourite restaurant for the food is profoundly hearty.

▸**B** *adverb.* Heartily. *non-standard.* **M18.**
▸**C** *noun.* **1** A hearty or vigorous person. **M19.**
2 *spec.* An extrovert, outgoing person involved in sport and social activities; an athlete as opp. to an aesthete. Orig. *Univ. slang.* **E20.**

A. POWELL Militarily moustached, bluff in demeanour, apparently a hearty of hearties.

■ **heartily** *adverb* **ME. heartiness** *noun* **M16.**

heat /hiːt/ *noun*.
[ORIGIN Old English *hǣtu* = Old Frisian *hēte*, Middle Dutch *hēte*, Old High German *heizī*, from West Germanic, from base of HOT *adjective*: also Old English *hǣte*.]
▸ **I** In literal use.
1 The quality which is felt as the opposite of cold and is expressed by temperature; the quality of being hot; *esp.* a perceptible degree of this quality, (high) temperature, warmth. OE. ▸**b** More fully ***vital heat*** etc. The normal high temperature of a living warm-blooded animal. ME.

A. REID Liquors . . evaporated by a gentle heat. B. MALAMUD He was being boiled alive in the smothering heat of the small . . cell. W. WHARTON The fire starts burning but it's not giving off enough heat.

2 a Hot weather or condition of the atmosphere; a hot spell. OE. ▸**b** A hot environment. *arch.* LME.

a A. P. STANLEY The chief resorts of the Bedouin tribes during the summer heats. E. LANGLEY An hour when . . the clay of the roads is burning and sickly with the heat.

3 (An instance of) abnormally high body temperature; the hot or burning sensation which this gives rise to. Freq., high temperature caused by sickness or fever. OE. ▸**b** An eruption of the skin, accompanied by a hot sensation. OE.

M. DRAYTON Her heat to cool, She bathes her in the pleasant Pool. J. CONRAD The essence of her tremors, her flushes of heat, and her shudders of cold.

4 a An exposure to warmth or heat. Now only *Scot.*, esp. in ***give oneself a heat***, ***get a heat***, warm oneself. ME. ▸**b** A single operation of heating, as of metal in a furnace; the amount of metal etc. heated in one operation. L16.

b J. MOXON If it be not . . thoroughly welded at the first Heat, you must reiterate your Heats.

†**5** In medieval physiology: heat as one of the four fundamental qualities of 'elements', bodily humours, etc.: see HOT *adjective* 2. Cf. COLD *adjective*, DRY *adjective*, MOIST *adjective*. ME–E17.
6 PHYSICS. Heat regarded as a form of energy arising from the random motion of molecules and capable of transmission by conduction, convection, or radiation: formerly held to be an elastic material fluid (***caloric***). Also, the amount of energy in this form required to bring about a process or involved in a process. E17.
▸ **II** *transf.* & *fig.* **7** Vehemence of feeling, passion; an instance of this. Formerly, an angry dispute. OE. ▸†**b** Passionateness of temperament, excitability. L17–E18.

WELLINGTON To keep alive heats and animosities. L. RITCHIE A lady, who spoke with some heat, and great volubility. G. A. BIRMINGHAM A mere heresy can be settled without heat or unpleasantness by a few scholars sitting round a table.

8 Sexual excitement or desire. Now only, (the period of) a female animal's readiness for mating; esp. in ***on heat***, (chiefly US) ***in heat***. ME.
9 Hotness or pungency of flavour. LME.

M. JAFFREY If you want the flavour of chillies without their heat.

10 *The* (most) intense or violent stage of an activity. Also, *the* excitement or pressure generated by an activity or event. L16.

W. H. PRESCOTT In the very heat of the war against the insurgent Catalans. *Practical Gardening* In the heat of the programme-making, he left it in the boot of his car.

11 A single course or round in a race or other contest. Also (more fully ***trial heat***), one of a series of preliminary contests in which inferior competitors are successively eliminated before the final contest. M17.
†**12** A run given to a racehorse as exercise before a race. L17–E18.
13 A state of intoxication induced by drink or drugs. Esp. in ***have a heat on***. *US slang*. E20.
14 A pistol. *slang* (orig. *US*). E20.
15 (Pursuit or intense activity by) the police; *gen.* pressure, harassment. Chiefly in ***the heat is on***, ***the heat is off***, ***turn on the heat***, and similar phrs. *slang* (orig. *US*). M20.

Toronto Life The heat is on to . . reinvent the family.

– PHRASES: **at a heat**, **at a single heat** in a single operation, at a go. *ATOMIC* **heat**. **black heat**: see BLACK *adjective*. **dead heat**: see DEAD *adjective* etc. **get a heat**, **give oneself a heat**: see sense 4a above. **in heat** in a hotbed; see also sense 8 above. **in the heat of the moment** without pause for thought, as a result of the vigorous action etc. then in progress. *LATENT* **heat**. **mechanical equivalent of heat**: see EQUIVALENT *adjective*. *MOLECULAR* **heat**. *PRICKLY* **heat**. *RADIANT* **heat**. **red heat**: see RED *adjective*. **specific heat**: see SPECIFIC *adjective*. **take heat**, **take the heat** *N. Amer. colloq.* be at the receiving end of people's resentment, get the blame. **trial heat**: see sense 11 above. **vital heat**: see sense 1b above. **waste heat**: see WASTE *noun*. **white heat**: see WHITE *adjective*.
– COMB.: **heat barrier** the limitation of the speed of an aircraft etc. by heat resulting from friction with the air; **heat capacity** thermal capacity; **heat death** PHYSICS a state of uniform distribution of energy to which the universe is thought to be tending as a corollary of the second law of thermodynamics (that entropy must always increase); **heat-drop** (*a*) a drop of rain ushering in a hot day; (*b*) a drop of sweat; **heat engine** any device for producing motive power from heat; **heat-exchanger** a device for the transfer of heat from one medium to another; **heat exhaustion** fatigue and collapse resulting from prolonged exposure to excessive or unaccustomed heat; **heatproof** *adjective* & *verb* (*a*) *adjective* able to resist great heat; (*b*) *verb trans.* make heatproof; **heat pump** a device in which mechanical energy is used to force the transfer of heat from a colder area to a hotter area, as in a refrigerator; **heat rash** = *prickly heat* s.v. PRICKLY; **heat-resistant** *adjective* = *heatproof adjective* above; **heat-seeker** (a missile incorporating) a heat-seeking device; **heat-seeking** *adjective* (of a missile etc.) that detects and homes in on infrared radiation emitted by a target; **heat shield** a device for protection from excessive heat, esp. to protect a spacecraft during re-entry to the earth's atmosphere; **heat sink** a device or substance for absorbing excessive or unwanted heat; **heatstroke** a condition marked by fever and often by unconsciousness, due to the failure of the body's temperature-regulating mechanism in circumstances of excessive exposure to heat; **heat treatment** (*a*) the use of heat to modify the properties of a material, esp. in metallurgy; (*b*) the therapeutic use of heat in various forms; **heat wave** a prolonged period of hot weather.

heat /hiːt/ *verb*. Pa. t. & pple **heated**, †**heat**; pa. pple also (now *dial.*) **het** /hɛt/. See also HET.
[ORIGIN Old English *hǣtan* = Middle Dutch & mod. Dutch *hēten*, Old High German *heizzen*, *heizen* (German *heizen*), Old Norse *heita*, from Germanic, from base repr. also by HOT *adjective*.]
▸ **I** *verb trans.* **1** Expose to heat; make hot or warm. Freq. foll. by *up*. OE. ▸**b** Cause to feel hot or warm. LME.

B. PYM I'll just go and heat up the soup. E. FEINSTEIN Their flat was heated by a small, sooty stove. **b** W. WARBURTON Men heated with wine.

2 *fig.* Inflame with passion; excite. ME.

LD MACAULAY Officers who heated each other into fury by talking against the Dutch.

▸ **II** *verb intrans.* **3** Rise in temperature; become hotter or warmer. (Foll. by *up*.) OE. ▸**b** Have or get a sensation of heat, grow hot. ME.

S. PURCHAS They set a kettle of water over the fire to heat.

4 *fig.* Become excited or impassioned. Of a condition (usu. foll. by *up*): intensify. OE.

J. BARNES He seemed to calm down as quickly as he had heated up. *Newsweek* Now competition is heating up.

■ **heated** *ppl adjective* (*a*) that has been made or become hot (***heated term*** (*US*), the hot season of the year); (*b*) fevered, inflamed; impassioned, animated, angry: L16. **heatedly** *adverb* in an impassioned or angry manner M19.

heater /ˈhiːtə/ *noun*. L15.
[ORIGIN from HEAT *verb* + -ER[1].]
1 A person who or thing which heats. L15.
2 *spec.* Any of various devices for imparting heat; *esp.* (*a*) a piece of iron made hot and placed in the cavity of a flat iron; (*b*) a stove, hot-air blower, or other gas or electric device for warming the air in a room, car, etc.; (*c*) = *IMMERSION* ***heater***; (*d*) ELECTRONICS a conductor used for indirect heating of the cathode of a thermionic valve. M17.
3 A firearm. *N. Amer. slang*. E20.
– COMB.: **heater-shaped** *adjective* (of a medieval shield) having the shape of a flat iron heater, i.e. triangular with curved sides.

heath /hiːθ/ *noun*.
[ORIGIN Old English *hǣþ*, corresp. to Old Saxon *hēþa*, Middle Low German, Middle Dutch *hēde*, Middle High German *heide* (Dutch *heide*, *hei*, German *Heide*), Old Norse *heiðr*, Gothic *haiþi*, from Germanic.]
1 (An area of) open uncultivated ground, esp. on acid sandy or peaty soil and covered by heather or related plants (see sense 2 below). OE.

A. YOUNG An uninteresting flat, with many heaths of ling.

native heath native country or territory.
2 Any of various dwarf shrubs of the family Ericaceae characteristic of heathland or moor; esp. *Erica cinerea* (more fully ***fine-leaved heath***) and *E. tetralix* (more fully ***cross-leaved heath***), common in dry and in boggy heath respectively. Also (now chiefly *dial.*), heather, *Calluna vulgaris*. OE. ▸**b** In biblical lang., in renderings of *Jer.* 17:6, 48:6: a desert plant of uncertain identity, perh. a tamarisk, or savin, *Juniperus sabina*. M16. ▸**c** With specifying word. Any of various plants resembling ericas and freq. growing in the same habitat. E17. ▸**d** More fully ***Australian heath***, ***Tasmanian heath***. Any of various heathlike plants of the genus *Epacris* (family Epacridaceae). *Austral. & NZ*. M19.
3 Either of two satyrid butterflies of the genus *Coenonympha*: *C. pamphilus* (the small heath), of rough grassland, and *C. tullia* (the large heath), of moors and bogs. E19.
– COMB.: **heath-bell** (the blossom of) any of several plants with bell-shaped flowers growing in heath; *esp.* harebell, *Campanula rotundifolia*; **heath-berry** any of several berry-bearing shrubs growing in heath; *esp.* bilberry or crowberry; **heath-bird** = *heath-fowl* below; **heath-cock** the male black grouse; **heath-cropper** a sheep or pony that grazes on open pasture or down; a person who inhabits a heath; **heath-fowl** *arch.* the black grouse, *Tetrao tetrix*; **heath-grass** a low-growing grass of acid soils, *Danthonia decumbens*; **heath-hen** the female black grouse; *N. Amer.* a variety of prairie chicken, now extinct; **heathland** heathy country; **heath-poult** the female or young of the black grouse; **heath speedwell** a creeping lilac-flowered speedwell, *Veronica officinalis*, of heaths and turfy pastures in Eurasia; **heath-thrush** the ring ouzel, *Turdus torquatus*.
■ **heathlike** *adjective* resembling (that of) heath or a heath M19.

heathen /ˈhiːð(ə)n/ *adjective* & *noun*.
[ORIGIN Old English *hǣþen* = Old Frisian *hēthin*, Old Saxon *hēþin* (Dutch *heiden*), Old High German *heidan* (German *heide*), Old Norse *heiðinn*, in Gothic repr. by *haiþnō* Gentile woman: gen. regarded as a specific Christian use (perh. as a loose rendering of Latin *paganus*, and orig. in Gothic) of a Germanic adjective meaning 'inhabiting open country, savage', repr. by the ethnic and personal names Greek *Khaideinoi* a people of W. Scandinavia (Ptolemy), Old English *Hǣþnum* (dat.), Old Norse *Heinir* (from *Heiðnir*), Old High German *theidanrīh*, from Germanic base of HEATH *noun*: see -EN[4]. Cf. PAGAN.]
▸ **A** *adjective*. **1** Of an individual or people: holding religious beliefs of a sort that are considered unenlightened, now esp. ones of a primitive or polytheistic nature; *spec.* not of the Christian, Jewish, or Muslim faiths. *derog.* OE.

T. MO Bring spoons, you heathen devil.

2 Of a thing: belonging to heathen people or races or their beliefs and customs. OE.

J. A. MICHENER The villagers were convinced that it honored a heathen goddess.

3 *transf.* Resembling heathen people in their (supposed) beliefs, behaviour, etc.; unenlightened, barbarous. M19.

R. W. EMERSON A country of extremes—dukes and chartists, Bishops of Durham and naked heathen colliers.

▸ **B** *noun*. **1** A heathen person: see sense A.1 above. *derog.* OE. ▸**b** *collect.* (usu. preceded by def. article). Heathens as a group. In biblical language: those who do not worship Israel's God, idolaters. OE.

SWIFT I was sorry to find more mercy in an heathen than in a brother Christian. **b** AV *Ps.* 33:10 The Lord bringeth the counsell of the heathen to nought. E. O'NEILL Like a missionary converting the heathen.

2 *transf.* An unenlightened, barbarous, or uncivilized person. E19.

DICKENS My ideas of civility were formed among Heathens.

■ **heathendom** *noun* (*a*) heathenism; (*b*) heathen people or countries collectively: OE. **heathenism** *noun* heathen or (*transf.*) unenlightened beliefs or practices E17. **heathenize** *verb trans.* & *intrans.* make or become heathen(ish) L17. **heathenly** *adverb* in the manner of the heathen LME. **heathenry** *noun* = HEATHENDOM L16.

heathenesse /hiːðəˈnɛs/ *noun*. *arch.*
[ORIGIN Old English *hǣþennes*, -*nys*, from HEATHEN + -NESS: because one of the two *n*'s was often omitted, sometimes interpreted as formed with -ESS[2].]
= HEATHENDOM.

heathenish /ˈhiːð(ə)nɪʃ/ *adjective*.
[ORIGIN Old English *hǣþenisc*, Old High German *heidanisc*, Old Norse *heiðneskr*. In mod. use prob. a new formation from HEATHEN *adjective* & *noun* + -ISH[1].]
1 = HEATHEN *adjective* 2. Now *rare*. OE.
†**2** = HEATHEN *adjective* 1. M16–E18.
3 Unworthy of a Christian, barbarous, uncivilized; *colloq.* objectionable, beastly. L16.

R. KIPLING The Gunner maps up a heathenish large detail for some hanky-panky in the magazines.

■ **heathenishly** *adverb* M16. **heathenishness** *noun* L16.

heather /ˈhɛðə/ *noun*.
[ORIGIN Old English *hadre*, (h)*eddre* (in place names), of unknown origin: assim. to HEATH.]
A dwarf shrub of the heath family, *Calluna vulgaris*, with terminal spikes of small purple flowers, freq. dominant over large areas of heathland and moor; ling. Also, any of several related or similar plants.
bell-heather: see BELL *noun*[1]. **take to the heather** SCOTTISH HISTORY become an outlaw.
– COMB.: **heather-bell** (the bell-shaped flower of) either of the heaths, *Erica tetralix* and *E. cinerea*; **heather-bleat**, **heather-bleater** [perh. orig. alt. of Old English *hæfer-blǣte* lit. 'goat-bleater'] *Scot. & N. English* the snipe; **heather honey** honey from the nectar of heather; **heather mixture** (a suit or garment made from) a fabric of interwoven varicoloured fibres suggestive of heather on a moor.
– NOTE: Orig. a Scottish and Border counties word, corresp. to *ling* of Yorkshire etc. and the southern & midland dial. *heath*; it is now the most general name for *Calluna vulgaris*.
■ **heathered** *adjective* covered with heather M19.

heathery /ˈhɛð(ə)ri/ *adjective*. L15.
[ORIGIN from HEATHER + -Y[1].]
Covered with or composed of heather.

Heath Robinson /hiːθ ˈrɒbɪns(ə)n/ *adjective* & (*rare*) *noun*. E20.
[ORIGIN W. *Heath Robinson* (1872–1944), Brit. humorous artist, whose illustrations often depicted such contraptions.]
(A contraption) having absurdly elaborate and ingenious machinery for performing some simple function. Cf. RUBE GOLDBERG.

C. J. STONE A dirigible ambling about in the still air like some Heath Robinson flying saucer.

■ Also **Heath-Robinsonish** *adjective* M20.

heathy /ˈhiːθi/ *adjective*. LME.
[ORIGIN from HEATH *noun* + -Y[1].]
Covered with heath; of the nature of heath.

H

heating /ˈhiːtɪŋ/ *noun*. LME.
[ORIGIN from HEAT *verb* + -ING[1].]
The action of HEAT *verb*; equipment for heating a building, room, etc.
CENTRAL heating.
– COMB.: **heating engineer** a person who installs and maintains (central) heating systems.

heaume /həʊm/ *noun*. *obsolete* exc. *hist*. L16.
[ORIGIN French from Old French *helme*: see HELM *noun*[1].]
A massive helmet reaching to the shoulders, worn in the 12th and 13th cents.

heave /hiːv/ *noun*. L16.
[ORIGIN from the verb.]
1 An act of heaving; an effort made to lift or move something; a swelling; a rhythmical rising that alternates with sinking; an utterance of a sigh with a deep breath or effort; a retch. L16.

B. CABLE And with . . a heave flung the officer out over the front parapet. *New Yorker* The doctors who had watched the mysterious disease . . had felt a heave of fear.

heave of the sea the force exerted by the swell of the sea on a ship's course.
2 In *pl*. A disease of horses characterized by laborious breathing. Cf. HOOVE, HOVEN *adjective & noun*. L18.
3 A horizontal displacement of a mineral vein or rock stratum. E19.

H

heave /hiːv/ *verb*. Pa. t. **heaved** /hiːvd/, (esp. NAUTICAL) **hove** /həʊv/. Pa. pple **heaved**, (esp. NAUTICAL) **hove**, **hoven** /ˈhəʊv(ə)n/.
[ORIGIN Old English *hebban* = Old Frisian *heva*, Old Saxon *hebbian* (Dutch *heffen*), Old High German *heffen* (German *heben*), Old Norse *hefja*, Gothic *hafjan*, from Germanic word rel. to Latin *capere* take.]
► **I** *verb trans*. **1** Lift or raise up. Now only (exc. *arch*. & *dial*.), lift, raise, or move with effort or force. Freq. foll. by *up*, *down*, etc. OE. ›**b** NAUTICAL. Haul up, raise, pull, cause (a ship) to move in a specified direction, by means of a rope; weigh (anchor); pull on (a rope). E17.

POPE Her trembling hand she heaves To rend her hair. S. MIDDLETON The congregation heaved itself to its feet. E. CRISPIN Fen went and heaved the motor-cycle in to the side of the lane. P. FITZGERALD Heaving up the two volumes of the *Shorter Oxford Dictionary*. **b** *Lifeboat* Martin first thought he might be able to heave the lifeboat in closer.

2 *fig*. Raise, lift. Formerly also, exalt, lift up, elevate, in dignity, station, etc. OE.

MILTON For the prevention of growing schisme the Bishop was heav'd above the Presbyter. W. IRVING The resolution . . heaved a load from off my heart.

†**3** *spec*. (Of a sponsor at baptism) lift (a child) from the font; *fig*. stand sponsor to; baptize, christen. ME–L16.
4 †**a** Lift and take away, carry off; remove; *criminals' slang* rob. ME–L17. ›**b** Throw, fling, hurl (esp. something heavy requiring effort). Now only NAUTICAL & *colloq*. L16. ›**c** Of a mineral vein or rock stratum: move away or displace (an intersecting vein or stratum). E18.

b C. KINGSLEY Tom was . . hiding behind a wall, to heave half a brick at his horse's legs.

5 a Cause to swell or rise; *spec*. cause bloat in (livestock). Now *dial*. LME. ›**b** Cause to rise repeatedly. E17.

b SIR W. SCOTT The death-pangs of long-cherished hope . . Convulsive heaved its chequered shroud.

6 Utter (a sigh, groan, etc.) with effort or with a deep breath which causes the chest to rise; draw (a breath) with effort. L15.

P. DE VRIES I heaved a long, defeated sigh, blowing out my cheeks. J. HARVEY He only sat . . heaving long shuddering breaths.

► **II** *verb intrans*. **7** Make an effort to lift or move something; push or pull with force. Formerly also, foll. by *at*: aim at, *fig*. strive after. ME. ›**b** NAUTICAL. Pull or haul *at* (a rope); move a ship, (of a ship) move, in a specified direction by such means. E17.

L. DEIGHTON He heaved desperately on the stick with one hand. J. UPDIKE They heaved at the snow in their driveways. **b** *transf*.: S. BECKETT Nothing will induce her to throw herself down till he actually heaves into view.

8 Rise, rear up or *up*. Now *rare* exc. as below. ME.

E. K. KANE This ice seems to heave up slowly against the sky.

9 Rise up above the general surface, expand; (now *dial*.) swell up. E17.

Daily Telegraph So violently did the soil heave when frozen after it was so damp.

10 Rise in alternation with sinking, as waves, or the chest in deep breathing. E17. ›**b** Pant; gasp *for* breath. L17.

D. H. LAWRENCE The sea heaved with a sucking noise inside the dock. R. P. JHABVALA Her chest . . was heaving . . with heavy sobs. M. PIERCY The ceiling above them heaved like a bullfrog's throat.

11 Make an effort to vomit, retch, gag. E17.

M. SCAMMELL A meatless, saltless, fatless, evil-smelling nettle soup that made his stomach heave.

– PHRASES, & WITH ADVERBS IN SPECIALIZED SENSES: **heave down** turn (a ship) over on one side for cleaning, repairing, etc. **heave in sight** (NAUTICAL & *colloq*.) become visible. **heave the gorge** retch, gag. *heave the log*: see LOG *noun*[1]. **heave to** *verb phr. trans*. & *intrans*. (**a**) *verb phr. trans*. bring (a vessel) to a standstill without anchoring; (**b**) *verb phr. intrans*. (of a vessel) be brought to a standstill in this way. **heaving line** NAUTICAL a line, usu. five to ten fathoms long and weighted at one end, used to cast a heavier line to another vessel or to the shore when coming alongside.
■ **heaving** *adjective* (**a**) that heaves; (**b**) *colloq*. (of a place) extremely crowded: E17.

heave-ho /hiːvˈhəʊ/ *interjection, noun, & verb*. LME.
[ORIGIN App. from HEAVE *verb* (imper.) + HO *interjection*[1].]
► **A** *interjection*. Expr. effort in heaving on a rope etc. Formerly used esp. by sailors. LME.
► **B** *noun*. **1** A cry of 'heave-ho!' LME.
2 A dismissal or rejection. Chiefly in ***give the heave-ho***, ***give the old heave-ho***, dismiss, reject, (a person or thing). *slang* (orig. *US*). M20.
► **C** *verb*. **1** *verb intrans*. Cry 'heave-ho!' M19.
2 *verb trans*. Move or lift with effort. *colloq*. M20.

heaven /ˈhɛv(ə)n/ *noun*.
[ORIGIN Old English *heofon*, earlier *hefen*, *heben*, corresp. to Old Saxon *hean*, Old Norse *himinn* (inflected stem *hifn-*), Gothic *himins*; parallel formations with *l-* suffix are Old Frisian *himul*, Old Saxon, Old High German *himil* (Dutch *hemel*, German *Himmel*); ult. origin unknown.]
1 The expanse in which the sun, moon, and stars are seen, having the appearance of a vast vault arched over the earth (now usu. in *pl*. exc. *poet*.); *fig*. an immense height, distance, extent, etc. OE. ›**b** *transf*. & *fig*. A canopy; the covering over a stage. L15.

R. L. STEVENSON After the sun is down . . , the heavens begin to fill with shining stars. **b** SHELLEY Under a heaven of cedar boughs.

2 The part of the atmosphere in which the clouds float, the winds blow, and the birds fly. Chiefly *poet*. OE. ›**b** The condition of this; the climate. Chiefly *poet*. L16.

H. BELLOC Clouds of a . . hurrying sort ran across the gentle blue of that heaven. DAY LEWIS I can still see the bubbles I blew . . towards the blue heaven. **b** DRYDEN Not tho' beneath the Thracian Clime we freeze; Or Italy's indulgent Heav'n forego.

3 The region of space beyond the clouds or the visible sky. Chiefly in ***heaven and earth*** the universe. OE. ›**b** *hist*. Each of the celestial spheres into which the regions of space were divided by medieval astronomers and cosmographers, the number varying from seven to eleven. ME.

TENNYSON All heaven bursts her starry floors.

4 (Often **H-**.) *sing*. & (now *rare*) *pl*. In Christian theology, the abode of God, the angels, and the beatified spirits, usu. regarded as beyond the sky; a state or condition of being or living with God after death; everlasting life. In Islamic theology, each of seven stages of blessed life after death. In Jewish religious thought, each of seven celestial regions. Also, the abode of any of various non-Christian gods. OE.

AV *Luke* 11:2 Our Father which art in heaven, Halowed be thy Name. W. C. WILLIAMS Is it any better in Heaven, my friend Ford, Than you found it in Provence?

5 (Usu. **H-**.) *sing*. & in *pl*. God, Providence; the gods. Freq. in exclamatory phrs. (see below). OE.
6 A place or state of supreme bliss. ME.

D. HEWETT It was heaven to get the weight off her legs.

– PHRASES & COMB.: **by heaven**: introducing a solemn or avowed declaration. *crystalline heaven*: see CRYSTALLINE *adjective* 1. ***for heaven's sake***: see SAKE *noun*[1]. ***good heavens***: see GOOD *adjective*. **heaven-born** *adjective* of divine origin or design. ***Heaven defend***: see DEFEND *verb*. ***Heaven forbid***: see FORBID *verb*. ***Heaven forfend***: see FORFEND *verb*. ***Heaven help you*** etc.: see HELP *verb*. ***Heaven knows***: see KNOW *verb*. **heaven of heavens** = ***seventh heaven*** below. **Heavens above!**, **Heavens alive!**: expr. surprise, astonishment, exasperation, etc. **heaven-sent** *adjective* providential. **heavens hard** etc. (*colloq*.) extremely hard etc. **heavens to Betsy!** *N. Amer*.: expr. astonishment, dismay, exasperation, etc. ***host of heaven***, ***hosts of heaven***: see HOST *noun*[1]. ***in Heaven's name***: see NAME *noun*. **move heaven and earth** make every possible effort (*to do*). ***pennies from heaven***: see PENNY *noun*. **seventh heaven** the highest of the seven Islamic heavens; ***in the seventh heaven***, in a state of extreme delight or exaltation. ***thank heaven(s)***: see THANK *verb*. **the heavens open** it begins to rain heavily. ***tree of heaven***: see TREE *noun*.
■ **heavenless** *adjective* (*rare*) M17. **heavenlike** *adjective* divine M16.

heaven /ˈhɛv(ə)n/ *verb trans*. E17.
[ORIGIN from the noun.]
Transport into heaven; make supremely happy; beatify.

heavenly /ˈhɛv(ə)nli/ *adjective & noun*.
[ORIGIN Old English *heofonlīć*, formed as HEAVEN *verb* + -LY[1].]
► **A** *adjective*. **1** Of, in, or belonging to heaven, the abode of God; of or from God; divine, sacred, holy. OE. ›**b** Of, in, or belonging to heaven, the abode of non-Christian gods. LME.

J. CONRAD As though I had got a heavenly mission to civilize you. C. CAUDWELL This Kingdom of Heaven was to be achieved by non-resistance, by heavenly forces and a general change of heart. **b** SHAKES. *Merch. V.* If two gods should play some heavenly match, And on the wager lay two earthly women.

2 Of or belonging to the sky. Now chiefly in ***heavenly body*** below. ME.

L. BINYON The stars . . Moving in marches upon the heavenly plain.

3 Of more than earthly or human beauty or excellence; *colloq*. wonderful, delightful. LME.

I. MURDOCH After the first few heavenly puffs the cigarette began to lose its charm. J. KRANTZ The sound of her heavenly chortling mingled with Billy's half-repressed yelps.

– SPECIAL COLLOCATIONS: ***heavenly body***: see BODY *noun*. ***the Heavenly City***: see CITY 2. ***heavenly host***: see HOST *noun*[1].
– COMB.: **heavenly-minded** *adjective* devout; **heavenly-mindedness** devoutness.
► **B** *noun*. In *pl*. [translating Greek *tois epouraniois* (Eph. 1:3, 3:10)] Heavenly places or things. M19.
■ **heavenliness** *noun* M16.

heavenly /ˈhɛv(ə)nli/ *adverb*. OE.
[ORIGIN formed as HEAVEN *verb* + -LY[2].]
1 From or by heaven; divinely (usu. modifying an adjective). OE.
†**2** To the extent of heaven. Only in ***heavenly wide***. L16–L17.

heavenward /ˈhɛv(ə)nwəd/ *adverb & adjective*. ME.
[ORIGIN from HEAVEN *noun* + -WARD.]
► **A** *adverb*. Towards heaven. ME.
► **B** *adjective*. Moving or directed towards heaven. L18.
■ Also **heavenwards** *adverb* M17.

heaver /ˈhiːvə/ *noun*. L16.
[ORIGIN from HEAVE *verb* + -ER[1].]
A person who or thing which heaves something; *spec*. (**a**) a labourer who lands goods at a dockyard; (**b**) a lever; a wooden bar for twisting or tightening a rope or strap on board ship.

heavily /ˈhɛvɪli/ *adverb*. OE.
[ORIGIN from HEAVY *adjective* + -LY[2].]
1 With heavy or laborious movement; without animation. OE.

P. ROTH He came heavily to his feet; slowly and heavily, like an elephant. A. BROOKNER She breathed heavily, her hand once more to her chest.

2 Forcibly, violently; strongly; severely; to a heavy degree. OE. ›**b** To a large extent; extensively. E19.

A. TREW Rain was falling more heavily now and the sky had darkened. W. WHARTON She's conscious but still heavily sedated. *New Statesman* They are . . all heavily into courgettes. P. ROTH Where the woman's English is heavily accented, Sisovsky's is only mildly flawed. **b** D. H. LAWRENCE He drank heavily now and again. G. GREENE They were noisy and heavily made-up and rather unconvincing. Z. MEDVEDEV Stalin had decided . . to invest heavily in Soviet science. J. VIORST I have drawn heavily on my own personal experiences.

3 With sorrow, grief, or displeasure. *arch*. OE.

CLARENDON Berkley . . took this refusal very heavily. R. LEHMANN 'Darling, you must do as you like,' he said heavily.

4 (As) with weight; massively, thickly, ponderously; oppressively. ME.

M. BARING A young woman dressed in black and heavily veiled. J. B. PRIESTLEY It bumped heavily against something. G. GREENE Time for a few days was hanging . . heavily on my hands. A. J. P. TAYLOR At six foot tall and heavily built, he was by no means beautiful.

bear heavily: see BEAR *verb*[1].

heaviness /ˈhɛvɪnɪs/ *noun*.
[ORIGIN Old English *hefignes*, formed as HEAVILY: see -NESS.]
1 Weight; weightiness; oppressiveness. OE.

V. S. NAIPAUL Brenda's heaviness, in hips and thighs, had . . suggested someone spoilt.

2 Oppressed condition of the body or mind; torpor, drowsiness; absence of animation. OE.

A. BROOKNER At this the heaviness lifted from his face.

3 Dejectedness. Formerly also, sadness; anger, displeasure. ME.

P. S. BUCK He thought of her with sadness that was not sorrow but only heaviness of memory.

4 Severity; force of impact. ME.

Heaviside layer /ˈhɛvɪsʌɪd ˌleɪə/ *noun phr*. E20.
[ORIGIN Oliver *Heaviside* (1850–1925), English physicist.]
= ***E-layer*** s.v. E, E II. Also called KENNELLY LAYER, ***Kennelly–Heaviside layer***.

heavisome /ˈhɛvɪs(ə)m/ *adjective*. *obsolete* exc. *dial*. LME.
[ORIGIN from HEAVY *adjective* & *noun* + -SOME[1].]
Doleful; dull, gloomy.

heavy /ˈhɛvi/ *adjective & noun*.
[ORIGIN Old English *hefiġ* = Old Saxon *heig* (Dutch *hevig*), Old High German *hebig*, Old Norse *hǫfugr*, *hǫfigr*, from Germanic (repr. by Old English *hefe* weight), from base of HEAVE *verb*.]
► **A** *adjective*. **I** Physically weighty.

1 Of great weight. OE. ▸**b** Weighty because of the quantity present; abundant; in large quantity or amount. LME. ▸**c** That does what is specified to excess. E19.

D. BAGLEY Mrs. Warmington collapsed on top of her, a warm, dead weight, flaccid and heavy. R. MACDONALD The heavy brown grocery bag was beginning to slip out of her arms. **b** B. W. ALDISS Saturday morning traffic into town was heavy. *Music Week* Hello Again has been picking up heavy Radio Two airplay. **c** M. PUZO Hagen's father, a heavy drinker, had become a hopeless drunkard. G. KEILLOR He was a heavy reader. He subscribed to four newspapers.

2 Of great relative density; dense. OE. ▸**b** Of bread, pastry, etc.: not properly risen; dense, compact. E19. **3** Weighed down; laden *with*. Formerly foll. by *in*. ME. ▸**b** At an advanced stage of pregnancy; heavily pregnant. LME.

T. GUNN For the grass is heavy / with water and meets over / the bright path he makes. W. HOLTBY The days were long, heavy with pain and weariness. W. BOYD The atmosphere in the compartment was heavy with tension.

4 (Of a class of goods, breed of animal, etc.) of more than a defined or usual weight; concerned with the manufacture, transport, etc., of these; (of ordnance) of the larger kind. E17. ▸**b** Of an army division etc.: carrying heavy arms or equipment. M19.

D. FRASER The British Army of 1915 . . was short of heavy and medium artillery. *Horse International* She . . turned her attention away from ponies towards the heavy horses. *Daily Telegraph* Heavy woollen tunics and overcoats.

▸ **II** Weighty in importance etc.
5 Weighty, important, serious; overly serious, dull, tedious. OE. ▸**b** (Of a theatrical part or production) sombre, serious, tragic; (of a person, speech, etc.) ponderously dignified, sternly repressive. E19. ▸**c** Of a newspaper: serious in tone. L19.

Australian Business In his tough voice normally reserved for heavy negotiations. K. ISHIGURO It had not been my intention to make heavy talk at the supper table. W. A. PERCY An opera new to New Orleans called *Lohengrin*, which . . was *very* heavy. **b** K. AMIS Alexander's tone and manner were entirely respectful, neither heavy nor frivolous.

6 Grave, severe; marked, extensive. OE. ▸**b** Serious, intense, profound. *colloq.* M20.

B. WEBB Sidney came down . . last week with a heavy cold. M. PUZO She had a heavy Italian accent. J. UPDIKE Little shops heavy on macramé and batik. **b** J. LENNON Anybody that sings with a guitar and sings about something heavy.

▸ **III** That weighs on or oppresses the senses or feelings.
7 Hard to bear or endure; grievous; causing sorrow, sad, distressing. OE. ▸**b** Troublesome, annoying, difficult to deal with; *esp.* violent. Now chiefly *colloq.* OE.

DEFOE This was a heavy piece of news to my nephew. W. SOYINKA Her sins had become heavy. B. EMECHETA He did not know why ones parents should be such a heavy responsibility. *New York Review of Books* The Depression was heavy on the country. **b** G. F. NEWMAN The more experienced protesters realised things might get heavy when they . . saw police transit vans.

8 Hard to perform or accomplish; requiring much effort or exertion. ME.

Boxing News World-rated cruiserweight Spenser Chavis made heavy work of outpointing Joey Parker.

9 Oppressive; overpowering. LME.

B. ENGLAND The night air was stiflingly heavy, the earth cold against his stomach. M. MOORCOCK The heavy scent of stocks and dying lilac ascended from the square.

▸ **IV** Mentally weighed down.
10 Weighed down by sorrow or grief; saddened, despondent; (of the face, music, etc.) expressing grief, doleful. ME.

R. POLLOK Who farther sings, must change the pleasant lyre To heavy notes of woe. S. RUSHDIE The power of lifting the heaviest hearts and making one think that nothing was insoluble.

11 Sleepy, drowsy, weary; dulled. LME.

A. MUNRO Her throat feels slightly raw and her head heavy.

▸ **V** Having the slow or clumsy action of something physically heavy.
12 Acting or moving slowly, clumsily, or with difficulty; slow, laboured, sluggish. ME. ▸**b** *spec.* in COMMERCE. Characterized by declining prices. M19.

TENNYSON If Time be heavy on your hands, Are there no beggars at your gate? D. H. LAWRENCE He heard Dawes's heavy panting, like a wild beast's. *Which?* Steering fairly heavy when parking or cornering hard.

13 Of a person: intellectually slow, lacking vivacity. ME.

STEELE A Set of heavy honest Men, with whom I have passed many Hours with much Indolence.

▸ **VI** Expressing the action of something physically heavy.
14 Having great momentum or force; striking or falling with force or violence. LME. ▸**b** Of music, esp. rock: having a strong bass component and a forceful rhythm. M20.

D. PRATER Despite high winds and heavy rain, he was on deck for the whole crossing. **b** *Sounds* Vocalist and Bassist for heavy but melodic band.

15 Of food: difficult to digest, rich. Of wine, beer, etc.: containing much alcohol. LME.

J. BUCHAN He . . ate a . . heavy tea about half-past four.

16 Of soil, ground, etc.: clayey, cloggy; difficult to travel over. L16.
▸ **VII** Having the appearance or sound of heaviness.
17 Having a loud and deep sound. LME. ▸**b** (Of a syllable) stressed; *spec.* (of a line in Old English verse) containing more than the normal number of stressed elements. L19.

SHELLEY Listen well If you hear not a deep and heavy bell.

18 Of the sky: overcast, gloomy, threatening rain, snow, etc. L16.
19 Having the appearance of heaviness; thick, substantial; coarse, lacking grace, delicacy, or elegance. E19.

M. PIERCY The black eyes glinted anger under the heavy lids. P. ROTH A large man, . . wearing heavy tortoise-shell glasses.

– PHRASES ETC.: *as heavy as lead*: see LEAD *noun*[1]. **heavier-than-air** *adjective* (of an aircraft) weighing more than the air it displaces. **heavy-armed** *adjective* bearing heavy weapons or armour. **heavy bag** a punchbag. ***heavy chemicals***: see CHEMICAL *noun*. **heavy-duty** *adjective* (of material etc.) designed to be unusually resistant to stresses in use. **heavy-footed** *adjective* ponderous. ***heavy going***: see GOING *noun* 4. **heavy-headed** *adjective* (*a*) having a large head; (*b*) sleepy, dull; stupid. **heavy-hearted** *adjective* sad, melancholy, doleful. **heavy hitter** *N. Amer. colloq.* a person who is significant or influential in a particular field. **heavy hydrogen** deuterium. **heavy industry**: concerned with the production of metal, machines, etc. **heavy man** *colloq.* a heavily built thug or criminal. **heavy metal** (*a*) a metal of high density; (*b*) a type of loud vigorous rock music with a strong (usu. fast) beat and a harsh or clashing musical style, freq. spectacularly performed. **heavy mob** *colloq.* (freq. with *the*) violent gangsters; a bunch of hired thugs. **heavy oil** any oil of a high relative density; orig., such an oil obtained from coal tar by distillation. **heavy petting** non-coital physical contact between two people involving stimulation of the genitals. **heavy sleeper**: difficult to rouse. **heavy spar** barytes. **heavy swell** (*a*) a strong swell of the sea; (*b*) *arch. slang* an exceedingly fashionable or stylish person. **heavy type** printed characters with unusually thick strokes. **heavy water** deuterium oxide, or a mixture of this with ordinary water. **heavy wet** *slang* malt liquor. ***lie heavy***: see LIE *verb*[1] 10. ***make heavy weather of***: see WEATHER *noun*. ***sit heavy on***: see SIT *verb*. **with a heavy hand** oppressively (cf. HEAVY-HANDED).
▸ **B** *noun*. **1** (Strong) beer or ale. Cf. ***heavy wet*** above. *slang*. E19.

Truck & Driver A pint of heavy costs 85p for drivers, 90p in the public bar.

2 a In *pl.* Heavy cavalry; heavy artillery. M19. ▸**b** A heavy bomber. M20.
3 Anything particularly large and heavy of its kind. M19.

Truck & Driver Wet trailer curtains were strapped down and the heavies began pulling out. *Strength Athlete* Bodyweight divisions . . range from the lightest . ., to the super heavies.

4 A serious or tragic theatrical part. L19. ▸**b** In *pl.* *The* serious newspapers or journals. M20.

S. FORD It's as good as playin' leading heavy in 'The Shadows of a Great City'. **b** *Punch* To be subsequently published in one of the glossies or . . in one of the heavies.

5 A heavily built person of violent disposition, a thug. Also, an important person. M20.

J. WAINWRIGHT One Saturday night, the heavies from some other outfit started to throw muscle. *Australian Business* BT Australia's heavies were on hand to celebrate BT Innovation's first 12 months of activity.

■ **heavi'osity** *noun* (*colloq.*) the quality of being serious, intense, or 'heavy', esp. in popular music L20.

heavy /ˈhɛvi/ *adverb*.
[ORIGIN Old English *hefiġe* = Old High German *hefigo*, *hevigo*, formed as HEAVY *adjective & noun*.]
= HEAVILY. Freq. qualifying adjectives, as ***heavy-laden***, ***heavy-pulling***, etc.

heavy-handed /hɛvɪˈhandɪd/ *adjective*. M17.
[ORIGIN from HEAVY *adjective* + HANDED *adjective*.]
1 Having heavy or weary hands. Now chiefly *transf.*, clumsy; lacking subtlety. M17.

K. CLARK Those critics who have maintained that he was a clumsy or heavy-handed painter. *Face* The heavy-handed irony of some sequences.

2 Oppressive; overbearing. L19.

City Limits Camden . . is becoming so heavy-handed in dealing with the attendant problems.

■ **heavy-handedness** *noun* L19.

heavyweight /ˈhɛvɪweɪt/ *noun & adjective*. M19.
[ORIGIN from HEAVY *adjective* + WEIGHT *noun*.]
▸ **A** *noun*. **1** A person (esp. a jockey), animal, or thing of more than the average weight. M19.

W. HOLTBY Thundering round the ring at agricultural shows on his huge heavyweights.

2 A weight at which boxing etc. matches are made, above middleweight (or cruiserweight) and usu. the heaviest weight, in the amateur boxing scale now being above 81 kg, though differing for professionals, wrestlers, and weightlifters, and according to time and place; a boxer etc., of this weight. L19.
3 A person of importance and influence. L19.

TV Guide (Canada) Casting heavyweights Charlton Heston and Barbara Stanwyck to help win viewers.

▸ **B** *adjective*. Particularly heavy of its kind; (of a boxer etc.) that is a heavyweight, of or pertaining to heavyweights. L19.

Times Heavyweight American and Continental trucks and buses.

– PHRASES: **light heavyweight** (of) a weight in boxing and some other sports above middleweight, in the amateur boxing scale now being between 75 and 81 kg; (designating) a boxer etc. of this weight; also called ***cruiserweight***.

Heb. *abbreviation*.
1 Hebrew.
2 Hebrews (New Testament).

hebdomad /ˈhɛbdəmad/ *noun*. Also (now *rare*) **-ade** /-eɪd/. M16.
[ORIGIN Late Latin from Greek *hebdomas*, *-ad-*, the number seven, period of seven days, from *hepta* seven: see -AD[1], -ADE.]
†**1** The number seven viewed collectively; a group of seven. M16–M19.
2 The space of seven days, a week, esp. with ref. to *Daniel* 9:24–7. E17.
3 In Gnosticism etc., a group of seven superhuman beings. Also, a title of the Demiurge. M19.

hebdomadal /hɛbˈdɒmməd(ə)l/ *adjective & noun*. E17.
[ORIGIN Late Latin *hebdomadalis*, from *hebdomas*, *-ad-*: see HEBDOMAD, -AL[1].]
▸ **A** *adjective*. †**1** Consisting of or lasting seven days. E–M17.
2 Meeting or occurring once a week; weekly. E18.
Hebdomadal Council the representative board of Oxford University, which meets weekly.
▸ **B** *noun*. A periodical appearing once a week; a weekly. *joc.* M19.
■ **hebdomadally** *adverb* E19.

hebdomadarian /hɛbdɒməˈdɛːrɪən/ *noun*. L19.
[ORIGIN from HEBDOMADARY + -IAN.]
= HEBDOMADARY *noun*.

hebdomadary /hɛbˈdɒməd(ə)ri/ *noun & adjective*. Also **H-**, (earlier) †**eb-**. LME.
[ORIGIN Late or ecclesiastical Latin *hebdomadarius*, formed as HEBDOMADAL: see -ARY[1].]
▸ **A** *noun*. ROMAN CATHOLIC CHURCH. A member of a chapter or convent, who takes his or her weekly turn in performing the sacred offices of the Church. LME.
▸ **B** *adjective*. Weekly; doing duty for a week. E17.
■ **hebdomary** *noun* = HEBDOMADARY *noun* LME.

hebdomade *noun* see HEBDOMAD.

Hebe /ˈhiːbi/ *noun*[1]. E17.
[ORIGIN Greek *hēbē* youthful beauty, *Hēbē* the Greek goddess of youth and spring, daughter of Zeus and Hera, and cupbearer of Olympus.]
1 A young woman resembling Hebe; a waitress. E17.
2 (**h-**.) Any of numerous New Zealand evergreen shrubs constituting the genus *Hebe* (formerly included in *Veronica*), of the figwort family, with spikes of blue, white, mauve, etc., flowers. M20.

Hebe /hiːb/ *noun*[2]. *derog. offensive*. Also **h-**. E20.
[ORIGIN Abbreviation of HEBREW *noun* 1.]
A Jew.

†**hebenon** *noun* var. of HEBONA.

hebephrenia /hiːbɪˈfriːnɪə/ *noun*. L19.
[ORIGIN from HEBE *noun*[1] + Greek *phrēn* mind + -IA[1].]
Orig., a form of insanity which occurs during puberty. Now, a form of schizophrenia characterized by incoherence, silliness, and inappropriate emotions.
■ **hebephrenic** /-ˈfrɛnɪk/ *adjective & noun* (a person) affected by hebephrenia E20. **hebephreniac** *noun* a person affected by hebephrenia L19.

Heberden's node /ˈhɛbəd(ə)nz nəʊd/ *noun phr.* L19.
[ORIGIN William *Heberden* (1710–1801), English physician.]
MEDICINE. A nodular enlargement of a terminal joint of a finger, due to osteoarthritis. Usu. in *pl.*

hebetate /ˈhɛbɪteɪt/ *verb trans. & intrans.* L16.
[ORIGIN Latin *hebetat-* pa. ppl stem of *hebetare*, from *hebes*, *hebet-* blunt, dull: see -ATE[3].]
Make or become dull or inert.
■ **hebe'tation** *noun* E17.

hebete /ˈhɛbiːt/ *adjective*. *rare*. M18.
[ORIGIN Latin *hebet-*, *hebes* blunt, dull.]
Dull, stupid, obtuse.

hebetude /ˈhɛbɪtjuːd/ *noun*. *literary*. E17.
[ORIGIN Late Latin *hebetudo*, formed as HEBETE: see -TUDE.]
Dullness, bluntness, lethargy.

hebona /ˈhɛbənə/ *noun*. Long *rare*. Also †**hebenon**. L16.
[ORIGIN Unknown.]
A poisonous juice or substance.

SHAKES. *Haml.* Upon my secure hour thy uncle stole, with juice of cursed hebona in a vial.

H

hebra /ˈhɛbrə/ *noun*. Also **chevra** /ˈxɛvrə/. Pl. **-ras**, **-roth** /-rəʊt/. L19.
[ORIGIN Hebrew *ḥebrāh* association, society.]
A small group formed by members of a Jewish community for religious and charitable purposes.

Hebraean /hɪˈbreɪən, -ˈbriːən/ *noun*. *rare*. Also **Hebrean**. E16.
[ORIGIN from Latin *Hebraeus*: see HEBREW, -AN.]
†1 A Jew. Only in E16.
†2 A Hebrew scholar. M17–E19.
3 A member of a Dutch religious sect whose beliefs were based on the meanings of hidden truths in Hebrew. *obsolete* exc. *hist.* L19.

Hebraic /hɪˈbreɪɪk/ *adjective*. LME.
[ORIGIN Christian Latin *Hebraicus* from late Greek *Hebraikos*, from *Hebra-* based on Aramaic *ʿibray*: see HEBREW, -IC.]
Pertaining or relating to the Hebrews or to their language; Hebrew.
■ **Hebraical** *adjective* (now *rare*) E17. **Hebraically** *adverb* in Hebrew fashion; in the manner of the Hebrews or their language, *spec.* with ref. to the fact that Hebrew is written from right to left: E18. †**Hebraician** *noun* = HEBRAIST 1 E17–E18.

Hebraise *verb* var. of HEBRAIZE.

Hebraism /ˈhiːbreɪɪz(ə)m/ *noun*. L16.
[ORIGIN French *hébraïsme* or mod. Latin *Hebraismus* = late Greek *Hebraismos*: see HEBREW, -ISM.]
1 A Hebrew idiom or expression, esp. one as used in some other language. L16.
2 A quality or attribute of the Hebrew people; Hebrew character or nature; the Hebrew system of thought or religion. M19.

Hebraist /ˈhiːbreɪɪst/ *noun*. M18.
[ORIGIN from Greek *Hebra-* stem of HEBRAIC + -IST.]
1 A Hebrew scholar; a person skilled in Hebrew. M18.
2 A person who maintains that the New Testament was written in Greek with Hebrew idioms. M19.
3 An adherent of Hebrew thought or religion. L19.
4 *hist.* A Palestinian Jew, as opp. to a Hellenistic or Grecian Jew. L19.
■ **Hebraˈistic** *adjective* M19.

Hebraize /ˈhiːbreɪʌɪz/ *verb*. Also **-ise**. M17.
[ORIGIN Late Greek *Hebraizein* speak Hebrew, imitate Jews, from *Hebra-*: see HEBRAIC, -IZE.]
1 *verb intrans.* Use a Hebrew idiom or expression. M17.
2 *verb trans.* Make Hebrew; give a Hebrew character to. E19.

Hebrean *noun* var. of HEBRAEAN.

Hebrew /ˈhiːbruː/ *noun & adjective*. ME.
[ORIGIN Old French *ebreu*, *ebrieu* (mod. *hébreu*) from medieval Latin *Ebreus* from Latin *Hebraeus* from late Greek *Hebraios* from Aramaic *ʿibrāy*, for Hebrew *ʿibrī* interpreted as 'one from the other side (of the river)', as if from *ʿēber* the region on the other or opposite side, from *ʿābar* cross or pass over.]
▸ **A** *noun*. **1** A member of a Semitic people living in ancient Palestine and having a descent traditionally traced from Abraham, Isaac, and Jacob; an Israelite, a Jew. In *pl.* (treated as *sing.*), the Epistle to the Hebrews, a book of the New Testament traditionally (but probably not rightly) included among the epistles of St Paul. ME.
2 The Semitic language spoken by the Hebrews, in which most of the books of the Hebrew Scriptures were written. Also, a modern form of this revived in the 19th cent.; the official language of the state of Israel. ME. ▸**b** Unintelligible speech. Cf. GREEK *noun* 8. *colloq.* E17.
▸ **B** *adjective*. **1** Belonging to, written in, or spoken in the language of the Hebrews. ME.
2 Of, belonging to, or characteristic of the Hebrews; Jewish. L15.
Hebrew Scriptures: see SCRIPTURE 1a.
■ **Hebrewdom** *noun* the Hebrew community; the quality of the Hebrew people: M19. **Hebrewess** *noun* (*rare*) a female Hebrew, a Jewess M16. **Hebrewism** *noun* (now *rare*) = HEBRAISM E17.

Hebrician /hiːˈbrɪʃ(ə)n/ *noun*. Now *rare* or *obsolete*. M16.
[ORIGIN formed as HEBRAIC + -ICIAN.]
†1 A Hebrew. M–L16.
2 A Hebrew scholar; a person skilled in Hebrew. L16.

Hebridean /hɛbrɪˈdiːən/ *adjective & noun*. Also **-ian**. E17.
[ORIGIN from *Hebrides* (see below) + -AN, -EAN.]
▸ **A** *adjective*. Of or pertaining to the Hebrides, a group of islands off the west coast of Scotland. E17.
▸ **B** *noun*. A native or inhabitant of the Hebrides. M17.
■ ˈ**Hebrid** *adjective* (*poet.*, *rare*) = HEBRIDEAN *adjective* M18.

Hecate /ˈhɛkəti/ *noun*. L16.
[ORIGIN Greek *Hekatē* fem. of *hekatos* far-darting (an epithet of Apollo), in Greek mythol. name of a goddess of Thracian origin identified with Artemis and the moon, and also with Persephone, the goddess of the infernal regions, and accordingly regarded as presiding over magic and witchcraft.]
A hag, a witch.

SHAKES. *1 Hen. VI* I speak not to that railing Hecate.

– NOTE: In Shakes. usually disyllabic (/ˈhɛkət/).

hecatomb /ˈhɛkətuːm/ *noun & verb*. L16.
[ORIGIN Latin *hecatombe* from Greek *hekatombē*, from *hekaton* hundred + *bous* ox.]
▸ **A** *noun*. **1** A great public sacrifice, strictly of a hundred oxen, among the ancient Greeks and Romans; *gen.* a religious sacrifice; a large number of animals set apart for sacrifice. L16.
2 *transf.* & *fig.* A sacrifice of many victims. L16.

T. PARNELL A hecatomb of reputations was that day to fall for her pleasure.

▸ **B** *verb trans.* Provide with a hecatomb. *rare*. M18.

hecatomped /hɛkəˈtɒmpɪd/ *adjective*. E18.
[ORIGIN Greek *hekatompedos*, from *hekaton* hundred + *ped-* ablaut var. of *pous*, *pod-* foot.]
Measuring a hundred feet (30.48 m) in length and breadth; that is a hundred feet square.
■ **hecatompedon** *noun* (*rare*) a temple of hecatomped dimensions (as the Parthenon at Athens) L18.

hecatontarchy /hɛkəˈtɒntɑːki/ *noun*. M17.
[ORIGIN Late Greek *hekatontarkhia* post or command of a centurion, from *hekatont(a)-* combining form, from *hekaton* hundred: see -ARCHY.]
Government by a hundred rulers.

heck /hɛk/ *noun*[1]. Chiefly *Scot.* & *N. English*. ME.
[ORIGIN Var. (from inflected forms) of HATCH *noun*[1]. Cf. HACK *noun*[3].]
1 A grating or frame of parallel bars in a river used to obstruct the passage of fish or solid bodies without obstructing the flow of water. Also = HATCH *noun*[1] 3. ME.
2 A rack of parallel spars used to hold fodder. ME.
at heck and manger in comfortable circumstances, in plenty.
3 The lower half of a divided door; a half-door, a gate, a wicket; = HATCH *noun*[1] 1. LME. ▸**b** A passage in a house; *esp.* one forming a screen or division. E19.
4 = HACK *noun*[3] 4. *obsolete* exc. *Scot.* LME.
5 A movable board at the back of a cart. E19.
6 A piece in a spinning wheel or warping mill by which the yarn or thread is guided to the reels. E19.

heck /hɛk/ *noun*[2]. *colloq.* *euphem.* L19.
[ORIGIN Alt. of HELL *noun*.]
1 In exclamatory or imprecatory phrs. (in which ***hell*** can always be substituted) expr. anger, annoyance, incredulity, dismay, etc., or merely emphatic. L19.

M. RENAULT What the heck does he want? *Guardian* Sometimes he sings for sheer fun and the heck of it. D. WESTHEIMER It's a heck of a responsibility.

2 As *interjection*. An exclam. of anger, annoyance, dismay, etc. M20.

heck /hɛk/ *verb intrans.* Now *rare*. M17.
[ORIGIN Imit.: cf. HACK *verb*[1].]
Make a short dry cough; = HACK *verb*[1] 9. Chiefly in ***hecking cough***.

heckberry *noun* var. of HAGBERRY.

heckelphone /ˈhɛk(ə)lfəʊn/ *noun*. Also **-phon**. E20.
[ORIGIN German *Heckelphon*, from Wilhelm *Heckel* (1856–1909), German instrument-maker + -PHONE.]
A baritone oboe.

heckle /ˈhɛk(ə)l/ *noun*. LME.
[ORIGIN North. & East Anglian form of HACKLE *noun*[2].]
▸ **I 1** = HACKLE *noun*[2] 5. LME.
2 = HACKLE *noun*[2] 1. LME.
3 ANGLING. = HACKLE *noun*[2] 2. E19.
▸ **II** [Prob. from the verb.]
4 **a** = HECKLER *noun* 2. L18. ▸**b** The action or an act of heckling a public speaker. E20.

heckle /ˈhɛk(ə)l/ *verb*. ME.
[ORIGIN from the noun Cf. HACKLE *verb*[3], HATCHEL.]
1 *verb trans.* Dress (flax or hemp) with a heckle, to split and straighten out the fibres for spinning; = HACKLE *verb*[3] 1. ME.
2 *verb trans.* & *intrans.* Interrupt (a public speaker) with aggressive questions or abuse, esp. in order to undermine the speaker or to weaken his or her argument. M17.

W. E. GOSSE On the hustings, Lord John Manners was a good deal heckled. B. EMECHETA They started to heckle and jeer.

3 *verb trans.* Chastise, scold. *dial.* E19.

heckler /ˈhɛklə/ *noun*. LME.
[ORIGIN from HECKLE *verb* + -ER[1].]
1 A dresser of flax or hemp. LME.
2 A person who heckles a public speaker. E19.

N. CHOMSKY The speakers . . were drowned out by hecklers and counterdemonstrators.

hecogenin /hɛkəʊˈdʒɛnɪn/ *noun*. M20.
[ORIGIN from mod. Latin *Hechtia* genus name of a source plant + -O- + GENIN.]
BIOCHEMISTRY. A steroid glycoside present in various plants and obtained commercially from sisal waste, used in the manufacture of cortisone and related steroids.

hectare /ˈhɛktɛː, -ɑː/ *noun*. E19.
[ORIGIN French, irreg. from Greek *hekaton* hundred + ARE *noun*[2]: see HECTO-.]
A metric unit of square measure equal to 100 ares (10000 m^2), or 2.471 acres.
■ **hectarage** *noun* extent of hectares; hectares collectively: L20.

hectic /ˈhɛktɪk/ *adjective & noun*. Also (earlier) †**etik**. LME.
[ORIGIN Old French *etique* from late Latin *hecticus* from Greek *hektikos* habitual, hectic, consumptive, from *hexis* habit, state of body or mind: see -IC. Assim. to Latin, or mod. French *hectique*.]
▸ **A** *adjective*. **1** MEDICINE. Belonging to or symptomatic of the bodily state or condition; *spec.* characteristic of or associated with tuberculosis or other wasting disease; showing tubercular symptoms such as flushed cheeks and hot dry skin. LME.

C. KINGSLEY A pretty, hectic girl of sixteen. E. LYALL The hectic beauty of one dying of consumption.

hectic fever a fever (often of regular daily occurrence) which accompanies tuberculosis or other wasting diseases. ***hectic flush***: see FLUSH *noun*[2] 4.
2 *fig.* **a** Wasting, consuming. *rare*. E17. ▸**b** Flushed, bright red. E19.

b F. KING A high cheekbone hectic with rouge.

†3 Habitual, constitutional. Only in M17.
4 (Now the usual sense.) Stirring, exciting, disturbing; characterized by a state of feverish excitement or activity. E20.

GODFREY SMITH Long periods of boredom broken by hectic spells of chaos. A. BROOKNER The streets now hectic with traffic and confusion.

▸ **B** *noun*. **1** A hectic fever. LME. ▸**b** *fig.* A consuming disturbance or obsession of the mind. LME.
2 A person affected with hectic fever. LME.
3 A hectic flush; *gen.* a flush, heightened colour. M18.
■ **hectical** *adjective* (*arch.*) E17. **hectically** *adverb* M18.

hecto- /ˈhɛktəʊ/ *combining form*.
[ORIGIN French, contr. of Greek *hekaton* hundred.]
Used with the sense 'one hundred', esp. to form units in the metric system, as ***hectogram***, ***hectolitre***, etc. Abbreviation ***h***.

hectocotylus /hɛktəʊˈkɒtɪləs/ *noun*. Pl. **-li** /-lʌɪ, -liː/. Also anglicized as **-cotyl**. M19.
[ORIGIN mod. Latin (see note below), formed as HECTO- + Greek *kotulē* cup, hollow thing.]
ZOOLOGY. A modified arm in male dibranchiate cephalopods which is adapted for the transfer of sperm to the female, in some species becoming detached and remaining in the body of the female.
■ **hectocotyliˈzation** *noun* the process of forming a hectocotylus L19. **hectocotylize** *verb trans.* (in *pass.*) become modified into a hectocotylus L19.

hectogram /ˈhɛktə(ʊ)gram/ *noun*. Also **-gramme**. L18.
[ORIGIN French *hectogramme*, formed as HECTO- + GRAM *noun*[2].]
A weight of 100 grams.

hectograph /ˈhɛktə(ʊ)grɑːf/ *noun & verb*. L19
[ORIGIN from HECTO- + -GRAPH.]
▸ **A** *noun*. An apparatus used for copying documents by means of a gelatin plate; the process of making copies with this apparatus. L19.
▸ **B** *verb trans.* Reproduce by means of a hectograph. L19.
■ **hectoˈgraphic** *adjective* L19.

hectolitre /ˈhɛktə(ʊ)liːtə/ *noun*. Also **-liter**. E19.
[ORIGIN French, formed as HECTO- + LITRE.]
A volume of 100 litres.

hectometre /ˈhɛktə(ʊ)miːtə/ *noun*. Also **-meter**. E19.
[ORIGIN French *hectomètre*, formed as HECTO- + METRE *noun*[2].]
A length of 100 metres.

hector /ˈhɛktə/ *noun*. Also **H-**. LME.
[ORIGIN Latin *Hector*, Greek *Hektōr* son of Priam and Hecuba, a Trojan hero, use as noun of adjective *hektōr* holding fast, from *ekhein* to hold.]
1 A valiant warrior. LME.
2 A swaggering fellow, a braggart, a bully. M17.

hector /ˈhɛktə/ *verb*. M17.
[ORIGIN from the noun.]
1 *verb intrans.* Play the bully; brag, bluster, domineer. M17.
2 *verb trans.* Intimidate by bluster or threats; domineer over; bully *out of*, *into*, etc. M17.
■ **hectoringly** *adverb* in a blustering or intimidatory manner E20.

heddle /hɛd(ə)l/ *noun*. E16.
[ORIGIN App. ult. from Old English alt. of *hefeld* HEALD *noun*.]
Any of the sets of small cords or wires between which the warp is passed in the loom before going through the reed, dividing the warp threads to allow the passage of the shuttle with the weft. Freq. in *pl.*

hedenbergite /ˈhɛd(ə)nbəgʌɪt/ *noun*. E19.
[ORIGIN from Ludwig *Hedenberg*, 19th-cent. Swedish mineralogist + -ITE[1].]
MINERALOGY. A black mineral of the clinopyroxene group, containing calcium and iron.

heder *noun* var. of CHEDER.

hedge /hɛdʒ/ *noun*.
[ORIGIN Old English *heġġ* = East Frisian *hegge*, Middle Dutch *hegghe* (Dutch *heg*), Old High German *hegga*, *hecka* (German *Hecke*) from Germanic base rel. to HAG *noun*[2], HAW *noun*[1], HAY *noun*[2].]
1 A closely planted line of bushes, small trees, or dead wood, esp. forming a boundary of a field, garden, road, etc. Also occas., a similar boundary of turf, stone, etc. OE. ▸**b** *transf.* Any line of objects forming a barrier, boundary, or partition. E16.

W. BOYD An ornamental rose garden separated from the lawn by a neat briar hedge. **b** H. MARTINEAU Hedges of police from our little street to the gates of the Abbey.

2 A barrier; a means of protection or defence. ME. ▸**b** *spec.* An act or means of hedging or protecting a bet or speculation. Cf. HEDGE *verb* 7. M18.

Atlantic Monthly Last year you wanted some extra money as a hedge against hard luck. **b** *Punch* A good unit trust group . . provides . . a hedge against inflation.

3 A fishing weir. LME.

– ATTRIB. & COMB.: In the senses 'living, working, occurring, etc., at the roadside; done under a hedge or clandestinely; inferior, paltry,' as ***hedge-doctor***, ***hedge-inn***, ***hedge-lawyer***, ***hedge-marriage***, ***hedge-parson***, ***hedge-poet***, etc. Special combs., as **hedge-bill** = *hedging-bill* s.v. HEDGING; ***hedge bindweed***: see BINDWEED 1. **hedge bird** (*a*) a bird that inhabits or frequents hedges; (*b*) a person born or brought up on or frequenting the roadside; a vagrant; a footpad; **hedge-clippers**: for trimming a hedge; **hedge-creeper** (now *rare* or *obsolete*) a vagrant; a thief; a peeping tom; **hedge-fence** a hedge serving as a fence; **hedge fund** an offshore investment fund that engages in speculation using credit or borrowed capital; **hedge garlic** = GARLIC ***mustard***; **hedge-hop** *verb intrans. & trans.* fly at a low altitude (over); **hedge-hyssop** any of various low-growing N. American marsh plants of the genus *Gratiola*, of the figwort family; earlier, a similar plant of central Europe, *G. officinalis*, once valued for its medicinal properties; ***hedge maple***: see MAPLE *noun* 1; **hedge mustard** a cruciferous roadside weed, *Sisymbrium officinale*, with small yellow flowers and adpressed pods; **hedge-parsley** any of several umbelliferous plants of the genus *Torilis*; *esp.* (in full ***upright hedge-parsley***) *T. japonica*, a common plant of hedgerows; **hedge-pig** a hedgehog; **hedge-priest** *derog.* (*hist.*) an illiterate priest of low status; **hedge-school** *hist.* (orig.) an open-air school, esp. in Ireland; (later) an inferior type of school; **hedge-side**: of a hedge (freq. *attrib.*); **hedge sparrow** the dunnock, *Prunella modularis*; ***hedge trimmer***: see TRIMMER *noun*; **hedge-wood** trees or bushes suitable for growing as hedges.

■ **hedgeless** *adjective* E19.

hedge /hɛdʒ/ *verb*. LME.

[ORIGIN from the noun.]

1 *verb trans.* Surround or enclose with a hedge or fence as a boundary or defence. (Foll. by *in*, *about*.) LME. ▸**b** Make into a hedge or barrier. M18.

2 *verb intrans.* Construct a hedge or hedges. LME.

3 *verb trans.* Surround or enclose as with a hedge or fence. LME. ▸**b** Hem in, confine, restrict. M16.

SHAKES. *Haml.* There's such divinity doth hedge a King. **b** *fig.*: I. D'ISRAELI The King was hedged in by the most thorny difficulties.

4 *verb trans.* Obstruct (as) with a hedge. M16.

5 *verb intrans.* Avoid committing oneself, refuse to face an issue, evade the question. Formerly also, turn from the direct path; leave a way of retreat. L16.

P. CUSHING The miller hedged and dodged, but being pressed hard he finally admitted the truth.

†**6** *verb trans.* With *in*: include within the limits of something else; *spec.* secure (a debt) by including it in another for which better security is obtained. E17–M18.

7 *verb trans.* Secure oneself against total loss on (a bet or speculation) by making similar transactions on the other side. L17. ▸**b** *verb trans. & intrans. spec.* Insure (one's commercial activities) against risk or loss by entering into contracts which balance one another. E20.

absol.: LD MACAULAY He had betted too deep on the Revolution and . . it was time to hedge.

■ **hedger** *noun* (*a*) a person who lays or trims hedges; (*b*) a person who hedges (senses 5 & 7 above): ME. **hedgingly** *adverb* in an evasive or non-committal manner L19.

hedgebote /ˈhɛdʒbəʊt/ *noun*. ME.

[ORIGIN from HEDGE *noun* + BOTE.]

LAW. = HAYBOTE.

hedgehog /ˈhɛdʒ(h)ɒg/ *noun*. LME.

[ORIGIN from HEDGE *noun* + HOG *noun*.]

1 Any of various spiny nocturnal insectivorous mammals of the family Erinaceidae (esp. the western European *Erinaceus europaeus*), noted for the ability to roll up into a ball when alarmed. LME.

†**2** *fig.* A person who disregards the feelings of others. L16–M17.

3 Any of various other spiny animals; *esp.* (*US*) the porcupine; ***sea hedgehog***, (*a*) a sea urchin; (*b*) the porcupine fish, *Diodon hystrix*. L16.

4 Any of various objects held to resemble a hedgehog in shape, appearance, etc., as (*a*) a type of dredging machine; (*b*) a pudding or cake shaped like a hedgehog; (*c*) a small self-contained fortified position bristling with defences on all sides; (*d*) a type of ship-borne multi-barrelled mortar firing a pattern of depth charges. L17.

5 *sing.* & in *pl.* (The fruits of) any of several plants with prickly seed vessels, esp. the corn buttercup *Ranunculus arvensis*. E18.

– COMB.: **hedgehog holly** a cultivated form of holly with leaves prickly on the upper surface.

■ **hedgehoggy** *adjective* resembling a hedgehog; prickly; (of a person) difficult to get on with: M19.

hedgerow /ˈhɛdʒrəʊ/ *noun*. OE.

[ORIGIN from HEDGE *noun* + REW, assim. to ROW *noun*¹.]

A hedge, esp. as used as the boundary of a field or road.

hedging /ˈhɛdʒɪŋ/ *verbal noun*. LME.

[ORIGIN from HEDGE *verb* + -ING¹.]

1 The laying, repairing, or trimming of hedges. LME.

2 (The trees, bushes, etc., forming) a hedge. LME.

3 The securing of, or limiting the possible loss on, a bet or financial speculation. M17.

4 Evasion; refusal to commit oneself. E18.

– COMB.: **hedging bill** a long-handled bill for cutting and trimming hedges.

hedgy /ˈhɛdʒi/ *adjective*. L16.

[ORIGIN from HEDGE *noun* or *verb* + -Y¹.]

†**1** Pertaining to or of the nature of a hedge. Only in L16.

2 Characterized by or having many hedges. M17.

3 Marked by hedging; evasive, non-committal. E20.

hedonic /hiːˈdɒnɪk, hɛ-/ *adjective & noun*. M17.

[ORIGIN Greek *hēdonikos*, formed as HEDONISM: see -IC.]

▸ **A** *adjective*. **1** Of or pertaining to pleasure; (chiefly *PSYCHOLOGY*) of, pertaining to, or involving pleasurable or painful sensations or feelings, considered as affects. M17. **hedonic tone** the degree of pleasantness or unpleasantness associated with an experience or state, esp. as referred to a continuum extending from pleasure to pain.

2 *ZOOLOGY.* Designating or relating to glands in reptiles and amphibians which serve to attract members of the opposite sex for mating. E20.

▸ **B** *noun*. †**1** A Cyrenaic. Only in L17.

2 In *pl.* The science of pleasure; that part of ethics which refers to pleasure. Now *rare*. M19.

hedonism /ˈhiːd(ə)nɪz(ə)m, ˈhɛ-/ *noun*. M19.

[ORIGIN from Greek *hēdonē* pleasure + -ISM.]

The doctrine or theory of ethics in which pleasure is regarded as the chief good or the proper aim. Freq. now also, devotion to or pursuit of pleasure.

hedonist /ˈhiːd(ə)nɪst, ˈhɛ-/ *noun*. M19.

[ORIGIN from Greek as HEDONISM + -IST.]

A person who regards pleasure as the chief good or the proper aim. Now freq., a pleasure-seeker.

D. ATHILL Deliberately frivolous as he was, a hedonist, an opportunist.

■ **hedoˈnistic** *adjective* M19. **hedoˈnistically** *adverb* L19.

hedonometer /hiːdɒˈnɒmɪtə, hɛ-/ *noun*. *joc.* E19.

[ORIGIN from Greek *hēdonē* + -METER.]

A (hypothetical) device for measuring pleasure.

-hedral /ˈhiːdr(ə)l, ˈhɛd-/ *suffix*.

[ORIGIN from (the same root as) -HEDRON + -AL¹.]

Forming adjectives (usu. corresp. to nouns in **-HEDRON**) in sense 'having or involving a specified number or kind of plane surfaces or faces' (***anhedral***, ***dihedral***, ***dodecahedral***, ***rhombohedral***).

-hedron /ˈhiːdrən, ˈhɛd-/ *suffix*. Pl. **-hedra** /ˈhiːdrə, ˈhɛd-/, **-hedrons**.

[ORIGIN from Greek *hedra* seat, base, after OCTAHEDRON etc.]

Forming nouns denoting geometrical solid figures or objects with various numbers or shapes of faces (***dodecahedron***, ***rhombohedron***).

hedrumite /ˈhɛdrəmʌɪt/ *noun*. L19.

[ORIGIN from *Hedrum* a village in Norway + -ITE¹.]

GEOLOGY. A hypabyssal porphyritic igneous rock having a trachytic texture and consisting essentially of a potash-feldspar with some pyribole and (usu.) nepheline.

hedychium /hɪˈdɪkɪəm/ *noun*. E19.

[ORIGIN mod. Latin *Hedychium* genus name, from Greek *hēdus* sweet + *khiōn* snow, with ref. to the fragrant white flowers of one species.]

= ***ginger lily*** s.v. GINGER *noun*.

heebie-jeebie /hiːbɪˈdʒiːbi/ *noun*. *slang* (orig. *US*). Also **heeby-jeeby**. E20.

[ORIGIN Unknown.]

sing. or (usu.) in *pl.*, with *the*: a state of nervous depression or apprehension; delirium tremens. Also formerly, a type of dance.

Weekly Dispatch Does this work never give you the heebie-jeebies? Does it never depress you?

heed /hiːd/ *noun*. ME.

[ORIGIN from the verb.]

1 Careful attention, observation, regard. Now chiefly in phrs. below. ME.

T. HERBERT Swimming so without heed, that some were in apparant danger.

give heed to, **pay heed to** pay attention to. **take heed (of)** take care, attend (to).

†**2** That which is heeded. *rare* (Shakes.). Only in L16.

■ **heedful** *adjective* careful, attentive, mindful, cautious M16. **heedfully** *adverb* M16. **heedfulness** *noun* M16. †**heedily** *adverb* carefully, with attention L16–M17. †**heediness** *noun* attentiveness, caution L16–E17. **heedless** *adjective* careless, inattentive, regardless, reckless L16. **heedlessly** *adverb* L17. **heedlessness** *noun* L16. †**heedy** *adjective* attentive, cautious M16–M17.

heed /hiːd/ *verb*.

[ORIGIN Old English *hēdan* = Old Saxon *hōdian* (Dutch *hoeden*), Old High German *huoten* (German *hüten*), from West Germanic base of Old Frisian, Middle Low German *hōde*, Old High German *huota*, German *Hut* care, keeping.]

1 *verb intrans.* Have a care, pay attention, take notice. Now chiefly *dial.* OE.

R. MACAULAY I did my best to warn her, but she wouldn't heed.

never heed *dial.* do not worry, never mind.

2 *verb trans.* Concern oneself about, take notice of, regard. ME.

V. WOOLF Mrs Ambrose alone heeded none of this stir. C. CHAPLIN When the fates deal in human destiny, they heed neither pity nor justice. K. CROSSLEY-HOLLAND My advice will help you if you heed it.

hee-haw /ˈhiːhɔː/ *noun & verb*. E19.

[ORIGIN Imit.]

▸ **A** *noun*. **1** (A representation of) a donkey's bray. E19.

2 A loud, coarse laugh. M19.

▸ **B** *verb intrans.* Utter a hee-haw, bray. E19.

heel /hiːl/ *noun*¹.

[ORIGIN Old English *hēla*, *hǣla* corresp. to Old Frisian *hēla*, Middle Dutch *hiele* (Dutch *hiel*), Old Norse *hæll*, from Germanic base of Old English *hōh* heel: see HOUGH *noun*.]

1 The hinder part of the human foot below the ankle. OE. ▸**b** The corresponding part of the foot or hind limb of an animal; *esp.* (*a*) the hinder part of the hoof; (*b*) a hind foot of a quadruped; (*c*) the hinder toe or hallux of a bird. OE. ▸**c** The foot as a whole. ME.

E. LINKLATER A muslin wrapper which fell loosely from her shoulders to her heels. M. FRAYN He . . raised himself on his toes, and let himself sink . . back on to his heels. **c** M. PRIOR He . . was carried off to bed: John held his heels, and Nan his head.

2 The heel or foot as an instrument of kicking, trampling, or oppression. OE. ▸**b** The armed, booted, or spurred heel, esp. as used in horsemanship. LME. ▸**c** *RUGBY.* A heeling of the ball from the scrummage. Cf. HEEL *verb*² 6. M20.

H. GEORGE Those classes upon whom the iron heel of modern civilisation presses.

3 The part of a sock or stocking which covers the heel; the part of a boot or shoe which supports or raises the heel. Also, in *pl.*, high-heeled shoes. ME. ▸**b** Either of the raised extremities of a horseshoe; a calkin. M19.

C. BEATON She wore . . white satin shoes whose Spanish Spike heels were fully six inches high. P. MATTHIESSEN I wear my . . socks upside down so that the hole in the heel sits on the top of my foot. *New York Times* 'Take off those heels,' my aunt says.

4 (The heels as) the hindmost part of a person or animal, esp. one pursued; hence, the means of flight. LME.

N. BAILEY One Pair of Heels is worth two Pair of Hands, that is, it is better to run for it.

5 The remains or end part of anything, as the crust of a loaf, the rind of a cheese, etc. LME.

D. L. SAYERS The heel of a stale loaf. P. V. PRICE The bottle heel or dregs can be filtered and used in cooking.

6 The concluding part of anything, as a period of time, a book, etc. L16.

S. O'FAOLÁIN It was so fine in the heel of the day.

7 The lower or handle end of anything, as the handle end of a violin bow, the inner end of the head of a golf club, the lower part of a ship's mast or rudder, etc. L16.

8 a The part of a bivalve shell which bears the hinge. L17. ▸**b** The vertical timber of a gate which bears the hinges. M19.

9 The broadest or thickest part of a wedge-shaped object. L19.

10 A projection resembling a heel in shape or position, as; (*a*) a small piece of older wood taken off with a cutting; (*b*) the small projecting part at the back of the bowl of a spoon. L19.

Practical Gardening Cuttings of young side-shoots . . preferably with a tiny heel of wood attached to each.

– PHRASES: *ACHILLES heel*. **at heel** = *to heel* below. **at one's heels**, **at the heels of** close behind, in close pursuit of or attendance on. **back on one's heels** into a state of discomfiture or astonishment. *beef to the heel(s)*: see BEEF *noun*. **bring to heel**, **come to heel** make or come to walk at heel; bring or come under control. *dig in one's heels*: see DIG *verb*. **down at heel**, **down at the heel** (*a*) (of a shoe) having the heels worn down; worn carelessly with the heel part crushed under the foot; (*b*) (of a person) wearing down-at-heel shoes; destitute, slovenly. ***hairy about the heels***, ***hairy at the heels***, ***hairy in the heels***: see HAIRY *adjective*. ***head over heels***: see HEAD *noun*. **heel-and-toe** *adverb*. (*a*) with proper walking action, esp. as required in race-walking; (*b*) with the action of heeling-and-toeing in driving a motor vehicle (see HEEL *verb*²). **heel of Italy** the SE extremity of Italy (which country resembles a leg and foot in shape). **heel of the hand** the part of the palm nearest the wrist. **heels over head** *arch.* = ***head over heels*** s.v. HEAD *noun*. **his heels** *CRIBBAGE* a score of two points by a dealer turning up a jack. ***hot on the heels of***: see HOT *adjective*. **in the heel of the hunt** *Irish* at the last minute; finally. **kick one's heels** be kept waiting. **lay by the heels** fetter, arrest, confine; *fig.* overthrow, disgrace. ***neck and heels***: see NECK *noun*¹. **on one's heels**, **on the heels of** = *at one's heels* above. **out at heels** with shoes worn out at the heel; destitute, in trouble or distress. **run heel** = HEEL *verb*² 8. **set by the heels** = *lay by the heels* above. ***show a clean pair of heels***: see CLEAN *adjective*. **take to one's heels** run away. **to heel** of a dog: following closely and obediently. **turn on one's heel** turn sharply round. **under the heel**

H

of dominated by. **upon one's heels**, **upon the heels of** = *at one's heels, at the heels of* above.

– COMB.: **heelball** (*a*) a polishing mixture of hard wax and (usu. black) colouring used by shoemakers; (*b*) this or a similar composition used to make rubbings of monumental brasses etc.; **heel bar** a shop or stall where shoes are mended while the customer waits; **heel bone** the calcaneum; **heel bug** a harvest mite, *Trombicula autumnalis*; skin disease in horses due to this; **heel cup** a (usu. soft rubber) insert in a sports shoe to prevent or alleviate bruising of the heel; **heel grip** (*a*) a stud or cleat on the heel of a boot etc. to give footing on slippery ground; (*b*) (freq. adhesive) padding inside a shoe heel to prevent it slipping or chafing; **heel-lift** any of the layers of leather etc. which make up the heel of a shoe; **heel-piece** *noun & verb* (*a*) *noun* a piece attached to or forming the heel of anything, as a shoe, a ship's mast, etc.; *fig.* an end piece or conclusion; (*b*) *verb trans.* put a heel piece on (a shoe); **heel plate** (*a*) the plate on the butt end of a gun stock; (*b*) a metal plate protecting the heel of a shoe; (*c*) a plate to support the heel of a skating boot; **heel-post** (*a*) the post to which a door or gate is fixed; (*b*) SHIPBUILDING a post supporting the outer end of a propeller shaft; **heel-rope** a rope attached to the heel of anything, as a spar or rudder; a hobble for a horse etc.; **heeltap** (*a*) = *heel-lift* above; (*b*) liquor left in the bottom of a glass after drinking; **heel-tap** *verb* (*a*) *verb trans.* add a piece of leather etc. to a shoe heel; (*b*) *verb intrans.* delay, dawdle.

▪ **heelless** /-l-l-/ *adjective* having no heel; not using the heel: M19.

heel /hiːl/ *noun*[2]. M18.
[ORIGIN from HEEL *verb*[1].]
NAUTICAL. An act (on the part of a ship) of heeling or inclining to one side; a lurch; extent of this measured from the vertical.

heel /hiːl/ *noun*[3]. *slang* (orig. *US*). E20.
[ORIGIN Prob. from HEEL *noun*[1].]
An untrustworthy or despicable person.

> L. P. HARTLEY She's lost her fiancé . . he was a heel and she's well rid of him.

heel /hiːl/ *verb*[1]. L16.
[ORIGIN Prob. from HIELD *verb*, the *d* being taken as a pa. ppl suffix.]
1 *verb intrans.* Of a ship etc.: lean to one side; lean or fall *over*, capsize, topple. L16.

> G. K. CHESTERTON The whole tree heeled over like a ship, smashing everyone in its fall. *Motor Cruiser* The boat . . heels until the . . tube is immersed.

2 *verb trans.* Cause (a vessel) to incline thus. Formerly also, lay (a vessel) on its side for hull repairs etc. L16.

> E. K. KANE The Rescue was heeled over considerably by the floes.

heel /hiːl/ *verb*[2]. E17.
[ORIGIN from HEEL *noun*[1].]
1 *verb intrans.* & (*rare*) *trans.* Perform (a dance etc.) involving tapping the ground rhythmically with the heels. E17.
2 *verb trans.* **a** Provide (a shoe, sock, etc.) with a heel or heel piece. E17. ▸**b** Arm (a gamecock) with a gaff or spur; (*slang*, orig. *US*) provide (a person) with something, esp. a weapon. M18.
3 *verb trans.* Catch or tether by the heel; bind the heels of. M17.
4 *verb intrans.* SHIPBUILDING. Rest or be placed with the heel or lower end *on* something. M19.
5 **a** *verb trans.* Urge (a horse etc.) *on* with the heels. M19. ▸**b** *verb trans.* GOLF. Strike (the ball) with the heel of the club. M19.
6 *verb trans. & intrans.* RUGBY. Send (the ball) out at the back of the scrummage with the heel. L19.
7 **a** *verb intrans.* Of a dog: follow obediently at a person's heels. Freq. in *imper.* L19. ▸**b** *verb trans.* Of a dog: chase or drive (cattle etc.) by running or nipping at their heels. Foll. by *up*: nip the heels of. L19.
8 *verb intrans.* Of hounds: follow a scent in the direction from which the quarry has come. L19.

– PHRASES: **heel and toe** (*a*) touch the ground with the heel and toe alternately in dancing; (*b*) operate the accelerator and brake pedals of a motor vehicle with one foot simultaneously in contact with both.

▪ **heeling** *noun* (*a*) the action of the verb; (*b*) the heel piece of a stocking; the (square) lower end of a ship's mast: L16.

heel *verb*[3] see HELE *verb*.

heelaman *noun* var. of HIELAMAN.

heeled /hiːld/ *adjective*. M16.
[ORIGIN from HEEL *noun*[1] or *verb*[2]: see -ED[1], -ED[2].]
1 Having a heel or similar projection; having a (specified) kind of heel, as ***high-heeled***, ***stiletto-heeled***, etc. M16.
2 *slang* (orig. *US*). ▸**a** Provided, equipped; armed. M19. ▸**b** Provided with money. Usu. preceded by *well*. L19.

> **b** G. MCINNES Dr. Crapp was a prominent dentist . . . He was therefore obviously well heeled.

heeler /ˈhiːlə/ *noun*[1]. M17.
[ORIGIN from HEEL *verb*[2] or *noun*[1] + -ER[1].]
1 A person who puts heels on shoes. M17. ▸**b** A person who fits spurs to a fighting cock. M19.
2 A person who trips up, undermines, or supplants another. M17.
3 A gamecock that uses its spurs in fighting. L18.
4 A fast runner; one who shows a clean pair of heels. E19. ▸**b** A light, fast sailing ship. E20.

> A. B. PATERSON Some horses, real heelers . . Beat our nags and won our money.

5 A person who follows a leader; a (disreputable) follower of a politician. *US*. L19.

> H. G. WELLS The specialist demagogue, sustained by his gang and his heelers, his spies and secret police.

6 A working dog which urges animals on by nipping at their heels. Also, a nip on the heels. *Austral. & NZ*. L19.
blue heeler: see BLUE *adjective*.
7 RUGBY. A player who heels the ball out of the scrummage. L19.

heeler /ˈhiːlə/ *noun*[2]. *colloq.* L19.
[ORIGIN from HEEL *verb*[1] + -ER[1].]
A lurch (of a vessel) to one side; a vessel inclined to lurch.

heemraad /ˈhɪəmrɑːt, ˈheɪm-, -rɑːd/ *noun*. Also **H-**, **-rad**. Pl. **-den** /-d(ə)n/. L18.
[ORIGIN Dutch, from *heem* village, home + *raad* council.]
hist. A local court or council in South Africa and also formerly in the Netherlands. Also, a member of such a body.

heeze /hiːz/ *noun*. *Scot. & N. English*. Also **heize**. E16.
[ORIGIN from the verb.]
An act of hoisting or raising; a lift.
▪ Also **heezy** /ˈhiːzi/ *noun* E18.

heeze /hiːz/ *verb trans.* *Scot. & N. English*. Also **heize**. E16.
[ORIGIN Var. of HOISE *verb*.]
Hoist, raise; push or pull *up*.

HEFCE *abbreviation*.
Higher Education Funding Council for England.

HEFCS *abbreviation*.
Higher Education Funding Council for Scotland.

HEFCW *abbreviation*.
Higher Education Funding Council for Wales.

heffalump /ˈhɛfəlʌmp/ *noun*. E20.
[ORIGIN coined by A. A. Milne in the children's book *Winnie-the-Pooh*.]
A child's word for an elephant.

> A. A. MILNE He and Piglet had fallen into a heffalump trap. *Guardian* Hannibal's heffalumps can hardly have had any such protection against the weather.

heft /hɛft/ *noun*[1]. LME.
[ORIGIN Prob. from HEAVE *verb* on the analogy of *cleave/cleft*, *weave/weft*, etc.]
▸ **I** **1** Weight, heaviness. Now *dial. & N. Amer.* LME.

> H. ROTH He was more on the lean side than supplied with heft. *Scientific American* Go ahead, pick it up. The heft tells you it's solid sterling silver.

2 The bulk, mass, or main part. *N. Amer. colloq.* E19.

> J. PICKERING A part of the crop of corn was good, but the heft of it was bad.

▸ **II** †**3** A heave, a strain. *rare* (Shakes.). Only in E17.
4 The act of lifting; a lift, a push. *dial.* L19.

> R. D. BLACKMORE The . . parson . . gave the stuck wheel such a powerful heft, that the whole cart rattled.

heft /hɛft/ *noun*[2]. *Scot. & N. English*. Also **haft** /hɑːft/. M18.
[ORIGIN Rel. to HEFT *verb*[1].]
1 A fixed place of residence. Now *rare* or *obsolete*. M18.
2 (The sheep in) a settled or accustomed pasturage. L18.

Heft /hɛft/ *noun*[3]. Pl. ***Hefte*** /ˈhɛftə/. L19.
[ORIGIN German.]
A number of sheets of paper fastened together to form a book; *spec.* a part of a serial publication, a fascicle.

heft *noun*[4] see HAFT *noun*[1].

heft /hɛft/ *verb*[1]. *Scot. & N. English*. Also **haft** /hɑːft/. L16.
[ORIGIN Prob. of Scandinavian origin (cf. Old Norse *hefða* gain possession by long occupation), infl. by HAFT *noun*[1], *verb*[1].]
1 *verb trans.* Fix, establish, settle; now chiefly *spec.*, accustom (sheep, cattle) to a pasturage. L16.
2 *verb intrans.* Become established; (of sheep, cattle) become accustomed to a pasturage. E18.

heft /hɛft/ *verb*[2]. M17.
[ORIGIN from HEFT *noun*[1].]
1 *verb trans.* Lift, hoist up; pick up and carry. M17.

> N. BAWDEN I develop . . lumbago from hefting my baggage at airports. P. CAREY He hefted the sledgehammer on to his shoulder.

2 *verb trans.* Lift or hold in order to feel the weight or balance of. E19.

> R. MACDONALD I lifted one of the pistols and hefted it in my hand. It was so light and so well balanced.

3 *verb intrans.* Weigh, have weight. M19.

> C. M. YONGE I do believe it is [gold]. Brass never would heft so much.

heft *verb*[3] see HAFT *verb*[1].

Hefte *noun* pl. of HEFT *noun*[3].

hefty /ˈhɛfti/ *adjective*. *colloq.* M19.
[ORIGIN from HEFT *noun*[1] + -Y[1].]
1 Weighty, heavy; brawny, strong. Also *fig.*, great, considerable. M19.

> P. H. GIBBS A . . hefty man who . . might have been a professional pugilist. A. MACLEAN A hefty tot of rum all round. *TV Times* One of these entitles you to some hefty reductions on the trains.

2 Rough, violent. *US & dial.* L19.
3 Easy to lift or handle. *rare*. L19.
▪ **heftily** *adverb* L20. **heftiness** *noun* E20.

hegberry *noun* var. of HAGBERRY.

Hegelian /heɪˈgiːlɪən, hɪ-, -ˈgeɪl-/ *adjective & noun*. M19.
[ORIGIN from *Hegel* (see below) + -IAN.]
▸ **A** *adjective*. Of or pertaining to Georg Hegel, German philosopher (1770–1831), or his philosophy of objective idealism. M19.
▸ **B** *noun*. A person who believes in or advocates Hegel's philosophy. M19.
▪ **Hegelianism** *noun* the philosophical system of Hegel M19. **Hegelianize** *verb trans.* make Hegelian L19. **Hegelism** /ˈheɪg(ə)lɪz(ə)m/ *noun* Hegelianism M19.

hegemon /ˈhɛgɪmɒn, ˈhiː-, -dʒɪ-/ *noun*. E20.
[ORIGIN Greek *hēgemōn* leader, from *hēgeisthai* to lead.]
A leading or paramount power; a dominant state or person.

> *Public Opinion* Japan . . asserting her ambition to become hegemon of a Far East on which white influence shall be reduced. *Observer* Peace talks crucial to Peking's plans to contain the 'hegemons' in the Kremlin almost stalled.

hegemonic /hɛdʒɪˈmɒnɪk, hɛgɪ-/ *adjective & noun*. M17.
[ORIGIN Greek *hēgemonikos* capable of command, from *hēgemōn*: see HEGEMON, -IC.]
▸ **A** *adjective*. Ruling, supreme, dominant. M17.
▸ **B** *noun*. The supreme part; the master principle. L17.
▪ Also **hegemonical** *adjective* = HEGEMONIC *adjective* E17.

hegemony /hɪˈdʒɛməni, -ˈgɛ-/ *noun*. M16.
[ORIGIN Greek *hēgemonia*, from *hēgemōn*: see HEGEMON, -MONY.]
1 Leadership or predominance, esp. by one member of a confederacy or union (orig. of the states of ancient Greece); a state etc. having this. M16.

> H. H. ASQUITH Attempting . . to secure for the Papal State the political hegemony of Italy. A. BRIGGS A new working-class hegemony, . . an attempt to build a paradise for the poor.

2 Dominance or undue influence exercised by a country (*spec.* the former USSR) over its weaker neighbour(s). L20.

> *Daily Telegraph* In Third World terms 'hegemony' has come generally to mean Soviet domination.

▪ **hegemonist** *noun* an advocate of a particular form of hegemony L19.

hegira /ˈhɛdʒɪrə/ *noun*. Also **H-**, **-jira**, **hijra** /ˈhɪdʒrə/. L16.
[ORIGIN medieval Latin from Arabic *hijra* departure from one's home and friends, from *hajara* separate, emigrate.]
1 The emigration of Muhammad from Mecca to Medina in 622; the Muslim era reckoned from this. L16.
2 Any exodus or departure. M18.

hegumen /hɪˈgjuːmən/ *noun*. Also **-nos** /-nɒs/. M17.
[ORIGIN (Late Latin *hegumenus* from) Greek *hēgoumenos*, use as noun of pres. pple of *hēgeisthai* lead, command.]
In the Greek Orthodox Church, the head of a religious house, corresponding to an abbot or prior; the leader of any religious community.

heh /heɪ/ *interjection*. LME.
[ORIGIN Natural exclam. Cf. HE *interjection*, HEIGH.]
Expr. emotion, inquiry, or surprise.

he he /hiː ˈhiː/ *interjection & verb*. As verb also **he-he**. OE.
[ORIGIN Redupl. of HE *interjection*.]
▸ **A** *interjection*. Also **he he he** etc. Repr. laughter, usu. affected or derisive. OE.
▸ **B** *verb intrans.* Laugh aloud (affectedly or derisively). M19.

†**hei** *interjection & noun* see HEIGH.

Heian /ˈheɪən/ *adjective*. L19.
[ORIGIN Japanese, from *Heian*-kyō (now Kyoto), former capital of Japan.]
Of, pertaining to, or designating a period in Japanese history from the late 8th to the late 12th cent.

heiau /ˈheɪaʊ/ *noun*. E19.
[ORIGIN Hawaiian.]
An ancient pagan temple (in Hawaii).

Heidelberg /ˈhʌɪd(ə)lbəːg/ *noun*. E20.
[ORIGIN A city in SW Germany.]
Used *attrib.* to designate a prehistoric jaw found at Mauer near Heidelberg in 1907, or the type of prehistoric human (*Homo heidelbergensis*) indicated by this jaw.

heifer /ˈhɛfə/ *noun*.
[ORIGIN Old English *heahfore*, *heafru*, *-fre*, of unknown origin.]
1 A young cow that has had no more than one calf; a female calf. OE.
2 **a** A wife. Now *rare* or *obsolete*. E17. ▸**b** A woman, a girl. *slang. derog.* M19.

heigh /heɪ/ *interjection & noun*. Also (earlier) †**hei**. ME.
[ORIGIN Natural exclam. Cf. HE *interjection*, HEH, HEY *interjection & noun*[2].]
▸ **A** *interjection*. Expr. encouragement or inquiry. Formerly also, expr. challenge, anger, derision, or concern. ME.

J. WESLEY Now, heigh for the Romans!

▸ **B** *noun*. An exclamation of *heigh!* L16.

heigh-ho /heɪˈhəʊ/ *interjection, noun, & verb*. Also (earlier) **hey-**. LME.
[ORIGIN from HEIGH, HEY *interjections* + HO *interjection*[1].]
▸ **A** *interjection*. Expr. boredom, weariness, disappointment, etc. Also (orig.), a meaningless refrain. LME.

D. CUSACK Heigho, it's a damn silly world. *Sunday Express* Two more butlers welcomed us aboard . . Heigh ho.

▸ **B** *noun*. An utterance of 'heigh-ho!'; a loud or audible sigh. L16.
▸ **C** *verb intrans*. Utter 'heigh-ho!'; sigh audibly. E19.

height /hʌɪt/ *noun*. Also †**-th**.
[ORIGIN Old English *hēhþu*, (West Saxon) *hīehþu* = Middle Dutch *hogede*, *hoochte* (Dutch *hoogte*), Old High German *hōhida*, Gothic *hauhiþa* from Germanic. Cf. HIGH *adjective*, -TH[1], -T[2].]
▸ **I 1** The highest part *of* anything; the top, summit. Now *rare*. OE.
2 The highest point of something abstract; the extremity, summit, zenith. OE.

D. BAGLEY The hurricane reached its height at eleven in the morning. M. SEYMOUR-SMITH He was now at the height of his fame. E. P. THOMPSON The price of wheat reached impossible heights.

3 The heavens. *obsolete* exc. *Scot*. OE.
4 A piece of high or rising ground; an eminence. LME.

M. MILNER The grey cliff bordering the valley . . that slopes down from the city's heights.

5 A high point or position. M16.

F. WELDON Mr. Allbright added golden syrup from a height, for the delight of seeing it fall.

▸ **II 6** Distance or measurement from the base to the top; altitude; stature (of a person); the elevation of an object above the ground or a recognized level, esp. sea level. ME. ▸**b** ASTRONOMY. Angular distance above the horizon; = ALTITUDE 1. Long *rare*. LME. ▸**c** TYPOGRAPHY. The distance from the foot of a piece of type to its face. Also *height to paper*. L17.

A. PATON The maize hardly reaches the height of a man. *fig*.: MILTON To attaine The highth and depth of thy Eternal wayes.

7 Great or considerable altitude or elevation. Now *rare*. ME.
†**8** Exalted rank or estate. ME–E18.
9 Haughtiness, pride. Also, loftiness of mind, magnanimity. *arch*. ME.

O. CROMWELL A very resolute answer, and full of height.

†**10** The diameter of a bullet; the bore of a gun. L16–L17.
†**11 a** GEOGRAPHY. = LATITUDE. L16–L17. ▸**b** More gen., position at sea alongside of or *off* some place. E17–M18.
12 High degree of any quality. *arch*. E17.

T. STANLEY Heighth of ambition causeth many men to go astray.

13 HERALDRY. Each of the rows of feathers into which a plume of more than one row of feathers is arranged. M19.
– PHRASES: **at its height** at its highest degree. *head for heights*: see HEAD *noun*. **height of land** *N. Amer*. a watershed, a ridge of high land dividing two river basins. *height to paper*: see sense 6c above. †**in height** (*rare*, Shakes.) = *at its height* above. †**in the height** (*rare*, Shakes.) in the highest degree. †**on height** (*a*) on high, aloft; (*b*) aloud. **the height of** the utmost degree of (fashion, folly, luxury, etc.). **to the height** (*obsolete* exc. *literary*) to the highest or utmost degree. †**upon height** = *on height* above. VIRTUAL *height*. *x-height*: see X, X 1.

height /hʌɪt/ *verb trans*. Now *rare* exc. *Scot*. LME.
[ORIGIN from the noun.]
1 Raise in amount, degree, quality, etc.; increase, augment; elevate, exalt. LME.
2 Make high, heighten; raise aloft or on high. L15.

heighten /ˈhʌɪt(ə)n/ *verb*. LME.
[ORIGIN from HEIGHT *noun* or *verb* + -EN[5].]
†**1** *verb trans*. Exalt; elate, excite; beautify. LME–L17.
2 *verb trans*. Make high or higher; give or add height to; *fig*. increase or augment in amount or degree. E16. ▸**b** *spec*. Make (a colour) more luminous or more intense. L16. ▸**c** Strengthen or augment the details of (a description, a story). M18.

E. A. FREEMAN That church . . had been simply repaired and heightened. M. M. KAYE The severity of the headgear only served to heighten the beauty of her features. D. WIGODER The atmosphere of suspicion . . was heightened by the theft. **b** J. GALSWORTHY His pleasant colour was heightened by exercise. J. BARNES A pen-and-ink drawing . . in sepia, heightened with white.

3 *verb intrans*. Become high or higher; increase in height. Now chiefly *fig*. increase in amount or intensity. M16.

E. B. PUSEY Obadiah's description heightens as it goes on.

■ **heightened** *ppl adjective* (*a*) raised, intensified, increased; (*b*) *spec*. (in HERALDRY) having another charge placed higher in the field: M17. **heightener** *noun* M17. **heightening** *noun* (*a*) the action of the verb; (*b*) a colouring which highlights or intensifies another colour: L16.

†**heighth** *noun* var. of HEIGHT *noun*.

heightism /ˈhʌɪtɪz(ə)m/ *noun*. L20.
[ORIGIN from HEIGHT + -ISM.]
Prejudice or discrimination against someone on the basis of his or her height.
■ **heightist** *noun & adjective*. L20.

heil /hʌɪl/ *interjection, noun, & verb*. E20.
[ORIGIN German, lit. 'well-being'.]
▸ **A** *interjection*. Used as an exclamation of greeting, salutation, or acclamation, esp. during or with ref. to the Nazi regime in Germany. E20.
heil Hitler! used by the Germans or their supporters during the Nazi regime as a greeting or an acclamation of the supremacy of Hitler.
▸ **B** *noun*. An exclamation of 'heil!' M20.
▸ **C** *verb*. **1** *verb intrans*. Make a Nazi salute. M20.
2 *verb trans*. Greet or hail esp. with a Nazi salute. M20.

Heilsgeschichte /ˈhaɪlsgəʃɪçtə/ *noun*. M20.
[ORIGIN German.]
THEOLOGY. Sacred history; *spec*. the history of the salvation of humankind by God; history seen as the working out of this salvation.

heimin /ˈheɪmɪn/ *noun*. L19.
[ORIGIN Japanese, from *hei* level, ordinary, common + *min* people.]
In Japanese feudal society, the common people, including peasants and traders, as opp. to the court aristocracy and samurai.

heimisch /ˈheɪmɪʃ/ *adjective*. M20.
[ORIGIN Yiddish *heymish* domestic, homelike.]
In Jewish speech: homely, unpretentious.

Heimlich manoeuvre /ˈhʌɪmlɪç məˈnuːvə/ *noun phr*. L20.
[ORIGIN Named after Henry J. *Heimlich* (b. 1920), US doctor, who developed the procedure.]
A first-aid procedure for dislodging an obstruction from a person's windpipe, in which a sudden strong pressure is applied on the abdomen between the navel and the ribcage.

Heimweh /ˈhaɪmveː/ *noun*. E18.
[ORIGIN German.]
Homesickness.

Heimwehr /ˈhaɪmveːr/ *noun*. M20.
[ORIGIN German, from *Heim* home + *Wehr* defence.]
hist. The German or Austrian Home Defence Force which existed between 1919 and 1938.

Heinie /ˈhʌɪni/ *noun*[1]. *N. Amer. slang*. Also **Hiney**. E20.
[ORIGIN from the German male name *Heinrich*.]
A German, a German soldier.

heinie /ˈhʌɪni/ *noun*[2]. *US colloq*. M20.
[ORIGIN Alt. of BEHIND *noun*.]
A person's buttocks.

heinous /ˈheɪnəs, ˈhiːnəs/ *adjective*. LME.
[ORIGIN Old French *haïneus* (mod. *haineux*), from *haïne* (mod. *haine*) from Old French & mod. French *haïr* from Frankish, rel. to HATE *verb*: see -OUS.]
1 Of a crime, an offence, or its perpetrator: highly criminal or wicked, utterly odious or atrocious. LME. ▸**b** *transf*. Of an accusation or charge: relating to a highly wicked person or deed. LME.

R. JEBB Heinous offenders, whose crimes afford proof of an incorrigibly bad disposition. E. HUXLEY To refuse a stranger . . food and shelter is a heinous crime.

†**2** Of words, feelings, etc.: full of hate, expressing hatred. LME–L16.
†**3** Grievous, grave, severe. M16–L17.
■ **heinously** *adverb* LME. **heinousness** *noun* M16.

heir /ɛː/ *noun*. ME.
[ORIGIN Old French *eir*, *heir* (later *hoir*) from arch. and late Latin *herem* for reg. *heredem*, accus. of *heres* heir.]
1 A person receiving or entitled by law to receive property or rank as the successor or legal representative of the former owner. ME.

J. BERGER On 2 June 1914 Francis Ferdinand, heir to the Hapsburg throne, was shot dead. R. DAVIES He never married & leaves no direct heirs.

2 *transf*. & *fig*. A person possessing or entitled to possess any gift or quality, orig. in succession to another. Now usu., a person to whom something, such as joy, punishment, etc., is morally due. ME.

J. GILBERT The first born of the human race became the heir of failure.

†**3** *fig*. An offspring, product. LME–L16.
– PHRASES & COMB.: *expectant heir*: see EXPECTANT *adjective*. *heir apparent*: see APPARENT *adjective* 2. **heir-at-law** a person who succeeds by right of blood; *esp*. (in English Law before 1926 and Scots Law before 1965) a person who succeeds in this way to an intestate's real property. **heir designate** a person who has been designated another's heir. **heir female** an heiress or an heir (male or female) whose rights are derived completely through the female line. **heir-general** an heir-at-law, *spec*. one who can be an heir female as distinct from exclusively an heir male. **heir in tail** a person who succeeds to an entailed estate by virtue of the deed of entail. **heir male** a male heir whose rights are derived completely through the male line. **heir of one's body**, **heir of the body** an heir who is a direct descendant. *heir-portioner*: see PORTIONER 1. *heir presumptive*: see PRESUMPTIVE 1.

■ **heirdom** *noun* succession by right of blood; the state or dignity of an heir; an inheritance: L16. **heirless** *adjective* without an heir LME. **heirship** *noun* the state, condition, or rights of an heir; right of inheritance: LME.

heir /ɛː/ *verb trans*. ME.
[ORIGIN from the noun.]
Inherit; be or make heir to; acquire by inheritance or succession.

heiress /ˈɛːrɪs, ɛːˈrɛs/ *noun*. M17.
[ORIGIN from HEIR *noun* + -ESS[1].]
A female heir.

B. T. BRADFORD Paula, Daisy's daughter, was . . heiress to her enormous retailing empire.

■ **heiress-ship** *noun* the state or position of an heiress M19.

heirloom /ˈɛːluːm/ *noun*. LME.
[ORIGIN from HEIR *noun* + LOOM *noun*[1].]
A chattel which under a will or by custom is inherited by an heir in the same way as real estate. Also, any piece of personal property or any quality, name, etc., which has been in a family for generations.

R. B. SHERIDAN Learning that had run in the family like an heir-loom! H. I. JENKINSON A glass cup . . a precious heirloom, and a harbinger of the family's fortunes.

heirmos *noun* var. of HIRMOS.

Heisenberg /ˈhʌɪz(ə)nbəːg/ *noun*. M20.
[ORIGIN Werner *Heisenberg* (1901–76), German physicist.]
PHYSICS. ***Heisenberg principle***, ***Heisenberg uncertainty principle***, ***Heisenberg's principle***, ***Heisenberg's uncertainty principle***, = UNCERTAINTY *principle*.

heist /hʌɪst/ *verb & noun*. *slang*. Chiefly *N. Amer*. M19.
[ORIGIN Repr. US local pronunc. of HOIST *verb*[1] or *noun*. Cf. HIST *verb*[2].]
▸ **A** *verb trans*. Rob, hold up; steal. M19.
▸ **B** *noun*. A hold-up, a robbery. M20.

Superman We pulled off a heist in Smallville and got away with it!

■ **heister** *noun* a robber, a thief, a hijacker E20.

heit *noun* var. of HAIT.

heitiki /heɪˈtɪki/ *noun*. *NZ*. M19.
[ORIGIN Maori, from *hei* hang + TIKI.]
A Maori greenstone neck ornament shaped like a human figure.

heize *noun*, *verb* vars. of HEEZE *noun*, *verb*.

hejira *noun* var. of HEGIRA.

hekistotherm /hɪˈkɪstəθəːm/ *noun*. L19.
[ORIGIN French *hékistotherme*, from Greek *hēkisto-s* least + *thermē* heat.]
BOTANY. A plant capable of growing at very low temperatures, such as the Arctic and Antarctic mosses and lichens.

hekte /ˈhɛkti/ *noun*. Pl. **-tae** /-tiː/. L19.
[ORIGIN Greek *hektē* the sixth (of a stater), fem. of *hektos* sixth.]
A Greek silver coin.

HeLa /ˈhiːlə/ *noun*. M20.
[ORIGIN from *Henrietta Lacks*, patient from whom the orig. tissue was taken.]
MEDICINE. (In full ***HeLa strain***) a strain of human epithelial cells maintained in tissue culture and derived orig. from cervical carcinoma tissue; ***HeLa cell***, a cell of this strain.

hélas /elɑːs/ *interjection*. LME.
[ORIGIN French, later form of *ha las*, *a las* ALAS.]
Expressing grief, sadness, regret, etc.
– NOTE: Formerly naturalized, but now only in representations or affectations of French.

held /hɛld/ *ppl adjective*. L16.
[ORIGIN pa. pple of HOLD *verb*.]
That is or has been held; (of breath) kept in; (of a note) sustained.

held *verb pa. t. & pple* of HOLD *verb*.

Heldentenor /ˌhɛldənteˈnoːr/ *noun*. Pl. **-tenöre** /-teˈnøːrə/. E20.
[ORIGIN German = hero tenor.]
A singer with a powerful tenor voice suited to heroic roles, esp. in Wagnerian opera.

†**hele** *noun* var. of HEAL *noun*.

hele /hiːl/ *verb*. Also **heal**, (now usual in sense 2(a)) **heel**.
[ORIGIN Old English *helian* = Old Saxon *bihellian*, Old High German *bihellen*, from West Germanic causative verb from Germanic base meaning 'conceal', rel. to Latin *celare*, Greek *kaluptein*.]
1 Conceal, hide; keep secret. *obsolete* exc. *Scot*. OE.
2 Cover over or in; *spec*. (*a*) (esp. foll. by *in*) cover (roots, seeds, etc.) with earth; (*b*) cover with slates or tiles, roof. ME.
■ **heling** *noun* (*a*) the action of the verb; (*b*) a covering; *esp*. (the materials of) a roof: ME.

helenium /hɛˈliːnɪəm/ *noun*. LME.
[ORIGIN mod. Latin (see below), from Greek *helenion*, perh. commemorating Helen of Troy.]
†**1** The herb elecampane, *Inula helenium*. LME–E17.

H

2 Any of various N. American plants of the genus *Helenium*, of the composite family, freq. grown for their yellow- or orange-rayed flowers. L18.

heli- /ˈhɛli/ *combining form* of HELI(COPTER *noun*.
■ **heliborne** *adjective* carried by helicopter M20. **helibus** *noun* a helicopter with room for a large number of passengers M20. **helipad** *noun* a landing pad for helicopters M20. **heliport** *noun* an airport or landing place for helicopters M20. **heli-skiing** *noun* skiing in which the skier is taken up the mountain by helicopter L20.

heliac /ˈhiːlɪak/ *adjective*. L18.
[ORIGIN Late Latin *heliacus* from Greek *hēliakos*, from *hēlios* sun: see -AC.]
= HELIACAL.

heliacal /hɪˈlʌɪək(ə)l/ *adjective*. M16.
[ORIGIN from medieval Latin *heliacus* (from Greek *hēliakos*, from *hēlios* sun) + -AL¹.]
Relating to the sun. Chiefly, in ancient astronomy: ***heliacal rising***, the first rising of a star after a period of invisibility due to conjunction with the sun (in a given year); ***heliacal setting***, the last setting of a star before a period of invisibility due to conjunction with the sun.
■ **heliacally** *adverb* M16.

helianthemum /hiːlɪˈanθɪməm/ *noun*. E19.
[ORIGIN mod. Latin (see below), from Greek *hēlios* sun + *anthemon* flower.]
Any of various chiefly Mediterranean shrubs and herbs constituting the genus *Helianthemum* (family Cistaceae), which includes the common rock rose, *H. nummularium*.

H

helianthus /hiːlɪˈanθəs/ *noun*. L18.
[ORIGIN mod. Latin, from Greek *hēlios* sun + *anthos* flower.]
Any of various plants constituting the genus *Helianthus*, of the composite family, which includes the common sunflower, *H. annuus*.

helical /ˈhɛlɪk(ə)l, ˈhiː-/ *adjective*. L16.
[ORIGIN from Latin HELIX + -AL¹.]
Having the form of a helix; spirally coiled.
■ **helically** *adverb* M17.

helices *noun pl.* see HELIX.

helichrysum /hɛlɪˈkrʌɪsəm/ *noun*. Also (now only ART etc.) **-son** /-sɒn/, **-sos** /-sɒs/. M16.
[ORIGIN Latin (see below), also *helichrysos*, from Greek *helikhrusos*, from HELIX + *khrusos* gold.]
1 A yellow-flowered Mediterranean plant known to the ancient Greeks, perhaps the helichrysum (sense 2) *Helichrysum stoechas*. M16.
2 Any of various plants with persistent flower heads (everlastings) constituting the genus *Helichrysum*, of the composite family, and found esp. in Australia and southern Africa. M17.

helicity /hiːˈlɪsɪti/ *noun*. M20.
[ORIGIN from Latin *helic-* HELIX + -ITY.]
1 PHYSICS. The projection of the spin angular momentum of a subatomic particle on the direction of its linear momentum. M20.
2 Chiefly BIOCHEMISTRY. Helical character. M20.

helicobacter /ˈhɛlɪkə(ʊ)baktə/ *noun*. L20.
[ORIGIN mod. Latin (see below), formed as HELICOGRAPH + BACTER(IUM.]
A bacterium of the genus *Helicobacter*, which causes chronic gastritis and peptic ulcer disease in humans.

helicograph /ˈhɛlɪkə(ʊ)grɑːf/ *noun*. M19.
[ORIGIN from Latin *helic-* HELIX + -O- + -GRAPH.]
An instrument for drawing spirals.

helicoid /ˈhɛlɪkɔɪd, ˈhiː-/ *noun & adjective*. L17.
[ORIGIN Greek *helikoeidēs*, from HELIX: see -OID.]
▸ **A** *noun*. **1** An object of spiral shape. *rare*. L17.
2 GEOMETRY. A surface generated by moving a straight line in the direction of an axis about which it simultaneously rotates. M19.
▸ **B** *adjective*. Esp. of a shell, inflorescence, etc.: having the form of a helix; spirally coiled. E18.
†**helicoid parabola** = ***parabolic spiral*** s.v. PARABOLIC *adjective* 2.
■ **heliˈcoidal** *adjective* = HELICOID *adjective* M19. **heliˈcoidally** *adverb* M20.

Helicon /ˈhɛlɪk(ə)n/ *noun*. L15.
[ORIGIN Latin from Greek *Helikōn* a mountain in Boeotia, Greece, formerly sacred to the Muses, often confused by 16th- and 17th-cent. writers with the springs of Aganippe and Hippocrene which rose in it. In sense 2 assoc. with HELIX.]
1 A source, region, etc. of poetic inspiration. L15.
Bookman Any question of his precise place in England's Helicon.
2 (**h-**.) A large kind of bass tuba made in spiral form. L19.
■ **Heliconian** /-ˈkəʊnɪən/ *adjective* of Helicon or the Muses M16.

helicopter /ˈhɛlɪkɒptə/ *noun & verb*. L19.
[ORIGIN French *hélicoptère*, from Greek HELIX + *pteron* wing.]
▸ **A** *noun*. An aircraft deriving both lift and propulsive power from horizontally revolving, usu. engine-driven, blades or rotors and capable of ascending and descending vertically. L19.
▸ **B** *verb trans. & intrans.* Transport or fly by helicopter. E20.
– COMB.: **helicopter view** *colloq.* (esp. in business) a general survey, an overview.

helictite /hɛˈlɪktʌɪt/ *noun*. L19.
[ORIGIN from Greek *heliktos* twisted, after *stalactite*.]
A distorted form of stalactite resembling a twig.

Heligoland trap /ˈhɛlɪgə(ʊ)land trap/ *noun phr.* M20.
[ORIGIN *Heligoland*, an island in the North Sea off the NW German coast, site of the earliest bird observatory.]
A long funnel-shaped enclosure of wire netting into which birds are driven for ringing.

helio /ˈhiːlɪəʊ/ *noun*¹ *& verb*. *colloq.* L19.
[ORIGIN Abbreviation.]
▸ **A** *noun*. Pl. **-os**. = HELIOGRAPH *noun* 4, 4b. L19.
▸ **B** *verb intrans. & trans.* = HELIOGRAPH *verb* 1. L19.

helio /ˈhiːlɪəʊ/ *noun*² *& adjective*. *colloq.* L19.
[ORIGIN Abbreviation.]
(Of) the colour heliotrope.

helio- /ˈhiːlɪəʊ/ *combining form* of Greek *hēlios* sun: see -O-.
■ **heliopause** *noun* (ASTRONOMY) the boundary which separates the heliosphere from outer space beyond the solar system L20. **helioseisˈmology** *noun* (ASTRONOMY) the study of the sun's interior by the observation and analysis of oscillations at its surface L20.

heliocentric /ˌhiːlɪə(ʊ)ˈsɛntrɪk/ *noun & adjective*. M17.
[ORIGIN from HELIO- + -CENTRIC.]
▸ †**A** *noun*. A person who believes that the sun is the centre of the universe. Only in M17.
▸ **B** *adjective*. **1** Considered as viewed from the centre of the sun; referred to the sun as centre. L17.
heliocentric latitude, **heliocentric longitude**: at which a planet etc. would appear if observed from the position of an observer at the sun's centre.
2 Having or representing the sun as the centre. Freq. opp. ***geocentric***. M19.
■ **heliocentrically** *adverb* as viewed from the centre of the sun E18. **heliocentricism** /-sɪz(ə)m/ *noun* a heliocentric theory of the universe M19.

heliodon /ˈhiːlɪədɒn/ *noun*. E20.
[ORIGIN from HELIO- + Greek *hodos* way, path.]
A mechanical apparatus for demonstrating the apparent motion of the sun.

heliodor /ˈhiːlɪədɔː/ *noun*. Also **-dore**. E20.
[ORIGIN German, from HELIO- + Greek *dōron* gift.]
A golden-yellow variety of beryl found in Namibia.

Heliogabalus /ˌhiːlɪəˈgab(ə)ləs/ *noun*. L16.
[ORIGIN Alt. of *Elagabalus* (from *Elah-Gabal* Syrian deity), the name assumed by Varius Avitus Bassianus, Roman Emperor 218–222, with assim. to HELIO-.]
A person resembling the emperor Elagabalus (Heliogabalus) in dissoluteness or moral depravity.
■ **Heliogabalian** /-gəˈbeɪlɪən/ *adjective* pertaining to or characteristic of Heliogabalus; highly dissolute: M19.

heliogram /ˈhiːlɪə(ʊ)gram/ *noun*. L19.
[ORIGIN from HELIO- + -GRAM.]
A message signalled by heliograph (HELIOGRAPH *noun* 4).

heliograph /ˈhiːlɪə(ʊ)grɑːf/ *noun & verb*. M19.
[ORIGIN from HELIO- + -GRAPH.]
▸ **A** *noun*. **1** A photograph or engraving made by heliography (sense 2). *obsolete* exc. *hist.* M19.
2 A photographic telescope for photographing the sun. M19.
3 An instrument for measuring the intensity of sunlight. M19.
4 An apparatus for signalling by means of a movable mirror which reflects flashes of sunshine. L19. ▸**b** A message sent by heliograph. L19.
▸ **B** *verb*. **1** *verb intrans. & trans.* Signal by means of a heliograph. L19.
2 *verb trans.* Photograph by heliography. *obsolete* exc. *hist.* L19.
■ **heliˈographer** *noun* L19.

heliography /hiːlɪˈɒgrəfi/ *noun*. M18.
[ORIGIN from HELIO- + -GRAPHY.]
1 (A) description of the sun. M18.
2 An early photographic process using iodine-sensitized silver plate and an asphalt or bitumen varnish. *obsolete* exc. *hist.* M19.
3 Signalling by means of a heliograph (HELIOGRAPH *noun* 4). L19.
■ **helioˈgraphic** *adjective* pertaining to heliography; ***heliographic latitude***, ***heliographic longitude***, the latitude, longitude, of points on the sun's surface, referred to the sun's equator and a meridian passing through the node of this with the ecliptic: E18. **helioˈgraphically** *adverb* by means of heliography L19.

†**heliogravure** *noun*. Only in L19.
[ORIGIN French *héliogravure*, formed as HELIO- + *gravure* engraving.]
= PHOTOGRAVURE.

Heliolithic /ˌhiːlɪəˈlɪθɪk/ *adjective*. *obsolete* exc. *hist.* E20.
[ORIGIN from HELIO- after *eolithic* etc.]
Of a (supposed) civilization: marked by megaliths and sun worship.

heliometer /hiːlɪˈɒmɪtə/ *noun*. M18.
[ORIGIN from HELIO- + -METER.]
ASTRONOMY. A refracting telescope with a split objective lens, used to measure angular distances between stars etc. (orig. to measure the sun's apparent diameter).
■ **helioˈmetric**, **helioˈmetrical** *adjectives* L19. **helioˈmetrically** *adverb* L19. **heliometry** *noun* L19.

helion /ˈhiːlɪɒn/ *noun*. M20.
[ORIGIN from HELIUM + -ON.]
NUCLEAR PHYSICS. The nucleus of a helium atom, (***a***) of the normal isotope ^{4}He, an alpha particle, consisting of two protons and two neutrons, (***b***) of the isotope ^{3}He, consisting of two protons and one neutron.

helioscope /ˈhiːlɪəskəʊp/ *noun*. L17.
[ORIGIN from HELIO- + -SCOPE.]
(A telescope fitted with) an apparatus for observing the sun without harm to the eyes, by means of smoked glass, reflectors, etc.
■ **helioˈscopic** *adjective* L19.

heliosphere /ˈhiːlɪəsfɪə/ *noun*. M20.
[ORIGIN from HELIO- + SPHERE *noun*.]
ASTRONOMY. The region of space, encompassing the solar system, in which the solar wind has a significant influence.
■ **helioˈspheric** *adjective* L20.

heliostat /ˈhiːlɪəstat/ *noun*. M18.
[ORIGIN mod. Latin *heliostata* or French *héliostat*, from HELIO- + Greek *statos* standing.]
An apparatus containing a movable mirror, used to reflect the sun's light in a fixed direction.

heliotherapy /ˌhiːlɪə(ʊ)ˈθɛrəpi/ *noun*. E20.
[ORIGIN from HELIO- + THERAPY.]
The use of sunbaths as a therapeutic treatment.

heliotrope /ˈhiːlɪətrəʊp, ˈhɛl-/ *noun & adjective*. Also (earlier) †**eliotropus** and other classical forms. OE.
[ORIGIN Latin *heliotropium*, medieval Latin also *eliotropus*, *-ius*, etc., from Greek *hēliotropion*, from *hēlios* sun + *-tropos* turning, *trepein* to turn.]
▸ **A** *noun*. **1** Orig., any of several plants whose flowers turn towards the sun, e.g. the sunflower, the marigold. Now, any plant of the genus *Heliotropium*, of the borage family, with cymes of small blue, purple, or white flowers; esp. *H. arborescens*, a S. American shrub grown for its fragrant flowers. OE. ▸**b** A scent imitating that of the heliotrope. M19. ▸**c** A bluish-purple colour like that of the heliotrope. L19.
winter heliotrope: see WINTER *noun*.
2 A green variety of chalcedony with veins of red jasper; bloodstone. LME.
3 An ancient kind of sundial, showing when the sun had reached the solstice. M17.
4 An apparatus with a telescope and a movable mirror for reflecting the sun's rays, used for signalling, esp. in geodesic operations. Cf. HELIOGRAPH *noun* 4. E19.
▸ **B** *adjective*. Of a heliotrope colour: see sense 1c above. L19.
■ **heliotroper** *noun* a person who operates a heliotrope (HELIOTROPE *noun* 4) M19.

heliotropic /ˌhiːlɪə(ʊ)ˈtrəʊpɪk, -ˈtrɒpɪk/ *adjective*. L19.
[ORIGIN from HELIOTROPISM + -IC.]
BOTANY. Exhibiting heliotropism; growing towards the light.
■ **heliotropically** *adverb* L19.

heliotropin /ˌhiːlɪəˈtrəʊpɪn/ *noun*. L19.
[ORIGIN from HELIOTROPIC + -IN¹.]
= PIPERONAL.

heliotropism /ˌhiːlɪə(ʊ)ˈtrəʊpɪz(ə)m/ *noun*. M19.
[ORIGIN from HELIO- + Greek *-tropos* turning + -ISM.]
BOTANY. The property of growing in a given direction in response to sunlight; *esp.* (in full ***positive heliotropism***) growth towards the light. Also ***negative heliotropism***, growth away from the light; ***transverse heliotropism***, growth in a direction at right angles to the light.

heliotype /ˈhiːlɪətʌɪp/ *noun*. L19.
[ORIGIN from HELIO- + -TYPE.]
hist. (A print made by) a variety of the collotype process.

heliozoan /ˌhiːlɪəˈzəʊən/ *noun & adjective*. L19.
[ORIGIN from mod. Latin *Heliozoa* noun pl. (see below), from Greek *hēlios* sun + *zōion* animal: see -AN.]
▸ **A** *noun*. Any of the chiefly freshwater protozoans constituting the class Heliozoa, related to radiolarians and having spherical cells with long slender radial pseudopodia and often a siliceous test. L19.
▸ **B** *adjective*. Of or pertaining to the class Heliozoa. L19.

helipterum /hɪˈlɪpt(ə)rəm/ *noun*. M19.
[ORIGIN mod. Latin (see below), from Greek *hēlios* sun + *pteron* wing, with ref. to the feathery pappus.]
Any of various Australian and southern African shrubs and herbs constituting the genus *Helipterum*, of the composite family, grown as everlastings.

helium /ˈhiːlɪəm/ *noun*. L19.
[ORIGIN from Greek *hēlios* sun + -IUM: the element was inferred to exist from an emission line in the sun's spectrum.]
A colourless odourless gaseous chemical element, atomic no. 2, which is the lightest of the noble gases and

is present in traces in the earth's atmosphere (symbol He).

helix /ˈhiːlɪks/ *noun*. Pl. **helices** /ˈhɛlɪsiːz, ˈhiː-/, **helixes**. **M16**.
[ORIGIN Latin *helix*, *helicis* from Greek *helix*, *helikos*.]
1 Chiefly ARCHITECTURE. A spiral ornament, a volute; *spec.* each of the eight smaller volutes under the abacus of a Corinthian capital. **M16**.
2 An object of coiled form, either round an axis (like a corkscrew) or, less usually, in one plane (like a watch spring); GEOMETRY a three-dimensional curve on a (notional) conical or cylindrical surface which becomes a straight line when the surface is unrolled into a plane. **E17**.
double helix: see DOUBLE *adjective & adverb*.
3 ANATOMY. The curved fold which forms the rim of the exterior ear. Cf. ANTHELIX. **L17**.
4 ZOOLOGY. Any spiral-shelled mollusc of the genus *Helix*, which includes the garden snail, *H aspersa*. **E19**.

hell /hɛl/ *noun*.
[ORIGIN Old English *hel(l)* = Old Frisian *helle*, Old Saxon *hell(j)a* (Dutch *hel*), Old High German *hella* (German *Hölle*), Old Norse *hel*, Gothic *halja* from Germanic base meaning 'cover, conceal': see HELE *verb*.]
1 (Often **H-**.) The abode of the dead; the place of departed spirits; the infernal regions regarded as a place of existence after death, the kingdom of Hades. **OE**. ▸**b** The kingdom or power of hell; *collect.* the inhabitants, wicked spirits, or powers of hell. **ME**. ▸**c** A devilish assembly. Long *rare*. **L16**.
2 (Often **H-**.) The infernal regions regarded as a place of torment or punishment; the abode of devils and condemned spirits. Freq. as an interjection or in exclamatory phrs. expr. annoyance, incredulity, dismay, etc., or merely emphatic (cf. HECK *noun*[2]). **OE**.

> *New Republic* Oh hell! Has it? Oh my god. Dear oh dear.

3 a A place compared to hell because of its darkness, discomfort, etc.; a place of confinement or punishment. **ME**. ▸**b** A place or state of wickedness, suffering, or misery; a place of turmoil and discord. **LME**.

> **b** I. HAY War is hell. H. E. BATES If the times had been bad for writers in 1926 . . they were now hell.

4 The den or base to which captives are carried in the games barley-break and prisoner's base. **M16**.
5 *hist.* A place in a tailor's shop into which shreds or offcuts of material are thrown. **L16**.
6 *hist.* A gaming house; a gambling booth. **L18**.
– PHRASES: **a — from hell** an exceptionally unpleasant or bad —. **a hell of a —** *colloq.* an infernal or very bad, great, etc., —. **all hell let loose** utter pandemonium. **as hell** very, exceedingly. **beat hell out of**, **knock hell out of**, etc., thrash, pound heavily; *fig.* achieve supremacy over. **for the hell of it** for amusement, for fun. **get hell** be severely reprimanded. **get the hell out (of)**, **get to hell out (of)** make a hasty retreat (from). **give a person hell** make a person uncomfortable, give a person a difficult time. **go to hell** (chiefly *interjection*) go away, make off. **go to hell and back** endure an extremely unpleasant or difficult experience. **hell and high water**, **hell or high water** any great obstacle or problem. **hell and Tommy** = *merry hell* below. **hell for leather** at breakneck speed. **hell on wheels** a terrible person or thing, *esp.* one of great speed or ferocity. **hell to pay** great trouble, discord, pandemonium, esp. as a result of previous action. ***knock hell out of***: see *beat hell out of* above. ***like a bat out of hell***: see BAT *noun*[3]. **like hell** very much, exceedingly; recklessly, desperately; *iron.* not at all, on the contrary. **merry hell** a disturbance, an upheaval; great trouble, great pain; ***play merry hell (with)*** = ***play hell (with)*** below. ***not a cat in hell's chance***: see CAT *noun*[1]. **not a chance in hell**, **not a hope in hell** no likelihood, no possibility. ***not a snowball's chance in hell***: see SNOWBALL *noun* 1. **play hell (with)** upset, confuse; cause trouble (for); make a fuss; cf. ***play merry hell (with)*** above. **raise hell** cause trouble, create chaos. **the — from hell** = ***a — from hell*** above. **the hell of a —** = ***a hell of a —*** above. **the hell you say** expr. surprise or disbelief. **till hell freezes (over)**, **until hell freezes (over)** until some date in the impossibly distant future; forever. **to hell and gone** a great distance; endlessly, for ever. **to hell with it**, **to hell with you** away to perdition; go away; expr. dismissal or an end of concern. ***until hell freezes (over)***: see ***till hell freezes (over)*** above. **what in hell . . . ?**, **what the hell . . . ?**, **who in hell . . . ?**, **who the hell . . . ?** (*a*) as an intensive: expr. incredulity, amazement, annoyance, etc., cf. ***who on earth*** s.v. EARTH *noun*[1]; (*b*) also simply ***what the hell***, expr. dismissal of a difficulty etc. **when hell freezes (over)** at some date in the impossibly distant future; never. ***who in hell . . . ?***, ***who the hell . . . ?***: see ***what in hell . . . ?*** above.
– COMB.: **hellbender** a large, grotesque N. American salamander, *Cryptobranchus alleganiensis*; **hell-bent** *adjective* recklessly determined *for* or *on*; **hell-born** *adjective* born of hell, of infernal origin; **hell-box** PRINTING a box for holding damaged or discarded type; **hell-bred** *adjective* bred or engendered in hell; **hell-broth** *rare* a broth of infernal character or for an infernal purpose; **hellcat** a spiteful or furious (esp. female) person; **hell-diver** *US* the pied-billed grebe, *Podilymbus podiceps*; **helldog** = HELLHOUND; **hell-driver** *slang* a person who drives a vehicle in a fast or daredevil manner; **hell-gate(s)** the portal or entrance of hell; **hell-hag** a diabolical or vile woman; **hellhole** an oppressive place; **hell-kite** *rare* a kite of hell; a person of hellish cruelty; **hellraiser** a person who causes trouble or creates chaos; ***Hell's Angel***: see ANGEL *noun* 2b; **hell's bells** an excl. of anger, annoyance, etc.; **hell's delight** pandemonium; **hell-ship**: with a reputation for cruelty and tyranny among the crew; ***hell's kitchen***: see KITCHEN *noun*; **hellweed** (*obsolete* exc. *dial.*) dodder.
■ **hellful** *noun* **M17**. **hell-like** *adjective* **M16**.

hell /hɛl/ *verb*. Now chiefly *slang*. **E17**.
[ORIGIN from the noun.]
†**1** *verb trans.* Place in or as in hell; condemn to suffer. **E–M17**.
2 *verb intrans.* Hurry, rush; *spec.* rush *around* or conduct oneself in an irresponsible or high-spirited way. **L19**.
3 *verb trans.* Make or turn into chaos or an inferno. **E20**.
4 *verb trans.* Cause trouble for, annoy. **E20**.

hellacious /hɛˈleɪʃəs/ *adjective & adverb*. *US slang*. **M20**.
[ORIGIN from HELL *noun* + *-acious* perh. after BODACIOUS.]
Terrific(ally), tremendous(ly), enormous(ly).

> A. MAUPIN This hellacious hailstorm which knocked down our tents.

Helladic /hɛˈladɪk/ *adjective & noun*. **E19**.
[ORIGIN Greek *Helladikos*, from *Hellas*, *Hellad-* Greece: see -IC.]
▸ **A** *adjective*. **1** Pertaining or relating to Greece or to Greek culture. **E19**.
2 ARCHAEOLOGY. Designating or pertaining to the Bronze Age cultures of Greece, lasting from *c* 2800–*c* 1200 BC. **E20**.
▸ **B** *noun*. ARCHAEOLOGY. The (period of) Bronze Age culture in Greece. **E20**.

hellebore /ˈhɛlɪbɔː/ *noun*. Also in Latin form **-rum** /-rəm/, **-rus** /-rəs/. **OE**.
[ORIGIN (Old French *ellebre*, *elebore* from) medieval Latin *eleborus*, Latin *(h)elleborus* from Greek *helleboros*: refashioned in 16 after prevailing Greek form.]
Orig., (the root of) either of two poisonous and purgative plants reputed in classical times to cure insanity, *Helleborus orientalis* and related species (more fully ***black hellebore***) and *Veratrum album* (more fully ***white hellebore***; cf. ***false hellebore*** below). Now, any of various early-flowering plants constituting the Eurasian genus *Helleborus*, of the buttercup family, with palmately divided leaves and petaloid sepals; esp. *H. viridis* (in full ***green hellebore***) and *H. foetidus* (in full ***stinking hellebore***), both green-flowered plants of calcareous woodland.
false hellebore any of various plants of the genus *Veratrum* of the lily family (see VERATRUM).
■ **helleborism** *noun* [Greek *helleborismos*] the treatment of insanity etc. by means of hellebore (*hist.*); the (excessive) ingestion of hellebore: **E17**.

helleborine /ˈhɛlɪbəriːn, -rʌɪn/ *noun*. **L16**.
[ORIGIN French, or Latin *(h)elleborine* from Greek *helleborinē* a plant like hellebore: see -INE[1].]
Any of various mainly woodland orchids of the genus *Epipactis*, chiefly with greenish sometimes self-fertilized flowers, and of the related genus *Cephalanthera*, with larger white or pink flowers.

Hellene /ˈhɛliːn/ *noun*. **M17**.
[ORIGIN Greek *Hellēn* a Greek.]
A Greek: an ancient Greek of genuine Grecian descent; a subject of the modern nation of Greece.

Hellenian /hɛˈlɛnɪən, hɛˈliː-/ *noun & adjective*. *rare*. **E17**.
[ORIGIN Greek *Hellēnios*, formed as HELLENIC: see -IAN.]
▸ **A** *noun*. A member of an ancient Thessalian tribe, an ancient Hellene. **E17**.
▸ **B** *adjective*. = HELLENIC *adjective*. **E19**.

Hellenic /hɛˈlɛnɪk, hɛˈliː-/ *adjective & noun*. **M17**.
[ORIGIN Greek *Hellēnikos*, from *Hellēn* HELLENE: see -IC.]
▸ **A** *adjective*. Of or pertaining to the Hellenes or the Greeks; native to or originating in Greece; characteristic of or attributed to Greece or to the Hellenes; *spec.* in ARCHAEOLOGY, relating to or denoting Iron Age and Classical Greek culture (between Helladic and Hellenistic). **M17**.
▸ **B** *noun*. **1** The Greek language. **M19**.
2 In *pl.* Writings on Greece or things Greek. **M19**.
■ **Hellenicize** /-sʌɪz/ *verb trans.* make Greek, Graecize **M19**.

Hellenise *verb* var. of HELLENIZE.

Hellenism /ˈhɛlɪnɪz(ə)m/ *noun*. **E17**.
[ORIGIN Greek *Hellēnismos*, from *Hellēnizein* Hellenize: see -ISM.]
1 A particular feature of the Greek language; a Greek phrase, idiom, or construction, esp. one as used in some other language; a Graecism. **E17**.

> I. D'ISRAELI When Greek was first studied . . it planted many a Hellenism in our language.

2 Conformity to Hellenic speech and ideas; imitation or adoption of Greek characteristics, esp. by the Jews of the Diaspora or the later Romans. **M19**.
3 Greek character or nature; Grecian culture. **M19**.
4 Greek nationality; the Hellenic race or world as a political entity. **L19**.

Hellenist /ˈhɛlɪnɪst/ *noun*. **E17**.
[ORIGIN Greek *Hellēnistēs*, from *Hellēnizein*: see HELLENISM, -IST.]
1 A person who uses the Greek language, but is not a Greek; *esp.* a Greek-speaking Jew of the Diaspora. **E17**.
2 A person skilled in Greek language or literature; a Greek scholar. **L17**.

Hellenistic /hɛlɪˈnɪstɪk/ *adjective*. **E18**.
[ORIGIN from HELLENIST + -IC.]
Of or pertaining to the Hellenists: using the Greek language or following Greek modes of thought or life; *spec.* of, pertaining to, or designating the period of Greek history and language from the death of Alexander the Great (323 BC) to the defeat of Antony and Cleopatra (31 BC).
■ **Helle'nistical** *adjective* **M17**. **Helle'nistically** *adverb* **M17**.

Hellenize /ˈhɛlɪnʌɪz/ *verb*. Also **-ise**. **E17**.
[ORIGIN Greek *Hellēnizein* speak Greek, make Greek, from *Hellēn* HELLENE: see -IZE.]
1 *verb intrans.* Use the Greek language; adopt Greek habits; live as or become a Hellenist. **E17**.
2 *verb trans.* Make Greek or Hellenistic in form or character. **L18**.
■ **Helleni'zation** *noun* **L19**. **Hellenizer** *noun* **M19**.

Hellenophile /ˈhɛlɪnə(ʊ)fʌɪl/ *adjective & noun*. Also **-phil** /-fɪl/. **L19**.
[ORIGIN from HELLENE + -O- + -PHIL, -PHILE.]
(A person who is) friendly towards or fond of Greece and things Greek.

heller /ˈhɛlə/ *noun*[1]. Also (earlier) †**haller**. **L16**. Pl. **-s**, same.
[ORIGIN German from Middle High German *häller*, *haller*, from (*Schwäbisch*) *Hall*, a town in Germany where this coin was first minted: see -ER[1].]
An old German or Austrian coin of low value. Also, = HALER.

heller /ˈhɛlə/ *noun*[2]. *slang* (chiefly *US*). **L19**.
[ORIGIN from HELL *verb* + -ER[1].]
A troublesome, reckless, or aggressive person; a hellion.

Hellerwork /ˈhɛləwəːk/ *noun*. **L20**.
[ORIGIN from the name of J. *Heller* (b. 1940), who developed it.]
A system involving deep tissue massage and exercise, designed to help correct posture, relieve pain, etc.

Hellespont /ˈhɛlɪspɒnt/ *noun*. **L16**.
[ORIGIN Greek *Hellēspontos*, ancient name for the Dardanelles, the strait linking the Aegean Sea and the Sea of Marmara, from *Hellē*, daughter of Athamas, said to have drowned there + *pontos* sea.]
Something which separates two lovers (with allusion to Leander's feat of swimming the Hellespont to be with Hero).
■ **Helle'spontine** *adjective* of, pertaining to, or situated on the Hellespont **M19**.

hellfire /ˈhɛlfʌɪə/ *noun & adjective*. **OE**.
[ORIGIN from HELL *noun* + FIRE *noun*.]
▸ **A** *noun*. **1** The fire or fires of hell. **OE**.

> *transf.*: A. MACLEAN Breathing hell-fire and brimstone in all directions.

2 (**H-**.) A member of a Hell-fire club (see below). *obsolete* exc. *hist.* **E18**.
▸ **B** *attrib.* or as *adjective*. **1** *hist.* ***Hell-fire club***, any of a number of clubs of reckless young men, popular at the beginning of the 18th cent. **E18**.
2 Esp. of preaching: concerned with or emphasizing the damnation of souls and the eternal punishments of hell. **M20**.

> R. CAMPBELL The hell-fire sermons of the local priest.

■ **hell-fired** *adjective* subjected to hellfire; chiefly *fig.* (*slang*) damned, confounded: **E18**.

hellgrammite /ˈhɛlgrəmʌɪt/ *noun*. *US*. Also **helg-**. **M19**.
[ORIGIN Unknown.]
The aquatic larva of an insect, *spec.* of the dobsonfly, *Corydalus cornutus*, used as bait by anglers.

hellhound /ˈhɛlhaʊnd/ *noun*. **OE**.
[ORIGIN from HELL *noun* + HOUND *noun*[1].]
1 A hound or dog of hell; *esp.* in CLASSICAL MYTHOLOGY, Cerberus, the watchdog of Hades. **OE**.
2 A fiend, a fiendish person. **LME**.

hellicat *adjective & noun* see HALLOCKIT.

hellier /ˈhɛljə/ *noun*. Now *dial.* **LME**.
[ORIGIN from HELE *verb*: see -IER.]
A slater, a tiler.

hellion /ˈhɛljən/ *noun*. *colloq.* Chiefly *N. Amer.* Also **-yon**. **M19**.
[ORIGIN Prob. var. of HALLION, assim. to HELL *noun*.]
A troublesome or disreputable person; a mischievous child.

hellish /ˈhɛlɪʃ/ *adjective & adverb*. **M16**.
[ORIGIN from HELL *noun* + -ISH[1].]
▸ **A** *adjective*. **1** Of or pertaining to hell; infernal. **M16**. ▸**b** Belonging to Hades. **L16**.
2 Of the nature or character of hell; worthy of hell; diabolical, fiendish. **M16**.
3 Exceedingly bad, long, fast, etc. *colloq.* **L18**.
▸ **B** *adverb*. Infernally, devilishly; *colloq.* exceedingly. **E17**.
■ **hellishing** *adjective & adverb* (*slang*, chiefly *Austral. & NZ*) = HELLISH *adjective* 3, *adverb* **M20**. **hellishly** *adverb* (*a*) in a hellish manner, infernally, devilishly; (*b*) *colloq.* exceedingly, very much: **L16**. **hellishness** *noun* **L16**.

hellite /ˈhɛlʌɪt/ *noun*. **E19**.
[ORIGIN from HELL *noun* + -ITE[1].]
1 The proprietor of a hell or gaming house. **E19**.
2 An inhabitant of hell. *rare*. **M19**.

hello /həˈləʊ, hɛ-/ *interjection, noun, & verb*. **L19**.
[ORIGIN Var. of HALLO. Cf. HULLO.]
▸ **A** *interjection*. Greeting or expr. surprise on encountering; beginning a telephone conversation. **L19**.

H

▸ **B** *noun*. Pl. **-os**. A shout of 'hello!'; an utterance of 'hello!' **L19**.
golden hello: see **GOLDEN** *adjective*.
▸ **C** *verb intrans*. Say or shout 'hello!' **L19**.

> T. MORRISON Lily Cary helloed from the porch of her house . . but he did not turn his head.

helluo /ˈhɛljʊəʊ/ *noun*. Pl. **-os**. **L16**.
[**ORIGIN** Latin *helluo*, *heluo*.]
A glutton, a gourmandizer.

helluva /ˈhɛləvə/ *adjective*. *non-standard*. **E20**.
[**ORIGIN** Repr. a pronunc.]
= ***a hell of a*** — s.v. **HELL** *noun*.

> C. E. MULFORD I got money—helluva lot of money. *Times* It's very unfortunate looking like him: he must have a helluva life.

hellward /ˈhɛlwəd/ *adverb & adjective*. **LME**.
[**ORIGIN** from **HELL** *noun* + **-WARD**.]
▸ **A** *adverb*. Towards hell; downward, towards the centre of the earth; towards the place of final punishment. **LME**.
▸ **B** *adjective*. Heading to hell. **E19**.

helly /ˈhɛli/ *adjective & adverb*. *obsolete* exc. *poet*. **OE**.
[**ORIGIN** from **HELL** *noun*: see **-LY**[1], **-LY**[2], **-Y**[1].]
▸ **A** *adjective*. Of or belonging to hell; of the nature of hell; hellish, infernal, devilish. **OE**.
▸ **†B** *adverb*. Hellishly, infernally. **E17–M18**.

H

hellyon *noun* var. of **HELLION**.

helm /hɛlm/ *noun*[1].
[**ORIGIN** Old English *helm* = Old Frisian, Old Saxon, Old High German (Dutch, German) *helm*, Old Norse *hjalmr*, Gothic *hilms*, from Germanic, from Indo-European base meaning 'cover, conceal': see **HELE** *verb*. Cf. **HEMMEL**.]
1 Armour for the head; a helmet. *arch*. **OE**. ▸**†b** *transf*. A knight. **ME–M16**. ▸**c** = **HELMET** *noun* 1b. **M19**.
†2 Jesus's crown of thorns. **OE–LME**.
3 The top or summit of something. *obsolete* exc. *dial*. **OE**. ▸**b** The head or cap of an alembic or retort. *obsolete* exc. *hist*. **L16**.
4 A roofed shelter for cattle etc. *N. English*. **E16**.
5 **a** More fully ***helm cloud***. In the Lake District, a cloud forming over a mountain top before or during a storm. **L18**. ▸**b** In full ***helm wind***. A violent wind associated with a helm cloud. **L18**.
■ **helmless** *adjective*[1] **E17**.

helm /hɛlm/ *noun*[2].
[**ORIGIN** Old English *helma* corresp. to Middle Low German *helm* handle, Old High German *helmo*, *halmo*, Old Norse *hjalmvǫlr* rudder-stick: prob. rel. to **HELVE**.]
1 *NAUTICAL*. The tiller or wheel by which the rudder is controlled. **OE**. ▸**b** Use of the helm; the space through which the helm is turned. **L19**.

> **b** A. MACLEAN Naseby gave the rudder maximum helm to port.

2 *fig*. The position of leadership or government. **OE**.

> *fig*.: A. L. ROWSE Chamberlain, who had succeeded Baldwin at the helm of the drifting country.

– **PHRASES**: **down helm**, **down with the helm** place the helm so as to bring the rudder to windward. **lee helm** helm put down. ***put the helm APORT***. ***right the helm***: see **RIGHT** *verb* 8. **take the helm** control the direction of a boat; *fig*. assume control. **up helm**, **up with the helm** place the helm so as to bring the rudder to leeward. **weather helm** helm put up.
■ **helmless** *adjective*[2] without a helm or rudder **E19**. **helmsman** *noun* the steersman **E17**. **helmsmanship** *noun* the function or practice of a helmsman **L19**. **helmswoman** *noun* a female steersman **L19**.

helm /hɛlm/ *verb*[1] *trans*. *arch*. or *poet*.
[**ORIGIN** Old English *helmian*, from **HELM** *noun*[1].]
Provide or cover with a helm.
■ **helmed** *ppl adjective* wearing a helm, helmeted **ME**.

helm /hɛlm/ *verb*[2] *trans*. **E17**.
[**ORIGIN** from **HELM** *noun*[2].]
1 Steer or guide (as) with a helm. **E17**.

> *Irish Press* Local boats helmed by Jack Roy and Roger Bannon set the pace.

2 Direct (a film). *N. Amer*. **M20**.

> *Premiere* He had helmed six features of his own.

■ **helmer** *noun* (*N. Amer.*) a film director **L20**.

helmet /ˈhɛlmɪt/ *noun & verb*. **LME**.
[**ORIGIN** Old French, from *helme* ult. formed as **HELM** *noun*[1]: see **-ET**[2].]
▸ **A** *noun*. **1** A piece of (usu. metal) armour for the head. **LME**. ▸**b** A representation of a helmet; *esp*. in *HERALDRY*, one placed above the shield in an achievement and supporting the crest, used to denote rank. **E17**. ▸**c** Any of various types of protective headgear as worn by police officers, firefighters, divers, motorcyclists, sports players, etc.; a felt or pith hat worn in hot climates. **M19**.
2 = **HELM** *noun*[1] 3b. *obsolete* exc. *hist*. **L16**.
3 A kind of fancy pigeon having distinctively coloured head plumage. **L17**.
4 In full ***helmet shell***. (The large thick shell of) any of various marine gastropods of the family Cassididae. **M18**.
5 *BOTANY*. The arched upper part of the calyx of certain flowers, esp. of labiates and orchids; = **GALEA**. **L18**.
– **COMB.**: **helmet-crest** (*a*) the crest of a helmet; (*b*) (in full ***bearded helmet-crest***) a crested hummingbird, *Oxypogon guerinii*, of northern S. America; ***helmet shell***: see sense 4 above.
▸ **B** *verb trans*. Equip with a helmet. Chiefly as ***helmeted*** *ppl adjective*. **M16**.
helmeted CURASSOW.
■ **helmetless** *adjective* **L19**. **helmet-like** *adjective* resembling (that of) a helmet **L19**.

Helmholtz /ˈhɛlmhɒlts/ *noun*. **M20**.
[**ORIGIN** H. L. F. von *Helmholtz* (1821–94), German physicist.]
Used *attrib*. to designate devices and concepts introduced by Helmholtz.
Helmholtz resonator a simple acoustic resonator consisting of a straight tube open at one end, with the other end connected to an enclosed cavity.

helminth /ˈhɛlmɪnθ/ *noun*. **M19**.
[**ORIGIN** Greek *helmins*, *helminth-* intestinal worm.]
Any of a diverse group of worms which are internal parasites of humans and other animals, as nematodes, flukes, etc.
■ **helminˈthiasis** *noun*, pl. **-ases** /-əsiːz/, infestation by helminths of any kind **E19**. **helˈminthic** *noun & adjective* †(*a*) *noun* an anthelmintic substance; (*b*) *adjective* of or pertaining to, or caused by helminths: **E18**.

helminthology /hɛlmɪnˈθɒlədʒi/ *noun*. **E19**.
[**ORIGIN** from **HELMINTH** + **-OLOGY**.]
The branch of zoology or medicine that deals with helminths and the diseases they cause.
■ **helminthoˈlogic**, **helminthoˈlogical** *adjectives* **E19**. **helminthologist** *noun* **E19**.

helophyte /ˈhɛləfʌɪt/ *noun*. **E20**.
[**ORIGIN** from Greek *helos* marsh + **-PHYTE**.]
ECOLOGY. A marsh plant; *spec*. one whose perennating buds are situated in the mud at the bottom of a pond, lake, etc.

helot /ˈhɛlət/ *noun*. **L16**.
[**ORIGIN** Latin *Helotes* pl. from Greek *Heilōtes* (pl. of *Heilōs*), also *Hilotae* from Greek *Heilōtai* (pl. of *Heilōtēs*): usu. derived from *Helos* a town in Laconia whose inhabitants were enslaved.]
GREEK HISTORY. **1** (**H-**.) A member of a class of serfs in ancient Sparta, intermediate in status between slaves and citizens. **L16**.
drunken Helot: forced to appear in a drunken state as a dreadful warning to Spartan youths.
2 *transf*. & *fig*. A serf, a slave. **E19**.

> P. D. JAMES Dalgliesh's helot, whose role was to take unobtrusive notes.

■ **helotage** *noun* = **HELOTISM** (a) **M19**. **helotism** *noun* (*a*) a system under which a class of the community is treated as inferior or subjugated; the condition of a helot; (*b*) *BIOLOGY* a form of symbiosis in which one organism is held to make use of another as if it were a slave; *esp*. the relationship of ants and aphids, or of fungus and alga in a lichen: **E19**. **helotize** *verb trans*. reduce to the condition of a helot **M19**. **helotry** *noun* (*a*) helots collectively; (*b*) the condition of a helot, slavery: **E19**.

help /hɛlp/ *noun*.
[**ORIGIN** Old English *help* = Old Frisian *helpe*, Old Saxon *helpa*, Old High German *helfa*, Old Norse *hjálp*, from Germanic base of **HELP** *verb*.]
1 The action of helping or being helped; the useful supplementing of action or resources; aid, assistance. **OE**. ▸**b** An act of helping, an aid or assistance. Now *rare* exc. as passing into sense 2. **ME**.

> K. VONNEGUT They . . have a tough job . . and they need all the help they can get. *Dumfries & Galloway Standard* It's an advanced communications system which summons help in an emergency. D. WIGODER They must all think me crazy and beyond help. **b** R. L. STEVENSON I'll ask you, later on, to give us a help.

2 A person who or thing which provides help; a source or means of assistance. **OE**. ▸**b** A domestic servant or employee; *collect*. servants, hired workers; the labour of hired workers. Formerly, an assistant, an ally. **ME**.

> AV *Ps*. 46:1 God is our refuge and strength: a very present helpe in trouble. J. S. BLACKIE Books are no doubt very useful helps to knowledge. **b** G. PALEY I was going to organize the help You know, the guards, the elevator boys. P. LIVELY She has taught herself to cook . . since the defection of the last of the village helps.

3 Cure, remedy. Now chiefly in ***there is no help for it***, there is no way of avoiding it. **OE**.

> DICKENS Poor Catherine and I are not made for each other, and there is no help for it.

4 A portion of food, a helping. **E19**.

> P. V. WHITE He agreed . . to accept another help of mutton.

– **COMB.**: **help desk** a service providing information and support to the users of a computer network; **helpline** a telephone service providing help with problems; **help-mate** *CHESS* a type of problem in which Black must assist White to give mate in a certain number of moves.

help /hɛlp/ *verb*. Pa. t. **helped**, (*arch*. & *US dial*.) **holp** /həʊlp/. Pa. pple **helped**, (*arch*. & *US dial*.) **holpen** /ˈhəʊlp(ə)n/.
[**ORIGIN** Old English *helpan* = Old Frisian *helpa*, Old Saxon *helpan* (Dutch *helpen*), Old High German *helfan* (German *helfen*), Old Norse *hjalpa*, Gothic *hilpan*, from Germanic.]
1 *verb trans*. & *intrans*. Provide (a person etc.) with what is needed for a purpose; aid, assist. Also, supply the needs of, succour. Freq. in *imper*., expr. a need for assistance. **OE**. ▸**b** With inf., with or without direct obj.: give help or assistance to *do* etc. or *to do* etc. **ME**.

> G. GREENE He felt as though he were in a strange country without any maps to help him. DAY LEWIS Help! I've a bee in my hair! **b** POPE He help'd to bury whom he help'd to starve. *Punch* Sir Kingsley Wood . . asked the House for £1,000,000,000 to help pay for the . . war. T. F. POWYS Someone had . . appeared to help Lord Bullman to open the gate. R. INGALLS Help me look for that one.

God help me, **God help you**, **Heaven help you**, etc., *interjection* expr. pity, anxiety, etc. **so help me (God)** (in an invocation or oath) as I keep my word, as I speak the truth, etc. (cf. **SWELP ME**).
2 *verb trans*. Benefit, do good to; be of use or service to; profit. **OE**. ▸**b** *verb intrans*. Be of use or service; avail. **OE**. ▸**c** *verb trans*. Make (an action, process, etc.) more effective; assist in achieving; promote, further. **LME**.

> J. WESLEY Mustard, and Juice of Scurvy Grass, help in a cold Scurvy. **b** T. MORRISON She actually wanted to help, to soothe. **c** J. R. GREEN The troubles of the time helped here as elsewhere the progress of the town.

3 *verb trans*. Relieve or cure (a disease etc.); remedy, amend. Long *arch*. **OE**. ▸**b** Succour in distress or misfortune; deliver, save (*from*, *of*); *spec*. cure of a disease. **ME**.
4 *verb refl*. Make an effort on one's own behalf; do what is needed for oneself; extricate oneself from a difficulty. **ME**.

> F. W. ROBINSON I don't think that I shall require your assistance, or that I shall be unable to help myself.

5 *verb trans*. Assist (a person etc.) to progress in a specified direction. **ME**. ▸**b** Foll. by *with*: assist (a person) to put, take, or get something (esp. an article of clothing) *on*, *off*, etc. **ME**. ▸**c** Give assistance in dealing *with*. **E19**.

> A. HIGGINS Leaning out the conductor helped her down, his hand at her elbow. J. STEINBECK He helped Curley out the door. **c** A. D. SEDGWICK If he sat there . . not helping with the water-cans, . . it was because he . . wanted to watch her.

help out, **help through** *spec*. assist in completing or enduring something, or out of a difficulty; supplement, eke out. **c help the police in their enquiries**, **help the police with their enquiries** be questioned (usu. as the chief suspect for a crime) by the police.
6 *verb trans*. Avoid, obviate, prevent, remedy; cause to be otherwise; refrain from, forbear. **LME**. ▸**b** With neg. omitted after a neg. expressed or implied. Be unavoidable. *colloq*. **M19**.

> J. BARZUN A man cannot help being intelligent, but he can easily help becoming intellectual. **b** C. H. SPURGEON I did not trouble myself more than I could help.

7 *verb trans*. Foll. by *to*: assist (a person) in obtaining, provide or present with; *refl*. (also *absol*. without *to*) provide oneself (with), take for oneself, *euphem*. take without permission, steal. Cf. sense 8. **LME**.
8 *verb trans*. Serve (a person) with food etc. (foll. by *to*); serve (food etc.). **L17**.

> G. GREENE I helped him to a glass of rum and awaited an explanation. *refl*.: I. MURDOCH Cheese and biscuits are on the table, so do help yourselves if you want any.

– **COMB.**: **helping hand** *fig*. an act of assistance; **help-yourself** *adjective* self-service.
■ **helpable** *adjective* able to be helped **L16**. **helper** *noun* (*a*) a person or thing which helps; (*b*) a person employed as an assistant; *spec*. a groom's assistant in a stable; *colloq*. an assistant minister (in Methodist and Scottish churches); (*c*) ***helper cell*** (*PHYSIOLOGY*) a T-lymphocyte that influences or controls the differentiation or activity of other cells of the immune system: **ME**. **helping** *noun* (*a*) the action of the verb; (*b*) *spec*. the action of serving food etc.; a portion of food, esp. as served at one time (cf. **HELP** *noun* 4): **ME**.

helpful /ˈhɛlpfʊl, -f(ə)l/ *adjective*. **LME**.
[**ORIGIN** from **HELP** *noun* + **-FUL**.]
Giving or productive of help; useful, profitable.
■ **helpfully** *adverb* **M19**. **helpfulness** *noun* (earlier in **UNHELPFULNESS**) **M17**.

helpless /ˈhɛlplɪs/ *adjective*. **ME**.
[**ORIGIN** from **HELP** *noun* + **-LESS**.]
1 Lacking help or assistance; needy. Often passing into sense 2. **ME**.

> *Which?* Some . . parts of a car are designed so that even if they do go wrong you aren't left helpless.

2 Unable to help oneself; incapable. **ME**.

> P. CAMPBELL Bill was so helpless with laughter that he missed me with the ruler altogether.

†3 That cannot be helped or remedied. **ME–L16**.
4 Unhelpful. Now *rare* or *obsolete*. **LME**.
■ **helplessly** *adverb* **L16**. **helplessness** *noun* **M18**.

helpmate /ˈhɛlpmeɪt/ *noun*. **E18**.
[**ORIGIN** from **HELP** *noun* or *verb* + **MATE** *noun*[2]; prob. infl. by **HELPMEET**.]
A companion who is a help or who gives help; a partner, esp. a husband or wife.

helpmeet /ˈhɛlpmiːt/ *noun*. **L17**.
[**ORIGIN** from *help meet* (two words) in *Genesis* 2:18, 20 (AV), 'an help meet for him' (**HELP** *noun* 2 + **MEET** *adjective* 3), taken as one word.]
A suitable helper; = **HELPMATE**.

helter-skelter /hɛltəˈskɛltə/ *adverb, noun, & adjective*. **L16.**
[**ORIGIN** A rhyming comb.; cf. *harum-scarum*.]
▸ **A** *adverb*. In disordered haste. *colloq*. **L16.**

S. BELLOW I've been writing letters helter-skelter in all directions.

▸ **B** *noun*. **1** Disordered haste; a hurried flight. *colloq*. **E18.**
2 A tower-shaped structure at a funfair etc., with an external spiral track down which one may slide on a mat. **E20.**
▸ **C** *attrib*. or as *adjective*. Characterized by disorderly haste or confusion. *colloq*. **L18.**

helve /hɛlv/ *noun & verb*.
[**ORIGIN** Old English *helfe*, (West Saxon) *hielfe*, corresp. to Old Saxon *helfi* (Middle Dutch *helf*, *helve*), Old High German *halp* from West Germanic, whence also **HALTER** *noun*[1]: cf. **HELM** *noun*[2].]
▸ **A** *noun*. **1** A handle or shaft of a weapon or tool. **OE.**
throw the helve after the hatchet, ***throw the hatchet after the helve***: see **HATCHET** *noun*.
2 In full ***helve-hammer***. A tilt hammer, the helve of which oscillates on bearings, so that it is raised by a cam carried by a revolving shaft, and falls by its own weight. **M19.**
▸ **B** *verb trans*. Provide or fit with a helve. Now *rare*. **LME.**

Helvetian /hɛlˈviːʃ(ə)n/ *adjective & noun*. **M16.**
[**ORIGIN** from Latin *Helvetia* Switzerland, from *Helvetius* pertaining to the Helvetii: see **-IAN**.]
▸ **A** *adjective*. Of or pertaining to the Helvetii; of or pertaining to Switzerland, Swiss. **M16.**
▸ **B** *noun*. One of the Helvetii; a native or inhabitant of Switzerland, a Swiss. **M16.**

Helvetic /hɛlˈvɛtɪk/ *adjective*. **E18.**
[**ORIGIN** Latin *Helveticus* pertaining to the Helvetii: see **HELVETIAN**, **-IC**.]
Swiss.

helvolic /hɛlˈvɒlɪk/ *adjective*. **M20.**
[**ORIGIN** from Latin *helvola* lit. 'yellowish', name of the mutant variety of fungus from which the acid was isolated: see **-IC**.]
BIOCHEMISTRY. ***helvolic acid***, an antibiotic acid produced by some strains of the fungus *Aspergillus fumigatus*.

helxine /hɛlkˈsʌɪni/ *noun*. **L19.**
[**ORIGIN** mod. Latin former genus name from Greek *helxinē* pellitory.]
A small creeping mat-forming plant of the nettle family, *Soleirolia soleirolii*, native to the western Mediterranean islands and grown elsewhere in rockeries. Also called ***mind-your-own-business***, ***mother of thousands***.

hem /hɛm/ *noun*[1].
[**ORIGIN** Old English *hem* corresp. to Old Frisian *hemme* enclosed land.]
1 The border or edge of a piece of cloth or clothing; (long *dial*.) the border or edge of anything. **OE.**

P. THEROUX Hetta . . was striding, lifting the hem of her coat with her knees.

2 *esp*. A border made on a piece of cloth by doubling or turning in the (usu. cut) edge and sewing it down; used for strengthening or preventing fraying. **M17.**

N. GORDIMER She was putting safety pins round the torn hem of a skirt.

– **COMB.**: **hemline** the edge of a skirt, coat, etc.; the height of this from the ground.

hem /həm, hɛm/ *noun*[2]. **M16.**
[**ORIGIN** from the interjection.]
An utterance of 'hem'.

C. BRONTË I heard a hem close at my elbow.

†**hem** *pronoun*. See also **'EM** *pronoun*. **OE–M17.**
[**ORIGIN** Old English *him*, *hiom*, *heom* dat. pl. in all genders of **HE** *pers. pronoun*; later supplanting the accus. *hi*; finally itself displaced by **THEM**.]
Them.

hem /hɛm/ *verb*[1]. Infl. **-mm-**. **LME.**
[**ORIGIN** from **HEM** *noun*[1].]
1 *verb trans*. Edge or border (cloth, a garment), esp. decoratively. Long *rare*. **LME.**

SPENSER All the skirt about Was hemd with golden fringe.

2 *verb trans. & intrans*. Turn and sew down the edge of (a garment or piece of cloth). **M16.**

T. HOOD One used to stitch a collar then, Another hemmed a frill.

3 *verb trans*. Enclose, confine, shut *in*. Also foll. by *round*, *up*. **M16.**

G. GREENE Two one-armed men and three one-legged men hemmed him round. M. IGNATIEFF Hemmed in on one side by older brothers . . and on the other by this father. D. WIGODER I couldn't physically escape from the grim walls which hemmed me in.

hem /hɛm/ *verb*[2]. Infl. **-mm-**. **L15.**
[**ORIGIN** Imit.]
1 *verb intrans*. Utter a hem, clear the throat; hesitate in speech esp. through indecision, disagreement, etc. Chiefly in ***hem and haw***. **L15.** ▸†**b** *verb trans*. Drown *out* (speech) with a cough. Also foll. by *over*. **M16–L17.**

HENRY MILLER He began to hem and haw, not knowing really what he wanted to say. I. WALLACE He hemmed and hawed, weaseling all the way.

2 *verb trans*. Clear *away* with a cough. *rare*. **E16.**

SHAKES. *A.Y.L.* These burs are in my heart . . Hem them away.

hem /həm, hɛm/ *interjection*. **E16.**
[**ORIGIN** Imit.: see **HEM** *verb*[2].]
Expr. hesitation or a desire to attract attention by a slight cough or clearing of the throat.

DICKENS Gardens are—hem—are not accessible to me.

hemagglutinate *verb*, **hemal** *adjective*, **hematite** *noun*, **hemato-** *combining form*, etc.: see **HAEMAGGLUTINATE** etc.

heme *noun* var. of **HAEM**.

hemelytron /hɛˈmɛlɪtrɒn/ *noun*. Pl. **-tra** /-trə/. **E19.**
[**ORIGIN** from **HEMI-** + Greek *elutron* sheath.]
ENTOMOLOGY. The forewing of a heteropteran insect, thickened at the base and membranous at the end.

hemeralopia /hɛmərəˈləʊpɪə/ *noun*. **E18.**
[**ORIGIN** mod. Latin, from Greek *hēmeralōps*, from *hēmera* day + *alaos* blind + *ōps* eye: see **-IA**[1]. Cf. **NYCTALOPIA**.]
1 Chiefly *MEDICINE*. A defect of vision (usu. congenital) in which there is poor vision in good light but comparatively good vision in poor light. Also called ***day blindness***. **E18.**
2 [By confusion.] = **NYCTALOPIA** 1. Now *rare*. **E19.**
▪ **hemeralopic** *adjective* affected with hemeralopia **L19.**

hemerobaptist /hɛm(ə)rə(ʊ)ˈbaptɪst/ *noun*. **L16.**
[**ORIGIN** ecclesiastical Latin *Hemerobaptista* from Greek *hēmerobaptistai* pl., from *hēmera* day + *baptistēs* baptist.]
hist. A member of a Jewish sect which practised daily baptism as a means of ritual purification.

hemerocallis /hɛm(ə)rə(ʊ)ˈkalɪs/ *noun*. **M17.**
[**ORIGIN** Greek *hēmerokallis* a lily that flowers for one day only, from *hēmera* day + *kallos* beauty.]
= ***day lily*** s.v. **DAY** *noun*.

hemerythrin *noun* see **HAEMERYTHRIN**.

hemi- /ˈhɛmi/ *prefix*.
[**ORIGIN** Greek *hēmi-* combining elem. corresp. to Latin **SEMI-**, from Indo-European base also of Old English *sam-* (cf. **SAND-BLIND**), Old Saxon *sām-*, Old High German *sāmi-*.]
Used in words adopted (ult.) from Greek, or as a productive prefix (esp. in scientific and technical subjects) in new formations usu. with Greek roots, with the sense 'half-, affecting one half, partial.' Cf. **SEMI-**.
▪ **hemiˈacetal** *noun* (*CHEMISTRY*) any of a class of compounds of formula R·CH(OH)(OR′), differing from acetals in having a hydroxyl instead of one alkoxy-group **L19.** **hemibranch** *noun* (*ICHTHYOLOGY*) an incomplete gill, having lamellae on one side only **L19.** **hemiˈcellulose** *noun* any of various polysaccharides of simpler composition than cellulose which occur as constituents of the cell walls of plants **L19.** **hemiˈchordate** *noun & adjective* (*a*) *noun* any member of the phylum Hemichordata of wormlike marine invertebrates, including the acorn worms and pterobranchs and orig. classified as chordates; (*b*) *adjective* of or pertaining to this phylum: **L19.** **hemicircle** *noun* a semicircle **E17.** **hemicoˈlectomy** *noun* (an instance of) surgical removal of the right or left half of the colon **E20.** **hemiˈcryptophyte** *noun* (*BOTANY*) a plant having perennial shoots and buds at ground level or within the surface layer of soil **E20.** **hemicyˈlindrical** *adjective* having the form of half a cylinder **M19.** **hemiˈhedral** *adjective* (*CRYSTALLOGRAPHY*) (of a crystal or crystal class) having half of the maximum number of faces or symmetry planes possible for a given crystal system **M19.** **hemiˈhedron** *noun*, pl. **-dra**, **-drons**, *CRYSTALLOGRAPHY* any hemihedral crystal **M19.** **hemiˈhedry** *noun* (*CRYSTALLOGRAPHY*) the property of being hemihedral **M19.** **hemiˈhydrate** *noun* (*CHEMISTRY*) a hydrate containing half a mole of water per mole of the compound **L19.** **hemiˈparasite** *noun* (*BOTANY*) a parasitic plant which can also live as a saprophyte (as certain fungi), or which also photosynthesizes (as mistletoe) **L19.** **hemiparaˈsitic** *adjective* pertaining to or of the nature of a hemiparasite **E20.** **hemipaˈresis** *noun* = **HEMIPLEGIA** **L19.** **hemipaˈretic** *adjective* = **HEMIPLEGIC** *adjective* **L19.** **hemipenis** *noun* (*ZOOLOGY*) each of the paired eversible copulatory organs in snakes and lizards **E20.** **hemisect** *verb trans*. bisect esp. longitudinally or into right and left halves **L19.** **hemiˈsection** *noun* the action or process of hemisecting **L19.** **hemispasm** *noun* a spasm affecting one side of the body only **L19.** †**hemitone** *noun* a semitone **L17–M18.** **hemiˈzygote** *noun* (*BIOLOGY*) a hemizygous organism **M20.** **hemiˈzygous** *adjective* (*BIOLOGY*) having a single unpaired allele at a particular genetic locus **E20.**

hemianopsia /ˌhɛmɪəˈnɒpsɪə/ *noun*. **L19.**
[**ORIGIN** from **HEMI-** + Greek **AN-**[5] + *opsis*: see **-IA**[1].]
Blindness covering one half of the normal field of vision.
▪ **hemianopia** /-ˈnəʊpɪə/ *noun* [**-OPIA**] = **HEMIANOPSIA** **L19.** **hemianopic** *adjective & noun* (*a*) *adjective* of, pertaining to, or characterized by hemianopia; (*b*) *noun* a person with hemianopia: **L19.**

hemic *adjective* see **HAEMIC**.

hemicrania /hɛmɪˈkreɪnɪə/ *noun*. **LME.**
[**ORIGIN** Old French *emigraine* or medieval Latin *emigrania* from late Latin *hemicrania* from Greek *hēmikrania*, formed as **HEMI-** + *kranion* skull: see **-IA**[1], **MEGRIM** *noun*[1], and **MIGRAINE**.]
A migraine; a headache, *esp*. one confined to one side of the head.

hemicycle /ˈhɛmɪsʌɪk(ə)l/ *noun*. **L15.**
[**ORIGIN** French *hémicycle* from Latin *hemicyclium* from Greek *hēmikuklion*, formed as **HEMI-** + *kuklos* circle.]
A semicircle; a semicircular structure.

J. ARCHER The hemicycle is a round bank of seats inside the theatre.

hemi-demi-semi- /ˈhɛmɪdɛmɪsɛmi/ *prefix*. Also as adjective **hemi-demi-semi**. **E20.**
[**ORIGIN** from **HEMI-** + **DEMI-** + **SEMI-**, after **HEMIDEMISEMIQUAVER**.]
Half-half-half-, an eighth of; slight(ly), insignificant(ly).

hemidemisemiquaver /ˈhɛmɪdɛmɪˌsɛmɪkweɪvə/ *noun*. **M19.**
[**ORIGIN** from **HEMI-** + **DEMISEMIQUAVER**.]
MUSIC. A note of half the value of a demisemiquaver, represented as a quaver with four hooks.

hemidesmus /hɛmɪˈdɛsməs/ *noun*. **L19.**
[**ORIGIN** mod. Latin (see below), from **HEMI-** + Greek *desmos* bond, with ref. to the partial fusion of the stamens.]
An Indian twining shrub, *Hemidesmus indicus* (family Asclepiadaceae), whose root is used as a substitute for sarsaparilla; a syrup prepared from this root.

hemimetabolous /ˌhɛmɪməˈtab(ə)ləs/ *adjective*. **L19.**
[**ORIGIN** from **HEMI-** + Greek *metabolos* changeable: see **-OUS**.]
ENTOMOLOGY. Of an insect: that undergoes incomplete metamorphosis, with no pupal stage in the transition from larva to adult. Cf. **HOLOMETABOLOUS**.

hemimorphic /hɛmɪˈmɔːfɪk/ *adjective*. **M19.**
[**ORIGIN** from **HEMI-** + Greek *morphē* shape + **-IC**.]
CRYSTALLOGRAPHY. Of a crystal: having unlike planes at the ends of the same axis.
▪ **hemimorphism** *noun* the property of being hemimorphic **L19.**

hemimorphite /hɛmɪˈmɔːfʌɪt/ *noun*. **M19.**
[**ORIGIN** from **HEMIMORPHIC** + **-ITE**[1].]
MINERALOGY. An orthorhombic hydrated zinc silicate, usu. occurring as white flattened prisms, one of the forms of calamine (cf. **SMITHSONITE**).

hemin *noun* see **HAEMIN**.

hemina /həˈmʌɪnə/ *noun*. Long *rare*. Also (earlier) †**emina**. **E17.**
[**ORIGIN** Latin from Greek *hēmina*, formed as **HEMI-**.]
A measure of corn; a liquid measure of approx. half a pint.

Hemingwayesque /ˌhɛmɪŋweɪˈɛsk/ *adjective*. **M20.**
[**ORIGIN** from Ernest *Hemingway* (1899–1961), US novelist + **-ESQUE**.]
Characteristic or in the style of the works of Hemingway.
▪ Also **Hemingˈwayan** *adjective* **M20.**

hemiola /hɛmɪˈəʊlə/ *noun*. Also **-lia** /-lɪə/. **LME.**
[**ORIGIN** medieval Latin *hemiolia* from Greek *hēmiolia*, *-lios* in the ratio of one and a half to one, formed as **HEMI-** + *holos* whole.]
In early music, an interval of a fifth (produced by shortening the string to two-thirds of its length); the substitution of three imperfect notes for two perfect ones. In modern music, the performance of two bars in triple metre as if they were notated as three bars in duple metre.

hemiopsia /hɛmɪˈɒpsɪə/ *noun*. **E19.**
[**ORIGIN** from **HEMI-** + Greek *opsis* sight: see **-IA**[1].]
= **HEMIANOPSIA**.
▪ **hemiopia** /-ˈəʊpɪə/ *noun* [**-OPIA**] = **HEMIANOPSIA** **M19.** **hemiopic** *adjective* = **HEMIANOPIC** *adjective* **L19.**

hemiplegia /hɛmɪˈpliːdʒə/ *noun*. **E17.**
[**ORIGIN** mod. Latin from Greek *hēmiplēgia*, formed as **HEMI-** + *plēgē* stroke: see **-IA**[1]. Cf. **DIPLEGIA**, **PARAPLEGIA**.]
Paralysis of one side of the body.
▪ **hemiplegiac** *noun & adjective* = **HEMIPLEGIC** **L18.** **hemiplegic** *noun & adjective* (a person) affected with hemiplegia **E19.** **ˈhemiplegy** *noun* (*rare*) = **HEMIPLEGIA** **M18.**

hemipode /ˈhɛmɪpəʊd/ *noun*. **M19.**
[**ORIGIN** mod. Latin *Hemipodius* former genus name, from Greek **HEMI-** + *pous*, *podos* foot.]
= ***button-quail*** s.v. **BUTTON** *noun*; ***Andalusian hemipode***, the little button-quail, *Turnix sylvatica* (as occurring in Iberia).

Hemiptera /hɪˈmɪpt(ə)rə/ *noun*. **E19.**
[**ORIGIN** mod. Latin, neut. pl. of *hemipterus*, formed as **HEMI-** + Greek *pteron* wing (with ref. to the partly hardened forewings of bugs): see **-A**[3].]
(Members of) a large order of insects characterized by having piercing and sucking mouthparts, and comprising two suborders, Heteroptera (bugs in the narrower sense) and Homoptera (cicadas, leafhoppers, aphids, scale insects, etc.).

hemipteran /hɪˈmɪpt(ə)rən/ *adjective & noun*. **L19.**
[**ORIGIN** from **HEMIPTERA** + **-AN**.]
▸ **A** *adjective*. Of, pertaining to, or characteristic of the Hemiptera. **L19.**
▸ **B** *noun*. A hemipteran insect. **L19.**
▪ **hemipterous** *adjective* = **HEMIPTERAN** *adjective* **E19.**

hemisphere /ˈhɛmɪsfɪə/ *noun*. **LME.**
[**ORIGIN** Old French *emisp(h)ere* (mod. *hémisphère*) and also Latin *hemisphaerium*, from Greek *hēmisphairion*, formed as **HEMI-** + *sphaira* sphere.]
1 a Half the celestial sphere, now *esp*. as divided by the equinoctial or the ecliptic. Formerly *esp*. that half of the celestial sphere seen above the horizon, the sky. **LME.** ▸**b** Either of the halves of the earth, esp. as divided by the equator (***Northern hemisphere***, ***Southern***

H

hemisphere) or longitudinally (***Eastern hemisphere***, ***Western hemisphere***: see below). M16.

a R. S. BALL The number of stars in the northern hemisphere alone is . . three hundred thousand. **b** J. D. MACDONALD The normal pattern in this hemisphere is for a storm to start near the equator. V. S. NAIPAUL A man from another hemisphere, another background.

b Eastern hemisphere: containing Europe, Asia, and Africa. **Western hemisphere**: containing America.
2 *fig.* A realm of thought, action, etc. E16.

P. E. DOVE To surmise the possibility, as beyond the hemisphere of my knowledge.

3 *gen.* A half sphere. M16.

A. R. AMMONS The dune thistle . . / opening thorny hemispheres / of yellow florets. A. GRAY The chamber was a perfect hemisphere.

MAGDEBURG HEMISPHERE.
4 A map of half the earth or the celestial globe. M17.
5 *ANATOMY.* Each of the halves of the cerebrum. More fully ***cerebral hemisphere***. E19.
■ **hemiˈspheral** *adjective* (*rare*) M19. **hemisphеˈrectomy** *noun* (an instance of) surgical removal of a cerebral hemisphere M20. **hemisphered** *adjective* (*rare*) shaped like a hemisphere M17.

hemispherical /hɛmɪˈsfɛrɪk(ə)l/ *adjective*. E17.
[ORIGIN from HEMISPHERE + -ICAL.]
1 Of the nature of or resembling a hemisphere; of or pertaining to a hemisphere. E17.
2 Concerned with, relating to, or extending over a hemisphere of the earth. L19.
■ **hemispheric** *adjective* = HEMISPHERICAL L16. **hemispherically** *adverb* M19.

H

hemispheroid /hɛmɪˈsfɪərɔɪd/ *noun*. E18.
[ORIGIN from HEMI- + SPHEROID.]
A half spheroid; a figure approaching a hemisphere.
■ **hemispheˈroidal** *adjective* having the form of a hemispheroid E18.

hemistich /ˈhɛmɪstɪk/ *noun*. L16.
[ORIGIN Late Latin *hemistichium* from Greek *hēmistikhion*, formed as HEMI- + STICH.]
Esp. in Old English verse, a half of a line of verse or a line of less than the usual length.

hemitrope /ˈhɛmɪtrəʊp/ *adjective & noun*. Now *rare* or *obsolete*. E19.
[ORIGIN from HEMI- + Greek *-tropos* turning.]
CRYSTALLOGRAPHY. ▸**A** *adjective*. Of a crystal: twinned. E19.
▸**B** *noun*. A twinned crystal. E19.
■ **hemitropic** /-ˈtrəʊpɪk, -ˈtrɒpɪk/ *adjective* L19. **hemiˈtropism** *noun* M19. **heˈmitropy** *noun* L19.

hemlock /ˈhɛmlɒk/ *noun & verb*.
[ORIGIN Old English *hymlic(e*, *hemlic*, of unknown origin. For the late Middle English alt. of the final syll. to *-lock*, cf. *charlock*.]
▸**A** *noun*. **1** A highly poisonous umbelliferous plant, *Conium maculatum*, with glaucous spotted stems, white flowers, and finely divided leaves; also (chiefly *US*) ***poison-hemlock***. Also *loosely*, any of several superficially similar tall umbellifers. OE. ▸**b** A draught prepared from hemlock, reputedly the poison given to Socrates. E17.

b KEATS A drowsy numbness pains My sense, as though of hemlock I had drunk.

water hemlock: see WATER *noun*.
2 More fully ***hemlock spruce***. Any of various coniferous trees of the genus *Tsuga* of N. America and Asia, with drooping branches recalling the leaves of *Conium maculatum*; *esp.* (in full ***western hemlock***) *T. heterophylla*, of western N. America. M17.
MOUNTAIN ***hemlock***.
– COMB.: ***hemlock spruce***: see sense 2 above; **hemlock water dropwort** a poisonous umbellifer of marshy places, *Oenanthe crocata*.
▸**B** *verb trans*. Poison with hemlock. M19.

L. ABERCROMBIE And with this stew Hemlock'd the wine of Heaven.

hemmel /ˈhɛm(ə)l/ *noun*. *N. English*. E18.
[ORIGIN Var. of HELM *noun*[1].]
A (partly covered) cowshed.

hemmer /ˈhɛmə/ *noun*. ME.
[ORIGIN from HEM *verb*[1] + -ER[1].]
1 A person who hems. ME.
2 A hemming attachment for a sewing machine. M19.

hemming /ˈhɛmɪŋ/ *noun*. LME.
[ORIGIN from HEM *verb*[1] + -ING[1].]
The action of HEM *verb*[1]. Formerly also, a hem, a border.

hemo- *combining form*, **hemoglobin** *noun*, **hemophilia** *noun*, **hemorrhage** *noun & verb*, etc.: see HAEMO- etc.

hemp /hɛmp/ *noun*.
[ORIGIN Old English *henep*, *hænep* = Old Saxon *hanap* (Dutch *hennep*), Old High German *hanaf* (German *Hanf*), Old Norse *hampr*, from Germanic word rel. to Greek *kannabis* (whence Latin *cannabis*; cf. CANVAS *noun*[1]).]
1 A herbaceous plant, *Cannabis sativa* (family Cannabaceae), native to central Asia, cultivated for its valuable fibre and the drug marijuana (see ***Indian hemp*** s.v. INDIAN *adjective*). OE.
2 The cortical fibre of this used for making rope and strong fabric. ME. ▸**b** *joc.* or *allus.* A rope for hanging a person. M16.

C. FRANCIS Hemp is strong, but it stretches a good deal when new and shrinks when wet. **b** SHAKES. *Hen. V* And let not hemp his windpipe suffocate.

3 With specifying word: any of various plants related to hemp or producing a similar fibre; the fibre produced by such a plant. L16.
African hemp, ***bowstring hemp***, ***Manila hemp***, ***sisal hemp***, etc.
4 The drug marijuana. L19.
– COMB.: **hemp agrimony** the plant *Eupatorium cannabinum*, of the composite family, found in damp bushy places and with heads of dull purplish flowers; **hempland** (now chiefly *dial.*) a piece of land on which hemp is or was grown; **hemp-nettle** any of several labiate weeds of the genus *Galeopsis*, with leaves like those of nettles; *esp.* the common *G. tetrahit*, which has purple, white, or varicoloured flowers. **hempseed** (*a*) the seed of hemp; †(*b*) (*rare*, Shakes.) a gallows bird.
■ **hempen** *adjective* of, pertaining to, or resembling hemp LME.

hempy /ˈhɛmpi/ *adjective & noun*. Also (*Scot. & N. English*) **hempie**. LME.
[ORIGIN from HEMP + -Y[1].]
▸**A** *adjective*. **1** Hempen. LME.
2 Mischievous, naughty; deserving to be hanged. *joc.* (*Scot. & N. English*). M18.
▸**B** *noun*. A hempy person, esp. a girl. *joc.* (*Scot. & N. English*). E18.

hemstitch /ˈhɛmstɪtʃ/ *noun & verb*. M19.
[ORIGIN from HEM *noun*[1] + STITCH *noun*[1].]
▸**A** *noun*. In *EMBROIDERY*, an ornamental stitch in drawn work involving drawing bundles of thread together and used esp. to hem a piece of work; *gen.* a stitch used to hem a garment etc. involving small widely spaced diagonal stitches designed to be invisible from the right side. M19.
▸**B** *verb trans*. Hem using this stitch. M19.

hen /hɛn/ *noun*.
[ORIGIN Old English *henn* = Old Frisian, Middle Low German *henne*, Old High German *henna* (German *Henne*), from West Germanic deriv. of Germanic base of Old English *hana* cock, rel. to Latin *canere* sing.]
1 A female bird; *esp.* the female of the domestic fowl; in *pl.* also, domestic fowls of both sexes. OE.
2 *fig.* **a** A wife, a woman: *spec.* (*Scot.*) as a familiar form of address to a woman or girl. *colloq.* E17. ▸**b** A coward. L19.

a I. BANKS Oh, hen! Are you all right?

3 Any of various bivalve molluscs; *esp.* (more fully ***hen-clam***) a large clam, *Spisula solidissima*, of the N. American Atlantic coast. Chiefly *N. Amer.* E17.
4 A female fish or crustacean. M18.
– PHRASES: **as scarce as hen's teeth** very scarce. ***like a hen on a hot girdle***: see GIRDLE *noun*[2]. **like a hen with one chicken** absurdly fussy.
– COMB.: **hen and chickens** (*a*) (in full ***hen-and-chickens daisy***) a freak form of the daisy, sometimes cultivated, in which smaller flower heads grow from the edge of the main flower head; (*b*) a kind of houseleek, *Sempervivum soboliferum*, with numerous offsets; (*c*) a kind of children's game; **hen-and-egg** *adjective* = ***chicken-and-egg*** s.v. CHICKEN *noun*[1]; **henbane** a plant of the nightshade family, *Hyoscyamus niger*, with amber purple-streaked flowers, noted for its poisonous and narcotic properties; the drug obtained from this plant; **henbit** either of two low-growing weeds with roundish shallowly lobed leaves: †(*a*) (more fully ***small hen***) the ivy-leaved speedwell, *Veronica hederifolia*; (*b*) (more fully ***hen dead-nettle***, formerly ***great hen***) a kind of dead-nettle, *Lamium amplexicaule*; ***hen-clam***: see sense 3 above; **hen coop**: for keeping fowls in; **hencote** (now *dial.*) a henhouse; **hen egg** a hen's egg; **hen-fruit**, **hen's fruit** (chiefly *US slang*) eggs; **hen harrier** a harrier, *Circus cyaneus*, inhabiting open country and moorland across much of the Palaearctic and New World; **hen-hawk** *US local* any of various large raptors reputed to attack poultry; †**hen heart** = sense 2b above; **hen-hearted** *adjective* lacking courage; **henhouse** a small shed for fowls to roost in; *fig.* an establishment inhabited chiefly by women; **hen night** *colloq.* a celebration held for a woman who is about to get married, attended only by women; **hen party** *colloq.* (orig. *derog.*) a social gathering of women only, *esp.* one held in honour of a woman about to marry; **hen-roost** a place where fowls roost at night; **hen-run** an enclosure for fowls; **hen-scratch** *verb intrans. & trans.* scratch in the manner of a hen; ***hen's fruit***: see ***hen-fruit*** above; **hensure** *adjective* (*joc.*) [after COCKSURE] = COCKSURE *adjective* 4; **henwife** (chiefly *Scot.*, *arch.*) a woman who keeps fowls; **hen yard** = ***hen-run*** above.
■ **hennery** *noun* an establishment or place where hens are reared or kept M19. **henny** *adjective & noun* (*a*) *adjective* of, pertaining to, or resembling a hen; (*b*) *noun* a male fowl resembling a hen: M19.

hen /hɛn/ *adverb*. Long *obsolete* exc. *dial.*
[ORIGIN Old English *heonan(e)* = Old Saxon, Old High German *hinan(a)* (German *hinnen*); also Old English *hina*, *heona* = Middle Low German, Middle Dutch *hēne* (Dutch *heen*), Old High German *hina* (German *hin*): West Germanic formations on the Germanic pronominal base of HE *pers. pronoun*.]
= HENCE *adverb*.
– NOTE: The 1st elem. of HENCE *adverb*.

†**henad** *noun*. L17–L18.
[ORIGIN Greek *henas*, *henad-* unit, from *hen* one: see -AD[1].]
In Platonic philosophy: a unit, a monad.

hence /hɛns/ *adverb, pronoun, & noun*. ME.
[ORIGIN from HEN *adverb* + -S[3]. The spelling *-ce* is phonetic, to retain the unvoiced sound denoted in the earlier spelling by *-s*. Cf. THENCE, WHENCE.]
▸**A** *adverb*. **I** Of place.
1 (Away) from here; to or at a distance from here; away. ME.
2 *spec.* From this world, from this life. ME. ▸†**b** In the next or another world. LME–E17.
go hence die.
3 *ellipt.* As a command: go hence. L16.

SHAKES. *Temp.* Hence! Hang not on my garments.

hence with — go away with —, take — away.
▸**II** Of time.
4 From this time forward. *arch. & poet.* LME. ▸**b** (At some time in the future) from now. L16.

b H. JAMES He wished he might see her ten years hence.

▸**III** Of result or consequence.
5 From this, as a source. L16.
6 For this reason, therefore. L16.

D. LARDNER Hence, the surface of the entire sphere is equal to the surface of the entire cylinder.

7 (As a result) from this fact or circumstance. E17.

A. BURGESS I was seven now, and hence had arrived at the age of reason. *Sunday Express* He is a member of the Upper House of Parliament (hence the Hon.).

▸**B** *pronoun & noun*. **1** ***from hence***, †***of hence***, from this place; from this world; from now on; from this circumstance. LME.
2 The other world; the future. *US*. L19.

E. W. NYE One who is now in the golden hence. F. LYNDE Developments may be safely predicted in the immediate hence.

henceforth /hɛnsˈfɔːθ, ˈhɛnsfɔːθ/ *adverb & pronoun*. LME.
[ORIGIN from HENCE + FORTH *adverb*.]
Also (arch.) ***from henceforth***. From now onwards.

M. SINCLAIR But that resource would henceforth be denied him.

henceforward /hɛnsˈfɔːwəd/ *adverb*. ME.
[ORIGIN formed as HENCEFORTH + FORWARD *adjective*.]
= HENCEFORTH.
■ **henceforwards** *adverb* = HENCEFORWARD *adverb* LME.

henchman /ˈhɛn(t)ʃmən/ *noun*. Pl. **-men**. ME.
[ORIGIN from Old English *heng(e)st* stallion, gelding + MAN *noun*.]
1 *hist.* A squire or page of honour to a person of great rank. ME.
2 The chief personal attendant of a Highland chief; *gen.* a trusty attendant of a leader. M18. ▸**b** A (political) supporter; a partisan. Freq. *derog.* M19.

b D. JACOBSON To have your enemies killed off by your henchmen, as any other tyrant would.

■ **henchwoman** *noun* L19.

†**hend** *verb trans*. ME–L16.
[ORIGIN Prob. from Old English *gehendan* handle, take hold of, from HAND *noun*. Cf. Old Norse *henda*.]
Seize, take; grasp, hold.

hendeca- /ˈhɛndɛkə, hɛnˈdɛkə/ *combining form*. Before a vowel **hendec-**. Also **en-** /ɛn-/.
[ORIGIN Greek *hendeka* eleven.]
Having or consisting of eleven; elevenfold; in *CHEMISTRY* (now *rare*) = UNDECA-.
■ **henˈdecagon** *noun* a plane figure with eleven sides and angles E18. **ˈhendecarchy** *noun* (*rare*) government by eleven people M17.

hendecasyllabic /ˌhɛndɛkəsɪˈlabɪk, hɛnˌdɛk-/ *adjective & noun*. Also **en-** /ɛn-/. E18.
[ORIGIN from Latin *hendecasyllabus* (see HENDECASYLLABLE) + -IC, after *disyllabic*, *trisyllabic*.]
▸**A** *adjective*. Of a line of poetry: consisting of eleven syllables. E18.
▸**B** *noun*. A hendecasyllabic line. Usu. in *pl.* M19.

hendecasyllable /ˌhɛndɛkəˈsɪləb(ə)l, hɛnˌdɛkə-/ *noun*. Also **en-** /ɛn-/. E17.
[ORIGIN Alt. (after SYLLABLE *noun*) of Latin *hendecasyllabus* from Greek *hendekasullabos* use as noun (sc. *stikhos* row, line of verse) of adjective = eleven-syllabled, formed as HENDECA- + *sullabē* SYLLABLE *noun*.]
PROSODY. A verse or line of eleven syllables.

hendiadys /hɛnˈdʌɪədɪs/ *noun*. L16.
[ORIGIN medieval Latin, from Greek *hen dia duoin* lit. 'one through two'.]
A figure of speech in which a single complex idea is expressed by two words usu. connected by *and* (e.g. *nice and warm* for *nicely warm*).

heneicosane /hɛˈnʌɪkəseɪn/ *noun*. L19.
[ORIGIN from Greek *hen-*, *heis* one + *eikosi* twenty + -ANE.]
CHEMISTRY. Any saturated hydrocarbon of formula $C_{21}H_{44}$, of which numerous isomers exist; *spec.* the unbranched isomer (also called *n-****heneicosane***).

henequen /ˈhɛnɪkɛn/ *noun*. Also **-quin**. E17.
[ORIGIN Spanish *jeniquen*, *geniquen*, from the Mexican name.]
A Mexican agave, *Agave fourcroydes*, grown for its leaf fibre; the fibre obtained from this plant.

henge /hɛn(d)ʒ/ *noun*[1]. M18.
[ORIGIN from STONE)HENGE.]
†**1** A stone that is suspended overhead or overhangs. Only in M18.

2 *ARCHAEOLOGY.* Any large circular monument usually of later Neolithic date, comprising a bank and internal ditch which may enclose stone or wooden structures. **M20.**

†**henge** *noun*[2] var. of **HINGE** *noun*.

Henle /ˈhɛnli/ *noun*. **M19.**
[**ORIGIN** F. G. J. *Henle* (1809–85), German anatomist.]
ANATOMY. Used in *possess.* to designate structures described by Henle.
Henle's layer, layer of Henle a layer of cubical cells in the inner root sheath of the hair follicle. **Henle's loop, loop of Henle** the part of a kidney tubule forming a loop within the renal medulla.

henna /ˈhɛnə/ *noun & verb*. **E17.**
[**ORIGIN** Arabic *ḥinnā'*: cf. **ALCANNA, ALKANET.**]
▸ **A** *noun*. A shrub of the purple loosestrife family, *Lawsonia inermis*, native from N. Africa to India; a preparation of its powdered leaves and shoots, used to stain the hair and, in the east, the fingernails etc. a reddish-yellow colour. **E17.**
▸ **B** *verb trans*. Dye or stain with henna. Chiefly as ***hennaed*** *ppl adjective*. **E20.**

Henoch /ˈhiːnɒk/ *noun*. **L19.**
[**ORIGIN** E. H. *Henoch* (1820–1910), German paediatrician.]
MEDICINE. **1** ***Henoch's purpura***, a form of Henoch–Schönlein purpura associated esp. with gastrointestinal symptoms. Cf. **SCHÖNLEIN** 1. **L19.**
2 ***Henoch–Schönlein purpura***, ***Henoch–Schönlein syndrome***, a form of purpura affecting mainly young children, esp. boys, involving a characteristic rash and gastrointestinal or rheumatic symptoms. **M20.**

henotheism /ˈhɛnəʊˌθiːɪz(ə)m/ *noun*. **M19.**
[**ORIGIN** from Greek *heno-* stem of *heis* one + *theos* god + **-ISM.**]
Belief in a single god of e.g. one's tribe, without assertion that there is only one god.
■ **henotheist** *noun* **L19.** **henotheˈistic** *adjective* **L19.**

henpeck /ˈhɛnpɛk/ *verb & noun*. *colloq*. **L17.**
[**ORIGIN** (Back-form.) from **HENPECKED.**]
▸ **A** *verb trans*. Of a wife: domineer over (her husband). Usu. in *pass*. **L17.**

N. BAWDEN Always the gentleman, hen-pecked by his harridan wife.

▸ **B** *noun*. *rare*.
1 A henpecked husband; a domineering wife. **M18.**
2 Domineering by a wife. **M19.**
■ **henpeckery** *noun* (*rare*) the state or condition of being henpecked **M19.**

henpecked /ˈhɛnpɛkt/ *adjective*. *colloq*. **L17.**
[**ORIGIN** from **HEN** *noun* + **PECKED** *ppl adjective* (alluding to the plucking of the domestic cock by his hens).]
Domineered over or ruled by a wife.

D. H. LAWRENCE A little red-faced man, rather beery and hen-pecked looking.

Henrician /hɛnˈrɪʃɪən, -ʃ(ə)n/ *noun & adjective*. *hist*. **L16.**
[**ORIGIN** medieval Latin *Henrician-*, from *Henricus* Henry: see **-IAN.**]
▸ **A** *noun*. A follower of any of various people named Henry; *spec*. (***a***) a follower of Henry of Lausanne, a religious and moral reformer of the 12th cent.; (***b***) a supporter of the ecclesiastical policy of Henry VIII, king of England (1509–47). **L16.**
▸ **B** *adjective*. Of or pertaining to Henry (see above) or the Henricians. **L19.**

Henri Deux /ɑ̃ri dø/ *adjectival phr*. **M19.**
[**ORIGIN** French = Henri II (see below).]
Designating (the style of) Renaissance art or architecture developed in France during the reign of Henri II, king of France 1547–59; *esp*. designating the purest style of the French Renaissance.

Henrietta /hɛnrɪˈɛtə/ *noun*. *obsolete* exc. *hist*. **M19.**
[**ORIGIN** Female name.]
In full ***Henrietta cloth***. A lightweight dress fabric, sometimes with a silk warp.

Henry /ˈhɛnri/ *noun*[1]. **M19.**
[**ORIGIN** Benjamin Tyler *Henry* (1821–98), Amer. inventor.]
Used *attrib*. to designate (parts of) a breech-loading magazine rifle introduced by Henry. See also **MARTINI** *noun*[1].

henry /ˈhɛnri/ *noun*[2]. Pl. **-ries, -rys. L19.**
[**ORIGIN** Joseph *Henry* (1797–1878), US physicist.]
PHYSICS. The SI unit of inductance, equal to the inductance of a circuit in which an electromotive force of one volt is produced by a current changing at the rate of one ampere per second. (Symbol H.)

Henry Clay /hɛnri ˈkleɪ/ *noun*. **M19.**
[**ORIGIN** *Henry Clay* (1777–1852), US statesman.]
A type of cigar.

Henry's law /ˈhɛnrɪz lɔː/ *noun phr*. **L19.**
[**ORIGIN** William *Henry* (1774–1836), English chemist.]
CHEMISTRY. The statement that the amount of a gas dissolved in a given quantity of liquid in conditions of equilibrium is directly proportional to the pressure of the gas in contact with the liquid.

†**hent** *noun*. **E16.**
[**ORIGIN** from the verb.]
1 The act of seizing; a grasp. Only in **E16.**
2 Something grasped in the mind; an idea. Only in **E17.**

hent /hɛnt/ *verb*. *arch*. & *dial*. Pa. t. & pple **hent**.
[**ORIGIN** Old English *hentan*, from Germanic weak grade of base of **HUNT** *verb*.]
1 *verb trans*. Seize, grasp; move; take (*away*, *off*, etc.), put (*on*). **OE.**
†**2** *verb trans*. Arrive at, reach, occupy. **ME–E17.**
†**3** *verb trans*. Get, take, receive, meet with; experience, suffer; apprehend. **ME–L16.**
†**4** *verb trans*. Seize, affect (as an influence or condition). **ME–E17.**
5 *verb intrans*. Go, depart. **L16.**

Hentenian /hɛnˈtiːnɪən/ *adjective*. **E20.**
[**ORIGIN** from *Henten* (see below) + **-IAN.**]
Designating editions of the Vulgate prepared at Louvain by John Henten or Hentenius (1499–1566), theologian of the Dominican order.

hentriacontane /ˌhɛntrʌɪəˈkɒnteɪn/ *noun*. **L19.**
[**ORIGIN** from Greek *hen-*, *heis* one + *triakonta* thirty + **-ANE.**]
CHEMISTRY. Any of a series of saturated hydrocarbons (alkanes) with the formula $C_{31}H_{64}$; *spec*. (also n-*hentriacontane*) the unbranched isomer, $CH_3(CH_2)_{29}CH_3$, found in paraffin wax.

heortology /hɪɔːˈtɒlədʒi/ *noun*. **E20.**
[**ORIGIN** German *Heortologie*, French *héortologie*, from Greek *heortē* feast: see **-OLOGY.**]
The branch of knowledge that deals with the religious feasts and seasons of the Christian year.
■ **heortologist** *noun* **E20.**

hep /hɛp/ *noun*[1]. *slang*. **E20.**
[**ORIGIN** from the adjective.]
The state of being hep; something that is hep.

hep *noun*[2] var. of **HIP** *noun*[2].

hep /hɛp/ *adjective*. *slang*. **E20.**
[**ORIGIN** Unknown. Cf. **HIP** *adjective*, *verb*[3].]
= **HIP** *adjective*

S. SELVON Tall Boy, I always thought you was hep, that you on the ball.

hep-cat = ***hip-cat*** s.v. **HIP** *adjective*.
■ **hepster** *noun* = ***hep-cat*** above (cf. **HIPSTER** *noun*[1]) **M20.**

hep /hɛp/ *verb trans*. Infl. **-pp-. M20.**
[**ORIGIN** from the adjective.]
Pep *up*.
■ **hepped** *ppl adjective* (***a***) pepped *up*; (***b***) (foll. by *on*) enthusiastic about: **M20.**

hep /hɛp/ *interjection*. **M19.**
[**ORIGIN** Perh. from the initials of Latin *Hierosolyma Est Perdita* (Jerusalem is destroyed).]
Usu. redupl. ***hep! hep!*** Used by (German) persecutors of Jews in the 19th cent.

hepar /ˈhiːpɑː/ *noun*. *obsolete* exc. *hist*. **L17.**
[**ORIGIN** Late Latin from Greek *hēpar* liver.]
Any of various sulphur compounds, generally of a reddish-brown colour and often in (former) medicinal use.
– **COMB.:** **hepar sulphur(is)** (***a***) a preparation containing potassium sulphide; (***b***) in *HOMEOPATHY*, calcium sulphide.

heparin /ˈhɛpərɪn/ *noun*. **E20.**
[**ORIGIN** formed as **HEPAR** + **-IN**[1].]
BIOCHEMISTRY. A sulphur-containing polysaccharide with anticoagulant properties, present in the blood and various bodily organs and tissues.
■ **heparini'zation** *noun* the process of heparinizing **M20.** **heparinize** *verb trans*. treat with heparin so as to inhibit blood clotting **M20.**

hepat- *combining form* see **HEPATO-**.

hepatic /hɪˈpatɪk/ *adjective & noun*. **LME.**
[**ORIGIN** Latin *hepaticus* from Greek *hēpatikos*, from *hēpar*, *hēpat-* liver: see **-IC.**]
▸ **A** *adjective* **I** †**1** Affected with a liver complaint. Only in **LME.**
2 Of or pertaining to the liver. **L16.**
3 Acting on the liver, good for the liver. **L17.**
▸ **II** **4** Of the colour of liver; dark reddish-brown. **LME.**
5 Sulphurous; containing sulphur. Cf. **HEPAR.** *arch*. **M17.**
▸ **B** *noun*. **1** A medicine that acts on the liver. **L15.**
2 = **LIVERWORT. L19.**
■ **hepatical** *adjective* (now *rare*) = **HEPATIC** *adjective* **E17.**

hepatica /hɪˈpatɪkə, hɛ-/ *noun*. Pl. **-cas**, (in sense 1) **-cae** /-kiː/. **LME.**
[**ORIGIN** medieval Latin (sc. *herba*) plant with liver-shaped parts or used for liver diseases, use as noun of fem. of Latin *hepaticus*: see **HEPATIC.**]
1 = **LIVERWORT** 1. Orig., (a herbalist's name for) the liverwort *Marchantia polymorpha*. **LME.**
2 Any of several spring-flowering woodland plants of northern temperate regions belonging to the genus *Hepatica*, allied to the anemone, with three-lobed leaves thought to resemble the liver. **L16.**
■ **hepatiˈcologist** *noun* a person who studies liverworts **L19.**

hepatico- /hɪˈpatɪkəʊ/ *combining form* of **HEPATIC**: see **-O-**. = **HEPATO-**.
■ **hepatiˈcostomy** *noun* (the surgical formation of) an opening in the main bile duct; an instance of this: **E20.**

hepatisation *noun* var. of **HEPATIZATION**.

hepatitis /hɛpəˈtʌɪtɪs/ *noun*. **E18.**
[**ORIGIN** mod. Latin, from Greek *hēpar*, *hēpat-* liver + **-ITIS.**]
MEDICINE. Inflammation of the liver; any of several diseases in which this occurs.
hepatitis A infectious hepatitis. **hepatitis B** serum hepatitis. **hepatitis C** a viral form of hepatitis transmitted in infected blood, causing chronic liver disease. **infectious hepatitis** a viral form of hepatitis transmitted in food, causing fever and jaundice. ***SERUM hepatitis***.

hepatization /hɛpətʌɪˈzeɪʃ(ə)n/ *noun*. Also **-isation. L18.**
[**ORIGIN** from Greek *hēpar*, *hēpat-* liver + **-IZATION.**]
†**1** *CHEMISTRY.* Treatment with hydrogen sulphide. Cf. **HEPATIC** *adjective* 5. Only in **L18.**
2 *MEDICINE.* Consolidation of lung tissue into a solid mass resembling liver tissue, occurring in lobar pneumonia. **E19.**
■ †**hepatize** *verb trans*. (*CHEMISTRY*) treat with hydrogen sulphide **L18–M19.**

hepato- /ˈhɛpətəʊ/ *combining form* of Greek *hēpar*, *hēpat-* liver: see **-O-**. Before a vowel also **hepat-**. Cf. **HEPATICO-**.
■ **hepaˈtectomy** *noun* (an instance of) surgical removal of all or part of the liver: **E20.** **hepatoˈcellular** *adjective* of or pertaining to the cells of the liver **M20.** **hepaˈtoma** *noun*, pl. **-mas**, **-mata** /-mətə/, a carcinoma of the epithelial cells of the liver **E20.** **hepatomeˈgalia** *noun* = **HEPATOMEGALY L19.** **hepatoˈmegaly** *noun* abnormal enlargement of the liver **E20.** **hepatoˈpancreas** *noun* (*ZOOLOGY*) a glandular organ of digestion in most crustaceans **L19.** **hepaˈtoscopy** *noun* divination by examination of the liver of an animal **E18.** ˌ**hepatoˌsplenomeˈgalia**, ˌ**hepatoˌsplenoˈmegaly** *nouns* abnormal enlargement of the liver and spleen **M20.** **hepatoˈtoxic** *adjective* toxic to liver cells **M20.** **hepatotoˈxicity** *noun* hepatotoxic character **M20.** **hepatoˈtoxin** *noun* any substance toxic to the liver **M20.**

hepatolenticular /ˌhɛpətəʊlɛnˈtɪkjʊlə/ *adjective*. **E20.**
[**ORIGIN** from **HEPATO-** + **LENTICULAR** (as affecting the lenticular (lentiform) nuclei of the basal ganglia of the brain).]
MEDICINE. ***hepatolenticular degeneration***, = ***Wilson's disease*** s.v. **WILSON** *noun*[2].

Hephaestian /hɪˈfiːstɪən/ *adjective*. **M17.**
[**ORIGIN** from *Hephaestus* (see below) + **-IAN.**]
Of, belonging to, or made by Hephaestus, Greek god of fire, identified by the Romans with Vulcan.

hephthemimer /hɛfθɪˈmɪmə/ *noun*. Also (earlier) in Latin form **-meris** /-mərɪs/. **E18.**
[**ORIGIN** Late Latin *hephthemimeres* (*-is*) from Greek *hephthēmimerēs* containing seven halves, from *hepta* seven + *hēmi-* half + *meros* part, *-merēs* -partite.]
CLASSICAL PROSODY. A group of seven half-feet; the part of a hexameter line preceding the caesura when this occurs in the middle of the fourth foot.
■ **hepthemimeral** *adjective* **L19.**

hepialid /hiːpɪˈalɪd/ *adjective & noun*. **L19.**
[**ORIGIN** mod. Latin *Hepialidae* (see below), from *Hepialus* genus name from Greek *hēpiolos* moth, perh. alt. by confusion with *ēpialos* nightmare: see **-ID**[3].]
ENTOMOLOGY. ▸**A** *adjective*. Of, pertaining to, or designating the family Hepialidae, comprising the swift moths. **L19.**
▸ **B** *noun*. A moth of this family. **L19.**

Hepplewhite /ˈhɛp(ə)lwʌɪt/ *noun*. **L19.**
[**ORIGIN** George *Hepplewhite* (d. 1786), English cabinetmaker.]
Used *attrib*. to designate an English style of furniture of the late 18th cent., characterized by lightness, delicacy, and graceful curves.

hepta- /ˈhɛptə/ *combining form*. Before a vowel **hept-**.
[**ORIGIN** Greek *hepta* seven.]
Having seven, sevenfold.
■ **heptachlor** *noun* a chlorinated hydrocarbon, $C_{10}H_5Cl_7$, used as an insecticide **M20.** **heptaˈhydrate** *noun* (*CHEMISTRY*) a hydrate containing seven moles of water per mole of the compound **L19.** **heptahyˈdrated** *adjective* (*CHEMISTRY*) hydrated with seven moles of water per mole of the compound **L19.** **heptamer** *noun* (*CHEMISTRY*) a compound whose molecule is composed of seven molecules of monomer **M20.** **heptaˈmeric** *adjective* (*CHEMISTRY*) of the nature of a heptamer, consisting of a heptamer or heptamers **L20.** **hepˈtangular** *adjective* having seven angles **E18.** **heptastich** *noun* a group of seven lines of verse **L19.** **heptasyˈllabic** *noun & adjective* (a metrical line) of seven syllables **L18.** **heptaˈtonic** *adjective* (*MUSIC*) consisting of seven notes **L19.** **heptaˈvalent** *adjective* (*CHEMISTRY*) having a valency of seven **L19.**

heptachord /ˈhɛptəkɔːd/ *adjective & noun*. **E18.**
[**ORIGIN** In senses A., B.1 from Greek *heptakhordos* seven-stringed from **HEPTA-** + *khordē* string (see **CORD** *noun*[1]). In sense B.2, 3 from **HEPTA-** + **CHORD** *noun*[1].]
MUSIC. ▸†**A** *adjective*. Seven-stringed. **E–M18.**
▸ **B** *noun*. **1** Any musical instrument of seven strings. **M18.**
2 The interval of a seventh. **M18.**
3 A scale of seven notes; the modern major or minor scale. **L18.**

heptacosane /hɛptəˈkəʊseɪn/ *noun*. Also (earlier) †**heptaicosane. L19.**
[**ORIGIN** from **HEPTA-** + Greek *eikosi* twenty + **-ANE.**]
CHEMISTRY. Any of a series of saturated hydrocarbons (alkanes) with the formula $C_{27}H_{56}$; *spec*. (also n-*heptacosane*) the unbranched isomer, $CH_3(CH_2)_{25}CH_3$.

H

heptad /ˈhɛptad/ *noun*. **M17.**
[**ORIGIN** Greek *heptad-*, *heptas*, from *hepta* seven: see **-AD**[1].]
1 A group of seven. **M17.**
2 *spec.* = **HEBDOMAD** 2. **L19.**
†**3** *CHEMISTRY.* A heptavalent element or group. Only in **L19.**

heptadecane /hɛptəˈdɛkeɪn/ *noun*. **L19.**
[**ORIGIN** from **HEPTA-** + Greek *deka* ten + **-ANE.**]
CHEMISTRY. Any of a series of saturated hydrocarbons (alkanes) with the formula $C_{17}H_{36}$; *spec.* (also n-*heptadecane*) the solid unbranched isomer, $CH_3(CH_2)_{15}CH_3$.
■ **heptadecaˈnoic** *adjective* = **MARGARIC** **L19.**

heptaglot /ˈhɛptəglɒt/ *noun & adjective*. **L17.**
[**ORIGIN** from Greek *hepta* seven + *glōtta* tongue, *glōttos* tongued, prob. after **POLYGLOT.**]
(A book) in seven languages.

heptagon /ˈhɛptəg(ə)n/ *noun*. **L16.**
[**ORIGIN** French *heptagone* or medieval Latin *heptagonum* use as noun of neut. sing. of late Latin *heptagonus* adjective from Greek *heptagonos* seven-cornered, formed as **HEPTA-**: see **-GON.**]
GEOMETRY. A plane figure with seven straight sides and seven angles.
■ **heptagonal** /hɛpˈtag(ə)n(ə)l/ *adjective* having the form of a heptagon; having seven sides: **E17.**

heptahedron /hɛptəˈhiːdrən, -ˈhɛd-/ *noun*. Pl. **-dra** /-drə/, **-drons.** **L17.**
[**ORIGIN** from **HEPTA-** + **-HEDRON.**]
A solid figure or object with seven plane faces.
■ **heptahedral** *adjective* having the form of a heptahedron; having seven faces: **M18.** †**heptahedrical** *adjective* = **HEPTAHEDRAL**: **M–L17.**

†**heptaicosane** *noun* var. of **HEPTACOSANE.**

heptamerous /hɛpˈtam(ə)rəs/ *adjective*. **M19.**
[**ORIGIN** from **HEPTA-** + Greek *meros* part + **-OUS.**]
Having seven parts.

heptameter /hɛpˈtamɪtə/ *noun*. **L19.**
[**ORIGIN** Late Latin *heptametrum* from Greek *heptametron*, from *hepta-* **HEPTA-** + *metron* measure, metre.]
PROSODY. A line of seven metrical feet.
■ **heptaˈmetrical** *adjective* **E19.**

heptane /ˈhɛpteɪn/ *noun*. **L19.**
[**ORIGIN** from **HEPTA-** + **-ANE.**]
CHEMISTRY. Any of a series of saturated hydrocarbons with the formula C_7H_{16}; *esp.* (also n-*heptane*) the unbranched isomer, $CH_3(CH_2)_5CH_3$.
■ **heptaˈnoic** *adjective* = **OENANTHIC** **E20.**

heptarch /ˈhɛptɑːk/ *noun*. **L17.**
[**ORIGIN** from **HEPTA-** + **-ARCH**, after **TETRARCH** *noun*.]
†**1** A seventh king (see *Revelation* 17:9–11). Only in **L17.**
2 A ruler of one of seven divisions of a country; *esp.* any of the rulers of the Anglo-Saxon Heptarchy. **E19.**

heptarchy /ˈhɛptɑːki/ *noun*. **L16.**
[**ORIGIN** from **HEPTA-** + **-ARCHY**, after **TETRARCHY.**]
Government by seven rulers; an aggregate of seven districts, each under its own ruler; *spec.* the supposed seven kingdoms of the Angles and Saxons in Britain in the 7th and 8th cents.
■ **hepˈtarchal** *adjective* **M19.** **hepˈtarchic** *adjective* **L18.** **hepˈtarchical** *adjective* **M19.**

heptateuch /ˈhɛptətjuːk/ *noun*. **L17.**
[**ORIGIN** Late Latin *heptateuchus* from Greek *heptateukhos*, from *hepta* seven + *teukhos* book.]
A volume consisting of seven books; ***the Heptateuch***, the first seven books of the Bible. Cf. **PENTATEUCH.**

heptathlon /hɛpˈtaθlɒn, -lən/ *noun*. **L20.**
[**ORIGIN** from **HEPTA-** + Greek *athlon* contest.]
An athletic contest, usu. for women, comprising seven different events for the competitor.
■ **heptathlete** *noun* a competitor in the heptathlon **L20.**

heptode /ˈhɛptəʊd/ *noun*. **M20.**
[**ORIGIN** from **HEPTA-** + **-ODE**[2].]
ELECTRONICS. A thermionic tube with seven electrodes.

heptoic /hɛpˈtəʊɪk/ *adjective*. **L19.**
[**ORIGIN** from **HEPTA-** + **-OIC.**]
CHEMISTRY. = **OENANTHIC.**

heptose /ˈhɛptəʊz, -s/ *noun*. **L19.**
[**ORIGIN** from **HEPTA-** + **-OSE**[2].]
CHEMISTRY. Any monosaccharide sugar with seven carbon atoms in its molecule.

heptyl /ˈhɛptʌɪl, -tɪl/ *noun*. **M19.**
[**ORIGIN** from **HEPTA-** + **-YL.**]
CHEMISTRY. A radical, $C_7H_{15}\cdot$, derived from a heptane. Usu. in *comb.*

her /həː, *unstressed* ə/ *pers. pronoun*[1], *3 sing. fem. objective (dat. & accus.)*, *& noun*.
[**ORIGIN** Old English *hire* dat. of *hīo*, *hēo* **HOO** *pronoun*, = Old Frisian *hiri*, Middle Dutch *hare*, *haer*, *hore*, Dutch *haar*, with inflection parallel to Old Saxon *iru*, Old High German *iru*, *iro* (German *ihr*), Gothic *izai*.]
▸ **A** *pronoun* **I 1** Objective (direct & indirect) of **SHE** *pronoun* (orig. of **HOO** *pronoun*): the female person or animal, or the animal conventionally regarded as female (as a cat, a hare, a rabbit), or the thing personified or conventionally treated as female or (in early use) grammatically feminine, previously mentioned or implied or easily identified. **OE.** ▸**b** Herself: direct (*arch.* exc. after prepositions) & indirect (*arch.* exc. *US dial.*) objective. **OE.**

> TENNYSON He stoops—to kiss her—on his knee. J. MASEFIELD All I ask is a tall ship and a star to steer her by. J. RHYS To get in the dig that will make him or her feel superior. E. BOWEN Suspiciousness made him send her frequent bunches of flowers, and post her . . little letters. J. BETJEMAN The Morris eight . . . Put her in reverse. O. MANNING Harriet looked uneasily about her. J. BALDWIN I love America . . and . . I insist on the right to criticize her. **b** C. KINGSLEY Then peevishly she flung her on her face.

her indoors *colloq.* (freq. *joc.*) one's wife, the woman with whom one lives. **herseems**, **-seemeth**, (pa. t. **-seemed**) *verb intrans. impers.* (long *arch.*) it seems, seemed, to her (modifying a sentence or parenthetically).
2 Subjective: she. Esp. pred. after *be* & after *than*, *as*. As subj. of a verb *W. Indian*. **L17.**

> OED I am sure it was her that told me.

not quite her (of a garment etc.) that does not suit her.
▸ **II 3** Repr. the English of Welsh or Gaelic speakers: he, him, his. **E16.**
▸ **B** *noun*. The female; a female. *colloq.* **M17.**

her /həː, *unstressed* ə/ *possess. pronoun*[2] *& adjective* (in mod. usage also classed as a **determiner**), *3 sing. fem.*
[**ORIGIN** Old English *hiere*, *hire* genit. of *hīo*, *hēo* **HOO** *pronoun*, = Old Frisian *hiri*, Middle Dutch *hare*, Dutch *haar*, with inflection parallel to Old Saxon *ira*, *iro*, *iru*, *ire*, Old High German *ira*, *iro*, Middle High German *ire*, *ir* (German *ihr*), Gothic *izōs*. Cf. **HERN** *pronoun*, **HERS** *pronoun*.]
▸ †**A** *pronoun*. **1** Genit. of **HOO** *pronoun*; of her. **OE–ME.**
2 = **HERS.** Only in **ME.**
▸ **B** *adjective* (*attrib.*). **1** Of her; of herself; which belongs or pertains to her(self). **OE.** ▸**b** In titles (as ***Her Ladyship***, ***Her Majesty***): that she is. **LME.**

> J. CONRAD It does not matter much to a ship having all the open sea before her bows. J. BUCHAN London at the turn of the century had not yet lost her Georgian air. E. WAUGH Then she went on her way to the scoutmaster's. P. KAVANAGH With her left hand she poked the fire with a long pot-stick and her handling of that pot-stick showed better than her talk her annoyance with her son. SCOTT FITZGERALD Her name was Irene Scheerer, and her father was one of the men who . . believed in Dexter. I. MURDOCH Laura was looking her most energetic and eccentric.

her own: see **OWN** *adjective & pronoun*. ***her watch***: see **WATCH** *noun*.
2 After a noun (esp. a personal name): substituting for the genit. inflection or possess. suffix **-'s**[1]. *arch.* **OE.**

> H. L'ESTRANGE The Excellency of our Church her burial office.

Heracleid /ˈhɛrəklʌɪd/ *noun*. **M19.**
[**ORIGIN** Greek *Hērakleidēs* (pl. *-dai*), Latin *Heraclides* (pl. *-dae*).]
Any of the descendants of Heracles (Hercules) from whom the Dorian aristocracy of the Peloponnese claimed descent. Usu. in *pl.*
■ **Heraˈcleidan** *adjective* of or pertaining to a Heracleid or the Heracleids **E19.**

Heracleitean *adjective & noun* var. of **HERACLITEAN.**

Heracleonite /hɛrəˈkliːənʌɪt/ *noun*. **M16.**
[**ORIGIN** from *Heracleon* (see below) + **-ITE**[1].]
A member of a sect of Gnostics founded by Heracleon (fl. AD 145–80), a disciple of Valentinus.

heracleum /hɛrəˈkliːəm, hɛˈraklɪəm/ *noun*. **L18.**
[**ORIGIN** mod. Latin, from Greek *hērakleia* a plant named after Heracles.]
Any of various tall umbelliferous plants constituting the genus *Heracleum*, which includes the cow parsnip or hogweed, *H. sphondylium*.

Heraclitean /hɛrəklʌɪˈtiːən/ *adjective & noun*. Also **-cleit-**. **E18.**
[**ORIGIN** from (Latin *Heraclitus* from) Greek *Hērakleiteios*, from *Hērakleitos* Heraclitus (see below): see **-AN.**]
▸ **A** *adjective*. Of or pertaining to (the theories of) the Greek philosopher Heraclitus of Ephesus (fl. *c* 500 BC), who maintained that all things are in a state of flux. **E18.**
▸ **B** *noun*. A follower of Heraclitus. **L19.**
■ **Heracliteanism** *noun* **L19.** **Heraˈclitic** *adjective* = **HERACLITEAN** *adjective* **L17.**

herald /ˈhɛr(ə)ld/ *noun*. **ME.**
[**ORIGIN** Old French *herau(l)t* (mod. *héraut*) from Germanic bases of **HERE** *noun*[1] and **WIELD** *verb*.]
1 *hist.* An official employed to make a ruler's proclamations and carry ceremonial messages between heads of state, or in tournaments, to convey challenges, marshal combatants, etc., or at Court, to arrange various state ceremonies, regulate the use of armorial bearings, settle questions of precedence, etc. Formerly also ***herald of arms***, ***herald at arms***. **ME.**

> C. THIRLWALL A herald came to demand an armistice. A. SETON The King's heralds had galloped throughout the country proclaiming the great tournament.

Windsor herald: see **WINDSOR** *adjective* 1.
2 *transf.* & *fig.* **a** A messenger, an envoy. Also in titles of newspapers. **LME.** ▸**b** A person who or thing which precedes and announces the approach of another; a precursor. **L16.**

> **a** W. COWPER A herald of God's love to pagan lands. **b** T. H. HUXLEY Earthquakes are often the heralds of volcanic eruptions.

a Catholic Herald, ***Glasgow Herald***, etc.
3 Any of the members of the College of Arms (**COLLEGE** *noun* 1) or (in Scotland) of the Court of the Lord Lyon directly senior to the pursuivants. **M16.** ▸**b** An expert in heraldry. **E19.**
Heralds' College: see **COLLEGE** 1. **Heralds' Office** the office of the College of Arms.
– **COMB.:** **herald-snake** a moderately venomous southern African snake, *Crotaphopeltis hotamboeia*, with red- or yellow-edged mouth.

herald /ˈhɛr(ə)ld/ *verb trans*. **LME.**
[**ORIGIN** Old French *herauder*, *heraulder*, etc., formed as **HERALD** *noun*.]
Proclaim the approach of; usher *in*. Chiefly *fig.*

> B. EMECHETA An envelope . . one of those horrible khaki-coloured ones that usually herald the gas bill. A. PRICE Any . . distant noise which might herald Audley's return.

heraldic /hɛˈraldɪk/ *adjective*. **L18.**
[**ORIGIN** from **HERALD** *noun* + **-IC**: cf. French *héraldique*.]
Of, pertaining to, or represented in heraldry.

> O. NEUBECKER Unlike its natural counterpart, the heraldic pelican has no bill pouch.

heraldic tyger: see **TIGER** *noun* 3.
■ **heraldical** *adjective* = **HERALDIC** **E17.** **heraldically** *adverb* **E19.**

heraldist /ˈhɛr(ə)ldɪst/ *noun*. **E19.**
[**ORIGIN** from **HERALD** *noun* + **-IST.**]
An expert in heraldry.

heraldry /ˈhɛr(ə)ldri/ *noun*. **L16.**
[**ORIGIN** from **HERALD** *noun* + **-RY.**]
1 The art or science of a herald; *spec.* that of blazoning armorial bearings and deciding the rights of people to bear arms. **L16.** ▸†**b** Heraldic law. *rare* (Shakes.). Only in **E17.** ▸†**c** Heraldic rank or title. Also, the practice of buying and selling precedence in a list of cases to be heard. **E17–M18.**

> **b** SHAKES. *Haml.* This Fortinbras; who by a Seal'd Compact, Well ratified by law and heraldry, Did forfeit . . all those his lands. **c** SHAKES. *All's Well* You are more saucy with lords . . than the commission of your birth and virtue gives you heraldry.

2 A heraldic emblazonment; heraldic devices collectively. **L16.**

> F. R. WILSON A series of panels filled alternately with heraldry and figures.

3 The office of herald or messenger. **L16.**
4 Ceremony characteristic of a herald. **M17.**

> J. S. MILL A writer . . announced, with all the pomp and heraldry of triumphant genius, a discovery.

†**heraldy** *noun*. **LME–M18.**
[**ORIGIN** from **HERALD** *noun* + **-Y**[3].]
= **HERALDRY.**

Herat /hɛˈrɑːt/ *adjective*. **E20.**
[**ORIGIN** A city in NW Afghanistan.]
Designating a type of carpet or rug made at Herat, or the small close design of leaf and rosette patterns characteristic of this.
■ **Herati** *noun & adjective* (**a**) *noun* a Herat carpet or rug; (**b**) *adjective* = **HERAT**: **E20.**

herb /həːb/ *noun*. **ME.**
[**ORIGIN** Old French *erbe* (mod. *herbe*) from Latin *herba* grass, green crops, herb. The spelling with *h* is recorded from the earliest times, but a pronunc. without initial aspirate was regular till **E19.**]
1 A plant whose stem does not become woody and persistent (as in a shrub or tree) but remains soft and succulent, and dies (completely or down to the root) after flowering. **ME.**
2 A (freq. aromatic) plant used for flavouring or scent, in medicine, etc. **ME.**

> R. INGALLS She sprinkled some herbs and salt on the top.

3 *collect.* Herbage. In later use *poet.* **LME.**

> W. OWEN Soon they topped the hill, and raced . . Over an open stretch of herb and heather.

†**4** The leafy part of a (herbaceous) plant, esp. as distinct from the root. **M17–L18.**
– **COMB. & PHRASES:** **herb beer** a drink made from herbs; ***herb bennet***: see **BENNET** *noun*[1]; **herb Christopher** [translating medieval Latin *herba Christophori* herb of St Christopher, early martyr] (**a**) a baneberry, *esp.* a common Eurasian baneberry, *Actaea spicata*; †(**b**) royal fern, *Osmunda regalis*; **herb-doctor** (chiefly *N. Amer.*) a doctor who treats diseases with herbs instead of conventional remedies; **herb Gerard** [named after St *Gerard* of Toul (*c* 935–94), formerly invoked against gout] the plant ground elder, *Aegopodium podagraria*; ***herb-grace***: see ***herb of grace*** below; ***herb mastic***: see **MASTIC** *noun* 3; **herb of grace**, **herb-grace** (now *arch.* & *dial.*) [app. after the formal coincidence of the name *rue* with **RUE** *verb*, *noun*[1] repent, repentance] the herb rue, *Ruta graveolens*; *gen.* any herb of valuable properties; **herb Paris** [translation of medieval Latin *herba paris*, prob. lit. 'herb of a pair', from the resemblance of the four leaves to a true-lover's knot] a woodland plant, *Paris quadrifolia* (of the lily family), bearing a

single greenish flower at the top of the stem, and just beneath it four large ovate leaves in the form of a cross; **herb Robert** [translation of medieval Latin *herba Roberti*: variously referred to Robert Duke of Normandy, to St Robert, and to St Rupert] a wild cranesbill common in hedges, *Geranium robertianum*, with bright pink flowers, reddish stems, and finely cut leaves; **herb tea** an infusion of herbs; **herb tobacco** a mixture of herbs smoked as a substitute for tobacco; **herb Trinity** *arch.* the hepatica, *Hepatica nobilis*, so called from its three-lobed leaves; ***herb* TWOPENCE**; **herb water** = ***herb tea*** above.

†**herba** *noun*. L16–E19.
[**ORIGIN** Italian (now *erba*), lit. 'grass'.]
A sort of grasscloth formerly imported from India.

herbaceous /hə:ˈbeɪʃəs/ *adjective*. M17.
[**ORIGIN** Latin *herbaceus* grassy, from *herba* **HERB**: see **-ACEOUS**.]
1 Of the nature of a herb (**HERB** 1); *esp.* not forming a woody stem but dying down to the root each year. M17.
herbaceous border a garden border containing esp. perennial flowering plants.
2 *BOTANY.* Resembling a leaf in colour or texture. Opp. ***scarious***. L18.

herbage /ˈhə:bɪdʒ/ *noun*. LME.
[**ORIGIN** Old French *erbage* (mod. *herbage*) from medieval Latin *herbaticum*, *-us* (also *herbagium*), from Latin *herba* **HERB**.]
1 Herbaceous vegetation; *esp.* grass and other low-growing plants used as pasture. LME.
2 *LAW.* The natural herbage of a piece of land as a species of property distinct from the land itself; the right of grazing one's cattle on another person's land. LME.
3 The green succulent parts of a herbaceous plant. E18.
■ **herbaged** *adjective* covered in herbage E18.

herbal /ˈhə:b(ə)l/ *noun*. E16.
[**ORIGIN** medieval Latin *herbalis* (sc. *liber*), from Latin *herba*: see **-AL**[1].]
1 *hist.* A book containing descriptions of plants, together with accounts of their properties and medicinal uses. E16.
2 A collection of herbs; *esp.* an album or collection of botanical specimens. Now *rare* or *obsolete*. L16.

herbal /ˈhə:b(ə)l/ *adjective*. E17.
[**ORIGIN** (French †*herbal* from) medieval Latin *herbalis*: see **HERBAL** *noun*.]
Pertaining to, consisting of, or made from a herb or herbs.
■ **herbally** *adverb* M20.

herbalist /ˈhə:b(ə)lɪst/ *noun*. L16.
[**ORIGIN** from **HERBAL** *noun* + **-IST**.]
1 A collector of or writer on plants or herbs. Now *spec.* an early botanical writer. L16.
2 A dealer in medicinal herbs; a person who prepares herbal remedies. Also, a person who practises or advocates the use of herbs to treat disease. L16. ▸**b** In S. Africa, a practitioner of traditional medicine. L16.
■ **herbalism** *noun* †(*a*) botany; (*b*) the use of herbs to treat disease: M17. **herbalize** *verb intrans.* (*arch.*) search for plants, esp. medicinal herbs L17.

herbaria *noun pl.* see **HERBARIUM**.

herbarise *verb* var. of **HERBARIZE**.

herbarist /ˈhə:bərɪst/ *noun*. *obsolete* exc. *hist.* L16.
[**ORIGIN** from Latin *herbaria* botany (see **HERBARIUM**) + **-IST**.]
An expert on or student of herbs or plants.
■ †**herbarism** *noun* botany L16–M19.

herbarium /hə:ˈbɛ:rɪəm/ *noun*. Pl. **-ria** /-rɪə/, **-riums**. L18.
[**ORIGIN** Late Latin, use as noun of adjective repr. by Latin *herbarius* botanist, *herbaria* (sc. *ars*) botany.]
A collection of dried botanical specimens systematically arranged for reference. Also, a room or building housing such a collection.

herbarize /ˈhə:bərʌɪz/ *verb intrans.* *arch.* Also **-ise**. L17.
[**ORIGIN** formed as **HERBARIST** + **-IZE**.]
= **HERBALIZE**, **HERBORIZE**.
■ **herbariˈzation** *noun* L17.

Herbartian /hə:ˈbɑ:tɪən/ *adjective* & *noun*. L19.
[**ORIGIN** from *Herbart* (see below) + **-IAN**.]
▸ **A** *adjective*. Pertaining to the German philosopher J. F. Herbart (1776–1841) or the system of psychology and teaching originated by him. L19.
▸ **B** *noun*. A follower of Herbart. L19.

herbary /ˈhə:bəri/ *noun*. M16.
[**ORIGIN** In sense 1 from Latin *herbarius*, in sense 2 from late Latin *herbarium*, in sense 3 from medieval Latin *herbarius*, *-um*, all from Latin *herba* **HERB**: see **-ARY**[1].]
†**1** A herbalist. Only in M16.
2 A herbarium. Now *rare* or *obsolete*. L16.
3 A herb garden. *arch.* M17.

herbed /hə:bd/ *adjective*. L20.
[**ORIGIN** from **HERB** *noun* + **-ED**[2].]
Flavoured with herbs.

herber *noun* see **ARBOUR**.

herbert /ˈhɛ:bət/ *noun*. *slang*. M20.
[**ORIGIN** Arbitrary use of a male forename.]
An undistinguished or foolish man or youth.

Independent An overweight scruffy herbert . . sticks his head round the door.

herbicide /ˈhə:bɪsʌɪd/ *noun*. L19.
[**ORIGIN** from Latin *herba* **HERB** + **-CIDE**.]
A substance toxic to plants and used to destroy unwanted vegetation, esp. weeds.
■ **herbiˈcidal** *adjective* M19.

herbivore /ˈhə:bɪvɔ:/ *noun*. M19.
[**ORIGIN** formed as **HERBIVOROUS** or from French *herbivore*.]
An animal, esp. a mammal, that feeds naturally on plants.

herbivorous /hə:ˈbɪv(ə)rəs/ *adjective*. M17.
[**ORIGIN** mod. Latin *herbivorus*, from Latin *herba* **HERB**: see **-I-**, **-VOROUS**.]
Of an animal, esp. a mammal: feeding naturally on plants.
■ **herˈbivory** *noun* herbivorous nature or habits M20.

herbless /ˈhə:blɪs/ *adjective*. L17.
[**ORIGIN** from **HERB** *noun* + **-LESS**.]
Devoid of herbage.

herblet /ˈhə:blɪt/ *noun*. E17.
[**ORIGIN** from **HERB** *noun* + **-LET**.]
An insignificant herb or herbaceous plant.

herborise *verb* var. of **HERBORIZE**.

herborist /ˈhə:bərɪst/ *noun*. *arch.* L16.
[**ORIGIN** French *herboriste*, from *herbe* **HERB** by assoc. with Latin *arbor* tree: cf. **HERBORIZE** & see **-IST**.]
An expert on or student of herbs or plants.

herborize /ˈhə:bərʌɪz/ *verb intrans.* *arch.* Also **-ise**. M17.
[**ORIGIN** French *herboriser*, formed as **HERBORIST** by assoc. with *arboriser* collect plants: see **-IZE**.]
†**1** Tend herbs; garden. *rare*. Only in M17.
2 Search for plants, esp. medicinal herbs. M18.
■ **herboriˈzation** *noun* a botanizing excursion L17.

herbose /hə:ˈbəʊs/ *adjective*. E18.
[**ORIGIN** Latin *herbosus*, from *herba* **HERB**: see **-OSE**[1].]
Having much herbage.

herbous /ˈhə:bəs/ *adjective*. E18.
[**ORIGIN** Latin *herbosus*: see **HERBOSE**, **-OUS**.]
Pertaining to or of the nature of a herb (**HERB** 1, 2).

herby /ˈhə:bi/ *adjective*. M16.
[**ORIGIN** from **HERB** + **-Y**[1].]
1 Covered with herbage or grass, having much herbage. M16.
2 Of the nature of or pertaining to a herbaceous plant or the leafy part of it. M16.
3 Flavoured with or redolent of (aromatic) herbs. L19.

Hercegovinian *adjective* & *noun* var. of **HERZEGOVINIAN**.

hercogamy /hə:ˈkɒgəmi/ *noun*. Also **herk-**. L19.
[**ORIGIN** from Greek *herkos* fence + **-GAMY**.]
BOTANY. A condition in which the stamens and stigmas of a flower are separated by physical barriers, so preventing self-pollination.
■ **hercoˈgamic**, **hercogamous** *adjectives* L19.

Herculean /hə:kjʊˈli:ən, hə:ˈkju:lɪən/ *adjective*. Also **h-**. L16.
[**ORIGIN** from Latin *Herculeus* (formed as **HERCULES**) + **-AN**: see **-EAN**.]
1 Of or pertaining to Hercules, the superhuman hero of classical mythology; resembling Hercules in strength etc., immensely powerful or vigorous. L16.

Q. BELL A man of Herculean stature. K. WILLIAMS We . . made a Herculean effort . . to put in all the new moves and dialogue. *transf.*: H. POWER The first (which is the main and Herculean-Argument).

2 Of a task: as hard to accomplish as were Hercules's twelve labours; immensely arduous. E17.

Horse & Rider Such Herculean tasks aren't beyond it.

Hercules /ˈhə:kjʊli:z/ *noun*. ME.
[**ORIGIN** Latin, alt. of Greek *Hēraklēs*, from *Hēra* wife of Zeus + *kleos* glory, lit. 'having or showing the glory of Hera'.]
1 *CLASSICAL MYTHOLOGY.* A hero of superhuman strength, usu. depicted as carrying a club, who was celebrated for accomplishing twelve extraordinary tasks or 'labours' imposed on him by Hera and who after death was ranked among the gods. ME. ▸**b** A representation of Hercules or a strong man. M17.
2 An exceptionally strong or muscular man. M16.
3 (The name of) a faint constellation of the northern hemisphere, between Draco and Ophiuchus. M16.
4 Any of several powerful machines; *esp.* a heavy weight used like the ram in a pile-driving machine. L18.
5 More fully ***Hercules beetle***. A very large S. American scarabaeid beetle, *Dynastes hercules*. E19.
– **PHRASES & COMB.**: ***Hercules beetle***: see sense 5 above. **Hercules braid** a heavily corded worsted braid, used for trimmings. **Hercules' club** either of two tall prickly shrubs or small trees of the US: (*a*) the southern prickly ash, *Zanthoxylum clava-herculis*, of the rue family; (*b*) the angelica tree, *Aralia spinosa*. **Hercules' Pillars** *arch.* = ***Pillars of Hercules*** below. **Hercules powder** *US* a powerful explosive used in mining. ***labour of Hercules***: see **LABOUR** *noun*. **Pillars of Hercules** the rocks (now Gibraltar and Ceuta) on either side of the Straits of Gibraltar, believed by the ancients to mark the western limits of the habitable world.

Hercynian /hə:ˈsɪnɪən/ *adjective*. L16.
[**ORIGIN** from Latin *Hercynia* (sc. *silva* wood) = Greek *Herkunios drumos*: see **-AN**.]
1 In ancient Greek and Roman writers, designating a vaguely defined area of forest-covered mountains between the Rhine and the Carpathians. L16.
2 *GEOLOGY.* **a** Designating or pertaining to one of the Devonian formations of the Harz Mountains. L19. ▸**b** Designating or pertaining to an episode of mountain-building in Europe in late Carboniferous and early Permian times. Also called ***Armorican***. L19.

hercynite /ˈhə:sɪnʌɪt/ *noun*. M19.
[**ORIGIN** formed as **HERCYNIAN** + **-ITE**[1].]
MINERALOGY. A black mineral of the spinel group consisting essentially of ferrous iron and aluminium oxides, usu. found as granules.

herd /hə:d/ *noun*[1].
[**ORIGIN** Old English *heord* = Middle Low German *herde*, Old High German *herta* (German *Herde*), Old Norse *hjǫrð*, Gothic *hairda*, from Germanic.]
1 A company of domestic animals, now esp. cattle, kept together. OE.

M. SHADBOLT He got stuck into the milking, and had the herd finished before dark.

flocks and herds: see **FLOCK** *noun*[1]. **ride herd on** *US* keep watch on.
2 A company of animals feeding and travelling together. ME.

B. LOPEZ Herds of musk oxen graze below a range of hills in clusters of three or four.

3 A large number of people, a crowd; a rabble. Now *derog.* LME.

C. THIRLWALL The legitimate chief was distinguished from the vulgar herd . . by his robust frame. SAKI That world where people are counted individually and not in herds.

the herd instinct gregariousness and mutual influence as a psychological factor.
– **COMB.**: **herd book** a pedigree book of cattle or pigs; **herd-grass**, **herd's-grass** *US* any of various grasses grown for hay or pasture, *esp.* timothy, *Phleum pratense*, and the red-top grass, *Agrostis capillaris*.

herd /hə:d/ *noun*[2].
[**ORIGIN** Old English *hirdi*, (West Saxon) *hierde* = Old Saxon *hirdi*, *herdi*, Old High German *hirti* (German *Hirte*), Old Norse *hirðir*, Gothic *hairdeis*, from Germanic base of **HERD** *noun*[1].]
1 A keeper of herds, a herdsman. Now usu. as 2nd elem. of comb. OE.
cowherd, ***swineherd***, etc.
2 A spiritual shepherd, a pastor. Long *obsolete* exc. *Scot.* OE.
†**3** A keeper, a guardian. OE–L16.

herd /hə:d/ *verb*[1]. ME.
[**ORIGIN** from **HERD** *noun*[2].]
†**1** *verb trans.* Keep safe, shelter. ME–M16.
2 *verb trans.* & (*rare*) *intrans.* Tend (sheep, cattle, etc.). LME.
3 *verb trans.* Drive (an animal, a person) in a particular direction. Passing into **HERD** *verb*[2] 3. L19.

D. MORRIS They were particularly adept at herding and driving prey during hunting manoeuvres. J. A. MICHENER They had herded nearly three thousand longhorns thirteen hundred miles. J. M. COETZEE They herd the captives along.

■ **herder** *noun* (now chiefly *N. Amer.*) a herdsman ME.

herd /hə:d/ *verb*[2]. LME.
[**ORIGIN** from **HERD** *noun*[1].]
1 *verb intrans.* Go in a herd, form a herd; move (*about*, *along*, etc.) as a herd; *derog.* (of people) live together, associate with. Freq. foll. by *together*, *with*. LME. ▸**b** Of things: gather, be assembled. *rare*. E18.

GOLDSMITH These animals are in general fond of herding and grazing in company. R. INGALLS They all herded forward over a bridge.

2 *verb intrans.* Join oneself to a company etc., go in company *with*. *arch.* LME.

THACKERAY Ethel herded not with the children of her own age.

3 *verb trans.* Place in or among a herd; gather (*together*) as a herd. Passing into **HERD** *verb*[1] 3. L16.

JONSON The rest, However great we are . . Are herded with the vulgar. B. TAYLOR Our mules had scattered far and wide . . and several hours elapsed before they could be herded. T. DREISER A sharp, almost January wind that herded the fallen leaves into piles.

herdboy /ˈhə:dbɔɪ/ *noun*. L18.
[**ORIGIN** from **HERD** *noun*[1], *noun*[2] + **BOY** *noun*.]
A boy who tends sheep, cattle, etc.; *US* a cowboy.

herderite /ˈhə:dərʌɪt/ *noun*. E19.
[**ORIGIN** from S. A. W. von *Herder* (1776–1838), German mining official + **-ITE**[1].]
MINERALOGY. A monoclinic phosphate and fluoride of beryllium and calcium, usu. occurring as colourless, yellowish, or greenish prisms or fibrous aggregates.

herdic /ˈhəːdɪk/ *noun. US* (now *hist.*). L19.
[ORIGIN from Peter *Herdic* (1824–88), Amer. inventor.]
A kind of small cab or carriage for public transport.

†**herdman** *noun.* Pl. **-men.** OE–M17.
[ORIGIN from HERD *noun*² + MAN *noun.*]
A herdsman.

herdsman /ˈhəːdzmən/ *noun.* Pl. **-men.** LME.
[ORIGIN Alt. of HERDMAN after *craftsman* etc.]
1 An owner or keeper of herds. LME.
2 (Usu. **H-**.) *The* constellation Boötes. L17.
■ **herdsmanship** *noun* L19.

herdswoman /ˈhəːdzwʊmən/ *noun.* Pl. **-women** /-wɪmɪn/. E19.
[ORIGIN formed as HERDSMAN + WOMAN *noun.*]
A female owner or keeper of herds.

Herdwick /ˈhəːdwɪk/ *noun.* ME.
[ORIGIN from HERD *noun*² + -WICK.]
†1 (Usu. **h-**.) A pasturage. ME–E19.
2 (An animal of) a hardy breed of sheep originating in Cumbria, NW England. Also ***Herdwick sheep.*** E19.

here /ˈhɛrə/ *noun*¹. Long *obsolete* exc. *hist.*
[ORIGIN Old English *here* = Old Frisian, Old Saxon, Old High German *heri* (Dutch, German *Heer*), Old Norse *herr*, Gothic *harjis*, from Germanic. Cf. HARRY *verb*, HARBOUR *noun*¹, HERIOT.]
A host, a multitude; an army; *esp.* the Danish invaders of England during the Anglo-Saxon period.

H

here /hɪə/ *adverb, noun*², & *pronoun.*
[ORIGIN Old English *hēr* = Old Frisian, Old Saxon *hēr*, Old High German *hiar* (Du, German *hier*), Old Norse *hér*, Gothic *her* (beside Old Frisian, Old Saxon *hir*), app. from Germanic base meaning 'this' (see HE *pronoun*). Cf. YERE.]
▸ **A** *adverb* **I 1** In this place or position. OE. ▸**b** Indicating the presence of something: in unemphatic use, chiefly preceding *is, was,* etc. LME. ▸**c** Imparting emphasis preceding a noun qualified by *this, these. dial. & colloq.* M18.

OED My brother, here, is ready to give information. E. HARDWICK Dearest M.: Here I am in Boston, .. looking out on a snowstorm. **b** MRS ALEXANDER I says, 'here's your tea, sir', but he made no answer. **c** DICKENS 'Now, with regard to this here robbery, master', said Blathers. 'What are the circumstances?'

2 In this world; in this life; on earth. Long *rare* exc. in ***here below.*** OE.

J. MONTGOMERY There is no union here of hearts, That finds not here an end.

3 At this point in an argument, a situation, etc.; at this juncture. OE.

Book of Common Prayer In Quires and Places where they sing, here followeth the Anthem. J. B. PRIESTLEY Here she was stopped by a cough.

4 In the matter in question, in this case. ME.

STEELE Here can then be no Injustice, where no one is injured. J. MORLEY Here more than anywhere else you need to give the tools to him who can handle them.

5 To this place or position. ME.

V. WOOLF When we got back here we found the room full of people. J. GATHORNE-HARDY A Hungarian who came over here to escape from Hitler in the late thirties.

▸ **II** As *interjection.*
6 I am present. OE.

SHAKES. *Mids. N. D.* Francis Flute, the bellows-mender .. Here, Peter Quince.

7 Calling attention or introducing a command or a remonstration. M17.

OED John! here! quick! J. KRANTZ Here, I almost forgot, .. your Christmas present.

– PHRASES: **here and now** *adverbial & noun phr.* (**a**) *adverbial phr.* at this very moment, immediately; (**b**) *noun phr.* the present reality. **here and there** in various places. **here below** in this life. **here goes!** expr. an intention to begin a bold act. ***here lies our way, here lies your way***: see WAY *noun.* ***here's how***: see HOW *noun.* ***here's looking at you***: see LOOK *verb.* ***here's mud in your eye!***: see MUD *noun*¹. **here's to** — I drink to the health of —. **here, there, and everywhere** in many different places. **here today, gone tomorrow** short-lived, merely transient. **here we are** *colloq.*: said on arrival at one's destination. **here we go again** *colloq.* the same, usu. undesirable, events are recurring. **here you are**: said on handing something to somebody. ***look here***: see LOOK *verb.* **neither here nor there** of no importance or relevance. ***same here***: see SAME *pronoun & noun.* ***see here***: see SEE *verb.*
– COMB.: **hereabout, hereabouts** *adverbs* †(**a**) about or concerning this thing etc.; (**b**) about or near this place; in the neighbourhood; **hereat** *adverb* †(**a**) at this place; (**b**) *arch.* as a result of this; **hereaway, hereaways** *adverbs* (now *dial. & US*) (**a**) hereabouts; (**b**) to this place, hither; **herefrom** *adverb* (now *rare* or *obsolete*) (**a**) from this place, from here; (**b**) from this circumstance, from this source; **hereon** *adverb* (long *rare* or *obsolete*) (**a**) herein; †(**b**) to this place, on here; (**c**) on this matter etc., on this basis; (**d**) = ***hereupon*** (b) below; **hereout** *adverb* (long *rare* or *obsolete*) (**a**) out of this place; †(**b**) from this source; **hereunder** *adverb* (*formal*) below (esp. in a book, document, etc.); **hereunto** *adverb* (*arch.*) to this document etc.; **hereupon** *adverb* †(**a**) on this subject, matter, etc.; (**b**) after this, in consequence of this; **herewith**, †**herewithal** *adverbs* (**a**) with this (esp. of an enclosure in a letter etc.); †(**b**) on this, with these words etc.; (**c**) *rare* by means of this, hereby.
▸ **B** *noun & pronoun.* This place or position. E17.

SHAKES. *Lear* Thou losest here, a better where to find. DICKENS You would rather not leave here till to-morrow morning. JOYCE Go away from here, he said rudely.

■ **hereness** *noun* the fact or condition of being here L17.

hereafter /hɪərˈɑːftə/ *adverb, noun, & adjective.*
[ORIGIN Old English *hēræfter*, from HERE *adverb* + AFTER *adverb.*]
▸ **A** *adverb.* **1** After this in order or position. OE.

W. CRUISE In consequence of the statute .. which will be stated hereafter.

2 At a future time, later on. ME.

B. JOWETT We cannot .. anticipate the details which will hereafter be needed. J. P. DONLEAVY Things could be different. Must control myself hereafter.

3 In the world to come. LME.

P. LIVELY You do not merely believe but *know* that there is a life hereafter.

▸ **B** *noun.* **1** The future. M16.

SYD. SMITH Leave hereafter to the spirit and the wisdom of hereafter.

2 The world to come. E18.

V. BRITTAIN I knew now that death was the end ... There was no hereafter.

▸ **C** *adjective.* To come, future. Now *rare.* L16.

A. SEWARD Claims .. to hereafter compensation.

hereby /hɪəˈbʌɪ/ *adverb.* ME.
[ORIGIN from HERE *adverb* + BY *preposition.*]
†1 By or near this place, close by. ME–M17.

SHAKES. *L.L.L.* Hereby, upon the edge of yonder coppice.

2 As a result of this, by this means. ME.

O. WILDE I hereby agree to assign you the rights in my play.

hereditable /hɪˈrɛdɪtəb(ə)l/ *adjective.* LME.
[ORIGIN French †*héréditable* or medieval Latin *hereditabilis*, from ecclesiastical Latin *hereditare*: see HEREDITAMENT, -ABLE.]
That may be inherited.
■ **heˌreditaˈbility** *noun* (*rare*) M19. **hereditably** *adverb* (now *rare*) L15.

hereditament /hɛrɪˈdɪtəm(ə)nt, hɪˈrɛdɪt-/ *noun.* LME.
[ORIGIN medieval Latin *hereditamentum*, from ecclesiastical Latin *hereditare* inherit, from *heres, hered-* HEIR *noun*: see -MENT.]
1 LAW. An item of property that can be inherited; real property. LME.
2 Inheritance. E16.

hereditary /hɪˈrɛdɪt(ə)ri/ *adjective & noun.* LME.
[ORIGIN Latin *hereditarius*, formed as HEREDITY: see -ARY¹.]
▸ **A** *adjective.* **1** Descending by inheritance. LME.

T. HARDY If knighthood were hereditary, .. from father to son, you would be Sir John now. A. MUNRO The ruler .. , not through hereditary right but through force of personality.

2 Transmitted from one generation to another. LME. ▸**b** Identical with or similar to what one's parents or precursors had. E17.

Practical Hairstyling & Beauty It is a hereditary trait which cannot be controlled. **b** E. YOUNG Long burnt a fixt hereditary hate, Between the crowns of Macedon and Thrace.

3 Holding one's position by inheritance. M17.

R. HOGGART These .. belong to the hereditary aristocracy of the neighbourhood. G. VIDAL The magians are the hereditary priests of the Medes and the Persians.

4 Of or pertaining to inheritance. L18.

R. N. KHORY Abnormal structures are the most obvious instances of hereditary transmission.

▸ **B** *noun.* A person who holds a position by inheritance. *rare.* M19.
■ **herediˈtarian** *noun* a person who considers that heredity has the primary influence on a person's or a group's development L19. **hereditarily** *adverb* E17. **hereditariness** *noun* M17.

heredity /hɪˈrɛdɪti/ *noun.* M16.
[ORIGIN Old French & mod. French *hérédité* or Latin *hereditas*, formed as HEIR *noun*: see -ITY.]
†1 Hereditary succession; an inheritance. Only in M16.
2 LAW. Hereditary character, quality, or condition. Now *rare* or *obsolete.* L18.

Athenaeum The heredity and independence of the fiefs .. shown to have commenced in .. the tenth century.

3 The tendency of like to beget like; the property of organic beings by which offspring have the nature and characteristics of their parents and ancestors; the genetic constitution of an individual. M19.

B. MACDONALD Gammy was a strong believer in heredity, particularly the inheritance of bad traits. R. MACDONALD Their basic trouble was genetic, and there's still not much we can do about heredity.

Hereford /ˈhɛrɪfəd/ *adjective & noun.* E19.
[ORIGIN from *Hereford* a city and county in the west of England where the breed originated.]
▸ **A** *adjective.* Designating, of, or pertaining to a breed of red and white beef cattle. E19.
▸ **B** *noun.* (An animal of) the Hereford breed of cattle. E19.

■ †**Herefordshire** *adjective* = HEREFORD *adjective* L18–M19.

heregeld /ˈhɛrɪgɛld/ *noun.* Long *obsolete* exc. *hist.*
[ORIGIN Old English *heregield*, from HERE *noun*¹ + *gield* payment (see GELD *noun*).]
The tribute paid by the Anglo-Saxons to the Danish army; Danegeld.

herein /hɪərˈɪn/ *adverb. formal.* OE.
[ORIGIN from HERE *adverb* + IN *adverb, preposition.*]
1 In this place; *esp.* in this book, document, etc.; into this place. OE.

J. RAY Herein were many vaulted or arched walks hewn out of the Rock. *Atlantic Monthly* 'Read this shit, man,' an attached note said. 'Essential knowledge herein'.

2 In this matter, case, etc.; in this particular. ME.

I. S. LEADAM He insists strongly that the king can be sued, herein opposing Bracton.

– COMB.: **hereinafter** below (in this document etc.); **hereinbefore** in a preceding part (of this document etc.).

herem *noun* var. of CHEREM.

†**heremite** *noun* var. of HERMIT.

herenach /ˈhɛrɪnɑːk/ *noun.* Also **er-** /ˈɛr-/. E17.
[ORIGIN Alt. of Irish *airchinneach*, Old Irish *airchinnech* chief man, principal, prince, leader, from *a(i)r* over + *ce(a)nn* head, cogn. with Welsh *arbennig*.]
hist. In the ancient Irish Church, a lay superintendent of church lands; the hereditary warden of a church.

hereof /hɪərˈɒv/ *adverb. formal.* OE.
[ORIGIN from HERE *adverb* + OF *preposition.*]
1 Of this, concerning this. OE.
†2 From this, from here. ME–L16.

hereright /hɪəˈrʌɪt/ *adverb. obsolete* exc. *dial.* ME.
[ORIGIN from HERE *adverb* + RIGHT *adverb.*]
Straightway.

Herero /hɛˈrɛːrəʊ, həˈrɪə-/ *noun & adjective.* M19.
[ORIGIN Bantu. Cf. OVAHERERO.]
▸ **A** *noun.* Pl. same, **-os.**
1 The Bantu language of any of several peoples of Namibia, Angola, and Botswana. M19.
2 A member of any of these peoples. L19.
▸ **B** *attrib.* or as *adjective.* Of or pertaining to the Herero or their language. M19.

heresiarch /hɛˈriːzɪɑːk/ *noun.* M16.
[ORIGIN ecclesiastical Latin *haeresiarcha* from ecclesiastical Greek *hairesiarkhēs* leader of a sect (Greek = leader of a school), formed as HERESY + -ARCH.]
A leader or founder of a heresy.

heresiography /ˌhɛrɪsɪˈɒgrəfi/ *noun.* M17.
[ORIGIN from Greek *hairesis* HERESY + -O- + -GRAPHY.]
A treatise on or the description of heresies.

heresiologist /ˌhɛrɪsɪˈɒlədʒɪst/ *noun.* E18.
[ORIGIN formed as HERESIOGRAPHY + -O- + -LOGIST.]
An expert in or student of heresies.
■ **heresiology** *noun* the branch of knowledge that deals with heresies M19.

heresy /ˈhɛrɪsi/ *noun.* ME.
[ORIGIN Old French (*h*)*eresie* (mod. *hérésie*) from Proto-Romance from ecclesiastical Latin *haeresis* (Latin = school of thought) from ecclesiastical Greek *hairesis* heretical sect (Greek = choice), from Greek *haireomai* choose from *hairein* take.]
1 Opinion or doctrine contrary to the orthodox doctrine of the Christian Church; an instance of this. ME.

R. MACAULAY [She] was a partial-diluvian, .. a heresy that the flood had not covered the whole earth. D. CUPITT Priscillian and a number of his followers were executed for heresy at Trier.

2 Opinion or doctrine contrary to the accepted doctrine of any subject; an instance of this. LME.

Sunday Express If winning is the name of the game, why is it heresy to suggest a soccer team to represent Great Britain?

3 Opinion or doctrine characterizing a particular individual or group; a school of thought, a sect. Now *rare.* LME.

heretic /ˈhɛrɪtɪk/ *noun & adjective.* ME.
[ORIGIN Old French & mod. French *hérétique*, from ecclesiastical Latin *haereticus* adjective & noun, from ecclesiastical Greek *hairetikos* heretical (Greek = able to choose) from Greek *haireomai*: see HERESY: see -IC.]
▸ **A** *noun.* **1** A person who holds an opinion or a doctrine contrary to the orthodox doctrine of the Christian Church. ME.

K. CLARK The northern heretics were insulting the Virgin, desecrating her sanctuaries.

2 A person who holds an opinion or a doctrine contrary to the accepted doctrine of any subject. L16.

SHAKES. *Much Ado* Thou wast ever an obstinate heretic in the despite of beauty.

▸ **B** *attrib.* or as *adjective.* = HERETICAL. *rare.* LME.

heretical /hɪˈrɛtɪk(ə)l/ *adjective.* LME.
[ORIGIN medieval Latin *hereticalis*, formed as HERETIC: see -ICAL.]
Of or pertaining to heresy or heretics; of the nature of heresy.
■ **heretically** *adverb* E17. **hereticalness** *noun* (long *rare* or *obsolete*) L17.

hereticate /hɪˈrɛtɪkeɪt/ *verb trans.* E17.
[ORIGIN medieval Latin *hereticat-* pa. ppl stem of *hereticare*, from *haereticus*: see HERETIC, -ATE[3].]
1 Pronounce (a person, a doctrine, etc.) to be heretical. E17.
2 Make a heretic of: esp. (*derog.*, now *hist.*) denoting the ceremony of deathbed inauguration said to have been practised by the Albigenses. M18.
■ **hereti'cation** *noun* M18.

hereto /hɪəˈtuː/ *adverb. formal.* ME.
[ORIGIN from HERE *adverb* + TO *preposition*.]
1 To this place. Long *rare* or *obsolete*. ME.
2 To this matter, subject, etc.; with regard to this point. ME.
3 Up to this time. Long *rare* or *obsolete*. ME.
4 (Annexed) to this document etc. M16.

heretofore /hɪətʊˈfɔː/ *adverb, adjective, & noun. formal.* LME.
[ORIGIN from HERE *adverb* + TOFORE.]
▸ **A** *adverb*. Before this time, formerly. LME.
▸ **B** *adjective*. Former, previous. Now *rare*. L15.
▸ **C** *noun*. Time past; the past. *rare*. E19.
■ **heretoforetime** *adverb* (*rare*) = HERETOFORE *adverb* L15.

heretoga /hɛrɪˈtəʊɡə/ *noun.*
[ORIGIN Old English *heretoga* = Old Frisian *hertoga*, Old Saxon *heritogo* (Dutch *hertog*), Old High German *herizogo* (German *Herzog*), Old Norse *hertogi*, from HERE *noun*[1] + *-toga*, from Germanic base of TEAM *noun*.]
hist. The leader of an army; the commander of the militia of a shire etc.

heriot /ˈhɛrɪət/ *noun.*
[ORIGIN Old English *heregeatwa*, *-geatwe* (whence medieval Latin *herietum -otum*, Anglo-Norman *heriet*), from HERE *noun*[1] + *geatwa* (Old Norse *gotvar* pl.) trappings.]
hist. A tribute, orig. the return of military equipment, later the best live beast or dead chattel or a money payment, made to a lord on the death of a tenant.
■ **heriotable** *adjective* subject or liable to the payment of heriots E17.

herisson /ˈhɛrɪs(ə)n/ *noun.* L16.
[ORIGIN French *hérisson*: see URCHIN.]
†1 A hedgehog. L16–E17.
2 FORTIFICATION. A barrier consisting of a revolving beam set with iron spikes. E18.

herit /ˈhɛrɪt/ *verb trans. rare.* LME.
[ORIGIN Old French *heriter* from ecclesiastical Latin *hereditare*.]
Inherit.

heritable /ˈhɛrɪtəb(ə)l/ *adjective.* LME.
[ORIGIN Old French & mod. French *héritable*, from *heriter* from ecclesiastical Latin *hereditare*: see HEREDITABLE.]
1 Able to be inherited; *esp.* in SCOTS LAW (now *hist.*) designating property which devolved on the heir-at-law as opp. to an executor (opp. ***movable***). LME. ▸**b** SCOTS LAW. Pertaining to or connected with heritable property. M16.
2 Transmissible from parent to offspring, hereditary. LME.
3 Capable of inheriting. LME.
■ **herita'bility** *noun* M19. **heritably** *adverb* LME.

heritage /ˈhɛrɪtɪdʒ/ *noun.* ME.
[ORIGIN Old French *(h)eritage* (mod. *héritage*), from *hériter*: see HERITABLE, -AGE.]
1 That which is or may be inherited; *fig.* the portion allotted to a specified person, group, etc. ME. ▸**b** SCOTS LAW (now *hist.*). Property consisting of land etc. that devolved on the heir-at-law as opp. to an executor. E16.

> SIR W. SCOTT Lord of a barren heritage. N. EZEKIEL God's love remains your heritage.

†2 The fact of inheriting; hereditary succession. ME–M16.
3 A gift which constitutes a proper possession; *spec.* God's chosen people; the ancient Israelites; the Church. ME.

> AV 1 *Pet.* 5:3 Neither as being lords over Gods heritage.

4 Inherited circumstances or benefits. E17.

> LYNDON B. JOHNSON My Texas background or my Southern heritage. J. BRODSKY She was carrying the heritage of her predecessors into the art of this century.

– ATTRIB. & COMB.: In the senses 'forming part of a national or cultural heritage', as ***heritage highway***, ***heritage train***, etc.; 'concerned with the conservation and use of the national or cultural heritage', as ***heritage group***, ***heritage industry***, etc. Special combs., as **heritage coast** a section of the UK coastline designated as aesthetically or culturally important and therefore protected from development; **heritage trail** a route linking places of historic interest; ***World Heritage Site***: see WORLD *noun*.

heritance /ˈhɛrɪt(ə)ns/ *noun.* LME.
[ORIGIN Old French, from *heriter*: see HERITABLE, -ANCE.]
Inheritance; heirship (*lit.* & *fig.*).

heritor /ˈhɛrɪtə/ *noun.* LME.
[ORIGIN Anglo-Norman *heriter* = Old French & mod. French *heritier*, formed as HEREDITARY, assim. to words in -OR.]
1 A person who inherits. LME.
2 SCOTS LAW. The proprietor of a heritable subject, esp. one who is liable for parochial dues. L15.
■ **heritress** *noun* an heiress, an inheritress M16. **heritrix** *noun* an heiress, a female heritor E16.

herkogamy *noun* var. of HERCOGAMY.

herky-jerky /ˈhəːkɪdʒəːki/ *adjective. N. Amer. slang.* L20.
[ORIGIN from JERKY *adjective*.]
Of a movement: occurring at an irregular rate, spasmodic.

herl /həːl/ *noun.* LME.
[ORIGIN Alt.]
= HARL *noun*[1].

herling /ˈhəːlɪŋ/ *noun. Scot. dial.* L17.
[ORIGIN Unknown.]
A salmon; a sea trout.

herm /həːm/ *noun.* Also (now *rare*) **herma** /ˈhəːmə/, pl. **-mae** /-miː/. L16.
[ORIGIN Latin *Herma*, from Greek *Hermēs*: see HERMES II.]
CLASSICAL ANTIQUITIES. A squared pillar surmounted by a head or bust (usu. that of Hermes), used as a boundary marker, signpost, etc.

Hermaic /həːˈmeɪɪk/ *adjective.* L17.
[ORIGIN Greek *Hermaikos* of or like Hermes: see HERMES, -IC.]
1 = HERMETIC. L17.
2 Of the nature of or resembling a herm. E19.

hermandad /ermanˈdað/ *noun.* Pl. ***-es*** /-ɛs/. M18.
[ORIGIN Spanish = brotherhood.]
hist. In Spain, a resistance group against oppression by the nobility; *spec.* a voluntary organization later reorganized as regular national police.

hermaphrodism /həːˈmafrədɪz(ə)m/ *noun.* Now *rare*. E19.
[ORIGIN French *hermaphrodisme*, irreg. from *hermaphrodite*, formed as HERMAPHRODITE: see -ISM.]
= HERMAPHRODITISM.

hermaphrodite /həːˈmafrədʌɪt/ *noun & adjective.* LME.
[ORIGIN Latin *hermaphroditus* from Greek *hermaphroditos*, orig. in Greek mythol. the name of the son of Hermes and Aphrodite, who became joined in one body with the nymph Salmacis.]
▸ **A** *noun*. **1** A human being or animal combining characteristics of both sexes. LME. ▸**b** *fig.* A person or thing combining two opposite qualities or functions; NAUTICAL a ship having the characters of two kinds of vessel, *esp.* a hermaphrodite brig. LME. ▸**c** A homosexual; an effeminate man. Long *rare*. L16.

> J. BRONOWSKI Males and females of the same species do not produce sexual monsters or hermaphrodites. **b** T. KEN He acts the Hermaphrodite of Good and Ill, But God detests his double Tongue and Will.

2 An animal having normally both male and female sexual organs, as many snails and earthworms. E18.
3 A flower in which both stamens and pistils are present; a plant having such flowers. E18.
▸ **B** *adjective*. **1** Combining the characteristics of or consisting of both sexes; combining two opposite qualities. L16.
hermaphrodite brig: see BRIG *noun*[1] 1.
2 Of the nature of or being a hermaphrodite. E17.

> B. TRAPIDO With my almost non-existent breasts and my narrow hips, I looked alluringly hermaphrodite.

■ **hermaphro'ditic**, **hermaphro'ditical** *adjectives* = HERMAPHRODITE *adjective* E17. **hermaphro'ditically** *adverb* L17.

hermaphroditism /həːˈmafrədɪtɪz(ə)m/ *noun.* E19.
[ORIGIN from HERMAPHRODITE + -ISM.]
The state or condition of being hermaphrodite.

hermeneut /ˈhəːmɪnjuːt/ *noun.* L19.
[ORIGIN Greek *hermēneutēs* agent noun from *hermēneuein* interpret, from *hermeneus* interpreter.]
An interpreter, esp. in the early Christian Church.

> *Listener* It is, he argues, not just medieval exegetes, rabbinic hermeneuts or Princeton professors who interpret.

hermeneutic /həːmɪˈnjuːtɪk/ *adjective.* L17.
[ORIGIN Greek *hermēneutikos*, formed as HERMENEUT: see -IC.]
Of or pertaining to (theories of) interpretation.

> *Journal of Theological Studies* Augustine holds Paul's conversion as the hermeneutic key to Pauline theology.

■ **hermeneutical** *adjective* = HERMENEUTIC *adjective* L18. **hermeneutically** *adverb* E19.

hermeneutics /həːmɪˈnjuːtɪks/ *noun pl.* (also treated as *sing.*). M18.
[ORIGIN mod. Latin *hermeneutica* from Greek *hermēneutikē* use as noun of fem. sing. of adjective *hermēneutikos*: see HERMENEUTIC, -ICS.]
The branch of knowledge that deals with (theories of) interpretation, esp. of Scripture.

> D. CUPITT Those who had sought the historical Jesus, . . had somehow assumed that exegesis was hermeneutics.

†**Hermes** *noun.* L15.
[ORIGIN Latin, Greek *Hermēs*: see below.]
▸ **I** [Latin *Hermes Trismegistus* irreg. translation of 'Thoth the very great', the Egyptian god regarded as the founder of alchemy, astrology, etc., and more or less identified with the Greek god Hermes: see branch II.] Used *attrib.* in ALCHEMY.
1 ***Hermes tree***, the mixture of substances acted upon by acids in the third stage of calcination. Only in L15.
2 ***Hermes seal***, a hermetic seal. E17–M18.
▸ **II** [Greek *Hermēs* Hermes, the son of Zeus and Maia in Greek mythol., represented as the god of science, commerce, etc., and the messenger of the gods; identified by the Romans with *Mercury*.]
3 The metal mercury. *rare* (Milton). Only in M17.

hermetic /həːˈmɛtɪk/ *adjective & noun.* M17.
[ORIGIN mod. Latin *hermeticus*, from (prob. after *magnes*, *magneticus* MAGNET) *Hermes Trismegistus*: see HERMES I.]
▸ **A** *adjective*. **1** Of or pertaining to Hermes Trismegistus or the theosophical etc. writings ascribed to him; *esp.* of, pertaining to, or concerned with occult science, esp. alchemy. M17.

> K. A. PORTER A hermetic society, with ritual greetings, secret handgrips . . and a jargon.

2 Airtight, hermetically sealed; *fig.* protected from outside agencies, esoteric, recondite. E18.

> E. BOWEN Her house was hermetic against the storm. C. THUBRON The Soviet Union was so vast and hermetic that it comprised all the conceivable world.

hermetic seal an airtight closure of a vessel by fusion, soldering, etc., orig. as used by alchemists.
3 (**H-**.) Of or pertaining to the god Hermes. L19.

> J. R. LOWELL [The Elizabethans] had the Hermetic gift of buckling wings to the feet of their verse.

▸ **B** *noun*. **1** A person skilled in hermetic science. L17.

> T. LEARY The ancient wisdom of gnostics, hermetics, sufis, Tantric gurus, yogis, occult healers.

2 In *pl.* Hermetism. *rare*. M19.
■ **hermetical** *adjective* = HERMETIC *adjective* 1, 2 E17. **hermetically** *adverb* by means of a hermetic seal; *fig.* closely, tightly: E17. **hermeticism** /-sɪz(ə)m/ *noun* = HERMETISM *noun* E20.

hermetism /ˈhəːmɪtɪz(ə)m/ *noun.* L19.
[ORIGIN from HERMET(IC *adjective* + -ISM.]
Hermetic or theosophical philosophy.
■ **hermetist** *noun* M19.

hermit /ˈhəːmɪt/ *noun.* Also (now chiefly ECCLESIASTICAL HISTORY) **eremite** /ˈɛrɪmʌɪt/, †**heremite**. ME.
[ORIGIN Old French *(h)ermite*, *eremite* (mod. *ermite*) or late Latin *eremita* (medieval Latin *her-*) from Greek *erēmitēs* from *erēmia* desert, from *erēmos* solitary, deserted.]
1 A person (esp. a man) who from religious motives has retired into solitary life; *esp.* an early Christian recluse. ME. ▸**b** A person who falsely claims to be a recluse; a beggar. *obsolete* exc. *hist.* LME. ▸†**c** A beadsman. L16–L17.

> H. MAUNDRELL Hermits retiring hither for Penance and Mortification. **c** SHAKES. *Tit. A.* As perfect As begging hermits in their holy prayers.

2 A member of any of various monastic orders. LME.
3 A person who lives in solitude or shuns human society from any motive; an animal, esp. a sheep, of solitary habit. M17.

> G. GORER The old and poor . . choose their own company; and these hermits are represented in every category. D. PRATER He was by no means a hermit, and went from time to time into town.

– COMB.: **hermit crab** any soft-bodied decapod crustacean of the family Paguridae, members of which occupy cast-off mollusc shells as protection for their hind parts; **hermit ibis** = WALDRAPP; **hermit thrush** a migratory N. American thrush, *Catharus guttatus*.
■ **hermitess** *noun* a female hermit M17. **hermithood** *noun* E20. **hermitish** *adjective* resembling or befitting a hermit E17. **hermitism** *noun* the state of being a hermit; the hermitic life: L19. †**hermitress** *noun* = HERMITESS E17–E19. **hermitry** *noun* the mode of life of a hermit L19. **hermitship** *noun* E19.

hermitage /ˈhəːmɪtɪdʒ, *in sense 3 also* əːmɪˈtɑːʒ/ *noun.* Also †**eremitage**. ME.
[ORIGIN Old French *(h)ermitage* (mod. *ermitage*), formed as HERMIT: see -AGE.]
1 The dwelling place of a hermit; a monastery. ME. ▸**b** The condition of a hermit. L16.
2 A solitary or secluded dwelling place. M17.

> Y. MENUHIN For a few years it was an idyllic summer holiday hermitage.

3 (Usu. **H-**.) A French wine produced near Tain l'Hermitage in the Rhône valley. L17.

> D. L. SAYERS Mellow with Hermitage and cigars.

Hermitian /həːˈmɪʃ(ə)n/ *adjective.* E20.
[ORIGIN from Charles *Hermite* (1822–1901), French mathematician + -IAN.]
MATH. Designating, pertaining to, or taking the form of, a matrix in which pairs of elements symmetrically placed with respect to the principal diagonal are complex conjugates.

hermitic /həːˈmɪtɪk/ *adjective.* Also (earlier, now chiefly ECCLESIASTICAL HISTORY) **ere-** /ɛrɪ-/. L15.
[ORIGIN Old French *heremitique*, formed as HERMIT: see -IC.]
Of, pertaining to, or characteristic of a hermit.

hermitical /həːˈmɪtɪk(ə)l/ *adjective.* Also (now chiefly ECCLESIASTICAL HISTORY) **ere-** /ɛrɪ-/. L16.
[ORIGIN from (the same root as) HERMITIC: see -ICAL.]
= HERMITIC.

H

hermodactyl /hɜːməˈdaktɪl/ *noun. obsolete* exc. *hist.* LME.
[ORIGIN medieval Latin *hermodactylus* from Greek *hermodaktulos* lit. 'Hermes' finger', formed as HERMES II + -O- + DACTYL.]
The dried bulbous root of some eastern plant, prob. of the genus *Colchicum*, formerly used in medicine; the plant itself. Usu. in *pl.*

hern *noun* see HERON.

hern /hɜːn/ *possess. pronoun.* Long *obsolete* exc. *dial.* ME.
[ORIGIN from HER *pronoun*[2] after *my* and *mine*, *thy* and *thine*, etc.]
= HERS. See note s.v. HERS.

hernia /ˈhɜːnɪə/ *noun.* Pl. **-ias**, **-iae** /-ɪiː/. LME.
[ORIGIN Latin.]
MEDICINE. An abnormal displacement and protrusion of an organ or tissue through an aperture in the wall of the cavity which contains it, esp. through the wall of the abdomen; a rupture.
SLIDING hernia. strangulated hernia: see STRANGULATED 1.
■ **hernial** *adjective* LME. **herniary** *adjective* M18. **herniˈated** *adjective* affected with or protruding as a hernia L19. **herniˈation** *noun* protrusion as a hernia L19.

hernio- /ˈhɜːnɪəʊ/ *combining form* of prec.: see -O-.
■ **hernioˈrrhaphy** *noun* (an instance of) surgical repair of a hernia and suturing of the opening E20. **herniˈotomy** *noun* (an instance of) surgical enlargement of the opening through which a strangulated hernia has protruded, to allow its reduction; *gen.* any operation on a hernia: E19.

H

hernsew, **hernshaw**, **hernshew** *nouns* vars. of HERONSHAW.

hero /ˈhɪərəʊ/ *noun.* Pl. **-oes**. M16.
[ORIGIN Latin *heros*, (pl.) *heroes* from Greek *hērōs*, (pl.) *hērōes*.]
1 *GREEK HISTORY.* A man of superhuman strength, courage, or ability, favoured by the gods; a demigod. M16.

> H. ALLEN Perhaps there were even gods and giants, heroes and demi-gods . . buried there.

2 A man, now also a woman, distinguished by the performance of extraordinarily brave or noble deeds; an illustrious warrior. L16.

> M. LOWRY He was an extremely brave man, no less than a hero. A. S. NEILL A hero is a man who can change his fear into positive energy.

3 A man, now also a woman, admired and venerated for his or her achievements and noble qualities in any field. M17.

> JILLY COOPER He still identifies with David Bailey as a great working-class hero. A. GHOSH Edison became one of his heroes.

4 The chief male character in a poem, story, play, etc. L17.

> J. BARTH I recall once reading a story that ended with the hero dead on the floor. *Star & Style* It wasn't clear as to who the real hero of the film was.

5 In full *hero sandwich*. A sandwich made with a large roll or small loaf and filled with meat, cheese, and mixed salad. *N. Amer.* M20.
– COMB.: *hero sandwich*: see sense 5 above; **hero's welcome** a rapturous welcome, like that given to a successful warrior; **hero-worship** *noun* & *verb* (**a**) *noun* the idealization of an admired person; *GREEK HISTORY* worship of the ancient heroes; (**b**) *verb trans.* worship as a hero, idolize; **hero-worshipper** a person engaging in or given to hero worship.
■ †**heroess** *noun* = HEROINE E17–E18. **heroify** /hɪˈrəʊɪfʌɪ/ *verb trans.* [cf. DEIFY] make a hero of, venerate as a hero E19. **heroˈology** *noun* (*rare*) a history of heroes L17. **heroship** *noun* L18.

heroa *noun* pl. of HEROON.

Herodian /hɛˈrəʊdɪən/ *noun* & *adjective.* LME.
[ORIGIN ecclesiastical Latin *Herodianus*, from ecclesiastical Greek *Hērōdianos*, pertaining to Herod, *Hērōdianoi* pl. followers of Herod (*Mark* 3:6): see -IAN.]
► **A** *noun.* A member of a Jewish political party supporting the dynasty of Herod, esp. Herod Antipas (4 BC–AD 39). LME.
► **B** *adjective.* Of or pertaining to Herod, King of Judaea (38–4 BC), or members of his family of the same name. M17.

Herodotean /hɛrɒdəˈtiːən/ *adjective.* M19.
[ORIGIN from *Herodotus* (see below): see -AN, -EAN.]
Of, pertaining to, or characteristic of (the work of) Herodotus, Greek historian of the 5th cent. BC.

heroic /hɪˈrəʊɪk/ *adjective* & *noun.* LME.
[ORIGIN Old French & mod. French *héroïque* or Latin *heroicus* from Greek *hērōikos* pertaining to heroes, from *hērōs*: see HERO, -IC.]
► **A** *adjective.* **1** Of an action, a quality, etc.: of, pertaining to, or characteristic of a hero; bold, daring, attempting great things; fit for a hero. LME.

> J. MASTERS He stood in a heroic posture, his legs braced and his revolver arm steady. M. PIERCY He didn't like shopping any better than she did, so his trip verged on the heroic. A. S. BYATT The heroic transatlantic crossings of certain butterflies.

2 Of a person: having the qualities of a hero. L16.

> B. WEBB She is heroic: as . . chieftain she would have led her people into battle and died fighting. E. FEINSTEIN She could distinguish no single heroic figure among the rebels—only a mob.

3 Of or pertaining to the heroes of (esp. Greek) antiquity; (of poetry etc.) dealing with heroes and their deeds, epic. L16.
the heroic age the period in Greek history before the return from Troy.
4 Of language: grand; high-flown, exaggerated. L16.
5 (Of a statue) of a size between life-size and colossal; unusually large or great, extravagant. L18.

> CLIVE JAMES A flyover of heroic ugliness . . was built over Circular Quay. E. FERBER Himself of heroic stature, he fitted well into the gorgeous and spectacular setting.

– SPECIAL COLLOCATIONS: **heroic couplet**: of rhyming iambic pentameters. **heroic verse** (a) verse used in heroic poetry, esp. the hexameter, the iambic pentameter, or the alexandrine.
► **B** *noun.* **1** A heroic verse. Usu. in *pl.* L16.
†**2** A heroic man; *esp.* a demigod. Only in 17.
3 In *pl.* High-flown or extravagant language; extravagantly or recklessly bold behaviour. E18.

> J. FIELD No extravagant expressions of emotion were tolerated. 'Scenes' and heroics were alike taboo. A. MACLEAN The only thing that heroics will get us is an early and watery grave.

heroical /hɪˈrəʊɪk(ə)l/ *adjective.* LME.
[ORIGIN formed as HEROIC: see -ICAL.]
†**1** = HEROIC *adjective* 1. LME–E19.
2 = HEROIC *adjective* 3. LME.
3 = HEROIC *adjective* 2. M16.
4 = HEROIC *adjective* 5. L18.
■ **heroicalness** *noun* (now *rare*) M17.

heroically /hɪˈrəʊɪk(ə)li/ *adverb.* L16.
[ORIGIN from HEROIC *adjective* or HEROICAL: see -ICALLY.]
In a heroic manner; by heroic means.

> M. SEYMOUR-SMITH He behaved heroically, . . and was even recommended for a Victoria Cross. P. ROTH His chin was not protruding heroically but slightly receding.

heroi-comical /hɪˌrəʊɪˈkɒmɪk(ə)l/ *adjective.* E18.
[ORIGIN from French *héroï-comique* + -AL[1]: see HEROIC, COMICAL.]
Combining the heroic with the comic.

> POPE The Rape of the Lock. An Heroi-comical Poem.

■ Also **heroi-comic** *adjective* M18.

heroin /ˈhɛrəʊɪn/ *noun.* L19.
[ORIGIN German, formed as HERO (from its effect on the user's perception of his or her personality) + -IN[1].]
A morphine derivative, diacetylmorphine, which is a sedative addictive drug (illicitly) used to produce intense euphoria.

heroine /ˈhɛrəʊɪn/ *noun.* M17.
[ORIGIN French *héroïne* or Latin *heroina* from Greek *hērōinē* fem. of *hērōs* HERO: see -INE[3].]
1 A woman distinguished and venerated for her extraordinary courage, fortitude, or noble qualities. M17.

> E. FEINSTEIN Marina waited . . for an autograph from the great actress—she had found a new heroine.

2 *GREEK HISTORY.* A demigoddess. M17.
3 The chief female character in a poem, story, play, etc. E18.

> R. ELLMANN In his first play, *Vera*, the heroine plans to kill the Czar.

– COMB.: **heroine-worship** the idealization of an admired woman.
■ **heroineship** *noun* M18. **heroinism** *noun* the conduct or qualities of a heroine L18.

heroism /ˈhɛrəʊɪz(ə)m/ *noun.* M17.
[ORIGIN After French *héroïsme* (17th cent.), from *héros* HERO.]
1 The action and qualities of a hero; exalted courage, intrepidity, or boldness; heroic conduct. M17.
2 A heroic action or trait. M19.

heroize /ˈhɪərəʊʌɪz/ *verb trans.* Also **-ise**. M18.
[ORIGIN from HERO + -IZE.]
Make a hero of; treat or represent as a hero; make heroic.

> *Times* Huntford also gives the lie to the official version, the heroized version of Scott's journey.

■ **heroiˈzation** *noun* M19.

herola *noun* var. of HIROLA.

heron /ˈhɛr(ə)n/ *noun.* Also (*arch., poet., & dial.*) **hern** /hɜːn/. ME.
[ORIGIN Old French (also *hairon* (mod. *héron*)) from Germanic (whence Old High German *heigaro*; cf. Old Norse *hegri*).]
Any of various large long-legged long-necked wading birds of the family Ardeidae; in Great Britain and Ireland, *esp.* the grey *Ardea cinerea*, widespread in the Old World.

> TENNYSON I come from haunts of coot and hern.

Goliath heron, *green heron*, *night heron*, *purple heron*, *white heron*, etc.
– COMB.: **heron's-bill** (now chiefly *US*) = **storksbill** s.v. STORK *noun*.
■ **heronry** *noun* a place where herons breed; a colony of herons: E17.

heronshaw /ˈhɛr(ə)nʃɔː/ *noun.* Now *arch.* & *dial.* Also **hern-** /hɜːn-/, **-sew** /-sjuː/, **-shew** /-ʃuː/. LME.
[ORIGIN Old French *heronceau*, earlier *-cel* dim. of *heron* HERON.]
A young or small heron; *gen.* a heron.
know a hawk from a heronshaw: see HAWK *noun*[1].

heroon /hɪˈrəʊɒn/ *noun.* Pl. **-roa** /-ˈrəʊə/. Also (earlier) **heroum** /hɪˈrəʊəm/. L18.
[ORIGIN Latin *heroum* from Greek *hērōon*, from *hērōios* of a hero, from *hērōs* HERO.]
Orig., a temple dedicated to a hero, often over his supposed tomb. Now, a sepulchral monument in the form of a small temple.

herp /hɜːp/ *noun.* M20.
[ORIGIN Abbreviation.]
= HERPTILE.

herpes /ˈhɜːpiːz/ *noun.* LME.
[ORIGIN Latin = shingles from Greek, lit. 'creeping', from *herpein* creep.]
Orig., any skin disease characterized by the formation of groups of vesicles. Now, (infection with) any of a small group of viruses affecting the skin and nervous system.
– COMB.: **herpes simplex** (infection with) a herpesvirus causing usu. localized inflammation, as conjunctivitis, cold sore, oral or vaginal inflammation, etc. **herpesvirus** any of a small group of viruses causing herpes. **herpes zoster** /ˈzɒstə, ˈzəʊ-/ [Latin *zoster*, Greek *zōstēr* girdle, shingles] shingles; the herpesvirus causing this (and also chickenpox).

herpetofauna /ˈhɜːpɪtə(ʊ)ˌfɔːnə/ *noun.* M20.
[ORIGIN formed as HERPETOLOGY + FAUNA.]
ZOOLOGY. The reptiles and amphibians of a particular region, habitat, or geological period.
■ **herpetoˈfaunal** *adjective* M20.

herpetology /hɜːpɪˈtɒlədʒi/ *noun.* E19.
[ORIGIN from Greek *herpeton* creeping thing + -OLOGY.]
The branch of zoology that deals with reptiles and amphibians.
■ **herpetoˈlogic** (chiefly *US*), **herpetoˈlogical** *adjectives* E19. **herpetoˈlogically** *adverb* L19. **herpetologist** *noun* E19.

herpolhode /ˈhɜːp(ə)lhəʊd/ *noun.* M19.
[ORIGIN from Greek *herpein* creep + *polos* pole + *hodos* way.]
GEOMETRY. A curve traced on a fixed plane by the point of contact of an ellipsoid rolling on the plane about an internal axis. Cf. POLHODE.

herptile /ˈhɜːptʌɪl/ *noun.* L20.
[ORIGIN Blend of HERPETOLOGY and REPTILE.]
A reptile or amphibian.

Herr /hɛː/ *noun.* Pl. **Herren** /ˈhɛːrən/ M17.
[ORIGIN German, from Old High German *hērro* compar. of *hēr* exalted.]
A title used in referring to or addressing a German or German-speaking man, corresponding to *Mr* or *sir*; a German or German-speaking man.

> W. S. CHURCHILL But Herr Hitler is not thinking only of stealing other people's territories.

Herrenvolk /ˈhɛːrənfɒlk, ˈhɛr(ə)n-, -fəʊk/ *noun.* M20.
[ORIGIN German = master-race, formed as HERR + FOLK.]
The German nation, viewed (esp. by the Nazis) as a race born to mastery; in extended usage, a group regarding itself as innately superior.

> G. B. SHAW Nations each of which regards itself as The Chosen Race or Herrenvolk.

herriment /ˈhɛrɪm(ə)nt/ *noun. Scot.* L18.
[ORIGIN from HARRY *verb* + -MENT.]
Harrying, ravaging, devastation.

herring /ˈhɛrɪŋ/ *noun.* Pl. same, **-s**.
[ORIGIN Old English *hǣring*, *hēring* = Old Frisian *hēreng*, Middle Low German *hērink*, *harink* (Dutch *haring*), Old High German *hāring* (German *Hering*), from West Germanic.]
Any of various chiefly marine fishes of the family Clupeidae, which includes several important food fishes; *spec.* a blue-backed silvery fish of the N. Atlantic, *Clupea harengus*, which forms shoals in coastal waters at spawning time. Also, the flesh of any of these fishes as food.
fall herring a herring of NW Atlantic coastal waters, *Alosa mediocris*. **lake herring** = CISCO. *MATJE herring*. RED HERRING. **round herring** a herring of NW Atlantic coastal waters, *Etrumeus teres*, with a slender body of round cross-section. *SMIG herring*.
– COMB.: **herring choker** *slang* (**a**) *Canad.* a native or inhabitant of the Maritime Provinces; (**b**) *US* a Scandinavian; **herring gull** a large gull, *Larus argentatus*, widespread and common on Palaearctic coasts; **herring-gutted** *adjective* (of a horse) being too narrow through the body behind the ribs; **herring pond** *joc.* the sea, *esp.* the N. Atlantic.
■ **herring-like** *adjective* E20.

herringbone /ˈhɛrɪŋbəʊn/ *noun*, *adjective*, & *verb.* Also **herring-bone**. L16.
[ORIGIN from HERRING + BONE *noun*.]
► **A** *noun.* **1** (A bone from) the skeleton of a herring. L16.
2 = ***herringbone stitch*** below. M18.
3 A zigzag pattern or arrangement, as of the weave of a cloth, or of stones, bricks, or tiles; cloth woven in a zigzag pattern. M19.
4 *SKIING.* A method of climbing a slope by walking with the skis pointed outwards. E20.
► **B** *attrib.* or as *adjective.* Resembling the bones of a herring; having a zigzag pattern; (of cloth) having a zigzag weave. M17.
– SPECIAL COLLOCATIONS & COMB.: **herringbone banding** a decorative border on furniture consisting of two diagonally grained strips of veneer laid side by side. **herringbone coralline** a

marine coelenterate of the genus *Halecium*, often growing on oyster shells. **herringbone gear** a gearwheel with two sets of teeth inclined at an acute angle to each other. **herringbone parlour** a milking parlour in which the cows stand at an angle to a central operator's pit. **herringbone stitch** an asymmetric cross stitch used in embroidery or for securing an edge.
▸ **C** *verb.* **1** *verb trans. & intrans.* Sew with herringbone stitch. L18.
2 *verb trans.* Mark with a herringbone pattern; ARCHITECTURE lay (stones, bricks, tiles etc.) in a herringbone design. L19.
3 *verb intrans.* SKIING. Climb a slope by pointing the skis outward. E20.

Herrnhuter /ˈhɛːnhuːtə, ˈhɛːr(ə)n-/ *noun.* M18.
[ORIGIN German, from *Herrnhut* (= the Lord's keeping) the first German settlement of the Moravian Church + -ER¹.]
A member of the Moravian Church.

hers /həːz/ *possess. pronoun.* ME.
[ORIGIN from HER *pronoun*² + possess. suffix -'s¹. Cf. HERN *possess. pronoun.*]
1 Her one(s), that or those belonging or pertaining to her. ME.
W. S. MAUGHAM Julia took his head in both her hands and pressed his lips with hers. E. BAKER Hers was the seventh folding chair in from the aisle. M. ROBERTS The garden is not hers . . but the landlord lets all the tenants use it.
get hers: see GET *verb*. *his and hers*: see HIS *pronoun*² 1.
2 *of hers*, belonging or pertaining to her. L15.
H. G. WELLS She asked me with that faint lisp of hers.
– NOTE: Orig. northern, the southern & midland equivalent being HERN *pronoun*.

†**hersall** *noun. rare* (Spenser). Only in L16.
[ORIGIN Abbreviation.]
= REHEARSAL.

Herschelian /həːˈʃɛlɪən/ *adjective.* L18.
[ORIGIN from Sir William *Herschel* (1738–1822), German-born English astronomer and discoverer of the planet Uranus + -IAN.]
ASTRONOMY. Of a (reflecting) telescope: having a concave mirror slightly inclined to the axis.

herse *noun* see HEARSE *noun*¹.

herself /həːˈsɛlf/ *pronoun.* OE.
[ORIGIN from HER *pronoun*¹ + SELF *adjective* (but long interpreted as HER *adjective* + SELF *noun*).]
▸ **I** *refl.* **1** Refl. form (indirect, direct, & after prepositions) of HER *pronoun*¹: (to, for, etc.) the female person or animal, or the thing personified or conventionally treated as female or (in early use) grammatically feminine, in question. OE.
H. JAMES Something she admitted herself shy about. J. CONRAD If you mean her to come with credit to herself and you. E. WAUGH I hope Doris is making herself useful about the house. P. ACKROYD Her reality . . was known only to herself.
▸ **II** *emphatic.* **2** In apposition to a personal noun (subjective or objective) or to a subjective pronoun: that particular female person or animal, etc., the female person in question personally. ME.
J. BRYCE The Saracen wasted the Mediterranean coasts, and sacked Rome herself. E. BLISHEN Mother herself was a Methodist. C. P. SNOW She told me herself she was old enough to know better than marry Max. I. MCEWAN Again, Caroline stared at Mary as though she herself could not be seen.
3 (Not appositional.) ▸**a** Subjective: she herself. Now *arch. & dial.* exc. *colloq.* after *be* & after *than*, *as* (cf. HER *pronoun*¹ 2). ME. ▸**b** Objective: the female person etc. in question herself. ME.
a T. HARDY Mrs. Garland acknowledged her friendship for her neighbour, with whom Anne and herself associated. C. RAYNER She had imagined . . the women as well endowed with beauty as herself.
– PHRASES: **be herself** (*a*) act in her normal unconstrained manner; (*b*) feel as well as she usually does (usu. in neg. contexts). **by herself** on her own.

hership /ˈhəːʃɪp/ *noun. Scot.* (now *arch.* or *hist.*). LME.
[ORIGIN from HERE *noun*¹ or stem of Old English *hergian* HARRY *verb* + -SHIP. Cf. Old Norse *herskapr* warfare, harrying.]
1 Harrying, pillage, plunder, devastation. LME.
2 Distress, poverty, or famine, caused by pillage etc. LME.
3 Booty, plunder; *esp.* cattle forcibly driven off. M16.

herstory /ˈhəːst(ə)ri/ *noun.* Orig. *US.* L20.
[ORIGIN from HER *pronoun*² + STORY *noun*¹, by analogy with *history*.]
History as written or perceived from a feminist or woman's point of view.

Hertfordshire kindness /ˌhɑː(t)fədʃə ˈkʌɪndnɪs/ *noun phr. arch.* M17.
[ORIGIN An English county.]
The returning of a toast by drinking to the person who has just toasted one.

Herts. *abbreviation.*
Hertfordshire.

†**hertwort** *noun* see HARTWORT.

Hertz /həːts/ *noun.* In sense 2 **h-**, pl. same. L19.
[ORIGIN H. R. *Hertz* (1857–94), German physicist.]
PHYSICS. **1** *Hertz waves*, = *Hertzian waves* below. *obsolete* exc. *hist.* L19.
2 A unit of frequency (now in the SI) equal to one cycle per second. Abbreviation ***Hz***. E20.
■ **Hertzian** *adjective* of or pertaining to Hertz or the phenomena discovered by him; ***Hertzian waves*** (*obsolete* exc. *hist.*), radio waves: L19.

Hertzsprung–Russell diagram /ˌhəːtssprʌŋˈrʌs(ə)l ˌdʌɪəgram/ *noun phr.* M20.
[ORIGIN from E. *Hertzsprung* (1873–1967), Danish astronomer + H. N. *Russell* (1877–1957), US astronomer.]
ASTRONOMY. A diagram in which the visual magnitudes of stars are plotted against their spectral types or surface temperatures.

Herzegovinian /ˌhɛːtsəgəˈvɪnɪən, ˌhəːt-/ *adjective & noun.* Also **Herce-**. L19.
[ORIGIN from *Herzegovina* (see below) + -IAN.]
Of or pertaining to, a native or inhabitant of, Herzegovina, a region in the Balkans now a part of Bosnia-Herzegovina.

Heshvan *noun* var. of HESVAN.

Hesiodic /hiːsɪˈɒdɪk/ *adjective.* E19.
[ORIGIN from *Hesiod* (Greek *Hēsiodos*) (see below) + -IC.]
Of, pertaining to, or resembling the poetical style of Hesiod, a Greek epic poet of *c* 700 BC, or of the school of poetry which followed him.

hesitance /ˈhɛzɪt(ə)ns/ *noun.* E17.
[ORIGIN formed as HESITANT: see -ANCE.]
Hesitation.

hesitancy /ˈhɛzɪt(ə)nsi/ *noun.* E17.
[ORIGIN Latin *haesitantia* (in late Latin = hesitation, delay) from *haesitant-*, formed as HESITANT: see -ANCY.]
(An instance of) hesitation, vacillation, or indecision.
G. VIDAL After many soft hesitancies, she came to the point. *Observer* The new dawn saw him working as an accounts clerk . . . but only after some hesitancy.

hesitant /ˈhɛzɪt(ə)nt/ *adjective.* LME.
[ORIGIN Latin *haesitant-* pres. ppl stem of *haesitare*: see HESITATE, -ANT¹.]
Hesitating, irresolute, undecided; (of speech) stammering.
M. L. KING From a hesitant leader with unsure goals to a strong figure with deeply appealing objectives. M. DRABBLE Stephan's narrative style was hesitant, oblique, slightly stammering.
■ **hesitantly** *adverb* M17.

hesitate /ˈhɛzɪteɪt/ *verb.* E17.
[ORIGIN Latin *haesitat-* pa. ppl stem of *haesitare* stick fast, be undecided, stammer, from *haes-* pa. ppl stem of *haerere* stick, hold fast: see -ATE³.]
1 *verb intrans.* Pause irresolutely; show or speak with indecision (*about*, *over*); be reluctant *to do*; be deterred by scruples. E17. ▸**b** Move in an indecisive or faltering manner. E20.
L. STEFFENS The items are so incredible that I hesitate to print them. J. MARQUAND A time when it is better to do something, even if it is wrong, than to hesitate. W. SOYINKA They would not hesitate to put an end to my life.
2 *verb intrans.* Stammer or falter in speech. E18.
3 *verb trans.* Express with hesitation. M18.
W. GODWIN I hesitated a confused and irresolute answer. SIR W. SCOTT 'I am not sure,' hesitated Edith.
■ **hesitative** *adjective* showing or given to hesitation L18. **hesitatively** *adverb* L19. **hesitatory** *adjective* (now *rare* or *obsolete*) hesitative M18.

hesitation /hɛzɪˈteɪʃ(ə)n/ *noun.* E17.
[ORIGIN Latin *haesitatio(n-)*, formed as HESITATE: see -ATION.]
1 The action or an act of hesitating; irresolute pausing or delay; a state of doubt with regard to action. E17.
LYNDON B. JOHNSON Any hesitation or wavering, any false step, any sign of self-doubt, could have been disastrous. H. BAILEY Vera had no hesitation about condemning what was going on.
2 Hesitancy in speech; stammering. E18.
R. WARNER The Air Vice-Marshal spoke without hesitation, . . in the manner of one who was delivering important instructions.
– COMB.: **hesitation-form** LINGUISTICS (a form representing) a sound uttered when hesitating or faltering in speech; **hesitation-step** a step in ballroom dancing which takes up more than one beat; **hesitation waltz**: characterized by the hesitation step.

Hesped /ˈhɛspɛd/ *noun.* M17.
[ORIGIN Hebrew.]
A funeral oration pronounced over the dead at a Jewish memorial service.

Hesper /ˈhɛspə/ *noun. poet.* E17.
[ORIGIN Latin HESPERUS.]
= HESPERUS.

Hesperian /hɛˈspɪərɪən/ *adjective & noun.* L15.
[ORIGIN Latin *hesperius*, Greek *hesperios*, from *Hesperia* (poet.) land of the west, formed as HESPERUS: see -AN, -IAN.]
▸ **A** *adjective.* **1** Western. *poet.* L15.
2 GREEK MYTHOLOGY. Of or pertaining to the Hesperides. L16.
3 = HESPERIID *adjective*. Now *rare*. M19.
▸ **B** *noun.* **1** A native or inhabitant of a western land. *arch. rare.* E17.
2 = HESPERIID *noun*. Now *rare*. M19.

hesperid *noun & adjective* var. of HESPERIID.

Hesperides /hɛˈspɛrɪdiːz/ *noun pl.* L16.
[ORIGIN Greek, pl. of *hesperis* (adjective) western, (noun) daughter of the west, land of the sunset, from *hesperos*: see HESPERUS.]
GREEK MYTHOLOGY. **1** (The islands containing) gardens with a tree of golden apples guarded by nymphs and popularly located beyond the Atlas mountains at the western border of Oceanus, the river encircling the world. L16.
2 The (three, four, or seven) nymphs, daughters of Hesperus (or, in earlier versions, of Night and Hades), who guarded the tree in these gardens. E17.

hesperidia *noun* pl. of HESPERIDIUM.

hesperidin /hɛˈspɛrɪdɪn/ *noun.* M19.
[ORIGIN formed as HESPERIDIUM + -IN¹.]
CHEMISTRY. A flavonoid glycoside obtained from the peel of citrus fruits.

hesperidium /hɛspəˈrɪdɪəm/ *noun.* Pl. **-ia** /-ɪə/. M19.
[ORIGIN formed as HESPERIDES + -IUM, with ref. to the mythical golden apples of the Hesperides.]
BOTANY. A form of berry with a tough leathery rind, as a citrus fruit.

hesperiid /hɛˈspɛrɪɪd/ *noun & adjective.* Also **hesperid** /ˈhɛspərɪd/. L19.
[ORIGIN mod. Latin *Hesperiidae* (see below), from *Hesperia* genus name: see -ID³.]
ENTOMOLOGY. ▸**A** *noun.* Any of numerous small butterflies of the family Hesperiidae, somewhat like moths; a skipper. L19.
▸ **B** *adjective.* Of, pertaining to, or designating this family. E20.

H

Hesperus /ˈhɛspərəs/ *noun. poet.* LME.
[ORIGIN Latin, from Greek *hesperos* (adjective) western, (noun) the evening star.]
The evening star.

Hessian /ˈhɛsɪən/ *adjective & noun.* Also **h-** (see below). L17.
[ORIGIN from *Hesse* (see below) + -IAN.]
▸ **A** *adjective.* **1** Of or pertaining to the former grand duchy, or the region or state, of Hesse in Germany. L17.
2 (**h-**.) Made of hessian. M20.
– SPECIAL COLLOCATIONS: **Hessian boot** a tasselled high boot fashionable in the early 19th cent., first worn by Hessian troops. **Hessian fly** [thought to have been brought to N. America in bedding by Hessian troops, *c* 1776] a gall midge, *Mayetiola destructor*, native to SE Europe and introduced elsewhere, whose larvae are destructive to wheat and other crops.
▸ **B** *noun.* **1** A native or inhabitant of Hesse; *hist.* a Hessian soldier. M18. ▸**b** A military or political hireling, a mercenary. *arch. US.* M19.
2 In *pl.* Hessian boots. E19.
3 (**h-**.) A strong coarse cloth made of hemp or jute. L19.

hessite /ˈhɛsʌɪt/ *noun.* M19.
[ORIGIN from G. H. *Hess* (1802–50), Swiss-born Russian scientist + -ITE¹.]
MINERALOGY. Silver telluride, crystallizing in the cubic system and usu. occurring as grey prisms with a metallic lustre.

hessonite *noun* var. of ESSONITE.

hest /hɛst/ *noun.*
[ORIGIN Old English *hǣs*, from Germanic base of Old English *hātan* call (see HIGHT *verb*) assim. to nouns in *-t*.]
1 Bidding, a command, an injunction. *arch.* OE.
SIR W. SCOTT Christian or heathen, you shall swear to do my hest. CARLYLE Standing like a hackney-coach . . at the hest of a discerning public.
†**2** A vow, a promise. ME–L16.
†**3** Will, purpose, determination. LME–M19.

†**hestern** *adjective.* L16–E18.
[ORIGIN Latin *hesternus*.]
Of yesterday; yester-.

hesternal /hɛˈstəːn(ə)l/ *adjective.* Now *rare*. M17.
[ORIGIN formed as HESTERN + -AL¹.]
Of yesterday, of yesterday's standing or date.

Hesvan /ˈhɛsv(ə)n/ *noun.* Also **Ches-** /ˈxɛs-/, **Hesh-** /ˈhɛʃ-/, & other vars. M19.
[ORIGIN Hebrew *ḥešwān* from earlier *marḥešwān*, from Akkadian *araḫ samna* eighth month.]
In the Jewish calendar, the second month of the civil and eighth of the religious year, usu. coinciding with parts of October and November.

Hesychast /ˈhɛsɪkast/ *noun.* M19.
[ORIGIN Late Greek *hēsukhastēs* hermit, from *hēsukhazein* be still, from *hēsukhos* still, quiet.]
ECCLESIASTICAL HISTORY. A member of a movement dedicated to the practice of interior prayer originating among the monks of Mount Athos in the 14th cent.

het /hɛt/ *noun & adjective.* L20.
[ORIGIN Abbreviation.]
= HETEROSEXUAL.

het /hɛt/ *ppl adjective.* LME.
[ORIGIN pa. pple of HEAT *verb* (cf. LEAD *verb*¹, LED *verb*).]
1 Heated, hot. Long *dial.* LME.
2 Excited, agitated; upset. Foll. by *up* (exc. *dial.*). M19.
P. LIVELY Being overtired and overstrained and generally het up.

hetaera /hɪˈtɪərə/ *noun*. Pl. **-ras**, **-rae** /-riː/. Also **hetaira** /hɪˈtʌɪrə/, pl. **-ras**, **-rai** /-rʌɪ/. **E19**.
[ORIGIN Greek *hetaira* fem. of *hetairos* companion.]
Esp. in ancient Greece: a mistress, a concubine; a courtesan, a prostitute.

hetaerism /hɪˈtɪərɪz(ə)m/ *noun*. Also **hetairism** /hɪˈtʌɪrɪz(ə)m/. **M19**.
[ORIGIN Greek *hetairismos* prostitution, from *hetairizein* be a prostitute, from *hetaira*: see HETAERA, -ISM.]
1 Concubinage as a recognized social system. **M19**.
2 *ANTHROPOLOGY*. Communal marriage as a social system. **L19**.

hetaerolite /hɪˈtɪərəlʌɪt/ *noun*. **L19**.
[ORIGIN from Greek *hetairos* companion (from having been orig. found associated with chlorophanite) + -LITE.]
MINERALOGY. A black, tetragonal, mixed oxide of zinc and manganese, usu. occurring as octahedral crystals and isostructural with hausmannite.

hetaira *noun* var. of HETAERA.

hetairai *noun pl.* see HETAERA.

hetairism *noun* var. of HETAERISM.

†**hetchel** *noun & verb* see HATCHEL.

hetero /ˈhɛt(ə)rəʊ/ *noun & adjective*. *colloq*. Pl. of noun **-os**. **M20**.
[ORIGIN Abbreviation.]
= HETEROSEXUAL *noun & adjective*.

H

hetero- /ˈhɛtərəʊ/ *combining form*. Before a vowel also **heter-**.
[ORIGIN from Greek *heteros* the other of two, other: see -O-.]
Used in words adopted from Greek and in English words modelled on these, and as a freely productive prefix, with the sense 'other, different'. Freq. opp. HOMO-, occas. opp. AUTO-[1], ISO-, ORTHO-.
■ **heteracanth** *adjective* (*ICHTHYOLOGY*) having the spines of the dorsal and anal fins alternately broader on one side than on the other **L19**. **heterauˈxesis** *noun* [Greek *auxēsis* growth] growth of different parts at unequal rates **L19**. **hetero-aˈgglutinin** *noun* an agglutinin that causes agglutination of cells of a different blood group, animal species, etc. **E20**. **hetero-agglutiˈnation** *noun* agglutination of cells brought about by a hetero-agglutinin **E20**. **heteroaroˈmatic** *adjective & noun* (*CHEMISTRY*) (**a**) *adjective* heterocyclic and aromatic; (**b**) *noun* a heteroaromatic compound: **M20**. **ˈhetero-atom** *noun* (*CHEMISTRY*) an atom, other than a carbon atom, in the ring of a cyclic compound **E20**. **heteroˈauxin** *noun* a growth-promoting hormone present in some plants and micro-organisms **M20**. **heteroˈblastic** *adjective* (**a**) *BOTANY* characterized by a marked difference between immature and adult forms; (**b**) *PETROGRAPHY* composed of grains of two or more distinct sizes: **L19**. **heteroˈcarpous** *adjective* producing fruit of different kinds **L19**. **heteroˈcercal** *adjective* [Greek *kerkos* tail] *ICHTHYOLOGY* designating or possessing a tail with unequal lobes, esp. with the spine deflected into the upper lobe **M19**. **heterochlaˈmydeous** *adjective* [Greek *khlamud-*, *khlamus* cloak] *BOTANY* having the calyx and corolla of different colour or texture **L19**. **heteroˈchromia** *noun* (*MEDICINE*) a difference in colour between two parts (esp. the irises of the eyes) that are usually the same colour **L19**. **heteroˈchromic** *adjective* characterized by or exhibiting heterochromia **E20**. **heteroˈchromous** *adjective* (chiefly *BOTANY*) of different colours **M19**. **heteroˈchronic** *adjective* occurring at different times; irregular; *esp.* (of a transplant) between individuals of different ages: **M19**. **heterocosm** *noun* a different or separate world **M20**. **heterocycle** *noun* (*CHEMISTRY*) a heterocyclic molecule or compound **E20**. **heteroˈcyclic** *noun & adjective* (*CHEMISTRY*) (a molecule or compound) containing a ring formed of atoms of more than one element **L19**. **heterocyst** *noun* a specialized cell of different structure present in certain algae and bacteria **L19**. **heteroˈdesmic** *adjective* (*CRYSTALLOGRAPHY*) containing chemical bonds of more than one kind **M20**. **heterodimer** *noun* (*CHEMISTRY*) a dimer composed of two different subunits **L20**. **heteroˈduplex** *adjective & noun* (*BIOCHEMISTRY*) (a molecule) containing or consisting of polynucleotide strands derived from two different parent molecules **M20**. **heteroecious** /hɛtəˈriːʃəs/ *adjective* [Greek *oikia* house] (of a fungus etc.) parasitic on different hosts at different stages of its life cycle **L19**. **heteroecism** /hɛtəˈriːsɪz(ə)m/ *noun* the condition of being heteroecious **L19**. **heteroˈglossia** *noun* the presence of two or more expressed viewpoints in a text or other artistic work **M20**. **heteroˈglossic** *adjective* involving heteroglossia **M20**. **heterograft** *noun* = HETEROTRANSPLANT *noun* **E20**. **heteroiˈmmune** *adjective* immune to an antigen derived from a different species **E20**. **heteroˈnuclear** *adjective* (*CHEMISTRY* etc.) (**a**) (of substitution) taking place on different rings in a polycyclic molecule; (**b**) composed of atoms whose nuclei are unalike: **E20**. **heteroˈphasia** *noun* [Greek *phasis* speech] the condition of saying or writing one word or phrase when another is meant, esp. as a result of brain damage etc. **M19**. **heteroˈphoria** *noun* a latent squint **L19**. **heteroˈphoric** *adjective* pertaining to or exhibiting heterophoria **L19**. **heteroˈpolar** *adjective* characterized by opposite or alternating polarity; *esp.* having armatures passing north and south magnetic poles alternately: **L19**. **heteroscеˈdastic** *adjective* [Greek *skedastos* able to be scattered, from *skedannunai* scatter] *STATISTICS* of unequal scatter or variation; having unequal variances: **E20**. **heteroscedaˈsticity** *noun* (*STATISTICS*) unequal variance **E20**. **heterospeˈcific** *adjective* (**a**) of different blood groups; (of a pregnancy) in which the mother's serum would agglutinate the red blood cells of the fetus; (**b**) derived from an organism of a different species: **E20**. **heteroˈsporic**, **heteˈrosporous** *adjectives* (*BIOLOGY*) producing two different kinds of spore **L19**. **heteˈrospory** *noun* (*BIOLOGY*) the condition of being heterosporous **L19**. **heterosuˈggestion** *noun* suggestion from another person (cf. AUTO-SUGGESTION) **E20**. **heterosyˈllabic** *adjective* belonging to a different syllable **E20**. **heteroˈthallic** *adjective* (*MYCOLOGY*) (of a fungus) having an incompatibility system such that only genetically different strains can undergo nuclear fusion during sexual reproduction **E20**. **heteroˈthallism** *noun* the state or condition of being heterothallic **E20**. **heteroˈthally** *noun* = HETEROTHALLISM **M20**. **heterotherm** *noun* a heterothermic animal **M20**. **heteroˈthermic** *adjective* displaying homeothermy and poikilothermy at different times **L19**. **heterothermy** *noun* heterothermic behaviour **M20**. **heteroˈtypic** *adjective* (*BIOLOGY*) designating or relating to the first of the two nuclear divisions of meiosis **L19**.

heterocaryotic *adjective* var. of HETEROKARYOTIC.

heterochromatic /ˌhɛtərəʊkrə(ʊ)ˈmatɪk/ *adjective*. **L19**.
[ORIGIN Sense 1 from HETERO- + CHROMATIC; sense 2 from HETEROCHROMATIN + -IC.]
1 Relating to or possessing more than one colour; pertaining to light or other radiation of more than one wavelength. **L19**.
2 Exhibiting heteropycnosis. **M20**.

heterochromatin /hɛtərə(ʊ)ˈkrəʊmətɪn/ *noun*. **M20**.
[ORIGIN from HETERO- + CHROMATIN.]
Heteropycnotic chromosome material.
■ **heterochromatiniˈzation** *noun* = HETEROCHROMATIZATION **M20**. **heterochromatinized** *adjective* = HETEROCHROMATIZED **M20**.

heterochromatization /ˌhɛtərə(ʊ)krəʊmətʌɪˈzeɪʃ(ə)n/ *noun*. Also **-isation**. **M20**.
[ORIGIN from HETEROCHROMAT(IN + -IZATION.]
(The extent of) a change of state of chromosome material in which it becomes heterochromatic and the action of the genes is modified or suppressed.
■ **heteroˈchromatized** *adjective* having undergone heterochromatization **M20**.

heteroclite /ˈhɛtərə(ʊ)klʌɪt/ *adjective & noun*. Orig. †**ethroclite**. **L15**.
[ORIGIN medieval Latin *ethroclitus* & late Latin *heteroclitus* from Greek *heteroklitos*, formed as HETERO- + *-klitos* bent, inflected, from *klinein* to lean, bend, inflect: see -ITE[2].]
▸ **A** *adjective*. **1** Deviating from the norm; abnormal, irregular, anomalous. **L15**.
2 *GRAMMAR*. Irregularly declined or inflected. **M17**.
▸ **B** *noun*. **1** A heteroclite person or thing. **L15**.
2 *GRAMMAR*. A heteroclite word, esp. a noun. **L16**.
■ **heteroˈclitic** *adjective & noun* = HETEROCLITE **M17**. †**heteroclitical** *adjective* = HETEROCLITE *adjective* **M17–L19**.

heterodont /ˈhɛt(ə)rə(ʊ)dɒnt/ *adjective & noun*. **L19**.
[ORIGIN from HETERO- + -ODONT.]
▸ **A** *adjective*. Having teeth of different kinds. **L19**.
▸ **B** *noun*. A heterodont animal. **L19**.

heterodox /ˈhɛt(ə)rə(ʊ)dɒks/ *noun & adjective*. **E17**.
[ORIGIN Late Latin *heterodoxus*, *-os* from Greek *heterodoxos*, formed as HETERO- + *doxa* opinion.]
▸ †**A** *noun*. An unorthodox opinion. Only in **17**.
▸ **B** *adjective*. Of an opinion or a person: unorthodox. **M17**.

> E. H. JONES Men .. tabooed by society because they were believed to be heterodox on questions of social policy.

heterodoxy /ˈhɛt(ə)rə(ʊ)dɒksi/ *noun*. **M17**.
[ORIGIN Greek *heterodoxia* error of opinion, formed as HETERODOX: see -Y[3].]
1 A heterodox opinion. **M17**.
2 The quality of being heterodox; deviation from what is considered to be orthodox. **M17**.

heterodyne /ˈhɛt(ə)rə(ʊ)dʌɪn/ *adjective, verb, & noun*. **E20**.
[ORIGIN from HETERO- + Greek *dunamis* power.]
▸ **A** *adjective*. Pertaining to, involving, or designating the production of beats by the combination of two oscillations of slightly different frequencies, esp. as a method of radio detection in which the incoming signal combines with an oscillation generated in the receiver, producing an audible signal. **E20**.
▸ **B** *verb*. **1** *verb trans*. Change the frequency of (a signal) by a heterodyne process. **E20**.
2 *verb intrans*. Combine in a heterodyne process. **M20**.
▸ **C** *noun*. A heterodyne receiver or oscillator. Now *rare*. **E20**.

heterogamete /hɛt(ə)rə(ʊ)ˈgamiːt/ *noun*. **L19**.
[ORIGIN from HETERO- + GAMETE.]
BIOLOGY. Either of a pair of conjugating gametes that differ in form or character.

heterogametic /ˌhɛt(ə)rə(ʊ)gəˈmɛtɪk, -ˈmiː-/ *adjective*. **E20**.
[ORIGIN from HETERO- + GAMETIC.]
BIOLOGY. Producing gametes that differ with respect to a sex chromosome.
■ **heteroˈgamety** *noun* the condition or state of being heterogametic **M20**.

heterogamic /hɛt(ə)rə(ʊ)ˈgamɪk/ *adjective*. **E20**.
[ORIGIN from HETEROGAMY + -IC.]
BIOLOGY. Characterized by heterogamy.

heterogamous /hɛtəˈrɒgəməs/ *adjective*. **M19**.
[ORIGIN from HETERO- + Greek *gamos* marriage + -OUS.]
1 *BOTANY*. Having flowers of different sexual types (male, female, and/or hermaphrodite) in the same inflorescence. **M19**.
2 *BIOLOGY*. Characterized by the alternation of generations. **L19**.
3 *BIOLOGY*. Involving, being, or producing heterogametes **L19**.

heterogamy /hɛtəˈrɒgəmi/ *noun*. **L19**.
[ORIGIN from HETERO- + -GAMY.]
1 *BIOLOGY*. Alternation of generations. **L19**.
2 *BIOLOGY*. The condition of producing heterogametes; heterogamous reproduction. **L19**.
3 *BOTANY*. Heterogamous condition. **L19**.

heterogene /ˈhɛt(ə)rə(ʊ)dʒiːn/ *adjective*. Long *rare* or *obsolete*. Orig. †**ethrogene**. **LME**.
[ORIGIN Greek *heterogenēs*: see HETEROGENEOUS.]
= HETEROGENEOUS.

heterogeneal /hɛt(ə)rə(ʊ)ˈdʒiːnɪəl, -ˈdʒɛn-/ *adjective & noun*. Now *rare*. **E17**.
[ORIGIN formed as HETEROGENEOUS + -AL[1].]
▸ **A** *adjective*. = HETEROGENEOUS. **E17**.
▸ †**B** *noun*. A heterogeneous person or substance. Only in **M17**.

heterogeneity /ˌhɛt(ə)rə(ʊ)dʒɪˈniːɪti/ *noun*. **M17**.
[ORIGIN medieval Latin *heterogeneitas*, formed as HETEROGENEOUS: see -ITY.]
1 The quality or condition of being heterogeneous. **M17**.
2 A heterogeneous element or constituent. Now *rare*. **M17**.

heterogeneous /hɛt(ə)rə(ʊ)ˈdʒiːnɪəs, -ˈdʒɛn-/ *adjective*. **E17**.
[ORIGIN from medieval Latin *heterogeneus*, from Greek *heterogenēs* of different kinds, formed as HETERO- + *genos* kind: see -OUS.]
1 Diverse in kind or nature; dissimilar, incongruous; *gen*. (now *rare*) anomalous, abnormal. **E17**.

> N. PODHORETZ An organization embracing people of such diverse and heterogeneous tastes.

2 Composed of different elements or constituents; not homogeneous. **M17**. ▸**b** *PHYSICAL CHEMISTRY*. Consisting of or involving more than one phase. **L19**. ▸**c** Of a nuclear reactor: not having the fuel uniformly mixed with the moderator and/or coolant. **M20**.

> I. COLEGATE Another sub-group in this apparently heterogeneous but in fact multifariously differentiated collection of men.

3 *MATH*. Of different kinds or degrees; consisting of terms of different dimensions. **M17**.
■ **heterogeneously** *adverb* **L18**. **heterogeneousness** *noun* **M17**.

heterogenesis /hɛt(ə)rə(ʊ)ˈdʒɛnɪsɪs/ *noun*. **M19**.
[ORIGIN from HETERO- + -GENESIS.]
BIOLOGY. **1** The origination or birth of an organism otherwise than from a similar organism as parent. **M19**.
2 *spec*. Alternation of generations. **M19**.

heterogenetic /ˌhɛt(ə)rə(ʊ)dʒɪˈnɛtɪk/ *adjective*. **L19**.
[ORIGIN from HETERO- + GENETIC.]
BIOLOGY. **1** Of, pertaining to, or characterized by heterogenesis or heterogeny. **L19**.
2 = HETEROPHILE *adjective*. **E20**.

heterogenous /hɛtəˈrɒdʒɪnəs/ *adjective*. **L17**.
[ORIGIN Alt. of HETEROGENEOUS; in sense 2 prob. directly from Greek *genos* race.]
1 Heterogeneous. Freq. considered *erron*. **L17**.
2 *MEDICINE*. †**a** = HOMOPLASTIC *adjective* 2. Only in **E20**. ▸**b** = HETEROPLASTIC *adjective* 2. **M20**.

heterogeny /hɛtəˈrɒdʒəni/ *noun*. **M17**.
[ORIGIN In sense 1 app. from HETEROGENE + -Y[3]; in senses 2 and 3 from HETERO- + -GENY.]
†**1** Heterogeneousness. Only in **M17**.
2 A heterogeneous collection or group. **M19**.
3 *BIOLOGY*. **a** Spontaneous generation. **M19**. ▸**b** the alternation of generations, esp. of a sexual and a parthenogenetic generation. **L19**.
■ **heterogenist** *noun* a supporter of the hypothesis of spontaneous generation **L19**.

heterogony /hɛtəˈrɒgəni/ *noun*. **L19**.
[ORIGIN from HETERO- + -GONY.]
1 = HETEROGENESIS. **L19**.
2 Allometry. **E20**.
■ **heteroˈgonic** *adjective* **E20**. **heterogonous** *adjective* **L19**.

heterography /hɛtəˈrɒgrəfi/ *noun*. **L18**.
[ORIGIN from HETERO- + -GRAPHY, after *orthography*.]
Unconventional or incorrect spelling.
■ **heteroˈgraphic** *adjective* of, pertaining to, or characterized by heterography **M19**. **heteroˈgraphically** *adverb* **L18**.

heterokaryotic /ˌhɛt(ə)rə(ʊ)karɪˈɒtɪk/ *adjective*. Also **-caryotic**. **E20**.
[ORIGIN from HETERO- + KARYO- + -OTIC.]
Chiefly *MYCOLOGY*. Having two or more genetically different nuclei within a common cytoplasm.
■ **heteroˈkaryon** *noun*, pl. **-ya**, a heterokaryotic cell, structure, or organism **M20**. **heterokaryosis** *noun* the state or condition of being heterokaryotic **E20**.

heterological /hɛt(ə)rə(ʊ)ˈlɒdʒɪk(ə)l/ *adjective*. **E20**.
[ORIGIN German *heterologisch*, formed as HETERO- + Greek LOGOS: see -ICAL.]
Of a word: not having the property which it denotes. Opp. AUTOLOGICAL.

heterologous /hɛtəˈrɒləgəs/ *adjective*. **M19**.
[ORIGIN from HETERO- + Greek *logos* relation, ratio: see LOGOS, -OUS.]
Not corresponding; consisting of different elements; derived from or pertaining to different species, bodies, etc. Opp. HOMOLOGOUS.

heterology /hɛtəˈrɒlədʒi/ *noun*. **M19**.
[ORIGIN formed as HETEROLOGOUS + -Y³.]
The quality or condition of being heterologous.

heterolysis /hɛtəˈrɒlɪsɪs/ *noun*. **E20**.
[ORIGIN from HETERO- + -LYSIS.]
1 *BIOLOGY*. The dissolution of cells of one kind by an agent produced by cells of another kind. **E20**.
2 *CHEMISTRY*. The splitting of a molecule into two oppositely charged ions. **M20**.
■ **heteroˈlytic** *adjective* characterized by or of the nature of heterolysis **E20**.

heteromerous /hɛtəˈrɒm(ə)rəs/ *adjective*. **E19**.
[ORIGIN from HETERO- + -MEROUS.]
1 *ENTOMOLOGY*. Of, pertaining to, or designating a group of beetles (sometimes classed as Heteromera) which typically have a reduced number of tarsal joints in the posterior pair of legs. **E19**.
2 *BOTANY*. **a** Of a lichen: having the algal and fungal components in separate layers. **L19**. ▸**b** Of a flower: having a different number of members in each whorl. Opp. ***isomerous***. **L19**.

heteromorph /ˈhɛt(ə)rə(ʊ)mɔːf/ *adjective & noun*. **L19**.
[ORIGIN formed as HETEROMORPHIC.]
(A thing that is) heteromorphous.

heteromorphic /hɛt(ə)rə(ʊ)ˈmɔːfɪk/ *adjective*. **M19**.
[ORIGIN from HETERO- + Greek *morphē* form: see -IC.]
BIOLOGY. **1** Differing in form; occurring in differing forms, esp. at different stages of life. **M19**.
2 Resulting from heteromorphosis. **L19**.

heteromorphism /hɛt(ə)rə(ʊ)ˈmɔːfɪz(ə)m/ *noun*. **M19**.
[ORIGIN formed as HETEROMORPHIC + -ISM.]
The quality or condition of being heteromorphic.

heteromorphosis /hɛt(ə)rə(ʊ)ˈmɔːfəsɪs, ˌhɛt(ə)rə(ʊ)mɔːˈfəʊsɪs/ *noun*. Pl. **-morphoses** /-ˈmɔːfəsiːz, -mɔːˈfəʊsiːz/. **L19**.
[ORIGIN from HETERO- + MORPHOSIS.]
BIOLOGY & MEDICINE. **1** Growth of abnormal tissue. **L19**.
2 Regeneration of an organ etc. different from that which has been damaged or lost. **L19**.

heteromorphous /hɛt(ə)rə(ʊ)ˈmɔːfəs/ *adjective*. **E19**.
[ORIGIN formed as HETEROMORPHIC: see -OUS.]
Of abnormal or irregular form.

heteronomous /hɛtəˈrɒnəməs/ *adjective*. **E19**.
[ORIGIN from HETERO- + Greek *nomos* law: see -OUS.]
1 Subject to different laws, *spec.* (*BIOLOGY*) of growth. **E19**.
2 Subject to an external law. **L19**.

D. CUPITT Morality was heteronomous, in being a matter of keeping to a sacred Law imposed upon you by another.

■ **heteronomously** *adverb* **E20**.

heteronomy /hɛtəˈrɒnəmi/ *noun*. **L18**.
[ORIGIN formed as HETERONOMOUS: see -Y³, -NOMY.]
1 Subjection to an external law or power. **L18**.
2 Presence of a different law or principle. **E19**.

heteronym /ˈhɛt(ə)rə(ʊ)nɪm/ *noun*. **L19**.
[ORIGIN from HETERO- + -NYM.]
1 Each of two or more words identical in spelling but distinct in sound and meaning. Cf. HOMONYM, SYNONYM. **L19**.
2 A word in one language which is a translation of the designation in another language. Opp. PARONYM 2. **L19**.

heteronymous /hɛtəˈrɒnɪməs/ *adjective*. **L17**.
[ORIGIN Greek *heterōnumos*, formed as HETERONYM: see -OUS.]
1 Designating correlatives which are denoted by unlike or unrelated terms, as *husband*, *wife*. Cf. SYNONYMOUS. **L17**.
2 Having the character of a heteronym. **L19**.
3 *ZOOLOGY*. Of animal horns: such that the right horn has a left-handed spiral core and vice versa. **E20**.

heteroousian /hɛt(ə)rəʊˈuːsɪən, -ˈaʊ-, -z-/ *noun & adjective*. Also **heterous-** /hɛtəˈruːs-, hɛtəˈraʊs-/, (esp. as noun) **H-**. **L17**.
[ORIGIN from Greek *heter(o)ousios* (formed as HETERO- + *ousia* essence, substance): see -IAN. Opp. HOMOIOUSIAN and HOMOOUSIAN.]
CHRISTIAN THEOLOGY & ECCLESIASTICAL HISTORY. ▸**A** *noun*. A person who believed the first and second persons of the Trinity to be different in essence or substance. **L17**.
▸**B** *adjective*. Of different essence or substance (esp. of the first and second persons of the Trinity). Also, of or pertaining to the heteroousians. **L17**.

heterophile /ˈhɛt(ə)rə(ʊ)fʌɪl/ *adjective & noun*. Also (esp. as noun) **-phil** /-fɪl/. **E20**.
[ORIGIN from HETERO- + -PHIL(E).]
▸**A** *adjective*. Able to react immunologically with sera etc. from organisms of another species. **E20**.
▸**B** *noun*. A polymorphonuclear leucocyte found in mammalian blood, stained by both acid and basic dyes. **M20**.
■ **heteroˈphilic** *adjective* = HETEROPHILE *adjective* **E20**.

heterophony /hɛtəˈrɒf(ə)ni/ *noun*. **M20**.
[ORIGIN Greek *heterophōnia* difference in note, formed as HETERO-: see -PHONY.]
A simultaneous performance of the same melody by different voices or instruments.
■ **heteroˈphonic** *adjective* different in sound **E20**.

heterophyllous /hɛt(ə)rə(ʊ)ˈfɪləs/ *adjective*. **E19**.
[ORIGIN from HETERO- + Greek *phullon* leaf: see -OUS.]
BOTANY. Bearing leaves of different forms on the same plant.
■ ˈ**heterophylly** *noun* the condition of being heterophyllous **L19**.

heteroplasia /hɛt(ə)rə(ʊ)ˈpleɪzɪə/ *noun*. **M19**.
[ORIGIN from HETERO- + -PLASIA. Cf. HETEROPLASTIC.]
Abnormal growth of tissue.

heteroplastic /hɛt(ə)rə(ʊ)ˈplastɪk/ *adjective*. **M19**.
[ORIGIN from HETERO- + PLASTIC *adjective & noun*³.]
BIOLOGY & MEDICINE. **1** Pertaining to or being an abnormal growth of tissue. **M19**.
2 Of a graft: between individuals of different species. **L19**.
■ **heteroplastically** *adverb* **E20**.

heteroplasty /ˈhɛt(ə)rə(ʊ)plasti/ *noun*. **M19**.
[ORIGIN from HETERO- + -PLASTY.]
BIOLOGY & MEDICINE. **1** The grafting of tissues between individuals of the same species. **M19**.
2 The grafting of tissues between individuals of different species. **E20**.

heteroploid /ˈhɛt(ə)rə(ʊ)plɔɪd/ *adjective*. **E20**.
[ORIGIN from HETERO- + -PLOID.]
BIOLOGY. Having a chromosome number other than that typical of the species.
■ **heteroploidy** *noun* heteroploid condition **E20**.

heteropod /ˈhɛt(ə)rə(ʊ)pɒd/ *noun & adjective*. **M19**.
[ORIGIN mod. Latin *Heteropoda* pl., formed as HETERO- + -POD.]
ZOOLOGY. ▸**A** *noun*. Pl. **heteropods**, in Latin form **Heteropoda** /hɛtəˈrɒpədə/. Any of a group of free-swimming prosobranch gastropods having the foot adapted for swimming. **M19**.
▸**B** *adjective*. Of or pertaining to this group. **L19**.

heteropteran /hɛtəˈrɒpt(ə)rən/ *noun & adjective*. **M19**.
[ORIGIN from mod. Latin *Heteroptera* (see below), formed as HETERO- + Greek *pteron* wing: see -AN.]
ENTOMOLOGY. ▸**A** *noun*. Any hemipteran insect of the suborder Heteroptera, which comprises the true bugs, i.e. those whose wings, where present, have hardened bases and membranous tips. Cf. HOMOPTERAN. **M19**.
▸**B** *adjective*. Of, pertaining to, or characteristic of the suborder Heteroptera. **E20**.
■ **heteropterous** *adjective* = HETEROPTERAN *adjective* **L19**.

heteropycnosis /ˌhɛt(ə)rə(ʊ)pɪkˈnəʊsɪs/ *noun*. Also **-pyknosis**. **E20**.
[ORIGIN from HETERO- + Greek *puknos* thick: see -OSIS.]
BIOLOGY. The condition in chromosome material of being more (or less) condensed than the majority of such material, and hence staining more (or less) intensely.
■ **heteropycnotic** *adjective* **M20**.

heterosexism /hɛt(ə)rə(ʊ)ˈsɛksɪz(ə)m/ *noun*. **L20**.
[ORIGIN from HETERO- + SEXISM.]
Discrimination or prejudice by heterosexuals against or towards homosexuals.
■ **heterosexist** *adjective* **L20**.

heterosexual /hɛt(ə)rə(ʊ)ˈsɛkʃʊəl/ *adjective & noun*. **L19**.
[ORIGIN from HETERO- + SEXUAL.]
▸**A** *adjective*. **1** Of, pertaining to, or characterized by sexual attraction towards the opposite sex; of, pertaining to, or involving sexual activity between members of the opposite sex. **L19**.

Daily Telegraph Co-educational schools probably tend to hasten heterosexual experimentation.

2 Pertaining to, characteristic of, or comprising both sexes. **E20**.

D. MORRIS The males . . find themselves in heterosexual groups instead of the old all-male parties.

▸**B** *noun*. A heterosexual person. **E20**.
■ **heterosexuˈality** *noun* the condition of being heterosexual; heterosexual characteristics: **E20**. **heterosexually** *adverb* **M20**.

heterosis /hɛtəˈrəʊsɪs/ *noun*. Pl. **-roses** /-ˈrəʊsiːz/. **M19**.
[ORIGIN Greek *heterōsis* alteration, from *heteros* different: see -OSIS.]
1 The use of one form of a noun, pronoun, etc., for another as a figure of speech. *rare*. **M19**.
2 *GENETICS*. The tendency of a crossbred individual to show qualities superior to those of both parents; hybrid vigour. **E20**.
■ **heterotic** *adjective* (*GENETICS*) pertaining to or exhibiting heterosis **E20**.

heterosite /ˈhɛt(ə)rə(ʊ)sʌɪt/ *noun*. **M19**.
[ORIGIN from Greek *heteros* different + -ITE¹.]
MINERALOGY. An orthorhombic hydrated phosphate of iron and manganese that occurs as dark violet to bright purple masses. Cf. PURPURITE.

heterostyled /ˈhɛt(ə)rə(ʊ)stʌɪld/ *adjective*. **L19**.
[ORIGIN from HETERO- + STYLE + -ED².]
BOTANY. In which the styles of different individual plants differ in length relative to the stamens.
■ **heteroˈstylism** *noun* the condition of being heterostyled **L19**. **heteroˈstylous** *adjective* = HETEROSTYLED **L19**. ˈ**heterostyly** *noun* = HETEROSTYLISM **L19**.

heterotaxy /ˈhɛt(ə)rə(ʊ)taksi/ *noun*. **M19**.
[ORIGIN from HETERO- + -TAXY.]
1 *ANATOMY & BOTANY*. Abnormal disposition of organs or parts. **M19**.
2 *GEOLOGY*. Lack of uniformity in stratification. **L19**.

heterotopia /hɛt(ə)rə(ʊ)ˈtəʊpɪə/ *noun*. Also anglicized as **heterotopy** /hɛtəˈrɒtəpi/. **L19**.
[ORIGIN mod. Latin, formed as HETERO- + Greek *-topia*, from *topos* place: see -IA¹, -Y³.]
BIOLOGY & MEDICINE. The presence of an organ or other tissue at a site where it is not normally found.

heterotopic /hɛt(ə)rə(ʊ)ˈtɒpɪk/ *adjective*. **L19**.
[ORIGIN formed as HETEROTOPIA + -IC.]
1 *BIOLOGY & MEDICINE*. Of, pertaining to, or displaying heterotopia. **L19**.
2 *ECOLOGY*. Occupying different environments; present in an environment different from that normally occupied. **L19**.
■ **heterotopically** *adverb* **E20**.

heterotransplant /*as noun* hɛt(ə)rə(ʊ)ˈtranspla:nt, -ˈtrɑːns-, -nz-; *as verb* -transˈplɑːnt, -trɑːns-, -nz-/ *noun & verb*. **E20**.
[ORIGIN from HETERO- + TRANSPLANT *noun*.]
MEDICINE & BIOLOGY. ▸**A** *noun*. A piece of tissue or an organ (to be) transplanted from one individual to another of a different species. Also, an operation in which such a transplantation is performed. **E20**.
▸**B** *verb trans*. Transplant from one individual to another of a different species. **E20**.
■ ˌ**heterotransplantaˈbility** *noun* ability to be heterotransplanted **M20**. ˌ**heterotransˈplantable** *adjective* able to be heterotransplanted **M20**. ˌ**heterotransplanˈtation** *noun* **E20**.

heterotroph /ˈhɛt(ə)rə(ʊ)trəʊf/ *noun*. Also **-trophe**. **E20**.
[ORIGIN from HETERO- + Greek *trophos* feeder.]
BIOLOGY. Any organism depending on an external energy supply contained in complex organic compounds.

heterotrophic /hɛt(ə)rə(ʊ)ˈtrəʊfɪk, -ˈtrɒfɪk/ *adjective*. **L19**.
[ORIGIN from HETERO- + -TROPHIC.]
BIOLOGY. Of an organism: deriving its nourishment from outside; not autotrophic.
■ **heterotrophically** *adverb* **M20**. **heterotrophism** *noun* **E20**. **heterotrophy** /ˈhɛt(ə)rə(ʊ)trəʊfi/ *noun* **L19**.

heterousian *noun & adjective* var. of HETEROOUSIAN.

heterozygote /hɛt(ə)rə(ʊ)ˈzʌɪgəʊt/ *noun & adjective*. **E20**.
[ORIGIN from HETERO- + ZYGOTE.]
BIOLOGY. ▸**A** *noun*. An individual having different alleles at one or more genetic loci. **E20**.
▸**B** *adjective*. Heterozygous. **E20**.
■ **heterozyˈgosity** *noun* the state or condition of being heterozygous **E20**. **heterozyˈgotic**, **heterozygous** *adjectives* having different alleles at one or more genetic loci, or *for* a given gene **E20**.

†**hethen** *adverb*. **ME–L15**.
[ORIGIN Old Norse *heðan* from the Germanic pronominal base of HE *pers. pronoun*.]
Hence.

hetman /ˈhɛtmən/ *noun*. **M18**.
[ORIGIN Polish, prob. from German *Hauptmann* (earlier *Heubtman*) headman, captain.]
hist. A Polish general; a Cossack military commander. Cf. ATAMAN.

heuch *noun* var. of HEUGH *noun*.

heuchera /ˈhɔɪkərə, ˈhjuːk-/ *noun*. **L18**.
[ORIGIN mod. Latin, from J. H. *Heucher* (1677–1747), German botanist.]
Any of various frequently cultivated plants of the N. American genus *Heuchera*, of the saxifrage family, with loose panicles of small esp. reddish flowers and heart-shaped leaves in basal tufts. Also called ***alum root***.

heugh /hjuːx/ *noun*. *Scot. & N. English*. Also **heuch**. **LME**.
[ORIGIN Var. of HOE *noun*¹.]
1 A precipice, a cliff. **LME**.
2 (The steep face of) an excavation or quarry; a mine. **LME**.
3 A ravine, a narrow glen. **L15**.

heugh /hjuː(x)/ *interjection*. Now *rare*. Also †**hewgh**. **E17**.
[ORIGIN Natural exclam.]
Expr. surprise.

heulandite /ˈhjuːləndʌɪt/ *noun*. **E19**.
[ORIGIN from Henry *Heuland* (1777–1856), English mineralogist + -ITE¹.]
MINERALOGY. A monoclinic hydrated silicate of aluminium and calcium belonging to the zeolite group, usu. occurring as elongated tabular crystals, white or faintly coloured with a pearly lustre.

heumite /ˈhjuːmʌɪt/ *noun*. **E20**.
[ORIGIN from *Heum* locality in southern Norway + -ITE¹.]
GEOLOGY. A brownish-black hypabyssal rock occurring as dykes and containing predominantly alkali feldspars, hornblende, and biotite.

heuretic /hjʊ(ə)ˈrɛtɪk/ *adjective & noun*. *rare*. **L17**.
[ORIGIN Greek *heuretikos* inventive, from *heuriskein* find: see -IC.]
(Designating or pertaining to) the branch of logic which deals with discovery or invention.

H

Heuriger /ˈhɔyrɪɡər/ *noun*. Also **-ge** /-ɡə/. Pl. **-gen** /-ɡən/. M20.
[ORIGIN Southern German & Austrian German = new (wine); vintner's establishment.]
1 Esp. in Austria: wine from the latest harvest. M20.
2 An establishment where such wine is served. M20.

heurism /ˈhjʊ(ə)rɪz(ə)m/ *noun*. E20.
[ORIGIN from HEURISTIC + -ISM.]
The educational practice or principle of training pupils to discover things for themselves.

heuristic /hjʊ(ə)ˈrɪstɪk/ *adjective & noun*. E19.
[ORIGIN Irreg. from Greek *heuriskein* find, after words in -ISTIC from verbs in *-izein* -IZE.]
▸ **A** *adjective*. **1** Serving to find out or discover something. E19.
2 Of or pertaining to heurism in education. L19.
3 Esp. COMPUTING. Designating or employing trial-and-error methods in problem-solving. M20.
▸ **B** *noun* **1** **a** Heuretic logic. E19. ▸**b** A heuristic method for attempting the solution of a problem; a rule or item of information used in such a process. M20.
2 In *pl.* (treated as *sing.*). The study and use of heuristic techniques in data processing. M20.
■ **heuristical** *adjective* = HEURISTIC *adjective* 2 M19. **heuristically** *adverb* M20.

heurte *noun* var. of HURT *noun*².

H

hevea /ˈhiːvɪə/ *noun*. L19.
[ORIGIN mod. Latin, from Quechua *hyeve*.]
Any of various S. American trees of the genus *Hevea*, of the spurge family; esp. *H. brasiliensis*, whose milky sap is a major source of rubber.

HEW *abbreviation*. *US*.
Department of Health, Education, and Welfare.

†**hew** *noun*. L16–E17.
[ORIGIN from the verb.]
An act of hewing; hacking, slaughter; a cut, a gash.

hew /hjuː/ *verb*. Pa. pple **hewn** /hjuːn/, **hewed**.
[ORIGIN Old English *hēawan* = Old Frisian *hawa*, *howa*, Old Saxon *hauwan* (Dutch *houwen*), Old High German *houwan* (German *hauen*), Old Norse *hǫggva*, from Germanic.]
1 *verb intrans*. Deal cutting blows (*at*, *among*, etc.). OE.
> TOLKIEN In a fury he hewed at them with his sword.

2 *verb trans*. *gen*. Chop or cut, with an axe, sword, etc. Freq. in *pass*. OE.
> C. KINGSLEY His casque and armour . . were hewn and battered by a hundred blows.

3 *verb trans*. Cut into shape with cutting or chopping blows of an axe etc. OE.
> C. THUBRON Some of the stones are hewn smooth, others left jagged.

rough-hew: see ROUGH *adverb*.
4 *verb trans*. Chop or cut *down* etc.; fell (timber); cut (coal) from a seam. OE.
> G. K. CHESTERTON The invaders were hewn down horribly with black steel. G. L. HARDING Those who hewed the stone from the local quarries.

5 *verb trans*. Sever (a part from the whole) with cutting blows, cut *away*, *off*, etc. OE.
> E. A. FREEMAN The fragments of rock left when the rest is hewn away.

6 *verb trans*. Make or produce by hewing. (Foll. by *out*, *into*, etc.) OE.
> B. MALAMUD Rough steps that had been hewn into the rocky hills.

hew one's way make a way for oneself by hewing.
7 *verb trans*. Divide with cutting blows; chop (a thing) into pieces. Now chiefly (*arch*.) in ***hew asunder***, ***hew in pieces***, ***hew to pieces***, etc. LME.
†**8** *verb trans*. & *intrans*. Of a horse etc.: strike (a foot etc.) *against*, *upon* another foot etc. in going. Cf. CUT *verb* 30. E16–E19.
9 *fig*. Conform *to*. *N. Amer*. L19.
> *New Yorker* Even Sandra Day O'Connor . . has not reliably hewed to the Reagan agenda.

hewer /ˈhjuːə/ *noun*. OE.
[ORIGIN from HEW *verb* + -ER¹.]
A person who hews (something); *spec*. one who cuts coal from a seam.
hewers of wood and drawers of water [*Joshua* 9:21] menial drudges; labourers.

hewgag /ˈhjuːɡaɡ/ *noun*. *US*. M19.
[ORIGIN Unknown.]
A toy musical instrument, in which a piece of parchment etc. is vibrated by blowing.

†**hewgh** *interjection* var. of HEUGH *interjection*.

hewn *verb pa. pple*: see HEW *verb*.

hex /hɛks/ *noun*¹. Chiefly *N. Amer*. M19.
[ORIGIN Pennsylvanian German from German *Hexe*. Cf. HEX *verb*, HAG *noun*¹.]
1 A witch; a woman resembling a witch. M19.
2 A magic spell, a curse. E20.
> B. KINGSOLVER He looks at his clothes real hard and says a hex before he puts them on.

hex /hɛks/ *noun*². M20.
[ORIGIN Abbreviation.]
NUCLEAR PHYSICS. Uranium hexafluoride, UF_6, as used in the separation of uranium isotopes by gaseous diffusion.

hex /hɛks/ *noun*³ & *adjective*. L20.
[ORIGIN Abbreviation.]
COMPUTING. = HEXADECIMAL *adjective & noun*.

hex /hɛks/ *verb*. Chiefly *N. Amer*. M19.
[ORIGIN Pennsylvanian German *hexe* from German *hexen*. Cf. HEX *noun*¹.]
1 *verb intrans*. Practise witchcraft. M19.
2 *verb trans*. Bewitch, cast a spell on. M20.

hexa- /ˈhɛksə/ *combining form*. Before a vowel **hex-**.
[ORIGIN Greek *hex*, *hexa-* six.]
Having six, sixfold.
■ **hexacanth** *adjective* [Greek *akantha* thorn] ZOOLOGY having six spines, rays, or hooks L19. **hexaˈchloraphane**, **-phene** *noun* a powder, $CH_2(C_6HCl_3OH)_2$, used as a disinfectant, esp. for the skin M20. **hexachloroˈethane**, **hexachloˈrethane** *noun* a toxic crystalline compound, $Cl_3C{\cdot}CCl_3$, used as an insecticide and anthelmintic and in smoke-producing mixtures L19. **hexaˈdactylism** *noun* the condition of having six digits on each hand or each foot L19. **hexaˈdecane** *noun* (CHEMISTRY) any of a series of saturated hydrocarbons (alkanes) with the formula $C_{16}H_{34}$, *spec*. (also n-*hexadecane*) = CETANE L19. **hexaˈdecapole** *noun* (PHYSICS) a multipole of order 4 L20. **hexadecimal** *adjective & noun* (COMPUTING) (*a*) *adjective* designating or pertaining to a system of numerical notation that uses 16 rather than 10 as a base; (*b*) *noun* the hexadecimal system; hexadecimal notation: M20. **hexaˈdecimally** *adverb* using hexadecimal notation M20. **heˈxagonous** *adjective* (BOTANY) hexagonal in cross-section L19. **hexaˈhydrate** *noun* (CHEMISTRY) a hydrate containing six moles of water per mole of compound E20. **hexahyˈdrated** *adjective* (CHEMISTRY) hydrated with six molecules of water per molecule of compound L19. **hexaˈhydric** *adjective* (CHEMISTRY) containing six hydroxyl groups in the molecule L19. **hexamer** *noun* (CHEMISTRY) a compound whose molecule is composed of six molecules of monomer M20. **hexaˈmeric** *adjective* (CHEMISTRY) of the nature of a hexamer, consisting of a hexamer or hexamers M20. **heˈxamerism** *noun* (BIOLOGY) the condition of being hexamerous E20. **heˈxamerous** *adjective* (BIOLOGY) having parts arranged in groups of six M19. **hexametaˈphosphate** *noun* a phosphate regarded as derived from an acid with the formula $(HPO_3)_6$; *spec*. a glassy sodium salt used industrially as a water softener: L19. **hexameˈthonium** *noun* (PHARMACOLOGY) a quaternary ammonium ion, containing six methyl groups; any of the salts of this ion, some of which have been used as ganglionic blocking agents in cases of severe hypertension: M20. **hexaˈmethylene** *noun* (CHEMISTRY) = CYCLOHEXANE L19. **hexamethyleneˈdiamine** *noun* (CHEMISTRY) a crystalline compound, $H_2N(CH_2)_6NH_2$, used in making nylon L19. **hexamethyleneˈtetramine** *noun* (CHEMISTRY) a heterocyclic crystalline compound, $(CH_2)_6N_4$, used in making phenol-formaldehyde resins and antiseptics L19. **heˈxandrous** *adjective* (BOTANY) having six stamens M19. **heˈxangular** *adjective* having six angles, hexagonal M17. **hexaˈpeptide** *noun* (BIOCHEMISTRY) a peptide with six amino acids in its molecule E20. **hexaˈpetalous** *adjective* having six petals E18. **hexarch** *adjective* (BOTANY) (of a vascular bundle) having six strands of xylem, formed from six points of origin E20. **hexaˈsepalous** *adjective* having six sepals L19. **hexastich** /ˈhɛksəstɪk/ *noun* a group of six lines of verse L16. **hexastyle** *noun & adjective* (a portico or facade) of six columns E18. **hexasyˈllabic** *adjective* of six syllables L19. **Hexateuch** *noun* the first six books of the Bible L19. **hexaˈtomic** *adjective* (CHEMISTRY, now *rare*) containing six replaceable hydrogen atoms or groups; hexavalent: M19. **hexatone** *noun* (MUSIC) an octave of six pitches M20. **hexaˈtonic** *adjective* (MUSIC) characterized by hexatones M20. **hexaˈvalent** *adjective* (CHEMISTRY) having a valency of six L19.

hexachord /ˈhɛksəkɔːd/ *noun*. L17.
[ORIGIN from HEXA- + CHORD *noun*¹.]
MUSIC. †**1** The interval of a sixth. L17–M18.
2 A diatonic scale of six notes with a semitone between the third and fourth, used at three different pitches in medieval music. M18.

hexad /ˈhɛksad/ *noun*. M17.
[ORIGIN Greek *hexad-*, *hexas* a group of six, from *hex* six: see -AD¹.]
1 The number six in the Pythagorean system; a series of six numbers. M17. ▸**b** A group of six. L19.
†**2** CHEMISTRY. A hexavalent element or group. M–L19.
■ **heˈxadic** *adjective*.

hexaemeron *noun* var. of HEXAMERON.

hexagon /ˈhɛksəɡ(ə)n/ *noun*. L16.
[ORIGIN Late Latin *hexagonum* from Greek *hexagōnon* use as noun of *hexagōnos* six-cornered, formed as HEXA-: see -GON.]
A plane figure with six straight sides and six angles.

hexagonal /hɛkˈsaɡ(ə)n(ə)l/ *adjective*. L16.
[ORIGIN from HEXAGON + -AL¹.]
1 Of or pertaining to a hexagon; having six sides and six angles. L16.
2 Of a solid: having a section which is a hexagon; constructed on a hexagon as base. M17.
3 Designating or pertaining to a crystal system referred to three coplanar axes of equal length separated by 60° and a fourth axis at right angles to these and of a different length; (of a mineral) crystallizing in this system. M19.
■ **hexagonally** *adverb* E18.

hexagram /ˈhɛksəɡram/ *noun*. M19.
[ORIGIN from HEXA- + -GRAM.]
1 Any of various figures composed of six straight lines; *spec*. one formed by two intersecting equilateral triangles whose angular points coincide with those of a hexagon. M19.
2 Each of 64 figures composed of six whole or broken parallel lines occurring in the ancient Chinese text *I Ching*. L19.

hexahedron /hɛksəˈhiːdrən, -ˈhɛd-/ *noun*. Pl. **-dra** /-drə/, **-drons**. L16.
[ORIGIN Greek *hexaedron* neut. sing. of *hexaedros*, formed as HEXA-: see -HEDRON.]
A solid figure or object with six plane faces.
■ **hexahedral** *adjective* having the form of a hexahedron; having six faces: E19. †**hexahedrical** *adjective*: only in L17.

hexakis- /ˈhɛksəkɪs/ *combining form*.
[ORIGIN Greek *hexakis* adverb.]
Six times (a number denoted by a second combining form), as ***hexakistetrahedron***.

hexameron /hɛkˈsam(ə)r(ə)n/ *noun*. Also **hexaem-** /hɛksəˈiːm-, -ˈɛm-/. L16.
[ORIGIN Late Latin *hexaemeron* (the title of a work by Ambrose) = Greek use as noun of *hexaēmeros* adjective, formed as HEXA- + *hēmera* day.]
The six days of the Creation; an account (as contained in Genesis) of this period.

hexameter /hɛkˈsamɪtə/ *noun & adjective*. LME.
[ORIGIN Latin, from Greek *hexametros* of six measures, formed as HEXA- + -METER.]
PROSODY. ▸**A** *noun*. A line of six metrical feet. LME.
dactylic hexameter: having five dactyls and a spondee or trochee, any of the first four feet, and sometimes the fifth, being replaceable by a spondee.
▸ **B** *attrib*. or as *adjective*. Hexametric. M16.
■ **hexaˈmetric** *adjective* of or pertaining to a hexameter; consisting of six metrical feet; composed in hexameters: L18. **hexaˈmetrical** *adjective* = HEXAMETRIC M18. **hexametrist** *noun* a person who composes or writes (in) hexameters L18. **hexametrize** *verb intrans*. & *trans*. compose or write (in) hexameters L18.

hexamitiasis /hɛksəmɪˈtʌɪəsɪs/ *noun*. Pl. **-ases** /-əsiːz/. M20.
[ORIGIN from mod. Latin *Hexamita* (see below), from HEXA- + Greek *mitos* thread: see -IASIS.]
Infection with, or a disease caused by, protozoa of the genus *Hexamita*; *esp*. an infectious, often fatal, enteritis of turkeys.

hexane /ˈhɛkseɪn/ *noun*. L19.
[ORIGIN from HEXA- + -ANE.]
CHEMISTRY. Any of five isomeric liquid alkanes with the formula C_6H_{14}; *esp*. (also n-***hexane***) the unbranched isomer, $CH_3(CH_2)_4CH_3$.
■ **hexaˈnoic** *adjective*: ***hexanoic acid***, a fatty acid, $CH_3(CH_2)_4COOH$, that is an oily liquid occurring in milk fat and in coconut and palm oil (also called ***caproic acid***) E20.

hexapla /ˈhɛksəplə/ *noun*. Also **hexaple** /ˈhɛksəp(ə)l/. E17.
[ORIGIN Greek (*ta*) *hexapla* (title of Origen's work) neut. pl. of *hexaplous* sixfold.]
A sixfold text in parallel columns, esp. of the Old or New Testament.
■ **hexaplar** *adjective* E19. **hexaˈplaric** *adjective* L19.

hexaploid /ˈhɛksəplɔɪd/ *adjective & noun*. E20.
[ORIGIN from HEXA- + -PLOID.]
BIOLOGY. ▸**A** *adjective*. (Of a cell) containing six sets of chromosomes; (of an individual) composed of hexaploid cells. E20.
▸ **B** *noun*. A hexaploid individual. E20.
■ **hexaploidy** *noun* hexaploid condition E20.

hexapod /ˈhɛksəpɒd/ *noun & adjective*. M17.
[ORIGIN Greek *heksapod-*, *hexapous*, formed as HEXA- + *pous* foot: see -POD.]
ZOOLOGY. ▸**A** *noun*. An animal with six feet, an insect; *spec*. an animal of the superclass Hexapoda, which comprises the true insects together with the Protura, Diplura, and Collembola treated as separate classes. M17.
▸ **B** *adjective*. Having six feet; of or pertaining to the superclass Hexapoda. M19.

hexapody /hɛkˈsapədi/ *noun*. M19.
[ORIGIN formed as HEXAPOD + -Y³, after *dipody*, *tetrapody*, etc.]
PROSODY. A line of verse consisting of six feet.

hexestrol *noun* var. of HEXOESTROL.

hexite /ˈhɛksʌɪt/ *noun*. L19.
[ORIGIN from HEXA- + -ITE¹.]
1 CHEMISTRY. = HEXITOL. L19.
2 A kind of high explosive. M20.

hexitol /ˈhɛksɪtɒl/ *noun*. L19.
[ORIGIN from HEX(OSE + -ITOL.]
Any of a class of hexahydric alcohols closely related to the hexoses.

hexobarbital /hɛksə(ʊ)ˈbɑːbɪtal/ *noun*. Chiefly *US*. M20.
[ORIGIN formed as HEXOBARBITONE + BARBITAL.]
PHARMACOLOGY. = HEXOBARBITONE.

hexobarbitone /hɛksə(ʊ)ˈbɑːbɪtəʊn/ *noun.* **M20.**
[ORIGIN from HEXA- + -O- + BARBITONE.]
PHARMACOLOGY. A short-acting barbiturate, $C_{12}H_{16}N_2O_3$, with hypnotic properties, used as a very short-acting anaesthetic.
– NOTE: A proprietary name for this drug is EVIPAN.

hexode /ˈhɛksəʊd/ *adjective & noun.* **L19.**
[ORIGIN from HEXA- + -ODE².]
▸ **A** *adjective.* **1** Designating a mode of telegraphy in which six messages can be sent simultaneously. **L19.**
2 Of a radio valve: having six electrodes. **M20.**
▸ **B** *noun.* A radio valve with six electrodes. **M20.**

hexoestrol /hɛkˈsiːstrɒl/ *noun.* Also **hexest-**. **M20.**
[ORIGIN from HEX(ANE + OESTR(US + -OL.]
A synthetic oestrogen, $C_{18}H_{22}O_2$, related to stilboestrol and used in hormone therapy.

hexogen /ˈhɛksə(ʊ)dʒ(ə)n/ *noun.* **E20.**
[ORIGIN German, formed as HEXA- + -GEN.]
= CYCLONITE.

hexokinase /hɛksə(ʊ)ˈkʌɪneɪz/ *noun.* **M20.**
[ORIGIN from HEXO(SE + KINASE.]
BIOCHEMISTRY. Any of various enzymes that catalyse the transfer of a phosphate group from ATP to a hexose as the first step in glycolysis.

hexon /ˈhɛksɒn/ *noun.* **M20.**
[ORIGIN from HEXA- + -ON.]
MICROBIOLOGY. A capsomere of the kind forming the majority of those in the capsid of an adenovirus, each of which is surrounded by six other capsomeres.

hexone /ˈhɛksəʊn/ *noun.* **L19.**
[ORIGIN from HEXA- + -ONE.]
1 In full ***hexone base***. Each of the three basic amino acids arginine, histidine, and lysine. **L19.**
2 Methyl isobutyl ketone as used industrially. **M20.**

hexosamine /hɛkˈsəʊsəmiːn/ *noun.* **E20.**
[ORIGIN formed as HEXOSAN + AMINE.]
CHEMISTRY. Any derivative of a hexose in which a hydroxyl group is replaced by an amino group.

hexosan /ˈhɛksəsan/ *noun.* **L19.**
[ORIGIN from HEXOSE + -AN.]
CHEMISTRY. A polysaccharide whose constituent monosaccharides are hexoses.

hexose /ˈhɛksəʊz, -s/ *noun.* **L19.**
[ORIGIN from HEXA- + -OSE².]
CHEMISTRY. Any monosaccharide sugar with six carbon atoms in its molecule, e.g. glucose and fructose.

hexuronic /hɛksjʊˈrɒnɪk/ *adjective.* **E20.**
[ORIGIN from HEXOSE + URONIC.]
hexuronic acid: any of a class of uronic acids derived from a hexose; *spec.* ascorbic acid.

hexyl /ˈhɛksʌɪl, -sɪl/ *noun.* **M19.**
[ORIGIN from HEXA- + -YL.]
CHEMISTRY. A radical, $C_6H_{13}\cdot$, derived from a hexose. Usu. in *comb.*
– COMB.: **hexylresorcinol** a crystalline derivative, $(HO)_2\cdot C_6H_3\cdot(CH_2)_5CH_3$, of resorcinol used as an anthelmintic and urinary antiseptic.

hey *noun*¹ var. of HAY *noun*⁴.

hey /heɪ/ *interjection & noun*². **ME.**
[ORIGIN Natural exclam. Cf. Old French *hai*, *hay*, Dutch, German *hei*, Swedish *hej*. Cf. also HEIGH.]
▸ **A** *interjection.* Attracting attention; expr. joy, surprise, or inquiry, or enthusiastic approval *for*. Freq. in comb. with redupl. words to form a meaningless refrain, as, ***hey-diddle-diddle***, ***hey-nonny-nonny***, etc. **ME.**

C. GEBLER Hey mother, the water's running down the back of my neck.

hey* COCKALORUM. *hey jingo: see JINGO *interjection* 1. ***hey presto***: see PRESTO *adverb*. ***hey, Rube!***: see RUBE 2.
▸ **B** *noun.* A cry of 'hey!' **LME.**

heyday /ˈheɪdeɪ/ *noun.* **L16.**
[ORIGIN from HEY-DAY *interjection*.]
1 A state of high spirits or passion. Now *rare*. **L16.**
2 The full bloom, flush, (of youth, vigour, prosperity, etc.). **M18.**

E. WAUGH The liturgy composed in the heyday of English prose style.

hey-day /ˈheɪdeɪ/ *interjection. arch.* **E16.**
[ORIGIN Cf. Low German *heida*, also *heidi* hurrah!]
Expr. joy, surprise, etc.

heyduck /ˈhʌɪdʊk, ˈheɪdʌk/ *noun. obsolete* exc. *hist.* **E17.**
[ORIGIN Czech, Polish, Serbian and Croatian *hajduk*, in Hungarian *hajdú*, (pl.) *-dúk*.]
In Hungary, a member of an ennobled military class; in Poland, a liveried personal follower of a noble. Also, a robber, a brigand.

hey-ho *interjection, noun, & verb* see HEIGH-HO.

Hezbollah /hɛzbəˈlɑː/ *noun.* Also **Hiz-** /hɪz-/, **-bullah**. **M20.**
[ORIGIN Persian *hezbollāh*, Arabic *ḥizbu-'llāh(i)* party of God, from *ḥizb* party + *allāh* ALLAH.]
A Shiite Muslim group, active esp. in Lebanon.
■ **Hezbollahi** *noun* a member or adherent of Hezbollah **L20.**

HF *abbreviation*¹.
High frequency.

hf *abbreviation*².
Half.

Hf *symbol.*
CHEMISTRY. Hafnium.

HFC *abbreviation.*
CHEMISTRY. Hydrofluorocarbon.

HG *abbreviation*¹.
1 Her, His, Grace.
2 Home Guard.

hg *abbreviation*².
Hectogram(s).

Hg *symbol.*
[ORIGIN mod. Latin *hydrargyrum*.]
CHEMISTRY. Mercury.

HGH *abbreviation.*
MEDICINE. Human growth hormone.

HGV *abbreviation.*
Heavy goods vehicle.

HH *abbreviation.*
1 Her, His, Highness.
2 His Holiness.
3 Double-hard (pencil lead).

hh. *abbreviation.*
Hands (units of 4 inches, the linear measure of a horse's height).

hhd *abbreviation.*
Hogshead(s).

HI *abbreviation. US.*
Hawaii; the Hawaiian Islands.

hi /hʌɪ/ *adjective. colloq.* **E20.**
[ORIGIN Repr. pronunc.]
High: esp. in special collocations & combs.
hi-fi, ***hi-hat***, ***hi-liter***, ***hi-tech***, etc.

hi /hʌɪ/ *interjection.* **LME.**
[ORIGIN Natural exclam. Cf. HEY *interjection*.]
1 Attracting someone's attention, or expr. encouragement or enthusiasm. **LME.**
2 = HELLO *interjection*. **M19.**
■ **hi-de-hi** /hʌɪdɪˈhʌɪ/ *interjection* greeting, encouraging, or expr. enthusiasm, esp. in a dance band, holiday camp, etc., (freq. answered with HO-DE-HO) **M20.** **hi-de-ho** /hʌɪdɪˈhəʊ/ *interjection & noun* (an exclam.) expr. joy or enthusiasm, esp. in a jazz or dance band **M20.**

hiant /ˈhʌɪənt/ *adjective. rare.* **E19.**
[ORIGIN Latin *hiant-* pres. ppl stem of *hiare* gape: see -ANT¹.]
Chiefly BOTANY. Gaping, having a wide aperture.

hiaqua /ˈhʌɪəkwə/ *noun.* **E19.**
[ORIGIN Chinook Jargon *hykwa*, *haikwa*, from Nootka *ḥi:xʷa:*.]
An ornament or necklace of large dentalium shells, formerly used as money by the natives of the N. Pacific coast of N. America.

hiatus /hʌɪˈeɪtəs/ *noun.* Pl. same, **-tuses**. **M16.**
[ORIGIN Latin = gaping, opening, from *hiare* gape.]
1 A physical break in continuity; a gaping chasm; an opening, an aperture. *rare* in *gen.* sense. **M16.** ▸**b** ANATOMY. Any of various natural openings or gaps. Usu. with specifying word. **L19.**
2 A gap or break in continuity, esp. in a series or an account; a missing link in a chain of events; *esp.* in GEOLOGY (the time value of) a break or unconformity in the stratigraphic sequence. **E17.** ▸**b** LOGIC. A missing link in a chain of argument, a gap in reasoning or evidence. **M19.**

M. SARTON There has been a long hiatus in this journal because I have had no days here alone. I. COLEGATE Lunch was a hiatus which separated the morning from the afternoon.

3 GRAMMAR & PROSODY. A break between two vowels which come together without an intervening consonant in successive words or syllables. **E18.**
– COMB.: **hiatus hernia** protrusion of an organ, esp. the stomach, through the oesophageal opening in the diaphragm.
■ **hiatal** *adjective* of or pertaining to a hiatus **E20.**

hiawa *noun* var. of HYAWA.

hiawaballi *noun* var. of HYAWABALLI.

Hib /hɪb/ *noun.* **L20.**
[ORIGIN Acronym, from Haemophilus influenzae b (see below).]
MEDICINE. Infection with the bacterium *Haemophilus influenzae* type *b*, a cause of acute meningitis, esp. in babies and young children. Freq. *attrib.*
Hib infection, ***Hib vaccine***, etc.

hibachi /hɪˈbatʃi, ˈhɪbətʃi/ *noun.* **M19.**
[ORIGIN Japanese, from *hi* fire + *hachi* bowl, pot.]
1 In Japan, a large earthenware pan or brazier in which charcoal is burnt to provide indoor heating. **M19.**
2 A type of esp. outdoor cooking apparatus similar to a barbecue. **M20.**

hibakusha /ˈhɪbəkuːʃə/ *noun.* Pl. same. **M20.**
[ORIGIN Japanese, from *hi* suffer + *baku* explosion + *sha* person.]
A survivor of an atomic explosion, *esp.* in *pl.*, the survivors of the atomic explosions at Hiroshima and Nagasaki in 1945.

hibernacle /ˈhʌɪbənak(ə)l/ *noun.* Also †**hy-**. **E18.**
[ORIGIN Latin *hibernaculum*: see HIBERNACULUM.]
A winter retreat, a hibernaculum.

hibernaculum /hʌɪbəˈnakjʊləm/ *noun.* Also †**hy-**. Pl. **-la** /-lə/. **L17.**
[ORIGIN Latin (usu. in pl. *-la*), from *hibernare* HIBERNATE: see -CULE.]
†**1** A greenhouse for wintering plants. Only in **L17.**
2 BOTANY & ZOOLOGY. A structure which protects (part of) a plant or animal during hibernation. **M18.**
3 ZOOLOGY. The place or nest in which an animal hibernates. **L18.**

hibernal /hʌɪˈbəːn(ə)l/ *adjective.* Also †**hy-**. **E17.**
[ORIGIN Late Latin *hibernalis*, from *hibernus* wintry: see -AL¹.]
Of, pertaining to, or proper to winter; appearing in winter.

D. MORTMAN She felt a radiating heat within and a hibernal chill without.

hibernate /ˈhʌɪbəneɪt/ *verb intrans.* Also †**hy-**. **E19.**
[ORIGIN Latin *hibernat-* pa. ppl stem of *hibernare*, from *hiberna* winter quarters, use as noun of neut. pl. of *hibernus* wintry: see -ATE³.]
1 Spend the winter in a state or location which mitigates its effects; (of an organism, esp. a mammal) pass the winter in a state of dormancy or torpor; (of a person, esp. an invalid) pass the winter in a mild climate. **E19.**

B. LOPEZ In winter, while the grizzly hibernates, the polar bear is out. . hunting.

2 *fig.* Remain in a torpid or inactive state; lie dormant. **M19.**

SOUTHEY Inclination would lead me to hibernate during half the year.

■ **hibernator** *noun* an animal which hibernates **L19.**

hibernation /hʌɪbəˈneɪʃ(ə)n/ *noun.* Also †**hy-**. **M17.**
[ORIGIN Latin *hibernatio(n-)*, formed as HIBERNATE: see -ATION.]
1 The action of wintering or passing the winter, esp. in a suitable place or condition. **M17.**
2 The condition of dormancy or torpor in which many plants and (esp.) animals spend the winter. **E19.**
3 *fig.* A period of dormancy or suspended activity; dormant condition. **E19.**

Hibernian /hʌɪˈbəːnɪən/ *adjective & noun.* Also †**Hy-**, (earlier) †**Ib-**. **E16.**
[ORIGIN from Latin *Hibernia* Ireland alt. of *I(u)verna*, *Iuberna* from Greek *I(w)ernē* from Celtic, whence also Irish *Ériu*, (accus.) *Éirinn* Erin, later Middle Irish *Éri*, whence Old English *Īraland* Ireland: see -AN, -IAN.]
▸ **A** *adjective.* Of or belonging to Ireland; Irish. **E16.**
▸ **B** *noun.* A native or inhabitant of Ireland; an Irishman, an Irishwoman. **M16.**

Hibernically /hʌɪˈbəːnɪk(ə)li/ *adverb.* **E19.**
[ORIGIN medieval or mod. Latin *Hibernicus* Irish, from *Hibernia*: see HIBERNIAN, -ICALLY.]
In an Irish manner; *esp.* (with ref. to speech) with an (apparent) illogicality or self-contradiction.

Hibernicise *verb* var. of HIBERNICIZE.

Hibernicism /hʌɪˈbəːnɪsɪz(ə)m/ *noun.* **M18.**
[ORIGIN formed as HIBERNIAN + -IC + -ISM.]
1 An idiom or expression characteristic of or attributed to Irish speech, *esp.* an Irish bull (see BULL *noun*⁴ 1). **M18.**
2 The condition of being Irish; Irish nationality. *rare.* **E19.**

Hibernicize /hʌɪˈbəːnɪsʌɪz/ *verb trans.* Also **-ise**. **E19.**
[ORIGIN formed as HIBERNICISM + -IC + -IZE.]
Make Irish in form or character.

Hibernize /hʌɪˈbəːnʌɪz/ *verb. rare.* Also **-ise**. **L18.**
[ORIGIN formed as HIBERNICISM + -IZE.]
1 *verb trans.* = HIBERNICIZE. **L18.**
2 *verb intrans.* Act as an Irishman or Irishwoman. **L18.**

Hiberno- /hʌɪˈbəːnəʊ/ *combining form.* **E19.**
[ORIGIN from medieval Latin *Hibernus* Irish, formed as HIBERNIAN: see -O-.]
Forming nouns and adjectives with the sense 'Irish and —' as ***Hiberno-English***, ***Hiberno-Latin***, ***Hiberno-Saxon***, etc.

hibiscus /hɪˈbɪskəs/ *noun.* **E18.**
[ORIGIN Latin from Greek *hibiskos*, identified by Dioscorides with *althaia* marshmallow, ALTHAEA.]
Any of numerous chiefly tropical herbaceous plants, shrubs, and trees of the genus *Hibiscus*, of the mallow family, with showy brightly coloured flowers, freq. grown for ornament; a flowering stem of such a plant. Also called ***rose mallow***.

hic /hɪk/ *interjection.* **L19.**
[ORIGIN Imit.]
Repr. the sound of a hiccup, esp. when made by a drunk person.

H

hiccius doccius /ˌhɪkʃɪəs ˈdɒkʃɪəs/ *noun & adjectival phr.* Now *rare*. L17.
[ORIGIN Perh. alt. of *hicce est doctus* 'here is the learned man', or a nonsense formula simulating Latin.]
▸ **A** *noun phr.* A formula uttered by a juggler when performing a trick; a feat of dexterity, a clever trick. L17.
▸ **B** *adjectival phr.* Accompanied by the formula 'hiccius doccius', magical, skilful. M18.

hiccough *noun, verb* vars. of HICCUP *noun, verb*.

hiccup /ˈhɪkʌp/ *noun*. Also **-cough**. L16.
[ORIGIN Imit.: cf. Old Norse *hixti* noun, *hixta* verb, Dutch *hik*, *hikken*, Swedish *hicka*, Danish *hik(ke)*, Russian *ikat'*, French *hoquet*. The form *hiccough* is due to assim. to COUGH *noun*. Cf. HICKET.]
1 An involuntary spasm of the respiratory muscles, consisting in a quick inspiratory movement of the diaphragm checked suddenly by closure of the glottis, producing a characteristic sound. Also (orig. *sing.*, now usu. in *pl.*: often with *the*), affliction with a succession of such spasms. L16.

P. P. READ The hiccups of suppressed laughter.

2 *fig.* A temporary minor setback or stoppage. M20.

J. HIGGINS The nonsense over Tanya Voroninova had been an unfortunate hiccup in his career.

– COMB.: **hiccup-nut** *S. Afr.* an ornamental scarlet-flowered shrub, *Combretum bracteosum* (family Combretaceae); its fruit, said to cause violent hiccups.
■ **hiccupy** *adjective* marked by hiccups M19.

H

hiccup /ˈhɪkʌp/ *verb*. Infl. **-p(p)-**. Also **-cough**. L16.
[ORIGIN from the noun.]
1 *verb intrans.* Make the sound (as) of a hiccup; suffer from hiccups. L16.

A. GHOSH She . . sat down again beside him, shivering and hiccuping.

2 *verb trans.* Express by or utter with hiccups, as a drunken person. (Foll. by *out*.) L18.

hic jacet /hɪk ˈdʒeɪsɛt, ˈjakɛt/ *noun phr.* E17.
[ORIGIN Latin, lit. 'here lies', the first two words of a Latin epitaph.]
An epitaph.

hick /hɪk/ *noun*[1] *& adjective*. *derog.* M16.
[ORIGIN Familiar by-form of male forename *Richard*: see DICK *noun*[1]. Cf. HOB *noun*[1], HODGE *noun*.]
▸ **A** *noun*. An ignorant countryman, a silly person. M16.

S. RUSHDIE He would pretend to be a hick just down from the villages.

▸ **B** *adjective*. Characteristic of a hick; unsophisticated, provincial. *colloq.* E20.

Listener Their books were freely available in the most hick little market town.

hick /hɪk/ *noun*[2] *& verb*. Now *rare*. E17.
[ORIGIN App. abbreviation of HICCUP *noun*, HICKET.]
▸ **A** *noun*. A hiccup. Also, a hesitation in speech. E17.
▸ **B** *verb intrans.* Hiccup. E17.

hickery-pickery /ˌhɪk(ə)rɪ ˈpɪk(ə)ri/ *noun. rare.* E19.
[ORIGIN Alt. of HIERA PICRA.]
= HIERA PICRA.

†**hicket** *noun*. M16–L17.
[ORIGIN formed as HICCUP *noun*: see -ET[1].]
= HICCUP *noun*.

hickey /ˈhɪki/ *noun*. Chiefly *N. Amer.* E20.
[ORIGIN Unknown.]
1 A small gadget or device. E20. ▸**b** Something of little consequence. E20.
2 A pimple; a mark left by a lovebite. *colloq.* M20.
3 PRINTING. A spot of foreign matter appearing on a negative, a proof, or a final printed sheet. M20.

hickle *noun* var. of HICKWALL.

hickory /ˈhɪkəri/ *noun & adjective*. L17.
[ORIGIN Abbreviation of POHICKORY.]
▸ **A** *noun*. **1** Any of various N. American trees of the genus *Carya*, of the walnut family, which have tough heavy wood, pinnate leaves, and a fruit consisting of a fleshy husk which splits into four and encloses a freq. edible nut. L17. ▸**b** In Australia: any of various trees with timber similar in quality to the N. American tree; *esp.* a kind of wattle, *Acacia implexa*. M19.
pignut hickory, *scaly-bark hickory*, *shagbark hickory*, etc.
2 The wood of the American hickory. L17. ▸**b** A stick, rod, etc., made from hickory wood. E19.
3 In full ***hickory nut***. The nut of the American hickory. L17.
▸ **B** *adjective*. **1** Made of or resembling the wood of the hickory; *fig.* hard, tough. M18.
2 Of a member of a religious sect: lacking in religious fervour or devotion, flexible. M19.

hickwall /ˈhɪkwɔːl/ *noun. dial.* Also **hickle** /ˈhɪk(ə)l/, & other vars. LME.
[ORIGIN Prob. imit. Cf. HIGH-HOLE, WITWALL, YAFFLE *noun*.]
A woodpecker; *esp.* the green woodpecker, *Picus viridis*.

hid /hɪd/ *ppl adjective*. Long *rare*. ME.
[ORIGIN pa. pple of HIDE *verb*[1].]
Hidden, concealed, secret.

hid *verb pa. t. & pple*: see HIDE *verb*[1].

hidage /ˈhʌɪdɪdʒ/ *noun. obsolete* exc. *hist.* ME.
[ORIGIN Anglo-Latin *hidagium*, from *hida* HIDE *noun*[2]: see -AGE.]
1 A tax payable to the royal exchequer, assessed at a certain quota for each hide of land. ME.
2 The assessed value or measurement of lands on which this tax was levied. M19.

hidalgo /hɪˈdalɡəʊ/ *noun*. Pl. **-os**. L16.
[ORIGIN Spanish, formerly also *hijo dalgo* contr. of *hijo de algo* lit. 'son of something'. Cf. FIDALGO.]
1 In Spain, a member of the lower nobility. L16.
2 *transf.* A person resembling a hidalgo; *spec.* one who is suited to be or aspires to be a member of the nobility. E19.

Hidatsa /hɪˈdatsə/ *noun & adjective*. L19.
[ORIGIN Hidatsa *hiratsa* lit. 'willow wood lodge'.]
▸ **A** *noun*. Pl. same, **-s**. A member of a Siouan people living on the Missouri river; the language of this people. Also called ***Gros Ventre***. L19.
▸ **B** *attrib.* or as *adjective*. Of or pertaining to the Hidatsa or their language. L19.

hidden /ˈhɪd(ə)n/ *ppl adjective*. M16.
[ORIGIN pa. pple of HIDE *verb*[1].]
1 Concealed, secret; occult. M16.

I. MURDOCH He had heard in her bantering voice the hidden whine of despair. B. EMECHETA The sound of . . tiny hidden insects harmonized with the landscape.

2 *spec.* ▸**a** MUSIC. Of a consecutive fifth or octave: suggested in part music when two parts separated by one of these intervals move in similar motion. M19. ▸**b** PROSODY. Of the quantity of a vowel: unable to be determined by scansion on account of the placing of the vowel (usu. before two consonants) in a word. L19.
– SPECIAL COLLOCATIONS: **hidden agenda** a concealed motive or reason behind the ostensible purpose of an action, statement, etc. **hidden hand** a secret or occult influence, esp. of a malignant character. **hidden reserves** extra profits, resources, etc., kept concealed in reserve.
■ **hiddenly** *adverb* in a hidden manner, secretly L16. **hiddenmost** *adjective* most hidden or secret L19. **hiddenness** /-n-n-/ *noun* the condition or state of being hidden; secrecy: LME.

hidden *verb pa. pple* of HIDE *verb*[1].

hiddenite /ˈhɪd(ə)nʌɪt/ *noun*. L19.
[ORIGIN from W. E. *Hidden* (1832–1918), US mineralogist + -ITE[1].]
MINERALOGY. A rare green variety of spodumene, prized as a gemstone.

hide /hʌɪd/ *noun*[1].
[ORIGIN Old English *hȳd* = Old Frisian *hēd*, Old Saxon *hūd* (Dutch *huid*), Old High German *hūt* (German *Haut*), Old Norse *húð*, from Germanic from Indo-European whence also Latin *cutis*, Greek *kutos*.]
1 The skin of an animal, raw or dressed; *esp.* (a) skin (as of one of the larger animals) which may be tanned into leather. OE.

C. FREEMAN The hides were sold for four dollars a skin to a tannery.

2 The human skin. Now *joc.* OE. ▸**b** *fig.* Impudence, effrontery, nerve. Chiefly *Austral. & NZ.* E20.

HENRY MILLER Huge spiked thongs that will flay the living hide off you.

3 (A piece of) animal hide used as material for clothing, shoes, etc. ME.
4 A whip made of animal hide. M19.
– PHRASES & COMB.: †**hide and hue** skin and complexion; the visible outer part of the body. **hide beetle** = *leather beetle* s.v. LEATHER *noun & adjective*. **neither hide nor hair (of someone)** nothing whatever (of someone). ***save one's hide***, ***save one's own hide***: see SAVE *verb*. **tan a person's hide** thrash or flog a person.
■ **hided** *adjective* (*a*) having a hide, esp. of a specified kind; (*b*) *rare* made of twisted hide: LME. **hideless** *adjective* LME.

hide /hʌɪd/ *noun*[2]. *obsolete* exc. *hist.*
[ORIGIN Old English *hīd* earlier *hīgid* from *hīg-*, *hīw-* (in comb.) = Old High German *hī-*, Old Norse *hý-*, Gothic *heiwa-* rel. to Latin *civis* citizen and to a Germanic *n*-stem in Old English *hīwan* (pl.), Old Frisian *hīuna* members of a household, Old High German *hī(w)un*, Old Norse *hjún* man and wife. See HIND *noun*[2].]
A measure of land in Anglo-Saxon and early Norman times, used esp. to specify the amount of land needed to support one free family and varying in extent from 60 to 120 acres (approx. 24 to 49 hectares) according to locality.

hide /hʌɪd/ *noun*[3]. ME.
[ORIGIN from HIDE *verb*[1].]
†**1** The action or an act of hiding; concealment. Only in ME.
2 A hiding place; *esp.* a place for observing or hunting wildlife without being seen. ME. ▸**b** *spec.* A cache. L19.

E. FIGES Having set an inviting trap, I lie in my hide, in wait.

hide /hʌɪd/ *verb*[1]. Pa. t. **hid** /hɪd/; pa. pple **hidden** /ˈhɪd(ə)n/, (*arch.*) **hid**.
[ORIGIN Old English *hȳdan* = Old Frisian *hēda*, Middle Dutch *hūden*, Low German *(ver)hüen*, from West Germanic.]
1 *verb trans.* Put or keep out of sight; conceal intentionally from the view or notice of others. OE. ▸†**b** Conceal in order to shield or protect. ME–E17.

S. BELLOW Hoards sugar and potatoes, hides money in his mattress.

2 *verb intrans. & refl.* Put or keep oneself out of sight, conceal oneself. OE.

N. SYMINGTON Little Carl hid behind a bush to listen to their conversation.

3 *verb trans.* Keep (a fact or matter) from the knowledge or observation of others; keep secret. ME.
4 *verb trans.* Keep (something) from view without intention of secrecy; cover up; obstruct the view of. ME.

V. S. NAIPAUL The four days of rain and mist that hid my surroundings from me.

– PHRASES, & WITH ADVERBS & PREPOSITIONS IN SPECIALIZED SENSES: †**all hid** hide-and-seek; the signal cry in hide-and-seek. **hide away** conceal (a person or thing). **hide one's face** (in biblical language) turn away, withdraw one's eyes, take no heed. **hide one's head** protect one's head, take shelter; keep out of sight, keep from shame. ***hide one's light under a bushel***: see BUSHEL *noun* 3. **hide out** remain in concealment. **hide up** (*a*) = ***hide away*** above; (*b*) = ***hide out*** above.
– COMB.: **hide-and-coop** *US* = ***hide-and-seek*** below; **hide-and-go-seek** *N. Amer.* = ***hide-and-seek*** below; **hide-and-seek** (*a*) a children's game in which one or more players seek a player or players in hiding; (*b*) a process or an attempt to find an evasive person or thing, or to evade a seeker; **hideout** *colloq.* a hiding place.
■ **hider** *noun* LME.

hide /hʌɪd/ *verb*[2] *trans.* M18.
[ORIGIN from HIDE *noun*[1].]
1 Remove the hide from; flay. *rare.* M18.
2 Beat the hide or skin of; flog, thrash. *colloq.* E19.

hideaway /ˈhʌɪdəweɪ/ *noun & adjective*. L19.
[ORIGIN from HIDE *verb*[1] + AWAY *adverb*.]
▸ **A** *noun*. **1** A person who hides himself or herself away; a fugitive. L19.
2 A small quiet restaurant etc.; a secluded place of entertainment. E20.
3 A place of concealment or retreat. M20.

V. GLENDINNING Rural and remote, her hideaway was the perfect setting for a rustic idyll.

▸ **B** *adjective*. That hides, that is hidden away. L19.

hidebind /ˈhʌɪdbʌɪnd/ *verb trans.* Now *rare*. Pa. t. & pple **-bound** /-baʊnd/. M17.
[ORIGIN from HIDE *noun*[1] + BIND *verb*, after *hidebound*.]
Make hidebound; confine, constrict.

hidebound /ˈhʌɪdbaʊnd/ *noun & adjective*. M16.
[ORIGIN from HIDE *noun*[1] + BOUND *adjective*[2].]
▸ **A** *noun*. Hidebound condition of cattle. Now *rare* or *obsolete*. M16.
▸ **B** *adjective*. **1** (Of a person) having the skin tightly stretched over the bones, esp. as the result of malnutrition; (of cattle) having the skin clinging close to the back and ribs as a result of bad feeding or ill health; (of a tree) having the bark so closely adherent and unyielding as to impede growth. L16.
2 *fig.* †**a** Of a person: stingy, niggardly, mean. L16–L17. ▸**b** Of a person, a mind, etc.: restricted in view or scope; narrow, cramped; bigoted. E17.

b R. L. STEVENSON An excellent fellow . . but a hide-bound pedant for all that. V. WOOLF I shall be debased and hidebound by the bestial and beautiful passion of maternity.

3 Having an edging or binding of hide. *rare.* M19.

hideland /ˈhʌɪdland/ *noun. obsolete* exc. *hist.* L16.
[ORIGIN from HIDE *noun*[2] + LAND *noun*[1].]
= HIDE *noun*[2].

hideling /ˈhʌɪdlɪŋ/ *adjective & noun*. Chiefly *dial.* M19.
[ORIGIN App. a derived use of HIDLINGS (the ending being confused with verbal nouns & ppl adjectives in *-ing*), also infl. by nouns in *-ling* as *changeling*: see -LING[2].]
▸ **A** *adjective*. Given to hiding or concealment. M19.
▸ **B** *noun*. A person or thing in the habit of hiding. L19.

hideosity /hɪdɪˈɒsɪti/ *noun*. LME.
[ORIGIN from HIDEOUS. + -ITY, after *curiosity* etc.]
(An embodiment of) hideousness, a very ugly object.

hideous /ˈhɪdɪəs/ *adjective & adverb*. ME.
[ORIGIN Anglo-Norman *hidous*, Old French *hidos*, *-eus* (mod. *hideux*), earlier *hisdos* from *hi(s)de* fear, ult. origin unknown: see -EOUS.]
▸ **A** *adjective*. **1** Frightful, repulsive, revolting, (to the senses or the mind), extremely ugly; *colloq.* unpleasant, displeasing. ME.

A. POWELL The Loathly Damsel, a hideous young woman riding upon a mule. R. INGALLS This is a hideous and freakish thing to have occurred. V. SETH That calendar is hideous.

2 Terrifying on account of size; immense. Now *rare* or *obsolete*. ME.

J. MORSE The great precipice below . . is so hideous.

▸ †**B** *adverb*. Hideously. M17–E18.
■ **hideously** *adverb* in a hideous manner; *colloq.* dreadfully, excessively: ME. **hideousness** *noun* (*a*) the quality of being hideous; †(*b*) horror, dread: ME.

hidey-hole /ˈhʌɪdɪhəʊl/ *noun. colloq.* (orig. *Scot.*). Also **hidy-**. E19.
[ORIGIN Alt. of ***hiding hole*** s.v. HIDING *noun*[1].]
A hiding place.

hiding /ˈhʌɪdɪŋ/ *noun*¹. ME.
[ORIGIN from HIDE *verb*¹ + -ING¹.]
1 The action of HIDE *verb*¹; the condition of being or remaining hidden; concealment. ME.

H. BASCOM Apata comes out of hiding and sneaks past the posted sentry.

be in hiding, **go into hiding** conceal oneself, esp. from the authorities.
†**2** A hidden or secret thing. *rare*. Only in ME.
3 A thing that hides; a means of concealment; a hiding place. LME.
– COMB.: **hiding hole** *rare* a hiding place; a place of concealment; **hiding place** a place of concealment; **hiding power** the capacity of paint or other colouring materials to obliterate certain surfaces.

hiding /ˈhʌɪdɪŋ/ *noun*². *colloq*. E19.
[ORIGIN from HIDE *verb*² + -ING¹.]
The action of HIDE *verb*²; a flogging, a thrashing, a beating; a punishment.

P. FERGUSON If it had been me . . doing that, I'd have got a hiding for it.

on a hiding to nothing in a position from which there can be no successful outcome.

hidlings /ˈhɪdlɪŋz/ *adverb, noun, & adjective*. *Scot. & N. English*. As adjective also **-ling** /-lɪŋ/. ME.
[ORIGIN from HID *ppl adjective* + -LING².]
▸ **A** *adverb*. In a hidden way, secretly. ME.
▸ **B** *noun*. **1** *in hidlings*, in secret, secretly. LME.
2 *pl*. Hiding places, secret places. E16.
3 *pl*. Secret or clandestine operations. E19.
▸ **C** *adjective*. Hidden, secret, underhand, clandestine. L18.

hidrosis /hɪˈdrəʊsɪs/ *noun*. M19.
[ORIGIN Greek *hidrōsis* sweating, from *hidrōs* sweat: see -OSIS.]
MEDICINE. (Excessive) sweating.

hidrotic /hɪˈdrɒtɪk/ *noun & adjective*. E18.
[ORIGIN medieval Latin *hidroticus* from Greek *hidrōtikos*, from *hidrōt-*, *hidrōs* sweat: see -IC. Cf. earlier HYDROTIC.]
MEDICINE. ▸ **A** *noun*. A drug or other agent that causes sweating. E18.
▸ **B** *adjective*. Of, pertaining to, or promoting sweating. E18.

hidy-hole *noun* var. of HIDEY-HOLE.

hie /hʌɪ/ *verb*. Now *arch*. or *poet*. Pa. t. & pple **hied** /hʌɪd/; pres. pple **hieing**, **hying**, /ˈhʌɪɪŋ/. OE.
[ORIGIN Unknown.]
†**1** *verb intrans*. Strive, exert oneself; pant. OE–ME.
2 *verb intrans. & refl*. Hasten, hurry, go quickly, (*to*). ME. ▸†**b** Advance quickly; make progress; prosper. ME–E17.

J. GRENFELL Now let us hie ourselves to the Low Countries. ALAN BENNETT Let us hie hence in yon Aston Martin.

†**3** *verb trans*. Cause to hasten; urge on; bring quickly; drive *away*. ME–L16.
4 *verb trans*. Make *one's way* quickly. ME.

hielaman /ˈhiːləmən/ *noun*. *Austral*. Also **heela-** & other vars. L18.
[ORIGIN Dharuk *yilimang*.]
A narrow shield made of bark or wood.

hield /hiːld/ *verb*. *obsolete* exc. *dial*. Also **heald**.
[ORIGIN Old English *hieldan* = Old Saxon *ofheldian*, Middle Dutch *helden* (Dutch *hellen*), from West Germanic base of Old English *heald* inclined, Old High German *halda* (German *Halde*), Old Norse *hallr* slope: cf. HEEL *verb*¹.]
▸ **I** *verb intrans*. **1** Bend downwards or to one side; lean, incline, slope; go down. OE.
2 Incline *to*; favour. ME.
▸ **II** *verb trans*. †**3** Cause to incline; bend, bow *down*. OE–LME.
4 Pour (liquid) by tilting the vessel that contains it. ME.

hiemal /ˈhʌɪɪm(ə)l/ *adjective*. Now *rare*. Also **hye-**. M16.
[ORIGIN Latin *hiemalis*, from *hiems* winter: see -AL¹.]
Of or belonging to winter.

hiemate /ˈhʌɪɪmeɪt/ *verb intrans*. Now *rare*. Also **hye-**. E17.
[ORIGIN Latin *hiemat-* pa. ppl stem of *hiemare*, from *hiems* winter: see -ATE³.]
Winter, hibernate.

hier- *combining form* see HIERO-.

Hieracite /ˈhʌɪrəsʌɪt/ *noun*. L16.
[ORIGIN Late Latin *hieracita*, from *Hierax* (see below) + -ITE¹.]
ECCLESIASTICAL HISTORY. A follower of the teachings of Hierax (fl. *c* AD 300), an Egyptian ascetic who denied bodily resurrection and believed in the necessity of celibacy for Christian perfection.

hieracium /hʌɪˈreɪʃɪəm/ *noun*. Pl. **-ia** /-ɪə/, **-iums**. M16.
[ORIGIN Latin from Greek *hierakion*, from *hierax* hawk: see -IUM.]
= ***hawkweed*** s.v. HAWK *noun*¹.

hiera picra /hʌɪrə ˈpɪkrə/ *noun phr*. LME.
[ORIGIN medieval Latin from Greek, from *hiera* sacred (name of many medicines) + *pikra* fem. of *pikros* bitter.]
PHARMACOLOGY. A purgative drug composed mainly of aloes and canella bark. Cf. HICKERY-PICKERY.

hierarch /ˈhʌɪrɑːk/ *noun*. Also (esp. in sense 2) **H-**. LME.
[ORIGIN medieval Latin *hierarcha* from Greek *hierarkhēs* high priest, from *hieros* sacred + *-arkhēs* -ARCH.]
1 A person who has authority in sacred matters; an ecclesiastical ruler or potentate; a chief priest; an archbishop. LME.

MILTON Their great Hierarch the Pope.

2 An archangel; Christ as commander of the celestial hierarchy. M16.

H. H. MILMAN Subject to the Hierarch of the Celestial Hierarchy.

■ **hieˈrarchal** *adjective* hierarchic M17.

hierarchic /hʌɪˈrɑːkɪk/ *adjective*. L17.
[ORIGIN medieval Latin *hierarchicus* from ecclesiastical Greek *hierarkhikos*, from *hierarkhēs* HIERARCH: see -IC.]
Of or belonging to a hierarch or a hierarchy.

hierarchical /hʌɪˈrɑːkɪk(ə)l/ *adjective*. L15.
[ORIGIN formed as HIERARCHIC + -AL¹.]
†**1** Belonging to the celestial hierarchy. Only in L15.
2 Belonging to a priestly hierarchy or a body of ecclesiastical rulers. M16.
3 Belonging to or according to a regular gradation of orders, classes, or ranks. M19.

hierarchically /hʌɪˈrɑːkɪk(ə)li/ *adverb*. E17.
[ORIGIN from HIERARCHIC or HIERARCHICAL: see -ICALLY.]
In a hierarchical manner.

hierarchize /ˈhʌɪrɑːkʌɪz/ *verb trans*. Also **-ise**. L19.
[ORIGIN from HIERARCH + -IZE.]
Arrange in a hierarchy or gradation of orders.

hierarchy /ˈhʌɪrɑːki/ *noun*. LME.
[ORIGIN Old French *ierarchie*, *gerarchie* (mod. *hiérarchie*) from medieval Latin *(h)ierarchia*, Greek *hierarkhia*, from *hierarkhēs*: see HIERARCH, -Y³. Latinized forms usual from 16.]
1 In Christian theology, each of three divisions of angelic beings (each comprising three orders) in the ninefold celestial system described in a 4th-cent. work attributed to Dionysius the Areopagite; angels collectively, the angelic host. LME. ▸**b** *transf*. Each of three divisions of other objects, esp. of heavenly bodies or beings. LME.
2 Rule or dominion esp. in sacred matters; priestly rule or government; a system of ecclesiastical rule. LME.
3 A body of ecclesiastical rulers; an organized body of priests or clergy in successive orders or grades. E17.

A. BRIGGS The hierarchy of the Church—from bishops to parish priests—survived everywhere.

4 A body of people, animals, or things ranked (in grades, orders, or classes) one above the other, esp. with respect to authority or dominance; *spec*. in logical and scientific classifications, a system or series of (esp. more or less inclusive) terms of successive rank. M17.

G. M. TREVELYAN At the top of the social hierarchy stood the Dukes.

■ **hierarchism** *noun* hierarchical practice and principles; hierarchical system: M19. **hierarchist** *noun* an adherent of a hierarchy or of hierarchical practice and principles M17.

hieratic /hʌɪˈratɪk/ *adjective*. M17.
[ORIGIN Latin *hieraticus* from Greek *hieratikos* priestly, sacerdotal, from *hierasthai* be a priest, from *hiereus* priest, *hieros* sacred: see -IC.]
1 Pertaining to or used by a priestly class; used in connection with sacred subjects; *spec*. designating a style of ancient Egyptian writing consisting of abridged forms of hieroglyphics. (Opp. ***demotic***.) M17. ▸**b** Appropriate to or characteristic of a sacred person or duty. M19. ▸**c** Of a style of art, esp. of ancient Greece or Egypt: adhering to early methods as laid down by religious tradition. M19.

C H. READ A hieratic art depending on a very exclusive priesthood.

hieratic paper papyrus of highest quality used for sacred writings in ancient Egypt.
2 Priestly, sacerdotal. M19.
■ **hieratical** *adjective* hieratic E17.

hieratite /ˈhʌɪrətʌɪt/ *noun*. L19.
[ORIGIN from *Hiera* ancient name of one of the Lipari Islands, now Vulcano: see -ITE¹.]
MINERALOGY. A greyish cubic phase of potassium hexafluorosilicate, K_2SiF_6, formed at high temperatures in volcanic vents.

hiero- /ˈhʌɪrəʊ/ *combining form* of Greek *hieros* sacred, holy: see -O-. Before a vowel also **hier-**.
Forming nouns and adjectives with the meaning 'holy', 'sacred'.
■ **hieˈrogamy** *noun* a sacred marriage L19. **hieˈrolatry** *noun* worship of saints; hagiolatry: E19.

hierocracy /hʌɪˈrɒkrəsi/ *noun*. L18.
[ORIGIN from HIERO- + -CRACY.]
1 The rule of priests or religious dignitaries; government by priests or ecclesiastics. L18.
2 A body of ruling priests or ecclesiastics. E19.
■ **hieroˈcratic** *adjective* M19.

hierodule /ˈhʌɪrədjuːl/ *noun*. M19.
[ORIGIN Late Latin *hierodulus* from Greek *hierodoulos* (masc. and fem.), from *hieron* (use as noun of neut. of *hieros* sacred) temple + *doulos* slave.]
GREEK HISTORY. A slave living in a temple and dedicated to the service of a god.

hieroglyph /ˈhʌɪrəglɪf/ *noun & verb*. L16.
[ORIGIN Back-form. from HIEROGLYPHIC, or after French *hiéroglyphe*.]
▸ **A** *noun*. **1** Any of the characters of the ancient Egyptian writing system; a figure of an object standing for a word, syllable, or sound in a kind of writing, esp. in the writing found on ancient Egyptian monuments and records; a writing consisting of these characters. L16.
2 *transf. & fig*. A figure, device, or sign, with a hidden meaning; a secret or enigmatic symbol; an emblem. M17. ▸**b** A piece of writing difficult to decipher. *joc*. L19.

A. C. SWINBURNE On your brows is written a mortal sentence, An hieroglyph of sorrow.

3 A person who makes hieroglyphic inscriptions. *rare*. M19.
▸ **B** *verb trans*. Represent by a hieroglyph; write in hieroglyphs. E17.
■ **hieroglyphed** *adjective* written in or inscribed with hieroglyphs L19. **hieˈroglyphist** *noun* a writer of hieroglyphs; a person versed in hieroglyphs: E19.

hieroglyphic /hʌɪrəˈglɪfɪk/ *noun, adjective, & verb*. L16.
[ORIGIN French *hiéroglyphique* or late Latin *hieroglyphicus* from Greek *hieroglyphikos*, from *hieros* (see HIERO-) + *gluphē* carving: see -IC. The adjective was used as a noun by Plutarch *ta hierogluphika* (sc. *grammata*) letters, writing, whence *hieroglyphics*.]
▸ **A** *noun*. **1** In *pl*. The characters or mode of writing used esp. by the ancient Egyptians and consisting of figures of objects directly or figuratively representing words, syllables, etc. Occas. *sing*., such a character. L16.
2 A picture standing for a word or idea, *esp*. one symbolizing something which it does not directly depict; a figure, device, or sign having a hidden meaning; an enigmatic symbol. L16. ▸**b** In *pl*. Characters or writing difficult to decipher. *joc*. M18.
▸ **B** *adjective*. **1** Of the nature of a hieroglyph, esp. an Egyptian one; written in or consisting of hieroglyphics. L16.

G. DANIEL This was a bilingual inscription and . . the Demotic and hieroglyphic writing could be deciphered.

2 *transf. & fig*. Having a hidden meaning; symbolical, emblematic. M17.
▸ †**C** *verb trans*. Infl. **-ck-**. Represent by or express as a hieroglyphic. E17–E18.

hieroglyphical /hʌɪrəˈglɪfɪk(ə)l/ *adjective*. L16.
[ORIGIN formed as HIEROGLYPHIC + -AL¹.]
1 Pertaining to or of the nature of hieroglyphics; *transf. & fig*. symbolical, emblematic. L16.
2 Difficult to decipher or make sense of. E17.

hierogram /ˈhʌɪrəgram/ *noun*. E17.
[ORIGIN from HIERO- + -GRAM.]
A sacred symbol; a hieroglyph.
■ **hierograˈmmatic**, **hierograˈmmatical** *adjectives* of the nature of, relating to, or consisting of hierograms M17. **hieroˈgrammatist** *noun* a hierogrammate L17.

hierogrammate /hʌɪrə(ʊ)ˈgramət/ *noun*. Also **-at**. M19.
[ORIGIN Greek *hierogrammateus* sacred scribe, from *hieros* (see HIERO-) + *grammateus* clerk, scribe.]
A writer of sacred records; *spec*. a writer of hieroglyphics.

hierograph /ˈhʌɪrəgrɑːf/ *noun*. M19.
[ORIGIN from HIERO- + -GRAPH.]
A sacred inscription or symbol; a hieroglyph.

hierography /hʌɪˈrɒgrəfi/ *noun*. M17.
[ORIGIN from HIERO- + -GRAPHY.]
1 A description of sacred things; a description of religions. M17.
†**2** Sacred writing; writing by hierograms. Only in M18.

hierology /hʌɪˈrɒlədʒi/ *noun*. E19.
[ORIGIN from HIERO- + -LOGY.]
†**1** A discourse on sacred things. Only in E19.
†**2** Hieroglyphic lore; the branch of archaeology that deals with Egyptian records. Only in M19.
3 Sacred literature or lore; the literature embodying the religious beliefs of a country or people. M19.
4 The branch of knowledge that deals with the history of religions. L19.
5 = HAGIOLOGY. L19.

hieromonach /hʌɪrə(ʊ)ˈmɒnək/ *noun*. Also **-monk** /-ˈmʌŋk/. L18.
[ORIGIN Greek *hieromonakhos* holy monk: see HIERO-, MONK *noun*¹.]
GREEK ORTHODOX CHURCH. A monk who is also a priest; a regular as opp. to a secular cleric.

Hieronymian /hʌɪrəˈnɪmɪən/ *noun & adjective*. M17.
[ORIGIN from *Hieronymus* (St Jerome, see below) + -IAN.]
▸ **A** *noun*. = HIERONYMITE *noun*. M17.
▸ **B** *adjective*. Of or pertaining to St Jerome (d. 420), the author of the Latin Vulgate translation of the Bible and one of the Doctors of the Church. L19.

hieronymite /hʌɪˈrɒnɪmʌɪt/ *noun & adjective*. E18.
[ORIGIN formed as HIERONYMIAN + -ITE¹.]
▸ **A** *noun*. A hermit of an order of St Jerome. E18.
▸ **B** *adjective*. Belonging to an order of St Jerome. M19.

H

hierophant /ˈhʌɪrə(ʊ)fant/ *noun*. L17.
[ORIGIN Late Latin *hierophanta*, *-es* from Greek *hierophantēs*, from *hieros* (see HIERO-) + *phan-* base of *phainein* reveal: see -ANT[1].]
1 *ANTIQUITIES*. An official expounder of sacred mysteries or ceremonies, esp. in ancient Greece; an initiating or presiding priest. L17.
2 *gen*. An expounder of sacred mysteries; an interpreter of an esoteric principle. E19.
M. LOWRY What did . . the hierophants of science know of the fearful potencies of . . evil?
■ **hieroˈphantic** *adjective* L18.

hieroscopy /hʌɪˈrɒskəpi/ *noun*. E18.
[ORIGIN Greek *hieroskopia*, from *hiera* sacrifices, victims + *-skopia* view.]
Divination from the observation of objects offered in religious sacrifices, or from sacred things.

Hierosolymitan /hʌɪrə(ʊ)ˈsɒlɪmʌɪt(ə)n/ *noun & adjective*. M16.
[ORIGIN Late Latin *Hierosolymitanus*, from *Hierosolyma* = Greek *Hierosoluma* Jerusalem: see -AN.]
Chiefly *hist*. ▸**A** *noun*. A native or inhabitant of Jerusalem. M16.
▸**B** *adjective*. Belonging to Jerusalem. E18.
■ **hierosolymite** *noun & adjective* Hierosolymitan M16.

hierurgy /ˈhʌɪrəːdʒi/ *noun*. Long *rare*. L17.
[ORIGIN Greek *hierourgia* religious service, from *hierourgos* sacrificing priest. Cf. LITURGY.]
A sacred performance; a religious observance or rite.

H

hi-fi /ˈhʌɪfʌɪ/ *adjective & noun*. *colloq*. M20.
[ORIGIN from HI *adjective* + abbreviation of FIDELITY, repr. ***high fidelity*** s.v. HIGH *adjective*.]
AUDIO. ▸**A** *adjective*. Of, pertaining to, or (esp.) designating equipment for the high-fidelity recording and reproduction of sound. M20.
▸**B** *noun*. (The design and use of) equipment for the high-fidelity recording and reproduction of sound; the use of such equipment as a hobby etc. M20.

higgle /ˈhɪɡ(ə)l/ *verb intrans*. M17.
[ORIGIN Var. of HAGGLE.]
1 Dispute over terms, *esp*. try to gain the advantage in bargaining; haggle. M17.
2 Conduct the trade of a higgler; buy and sell; sell goods from door to door. L18.
■ **higgling** *verbal noun* (**a**) the action of the verb; (**b**) the occupation of a higgler: E18.

higgledy-piggledy /ˌhɪɡ(ə)ldiˈpɪɡ(ə)ldi/ *adverb, noun, & adjective*. L16.
[ORIGIN Rhyming jingle prob. based on PIG *noun*[1] with ref. to swine herding together.]
▸**A** *adverb*. Without any order of position or direction; in utter confusion or disorder. L16.
J. L. WATEN The new-comers' wagon was piled higgledy-piggledy with stretchers, chairs, wooden boxes, pots and pans.
▸**B** *noun*. A confusion; a disorderly jumble. M17.
▸**C** *adjective*. Void of order or regular plan; confused, jumbled. M19.
L. EDEL The entire work . . offers us the data in higgledy-piggledy disorder.

higgler /ˈhɪɡlə/ *noun*. M17.
[ORIGIN from HIGGLE *verb* + -ER[1].]
A person who higgles in bargaining; an itinerant dealer, *esp*. one who buys poultry or dairy produce in exchange for small commodities.

Higgs /hɪɡz/ *noun*. L20.
[ORIGIN P. W. Higgs (b. 1929), English physicist.]
PHYSICS. In full ***Higgs boson***, ***Higgs particle***. A subatomic particle whose existence is predicted by the quantum theory of spontaneous symmetry-breaking.

high /hʌɪ/ *adjective, adverb, & noun*.
[ORIGIN Old English *hēah* (*hēag-*) = Old Frisian *hāch*, Old Saxon, Old High German *hōh* (Dutch *hoog*, German *hoch*), Old Norse *hár*, Gothic *hauhs*, from Germanic.]
▸**A** *adjective* **I 1** Of great or above average or (*pred*.) specified vertical extent or magnitude. OE. ▸**b** Standing out from a surface, in relief. OE. ▸**c** *spec*. in *TYPOGRAPHY*. Designating type which stands higher than the rest of the forme. L17. ▸**d** Esp. of clothing: extending above the normal or average level. E19.
SWIFT The common size of the natives is somewhat under six inches high. T. HARDY The granary . . stood on stone staddles, high enough for persons to walk under. E. WELTY Her high heels tilted her nearly to tiptoe. J. G. BALLARD To calculate the height of . . the highest building by pacing out its shadow on the ground. A. MUNRO The house we lived in had big, high rooms.
2 Situated far above the ground or a specified level; designating the upper or inland part of a country or district (chiefly in place names). OE. ▸**b** *pred*. Situated at a specified distance above some level. M17.
G. GREENE She had high prominent cheek-bones. J. STEINBECK The high slopes of this mountain were swaddled with pines. J. WAIN High up, but not at the top. **b** R. S. ROBINSON The limit of atmospheric air, supposed to be forty-five miles high.
3 Of a physical action: extending to or from, or performed at, a considerable distance above the ground or some other level. L16.
New Yorker He climbed up the ladder to the high-diving platform.
4 Esp. of a river, lake etc.: above the usual vertical measurement; deep. L18.
5 *PHONETICS*. Of a sound: produced with part of the tongue raised close to the palate. M19.
▸**II** *fig*. **6** Of exalted rank, position, or quality; superior, noble; elevated; luxurious. OE. ▸**b** Haughty, arrogant, overbearing; angry. Now chiefly *dial*. ME. ▸**c** Important; serious, grave. ME. ▸**d** Advanced, abstruse. *obsolete* exc. in special collocations (see below). LME. ▸**e** *BIOLOGY*. Having a highly developed or complex organization, *spec*. through evolutionary advance. Earlier in HIGHER *adjective* 2b. L19.
F. NORRIS He now should follow his best, his highest, his most unselfish impulse. J. CONRAD I know the wife of a very high personage in the Administration. W. GOLDING My status there was not precisely as high as I had suggested. P. ROTH He loses his job . . because somebody high up wants to be rid of the stupid Vice-Minister. **b** D. JACOBSON He . . tried to take a high line with me, looking haughty and indifferent. **c** SIR W. SCOTT When tidings of high weight were borne To that lone island's shore.
7 Chief, principal, main. *obsolete* exc. in special collocations (see below). ME.
8 (Of a quality, condition, etc.) great, intense; strong; violent; (of a quantity or value) greater than what is regarded as normal; (of a temperature) more likely to promote melting and the emission of radiation. Formerly also, (of a voice) raised, loud. ME. ▸**b** Extreme in opinion; *spec*. = HIGH CHURCH *adjectival phr*. L17. ▸**c** Expensive, costly; (of a card game) played for large stakes. E18. ▸**d** Of latitude: at a great distance from the equator. M18. ▸**e** *NAUTICAL*. Of a ship or its head: pointing close to the wind. M19.
E. WAUGH He played poker for high stakes. W. S. MAUGHAM He had high fever, and looked very much as if he were going to die. W. S. CHURCHILL In a time of high crisis he could play a decisive rôle. R. INGALLS Dorothy did not set the sound very high. J. GATHORNE-HARDY Diabetes is statistically high in Lincolnshire. **b** G. GREENE He learns the truth, takes a high moral line about deception. P. ACKROYD The services . . were as 'high' as possible without bearing the taint of Romanism. **c** G. SANTAYANA The thing was well worth the money, even if the tickets came rather high.
9 Of a time or season: far advanced, fully reached, at its peak of activity. ME. ▸**b** *spec*. Of a period (in the past): remote in time, ancient, *esp*. at its peak of development. E17. ▸**c** (Esp. of meat) smelling and beginning to go bad; (of game) slightly decomposed and so ready to cook. E19.
S. BEDFORD High time some of us were baptized. M. SHADBOLT It was a high hot summer before they got down to Telka. **b** A. BRIGGS The period from 1851–1867 was the period of high-Victorian England. **c** J. RABAN The room was high with the thin stink of their preservative. T. MO Disease from dead bodies, Sir. He'll be high by noon.
10 Of a voice, musical note, etc.: acute in pitch, shrill. LME.
G. GREENE A saloon car with a high yapping horn. B. EMECHETA The high laughter of the Shavi women.
11 Elated, merry (chiefly in ***high spirits***, ***high-spirited*** below); *spec*. (*slang*) intoxicated by or *on* alcohol or drugs. E17.
P. BOWLES You know, I think I'm getting quite high. J. HELLER She is at least a little bit high on wine or whiskey. *Midweek Truth* (*Melbourne*) She was high on heroin.
▸**B** *adverb*. **1** At or to a great distance upward; in or into a high position; far up. OE.
M. ROBERTS She walks down the street as proud as a queen, holding her head high. H. BASCOM Twelve o'clock. The sun stands high.
2 In or to a high degree, rank, etc.; to a great extent; at or to a high price. Formerly also, loudly. ME. ▸**b** Richly, luxuriously. E17. ▸**c** At or to a high latitude; far from the equator. M17.
LD MACAULAY Lewis consented to go as high as twenty-five thousand crowns. H. BELLOC A courtier who had risen high in the State by flattery and cowardice. B. EMECHETA Malaria would make a child's temperature run high. **b** R. CARVER He . . always had money and lived high.
†**3** Haughtily, arrogantly, overbearingly. LME–M19.
4 At or to a high pitch in sound. LME.
R. DAHL The woman's voice, raised high in anger, or pain.
5 Far back in time, early. Formerly also, far on in time, late. Now *rare*. E16.
▸**C** *noun*. **1** A high place or region; *spec*. an area of high barometric pressure. ME.
A. ALVAREZ The weather forecaster talked . . of a high over the Atlantic and continuing fine weather.
2 The highest card dealt or drawn. Chiefly in ***high-low-jack (and the game)*** = ALL FOURS 2. E19.
3 A high level exceeding that previously attained, a record. E20.
St Louis Post-Dispatch Kinloch's population has shrunk to 4,455 from a high of 10,000.
4 High school. *N. Amer. colloq*. E20.
New Yorker I started playing drums in junior high.
5 High gear. E20.
6 A euphoric state (as) induced by the taking of a drug or drugs. *slang*. M20.
J. GASKELL They think it's the smoke talking, and they feel it's the sign of a good high. J. O'FAOLAIN Yeats had managed to get a remarkable high out of his failures with women.
— PHRASES ETC.: **ace high**, **King high**, **Queen high**, etc., *CARDS* having the specified card as the highest-ranking card. **a high old time** *colloq*. a most enjoyable time. ***at high wish***: see WISH *noun*. ***blow high, blow low***: see BLOW *verb*[1]. ***friends in high places***: see FRIEND *noun*. **from on high** from heaven or a high place. ***hang as high as Haman***. ***hell and high water***: see HELL *noun*. **High Admiral** *NAUTICAL* a chief officer of admiral's rank. **high altar** the principal altar of a church. **high and dry** (**a**) *NAUTICAL* (of a ship) out of the water; above the high-water mark; (**b**) *fig*. out of the current of events; stranded. **high and low** *adjective & noun* (people) of all conditions. **high and low** *adverb* everywhere, esp. in ***search high and low*** etc. **high and mighty** (**a**) *colloq*. arrogant; (**b**) *arch*. of exalted rank. **high as a kite** intoxicated. **highbinder** *US* (**a**) a hired thug or assassin; (**b**) a swindler; a fraudulent politician; (**c**) a member of a Chinese-American secret society resembling the Mafia. **highboard** *adjective* of or relating to diving from a high diving board. **high-born** *adjective* of noble birth. **highboy** *N. Amer*. a chest of drawers on a stand or table with drawers. **high-bred** *adjective* (**a**) (of an animal) bred from superior stock; (**b**) (of a person) of good family and upbringing, well-bred. **high-brown** *noun & adjective* (*US*) (a person) of mixed black and white parentage, having a pale brown skin. **high camp** sophisticated camp (cf. CAMP *noun*[3]). **high card** a card that outranks others; *esp*. an ace or a court card. **high chair** an infant's chair for use at meals, having long legs, and a tray acting as both table and restraint. **high-class** *adjective* of high quality. ***high* COCKALORUM**. **high colour** a flushed or florid complexion. **High Commission** an embassy from one Commonwealth country to another. **High Commissioner** the head of such an embassy. **high-concept** *noun & adjective* (having or designating) a striking and easily communicable idea, esp. a plot for a film or television show. ***High Constable***: see CONSTABLE 4. **high country** *NZ* hilly country (esp. in the South Island) used for sheep-farming. **high court** a supreme court of justice; ***High Court*** (***of Justice***), the supreme court of justice for civil cases in England and Wales. ***High Court of Chancery***: see CHANCERY 2. ***High Court of Justiciary***: see JUSTICIARY *noun*[2]. **high day** the day of a religious festival. **high-definition** *adjective* designating or providing a relatively clear or distinct image. ***High Dutch***: see DUTCH *noun*[1], *adjective*. **high-end** *adjective* of, pertaining to, or associated with the most expensive section of the market. **high enema**: delivered into the colon. ***highest good***: see GOOD *noun*. ***high explosive***: see EXPLOSIVE *noun*. **high farming** the extensive use of fertilizers in land cultivation. **high fashion** = HAUTE COUTURE. **high fidelity** *AUDIO* (the reproduction of) high-fidelity sound. **high-fidelity** *adjective* (*AUDIO*) designating, pertaining to, or characterized by relatively accurate reproduction of sound with little distortion (cf. HI-FI). **high finance**: concerned with large sums. **high-five** *noun & adjective* (*N. Amer. slang*) (**a**) *noun* a gesture of celebration or greeting in which two people slap each other's palms with their arms extended over their heads; (**b**) *verb trans*. greet with a high-five. **high forest** a forest composed wholly or chiefly of trees raised from seed; *gen*. a forest composed of tall trees. **high frequency** *spec*. a frequency of vibration or oscillation having a relatively large number of cycles per second; in *TELECOMMUNICATIONS* etc., a frequency in the range from 3 to 30 megahertz. **high gear** a gear of a motor vehicle providing a high ratio between the speed of the driven wheels and that of the driving mechanism and so a high speed to the vehicle itself. ***High German***: see GERMAN *noun*[1] & *adjective*[1]. **high-grade** *adjective & verb* (**a**) *adjective* of high quality; *spec*. (of ore) rich in metal value and commercially profitable; (**b**) *verb trans. & intrans*. steal (high-grade ore). **high ground** (**a**) ground that is naturally elevated and therefore strategically advantageous; (**b**) *the* position of (esp. moral) superiority in a debate etc. **high-headed** *adjective* proud, arrogant. **high-hearted** *adjective* (*arch*.) courageous. **high heels** high-heeled shoes. **high holiday** the Jewish New Year or Day of Atonement. **high hurdles** a race in which runners jump over hurdles 42 inches (107 cm) high. **high-impact** *adjective* (**a**) that causes a great impact; that has a great effect or makes a strong impression; (**b**) (of plastic etc.) able to withstand a large impact without breaking; (**c**) (of exercises, typically aerobics) that place a great deal of stress on the body. ***high jinks***: see JINK *noun* 1. **high jump** *noun & verb* (**a**) *noun* an athletic event consisting of jumping over a high bar without dislodging it; ***for the high jump***, on trial and likely to be sentenced to hanging, on a misdemeanour charge and likely to receive punishment, likely to be dismissed; (**b**) *verb intrans*. make or take part in a high jump. **high jumper** an athlete who performs or specializes in the high jump. **high-jumping** the action of performing the high jump. **high-key** *adjective* (*PHOTOGRAPHY*) consisting of light tones. **high-keyed** *adjective* of a high pitch; *fig*. tense, nervous. **high kick** a dancer's kick high in the air. **high-level** *adjective* (**a**) (of negotiations etc.) conducted by high-ranking people; (**b**) (of a computer language) having each instruction corresponding to many instructions in machine code. **high life** (**a**) a luxurious existence ascribed to the upper classes; (**b**) a W. African type of dance music. **high living** = ***high life*** (**a**) above. ***high mass***: see MASS *noun*[1]. **high-maintenance** *adjective* (*colloq*.) (of a person) demanding a lot of attention. **high-melting** *adjective* melting at a relatively high temperature. **high men** dice loaded to turn up high numbers. **high noon** (**a**) midday; (**b**) [popularized by the film *High Noon* (1952)] an event or confrontation which is likely to decide the final outcome of a situation. **high-octane** *adjective* (of petrol etc.) having good anti-knock properties. **high opinion** a favourable opinion *of*. **high-pass** *adjective* (*ELECTRONICS*) designating

a filter that attenuates only those components with a frequency lower than some cut-off frequency. **high-pitched** *adjective* (**a**) (of a sound) high; (**b**) (of a roof) steep; (**c**) (of style etc.) elevated. **high point** the maximum or best state reached; a noteworthy or outstanding feature. **high polymer** a polymer having a high molecular weight. **high post** BASKETBALL an offensive position on the court, near to the free-throw line. **high-powered** *adjective* (**a**) having great power or energy; (**b**) *fig.* important, influential. **high pressure** (**a**) a high degree of activity, exertion, or coercion; (**b**) a condition of the atmosphere with the pressure above average. **high-pressure** *verb trans.* pressurize. **high priest** (**a**) a chief priest, *esp.* (*hist.*) a Jewish one; (**b**) the head of a cult. **high priestess** a chief priestess. **high profile** a conspicuous public image or way of behaving; exposure to attention or publicity. **high-profile** *adjective* having a high profile. **high-ranking** *adjective* of high rank, senior. **high-reaching** *adjective* aspiring, ambitious. ***high relief***: see RELIEF *noun*[2] 1. **high-rise** *adjective & noun* (**a**) *adjective* (of a building) having many storeys; (**b**) *noun* a high-rise building, esp. a block of flats. **high-risk** *adjective* involving or exposed to danger. **high road** (**a**) a main road; (**b**) a direct route to. **high roller** *N. Amer. slang* a person who gambles for high stakes or spends extravagantly. **high school** (**a**) a secondary school with a curriculum similar to that of a grammar school; *N. Amer.* a secondary school; (**b**) = HAUTE ÉCOLE. **high sea(s)** open sea(s), the sea(s) as not within any country's jurisdiction. **high season** the period of the greatest number of visitors at a resort etc. **high-set** *adjective* (*arch.*) (of sound) high-pitched. ***high sheriff***: see SHERIFF *noun* 1. **high sign** *US colloq.* a surreptitious gesture indicating that all is well or that the coast is clear. **high-sounding** *adjective* (of speech etc.) pretentious, bombastic. **high-speed** *adjective* (**a**) produced or able to operate at high speed; (**b**) (of steel) suitable for cutting tools even when red-hot. **high-spirited** *adjective* vivacious; cheerful. **high spirits** vivacity; energy; cheerfulness. **high spot** *colloq.* a notable place or feature, an enjoyable moment or experience. **high-stepper** (**a**) a horse that lifts its feet high when walking or trotting; (**b**) a stately or high-class person. ***High Steward***: see STEWARD *noun*. **high-strung** *adjective* = HIGHLY *strung*. **high table** a table on a platform at a public dinner, or for the fellows of a college. ***high tea***: see TEA *noun* 5(b). **high tech** *noun & adjective* (**a**) *noun* = **high technology** below; (**b**) *adjective* (of interior design etc.) imitating functional styles more usual in industry etc.; *gen.* involved in, employing, or requiring high technology. **high technology** advanced technological development or equipment, esp. in electronics. **high-tensile** *adjective* (of metal) having great tensile strength. ***high tension***: see TENSION *noun* 4. **high-test** *adjective* (*US*) (**a**) (of petrol) high-octane; (**b**) meeting very high standards. **high tide** the time or level of the tide at its flood. **high-toned** *adjective* stylish; pretentious; dignified; superior. ***high treason***: see TREASON *noun* 2a. **high-up** *colloq.* a person of high rank (cf. HIGHER *noun* 1). **high voltage** electrical potential causing some danger of injury or damage. **high water** (the time of) the tide at its fullest; ***high-water mark***, the level reached at high water or in a flood, *fig.* the maximum recorded value or highest point of excellence. **high, wide, and handsome** in a carefree or stylish manner. **high wine**: containing a high percentage of alcohol. **high wire** a high tightrope. **highwood** a forest of tall trees. **high words** angry talk. **high yaller**, **high yellow** *US, offensive* a person with one black and one white parent and having a palish skin. ***hold one's head high***: see HOLD *verb*. ***how is that for high***: see HOW *adverb*. ***in high feather***: see FEATHER *noun*. ***in high gig***: see GIG *noun*[1]. **in the highest** (**a**) in the heavens; (**b**) in the highest degree. ***King high***: see ***ace high*** above. ***live high off the hog***, ***live high on the hog***: see HOG *noun*. ***Lord High Commissioner***: see COMMISSIONER 1. **on high** in or to heaven or a high place. ***on one's high horse***: see HORSE *noun*. ***on the high gig***: see GIG *noun*[1]. **play high** (**a**) play for high stakes; (**b**) play a card of high value. ***Queen high***: see ***ace high*** above. ***ride high***: see RIDE *verb*. **run high** (**a**) (of the sea) have a strong current with high tide; (**b**) (of feelings) be strong. **the High** *colloq.* the High Street, esp. in Oxford. ***the high command***, ***the higher command***: see COMMAND *noun* 2b. **the Most High** God.

†high *verb*.
[ORIGIN Old English *hēan*, formed as HIGH *adjective*. Cf. Old High German *hōhen*, Gothic *hauhjan*.]
1 *verb trans.* Make high or higher; raise, lift up, exalt. OE–M18.
2 *verb intrans.* Become high or higher; rise. ME–M17.

highball /ˈhʌɪbɔːl/ *noun & verb*. *N. Amer.* L19.
[ORIGIN from HIGH *adjective* + BALL *noun*[1].]
▸ **A** *noun*. **1** A spirit (esp. whisky) and soda etc. served usu. with ice in a tall glass; a drink of this. L19.

R. LARDNER Will you take yours straight or in a highball?

2 A railway signal to proceed (orig. made by lifting up a ball); *gen.* a signal to go ahead, a clear way. Also ***highball signal***. L19.
▸ **B** *verb*. **1** *verb intrans.* Signal a train to proceed. E20.
2 *verb intrans. & trans.* (with *it*). Go or travel at speed. Freq. foll. by *along*, *out*, etc. E20. ▸**b** *verb trans.* Drive (a vehicle) at speed. M20.

R. LINDNER The train highballed out of the city.

highbrow /ˈhʌɪbraʊ/ *noun & adjective*. *colloq.* (orig. *US*). L19.
[ORIGIN Back-form. from HIGHBROWED.]
▸ **A** *noun*. A person with (esp. consciously) superior intellectual or cultural interests. L19.

L. MACNEICE A fall in the standard of intellectual living And nothing left that the highbrow cared about.

▸ **B** *adjective*. Designed for, appealing to, or characteristic of a highbrow. L19.

F. SPALDING A highbrow seriousness that limits its appeal.

■ **highbrowish** *adjective* E20. **highbrowism** *noun* intellectual superiority E20.

highbrowed /ˈhʌɪbraʊd/ *adjective*. M19.
[ORIGIN from HIGH *adjective* + BROW *noun*[1] + -ED[2].]
1 Having a high forehead. M19.
2 = HIGHBROW *adjective*. E20.

High Church /hʌɪ ˈtʃəːtʃ/ *noun & adjectival phr.* E18.
[ORIGIN from HIGH *adjective* + CHURCH *noun*, after HIGH CHURCHMAN.]
▸ **A** *noun phr.* (The principles of) a section of the Church of England emphasizing ritual, priestly authority, and sacraments. E18.
▸ **B** *adjectival phr.* Of, pertaining to, or characteristic of this section or its principles. E18.
■ **High-ˈChurchism** *noun* High Church principles, doctrine, or practice L18.

High Churchman /hʌɪ ˈtʃəːtʃmən/ *noun phr.* Pl. **High Churchmen**. L17.
[ORIGIN from HIGH *adjective* + CHURCHMAN.]
An advocate of High Church principles.
■ **High-Churchmanship** *noun* = HIGH-CHURCHISM L19.

higher /ˈhʌɪə/ *adjective, adverb, & noun*.
[ORIGIN Old English *hēr(r)a*, (West Saxon) *hīer(r)a*, later conformed to HIGH *adjective*: see -ER[3].]
▸ **A** *adjective*. **1** Compar. of HIGH *adjective*. OE.
2 *spec.* Superior to the common or ordinary sort, passing beyond the ordinary limits. M19. ▸**b** BIOLOGY. Of an organism or group: more advanced, complex in organization. M19.
– PHRASES & COMB.: **higher court** LAW a court superior in the judicial hierarchy, and thus often having the power to overrule the decisions of courts which are beneath it. **higher education**: beyond school, at university, etc. **higher mathematics** advanced mathematics as taught at university etc. ***higher orders***: see ORDER *noun* 5. ***the higher command***: see COMMAND *noun* 2b. ***the higher criticism***: see CRITICISM 2.
▸ **B** *adverb*. Compar. of HIGH *adverb*. OE.
▸ **C** *noun*. **1** A person of higher rank; a superior. Chiefly (*colloq.*) in ***higher-up*** (cf. ***high-up*** s.v. HIGH *noun*). ME.
2 (**H-**.) (A pass in) an examination leading to the Scottish Certificate of Education, Higher Grade. E20.
■ **highermost** *adjective & adverb* (*rare*) highest E17.

higher /ˈhʌɪə/ *verb trans.* *rare* exc. *N. English*. E18.
[ORIGIN from HIGHER *adjective, adverb, & noun*: cf. LOWER *verb*[1].]
Make higher, raise.

highfalutin /hʌɪfəˈluːtɪn/ *adjective & noun*. *colloq.* Also **-ing** /-ɪŋ/. M19.
[ORIGIN Perh. from HIGH *adjective* + *fluting* pres. pple of FLUTE *verb*.]
Absurdly pompous or pretentious (speech, writing, etc.).
■ **highfalutiˈnation** *noun* M19.

high-flier *noun* var. of HIGH-FLYER.

high-flown /hʌɪˈfləʊn/ *adjective*. M17.
[ORIGIN Orig. from HIGH *adverb* + FLOWN *ppl adjective*[2]; later assoc. with FLOWN *ppl adjective*[1].]
1 Of language, style, etc.: extravagant, bombastic. M17.

M. MEYER This powerful melodrama, written in high-flown prose. *Guardian* Many were irritated by the high-flown claims being made.

†2 Extreme in opinion. L17–E18.

high-flyer /hʌɪˈflʌɪə, ˈhʌɪflʌɪə/ *noun*. Also **-flier**. L16.
[ORIGIN from HIGH *adverb* + FLYER *noun*.]
1 A person who or thing which flies high. L16.

BROWNING All ye highfliers of the feathered race, Swallows and curlews!

2 An ambitious or successful person. M17. ▸**b** A person with extreme views. L17.

P. LIVELY He's not headmaster . . for nothing, he knows a high-flyer when he sees one.

3 A high-class prostitute. *slang* (now *hist.*). L17.
†4 A fast stagecoach. E–M19.
5 In full ***high-flyer walnut***. A variety of walnut. Now *rare*. E19.
6 A moth of the genus *Hydriomena*. M19.
July high-flyer: see JULY *noun*[1].
7 A speculative financial investment giving an above average return. *slang*. M20.

Fortune Its stock was a highflier on the volatile Hong Kong Stock Exchange.

high-flying /ˈhʌɪflʌɪɪŋ, hʌɪˈflʌɪɪŋ/ *adjective*. L16.
[ORIGIN from HIGH *adverb* + FLYING *ppl adjective*.]
1 Reaching great heights; ambitious; having great potential. L16. ▸**b** Extreme. L17.

T. HEALD The general had tried to encourage high-flying state school applicants. *Times* The once high-flying shares of . . Britain's biggest housebuilder fell to a 1983/84 low yesterday.

2 That flies high. E17.

Highgate resin /hʌɪgeɪt ˈrɛzɪn/ *noun phr.* E19.
[ORIGIN See below.]
A fossil resin similar to copal, found in clay at Highgate Hill, London.

high-handed /hʌɪˈhandɪd/ *adjective*. E17.
[ORIGIN from HIGH *adjective* + HANDED *adjective*.]
Overbearing; disregarding the feelings of others, imperious.

R. SUTCLIFF He was annoyed by the man's high-handed manner. K. ISHIGURO That there was something high-handed about these arrangements there was no denying.

■ **high-handedly** *adverb* L19. **high-handedness** *noun* L19.

high-hat /ˈhʌɪhat/ *noun, adjective, & verb*. In sense A.2 also **hi-hat**. L19.
[ORIGIN from HIGH *adjective* + HAT *noun*.]
▸ **A** *noun*. **1** A tall hat; *esp.* a top hat; *fig.* a supercilious or snobbish person. L19.
2 A pair of foot-operated cymbals. M20.
▸ **B** *adjective*. Supercilious, snobbish, overbearing. E20.

H. ROBBINS Some people say you're getting very high-hat since you lived on Riverside Drive. A. COOKE Chaplin . . went at once into his act of the high-hat millionaire commanding empires.

▸ **C** *verb trans. & intrans.* Infl. **-tt-**. Assume or treat with a superior or condescending attitude. Chiefly *US*. E20.

C. E. MERRIAM Dever's dignity was mistaken by some for 'high-hatting.' T. K. WOLFE Some of the boys felt that rocket pilots . . were high-hatting them.

high-hole /ˈhʌɪhəʊl/ *noun*. *US*. M19.
[ORIGIN Cogn. of HICKWALL by popular etymology.]
= HICKWALL.

highland /ˈhʌɪlənd/ *noun & adjective*. OE.
[ORIGIN from HIGH *adjective* + LAND *noun*[1].]
▸ **A** *noun*. Orig., a high headland or cliff. Now chiefly (in *pl.*), an area of high land, a mountainous region of a country; spec. ***the Highlands***, the mountainous northern region of Scotland. OE.

H

L. MACNEICE The Highlands and Islands had now a permanent focus for the age-old nostalgia of Gaeldom.

White Highlands: see WHITE *adjective*.
▸ **B** *adjective*. Of or pertaining to high land or a mountainous region; *spec.* (**H-**) of, pertaining to, or characteristic of (the people of) the Scottish Highlands. LME.

R. BURNS There's naething here but Highland pride, And Highland scab and hunger. *New Yorker* In . . Bhutan . . rice—highland red rice, the highest-altitude rice on earth—is the staple.

the Highland clearances: see CLEARANCE 1.
– SPECIAL COLLOCATIONS & COMB.: **Highland bonnet** a Scotch cap. **Highland cattle** (animals of) a small shaggy-haired breed of cattle with long spreading horns, developed in the Scottish Highlands (also called ***West Highland cattle***, ***kyloes***). **Highland dress** the kilt, sporran, plaid, etc. ***Highland fling***: see FLING *noun* 2b. **Highland games** a meeting consisting of athletic events, piping, and dancing, orig. and esp. as held in various Highland centres, esp. Braemar. **Highlandman** a male native or inhabitant of the Scottish Highlands. **Highland terrier** = WEST HIGHLAND 2.
■ **highlandish** *adjective* (*rare*) of the nature of high land; like the Scottish Highlands: M17.

highlander /ˈhʌɪləndə/ *noun*. E17.
[ORIGIN from HIGHLAND + -ER[1].]
1 A native or inhabitant of high or mountainous land; *spec.* (**H-**) a native or inhabitant of the Scottish Highlands. Also (**H-**), a soldier of any of the Highland regiments of the British army. E17.
2 An animal of the Highland breed of cattle. L18.

highlight /ˈhʌɪlʌɪt/ *noun & verb*. M17.
[ORIGIN from HIGH *adjective* + LIGHT *noun*.]
▸ **A** *noun*. **1** A light area or one seeming to reflect the light in a painting, photograph, etc. Freq. in *pl.* M17.

C. HAYES A neutral mid-tone into which both shadows and highlights could be painted.

2 A moment or detail of vivid interest or action; an outstanding feature. M19.

Times Highlights from one of tonight's top soccer matches. D. PRATER At the end of the month was to come the highlight of the visit.

3 A bright (esp. artificial) tint in parts of the hair that catches the light. Usu. in *pl.* M20.

City Limits For my cut and highlights, I had a brief consultation with the women.

▸ **B** *verb trans.* **1** Bring into prominence; draw attention to; *spec.* mark with a highlighter. M20.

E. HUXLEY Immigrants . . haven't really brought new problems with them, . . they've highlighted and sharpened up the problems we . . have. *Practical Householder* Wooden mouldings inside the ceiling perimeter can be highlighted in white gloss or strong colour.

2 Tint or bleach (parts of the hair) so as to catch the light. M20.

Hair This tousled style is scrunch dried and highlighted to enhance the shape.

highlighter /ˈhʌɪlʌɪtə/ *noun*. Also (earlier & as US proprietary name) **Hi-liter**. M20.
[ORIGIN from HIGHLIGHT *verb* + -ER[1].]
1 A marker pen which emphasizes a printed word etc. by overlaying it with a transparent (usu. fluorescent) colour. M20.
2 A cosmetic that is lighter than the wearer's foundation or skin, used to emphasize features such as the eyes or cheekbones. L20.

high-lone /ˈhʌɪləʊn/ *adverb*. Now *obsolete* exc. *US dial.* L16.
[ORIGIN Alt. of ALONE, with HIGH *adverb* as intensifier.]
Quite alone, without support.

SHAKES. *Rom. & Jul.* For then she could stand high-lone.

highly /ˈhʌɪli/ *adverb*. OE.
[ORIGIN from HIGH *adjective* + -LY².]
1 In a high place; on high. Long *rare* or *obsolete*. OE.
2 In or to a high rank. Now *rare*. OE.

G. MACKENZIE She is one of the Heads and highly situate.

3 In or to a high degree, amount, or extent; greatly, extremely; at a high price or rate. Formerly also, loudly. OE. ▸**b** To a high degree of artistic quality; elaborately. E18.

E. BOWEN These two showed how highly they rated their fortune. M. AMSTERDAM A highly-publicized Hollywood 'sex-pot' was stopping at a New York hotel. K. VONNEGUT He was highly literate, well read, and the author of various pamphlets. M. DRABBLE Eating . . was to be a highly fashionable occupation, in the early 1980s. **b** W. PALEY The hinges in the wings of an earwig . . are as highly wrought as if the Creator had nothing else to finish.

highly strung *adjective* very sensitive or nervous.
4 With high approval; favourably, honourably. ME.

E. WAUGH D'you read his paper? . . It's highly thought of. G. WINOKUR He was . . highly regarded and famous.

5 With stateliness, solemnly; proudly, angrily. Formerly also, seriously, earnestly. Now *rare* or *obsolete*. ME.

high-minded /hʌɪˈmʌɪndɪd/ *adjective*. E16.
[ORIGIN from HIGH *adjective* + MINDED *adjective*.]
1 Haughty, arrogant. *arch.* E16.
2 Characterized by high principles; magnanimous. M16.

S. BELLOW He had a weakness for high-minded people, for people with moral principles. P. ROTH Two high-minded boys who were putting away their earnings for an education.

■ **high-mindedly** *adverb* E19. **high-mindedness** *noun* L16.

highmost /ˈhʌɪməʊst/ *adjective*. *obsolete* exc. *dial.* L16.
[ORIGIN from HIGH *adjective* + -MOST.]
Highest.

high-muck-a-muck /ˈhʌɪmʌkəmʌk/ *noun*. *N. Amer. colloq.* M19.
[ORIGIN Prob. from Chinook Jargon *hiyu muckamuck* plenty of food, from Nootka *ḥayo* ten + *ma·ho·maq-* choice whalemeat, with substitution of HIGH *adjective*.]
A person of great self-importance.

highness /ˈhʌɪnɪs/ *noun & verb*. OE.
[ORIGIN from HIGH *adjective* + -NESS.]
▸ **A** *noun*. **1** The quality or condition of being high. Formerly also a high place, a summit. Now *rare* exc. *fig.* OE. ▸**b** *spec.* (**H-**.) An honorific title given to a person of royal etc. rank. (Chiefly modified by possess. adjective.) LME. **b** ***Imperial Highness***, ***Royal Highness***, ***Serene Highness***, etc.
†**2** Haughtiness, arrogance. ME–M17.
▸ **B** *verb trans.* Address with the title of 'Highness'. *rare*. M17.

high street /ˈhʌɪ striːt/ *noun & adjectival phr.* OE.
[ORIGIN from HIGH *adjective* + STREET *noun*.]
▸ **A** *noun phr.* A main road; *esp.* the principal shopping street of a town. OE.
▸ **B** *attrib.* or as *adjective*. Of, relating to, or characteristic of a high street; designed for, targeted at, or readily available to the general public. M20.

highstrikes /ˈhʌɪstrʌɪks/ *noun pl. joc. colloq.* M19.
[ORIGIN Alt., after HIGH *adjective* + STRIKE *noun*¹ + -S¹.]
Hysterics.

hight /hʌɪt/ *noun*. *obsolete* exc. *Scot.* ME.
[ORIGIN from the verb.]
†**1** A command, an order. Only in ME.
2 A promise, a vow. ME.

hight /hʌɪt/ *verb*. *arch.* Long only as pa. t. & pple **hight**.
[ORIGIN Old English *hātan* = Old Frisian *hēta*, Old Saxon *hētan*, Old High German *heizzan* (German *heissen* call, bid, be called), Old Norse *heita*, Gothic *haitan*, from a base repr. by Latin *ciere* summon, CITE *verb*.]
1 *verb trans.* Command, bid, order. Long *rare*. OE.
2 *verb trans.* Promise, vow. *obsolete* exc. *Scot.* OE.
3 *verb trans.* Call, name. OE.

E. BIRNEY That sea is hight Time.

4 *verb intrans.* Be called, have as a name. OE.

LONGFELLOW Father he hight.

†**5** *verb trans.* Direct; commit; designate; mean. *rare* (Spenser). Only in L16.

hightail /ˈhʌɪteɪl/ *verb intrans. & trans.* (with *it*). *N. Amer. colloq.* E20.
[ORIGIN from HIGH *adjective* + TAIL *noun*¹, with allus. to the erect tails of animals in flight.]
Move (away) at high speed.

highty-tighty *noun, adjective, & interjection* var. of HOITY-TOITY.

highveld /ˈhʌɪvɛlt, -f-/ *noun*. L19.
[ORIGIN Partial translation of Afrikaans *hoëveld*, from *hoë* attrib. form of *hoog* high + VELD.]
(A region of) veld situated at a high altitude; *spec.* the region in Transvaal, South Africa, between 1200 and 1800 metres (4000 and 6000 feet) above sea level.

highway /ˈhʌɪweɪ/ *noun*. OE.
[ORIGIN from HIGH *adjective* + WAY *noun*.]
1 A public road; *spec.* a main road forming the direct route between one town etc. and another. OE. ▸**b** A main route by land or water; a well-used track. LME. ▸**c** COMPUTING. A main route or path along which signals from any of several sources travel to any of several destinations; a bus. M20.

J. GARDNER There'd been a road through there, twenty . . years ago, but they'd moved the highway now. *Medway Extra* Kent County Council's highways department is carrying out carriageway reconstruction.

divided highway. **King's highway**, **Queen's highway** a public road regarded as being under the monarch's protection.
2 *fig.* The ordinary or direct course of action; a course of conduct leading directly to some end. L16.

B. JOWETT That state . . I perceive to be on the highway to ruin.

– COMB.: **Highway Code** the official book of guidance for road users; **highwayman** *hist.* a (usu. mounted) man who robbed passengers on a highway.

higlif /iglif/ *noun*. E20.
[ORIGIN Repr. a French pronunc. of *high life*.]
English high society (seen from the point of view of the French or other Europeans).

HIH *abbreviation*.
Her, His, Imperial Highness.

hi-hat *noun* see HIGH-HAT.

hijab /ˈhɪdʒab/ *noun*. L19.
[ORIGIN Persian from Arabic *ḥajaba* to veil.]
A head covering worn in public by some Muslim women; the religious code which governs the wearing of such clothing.

hijack /ˈhʌɪdʒak/ *verb & noun*. Also **hi-jack**. E20.
[ORIGIN Unknown.]
▸ **A** *verb trans.* Steal (goods, formerly *spec.* contraband etc.) in transit; seize control of (a means of transport, e.g. a lorry with goods, an aircraft in flight, etc.) by force; re-route (an aircraft etc.) *to* a new destination in this way. E20.

A. W. SHERRING A stack of old banknotes leaves Central Post at three . . . The van will be hijacked. *transf.*: *Daily Telegraph* When a virus enters a cell it hijacks it, and makes it do what it wants. *Woman's Own* The charter companies have hi-jacked some of the trimmings they provide.

▸ **B** *noun*. The action or an act of hijacking. M20.

C. BONINGTON We were taking risks not just of hi-jacks but also of accidents.

■ **hijacker** *noun* a person who hijacks something E20.

hijra *noun* var. of HEGIRA.

hikayat /hɪˈkʌɪjat/ *noun*. E19.
[ORIGIN Malay from Arabic *ḥikāya(t)* story, narrative.]
In classical Malay literature, a prose narrative combining fact and romance.

hike /hʌɪk/ *verb & noun*. *colloq.* (orig. *dial.*). E19.
[ORIGIN Unknown.]
▸ **A** *verb*. **1** *verb intrans.* Walk vigorously or laboriously; go for a long walk or walking tour for pleasure or exercise. E19. ▸**b** *verb trans.* Traverse (a distance) in this way. M20.

E. FEINSTEIN She . . spent some days hiking about the hills of France. **b** J. BARTH I walked out to the road and hiked two miles to a telephone.

hitch-hike: see HITCH *verb*.
2 *verb trans.* Force to move, shove; hoist, pull; increase (a price etc.). Also foll. by *up*. M19. ▸**b** *verb intrans.* Be or become hitched *up*. L19.

E. BIRNEY Gilda . . hiked the strap of her shiny plastic bag higher on her shoulder. *Listener* Market restrictions . . have hiked the price of Japanese recorders. **b** *Saturday Evening Post* When I sit down, it hikes up.

▸ **B** *noun*. **1** A vigorous or laborious walk; a long walk or walking tour undertaken for pleasure or exercise. M19.

H. L. WILSON What's the matter with him and Lon taking a swift hike down to New York?

2 An increase (in prices etc.). Chiefly *N. Amer.* M20.

Scientific American There will be no hikes in electricity rates until the 1990's.

■ **hiker** *noun* E20.

hikoi /ˈhiːkɔɪ/ *noun*. *NZ*. L20.
[ORIGIN Maori.]
A communal march or walk, esp. as a form of protest or to support a cause.

hila *noun* pl. of HILUM.

hilar /ˈhʌɪlə/ *adjective*. M19.
[ORIGIN from HILUM + -AR¹.]
Of or pertaining to a hilum or hilus.

Hilaria /hɪˈlɛːrɪə/ *noun*. M18.
[ORIGIN Latin, neut. pl. of *hilaris*: see HILARITY, -IA².]
CLASSICAL HISTORY. In ancient Rome etc., a festival in honour of Cybele celebrated at the vernal equinox.

hilarious /hɪˈlɛːrɪəs/ *adjective*. E19.
[ORIGIN from Latin *hilaris* (see HILARITY) + -OUS.]
1 Mirthful, joyous; causing merriment. E19.

SIR W. SCOTT In answer to my hilarious exhortations to confidence. O. MANNING Laughing as though Yakimov's speech had been one of hilarious impropriety.

2 Boisterously merry. M19.

B. PYM I was *very* happy and hilarious, cracking many jokes.

■ **hilariously** *adverb* M19. **hilariousness** *noun* M19.

hilarity /hɪˈlarɪti/ *noun*. LME.
[ORIGIN French *hilarité* from Latin *hilaritas*, from *hilaris*, (-*us*) from Greek *hilaros* cheerful: see -ITY.]
1 Cheerfulness; calm joy. LME.

SOUTHEY The pleasure which they partake conduces . . to health and present hilarity.

2 Boisterous merriment. M19.

C. STEAD There was wild hilarity, kind Bonnie and Jinny stuffing their hands into their mouths.

Hilary /ˈhɪləri/ *noun*. LME.
[ORIGIN from *Hilarius*, bishop of Poitiers (d. 367), with Anglican feast day 13 January.]
In full ***Hilary term***. A university etc. term beginning in January; a term or session of the High Court beginning in January.

Hilbert space /ˈhɪlbət speɪs/ *noun*. E20.
[ORIGIN from D. *Hilbert* (1862–1943), German mathematician + SPACE *noun*.]
MATH. A normed space having an infinite number of dimensions with each point at a finite distance from the others.

Hildebrandine /ˈhɪldɪbrandʌɪn/ *adjective*. M17.
[ORIGIN from *Hildebrand* (see below) + -INE¹.]
Of, or pertaining to, the policy of Hildebrand (Pope Gregory VII 1073–85), who asserted the power of the papacy and hierarchy and insisted on clerical celibacy.

hilding /ˈhɪldɪŋ/ *noun & adjective*. Long *arch. & dial.* L16.
[ORIGIN Unknown.]
▸ **A** *noun*. †**1** A worthless or vicious animal, esp. a horse. L16–E19.
2 A contemptible or worthless person. L16.
▸ **B** *attrib.* or as *adjective*. Of a person or an animal: worthless, contemptible. L16.

hili *noun* pl. of HILUS.

Hi-liter *noun* see HIGHLIGHTER.

hill /hɪl/ *noun*.
[ORIGIN Old English *hyll* = Old Frisian *hel*, Low German *hull*, Middle Dutch *hille*, *hil*, *hul*, from West Germanic (of the Low German area) from Indo-European base also of Latin *collis*, Greek *kolōnos*, *kolōnē* hill.]
1 A natural elevation of the earth's surface; a small mountain; *fig.* something not easily surmounted or overcome. OE.

MILTON About me round I saw Hill, Dale, and shadie Woods. L. GORDON From that hill, they could see both coasts of Cornwall. *fig.*: C. WESLEY O'er Hills of Guilt and Seas of Grief, He leaps.

2 A heap or mound of earth, sand, etc., raised by human or other agency. Freq. with specifying word. ME. ▸**b** A heap formed round a plant by banking up soil. Also, a cluster of plants on level ground. Chiefly *US*. L16. ▸**c** The rising ground on which ruffs assemble at the breeding season; an assemblage of ruffs. L18. ▸**d** HERALDRY. A charge representing a hill. E19.

W. COWPER The wain . . appears a moving hill of snow.

anthill, *dunghill*, *molehill*, etc.
– PHRASES: ***hill of beans***: see BEAN *noun*. **old as the hills** very ancient. **over the hill** *colloq.* (**a**) past the prime of life; declining; (**b**) past the crisis. **the Hill** *N. Amer. colloq.* the US Senate; the Canadian federal parliament or government. **the hills** *Indian* the low mountains of the northern part of the Indian subcontinent, esp. as the location of hill stations. **up hill and down dale** up and down in every direction, taking the country or (*fig.*) the situation as it comes. ***up the wooden hill***: see WOODEN *adjective*.
– COMB.: **hill and dale** *adjective* (of a gramophone record) with undulations made by a cutting stylus that moved in a vertical plane (opp. ***lateral-cut*** s.v. LATERAL *adjective*); **hillbilly** *US* (**a**) *colloq.* (freq. *derog.*) a person from a remote rural area in a southern state; (**b**) folk music of or like that of the southern US; **hill climb** the action or an act of climbing hills; *spec.* a race for motor vehicles over hilly ground; **hill country** *NZ* hilly country in the North Island used esp. for sheep-farming; ***Hill DAMARA***; **hill-folk** *arch.* hillmen; **hill fort** a fort built on a hill, *esp.* a prehistoric hilltop fortification; **hillman** (**a**) *gen.* an inhabitant or frequenter of hills or hilly country; (**b**) *hist.* a Scottish Covenanter, a Cameronian; (**c**) an elf, a troll; **hillside** the lateral slope of a hill; **hillstar** any of a number of hummingbirds, esp. of the genus *Oreotrochilus*, that live at high altitude in the Andes or other mountains; **hill station** *Indian* a government settlement, esp. for holidays etc. during the hot season, in the low mountains of the northern part of the Indian subcontinent; **hilltop** the summit of a hill;

hillwalker a person who engages in hillwalking; **hillwalking** the pastime of walking in hilly country.

hill /hɪl/ *verb*[1] *trans. obsolete* exc. *dial.* ME.
[ORIGIN Corresp. to Old English *behylian*, corresp. to Old Saxon *bihullean*, Old High German *hullen* (German *hüllen*), Old Norse *hylja*, Gothic *huljan*, from Germanic weak grade of HELE *verb*.]
1 Cover (up), protect. ME.
†2 Cover from sight, conceal. Only in ME.
■ **hilling** *noun* (*a*) covering; hiding; protection; (*b*) a covering: ME.

hill /hɪl/ *verb*[2]. M16.
[ORIGIN from HILL *noun*, in branch II infl. by HILL *verb*[1].]
▸**I** †1 *verb intrans.* Ascend; rise in or on a slope. Only in M16.
2 *verb trans.* Form into a hill; heap up. L16.
3 *verb trans.* Surround with hills; cover with hills. *rare.* E17.
4 *verb intrans.* Of ruffs: assemble on rising ground at the breeding season. L18.
▸**II** 5 *verb trans.* Bank *up* (plants) with soil. L16.

hillo /ˈhɪləʊ/ *interjection & noun*. Also **hilloa** /ˈhɪləʊ, hɪˈləʊ/. E17.
[ORIGIN Var. of HOLLO *interjection & noun*.]
▸**A** *interjection.* Commanding or attempting to attract attention. Also = HELLO *interjection*. E17.
▸**B** *noun.* Pl. **-os**. A shout of 'hillo!' E19.

hillock /ˈhɪlək/ *noun & verb*. ME.
[ORIGIN from HILL *noun* + -OCK.]
▸**A** *noun.* **1** A small hill. ME.
2 A small mound or heap. LME.
†3 A protuberance; the raised portion of a surface. E16–M17.
▸**B** *verb trans.* Form into a hillock, heap up. Usu. in *pass.* Now *arch.* or *poet.* L18.
■ **hillocky** *adjective* E18.

hilly /ˈhɪli/ *adjective*. LME.
[ORIGIN from HILL *noun* + -Y[1].]
1 Characterized by hills; having many hills. LME.

W. BLACK The hillier regions of Dumfriesshire.

2 Resembling a hill; steep. LME.

G. CHARLES A hilly street with high, iron railings. T. MORRISON He could barely see the hilly outline of the island.

†3 Inhabiting or frequenting a hill or hills. Only in 17.
■ **hilliness** *noun* E17.

hilo /ˈhiːləʊ/ *noun*. Pl. **-os**. M19.
[ORIGIN Spanish = thread, from Latin *filum*.]
A thin vein of ore.

hilsa /ˈhɪlsə/ *noun*. E19.
[ORIGIN Hindi.]
An anadromous Indian food fish, *Alosa sapidissima*, of the herring family. Also ***Indian shad***.

hilt /hɪlt/ *noun & verb*.
[ORIGIN Old English *hilt(e)*, corresp. to Old Saxon *hilte*, *helta*, Middle Low German *hilte*, Middle Dutch *helte*, Old High German *helza*, Old Norse *hjalt*, from Germanic: ult. origin unknown.]
▸**A** *noun.* **1** The handle of a sword or dagger. (Formerly also in *pl.* with sing. sense.) OE.

P. L. FERMOR Their hands on the hilts of their broadswords tilted up the scabbards behind them.

2 The handle of some other weapon or tool. LME.

A. W. KINGLAKE Unnecessary . . to shew even the hilt of his pistol.

– PHRASES: †**by these hilts**: expr. assertion. **to the hilt**, **up to the hilt** completely.
▸**B** *verb trans.* Provide with a hilt. E19.
■ **hilted** *adjective* (*a*) possessing a hilt; (*b*) HERALDRY having a hilt of a different tincture from the corresponding blade: OE.

hilum /ˈhʌɪləm/ *noun*. Pl. **-la** /-lə/. M17.
[ORIGIN Latin *hilum* little thing, trifle, once thought to mean 'that which adheres to a bean'.]
†1 A very minute thing. Only in M17.
2 BOTANY. The scar of a seed, marking the point where it was attached to the fruit by the funicle. M18. ▸**b** A point in a starch granule around which the layers of starch are arranged. M19.
3 ANATOMY. = HILUS. *rare.* L19.

hilus /ˈhʌɪləs/ *noun*. Pl. **hili** /ˈhʌɪlʌɪ/. M19.
[ORIGIN mod. Latin, alt. of HILUM.]
ANATOMY. An indentation in the surface of an organ, as the kidney or spleen, where blood vessels, ducts, nerve fibres, etc., enter or leave it.

HIM *abbreviation.*
Her, His, Imperial Majesty.

him /hɪm, *unstressed* ɪm/ *pers. pronoun, 3 sing. masc.* (& †*neut.*) *objective* (*dat. & accus.*), & *noun*.
[ORIGIN Old English *him* = Old Frisian *him*, Middle Dutch *hem(e)*, *him* (Dutch *hem*), from Germanic base of HE *pronoun*, with inflection parallel to Old Saxon, Old High German *imu*, *imo* (German *ihm*), from base also of Latin *is* he, *id* it, Gothic *is*, *ita*, Old High German *er*, *ez*, German *er*, *es*. Cf. IT *pronoun*, UN *pronoun*[1].]
▸**A** *pronoun.* **1** Objective (direct & indirect) of HE *pronoun*: the (male) person or animal, or the thing personified or conventionally treated as male or (in early use) grammatically masculine, previously mentioned or implied or easily identified. OE. ▸**b** Himself: direct (*arch.* exc. after prepositions) & indirect (*arch. & US dial.*) objective. OE.

MILTON The Sun was sunk, and after him the Starr Of Hesperus. SCOTT FITZGERALD Dexter . . collected what money was due him . . and walked home. S. T. WARNER They sat on the lawn and watched him unpacking. J. BUCHAN The lover of gossip will find nothing to please him. I. MURDOCH God is . . important in Pattie's life and she is comforted when other people believe in Him. G. VIDAL Peter admired his father without liking him. R. P. JHABVALA I . . smartly boxed his ears for him. **b** BYRON He who hath bent him o'er the dead. D. H. LAWRENCE In the depths of him, he too didn't want to go. D. A. DYE If he could . . kill him a few gooks . . he'd shed the New Guy image.

himseems, **-seemeth**, (pa. t. **-seemed**) *verb intrans. impers.* (long *arch.*) it seems, seemed, to him (modifying a sentence or parenthetically).
†2 Objective of IT *pronoun*. ME–E17.
3 Subjective: he. Esp. pred. after *be* & after *than*, *as*. As subj. of a verb *W. Indian*. LME.

S. JOHNSON No man had ever more discernment than him, in finding out the ridiculous. R. H. BARHAM They all cried, 'That's him!' E. BRODBER Him will have to repair it.

▸**B** *noun.* The male; a male; a man. *colloq.* L19.

W. S. GILBERT 'Mr F. shall introduce him' 'It ain't a him, it's a her.'

Himalayan /hɪməˈleɪən/ *adjective*. M19.
[ORIGIN from *Himalaya* mountains in Nepal (Sanskrit, from *hima* snow + *ālaya* abode) + -AN.]
Of, pertaining, or belonging to the Himalayas; *fig.* enormous, vast.
Himalayan balsam: see BALSAM *noun* 6(b). ***Himalayan*** MONAL.

himation /hɪˈmatɪɒn/ *noun*. M19.
[ORIGIN Greek.]
In ancient Greece, an outer garment worn over the left shoulder and under the right.

himbo /ˈhɪmbəʊ/ *noun. joc. slang*. Pl. **-os**. L20.
[ORIGIN Blend of HIM + BIMBO *noun*.]
An attractive but unintelligent man.

himp /hɪmp/ *verb intrans.* Long *obsolete* exc. *dial.* L16.
[ORIGIN Corresp. to German dial. *humpen*, *hümpen*, *himpen*, Danish dial. *hompen* hobble.]
Limp.

himself /hɪmˈsɛlf/ *pronoun*. OE.
[ORIGIN from HIM + SELF *adjective* (but long interpreted as SELF *noun*: cf. HIS-SELF).]
▸**I** *emphatic.* **1** In apposition to a personal noun (subjective or objective) or to a subjective pronoun: that particular (male) person or animal, that particular thing personified or conventionally treated as male or (in early use) grammatically masculine; the (male) person in question personally. OE.

I. MURDOCH 'The great man himself!' said Nick Fawley. O. MANNING Yesterday he received a summons from the King himself. N. O. BROWN Freud himself added politics in his later writings. G. GREENE He never himself asked a question and his discretion seemed to rebuke our . . curiosity. E. HEATH He himself had been born in the North and come to the South. D. CECIL George Austen educated his sons himself.

2 (Not appositional.) ▸**a** Subjective: he himself (formerly also, it itself). Now *arch.* & *dial.* exc. *colloq.* after *be* & after *than*, *as*, (cf. HIM 3). OE. ▸**b** Objective: the (male) person etc. in question himself. E16.

a TENNYSON The dagger which himself Gave Edith. G. GREENE He was full of the conventions of a generation older than himself. P. KAVANAGH Every evening himself and Eusebius went down the road. **b** J. C. POWYS That had been quite long enough for himself and Lady Val.

▸**II** *refl.* **3** Refl. form (indirect, direct, & after prepositions) of HIM: (to, for, etc.) the (male) person in question himself. OE.

JOYCE His conversation was mainly about himself: what he had said . . to settle the matter. S. T. WARNER He had seen himself setting foot upon the island alone. O. MANNING He was going to prove himself the saviour of his country. R. P. JHABVALA The Nawab . . threw himself far back in his chair. C. P. SNOW Humphrey bought himself a second pint of bitter.

– PHRASES: **be himself** (*a*) act in his normal unconstrained manner; (*b*) feel as well as he usually does (usu. in neg. contexts). **by himself** on his own.

Himyarite /ˈhɪmjərʌɪt/ *noun*. M19.
[ORIGIN from *Himyar*, a traditional king of Yemen + -ITE[1]. Cf. earlier HOMERITE.]
A member of an ancient people in the southern part of the Arabian peninsula.
■ **Himyaˈritic** *adjective* of or pertaining to the Himyarites or their language M19.

hin /hɪn/ *noun*. Also **H-**. LME.
[ORIGIN Biblical Hebrew *hīn*.]
A Hebrew liquid unit of capacity equal to approx. 5 litres, about one gallon.

†**hin** *pronoun* see UN *pronoun*[1].

hinaki /ˈhiːnakiː/ *noun*. *NZ*. Pl. same, **-s**. M19.
[ORIGIN Maori.]
A wicker eel pot.

hinau /ˈhɪnaʊ/ *noun*. M19.
[ORIGIN Maori.]
A New Zealand evergreen tree, *Elaeocarpus dentatus* (family Elaeocarpaceae), which yields a black dye.

Hinayana /hiːnəˈjɑːnə/ *noun*. M19.
[ORIGIN Sanskrit, from *hīna* lesser, little + *yāna* vehicle.]
= THERAVADA.

hincty /ˈhɪŋkti/ *adjective*. *US slang*. E20.
[ORIGIN Unknown.]
Conceited, snobbish, stuck-up.

hind /hʌɪnd/ *noun*[1].
[ORIGIN Old English *hind*, corresp. to Old Saxon *hind*, Middle Dutch & mod. Dutch *hinde*, Old High German *hinta* (German *Hinde*), Old Norse *hind*, from Germanic from Indo-European base with the sense 'hornless' repr. also by Greek *kemas* young deer.]
1 A female deer; *spec.* the female of the red deer, esp. in or after its third year. OE.
2 Any of several large edible groupers of the genus *Epinephelus* with spotted markings. M18.

hind /hʌɪnd/ *noun*[2]. Also (earlier) †**hine**.
[ORIGIN Old English *hī(g)na* genit. pl. of *hīgan*, *hīwan* (cf. HIDE *noun*[2]), as in *hīna fæder* paterfamilias. For the parasitic *d* cf. SOUND *noun*[2].]
†1 In *pl.* (Household) servants, domestics. OE–LME.
2 A servant, *esp.* an agricultural worker. Also, a bailiff, a steward. *arch.* ME. ▸**b** A skilled farmworker having a degree of responsibility and provided with tied accommodation. *Scot.* L16.
3 *transf.* A rustic; a boor. *arch.* ME.
4 A boy, a lad; a person, a fellow. Long *arch. rare.* ME.

hind /hʌɪnd/ *adjective & noun*[3]. ME.
[ORIGIN Perh. abbreviation of Old English *behindan* BEHIND. Cf. HINDER *adjective & noun*.]
▸**A** *adjective.* Situated behind or at the back; posterior, rear. Freq. opp. ***front***, ***fore***. ME.

T. ROETHKE The hind part of the worm wriggles the most. B. LOPEZ Ground sloths that stood as tall on their hind legs as modern giraffes.

on one's hind legs *joc.* standing up to make a speech. ***suck the hind teat***, ***suck the hind tit***: see SUCK *verb*. ***talk the hind leg(s) off a*** DONKEY.
▸**B** *ellipt.* as *noun*. A hind leg etc. L19.

D. L. SAYERS You know you've got a loose shoe on your rear hind.

– SPECIAL COLLOCATIONS & COMB.: **hindbrain** ANATOMY the part of the brain comprising the cerebellum, pons, and medulla oblongata; = RHOMBENCEPHALON. **hindgut** ANATOMY & ZOOLOGY the posterior part of the gut, in vertebrates including the large intestine. **hindhead** *arch.* the back of the head. **hindquarters** the hind legs and the adjoining parts of a quadruped. **hindside** the back part of something. **hindwing** either of the posterior wings of an insect.
■ **hindward** *adverb & adjective* (*rare*) (*a*) *adverb* backward, to the rear; (*b*) *adjective* backward: ME.

hindberry /ˈhʌɪndb(ə)ri/ *noun*. *obsolete* exc. *N. English*. OE.
[ORIGIN from HIND *noun*[1] + BERRY *noun*[1]: so called because growing in woods and assumed to be eaten by deer.]
The fruit of the (wild) raspberry, *Rubus idaeus*.

Hindenburg line /ˈhɪnd(ə)nbəːɡ lʌɪn/ *noun phr.* E20.
[ORIGIN Paul von *Hindenburg* (1847–1934), German Field Marshal and statesman.]
hist. A line of fortifications in NE France constructed by the German forces in 1916–17.

hinder /ˈhʌɪndə/ *adjective & noun*. ME.
[ORIGIN Perh. deduced from Old English *hinderweard* backward and taken as compar. of HIND *adjective*.]
▸**A** *adjective.* **1** Situated behind, at the back, or in the rear; posterior. ME.

H. READ The female of the species emitted a luminous glow from the hinder end of their bodies.

2 Of (a period of) time: most recently past, last. *Scot.* LME.
†3 Latter (opp. ***former***). LME–M17.
– SPECIAL COLLOCATIONS: **hinder end** *Scot. & N. English* (*a*) the latter end, esp. of life; (*b*) the rear or back of something.
▸**B** *noun.* Usu. in *pl.* Hindquarters, buttocks; hind legs. M19.
■ **hinderling** *noun* †(*a*) a backward direction; †(*b*) a person at the rear; (*c*) *Scot.* (in *pl.*) the buttocks: OE. **hindermost** *adjective* (*arch.*) = HINDMOST *adjective* LME.

hinder /ˈhɪndə/ *verb*.
[ORIGIN Old English *hindrian* = Middle Low German, Middle Dutch *hinderen*, Old High German *hintarōn* (German *hindern*), Old Norse *hindra*, from Germanic, from a base repr. by Old English *hinder* below, Old Saxon *hindiro*, Old High German *hintar*, Gothic *hindar* (preposition) beyond.]
†1 *verb trans.* Do harm to; injure, damage. OE–L18. ▸**b** Disparage, slander, belittle. LME–L16.
2 *verb trans.* Keep back, delay; impede, obstruct; prevent. (Foll. by *from*, *in*.) LME.

S. PEPYS These pleasures do hinder me in my business. J. G. HOLLAND What's to hinder other people from liking one another? F. SPALDING Economic difficulties hindered the Labour Government's attempts at social reform.

3 *verb intrans.* Delay or frustrate action; be an obstacle. LME.

CARLYLE It is not the dark place that hinders, but the dim eye.

■ **hinderer** *noun* LME. **hindersome** *adjective* (*Scot. & N. English*) tending to hinder, obstructive L16.

H

Hindi /ˈhɪndi/ *noun & adjective*. E19.
[ORIGIN Urdu *hindī*, from *Hind* India.]
▸ **A** *noun*. A group of Indo-Aryan dialects of the northern part of the Indian subcontinent; a literary form of Hindustani with Sanskrit-based vocabulary and Devanagari script, one of the official languages of the Republic of India. E19.
▸ **B** *adjective*. Of or pertaining to the northern part of the Indian subcontinent; of or pertaining to Hindi. E19.

Hindki /ˈhɪndkiː/ *noun*. E19.
[ORIGIN from Urdu *Hind* India + unexpl. suffix *-ki*.]
A member of a people of the NW part of the Indian subcontinent and Afghanistan; the Indo-Aryan language of this people.

hindmost /ˈhʌɪn(d)məʊst/ *adjective*. LME.
[ORIGIN from HIND *adjective* + -MOST.]
1 Furthest behind; last in position; most remote. LME.
C. M. YONGE The hindmost declared they would not stop till they were even with the front.
devil take the hindmost: see DEVIL *noun*.
2 Last in order or time. Chiefly *Scot*. LME.
J. M. BARRIE For the hinmost years o' his life.

Hindoo *noun & adjective* see HINDU.

Hindooism *noun* see HINDUISM.

H

Hindoostanee *noun & adjective* see HINDUSTANI.

hindrance /ˈhɪndr(ə)ns/ *noun*. LME.
[ORIGIN from HINDER *verb* + -ANCE.]
†**1** Injury, damage, disadvantage. LME–L16.
2 (An) obstruction; an obstacle, an impediment. E16.
P. LARKIN Hardy built a private entrance . . so that he could enter and leave the house without hindrance. JANET MORGAN In discovering what happened . . the press is as much of a hindrance as a help.
let or hindrance: see LET *noun*[1]. STERIC ***hindrance***.

hindsight /ˈhʌɪn(d)sʌɪt/ *noun*. M19.
[ORIGIN from HIND *adjective* + SIGHT *noun*.]
1 Seeing what has happened and what ought to have been done after the event; wisdom after the event. (Opp. ***foresight***.) M19.
G. F. KENNAN We can see today, with the advantage of hindsight, that the . . possibilities . . were extremely limited. A. MACLEAN Hindsight and bitter experience make for a splendid conductor to belated wisdom.
2 The sight nearest the rear of a gun. M19.
kick the hindsight(s) off, **kick the hindsight(s) out of**, **knock the hindsight(s) off**, **knock the hindsight(s) out of** *US colloq*. dispose of or demolish (a person) completely.

Hindu /ˈhɪnduː, hɪnˈduː/ *noun & adjective*. Also (*arch*.) **-doo**. M17.
[ORIGIN Urdu from Persian *hindū*, formerly *hindō*, from *Hind* India.]
▸ **A** *noun*. A native or inhabitant of (orig. the northern part of) the Indian subcontinent, *esp*. one adhering to Hinduism; an adherent of Hinduism. M17.
▸ **B** *adjective*. Of, pertaining to, or characteristic of the Hindus or Hinduism. L17.
■ **Hinduize** *verb trans*. make Hindu in appearance, customs, or religion M19.

Hinduism /ˈhɪnduːɪz(ə)m/ *noun*. Also (*arch*.) **-dooism**. E19.
[ORIGIN from HINDU + -ISM.]
A system of religious beliefs and social customs, with adherents esp. in India, with a belief in reincarnation, the worship of several gods, and an ordained caste system, as the basis of society.

Hindustani /hɪndʊˈstɑːni/ *noun & adjective*. Also (*arch*.) **Hindoostanee**. E17.
[ORIGIN Urdu from Persian *hindūstānī*, from *hindū*, formerly *hindō*, + *-stān* country + adjectival suffix *-ī*.]
▸ **A** *noun*. **1** A language based on the Hindi dialect of the Delhi region with an admixture of Arabic, Persian, etc., current as the standard language and lingua franca in much of northern India and Pakistan; *arch*. Urdu. E17.
2 A native or inhabitant of (the northern part of) the Indian subcontinent. *arch*. E19.
▸ **B** *adjective*. Of, pertaining to, or characteristic of the Hindustani language or the Hindustanis. E19.
– NOTE: The usual term in 18 and 19 for the native language of NW India. The usual modern term is *Hindi* (or *Urdu* in Muslim contexts), although *Hindustani* is still used to refer to the dialect of Hindi spoken around Delhi.

†**hine** *noun* see HIND *noun*[2].

†**hine** *pronoun* see UN *pronoun*[1].

Hiney *noun* var. of HEINIE.

hing /hɪŋ/ *noun*. L16.
[ORIGIN Hindi *hīg* from Sanskrit *hiṅgu*.]
= ASAFOETIDA.

hinge /hɪn(d)ʒ/ *noun*. Also (earlier) †**henge**. ME.
[ORIGIN from base of HANG *verb*, cf. Middle & mod. Low German *henge* hinge. Cf. HINGLE.]
▸ **I 1** The movable joint or mechanism by which a door etc. is hung on its side post to permit opening and shutting; a similar mechanism providing for turning in other linked objects. ME. ▸**b** A natural movable joint acting in a similar manner, *esp*. that of a bivalve shell. E18. ▸**c** More fully ***stamp hinge***. A small piece of gummed transparent paper used for fixing a postage stamp in an album etc. L19.
A. CARTER The door swung silently inward on well-oiled hinges.
2 The axis of the earth; the two poles about which the earth revolves; *loosely* (in *pl*.), the four cardinal points. Long *arch. rare*. LME.
MILTON The winds . . rushed abroad From the four hinges of the world.
3 The central principle, cardinal or critical point, on which everything turns or relies. E17.
SWIFT We usually call reward and punishment the two hinges upon which all government turns. J. B. MARSDEN The nature of the sacraments . . was the hinge of the whole controversy with Rome.
▸ **II 4** Now *dial*. The pluck (heart, liver, and lungs) of an animal, as used for food. LME.
– COMB.: **hinge-pin**: that fastens together the parts of a hinge.
■ **hingeless** *adjective* E17.

hinge /hɪn(d)ʒ/ *verb*. Pres. pple **hinging**, **hingeing**. E17.
[ORIGIN from the noun.]
1 *verb trans*. Bend (esp. the knee) as a hinge. *rare*. E17.
SHAKES. *Timon* Be thou a flatterer now, and . . hinge thy knee.
2 *verb intrans*. **a** Depend decisively *on*. E18. ▸**b** Of a part of a structure: turn (as) on a hinge. L19.
a C. THIRLWALL The point on which the decision must finally hinge. **b** D. ATTENBOROUGH When the muscle contracts between these two attachment points, the limb hinges.
3 *verb trans*. Attach or hang (as) with a hinge. Cf. earlier HINGED. M18.
fig.: GOLDSMITH The vulgar . . whose behaviour . . is totally hinged upon their hopes and fears.

hinged /hɪŋ(d)ʒd/ *adjective*. E17.
[ORIGIN from HINGE *noun* or *verb*: see -ED[2], -ED[1].]
Having a hinge or hinges; turning on a hinge or hinges.

hingle /ˈhɪŋg(ə)l/ *noun*. Now *Scot. & dial*. ME.
[ORIGIN from base of HINGE *verb*: see -LE[1] and cf. Middle Low German, Middle High German *hengel*, Dutch *hengel* fishing rod, handle, *hengsel* hinge, handle.]
A hinge; *esp*. the part of a hinge attached to a door etc.

Hinglish /ˈhɪŋglɪʃ/ *noun*. M20.
[ORIGIN Blend of HINDI and ENGLISH: see -LISH.]
A blend of Hindi and English, *esp*. a variety of English used by speakers of Hindi, characterized by frequent use of Hindi vocabulary or constructions.

hinin /ˈhɪnɪn/ *noun*. Pl. same. L19.
[ORIGIN Japanese, lit. 'non-human', from *hi* not + *nin* person.]
A member of an outcast group in Japan. Cf. ETA *noun*[2].

hinky /ˈhɪnki/ *adjective*. *US colloq*. M20.
[ORIGIN Uncertain: perh. rel. to Scot. †*hink* faltering, hesitation.]
Of a person: suspicious; disreputable; nervous, uneasy. Also, of a thing: unreliable, problematic.

hinnible /ˈhɪnɪb(ə)l/ *adjective*. *rare*. M17.
[ORIGIN Late Latin *hinnibilis*, from *hinnire* neigh: see -IBLE.]
Capable of neighing.

hinnie *noun* var. of HINNY *noun*[2].

hinny /ˈhɪni/ *noun*[1]. E17.
[ORIGIN Latin *hinnus* from Greek *hinnos*, *ginnos*: assim. to HINNY *verb*.]
An animal born of a mating between a female ass and a stallion.

hinny /ˈhɪni/ *noun*[2]. *Scot. & N. English*. Also **hinnie**. E19.
[ORIGIN Var. of HONEY *noun*.]
= HONEY *noun* 3.
singing hinny a currant cake baked on a griddle.

hinny /ˈhɪni/ *verb intrans*. LME.
[ORIGIN Old French & mod. French *hennir* from Latin *hinnire* neigh (to which it was assim.).]
Neigh, whinny.

hinoki /hɪˈnəʊki/ *noun*. E18.
[ORIGIN Japanese, lit. 'fire-making tree'.]
(The timber of) a tall Japanese cypress, *Chamaecyparis obtusa*.

hint /hɪnt/ *noun*. E17.
[ORIGIN Prob. alt. of HENT *noun*.]
†**1** An occasion, an opportunity. E17–E19.
SIR W. SCOTT It is my hint to speak.
2 A slight indication; a covert or indirect suggestion. (Foll. by *of*.) E17. ▸**b** A small piece of practical information, a tip. L18.
G. VIDAL The hint of a sneer in his voice excited me. J. M. ROBERTS Trivial facts are often the best hints to what is going on. **b** R. MACAULAY Audrey gave them household hints.
– PHRASES: ***broad hint***: see BROAD *adjective*. ***drop a hint***: see DROP *verb*. ***take a hint***: see TAKE *verb*.

hint /hɪnt/ *verb*. M17.
[ORIGIN from the noun.]
1 *verb trans*. Give a hint of; suggest or indicate indirectly or covertly (*that*); express (something) by a hint or hints. M17.
DICKENS 'I'm sure he is very rich, Fred,' hinted Scrooge's niece. E. M. FORSTER Already at Rome he had hinted to her that they might be suitable for each other. R. G. COLLINGWOOD Nothing was definitely said, but a great deal was hinted.
2 *verb intrans*. Foll. by *about*, *at*, etc.: give a hint of; refer indirectly to. L17.
J. CONRAD A few books, with titles hinting at impropriety.
■ **hinter** *noun* M17.

hinterland /ˈhɪntəland/ *noun*. L19.
[ORIGIN German, from *hinter-* behind + *Land* land.]
The often deserted or uncharted district behind a coast or river's banks; an area served by a port or other centre; a remote or fringe area.
Guardian As Clydeside developed . . it attracted labour from its own hinterland and from . . Ireland. H. BASCOM The turbulence of the dangerous hinterlands of rivers and creeks. *fig*.: M. K. BRADBY Unexplored territories . . in the hinterland of their own minds.

hip /hɪp/ *noun*[1].
[ORIGIN Old English *hype* = Middle Dutch *hōpe*, *hüpe* (Dutch *heup*), Old High German *huf*, (pl.) *huffi* (German *Hüfte*), Gothic *hups*, (pl.) *hupeis*, from Germanic base rel. to HOP *verb*[1].]
1 The projection of the pelvis and the upper part of the thigh in human beings and quadrupeds; *sing*. & in *pl*., the circumference of the body at the buttocks. Also, the hip joint. OE.
W. WHARTON She stands at the edge of the water, with hands on hips. *attrib*.: B. BAINBRIDGE He's had a hip replacement. He's got a steel ball-and-socket thing.
be joined at the hip *colloq*. (of two people) be inseparable. **hip and thigh** unsparingly (see ***smite hip and thigh*** below). **on the hip** *arch*. at a disadvantage. ***shoot from the hip***: see SHOOT *verb*. **smite hip and thigh** punish unsparingly.
2 ARCHITECTURE. The arris of a roof from the ridge to the eaves; the triangular area of a sloping roof rising from the end of a rectangular building to meet a longitudinal ridge. LME.
J. S. FOSTER The hip has an external angle greater than 180 degrees.
– COMB.: **hip bath** a bath in which a person can sit immersed up to the hips; **hip bone** a bone forming the hip, *esp*. the ilium; **hip-boots**: reaching up to the hips; **hip flask** a flask for spirits etc. (designed to be) carried in the hip pocket; ***hip girdle***: see GIRDLE *noun*[1] 4a; **hip-hole** a hollow dug in the ground to accommodate the hip, for greater comfort when sleeping on the ground; **hip-huggers** hip-hugging trousers; **hip-hugging** *adjective* (of trousers etc.) fitting closely to the hips; **hip joint** the articulation of the head of the thigh bone with the hip bone; **hip-length** *adjective* (of a garment) reaching down to the hips; **hip pocket** a pocket in trousers, a skirt, etc. just behind the hip; **hip roof**: with the ends as well as the sides inclined; **hipshot** *adjective* having a dislocated hip; lame, disabled; **hip-tile**: specially shaped to be used at the hip of a roof.
■ **hipless** *adjective* (*rare*) L19.

hip /hɪp/ *noun*[2]. Also **hep** /hɛp/.
[ORIGIN Old English *hēope*, *hīope*, corresp. to Old Saxon *hiopo* (Dutch *joop*), Old High German *hiufa* (German *Hiefe*), from West Germanic.]
The fruit of the (esp. wild) rose.
J. H. B. PEEL Country lanes are lined . . with hips and haws.

hip /hɪp/ *noun*[3]. *arch. colloq*. Also **hyp**. Pl. **-p(p)s**. E18.
[ORIGIN from HYP(OCHONDRIA. Cf. HIP *verb*[3], HYPO *noun*[1].]
sing. & in *pl*. Depression, low spirits.
C. JOHNSTON That . . sentimental strain gives me the hip.

hip /hɪp/ *noun*[4] *& interjection*. M18.
[ORIGIN Unknown.]
(A cry or shout) introducing a cheer, chiefly in ***hip hip hurray***. Formerly also, (a cry or shout) attracting a person's attention.

hip /hɪp/ *adjective*. *slang* (orig. *US*). E20.
[ORIGIN Unknown. Cf. HEP *adjective*.]
Following the latest fashion in esp. popular and jazz music, clothes, etc., stylish; understanding, aware, (freq. foll. by *to*).
E. JONG He . . threw in a four-letter word to show how hip he was. S. NAIPAUL And now specially for you cool cats out there something real hip.
– COMB.: **hip-cat** a person who is hip.
■ **hipness** *noun* M20.

hip /hɪp/ *verb*[1]. Long *dial*. Infl. **-pp-**. ME.
[ORIGIN Corresp. to Middle Low German, Dutch *huppen*, Low German *hüppen*, Middle & mod. High German *hüpfen*, vars. of corresponding forms of HOP *verb*[1].]
1 *verb intrans*. Hop. ME. ▸†**b** Limp, hobble. Only in LME.
2 *verb trans*. Miss, skip, leave out. M18.

hip /hɪp/ *verb*[2] *trans.* Infl. **-pp-**. E17.
[ORIGIN from HIP *noun*[1].]
1 Dislocate or injure the hip of (a person or an animal, esp. a horse). Usu. in *pass.* Cf. earlier HIPPED *adjective*[1] 2. Now chiefly *dial.* E17.
2 Form (a roof) with a hip or sloping edge. Usu. in *pass.* Cf. HIPPED *adjective*[1] 3. M17.
3 Carry on the hip. *US.* E19.

hip /hɪp/ *verb*[3] *trans. arch. colloq.* Infl. **-pp-**. M19.
[ORIGIN from HIP *noun*[3] or back-form. from HIPPED *adjective*[2].]
Depress, dispirit, sadden.

hip /hɪp/ *verb*[4] *trans. rare.* Infl. **-pp-**. E19.
[ORIGIN from HIP *noun*[4].]
Shout 'hip' at.
J. H. B. PEEL To hear the farmer yipping and hipping his collie.

hip /hɪp/ *verb*[5] *trans. slang* (orig. *US*). Infl. **-pp-**. M20.
[ORIGIN from HIP *adjective*.]
Make (a person) hip; inform, tell, (a person). Cf. earlier HIPPED *adjective*[3].
J. KEROUAC Sand must have hipped him quietly . . what was happening with the lovers.

hipe /hʌɪp/ *noun & verb.* E19.
[ORIGIN Perh. from HIP *noun*[1].]
CUMBERLAND WRESTLING. ▶**A** *noun.* A throw involving an opponent's being lifted over the thigh. E19.
▶**B** *verb trans.* Throw (an opponent) by such a move. E19.

hip-hop /hɪpˈhɒp/ *adverb.* L17.
[ORIGIN from HIP *verb*[1] + HOP *verb*[1].]
With a hopping movement; with successive hops.

hip hop /ˈhɪphɒp/ *noun.* L20.
[ORIGIN Redupl. of *hip*: cf. HIP *adjective*, BEBOP, HOP *noun*[2].]
A style of popular music of US black and Hispanic origin, featuring rap with an electronic backing. Also, an associated youth subculture.
■ **hip-hopper** *noun* a fan of hip hop L20.

hipp- *combining form* see HIPPO-.

hipparch /ˈhɪpɑːk/ *noun.* M17.
[ORIGIN Greek *hipparkhos*, from *hippos* horse + *-arkhos* -ARCH.]
GREEK HISTORY. A commander of cavalry.

hippeastrum /hɪpɪˈastrəm/ *noun.* E19.
[ORIGIN mod. Latin, from Greek *hippeus* horseman + *astron* star.]
Any of various tropical American bulbous plants of the genus *Hippeastrum* (family Amaryllidaceae), with showy freq. bright red or crimson flowers. Also called ***Barbados lily***.

hipped /hɪpt/ *adjective*[1]. LME.
[ORIGIN from HIP *noun*[1] + -ED[2].]
1 Of a person etc.: having hips (of a specified kind). LME.
A. TYLER Their wide-hipped khaki skirts.
2 Having the hip injured or dislocated. Now chiefly *dial.* M16.
3 Of a roof: constructed with a hip or hips. Cf. HIP *verb*[2] 2. E19.
M. GIROUARD The house is 'Queen Anne' in . . its . . hipped roof with gables.

hipped /hɪpt/ *adjective*[2]. *arch. colloq.* Also **hypped**, †**hypt**. E18.
[ORIGIN from HIP *noun*[3] + -ED[2].]
Depressed, low-spirited.
LONGFELLOW What with his bad habits and his domestic grievances he became completely hipped.

hipped /hɪpt/ *adjective*[3]. E20.
[ORIGIN from HIP *adjective* or *verb*[5]: see -ED[1].]
Well-informed, knowing, up-to-date, *au fait*; enthusiastic about, keen, fond, (foll. by *on*).
R. MACDONALD He's been hipped on this subject for years.

hippety-hop /hɪpətɪˈhɒp/ *adverb & noun.* Also (as adverb) **-hoppety** /-ˈhɒpəti/. E19.
[ORIGIN from HIP-HOP *adverb*, with fanciful ending. Cf. HOPPITY *adverb & adjective*.]
▶**A** *adverb.* = HIP-HOP *adverb*. E19.
▶**B** *noun.* A small hop or skip. M20.

hippiatrics /hɪpɪˈatrɪks/ *noun pl. rare.* M17.
[ORIGIN Greek *hippiatrikos* from *hippiatros* veterinary surgeon, from *hippos* horse + *iatros* healer, physician: see -ICS.]
The treatment of diseases of horses.

hippic /ˈhɪpɪk/ *adjective. rare.* M19.
[ORIGIN Greek *hippikos*, from *hippos* horse: see -IC.]
Of or pertaining to horses or (esp.) horse-racing.

hippie *noun & adjective* var. of HIPPY *noun & adjective*[1].

hippiedom /ˈhɪpɪdəm/ *noun.* Also **hippy-**. M20.
[ORIGIN from *hippie* var. of HIPPY *noun* + -DOM.]
The condition or fact of being a hippy; the domain of hippies.

hippish /ˈhɪpɪʃ/ *adjective. arch. colloq.* Also †**hy-**. E18.
[ORIGIN from HIP *noun*[3] + -ISH[1].]
Depressed, low-spirited.
■ **hippishness** *noun* L18.

hippo /ˈhɪpəʊ/ *noun. colloq.* Pl. **-os**. L19.
[ORIGIN Abbreviation.]
= HIPPOPOTAMUS.

hippo- /ˈhɪpəʊ/ *combining form* of Greek *hippos* horse: see -O-. Before a vowel **hipp-**.
Forming nouns and adjectives with the sense 'of or pertaining to horses'.
■ **hiˈppologist** *noun* an expert on or student of horses L19. **hiˈppology** *noun* (*rare*) the branch of knowledge that deals with horses M19. **hippomobile** *noun* (*hist.*) a horse-drawn vehicle E20. **hiˈppophagy** *noun* the practice of eating horseflesh E19. **hippophil(e)** *noun* a lover of horses M19. **hippoˈphobia** *noun* fear of horses M19. **hiˈppotomist** *noun* a person skilled in horse anatomy M18.

hippoboscid /hɪpəˈbɒsɪd/ *noun & adjective.* L19.
[ORIGIN mod. Latin *Hippoboscidae* (see below), from HIPPO- + Greek *boskein* feed: see -ID[2].]
▶**A** *noun.* Any bloodsucking dipteran fly of the family Hippoboscidae, parasitic on mammals and birds. L19.
▶**B** *adjective.* Of, pertaining to, or designating this family. E20.

hippocamp /ˈhɪpəkamp/ *noun.* Now *rare.* E17.
[ORIGIN from HIPPOCAMPUS.]
= HIPPOCAMPUS 2.

hippocampus /hɪpə(ʊ)ˈkampəs/ *noun.* Pl. **-pi** /-pʌɪ/. L16.
[ORIGIN Latin from Greek *hippokampos*, from *hippos* horse + *kampos* sea monster.]
1 A fish of the genus *Hippocampus*; a sea horse. L16.
2 A mythical sea monster, half horse and half fish or dolphin, represented as drawing the chariot of Neptune etc.; a representation of this. E17.
3 ANATOMY. A swelling on the floor of each lateral ventricle of the brain, containing folded cortical tissue and forming part of the limbic system. E18.
■ **hippocampal** *adjective* of or pertaining to the hippocampus of the brain; *esp.* designating the part of the limbic system formed by the hippocampus and associated cortical tissue: M19.

hippocentaur /hɪpə(ʊ)ˈsɛntɔː/ *noun.* E16.
[ORIGIN Latin *hippocentaurus* from Greek *hippokentauros*, from *hippos* horse + *kentauros* CENTAUR.]
= CENTAUR.

hippocras /ˈhɪpəkras/ *noun.* LME.
[ORIGIN Old French *ipo-*, *ypocras*, forms of Latin *Hippocrates* (see HIPPOCRATES' SLEEVE), used for medieval Latin *vinum Hippocraticum* wine strained through a filter called 'Hippocrates' sleeve' (see HIPPOCRATES' SLEEVE).]
1 *hist.* Wine flavoured with spices. LME.
T. H. WHITE Would you like a glass of hippocras, or some perry?
†**2** In full ***Hippocras bag***. = HIPPOCRATES' SLEEVE. Only in 17.

†**Hippocrates' sleeve** *noun phr.* E17–L18.
[ORIGIN translating Latin *manica Hippocratis*, from *Hippocrates* a Greek physician (c 460–c 377 BC).]
A conical bag of cotton, linen, or flannel, used as a filter. Also called ***Hippocras bag***.

Hippocratic /hɪpəˈkratɪk/ *adjective.* In sense 2 also **h-**. E17.
[ORIGIN medieval Latin *Hippocraticus*, from *Hippocrates*: see HIPPOCRATES' SLEEVE, -IC.]
†**1** ***Hippocratic wine***, = HIPPOCRAS 1. Only in 17.
2 Of the face: shrunken and livid (as) on the point of death (as described by Hippocrates). E18.
3 Of or according to Hippocrates; *spec.* designating an oath stating the code of professional medical conduct and ethics, formerly taken by those beginning medical practice. M19.
■ **Hippocratian** /-ˈkreɪʃ(ə)n/ *adjective* = HIPPOCRATIC M19. **Hippocratical** *adjective* = HIPPOCRATIC E17.

Hippocrene /ˈhɪpəkriːn/ *noun.* E17.
[ORIGIN Latin *Hippocrene*, Greek *Hippokrēnē* or *Hippou krēnē* (lit. 'fountain of the horse'), a fountain on Mount Helicon sacred to the Muses, fabled to have been produced by a stroke of Pegasus' hoof.]
Poetic or literary inspiration.
KEATS O for a beaker . . Full of the true, the blushful Hippocrene.

hippodame /ˈhɪpədeɪm/ *noun.* Long *rare* or *obsolete*. L16.
[ORIGIN Greek *hippodamos*, from *hippos* horse + *damos* a tamer.]
†**1** [By confusion.] = HIPPOCAMPUS 2. *rare* (Spenser). Only in L16.
2 A horsebreaker. E17.

hippodrome /ˈhɪpədrəʊm/ *noun & verb.* L16.
[ORIGIN Old French & mod. French, or Latin *hippodromus* from Greek *hippodromos*, from *hippos* horse + *dromos* race, course.]
▶**A** *noun.* **1** In ancient Greece and Rome, a course for chariot races or horse races. Also, a modern circus. L16.
2 (**H-**.) (The name of) a theatre used for various stage entertainments. L19.
3 A race or contest in which the result is prearranged or fixed. *US slang.* L19.
▶**B** *verb intrans.* Prearrange or fix the result of a race or contest. Chiefly as ***hippodroming*** *verbal noun. US slang.* M19.

hippogriff /ˈhɪpə(ʊ)grɪf/ *noun.* Also †**-gryph**. M17.
[ORIGIN French *hippogriffe* from Italian *ippogrifo*, formed as HIPPO- + Italian *grifo* griffin, from late Latin *gryphus* GRIFFIN *noun*[1].]
A mythical creature with the body and hindquarters of a horse and the wings and head of an eagle; a representation of this.
■ Also †**hippogriffin** *noun* M17–M19.

hippomanes /hɪˈpɒməniːz/ *noun.* E17.
[ORIGIN Greek, formed as HIPPO- + *man-* base of *mainesthai* be mad.]
A growth said to occur on the head of a newborn foal, used in antiquity as an aphrodisiac.

hippopotamus /hɪpəˈpɒtəməs/ *noun.* Pl. **-muses**, **-mi** /-mʌɪ/. ME.
[ORIGIN Old French *ypotame*, medieval Latin *ypotamus*, or its source Latin *hippopotamus* from Greek *hippopotamos*, earlier *hippos ho potamios* horse of the river.]
A very large heavy short-legged artiodactyl mammal of the family Hippopotamidae; spec. *Hippopotamus amphibius*, which lives in or near rivers and lakes in tropical African grassland and is a gregarious semi-aquatic herbivore having a wide tusked mouth and thick, almost hairless skin.
pygmy hippopotamus: see PYGMY *adjective*.
■ **hippopoˈtamian** *adjective* of, belonging to, or suggestive of a hippopotamus M19. **hippopoˈtamic** *adjective* = HIPPOPOTAMIAN L18. **hippopotamid** *noun & adjective* (ZOOLOGY) (**a**) *noun* any animal of the family Hippopotamidae; (**b**) *adjective* of, pertaining to, or designating this family: L19. **hippopotamine** *adjective* = HIPPOPOTAMIAN L19.

hipps *noun pl.* see HIP *noun*[3].

hippuric /hɪˈpjʊərɪk/ *adjective.* M19.
[ORIGIN from Greek *hippos* horse + *ouron* urine + -IC.]
BIOCHEMISTRY. ***hippuric acid***, a benzoyl derivative of glycine, $C_6H_5CONHCH_2COOH$, found in urine (esp. of herbivores).

hippurite /ˈhɪpjʊrʌɪt/ *noun.* E19.
[ORIGIN from mod. Latin genus name *Hippurites* from Greek *hippouros* having a tail like a horse, from *hippos* horse + *oura* tail: see -ITE[1].]
= RUDIST *noun*.

hippus /ˈhɪpəs/ *noun.* L17.
[ORIGIN mod. Latin from Greek *hippos* tremor of the eyes.]
OPHTHALMOLOGY. Spasmodic or rhythmic contraction of the pupil of the eye, a symptom of some neurological conditions.

hippy /ˈhɪpi/ *noun & adjective*[1]. Orig. *US colloq.* Also **hippie**. M20.
[ORIGIN from HIP *adjective* + -Y[6], -IE. Cf. YIPPIE.]
▶**A** *noun.* A person of an unconventional appearance, typically with long hair, jeans, beads, etc., often associated with hallucinogenic drugs and a rejection of conventional values. M20.
T. LEARY Every visible hippy, barefoot, beflowered, beaded.
▶**B** *adjective.* Of, pertaining to, or characteristic of a hippy or hippies. M20.
J. UPDIKE Hippie Ph.D's who've gone to work in the crafts to spite their fathers.
■ **hippieness** *noun* M20.

hippy /ˈhɪpi/ *adjective*[2]. E20.
[ORIGIN from HIP *noun*[1] + -Y[1].]
Having large hips.

hippydom *noun* var. of HIPPIEDOM.

hipster /ˈhɪpstə/ *noun*[1]. *slang* (orig. *US*). M20.
[ORIGIN from HIP *adjective* + -STER.]
A person who is hip.
P. GOODMAN The hipster will often boast: he knows the score, he is ahead of the game.

hipster /ˈhɪpstə/ *adjective & noun*[2]. M20.
[ORIGIN from HIP *noun*[1] + -STER.]
▶**A** *adjective.* Of a garment, esp. a pair of trousers: hanging from the hips rather than from the waist. M20.
▶**B** *noun.* In *pl.* Hipster trousers. M20.

Hirado /hɪˈrɑːdəʊ/ *adjective.* Also **-to** /-təʊ/. L19.
[ORIGIN An island off the NW coast of Kyushu, Japan.]
Designating a form of Hizen ware manufactured on Hirado.

hiragana /hɪrəˈgɑːnə/ *noun.* Also **-kana** /-ˈkɑːnə/. E19.
[ORIGIN Japanese, from *hira* plain + KANA.]
The form of kana normally used in Japanese, derived from the cursive style of writing. Cf. KATAKANA.

Hirato *adjective* var. of HIRADO.

hircarra /həːˈkɑːrə/ *noun.* Now *rare.* Also **-rah**. M18.
[ORIGIN Persian & Urdu *harkārah* messenger.]
In the Indian subcontinent, a spy, a messenger.

hircine /ˈhəːsʌɪn/ *adjective.* M17.
[ORIGIN Latin *hircinus*, from *hircus* he-goat: see -INE[1].]
Of, belonging to, or resembling a goat; goatlike.

hircocervus /həːkə(ʊ)ˈsəːvəs/ *noun.* LME.
[ORIGIN Late Latin, from *hircus* he-goat + *cervus* stag.]
A mythical animal, half goat, half stag; a representation of this.

hirdy-girdy /ˈhəːdɪgəːdi/ *noun & adverb. Scot. & N. English.* E16.
[ORIGIN Imit.: cf. HURDY-GURDY.]
▶**A** *noun.* Uproar, disorder. E16.
▶**B** *adverb.* In or into disorder. L16.

H

hire /ˈhʌɪə/ *noun*.
[ORIGIN Old English *hȳr* = Old Frisian *hēre*, Old Saxon *hūria*, Middle Low German, Middle Dutch *hūre* (Dutch *huur*), from West Germanic.]
1 Payment under contract for the use of something. OE.
D. WIGODER Regent's Park . . with its rowing boats for hire. *attrib.*: *Sunday Express* Avis . . has hire prices from about £15 per day.
2 Payment under contract for personal service; wages. ME.
AV *Luke* 10:7 The labourer is worthy of his hire.
3 *fig.* Reward, recompense, payment, (for work, service, etc.). ME.
4 The action of hiring or fact of being hired; engagement on agreed terms of payment for use, service, etc. E17.
OED To arrange for the hire of a horse.
5 One who is hired; an employee. *US*. L20.
– PHRASES: **for hire** available to be hired. **on hire** available to be hired, that has been hired.
– COMB.: **hire car**: available for hire; **hireman** (now only *Scot.*) a hired servant; **hire purchase**, **hire-purchase system**: by which something hired becomes the hirer's after a certain number of payments.
■ **hireless** *adjective* (now *rare*) without hire; unhired: M17.

hire /ˈhʌɪə/ *verb*.
[ORIGIN Old English *hȳrian* = Old Frisian *hēra*, Middle Low German, Middle Dutch *hūren* (Dutch *huren*).]
1 *verb trans.* Employ (a person) for wages; take on (an employee) for an agreed remuneration (now chiefly *N. Amer.*). OE. ▸**b** Engage, induce, (a person) to do something by a (promise of) payment or reward; bribe. LME. ▸**c** Borrow (money). *US*. L18.
W. S. CHURCHILL With his revenues he could hire Swiss infantry. N. MAILER Remind me to hire you if I need a lawyer. **b** LD MACAULAY A popish priest was hired with the promise of the mitre of Waterford to preach . . against the Act.
hire and fire engage and dismiss.
2 *verb trans.* Procure (*from* a person) the temporary use of (a thing) for stipulated payment. ME.
V. GLENDINNING He and Martha hired a car in Naples.
3 *verb trans.* Grant (*out*, *to* a person) the temporary use or employment of (a thing, a person, etc.) for stipulated payment. LME. ▸**b** *verb intrans.* Foll. by *out*: engage oneself as a servant for wages. *N. Amer.* M19.
TENNYSON He . . hired himself to work within the fields. **b** C. A. DAVIS I had hired out here this summer.
■ **hireable**, **hirable** *adjective* able to be hired M19. **hired** *ppl adjective* (**a**) that has been hired; (**b**) **hired girl**, **hired man**, etc. (*N. Amer.*) a domestic servant (formerly a free person as opp. to a slave) esp. on a farm: ME. **hirer** *noun* LME.

hireling /ˈhʌɪəlɪŋ/ *noun & adjective*. Usu. *derog.* OE.
[ORIGIN from HIRE *noun* + -LING¹.]
▸ **A** *noun*. **1** A person who serves for hire; one motivated chiefly by reward or material remuneration; a mercenary. OE.
BYRON Baser hirelings, who live by lies on good men's lives. A. DUGGAN I hoped that the infantry of the line would do better than our Arab hirelings.
2 A hired horse. L19.
▸ **B** *attrib.* or as *adjective*. Of or pertaining to a hireling; serving for hire; mercenary. L16.
– NOTE: Rare in OE; not recorded again until 16, when formed afresh, prob. after Dutch *huurling*.

†Hiren *noun*. L16–E17.
[ORIGIN A character in Peele's play 'The Turkish Mahamet and Hyrin the fair Greek': alt. of *Irene*, French *Irène*.]
A prostitute or seductive woman.

hirmos /ˈhəːmɒs/ *noun*. Also **heirmos**. Pl. **-moi** /-mɔɪ/, **-mi** /-miː/. M19.
[ORIGIN Greek *heirmos* series, connection.]
In the hymnology of the Orthodox Church, a model stanza forming a pattern for the other stanzas.

hirola /hɪˈrəʊlə/ *noun*. Also **her-**. L19.
[ORIGIN Galla.]
A small antelope, *Damaliscus hunteri*, native to Kenya and Somalia. Also called ***Hunter's hartebeest***.

hirondelle /hɪrɒnˈdɛl/ *noun*. *obsolete* exc. HERALDRY. E17.
[ORIGIN French.]
A swallow; a charge representing this.

hirple /ˈhəːp(ə)l/ *verb intrans.* Chiefly *Scot. & N. English*. L15.
[ORIGIN Unknown.]
Walk or move with a gait between walking and crawling; walk lamely, hobble.

Hirschsprung's disease /ˈhɪəʃprʊŋz dɪˌziːz/ *noun phr.* E20.
[ORIGIN from Harald *Hirschsprung* (1830–1916), Danish paediatrician.]
MEDICINE. Congenital absence of the ganglion cells in a segment of the colon and rectum, causing failure of peristalsis and colonic dilatation by faeces. Formerly also, any abnormal dilatation of the colon.

hirsel /ˈhəːs(ə)l/ *noun & verb*. Orig. *Scot. & N. English*. LME.
[ORIGIN from Old Norse *hirzla* safe-keeping, from *hirða* herd sheep from Germanic base of HERD *noun*².]
▸ **A** *noun*. **1** The collection of sheep under a shepherd's charge or on an individual farm; *fig.* a spiritual flock. *Scot. & N. English*. LME.
2 A company to look after; a collection of persons or things of one kind. *Scot. & N. English*. LME.
3 The ground occupied by a flock of sheep. E19.
Punch The Scottish hirsel (where the flock grazes all the year round on one hill).
▸ **B** *verb trans.* Form into a hirsel or hirsels. *Scot. & N. English*. L18.

hirsle /ˈhəːs(ə)l/ *verb*. *Scot. & N. English*. E16.
[ORIGIN Unknown.]
1 *verb intrans.* Move or slide esp. with grazing or friction. E16.
2 *verb trans.* Move (something) with much effort. E18.

hirst *noun* var. of HURST.

hirsute /ˈhəːsjuːt/ *adjective*. E17.
[ORIGIN Latin *hirsutus* rough, shaggy, rel. to synon. *hirtus*.]
1 Having rough or shaggy hair; hairy, shaggy; *transf.* & *fig.* rough, untrimmed. E17.
A. S. BYATT Like many hirsute men he had thinned a little on top. Z. MDA A very prosperous and very hirsute farmer with a beer belly.
2 BOTANY & ZOOLOGY. Covered with long soft or moderately stiff hairs. E17.
3 Of or pertaining to hair; of the nature of or consisting of hair. E19.
■ **hirsuteness** *noun* E17. **hirsutism** *noun* abnormal hairiness E20.

hirudin /hɪˈruːdɪn/ *noun*. E20.
[ORIGIN from Latin *hirudo* leech + -IN¹.]
An anticoagulant protein found in the saliva of leeches and in some snake venoms, which inhibits the action of thrombin in blood-clotting.

hirudinean /hɪrʊˈdɪnɪən/ *noun*. M19.
[ORIGIN from mod. Latin *Hirudinea* (see below), from *hirudo* leech: see -AN.]
ZOOLOGY. An annelid of the class Hirudinea, which comprises the leeches.

hirundine /ˈhɪrʌndʌɪn, hɪˈrʌndʌɪn/ *adjective & noun*. M19.
[ORIGIN from Latin *hirundo* swallow + -INE¹.]
▸ **A** *adjective*. Of, pertaining to, or characteristic of a swallow. M19.
▸ **B** *noun*. A bird of the swallow family Hirundinidae. L20.

his /hɪz, *unstressed* ɪz/ *possess. pronoun*¹ & *adjective* (in mod. usage also classed as a **determiner**), *3 sing. masc.* (& †*neut.*).
[ORIGIN Old English *his* genit. of HE *pronoun*, IT *pronoun*, with inflection parallel to Old Saxon, Gothic *is*, Old High German *es* (cf. HIM). Cf. HIS *pronoun*², HISN.]
▸ †**A** *pronoun*. Genit. of HE *pronoun*; of him. OE–LME.
▸ **B** *adjective* (*attrib.*). **1** Of him; of himself; which belongs or pertains to him(self). OE. ▸**b** In titles (as ***His Lordship***, ***His Majesty***): that he is. M16.
KEATS The owl, for all his feathers, was a-cold. T. HARDY He went out and resumed his painting. G. GREENE He can't open his mouth without lying. J. C. POWYS Giants of his size were very rare among Mongolian Tartars. E. J. HOWARD He parked his car outside the mews in Hillsleigh Road. A. S. J. TESSIMOND For X is never annoyed Or shocked; has read his Jung and knows his Freud. G. GORDON He touched nothing that any other child had made, only his and Patrick's work. E. BLISHEN She remembered his making a doll's house for his daughters.
his own: see OWN *adjective & pronoun*. ***his watch***: see WATCH *noun*.
2 Its. Long *obsolete* exc. in personification, passing into sense 1. OE.
3 After a noun (esp. a personal name): substituting for the genit. inflection or possess. suffix **-'S**¹. *arch.* OE.
CARLYLE It were better for you . . to keep out of Pandarus his neighbourhood.

his /hɪz, *unstressed* ɪz/ *possess. pronoun*². OE.
[ORIGIN Absol. use of HIS *pronoun*¹ & *adjective*. Cf. HISN.]
1 His one(s), that or those belonging or pertaining to him. In early use also, its. OE.
J. CONRAD His was the soul of obedience. E. WAUGH A tone of voice, . . a swift, epicene felicity of wit, . . these had been his. I. MURDOCH He took her ungloved hand in his.
get his: see GET *verb*. **his and hers** (a pair of matching items intending to be) a husband's and a wife's or a man's and a woman's.
2 ***of his***, belonging or pertaining to him or, in early use, it. ME.

hish /hɪʃ/ *verb intrans.* Now only *Scot. & dial.* LME.
[ORIGIN Imit.: cf. HISS *verb*.]
Hiss, make a hissing noise (*at*).

hisn /ˈhɪz(ə)n/ *possess. pronoun*. Long *obsolete* exc. *dial.* LME.
[ORIGIN from HIS *pronoun*² after *my* and *mine*, *thy* and *thine*, etc.]
His one(s), that or those belonging or pertaining to him.

Hispanic /hɪˈspanɪk/ *adjective & noun*. L16.
[ORIGIN Latin *Hispanicus*, from *Hispania* Spain: see -IC.]
▸ **A** *adjective*. Of or pertaining to Spain (and Portugal); of or pertaining to Spain and Spanish-speaking countries. L16.
▸ **B** *noun*. A Spanish-speaking person, esp. one of Latin American descent, living in the US. Usu. in *pl.* L20.
■ **Hispanically** *adverb* M19.

Hispanicise *verb* var. of HISPANICIZE.

Hispanicism /hɪˈspanɪsɪz(ə)m/ *noun*. M19.
[ORIGIN from HISPANIC + -ISM.]
A Hispanic idiom or characteristic.

Hispanicist /hɪˈspanɪsɪst/ *noun*. M20.
[ORIGIN formed as HISPANICISM + -IST.]
= HISPANIST.

Hispanicize /hɪˈspanɪsʌɪz/ *verb trans.* Also **-ise**. L19.
[ORIGIN from HISPANIC + -IZE.]
Make Hispanic in form or character.
■ **Hispaniciˈzation** *noun* M20.

hispaniolize /hɪˈspanɪəlʌɪz/ *verb trans.* Long *rare*. Also **-ise**. L16.
[ORIGIN from Spanish *españolar* make Spanish + -IZE, with assim. to Latin *Hispania* Spain.]
= HISPANIZE.

hispanise *verb* var. of HISPANIZE.

Hispanism /ˈhɪspənɪz(ə)m/ *noun*. M20.
[ORIGIN from Latin *Hispania* Spain + -ISM.]
= HISPANICISM.

Hispanist /ˈhɪspənɪst/ *noun*. M20.
[ORIGIN formed as HISPANISM + -IST.]
An expert in or student of Spanish literature, language, and civilization.

hispanize /ˈhɪspənʌɪz/ *verb trans.* Also **-ise**. E17.
[ORIGIN from Latin *Hispanus* Spanish, Spaniard + -IZE.]
Make (esp. a person) Spanish in culture, speech, or sympathies.
■ **hispaniˈzation** *noun* M20.

Hispano- /hɪˈspanəʊ/ *combining form*.
[ORIGIN from Latin *Hispanus* Spanish: see -O-.]
Forming nouns and adjectives with the sense 'Spanish and —', as ***Hispano-American***, ***Hispano-Arab***, ***Hispano-Arabic***, ***Hispano-Gothic***, etc.

Hispanophile /hɪˈspanəfʌɪl/ *noun*. Also **-phil** /-fɪl/. E20.
[ORIGIN from HISPANO- + -PHIL.]
A lover of Spain and Spanish culture.

Hisperic /hɪˈspɛrɪk/ *adjective*. E20.
[ORIGIN from medieval Latin *Hisperica* (see below). Cf. German *hisperisch*.]
Designating a variety of medieval Latin, of which the group of documents entitled *Hisperica Famina* (probably of the 6th cent.) is a notable example, characterized by a highly artificial vocabulary, with many borrowed words.

hispid /ˈhɪspɪd/ *adjective*¹. M17.
[ORIGIN Latin *hispidus*: see -ID¹. Cf. Old French & mod. French *hispide*.]
Now chiefly BOTANY. Covered with short stiff hairs or bristles; bristly.
■ **hiˈspidity** *noun* M17.

hispid /ˈhɪspɪd/ *adjective*² & *noun*. E20.
[ORIGIN from mod. Latin *Hispidae* (former family name), from *Hispa* (genus name), formed as HISPID *adjective*¹: see -ID³.]
ENTOMOLOGY. ▸**A** *adjective*. Of, pertaining to, or designating the subfamily Hispinae of leaf beetles. E20.
▸ **B** *noun*. A leaf beetle of this subfamily. E20.

hi-spy *noun phr.* see I-SPY.

hiss /hɪs/ *noun*. E16.
[ORIGIN from the verb.]
1 A sharp sibilant sound (as of *s*); *spec.* such a sound made to express disapproval or derision. E16.
B. BAINBRIDGE The murmurings of their voices and the hiss of the gas fire merged. M. MEYER His first production there had been repeatedly interrupted by boos, hisses and cries.
2 PHONETICS. A sibilant. L19.

hiss /hɪs/ *verb*. LME.
[ORIGIN Imit. Cf. HISH.]
1 *verb intrans.* Of a person, animal, or thing: make a sharp sibilant sound (as of *s*). Of a person: make such a sound to express disapproval or derision (foll. by *at*). LME.
R. L. STEVENSON I saw snakes, and one . . hissed at me. W. VAN T. CLARK In the silence the fire crackled and hissed when the snow fell into it. *Independent* People in the public gallery have started to hiss when Barbie's defence counsel speaks.
hissing adder *US* a hognose snake.
2 *verb trans.* Drive away by hissing. (Foll. by *away*, *down*, *off*, *out*.) E16.
R. H. SHERARD The first performance of 'Faust', which was hissed off the stage.
3 *verb trans.* Express disapproval of by hissing. L18.
4 *verb trans.* Express by hissing or with a hiss. L18.
F. HOWERD The orchestra leader hissed from the pit: 'Do something, or get off!'

■ **hisser** *noun* LME. **hissing** *noun* (*a*) the action of the verb; (*b*) *arch.* something that causes or is the object of expressed disapproval or scorn: LME. **hissingly** *adverb* in a hissing manner E17.

his-self /hɪzˈsɛlf/ *pronoun.* Now *dial.* & *colloq.* ME.
[ORIGIN from HIS *adjective* + SELF *noun* (reinterpreting *self* in HIMSELF).]
= HIMSELF.

hissy /ˈhɪsi/ *adjective* & *noun.* E20.
[ORIGIN from HISS *noun* + -Y³; *hissy fit* is perh. alt. of *hysterics*.]
▸ **A** *adjective.* Consisting of, accompanied by, or resembling a hiss. E20.
▸ **B** *noun.* More fully ***hissy fit***. An angry outburst; a temper tantrum. *US colloq.* M20.

hist /hɪst/ *verb*¹. Now *poet.* E17.
[ORIGIN from the interjection.]
1 *verb trans.* Incite, urge (*on*). E17.
†**2** *verb trans.* Summon with the exclamation 'hist!'; summon silently. M17–L18.
3 *verb intrans.* Be silent. M19.

hist /hʌɪst/ *verb*² *trans.* Chiefly *US.* Also **h'ist**, **hyst**. M19.
[ORIGIN Var. of HOIST *verb*¹. Cf. HEIST *verb*.]
Raise aloft (= HOIST *verb*¹ 1); steal, hijack.

hist /hɪst/ *interjection.* L16.
[ORIGIN Natural exclam. Cf. ST, WHISHT.]
Calling attention, enjoining silence, inciting a dog etc.

Histadrut /ˈhɪstʌdruːt/ *noun.* Also †**-druth**. E20.
[ORIGIN mod. Hebrew *ha-histaddĕrūṯ* the federation: in full *ha-histaddĕrūṯ ha-kĕlālīṯ šel hā-ʿōbĕdīm bĕ-ʾereṣ Yiśrāʾēl* the general federation of workers in the land of Israel.]
A labour organization in the state of Israel, the General Federation of Labour, founded in 1920, and having a large membership of industrial and agricultural workers.

histamine /ˈhɪstəmiːn/ *noun.* E20.
[ORIGIN from HIST(IDINE + AMINE.]
BIOCHEMISTRY. A heterocyclic amine, $C_5H_9N_3$, widespread in animal and plant tissues, which is formed by decarboxylation of histidine, stimulates gastric secretion, smooth muscle contraction, and vasodilation, and is released by mast cells in response to wounding and in inflammatory, allergic, and anaphylactic reactions. Cf. ANTIHISTAMINE.

hister /ˈhɪstə/ *noun.* L18.
[ORIGIN mod. Latin (see below) from Latin = actor (from the beetle's pretence of death when alarmed).]
Any of numerous small carnivorous or scavenging beetles of the family Histeridae; *esp.* any of the genus *Hister*. Also ***hister beetle***.
■ **histerid** *adjective* & *noun* (*a*) *adjective* of or pertaining to the family Histeridae; (*b*) *noun* any beetle of this family: E20.

histidine /ˈhɪstɪdiːn/ *noun.* L19.
[ORIGIN from Greek *histos* tissue, web + -IDINE.]
BIOCHEMISTRY. A weakly basic heterocyclic amino acid, $C_6H_9N_3O_2$, which occurs in proteins, often at catalytic sites, and is an imidazole derivative.

histiocyte /ˈhɪstɪəsʌɪt/ *noun.* E20.
[ORIGIN from Greek *histion* dim. of *histos* tissue, web + -CYTE.]
PHYSIOLOGY. A macrophage found in connective tissue and becoming motile when stimulated.
■ **histioˈcytic** *adjective* E20. **histiocyˈtosis** *noun*, pl. **-toses** /-ˈtəʊsiːz/, MEDICINE any of a number of conditions involving proliferation of histiocytes E20.

histioid /ˈhɪstɪɔɪd/ *adjective.* Now *rare* or *obsolete.* M19.
[ORIGIN from Greek *histion* dim. of *histos* tissue, web: see -OID.]
= HISTOID.

histo- /ˈhɪstəʊ/ *combining form* of Greek *histos* tissue, web: see -O-.
■ **histoˈchemical** *adjective* of or pertaining to histochemistry L19. **histoˈchemically** *adverb* by histochemical means M20. **histoˈchemistry** *noun* the branch of science that deals with the chemical properties of tissues and cells, esp. by microscopic examination with staining; the histochemical properties *of* a thing: M19. **histocomˈpatibility** *noun* (MEDICINE) compatibility between the tissue of different individuals, so that one accepts a graft from the other without giving an immune reaction M20. **histocomˈpatible** *adjective* exhibiting histocompatibility M20. **histoˈgenesis** *noun* the production and differentiation of organic tissue M19. **histogeˈnetic** *adjective* of or pertaining to histogenesis M19. **histogeˈnetically** *adverb* as regards histogenesis L19. **hiˈstogeny** *noun* = HISTOGENESIS M19. **hiˈstolysis** *noun* the disintegration of organic tissue M19. **histoˈlytic** *adjective* of or pertaining to histolysis M19. **histopathoˈlogic** *adjective* (chiefly *US*) = HISTOPATHOLOGICAL E20. **histopathoˈlogical** *adjective* characterized by or characteristic of diseased tissue; of or pertaining to histopathology: M20. **histopathoˈlogically** *adverb* as regards histopathology; by histopathological means: E20. **histopaˈthologist** *noun* an expert in or student of histopathology E20. **histopaˈthology** *noun* the branch of medicine that deals with the tissue changes associated with disease; the tissue changes characteristic *of* a disease: L19. **histoˈplasmin** *noun* (MEDICINE) a sterile culture of the fungus *Histoplasma capsulatum*, used in skin tests for histoplasmosis M20. **histoplasˈmosis** *noun* infection with *Histoplasma capsulatum* (a fungus found esp. in the droppings of birds and bats in humid areas), which may be a transient benign infection of the lungs or a disseminated usu. fatal disease of the reticuloendothelial system E20. **histosol** *noun* (SOIL SCIENCE) a soil of an order comprising peaty soils, with a deep surface layer of purely organic material L20.

histogen /ˈhɪstə(ʊ)dʒ(ə)n/ *noun.* E20.
[ORIGIN from HISTO- + -GEN.]
BOTANY. Each of three layers (dermatogen, periblem, and plerome) supposedly distinguishable in an apical meristem, which is now usu. regarded as comprising tunica and corpus. Chiefly in ***histogen theory***.

histogram /ˈhɪstəgram/ *noun.* L19.
[ORIGIN from Greek *histos* mast, web + -GRAM.]
A diagram consisting of a number of rectangles or lines drawn (usu. upwards) from a base line, their heights representing frequencies of a series of values (or value ranges) of a quantity.

histoid /ˈhɪstɔɪd/ *adjective.* L19.
[ORIGIN from Greek *histos* tissue, web + -OID.]
MEDICINE. Resembling (ordinary) tissue.

histology /hɪˈstɒlədʒi/ *noun.* M19.
[ORIGIN from HISTO- + -LOGY. Cf. French *histologie* (E19).]
The branch of science that deals with the structure and composition of organic tissue, esp. on a microscopic scale; the histological properties *of* a thing.
■ **histoˈlogic** *adjective* (chiefly *US*) L19. **histoˈlogical** *adjective* M19. **histoˈlogically** *adverb* as regards histology M19. **histologist** *noun* M19.

histomap /ˈhɪstəmap/ *noun.* M20.
[ORIGIN from HISTO(RY *noun* + MAP *noun*¹.]
A diagram representing the historical development of a religion or a civilization.

histone /ˈhɪstəʊn/ *noun.* L19.
[ORIGIN German *Histon*, perh. from Greek *histanai* arrest or *histos* web, tissue: see -ONE.]
Any of a group of simple basic water-soluble proteins that occur associated with DNA in the cell nuclei of eukaryotes.

historian /hɪˈstɔːrɪən/ *noun.* LME.
[ORIGIN Old French & mod. French *historien*, from Latin *historia* after *logicien* etc.: see -AN, -IAN.]
1 A writer of history, *esp.* a critical analyst, as opp. to a chronicler or compiler; a person learned in history; a student of history. (Freq. with specifying word.) LME.

> R. SCRUTON Historians discuss the origins of the state. M. SEYMOUR-SMITH When literary historians come to record the development of modernism . . they ignore Graves.

ancient historian, ***economic historian***, ***French historian***, ***Marxist historian***, ***medieval historian***, ***modern historian***, ***social historian***, etc.

†**2** A storyteller. L16–M17.

historiated /hɪˈstɔːrɪeɪtɪd/ *adjective.* L19.
[ORIGIN Repr. French *historié* (in same sense) pa. pple of Old French & mod. French *historier* †illustrate, from medieval Latin *historiare* as HISTORY *noun*: see -ATE³, -ED¹.]
Decorated with figures of people, animals, etc. Cf. FLORIATED, STORIATED.

historic /hɪˈstɒrɪk/ *adjective* & *noun.* E17.
[ORIGIN French *historique* or directly from Latin *historicus* from Greek *historikos*, from *historia* HISTORY *noun*: see -IC.]
▸ **A** *adjective.* **1** = HISTORICAL *adjective* 1. *arch.* E17.

> TENNYSON A hoard of tales that dealt with knights, Half-legend, half-historic.

2 = HISTORICAL *adjective* 3. L17.

> M. EDWARDES The historic expectations of the motor industry worker who had grown used to seeing his income rise. *Times Lit. Suppl.* Russian artists . . were fixated by the historic genre.

3 Of great historical importance or fame; having a significance due to connection with historical events. L18.

> P. GAY Certain historic acts—Napoleon invading Russia . . or Britain abandoning the gold standard in 1931. B. EMECHETA Asaba is . . an old and a very historic town.

4 GRAMMAR. Designating any of various tenses and moods used in the narration of past events, esp. the Latin and Greek imperfect and pluperfect, the Greek aorist, and the Latin perfect used in the sense of the latter. M19.
historic infinitive the infinitive when used instead of the indicative. **historic present** the present tense when used instead of the past in vivid narration. ***past historic***: see PAST *adjective* & *noun*.
▸ **B** *noun.* †**1** A historian. Only in E17.
2 = HISTORICAL *noun.* *rare.* M19.

historical /hɪˈstɒrɪk(ə)l/ *adjective* & *noun.* LME.
[ORIGIN formed as HISTORIC: see -ICAL.]
▸ **A** *adjective.* **1** Of, belonging to, or pertaining to history, esp. as opp. to prehistory or to fiction or legend; of the nature of or in accordance with history. LME.

> E. DOWDEN This historical Oldcastle is better known as Lord Cobham. *Sunday Express* The guide provides . . the historical background to the early English colonies.

2 Relating to or concerned with (events of) history. E16. ▸**b** (Of the study of a subject) based on history or an analysis of development in course of time; in connection with history, from the historian's point of view; belonging to the past, not to the present. L19.

> J. B. MOZLEY By the historical imagination I mean the habit of realizing past time. **b** O. JESPERSEN Descriptive linguistics can never be rendered superfluous by historical linguistics. *American Speech* The utility of full-text data bases for historical-lexicographical research.

b ***historical grammar***: see GRAMMAR *noun*.
3 Of a novel, a writer, etc.: dealing with events of history; depicting or describing events of history. L16.

> *Observer* Philip Woodruff's *Colonel of Dragoons* . . a very model of what historical fiction ought to be.

4 = HISTORIC *adjective* 3. M19.

> M. PATTISON It is the old historical lands of Europe that the lover of history longs to explore.

5 = HISTORIC *adjective* 4. *rare.* M19.
▸ **B** *noun.* A historical work etc.; *esp.* a historical novel. M17.

> A. BLAISDELL Donaldson was yawning over a paper-back historical.

■ **historicalness** *noun* M17.

historically /hɪˈstɒrɪk(ə)li/ *adverb.* M16.
[ORIGIN from HISTORIC or HISTORICAL: see -ICALLY.]
In a historic or historical manner, *esp.* relatively to the past.

> *Economist* The yields on copper shares are at historically high levels.

historicise *verb* var. of HISTORICIZE.

historicism /hɪˈstɒrɪsɪz(ə)m/ *noun.* L19.
[ORIGIN from HISTORIC + -ISM: translating German *Historismus*.]
1 The theory that social and cultural phenomena are determined by history. L19.
2 The belief that historical events are governed by laws. E20.
3 The tendency to regard historical development as the most basic aspect of human existence, and historical thinking as the most important type of thought. M20.
4 Excessive regard for the values or styles of the past. M20.
■ **historicist** *noun* & *adjective* (*a*) *noun* an adherent of historicism; (*b*) *adjective* of or pertaining to historicism or historicists: M20.

historicity /hɪstəˈrɪsɪti/ *noun.* L19.
[ORIGIN from HISTORIC + -ITY, after *authenticity*.]
Historic quality or character; *esp.* the historical genuineness or accuracy of an alleged event etc.

historicize /hɪˈstɒrɪsʌɪz/ *verb trans.* Also **-ise**. M19.
[ORIGIN formed as HISTORICITY + -IZE.]
Make or represent as historical.
■ **historicizer** *noun* M20.

historico- /hɪˈstɒrɪkəʊ/ *combining form.*
[ORIGIN from Greek *historikos* historic, historical: see -O-.]
Forming adjectives and nouns with the sense 'historically —', 'historical (and) —', as ***historico-critical***, ***historico-geographical***, ***historico-philology***.

historied /ˈhɪst(ə)rɪd/ *adjective.* E19.
[ORIGIN from HISTORY *noun*, *verb*: see -ED², -ED¹.]
1 Having a history of a specified kind; recorded or celebrated in history. Chiefly *literary.* E19.
2 Decorated with figures, historiated. Cf. HISTORY *verb* 2. L19.

historiette /ˌhɪstɔːrɪˈɛt/ *noun.* Now *arch.* or *joc.* E18.
[ORIGIN French from Italian †*istorietta* (now *storietta*), from †*istoria*, *storia* story: see -ETTE.]
An anecdote, a short story or history.

historify /hɪˈstɒrɪfʌɪ/ *verb.* L16.
[ORIGIN from HISTORY *noun*: see -FY.]
1 *verb trans.* Relate the history of; record or celebrate in history. L16.
2 *verb intrans.* Write history; utter or write narrative. E17.

historio- /hɪˈstɔːrɪəʊ/ *combining form.*
[ORIGIN Greek, from *historia* HISTORY *noun*: see -O-.]
Forming adjectives with the sense 'historical and —', as ***historio-cultural***, ***historio-patriotic***, ***historiopoeic***, etc.

†**historiograph** *noun.* LME–M18.
[ORIGIN formed as HISTORIO-: see -GRAPH.]
A historiographer.

historiographer /ˌhɪstɔːrɪˈɒgrəfə, -stɒr-/ *noun.* L15.
[ORIGIN Old French & mod. French *historiographe* or late Latin *historiographus* from Greek *historiographos*, from *historia* HISTORY *noun*: see -O-, -GRAPHER.]
1 A writer of history, *esp.* the official historian of a court etc. L15.
2 A person who describes or gives a systematic account of some natural object or objects; a writer of natural history. *arch.* M16.
■ **historiographership** *noun* the position of a historiographer E19.

historiography /ˌhɪstɔːrɪˈɒgrəfi, -stɒr-/ *noun.* M16.
[ORIGIN medieval Latin from Greek *historiographia*, formed as HISTORIO-: see -GRAPHY.]
The writing of history; written history; the study of history-writing.
■ **historioˈgraphic** *adjective* of or pertaining to the writing of history E19. **historioˈgraphical** *adjective* M17. **historioˈgraphically** *adverb* L19.

H

historiology /ˌhɪstɔːrɪˈɒlədʒi, -stɒr-/ *noun*. L16.
[ORIGIN from HISTORY *noun* + -OLOGY.]
The knowledge or study of history.

historize /ˈhɪstərʌɪz/ *verb*. Now *rare* or *obsolete*. Also **-ise**. L16.
[ORIGIN from HISTORY *noun* + -IZE.]
1 *verb trans.* Tell the history of; narrate as history. L16.
2 *verb intrans.* Compose history or narrative; act as a historian. M17.

history /ˈhɪst(ə)ri/ *noun*. LME.
[ORIGIN Latin *historia* from Greek = learning or knowing by enquiry, narrative, history, from *histōr* learned, wise man, ult. from Indo-European base also of WIT *verb*.]
1 A narration of (in later use, esp. professedly true) incidents; a narrative, a story. *obsolete* exc. as passing into sense 2. LME.

T. MEDWIN Some . . pairs of pistols, about most of which there were histories.

2 *spec.* The continuous methodical record of important or public events, esp. those connected with a particular country, individual, etc. LME.

E. WILSON The first volume or two of Michelet's history, dealing with the early races of Gaul.

3 The branch of knowledge that deals with past events; the formal record or study of past events, esp. human affairs. Freq. with specifying word. LME.

E. A. FREEMAN History is the science of man in his character as a political being. D. FRASER The name of Dowding . . was soon to take its place in history. C. HOPE Then you understand that history deceives us.

economic history, ***French history***, ***Marxist history***, ***medieval history***, ***modern history***, ***social history***, etc.
4 Orig., a story represented dramatically. Later, a historical play. LME.

E. DOWDEN Both parts of *Henry IV* consist of a comedy and a history fused together.

5 A story represented pictorially; a historical picture. LME.

Listener A race that . . converted the classical 'history' into a kind of privileged leg show.

6 A systematic account of natural phenomena etc. Now chiefly in ***natural history*** s.v. NATURAL *adjective*. M16.
7 †**a** A series of events (of which the story has been or might be told). L16–L17. ▸**b** The whole train of events connected with a nation, person, thing, etc.; an eventful past career. M17. ▸**c** The aggregate of past events; the course of human affairs. M17.

a A. LOVELL Many Figures in Bass Relief, representing several sacred Histories. **b** D. W. GOODWIN Women who give a history of 'heavy' drinking during pregnancy. J. VIORST People having strikingly similar histories may emerge from them in strikingly different ways. **c** ISAIAH BERLIN History alone—the sum of empirically discovered data—held the key.

– PHRASES & COMB.: ***ancient history***: see ANCIENT *adjective* 1c. **be history** cease to exist or be perceived as relevant to the present. ***case history***: see CASE *noun*[1]. **drum-and-trumpet history** *derog.*: in which undue prominence is given to battles and wars. **go down in history** be recorded in history, be remembered. **history-sheeter** *Indian* a person with a criminal record. **make history** (*a*) influence the course of history; (*b*) do something memorable. ***natural history***: see NATURAL *adjective*. **the rest is history** a concluding statement used to indicate that the events succeeding those already related are so well known that they need not be recounted again.

history /ˈhɪst(ə)ri/ *verb trans.* Long *rare*. LME.
[ORIGIN Old French & mod. French *historier* from medieval Latin *historiare* (in both senses), from Latin *historia* HISTORY *noun*, sense 2 partly through Italian *istoriare*, *-ato*.]
†**1** Relate in a history or narrative. LME–L16.
2 Decorate with figures, make historiated. Usu. in *pass.* Cf. HISTORIED 2. L16.

histrio /ˈhɪstrɪəʊ/ *noun*. Long *arch. rare*. Pl. **-os**. M17.
[ORIGIN Latin: see HISTRION.]
= HISTRION.

histrion /ˈhɪstrɪən/ *noun*. Now *rare*. M16.
[ORIGIN French, or Latin *histrio(n-)* actor.]
An actor.

histrionic /hɪstrɪˈɒnɪk/ *adjective* & *noun*. M17.
[ORIGIN Late Latin *histrionicus*, from Latin *histrio(n-)* actor: see -IC. Cf. HISTRIONICAL (earlier).]
▸**A** *adjective*. **1** Theatrical in character or style, dramatically exaggerated, stagy; hypocritical. M17.

H. JAMES Madame Carré gave one of her histrionic stares, throwing back her head.

2 Of or pertaining to actors or acting; dramatic. M18.

J. SYMONS His histrionic ability might have moved him to become an actor.

▸**B** *noun*. **1** An actor. M19.
2 In *pl.* Theatricals, theatrical art; pretence, insincere actions done merely to impress others. M19.

L. NKOSI The exultant, most extravagant histrionics of the prosecution.

■ **histrionicism** /-sɪz(ə)m/ *noun* histrionic action; histrionism: L19.

histrionical /hɪstrɪˈɒnɪk(ə)l/ *adjective*. M16.
[ORIGIN from (the same root as) HISTRIONIC: see -ICAL.]
1 = HISTRIONIC *adjective* 1. M16.
2 = HISTRIONIC *adjective* 2. L16.

histrionically /hɪstrɪˈɒnɪk(ə)li/ *adverb*. M17.
[ORIGIN from HISTRIONIC *adjective* or HISTRIONICAL: see -ICALLY.]
In a histrionic manner.

histrionism /ˈhɪstrɪənɪz(ə)m/ *noun*. L17.
[ORIGIN from HISTRION or directly from Latin *histrio(n-)*: see -ISM.]
Theatrical practice, action, or style; an instance of this.

hit /hɪt/ *noun*. LME.
[ORIGIN from the verb.]
1 A blow; a shot etc. that hits its target; a stroke in many sports; a collision, an impact. LME. ▸**b** A killing, a robbery. *slang* (orig. *US*). L20.

b D. MACKENZIE I . . called the whole thing off. Someone else must have made the hit.

base hit, ***safe hit***, ***square hit***, etc. ***direct hit***: see DIRECT *adjective*.
2 A stroke of sarcasm or censure (*at*). M17.

A. HELPS In Hudibras there is a sly hit at the sayings of the philosophers.

3 A stroke of good fortune; a lucky chance. M17.
look to one's hits, **mind one's hits** *arch.* look to one's chances.
4 BACKGAMMON. A game; a win in which the loser has already borne off one or more men. Also, the act of hitting a blot (cf. HIT *verb* 11). L17.
5 An abundant crop of fruit. *dial.* L18.
6 A successful attempt; *esp.* a popular success in public entertainment. Freq. *attrib.* E19. ▸**b** A striking or effective expression; a telling phrase. M19. ▸**c** A successful guess. M19. ▸**d** COMPUTING. An instance of identifying an item of data which matches the requirements of a search. M20. ▸**e** COMPUTING. A connection made to a Web server. L20.

J. LE CARRÉ An elderly pianist was playing a medley of hits from the Fifties. D. PIPER As a theatrical spectacular there, it proved almost the smash hit of the century. *Melody Maker* Also, that nice Gary Kemp tells how to write light-operatic hit singles.

be a hit with, **make a hit with** be successful or popular with.
7 A dose of something, esp. a narcotic drug; the action of obtaining or administering such a dose. M20.

Daily Telegraph In San Francisco's Haight-Ashbury district, the hippie Mecca, the price of one 'hit' has dropped. *Southerly* Somebody hands me a joint and I take a hit.

– COMB.: **hit list** *slang* a list of prospective victims esp. of assassination or concerted action; **hitmaker** *colloq.* a successful singer or producer of popular music; **hit man** *slang* a hired assassin; **hit-mark** *slang* (orig. *US*) the scar from an injection of a drug, esp. a narcotic drug; **hit parade** *colloq.* a list of the best-selling records of popular music; **hit squad** a group of assassins or kidnappers.

†**hit** *pers. pronoun* see IT *pers. pronoun*.

hit /hɪt/ *verb*. Infl. **-tt-**. Pa. t. & pple **hit**. LOE.
[ORIGIN Old Norse *hitta* light upon, meet with (Swedish *hitta*, Danish *hitte*): ult. origin unknown.]
▸**I** **1** *verb trans.* Come upon, light on, meet with, find. Now freq. (*colloq.*, esp. *N. Amer.*), go to, start or set out on. LOE.

J. WAIN It was still night when I hit the outskirts of London. M. AMIS I hit a topless bar on Forty-Fourth. *New Yorker* You hit forty and have a couple of kids and a mortgage.

2 *verb intrans.* Foll. by *on*, *upon*: come on, light on, meet with, find, esp. by chance. ME.

A. J. P. TAYLOR By chance I had hit on a good subject.

3 *verb intrans.* Attain a desired object, succeed; work out as intended. *obsolete* exc. *dial.* LME. ▸**b** Foll. by *off*: produce successfully; succeed in attaining or discovering. L17.

SHAKES. *Merch. V.* Hath all his ventures fail'd? What, not one hit? **b** M. A. KELTY You need to be rather au fait at hitting off a sonnet. *Sporting Magazine* The hounds again hit off the scent.

4 *verb trans.* Suit, fit, be agreeable to. L16. ▸†**b** *verb intrans.* Coincide or agree *with*. E17–E18. ▸**c** *verb intrans.* Agree together. *obsolete* exc. *dial.* E17.

R. W. CHURCH In the hope . . of hitting her taste on some lucky occasion. **b** DEFOE The Scheme hit so exactly with my Temper. **c** T. NEVILE Believe me, contraries will never hit.

5 *verb trans.* Represent or imitate exactly. Freq. foll. by *off*. E17.

J. L. MOTLEY One of the most difficult things in painting is to hit the exact colour.

▸**II** **6** *verb intrans.* Give or direct a blow or blows; strike *at* or *out*. ME. ▸**b** *verb trans.* In various sports, strike (a ball etc.) with a bat, stick, etc., score (a goal) or make (a pass) by so doing; CRICKET score (a number of runs) by batting (foll. by *off*, *up*); strike a ball from (the bowler). M19.

E. WELTY Fay struck out with her hands, hitting at Major Bullock and Mr. Pitts and Sis.

7 *verb trans.* Strike (a person or thing) with a blow or missile; deliver (a blow or stroke); strike (a person etc. a blow etc.). ME. ▸**b** Knock (a part of the body) *on* or *against* something. M17. ▸**c** Kill, attack, rob. *slang* (orig. *US*). M20.

DAY LEWIS I hit him a too effective blow during one of our rough-and-tumbles. H. KISSINGER Our bombing had accidentally hit four Soviet merchant ships. E. WELTY He reached out and without any warning hit Max in the jaw with his fist. **b** P. F. BOLLER The man fell, . . hit his head against the bar and was knocked unconscious. **c** D. E. WESTLAKE If they're cops, maybe it's not . . a good idea to have them hit.

8 *verb trans.* & *intrans.* Of a moving object: strike against or *against*, collide (with), crash (into). LME.

B. HARRIS When we endeavour to shun one . . Sand-bank, we hit against another. R. INGALLS He didn't come back because he had been hit by a car. *fig.*: TENNYSON The sun, that now . . hit the Northern hills.

9 *verb trans.* Cast, throw. *obsolete* exc. *dial.* LME.
10 *verb trans.* & *intrans. fig.* Affect the feelings, conscience, etc., of (a person), esp. deeply or painfully; hurt. LME.

W. WHARTON Inflation's really hit hard here. H. BASCOM I understand how Uncle Joel's death must have hit you.

11 *verb trans.* BACKGAMMON. Take (an opponent's unguarded piece) temporarily out of play by landing one's own piece on the same point, freq. in ***hit a blot*** (see BLOT *noun*[2]); *fig.* discover a weak point. L16.
12 *verb trans.* & *intrans.* with (*out*) *at*. Criticize, ridicule. M19.

Daily Express He hit out at pay deals which were pushing up wages.

13 *verb trans.* Occur forcefully to (a person); affect in a particular way; have an impact on. L19.

W. GASS Like something you see once and it hits you so hard you never forget it. W. SOYINKA I'm asking you what it sounded like. How did the words hit you?

14 *verb trans.* Use (to excess), indulge in. Chiefly in phrs. below. *colloq.* (chiefly *US*). L19.

Daily Telegraph The first thing I do is hit the tub.

15 *verb trans.* Ask (a person) for; beg. Also foll. by *up*. *N. Amer.* & *NZ slang*. E20.

R. INGALLS They may be planning to hit us for a little loan.

16 *verb trans.* & *intrans.* Give a drug, esp. a narcotic drug, or an alcoholic drink to (a person). M20.

A. TYLER 'Hit me again,' the robber told the bartender, holding out his glass.

17 *verb intrans.* Foll. by *on*: make sexual advances towards. *N. Amer. colloq.* M20. ▸**b** Attempt to get something, esp. money, from (someone). L20.

J. MCINERNEY As soon as Skip clears out this guy . . sits down and starts hitting on me.

▸**III** **18** *verb trans.* Set *out* for; set off in a particular direction. Now chiefly *US*. LME.
– PHRASES, & WITH ADVERBS IN SPECIALIZED SENSES: ***hard hit***: see HARD *adverb*. ***hit a blot***: see BLOT *noun*[2]. **hit back** retaliate. **hit below the belt** (*a*) esp. in BOXING, give (a person) a foul blow; (*b*) *fig.* treat or behave unfairly. ***hit for six***: see SIX *noun* 4. **hit home** make a salutary impression. **hit in** POLO hit the ball into the field of play. **hit it** (*a*) come to exactly the right place, point, or conclusion; (*b*) (now *rare*) agree or be congenial, get on; (*c*) ***hit it off***, agree or be congenial, get on (*with*, *together*). ***hit one in the eye***: see EYE *noun*. **hit the booze**, **hit the bottle**, etc., drink to excess. ***hit the breeze***: see BREEZE *noun*[2]. **hit the bricks** *US slang* go on strike. ***hit the ceiling***: see CEILING *noun*. **hit the deck** *colloq.* (*a*) go to bed; (*b*) land an aircraft; (*c*) fall to the ground; (*d*) get out of bed, get up. ***hit the gong***: see GONG *noun* 3. **hit the ground running** start something (esp. when newly appointed or elected) and proceed at a fast pace with enthusiasm. **hit the hay** *colloq.* go to bed. ***hit the headlines***: see HEADLINE 3b. **hit the jackpot** be remarkably lucky, esp. in winning a large prize. **hit the nail on the head** state the truth exactly. **hit the pipe** *US slang* smoke opium. **hit the road** *slang* (chiefly *US*) set off, depart. ***hit the roof***: see ROOF *noun*. ***hit the sack***: see SACK *noun*[1] 1c. ***hit the silk***: see SILK *noun* 6. **hit the trail** *slang* (chiefly *US*) = ***hit the road*** above. **hit wicket** CRICKET be out by striking the wicket with the bat etc. in playing a stroke. **not know what hit one**, **wonder what hit one** be killed instantly, be knocked out or stunned; *fig.* be amazed.
– COMB.: **hit-and-miss** *adjective* (*a*) aimed or done carelessly, at random, or haphazardly; (*b*) designating ventilators etc. in which the flow of air etc. is controlled by the coincidence or otherwise of apertures in two plates which can move relative to each other; **hit-and-run** *adjective* (*a*) designating a motor accident in which the vehicle involved does not stop, or a driver, vehicle, victim, etc., involved in such an accident; (*b*) designating an attack or attacker using swift action followed by immediate withdrawal; (*c*) BASEBALL with the departure of a runner from his or her base as soon as the pitcher begins to throw; **hit-in** POLO the hitting of the ball into the field of play; **hit-or-miss** *adjective* = ***hit-and-miss*** above. **hit-out** (*a*) HOCKEY a pass awarded to a defending team to restart play after the ball has been sent over the goal line (without a goal being scored) by the attacking team; (*b*) *Austral.* & *NZ slang* a brisk gallop.
■ **hitter** *noun* one who hits or strikes, as in boxing, cricket, baseball, etc. E19.

hitch /hɪtʃ/ *noun*. M17.
[ORIGIN from HITCH *verb*.]
1 A short abrupt movement, pull, or push; a jerk. M17.
2 MINING. A slight fault or dislocation in strata. M17.
3 A limp, a hobble; a fault in a horse's gait. M17. ▸**b** The act of hopping; a hop. *Scot.* & *dial.* L18.
4 An accidental or temporary stoppage; an interruption, an impediment. M18.

E. WAUGH The service passed off without a hitch. L. MACNEICE Loath to meet his fate, he cowers and prays For some last-minute hitch.

technical hitch: see TECHNICAL *adjective*.

5 Any of various (specified) kinds of noose or knot used to fasten one thing temporarily to another. (Earliest in CLOVE HITCH.) **M18.** ▸**b** A contrivance for fastening something; a catch. **L19.**

half hitch *NAUTICAL* a knot formed by passing the end of a rope round its standing part and then through the bight.

6 The action of catching or fastening in a temporary way. **E19.** ▸**b** A method of harnessing a horse or team; a vehicle with its horse(s). *N. Amer.* **L19.**

b *Horse International* Each pair of horses in the eight-horse hitch has a specific job.

7 A period of service (as in the armed forces); a spell, a term. *slang* (chiefly *N. Amer.*). **M19.**

J. KEROUAC Another hitch in prison and you'll be put away for life.

8 = HITCHHIKE *noun*. *colloq.* **M20.**

J. DOS PASSOS Getting hitches all over the place on graintrucks.

– COMB.: **hitch and kick**, **hitch-kick** (*a*) *GYMNASTICS* a scissor jump landing on the take-off foot; (*b*) *ATHLETICS* a style of long jump in which the jumper makes two or more strides in the air before landing feet together.

hitch /hɪtʃ/ *verb*. **ME.**

[ORIGIN Unknown. Cf. HOTCH *verb*.]

1 *verb trans.* Move or lift *up* with a jerk; shift a little or aside. **ME.** ▸**b** *verb intrans.* Move jerkily; shift one's position a little. Formerly also, jerk the body up and down. **E16.** ▸**c** *verb trans.* & *intrans. fig.* Move into some position; *spec.* insert or interpolate (a passage etc.) in a literary work, esp. in order to expose or ridicule. Also foll. by *in*, *into*. *arch.* **M18.**

T. SHARPE Sir Godber hitched his chair forward. K. WILLIAMS I hitched up my sodden trousers and sat down. **b** E. WELTY 'I can see him coming . . ,' said Aunt Nanny, hitching forward in her rocker. **c** J. ADAMS If . . the letter should be caught and hitched into a newspaper.

2 *verb intrans.* Limp, hobble. Also (*Scot.* & *dial.*), hop. **E16.** ▸**b** Of a horse: strike the feet together in going; brush. **L17.**

fig.: *Examiner* A hitching verse or hobbling rhyme.

3 *verb intrans.* Catch on something; become caught or stopped by an obstruction. **L16.**

W. IRVING The lariat hitched on one of his ears, and he shook it off. *fig.*: SIR W. SCOTT Despatched all my sheriff processes, save one, which hitches for want of some papers.

4 *verb trans.* Catch as with a noose, loop, or hook; fasten, esp. temporarily and against force acting in one direction. **E17.**

R. OWEN Sometimes the crab hitches one of its claws into some crack or fissure. Z. GREY Several cowboy broncos stood hitched to a railing.

5 a *verb intrans.* Foll. by *up*: harness a draught animal or team to a vehicle. **E19.** ▸**b** *verb trans.* Harness (a draught animal or team, a vehicle). Foll. by *up*. **M19.**

a E. E. HALE He would hitch up at once and drive over to Elyria. *fig.*: J. O'FAOLAIN You never knew what class of customer Michael would hitch up with. **b** W. CATHER Old Ivar was hitching the horses to the wagon.

6 *verb trans.* & *intrans.* Obtain (a lift, a ride) in or on (a vehicle); travel by this means, hitchhike. **L19.**

T. PYNCHON Let me hitch a ride with you guys. N. GORDIMER Don't send an air ticket or the train fare. I'll hitch.

– PHRASES: **get hitched** (**up**) *colloq.* get married **hitch horses** (**together**) *US colloq.* get on well together, act in harmony. **hitch one's wagon to a star** make use of powers higher than one's own.

– COMB.: **hitching post**, **hitching rail** a fixed post, rail, for tethering a horse; **hitch pin**: to which the fixed end of a piano string is fastened.

■ **hitcher** *noun* (*a*) a person who or thing which hitches one thing to another; (*b*) a hitchhiker: **M17.**

Hitchcock /ˈhɪtʃkɒk/ *adjective*. **E19.**

[ORIGIN L. H. *Hitchcock* (1795–1852), Amer. furniture manufacturer.]

Designating a type of wooden chair, typically painted with stencilled decoration, as made in Hitchcock's factory at Barkhamsted, Connecticut.

Hitchcockian /hɪtʃˈkɒkɪən/ *adjective*. **M20.**

[ORIGIN from *Hitchcock* (see below) + -IAN.]

Characteristic of or resembling Sir Alfred Hitchcock, British director of suspense films (1899–1980), or his work.

hitchhike /ˈhɪtʃhʌɪk/ *verb* & *noun*. Orig. *US*. Also **hitch-hike**. **E20.**

[ORIGIN from HITCH *verb* + HIKE *verb*.]

▸ **A** *verb intrans.* Travel, obtain transport, by begging a free ride in a passing vehicle. **E20.**

J. GATHORNE-HARDY I would . . hitch-hike and get a lift with someone I'd never seen before.

▸ **B** *noun*. A journey made by hitchhiking. **E20.**

■ **hitchhiker** *noun* **E20.**

hithe /hʌɪð/ *noun*. Long *obsolete* exc. *hist.* & in place names. Also **hythe**.

[ORIGIN Old English *hȳþ*, Old Saxon *hūþ*, Middle Low German *-hude* (in place names), of unknown origin.]

A port, a haven, *esp.* a small landing place in a river.

hither /ˈhɪðə/ *adverb*, *adjective*, & *verb*. Chiefly *literary*.

[ORIGIN Old English *hider*, corresp. to Old Norse *heðra* here, hither, Gothic *hidrē*, from Germanic demonstr. base of HE *adjective*, HENCE *adverb*, HERE *adverb*, + suffix appearing in Latin *citra* on this side. Cf. THITHER, WHITHER *adverb* etc.]

▸ **A** *adverb*. **1** To or towards this place, here. **OE.** ▸**b** To or on this side. *rare*. **M19.**

R. CROWLEY Come hither unto me. T. GRAY Till my return hither yesterday.

come-hither: see COME *verb*. **hither and thither**, **hither and yon** this way and that, here and there, to and fro.

†**2** Up to this point (of time, a discourse, etc.); thus far, hitherto. **LME–E17.**

†**3** To this end or result; to this subject or category. **M16–L17.**

▸ **B** *adjective*. Situated on this side; the nearer (of two). **ME.**

– COMB.: **hitherside** this side, the nearer side.

▸ **C** *verb intrans.* Come hither. Chiefly in ***hither and thither***, go to and fro. **M19.**

■ **hithermost** *adjective* nearest **M16.**

hitherto /hɪðəˈtuː, ˈhɪðətuː/ *adverb* & *adjective*. **ME.**

[ORIGIN from HITHER *adverb* + TO *preposition*.]

▸ **A** *adverb*. **1** Up to this time, until now, as yet. **ME.**

HOBBES Except the vulgar be better taught than they have hetherto been. S. MORLEY Evening sing-songs produced some hitherto hidden talents. *Sunday (Kolkata)* The minimum time between . . issues would now be 24 months against 36 months hitherto.

2 Up to this point (in space, a discourse, writing, etc.); thus far. *arch.* **ME.**

S. JOHNSON Hitherto shall ye come and no further.

†**3** To this end or purpose; to this class or subject. **E–M17.**

▸ **B** *adjective*. Existing at or until this time. *rare*. **L18.**

hitherward /ˈhɪðəwəd/ *adverb*. *arch.* **LOE.**

[ORIGIN from HITHER + -WARD.]

1 Towards this place, in this direction, hither. **LOE.** ▸**b** On this side (*of*). **M19.**

†**2** Up to this time, until now. **ME–M16.**

■ Also **hitherwards** *adverb* **ME.**

Hitler /ˈhɪtlə/ *noun*. **M20.**

[ORIGIN Adolf *Hitler* (1889–1945), leader of the Nazi Party and Chancellor of the German Reich. Cf. FÜHRER.]

1 Used *attrib.* and in *possess.* with ref. to Hitler's rule or personal characteristics. **M20.**

Hitler moustache a small square moustache as worn by Hitler. **Hitler salute** = *Nazi salute* s.v. NAZI *adjective*. **Hitler's war** the Second World War. **Hitler Youth** (**Movement**) the young persons' organization of the Nazi party, membership of which was compulsory under the Third Reich.

2 A tyrannical ruler or leader; a dictatorial person (freq. in ***little Hitler***). **M20.**

■ **Hitlerian** /hɪtˈlɪərɪən/ *adjective* of, pertaining to, or characteristic of Hitler **M20.** **Hitlerism** *noun* the political principles or policy of the Nazi party in Germany **M20.** **Hitlerist** *noun* & *adjective* (*a*) *noun* a follower of Hitler; (*b*) *adjective* resembling Hitler or his followers: **M20.** **Hitleˈristic** *adjective* somewhat Hitlerist **M20.** **Hitlerite** *noun* & *adjective* = HITLERIST **M20.**

Hittite /ˈhɪtʌɪt/ *noun* & *adjective*. **M16.**

[ORIGIN from Hebrew *Ḥittī(m*, Hittite *Ḫatti* + -ITE[1].]

▸ **A** *noun*. **1** In biblical use, a member of a Canaanite or Syrian tribe, perhaps a part of sense 2. **M16.**

2 A member of a powerful ancient (non-Semitic) people of Asia Minor or Syria, or of their subject peoples. **L19.** ▸**b** The Indo-European language of this people. **L19.**

▸ **B** *adjective*. Of or pertaining to the Hittites or their language. **L19.**

■ **Hittiˈtologist** *noun* an expert in or student of Hittite philology, archaeology, or history **M20.** **Hittiˈtology** *noun* the branch of knowledge that deals with Hittite philology, archaeology, or history **M20.**

hitty-missy /hɪtɪˈmɪsi/ *adverb* & *adjective*. Now *rare*. **M16.**

[ORIGIN Perh. from *hit I, miss I*: cf. WILLY-NILLY.]

▸ **A** *adverb*. Hit or miss, haphazardly, at random. **M16.**

▸ **B** *adjective*. Random, haphazard. **L19.**

HIV *abbreviation*.

Human immunodeficiency virus (the retrovirus which causes Aids).

HIV-positive *adjective* having had a positive result in a blood test for HIV.

hive /hʌɪv/ *noun*.

[ORIGIN Old English *hȳf* from Germanic base of Old Norse *húfr* ship's hull: cf. Latin *cupa* barrel.]

▸ **I 1** An artificial structure to house a colony of bees. Also ***beehive***. **OE.** ▸**b** *fig.* A storehouse of sweet things. **M17.**

T. HOOPER Bees have been kept . . in earthenware pipes, straw skeps, wooden boxes and all types of hive. **b** G. HERBERT Must he leave that nest, that hive of sweetnesse.

2 Something resembling this structure in (esp. domed) shape or design. **M16.**

3 A structure to house any gregarious livestock. *rare*. **M17.**

4 A place swarming with busy occupants. **M17.** ▸**b** A place from which multitudes of people emerge. **L18.**

J. HIGGINS The place was a hive of activity, workmen everywhere. **b** J. PRIESTLEY They no longer send forth those swarms of people . . which made them be called the northern hive.

▸ **II 5** Bees in a hive collectively. **LME.**

SHAKES. *2 Hen. VI* The commons, like an angry hive of bees That want their leader, scatter up and down.

6 A swarm of people, a multitude. **M19.**

hive /hʌɪv/ *verb*. **LME.**

[ORIGIN from the noun.]

1 *verb trans.* House (bees) in a hive; place (a swarm) in a hive. **LME.** ▸**b** Give shelter to, house snugly. **L16.**

Beekeeping Smoke is used to subdue, . . bees . . when taking and hiving a swarm. **b** C. BRASCH I think of you Hived in another cell of this same House of pain and healing.

2 *verb intrans.* Enter a hive; live together as bees in a hive. **LME.**

H. VAUGHAN Where bees at night get home and hive. POPE We are . . forc'd to . . get into warmer houses and hive together in cities.

3 *verb trans.* Hoard or store *up*, as honey in a hive. **L16.**

BYRON And hiving wisdom with each studious year.

4 a *verb intrans.* Foll. by *off*: swarm off like bees; break away or separate from a group. **M19.** ▸**b** *verb trans.* Foll. by *off*: remove from a larger unit or group; form into or assign (work) to a subsidiary department or company; denationalize or privatize (an industry etc.). **M20.**

a *Nature* Experimental psychology . . has hived off from physiology. **b** *Sunday Mail (Brisbane)* The ginger beer plant was preserved, and new ones could be hived off at this stage. *Fremdsprachen* The Arts Council itself cannot be hived off like British Telecommunications.

hives /hʌɪvz/ *noun* (treated as *sing.* or *pl.*). Orig. *Scot.* **E16.**

[ORIGIN Unknown.]

MEDICINE. Orig., any of various conditions, esp. of children, characterized by a rash. Now *spec.* urticaria.

hiya /ˈhʌɪjə/ *interjection*. *colloq.* Also **hi-ya**, **hiyah**. **M20.**

[ORIGIN App. contr. of *how are you*, infl. by HI *interjection* 2.]

As a word of greeting: hello.

R. CHANDLER Hiya, babe. Long time no see.

Hizbollah, **Hizbullah** *nouns* vars. of HEZBOLLAH.

Hizen /hiːˈzɛn/ *noun* & *adjective*. **L19.**

[ORIGIN A former province in the north-west of Kyushu in Japan.]

(Designating) a class of high-quality porcelains characterized by rich decoration and delicate colouring, and including Hirado, Imari, and Nabeshima ware.

hizz /hɪz/ *verb intrans.* Now *rare*. **L16.**

[ORIGIN Imit.: cf. HISS *verb*.]

= HISS *verb*.

HK *abbreviation*.

1 Hong Kong.

2 House of Keys.

HL *abbreviation*[1].

House of Lords.

hl *abbreviation*[2].

Hectolitre(s).

HM *abbreviation*[1].

1 Headmaster.

2 Headmistress.

3 Heavy metal (music).

4 Her Majesty('s), His Majesty('s).

hm *abbreviation*[2].

Hectometre(s).

HMAS *abbreviation*.

Her, His, Majesty's Australian Ship.

HMCS *abbreviation*.

Her, His, Majesty's Canadian Ship.

HMG *abbreviation*.

Her, His, Majesty's Government.

HMI *abbreviation*.

Her, His, Majesty's Inspector (of Schools).

HMNZS *abbreviation*.

Her, His, Majesty's New Zealand Ship.

HMO *abbreviation*. Chiefly *US*.

Health Maintenance Organization.

Hmong /hmɒŋ/ *noun* & *adjective*. **M20.**

[ORIGIN Hmong.]

▸ **A** *noun*. Pl. same. A member of a people of the mountains of southern China and Indo-China; the language of this people. Also called ***Miao***. **L20.**

▸ **B** *adjective*. Of or pertaining to this people or their language. **L20.**

HMS *abbreviation*.

Her, His, Majesty's Ship.

HMSO *abbreviation.*
Her, His, Majesty's Stationery Office.

HMV *abbreviation.*
His Master's Voice (proprietary name).

HNC *abbreviation.*
Higher National Certificate.

HND *abbreviation.*
Higher National Diploma.

Ho *symbol.*
CHEMISTRY. Holmium.

ho /həʊ/ *noun*[1]. Pl. **hos**. LME.
[ORIGIN from HO *interjection*[1].]
A cry of 'ho'.

ho /həʊ/ *noun*[2]. Now *rare*. Pl. **hos**. LME.
[ORIGIN from HO *interjection*[2].]
(A) halt; (a) pause; (a) limit.

SWIFT When your tongue runs, there's no ho with you.

Ho /həʊ/ *noun*[3] *& adjective*. Pl. of noun **Hos**. M19.
[ORIGIN Ho, contr. of *horo* man.]
Of or pertaining to, a member of, a people of the state of Bihar in India; (of) the language of this people, one of the principal dialects of central India, belonging to the Kolarian group.

ho /həʊ/ *noun*[4]. *US black English, derog.* Also **hoe**. M20.
[ORIGIN Alt. of WHORE.]
A prostitute. Also, (as a term of abuse) a sexually promiscuous woman; *gen.* a woman. M20.

ho /həʊ/ *interjection*[1]. See also HO HO. ME.
[ORIGIN Natural exclam. Cf. HA *interjection*, HOW *interjection*[1], etc.]
1 Expr. surprise, admiration, triumph, or derision. ME.

Times Lit. Suppl. If it be philistine to prefer gourmet dishes . . to a poetry reading . . , then ho for Philistia!

2 Commanding or attempting to attract attention. LME. ▸**b** Used after the name of a place or thing to which attention is called, esp. as a destination. L16.

LD MACAULAY Ho! gunners, fire a loud salute. **b** C. KINGSLEY Thou too shalt forth, and westward ho, beyond thy wildest dreams. ALAN BENNETT They are rubbish, waste, junk . . . Dustbin ho!

3 Used as the 2nd elem. of other interjections, as ***heave-ho***, ***heigh-ho***, ***what ho***, etc. LME.
■ **ho-de-ho** /həʊdɪˈhəʊ/ *interjection* responding to the greeting HI-DE-HI M20.

ho /həʊ/ *interjection*[2]. Now *rare*. LME.
[ORIGIN Old French = halt! stop! Cf. WHOA.]
Ordering or requesting a person or animal to stop.
wo ho, ***wo ho ho***, ***wo ha ho***: see WO *interjection* 1.

ho. *abbreviation.*
House.

Hoabinhian /həʊəˈbɪnɪən/ *adjective & noun*. M20.
[ORIGIN from *Hoabinh* a village in Vietnam where the first major site was found + -IAN.]
(Designating or pertaining to) a Mesolithic and Neolithic culture of parts of SE Asia, characterized by stone tools.

hoactzin *noun* var. of HOATZIN.

hoagie /ˈhəʊgi/ *noun*. *N. Amer.* M20.
[ORIGIN Unknown.]
A long loaf or roll filled with meat, cheese, salad, etc.

hoar /hɔː/ *adjective, noun, & verb*.
[ORIGIN Old English *hār* = Old Saxon, Old High German *hēr* old, venerable (German *hehr* august, stately, sacred), Old Norse *hárr* hoary, old from Germanic, from Indo-European stem meaning 'shine'.]
▸ **A** *adjective*. **1** Grey-haired or (of a thing) grey with age; ancient, venerable. OE.

R. JEFFERIES A very old hare, quite hoar with age. H. C. ADAMS To trace legends back to yet more hoar antiquity.

2 Esp. of hair, or of a thing covered with frost: grey, greyish-white. OE.

COLERIDGE Whose beard with age is hoar. W. DE LA MARE A north-ern wind had frozen the grass; its blades were hoar with crystal rime.

3 Of a tree or wood: grey from absence of foliage or because covered in lichen. Long *arch. & poet.* ME.
4 Grey with mould; mouldy, musty. *obsolete* exc. *dial.* LME.
– COMB.: **hoar frost** frozen (in METEOROLOGY, distinctly crystalline) water vapour deposited in clear still weather on grass etc.; **hoarhead** *arch.* a hoary head; an old or grey-haired person; **hoar-headed** *adjective* grey-haired; **hoarstone** an ancient stone, esp. as marking a boundary.
▸ **B** *noun*. †**1** A grey-haired person. OE–ME.
2 Hoariness; hoary appearance; hoar frost. LME.
▸ †**C** *verb trans. & intrans.* Make or become hoary. OE–M18.

hoard /hɔːd/ *noun*[1].
[ORIGIN Old English *hord* = Old Saxon *hord*, *horþ* treasure, secret place, Old High German *hort*, Old Norse *hodd*, Gothic *huzd*, from Germanic.]
1 A collection, esp. of valuable items, hidden or stored for preservation or future use; a stock, a store, esp. of money; an amassed stock of facts etc. OE.

D. WILSON A large hoard of coins was discovered. WORDSWORTH A hoard of grievances.

2 A place in which items are hoarded; a hiding place; a treasury. *obsolete* exc. *hist.* ME.

hoard /hɔːd/ *noun*[2]. Now *rare* or *obsolete*. M18.
[ORIGIN Prob. ult. from Anglo-Norman *hourdis*, *hurdis* (taken as pl.) from Old French *hourd*, *hort* (from Frankish, = Old High German *hurt* HURDLE *noun*) + *-is* from Latin *-itius* (see -ICE[1]).]
= HOARDING *noun*[2].

hoard /hɔːd/ *verb*. OE.
[ORIGIN from HOARD *noun*[1].]
1 *verb trans.* Collect and hide or store (esp. valuable items) for preservation, security, or future use; treasure *up* (esp. money); store in the mind etc. OE.

D. BOGARDE She hoards everything. Envelopes, string, elastic bands and so on. *fig.*: BURKE Revenge will be smothered and hoarded.

2 *verb intrans.* Hoard things. OE.

TENNYSON A savage race, That hoard, and sleep, and feed, and know not me.

■ **hoarder** *noun* †(**a**) the keeper of a hoard, a treasurer; (**b**) a person who hoards (esp. money): OE.

hoarding /ˈhɔːdɪŋ/ *noun*[1]. L16.
[ORIGIN from HOARD *verb* + -ING[1].]
1 The action of HOARD *verb*. L16.
2 In *pl.* Things hoarded. E18.

hoarding /ˈhɔːdɪŋ/ *noun*[2]. E19.
[ORIGIN from HOARD *noun*[2] + -ING[1].]
A temporary fence (of boards) round a building during erection or repair, often used for displaying advertisements or notices; a structure for displaying advertisements.

hoarse /hɔːs/ *adjective & adverb*.
[ORIGIN Old English *hās* = Old Frisian *hās*, Middle Low German *hēs*, *hēsch* (Dutch *heesch*), Old High German *heis(i*, Middle & mod. High German *heiser*, from Germanic: ult. origin unknown. Superseded in Middle English by forms with *-r-* from Old Norse cognate.]
▸ **A** *adjective*. (Of a voice or (chiefly *poet.*) other sound) rough and deep-sounding, husky, croaking, harsh; having such a voice or sound. OE.

DICKENS Cloisterham, with its hoarse cathedral bell. OUIDA The hoarse sound of the sea surging amongst the rocks. L. M. MONTGOMERY She lay . . feverish and restless, while her hoarse breathing could be heard all over the house. I. COMPTON-BURNETT I have been calling until I am hoarse. R. OWEN He grins, and drinks wine to soothe a voice hoarse from poetry readings.

▸ **B** *adverb*. Hoarsely. *rare*. E18.
■ **hoarsely** *adverb* LME. **hoarseness** *noun* OE.

hoarse /hɔːs/ *verb intrans. & trans. obsolete* exc. *dial.* OE.
[ORIGIN from the adjective.]
Hoarsen. Latterly only foll. by *up*.

hoarsen /ˈhɔːs(ə)n/ *verb*. M18.
[ORIGIN from HOARSE *adjective* + -EN[5].]
1 *verb trans.* Make hoarse. M18.
2 *verb intrans.* Be or become hoarse. L18.

hoary /ˈhɔːri/ *adjective*. LME.
[ORIGIN from HOAR *adjective* or *noun* + -Y[1].]
1 (Of hair) grey or white with age; grey-haired; ancient, venerable. Also, old and trite. LME.

Independent 'Being part of a team' is a hoary old cliché.

2 Grey, greyish-white, esp. with frost. L15.
†**3** Mouldy, musty. M16–L17.
4 BOTANY & ZOOLOGY. Covered with short dense white or whitish hairs. L16.
hoary marmot a large stocky greyish-brown marmot, *Marmota caligata*, of mountains in north-western N. America (also called ***siffleur***, ***whistler***). ***hoary*** PUCCOON.
■ **hoariness** *noun* LME.

hoast /həʊst/ *noun & verb*. Chiefly *Scot. & N. English*. ME.
[ORIGIN Old Norse *hóste* = Middle Low German *hōste*, Middle Dutch *hoeste*, Old High German *huosto* (German *Husten*), from Germanic.]
▸ **A** *noun*. A cough. ME.
▸ **B** *verb*. **1** *verb intrans.* Cough. LME.
2 *verb trans.* Cough *up* or *out*. E16.

Hoastman /ˈhəʊstmən/ *noun*. *local*. Pl. **-men**. E16.
[ORIGIN from HOST *noun*[2] II + MAN *noun*.]
Orig., a member of a guild in Newcastle upon Tyne who had the duty of receiving visiting merchants. Later, a member of a body controlling the sale of coal. Now, a member of the premier civic corporation.

hoatzin /həʊˈatsɪn/ *noun*. Also (earlier) **hoactzin** /-kt-/. M17.
[ORIGIN Amer. Spanish from Nahuatl *uatzin*, prob. imit.]
A large crested bird of S. American rainforests, *Opisthocomus hoazin*, of uncertain affinities, the young of which climb by means of claws on the wings.

hoax /həʊks/ *verb & noun*. L18.
[ORIGIN Prob. contr. of HOCUS *verb*.]
▸ **A** *verb*. **1** *verb trans.* Deceive by way of a joke, play a trick or joke on. L18.
2 *verb intrans.* Perpetrate a hoax. E19.
▸ **B** *noun*. A mischievous or humorous deception; a trick, a joke. E19.

Sunday Express There was also a hoax involving a tailor's dummy dressed as a Russian officer. *attrib.*: R. INGALLS There had been a hoax call about a bomb at some large public building.

■ **hoaxer** *noun* E19.

hob /hɒb/ *noun*[1]. LME.
[ORIGIN from *Hob* by-form of *Rob*, abbreviation of the names *Robert*, *Robin*: cf. HICK *noun*[1], HOBBY *noun*[1], HODGE *noun*.]
1 (Also **H-**.) (A name for) a country fellow, a rustic. Now *dial.* LME.
2 A hobgoblin, a sprite; *spec.* (also **H-**) Robin Goodfellow. Now *rare*. LME.
3 A male ferret. Also ***hob ferret***. L17.
– PHRASES: **play hob**, **raise hob** (chiefly *US*) cause mischief.

hob /hɒb/ *noun*[2]. L16.
[ORIGIN Alt. of HUB *noun*[1].]
▸ **I** **1** A peg or pin used as a mark or target in games, esp. quoits. Also, a game using these. L16.
2 = HOBNAIL *noun* 1. L17.
3 The shoe of a sledge. L18.
4 A (rotating) cutting tool used for cutting gears, worm-wheels, etc. Also, a pattern for making a mould or die in cold metal. L19.
▸ **II** **5** A side casing of a fireplace, having a surface level with the top of the grate. Cf. earlier HUB *noun*[1] 1. L17.
6 The top surface of a cooker or a separate cooking surface equipped with hotplates or burners. Also, a level support or set of supports on which a pan etc. is rested over a hotplate or burner on a cooker. M20.

hob /hɒb/ *verb*[1] *intrans.* Infl. **-bb-**. E17.
[ORIGIN formed as HOB *adverb & noun*[3].]
†**1** 3 *sing. pres. subjunct.* Give (in **hob, nob**, give or take). *rare* (Shakes.). Only in E17.
2 ***hob and nob***, ***hob or nob***: ▸**a** = HOBNOB *verb* 1. M18. ▸**b** = HOBNOB *verb* 2. E19.

hob /hɒb/ *verb*[2] *trans.* Infl. **-bb-**. M19.
[ORIGIN from HOB *noun*[2].]
1 Equip with hobnails. M19.
2 Cut or form by means of a hob (HOB *noun*[2] 4). L19.

hob /hɒb/ *adverb & noun*[3]. M17.
[ORIGIN Var. of HAB.]
1 See HOB-NOB *adverb*. M17.
2 ***hob and nob***, ***hob or nob***: expr. good wishes to another person before drinking. ***drink hob and nob***, ***drink hob or nob***, drink to each other alternately, with clinking of glasses. *arch.* M18.
– COMB.: **hob-and-nob** *adjective* (*arch.*) companionable, on intimate terms; **hob-or-nob** *arch.* = HOB-NOB *noun* 2.

hobbadehoy *noun* var. of HOBBLEDEHOY.

Hobbesian /ˈhɒbzɪən/ *adjective*. L18.
[ORIGIN from *Hobbes* (see below) + -IAN.]
Of or pertaining to the English political philosopher Thomas Hobbes (1588–1679) or his philosophy.

†**Hobbian** *adjective & noun*. L17.
[ORIGIN from *Hobb(es* (see HOBBESIAN) + -IAN.]
▸ **A** *adjective*. = HOBBESIAN. Only in L17.
▸ **B** *noun*. = HOBBIST *noun*. L17–M19.
■ †**Hobbianism** *noun* = HOBBISM M17–E18.

Hobbism /ˈhɒbɪz(ə)m/ *noun*. L17.
[ORIGIN from *Hobb(es* (see HOBBESIAN) + -ISM.]
The philosophy or principles of Thomas Hobbes.
■ **Hobbist** *noun & adjective* (**a**) *noun* an advocate or follower of Hobbes's philosophy; (**b**) *adjective* = HOBBESIAN: L17.

hobbit /ˈhɒbɪt/ *noun*. M20.
[ORIGIN Invented word: said by Tolkien to mean 'hole-builder'.]
In the stories of J. R. R. Tolkien (1892–1973): a member of a fictional race related to humans, characterized by their small size and hairy feet.

hobble /ˈhɒb(ə)l/ *noun*. E18.
[ORIGIN from the verb.]
1 The action of hobbling; an uneven, unsteady, or feeble gait. E18.

SWIFT One of his heels higher than the other; which gives him a hobble in his gait.

2 An awkward situation. Now *arch. & dial.* L18.

B. FRANKLIN A fine Hobble they are all got into by their unjust and blundering Politics.

3 A rope, strap, block of wood, etc., used for hobbling a horse or similar animal. Usu. in *pl.* Cf. HOPPLE *noun*. L18.

fig.: P. CAREY City women . . released from the hobble of high heels.

4 In full ***hobble skirt***. A close-fitting skirt so narrow at or near the hem as to impede walking. E20.
– COMB.: **hobblebush** a N. American viburnum, *Viburnum alnifolium*, with clusters of white flowers and purple-black berries; **hobble chain** (chiefly *Austral.*) a chain used for hobbling a horse etc.; ***hobble skirt***: see sense 4 above.

hobble /ˈhɒb(ə)l/ *verb*. ME.
[ORIGIN Prob. of Low German origin (cf. early Dutch *hobbelen* toss, rock from side to side, halt, stammer, frequentative of *hobben*). In sense 5 var. of HOPPLE *verb*.]

1 *verb intrans.* Move unsteadily, esp. up and down; wobble. Formerly also (of a boat) rise and fall on the sea. Now *rare*. ME.
2 *verb intrans.* Walk with an uneven, unsteady, or feeble gait; limp. LME. ▸**b** Dance, esp. clumsily. Now *rare* or *obsolete*. M16.

D. M. THOMAS An old and stooping nun had hobbled out with a basket of linen to wash.

3 *verb intrans.* Proceed haltingly or lamely in action or speech. Now *rare*. E16.
4 *verb trans.* Cause to hobble; *esp.* hinder, interfere with, foil, perplex. M18.

A. COOKE The endless tedious chores that hobble the days and nights of royalty. *Nature* Progress on the clean-up is . . being hobbled by . . financial difficulties.

5 *verb trans.* Tie or fasten together the legs of (a horse etc.) to prevent it straying, kicking, etc., or to regulate its pace in a race; tie or fasten together (the legs of a horse etc.) with this purpose. M18.

A. HALEY He remembered awakening . . and finding himself gagged, . . and his ankles hobbled with knotted rope.

■ **hobblingly** *adverb* in a hobbling manner E17.

hobbledehoy /ˈhɒb(ə)ldɪˌhɔɪ/ *noun. colloq.* Also **hobbade-** /ˈhɒbədɪ-/ & other vars. M16.
[ORIGIN Unknown.]
A clumsy or awkward person, esp. a youth.

MOLLIE HARRIS Some of the town kids looked upon us as a bunch of hobbledehoys.

■ **hobbledeˈhoydom** *noun* the condition of a hobbledehoy, adolescence L19. **hobbledeˈhoyhood** *noun* = HOBBLEDEHOYDOM M19. **hobbledeˈhoyish** *adjective* like a hobbledehoy E19. **hobbledeˈhoyism** *noun* = HOBBLEDEHOYDOM M19.

hobbler /ˈhɒblə/ *noun*[1]. *obsolete* exc. *hist.* ME.
[ORIGIN Anglo-Norman *hobeleor*, *-lour* = Anglo-Latin *hobellarius*, irreg. formed as HOBBY *noun*[1]: see -ER[2].]
A retainer maintaining a small horse or pony for military service; a light horseman.

hobbler /ˈhɒblə/ *noun*[2]. L16.
[ORIGIN from HOBBLE *verb* + -ER[1].]
†**1** A child's top that wobbles or spins unsteadily. L16–M19.
2 A person who hobbles. *rare*. M17.
3 An unlicensed boatman or pilot, a hoveller. *obsolete* exc. *hist.* M19.

hobby /ˈhɒbi/ *noun*[1]. LME.
[ORIGIN By-form of *Robbie* abbreviation of the name *Robert*: cf. HOB *noun*[1].]
1 A small horse, a pony. *arch.* LME.
2 = HOBBY HORSE *noun* 4. L17.
3 = HOBBY HORSE *noun* 1. M18.
4 A favourite subject or occupation that is not one's main business; a spare-time activity followed for pleasure or relaxation. Cf. earlier HOBBY HORSE 5. E19.

P. G. WODEHOUSE Kirk's painting had always been more of a hobby with him than a profession. M. IGNATIEFF Trade and industry were interesting hobbies but not serious vocations.

5 *hist.* = VELOCIPEDE 1. E19.
– COMB.: **hobby farm** (chiefly *N. Amer.*) a small farm operated primarily for pleasure rather than profit.
■ **hobbyism** *noun* pursuit of or devotion to a hobby or spare-time activity M19. **hobbyist** *noun* a person pursuing or devoted to a hobby or spare-time activity L19.

hobby /ˈhɒbi/ *noun*[2]. LME.
[ORIGIN Old French *hobé*, *hobet* dim. of *hobe* falcon (cf. French *hobereau*), prob. rel. to *hobeler* from Middle Dutch *hobbelen* turn, roll.]
A migratory Old World falcon, *Falco subbuteo*, formerly used for hunting small birds. Also (with specifying word), any of a number of similar falcons.

hobby horse /ˈhɒbɪ hɔːs/ *noun & verb phr.* ME.
[ORIGIN from HOBBY *noun*[1] + HORSE *noun*.]
▸**A** *noun phr.* **1** A figure of a horse (made of wicker etc.) fastened around the waist or over the head of a performer in a morris dance, pantomime, etc. ME.
†**2** = HOBBY *noun*[1] 1. L16–E17.
†**3** A person who behaves in a ridiculous way; a jester, buffoon. Also, a lustful person; a prostitute. L16–E17.
4 a A toy consisting of a stick with a horse's head at one end, for a child to bestride. L16. ▸**b** A horse on a merry-go-round; a rocking horse. M18.
5 Orig., = HOBBY *noun*[1] 4. Now usu., a topic to which a person constantly recurs or in which he or she shows an obsessive interest. L17.

C. MCCULLOUGH He also had a tendency to be downright boring once he climbed aboard his hobbyhorse.

6 *hist.* = HOBBY *noun*[1] 5. E19.
▸**B** *verb intrans.* (With hyphen.) Perform as a hobby horse; move like a hobby horse. E19.
■ **hobby-ˈhorsical** *adjective* constantly recurring to the same topic, devoted to a hobby, crotchety, whimsical M18.

hobday /ˈhɒbdeɪ/ *verb trans.* Also **H-**. M20.
[ORIGIN F. T. *Hobday* (1869–1939), Brit. veterinary surgeon.]
Operate on the larynx of (a horse) to improve its breathing.

hobgoblin /ˈhɒbɡɒblɪn/ *noun, adjective, & verb.* M16.
[ORIGIN from HOB *noun*[1] + GOBLIN *noun*[1].]
▸**A** *noun.* A mischievous imp or sprite, *spec.* Robin Goodfellow; something to be feared superstitiously, a bogey, a bugbear. M16.
▸**B** *attrib.* or as *adjective*. Of, pertaining to, or resembling a hobgoblin. E17.
▸**C** *verb trans.* Terrify or pursue as a hobgoblin. Chiefly *joc.* E18.

hobnail /ˈhɒbneɪl/ *noun, adjective, & verb.* L16.
[ORIGIN from HOB *noun*[2] + NAIL *noun*.]
▸**A** *noun.* **1** A nail with a large head and short tang, used to reinforce the soles of heavy boots and shoes. L16.
2 A person wearing hobnailed boots; a rustic, labourer. Now *rare*. M17.
– COMB.: **hobnail liver** MEDICINE: having many small knobbly projections due to cirrhosis.
▸**B** *attrib.* or as *adjective*. Rustic, boorish. E17.
▸**C** *verb trans.* Provide or reinforce with hobnails. M17.

hobnailed /ˈhɒbneɪld/ *adjective.* L16.
[ORIGIN from HOBNAIL *noun* or *verb*: see -ED[2], -ED[1].]
1 Rustic, boorish. Now *rare*. L16.
2 Provided or reinforced with hobnails. E17.
– SPECIAL COLLOCATIONS: **hobnailed liver** = *hobnail liver* s.v. HOBNAIL *noun*.

hobnob /ˈhɒbnɒb/ *verb.* Also **hob-nob**. Infl. **-bb-**. E19.
[ORIGIN from *hob and* (or *or*) *nob*: see HOB *verb*[1] 2.]
1 *verb intrans.* Drink to each other, drink together. *arch.* E19.
2 *verb intrans. & trans.* (with *it*). Be on familiar terms (*with*); talk informally (*with*). M19.

C. S. FORESTER There were advantages . . in hobnobbing with generals.

hob-nob /ˈhɒbnɒb/ *noun.* M18.
[ORIGIN from (the same root as) HOBNOB *verb*.]
†**1** Any phrase or toast used in drinking together. M–L18.
2 A drinking to each other or together. *arch.* E19.
3 An intimate conversation, a tête-à-tête. L19.

hob-nob /ˈhɒbnɒb/ *adverb. obsolete* exc. *dial.* Also (earlier) **hab-nab** /ˈhabnab/, **habs-nabs** /ˈhabznabz/. L16.
[ORIGIN See HAB.]
However it may turn out, anyhow; in random fashion, by chance, by one means or another; hit or miss, succeed or fail.

hobo /ˈhəʊbəʊ/ *noun & verb.* Chiefly *N. Amer.* L19.
[ORIGIN Unknown.]
▸**A** *noun.* Pl. **-o(e)s**. A wandering workman or tramp. L19.

D. CARNEGIE He . . became a hobo, . . slept in haystacks, begged his food from door to door.

▸**B** *verb intrans. & trans.* with *it*. Be or behave like a hobo; wander. E20.

hobohemia /həʊbəʊˈhiːmɪə/ *noun.* E20.
[ORIGIN Blend of HOBO *noun* and *Bohemia*.]
A community of hoboes; a district in which hoboes live.
■ **hobohemian** *adjective & noun* (of, pertaining to, or resembling) a hobo E20.

hoboy *noun* see HAUTBOY.

Hobson-Jobson /hɒbs(ə)nˈdʒɒbs(ə)n/ *noun.* L19.
[ORIGIN Title of a famous collection (1886) of Anglo-Ind. words by Yule & Burnell, repr. alt. (by Brit. hearers) of Arabic *Yā Ḥasan! Yā Ḥusayn!* O Hasan! O Husain!, a cry used by Muslims at the ceremonies held at Muharram.]
Assimilation of adopted foreign words to the sound pattern of the adopting language. Chiefly in ***the law of Hobson-Jobson***.

Hobson's choice /hɒbs(ə)nz ˈtʃɔɪs/ *noun phr.* M17.
[ORIGIN T. *Hobson* (1554–1631), a Cambridge carrier who gave his customers a choice between the next horse or none at all.]
The option of taking what is offered or nothing; no choice.

Hobthrush /ˈhɒbθrʌʃ/ *noun. obsolete* exc. *dial.* Also **-thrust** /-θrʌst/, **-thurst** /-θəːst/. L16.
[ORIGIN from HOB *noun*[1] + THURSE with metathesis.]
1 A hobgoblin. L16.
2 A rustic. *derog.* L17.

hoc /hɒk/ *noun. obsolete* exc. *hist.* Also **hock**. M17.
[ORIGIN French, prob. from Latin = this (neut.).]
A card game in which players may assign whatever value they choose to certain privileged cards.

hoch /hoːx/ *interjection & noun.* M19.
[ORIGIN German, abbreviation of *hoch lebe* long live.]
(An instance of the German exclamation) expr. loyal approval.

hocheur /hɒˈʃəː; *foreign* ɔʃœːr (*pl. same*)/ *noun.* M19.
[ORIGIN French, from *hocher* nod + *-eur* -OR.]
The spot-nosed monkey, *Cercopithecus nictitans*, of W. African rainforests, olive and black with a white spot on the nose. Also ***hocheur monkey***.

hochgeboren /ˈhoːxɡəboːrən/ *noun & adjective.* Pl. of noun same. E20.
[ORIGIN German.]
(A person who is) high-born.

hock /hɒk/ *noun*[1]. Long *obsolete* exc. in HOLLYHOCK. OE.
[ORIGIN Unknown.]
Any of various plants of the mallow family, *esp.* the common mallow, *Malva sylvestris*, and the hollyhock, *Alcea rosea*.

hock /hɒk/ *noun*[2]. LME.
[ORIGIN Var. of HOUGH *noun*.]
1 The joint in the hind leg of a quadruped between the tibia and the metatarsus, the angle of which points backwards. LME.
2 A knuckle of meat, esp. pork. Cf. HOUGH *noun* 3. E18.

hock /hɒk/ *noun*[3]. M16.
[ORIGIN Perh. var. of HOOK *noun*.]
A rod, stick, or chain with a hook at the end.

hock /hɒk/ *noun*[4]. E17.
[ORIGIN Abbreviation formed as HOCKAMORE.]
A white wine from the Rhine region (orig. from Hochheim on the River Main, Germany); *loosely* any dry white wine.

hock /hɒk/ *noun*[5]. Chiefly *US*. M19.
[ORIGIN Perh. abbreviation of HOCKELTY.]
In faro, the last card remaining in the box after all the others have been dealt.
from soda card to hock, **from soda to hock** from the top card to the last in the deal, from beginning to end.

hock /hɒk/ *noun*[6]. *slang* (chiefly *N. Amer.*). M19.
[ORIGIN Dutch *hok* hutch, hovel, prison, (slang) credit, debt.]
Pawn, pledge; debt. Also, prison. Chiefly in ***in hock***.

Collier's My cash was gone, and I was in hock for the next three years. G. CLARE There was never enough money to get her brooch out of hock again.

– COMB.: **hock-shop** a pawnshop.

hock *noun*[7] var. of HOC.

hock /hɒk/ *verb*[1]. *obsolete* exc. *hist.* LME.
[ORIGIN from HOCK-.]
1 *verb intrans.* Collect money (often by roughly humorous methods) for parish purposes at Hocktide; celebrate Hocktide. LME.
2 *verb trans.* Tie up or otherwise beset (a person) to extract money at Hocktide. E18.
– COMB.: **hocking ale**: brewed for the Hocktide festival.

hock /hɒk/ *verb*[2] *trans.* L16.
[ORIGIN from HOCK *noun*[2].]
Disable by cutting the tendons of the ham or hock; hamstring.

hock /hɒk/ *verb*[3] *trans. slang* (chiefly *N. Amer.*). L19.
[ORIGIN from HOCK *noun*[6].]
Pawn.

Hock- /hɒk/ *combining form.* Now chiefly *hist.* Also as separate word. ME.
[ORIGIN Unknown.]
Designating days of or events connected with the beginning of the second week after Easter, formerly important for the payment of rents etc., the collection of money (often by roughly humorous methods) for parish purposes, and as the beginning of the summer half of the rural year.
Hock-day the second Tuesday after Easter Sunday; in *pl.* also, the second Monday and Tuesday after Easter Sunday. **Hock Monday** the second Monday after Easter Sunday. **Hock-money** money collected for parish purposes during Hocktide. **Hocktide** the period comprising the second Monday and Tuesday after Easter Sunday. **Hock Tuesday** the second Tuesday after Easter Sunday.

†**Hockamore** *noun.* L17–M18.
[ORIGIN Alt. of German *Hochheimer (Wein)* wine of Hochheim on the River Main, Germany.]
= HOCK *noun*[4].

hock-cart /ˈhɒk-kɑːt/ *noun. obsolete* exc. *hist.* M17.
[ORIGIN Prob. from elem. rel. to HOCKEY *noun*[2], HORKEY + CART *noun*.]
The cart which carried home the last load of a harvest.

hockelty /ˈhɒk(ə)lti/ *noun.* Chiefly *US*. Now *rare*. Also **hocklety**, (earlier) **hockly** /ˈhɒkli/. E19.
[ORIGIN Uncertain: 1st elem. perh. rel. to HOC.]
In faro: the last card but one in the deal which forms part of the banker's gain; also = HOCK *noun*[5].

hocket /ˈhɒkɪt/ *noun.* ME.
[ORIGIN French *hoquet* hiccup, in Old French shock, sudden interruption, hitch.]
†**1** A hitch, an obstacle; an interruption; a trick. Only in ME.
†**2** *The* hiccups. Only in E17.
3 MUSIC. A device of medieval polyphony whereby a melody is divided between two or more contrapuntal voice parts which alternate with rests to produce a spasmodic effect. L18.

hockey /ˈhɒki/ *noun*[1]. E16.
[ORIGIN Unknown.]
▸**I 1** An outdoor team game played with sticks hooked at one end with which the players drive a ball towards goals at opposite ends of the field. Also more fully (esp. in N. America to distinguish it from sense 2) ***field hockey***. E16.

2 A variant of this game played on ice in skates with sticks hooked or (now usu.) angled at one end and a rubber disc or puck. Also more fully (esp. outside N. America to distinguish it from sense 1) ***ice hockey***. L19.
▸ **II 3** A stick or club used in hockey. Chiefly *US*. M19.
– COMB.: **hockey stick** a stick hooked or angled at one end, used in hockey.
■ **hockeyist** *noun* (*N. Amer.*) a person who plays ice hockey L19.

hockey *noun*² var. of HORKEY.

hockey *noun*³ see OCHE.

hocklety, hockly *nouns* see HOCKELTY.

hocus /ˈhəʊkəs/ *noun*. M17.
[ORIGIN Abbreviation of HOCUS-POCUS *noun & adjective*.]
▸ **I** †**1** A conjuror, a juggler. M–L17.
†**2** A cheat, an impostor. Only in L17.
3 A stupid person. *Scot.* L18.
▸ **II 4** Jugglery, trickery, deception. *arch.* M17.

hocus /ˈhəʊkəs/ *verb trans*. Infl. **-ss-**, **-s-**. L17.
[ORIGIN from the noun.]
1 Play a trick on; hoax. L17.
2 Stupefy with drugs, esp. for a criminal purpose; drug (a drink). Cf. LOCUS *verb*. M19.

hocus-pocus /həʊkəsˈpəʊkəs/ *noun & adjective*. E17.
[ORIGIN from pseudo-Latin *hax pax max Deus adimax*, used as magical formula.]
▸ **A** *noun*. †**1** A conjuror, a juggler; a trickster. E17–M18.
2 (As *interjection* used as) a formula of conjuring or magical incantation. E17.
3 A juggler's trick; conjuring; sleight of hand; trickery, deception. M17.

J. F. KENNEDY Englishmen, with their balanced budgets and sound economy, had watched the German financial hocus-pocus with amazement.

▸ **B** *attrib.* or as *adjective*. Juggling; cheating, tricky. Now *rare*. M17.

hocus-pocus /həʊkəsˈpəʊkəs/ *verb*. Infl. **-ss-**, **-s-**. L17.
[ORIGIN from HOCUS-POCUS *noun & adjective*.]
1 *verb intrans.* Act the conjuror, juggle; play tricks, practise deception. L17.
2 *verb trans.* Play tricks on; transform as if by jugglery. L18.

hod /hɒd/ *noun*. L16.
[ORIGIN Var. of HOT *noun*¹.]
1 A builder's open receptacle, now usu. a trough on a staff, for carrying mortar, bricks, or stones; the quantity that such a receptacle will contain, a hodful. L16.
2 A receptacle for carrying or holding coal; a coal scuttle. E19.
– COMB.: **hodman** a building worker who carries a hod; now chiefly *fig.*, an unskilled worker, a literary hack.
■ **hodful** *noun* the quantity that a hod will contain; (somewhat *derog.*) a large quantity: E19.

hod /hɒd/ *verb intrans. Scot.* Infl. **-dd-**. L18.
[ORIGIN Imit.]
Bob up and down in riding; jog.

hodad /ˈhəʊdad/ *noun*. *Surfing slang*. M20.
[ORIGIN Unknown.]
An ill-mannered or boastful surfer.

hodden /ˈhɒd(ə)n/ *noun & adjective*. *Scot.* Now *arch.* or *hist.* L16.
[ORIGIN Unknown.]
(Made of) woollen cloth of a coarse quality such as was made on hand looms.
hodden grey (of) grey hodden made without dyeing from a combination of black and white fleeces, taken as typical rustic garb.

hoddy-doddy /ˈhɒdɪˌdɒdi/ *noun & adjective*. *obsolete* exc. *dial.* In sense A.3 also †**-dod**. M16.
[ORIGIN Perh. child's redupl. of *dod* in DODMAN.]
▸ **A** *noun*. **1** A short and dumpy person. M16.
†**2** A cuckold; a henpecked man; a simpleton. L16–M17.
3 A small snail. E17.
4 A revolving light. *dial.* L18.
▸ **B** *adjective*. **1** Confused; giddy; drunk. L18.
2 Short and dumpy; clumsy. E19.

hoddy-noddy /ˈhɒdɪˌnɒdi/ *noun*. *rare*. E17.
[ORIGIN Redupl. of NODDY *noun*¹ & *adjective*: cf. HODDY-DODDY.]
A fool, a simpleton.

Hodegetria /həʊdɪˈgiːtrɪə/ *noun*. L19.
[ORIGIN Greek *hodēgētria* lit. 'the indicator of the way'.]
An iconographical depiction of the Virgin and Child in which the Virgin with her right hand indicates the Child, who is on her left arm.

Hodge /hɒdʒ/ *noun*. LME.
[ORIGIN By-form of the male first name *Roger*: cf. HICK *noun*¹, HOB *noun*¹.]
(A name for) a typical English agricultural labourer, a rustic.

hodgepodge /ˈhɒdʒpɒdʒ/ *noun, adjective, & verb*. Also (earlier) †**-potch**. LME.
[ORIGIN Var. of HOTCHPOTCH, prob. with assim. to HODGE. Cf. HODGEPOT, HOTCHPOT.]
▸ **A** *noun*. **1** = HOTCHPOTCH *noun* 1. LME. ▸**b** A clumsy mixture of ingredients. E17.
2 = HOTCHPOTCH *noun* 2. E17.
▸ **B** *attrib.* or as *adjective*. = HOTCHPOTCH *adjective*. E17.
▸ **C** *verb trans.* = HOTCHPOTCH *verb*. M18.

hodgepot /ˈhɒdʒpɒt/ *noun*. Long *rare*. LME.
[ORIGIN Var. of HOTCHPOT, prob. with assim. to HODGE. Cf. HODGEPODGE.]
1 = HOTCHPOTCH *noun* 2. LME.
2 = HOTCHPOT *noun* 3. E18.

†**hodgepotch** *noun* see HODGEPODGE.

†**hodge-pudding** *noun*. *rare* (Shakes.). Only in L16.
[ORIGIN from HODGE(PODGE *noun* + PUDDING *noun*.]
A pudding made of a medley of ingredients.

Hodgkin's disease /ˈhɒdʒkɪnz dɪˌziːz/ *noun phr.* M19.
[ORIGIN from Thomas *Hodgkin* (1798–1866), English physician.]
MEDICINE. A malignant but often curable disease of the lymphatic system causing painless swelling of the lymph nodes, liver, and spleen.

hodiern /ˈhɒdɪəːn, ˈhəʊ-/ *adjective*. Long *rare*. E16.
[ORIGIN Latin *hodiernus*, from *hodie* today.]
= HODIERNAL.

hodiernal /hɒdɪˈəːn(ə)l, həʊ-/ *adjective*. M17.
[ORIGIN formed as HODIERN + -AL¹.]
Of or belonging to the present day.

hodmandod /ˈhɒdməndɒd/ *noun*. *obsolete* exc. *dial.* L16.
[ORIGIN Redupl. var. of DODMAN: cf. HODDY-DODDY. In sense 2 alt. of HOTTENTOT.]
1 A snail; *fig.* a deformed person. L16.
†**2** A Nama. L17–E18.

hodograph /ˈhɒdəgrɑːf/ *noun*. M19.
[ORIGIN from Greek *hodos* way + -GRAPH.]
A curve constructed by extending from a fixed point lines representing in magnitude and direction the velocity of a moving particle, or some other vector quantity.

hodometer *noun* var. of ODOMETER.

hodometrical /hɒdəˈmɛtrɪk(ə)l/ *adjective*. M18.
[ORIGIN from Greek *hodos* way + *metrikos* metric + -AL¹.]
NAUTICAL. Relating to the measurement of a ship's progress.

hodoscope /ˈhɒdəskəʊp/ *noun*. E20.
[ORIGIN from Greek *hodos* way + -SCOPE.]
1 A form of microscope for examining light paths in a crystal. Now *rare* or *obsolete*. E20.
2 PHYSICS. An array of particle detectors used for observing the paths of cosmic-ray and other particles. M20.

hoe /həʊ/ *noun*¹. Now only in place names.
[ORIGIN Old English *hōh*, *hō* from Germanic. Perh. same word as HOUGH *noun*. See also HEUGH *noun*.]
A projecting ridge of land, a promontory.
Plymouth Hoe etc.

hoe /həʊ/ *noun*². *obsolete* exc. *dial.* Also †**how**.
[ORIGIN Old English *hogu* corresp. to Old High German *hugu*, *hugi*, Old Saxon *hugi* (Dutch *heug*), Old Norse *hugr*, Gothic *hugs* thought, from Germanic.]
Care, anxiety, trouble.

hoe /həʊ/ *noun*³. ME.
[ORIGIN Old French *houe* from Old Frankish = Old High German *houwa* (German *Haue*) rel. to HEW *verb*.]
A tool consisting of a thin blade attached to a long handle, used for loosening the surface of the ground, digging up weeds, etc.
Dutch hoe: see DUTCH *adjective*. **draw hoe** a hoe used with a pulling action.
– COMB.: **hoecake** *US* a cake of maize flour of a type orig. baked on the blade of a hoe.
■ **hoeful** *noun* as much as can be lifted on a hoe M19.

hoe *noun*⁴ var. of HO *noun*⁴.

hoe /həʊ/ *verb*. LME.
[ORIGIN from HOE *noun*³.]
1 *verb intrans.* Use a hoe; work with a hoe. LME.
2 *verb trans.* Break or loosen (ground) with a hoe. Also foll. by *up*. M17.
3 *verb trans.* Weed (crops) with a hoe; thin *out*, dig *up*, etc. (plants) with a hoe. L17.
– PHRASES, & WITH ADVERBS & PREPOSITIONS IN SPECIALIZED SENSES: ***a hard row to hoe***: see ROW *noun*¹. **hoe in** *Austral. & NZ slang* eat eagerly. **hoe into** *Austral. & NZ slang* attack (food, a person, a task).
■ **hoer** *noun* M18.

hoedown /ˈhəʊdaʊn/ *noun*. Chiefly *N. Amer.* M19.
[ORIGIN from HOE *verb* + DOWN *adverb*.]
A lively folk dance; a tune for such a dance; a social gathering for dancing hoedowns etc.

hoernesite /ˈhəːnəsʌɪt/ *noun*. Also **hör-**. M19.
[ORIGIN from Moritz *Hörnes* (1815–68), Austrian mineralogist + -ITE¹.]
MINERALOGY. A monoclinic hydrated arsenate of magnesium, usu. occurring as groups of white crystals.

hoey /ˈhəʊi/ *noun*. Now *rare* or *obsolete*. M19.
[ORIGIN Chinese *hui* association, society, club.]
A (secret) society or association of Chinese, esp. in an English-speaking community.

Hoffmann /ˈhɒfmən/ *noun*. M18.
[ORIGIN German surname: in sense 1 Friedrich *Hoffmann* (1660–1742), physician; in sense 2 Johann *Hoffmann* (1857–1919), neurologist.]
1 PHARMACOLOGY. ***Hoffmann's anodyne***, a mineral solution of alcohol and ether. M18.
2 MEDICINE. ***Hoffmann's sign***, increased sensitivity of the sensory nerves to mechanical stimulation. E20.

Hofmann /ˈhɒfmən/ *noun*. M19.
[ORIGIN August Wilhelm von *Hofmann* (1818–92), German chemist.]
CHEMISTRY. Used *attrib.* and in *possess.* to designate substances, methods, etc., discovered or devised by Hofmann.
Hofmann degradation (*a*) = *Hofmann reaction* below; (*b*) the pyrolysis of a quaternary ammonium hydroxide to yield a tertiary amine and an alkene. **Hofmann reaction**, **Hofmann rearrangement** the elimination of a carbonyl group from an acid amide when heated in a solution of sodium hypochlorite or a similar compound, yielding a primary amine. **Hofmann's violet** any of a group of basic rosaniline dyes formerly used to dye fabrics.

hog /hɒg/ *noun*. Also (now only in sense 4) **hogg**. LOE.
[ORIGIN Perh. of Celtic origin: cf. Welsh *hwch*, Cornish *hoch* pig, sow.]
▸ **I 1** A domesticated pig; *esp.* a castrated male reared for slaughter. LOE.

W. STYRON I could hear Travis's hogs grunting sleepily in their pen.

2 Any (wild) pig of the domesticated species, *Sus scrofa*. L15.
3 With specifying word: any of various other animals of the pig family Suidae or otherwise held to resemble the pig. L16.
groundhog, *wart hog*, etc.
▸ **II 4** A young sheep, *esp.* one from the time it ceases to be a lamb until its first shearing. Now chiefly *Scot. & dial.* ME. ▸**b** The first fleece shorn from such a sheep. Chiefly *dial.* M19.

Yorkshire Post Best Cheviot hogs and wethers are five per cent. cheaper.

5 Any of various farm animals of a year old; a yearling. Usu. more fully ***hog-bull***, ***hog-colt***, etc. L16.
▸ **III 6** A coarse, filthy, gluttonous, or inconsiderate person. Cf. ROAD HOG. LME.

SHAKES. *Rich. III* Thou elvish-mark'd, abortive, rooting hog.

7 A shilling; *US* a ten-cent piece. *arch. slang.* L17.
8 NAUTICAL. A scrubbing brush for cleaning a ship's bottom. M18.
9 CURLING. A stone lacking sufficient impetus to carry it over the distance line or hog score; the distance line itself. L18.
10 A machine for grinding (esp. refuse) wood into chips for fuel. L19.
11 A railway locomotive for hauling freight. *US slang.* L19.
12 A large motorcycle. *US slang.* M20.
– PHRASES: **go the whole hog** *colloq.* do a thing completely or thoroughly. **hog in armour** a person who is ill at ease. **hog on ice** *N. Amer. colloq.* an insecure person. **live high off the hog**, **live high on the hog** (orig. *US*) live luxuriously.
– COMB.: **hog badger** a yellowish-grey badger, *Arctonyx collaris*, of East Asian forests, having an elongated mobile snout; **hog cholera** *US* swine fever; **hog deer** a small, short-legged deer, *Cervus porcinus*, native to southern Asian grassland; **hog gum** a gum obtained from any of various West Indian trees, esp. *Rhus metopium* (family Anacardiaceae) and *Symphonia globulifera* (family Guttiferae); ***hog-gum tree***, any of the trees producing this gum; **hog-head** *US slang* the driver of a locomotive; **hog heaven** (*colloq.*, orig. *US*) a place or condition of foolish or idle bliss; †**hogherd** a swineherd; **hog-killing** *US* the time when pigs are killed; *fig.* a time of special enjoyment; **hog-Latin** any incomprehensible language; esp. = ***pig Latin*** s.v. PIG *noun*¹; **hog line** = ***hog score*** below; **hog louse** a woodlouse; cf. ***pig louse*** (a) s.v. PIG *noun*¹; **hognose (snake)** any of several harmless colubrid snakes constituting the N. American genus *Heterodon*, which have an upturned snout and defensive behaviour including hissing, flattening the head, inflating the body, and feigning death; **hog-nosed** *adjective* having a flattened or upturned snout suggesting that of a hog (***hog-nosed bat***, a tailless colonial bat, *Craseonycteris thonglongyai*, of west Thailand, the smallest known bat; ***hog-nosed snake*** = ***hognose*** above); **hognut** = ***pignut*** (a) s.v. PIG *noun*¹; ***hog peanut***: see PEANUT 1; **hog-pen** *N. Amer.* a pigsty; **hog plum** (the plumlike fruit of) any of several trees, esp. (*W. Indian*) *Spondias mombin* (family Anacardiaceae) and (*US*) *Ximenia americana* (family Olacaceae); **hog score** CURLING either of two lines drawn across each end of a rink at one-sixth of the rink's length from the tee, over which a stone must cross to count in the game; **hog's fennel** a tall umbelliferous plant, *Peucedanum officinale*, with yellowish flowers and finely divided leaves like those of fennel; **hogskin** *noun & adjective* (made of) pigskin; **hog's pudding** the entrails of a hog, filled with either a sweet or savoury stuffing; **hog-sucker** any fish of the N. American genus *Hypentelium*; **hog-tie** *verb trans.* (*N. Amer.*) secure by fastening the hands and feet or all four feet together; restrain, impede; **hog-tight** *adjective* (of a fence) close or narrow enough to stop pigs forcing a way through; **hog-trough** a trough for hogs to feed out of; **hog-wash** kitchen swill etc. for pigs; *fig.* worthless stuff, nonsense; **hogweed** any of various plants on which hogs feed or are fed; *spec.* (*a*) any of several coarse umbelliferous plants of the genus *Heracleum*, esp. cow parsnip, *H. sphondylium*; (*b*) *W. Indian* any of various plants of the genus *Boerhavia* (family Nyctaginaceae); **hog-wild** *adjective* (*US colloq.*) absolutely wild or furious; **hog-yoke** a wooden frame for a hog's neck, used to prevent it from going through hedges.

hog /hɒɡ/ *verb*. Infl. **-gg-**. M17.
[ORIGIN from the noun.]
▸ **I 1** *verb trans.* NAUTICAL. Clean the bottom of (a ship) with a hog. Now *rare*. M17.
2 *verb trans.* CURLING. Play (a stone) without enough force for it to cross the hog score. E19.
▸ **II 3** *verb trans.* Cut (a horse's mane) short so that it stands up like a hog's bristles. M18.
4 *verb trans.* Arch (the back); cause (a boat, plank, etc.) to rise archwise in the centre and sag at the ends as a result of strain. L18. ▸**b** *verb intrans.* Arch the back; (of a ship) rise archwise in the centre. L18.

WELLINGTON Draught bullocks . . . stick in the mud, hog their backs, droop their heads and die.

5 *verb trans.* Appropriate greedily or selfishly; take an unduly large share of for oneself, monopolize. *colloq.* L19. ▸**b** *verb trans.* Eat (something) greedily. *colloq.* E20. ▸**c** *verb trans.* with *it* & *intrans.* Behave as a road hog, monopolize the road. E20.

A. BROOKNER My mother . . hogged all the attention at my wedding. *Brides & Setting up Home* Who hogs the duvet is no longer a problem. **b** C. THUBRON A modern restaurant where I hogged down two bowls of the meat soup.

▸ **III 6** *verb trans.* Keep (a lamb) over winter for sale the following year. Now chiefly *Scot.* E19.
7 *verb trans.* Feed swine on (a crop or crop-covered land). Also foll. by *down*, *off*. *US colloq.* M19.
– COMB.: **hog-mane** a hogged mane; **hog-maned** *adjective* having a hog-mane.

hogan /ˈhəʊɡ(ə)n/ *noun*[1]. L19.
[ORIGIN Navajo.]
An American Indian (esp. Navajo) hut made from logs, earth, etc.

hogan *noun*[2] var. of HOGEN.

Hogan Mogan *noun & adjective* var. of HOGEN MOGEN.

Hogarthian /həʊˈɡɑːθɪən/ *adjective*. L18.
[ORIGIN from *Hogarth* (see below) + -IAN.]
Of, pertaining to, or characteristic of the English satirical painter and caricaturist William Hogarth (1697–1764) or his style of painting.

hogback /ˈhɒɡbak/ *noun*. Also **hog's back** /ˈhɒɡz bak/. M17.
[ORIGIN from HOG *noun* + BACK *noun*[1].]
1 A back like that of a hog. M17.
2 A thing shaped like a hog's back; *esp.* a sharply crested hill ridge. E19.

C. G. D. ROBERTS The lake lay . . sheltered . . by a high hog-back of dark green spruce.

3 A rectangular tomb with a curved or pitched roof. L19.
▪ **hogbacked** *adjective* (*a*) having a back like that of a hog; (*b*) having a rise in the middle like a hog's back: M17.

hogen /ˈhəʊɡ(ə)n/ *noun & adjective*. Also **-an**. M17.
[ORIGIN Abbreviation of HOGEN MOGEN.]
▸ **A** *noun*. Also **H-**.
†**1** A Netherlander. M–L17.
2 A strong type of beer. Cf. earlier HOGEN MOGEN *adjective* 3. E18.
▸ †**B** *adjective*. Excellent; high and mighty. L17–M18.

Hogen Mogen /ˌhəʊɡ(ə)n ˈməʊɡ(ə)n/ *noun & adjective*. Also **Hogan Mogan**, **h- m-**. M17.
[ORIGIN from Dutch *Hoogmogendheiden* High Mightinesses, the title of the States General.]
▸ **A** *noun*. Pl. same, **-s**.
†**1** The States General of the Netherlands; *pl.* the members of this. Also, any person, council, or authority affecting power. M17–E18.
2 A Netherlander. *derog.* Now *rare*. L17.
▸ **B** *adjective*. **1** Dutch. *derog.* Now *rare*. M17.
†**2** Affecting power; high and mighty. M17–E18.
†**3** Of an alcoholic drink, esp. beer: strong. Cf. HOGEN *noun* 2. Only in M17.

hogfish /ˈhɒɡfɪʃ/ *noun*. Pl. **-es** /-ɪz/, (usu.) same. L16.
[ORIGIN from HOG *noun* + FISH *noun*[1].]
†**1** A manatee. L16–E17.
†**2** A porpoise. Only in 17.
3 a The orange scorpionfish, *Scorpaena scrofa*, of the Mediterranean and eastern Atlantic. Now *rare* or *obsolete*. E17. ▸**b** Any of various fishes of American waters; *esp.* (*a*) a large edible wrasse, *Lachnolaimus maximus*; (*b*) a pigfish, *Orthopristis chrysoptera*. M18.

hogg *noun* see HOG *noun*.

†**hoggaster** *noun*. Also **hogster**. LME.
[ORIGIN medieval Latin *ho(c)gaster* (whence also Anglo-Norman *hogastre*), from HOG *noun* + Latin -ASTER, as in late Latin *porcastra* young pig, medieval Latin *porcaster* piglet.]
1 A boar in its third year. LME–M19.
2 A young sheep. E18–L19.

hogger /ˈhɒɡə/ *noun*. *US slang*. E20.
[ORIGIN from HOG *noun* + -ER[1].]
A locomotive engineer.

hoggerel /ˈhɒɡ(ə)r(ə)l/ *noun*. Now *dial.* M16.
[ORIGIN from HOG *noun*: see -REL. Cf. Anglo-Latin *hogerellus*.]
A young sheep in its second year.

hoggery /ˈhɒɡ(ə)ri/ *noun*. M17.
[ORIGIN from HOG *noun* + -ERY.]
1 A place where hogs are kept; a piggery. M17.
2 Hoggishness. *rare*. M19.

hogget /ˈhɒɡɪt/ *noun*. LME.
[ORIGIN from HOG *noun* + -ET[1]. Cf. Anglo-Latin *hogettus*.]
1 A young boar in its second year. Now *rare* or *obsolete*. LME.
2 A yearling sheep; *esp.* (*NZ*) a lamb from when it is weaned to its first shearing. LME.
3 A year-old colt. *dial.* L18.

hoggin /ˈhɒɡɪn/ *noun*. M19.
[ORIGIN Unknown.]
A mixture of sand and gravel; sifted gravel.

hoggish /ˈhɒɡɪʃ/ *adjective*. L15.
[ORIGIN from HOG *noun* + -ISH[1].]
Of, pertaining to, or characteristic of a hog; filthy; gluttonous; selfish, mean.
▪ **hoggishly** *adverb* L16. **hoggishness** *noun* E17.

hoglike /ˈhɒɡlʌɪk/ *adjective*. E19.
[ORIGIN from HOG *noun* + -LIKE.]
Like (that of) a hog, hoggish.

hogling /ˈhɒɡlɪŋ/ *noun*. LME.
[ORIGIN from HOG *noun* + -LING[1].]
1 A young or small pig. LME.
2 A kind of pastry turnover. *dial.* E19.

Hogmanay /ˈhɒɡmənеɪ, hɒɡməˈneɪ/ *noun*. *Scot. & N. English.* E17.
[ORIGIN Corresp. in meaning and use to Old French *aguillanneuf* last day of the year, (the cry for) new-year's gift, of which the Norman form *hoguinané* may be the immediate source of the English word.]
(The celebration of) the last day of the year; (the cry for) the former customary gift of an oatmeal cake etc. demanded by children on this day.

hogo /ˈhəʊɡəʊ/ *noun*. Pl. **-os**. M17.
[ORIGIN Anglicized from French HAUT-GOÛT.]
†**1** A strong or piquant flavour; a highly flavoured dish. M–L17.
2 An offensive smell; a stench, a stink. M17.

Times Amid the hogo of stale sweat and embrocation, Setter stretched himself back on a bench.

hog's back *noun* see HOGBACK.

hogshead /ˈhɒɡzhɛd/ *noun*. LME.
[ORIGIN from HOG *noun* + -'S[1] + HEAD *noun*, (for unkn. reason).]
1 A large cask; *spec.* one of a definite capacity, varying according to the commodity. LME.
2 A liquid or dry measure, varying according to the commodity; *esp.* (*a*) a liquid measure of beer equal to 54 imperial gallons (245.48 litres) or 64.85 US gallons; (*b*) a liquid measure of wine equal to 52.5 imperial gallons (238.67 litres) or 63 US gallons. LME.
3 A person resembling a hog in conduct or behaviour. *derog.* E16.

†**hogster** *noun* var. of HOGGASTER.

hohlflute /ˈhəʊlfluːt/ *noun*. M17.
[ORIGIN Partial translation of German *Hohlflöte* lit. 'hollow flute': see FLUTE *noun*[1].]
An open 8-ft flute stop in an organ, having a soft hollow tone.

ho ho /həʊ ˈhəʊ/ *interjection*. Also **ho ho ho**, **ho-ho(-ho)**. M16.
[ORIGIN Redupl. of HO *interjection*[1].]
Expr. derision or repr. derisive laughter. Also, expr. surprise or triumph.

ho-ho bird /ˈhəʊhəʊ bəːd/ *noun phr.* E20.
[ORIGIN from Chinese *ho-ho* + BIRD *noun*.]
A mythical Chinese bird resembling a pheasant, freq. used as an emblem of courage.

Hohokam /həʊhəʊˈkɑːm/ *noun & adjective*. L19.
[ORIGIN Pima *hú̆hukam* old one.]
▸ **A** *noun*. Pl. same. A member of an extinct N. American Indian people; the culture of this people, characterized by irrigated agriculture and houses built in pits, and flourishing in Arizona after *c* 450. L19.
▸ **B** *adjective*. Of or pertaining to this people or culture. M20.

ho-hum /həʊˈhʌm/ *interjection, noun, & adjective*. E20.
[ORIGIN from HO *interjection*[1] + HUM *interjection*, suggestive of a yawn.]
▸ **A** *interjection*. Expr. boredom. E20.
▸ **B** *noun*. An utterance of 'ho-hum!'; a boring statement etc. M20.
▸ **C** *adjective*. Dull, routine, boring. M20.

hoick /hɔɪk/ *verb*[1] & *noun*. *slang*. Also **hoik**. L19.
[ORIGIN Perh. var. of HIKE *verb*.]
▸ **A** *verb trans.* Lift or bring (*out* etc.), esp. with a jerk; yank. L19.

R. RENDELL Can you imagine him hoicking her out of bed.

▸ **B** *noun*. A jerky lift or pull; CRICKET a jerky hoisted shot. L19.

J. HERRIOT The Hedwick lads . . gave a great hoick at the ball.

hoick *verb*[2] see HOICKS.

hoicks /hɔɪks/ *interjection, verb, & noun*. Also **hoick** /hɔɪk/. E17.
[ORIGIN Unknown: cf. YOICKS.]
▸ **A** *interjection*. Inciting a hound or hounds to the chase. E17.
▸ **B** *verb trans. & intrans.* Incite with or cry 'hoicks!' M18.
▸ **C** *noun*. A cry of 'hoicks!' L18.

hoik *verb & noun* var. of HOICK *verb*[1] & *noun*.

hoi polloi /hɔɪ ˈpɒlɔɪ, pɒˈlɔɪ/ *noun phr.* M17.
[ORIGIN Greek = the many.]
The majority, the masses; the rabble. Freq. with *the*.

Newsweek They're trying to get rid of the hoi polloi and make Venice into a country club for the wealthy.

– NOTE: Orig. in Greek characters; recorded in transliterated form from M19. Strictly, should be used without 'the', as *hoi* is the Greek definite article (nominative masculine pl.), but *the hoi polloi* is now largely accepted in standard English.

hoise /hɔɪz/ *verb*. *obsolete* exc. *dial.* & after Shakes. Pa. t. & pple **hoised**, **hoist** /hɔɪst/. L15.
[ORIGIN Prob. from Dutch †*hijschen* (now *hijsen*) or Low German *hissen*, *hiesen* (whence also French *hisser*), but recorded earlier. Cf. HEEZE *verb*.]
1 *verb trans.* = HOIST *verb*[1] 1. L15.
†**2** *verb intrans.* = HOIST *verb*[1] 4. M–L16.
†**3** *verb trans.* Lift and move; remove. L16–M18.
†**4** *verb trans.* Raise in degree, quality, or price. L16–M18.
– PHRASES (of pa. pple): **hoist with one's own petard** [after Shakes. *Haml.*] blown up by one's own bomb, ruined by one's own devices against others.

hoisin /ˈhɔɪzɪn/ *noun*. M20.
[ORIGIN Chinese (Cantonese) *hói sìn* (*jeung*) (sauce for) seafood.]
In full ***hoisin sauce***. A sweet, spicy, dark red sauce made from soya beans, vinegar, sugar, garlic, and various spices, widely used in southern Chinese cooking.

hoist /hɔɪst/ *noun*. M17.
[ORIGIN from the verb. Cf. HEIST *noun*.]
▸ **I 1** An act of hoisting or raising something aloft; a lift (*up*), a raise. M17.

S. R. CROCKETT As one gets to the edge of a wall when a comrade gives a hoist up. *Sunday Times* Expect a big hoist in the dividend when Lonrho reports its full-year figures.

2 Orig., housebreaking. Now, shoplifting. Chiefly in ***on the hoist***. *slang*. E19.
▸ **II 3** The middle part of a ship's mast; the perpendicular height of a sail or flag; the fore edge of a staysail; the part of a flag nearest to the mast or staff. M18.
4 Something hoisted; a group of flags raised as a signal. E19.
5 A device or mechanism for hoisting; a goods elevator. M19. ▸**b** In full ***rotary hoist***. A rotary clothes drier. *Austral.* M20.

T. PYNCHON Turns out the only way down is by a cable, hooked to an overhead hoist. **b** A. LUBBOCK The . . washing blowing . . from the rotary hoists in their back gardens.

hoist /hɔɪst/ *verb*[1]. See also HEIST *verb*, HIST *verb*[2]. L15.
[ORIGIN Alt. of HOISE *verb*, perh. after the pa. t. & pple.]
1 *verb trans.* Raise aloft, lift or set up; raise by means of a rope or pulley and tackle, or other mechanical device. Also foll. by *up*. L15. ▸**b** Chiefly *hist.* Lift up (a person) on the back of another for a flogging. E19.

W. WHARTON They hoisted the trees on top of their . . station wagon and drove off. D. BAGLEY They were hoisted up by the winch one at a time. J. G. BALLARD The Rising Sun was ceremonially hoisted to the mast of the USS *Wake*.

†**2** *verb trans.* Lift and move; remove; carry *away*. M16–M18.

T. NASHE She saw her mistris . . hoysted away to hell or to heaven.

3 *verb trans.* Raise in degree or quality; exalt, elevate. Now *rare*. M17.
4 *verb intrans.* Be raised, rise aloft. M17.
5 *verb trans. & intrans.* Orig., break into (a building). Now, steal, esp. by shoplifting. (Cf. earlier HOISTER 1.) *slang*. L18.

J. L. WATEN I know where we can hoist a car.

hoist *verb*[2] *pa. t. & pple*: see HOISE.

hoister /ˈhɔɪstə/ *noun*. E18.
[ORIGIN from HOIST *verb*[1] + -ER[1]. Cf. HEISTER.]
1 Orig., a housebreaker. Now, a shoplifter, a pickpocket. *slang*. E18.
2 A person who hoists a flag etc., a contrivance for hoisting something. M19.

hoit /hɔɪt/ *verb intrans. obsolete* exc. *dial.* L16.
[ORIGIN Unknown.]
1 Indulge in riotous mirth; (of a woman) behave boisterously. L16.
2 Move clumsily; limp. *Scot.* L18.

hoity-toity /hɔɪtɪˈtɔɪti/ *noun, adjective, & interjection*. Also **highty-tighty** /hʌɪtɪˈtʌɪti/. M17.
[ORIGIN Redupl. of HOIT; later infl. by *high*, *height*.]
▸ **A** *noun*. **1** Orig., riotous or giddy conduct. Later, haughty behaviour, an assumption of superiority. *arch.* M17.

H

2 A lively or unruly girl. Long *obsolete* exc. *dial.* L17.
▸ **B** *adjective.* Orig. (*arch.*) frolicsome. Later, haughty, petulant. L17.

R. FRAME They don't like hoity-toity kids . . . Makes them sick. Stuck-up little madams.

▸ **C** *interjection.* Expr. surprised protest at undue presumption, petulance, etc. L17.

HENRY FIELDING Hoity-toity! . . madam is in her airs, I protest.

■ **hoity-toityness** *noun* E19.

Hokan /ˈhəʊk(ə)n/ *noun & adjective.* E20.
[ORIGIN from Hokan *hok* approximate form of 'two' + -AN.]
(Designating or pertaining to) a group of languages spoken by certain N. American Indian peoples of the west coast of the US.

hoke /həʊk/ *verb trans. slang.* E20.
[ORIGIN Back-form. from HOKUM.]
Overact (a part). Also foll. by *up*.

hokey /ˈhəʊki/ *noun. slang.* Now *rare.* E19.
[ORIGIN Unknown.]
Only in ***by hokey***, ***by the hokey*** (***fiddle***): used as an oath or to express emphasis.

hokey /ˈhəʊki/ *adjective. slang* (chiefly *N. Amer.*). M20.
[ORIGIN from HOKE or HOKUM + -Y¹.]
Involving hokum, sentimental, overacted.

H

hokey-cokey /həʊkɪˈkəʊki/ *noun.* M20.
[ORIGIN Unknown.]
A kind of communal dance characterized by raising the hands in the air and shaking them while bowing and lowering them.

hokey-pokey /həʊkɪˈpəʊki/ *noun. colloq.* M19.
[ORIGIN In sense 1 alt. of HOCUS-POCUS *noun*; other uses of unknown origin.]
1 Deception, trickery. M19.
2 A kind of cheap ice cream sold by street vendors. L19.
3 A brittle porous kind of toffee. *NZ.* M20.

hoki /ˈhəʊki/ *noun.* L19.
[ORIGIN Maori.]
An edible marine fish resembling a hake, *Macrouronus novaezelandiae* (family Macruronidae), found off the southern coasts of New Zealand; the flesh of this as food.

Hokkien /həʊˈkiːn/ *adjective & noun.* M19.
[ORIGIN Amoy *hok kian*.]
▸ **A** *adjective.* Of or pertaining to a people of SE China, or their dialect of southern Min Chinese. M19.
▸ **B** *noun.* **1** A member of a people traditionally inhabiting SE China. E20.
2 A dialect of southern Min Chinese that is also spoken in Malaysia, Singapore, Taiwan, and the Philippines. M20.

hokku /ˈhɒkuː/ *noun.* Pl. same, -S. L19.
[ORIGIN Japanese = opening verse (of a linked sequence of comic verses).]
= HAIKU.

hokonui /ˈhɒkənuːi/ *noun. NZ.* M20.
[ORIGIN Maori place name.]
Illicitly distilled spirits.

hokum /ˈhəʊkəm/ *noun. slang* (orig. *US*). E20.
[ORIGIN Unknown.]
Sentimental, popular, sensational, or unreal situations, dialogue, etc., in a film or play etc.; bunkum.

CLIVE JAMES The ideal biographer's innocent nostrils have detected the odd whiff of hokum. *TV Times* Hard-to-swallow science fiction hokum about a mummy escaping from a sarcophagus.

hol- *combining form* see HOLO-.

holarctic /həʊˈlɑːktɪk/ *adjective & noun.* Also **H-**. L19.
[ORIGIN from HOLO- + ARCTIC *adjective.*]
▸ **A** *adjective.* Of, pertaining to, or (usu. **H-**) designating the biogeographical region which includes the cold and temperate zones of the northern hemisphere (i.e. both Nearctic and Palaearctic regions). Of an animal: inhabiting or (esp.) distributed throughout this region; circumpolar. L19.
▸ **B** *ellipt.* as *noun.* (Usu. **H-**.) The Holarctic region. L20.

Holbein /ˈhɒlbʌɪn, ˈhəʊl-/ *adjective.* L19.
[ORIGIN from Hans *Holbein* (1497–1543), German painter.]
Designating or pertaining to a style of embroidery etc. embodying qualities or decoration characteristic of Holbein or his work.
■ **Holbeinesque** *adjective* resembling the work of Holbein L19.

holcus /ˈhɒlkəs/ *noun.* L18.
[ORIGIN mod. Latin from Greek *holkos* a kind of grass.]
Any of various grasses of the genus *Holcus*, which includes the common pasture grass Yorkshire fog or meadow soft-grass, *H. lanatus*.

hold /həʊld/ *noun*¹. See also HOLT *noun*². OE.
[ORIGIN Partly from HOLD *verb*, partly from Old Norse *hald* hold, support, custody.]
▸ **I 1** †**a** The action or fact of keeping or guarding; occupation, possession; rule. OE–L16. ▸**b** Tenure. (Earlier in senses of COPYHOLD, FREEHOLD.) *obsolete* exc. *dial.* M17.

2 The action or an act of keeping something in one's hand or grasping; grasp (*lit.* & *fig.*), a controlling influence. Also, an opportunity of holding, something to hold by. ME. ▸**b** *spec.* A manner of holding in wrestling etc. E18.

L. STEPHEN The hold was generally firm when the fissures were not filled with ice. L. GORDON Leslie Stephen's hold on his . . daughter's imagination was the result . . of the education he gave her. A. MCCOWEN My father . . tried to break the Conservative hold on the Royal Borough.

catch hold of: see CATCH *verb*. ***get hold of*** (**a**) take into one's grasp (*lit.* & *fig.*); (**b**) get possession of, obtain; (**c**) get into contact with (a person). ***lay hold of***, ***lay hold on***: see LAY *verb*¹. ***take hold*** (**a**) ***take hold of***, take into one's grasp; (**b**) (of a custom or habit) become established. **b *no holds barred***, ***with no holds barred*** (with) no restrictions, all methods being permitted.

3 Confinement, custody, imprisonment. Long *arch. rare.* ME.

J. BRAMHALL Father Oldcorne being in hold for the powder treason.

4 †**a** Retention, restraint. ME–L17. ▸**b** A delay, a pause, a postponement. M20. ▸**c** A facility whereby an incoming telephone connection is held automatically until a specified recipient can take the call; freq. in ***on hold***. M20.

a HENRY MORE And this is a good hold to the Church from relapsing into Heathenism again. **b** *New Scientist* Unless there has been a last-minute 'hold' . . the first . . *Mariner* spacecraft should . . be on its way. **c** D. E. WESTLAKE I put him on hold and called Mr Clarebridge. *fig.*: *Ottawa Journal* Our sex life is on hold until after the 10 p.m. sportscast.

†**5** Contention, struggle; resistance. E16–M17.

E. JOHNSON Great hold and keepe there was about choice of Magistrates this yeare.

▸ **II** †**6** A support, a defence. OE–ME.
†**7** Property held, a holding; *spec.* a tenement. Cf. COPYHOLD, FREEHOLD, LEASEHOLD, etc. ME–L16.
8 A place of refuge or shelter; *esp.* an animal's lurking place. ME.

F. FRANCIS Reed or rush beds, . . all of which are favourite holds.

9 A fortress, a stronghold. *arch.* ME.

LYTTON A rude fortress . . out of the wrecks of some greater Roman hold.

10 a A thing that holds something, a receptacle. E16. ▸**b** Something which is grasped; something by or with which an object is grasped. L16.

b J. SPENCER To conclude it a falling cause which catcheth at such weak and unfaithful holds. F. MARRYAT Sharks . . watched with upturned eyes . . the snapping of the frail hold that supported me.

11 MUSIC. A pause. Now chiefly *US.* L17.
12 A prison cell. E18.
13 The retention of an image in a film shot. E20.

hold /həʊld/ *noun*². Long *obsolete* exc. *hist.* OE.
[ORIGIN Old Norse *hǫldr*, identified with Old English *hæleþ*, German *Held* hero, in Norse law a yeoman of higher rank, the owner of allodial land, (poet.) a man.]
In the Anglo-Saxon period, a high-ranking officer in the Danelaw.

hold /həʊld/ *noun*³. L16.
[ORIGIN Alt., by assim. to HOLD *verb*, of HOLL *noun*, HOLE *noun*¹.]
A compartment in a ship or aircraft below the (lower) deck, where cargo is stored.

T. HEGGEN The ship was simultaneously unloading cargo from three holds.

hold /həʊld/ *verb.* Pa. t. **held** /hɛld/; pa. pple **held** /hɛld/, (*arch.*) **holden** /ˈhəʊld(ə)n/.
[ORIGIN Old English *haldan* (*healdan*) = Old Frisian *halda*, Old Saxon *haldan* (Dutch *houden*), Old High German *haltan* (German *halten*), Old Norse *halda*, Gothic *haldan*, from Germanic orig. strong verb with the senses watch (cf. BEHOLD), look after, pasture (cattle).]
▸ **I** *verb trans.* †**1** Keep watch over (sheep etc.); rule (people). OE–ME.
2 Prevent from getting away; keep fast, grasp, have a grip on. Freq. with adverbial extension. OE. ▸**b** CRICKET etc. Catch (a ball), esp. particularly skilfully. M18. ▸**c** SPORT. Prove a match for; restrict (an opponent) *to* (a draw etc.). L19.

E. AMADI Oyia held her in a vice-like grip. R. INGALLS She held his hand. **c** *Racing Post* Heiress Green . . held Another Earl by a head in the Coolmine Race.

roadholding: see ROAD *noun*.

3 Keep from falling; support in or with the hands, arms, etc. OE. ▸†**b** *fig.* Uphold, support. OE–E16. ▸**c** Grasp so as to control (*lit.* & *fig.*). L16. ▸†**d** Bear (a particular treatment). L16–M17.

New Yorker She was holding the baby. 'Would you like to hold him, Beverly?' M. AMIS I held the telephone at arm's length, and stared at it. **c** T. BIDDLECOMBE Going to the first fence there was no way I was going to hold the horse. **d** SHAKES. *Coriol.* Now humble as the ripest mulberry That will not hold the handling.

4 Have or keep within it; contain or be able to contain; have the capacity for; (of a person) consume (liquor etc.) without undue intoxication. OE.

V. WOOLF Crumpling the bag which had held the cherries. S. LEWIS Their favourite motion-picture theatre was the Château, which held three thousand spectators. G. GREENE They were . . crushed at a small table, just large enough to hold three whiskies. D. BALLANTYNE It's Betty that can't hold the liquor.

5 Have or keep as one's own; possess, be the owner, occupant, incumbent, or tenant of; have gained as a qualification or honour. OE. ▸**b** Keep possession of (a place etc.) against attack. ME. ▸**c** Be in (a place); retain possession or occupation of; dominate; engross, retain the attention of. ME.

P. MASSINGER I hold my dukedom from you, as your vassal. SIR W. SCOTT My Sovereign holds in ward my land. A. CARNEGIE We held the record and many visitors came to marvel at the marvel. C. HILL Arminians held all the best bishoprics and deaneries. N. SYMINGTON For the next three years he held posts in different hospitals. *Soldier* He also holds the Long Service and Good Conduct Medal. **b** SLOAN WILSON A very small island which the British had held for two months. **c** MILTON The star, that bids the shepherd fold, Now the top of heaven doth hold. J. R. SEELEY The intoxication of the Marengo campaign still held him. K. AMIS The journal held no more than half his attention. S. BELLOW He checked their smiles, holding them all with his serious, worn, blue gaze. R. CARVER He spent his time repairing things, now that he could no longer hold a job in the aerospace industry. *Stage & Television Today* Carr . . is a gifted, confident comedian who held the audience.

6 Not let go; keep, retain; keep (a person etc.) in a specified place, condition, etc. (cf. sense 11 below); make (a person) adhere *to* (terms, a promise, etc.). OE. ▸†**b** Continue to occupy; remain in (a place); not leave. LME–L18. ▸**c** Keep back, detain, delay. Also (orig. *US*) detain (a person) in custody. L19.

R. BUSH Vivienne held him to standards of emotional forthrightness he wished to but could not sustain. A. TREW A beam of light . . pierced the darkness, picked up the skimmer and held it. **b** W. A. OSBALDISTONE The hare will hold the highways more than at any other time. **c** J. RATHBONE There were no convictions, but she had been held for questioning on three occasions. J. CHEEVER I don't want you to hold dinner for me.

7 Keep together; keep in existence or operation, carry on; conduct (a meeting); observe, celebrate, (a festival etc.); engage in (a conversation); keep (company, silence, etc.); use (insolent etc.) language. OE.

P. KAVANAGH Peter walked in the garden . . and there held commune with the spirits of wealth and influence. P. ACKROYD The seance was to be held near Ealing Common.

†**8** Keep unbroken or inviolate; abide by (a command, a promise, etc.). OE–E17.

SHAKES. *Merry W.* To Master Brook you yet shall hold your word.

9 Restrain, refrain from; *colloq.* withhold, cease, stop. OE.

T. JEFFERSON The only restraining motive which may hold the hand of a tyrant. DICKENS I wish you'd hold your noise!

10 a Have in mind, entertain (a feeling, sentiment, etc.). *arch.* OE. ▸**b** Accept the truth of (a belief, doctrine, etc.); think or believe *that*, believe to be or *to be*, regard *as*, (*arch.* also *for*). ME. ▸**c** Have a specified feeling towards. ME. ▸**d** Of a judge or court: lay down, decide. M17.

a H. W. TORRENS The first . . who acknowledged the . . theory and held great account of those who practised it. **b** J. CONRAD A kind of railway contractor . . who held the doctor for an ass. I. MURDOCH It may be relevant here to add that I hold no religious beliefs whatever. C. RYCROFT He also held that most of the dreams of adults express repressed erotic wishes. W. GOLDING Words I must ever hold sacred. A. BRIGGS Wives . . were held to be subordinate to their husbands. **c** T. S. ELIOT They hold these monkeys in peculiar veneration. **d** *Independent* The justices held that they could not grant a protection order.

11 Keep (one's body, head, etc.) in a particular attitude or position. ME.

W. C. RUSSELL She held her face averted. D. HAMMETT She held her small body stiffly erect.

12 Oblige, constrain. Long *arch. rare.* ME.

S. WILLIAMS They could not view themselves as holden . . to submit.

†**13** Offer or accept as a wager, bet. LME–M18.

T. D'URFEY I'll hold ye five Guineas to four.

▸ **II** *verb intrans.* **14** Maintain one's position (against an adversary); (of a place) be held or occupied, hold out. OE.

SHAKES. *Ant. & Cl.* Our force by land Hath nobly held.

15 Continue in a (specified) state or course; last. ME. ▸**b** Be or remain valid, apply. ME. ▸**c** Of the weather: continue fine. L19.

I. BANKS My luck holds. Miss Arrol is in. H. WEINZWEIG He could come back next week, to see if the tuning held. **b** H. R. MILL This law does not hold for gases. **c** L. WHISTLER The weather held, and with the may bushes lathered in blossom the scene grew unearthly.

16 Maintain a hold, cling. ME. ▸†**b** In *imper.* Here, take this. L15–E17. ▸**c** Of a female animal: retain the seed of the male; conceive. E17. ▸**d** BOXING. Grasp an opponent with the hands, in contravention of the rules. E20. ▸**e** Be in possession of illicit drugs. *US slang.* M20.

TENNYSON There was no anchor, none, To hold by. **b** SHAKES. *Macb.* Hold, take my sword. **d** *Times* The referee had to speak to both men for holding.

17 Maintain an attachment *to*; adhere *to*, abide *by*, (a choice, purpose, etc.). ME.

J. BUCHAN In a pedestrian world he held to the old cavalier grace. P. GAY Freud persisted in holding to the cardinal ideas of psychoanalysis all his life.

18 Hold property by tenure; derive title to something (*of* or *from* a superior). Also *fig.*, (foll. by *of*, †*on*) depend on, belong or pertain to. ME.

W. LONGMAN Men holding by knight's service. W. S. LILLY No wonder, for genius holds of the noumenal.

19 Foll. by *with*: maintain allegiance to, side with; *colloq.* approve of (usu. in neg. contexts). ME.

M. HANMER Some there were, that held with both sides. *Cornhill Magazine* I don't hold with him buying flowers when his children haven't got enough to eat.

†**20** Avail, be of use. (Usu. in neg. & interrog. contexts.) Only in ME.

21 Keep going (in a specified direction); continue *on* (one's way etc.). ME.

CONAN DOYLE I've held on my course when better men . . have asked me to veil topsails. *Field* Instead of holding to Oakhill Wood, the pack bore to the right.

22 Remain unbroken; not give way. LME.

Illustrated London News The helm was perfectly sound, and the lashings held bravely.

23 Take place; occur, prevail. *arch.* LME.

SHAKES. *Rich. II* What news from Oxford? Do these justs and triumphs hold?

24 Restrain oneself. *arch.* L16.

SHELLEY 'Hold, hold!' He cried,—'I tell thee 'tis her brother!'

25 Have a capacity (now *rare*); HUNTING (of a covert) contain game. L16.

Hounds A cold, raw day with little scent and the coverts that normally hold were bare.

– PHRASES, & WITH ADVERBS IN SPECIALIZED SENSES: (A selection of cross-refs. only is included: see esp. other nouns.) **hold a candle to the Devil** *arch.* serve or assist a wicked person, be active in wickedness. ***hold a person's hand***: see HAND *noun*. ***hold a person's nose to the grindstone***: see GRINDSTONE *noun*. ***hold at bay***: see BAY *noun*[1] 2. ***hold a torch for***: see TORCH *noun*. ***hold a wolf by the ears***: see WOLF *noun*. **hold back** (*a*) impede the progress of; restrain; (*b*) keep (a thing) to or for oneself; (*c*) refrain or shrink (*from*). ***hold cheap***: see CHEAP *adjective*. ***hold court***: see COURT *noun*[1]. ***hold dear***: see DEAR *adjective*[1]. **hold down** (*a*) repress (*lit.* & *fig.*); (*b*) *colloq.* be competent enough to keep (one's job etc.). **hold everything!** = *hold it!* below. **hold forth** †(*a*) keep up, go on with; †(*b*) go on, proceed; (*c*) offer (an inducement etc.); (*d*) (usu. *derog.*) speak at length or tediously, preach. **hold good** be valid; apply. ***hold hands***: see HAND *noun*. **hold hard** (*a*) pull hard at the reins in order to stop a horse; (*b*) in *imper.* (*colloq.*) stop! wait! ***hold harmless***: see HARMLESS 3. **hold in** (*a*) keep in check, confine; (*b*) continue in a particular state etc.; restrain oneself, refrain. ***hold in DEMESNE***. **hold it!** cease action or movement. **hold it against** regard it to the discredit of (*that*). **hold it good** think it advisable (*to do*). **hold off** *verb phr. trans.* & *intrans.* delay; not begin; keep at a distance. **hold on** (*a*) *verb phr. trans.* keep in place on something; †(*b*) *verb phr. trans.* continue, keep up; (*c*) *verb phr. intrans.* keep one's grasp of something, not let go; (*d*) *verb phr. intrans.* continue, go on; (*e*) *verb phr. intrans.* (*colloq.*) wait a moment (freq. in *imper.*); (*f*) *verb phr. intrans.* (when telephoning) not ring off. ***hold one's BREATH***. ***hold one's ground***: see GROUND *noun*. **hold one's head high** behave proudly and confidently. **hold one's horses** *colloq.* stop; slow down. ***hold one's nose***: see NOSE *noun*. ***hold one's own***: see OWN *adjective* & *pronoun*. ***hold one's peace***: see PEACE *noun*. **hold one's serve**, **hold one's service** in tennis etc., win a game in which one is the server. ***hold one's tongue***: see TONGUE *noun*. ***hold one's way***: see WAY *noun*. ***hold one's whistle***: see WHISTLE *noun* 2. **hold out** (*a*) *verb phr. trans.* stretch out, proffer, (a hand etc.); offer (an inducement etc.); (*b*) *verb phr. trans.* represent *to be*; (*c*) *verb phr. trans.* (now *rare*) keep out, exclude; (*d*) *verb phr. trans.* keep up, continue; formerly also, bear or sustain to the end; (*e*) *verb phr. trans.* occupy or defend to the end; (*f*) *verb phr. intrans.* maintain resistance; persist, last; continue to make a demand *for*; (*g*) ***hold out on*** (*colloq.*), refuse something to (a person). **hold over** (*a*) LAW remain in possession of land after the expiration of a tenancy; remain in office etc. beyond the regular term; (*b*) keep for future consideration, postpone. **hold over (a person)** threaten (a person) constantly with. **hold serve**, **hold service** = *hold one's serve* above. ***hold the baby***: see BABY *noun* 1. ***hold the bag***: see BAG *noun*. ***hold the clock on***: see CLOCK *noun*[1]. ***hold the field***: see FIELD *noun*. ***hold the fort***: see FORT *noun* 1. **hold the line** (*a*) not yield; (*b*) maintain a telephone connection. **hold the stage** dominate a conversation etc. **hold to bail** LAW bind by bail. **hold together** (cause to) cohere. **hold to ransom** keep (a person) prisoner until a ransom is paid; demand concessions from by threats, esp. of industrial action. **hold true** = *hold good* above. **hold up** (*a*) maintain (the head etc.) erect; *fig.* support, sustain; (*b*) exhibit, display; subject openly to (contempt, derision, etc.); (*c*) let alone, give up; keep back, withhold; (*d*) stop and rob by violence or threats; (*e*) arrest the progress of, obstruct; (*f*) not fall, keep up; (*g*) hold out, endure; †(*h*) give in, surrender; (*i*) (of the weather) remain fine, not rain. **hold water** (*a*) not let water through or out; *fig.* (of reasoning) be sound, bear examination; (*b*) stop a boat by holding the blades of the oars flat against the boat's way. ***not able to hold a candle***, ***not fit to hold a candle***: see CANDLE *noun*. ***hold wedlock***: see WEDLOCK *noun* 1. ***Texas Hold 'Em***. **there is no holding him**, **there is no holding her**, etc., he, she, etc., is restive, high-spirited, determined, etc. ***too hot to hold one***: see HOT *adjective*.

holdall /ˈhəʊldɔːl/ *noun*. M19.
[ORIGIN from HOLD *verb* + ALL *pronoun*.]
A portable case or bag for miscellaneous articles.

holdback /ˈhəʊl(d)bak/ *noun*. L16.
[ORIGIN from HOLD *verb* + BACK *adverb*.]
1 Something that holds one back, a hindrance. L16. **2** An iron or strap on the shaft of a horse-drawn vehicle to which the breeching of the harness is attached. M19.

hold-down /ˈhəʊl(d)daʊn/ *noun*. L19.
[ORIGIN from HOLD *verb* + DOWN *adverb*.]
1 A device to prevent material or apparatus from moving or shaking. L19. **2** A judo grip or move in which the opponent is held down on the ground. M20.

holden *verb pa. pple*: see HOLD *verb*.

holder /ˈhəʊldə/ *noun*[1]. ME.
[ORIGIN from HOLD *verb* + -ER[1].]
▸ **I 1** A person who holds or grasps something. ME.

DICKENS The holder of a horse at Tellson's door.

2 A person who occupies or possesses something; *spec.* (*a*) the occupant of a post, position, office, etc., the current possessor of a (hereditary) title; (*b*) SPORT a person who has set a current record, the winner of a challenge cup; (*c*) the owner of a bank account, credit card, company shares, etc. ME.

E. ARBER The present holder of the farm. *Times* The effect on the players was clearly seen when L. Hoad, the holder, beat R. Bedard.

freeholder, ***householder***, ***jobholder***, ***smallholder***, etc. ***account holder***, ***cardholder***, ***shareholder***, etc.

3 a A canine tooth. *rare*. L17. ▸**b** In various animals, an organ of attachment or for grasping. L18. **4** A contrivance for holding something. M19.

cigarette-holder, ***kettle-holder***, ***penholder***, etc.

▸ **II 5** Something of which hold is taken. L18.

– COMB.: **holderbat** a type of bracket for fastening a pipe to a wall etc., consisting of two semicircular parts that are clamped round the pipe and a projection on one of the parts that is built into the wall.

holder /ˈhəʊldə/ *noun*[2]. L15.
[ORIGIN from HOLD *noun*[3] + -ER[1].]
A workman employed in a ship's hold.

holdfast /ˈhəʊl(d)fɑːst/ *adjective* & *noun*. M16.
[ORIGIN from HOLD *verb* + FAST *adverb*.]
▸ **A** *adjective*. That holds fast (*lit.* & *fig.*); persistent. M16.
▸ **B** *noun*. **1** A thing affording a secure hold or support. M16.
2 The action or fact of holding fast; firm or secure grasp. M16.
3 A thing that holds something fast; a staple, bolt, clamp, etc., securing an object to a wall. L16. ▸**b** A rootlike or disc-shaped organ of attachment in some algae (esp. seaweeds) and fungi. M19.
4 †**a** A stingy person, a miser. L16–E18. ▸**b** (A name for) a dog that holds tenaciously. Now chiefly in proverb ***Brag is a good dog, but Holdfast is better***. L16.

holding /ˈhəʊldɪŋ/ *noun*. ME.
[ORIGIN from HOLD *verb* + -ING[1].]
▸ **I 1** The action of HOLD *verb*. Also foll. by adverb. ME. ▸**b** *spec.* The tenure of land. LME. ▸†**c** Consistency. *rare* (Shakes.). Only in E17.
2 Something which holds or lays hold; an attachment; a means of influencing. L18.
▸ **II 3** An opinion held, a tenet. Now chiefly US LAW, a ruling on a point of law. LME.
†**4** The burden of a song. L16–E17.
5 a Property held, *esp.* stocks or shares. L16. ▸**b** Land held by legal right. M17. ▸**c** The hand held by a card player. E20.

b *smallholding*.

– COMB.: **holding company** a company created to hold the shares of other companies, which it then controls; **holding ground** a bottom in which an anchor will hold; anchorage (*lit.* & *fig.*); **holding operation** a manoeuvre designed to maintain the status quo; **holding paddock** *Austral.* & *NZ* a paddock where sheep or cattle are kept until required for droving etc.; **holding pattern** a flight path maintained by an aircraft awaiting permission to land.

holdout /ˈhəʊldaʊt/ *noun*. L19.
[ORIGIN from HOLD *verb* + OUT *adverb*.]
1 A card sharper's mechanical device for concealing cards. *arch. slang*. L19.
2 The action of holding out for something; a person who holds out for something, esp. higher pay. Chiefly *N. Amer.* M20.
3 The ability of paint or ink to dry normally on an imperfect surface. M20.

holdover /ˈhəʊldəʊvə/ *noun*. L19.
[ORIGIN from HOLD *verb* + OVER *adverb*.]
1 A person who remains in office etc. beyond the regular term. L19.
2 Something left over, a relic. *N. Amer.* E20.

hold-up /ˈhəʊldʌp/ *noun*. M19.
[ORIGIN from HOLD *verb* + UP *adverb*[1].]
1 A check to progress; a stoppage or delay of traffic etc. M19.
2 A robbery, esp. with the use of violence or threats. L19.

hole /həʊl/ *noun*[1].
[ORIGIN Old English *hol* (repr. inflected forms with lengthened vowel) = Old Norse *hol*, orig. use as noun of neut. sing. of *hol* HOLL *adjective* = Old Frisian, Old Saxon, Middle Dutch & mod. Dutch, Old High German *hol* (German *hohl*), Old Norse *holr*, from Germanic base repr. by Old High German *huli*, German *Höhle*, Old English *hylu*, Old Norse *hola* hollow, hole, *hylr* deep place, pool, ult. from Indo-European base meaning 'cover, conceal': see HELE *verb*. Rel. also to HELL *noun*, HELM *noun*[1], HOLD *noun*[3], HOLL *noun*, HOLLOW *noun*[1], HOWE *noun*[2].]
▸ **I** A hollow place, a cavity.
1 An empty place or cavity in a solid body or in the ground; a pit; a cave; a deep place in a pond, stream, etc.; *spec.* an animal's den or burrow. OE. ▸**b** A deep hollow in the surface of the body, as an eye socket. ME.

DAY LEWIS I came to know . . the holes and corners, where each of them deposited her eggs. JONATHAN MILLER If you poke your tongue into a hole in . . your teeth, the hole feels enormous. B. EMECHETA Mendoza has seen to it that you have more water holes.

2 a A secret place; a hiding place. *obsolete* exc. in ***priest's hole*** s.v. PRIEST. ME. ▸**b** A dungeon, a prison cell; *esp.* a cell used for solitary confinement. M16. ▸**c** A small, unpleasant, dreary or dingy place. E17.

c P. BOWLES Dahar's a filthy hole. S. MIDDLETON Nobody would want to live in a dead-and-alive hole like this.

3 a A valley. Chiefly in place names. ME. ▸**b** A small bay, a cove. *Scot.* & *US*. M17.
4 The hold of a ship. (Earlier as HOLL *noun* 2.) Now *rare*. L15.
5 A cavity into which a ball etc. must be got in various games, esp. golf; each of the pockets of a billiard table or pool table. L16.
6 GOLF. Each of the divisions of a course from each tee to each green; the play on this; a point scored by a player driving the ball from one hole to another with the fewest strokes. M18.
7 An awkward situation, a fix, a scrape. *colloq.* M18.

B. BAINBRIDGE You got me out of a hole . . I'm very grateful.

8 CHESS. A square no longer protected by a defender's pawns and so easily available to attacking pieces. L19.
9 PHYSICS. A position from which an electron is absent, esp. in an energy band in a crystal lattice; such a vacancy regarded as a mobile carrier of a positive charge. E20.
▸ **II** A perforation, an opening, etc.
10 An aperture passing through something; an opening, a perforation. OE.

G. ORWELL Large, dirty toes were sticking out of the holes in his socks.

11 The orifice of an organ or part of the body; *spec.* (*slang*) the mouth, the anus, the vagina; *transf.* sexual intercourse. ME.

L. COHEN Don't give me all this diamond shit, shove it up your occult hole. T. PARKER I never thought the day'd come when I'd pass by a chance to have a bit of hole.

– PHRASES: ***a round peg in a square hole***, ***a square peg in a round hole***: see PEG *noun*[1]. ***black hole***: see BLACK *adjective*. ***burn a hole in one's pocket***: see BURN *verb* 9b. **hole in the heart** a congenital defect in the heart membrane. **hole in one** GOLF a first shot from the tee that enters the hole. **hole in the wall** (*a*) a small dingy place; *esp.* a business or (*US*) a place where alcoholic drinks are sold illegally; (*b*) an automatic cash dispenser installed in the outside wall of a bank. **in holes** worn so much that holes have formed. **in the hole** in debt. **make a hole in** use a large amount of. **make a hole in the water** commit suicide by drowning. **need like a hole in the head** have no need or desire at all for (something). **pick holes in** find fault with. **the hole** *slang* solitary confinement; (see also *in the hole* above). ***toad in the hole***: see TOAD 1. ***white hole***: see WHITE *adjective*.

– COMB.: **hole-and-corner** *adjective* secret; underhand; **hole card** in stud poker, a card which has been dealt face down; **hole-proof** *adjective* (of a material) treated so as to be resistant to wear; **hole punch** a device for piercing a hole or holes, esp. one for punching holes in paper so as to allow for filing or binding; **hole saw** = *crown saw* s.v. CROWN *noun*.

†**hole** *adjective*, *noun*[2], *adverb*, & *interjection* see WHOLE.

hole /həʊl/ *verb*.
[ORIGIN Old English *holian* = Old High German *holōn*, Gothic *-hulōn*, from Germanic base of HOLL *adjective*: see HOLE *noun*[1].]
1 *verb trans.* Make a hole or holes in, hollow out; dig (the ground); *spec.* (NAUTICAL) pierce the side of (a ship). OE.

E. DIEHL After the boards have been cut to size, they are holed-out and laced onto the book. SNOO WILSON I've got to get him before we get holed by a Russian submarine.

2 *verb intrans.* Make a hole or holes; dig *through* from one mine-working to another. ME.
3 *verb intrans.* Become full of holes through wear. E17.
4 *verb intrans.* Go into a hole, esp. for hibernation; *esp.* (*N. Amer. colloq.*) hide oneself, lie in wait, seek shelter. Usu. foll. by *out*, *up*. E17.

E. BIRNEY Or you could hole out in Canada in an igloo or something. T. O'BRIEN I holed up in the bathroom.

H

5 *verb trans.* Put into a hole; put in prison; hide. E17.
6 *verb trans.* GOLF & BILLIARDS etc. Drive (a ball) or play (a shot) into a hole or pocket. L17. ▸**b** *verb intrans.* GOLF. Drive the ball into the hole. Usu. foll. by *out.* M19. ▸**c** *verb intrans.* CRICKET. (Of a batsman) be dismissed by hitting a catch to a (usu. specified) fielder or position. Foll. by *out.* L20.

JO GRIMOND His brother . . holed a putt of awkward length to win the Calcutta Cup. **b** N. BLAKE Holed out in one. *Golf Monthly* He . . gave a strong hint of . . greater things to come by holing for a birdie. **c** *Times* 47 runs were added in seven overs before Lloyds holed out to deep mid-wicket.

7 *verb trans.* MINING. Sink (a shaft), drive (a tunnel) through; undercut (coal) in a seam. E18.
■ **holeable** *adjective* (GOLF) (of a stroke, esp. a putt) capable of sending the ball into the hole E20. **holer** *noun* a person who makes or bores a hole; *spec.* a collier who undercuts a coal seam: LME. **holing** *noun* (*a*) the action of the verb; (*b*) MINING a wedge-shaped section of a coal seam or floor removed to undermine or loosen it: LME.

holed /həʊld/ *adjective.* LME.
[ORIGIN from HOLE *noun*[1], *verb*: see -ED[2], -ED[1].]
Having a hole or holes.

holey /ˈhəʊli/ *adjective.* ME.
[ORIGIN from HOLE *noun*[1] + -Y[1].]
Full of holes.

J. RABAN Shoes which let the sand into their holey socks.

holey dollar AUSTRAL. HISTORY a coin originally worth 5s. current in parts of Australia from 1813 to about 1830, made by punching a circular piece out of the centre of a Spanish dollar.

Holi /ˈhəʊliː/ *noun.* Also (earlier) †**Hoolee**. L17.
[ORIGIN Hindi *holī*.]
The Hindu spring festival in honour of Krishna the amorous cowherd.

holiday /ˈhɒlədeɪ, ˈhɒlɪ-, -di/ *noun & adjective.*
[ORIGIN Old English *hāligdæg*, late Old English *hālidæg*, found beside *hālig dæg* HOLY DAY.]
▸ **A** *noun.* **1** = HOLY DAY. Now *rare.* OE.
2 A day of festivity or recreation, on which no work is done; *sing.* & in *pl.*, a period of such recreation, a vacation. ME. ▸**b** *gen.* Festivity, recreation. E16.

A. TROLLOPE Glomax thought that Tony had been idle, and had made a holiday of the day. A. S. BYATT He was sure she would find a nice holiday abroad very restorative. J. MORTIMER Separated at school the boys remained apart during the holidays. **b** T. KENEALLY To see the distinctive hills . . gave them an unwarranted sense of holiday.

3 Chiefly NAUTICAL. A patch or area unintentionally left uncoated in painting etc. L18.
4 A short period during which the payment of instalments, tax, etc. may be suspended. Usu. with specifying word. E20.
– PHRASES ETC.: *busman's holiday*: see *busman* s.v. BUS *noun*. *blind-man's holiday*: see BLIND *adjective*. *half holiday*: see HALF-. *high holiday*: see HIGH *adjective*. **make holiday** *arch.* have a break from work. **on holiday**, **on one's holidays** in the course of a holiday or vacation. *Roman holiday*: see ROMAN *adjective*. **take a holiday** have a break from work. *whole holiday*: see WHOLE.
– COMB.: **holiday camp** a camp for holidaymakers with accommodation, entertainment, and facilities on site; **holiday centre** a place with many tourist attractions; **holiday home** a house or second home where people may spend holidays; **holiday loading** *Austral.* an addition to holiday pay to compensate for lost overtime earnings; **holidaymaker** a person on holiday; **holiday village** a complex for holidaymakers with cottages, shops, entertainment, etc., on site.
▸ **B** *attrib.* or as *adjective.* Of, pertaining to, or characteristic of a holiday; festive; idle, jesting. LME.

SHAKES. *A.Y.L.* They are but burs . . thrown upon thee in holiday foolery.

holiday /ˈhɒlədeɪ, ˈhɒlɪ-, -di/ *verb intrans.* M19.
[ORIGIN from HOLIDAY *noun & adjective.*]
Spend a holiday.

R. P. GRAVES He was holidaying in a hotel with a magnificent view.

■ **holidayer** *noun* L19.

holily /ˈhəʊlɪli/ *adverb.* OE.
[ORIGIN from HOLY *adjective* + -LY[2].]
1 With sanctity or devoutness; in a holy manner. OE.
2 Sacredly; solemnly. Now *rare* or *obsolete.* LME.

holiness /ˈhəʊlɪnɪs/ *noun & adjective.* OE.
[ORIGIN from HOLY *adjective* + -NESS.]
▸ **A** *noun.* **1** The quality of being holy; sanctity; saintliness. OE.

P. ROTH In the old parables about the spiritual life, there were searches for a kind of holiness.

†**2** A holy place or thing. OE–ME.
3 (Usu. **H-**.) With possess. adjective (as ***his holiness*** etc.): a title of respect given to the Pope and (formerly) any of various high ecclesiastical dignitaries. LME.

R. BOLT His present Holiness is . . a strikingly corrupt old person.

▸ **B** *attrib.* or as *adjective.* Designating or pertaining to any of various religious sects or Churches which emphasize sanctification, spiritual purity, and perfectionism. Chiefly *US.* L19.

holinight /ˈhɒlɪnʌɪt/ *noun.* ME.
[ORIGIN from HOLY *adjective* + NIGHT *noun*, after HOLIDAY *noun.*]
†**1** The eve of a holy festival. Only in ME.
2 A night of festivity or pleasure. *rare.* E19.

holism /ˈhəʊlɪz(ə)m, ˈhɒl-/ *noun.* E20.
[ORIGIN from HOLO- + -ISM. Cf. WHOLISM.]
The theory or principle of a tendency in nature to form or produce organized wholes which are more than the mere sum of the component units; *spec.* the application of this theory in medicine, involving the treatment of the whole person rather than the physical symptoms alone.
■ **hoˈlistic** *adjective* (*a*) of or pertaining to holism; (*b*) whole, complete, comprising or involving all parts, aspects, etc.: E20. **hoˈlistically** *adverb* as a whole E20.

†**holk** *verb* see HOWK.

holl /həʊl/ *noun. obsolete* exc. *dial.* See also HOWE *noun*[2].
[ORIGIN Old English *hol* HOLE *noun*[1], repr. orig. uninflected form with short vowel (later with diphthong). Cf. HULL *noun*[2].]
1 A hole, a hollow place, a dip, a valley. OE.
†**2** A ship's hold. ME–E17.
3 The middle or depth (of winter or night). *Scot. & N. English.* LME.

holl /həʊl/ *adjective. obsolete* exc. *dial.*
[ORIGIN Old English *hol*: see HOLE *noun*[1].]
1 Hollow, concave, empty. OE.
2 Deeply excavated or dug; lying in a hollow. OE.

holla /ˈhɒlə/ *verb intrans. & trans.* Pa. t. & pple **-aed**, **-a'd**. L16.
[ORIGIN Partly var. of HOLLO *verb*, partly from HOLLA *interjection & noun.*]
= HOLLO *verb.*

holla /ˈhɒlə, *occas.* hɒˈlɑː/ *interjection & noun.* E16.
[ORIGIN French *holà*, from *ho* HO *interjection*[2] + *là* there. Cf. HOLLO *interjection & noun* etc.]
▸ **A** *interjection.* †**1** Stop! Cease! E16–L17.
2 Commanding or attempting to attract attention. L16.
3 Expr. pleasure, satisfaction, encouragement, etc. E18.
▸ **B** *noun.* A shout of 'holla!' L16.

hollabaloo *noun, interjection, & verb* var. of HULLABALOO.

holland /ˈhɒlənd/ *noun & adjective.* ME.
[ORIGIN *Holland*, a former province of the Netherlands (now freq. also used as the name of the whole country), from Dutch, earlier *Holtlant*, from *holt* wood + *-lant* land, describing the Dordrecht district.]
▸ **A** *noun.* Any smooth hard-wearing linen fabric, orig. a kind produced in the Netherlands (Holland). ME.
▸ **B** *attrib.* or as *adjective.* **1** (**H-**.) Of, pertaining to, or produced in the Netherlands. LME.
2 Made of holland. M16.
– PHRASES: *brown holland*: see BROWN *adjective*.

hollandaise /hɒlənˈdeɪz, *attrib. also* ˈhɒləndeɪz/ *noun & adjective.* M19.
[ORIGIN French, fem. of *hollandais* Dutch, from *Hollande* Holland.]
(Designating) a sauce made with butter, egg yolks, vinegar or white wine, and lemon juice, usu. served with fish.

Hollander /ˈhɒləndə/ *noun.* LME.
[ORIGIN formed as HOLLAND + -ER[1].]
1 A native of the Netherlands (Holland); a Netherlander. Now chiefly *spec.*, a South African colonist or immigrant of Dutch birth or descent. LME.
2 *hist.* A Dutch ship. L16.
3 A machine, invented in the Netherlands, for making paper pulp from rags. L19.

Hollands /ˈhɒləndz/ *noun. arch.* L18.
[ORIGIN from Dutch †*hollandsch genever* (now *hollands jenever*) Dutch gin: see GENEVER.]
Dutch gin, genever. Also ***Hollands gin***.

Hollantide /ˈhɒl(ə)ntʌɪd/ *noun.* Now chiefly *Irish.* L16.
[ORIGIN Alt.]
= ***Hallowtide*** s.v. HALLOW *noun*[1].

holler /ˈhɒlə/ *noun.* Chiefly *dial. & N. Amer. colloq.* E19.
[ORIGIN Partly var. of HOLLO *noun*, partly from the verb.]
A shout, esp. of protest or complaint; a protest, a complaint; a work song of southern states of the US.
a whoop and a holler: see WHOOP *noun* 1.

holler /ˈhɒlə/ *verb intrans. & trans.* Chiefly *dial. & N. Amer. colloq.* L17.
[ORIGIN Var. of HOLLO *verb.*]
Cry out, shout, esp. in protest or complaint.

G. PALEY You always start hollering if I don't do what you tell me. J. BARTH 'Toddy!' one of my companions hollered from down a hallway. W. WHARTON With the sound of babies hollering to be fed . . it makes quite a racket.

Hollerith /ˈhɒlərɪθ/ *noun.* L19.
[ORIGIN Herman *Hollerith* (1860–1929), Amer. inventor.]
Used *attrib.* to designate the system of using punched cards in accounting, statistics, etc., or such cards themselves.

hollin /ˈhɒlɪn/ *noun.* Now *arch. & dial.*
[ORIGIN Old English *hole(g)n* rel. to Old Saxon, Old High German *hulis* (Middle High German *huls*, German *Hulst*), Old Frankish source of French *houx*, and further to Welsh *celyn*, Old Irish *cuilenn*, Gaelic *cuilionn.*]
Holly.

hollo /ˈhɒləʊ/ *verb.* Also **holloa** /ˈhɒləʊ, hɒˈləʊ/, (now *rare*) **hollow**. LME.
[ORIGIN Prob. var. of HALLOW *verb*[2]. See also HALLO, HALLOO *verb*, HOLLER *verb.*]
1 *verb intrans. & trans.* Call out or yell to attract attention, express surprise, give encouragement, etc. LME.
2 *verb trans.* Call after or to. E17.
3 *verb trans.* Drive *away*, call *in*, *off*, etc., by holloing. E17.

hollo /ˈhɒləʊ/ *interjection & noun.* Also **holloa** /ˈhɒləʊ, hɒˈləʊ/, (now *rare*) **hollow**. L16.
[ORIGIN Rel. to HOLLA *interjection & noun.* See also HALLO, HILLO, HOLLER *noun.*]
▸ **A** *interjection.* Commanding or attempting to attract attention. Also expr. pleasure, satisfaction, encouragement, etc. L16.
▸ **B** *noun.* A shout of 'hollo!'; a loud shout. L16.

holloa *verb, interjection & noun* var. of HOLLO *verb, interjection & noun.*

hollow /ˈhɒləʊ/ *noun*[1].
[ORIGIN Old English *holh* obscurely rel. to *hol* HOLE *noun*[1], HOLL *noun*. Re-formed M16 from the adjective (obsolete from early ME).]
1 A concave formation or place dug out or resembling one dug out; a depression on any surface; an internal cavity (with or without an opening), an empty space. OE.

E. BOWEN A large double bed with a hollow in the middle. E. O'BRIEN The hollows in his face made him seem thinner than he actually was.

in the hollow of one's hand *fig.* entirely subservient to one.
2 *spec.* A depression on the earth's surface; a dip, a valley, a basin. ME.

K. MANSFIELD Down below in the hollow the little cottages were in deep shade.

3 BOOKBINDING. A strip of thick paper glued to the boards and back of a book in order to strengthen its spine. L19.
OXFORD *hollow.*

hollow *noun*[2] see HOLLO *noun.*

hollow /ˈhɒləʊ/ *adjective & adverb.* ME.
[ORIGIN from HOLLOW *noun*[1].]
▸ **A** *adjective.* **1** Having a hole or empty space inside; not solid. Formerly also, porous or open in texture or composition. ME. ▸**b** Having an empty space below. M17.

W. WHARTON The feather has a hollow shaft. *fig.*: L. GORDON Lily's very body felt stark and hollow with longing.

2 Having a hole or depression on the surface; sunken, indented. ME. ▸**b** Of the sea: having deep troughs. E17.

G. GREENE The men trudging to Castile for work . . , bony wrists and hollow chests, incredible rags. U. LE GUIN The stone plain was . . hollow, like a huge bowl full of sunlight. S. ROE She eats very little . . . Her cheeks are hollow.

3 Empty; *transf.* having an empty stomach, hungry, lean. LME.

SHAKES. *Merry W.* As jealous as Ford, that search'd a hollow walnut for his wife's leman.

4 *fig.* Lacking substance or value; insincere, false; cynical. E16.

C. G. WOLFF Raucous laughter pursues us . . hollow, mocking, derisive. KARL MILLER The hollow enthusiasm which many people profess for music. *Times* If Seb had competed it would have been a hollow victory over him.

5 Of a sound: echoing, as if made in or on a hollow container. M16.

E. LANGLEY An emaciated boy with a hollow cough and that easy-going look of the consumptive. S. SASSOON A hollow cry of hounds like lonely bells.

▸ **B** *adverb.* **1** Hollowly. Now *rare* exc. in comb. & in ***ring hollow***, sound insincere or unconvincing. L15.
2 Thoroughly, completely. *colloq.* M17.

GEO. ELIOT She beats us younger people hollow.

– SPECIAL COLLOCATIONS & COMB.: **hollow-eyed** *adjective* with eyes (apparently) deeply sunken from fatigue etc. **hollow-ground** *adjective* ground so as to have a concave surface. **hollow heart** a condition of potatoes in which a cavity is formed in the centre of the tuber by overripid growth. **hollow horn** *US* listlessness and weakness in cattle, erroneously believed to be due to hollow horns. **hollow square** MILITARY HISTORY a body of infantry drawn up in a square with a space in the middle.

hollow /ˈhɒləʊ/ *verb*[1]. LME.
[ORIGIN from the adjective.]
1 *verb trans.* Make hollow or concave; form or bend into a hollow or concave shape. Also foll. by *out.* LME.

V. WOOLF The breeze blew out her match. Giles hollowed his hand and lit another. J. M. COETZEE The bowls we ate . . from were crude blocks of wood hollowed out by scraping and burning.

2 *verb trans.* Form by making a hollow. Freq. foll. by *out.* M17.

M. MEYER A huge natural cave hollowed into the rock.

3 *verb intrans.* Become hollow or concave. M19.

K. ISHIGURO Kuroda's face . . had hollowed out around the cheekbones.

hollow *verb*² see HOLLO *verb*.

hollow *interjection* see HOLLO *interjection*.

hollow-hearted /hɒləʊˈhɑːtɪd/ *adjective*. M16.
[ORIGIN from HOLLOW *adjective* + HEARTED *adjective*.]
Insincere, false.
■ **hollow-heartedness** *noun* M16.

hollowly /ˈhɒləʊli/ *adverb*. M16.
[ORIGIN from HOLLOW *adjective* + -LY².]
In a hollow manner; with a hollow sound or voice; insincerely.

J. WYNDHAM A louder voice echoing hollowly in the corridors.

hollowness /ˈhɒləʊnɪs/ *noun*. LME.
[ORIGIN from HOLLOW *adjective* + -NESS.]
1 The quality or condition of being hollow. LME.
†**2** A hollow formation or place. LME–E18.

hollow-ware /ˈhɒləʊwɛː/ *noun*. L17.
[ORIGIN from HOLLOW *adjective* + WARE *noun*².]
Hollow articles of wood, china, or esp. metal, as pots, kettles, etc. Opp. ***flatware***.

holluschickie /ˈhɒləstʃɪki/ *noun pl.* L19.
[ORIGIN Russian *kholostyaki* bachelors.]
Young 'bachelor' male fur seals.

holly /ˈhɒli/ *noun*. ME.
[ORIGIN Reduced form of Old English *hole(g)n* HOLLIN.]
1 Any of several evergreen shrubs or small trees of the genus *Ilex* (family Aquifoliaceae); *esp.* one of the common European species *I. aquifolium*, with tough dark green glossy leaves with indented edges usu. set with sharp stiff prickles at the points, and bearing small white flowers succeeded by red berries, much used for Christmas decoration. Also, the American holly, *I. opaca*, a similar tree of the US. Also ***holly bush***, ***holly tree***. ME.
2 Any of various plants resembling the holly in some way, esp. in having prickly leaves. Usu. with specifying word. ME.
knee-holly: see KNEE *noun*. *sea holly*: see SEA *noun*.
– COMB.: **holly blue** a butterfly, *Celastrina argiolus*, whose caterpillars feed in spring on buds etc. of holly (the late summer brood feeding on ivy); **holly fern** a mountain fern, *Polystichum lonchitis*, having stiff glossy fronds with spine-tipped teeth; **holly oak** = ***holm oak*** s.v. HOLM *noun*² 2.

holly *adverb* see WHOLLY.

hollyhock /ˈhɒlɪhɒk/ *noun*. ME.
[ORIGIN from HOLY *adjective* + HOCK *noun*¹: cf. the Welsh name (dating from 16th cent.) *hocys bendigaid* lit. 'blessed mallow'.]
Orig., the marsh mallow, *Althaea officinalis*, of the mallow family. Now, (a flowering stem of) a related garden plant, *Alcea rosea*, with very tall stout stems bearing numerous large blooms on very short stalks.

Hollywood /ˈhɒlɪwʊd/ *noun & adjective*. E20.
[ORIGIN A district of Los Angeles in California, the principal centre of the US film industry.]
▸ **A** *noun*. The American film industry or its products. E20.

H. G. WELLS There was a vast editor's desk, marvellously equipped, like a desk out of Hollywood.

▸ **B** *adjective*. Of, pertaining to, or characteristic of Hollywood. E20.

C. MORLEY Those black and white yachting shoes . . were definitely Hollywood.

Hollywood ending a conventional ending in a film, novel, etc., esp. one that is sentimental or improbably positive.
■ **Hollywoodean**, **Hollywoodian** *adjectives* = HOLLYWOOD *adjective* M20. **Hollywoodish** *adjective* somewhat resembling or characteristic of a Hollywood film E20. **Hollywoodism** *noun* a style or idiom characteristic of Hollywood M20. **Hollywoodize** *verb trans.* make typically Hollywoodian M20.

holm /həʊm/ *noun*¹. Also **holme**. OE.
[ORIGIN Old Norse *holmr* islet in a bay, lake, or river, meadow on the shore, corresp. to Old Saxon *holm* hill.]
1 An islet, esp. in a river or near the mainland. OE.
2 A flat low-lying piece of ground by a river, submerged in time of flood. ME.

holm /həʊm/ *noun*². ME.
[ORIGIN Alt. of HOLLIN.]
1 The holly. *obsolete* exc. *dial.* ME.
2 Now usu. more fully ***holm oak***. A kind of oak, *Quercus ilex*, common in Mediterranean countries, with dark evergreen sometimes spiny-toothed leaves. Also called ***evergreen oak***, ***ilex***. LME.
– COMB.: *holm oak*: see sense 2 above; **holm tree** (*a*) (*obsolete* exc. *dial.*) the holly; (*b*) (now *rare*) the holm oak.

holme *noun* var. of HOLM *noun*¹.

Holmesian /ˈhəʊmzɪən/ *adjective*. E20.
[ORIGIN from *Holmes* (see below) + -IAN.]
Of, pertaining to, or characteristic of Sherlock Holmes, the amateur detective in the stories of A. Conan Doyle (1859–1931).

C. WAUGH To uncover . . plots with the aid of magnifying glass, pipe and Holmesian costume.

holmgang /ˈhəʊmgaŋ/ *noun*. M19.
[ORIGIN Old Norse *holmganga* 'going to the holm', on which a duel was fought.]
hist. A duel to the death, as practised by ancient Germanic peoples.

S. HEANEY That holmgang Where two berserks dub each other to death For honour's sake.

Holmgren /ˈhəʊ(l)mgrən/ *noun*. L19.
[ORIGIN A. F. *Holmgren* (1831–97), Swedish physiologist.]
Holmgren's test, a test for colour blindness in which the subject is required to match differently coloured pieces of wool (***Holmgren's wools***).

holmium /ˈhəʊlmɪəm/ *noun*. L19.
[ORIGIN from *Holmia* Latinized form of *Stockholm*, Swedish capital city: see -IUM.]
A soft silvery metallic chemical element of the lanthanide series, atomic no. 67 (symbol Ho).
■ **holmia** *noun* holmium oxide, Ho_2O_3, a pale yellow solid L19.

holmquistite /ˈhəʊmkwɪstʌɪt, -kvɪst-/ *noun*. E20.
[ORIGIN from Per Johan *Holmquist* (1866–1946), Swedish geologist + -ITE¹.]
MINERALOGY. A rare blue or violet orthorhombic amphibole containing lithium.

holo /ˈhɒləʊ/ *noun & adjective*. *colloq.* L20.
[ORIGIN Abbreviation.]
▸ **A** *noun*. Pl. **-os**. A hologram. L20.
▸ **B** *adjective*. Holographic. L20.

holo- /ˈhɒləʊ/ *combining form*. Before a vowel also **hol-**.
[ORIGIN Greek *holos* whole, entire.]
Complete, whole; completely, wholly. Cf. HEMI-, MERO-¹.
■ **hoˈlandric** *adjective* inherited solely in the male line (on the Y chromosome) M20. **holo-alphaˈbetic** *adjective* containing the whole alphabet L20. **holoˈaxial** *adjective* (CRYSTALLOGRAPHY) (of a crystal class) having one or more (esp. all compatible) axes of symmetry, but no plane or centre of symmetry E20. **holoˈbenthic** *adjective* (BIOLOGY) living at the bottom of the sea at all stages of the life cycle E20. **holoˈblastic** *adjective* (of an ovum) undergoing complete cleavage L19. **holobranch** *noun* (ICHTHYOLOGY) a complete gill having lamellae on both sides E20. **holoˈcarpic** *adjective* (MYCOLOGY) designating a thallus the whole of which is transformed into a reproductive structure at maturity; possessing such a thallus: E20. **holoˈcephalan**, **holoceˈphalian** *nouns & adjectives* (*a*) *noun* a cartilaginous fish of the subclass Holocephali, which comprises the chimaeras or ratfishes; (*b*) *adjective* of, pertaining to, or characteristic of (a fish of) the order Holocephali: M20. **holocrine** *adjective* (PHYSIOLOGY) of, pertaining to, or designating a gland in which secretion occurs by total disintegration of the cell E20. **holoˈcrystalline** *adjective* (PETROGRAPHY) wholly composed of (esp. large) crystals L19. **holoenˈdemic** *adjective* (MEDICINE) permanently affecting most or all of a population M20. **holoˈenzyme** *noun* the active complex of an enzyme with its coenzyme M20. **hologamete** *adjective* (BIOLOGY) (in some protists) a gamete morphologically similar to an ordinary individual and not formed by special fission E20. **hoˈlogamous** *adjective* (BIOLOGY) (of certain unicellular organisms) reproducing by sexual fusion of two ordinary individuals acting as gametes E20. **hoˈlogamy** *noun* reproduction by hologamous fusion E20. **holoˈhedral** *adjective* (CRYSTALLOGRAPHY) (of a crystal or crystal class) having the maximum possible symmetry for a given crystal system M19. **holoˈhedron** *noun*, pl. **-dra**, **-drons**, CRYSTALLOGRAPHY any holohedral crystal L19. †**holometer** *noun* a pantometer L17–M19. **holoˈmorphic** *adjective* (MATH.) (of a function of a complex variable) having a derivative at all points of the domain; analytic: L19. **holophote** *noun* [Greek *phōt-*, *phōs* light] an apparatus for making nearly all of the light from a lamp available (as in a lighthouse) M19. **holophyˈletic** *adjective* (BIOLOGY) (of a taxon) including all descendants of the common ancestor (cf. MONOPHYLETIC) M20. **holophytic** /-ˈfɪtɪk/ *adjective* (BIOLOGY) of, pertaining to, or designating a plant or protozoan which obtains organic nutrients by photosynthesis L19. **holoˈplankton** *noun* (BIOLOGY) holoplanktonic organisms (cf. MEROPLANKTON) E20. **holoplankˈtonic** *adjective* (BIOLOGY) (of aquatic organisms) passing all stages of the life cycle as plankton L19. **holopneustic** /hɒlə(ʊ)ˈpnjuːstɪk/ *adjective* [Greek *-pneustos* breathing] ENTOMOLOGY having eleven or (usu.) ten pairs of spiracles, all fully functional L19. **hoˈloptic** *adjective* (ENTOMOLOGY) having the eyes meeting at the midline L19. **holoseˈriceous** *adjective* (BOTANY & ENTOMOLOGY) wholly covered with a silky pubescence M19. **hoˈlostean** *noun & adjective* [Greek *osteon* bone] (*a*) *noun* any member of a group (Holostei) of bony fishes intermediate between chondrosteans and teleosts, and including the extant bowfin and gar pike, and many fossil forms; (*b*) *adjective* of, pertaining to, or characteristic of (a fish of) the group Holostei: L19. **holoˈstylic** *adjective* (ZOOLOGY) having the upper jaw fused to the cranium M20. **holosyˈmmetrical**, **holosysteˈmatic** *adjectives* = HOLOHEDRAL L19. **holoˈzoic** *adjective* (BIOLOGY) of, pertaining to, or designating an organism which ingests organic nutrients from other organisms L19.

holocaine /ˈhɒləkeɪn/ *noun*. L19.
[ORIGIN from HOLO- + -CAINE.]
PHARMACOLOGY. = PHENACAINE.

holocaust /ˈhɒləkɔːst/ *noun*. In sense 4 also **H-**. ME.
[ORIGIN Old French & mod. French *holocauste* from late Latin *holocaustum* from Greek *holokauston*, formed as HOLO- + *kaustos* var. of *kautos* burnt, from *kau-* base of *kaiein* burn.]
1 A sacrifice wholly consumed by fire. ME.
2 A complete or large-scale sacrifice. L15.
3 A complete or wholesale destruction, esp. by fire; a great slaughter or massacre. L17.

W. STYRON His stable . . burned to the ground in one horrid and almost instantaneous holocaust. B. CASTLE The bombing holocaust in Birmingham . . has shaken the country.

nuclear holocaust: see NUCLEAR *adjective*.

4 spec. *The* (period of the) mass murder of the Jews (or *transf.* of other groups) by the Nazis in the Second World War. M20.

F. FORSYTH Yad Vashem, . . the shrine to six million . . Jews who died in the holocaust. M. FRENCH My students . . don't even care about World War II or the Holocaust.

– COMB.: **Holocaust denial** the mistaken belief or assertion that the Holocaust did not happen, or was greatly exaggerated.
■ **holoˈcaustal** *adjective* (*rare*) = HOLOCAUSTIC E19. **holoˈcaustic** *adjective* of the nature of or pertaining to a holocaust L19.

Holocene /ˈhɒləsiːn/ *adjective & noun*. L19.
[ORIGIN French, formed as HOLO- + Greek *kainos* new, recent.]
GEOLOGY. ▸**A** *adjective*. Of, pertaining to, or designating the most recent geological epoch, subsequent to the Pleistocene and forming with it the Quaternary period; = RECENT *adjective* 4. L19.
▸ **B** *noun*. The Holocene epoch; the series of rocks dating from this time. E20.

hologram /ˈhɒləgram/ *noun*. M20.
[ORIGIN from HOLO- + -GRAM.]
PHYSICS. A pattern produced by interference between light reflected (or diffracted or transmitted) by an object and other light with the same or a related phase; a photograph of such a pattern, which can be illuminated so as to produce a spatial image of the object used.

holograph /ˈhɒləgrɑːf/ *noun & adjective*. E17.
[ORIGIN French *holographe* or late Latin *holographus* from Greek *holographos*: see HOLO-, -GRAPH.]
▸ **A** *noun*. A document etc. wholly written by hand by the person named as its author. E17.
▸ **B** *adjective*. (Of a document etc.) wholly written by the hand of the person named as the author; *spec.* in *Scot.* & *US* LAW, (of a will) written by the hand of and signed by the testator and thereby valid. E18.

holograph /ˈhɒləgrɑːf/ *verb trans.* M20.
[ORIGIN Back-form. from HOLOGRAPHY, after PHOTOGRAPH *verb*, TELEGRAPH *verb*.]
PHYSICS. Record as a hologram.

holographic /hɒləˈgrafɪk/ *adjective*. E18.
[ORIGIN from HOLOGRAPH *noun*, HOLOGRAPHY + -IC.]
1 = HOLOGRAPH *adjective*. E18.
2 PHYSICS. Of or pertaining to holography; produced by or involving holography. M20.
■ **holographically** *adverb* (PHYSICS) by means of holography M20.

holography /hɒˈlɒgrəfi/ *noun*. E19.
[ORIGIN from HOLO- + -GRAPHY; in sense 2 after *photography*, *telegraphy*, etc.]
1 Writing wholly by one's own hand. E19.
2 PHYSICS. The process or science of producing and using holograms. M20.

holoku /hɒˈləʊkuː/ *noun*. L19.
[ORIGIN Hawaiian.]
A long gown with a train, as worn in Hawaii.

holometabolous /ˌhɒləʊməˈtabələs/ *adjective*. L19.
[ORIGIN from HOLO- + Greek *metabolos* changeable: see -OUS.]
ENTOMOLOGY. Of an insect: that undergoes complete metamorphosis to the adult from a morphologically distinct larval stage. Cf. HEMIMETABOLOUS.

holoparasite /hɒlə(ʊ)ˈparəsʌɪt/ *noun*. L19.
[ORIGIN from HOLO- + PARASITE *noun*.]
BIOLOGY. An obligate parasite, unable to exist apart from its host.
■ **holoparaˈsitic** *adjective* E20. **holoˈparasitism** *noun* E20.

Holophane /ˈhɒləfeɪn/ *noun*. Also **h-**. L19.
[ORIGIN from HOLO- + Greek *phanein* shine, appear.]
(Proprietary name for) (a type of lampshade made of) glass specially fluted or ribbed to refract and reflect the light with little loss.

holophrase /ˈhɒləfreɪz/ *noun*. L19.
[ORIGIN from HOLO- + PHRASE *noun*.]
A single word expressing a whole phrase or combination of ideas.

holophrasis /hɒˈlɒfrəsɪs/ *noun*. Pl. **-phrases** /-ˈfreɪsiːz/. M19.
[ORIGIN from HOLO- + Greek *phrasis* speech, phrase.]
The use of a single word to express a whole phrase or combination of ideas.

holophrastic /hɒlə(ʊ)ˈfrastɪk/ *adjective*. M19.
[ORIGIN from HOLO- + Greek *phrastikos*, from *phrazein* tell: see -IC.]
Of a particular language or a stage in language acquisition: characterized by holophrasis.

holothuria /hɒlə(ʊ)ˈθjʊərɪə/ *noun*. Pl. **-iae** /-ɪiː/, **-ias**. L18.
[ORIGIN mod. Latin *Holothuria* genus name from Latin *holothurion* some marine creature from Greek, of unknown origin.]
ZOOLOGY. A holothurian. Formerly also, any of several other elongate aquatic invertebrates. Now only as mod. Latin genus name.

holothurian /hɒlə(ʊ)ˈθjʊərɪən/ *noun & adjective*. M19.
[ORIGIN formed as HOLOTHURIA + -AN.]
ZOOLOGY. ▸**A** *noun*. Any elongate, bilaterally symmetrical echinoderm of the class Holothuroidea, having a leathery integument and a diffuse skeleton of calcitic spicules; a sea cucumber. M19.

H

▶ **B** *adjective*. Of or pertaining to the class Holothuroidea. L19.

holotype /ˈhɒlətʌɪp/ *noun*. L19.
[ORIGIN from HOLO- + -TYPE.]
TAXONOMY. A single specimen chosen to represent a new species by the first author to describe it and with which the specific epithet remains associated during any taxonomic revision.
■ **holoˈtypic** *adjective* M20.

holp *verb pa. t.*: see HELP *verb*.

holpen *verb pa. pple*: see HELP *verb*.

hols /hɒlz/ *noun pl. colloq.* E20.
[ORIGIN Abbreviation.]
Holidays.

A. T. ELLIS He's going off on his hols for a couple of weeks.

Holstein /ˈhɒlstʌɪn/ *adjective & noun*. Chiefly *N. Amer.* M19.
[ORIGIN A region in northern Germany.]
= FRIESIAN.

Holsteinian /hɒlˈstʌɪnɪən/ *adjective & noun*. M20.
[ORIGIN from HOLSTEIN + -IAN.]
GEOLOGY. (Designating or pertaining to) an interglacial stage of the Pleistocene in northern Europe, preceding the Saale glaciation.

H

holster /ˈhəʊlstə, ˈhɒl-/ *noun & verb*. M17.
[ORIGIN Corresp. to and contemporary with Dutch *holster*, perh. ult. from Germanic base of HELE *verb*: see -STER.]
▶ **A** *noun*. A (usu. leather) case or holder for a pistol or occas. a larger gun, fixed to a saddle or worn on a belt or under the arm. Also, any such case designed for convenient holding or carrying, esp. of a piton hammer or ice axe in mountaineering. M17.

P. CAMPBELL The butt of an immense gun stood out from the holster strapped to his side. *Climber* Tools are slid into holsters, over-mitts removed and I pretend it's summer.

▶ **B** *verb trans.* Put (a pistol etc.) into a holster. Chiefly *US*. M20.

T. MO He still had his pistol out but holstered it again.

holt /həʊlt/ *noun*[1].
[ORIGIN Old English *holt* = Old Frisian, Old Saxon, Old Norse *holt*, Middle Dutch *hout*, Old & mod. High German *holz*, from Germanic, from Indo-European base repr. by Greek *klados* twig.]
1 A wood, a copse. Now *arch. & dial.* OE. ▸**b** A plantation, esp. of osiers. *local*. E17.
2 A wooded hill. M16.

holt /həʊlt/ *noun*[2]. LME.
[ORIGIN Var. of HOLD *noun*[1].]
1 Hold, grip. Now *dial. & US colloq.* LME.
2 The lair or den of an animal, esp. an otter or fish. L16.

holus-bolus /həʊləsˈbəʊləs/ *adverb*. Orig. *dial.* M19.
[ORIGIN Uncertain: pseudo-Latin for 'whole bolus' or joc. repr. assumed Greek *holos bōlos* whole lump (see BOLUS).]
All in a lump, altogether.

Times An insurance company can be swallowed holus-bolus like a sprat by a hungry predator.

holy /ˈhəʊli/ *adjective & noun*.
[ORIGIN Old English *hālig*, *-ēg* = Old Frisian *hēlich*, Old Saxon *hēlag*, *-eg*, Old High German *heilag* (Dutch, German *heilig*), Old Norse *heilagr*, from Germanic base of WHOLE.]
▶ **A** *adjective*. **1** Of a thing, place, etc.: kept or regarded as sacred; set apart for religious use or observance; consecrated. OE.

G. VIDAL The holy capital of the Middle Kingdom.

2 Of a god or icon: (to be) held in religious veneration or reverence; *spec.* in the Christian Church, free from all contamination of sin and evil, morally and spiritually perfect (cf. sense 4). OE.

AV *Ps.* 22:3 But thou art holy, O thou that inhabitest the praises of Israel.

3 (Of a person) (regarded as) specially belonging to, empowered by, or devoted to God; (of a thing) pertaining to, originating from, or sanctioned by God or the Trinity. Formerly also, (of a person) religiously devoted *to* (anything). OE. ▸**b** *gen.* Of surpassing excellence; having mysterious power. Also with intensive force (*colloq.*), absolute, complete. L16.

S. MORLEY The players . . seemed . . to be regarding their work as a kind of holy calling. **b** G. KEILLOR If any of his children had done it he would have given them holy hell.

4 Pious, devout; *esp.* of godly character and life, saintly, morally and spiritually clean; *colloq.* sanctimonious. OE.

JONATHAN ROSS She said again, in that holy voice, [etc.]. *absol.*: T. ARNOLD For a moment it must overwhelm the mind of the holiest.

5 Used with following noun as an oath or expletive, as ***holy cow!***, ***holy mackerel!***, ***holy Moses!***, ***holy smoke!***, etc. M19.

– SPECIAL COLLOCATIONS, PHRASES, & COMB.: **holier-than-thou** *adjective* (*colloq.*) self-righteous, characterized by an attitude of superior sanctity. **Holy Alliance** *hist.* an alliance formed between Russia, Austria, and Prussia in 1815 on the basis of proposed common Christian principles of government. **holy basil** an Indian basil, *Ocimum sanctum*, regarded by Hindus as sacred to Vishnu. **holy bread** (**a**) the bread provided for the Eucharist; the bread consecrated in the Eucharist; (**b**) ordinary bread blessed and distributed after the Eucharist to non-communicants. ***Holy Church***: see CHURCH *noun*. **Holy City** (**a**) a city held sacred by the adherents of a religion, *esp.* Jerusalem; (**b**) Heaven. ***Holy Communion***: see COMMUNION 5. **holy Cross** the Cross on which Jesus died; ***Holy Cross Day***, the festival of the Exaltation of the Cross, 14 September. **Holy Family** the young Jesus with his parents (often with St John Baptist and St Anne) as grouped in art. ***Holy Father***: see FATHER *noun*. †**holy fire** erysipelas. ***Holy Grail***: see GRAIL *noun*[2]. **holy grass** a fragrant grass, *Hierochloe odorata*, which in Prussia was dedicated to the Virgin Mary and strewn on church floors. ***Holy Innocents' Day***: see INNOCENT *noun*. **Holy Joe** (orig. *nautical slang*) a clergyman; a pious person. ***Holy Lamb***: see LAMB *noun*. **Holy Land** [translating medieval Latin *terra sancta*, French *la terre sainte*] W. Palestine, esp. Judaea; a region similarly revered in religions other than Christianity. **holy laugh** a laugh by a person in a state of religious fervour. **holy loaf** (now *rare*) = ***holy bread*** above. **Holy Name** *ROMAN CATHOLIC CHURCH* the name of Christ as an object of formal devotion. **Holy Office** *hist.* the Inquisition. ***holy orders***: see ORDER *noun* 2a. **holy place** the outer chamber of the sanctuary in a synagogue; in *pl.*, places to which religious pilgrimage is made. **holy roller** *slang* a member of a religious group characterized by frenzied excitement or trances. ***Holy Roman Empire***: see ROMAN *adjective*. **Holy Rood** *arch.* (a representation of) the Cross of Jesus; ***Holy Rood Day***, (**a**) the festival of the Invention of the Cross, 3 May; (**b**) = ***Holy Cross Day*** above. **Holy Saturday** Saturday in Holy Week. ***Holy Scripture***: see SCRIPTURE. ***Holy See***: see SEE *noun*[1] 2b. **holy souls** the blessed dead. **Holy Spirit** the third person of the Trinity; God as spiritually active; = HOLY GHOST 1; ***God the Father, God the Son, and God the Holy Spirit***: see GOD *noun*. ***holy terror***: see TERROR *noun* 2b. **Holy Thursday** *ANGLICAN CHURCH* (*arch.* or *hist.*) Ascension Day; *ROMAN CATHOLIC CHURCH* Maundy Thursday. **holytide** *arch.* a holy day or season, a day or season of religious observance. ***Holy Trinity***: see TRINITY. **holy war**: waged in support of a religious cause. **Holy Week** [after Italian *la settimana santa*, French *la semaine sainte*] the week before Easter Sunday. **holy Willie** a hypocritically religious person. ***Holy Writ***: see WRIT *noun* 1. ***Holy Write***: see WRITE *noun* 1. ***the Holy Innocents***: see INNOCENT *noun*. ***the Holy Sacrament***: see HOLY *adjective*. ***the Holy Sepulchre***: see SEPULCHRE *noun* 1. ***the holy table***: see TABLE *noun* 13(b).

▶ **B** *noun*. **1** That which is holy; a holy thing. OE.
holy of holies (**a**) *JEWISH ANTIQUITIES* the inner chamber of the sanctuary in the Jewish Temple, separated by a veil from the outer chamber; (**b**) an innermost shrine; a thing regarded as most sacred.
†**2** A holy person, a saint. LME–M17.

holy day /ˈhəʊli deɪ/ *noun phr.*
[ORIGIN Old English *hālig dæg*. Cf. HOLIDAY *noun & adjective*.]
A day consecrated or set apart for religious observance, usu. in commemoration of some sacred person or event; a religious festival. Cf. HOLIDAY *noun* 1.

Holy Ghost /həʊli ˈɡəʊst/ *noun phr.*
[ORIGIN Old English *se hālga gāst*, *hālig gāst*, translating ecclesiastical Latin *spiritus sanctus*.]
1 *CHRISTIAN THEOLOGY*. = ***Holy Spirit*** s.v. HOLY *adjective*. OE.
God the Father, God the Son, and God the Holy Ghost: see GOD *noun*.
2 A figure of a dove as a symbol of this. Long *rare* or *obsolete*. E16.
– COMB.: **Holy Ghost flower**, **Holy Ghost plant** a tropical American orchid, *Peristeria elata*, so called because part of the flower is thought to resemble a dove; also called ***dove-flower***.

holystone /ˈhəʊlɪstəʊn/ *noun & verb*. E19.
[ORIGIN Prob. from HOLY *adjective* + STONE *noun*, perh. so called because used while kneeling.]
▶ **A** *noun*. A piece of soft sandstone used for scouring the decks of ships. E19.
▶ **B** *verb trans.* Scour with a holystone. E19.

T. MO He is on a deck holystoned white as any man-of-war's.

holy water /həʊli ˈwɔːtə/ *noun phr.*
[ORIGIN Old English *hāligwæter* translating ecclesiastical Latin *aqua benedicta* blessed water.]
Water blessed by a priest and used in various rites etc. esp. of purification; water dedicated to holy uses.
– COMB.: **holy-water sprinkle**, **holy-water sprinkler** (**a**) an aspergillum; (**b**) *hist.* a kind of club fitted with spikes.

hom /həʊm/ *noun*. Also **haoma**, **homa**, /ˈhəʊmə/. M19.
[ORIGIN Persian *ḥōm*, *hūm* (Avestan *haoma*) = Sanskrit SOMA *noun*[1].]
(The juice of) the sacred plant of the ancient Persians and Parsees.

hom- *combining form* see HOMO-.

homage /ˈhɒmɪdʒ/ *noun*. ME.
[ORIGIN Old French *(h)omage* (mod. *hommage*) from medieval Latin *hominaticium*, from Latin *homo*, *homin-* man: see -AGE.]
1 In *FEUDAL LAW*, formal public acknowledgement of allegiance, by which a tenant or vassal declared himself the man of the king or lord from whom he held land, and bound himself to his service; *gen.* acknowledgement of a person's superior worth, rank, beauty, etc.; dutiful reverence. Freq. in ***do homage*** (***to***), ***pay homage*** (***to***), ***render homage*** (***to***). ME.

N. MONSARRAT The crowd came forward to kneel in homage. E. FEINSTEIN Poets as disparate as Yevtushenko and Brodsky have paid homage to her.

2 A body of people owing allegiance; *spec.* the body of tenants attending, or the jury in, a manorial court. ME.

3 An act of homage; a payment of money etc. made as an acknowledgement of vassalage. L16.

J. UPDIKE Proust pens homages to such modern inventions as the railroad.

homage /ˈhɒmɪdʒ/ *verb*. Now *rare*. LME.
[ORIGIN from the noun.]
1 †**a** *verb intrans.* Pay homage. LME–M17. ▸**b** *verb trans.* Pay homage to. M17.
†**2** *verb trans.* Give or pay as a token of homage. L16–M17.
■ †**homageable** *adjective* bound to pay homage M17–M18.

homager /ˈhɒmɪdʒə/ *noun*. Now *arch.* or *hist.* LME.
[ORIGIN Old French *homag(i)er*, formed as HOMAGE *noun*: see -ER[2].]
A person who owes homage or holds land by it; *spec.* (*ENGLISH LAW*, now *hist.*) a manorial tenant.

fig.: SHAKES. *Ant. & Cl.* Thou blushest, Antony, and that blood of thine Is Caesar's homager.

homalographic *adjective* var. of HOMOLOGRAPHIC.

hombre /ˈɒmbreɪ, -bri/ *noun*. M19.
[ORIGIN Spanish = man, from Latin *homo*, *homin-* human being: cf. OMBRE.]
In Spain and Spanish-speaking countries, a man; *gen.* (chiefly *US slang*) a man, a guy.

American Speech Cowboys living a rough and hardy existence occasionally develop into 'tough hombres'.

Homburg /ˈhɒmbəːɡ/ *noun*. L19.
[ORIGIN *Homburg*, a town near Wiesbaden, western Germany.]
In full ***Homburg hat***. A soft felt hat with a curved brim and dented crown, first worn at Homburg.

home /həʊm/ *noun & adjective*.
[ORIGIN Old English *hām*, corresp. to Old Frisian *hām*, *hēm*, Old Saxon *hēm* (Dutch *heem*), Old & mod. High German *heim*, Old Norse *heimr*, Gothic *haims*, from Germanic.]
▶ **A** *noun*. †**1** A collection of dwellings; a village, a town. OE–ME.
2 The place where one lives permanently, esp. as a member of a family or household; a fixed place of residence. Freq. without article or possessive, esp. as representing the centre of family life. OE. ▸**b** The family or social unit occupying a home. Freq. with descriptive adjective, as ***broken home***, ***happy home***. L19. ▸**c** The furniture or contents of a home. L19. ▸**d** A private house, a dwelling house. L19.

G. B. SHAW When their business compels them to be away from home. LYNDON B. JOHNSON Every family in America deserves a decent home, whether a farmhouse or a city apartment. M. IGNATIEFF Home is the place we have to leave in order to grow up. G. STEIN Stray dogs and cats Anna always kept until she found them homes. **d** N. MAILER Now he had a home instead of an apartment.

holiday home, ***mobile home***, ***motor home***, etc.

3 Usu. without article or possessive: (an affectionate term for) the country of one's origin; *esp.* Great Britain or England regarded as the mother country among citizens living abroad or (now chiefly *arch.* or *hist.*) inhabitants of what were in the past its colonies or dependencies. ME.

S. HARVESTER Members could . . sit quiet under lazy fans while they read the latest newspapers . . from home.

4 A place or region to which one naturally belongs or where one feels at ease. Also ***spiritual home***. M16.

Contemporary Review In the Church of England he found a satisfying home.

5 A place where a thing flourishes or from which it originates. E18.

M. ARNOLD Oxford . . . home of lost causes and forsaken beliefs!

6 An institution looking after people etc. who need care or have no home of their own. M19. ▸**b** *spec.* Such an institution for mentally ill or mentally disabled people. *colloq.* M20.

G. STEIN They sent her where she would be taken care of, a home for poor consumptives. **b** A. MCCOWEN His brain collapsed and he finished his days in a home.

convalescent home, ***dogs' home***, ***mental home***, ***nursing home***, ***old people's home***, etc.

7 *SPORTS & GAMES*. An area where a player is free from attack. Also, the point aimed at, the goal. M19.
8 *LACROSSE*. Each of the three players stationed nearest their opponents' goal. M19.
9 *ellipt.* A home win. L20.
– PHRASES: **at home** (**a**) in one's own home; one's neighbourhood, town, country, etc.; *arch.* in the mother country, in Britain; (**b**) at ease as if in one's own home; well-informed, familiar (*in*, *on*, *with*); (**c**) available to callers; see also AT-HOME *noun*; (**d**) on a team's own ground (opp. ***away***). **close to home** = ***near home*** below. ***eat out of house and home***: see EAT *verb*. ***hearth and home***: see HEARTH *noun*. **home away from home** *N. Amer., Austral., & NZ* = ***home from home*** below. **home from home** a place other than one's home where one feels at home; a place providing home-like amenities. ***house and home***: see HOUSE *noun*[1]. ***last home***: see LAST *adjective*. ***long home***: see LONG *adjective*[1]. **near home** near one's home, country, etc.; *fig.* affecting one closely. ***not at home***: see NOT *adverb*. ***second home***: see SECOND *adjective*. ***starter home***. *STATELY* ***home***. **to home** *dial. & US* at home. ***walk home***: see WALK *verb*[1].

▸ **B** *attrib.* or as *adjective* (freq. hyphenated, not *pred.* except formerly in sense 3).

1 Of, relating to, or associated with (one's) home, domestic; used, performed, carried on, etc., at home. **M16.** ▸**b** Adjoining or surrounding one's home, or the chief house on an estate. **M17.**

S. SMILES Its citizens had no true family or home life. I. NOVELLO Keep the home-fires burning. **b** A. TROLLOPE An inner gate, leading from the home paddock, through the gardens.

home comforts, *home computer*, *home cooking*, etc.

2 Relating to, produced or carried on in, originating from, one's country or nation. Opp. ***foreign***. **L16.** ▸**b** Dealing with the affairs of one's own country (opp. those of foreign countries) or (chiefly *hist.*) with the mother country (opp. its colonies). **L18.** ▸**c** Of a team, player, etc.: belonging to the country, locality, etc., in which a sporting event takes place. Of a match, victory, etc.: played, experienced, etc., by a team on its own ground. **L19.**

Time Entente Cordiale . . was probably intended as French propaganda for home consumption. H. WILLIAMSON The least we civilians can do is to hold the Home Front. **b** *Listener* The Ministry of Defence is classified as a home rather than an 'overseas' department. **c** *Times* The biggest single event of the British season will bring together five home riders, four Danes, three Swedes.

home industry, *home market*, *home produce*, etc.

3 That strikes home; searching, effective. (Passing into adverb.) **E17.**

HOR. WALPOLE That negociation not succeeding, the Duchess made a more home push.

4 *SPORTS & GAMES.* Of, pertaining to, or situated at or near home (sense A.7 above); reaching or enabling a player to reach home. **M19.**

— COMB. & SPECIAL COLLOCATIONS: With ppl adjectives in sense '(for use) at home', as ***home-baked***, ***home-based***, ***home-born***, ***home-brewed***, ***home-cured*** [CURE *verb* 8], ***home-produced***. **home base** = ***home plate*** below; **home bird**, **homebody** a person who likes to stay at home; **homeboy** (orig. & chiefly *black English*) (*a*) a man coming from the same district, town, or community as the speaker; (*b*) a performer of rap music; **home-bred** *adjective* (*a*) reared at home; indigenous; (*b*) *fig.* having no culture or breadth of experience; **home brew** (*a*) beer or other alcoholic drink brewed at home; (*b*) *Canad.* a player of professional football etc. born or brought up where his team is based; **Home Counties** the counties (esp. Surrey, Kent, Essex, and formerly Middlesex) closest to London; **home economics** the study of household management, domestic science; **home economist** a student of or specialist in home economics; **home farm** a farm reserved and worked by the owner of an estate which contains other farms; **home-felt** *adjective* felt intimately; **homefolks** *colloq.* (chiefly *US*) the people from or near one's home, one's family and neighbours; **homegirl** (orig. & chiefly *black English*) (*a*) a woman coming from the same district, town, or community as the speaker; (*b*) a female performer of rap music; **home-grown** *adjective* raised or cultivated on one's own land; *fig.* native, indigenous; **home guard** (a member of) a local volunteer force; *spec.* (with cap. initials) (a member of) the British citizen army organized 1940–57 to defend the country against invaders; **home help** a person who helps with household work, *spec.* one deputed by a local authority to assist an elderly or infirm person; **home-keeping** *adjective* that stays at or takes care of a home; **home key** *MUSIC* the basic key in which a work is written; **homeland** (*a*) one's native land; *esp.* Great Britain; (*b*) *S. AFR. HISTORY* an area reserved for members of a particular (indigenous African) ethnic or linguistic group (the official name for a Bantustan); **home language** one's native language; **home-leave** leave, esp. long leave, granted to officials etc. serving overseas; **home loan**: advanced to a person to assist in buying a house, flat, etc., to live in; **home-lot** *US* a building plot; **home-made** *adjective* made in one's own home or by one's own hands; crude or simple in construction; **homemaker** a person, esp. a housewife, who creates a (pleasant) home; **homemaking** the activity of a homemaker; **home movie**: made at home or showing the activities of one's family circle; **Home Office** (the building used for) the British government department dealing with law and order, immigration, etc., in England and Wales; **homeowner** a person who owns his or her home; **home page** *COMPUTING* an individual's or organization's introductory document on the World Wide Web; **home perm** a permanent hair wave made with equipment for home use; ***home plate***: see PLATE *noun* 15; **home port**: from which a ship sails or is registered; **home range** *ZOOLOGY* the area over which an animal regularly travels in search of food etc., and which may overlap with those of neighbouring animals of the same species (cf. TERRITORY 1d); **homeroom** *N. Amer.* a schoolroom where pupils of the same grade assemble at the beginning of school; **home rule** (a movement for) the government of a colony, dependent country, etc., by its own citizens; *spec.* (with cap. initials) the movement advocating devolved government for Ireland, *c* 1870–1914; **home run** *BASEBALL* a hit that allows the batter to make a complete circuit of the bases; **home-school** *verb trans.* educate (a child, esp. one's own) at home; **home-schooler** (*a*) a child who is educated at home; (*b*) a parent or other person who educates a child or children at home; **home science** (chiefly *NZ*) home economics, domestic science; **Home Secretary** (in Britain) the Secretary of State for the Home Department, the government minister in charge of the Home Office; **Home Service** *hist.* one of the programme services of the BBC (renamed *Radio 4*); **homesick** *adjective* depressed by a longing for home during an absence from it; **homesickness** the condition of being homesick; **home signal**: indicating whether or not a train may proceed into a station or to the next section of a line; **homesite** (chiefly *N. Amer. & Austral.*) a building plot; **home straight**, (*N. Amer.*) **home stretch** the concluding stretch of a racecourse; **home thrust** *FENCING* (now *rare*) a thrust which reaches the mark aimed at; *fig.* a direct remark or criticism which touches a person's feelings or consciousness; **home town**: of one's birth or early life or present fixed residence; **home truth** a wounding mention of a person's weakness; ***home unit***: see UNIT *noun*[1] 7; **homework** work (to be) done at home; *esp.* lessons done at home by a schoolchild (***do one's homework*** (*fig.*), brief oneself before a meeting etc.).

home /həʊm/ *verb.* **E17.**

[ORIGIN from HOME *noun*, HOME *adverb*.]

†**1** *verb intrans.* *NAUTICAL.* Foll. by *in*: = ***tumblehome*** (see TUMBLE *verb*). Only in **E17.**

2 *verb intrans.* Go home. Chiefly, of an animal: return by instinct to its territory after leaving it or being removed from it; (of a carrier pigeon) fly back to or arrive at its loft after being released at a distant point. **M18.** ▸**b** *verb trans.* Train (a pigeon) to fly home. **E20.**

3 *verb trans.* Provide (esp. a pet) with a home. **E19.**

Maidenhead Advertiser If we have a dog that has, perhaps, turned on a child, then we home it where there are no children.

4 *verb intrans.* Have one's home, dwell. *poet.* **M19.**

5 *verb intrans.* (Of an aircraft, missile, etc.) be guided (*in*) by a landmark, radio beam, etc.; *fig.* direct one's attention, seek out. Foll. by *on*, *on to*, etc., the destination, target, object of attention, etc. **E20.**

Daily Telegraph The other helicopter located the dinghy by homing in on . . the emergency distress [call]. *New Scientist* Mexico's Professor S. F. Beltran homed in on education as a critical need.

homing device an automatic device for guiding an aircraft, missile, etc.

home /həʊm/ *adverb.* **OE.**

[ORIGIN Orig. accus. of HOME *noun*, as the case of destination after a verb of motion.]

1 To one's home; to the house, district, country, etc., where one lives. Also, to one's family circle. **OE.** ▸**b** To one's grave. **E16.** ▸**c** With ellipsis of verb: go, drive, etc., home. **L16.**

D. H. LAWRENCE He worked automatically till it was time to go home. M. CALLAGHAN He liked to explain that he was doing well. He wrote home about it.

c *Home, James, and don't spare the horses.*

†**2** To one's normal or natural condition; to one's senses, right mind, etc. **E16–M17.**

F. QUARLES Call home thy selfe: Inspect thy selfe anew.

3 To the mark aimed at, to the maximum extent of penetration etc., (esp. in ***drive home***, ***hammer home***, ***press home***, ***ram home***, etc.). Freq. *fig.*, into a person's feelings or consciousness; formerly more *gen.*, fully, effectively. **M16.** ▸**b** *NAUTICAL.* Directly to the shore. **L18.**

SHAKES. *Ant. & Cl.* Speak to me home; mince not the general tongue. DEFOE The witnesses swear so home against you. J. FOWLES I slammed the door and got the bolts home. P. ACKROYD She decided not to press home her advantage. *Survival Weaponry* Screw the magazine cap fully home.

4 Expr. the result of motion: arrived at one's home after an absence. Also *fig.*, successfully arrived at, or within sight of, the end of a difficult enterprise, (more emphatically ***home and dry***, (*Austral. & NZ*) ***home and dried***, ***home and hosed***). **L16.** ▸**b** With no implication of motion: in one's home, at home. *N. Amer.* **M19.**

E. BOWEN Elsie came in—home from a tennis party. **b** A. COOKE He would give his . . servants the sternest orders that he was home to nobody.

5 To or arrived in the mother country (from a colony or overseas possession). **E17.**

J. GAIRDNER The Regent Bedford . . wrote home to the government in England.

6 *NAUTICAL.* Towards or into the ship. Also, with ref. to an anchor: away from its hold, so as to drag. **E17.**

7 *SPORTS & GAMES.* To or arrived at the home (HOME *noun* 7) or goal. **L18.**

Dumfries Courier Hardy Lad is the new racing hero . . after romping home at 28–1 odds.

— PHRASES: **bring oneself home** recoup one's (financial) losses. **bring something home to** make (a person) fully aware of something. **call home** *dial.* call the marriage banns of. **come home** = ***bring oneself home*** above. **come home to** (*a*) become fully realized by; (*b*) touch or affect intimately. ***come home to roost***: see ROOST *noun*[1]. †**come short home** fail to reach one's objective, come to grief. ***down home***: see DOWN *preposition*. ***down-home***: see DOWN-. **go home** *spec.* (*dial.*) die. **nothing to write home about**, **not much to write home about**, etc., *colloq.* nothing etc. to boast about, nothing etc. special. ***till the cows come home***: see COW *noun*[1]. ***tumblehome***: see TUMBLE *verb* 11. ***when a person's ship comes home***: see SHIP *noun* 1.

homecoming /ˈhəʊmkʌmɪŋ/ *noun.* **LME.**

[ORIGIN from HOME *adverb* + COMING *noun*.]

A coming home, an arrival at home. Also, a reunion, *spec.* (*US*) of former students of a college or university.

homeish *adjective* var. of HOMISH.

homeless /ˈhəʊmlɪs/ *adjective & noun.* **E17.**

[ORIGIN from HOME *noun* + -LESS.]

▸ **A** *adjective.* **1** Of a person or (*transf.*) his or her condition etc.: having no home or permanent place to live in. **E17.**

2 Affording no home, inhospitable. *rare.* **L18.**

▸ **B** *noun pl.* *The* people who are homeless as a class. **M20.**

Soldier Their first priority is housing the homeless.

■ **homelessness** *noun* **M19.**

homelike /ˈhəʊmlʌɪk/ *adjective.* **E19.**

[ORIGIN from HOME *noun* + -LIKE.]

Resembling or suggestive of home; homely.

homeling /ˈhəʊmlɪŋ/ *noun.* Long *arch. rare.* **L16.**

[ORIGIN from HOME *noun* + -LING[1].]

A home-born inhabitant, a native.

homely /ˈhəʊmli/ *adjective.* **ME.**

[ORIGIN from HOME *noun* + -LY[1].]

1 Friendly, intimate; at home *with*. Long *arch. & dial. rare.* **ME.**

R. W. EMERSON The end of friendship is a commerce, the most strict and homely that can be joined.

†**2** Of or belonging to a home or household; domestic. **LME–L16.**

3 Kindly, sympathetic. Now *Scot.* **LME.**

4 Characteristic or suggestive of home, esp. in its cosiness, lack of formality, etc.; unsophisticated, plain, simple, unpretentious. **LME.**

J. B. PRIESTLEY Her speech was far homelier . . and any suggestion of the great lady had completely vanished. A. WILSON She's a very nice, homely Lancashire body, but not stylish at all. M. MEYER The gift of making the place they lived in homely.

5 Of a person, the features: plain or unattractive in appearance. Now *N. Amer.* **LME.**

M. TWAIN She is not beautiful, she is homely.

■ **homelily** *adverb* (now *rare* or *obsolete*) **L15.** **homeliness** *noun* **ME.**

†**homely** *adverb.* **ME.**

[ORIGIN from HOME *noun* + -LY[2].]

1 Familiarly, intimately. **ME–M17.**

2 In a kindly manner. **LME–L16.**

3 Plainly, simply, unpretentiously. **LME–L18.**

4 Directly, without circumlocution. **LME–L17.**

homelyn /ˈhəʊmlɪn/ *noun.* **M17.**

[ORIGIN Unknown.]

A coastal fish of the skate family, *Raja montagui*. Also called ***spotted ray***.

homeo- *combining form*, var. of HOMOEO-.

homeobox /hɒmɪə(ʊ)ˈbɒks, həʊm-/ *noun.* Also **homoeo-**. **L20.**

[ORIGIN from HOMEO(TIC + BOX *noun*[2] (as first discovered in homeotic genes of *Drosophila* fruit flies).]

GENETICS. Any of a class of closely similar sequences which occur in various genes and are involved in regulating embryonic development in a wide range of species.

— COMB.: **homeobox gene** a gene containing a homeobox.

homeopath /ˈhəʊmɪəpaθ, ˈhɒm-/ *noun.* Also **homoeo-**. **M19.**

[ORIGIN German *Homöopath*: see HOMEOPATHY.]

A person who practises or advocates homeopathy.

homeopathic /həʊmɪə(ʊ)ˈpaθɪk, hɒm-/ *adjective.* Also **homoeo-**. **M19.**

[ORIGIN German *homöopathisch*: see HOMEOPATHY, -IC.]

1 Of or pertaining to homeopathy; practising or advocating homeopathy. **M19.**

2 Extremely small, as the doses in homeopathy. Chiefly *joc.* **M19.**

C. M. DAVIES The chapel was homœopathic in its dimensions.

homeopathy /həʊmɪˈɒpəθi, hɒm-/ *noun.* Also **homoeo-**, (earlier) †**-pathia**. **E19.**

[ORIGIN German *Homöopathie*, from Greek *homoios* like + *-patheia* -PATHY.]

A system of medicine in which diseases are treated by the administration (usu. in extremely small doses) of salts, drugs, etc., which would in larger doses cause the symptoms of the disease so treated.

■ **homeopathist** *noun* = HOMEOPATH **M20.**

homeosis /hɒmɪˈəʊsɪs/ *noun.* Also **homoeosis**. Pl. **-oses** /-ˈəʊsiːz/. **L19.**

[ORIGIN Greek *homoiōsis* a becoming like, from *homoios* like.]

BIOLOGY. In a segmented animal, the replacement of part of one segment by a structure characteristic of another segment, esp. in regeneration or by mutation. Also, an analogous process in plants.

■ **homeotic** /-ˈɒtɪk/ *adjective* exhibiting, characterizing, or inducing homeosis **L19.**

homeostasis /hɒmɪəʊˈsteɪsɪs, həʊm-/ *noun.* Also **homoeostasis**. **E20.**

[ORIGIN from HOMEO- + Greek *stasis* standing still, stationariness.]

Maintenance of a dynamically stable state within a system by means of internal regulatory processes that counteract external disturbance of the equilibrium; the state so maintained; *spec.* in *PHYSIOLOGY*, maintenance of relatively constant conditions in the body.

■ ˈ**homeostat** *noun* a system which maintains a steady state by internal processes **M20.** **homeostatic** *adjective* of, pertaining to, or maintained by homeostasis **E20.**

homeothermic /ˌhɒmɪəʊˈθəːmɪk/ *adjective*. Also **homoio-, homoeo-** /ˌhɒmɔɪəʊ-/. L19.
[ORIGIN from *homoio-* var. of HOMOEO- + THERMIC.]
ZOOLOGY & PHYSIOLOGY. Maintaining an almost constant body temperature, independent of that of the surroundings. Opp. POIKILOTHERMIC *adjective*.
▪ **homeotherm** *noun* a homeothermic animal L19. ˈ**homeothermy** *noun* M20.

homer /ˈhəʊmə/ *noun*[1]. Also **cho-** /ˈkəʊ-/. M16.
[ORIGIN Hebrew *ḥōmer* lit. 'heap'.]
A Hebrew measure of capacity equal to ten ephahs (about 400 litres). Also called *cor*.

homer /ˈhəʊmə/ *noun*[2] *& verb*. M19.
[ORIGIN from HOME *verb* + -ER[1].]
▸ **A** *noun*. **1** *BASEBALL*. A home run. M19.
2 A homing pigeon. L19.
3 A homing device. M20.
▸ **B** *verb intrans*. *BASEBALL*. Hit a home run. M20.

Homeric /həʊˈmɛrɪk/ *adjective*. E17.
[ORIGIN Latin *Homericus* from Greek *Homērikos*, from *Homēros* Homer: see below, -IC.]
1 Of, relating to, or characteristic of Homer, the traditional author of two ancient epics, the *Iliad* and the *Odyssey*, the poems ascribed to him, or the age with which they deal; like or in the style of Homer. E17.
2 On a scale worthy of Homer; epic, tremendous. M20.
– SPECIAL COLLOCATIONS: **Homeric laughter**: irrepressible (like that of Homer's gods at the sight of Hephaestus). **Homeric question**: regarding the authorship of the *Iliad* and the *Odyssey*.
▪ †**Homerical** *adjective* = HOMERIC L16–L18. **Homerically** *adverb* M19. †**Homerican** *adjective* = HOMERIC L17–E19.

H

Homerist /ˈhəʊmərɪst/ *noun*. L16.
[ORIGIN Latin *Homerista* from Greek *Homēristēs*, from *Homēros*: see HOMERIC, -IST.]
An imitator of Homer; a Homeric scholar or rhapsodist.

Homerite /ˈhəʊmərʌɪt/ *noun*. Now *rare* or *obsolete*. E17.
[ORIGIN Greek *Homēritai* pl., formed as HIMYARITE: see -ITE[1].]
= HIMYARITE.

Homerology /həʊməˈrɒlədʒi/ *noun*. L19.
[ORIGIN from *Homer* (see HOMERIC) + -OLOGY.]
The branch of knowledge that deals with Homer and the Homeric poems, their authorship, date, etc.
▪ **Homerologist** *noun* L19.

homespun /ˈhəʊmspʌn/ *adjective & noun*. L16.
[ORIGIN from HOME *noun* + SPUN *ppl adjective*.]
▸ **A** *adjective*. **1** Spun at home. L16.
2 *fig*. Simple, homely, unsophisticated, practical. E17.

> J. P. MAHAFFY The plainest homespun morality. L. STEPHEN Crabbe was one of those simple, homespun characters.

▸ **B** *noun*. **1** A person who wears homespun cloth; a rustic. *arch*. L16.

> SHAKES. *Mids. N. D.* What hempen homespuns have we swagg'ring here.

2 Cloth made of yarn spun at home. Also, a material resembling this. E17. ▸**b** *transf*. Something of plain or homely style. M19.

> **b** *Athenaeum* Instead of being . . of superfine quality in one part, and arrant home-spun in another.

homestall /ˈhəʊmstɔːl/ *noun*. Now *dial*. OE.
[ORIGIN from HOME *noun* + *steall* position, place.]
1 = HOMESTEAD *noun*. OE.
2 A farmyard. M17.

homestead /ˈhəʊmstɛd/ *noun & verb*. OE.
[ORIGIN from HOME *noun* + STEAD *noun*.]
▸ **A** *noun*. **1** Orig., the place in which a person or group lives; a settlement. In later use, a home. OE.
2 *N. Amer.* ▸**a** A piece of land adequate for the residence and support of a family. M17. ▸**b** A piece of land (usu. 160 acres, approx. 65 hectares) granted to a settler to live on, esp. (*US*) under the Homestead Act of Congress (1862). E19.
3 A house with its dependent buildings etc.; *esp*. a farmstead. L17.
4 In Australia and New Zealand: the owner's residence on a sheep or cattle station. Also (*NZ*), a place from which a run is worked. M19.
– COMB.: **homestead exemption law** *US* a law exempting a homestead from seizure or forced sale for debt.
▸ **B** *verb trans. & intrans*. Settle, live on, (land) as a homestead. *N. Amer.* L19.
▪ **homesteader** *noun* the holder of a homestead; *spec*. (*N. Amer.*) a person holding land acquired by settlement, esp. (*US*) under the Homestead Act of 1862: L19. **homesteading** *noun* (**a**) a farmstead; (**b**) *N. Amer.* the granting of land to settlers, esp. (*US*) under the Homestead Act of 1862; (**c**) settling or living on land as a homestead: M19.

homester /ˈhəʊmstə/ *noun*. *rare*. M19.
[ORIGIN from HOME *noun* + -STER.]
1 A stay-at-home. M19.
2 A member of the home team in a sporting match. L19.

homeward /ˈhəʊmwəd/ *adverb & adjective*. OE.
[ORIGIN from HOME *noun* + -WARD.]
▸ **A** *adverb*. In the direction of one's place of residence or native country; towards home. OE.
– COMB.: **homeward-bound** *adjective* (esp. of a ship) preparing to go home, on the way home.
▸ **B** *adjective*. Directed or going homeward. M16.

homewards /ˈhəʊmwədz/ *adverb*. OE.
[ORIGIN from HOME *noun* + -WARDS.]
= HOMEWARD *adverb*.

homey *noun* var. of HOMIE.

homey /ˈhəʊmi/ *adjective*. *colloq*. Also **homy**. M19.
[ORIGIN from HOME *noun* + -Y[1].]
Resembling or suggestive of home; homely.

> D. ACHESON This homey chat between their shirt-sleeved diplomats at work.

homeyness /ˈhəʊmɪnɪs/ *noun*. Also **hominess**. L19.
[ORIGIN from HOMY *adjective* + -NESS.]
The quality of being homey, homeliness.

homicidal /hɒmɪˈsʌɪd(ə)l/ *adjective*. E18.
[ORIGIN from HOMICIDE + -AL[1].]
Of, pertaining to, or tending to homicide; having an impulse towards homicide; murderous.
homicidal mania insanity characterized by impulses to commit murder.
▪ **homiˈcidally** *adverb* L19.

homicide /ˈhɒmɪsʌɪd/ *noun*. ME.
[ORIGIN Old French & mod. French, from (sense 1) Latin *homicidium*, (sense 2) Latin *homicida*, both from shortened stem of *homo*, *homin-* human being: see -CIDE.]
1 The killing, by a human being, of a human being. ME. **excusable homicide**: incurring blame, but no criminal liability because in self-defence or by misadventure. **justifiable homicide**: incurring neither blame nor criminal liability because in the execution of one's duty. **unlawful homicide**: incurring criminal liability because done with malice aforethought or culpable neglect.
2 A person who kills a human being. In early use often *spec*. a murderer. LME.

homie /ˈhəʊmi/ *noun*. *slang*. Also **homey**. E20.
[ORIGIN from HOME *noun* + -IE.]
1 A British immigrant, *esp*. one recently arrived. *NZ*. *arch*. E20.
2 A homeboy or homegirl. Chiefly *US*. M20.

homilete /ˈhɒmɪliːt/ *noun*. *US*. L19.
[ORIGIN Greek *homilētēs* disciple, scholar, from *homilein*: see HOMILETIC.]
= HOMILIST.

homiletic /hɒmɪˈlɛtɪk/ *adjective & noun*. M17.
[ORIGIN Late Latin *homileticus* from Greek *homilētikos*, from *homilētos* verbal adjective of *homilein* consort or hold converse with, from *homilos* crowd: see -IC.]
▸ **A** *adjective*. Of the nature of or characteristic of a homily. M17.
▸ **B** *noun*. In *pl*. & †*sing*. The art of preaching. M19.
▪ **homiletical** *adjective* †(**a**) relating to social intercourse; sociable; (**b**) = HOMILETIC *adjective*: M17. **homiletically** *adverb* M19.

homiliary /hɒˈmɪlɪəri/ *noun*. M19.
[ORIGIN medieval Latin *homiliarium*, *homiliarius* (sc. *liber* book), from ecclesiastical Latin *homilia* HOMILY: see -ARY[1]. Cf. Old French *omiliaire*.]
A book of homilies.

homilise *verb* var. of HOMILIZE.

homilist /ˈhɒmɪlɪst/ *noun*. E17.
[ORIGIN from HOMILY + -IST.]
A person who writes or delivers homilies; a preacher.

homilite /ˈhɒmɪlʌɪt/ *noun*. L19.
[ORIGIN from Greek *homilia* association + -ITE[1].]
MINERALOGY. A black or brown monoclinic borosilicate of calcium also containing iron and magnesium.

homilize /ˈhɒmɪlʌɪz/ *verb intrans*. Also **-ise**. E17.
[ORIGIN from HOMILY + -IZE.]
Preach, sermonize, discourse.

homily /ˈhɒmɪli/ *noun*. LME.
[ORIGIN Old French *omelie* (mod. *homélie*) from ecclesiastical Latin *homilia* from Greek = converse, discourse, (eccl.) sermon, from *homilos* crowd: see -Y[3]. Finally assim. to Latin in 16.]
1 A religious discourse, a sermon. Now *spec*. a practical discourse aimed at the spiritual edification of a congregation (rather than an exposition of a point of doctrine). LME.
2 *transf*. A tedious (esp. moralizing) discourse; a lecture. L16.

> J. BRAINE As each bottle [of wine] was brought out he treated me to a short homily on the reasons for his choice.

hominess *noun* var. of HOMEYNESS.

homing /ˈhəʊmɪŋ/ *adjective*. M19.
[ORIGIN from HOME *verb* + -ING[2].]
That goes home; *spec*. (of a pigeon) trained to fly back to its loft from a distance, bred for long-distance racing.

hominid /ˈhɒmɪnɪd/ *noun & adjective*. L19.
[ORIGIN mod. Latin *Hominidae* (see below), from *homo*, *homin-* human being: see -ID[3].]
▸ **A** *noun*. A primate of the family Hominidae, which includes human beings (*Homo sapiens*), and several fossil forms. L19.
▸ **B** *adjective*. Belonging to or characteristic of a hominid or the Hominidae. E20.

hominin /ˈhɒmɪnɪn/ *noun & adjective*. L20.
[ORIGIN mod. Latin *Hominini* (see below), formed as HOMININE + -*in* var. of -INE[1].]
▸ **A** *noun*. A member of a species regarded as human or very closely related to humans, in many modern classifications placed in the tribe Hominini. L20.
▸ **B** *adjective*. Of or pertaining to hominins; belonging to the tribe Hominini. L20.
– NOTE: Some authors regard the tribe Hominini as including the genus Homo and the Australopithecines, thus making *hominin* equivalent to *hominid*; others define the tribe so as to include the chimpanzees, and sometimes also the gorillas.

hominine /ˈhɒmɪnʌɪn/ *adjective & noun*. L19.
[ORIGIN from Latin *homo*, *homin-* human being + -INE[1]. Cf. ASININE.]
▸ **A** *adjective*. Pertaining to human beings, zoologically considered; hominid; *spec*. designating larger-brained hominids (opp. smaller-brained australopithecines). L19.
▸ **B** *noun*. A hominine primate. M20.

hominivorous /hɒmɪˈnɪv(ə)rəs/ *adjective*. M19.
[ORIGIN from Latin *homin-*, *homo* human being + -VOROUS.]
That feeds on human beings.

hominization /ˌhɒmɪnʌɪˈzeɪʃ(ə)n/ *noun*. Also **-isation**. M20.
[ORIGIN French *hominisation*, from Latin *homo*, *homin-* human being: see -IZATION.]
In evolution: the development of the higher characteristics that are thought to distinguish humans from other animals.

hominoid /ˈhɒmɪnɔɪd/ *adjective & noun*. E20.
[ORIGIN from Latin *homo*, *homin-* human being + -OID.]
▸ **A** *adjective*. Of human (rather than apelike) form; *spec*. belonging to or characteristic of (a member of) the Hominoidea (see below). E20.
▸ **B** *noun*. An animal resembling a human; *spec*. a primate of the superfamily Hominoidea, which includes humans and the anthropoid apes. E20.

hominy /ˈhɒmɪni/ *noun*. E17.
[ORIGIN Contr. of Virginia Algonquian *uskatahomen*. Cf. ROCKAHOMINY.]
Maize hulled and ground and prepared for food by being boiled with water or milk.

homish /ˈhəʊmɪʃ/ *adjective*. Also **homeish**. M16.
[ORIGIN from HOME *noun* + -ISH[1].]
†**1** Belonging to home; domestic. M–L16.
2 Homelike, homely. L18.
▪ **homishness** *noun* M19.

homme /ɔm/ *noun*. Pl. pronounced same. E18.
[ORIGIN French.]
The French for 'man', occurring in various phrases used in English.
▪ ***homme d'affaires*** /dafɛːr/, pl. ***hommes d'affaires*** (pronounced same), a businessman, an agent, a lawyer E18. ***homme moyen*** /mwajɛ̃/, pl. **-s -s** (pronounced same), an average man; ***homme moyen sensuel*** /sɑ̃sɥɛl/, the average sensual man: L19.

homo /ˈhəʊməʊ, ˈhɒməʊ/ *noun*[1]. Pl. **-os**. L16.
[ORIGIN Latin = man.]
1 A human being. L16.
2 (**H-**.) The genus to which human beings and certain of their fossil ancestors belong. Also with Latin specific epithets in names of (proposed) species, and with Latin or mock-Latin adjectives (in imitation of zool. nomenclature) in names intended to personify some aspects of human life or behaviour. L18.

> *Times* Symbolizing . . this concept of *homo turisticus*, the new Hilton hotel. *English Studies* An arraignment of Walter Pater in his quality of *homo aestheticus*.

homo faber /ˈfeɪbə/ [Latin = maker] the human species regarded as makers of tools. **Homo sapiens** /ˈsapɪɛnz/ [Latin = wise] modern humans regarded as a species. **the genus Homo** humankind.

homo /ˈhəʊməʊ/ *noun*[2] *& adjective*. *colloq*. (usu. *derog*.). Pl. of noun **-os**. E20.
[ORIGIN Abbreviation.]
= HOMOSEXUAL *noun & adjective*.

homo- /ˈhɒməʊ, ˈhəʊməʊ/ *combining form*. Before a vowel also **hom-**.
[ORIGIN from Greek *homos* same: see -O-.]
1 Used in words adopted from Greek and in English words modelled on these, and as a freely productive prefix, with the sense 'same, equal'. Freq. opp. HETERO-.
2 [Extracted from HOMOLOGUE.] *CHEMISTRY*. Forming names of compounds which are homologues (usu. by addition of $\cdot CH_2\cdot$) of those whose names follow, as ***homatropine***, ***homocitrate***, ***homoserine***, etc.
▪ **homacanth** *adjective* (*ICHTHYOLOGY*) having the spines of the dorsal and anal fins symmetrical L19. **homoˈcercal** *adjective* [Greek *kerkos* tail] *ICHTHYOLOGY* designating or possessing a tail with equal lobes, esp. with the spine deflected into the upper lobe M19. **homochlaˈmydeous** *adjective* [Greek *khlamud-*, *khlamus* cloak] *BOTANY* having the outer and inner layers of the perianth alike, not differentiated into sepals and petals L19. **homoˈchromous** *adjective* (chiefly *BOTANY*) of uniform colour M19. **homochromy** *noun* (*ZOOLOGY*) cryptic coloration L19. **homoclime**

noun (GEOGRAPHY) any of several places or regions having a similar climate E20. **homo'cyclic** *adjective* (CHEMISTRY) containing or designating a ring formed of atoms of a single element E20. **homo'cysteine** *noun* (BIOCHEMISTRY) an amino acid, $HSCH_2CH_2CH(NH_2)COOH$, formed as an intermediate in the metabolism of methionine and cysteine M20. **homo'desmic** *adjective* (CRYSTALLOGRAPHY) containing only a single kind of chemical bond M20. **homodimer** *noun* (CHEMISTRY) a dimer of two identical subunits L20. **homodont** *adjective* (ZOOLOGY) of or possessing teeth all of the same type (as reptiles) L19. **homoge'netic** *adjective* having a common descent or origin L19. **homogen'tisic** *adjective* (CHEMISTRY): ***homogentisic acid***, an organic acid, intermediate in the metabolism of aromatic amino acids and excreted by persons with alkaptonuria; 2,5-dihydroxyphenylacetic acid: L19. **homograft** *noun* = HOMOTRANSPLANT *noun* E20. **homo'lateral** *adjective* (chiefly MEDICINE) on or affecting the same side (of the body) E20. **homo'lecithal** *adjective* (of an egg or egg cell) having the yolk uniformly distributed throughout the cytoplasm L19. **homo'nuclear** *adjective* (CHEMISTRY etc.) (***a***) (of substitution) taking place on the same ring in a polycyclic molecule; (***b***) composed of atoms whose nuclei are identical: M20. **homo'polar** *adjective* characterized by equal or constant polarity L19. **homosce'dastic** *adjective* [Greek *skedastos* able to be scattered, from *skedannunai* scatter] STATISTICS of equal scatter or variation; having equal variances: E20. **homosceda'sticity** *noun* (STATISTICS) equal or constant variance E20. **ho'mosporous** *adjective* (BIOLOGY) producing only one kind of spore L19. **ho'mospory** *noun* (BIOLOGY) homosporous condition E20. **homo'thallic** *adjective* (MYCOLOGY) having self-fertile thalli E20. **homo'thallism** *noun* the state or condition of being homothallic E20. **homo'thally** *noun* = HOMOTHALLISM M20. **homotherm** *noun* = HOMEOTHERM M20. **homo'thermic** *adjective* = HOMEOTHERMIC L19.

homocaryotic *adjective* var. of HOMOKARYOTIC.

homocentric /hɒmə(ʊ)'sɛntrɪk, həʊm-/ *noun & adjective*[1]. E17.
[ORIGIN mod. Latin *homocentricus*, formed as HOMO- + Greek *kentrikos*: see -CENTRIC.]
▸ †**A** *noun*. ASTRONOMY. A sphere or circle concentric with another or with the earth. Only in E17.
▸ **B** *adjective*. **1** ASTRONOMY. Concentric. *obsolete* exc. *hist.* L17.
2 PHYSICS. Of rays: either parallel, or passing through a single focal point (or appearing to do so when extended). L19.

homocentric /həʊmə(ʊ)'sɛntrɪk, hɒm-/ *adjective*[2]. E20.
[ORIGIN from Latin HOMO *noun*[1] + -CENTRIC.]
= ANTHROPOCENTRIC.

homocline /'hɒmə(ʊ)klʌɪn/ *noun*. E20.
[ORIGIN from HOMO- + CLINE, as *anticlyne*, *syncline*, etc.]
GEOLOGY. A set of strata dipping throughout in the same general direction. Cf. MONOCLINE.
■ **homo'clinal** *adjective* of, pertaining to, or associated with a homocline E20.

homoe- *combining form* see HOMOEO-.

Homoean /hɒ'miːən/ *adjective & noun*. M19.
[ORIGIN from mod. Latin *homoeus* from Greek *homoios* like, similar + -AN.]
ECCLESIASTICAL HISTORY. Designating or pertaining to, a member of, a group of Arians which developed *c* 355 and repudiated both the Homoousion and the Homoiousion, maintaining simply that in the Trinity the Son is 'like' the Father.

homoeo- /'hɒmɪəʊ, 'həʊm-/ *combining form* of Greek *homoios* like, similar: see -O-. Also **homeo-**, **homoio-**, before a vowel **homoe-**, **homoi-**.
■ **homoeo'blastic** *adjective* (PETROGRAPHY) (of metamorphic rocks) composed of grains equal in size E20. **homoeo'crystalline** *adjective* (PETROGRAPHY) composed of crystals of roughly equal size L19. **homoeo'geneous** *adjective* [after HOMOGENEOUS] of a similar kind L19.

homoeobox *noun* var. of HOMEOBOX.

homoeomerous /hɒmɪ'ɒm(ə)rəs/ *adjective*. Also (in BOTANY usu.) **homoi-** /hɒmɔɪ-/. L19.
[ORIGIN from HOMOEO- + Greek *meros* part: see -OUS.]
Having or consisting of similar parts; *spec.* in BOTANY, (of lichen) having the algal and fungal cells uniformly distributed (opp. ***heteromerous***).

homoeomery /hɒmɪ'ɒm(ə)ri/ *noun*. Also **homoi-** /hɒmɔɪ-/, **-omeria** /-ɒ'mɛrɪə/. L17.
[ORIGIN from Latin *homoeomeria* from Greek *homoiomereia*, from *homoiomerēs* consisting of like parts, from *homoios* like + *meros* part: see -Y[3].]
hist. The theory (propounded by Anaxagoras) that the ultimate particles of matter are homogeneous. Also, in *pl.*, the ultimate particles of matter, regarded as homogeneous.

homoeomorph /'hɒmɪəmɔːf, 'həʊm-/ *noun*. Also **homeo-**. L19.
[ORIGIN from HOMOEO- + Greek *morphē* shape, form.]
A chemical substance, fossil species, or topological figure which exhibits homoeomorphism or homoeomorphy.

homoeomorphic /hɒmɪə(ʊ)'mɔːfɪk, həʊm-/ *adjective*. Also (in MATH. usu.) **homeo-**. E20.
[ORIGIN formed as HOMOEOMORPH + -IC.]
Of the same kind or form; homoeomorphous; *spec.* in MATH., topologically equivalent to another figure, space, etc.

homoeomorphism /hɒmɪə(ʊ)'mɔːfɪz(ə)m, həʊm-/ *noun*. Also (in sense 2 usu.) **homeo-**. M19.
[ORIGIN formed as HOMOEOMORPH + -ISM.]
1 CRYSTALLOGRAPHY. The condition of being homoeomorphous; possession of similar crystal structures. M19.
2 MATH. The condition of being homoeomorphic; topological equivalence. E20.

homoeomorphous /hɒmɪə(ʊ)'mɔːfəs, həʊm-/ *adjective*. Also **homeo-**. M19.
[ORIGIN formed as HOMOEOMORPH + -OUS.]
1 CRYSTALLOGRAPHY. Of chemical substances: having a similar crystal form and habit though different chemical composition. M19.
2 PALAEONTOLOGY. Exhibiting homoeomorphy; superficially similar. L19.

homoeomorphy /'hɒmɪəmɔːfi, 'həʊm-/ *noun*. Also **homeo-**. L19.
[ORIGIN formed as HOMOEOMORPH + -Y[3].]
PALAEONTOLOGY. A superficial or deceptive resemblance between two fossils or fossil species; *esp.* resemblance due to convergent evolution.

homoeopath, **homoeopathy**, etc. *nouns* vars. of HOMEOPATH, HOMEOPATHY, etc.

homoeosis *noun* var. of HOMEOSIS.

homoeostasis *noun* var. of HOMEOSTASIS.

homoeoteleuton /hɒ,miːətɪ'ljuːt(ə)n/ *noun*. Also **homoi-** /,hɒmɔɪ-/. L16.
[ORIGIN Late Latin from Greek *homoioteleuton* (sc. *rhēma* word), from *homoios* like + *teleutē* ending.]
1 A rhetorical figure consisting in the use of a series of words with the same or similar endings. *rare*. L16.
2 (An error in copying caused by) the occurrence of similar endings in two neighbouring words, lines, etc. M19.

homo-erotic /,hɒməʊɪ'rɒtɪk, 'həʊm-/ *adjective & noun*. E20.
[ORIGIN from HOMO- + EROTIC *adjective & noun*.]
= HOMOSEXUAL.
■ **homo-eroticism** /-sɪz(ə)m/ *noun* M20. **homo-erotism** *noun* E20.

homogametic /hɒməgə'mɛtɪk, -'miː-; həʊm-/ *adjective*. E20.
[ORIGIN from HOMO- + GAMETIC.]
BIOLOGY. Producing gametes that all have the same kind of sex chromosome.
■ **homo'gamety** *noun* the condition or state of being homogametic M20.

homogamous /hɒ'mɒgəməs/ *adjective*. M19.
[ORIGIN from HOMO- + Greek *gamos* marriage + -OUS.]
BOTANY. **1** Of a plant: having all the florets of a capitulum or spikelet hermaphrodite, or of the same sex. M19.
2 Of a flower: having the anthers and stigmas maturing together, so as to permit self-fertilization. Cf. DICHOGAMOUS. M19.

homogamy /hɒ'mɒgəmi/ *noun*. L19.
[ORIGIN formed as HOMOGAMOUS + -GAMY.]
1 BOTANY. The condition of being homogamous; the possession of homogamous flowers. L19.
2 BIOLOGY. Breeding between individuals similar in some characteristic; inbreeding. L19.
■ **homo'gamic** *adjective* (BIOLOGY) of or pertaining to homogamy E20.

homogene /'hɒmədʒiːn, 'həʊm-/ *adjective & noun*. Now *rare* or *obsolete*. M16.
[ORIGIN Greek *homogenēs*: see HOMOGENEOUS.]
▸ **A** *adjective*. Homogeneous. M16.
▸ **B** *noun*. A homogeneous thing. E18.

homogeneal /hɒmə(ʊ)'dʒiːnɪəl, -'dʒɛn-; həʊm-/ *adjective & noun*. Now *rare*. E17.
[ORIGIN medieval Latin *homogenealis*, from *homogeneus* (see HOMOGENEOUS) + *-alis* -AL[1].]
▸ **A** *adjective*. Homogeneous. E17.
▸ **B** *noun*. A homogeneous thing. M17.

homogeneate /hɒmə(ʊ)'dʒiːnɪeɪt, -'dʒɛn-; həʊm-/ *verb trans*. *rare*. M17.
[ORIGIN from medieval Latin *homogeneus* (see HOMOGENEOUS) + -ATE[3].]
Make homogeneous.

homogeneity /,hɒmə(ʊ)dʒɪ'niːɪti, -'neɪɪti; ,həʊm-/ *noun*. E17.
[ORIGIN medieval Latin *homogeneitas*, from *homogeneus*: see HOMOGENEOUS, -ITY.]
The quality or condition of being homogeneous.

P. BOWLES The men . . all wore . . white turbans . . which lent the scene a strong aspect of homogeneity.

homogeneous /hɒmə(ʊ)'dʒiːnɪəs, -'dʒɛn-; həʊm-/ *adjective*. M17.
[ORIGIN from medieval Latin *homogeneus*, from Greek *homogenēs* of the same kind, formed as HOMO- + *genos* kind: see -OUS.]
1 Of the same kind, nature, or character; alike, similar, congruous. M17.
2 Consisting of parts or elements of the same kind; of uniform character throughout. M17. ▸**b** PHYSICS. Of light or other radiation: monochromatic. L18. ▸**c** PHYSICAL CHEMISTRY. Consisting of, or involving a single phase. L19. ▸**d** Of a nuclear reactor: having the fuel uniformly mixed with the moderator. M20.
3 MATH. Of the same kind or degree; consisting of terms of the same dimensions. L17.
homogeneous coordinates: replaced by their ratios such that equations in the system are homogeneous.
■ **homogeneously** *adverb* M17. **homogeneousness** *noun* M17.

homogenize /hə'mɒdʒənʌɪz/ *verb*. Also **-ise**. L19.
[ORIGIN from HOMOGENE + -IZE.]
1 *verb trans*. Make homogeneous or uniform; incorporate into a whole of uniform composition. L19. ▸**b** Subject (milk, cream, or another emulsion) to a process by which suspended droplets are broken up and dispersed through the liquid, so preventing separation of the constituents. E20. ▸**c** METALLURGY. Render (an alloy) more uniform in composition by heating and slow cooling. E20. ▸**d** Prepare a suspension of cell constituents from (tissue) by physical treatment (as grinding) in a liquid. M20.
2 *verb intrans*. Become homogeneous. M20.
■ **homogenized** *ppl adjective* (***a***) that has been homogenized; *esp.* (of milk etc.) having the globules of fat reduced in size and distributed throughout the liquid; (***b***) (of abstract notions) not readily differentiated; similar in nature: E20. **homogenizer** *noun* a machine or apparatus designed to homogenize some material (as milk or tissue) L19.

homogenous /hə'mɒdʒɪnəs/ *adjective*[1]. *arch*. L19.
[ORIGIN from HOMO- + Greek *genos* race + -OUS.]
Homogenetic.

homogenous /hə'mɒdʒɪnəs/ *adjective*[2]. Freq. considered *erron*. M20.
[ORIGIN Alt. of HOMOGENEOUS, prob. after *homogenize* etc.]
Homogeneous.

homogeny /hə'mɒdʒəni/ *noun*. E17.
[ORIGIN In sense 1 from mod. Latin *homogenia* from Greek *homogeneia*, from *homogeneus*: see HOMOGENEOUS, -Y[3]. In sense 2 from HOMO- + -GENY.]
†**1** Homogeneity. Only in E17.
2 BIOLOGY. Correspondence of structure due to common descent. *rare*. L19.

homograph /'hɒməgrɑːf; 'həʊm-/ *noun*. E19.
[ORIGIN from HOMO- + -GRAPH.]
†**1** A system of signalling. Only in E19.
2 Each of a set of words having the same written form but of different origin, meaning, or pronunciation. Also, a homonym. L19.

homographic /hɒmə'grafɪk, həʊm-/ *adjective*. M19.
[ORIGIN from HOMO- + -GRAPHIC, in sense 1 through French *homographique*.]
1 GEOMETRY. Having the same anharmonic ratio or system of anharmonic ratios, as two figures of the same thing in different perspectives; belonging or relating to such figures. M19.
2 Designating or pertaining to a spelling system having a one-to-one relationship between character and sound. M19.
3 Of, pertaining to, or consisting of homographs. L19.

homoi(o)- *combining forms* see HOMOEO-.

homoiomerous *adjective*, **homoiomery** *noun* vars. of HOMOEOMEROUS, HOMOEOMERY.

homoiosmotic /,hɒmɔɪɒz'mɒtɪk/ *adjective*. Also **homeo-osmotic** /,hɒmɪəʊɒz'mɒtɪk/, **homoio-osmotic** /,hɒmɔɪəʊɒz'mɒtɪk/. M20.
[ORIGIN from *homoio-* var. of HOMOEO- + OSMOTIC.]
ZOOLOGY. Maintaining a more or less constant concentration of solutes in the body fluids independent of variations of concentration in the surrounding medium.
■ **homoiosmosis** *noun* M20.

homoioteleuton *noun* var. of HOMOEOTELEUTON.

homoiousian /hɒmɔɪ'uːsɪən, -'aʊ-, -z-/ *adjective & noun*. Also (esp. as noun) **H-**. L17.
[ORIGIN from ecclesiastical Latin *homoeusius* from Greek *homoiousios* of like essence, from *homoios* like, similar + *ousia* essence, substance: see -IAN. Opp. HETEROOUSIAN and HOMOOUSIAN.]
CHRISTIAN CHURCH. ▸**A** *adjective*. Of like but not identical essence or substance (esp. of the first and second persons of the Trinity). Also (*hist.*), of or pertaining to the homoiousians. L17.
▸ **B** *noun*. *hist.* A person who believed the first and second persons of the Trinity to be of like but not identical essence or substance; a semi-Arian. M18.

Homoiousion /hɒmɔɪ'uːsɪən, -'aʊ-, -z-/ *noun*. M19.
[ORIGIN ecclesiastical Greek, neut. of *homoiousios*: see HOMOIOUSIAN. Cf. HOMOOUSION.]
ECCLESIASTICAL HISTORY. *The* doctrine that the first and second persons of the Trinity are of like but not identical essence or substance.

homokaryotic /,hɒmə(ʊ)karɪ'ɒtɪk, ,həʊm-/ *adjective*. Also **-caryotic**. E20.
[ORIGIN from HOMO- + KARYO- + -OTIC.]
Chiefly MYCOLOGY. Having two or more genetically identical nuclei within a common cytoplasm.

H

■ **homo'karyon** *noun*, pl. **-ya**, a homokaryotic cell, structure, or organism M20. **homokary'osis** *noun* the state or condition of being homokaryotic E20.

homolog *noun* see HOMOLOGUE.

homologate /hə'mɒləɡeɪt/ *verb trans.* E16.
[ORIGIN medieval Latin *homologat-* pa. ppl stem of *homologare* agree, after Greek *homologein* confess, acknowledge: see -ATE[3].]
1 Express agreement with; approve; acknowledge; confirm, ratify. Chiefly *Scot.* E16.
2 *spec.* Confirm as an official specification of performance; approve (a car, boat, engine, etc.) for sale in a particular market or for use in a particular class of racing. M20.
■ **homolo'gation** *noun* M17.

homological /hɒmə'lɒdʒɪk(ə)l, həʊm-/ *adjective.* M19.
[ORIGIN from HOMOLOGY + -ICAL.]
1 Homologous; pertaining to or characterized by homology. M19.
2 PHILOSOPHY. = AUTOLOGICAL *adjective.* M20.
■ **homologically** *adverb* M19.

homologize /hɒ'mɒlədʒʌɪz/ *verb.* Also **-ise**. M18.
[ORIGIN from HOMOLOGOUS + -IZE.]
1 *verb intrans.* Be homologous; correspond. M18.
2 *verb trans.* Make or show to be homologous. E19.
■ **homologizer** *noun* (*rare*) E18.

homologous /hɒ'mɒləɡəs/ *adjective.* M17.
[ORIGIN from medieval Latin *homologus* from Greek *homologos* agreeing, consonant, from *homos* same + *logos* relation, ratio: see LOGOS, -OUS.] **I** *gen.* **1** Having the same relation, structure, relative position, etc.; corresponding. M17.
▸ **II** *spec.* **2** MATH. Of elements (as lines, points, terms, etc.): having similar or analogous positions or roles in distinct figures or functions. Also, of figures, expressions, etc.: showing one-to-one correspondence between elements; equivalent. M17.
3 a BIOLOGY. Of organs, parts, or traits: orig., having the same fundamental structure, organization, or mode of development. Now *esp.* having a common evolutionary origin. M19. ▸**b** MEDICINE. Of a tumour: having the same form as normal tissue of the part. *obsolete* exc. *hist.* L19. ▸**c** CYTOLOGY. Of chromosomes: pairing at meiosis and (usu.) identical in morphology and in arrangement of genetic loci. E20. ▸**d** MEDICINE & ZOOLOGY. Derived from or involving conspecific organisms; *spec.* involving or containing antibodies and their specific antigens. E20.

> **a** E. C. MINKOFF The human arm, . . the bird's wing, and the pectoral fins of certain fishes are all homologous.

4 CHEMISTRY. Of a series of (esp. organic) compounds: differing successively by addition of some constituent (esp. $\cdot CH_2 \cdot$), and showing graded physical and chemical properties. M19.

homolographic /hɒmələ'ɡrafɪk/ *adjective.* Also **homalo-**. M19.
[ORIGIN Alt. of Greek *homalos* even, level + -O- + -GRAPHIC: assim. to HOMO-.]
GEOGRAPHY. Designating a method of projection in which equal areas on the earth's surface are represented by equal areas on the map.

homologue /'hɒməlɒɡ/ *noun.* Also ***-log**. M19.
[ORIGIN French, from Greek *homologos*: see HOMOLOGOUS.]
A thing which is homologous; a homologous organ, compound, etc.

homology /hɒ'mɒlədʒi/ *noun.* E17.
[ORIGIN Late Latin *homologia* from Greek *homologia* agreement, assent, from *homologos*: see HOMOLOGOUS, -Y[3].]
1 The quality or condition of being homologous; sameness of relation; (an instance of) correspondence. E17.
2 BIOLOGY. **a** Orig., correspondence in fundamental structure of an organ, part, etc. Now chiefly, correspondence in evolutionary origin (of organs, parts, etc.). M19. ▸**b** An instance of this. M19.

homolysis /hɒ'mɒlɪsɪs/ *noun.* M20.
[ORIGIN from HOMO- + -LYSIS.]
CHEMISTRY. The splitting of a molecule into two neutral atoms or radicals.
■ **homo'lytic** *adjective* of the nature of or involving homolysis M20.

homomorph /'hɒməmɔːf, 'həʊm-/ *noun.* L19.
[ORIGIN from HOMO- + Greek *morphē* form.]
A thing (as a letter, a word, a system) having the same form as another.

homomorphic /hɒmə(ʊ)'mɔːfɪk, həʊm-/ *adjective.* L19.
[ORIGIN formed as HOMOMORPH + -IC.]
▸ **I** *gen.* **1** Of the same or similar form; of, relating to, or consisting of things of the same or similar form. L19.
▸ **II** *spec.* **2 a** BIOLOGY. Of organisms or organs: having external resemblance but not related in structure or origin. L19. ▸**b** BOTANY. Designating (the self-fertilization of) flowers with stamens and pistils of equal length. L19. ▸**c** ENTOMOLOGY. Having larvae resembling the adults; hemimetabolous. L19. ▸**d** ZOOLOGY. Of animal colonies: having the constituent individuals all alike. L19. ▸**e** CYTOLOGY. Of homologous chromosomes: the same in size and form. E20.
3 MATH. Relating to, produced by, or designating a homomorphism; giving rise *to* a second set by a homomorphism. M20.

homomorphism /hɒmə(ʊ)'mɔːfɪz(ə)m, həʊm-/ *noun.* M19.
[ORIGIN formed as HOMOMORPH: see -ISM.]
1 Resemblance of form. *rare.* M19.
2 MATH. A transformation of one set into another that preserves in the second set the relations between elements of the first. M20.

homomorphous /hɒmə(ʊ)'mɔːfəs, həʊm-/ *adjective.* M19.
[ORIGIN formed as HOMOMORPH + -OUS.]
Of the same or similar form, homomorphic.

homonym /'hɒmənɪm/ *noun.* L17.
[ORIGIN Latin *homonymum* from Greek *homōnumon* neut. of *homōnumos* HOMONYMOUS: see -NYM.]
1 Each of two or more words having the same written form but of different meaning and origin, a homograph. Also, a homophone. L17.
2 A person or thing having the same name as another; a namesake. M19.
3 BIOLOGY. A Latin genus name or binomial applied to more than one organism (the earlier use having precedence). L19.
■ **homo'nymic** *adjective* M19. **homo'nymity** *noun* homonymy L20.

homonymous /hə'mɒnɪməs/ *adjective.* E17.
[ORIGIN from Latin *homonymus* from Greek *homōnumos*, formed as HOMO- + *onuma* name: see -NYM, -OUS.]
1 Employing the same name for different things, equivocal, ambiguous. E17.
2 Having the same name. M17.
3 Having the same written or spoken form but differing in meaning and origin. L19.
4 ZOOLOGY. Of animal horns: such that the right and left horns have right-handed and left-handed spiral cores respectively. E20.
■ **homonymously** *adverb* M18.

homonymy /hə'mɒnɪmi/ *noun.* L16.
[ORIGIN Late Latin *homonymia* from Greek *homōnumia*, from *homōnumos*: see HOMONYMOUS, -Y[3].]
The quality or state of being homonymous.

homoousian /hɒməʊ'uːsɪən, -'aʊ-, -z-; həʊməʊ-/ *noun* & *adjective.* Also **homousian** /hɒ'muː-, -'maʊ-/, (esp. as noun) **H-**. M16.
[ORIGIN ecclesiastical Latin *homousianus*, from *hom(o)usius* from Greek *hom(o)ousios*, formed as HOMO- + *ousia* essence, substance: see -IAN. Opp. HETEROOUSIAN and HOMOIOUSIAN.]
CHRISTIAN CHURCH. ▸**A** *noun.* A person who believes the three persons of the Trinity to be of identical essence or substance; an orthodox Trinitarian. M16.
▸ **B** *adjective.* Of identical essence or substance (esp. of the three persons of the Trinity). Also, of or pertaining to the homoousians. L17.

Homoousion /hɒməʊ'uːsɪən, -'aʊ-, -z-; həʊməʊ-/ *noun.* L18.
[ORIGIN ecclesiastical Greek, neut. of *homoousios*: see HOMOOUSIAN. Cf. HOMOIOUSION.]
CHRISTIAN CHURCH. *The* doctrine that the first and second persons of the Trinity are of identical essence or substance.

homoousios /hɒməʊ'uːsɪəs, -'aʊ-, -z-; həʊməʊ-/ *adjective.* M19.
[ORIGIN Greek: see HOMOOUSIAN.]
= HOMOOUSIAN *adjective.*

homophile /'hɒməfʌɪl, 'həʊm-/ *noun* & *adjective.* M20.
[ORIGIN from HOMO- + -PHILE.]
= HOMOSEXUAL *adjective* & *noun.*

homophobia /hɒmə'fəʊbɪə, həʊmə-/ *noun*[1]. *rare.* E20.
[ORIGIN from Latin HOMO *noun*[1] + -PHOBIA.]
Fear or hatred of the male sex or humankind.

homophobia /hɒmə'fəʊbɪə, həʊmə-/ *noun*[2]. M20.
[ORIGIN from HOMO(SEXUAL *adjective* & *noun* + -PHOBIA.]
Fear or hatred of homosexuals and homosexuality.
■ **'homophobe** *noun* a person who is afraid of or hostile to homosexuals and homosexuality L20. **homophobic** *adjective* & *noun* (**a**) *adjective* afraid of or hostile to homosexuals and homosexuality; (**b**) *noun* = HOMOPHOBE: L20.

homophone /'hɒməfəʊn/ *adjective* & *noun.* E17.
[ORIGIN Greek *homophōnos*, formed as HOMO-, -PHONE.]
▸ **A** *adjective.* Pronounced the same. *rare.* E17.
▸ **B** *noun.* Each of a set of words pronounced the same but of different meaning, origin, or spelling. Also, each of a set of symbols denoting the same sound or group of sounds. E17.

homophonic /hɒmə'fɒnɪk, həʊm-/ *adjective.* L19.
[ORIGIN formed as HOMOPHONE + -IC.]
1 MUSIC. Characterized by having one melodic part, to which the other parts provide harmonic accompaniment. L19.
2 = HOMOPHONOUS 2. M20.

homophonous /hə'mɒf(ə)nəs/ *adjective.* M18.
[ORIGIN formed as HOMOPHONE + -OUS.]
1 MUSIC. = HOMOPHONIC 1. M18.
2 Having the same pronunciation but differing in meaning, origin, or spelling. E19.

homophony /hə'mɒf(ə)ni/ *noun.* M18.
[ORIGIN Greek *homophōnia* unison formed as HOMOPHONE: see -PHONY.]
1 MUSIC. Homophonic music or style; a homophonic composition. M18.
2 The quality or state of being homophonous with regard to pronunciation. M19.

homoplastic /hɒmə(ʊ)'plastɪk, həʊm-/ *adjective.* L19.
[ORIGIN from HOMO- + Greek *plastos* moulded + -IC.]
1 BIOLOGY. Of a trait or character: having a similar structure but not a common origin; analogous. L19.
2 BIOLOGY & MEDICINE. Of or involving tissue grafted from one individual to (the equivalent site in) another of the same species. E20.
■ **'homoplasty** *noun* homoplastic transplantation E20.

homoplasy /'hɒməpleɪsi, 'həʊm-/ *noun.* L19.
[ORIGIN formed as HOMOPLASTIC + Greek *plasia*: see -PLASIA, -Y[3].]
BIOLOGY. (An instance of) similarity of structure produced independently (as) by the operation of similar circumstances.

homopteran /hɒ'mɒpt(ə)rən/ *noun* & *adjective.* M19.
[ORIGIN from mod. Latin *Homoptera* (see below), formed as HOMO- + Greek *pteron* wing: see -AN.]
ENTOMOLOGY. ▸**A** *noun.* Any hemipteran insect of the suborder Homoptera of chiefly plant-sucking bugs with wings of uniform texture, including aphids, scale insects, cicadas, etc. Cf. HETEROPTERAN. M19.
▸ **B** *adjective.* Of, pertaining to, or characteristic of the suborder Homoptera. E20.
■ **homopterous** *adjective* = HOMOPTERAN *adjective* E19.

homorganic /hɒmɔː'ɡanɪk/ *adjective.* M19.
[ORIGIN from HOMO- + ORGANIC *adjective.*]
PHONETICS. Produced by the same vocal organ or organs; sharing a specific place of articulation.

homosexual /hɒmə(ʊ)'sɛkʃʊəl, həʊm-/ *adjective* & *noun.* L19.
[ORIGIN from HOMO- + SEXUAL.]
▸ **A** *adjective.* Sexually attracted to people of one's own sex; of, pertaining to, or characterized by sexual attraction between people of the same sex. L19.
▸ **B** *noun.* A person who is sexually attracted (often exclusively) to people of his or her own sex. E20.
■ **homosexualist** *noun* a homosexual E20. **homosexually** *adverb* E20.

homosexuality /ˌhɒmə(ʊ)sɛkʃʊ'alɪti, ˌhəʊm-/ *noun.* L19.
[ORIGIN from HOMOSEXUAL + -ITY.]
The quality or condition of being homosexual; homosexual character, behaviour, or activity.

homostyled /'hɒmə(ʊ)stʌɪld, 'həʊm-/ *adjective.* L19.
[ORIGIN from HOMO- + STYLE + -ED[2].]
BOTANY. Having the styles in different individuals of the same length relative to the stamens.
■ **homo'stylous** *adjective* homostyled L19. **'homostyly** *noun* the state or condition of being homostylous L19.

homotopic /hɒmə(ʊ)'tɒpɪk, həʊm-/ *adjective.* L19.
[ORIGIN from HOMO- + Greek *topos* place + -IC.]
1 Relating to corresponding parts or places. *rare.* L19.
2 MATH. Related by a homotopy *to* another path, complex, etc. E20.

homotopy /'hɒmətəʊpi, hɒ'mɒtəpi/ *noun.* E20.
[ORIGIN formed as HOMOTOPIC: see -Y[3].]
MATH. (The property which characterizes) a mapping that deforms one path continuously into another, such that all intermediates lie within the topological space of which the two given paths are subspaces.

homotransplant /*as noun* hɒmə(ʊ)'transplɑːnt, -'trɑːns-, -nz-; həʊm-; *as verb* -trans'plɑːnt, -trɑːns-, -nz-/ *noun* & *verb.* E20.
[ORIGIN from HOMO- + TRANSPLANT *noun.*]
MEDICINE & BIOLOGY. ▸**A** *noun.* A piece of tissue or an organ (to be) transplanted from one individual to another of the same species. Also, an operation in which such a transplantation is performed. E20.
▸ **B** *verb trans.* Transplant from one individual to another of the same species. M20.
■ **homotransplan'tation** *noun* E20.

homozygote /hɒmə(ʊ)'zʌɪɡəʊt, həʊm-/ *noun* & *adjective.* E20.
[ORIGIN from HOMO- + ZYGOTE.]
BIOLOGY. ▸**A** *noun.* An individual that has identical alleles at one or more genetic loci; a Mendelian hybrid that is not a heterozygote and so breeds true. E20.
▸ **B** *adjective.* Homozygous. E20.
■ **homozy'gosity** *noun* (**a**) the state or condition of being homozygous; (**b**) the degree to which an individual is homozygous: E20. **homozy'gotic** *adjective* of or pertaining to homozygosis; homozygous: E20. **homozygous** *adjective* having identical alleles at one or more genetic loci, or *for* a given gene E20.

homuncio /hɒˈmʌnsɪəʊ/ *noun*. Now *rare* or *obsolete*. Pl. **-o(e)s**. LME.
[ORIGIN Latin, dim. of *homo* man.]
= HOMUNCULUS.

homunculus /hɒˈmʌŋkjʊləs/ *noun*. Pl. **-li** /-lʌɪ, -liː/. M17.
[ORIGIN Latin, dim. of *homo* man: see -CULE.]
A small or diminutive person, a dwarf; *hist.* a fetus considered as a fully formed human being.

HENRY MORE There is an artificiall way of making an Homunculus, and.. the Fairies.. had some such originall. E. JONG An Herbal Remedy, swiftly swallow'd, which would loose the dread Homunculus from the womb.

■ **homuncular** *adjective* diminutive, dwarfish E19. **homuncule** /hɒˈmʌŋkjuːl/ *noun* (now *rare*) = HOMUNCULUS L17.

homy *adjective* var. of HOMEY *adjective*.

hon /hʌn/ *noun*. *colloq.* E20.
[ORIGIN Abbreviation.]
= HONEY *noun* 3 (chiefly as a form of address).

Hon. *abbreviation*.
1 Honorary.
2 Honourable.

honcho /ˈhɒntʃəʊ/ *noun & verb*. *slang*. Chiefly *N. Amer.* M20.
[ORIGIN Japanese *hanchō* group leader.]
► **A** *noun*. Pl. **-os**. The leader of a small group or squad; a person who is in a position of power; a strong leader. M20.

JULIA PHILLIPS Dr Morse is the head honcho, the guy Howard Koch had called to get me in quick.

► **B** *verb trans.* Oversee; be in charge of (a situation). M20.

honda /ˈhɒndə/ *noun*. *US*. Also **-do** /-dəʊ/, pl. **-os**, **-du** /-duː/. L19.
[ORIGIN Prob. from Spanish *hondón* eyelet, infl. by Spanish *honda* sling.]
The eye at the end of a lasso through which the rope passes to form a loop.

Honduran /hɒnˈdjʊər(ə)n/ *adjective & noun*. E20.
[ORIGIN from *Honduras* (see below) + -AN.]
► **A** *adjective*. Of, pertaining to, or characteristic of the Central American country of Honduras or (formerly) of nearby British Honduras (now Belize). E20.
► **B** *noun*. A native or inhabitant of Honduras or (formerly) British Honduras. M20.
■ Also **Honduranean**, **-ian** /hɒndjʊˈreɪnɪən/ *adjective & noun* (now *rare*) L19.

hone /həʊn/ *noun*.
[ORIGIN Old English *hān* = Old Norse *hein*, from Germanic.]
†1 A stone, a rock. OE–ME.
2 A whetstone used for giving a fine edge to cutting tools. ME.
3 The stone of which whetstones are made. Also ***hone stone***. E18.

hone /həʊn/ *verb*[1] *intrans. dial. & US.* LME.
[ORIGIN Old French *hogner*, *-ier* grumble.]
1 Whine or pine *for*; hanker *after*. LME.
2 Grumble, whine, moan. E17.

hone /həʊn/ *verb*[2] *trans.* E19.
[ORIGIN from HONE *noun*.]
Sharpen on a hone or whetstone; *transf. & fig.* sharpen, streamline, focus. (Foll. by *up*.)

C. MCCULLOUGH Colonial axes had only one blade, honed to hair-splitting sharpness. A. PRICE Desperation honed up her wits to a razor edge.

honest /ˈɒnɪst/ *adjective & adverb*. ME.
[ORIGIN Old French (*h*)*oneste* (mod. *honnête*) from Latin *honestus*, from *honos*, *honor* HONOUR *noun*.]
► **A** *adjective* **1** †**a** Of a person: held in honour; holding an honourable position; respectable. ME–L17. ▸**b** Blameless but undistinguished. Chiefly *iron.* M16.

b J. T. BROCKETT Now, my honest man, you have been convicted of felony.

2 Of a thing, action, condition, etc.: bringing or deserving honour, honourable, decent, worthy, respectable; without disgrace or blemish. ME.

Globe & Mail (Toronto) When the thermometer really plunges, this is an honest garment. G. GREENE Men who've never done a stroke of honest work, talkers, scribblers.

3 **a** Of an action, one's feelings, etc.: showing sincerity of character or intention; fair, straightforward; free from fraud. ME. ▸**b** Of a thing: exactly as it appears; genuine, unadulterated. L16. ▸**c** Of money or gain: acquired by fair means; legitimate. L17.

a THACKERAY The very best and honestest feelings of the man came out in these artless pourings of paternal feeling. **b** U. BENTLEY It was not an honest gas fire, but one of those.. with coals fashioned out of fibre glass.

4 Of a person: marked by uprightness or probity; fair and righteous in speech and act; fundamentally sincere, or truthful; not lying, cheating, or stealing. LME. ▸†**b** *gen.* Of good moral character; virtuous, well-disposed. LME–E18. ▸**c** Of a woman: chaste, virtuous. *arch.* LME.

P. ROTH Far from being 'exploitive', I am just one of the few honest people around.

5 Ingenuous; without disguise; open, frank, truthful. M17.

D. H. LAWRENCE Sam, seeing her look at him, distorted his honest features. J. O'HARA I went to the boxing match, and to be completely frank and honest, I enjoyed myself.

– PHRASES: **earn an honest penny** = *turn an honest penny* below. **make an honest woman of** *colloq.* marry (esp. a pregnant woman). **turn an honest penny** earn money by fair means, make one's livelihood by hard work.

– SPECIAL COLLOCATIONS & COMB.: **honest broker** an impartial mediator in international, industrial, etc., disputes (orig. *spec.* Otto von Bismarck, under whom Germany was united). ***honest Injun***. **Honest John** (*a*) an honest person; (*b*) *hist.* an American missile designed to carry a nuclear warhead. **honest-to-God**, **honest-to-goodness** *adjectives & adverbs* (*colloq.*) genuine(ly), real(ly).

► **B** *adverb*. Honestly; *esp.* (*colloq.*) really, genuinely, in truth. L16.

ARNOLD BENNETT 'But I'm not sarcastic!' he protested. 'Honest?'.. 'Honest!' he solemnly insisted.

honestly /ˈɒnɪstli/ *adverb*. ME.
[ORIGIN from HONEST + -LY[2].]
1 In an honourable or respectful manner; worthily, decently. ME.

Practical Woodworking Honestly built in sound and suitable materials they have served several generations.

†2 Chastely, virtuously. ME–L17.
3 With upright conduct; without fraud, by honest means; sincerely, fairly, openly. LME. ▸**b** Really, genuinely, in truth. As *interjection* also expr. exasperation. L19.

B. JOWETT He does not like honestly to confess that he is talking nonsense. **b** R. LEHMANN It isn't amusing to be poor, darling. You wouldn't like it, honestly. *Courier & Advertiser (Dundee)* Honestly, some of these drivers should have their heads seen to!

honesty /ˈɒnɪsti/ *noun*. ME.
[ORIGIN Old French (*h*)*onesté* from Latin *honestas*, from *honestus* HONEST *adjective*: see -TY[1].]
► **I** The quality of being honest.
†1 Honour gained or conferred; repute, respect; respectability. ME–E17.
2 Appropriateness; decency, decorum. *obsolete* exc. *Scot.* LME.
†3 **a** Moral excellence; honourable character; *spec.* virtue, chastity, esp. of a woman. LME–M17. ▸**b** Generosity, liberality, hospitality. LME–E19.
4 Integrity, uprightness, truthfulness, sincerity. L16.

E. M. FORSTER He had a strong regard for honesty, and his word, once given, had always been kept.

► **II 5** A cruciferous plant, *Lunaria annua*, much grown for its purple or white flowers and round semi-transparent seed pods. L16.

– PHRASES: ***in the way of honesty***: see WAY *noun*.

honewort /ˈhəʊnwəːt/ *noun*. M17.
[ORIGIN from unkn. 1st elem. + WORT *noun*[1].]
Orig., corn parsley, *Petroselinum segetum*. Now, the related plant *Trinia glauca*, a small European umbellifer found in limestone turf in SW England; *N. Amer.* a woodland plant of the same family, *Cryptotaenia canadensis*.

honey /ˈhʌni/ *noun & adjective*. See also HINNY *noun*[2].
[ORIGIN Old English *hunig* = Old Frisian *hunig*, Old Saxon *honeg*, *-ig*, Old High German *honag*, *-ang* (Dutch, German *Honig*), Old Norse *hunang*, from Germanic.]
► **A** *noun*. **1** A sweet viscid fluid of various shades of yellow or gold, which is the nectar of flowers collected and worked up for food by insects, esp. by the honeybee. OE. ▸**b** A colour resembling that of honey. E19.
2 A juice which has similar qualities to honey; nectar; the juice of dates etc. LME.
3 A term of endearment: sweetheart, darling. Also, a beloved person, a sweetheart. Now chiefly *N. Amer.* LME. ▸**b** A good specimen of its kind; an excellent person or thing. *colloq.* L19.

J. HELLER 'Be thankful you've got me,' she insisted. 'I am, honey'. *Blues & Soul* You can just curl up with your honey and listen to it. **b** M. HOWARD She will write him a honey of a book.

4 *fig.* Sweetness, beauty, eloquence. L16.
5 A spoiled child; a person who is difficult to please. *US slang.* M20.

– PHRASES: ***bees and honey***: see BEE *noun*[1]. ***milk and honey***: see MILK *noun*. ***palm honey***: see PALM *noun*[1]. ***sugar and honey***: see SUGAR *noun* 2b. **virgin honey** liquid honey that flows or is centrifugally extracted from the combs.

– COMB.: **honey ant** = HONEYPOT 4; **honey badger** = RATEL; **honey bag** a bag containing honey; *spec.* = ***honey stomach*** below; **honey-bear** (*a*) the kinkajou, *Potos flavus*; (*b*) the sloth bear, *Melursus ursinus*; **honeybee** the common hive bee, *Apis mellifera*; **honey bucket** *N. Amer. slang* a container for excrement; **honeybun**, **honeybunch** *colloq.* = sense 3 above; **honey buzzard** any of several hawks of the genus *Pernis*, *esp.* a migratory Eurasian hawk, *P. apivorus*, which feeds extensively on the contents of the nests of bees and wasps; **honey chile** /tʃʌɪl/ *Southern US colloq.* (chiefly *black English*) [repr. a pronunc. of *child*] = sense 3 above; **honeycreeper** (*a*) any of various passerine birds of the family Drepanididae, native to the Hawaiian Islands; (*b*) any of various neotropical tanagers, esp. of the genera *Cyanerpes* and *Chlorophanes*, which feed on nectar; **honey drop** a drop of honey or of something sweet and delicious; **honeyeater** an animal etc. that feeds on honey; *esp.* any of various mainly Australasian passerine birds of the family Meliphagidae, with a long tongue used to take nectar from flowers; **honey-flow** (the period of) the secretion of honey or nectar by flowers; **honey flower** any of various plants yielding abundant nectar; *esp.* (*a*) any of several southern African shrubs of the genus *Melianthus* (family Melianthaceae), grown for their large flowers and pinnate leaves; (*b*) an Australian shrub, *Lambertia formosa* (family Proteaceae); **honey fungus** a fungus, *Armillaria mellea*, which attacks the roots of trees etc. and produces honey-coloured toadstools; **honey gilding** a dull gilding of gold leaf and honey used to decorate porcelain; the process of applying such gilding; **honeyguide** (*a*) any of various small tropical birds of the largely African family Indicatonidae, which feed on insects, honey, and beeswax, and can serve to reveal the location of bees' nests; (*b*) a marking on a flower which serves to direct pollinating insects to the nectaries; **honey-lipped** *adjective* sweet or soft in speech; sweet talking, insincere; **honey locust** a spiny N. American leguminous tree, *Gleditsia triacanthos*; †**honey-month** [after HONEYMOON] the first month after marriage; **honey mouse** = *honey possum* below; †**honey-mouthed** *adjective* = *honey-lipped* above; **honey-myrtle** *Austral.* = MELALEUCA; **honey possum** a small nectar-eating marsupial, *Tarsipes spencerae*, of SW Australia; **honey sac**, **honey stomach** the crop of a bee, in which nectar is stored during conversion to honey; **honeystone** = MELLITE; **honeysucker** a honeyeater or other bird etc. that feeds on honey or nectar; **honey-sweet** *adjective & noun* (*a*) *adjective* sweet as honey; (*b*) *noun* = sense 3 above; **honey-tongued** *adjective* speaking sweetly, softly, or winningly; **honeywort** any of several plants of the genus *Cerinthe*, of the borage family, esp. *C. major*, with glaucous leaves and drooping bell-shaped flowers, grown as bee plants.

► **B** *adjective*. Resembling or of the nature of honey; sweet; honeyed; lovable, dear. LME.
■ **honeyish** *adjective* (*rare*) somewhat like honey, rather sweet or pleasing M17. **honeyless** *adjective* E17.

honey /ˈhʌni/ *verb*. Pa. t. & pple **honeyed**, **honied**. LME.
[ORIGIN from the noun.]
1 *verb trans.* Make sweet with or as with honey; sweeten. LME.
2 *verb trans.* Address as 'honey'; use endearing terms to. Chiefly *US*. E17.
3 *verb intrans.* Use honeyed or endearing words; talk fondly or sweetly, use flattery. E17.
4 *verb trans.* Coax, cajole; flatter. E17.

honeybird /ˈhʌnɪbəːd/ *noun*. LME.
[ORIGIN from HONEY *noun* + BIRD *noun*.]
†1 A bee. LME–E17.
2 Any of various birds feeding on nectar or honey; *esp.* a honeyeater or a honeyguide. M18.

honeycomb /ˈhʌnɪkəʊm/ *noun & adjective*. OE.
[ORIGIN from HONEY *noun* + COMB *noun*[1].]
► **A** *noun*. **1** A structure of wax containing two series of hexagonal cells separated by thin partitions, formed by bees for the reception of honey and their eggs; *fig.* a receptacle for sweet things. OE.
†2 = HONEY *noun* 3. LME–M16.
3 A cavernous flaw in metalwork, esp. in a gun. M16.
4 The reticulum or second stomach of a ruminant. Also ***honeycomb tripe***. E18.
5 **a** Decorative or other work with a hexagonal or cellular arrangement like a honeycomb. M19. ▸**b** A sturdy material consisting of a network of open-ended cells bonded together. M20.
► **B** *attrib.* or as *adjective*. Resembling or suggestive of a honeycomb; having a hexagonal or cellular pattern or arrangement. E18.

– SPECIAL COLLOCATIONS & COMB.: **honeycomb quilt**: with a raised hexagonal pattern; **honeycomb ringworm** = FAVUS. ***honeycomb tripe***: see sense 4 above. **honeycomb wall** a wall with numerous small openings at regular intervals.

honeycomb /ˈhʌnɪkəʊm/ *verb*. L18.
[ORIGIN from the noun.]
1 *verb trans. & intrans.* Make or become like a honeycomb with cells, cavities, or perforations; make or become cavernous, hollow, or insubstantial. L18.

SLOAN WILSON They had honeycombed the island with tunnels and caves.

2 *verb trans. fig.* Penetrate throughout so as to make hollow, rotten, etc.; undermine. M19.

F. L. ALLEN The colleges were honeycombed with Bolshevism.

3 *verb trans.* Mark with a honeycomb pattern. L19.
4 *verb trans.* Build as a honeycomb wall. E20.
■ **honeycombing** *noun* (*a*) the action of the verb; (*b*) a defective condition of wood characterized by cracks and holes: L19.

honeycombed /ˈhʌnɪkəʊmd/ *adjective*. E17.
[ORIGIN from HONEYCOMB *verb*, *noun* + -ED[1], -ED[2].]
1 Having perforations, excavations, or cavernous parts like a honeycomb; *esp.* having numerous small cells. E17.
2 Marked with a honeycomb pattern. L19.

honeydew /ˈhʌnɪdjuː/ *noun*. L16.
[ORIGIN from HONEY *noun* + DEW *noun*.]
1 A sweet, sticky substance exuded by aphids, found on the leaves and stems of plants (orig. believed to be akin to dew). L16.

H

2 An ideally sweet or luscious substance; the nectar of flowers; honey. Now chiefly *poet.* **E17.**
3 A kind of tobacco sweetened with molasses. **M19.**
– COMB.: **honeydew melon** a cultivated variety of the melon, *Cucumis melo*, with smooth ivory or pale yellow skin and sweet green flesh.

honeyed /ˈhʌnɪd/ *adjective.* Also **honied**. **LME.**
[ORIGIN from HONEY *noun* + -ED².]
1 Having much honey, laden with honey; consisting of or containing honey. **LME.**
2 *fig.* Sweet; sweet-sounding, mellifluous. **LME.**

honey-fuggle /ˈhʌnɪfʌg(ə)l/ *verb. US colloq.* Also **-fugle** /-fjuːg(ə)l/. **E19.**
[ORIGIN from HONEY *noun* + FUGLE *verb*¹.]
1 *verb trans.* Dupe, deceive, swindle. **E19.** ▸**b** Obtain by duplicity or wheedling. **E20.**
2 *verb intrans.* Act in an underhand or indirect way in order to deceive or obtain by duplicity. **M19.**

honeymoon /ˈhʌnɪmuːn/ *noun & verb.* **M16.**
[ORIGIN from HONEY *noun* + MOON *noun*, orig. with ref. to waning affection, not to period of a month.]
▸ **A** *noun.* **1** Orig., the first month after marriage. Now usu., a holiday spent together by a newly married couple. **M16.**
2 *transf.* (The period of) the first warmth of newly established friendly relations. **L16.**

Guardian The Government has had its honeymoon, free from captious criticism.

– COMB. & PHRASES: **honeymoon couple** a newly married couple; **second honeymoon** a romantic holiday or trip taken by a couple who have been married for some time; *transf.* a period of renewed friendly relations.
▸ **B** *verb intrans.* Spend a honeymoon. **E19.**
■ **honeymooner** *noun* **L19.**

honeypot /ˈhʌnɪpɒt/ *noun.* **L15.**
[ORIGIN from HONEY *noun* + POT *noun*¹.]
1 A pot in which honey is stored. **L15.**
2 The female external genitals. *slang.* **E18.**
3 In *pl.*, a children's game in which one player clasps hands under his or her thighs and is carried like a honeypot by others; *sing.* the posture with the hands clasped under the thighs. **E19.**
4 More fully ***honeypot ant***. A worker ant distended with surplus food which can be regurgitated when needed by the colony; any of various kinds of ant which store food in this way. **L19.**
5 A person or thing which tempts or attracts attention; *spec.* an attractive woman. **E20.**

honeysuck /ˈhʌnɪsʌk/ *noun.* Long *obsolete* exc. *dial.* **OE.**
[ORIGIN from HONEY *noun* + SUCK *verb*.]
= HONEYSUCKLE 1, 2.

honeysuckle /ˈhʌnɪsʌk(ə)l/ *noun.* **ME.**
[ORIGIN App. an extension of HONEYSUCK.]
1 *sing.* & in *pl.* The tubular flowers of certain plants, esp. red clover, *Trifolium pratense*, and white clover, *T. repens*, sucked for the nectar contained in them; any of the plants bearing these flowers. Now *dial.* **ME.**
2 A twining shrub of woods and hedges, *Lonicera periclymenum* (family Caprifoliaceae), with fragrant trumpet-shaped typically pale yellow pink-tinged flowers (also ***common honeysuckle***; also called **woodbine**); *gen.* any plant of this or related genera. Also, the flower of these plants. **LME.**

T. KEN Sweet Honeysuckles round the Branches twin'd.

fly honeysuckle either of two erect honeysuckles bearing flowers in pairs, the European *Lonicera xylosteum* and the N. American *L. canadensis*. **trumpet honeysuckle** a N. American climbing honeysuckle, *Lonicera sempervirens*, with evergreen foliage and scarlet flowers.
3 Chiefly ARCHITECTURE. A design or ornament resembling a sprig or flower of honeysuckle. **M16.**
4 With or without specifying word: any of various plants thought to resemble the honeysuckle (or clover), esp. in abundance of nectar; *esp.* (***a***) *Austral.* = BANKSIA; (***b***) *N. Amer.* a kind of columbine, *Aquilegia canadensis*; (***c***) *NZ* = REWA-REWA. **L16.**
French honeysuckle an ornamental Italian leguminous plant, *Hedysarum coronarium*, with flowers like those of sainfoin. ***swamp honeysuckle***: see SWAMP *noun*.
5 The colour of honeysuckle flowers, which combines pale yellow and pink. **L19.**
■ **honeysuckled** *adjective* overgrown or scented with honeysuckle **M17.**

hong /hɒŋ/ *noun.* **E18.**
[ORIGIN Chinese *háng*, (Cantonese) *hòhng* row, trade.]
1 In China, a series of rooms or buildings used as a warehouse, factory, etc. *esp.* one of the foreign factories formerly maintained at Canton. Also in Hong Kong, a trading establishment. **E18.**
2 *hist.* The corporation of Chinese merchants at Canton who had a monopoly of trade with Europeans. **L18.**

hongi /ˈhɒŋi/ *noun & verb. NZ.* **L18.**
[ORIGIN Maori.]
▸ **A** *noun.* The touching or pressing together of noses as a Maori greeting. **L18.**
▸ **B** *verb intrans. & trans.* Press noses in greeting (a person). **M19.**

honied *adjective* var. of HONEYED *adjective*.

honied *verb pa. t. & pple*: see HONEY *verb*.

honi soit qui mal y pense /ɔni swa ki mal i pɑ̃s/ *noun phr.* **ME.**
[ORIGIN French.]
Shame on him who thinks evil of it (the motto of the Order of the Garter).

Honiton /ˈhɒnɪt(ə)n, ˈhʌn-/ *adjective.* **M19.**
[ORIGIN A town in Devon.]
Designating or pertaining to a type of lace orig. made in Honiton consisting of floral sprigs hand sewn on to fine net or joined by bars of other lacework.

honk /hɒŋk/ *noun & verb.* **M19.**
[ORIGIN Imit.]
▸ **A** *noun.* **1** The cry of the wild goose. **M19.**
2 Also redupl. **honk-honk**. The harsh sound of a motor horn. **E20.**
▸ **B** *verb.* **1** *verb intrans.* Make or emit a honk. **M19.**
2 *verb trans.* Utter with a honk; move or alert with a honk on a horn. **E20.**

honker /ˈhɒŋkə/ *noun.* **L19.**
[ORIGIN from HONK + -ER¹.]
1 A wild goose. **L19.**
2 A person who makes a honking noise. **L19.**
3 The horn of a motor vehicle. **E20.**
4 A nose. *slang.* **M20.**

honkers /ˈhɒŋkəz/ *adjective. slang.* **M20.**
[ORIGIN Unknown.]
Drunk.

honky /ˈhɒŋki/ *noun & adjective. US black slang. derog.* **M20.**
[ORIGIN Unknown.]
▸ **A** *noun.* A white person; *collect.* white people. **M20.**
▸ **B** *adjective.* Of a person: white. **L20.**

honky-tonk /ˈhɒŋkɪtɒŋk/ *noun & adjective. colloq.* (orig. *US*). **L19.**
[ORIGIN Unknown.]
▸ **A** *noun.* **1** A tawdry drinking saloon, dancehall, or gambling house; a cheap nightclub. **L19.**
2 Ragtime music or jazz of a type played in honky-tonks, esp. on the piano. **M20.**
▸ **B** *adjective.* Of or pertaining to (a) honky-tonk; *esp.* (of a piano) tinny-sounding, out of tune. **M20.**

honnête homme /ɔnɛt ɔm/ *noun phr.* Pl. **-s -s** (pronounced same). **M17.**
[ORIGIN French.]
A decent, cultivated man of the world.

honor *noun, verb* see HONOUR *noun, verb*.

honorable *adjective & noun* see HONOURABLE.

†**honorance** *noun.* **ME–E18.**
[ORIGIN Old French, formed as HONOUR *verb*: see -ANCE.]
The action of honouring.

honorand /ˈɒnərand/ *noun.* **M20.**
[ORIGIN Latin *honorandus* gerundive of *honorare* HONOUR *verb*: see -AND.]
A person to be honoured, esp. with an honorary degree.

honorarium /ɒnəˈrɛːrɪəm/ *noun.* Pl. **-iums**, **-ia** /-ɪə/. **M17.**
[ORIGIN Latin *honorarium* gift made on being admitted to a post of honour, use as noun of neut. of *honorarius* HONORARY *adjective*: see -ARIUM.]
A (voluntary) fee, esp. for professional services nominally rendered without payment.

A. HAILEY Acceptance by one high-ranking FDA official of 'honorariums' totalling $287,000 from a drug firm source.

honorary /ˈɒn(ə)rəri/ *noun.* Now *rare.* **E17.**
[ORIGIN Orig. formed as HONORARIUM; later from HONORARY *adjective*.]
An honorarium; an honorary distinction; a holder of an honorary post.

honorary /ˈɒn(ə)rəri/ *adjective.* **E17.**
[ORIGIN Latin *honorarius*, from *honor* HONOUR *noun*: see -ARY¹.]
1 Of a title, position, etc.: conferred as an honour, esp. without the usual requirements, functions, etc. **E17.**

DAY LEWIS The honorary membership of the Incorporated Society of Musicians which I was given.

2 Of a person: holding an honorary title or position. **E18.**

R. P. JHABVALA He was, after all, only the paid secretary, whereas she was the honorary one.

3 Of an obligation etc.: depending on honour, not legally enforceable. **L18.**
– SPECIAL COLLOCATIONS: ***honorary alderman***: see ALDERMAN 3. ***honorary canon***: see CANON *noun*² 2. ***honorary degree***: see DEGREE *noun*. **honorary secretary**, **honorary treasurer**, etc.: serving without pay.

honoree /ɒnəˈriː/ *noun.* Orig. *US.* **M20.**
[ORIGIN from HONOR *verb* + -EE¹.]
A person who is honoured in some way.

honorer *noun* see HONOURER.

honorial /ɒˈnɔːrɪəl/ *adjective.* **E19.**
[ORIGIN from HONOR *noun* + -IAL.]
Chiefly *hist.* Of or pertaining to an honour (HONOUR *noun* 6); of or pertaining to an honorific title.

honorific /ɒnəˈrɪfɪk/ *adjective & noun.* **M17.**
[ORIGIN Latin *honorificus*, from *honor*: see HONOUR *noun*, -FIC.]
▸ **A** *adjective.* Of a word, phrase, etc.: implying or expressing respect. **M17.**

A. BURGESS The honorific Mr was used, to the disgust of the NCOs.

▸ **B** *noun.* An honorific word or phrase. **L19.**

J. A. MICHENER His voluntary use of the Polish honorific proved the sincerity of his evaluation.

honorificabilitudinitatibus /ɒˌnɔːrɪfɪˌkɑːbɪlɪˌtjuːdɪnɪˈtɑːtɪbəs/ *noun. joc. rare.* **L16.**
[ORIGIN medieval Latin.]
Honourableness.
■ Also **honorificabilituˈdinity** *noun* **M17.**

honoris causa /ɒˌnɔːrɪs ˈkauzə/ *adverbial phr.* **E17.**
[ORIGIN Latin = for the sake of honour.]
As a mark of esteem, esp. in reference to an honorary degree.

honorless *adjective* see HONOURLESS.

honour /ˈɒnə/ *noun.* Also ***honor**. **ME.**
[ORIGIN Anglo-Norman *anur*, *anour*, Old French *(h)onor*, *(h)onur*, earlier *enor* (mod. *honneur*), from Latin *honor*, *honor-*: see -OUR.]
1 High respect, esteem, deferential admiration; an expression of this; glory, credit, reputation, good name. **ME.** ▸**b** *spec.* The chastity or purity of a woman; a woman's reputation for this. **LME.**

R. BOLT Your majesty does my house more honour than I fear my household can bear. M. IGNATIEFF Family honour could be rebuilt: father's debts could be paid off. **b** SHAKES. *Temp.* Till thou didst seek to violate The honour of my child.

2 Nobleness of mind or spirit; magnanimity; uprightness; adherence to what is due or correct according to some conventional or accepted standard of conduct. **ME.** ▸**b** A promise, an assurance. *arch.* **M17.**
3 Exalted rank or position; distinction. **ME.** ▸**b** (**H-.**) With possess.: a title of respect given to a County Court etc. judge, a US mayor, and (now only in Irish speech) to any person of rank. **M16.**

S. MORLEY I must claim the honour of being one of his first stage directors.

4 A thing conferred or done as a mark of respect or distinction, *esp.* a title of rank. **ME.** ▸†**b** A bow or curtsy. **M16–E19.** ▸**c** In *pl.* Civilities or courtesies rendered to a guest etc. Chiefly in ***do the honours***. **M17.** ▸**d** In *pl.* A special distinction for outstanding proficiency in an examination; in higher education, a degree or course of degree studies more specialized than that for an ordinary degree. **L18.** ▸**e** A privilege, a special right; *spec.* in GOLF, the right of driving off first. **L19.**

R. L. FOX He was promptly recognised as a ruler of the Thessalians, a remarkable honour for an outsider. K. M. E. MURRAY It was almost the only royal Birthday honour of which the newspapers had approved. **e** E. CRANKSHAW His was the honour of discovering the young Turgenev in 1847.

5 A source or cause of distinction; a person who or thing which does credit *to* another. **ME.**

I. MACLAREN You are an honour to our profession.

6 LAW. A seigniory of several manors under one baron or lord paramount. *obsolete* exc. *hist.* **ME.**
7 CARDS. In whist, any of the ace, king, queen, and jack of trumps; in bridge, any of these and the ten also, or the four aces at no trumps. **M17.**
– PHRASES: ***affair of honour***: see AFFAIR 1. **code of honour** the rules forming a conventional standard of conduct. ***Companion of Honour***: see COMPANION *noun*¹. ***debt of honour***: see DEBT *noun*. ***field of honour***: see FIELD *noun*. **funeral honours** observances of respect at a funeral. ***give the honour of the flag***: see FLAG *noun*⁴. ***guest of honour***: see GUEST *noun* 1. **honour bright** *interjection* (*colloq.*) protesting one's sincerity. **honours are even** the contest is equal. **honours of war** privileges granted to a capitulating force, e.g. that of marching out with colours flying. **in honour bound** under a moral obligation (*to do*). **in honour of** as a celebration of, as an expression of respect or admiration for. ***lap of honour***: see LAP *noun*³. **last honours** = ***funeral honours*** above. **law of honour** = ***code of honour*** above. ***Legion of Honour***: see LEGION *noun*. ***maid of honour***: see MAID *noun*. ***matron of honour***: see MATRON *noun*. **military honours** marks of respect paid by troops at the burial of a soldier, to royalty, etc. **on my honour**, **upon my honour** *interjection* protesting one's sincerity. **on one's honour** under a moral obligation (*to do*). ***parole of honour***: see PAROLE *noun & adjective* 2(a). ***point of honour***: see POINT *noun*¹. ***roll of honour***: see ROLL *noun*¹. ***upon my honour***: see ***on my honour*** above. ***word of honour***: see WORD *noun*.
– COMB.: **honour killing** the killing of a relative (esp. a girl or woman) who is perceived to have brought dishonour upon the family; **honour point** HERALDRY the point halfway between the top of a shield and the fesse point; **honours course** a course at a university etc. leading to an honours degree; **honours degree** (a course leading to) a degree with honours; **honours list** (***a***) a list of successful candidates in an examination for an honours degree; (***b***) a list of people awarded honours by the British

monarch, as at New Year; **honours school** a branch of study at a university etc. in which an honours degree may be taken; **honour system** a system of examinations etc. without supervision, relying on the honour of those concerned; **honour-trick** BRIDGE = *quick trick* s.v. QUICK *adjective*.

honour /ˈɒnə/ *verb trans.* Also ***honor**. ME.
[ORIGIN Old French *onorer*, *onurer* (mod. *honorer*) from Latin *honorare*, from *honor*- HONOUR *noun*.]
†**1** Pay respect or do honour to by some outward action; do homage to. ME–L17.
SHAKES. *Ven. & Ad.* Till I have honoured you with some graver labour.
2 Regard with honour, respect highly, reverence. ME.
E. WAUGH Women are naturally Bohemian, while men honour convention. A. BURGESS Honour thy father, though not necessarily thy stepfather.
3 Confer honour upon; grace. ME.
K. AMIS Are you sure Alexander is to honour us with his company this evening?
4 Accept or pay (a bill or cheque) when due; fulfil (an obligation), abide by the terms of (an agreement). E18.
B. MAGEE Necessary order should rest not on force but on consent and the honouring of agreements. J. C. OATES And there was some question about Goodheart's honouring their IOU.

honourable /ˈɒn(ə)rəb(ə)l/ *adjective.* Also ***honor-**. ME.
[ORIGIN Old French & mod. French from Latin *honorabilis*, from *honorare*: see HONOUR *verb*, -ABLE.]
▸ **A** *adjective.* **1** Worthy of being honoured; entitled to honour or respect. ME. ▸†**b** Respectable in quality or amount; befitting a person of honour. ME–M17.
B. JOWETT The soul which came from heaven is more honourable than the body which is earth-born.
2 Characterized by honour; virtuous, upright, honest; bringing honour to the possessor. ME. ▸**b** Consistent with honour. M16.
SHAKES. *Two Gent.* The match Were rich and honourable. R. C. SHERRIFF An honourable man whose word was his bond. **b** J. STEINBECK She was surrounded, and there was no honourable way out save death.
3 Holding a position of honour or rank. ME. ▸**b** (**H-**.) Used as a title indicating eminence or distinction, given e.g. to the younger sons of Earls, children of Viscounts and Barons, maids of honour, Justices of High Court without higher title, Lords of Session, members of Government in Dominions, Colonies and Commonwealth states, to Members of Parliament by one another, and in the US to members of Congress, Cabinet ministers, judges, etc. LME.
LD MACAULAY This man, named Edward Petre, was descended from an honourable family.
b Most Honourable the title of Marquesses, members of the Privy Council, and holders of the Order of the Bath. **Right Honourable** the title of Earls, Viscounts, Barons, Privy Counsellors, Lords (Justices) of Appeal, the Lord Mayor of London, York, or Belfast, Lord Provost of Edinburgh or Glasgow, etc.
4 Showing or doing honour. LME.
BOSWELL An honourable monument to his memory.
– SPECIAL COLLOCATIONS: **honourable discharge** *US* a discharge or release from the armed forces at the end of a period of honourable service. **honourable intentions** *colloq.*: to marry the woman one is courting. **honourable mention** an award of merit to a candidate in an examination, a work of art, etc., not entitled to a prize.
▸ **B** *noun.* An honourable person; *spec.* a person with the title Honourable. LME.
D. LESSING Marion's mother being the widow of a general, and her sisters all ladies or honourables.
■ **honouraˈbility** *noun* (*rare*) LME. **honourableness** *noun* M16. **honourably** *adverb* ME.

honourer /ˈɒnərə/ *noun.* Also ***honor-**. ME.
[ORIGIN from HONOUR *verb* + -ER[1].]
A person who honours someone or something. In early use also, a worshipper.

honourless /ˈɒnəlɪs/ *adjective.* Also ***honor-**. M16.
[ORIGIN from HONOUR *noun* + -LESS.]
Lacking honour; unworthy of honour.

Hon. Sec. *abbreviation.*
Honorary Secretary.

Honved /ˈhɒnveɪd/ *noun.* M19.
[ORIGIN Hungarian, from *hon* home + *véd* defend.]
(A member of) the Hungarian second-line formation during the revolutionary war of 1848–9, or later, the militia reserve.

honyock, **honyocker** *nouns* vars. of HUNYAK.

hoo /huː/ *noun*[1]. Long *obsolete* exc. *Scot.* Also **how** /haʊ/, (earlier) †**houve**.
[ORIGIN Old English *hūfe* = Middle Low German, Middle Dutch *hūve* (Dutch *huif*), Old High German *hūba* (German *Haube*), from Germanic, from base repr. also by HIVE *noun*.]
1 A covering for the head; a cap, *spec.* a nightcap. OE.
2 A child's caul. M16.

hoo /(h)uː/ *pers. pronoun.* Long *obsolete* exc. *dial.*
[ORIGIN Old English *hīo*, *hēo* fem. of HE *pronoun*.]
= SHE *pers. pronoun.*

hoo /huː/ *interjection, verb, & noun*[2]. Also redupl. **hoo-hoo**. OE.
[ORIGIN Partly natural exclam., partly imit. See also WHOO *verb*, *interjection & noun*.]
▸ **A** *interjection.* **1** Expr. surprise or requesting attention etc. OE.
2 Repr. the hoot of an owl or the sough of the wind. L15.
▸ **B** *verb intrans.* Give a cry of 'hoo!'; (of an owl) hoot; (of the wind) sough. L18.
▸ **C** *noun.* A call or cry of 'hoo!' M19.

hooch /huːtʃ/ *noun*[1]. *colloq.* (chiefly *N. Amer.*). Also **hootch**. L19.
[ORIGIN Abbreviation of HOOCHINOO.]
Alcoholic liquor; *esp.* inferior or illicit alcoholic liquor.
D. LODGE 'Duty-free hooch,' said Morris Zapp, taking a half-bottle of Scotch from his . . pocket.

hooch /huːtʃ/ *noun*[2]. *military slang.* Also **hoochie** /ˈhuːtʃi/, **hootch**. M20.
[ORIGIN Perh. from Japanese *uchi* dwelling.]
A dugout; a shelter, *esp.* a temporary or insubstantial one.
New York Times His decision to remove the United States Marines from their hooches at the Beirut airport.

Hoochinoo /ˈhuːtʃɪnuː/ *noun.* In sense 2 also **h-**. Pl. same. L19.
[ORIGIN Tlingit *xutsnu:wú* (place name), lit. 'brown bear's fort'.]
1 A member of a Tlingit people of Admiralty Island, Alaska. L19.
2 = HOOCH *noun*[1]. L19.

hood /hʊd/ *noun*[1] *& verb.*
[ORIGIN Old English *hōd* = Old Frisian *hōd*, Middle Dutch *hoet* (Dutch *hoed*), Old High German *huot* (German *Hut* hat), from West Germanic base rel. to that of HAT *noun*.]
▸ **A** *noun.* **1** A covering for the head and neck (sometimes also the shoulders) with an opening for the face, either forming part of a coat, cloak, etc., or separate. OE.
B. LOPEZ A movement of my head shifted the hood of my parka slightly.
three faces in a hood, ***three faces under a hood***: see THREE *adjective*.
2 *spec.* A hood worn as a mark of official or professional dignity, usu. thrown back on the shoulders; *esp.* such a hood worn with an academic gown, coloured or ornamented to indicate degree, faculty, etc.; the ornamental attachment on the back of a cope, orig. shaped and used like a hood. ME.
D. L. SAYERS His surplice and Oxford hood over one arm.
3 The part of a suit of armour for covering the head, a helmet or a flexible covering worn under a helmet, (*obsolete* exc. *hist.*). Now also, a helmet-like covering for the entire head as protection against fumes, radiation, etc. ME.
Observer The burnproof transparent hood covers the entire head.
4 A leather covering for a hawk's head to keep it quiet when not hunting. LME.
5 Something resembling a hood in shape or use; a covering, a protection; *spec.* (**a**) the cover of a carriage; *esp.* a folding waterproof cover of a pram, (convertible) car, etc.; (**b**) a canopy to remove fumes from a cooker etc. or to protect the user of machinery; (**c**) a tube attached to the front of a camera lens to protect it from strong or extraneous light; (**d**) (chiefly *N. Amer.*) the bonnet of a motor vehicle; (**e**) the upper part of the corolla or calyx in some flowers; (***f***) a flap of skin or a marking on the head of any of various animals, as the cobra. E17.
F. O'CONNOR He got out and opened the hood of the truck and began to study the motor. J. S. FOSTER Control of the . . air supply can be effected by a hood . . above the fire bed. P. LEACH Put the pram hood up and turn its back to the breeze.
– COMB.: **hood-end** NAUTICAL the end of a plank fitting into the stem and stern rabbeting; **hood mould**, **hood moulding** ARCHITECTURE a dripstone.
▸ **B** *verb trans.* Cover or protect (as) with a hood. ME.
W. WHARTON He listens, bright blue eyes hooded with fine red eyelashes. *New Yorker* Mrs. Wetten was forced into a car, hooded, taken to a cell.

hood /hʊd/ *noun*[2]. *slang.* M20.
[ORIGIN Abbreviation of HOODLUM.]
A gunman, a gangster; a hoodlum.
J. DIDION She was sitting in a park watching some hoods rifling cars. D. CAUTE In my Bronx you were either a gangster or you fought the hoods.

hood /hʊd/ *noun*[3]. *US slang.* Also **'hood**. L20.
[ORIGIN Aphet.]
= NEIGHBOURHOOD 2.

-hood /hʊd/ *suffix.*
[ORIGIN Old English *-hād* = Old Saxon *-hēd*, Old & mod. High German *-heit*, orig. a Germanic noun meaning 'person, sex, condition, rank, quality', repr. by Old English *hād*, Old Saxon *hēd*, Old High German *heit*, Old Norse *heiðr* honour, worth, Gothic *haidus* kind, manner.]
Forming nouns of condition or quality or indicating a collection or group from nouns and adjectives, as ***childhood***, ***falsehood***, ***sisterhood***.

hooded /ˈhʊdɪd/ *adjective.* LME.
[ORIGIN from HOOD *noun*[1], *verb*: see -ED[2], -ED[1].]
1 Wearing a hood; covered (as) with a hood. LME. ▸**b** Of a garment: having a hood attached to or forming part of it. L16.
E. BLISHEN Mr. Trellis, gowned and hooded, was the first speechmaker. R. HUNTFORD A great bearded figure with high cheekbones and hooded, . . like a Viking chieftain. **b** *New Yorker* Hooded homespun cassocks.
2 *gen.* Having or provided with a hood or protective covering. E16.
D. WELCH Against one wall stood a huge Chinese bed hooded grimly in dark blue cotton. *Practical Gardening* Hooded flowers appear from April to June.
hooded crow: see CROW *noun*[1] 1. **hooded seal** a seal, *Cystophora cristata*, of the Arctic and N. Atlantic Oceans, grey with black blotches, the male of which has inflatable nasal sacs used in display.
3 *fig.* Covered, concealed. M17.

hoodia /ˈhʊdɪə/ *noun.* M19.
[ORIGIN mod. Latin (genus name), from *Hood*, the name of an English plant grower.]
A cactus-like succulent plant native to southern Africa; a compound derived from hoodia which acts as an appetite suppressant.

hoodie /ˈhʊdi/ *noun.* L18.
[ORIGIN from HOOD *noun*[1] + -IE.]
1 A hooded crow. Also ***hoodie-crow***. L18.
2 (Also **hoody**.) A hooded sweatshirt, jacket, or other top. L20. ▸**b** A person, esp. a youth, wearing a hooded sweatshirt or other top. *colloq.* L20.

hooding /ˈhʊdɪŋ/ *noun.* LME.
[ORIGIN from HOOD *noun*[1], *verb* + -ING[1].]
†**1** *collect.* Hoods as a mark of official or professional dignity. Only in LME.
2 The putting on or wearing of a hood. L16.
3 NAUTICAL. = ***hood-end*** s.v. HOOD *noun*[1]. E17.

hoodless /ˈhʊdlɪs/ *adjective.* LME.
[ORIGIN from HOOD *noun*[1] + -LESS.]
Without a hood.

hoodlum /ˈhuːdləm/ *noun.* Orig. *US slang.* L19.
[ORIGIN Unknown.]
A street hooligan; a young thug.
J. K. TOOLE An old aunt had been robbed of fifty cents by some hoodlums. R. ELLMANN This childhood memory, in which a child dies and a hoodlum rises up in his place.
■ **hoodlumism** *noun* the conduct or methods of a hoodlum L19.

hoodman /ˈhʊdmən/ *noun. arch.* Pl. **-men**. LME.
[ORIGIN HOOD *noun*[1] + MAN *noun*.]
A hooded man; the blindfolded player in blind man's buff. Now only in ***hoodman blind***, blind man's buff.

hoodoo /ˈhuːduː/ *noun, adjective, & verb.* Orig. *US.* L19.
[ORIGIN App. alt. of VOODOO.]
▸ **A** *noun.* **1** A person who practises voodoo. L19.
R. TALLANT I heard people say hoodoos was cannibals and used to eat babies.
2 (A hidden cause of) bad luck; a person or thing supposed to bring bad luck. L19.
L. VAN DER POST By nightfall everyone . . seemed convinced there was a permanent hoodoo on us. *Independent* McEvoy's hoodoo at the . . championship . . struck again—and . . he was knocked out.
3 A fantastic pinnacle or column of rock formed by erosion or other natural agency. L19.
▸ **B** *adjective.* Unlucky. L19.
▸ **C** *verb trans.* Bewitch; bring bad luck to. L19.
W. A. PERCY He had been hoodooed by a witch-doctor and was going to die.
■ **hoodooism** *noun* the practice of hoodoo rites L19.

hoodwink /ˈhʊdwɪŋk/ *verb & noun.* M16.
[ORIGIN from HOOD *noun*[1] + WINK *verb*[1].]
▸ **A** *verb trans.* **1** Cover the eyes (of a person) with a hood etc. to prevent vision; blindfold. *arch.* M16.
2 Cover up from sight. Long *rare.* L16.
3 Deceive, delude. E17.
W. H. AUDEN Expert impersonator and linguist, proud of his power To hoodwink sentries. P. HOWARD The rest of the Old Gang combining to hoodwink the public and turn a blind eye on Hitler.
▸ **B** *noun.* **1** A blindfold; *fig.* a deception. Now *rare.* L16.
†**2** Blind man's buff. L16–E17.

hoody *noun* var. of HOODIE 2.

H

hooer /ˈhuːə/ *noun*. *Austral. & NZ colloq.* M20.
[ORIGIN Repr. a pronunc. of WHORE *noun*.]
1 A whore, a prostitute. M20.
2 A thoroughly unpleasant or contemptible person. M20.

hooey /ˈhuːi/ *noun*. *colloq.* (orig. *US*). E20.
[ORIGIN Unknown.]
Nonsense, humbug.

W. WHARTON They give out reams of hooey about how *lucky* we are.

hoof /huːf/ *noun*. Pl. **hoofs**, **hooves** /huːvz/.
[ORIGIN Old English *hōf* = Old Frisian, Old Saxon *hōf* (Dutch *hoef*), Old High German *huof* (German *Huf*), Old Norse *hófr*, from Germanic base rel. to synon. Sanskrit *śapha*, Avestan *safa*.]
1 (The horny casing of) the toe or foot of an ungulate mammal, esp. a horse. OE. ▸**b** Horny or calloused skin on the hands etc. Long *dial.* LME. ▸**c** The cloven hoof attributed to the Devil. M17.

E. LANGLEY I heard the little hard hooves of his mare come scuttling across the dry hill.

2 A hoofed animal, as the smallest unit of a herd. M16.
3 The human foot. *joc.* or *derog.* L16.

A. PRICE It's through the family that Danny has got his dirty little hoof into the door.

– PHRASES: ***divide the hoof***: see DIVIDE *verb* 1. **on the hoof** (*a*) (of cattle) not yet slaughtered; (*b*) (of an action) extempore. ***pad the hoof***: see PAD *verb*[1].
– COMB.: **hoof-and-mouth disease** foot-and-mouth disease; **hoof-pick** a hooked implement for removing stones from a horse's hoof; **hoof stick** an instrument with a head shaped like a horse's hoof used for manicuring the nails.
■ **hoofless** *adjective* E18.

H

hoof /huːf/ *verb*. M17.
[ORIGIN from the noun.]
1 *verb intrans. & trans.* (with *it*). Go on foot. M17.

W. WHARTON Marty, my daughter, lives near the garage so Billy and I hoof it over there.

2 *verb trans.* Strike with the hoof; *slang* dismiss, expel, kick *out*. M19.

D. L. SAYERS They'd hoof me out of the Club if I raised my voice beyond a whisper. *Rugby News* Mesnel kicked like the proverbial golfing gorilla, hoofing the ball as far as he could.

3 *verb intrans. & trans.* (with *it*). Dance, *spec.* tap dance, esp. routinely or as a profession. E20.

A. GILBERT A pretty nifty dancer himself.. and still able to hoof it quite neatly. W. ALLEN I was his best dancer... The other girls just hoofed.

■ **hoofer** *noun* (*slang*) a dancer, *esp.* a professional dancer E20.

hoofed /huːft/ *adjective*. Also **hooved** /huːvd/. LME.
[ORIGIN from HOOF *noun* + -ED[2].]
Having hoofs.

hoofy /ˈhuːfi/ *adjective*. L17.
[ORIGIN from HOOF *noun* + -Y[1].]
Having a hoof or hoofs.

hoo-ha /ˈhuːhɑː/ *noun*. *colloq.* Also **-hah**. M20.
[ORIGIN Unknown.]
A commotion, an uproar; trouble.

B. GOOLDEN I don't think Mummy will make much of a hoo-ha if she knows it's not for long. E. FAIRWEATHER One can imagine the hoo-ha if such an innovation were suggested here.

hoo-hoo *interjection, verb, noun* see HOO *interjection, verb, & noun*[2].

hook /hʊk/ *noun*.
[ORIGIN Old English *hōc* = Old Frisian, Middle Low German, Middle Dutch *hōk* (Dutch *hoek*) corner, angle, point of land, rel. to Old English *haca* bolt, Old Saxon *haco* (Middle Dutch *hake*, Dutch *haak*) Old High German *hāko* (German *Haken*) hook, Old Norse *haki*.]
1 A piece of metal or other material bent back at an angle or with a round bend, for catching hold of things, or for hanging things on; such a hook attached to a pole etc. OE. ▸**b** *spec.* A bent piece of thin wire, usu. barbed, attached to a fishing line to carry bait (also ***fish hook***); *fig.* a baited trap, a snare, a lure. OE. ▸**c** A small piece of bent and flattened metal or plastic used with a loop or 'eye' as a fastener or closure on a garment. Freq. in ***hook and eye***. E16.

J. CARY The stable lantern hung from a bacon hook in the beam. *fig.*: *City Limits* The sociology becomes just a hook for some sly and witty observations. **b** T. WYATT Farewell, Loue.. Thy bayted hokes shall tangle me no more.

boat-hook, ***coat-hook***, ***meat-hook***, ***pot-hook***, etc.
2 A curved sharp-edged cutting tool, esp. as used for reaping, mowing, and shearing. OE.
grass hook, ***pruning hook***, ***reaping hook***, etc.
3 The pin in the fixed part of the hinge on which a door or gate is hung. ME. ▸**b** Orig., a hook, now, a cradle on which a telephone receiver rests. L19.
4 The barb of an arrow; the fluke of an anchor. ME.
5 SHIPBUILDING. A curved piece of timber used to strengthen an angular framework. ME.
6 A sharp bend or angle in the length of something; *esp.* a bend in a river. Also, a projecting piece of land, a spit, a headland. Earliest in place names. ME.

J. L. MOTLEY This narrow hook of land, destined.. to be the cradle of a considerable empire.

†**7** A shepherd's crook, a bishop's crozier. LME–L17.
8 A ball or bowl's deviation from a straight line; the action or an act of hooking a ball (see HOOK *verb* 8). E17.
9 ZOOLOGY & BOTANY. Any recurved and pointed appendage in a plant or animal. M17.
10 A hook-shaped symbol or character, esp. in handwriting. M17. ▸†**b** In *pl.* Brackets. Also, inverted commas. L17–E19. ▸**c** MUSIC. A transverse line added to the stem of the ascender in the symbol for a quaver, semiquaver, etc. L18. ▸**d** LOGIC. (A name for, or reading of) the sign ⊃, used as the implication sign. Also called ***horseshoe***. M20.
11 A finger, a hand. Usu. in *pl. slang*. E19. ▸**b** A thief, a pickpocket. *slang*. M19.
12 BOXING. A short swinging blow with the elbow bent. L19.

F. MUIR He.. let loose a right hook that would have felled an ox.

13 A memorable or catchy passage in a piece of popular music. L20.
– PHRASES: **by hook or by crook** by one means or another, by fair means or foul. **hook, line, and sinker** entirely, without reservations. **get one's hooks into**, **get one's hooks on** get hold of; get a hold over. **off the hook** (*a*) *colloq.* no longer in difficulty or trouble; (*b*) (of a telephone receiver) not on its rest, thus preventing incoming calls. **off the hooks** *colloq.* dead; ***pop off the hooks***, die. **on one's own hook** *slang* on one's own account; at one's own risk. **on the hook** *colloq.* ensnared; in someone's power or grasp; addicted. **put the hooks in** *Austral. slang* ask (someone) for a loan. **sling one's hook**, **take one's hook** *slang* leave, go away, make off.
– COMB.: **hook-and-eye** *verb trans.* fasten (as) with a hook and eye; **hook-and-ladder** *noun & adjective* (*US*) (designating a fire engine etc. with) an apparatus of ladders and hooks used by firefighters; **hook-bill** a curved bill; **hook-billed** *adjective* having a curved bill; **hook-bolt**: with a hook at one end and threaded at the other; **hook-bone** the projecting upper part of the thigh bones of cattle near the hip joint; **hook gauge**: for determining the surface level of water; **hook-ladder**: having hooks at one end by which it can be suspended; **hook nose** an aquiline nose; **hook-nosed** *adjective* having an aquiline nose; **hook-pin**: having a hooked head, used to pin together the frame of a roof or floor; **hook-pot** NAUTICAL a (tin) pot or mug designed to hang on the bars of the galley range; **hook rug** a rug made by pulling yarn, canvas, etc., through a canvas ground on a hook; **hook shop** *slang* a brothel; **hook shot** BASKETBALL a twisting shot started with the player's back to the basket, and completed as he (or she) pivots round towards the basket; **hook stroke** CRICKET a stroke played by hitting a short-pitched ball, after it has risen, round to leg with a horizontal swing of the bat; **hooktip** any of various moths of the family Drepanidae having a curved point to the forewings; **hookworm** any of various nematode worms infesting the gut of people and animals, esp. in the tropics, and causing severe anaemia; the disease caused by hookworm infestation.
■ **hookless** *adjective* L18. **hooklike** *adjective* resembling (that of) a hook, shaped like a hook E17.

hook /hʊk/ *verb*. ME.
[ORIGIN from the noun.]
▸ **I 1** *verb trans.* Make hooklike or hooked; bend, crook. *rare*. ME.
2 *verb trans.* Catch (a fish) with a hook. ME. ▸**b** *verb trans. fig.* Catch, secure; captivate, ensnare. L17. ▸**c** *verb intrans.* Solicit as a prostitute. *slang*. M20.

R. BRAUTIGAN I have lost every trout I ever hooked. **b** F. J. FURNIVALL A man trying to hook a well-off widow.

▸ **II 3** *verb intrans.* Have a hooked shape; bend or curve sharply. ME.

W. HOLTBY A big pale face rather like Mussolini's—only his nose hooks a bit.

4 *verb intrans. & trans.* (with *it*). Make off, run away, esp. surreptitiously. (Foll. by *off*, *out*.) *colloq.* ME.

F. SARGESON If Ted saw her coming.. he'd hook off if he could before she got near.

5 *verb intrans.* Attach oneself or be attached (as) with a hook; fasten (as) with a hook or hooks. L16. ▸**b** Foll. by *up*: establish a link or connection; meet or form a relationship. *colloq.* E20.

THACKERAY He hooked on to my arm as if he had been the Old Man of the Sea. J. K. TOOLE The long red beard that hooked over his ears by means of wires. **b** *Rolling Stone* They'd all hook up later out there in the parking lot. I. RANKIN So every time we went across, he hooked up with her.

6 *verb trans.* Catch hold of or grasp (as) with a hook; attach or secure (as) with a hook or hooks; connect or fasten together with hooks, or hooks and eyes. (Foll. by *in*, *on*, *up*, etc.) L16. ▸**b** *verb trans.* Make (a rug) using a hook to pull yarn, rag, etc., through a canvas ground. L19.

A. TYLER He hooked his thumbs in his belt. C. PHILLIPS Bertram hooked both feet around the bar of his chair.

7 *verb trans.* Snatch (as) with a hook; take by stealth; steal. E17.
8 *verb trans. & intrans.* **a** Strike (a ball) so that it deviates from a straight line; GOLF drive (the ball) wide in the direction of the follow-through; CRICKET hit (a fast, short-pitched ball) round to leg from shoulder height with a horizontal or rising swing of the bat. M19. ▸**b** RUGBY. Secure and propel (the ball) backward with the foot in the scrummage. E20.
9 *verb trans.* Provide with a hook. M19.
10 *verb trans. & intrans.* BOXING. Strike (an opponent) with the elbow bent and rigid. L19.
– COMB.: **hook-up** *colloq.* a connection or link, esp. of radio or television broadcasting facilities.

hookah /ˈhʊkə/ *noun*. M18.
[ORIGIN Urdu from Arabic *ḥuqqa* small box, container, pot, jar.]
A pipe for smoking tobacco, marijuana, etc., with a long flexible tube connected to a container of water, through which the smoke is drawn from the tobacco etc.

Hooke /hʊk/ *noun*. E19.
[ORIGIN Robert *Hooke* (1635–1703), English inventor and natural philosopher.]
Used ***attrib.*** and in ***possess.*** to designate devices or concepts introduced by Hooke.
Hooke coupling, **Hooke joint**, **Hooke's coupling**, **Hooke's joint** a kind of universal joint for transmitting rotary motion between shafts. **Hooke's law**: that the strain in an elastic solid is proportional to the applied stress producing it.
■ **Hookean** /-ɪən/ *adjective* that obeys Hooke's law M20.

hooked /hʊkt/ *adjective*. OE.
[ORIGIN from HOOK *noun*, *verb*: see -ED[2], -ED[1].]
1 Shaped like a hook. OE.

A. MASON The black eyes were piercing,.. the nose hooked, dominant and uncompromising.

2 Provided or equipped with a hook or hooks. ME.
3 Made, caught, etc., (as) with a hook. E17. ▸**b** *pred.* Addicted, captivated. (Foll. by *on*.) E20.

b D. W. GOODWIN By now I was hooked.. I had been sneaking drinks for years. *Listener* Haunted by the death of his friends, and hopelessly hooked on drugs and drink.

hooker /ˈhʊkə/ *noun*[1]. M16.
[ORIGIN from HOOK *verb* + -ER[1].]
1 A thief (orig., who snatched things using a hook). *slang*. M16.
2 *gen.* A person who or thing which hooks. M19.
3 A prostitute. *colloq.* M19.
4 RUGBY. A player in the front row of the scrummage whose function it is to obtain the ball for his team by hooking it. E20.

hooker /ˈhʊkə/ *noun*[2]. M17.
[ORIGIN Dutch *hoeker*, from *hoek* HOOK *noun* (in earlier *hoekboot*): see -ER[1].]
Orig., a two-masted Dutch coasting or fishing vessel. Later also, a one-masted fishing smack from Ireland or SW England. Now usu., an old or fondly regarded boat.

hooker /ˈhʊkə/ *noun*[3]. *dial. & N. Amer. colloq.* M19.
[ORIGIN Unknown.]
A glass or drink of whisky, brandy, etc. Freq. in ***stiff hooker***.

Hooker's green /ˈhʊkəz ˈɡriːn/ *noun phr.* M19.
[ORIGIN William *Hooker* (1779–1832), botanical artist.]
A bright green colour used in watercolour painting.

hookey /ˈhʊki/ *noun*. *colloq.* (orig. *N. Amer.*). Also **hooky**. M19.
[ORIGIN Perh. from HOOK *verb* 4 + *-ey* -Y[6].]
1 Truanting. Chiefly in ***play hookey***, play truant. M19.

P. G. WODEHOUSE He's played hookey from the choir so often.

2 In full ***blind hookey***. A guessing game using cards. M19.

Hookey /ˈhʊki/ *interjection*. *arch.* E19.
[ORIGIN Unknown. Cf. WALKER *interjection*.]
In full ***Hookey Walker***. Expr. incredulity.

hooklet /ˈhʊklɪt/ *noun*. M19.
[ORIGIN from HOOK *noun* + -LET.]
A small hook.

hooky *noun* var. of HOOKEY *noun*.

hooky /ˈhʊki/ *adjective*. M16.
[ORIGIN from HOOK *noun* + -Y[1].]
1 Having a hook or hooks, full of hooks; hooked. M16.
2 Of a popular song: catchy, memorable. *colloq.* L20.
3 Obtained illegally, stolen; counterfeit. *slang*. L20.

Hoolee *noun* see HOLI.

hooley /ˈhuːli/ *noun*. Chiefly *Irish*. L19.
[ORIGIN Unknown.]
A wild or noisy party.

hooligan /ˈhuːlɪɡ(ə)n/ *noun*. L19.
[ORIGIN Perh. from *Hooligan* surname of a fictional rowdy Irish family in a music hall song, and a character in a cartoon.]
A young thug or vandal; a member of a gang of troublemakers.

M. GIROUARD Local hooligans threw stones at the new schools.

■ **hooliganism** *noun* the behaviour or activity characteristic of hooligans; vandalism: L19.

hoolock /ˈhuːlək/ *noun*. E19.
[ORIGIN Perh. from Bengali: imit. (from the animal's cry).]
A gibbon of Assam and SE Asia, *Hylobates hoolock*, with white eyebrows and (in the male) black and (in the female) golden fur. Also called ***white-browed gibbon***.

hooly /ˈhuːli/ *adverb & adjective*. *Scot. & N. English*. ME.
[ORIGIN Prob. from Old Norse: cf. *hófligr* moderate, *hógligr* easy, gentle.]
▸ **A** *adverb*. Gently, cautiously, slowly. ME.
▸ **B** *adjective*. Gentle, cautious, slow. LME.

hoon /huːn/ *noun*^{1} *& verb*. *Austral. slang*. M20.
[ORIGIN Unknown.]
(Behave like) a lout or idiot.

hoon *noun*^{2} var. of HUN *noun*^{2}.

hoop /huːp/ *noun*^{1}.
[ORIGIN Late Old English *hōp* = Old Frisian *hōp*, Middle Dutch *hoop* (Dutch *hoep*) from West Germanic, rel. to Old Norse *hóp* small land-locked bay.]
▸ **I** **1** A measure for grain, salt, etc. *obsolete* exc. *hist*. LOE.
2 A circular band or ring of metal, wood, etc., esp. for binding together the staves of casks, barrels, tubs, etc. ME.
fig.: SHAKES. *Haml*. Those friends thou hast, . . Grapple them to thy soul with hoops of steel.
†**3** Each of the bands on a quart pot; the amount of liquor contained between two of these. L16–E17.
▸ **II** **4** Anything having a structure or appearance that resembles a hoop; a circle, a ring, an arc. LME.
5 A finger ring; a circular earring. E16.
6 Each of a set of circles of flexible material used to spread out a skirt; a hoop petticoat or skirt. M16.
7 A circle of wood, plastic, or metal rolled along as a toy or used in various exercises, esp. by children. M17.
H. ALLEN He began to drive his hoop . . in skilful narrowing circles about the man.
8 A metal ring for holding cake mixture during baking. M18.
9 A circular wooden frame in which a cheese is moulded. L18.
10 A ring, often with paper stretched over it, through which acrobats or performing animals leap. L18.
be put through the hoop(s), **go through the hoop(s)**, **jump through the hoop(s)** undergo an ordeal.
11 A band in contrasting colour on a jockey's blouse, sleeves, or cap; *Austral*. a jockey. L19.
12 (The round metal frame of) the basket used in basketball. L19.
13 Each of the arches through which the ball must be driven in croquet. L19.
– COMB.: **hoop-back** (a chair with) a hooped back; **hoop iron**: in long thin strips for binding casks etc.; **hoop petticoat** (*a*) a petticoat spread out by hoops; (*b*) (in full ***hoop-petticoat narcissus***, ***hoop-petticoat daffodil***) a kind of narcissus, *Narcissus bulbocodium*, with long tubular corona and narrow reversed perianth segments; **hoop pine** an eastern Australian conifer, *Araucaria cunninghamii*, yielding a valuable timber; **hoop ring** a finger ring; **hoop skirt**: spread out by hoops; **hoop-snake** an American snake popularly believed to roll like a hoop, usu. identified with the mud snake *Farancia abacura*.

†**hoop** *noun*^{2}. L15–E18.
[ORIGIN French *huppe*, from Latin *upupa* HOOPOE.]
A hoopoe; occas., by confusion, a lapwing.

hoop *noun*^{3} *& interjection* see WHOOP *noun*, *interjection*.

hoop /huːp/ *verb*^{1} *trans*. LME.
[ORIGIN from HOOP *noun*^{1}. Cf. earlier HOOPER *noun*^{1}.]
Fasten round (as) with a hoop or hoops.
SHAKES. *Wint. T*. If ever henceforth thou . . hoop his body more with thy embraces. L. DURRELL A man hooping a barrel.

hoop *verb*^{2} var. of WHOOP *verb*.

Hoopa *noun & adjective* var. of HUPA.

hooped /huːpt/ *adjective*. M16.
[ORIGIN from HOOP *noun*^{1}, *verb*^{1}: see -ED^2, -ED^1.]
Having or fastened with a hoop or hoops; made with a hoop; shaped like a hoop.

hooper /ˈhuːpə/ *noun*^{1}. ME.
[ORIGIN from HOOP *noun*^{1} or *verb*^{1} + -ER^1.]
A person who makes hoops, or who fits hoops on barrels etc.; a cooper.

hooper *noun*^{2} see WHOOPER.

hooping *verbal noun*, *ppl adjective* see WHOOPING *verbal noun*, *ppl adjective*.

hoopla /ˈhuːplɑː/ *noun*. E20.
[ORIGIN from HOOP *noun*^{1} + LA *interjection*, prob. after HOUP-LA.]
1 A game in which rings are thrown in an attempt to encircle one of various prizes. E20.
2 Extravagant publicity or fuss, commotion. *colloq*., chiefly *N. Amer*. M20.
T. CLANCY Despite all the hoopla in the press, they aren't quite there yet, technologically.

hoop-la *interjection & noun* var. of HOUP-LA.

hoopoe /ˈhuːpuː, -pəʊ/ *noun*. M17.
[ORIGIN Alt. of HOOP *noun*^{2}, after Latin *upupa* (imit., from the bird's cry).]
A medium-sized, short-legged perching bird of Africa and Eurasia, *Upupa epops*, having a long, downcurved beak, a prominent crest, and pinkish-brown plumage with black and white striped wings and tail.

hoopster /ˈhuːpstə/ *noun*. *N. Amer. colloq*. E20.
[ORIGIN from HOOP *noun*^{1} + -STER.]
A basketball player.

hooptie /ˈhuːpti/ *noun*. *US slang*. M20.
[ORIGIN Unknown.]
A car, *esp*. one that is old or dilapidated.

hoor /hɔː, hʊə/ *noun*. *Irish & Scot*. M20.
[ORIGIN Repr. a pron. of WHORE.]
A prostitute. Also, a disliked person of either sex.

hooray /hʊˈreɪ; attrib. ˈhuːreɪ/ *noun*, *interjection*, *& verb*. Also **hurray**. L17.
[ORIGIN Alt. of HURRAH. Cf. HURROO.]
▸ **A** *noun*. A shout of 'hooray!', a cheer. L17.
▸ **B** *interjection*. **1** Expr. approval, encouragement, enthusiasm, or delight. L18.
2 Goodbye. *Austral. & NZ colloq*. L19.
▸ **C** *verb intrans*. Shout 'hooray!' L18.
– COMB.: **Hooray Henry** a rich but ineffectual young man, *esp*. one who is fashionable, extroverted, and conventional.

hooroo *interjection* see HURROO.

hooroosh /hʊˈruːʃ/ *noun & verb*. Also **hurroosh**. M19.
[ORIGIN Imit.]
▸ **A** *noun*. A cry or noise of excitement or confusion. M19.
▸ **B** *verb intrans. & trans*. Shoo. M19.

hoose /huːz/ *noun & verb*. Also **hooze**. L18.
[ORIGIN Perh. ult. from base of WHEEZE.]
▸ **A** *noun*. Chronic bronchitis in farm animals caused by parasitic nematodes; = HUSK *noun*^{2}. L18.
▸ **B** *verb intrans*. Cough, wheeze. *dial*. M19.

hoosegow /ˈhuːsgaʊ/ *noun*. *US slang*. E20.
[ORIGIN S. Amer. or Mexican Spanish *juzgao* = *juzgado* tribunal from Latin *judicatum* pa. pple of *judicare* JUDGE *verb*.]
A prison.

hoosh /huːʃ/ *interjection & verb*. L19.
[ORIGIN Natural exclam. Cf. SHOO *interjection & verb*.]
▸ **A** *interjection*. Encouraging or inciting an animal etc. to move; shoo! L19.
T. HARDY Saying 'Hoosh!' to the cocks and hens when they go upon your seeds.
▸ **B** *verb*. **1** *verb trans*. Drive (as) with the word 'hoosh!', shoo. (Foll. by *off*, *out*, etc.) E20.
A. THIRKELL Oh, she's dressing, and Aunt Palmer hooshed me out.
2 *verb intrans*. Move rapidly. M20.

hooshtah /ˈhuːʃtɑː/ *interjection & verb*. L19.
[ORIGIN Natural exclam.]
▸ **A** *interjection*. Encouraging or ordering a camel to move, esp. to get down on its knees for mounting or dismounting. L19.
▸ **B** *verb trans*. Direct with the word 'hooshtah!' E20.

Hoosier /ˈhuːʒɪə/ *noun & adjective*. *US*. E19.
[ORIGIN Unknown.]
▸ **A** *noun*. **1** (A nickname for) a native or inhabitant of the state of Indiana. E19.
2 An inexperienced, awkward, or unsophisticated person. M19.
▸ **B** *attrib*. or as *adjective*. Of, pertaining to, or characteristic of Indiana. M19.

hoot /huːt/ *noun*^{1}. LME.
[ORIGIN from the verb.]
1 A loud inarticulate exclamation, a shout, *spec*. of derision or disapproval. LME. ▸**b** A sound produced by a vehicle's horn, a siren, etc., esp. as a signal or warning. E20. ▸**c** A shout of laughter; a joke, an amusing situation, person, or thing. M20.
C. G. LELAND I heard certain mutterings and hoots among the students. **b** H. GARNER A long hoarse hoot of the factory whistle announced the lunch break. **c** D. HALLIDAY Janey can imitate anybody. So can I . . . We'd have the whole form in hoots of laughter.
2 An owl's cry. L18.
3 The smallest amount; a scrap, a whit. Chiefly in ***not care a hoot***, ***not care two hoots***, ***not give a hoot***, ***not matter two hoots***, etc. Cf. earlier HOOTER 2. L19.
D. PARKER She paid no attention to her birthdays—didn't give a hoot about them.
– COMB.: **hoot owl** any of various owls with a hooting call, as the tawny owl or (*US*) the barred owl.

hoot /huːt/ *noun*^{2}. *Austral. & NZ slang*. E19.
[ORIGIN Maori UTU.]
Money, esp. paid as recompense.

hoot /huːt/ *verb*. ME.
[ORIGIN Perh. imit.]
1 *verb intrans*. Make loud expressive sounds, esp. of derision or disapproval; make a loud sound on a horn etc. ME. ▸**b** Laugh loudly. *colloq*. E20.
W. IRVING A troop of strange children ran at his heels, hooting at him. C. MACKENZIE Visibility was hardly as much as twenty yards and he drove . . slowly, hooting almost continuously. W. WHARTON The whole crowd was hollering and hooting, whistling, throwing paper . . into the ring. **b** R. GITTINGS The class hooted with pleasure at the prospect of a free day.
2 *verb trans*. Assail with shouts or sounds of derision, disapproval, or contempt; drive *out*, *away*, etc., by hooting. ME.
LD MACAULAY His play had not been hooted from the boards. *Observer* In the shadiest lanes we were . . hooted out of the way.
3 *verb intrans*. Of a bird, esp. an owl: make its natural cry, call. L15.
H. BASCOM Outside, the owl hoots spookily from across the swamps.
4 *verb trans*. Vocalize or express by a hoot or hoots. L17.
5 *verb intrans*. Of a horn, siren, etc.: sound, emit noise as a signal or warning. L19.
R. KIPLING Through the yelling Channel tempest when the siren hoots and roars. R. C. HUTCHINSON An omnibus hooted as it passed the house.
6 *verb trans*. Sound a hoot on (a horn etc.). M20.

hoot /huːt/ *interjection*. *Scot. & N. English*. M16.
[ORIGIN Natural exclam.]
= HOOTS.

hootch *noun*^{1}, *noun*^{2} vars. of HOOCH *noun*^{1}, *noun*^{2}.

hootchy-kootchy /huːtʃɪˈkuːtʃi/ *noun & adjective*. Also **hootchie-kootchie**; **-cootchy**. L19.
[ORIGIN Unknown.]
▸ **A** *noun*. An erotic dance. L19.
▸ **B** *attrib*. or as *adjective*. Erotic; indecent, suggestive. L19.

H

hootenanny /ˈhuːt(ə)nani/ *noun*. *colloq*. Chiefly *US*. E20.
[ORIGIN Unknown.]
1 A gadget. *rare*. E20.
2 An informal party, esp. with folk music. M20.

hooter /ˈhuːtə/ *noun*. L17.
[ORIGIN from HOOT *verb* + -ER^1.]
1 A person or animal that hoots; *esp*. an owl. L17.
2 = HOOT *noun*^{1} 3. *US colloq*. M19.
3 A siren, a steam whistle, esp. as a signal for work to begin or cease; a horn, esp. of a motor vehicle. L19.
D. H. LAWRENCE They will hear far, far away the last factory hooter.
4 A person's nose. *slang*. M20.
5 In *pl*. A woman's breasts. *N. Amer. slang*. M20.

hoots /huːts/ *interjection*. *Scot. & N. English*. E19.
[ORIGIN from HOOT *interjection* + -S^3.]
Expr. dissatisfaction or impatience; contradicting or dismissing a statement.

hoove /huːv/ *noun*. M19.
[ORIGIN Alt.]
= HOVEN *noun*. Cf. HEAVE *noun* 2.

hooved *adjective* var. of HOOFED.

Hoover /ˈhuːvə/ *noun & verb*. Also (esp. as verb) **h-**. E20.
[ORIGIN W. H. *Hoover* (1849–1932), Amer. industrialist.]
▸ **A** *noun*. (Proprietary name for) a vacuum cleaner. E20.
▸ **B** **1** *verb trans. & intrans*. Clean (a floor etc.) with a vacuum cleaner. E20.
2 *verb trans*. Consume voraciously; devour completely. L20.
Rugby News Judging by the amount of beer they hoovered up . . Worthing soon drowned their sorrows. *Organic Gardening* Green woodpeckers hoover up ants on the lawn.

Hooverville /ˈhuːvəvɪl/ *noun*. *US*. M20.
[ORIGIN from Herbert C. *Hoover* (1874–1964), US President 1929–33 + -VILLE: temporary accommodation was provided for unemployed workers in the economic depression of the early 1930s (during Hoover's presidency).]
(A name for) a shanty town.

hooves *noun pl*. see HOOF *noun*.

hooze *noun & verb* var. of HOOSE.

hop /hɒp/ *noun*^{1}. LME.
[ORIGIN Middle Low German, Middle Dutch *hoppe* (Dutch *hop*), in Old Saxon *feldhoppo* = late Old High German *hopfo* (German *Hopfen*).]
1 In *pl*. & †*collect. sing*. The ripened conelike spikes of the female hop plant (see sense 2 below), used to give a bitter flavour to malt liquors, and as a tonic and soporific. LME. ▸**b** *sing*. & (usu.) in *pl*. Beer. Chiefly *Austral. & NZ slang*. M20.
2 A twining dioecious plant, *Humulus lupulus*, of the hemp family, with rough lobed leaves and small green flowers, the female becoming enlarged and conelike in seed, found in damp bushy places and much cultivated as a source of hops. Also ***hop plant***. M16.
3 A narcotic drug; *spec*. opium. L19.
– COMB.: **hop back** [BACK *noun*^{2}] a vessel with a perforated bottom for straining off the hops in the manufacture of beer; **hop bind**, **hop bine** the climbing stem of the hop; **hopbush** any of various Australian shrubs of the genus *Dodonaea*, of the soapberry family; **hop-dog** a tool for drawing hop poles out of the ground; **hop-fly** an aphid, *Phorodon humuli*, destructive to hops; **hop garden**, **hop ground** a piece of ground where hops are grown; **hophead** (*a*) *slang* (chiefly *US*) a drug addict; (*b*) *Austral. & NZ slang* a drunkard; ***hop*** HORNBEAM; **hop joint** *slang* an opium den; **hop-picker** a labourer or machine employed to pick hops; **hop-pillow**: stuffed with hops, to induce sleep; ***hop plant***: see sense 2 above; **hop pole**: on which a hop plant is trained; **hopsack**, **hopsacking** (*a*) (a sack or sacking for hops made from) a coarse material made from hemp etc.; (*b*) a coarse clothing fabric of a loose plain weave; **hop toy** *slang* a container used in smoking

opium; **hop tree** a N. American shrub, *Ptelea trifoliata*, of the rue family, with bitter fruit which has been used in brewing as a substitute for hops; **hop trefoil** a yellow-flowered clover, *Trifolium campestre*, whose withered flower heads resemble the cones of the hop; **hopyard** = *hop garden* above.

hop /hɒp/ *noun*². E16.
[ORIGIN from HOP *verb*¹.]
1 An act or the action of hopping; a short spring or leap, esp. on one foot; a leap or step in dancing. E16. ▸**b** A distance traversed in an aircraft or vehicle at one stretch; a stage of a flight or journey. E20. ▸**c** RADIO. A transmission path from one point on the earth to another that involves a single reflection from some region of the atmosphere. M20.

b C. A. LINDBERGH The first hop was from Americus to Montgomery, Alabama.

2 An informal dance. *colloq.* E18.

Listener Taking a girl to the Saturday-night hop in my village.

– PHRASES: ***Aztec hop***: see AZTEC *adjective*. **go on the hop** *slang* play truant. **hop, skip, and jump**, **hop, step, and jump** (*a*) the action of making these three (or similar) movements in succession, *spec.* as an athletic exercise or contest (= ***triple jump*** s.v. TRIPLE *adjective*); (*b*) a short distance. ***long hop***: see LONG *adjective*¹. **on the hop** *colloq.* (*a*) unprepared (esp. in ***caught on the hop***); (*b*) bustling about. **play the hop** = *go on the hop* above.

H

Hop /hɒp/ *noun*³. *Austral. slang.* E20.
[ORIGIN Rhyming slang for COP *noun*⁴.]
More fully ***John Hop***. A police officer.

hop /hɒp/ *verb*¹. Infl. **-pp-**. Pa. t. & pple **hopped**, (*arch.*) **hopt**.
[ORIGIN Old English *hoppian*, corresp. to Middle High German (German dial.) *hopfen*, Old Norse *hoppa*, from Germanic base repr. also by Old English *hoppetan*, German *hopsen*, a var. of which appears in HIP *verb*¹.]
1 *verb intrans.* Spring or leap a short distance once or in a succession of movements; *colloq.* make a quick change of position or location. OE. ▸**b** *spec.* Of a small animal or bird: move by leaps with all feet at once, as opp. to walking or running. LME. ▸**c** Of a person: spring or leap on one foot; move forward by a succession of leaps on one foot. E18. ▸**d** Limp. E18. ▸**e** With adverbial extension: get lightly or quickly *in*, *into* (a motor vehicle etc.), *on*, *on to* (a bicycle, bus, etc.), *out*, *out of* (a motor vehicle etc.). *colloq.* E20.

New Yorker He used to be a pilot himself.. when he was a.. seed salesman and would hop about calling on prospects. **b** B. EMECHETA The.. parrots hopped about in their cages.

2 *verb intrans.* Dance. Now *rare* or *obsolete*. ME.
3 *verb trans.* Hop about, along, or over; pass quickly between each of a succession of. L18.

C. G. TURNER Twice daily [the cow] hopped the fence.

cloud hopping, ***hedge-hopping***, etc.
4 *verb trans.* Jump on to (a moving vehicle); obtain (a ride, a lift) by jumping on to a moving vehicle; catch (a train etc.). *colloq.* E20.

J. KEROUAC I used to hop freights at least once a month.

– PHRASES, & WITH ADVERBS IN SPECIALIZED SENSES: **hop into bed** have (casual) sexual intercourse (*with*). **hop it** *slang* go away. **hop off** (*a*) *slang* die; (*b*) depart, *spec.* in an aircraft; (*c*) *colloq.* get off a bicycle, bus, etc. **hop, skip, and jump**, **hop, step, and jump** make these three movements in succession, perform the triple jump. ***hop the perch***: see PERCH *noun*². **hop the stick**, **hop the twig** *slang* depart suddenly, die. **hop the wag** *slang* play truant.
– COMB.: **hop-o'-my-thumb** [o' = on] a dwarf, a pygmy. **hop-toad** *US* a toad.

hop /hɒp/ *verb*². Infl. **-pp-**. L16.
[ORIGIN from HOP *noun*¹.]
1 *verb trans.* Impregnate or flavour with hops. Usu. in *pass.* L16.
2 *verb intrans.* Pick hops. Chiefly as ***hopping*** *verbal noun*. E18.
3 *verb intrans.* Of the hop plant: produce hops. M19.
4 *verb trans.* Foll. by *up*: stimulate or intoxicate with a narcotic drug. Cf. earlier HOPPED 2. *US slang.* M20.

hope /həʊp/ *noun*¹.
[ORIGIN Late Old English *hopa*, also *tōhopa*, corresp. to Old Low German *tōhopa*, Old Frisian, Middle Low German, Middle Dutch *hope* (Dutch *hoop*). Orig. belonging to Low German areas, whence it spread to High German (Middle High German *hoffe*) and Scandinavian (Swedish *hopp*, Danish *haab*): of unknown origin.]
1 Expectation of something desired, a feeling of expectation and desire combined (in *pl.* also with sing. sense); *iron.* an expectation which has little or no chance of fulfilment. (Foll. by *of* (a thing, *doing*), *that*, *to do*.) LOE. ▸†**b** Expectation (without implication of desire); prospect. LME–M16.

TENNYSON And still we follow'd.. In hope to gain upon her flight. V. BRITTAIN My hopes of ever escaping from provincial young-ladyhood were almost abandoned. B. EMECHETA After he had completely given up hope, a miracle.. happened. T. PYNCHON Always baiting his master in hopes of getting a .. stripe or two across those.. buttocks. C. EGLETON 'Make sure you get the right mix of weapons and explosives.' 'You've got a hope'. *personified*: HANNAH MORE Fair Hope, with smiling face but ling'ring foot.

2 (A feeling of) trust or confidence. *arch.* LOE.

G. MACDONALD Though the sky be dim, My hope is in the sky.

3 A person who or thing which gives cause for hope; an object or ground of hope; (a) probability; (a) promise. ME.

POPE Her tender mother's only hope and pride. SHELLEY Staking his very life on some dark hope.

– PHRASES: ***hope against hope***: see HOPE *verb* 1. **not a hope** *colloq.* no chance at all (also ***not a hope in hell***: see HELL *noun*). ***pin one's hopes on***: see PIN *verb*. ***pious hope***: see PIOUS *adjective* 1. **some hope!**, **some hopes!**, **what a hope!** *colloq.* little or no chance. ***white hope***: see WHITE *adjective*.
– COMB.: **hope chest** (chiefly *N. Amer.*) = ***bottom drawer*** s.v. BOTTOM *adjective*.

hope /həʊp/ *noun*².
[ORIGIN Late Old English *hop* = Middle Low German *hop* (in place names), Middle Dutch *hop* bay: origin unknown.]
1 A piece of enclosed land. Now *rare* or *obsolete*. LOE.
2 A small valley, *esp.* one branching up from a main valley to higher ground. Chiefly *Scot.* & *N. English*. LME.
3 An inlet, a small bay; a harbour. Chiefly *Scot.* & *dial.* LME.

hope /həʊp/ *verb*.
[ORIGIN Late Old English *hopian* = Old Frisian *hopia*, Middle Dutch & mod. Dutch *hopen* (orig., like HOPE *noun*¹, belonging to Low German areas), whence Middle High German, German *hoffen*.]
1 *verb intrans.* Entertain expectation of something desired. (Foll. by *for*.) LOE. ▸†**b** Look for, expect (without implication of desire). Foll. by *to*, *for*. *rare*. ME–L16.

E. O'BRIEN She hoped, the way children hope, for a happy ending to this courtship.

hope against hope cling to a mere possibility.
2 *verb intrans.* Trust, have confidence, (*in*). *arch.* LOE.
3 *verb trans.* Expect and desire (a thing (*arch.*), *that*, *to do*); feel fairly confident *that*; intend, if possible, *to do*. LOE.

S. ROGERS With looks that asked yet dared not hope relief. C. P. SNOW He was hoping that Kate and Humphrey could go round to his house. I. MURDOCH Adelaide.. hoped to become a buyer.

cross my heart (***and hope to die***): see HEART *noun*.
†**4** *verb trans.* Expect or anticipate (without implication of desire); suppose, think, suspect. ME–M17.
■ **hoped** *ppl adjective* expected with desire (now usu. ***hoped-for***). L16. **hoper** *noun* LME. **hopingly** *adverb* (*rare*) with hope, hopefully. E17.

hopeful /ˈhəʊpfʊl, -f(ə)l/ *adjective* & *noun*. ME.
[ORIGIN from HOPE *noun*¹ + -FUL.]
▸ **A** *adjective*. **1** Full of hope; feeling or entertaining hope. ME. ▸**b** Expressing hope. E17.

T. HERBERT Hopeful of some reward. J. BUCHAN Gazing at his companion as a hopeful legatee might gaze at a lawyer engaged in reading a will. **b** J. B. PRIESTLEY In the original itinerary I sketched for myself.. there were hopeful references to places like Newmarket.

2 Inspiring hope, promising; *iron.* likely to disappoint hopes. M16.
▸ **B** *noun*. A person, esp. (more fully ***young hopeful***) a young person, likely to succeed or *iron.* to be disappointed; a person who hopes to achieve something. E18.

R. HUNTFORD Like many another hopeful, he was rushing to strike while the iron was hot.

■ **hopefulness** *noun* E17.

hopefully /ˈhəʊpfʊli, -f(ə)li/ *adverb*. E17.
[ORIGIN from HOPEFUL + -LY².]
1 In a hopeful manner; with a feeling of hope; promisingly. E17.

V. GLENDINNING She was desperate to get *The Freewoman* re-established, and hopefully collected donations.

2 (Modifying a sentence.) It is hoped (that). (Considered *erron.* by some.) E20.

Lebende Sprachen Machines will hopefully enable the scientist to find quickly the information he needs. *Observer* Hopefully, they too will be pleasantly surprised.

hopeless /ˈhəʊplɪs/ *adjective*. M16.
[ORIGIN from HOPE *noun*¹ + -LESS.]
1 Having or feeling no hope; despairing. M16.

G. GREENE He seemed too tired to hurry, too hopeless to have an object in hurrying.

2 Admitting no hope, despaired of, irremediable. M16. ▸**b** Ineffectual; incompetent, stupid. M19.

C. G. WOLFF She.. fell so ill with typhoid fever that her case was considered hopeless. **b** C. S. FORESTER Only a couple of hands were necessary to show up Simpson as a hopeless whist player.

†**3** Unhoped-for, unexpected. L16–E17.
■ **hopelessly** *adverb* E17. **hopelessness** *noun* E19.

Hopi /ˈhəʊpi/ *noun* & *adjective*. L19.
[ORIGIN Hopi.]
▸ **A** *noun*. Pl. same, **-s**. A member of a group of N. American Indians living chiefly in NE Arizona; the Uto-Aztecan language of this people. L19.
▸ **B** *attrib.* or as *adjective*. Of or pertaining to the Hopi or their language. E20.

Hopkinsian /hɒpˈkɪnzɪən/ *noun* & *adjective*. L18.
[ORIGIN from Samuel *Hopkins* (see below) + -IAN.]
(An adherent) of the modified Calvinism of the New England theologian Samuel Hopkins (1721–1803).
■ **Hopkinsianism** *noun* the theological system of Samuel Hopkins E19.

hoplite /ˈhɒplʌɪt/ *noun*. E18.
[ORIGIN Greek *hoplitēs*, from *hoplon* weapon, *hopla* arms: see -ITE¹.]
A heavy-armed foot soldier of ancient Greece.

hopo /ˈhəʊpəʊ/ *noun*. Pl. **-os**. M19.
[ORIGIN Of African origin.]
A trap for game, consisting of two converging hedges with a pit at the angle.

hopped /hɒpt/ *adjective*. M17.
[ORIGIN from HOP *noun*¹, *verb*²: see -ED², -ED¹.]
1 Impregnated, mixed, or flavoured with hops. M17.
2 Stimulated or intoxicated by a narcotic drug (usu. foll. by *up*). Foll. by *up* also, excited, enthusiastic, (of a motor vehicle etc.) modified to give improved performance. *US slang.* E20.

hopper /ˈhɒpə/ *noun*¹. ME.
[ORIGIN from HOP *verb*¹ + -ER¹. Connection of sense 4 unkn.]
1 A person who hops, leaps, or dances. ME. ▸**b** BASEBALL. A ball which having been struck rebounds from the ground. *US slang.* M20.
2 An animal characterized by hopping; *esp.* an insect that hops, as a grasshopper, a flea, a cheese maggot, a young locust. ME.
3 In milling, a cone-shaped receptacle, orig. operated with a hopping motion, used to receive the material to be ground; any of various devices that resemble this in use or shape. ME.
4 A basket, *esp.* one used by a sower for carrying seed. Now only *Scot.* & *dial.* ME.
5 A barge which carries away mud or gravel from a dredging machine and discharges it at sea through an opening in its bottom. M18.
6 A railway truck able to discharge coal, gravel, etc., through its floor. M19.
7 A funnel-shaped or conical hollow. M19.
8 A mechanism in a piano which regulates the movement of the hammer of a key. Also called ***grasshopper***. M19.
– COMB.: **hopper barge** = sense 5 above; **hopper car** = sense 6 above; **hopper dredge**, **hopper dredger** a vessel combining the functions of a hopper and a dredger.

hopper /ˈhɒpə/ *noun*². E18.
[ORIGIN from HOP *verb*² + -ER¹.]
A hop-picker.

hopperdozer /ˈhɒpədəʊzə/ *noun*. *US*. L19.
[ORIGIN from HOPPER *noun*¹, perh. after *bulldozer*.]
A device for catching and destroying insects, consisting of a movable pen or frame filled or smeared with a poisonous or glutinous substance.

hoppergrass /ˈhɒpəgrɑːs/ *noun*. Chiefly *US dial.* E19.
[ORIGIN Alt.]
A grasshopper.

hoppet /ˈhɒpɪt/ *noun*. Chiefly *N. English*. L17.
[ORIGIN Uncertain: perh. from HOPPER *noun*¹ + -ET¹.]
1 A basket, *esp.* a small handbasket. L17.
2 A large bucket used for raising and lowering men and materials in a mine shaft. M19.

hoppety *adverb* & *adjective* var. of HOPPITY *adverb* & *adjective*.

hopping /ˈhɒpɪŋ/ *noun*. ME.
[ORIGIN from HOP *verb*¹ + -ING¹.]
1 The action of HOP *verb*¹. ME.
2 A dance; a festival with dancing. Now *dial.* ME.

hopping /ˈhɒpɪŋ/ *adjective* & *adverb*. L16.
[ORIGIN from HOP *verb*¹ + -ING².]
▸ **A** *adjective*. **1** That hops. L16.

BURKE The little shrivelled, meagre, hopping, though loud and troublesome insects of the hour. H. G. WELLS The hopping inconsecutiveness of English conversation.

Hopping Dick *W. Indian* the common white-chinned thrush of Jamaica, *Turdus aurantius*. **hopping john** in the southern US and W. Indies, a stew of rice with peas or bacon or other ingredients.
2 Very angry, furious, 'hopping mad'. L19.

W. HILDICK I was mad, real hopping!

3 Very active, busy, lively. *colloq.* (chiefly *N. Amer.*). E20.

N. MAILER You have two sons to take care of. That must keep you hopping. *Philadelphia Inquirer* The Devon Horse Show Grounds will be hopping.

▸ **B** *adverb*. So as to hop; extremely. Chiefly in ***hopping mad***, very angry, furious. L17.

W. P. KELLER Building a hopping big fire to burn the rubbish.

hoppity /ˈhɒpɪti/ *noun*. L19.
[ORIGIN from HOP *verb*¹.]
= HALMA.

hoppity /ˈhɒpɪti/ *adverb & adjective*. Also **-ety**. Also redupl. **hoppity-hop**, **hoppity-hoppity**. E19.
[ORIGIN from HOP *verb*[1]. Cf. HIPPETY-HOP.]
▸ **A** *adverb*. In a hopping or limping manner, unevenly. E19.
▸ **B** *adjective*. Hopping, full of movement; limping. L19.

hopple /ˈhɒp(ə)l/ *noun*. M17.
[ORIGIN from the verb.]
A device for hoppling animals; *transf.* a fetter; = HOBBLE *noun* 3.

hopple /ˈhɒp(ə)l/ *verb trans*. L16.
[ORIGIN Prob. of Low German origin: cf. early Flemish *hoppelen* = Middle Dutch *hobelen* jump, dance: see HOBBLE *verb*.]
Fasten together the legs of (an animal) to prevent straying; *transf.* fetter (a person); = HOBBLE *verb* 5.

Hoppo /ˈhɒpəʊ/ *noun*. Pl. **-os**. E18.
[ORIGIN Prob. from Chinese *hùbù* the Ministry of Revenue in feudal China.]
hist. In China: the board of revenue or customs; (in full ***Hoppo-man***) an officer of the customs.

Hoppus /ˈhɒpəs/ *noun*. Also **h-**. L19.
[ORIGIN Edward *Hoppus*, 18th-cent. English surveyor.]
Used **attrib.** and in **possess.** to designate a method of measuring the cubic content of round timber.
Hoppus foot a unit of timber volume equal to approximately 1.27 cu. ft (0.0360 cu. metre).

hoppy /ˈhɒpi/ *noun*[1]. *US slang*. E20.
[ORIGIN from HOP *noun*[1] + -Y[6].]
An opium addict; a hophead.

hoppy /ˈhɒpi/ *noun*[2]. *colloq.* E20.
[ORIGIN from HOP *noun*[2] + -Y[6].]
A lame person.

hoppy /ˈhɒpi/ *adjective*[1]. L19.
[ORIGIN from HOP *noun*[1] + -Y[1].]
1 Tasting or smelling of hops; beery. L19.
2 Of, pertaining to, or characterized by drugs or drug-taking. *US slang*. M20.

hoppy /ˈhɒpi/ *adjective*[2]. *colloq.* E20.
[ORIGIN from HOP *noun*[2] + -Y[1].]
Characterized by or inclined to hopping; lively; limping, lame.

hopscotch /ˈhɒpskɒtʃ/ *noun*. E19.
[ORIGIN from HOP *verb*[1] + SCOTCH *noun*[1].]
A children's game involving hopping on one foot over lines or between compartments marked on the ground, over or into which a flat stone or similar object has been cast for retrieval.

J. L. WATEN I joined the . . game of hopscotch on white squares drawn in chalk on the footpath.

■ Also †**hop-scot** *noun* (*rare*): only in L18.

hopshackle /ˈhɒpʃak(ə)l/ *verb & noun*. *obsolete* exc. *dial.* E16.
[ORIGIN Unknown.]
▸ **A** *verb trans.* = HOBBLE *verb* 5. E16.
▸ **B** *noun*. = HOBBLE *noun* 3. M16.

†**hopt** *verb pa. t. & pple*: see HOP *verb*[1].

Hopton wood /ˈhɒptən ˈwʊd/ *noun & adjectival phr.* L19.
[ORIGIN A wood and neighbouring quarries near Wirksworth, Derbyshire.]
(Designating) a pale limestone used for building and decorative purposes.

hora /ˈhɔːrə/ *noun*. Also **horah**. L19.
[ORIGIN Romanian *horă*, Hebrew *hōrāh*.]
A Romanian and Israeli ring dance; a piece of music for this dance; a song to which it is performed.

horae /ˈhɔːriː/ *noun*. L19.
[ORIGIN Latin, pl. of *hora* HOUR.]
A book of hours.

horah *noun* var. of HORA.

horal /ˈhɔːr(ə)l/ *adjective*. E18.
[ORIGIN Late Latin *horalis*, from Latin *hora* HOUR: see -AL[1].]
Of or pertaining to an hour or hours.

horary /ˈhɔːrəri/ *noun*. *rare*. M17.
[ORIGIN mod. Latin *horarium* book of hours, use as noun of neut. sing. of medieval Latin *horarius*: see HORARY *adjective*.]
†**1** *ECCLESIASTICAL*. A book containing the offices for the canonical hours. M17–L18.
2 An hourly account or narrative; a timed programme or plan. M19.

horary /ˈhɔːrəri/ *adjective*. E17.
[ORIGIN medieval Latin *horarius*, from Latin *hora* HOUR: see -ARY[1].]
1 Occurring every hour, hourly. E17.
†**2** Lasting only for an hour, of a short duration. Only in 17.
3 Of, relating to, or indicating the hours. M17.
4 *ASTROLOGY*. Of or pertaining to observation of the sky and planets at a particular moment. M17.
horary question: the answer to which is obtained by erecting a figure of the sky and planets for the moment at which it is propounded.

Horatian /həˈreɪʃ(ə)n, -ʃɪən/ *adjective*. E17.
[ORIGIN Latin *Horatianus*, from Quintus *Horatius* Flaccus (see below): see -AN.]
Of, pertaining to, or resembling the Roman poet Horace (Quintus Horatius Flaccus, 65–8 BC) or his work.

horchata /ɔrˈtʃata, ɔːˈtʃɑːtə/ *noun*. Also **or-**. M19.
[ORIGIN Spanish.]
In Spain and Latin American countries, an almond-flavoured soft drink.

horde /hɔːd/ *noun*. M16.
[ORIGIN Polish *horda* (whence French, German, Dutch *horde*, Swedish *hord*), corresp. to Russian *orda*, Italian, Romanian *orda*, all ult. from Turkish *ordu* (royal) camp: cf. URDU.]
1 A tribe or troop of Tartar or other nomads. M16. ▸**b** *ANTHROPOLOGY*. A loosely knit social group consisting of about five families. L19.
Golden Horde (a state established by) a Mongol and Turkish host under Mongol leadership which overran Asia in the 13th cent., and maintained control of the centre of the continent until the end of the 15th cent.
2 A numerous company; a gang, a troop. Usu. *derog.* E17.

BURKE I hardly shall allow that with the horde of regicides we could . . obtain anything . . deserving the name of peace. DAY LEWIS He . . was . . inclined to separate himself from the horde of relations . . which littered Dublin.

hordeolum /hɔːdɪˈəʊləm/ *noun*. Pl. **-la** /-lə/. E19.
[ORIGIN Alt. of late Latin *hordeolus* sty, dim. of Latin *hordeum* barley.]
MEDICINE. A sty on the eyelid.

horehound /ˈhɔːhaʊnd/ *noun*. OE.
[ORIGIN formed as HOAR + *hūne* the plant *Marrubium*, of unknown origin. For the parasitic *d* cf. BOUND *adjective*[1], SOUND *noun*[2].]
1 More fully ***white horehound***. An aromatic labiate plant, *Marrubium vulgare*, with white flowers and cottony pubescence, formerly grown as a herb. Also, an extract or confection of this plant, used as a herbal remedy. OE.
2 ***black horehound***, a fetid purple-flowered labiate plant, *Ballota nigra*, common by roadsides. M16.

Hori /ˈhɔːri/ *noun*. *Austral. & NZ offensive*. M20.
[ORIGIN Maori form of the name 'George'.]
A Maori.

horizon /həˈrʌɪz(ə)n/ *noun & verb*. LME.
[ORIGIN Old French *orizon(te)* (mod. *horizon*) from late Latin *horizon*, *horizont-* from Greek *horizōn* use as noun (sc. *kuklos* circle) of pres. pple of *horizein* bound, limit, define, from *horos* boundary.]
▸ **A** *noun*. **1** The boundary of that part of the earth's surface visible from a given viewpoint; the line at which earth and sky appear to meet. Also (more fully ***apparent horizon***, ***sensible horizon***, ***visible horizon***), the circle where the earth's surface touches a cone whose vertex is at the observer's eye. LME.

K. GRAHAME The great ring of Downs that barred his vision . . his simple horizon. E. J. HOWARD He couldn't see the horizon, the sky just seemed to come down into the sea.

on the horizon *fig.* (of an event etc.) just imminent or becoming apparent.
2 *fig.* †**a** The dividing line between two regions of existence. Only in LME. ▸**b** The boundary of any sphere of thought, action, etc.; the limit of mental perception, experience, interest, etc. Formerly also, the sphere so bounded or limited. E17.

b J. RUSKIN Their range necessarily includes the entire horizon of man's action. C. PRIEST Children lack a world perspective; their horizons are narrow.

3 *ASTRONOMY*. More fully ***celestial horizon***, ***rational horizon***, ***true horizon***. A great circle of the celestial sphere, the plane of which passes through the centre of the earth and is parallel to that of the apparent horizon of a given place. LME. ▸**b** The celestial hemisphere within the horizon of a place. L16.

T. HERBERT For the Æquator is Horizon to both Poles. **b** SIR W. SCOTT The burning Sun of Syria had not yet attained its highest point in the horizon.

4 A representation of the horizon; *esp.* the broad ring in which an artificial globe is fixed, the upper surface of which represents the plane of the rational horizon (see sense 3 above). L16.
artificial horizon: see ARTIFICIAL *adjective* 2.
5 **a** *GEOLOGY*. A plane, interface between strata, or characteristic thin stratum, identifiable over a wide area and assumed originally continuous. M19. ▸**b** *SOIL SCIENCE*. Any of several layers in the soil lying roughly parallel to the surface and having distinguishable physical and chemical properties. Also ***soil horizon***. E20. ▸**c** *ARCHAEOLOGY*. A level at which a particular group of remains is found, or which is taken as representing a particular culture or cultural period. E20.
b A horizon a surface horizon of mixed organic and mineral matter. **B horizon** a horizon of mineral material below the A (and E) horizons, in which certain minerals accumulate by illuviation. **C horizon** a horizon underlying the B horizon, consisting of unconsolidated or unaltered material. **E horizon** an eluvial horizon underlying the A horizon, with less organic matter.
6 *EMBRYOLOGY*. Any of a numbered sequence of stages in the development of the human embryo. M20.
7 In horizon mining, a system of approximately horizontal tunnels lying in the same horizontal plane; the plane containing these tunnels. M20.
– COMB.: **horizon-blue** *noun & adjective* [French *bleu horizon*] (of) a light shade of blue, the colour of the French Army uniform during and after the First World War; **horizon glass** *NAUTICAL* a small glass fixed on the frame of a quadrant or sextant, half of which is clear glass for direct observation of the horizon and half of which is silvered to bring the reflected image of an observed body into optical coincidence with the horizon; **horizon mining** a method of working inclined seams from systems of approximately horizontal tunnels lying in the same horizontal plane.
▸ **B** *verb trans.* Provide or bound with a horizon. Usu. in *pass.* L18.
■ **horizonless** *adjective* M19.

horizontal /hɒrɪˈzɒnt(ə)l/ *adjective & noun*. M16.
[ORIGIN French, or mod. Latin *horizontalis*, from late Latin *horizon*, *horizont-*: see HORIZON, -AL[1].]
▸ **A** *adjective*. **1** Of or belonging to the horizon; at the horizon. M16.

G. BERKELEY He will . . declare the horizontal moon shall appear greater than the meridional.

2 Parallel to the plane of the horizon; at right angles to the vertical. M17. ▸**b** Designating a device or structure which works or lies in a horizontal direction. L17.

D. ATTENBOROUGH Their upright stems sprang from a horizontal one . . lying along the ground.

b horizontal bar a round bar fixed horizontally some distance above the ground for gymnastic exercise. ***horizontal pendulum***: see PENDULUM *noun*.
3 **a** Uniform; producing or based on uniformity. Chiefly *US*. M19. ▸**b** Involving (the combining of) firms engaged in the same stage or type of production. E20. ▸**c** Involving social groups of equal status etc. M20.

a *Congressional Globe* The Democratic bill made a horizontal cut of 20 per cent.

4 *MUSIC*. Involving the relationship of notes or chords as they are played, read horizontally. L19.
▸ **B** *noun*. †**1** The horizon. *rare*. Only in M16.
2 A horizontal line, plane, etc. L17.

Listener Bonnard derived his use of horizontals and verticals within the picture from Gauguin.

3 A Tasmanian evergreen tree, *Anodopetalum biglandulosum* (family Cunoniaceae), in which the stems and branches bend over into a horizontal position, so as to create an impenetrable mat. L19.
4 [translation of HORIZONTALE.] More fully ***grand horizontal*** = HORIZONTALE. *slang*. E20.
■ **horizontalism** *noun* the quality of being, or of having some part, horizontal M19. **horizonˈtality** *noun* the condition or quality of being horizontal; horizontal position: M18. **horizontaliˈzation** *noun* the action or an act of making horizontal L19. **horizontalize** *verb trans.* place in a horizontal position, make horizontal M19. **horizontally** *adverb* M17. **horizontalness** *noun* M19.

horizontale /ɔrizɔ̃tal/ *noun*. *slang*. Pl. pronounced same. L19.
[ORIGIN French.]
More fully ***grande horizontale*** /grɑ̃ːd/ (pl. ***grandes*** /grɑ̃ːd/). A prostitute.

New Yorker He is over-shadowed . . by Aunt Augusta, the still unretired *grande horizontale* of seventy-three.

horkey /ˈhɔːki/ *noun*. *dial.* (*obsolete* exc. *hist.*). Also **hockey** /ˈhɒki/. M16.
[ORIGIN Unknown.]
The festival of harvest home.

Horlicks /ˈhɔːlɪks/ *noun*. Also **Horlick's**, (in sense 2) **h-**. L19.
[ORIGIN from W. *Horlick* (1846–1936), British-born Amer. industrialist, its first manufacturer + -'S[1].]
1 (Proprietary name for) a malted milk powder; the drink made from this. L19.
2 A mess, a muddle. Chiefly in ***make a Horlicks of***. *slang*. L20.

horme /ˈhɔːmi/ *noun*. Also **-mé**. L17.
[ORIGIN Greek *hormē* impulse. Introduced in current use by Jung.]
†**1** A passion, an impulse. *rare*. Only in L17.
2 *PSYCHOLOGY*. Vital or purposeful energy. E20.
■ **hormic** *adjective* of, pertaining to, or characterized by horme E20.

hormesis /hɔːˈmiːsɪs/ *noun*. M20.
[ORIGIN Greek *hormēsis* rapid motion, eagerness, from *hormáein* set in motion, urge on.]
BIOLOGY. The phenomenon of a substance or other agent having a beneficial physiological effect at low levels of exposure even though it is toxic or otherwise harmful at higher levels.

hormogone /ˈhɔːməgəʊn/ *noun*. Also **-gon** /-gən/. L19.
[ORIGIN from HORMOGONIUM.]
BOTANY. = HORMOGONIUM.

hormogonium /hɔːməˈgəʊnɪəm/ *noun*. Pl. **-nia** /-nɪə/. L19.
[ORIGIN mod. Latin, from Greek *hormos* chain, necklace + *gonos* generation.]
BOTANY. In certain cyanobacteria, a short filament of rounded cells which detaches to form a new organism.

hormone /ˈhɔːməʊn/ *noun*. E20.
[ORIGIN from Greek *hormōn* pres. pple of *horman* set in motion (from *hormē* onset, impulse), assim. to -ONE.]
PHYSIOLOGY. **1** Any of numerous organic compounds produced by specialized cells in a living organism and transported in tissue fluids to regulate the action of specific

H

cells or tissues; any synthetic compound having such an effect. **E20.**

2 Any of numerous organic compounds produced by plants which regulate growth and other physiological activities; any synthetic compound having such an effect. **E20.**

– COMB.: **hormone replacement (therapy)** treatment with oestrogenic hormones to alleviate certain menopausal symptoms.

■ **horˈmonal** *adjective* of, involving, or effected by a hormone or hormones; *colloq.* having one's behaviour or mood influenced by one's sex hormones: **E20. horˈmonally** *adverb* **M20. horˈmonic** *adjective* (*rare*) = HORMONAL **E20. hormonize** *verb trans.* treat with a hormone **M20. hormoˈnology** *noun* (*rare*) endocrinology **E20.**

horn /hɔːn/ *noun & adjective.*

[ORIGIN Old English *horn* corresp. to Old Frisian, Old Saxon, Old High German, Old Norse *horn* (Dutch, German *Horn*), Gothic *haurn*, from Germanic, rel. to Latin *cornu*, Greek *keras*.]

▸ **A** *noun* **I 1** A non-deciduous bony outgrowth with (usu.) a keratinous sheath, often curved and pointed, found in pairs on the head of cattle, sheep, goats, and related mammals, and often used for display or combat. Also, the wholly keratinous outgrowth on the snout of a rhinoceros, found single or one behind another. **OE.** ▸**b** A horned animal. Also (*sing.* & in *pl.*), cattle. Long *rare.* **ME.** ▸**c** (The stars in) a part of the constellation Aries (the Ram) or of Taurus (the Bull). Long *rare.* **LME.**

S. BECKETT A young boy holding a goat by a horn. **b** SHAKES. *L.L.L.* My lady goes to kill horns.

2 An antler of a deer. **OE.**

3 In biblical and derived uses, a horn as a symbol of power and might or as a means of defence or resistance. **OE.**

AV *2 Sam.* 22:3 Hee is my Shield, and the horne of my Saluation.

4 A projection on the head of any of various animals, as a snail's tentacle, an insect's antenna, the crest of the horned owl, etc. **ME.** ▸**b** An erect penis; an erection. *coarse slang.* **L18.** ▸**c** A person's nose. *joc.* **M19.**

SHAKES. *L.L.L.* The tender horns of cockled snails. T. MEDWIN The beetle being somewhat restless, they pinioned down his horns . . to the ground.

5 (The representation of) an animal's horn as appearing on the head of a person, a supernatural (esp. evil) being, etc. **LME.**

P. THOMPSON Horns and a tail would not be more decisive to a frightened child at midnight.

6 A horn as fancifully said to be worn by a cuckold. **LME.**

J. BARTH When the horns on Harrison's brow were . . a few days old, . . I contrived to lengthen them a bit.

7 The tusk of a narwhal. Formerly also, the tusk of an elephant. **E17.**

▸ **II 8** A vessel made out of or shaped like the horn of cattle or other animals, for holding liquid, powder, etc.; a drinking vessel; a powder flask. **OE.**

T. H. WHITE The butler . . poured another horn, which Lancelot drained.

9 An animal's horn used as a wind instrument. Now usu. a wind instrument more or less resembling a horn in shape, usu. made of brass (freq. with specifying word). **OE.** ▸**b** An 8-foot reed stop in an organ. *rare.* **E18.** ▸**c** A trumpet; *gen.* a wind instrument. *Jazz slang.* **M20.** ▸**d** The player of a horn. **M20.**

E. LINKLATER I hear the pizzicati of the strings under wood-wind and horns. **c** G. AVAKIAN Each of these trio cuttings ends with Bix picking up his horn to play the coda.

bugle-horn, hunting horn, post horn, etc.

10 The wind instrument as used in forms of legal process, as the proclamation of outlawry. *obsolete* exc. SCOTTISH HISTORY. **LME.**

11 A cone-shaped apparatus (esp. part of an early gramophone etc.) for the collection or amplification of sound. **L19.** ▸**b** RADIO. A hollow waveguide expanded towards the open end to act as a transmitting or receiving aerial. **M20.**

J. MASTERS I remember their playing an old gramophone with a huge horn.

12 An instrument for sounding a warning signal. **E20.**

D. DELILLO A car came towards us, horn blowing.

fog-horn, motor horn, etc.

13 A horn-shaped pastry case (to be) filled with cream etc. **E20.**

14 The telephone. Chiefly in ***on the horn***. *US colloq.* **M20.**

D. C. COOKE I've been on the horn half the night trying to get you.

▸ **III 15** A horn-shaped projection at each corner of the altar in the Jewish Temple; *rare* either of the two outer corners of a church altar. **OE.**

AV *Exod.* 27:2 Thou shalt make an Altar . . and thou shalt make the hornes of it upon the foure corners thereof.

16 Each of the extremities of the moon or other crescent; a cusp. **OE.** ▸**b** Each tip or end of a bow. **E17.**

MILTON From the hornes Of Turkish Crescent. J. THOMSON The moon Wears a wan circle round her blunted horns.

17 ARCHITECTURE. Orig. (*rare*) a pinnacle, a gable. Later, an Ionic volute, a projection of an abacus. **OE.**

18 Chiefly *hist.* A horn-shaped appendage or ornament worn as (part of) a headdress. **ME.**

19 Either of the two wings of an army. **ME.**

E. DACRES Quintius seeing one of the hornes of his Army beginning to fayle.

20 A pointed or tapering projection. **ME.** ▸**b** AERONAUTICS. A projection from an aileron or other control surface, for attachment of a controlling wire, or to improve the balance of the surface. **E20.**

Athenaeum The extreme western horn of Brittany.

21 Either of two (or more) lateral projections; *esp.* an arm or branch of a bay, a river, etc. **LME.** ▸**b** ANATOMY. A cornu. **LME.**

W. MORRIS Within the long horns of a sandy bay. **b** J. M. DUNCAN The fœtus developed in a uterine horn.

22 NAUTICAL. Each of the extremities of a piece of rigging etc. **L18.**

23 In *pl.* The awns of barley. *dial.* **E19.**

24 Each of the curved projections of (part of) a particular mechanism, device, etc. **L19.** ▸**b** ELECTRICITY. Each of the conducting rods in a horn gap or horn arrester. **E20.**

▸ **IV 25** A hard, keratinous epidermal structure or growth, as a hoof, a nail, a corn, a callosity. **LME.**

26 The compacted keratinous material of which animals' horns are composed. **LME.**

Horse & Hound Oil feeds the hoof and helps to stimulate the growth of healthy horn. E. LINKLATER Faces behind heavy spectacles of tortoise-shell or horn.

27 A thing made from horn. **L15.** ▸**b** The substance of which part of the face of a wooden golf club is made. **M18.**

E. TOPSELL To make hafts for knives, or else horns for Spectacles.

▸ **V 28** Either alternative of a dilemma. **M16.**

– PHRASES ETC.: ***bass-horn***: see BASS *adjective*. **draw in one's horns** (*a*) restrain one's ambition or ardour, draw back; (*b*) restrict one's expenditure. **English horn** the cor anglais. **French horn** an orchestral wind instrument with a coiled tube, valves, and wide bell, usu. made of brass. ***gate of horn***: see GATE *noun*[1]. ***Golden Horn***: see GOLDEN *adjective*. ***greenhorn***: see GREEN *adjective*. ***hollow horn***: see HOLLOW *adjective*. **Horn of Africa** the peninsula of NE Africa separating the Gulf of Aden from the main part of the Indian Ocean. **horn of plenty** (*a*) a cornucopia; (*b*) an edible woodland mushroom, *Craterellus cornucopioides*, with a funnel-shaped cap that bears spores on its greyish outer surface. **lift up the horn** *arch.* exalt oneself; offer resistance. ***lock horns***: see LOCK *verb*[1] 4a. **on the horns of a dilemma** faced with a decision involving equally unfavourable alternatives. **pull in one's horns** = ***draw in one's horns*** above. **put to the horn** SCOTTISH HISTORY declare outlaw (by blowing three blasts on a horn). ***shoehorn***: see SHOE *noun*. ***take the bull by the horns***: see BULL *noun*[1] 1. **the Horn** Cape Horn. ***wear the horn(s)***: see WEAR *verb*[1]. ***Wiltshire Horn***: see WILTSHIRE 1. **wind a horn** *arch.* blow a horn.

▸ **B** *attrib.* or as *adjective*. Made of horn. **LME.**

– COMB. & SPECIAL COLLOCATIONS: **horn antenna** = sense A.11b above; **horn arrester** ELECTRICITY a horn gap designed to protect power lines from lightning arcs and other voltage surges; **horn-band** a band of musicians playing horns; **hornbeak** (now *dial.*) = ***horn-fish*** (a) below; †**horn-beast** an animal with horns; **horn beetle** a beetle with stout curved jaws or processes on the head, esp. (*a*) *US* a black woodland beetle, *Popilius disjunctus*; †(*b*) a stag beetle; **hornbill** any bird of the family Bucerotidae of tropical Asia and Africa, having a large downcurved bill with a ridge or elaborate casque along the top; **hornbook** *hist.* a paper containing the alphabet, the Lord's Prayer, etc., orig. mounted on a wooden tablet with a handle, and protected by a thin plate of horn; **horn-bug** *US* = ***horn beetle*** above; **horn cell** ANATOMY (now *rare*) any of the ganglion cells of the cornua of the spinal cord; **horn-fish** (*a*) a garfish; †(*b*) *Canad.* a sauger; **horn-fly** a small black bloodsucking fly, *Haematobia irritans*, which hovers esp. around the heads of cattle; **horn gap** ELECTRICITY a pair of rod conductors diverging from a small gap, so as to attract and extinguish any electric arc struck across the gap; **horn-mad** *adjective* (*arch.*) (*a*) (orig. of horned beasts) mad with rage; (*b*) *slang* lecherous; **horn-man** a man with a horn; *spec.* in Jamaica among the Maroons, a man who blew warning etc. signals on a horn; **horn-owl** = HORNED ***owl***; **horn poppy** = HORNED ***poppy***; **hornpout** the brown bullhead, *Ictalurus nebulosus*, introduced into western Europe from N. America in the 19th cent.; **horn-rimmed** *adjective* (esp. of spectacles) having rims made of horn or a substance resembling it; **horn-rims** horn-rimmed spectacles; **horn-ring** a circular attachment to the steering wheel of a motor vehicle by which the horn may be readily sounded; **horn silver** [translating German *Hornsilber*] MINERALOGY native silver chloride, AgCl, crystallizing in the cubic system and having a dull lustre; cerargyrite; **horn-snake** an American snake with a spinelike tail; *esp.* the mud snake, *Farancia abacura*; **horn spectacles** = ***horn-rims*** above; **hornstone** [translating German *Hornstein*] (*a*) chert; (*b*) hornfels; **horntail** a woodwasp of the hymenopteran family Siricidae; **hornwork** (*a*) FORTIFICATION an outwork consisting of two demi-bastions connected by a curtain and joined to the main work by two parallel wings; (*b*) work done in horn; articles made of horn; †(*c*) cuckoldry; **hornworm** *N. Amer.* any of several hawkmoth larvae having a hornlike spike on the tail, esp. the vegetable pests *Manduca sexta* (more fully ***tobacco hornworm***) and *M. quinquemaculata* (more fully ***tomato hornworm***); **hornwort** any of several submerged aquatic plants of the genus *Ceratophyllum* (family Ceratophyllaceae), with dense whorls of forked leaves; **hornwrack** any colonial bryozoan or sea mat (esp. *Flustra*) resembling seaweed and occasionally washed ashore.

■ **hornen** *adjective* (long *obsolete* exc. *dial.*) made of horn **LME. hornful** *noun* as much as a horn (esp. a drinking horn) will hold **E17. hornless** *adjective* **LME. hornlessness** *noun* **L19. hornlike** *adjective* resembling horn or a horn **L16.**

horn /hɔːn/ *verb.* **LME.**

[ORIGIN from the noun.]

1 *verb trans.* **a** Provide with horn or horns. **LME.** ▸**b** Cuckold. Cf. HORN *noun* 4b. **M16.**

2 *verb trans.* Put to the horn; outlaw. *obsolete* exc. SCOTTISH HISTORY. **E16.**

3 *verb trans.* Butt or (esp.) gore with the horns. **L16.** ▸**b** *verb intrans.* Foll. by *in*: intrude (*on*), interfere. *slang.* **E20.**

4 *verb trans.* Adjust (the frame of a ship) at right angles to the line of the keel. **M19.**

5 *verb intrans.* Blow a horn; progress blowing a horn. **L19.**

hornbeam /ˈhɔːnbiːm/ *noun.* **LME.**

[ORIGIN from HORN *noun* + BEAM *noun*.]

(The hard tough wood of) any of several trees of the genus *Carpinus*, of the birch family, resembling the beech, esp. the European *C. betulus* and the N. American *C. caroliniana*.

hop hornbeam either of two trees of the genus *Ostrya* (*O. carpinifolia* of southern Europe, *O. virginiana* of N. America) related to the hornbeam (so called from the resemblance of the ripe catkins to hops).

hornblende /ˈhɔːnblɛnd/ *noun.* **L18.**

[ORIGIN German, from *Horn* HORN *noun* + BLENDE.]

MINERALOGY. A dark green or brown, monoclinic, basic aluminosilicate of calcium, sodium, magnesium, and iron, which is a mineral of the amphibole group and is a common constituent of igneous and metamorphic rocks, the crystals usu. being columnar prisms.

■ **hornˈblendic** *adjective* **E19.**

hornblendite /ˈhɔːnblɛndʌɪt/ *noun.* Also †**-yte.** **L19.**

[ORIGIN from HORNBLENDE + -ITE[1].]

PETROGRAPHY. A granular rock composed largely or entirely of hornblende.

horned /hɔːnd/ *adjective.* **ME.**

[ORIGIN from HORN *noun*, *verb*: see -ED[2], -ED[1].]

1 Wearing or having a horn or horns, *spec.* designating animals and plants distinguished in this way. **ME.**

H. W. TORRENS A peculiar horned or crested helmet. C. BOWEN Bull to the horned herd, and the corn to a fruitful plain.

yellow horned: see YELLOW *adjective*.

2 Crescent-shaped. **LME.**

W. HOLTBY She . . drove out, under a small horned moon.

3 Made of horn; provided or fitted with horn. **LME.**

– SPECIAL COLLOCATIONS & PHRASES: **horned adder** = ***horned viper*** below. **horned cairn** ARCHAEOLOGY a type of long barrow with an enclosed forecourt peculiar to Scotland and Ireland. **horned dace** *US* a small freshwater cyprinid fish, *Semotilus atromaculatus*. **horned frog** (*a*) = ***horned toad*** (a) below; (*b*) a S. American frog of the genus *Ceratophrys*, having hornlike projections on its eyelids. **horned grebe** (chiefly *US*) = ***Slavonian grebe*** s.v. SLAVONIAN *adjective* 2. **horned helmet** a large gastropod mollusc, *Cassis cornuta*, or its shell, from which cameos are cut. **horned lark** (*a*) a brown and white lark, *Eremophila bilopha*, having two black tufts on the head and found in N. African and Arabian deserts (also **Temminck's horned lark**); (*b*) (chiefly *N. Amer.*) = ***shorelark*** s.v. SHORE *noun*[1]. **horned lizard** = ***horned toad*** below. **horned owl** an owl having hornlike feathers over the ears; now *esp.* a large American owl, *Bubo virginianus*. **horned pondweed** an aquatic plant, *Zannichellia palustris* (family Zannichelliaceae), with filiform leaves, small axillary flowers, and beaked achenes. **horned poppy** any of several glaucous poppies of the genus *Glaucium*, with very long curved capsules; *esp.* (more fully ***yellow horned poppy***) *G. flavum*, a native of shingle beaches. **horned pout** = ***hornpout*** s.v. HORN *noun*. **horned rattlesnake** = SIDEWINDER *noun*[2]. **horned screamer** a large greenish-black screamer (bird), *Anhima cornuta*, of S. American tropical grasslands, having a hornlike quill on the forehead. **horned snake** (*a*) = ***horn-snake*** s.v. HORN *noun*; (*b*) = ***horned viper*** below. **horned sungem**: see SUN *noun*[1]. †**horned syllogism** LOGIC the dilemma. **horned toad** (*a*) a small spiny American lizard of the genus *Phrynosoma*, esp. *P. cornutum*, sometimes kept as a pet; (*b*) any of several large Old World toads that have a fleshy 'horn' above the eye. **horned viper** a venomous N. African desert viper, *Cerastes cerastes*, having a spine over each eye. ***Wiltshire Horned sheep***: see WILTSHIRE 1.

horner /ˈhɔːnə/ *noun.* **ME.**

[ORIGIN from HORN *noun* or *verb* + -ER[1].]

1 A maker of articles of horn, as spoons, combs, etc. **ME.**

2 A person who blows a horn. **LME.**

†**3** A person outlawed by being put to the horn. *Scot.* **M–L16.**

†**4** A person who has cuckolded another. **L16–E18.**

hornero /ɔːˈnɛːrəʊ/ *noun.* Pl. **-os.** **L19.**

[ORIGIN Spanish = baker.]

Any of various S. American birds of the genus *Furnarius*, esp. *F. rufus* (more fully ***rufous hornero***). Also called ***ovenbird***.

Horner's syndrome /ˈhɔːnəz ˌsɪndrəʊm/ *noun phr.* **E20.**

[ORIGIN from J. F. *Horner* (1831–86), Swiss ophthalmologist.]

MEDICINE. A condition marked by a contracted pupil, drooping upper eyelid, and local inability to sweat on one side of the face, caused by damage to sympathetic nerves on that side of the neck.

hörnesite *noun* var. of HOERNESITE.

hornet /ˈhɔːnɪt/ *noun*.
[ORIGIN Old English *hyrnet(u)* rel. to Old High German *hornuz* (German *Hornisse*), Old Saxon *hornut*; later forms infl. by Middle Dutch, Middle High German *hornte*; perh. ult. from base of HORN *noun*: see -ET[2].]
1 Any of various large social wasps of the family Vespidae, esp. the red and yellow European *Vespa crabro*, which has a severe sting. OE.
2 *transf. & fig.* A persistent and virulent attacker. Esp. in ***a hornets' nest***, ***a nest of hornets***, etc., trouble or opposition encountered or stirred up. L16.
– COMB.: **hornet clearwing** = *hornet moth* below; †**hornet fly** a robber fly; **hornet moth** either of two European wood-boring clearwing moths, *Sphecia bombeciformis* and *Sesia apiformis*, which resemble hornets.

hornfels /ˈhɔːnfɛls/ *noun & verb*. M19.
[ORIGIN German = horn rock.]
GEOLOGY. ▸**A** *noun*. A dark, fine-grained, non-schistose rock composed mainly of quartz, mica, and feldspars, and formed by contact metamorphism. M19.
▸**B** *verb trans.* Metamorphose (a rock) into hornfels. E20.

hornify /ˈhɔːnɪfʌɪ/ *verb trans*. E17.
[ORIGIN from HORNY: see -FY.]
1 Cuckold. Long *rare* or *obsolete*. E17.
2 Make horny or hornlike in texture. Usu. in *pass.* L17.

hornito /hɔːˈniːtəʊ/ *noun*. Pl. **-os**. M19.
[ORIGIN Amer. Spanish, dim. of *horno* (from Latin *furnus*) oven, furnace.]
GEOLOGY. A driblet cone formed by successive ejections through a vent in a lava flow.

hornpipe /ˈhɔːnpʌɪp/ *noun*. LME.
[ORIGIN from HORN *noun & adjective* + PIPE *noun*[1].]
1 *hist.* A wind instrument made wholly or partly of horn. LME.
2 A lively and vigorous dance, usu. for one person, orig. to the accompaniment of the wind instrument, and esp. associated with the merrymaking of sailors. L15.
3 A piece of music for this dance. L18.

hornswoggle /ˈhɔːnswɒɡ(ə)l/ *verb trans. slang* (orig. *US*). E19.
[ORIGIN Unknown.]
Get the better of; cheat, hoax; humbug.

horny /ˈhɔːni/ *adjective & noun*. LME.
[ORIGIN from HORN *noun* + -Y[1].]
▸**A** *adjective* **I 1** *gen.* Of or like horn; keratinous. LME.
2 Semi-opaque like horn. M17.
3 Hard as horn. L17.
4 Sexually excited; lecherous. Also, arousing sexual excitement. *slang*. L19.
▸**II 5** Wearing or having a horn or horns. M16.
– COMB.: **horny-handed** *adjective* having hands calloused by manual labour.
▸**B** *noun*. **1** A police officer. *slang*. M18.
2 (With cap. initial, usu. **Hornie**.) The Devil. *colloq.* (chiefly *Scot.*). L18.
3 A cow, a bullock. *Scot. & Austral. slang*. E19.
■ **hornily** *adverb* L19. **horniness** *noun* L19.

horography /hɒˈrɒɡrəfi/ *noun*. Now *rare*. E18.
[ORIGIN French *horographie*, from Greek *hōra* time, season + *-graphia* -GRAPHY.]
The art of making or constructing dials.

horologe /ˈhɒrəlɒdʒ/ *noun*. *arch*. LME.
[ORIGIN Old French *or(i)loge* (mod. *horloge*) from Latin *horologium* timepiece, from Greek *hōrologion* dim. of *hōrologos*, from *hōra* time, hour + *-logos* telling (see -LOGUE).]
An instrument for telling the time; a dial, an hourglass, a clock.

horologer /hɒˈrɒlədʒə/ *noun*. ME.
[ORIGIN Anglo-Norman *orloger*, Old French *orlogier*, formed as HOROLOGE: see -ER[2]. Reintroduced in 19, from HOROLOGE.]
Orig., a person who proclaimed the time of day to others, or maintained a timepiece. Now, a clockmaker.

horologic /hɒrəˈlɒdʒɪk/ *adjective*. M17.
[ORIGIN Late Latin *horologicus* from Greek *hōrologikos*, from *hōrologos*: see HOROLOGE, -IC. Cf. HOROLOGICAL.]
Of or pertaining to horology.

horological /hɒrəˈlɒdʒɪk(ə)l/ *adjective*. LME.
[ORIGIN formed as HOROLOGIC: see -AL[1].]
Of or pertaining to horology or (the use of) a horologe; measuring or recording time.

horologion /hɒrəˈləʊdʒɪən, -ˈlɒdʒ-/ *noun*. E18.
[ORIGIN Greek *hōrologion*: see HOROLOGE.]
In the Orthodox Church, a liturgical book containing the offices for the canonical hours, corresponding more or less to the Western breviary.

horologist /hɒˈrɒlədʒɪst/ *noun*. L18.
[ORIGIN from HOROLOGE or HOROLOGY *noun*[2] + -IST.]
A person skilled in horology; a maker of clocks or watches.

horologium /hɒrəˈləʊdʒɪəm, -ˈlɒdʒ-/ *noun*. M17.
[ORIGIN Latin: see HOROLOGE.]
1 = HOROLOGE. M17.
2 = HOROLOGION. E18.
3 (Usu. **H-**.) (The name of) an inconspicuous constellation of the southern hemisphere, between Hydrus and Eridanus; the Clock. E19.

†**horology** *noun*[1]. LME–M19.
[ORIGIN from HOROLOGIUM *noun*: see -Y[3].]
= HOROLOGE.

horology /hɒˈrɒlədʒi/ *noun*[2]. E19.
[ORIGIN from Greek *hōra* time, hour + -OLOGY.]
The study or science of measuring time; the construction of clocks, watches, etc.

horometry /hɒˈrɒmɪtri/ *noun*. L16.
[ORIGIN formed as HOROLOGY *noun*[2] + -METRY.]
The measurement of time.
■ **horoˈmetrical** *adjective* of or pertaining to horometry L17.

horopter /hɒˈrɒptə/ *noun*. E18.
[ORIGIN from Greek *horos* limit + *optēr* a person who looks.]
OPTICS. A line or surface containing all those points in space of which images fall on corresponding points of the retinas of the two eyes.

horoscopal /hɒˈrɒskəp(ə)l/ *adjective*. M17.
[ORIGIN from Latin *horoscopus* HOROSCOPE + -AL[1].]
Of or pertaining to a horoscope.

horoscope /ˈhɒrəskəʊp/ *noun & verb*. OE.
[ORIGIN In early use from Latin *horoscopus* from Greek *hōroskopos* nativity, horoscope, etc., from *hōra* time, hour + *skopos* observer (cf. SCOPE *noun*[1]); later from Old French & mod. French.]
▸**A** *noun*. An observation of the sky and the configuration of the planets at a particular moment, esp. at a person's birth; a diagram showing such a configuration of the planets; a prediction of a person's future based on this. Formerly also *spec.*, the ascendant. OE.

> R. DAVIES Request for my birth date and hour, as he would . . cast my horoscope.

▸**B** *verb trans. & intrans.* Cast the horoscope of (a person). *rare*. E17.
■ **horoscoper** *noun* (now *rare*) an astrologer M16. **horoˈscopic** *adjective* M19. **horoˈscopical** *adjective* L18. **hoˈroscopy** *noun* the casting of horoscopes M17.

horrendous /həˈrɛndəs/ *adjective*. M17.
[ORIGIN from Latin *horrendus* gerund. of *horrere* (see HORRIBLE) + -OUS. Cf. *tremendous*, *stupendous*.]
Horrible, horrifying; awful, frightful.

> B. GUEST The translations were mostly horrendous, . . stale and florid. S. MORLEY Niven had just lost his first wife in a horrendous fall down . . cellar stairs.

■ **horrendously** *adverb* M20. **horrendousness** *noun* L20.

horrent /ˈhɒr(ə)nt/ *adjective*. Chiefly *poet*. M17.
[ORIGIN Latin *horrent-* pres. ppl stem of *horrere*: see HORRIBLE, -ENT.]
1 Of hair: standing on end, bristling. M17.

> A. BURGESS Things went on in Manchester . . which would make our hair horrent.

2 Shuddering; feeling horror. E18.

horribile dictu /hɒˌrɪbɪleɪ ˈdɪktuː, hɒˌriːbɪli/ *adverbial phr.* M19.
[ORIGIN mod. Latin, by analogy with MIRABILE DICTU.]
Horrible to relate.

horribility /hɒrɪˈbɪlɪti/ *noun*. Long *rare*. LME.
[ORIGIN Old French *horribleté*, from *horrible*: see HORRIBLE, -ITY. Cf. medieval Latin *horribilitas*. In mod. use from HORRIBLE.]
Horribleness. Formerly also, something horrible.

horrible /ˈhɒrɪb(ə)l/ *adjective, noun, & adverb*. ME.
[ORIGIN Old French *orrible*, (also mod.) *horrible* from Latin *horribilis*, from *horrere* (of hair) stand on end, tremble, shudder: see -IBLE.]
▸**A** *adjective*. Exciting, or likely to excite, horror; repulsive, hideous, shocking; *colloq.* excessive, frightful, unpleasant. ME.

> V. WOOLF I should stand in a queue and smell sweat, and scent as horrible as sweat. J. F. LEHMANN It was horrible to me to imagine them being trained to kill young Englishmen. R. DAVIES The horrible children had become more tolerable since last he saw them. R. INGALLS The weather there was horrible.

▸**B** *noun*. A horrible person or thing; that which is horrible. Formerly also, something exciting horror. LME.

> H. MELVILLE Such a waggish leering as lurks in all you horribles! CONAN DOYLE There is but one step from the grotesque to the horrible.

▸**C** *adverb*. Horribly. Now *rare*. LME.
■ **horribleness** *noun* (*a*) the quality of being horrible; †(*b*) a feeling of horror: LME. **horribly** *adverb* in a horrible manner; exceedingly: ME.

horrid /ˈhɒrɪd/ *adjective & adverb*. L16.
[ORIGIN Latin *horridus*, from *horrere*: see HORRIBLE, -ID[1].]
▸**A** *adjective*. **1** Rough, bristling. *literary*. L16.

> POPE Ye grots and caverns shagg'd with horrid thorn!

2 Exciting horror; repulsive, horrible, frightful. Now chiefly *colloq.*, disagreeable, objectionable. E17.

> DRYDEN An horrid stillness first invades the ear, And in that silence we the tempest fear. P. G. WODEHOUSE You've grown a beard, and it looks perfectly horrid. R. WEST There have been a lot of horrid little boys since the world began.

▸**B** *adverb*. Horridly. *colloq.* E17.
■ **horridly** *adverb* in a horrid manner, to a horrid degree, objectionably E17. **horridness** *noun* E17.

horridity /hɒˈrɪdɪti/ *noun*. E17.
[ORIGIN medieval Latin *horriditas*, formed as HORRID: see -ITY. Cf. French †*horridité*.]
†**1** A shudder of horror. Only in E17.
2 The quality of being horrid; something horrid. *rare*. M17.

horrific /hɒˈrɪfɪk/ *adjective*. M17.
[ORIGIN French *horrifique* or Latin *horrificus*, from *horrere*: see HORRIBLE, -FIC.]
Exciting horror; horrifying.

> J. GATHORNE-HARDY Dr Locking now recounted a horrific tale of *a whole year* devoted to Latin. N. SYMINGTON During this time she was also plagued by horrific nightmares.

■ **horrifically** *adverb* L17.

horrification /ˌhɒrɪfɪˈkeɪʃ(ə)n/ *noun*. E19.
[ORIGIN from HORRIFY after *magnify*, *magnification* etc.: see -FICATION.]
1 A horrifying or objectionable thing. Now *rare*. E19.
2 The action of horrifying; the state of being horrified. L19.

horrify /ˈhɒrɪfʌɪ/ *verb trans*. L18.
[ORIGIN Latin *horrificare*, from *horrificus*: see HORRIFICATION, -FY.]
Excite horror in; shock, scandalize.

> A. C. BOULT She was horrified one day to find three granddaughters turning cartwheels across the room. J. HELLER She is . . ready to take chances that horrify even me.

■ **horrifiedly** *adverb* in a horrified manner E20.

horripilation /hɒˌrɪpɪˈleɪʃ(ə)n/ *noun*. *literary*. M17.
[ORIGIN Late Latin *horripilatio(n-)*, from Latin *horripilat-* pa. ppl stem of *horripilare* become bristly or hairy, from *horrere* (see HORRIBLE) + *pilus* hair: see -ATION.]
Erection of the hairs on the skin caused by cold, fear, etc.; the condition of having goose pimples.
■ **hoˈrripilate** *verb trans. & intrans.* (cause to) have bristling hairs or goose pimples E17. **hoˈrripilant** *adjective* causing bristling hairs or goose pimples M19.

horrisonant /hɒˈrɪs(ə)nənt/ *adjective*. L16.
[ORIGIN from Latin *horrere* (see HORRIBLE) + *sonant-* sounding, from *sonare* to sound: see -ANT[1].]
Having a horrible sound.

horror /ˈhɒrə/ *noun & adjective*. ME.
[ORIGIN Old French *(h)orrour* (mod. *horreur*) from Latin *horror*, from *horrere*: see HORRIBLE, -OR.]
▸**A** *noun*. **1** (A painful feeling of) intense loathing and fear; a terrified and revolted shuddering; a strong aversion or an intense dislike (*of*); *colloq.* dismay (*at*). ME. ▸†**b** (A feeling of) awe. L16–E18.

> V. BRITTAIN The older generation held up outraged hands in horror at such sacrilege. H. E. BATES I felt . . pure cold horror hit me more savagely than the wind.

2 The quality of exciting intense loathing and fear; a person who or thing which excites such feelings; *colloq.* a mischievous person, esp. a child. Also, a genre of literature etc. designed to excite pleasurable feelings of horror by the depiction of the supernatural, violence, etc. LME.

> E. HALL Took the horrors for a drive, and . . Sydney and Cornelia could not behave themselves. S. BELLOW Many of the things that terrified people lost their horror when a doctor explained them. E. AMADI Port Harcourt still bore the marks of the horrors of war.

chamber of horrors a place full of horrors (orig., the room containing effigies of notorious murderers and their victims, methods of execution, etc., in Madame Tussaud's waxworks).
3 a An attack of shuddering or shivering, esp. as symptomatic of some disease. Now *rare*. LME. ▸**b** ***the horrors***, a fit of horror or depression, *spec.* as in delirium tremens. M18. ▸**c** In *pl.* as *interjection*. Expr. shock, dismay, etc. L19.
4 Roughness, ruggedness. Now *poet.* L17.
– COMB.: **horror-stricken**, **horror-struck** *adjectives* horrified, shocked.
▸**B** *attrib.* or as *adjective*. Of literature, a film, etc.: designed to excite pleasurable feelings of horror by the depiction of the supernatural, violence, etc. M20.

> *Variety* Recently showed . . horror films and Sino-Japanese War cruelty shots.

horror comic a periodical like a comic but with much violence and sensationalism.

horror vacui /hɒrə ˈvakjuːʌɪ/ *noun phr.* M19.
[ORIGIN mod. Latin = the horror of a vacuum.]
(A) fear or dislike of leaving empty spaces in an artistic composition etc.

> E. LUCIE-SMITH Nudes . . fill the whole picture-space as if the artist suffered from horror vacui.

hors concours /ɔr kɔ̃kuːr/ *adverbial & pred. adjectival phr.* L19.
[ORIGIN French = out of the competition.]
Not competing for a prize; without a rival.

> *Tablet* A work such as . . would, were it shown in the *Salon*, range him Hors Concours. V. NABOKOV Most husbands are fools, but that one was *hors concours*.

H

hors de combat /ɔr də kɔ̃ba/ *adverbial & pred. adjectival phr.* **M18.**
[**ORIGIN** French = out of the fight.]
Out of the fight; out of the running; in an injured or disabled condition.

hors d'oeuvre /ɔː ˈdəːv, ɔː ˈdəːvr(ə)/ *noun phr.* Pl. same, **hors d'oeuvres.** **M18.**
[**ORIGIN** French, lit. 'outside the work'.]
An extra dish served as an appetizer before or (occas.) during a meal; a starter; in *pl.* also, (usu. mixed) items of food served as such a dish.

horse /hɔːs/ *noun.* Pl. **-s**, (see below) same.
[**ORIGIN** Old English *hors* = Old Frisian *hors, hars, hers*, Old Saxon *hros, hers* (Middle Low German *ros, ors*, Middle Dutch *ors*, Dutch *ros*), Old High German *(h)ros* (Middle High German *ros, ors*, German *Ross*), Old Norse *hross*, from Germanic. See also **HOSS.**]
▸ **I 1** Pl. **-s**, (esp. after a numeral, now *rare*) same. A solid-hoofed perissodactyl ungulate mammal, *Equus caballus*, having a short coat and long mane and tail, native to central Asia but long domesticated as a draught animal and esp. for riding; *esp.* a member of a relatively large breed of this, *spec.* one of 15 hands or above (cf. **PONY** *noun* 1). Also (esp. in **ZOOLOGY**), any member of the family Equidae. **OE.** ▸**b** The adult male of this; a stallion or gelding. **LME.**
Arabian horse, carthorse, draught horse, great horse, liberty horse, racehorse, saddle horse, warhorse, wild horse, etc.
2 A representation, figure, or model of a horse. **ME.**
F. WISE The Horse was the Standard which the Saxons used.
hobbyhorse, rocking horse, etc.
3 In pl. ***horse***, †***horses***. Cavalry soldiers. **LME.**
E. LINKLATER Horse, foot, and guns they came, an army with banners.
4 A person as resembling a horse in some way. Now chiefly as a familiar form of address in ***old horse***. **E16.**
SHAKES. *1 Hen. IV* If I tell thee a lie, spit in my face, call me horse.
▸ **II** A thing.
5 Any of various devices on which a person rides or sits astride, used as conveyances, or for carrying or hauling; *spec.* (***a***) *hist.* a wooden frame having a sharp ridge on which delinquent soldiers were made to sit; (***b***) a piece of gymnastic apparatus for vaulting over (also ***vaulting horse***); (***c***) a board or seat on a rope on which a person is lowered down a shaft; (***d***) a low wooden stool used in various trades; (***e***) a tractor; a locomotive. **LME.**
6 Any of various small devices (chiefly wedges, vices, or clamps) used in various trades. **LME.**
7 **NAUTICAL.** Any of various ropes or bars; *spec.* (***a***) a rope or track on which a sail runs; (***b***) a rope or bar providing footing or protection for sailors, *spec.* a rope along the yards on which sailors stand when handling the sails. **E17.**
8 A frame or structure, usu. one with legs, on which something is mounted or supported. **E18.**
C. MORFIT A horse . . formed of two uprights and two crossbars, solidly joined together.
clothes horse, sawhorse, etc.
9 A lottery ticket hired out by the day. *obsolete* exc. *hist.* **E18.**
10 a **MINING.** An obstruction (as a mass of rock or earth) or fault in a vein. **L18.** ▸**b** A shoal, a sandbank. Chiefly *dial.* **E20.**
11 Work charged for before it is carried out. *slang.* Now *rare* or *obsolete.* **L18.**
12 (A unit of) horsepower. *colloq.* **M19.**
Motocross Rider Judging an engine on how many horses escape from it.
13 = **PONY** *noun* 3. *US slang.* **L19.**
14 Heroin. *slang* (orig. *US*). **M20.**
J. BALDWIN His first taste of marijuana, his first snort of horse.
– **PHRASES ETC.**: ***back the wrong horse***: see **BACK** *verb* 5. ***break a horse (to the rein)***: see **BREAK** *verb.* **change horses in midstream** change one's ideas, plans, etc., in the middle of a project or process. ***dark horse***: see **DARK** *adjective.* ***dead horse***: see **DEAD** *adjective* etc. ***devil's coach horse***: see **DEVIL** *noun.* **eat like a horse** eat heartily or greedily. ***Flemish horse***: see **FLEMISH** *adjective.* ***flog a dead horse***: see **DEAD** *adjective* etc. ***Flying Horse***: see **FLYING** *ppl adjective.* **frighten the horses** cause consternation or dismay; shock. **from the horse's mouth** (of information etc.) from the person directly concerned or another authoritative source. ***hitch horses (together)***: see **HITCH** *verb.* ***hold one's horses***: see **HOLD** *verb.* ***horse and hattock***: see **HATTOCK** *noun.* **horse of another colour** a thing significantly different. **horses for courses** the matching of tasks and talents. ***iron horse***: see **IRON** *adjective.* ***light horse***: see **LIGHT** *adjective*[1]. ***Little Horse***: see **LITTLE** *adjective.* ***look a gift-horse in the mouth***: see **GIFT** *noun.* ***one-horse***: see **ONE** *adjective.* **on one's high horse** *colloq.* behaving with pretentiousness or arrogance. ***put the cart before the horse***: see **CART** *noun.* ***sea horse***: see **SEA** *noun.* **swap horses in midstream** = ***change horses in midstream*** above. **to horse** *imper.* mount your horses. ***Trojan horse***: see **TROJAN** *adjective* 1. ***white horse***: see **WHITE** *adjective.* ***wild horse***: see **WILD** *adjective, noun, & adverb.* ***wooden horse***: see **WOODEN** *adjective.* ***workhorse***: see **WORK** *noun.*
– **COMB.**: **horse-and-buggy** *adjective* (*N. Amer.*) old-fashioned, bygone; **horse ant** the large European wood ant, *Formica rufa*; **horse-balm** a lemon-scented labiate plant of N. America, *Collinsonia canadensis*; **horsebane** a poisonous umbelliferous plant of watery places, *Oenanthe aquatica*, also called ***fine-leaved water dropwort***; **horsebean** any of several leguminous plants grown as fodder, esp. *Vicia faba* and (in tropical America) *Canavalia ensiformis*; **horse block** a small platform of stone or wood for mounting a horse; **horse-boat** (***a***) (chiefly *hist.*) a ferryboat for carrying horses or carriages; (***b***) **N. AMER. HISTORY** a paddle boat powered by horses working a treadmill; (***c***) a type of landing craft; **horsebox** a closed vehicle for transporting a horse or horses; ***horse brass***: see **BRASS** *noun* 2d; **horse-bread** *hist.* bread fed to horses, made of beans, bran, etc.; **horsebreaker** (***a***) a person who breaks in horses; (***b***) *hist.* a courtesan (freq. in ***pretty horsebreaker***); **horse-car** *US* (chiefly *hist.*) a horse-drawn tramcar or railway car; **horse cloth**: used to cover a horse, or as part of its trappings; **horse collar** a thickly padded collar forming part of a draught horse's harness (***grin through a horse collar***: see **GRIN** *verb*[2]); **horse-colt** a young male horse; **horse-comb** a comb for use on a horse, a curry comb; **horse-coper** a dealer in horses; ***horse-*CORSER**; **horse cubes** concentrated food in pellet form for horses; **horse daisy** *dial.* = ***ox-eye daisy*** s.v. **OX-EYE** 1(c); **horse-doctor** a veterinary surgeon attending horses; **horse-drawn** *adjective* (of a vehicle) pulled by a horse or horses; **horse-eye bean** (the seeds of) the W. Indian leguminous vine *Mucuna urens*, so called from the black hilum of the seeds; **horse fair** a (yearly) market for the sale of horses; **horsefeathers** *N. Amer. slang* nonsense; **horse-fish** any of various fishes having a horselike head, as the sea horse, the look-down; *spec.* a brownish fish with long joined dorsal spines, *Congiopodus torvus*, of deep southern African waters; **horsefly** any of various tabanid flies (esp. of the genus *Tabanus*), the females of which suck blood; also, any of various other bloodsucking flies, as the forest fly *Hippobosca equina*; **horse-foal** a male foal; **horse-foot (crab)** *US* a horseshoe crab; **horse-gear** *collect.* harness or trappings for horses; **horse-godmother** *arch. & dial.* a large coarse-looking woman; **horse-head** (***a***) a horse's head; a head like that of a horse; (***b***) = ***horse-fish*** above; **horsehide** *noun & adjective* (made of) leather made from the hide of a horse; **horse hoe** *noun & verb* (***a***) *noun* an early horse-drawn cultivator; (***b***) *verb trans. & intrans.* work with a horse hoe; **horse-hoer** a person who horse-hoes; **horse-hoof** (now *dial.*) coltsfoot; **horse-jockey** (now *rare*) (***a***) a jockey in horse races; (***b***) *US* a dealer in horses; **horse latitudes** a belt of calms in each hemisphere between the trade winds and the westerlies; **horse laugh** a loud coarse laugh; **horseleech** a large predatory leech of the genus *Haemopis*; *fig.* = **LEECH** *noun*[2] 2; **horse-litter** (***a***) *hist.* a litter hung on poles and carried between two horses, one in front, one behind; (***b***) straw etc. used as bedding for horses; this when soiled used as manure; **horse-load** (now *rare*) (***a***) a quantity (formerly occas. a specific weight) constituting a pack load for a horse; *loosely* a large load or quantity; **horse mackerel** (***a***) any of several large carangid fishes, *esp.* the scad, *Trachurus trachurus*; also *attrib.*, designating the family Carangidae; (***b***) (chiefly *N. Amer.*) any of various large tunnies or similar fishes; **horse manure** (***a***) horse dung and soiled straw etc. used as manure; (***b***) = ***horseshit*** below; **horse-master** a person who owns, manages, or breaks in horses; a person skilled in managing horses; **horse-mastership** skill in managing horses; **horse-meat** †(***a***) fodder for horses; (***b***) horseflesh as food; **horse-mill** a mill driven by a horse or horses, usu. by one walking in a circle or in a wheel; **horsemint** any of several coarse spicate mints, esp. hairy variants and hybrids of spearmint, *Mentha spicata*; *US* = ***wild bergamot*** s.v. **BERGAMOT** *noun*[2] 3(b); **horse mushroom** an edible mushroom, *Agaricus arvensis*, larger and coarser than the field mushroom, *A. campestris*; **horse mussel** †(***a***) a freshwater mussel; (***b***) a large marine mussel of the genus *Modiolus*, esp. *M. modiolus*; **horse-nail** a nail for a horseshoe; **horse opera** *N. Amer. slang* a western film; **horse pistol** a large pistol carried at the pommel of the saddle by a rider; **horseplay** †(***a***) play in which a horse is used or takes part, flamboyant horsemanship; (***b***) boisterous play; **horse-plum** (***a***) a coarse red variety of plum; (***b***) *US* either of two N. American wild plums, *Prunus americana* and *P. nigra*; **horse-pond** *noun & verb* (***a***) *noun* a pond for watering and washing horses, proverbial as a place for ducking obnoxious people; (***b***) *verb trans.* (now *rare*) duck in or drag through a horse pond; **horse-pox** a mild viral disease affecting horses; **horse race** a race between horses with riders; **horse racer** a person who participates in horse-racing; **horse-racing** the sport of conducting horse races; **horse's ass** *N. Amer. slang* a fool; **horse sense** *colloq.* (orig. *US*) plain common sense; **horseshit** *fig.* (*N. Amer. slang*) nonsense, rubbish; **horse sickness** a usu. fatal viral disease of horses, esp. in southern Africa (also ***African horse-sickness***); **horse's neck** (orig. *US*) a drink of ginger ale flavoured with lemon peel, usu. with whisky, brandy, or gin; **horse-soldier** a soldier mounted on a horse; **horse's tail** a hairstyle in which the hair is tied at the back and hangs down like a horse's tail, a ponytail; **horse-trading** (***a***) *N. Amer.* dealing in horses; (***b***) shrewd bargaining; **horse walker** a mechanically rotating arm to which horses are tied for the purpose of exercise; **horse-way** (now *rare*) a bridleway; **horsewhip** *noun & verb* (***a***) *noun* a whip used in driving and controlling horses; (***b***) *verb trans.* beat with a horsewhip; chastise.
■ **horselike** *adjective* resembling (that of) a horse **M16.**

horse /hɔːs/ *verb.* **OE.**
[**ORIGIN** from the noun.]
1 *verb trans.* Provide (a person, a vehicle) with a horse or horses. **OE.**
T. CORYAT Maron of Turin, who horsed our Company from Lyons to Turin. G. WASHINGTON We set out with less than thirty carriages . . all of them strongly horsed.
2 *verb intrans.* Mount or go on horseback. **LME.**
M. BRADBURY Two rodeo riders horsed showily down the street.
3 a *verb trans.* Of a stallion: mate with (a mare). **LME.** ▸**b** *verb intrans.* Of a mare: be in heat, desire the stallion. Freq. as ***horsing*** *pres. pple.* Chiefly *US dial. & Austral.* **L16.**
†**4** *verb trans.* Raise or hoist up. **LME–M17.**
S. PURCHAS Three of them stole a horse . . but were therefore horsed on a Gibbet.
5 *verb trans.* Carry on a person's back; lift on someone's back in order to be flogged. *arch.* **M16.**
THACKERAY The biggest boy . . horsed me—and I was flogged.
†**6** *verb trans.* Sit astride, bestride. *rare* (Shakes.). Only in **E17.**
†**7** *verb trans.* **NAUTICAL.** Of a tide or current: carry or sweep along. **L17–E18.**
G. SHELVOCKE We were in eminent danger of being horsed by the current upon two rocks.
8 *verb trans.* Make fun of, ridicule, tease. *US.* **E20.**
9 *verb intrans.* Indulge in horseplay; fool *about* or *around*. Also, be promiscuous, sleep *around*. *colloq.* **E20.**
W. G. HARDY Peter horsed around and ducked Elise and she ducked him. S. KAUFFMANN It isn't as if I didn't love her . . . Then why do I have to go horsing around with dames?

horseback /ˈhɔːsbak/ *noun & adverb.* **LME.**
[**ORIGIN** from **HORSE** *noun* + **BACK** *noun*[1].]
▸ **A** *noun.* **1** A horse's back. Now only in ***on horseback***, (***a***) mounted on a horse; (***b***) on to a horse. **LME.**
LD MACAULAY In an age when even princesses performed their journeys on horseback. OED He had some difficulty in climbing on horseback.
devils on horseback: see **DEVIL** *noun.*
2 **GEOLOGY.** A low sharp ridge of gravel, sand, or rock, *esp.* an esker or kame. *US.* **M19.**
– **COMB.**: **horseback opinion** *US*: given without opportunity to consider the matter; **horseback-riding** (chiefly *N. Amer.*) horse-riding.
▸ **B** *adverb.* On horseback. **E18.**
M. AMSTERDAM I love to ride horseback.

horse chestnut /hɔːs ˈtʃɛsnʌt/ *noun phr.* **L16.**
[**ORIGIN** from **HORSE** *noun* + **CHESTNUT** *noun*, translating mod. Latin †*Castanea equina*: cf. German *Rosskastanie*.]
1 Any of various trees constituting the genus *Aesculus* (family Hippocastanaceae), with large palmate leaves and panicles of white, pink, or red flowers; esp. *A. hippocastanum*, a widely planted tree, native to the Balkans. **L16.**
2 The hard shiny dark brown seed (enclosed in a prickly fruit) of the horse chestnut, resembling that of the sweet chestnut but with a coarse bitter taste. Also called (esp. by children) ***conker***. **E17.**

horseflesh /ˈhɔːsflɛʃ/ *noun.* **LME.**
[**ORIGIN** from **HORSE** *noun* + **FLESH** *noun*.]
1 Horses collectively, esp. with regard to riding, driving, or racing. **LME.**
2 The flesh of a horse, esp. as food. **M16.**
3 In full ***horseflesh mahogany***. The sabicu tree, *Lysiloma latisiliqua*, of the W. Indies; the wood of this tree. **L18.**

horse guard /ˈhɔːs gɑːd/ *noun phr.* Also **horse-guard.** **M17.**
[**ORIGIN** from **HORSE** *noun* + **GUARD** *noun*.]
▸ **I** *gen.* **1** A member of a body of cavalry selected for special guard duties. **M17.**
2 A person or persons set to guard horses. *N. Amer.* **E19.**
▸ **II** *spec.* (With cap. initials.)
3 In *pl.* A cavalry brigade of the British Household troops, the Life Guards and (esp.) Royal Horse Guards (the Blues), now an armoured-car regiment providing a mounted squadron for ceremonial purposes, and merged with the Dragoon Guards in the Household Cavalry Regiment. **M17.**
4 In *pl.* & †*sing.* The headquarters of this brigade in Whitehall, London. **M17.**
5 In *pl.* The personnel of the office of the commander-in-chief of the British army and the military, as opp. to the civil, authorities. Now *arch.* or *hist.* **E19.**

horsehair /ˈhɔːshɛː/ *noun & adjective.* **ME.**
[**ORIGIN** from **HORSE** *noun* + **HAIR** *noun*.]
▸ **A** *noun.* (A strand of) the hair of a horse's mane or tail. **ME.**
▸ **B** *attrib.* or as *adjective.* Of horsehair; stuffed with horsehair. **L18.**
horsehair worm, (*US*) **horsehair snake** a hair worm of the phylum Nematomorpha.

horseless /ˈhɔːslɪs/ *adjective.* **L17.**
[**ORIGIN** from **HORSE** *noun* + **-LESS**.]
Having no horse.
horseless carriage *arch.* a car.

horseman /ˈhɔːsmən/ *noun.* Pl. **-men.** **ME.**
[**ORIGIN** from **HORSE** *noun* + **MAN** *noun*.]
1 A (skilled) rider on horseback. **ME.** ▸**b** A mounted soldier. Now chiefly *hist.* **ME.** ▸**c** A knight. *obsolete* exc. *hist.* **L16.**
JAS. HARRIS These Spanish Arabians . . were great horsemen, and particularly fond of their horses.
b light horseman: see **LIGHT** *adjective*[1].
2 A stableman, a groom. **LME.**
RIDER HAGGARD The agricultural labourer . . works from six to six . . horsemen and cattlemen work longer.
■ **horsemanship** *noun* skill in riding or managing horses **M16.**

H

horse-marine /ˈhɔːsməriːn/ *noun*. **E19**.
[**ORIGIN** from **HORSE** *noun* + **MARINE** *noun*.]
1 In *pl.*, an imaginary corps of mounted marine soldiers (out of their natural element); *sing.* a person unsuited to the work in hand, a landlubber at sea. *joc.* **E19**.
tell that to the horse-marines *colloq.*: indicating incredulity.
2 A person who leads and attends to a barge horse. **M19**.
3 A marine mounted on horseback; a cavalryman doing a marine's work. **L19**.

horsepower /ˈhɔːspaʊə/ *noun*. Pl. same. **E19**.
[**ORIGIN** from **HORSE** *noun* + **POWER** *noun* (from the supposed rate of work of a horse).]
(Power as measured in terms of) a unit of rate of performing work, equivalent to 550 foot-pounds per second, (in the US) 746 watts or about 550 foot-pounds per second.

F. MARRYAT She . . preferred the three-horse power of the schuyt to the hundred-horse power of the steam-packet. *fig.*: R. W. EMERSON Enthusiasm is the leaping lightning, not to be measured by the horse-power of the understanding.

brake horsepower the power available at the shaft of an engine, measurable by means of a brake. **indicated horsepower** the power produced within the cylinders of an engine, as shown by an indicator.

horseradish /ˈhɔːsradɪʃ/ *noun*. **L16**.
[**ORIGIN** from **HORSE** *noun* + **RADISH**.]
A white-flowered cruciferous plant, *Armoracia rusticana*, cultivated for its root; the thick pungent rootstock of this plant, which is scraped or grated as a condiment, and made into a sauce.
– **COMB.**: **horseradish tree** an Indian tree, *Moringa oleifera* (family Moringaceae), with oil-yielding seeds (ben nuts) and a root smelling of horseradish; also called ***drumstick tree***.

horseshoe /ˈhɔːsʃuː, -ʃʃ-/ *noun & adjective*. **ME**.
[**ORIGIN** from **HORSE** *noun* + **SHOE** *noun*.]
▸**A** *noun*. **1** A shoe for a horse, now formed of a narrow band of iron etc. shaped to the outline of the hard part of the hoof and secured by nails driven through the hoof wall. Also, this or a representation of this as a good-luck charm. **ME**. ▸**b** In *pl.* A game resembling quoits in which horseshoes are thrown at a peg. Chiefly *N. Amer.* **E19**.
2 Something shaped like a horseshoe or a circular arc larger than a semicircle. **L15**. ▸**b** *LOGIC*. = **HOOK** *noun* 10d. **E20**.

B. STOKER I read that every known superstition . . is gathered into the horseshoe of the Carpathians. *Road Racer* Spencer leapt away from the flag, and led round the first horseshoe.

3 = ***horseshoe-vetch*** below. Now *rare*. **L16**.
▸**B** *attrib.* or as *adjective*. Having the shape of a horseshoe. **L18**.

M. TWAIN The water cuts the alluvial banks of the 'lower' river into deep horseshoe curves. *Graphic* The delegates took their places . . at a horseshoe table.

– **COMB. & SPECIAL COLLOCATIONS**: **horseshoe bat** any of various mainly tropical Old World bats of the genus *Rhinolophus* and family Rhinolophidae, usu. having a horseshoe-shaped ridge on the nose; **horseshoe crab** any of several large marine arthropods, the only members of the chelicerate class Merostomata (subclass Xiphosura), having a horseshoe-shaped carapace and a long tail spine, *esp.* the N. American *Limulus polyphemus*; a king crab; **horseshoe-vetch** a leguminous plant of calcareous grassland, *Hippocrepis comosa*, with heads of bright yellow flowers and pods breaking into horseshoe-shaped segments.

horse-shoe /ˈhɔːsʃuː, -ʃʃ-/ *verb*. Pres. pple & verbal noun **-shoeing**. **LME**.
[**ORIGIN** Partly from **HORSESHOE**, partly from **HORSE** *noun* + **SHOE** *verb*.]
1 *verb intrans.* Shoe horses; make horseshoes. Chiefly as ***horse-shoeing*** *verbal noun*. **LME**.
2 *verb trans.* Make horseshoe-shaped. *rare*. **M19**.
■ **horse-shoer** *noun* **L16**.

horsetail /ˈhɔːsteɪl/ *noun*. **ME**.
[**ORIGIN** from **HORSE** *noun* + **TAIL** *noun*[1].]
1 The tail of a horse. **ME**. ▸**b** This as formerly used in Turkey as a decoration, a military standard, or a symbol of a pasha's rank. **E17**. ▸**c** A fine strong sewing silk. **L19**. ▸**d** A ponytail; = ***horse's tail*** s.v. **HORSE** *noun*. **M20**.
2 Any of the flowerless plants constituting the nearly worldwide genus *Equisetum* (family Equisetaceae), which are related to the ferns and have hollow jointed grooved stems and leaves reduced to nodal sheaths. **M16**.
rough horsetail: see **ROUGH** *adjective*.

horsewoman /ˈhɔːswʊmən/ *noun*. Pl. **-women** /-wɪmɪn/. **L16**.
[**ORIGIN** from **HORSE** *noun* + **WOMAN** *noun*.]
A (skilled) female rider.
■ **horsewomanship** *noun* a woman's skill in riding or managing horses **M19**.

horsey *noun, adjective* vars. of **HORSIE, HORSY**.

horsfordite /ˈhɔːsfədʌɪt/ *noun*. **L19**.
[**ORIGIN** from E. N. *Horsford* (1818–93), US chemist + **-ITE**[1].]
MINERALOGY. A brittle, silvery-white antimonide of copper.

horsiculture /ˈhɔːsɪkʌltʃə/ *noun*. *derog.* **L20**.
[**ORIGIN** from **HORSE** *noun* + **-CULTURE** after *horticulture*.]
The commercial development of farmland for the pasturing of horses or equestrian activities.

horsie /ˈhɔːsi/ *noun*. Also **horsey**. **E20**.
[**ORIGIN** from **HORSE** *noun* + **-IE**, **-Y**[6].]
A child's word for a horse.

horst /hɔːst/ *noun*. **L19**.
[**ORIGIN** German = heap, mass.]
GEOLOGY. A block of the earth's surface bounded by faults on some or all sides and raised relative to the surrounding land.

Horst Wessel /hɔːst ˈvɛs(ə)l/ *noun phr.* **M20**.
[**ORIGIN** German writer of the words (1907–30).]
More fully ***Horst Wessel Lied***, ***Horst Wessel song***. The official anthem of the German Nazi party.

horsy /ˈhɔːsi/ *adjective*. Also **horsey**. **L16**.
[**ORIGIN** from **HORSE** *noun* + **-Y**[1].]
1 Of, pertaining to, or resembling a horse or horses. **L16**.

X. HERBERT Soon he heard a horsy snort and clink of hobbles.

2 Concerned with or devoted to horses or horse-racing; affecting the dress and language of a groom or jockey. **M19**.

P. LEVI Horsy people and hunting people seem to many of my friends painfully conventional.

3 Of a mare: in heat, ready to mate. **L19**.
■ **horsily** *adverb* **L19**. **horsiness** *noun* **M19**.

hortal /ˈhɔːt(ə)l/ *adjective*. *rare*. **E18**.
[**ORIGIN** from Latin *hortus* garden + **-AL**[1].]
Of a plant: cultivated; of garden origin.

hortation /hɔːˈteɪʃ(ə)n/ *noun*. **M16**.
[**ORIGIN** Latin *hortatio(n-)*, from *hortat-* pa. ppl stem of *hortari* exhort: see **-ATION**.]
Exhortation.

hortative /ˈhɔːtətɪv/ *adjective & noun*. **E17**.
[**ORIGIN** Latin *hortativus*, from *hortat-*: see **HORTATION**, **-IVE**.]
▸**A** *adjective*. Exhortative. **E17**.

J. MCPHEE When he is being pedagogical, the voice goes up . . , and becomes hortative and sharp.

▸**B** *noun*. A hortative speech. **E17**.

hortatory /ˈhɔːtət(ə)ri/ *adjective*. **L16**.
[**ORIGIN** Late Latin *hortatorius*, from *hortat-*: see **HORTATION**, **-ORY**[2].]
Exhortatory.

T. MO The vocabulary . . appears couched imperatively and in a hortatory tone.

hortensia /hɔːˈtɛnsɪə/ *noun*. **L18**.
[**ORIGIN** mod. Latin, from *Hortense*, wife of J.-A. Lepaute (1720–c 1787), French clockmaker.]
A variety of the common hydrangea, *Hydrangea macrophylla*, in which all the flowers are of the sterile showy type.

horti conclusi *noun phr.* pl. of **HORTUS CONCLUSUS**.

horticulture /ˈhɔːtɪkʌltʃə/ *noun*. **L17**.
[**ORIGIN** from Latin *hortus* garden, after **AGRICULTURE**.]
The art of garden cultivation or management.
■ **hortiˈcultural** *adjective* **L18**. **hortiˈculturalist** *noun* = **HORTICULTURIST** **L20**. **hortiˈculturally** *adverb* with regard to horticulture **L19**. **hortiˈculturist** *noun* a gardener, a specialist in horticulture **E19**.

hortulan /ˈhɔːtjʊlən/ *adjective*. Now *rare*. **M17**.
[**ORIGIN** Latin *hortulanus*, from *hortulus* dim. of *hortus* garden: see **-ULE**, **-AN**. Cf. **ORTOLAN**.]
Of or pertaining to a garden or gardening.

hortus conclusus /ˌhɔːtəs kənˈkluːsəs/ *noun phr.* Pl. ***horti conclusi*** /hɔːtʌɪ kənˈkluːsʌɪ, -tiː -siː/. **E17**.
[**ORIGIN** Latin = enclosed garden: see *Song of Solomon* 4:12.]
1 An enclosed inviolate garden; freq., in spiritual and exegetical tradition, as symbolic of the soul, the Christian Church, or the virginity of Mary. **E17**.
2 A painting of the Madonna and Child in an enclosed garden. **M19**.

hortus siccus /ˌhɔːtəs ˈsɪkəs/ *noun phr.* Pl. **horti sicci** /hɔːtʌɪ ˈsɪkʌɪ, -tiː -kiː/. **L17**.
[**ORIGIN** Latin = dry garden.]
An arranged collection of dried plants; *fig.* a collection of uninteresting facts etc.

Hos. *abbreviation*.
Hosea (in the Bible).

hosanna /həʊˈzanə/ *interjection, noun, & verb*. Also **-ah**. **OE**.
[**ORIGIN** Late Latin (h)*osanna* from Greek *hōsanna* from Rabbinic Hebrew *hōšaʿnā*, abbreviation of biblical *hōšīʿā-nnā* save, (we) pray (*Psalms* 118:25).]
▸**A** *interjection*. Appealing for deliverance or praising God, *spec.* in Jewish liturgical or Christian use. **OE**.
▸**B** *noun*. A cry or shout of 'hosanna!'; a shout of praise or adoration. **M17**.
▸**C** *verb trans.* Address, applaud, or escort with cries of 'hosanna!' **L17**.
– **COMB.**: **Hosanna Sunday** *arch.* Palm Sunday.

Hosay /həʊˈzeɪ/ *noun*. **L20**.
[**ORIGIN** Repr. a pronunc. of *Husain*.]
An annual Shiite Muslim festival in the West Indies, commemorating the death of Husain, grandson of Muhammad.

hose /həʊz/ *noun*. Pl. **hose**, (in branch I, *arch.*) **hosen** /ˈhəʊz(ə)n/, (now only in branch II, where usual) **hoses**.
[**ORIGIN** Old English *hosa*, *-e* = Old Saxon, Old High German, Old Norse *hosa* (Dutch *hoos* stocking, water-hose, German *Hose(n)* trousers), from Germanic. In sense 3 prob. from Dutch.]
▸**I** **1** In *pl.* & †*sing.*, an article of clothing for the leg, sometimes also covering the foot. Now *spec.* in *pl.*, stockings. **OE**. ▸**b** *hist.* In *pl.* Covering for the legs forming part of a suit of armour; greaves. **ME**.

H. WILSON Her hose had been laddered.

half-hose: see **HALF-**. ***wear yellow hose***: see **WEAR** *verb*[1].
2 *hist.* In *pl.* Clothing for the legs and groin, breeches. **LME**.
▸**II** **3** A flexible tube or pipe used for the conveyance of water for watering plants, putting out fires, dispersing rioters, etc. **ME**.

B. PYM Dulcie could see her neighbour . . watching her hose watering the lawn.

fire hose, ***water hose***, etc.
4 A sheath or sheathing part; *spec.* the sheath enclosing an ear of corn, the sheath or spathe of an arum. *obsolete* exc. *dial.* **LME**.
†**5** The bag at the lower end of a trawl net etc. **L15–M17**.
6 A socket in a metal tool, golf club, etc., into which a handle or shaft is fitted. **L16**.
– **COMB.**: **hose company** *US* a company in charge of a fire hose; **hose-in-hose** *adjective & noun* (**a**) *adjective* (esp. of a polyanthus or other primula) having a petaloid calyx, and so appearing to have one corolla within another; (**b**) *noun* a flower of this form; **hosenet** (chiefly *Scot.*, now *rare*) a kind of small net; *fig.* a situation from which escape is difficult; **hosepipe** *noun & verb* (**a**) *noun* = sense 3 above; (**b**) *verb trans.* spray with water from a hose.
■ **hoseless** *adjective* **L16**.

H

hose /həʊz/ *verb trans.* **ME**.
[**ORIGIN** from the noun.]
1 Provide with hose or stockings. **ME**.
2 Spray or drench with water etc. from a hose. Also foll. by *down*. **L19**.

H. FAST Jack Harvey had cleaned the deck and hosed it down.

hosel /ˈhəʊz(ə)l/ *noun*. **L16**.
[**ORIGIN** Dim. of **HOSE** *noun*, in the dial. sense 'sheathing'.]
The socket of a golf club head into which the shaft fits.

hosen *noun pl.* see **HOSE** *noun*.

hoser /ˈhəʊzə/ *noun*. *Canad. slang*. **L20**.
[**ORIGIN** Uncertain; perh. from slang *hose* the penis.]
A foolish, uncultivated, or unintelligent person.

hosier /ˈhəʊzɪə/ *noun*. **ME**.
[**ORIGIN** from **HOSE** *noun* + **-IER**.]
A person who makes or deals in hose or stockings, or in these and knitted or woven underwear. Occas. more widely, a men's outfitter, a haberdasher.

hosiery /ˈhəʊzɪəri, -ʒəri/ *noun*. **L18**.
[**ORIGIN** from **HOSE** *noun* + **-ERY**.]
1 Hose collectively; the goods in which a hosier deals. **L18**.
2 The business or trade of a hosier. **L18**.

hospice /ˈhɒspɪs/ *noun*. **E19**.
[**ORIGIN** Old French & mod. French from Latin *hospitium* hospitality, lodging, from *hospes*, *hospit-* **HOST** *noun*[2].]
1 A house of rest and entertainment for travellers or strangers, *esp.* one belonging to a religious order. **E19**.
2 A home for the destitute or sick; *spec.* a nursing home for the care of the dying. **L19**.

hospitable /hɒˈspɪtəb(ə)l, ˈhɒspɪt-/ *adjective*. **L16**.
[**ORIGIN** French, from †*hospiter* receive a guest, from medieval Latin *hospitare*, from Latin *hospit-*, *hospes* **HOST** *noun*[2]: see **-ABLE**.]
1 Offering welcome and entertainment to strangers; extending or disposed to extend a generous hospitality to guests and visitors. **L16**.

E. TEMPLETON The English are very hospitable, they are bound to make you welcome. A. L. ROWSE In Elizabeth Mayer's hospitable house.

2 *transf.* Disposed to receive or welcome something readily, receptive *to*. Also, of an environment: pleasant and favourable for living in. **M17**.

E. SIMPSON I had emerged unscathed. Hospitable to happiness, tenacious in adversity. *Chicago Tribune* Mars itself might be 'terraformed' to make it more hospitable to humans.

■ **hospitableness** *noun* **E17**. **hospitably** *adverb* **E18**.

hospitage /ˈhɒspɪtɪdʒ/ *noun*. *rare*. **L16**.
[**ORIGIN** medieval Latin *hospitagium*, from Latin *hospes*, *hospit-* **HOST** *noun*[2]: see **-AGE**.]
†**1** The position of a guest. Only in **L16**.
†**2** Lodging or entertainment as a guest. Only in **E17**.
3 A place of hospitality. **M19**.

hospital /ˈhɒspɪt(ə)l/ *noun*. **ME**.
[**ORIGIN** Old French (mod. *hôpital*) from medieval Latin *hospitale* use as noun of Latin *hospitalis*: see **HOSPITAL** *adjective*.]
1 *hist.* A house for the reception and entertainment of pilgrims, travellers, or strangers; any of the establishments of the Knights Hospitaller. **ME**.

2 A charitable institution for the housing and maintenance of the needy; an asylum for the destitute, infirm, or aged. Now chiefly in surviving proper names. ME. ▸†**b** *gen.* A place of lodging. Only in **16.** ▸†**c** A house for lodging students in a university; a hostel or hall. M16–E18. ▸**d** A charitable institution for the education etc. of the young. Now only *SCOTS LAW* (*hist.*) and in surviving proper names, (as ***Christ's Hospital***, a public school formerly in London). M16.

3 An institution or establishment providing medical or surgical treatment for the ill or wounded. M16. ▸**b** An establishment for the treatment of sick or injured animals. E17.

cottage hospital, ***eye hospital***, ***general hospital***, ***isolation hospital***, etc. **in hospital**, (*US*) **in the hospital** receiving treatment, *spec.* as an inpatient, at a hospital. ***walk the hospitals***: see WALK *verb*[1].

– COMB.: **hospital ball** = *hospital pass* below; **hospital bed** (*a*) a bed for a patient in a hospital, usu. higher than an ordinary bed to facilitate nursing; (*b*) an available place for an inpatient at a hospital; **hospital blue(s)** the uniform worn by wounded soldiers in the First and Second World Wars; **hospital corners** a way of tucking sheets, used by nurses; **hospital fever** typhus acquired in overcrowded, insanitary conditions in a hospital; **hospital gangrene**: caused by sepsis in a hospital; ***hospital gown***: see GOWN *noun* 4; **hospital pass** in *FOOTBALL* etc., a pass to a player likely to be tackled heavily as soon as it is received; **hospital ship**: to receive sick and wounded seamen, or to take sick and wounded soldiers home; **hospital train**: taking wounded soldiers from a battlefield.

H

†**hospital** *adjective.* LME–E19.

[ORIGIN Latin *hospitalis* hospitable, from *hospes*, *hospit-* HOST *noun*[2]: see -AL[1].]

Hospitable; *spec.* (as an epithet of Jove) protecting the rights of hospitality.

hospitaler *noun* see HOSPITALLER.

hospitalise *verb* var. of HOSPITALIZE.

hospitalism /ˈhɒspɪt(ə)lɪz(ə)m/ *noun.* M19.

[ORIGIN from HOSPITAL *noun* + -ISM.]

The system of medical treatment in hospitals, esp. formerly in overcrowded and unhygienic conditions.

hospitality /hɒspɪˈtalɪti/ *noun.* LME.

[ORIGIN Old French & mod. French *hospitalité* from Latin *hospitalitas*, *-tat-*, from *hospitalis*: see HOSPITAL *adjective*, -ITY.]

1 The act or practice of being hospitable; the reception and entertainment of guests, visitors, or strangers; *transf.* receptiveness to new ideas etc. LME.

P. ROTH Thanks to your hospitality we are getting nicely drunk here.

enjoy Her Majesty's hospitality, **enjoy His Majesty's hospitality** *slang* spend time in prison (in the UK).

†**2** A hospitable institution or foundation; a hospital. M16–M18.

†**3** The quality of being hospitable. Only in E18.

– COMB.: **hospitality room**, **hospitality suite** a room, suite, in a hotel or television studio set aside for the entertainment of guests.

hospitalize /ˈhɒspɪt(ə)lʌɪz/ *verb trans.* Also **-ise**. M17.

[ORIGIN from HOSPITAL *noun* + -IZE.]

Admit to or treat in a hospital.

– NOTE: App. not recorded between M17 and E20.

■ **hospitaliˈzation** *noun* E20.

hospitaller /ˈhɒspɪt(ə)lə/ *noun.* Also *-**aler**. ME.

[ORIGIN Old French *hospitalier* from medieval Latin *hospitalarius* (also *-aris*), from *hospitale*: see HOSPITAL *noun*, -ER[2].]

1 (**H-**.) More fully ***Knight Hospitaller*** (pl. ***Knights Hospitaller***, ***Knights Hospitallers***). A member of a military religious order founded as the Knights of the Hospital of St John at Jerusalem in the 11th cent. Usu. in *pl.*, this order. ME.

2 *gen.* A member of a charitable religious order. LME.

3 In a religious house or hospice, the person with responsibility for receiving and attending to visitors, pilgrims, and strangers. LME.

4 In some London hospitals: formerly, the chief resident official, whose responsibilities included religious superintendence; now, the hospital chaplain. M16.

hospitia *noun* pl. of HOSPITIUM.

†**hospitious** *adjective.* L16–L18.

[ORIGIN from Latin *hospitium* (see HOSPICE) + -OUS.]

Hospitable.

hospitium /hɒˈspɪʃɪəm/ *noun.* Pl. **-tia** /-ʃɪə/. M17.

[ORIGIN Latin: see HOSPICE.]

= HOSPICE 1.

hospodar /ˈhɒspədɑː/ *noun.* Also (as a title) **H-**. L16.

[ORIGIN Romanian *hospodár*, from Ukrainian *hospodár* = Russian *gospodar'*, from *gospod'* lord.]

hist. A lord: *spec.* the title of the former governors of Wallachia and Moldavia under the Ottoman Porte.

hoss /hɒs/ *noun. dial. & US.* E19.

[ORIGIN Repr. a pronunc. of HORSE *noun*.]

A horse.

host /həʊst/ *noun*[1]. ME.

[ORIGIN Old French *(h)ost*, *(h)oost* from Latin *hostis* stranger, enemy, (in medieval Latin) army: cf. GUEST *noun*.]

1 An armed company or multitude of men; an army. Now *arch. & literary.* ME.

C. C. TRENCH Well might Marshal Noailles tremble when he saw the host arranged against him, commanded moreover by the King of England in person.

2 *transf.* A great company; a multitude, a large number, (*of*). LME.

J. T. STORY We've got hosts of primroses. D. ACHESON Two long talks . . on a host of matters of common concern to us both.

– PHRASES: **be a host in oneself** be able to do as much as several ordinary people. **heavenly host**, **host of heaven**, **hosts of heaven** (*a*) in biblical use, the angels that attend on God; (*b*) the sun, the moon, and the stars. **Lord of hosts**, **Lord God of hosts** God as Lord over earthly or heavenly armies.

host /həʊst/ *noun*[2]. ME.

[ORIGIN Old French *(h)oste* (mod. *hôte*) from Latin *hospis*, *hospit-* host, prob. from *hostis*: see HOST *noun*[1].]

▸ **I 1** A person who lodges or receives and entertains another as a guest, esp. in his or her own home; a compère or presenter of a television programme. ME.

DAY LEWIS I feel more at home as a guest than as a host. P. F. BOLLER For eight years he acted as host and occasional star of . . a half-hour TV series.

2 A person who lodges or entertains another for payment; a person who keeps a lodging house; the landlord or landlady of an inn or public house. ME. ▸**b** The presenter of a television or radio programme. M20.

W. HOLTBY These might be the new host and hostess of the Nag's Head. **b** TONY PARSONS I thought you once told me that it was good television if the guest attacked the host.

mine host the landlord or landlady of an inn or public house. **reckon without one's host** neglect a difficulty, opposition, etc.

3 *BIOLOGY.* An animal or plant on or in which a parasite or commensal organism lives. M19.

4 a *GEOLOGY.* The rock or mineral mass of which a distinct substance such as an ore is a minor component. L19. ▸**b** *PHYSICS & CHEMISTRY.* A crystal lattice or molecular structure that contains a foreign ion, atom, or molecule. M20.

5 *BIOLOGY & MEDICINE.* An animal or person that is the recipient of tissue transplanted from another. E20.

6 In full ***host computer***. A computer which mediates (usu. multiple) access to databases mounted on it or provides other services to a computer network. M20.

▸ **II 7** A guest. Long *obsolete* exc. in HOASTMAN & in ***host-house*** (dial.), an inn, a hostelry. ME.

■ **hostless** *adjective* (*rare*) without a host; inhospitable: L16.

host /həʊst/ *noun*[3]. ME.

[ORIGIN Old French *(h)oiste* from Latin *hostia* sacrificial animal, victim, (in late Latin) eucharistic sacrifice. Cf. HOSTIE *noun*[1].]

†**1** A sacrificial victim; a sacrifice, *spec.* with reference to Christ. ME–M17.

2 *ECCLESIASTICAL.* The bread consecrated in the Eucharist regarded as the body of Christ sacrificially offered; a wafer before or after consecration. ME.

†**host** *noun*[4]. LME–L16.

[ORIGIN Perh. from Old French *(h)osté* var. of *(h)ostel* HOSTEL *noun*.]

A place of lodging, an inn.

at host put up at an inn.

host /həʊst/ *verb*[1]. ME.

[ORIGIN from HOST *noun*[1].]

1 *verb trans.* Gather into a host; assemble in battle array, encamp. Long *obsolete* exc. as HOSTING. ME.

†**2** *verb intrans.* Be assembled or gather in a host. LME–L18.

host /həʊst/ *verb*[2]. LME.

[ORIGIN from HOST *noun*[2].]

▸ **I 1** *verb trans.* **a** Receive (a person) into one's house, town, or country and entertain as a guest. LME. ▸**b** Be host at (a party, dinner, etc.); compère or present (a television programme etc.). M20.

a *John o' London's* A sense of deep and humble respect for the people and the country who had hosted them. **b** S. BRETT Alexander Harvey hosted the most successful chat-show in the country. D. DELILLO David was hosting a . . party at his house.

2 *verb intrans.* Play the host, be host. M19.

Time Critic John Crosby . . will host.

▸ †**II 3** *verb intrans.* Be a guest; lodge. LME–M17.

hosta /ˈhɒstə/ *noun.* E19.

[ORIGIN mod. Latin, from N. T. *Host* (1761–1834), Austrian physician: see -A[1].]

Any plant of the east Asian genus *Hosta* (family Agavaceae), comprising lily-like plants widely cultivated for their broad often variegated leaves. Also called ***plantain lily***.

hostage /ˈhɒstɪdʒ/ *noun*[1]. ME.

[ORIGIN Old French & mod. French *(h)ostage* (now *otage*) from Proto-Romance, from late Latin *obsidiatus* hostageship, from *obses*, *obsid-* hostage, from *ob* OB- + base of *sedere* sit: see -AGE.]

†**1** (The state of a person or persons handed over in) pledge or security for fulfilment of an undertaking. Chiefly in ***in hostage***, ***into hostage***, ***to hostage***. ME–E18.

2 A person given or seized and held as a pledge or security for fulfilment of an undertaking or imposed condition. ME.

M. PUZO Maybe Sollozzo figures to snatch you and hold you for a hostage to make a deal. J. CLAVELL Toranaga's war had begun when he was six and had been ordered as hostage into the enemy camp.

hold hostage hold as a hostage (*lit. & fig.*).

3 A pledge, a security. ME.

hostage to fortune an acquisition, commitment, etc., regarded as endangered by unforeseen circumstances.

■ **hostageship** *noun* the condition of being a hostage M19.

†**hostage** *noun*[2]. LME–M19.

[ORIGIN Old French *(h)ostage*, formed as HOST *noun*[2] + -AGE.]

A hotel, a hostelry, an inn.

hostel /ˈhɒst(ə)l/ *noun.* ME.

[ORIGIN Old French *(h)ostel* (mod. *hôtel* HOTEL) from medieval Latin *hospitale* HOSPITAL *noun*.]

†**1** A place to stay; a lodging. ME–E17.

†**2** Lodging, entertainment. Only in ME.

3 A public house of lodging and entertainment for strangers and travellers; an inn, a hotel. *arch.* ME. ▸**b** A youth hostel. E20.

CONAN DOYLE After we had deposited our suit-cases at the ancient hostel.

4 A house of residence for students at a university or on a course, esp. at a non-residential college, or for some other special class of people. M16.

C. HOPE The nearby hostel for homeless boys.

†**5** A town mansion. L16–L17.

hostel /ˈhɒst(ə)l/ *verb.* Infl. **-ll-**, ***-l-**. ME.

[ORIGIN from the noun.]

†**1** *verb trans.* Provide with lodging. Only in ME.

2 *verb intrans.* Lodge (*at*). Long *obsolete* exc. *dial.* ME.

3 *verb intrans.* Lodge at youth hostels, take a holiday lodging at youth hostels. Chiefly as ***hostelling*** *verbal noun.* M20.

hosteler /ˈhɒst(ə)lə/ *noun.* Also (esp. in sense 5) **-eller**. See also HOSTLER. ME.

[ORIGIN Anglo-Norman, = Old French *(h)ostelier* (mod. *hôtelier*), formed as HOSTEL *verb*: see -ER[2]. In sense 5 from HOSTEL *noun* or *verb* + -ER[1].]

1 A person who receives, lodges, or entertains guests and strangers, esp. in a religious house or monastery. *obsolete* exc. *hist.* ME.

2 A keeper of a hostelry or inn; an innkeeper. *arch.* LME.

†**3** An ostler. LME–L15.

†**4** A student who lives in a hostel. L16–M17.

5 A person who stays in a youth hostel; a person youth-hostelling. Also ***youth-hosteler***. M20.

hostelry /ˈhɒst(ə)lri/ *noun.* LME.

[ORIGIN Old French *(h)ostelerie* (mod. *hôtellerie*), from *(h)ostelier*: see HOSTELER, -ERY.]

1 A house where lodging and entertainment are provided; an inn, a hostel. Now *arch.* or *literary.* LME.

2 The business of a hostel. *rare.* L16.

hostess /ˈhəʊstɪs, -ɛs, həʊˈstɛs/ *noun & verb.* ME.

[ORIGIN Old French *(h)ostesse* (mod. *hôtesse*), from *(h)oste* HOST *noun*[2]: see -ESS[1].]

▸ **A** *noun.* **1** A woman who lodges or entertains guests; a woman who acts as a host. ME.

Radio Times The BBC was looking for two hostess-announcers for television. S. SPENDER She was a great hostess and patroness.

2 A woman who keeps a public place of lodging and entertainment; the landlady of an inn or public house. ME.

3 A woman employed to entertain customers at a nightclub etc.; *euphem.* a prostitute. M20.

4 A woman employed to attend to passengers on an aircraft (also ***air hostess***), train, etc. M20.

– COMB.: **hostess apron**, **hostess dress**, **hostess pyjamas**, etc.: suitable for wearing to receive guests; **hostess trolley**: for holding (and keeping hot) food to be served at table.

▸ **B** *verb intrans. & trans.* Be the hostess of (a party etc.); act as hostess (at). E20.

■ **hostessy** *adjective* pertaining to or typical of a hostess; hospitable: M20.

hostie /ˈhəʊsti/ *noun*[1]. Now *arch. rare.* L15.

[ORIGIN Old French & mod. French from Latin *hostia*: see HOST *noun*[3].]

†**1** = HOST *noun*[3] 1. L15–L17.

2 = HOST *noun*[3] 2. L16.

hostie /ˈhəʊsti/ *noun*[2]. *Austral. & NZ colloq.* M20.

[ORIGIN from HOSTESS: see -IE.]

A hostess; *spec.* an air hostess.

hostile /ˈhɒstʌɪl/ *adjective & noun.* L16.

[ORIGIN French, or Latin *hostilis*, from *hostis* stranger, enemy: see -ILE.]

▸ **A** *adjective.* **1** Of or pertaining to an enemy; pertaining to or engaged in hostilities. L16.

POPE Thus . . from the din of war, Safe he return'd without one hostile scar. WELLINGTON The operations of hostile armies.

2 Of the nature or disposition of an enemy; unfriendly, antagonistic. L16. ▸**b** Angry. *Austral. & NZ colloq.* M20.

J. STEINBECK Her hostile eyes glared at him. E. ROOSEVELT Their questions were so hostile as to give the impression that the witness had been . . prejudged a criminal. E. FEINSTEIN No good writer could be hostile to the Revolution.

hostile witness *LAW* a witness who is (contrary to the usual practice) allowed to be asked leading questions in the nature of cross-examination.

3 Of a thing: contrary, adverse, opposed, (*to*). E19. ▸**b** Of a takeover bid: liable to be opposed by the management of the target company. L20.

W. LIPPMANN As industrial organization becomes bigger, it must become more inflexible, until . . it is hostile to invention, enterprise, competition, and change.

▸ **B** *noun.* A hostile person; *spec.* (*US HISTORY*) a N. American Indian unfriendly to settlers. M19.

■ **hostilely** *adverb* E17.

hostilise *verb* var. of HOSTILIZE.

hostility /hɒˈstɪlɪti/ *noun.* LME.

[ORIGIN French *hostilité* or late Latin *hostilitas*, from *hostilis*: see HOSTILE, -ITY.]

1 The state of being hostile; hostile action exercised by one community, state, or power against another, *esp.* war; (a feeling of) unfriendliness, antagonism, or opposition. LME.

N. MOSLEY His first wife . . had suffered much public hostility due to his politics. *New Republic* Nor does the new openness to religion signify a hostility to science.

2 In *pl.* Hostile acts, *spec.* acts of war. E17.

L. STRACHEY Victoria's martial ardour was not to be side-tracked by hostilities against Lord Derby; hostilities against Russia were what she wanted.

hostilize /ˈhɒstɪlʌɪz/ *verb trans. rare.* Also **-ise**. L18.

[ORIGIN from HOSTILE *adjective* + -IZE.]

Make hostile. Chiefly as ***hostilized*** *ppl adjective.*

hosting /ˈhəʊstɪŋ/ *noun. obsolete* exc. *hist.* LME.

[ORIGIN from HOST *verb*[1] + -ING[1].]

The raising of a host or armed multitude, hostile encounter or array; a military expedition, esp. in Ireland.

hostler /ˈ(h)ɒslə/ *noun.* See also OSTLER. LME.

[ORIGIN Syncopated form of HOSTELER.]

1 = OSTLER. LME.

2 A person in charge of locomotives when not in use. *US.* L19.

†**hostry** *noun.* LME–L19.

[ORIGIN Old French *host(e)rie*, formed as HOST *noun*[2]: see -ERY.]

= HOSTELRY.

hot /hɒt/ *noun*[1]. *obsolete* exc. *dial.* Also **hott**, (branch II) †**hutt**. ME.

[ORIGIN Old French & mod. French *hotte*, prob. of Germanic origin: cf. HOD *noun*. Branch II may be a different word.]

▸ **I 1** A kind of basket for carrying earth, sand, lime, manure, etc. *N. English.* ME.

2 A small heap (of dust, sand, etc.). *Scot. & N. English.* E18.

▸ **II** †**3** A padded sheath for the spur of a fighting cock. E17–E19.

hot /hɒt/ *noun*[2]. ME.

[ORIGIN Absol. use of HOT *adjective.*]

1 a Hot condition, heat. Now only (*dial.*), a spell of hot weather. ME. ▸**b** ***walk hots***, lead a horse around to cool it down after a race or exercise. M20.

2 Hot water. Chiefly in ***hot and cold***. E20.

3 ***the hots***, a strong sexual desire. Esp. in ***have the hots for***. *slang.* M20.

hot /hɒt/ *adjective.* Compar. & superl. **-tt-**.

[ORIGIN Old English *hāt* = Old Frisian, Old Saxon *hēt* (Dutch *heet*), Old High German *heiz* (German *heiss*), Old Norse *heitr*, from Germanic.]

1 Having or giving out a high degree of heat; of or at a high temperature, very warm. OE. ▸**b** (Of food or drink) prepared by heating and consumed before it has time to cool; *fig.* recent, fresh in people's minds. ME. ▸**c** Of metal, esp. iron: sufficiently high above melting point to flow readily. L19. ▸**d** At a high voltage, live. E20. ▸**e** Radioactive. Also, (of an atom, molecule, etc.) possessing extra energy in some form (nuclear, electronic, vibrational, etc.); excited. *colloq.* M20.

J. CONRAD A grey rock which smokes like a hot cinder after a shower. J. STEINBECK The hot sun beat on the earth. DAY LEWIS We were there during the phenomenally hot July of 1911. **b** E. O'BRIEN He had brought her some croissants hot from the oven.

2 *hist.* Designating a quality associated with heat and regarded in medieval and later times as one of the four qualities inherent in all things. Cf. ***cold***, ***dry***, ***moist***. OE.

3 At a high emotional pitch; *esp.* enthusiastic (*for*), keen (*on*). Also, following closely in pursuit. OE. ▸**b** Lustful, amorous, sexually aroused. Of a book, play, etc.: erotic, salacious. ME. ▸**c** Very angry, indignant. Also = ***hot-tempered*** below. ME.

R. BRAUTIGAN He ran around the house, . . with the dog hot after him. E. JONG 'Why are you a feminist?' I . . asked a guy . . who is very hot for the movement. JILLY COOPER The middle classes are obsessively hot on table manners. **b** F. M. COLBY A hot young satyr in pursuit of nymphs. *Music Week* No 'hot' videos required. **c** T. MORRISON More words were exchanged, hot words and dark.

4 Attended with feverish or violent exertion; (of a contest, debate, etc.) fiercely contested, intense. Formerly also, of an epidemic: raging violently. OE.

DEFOE The Plague grows hot in the City. A. BURGESS The Stage Society was able, after months of hot argument, to agree.

5 Producing an effect as of heat or burning, esp. on the nerves of taste or on the mucous membrane; pungent, biting, acrid. ME.

H. DAY I had some curry . . which was so hot that it well nigh took the skin off my tongue.

6 a Feeling an uncomfortable sensation of heat. Usu. *pred.* LME. ▸**b** Producing or accompanied by (excessive) sensations of heat. M16.

a C. PHILLIPS He began to feel hot as the climb became harder. **b** J. PURCELL Violent Hot Pains in the Lower-Belly. A. SILLITOE His uniform was too hot, and he unbuttoned the tunic.

7 Difficult or awkward to deal with; *spec.* (***a***) (of circumstances, a situation) uncomfortable, dangerous; (***b***) (of a hit, return, etc., in a ball game) difficult for an opponent to cope with; (***c***) *criminals' slang* (of property) stolen and hard to dispose of because easily identifiable; (of a person) wanted by the police; (***d***) (orig. *US*) (of goods, an area of work, etc.) affected by a trade-union dispute. E17.

G. F. KENNAN The place was well selected from the standpoint of making a getaway if things became hotter.

8 a *HUNTING.* Of a scent: fresh, strong, intense. M17. ▸**b** Of a participant in a children's seeking or guessing game: very close to finding or guessing what is sought. L19.

9 Of a shade of colour: (unpleasantly) intense. E19.

C. MCCULLERS His socks and tie were a hot red.

10 Exceptionally good, skilful, or successful. Freq. in neg. contexts. *colloq.* L19.

Daily Express The Deutsches have some pretty hot snipers. W. BOYD A pair of opera glasses . . that I use to see better—my eyesight's not too hot.

11 a *RACING.* Of a favourite: strongly fancied. *slang.* L19. ▸**b** Currently popular or in demand. M20.

b *Standard* Eddie Murphy has firmly established himself as America's hottest box office comedian. *Hairdo Ideas* One of the hottest trends this season are hair extensions.

12 a Of information etc.: completely new; *esp.* novel and exciting. E20. ▸**b** Of a Treasury note: just issued. E20.

a B. SCHULBERG The idea is so hot I don't want to give anybody time to steal it. N. BARBER If you get onto something hot . . phone me.

13 Of jazz etc.: strongly rhythmic and emotional. Opp. COOL *adjective* 5. Orig. *US.* E20.

14 Of a vehicle: fast or powerful, esp. in relation to its size. *colloq.* M20.

– PHRASES ETC.: **a bit hot** *Austral. slang* somewhat unreasonable. ***blow hot and cold***: see BLOW *verb*[1]. ***boiling hot***: see BOILING *adverb*. ***get it hot (and strong)***: see GET *verb*. ***give it hot to***, ***give it hot and strong to***: see GIVE *verb*. **go hot and cold** feel alternately hot and cold owing to fear etc. **hot and bothered** in a state of exasperated agitation. **hot and hot** *arch.* (of food) served piping hot. ***hot dark matter***: see ***dark matter*** s.v. DARK *adjective*. **hot on the heels of** in close pursuit of. **hot to trot** ready and eager to engage in an activity. **hot under the collar** feeling anger, resentment, or embarrassment. ***like a cat on hot bricks***: see CAT *noun*[1]. **not so hot**, **not too hot** *colloq.* only mediocre, indifferent in performance, health, etc. ***piping hot***: see PIPING *adverb*. ***red-hot***: see RED *adjective*. **too hot to hold one** (of a place) not safe to remain in (because of past misconduct etc.). ***white-hot***: see WHITE *adjective*.

– SPECIAL COLLOCATIONS & COMB.: **hot air** *fig.* (*colloq.*) pretentious or unsubstantial statements or claims. **hot-air** *adjective* of or making use of heated air (esp. in ***hot-air balloon***). **hot bath**: in hot water. **hot blast**: of heated air forced into a furnace. **hot-blooded** *adjective* ardent, passionate. **hot bottle** = ***hot-water bottle*** below. **hotbrain** *arch.* = HOTHEAD. **hot-brained** *adjective* (*arch.*) = HOT-HEADED. **hot button** *US colloq.* (***a***) an emotionally or politically sensitive topic or issue; (***b***) a commercially attractive feature of a new product. **hot cake** (***a***) *US* a griddle cake; (***b***) ***go like hot cakes***, ***sell like hot cakes***, be sold extremely fast, be a popular commodity. **hot cathode**: heated to emit electrons thermionically. ***hot chisel***: see CHISEL *noun*[1] 1. **hot cockles** (*obsolete* exc. *dial.*) a rustic game in which one player is blindfolded and has to guess which of the others struck him or her. ***hot coppers***: see COPPER *noun*[1] 6. ***hot cross bun***: see CROSS-. **hot cupboard** an airing cupboard; a cupboard in which crockery is made warm for a meal. **hot-desking** the practice in an office of allocating desks to workers when they are required or on a rota system, rather than giving workers their own desks. **hot-dipped** *adjective* coated in metal, either by being dipped in the molten metal or by being dipped hot in a bath of liquid. **hot flash**, **hot flush** a feeling of feverish heat, esp. as a menopausal symptom. ***hot gospeller***: see GOSPELLER. **hot key** *COMPUTING*: that initiates a complex operation. **hot laboratory**: designed for the safe handling of radioactive material. **hotline** a direct exclusive telecommunications link, esp. for use by heads of government in emergencies. **hot-link** *noun & verb* (*COMPUTING*) (***a***) *noun* a connection between documents or applications, which enables material from one source to be incorporated into another (*spec.* one providing for automatic updating); a hypertext link; (***b***) *verb trans.* connect (two documents) by means of a hot-link. **hotlist** (***a***) a list of stolen items or of persons who have committed an offence; (***b***) a list of important, popular, or favourite things. **hot-metal** *adjective* (*PRINTING*, chiefly *hist.*) using metal type or slugs cast by a (Linotype, Monotype, etc.) composing machine. **hot money** capital transferred from one country to another for the sake of high interest rates or to avoid the effects of currency devaluation. **hot pants** (***a***) *US slang* an uncontrollable sexual passion (esp. in ***have hot pants for***, ***have got hot pants for***); (***b***) *slang* a sexually insatiable person; (***c***) brief shorts worn by young women, esp. as a fashion in the early 1970s. **hotplate** (***a***) a heated flat surface on a stove or electric cooker; (***b***) a low flat-topped portable device for keeping food warm. ***hot potato***: see POTATO *noun*. **hot-press** *noun & verb* (***a***) *noun* a press of glazed boards and hot metal plates for smoothing paper or cloth or making plywood; (***b***) *verb trans.* press (paper etc.) in a hot-press. **hot-presser** a person who hot-presses paper etc. **hot pursuit** close pursuit, *spec.* of a criminal etc. across an international frontier. **hot rod** (***a***) a motor vehicle specially modified to give high power and speed; (***b***) = ***hot-rodder*** below. **hot-rod** *verb intrans.* drive a hot rod. **hot-rodder** a driver of a hot rod. **hot seat** *slang* (***a***) *US* the electric chair; (***b***) *fig.* a position of difficult responsibility. ***hot shoe***: see SHOE *noun*. **hot-short** *adjective* (of metal) brittle in its hot state (opp. ***cold-short*** *adjective*). **hot-shortness** hot-short quality or condition. **hot shower**: in hot water. **hot spot** (***a***) a small area in a surface or body that is at a higher temperature than its surroundings; (***b***) a lively nightclub; (***c***) a place of danger or military activity; (***d***) a place in a public building that is equipped with a device enabling computer users to make a wireless connection to the Internet. **hot spring** a spring of naturally hot water. **hot-stove** *adjective* (*N. Amer.*) designating a discussion about a favourite sport, esp. baseball, carried on during the off season. **hot stuff** (***a***) sexually explicit material; (***b***) (a designation of) a woman reputed to be highly sexed; (***c***) (a designation of) a person or thing of outstanding quality. **hot tap**: dispensing hot water. **hot tear** *METALLURGY* a split produced in a casting as the hot metal cools. **hot-tempered** *adjective* impulsively angry, short-tempered. **hot ticket** *colloq.* a person or thing that is much in demand. **hot tip** *colloq.* an unusually reliable tip for the winner of a race etc. **hot tub** a wooden tub, freq. accommodating several people, filled with hot aerated water for recreation or physical therapy. **hot tube** in some early internal-combustion engines, a closed tube which projected from the cylinder and was heated externally by a flame, so that it ignited the mixture forced into it during the compression stroke. **hot war** an open war, involving active hostilities. **hot water** *fig.* (*colloq.*) trouble, difficulty (chiefly in ***in hot water***, ***into hot water***). **hot-water** *adjective* using or containing heated water; ***hot-water bottle***, (*US*) ***hot-water bag***, a container, now usu. made of rubber, filled with hot water, esp. to warm a bed. **hot well** (***a***) = ***hot spring*** above; (***b***) a reservoir in a condensing steam engine. **hot wind**: heated by passing over plains or prairies. **hot-wire** *adjective* operated by the expansion of heated wire. **hot-work** *verb trans.* work (metal), e.g. by rolling, forging, etc., while it is still hot and above the temperature at which recrystallization takes place.

■ **hotly** *adverb* LME. **hotness** *noun* M16. **hottish** *adjective* L16.

hot /hɒt/ *verb.* Infl. **-tt-**.

[ORIGIN Old English *hātian*, from *hāt* HOT *adjective*: later formed afresh from the adjective.]

1 *verb intrans.* Become hot or (*fig.*) intense, lively, dangerous, etc. Now only foll. by *up*. OE.

E. MANNIN Immediately the day hotted up with the return of the sun. *Guardian* The . . takeover battle for control of John Waddington will hot up this week.

2 *verb trans.* Make (esp. precooked food) hot; heat, warm up. Now usu. foll. by *up*. Now *colloq.* ME.

J. GALSWORTHY Let me hot up your stew.

3 *verb trans.* Foll. by *up*: make intense, lively, (unpleasantly) exciting, etc. E20.

J. CAREW The drummerboys hotted up the rhythm. *Guardian* The need to avoid actions which would 'hot up this cod war'.

4 a *verb trans.* Increase the power of (a car, engine, etc.) so that it is capable of higher speeds. Usu. in *pass.* E20. ▸**b** *verb intrans.* Drive recklessly in a stolen car. Chiefly as ***hotting*** *verbal noun.* L20.

– NOTE: Sense 1 long obsolete before reintroduction in 20.

hot /hɒt/ *adverb.*

[ORIGIN Old English *hāte* = Old Saxon *hēto*, Old High German *heizo*: afterwards levelled with the adjective.]

Hotly; with or to great heat; eagerly, violently, angrily, etc.

SHAKES. *3 Hen. VI* The sun shines hot. BYRON Fast and hot Against them pour'd the ceaseless shot.

hotbed /ˈhɒtbɛd/ *noun.* E17.

[ORIGIN from HOT *adjective* + BED *noun*.]

1 A bed of earth heated by fermented manure, for raising or forcing plants. E17.

2 *fig.* A place that favours the rapid growth of a (usu. undesirable) condition etc. M18.

M. COX The monasteries were not hotbeds of crime and luxury.

3 A bed in a dosshouse etc. which is slept in by two or more people in shifts; a dosshouse. *US slang.* M20.

hotch /hɒtʃ/ *verb & noun. Scot. & N. English.* LME.

[ORIGIN Corresp. to Dutch *hotsen*, *hossen* to jog, to jolt, Middle High German (German dial.) *hotzen* move up and down.]

▸ **A** *verb.* **1** *verb intrans.* Jerk up and down; move forward in short leaps. Also, move impatiently, fidget. LME.

H

2 *verb intrans.* Swarm (*with*). **L18.**

A. GRAY These nights the sky was just hotching with stars.

3 *verb trans.* Shake with a jerky motion. **E19.**
▸**B** *noun.* A jerk, a jolt. **E18.**

hotcha /ˈhɒtʃə/ *adjective. slang* (now *rare*). **M20.**
[ORIGIN Fanciful extension of HOT *adjective*.]
1 (Sexually) attractive. Also as *interjection*, expr. enthusiastic approval. **M20.**
2 = HOT *adjective* 13. **M20.**

Hotchkiss /ˈhɒtʃkɪs/ *adjective.* **L19.**
[ORIGIN B. B. *Hotchkiss* (1826–85), US inventor.]
Designating a revolving cannon, types of rifle, etc., invented by B. B. Hotchkiss, and a machine gun developed by his successors.

hotchpot /ˈhɒtʃpɒt/ *noun & adjective.* **LME.**
[ORIGIN Anglo-Norman, Old French & mod. French *hochepot*, from *hocher* to shake, prob. from Low German, + POT *noun*[1]. Cf. HOTCHPOTCH, HODGEPODGE.]
▸**A** *noun.* **1** = HOTCHPOTCH *noun* 1. **LME.**
2 = HOTCHPOTCH *noun* 2. **LME.**
3 ENGLISH LAW. The bringing together of properties in order to secure equality of division, esp. as practised in certain cases in the distribution of the property of an intestate parent. **M16.**
▸**B** *attrib.* or as *adjective.* = HOTCHPOTCH *adjective.* **L16.**

hotchpotch /ˈhɒtʃpɒtʃ/ *noun, adjective, & verb.* **LME.**
[ORIGIN Alt., by rhyming assim., of HOTCHPOT. Cf. HODGEPODGE *noun*.]
▸**A** *noun.* **1** A mixture of heterogeneous things, a confused medley. **LME.**

H. CARPENTER This final fantasy, with its .. hotchpotch of gnostic religions and sinister folklore.

2 A dish containing a number of different ingredients; *spec.* a mixed stew, esp. of mutton and various vegetables. **L16.**
3 = HOTCHPOT *noun* 3. **E17.**
▸**B** *attrib.* or as *adjective.* Of the nature or composition of a hotchpotch; heterogeneous, confused, disorderly. **L16.**
▸**C** *verb trans.* Make a hotchpotch of, mix up. **L16.**

hot dog /ˈhɒt dɒg/ *adjectival & noun phr.* Also **hot-dog**. **L19.**
[ORIGIN from HOT *adjective* + DOG *noun*.]
▸**A** *adjectival phr.* Outstandingly good, first-rate. Also as *interjection*, expr. delighted approval. *N. Amer. slang.* **L19.**
▸**B** *noun phr.* **1** A person outstandingly proficient in a sport etc., *esp.* one who gives a flamboyant display of his or her skill. *N. Amer. slang.* **E20.**
2 A hot frankfurter sandwiched in a soft roll. **E20.**

hotel /həʊˈtɛl, əʊ-/ *noun.* **M17.**
[ORIGIN French *hôtel*, later form of *hostel*: see HOSTEL *noun*.]
1 In France and French-speaking countries: ▸**a** ***hotel-Dieu*** /djø/, a hospital. **M17.** ▸**b** ***hotel de ville*** /də vil/, a town hall. **M18.** ▸**c** ***hotel garni*** /garni/, a lodging house providing bed and breakfast only; also, a furnished apartment. **L18.** ▸**d** ***hotel particulier*** /partikylje/, a large privately owned town house or block of flats. **M20.**
2 A large town mansion of an (orig. French) aristocrat or person of position. Now only *hist.* & in names of surviving mansions. **L17.**
3 An establishment, esp. of a comfortable or luxurious kind, where paying visitors are provided with accommodation, meals, and other services. **M18.**
family hotel, ***private hotel***, ***residential hotel***, ***temperance hotel***, etc.
4 A public house or other place serving alcoholic drink. *Canad., Austral., & NZ colloq.* **E19.**
■ **hoteldom** *noun* the world of hotels **E20.** **hotelling** *noun* the short-term provision of office space to a temporary employee, a consultant, etc.; short-term letting of surplus office space to employees from other companies: **L20.**

hotelier /həʊˈtɛlɪeɪ, -ɪə/ *noun.* **E20.**
[ORIGIN French *hôtelier*: see HOSTELER.]
A person who owns or runs a hotel or group of hotels.

hotfoot /ˈhɒtfʊt/ *noun.* **M19.**
[ORIGIN Sense 1 from the adverb. Sense 2 from HOT *adjective* + FOOT *noun*.]
1 Prompt or rapid action or movement; a quick escape. Chiefly in ***do a hotfoot***, ***give the hotfoot to***. *US slang.* **M19.**
2 An act of beating a person on the bare soles or of inserting a lighted match between the soles and uppers of the shoes, either to rouse from sleep or (in the latter case) as a practical joke. **E20.**

hotfoot /ˈhɒtfʊt, hɒtˈfʊt/ *adverb, verb, & adjective.* **ME.**
[ORIGIN from HOT *adjective* + FOOT *noun*.]
▸**A** *adverb.* With eager or rapid pace; in great haste. **ME.**
▸**B** *verb intrans. & trans.* (with *it*). Go hotfoot, hasten. **L19.**
▸**C** *adjective.* Travelling hotfoot or in haste. **E20.**

hothead /ˈhɒthɛd/ *noun.* **M17.**
[ORIGIN from HOT *adjective* + HEAD *noun*.]
A hot-headed person.

hot-headed /hɒtˈhɛdɪd/ *adjective.* **M17.**
[ORIGIN from HOT *adjective* + HEAD *noun* + -ED[2].]
Having an impetuous or fiery temperament; impulsive, headstrong.
■ **hot-headedly** *adverb* **L19.** **hot-headedness** *noun* **M19.**

hothouse /ˈhɒthaʊs/ *noun, adjective, & verb.* **E16.**
[ORIGIN from HOT *adjective* + HOUSE *noun*[1].]
▸**A** *noun.* †**1** A bathhouse with hot baths, vapour baths, etc. Also, a brothel. **E16–M18.**
2 A heated chamber or building for drying something. **M16.**
†**3** A hospital for slaves etc. on a plantation. *W. Indian.* **E18–M19.**
4 A heated building with a glass roof and sides for growing plants out of season or in a colder climate. **M18.**
▸**B** *adjective.* Characteristic of or raised in a hothouse. Freq. *fig.*, tender from overprotection; excessively artificial. **E19.**

J. S. MILL Modern German art .. appears to me a feeble, hot-house product. *Listener* Opera will never cease to be a hothouse plant in this country.

▸**C** *verb trans.* Raise (as) in a hothouse; raise in an artificial environment; force the development of. **M19.**

A. S. NEILL Every child has been hothoused into an adult long before he has reached adulthood.

†**hoti** *noun.* Pl. **hoties**. **M17.**
[ORIGIN Greek = that, because.]
1 = DIOTI. Only in **M17.**
2 A statement of fact, a thing asserted. **M17–M18.**

Hotnot /ˈhɒtnɒt/ *noun. S. Afr. slang* (*derog. & offensive*). **E20.**
[ORIGIN Afrikaans & Dutch, contr. of HOTTENTOT.]
A coloured person (COLOURED *adjective* 4b).

hotpot /ˈhɒtpɒt/ *noun.* **L17.**
[ORIGIN from HOT *adjective* + POT *noun*[1].]
1 A hot drink composed of ale and spirits, or ale sweetened and spiced. *dial.* **L17.**
2 A stew of meat or fish and potatoes (and often other vegetables). Also, a Chinese, Mongolian, etc. dish consisting of thinly sliced meat, vegetables, etc., dipped in boiling soup by the diner. **M19.**
Lancashire hotpot, ***Mongolian hotpot***.

hotshot /ˈhɒtʃɒt/ *noun & adjective.* **L16.**
[ORIGIN from HOT *adjective* + SHOT *noun*[1].]
▸**A** *noun.* †**1** A reckless shooter with a firearm; a hothead. **L16–M17.**
†**2** A ball of clay and coal, used as fuel. Also, a type of incendiary shell or bomb. **L17–L19.**
3 A fast or express goods train; a fast motor vehicle, aeroplane, etc. *US slang.* **E20.**
4 An important or exceptionally able person; a person who has gained sudden prominence. *colloq.* **M20.**

S. BELLOW He's on the make everywhere and cultivates all the Chicago hot-shots. *Globe & Mail (Toronto)* He wasn't a showoff and didn't perceive himself to be a hotshot.

5 An exceptionally good shot or aim in a sport, as snooker, basketball, etc. *colloq.* **M20.**
▸**B** *attrib.* or as *adjective.* **1** Of a goods train etc.: fast, express, non-stop. *US slang.* **M20.**
2 Important; expert, exceptionally able; suddenly prominent. *colloq.* **M20.**

A. MILLER Let's face it: he's no hot-shot selling man. W. WHARTON I go to all the museums in Paris. I look at every hotshot object they have to show me.

hotspur /ˈhɒtspəː, -spə/ *noun & adjective.* **LME.**
[ORIGIN from HOT *adjective* + SPUR *noun*[1].]
▸**A** *noun.* A person whose spur is hot with impetuous riding; *transf.* an impetuous or reckless person. Chiefly as the nickname of Sir Henry Percy (1364–1403), English rebel. **LME.**
▸**B** *adjective.* Fiery, impetuous. **L16.**

hotsy-totsy /hɒtsɪˈtɒtsi/ *adjective. slang* (orig. *US*). **E20.**
[ORIGIN Fanciful formation from HOT *adjective*, by Billie De Beck, Amer. cartoonist.]
Satisfactory, just fine.

F. POPCORN It's .. no longer hotsy-totsy to get stinking drunk.

Hottentot /ˈhɒt(ə)ntɒt/ *noun & adjective.* Now considered *offensive* in reference to the people. **L17.**
[ORIGIN Dutch, prob. orig. a repetitive formula in a Nama dancing song, transferred by Dutch seamen to the people themselves.]
▸**A** *noun.* Pl. same, **-s**.
1 A member of a Khoikhoi people. **L17.**
2 An ignorant or savage person. Now *rare.* **E18.**
3 Any of several southern African marine fishes of the genus *Pachymetopon*, esp. *P. blochii.* **M19.**
4 Any of the Khoikhoi languages, *esp.* Nama. **M19.**
▸**B** *attrib.* or as *adjective.* Of or pertaining to the Khoikhoi or their languages. **E18.**
– SPECIAL COLLOCATIONS & PHRASES: **Hottentot bread** = *elephant's foot* s.v. ELEPHANT. **Hottentot cherry** a southern African evergreen shrub or small tree, *Maurocenia frangularia*, of the spindle tree family. **Hottentot fig** a succulent plant, *Carpobrotus edulis*, of the mesembryanthemum family. **Hottentot fish** = sense A.3 above. **Hottentot god** a praying mantis (formerly venerated by the Nama people). **Hottentot's bread** = *Hottentot bread* above. **Hottentot's god** = *Hottentot god* above. **Hottentot's tea**, **Hottentot tea** a shrubby everlasting, *Helichrysum orbiculare*, infused as a drink by the Nama people.
– NOTE: Now regarded as offensive with reference to people: *Khoikhoi* or the names of the particular peoples are preferred.

hotter /ˈhɒtə/ *verb intrans. Scot. & N. English.* **L18.**
[ORIGIN Perh. rel. to Middle Dutch *hotten*, Flemish *hotteren* shake up: see -ER[5].]
1 Vibrate, shake, rattle, clatter; totter. **L18.**
2 Cluster in a confused mass, swarm. **E19.**

hottie /ˈhɒti/ *noun. colloq.* Also **hotty**. **E20.**
[ORIGIN from HOT *adjective* + -IE, -Y[6].]
†**1** An important person. *Austral. & NZ.* Only in **E20.**
2 A hot-water bottle. **M20.**
3 A sexually attractive young man or woman. *US.* **L20.**

houbara /huːˈbɑːrə/ *noun.* **E19.**
[ORIGIN (mod. Latin from) Arabic *hubārā*.]
A kind of bustard, *Chlamydotis* (formerly *Houbara*) *undulata*, found in N. Africa and the Middle East.

Houdan /ˈhuːd(ə)n/ *noun.* **L19.**
[ORIGIN A town in the French department of Seine-et-Oise.]
(A bird of) a French breed of fowl marked by black and white plumage, a heavy crest, and prolific laying.

Houdini /huːˈdiːni/ *adjective & noun.* **E20.**
[ORIGIN Harry *Houdini*, professional name of Erich Weiss (1874–1926), US escapologist.]
▸**A** *adjective.* Characteristic or worthy of Houdini; involving ingenious escape. **E20.**
▸**B** *noun.* An ingenious escape; a person etc. clever at escaping. **M20.**

hougan *noun* var. of HOUNGAN.

hough /hɒk, hɒx/ *noun.* Long chiefly *Scot.* See also HOCK *noun*[2].
[ORIGIN Old English *hōh* from Germanic, shortened as 1st elem. of *hōhsinu* (= ***hough-sinew*** below). Cf. HOE *noun*[1].]
1 Orig., a person's heel. Later, (the part of the thigh adjacent to) the hollow part behind a person's knee joint. **OE.**
2 = HOCK *noun*[2] 1. **LME.**
3 A joint of meat consisting of the part extending from the hock some way up the leg. Cf. HOCK *noun*[2] 2. **LME.**
– COMB.: †**hough-sinew** *noun & verb* [corresp. to Old Norse *hásin*] (*a*) *noun* a person's hamstring, an animal's Achilles tendon; (*b*) *verb trans.* hamstring.

hough /hɒk/ *verb trans.* **LME.**
[ORIGIN from the noun.]
Disable by cutting a hamstring or hamstrings; hamstring.
■ **hougher** *noun* a person who hamstrings someone or something, *esp.* (IRISH HISTORY) one who hamstrings cattle as an agrarian outrage: **L16.**

houghmagandie /hɒkməˈgandi, hɒx-/ *noun.* Chiefly *Scot.* (now *rare*). Also **-gandy**. **L17.**
[ORIGIN Fanciful formation, perh. from HOUGH *noun* + CANTY *adjective*.]
Fornication.

houhere /ˈhəʊhɛri/ *noun.* **L19.**
[ORIGIN Maori, from *hou* bind together + *here* tie.]
Any of several small New Zealand trees constituting the genus *Hoheria*, of the mallow family, whose bark supplies a fibre resembling raffia.

houmous *noun* var. of HUMMUS.

hound /haʊnd/ *noun*[1].
[ORIGIN Old English *hund* = Old Frisian, Old Saxon *hund* (Dutch *hond*), Old High German *hunt* (German *Hund*), Old Norse *hundr*, Gothic *hunds*, from Germanic, from Indo-European base repr. also by Old Irish & mod. Irish *cú* (genit. *con*), Greek *kuōn* (genit. *kunos*).]
1 *gen.* A dog. *arch.* exc. *Scot.* **OE.** ▸**b** *transf.* A detested, mean, or contemptible person. **OE.**

LONGFELLOW A traveller, by the faithful hound, Half-buried in the snow was found. **b** BROWNING Miserable hound! This comes of temporising, as I said!

2 A dog used for hunting, *esp.* one that tracks by scent; *spec.* a foxhound. **ME.** ▸**b** *transf.* A player in the game of hare and hounds who follows the 'scent' laid down. Cf. HARE *noun*[1] 2b. **M19.**
bloodhound, ***deerhound***, ***foxhound***, ***greyhound***, ***otter hound***, ***Walker hound***, ***Welsh hound***, etc. **the hounds** a pack of fox-hounds; ***follow the hounds***: see FOLLOW *verb*; ***hold with the hare and hunt with the hounds***, ***run with the hare and hunt with the hounds***: see HARE *noun*[1]. **ride to hounds** go fox-hunting on horseback.
3 Orig. more fully †***houndfish***. A small shark, a dogfish. Now only with specifying word (see below). **LME.**
nurse-hound: see NURSE *noun*[2]. ***rough hound***: see ROUGH *adjective*. ***smooth hound***: see SMOOTH *adjective & adverb*.
4 The long-tailed duck, *Clangula hyemalis*, with a cry thought to resemble that of a pack of hounds. *Canad.* **E17.**
5 (As 2nd elem. of comb.) A person keen in the pursuit of the thing specified. Esp. ***news-hound***. **E20.**

City Limits Camden Lock offers the best opportunity for the equipment hound.

– COMB.: **hound-dog** *US colloq.* = sense 2 above; **houndfish** †(*a*) see sense 3 above; (*b*) any of several garfish of the genus *Tylosurus*; †**houndsfoot** *noun & adjective* (characteristic of) a worthless fellow; **hound's tongue** any of several plants of the genus *Cynoglossum*, of the borage family, esp. *C. officinale*, with dull red flowers and usu. bristly stems; also called ***dog's tongue***;

houndstooth *noun & adjective* (of) a check pattern with notched corners suggestive of a canine tooth.

■ **houndish** *adjective* of the nature of or characteristic of a hound LME.

hound /haʊnd/ *noun*². L15.

[ORIGIN Alt. (with parasitic *-d*, as in SOUND *noun*²) of earlier HUNE: infl. by HOUND *noun*¹.]

1 *NAUTICAL*. Each of one or more wooden projections below a masthead, supporting (in smaller vessels) the shrouds by which a mast is stayed laterally, or formerly (in larger ships) the trestletrees. Usu. in *pl.* L15.

2 Each of two or more wooden bars connecting the forecarriage of a springless carriage. *dial. & US*. M19.

hound /haʊnd/ *verb trans.* LME.

[ORIGIN from HOUND *noun*¹.]

†**1** *refl.* Of a dog: copulate. (Foll. by *on* the bitch.) Only in LME.

2 Hunt (as) with hounds; *spec.* (*US*) track or drive (a deer etc.) with hounds until it is brought under the hunter's gun. E16.

3 Set on (a dog); *transf.* incite (a person) to the attack. M16.

J. L. MOTLEY It was idle . . to hound the rabble upon them as tyrants and mischief-makers.

4 Harass or persecute relentlessly; drive *away*, *out*, etc., by persistent harassment. L16.

HARPER LEE Whoever breaks it is hounded from our midst as unfit to live with. R. INGALLS He was fed up with being hounded by reporters.

hounding /ˈhaʊndɪŋ/ *noun*. M19.

[ORIGIN from HOUND *noun*² + -ING¹, perh. after BUNTING *noun*², COAMING.]

NAUTICAL. The lower part of a mast, below the hounds.

houngan /ˈhuːŋg(ə)n/ *noun*. Also **hougan** /ˈhuːg(ə)n/ E20.

[ORIGIN Fon *hun* vodun deity + *ga* chief.]

A voodoo priest.

houp-la /ˈhuːplɑː/ *interjection & noun*. Also **hoop-la**. L19.

[ORIGIN French *houp-là!*, from *houp* interjection + *là* there.]

▸ **A** *interjection*. Accompanying or drawing attention to a quick or sudden movement. L19.

▸ **B** *noun*. An exclamation of 'houp-la!' L19.

houppelande /ˈhuːplənd/ *noun*. Also †**houpland**. LME.

[ORIGIN French, of uncertain origin: cf. Spanish *hopalanda*.]

hist. A medieval tunic or gown, freq. with full sleeves and a long train.

hour /ˈaʊə/ *noun*. ME.

[ORIGIN Anglo-Norman *ure*, Old French *ore*, *eure* (mod. *heure*) from Latin *hora* from Greek = season, time of day, hour.]

1 A space of time containing sixty minutes; the twenty-fourth part of a civil day. Formerly (more fully ***planetary unequal hour***, ***unequal hour***), the twelfth part of a natural day, whatever its length. ME. ▸**b** In *pl.* with preceding numeral, denoting the number of hours that have elapsed between midnight and the following noon or between noon and the following midnight, and so indicating the time of day (chiefly *Scot.*, *arch.*). In recent use (chiefly *MILITARY*), indicating the number of hours and minutes (usu. expressed in figures) past midnight, as measured on the twenty-four hour clock. LME. ▸**c** The distance the sun moves above the horizon in an hour; the height of the sun at a particular time after sunrise. *US*. M17. ▸**d** The distance one can travel in an hour by a (stated or implied) means. Also, (as 2nd elem. of comb.) the amount of energy or work of the specified kind produced or done in an hour. L18.

SCOTT FITZGERALD We sped along . . at fifty miles an hour. M. DRABBLE A couple of hours of any party is enough for me. **b** J. K. HUNTER When it cam' near to ten hours at e'en. *Punch* It is 21.00 hours on the last day of our month's training. **c** M. H. NORRIS The sun was an hour high. **d** *New Yorker* Two years ago, . . I moved to a farm, an hour from Canada.

d ampère-hour, ***horsepower-hour***, ***man-hour***, ***watt-hour***, etc.

2 A short indefinite period of the day, more or less than an hour; *esp.* one set aside for a specified activity. Freq. in *pl.* ME. ▸**b** In *pl.* The part of a day during which a person has to work. E19. ▸**c** In *pl.* The part of a day when a shop etc. is open, a doctor available for consultation, etc. Esp. in ***after hours***, ***during hours***, ***out of hours***. M19. ▸**d** A scheduled radio or TV feature, orig. an hour long. Esp. in ***children's hour*** (see CHILD *noun*). M20.

E. DARWIN In dreams, we cannot compare them with our previous knowledge . . , as we do in our waking hours. J. K. JEROME The boy does not . . prepare for the French or English hour any exhibition of homely wit. **b** J. S. MILL A reduction of hours without any diminution of wages.

lunch hour, ***office hours***, ***school hours***, etc.

3 The point of time at which each of the twelve or twenty-four hours measured by a timepiece ends and the next begins (in general or of each of a given succession of hours); the time on the clock; *gen.* any definite point in a day. ME. ▸**b** In *pl.* One's habitual time of getting up or (esp.) going to bed. Usu. with specifying adjective, as *early*, *late*, *regular*. E17.

J. BUCHAN At the moment the clock . . struck the hour of seven. J. MARQUAND I looked at my watch and found . . that the hour was getting on to half-past eight. DAY LEWIS This took place every morning at a given hour. **b** R. B. SHERIDAN Their regular hours stupefy me—not a fiddle nor a card after eleven!

4 A particular moment when an event etc. occurs; *spec.* the moment of one's death. Also, *the* time to act etc. ME. ▸**b** *The* present occasion, *the* time in question. Chiefly in ***of the hour***. L19.

LD MACAULAY To hasten the hour of his own return. G. B. SHAW The law failed them in their hour of need. E. O'NEILL He knew . . his hour was near. **b** J. RUSKIN There are good books for the hour, and good ones for all time.

5 *ECCLESIASTICAL*. In *pl.* The prayers or offices appointed to be said at certain stated times of day allotted to prayer. Also (usu. treated as *sing.*), a book containing these (more fully ***book of hours***). ME.

6 *MYTHOLOGY* (**H-**.) Female divinities presiding over the changes of the seasons. E17.

7 *ASTRONOMY & GEOGRAPHY*. An angular unit of right ascension or longitude equal to 1/24 of a great circle (15 degrees). L18.

– PHRASES: **at all hours** at every hour of the day, no matter how early or late. **by the hour** for many hours at a time. ***canonical hour***: see CANONICAL *adjective* 1. *ELEVENTH*-***hour***. ***evil hour***: see EVIL *adjective*. *FORTY* **hours**. ***happy hour***: see HAPPY *adjective*. ***one's finest hour***: see FINE *adjective*. **on the hour** (*a*) exactly at the hour named; (*b*) at the very beginning of every hour within a specified period. ***planetary hour***: see sense 1 above. ***small hours***: see SMALL *adjective*. ***solar hour***: see SOLAR *adjective*¹. ***the witching hour***: see WITCHING 2. **till all hours** until very late in the evening. ***unequal hour***: see sense 1 above. ***wait the hour***: see WAIT *verb*. ***wee hours***, ***wee small hours***: see WEE *adjective*. ***zero hour***: see ZERO *noun* 5.

– COMB.: **hour-angle** the angular distance measured westwards along the celestial equator from the observer's meridian to the hour-circle of a particular celestial object; **hour-circle** (*a*) any great circle of the celestial sphere passing through the poles; *esp.* any of 24 such marked on a globe etc. at intervals of one hour of right ascension; (*b*) a graduated circle on a globe, telescope, etc., marked with divisions of one hour of right ascension or longitude; **hour hand** the short hand of a clock or watch, which indicates the hours; **hour-long** *adjective & adverb* (*a*) *adjective* lasting for one hour; (*b*) *adverb* for one hour.

■ **houred** *adjective* †(*a*) *rare* definite; (*b*) (as 2nd elem. of comb.) of the specified number of hours: L15.

hourglass /ˈaʊəglɑːs/ *noun & adjective*. E16.

[ORIGIN from HOUR + GLASS *noun*.]

▸ **A** *noun*. A device for measuring time, consisting of two glass etc. bulbs joined by a narrow neck, the upper bulb containing grains of sand which travel into the lower bulb in the space of an hour; *fig.* (*arch.*) the space of an hour, a strictly finite period of time. E16.

▸ **B** *attrib.* or as *adjective*. Shaped like an hourglass, constricted or narrowed in the middle. E19.

houri /ˈhʊəri/ *noun*. M18.

[ORIGIN French from Persian *hūrī* from Arabic *hūr* pl. of *'ahwar*, fem. *ḥawrā'* having eyes with marked contrast of white and black.]

Any of the virgins of the Muslim paradise, promised as wives to believers; *transf.* a voluptuously beautiful woman.

hourly /ˈaʊəli/ *adjective*. E16.

[ORIGIN from HOUR *noun* + -LY¹.]

1 Of an hour's duration; very brief. *rare*. E16.

2 Occurring, performed, etc., every hour; paid etc. by the hour. M16.

hourly /ˈaʊəli/ *adverb*. L15.

[ORIGIN from HOUR *noun* + -LY².]

1 Every hour, by the hour. Also, very frequently, continually. L15.

GIBBON The barbarians were hourly expected at the gates of Rome.

†**2** For the duration of an hour, briefly, quickly. E–M16.

house /haʊs/ *noun*¹ *& adjective*.

[ORIGIN Old English *hūs* = Old Frisian, Old Saxon, Old High German (Dutch *huis*, German *Haus*), Old Norse *hús*, Gothic *-hūs* (only in *gudhūs* temple), from Germanic: ult. origin unknown.]

▸ **A** *noun*. Pl. **houses** /ˈhaʊzɪz/.

1 A building for human habitation, a dwelling, a home; *spec.* a self-contained unit having a ground floor and one or more upper storeys (as opp. to a bungalow, flat, etc.). OE. ▸**b** A part of a building occupied by one tenant or family. *Scot. & dial.* OE. ▸**c** The living room of a house. *dial.* L17.

J. STEINBECK The rich people who lived in the stone and plaster houses of the town.

apartment house, ***council house***, ***country house***, ***doll's house***, ***farmhouse***, ***manor house***, ***mansion-house***, ***town house***, ***Wendy house***, etc.

2 (As 2nd elem. of comb. or with other specification.) A building accommodating or frequented by people that is other than an ordinary private dwelling; a building or place where a specified occupation, activity, etc., is pursued, or where refreshment of a specified kind is provided. OE. ▸**b** *spec.* A building occupied by a religious community; a monastery, a convent; the religious community itself. ME. ▸**c** A university college. Now *rare* exc. in ***the House***, Christ Church, Oxford, ***Peterhouse***, St Peter's College, Cambridge. M16. ▸**d** A building in which a legislative or deliberative assembly meets; the assembly itself; *the* British House of Commons. M16. ▸**e** A place of business; a business establishment, a firm; *spec.* a printing or publishing firm, a couture or fashion establishment. Also, *the* Stock Exchange. L16. ▸**f** A building where public refreshment is provided; an inn, a tavern, a public house. Also as ***interjection***, demanding service at a bar, dining table, etc. M17. ▸**g** A theatre, a cinema; a performance or showing (usu. specified, as *first*, *second*, etc.) in a theatre or cinema; the audience in a theatre or cinema or at a (specified) performance or showing. M17. ▸**h** A brothel. E19. ▸**i** A boarding house of a public school; a division of a school for organizational purposes, as for competitive games; the pupils in such a boarding house or division. M19. ▸**j** An establishment for gambling, a casino; the management of such an establishment (against which bets are placed). E20.

f J. P. DONLEAVY Can't serve you, sir, rules of the house, you've had enough to drink. **g** J. AGATE The play . . is being played to packed houses.

alehouse, ***almshouse***, ***bakehouse***, ***bathhouse***, ***bawdy-house***, ***boarding house***, ***clubhouse***, ***coffee house***, ***courthouse***, ***custom house***, ***dosshouse***, ***dwelling house***, ***guardhouse***, ***guest house***, ***lodging house***, ***madhouse***, ***meeting house***, ***opera house***, ***playhouse***, ***slaughterhouse***, ***summer house***, ***wash house***, ***whorehouse***, ***workhouse***, etc. **d** ***House of Commons***, ***House of Delegates***, ***House of Keys***, ***House of Lords***, ***House of Representatives***, ***Lower House***, ***Upper House***, etc.

H

3 A place of worship (considered as the home of a god); a temple, a church. OE.

4 The natural habitation of an animal, a den, a burrow, a nest; *esp.* the shell of a snail, tortoise, etc. OE.

J. ALDAY Snayles . . beare with them their houses easely on their backes.

5 *gen.* A place of abode or rest. OE.

W. COWPER A heavenly mind May be indifferent to her house of clay. SIR W. SCOTT The peaceful house of death.

6 *collect.* The inhabitants of a house; a household, a family. OE.

OED The whole house was down with influenza.

7 The line of descent of a family; a dynasty, a lineage, *esp.* one of high rank or fame. OE.

J. RUSKIN To read the shields, and remember the stories, of the great houses of England.

House of Hanover, ***House of Stuart***, etc.

8 (Chiefly as 2nd elem. of comb.) A building for the keeping of animals or plants or for the storage or protection of something; a building for the production of something specified. ME.

coach house, ***coalhouse***, ***doghouse***, ***glasshouse***, ***greenhouse***, ***henhouse***, ***hothouse***, ***ice house***, ***lighthouse***, ***outhouse***, ***powerhouse***, ***storehouse***, ***warehouse***, ***wheelhouse***, etc.

9 *ASTROLOGY*. **a** Each of the twelve divisions of the ecliptic fixed with respect to the horizon. Also ***mundane house***. LME. ▸**b** Any of the signs of the zodiac considered as the seat of the greatest influence of a particular planet. Cf. MANSION 5. LME.

10 †**a** Each square of a chessboard. M16–E19. ▸**b** *CURLING*. The space within the outermost circle drawn round either tee. L19.

11 Bingo, lotto, tombola, esp. as played for money; (the call announcing or the prize for) the winning of the game. E20.

12 A form of popular dance music characterized by the use of synthesized sounds and a fast beat. L20.

– PHRASES: **(as) safe as houses** perfectly safe. ***big house***: see BIG *adjective*. **bow down in the house of Rimmon**, **worship in the house of Rimmon** [after *2 Kings* 5:18] pay lip service to a principle; sacrifice one's principles for the sake of conformity. ***bring down the house***: see BRING *verb*. **clean house** *US* do housework; *fig.* wipe out corruption, inefficiency, etc. **daughter of the house** a daughter of the family. ***dead house***: see DEAD *adjective* etc. ***disorderly house***: see DISORDERLY *adjective*. ***eat out of house and home***: see EAT *verb*. ***free house***: see FREE *adjective*. ***full house***: see FULL *adjective*. **go all round the houses**, **go round the houses** *fig.* beat about the bush; arrive at the point in a roundabout way. ***great house***: see GREAT *adjective*. *HALFWAY* ***house***. **house and home** *emphatic* home. **house of call** *arch.* a place where carriers call for commissions, where a person may be heard of, etc.; a house one visits regularly. **house of cards** a structure built of playing cards balanced together; *fig.* an insubstantial or precarious structure, an insecure or overambitious scheme. ***house of correction***: see CORRECTION 3. **house of God** a church, a temple. **house of ill fame**, **house of ill repute** *arch.* a brothel. **house of office** *arch.* a privy, a lavatory. **house of prayer** a church, a temple. ***house of*** *RELIGION*. ***house of the ascendant***: see ASCENDANT *noun* 1. ***House of Windsor***: see WINDSOR *noun* 2. ***Houses of Parliament***: see PARLIAMENT *noun*. **keep a House** secure the presence of enough members for a quorum in the House of Commons. **keep house** maintain, provide for, or manage a household. **keep the house**, **keep one's house**, **keep to the house**, **keep to one's house** not go outdoors, esp. because of illness. **like a house on fire** vigorously, fast; successfully, excellently. **make a House** = ***keep a House*** above. ***man of the house***: see MAN *noun*. ***move house***: see MOVE *verb*. **on the house** (esp. of a drink) at the publican's or management's expense, free. **open house** general hospitality (***keep open house***, provide this). **play house** play at being a family in its home. PUBLIC HOUSE. **put one's house in order**, **set**

one's house in order make necessary reforms; settle one's arrangements. ***safe as houses***: see ***as safe as houses*** above. ***set one's house in order***: see ***put one's house in order*** above. **set up house** begin to live in a separate dwelling. **son of the house** a son of the family. **the House** (*a*) see senses 2c, d, e above; (*b*) *euphem.* (*hist.*) the workhouse. **the House of Windsor** the present British Royal Family. ***the lady of the house***: see LADY *noun*. **the Lord's house** a church, a temple. ***throw the house out of the window***: see WINDOW *noun*. ***White House***: see WHITE *adjective*. ***white house***: see WHITE *adjective*. ***worship in the house of Rimmon***: see ***bow down in the house of Rimmon*** above.

▸ **B** *attrib.* or as *adjective* (freq. with hyphen).

1 *gen.* Of or pertaining to a house or a household; used or kept in or about a house; domestic. **OE.**

J. AUSTEN The loud noise of the house-bell. J. CARLYLE My house-money is utterly done. B. KIMENYE His house servant was away on leave, and the drawbacks of bachelorhood were making themselves acutely felt. R. LUDLUM His clumsy, long-haired house cat had knocked over a stray glass.

2 Of or pertaining to a house at a school. **M19.**

3 Of or pertaining to a commercial house or business establishment; (of a magazine etc.) published by a particular firm or society and dealing mainly with its activities; (of a wine etc.) selected and recommended by a restaurant etc. as a reasonable buy; (of a band, group, etc.) resident or regularly performing (in a club etc.). **E20.**

T. HILTON *The Germ* was the first house journal of a self-consciously avant-garde artistic group. O. LANCASTER The house burgundy at five bob a bottle.

H

– COMB. & SPECIAL COLLOCATIONS: **house agent** an agent for the sale and letting of houses, an estate agent; **house arrest** detention in one's own house etc., not in prison; **house-arrest** *verb trans.* put under house arrest; **houseboat** a boat fitted up for living in, usu. on inland waters; **housebote** [BOOT *noun*[1]] *LAW* (a tenant's right to) timber from the landlord's estate for house repairs; **housebound** *adjective* unable to leave one's house through illness etc.; **houseboy** a boy or man as a servant in a house, esp. in Africa; **house-burn** *verb intrans.* (of tobacco) become damaged or spoilt by disease during the curing process; **house call** a visit made to a patient in his or her own home by a doctor etc.; **housecarl** [CARL *noun*] *hist.* (before the Norman Conquest) a member of the bodyguard of a Danish or English king or noble; **house church** (*a*) a charismatic Church independent of traditional denominations; (*b*) a group meeting in private houses as part of the activities of a Church; **house-clean** *verb trans. & intrans.* clean (the interior of a house); **housecoat** a woman's informal coat dress, esp. for wearing in the home; **house colours** a badge, cap, etc. awarded for representing a house of a school, esp. in a sporting event; **housecraft** (skill in) household management; **house detective** a private detective employed on the premises by a hotel, business, etc.; **house-dog** a dog kept as a pet or to guard a house; **housefather** the father of a household or family; a man in charge of a house, esp. of a home for children; **house flag** a flag indicating to what firm a ship belongs; **housefly** the common fly of houses and farms, *Musca domestica*, a dipteran insect which lays its eggs in excrement and decaying organic matter, and spreads disease; **house-girl** a female domestic servant, formerly esp. a slave; **house guest**: staying in a private house; **house-heating** (*a*) the heating of a house; (*b*) (chiefly *Scot.*) a house-warming party etc.; **house-hunting** looking for a house to live in; **house husband** a husband who carries out the household duties traditionally carried out by a wife; **house-lamb** (now *rare*) a lamb kept in or near a house as a pet or for fattening for the table; the meat from such a lamb; **houseleek** a plant of the stonecrop family, *Sempervivum tectorum*, with pink flowers and dense rosettes of fleshy leaves, formerly much planted on roofs as a protection against lightning; **house lights**: in the auditorium of a theatre; **house longhorn** a wood-boring beetle, *Hylotrupes bajulus*, of the family Cerambycidae; **house-lot** *N. Amer.* a building plot; **house-manager** the manager of a theatre, cinema, club, etc.; **house martin** an Old World swallow, *Delichon urbica*, which builds mud nests on house walls, rocky cliffs, etc.; **housemaster** a master of a house; *spec.* a male teacher in charge of a house in a school; **housemastership** the position or office of a housemaster; **housemate** a person who shares a house with another or others; **housemistress** a mistress of a house; *spec.* a female teacher in charge of a house in a school; **housemother** the mother of a household or family; a woman in charge of a house, esp. of a home for children; **house mouse** a usually grey mouse, *Mus musculus*, which lives close to human habitation in most parts of the world and eats almost anything; **house music** = sense A.12 above; **house officer** a (usu. resident) doctor of one of the more junior grades in a hospital; **houseparent** a housemother or housefather; esp. of a home for children; **house party** (a gathering of) guests staying at a house; **house physician** a resident physician in a hospital, usu. of the most junior grade; **house-place** *dial.* a combined living room and kitchen in a farmhouse etc.; **house plant** a plant that is suitable for growing indoors; **house-proud** *adjective* attentive to, or unduly occupied with, the care and appearance of the home; **house-raising** *US* (chiefly *hist.*) a gathering of people to help a neighbour construct a house; **house-rent party** *US* (*a*) a party held to raise money to pay the rent of a house; (*b*) a jam session in a house or apartment; **houseroom** accommodation or space in a house (***not give houseroom to***, not tolerate having or keeping); **house row** *hist.* a row or street of houses; **house-sitter** a person who temporarily lives in a house by arrangement during an absence by the usual occupant(s); **house snake** (*a*) any of several N. American colubrid snakes of the genera *Elaphe* and *Lampropeltis*; (*b*) a southern African colubrid snake of the genus *Boaedon*; (*c*) a snake kept as a household god; **house sparrow** the common sparrow, *Passer domesticus*, a small noisy gregarious bird native to Eurasia but now found close to human habitation in most areas other than the Far East; **house style** a particular printer's or publisher's etc. preferred way of presenting text, including rules for spelling, punctuation, etc.; the distinctive style, esp. in artistic presentation, of a firm etc.; **house surgeon** a resident surgeon in a hospital, usually of the most junior grade; **house-to-house** *adjective* visiting or performed in turn at each of a series of houses; **housetop** the top or roof of a house; ***cry from the housetops***, ***proclaim from the housetops***, etc. [with allus. to *Luke* 12:3], announce publicly, announce loudly; **housewares** (chiefly *N. Amer.*) utilitarian household items, esp. kitchen utensils; **house-warming** (*a*) the warming of a house; (*b*) a party or other entertainment celebrating a move to a new home (also ***house-warming party*** etc.); **housework** cleaning, cooking, and other domestic work undertaken in a house; **housewright** *arch.* a house-builder.

house /haʊs/ *noun*[2]. Now *rare*. **ME.**

[ORIGIN Old French *houce* (mod. *housse*) from medieval Latin *hultia* from Germanic (whence Middle Dutch *hulfte* pocket for bow and arrow, Middle High German *hulft* covering).]

A textile covering, *spec.* one attached to a saddle to cover the back and flanks of the horse. Cf. HOUSING *noun*[2].

house /haʊs/ *noun*[3]. Orig. *US*. **L20.**

[ORIGIN Prob. from The Ware*house*, a Chicago nightclub.]

In full ***house music***. A type of popular music characterized by the extensive use of synthetic sounds produced electronically, sparse vocals, and a fast beat.

house /haʊz/ *verb*[1].

[ORIGIN Old English *hūsian* = Middle Low German, Middle Dutch *hūsen*, Old High German *hūsōn* (Dutch *huizen*, German *hausen*), Old Norse *húsa*, from Germanic base of HOUSE *noun*[1].]

▸ **I** *verb trans.* **1** Take or put into a house; provide with a house or houses; keep or store in a house etc. **OE.** ▸**b** *refl.* Enter a house; take shelter in a house. **LME.** ▸†**c** Drive or pursue into a house. **L16–E18.**

A. J. P. TAYLOR He . . housed us without a moment's fuss. **b** E. FEINSTEIN A small friendly square around which many Russians housed themselves.

2 Place or enclose as in a house; cover as with a roof; harbour, lodge; contain, as a house does; give shelter to. **LME.**

L. DURRELL A small observatory which housed a telescope of thirty magnifications. K. TYNAN The difficulty of finding out what theatre is housing the play you want to see. *Antiquarian Horology* A clock-case which houses a clock by Thomas Fayrer of Lancaster. J. A. MICHENER The mound now housed a town of a hundred mud-brick houses.

3 *NAUTICAL.* Place in a secure or sheltered position. **M18.**

4 Fix (a piece of wood, etc.) in a socket, joint, or mortise. **M19.**

▸ **II** *verb intrans.* †**5** Build a house or houses. **ME–L15.**

6 Live or take shelter (as) in a house. **L16.**

R. L. STEVENSON An old gentleman . . housed with them for a while during our stay.

house /haʊz/ *verb*[2] *trans.* Now *rare*. **E16.**

[ORIGIN from HOUSE *noun*[2].]

Cover (a horse) with a textile house or housing.

housebreak /ˈhaʊsbreɪk/ *verb*. Pa. t. (*rare*) **-broke** /-brəʊk/, pa. pple & ppl adjective **-broken** /-brəʊk(ə)n/. **ME.**

[ORIGIN from HOUSE *noun*[1] + BREAK *verb*.]

1 *verb intrans.* Break into a house with intent to steal etc. Chiefly as HOUSEBREAKING. **ME.**

2 *verb trans.* = HOUSE-TRAIN. Freq. in *pass.* Chiefly *N. Amer.* **E20.**

housebreaker /ˈhaʊsbreɪkə/ *noun*. **LME.**

[ORIGIN from HOUSE *noun*[1] + BREAKER *noun*[1].]

1 A person who breaks into a house with intent to steal etc. (in *LAW* formerly in the daytime only: cf. BURGLAR). **LME.**

2 A person employed in demolishing houses. **L19.**

housebreaking /ˈhaʊsbreɪkɪŋ/ *noun*. **E17.**

[ORIGIN from HOUSE *noun*[1] + BREAKING *noun*.]

The act of breaking into a house with intent to steal etc. (in *LAW* formerly in the daytime only: cf. BURGLARY).

houseful /ˈhaʊsfʊl, -f(ə)l/ *noun*. **ME.**

[ORIGIN from HOUSE *noun*[1] + -FUL.]

As much or as many as a house will hold.

household /ˈhaʊshəʊld/ *noun & adjective*. **LME.**

[ORIGIN from HOUSE *noun*[1] + HOLD *noun*[1].]

▸ **A** *noun*. **1** *collect.* The people living in a house, *esp.* a family in a house; a domestic establishment. **LME.**

V. GLENDINNING The Fairfield household moved back to London. E. FEINSTEIN After his second wife's death, the household of Professor Tsvetayev split up.

the Household *spec.* the royal household.

†**2** The maintaining of a house or family; housekeeping. **LME–L16.**

†**3** *collect.* The contents of a house; household goods and furniture. **LME–E18.**

▸ **B** *attrib.* or as *adjective*. **1** Of or pertaining to a household; domestic. **LME.**

2 Intimate, homely. *arch.* **LME.**

L. STERNE Good plain household judgment.

– SPECIAL COLLOCATIONS & COMB.: **household appliance** a piece of equipment used in the house. **household book** a book for the keeping of household accounts. **household bread** *hist.* bread of an ordinary quality for household use. **household effects** the movable contents of a house. **household franchise** *hist.* the right of voting in elections consequent on being a householder. **household gods** (*a*) gods presiding over a household, *esp.* (*ROMAN HISTORY*) the lares and penates; (*b*) the essentials of home life. **household management** the management of domestic affairs, esp. as a subject of study. **household name** a well-known person. **household science** (chiefly *N. Amer.*) the study of household management, domestic science. **household stuff** *arch.* = ***household effects*** above. **household troops** (in Britain) troops nominally employed to guard the monarch. **household word** a well-known name or saying.

■ **householdry** *noun* (*arch.*) management of a household, housekeeping **L16.**

householder /ˈhaʊshəʊldə/ *noun*. **LME.**

[ORIGIN from HOUSE *noun*[1] + HOLDER *noun*[1].]

A person who owns or rents a house, flat, etc., as his or her own dwelling (*hist.* with a type of occupancy bringing entitlement to the franchise); a head of a household or family.

■ **householdership** *noun* **E19.**

householding /ˈhaʊshəʊldɪŋ/ *noun*. Now *rare*. **LME.**

[ORIGIN from HOUSE *noun*[1] + HOLDING *noun*.]

(Formerly) management or (later) occupancy of a house.

housekeep /ˈhaʊskiːp/ *verb intrans. colloq.* Pa. t. & pple **-kept** /-kɛpt/. **M19.**

[ORIGIN Back-form. from HOUSEKEEPER or HOUSEKEEPING *noun*. Cf. earlier HOUSEKEEPING *adjective* 1.]

Act as a housekeeper (*for*); keep house.

housekeeper /ˈhaʊskiːpə/ *noun*. **LME.**

[ORIGIN from HOUSE *noun*[1] + KEEPER *noun*.]

†**1** = HOUSEHOLDER. **LME–M19.**

†**2** With qualifying adjective: a *good* etc. person in offering hospitality. **M16–E18.**

3 A person in charge of a house, office, etc.; a caretaker. **M16.** ▸†**b** A guard dog. Only in **L17.**

4 *spec.* A person, esp. a woman, who manages the affairs of a household or (now) the cleaning of a hotel etc.; (with qualifying adjective) a *good* etc. person at managing household affairs. Formerly also, a person engaged in a domestic occupation. **L16.**

5 A person who keeps to the house, or stays at home. *rare*. **E18.**

housekeeping /ˈhaʊskiːpɪŋ/ *noun*. **M16.**

[ORIGIN from HOUSE *noun*[1] + KEEPING *noun*.]

1 Maintenance of a household, keeping a house; management of household affairs, *transf.* management of an organization's finances etc. **M16.**

C. ODETS We've set up housekeeping together, Joe. *Abingdon Herald* The Vale's financial strategy, based on continued good housekeeping and further capital investment.

†**2** Hospitality. Usu. with qualifying adjective. **M16–M19.**

3 Money set aside or given for housekeeping expenses, housekeeping money. *colloq.* **M20.**

J. PORTER If I ask you for a bit more housekeeping, that's a different story.

4 Those operations of a computer, an organization, etc., which make its work possible but do not directly constitute its performance, e.g. maintenance and record-keeping. **M20.**

– COMB. (see also HOUSEKEEPING *adjective* 2): **housekeeping allowance**, **housekeeping money**: set aside or given for housekeeping expenses.

housekeeping /ˈhaʊskiːpɪŋ/ *adjective*. **M16.**

[ORIGIN Sense 1 from HOUSE *noun*[1] + *keeping* pres. pple of KEEP *verb*; sense 2 the noun used attrib.]

1 That keeps a house or maintains a household. Now *rare*. **M16.**

2 Designating holiday or rented accommodation providing equipment for housekeeping; self-catering. *N. Amer.* **M20.**

housekept *verb pa. t. & pple* of HOUSEKEEP.

housel /ˈhaʊz(ə)l/ *noun & verb*. *obsolete* exc. *hist.*

[ORIGIN Old English *hūsl* (whence Old Norse *húsl*) = Gothic *hunsl* sacrifice, offering: ult. origin unknown.]

▸ **A** *noun*. (The administration or receiving of) the Eucharist. **OE.**

▸ **B** *verb trans.* Infl. **-ll-**, **-l-**. Administer the Eucharist to; in *pass.*, receive the Eucharist. **OE.**

■ **houseling** *noun & adjective* (*a*) *noun* the action of the verb; (*b*) *adjective* (*attrib.*) used at the celebration of the Eucharist: **OE.**

houseless /ˈhaʊslɪs/ *adjective*. **LME.**

[ORIGIN from HOUSE *noun*[1] + -LESS.]

Without a house; homeless.

■ **houselessness** *noun* **E19.**

housemaid /ˈhaʊsmeɪd/ *noun & verb*. **L17.**

[ORIGIN from HOUSE *noun*[1] + MAID *noun*.]

▸ **A** *noun*. A female domestic servant, *esp.* one in charge of reception rooms and bedrooms. **L17.**

housemaid's closet, **housemaid's cupboard**: where cleaning materials are kept. **housemaid's knee** swelling of the bursa in front of the kneecap, often the result of frequent kneeling.

▸ **B** *verb trans.* Look after in the manner of a housemaid; put in order. **M19.**

P. DEVLIN One of his [the trial judge's] jobs is to housemaid the case . . . To get the evidence as clean and tidy as he can.

houseman /ˈhaʊsmən/ *noun*. Pl. **-men**. L18.
[ORIGIN from HOUSE *noun*[1] + MAN *noun*.]
1 A married labourer on a Norwegian farm. *rare*. L18.
2 (**H-**.) A member of Christ Church, Oxford ('the House'). M19.
3 A man responsible for general duties in a house, hotel, etc. M19.
4 A house physician or house surgeon, in Britain now usu. a qualified junior doctor working under supervision in a hospital before being fully registered as an independent medical practitioner. M20.
■ **housemanship** *noun* the position of being a houseman in a hospital M20.

house-train /ˈhaʊstreɪn/ *verb trans*. E20.
[ORIGIN from HOUSE *noun*[1] + TRAIN *verb*.]
Train (a domestic animal, an infant) to be clean in the house, teach where to urinate and defecate; *joc. colloq.* teach good manners or tidiness to. Usu. in *pass.*

housewife /ˈhaʊswʌɪf/, *in sense 3 & dial.* ˈhʌzɪf/ *noun*. Pl. **-wives** /-wʌɪvz/. Also (now only in sense 3) **hussive** /ˈhʌzɪv/, (esp. in sense 2) †**huswife**. ME.
[ORIGIN from HOUSE *noun*[1] + WIFE *noun*. See also HUSSY.]
1 A (married) woman who looks after the domestic affairs of her household, esp. as her principal occupation; (with qualifying adjective) a *good* etc. domestic manager. ME.
†**2** = HUSSY 3. M16–E18.
3 A small case for sewing equipment. M18.
■ **housewifeship** *noun* (chiefly *Scot. & N. English*) housewifery ME. **housewifish** *adjective* housewifely M19.

housewife /ˈhaʊswʌɪf/ *verb*. Now *rare*. M16.
[ORIGIN from the noun.]
1 *verb intrans. & trans.* (with *it*). Be a (good) housewife; manage a household, esp. skilfully and economically. M16.
2 *verb trans.* Manage as a (good) housewife, skilfully and economically. M17.

DEFOE I must housewife the money.

housewifely /ˈhaʊswʌɪfli/ *adjective*. LME.
[ORIGIN formed as HOUSEWIFE *verb* + -LY[1].]
Pertaining to or characteristic of a (good) housewife; skilful and economical in managing household affairs.
■ **housewifeliness** *noun* M16.

housewifery /ˈhaʊswɪfri/ *noun*. LME.
[ORIGIN formed as HOUSEWIFE *verb* + -RY.]
1 (Skill in) household management, housecraft; housekeeping. LME. ▸†**b** Thrift, economy. M17–L18.
†**2** *collect.* Articles of household use. M16–E19.

housewives *noun* pl. of HOUSEWIFE *noun*.

housey /ˈhaʊsi/ *noun*. *colloq.* Also **housie**. M20.
[ORIGIN Abbreviation of HOUSEY-HOUSEY.]
= HOUSE *noun*[1] 11.

housey-housey /haʊsɪˈhaʊsi/ *noun*. Also **housie-housie**. M20.
[ORIGIN from HOUSE *noun*[1] + -Y[6].]
= HOUSE *noun*[1] 11.

housie(-housie) *nouns* vars. of HOUSEY(-HOUSEY).

housing /ˈhaʊzɪŋ/ *noun*[1]. ME.
[ORIGIN from HOUSE *noun*[1] or *verb*[1] + -ING[1].]
▸ **I** **1** Shelter (like that of a house); lodging. ME.

C. MATHER Their housing is nothing but a few mats tyed about poles fastened in the earth.

2 Property consisting of houses; houses or buildings, collectively; *spec.* outbuildings attached to a house. LME. ▸**b** A house, a building. Long *rare*. LME.

J. KRANTZ I'll never accept the idea that public housing can't be beautiful.

3 ARCHITECTURE. A canopied niche for a statue or other image. Long *obsolete* exc. *hist*. LME.
4 NAUTICAL. A covering or roofing for a ship. E19.
5 CARPENTRY. A recess or groove in one piece of timber etc. for another to fit into. E19.
6 A massive metal frame or pillar that supports one end of a set of rolls in a rolling mill. M19.
7 A structure that supports and encloses the bearings at the end of an axle or shaft, a journal box; a rigid casing that encloses and protects any piece of moving or delicate equipment. L19.
▸ **II** **8** The action of HOUSE *verb*[1]; *esp.* provision of houses. LME.
– COMB.: **housing association** an association aiming to provide housing at (relatively) low cost; **housing development** the act or process of planning and building a (large) group of houses; a housing estate; **housing estate** a residential area planned as a unit, and often having its own shops and other facilities; **housing list** a waiting list for council houses; ***housing project***: see PROJECT *noun* 6c; **housing scheme** a housing estate, esp. of council houses.

housing /ˈhaʊzɪŋ/ *noun*[2]. LME.
[ORIGIN from HOUSE *noun*[2] or *verb*[2] + -ING[1].]
A covering, esp. of cloth; *spec.* a covering put on a horse etc. for protection or ornament, trappings. Freq. in *pl.*

houstonia /huːˈstəʊnɪə/ *noun*. E19.
[ORIGIN mod. Latin (see below), from William *Houston*, Scot. botanist (d. 1733): see -IA[1].]
Any of various N. American plants of the former genus *Houstonia*, of the madder family, now included in the genus *Hedyotis*; *esp.* the bluets, *Hedyotis* (formerly *Houstonia*) *caerulea*.

houting /ˈhaʊtɪŋ/ *noun*. L19.
[ORIGIN Dutch from Middle Dutch *houtic*, of uncertain origin.]
Either of two whitefish, valued in places for food, either (***a***) the rare anadromous form *Coregonus oxyrhynchus*, of Baltic coasts and rivers, or (***b***) the variable freshwater form *Coregonus lavaretus*, which occurs in lakes of northern Europe and Asia. Cf. GWYNIAD, LAVARET, POWAN, SKELLY *noun* 1.

†**houve** *noun* see HOO *noun*[1].

houyhnhnm /ˈhʊɪnɪm, ˈhwɪnɪm/ *noun*. E18.
[ORIGIN The name (intended to suggest the neigh of a horse) of a fictional race of reasoning horses in Swift's *Gulliver's Travels*.]
A horse considered as having human characteristics.

Hova /ˈhəʊvə, ˈhɒvə/ *noun & adjective*. M19.
[ORIGIN Malagasy.]
▸ **A** *noun*. Pl. **-s**, same. A member of the dominant people of Madagascar; the dialect of Malagasy spoken by this people. M19.
▸ **B** *attrib.* or as *adjective*. Of or pertaining to the Hovas or their dialect. L19.

hove /həʊv/ *verb*[1] *intrans*. Long *arch. rare*. ME.
[ORIGIN Unknown: superseded by HOVER *verb*.]
1 Hover, as a bird etc. ME.
2 Wait, linger, stay, remain; *spec.* remain on horseback. ME.
†**3** Float or soar *on* or *by*; move away; be borne (on horseback). ME–M17.

hove /həʊv/ *verb*[2]. Now chiefly *Scot*. LME.
[ORIGIN App. from pa. t. & pple of HEAVE *verb*.]
†**1** *verb trans.* Raise, lift. LME–L16.
2 *verb intrans.* Rise, swell up. L16.
3 *verb trans.* Cause to swell up, inflate. E17.

hove *verb*[3] *pa. t. & pple*: see HEAVE *verb*.

hovel /ˈhɒv(ə)l/ *noun*[1]. LME.
[ORIGIN Perh. of Low German origin.]
1 An open shed or an outhouse used for sheltering cattle, storing grain, etc. Now chiefly *dial*. LME. ▸**b** A stack of corn, a heap of hay, etc. Now *dial*. L16.
2 A simple, roughly constructed, or (esp.) squalid dwelling. LME.
3 ARCHITECTURE. A canopied niche for a statue or other image. Long *obsolete* exc. *hist*. LME.
4 A conical construction enclosing a kiln. E19.

hovel /ˈhɒv(ə)l/ *noun*[2]. Now *rare*. L17.
[ORIGIN Middle Dutch *hövel*, Dutch *heuvel*.]
The bump on the top of a whale's head.

hovel /ˈhɒv(ə)l/ *verb trans*. Infl. **-ll-**, *-**l**-. L16.
[ORIGIN from HOVEL *noun*[1].]
1 Shelter (as) in a hovel. L16.
2 Shape (a chimney) like a hovel or open shed. E19.

hoveller /ˈhɒv(ə)lə/ *noun*. M18.
[ORIGIN Unknown.]
hist. **1** An unlicensed boatman, esp. on the Kentish coast; *spec.* one who went out to wrecks. M18.
2 A boat used by a hoveller. M19.

hoven /ˈhəʊv(ə)n/ *adjective & noun*. M16.
[ORIGIN pa. pple of HEAVE *verb*.]
▸ **A** *adjective*. Swollen, bloated. Now *dial*. M16.
▸ **B** *noun*. Distension of the stomachs of cattle with gas, usu. owing to overfeeding on clover etc.; bloat. Cf. HEAVE *noun* 2, HOOVE. M19.

hoven *verb pa. pple*: see HEAVE *verb*.

hover /ˈhɒvə/ *verb & noun*. LME.
[ORIGIN from HOVE *verb*[1] + -ER[5].]
▸ **A** *verb*. **I** *verb intrans.* **1** (Of a bird, esp. a hawk etc., or an insect) hang or remain suspended in the air by rapidly beating the wings; hang in the air with a wavering or fluttering movement. (Foll. by *over*, *about*.) LME. ▸**b** Of a helicopter or other aircraft: maintain a stationary position in the air. L19. ▸**c** Of a hovercraft: be supported, esp. in a stationary position, on the air cushion. M20.

HUGH WALPOLE A faint red glow hovered over the dark, heaving water. A. J. CRONIN He . . turned out the lamp, around which great moths were hovering in the languid air. B. HINES Persistently this time, hovering then dropping vertically in short bursts. **b** A. CARTER The whirring helicopter hovered over a crag where eagles nested.

2 Be in an indeterminate or irresolute state, waver, (*between*); (*obsolete* exc. *Scot.*) wait, delay, hesitate. LME.

P. G. WODEHOUSE He felt that he hovered on the brink of some strange revelation. TOLKIEN He lost count of time, hovering between sleep and waking. C. POTOK He hovered tenuously between life and death for three days. *Scientific American* A climate where the thermometer regularly hovers around 40 °C.

3 Linger about or round (a person or place); move restlessly about. (Foll. by *about*, *round*.) L16.

J. M. BARRIE He hovered around the table as if it would be unsafe to leave us. D. M. THOMAS Kolya was edging towards the door impatiently, but Lisa hovered, doubtful.

▸ **II** *verb trans.* **4** Cover, protect; *esp.* (of a bird) cover (the young) with its body. *arch.* LME.
†**5** Of a bird: flap (the wings) in order to hang in the air. L16–L17.
6 Maintain (an aircraft) in a hovering state. M20.

Daily Telegraph It is feasible to fly a Sea Harrier and hover it to an accuracy of 2 ft.

▸ **B** *noun*. **1** Indecision; an instance or state of indecision. E16.
2 An overhanging shelter; *spec.* an overhanging stone or bank under which fish hide. Also, a shelter used in the brooding of chickens. Chiefly *dial.* E17.
3 An act or state of hovering. L19.
4 A floating island of vegetation or a bed of reeds. Chiefly *dial.* L19.
– COMB.: **hovercraft** a vehicle or craft supported by a cushion of air ejected downwards against the surface (of land or sea); **hoverfly** any fly of the dipteran family Syrphidae, the members of which resemble wasps but are stingless and often hover in the air; **hover-mower** a lawnmower supported and moving on a cushion of air; **hoverport** a port used by hovercraft; **hovertrain** a train progressing along a concrete track on an air cushion like a hovercraft.
■ **hoverer** *noun* E17. **hoveringly** *adverb* in a hovering manner E19.

how /haʊ/ *noun*[1] *& interjection*[1]. LME.
[ORIGIN Natural exclam.]
1 (An utterance of the exclamation) attracting attention etc. *obsolete* exc. *dial.* in ***how way!***, come on! LME.
2 An exclamation of sailors in hauling. LME.
hale and how: see HALE *noun*[3].

how /haʊ/ *noun*[2]. M16.
[ORIGIN from HOW *adverb*.]
(A question as to) the way or manner (of doing something).

W. GOLDING The Marxist is . . right to insist on the *how* of Utopia even if . . hazy about the what and when. R. F. HOBSON The 'how,' the manner of psychotherapy, can be prepared for.

how /haʊ/ *noun*[3] *& interjection*[2]. E19.
[ORIGIN Cf. Sioux *háo*, Omaha *hou*.]
Used in greeting or welcoming, by or in imitation of N. American Indians; an utterance of 'how!'

†**how** *noun*[4] var. of HOE *noun*[2].

how *noun*[5] var. of HOO *noun*[1].

how *noun*[6], *noun*[7] see HOWE *noun*[1], *noun*[2].

how /haʊ/ *adverb*.
[ORIGIN Old English *hū* = Old Frisian *hū*, *hō*, Old Saxon *(h)wō*, *hwuo* (Middle Low German *woe*, Dutch *hoe*), Old High German *wuo*, from West Germanic adverb from base of WHO, WHAT.]
An adverb primarily interrog., used also in exclams., and in conjunctive and relative constructions.
1 In what way or manner; by what means; in whatever way; by whatever means. Used in qualifying verbs in dependence on verbs of saying, asking, perceiving, etc., on nouns like *heed*, *care*, and related adjectives, on prepositions, and following an infinitive. OE. ▸**b** Used in weakened sense 'that' following verbs of saying, perceiving, etc. OE.

T. HARDY He does not love you, but you love him—is that how it is? W. S. MAUGHAM She asked herself . . how on earth she was to endure the slow passing of the hours. SCOTT FITZGERALD Well, how can any one tell what's eccentric and what's crazy? J. KRANTZ No gigolo . . was going to tell him how to run his business. H. CARPENTER He wanted to understand machinery and to know how it worked. W. GOLDING What an audience wants to hear from a novelist is how he writes. P. ROTH Look at him! Look at how he dresses. *ellipt.*: E. BOWEN I say, *Father*, about tomorrow, how if I telephoned H.Q. for a lay reader? A. MACLEAN 'A mistake, but easy enough to put right.' 'How?' *Independent* There is likely to be uncertainty . . over what to assess and how. **b** D. WELCH He told us how, as a child, he had once eaten swan for dinner. I. MURDOCH Did she show you her rings, how they were diamonds my father got for us?

2 To what degree or extent. Used in qualifying adjectives or adverbs, or verbs of liking. OE. ▸†**b** = HOWEVER 2. In later use, only correlative to *so*. ME–L19. ▸†**c** As . . . as. LME–M18.

T. HARDY Why, how late you are, Ethelberta, and how heated you look! W. S. MAUGHAM If he only knew how I adore him! M. SINCLAIR Her mother sat down to show how tired she was. I. MURDOCH How long are you planning to stay with us? K. VONNEGUT I suppose I should tell you how old I am too. **b** T. VENNER By how much the younger they are, by so much the moyster they are. W. GOODALL Cecil . . had all in readiness to be published how soon the Duke should be beheaded.

3 *interrog.* What. Used esp. as a request for repetition of a question or statement. *arch. & US dial.* exc. in ***how about***, ***how's about*** s.v. ABOUT *preposition* 6. OE. ▸**b** *interrog.* By what name; to what effect, with what meaning. Now chiefly, what, why (*colloq.*). ME.

A. PRICE How's that again, Elizabeth? . . This fellow you talked to—? **b** J. CONRAD How is it that you let Tait's people put us off with a defective lock?

4 In what condition or state; in whatever condition or state. Used in qualifying verbs. ME.

> T. HARDY But I had a great wish to see you, and inquire how you were. R. LEHMANN How are you?.. You're looking awfully well. L. W. MEYNELL 'How's tricks?' he enquired. 'I'm fine. I slept like a top.'

5 At what rate or price. *arch.* LME.

> SHAKES. 2 *Hen. IV* How a score of ewes now?.. A score of good ewes may be worth ten pounds.

– PHRASES & COMB.: **and how!** *colloq.* (*iron.* or *emphatic*) very much so; and no mistake. ***as how***: see AS *adverb* etc. **here's how!** I drink to your good health. ***how about***, ***how about that?***: see ABOUT *preposition* 6. **how come?** *colloq.* how did (or does) it come about (*that*). **how do?** *colloq.* how do you do; hello. **how do you do?**, (*arch.* & *dial.*) **how do ye?** or **how d'ye?**: a formal greeting enquiring as to a person's health etc. **how-do-you-do**, **how-d'ye-do** (*a*) an enquiry of 'how do you do?'; (*b*) an awkward or embarrassing situation. ***how goes it***, ***how is it going***, ***how are things going?***: see GO *verb*. **how is that for high?**, **how is that for queer?** *colloq.* isn't that amazing?, isn't that surprising? **how many** what number. **how much** (*a*) what amount; (*b*) what price; (*c*) *joc.* what? pardon? **how now?** *arch.* how is it now? what is the meaning of this? ***how say you?***: see SAY *verb*[1]. **how so?** how can you show that that is so? **how — soever** to whatever degree or extent. ***how's about***: see ABOUT *preposition* 6. **how's that?** (*a*) what is your opinion of that?; (*b*) CRICKET (said to an umpire) is the batsman out or not? (cf. OWZAT). ***how the other half lives***: see HALF *noun*. ***how the wind blows***, ***how the wind lies***: see WIND *noun*[1]. ***how the world wags***: see WAG *verb*. **how-to** *adjective* (*colloq.*) instructive; of the nature of a manual.

H

howardite /ˈhaʊədʌɪt/ *noun*. M19.
[ORIGIN from E. *Howard* (fl. 1802), English chemist + -ITE[1].]
1 MINERALOGY. A supposed silicate of iron and magnesium occurring in some meteorites. M19.
2 ASTRONOMY. Any of a group of achondritic meteorites principally composed of hypersthene and anorthite. L19.

howbeit /haʊˈbiːɪt/ *adverb & conjunction*. Now *arch.* or *literary*. LME.
[ORIGIN from HOW *adverb* + BE + IT *pronoun* (orig. as three words with pa. t. *how were it*).]
▸ **A** *adverb*. Nevertheless; however. LME.
▸ **†B** *conjunction*. Though, although. LME–M17.

howdah /ˈhaʊdə/ *noun*. L18.
[ORIGIN Urdu *haudah* from Arabic *hawdaj* a litter carried by a camel.]
A seat for two or more, usu. with a canopy, carried on an elephant's back.
■ **howdahed** *adjective* carrying a howdah E19.

howdie /ˈhaʊdi/ *noun*. *Scot.* & *N. English*. Also **-dy**. L17.
[ORIGIN Unknown.]
A midwife.

howdy /ˈhaʊdi/ *noun*[1] & *interjection*. *colloq.* (chiefly *US*). E19.
[ORIGIN Alt. of ***how d'ye?*** s.v. HOW *adverb*.]
(A greeting of) how do you do?; (a) hello.

> T. MORRISON It was like talking to somebody's cousin who just stepped by to say howdy.

howdy *noun*[2] var. of HOWDIE.

howe /haʊ/ *noun*[1]. Also (earlier, now only in sense 1) **how**. ME.
[ORIGIN Old Norse *haugr* mound, cairn, from Germanic base of HIGH *adjective*.]
1 A hill. Now only in northern place names. ME.
2 An artificial mound; *esp.* a tumulus, a barrow. M17.

howe /haʊ/ *noun*[2]. *Scot.* & *N. English*. Also (earlier) **how**. LME.
[ORIGIN Var. of HOLL *noun*.]
†1 A hole. *rare*. LME–L16.
†2 = HOLL *noun* 2. E16–M17.
3 A hollow place; a depression. M16.

howe /haʊ/ *adjective & adverb*. *Scot.* & *N. English*. LME.
[ORIGIN Var. of HOLL *adjective*.]
Hollow(ly).

howe'er *adverb* see HOWEVER.

howel /ˈhaʊəl/ *noun & verb*. E19.
[ORIGIN Prob. of Low German origin: cf. Middle Low German *hövel*, Low German *Höwel* plane.]
▸ **A** *noun*. A plane with a convex sole, used by a cooper for smoothing the inside of a cask etc. E19.
▸ **B** *verb trans.* Infl. **-l(l)-**. Plane or smooth with a howel. M19.

however /haʊˈɛvə/ *adverb*. Also contr. **-e'er** /-ˈɛː/. LME.
[ORIGIN from HOW *adverb* + EVER *adverb*.]
▸ **I 1** In whatever manner; by whatever means. Used in qualifying verbs. LME.

> M. KEANE However she had done it, she had alerted the busy Abbot.

2 To whatever degree or extent. Used in qualifying adjectives or adverbs. LME.

> V. WOOLF I am sure however many years I keep this diary, I shall never find a winter to beat this. C. P. SNOW Whatever Sheriff did, however inconsequently he behaved, would only strengthen her love. E. FIGES However tired she felt, she would have to make an effort. L. GORDON However much Virginia criticised the Victorians.. she was nostalgic for their manners.

†3 In any case, at any rate. L16–M18.

> J. BUTLER Till we know the Whole, or, however, much more of the Case.

4 For all that, nevertheless, notwithstanding; but; *arch.* however much, notwithstanding that. Used in qualifying a whole clause or sentence. L16.

> G. GREENE One must not exaggerate his knowledge, however. A. GARLAND There weren't, however, any fish to be seen. *Which?* However, a couple of the computers we looked at had drawbacks.

▸ **II** *interrog.* **5** (Also as two words.) Used with emphatic force in place of *how* in a question. L19.

howff /haʊf/ *noun & verb*. *Scot.* M16.
[ORIGIN Unknown.]
▸ **A** *noun*. **1** The main burial ground at Dundee (*hist.*); *gen.* any cemetery. M16.
2 A favourite meeting place, a haunt. E18.
▸ **B** *verb intrans.* Frequent, haunt. E19.

howgozit /haʊˈgəʊzɪt/ *noun*. M20.
[ORIGIN Alt. of ***how goes it?*** s.v. GO *verb*.]
A graph showing how much fuel an aircraft has left in relation to that needed to reach the destination or to return to the point of departure.

howish /ˈhaʊɪʃ/ *adjective*. *obsolete* exc. *dial.* L17.
[ORIGIN from HOW *adverb* + -ISH[1].]
Vaguely unwell; having a vague sense of illness.

†howitz *noun*. Also **haubitz**. Pl. **-es**, same. L17–L18.
[ORIGIN German *Haubitze*, †*Hau(f)enitz* from Czech *houfnice* sling, catapult.]
= HOWITZER.

howitzer /ˈhaʊɪtsə/ *noun*. L17.
[ORIGIN Dutch *houwitser* from German *Haubitze*: see HOWITZ, -ER[1].]
A short relatively light gun for the high-angle firing of shells at a low velocity.

howk /haʊk/ *verb*. Now chiefly *dial.* Also (earlier) **†holk**. LME.
[ORIGIN Cogn. with Middle Low German *holken*, Low German *holken*, *hölken* hollow, from base of HOLL *adjective* + dim. formative *-k*, as in *talk* etc.]
1 *verb trans.* Hollow out by digging; excavate; dig out or up; unearth. LME.

> B. MARSHALL Deep in their trenches the hairy men stood, howking out the brown earth. W. MCILVANNEY Ah canny see beyond the seam that Ah'm tryin' tae howk.

2 *verb intrans.* Dig; search about; find. E16.

> R. KIPLING Dan hiked and howked with a boat-hook (the brook was too narrow for sculls).

howl /haʊl/ *noun*. L16.
[ORIGIN from the verb.]
1 A long loud doleful cry of a dog, wolf, etc.; a loud cry of pain, anguish, or laughter; a yell of derision. L16.

> J. KRANTZ Dolly clutched her belly and gave a sudden grunting howl. P. HOWARD The attitude of *The Times* provoked howls of indignation.

2 A wailing noise of an inanimate agent; *spec.* such a noise produced in a loudspeaker as a result of electrical or acoustic feedback. M19.

howl /haʊl/ *verb*. ME.
[ORIGIN Corresp. to Middle Low German, Middle Dutch *hūlen* (Dutch *huilen*), Middle High German *hiulen*, *hiuweln* (German *heulen*) rel. to Old High German *hūwila* (Middle High German *hiuwel*) owl; perh. immed. from OWL *noun* (cf. also Latin *ululare* howl, *ulula* owl, Greek *hulan* bark).]
1 *verb intrans.* (Of a dog, wolf, etc.) emit a long loud doleful cry; (of a person) utter a long loud cry of pain, derision, laughter, etc.; (esp. of a child) cry or weep loudly. Formerly also, (of an owl) hoot. ME. ▸**b** Of an inanimate agent, esp. the wind or a storm: make a prolonged wailing noise. L17.

> C. CHAPLIN At night from my bedroom I would listen to the coyotes howling. V. S. PRITCHETT They were howling with grief, the tears drenched their faces as they rocked in.. sorrow. V. GLENDINNING The audience, after howling with derision during the first act, ended up applauding wildly. **b** T. C. WOLFE And the great winds howl and swoop across the land. I. BANKS The trains howl like lost souls.

2 *verb trans.* Utter (words) with howling. M16.

> SHAKES. *Macb.* But I have words That would be howl'd out in the desert air.

3 *verb trans.* Foll. by *down*: prevent (a speaker, words) from being heard by howls of derision. L19.

> A. BURGESS There was no noise of disagreement save from myself, and I was easily howled down.

howler /ˈhaʊlə/ *noun*. E19.
[ORIGIN from HOWL *verb* + -ER[1].]
1 More fully ***howler monkey***. Any of several S. American cebid monkeys constituting the genus *Alouatta*, which have long prehensile tails and make loud howling noises. E19.
2 A person hired to cry or wail at a funeral or a person's deathbed. Now *rare*. M19.
3 A glaring blunder. *colloq.* L19.

> E. JONG Herr Hummel.. spoke English well, but he made occasional howlers.

howlet /ˈhaʊlɪt/ *noun*. *dial.* (chiefly *Scot.*). L15.
[ORIGIN Dim. of OWL *noun* with assim. to HOWL *verb*: see -ET[1]. Cf. OWLET.]
An owl, an owlet.

howling /ˈhaʊlɪŋ/ *noun*. LME.
[ORIGIN from HOWL *verb* + -ING[1].]
1 The action of HOWL *verb*; an instance of this. LME.
2 *spec.* The production of a wailing noise in a loudspeaker by feedback. E20.

howling /ˈhaʊlɪŋ/ *adjective & adverb*. L16.
[ORIGIN from HOWL *verb* + -ING[2].]
▸ **A** *adjective*. **1** That howls. L16.
howling baboon = HOWLER 1. ***howling*** DERVISH. **howling monkey** = HOWLER 1.
2 Filled with howling; bleak, dreary. L16.
howling wilderness *biblical* a dreary wilderness.
3 Extreme, glaring; great. *colloq.* M19.

> *Times* The Frankie marketing campaign was a howling success. *Listener* If he wasn't guilty of (at best) howling incompetence, somebody in his administration was.

▸ **B** *adverb*. Extremely; completely. *colloq.* L19.

> R. KIPLING He'll be howling drunk to-night.

■ **howlingly** *adverb* L16.

Howship /ˈhaʊʃɪp/ *noun*. L19.
[ORIGIN J. *Howship* (1781–1841), English surgeon.]
ANATOMY. ***Howship's lacuna***, ***†lacuna of Howship***, each of the microscopic pits on the surface of bony tissue undergoing resorption.

howsoever /haʊsəʊˈɛvə/ *adverb*. *arch.* Also contr. **-e'er** /-ˈɛː/. LME.
[ORIGIN from HOW *adverb* + SO *adverb* + EVER *adverb*.]
1 = HOWEVER 1. LME.
†2 = HOWEVER 3. L16–M17.
†3 = HOWEVER 4. L16–E18.
4 = HOWEVER 2. L17.

howsomever /haʊs(ə)mˈɛvə/ *adverb*. ME.
[ORIGIN from HOW *adverb* + SOME *adverb* + EVER *adverb*; parallel formation with HOWSOEVER.]
†1 = HOWEVER 1. ME–E17.
2 = HOWEVER 4. Now chiefly *dial.* & *N. Amer. colloq.* M16.

> W. GOLDING Howsomever we must play our game as long as we can.

howtowdie /haʊˈtaʊdi/ *noun*. *Scot.* E19.
[ORIGIN Prob. from Old French *hétoudeau*, *estaudeau* a young chicken for the pot.]
(A) boiled chicken served with spinach and poached eggs.

howzat *interjection* var. of OWZAT.

†hox *noun & verb*. LME.
[ORIGIN Prob. abbreviation from ***hough-sinew*** s.v. HOUGH *noun*.]
▸ **A** *noun*. A hamstring. Only in LME.
▸ **B** *verb trans.* Hamstring. LME–M18.

Hoxnian /ˈhɒksnɪən/ *adjective & noun*. M20.
[ORIGIN from *Hoxne*, a village in Suffolk + -IAN.]
GEOLOGY. (Designating or pertaining to) an interglacial stage of the Pleistocene in Britain, preceding the Wolstonian glaciation and identified with the Holsteinian of northern Europe.

hoy /hɔɪ/ *noun*[1]. ME.
[ORIGIN Middle Dutch *hoei* var. of *hoede*, *heude* (mod. *heu*), of unknown origin.]
hist. A small sailing vessel, usu. rigged as a sloop, for carrying passengers and goods, esp. for short coastal journeys.
– COMB.: **hoyman** a man in charge of a hoy.

hoy /hɔɪ/ *interjection, verb, & noun*[2]. LME.
[ORIGIN Natural exclam. Cf. AHOY, OI *interjection*[1] & *noun*.]
▸ **A** *interjection*. Attracting attention, driving animals; NAUTICAL hailing or calling aloft. LME.
▸ **B** *verb trans.* Urge on, summon, with a cry or cries of 'hoy!' M16.

> J. FOWLES He saw a man hoying a herd of cows away from a low byre.

▸ **C** *noun*. A cry of 'hoy!' M17.

hoya /ˈhɔɪə/ *noun*. M19.
[ORIGIN mod. Latin (see below), from Thomas *Hoy*, English gardener (d. 1821): see -A[1].]
Any of various chiefly climbing or twining plants of the genus *Hoya* (family Asclepiadaceae), natives of the Far East, bearing dense umbels of fleshy or waxy pink, white, or yellow flowers. Also called ***wax flower***, ***wax plant***.

hoyden /ˈhɔɪd(ə)n/ *noun & adjective*. L16.
[ORIGIN Prob. from Middle Dutch & mod. Dutch *heiden* HEATHEN, gypsy.]
▸ **A** *noun*. **†1** A rude or ignorant fellow. L16–E18.
2 A noisy, rude, or (esp.) boisterous girl or woman. L17.

> B. GUEST She leaped over stiles in the fields, a hoyden, careless of her dress.

▸ **B** *attrib.* or as *adjective*. Pertaining to or characteristic of a hoyden. E18.
■ **hoydenish** *adjective* behaving like or having the character of a hoyden; = HOYDEN *adjective*: L18.

hoyden /ˈhɔɪd(ə)n/ *verb intrans.* Now *rare*. E18.
[ORIGIN from the noun.]
Behave like a hoyden.

hoyle /hɔɪl/ *noun*[1]. Now *rare*. E17.
[ORIGIN Unknown.]
ARCHERY. A short distance mark used esp. when shooting at rovers.

Hoyle /hɔɪl/ *noun*[2]. E20.
[ORIGIN Edmond *Hoyle* (1672–1769), English author of several works on card games.]
A book of rules on card games. Chiefly in ***according to Hoyle***, according to the highest authority, in accordance with strict rules.

h.p. *abbreviation*. Also **HP**.
1 High pressure.
2 Hire purchase.
3 Horsepower.

HPV *abbreviation*.
MEDICINE. Human papillomavirus.

HQ *abbreviation*.
Headquarters.

HR *abbreviation*[1].
1 House of Representatives. *US*.
2 Human Resources (the personnel department of an organization).

hr *abbreviation*[2].
hour.

HRH *abbreviation*.
Her, His, Royal Highness.

hrs *abbreviation*.
Hours.

HRT *abbreviation*.
Hormone replacement therapy.

hryvna /ˈhrɪvnjə/ *noun*. Also **-nia**. Pl. same, **-as**. L20.
[ORIGIN Ukrainian *gryvnya* 3-kopek coin of pre-independent Ukraine, from Old Russian *grivina* necklace, ring, coin.]
The basic monetary unit of Ukraine, equal to 100 kopiykas.

Hs *symbol*.
CHEMISTRY. Hassium.

HSH *abbreviation*.
Her, His, Serene Highness.

Hsiang *noun* var. of XIANG.

HT *abbreviation*.
High tension.

HTLV *abbreviation*.
Human T-cell lymphotropic (or lymphocyte) virus.

HTML *abbreviation*.
COMPUTING. Hypertext Markup Language, a standardized system for tagging text files to achieve font, colour, graphic, and hyperlink effects on World Wide Web pages.

HTTP *abbreviation*.
COMPUTING. Hypertext Transport (or Transfer) Protocol, the data transfer protocol used on the World Wide Web.

HUAC /ˈhjuːak/ *abbreviation*. *US*.
House (of Representatives) Un-American Activities Committee.

huaca /ˈwɑːkə/ *noun*. Also (earlier) †**gua-**. E17.
[ORIGIN Spanish *huaca*, *guaca* from Quechua *waca* god of the house.]
1 The all-pervading spirit thought by some Peruvian Indians to be disseminated through the whole world; any material object thought to be the abode of such a spirit. E17.
2 A prehistoric Peruvian tomb or temple. M19.

huaco /ˈwɑːkəʊ/ *noun*. Also **gua-** /ˈgwɑː-/. Pl. **-os**. M20.
[ORIGIN Alt. of HUACA.]
In Peru, Bolivia, and Chile, a piece of ancient Indian pottery.

huarache /wəˈrɑːtʃi/ *noun*. Also **gua-** /gwə-/. L19.
[ORIGIN Mexican Spanish.]
A leather-thonged sandal, orig. worn by Mexican Indians.

Huastec /ˈwɑːstɛk/ *noun*. Also **-teca** /-tɛkə/, **Huax-** /ˈwɑːks-/. Pl. **-s**, same. M19.
[ORIGIN Spanish *huasteco*, *huaxteco*.]
A member of an Indian people inhabiting parts of Mexico; the Mayan language of this people.

hub /hʌb/ *noun*[1]. E16.
[ORIGIN Unknown. Cf. HOB *noun*[2].]
†**1** = HOB *noun*[2] 5. E16.
2 The central solid part of a wheel, from which the spokes radiate, and which rotates on or with the axle. M17.
up to the hub *US* as far as possible.
3 A bump in the ground. Now *US* & *dial.* M17.
4 *fig.* The central point of an activity, interest, etc. M19.

> R. P. GRAVES The critic Edmund Gosse, who lived at the very hub of London's literary life.

5 A cylindrical piece of steel on which the design for a coin is engraved in relief. M19.
– COMB.: **hub brake**: that acts on the hub of a wheel; **hubcap** a cover for the hub of a vehicle's wheel.
■ **hubless** *adjective* L20.

hub /hʌb/ *noun*[2]. E19.
[ORIGIN Abbreviation.]
= HUBBY *noun*.

hubba hubba /ˈhʌbəhʌbə/ *interjection & noun*. *N. Amer. slang*. M20.
[ORIGIN Unknown.]
▸ **A** *interjection*. Expr. approval, excitement, or enthusiasm. M20.
▸ **B** *noun*. Nonsense; ballyhoo. M20.

Hubbard /ˈhʌbəd/ *noun*. Chiefly *N. Amer.* M19.
[ORIGIN Prob. a personal name.]
In full ***Hubbard squash***. A large green or yellow variety of the winter squash (*Cucurbita maxima*).

Hubble /ˈhʌb(ə)l/ *noun*. M20.
[ORIGIN Edwin P. *Hubble* (1889–1953), US astronomer.]
Used *attrib.* and in *possess.* to designate concepts arising from the work of Hubble.
Hubble constant, **Hubble's constant** the ratio of the recessional speed of a galaxy to its distance; the reciprocal of this, interpretable as the time elapsed since the universe started to expand (at constant rate) from a single point. **Hubble's law**, **Hubble law**: that the redshifts in the spectra of distant galaxies (and hence their speeds of recession) are proportional to their distance.

hubble-bubble /ˈhʌb(ə)lbʌb(ə)l/ *noun*. E17.
[ORIGIN Imit. redupl. of BUBBLE *noun*.]
1 A hubbub; confused talk; a bubbling sound. E17.
2 A rudimentary form of hookah, the water being held in a coconut shell or similar receptacle. M17.

hubbub /ˈhʌbʌb/ *noun*. M16.
[ORIGIN Perh. from Irish: cf. Irish *ababú!* used in battle-cries, Gaelic *ub! ub! ubub!* expr. aversion or contempt, *ubh ubh!* expr. disgust or amazement.]
1 A confused noise of a crowd shouting or talking; the shouting of a war cry; noisy turmoil; (a) confusion, (a) disturbance; a row. M16.

> P. MEDAWAR The hubbub that broke out after the publication of the Origin of Species.

2 A game similar to dice, formerly played by American Indians in New England. *obsolete* exc. *hist.* M17.
■ **hubbuboo**, **-aboo** /ˈhʌbəbuː/ *noun* a confused yelling, esp. as a war cry; a tumult: L16.

hubby /ˈhʌbi/ *noun*. *colloq.* L17.
[ORIGIN Abbreviation.]
A husband.

hubby /ˈhʌbi/ *adjective*. *US*. Now *rare*. M19.
[ORIGIN from HUB *noun*[1] + -Y[1].]
Of a road: full of bumps.

hübnerite /ˈhjuːbnərʌɪt/ *noun*. Also ***hueb-**. M19.
[ORIGIN from A. *Hübner*, 19th-cent. German miner + -ITE[1].]
MINERALOGY. Manganese tungstate, $MnWO_4$, occurring as a monoclinic mineral in red-brown crystals and forming a series with ferberite.

hubris /ˈhjuːbrɪs/ *noun*. L19.
[ORIGIN Greek.]
Presumption, insolence, (orig. towards the gods); pride, excessive self-confidence.

> ALDOUS HUXLEY Hubris against the essentially divine order of Nature would be followed by its appropriate nemesis.
> S. J. GOULD By what hubris do we consider ourselves any bigger in a universe of such vastness?

■ **huˈbristic** *adjective* insolent, contemptuous, proud M19. **huˈbristically** *adverb* with hubris; in a presumptuous manner: E20.

Hubshee /ˈhʌbʃiː/ *noun & adjective*. Now *rare*. Also **-shi**. E17.
[ORIGIN Persian & Urdu *ḥab(a)šī*, Arabic *ḥabašī*, from *Ḥabaš(a)* (people of) Ethiopia.]
▸ **A** *noun*. An Ethiopian, an Abyssinian. E17.
▸ **B** *adjective*. Ethiopian, Abyssinian. L17.

huchen /ˈhuːk(ə)n, ˈhuːxən/ *noun*. E20.
[ORIGIN German.]
A large slender salmonid fish, *Hucho hucho*, of the Danube river system.
■ †**hucho** *noun* [from the Latin name] = HUCHEN: only in 19.

huck /hʌk/ *noun*. *obsolete* exc. *dial.* LME.
[ORIGIN Uncertain: perh. rel. to Middle Low German, Middle Dutch *hūken*, *hukken* sit bent, crouch, from Germanic base meaning 'be bent'.]
The hip, the haunch.
– COMB.: **huck-bone** = *huckle-bone* s.v. HUCKLE *noun*.

huck /hʌk/ *verb intrans.* Long *obsolete* exc. *dial.* ME.
[ORIGIN Prob. ult. from Germanic base also of HUCKSTER *noun*.]
Haggle, bargain.

huckaback /ˈhʌkəbak/ *noun & adjective*. L17.
[ORIGIN Unknown.]
(Made of) a strong linen or cotton fabric used for towels etc., having the weft threads thrown alternately up to form a rough surface.

hucker-mucker *noun*, *adjective*, & *adverb* see HUGGER-MUGGER *noun, adverb, & adjective*.

huckle /ˈhʌk(ə)l/ *noun*. E16.
[ORIGIN Dim. of HUCK *noun*: see -LE[1].]
The hip, the haunch.
– COMB.: **huckle-back** a humpback; **huckle-backed** *adjective* humpbacked; **huckle-bone** (*a*) the bone of the hip, or (occas.) the head of the femur; (*b*) the astragalus bone of the hock joint in a quadruped, used in games or divination; a knuckle bone.

huckleberry /ˈhʌk(ə)lb(ə)ri/ *noun*. L16.
[ORIGIN Perh. from HUCKLE *noun* + BERRY *noun*[1].]
1 Any of various low N. American shrubs of the genus *Gaylussacia*, esp. *G. baccata*, of the heath family, which are valued for their tart edible fruits; the fruit of such a plant. Also = ***blueberry*** s.v. BLUE *adjective*. L16.
2 In British use: the bilberry, *Vaccinium myrtillus*. M19.
– NOTE: Despite the lateness and paucity of the evidence for sense 2, it is likely that this was the original sense.

huckster /ˈhʌkstə/ *noun*. ME.
[ORIGIN Prob. of Low German origin and rel. to HUCK *verb*: see -STER.]
1 A retailer in a small shop or at a stall; a pedlar, a hawker. ME.

> L. DURRELL The hucksters set up their stalls in preparation for some familiar village fete.

2 A mercenary person ready to make a profit out of anything. LME.
3 A publicity agent or advertising copywriter, esp. for radio or television. *US*. M20.
– PHRASES: †**in huckster's hands** likely to be roughly used or lost.
■ **hucksterdom** *noun* L19. **hucksterism** *noun* (usu. *derog.*) the theory or practice of being a huckster M20. **huckstery** *noun* the trade or place of trade of a huckster; petty bargaining; in *pl.*, the goods of a huckster: LME.

huckster /ˈhʌkstə/ *verb*. L16.
[ORIGIN from the noun.]
1 *verb intrans.* Bargain, haggle. L16.
2 *verb trans.* Deal in, retail, (esp. in small quantities); bargain over. M17.
■ **huckisterer** *noun* E18. **hucksteress**, **-tress** *noun* a female huckster E17.

HUD *abbreviation*.
Head-up display.

hud /hʌd/ *noun*. *obsolete* exc. *dial.* LME.
[ORIGIN Perh. from Germanic base of HIDE *verb*[1]: cf. HUDDLE *verb*.]
The husk or covering of a seed; the pod of a legume.

†**hudder-mudder** *noun*. LME–L16.
[ORIGIN Redupl., with 1st elem. prob. rel. to HUDDLE *verb*: cf. later HUGGER-MUGGER *noun*.]
Concealment; secrecy. Chiefly in ***in hudder-mudder***, secretly, clandestinely.

huddle /ˈhʌd(ə)l/ *noun*. L16.
[ORIGIN Prob. from the verb.]
1 A crowded or confused mass of people or things. L16.

> B. MOORE In the distance, a huddle of slate rooftops. P. ROTH A huddle of graduate students waiting shyly . . to ask the writer serious questions.

2 Confusion; disorderly haste. E17.
3 A close or secret conference. Freq. in ***go into a huddle***. *colloq.* E20. ▸**b** *spec.* In any of various team games, esp. American football, a brief gathering of players during a game to receive instructions. M20.

> F. ASTAIRE We immediately went into huddles . . to hear and discuss the material which they had written.

4 BRIDGE. A pause during which a player considers his or her next call or play. M20.

huddle /ˈhʌd(ə)l/ *verb*. L16.
[ORIGIN Perh. of Low German origin and ult. from Germanic base of HIDE *verb*[1]: cf. HUD.]
▸ **I** *verb trans.* †**1** Hide; hush *up*. L16–E19.
2 Heap *up*, mix, or crowd *together* closely or in a disordered manner; push in a disorderly mass *into*, *out of*, *through*, etc.; put (clothes) on or *on* hurriedly or untidily. L16. ▸**b** Hunch, coil, (oneself) *over*, *up*, etc. M18.

> SIR W. SCOTT The Friar . . had huddled a friar's frock over his green cassock. R. L. STEVENSON The bar-keeper led us upstairs to a room . . with . . chairs huddled into one corner.
> W. S. CHURCHILL They were huddling and clumping themselves together for mutual protection. **b** CONAN DOYLE I found him huddled up in his arm-chair with updrawn knees.

3 Hurry (*over*, *through*); hurry the completion of, botch *up* through haste. Now *rare* or *obsolete*. M17.
4 Hug. Now *dial.* M17.

H

▸ **II** *verb intrans.* **5** Gather or crowd closely or in disorder; hunch up; nestle closely in a hunched position. Freq. foll. by *together, up*. L16.

> H. ROTH They huddled together as if for protection. P. L. FERMOR Villages that huddled round the shingle roofs of churches. B. CHATWIN After dark, she would huddle over the fire.

†**6** Hurry in disorder or confusion. M17–M18.
■ **huddlement** *noun* huddled condition, huddling M19. **huddler** *noun* (*rare*) E17.

†**huddle** *adverb & adjective*. M16.
[ORIGIN Rel. to the verb.]
▸ **A** *adverb*. Confusedly; in a crowded mass; in disorderly haste. M16–E17.
▸ **B** *adjective*. Huddled, confused, crowded. E17–E18.

hudibrastic /hjuːdɪˈbrastɪk/ *adjective & noun*. E18.
[ORIGIN from *Hudibras* (see below) after *fantastic* etc.]
▸ **A** *adjective*. In the metre or manner of *Hudibras*, a mock-heroic satirical poem by Samuel Butler, published 1663–78. E18.
▸ **B** *noun*. (A) Hudibrastic language, verse, or style. M18.
■ **hudibrastically** *adverb* L19.

Hudson Bay /hʌds(ə)n ˈbeɪ/ *noun phr.* Also **Hudson's Bay** /ˈhʌds(ə)nz/. L19.
[ORIGIN See HUDSONIAN. Var. from the Hudson's Bay Company.]
In full ***Hudson Bay blanket***. A durable woollen blanket of a kind orig. sold by the Hudson's Bay Company and freq. used as material for coats.

H

Hudsonian /hʌdˈsəʊnɪən/ *adjective*. M19.
[ORIGIN from *Hudson* Bay, from its discoverer Henry *Hudson* (d. 1611), English navigator: see -IAN.]
Of or pertaining to Hudson Bay in Canada and the surrounding land; *esp.* designating the biogeographical zone represented by the territory around the bay (north of the tree line from Labrador to Alaska).
Hudsonian curlew *N. Amer.* a whimbrel, *Numenius phaeopus* (of the N. American subspecies). **Hudsonian godwit** a New World godwit, *Limosa haemastica*, breeding in NW Canada.

hue /hjuː/ *noun*[1].
[ORIGIN Old English *hēw, hēow, hīw, hiew* = Old Norse *hý* down on plants (Swedish *hy* skin, complexion), Gothic *hiwi* form, appearance, from Germanic base of unknown origin.]
1 Form, shape, figure; appearance, aspect; species. Long *obsolete* exc. *Scot.* OE. ▸†**b** An apparition. OE–E17.
2 Colour. OE. ▸**b** Variety, tint, or quality of a colour. M19. ▸**c** That attribute of a colour by which it is recognized as a red, a green, etc., and which is dependent on its dominant wavelength, and independent of intensity or lightness. M19.

> SLOAN WILSON The rocks were . . tinged with a dull red hue. B. BREYTENBACH Their cheeks have the hue of tomatoes.

3 Complexion of the face or skin; *fig.* character, aspect. ME.

> ISAIAH BERLIN Muddle-headed men of good will and quacks and false prophets of every hue.

hide and hue: see HIDE *noun*[1].
■ **hueless** *adjective* colourless, pallid OE.

hue /hjuː/ *noun*[2]. *obsolete* exc. in HUE AND CRY. LME.
[ORIGIN Old French *hu*, from *huer* HUE *verb*[2].]
Outcry, shouting, clamour, esp. during battle or hunting.

hue /hjuː/ *verb*[1] *trans.* Pres. pple & verbal noun **hu(e)ing**. OE.
[ORIGIN from HUE *noun*[1].]
1 Form, fashion, give an external appearance to; colour. Chiefly as ***hued*** *ppl adjective*. OE.
†**2** Depict, describe vividly. Only in ME.

hue /hjuː/ *verb*[2]. Now *local*. Pres. pple & verbal noun **hu(e)ing**. ME.
[ORIGIN Old French & mod. French *huer* shout as in battle or hunting: of imit. origin.]
1 *verb intrans.* Shout, make an outcry; *spec.* in hunting, and in guiding a seine-fishing operation. ME.
2 *verb trans.* Assail, drive, or guide with shouts. L16.
■ **huer** *noun* M16.

hue and cry /hjuː (ə)n(d) ˈkrʌɪ/ *noun & verb phr.* Also **hue-and-cry**. LME.
[ORIGIN Legal Anglo-Norman *hu e cri*, i.e. *hu* outcry, HUE *noun*[2], *e* and, *cri* CRY *noun*.]
▸ **A** *noun*. **1** LAW (now *hist.*). ▸**a** An outcry calling for the pursuit of a felon; the pursuit of a felon with such an outcry. LME. ▸**b** A proclamation for the capture of a criminal or the recovery of stolen property. E17. ▸**c** An official publication in which details of offences committed and offenders sought are given. E19.

> W. COWPER They raised the hue and cry:—'Stop thief! stop thief!—a highwayman!'

2 *gen.* A shout of pursuit or attack; a cry or general expression of alarm or opposition. L15.

> H. EVANS There was, none the less, an immediate hue and cry in the press and Parliament.

▸ **B** *verb*. **1** *verb intrans.* Raise a hue and cry; make an outcry. M18.
2 *verb trans.* Pursue with hue and cry. M19.

huebnerite *noun* see HÜBNERITE.

huegelite *noun* see HÜGELITE.

huerta /ˈhwɛːtə/ *noun*. M19.
[ORIGIN Spanish.]
In Spain and Spanish-speaking countries: a piece of irrigated land; an orchard.

huet-huet /ˈhuːɪthuːɪt/ *noun*. Also **guidguid** /ˈgwɪdgwɪd/. M19.
[ORIGIN Imit.]
Either of two S. American birds of the tapaculo family, *Pteroptochos tarnii* and *P. castaneus*.

huevos rancheros /ˌ(h)wɛvɒs ranˈtʃɛːrɒs/ *noun phr. pl.* L20.
[ORIGIN Spanish = rancheros' eggs.]
Fried or poached eggs served on a tortilla with a spicy tomato sauce.

huff /hʌf/ *noun*. L16.
[ORIGIN from the verb.]
1 A sudden rush *of* anger or arrogance. Now usu., a fit of pique or offended dignity. L16.

> *Listener* It seems a pity that this new era . . should be accompanied by an international huff-and-puff over priorities. A. WEST The medical man . . leaves in a huff when his advice is turned down.

†**2** A person puffed up with self-importance; a swaggerer, a bully. Also, (a display of) self-importance. E17–E18.
3 A puff of wind. *obsolete* exc. in ***huff and puff***, passing into sense 1. E17.
4 DRAUGHTS. The removal of an opponent's piece for missing or ignoring the opportunity to take one of one's own pieces (orig. accompanied by blowing on the piece). L19.

huff /hʌf/ *verb*. L16.
[ORIGIN formed as HUFF *interjection*.]
1 *verb intrans.* Blow, puff. *obsolete* exc. in ***huff and puff***, passing into sense 2. L16.

> W. D. SNODGRASS We huff like windy giants / scattering with our breath / gray-headed dandelions. *fig.*: A. F. DOUGLAS-HOME Tom Steele puffed and huffed and threatened to sue me.

2 *verb intrans.* Puff or swell with pride or arrogance; speak arrogantly, bluster. Cf. earlier HUFFER *noun*. L16. ▸**b** *verb trans.* Bully or scold (*into, off, to*, etc.); treat with arrogance or contempt. Now *rare* or *obsolete*. L17.
3 a *verb intrans.* Swell with anger or irritation; take offence. Now *rare*. L16. ▸**b** *verb trans.* Offend the dignity of; cause to take offence, put into a huff. L18.

> **a** W. BURKITT Some would have huffed at it as a rude affront.

4 †**a** *verb trans.* Blow or puff (*up*); inflate, cause to swell. E17–E18. ▸**b** *verb intrans.* Swell (up). *obsolete* exc. *dial.* M17.
5 *verb trans.* DRAUGHTS. Remove (an opponent's piece) for missing or ignoring the opportunity to take one of one's own pieces (orig. accompanied by blowing on the piece). L17.
6 *verb trans.* Sniff fumes from (petrol or solvents) for a euphoric effect. *N. Amer. slang*. L20.
■ **huffingly** *adverb* in a huffing manner E17.

†**huff** *interjection*. Also **huffa**. LME–E17.
[ORIGIN Imit. of blowing or puffing: cf. PUFF *noun, verb*.]
Expr. a swaggering, boastful, or bullying personality (esp. on the theatrical stage).

huff-cap /ˈhʌfkap/ *adjective & noun*. *arch.* L16.
[ORIGIN from HUFF *verb* + CAP *noun*[1].]
▸ **A** *adjective*. **1** Of drink: heady, strong. L16.
2 Blustering, swaggering. L16.
▸ **B** *noun*. **1** (A drink made from) strong ale. L16.
2 A swaggering or blustering person. E17.

huff-duff /ˈhʌfdʌf/ *noun*. M20.
[ORIGIN from initial letters of *high-frequency direction finder*.]
hist. (Equipment for) radio direction-finding (esp. in the Second World War).

huffer /ˈhʌfə/ *noun*. M16.
[ORIGIN from HUFF *verb* + -ER[1].]
A person who huffs; formerly *esp.* a boastful or swaggering person.

huffish /ˈhʌfɪʃ/ *adjective*. M18.
[ORIGIN from HUFF *noun* + -ISH[1].]
Arrogant; petulant, piqued.
■ **huffishly** *adverb* M18. **huffishness** *noun* M18.

huffkin /ˈhʌfkɪn/ *noun*. *local*. L18.
[ORIGIN Unknown.]
A type of teacake made chiefly in Kent.

huffle /ˈhʌf(ə)l/ *verb trans. & intrans.* *obsolete* exc. *dial.* L16.
[ORIGIN from HUFF *verb* + -LE[3].]
Blow; inflate, swell.

huffy /ˈhʌfi/ *adjective*. L17.
[ORIGIN from HUFF *noun* + -Y[1].]
Quick to take offence or go into a huff; touchy.

> N. BAWDEN I heard myself being huffy and whining and spiteful. J. UPDIKE I'm crazy about that huffy frozen look you get . . when you get defensive.

■ **huffily** *adverb* M19. **huffiness** *noun* L17.

hug /hʌg/ *noun*. E17.
[ORIGIN from the verb.]
1 A squeezing grip in wrestling. Chiefly in ***Cornish hug***. E17.
2 A tight embrace, usu. of affection; a rough grasp with the arms; the squeeze of a bear. M17.

> C. POTOK Manya . . smothered me with a hug that pushed the air from my lungs. *Independent* It was hugs, laughter and tears as they celebrated.

hug /hʌg/ *verb*. Infl. **-gg-**. M16.
[ORIGIN Prob. of Scandinavian origin: cf. Old Norse *hugga* (Norwegian *hugge*) comfort, console, rel. to *hugr* thought, feeling, interest, *hugða* interest, affection, *hugsa* think.]
1 *verb trans.* Clasp in the arms, embrace, usu. affectionately; (of a bear etc.) squeeze with the forelegs. M16. ▸**b** Show fondness for; *spec.* court in order to get patronage. Cf. HUGGERY. E17. ▸**c** Cling emotionally or intellectually to (a belief etc.). M17.

> V. WOOLF A son who was hugged to death by a bear. E. CALDWELL Wayne put his arms around her and hugged her tightly against his chest. **c** T. MOORE Faith . . once wedded fast To some dear falsehood, hugs it to the last.

hug-me-tight a knitted close-fitting usu. sleeveless woollen wrap.
2 *verb intrans.* Embrace tightly, cuddle. L16.

> POPE Tis a Bear's talent not to kick but hug.

3 *verb refl.* Congratulate (oneself). E17. ▸†**b** Cherish (oneself); make (oneself) comfortable. M17–M18.

> G. W. LE FEVRE We hugged ourselves with the idea that we had done right.

4 *verb trans.* Keep as close as possible to (a shore etc.). E19.

> C. PHILLIPS This one road hugged the perimeter of the island. *Hairdo Ideas* Hair is scissored to hug the head.

huge /hjuːdʒ/ *adjective*. ME.
[ORIGIN Aphet. from Old French *ahuge, ahoge, ahoege*: ult. origin unknown.]
Very great, large, or big; immense, enormous, vast.

> R. LINDNER They were, he remembers, big people with heavy hands and huge feet. E. REVELEY You seem to regard the—ah—gulf . . of your ignorance as so huge. *Star & Style* This was a big film with a huge cast.

■ **hugely** *adverb* LME. **hugeness** *noun* LME.

hügelite /ˈhjuːgəlʌɪt/ *noun*. Also ***huegelite**. E20.
[ORIGIN from German *Hügel* (family name) + -ITE[1].]
MINERALOGY. A brown or orange monoclinic hydrated arsenate of lead and uranium (orig. supposed a vanadate of lead and zinc).

hugeous /ˈhjuːdʒəs/ *adjective*. Now *rare*. LME.
[ORIGIN from HUGE + -OUS.]
= HUGE.
■ **hugeously** *adverb* M17.

huggable /ˈhʌgəb(ə)l/ *adjective*. L19.
[ORIGIN from HUG *verb* + -ABLE.]
Such as invites hugging; cuddly.

hugger /ˈhʌgə/ *noun*. L17.
[ORIGIN from HUG *verb* + -ER[1].]
A person who hugs.

hugger-mugger /ˈhʌgəmʌgə/ *noun, adverb, & adjective*. Also (earlier & now *dial.*) **hucker-mucker** /ˈhʌkəmʌkə/. E16.
[ORIGIN Redupl., with 1st elem. prob. rel. to HUDDLE *verb* and 2nd elem. to MUCKER *verb*[1]: cf. earlier HUDDER-MUDDER.]
▸ **A** *noun*. **1** Concealment, secrecy. Chiefly in ***in hugger-mugger***, secretly, clandestinely. *arch.* E16.

> S. BUTLER In Hugger-mugger hid.

2 Disorder, confusion; a muddle. L17.

> *Times Lit. Suppl.* The . . Carthusians, revolting against the gregarious hugger-mugger of the older orders, were . . serious writers.

▸ **B** *adverb*. **1** Secretly, clandestinely. Now chiefly *dial.* E16.
2 In disorder or confusion, in a muddle. L19.

> V. GLENDINNING Rich and poor lived here hugger-mugger, literally on top of one another.

▸ **C** *adjective*. **1** Secret, clandestine. L17.

> A. SILLITOE There was no longer the hugger-mugger anecdote, or any juicy elbow-gripping gossip.

2 Disorderly, confused; makeshift. M19.

> H. NICOLSON It entailed . . living a rather hugger-mugger existence in Berlin.

hugger-mugger /ˈhʌgəmʌgə/ *verb*. Now *rare*. E19.
[ORIGIN from HUGGER-MUGGER *noun, adverb, & adjective*.]
1 *verb trans.* Keep secret or concealed. E19.
2 *verb intrans.* Proceed in a clandestine manner; behave in a confused or muddled way. E19.

huggery /ˈhʌg(ə)ri/ *noun*. L18.
[ORIGIN from HUG *verb* or HUGGER: see -ERY.]
The action or practice of hugging; *spec.* the action of a barrister in courting a solicitor etc. in the hope of employment.

huggle /ˈhʌɡ(ə)l/ *verb trans. & intrans.* Now chiefly *dial.* L16.
[ORIGIN Perh. iterative of HUG *verb*: see -LE[3].]
Hug.

Hughie /ˈhjuːi/ *noun. Austral. & NZ slang.* E20.
[ORIGIN Dim. of male forename *Hugh*: see -IE, -Y[6].]
The imaginary being responsible for the weather. Chiefly in ***send her down, Hughie!***

Hugo /ˈhjuːɡəʊ/ *noun.* Pl. **-os**. M20.
[ORIGIN from *Hugo* Gernsback (1884–1967), US science-fiction magazine editor.]
Any of several awards presented annually to writers of the best new science fiction.

hugsome /ˈhʌɡs(ə)m/ *adjective.* L19.
[ORIGIN from HUG *verb* + -SOME[1].]
= HUGGABLE.

Huguenot /ˈhjuːɡənəʊ, -nɒt/ *noun & adjective. hist.* M16.
[ORIGIN French, alt. (by assim. to the name of Besançon *Hugues* (c 1491–1532), Genevese burgomaster) of †*eiguenot*, pl. †*aignos*, †*hugenaulx*, from Dutch *eedgenot* from Swiss German *Eidgenosse* confederate, from *Eid* OATH *noun* + *Genosse* associate.]
▶**A** *noun.* A French Protestant of the 16th and 17th cents. M16.
▶**B** *attrib.* or as *adjective.* Of or pertaining to the Huguenots. L17.
■ **Huguenotism** *noun* French Protestantism in the 16th and 17th cents. E17.

†**hugy** *adjective.* LME–E19.
[ORIGIN from HUGE + -Y[1].]
Huge.

huh /hʌ, hə/ *interjection.* E17.
[ORIGIN Natural exclam.]
Expr. surprise, derision, or enquiry.

W. WHARTON Hey, Margolis, give us other guys a chance, huh? R. JARRELL Huh! . . I'll tell 'em.

huhu /ˈhuːhuː/ *noun.* Chiefly *NZ.* M19.
[ORIGIN Maori.]
A common large New Zealand beetle, *Prionoplus reticularis*, or its larva (more fully ***huhu grub***) found in decaying wood and eaten locally.

huh-uh *interjection & adverb* var. of UH-UH.

hui /ˈhuːi/ *noun.* M19.
[ORIGIN Maori & Hawaiian.]
In New Zealand, a large social or ceremonial gathering, a meeting, a conference; in Hawaii, a formal club or association.

huia /ˈhuːɪə/ *noun.* M19.
[ORIGIN Maori: imit.]
A black New Zealand wattlebird, *Heteralocha acutirostris* (now extinct), having white-tipped feathers formerly prized by Maori as marks of rank.

Huichol /wɪˈtʃəʊl/ *noun & adjective.* E20.
[ORIGIN Spanish from Huichol.]
▶**A** *noun.* Pl. same, **-s**. A member of a Mexican Indian people; the language of this people. E20.
▶**B** *attrib.* or as *adjective.* Of or pertaining to the Huichol or their language. E20.

huitain /ˈwiːteɪn/ *noun. rare.* L16.
[ORIGIN French, from *huit* eight + *-ain* -AN.]
A set or series of eight lines of verse.

Huk /hʌk/ *noun.* M20.
[ORIGIN Abbreviation of Tagalog *Hukbalahap*, from initial syllables of *hukbó* army + *bayan* people, country + *laban* against + *Hapón* Japanese (i.e. *hukbó ng bayan laban sa Hapón* people's army against the Japanese).]
A guerrilla movement in the Philippines, orig. against the Japanese in the Second World War, later popularly identified with Communism.

huke /hjuːk/ *noun. obsolete* exc. *hist.* LME.
[ORIGIN Old French *h(e)uque*, in medieval Latin *huca*, corresp. to Middle Dutch *hûke*, *heuke* (Dutch *huik*), Middle Low German *hoike*, etc.: ult. origin unknown.]
A kind of hooded cloak; later, a tight-fitting garment worn chiefly by women.

hula /ˈhuːlə/ *noun & verb intrans.* Also **hula-hula**. E19.
[ORIGIN Hawaiian.]
(Perform) a Hawaiian dance with six basic steps and gestures symbolizing or imitating natural phenomena, historical events, etc.
– COMB.: **hula hoop**, (US proprietary) **Hula-Hoop** a plastic or wooden hoop for spinning round the body by movement of the waist and hips; **hula skirt** a grass skirt as worn by a hula dancer.

hulan *noun* var. of UHLAN.

†**hulch** *adjective.* E17–M18.
[ORIGIN Unknown.]
Hunched; humpy. Freq. in ***hulch-backed*** *adjective.*

huldee *noun* var. of HALDI.

hule /ˈuːli/ *noun.* Also **ule**, **ulli**. E17.
[ORIGIN Mexican Spanish *(h)ule* from Nahuatl *ulli*, *olli*.]
Any of several rubber-yielding trees of the tropical American genus *Castilla*, of the mulberry family, esp. *C. elastica* of Central America; the crude rubber obtained from such trees.

hulk /hʌlk/ *noun*[1].
[ORIGIN Old English *hulc* prob. dim. formation from weak grade of *helan*: see HULL *noun*[1].]
1 A hut, a hovel. Long *obsolete* exc. *dial.* OE.
2 The hull or husk of a fruit, grain, etc. Long *obsolete* exc. *dial.* LME.

hulk /hʌlk/ *noun*[2].
[ORIGIN Late Old English *hulc* (in Anglo-Latin *hulcus*), prob. reinforced in Middle English by Middle Low German *hulk*, *holk(e*, Middle Dutch *hulke*, *hulc* (Dutch *hulk*) = late Old High German *holko* (German *Hulk*, *Holk*), whence Old French *hulque*; prob. of Mediterranean origin: cf. Greek *holkas* cargo ship.]
1 A large cargo or transport ship (*arch.*); any large unwieldy boat. LOE. ▸†**b** The hull of a ship. M17–E19. ▸**c** The body of a dismantled ship, esp. used as a storehouse or temporary quarters; *spec.* (*hist.*) such a ship used as a prison. L17.
2 A big unwieldy person; a bulky or unwieldy mass. LME.

M. GEE Rawdon himself was there . . a hulk of a man with tall boots.

■ **hulky** *adjective* = HULKING L18.

hulk /hʌlk/ *verb.* L18.
[ORIGIN from HULK *noun*[2].]
▶**I 1** *verb intrans.* Behave in a clumsy or idle way. L18.
2 *verb intrans.* Appear like a hulk, be bulky or massive; rise *up* like a hulk. L19.

A. TYLER We . . came upon the car: hulking in the dark.

▶**II 3** *verb trans.* Accommodate (sailors) temporarily on a hulk. Formerly also, condemn to the hulks. E19.

hulking /ˈhʌlkɪŋ/ *adjective.* L17.
[ORIGIN from HULK *noun*[2] + -ING[2].]
Massive, bulky; unwieldy, clumsy due to bulk; idle.

P. BOWLES Look at that hulking boy. He's never done a day's work in his life. J. CAREY The hulking London footman making a darkness in the cabin as he stoops through it.

hull /hʌl/ *noun*[1].
[ORIGIN Old English *hulu* from weak grade of *helan* to cover, whence also Old English *hylma*, Old High German *hulla* mantle, head covering (German *Hülle*) and Dutch *huls*, Old High German *hulsa* (German *Hülse* husk, pod): cf. HOLE *noun*[1], HULL *noun*[2].]
1 The outer covering, rind, shell, pod, or husk of any fruit or seed. OE. ▸**b** Bran. *rare.* LME. ▸**c** The calyx which persists at the base of some fruits, as strawberries. Also, the core of a fruit, as an apple, a raspberry, etc. L19.
2 A sty or pen for animals. Formerly also, a hut, a hovel. *Scot. & N. English.* ME.
3 Something that encases or encloses; a covering; *spec.* (now *rare*) the membrane enclosing the heart, the pericardium; in *pl.* (now chiefly *Scot.*), clothes. E17.

hull /hʌl/ *noun*[2]. LME.
[ORIGIN Perh. var. of HOLL *noun* or same word as HULL *noun*[1].]
The body or frame of a ship or boat, apart from the masts etc.; the frame of an airship, seaplane, etc.
hull down (of a ship) so far away that the hull is below the horizon; (of a tank) concealed apart from the gun turret.

hull /hʌl/ *verb*[1] *trans.* LME.
[ORIGIN from HULL *noun*[1].]
Remove the hull, shell, or husk of; strip off the outer covering.

hull /hʌl/ *verb*[2]. M16.
[ORIGIN from HULL *noun*[2].]
†**1** *verb intrans.* Of a ship: move by the force of the wind or current on the hull alone; drift. M16–E18.
2 *verb trans.* Strike (a ship) in the hull with cannon shot etc. E18.

hullabaloo /hʌləbəˈluː/ *noun, interjection, & verb.* Also **halla-**, **holla-**. M18.
[ORIGIN Redupl. of HULLO, HALLO, etc.]
▶**A** *noun.* (An) uproar, (a) clamour; noisy confusion. M18.

J. HERSEY A terrible hullabaloo of hammering, wedging, ripping, and splitting. W. GOLDING The excitement, the hullabaloo, the world interest of Tutankhamun's tomb.

▶**B** *interjection.* Used to attract attention. *rare.* M19.
▶**C** *verb intrans.* Make a hullabaloo. M19.

hullo /həˈləʊ, hʌ-/ *interjection.* Also **hulloa**, (*joc. & colloq.*) **'ullo** /əˈləʊ/. M19.
[ORIGIN Var. of HALLO *interjection.*]
= HELLO *interjection.*

Listener If, when you take off the receiver, you say 'Hullo!' . . you might be saying 'Hullo!' to a total stranger.

†**hullock** *noun.* M16–E18.
[ORIGIN Unknown.]
A small part of a sail let out in a gale to keep a ship's head to the sea.

hully gee /hʌlɪ ˈdʒiː/ *interjection.* Chiefly *US.* L19.
[ORIGIN Alt. of *Holy Jesus.*]
Expr. surprise or delight.

hully gully /hʌlɪ ˈɡʌli/ *noun phr.* M20.
[ORIGIN Unknown.]
A dance that is a modification of the frug, popular in the 1960s.

hulver /ˈhʌlvə/ *noun. obsolete* exc. *dial.* ME.
[ORIGIN Old Norse *hulfr.*]
Holly.

hulwa *noun* var. of HALVA.

hum /hʌm/ *noun*[1] & *interjection.* LME.
[ORIGIN Rel. to or formed as HUM *verb*[1].]
▶**A** *noun* **I 1** A slight inarticulate vocal sound usu. uttered in hesitation, embarrassment, approval, dissent, etc. Freq. in ***hums and ha's***, ***hums and haws***. LME.
2 A low continuous non-sibilant sound (as) made by a bee, a spinning top, working machinery, etc.; an indistinct sound produced by a blend of distant noises, a murmur; *transf.* a rumour. L16. ▸**b** MEDICINE. In full ***venous hum***. A continuous humming sound heard on auscultation of the jugular vein, esp. in some anaemic patients, due to increased blood flow. M19. ▸**c** ELECTRONICS. Unwanted low-frequency variation in current or voltage (as from the alternating mains current) which causes a humming sound in a loudspeaker; the sound so produced. E20.

N. BAWDEN I have found . . the persistent hum of the traffic . . remarkably soothing. R. INGALLS A low hum given off by the museum's slide projector. *Observer* All of a sudden . . a 'hum' goes round about some politician or other.

3 An instance of humming (a tune). M17.
▶**II** †**4** A type of strong ale. Cf. HUMMING 2b. E17–E18.
5 A bad smell, a stink. E20.
▶**B** *interjection.* Expr. hesitation, embarrassment, dissent, etc. Cf. HA *interjection* 3. M16.

hum /hʌm/ *noun*[2]. *slang.* M18.
[ORIGIN Abbreviation of HUMBUG. Cf. HUMDUDGEON.]
1 A hoax, a sham. *arch.* M18.
2 A scrounger, a persistent borrower. *Austral.* E20.

hum /hʌm/ *noun*[3]. E20.
[ORIGIN Croatian.]
PHYSICAL GEOGRAPHY. A steep-sided hill, of roughly circular cross-section, characteristic of karst topography. Cf. MOGOTE, PEPINO.

hum /hʌm/ *verb*[1]. Infl. **-mm-**. LME.
[ORIGIN Imit.: cf. BUM *verb*[1], Middle High German (German dial.) *hummen*, German *summen*, *brummen*, Dutch *brommen*.]
1 *verb intrans.* Utter 'hum' in hesitation, embarrassment, etc. Chiefly in ***hum and ha***, ***hum and haw***. LME.

J. KELMAN They hummed and hawed and I could tell they weren't too interested.

2 *verb intrans.* Make a low continuous non-sibilant sound. LME. ▸**b** *verb intrans.* Emit or produce an indistinct noise; *colloq.* be in a state of activity. M18.

E. L. DOCTOROW The car moved through the city, its motor humming in the warm afternoon. H. BASCOM Bullets like supersonic bees now hum through the darkness. **b** J. CONRAD The growling voices hummed steady amongst bursts of laughter. *Times* There was an initial shock . . but things are humming at the Mirror now.

3 *verb trans. & intrans.* Sing (a tune etc.) with closed lips and without articulation. L15. ▸†**b** *verb trans.* Express approval or disapproval of (a person or thing) by humming. M17–M18. ▸**c** *verb trans.* Bring (a person) into a specified state by humming. E19.

W. WHARTON Doris starts humming to the music. E. O'BRIEN They glide through their own hallways, whistling or humming a familiar, guarded tune. **c** J. CLARE The busy bee hath humm'd himself to rest.

4 *verb intrans.* Smell unpleasant, stink. E20.

Daily Telegraph When the wind drops this stuff really hums.

hum /hʌm/ *verb*[2]. *slang.* Infl. **-mm-**. M18.
[ORIGIN Abbreviation of HUMBUG.]
1 *verb trans.* Hoax, deceive, take in. Now *arch. & dial.* M18.
2 *verb trans. & intrans.* Scrounge, cadge. *Austral.* E20.

huma /ˈhuːmə/ *noun.* M19.
[ORIGIN Persian & Urdu *humā* phoenix.]
A mythical bird similar to the phoenix, supposed to bring luck to any person over whom it hovers on its restless flights.

human /ˈhjuːmən/ *adjective & noun.* Also (earlier) †**humane**. See also HUMANE. LME.
[ORIGIN Old French & mod. French *humain(e)* from Latin *humanus* rel. to *homo* man.]
▶**A** *adjective* **I 1** Of, pertaining to, or characteristic of humankind or people; belonging to humankind; of or belonging to the species *Homo sapiens*. LME.

V. WOOLF Now we wake the sleeping daws who have never seen a human form. I. ASIMOV Baley wondered if . . they would accept *anything* in human appearance as a man. M. AMSTERDAM There is definitely no human life on the planet, Mars. F. FITZGERALD Groups of students formed human roadblocks across the avenues leading into the city. R. WEST We obeyed that mysterious human impulse to smile . . at . . a fellow-creature occupied in baseness. M. GEE We have the cerebral cortex, the part that makes us human. *National Trust Magazine* Conservation . . is a key to the well-being of the human race.

2 *spec.* ▸**a** Of, pertaining to, or characteristic of (the faculties of) human beings as opp. to gods or God; fallible; mundane. M16. ▸**b** Of, pertaining to, or characteristic of the activities, relationships, etc., of human beings, esp. as distinct from those of lower animals, machines, mere objects, etc. M18. ▸**c** Having or showing the (esp. better) qualities distinctive of or attributed to human beings. M19.

a POPE To err is humane, to forgive divine. J. GATHORNE-HARDY The GPs make a slip, they're only human. **b** *Observer* Much of British management does not seem to understand the human factor. **c** B. CASTLE I get very fond of my civil servants . . . The outside world has no idea how human they are. M. ESSLIN Bérenger, its hero, is a Chaplinesque little man, simple, awkward, but human.

3 *ASTROLOGY.* Of a zodiacal sign: having the form of a man, woman, or child. M17.

▸ **II** See HUMANE.

– SPECIAL COLLOCATIONS: **human animal** the human being viewed as one member of the animal kingdom. **human being** a person; a man, a woman, a child; a member of the species *Homo sapiens*. **human capital** the skills, knowledge, and experience possessed by an individual or population, viewed in terms of their value or cost to an organization or country. ***human ecology***. **human engineering** (the study of) the management of industrial labour, esp. concerning the relationships between machines and human beings. ***human equation***: see EQUATION 4. ***human geography***. **human interest** reference to human experience and emotions etc., esp. in a news story etc. **human nature** the general characteristics and feelings attributed to human beings. **human papillomavirus** a virus with subtypes that cause diseases in humans ranging from common warts to cervical cancer. **human race** the division of living creatures to which people belong; humankind. **human relations**: with or between people or individuals. **human resources** people (esp. personnel or workers) as a significant asset of a business etc. **human rights**: held to be justifiably claimed by any person. **human shield** a person or group of persons placed in a potential line of fire in order to deter attack.

▸ **B** *noun*. **1** A human being. M16.

B. EMECHETA The centre apartment slept both the humans as well as the animals.

2 That which is human. E20.

▪ **humanhood** *noun* human character M19.

humanation /hjuːməˈneɪʃ(ə)n/ *noun*. *rare*. M17.
[ORIGIN Late Latin *humanatio(n-)*, from *humanare* to incarnate, from *humanus* HUMAN *adjective*: see -ATION.]
Incarnation.

humane /hjʊˈmeɪn/ *adjective & noun*. See also HUMAN. LME.
[ORIGIN Earlier form of HUMAN.]

▸ **A** *adjective* **I 1** See HUMAN. LME.

▸ **II 2** In early use, civil, courteous, or obliging towards others. Now only, characterized by sympathy with or consideration for others; compassionate; benevolent. (Earlier in HUMANELY.) E16. ▸**b** Inflicting the minimum of pain. E20.

R. C. TRENCH It is just in man to be merciful . . to be humane is human. J. M. MURRY The humane and generous wisdom which seems to have been his birthright.

b humane killer an instrument for the painless slaughter of animals.

3 Of a branch of study: intended to civilize or refine; elegant. L17.

▸ †**B** *noun*. See HUMAN.

humanely /hjʊˈmeɪnli/ *adverb*. Also †**humanly**. L15.
[ORIGIN from HUMANE *adjective* + -LY².]
In a humane manner, compassionately. Formerly also = HUMANLY.

humaneness /hjʊˈmeɪn-nɪs/ *noun*. E19.
[ORIGIN formed as HUMANELY + -NESS.]
Humane quality or condition; compassionateness.

humanics /hjʊˈmanɪks/ *noun*. M19.
[ORIGIN from HUMAN *adjective & noun* + -ICS.]
The branch of knowledge that deals with human affairs.

humanify /hjʊˈmanɪfʌɪ/ *verb trans*. E17.
[ORIGIN from HUMAN *adjective* + -I- + -FY.]
Make human.

▪ **humanifiˈcation** *noun* L19.

humanise *verb* var. of HUMANIZE.

humanism /ˈhjuːmənɪz(ə)m/ *noun*. E19.
[ORIGIN In sense 1 from HUMAN *adjective* + -ISM; in other senses from HUMANIST.]

†**1** Belief in the humanity but not the divinity of Christ. Only in E19.

2 The quality of being human; devotion to human interests or welfare. M19.

3 Devotion to studies promoting human culture; literary culture, *esp.* that of the Renaissance humanists. M19.

4 a *PHILOSOPHY & THEOLOGY.* An outlook or system of thought concerned with human rather than divine or supernatural matters. M19. ▸**b** *PHILOSOPHY.* A belief or outlook emphasizing common human needs and seeking solely rational ways of solving human problems, and concerned with humankind as responsible and progressive intellectual beings. E20.

humanist /ˈhjuːmənɪst/ *noun & adjective*. L16.
[ORIGIN French *humaniste* from Italian *umanista*, from *umano* from Latin *humanus*: see HUMAN, -IST.]

▸ **A** *noun*. **1** A classical scholar, a Latinist (*arch.*); *spec.* (*hist.*) a student of Roman and Greek literature and antiquities, esp. during the Renaissance. L16.

2 A person concerned with or interested in human affairs; a humanitarian. E17.

3 *PHILOSOPHY.* An adherent of humanism. E20.

▸ **B** *attrib.* or as *adjective*. *PHILOSOPHY.* Of or pertaining to humanism. E20.

humanistic /hjuːməˈnɪstɪk/ *noun & adjective*. E18.
[ORIGIN from HUMANIST + -IC.]

▸ **A** *noun*. In *pl.* Classical studies. *rare*. E18.

▸ **B** *adjective*. **1** *hist.* Of or pertaining to the Renaissance humanists. M19.

2 *PHILOSOPHY.* Of, pertaining to, or characteristic of humanism. E20.

humanistical /hjuːməˈnɪstɪk(ə)l/ *adjective*. E18.
[ORIGIN formed as HUMANISTIC + -ICAL.]
= HUMANISTIC *adjective*.

▪ **humanistically** *adverb* L19.

humanitarian /hjʊˌmanɪˈtɛːrɪən/ *noun & adjective*. E19.
[ORIGIN from HUMANIT(Y + -ARIAN, after *equalitarian*, *unitarian*, etc.]

▸ **A** *noun*. **1** A person believing in the humanity but not the divinity of Christ. Now *rare*. E19.

2 A person concerned with human welfare; a person advocating or practising humane action; a philanthropist. M19.

E. J. HOWARD He was regarded as a . . humanitarian, someone . . who cared what happened to society.

3 *PHILOSOPHY.* A person believing in the primary importance of the advancement or welfare of the human race. M19.

▸ **B** *adjective*. Of, pertaining to, or holding the views of a humanitarian; concerned with or seeking to promote human welfare. M19.

G. M. TREVELYAN This greater sensitiveness to evils . . was part of the general humanitarian movement.

▪ **humanitarianism** *noun* humanitarian principles or practice M19.

humanitary /hjʊˈmanɪt(ə)ri/ *adjective*. *rare*. M19.
[ORIGIN formed as HUMANITARIAN + -ARY¹. Cf. French *humanitaire*.]

1 Of or pertaining to the human race. M19.

2 Humanitarian, philanthropic. L19.

humanitas /hjʊˈmanɪtɑːs/ *noun*. M20.
[ORIGIN Latin *humanitas*.]
Humanity.

humanity /hjʊˈmanɪti/ *noun*. LME.
[ORIGIN Old French & mod. French *humanité* from Latin *humanitas*, from *humanus*: see HUMAN, -ITY.]

▸ **I** Rel. to HUMAN.

1 The quality, condition, or fact of being human. LME. ▸**b** In *pl.* Human attributes. Also, human affairs. E19.

New York Voice They denounced slavery as a sin, asserted the humanity of the blacks.

2 The human race; human beings collectively. LME.

Observer Most of humanity is sensitive about apartheid because most of humanity is black. P. LIVELY The trams so loaded with humanity that they looked like a beeswarm.

▸ **II** Rel. to HUMANE.

3 The quality of being humane; kindness, benevolence. LME. ▸**b** An act of humanity. Usu. in *pl.* Now *rare*. L16.

G. M. TREVELYAN The sentiment of humanity was now a great force in politics. T. KENEALLY For his humanity he had been honoured by the Israeli government.

4 Learning or literature concerned with human culture, *esp.* (now in *pl.*) the branch of knowledge that deals with the Latin and Greek classics; *sing.* (in Scottish universities) Latin as a subject of study. L15.

R. HAYMAN Law students at Prague were obliged to devote one term to the humanities. Z. MEDVEDEV The humanities—philosophy, history, law, literature, linguistics, etc.—remained in the old university buildings.

humanize /ˈhjuːmənʌɪz/ *verb*. Also **-ise**. E17.
[ORIGIN French *humaniser*, from Latin *humanus*: see HUMAN, -IZE.]

1 *verb trans.* Make human; give a human character to; represent in human form. E17. ▸**b** *spec.* Render (cow's milk) more similar to human milk and hence more suitable for consumption by infants. L19.

Times Nash . . was rendering a humanized version of a young lady goat with his usual facility.

2 *verb trans.* Make humane; soften, refine, civilize. M17. ▸**b** *verb intrans.* Become humane; cause humanization. L18.

▪ **humaniˈzation** *noun* E19. **humanizer** *noun* L18.

humankind /hjuːmənˈkʌɪnd/ *noun*. L16.
[ORIGIN from HUMAN *adjective* + KIND *noun*, after MANKIND.]
The human race; = MANKIND *noun* 1.

humanly /ˈhjuːmənli/ *adverb*. See also HUMANELY. L15.
[ORIGIN from HUMAN *adjective* + -LY².]

1 With human kindness or feeling. L15.

J. R. LOWELL If he had not felt intensely and humanly.

2 From a human point of view; within the range of human power; by human means; in accordance with human nature. L16.

B. BETTELHEIM A . . desire to destroy opposition is rationally understandable, though humanly we do not condone it. E. BOWEN By as soon as was humanly possible after six o'clock she was back home.

humanness /ˈhjuːmən-nɪs/ *noun*. E18.
[ORIGIN formed as HUMANLY + -NESS.]
The quality, condition, or fact of being human.

humanoid /ˈhjuːmənɔɪd/ *adjective & noun*. E20.
[ORIGIN from HUMAN + -OID.]
(An animal or thing) with human form or character.

New Scientist Evolving humanoids grew more intelligent at about the time they began using tools to hunt. *Sun* The humanoid robots familiar to us from fiction are worlds apart from today's industrial models.

humantin /hjʊˈmantɪn/ *noun*. E20.
[ORIGIN French, of unknown origin.]
A shark, *Oxynotus centrina*, of the Mediterranean Sea and Portuguese coasts, having high, angular, spiny dorsal fins.

humate /ˈhjuːmeɪt/ *noun*. M19.
[ORIGIN from HUMIC + -ATE¹.]
CHEMISTRY. A salt of any of the humic acids.

hum-bird /ˈhʌmbəːd/ *noun*. Now *US*. M17.
[ORIGIN from HUM *noun*¹ or *verb*¹ + BIRD *noun*.]
The hummingbird.

humble /ˈhʌmb(ə)l/ *adjective*¹ *& verb*¹. ME.
[ORIGIN Old French *umble*, (also mod.) *humble* from Latin *humilis* low, lowly, base, from *humus* ground, earth, rel. to *homo* man.]

▸ **A** *adjective*. **1** Having or showing a low estimate of one's own importance; (of an action, thought, etc.) offered with or affected by such an estimate; lacking assertion, deferential. ME.

J. LONDON He was humble and meek, filled with self-disparagement and abasement. J. BUCHAN You're a great man. I offer you my humble congratulations. K. AMIS He muttered something and looked suitably humble, grateful and so on.

2 Of lowly rank or condition; modest; (of a thing) of modest dimensions, pretensions, etc. LME.

DAY LEWIS A love which had its humble beginnings in the harmonium at Monart. A. THWAITE Getting any . . place in the Civil Service, however humble, involved the exercise of patronage.

3 Of a plant: low-growing (now chiefly *fig.* and passing into sense 1). Formerly also, (of land) low-lying. L16.

– PHRASES: **eat humble pie** [with punning ref. to ***umble pie*** s.v. UMBLES as an inferior dish] make a humble apology; accept humiliation. **your humble (servant)** *arch.*: used in subscription of a letter or as a form of ironical courtesy.

▸ **B** *verb*. **1** *verb refl.* & †*intrans.* Lower oneself in respect or submission; bow. *arch.* LME.

S. PURCHAS All the people did humble themselves, laying earth upon their heads.

2 *verb trans.* Lower in dignity, position, etc.; abase; make humble in spirit. L15.

BARONESS ORCZY She would crush her own pride, humble it before him.

▪ **humbleness** *noun* LME. **humbler** *noun* E17. **humblingly** *adverb* in a humbling manner M19. **humbly** *adverb* LME.

humble *adjective*², *verb*², *& noun* var. of HUMMEL.

humble-bee /ˈhʌmb(ə)lbiː/ *noun*. LME.
[ORIGIN Prob. from Middle Low German *hummelbē*, *homelbē*, from *hummel* hum, buzz = Middle Dutch & mod. Dutch *hommel*, Old High German *humbal* (German *Hummel*) + *bē* BEE *noun*¹. Cf. BUMBLEBEE.]
= BUMBLEBEE.

humble-jumble /ˈhʌmb(ə)ldʒʌmb(ə)l/ *noun*. *rare*. M16.
[ORIGIN A rhyming formation on JUMBLE *noun*¹.]
= JUMBLE *noun*¹.

†**humblesse** *noun*. LME–M18.
[ORIGIN Old French *(h)umblesse*, from *(h)umble*: see HUMBLE *adjective*¹ *& verb*¹, -ESS².]
Humbleness, humility.

Humboldtian /hʌmˈbəʊltɪən/ *adjective*. E20.
[ORIGIN from *Humboldt* (see below) + -IAN.]
Of, pertaining to, or characteristic of the German philosopher K. Wilhelm von Humboldt (1767–1835) or his work.

humboldtine /ˈhʌmbəʊltʌɪn/ *noun*. E19.
[ORIGIN from F. H. A. von *Humboldt* (1769–1859), German traveller + -INE⁵.]
MINERALOGY. Ferrous oxalate, which forms yellow crystals of the monoclinic system.

humbucker /ˈhʌmbʌkə/ *noun*. L20.
[ORIGIN from HUM *noun*¹ + BUCK *verb*⁴ + -ER¹.]
An electric guitar pick-up containing two magnetic coils rather than a single one, which gives a high output and minimizes hum from electrical interference.

humbug /ˈhʌmbʌɡ/ *noun & verb.* M18.
[ORIGIN Unknown.]
▸ **A** *noun.* †**1** A hoax, a trick. M–L18.
2 A deceiver; a fraud, a sham. M18.
G. K. CHESTERTON That old gentleman . . —that venerable humbug was not really a philosopher. M. SCHORER His announced purpose is, we admit, a pious humbug.
3 Deception, pretence; nonsense, rubbish. E19.
I. MURDOCH The theatre is humbug. But who wants it to be like life, it's escape. A. L. ROWSE This was Hitler's propaganda line, bemusing the British with humbug about his pacific intentions.
4 A boiled sweet, usu. peppermint-flavoured, with a chewy centre and coloured stripes, and freq. pillow-shaped. E19.
▸ **B** *verb.* Infl. **-gg-**.
1 *verb trans.* Delude (*into* doing); cheat or trick (*out of* something). M18.
J. M. SYNGE If it's not humbugging me you are, I'm thinking that I'll surely stay.
2 *verb intrans.* Deceive, cheat; be a fraud or sham. M18.
3 Flounder *about*, make poor progress. Chiefly *local. US.* M19.
■ **humbuggable** *adjective* E19. **humbugger** *noun* M18. **humˈbuggery** *noun* the action or practice of humbugging M19.

humdinger /hʌmˈdɪŋə/ *noun.* E20.
[ORIGIN Prob. from HUM *verb*[1] + DINGER.]
1 A remarkable or outstanding person or thing; something exciting or thrilling. *slang* (orig. *US*). E20.
J. L. CARR Anyway, this Roscoe was a humdinger, a truly Great American. *Gridiron Pro* The game was a humdinger, with the lead switching first one way, then the other.
2 ELECTRONICS (chiefly *hist.*). A voltage divider introduced into the heater circuit of a valve in order to reduce hum by biasing. M20.

humdrum /ˈhʌmdrʌm/ *adjective, noun, & verb.* M16.
[ORIGIN Prob. redupl. of HUM *verb*[1].]
▸ **A** *adjective.* **1** Lacking variety; routine; dull, monotonous. M16.
J. F. LEHMANN The quiet, humdrum respectable façade of the neighbourhood dropped away. J. GATHORNE-HARDY They think it's going to be a glamorous life, and they find it's . . humdrum.
†**2** Undecided, irresolute. M17–E18.
▸ **B** *noun.* **1** A humdrum person or thing. *arch.* L16.
2 Dullness, monotony. L16.
GEO. ELIOT She was living with some intensity, and escaping humdrum.
▸ **C** *verb intrans.* & †*trans.* with *it.* Infl. **-mm-**. Proceed or act in a humdrum manner. *arch.* M18.
■ **humˈdrummery** *noun* = HUMDRUM *noun* 2 M19. **humˈdrumness** *noun* = HUMDRUM *noun* 2 L19.

humdudgeon /hʌmˈdʌdʒ(ə)n/ *noun. colloq.* Now *rare.* L18.
[ORIGIN Cf. HUM *noun*[2] and DUDGEON *noun*[2].]
Bad temper, sulking; a fuss.

Humean /ˈhjuːmɪən/ *adjective & noun.* Also **Humian**. E19.
[ORIGIN from *Hume* (see below) + -AN, -EAN, -IAN.]
▸ **A** *adjective.* Of or pertaining to the Scottish philosopher and historian David Hume (1711–76) or his philosophy. E19.
▸ **B** *noun.* An adherent or student of the philosophy of Hume. L19.
■ **Humism** *noun* the philosophy or beliefs of Hume M19. **Humist** *noun* = HUMEAN *noun* L19.

humect /hjʊˈmɛkt/ *verb.* Now *rare.* LME.
[ORIGIN Latin *(h)umect-* pa. ppl stem of *(h)umectare*, from *(h)umectus* moist, wet, from *(h)umere* be moist.]
1 *verb trans.* Moisten, make wet. LME.
2 *verb intrans.* Become moist or wet. Long *rare* or *obsolete.* LME.
■ **humective** *noun* (*rare*) a humectant LME.

humectant /hjʊˈmɛkt(ə)nt/ *adjective & noun.* M17.
[ORIGIN Latin *(h)umectant-* pres. ppl stem of *(h)umectare*: see HUMECT, -ANT[1].]
▸ **A** *adjective.* **1** Moistening, wetting. Long *rare* or *obsolete.* M17.
2 That retains moisture. M20.
▸ **B** *noun.* **1** A moistening agent. E19.
2 A substance, *spec.* a food additive, used to reduce the loss of moisture. M19.

humectate /hjʊˈmɛkteɪt/ *verb trans.* Now *rare.* M17.
[ORIGIN Latin *(h)umectat-* pa. ppl stem of *(h)umectare*: see HUMECT, -ATE[3].]
= HUMECT 1.
■ **humecˈtation** *noun* (*a*) the action of moistening, the condition of being moistened; †(*b*) liquefaction: LME.

humeral /ˈhjuːm(ə)r(ə)l/ *adjective.* L16.
[ORIGIN French *huméral* or mod. Latin *humeralis*, from Latin HUMERUS: see -AL[1].]
1 Of or pertaining to the humerus of a human or other vertebrate. L16.
2 ZOOLOGY. Of or pertaining to (the region of) the humerus of an insect or other invertebrate. See HUMERUS 2. E19.
3 Of or pertaining to the shoulder. M19.
humeral veil (in the Roman Catholic and Anglican Churches) an oblong scarf worn over the shoulders to veil the Blessed Sacrament in certain services.

humerus /ˈhjuːm(ə)rəs/ *noun.* Pl. **-ri** /-rʌɪ/. LME.
[ORIGIN Latin.]
ANATOMY & ZOOLOGY. **1** The bone of the upper arm or forelimb in humans and other tetrapod vertebrates, articulating at the shoulder and elbow. LME.
2 Chiefly ENTOMOLOGY. Any of various structures in insects etc. involving or in the region of the posterolateral angle of the thorax, the anterolateral angle of the wing case, the femur of the front leg, etc. E19.

†**humet** *adjective.* M17–M18.
[ORIGIN Abbreviation.]
= HUMETTY.

humetty /hjʊˈmɛti/ *adjective.* L16.
[ORIGIN Old French, dim. of *heaume* tiller of a rudder: see -ET[1], -Y[5].]
HERALDRY. Designating an ordinary of which the extremities are cut off so as not to reach the sides of the shield.

humhum /ˈhʌmhʌm/ *noun. obsolete* exc. *hist.* E17.
[ORIGIN Unknown.]
Any of various fabrics; *esp.* a coarse Indian cotton cloth.

Humian *adjective & noun* var. of HUMEAN.

humic /ˈhjuːmɪk/ *adjective.* M19.
[ORIGIN from HUMUS + -IC.]
Of, pertaining to, or contained in humus; rich in humus; derived from plant remains.
humic acid CHEMISTRY any of various complex organic acids formed in soil by decomposition of plant material. **humic coal**: derived from peat.

humicubation /ˌhjuːmɪkjʊˈbeɪʃ(ə)n/ *noun.* Now *rare.* M17.
[ORIGIN mod. Latin *humicubatio(n-)*, from Latin *humi* on the ground + *cubatio(n-)* (from *cubare* lie down): see -ATION.]
The action or an act of lying down on the ground, esp. as a sign of penitence or humiliation.

humid /ˈhjuːmɪd/ *adjective.* LME.
[ORIGIN French *humide* or Latin *(h)umidus*, from *(h)umere* be moist: see -ID[1].]
Slightly wet as with steam, mist, etc.; moist, damp.
D. BAGLEY The warm air rises, heavy and humid, full of water vapour. A. BROOKNER The warmth was humid, promising showers.
■ **humidly** *adverb* L19. **humidness** *noun* E18.

humidify /hjʊˈmɪdɪfʌɪ/ *verb trans.* L19.
[ORIGIN from HUMID + -I- + -FY.]
Make humid, make or keep moist.
■ **humidifiˈcation** *noun* the process of making the atmosphere etc. moist, esp. by means of a humidifier: L19. **humidifier** *noun* a machine or device for keeping the atmosphere moist: L19.

humidistat /hjʊˈmɪdɪstat/ *noun.* E20.
[ORIGIN from HUMIDI(TY + -STAT.]
A machine or device which automatically regulates the humidity of the air in a room or building.

humidity /hjʊˈmɪdɪti/ *noun.* LME.
[ORIGIN Old French & mod. French *humidité* or Latin *humiditas*, from *humidus* HUMID: see -ITY.]
1 The state or quality of being humid; moistness, dampness; *esp.* a specific degree of moisture in the atmosphere. LME.
J. S. FOSTER This detail should be used only in . . buildings . . not liable to high internal humidity.
absolute humidity METEOROLOGY: measured as the mass of water vapour in a given volume of air, usu. expressed in grams per cubic metre. **relative humidity** METEOROLOGY: expressed as the ratio of the mass of water vapour in a volume of air to the value for saturated air at the same temperature.
2 Moisture, fluid, damp. LME. ▸**b** In *pl.* The fluids of animal and plant bodies. Long *rare* or *obsolete.* LME.
Practical Hairstyling & Beauty Central heating and air-conditioning . . takes humidity out of the air.

humidor /ˈhjuːmɪdɔː/ *noun.* E20.
[ORIGIN from HUMID after *cuspidor.*]
A box or room etc. for keeping cigars and tobacco moist.

humification /ˌhjuːmɪfɪˈkeɪʃ(ə)n/ *noun.* L19.
[ORIGIN formed as HUMIFY *verb*[2]: see -FICATION.]
The process by which plant remains are converted into humus; the resultant state of being humified.

humify /ˈhjuːmɪfʌɪ/ *verb*[1] *trans. rare.* M17.
[ORIGIN Late Latin *(h)umificare*, from *(h)umificus*, from *(h)umidus*: see HUMID, -FY.]
= HUMIDIFY.

humify /ˈhjuːmɪfʌɪ/ *verb*[2]. E20.
[ORIGIN from HUM(US: see -FY. Cf. earlier HUMIFICATION.]
1 *verb trans.* Convert (plant remains) into humus. E20.
2 *verb intrans.* Of plant remains: be converted into humus. E20.

humiliate /hjʊˈmɪlɪeɪt/ *verb trans.* M16.
[ORIGIN Late Latin *humiliat-* pa. ppl stem of *humiliare*, from *humilis* HUMBLE *adjective*[1]: see -ATE[3].]
1 Make humble in position, state, or feeling; humble. Long *rare.* M16.
ROBERT BURTON How much we ought to . . examine and humiliate our selves.
2 Injure the dignity or self-respect of. M18.
J. GALSWORTHY It was humiliating to be treated like a child! R. P. GRAVES Housman was bitterly humiliated by his failure.
■ **humiliatingly** *adverb* in a humiliating manner L18. **humiliator** *noun* (*rare*) a person who humiliates another M19.

humiliation /hjʊˌmɪlɪˈeɪʃ(ə)n, ˌhjuːmɪlɪ-/ *noun.* LME.
[ORIGIN Old French & mod. French from late Latin *humiliatio(n-)*, formed as HUMILIATE: see -ATION.]
The action or an act of humiliating; the state or condition of being humiliated. Formerly also, humility.
P. H. GIBBS Patricia had a sudden feeling of humiliation and shame and anger. A. CLARE Mentally ill patients . . have been exposed to the most extraordinary physical and mental humiliations.

humility /hjʊˈmɪlɪti/ *noun.* ME.
[ORIGIN Old French & mod. French *humilité* from Latin *humilitas*, from *humilis* HUMBLE *adjective*[1]: see -ITY.]
1 The quality of being humble; humbleness, meekness. ME. ▸**b** An act of self-abasement. *rare.* E17.
P. G. HAMERTON The humility which acknowledges present insufficiency. R. PARK Out of her wickedness and pride had come tolerance, patience and humility.
2 Humble condition, rank, or position; unpretentiousness. E17.
C. LAMB I made a sort of apology for the humility of the fare.
3 Any of several snipe of the north-eastern US. *US local.* M17.

humite /ˈhjuːmʌɪt/ *noun.* E19.
[ORIGIN from A. *Hume* (1749–1838), English scientist + -ITE[1].]
MINERALOGY. An orthorhombic silicate of magnesium, also containing fluoride and hydroxide; any of a group of magnesium silicates isomorphous with this.

humlie /ˈhʌmli/ *noun. Scot.* E19.
[ORIGIN from HUMMEL + -IE.]
A hornless cow.

hummable /ˈhʌməb(ə)l/ *adjective.* M20.
[ORIGIN from HUM *verb*[1] + -ABLE.]
That may be hummed; suitable for humming, catchy.

hummel /ˈhʌm(ə)l/ *adjective, verb, & noun.* Chiefly *Scot. & N. English.* Also **humble** /ˈhʌmb(ə)l/. L15.
[ORIGIN Corresp. to Low German *hummel*, *hommel* hornless animal; prob. connected with HAMBLE *verb.*]
▸ **A** *adjective.* **1** Of barley etc.: awnless. L15.
2 Of a cow, stag, etc.: hornless. M16.
▸ **B** *verb trans.* Infl. **-ll-**.
1 Deprive (cattle, stags, etc.) of horns. Chiefly as ***hummelled*** *ppl adjective.* L16.
2 Remove the awns from (barley etc.). M18.
▸ **C** *noun.* A hornless stag. M19.
■ **hummeller** *noun* a machine for removing the awns from barley etc. L18.

hummer /ˈhʌmə/ *noun*[1]. E17.
[ORIGIN from HUM *verb*[1] + -ER[1].]
1 a An insect that hums. Also, a hummingbird. E17. ▸**b** A person who hums (a tune); a person who expresses doubt, hesitation, etc., by uttering 'hum'. M18.
2 A person or thing characterized by extreme activity, energy, etc. *colloq.* L17. ▸**b** A person or thing of extraordinary excellence. *colloq.* L19.

hummer /ˈhʌmə/ *noun*[2]. M18.
[ORIGIN from HUM *verb*[2] + -ER[1].]
†**1** A hoaxer. M–L18.
2 A scrounger. *Austral. colloq.* E20.
3 False or mistaken arrest. *slang.* M20.

Hummer /ˈhʌmə/ *noun*[3]. *N. Amer.* L20.
[ORIGIN from *hum-* in HUMVEE + -ER[6].]
= HUMVEE.

humming /ˈhʌmɪŋ/ *adjective.* E17.
[ORIGIN from HUM *verb*[1] + -ING[2].]
1 That hums or makes a low continuous murmuring sound. E17.
2 Of extraordinary activity, intensity, or magnitude; vigorous; striking. *colloq.* M17. ▸**b** Of liquor: strong. Cf. HUM *noun*[1] 4. *arch. colloq.* L17.
– COMB.: **hummingbird** any of numerous small American birds of the family Trochilidae, having usu. long, thin bills and iridescent plumage, which feed from flowers while hovering; ***hummingbird hawkmoth***, a day-flying hawkmoth, *Macroglossum stellatarum*, that makes an audible hum while hovering in front of flowers to feed on nectar; **humming top** a spinning top that makes a humming sound.
■ **hummingly** *adverb* E20.

hummock /ˈhʌmək/ *noun.* Earlier †**hammock**. See also HAMMOCK *noun*[2]. M16.
[ORIGIN Unknown.]
1 Orig. (NAUTICAL), a small eminence seen on the coast by approaching sailors. Later, any more or less rounded protuberance rising above the level of the surrounding ground; a hillock, a knoll. M16. ▸**b** A coastal sandhill. L18. ▸**c** A mound or ridge in an ice field. E19.

H

J. FOWLES The excavation of the harmless hummocks of earth that pimpled his three thousand Wiltshire acres. **c** JOHN ROSS We proceeded over . . the sea of ice, and, passing some hummocks, arrived at the . . cape.

2 See HAMMOCK *noun*².

■ **hummocked** *adjective* formed into hummocks, hummocky M19.

hummocky /ˈhʌməki/ *adjective*. M18.
[ORIGIN from HUMMOCK + -Y¹.]
1 Having many hummocks, characterized by hummocks. M18.

P. D. JAMES The garden, twenty yards of unmown grass, hummocky as a field.

2 Resembling a hummock. L18.

J. GEIKIE Even the projecting masses of rock . . present a rounded hummocky aspect.

hummum *noun* var. of HAMMAM.

hummus /ˈhʊməs/ *noun*. Also **houmous**. M20.
[ORIGIN Arabic *hummuṣ*.]
Ground chickpeas mixed with tahini, garlic, and lemon juice, served as a starter or dip.

humongous /hjuːˈmʌŋgəs/ *adjective*. *slang* (orig. *US*). Also **-mungous**. L20.
[ORIGIN Unknown. Cf. HUGEOUS, MONSTROUS, STUPENDOUS, etc.]
Extremely large, huge, enormous.

H

humor *noun, verb* see HUMOUR *noun, verb*.

humoral /ˈhjuːm(ə)r(ə)l/ *adjective*. LME.
[ORIGIN Old French & mod. French, or medieval Latin *humoralis*, from Latin *humor* HUMOUR *noun*: see -AL¹.]
MEDICINE (chiefly *hist.*). **1** Of or relating to body fluids, esp. as opp. to cells. LME.
2 Of diseases: caused by or attributed to a disordered state of body fluids or (formerly) the bodily humours. M16.
3 Of or pertaining to the bodily humours. L18.

humored *adjective* see HUMOURED.

humoresque /hjuːməˈrɛsk/ *noun*. L19.
[ORIGIN German *Humoreske*, from *Humor* humour + *-eske* -ESQUE.]
MUSIC. A short light capricious composition.

humorise *verb* var. of HUMORIZE.

humorism /ˈhjuːm(ə)rɪz(ə)m/ *noun*. M19.
[ORIGIN from HUMOUR *noun* + -ISM.]
▸ **I 1** Humorous style or manner. *rare*. M19.
2 A humorous saying or remark. L19.
▸ **II 3** MEDICAL HISTORY. The doctrine or theory of the relation of the bodily humours to temperament and disease. Cf. SOLIDISM. M19.

humorist /ˈhjuːm(ə)rɪst/ *noun*. L16.
[ORIGIN from HUMOUR *noun* + -IST.]
†**1** A person subject to humours or fancies; a whimsical person. L16–M19.
2 A witty or facetious person; a humorous talker, actor, or writer. L16.
†**3** A person given to humouring or indulging himself or herself or another. Only in 17.
■ **humoˈristic** *adjective* E19.

humorize /ˈhjuːm(ə)rʌɪz/ *verb*. Also **-ise**. L16.
[ORIGIN from HUMOUR *noun* + -IZE.]
†**1** *verb intrans.* Agree with the humour of a person or thing. Only in L16.
2 *verb intrans.* Speak or think humorously; make humorous remarks. E17.
3 *verb trans.* Make (something) humorous. *rare*. L19.

humorous /ˈhjuːm(ə)rəs/ *adjective*. LME.
[ORIGIN from HUMOUR *noun* + -OUS.]
†**1** Of, pertaining to, the bodily humours; humoral. LME–M19.
†**2** Moist, humid, damp. L15–E17.
3 Subject to or influenced by humour or mood; fanciful, capricious, whimsical. Now *rare*. L16. ▸†**b** Moody, peevish. E17–M19.
4 Full of, characterized by, or showing (a sense of) humour; amusing, comic, funny. E18.

A. CHRISTIE His eyes had an agreeable and humorous twinkle. A. BOURDAIN Humorous anecdotes of New York City.

■ **humorously** *adverb* L16. **humorousness** *noun* E17.

humorsome *adjective* see HUMOURSOME.

humour /ˈhjuːmə/ *noun*. Also ***-or**. ME.
[ORIGIN Anglo-Norman *(h)umour*, Old French *(h)umor*, *-ur* (mod. *humeur*) from Latin *(h)umor*, from *(h)umere*: see HUMID, -OUR.]
▸ **I 1** *hist.* The body fluid of a plant or animal; *spec.* (also ***cardinal humour***) each of the four fluids (blood, phlegm, choler, and melancholy) formerly (in Galen's theory) held to determine a person's physical and mental qualities. ME. ▸**b** In *pl.* The qualities (of a specified kind) determined by these fluids. Long *arch.* E17. ▸†**c** The particular constitution of a material substance. M17–E18.

J. BRONOWSKI The Greek elements were also the four humours which the human temperament combines. **c** S. SWITZER To wonder how Sea-Water shall be thus stripped of its pristine humour.

2 Either of the transparent fluids which fill parts of the eyeball; the aqueous humour; the vitreous humour. LME.
†**3** Moisture; vapour. LME–L17.

SHAKES. *Jul. Caes.* To walk unbraced and suck up the humours Of the dank morning.

▸ **II 4** Mental disposition (orig. as held to have been determined by the bodily humours); temperament. L15. ▸†**b** Character, style, or spirit (of a musical or literary composition etc.). L16–E18.

SHAKES. *Tam. Shr.* Thus I'll curb her mad and headstrong humour.

5 State of mind, mood. Formerly also, habitual frame of mind. E16. ▸**b** An excited state of public feeling. Now *rare*. E17.

P. BOWLES With all the venom of which a foul humour is capable. **b** CARLYLE Friedrich is deeply unaware of the humour he has raised against himself.

6 A particular inclination; a whim, a caprice. Also, (the state of mind characterized by) an inclination *for doing* or a fancy *to do* something. M16. ▸**b** In *pl.* Moods or fancies exhibited in action; vagaries; odd or whimsical traits. Now passing into sense 7. M16.

BURKE All which had been done . . was the effect not of humour, but of system. **b** N. HAWTHORNE Mariners . . who had come ashore to see the humors of Election Day.

7 A quality of action, speech, etc., which causes amusement; facetiousness, comicality; (more fully ***sense of humour***) the faculty of perceiving and enjoying what is ludicrous or amusing; a sense of the ludicrous or amusing. L16.

SWIFT The priest . . shew'd some humour in his face. L. DEIGHTON Much of the book's humour came from its deadpan style. V. GLENDINNING She extracted surreal and sometimes ribald humour from the most unlikely situations.

– PHRASES: ***aqueous humour***: see AQUEOUS 1. ***cardinal humour***: see sense 1 above. ***crystalline humour***: see CRYSTALLINE *adjective* 1. ***glassy humour***: see GLASSY *adjective* 1. ***glazy humour***: see GLAZY 1. **out of humour** displeased. ***radical humour***: see RADICAL *adjective* 2a. ***sense of humour***: see sense 7 above. VITREOUS ***humour***.
■ **humourless** *adjective* devoid of humour M19. **humourlessness** *noun* L19.

humour /ˈhjuːmə/ *verb*. Also ***-or**. L16.
[ORIGIN from the noun.]
1 *verb trans.* Comply with the humour of; gratify, indulge. L16.

W. GERHARDIE He felt he wanted to humour them as one is inclined to humour . . , unreasonable children.

2 *verb trans.* Comply with the peculiar nature or exigencies of; adapt to; make concessions to. L16.

J. MOORE The path is continually winding to humour the position of the mountains.

†**3** *verb intrans.* Exercise one's fancy, imagine. Only in E17.
4 *verb trans.* Give a particular character, style, or (now) turn or direction to. M17.

R. L. STEVENSON The patroon humoured his boat nearer in.

humoured /ˈhjuːməd/ *adjective*. Also ***-or-**. L16.
[ORIGIN from HUMOUR *noun* + -ED².]
Having a disposition of a specified kind. Now only in *comb.* as ***good-humoured***, ***ill-humoured***, etc.

humoursome /ˈhjuːməs(ə)m/ *adjective*. Also ***-or-**. M17.
[ORIGIN from HUMOUR *noun* + -SOME¹.]
Capricious, peevish.
■ **humoursomely** *adverb* M17. **humoursomeness** *noun* M17.

humous /ˈhjuːməs/ *adjective*. M19.
[ORIGIN from HUM(US: see -OUS.]
Present in or of the nature of humus; rich in humus.

hump /hʌmp/ *noun*. M17.
[ORIGIN Prob. rel. to Low German *humpe*, Dutch *homp* lump, hunk. Branch II directly from HUMPBACK.]
▸ †**I 1** A complaint. Also, a slight, a snub (chiefly in ***humps and grumps***). M17–M18.
▸ **II 2** A protuberance, esp. on the back, as a deformity or (in the camel etc.) as a natural feature. E18. ▸**b** A humpbacked person. *rare*. E18. ▸**c** The flesh of an animal's hump considered as food. E19.
3 ***the hump***, a fit of annoyance or bad temper. *colloq.* E18.

E.M. FORSTER That tune fairly gives me the hump. *Daily Star* He's said to get the hump because she flirts with other men.

4 A rounded raised mass of earth etc. E19. ▸**b** A mound in a railway yard over which vehicles are pushed so as to run down the other side by gravity to a siding etc. E20. ▸**c** A mountain barrier high enough to make land and air travel difficult. Chiefly *US*. E20. ▸**d** The critical point in an undertaking, ordeal, etc. Chiefly in ***over the hump***. E20.
5 A walk or hike with a load on one's back. *Austral. & NZ slang*. M19.
6 Copulation; a partner, esp. a woman, in copulation. *coarse slang*. M20.
– PHRASES: **get a hump on** *US colloq.* hurry. **live on one's hump** be self-sufficient. **over the hump** over the worst, well begun. VISCERAL ***hump***.

– COMB.: **hump bridge** = HUMPBACK ***bridge***; **hump-shouldered** *adjective* (long *rare*) having a humped shoulder; **hump speed** AERONAUTICS the speed of a seaplane or hovercraft at which the drag due to the water is at its maximum.
■ **humpless** *adjective* M19.

hump /hʌmp/ *verb*. L17.
[ORIGIN from the noun.]
1 *verb trans. & intrans.* Make (oneself, one's back, etc.) humped or hump-shaped, esp. as a result of vexation; progress by assuming a humped form. L17.

S. R. CROCKETT Sal humped up the shoulder . . and turned sharply away from him. E. FIGES I was aware of . . coughing coming from humped bedclothes.

2 *verb trans. & intrans.* Copulate (with). *coarse slang*. L18.

R. PRICE Maybe he's the scoundrel that was humping that gal when you caught them, Macey?

3 *verb trans.* Hoist up, shoulder, carry esp. on one's back, (a load, pack, etc.); transport with difficulty. Chiefly *Austral. & NZ slang*. M19.

K. WATERHOUSE I . . went downstairs, humping my parcel with me. K. CROSSLEY-HOLLAND They humped their boats overland on pine rollers.

hump bluey: see BLUEY *noun* 2.
4 *verb refl. & intrans.* Exert (oneself), make an effort; hurry. *slang*. M19.

M. WOODHOUSE I . . humped myself into my coat.

5 *verb trans.* Annoy, depress. *colloq.* M19.

A. BEARDSLEY Letter writing humps me dreadfully.

■ **humper** *noun* M19.

humpback /ˈhʌmpbak; *in sense A.1 also* hʌmpˈbak/ *noun & adjective*. L17.
[ORIGIN Prob. formed as HUMP *noun* + BACK *noun*¹: repl. earlier synon. *crump-back* and perh. infl. by *hunchback*.]
▸ **A** *noun*. **1** A back with a hump; a humped back. L17.
2 A person with a humped back, a hunchback. E18.
3 a = ***humpback whale*** below. E18. ▸**b** = ***humpback salmon*** below. L19.
▸ **B** *adjective*. Having a back with a hump. E18.
humpback bridge a small bridge with a steep ascent and descent. **humpback salmon** a medium-sized migratory salmon, *Oncorhynchus gorbuscha*, of the Pacific and (more recently) Atlantic Oceans, the male of which has a humped back at spawning time; also called ***gorbuscha***, ***pink salmon***. **humpback sucker** *US* a freshwater fish, *Xyrauchen texanus*, of the Colorado basin. **humpback whale** a large black baleen whale with white-marked flippers, *Megaptera novaeangliae* (family Balaenopteridae), having a fleshy pad on the back and a complex mating call.
■ **humpbacked** *adjective* having a humpback L17.

humped /hʌm(p)t/ *adjective*. E18.
[ORIGIN from HUMP *noun* + -ED².]
Having a hump; hump-shaped; having a rounded back.

humph /hʌmf, *as interjection also* h(ə)mf/ *interjection, verb, & noun*. M16.
[ORIGIN Natural exclam.]
▸ **A** *interjection*. Expr. doubt or dissatisfaction. Formerly also, giving a warning. M16.
▸ **B** *verb intrans.* Utter 'humph'. L17.
▸ **C** *noun*. An utterance of 'humph'. E19.

humpty /ˈhʌm(p)ti/ *adjective & noun*. E19.
[ORIGIN App. irreg. from HUMP *noun* or HUMPED *adjective*, perh. also infl. by HUMPTY-DUMPTY *noun*².]
▸ **A** *adjective*. Humped, humpbacked. E19.
▸ **B** *noun*. A low padded cushion seat. E20.

humpty-dumpty /hʌm(p)tɪˈdʌm(p)ti/ *noun*¹. L17.
[ORIGIN Uncertain: perh. rel. to HUM *noun*¹ 4.]
A drink made from ale boiled with brandy.

Humpty-Dumpty /hʌm(p)tɪˈdʌm(p)ti/ *noun*² *& adjective*. L18.
[ORIGIN Perh. from HUMPY *adjective* + DUMPY *adjective*² *& noun*: *-t-* unexpl.]
▸ **A** *noun*. A short dumpy person; (with reference to a nursery-rhyme character, whose name is taken to refer to an egg) a person who or thing which once overthrown cannot be restored; (with reference to a character of that name in Lewis Carroll's *Through the Looking Glass*) a person who makes things mean what he or she chooses. L18.
▸ **B** *adjective*. Short and fat; resembling or pertaining to the nursery-rhyme character Humpty-Dumpty. L18.

humpy /ˈhʌmpi/ *noun*¹. *Austral.* M19.
[ORIGIN Yagara (an Australian Aboriginal language of SE Queensland) *ngumbi*, infl. by HUMP *noun*.]
A hut; *esp.* an Aboriginal hut.

humpy /ˈhʌmpi/ *noun*². *Austral. slang*. M20.
[ORIGIN from HUMP *noun* + -Y⁶.]
A camel.

humpy /ˈhʌmpi/ *adjective*. E18.
[ORIGIN from HUMP *noun* + -Y¹.]
1 Having a hump or humps; resembling a hump. E18.
2 Out of humour, annoyed, depressed. L19.
■ **humpiness** *noun* L19.

humstrum /ˈhʌmstrʌm/ *noun*. Now *rare*. M18.
[ORIGIN from HUM *verb*[1] + STRUM *verb*.]
A roughly made or out-of-tune musical instrument; a hurdy-gurdy.

humulone /ˈhjuːmjʊləʊn/ *noun*. Also **-on** /-ɒn/. E20.
[ORIGIN from mod. Latin *Humulus* genus name of the hop plant after German *Humulon*: see -ONE.]
CHEMISTRY. A yellow crystalline cyclic ketone, $C_{21}H_{30}O_5$, that is one of the bitter-tasting constituents of hops and has antibiotic activity. Cf. LUPULONE.

humungous *adjective* var. of HUMONGOUS.

humus /ˈhjuːməs/ *noun*. L18.
[ORIGIN Latin = soil.]
The organic constituent of soil, formed by the decomposition of plant materials.

Humvee /ˈhʌmviː/ *noun*. Chiefly *N. Amer*. L20.
[ORIGIN Alt. from the initials of *high-mobility multipurpose vehicle*.]
(Proprietary name for) a modern military jeep.

Hun /hʌn/ *noun*[1].
[ORIGIN Old English *Hūne*, *Hūnas* (pl.), corresp. to Middle High German *Hiunen* (German *Hunnen*), Old Norse *Húnar*, *Hýnar*, from late Latin *Hunni*, *Huni*, also *Chunni*, *Chuni* from Greek *Hounnoi* from Sogdian *xwn* (whence also Sanskrit *Hūṇa*) = Chinese *Xiōngnú* (Wade–Giles *Hsiung-nu*).]
1 *hist*. A member of a warlike nomadic people of Asian origin who invaded Europe *c* 375 and who later, under their king Attila, overran and ravaged a great part of it. OE.
White Hun: see WHITE *adjective*.
2 *transf*. A wanton destroyer of the beauties of nature or art; *gen*. a person of brutal conduct or character. E19.
3 Chiefly during the First World War: a German. *slang*. *derog*. E20.

hun /huːn/ *noun*[2]. Also **hoon**. E19.
[ORIGIN Sanskrit *hūna*.]
hist. In the Indian subcontinent: a gold coin, the pagoda.

Hunanese /huːnəˈniːz/ *adjective & noun*. M20.
[ORIGIN from *Hunan* (see below) + -ESE.]
▸ **A** *adjective*. Of, pertaining to, or characteristic of the southern Chinese province of Hunan or the form of Chinese spoken there. M20.
▸ **B** *noun*. Pl. same.
1 A native or inhabitant of Hunan. M20.
2 The form of Chinese spoken in Hunan. M20.

hunch /hʌn(t)ʃ/ *noun*. M17.
[ORIGIN from the verb; in sense 3 app. inferred from HUNCHBACKED *adjective*. Sense 2 may be another word: cf. HUNK *noun*[1].]
1 A push, a shove. *obsolete* exc. *Scot*. M17.
2 A thick or clumsy piece; a hunk. L18.
3 A protuberance on the back etc.; a hump. E19.
4 A hint. *US colloq*. M19.
5 An intuitive feeling. *colloq*. (orig. *US*). L19.

HENRY MILLER I have a hunch as to who took that money, but I'm not absolutely sure. R. C. A. WHITE Jurors . . try cases according to the evidence and not on personal whims or hunches.

hunch /hʌn(t)ʃ/ *verb*. L15.
[ORIGIN Rel. to HUNCHBACK, HUNCHBACKED.]
1 *verb trans*. Give a push to, shove, thrust. Now chiefly *dial*. & *US*. L15. ▸**b** Nudge to attract the attention of. *US* (*obsolete* exc. *dial*.). M19.

J. DICKEY Lewis . . tried to hunch the canoe free with his weight.

2 *verb intrans*. **a** Give a push, shove. *obsolete* exc. *Scot*. L16. ▸**b** Push or lunge forward. *US*. E20.
3 *verb trans*. Thrust out or up (esp. the shoulders) to form a hump; arch convexly. Usu. in *pass*. L17. ▸**b** *verb intrans*. Sit in or lower oneself into a bent or huddled position. Chiefly *N. Amer*. M20.

D. WELCH The others gathered round, bending their heads and hunching their shoulders like a rugger scrum. P. ACKROYD An engraving of Faust sitting hunched at his desk. **b** J. STEINBECK Lennie hunched down on the little barrel. A. TYLER Don't *hunch*. Sit straight.

hunchback /ˈhʌn(t)ʃbak, *in sense A.1 also* hʌn(t)ʃˈbak/ *noun & adjective*. E18.
[ORIGIN Back-form. from HUNCHBACKED.]
▸ **A** *noun*. **1** A hunched or protuberant back; *spec*. kyphosis. E18.
2 A person with such a deformity; a hunchbacked person. E18.
▸ **B** *adjective*. Hunchbacked. M19.

hunchbacked /ˈhʌn(t)ʃbakt/ *adjective*. L16.
[ORIGIN from elem. of unknown origin + BACK *noun*[1] + -ED[2].]
Having a protuberant or crooked back; affected with kyphosis.

hunched /hʌn(t)ʃt/ *adjective*. M17.
[ORIGIN from HUNCH *noun*, *verb*: see -ED[2], -ED[1].]
Having a hump, bowed into a hump, hunchbacked; *fig*. stuck-up, arrogant.

hundred /ˈhʌndrəd/ *noun & adjective* (in mod. usage also classed as a **determiner**), (**cardinal numeral**).
[ORIGIN Late Old English *hundred* = Old Frisian *hundred*, Old Saxon *hunderod* (Dutch *honderd*), Middle High German, German *hundert*, Old Norse *hundrað*, from Germanic, from base meaning 'hundred' rel. to Latin *centum* + base meaning 'number' (cf. Gothic *raþjō* number, account).]
▸ **A** *noun*. In senses 1 and 4 pl. now always same after a numeral and often after a quantifier, otherwise **-s**; as *sing*. usu. preceded by *a* (earlier *an*), in emphatic use *one*.
1 A number equal to ten times ten units *of* a specified category or group (now almost always definite, as *a hundred of the, those*, etc., *one hundred of her, his mother's*, etc.; orig. with *genit. pl.*); a number equal to ten times ten persons or things identified contextually, as years of age, pounds, dollars, points or runs in a game, chances (in giving odds), etc.; *pl*. after a quantifier, multiples of ten times ten such people or things. Usu. treated as *pl*. LOE. ▸**b** In *pl*. without specifying word: several hundred; *hyperbol*. large numbers. (Foll. by *of*.) ME.

B. G. GERBIER About one hundred of Leagues. *Times* Tickets fabricated by the hundred. OED He lost several hundred of his men. E. O'NEILL I'll live to a hundred. J. LE CARRÉ They . . offered him six hundred a year. **b** C. DARWIN For many, perhaps for hundreds of generations. SCOTT FITZGERALD Gatsby's notoriety, spread about by the hundreds who had accepted his hospitality. V. GLENDINNING Dame Rebecca had hundreds of friends.

a hundred per cent, **one hundred per cent** (*a*) (orig. *US*) complete(ly), thorough(ly); (*b*) completely fit or well. ***a hundred in the water bag***: see WATER *noun*. **a hundred to one** a very strong probability. FIVE ***hundred***. ***one hundred per cent***: see ***a hundred per cent*** above. **b hundreds and thousands** tiny coloured balls of sugar used chiefly for decorating cakes etc.

2 A group or set of a hundred; *spec*. (*a*) a hundredweight; (*b*) (*obsolete* exc. *dial*.) a hundred years, a century. LOE.
3 *hist*. In England (and later Ireland): a subdivision of a county having its own court. Formerly also, such a court. Cf. WAPENTAKE. LOE. ▸**b** A subdivision of a county in the state of Delaware, and in colonial times also in Virginia, Maryland, and Pennsylvania. See also CHILTERN HUNDREDS. E17.
4 Ten times ten as an abstract number, the symbol(s) or figure(s) representing this (100 in arabic numerals, c, C, in roman); *pl*. after a numeral, that number of multiples of ten times ten as an abstract number, the symbol(s) or figure(s) representing any such number (as 900). ME. ▸**b** In *pl*. The digit denoting the number of hundreds. LME. ▸**c** The hundredth of a set or series with numbered members, the one designated one hundred, (usu. ***number one hundred***, ***number a hundred***, or with specification, as ***Psalm One Hundred***). E17.
5 In the sale of certain commodities, esp. herring and other fishes: a quantity greater than a hundred (*of*). Esp. in ***great hundred***, ***long hundred***, six score, 120. LME.
6 In *pl*. The numbers from 100 to 109 (or 199) inclusive, esp. as denoting years of a decade or century or units of a scale of temperature. E20.

SCOTT FITZGERALD The dark . . saloons of the faded-gilt nineteen-hundreds.

7 In *pl*. (After a numeral.) Used to represent the two noughts in a figure expressing the exact hour, in expressing time by the twenty-four hour clock, as ***twenty hundred hours*** = 20.00 hours, 8 p.m. M20.
▸ **B** *adjective*. After an article, possessive, etc.: ten times ten (a cardinal numeral represented by 100 in arabic numerals, c, C in roman); *hyperbol*. a great many. After a numeral or quantifier: multiples of ten times ten. LOE.

G. B. SHAW Anything from sixpence to several hundred guineas. E. O'NEILL Do you suppose I wouldn't prevent that—for a hundred reasons? E. WAUGH The whole place hummed from its hundred ventilators. S. HILL A house two hundred yards across the green.

a hundred and one *hyperbol*. a countless number of. **not a hundred miles from** *joc*. very close to (this place etc.). **the Hundred Days** the period of the restoration of Napoleon Bonaparte, after his escape from Elba. **the Hundred Flowers** (the period of) an ideological movement in Communist China in the summer of 1957, when people were invited to voice their criticisms of the regime. **the Hundred Years War**, **the Hundred Years' War** the intermittent war between England and France from 1337 to 1453, arising out of the claim of the English kings to the French crown.

– COMB.: Forming compound numerals (cardinal or ordinal) with numerals below 100, as **120** (read ***a hundred and twenty***, ***one hundred and twenty***, (N. Amer.) also ***a hundred twenty***, ***one hundred twenty***), **120th** (read ***hundred and twentieth***, ***one hundred and twentieth***), or (cardinals) with multiples of 1000, as **1200** (read ***one thousand two hundred*** or, esp. in dates, ***twelve hundred***). Special combs., as **hundred-per-center** *N. Amer*. a thoroughgoing or uncompromising person; **hundred-pounder** a cannon throwing a shot that weighs one hundred pounds.

hundredal /ˈhʌndrəd(ə)l/ *adjective*. M19.
[ORIGIN from HUNDRED *noun* + -AL[1].]
Relating to a territorial hundred.

hundredary /ˈhʌndrəd(ə)ri/ *noun*. E18.
[ORIGIN medieval Latin *hundredarius*, formed as HUNDREDER + *-arius* -ARY[1].]
= HUNDREDER *noun* 1.

hundreder /ˈhʌndrədə/ *noun*. Also **-dor**. LME.
[ORIGIN from HUNDRED *noun* + -ER[2], -OR.]
hist. **1** The chief officer of a territorial hundred. LME.
2 An inhabitant of a territorial hundred, *esp*. one liable to be empanelled on a jury. E16.

hundredfold /ˈhʌndrədfəʊld/ *noun & adjective*. OE.
[ORIGIN from HUNDRED + -FOLD.]
▸ **A** *noun*. A hundred times the amount or number. Freq. used adverbially. OE.
▸ **B** *adjective*. A hundred times as much or many. Now *rare* or *obsolete*. ME.

hundredor *noun* var. of HUNDREDER.

hundredth /ˈhʌndrətθ, -rədθ/ *adjective & noun*. ME.
[ORIGIN from HUNDRED + -TH[2].]
▸ **A** *adjective*. Next in order after the ninety-ninth, that is number one hundred in a series, (represented by 100th). Also ***one-hundredth***. ME.

K. VONNEGUT I am here to congratulate *The Cornell Daily Sun* on its one-hundredth anniversary.

hundredth part *arch*. = sense B.1 below.
▸ **B** *noun*. **1** Each of a hundred parts into which something is or may be divided, a fraction which when multiplied by one hundred gives one, (= ***hundredth part*** above). L18.
2 The hundredth person or thing in a category, series, etc., identified contextually; *spec*. in ***Old Hundredth***, (the tune of) the hymn beginning 'All people that on earth do dwell', an early metrical version of Psalm 100 (99 in the Vulgate). M19.

hundredweight /ˈhʌndrədweɪt/ *noun*. Pl. same (after numeral or quantifier), **-s**. E16.
[ORIGIN from HUNDRED + WEIGHT *noun*.]
An avoirdupois weight equal to 112 pounds, approx. 50.80 kg, (more fully ***long hundredweight***) or (*US*) 100 pounds, approx. 45.36 kg, (more fully ***short hundredweight***). Also, a metric weight equal to 50 kilograms, approx. 110.2 lb, (more fully ***metric hundredweight***). Abbreviation ***cwt***.

H

†**hune** *noun*. ME–M18.
[ORIGIN Orig. app. from Old Norse *húnn* knob at the top of a masthead; in later use prob. from French *hune* (from Norse) in same sense: cf. HOUND *noun*[2].]
= HOUND *noun*[2] 1.

hung /hʌŋ/ *adjective*. LME.
[ORIGIN pa. pple of HANG *verb*.]
1 Provided or decorated *with* hanging things. LME. ▸**b** Of a male: having (esp. large) sexual organs. Chiefly with qualifying adverb or phr., as ***hung like a bull***, ***hung like a donkey***, ***well hung***, etc. *slang*. M17.

O. MANNING Tramway cars, hung with passengers like swarming bees.

2 Suspended, attached so as to hang. M16. ▸**b** Of meat: suspended in the air to mature or dry. M17.
3 a Of a jury: unable to agree on a verdict. *US*. M19. ▸**b** Of an elected body: in which no political party has an overall majority. L20.
4 Usu. ***hung-over***. Suffering from the after-effects of excess alcohol or drugs, having a hangover. M20.
5 ***hung up***; confused, bewildered; (foll. by *on*) obsessed or preoccupied with. *slang*. M20.

E. JONG He was all hung up on Jewish girls. G. PRIESTLAND He was not one to . . get hung up on personal taboos.

†**Hungar** *noun*. LME.
[ORIGIN Middle High German *Ungar*, medieval Latin *Hungarus*.]
1 A Hungarian. LME–E17.
2 A gold coin of Hungary. Also ***Hungar-dollar***. L15–M18.

Hungarian /hʌŋˈgɛːrɪən/ *adjective & noun*. E16.
[ORIGIN from medieval Latin *Hungaria* Hungary, from *(H)ungari*, *Ungri*, *Ugri* (cf. UGRIC), medieval Greek *Ouggroi*, Middle High German *Ungar-n*, name applied to the Hungarians, who called themselves Magyars: see -AN.]
▸ **A** *adjective*. **1** Of, pertaining to, or native to Hungary, a country in central Europe. E16.
Hungarian cap the shell of a marine gastropod mollusc, *Capulus ungaricus*. †**Hungarian grass** = ***Hungarian millet*** below. **Hungarian millet** = FOXTAIL ***millet***. **Hungarian turnip** (the swollen stem base of) the kohlrabi, *Brassica oleracea* var. *gongylodes*.
†**2** [With play on HUNGRY *adjective*.] Thievish, marauding; needy, beggarly. *slang*. L16–E17.

SHAKES. *Merry W.* O base Hungarian wight! Wilt thou the spigot wield?

▸ **B** *noun*. **1** A native or inhabitant of Hungary, a Magyar. Also, a Hungarian horse. M16.
2 The Finno-Ugric language spoken by inhabitants of Hungary, and now its official language. M17.

Hungary /ˈhʌŋg(ə)ri/ *noun*. LME.
[ORIGIN See HUNGARIAN.]
Used *attrib*. to designate things found in, obtained from, or associated with Hungary.
Hungary water a preparation distilled from rosemary flowers, formerly popular as a lotion and restorative.

hunger /ˈhʌŋgə/ *noun*.
[ORIGIN Old English *hungor*, *-ur* = Old Saxon, Old High German *hungar* (Dutch *honger*, German *Hunger*), Old Norse *hungr*, from Germanic.]
1 The uneasy or painful sensation caused by lack of food; craving appetite. Also, the exhausted condition caused by lack of food. OE.

A. GRAY He had been foodless for two days and ached with hunger.

2 (A) famine. *arch.* OE.
3 *gen.* A strong desire or craving (*for* etc.); a hankering *after*. LME.

GEO. ELIOT This need of love—this hunger of the heart. T. KENEALLY He had a hunger for a thin, consumptive black girl called Tessie.

– COMB.: **hunger-bitten** *adjective* (*arch.*) pinched with hunger, famished; **hunger march**: undertaken by a body of the unemployed etc. to call attention to their condition; **hunger marcher** a person who goes on a hunger march; †**hunger-starve** *verb trans.* famish, starve; **hunger strike** the refusal of food as a form of protest, esp. by a prisoner; **hunger striker** a person who takes part in a hunger strike; **hunger-weed** the corn buttercup, *Ranunculus arvensis*.

hunger /ˈhʌŋɡə/ *verb*.
[ORIGIN Old English *hyngran*, *hyngrian* (= Old Saxon *gihungrian*, Gothic *huggrjan*), from Germanic base of HUNGER *noun*; assim. in Middle English to the noun.]
†**1** *verb intrans. impers.* as in ***me hungreth***, it hungers me, I am hungry. OE–LME.
2 *verb intrans.* Feel or suffer hunger through lack of food, be hungry. *arch.* OE.
†**3** *verb trans.* Have a hunger or craving for; desire with longing. OE–M16.
4 *verb intrans. gen.* Have a strong desire or craving *for*, *to do*; hanker *after*. LME.

E. WAUGH Basil is a Philistine and a crook . . and yet . . I hunger for his company. B. MALAMUD He hungered to explain who he was.

5 *verb trans.* Subject to hunger, starve; drive *out* by hunger, starve *out*. Now *rare*. L16.
■ **hungerer** *noun* LME.

hungered /ˈhʌŋɡəd/ *adjective*. *arch.* LME.
[ORIGIN Partly aphet. from AHUNGERED, partly pa. pple of HUNGER *verb*: see -ED[1].]
Hungry; famished, starved.

hungerly /ˈhʌŋɡəli/ *adjective*. Now *rare* or *obsolete*. LME.
[ORIGIN from HUNGER *noun* + -LY[1].]
Having a hungry or famished look.

hungerly /ˈhʌŋɡəli/ *adverb*. Now *rare* or *obsolete*. M16.
[ORIGIN from HUNGER *noun* + -LY[2].]
Hungrily, greedily.

hungry /ˈhʌŋɡri/ *adjective*.
[ORIGIN Old English *hungrig* = Old Frisian *hungerig*, Old High German *hung(a)rag* (German *hungrig*), from West Germanic, from base of HUNGER *noun*: see -Y[1].]
1 Feeling pain or discomfort from the lack of food; having a keen appetite. OE. ▸**b** Indicating or marked by hunger; belonging to a hungry person. LME.

I. MURDOCH She felt very hungry, having had no lunch. W. BRONK Yes, I'm hungry, I'll eat anything. **b** SHAKES. *Jul. Caes.* Yond Cassius has a lean and hungry look.

2 Having a strong desire or craving (*for*, †*after*); *spec.* eager for money, profits, etc.; *Scot.*, *Austral.*, & *NZ* mean, stingy. ME.

H. D. TRAILL The conveyance of prize-money . . into Charles's always hungry pocket. E. BOWEN She heard a great hum from the waiting plane hungry for flight. M. BINCHY He was hungry for every detail of her.

3 Of a period, place, etc.: marked by famine or scarcity of food. Now *rare* exc. in ***hungry forties*** below. ME.

S. ROWLANDS When thou art hording vp thy foode, Against these hungry dayes.

4 a Of air etc.: that produces a keen appetite. *rare*. LME. ▸**b** Of a meal: eaten with a hearty appetite. Now *rare* or *obsolete*. M16.
5 Of food etc.: that does not satisfy the hunger. Now *rare*. M16.
6 Esp. of land, soil, etc.: deficient in nutrients, poor, infertile. Also, of a river: not supplying food for fish. L16.

M. B. KEATINGE Flat tracts of hungry pasture ground.

– SPECIAL COLLOCATIONS: **hungry forties** the decade 1840–9 in Britain, a period of great distress and scarcity of food among the poor. **hungry rice** (the seed of) a kind of millet, *Digitaria exilis*, grown in arid areas of W. Africa; also called *fundi*.
■ **hungrily** *adverb* LME. **hungriness** *noun* M16.

hunk /hʌŋk/ *noun*[1]. E19.
[ORIGIN Prob. of Low Dutch origin: cf. Western Flemish *hunke*. Cf. HUNCH *noun*.]
1 A large piece cut off from a loaf, a cheese, etc.; a thick or clumsy piece. E19.
2 A large or solidly built person, esp. a man; a muscular or ruggedly handsome man, a sexually desirable man. *colloq.* M20.

hunk /hʌŋk/ *noun*[2] & *adjective*. *US*. M19.
[ORIGIN Dutch *honk*: cf. West Frisian *honck(e)*, place of refuge.]
▸ †**A** *noun*. In children's games (in New York): a position where a player is safe, the goal or 'home'. Esp. ***be on hunk***, ***reach hunk***. M–L19.
▸ **B** *adjective*. (*slang*). **1** = HUNKY-DORY. Now *rare*. M19.
2 Even, on even terms. In ***get hunk*** (***with***). M19.

hunk /hʌŋk/ *noun*[3]. *N. Amer. slang. derog.* Now *rare*. L19.
[ORIGIN Prob. alt. of HUNG(ARIAN. Cf. BOHUNK.]
= HUNKY *noun*.

hunker /ˈhʌŋkə/ *noun*. *US*. Now *arch.* or *hist.* Also **H-**. M19.
[ORIGIN Unknown.]
A member of a conservative faction of the Democratic Party (orig. that in New York in the 1840s); *transf.* (*colloq.*) a person of old-fashioned or conservative outlook.
■ **hunkerish** *adjective* conservative, old-fashioned M19. **hunkerism** *noun* the views or policies of hunkers M19.

hunker /ˈhʌŋkə/ *verb intrans.* Chiefly *Scot.* & *N. Amer.* E18.
[ORIGIN Cf. Middle Dutch *hucken*, Middle Low German *hûken* (Dutch *huiken*, German *hocken*), Old Norse *húka*.]
1 Squat (*down*) so that the haunches nearly touch the heels; crouch *down* for shelter or concealment. Also, station oneself in a hunched or huddled position. E18.

K. TENNANT Kelly . . hunkered down by the sunny office wall. A. TYLER He played the drums intently . . sitting very straight instead of hunkering over.

2 *fig.* Foll. by *down*. Apply oneself, knuckle down. Orig. *US*. E18.

hunkers /ˈhʌŋkəz/ *noun pl.* Orig. *Scot.* M18.
[ORIGIN from (the same root as) HUNKER *verb*.]
The haunches, the hams.
on one's hunkers, **upon one's hunkers** in a squatting position; *fig.* in a desperate situation, on one's last legs.

hunkey, **hunkie** *nouns* vars. of HUNKY *noun*.

hunks /hʌŋks/ *noun*. *derog.* E17.
[ORIGIN Unknown.]
A surly cross-grained old person; a stingy person, a miser. Freq. in ***old hunks***.

hunky /ˈhʌŋki/ *noun*. *N. Amer. slang. derog.* Also **hunkey**, **hunkie**. E20.
[ORIGIN from (the same root as) HUNK *noun*[3] + -Y[6], -IE. Cf. BOHUNK.]
(A nickname given to) an immigrant to N. America from Hungary or the Slavonic countries of Europe, *esp.* one of inferior class.

†**hunky** *adjective*[1]. *US slang*. M19–E20.
[ORIGIN from HUNK *noun*[2] + -Y[1].]
= HUNKY-DORY.

hunky /ˈhʌŋki/ *adjective*[2]. *colloq.* E20.
[ORIGIN from HUNK *noun*[1] + -Y[1].]
Thickset, solidly built; *esp.* (of a man) ruggedly handsome, sexually desirable.

hunky-dory /hʌŋkɪˈdɔːri/ *adjective*. *slang* (orig. *US*). Also **-rey**. M19.
[ORIGIN from (the same root as) HUNKY *adjective*[1] + *dory* of unknown origin.]
In a safe or good position or condition; satisfactory, fine.

Hunnish /ˈhʌnɪʃ/ *adjective*. M17.
[ORIGIN from HUN + -ISH[1].]
Of, pertaining to, or resembling the Huns; wantonly destructive.

hunsup *noun* see HUNT'S-UP.

†**hunt** *noun*[1]. OE–E19.
[ORIGIN Old English *hunta* from Germanic.]
A hunter, a huntsman. In later use only in the title ***common hunt***, an official appointed to look after a Lord Mayor's kennel.
– NOTE: Surviving in the surname *Hunt*.

hunt /hʌnt/ *noun*[2]. LME.
[ORIGIN from HUNT *verb*.]
1 The action or an act of hunting game for sport or food. LME. ▸**b** A diligent or energetic search or pursuit. E17. ▸**c** *TELEPHONY*. An automatic search for a free line. E20.

b G. GORER The papers . . were much taken up with the hunt for the missing Coronation Stone. *Medway Extra* A twice-a-year hunt to recruit more staff.

2 a A body of people (sometimes including their horses and hounds) engaged in hunting wild animals or game, esp. foxes. Also, a body of people meeting regularly to hunt. L16. ▸†**b** Game pursued or killed in hunting. L16–E17. ▸**c** The district over which a pack of hounds hunts. M19.

a G. M. TREVELYAN Very few joined a Hunt who were not resident in the County. **c** *Field* Every landowner within the hunt should be careful to preserve foxes.

3 In change-ringing: a movement of bells through a fixed succession of positions. Formerly, the first or treble bell in a set of bells. L17.
4 An oscillatory motion. E20.
– COMB.: **hunt ball** a ball or dance given by members of a hunt; **hunt saboteur** a person whose intention is to disrupt a hunt in the interests of animal welfare.

hunt /hʌnt/ *verb*.
[ORIGIN Old English *huntian*, from Germanic weak grade of base of HENT *verb*.]
1 *verb intrans.* & *trans.* Pursue (wild animals or game) for food or sport; *spec.* (chiefly in England) pursue (esp. foxes) with hounds; *N. Amer.* shoot (game). Also, of an animal: pursue (prey). OE.

J. BUCHAN He used to hunt with the Pytchley. T. F. POWYS An old dog-fox who had been hunted many times before. J. RABAN The bustards . . were hunted with falcons.

2 a *verb intrans.* Make a diligent or energetic search, look *about*. (Foll. by *for*, *after*.) ME. ▸**b** *verb trans.* Make a diligent or energetic search for, look eagerly for. Now chiefly *US*. LME. ▸**c** *verb intrans.* *TELEPHONY*. Of a selector or switch: search automatically for a free line (and make connection with it). (Foll. by *for* a line, *over* lines.) E20.

a E. M. FORSTER She hunted in the grass for her knitting-needle. C. STEAD She hunted high and low and found nothing but peanut-butter jars. **b** A. TYLER I'm hunting Oliver Jamison . . . You know him?

3 *verb trans.* Drive *away* or *from* a place, etc., by pursuit or harassment. ME. ▸**b** *fig.* Pursue vexatiously; pester, dog. L16.

b N. HAWTHORNE These pests had hunted the two travellers at every stage of their journey.

4 *verb trans.* Scour (a district) in pursuit of game, esp. foxes. LME.

G. J. WHYTE-MELVILLE When he . . hunted the Cottesmore country.

5 *verb trans.* Follow up (a trail) in the manner of a hound. L16.

J. TYNDALL I hunted the seams still farther up the glacier.

6 *verb trans.* Direct (hounds) in a hunt; ride (a horse) in a hunt. E17.
7 *verb trans.* & *intrans.* In change-ringing: alter the position of (a bell), (of a bell) have its position altered, through a fixed succession of changes. (Foll. by *up*, *down*.) L17.
8 *verb intrans.* (Of a generator, engine, etc.) run alternately too fast and too slow; *gen.* (of any machine, system, etc.) oscillate (undesirably) *about* a desired speed, position, or state. L19.
– PHRASES, & WITH ADVERBS IN SPECIALIZED SENSES: **hunt away** *NZ* (of a dog) drive sheep forward. ***hunt counter***: see COUNTER *adverb*. **hunt down** (***a***) pursue or search for relentlessly until caught or apprehended; (***b***) *NZ* drive (sheep) down from higher ground. **hunt out** drive from cover by hunting; *fig.* bring to light by persistent searching. ***hunt riot***: see RIOT *noun*. ***hunt the fox***: see FOX *noun*. **hunt up** search energetically for until one finds.
– COMB. (in names of various games): **hunt the hare** = ***fox and hounds*** s.v. FOX *noun*; **hunt the lady** a card game of the whist family; **hunt the slipper** a game in which all the players but one sit in a ring and pass a slipper covertly from one to another, the remaining player having to find the player in possession of it; **hunt the thimble** a game in which one player hides a thimble which the other players then have to locate; **hunt the whistle** a game in which a player is blindfolded and is told to look for a whistle, which has actually been fastened to his or her own clothing.
■ **huntable** *adjective* M19. **hunted** *adjective* that is hunted; looking or behaving as if being pursued, worn and harassed: L16.

huntaway /ˈhʌntəweɪ/ *noun*. *NZ*. E20.
[ORIGIN from *hunt away* s.v. HUNT *verb*.]
A dog trained to drive sheep forward.

hunter /ˈhʌntə/ *noun*. ME.
[ORIGIN from HUNT *verb* + -ER[1].]
1 A person engaged in the pursuit of wild animals or game; a person who hunts. ME. ▸**b** A person who searches or seeks diligently or energetically for something. Usu. in *comb.*, as ***fortune-hunter***. LME.
White hunter: see WHITE *adjective*.
2 a A dog good at or used in hunting. E17. ▸**b** A horse bred for its stamina in hunting, its ability to jump, etc.; a horse used in hunting. L17.
3 An animal that hunts its prey; *spec.* (***a***) = ***hunting spider*** s.v. HUNTING *ppl adjective*; (***b***) a Jamaican cuckoo, *Piaya pluvialis*. M17.
4 = ***hunting-watch*** s.v. HUNTING *noun*. M19.
half-hunter a watch with a hinged cover protecting the outer part of the glass.
– COMB.: **hunter-gatherer** a member of a people whose mode of subsistence is based on hunting land and sea animals and collecting wild plants, small land fauna, fish, and shellfish; **hunter-killer** *adjective* (of a naval vessel or group of vessels) equipped to locate and destroy enemy vessels, esp. submarines; **hunterman** (*US*, *W. Indian*, etc.) = sense 1 above; **hunter's green** a dark slightly yellowish green; **hunter's moon** the next full moon after a harvest moon; **hunter trials** a competition for horses used in hunting, with obstacles to simulate the conditions of a hunt.

hunting /ˈhʌntɪŋ/ *noun*. OE.
[ORIGIN from HUNT *verb* + -ING[1].]
1 The action of HUNT *verb*; *esp.* the action or sport of pursuing game; an act or instance of hunting, a hunt. OE.
†**2** Game killed in hunting. ME–E17.
– COMB. (partly also from HUNTING *ppl adjective*): **hunting box** a small house or lodge for use during the hunting season; **hunting case** a watch case with a hinged cover to protect the glass (orig. against accidents in hunting); **hunting cat** = ***hunting leopard*** below; ***hunting crop***: see CROP *noun* 4; **hunting dog** (***a***) a dog used for hunting game; in *pl.* (***Hunting Dogs***) *the* constellation Canes Venatici; (***b***) a southern African animal of the dog family, *Lycaon pictus*, which hunts its prey in packs; **hunting ground** a district or place where hunting or searching is carried on; ***happy hunting ground(s)***, (among N. American Indians) a fabled country full of game to which warriors go after death; *fig.* a fruitful place for collecting, making acquisitions, etc.; **hunting horn** (***a***) a straight horn blown to give signals in hunting; (***b***) = ***leaping-***

H

horn s.v. LEAPING *verbal noun*; **hunting leopard** the cheetah, in Asia tamed and used for hunting; **hunting lodge** a lodge for use during the hunting season; ***hunting pink***: see PINK *noun*[4]; **hunting shirt** *US* an ornamented shirt orig. of deerskin, worn by trappers, hunters, etc.; **hunting watch** a watch having a hunting case to protect the glass.

hunting /ˈhʌntɪŋ/ *ppl adjective*. ME.
[ORIGIN from HUNT *verb* + -ING[2].]
That hunts; that pursues game or prey.
– SPECIAL COLLOCATIONS (see also HUNTING *noun*): **hunting spider** a spider that hunts its prey instead of lying in wait.

Huntingdonian /hʌntɪŋˈdəʊnɪən/ *adjective & noun*. L18.
[ORIGIN from *Huntingdon* (see below) + -IAN.]
(A person) belonging to the Countess of Huntingdon's Connexion, a Calvinistic Methodist sect founded by Selina, Countess of Huntingdon (1707–91).

Huntington /ˈhʌntɪŋt(ə)n/ *noun*. L19.
[ORIGIN George *Huntington* (1851–1916), US neurologist.]
MEDICINE. ***Huntington's chorea***, ***Huntington's disease***, a hereditary disease with progressive brain-cell degeneration, causing spasmodic body movements and progressive dementia.

huntite /ˈhʌntʌɪt/ *noun*. M20.
[ORIGIN from Walter F. *Hunt* (1882–1975), US mineralogist + -ITE[1].]
MINERALOGY. A mixed carbonate of magnesium and calcium, crystallizing in the trigonal system and usu. occurring as a white powder.

huntress /ˈhʌntrɪs/ *noun*. LME.
[ORIGIN from HUNTER *noun* + -ESS[1].]
1 A woman (or goddess) who hunts. LME.
2 A mare used in hunting. M19.

Hunts. *abbreviation*.
Huntingdonshire (a former county in England).

huntsman /ˈhʌntsmən/ *noun*. Pl. **-men**. M16.
[ORIGIN from HUNT *noun*[1] + -'S[1] + MAN *noun*.]
A man who hunts, a hunter; *spec.* a person in charge of a pack of hounds (esp. foxhounds), who directs the pursuit of wild animals and game.
– COMB.: **huntsman's cup** = ***pitcher plant*** s.v. PITCHER *noun*[1]; **huntsman spider** any of various spiders of the family Sparassidae, widespread in warmer regions of the world.
■ **huntsmanship** *noun* M17.

hunt's-up /ˈhʌntsʌp/ *noun*. Now *rare* or *obsolete*. Also (long *dial.*) **hunsup** /ˈhʌnsʌp/. L16.
[ORIGIN from *The hunt is up*, the words of an old song sung or (its tune) played to rouse huntsmen in the morning, and also as a dance.]
1 An early morning song, a song or tune to rouse sleepers. L16.
2 A disturbance, an uproar. E17.

huntswoman /ˈhʌntswʊmən/ *noun*. Pl. **-women** /-wɪmɪn/. E17.
[ORIGIN from HUNT *noun*[1] + -'S[1] + WOMAN *noun*.]
A woman who hunts, a female hunter.

hunyak /ˈhʌnjak/ *noun*. *US slang*. *derog.* Also **honyock** /ˈhɒnjɒk/, **honyocker** /ˈhɒnjɒkə/. E20.
[ORIGIN Alt. of HUNGARIAN after *Polack*.]
= HUNKY *noun*.

Huon pine /ˈhjuːɒn ˈpʌɪn/ *noun phr.* E19.
[ORIGIN A river in the south of Tasmania.]
(The timber of) a large Tasmanian evergreen conifer, *Dacrydium franklinii*.

hup /hʌp/ *interjection & verb*. As interjection also **hupp**. M18.
[ORIGIN Cf. Dutch *hop!* gee-up.]
▸ **A** *interjection*. Encouraging a horse etc. to go faster: gee-up. M18.
▸ **B** *verb*. Infl. **-pp-**.
1 *verb intrans.* Shout 'hup!' E19.
2 *verb trans.* Direct or turn (a horse) to the right. M19.

Hupa /ˈhuːpə, -pɔː/ *noun & adjective*. Also **Hoopa**. M19.
[ORIGIN Yurok *hupǫ̂* the name for this people.]
▸ **A** *noun*. Pl. **-s**, same. A member of an Athabaskan people in California; the language of this people. M19.
▸ **B** *attrib.* or as *adjective*. Of or pertaining to the Hupas or their language. L19.

hupp *interjection* var. of HUP *interjection*.

hurcheon /ˈhəːtʃ(ə)n/ *noun*. Long *obsolete* exc. *Scot.* & *N. English*. ME.
[ORIGIN Old Northern French *herichon*: see URCHIN.]
1 A hedgehog. ME.
2 a A slovenly person; a hag. M18. ▸**b** A mischievous person; an urchin. *rare*. L18.

hurdie /ˈhəːdi/ *noun*. *Scot.* M16.
[ORIGIN Unknown.]
A buttock, a hip, a haunch. Usu. in *pl.*

hurdle /ˈhəːd(ə)l/ *noun & verb*.
[ORIGIN Old English *hyrdel* from Germanic, from base repr. also by Old Saxon *hurþ*, Middle Low German *hurt*, *hort*, Middle Dutch & mod. Dutch *horde*, Old High German *hurt* (German *Hürde*) hurdle, Old Norse *hurð*, Gothic *haurds* door, from Indo-European (whence also Greek *kartalos* basket, Latin *cratis* hurdle): see -LE[1].]
▸ **A** *noun*. **1** A portable rectangular frame strengthened by bars or withes, now esp. with horizontal bars, uprights, and a diagonal strengthening bar, used for temporary fencing or enclosure. OE.
2 A framework laid on marshy ground etc. to provide a path or bridge; a framework, often covered with earth etc., used to stop a gap in fortifications, or protect a position from enemy fire. ME.
3 *hist.* A frame or sledge on which a traitor was drawn through the streets to execution. LME.
4 An upright frame to be jumped over in a race; in *pl.*, a race over hurdles (for athletes or horses). M19. ▸**b** An obstacle, a difficulty. E20.

> **b** *Radio Times* Andrew Cooper describes the hurdles to be cleared . . to win . . a seat on the Board.

– COMB.: **hurdle race** a race over hurdles; **hurdle racing** the sport of racing over hurdles.
▸ **B** *verb*. **1** *verb trans.* Construct like a hurdle or with hurdles. Chiefly as ***hurdled*** *ppl adjective*. M16.
2 *verb trans.* Enclose with hurdles; mark *off* etc. with hurdles. M17.
3 *verb intrans.* Run a race over hurdles; jump hurdles as an athletic activity. L19. ▸**b** *verb trans.* & *intrans.* Jump over (an obstacle) as if it were a hurdle. L19.

> *Daily Mail* When Lord Burghley hurdled easily to victory. **b** B. HINES Long enough for Billy to hurdle the upturned settee.

hurdler /ˈhəːdlə/ *noun*. ME.
[ORIGIN from HURDLE + -ER[1].]
1 A person who makes hurdles. ME.
2 A person who or horse which races over hurdles. L19.

hurdy-gurdy /ˈhəːdɪˌɡəːdi/ *noun*. M18.
[ORIGIN Imit. of the sound of the instrument: cf. HIRDY-GIRDY.]
1 A musical instrument producing a droning sound, played by turning a handle, *esp.* one with a rosined wheel turned by the right hand to sound drone strings, and with keys played by the left hand; *colloq.* a barrel organ. M18.
2 In full ***hurdy-gurdy wheel***. A wheel driven by a tangential jet of water under pressure, which strikes a series of buckets on the circumference. *US*. M19.
– COMB.: **hurdy-gurdy girl** *N. AMER. HISTORY* a dance hostess, esp. in a hurdy-gurdy house; **hurdy-gurdy house** *N. AMER. HISTORY* a disreputable dancehall.

hure /hjʊə/ *noun*. ME.
[ORIGIN Old French & mod. French = †hair of the head, †head of man or animal, (mod.) head of certain animals, corresp. to medieval Latin *hura* rough cap: ult. origin unknown.]
1 A cap. Long *obsolete* exc. *dial.* ME.
2 The head of a boar, wolf, or bear. *rare*. M19.

hurkle /ˈhəːk(ə)l/ *verb intrans.* Long *obsolete* exc. *Scot.* & *dial.* ME.
[ORIGIN Cf. Middle & mod. Low German, Dutch *hurken* to squat.]
Draw the limbs closely together, esp. with pain or cold; shrink, cower, crouch; move in a crouching or cowering manner.

hurl /həːl/ *noun*. LME.
[ORIGIN from the verb.]
1 a A rush or swirl of water; rushing water. *rare*. LME. ▸**b** A noisy rush or fall, esp. of stones etc. down a slope. *Scot.* M16.
†**2** Strife; commotion. LME–M17.
3 The action or an act of hurling; a violent throw or cast. M16.
4 A ride in a wheeled vehicle; a drive. *Scot.* E19.

hurl /həːl/ *verb*. ME.
[ORIGIN Prob. imit.: cf. Low German *hurreln* toss, throw, push, dash.]
1 *verb intrans.* Move or be moved with violence or impetuosity. *arch.* exc. *Scot.* ME.

> J. THOMSON The very streams . . impatient, seem To hurl into the covert of the grove.

2 *verb trans.* Move or drive with violence or impetuous force. ME. ▸**b** *refl.* Throw or move oneself violently or impetuously. LME.

> D. ADAMS Zaphod was . . hurled bodily backwards. **b** R. KIPLING Like . . a swimmer before sharks, who hurls himself half out of the water.

3 *verb trans.* Throw or cast with violence; fling; throw down. ME.

> W. SOYINKA Her husband was about to be . . hurled from the church tower. G. SWIFT He hurls the bottle in a lofty, arcing trajectory into the river.

†**4** *verb trans.* Drag or pull violently. ME–M17.
†**5** *verb intrans.* Strive, contend. Only in LME.
6 *verb trans.* Utter forcefully (words, abuse, etc.); dart (a glance, a ray or beam, etc.). M16.

> MILTON Hurling defiance toward the vault of Heav'n. H. E. MANNING The accusations that may be hurled at you.

7 *verb trans.* & *intrans.* Drive (a vehicle), drive in (a vehicle); wheel (a barrow etc.). Earliest in ***hurlbarrow***, a wheelbarrow. *Scot.* & *N. English*. M16.

> A. GRAY Thaw and his mother . . sat in buses at night hurling through unseen country.

8 *verb intrans.* Play hurley or hurling. L16.

†**hurlbat** *noun* see WHIRLBAT.

hurler /ˈhəːlə/ *noun*[1]. ME.
[ORIGIN from HURL *verb* + -ER[1].]
1 *gen.* A person who hurls something. ME.
2 A player at hurley or hurling. L16.
3 A pitcher at baseball. *N. Amer. slang*. E20.

Hurler /ˈhəːlə/ *noun*[2]. M20.
[ORIGIN G. *Hurler* (1889–1965), German paediatrician.]
MEDICINE. ***Hurler disease***, ***Hurler syndrome***, ***Hurler's disease***, ***Hurler's syndrome***, a form of mucopolysaccharidosis caused by the faulty metabolism of glycosaminoglycans, producing a characteristic facial appearance, short limbs, and a protruding abdomen. Also called ***gargoylism***.

hurley /ˈhəːli/ *noun*. E19.
[ORIGIN from HURL *verb* + *-ey*, -Y[6].]
An Irish form of hockey; a broad stick (of the type) used in this. Cf. earlier HURLING 2a.

hurling /ˈhəːlɪŋ/ *noun*. LME.
[ORIGIN from HURL *verb* + -ING[1].]
1 The action of HURL *verb*; throwing, casting, esp. with violence. LME.
2 a The game of hurley. LME. ▸**b** *hist.* A game, played esp. in Cornwall, in which two parties attempt to hurl or carry a ball to a distant goal. E17.
†**3** Strife; commotion. LME–M17.
†**4** (The sound of) the violent rushing of wind. LME–M17.

hurly /ˈhəːli/ *noun*. Now *rare*. L16.
[ORIGIN from HURL *verb* + -Y[6].]
Commotion, uproar; strife.

hurly-burly /ˈhəːlɪˌbəːli/ *noun, adverb, verb, & adjective*. ME.
[ORIGIN Redupl. of HURL *verb*.]
▸ **A** *noun*. Commotion, uproar, confusion; struggle, strife; (now *rare*) an instance of this. ME.

> SHAKES. *Macb.* When the hurlyburly's done, When the battle's lost and won. *House & Garden* Kitchen gadgetry remains indispensable to the hurly-burly of twentieth-century life.

▸ †**B** *adverb*. In commotion or confusion. M16–E18.
▸ **C** *verb*. †**1** *verb trans.* Hurl about; throw into confusion. M16–L17.
2 *verb intrans.* Make an uproar. Now *rare*. L16.
▸ **D** *adjective*. Characterized by commotion, uproar, struggle, or confusion. L16.

Huron /ˈhjʊər(ə)n/ *noun & adjective*. M17.
[ORIGIN French, formed as HURE.]
▸ **A** *noun*. Pl. **-s**, same. A member of an Iroquoian people formerly inhabiting an area near Lake Huron; the language of this people. M17.
▸ **B** *attrib.* or as *adjective*. Of or pertaining to this people or their language. L18.

hurr /həː/ *verb intrans.* *obsolete* exc. *dial.* LME.
[ORIGIN Imit.]
Make or utter a vibrating or trilling sound; buzz, snarl.

hurrah /hʊˈrɑː/ *noun, interjection, adjective, & verb*. Also **hurra**. See also HOORAY. L17.
[ORIGIN Alt. of HUZZA.]
▸ **A** *noun*. **1** A shout of 'hurrah!'; a cheer. L17.
last hurrah: see LAST *adjective*.
2 ***hurrah's nest***, a state of confusion or disorder. *US colloq.* E19.
▸ **B** *interjection*. Expr. approval, encouragement, enthusiasm, or delight. E18.
▸ **C** *attrib.* or as *adjective*. Characterized by loud cheering, (wildly or blindly) enthusiastic; expressing enthusiasm or joy. M19.
▸ **D** *verb*. **1** *verb intrans.* Shout 'hurrah!' M19.
2 *verb trans.* Welcome or encourage with shouts of 'hurrah!' M19.

hurray *noun, interjection, & verb* var. of HOORAY.

†**hurrer** *noun*. Also **-ier**. LME–M18.
[ORIGIN from HURE *noun* 1 + -ER[1], -IER.]
A maker of or dealer in hats and caps.

Hurri /ˈhʌri/ *noun*. Also **Harri**, **Kh-**. Pl. same. E20.
[ORIGIN Hittite & Assyrian *Ḫarri*, *Ḫurri*.]
A member of a people, originally from Armenia, who settled in northern Mesopotamia and Syria in the second and third millennia BC and were later absorbed by the Hittites and Assyrians.

Hurrian /ˈhʌrɪən/ *adjective & noun*. Also **Harrian**, **Kh-**. E20.
[ORIGIN from HURRI + -AN.]
▸ **A** *adjective*. Of or pertaining to the Hurri or their language. E20.
▸ **B** *noun*. **1** The language (written in cuneiform) of the Hurri. E20.
2 A member of the Hurri. M20.

H

hurricane /ˈhʌrɪk(ə)n, -keɪn/ *noun & verb*. Also (earlier) †**furacan**, †**furicano**, †**hurricano**, (pl. **-o(e)s**), & other vars. M16.
[ORIGIN Spanish *huracán* & Portuguese *furacão* prob. from Taino *hurakán* god of the storm.]
▸ **A** *noun*. **1** A tropical cyclone, *esp.* a W. Indian one; any violent and destructive storm; METEOROLOGY a wind of hurricane force. M16. ▸**b** A space from which trees etc. have been cleared by a hurricane. M18.
†**2** (As *hurricano*.) A waterspout. Only in E17.
3 A violent rush or commotion; a storm of words, noises, etc. M17.
†**4** A large crowded assembly of fashionable people at a private house. M18–E19.
– COMB.: **hurricane bird** a frigate bird; **hurricane deck** a light upper deck on a ship etc.; **hurricane force** force 12 on the Beaufort scale, corresponding to a wind speed of 64 knots (about 74 mph); **hurricane house** a shelter at the masthead or on deck; **hurricane lamp**, **hurricane lantern** a lamp designed to resist a high wind; **hurricane wind** a wind associated with a tropical cyclone; a wind of hurricane force.
▸ **B** *verb intrans. & trans.* Whirl like a hurricane. L17.

G. BOYCOTT A great swirl of dust . . , most of which seemed to hurricane into the Press box.

hurried /ˈhʌrɪd/ *adjective*. M17.
[ORIGIN from HURRY *verb* + -ED[1].]
Carried along or performed with a rapidity due to pressure of circumstances, excitement, or lack of time; characterized by hurry; hasty.

O. MANNING He came over at a hurried trot. M. RULE Intriguing signs of hurried and makeshift alterations.

■ **hurriedly** *adverb* E19. **hurriedness** *noun* M19.

hurrier /ˈhʌrɪə/ *noun*[1]. E17.
[ORIGIN from HURRY *verb* + -ER[1].]
A person who or thing which hurries.

†**hurrier** *noun*[2] var. of HURRER.

hurroo /hʊˈruː/ *interjection & noun*. In sense 2 also **hooroo**. E19.
[ORIGIN Alt. of HOORAY, HURRAH.]
1 *interjection & noun* (A shout) expr. triumph or excitement. E19.
2 *interjection*. Goodbye. *Austral. colloq.* E20.

hurroosh *noun & verb* var. of HOOROOSH.

hurry /ˈhʌri/ *noun*. E17.
[ORIGIN Prob. ult. imit.: in sense 1 perh. alt. of HURLY. Cf. HURR *verb*, HURRY *verb*.]
1 (An instance of) physical, social, or political disturbance; commotion. *obsolete* exc. *Scot. & Irish*. E17. ▸†**b** A confused crowd, a mob. E17–E18.

J. WESLEY A poor man began to make some tumult . . . 'Constables, take him away.' They did so, and the hurry was over.

†**2** (An instance of) mental agitation, excitement. E17–E19.

S. RICHARDSON I should not be admitted into her presence, till the hurries she was in had subsided.

3 Rapidity due to pressure of circumstances, excitement, or lack of time; great haste; eagerness to get a thing done quickly; eagerness *for*, *to do*; an action or state characterized by this, a rush. M17. ▸**b** (In neg. & interrog. contexts.) Need or reason for haste; urgency. M19.

LONGFELLOW A hurry of hoofs in a village street. M. BARING Coming down to dinner in a frantic hurry, thinking I was late. A. BURGESS The final issue . . lacked panache and it betrayed hurry. B. EMECHETA The hurry towards the kitchen had now begun. **b** A. CHRISTIE There was no hurry now. The urgency had gone . . It only needed patience.

not — in a hurry *colloq.* not do the specified thing very soon, not do willingly or easily.
– COMB.: **hurry call** a call for help in an emergency.
■ **hurrygraph** *noun* (*US*, now *rare*) a hurried sketch or impression M19.

hurry /ˈhʌri/ *verb*. L16.
[ORIGIN Imit.: cf. HURR *verb*, WHIRR *verb*; Middle High German, German *hurren* move quickly, Dutch *herrie* agitation.]
1 *verb trans.* Carry or take with great or undue haste, esp. because of pressure of circumstances, excitement, or lack of time. (Foll. by *away*, *into*, *into doing*, *out*, etc.) L16.

C. JOHNSTON My master was seized and hurried away to a prison. J. PITTS Drinking hurries Men on to the worst of Vices.

2 *verb intrans.* Move or act with great or undue haste or with an effort at speed. L16.

R. KIPLING Hurrying north on news of a job, and wasting no time by the road. J. STEINBECK The rabbits hurried noiselessly for cover.

3 *verb trans.* Agitate, disturb, excite; harass, worry. *obsolete* exc. *dial.* E17.

ISAAC TAYLOR So under the influence of the imagination as to have their sleep hurried with visions.

4 *verb trans.* Urge to greater speed; hasten (unduly) the action or progress of. E18.

R. FORD Nor is there any good to be got in trying to hurry man or beast in Spain. R. L. STEVENSON The motion and the close air . . hurried our departure. P. BARKER She tended . . to hurry Muriel along the road to recovery long before Muriel was ready.

5 *verb trans.* Put *away*, *on*, *out*, etc., hurriedly. E19.

L. M. MONTGOMERY 'He's gone . . for the doctor,' said Anne, who was hurrying on hood and jacket.

– WITH ADVERBS IN SPECIALIZED SENSES: **hurry along**, **hurry up** *colloq.* (cause to) make haste, move or act faster.
■ **hurryingly** *adverb* in a hurry; by hurrying: M18.

hurry-scurry /ˈhʌrɪskʌri/ *adverb, adjective, noun & verb*. *colloq.* M18.
[ORIGIN Redupl. of HURRY *verb*, perh. infl. by *scud*, or *scuttle*.]
▸ **A** *adverb*. In disorderly haste, in hurry and confusion. M18.

E. ELMHIRST A whistling coal train drove these horsemen hurry-scurry out of its way.

▸ **B** *adjective*. Characterized by hurry and confusion. M18.
▸ **C** *noun*. Hurry and confusion; disorderly haste, rush. M18.

A. CARLYLE An alarm was beat in the camp, which occasioned a great hurry-scurry in the courtyard.

▸ **D** *verb intrans. & trans.* (Cause to) move or act in confusion and hurry; rush. L18.

W. COMBE She was among those busy wives, Who hurry-scurry through their lives.

hurry-up /ˈhʌrɪʌp/ *adjective & noun*. *colloq.* L19.
[ORIGIN from *hurry up* s.v. HURRY *verb*.]
▸ **A** *attrib. adjective*. Used or arising in an emergency; involving or requiring haste. *US*. L19.
▸ **B** *noun*. (An) encouragement or a demand to hurry up. E20.

hurst /həːst/ *noun*. Also **hirst**.
[ORIGIN Old English *hyrst* from base repr. also by Old Saxon, Old High German *hurst*, (also mod. German) *horst*.]
▸ **I 1** A hillock, knoll, or bank, *esp.* a sandy one. OE. ▸**b** A sandbank; a ford formed by a bed of sand or shingle. LME.
2 A wooded hillock or rise; a copse, a wood. OE.
▸ **II 3** The frame of a pair of millstones. L16.

hurt /həːt/ *noun*[1]. ME.
[ORIGIN Old French, formed as HURT *verb*.]
†**1** A knock or blow causing a wound, injury, or damage. ME–M19.

R. W. EMERSON You admire this tower of granite, weathering the hurts of so many ages.

2 A physical injury, a wound; bodily or material damage. *arch.* ME.

LD MACAULAY He ordered his own surgeon to look to the hurts of the captive.

3 An injury of any kind; harm, wrong. Now *spec.* mental pain, emotional distress. ME.

S. PEPYS But [I] do not think that all this will redound to my hurt. H. ROBBINS The sudden look of hurt that flashed across her face. D. PRATER His first act was to write . . expressing his deep hurt at this dismissal.

hurt /həːt/ *noun*[2]. Also **heurte**. M16.
[ORIGIN French †*heurte*. Cf. GOLPE.]
HERALDRY. A roundel azure (usu. held to represent a hurtleberry).

hurt /həːt/ *noun*[3]. Now *dial.* M16.
[ORIGIN Unknown. Cf. earlier HURTLEBERRY. See also WHORT.]
= HURTLEBERRY.

hurt /həːt/ *verb*. Pa. t. & pa. pple **hurt**, (*dial.*) **hurted**. ME.
[ORIGIN Old French *hurter* (mod. *heurter*) from Proto-Gallo-Romance, perh. of Germanic origin.]
▸ **I** *verb trans.* †**1** Knock, strike, dash, (when so as to wound or injure passing into sense 2). ME–M17.

CAXTON Thone hurted the other soo harde thei felle doun. J. WINTHROP The Elizabeth Dorcas . . being hurt upon a rock . . lost sixty passengers at sea.

2 Injure physically; inflict bodily pain on, wound; cause bodily or material damage to (a person or animal, *arch.* a thing). ME. ▸**b** Of an injured limb etc.: be a source of pain to (a person or animal). M19.

J. BERGER He has broken both his legs, but . . he isn't badly hurt otherwise.

3 Give mental pain to, cause emotional distress to; upset, offend, (a person, feelings, etc.). ME.

DAY LEWIS He put on a hurt expression which . . succeeded in piercing me with guilt. J. HELLER He makes fun of me and often hurts my feelings.

4 *gen.* Injure or harm in any way; be prejudicial or detrimental to; wrong. ME.

E. NESBIT I don't think it hurts Albert to enjoy himself too. P. BOWLES It's fine old cognac. It won't hurt you. *Gentleman (Mumbai)* Sanctions will hurt poor blacks more than rich whites.

▸ **II** *verb intrans.* †**5** Strike or dash (*against* etc.); come into collision. ME–E17.
6 (Of a limb etc.) suffer injury or pain, be a source of pain; (of a person) suffer pain or distress, *transf.* (of a country etc.) experience difficulties or misfortune; *US* have a dire need *for*. ME.

C. POTOK My head doesn't hurt at all, and the wrist is a lot less sore. A. F. LOEWENSTEIN She was hurting bad, . . We just got that codeine into her. *Fortune* He knew the industry was hurting for trained personnel.

7 Cause hurt or pain; be harmful, damaging, or detrimental. LME.

M. AMIS My shoes, they're too tight—they hurt more every day. *Company* It didn't hurt that his stepfather was . . a descendant of the founders of MGM studios.

hurter /ˈhəːtə/ *noun*[1]. ME.
[ORIGIN Anglo-Norman *hurt(o)ur* (in Anglo-Latin *hurtur(i)um*), formed as HURT *verb*: see -OUR, -ER[2].]
1 (A strengthening piece on) the shoulder of an axle, against which the nave of the wheel strikes. ME.
2 An attachment on a gun carriage to restrict its movement or prevent it from damaging a parapet etc. E19.

hurter /ˈhəːtə/ *noun*[2]. LME.
[ORIGIN from HURT *verb* + -ER[1].]
A person who or thing which causes hurt or injury.

hurtful /ˈhəːtfʊl, -f(ə)l/ *adjective*. LME.
[ORIGIN from HURT *noun*[1] + -FUL.]
Causing hurt; harmful, detrimental; wounding to the feelings.
■ **hurtfully** *adverb* M16. **hurtfulness** *noun* E17.

hurtle /ˈhəːt(ə)l/ *noun*. *literary*. L18.
[ORIGIN from the verb.]
The action or an act of hurtling.

hurtle /ˈhəːt(ə)l/ *verb*. ME.
[ORIGIN from HURT *verb* + -LE[3].]
▸ **I** *verb trans.* **1** Strike, knock, (a thing *against*, a thing †*down*, things *together*); strike against, collide with. Now *rare* exc. as passing into sense 2. ME.

LYTTON His emotions . . so hurtling one the other.

2 Drive violently or swiftly; hurl, cast; *rare* brandish. LME.

Boy's Own Paper Pieces of ice are being . . hurtled into the air.

▸ **II** *verb intrans.* **3** Strike *against*, *together*, esp. with violence or noise; collide; clash. Now *rare* exc. as passing into sense 4. ME.

J. R. GREEN Where knights have hurtled together.

4 Move with a clattering or rattling sound; dash, rush, hurry, esp. noisily; move or travel rapidly. E16.

SHAKES. *Jul. Caes.* The noise of battle hurtled in the air. B. HECHT His streetcar . . had hurtled wildly through the streets. R. P. JHABVALA The mountains themselves crumble off in chunks which hurtle down.

■ **hurtlingly** *adverb* (*rare*) in a hurtling manner L19.

hurtleberry /ˈhəːt(ə)lb(ə)ri/ *noun*. LME.
[ORIGIN from elem. of unknown origin + BERRY *noun*[1]: earlier than synon. HURT *noun*[3] and WHORT, WHORTLEBERRY.]
(The berry of) any of various dwarf shrubs of the genus *Vaccinium*, of the heath family, *esp.* (in Britain) the bilberry, *V. myrtillus*; *N. Amer.* = HUCKLEBERRY *noun* 1.

hurtless /ˈhəːtlɪs/ *adjective*. LME.
[ORIGIN from HURT *noun*[1] + -LESS.]
1 Unhurt. Now *rare*. LME.
2 Causing no hurt, harmless. M16.
■ **hurtlessly** *adverb* (*rare*) L16. **hurtlessness** *noun* (*rare*) L16.

hurtsome /ˈhəːts(ə)m/ *adjective*. Chiefly *Scot.* M16.
[ORIGIN from HURT *noun*[1] + -SOME[1].]
Hurtful, harmful.

husband /ˈhʌzbənd/ *noun*. LOE.
[ORIGIN Old Norse *húsbóndi* master of a house, husband, from *hús* HOUSE *noun*[1] + *bóndi* occupier and tiller of the soil: see BOND *noun*[1].]
▸ **I** †**1** The master of a house; the male head of a household. LOE–ME.
2 A married man esp. in relation to his wife. ME.

W. TREVOR Her husband . . had married her . . . in the church of St. Cyril. *transf.*: E. TOPSELL A Bull is the husband of a Cow.

COMPLAISANT *husband*.
▸ **II 3** The manager of a household or establishment; a steward. *obsolete* exc. in ***ship's husband*** below. LOE.

H. FINCH The King hath a proper Court . . . The Judges whereof are called Barons, or housebands.

ship's husband an agent appointed by a ship's owners to see that a ship in port is well provided in all respects.
†**4** A tiller and cultivator of the soil, a farmer. Also, a manorial tenant (cf. HUSBANDLAND). ME–M18.

J. TULL Once in seven Years, the worst Husbands have the best Corn.

5 †**a** A good manager of his affairs. LME–L16. ▸**b** With qualifying adjective: a *good*, *bad*, etc., manager of his affairs. *arch.* E16.

b DEFOE I had been so good a husband of my rum that I had a great deal left. M. R. JAMES The next abbot was a bad husband to the Abbey.

■ **husbandhood** *noun* the state or position of a husband, the fact of being a husband LME. **husbandless** *adjective* without a husband; unmarried; widowed: LME. **husbandlike** *adjective &*

adverb after the manner of a husband M16. **husbandom** *noun (rare)* = HUSBANDHOOD L19. **husbandship** *noun* (**a**) *rare* husbandly behaviour; (**b**) the fact or condition of being the husband *of*: L18.

husband /ˈhʌzbənd/ *verb trans.* LME.
[ORIGIN from the noun.]
▸ **I 1** Till (the ground); cultivate (plants). *arch.* LME.
L. MORRIS The grain scarce husbanded by toiling hands Upon the sunlit plain.
2 Administer as a good steward; manage thriftily; use economically (*lit. & fig.*). LME.
C. BRONTË Husbanding my monthly allowance. R. GITTINGS He had the sufferer's gift of husbanding his energy.
▸ **II 3** Provide (a woman) with a husband; mate. *arch.* M16.
S. ROWLANDS I am husbanded with such a Clowne.
4 Behave as a husband to, marry (a woman). *arch.* E17.
G. MEREDITH He had been ready to perform the duty of husbanding the woman.
■ **husbander** *noun (rare)* E17.

husbandland /ˈhʌzbəndlənd/ *noun.* LME.
[ORIGIN from HUSBAND *noun* or Old Norse *húsbóndi* freeholder + LAND *noun*[1].]
hist. In N. England and Scotland, the holding of a manorial tenant; the land occupied and cultivated by the tenants of a manor as opp. to the demesne lands.

husbandly /ˈhʌzbəndli/ *adjective.* LME.
[ORIGIN from HUSBAND *noun* + -LY[1].]
†**1** Thrifty, economical. LME–M18.
O. BLACKALL He . . is nevertheless oblig'd to be frugal and husbandly.
2 †**a** Of plants: cultivated. M–L16. ▸**b** Pertaining or appropriate to a husbandman or husbandry. Now *rare* or *obsolete*. L16.
3 Pertaining or appropriate to a woman's husband; marital. L16.
Daily Telegraph Every mother with a daughter knows the husbandly potential of every other mother's son.

husbandly /ˈhʌzbəndli/ *adverb.* Now *rare* or *obsolete.* L15.
[ORIGIN formed as HUSBANDLY *adjective* + -LY[2].]
Thriftily, economically.

husbandman /ˈhʌzbəndmən/ *noun.* Pl. **-men.** ME.
[ORIGIN from HUSBAND *noun* + MAN *noun*.]
1 A man who tills or cultivates the ground; a farmer. Formerly also, the holder of a husbandland. *arch.* ME.
†**2** The male head or manager of a household. Only in ME. ▸**b** A married man, a husband. *rare.* Only in LME.

husbandry /ˈhʌzbəndri/ *noun.* ME.
[ORIGIN from HUSBAND *noun* + -RY.]
†**1** The administration and management of a household; domestic economy. ME–M17. ▸†**b** *gen.* Occupation, business. E–M17.
SHAKES. *Merch. V.* Lorenzo, I commit into your hands The husbandry and manage of my house.
2 Tillage or cultivation of the ground; agriculture; farming. ME.
C. FRANCIS Good management and wise husbandry are the cornerstones of bountiful harvesting. Z. MEDVEDEV There are . . . agricultural research institutes, one of which studies sheep and goat husbandry.
animal husbandry the science of breeding and caring for farm animals. **crop husbandry** the science of growing and harvesting crops.
†**3** Household goods; agricultural produce; land under cultivation; the body of husbandmen on an estate. ME–L17.
SHAKES. *Hen. V* All her husbandry doth lie on heaps, corrupting in its own fertility.
4 a Careful management, thrift, economy. LME. ▸**b** With qualifying adjective: *good*, *bad*, etc., management of resources. M16.
a R. W. EMERSON Reform has no gratitude, no prudence, no husbandry. **b** BOLINGBROKE The excessive ill husbandry practiced from the very beginning of King William's reign.

†**huseau** *noun.* LME–E18.
[ORIGIN French †*houseau* dim. of Old French (& French dial.) *house*, *heuse*, *husse* boot.]
A boot, a legging.

hush /hʌʃ/ *noun*[1]. E17.
[ORIGIN from HUSH *verb*[1].]
1 An utterance of 'hush!' E17.
2 Suppression of sound; stillness; silence; an instance of this. L17. ▸**b** Suppression of discussion, information, etc. L19.
E. FIGES A hush fell as the conversation died. C. PHILLIPS The . . hush of a late afternoon in the Caribbean overtook him. **b** *attrib.*: T. E. LAWRENCE There is a 'Hush' policy over the Red Sea and Arabia.
3 PHONETICS. A palatal or palato-alveolar fricative (as /ʃ/ or /ʒ/). M20.
– COMB.: **hush money**: paid to prevent the disclosure of a discreditable affair.
■ **hushful** *adjective* silent, still L19. **hushfully** *adverb* M19.

hush /hʌʃ/ *noun*[2]. Chiefly *N. English.* E19.
[ORIGIN from HUSH *verb*[3].]
A gush or rush of water, *esp.* one artificially produced.

hush /hʌʃ/ *adjective.* E17.
[ORIGIN Alt. of HUSHT *adjective*, also infl. by HUSH *verb*[1], *interjection*. In sense 2 merging with attrib. use of HUSH *noun*[1].]
1 Silent, still, quiet, hushed. *arch.* E17.
LONGFELLOW Hush sat the listening bench.
2 Secret. Cf. HUSH-HUSH *adjective. colloq.* M20.
J. WYNDHAM I don't know what goes on . . but I do know that it is very hush.

hush /hʌʃ/ *verb*[1]. M16.
[ORIGIN Prob. back-form. from HUSHT *adjective* regarded as a pa. pple: cf. HUSH *adjective*. See also HUSH-HUSH *verb*.]
▸ **I** *verb trans.* **1** Make silent, quiet, or still. Also foll. by *up*. M16.
T. O'BRIEN The child was talking . . ., then the young woman hushed her. G. CLARE Voices had to be hushed, movements subdued.
hush one's mouth *US dial.* be quiet, stop talking.
2 Calm (disturbance, disquiet, etc.); allay, lull, pacify. M17.
H. MANN I do sincerely congratulate you, that the disturbance is hushed.
3 Suppress public mention of (an affair); keep (an event, news, etc.) from becoming known. Freq. foll. by *up*. M17.
STEELE It had indeed cost him a Hundred Pounds to hush the affair. L. VAN DER POST Evil verily does not decrease by being hushed up as a non-reality.
▸ **II** *verb intrans.* **4** Become silent, quiet, or still. Freq. in *imper.*: see HUSH *interjection*. Also foll. by *up*. M16.
A. SETON The crowd hushed and listened avidly. *New Yorker* Hush up! You want these bitches to hear you?

hush /hʌʃ/ *verb*[2] *trans.* Now *dial.* E17.
[ORIGIN Alt. of SH *interjection & verb*. Cf. SHOO, German *husch* shoo!]
Shoo away (birds etc.).

hush /hʌʃ/ *verb*[3] *trans.* Chiefly *N. English.* M18.
[ORIGIN Imit.]
Send or release (water) with a rush.

hush /hʌʃ/ *interjection.* E17.
[ORIGIN Partly var. of HUSHT *interjection*, partly imper. of HUSH *verb*[1].]
Demanding silence or quiet.

hushaby /ˈhʌʃəbʌɪ/ *interjection.* Also **-bye.** M18.
[ORIGIN from HUSH *verb*[1] or *interjection* + *-a-* + *-by* as in BYE-BYE *interjection*. Cf. *lullaby*, *rock-a-bye*.]
Lulling a child: hush and sleep.

hushed /hʌʃt/ *adjective.* E17.
[ORIGIN (Alt. of HUSHT *adjective* after) pa. pple of HUSH *verb*[1]: see -ED[1].]
Silenced, quieted, stilled.
■ **hushedly** /ˈhʌʃɪdli/ *adverb* in a hushed manner M19.

hush-hush /hʌʃˈhʌʃ/ *adjective. colloq.* E20.
[ORIGIN from redupl. of HUSH *interjection*.]
(To be kept) highly secret.
A. S. BYATT I worked for British Intelligence, . . . On some very hush-hush research.

hush-hush /hʌʃˈhʌʃ/ *verb trans.* M19.
[ORIGIN Redupl. of HUSH *verb*[1].]
Silence, quiet (by saying 'hush!' to).

hushion /ˈhʌʃ(ə)n/ *noun. Scot.* L18.
[ORIGIN Perh. from HUSEAU: see -ION.]
A stocking without a foot.

hush puppy /ˈhʌʃ pʌpi/ *noun phr. US.* E20.
[ORIGIN from HUSH *verb*[1] + PUPPY *noun*.]
A kind of quickly fried maize bread.

husht /hʌʃt/ *adjective. arch.* LME.
[ORIGIN Orig. from HUSHT *interjection*, later taken as a pa. pple (whence HUSH *verb*[1]). See also HUSHED *adjective*.]
Silent, still, quiet; made silent, hushed.

husht /hʌʃt/ *interjection.* Now *dial.* Also †**hust.** LME.
[ORIGIN Natural exclam. Cf. HUSH, WHISHT, WHIST *interjections*.]
= HUSH *interjection*.

husk /hʌsk/ *noun*[1]. LME.
[ORIGIN Prob. from Low German *hüske* little house, core of fruit, sheath = Middle Dutch *hūskijn* (Dutch *huisken*) dim. of *hūs* HOUSE *noun*[1].]
1 The dry outer covering of some fruits and seeds, esp. grain, nuts, etc.; *N. Amer.* the outer covering of an ear of maize. LME. ▸†**b** The calyx of a flower. M16–E18.
AV *Luke* 15:16 And he would faine haue filled his belly with the huskes that the swine did eate. D. ATTENBOROUGH It bears numerous seeds, . . that are easily plucked and winnowed from their husks.
2 The outside part of something, esp. when worthless. LME.
J. R. LOWELL He . . gave us ravishing glimpses of an ideal under the dry husk of our New England. R. SUTCLIFF Some sitting like zombies. The husks of men, blind and leaden with exhaustion.
3 An insect's cocoon. Formerly, an elytron. *obsolete* exc. *poet.* M16.

husk /hʌsk/ *noun*[2]. E18.
[ORIGIN Prob. partly from HUSK *verb*[2], partly from HUSK *noun*[1], HUSKY *adjective*[2].]
1 Bronchitis in cattle, sheep, or swine caused by parasitic infestation, usu. marked by a husky cough. E18.
2 Huskiness. E19.

†**husk** *noun*[3] see HUSS.

husk /hʌsk/ *verb*[1] *trans.* M16.
[ORIGIN from HUSK *noun*[1].]
Remove the husk or husks from.

husk /hʌsk/ *verb*[2]. L16.
[ORIGIN Prob. partly imit., partly from HUSK *noun*[1], HUSKY *adjective*[2].]
1 *verb intrans.* Of a farm animal: cough as when suffering from husk. *local.* L16.
2 *verb intrans.* Of the voice: be or become husky. E20.
3 *verb trans.* Utter huskily. L20.

huskanaw /ˈhʌskənɔː/ *noun & verb. hist.* E18.
[ORIGIN Virginia Algonquian.]
▸**A** *noun.* An initiation rite for American Indian youths at puberty involving solitary confinement and the use of narcotics. E18.
▸ **B** *verb trans.* Cause to undergo this rite. E18.

huske /hʌsk/ *noun.* Long *arch. rare.* L15.
[ORIGIN Unknown.]
A company of hares.

husked /hʌskt/ *adjective.* L16.
[ORIGIN from HUSK *noun*[1], *verb*[1]: see -ED[2], -ED[1].]
†**1** Provided or covered with a husk. L16–L17.
2 Stripped of the husk; hulled. E17.

husker /ˈhʌskə/ *noun.* L18.
[ORIGIN from HUSK *verb*[1] + -ER[1].]
A person who or thing which removes husks; *N. Amer.* a participant in a husking bee.

huskie *noun & adjective* var. of HUSKY *noun*[1] & *adjective*[1].

husking /ˈhʌskɪŋ/ *noun.* L17.
[ORIGIN from HUSK *verb*[1] + -ING[1].]
The action of HUSK *verb*[1]; an instance of this; *N. Amer.* (more fully ***husking bee***) a gathering of neighbours etc. at a farm to remove husks from maize.

husky /ˈhʌski/ *noun*[1] & *adjective*[1]. Also **-ie**, **H-.** M19.
[ORIGIN Perh. ult. from abbreviation of Cree *a:yaskime·w* or a related form: cf. ESKIMO.]
▸ **A** *noun.* **1** The Eskimo language; an Eskimo. *colloq.* (now *offensive*). M19.
2 A powerful dog with a thick coat, used in the Arctic for pulling sledges. L19.
▸ **B** *adjective.* Eskimo. *colloq.* (now usu. *derog.*) exc. in ***husky dog***, = sense A.2 above. M19.

husky /ˈhʌski/ *adjective*[2] & *noun*[2]. M16.
[ORIGIN from HUSK *noun*[1] + -Y[1].]
▸ **A** *adjective.* **1** Full of or consisting of husks; of the nature of a husk. M16.
R. GRAVES On the tree a husky fruit.
2 Dry as a husk, arid (*lit. & fig.*). L16.
DISRAELI His translation is hard, dry, and husky, as the outside of a cocoa-nut.
†**3** Having or consisting of a cocoon. M17–M18.
4 Dry in the throat, hoarse; low-pitched and somewhat rough. E18.
L. DEIGHTON Jean's voice was husky, a bit edgy and rasplike. N. MAILER She had a rich husky voice.
5 Tough, strong, hefty. *colloq.* (orig. *N. Amer.*). M19.
D. DELILLO A husky blond Nebraskan.
▸ **B** *noun.* A strong stoutly built person; one whose appearance suggests strength and force. *N. Amer. colloq.* M19.
■ **huskily** *adverb* M19. **huskiness** *noun* L18.

huso /ˈhuːsəʊ/ *noun.* Pl. **-os.** ME.
[ORIGIN medieval Latin from Old High German *hūso*. Cf. HAUSEN.]
The beluga, *Huso huso*.

huspil /ˈhʌsp(ə)l/ *verb trans.* Long *obsolete* exc. *dial.* Also **-pel.** Infl. **-ll-.** LME.
[ORIGIN French *houspiller* maltreat by dragging about and shaking, alt. of earlier *hous(se)pigner*, from *housse* (see HOUSE *noun*[2]) + *p(e)igner* to comb.]
Treat with violence; maltreat; despoil; harass.

huss /hʌs/ *noun.* Orig. †**husk.** LME.
[ORIGIN Unknown.]
A dogfish; *esp.* (**a**) (more fully ***bull huss***) the nurse hound, *Scyliorhinus stellaris*; (**b**) (more fully ***robin huss***) the lesser-spotted dogfish, *S. canicula*.

hussar /hʊˈzɑː/ *noun.* M16.
[ORIGIN Hungarian *huszár* †freebooter, light horseman from early Serbian *husar*, *gusar*, *hursar* from Italian *corsaro* CORSAIR.]
Orig., a Hungarian light horseman of the 15th cent. Later, a soldier of a light cavalry regiment.

Husserlian /hʊˈsəːlɪ(ə)n/ *adjective.* M20.
[ORIGIN from *Husserl* (see below) + -IAN.]
Of, pertaining to, or characteristic of the German philosopher Edmund Husserl (1859–1938) or his work, esp. in phenomenology.

H

Hussite /ˈhʌsʌɪt/ *noun & adjective*. **M16**.
[ORIGIN mod. Latin *Hussita* (usu. pl.) from John *Huss* or *Hus* (see below), from *Husinec* his native village: see -ITE¹.]
▸ **A** *noun*. A follower of John Huss (*c* 1372–1415), a Bohemian religious reformer who became a national hero after being burned at the stake. **M16**.
▸ **B** *attrib.* or as *adjective*. Of or pertaining to Huss, his beliefs, or his teachings. **M19**.
■ **Hussitism** *noun* **L19**.

hussive *noun* see HOUSEWIFE *noun*.

hussy /ˈhʌsi, ˈhʌzi/ *noun*. Also **huzzy** /ˈhʌzi/. **LME**.
[ORIGIN Contr. of HOUSEWIFE *noun*: cf. GOODY *noun*¹.]
†**1** = HOUSEWIFE *noun* 1. **LME–E19**.
2 = HOUSEWIFE *noun* 3. *obsolete* exc. *dial.* **E16**.
3 An impudent or immoral girl or woman. **M17**.
E. O'BRIEN She wished that her daughter had not grown into the cruel feelingless hussy . . she was.

†**hust** *interjection* var. of HUSHT *interjection*.

husting /ˈhʌstɪŋ/ *noun*. Pl. **hustings**. **LOE**.
[ORIGIN Old Norse *húsþing* house of assembly (held by a king etc. with his immediate followers as opp. to a general assembly): see HOUSE *noun*¹, THING *noun*².]
1 A deliberative assembly, *esp.* one summoned by a king etc.; a council. Long *obsolete* exc. *hist.* **LOE**.
2 *sing.* & in *pl.* The most ancient and highest court in the City of London presided over nominally by the Lord Mayor and Sheriffs and actually by the Recorder of London. Formerly also (in *pl.* treated as *sing.*), the part of the Guildhall where this court was held. Also ***Court of Husting***. **LOE**.
3 In *pl.* (now usu. treated as *sing.*). Orig. (now *hist.*), the platform from which (before 1872) parliamentary candidates were nominated and electors addressed. Later, the proceedings of an election (for Parliament etc.). **E18**.
H. MARTINEAU The Church question was the leading one on the hustings. *Sunday (Kolkata)* At the hustings, her party somehow scraped through.

hustle /ˈhʌs(ə)l/ *noun*. **L17**.
[ORIGIN from the verb.]
1 The action of shaking together. Chiefly in ***pitch-and-hustle***, = ***hustle-cap*** s.v. HUSTLE *verb*. Long *rare* or *obsolete*. **L17**.
2 The act of pushing or jostling roughly; forceful or strenuous activity; push, drive; bustle. **E19**.
E. AMADI She could not cope with all the hustle and pressures of business.
get a hustle on *US* hurry up, get a move on.
3 A swindle, a means of deception or fraud. Also, a source of income, a paid job. *slang* (orig. *US*). **M20**.
MALCOLM X Hustles being used to avoid the draft. R. PHARR I got me a good hustle I write over $200 worth of numbers a day.

hustle /ˈhʌs(ə)l/ *verb*. **L17**.
[ORIGIN Middle Dutch & mod. Dutch *husselen*, *hutselen* shake, toss, frequentative of *hutsen* = Middle High German *hutzen* (cf. *hussen* run, *hutschen* push), from Germanic imit. base.]
▸ **I** *verb trans.* †**1** Shake to and fro, shake about; toss (money) in the game of hustle-cap (see below). **L17–M19**.
2 Push roughly, jostle, esp. in order to rob; thrust (a person) *into*, *out of*, *through*, etc.; impel unceremoniously *into* an action etc.; cause to hurry. **M18**.
SMOLLETT I was hussled by those rebellious rapscallions. R. K. NARAYAN Banks . . could not be hustled; they had their own pace of work. W. WHARTON He grabs me by the arm and hustles me down a tunnel. D. LESSING White clouds . . were being ripped and hustled and rolled across a mauve silk sky. *New Yorker* Transvestites hustled white men in business suits.
3 Obtain or produce by forceful action; steal, swindle. Also foll. by *up*. *US colloq.* **M19**.
P. MANSFIELD Perhaps they can hustle up some coffee.
4 Sell or serve (goods etc.), esp. aggressively. *N. Amer. slang.* **L19**.
P. BOOTH I'm afraid they make poor Nixon look like he's hustling real estate.
▸ **II** *verb intrans.* **5** Crowd together, jostle each other; push one's way; push roughly *against*. **E19**.
M. KINGSLEY The woman will accuse some man of having hustled against her. M. S. GATTY The tortoise began to hustle under the leaves and rubbish.
6 Move hastily, hurry, bustle. **E19**.
K. KESEY I'll have to hustle to catch up.
7 Engage in prostitution. *slang.* **E20**.
R. BRAUTIGAN She was hustling for a spade pimp.
– COMB.: **hustle-cap** (now *rare* or *obsolete*) a form of pitch-and-toss, in which the coins were shaken in a cap or hat before being tossed.

hustlement /ˈhʌs(ə)lm(ə)nt/ *noun*. Long *obsolete* exc. *dial.* **LME**.
[ORIGIN Old French *(h)ostillement* furniture, from *hostiller* furnish, equip, from *(h)ostil(le)* (mod. *outil*) tool: see -MENT.]
1 Household furniture. Usu. in *pl.*, household goods. **LME**.
2 Lumber; a miscellaneous collection; in *pl.*, odds and ends. **M17**.

hustler /ˈhʌslə/ *noun*. **E19**.
[ORIGIN from HUSTLE *verb* + -ER¹.]
A person who hustles; someone making a dishonest living, a thief, a pimp; (orig. *US*) an energetic person, *esp.* a (forcefully persuasive) salesman; *slang* a prostitute.
J. K. JEROME I don't want to appear a hustler, . . but it feels to me like hours since I asked you how the catastrophe really occurred. P. HOWARD Successful hustlers in modern methods of mass book-selling.

†**huswife** *noun* see HOUSEWIFE *noun*.

hut /hʌt/ *noun*. **M16**.
[ORIGIN French *hutte* from Middle & mod. High German *hütte*.]
1 a MILITARY. A temporary wooden etc. house for troops. **M16**. ▸**b** A small, simple, or crude house or shelter, *esp.* one made of mud, turf, etc., or constructed for temporary use; *Austral. & NZ* a dwelling for the use of stockmen, shearers, etc. **M17**.
2 The back end or body of the pin closing the breech of a musket. **M19**.
– COMB.: **hut-circle** ARCHAEOLOGY a ring of stones or earth or some other circular feature interpreted as the site of a prehistoric hut.

hut /hʌt/ *verb*. Infl. **-tt-**. **M17**.
[ORIGIN French *(se) hutter* make a hut for one's lodging, formed as HUT *noun*.]
1 *verb trans.* Place (troops etc.) in a hut or huts; provide with a hut or huts. **M17**.
2 *verb intrans.* Lodge or take shelter in a hut or huts. **L18**.

hutch /hʌtʃ/ *noun*. **ME**.
[ORIGIN Old French & mod. French *huche*, (dial.) *huge* from medieval Latin *hutica* (Anglo-Norman *hugia*): ult. origin unknown.]
1 A chest for storage, a coffer; *spec.* (*N. Amer.*) a (kitchen) sideboard with open shelves above for plates etc., a dresser. Now chiefly *N. Amer.* **ME**.
2 A cage; *spec.* a cage or box for small animals, a boxlike pen for rabbits etc. (also ***rabbit hutch*** etc.). **LME**.
3 A hut, a cabin, a small house. *derog.* **E17**.
4 *techn.* Any of various boxlike devices or containers; *esp.* (*a*) a box for sifting flour etc. (also ***bolting hutch***); (*b*) a low carriage or wagon used in agriculture, mining, etc. **E17**. ▸**b** A quantity (of coal, ore, etc.) held by a hutch. **L17**.
– COMB.: **hutch table** *N. Amer.* a combination table and chest which converts into a chair or a settee.

hutch /hʌtʃ/ *verb*. **L16**.
[ORIGIN from the noun.]
1 *verb trans.* Put or store in a hutch (*lit.* & *fig.*). **L16**.
MILTON In her own loins She hutched the all-worshipped ore.
2 *verb intrans.* & *trans.* Crouch, squat; hunch, huddle, (*up*); lower (oneself) into or move with a crouching, bent, or huddled posture; hitch (one's chair etc.) forward. Chiefly *dial.* **L19**.
D. H. LAWRENCE Long smooth thighs Hutched-up for warmth. W. GOLDING He hutched to the very edge and let his legs hang over. B. HINES Billy hutched his chair up and leaned forward over his desk.

Hutchinson /ˈhʌtʃɪns(ə)n/ *noun*. **L19**.
[ORIGIN J. *Hutchinson* (1828–1913), English surgeon.]
MEDICINE. **1** ***Hutchinson's tooth***, ***Hutchinson tooth***, (the possession of) a permanent incisor with a narrow notched biting edge, found in children with congenital syphilis. Usu. in *pl.* **L19**.
2 ***Hutchinson's triad***, ***Hutchinson triad***, Hutchinson's teeth, interstitial keratitis, and one form of deafness, jointly diagnostic of congenital syphilis. **L19**.

Hutchinsonian /hʌtʃɪnˈsəʊnɪən/ *adjective & noun*. **M18**.
[ORIGIN from *Hutchinson* (see below) + -IAN.]
▸ **A** *adjective*. **1** ECCLESIASTICAL HISTORY. Of or pertaining to John Hutchinson (1674–1737), a writer on natural philosophy who interpreted the Bible mystically and opposed Newtonian philosophy. Also, of or pertaining to Anne Hutchinson (1591–1643), an antinomian teacher in New England. **M18**.
2 MEDICINE. (Also **h-**.) Designating an incisor notched in the manner of Hutchinson's teeth. **E20**.
▸ **B** *noun*. ECCLESIASTICAL HISTORY. An adherent of John Hutchinson or of Anne Hutchinson. **M18**.

hutia /hʌˈtiːə/ *noun*. **M16**.
[ORIGIN Spanish from Taino *huti*, *cuti*.]
A rodent of the family Capromyidae, comprising W. Indian animals resembling cavies and related to the coypu.

hutment /ˈhʌtm(ə)nt/ *noun*. **L19**.
[ORIGIN from HUT *verb* + -MENT.]
Accommodation or lodging in huts; a hutted encampment.

hutt *noun* see HOT *noun*¹.

Hutterite /ˈhʌt(ə)rʌɪt/ *noun & adjective*. **L19**.
[ORIGIN from Jacob *Hutter* (d. 1536), a Moravian Anabaptist + -ITE¹.]
CHRISTIAN CHURCH. ▸**A** *noun*. A member of an Anabaptist sect established in Moravia by Jacob Hutter, or of any of various N. American sects originating among immigrants holding similar beliefs. **L19**.
▸ **B** *adjective*. Of, pertaining to, or holding the doctrines of, the Hutterites. **M20**.
■ **Hutterian** /hʌˈtɪərɪən/ *adjective* = HUTTERITE *adjective* **E20**.

Huttonian /hʌˈtəʊnɪən/ *adjective & noun*. **E19**.
[ORIGIN from *Hutton* (see below) + -IAN.]
GEOLOGY (now *hist.*).
▸ **A** *adjective*. Designating or pertaining to the ideas of James Hutton (1726–97), Scottish geologist, involving plutonism and uniformitarianism. **E19**.
▸ **B** *noun*. An adherent of Hutton's views. **E19**.

Hutu /ˈhuːtuː/ *noun & adjective*. **M20**.
[ORIGIN Bantu.]
▸ **A** *noun*. Pl. same, **Bahutu** /bəˈhuːtuː/. A member of a Bantu-speaking people forming the majority of the population of Rwanda and of Burundi. **M20**.
▸ **B** *adjective*. Of or pertaining to the Bahutu. **M20**.

hutung /ˈhʊtʊŋ/ *noun*. **E20**.
[ORIGIN Chinese (Pekinese) *hútòngr*.]
In northern Chinese cities, a narrow side street, an alley.

Huweitat /hʊˈweɪtɑːt/ *noun & adjective*. **E19**.
[ORIGIN Arabic *(al-)Ḥuwayṭāt* Arab tribes in NW Saudi Arabia.]
▸ **A** *noun*. Pl. same. A member of a Bedouin tribe of northern Saudi Arabia. **E19**.
▸ **B** *adjective*. Of or pertaining to this tribe. **M19**.

Huxham /ˈhʌks(ə)m/ *noun*. **L18**.
[ORIGIN J. *Huxham* (1692–1768), English physician.]
PHARMACOLOGY. In full ***Huxham's tincture (of bark)***. Compound tincture of cinchona bark, formerly used as a bitter tonic and febrifuge.

Huxleyan /ˈhʌkslɪən/ *adjective*. Also **-leian**. **L19**.
[ORIGIN from *Huxley* (see below): see -AN, -IAN.]
1 Of, pertaining to, or characteristic of T. H. Huxley (1825–95), English Darwinian biologist, humanist, and educational reformer. **L19**.
2 Of, pertaining to, or characteristic of his grandson Aldous Huxley (1894–1963), English novelist, or his work. **M20**.

Huygens /ˈhʌɪgənz/ *noun*. Also **-ghens**. **M19**.
[ORIGIN C. *Huygens* (1629–95), Dutch physicist.]
1 ***Huygens' principle***, a principle of wave propagation, that each point on a wave front can be regarded as a source of new waves, the overall effect of which constitutes the propagation of the wave front. **M19**.
2 ***Huygens construction***, ***Huygens' construction***, the geometrical construction for finding the position of a wave front using Huygens' principle. **M19**.
3 ***Huygens eyepiece***, ***Huygens' eyepiece***, a negative eyepiece of an optical instrument, consisting of two planoconvex lenses with their plane side towards the observer. (Earlier called ***Huygenian eyepiece***.) **E20**.
■ **Huygenian** /hʌɪˈgiːnɪən/ *adjective* of or pertaining to Huygens; ***Huygenian eyepiece*** = HUYGENS ***eyepiece***: **E18**.

huzoor /hʌˈzʊə, hʊ-/ *noun*. *arch.* Also (as a title) **H-**. **L18**.
[ORIGIN Persian & Urdu *ḥużūr* from Arabic *ḥuḍūr* presence, from *ḥaḍara* be present.]
An Indian potentate. (Chiefly a title used by Indians in respectful address.)

huzz /hʌz/ *verb intrans.* **M16**.
[ORIGIN Imit.]
Buzz.

huzza /hʌˈzɑː, hʊˈzɑː/ *noun*, *interjection*, & *verb*. *arch.* **L16**.
[ORIGIN Perh. orig. a sailor's cry when hauling (see HOISE), but cf. also German *Hussa* a cry of pursuit and exultation. See also HURRAH.]
▸ **A** *noun*. A shout of 'huzza!', a cheer. **L16**.
▸ **B** *interjection*. Expr. approval, encouragement, enthusiasm, or delight. **L17**.
▸ **C** *verb*. **1** *verb intrans.* Shout 'huzza!' **L17**.
2 *verb trans.* Welcome or encourage with shouts of 'huzza!' **L17**.

huzzy *noun* var. of HUSSY.

h.w. *abbreviation*.
Hit wicket.

HWM *abbreviation*.
High-water mark.

Hy *abbreviation*.
Henry.

hyacinth /ˈhʌɪəsɪnθ/ *noun*. Also †**hyacine** (Spenser). **M16**.
[ORIGIN French *hyacinthe* fr. Latin *hyacinthus* from Greek *huakinthos*, of pre-Hellenic origin: cf. earlier JACINTH.]
1 Orig. (now CLASSICAL HISTORY), a blue gem, perh. the sapphire. Now, the reddish-orange variety of zircon; also, a similar-coloured form of garnet or topaz. **M16**.
2 A flower whose dark markings were interpreted as the Greek word *aiai*, an exclamation of grief, and which was fabled to have sprung from the blood of Hyacinthus, a youth inadvertently killed by Apollo: variously identified with the martagon lily, a kind of iris, etc. Now CLASSICAL HISTORY or *poet.* **L16**.
3 (A flowering stem of) any of various bulbous plants of the genus *Hyacinthus*, of the lily family, with dense

H

racemes of bell-shaped flowers; esp. *H. orientalis*, native to SW Asia, much grown for its fragrant flowers. Also, any of various related or similar plants. **L16.**

4 A blue-black variety of the domestic pigeon with white markings. **M19.**

– PHRASES: **Cape hyacinth** = *summer hyacinth* below. **feather hyacinth** a sport of the tassel hyacinth in which all the flowers are sterile and divided into shreds. **grape hyacinth** any of various spring-flowering bulbs of the Mediterranean genus *Muscari*, of the lily family, much grown for their racemes of small ball-like blue flowers. **hyacinth of Peru** a bulbous plant of the lily family, *Scilla peruviana*, native to the Mediterranean, with dense racemes of blue-violet flowers. **Roman hyacinth** a smaller, earlier variant of *Hyacinthus orientalis*. **starch hyacinth** a kind of grape hyacinth with dark blue scented flowers. **summer hyacinth** a tall southern African plant of the lily family, *Galtonia candicans*, with fragrant white flowers. **tassel hyacinth** a kind of grape hyacinth, *Muscari comosum*, with a raceme of fertile brownish flowers bearing showy sterile purple-blue flowers at the top. **water hyacinth** a tropical American aquatic plant, *Eichhornia crassipes* (family Pontederiaceae), with large violet-blue flowers, a serious weed in waterways in warmer parts of the world. **wild hyacinth** either of two plants of the lily family: (**a**) (chiefly *Scot.*) the (English) bluebell, *Hyacinthoides non-scripta*; (**b**) *US* a meadow plant, *Camassia scilloides*, with starry pale blue flowers. **wood hyacinth** (chiefly *Scot.*) = *wild hyacinth* (a).

– COMB.: **hyacinth bean** = LABLAB.

hyacinthine /hʌɪəˈsɪnθʌɪn/ *adjective*. **M17.**
[ORIGIN Latin *hyacinthinus* from Greek *huakinthinos*, from *huakinthos*: see -INE[2].]

1 Of the colour of a hyacinth (the gem or the flower). Chiefly *poet. & rhet.*, as an epithet of hair. **M17.**

2 Consisting of or decorated with hyacinths (the flower). *poet.* **L17.**

■ Also **hyacinthian** *adjective* **E18.**

Hyades /ˈhʌɪədiːz/ *noun pl.* **LME.**
[ORIGIN Greek *Huades*, according to popular etym. from *huein* to rain but perh. actually from *hus* pig, SWINE (the Latin name being *Suculae* little pigs).]

(The name of) a group of stars near the Pleiades in the constellation Taurus, the heliacal rising of which was once thought to foretell rain.

hyaena *noun* var. of HYENA.

hyaenid /hʌɪˈiːnɪd/ *noun & adjective*. **M20.**
[ORIGIN mod. Latin *Hyaenidae* (see below), from Latin HYAENA: see -ID[3].]

▸ **A** *noun*. An animal of the family Hyaenidae, which comprises the hyenas and the aardwolf. **M20.**

▸ **B** *adjective*. Of, pertaining to, or designating this family. **L20.**

hyaenodon /hʌɪˈiːnədɒn/ *noun*. **M19.**
[ORIGIN mod. Latin (see below), from Latin *hyaena* hyena + -ODON.]

A large, heavily built carnivorous mammal of the genus *Hyaenodon*, occurring in the Oligocene epoch.

hya-hya /hʌɪəˈhʌɪə/ *noun*. **M19.**
[ORIGIN Guyanese name.]

A Guyanese evergreen tree, *Couma utilis*, of the dogbane family, with a drinkable latex.

hyaline /ˈhʌɪəlɪn, -iːn, -ʌɪn/ *adjective & noun*. In sense B.2 also **-in** /-ɪn/. **M17.**
[ORIGIN Latin *hyalinus* from late Greek *hualinos*, from *hualos* glass: see -INE[2].]

▸ **A** *adjective*. Transparent, translucent; glassy. Orig. *poet.*, now chiefly ANATOMY & MEDICINE. **M17.**

hyaline cartilage a translucent bluish-white kind of cartilage, present in joints and the respiratory tract and forming much of the fetal skeleton. **hyaline degeneration** hyalinization. **hyaline membrane disease** a condition in some babies, esp. premature ones, in which the lung spaces are lined with a membrane that inhibits adequate respiration.

▸ **B** *noun*. **1** A translucent substance such as the smooth sea or the clear sky. *poet.* **M17.**

2 ANATOMY & ZOOLOGY. A clear translucent substance, such as that in hydatid cysts. **M19.**

Zenker's hyaline degeneration: see ZENKER *noun*[1].

■ **hyaliniˈzation** *noun* (MEDICINE) a change of tissue into a homogeneous translucent often firm mass (also called ***hyaline degeneration***) **E20. hyalinized** *adjective* (MEDICINE) having the appearance that results from hyalinization **E20. hyaliˈnosis** *noun*, pl. **-noses** /-nəʊsiːz/, MEDICINE = HYALINIZATION **L19.**

hyalite /ˈhʌɪəlʌɪt/ *noun*. **L18.**
[ORIGIN from Greek *hualos* glass + -ITE[1].]

A clear colourless variety of opal occurring as globules.

hyalo- /ˈhʌɪələʊ/ *combining form* of Greek *hualos* glassy: see -O-.

■ **hyaloˈclastite** *noun* (GEOLOGY) (a) material formed as a result of lava coming into contact with water, solidifying, and shattering **M20. hyalopiˈlitic** *adjective* [Greek *pilos* felt] GEOLOGY characterized by needle-like microlites in a glassy matrix **L19. hyaloplasm** *noun* (BIOLOGY) the clear finely structured ground substance of cytoplasm **L19.**

hyaloid /ˈhʌɪəlɔɪd/ *adjective & noun*. **M19.**
[ORIGIN French *hyaloïde* or late Latin *hyaloides* from Greek *hualoeidēs* like glass, from *hualos* glass: see -OID.]

ANATOMY. ▸ **A** *adjective*. Of, pertaining to, or designating a thin transparent membrane enclosing the vitreous humour of the eye. **M19.**

▸ **B** *noun*. The hyaloid membrane. **M19.**

hyaluronic /ˌhʌɪəljʊəˈrɒnɪk/ *adjective*. **M20.**
[ORIGIN from HYALOID + URONIC.]

BIOCHEMISTRY. ***hyaluronic acid***, a viscous glycosaminoglycan found in synovial fluid, vitreous humour, bacterial capsules, etc., and composed of glucosamine and glucuronic acid.

■ **hyaˈluronate** *noun* a salt of hyaluronic acid **M20. hyaluronidase** *noun* an enzyme which depolymerizes hyaluronic acid, so reducing its viscosity and making tissue containing it more permeable **M20.**

hyawa /ˈhʌɪəwə/ *noun*. Also **hiawa**. **E19.**
[ORIGIN Arawak *hayäawa*.]

Any of several balsam-yielding trees and shrubs of Guyana, esp. *Protium heptaphyllum*, of the myrrh family.

hyawaballi /hʌɪəwəˈbali/ *noun*. Also **hiawa-**. **M19.**
[ORIGIN Arawak, formed as HYAWA + *-bali* suffix for a tree.]

A Guyanese timber tree, *Tetragastris panamensis*, related to the hyawas.

†**hybernacle**, **hybernaculum** *nouns*, †**hybernal** *adjective*, †**hybernate** *verb*, **hybernation** *noun*, †**Hybernian** *adjective & noun* vars. of HIBERNACLE, HIBERNACULUM, etc.

Hyblaean /hʌɪˈbliːən/ *adjective*. Also **Hyblean**. **E17.**
[ORIGIN from Latin *Hyblaeus* (from *Hybla*, Greek *Hublē*) + -AN: see -EAN.]

Of or pertaining to Hybla in Sicily, famous in ancient times for its honey; *poet.* honeyed, sweet. Cf. HYMETTIAN.

hybodont /ˈhɪbədɒnt/ *noun & adjective*. **M19.**
[ORIGIN from Greek *hubos* hump, humpbacked + -ODONT.]

(Of, characteristic of, or designating) an extinct elasmobranch fish of the family Hybodontidae or the order Hybodontiformes, from which present-day sharks are thought to be descended.

hybrid /ˈhʌɪbrɪd/ *noun & adjective*. **E17.**
[ORIGIN Latin *hybrida*, (*h*)*ibrida*.]

▸ **A** *noun*. **1** An animal or plant that is the offspring of individuals of different kinds (usually, different species). **E17.**

> ANTHONY HUXLEY Showy man-made hybrids seen in florists' shops.

2 A person of mixed descent or mixed ancestry. Now *offensive*. **M17.**

3 A thing derived from heterogeneous sources or composed of incongruous elements; PHILOLOGY a word formed of elements from different languages; GEOLOGY a hybrid rock. **M19.**

> R. F. HOBSON A psychotherapist is a kind of hybrid . . : a quasi-scientist, a quasi-artist.

▸ **B** *adjective*. **1** Of mixed character, heterogeneous; derived from unlike sources; (of a parliamentary bill) treated in some respects as a public bill and in others as a private one; (of a computer) employing both digital and analogue methods; (of rock) formed by the mixing of two magmas, or by the incorporation of solid rock into magma. **E18.**

2 Bred or produced as a hybrid. **L18.**

– SPECIAL COLLOCATIONS: **hybrid perpetual** any rose of a group of formerly popular garden hybrids, derived in part from the Bourbon rose. **hybrid swarm** ECOLOGY a variable population resulting from the hybridization of neighbouring species. **hybrid tea** any rose of a group of hybrids now much grown, evolved from crosses between hybrid perpetuals and the tea rose, *Rosa* × *odorata*. **hybrid vigour** = HETEROSIS 2.

■ **hybridism** *noun* (**a**) the fact or condition of being hybrid; (**b**) the production of hybrids: **M19. hybridist** *noun* a hybridizer **M19. hyˈbridity** *noun* = HYBRIDISM (a) **M19.**

hybridization /ˌhʌɪbrɪdʌɪˈzeɪʃ(ə)n/ *noun*. Also **-isation**. **M19.**
[ORIGIN from HYBRIDIZE + -IZATION.]

1 The production of hybrids by crossbreeding or cross-fertilization. **M19.**

2 *gen.* The action or result of hybridizing something; BIOLOGY the fusion of two somatic cells of different karyotypes to form a cell with nuclear material of both; BIOCHEMISTRY the process of combining into polymers complementary subunits of different but related substances, e.g. DNA and RNA. **E20.**

Southern hybridization = SOUTHERN BLOT.

hybridize /ˈhʌɪbrɪdʌɪz/ *verb*. Also **-ise**. **M19.**
[ORIGIN from HYBRID + -IZE.]

1 *verb trans.* Subject to crossbreeding, cause to produce hybrids. **M19.** ▸**b** Combine (things of different kinds); combine *with* a thing of a different kind; subject to hybridization. **M20.**

> **b** *Listener* A new series . . hybridising chat show and fly-on-the-wall documentary. S. L. WOLFE Experiments in which RNA is hybridized with its DNA template.

2 *verb intrans.* Produce a hybrid; interbreed (*with*). **M19.**

■ **hybridizable** *adjective* **M19. hybridized** *adjective* obtained by hybridization; *techn.* hybrid: **M19. hybridizer** *noun* a person who produces hybrids, esp. plant hybrids **M19.**

hybridoma /hʌɪbrɪˈdəʊmə/ *noun*. Pl. **-mas**, **-mata** /-mətə/. **L20.**
[ORIGIN from HYBRID + -OMA.]

A culture of cells produced by hybridization; *spec.* one in which myeloma cells are hybridized with antibody-producing lymphocytes, used to produce monoclonal antibodies.

hybridous /ˈhʌɪbrɪdəs/ *adjective*. Now *rare* or *obsolete*. **L17.**
[ORIGIN from HYBRID *noun* + -OUS.]

Hybrid.

hybris /ˈhʌɪbrɪs/ *noun*. **E20.**
[ORIGIN Greek HUBRIS.]

= HUBRIS.

Hydah *noun & adjective* var. of HAIDA.

hydantoin /hʌɪˈdantəʊɪn/ *noun*. **M19.**
[ORIGIN from Greek *hudōr* water + ALL)ANTOIC + -IN[1].]

CHEMISTRY & PHARMACOLOGY. A cyclic derivative of urea, used esp. in the synthesis of a class of anticonvulsants; glycolylurea, HN·CONH·$COCH_2$. Also, an anticonvulsant of this class.

hydathode /ˈhʌɪdəθəʊd/ *noun*. **L19.**
[ORIGIN from Greek *hudat-*, *hudōr* water + *hodos* way: cf. -ODE[2].]

A pore in a plant, esp. in a leaf, which exudes water.

hydatid /ˈhʌɪdətɪd/ *noun*. **L17.**
[ORIGIN mod. Latin *hydatid-*, *hydatis* from Greek *hudatid-*, *-is* drop of water, watery vesicle, from *hudat-*, *hudōr* water: see -ID[2].]

Orig., a cyst containing watery fluid. Now, a fluid-filled cyst or a jelly-filled cluster of cysts produced by and containing a larva of the tapeworms *Echinococcus granulosus* or *E. multilocularis*, and occurring in dogs, sheep, etc., whence it is caught by humans; a tapeworm so encysted. Freq. *attrib.*

– COMB.: **hydatid disease**: caused by a hydatid, with very variable symptoms and effects.

■ **hydaˈtidiform** *adjective* having the form of a hydatid; ***hydatidiform mole***, (the condition of having) a cluster of fluid-filled vesicles in the womb as a result of the degeneration of chorionic tissue during pregnancy: **M19. hydatiˈdosis** *noun* hydatid disease **E20.**

Hyde /hʌɪd/ *noun*. **L19.**
[ORIGIN The evil personality assumed by Dr Jekyll in R. L. Stevenson's story 'Strange Case of Dr Jekyll and Mr Hyde' (1886).]

An unsuspected or hidden evil side to a person's character. Cf. JEKYLL.

hydel /ˈhʌɪdɛl/ *adjective*. **M20.**
[ORIGIN Abbreviation.]

Hydroelectric.

Hyde Park /hʌɪd ˈpɑːk/ *adjectival phr.* **L19.**
[ORIGIN A park in London.]

Designating or employing impromptu controversial oratory of a kind traditionally associated with Speakers' Corner in Hyde Park.

hydnocarpus /hɪdnə(ʊ)ˈkɑːpəs/ *noun*. **E20.**
[ORIGIN mod. Latin, from Greek *hudnon* truffle + *karpos* fruit, from the appearance of the fruit.]

Any of various tropical Asiatic trees of the genus *Hydnocarpus* (family Flacourtiaceae), several of which (esp. *H. pentandra* and *H. kurzii*) are a source of chaulmoogra oil. Also ***hydnocarpus tree***.

■ **hydnocarpate** *noun* a salt or ester of hydnocarpic acid **E20. hydnocarpic** *adjective*: ***hydnocarpic acid***, an alicyclic acid, $C_5H_7(CH_2)_{10}COOH$, glycerides of which are the chief constituents of chaulmoogra oil and hydnocarpus oil **E20.**

hydr- *combining form* see HYDRO-.

hydra /ˈhʌɪdrə/ *noun & adjective*. **LME.**
[ORIGIN (Old French (*h*)*ydre*, *idre* from) Latin *hydra* from Greek *hudra* water snake.]

▸ **A** *noun*. **1** GREEK MYTHOLOGY. (Also **H-**.) A monster with many heads, which grew again as fast as they were cut off. **LME.**

2 (Usu. **H-**.) (The name of) a long faint constellation extending from Cancer to Centaurus; the Sea Serpent. Also ***the Hydra***. Cf. HYDRUS 2. **LME.**

3 A thing or person likened to the mythological hydra in its baneful character, its multifarious aspects, or the difficulty of its extirpation. **L15.**

4 Any terrible serpent or reptile. *rhet.* **M16.**

5 A water snake. **E17.**

6 Any of several hydrozoans of the genus *Hydra* that live as solitary polyps attached to pond plants and reproduce by budding and sexually. **L18.**

– COMB.: **hydra-headed** *adjective* having many heads like the mythological hydra; chiefly *fig.*, having the character of a hydra (sense 3 above); **hydratuba** /-tjuːbə/ [Latin] the trumpet-shaped larva of certain jellyfishes.

▸ **B** *attrib.* or as *adjective*. As multifarious or as difficult to extirpate as the mythological hydra. **L16.**

> M. ROBINSON They are the hydra assailants which return with every hour.

hydracid /hʌɪˈdrasɪd/ *noun*. Also †**hydro-acid**. **E19.**
[ORIGIN from HYDRO- + ACID *noun*.]

CHEMISTRY. Orig., an acid that contains hydrogen. Now, one that does not contain oxygen.

hydraelaeon *noun* var. of HYDRELAEON.

hydraemia /hʌɪˈdriːmɪə/ *noun*. Also ***-remia**. **M19.**
[ORIGIN from HYDRO- + -AEMIA.]

Thinness of the blood.

■ **hydraemic** *adjective* **L19.**

hydraform *adjective* var. of HYDRIFORM.

H

hydragogue /ˈhʌɪdrəgɒg/ *adjective & noun*. M17.
[ORIGIN Late Latin *hydragogus* adjective from Greek *hudragōgos* conveying water, from *hudr-* HYDRO- + *agein* to lead.]
(A medicine or drug) that causes accumulations of water or serum to disperse.
■ **hydraˈgogic** *adjective* E18.

hydralazine /hʌɪˈdraləziːn/ *noun*. Also **-ll-**. M20.
[ORIGIN from HYDRA(ZINE + PHTH)ALAZINE.]
PHARMACOLOGY. A sympatholytic drug, $C_8H_5N_2NHNH_2$, used to treat hypertension.

hydramnios /hʌɪˈdramnɪɒs/ *noun*. Also **-on** /-ɒn/. M19.
[ORIGIN from HYDRO- + AMNIOS, AMNION.]
Excessive accumulation of amniotic fluid during pregnancy.

hydrangea /hʌɪˈdreɪn(d)ʒə/ *noun*. M18.
[ORIGIN mod. Latin *hydrangea*, formed as HYDRO- + Greek *aggeion* vessel, with ref. to the cup-shaped seed-capsule.]
Any of various ornamental shrubs, chiefly of Japanese and Chinese origin, of the genus *Hydrangea* (family Hydrangeaceae); esp. *H. macrophylla*, with large round clusters of blue, pink, etc., flowers.

hydrant /ˈhʌɪdr(ə)nt/ *noun*. Orig. *US*. E19.
[ORIGIN Irreg. from HYDRO- + -ANT[1].]
A pipe with a valve for drawing water directly from a main; *esp.* (also ***fire hydrant***) one in the street to which a fire hose can be attached.

hydranth /ˈhʌɪdranθ/ *noun*. L19.
[ORIGIN from HYDRA + Greek *anthos* flower.]
ZOOLOGY. A nutritive zooid in a colony of hydrozoans.

hydrapulper /ˈhʌɪdrəpʌlpə/ *noun*. M20.
[ORIGIN from alt. of HYDRO- + PULPER.]
A tank in which rotating vanes break up the fibres of wood pulp or other paper stock in water.

hydrarch /ˈhʌɪdrɑːk/ *adjective*. E20.
[ORIGIN from HYDR(O- + Greek *arkhē* beginning.]
ECOLOGY. Of a succession of plant communities: originating in a watery habitat.

hydrargyria /hʌɪdrɑːˈdʒɪrɪə/ *noun*. Now *rare*. E19.
[ORIGIN from HYDRARGYRUM + -IA[1].]
Mercury poisoning.

hydrargyrum /hʌɪˈdrɑːdʒɪrəm/ *noun*. Now *rare* or *obsolete*. M16.
[ORIGIN mod. Latin from Latin *hydrargyrus* from Greek *hudrarguros* artificial quicksilver, from *hudr-* HYDRO- + *arguros* silver.]
Mercury (the element).

hydrase /ˈhʌɪdreɪz/ *noun*. M20.
[ORIGIN from HYDRO- + -ASE.]
BIOCHEMISTRY. An enzyme which catalyses the addition of water to a substrate or its removal from it. Cf. HYDRATASE.

hydrastis /hʌɪˈdrastɪs/ *noun*. M19.
[ORIGIN mod. Latin, of unknown origin.]
(An extract of) the dried rhizome of goldenseal, *Hydrastis canadensis*, formerly used as a stomachic and to control uterine bleeding; the plant itself.
■ **hydrastine** /-iːn/ *noun* the alkaloid that is the active constituent of hydrastis M19.

hydratase /ˈhʌɪdrəteɪz/ *noun*. E20.
[ORIGIN from HYDRATE *verb* + -ASE.]
= HYDRASE.

hydrate /ˈhʌɪdreɪt/ *noun*. E19.
[ORIGIN French, from Greek *hudr-*, *hudor* water: see -ATE[2].]
A compound in which water is chemically combined with another compound or an element.

hydrate /ˈhʌɪdreɪt, hʌɪˈdreɪt/ *verb*. M19.
[ORIGIN from the noun.]
1 *verb trans.* Cause to combine chemically with water; cause to absorb water. M19.
2 *verb intrans.* Undergo hydration. E20.
■ **hyˈdratable** *adjective* M20. **hyˈdration** *noun* the action of hydrating something; the condition of being hydrated: M19. **hydrator** *noun* a hydrating agent M20.

hydrated /ˈhʌɪdreɪtɪd, hʌɪˈdreɪtɪd/ *adjective*. E19.
[ORIGIN from HYDRATE *noun*, *verb* + -ED[2], -ED[1].]
Chemically combined with water or its elements; (of a mineral etc.) containing water of crystallization.

hydraulic /hʌɪˈdrɔːlɪk, -ˈdrɒl-/ *adjective & noun*. E17.
[ORIGIN Latin *hydraulicus* from Greek *hudraulikos*, from *hudr-* HYDRO- + *aulos* pipe: see -IC. Cf. French *hydraulique* (15).]
▸ **A** *adjective*. **1** Involving or pertaining to water or other liquid conveyed through pipes or channels, esp. by mechanical means; of or pertaining to hydraulics. E17.

> JULIETTE HUXLEY Squirted by hydraulic pressure out of the water-cushion in which it has grown to maturity. A. H. COMPTON His degree in hydraulic engineering. *Engineering* Experiments . . on the hydraulic transport of coal.

2 Of machinery or a mechanism: operated or controlled by water power or (more usually) by a liquid conveyed under pressure through pipes. E17.

> J. CRACE We . . bumped on the saloon's hydraulic suspension over the last few kilometres. A. TREW Gregorowski moved into the loader seat, checked the hydraulic controls.

3 **a** Of cement or other material: that hardens under water. E19. ▸**b** Of a liquid: used or suitable for use in hydraulic mechanisms. M20.

> **b** *Drive* It is advisable to change hydraulic fluid every eighteen months or 24,000 miles.

– SPECIAL COLLOCATIONS: **hydraulic brake** (*a*) a brake that uses a piston or rotor in a liquid-filled chamber to produce the slowing down; (*b*) a brake on a vehicle that is actuated hydraulically but operates through friction. **hydraulic intensifier** a device for obtaining an increase in pressure in a hydraulic system, by means of connected pistons with different areas. **hydraulic mining**: in which a powerful jet of water is used to wear down a bed of gravel etc. and carry the debris away for processing, or to extract coal from an underground seam. **hydraulic organ** = HYDRAULUS. **hydraulic press** a machine in which a force acting on a liquid, e.g. by means of a piston, produces elsewhere a larger force on a larger area of liquid. **hydraulic ram** (*a*) a device in which a falling body of water is brought to rest and its kinetic energy used to raise some of the water above its original level or produce water at increased pressure; (*b*) the larger or working piston of a hydraulic press.

▸ **B** *noun* **1** †**a** A hydraulic organ. E–M17. ▸**b** A hydraulic press or other machine. E18.
2 In *pl.* (treated as *sing.*). The branch of science and engineering that deals with the flow of liquids through pipes or channels, esp. as a source of mechanical force or control; hydrodynamics, fluid mechanics. L17.
■ †**hydraulical** *adjective* = HYDRAULIC *adjective* M17–L18. **hydraulically** *adverb* by hydraulic means L19. **hydraulician** /-ˈlɪʃ(ə)n/ *noun* an expert in hydraulics L19. **hydrauˈlicity** *noun* the property or quality of hardening under water M19.

hydraulic /hʌɪˈdrɔːlɪk, -ˈdrɒl-/ *verb trans*. Infl. **-ic(k)-**. M19.
[ORIGIN from HYDRAULIC *adjective & noun*. For the inflection with *k* cf. *frolicking*, *trafficking*, etc.]
Work or obtain by the methods of hydraulic mining.

hydraulis *noun* var. of HYDRAULUS.

†**hydraulo-pneumatical** *adjective*. M17–M18.
[ORIGIN from HYDRAULIC *adjective & noun* + -O- + PNEUMATICAL.]
Of or pertaining to hydraulics and pneumatics.

hydraulus /hʌɪˈdrɔːləs/ *noun*. Also **-lis** /-lɪs/. L19.
[ORIGIN Latin from Greek *hudraulos*, *-lis*, from *hudr-* HYDRO- + *aulos* pipe.]
The pipe organ of classical times, in which an even tone was ensured by using water pressure to maintain a constant airflow to the pipes. Also called ***water-organ***.

hydrazide /ˈhʌɪdrəzʌɪd/ *noun*. L19.
[ORIGIN formed as HYDRAZINE + -IDE.]
CHEMISTRY. Any compound of the formula $RCO{\cdot}HN{\cdot}NH_2$, where a hydrogen atom of hydrazine is replaced by an organic acid radical. Also, any substituted derivative of such a compound.

hydrazine /ˈhʌɪdrəziːn/ *noun*. L19.
[ORIGIN from HYDRO- + AZO- + -INE[5].]
CHEMISTRY. A colourless fuming liquid, $H_2N{\cdot}NH_2$, used as a strong reducing agent and as a rocket propellant. Also, any substituted derivative of this.
■ **hydrazinium** /hʌɪdrəˈzɪnɪəm/ *noun* (*a*) the ion $H_2N{\cdot}NH_3^+$; (*b*) the ion $H_3N^+{\cdot}NH_3^+$: E20.

hydrazoic /hʌɪdrəˈzəʊɪk/ *adjective*. L19.
[ORIGIN from HYDRO- + AZO- + -IC.]
CHEMISTRY. ***hydrazoic acid***, a colourless volatile explosive liquid, N_3H, with a foul smell.
■ **hydrazoate** *noun* an azide E20.

hydrazone /ˈhʌɪdrəzəʊn/ *noun*. L19.
[ORIGIN from HYDRAZ(INE + -ONE.]
CHEMISTRY. Any compound containing the group :N–NH$_2$ or the substituted groups :N–NHR or :N–NRR′.
■ **hydrazonium** /hʌɪdrəˈzəʊnɪəm/ *noun* (*a*) = HYDRAZINIUM (a),(b); (*b*) an ion of the type $R{=}N{\cdot}NH_3^+$; a substituted derivative of such an ion: L19.

hydrelaeon /hʌɪdrəˈliːɒn/ *noun*. Long *rare* or *obsolete*. Also **hydrae-**, **-leon**, **-laeum** /-ˈliːəm/, & other vars. M16.
[ORIGIN Greek *hudrelaion*, from *hudr-* HYDRO- + *elaion* oil.]
A medicinal mixture of water and oil.

hydremia *noun* see HYDRAEMIA.

hydria /ˈhʌɪdrɪə, ˈhɪd-/ *noun*. Pl. **-iae** /-ɪiː/. ME.
[ORIGIN (Old French *idr(i)e* from) Latin from Greek *hudria*.]
Formerly, a water pot. Now (ARCHAEOLOGY), a three-handled pitcher of ancient Greece.

hydric /ˈhʌɪdrɪk/ *adjective*[1]. Now *rare*. M19.
[ORIGIN from HYDR(OGEN + -IC.]
CHEMISTRY. Of or containing hydrogen in chemical combination.

hydric /ˈhʌɪdrɪk/ *adjective*[2]. E20.
[ORIGIN from HYDRO- + -IC.]
ECOLOGY. Of a habitat: containing plenty of moisture; damp.

hydride /ˈhʌɪdrʌɪd/ *noun*. M19.
[ORIGIN from HYDRO- + -IDE.]
CHEMISTRY. Formerly = HYDRATE *noun*. Now, a binary compound of hydrogen with another element, esp. a metal.
■ **hyˈdridic** *adjective* (of a hydrogen atom) having a negative charge M20.

hydriform /ˈhʌɪdrɪfɔːm/ *adjective*. Also **hydra-** /ˈhʌɪdrə-/. E19.
[ORIGIN from HYDRA (+ -I-) + -FORM.]
Having the form of a hydrozoan hydra or the hydra of mythology.

hydriodic /hʌɪdrɪˈɒdɪk, -drʌɪ-/ *adjective*. E19.
[ORIGIN from HYDR(OGEN + IOD(INE + -IC.]
CHEMISTRY. ***hydriodic acid***, a colourless or pale yellow liquid that is an aqueous solution of the gas hydrogen iodide, HI, and a strong acid and reducing agent.

hydrion /ˈhʌɪdrʌɪən, -drɪɒn/ *noun*. E20.
[ORIGIN Contr. of *hydrogen ion*.]
CHEMISTRY. The hydrogen ion, the proton.

hydro /ˈhʌɪdrəʊ/ *noun*[1]. Pl. **-os**. L19.
[ORIGIN Abbreviation of *hydropathic*.]
A clinic, hotel, etc., providing hydropathic treatment.

hydro /ˈhʌɪdrəʊ/ *noun*[2]. Pl. **-os**. E20.
[ORIGIN Abbreviation of *hydroelectric*.]
Hydroelectric power, hydroelectricity; *Canad.* (a supply of, a company supplying) mains electricity.

hydro- /ˈhʌɪdrəʊ/ *combining form*. Before a vowel also **hydr-**.
[ORIGIN Greek *hudro-* combining form of *hudōr* water: see -O-. In senses 3 & 4 partly from the definientia, which are themselves from Greek *hudro-*.]
1 Water; liquid.
2 MEDICINE. (An accumulation of) watery or serous fluid.
3 CHEMISTRY. Hydrogen.
4 ZOOLOGY. Hydrozoa, hydrozoan; hydroid.
■ **hydro-aroˈmatic** *adjective & noun* (CHEMISTRY) (a compound) having one or more benzene rings which are partly or completely hydrogenated (reduced) E20. **hydrobioˈlogic** *adjective* = HYDROBIOLOGICAL E20. **hydrobioˈlogical** *adjective* of or pertaining to hydrobiology M20. **hydrobiˈologist** *noun* an expert in or student of hydrobiology E20. **hydrobiˈology** *noun* the branch of biology that deals with aquatic plants and animals E20. **hydroˈborate** *noun & verb* (CHEMISTRY) (*a*) *noun* = BOROHYDRIDE; (*b*) *verb trans.* add a boron compound to (another compound) by hydroboration: M20. **hydroboˈration** *noun* (CHEMISTRY) a reaction of the type :BH + :C=C: → :B(C:)CH:, where a boron–hydrogen pair of atoms is added across a double or triple bond between a carbon atom and another atom; the process of subjecting to such a reaction: M20. **hydroˈbromic** *adjective* (CHEMISTRY): ***hydrobromic acid***, a strong acid that is a colourless or pale yellow aqueous solution of the gas hydrogen bromide, HBr M19. **hydrocast** *noun* (OCEANOGRAPHY) a long cable with sampling bottles attached at intervals; an operation in which this is used: M20. ˌ**hydrochloroˈfluorocarbon** *noun* any of a class of partly chlorinated and fluorinated hydrocarbons, used as less ozone-destructive substitutes for CFCs (abbreviation *HCFC*) L20. **hydrochloroˈthiazide**, **hydrochlorthiazide** *noun* (PHARMACOLOGY) a sulphonamide drug, $C_7H_8ClN_3O_4S_2$, related to chlorothiazide and used to treat oedema and hypertension M20. **hydrochore** *noun* a hydrochoric plant E20. **hydrochoric** /-ˈkɔːrɪk/ *adjective* [Greek *khōrein* spread] involving or characterized by the dispersal of plant seeds by water M20. **hydrochorous** /-ˈkɔːrəs/ *adjective* hydrochoric E20. **hydroˈcolloid** *noun & adjective* (designating) a substance that yields a gel on the addition of water, or the gel itself E20. **hydrocoˈlloidal** *adjective* = HYDROCOLLOID *adjective* E20. **hydrocool** *verb trans.* dip (fruit or vegetables) in chilled water soon after harvesting and packing, in order to preserve their freshness M20. **hydrocooler** *noun* an apparatus for hydrocooling M20. **hydrocrack** *verb trans.* crack (crude oil or a heavy distillate) by the action of a catalyst and hydrogen at a high temperature and pressure M20. **hydrocracker** *noun* an apparatus or plant where hydrocracking is carried out M20. **hydrodesulphuriˈzation**, (*US* & CHEMISTRY) **-sulf-** *noun* the removal of sulphur from crude oil or an oil product by the action of a catalyst and hydrogen at a moderately high temperature and pressure M20. **hydrodeˈsulphurize**, (*US* & CHEMISTRY) **-sulf-** *verb trans.* subject to hydrodesulphurization M20. **hydrodeˈsulphurizer**, (*US* & CHEMISTRY) **-sulf-** *noun* an apparatus where hydrodesulphurization is carried out M20. **hydro-engiˈneering** *noun* civil engineering as applied to the construction of dams, canals, etc. L20. **hydro-explosion** *noun* a volcanic explosion caused by hot magma or lava coming into contact with water and producing steam M20. **hydro-extract** *verb trans.* dry in a hydro-extractor L19. **hydro-extraction** *noun* the process of spinning textiles etc. in a hydro-extractor L19. **hydro-extractor** *noun* an industrial machine for drying textiles etc. by spinning them in a perforated drum M19. **hydrofining** *noun* the process of stabilizing a petroleum product and reducing its sulphur content by the action of a catalyst and hydrogen at a relatively low temperature and pressure M20. **hydrofluoroˈcarbon** *noun* (CHEMISTRY) any of a class of partly chlorinated and fluorinated hydrocarbons, used as an alternative to CFCs in foam production, refrigeration, and other processes M20. **hydroflumeˈthiazide** *noun* (PHARMACOLOGY) a drug, $C_8H_8F_3N_3O_4S_2$, analogous to hydrochlorothiazide and with similar uses M20. **hydroform** *verb trans.* subject (petroleum naphtha) to a process in which paraffins and alicyclic compounds are converted to aromatic compounds by the action of a catalyst and hydrogen at a high temperature and moderate pressure M20. **hydroˈformate** *noun* a petroleum product obtained by hydroforming M20. **hydroformer** *noun* an apparatus or plant where hydroforming is carried out M20. **hydroformyˈlation** *noun* (CHEMISTRY) the catalytic addition of carbon monoxide and hydrogen to an olefin to produce an aldehyde M20. **hydrofracture** *verb trans.* fracture (rock) by injecting water under pressure L20. **hydrofuge** *adjective & noun* (a substance) that repels or is impervious to water M19. **hydrogasifiˈcation** *noun* the production of methane directly from coal by treatment with hydrogen or hydrogen and steam at a high temperature and pressure. M20. **hydroˈgasifier** *noun* an apparatus in which hydrogasification is carried out M20. **hydrogel** *noun* a gel or gelatinous precipitate in which the liquid constituent is water M19. **hydrogeoˈlogical** *adjective* of or pertaining to hydrogeology L19.

hydroge'ologist *noun* an expert in or student of hydrogeology **M20.** **hydroge'ology** *noun* the branch of geology that deals with the movement, effects, properties, etc., of underground water and surface water; the hydrogeological features *of* a thing: **E19.** **hydro'kineter** *noun* [Greek *kinētēs*, -*tēr* initiator, agitator] a device for heating water at the bottom of large boilers by injecting surplus steam **L19.** **hydroki'netic** *adjective* pertaining to or involving the motion of liquids or a liquid **L19.** **hydrolith** *noun* calcium hydride, as a convenient source of hydrogen (evolved when water is added) **E20.** **hydromag'netic** *adjective* = MAGNETOHYDRODYNAMIC **M20.** **hydromag'netics** *noun* = MAGNETOHYDRODYNAMICS **M20.** **hydro'mania** *noun* an abnormal craving for water; an enthusiasm about water: **L18.** **hydromassage** *noun* massage using jets of water, as a health or beauty treatment **M20.** **hydrome'chanical** *adjective* pertaining to hydromechanics **E19.** **hydrome'chanics** *noun* the mechanics of liquids; hydrodynamics, esp. in relation to mechanical devices: **M19.** **hydrome'dusa** *noun*, pl. **-sae**, **-sas**, the medusoid phase in the life cycle of many hydrozoans **L19.** **hydrome'dusan** *adjective & noun* (*a*) (of or pertaining to) a hydromedusa; †(*b*) (of or pertaining to) a hydrozoan (of a taxon Hydromedusae): **L19.** **hydrometa'llurgical** *adjective* of or pertaining to hydrometallurgy **L19.** **hydrometallurgy** /-mɪ'tal-, -'mɛt(ə)l-/ *noun* metallurgical processes in which chemical reactions in water, such as leaching or precipitation, are used to extract or assay metals **M19.** **hydro'meteor** *noun* an atmospheric phenomenon or entity involving water or water vapour **M19.** **hydrometeoro'logical** *adjective* of or pertaining to hydrometeorology **L19.** **hydrometeo'rology** *noun* (*a*) *rare* the branch of meteorology that deals with hydrometeors; (*b*) meteorology as it relates to or is applied to hydrological matters: **M19.** **hydrone'phrosis** *noun* distension of the renal pelvis with urine, usually as a result of an obstructed outflow **M19.** **hydrone'phrotic** *adjective* of, characteristic of, or affected with hydronephrosis **M19.** **hydronym** *noun* a name of a body of water, such as a river or sea **M20.** **hydro'nymic** *adjective* of, pertaining to, or designating a hydronym **M20.** **hy'dronymy** *noun* the branch of knowledge that deals with hydronyms; hydronyms collectively: **M20.** †**hydro-oxygen** *noun* oxy-hydrogen: only in **M19.** **hydroperi'cardium** *noun* (MEDICINE) (the condition of having) an accumulation of watery fluid within the pericardium **M19.** **hydrope'roxide** *noun* (CHEMISTRY) any compound containing the hydroperoxyl group in its molecule **E20.** **hydrope'roxyl** *noun* (CHEMISTRY) the radical HO·O·; usu. *attrib.*: **M20.** **hydroplant** *noun* a hydroelectric generating station **E20.** **hydropneu'matic** *adjective* (of apparatus) involving the action of both water and air; partly hydraulic and partly pneumatic: **L18.** **hydropower** *noun* hydroelectric power **M20.** **hydro'quinone** *noun* a substance formed by the reduction of quinone, used as a photographic developer; 1,4-dihydroxybenzene, $C_6H_4(OH)_2$: **M19.** **hydro'salpinx** *noun*, pl. **-salpinges** /-sal'pɪndʒiːz/, [Greek SALPINX: cf. SALPINGO-] MEDICINE (the condition of having) an accumulation of watery fluid in the Fallopian tubes **M19.** **hydrosere** *noun* (ECOLOGY) a plant succession originating in a wet habitat **E20.** **hydroski** *noun* a hydrofoil on a seaplane or amphibious aircraft that skims the surface of the water during take-off and provides extra lift **M20.** **hydrosome** *noun* (ZOOLOGY) the body of a colonial hydrozoan **M19.** **hydrospeed**, **hydrospeeding** *nouns* a sport or leisure activity that involves jumping into fast-flowing white water and being carried along at high speed while buoyed up by a float **L20.** **hydrosphere** *noun* the waters of the earth's surface **L19.** **hydrospire** *noun* (ZOOLOGY) any of a number of respiratory tubes or pouches in blastoids **M19.** **hydro'theca** *noun*, pl. **-cae**, ZOOLOGY in some colonial hydrozoans, a cuplike extension of the perisarc that partly encloses a hydranth **L19.** **hydro'thorax** *noun* (MEDICINE) (the condition of having) an accumulation of fluid in one or both of the pleural cavities **L18.** **hydrotreat** *verb trans.* subject to hydrotreatment **M20.** **hydrotreater** *noun* an apparatus or plant where hydrotreatment is carried out **M20.** **hydrotreatment** *noun* the treatment of petroleum products with hydrogen in the presence of a catalyst, esp. at a higher temperature and pressure than in hydrofining **M20.** **hydrovane** *noun* (*a*) = HYDROPLANE *noun* 1; (*b*) = HYDROFOIL 1: **E20.** **hydrowire** *noun* a cable used for hydrocasts **M20.** **hydrozincite** *noun* (MINERALOGY) a monoclinic basic carbonate of zinc that is a secondary mineral occurring as light-coloured crusts on zinc deposits **M19.**

†**hydro-acid** *noun* var. of HYDRACID.

†**hydro-aeroplane** *noun*. **E–M20.**
[ORIGIN from HYDRO- + AEROPLANE *noun*.]
A seaplane. Cf. HYDROPLANE *noun* 3.

hydrocarbon /hʌɪdrə(ʊ)'kɑːb(ə)n/ *noun*. **E19.**
[ORIGIN from HYDRO- + CARBON *noun*.]
CHEMISTRY. A compound that contains hydrogen and carbon only; a substituted derivative of such a compound.

> *Nature* A much greater threat is posed by toxic chlorinated hydrocarbons such as DDT.

■ **,hydrocarbo'naceous** *adjective* of the nature of or containing a hydrocarbon **M19.**

hydrocarbonate /hʌɪdrə(ʊ)'kɑːbəneɪt/ *noun*. **E19.**
[ORIGIN from HYDRO- + CARBONATE *noun*.]
CHEMISTRY. †**1** A hydrocarbon, *spec.* methane. Only in **E19.**
2 A double salt consisting of a hydrate and a carbonate. Now *rare* or *obsolete*. **M19.**
3 A carbohydrate. *rare*. **L19.**

hydrocarbonous /hʌɪdrə(ʊ)'kɑːbənəs/ *adjective*. Now *rare* or *obsolete*. **L18.**
[ORIGIN from HYDRO- + CARBON *noun* + -OUS.]
Hydrocarbonaceous.

†**hydrocarburet** *noun*. **E–M19.**
[ORIGIN from HYDRO- + CARBURET *noun*.]
CHEMISTRY. = HYDROCARBONATE 1.
■ †**hydrocarburetted** *adjective* formed by the combination of hydrogen and carbon **E–M19.**

hydrocele /'hʌɪdrə(ʊ)siːl/ *noun*. **M16.**
[ORIGIN (French *hydrocèle* from) Latin *hydrocele* from Greek *hudrokēlē*, from *hudro-* HYDRO- + *kēlē* tumour.]
1 MEDICINE. An abnormal accumulation of fluid at a site in the body, esp. between the layers of serous membrane around a testicle. **M16.**
2 See HYDROCOEL.

hydrocephalus /hʌɪdrə'sɛf(ə)ləs, -'kɛf-/ *noun*. **L17.**
[ORIGIN mod. Latin from Greek *hudrokephalon*, from *hudr-* HYDRO- + *kephalē* head.]
MEDICINE. A condition in which excessive cerebrospinal fluid accumulates in the cranial cavity, occurring esp. in young children, when it causes enlargement of the head and sometimes brain damage (also called ***water on the brain***); the fluid accumulation itself.
■ **hydroce'phalic** *adjective & noun* (*a*) *adjective* pertaining to, characteristic of, or affected with hydrocephalus; (*b*) *noun* a person with hydrocephalus: **E19.** **hydrocephaloid** *adjective* designating a condition in which there are symptoms resembling those of hydrocephalus without any accumulation of cerebrospinal fluid **M19.** **hydrocephalous** *adjective* **M19.**

hydrocephaly /hʌɪdrə'sɛf(ə)li, -'kɛf-/ *noun*. **L19.**
[ORIGIN from HYDROCEPHALUS: see -Y[3].]
= HYDROCEPHALUS.

hydrochloric /hʌɪdrə(ʊ)'klɒrɪk, -'klɔːrɪk/ *adjective*. **E19.**
[ORIGIN from HYDRO- + CHLORIC.]
CHEMISTRY. ***hydrochloric acid***, a colourless or faintly yellow liquid that is an aqueous solution of the gas hydrogen chloride, HCl, and a strong, highly corrosive acid; formerly called ***muriatic acid***, ***spirit of salt***.
■ †**hydrochlorate** *noun* a chloride; a hydrochloride: only in **19.** **hydrochloride** *noun* a compound of hydrochloric acid with an organic base or (formerly) with an element **E19.**

hydrocoel /'hʌɪdrəsiːl/ *noun*. Also **-coele**, **-cele**. **L19.**
[ORIGIN from HYDRO- + Greek *koilia* body cavity.]
ZOOLOGY. The water-vascular system of an echinoderm.

hydrocortisone /hʌɪdrə(ʊ)'kɔːtɪzəʊn/ *noun*. **M20.**
[ORIGIN from HYDRO- + CORTISONE.]
A glucocorticoid hormone, $C_{21}H_{30}O_5$, that is used to treat inflammatory and allergic conditions.

hydrocyanic /hʌɪdrə(ʊ)sʌɪ'anɪk/ *adjective*. **E19.**
[ORIGIN from HYDRO- + CYANIC.]
CHEMISTRY. ***hydrocyanic acid***, a weak acid, HCN, that is a volatile colourless poisonous explosive liquid with a smell of bitter almonds and is used in many industrial processes. Also called ***prussic acid***.
■ †**hydrocyanate** *noun* a cyanide **E–M19.**

hydrodictyon /hʌɪdrə(ʊ)'dɪktɪɒn/ *noun*. **M19.**
[ORIGIN from HYDRO- + Greek *diktuon* net.]
Any of the green algae of the genus *Hydrodictyon*, which combine in colonies of multinucleate cells to form pentagonal and hexagonal meshes on the surface of water; popularly called ***water-net***.

hydrodynamic /ˌhʌɪdrə(ʊ)dʌɪ'namɪk/ *adjective*. **E19.**
[ORIGIN mod. Latin *hydrodynamicus*, formed as HYDRODYNAMICS: see -IC.]
Of or pertaining to hydrodynamics or its subject matter.
■ **hydrodynamical** *adjective* = HYDRODYNAMIC **M19.** **hydrodynamically** *adverb* from the point of view of hydrodynamics; by means of hydrodynamic forces: **M20.**

hydrodynamician /ˌhʌɪdrə(ʊ)dʌɪnə'mɪʃ(ə)n/ *noun*. **E20.**
[ORIGIN formed as HYDRODYNAMICIST + -ICIAN.]
= HYDRODYNAMICIST.

hydrodynamicist /ˌhʌɪdrə(ʊ)dʌɪ'namɪsɪst/ *noun*. **M20.**
[ORIGIN from HYDRODYNAMICS + -IST.]
An expert in or student of hydrodynamics.

hydrodynamics /ˌhʌɪdrə(ʊ)dʌɪ'namɪks/ *noun*. **L18.**
[ORIGIN mod. Latin *hydrodynamica*, formed as HYDRO- + Greek *dunamikos* DYNAMIC: see -ICS.]
The branch of physical science that deals with the motion of fluids, esp. liquids, and (in mod. use) with the forces acting on them and on bodies immersed in them.

hydroelectric /ˌhʌɪdrəʊɪ'lɛktrɪk/ *adjective*. **E19.**
[ORIGIN from HYDRO- + ELECTRIC.]
†**1** Of, pertaining to, or designating an electric current produced by a galvanic cell. **E–M19.**
2 Designating a machine for generating electricity by the friction of water or steam. *obsolete* exc. *hist.* **M19.**
3 Generating electricity by utilizing the energy of falling or flowing water; pertaining to such generation; (of electricity) generated in this way. **L19.**

> *Daily Telegraph* Brazil wants to build a huge hydro-electric dam on . . the River Parana.

■ **hydroelectrical** *adjective* = HYDROELECTRIC 3 **E20.** **hydroelectrically** *adverb* by hydroelectric means **E20.** **ˌhydroelec'tricity** *noun* †(*a*) galvanic electricity; (*b*) electricity generated hydroelectrically: **E19.**

hydrofluoric /hʌɪdrə(ʊ)'flʊərɪk/ *adjective*. **E19.**
[ORIGIN from HYDRO- + FLUORIC.]
CHEMISTRY. ***hydrofluoric acid***, a colourless fuming liquid that is an aqueous solution of the gas hydrogen fluoride, HF, and is sufficiently corrosive to attack glass.

hydrofoil /'hʌɪdrə(ʊ)fɔɪl/ *noun*. **E20.**
[ORIGIN from HYDRO- + FOIL *noun*[1] after *aerofoil*.]
1 A structure analogous to an aerofoil but attached underneath a boat to produce lift or to act as a stabilizer. **E20.**
2 A boat fitted with hydrofoils to lift its hull clear of the water at speed. Also more fully ***hydrofoil boat***. **M20.**

hydrogen /'hʌɪdrədʒ(ə)n/ *noun*. Also †**-gene**. **L18.**
[ORIGIN French *hydrogène*, from Greek *hudr-* HYDRO-: see -GEN.]
The simplest and lightest chemical element, atomic no. 1, a colourless flammable gas which is the commonest element in the universe and which occurs combined with oxygen in water and with carbon in organic compounds (symbol H).
– COMB.: **hydrogen bomb** an immensely powerful bomb in which hydrogen nuclei combine to form helium nuclei and release energy in an uncontrolled self-sustaining fusion reaction; also called an ***H-bomb***; **hydrogen bond** CHEMISTRY a weak bond formed by the electrostatic attraction between a strongly electronegative atom and a hydrogen atom covalently linked to another electronegative atom; **hydrogen cyanide** hydrocyanic acid, esp. as a vapour; **hydrogen ion** the positive ion (a proton) formed when a hydrogen atom loses its electron; a solvated form of this, *esp.* the hydrated ion H_3O^+ (cf. HYDRONIUM); **hydrogen peroxide** a colourless viscous unstable liquid, H_2O_2, with both oxidizing and reducing properties; **hydrogen sulphide** (*a*) a colourless flammable poisonous gas, H_2S, which has a smell of rotten eggs and is produced by putrefying organic matter; (*b*) (also **hydrogensulphide**) = HYDROSULPHIDE.
■ **hydrogen-like** *adjective* (of an atom) consisting of a nucleus to which is bound a single negatively charged particle; characteristic of such an atom: **E20.**

hydrogenase /hʌɪ'drɒdʒəneɪz/ *noun*. **E20.**
[ORIGIN from HYDROGEN + -ASE.]
BIOCHEMISTRY. An enzyme which catalyses the addition of hydrogen to an organic substrate, found esp. in some micro-organisms.

hydrogenate /hʌɪ'drɒdʒəneɪt, 'hʌɪdrədʒəneɪt/ *verb trans.* **E19.**
[ORIGIN formed as HYDROGENASE + -ATE[3].]
Cause to combine chemically with hydrogen.
■ **hydroge'nation** *noun* the state of being hydrogenated; the process of hydrogenating a substance: **E19.** **hydrogenator** *noun* a vessel or apparatus in which hydrogenation is carried out **E20.**

hydrogenic /hʌɪdrə(ʊ)'dʒɛnɪk/ *adjective*. **M19.**
[ORIGIN Partly from HYDRO- + -GENIC, partly from HYDROGEN + -IC.]
1 GEOLOGY. (Of soil) formed with water as the dominant influence; (of rock etc.) = HYDROGENOUS 2. **M19.**
2 PHYSICS. = HYDROGEN-LIKE. **M20.**

hydrogenite /hʌɪ'drɒdʒənʌɪt/ *noun*. **E20.**
[ORIGIN formed as HYDROGENIZE + -ITE[1].]
Either of two powders formulated to be convenient sources of hydrogen, one when water is added, the other when ignited.

hydrogenize /hʌɪ'drɒdʒənʌɪz, 'hʌɪdrə-/ *verb trans.* Also **-ise**. **E19.**
[ORIGIN from HYDROGEN + -IZE.]
= HYDROGENATE.

hydrogenolysis /hʌɪdrədʒə'nɒlɪsɪs/ *noun*. Pl. **-lyses** /-lɪsiːz/. **M20.**
[ORIGIN formed as HYDROGENIZE + -O- + -LYSIS, after *hydrolysis*.]
CHEMISTRY. A reaction in which a bond to a carbon atom is broken and a hydrogen atom added to each of the previously bonded atoms.
■ **ˌhydrogeno'lytic** *adjective* **M20.**

hydrogenosome /hʌɪdrə(ʊ)'dʒɛnəsəʊm/ *noun*. **L20.**
[ORIGIN formed as HYDROGENIZE + -O- + -SOME[3].]
BIOLOGY. An organelle in some protozoans which oxidizes pyruvate anaerobically, producing hydrogen.

hydrogenous /hʌɪ'drɒdʒɪnəs/ *adjective*. **L18.**
[ORIGIN Partly from HYDROGEN + -OUS, partly from HYDRO- + -GENOUS.]
1 Containing or consisting of hydrogen. **L18.**
2 GEOLOGY. Of rock, mineral deposits, etc.: formed in or by water. **L19.**
■ **hydrogenously** *adverb* **L20.**

hydrograph /'hʌɪdrəgrɑːf/ *noun*. **L19.**
[ORIGIN from HYDRO- + -GRAPH.]
A graphical record showing the variation in a river's height, speed, or the like at a particular point.

hydrography /hʌɪ'drɒgrəfi/ *noun*. **M16.**
[ORIGIN from HYDRO- + -GRAPHY, after *geography*.]
1 The branch of science that deals with seas, lakes, rivers, etc., including the mapping of them, their currents and tides, and (formerly) the principles of navigation; a book in which such bodies of water are scientifically described. **M16.**
2 The hydrographic features *of* a region. **M19.**
■ **hydrographer** *noun* an expert in or student of hydrography; *esp.* a person who makes hydrographic surveys and charts of the sea and its currents: **M16.** **hydro'graphic** *adjective* of or pertaining to hydrography **M17.** **hydro'graphical** *adjective* = HYDROGRAPHIC **L16.** **hydro'graphically** *adverb* as regards hydrography or hydrographic features **E18.**

†**hydroguret** *noun*. Only in **19**.
[ORIGIN from HYDROG(EN after *sulphuret*.)]
CHEMISTRY. A hydride.
■ †**hydroguretted** *adjective* combined with hydrogen: only in **E19**.

hydroid /ˈhʌɪdrɔɪd/ *adjective & noun*. **M19**.
[ORIGIN from HYDRA + -OID.]
ZOOLOGY. ▸**A** *adjective*. **1** Designating or pertaining to any coelenterate of the hydrozoan order Hydroida, which has the polyp phase prominent. **M19**.
2 Of, pertaining to, or belonging to the polypoid phase in the life cycle of hydrozoans. **L19**.
▸**B** *noun*. A hydroid individual or colony. **M19**.

hydrol /ˈhʌɪdrɒl/ *noun*. **L19**.
[ORIGIN from HYDRO- + -OL; sense 3 perh. from HYDROLYSIS.]
CHEMISTRY. **1** Any substituted derivative of benzhydrol, *esp*. Michler's hydrol. **L19**.
2 A dark viscous liquid left as a mother liquor when starch is subjected to acid hydrolysis and dextrose is allowed to crystallize out. **E20**.
3 The simple water molecule, H_2O. **E20**.

hydrolase /ˈhʌɪdrəleɪz/ *noun*. **E20**.
[ORIGIN from HYDROL(YSIS + -ASE.]
BIOCHEMISTRY. An enzyme which causes hydrolysis.

hydrolise, **hydrolize** *verbs* see HYDROLYSE.

H

hydrology /hʌɪˈdrɒlədʒi/ *noun*. **L17**.
[ORIGIN mod. Latin *hydrologia*, formed as HYDRO- + -LOGY.]
1 The branch of medicine that deals with treatment by baths and waters. *rare*. **L17**.
2 The branch of science that deals with the water on and under the earth's surface and in the atmosphere; the hydrologic features *of* a region. **L17**.
■ **hydroˈlogic** *adjective* of or pertaining to hydrology (***hydrologic cycle***, the continual movement of water between the different kinds of place in which it occurs, such as the atmosphere, rivers, seas, plants and animals, etc.) **L19**. **hydroˈlogical** *adjective* = HYDROLOGIC **L17**. **hydroˈlogically** *adverb* as regards hydrology or hydrologic matters **M20**. **hydrologist** *noun* **M19**.

hydrolube /ˈhʌɪdrəl(j)uːb/ *noun*. **M20**.
[ORIGIN from HYDRO- + -*lube* repr. *lubricant* (cf. LUBE).]
Any of various non-flammable hydraulic fluids based on water and glycol.

hydrolysate /hʌɪˈdrɒlɪseɪt/ *noun*. Also ***-lyz-** /-lɪz-/. **E20**.
[ORIGIN from HYDROLYSE + -ATE².]
CHEMISTRY. A product of hydrolysis.

hydrolyse /ˈhʌɪdrəlʌɪz/ *verb*. Also ***-lyze**, (*non-standard*) **-lise**, **-lize**. **L19**.
[ORIGIN from HYDROLYSIS after *analysis*, *analyse*.]
CHEMISTRY. **1** *verb trans*. Subject to or decompose by hydrolysis. **L19**.
2 *verb intrans*. Undergo hydrolysis. **E20**.
■ **hydrolysable** *adjective* **E20**.

hydrolysis /hʌɪˈdrɒlɪsɪs/ *noun*. Pl. **-lyses** /-lɪsiːz/. **L19**.
[ORIGIN from HYDRO- + -LYSIS.]
CHEMISTRY. Any reaction in which a compound is decomposed and the hydrogen and hydroxyl of the water molecule become attached to separate products (AB + $H_2O \to$ AH + BOH); an analogous decomposition of an organic compound by an acid or alkali; a reaction between a water molecule and an ion that gives a hydrogen or hydroxyl ion.
■ **hydroˈlytic** *adjective* **L19**. **hydroˈlytically** *adverb* by means of or as regards hydrolysis **E20**.

hydrolyst /ˈhʌɪdrəlɪst/ *noun*. Now *rare*. **L19**.
[ORIGIN from HYDROLYSIS after *analyse*, *analyst*.]
CHEMISTRY. A hydrolytic agent.

hydrolyze *verb* see HYDROLYSE.

hydromancy /ˈhʌɪdrəmansi/ *noun*. **LME**.
[ORIGIN Old French & mod. French *hydromancie* or late Latin *hydromantia*, formed as HYDRO-: see -MANCY.]
Divination by signs derived from water.

hydromantic /hʌɪdrəˈmantɪk/ *noun & adjective*. Now *rare* or *obsolete*. **L16**.
[ORIGIN medieval Latin *hydromanticus*, from late Latin *hydromantia* HYDROMANCY: see -IC.]
▸**A** *noun*. †**1** Hydromancy. Only in **L16**.
2 A person skilled in hydromancy. **M17**.
▸**B** *adjective*. Of or pertaining to hydromancy. **M17**.

hydromel /ˈhʌɪdrəmɛl/ *noun*. **LME**.
[ORIGIN Latin *hydromeli* (*-mel*) from Greek *hudromeli*, from *hudro-* HYDRO- + *meli* honey.]
A mixture of honey and water; mead.

hydrometer /hʌɪˈdrɒmɪtə/ *noun*. **M18**.
[ORIGIN from HYDRO- + -METER.]
1 An instrument for finding the relative density of a liquid (sometimes also that of a solid) and hence the strength of a solution or mixture. **M18**.
2 An instrument for finding the speed of a current or a boat. **M18**.
■ **hydroˈmetric** *adjective* **E19**. **hydroˈmetrical** *adjective* **L18**. **hydrometry** *noun* (the branch of hydrostatics that deals with) the measurement of relative density by means of a hydrometer **E18**.

hydronium /hʌɪˈdrəʊnɪəm/ *noun*. **E20**.
[ORIGIN from HYDR(OX)ONIUM.]
CHEMISTRY. More fully ***hydronium ion***. The hydrated hydrogen ion, H_3O^+. Cf. ***HYDROGEN ion***.

hydropathy /hʌɪˈdrɒpəθi/ *noun*. **M19**.
[ORIGIN from HYDRO- + -PATHY.]
The treatment of disorders by the application of water, internally as well as externally.
■ **ˈhydropath** *noun* (**a**) = HYDROPATHIST; (**b**) = HYDROPATHIC *noun*: **M19**. **hydroˈpathic** *adjective & noun* (**a**) *adjective* of, pertaining to, or of the nature of hydropathy; practising hydropathy; (**b**) *noun* an establishment where hydropathy is offered: **M19**. **hydropathist** *noun* a person who practises or advocates hydropathy **M19**. **hydropathize** *verb intrans*. undergo hydropathy **M19**.

hydrophane /ˈhʌɪdrəfeɪn/ *noun*. **L18**.
[ORIGIN from HYDRO- + Greek *-phanēs* apparent, *phanos* bright, clear, from *phainein* to show.]
A white variety of opal that absorbs water and becomes more translucent on immersion.
■ **hyˈdrophanous** *adjective* becoming more translucent on immersion **L18**.

hydrophile /ˈhʌɪdrəfʌɪl/ *adjective*. Also **-phil** /-fɪl/. **E20**.
[ORIGIN from HYDRO- + -PHIL.]
= HYDROPHILIC.

hydrophilic /hʌɪdrə(ʊ)ˈfɪlɪk/ *adjective*. **E20**.
[ORIGIN from HYDRO- + Greek *philos* loving + -IC.]
Having an affinity for water; readily absorbing or wetted by water; (of a colloid) readily forming or remaining as a hydrosol.
■ **hydrophilicity** /-ˈlɪs-/ *noun* hydrophilic quality **M20**.

hydrophilous /hʌɪˈdrɒfɪləs/ *adjective*. **M19**.
[ORIGIN from HYDRO- + -PHILOUS.]
1 Fond of water; *spec*. growing or living in water. *rare*. **M19**.
2 Of a plant: pollinated by the agency of water. **L19**.
■ **hydrophily** *noun* pollination by the agency of water **E20**.

hydrophobe /ˈhʌɪdrəfəʊb/ *noun & adjective*. **L19**.
[ORIGIN French from Latin *hydrophobus*, Greek *hudrophobos*, from Greek *hudro-* HYDRO- + *phobos* fear.]
▸**A** *noun*. **1** A person with hydrophobia. *rare*. **L19**.
2 A hydrophobic substance. **E20**.
▸**B** *adjective*. = HYDROPHOBIC *adjective* 2. **E20**.

hydrophobia /hʌɪdrə(ʊ)ˈfəʊbɪə/ *noun*. **LME**.
[ORIGIN Late Latin *hydrophobia* from Greek *hudrophobia*, from *hudrophobos*: see HYDROPHOBE, -IA¹.]
1 A strong aversion to or fear of water arising from the spasms that a rabid person suffers when attempting to drink; rabies itself. **LME**.
2 *gen*. A fear or dislike of water; *fig*. madness. **M18**.
■ **hydrophobial** *adjective* (now *rare* or *obsolete*) **M17**. **hyˈdrophobous** *adjective* (now *rare* or *obsolete*) **L17**.

hydrophobic /hʌɪdrə(ʊ)ˈfəʊbɪk/ *adjective*. **E19**.
[ORIGIN Late Latin *hydrophobicus* from Greek *hudrophobikos*, from *hudrophobia*: see HYDROPHOBIA, -IC.]
1 Of, pertaining to, or affected with hydrophobia. **E19**.
2 Tending to repel or not to absorb water; (of a colloid) not readily forming or remaining as a hydrosol. **E20**.
– NOTE: Recorded in **LME** as a noun in Latin form.
■ **hydrophobical** *adjective* (long *rare* or *obsolete*) = HYDROPHOBIC 1 **M17**. **hydrophobically** *adverb* in a manner that involves hydrophobic properties **M20**. **hydrophobicity** /-ˈbɪs-/ *noun* hydrophobic or water-repellent quality **M20**. **hyˈdrophobist** *noun* (*joc*.) a person who scorns non-alcoholic drinks **M19**.

hydrophone /ˈhʌɪdrəfəʊn/ *noun*. **M19**.
[ORIGIN from HYDRO- + -PHONE.]
1 *MEDICINE*. A bag of water placed between a stethoscope and the patient's chest in order to intensify the sounds heard. Now *rare* or *obsolete*. **M19**.
2 A transducer which detects sound waves transmitted through water and produces corresponding electrical signals which can drive a loudspeaker etc. **L19**.

> P. ZIEGLER Mountbatten claimed to have picked up traces of the U-boat on his hydrophone.

hydrophyte /ˈhʌɪdrəfʌɪt/ *noun*. **M19**.
[ORIGIN from HYDRO- + -PHYTE.]
A plant that grows in water or needs a waterlogged environment.
■ **hydrophytic** /-ˈfɪtɪk/ *adjective* **E20**.

hydropic /hʌɪˈdrɒpɪk/ *adjective & noun*. **LME**.
[ORIGIN Old French *ydropique*, *-ike* from Latin *hydropicus* from Greek *hudropikos*, from *hudrops* HYDROPS: see -IC. In 16 conformed (along with French *hydropique*) to Latin spelling.]
▸**A** *adjective*. **1** Oedematous, dropsical. **LME**.
†**2** *fig*. Insatiable; very thirsty. **LME–M18**.
3 Containing a lot of water; swollen. **M17**.
†**4** That cures dropsy. **L17–E18**.
– SPECIAL COLLOCATIONS: **hydropic degeneration**: in which a cell is swollen with so much excess water that its cytoplasm appears clear and homogeneous.
▸**B** *noun*. **1** A person with dropsy. Formerly, *the* dropsical people as a class. Now *rare*. **LME**.
2 A medicine for curing dropsy. Long *rare* or *obsolete*. **L17**.
■ **hydropical** *adjective* (now *rare* or *obsolete*) = HYDROPIC *adjective* 1,2,3 **M16**.

hydroplane /ˈhʌɪdrəpleɪn/ *noun & verb*. **E20**.
[ORIGIN from HYDRO- + PLANE *noun*³ (in sense 2 after *aeroplane*).]
▸**A** *noun*. **1** A movable horizontal vane (usu. one of several) projecting from the side of a submarine and used to steer it vertically and to provide stability. **E20**.
2 A motor boat with a specially shaped bottom to make it rise partly out of the water at speed. Also = HYDROFOIL 2. Also ***hydroplane boat***. **E20**.
3 A seaplane. Cf. HYDRO-AEROPLANE. *obsolete* exc. *hist*. **E20**.
▸**B** *verb intrans*. **1** Travel in a hydroplane boat. **E20**.
2 Of a boat or seaplane: rise out of the water at speed (without leaving it). **E20**.
3 Of a motor vehicle: aquaplane. Chiefly *US*. **M20**.

hydroponics /hʌɪdrə(ʊ)ˈpɒnɪks/ *noun*. **M20**.
[ORIGIN from HYDRO- + Greek *ponos* work + -ICS.]
The technique of growing plants without soil, in beds of sand, gravel, etc., flooded with nutrient solution.
■ **hydroponic** *adjective* pertaining to or grown by hydroponics **M20**. **hydroponically** *adverb* **M20**. **hydroponicist** /-sɪst-/ *noun* a person who practises hydroponics **M20**. **hydroponicum** *noun* a place or structure in which hydroponics is practised **M20**.

hydropot /ˈhʌɪdrəpɒt/ *noun*. **E18**.
[ORIGIN mod. Latin *hydropota* from Greek *hudropotēs* water-drinker, from *hudro-* HYDRO- + *potēs* drinker.]
A person who drinks only water; a teetotaller.
■ †**hydropotic** *adjective* (*rare*): only in **E17**.

hydrops /ˈhʌɪdrɒps/ *noun*. **LME**.
[ORIGIN Latin from Greek *hudrōps*, from *hudr-*, *hudōr* water.]
Oedema, dropsy. Now chiefly in ***hydrops fetalis*** below.
hydrops fetalis /fiːˈtaːlɪs/ [mod. Latin = of the fetus] the severest form of haemolytic disease of the newborn, in which the infant is grossly oedematous and anaemic and usually dies before birth or soon afterwards.

hydropsy /ˈhʌɪdrɒpsi/ *noun*. Now *rare* or *obsolete*. **ME**.
[ORIGIN Old French *idropesie* from medieval Latin (*h*)*ydropsia*, for Latin *hydropisis* from Greek *hudrōpiasis*, from *hudrōps* HYDROPS: see -IASIS. Cf. DROPSY.]
Oedema, dropsy.

hydroptic /hʌɪˈdrɒptɪk/ *adjective*. *arch*. **E17**.
[ORIGIN from HYDROPSY after *epilepsy*, *epileptic*, etc.]
= HYDROPIC *adjective* 1,2,3.

hydroscope /ˈhʌɪdrəskəʊp/ *noun*. **L17**.
[ORIGIN Greek *hudroskopos* water-seeker, *hudroskopion* water clock, from *hudro-* HYDRO-: see -SCOPE.]
†**1** = HYGROSCOPE. Only in **L17**.
2 *hist*. A water clock consisting of a graduated cylinder from which water trickled through an aperture in the bottom. **E18**.
3 A tube closed with clear glass or plastic at one end for looking below the surface of water. **E20**.

hydroscopic /hʌɪdrə(ʊ)ˈskɒpɪk/ *adjective*. **L19**.
[ORIGIN from HYDRO- after *hygroscopic*.]
= HYGROSCOPIC 3.

hydrosol /ˈhʌɪdrəsɒl/ *noun*. **M19**.
[ORIGIN from HYDRO- + SOL(UTION.]
A sol in which the liquid constituent is water.

hydrostat /ˈhʌɪdrəstat/ *noun*. **M19**.
[ORIGIN from HYDRO- + -STAT.]
1 An apparatus for preventing the explosion of boilers. *rare*. **M19**.
2 An electrical device for detecting the presence of water. **L19**.

hydrostatic /hʌɪdrə(ʊ)ˈstatɪk/ *adjective*. **L17**.
[ORIGIN Prob. from Greek *hudrostatēs* hydrostatic balance, (in medieval Greek) fire engine, from *hudro-* HYDRO- + STATIC.]
1 Pertaining to the equilibrium of liquids or the pressure of stationary liquids; pertaining to hydrostatics. **L17**.

> B. STEWART The hydrostatic pressure of the column of mercury.

2 Involving or employing the pressure of water or other liquid. **M18**.
hydrostatic balance: for finding the relative density of an object by weighing it in water. **hydrostatic press** = ***hydraulic press*** s.v. HYDRAULIC *adjective*.
■ **hydrostatical** *adjective* (now *rare*) = HYDROSTATIC **M17**. **hydrostatically** *adverb* by hydrostatic means; as regards hydrostatics: **M17**.

hydrostatician /ˌhʌɪdrəʊstəˈtɪʃ(ə)n/ *noun*. **M17**.
[ORIGIN from HYDROSTATICS + -IAN.]
An expert in or student of hydrostatics.

hydrostatics /hʌɪdrə(ʊ)ˈstatɪks/ *noun pl*. (treated as *sing*. or †*pl*.). **M17**.
[ORIGIN from HYDRO- + STATICS or STATIC *noun*: see -ICS.]
The branch of mechanics that deals with the properties and behaviour of stationary liquids.

†**hydrosulphate** *noun*. Also **-sulf-**. Only in **19**.
[ORIGIN from HYDRO- + SULPHATE *noun*.]
CHEMISTRY. = HYDROSULPHIDE.

hydrosulphide /hʌɪdrə(ʊ)ˈsʌlfʌɪd/ *noun*. Also **-sulf-**. **M19**.
[ORIGIN from HYDRO- + SULPHIDE *noun*.]
CHEMISTRY. Any acid salt formed by replacing a hydrogen atom of hydrogen sulphide by a metal atom. Also called ***hydrogensulphide***.
■ Also †**hydrosulphuret** *noun*: only in **E19**.

hydrosulphite /hʌɪdrə(ʊ)ˈsʌlfʌɪt/ *noun*. Also (*US & CHEMISTRY*) **-sulf-**. L19.
[ORIGIN from HYDRO- + SULPHITE.]
CHEMISTRY. A salt of hydrosulphurous acid; *esp.* the sodium salt, $Na_2S_2O_6{\cdot}2H_2O$, used as a reagent.

†**hydrosulphuric** *adjective*. Also **-sulf-**. Only in 19.
[ORIGIN from HYDRO- + SULPHURIC.]
CHEMISTRY. ***hydrosulphuric acid***, = SULPHYDRIC.

hydrosulphurous /hʌɪdrə(ʊ)ˈsʌlf(ə)rəs, -ˈsʌlfjʊr-/ *adjective*. Also **-sulf-**. M19.
[ORIGIN from HYDRO- + SULPHUROUS.]
CHEMISTRY. ***hydrosulphurous acid***: an unstable acid, $H_2S_2O_4$, that is known only in solution and is a strong reducing agent; formerly, dithionic acid, $H_2S_2O_6$.

hydrotherapy /hʌɪdrə(ʊ)ˈθɛrəpi/ *noun*. L19.
[ORIGIN from HYDRO- + THERAPY.]
The treatment of disorders by the application of water, esp. externally by immersion.
■ ˌ**hydrotheraˈpeutic** *adjective* of or pertaining to hydrotherapeutics or hydrotherapy L19. ˌ**hydrotheraˈpeutics** *noun* hydrotherapy; the branch of medicine that deals with this: M19. **hydrotherapic** *adjective* L19.

hydrothermal /hʌɪdrə(ʊ)ˈθəːm(ə)l/ *adjective*. M19.
[ORIGIN from HYDRO- + Greek *thermos* hot + -AL[1].]
Of, produced by, or designating naturally hot underground water that has geological effects.

F. H. POUGH Hydrothermal solutions, from which so many minerals are deposited.

hydrothermal vent an opening in the sea floor out of which comes hot or warm water.
■ **hydrothermally** *adverb* by hydrothermal action M20.

hydrotic /hʌɪˈdrɒtɪk/ *adjective & noun*. Long *rare* or *obsolete*. L17.
[ORIGIN formed as HIDROTIC with spelling conformed to HYDRO-.]
MEDICINE. ▸**A** *adjective*. = HIDROTIC *adjective*. L17.
▸**B** *noun*. = HIDROTIC *noun*; = HYDRAGOGUE *noun*. L17.
■ **hydrotical** *adjective* M17.

hydrotropic /hʌɪdrə(ʊ)ˈtrəʊpɪk, -ˈtrɒpɪk/ *adjective*. L19.
[ORIGIN from HYDRO- + -TROPIC.]
1 *BOTANY*. Exhibiting hydrotropism. L19.
2 *CHEMISTRY*. Exhibiting, causing, or caused by hydrotropy. E20.
■ **hydrotropically** *adverb* (*a*) *BOTANY* in a manner that results in movement towards moisture; (*b*) *CHEMISTRY* as regards hydrotropy: E20. **hyˈdrotropism** *noun* (*BOTANY*) the property on the part of a plant root etc. of turning or bending under the influence of nearby moisture L19. **hyˈdrotropy** *noun* (*CHEMISTRY*) the phenomenon whereby a substance that is only slightly soluble in water will dissolve readily in certain aqueous solutions E20.

hydrous /ˈhʌɪdrəs/ *adjective*. E19.
[ORIGIN from Greek *hudr-* HYDRO- + -OUS.]
Of a chemical or mineral: containing water.

hydroxide /hʌɪˈdrɒksʌɪd/ *noun*. M19.
[ORIGIN from HYDRO- + OXIDE.]
CHEMISTRY. A compound containing the hydroxyl group or the hydroxide ion.
– COMB.: **hydroxide ion** the negatively charged ion OH^-.

hydroxo- /hʌɪˈdrɒksəʊ/ *combining form*. Also as attrib. adjective **hydroxo**. E20.
[ORIGIN from HYDROX(YL + -O-.]
CHEMISTRY. Containing or designating a coordinated hydroxyl group; containing a hydroxide ion.
■ **hydroxocoˈbalamin** *noun* (*BIOCHEMISTRY*) an analogue of cyanocobalamin in which a hydroxide ion replaces the cyanide ion M20.

hydroxonium /hʌɪdrɒkˈsəʊnɪəm/ *noun*. E20.
[ORIGIN from HYDRO- + OXONIUM.]
CHEMISTRY. More fully ***hydroxonium ion***. = HYDRONIUM.

hydroxy- /hʌɪˈdrɒksi/ *combining form*. Also as attrib. adjective **hydroxy**.
[ORIGIN from HYDROXYL.]
CHEMISTRY. Containing the hydroxyl group, often in place of a hydrogen atom.
■ **hydroxyˈapatite** *noun* a mineral of the apatite group that is rare in the ground but is the principal inorganic constituent of tooth enamel and bone E20. **hydroxybenˈzoic** *adjective* designating three acids, $HO{\cdot}C_6H_4{\cdot}COOH$, derived from benzoic acid in which a hydroxyl group is attached to the ring, *spec.* the *ortho* isomer (also called ***salicylic acid***) L19. **hydroxyˈlysine** *noun* (*BIOCHEMISTRY*) an amino acid occurring chiefly as a constituent of collagen E20. **hydroxyproˈgesterone** *noun* (*PHARMACOLOGY*) any of various synthetic hydroxylated derivatives of progesterone, *esp.* one given to supplement a natural deficiency of progesterone M20. **hydroxyˈproline** *noun* (*BIOCHEMISTRY*) any of various hydroxylated derivatives of proline, *esp.* one that is an amino acid and a constituent of collagen and elastin E20. **hydroxyˈtryptamine** *noun* (*BIOCHEMISTRY*) any of various derivatives of tryptamine in which a hydroxyl group is attached to the benzene ring, *spec.* = SEROTONIN M20. **hydroxyuˈrea** *noun* any of several compounds $CH_4N_2O_2$, *esp.* (*PHARMACOLOGY*) one given orally in some forms of leukaemia E20. **hydroxyzine** /-ziːn/ *noun* (*PHARMACOLOGY*) a derivative of piperazine given as a minor tranquillizer M20.

hydroxyl /hʌɪˈdrɒksɪl, *uncombined also* -sʌɪl/ *noun*. M19.
[ORIGIN from HYDRO- + OXY- + -YL.]
CHEMISTRY. More fully ***hydroxyl group***, ***hydroxyl radical***. The neutral or positively charged group ·OH. Also, the (negative) hydroxide ion.
– COMB.: **hydroxylapatite** = HYDROXYAPATITE.
■ **hydroxylase** /-z/ *noun* (*BIOCHEMISTRY*) an enzyme which catalyses hydroxylation M20. **hydroxylate** *verb trans. & intrans.* (*a*) *verb trans.* introduce a hydroxyl group into; (*b*) *verb intrans.* accept a hydroxyl group: E20. **hydroxyˈlation** *noun* the introduction of a hydroxyl group into a molecule or compound L19. **hydroxylic** /-drɒkˈsɪlɪk/ *adjective* of or containing a hydroxyl group L19.

hydroxylamine /hʌɪˈdrɒksɪləˌmiːn, hʌɪˌdrɒksɪˈlamiːn, hʌɪdrɒkˈsʌɪləmiːn/ *noun*. M19.
[ORIGIN from HYDROXYL + AMINE.]
A compound, NH_2OH, which forms unstable deliquescent crystals that detonate on heating and is used in stable solution as a reducing agent and reagent.

hydrozoan /hʌɪdrə(ʊ)ˈzəʊən/ *noun & adjective*. L19.
[ORIGIN from mod. Latin *Hydrozoa* (see below), from HYDRO- + Greek *zōia* pl. of *zōion* animal.]
ZOOLOGY. ▸**A** *noun*. A coelenterate of the class Hydrozoa, comprising organisms that are mostly marine and colonial with polyp and medusoid stages in the life cycle. L19.
▸**B** *adjective*. Of or pertaining to the class Hydrozoa. L19.
■ **hydrozoic** *adjective* M19. **hydrozoon** *noun*, pl. **-zoa**, = HYDROZOAN *noun* (usu. in *pl.*) M19.

†**hydruret** *noun*. Only in 19.
[ORIGIN from HYDR(OGEN + -URET.]
CHEMISTRY. A hydride.

Hydrus /ˈhʌɪdrəs/ *noun*. In sense 1 **h-**; pl. **-dri** /-drʌɪ/. M17.
[ORIGIN Latin from Greek *hudros* water snake.]
1 A mythical water snake or sea serpent. *rare*. M17.
2 (The name of) a constellation of the southern hemisphere between the star Achernar and the pole; the Water Snake. Cf. HYDRA *noun* 2. E18.

hyemal *adjective* var. of HIEMAL.

hyemate *verb* var. of HIEMATE.

†**hyemnal** *adjective*. L17–L18.
[ORIGIN from HIEMAL, perh. after *autumnal*.]
= HIEMAL.

hyena /hʌɪˈiːnə/ *noun*. Also **hyaena**. ME.
[ORIGIN (Old French *hyene* from) Latin *hyaena* from Greek *huaina* use of fem. of *hus*, *hu-* pig, SWINE with ending as in *leaina* lioness.]
1 a Any of several carnivorous scavenging animals somewhat resembling a dog, but with the hind limbs shorter than the forelimbs, and belonging to the genera *Hyaena* and *Crocuta* (family Hyaenidae). ME. ▸**b** The thylacine, the Tasmanian wolf. Chiefly *Austral.* (now *rare*). E19.
a brown hyena *Hyaena brunnea*, of southern Africa. **laughing hyena** the spotted hyena; also (now *rare*), the striped hyena. **spotted hyena** *Crocuta crocuta*, of sub-Saharan Africa. **striped hyena** *Hyaena hyaena*, of Africa and SW Asia.
2 *fig.* A person who is cruel, treacherous, and rapacious, or is otherwise likened to a hyena. E17.
†**3** A mythical stone said to be taken from the eye of the hyena. E17–M19.
– COMB.: **hyena dog** = ***hunting dog*** (b) s.v. HUNTING *noun*.
■ **hyenaism** *noun* behaviour characteristic of a hyena M19.

hyetograph /ˈhʌɪɪtəgrɑːf/ *noun*. L19.
[ORIGIN from Greek *huetos* rain + -GRAPH.]
1 A chart or map of rainfall. L19.
2 A kind of recording rain gauge. M20.
■ **hyetoˈgraphic** *adjective* M19. **hyetoˈgraphical** *adjective* L19.

hygeen /hɪˈdʒiːn/ *noun*. Also **hajeen** /həˈdʒiːn/. E17.
[ORIGIN Arabic *hajīn*.]
A riding dromedary.

Hygeia /hʌɪˈdʒiːə/ *noun*. E18.
[ORIGIN Greek *hugeia* late form of *hugieia* health, *Hugieia* goddess of health, from *hugiēs* healthy.]
The personification of health; a system of sanitation or medical practice.
■ **hygeian**, **H-** *adjective* pertaining to Hygeia, health, or sanitation; healthy: M18. ˈ**hygeist**, **H-** *noun* an expert in hygiene E18.

hygiastic /hʌɪdʒɪˈastɪk/ *adjective*. L17.
[ORIGIN Greek *hugiastikos* curative, from *hugiazein* heal, from *hugiēs* healthy: see -IC.]
Relating to health, sanitary, hygienic.

hygiene /ˈhʌɪdʒiːn/ *noun*. Orig. in Latin & Greek forms †**hygie(i)na**, †**hygieine**. L16.
[ORIGIN (French *hygiène* from mod. Latin *hygieina* from) Greek *hugieinē* (sc. *tekhnē* art), use as noun of fem. of *hugienos* healthful, from *hugiēs* healthy.]
The branch of knowledge that deals with the maintenance of health, esp. the conditions and practices conducive to it; the conditions and practices of a place or person in so far as they promote health.

A. GHOSH A campaign to teach people the principles of hygiene. *Which?* The standard of hygiene and efficiency in the salon generally—dirty towels, combs, and other equipment. *New York Times* Food service workers should follow established standards of good personal hygiene.

mental hygiene: see MENTAL *adjective*[1].
■ **hyˈgienic** *adjective* pertaining to hygiene; conducive to health, clean and sanitary: M19. **hyˈgienically** *adverb* (earlier in UNHYGIENICALLY) in a hygienic manner; as regards hygiene: L19. **hyˈgienics** *noun* hygiene as a branch of knowledge M19. **hyˈgienist** *noun* (*a*) an expert in hygiene; (*b*) = DENTAL ***hygienist***: M19.

hygro- /ˈhʌɪgrəʊ/ *combining form*.
[ORIGIN Greek *hugro-*, from *hugros* wet, moist, fluid: see -O-.]
Moisture.
■ ˈ**hygrograph** *noun* an instrument that produces a graphical record of atmospheric humidity M19. **hyˈgrology** *noun* the branch of physics that deals with humidity and evaporation L18. ˈ**hygrophile** *noun* a hygrophilous plant M19. **hyˈgrophilous** *adjective* (of a plant) growing in damp environments M19. ˈ**hygrophyte** *noun* a plant that grows in damp (but not aquatic) environments E20. **hygrophytic** /-ˈfɪtɪk/ *adjective* designating or pertaining to a hygrophyte or hygrophytes M20. ˈ**hygrostat** *noun* = HUMIDISTAT E20. **hygroˈthermograph** *noun* an instrument that produces a graphical record of atmospheric humidity and temperature E20.

hygroma /hʌɪˈgrəʊmə/ *noun*. Pl. **-mas**, **-mata** /-mətə/. E19.
[ORIGIN from HYGRO- + -OMA.]
MEDICINE. A sac, cyst, or tumour filled with watery fluid.

hygrometer /hʌɪˈgrɒmɪtə/ *noun*. L17.
[ORIGIN from HYGRO- + -METER, or from French *hygromètre*.]
An instrument for measuring the humidity of the air or other gas. Formerly also, a hygroscope.

hygrometric /hʌɪgrə(ʊ)ˈmɛtrɪk/ *adjective*. L18.
[ORIGIN from (the same root as) HYGROMETER: see -IC.]
1 = HYGROSCOPIC 1. L18.
2 Pertaining to humidity or its measurement. E19.
3 = HYGROSCOPIC 3. M19.
■ **hygrometrical** *adjective* = HYGROMETRIC L18. **hygrometrically** *adverb* E19. **hyˈgrometry** *noun* the branch of science that deals with the measurement of humidity L18.

hygroscope /ˈhʌɪgrə(ʊ)skəʊp/ *noun*. M17.
[ORIGIN from HYGRO- + -SCOPE.]
An instrument which gives a qualitative indication of atmospheric humidity without measuring it.

hygroscopic /hʌɪgrə(ʊ)ˈskɒpɪk/ *adjective*. L18.
[ORIGIN from (the same root as) HYGROSCOPE + -IC.]
1 Of a substance: tending to absorb moisture from the air. L18.
2 Pertaining to humidity or its detection. L18.
3 Of water: present as moisture in soil as a result of humidity in the air to which it is exposed. M19.
■ **hygroscopical** *adjective* L18. **hygroscopically** *adverb* E19. **hygroscopicity** /ˌhʌɪgrə(ʊ)skɒˈpɪsɪti/ *noun* hygroscopic quality; the property of a substance of retaining moisture: M19.

hying *verb pres. pple* of HIE *verb*.

Hyksos /ˈhɪksɒs/ *noun & adjective*. E17.
[ORIGIN Greek *Huksōs* from Egyptian *heqa khoswe* foreign rulers.]
▸**A** *noun pl.* A nomadic people of mixed Semitic and Asian descent who invaded Egypt in the 18th cent. BC and ruled it until the 16th cent. BC. E17.
▸**B** *adjective*. Designating, of, or pertaining to the Hyksos. L19.

hyla /ˈhʌɪlə/ *noun*. M19.
[ORIGIN mod. Latin from Greek *hulē*: see HYLE.]
A tree frog of the genus *Hyla*.

†**hylarchic** *adjective*. L17–E18.
[ORIGIN from HYLE + -ARCH + -IC.]
Ruling over matter.

hyle /ˈhʌɪliː/ *noun*. LME.
[ORIGIN Late Latin from Greek *hulē* wood, timber, material, matter. Cf. Old French *hyle*.]
Matter, substance; *spec.* the primordial matter of the universe. Cf. YLEM.

hyleg /ˈhʌɪlɛg/ *noun*. E17.
[ORIGIN Persian *haylāj* celestial indicator of the length of a newborn child's life.]
ASTROLOGY. The giver of life in a nativity.
■ †**hylegial** *adjective* M17–M18.

hylic /ˈhʌɪlɪk/ *adjective*. M19.
[ORIGIN Late Latin *hylicus* from Greek *hulikos*, from *hulē* HYLE: see -IC.]
Pertaining to matter, material.
■ **hylicist** /-sɪst/ *noun* a materialist L19.

hylo- /ˈhʌɪləʊ/ *combining form*.
[ORIGIN Greek *hulo-* combining form of *hulē*: see HYLE, -O-.]
1 Wood; forest.
2 Matter.
■ **hyˈlobatid** *noun* [Greek *-batēs* walker] an animal of the family Hylobatidae, comprising the gibbons L20. **hyˈlology** *noun* a doctrine concerning matter; a branch of knowledge that deals with matter: M19. **hyloˈmorphic** *adjective* (*PHILOSOPHY*) of or pertaining to hylomorphism L19. **hyloˈmorphism** *noun* (*PHILOSOPHY*) the doctrine that matter is the first cause of the universe and that physical objects result from the combination of matter with form L19. **hyˈlophagous** *adjective* (of an insect) feeding on wood L19. **hyloˈtheism** *noun* the doctrine that God and matter are identical; material pantheism: E19. **hyloˈzoic** *adjective* of, pertaining to, or advocating hylozoism L17. **hyloˈzoism** *noun* the doctrine that all matter has life, or that life is merely a property of matter L17. **hyloˈzoist** *noun* a person who advocates hylozoism L17. **hylozoˈistic** *adjective* = HYLOZOIC L19.

hymen /ˈhʌɪmən/ *noun*[1]. L16.
[ORIGIN Latin from Greek *Humēn* the god of marriage.]
1 (**H-**.) Marriage personified. L16.
2 (Usu. **H-**.) Marriage; a wedding. Now *rare*. E17.
3 = HYMENEAL *noun* 2. *rare*. E17.

H

hymen /ˈhʌɪmən/ *noun*². M16.
[ORIGIN Latin from Greek *humēn* membrane (also, seed vessel of a plant).]
A mucous membrane which partly closes the entrance to the vagina and is broken usu. at a woman's first experience of sexual intercourse.
■ **hymenal** *adjective* = HYMENEAL *adjective*² L19.

hymeneal /hʌɪməˈniːəl/ *adjective*¹ & *noun*. E17.
[ORIGIN from Latin *hymenaeus* from Greek *humenaios*: see -AL¹.]
► **A** *adjective*. Pertaining to marriage. E17.
► **B** *noun*. **1** In *pl.* A wedding; nuptials. M17.
2 A wedding hymn. E18.
■ **hymeneally** *adverb* M19.

hymeneal /hʌɪməˈniːəl/ *adjective*². E20.
[ORIGIN from HYMEN *noun*² + -AL¹, perh. after HYMENEAL *adjective*¹.]
Of or pertaining to a woman's hymen.

hymenean /hʌɪməˈniːən/ *adjective* & *noun*. Now *rare*. E17.
[ORIGIN formed as HYMENEAL *adjective*¹ + -AN.]
► **A** *adjective*. = HYMENEAL *adjective*¹. E17.
► †**B** *noun*. = HYMENEAL *noun* 2. Only in M17.

hymenial /hʌɪˈmiːnɪəl/ *adjective*¹. E18.
[ORIGIN from HYMEN *noun*¹ + -IAL or alt. of HYMENEAL *adjective*¹.]
= HYMENEAL *adjective*¹.

hymenial /hʌɪˈmiːnɪəl/ *adjective*². L19.
[ORIGIN from HYMENIUM + -AL¹.]
Of or pertaining to the hymenium of a fungus.

H

hymenium /hʌɪˈmiːnɪəm/ *noun*. E19.
[ORIGIN Greek *humenion* dim. of *humēn*: see HYMEN *noun*².]
A spore-producing layer containing asci or basidia in some higher fungi.

hymenopter /hʌɪməˈnɒptə/ *noun*. E19.
[ORIGIN French *hyménoptère* formed as HYMENOPTERA.]
= HYMENOPTERAN *noun*.

Hymenoptera /hʌɪməˈnɒpt(ə)rə/ *noun pl.* Also **h-**. L18.
[ORIGIN mod. Latin from neut. pl. of Greek *humenopteros* membrane-winged, from *humen-*, *humēn* (see HYMEN *noun*²) + *pteron* wing: see -A³.]
(Members of) a large order of insects (including bees, wasps, and ants) characterized by two pairs of wings and in females an ovipositor adapted for stinging, piercing, or sawing.

R. F. CHAPMAN In some larval Diptera and Hymenoptera the antennae are very small.

■ **hymenopterous** *adjective* of or pertaining to the Hymenoptera E19.

hymenopteran /hʌɪməˈnɒpt(ə)rən/ *noun* & *adjective*. M19.
[ORIGIN from HYMENOPTERA + -AN.]
► **A** *noun*. A hymenopterous insect. M19.
► **B** *adjective*. Hymenopterous. E20.

Hymettian /hʌɪˈmɛtɪən/ *adjective*. E17.
[ORIGIN from Latin *Hymettius*, from *Hymettus*, Greek *Humēttos*: see -IAN.]
Of or belonging to Mount Hymettus in Attica, famous in ancient times for its honey and marble; *poet.* honeyed, sweet. Cf. HYBLAEAN.

Hymie /ˈhʌɪmi/ *noun*. *US slang* (*derog.* & *offensive*). L20.
[ORIGIN Colloq. abbreviation of Jewish man's name *Hyman*.]
A Jew.

hymn /hɪm/ *noun* & *verb*. OE.
[ORIGIN (Old French *ymne* from) Latin *hymnus* from Greek *humnos* song in praise of a god or hero, in Septuagint rendering various Hebrew words, and hence in New Testament and other Christian writings.]
► **A** *noun*. **1** A song of praise to God; *spec.* a metrical composition sung during a religious service and consisting of something other than the text of the Bible. OE.

W. SOYINKA Nothing but the sound of hymns at morning and evening prayers had been heard.

2 A song or other composition which praises a god or other exalted being or thing. LME.

D. PRATER Since his admiration . . had first been awakened, Rilke's letters had contained many a hymn to Rodin.

hymn of hate a tirade against a person or thing.
– COMB.: **hymn book** a book of hymns.
► **B** *verb*. **1** *verb trans.* Praise or celebrate in a hymn. M17.

W. DE LA MARE Within the eternal peace of God they stood, Hymning his glory. O. NASH Some singers sing of ladies' eyes, . . coarse ones hymn their hips.

2 *verb trans.* Sing as a hymn; express in a hymn. E18.

British Medical Journal It started in the 'fifties, hymning the praise . . of competition, and of private enterprise.

3 *verb intrans.* Sing a hymn or hymns. E18.
■ **hymner** /ˈhɪm(n)ə/ *noun* a singer of hymns E19. **hymnic** /ˈhɪmnɪk/ *adjective* of, or of the nature of, a hymn or hymns L16. **hymnist** /ˈhɪmnɪst/ *noun* a composer of hymns E17. **hymnless** *adjective* E19.

hymnal /ˈhɪmn(ə)l/ *noun* & *adjective*. L15.
[ORIGIN from Latin *hymnus* (see HYMN) + -AL¹. The noun use repr. a medieval Latin *hymnale*.]
► **A** *noun*. A hymn book; a collection of hymns. L15.
► **B** *adjective*. Of a hymn or hymns. M17.

hymnary /ˈhɪmnəri/ *noun*. L19.
[ORIGIN medieval Latin *hymnarium*, formed as HYMN: see -ARY¹.]
= HYMNAL *noun*.

hymnody /ˈhɪmnədi/ *noun*. E18.
[ORIGIN medieval Latin *hymnodia* from Greek *humnōidia* singing of hymns: cf. PSALMODY.]
1 The singing or composition of hymns. E18.
2 Hymns collectively; the body of hymns belonging to a period, country, church, etc. M19.

Presbyterian Herald A massive tune—one of the finest things in all hymnody.

■ **hymnodist** *noun* a person who is skilled in hymnody; a hymnist: E18.

hymnographer /hɪmˈnɒɡrəfə/ *noun*. E17.
[ORIGIN from Greek *humnographos* hymn-writer + -ER¹: see -GRAPHER.]
A composer of hymns.

hymnography /hɪmˈnɒɡrəfi/ *noun*. M19.
[ORIGIN from (the same root as) HYMNOGRAPHER + -GRAPHY.]
The literary history and bibliography of hymns.

hymnology /hɪmˈnɒlədʒi/ *noun*. M17.
[ORIGIN Orig. from Greek *humnologia* hymn-singing, medieval Latin *hymnologia* praise in song, but in mod. use from HYMN *noun* + -OLOGY.]
†**1** The singing of hymns. M17–M19.
2 The branch of knowledge that deals with hymns; hymns collectively or as a literary form. E19.
3 The composition of hymns. M19.
■ **hymnoˈlogic**, **hymnoˈlogical** *adjectives* L19. **hymnoˈlogically** *adverb* as regards hymnology L19. **hymnologist** *noun* a composer of hymns; an expert in or student of hymnology: L18.

hyne /hʌɪn/ *adverb*. Now *Scot.* & *dial.* LME.
[ORIGIN Contr. of HETHEN.]
Hence.

hyoid /ˈhʌɪɔɪd/ *adjective* & *noun*. E19.
[ORIGIN French *hyoïde* from mod. Latin *hyoides* from Greek *huoeidēs* shaped like the letter upsilon, from *hu* (name of) the letter υ: see -OID.]
ANATOMY & ZOOLOGY. ► **A** *adjective*. Designating a bone (U-shaped in humans) or a group of bones which supports the tongue, being situated at its base above the thyroid cartilage. E19.
hyoid arch the second visceral arch in lower vertebrates and the embryos of higher vertebrates.
► **B** *noun*. The hyoid bone. L19.

hyoidean /hʌɪˈɔɪdɪən/ *adjective*. M19.
[ORIGIN from mod. Latin *hyoideus*, from *hyoides*: see HYOID, -AN.]
ANATOMY & ZOOLOGY. Of or pertaining to the hyoid.

hyolithid /hʌɪəˈlɪθɪd/ *adjective* & *noun*. M20.
[ORIGIN from mod. Latin *Hyolitha*, from Greek *huoeidēs* (see HYOID) + *lithos* stone: see -ID³.]
(Pertaining to or designating) a marine invertebrate of Palaeozoic times that was bilaterally symmetric with a conical shell and was probably a kind of mollusc.

hyomandibular /ˌhʌɪə(ʊ)manˈdɪbjʊlə/ *adjective* & *noun*. L19.
[ORIGIN from Greek *huoeidēs* (see HYOID) + MANDIBULAR.]
ANATOMY & ZOOLOGY. ► **A** *adjective*. Pertaining to the hyoid bone or hyoid arch and the mandible. L19.
hyomandibular bone the dorsal component of the hyoid arch in vertebrates, which in fishes supports the jaws and in land animals is modified into an auditory ossicle.
► **B** *noun*. The hyomandibular bone. L19.

hyoscine /ˈhʌɪəsiːn/ *noun*. L19.
[ORIGIN from HYOSC(YAMUS + -INE⁵.]
Scopolamine; *spec.* the naturally occurring laevorotatory isomer.

hyoscyamia /ˌhʌɪə(ʊ)sʌɪˈeɪmɪə/ *noun*. Now *rare* or *obsolete*. E19.
[ORIGIN formed as HYOSCYAMINE after *ammonia*.]
= HYOSCYAMINE.

hyoscyamine /hʌɪə(ʊ)ˈsʌɪəmiːn/ *noun*. E19.
[ORIGIN from HYOSCYAMUS + -INE⁵.]
A poisonous alkaloid, $C_{17}H_{23}NO_3$; *spec.* the laevorotatory isomer, occurring in henbane and other solanaceous plants and used medicinally like atropine for its anticholinergic properties.

hyoscyamus /hʌɪə(ʊ)ˈsʌɪəməs/ *noun*. E17.
[ORIGIN mod. Latin from Greek *huoskuamos*, from *huos* genit. of *hus* swine + *kuamos* bean.]
A medicinal extract or tincture of henbane.

hyp *noun* var. of HIP *noun*³.

hyp- *combining form* see HYPO-.

hypabyssal /hʌɪpəˈbɪs(ə)l/ *adjective*. L19.
[ORIGIN from HYP- + ABYSSAL.]
GEOLOGY. Of igneous rock: formed from magma that has intruded into and solidified among other rocks not far below the earth's surface.

hypacusis /hʌɪpəˈk(j)uːsɪs/ *noun*. Also **-cou-**, **-ku-**, **-usia** /-uːsɪə/. L19.
[ORIGIN from HYPO- + Greek *akousis* hearing.]
Diminished acuteness of hearing.

hypaesthesia /ˌhʌɪpiːsˈθiːzɪə, -pɛs-/ *noun*. Also ***-pes-**. L19.
[ORIGIN from HYPO- + Greek *aisthēsis* sensation: see -IA¹.]
Abnormally low sensitivity of the body or mind, esp. of the skin.
■ **hypaesthetic** *adjective* M20.

hypaethral /hʌɪˈpiːθr(ə)l, hɪ-/ *adjective*. Also **-peth-**. L18.
[ORIGIN from Latin *hypaethrus* from Greek *hupaithros*, formed as HYPO- + *aithēr* air, ETHER *noun*¹: see -AL¹.]
1 ARCHITECTURE. Open to the sky; having no roof. Opp. CLEITHRAL. L18.
2 Open-air. L19.

hypakusis *noun* var. of HYPACUSIS.

hypalgesia /hʌɪpalˈdʒiːzɪə/ *noun*. L19.
[ORIGIN from HYP- + Greek *algēsis* sense of pain + -IA¹.]
Abnormally low sensitivity to pain.
■ **hypalˈgesic** *adjective* characterized by or tending to produce hypalgesia E20.

hypallage /hʌɪˈpalədʒiː, hɪ-/ *noun*. L16.
[ORIGIN Late Latin from Greek *hupallagē*, formed as HYPO- + *allag-* stem of *allassein* to exchange, from *allos* other.]
RHETORIC. A figure of speech in which there is a transposition of the natural relations of two elements of a proposition or a transference of an epithet.

Hypalon /ˈhʌɪp(ə)lɒn/ *noun*. M20.
[ORIGIN Unknown.]
(Proprietary name for) a synthetic rubber consisting of chlorinated and sulphonated polyethylene.

hypanthium /hɪˈpanθɪəm, hʌɪ-/ *noun*. M19.
[ORIGIN mod. Latin, formed as HYPO- + Greek *anthos* flower + -IUM.]
BOTANY. A cuplike or tubular enlargement of the receptacle, loosely surrounding the gynoecium (in a perigynous flower) or united with it (in an epigynous flower).
■ **hypanthial** *adjective* L19.

hyparterial /hʌɪpɑːˈtɪərɪəl/ *adjective*. L19.
[ORIGIN from HYP- + ARTERIAL.]
ANATOMY. Of a branch of a bronchus: situated below the pulmonary artery.

hypaspist /hɪˈpaspɪst, hʌɪ-/ *noun*. E19.
[ORIGIN Greek *hupaspistēs* lit. 'shield-bearer', formed as HYPO- + *aspis* shield.]
GREEK HISTORY. A member of a distinguished body of troops in the Macedonian army that included the foot guards.

hypate /ˈhɪpətiː/ *noun*. E17.
[ORIGIN Latin from Greek *hypatē* (sc. *khordē* string), fem. of *hupatos* uppermost, last.]
In ancient Greek music, the fixed lowest note of a lower tetrachord.

hypaxial /hɪˈpaksɪəl, hʌɪ-/ *adjective*. L19.
[ORIGIN from HYP- + AXIAL.]
ANATOMY & ZOOLOGY. Situated on the lower or ventral side of the vertebral axis.

hype /hʌɪp/ *noun*¹ & *verb*¹. *slang* (orig. *US*). E20.
[ORIGIN Unknown.]
► **A** *noun*. **1** An instance of short-changing; a person who short-changes people. E20.
2 Cheating, deception; a confidence trick, a swindle; persuasive talk; promotional publicity, esp. of an extravagant or intensive nature. M20.

Publishers Weekly They carried off the biggest money-making hype in sports history. *Newsweek* Despite some media hype Frost insists his series really 'breaks some new ground'.

► **B** *verb trans.* **1** Short-change; cheat, deceive, esp. by persuasive talk. E20.

J. HYAMS His sales technique was to hype the kids.

2 Promote with extravagant or intensive publicity. Also foll. by *up*. L20.

National Observer (US) Scientists hype up low-tar tobacco.

hype /hʌɪp/ *noun*² & *verb*². *slang* (orig. *US*). E20.
[ORIGIN Abbreviation of HYPODERMIC. Cf. HYPO *noun*³ & *verb*.]
► **A** *noun*. **1** A drug addict. E20.
2 **a** A hypodermic injection. E20. ► **b** A hypodermic needle or syringe. M20.
► **B** *verb trans.* Stimulate; excite, work up. Chiefly as ***hyped*** *pa. pple* & foll. by *up*. M20.

hyper /ˈhʌɪpə/ *noun*¹. L17.
[ORIGIN Abbreviation.]
†**1** = HYPERCRITIC *noun* 1. Only in L17.
2 = HYPER-CALVINIST. M19.

hyper /ˈhʌɪpə/ *noun*². *US slang*. E20.
[ORIGIN from HYPE *verb*¹ + -ER¹.]
A person who gives short change.

hyper /ˈhʌɪpə/ *adjective*. *slang*. M20.
[ORIGIN Abbreviation of HYPERACTIVE.]
Hyperactive, excitable; very highly strung; extraordinarily energetic.

M. BISHOP As tired as he was, he was too hyper to stretch out for some shut-eye. E. CURRIE My parents . . thought I was just a hyper kid.

hyper- /ˈhʌɪpə/ *combining form.*
[ORIGIN Greek *huper-*, from *huper* preposition & adverb, over, beyond, overmuch, above measure.]

1 Over, beyond, above, (*lit.* & *fig.*). Chiefly in adjectives, as ***hyperconstitutional***, ***hyperphysical***. ▸**b** MUSIC. In names of modes, denoting (***a***) each of a set of modes in ancient Greek music which began at a definite interval above the ordinary Aeolian etc. modes; (***b***) the authentic (Aeolian etc.) modes in medieval music as contrasted with the plagal (hypo-aeolian etc.) modes.

2 To excess, excessively; exceedingly. Chiefly in adjectives (& derived adverbs) & nouns, as ***hyperaccurate***, ***hypermodest***; ***hyperconservatism***, ***hyperscrupulosity***.

3 More than, greater than, as ***hyperfocal***, ***hypersonic***; (esp. MEDICINE) more than normal, as ***hyperacidity***. ▸**b** CHEMISTRY. In nouns denoting a compound in which a specified element is present in a higher proportion. Now largely superseded by PER-[1]. ▸**c** MATH. In nouns denoting an analogue in a space of four or more dimensions of a solid or figure of three-dimensional space.

■ **hyper'acid** *adjective* abnormally acid, characterized by hyperacidity L19. **hypera'cidity** *noun* a condition in which the gastrointestinal tract, esp. the stomach, is too acid, causing a burning sensation L19. **hypera'cute** *adjective* abnormally acute; MEDICINE (of tissue rejection) occurring within 48 hours of grafting: L19. **hyperalgesia** /-ˈdʒiːzɪə/ *noun* abnormally great sensitivity to pain L19. **hyperalgesic** /-ˈdʒiːzɪk/ *adjective* characterized by hyperalgesia L19. **hyperalgic** /-ˈaldʒɪk/ *adjective* = HYPERALGESIC M20. **hyperalimen'tation** *noun* (MEDICINE) intravenous supply of nutrients to patients incapable of normal digestion M20. **hypercal'caemia** *noun* (MEDICINE) an abnormally high concentration of calcium in the blood E20. **hypercal'caemic** *adjective* (MEDICINE) of or affected with hypercalcaemia M20. **hyper'capnia** *noun* [Greek *kapnos* smoke] MEDICINE an abnormally high concentration of carbon dioxide in the blood E20. **hyper'capnic** *adjective* (MEDICINE) of, pertaining to, or affected with hypercapnia M20. **hyperca'tharsis** *noun* (MEDICINE) excessive or violent purging, esp. by means of drugs L17. **hyper'cellular** *adjective* (MEDICINE) exhibiting hypercellularity M20. **hypercellu'larity** *noun* (MEDICINE) an excessive number of cells at a site in the body E20. **hyperchlor'hydria** *noun* (MEDICINE) an abnormally high concentration of hydrochloric acid in the gastric juice L19. **hyperchlor'hydric** *adjective* (MEDICINE) of, pertaining to, or characterized by hyperchlorhydria E20. **hypercholeste'raemia** *noun* (MEDICINE) = HYPERCHOLESTEROLAEMIA L19. **hypercholestero'laemia** *noun* (MEDICINE) an abnormally high concentration of cholesterol in the blood E20. **hypercholestero'laemic** *adjective* (MEDICINE) of or affected with hypercholesterolaemia E20. **hypercoagula'bility** *noun* (MEDICINE) an excessive tendency (of the blood) to coagulate M20. **hyperco'agulable** *adjective* (MEDICINE) characterized by hypercoagulability M20. **hypercolour** *noun* (PARTICLE PHYSICS) a hypothetical quantized property of bosons which is thought to form a strong interaction, analogous to the colour force L20. **hypercolumn** *noun* (ANATOMY & ZOOLOGY) an array of columns of neurons in the visual cortex of the brain L20. **hyper'complex** *adjective* (***a***) MATH. designating numbers such as quaternions that are generalizations of complex numbers for which multiplication is not commutative nor necessarily associative; (***b***) ANATOMY designating neurons of the visual cortex that respond only to visual stimuli satisfying certain conditions of orientation, size, etc.: L19. **hyper'conjugated** *adjective* (PHYSICAL CHEMISTRY) exhibiting hyperconjugation M20. **hyperconju'gation** *noun* (PHYSICAL CHEMISTRY) a direct attraction between the electrons of a methyl or substituted methyl group and the electrons of an adjacent conjugated system M20. **hyper'conscious** *adjective* acutely or excessively aware E20. **hyperco'rrect** *adjective & verb* (LINGUISTICS) (***a***) *adjective* (of a spelling, pronunciation, etc.) erroneous through being falsely modelled on an apparently analogous prestigeful form; (***b***) *verb trans. & intrans.* alter by or practise hypercorrection: E20. **hyperco'rrection** *noun* (LINGUISTICS) the use, or an instance, of hypercorrect spelling etc. M20. **hyperco'rrectness** *noun* (LINGUISTICS) the use of hypercorrect spelling etc. M20. **hypercube** *noun* (MATH.) an analogue in four or more dimensions of a cube in three dimensions E20. **hyper'diploid** *adjective & noun* (GENETICS) (***a***) *adjective* having one or a few chromosomes in excess of those of a diploid set; containing such cells; (***b***) *noun* a hyperdiploid individual: M20. **hyperdiploidy** *noun* (GENETICS) the condition of being hyperdiploid M20. **hyper'emesis** *noun* excessive vomiting, e.g. during pregnancy M19. **hyperen'demic** *adjective* (MEDICINE) permanently present in an area and affecting many individuals M20. **hypereu'tectic** *adjective* (of an alloy of iron) containing more carbon than the 4.3 per cent present in the eutectic composition E20. **hypereu'tectoid** *adjective* (of steel) containing more carbon than the 0.8 per cent present in the eutectoid composition E20. **hyperexcita'bility** *noun* the state or property of being hyperexcitable L19. **hyperex'citable** *adjective* abnormally excitable L19. **hyperex'tend** *verb trans.* (MEDICINE) bend (a limb, digit, etc.) so that it makes an abnormally great angle L19. **hyperextensi'bility** *noun* (MEDICINE) the property of being hyperextensible M20. **hyperex'tensible** *adjective* (MEDICINE) able to be hyperextended M20. **hyperex'tension** *noun* (MEDICINE) the state of being hyperextended; the action or an act of hyperextending a limb etc.: L19. **hyperfine** *adjective* (PHYSICS) designating or pertaining to (the presence of) closely spaced groups of lines in atomic spectra produced by coupling between the magnetic moment of the nucleus and the electromagnetic field of the orbital electrons E20. **hyper'focal** *adjective* designating or pertaining to the distance on which a camera must be focused for objects to be in focus over the greatest range of distances E20. **hyperform** *noun* (LINGUISTICS) a hypercorrect spelling or pronunciation M20. **hyperfunction** *noun & verb* (MEDICINE) (***a***) *noun* overactivity or overproduction in a gland etc.; (***b***) *verb intrans.* exhibit hyperfunction: E20. **hyper'functional** *adjective* (MEDICINE) exhibiting hyperfunction M20. **hypergamma,globuli'naemia** *noun* (MEDICINE) an abnormally high concentration of gamma globulin in the blood M20. **hypergamma,globuli'naemic** *adjective* (MEDICINE) characterized by hypergammaglobulinaemia L20. **hy'pergamous** *adjective* (ANTHROPOLOGY) of or pertaining to hypergamy L19. **hy'pergamy** *noun* (ANTHROPOLOGY) (the custom of) marriage to a person, esp. a husband, of superior standing L19. **hypergeo'metric** *adjective* (MATH.) designating or pertaining to a series of the kind 1, abx/c, $a(a+1)b(b+1)x^2/2!c^2$, etc. L19. **hypergeo'metrical** *adjective* (MATH.) = HYPERGEOMETRIC E19. **hypergeusia** /-ˈgjuːzɪə, -sɪə/ *noun* [Greek *geusis* taste] MEDICINE increased acuteness of the sense of taste L19. **hyper'gluon** *noun* (PARTICLE PHYSICS) a hypothetical particle bearing the same relation to hypercolour that gluons do to colour L20. **hypergly'caemia** *noun* (MEDICINE) an abnormally high concentration of sugar in the blood L19. **hypergly'caemic** *adjective* (MEDICINE) of, pertaining to, or characterized by hyperglycaemia E20. **hyperhi'drosis** *noun* (MEDICINE) excessive sweating M19. **hyperin'flation** *noun* a very high rate of monetary inflation M20. **hyperin'flationary** *adjective* of or pertaining to hyperinflation M20. **hyperinsuli'naemia** *noun* (MEDICINE) an abnormally high concentration of insulin in the blood E20. **hyperinsuli'naemic** *adjective* (MEDICINE) characterized by hyperinsulinaemia M20. **hyper'insulinism** *noun* (MEDICINE) excessive production of insulin by the pancreas; hyperinsulinaemia: E20. **hyperirrita'bility** *noun* (MEDICINE) abnormally high sensitivity to stimuli, esp. nervous stimuli E20. **hyper'irritable** *adjective* (MEDICINE) characterized by hyperirritability E20. **hyperka'laemia** *noun* [mod. Latin *kalium* potassium] MEDICINE an abnormally high concentration of potassium in the blood M20. **hyperka'laemic** *adjective* (MEDICINE) characterized by hyperkalaemia M20. **hyperkera'tosis** *noun*, pl. **-toses** /-ˈtəʊsiːz/, MEDICINE †(***a***) staphyloma of the cornea; (***b***) a thickening of the outer layer of the skin: M19. **hyperkera'totic** *adjective* (MEDICINE) of or characterized by hyperkeratosis M20. **hyperki'nesia** *noun* (MEDICINE) = HYPERKINESIS M19. **hyperki'nesis** *noun* (MEDICINE) an abnormal degree of muscular or bodily activity; *spec.* (***a***) muscle spasm; (***b***) a disorder of children marked by hyperactivity and an inability to attend: M19. **hyperki'netic** *adjective* (MEDICINE) characterized by hyperkinesis L19. **hyperlink** *noun & verb* (COMPUTING) (***a***) *noun* a link from a hypertext file or document to another location or file, typically activated by clicking on a highlighted word or image at a particular location on the screen; (***b***) *verb trans.* link (a file) in this way: L20. **hyperli'paemia** *noun* (MEDICINE) an abnormally high concentration of fats or lipids in the blood L19. **hyperli'paemic** *adjective* (MEDICINE) of or characterized by hyperlipaemia M20. **hyperlipi'daemia** *noun* (MEDICINE) = HYPERLIPAEMIA M20. **hyperlipi'daemic** *adjective* (MEDICINE) = HYPERLIPAEMIC M20. **hypermeta'bolic** *adjective* of or involving hypermetabolism M20. **hyperme'tabolism** *noun* metabolism at a high rate M20. **hypermeta'morphic** *adjective* (ENTOMOLOGY) undergoing metamorphosis through two or more larval stages L19. **hyperm'nesia** *noun* [Greek *mnēsis* memory] unusual power of memory M19. **hyperm'nesic** *adjective* pertaining to hypermnesia; accompanied by exceptionally vivid or detailed memories: M20. **hyper'mobile** *adjective* characterized by or exhibiting hypermobility E20. **hypermo'bility** *noun* abnormally great freedom of movement or flexibility in a joint E20. **hyper'modern** *adjective* excessively modern; *spec.* in CHESS, of or pertaining to the strategy of controlling the centre of the board with pieces at a distance (first used in the early 20th cent.): E20. **hypermorph** *noun* (GENETICS) an allele that is functionally more effective than a corresponding wild-type allele M20. **hyper'morphic** *adjective* (GENETICS) designating, of, or pertaining to a hypermorph M20. **hyper'mutable** *adjective* (GENETICS) of or in a state in which mutation is abnormally frequent M20. **hyperna'traemia** *noun* (MEDICINE) an abnormally high concentration of sodium in the blood M20. **hyperna'traemic** *adjective* (MEDICINE) characterized by hypernatraemia M20. **hyper'oestrogenism** *noun* (MEDICINE) excessive production of oestrogens by the body M20. **hyperosmo'lality** *noun* (MEDICINE) = HYPEROSMOLARITY M20. **hyperos'molar** *adjective* (MEDICINE) accompanied by or characterized by hyperosmolarity M20. **hyperosmo'larity** *noun* (MEDICINE) an abnormally high osmotic pressure of the blood serum of a person M20. **hyperpara'thyroid** *adjective* (MEDICINE) of, affected with, or accompanied by hyperparathyroidism M20. **hyperpara'thyroidism** *noun* (MEDICINE) a condition in which there is an abnormally high concentration of parathyroid hormone in the blood, resulting in loss of calcium from the bones, which become soft E20. **hyperphagia** /-ˈfeɪdʒɪə, -dʒə/ *noun* (MEDICINE) an abnormally great desire for food; excessive eating: M20. **hyperphagic** /-ˈfadʒɪk/ *adjective* (MEDICINE) of or exhibiting hyperphagia M20. **hyperpha'langia**, **hyperpha'langism**, **hyper'phalangy** *nouns* (MEDICINE & ZOOLOGY) the condition of having an additional digital phalanx, esp. in the absence of polydactyly L19. **hyper'phoria** *noun* (MEDICINE) latent strabismus in which there is a tendency for one eye to be directed above (or below) the line of sight of the other L19. **hyper'phoric** *adjective* (MEDICINE) of or affected with hyperphoria L19. **hyperphospha'taemia** *noun* (MEDICINE) an abnormally high concentration of phosphate (or other phosphorus compounds) in the blood E20. **hyperphospha'taemic** *adjective* (MEDICINE) pertaining to or characterized by hyperphosphataemia M20. **hyperpigmen'tation** *noun* (MEDICINE) excessive pigmentation of the skin L19. **hyperpi'tuitarism** *noun* (MEDICINE) increased hormone secretion by the pituitary E20. **hyperpi'tuitary** *adjective* (MEDICINE) of, pertaining to, or affected with hyperpituitarism E20. **hyperplane** *noun* (MATH.) an analogue in four or more dimensions of a plane in three dimensions E20. **hyperploid** *adjective & noun* (GENETICS) (***a***) *adjective* having one or a few chromosomes in excess of those of a haploid or polyploid set; containing such cells; (***b***) *noun* a hyperploid individual: M20. **hyperploidy** *noun* (GENETICS) the condition of being hyperploid M20. **hyperpolari'zation** *noun* (PHYSIOLOGY) an increase in the potential difference across the membrane of a nerve fibre M20. **hyper'polarize** *verb* (PHYSIOLOGY) (***a***) *verb trans. & intrans.* produce hyperpolarization (in); (***b***) *verb intrans.* undergo hyperpolarization: M20. **hyperprolacti'naemia** *noun* (MEDICINE) an abnormally high concentration of prolactin in the blood L20. **hyperprolacti'naemic** *adjective* (MEDICINE) of or characterized by hyperprolactinaemia L20. **hyperpy'retic** *adjective* (MEDICINE) of hyperpyrexia L19. **hyperpy'rexia** *noun* (MEDICINE) fever marked by an exceptionally high temperature L19. **hyperpy'rexial** *adjective* (MEDICINE) hyperpyretic L19. **hyper'realism** *noun* = PHOTOREALISM L20. **hyper'realist** *noun* a person who practises hyperrealism L20. **hyper'rhythmical** *adjective* = HYPERMETRIC E17. **hyper'saline** *adjective* (of natural water) more salty than typical seawater M20. **hypersa'linity** *noun* the condition of being hypersaline M20. **hyperse'crete** *verb intrans.* (MEDICINE) produce an increased amount of secretion (chiefly as ***hypersecreting*** *ppl adjective.*) E20. **hyperse'cretion** *noun* (MEDICINE) increased secretion M19. **hyper'sexed** *adjective* having an exceptionally strong sexual instinct M20. **hyper'sexual** *adjective* exhibiting or associated with hypersexuality M20. **hypersexu'ality** *noun* a condition in which the sexual instinct is exceptionally strong E20. **hyper'somnia** *noun* a condition in which a person has abnormally long or frequent periods of sleep, or sleeps abnormally deeply L19. **hyper'somnic** *adjective* causing hypersomnia; hypersomnolent: E20. **hyper'somnolence** *adjective* = HYPERSOMNIA L20. **hyper'somnolent** *adjective* of or affected with hypersomnia M20. **hypersphere** *noun* (MATH.) an analogue in four or more dimensions of a sphere in three dimensions E20. **hyper'spherical** *adjective* (MATH.) of or pertaining to a hypersphere L19. **hyper'splenic** *adjective* (MEDICINE) of or characterized by hypersplenism M20. **hyper'splenism** *noun* (MEDICINE) a condition in which there is a reduced number of circulating blood cells accompanied by an enlarged spleen E20. **hyper'static** *adjective* (of an engineering structure) having more members or supports than the minimum required for stability M20. **hyper'telorism** *noun* [Greek *tēle* at a distance + *orizein* to separate from] MEDICINE a developmental abnormality in which the eyes are abnormally far apart E20. **hyper'tensin** *noun* (BIOCHEMISTRY) = ANGIOTENSIN M20. **hyper'thyroid** *adjective* (MEDICINE) affected with or symptomatic of hyperthyroidism E20. **hyperthy'roidic** *adjective* (MEDICINE) = HYPERTHYROID E20. **hyper'thyroidism** *noun* (MEDICINE) a condition in which the thyroid produces more hormone than normal, resulting in an increased rate of metabolism and often loss of weight, restlessness, and emotional instability E20. **hyper'trichosis** /-trɪˈkəʊsɪs/ *noun* [TRICHO-[1]] excessive growth of hair L19. **hypertriglyceri'daemia** *noun* (MEDICINE) an abnormally high concentration of triglycerides in the blood M20. **hypertriglyceri'daemic** *adjective* (MEDICINE) of or affected with hypertriglyceridaemia M20. **hyper'tropia** *noun* (MEDICINE) strabismus in which one eye is directed above or below the line of sight of the other L19. **hyper'urban** *adjective* exhibiting hyperurbanism E20. **hyper'urbanism** *noun* a manner of speech arising from an effort to avoid provincialism; a hypercorrect form of speech or phrase resulting from this effort: E20. **hyperuri'caemia** *noun* (MEDICINE) an abnormally high concentration of uric acid in the blood L19. **hyperuri'caemic** *adjective* (MEDICINE) of or affected with hyperuricaemia M20. **hyperve,locity** *noun* a speed that is very great; usu. *attrib.*: M20. **hypervitami'nosis** *noun*, pl. **-noses** /-ˈnəʊsiːz/, MEDICINE any condition caused by an excessive intake of a vitamin, esp. over a prolonged period E20. **hyper'weak** *adjective* (PHYSICS) designating a hypothetical fifth interaction M20.

hyperacousis *noun* var. of HYPERACUSIS.

hyperactive /hʌɪpərˈaktɪv/ *adjective.* M19.
[ORIGIN from HYPER- + ACTIVE.]
Abnormally active, very active; *spec.* (of a person, esp. a child) unable to relax or be quiet.
■ **hyperac'tivity** *noun* L19.

hyperacusis /hʌɪpərəˈk(j)uːsɪs/ *noun.* Also **-cou-**, **-ku-**, **-usia** /-uːsɪə/. E19.
[ORIGIN from HYPER- + Greek *akousis* hearing.]
Abnormally acute hearing, often with pain from moderately loud sounds.

hyperaemia /hʌɪpərˈiːmɪə/ *noun.* Also ***-rem-**. M19.
[ORIGIN from HYPER- + -AEMIA.]
The presence of more than the normal amount of blood in a part of the body.
■ **hyperaemic** *adjective* M19.

hyperaesthesia /hʌɪpəriːsˈθiːzɪə, -ɛsˈθiː-/ *noun.* Also ***-res-**. M19.
[ORIGIN from HYPER- + Greek *aisthēsis* sensation: see -IA[1].]
Abnormally great sensitivity of the body or mind, esp. of the skin.

hyperaesthetic /hʌɪpəriːsˈθɛtɪk, -ɛsˈθɛ-/ *adjective.* Also ***-res-**. M19.
[ORIGIN from HYPER- + Greek *aisthētikos*: see AESTHETIC.]
1 Characterized by hyperaesthesia. M19.
2 Excessively aesthetic. L19.

hyperakusis *noun* var. of HYPERACUSIS.

†**hyperaspist** *noun.* E17–M18.
[ORIGIN Greek *huperaspistēs*, from *huperaspizein* hold a shield over, formed as HYPER- + *aspis* shield.]
A defender, a champion.

hyperbaric /hʌɪpəˈbarɪk/ *adjective.* M20.
[ORIGIN from HYPER- + Greek *baros* heavy + -IC.]
1 MEDICINE. Of a solution for spinal anaesthesia: denser than cerebrospinal fluid. M20.
2 Designating, employing, or pertaining to gas at a greater pressure than its partial pressure in the atmosphere, or at greater than atmospheric pressure. M20.

> *Offshore* A new record for hyperbaric welding . . at a simulated depth of 300 metres. L. OLIVIER Two surgeons . . decided that the best thing for me would be hyperbaric oxygen irradiation.

hyperbaton /hʌɪˈpəːbətɒn/ *noun.* M16.
[ORIGIN Latin from Greek *huperbaton* overstepping, from *huperbainein*, formed as HYPER- + *bainein* walk.]
GRAMMAR & RHETORIC. A figure of speech in which the logical order of words or phrases is inverted, esp. for the sake of emphasis.

hyperbola /hʌɪˈpəːbələ/ *noun.* Pl. **-las**, **-lae** /-liː/. M17.
[ORIGIN mod. Latin from Greek *huperbolē*: see HYPERBOLE.]
MATH. A conic section consisting of two identical curves formed where a plane intersects a double cone and makes a smaller angle with the axis of the cone than the

H

side of the cone makes; either of these curves individually, which consist of two infinitely long arms that are asymptotic to two straight lines that intersect midway between the two curves; a curve that is the graph of an equation of the type $x^2/a^2 - y^2/b^2 = 1$.

hyperbole /hʌɪˈpəːbəli/ *noun*. LME.
[ORIGIN Latin from Greek *huperbolē* excess, exaggeration, formed as HYPER- + *ballein* to throw.]
1 A figure of speech consisting in exaggerated or extravagant statement, used to express strong feeling or produce a strong impression and not meant to be taken literally; an instance of this. LME. ▸**b** *gen.* Excess, extravagance. *rare*. M17.

G. K. CHESTERTON Received with extravagant but dignified bows, and hyperboles of thanks. T. COLLINS The place was a residence, but by no stretch of hyperbole could you call it a home.

†**2** = HYPERBOLA. L16–E18.

hyperbolic /hʌɪpəˈbɒlɪk/ *adjective*. M17.
[ORIGIN Late Latin *hyperbolicus* from Greek *huperbolikos*, from *huperbolē* HYPERBOLE: see -IC.]
1 = HYPERBOLICAL 1. M17.
2 Of, belonging to, or of the form of a hyperbola; related mathematically to the hyperbola. L17.
hyperbolic COSINE. **hyperbolic function** each of a set of functions that bear the same algebraic relation to a rectangular hyperbola as the trigonometric functions do to a circle. **hyperbolic geometry** a non-Euclidean geometry defined so that a line may have more than one parallel through a given point. **hyperbolic navigation**: in which the position of a receiver is on the intersection of two hyperbolas, each determined by the difference at the receiver between signals transmitted in synchronism by one or other of two pairs of radio stations. *hyperbolic sine*: see SINE 2. *hyperbolic tangent*: see TANGENT *noun* 1.
▪ **hyperbolicity** /-ˈlɪsɪti/ *noun* the property of being hyperbolic M20.

hyperbolical /hʌɪpəˈbɒlɪk(ə)l/ *adjective*. LME.
[ORIGIN formed as HYPERBOLIC + -AL[1].]
1 Of the nature of, involving, or using hyperbole; exaggerated, extravagant (in language or expression). LME. ▸†**b** Extravagant in character or behaviour; excessive; enormous. L16–M19.
2 = HYPERBOLIC 2. M16.
▪ **hyperbolically** *adverb* with hyperbole or exaggeration M16.

hyperbolism /hʌɪˈpəːbəlɪz(ə)m/ *noun*. M17.
[ORIGIN formed as HYPERBOLIZE + -ISM. In sense 2 from mod. Latin *hyperbolismus*.]
1 The use of or fondness for hyperbole; (an instance of) exaggerated style. M17.
2 MATH. A curve whose equation is obtained from that of another curve by substituting *xy* for *y*. Now *rare*. M19.
▪ **hyperbolist** *noun* a person given to the use of hyperbole M17.

hyperbolize /hʌɪˈpəːbəlʌɪz/ *verb*. Also **-ise**. L16.
[ORIGIN from HYPERBOLE + -IZE.]
1 *verb intrans.* Use hyperbole; exaggerate. L16.
2 *verb trans.* Express or represent hyperbolically, exaggerate. Formerly also, praise extravagantly. L16.

hyperboloid /hʌɪˈpəːbəlɔɪd/ *noun*. M18.
[ORIGIN from HYPERBOLA + -OID.]
MATH. A curved solid or surface for which the cross-sections parallel to one axis are hyperbolas and those parallel to either of the other two axes are ellipses or circles.
▪ **hyperboˈloidal** *adjective* L19.

†**Hyperboreal** *adjective*. *rare*. L16–L18.
[ORIGIN from HYPER- + BOREAL.]
= HYPERBOREAN *adjective* 1.

Hyperborean /hʌɪpəbɔːˈriːən, -ˈbɔːrɪən/ *noun* & *adjective*. LME.
[ORIGIN Late Latin *hyperboreanus* = classical Latin *hyperboreus* from Greek *huperbore(i)os*, formed as HYPER- + *boreios* northern, *boreas* BOREAS: see -AN.]
▸**A** *noun*. A member of a race of people who in Greek mythology lived in a land of sunshine and plenty beyond the north wind, worshipping Apollo; (also **h-**) a person who lives in the extreme north of the earth. LME.
▸**B** *adjective*. **1** (Also **h-**.) Of, pertaining to, or characterizing the extreme north of the earth or (*joc.* & *colloq.*) of a particular country. L16.
2 Of or pertaining to the Hyperboreans of mythology. E17.

hyper-Calvinist /hʌɪpəˈkalvɪnɪst/ *noun*. M19.
[ORIGIN from HYPER- + CALVINIST.]
THEOLOGY. A person who holds a doctrine (esp. of predestination) more Calvinistic than Calvin's own.
▪ **hyper-Calvinism** *noun* L19. **hyper-Calviˈnistic** *adjective* L19.

hypercatalectic /ˌhʌɪpəkatəˈlɛktɪk/ *noun* & *adjective*. E17.
[ORIGIN Late Latin *hypercatalecticus* from Greek *huperkatalēktos*, formed as HYPER- + *katalēktikos*: see CATALECTIC.]
▸†**A** *noun*. A hypercatalectic line, verse, or colon. Only in E17.
▸**B** *adjective*. PROSODY. Of a line, verse, or colon: having an extra syllable after the last complete dipody. Of a syllable: constituting such a syllable. E18.

hypercharge /ˈhʌɪpətʃɑːdʒ/ *noun*. M20.
[ORIGIN from *hyper(onic) charge*.]
PARTICLE PHYSICS. A property of hadrons that is conserved in strong interactions, represented by a quantum number Y whose value for each particle of a charge multiplet is equal to twice the average charge quantum number of the multiplet.

hyperchromasia /hʌɪpəkrəˈmeɪzɪə/ *noun*. L19.
[ORIGIN from HYPER- + -CHROMASIA.]
1 MEDICINE. **a** Excessive pigmentation of the skin. L19. ▸**b** = HYPERCHROMIA. E20.
2 CYTOLOGY. The presence of an abnormally large amount of chromatin in a cell or nucleus. M20.
▪ **hyperchromatic** /-ˈmat-/ *adjective* characterized by or exhibiting hyperchromasia; hyperchromic: L19.

hyperchromatosis /ˌhʌɪpəkrəʊməˈtəʊsɪs/ *noun*. Pl. **-toses** /-ˈtəʊsiːz/. L19.
[ORIGIN from HYPER- + CHROMATO-, CHROMAT(IN + -OSIS.]
1 CYTOLOGY. The presence of an abnormally large number of chromosomes or amount of chromatin in a nucleus; hyperchromasia. L19.
2 MEDICINE. = HYPERCHROMASIA 1a. L19.

hyperchromia /hʌɪpəˈkrəʊmɪə/ *noun*. M20.
[ORIGIN formed as HYPERCHROMIC + -IA[1].]
MEDICINE. A hyperchromic condition of the blood.

hyperchromic /hʌɪpəˈkrəʊmɪk/ *adjective*. L19.
[ORIGIN from HYPER- + Greek *khrōma* colour + -IC.]
1 CYTOLOGY. Characterized by or exhibiting hyperchromasia. L19.
2 MEDICINE. Characterized by or designating red cells that contain more than the usual amount of haemoglobin and show little central pallor. E20.
3 Characterized by or exhibiting an increase in the extent to which light, esp. ultraviolet light, is absorbed. M20.
▪ **hyperchromicity** /-ˈmɪs-/ *noun* the property of being hyperchromic M20.

hypercritic /hʌɪpəˈkrɪtɪk/ *noun* & *adjective*. L16.
[ORIGIN mod. Latin *hypercriticus*, formed as CRITIC *noun*[1]: see HYPER-.]
▸**A** *noun*. †**1** Hypercriticism; a minute criticism; a critique. L16–M18.
2 A hypercritical person. Formerly, a master critic. M17.
▸**B** *adjective*. = HYPERCRITICAL. E19.

hypercritical /hʌɪpəˈkrɪtɪk(ə)l/ *adjective*. E17.
[ORIGIN from HYPER- + CRITICAL.]
Apt to give excessive adverse criticism, esp. on trivial points; extremely or unduly critical.
▪ **hyperˈcritically** *adverb* E18.

hypercriticism /hʌɪpəˈkrɪtɪsɪz(ə)m/ *noun*. L17.
[ORIGIN from HYPER- + CRITICISM.]
Excessive criticism; criticism that is unduly severe.

hypercriticize /hʌɪpəˈkrɪtɪsʌɪz/ *verb trans.* & *intrans.* Also **-ise**. E18.
[ORIGIN from HYPER- + CRITICIZE.]
Criticize excessively or unduly; be hypercritical.

hyperdisyllable /hʌɪpəˈdʌɪsɪləb(ə)l/ *noun* & *adjective*. L17.
[ORIGIN from HYPER- + DISYLLABLE. Cf. late Greek *huperdisullabos*.]
(A word) consisting of more than two syllables.

hyperdrive /ˈhʌɪpədrʌɪv/ *noun*. M20.
[ORIGIN from HYPER- + DRIVE *noun*, perh. suggested by HYPERSPACE, OVERDRIVE *noun*.]
In science fiction: a fictitious device by which a spaceship is enabled to travel to a distant point in a shorter time than light would take to reach it; the state of so travelling.

hyperdulia /hʌɪpədjʊˈlʌɪə/ *noun*. M16.
[ORIGIN medieval Latin *hyperdulia*, formed as HYPER-, DULIA.]
ROMAN CATHOLIC CHURCH. The veneration properly given to the Virgin Mary, higher than dulia but less than latria.
▪ **hyperdulic** *adjective* of the nature of hyperdulia M19. **hyperdulical** *adjective* = HYPERDULIC M17.

hyperemia *noun* see HYPERAEMIA.

hyperesthesia *noun*, **hyperesthetic** *adjective* see HYPERAESTHESIA etc.

hypergelast /hʌɪˈpəːdʒɪlast/ *noun*. L19.
[ORIGIN from HYPER- + Greek *gelastēs* laugher, from *gelan* to laugh.]
A person who laughs excessively.

hypergolic /hʌɪpəˈgɒlɪk/ *adjective*. M20.
[ORIGIN from German *Hypergol*, prob. from Greek *ergon* work + -OL + -IC.]
Of a rocket propellant: igniting spontaneously on contact with the oxidizer or another propellant.
▪ **hypergol** *noun* a hypergolic rocket propellant M20.

hypericin /hʌɪˈpɛrɪsɪn/ *noun*. M20.
[ORIGIN from HYPERICUM + -IN[1].]
PHARMACOLOGY. A quinone, $C_{30}H_{14}O_8$, found in the leaves and flowers of St John's wort, which is credited with anti-depressant, cytotoxic, and antiviral properties and is used in herbal remedies for depression.

hypericum /hʌɪˈpɛrɪkəm/ *noun*. Also †**-con**. LME.
[ORIGIN Latin *hypericum*, *-con* from Greek *hupereikon*, from *huper* over + *ereikē* heath.]
1 Any of various herbaceous plants or small shrubs of the genus *Hypericum* (family Guttiferae), with pentamerous usu. yellow flowers, stamens in bundles, and leaves usu. with glandular dots beneath. Also called ***St John's wort***, ***rose of Sharon***. LME.
†**2** A medicinal preparation made from this plant. LME–L17.

hyperinosis /hʌɪpərɪˈnəʊsɪs/ *noun*. Now *rare* or *obsolete*. Pl. **-noses** /-ˈnəʊsiːz/. M19.
[ORIGIN from HYPER- + Greek *inos*, *is* fibre + -OSIS.]
MEDICINE. An abnormally high concentration of fibrinogen in the blood.
▪ **hyperinotic** /-ˈnɒtɪk/ *adjective* M19.

hypermarket /ˈhʌɪpəmɑːkɪt/ *noun*. L20.
[ORIGIN from HYPER- + MARKET *noun* as translation of French *hypermarché*, from *marché* market, after *supermarché* SUPERMARKET.]
A very large self-service shop or complex of shops that sells a wide range of goods and is usually sited outside a town near a large car park.

hypermedia /hʌɪpəˈmiːdɪə/ *noun*. M20.
[ORIGIN from HYPER- + MEDIA *noun*[2].]
COMPUTING. A method of structuring information in different media for presentation to a user (usu. via a workstation) whereby related items of information are interconnected. Cf. HYPERTEXT.

hypermetric /hʌɪpəˈmɛtrɪk/ *adjective*. M19.
[ORIGIN from HYPER- + METRIC *adjective*[2].]
PROSODY. (Of a verse or line) containing an extra syllable; designating such a syllable.
▪ Also **hyperˈmetrical** *adjective* M18.

hypermetropia /hʌɪpəmɪˈtrəʊpɪə/ *noun*. M19.
[ORIGIN from Greek *hupermetros* beyond measure (formed as HYPER- + *metron* measure) + -OPIA.]
The condition in which rays from distant objects are focused behind the retina instead of on it when the eye is relaxed, and the eye cannot be focused on objects near it; long-sightedness.
▪ **hyperˈmetrope** *noun* a person with hypermetropia M19. **hypermetropic** /-ˈtrəʊpɪk, -ˈtrɒpɪk/ *adjective* pertaining to or affected with hypermetropia M19.

hypernym /ˈhʌɪpənɪm/ *noun*. L20.
[ORIGIN from HYPER- after *hyponym*.]
LINGUISTICS. A word whose meaning is implied by another and in terms of which the other word can be defined (e.g. *building* in relation to *house* or *hotel*).

hyperon /ˈhʌɪp(ə)rɒn/ *noun*. M20.
[ORIGIN from HYPER- + -ON.]
PARTICLE PHYSICS. A baryon other than a proton or neutron.
xi hyperon: see XI 2.
▪ **hypeˈronic** *adjective* M20.

hyperoodon /hʌɪpərˈəʊədɒn/ *noun*. M19.
[ORIGIN from Greek *huperōios* superior or *huperōiē* palate + -ODON.]
A bottlenose whale (genus *Hyperoodon*).

hyperopia /hʌɪpərˈəʊpɪə/ *noun*. L19.
[ORIGIN from HYPER- + -OPIA.]
= HYPERMETROPIA.
▪ **hyperope** /ˈhʌɪpərəʊp/ *noun* = HYPERMETROPE M20. **hyperopic** /-ˈɒpɪk/ *adjective* L19.

hyperostosis /hʌɪpərɒˈstəʊsɪs/ *noun*. Pl. **-stoses** /-ˈstəʊsiːz/. M19.
[ORIGIN from HYPER- + Greek *osteon*, *osto-* bone + -OSIS.]
A non-tumorous localized overgrowth of bone; excessive production of bone tissue.
▪ **hyperostotic** /-ˈstɒtɪk/ *adjective* M19.

hyperoxygenate /hʌɪpərˈɒksɪdʒəneɪt/ *verb trans.* L18.
[ORIGIN from HYPER- + OXYGENATE.]
Cause to contain or (now *rare*) combine with an increased proportion of oxygen; supersaturate (blood) with oxygen. Chiefly as ***hyperoxygenated*** pa. pple.

W. GOLDING The Dôle and the hyperoxygenated air did their work and I fell asleep.

▪ **ˌhyperoxygeˈnation** *noun* the action of hyperoxygenating something; the state of being hyperoxygenated: L18.

hyperparasite /hʌɪpəˈparəsʌɪt/ *noun*. L19.
[ORIGIN from HYPER- + PARASITE *noun*.]
BIOLOGY. A parasite whose host is itself a parasite.
▪ **hyperparaˈsitic** *adjective* parasitic on or in a parasite M19. **hyperparasitism** *noun* the condition of being hyperparasitic L19.

hyperper /hʌɪˈpəːpə/ *noun*. L16.
[ORIGIN medieval Latin *hyperperum*, *-pyrum* from Greek *huperpuron*, formed as HYPER- + *pur* FIRE *noun*.]
The Byzantine gold solidus.

hyperphysical /hʌɪpəˈfɪzɪk(ə)l/ *adjective*. E17.
[ORIGIN from HYPER- + PHYSICAL.]
Above or beyond what is physical; supernatural.

hyperplasia /hʌɪpəˈpleɪzɪə/ *noun*. M19.
[ORIGIN from HYPER- + -PLASIA.]
MEDICINE. Enlargement of tissue (usu. abnormal but non-tumorous) as a result of an increase in the number of cells. Cf. HYPERTROPHY *noun*
▪ **hyperplastic** /-ˈplastɪk/ *adjective* exhibiting or accompanied by hyperplasia L19.

hyperpnoea /hʌɪpəpˈniːə/ *noun*. Also *-**pnea**. M19.
[ORIGIN from HYPER- + Greek *pnoē* breathing: see -A[1].]
Deep or rapid breathing.
■ **hyperpnoeic** *adjective* of or exhibiting hyperpnoea E20.

hypersensitise *verb* var. of HYPERSENSITIZE.

hypersensitive /hʌɪpəˈsɛnsɪtɪv/ *adjective*. L19.
[ORIGIN from HYPER- + SENSITIVE.]
1 Sensitive to an abnormal or excessive degree; (of a person) easily hurt or offended, oversensitive. L19.
2 MEDICINE. Of an individual: having an adverse bodily reaction to a particular substance in doses that do not affect most individuals. L19.
3 Of a photographic film etc.: hypersensitized. M20.
■ **hypersensitiveness** *noun* L19. **hypersensiˈtivity** *noun* E20.

hypersensitize /hʌɪpəˈsɛnsɪtʌɪz/ *verb trans*. Also -**ise**. L19.
[ORIGIN from HYPER- + SENSITIZE.]
Make hypersensitive; PHOTOGRAPHY increase the speed of (a film etc.) by a special process before it is used.
■ ˌ**hypersensitiˈzation** *noun* the action or process of hypersensitizing someone or something; the state of being hypersensitized: E20.

hypersonic /hʌɪpəˈsɒnɪk/ *adjective*. M20.
[ORIGIN from HYPER- + SONIC, after *supersonic*, *ultrasonic*.]
1 Designating, of, or pertaining to sound waves or vibrations with a frequency greater than about 1000 million Hz. M20.
2 Designating, involving, or pertaining to speeds greater than about five times the speed of sound; (of aircraft) able to fly at such speeds. Cf. SUPERSONIC. M20.
■ **hypersonically** *adverb* at a hypersonic speed L20. **hypersonics** *noun* the branch of science and technology that deals with hypersonic phenomena, esp. hypersonic flight M20.

hyperspace /ˈhʌɪpəspeɪs/ *noun*. M19.
[ORIGIN from HYPER- + SPACE *noun*.]
1 Space of more than three dimensions; any non-Euclidean space. M19.
2 SCIENCE FICTION. A hypothetical space–time continuum, through which motion and communication at effective speeds greater than that of light are supposed to be possible. Also called *subspace*. M20.

D. ADAMS An old drinking game that Ford learned to play in the hyperspace ports . . in the star system of Orion Beta.

■ **hyperˈspatial** *adjective* of or occurring in hyperspace E20. **hyperspatiˈality** *noun* the property of being hyperspatial; travel in hyperspace: E20.

hypersthene /ˈhʌɪpəsθiːn/ *noun*. E19.
[ORIGIN French *hypersthène*, formed as HYPERSTHENIA, from its being harder than hornblende.]
MINERALOGY. A rock-forming orthorhombic silicate of magnesium and ferrous iron that is a member of the pyroxene group and is green, yellow, brown, or black in colour.
■ **hypersthenite** *noun* orig., norite; now, a pyroxenite composed almost wholly of hypersthene: M19.

hypersthenia /hʌɪpəsˈθiːnɪə/ *noun*. M19.
[ORIGIN from HYPER- + Greek *sthenos* strength + -IA[1].]
An abnormal degree of bodily strength or vitality.

hypersthenic /hʌɪpəsˈθɛnɪk/ *adjective*[1]. M19.
[ORIGIN from HYPERSTHENE + -IC.]
MINERALOGY. Pertaining to or containing hypersthene.

hypersthenic /hʌɪpəsˈθɛnɪk/ *adjective*[2]. L19.
[ORIGIN from HYPERSTHENIA + -IC.]
Exhibiting or characterized by hypersthenia.

hypertely /hʌɪˈpəːtɪli, ˈhʌɪpətɛli/ *noun*. L19.
[ORIGIN German *Hypertelie*, from Greek *huperteleios* beyond completeness, formed as HYPER- + *telos* end.]
ZOOLOGY. Extreme development of a characteristic beyond the degree to which it is apparently useful.
■ **hyperˈtelic** *adjective* M20.

hypertension /hʌɪpəˈtɛnʃ(ə)n/ *noun*. L19.
[ORIGIN from HYPER- + TENSION *noun*.]
1 Abnormally or excessively high pressure of arterial blood or intra-ocular fluid, *spec.* the former. L19.

B. EMECHETA They were . . sending themselves to early graves with hypertension.

2 A state of great emotional or nervous tension. M20.
■ **hypertensive** *adjective & noun* (*a*) *adjective* of, exhibiting, or associated with hypertension; tending to increase a person's blood pressure; (*b*) *noun* a person with (arterial) hypertension: E20.

hypertext /ˈhʌɪpətɛkst/ *noun*. M20.
[ORIGIN from HYPER- + TEXT *noun*.]
COMPUTING. A body of text, graphic material, etc., stored in a machine-readable form and structured in such a way that a reader can cross-refer between related items of information.
■ **hyperˈtextual** *adjective* L20.

hyperthermia /hʌɪpəˈθəːmɪə/ *noun*. L19.
[ORIGIN from HYPER- + Greek *thermē* heat + -IA[1].]
The condition of having a body temperature substantially above the normal, whether through natural causes or artificially induced.
■ **hyperthermic** *adjective* of or exhibiting hyperthermia L19.

hypertonia /hʌɪpəˈtəʊnɪə/ *noun*. M19.
[ORIGIN from HYPER- + Greek *tonos* TONE *noun* + -IA[1].]
MEDICINE. The condition of being hypertonic.

hypertonic /hʌɪpəˈtɒnɪk/ *adjective*. M19.
[ORIGIN from HYPER- + TONIC *adjective*.]
1 MEDICINE. (Of muscle) in a state of abnormally great tone or tension; of or characterized by muscle in such a state. M19.
2 PHYSIOLOGY. Having a higher osmotic pressure than some particular fluid (usually that in a cell, or a body fluid). L19.
■ **hypertonicity** /-ˈnɪsɪti/ *noun* the condition of being hypertonic; the extent to which a solution has a higher osmotic pressure than another: L19.

hypertonus /hʌɪpəˈtəʊnəs/ *noun*. L19.
[ORIGIN from HYPER- + TONUS.]
1 Hypertension of the intra-ocular fluid. Now *rare*. L19.
2 = HYPERTONIA. E20.

hypertrophy /hʌɪˈpəːtrəfi/ *noun & verb*. M19.
[ORIGIN from HYPER- + -TROPHY.]
▸ **A** *noun*. Enlargement of tissue (usu. abnormal but non-tumorous), now *spec.* as a result of an increase in the size of cells (cf. HYPERPLASIA); *fig.* excessive development. M19.

I. DEUTSCHER We have here a historic hypertrophy of practice and an atrophy of thought.

▸ **B** *verb*. 1 *verb trans*. Affect with hypertrophy. Now *rare*. M19.
2 *verb intrans*. Undergo hypertrophy. L19.
■ **hypertrophic** /-ˈtrɒfɪk, -ˈtrəʊfɪk/ *adjective* of the nature of, affected with, or producing hypertrophy M19. **hypertrophically** /-ˈtrɒf-, -ˈtrəʊf-/ *adverb* in a hypertrophic manner, to a hypertrophic degree L19. **hypertrophied** *adjective* affected with hypertrophy; *fig.* overgrown, excessive: M19. **hypertrophous** *adjective* (now *rare*) affected with hypertrophy M19.

hyperventilate /hʌɪpəˈvɛntɪleɪt/ *verb*. M20.
[ORIGIN from HYPER- + VENTILATE, or back-form. from HYPERVENTILATION.]
1 *verb intrans*. Breathe deeply or rapidly. M20.
2 *verb trans*. Produce hyperventilation in. M20.
■ ˌ**hyperventiˈlation** *noun* an increased or excessive exposure of the lungs to oxygen, resulting in an increased loss of carbon dioxide from the blood; the action of bringing this about: E20.

hypethral *adjective* var. of HYPAETHRAL.

hypha /ˈhʌɪfə/ *noun*. Pl. -**phae** /-fiː/. M19.
[ORIGIN mod. Latin from Greek *huphē* web.]
A filament in the mycelium of a fungus; any of the vertical unbranched filaments in the medulla of certain brown algae, believed to be conducting elements.
■ **hyphal** *adjective* L19.

hyphaema /hʌɪˈfiːmə/ *noun*. Also *-**phema**. L19.
[ORIGIN from HYPO- + Greek *haima* blood.]
MEDICINE. The presence of blood in the anterior chamber of the eye, in front of the iris.

hyphen /ˈhʌɪf(ə)n/ *noun & verb*. E17.
[ORIGIN Late Latin from late Greek *huphen* the sign ‿, use as noun of *huphen* together, from *huph-*, *hupo* HYPO- + *hen* neut. of *heis* one.]
▸ **A** *noun*. 1 A punctuation mark used to connect two words together, to indicate the division of a word between two successive lines, and to indicate a missing or implied element, and now represented as a short raised horizontal line. E17.

DAY LEWIS I do not use the hyphen in my surname.

double hyphen: see DOUBLE *adjective & adverb*. *soft hyphen*: see SOFT *adjective*.
2 *transf.* A short pause between two syllables in speaking. M19.
3 A narrow connecting link or passage. M19.
▸ **B** *verb trans*. Join by a hyphen; write (a compound) with a hyphen. E19.
■ **hyphenless** *adjective* M20.

hyphenate /ˈhʌɪfəneɪt/ *verb trans*. L19.
[ORIGIN from HYPHEN + -ATE[3].]
= HYPHEN *verb*.
■ **hyphenated** *ppl adjective* (*a*) joined by a hyphen; (*b*) designating a person with dual nationality or mixed background or ancestry (describable by a hyphenated term such as *Anglo-American*), and any person whose patriotic allegiance is assumed to be divided: M19.

hyphenation /hʌɪfəˈneɪʃ(ə)n/ *noun*. L19.
[ORIGIN from HYPHENATE + -ATION.]
The use of the hyphen to join words or divide a word; *esp.* in printing, the division of words at the end of lines, marked with hyphens.

hyphenism /ˈhʌɪfənɪz(ə)m/ *noun*. *US*. E20.
[ORIGIN from HYPHEN + -ISM.]
The state of being a hyphenated American; the attitude or conduct implied by this.

hyphenize /ˈhʌɪfənʌɪz/ *verb trans*. Also -**ise**. M19.
[ORIGIN from HYPHEN + -IZE.]
= HYPHEN *verb*.
■ **hypheniˈzation** *noun* = HYPHENATION M19.

hyphomycete /hʌɪfə(ʊ)ˈmʌɪsiːt/ *noun*. Orig. only in pl. -**mycetes** /-ˈmʌɪsiːts, -mʌɪˈsiːtiːz/. M19.
[ORIGIN Anglicized sing. of mod. Latin *Hyphomycetes* (see below), from Greek *huphē* web + *mukētes* fungi.]
MYCOLOGY. An imperfect fungus of the class Hyphomycetes, comprising filamentous moulds that bear naked asexual spores.
■ **hyphomyˈcetous** *adjective* L19.

hypidiomorphic /hɪˌpɪdɪəˈmɔːfɪk/ *adjective*. L19.
[ORIGIN from HYP- + IDIOMORPHIC.]
Of a rock texture or rock mineral: characterized by crystals that are incompletely developed.

hypinosis /hɪpɪˈnəʊsɪs/ *noun*. Now *rare* or *obsolete*. Pl. -**noses** /-ˈnəʊsiːz/. M19.
[ORIGIN from HYP- + Greek *inos*, *is* fibre + -OSIS.]
MEDICINE. An abnormally low concentration of fibrinogen in the blood.

hypna *noun* pl. of HYPNUM.

hypnagogic /hɪpnəˈgɒgɪk, -ˈgɒdʒɪk/ *adjective*. Also **hypno-**. L19.
[ORIGIN French *hypnagogique*, formed as HYPNO- + Greek *agōgos* leading, from *agein* lead: see -IC.]
That accompanies the process of falling asleep.

†**hypnale** *noun*. LME–M18.
[ORIGIN Late Latin from Greek *hupnaleē* fem. of *hupnaleos* sending to sleep, from *hupnos* sleep.]
A snake whose bite was supposed to induce a fatal sleep.

hypno- /ˈhɪpnəʊ/ *combining form* of Greek *hupnos* sleep, also used in the sense 'hypnosis, hypnotism': see -O-.
■ **hypnoaˈnalysis** *noun* psychoanalysis performed while the subject is hypnotized; = HYPNOTHERAPY *noun* below: E20. **hypnoanaˈlytic** *adjective* of or involving hypnoanalysis E20. **hypnoˈanalyst** *noun* a person who uses hypnoanalysis M20. **hypnoˈgenic** *adjective* producing hypnosis; producing sleep: L19. **hypnoˈlogical** *adjective* of or pertaining to hypnology M19. **hypˈnologist** *noun* an expert in hypnology M19. **hypˈnology** *noun* the science of the phenomena of sleep and hypnosis M19. **hypnoˈpaedia** *noun* [Greek *paideia* education] learning by being exposed to spoken lessons while asleep; teaching by this method: M20. **hypnoˈpaedic** *adjective* of or involving hypnopaedia M20. **hypnoˈpompic** *adjective* [Greek *pompē* sending away] that accompanies the process of waking up E20. **hypnotheraˈpeutic** *adjective* of or involving hypnotherapy L19. **hypnoˈtherapist** *noun* a person who uses hypnotherapy M20. **hypnoˈtherapy** *noun* psychotherapy that involves the use of hypnotism L19.

hypnogogic *adjective* var. of HYPNAGOGIC.

hypnoid /ˈhɪpnɔɪd/ *adjective*. L19.
[ORIGIN from HYPNO- + -OID.]
PSYCHOLOGY. Designating a state of consciousness marked by heightened suggestibility.
■ Also **hypˈnoidal** *adjective* L19.

hypnosis /hɪpˈnəʊsɪs/ *noun*. L19.
[ORIGIN from HYPNO- + -OSIS.]
1 A state of consciousness in which a person appears to lose all power of voluntary action or thought and to be highly responsive to suggestions and directions from the hypnotist. L19.

D. ADAMS You have been under hypnosis for a little less than an hour.

2 Artificially produced sleep or sleepiness. L19.

hypnotic /hɪpˈnɒtɪk/ *adjective & noun*. E17.
[ORIGIN French *hypnotique* from late Latin *hypnoticus* from Greek *hupnōtikos* putting to sleep, narcotic, from *hupnoun* put to sleep, from *hupnos* sleep: see -IC.]
▸ **A** *adjective*. 1 Inducing sleep; soporific. E17.
2 Of, pertaining to, or of the nature of hypnosis; accompanied by or producing hypnosis. M19.

D. DELILLO He bobbed his head, speaking in a soft hypnotic singsong. U. BENTLEY We all slowly came to out of a hypnotic trance.

3 Susceptible to hypnotism; hypnotizable. L19.
▸ **B** *noun*. 1 An agent that produces sleep; *spec.* a sedative or soporific drug. L17.
2 A person under or open to the influence of hypnotism. L19.
■ **hypnotically** *adverb* in a hypnotic manner; by means of hypnotism: L17.

hypnotise *verb* var. of HYPNOTIZE.

hypnotism /ˈhɪpnətɪz(ə)m/ *noun*. M19.
[ORIGIN Orig. coined as *neuro-hypnotism*, from NEURO- + HYPNOT(IC + -ISM, and shortened a year later.]
1 The action or process of hypnotizing a person; the branch of knowledge that deals with this and with the hypnotic state. M19.
2 = HYPNOSIS 1. M19.
3 = HYPNOSIS 2. M19.

hypnotist /ˈhɪpnətɪst/ *noun*. M19.
[ORIGIN formed as HYPNOTISM + -IST.]
A person who studies or practises hypnotism; a hypnotizer.

hypnotize /ˈhɪpnətʌɪz/ *verb trans*. Also -**ise**. M19.
[ORIGIN formed as HYPNOTISM + -IZE.]
1 Put into a hypnotic state. M19.
2 Fascinate, beguile; capture the mind or fancy of; lead *into* something as if by hypnosis. L19.

A. COOKE The press was simply hypnotised by long habit into seeing . . no idiosyncrasy in the Royal Family. F. HOWERD Absolutely hypnotised by the fairyland magic of *Cinderella*.

■ **hypnotiza'bility** *noun* L19. **hypnotizable** *adjective* L19. **hypnoti'zation** *noun* (now *rare*) the action or process of hypnotizing a person; the state of being hypnotized: L19. **hypnotizer** *noun* a hypnotist L19.

hypnum /ˈhɪpnəm/ *noun*. Pl. **-na** /-nə/, **-nums**. M18.
[ORIGIN mod. Latin (see below), from Greek *hupnon* a kind of lichen.]
Any of various pleurocarpous mosses of the genus *Hypnum* (order Hypnobryales), which form dense green mats on tree trunks, in grassland, etc.

†**hypo** *noun*[1]. E18–M19.
[ORIGIN Abbreviation of HYPOCHONDRIA. Cf. HIP *noun*[3].]
Depression, low spirits.

hypo /ˈhʌɪpəʊ/ *noun*[2]. M19.
[ORIGIN Abbreviation of HYPOSULPHITE.]
Sodium thiosulphate as used as a fixer in photography.

hypo /ˈhʌɪpəʊ/ *noun*[3] & *verb*. *slang*. E20.
[ORIGIN Abbreviation of HYPODERMIC. Cf. HYPE *noun*[2] & *verb*[2].]
▸ **A** *noun*. Pl. **-os**. A hypodermic needle or injection; a drug addict. E20.
▸ **B** *verb trans.* & *intrans.* Administer a hypodermic injection (to); *fig.* stimulate. E20.

hypo- /ˈhʌɪpəʊ/ *combining form*. Before a vowel also **hyp-**.
[ORIGIN Greek *hup(o)-*, from *hupo* preposition & adverb, under.]
1 Under, underneath, below; prepositionally, as ***hypodermic*** (under the skin); adverbially, as ***hypoblast*** (a layer underneath). ▸**b** *MUSIC*. In names of modes, denoting (***a***) each of a set of modes in ancient Greek music which began at a definite interval below the ordinary Aeolian etc. modes; (***b***) the plagal modes in medieval music, which have a compass a fourth below that of the corresponding authentic modes.
2 Slightly, slight, partial; as ***hypomania***, ***hypoplasia***.
3 Less than, as ***hypoploid***; (esp. *MEDICINE*) less than normal, as ***hypoacidity***; to a lesser degree, as ***hyposensitize***. ▸**b** *CHEMISTRY*. In nouns and adjectives denoting a compound that contains an element in lower oxidation state or has a lower oxygen content, as ***hypochlorous***.

■ **hypoa'cidity** *noun* abnormally low acidity, esp. of gastric juice E20. **hypo'active** *adjective* (*MEDICINE*) exhibiting hypoactivity M20. **hypoac'tivity** *noun* (*MEDICINE*) diminished activity, *esp.* diminished secretory activity of a gland E20. **hypoaes'thesia** *noun* = HYPAESTHESIA E20. **hypoal'gesia** *noun* = HYPALGESIA E20. **hypo'baric** *adjective* (*MEDICINE*) (of a solution for spinal anaesthesia) less dense than cerebrospinal fluid M20. **hypoblast** *noun* (*BIOLOGY*) endoderm, *esp.* that of an embryo L19. **hypo'blastic** *adjective* (*BIOLOGY*) of or pertaining to the hypoblast L19. **hypo'branchial** *adjective* (*ZOOLOGY*) situated below the gills M19. **hypo'bromite** *noun* (*CHEMISTRY*) a salt of hypobromous acid M19. **hypo'bromous** *adjective* (*CHEMISTRY*): ***hypobromous acid***, an unstable acid, HBrO, that has strong oxidizing properties and is used as a bactericide M19. **hypocal'caemia** *noun* (*MEDICINE*) an abnormally low concentration of calcium in the blood E20. **hypocal'caemic** *adjective* (*MEDICINE*) of or affected with hypocalcaemia M20. **hypo'capnia** *noun* [Greek *kapnos* smoke] *MEDICINE* an abnormally low concentration of carbon dioxide in the blood E20. **hypo'capnic** *adjective* (*MEDICINE*) of, pertaining to, or affected with hypocapnia L20. **hypo'cellular** *adjective* (*MEDICINE*) exhibiting hypocellularity M20. **hypocellu'larity** *noun* (*MEDICINE*) a diminution in the number of cells present at a site in the body M20. **hypochlor'hydria** *noun* (*MEDICINE*) an abnormally low concentration of hydrochloric acid in the gastric juice L19. **hypochlor'hydric** *adjective* (*MEDICINE*) of, pertaining to, or characterized by hypochlorhydria E20. **hypocone** *noun* (*ZOOLOGY*) a cusp on the posterior lingual corner of the tribosphenic upper molar tooth L19. **hypo'conid** *noun* (*ZOOLOGY*) a cusp on the posterior buccal corner of the tribosphenic lower molar tooth L19. **hypocotyl** /-ˈkɒtɪl/ *noun* the part of the stem of an embryo plant beneath the stalks of the cotyledons and directly above the root L19. **hypo'cretin** *noun* (*BIOCHEMISTRY*) = OREXIN 2 L20. **hypodigm** /-dʌɪm, -dɪm/ *noun* [Greek *hupodeigma* example] *TAXONOMY* the material on which the description of a species is based M20. **hypo'diploid** *adjective* & *noun* (*GENETICS*) (***a***) *adjective* having one or a few chromosomes less than the number in a diploid set; containing such cells; (***b***) *noun* a hypodiploid individual: M20. **hypo'diploidy** *noun* (*GENETICS*) the condition of being hypodiploid M20. **hypo'dorian** *adjective* & *noun* (*MUSIC*) (designating) a mode with a lower range than the Dorian but the same final M17. **hypoeu'tectic** *adjective* (of an alloy of iron) containing less carbon than the 4.3 per cent present in the eutectic composition E20. **hypoeu'tectoid** *adjective* (of steel) containing less carbon than the 0.8 per cent present in the eutectoid composition E20. **hypofunction** *noun* & *verb* (*MEDICINE*) (***a***) *noun* diminished or insufficient activity or production in a gland etc.; (***b***) *verb intrans.* exhibit hypofunction: E20. **hypo'functional** *adjective* (*MEDICINE*) exhibiting hypofunction M20. **hypogamma,globuli'naemia** *noun* (*MEDICINE*) an abnormally low concentration of gamma globulins in the blood M20. **hy'pogamous** *adjective* (*ANTHROPOLOGY*) of or pertaining to hypogamy M20. **hy'pogamy** *noun* (*ANTHROPOLOGY*) (the custom of) marriage to a person, esp. a husband, of lower social standing M20. **hypogeusia** /-ˈɡjuːzɪə, -sɪə/ *noun* [Greek *geusis* taste] *MEDICINE* diminished acuteness of the sense of taste L19. **hypogly'caemia** *noun* (*MEDICINE*) an abnormally low concentration of sugar in the blood L19. **hypogly'caemic** *adjective* & *noun* (*MEDICINE*) (***a***) *adjective* pertaining to or characterized by hypoglycaemia; (of a drug etc.) promoting the reduction of blood-sugar levels; (***b***) *noun* a hypoglycaemic person: E20. **hy'pognathous** *adjective* (***a***) (of a bird or a bird's bill) having the lower mandible longer than the upper; (***b***) (of an insect) having the head ventral and the mouth directed ventrally: L19. **hypo'gonadal** *adjective* (*MEDICINE*) characterized by hypogonadism M20. **hypo'gonadism** *noun* (*MEDICINE*) reduction or absence of gonadal activity, esp. of hormone secretion E20. **hypogonadotrophic** /-ˈtrəʊfɪk, -ˈtrɒfɪk/ *adjective* (*MEDICINE*) caused or characterized by a diminished secretion of gonadotrophic hormones M20. **hypoka'laemia** *noun* [mod. Latin *kalium* potassium] *MEDICINE* an abnormally low concentration of potassium in the blood M20. **hypoka'laemic** *adjective* (*MEDICINE*) characterized by hypokalaemia M20. **hypoki'nesis** *noun* (*MEDICINE*) an abnormally reduced amount of muscular or bodily activity L19. **hypoki'netic** *adjective* (*MEDICINE*) characterized by hypokinesis L19. **hypolem'niscus** *noun*, pl. **-sci**, a critical mark in the form of a lemniscus without its upper dot E18. **hypo'lydian** *adjective* & *noun* (*MUSIC*) (designating) a mode with a lower range than the Lydian mode but the same final E17. **hypomagne'saemia** *noun* (*MEDICINE* & *VETERINARY MEDICINE*) an abnormally low concentration of magnesium in the blood, important in cattle as the cause of grass tetany M20. **hypomagne'saemic** *adjective* (*MEDICINE* & *VETERINARY MEDICINE*) caused or characterized by hypomagnesaemia M20. **hypo'mania** *noun* (*PSYCHIATRY*) a mild form of mania, characterized by elation and quickness of thought and often occurring as part of the cycle of manic depressive illness of cyclothymia L19. **hypo'maniac** *noun* (*PSYCHIATRY*) = HYPOMANIC *noun* E20. **hypomanic** *adjective* & *noun* (*PSYCHIATRY*) (***a***) *adjective* of or affected with hypomania; (***b***) *noun* a hypomanic person: E20. **hypomixo'lydian** *adjective* & *noun* (*MUSIC*) (designating) a mode with a lower range than the mixolydian but the same final M18. **hypomorph** *noun* (*GENETICS*) an allele that is functionally less effective than a corresponding wild-type allele M20. **hypo'morphic** *adjective* (*GENETICS*) designating, of, or pertaining to a hypomorph M20. **hypo'nastic** *adjective* (*BOTANY*) characterized by hyponasty L19. **hyponasty** *noun* [Greek *nastos* pressed] *BOTANY* a tendency in part of a plant to grow more rapidly on the underside, so that it curves upwards L19. **hypona'traemia** *noun* (*MEDICINE*) an abnormally low concentration of sodium in the blood M20. **hypona'traemic** *adjective* (*MEDICINE*) characterized by hyponatraemia M20. **hyponome** /ˈhɪpənəʊm/ *noun* [Greek *huponomē* underground passage] *ZOOLOGY* the funnel through which a cephalopod expels a jet of water as a means of locomotion L19. **hypopara'thyroid** *adjective* affected with or accompanied by hypoparathyroidism E20. **hypopara'thyroidism** *noun* (*MEDICINE*) a condition in which there is an abnormally low concentration of parathyroid hormone in the blood, resulting in hypocalcaemia and hypophosphataemia with consequent tetany and other signs of neuromuscular excitability E20. **hypopha'langism**, **hypo'phalangy** *nouns* (*MEDICINE* & *ZOOLOGY*) the absence of one or more digital phalanges E20. **hypo'phoria** *noun* (*MEDICINE*) latent strabismus in which there is a tendency for one eye to be directed below the line of sight of the other M20. **hypophospha'taemia** *noun* (*MEDICINE*) an abnormally low concentration of phosphate (or other phosphorus compounds) in the blood M20. **hypophospha'taemic** *adjective* (*MEDICINE*) pertaining to or characterized by hypophosphataemia M20. **hypo'phosphate** *noun* (*CHEMISTRY*) a salt of hypophosphoric acid M19. **hypo'phosphite** *noun* (*CHEMISTRY*) a salt of hypophosphorous acid E19. **hypophos'phoric** *adjective* (*CHEMISTRY*) designating an unstable tetrabasic crystalline acid, $H_4P_2O_6$ M19. **hypo'phosphorous** *adjective* (*CHEMISTRY*) designating a monobasic acid, H_3PO_2, that is a colourless oily liquid or a deliquescent crystalline solid E19. **hypo'phrygian** *adjective* & *noun* (*MUSIC*) (designating) a mode with a lower range than the Phrygian but the same final M17. **hypopigmen'tation** *noun* (*MEDICINE*) inadequate pigmentation of the skin E21. **hypopi'tuitarism** *noun* (*MEDICINE*) diminished hormone secretion by the pituitary E20. **hypopi'tuitary** *adjective* (*MEDICINE*) of, pertaining to, or affected with hypopituitarism E20. **hypoploid** *adjective* & *noun* (*GENETICS*) (***a***) *adjective* having one or a few chromosomes missing from a haploid or polyploid set; containing such cells; (***b***) *noun* a hypoploid individual: M20. **hypoploidy** *noun* (*GENETICS*) the condition of being hypoploid M20. **hypose'cretion** *noun* (*MEDICINE*) diminished secretion E20. **hy'posmia** *noun* (*MEDICINE*) a poor or non-existent sense of smell L19. **hypo'splenic** *adjective* (*MEDICINE*) of or characterized by hyposplenism M20. **hypo'splenism** *noun* (*MEDICINE*) a condition in which there is hypofunction of the spleen and a changed blood picture E20. **hypostome** *noun* [Greek *stoma* mouth] *ZOOLOGY* any of several structures associated with the mouth in different invertebrates M19. **hypostyle** *adjective* having a roof supported by pillars M19. **hypo'thallus** *noun* (*BOTANY*) (***a***) the layer of filaments on which the thallus of a lichen is developed; (***b***) the sheetlike base of the fruiting body of a myxomycete: M19. **hypo'thecium** *noun* (*BOTANY*) a mass of hyphae filling the lower part of the apothecium of a discomycetous fungus M19. **hypo'thyroid** *adjective* (*MEDICINE*) affected with or symptomatic of hypothyroidism E20. **hypothy'roidic** *adjective* (*MEDICINE*) = HYPOTHYROID E20. **hypo'thyroidism** *noun* (*MEDICINE*) a condition in which the thyroid produces less hormone than normal, resulting in a reduced rate of metabolism and in severe cases cretinism (if congenital) or myxoedema (if acquired) E20. **hypotrichosis** /-trɪˈkəʊsɪs/ *noun* [TRICHO-[1]] partial or complete absence of hair L19. **hypotrichous** /hʌɪˈpɒtrɪkəs/ *adjective* (*ZOOLOGY*) designating ciliates belonging to the order Hypotricha of the order Spirotricha, characterized by cilia largely restricted to the ventral surface L19. **hypo'trochoid** *noun* a curve traced by a point on a radius or extended radius of a circle that rolls inside another circle M19. **hypoventi'lation** *noun* a diminished or insufficient exposure of the lungs to oxygen, resulting in a reduced oxygen content or an increased carbon dioxide content of the blood M20. **hypovitami'nosis** *noun*, pl. **-noses** /-ˈnəʊsiːz/, *MEDICINE* any condition caused by a vitamin deficiency in the diet E20. **hypovo'laemia** *noun* (*MEDICINE*) a decreased volume of circulating blood in the body E20. **hypovo'laemic** *adjective* (*MEDICINE*) affected or associated with hypovolaemia M20. **hypo'xaemia** *noun* (***a***) *MEDICINE* an abnormally low concentration of oxygen in the blood; (***b***) *ECOLOGY* oxygen deficiency in a biotic environment: L19. **hypoxanthine** /-ˈzanθiːn/ *noun* 6-hydroxypurine, $C_5H_4N_4O$, an intermediate in the metabolism of purines in animals which also occurs in plant tissues M19. **hy'poxia** *noun* (*MEDICINE*) a deficiency of oxygen reaching the tissues M20. **hy'poxic** *adjective* (*MEDICINE*) of, pertaining to, or exhibiting hypoxia M20.

hypoacusis /hʌɪpəʊəˈk(j)uːsɪs/ *noun*. Also **-cou-**, **-ku-**. M20.
[ORIGIN from HYPO- + Greek *akousis* hearing.]
= HYPACUSIS.
■ Also **hypoa'cusia** *noun* M20.

hypo-allergenic /ˌhʌɪpəʊaləˈdʒɛnɪk/ *adjective*. M20.
[ORIGIN from HYPO- + ALLERGENIC.]
Having little tendency to cause an allergic reaction; specially prepared or treated so as to cause no reaction in persons allergic to the normal product.

hypocaust /ˈhʌɪpə(ʊ)kɔːst/ *noun*. L17.
[ORIGIN Latin *hypocaustum* from Greek *hupokauston* room or place heated from below, formed as HYPO- + *kau-*, *kaiein* to burn.]
ROMAN ANTIQUITIES. In houses of Roman times, a hollow space under the floor where hot air was sent from a furnace to provide underfloor heating.
■ **hypocausted** *adjective* provided with a hypocaust L19.

hypocentre /ˈhʌɪpə(ʊ)sɛntə/ *noun*. Also ***-ter**. E20.
[ORIGIN from HYPO- + CENTRE *noun*.]
1 The point within the earth where an earthquake originates. E20.
2 = ***ground zero*** (a) s.v. GROUND *noun*. M20.
■ **hypocentral** *adjective* M20.

hypochlorous /hʌɪpə(ʊ)ˈklɔːrəs/ *adjective*. M19.
[ORIGIN from HYPO- + CHLOROUS.]
CHEMISTRY. ***hypochlorous acid***, an unstable weak acid, HOCl, that exists only in dilute aqueous solution, has strong oxidizing properties, and is used in bleaching and water treatment.
■ **hypochlorite** *noun* a salt of hypochlorous acid M19.

hypochonder /hʌɪpə(ʊ)ˈkɒndə/ *noun*. Now *rare* or *obsolete*. Also **-dre**. M16.
[ORIGIN Old French & mod. French *hypocondre* from late Latin *hypoc(h)ondria*: see HYPOCHONDRIA.]
= HYPOCHONDRIUM.

hypochondria /hʌɪpə(ʊ)ˈkɒndrɪə/ *noun*. See also HYPOCHONDRIUM. LME.
[ORIGIN Late Latin *hypoc(h)ondria* pl. from Greek *hupokhondria* pl., *-khondrion* sing., use as noun of *hupokhondrios* adjective, formed as HYPO- + *khondros* gristle, cartilage, esp. that of the breastbone.]
1 The part of the abdomen lying under the ribs on either side of the epigastric region. Formerly also, the viscera situated there (the liver, gall bladder, spleen, etc.), regarded as the seat of melancholy and 'vapours'. LME.
2 Depression or low spirits for which there is no real cause. M17. ▸**b** A person's unfounded belief that he or she is ill; persistent anxiety about or preoccupation with one's health. L19.

hypochondriac /hʌɪpə(ʊ)ˈkɒndrɪak/ *adjective* & *noun*. L16.
[ORIGIN French *hypocondriaque* from Greek *hupokhondriakos* affected in the hypochondria, from *hupokhondria*: see HYPOCHONDRIA, -AC. Cf. medieval Latin *hypochondriaca*.]
▸ **A** *adjective*. **1** Affected with or disposed to hypochondria. L16.
2 (Of an illness or symptom) affecting the hypochondria; *arch.* of the nature of depression or low spirits. L16.
3 *MEDICINE*. Situated on or near a hypochondrium. E18.
▸ **B** *noun*. †**1** = HYPOCHONDRIA 2. L16–L18.
2 A person affected with or disposed to hypochondria. M17.

C. P. SNOW He . . cherished his afflictions like a hypochondriac.

■ **hypochondriacal** /-ˈdrʌɪ-/ *adjective* (***a***) = HYPOCHONDRIAC *adjective* 1, 2; (***b***) *rare* = HYPOCHONDRIAC *adjective* 3: E17. **hypochondriacally** /-ˈdrʌɪ-/ *adverb* in the manner of a hypochondriac; with hypochondria: E19. **hypochondriacism** /-ˈdrʌɪ-/ *noun* = HYPOCHONDRIA 2 E18.

hypochondrial /hʌɪpə(ʊ)ˈkɒndrɪəl/ *adjective*. E17.
[ORIGIN from HYPOCHONDRIA + -AL[1].]
MEDICINE. Situated on or near, or affecting, a hypochondrium.

Lancet The patient presented with a painful right hypochondrial mass.

hypochondriasis /ˌhʌɪpə(ʊ)kɒnˈdrʌɪəsɪs/ *noun*. Pl. **-ases** /-əsiːz/. M18.
[ORIGIN from HYPOCHONDRIA + -IASIS.]
Hypochondria, esp. as a pathological state.

hypochondric /hʌɪpə(ʊ)ˈkɒndrɪk/ *adjective*. *rare*. L17.
[ORIGIN formed as HYPOCHONDRIASIS + -IC.]
= HYPOCHONDRIAC *adjective*.
■ Also **hypochondrical** *adjective* (long *rare* or *obsolete*) M17.

hypochondrium /hʌɪpə(ʊ)ˈkɒndrɪəm/ *noun*. Pl. **-ums**, HYPOCHONDRIA. M17.
[ORIGIN Back-form. from HYPOCHONDRIA.]
The part of the hypochondria lying to the left or the right of the epigastric region.

Lancet A mass in his left hypochondrium suggested pseudocyst of pancreas.

†**hypochondry** *noun*. Also **-condry**. LME.
[ORIGIN formed as HYPOCHONDRIA: see -Y[3].]
1 = HYPOCHONDRIUM Usu. in *pl.* LME–L17.
2 = HYPOCHONDRIA 2. M17–L19.

hypochoristic *adjective* var. of HYPOCORISTIC.

hypochromasia /hʌɪpə(ʊ)krəˈmeɪzɪə/ *noun*. E20.
[ORIGIN from HYPO- + -CHROMASIA.]
MEDICINE. = HYPOCHROMIA 2.
■ **hypochromatic** /-ˈmat-/ *adjective* (***a***) *rare* (of the skin) deficient in pigment; (***b***) = HYPOCHROMIC 1: L19.

hypochromatosis /ˌhʌɪpə(ʊ)krəʊmə'təʊsɪs/ *noun*. E20.
[ORIGIN from HYPO- + CHROMATO-, CHROMAT(IN + -OSIS.]
CYTOLOGY. The presence of an abnormally small number of chromosomes or amount of chromatin in a nucleus.

hypochromia /hʌɪpə(ʊ)'krəʊmɪə/ *noun*. L19.
[ORIGIN formed as HYPOCHROMIC + -IA[1].]
MEDICINE. **1** Paleness of the skin. L19.
2 A hypochromic condition of the blood. M20.

hypochromic /hʌɪpə(ʊ)'krəʊmɪk/ *adjective*. E20.
[ORIGIN from HYPO- + Greek *khrōma* colour, or HYPOCHROMIA, + -IC.]
1 *MEDICINE*. Characterized by or designating red cells that contain less than the usual amount of haemoglobin and show an increased central pallor. E20.

J. W. LINMAN Most hypochromic anemias are caused by iron lack.

2 Characterized by or exhibiting a decrease in the extent to which light, esp. ultraviolet light, is absorbed. M20.
■ **hypochromicity** /-'mɪsɪti/ *noun* the property of being hypochromic M20.

†**hypocistis** *noun*. LME–M18.
[ORIGIN medieval Latin from Greek *hupokistis*, formed as HYPO- + *kistos* CISTUS.]
A former tonic and astringent consisting of the solidified juice of *Cytinus hypocistis*, a plant of southern Europe parasitic on cistus.

hypocoristic /ˌhʌɪpə(ʊ)kə'rɪstɪk/ *adjective* & *noun*. Also **-chor-**. M18.
[ORIGIN Greek *hupokoristikos*, from *hupokorizesthai* play the child, formed as HYPO- + *korē* child: see -ISTIC.]
▸ **A** *adjective*. Of the nature of a pet name; pertaining to the habit of using endearing or euphemistic terms. M18.
▸ **B** *noun*. A pet name, a familiar name. L19.
■ **hypocorism** *noun* = HYPOCORISTIC *noun* M19. †**hypocoristical** *adjective*: only in E17. **hypocoristically** *adverb* M17.

hypocrateriform /ˌhɪpə(ʊ)krə'tɪərɪfɔːm/ *adjective*. M18.
[ORIGIN mod. Latin *hypocrateriformis*, from Greek *hupokratērion* stand of a large mixing bowl, from HYPO- + *kratēr* CRATER: see -FORM.]
BOTANY. = *SALVER-shaped*.

hypocrise /'hɪpəkrʌɪz/ *verb intrans. rare*. L16.
[ORIGIN French *hypocriser* or back-form. from HYPOCRISY.]
Practise hypocrisy.

hypocrisis /hɪ'pɒkrɪsɪs/ *noun*. ME.
[ORIGIN Latin: see HYPOCRISY.]
Hypocrisy, dissembling, feigning; a false or deceitful show.

hypocrisy /hɪ'pɒkrɪsi/ *noun*. ME.
[ORIGIN Old French *ypocrisie* (mod. *hypo-*), irreg. from ecclesiastical Latin *hypocrisis* from Greek *hupokrisis* acting of a theatrical part, from *hupokrinesthai* answer, play a part, pretend, formed as HYPO- + *krinein* decide, determine, judge. The etymological spelling with *h-* became current (as in French) in 16.]
The practice of falsely presenting an appearance of virtue or falsely professing a belief to which one's own character or conduct does not conform; dissimulation, pretence; an instance of this.

P. USTINOV The hypocrisy which permits selfish policies to be propounded in expressions of high-mindedness. R. H. TAWNEY To talk of holiness and to practise injustice is mere hypocrisy.

hypocrital /hɪ'pɒkrɪt(ə)l/ *adjective*. Now *rare*. M17.
[ORIGIN from HYPOCRITE + -AL[1].]
= HYPOCRITICAL.

hypocrite /'hɪpəkrɪt/ *noun* & *adjective*. ME.
[ORIGIN Old French *ypocrite*, *ipo-* (mod. *hypo-*) from ecclesiastical Latin *hypocrita* from Greek *hupokritēs* actor, dissembler, pretender, from *hupokrinesthai*: see HYPOCRISY.]
▸ **A** *noun*. A person who falsely professes to be virtuously or religiously inclined or to have feelings or beliefs of a higher order than is the case; a person given to hypocrisy. ME.

M. MEDVED Another holy hypocrite hides his private prurience behind a mask of public piety.

▸ **B** *adjective*. = HYPOCRITICAL. LME.

hypocritic /hɪpə'krɪtɪk/ *adjective*. M16.
[ORIGIN medieval Latin *hypocriticus* from Greek *hypokritikos* pertaining to (an actor's) delivery, from *hupokrisis*: see HYPOCRISY, -IC.]
= HYPOCRITICAL.

hypocritical /hɪpə'krɪtɪk(ə)l/ *adjective*. M16.
[ORIGIN formed as HYPOCRITIC: see -ICAL.]
Of an action: of the nature of or characterized by hypocrisy. Of a person: given to hypocrisy, having the character of a hypocrite.

J. TORRINGTON But there I'd been, exchanging a hypocritical handshake, mouthin how good it was to see'm again.

■ **hypocritically** *adverb* M16.

hypocycloid /hʌɪpə(ʊ)'sʌɪklɔɪd/ *noun*. M19.
[ORIGIN from HYPO- + CYCLOID.]
A curve traced by a point on the circumference of one circle as it rolls round the inside of another circle. Cf. EPICYCLOID.
■ **hypocy'cloidal** *adjective* L19.

hypoderma /hʌɪpə(ʊ)'dəːmə/ *noun*. Pl. **-mata** /-mətə/. E19.
[ORIGIN from HYPO- + Greek *derma* skin.]
†**1** *ZOOLOGY*. A membrane lining the underside of the elytra of Coleoptera. Only in E19.
2 *BOTANY*. = HYPODERMIS 1. L19.

hypodermal /hʌɪpə(ʊ)'dəːm(ə)l/ *adjective*. M19.
[ORIGIN from HYPODERMA, HYPODERMIS + -AL[1].]
Of or pertaining to hypodermis.

hypodermatic /ˌhʌɪpə(ʊ)dəː'matɪk/ *adjective*. Now *rare* or *obsolete*. M19.
[ORIGIN from HYPO- + DERMATO- + -IC.]
†**1** *ANATOMY*. = HYPODERMIC *adjective* 2. Only in M19.
2 = HYPODERMIC *adjective* 1. L19.
■ **hypodermatically** *adverb* L19.

hypodermic /hʌɪpə(ʊ)'dəːmɪk/ *adjective* & *noun*. M19.
[ORIGIN from HYPO- + Greek *derma* skin + -IC.]
▸ **A** *adjective*. **1** Involving, pertaining to, or designating the introduction of a drug etc. by injection under the skin. M19.

Times Hospital waste such as blood samples and hypodermic needles.

2 *ANATOMY*. Situated beneath the skin; pertaining to the region beneath the skin. L19.
▸ **B** *noun*. A hypodermic injection; a hypodermic syringe. L19.
■ **hypodermically** *adverb* M19.

hypodermis /hʌɪpə(ʊ)'dəːmɪs/ *noun*. M19.
[ORIGIN from HYPO- + *-dermis*, after *epidermis*.]
1 *BOTANY*. A layer of cells immediately below the epidermis of a plant, *esp*. one of a different origin. Also, the inner layer of the capsule of mosses. M19.
2 *ZOOLOGY*. A layer of cells below the cuticle of arthropods. L19.

hypogaeal *adjective*, **hypogaeum** *noun* vars. of HYPOGEAL, HYPOGEUM.

hypogastric /hʌɪpə(ʊ)'gastrɪk/ *adjective* & *noun*. M17.
[ORIGIN French *hypogastrique*, from *hypogastre* hypogastrium formed as HYPOGASTRIUM: see -IC.]
ANATOMY. ▸**A** *adjective*. Pertaining to, situated in, or designating the region of the hypogastrium. M17.
▸ **B** *noun*. †**1** In *pl*. The hypogastric arteries. *rare*. Only in L18.
2 A hypogastric nerve (connecting the superior and inferior hypogastric plexuses). L19.
■ Also †**hypogastrical** *adjective* (*rare*): only in E17.

hypogastrium /hʌɪpə(ʊ)'gastrɪəm/ *noun*. L17.
[ORIGIN mod. Latin from Greek *hupogastrion*, formed as HYPO- + *gastr-*, *gastēr* belly: see -IUM.]
ANATOMY. The lowest part of the abdomen, below the navel; *esp*. the middle of this, between the iliac regions.

hypogea *noun* pl. of HYPOGEUM.

hypogeal /hʌɪpə(ʊ)'dʒiːəl/ *adjective*. Also **-gaeal**. L17.
[ORIGIN formed as HYPOGEAN + -AL[1].]
= HYPOGEAN.
■ Also **hypogeous** *adjective* M19.

hypogean /hʌɪpə(ʊ)'dʒiːən/ *adjective*. M19.
[ORIGIN from late Latin *hypogeus* from Greek *hupogeios* underground, formed as HYPO- + *gē* earth: see -AN.]
Occurring or growing beneath the surface of the earth; underground.

hypogee /'hɪpədʒiː/ *noun*. *rare*. M17.
[ORIGIN French *hypogée* or Latin *hypogeum* HYPOGEUM.]
= HYPOGEUM.

hypogene /'hʌɪpədʒiːn/ *adjective*. M19.
[ORIGIN from HYPO- + -GENE.]
GEOLOGY. Formed or occurring beneath the surface of the earth.
■ Also **hypo'genic** *adjective* L19.

hypogeum /hʌɪpə(ʊ)'dʒiːəm/ *noun*. Also **-gaeum**. Pl. **-g(a)ea** /-dʒiːə/. M17.
[ORIGIN Latin *hypogeum*, *-gaeum* from Greek *hupogeion*, *-gaion* use as noun of neut. sing. of *hupogeios*: see HYPOGEAN.]
An underground chamber or vault.

hypoglossal /hʌɪpə(ʊ)'glɒs(ə)l/ *adjective* & *noun*. M19.
[ORIGIN from HYPOGLOSSUS + -AL[1].]
ANATOMY. ▸**A** *adjective*. Designating or pertaining to the twelfth pair of cranial nerves, which supply the muscles of the tongue. M19.
▸ **B** *noun*. Either of the hypoglossal nerves. M19.

hypoglossus /hʌɪpə(ʊ)'glɒsəs/ *noun*. *rare*. E19.
[ORIGIN from HYPO- + Greek *glōssa* tongue.]
ANATOMY. = HYPOGLOSSAL *noun*.

hypogynous /hɪ'pɒdʒɪnəs/ *adjective*. E19.
[ORIGIN from mod. Latin *hypogynus*, formed as HYPO- + Greek *gunē* woman (used for 'pistil'): see -OUS.]
BOTANY. Of a stamen, petal, or sepal: inserted on the receptacle below the gynoecium. Of a flower: having its parts so inserted. Cf. EPIGYNOUS, PERIGYNOUS.
■ **hypogyny** *noun* hypogynous condition L19.

hypoid /'hʌɪpɔɪd/ *adjective* & *noun*. E20.
[ORIGIN Uncertain: perh. from HYP(ERBOL)OID or *hy(perbolic parabol)oid*.]
MECHANICS. ▸**A** *adjective*. **1** Designating a gear similar to a spiral bevel gear but with the pinion offset from the centre line of the wheel, to connect non-intersecting shafts. E20.
2 Suited for or employing a hypoid gear. M20.

Practical Motorist The rear final drive should be drained and refilled . . using hypoid API GLS oil.

▸ **B** *noun*. A hypoid gear. M20.

hypolimnion /hʌɪpə(ʊ)'lɪmnɪən/ *noun*. Pl. **-nia** /-nɪə/. E20.
[ORIGIN from HYPO- + Greek *limnion* dim. of *limnē* lake.]
The lower, cooler layer of water below the thermocline in a stratified lake.
■ **hypolim'netic** *adjective* E20. **hypolimnial** *adjective* M20.

hypomochlion /hɪpə(ʊ)'mɒklɪən/ *noun*. *rare*. M17.
[ORIGIN Latin from Greek *hupomokhlion*, formed as HYPO- + *mokhlos*, *-lion* lever.]
A fulcrum.

hyponitrous /hʌɪpə(ʊ)'nʌɪtrəs/ *adjective*. E19.
[ORIGIN from HYPO- + NITROUS.]
CHEMISTRY. ***hyponitrous acid***, a weak unstable crystalline acid, $H_2N_2O_2$, which explodes when heated.
■ **hyponitrite** *noun* a salt of hyponitrous acid M19.

hyponym /'hʌɪpə(ʊ)nɪm/ *noun*. E20.
[ORIGIN from HYPO- + -NYM.]
1 *TAXONOMY*. A name made invalid by the lack of adequate contemporary description of the taxon it was intended to designate. E20.
2 *LINGUISTICS*. A word whose meaning implies or is included in that of another (e.g. *scarlet* and *tulip*, in relation to *red* and *flower* respectively). M20.

hyponymy /hʌɪ'pɒnɪmi/ *noun*. M20.
[ORIGIN from HYPO- after SYNONYMY.]
LINGUISTICS. The relation of a word to another word of which the former is a hyponym.

hypopharyngeal /ˌhʌɪpə(ʊ)fə'rɪn(d)ʒɪəl, -far(ə)n'dʒiːəl/ *adjective*. M19.
[ORIGIN Partly from HYPO- + PHARYNGEAL, partly from HYPOPHARYNX.]
1 *ZOOLOGY* & *ANATOMY*. Situated below the pharynx or in the hypopharynx. M19.
2 *ENTOMOLOGY*. Pertaining to the hypopharynx. L19.

hypopharynx /hʌɪpə(ʊ)'farɪŋks/ *noun*. E19.
[ORIGIN French, formed as HYPO-, PHARYNX.]
1 *ENTOMOLOGY*. A sensory structure projecting from the labium of an insect and usually incorporating salivary apertures. E19.
2 *ANATOMY*. The lower part of the pharynx (into which the larynx opens), between the epiglottis and the top of the oesophagus. E20.

hypophyllous /hʌɪ'pɒfɪləs/ *adjective*. E19.
[ORIGIN from HYPO- + Greek *phullon* leaf + -OUS.]
BOTANY. Growing under, or on the underside of, a leaf.

hypophysectomy /ˌhʌɪpə(ʊ)fɪ'sɛktəmi/ *noun*. E20.
[ORIGIN formed as HYPOPHYSIOTROPIC + -ECTOMY.]
Surgical removal of the hypophysis; an instance of this.
■ **hypophy'sectomize** *verb trans*. perform hypophysectomy on E20.

hypophysiotropic /ˌhʌɪpə(ʊ)fɪzɪə'trəʊpɪk, -'trɒpɪk/ *adjective*. Also **-troph-** /-'trəʊf-/. M20.
[ORIGIN from HYPOPHYSIS + -O- + -TROPIC.]
PHYSIOLOGY. Regulating the activity of the hypophysis.

hypophysis /hʌɪ'pɒfɪsɪs/ *noun*. Pl. **-yses** /-ɪsiːz/. L17.
[ORIGIN mod. Latin from Greek *hupophusis* offshoot, outgrowth, formed as HYPO- + *phusis* growth.]
†**1** Cataract in the eye. *rare* (only in Dicts.). L17–L19.
2 *ANATOMY*. The pituitary gland. Also, one or other lobes of this gland; both lobes together with the infundibulum. Also ***hypophysis cerebri*** /'sɛrɪbriː/. E19.
■ †**hypophysal** *adjective*: only in L19. **hypophyseal**, **hypophysial** /hʌɪpə(ʊ)'fɪzɪəl, hʌɪpə(ʊ)fɪ'siːəl/ *adjectives* L19.

hypoplasia /hʌɪpə(ʊ)'pleɪzɪə/ *noun*. L19.
[ORIGIN from HYPO- + -PLASIA.]
MEDICINE. Incomplete growth or development of a part.

hypoplastic /hʌɪpə(ʊ)'plastɪk/ *adjective*. L19.
[ORIGIN from HYPO(PLASIA + -PLASTIC.]
MEDICINE. Of an organ or tissue: undersized or underdeveloped at maturity as a result of hypoplasia.
hypoplastic anaemia: due to an insufficient production of red blood cells.

hypopyon /hʌɪ'pəʊpɪən/ *noun*. E18.
[ORIGIN Greek *hupopuon* ulcer, neut. of *hupopuos* tending to suppuration, formed as HYPO- + *puon* pus.]
MEDICINE. The presence of pus in the anterior chamber of the eye, in front of the iris.

hyporchem /'hɪpɔːkɛm, 'hʌɪp-/ *noun*. Also **-chema** /-'kiːmə/, pl. **-mata** /-mətə/. E17.
[ORIGIN Greek *huporkhēma*, formed as HYPO- + *orkheesthai* to dance.]
GREEK HISTORY. A choral hymn to Apollo which was accompanied by dancing and pantomimic action.

H

hyposarca /hɪpə(ʊ)ˈsɑːkə, hʌɪp-/ *noun. rare.* LME.
[ORIGIN medieval Latin from Greek *hupo sarka* under the flesh.]
= ANASARCA.

hyposcenium /hʌɪpə(ʊ)ˈsiːnɪəm, hɪp-/ *noun.* M18.
[ORIGIN mod. Latin, based, after *proscenium*, on Greek *huposkēnia* parts beneath the stage, formed as HYPO- + *skēnē* stage: see -IUM.]
GREEK ANTIQUITIES. The low wall supporting the front of the stage in a Greek theatre.

hyposensitize /hʌɪpə(ʊ)ˈsɛnsɪtʌɪz/ *verb trans.* Also **-ise**. M20.
[ORIGIN from HYPO- + SENSITIZE.]
MEDICINE. Subject to hyposensitization.
■ ˌ**hyposensitiˈzation** *noun* the process of reducing the sensitivity of a hypersensitive individual by special treatment; a state of reduced sensitivity so produced: E20.

hypospadias /hʌɪpə(ʊ)ˈspeɪdɪəs, hɪp-/ *noun.* E19.
[ORIGIN Greek *hypospadias* person with hypospadias, app. formed as HYPO- + *span* to draw.]
A congenital malformation of the penis in which the urethra opens on its underside.
■ **hypospadiac** *adjective* M19. **hypospadial** *adjective* L19.

hypostasis /hʌɪˈpɒstəsɪs/ *noun.* Pl. **-ases** /-əsiːz/. Also (*rare*) anglicized as †**hypostasy**. E16.
[ORIGIN ecclesiastical Latin from Greek *hupostasis* sediment, foundation, subject matter, (later) substance, existence, essence, personality, formed as HYPO- + *stasis* standing.]
1 THEOLOGY. A person; *spec.* (**a**) the single person of Christ, as opp. to his two natures, human and divine; (**b**) each of the three persons of the Trinity, which are of the same 'substance'. E16.
2 MEDICINE. **a** A sediment, esp. in urine. Long *rare* or *obsolete*. M16. ▸**b** The accumulation of blood or other fluid in a dependent part of the body. M19.

b D. L. SAYERS The hypostasis produced by his having lain a whole week face downwards in the cellar.

3 †**a** A base or foundation on which something abstract rests. L16–E17. ▸**b** PHILOSOPHY. An underlying reality, substance, as opp. to attributes ('accidents') or as distinguished from what is unsubstantial. E17. ▸**c** Essence, essential principle. L17.
4 GENETICS. [Back-form. from HYPOSTATIC.] Inhibition of the expression of a gene by another at a different locus. E20.
5 LINGUISTICS. The citing of a word, element, etc., as an example or model; the word etc. so cited. M20.

hypostasize /hʌɪˈpɒstəsʌɪz/ *verb trans.* Also **-ise**. E19.
[ORIGIN from HYPOSTASIS + -IZE.]
Make into or represent as a substance or a concrete reality; embody, personify.
■ **hypostasiˈzation** *noun* L19.

hypostatic /hʌɪpə(ʊ)ˈstatɪk/ *adjective.* L15.
[ORIGIN medieval Latin *hypostaticus* from Greek *hupostatikos* pertaining to substance, substantial, personal, from *hupostatos* set under, supporting.]
1 THEOLOGY. Of or pertaining to hypostasis (see HYPOSTASIS 1). Chiefly in ***hypostatic union***. L15.
2 MEDICINE. Of the nature of or caused by hypostasis. M19.
3 GENETICS. Of a gene: affected by hypostasis; not expressed owing to the effect of another gene at a different locus. E20.

hypostatical /hʌɪpə(ʊ)ˈstatɪk(ə)l/ *adjective.* M16.
[ORIGIN formed as HYPOSTATIC + -AL¹.]
1 THEOLOGY. = HYPOSTATIC 1. M16.
†**2** Of a principle of matter: elemental. M17–E18.
■ **hypostatically** *adverb* in a hypostatic manner; in actual substance or personality: L16.

hypostatize /hʌɪˈpɒstətʌɪz/ *verb trans.* Also **-ise**. E19.
[ORIGIN from Greek *hupostatos*: see HYPOSTATIC, -IZE.]
= HYPOSTASIZE.
■ **hypostatiˈzation** *noun* hypostasization L19.

†**hyposulphate** *noun.* Also **-sulf-**. Only in 19.
[ORIGIN from HYPO- + SULPHATE *noun*.]
CHEMISTRY. = DITHIONATE.

hyposulphite /hʌɪpə(ʊ)ˈsʌlfʌɪt/ *noun.* Also (*US* & CHEMISTRY) **-sulf-**. E19.
[ORIGIN French, formed as HYPO-, SULPHITE.]
1 CHEMISTRY. A thiosulphate, *esp.* sodium thiosulphate as used in photography. E19.
2 = HYDROSULPHITE. L19.

†**hyposulphuric** *adjective.* Also **-sulf-**. Only in 19.
[ORIGIN French *hyposulphurique*, formed as HYPO-, SULPHURIC.]
CHEMISTRY. = DITHIONIC.

hyposulphurous /hʌɪpə(ʊ)ˈsʌlf(ə)rəs/ *adjective.* Also **-sulf-**. E19.
[ORIGIN from HYPO- + SULPHUROUS.]
†**1** = THIOSULPHURIC. Only in 19.
2 = HYDROSULPHUROUS. L19.

hypotaxis /hʌɪpə(ʊ)ˈtaksɪs/ *noun.* L19.
[ORIGIN Greek *hupotaxis* subjection, from *hupotassein* arrange under, formed as HYPO- + *tassein* arrange.]
GRAMMAR. The subordination of one clause to another. Opp. PARATAXIS.
■ **hypotactic** *adjective* of, pertaining to, or exhibiting hypotaxis; subordinate: L19.

hypotension /hʌɪpə(ʊ)ˈtɛnʃ(ə)n/ *noun.* L19.
[ORIGIN from HYPO- + TENSION *noun*.]
Abnormally or excessively low pressure of arterial blood or intra-ocular fluid, *spec.* the former.
■ **hypotensive** *adjective* of, exhibiting, or associated with hypotension; tending to reduce a person's blood pressure: E20.

†**hypotenusa** *noun* see HYPOTENUSE.

hypotenusal /hʌɪˌpɒtɪˈnjuːʃ(ə)l, -s(ə)l/ *adjective & noun.* Now *rare*. Also †**-then-**. L16.
[ORIGIN Late Latin *hypotenusalis*, formed as HYPOTENUSE: see -AL¹.]
▸ **A** *adjective.* Pertaining to or of the nature of a hypotenuse; forming a hypotenuse. L16.
▸ †**B** *noun.* A hypotenuse. Only in M17.

hypotenuse /hʌɪˈpɒtɪnjuːz, -s/ *noun.* Also †**-then-**, & in Latin form †**-tenusa**. L16.
[ORIGIN Latin *hypotenusa* from Greek *hupoteinousa* subtending (*sc.* line) fem. pres. pple of *hupoteinein* stretch under, formed as HYPO- + *teinein* to stretch.]
The longest side of a right-angled triangle.

hypothalamus /hʌɪpə(ʊ)ˈθaləməs/ *noun.* Pl. **-mi** /-mʌɪ, -miː/. L19.
[ORIGIN from HYPO- + THALAMUS.]
ANATOMY. The lower part of the diencephalon in vertebrates, which in mammals controls autonomic functions such as temperature and hunger and regulates the hormonal activity of the adenohypophysis.
■ **hypothalamic** /-ˈθaləmɪk, -θəˈlamɪk/ *adjective* L19. **hypothalamo-hypoˈphysial**, **-eal** *adjective* of, pertaining to, or connecting the hypothalamus and the hypophysis M20.

hypothec /hʌɪˈpɒθɪk/ *noun.* Also (now only with ref. to Roman law) in Latin form **hypotheca** /hʌɪpə(ʊ)ˈθiːkə/. E16.
[ORIGIN French *hypothèque* from late Latin *hypotheca* from Greek *hupothēkē* deposit, pledge, from *hupotithenai* deposit as a pledge, formed as HYPO- + *tithenai* to place.]
In the law of Scotland, the Channel Islands, and ancient Rome: a creditor's right established over a debtor's property that continues in the debtor's possession.
■ **hypothecal** *adjective* (now *rare* or *obsolete*) = HYPOTHECARY E17.

hypotheca /hʌɪpə(ʊ)ˈθiːkə/ *noun*¹. L19.
[ORIGIN from HYPO- + THECA.]
BOTANY. The inner of the two valves of a diatom.

hypotheca *noun*² see HYPOTHEC.

hypothecary /hʌɪˈpɒθɪk(ə)ri/ *adjective.* M17.
[ORIGIN Late Latin *hypothecarius*, from *hypotheca* HYPOTHEC: see -ARY¹.]
ROMAN & SCOTS LAW. Of, pertaining to, or of the nature of a hypothec.

hypothecate /hʌɪˈpɒθɪkeɪt/ *verb trans.* E17.
[ORIGIN medieval Latin *hypothecat-* pa. ppl stem of *hypothecare*, from *hypotheca*: see HYPOTHEC, -ATE³.]
1 Give or pledge as security; pawn; mortgage; pledge (money) by law to a specific purpose. E17.
2 = HYPOTHESIZE 2. E20.
■ **hypotheˈcation** *noun* L17. **hypothecator** *noun* E19.

†**hypothenusal** *adjective*, †**hypothenuse** *noun* vars. of HYPOTENUSAL etc.

hypothermia /hʌɪpə(ʊ)ˈθəːmɪə/ *noun.* L19.
[ORIGIN from HYPO- + Greek *thermē* heat + -IA¹.]
The condition of having a body temperature substantially below the normal, whether through natural causes or artificially induced.
■ **hypothermic** *adjective* of or exhibiting hypothermia L19.

hypothesis /hʌɪˈpɒθɪsɪs/ *noun.* Pl. **-theses** /-θɪsiːz/. L16.
[ORIGIN Late Latin from Greek *hupothesis* foundation, base, formed as HYPO- + *thesis* placing.]
1 A proposition put forward merely as a basis for reasoning or argument, without any assumption of its truth. L16.
†**2** A subordinate thesis forming part of a more general one; a particular case of a general proposition; a detailed statement. L16–E18.
3 A supposition, an assumption; *esp.* one made as a starting point for further investigation or research from known facts. E17.

E. O'BRIEN The midwife . . repeated the hypothesis that if men had to give birth there would not be a child born. R. RENDELL That was what he thought had happened. It would do as a working hypothesis. G. A. BIRMINGHAM Have you any other hypothesis which meets the facts of the case better?

continuum hypothesis, ***Whorfian hypothesis***, ***zeta hypothesis***, etc.

4 A groundless assumption; a guess. E17.
5 An actual or possible situation considered as a basis for action. L18.
■ **hypothesist** *noun* a person who hypothesizes L18.

hypothesize /hʌɪˈpɒθɪsʌɪz/ *verb.* Also **-ise**. M18.
[ORIGIN from HYPOTHES(IS + -IZE.]
1 *verb intrans.* Frame a hypothesis or supposition. M18.
2 *verb trans.* Make a hypothesis of; put forward as a hypothesis; postulate, assume. M19.

M. T. TSUANG It has been hypothesized that the submissive twins may be . . more dependent on their parents. *Journal of Social Psychology* Hypothesizing an inverse relationship between task sophistication and conforming behavior.

■ **hypothesizer** *noun* M19.

hypothetic /hʌɪpə(ʊ)ˈθɛtɪk/ *adjective & noun.* L17.
[ORIGIN Latin *hypotheticus* from Greek *hupothetikos*, from *hupothesis*: see HYPOTHESIS, -IC.]
▸ **A** *adjective.* = HYPOTHETICAL *adjective*. L17.
▸ **B** *noun.* †**1** A hypothetical statement, a hypothesis; a hypothetical proposition or syllogism. L17–E18.
2 In *pl.* The making of hypotheses; hypothesizing. L19.

hypothetical /hʌɪpə(ʊ)ˈθɛtɪk(ə)l/ *adjective & noun.* L16.
[ORIGIN formed as HYPOTHETIC + -AL¹.]
▸ **A** *adjective.* **1** Involving, based on, or pertaining to a hypothesis; LOGIC designating a proposition having the form *if p then q* or a syllogism containing such a proposition; GRAMMAR expressing a conjecture, supposition, or condition. L16.

R. S. BALL The . . line which divides the truths that have been established . . from those parts of the science which . . [are] more or less hypothetical. R. B. LONG The verb forms used as hypothetical subjunctives are forms belonging to the four past tenses.

hypothetical imperative ETHICS a moral obligation that applies only if one desires the goal (opp. ***categorical imperative***).

2 Concerning which a hypothesis is made; supposed or assumed but not necessarily real or true. E17.

J. TYNDALL Any other obstacle will produce the same effect as our hypothetical post.

▸ **B** *noun.* **1** LOGIC. A hypothetical proposition or syllogism. M17.
2 GRAMMAR. A hypothetical word, phrases, or clause. M20.

hypothetically /hʌɪpə(ʊ)ˈθɛtɪk(ə)li/ *adverb.* E17.
[ORIGIN from HYPOTHETICAL + -LY².]
In a hypothetical manner or form; by hypothesis; supposedly.

hypotheticate /hʌɪpə(ʊ)ˈθɛtɪkeɪt/ *verb trans.* E20.
[ORIGIN from HYPOTHETIC(AL + -ATE³.]
= HYPOTHESIZE 2.
■ **hypothetiˈcation** *noun* L20.

hypothetico-deductive /hʌɪpəˌθɛtɪkəʊdɪˈdʌktɪv/ *adjective.* E20.
[ORIGIN from HYPOTHETICAL + -O- + DEDUCTIVE.]
PHILOSOPHY. Making use of or consisting in the testing of the consequences of hypotheses as a means of determining whether the hypotheses themselves are false or can be accepted.
■ **hypothetico-deductively** *adverb* M20. **hypothetico-deductivism** *noun* L20.

hypotonia /hʌɪpə(ʊ)ˈtəʊnɪə/ *noun.* Also anglicized as **hypotony** /hʌɪˈpɒtəni/. L19.
[ORIGIN from HYPO- + Greek *tonos* TONE *noun* + -IA¹, -Y³.]
MEDICINE. **1** A state of reduced pressure of the intra-ocular fluid. L19.
2 The condition of being hypotonic. L19.

hypotonic /hʌɪpə(ʊ)ˈtɒnɪk/ *adjective.* L19.
[ORIGIN from HYPO- + TONIC.]
1 PHYSIOLOGY. Having a lower osmotic pressure than some particular fluid (usually that in a cell, or a body fluid). L19.
2 Of the eye: having a reduced intra-ocular pressure. E20.
3 MEDICINE. (Of muscle) in a state of abnormally low tone or tension; of or characterized by muscle in this state. E20.
■ **hypotonically** *adverb* with a hypotonic solution M20. **hypotonicity** /-ˈnɪsɪti/ *noun* the condition of being hypotonic; the extent to which a solution has a lower osmotic pressure than another: E20.

hypotonus /hʌɪpə(ʊ)ˈtəʊnəs/ *noun.* L19.
[ORIGIN from HYPO- + TONUS.]
MEDICINE. = HYPOTONIA.

hypotony *noun* see HYPOTONIA.

hypotrachelium /ˌhɪpə(ʊ)trəˈkiːlɪəm/ *noun.* Also **-lion** /-lɪən/. M16.
[ORIGIN Latin from Greek *hupotrakhēlion*, formed as HYPO- + *trakhēlos* neck: see -IUM.]
ARCHITECTURE. The lower part or neck of the capital of a column; in the Doric order, the groove or sinking between the neck of the capital and the shaft.

hypotyposis /hɪpətʌɪˈpəʊsɪs/ *noun.* Pl. **-poses** /-ˈpəʊsiːz/. L16.
[ORIGIN Greek *hupotupōsis* sketch, outline, pattern, from *hupotupoun* to sketch, from *tupos* TYPE *noun*: see -OSIS.]
RHETORIC. (A) vivid description of a scene, event, or situation.

hypped, †**hyppish** *adjectives* vars. of HIPPED *adjective*², HIPPISH.

hypsarrhythmia /hɪpsəˈrɪθmɪə/ *noun.* M20.
[ORIGIN from HYPSI-, HYPSO- + ARRHYTHMIA.]
MEDICINE. (The condition of having) a grossly disturbed EEG pattern of the kind associated with infantile spasms.
■ **hypsarrhythmic** *adjective* L20.

hypsi- /ˈhɪpsi/ *combining form.*
[ORIGIN Repr. Greek *hupsi-* on high, aloft: see -I-.]
Used in senses 'high', 'height'.
■ **hypsiceˈphalic** *adjective* (ANTHROPOLOGY) having a skull that is high and broad in relation to its anteroposterior length L19. **hypsiconch** /-kɒŋk/, **hypsiˈconchic** *adjectives* (ANTHROPOLOGY) in which the orbit of the eye is high in relation to its width E20. **hypsiconchous** /-ˈkɒŋk-/ *adjective* (ANTHROPOLOGY) = HYPSICONCH(IC) L19. **hypsiconchy** /-kɒŋki/ *noun* (ANTHROPOLOGY) the condition of being hypsiconchic E20. **hypsiˈthermal** *adjective* designating a period of the Holocene when the northern hemisphere was relatively warm, usually put at about 8000 to 1000 BC M20.

hypsilophodont /hɪpsɪˈlɒfədɒnt/ *adjective & noun.* L19.
[ORIGIN from Greek *hupsilophos* high-crested (formed as HYPSI- + LOPHO-) + -ODONT.]
PALAEONTOLOGY. (Designating) any hypsilophodontid, *esp.* one of the genus *Hypsilophodon*, of Lower Cretaceous times.
■ ˌ**hypsilophoˈdontid** *adjective & noun* (designating) any of a family of ornithischian dinosaurs of Middle Jurassic to late Cretaceous times which had powerful jaws and chisel-like teeth L20.

Hypsistarian /hɪpsɪˈstɛːrɪən/ *adjective & noun.* E18.
[ORIGIN from Greek *Hupsistarios*, from *hupsistos* highest: see -AN.]
ECCLESIASTICAL HISTORY. ▸**A** *adjective.* Belonging to a 4th-cent. sect which worshipped God under the name of 'Most High' rather than 'Father'. E18.
▸**B** *noun.* A member of this sect. E18.
■ Also †**Hypsistary** *noun*: only in E17.

hypso- /ˈhɪpsəʊ/ *combining form* repr. rare Greek *hupso-* (= *hupsi-*: see HYPSI-) or *hupsos* height: see -O-.
■ **hypsochrome** *adjective & noun* (CHEMISTRY) (*a*) = HYPSOCHROMIC; (*b*) *noun* a hypsochromic atom or group: L19. **hypsoˈchromic** *adjective* (CHEMISTRY) causing or characterized by a lightening of colour or a shift of the absorption spectrum towards shorter wavelengths L19. **hypsodont** *adjective* (of a tooth) having a high crown and short root L19. **hypsoˌdonty** *noun* the condition of being hypsodont or of having hypsodont teeth M20. **hypsoˈgraphic** *adjective* of or pertaining to hypsography (*hypsographic curve*, a curve representing the proportion of the earth's surface, or of a specified part of it, that lies above each of a series of altitudes) L19. **hypsoˈgraphical** *adjective* hypsographic L19. **hypˈsography** *noun* the branch of geography that deals with the relative altitudes of different parts of the earth's surface and with their determination L19. **hypˈsometer** *noun* an instrument for estimating height above sea level from the temperature at which water boils M19. **hypsoˈmetric** *adjective* of or pertaining to hypsometry (*hypsometric curve*, a hypsographic curve) M19. **hypsoˈmetrical** *adjective* hypsometric M19. **hypsoˈmetrically** *adverb* by hypsometric methods; with a hypsometer: M19. **hypˈsometry** *noun* the branch of science that deals with the measurement of altitude; the hypsometric features of a region: L16.

†**hypt** *adjective* var. of HIPPED *adjective*[2].

hyraces *noun pl.* see HYRAX.

hyraceum /hʌɪˈreɪsɪəm/ *noun.* Also **-cium**. M19.
[ORIGIN from *hyrac-* combining form of HYRAX.]
A secretion of the African rock hyrax, *Procavia capensis*, formerly used as a fixative for perfume.

hyracotherium /hʌɪrəkə(ʊ)ˈθɪərɪəm/ *noun.* M19.
[ORIGIN mod. Latin, from *hyraco-* combining form of HYRAX + Greek *thērion* wild animal.]
PALAEONTOLOGY. A member of the extinct Eocene genus *Hyracotherium*, which comprised small mammals ancestral to the horse.

hyrax /ˈhʌɪraks/ *noun.* Pl. **hyraxes**, **hyraces** /ˈhʌɪrəsiːz/. M19.
[ORIGIN mod. Latin from Greek *hurax*, *hurak-* shrew-mouse.]
A mammal of the order Hyracoidea, comprising small stumpy animals of Africa and the Middle East which resemble rodents but are actually related to ungulates and sirenians, having feet with nails like hoofs.
rock hyrax: see ROCK *noun*[1].

Hyrcan /ˈhəːk(ə)n/ *noun & adjective.* M16.
[ORIGIN Latin *Hyrcanus* from Greek *Hurkanos*.]
▸**A** *noun.* = HYRCANIAN *noun.* M16.
▸**B** *adjective.* = HYRCANIAN *adjective.* L16.

Hyrcanian /həːˈkeɪnɪən/ *noun & adjective.* M16.
[ORIGIN from Latin *Hyrcania* from Greek *Hurkania*: see -AN.]
▸**A** *noun.* A native or inhabitant of Hyrcania, an ancient region bordering the Caspian Sea which was noted for its wildness. M16.
▸**B** *adjective.* Of or pertaining to Hyrcania. L16.

hyson /ˈhʌɪs(ə)n/ *noun.* M18.
[ORIGIN Chinese *xīchūn* (Wade–Giles *hsi-ch'un*) lit. 'bright spring'.]
A kind of Chinese green tea. Also ***hyson tea***.

Hy-spy *noun* var. of I-SPY.

hyssop /ˈhɪsəp/ *noun.*
[ORIGIN Old English (*h*)*ysope*, reinforced in Middle English by Old French *ysope*, *isope*, later assim. to the source, Latin *hyssopus*, *-um* from Greek *hussōpos*, *-on*, of Semitic origin (cf. Hebrew *'ēzōḇ*).]
1 An aromatic bitter-tasting labiate herb, *Hyssopus officinalis*, native to the Mediterranean region, with spikes of small blue flowers. OE. ▸**b** With specifying word: any of various plants of the Labiatae and allied families thought to resemble hyssop. L16.
b giant hyssop any of various tall labiate plants of the Asian and N. American genus *Agastache*. ***hedge-hyssop***: see HEDGE *noun*. **water hyssop** a tropical aquatic plant, *Bacopa monnieri*, of the figwort family.
2 In biblical translations and allusions: a low-growing plant of uncertain identity, the twigs of which were used by the Hebrews for sprinkling in ritual purification; a bundle of these twigs. OE. ▸**b** A holy-water sprinkler. M19.

> AV *Ps.* 51:7 Purge me with hyssope, and I shal be cleane.

hyst *verb* var. of HIST *verb*[2].

hysterectomy /hɪstəˈrɛktəmi/ *noun.* L19.
[ORIGIN from HYSTERO- + -ECTOMY.]
Surgical removal of the uterus; an instance of this.

> J. ARCHER A hysterectomy prevented Arlene from bearing him any more children.

■ **hysterectomize** *verb trans.* perform a hysterectomy on E20.

hysteresis /hɪstəˈriːsɪs/ *noun.* Pl. **-reses** /-ˈriːsiːz/. L19.
[ORIGIN Greek *husterēsis* short-coming, deficiency, from *husterein* be behind, come late, from *husteros* late.]
The phenomenon whereby changes in some property of a physical system lag behind changes in the phenomenon causing it, *esp.* the lag of magnetization behind magnetizing force when the latter is varying; any dependence of the value of a property on the past history of the system.
– COMB.: **hysteresis curve**, **hysteresis loop**: showing how a property varies when the phenomenon causing it varies from one value to another and back again; **hysteresis loss** the energy dissipated as heat in a system as a result of hysteresis.
■ **hysteresial** *adjective* L19.

hysteretic /hɪstəˈrɛtɪk/ *adjective.* L19.
[ORIGIN Prob. from HYSTERESIS after *synthesis*, *synthetic*, etc., but cf. Greek *husterētikos* which comes on later.]
Of, pertaining to, or exhibiting hysteresis.
■ **hysteretically** *adverb* by means or as a result of hysteresis E20.

hysteria /hɪˈstɪərɪə/ *noun.* E19.
[ORIGIN formed as HYSTERIC + -IA[1].]
1 A syndrome (formerly regarded as a disease peculiar to women) whose symptoms include shallow volatile emotions, overdramatic behaviour, susceptibility to suggestion, and amnesia, with physical symptoms such as anaesthesia, tremor, and convulsions that cannot be attributed to any physical pathology. E19.
conversion hysteria. **dissociative hysteria**: in which the principal manifestation is psychological symptoms (rather than physical ones).
2 Wild uncontrollable excitement or emotion. M19.

> *Observer* There is a war hysteria in this country now.

hysteric /hɪˈstɛrɪk/ *adjective & noun.* M17.
[ORIGIN Latin *hystericus* from Greek *husterikos* belonging to or suffering in the uterus, hysterical, from *hustera* uterus (see -IC), hysteria being formerly regarded as a disease of women due to a disturbance of the uterus.]
▸**A** *adjective.* **1** = HYSTERICAL *adjective.* M17.
hysteric passion (now *rare* or *obsolete*) hysteria.
†**2** Of a medicine: good for hysteria or uterine disorders. L17–M18.
▸**B** *noun.* †**1** A medicine that is good for hysteria or uterine disorders. L17–M18.
2 *sing.* & (now usu.) in *pl.* A hysterical fit or convulsion; *colloq.* overwhelming mirth; a display of uncontrolled laughter, sorrow, or anger. E18.

> S. MIDDLETON When I get back home Irene's broken down, near hysterics. A. T. ELLIS I'm going to have hysterics. I'm going to stand in this stream and scream. D. LODGE She . . burst into uncontrollable hysterics and began throwing crockery at the wall.

3 A person subject to or affected with hysteria. M18.
■ **hystericism** /-sɪz(ə)m/ *noun* the condition of being hysterical; hysteria: E18.

hysterical /hɪˈstɛrɪk(ə)l/ *adjective & noun.* E17.
[ORIGIN formed as HYSTERIC + -AL[1].]
▸**A** *adjective.* **1** Affected with hysteria or hysterics; of, pertaining to, or characteristic of hysteria. E17.

> W. WHARTON We all get hysterical, start dancing around in the garden. B. T. BRADFORD Her hysterical tantrums and rivers of tears.

2 Extremely amusing. *colloq.* L20.

> *Observer* All nuns are amusing but nuns who tap-dance are hysterical.

▸**B** *noun.* †**1** = HYSTERIC *noun* 1. M–L17.
2 In *pl.* Hysterics. *rare.* M19.
3 = HYSTERIC *noun* 3. L19.

hysterically /hɪˈstɛrɪk(ə)li/ *adverb.* E18.
[ORIGIN from HYSTERIC *adjective* or HYSTERICAL *adjective*: see -ICALLY.]
In a hysterical manner; in a fit of hysterics.

hysterica passio /hɪˌstɛrɪkə ˈpasɪəʊ/ *noun phr.* E17.
[ORIGIN Latin, formed as HYSTERIC + *passio* passion.]
= HYSTERIA 1.

hystericky /hɪˈstɛrɪki/ *adjective. US colloq.* E19.
[ORIGIN from HYSTERIC + -Y[1].]
= HYSTERICAL *adjective* 1.

hystero- /ˈhɪstərəʊ/ *combining form* of Greek *hustera* uterus and of HYSTERIA: see -O-.
■ **hystero-ˈepilepsy** *noun* hysteria accompanied by epileptiform attacks L19. **hystero-epiˈleptic** *noun & adjective* (a person) prone to hystero-epilepsy L19. **hysteroˈgenic** *adjective* (now *rare*) designating an area of skin in some individuals pressure on which produces hysteria L19. **hysterosalˈpingogram** *noun* a radiograph of the uterus and Fallopian tubes L20. **hysterosalpinˈgography** *noun* radiography of the uterus and the Fallopian tubes following the injection of a radio-opaque fluid M20. **hysteroscope** *noun* a tubular instrument that can be inserted along the vagina into the uterus so that observations of its interior can be made or (now) operations performed on it E20. **hysteroˈscopic** *adjective* of or pertaining to hysteroscopy M20. **hysteroˈscopically** *adverb* by means of hysteroscopy L20. **hysteˈroscopy** *noun* use of, or examination with, a hysteroscope M20. **hysterotome** *noun* an instrument for performing hysterotomy M19. **hysteˈrotomy** *noun* (an instance of) surgical incision into (or removal of) the uterus E19.

hysteroid /ˈhɪstərɔɪd/ *adjective & noun.* M19.
[ORIGIN from HYSTERIA + -OID.]
▸**A** *adjective.* Resembling (that of) hysteria. M19.
▸**B** *noun.* A person prone to hysteria. M20.

†**hysterology** *noun.* E17–M19.
[ORIGIN Late Latin *hysterologia* from Greek *husterologia*, from *husteros* later: see -OLOGY.]
RHETORIC. Hysteron proteron. Also, anticlimax.

hysteron proteron /ˌhɪstərɒn ˈprɒtərɒn/ *noun, adverbial, & adjectival phr.* M16.
[ORIGIN Late Latin from Greek *husteron proteron* latter (put in place of) former.]
▸**A** *noun phr.* **1** RHETORIC. A figure of speech in which what should come last is put first. M16.
2 *gen.* Position or arrangement of things in the reverse of their natural or rational order. L16.
▸†**B** *adverbial phr.* In a topsy-turvy way. Only in E17.
▸**C** *adjectival phr.* Involving or employing hysteron proteron. M17.

hystricomorph /ˈhɪstrɪkə(ʊ)mɔːf/ *noun.* L19.
[ORIGIN mod. Latin *Hystricomorpha* (see below), from Latin *hystric-*, *hystrix-* porcupine from Greek *hustrix*: see -MORPH.]
A rodent of the suborder Hystricomorpha, which includes the porcupines.
■ **hystricoˈmorphic**, **hystricoˈmorphine** *adjectives* E19.

hyte /hʌɪt/ *adjective. Scot.* E18.
[ORIGIN Unknown.]
1 Mad, crazy. E18.
2 Excessively keen. L18.

hythe *noun* var. of HITHE.

hyther /ˈhʌɪθə/ *noun.* E20.
[ORIGIN from HY(DRO- + THER(MO-.]
METEOROLOGY. A quantity determined from temperature and humidity to represent the discomfort they jointly cause; a unit on a scale of 0 to 10 expressing this.

hythergraph /ˈhʌɪθəgrɑːf/ *noun.* E20.
[ORIGIN from Greek *hy(etos* rain + *ther(mē* heat + -GRAPH.]
A diagram in which temperature and either humidity or precipitation are shown for different occasions, esp. monthly throughout a year.

Hz *abbreviation.*
Hertz.

H

Ii

I, i /ʌɪ/.
The ninth letter of the modern English alphabet, repr. the Semitic consonant yod, which was adopted by Greek as iota, repr. a vowel. In Latin the letter represented both a high front vowel (long and short) and a palatal semivowel or continuant /j/; subsequently in Proto-Romance it also represented a palatal or palato-alveolar affricate /dʒ/, into which the semivowel had developed. In the 17th cent. a differentiation was made in the Roman alphabet, the consonant being represented by J, j (in its origin merely a variant form of I, i in certain positions), and the vowel by I, i. In English the quality of the short vowel represented by I, i has not significantly changed since Old English, but in the mod. period the long vowel has developed into a diphthong with a short high front vowel as its second elem.: for this and other values of this letter see the Key to the Pronunciation. Pl. **I's**, **Is**, **ies**.
▸ **I 1** The letter and its sound.
dot the i's (and cross the t's): see **DOT** *verb*.
2 The shape of the letter.
I-beam a girder of I-shaped section. **I-shaped** having a shape or cross-section like the capital letter I; having a long straight central piece with a right-angled crosspiece at each end.
▸ **II** Symbolical uses.
3 Used to denote serial order; applied e.g. to the ninth group or section, sheet of a book, etc.
4 *LOGIC*. (Cap. I.) A particular affirmative proposition.
5 The ninth hypothetical person or example.
6 The roman numeral for 1.
IV, **IX** the roman numerals for 4, 9.
7 *MATH*. (Italic *i*.) The imaginary quantity $\sqrt{-1}$, the square root of minus one. Cf. **J**, **J** 6b.
8 *ANATOMY & ZOOLOGY*. [Initial letter of *isotropic*.] ***I band***, a light transverse band in a myofibril of striated muscle, which consists only of actin filaments and becomes narrower on contraction. Cf. **A**, **A** 11.
▸ **III 9** Abbreviations: **I.** = Institute; Institution; Island(s); Isle(s). **I** (*CHEMISTRY*) = iodine.
– **NOTE**: The dot over the lower-case *i* is derived from a diacritic mark, like an acute accent, used in Latin manuscripts to indicate the *i* in positions in which it might have been mistaken for part of another letter. The same cause led finally in English to a scribal convention that *i* must not be used as a final letter, but must in this position be changed to *y*, though in inflected forms, where the *i* was not final, it was retained (hence *city*, *cities*, *duty*, *dutiful*, etc.).

I /ʌɪ/ *pers. pronoun, 1 sing. subjective (nom.), & noun*[1].
[**ORIGIN** Old English *ić* = Old Frisian, Old Saxon (Dutch) *ik*, Old High German *ih* (German *ich*), Old Norse *ek*, Gothic *ik*, from Germanic, cogn. with Latin *ego*, Greek *egō(n)*, Sanskrit *aham*, Avestan *azəm*, Old Church Slavonic (*j*)*azŭ* (Russian *ya*), Lithuanian *eo*, Latvian, Old Prussian, Armenian *es*. Cf. **ME** *pronoun*, **MY** *adjective*.]
▸ **A** *pronoun*. **1** Used by the speaker or writer referring to himself or herself, as the subject of predication or in attributive or predicative agreement with that subject. **OE**.

> **DRYDEN** Wretched I, to love in vain. **TENNYSON** Her sweet 'I will' has made you one. **D. BARNES** So I, doctor Matthew Mighty O'Connor, ask you to think of the night the day long. **E. BOWEN** No one would be gladder than I would if things ran smoothly. **G. GREENE** He had been consulted as well as I. J. **SIMMS** I am saying, am I not, that I no longer loved Kiyoko.

I Am God as self-existent; *loosely* an important or self-important person.
2 Objective: me. Esp. when separated from the governing verb or preposition by other words. Now *non-standard*. **L16**.

> **T. HARDY** Nothing's known to poor I! *Oxford Mail* After showing photographer Bill Radford and I her stitching skill.

3 Used, esp. among Rastafarians, in place of other pronouns to refer to oneself or people in general. Also ***I and I***, ***I man***. *W. Indian*. **L20**.
▸ **B** *noun*. **1** A self, a person identical with oneself. Chiefly in ***another I***, a second self. Now *rare*. **M16**.
2 The pronoun 'I' as a word. **L16**.
3 *METAPHYSICS*. The subject or object of self-consciousness, *the* ego. **E18**.
4 The narrator of a work of fiction, appearing on his or her own account. **M20**.

> **G. GREENE** Many readers assume . . that an 'I' is always the author.

†**I** *adverb, interjection, & noun*[2] see **AYE** *adverb*[2], *interjection, & noun*[2].

i' *preposition* see **IN** *preposition*.

†**i-** *prefix*[1].
Repr. Old English *ġe-* (see **Y-**), forming collective nouns, deriv. adjectives, adverbs, and verbs, esp. used with the pa. pple of verbs.

i- *prefix*[2] see **IN-**[3].

-i /*from Italian* i; *from Latin* ʌɪ, iː/ *suffix*[1].
Repr. Latin pl. ending of masc. nouns in *-us* and *-er* and Italian pl. ending of masc. nouns in *-o* and *-e*, adopted unchanged as English pl., as ***foci***, ***timpani***, ***dilettanti***.

-i /i/ *suffix*[2].
Repr. an adjectival suffix in Semitic and Indo-Iranian langs., and forming adjectives and nouns from the names of regions in or near the Middle East, as ***Azerbaijani***, ***Israeli***, ***Pakistani***.

-i- /ɪ/ *combining form (connective)*.
Repr. Latin *-i-* as a stem vowel or connective, adopted in English through French or directly from Latin, forming the connecting vowel esp. of words in **-ANA**, **-FEROUS**, **-FIC**, **-FORM**, **-FY**, **-GEROUS**, **-VOROUS**: cf. **-O-**.

IA *abbreviation*.
1 Institute of Actuaries.
2 Iowa.

Ia. *abbreviation*.
Iowa.

-ia /ɪə/ *suffix*[1].
Repr. Greek & Latin nom. sing. ending of fem. nouns (in Greek esp. freq. as the ending of abstract nouns from adjectives in *-os*), adopted unchanged in English, as ***hydrophobia***, ***mania***, ***militia***; hence in mod. Latin terms (as ***Utopia***), *spec.* (***a***) *MEDICINE* in nouns denoting states and disorders, as ***hysteria***, ***diphtheria***; (***b***) *BOTANY & ZOOLOGY* in names of genera, as *Dahlia*, *Latimeria*, and those of higher taxa also, as *Reptilia*, *Cryptogamia*; (***c***) in names of countries, as ***Australia***, ***India***; (***d***) (after *ammonia*) in names of alkaloids, as ***morphia***: now superseded by **-INE**[5]. Cf. **-A**[1], **-Y**[3].

-ia /ɪə/ *suffix*[2].
Repr. Greek pl. ending of neut. nouns in *-ion* and Latin pl. ending of neut. nouns in *-ium* or *-e*, adopted unchanged as English pl. of collective nouns, as ***juvenilia***, ***paraphernalia***, ***regalia***, and (*ZOOLOGY*) in mod. Latin forming the names of classes, as *Mammalia*, *Reptilia*: cf. **-A**[3].

IAA *abbreviation*.
Indoleacetic acid.

IAAF *abbreviation*.
International Amateur Athletics Federations.

IAEA *abbreviation*.
International Atomic Energy Agency.

-ial /ɪəl/ *suffix*.
Repr. French *-iel* or Latin *-ialis*, *-iale* in adjectives formed from noun stems in *-io-*, *-ia-*, as *curialis*, *tibialis*; extensively used in medieval Latin, French, and English to form deriv. adjectives from Latin adjectives in *-is*, *-ius*, as ***celestial*** from Latin *caelestis*, ***dictatorial*** from Latin *dictatorius*, etc.: cf. **-AL**[1].

iamb /ˈʌɪam(b)/ *noun*. **M19**.
[**ORIGIN** Anglicized from **IAMBUS**.]
= **IAMBUS**.

iambi *noun pl.* see **IAMBUS**.

iambic /ʌɪˈambɪk/ *adjective & noun*. **M16**.
[**ORIGIN** French *iambique* from late Latin *iambicus* from Greek *iambikos*, from *iambos*: see **IAMBUS**, **-IC**.]
PROSODY. ▸ **A** *adjective*. **1** Consisting of, characterized by, or based on iambuses. **M16**.
2 Of a poet: using iambic metres. **L16**.
▸ **B** *noun*. An iambic foot, verse, or poem. Usu. in *pl.* **L16**.
■ **iambical** *adjective* (long *rare* or *obsolete*) = **IAMBIC** *adjective* **L16**. **iambically** *adverb* (*rare*) **M19**.

iambographer /ʌɪamˈbɒgrəfə/ *noun*. *rare*. **E17**.
[**ORIGIN** from Greek *iambographos*, from *iambos*: see **IAMBUS**, **-O-**, **-GRAPHER**.]
A writer of iambics.

iambus /ʌɪˈambəs/ *noun*. Pl. **-buses**, **-bi** /-bʌɪ/. **L16**.
[**ORIGIN** Latin from Greek *iambos* iambus, lampoon, from *iaptein* assail in words (the iambic trimeter having been first used by Greek satirists).]
PROSODY. A metrical foot consisting of one short followed by one long syllable or (in English etc.) of one unstressed followed by one stressed syllable.

-ian /ɪən/ *suffix*.
1 Repr. Latin *-ianus*, from *-anus* **-AN** added to noun stems in *-i-*; in English forming adjectives & nouns adopted or formed from Latin, as ***antediluvian***, ***barbarian***, ***equestrian***, ***patrician***, and from proper names of persons and places, as ***Bostonian***, ***Churchillian***, ***Georgian***, ***Oxonian***: see **-I-**, **-AN**. In some nouns, as ***theologian***, *-ian* is a refash. of French *-ien*.
2 [from **MAGNES)IAN**, **MANGANES)IAN**.] *MINERALOGY*. Replacing the ending of English or Latin names of elements to form adjectives with the sense 'having a small proportion of a constituent element replaced by the element concerned'.

-iana /ɪˈɑːnə/ *suffix*.
Repr. a euphonic var. of **-ANA**, after Latin words ending in *-iana*: see **-I-**, **-ANA**.

Iapygian /ʌɪəˈpɪdʒɪən/ *noun & adjective*. **L18**.
[**ORIGIN** from Latin *Iapygius*, from *Iapyg-*, *Iapyx* a son of Daedalus said to have ruled over southern Italy: see **-IAN**.]
▸ **A** *noun*. A member of a people inhabiting Iapygia, the name given by the ancient Greeks to the area comprising the peninsula of Apulia in southern Italy; the language of this people. **L18**.
▸ **B** *adjective*. Of or pertaining to Iapygia or the Iapygians. **M19**.

-iasis /ˈʌɪəsɪs/ *suffix*.
[**ORIGIN** from **-I-** + Latin or Greek *-asis* used to form nouns of state or process.]
Forming the names of diseases, as ***elephantiasis***, ***leishmaniasis***, ***psoriasis***.

IATA /ʌɪˈɑːtə/ *abbreviation*.
International Air Transport Association.

Iatmul /ˈjatmʊl/ *noun & adjective*. **M20**.
[**ORIGIN** Iatmul.]
▸ **A** *noun*. Pl. same. A member of a people of NW Papua New Guinea; the language of this people. **M20**.
▸ **B** *attrib.* or as *adjective*. Of or pertaining to the Iatmul or their language. **M20**.

iatraliptic /ʌɪˌatrəˈlɪptɪk/ *adjective & noun*. *rare*. **M17**.
[**ORIGIN** Latin *iatralipticus* from Greek *iatraleiptikos*, from *iatraleiptēs*, from *iatros* (see **IATRO-**) + *aleiptēs* anointer: see **-IC**.]
▸ **A** *noun*. A physician who uses unguents to effect cures. **M17**.
▸ **B** *adjective*. Consisting of the curative use of unguents. **E18**.

iatric /ʌɪˈatrɪk/ *adjective*. *rare*. **M19**.
[**ORIGIN** Greek *iatrikos*, from *iatros* physician: see **IATRO-**, **-IC**.]
Of or pertaining to a physician or medicine; medical; medicinal.
■ **iatrical** *adjective* **L17**.

iatro- /ʌɪˈatrəʊ/ *combining form*.
[**ORIGIN** Greek, from *iatros* physician, from *iasthai* heal: see **-O-**.]
Of or pertaining to physicians or medicine.
■ **iatroˈchemical** *adjective* of, pertaining to, or advocating iatrochemistry **M19**. **iatroˈchemist** *noun* an advocate of iatrochemistry **M17**. **iatroˈchemistry** *noun* the theory or school of thought that was adopted by Paracelsus and others in the 16th and 17th cents., according to which medicine and physiology were to be understood in terms of chemistry **M19**.

iatrogenic /ʌɪˌatrə(ʊ)ˈdʒɛnɪk/ *adjective*. **E20**.
[**ORIGIN** from **IATRO-** + **-GENIC**.]
(Of a disease, symptom, etc.) induced unintentionally by a physician's treatment, examination, etc.; of or pertaining to the inducing of disease etc. in this way.

> *British Medical Bulletin* The epidemic of iatrogenic deaths in asthmatic children.

■ **iatrogenically** *adverb* **M20**. **iatrogenicity** /-ˈnɪsɪti/ *noun* iatrogeny **M20**. **iaˈtrogeny** *noun* the iatrogenic production of disease etc. **E20**.

iatromathematical /ʌɪˌatrə(ʊ)maθ(ə)ˈmatɪk(ə)l/ *adjective*. **E17**.
[**ORIGIN** from mod. Latin *iatromathematicus* from Greek *iatromathēmatikos*, formed as **IATRO-** + *mathēmatikos*: see **MATHEMATIC**, **-AL**[1].]
HISTORY OF SCIENCE. †**1** Practising medicine in conjunction with astrology. Only in **E17**.
2 Of, pertaining to, or advocating iatromathematics. **M19**.
■ **iatromathematically** *adverb* **E17**. **iatromathemaˈtician** *noun* an advocate or adherent of iatromathematics **E18**. **iatromathematics** *noun* †(***a***) a work on medicine and astrology; (***b***) a theory or school of thought that arose in Italy in the 17th cent., according to which medicine and physiology were to be explained in terms of mathematics and mechanics: **M17**.

iatromechanical /ʌɪˌatrə(ʊ)mɪˈkanɪk(ə)l/ *adjective*. M19.
[ORIGIN from IATRO- + MECHANICAL.]
HISTORY OF SCIENCE. = IATROMATHEMATICAL 2.
■ **iatromechanic**, **iatromechanician** /-mɛkəˈnɪʃ(ə)n/ *nouns* an iatromathematician M19. **iatromechanics**, **iatroˈmechanism** *nouns* iatromathematics L19. **iatroˈmechanist** *noun* an iatromathematician M20.

iatrophysical /ʌɪˌatrə(ʊ)ˈfɪzɪk(ə)l/ *adjective*. L19.
[ORIGIN from IATRO- + PHYSICAL.]
HISTORY OF SCIENCE. = IATROMATHEMATICAL 2.
■ **iatrophysicist** /-sɪst/ *noun* an iatromathematician L19. **iatrophysics** *noun* iatromathematics L19.

IB *abbreviation*.
International Baccalaureate.

IBA *abbreviation*.
hist. Independent Broadcasting Authority.

Iban /ˈiːban, iːˈban/ *noun & adjective*. E20.
[ORIGIN Iban.]
▸ **A** *noun*. A member of a people of Sarawak (also called ***Sea Dyaks***); the Indonesian language of this people. E20.
▸ **B** *adjective*. Of or pertaining to this people or their language. E20.

Ibanag /ˈiːbənɑːɡ/ *noun & adjective*. L19.
[ORIGIN Ibanag.]
▸ **A** *noun*. A member of a people inhabiting Luzon in the Philippines; the Austronesian language of this people. L19.
▸ **B** *adjective*. Of or pertaining to this people or their language. M20.

Iberian /ʌɪˈbɪərɪən/ *adjective & noun*. E16.
[ORIGIN from Latin *Iberia* the country of the *Iberi* or *Iberes*, from Greek *Ibēres*, (i) Spaniards, (ii) a people of the S. Caucasus: see -IAN.]
▸ **A** *adjective*. **1** Of, pertaining to, or designating the peninsula of SW Europe occupied by Spain and Portugal or the (present or former) Iberians. E16.
2 Of or pertaining to ancient Iberia in Asia, a region approximately corresponding to modern Georgia. *rare*. L17.
3 Of or pertaining to the Iberians of Neolithic Britain. L19.
▸ **B** *noun* **1** **a** A native or inhabitant of Spain or Portugal; a Spaniard, a Portuguese. E17. ▸**b** A native or inhabitant of the Iberian peninsula in pre-Roman and Roman times. M19. ▸**c** The language or languages spoken by the ancient Iberians. L19.
2 A native or inhabitant of ancient Iberia in Asia. Long *rare* or *obsolete*. E17.
3 An inhabitant of Britain in Neolithic times regarded as belonging to a branch of the Iberians of Continental Europe. L19.

iberis /ʌɪˈbɪərɪs/ *noun*. M18.
[ORIGIN mod. Latin (see below), prob. from Greek *ibēris* a kind of pepperwort.]
Any of various low-growing cruciferous plants of the chiefly Mediterranean genus *Iberis*, bearing flattened heads of white, pink, or purple flowers and frequently grown as garden plants; = CANDYTUFT.

†**Ibernian** *adjective & noun* see HIBERNIAN.

Ibero- /ʌɪˈbɪərəʊ/ *combining form* of IBERIAN: see -O-.
■ **Ibero-Aˈmerican** *adjective & noun* (a) Spanish-American; (a) Latin American: E20. **Ibero-Cauˈcasian** *adjective & noun* (of) a group of languages spoken in the region of the Caucasus and ancient Iberia in Asia (see IBERIAN *adjective* 2) M20.

ibex /ˈʌɪbɛks/ *noun*. E17.
[ORIGIN Latin.]
A goat antelope, *Capra ibex*, with thick curved ridged horns and a chin beard and occurring chiefly in mountainous parts of NE Africa and central Asia. Also (in full ***Spanish ibex***), a related animal of the Pyrenees, *Capra pyrenaica*.
Siberian ibex: see SIBERIAN *adjective*. WALIA ***ibex***.

IBF *abbreviation*.
International Boxing Federation.

Ibibio /ɪbɪˈbiːəʊ/ *noun & adjective*. E19.
[ORIGIN Ibibio.]
▸ **A** *noun*. Pl. same, **-os**. A member of a people of southern Nigeria; the Niger-Congo language of this people. E19.
▸ **B** *attrib*. or as *adjective*. Of or pertaining to the Ibibio or their language. M19.

Ibicencan /ɪbɪˈθɛŋk(ə)n/ *noun & adjective*. M20.
[ORIGIN from Spanish *ibicenca* native or inhabitant of Ibiza + -AN.]
▸ **A** *noun*. A native or inhabitant of Ibiza (see IBIZAN). M20.
▸ **B** *adjective*. Of or pertaining to Ibiza. M20.
Ibicencan hound = IVICENE *noun*.

Ibicenco /ɪbɪˈθɛŋkəʊ/ *noun & adjective*. Pl. of noun **-os**. E20.
[ORIGIN Spanish *ibicenco* pertaining to Ibiza (see IBIZAN).]
= IBICENCAN.

ibid. /ˈɪbɪd/ *adverb*. M17.
[ORIGIN Abbreviation of Latin: see IBIDEM.]
= IBIDEM.

ibidem /ˈɪbɪdɛm, ɪˈbʌɪdɛm/ *adverb*. M18.
[ORIGIN Latin = in the same place, from *ibi* there + demonstr. suffix *-dem*, as in *idem*, *tandem*, etc.]
In the same book, chapter, passage, etc.

-ibility /ɪˈbɪlɪti/ *suffix*.
[ORIGIN French *-ibilité* from Latin *-ibilitas*.]
Forming nouns from adjectives in **-IBLE**, as ***credibility***, ***possibility***: see -ITY.

ibis /ˈʌɪbɪs/ *noun*. Pl. **ibises**; (now *rare*) **ibides** /ˈʌɪbɪdiːz/, **ibes** /ˈʌɪbiːz/. LME.
[ORIGIN Latin (genit. *ibis*, *ibidis*, pl. *ibes*) from Greek.]
1 Any of a group of gregarious wading birds of warm and tropical climates which have a long thin decurved bill, a long neck, and long legs, and which with the spoonbills constitute the family Threskiornithidae. LME.
sacred ibis a white ibis, *Threskiornis aethiopica*, native to Africa and Madagascar and venerated by the ancient Egyptians. ***scarlet ibis***: see SCARLET *adjective*.
2 *ANGLING*. Orig., a kind of artificial fly made with a feather dyed red. Now usu., such a feather. M19.

Ibizan /ɪˈbiːθ(ə)n/ *adjective & noun*. E20.
[ORIGIN from *Ibiza* (see below) + -AN.]
▸ **A** *adjective*. Of or pertaining to Ibiza, the westernmost of the Balearic Islands in the western Mediterranean. E20.
Ibizan hound = IVICENE *noun*.
▸ **B** *noun*. **1** The Catalan dialect of Ibiza. M20.
2 An Ibizan hound. L20.

-ible /ɪb(ə)l/ *suffix*.
[ORIGIN from Latin *-ibilis* adjectival suffix, the form taken by the suffix *-bilis* (see -BLE) when added to Latin consonantal stems (verbal or ppl) and some *e-* and *i-* stems.]
Forming adjectives with the senses 'able to be, suitable for being', as ***audible***, ***compressible***, ***edible***, and (formerly) 'able to, causing', as ***horrible***, ***passible***, ***terrible***. Freq. displaced by **-ABLE** in words that have come through French, or that are looked on as formed directly on an English verb.

Iblis *noun* var. of EBLIS.

IBM *abbreviation*.
International Business Machines (proprietary name).

Ibo *noun & adjective* var. of IGBO.

ibotenic /iːbəʊˈtɛnɪk/ *adjective*. M20.
[ORIGIN from Japanese *iboten(gutake* the mushroom *Amanita strobiliformis* from which the acid was first isolated, + -IC.]
BIOCHEMISTRY. ***ibotenic acid***, an isoxazole found in certain mushrooms, used as an insecticide and as a selective neurotoxin.
■ **ibotenate** *noun* a salt of ibotenic acid L20.

IBRD *abbreviation*.
International Bank for Reconstruction and Development.

IBS *abbreviation*.
Irritable bowel syndrome.

Ibsenism /ˈɪbs(ə)nɪz(ə)m/ *noun*. L19.
[ORIGIN from *Ibsen* (see below) + -ISM.]
The dramatic principles and aims of the works of the Norwegian dramatist and poet Henrik Ibsen (1828–1906) and his followers, in which social conventions are examined and criticized.
■ **Ibsenish** *adjective* resembling events in Ibsen's plays L19. **Ibsenist** *noun & adjective* (*a*) *noun* an admirer, student, or imitator of Ibsen; (*b*) *adjective* of or pertaining to Ibsenism or Ibsenists; typical of Ibsen's plays: L19. **Ibsenite** *noun & adjective* = IBSENIST L19.

ibuprofen /ʌɪbjuːˈprəʊf(ə)n/ *noun*. M20.
[ORIGIN from I(SO- + BU(TYL + PRO(PIONIC + alt. of PHEN(YL, elems. of the systematic name (see below).]
An anti-inflammatory and analgesic drug used to treat arthritis; 2-(4-isobutylphenyl)propionic acid, $C_{13}H_{18}O_2$.

IC *abbreviation*.
Integrated circuit.

i/c *abbreviation*.
1 In charge.
2 In command.
3 Internal combustion.

-ic /ɪk/ *suffix*. Also †**-ick**, †**-ique**.
[ORIGIN Repr. French *-ique*, its source Latin *-icus*, & its source Greek *-ikos*.]
1 In adjectives from French, Latin (esp. late Latin), or Greek, as ***civic***, ***classic***, ***historic***, or formed directly in English, as ***artistic***, ***Icelandic***, with the general sense 'of or pertaining to'. ▸**b** Forming part of compound suffixes, as **-ATIC**, **-ETIC**, **-FIC**, **-OLOGIC**. ▸**c** *CHEMISTRY*. In adjectives denoting a higher valence or degree of oxidation than those ending in *-ous*, as ***ferric***, ***sulphuric***.
2 In Greek, adjectives in *-ikos* were used absol. as nouns, which in medieval Latin gave words in *-ica* which could be taken as fem. sing. or as neut. pl. In English before the 16th cent. words of this class had the sing. form, and in some, as ***logic***, ***magic***, ***rhetoric***, the sing. has been retained; others have *-ic* after French or German, as ***dialectic***. More often such words now end in **-ICS**.
3 In nouns that are English adjectives used absol., as ***cosmetic***, ***emetic***; ***epic***, ***lyric***; ***domestic***, ***mechanic***, ***rustic***.

icaco /ɪˈkɑːkəʊ/ *noun*. Pl. **-o(e)s**. M18.
[ORIGIN Spanish *(h)icaco* from Taino *hikako*.]
An evergreen tree, *Chrysobalanus icaco*, native to tropical America and the W. Indies and bearing white flowers; the fruit of this tree. Also called ***coco-plum***.

-ical /ɪk(ə)l/ *suffix*.
1 In adjectives from late or medieval Latin words in *-icalis* (formed by adding *-alis* to nouns in *-icus* or *-ice*), as ***clerical***, ***grammatical***, or formed directly in English from nouns in *-ic*, Latin adjectives in *-icus*, & French adjectives in *-ique*, as ***domestical***, ***fanatical***, ***philosophical***, ***theoretical***: see **-AL**[1]. To many adjectives in *-ical* there corresponds another in *-ic*, that in *-ical* usually being the earlier and the more commonly used.
2 In compound suffixes, as **-OLOGICAL**.

-ically /ɪk(ə)li/ *suffix*.
[ORIGIN from -ICAL + -LY[2].]
Forming adverbs corresp. to adjectives in *-ic* and *-ical*.

ICAO *abbreviation*.
International Civil Aviation Organization.

Icarian /ɪˈkɛːrɪən/ *adjective*. M16.
[ORIGIN from Latin *Icarius* (= Greek *Ikarios*), formed as ICARUS: see -IAN.]
Of, pertaining to, or characteristic of Icarus; rashly ambitious or presumptuous.
†**Icarian Sea** the Aegean Sea.

Icarus /ˈɪk(ə)rəs/ *noun*. L16.
[ORIGIN Latin (see below) from Greek *Ikaros*.]
A person who is rashly ambitious or presumptuous, or who resembles in some other way Icarus the son of Daedalus in Greek mythology, who flew so high that the sun melted the wax with which his wings were fastened, so that he fell to his death in the Aegean Sea.

ICBM *abbreviation*.
Intercontinental ballistic missile.

ICC *abbreviation*.
1 Indian Claims Commission. *US*.
2 International Chamber of Commerce.
3 International Cricket Council.
4 Interstate Commerce Commission. *US*.

ICE *abbreviation*.
1 Institution of Civil Engineers.
2 Internal-combustion engine.

ice /ʌɪs/ *noun*.
[ORIGIN Old English *īs* = Old Frisian, Old Saxon, Old High German *īs* (Dutch *ijs*, German *Eis*), Old Norse *íss*, from Germanic, with analogues in Iranian langs.]
1 Frozen water, a brittle transparent crystalline solid. OE. ▸**b** A mass or body of ice. Usu. in *pl*. OE.
2 ***the ice***, the sheet or layer of ice on something, esp. a pond, river, etc. ME.

> B. LOPEZ No ship . . had been able to breach the ice in Davis Strait.

3 *fig*. Complete absence of warm feeling; cold-heartedness; reserve. L16.

> M. IGNATIEFF She watched . . as the ice formed at the heart of her marriage.

4 **a** (An) ice cream. E18. ▸**b** Icing for cakes etc. E18.
5 **a** Diamonds; jewellery. *slang*. E20. ▸**b** Profit from the illegal sale of theatre, cinema, etc., tickets. *US slang*. E20. ▸**c** Protection money. *slang*. M20.
– PHRASES: ***as cold as ice***: see COLD *adjective*. ***black ice***: see BLACK *adjective*. **break the ice** *fig*. make a beginning; break through reserve or stiffness. ***cut ice***: see CUT *verb*. ***dry ice***: see DRY *adjective*. ***fast ice***: see FAST *adjective*. ***hog on ice***: see HOG *noun*. ***inland ice***: see INLAND *adjective*. **like ice** (of a room, one's extremities, etc.) very cold. MOUNTAIN ***of ice***. **on ice** (*a*) (of an entertainment, sport, etc.) performed by skaters; (*b*) (of a bottle etc.) on or in ice to cool the contents; (*c*) *colloq*. held in reserve; postponed for attention at a later date. **on thin ice** in a risky situation. ***skate on thin ice***: see SKATE *verb*.
– COMB.: **ice age** a glacial period, esp. one of those in the Pleistocene epoch (***little ice age***: see LITTLE *adjective*); **ice axe** a tool used by mountaineers for cutting footholds in ice; **ice bag** an ice-filled rubber bag for medical use; **ice beer** a type of strong lager brewed at sub-zero temperatures so that ice crystals form, which are then strained off to remove impurities and excess water; **ice bird** (*a*) any of several prions; (*b*) the little auk; ***iceblink***: see BLINK *noun* 5a; **iceblock** (*a*) a block of ice; (*b*) *Austral. & NZ* an ice lolly; **ice blue** a very pale blue; **ice bolt** a bolt or dart of ice; an avalanche; *fig*. a sudden chill; **ice-bound** *adjective* held fast or confined by ice; **icebox** (*a*) a box for holding ice; (*b*) a box kept cold by ice; (*c*) *US* a refrigerator; (*d*) a compartment in a refrigerator for making and storing ice; **ice bucket** = ***ice pail*** below; **ice cap** (*a*) a permanent layer of ice covering a tract of land (esp. a polar region) or the top of a mountain; (*b*) a bag of crushed ice applied to the head; **ice chest** = *icebox* (a) above; **ice-cold** *adjective* as cold as ice; **ice cube** a small block of ice made in a refrigerator, used for chilling drinks; **ice dancing** a form of ice skating incorporating choreographed dance moves, typically performed by skaters in pairs; **icefall** (*a*) a steep part of a glacier resembling a frozen waterfall; (*b*) an avalanche of ice; **ice field** an extensive flat expanse of ice, esp. in polar regions; **icefish** *noun & verb* (*a*) *noun* a capelin; (*b*) *verb intrans*. fish through holes in the ice on a lake or river (chiefly as ***ice-fishing*** *verbal noun*); ***ice floe***: see FLOE; **ice flower** a delicate pattern of ice crystals formed by frost, esp. on a window; **ice fog** fog in which the obscuring matter is minute ice crystals suspended in the air; **ice foot** [Danish *isfod*] (*a*) a belt of ice on the sea next to the coast in Arctic regions; (*b*) the edge of an ice floe; **ice front** the margin of a glacier, ice shelf, or ice sheet; ***ice hockey***: see HOCKEY *noun*[1] 2; **ice house** (*a*) a building, often partly or wholly underground, in which to store ice; (*b*) a small shelter built out of ice; ***ice lolly***: see LOLLY *noun*[2] 1; **ice machine**: for making ice from water; **ice master** a pilot or sailing master who

has experience of navigating among ice floes; **ice pack** (**a**) (a mass of) pack ice; (**b**) a quantity of ice wrapped up and applied to the body for medical etc. purposes; **ice pail** a pail to hold ice for cooling bottles of wine; **ice pan** a small slab of floating ice; **ice pick** (**a**) a needle-like implement with a handle for splitting table ice; (**b**) a mountaineer's pick; **ice piton** a piton to assist climbing on ice; **ice plant** (**a**) any of various succulent plants of the mesembryanthemum family, native to southern Africa, esp. *Mesembryanthemum crystallinum*, whose leaves are covered with pellucid watery vesicles looking like ice crystals; (**b**) a tall freq. cultivated pink-flowered stonecrop, *Sedum spectabile*, with glaucous fleshy leaves; ***ice rink***: see RINK *noun* 3; **ice sheet** a permanent layer of ice covering an extensive tract of land, esp. a polar region; **ice shelf** a floating sheet of ice permanently attached to a land mass; **ice show** an entertainment performed by skaters on ice; **ice skate** a skate consisting of a boot with a blade beneath, for skating on ice; **ice-skate** *verb intrans.* skate on ice; **ice skater** a person who skates on ice; **ice storm** a storm of freezing rain that leaves a deposit of ice; **ice water**: obtained from or cooled by ice; **ice-wool** = EIS WOOL; **ice-work** (**a**) ornamentation executed in ice, or having the appearance of ice; frosted work; (**b**) work done by glaciers or icebergs; (**c**) (the technique of) climbing on icy surfaces; **ice worm** a small oligochaete worm, *Mesenchytraeus solifugus*, found in N. American glaciers and ice fields; **ice yacht** a lightly built boat with runners and a sail for travelling at speed over ice.

▪ **iceless** *adjective* free of ice; not covered by ice: M19.

ice /ʌɪs/ *verb*. LME.
[ORIGIN from the noun.]
1 *verb trans.* **a** Cover with ice. Foll. by *over*, *up*. Usu. in *pass.* LME. ▸**b** Convert into ice. M17.

Times A snowstorm was encountered and the aircraft became badly iced-up.

2 *verb trans.* Cover or decorate (a cake etc.) with icing. E17.
3 *verb trans.* Chill with ice; cool (esp. wine) by placing in ice. E19.
4 *verb trans.* Make cold. Chiefly *fig.* E19. ▸**b** Kill. *US slang*. M20.
5 *verb intrans.* Turn to ice; become covered with ice. Also foll. by *over*, *up*. M19.

C. A. LINDBERGH The turn indicator's icing up. E. JONG Pipes froze. The driveway iced over.

-ice /ɪs/ *suffix*[1].
Forming (esp. abstract) nouns and repr. Old French *-ice* (mod. *-ise*), of non-popular origin, from Latin *-itia*, *-itius*, *-itium*; e.g. ***avarice***, ***novice***, ***police***, ***precipice***, ***service***.
– NOTE: The ending has various other origins, partly through assim. to the above, as in *accomplice*, *apprentice*, *bodice*, *poultice*.

-ice /ɪsi/ *suffix*[2]. Also **-icè**.
In medieval Latin forming adverbs from adjectives, adopted esp. when from names of peoples or languages, as ***anglice***, ***gallice***, and in English occas. forming jocular nonce words.

iceberg /ˈʌɪsbəːg/ *noun*. L18.
[ORIGIN Middle Dutch & mod. Dutch *ijsberg*, whence also German *Eisberg*, Swedish *isberg*, Danish *isbjerg*: see ICE noun, BARROW noun[1].]
†**1** A glacier which comes close to the coast and is seen from the sea as a hill. L18–M19.
2 A very large mass of ice floating loose in the sea after becoming detached from a glacier or ice sheet. E19.
3 *fig.* An unfeeling or unemotional person. M19.
4 *fig.* Something of which the greater part is unknown or not recognized. M20.
tip of the iceberg a known or recognizable part of something (esp. a difficulty) evidently much larger.
– COMB.: **iceberg lettuce** any of various crisp pale cabbage lettuces.

iceboat /ˈʌɪsbəʊt/ *noun & verb*. M18.
[ORIGIN from ICE noun + BOAT noun.]
▸ **A** *noun*. **1** A boat mounted on runners for travelling on ice; *spec.* an ice yacht. M18.
2 = ICE-BREAKER 2. M19.
3 A fishing vessel with facilities for the refrigeration of fish. *US*. L19.
▸ **B** *verb intrans.* Travel in an iceboat or ice yacht. Chiefly as ***iceboating*** *verbal noun*. L19.
▪ **iceboater** *noun*. E20.

ice-breaker /ˈʌɪsbreɪkə/ *noun*. E19.
[ORIGIN from ICE noun + BREAKER noun[1].]
1 A thing which breaks up moving ice so as to diminish its impact; *spec.* a structure protecting the upstream end of a bridge pier. E19.
2 A ship specially built or adapted for breaking a channel through ice. L19.
3 *fig.* Something that breaks the ice on a social occasion etc. L19.

ice cream /ʌɪsˈkriːm/ *noun phr.* M18.
[ORIGIN Alt. of *iced cream* s.v. ICED 1.]
A semi-solid or semi-liquid foodstuff made from sweetened and flavoured milk fat, stirred to incorporate air, and frozen; a portion of this.
– COMB.: ***ice-cream float***: see FLOAT noun 9; **ice-cream parlour** a cafe where ice cream is sold.

iced /ʌɪst/ *adjective*. L17.
[ORIGIN from ICE noun, verb: see -ED[2], -ED[1].]
1 Covered or chilled with ice. L17.

M. PIERCY Why don't you bring us iced tea?

†**iced cream** ice cream. ***iced lolly***: see LOLLY noun[2] 1.

2 Covered with icing; (of fruit) glacé. M19.

Iceland /ˈʌɪslənd/ *noun*. Also †**Island**. M16.
[ORIGIN See sense 2. Branch II directly from ICE noun + LAND noun[1].]
▸ **I 1** In full ***Iceland dog***, (arch.) ***Iceland cur***. A shaggy sharp-eared white dog, formerly in favour as a lapdog in England. M16.
2 Used *attrib.* in the names of things associated with Iceland, an island republic in the N. Atlantic, near the Arctic Circle. L18.
Iceland falcon a usu. pale grey gyrfalcon from Iceland. **Iceland gull** a grey and white Arctic gull, *Larus glaucoides*. **Iceland lichen**, **Iceland moss** an Arctic and Alpine lichen, *Cetraria islandica*, which can be boiled to make an edible jelly. **Iceland poppy** an Arctic poppy, *Papaver nudicaule*, with leafless stems and white yellow-based petals; any of the garden poppies, with variously coloured flowers, derived from this or the related *P. alpinum* group, of European mountains. **Iceland spar** a transparent variety of calcite with strong double refraction.
▸ **II 3** (**i-**.) A country covered with ice; the realm of perpetual ice. M19.
▪ **Icelander** *noun* a native or inhabitant of Iceland E17. **Iceˈlandish** *adjective* Icelandic E18.

Icelandic /ʌɪsˈlandɪk/ *adjective & noun*. L17.
[ORIGIN from ICELAND + -IC.]
▸ **A** *adjective*. Of or pertaining to Iceland or its people or language. L17.
▸ **B** *noun*. The Germanic language of Iceland. L18.
Old Icelandic: see OLD adjective.

iceman /ˈʌɪsmən/ *noun*. Pl. **-men**. M19.
[ORIGIN from ICE noun + MAN noun.]
1 A person skilled in traversing ice in Alpine or polar regions. M19.
2 A person responsible for looking after the ice on an ice rink. M19.
3 A person who deals in or sells ice. *N. Amer.* M19.
4 A person who makes ice cream. L19.
▪ **icemanship** *noun* skill in traversing ice L19.

Icenian /ʌɪˈsiːnɪən/ *noun & adjective*. L16.
[ORIGIN from Latin *Iceni* the Icenians + -AN.]
▸ **A** *noun*. A member of a tribe of ancient Britons inhabiting the area of SE England represented by Norfolk and Suffolk and to which Boudicca belonged. L16.
▸ **B** *adjective*. **1** Of or pertaining to the Icenians or the area they inhabited. M18.
2 GEOLOGY. Designating or pertaining to certain early Pleistocene beds of Norfolk and Suffolk. L19.
▪ **Iˈcenic** *adjective* = ICENIAN *adjective* 1 L19.

ichabod /ˈɪkəbɒd/ *interjection*. E19.
[ORIGIN With allus. to *1 Samuel* 4:21, where Eli's daughter-in-law names her child Ichabod, saying 'The glory is departed from Israel.']
Expr. regret at former glories or higher standards.

I.Chem.E. *abbreviation*.
Institution of Chemical Engineers.

ichneumon /ɪkˈnjuːmən/ *noun*. L15.
[ORIGIN Latin from Greek *ikhneumōn* lit. 'tracker', from *ikhneuein* to track, from *ikhnos* track, footprint.]
1 The Egyptian mongoose, *Herpestes ichneumon*, found over much of Africa and parts of southern Europe, and noted for destroying crocodile eggs. L15.
2 More fully ***ichneumon fly***. Any of the family Ichneumonidae of hymenopterous insects, which mostly lay their eggs in other insects, esp. caterpillars. M17.
▪ **ichneumoned** *adjective* infested with ichneumon flies M19.

ichnofossil /ˈɪknəʊfɒs(ə)l, -sɪl/ *noun*. M20.
[ORIGIN from Greek *ikhnos* (see ICHNOGRAPHY) + FOSSIL noun.]
A trace fossil.

ichnography /ɪkˈnɒgrəfi/ *noun*. L16.
[ORIGIN French *ichnographie* or Latin *ichnographia* from Greek *ikhnographia*, from *ikhnos* track, footprint: see -GRAPHY.]
A ground plan; a plan, a map.
▪ **ichnoˈgraphic** *adjective* L17. **ichnoˈgraphical** *adjective* L16.

ichnology /ɪkˈnɒlədʒi/ *noun*. M19.
[ORIGIN from Greek *ikhnos* track, footprint + -LOGY.]
The branch of palaeontology that deals with fossil footprints; the features of a region that belong to this.
▪ **ichnoˈlogical** *adjective* M19.

icho *noun* var. of ICHU.

ichoglan /ˈɪtʃəglan/ *noun*. L17.
[ORIGIN Obsolete Turkish, from *ich* interior + *oğlan* young man.]
hist. A page-in-waiting in the palace of the Sultan of Turkey.

ichor /ˈʌɪkɔː/ *noun*. M17.
[ORIGIN Greek *ikhōr*.]
1 Blood; a liquid likened to the blood of animals. Now *literary*. M17.

J. FULLER The sweat gathered . . as if some precious ichor of the spirit were being pressed.

2 MEDICINE. A watery discharge from a wound or sore. *arch.* M17.
3 GREEK MYTHOLOGY. A fluid supposed to flow like blood in the veins of the gods. L17.
4 GEOLOGY. An emanation from magma supposed by some to cause granitization. E20.
▪ †**ichorose** *adjective* ichorous E–M18. **ichorous** *adjective* of the nature of ichor; containing ichor: M17.

ichthammol /ˈɪkθəmɒl/ *noun*. E20.
[ORIGIN from ICHTH(Y)OL with insertion of AMM(ONIA).]
PHARMACOLOGY. A dark viscous liquid obtained by sulphonating ichthyol and neutralizing the product with ammonia, used to treat eczema.

ichthus /ˈɪkθəs/ *noun*. E20.
[ORIGIN Greek *ikhthus* fish, an early symbol of Christianity: the initial letters of the word are sometimes taken as short for Iesous Christos, Theou Uios, Sōtēr (Jesus Christ, son of God, saviour).]
An image of a fish used as a symbol of Christianity.

ichthyic /ˈɪkθɪɪk/ *adjective*. M19.
[ORIGIN Greek *ikhthuikos* fishy, from *ikhthus* fish: see -IC.]
Of, pertaining to, or characteristic of a fish or fishes; piscine.

ichthyo- /ˈɪkθɪəʊ/ *combining form* of Greek *ikhthus* fish: see -O-.
▪ **ichthyoˈdorulite** *noun* [Greek *doru* spear] the fossil spine of a fish or fishlike animal M19. **ichthyolite** *noun* a fossil fish E19. **ichthyoˈlogic** *adjective* ichthyological M19. **ichthyoˈlogical** *adjective* of or pertaining to ichthyology E18. **ichthyˈologist** *noun* an expert in or student of ichthyology E18. **ichthyˈology** *noun* the branch of zoology that deals with fishes; the features or characteristics of a district that belong to this: M17.

ichthyocolla /ɪkθɪə(ʊ)ˈkɒlə/ *noun*. E17.
[ORIGIN Greek *ikhthuokolla*, formed as ICHTHYO- + *kolla* glue.]
Fish-glue, isinglass.

ichthyoid /ˈɪkθɪɔɪd/ *adjective & noun*. M19.
[ORIGIN from ICHTHYO- + -OID.]
▸ **A** *adjective*. Resembling a fish. M19.
▸ **B** *noun*. A fishlike vertebrate; an amphibian. Now *rare* or *obsolete*. M19.

Ichthyol /ˈɪkθɪɒl/ *noun*. Also **i-**. L19.
[ORIGIN from ICHTHYO- + -OL.]
(Proprietary name for) a brownish-yellow syrupy liquid obtained by the dry distillation of bituminous rocks containing the remains of fossil fishes, formerly used like ichthammol. Also = ICHTHAMMOL.

†**ichthyophagan** *noun*. *rare*. L15–E17.
[ORIGIN from Latin *ichthyophagus* sing. of *ichthyophagi*: see ICHTHYOPHAGI, -AN.]
An ichthyophagist.

ichthyophagi /ɪkθɪˈɒfədʒʌɪ/ *noun pl.* M16.
[ORIGIN Latin from Greek *ikhthuophagoi* a fish-eating people, formed as ICHTHYO- + *-phagos* eating: see -PHAGOUS.]
Eaters of fish.

ichthyophagian /ɪkθɪə(ʊ)ˈfeɪdʒɪən/ *noun & adjective*. *rare*. L15.
[ORIGIN formed as ICHTHYOPHAGI + -AN.]
▸ **A** *noun*. An ichthyophagist. L15.
▸ **B** *adjective*. Characterized by ichthyophagy. M19.

ichthyophagous /ɪkθɪˈɒfəgəs/ *adjective*. E19.
[ORIGIN from Latin *ichthyophagus* from Greek *ikhthuophagos*, formed as ICHTHYO- + *-phagos* eating + -OUS.]
That feeds on or eats fish.

ichthyophagy /ɪkθɪˈɒfədʒi/ *noun*. M17.
[ORIGIN French *ichthyophagie* from Greek *ikhthuophagia* fish diet, from *ikhthuophagos*: see ICHTHYOPHAGOUS, -PHAGY.]
The practice of feeding on or eating fish.
▪ **ichthyophagist** *noun* an eater of fish E18.

ichthyornis /ɪkθɪˈɔːnɪs/ *noun*. L19.
[ORIGIN mod. Latin, from ICHTHYO- + Greek *ornis* bird: the bird was orig. thought to have had teeth.]
An extinct gull-like bird of Cretaceous times characterized by amphicoelous dorsal vertebrae like those of a reptile.

ichthyosaur /ˈɪkθɪəsɔː/ *noun*. M19.
[ORIGIN from mod. Latin *Ichthyosauria* pl., formed as ICHTHYO-: see -SAUR.]
Any of a group of extinct marine reptiles of Mesozoic times somewhat resembling porpoises, with paddle-like limbs and a caudal fin.
▪ **ichthyoˈsaurian** *adjective & noun* M19. **ichthyoˈsaurus** *noun*, pl. **-ri** /-rʌɪ, -riː/, an ichthyosaur, *spec.* one of the genus *Ichthyosaurus* M19.

ichthyosis /ɪkθɪˈəʊsɪs/ *noun*. Pl. **-oses** /-ˈəʊsiːz/. E19.
[ORIGIN mod. Latin, from ICHTHYO- + -OSIS.]
MEDICINE. A condition or disease in which the epidermis becomes dry, tough, and scaly.
▪ **ichthyotic** /-ˈɒtɪk/ *adjective* subject to or affected with ichthyosis L19.

ichu /ˈiːtʃuː/ *noun*. Also ***icho*** /ˈiːtʃəʊ/. E17.
[ORIGIN Quechua.]
A coarse highland grass, *Stipa ichu*, of Central and S. America, used for thatching.

ICI *abbreviation*.
Imperial Chemical Industries.

-ician /ˈɪʃ(ə)n/ *suffix*.
[ORIGIN Old French & mod. French *-icien*, from *-ique* -IC + *-ien* -IAN, or directly from -IC, -ICS + -IAN.]
Forming nouns denoting a person skilled in or practising an art or science whose name ends in *-ic(s)*, as ***arithmetician***, ***magician***, ***politician***, ***statistician***, etc. Occas. by analogy forming nouns from bases not ending in *-ic(s)*, as ***geometrician***. Cf. also PATRICIAN.

icicle /ˈʌɪsɪk(ə)l/ *noun*. ME.
[ORIGIN from ICE *noun* + ICKLE *noun*, after Middle Swedish *isikil* (= Middle Danish *isegel*); cf. Norwegian *isjøkel*, *-jokkel*.]
1 A hanging tapering length of ice produced by the freezing of successive drops of water trickling from the point of attachment. ME.

E. O'BRIEN I watched the snow . . and saw the icicles extend from the roof. *fig.*: K. MANSFIELD I am writing with two icicles for fingers.

2 A stalactite. M17.
3 A needle-shaped crystal. E18.
■ **icicled** *adjective* (*a*) overhung with icicles; †(*b*) congealed, frozen: M17.

icily /ˈʌɪsɪli/ *adverb*. M19.
[ORIGIN from ICY + -LY².]
In an icy manner; coldly.

fig.: E. GASKELL A tone which he meant to be icily indifferent.

iciness /ˈʌɪsɪnɪs/ *noun*. L16.
[ORIGIN from ICY + -NESS.]
The quality or state of being icy; extreme cold; frigidity. Chiefly *fig.*

icing /ˈʌɪsɪŋ/ *noun*. E18.
[ORIGIN from ICE *verb* + -ING¹.]
1 Sugar paste for coating or decorating cakes etc.; the process of making or applying such a paste; *fig.* (in full ***icing on the cake***) an unlooked-for or incidental benefit. E18.
fondant icing, ***glacé icing***, ***royal icing***, etc.
2 The process of chilling or preserving with ice. M19.
3 The (usu. unintended) formation of ice on a surface. Freq. foll. by *up*. L19.
– COMB.: **icing sugar** finely powdered sugar for making icing.

-icity /ˈɪsɪti/ *suffix*.
[ORIGIN French *-icité* from Latin *-icitat-*, *-tas* suffix combining *-tat-* (see -TY¹) with adjective stems in *-ic(i)-*, as *rusticitas* from *rusticus*.]
Forming abstract nouns, also, by analogy, from adjectives of any origin in *-ic*, as ***electricity***, ***publicity***, etc.

ICJ *abbreviation*.
International Court of Justice.

†**-ick** *suffix* var. of -IC.

icker /ˈɪkə/ *noun*. *Scot*. E16.
[ORIGIN Alt. of EAR *noun*².]
An ear of corn.

ickle /ˈɪk(ə)l/ *noun*. *obsolete* exc. *dial*.
[ORIGIN Old English *gicel(a)* cogn. with Old Norse *jǫkull* icicle, glacier from Germanic. Cf. JOKUL.]
An icicle.

ickle /ˈɪk(ə)l/ *adjective*. M19.
[ORIGIN Hypocoristic form of LITTLE *adjective*.]
In childish use: little.

P. HOBSON She changed her role. Now she was Daddy's ickle girl.

icky /ˈɪki/ *adjective*. *colloq*. E20.
[ORIGIN Uncertain: perh. rel. to SICK *adjective* and ICKLE *adjective*.]
Distastefully sentimental or sweet; sickly; sticky; nasty, repulsive.

Harper's Bazaar Roast chestnuts or icky home-made fudge. B. T. BRADFORD Gran would have a fit because she'd consider it icky, bad form.

– COMB.: **icky-boo** *adjective* ill, sick.

†**icod** *interjection*. L17–L18.
[ORIGIN formed as AGAD.]
= EGAD.

icon /ˈʌɪkɒn, -k(ə)n/ *noun*. Also **ikon**. M16.
[ORIGIN Latin from Greek *eikōn* likeness, image, similitude.]
†**1** RHETORIC. A simile. M16–L17.
2 †**a** A portrait, a picture; *esp.* one of an animal or plant in a book of natural history. L16–E18. ▸**b** ECCLESIASTICAL. An image in traditional Byzantine style of Jesus or a holy person that is used ceremonially and venerated in the Orthodox Church. M19. ▸**c** COMPUTING. A small symbolic picture on a VDU screen, *esp.* one that may be selected with a cursor to exercise an option that it represents. L20.
3 A statue. L16.
4 A realistic description in writing. *rare*. L16.
5 PHILOSOPHY. A sign with some factor in common with the object it represents. E20.
6 A person or thing regarded as a representative symbol of a culture, movement, etc.; someone or something afforded great admiration or respect. M20.

D. BOLGER He's not just any American. He is an icon. C. BATEMAN He can become a gay icon.

■ **iˈconify** *verb trans*. (COMPUTING) reduce (a window on a VDU screen) to an icon L20. **iconize** *verb trans*. †(*a*) form into an image; (*b*) COMPUTING = ICONIFY: L17.

iconic /ʌɪˈkɒnɪk/ *adjective*. M17.
[ORIGIN Latin *iconicus* from Greek *eikonikos*, from *eikōn* ICON: see -IC.]
Of, pertaining to, or resembling an icon; of the nature of an icon; ART designating ancient Greek statues of victorious athletes executed in a conventional style.

N. HORNBY He had made himself unpackageable . . possibly the very last star of any iconic stature to do so. B. STERLING It's a face that is almost iconic.

■ **iconical** *adjective* (*rare*) = ICONIC M17. **iconically** *adverb* M20. **iconicity** /-ˈnɪsɪti/ *noun* the relation of similarity between a sign and its object M20.

iconism /ˈʌɪkɒnɪz(ə)m/ *noun*. M16.
[ORIGIN Late Latin *iconismus* from Greek *eikonismos* delineation, from *eikonizein* represent, from *eikōn* ICON: see -ISM.]
†**1** Representation by an image; imagery. M16–L17.
2 PHILOSOPHY. The quality of being an icon. L20.

icono- /ˈʌɪkənəʊ/ *combining form*.
[ORIGIN Greek *eikono-*, from *eikōn* ICON: see -O-.]
Image; icon.
■ **iconoˈdule** *noun* = ICONODULIST L19. **iconoˈdulist** *noun* a person who venerates religious images or advocates their veneration E18. **iconoˈmetric** *adjective* employing or forming part of iconometry L19. **iconoˈmetrical** *adjective* iconometric E20. **iconoˈmetrically** *adverb* in or by means of iconometry E20. **icoˈnometry** *noun* the process of taking measurements from photographs of an area and using them to make a map of it L19. **iconophil(e)** *noun & adjective* (*a*) *noun* a connoisseur or collector of book illustrations, engravings, etc.; ECCLESIASTICAL a person who uses or advocates the use of religious images or icons; (*b*) *adjective* designating an iconophile: L19. **iconoˈphobia** *noun* hatred of religious images or icons E20.

iconoclasm /ʌɪˈkɒnəklaz(ə)m/ *noun*. L18.
[ORIGIN from ICONOCLAST after *enthusiast*, *enthusiasm*, etc.]
Destruction of or opposition to religious images; the action of an iconoclast.

iconoclast /ʌɪˈkɒnəklast/ *noun & adjective*. M17.
[ORIGIN medieval Latin *iconoclastes* from ecclesiastical Greek *eikonoklastēs*, formed as ICONO- + *klan* to break.]
▸ **A** *noun*. **1** A destroyer or opponent of religious images or icons; *spec.* (*hist.*) (*a*) a member of the movement against the use and veneration of images in the Orthodox Church in the 8th and 9th cents.; (*b*) a Puritan of the 16th or 17th cent. M17.
2 A person who attacks a cherished belief or respected institution. M19.

H. R. REYNOLDS Respectable vices . . need nothing so much as the stern iconoclast.

▸ **B** *attrib.* or as *adjective*. Iconoclastic. Now *rare*. L17.
■ **iconoˈclastic** *adjective* of or pertaining to iconoclasts or iconoclasm M17. **iconoˈclastically** *adverb* M19.

iconography /ʌɪkəˈnɒgrəfi/ *noun*. E17.
[ORIGIN Greek *eikonographia* sketch, description, formed as ICONO-: see GRAPHY.]
†**1** A drawing, a plan. Only in 17.
2 The representation of a subject by illustrations; a book of illustrations; a collection of portraits of a particular subject. Also, the visual images and symbols of a work of art, a cult, etc.; (the interpretation of) the significance of these; iconology. L17.

D. PIPER It can be compared with other portraits of Prias, who has quite a rich iconography. *Library* An iconography of Don Quixote, 1605–1895.

■ **iconographer** *noun* an artist, an illustrator L19. **iconoˈgraphic**, **iconoˈgraphical** *adjectives* of or pertaining to iconography; representing by visual images: M19. **iconoˈgraphically** *adverb* M20. **iconographist** *noun* (*rare*) an iconographer M19.

iconolatry /ʌɪkəˈnɒlətri/ *noun*. E17.
[ORIGIN ecclesiastical Greek *eikonolatreia*, formed as ICONO-: see -LATRY.]
The worship of religious images or icons.
■ **iconolater** *noun* a person who practises iconolatry M17.

iconology /ʌɪkəˈnɒlədʒi/ *noun*. M18.
[ORIGIN from ICONO- + -LOGY.]
1 The branch of knowledge that deals with visual imagery and its symbolism and interpretation. M18.
2 Symbolism, symbolic representation. M19.
■ **iconoˈlogical** *adjective* M19.

iconomachy /ʌɪkəˈnɒməki/ *noun*. L16.
[ORIGIN from ecclesiastical Greek *eikonomakhein* to fight against images, formed as ICONO-: see -MACHY.]
A war against images; hostility to images, esp. their use in worship.

iconoscope /ʌɪˈkɒnəskəʊp/ *noun*. M19.
[ORIGIN from ICONO- + -SCOPE.]
†**1** An optical instrument for giving an impression of relief when viewing flat images. M19–E20.
2 An early television camera tube in which an electron beam scanned a photoemissive surface bearing the optical image, the current from which varied according to the brightness of the various points on the surface. M20.

iconostas /ʌɪˈkɒnəstas/ *noun*. M19.
[ORIGIN Russian *ikonostas* formed as ICONOSTASIS.]
= ICONOSTASIS.

iconostasis /ʌɪkəˈnɒstəsɪs/ *noun*. Pl. **-ases** /-əsiːz/. M19.
[ORIGIN mod. Greek *eikonostasis*, formed as ICONO- + STASIS.]
A screen separating the sanctuary or altar from the nave in some Orthodox churches and bearing icons.

icos- /ˈʌɪkɒs/ *combining form*. Also **icosa-** /ʌɪˈkɒsə/, **icosi-** /ʌɪˈkɒsi/. See also EICOS-.
[ORIGIN Greek *eikosi*.]
Twenty.
■ **iˌcosidodecaˈhedron** *noun*, pl. **-dra**, **-drons**, a solid bounded by twenty equilateral triangles and twelve regular pentagons L16. **iˌcositetraˈhedron** *noun*, pl. **-dra**, **-drons**, a solid with 24 faces M19.

icosahedron /ˌʌɪkɒsəˈhiːdrən, -ˈhɛd-/ *noun*. Also †**-drum**, †**eic-**. Pl. **-dra** /-drə/, **-drons**. L16.
[ORIGIN Late Latin *icosahedrum* (medieval Latin also *-hedron*) from Greek *eikosaedron*, formed as ICOS-: see -HEDRON.]
A solid figure or object with twenty plane faces; *esp.* (more fully ***regular icosahedron***) one with twenty equal equilateral triangular faces.
■ **icosahedral** *adjective* having the form of an icosahedron; having twenty faces: E19. **icosahedrally** *adverb* so as to form icosahedra L20.

icosane *noun* var. of EICOSANE.

icosi- *combining form* var. of ICOS-.

ICRC *abbreviation*.
International Committee of the Red Cross.

ICS *abbreviation*.
hist. Indian Civil Service.

-ics /ɪks/ *suffix*.
[ORIGIN from -IC + -S¹, repr. French *-iques*, medieval Latin *-ica*, Greek *-ika*: in earliest use in names of treatises.]
Forming nouns denoting a branch of knowledge (as ***economics***, ***ethics***) or a treatise on one, or a field or kind of activity (as ***politics***, ***acrobatics***).

ICSU *abbreviation*.
International Council of Scientific Unions.

ICT *abbreviation*.
Information and computing technology.

ictal /ˈɪkt(ə)l/ *adjective*. M20.
[ORIGIN from ICTUS + -AL¹.]
MEDICINE. Pertaining to or caused by an ictus.

icteric /ɪkˈtɛrɪk/ *adjective & noun*. L16.
[ORIGIN Latin *ictericus* from Greek *ikterikos*, from *ikteros* jaundice: see -IC.]
▸ **A** *adjective*. Associated with or caused by jaundice; affected with or by jaundice. L16.
▸ **B** *noun*. A person with jaundice. Now *rare* or *obsolete*. M17.
■ **icterical** *adjective* (now *rare* or *obsolete*) M17.

icterine /ˈɪkt(ə)rʌɪn/ *adjective*. M19.
[ORIGIN from ICTERUS + -INE¹.]
ZOOLOGY. Yellow. Chiefly in ***icterine warbler***, a yellow-breasted warbler, *Hippolais icterina*, of Continental Europe, found esp. in parks and gardens.

icteritious /ɪktəˈrɪʃəs/ *adjective*. E17.
[ORIGIN from late Latin *icteritia* jaundice (formed as ICTERUS) + -OUS.]
Jaundiced.

icterogenic /ɪkt(ə)rə(ʊ)ˈdʒɛnɪk/ *adjective*. E20.
[ORIGIN from ICTERUS + -O- + -GENIC.]
Causing jaundice.

icterus /ˈɪkt(ə)rəs/ *noun*. E18.
[ORIGIN Latin from Greek *ikteros*.]
1 Jaundice. E18.
2 A yellow discoloration of normally green plant tissue. E19.

ictic /ˈɪktɪk/ *adjective*. *rare*. M19.
[ORIGIN from ICTUS + -IC.]
1 Of the nature of a sudden blow. M19.
2 Pertaining to or due to ictus or stress. L19.

ictus /ˈɪktəs/ *noun*. E18.
[ORIGIN Latin, from *ict-* pa. ppl stem of *icere* to strike.]
1 MEDICINE. **a** The beat of the pulse. E18. ▸**b** A stroke; a seizure, a fit; any sudden event involving the nervous system. L19.
2 PROSODY. Rhythmical or metrical stress. M18.

ICU *abbreviation*.
Intensive-care unit.

icy /ˈʌɪsi/ *adjective*. OE.
[ORIGIN from ICE *noun* + -Y¹.]
1 Characterized by ice, having much ice; covered with ice. OE.

I

2 Resembling ice; bitterly cold; slippery. **L16.** ▸**b** *fig.* Cold in manner; unfriendly, hostile. **L16.**

P. S. BUCK A continual icy wind blew. **b** L. M. MONTGOMERY She passed him by with an icy contempt.

b *the icy* MITT.

3 Consisting of ice. **E17.**

ID *abbreviation.*
1 Idaho.
2 Identification.

Id *noun*[1]. A var. of EID.

id /ɪd/ *noun*[2]. *obsolete* exc. *hist.* **L19.**
[ORIGIN from Greek *idios* own, private, or contr. of IDIOPLASM.]
BIOLOGY. In Weismann's theory of heredity: a unit of germ plasm.

id /ɪd/ *noun*[3]. **E20.**
[ORIGIN Latin = it, translating German *es*.]
PSYCHOANALYSIS. The inherited instinctive impulses of the individual, forming part of the unconscious and, in Freudian theory, interacting in the psyche with the ego and the superego.

L. TRILLING A plea being made on behalf of the anarchic and self-indulgent id.

id. /ɪd/ *noun & adverb.* **L17.**
[ORIGIN Abbreviation of Latin *idem*.]
= IDEM.

i.d. *abbreviation.*
Inner diameter.

-id /ɪd/ *suffix*[1] (not productive).
Repr. French *-ide*, Latin *-idus*, forming adjectives chiefly from verbs with *e-* stems, as ***acidus*** ACID *adjective* from *acere* be sour; occas. from verbs with *i-* or consonant stems, and from nouns, as ***fluidus*** FLUID *adjective* from *fluere* flow, ***morbidus*** MORBID from *morbus* disease.

-id /ɪd/ *suffix*[2].
Corresp. to French *-ide*, forming nouns derived from Latin nouns in *-id*, *-is*, adopted from Greek nouns in *-ida*, *-is*, as ***carotid***, ***chrysalid***, ***pyramid***; in *BIOLOGY* forming names of structural constituents, as ***plastid***; in *BOTANY* forming nouns denoting plants belonging to the family typified by a certain genus, as ***amaryllid*** from *Amaryllis* (family Amaryllidaceae).

-id /ɪd/ *suffix*[3].
Corresp. to French *-ide*, repr. Latin *-ides* (pl. *-idae*, *-ida*), from Greek patronymic suffix *-idēs*. Forming nouns and corresp. adjectives with the senses 'member of a specified family or dynasty,' as ***Seleucid***, ***Sassanid***; in *ZOOLOGY*, 'member of a specified family (in *-idae*) or class (in *-ida*),' as ***canid***, ***arachnid***; in *ASTRONOMY*, 'meteor in a group with its radiant in a specified constellation,' as ***Leonid***, or 'star of a class like one in a specified constellation', as ***cepheid***.

-id /ɪd/ *suffix*[4].
[ORIGIN Arbitrary.]
Used in nomenclature of mammalian teeth, to form names of structures in the teeth of the lower jaw, as ***hypoconid***.

†-id *suffix*[5] see -IDE.

IDA *abbreviation.*
International Development Association.

Idaean /ʌɪˈdiːən/ *adjective.* **L16.**
[ORIGIN from Latin *Idaeus* (from *Ida*, *Ide*), Greek *Idaios* (from *Idē*) + -AN.]
Of, belonging to, or dwelling on Mount Ida in Asia Minor near the ancient city of Troy, or Mount Ida in Crete, the supposed birthplace of Zeus.

Idahoan /ˈʌɪdəhəʊən/ *noun.* **E20.**
[ORIGIN from *Idaho* (see below) + -AN.]
A native or inhabitant of Idaho, a state of the US.

Idalian /ʌɪˈdeɪlɪən/ *adjective.* **L16.**
[ORIGIN from Latin *Idalius*, from *Idalium* (see below) + -AN.]
Of or belonging to the ancient town of Idalium in Cyprus, where the goddess Aphrodite was worshipped.

-idan /ɪdən/ *suffix.*
[ORIGIN from -ID[3] + -AN.]
ZOOLOGY. Forming adjectives and nouns with the senses 'of or pertaining to', 'a member of' a particular family (in *-idae*) or class (in *-ida*), as ***arachnidan***, ***carabidan***.

IDB *abbreviation.*
Illicit diamond-buying.

iddingsite /ˈɪdɪŋzʌɪt/ *noun.* **L19.**
[ORIGIN from Joseph P. *Iddings* (1857–1920), US geologist + -ITE[1].]
MINERALOGY. A brownish mixture of silicates formed by alteration of olivine.

ide /ʌɪd/ *noun*[1]. **M19.**
[ORIGIN mod. Latin *idus*, from Swedish *id*.]
= ORFE *noun*.

ide *noun*[2] see IDES.

-ide /ʌɪd/ *suffix.* Also †**-id**.
[ORIGIN from OX)IDE.]
CHEMISTRY. Added to the (abbreviated) name of an element, radical, etc., to form nouns denoting binary compounds (***chloride***, ***cyanide***, ***halide***, ***sulphide***), or other kinds of compound (***amide***, ***anhydride***, ***peptide***, ***saccharide***) or element (***lanthanide***).
– NOTE: In full names of binary compounds the suffix attaches to the more electronegative element (***sodium chloride***, ***calcium carbide***).

idea /ʌɪˈdɪə/ *noun.* Also (now *rare* exc. *dial.*) **idee** /ʌɪˈdiː/. **LME.**
[ORIGIN Latin from Greek = look, semblance, form, kind, nature, ideal form, model, from base of *idein* see.]
▸ **I** An archetype, a pattern, a standard.
1 In Platonic philosophy: an eternally existing pattern of any class, of which the individual members are imperfect copies. **LME.**
2 The conception of something at its highest perfection or most complete stage of development; a standard of perfection, an ideal. **L16.** ▸†**b** A person or thing as an ideal. **L16–M17.**

E. B. BROWNING Thou [Lucifer] shalt be an Idea to all souls . . whence to mark despair.

3 The conception of a standard to be aimed at; the plan or design according to which something is created or constructed. Now passing into sense 4. **L16.** ▸†**b** A preliminary sketch or plan; a basic outline. **M17–M18.**

F. MYERS The ground-plan of the Universe—the idea according to which it is.

4 A conception of something to be done or achieved; an intention, a plan of action. **L16.**

D. L. SAYERS That was an ingenious idea nobody had yet thought of. W. S. BURROUGHS If you have your own ideas for a new model the designers will make it. W. MAXWELL He didn't think the party was at all a good idea.

▸ †**II** Form, image, nature.
5 A likeness, an image, a representation; shape, form; nature, character. **M16–M18.**
▸ **III** Mental image or conception.
†**6** A mental image of something previously seen or known and recalled by the memory. **L16–M18.**

HENRY FIELDING Though I despaired of possessing you . . I doted still on your charming idea.

7 Something imagined; a conception having no basis in reality; *gen.* a picture or notion of anything conceived in the mind. **L16.**

C. DAY The idea of playing in public sent cold chills down Julie's back. A. LURIE The idea . . which seemed so lovely last autumn, has become a cold, exhausting reality. A. DAVIS The preview trip to the school completely shattered my ideas of what schools were . . like.

8 A product of mental activity existing in the mind; an item of knowledge or belief; a thought; a way of thinking. **M17.** ▸**b** A vague or indefinite notion, belief, or opinion; a supposition, an impression. Also, a person's conception *of* an ideal, typical, or adequate example of the person or thing specified. **E18.**

P. BOWLES 'I wonder if . . I'm a coward?' he thought . . . The idea saddened him. S. SPENDER The three great political ideas of our time—Fascism, Communism, and Liberal-Socialism. A. CLARE There is a poverty of ideas and mental imagery. **b** H. JAMES To sit on a balcony, eating ices—that's my idea of heaven. B. LOPEZ Even officers of the British whaling fleet had little idea where a meteorite might come from. A. MUNRO He . . had some idea of doing work in underdeveloped countries.

▸ **IV** *PHILOSOPHY.* **9** In the philosophy of Descartes and Locke: whatever is in the mind and directly present to cognitive consciousness; the immediate object of thought or mental perception. **M17.**
10 (In the philosophy of Kant) a conception of reason transcending all experience, as opp. to a conception of the understanding which is confined by experience; (in the philosophy of Hegel) the absolute truth of which all phenomenal existence is the expression. **M19.**
– PHRASES: *FIXED* ***idea***. **get ideas**, **have ideas** *colloq.* be ambitious, rebellious, etc. **give a person ideas** (***a***) create a false impression of sexual promiscuity; (***b***) = ***put ideas into a person's head*** below. ***have ideas***: see ***get ideas*** above. **have no idea** *colloq.* (***a***) not know at all; (***b***) be completely incompetent. **man of ideas** a resourceful man. **put ideas into a person's head** suggest ambitions etc. that he or she would not otherwise have thought of. **that's an idea** *colloq.* that proposal etc. is worth considering. **that's the idea!** *colloq.* you are beginning to understand how to proceed. **the big idea** (usu. *iron.*) the important intention or scheme. **the very idea!** *colloq.*: an exclamation of disapproval or disagreement. **woman of ideas** a resourceful woman.
■ **idea'd** *adjective* having an idea or ideas, esp. of a specified kind **M18.** **idealess** *adjective* lacking ideas; meaningless: **E19.**

ideal /ʌɪˈdɪəl, -ˈdiːəl/ *adjective & noun.* **LME.**
[ORIGIN Late Latin *idealis*, from Latin IDEA: see -AL[1]. Partly through French *idéal*.]
▸ **A** *adjective.* **1** In Platonic philosophy: pertaining to or existing as an archetype. **LME.**
2 Regarded as perfect or supremely excellent; representing a perfect example. **E17.**

K. AMIS This isn't the ideal time to ask you. I. MURDOCH You were a sort of ideal figure, and . . I never thought they were as good as you.

3 Existing only as an idea, confined to the imagination, imaginary; visionary, not practical. **E17.** ▸**b** *MATH.* Of a number or quality: having no actual existence, but assumed for some purpose in a system of complex numbers; *spec.* in *GEOMETRY*, introduced in order to do away with exceptions to generalizations. **M19.**

T. HARDY The doctor . . much preferred the ideal world to the real.

4 Of, pertaining to, or of the nature of an idea or conception; representing an idea. **M17.** ▸**b** *PHILOSOPHY.* Regarding ideas as the only real entities; idealistic. **M18.**

H. T. BUCKLE Starting from the so called nature of things, his first steps were ideal.

– SPECIAL COLLOCATIONS: **ideal construction** *PHILOSOPHY* a mental conception formed by abstracting properties found in experience and recombining or developing them. **ideal fluid** a hypothetical fluid that has no viscosity and is incompressible. **ideal gas** a hypothetical gas which consists of molecules occupying negligible space and exerting no mutual attraction, and therefore obeys simple laws. **ideal type** *SOCIOLOGY* a hypothetical construct made up of the essential features of a social or historical phenomenon or generalized concept and used in comparison or classification of what actually occurs.
▸ **B** *noun.* **1** A conception of something in its highest perfection, esp. as a thing to be aimed at; a perfect example or specimen; a standard of perfection or excellence. **L15.** ▸**b** An actual thing as a standard for imitation. **M19.**

D. H. LAWRENCE We have an ideal of a perfect world. A. TOFFLER Maximum individual choice is regarded as the democratic ideal. **b** E. LANGLEY I should be to him the flawless love, the ideal of faithfulness. C. FRANCIS The Battle of Trafalgar . . the glorified ideal of everything that is brave . . in the fighting sailor.

2 *MATH.* A subring that contains all products of the form *rx* and *xr*, where *r* and *x* are elements of the ring and subring respectively. **L19.**

idealise *verb* var. of IDEALIZE.

idealism /ʌɪˈdɪəlɪz(ə)m, -ˈdiːə-/ *noun.* **L18.**
[ORIGIN French *idéalisme* or German *Idealismus*, formed as IDEAL: see -ISM.]
1 *PHILOSOPHY.* Any of various systems of thought in which the object of external perception is held to consist of ideas not resulting from any unperceived material substance. Opp. REALISM 1b. **L18.**
2 The representation of things in an ideal form; the practice of forming or pursuing ideals. **E19.** ▸**b** An example of this practice; an ideal. **E19.**

New York Times Congress is an institution of compromises, and that's the antithesis of idealism.

idealist /ʌɪˈdɪəlɪst, -ˈdiːə-/ *noun.* **E18.**
[ORIGIN from IDEAL + -IST.]
1 *PHILOSOPHY.* An advocate of a doctrine of idealism. **E18.**

B. RUSSELL Idealists tell us that what appears as matter is really something mental.

2 A person who idealizes someone or something. **E19.**

E. BLISHEN He is not an idealist . . that chooses to invest life with a general cloudy glory.

3 A person who forms or pursues (esp. impractical) ideals. **E19.**

A. G. GARDINER For the cynic is often the idealist turned sour. P. H. GIBBS We were the starry-eyed idealists talking peace when there was no peace.

■ **idea'listic** *adjective* of, pertaining to, or characteristic of an idealist **E19.** **idea'listically** *adverb* **L19.**

ideality /ʌɪdɪˈalɪti/ *noun.* **E18.**
[ORIGIN from IDEAL + -ITY.]
†**1** The faculty of forming ideas or archetypes. *rare.* Only in **E18.**
2 The faculty of imagining things. **E19.**
3 The quality of being ideal or imaginary; an imaginary or idealized thing. **E19.**

E. B. BROWNING I have had visions before . . and have called idealities realities all my life long. L. MUMFORD The belief in such ideality was almost a Quaker heresy.

idealize /ʌɪˈdɪəlʌɪz, -ˈdiːə-/ *verb.* Also **-ise**. **L18.**
[ORIGIN from IDEAL + -IZE.]
1 *verb trans. & intrans.* Represent or perceive (a person or thing) in an ideal form; exalt (a person or thing) to an ideal state of perfection. **L18.**

R. A. KNOX We . . differ from the animals in our capacity for idealizing . . the relations of the sexes. B. GUEST As long as H.D. lived she was idealized by Bryher as her heroine.

2 *verb intrans.* Form ideals. **L18.**
■ **ideali'zation** *noun* the action of idealizing; an idealized thing: **L18.** **idealizer** *noun* **E19.**

ideally /ʌɪˈdɪəli, -ˈdiːəli/ *adverb.* **L16.**
[ORIGIN from IDEAL *adjective* + -LY[2].]
1 In the imagination, imaginarily. **L16.**

W. B. CARPENTER The unexpected conclusion . . that more than three dimensions in space are ideally possible.

2 In relation to a general plan or archetype. **M17.**
3 In the highest conceivable perfection; in the most excellent way; as the best possible state of things. **M19.**

J. KOSINSKI You are a man ideally suited to provide the country with an explanation. *Practical Health* Ideally, eat a lot at the start of the day.

ideate /ʌɪˈdɪət/ *noun*. **L17.**
[ORIGIN formed as IDEATE *verb*: see -ATE[1].]
The external object of which an idea is formed.

ideate /ˈʌɪdɪeɪt/ *adjective*. **E20.**
[ORIGIN formed as IDEATE *verb*: see -ATE[2].]
1 Produced by or deriving its existence from a Platonic idea. *rare*. **E20.**
2 Concerned with ideas as opp. to reality. **M20.**

ideate /ˈʌɪdɪeɪt/ *verb*. **E17.**
[ORIGIN medieval Latin *ideat-* pa. ppl stem of *ideare* form an idea or conception of, from Latin IDEA: see -ATE[3].]
1 *verb trans.* Form an idea of, imagine. **E17.**

K. CLARK The arc whose ideated centre is a nodal point in the composition.

2 *verb intrans.* Form ideas, think. **M19.**

ideation /ʌɪdɪˈeɪʃ(ə)n/ *noun*. **E19.**
[ORIGIN from IDEATE *verb* + -ATION.]
The action of ideating; the formation of ideas or mental images.

ideational /ʌɪdɪˈeɪʃ(ə)n(ə)l/ *adjective*. **M19.**
[ORIGIN from IDEATION + -AL[1].]
1 Of or pertaining to ideation or the formation of ideas. **M19.**
2 SOCIOLOGY. Designating a culture which emphasizes spiritual values and ideals above material values. Cf. SENSATE *adjective* 4. **M20.**
■ **ideationally** *adverb* **L19.**

idee *noun* see IDEA.

idée fixe /ide fiks, iːdeɪ ˈfiːks/ *noun phr.* Pl. **-s -s** (pronounced same). **M19.**
[ORIGIN French = fixed idea.]
An idea that dominates the mind, an obsession.

E. CRANKSHAW Rigid adherence to dogmatic principle degenerated into a series of *idées fixes*.

idée reçue /ide rəsy, ˌiːdeɪ rəˈsjuː/ *noun phr.* Pl. **-s -s** (pronounced same). **M20.**
[ORIGIN French = received idea.]
A generally accepted notion or opinion.

idem /ˈɪdɛm, ˈʌɪ-/ *noun & adverb*. **LME.**
[ORIGIN Latin.]
(In) the same author, work, etc.

idempotent /ʌɪdɛmˈpəʊt(ə)nt, ʌɪˈdɛmpət(ə)nt/ *adjective*. **L19.**
[ORIGIN from Latin *idem* same + POTENT *adjective*[2].]
MATH. Of an element, matrix, etc.: unchanged in value after multiplication by itself. Also, (of a set) containing idempotent elements; (of a statement) expressing idempotency.
■ **idemˈpotence**, **idemˈpotency** *nouns* the property of being idempotent **M20.**

idem sonans /ʌɪdɛm ˈsəʊnanz/ *noun & adjectival phr.* **M19.**
[ORIGIN Latin = sounding the same.]
LAW (chiefly *US*).
▸ **A** *noun*. The occurrence in a document of a material word or name misspelled but having the sound of the word or name intended. **M19.**
▸ **B** *adjective*. Homophonous *with*. **M19.**

-idene /ɪdiːn/ *suffix*.
[ORIGIN from ETHYL)IDENE.]
CHEMISTRY. Forming names of divalent organic radicals in which both valencies derive from the same atom, as ***propylidene***.

ident /ʌɪˈdɛnt/ *noun*. *colloq.* **M20.**
[ORIGIN Abbreviation.]
= IDENTIFICATION; *spec.* a short sequence shown on television between programmes to identify the channel.

ident *adjective* var. of EIDENT.

identic /ʌɪˈdɛntɪk/ *adjective*. **M17.**
[ORIGIN medieval Latin *identicus*, from *ident-*: see IDENTITY, -IC.]
1 = IDENTICAL *adjective* 1, 2. **M17.**
2 In diplomats' use: designating action or language in which two or more powers or countries agree to use precisely the same form in their relations with some other. **M19.**
identic note: containing a uniformly worded expression of opinion from two or more powers or countries to another.

identical /ʌɪˈdɛntɪk(ə)l/ *adjective & noun*. **L16.**
[ORIGIN formed as IDENTIC: see -AL[1], -ICAL.]
▸ **A** *adjective*. **1** LOGIC. Designating a proposition whose terms express an identity or denote the same thing, as *man is man*. **L16.**
2 Of a thing or set of things viewed at different times: the very same. **M17.**

B. H. MALKIN This is the very identical man.

3 Of two or more separate things: agreeing in every detail. **L17.**

C. SAGAN The inside of the Earth and the outside of Venus are alike but not identical. I. MURDOCH They began to sing, swaying . . in an identical rhythm, as if . . joined together.

identical twin: developed from a single fertilized ovum and therefore of the same sex as and very similar to his or her sibling; a monozygotic twin.
4 MATH. Of the nature of or expressing an identity. **L19.**
▸ **B** *noun*. **1** An identical thing or feature. **L17.**
2 An identical twin. **M20.**
■ **identically** *adverb* **M17.** **identicalness** *noun* **E18.**

identifiable /ʌɪˈdɛntɪfʌɪəb(ə)l/ *adjective*. **E19.**
[ORIGIN from IDENTIFY + -ABLE.]
Able to be identified.
■ **identifiaˈbility** *noun* **L19.**

identification /ʌɪˌdɛntɪfɪˈkeɪʃ(ə)n/ *noun*. **M17.**
[ORIGIN Orig. from medieval Latin *identificatio(n-)*, from *identificat-* pa. ppl stem of *identificare* (see IDENTIFY); later from IDENTIFY: see -FICATION.]
1 The action or an act of identifying, the fact of being identified. **M17.**

N. ALGREN If you sent a man to prison on a wrong identification you're a criminal yourself. J. K. GALBRAITH Political identification with those of the lowest estate has anciently brought . . reproaches. *Lancashire Evening Telegraph* After formal identification of the body . . , the inquest was adjourned.

2 Documentary evidence, as a passport, driving licence, etc., serving to identify a person. **M20.**

Globe & Mail (Toronto) My driver's licence, draft card, student I.D., and all other identification I had on me.

– COMB.: **identification bracelet**, **identification card**, **identification disc**, etc.: worn or carried and bearing a name, assigned number, etc., identifying the wearer or carrier; **identification parade** an assembly of people among whom a suspect is to be identified.
■ **identificational** *adjective* of or involving identification **M20.** **identificatory** *adjective* serving to identify **M20.**

identify /ʌɪˈdɛntɪfʌɪ/ *verb*. **M17.**
[ORIGIN medieval Latin *identificare*, from *ident-*: see IDENTITY, -FY.]
1 *verb trans.* Regard or treat as identical (*with*). Now chiefly passing into sense 3b. **M17.** ▸†**b** *verb intrans.* Be or become identical. **L17–M19.**

GIBBON Osiris, whom he identifies with Serapis.

2 *verb trans.* Establish the identity of; establish who or what a given person or thing is; recognize. **M18.** ▸**b** TAXONOMY. Refer (a specimen) to its proper species etc. **L18.**

D. CUSACK She threw herself under a bus. We have to go—to identify her. R. LARDNER Rita . . identified Bob by the initials on his suitcase. B. EMECHETA She herself could not identify what it was that was unsettling her.

3 *verb trans. & intrans.* Foll. by *with*: regard (a person, oneself) as sharing the same characteristics, interests, principles, experiences, etc., with; feel (oneself) to be a part of; model (oneself) on. **L18.** ▸**b** *verb trans.* Associate (a person or thing) very closely or inseparably *with* (a person, event, etc.). Usu. in *pass.* **M19.**

A. STORR Some depressives become expert at identifying themselves with others. D. LESSING She . . did not identify particularly with any aspect of being Jewish. **b** J. BUCHAN I identified appreciation with enjoyment. *Listener* The Mandelas are identified with the struggle of black people for rights in South Africa.

■ **identifier** *noun* (**a**) a person who or thing which identifies; (**b**) COMPUTING a character or sequence of characters devised to identify or refer to a set of data, an element in a program, etc.: **L19.**

Identikit /ʌɪˈdɛntɪkɪt/ *noun & adjective*. Also **i-**. **M20.**
[ORIGIN Blend of IDENTITY and KIT *noun*[1].]
▸ **A** *noun*. (Proprietary name for) a reconstructed picture of a person (esp. a suspect sought by police) assembled from features described by a witness or witnesses. **M20.**
▸ **B** *adjective*. Having typical features and few unique ones; formulaic or standardized. Chiefly *derog.* **M20.**

W. HOLDEN A cluster of Identikit blondes . . stood nearby sipping their drinks.

Identitätsphilosophie /idɛntiˈtɛːtsfilozoˌfiː/ *noun*. **M19.**
[ORIGIN German = identity-philosophy.]
PHILOSOPHY. A system or doctrine that assumes the fundamental identity of spirit and nature.

identity /ʌɪˈdɛntɪti/ *noun*. **L16.**
[ORIGIN Late Latin *identitas*, from Latin *idem* same, prob. after *entitas* ENTITY, but perh. assoc. with *identidem* repeatedly: thus *ident-* was established as the combining form of *idem*. Cf. IDENTIC, IDENTIFY.]
1 The quality or condition of being identical in every detail; absolute sameness; an instance or example of this. Also, the fact of being identified *with*. **L16.**

H. FAWCETT There is no identity of interests between the employers and employed. D. MACDONALD The letter to Lang did express . . his feeling of identity with the masses.

mistaken identity error as regards who a person is.
2 The condition or fact of a person or thing being that specified unique person or thing, esp. as a continuous unchanging property throughout existence; the characteristics determining this; individuality, personality. **M17.**

SAKI To disguise one's identity in a neighbourhood where one was entirely unknown seemed . . rather meaningless. H. ARENDT The Jews . . had been able to keep their identity through the centuries. *Sunday Express* The victory sparking off a new sense of pride in national identity.

3 MATH. **a** An equation which holds for all values of its variables. **M19.** ▸**b** An element of a set which, if combined with another by a (specified) binary operation, leaves the second element unchanged. **L19.** ▸**c** A transformation which gives rise to the same elements as those to which it is applied. **E20.**
4 In full ***old identity***. A person long resident or well known in a place. *Austral. & NZ*. **M19.**

New Zealand Woman's Weekly Havelock North identity Mrs C. E. Turner-Williams . . at 98 stitches happily on.

– COMB.: **identity card** an identification card; **identity crisis** PSYCHOLOGY a period of emotional disturbance in which a person has difficulty in determining his or her identity and role in relation to society, esp. as part of the maturing process; **identity element** = sense 3b above; **identity matrix** MATH.: in which all the elements of the principal diagonal are ones and all other elements are zeros, so that its product with any matrix is identical with the latter; **identity parade** an identification parade; **identity politics** a tendency for people of a particular religion, race, social background, etc., to form exclusive political alliances, moving away from traditional broad-based party politics; **identity theft** the fraudulent practice of using another person's name and personal information in order to obtain credit, loans, etc.

ideo- /ˈʌɪdɪəʊ, ˈɪdɪəʊ/ *combining form* of Greek IDEA: see -O-.
■ **ideokiˈnetic** *adjective* (MEDICINE) designating a form of apraxia in which an action cannot be performed on request despite retention of the necessary motor ability and understanding **E20.** **ideoˈmotor** *adjective* (BIOLOGY & MEDICINE) (**a**) denoting or relating to a motor action stimulated by an idea; (**b**) = IDEOKINETIC: **L19.** **ideophone** *noun* (LINGUISTICS) an onomatopoeic or sound-symbolic word or class of words **L19.** **ideoˈphonic** *adjective* (LINGUISTICS) onomatopoeic, sound-symbolic **M20.** **ideoplasm** *noun* = ECTOPLASM 2 **E20.** **ideoplastic** *adjective* designating physiological or artistic processes supposed to be moulded by mental impressions or suggestions; also *spec.*, ectoplasmic: **E20.**

ideogram /ˈɪdɪəgram, ˈʌɪd-/ *noun*. **M19.**
[ORIGIN from IDEO- + -GRAM.]
An ideograph.
■ **ideoˈgrammic** *adjective* of the nature of an ideogram; expressed by symbols: **E20.**

ideograph /ˈɪdɪəgrɑːf, ˈʌɪd-/ *noun*. **M19.**
[ORIGIN from IDEO- + -GRAPH.]
A character symbolizing the idea of a thing without expressing the sequence of sounds in its name, as a numeral, any of various Chinese characters, etc.
■ **ideoˈgraphic** *adjective* of the nature of an ideograph; pertaining to or composed of ideographs: **E19.** **ideoˈgraphical** *adjective* ideographic **M19.** **ideoˈgraphically** *adverb* **E19.**

ideologist /ʌɪdɪˈɒlədʒɪst, ɪd-/ *noun*. **L18.**
[ORIGIN French *idéologiste*, formed as IDEO- + -LOGIST.]
1 A person who studies the origin and nature of ideas. *arch.* **L18.**
2 A theorist; a visionary, an idealist. **M19.**
3 A proponent or an adherent of an ideology. **L19.**

ideologue /ˈʌɪdɪəlɒg, ˈɪd-/ *noun*. **E19.**
[ORIGIN French *idéologue*, formed as IDEO- + -LOGUE.]
A theorist, a visionary; a proponent or adherent of an ideology.

D. HALBERSTAM He was not an ideologue of the left, but he was sympathetic to it.

ideology /ʌɪdɪˈɒlədʒi, ɪd-/ *noun*. **L18.**
[ORIGIN French *idéologie*, formed as IDEO- + -LOGY.]
1 The branch of philosophy or psychology dealing with the origin and nature of ideas. *arch.* **L18.**
2 Ideal or abstract (esp. impractical) speculation. *arch.* **E19.**
3 A system of ideas or way of thinking pertaining to a class or individual, esp. as a basis of some economic or political theory or system, regarded as justifying actions and esp. to be maintained irrespective of events. Freq. with specifying word. **E20.**

A. KOESTLER Transformed the founders' once fluid ideas into rigid ideologies. E. P. THOMPSON The working-class ideology . . put an exceptionally high value upon . . personal liberty.

■ **ideoˈlogical** *adjective* pertaining to or of the nature of an ideology **L18.** **ideoˈlogically** *adverb* **M19.** **ideologize** *verb trans.* interpret ideologically; give an ideological character to: **M19.**

ides /ʌɪdz/ *noun pl.* Rarely in sing. **ide**. Also **I-**. **LOE.**
[ORIGIN Old French & mod. French from Latin *idus* (pl.), of unknown origin.]
The eighth day after the nones in the ancient Roman calendar: the 15th day of March, May, July, and October, and the 13th of the other months.

id est /ɪd ˈɛst/ *adverbial phr.* **L16.**
[ORIGIN Latin = that is.]
That is to say. Usu. abbreviated to ***i.e.***

I

-idin /ɪdɪn/ *suffix.*
[ORIGIN from -IDE + -IN[1].]
CHEMISTRY. Forming names of anthocyanidins (*delphinidin*, *pelargonidin*).

-idine /iːdiːn, ɪdɪn/ *suffix.*
[ORIGIN from -IDE + -INE[5].]
CHEMISTRY. Forming names of usu. cyclic organic compounds containing nitrogen, esp. amino derivatives (***toluidine***, ***guanidine***), heterocycles (***piperidine***, ***pyridine***), and pyrimidine nucleosides (***thymidine***).

idio- /ˈɪdɪəʊ/ *combining form* of Greek *idios* own, personal, private, distinct: see -O-.
■ **idioˈglossia** *noun* lallation; idiolalia: L19. **idiogram** *noun* (*CYTOLOGY*) a diagram representing the chromosome complement of a cell or individual; a karyotype: E20. **idiograph** *noun* [Greek *idiographon*] one's signature or personal mark E17. **idioˈgraphic** *adjective* concerned with the individual, pertaining to or descriptive of single and unique facts and processes (opp. NOMOTHETIC) E20. **idioˈlalia** *noun* the speaking of an invented or private language M20. **idiophone** *noun* a percussion instrument that consists of elastic material (e.g. metal, wood), itself capable of producing sound M20. **idioˈphoneme** *noun* (*LINGUISTICS*) a phoneme in individual speech M20. **idiophoˈnemic** *adjective* (*LINGUISTICS*) of or pertaining to an idiophoneme M20. **idioplasm** *noun* (*obsolete* exc. *hist.*) germ plasm, genetic material L19. **idioˈrrhythmic**, **idiorhythmic** *noun & adjective* [Greek *idiorruthmos*] (a member of a monastic institution) allowing freedom to the individual (opp. COENOBITIC) M19. **idiosome** *noun* †(*a*) a supposed ultimate unit of living matter; (*b*) = IDIOZOME: L19. **idiovenˈtricular** *adjective* (*MEDICINE*) (esp. of a rhythm) proper to the ventricle of the heart alone E20. **idiozome** *noun* [Greek *zōma* band, girdle, loincloth] *CYTOLOGY* a rounded cytoplasmic structure in developing animal germ cells L19.

idioblast /ˈɪdɪə(ʊ)blast/ *noun.* L19.
[ORIGIN from IDIO- + -BLAST.]
1 *BOTANY.* A cell of distinctly different nature from the surrounding tissue. L19.
2 *PETROGRAPHY.* A mineral crystal which has grown with its own characteristic crystal faces in metamorphic rock. Opp. ***xenoblast***. E20.
■ **idioˈblastic** *adjective* pertaining to, composed of, or of the nature of an idioblast or idioblasts E20.

idiocy /ˈɪdɪəsi/ *noun.* E16.
[ORIGIN from IDIOT (perh. partly after *lunacy*): see -CY. Cf. Greek *idiōteia* uncouthness, lack of education.]
1 The state or condition of being an idiot; extremely low intelligence (now *obsolete* in *MEDICINE* use); stupidity, foolishness. E16.

S. MORLEY An act of such wanton idiocy.

2 A stupid or foolish action, remark, etc. M20.

C. PETERS He is sharp, too, on the idiocies of historical novels.

idiolect /ˈɪdɪəlɛkt/ *noun.* M20.
[ORIGIN from IDIO- + DIA)LECT.]
The linguistic system of an individual, differing in some details from that of all other speakers of the same dialect or language.
■ **idioˈlectal** *adjective* M20.

idiom /ˈɪdɪəm/ *noun.* L16.
[ORIGIN French *idiome* or late Latin *idioma* from Greek = property, peculiar phraseology, from *idiousthai* make one's own, from *idios* own, private.]
1 The language of a people or country. Now usu., the language of a particular area or group of people, dialect. L16.

R. GODFREY The writings of Glauber, which were translated into the English Idiom. GIBBON On the spot I read . . the classics of the Tuscan idiom.

Idiom Neutral: see NEUTRAL *noun* 4.
2 The specific character or property of a language or dialect; natural or individual manner of expression of a language or dialect. L16.

T. SHERLOCK To bring anything to light . . is . . in the Idiom of the English Tongue. *fig.*: LD MACAULAY Not so close as to destroy the idioms of national opinion and feeling.

3 A form of expression, grammatical construction, phrase, etc., peculiar to a person or language; a phrase etc. which is understood by speakers of a particular language despite its meaning's not being predictable from that of the separate words. E17. ▸**b** A characteristic mode of expression in music, art, writing, etc.; an instance of this. E20.

b J. AGATE The music . . is written in a fascinating idiom. K. CLARK In his figure drawings he mastered . . the idiom of the time.

idiomatic /ɪdɪəˈmatɪk/ *adjective.* E18.
[ORIGIN Greek *idiōmatikos* peculiar, characteristic, from *idiōmat-*, *-ma*: see IDIOM, -ATIC.]
1 Peculiar to or of the nature of an idiom; conforming to idiom; vernacular, colloquial. E18.

JANET MORGAN It was from her that Agatha learnt her idiomatic and fluent French.

2 Given to or distinguished by the use of idioms. M19.
■ **idiomatical** *adjective* (now *rare*) = IDIOMATIC E18. **idiomatically** *adverb* E18. **idiomaˈticity** *noun* the quality or state of being idiomatic M20.

idiomorphic /ɪdɪə(ʊ)ˈmɔːfɪk/ *adjective.* L19.
[ORIGIN from IDIO- + -MORPH + -IC.]
PETROGRAPHY. Of a crystal: euhedral. Of a rock: containing euhedral crystals.
■ **idiomorphically** *adverb* L19. **idiomorphism** *noun* the condition of being idiomorphic E20.

idiopathetic /ˌɪdɪə(ʊ)pəˈθɛtɪk/ *adjective. rare.* M17.
[ORIGIN formed as IDIOPATHIC after SYMPATHETIC.]
= IDIOPATHIC.

idiopathic /ɪdɪə(ʊ)ˈpaθɪk/ *adjective.* M17.
[ORIGIN from IDIO- + -PATHY + -IC.]
MEDICINE. Of a disease: not consequent on or symptomatic of another disease; having no known cause.
■ **idiˈopathy** *noun* (an) idiopathic disease L17.

idiosyncrasy /ɪdɪə(ʊ)ˈsɪŋkrəsi/ *noun.* E17.
[ORIGIN Greek *idiosugkrasia*, *-krasis*, from *idios* IDIO- + *sugkrasis* commixture, tempering, from *sun-* SYN- + *krasis* CRASIS.]
1 Orig., the physical constitution peculiar to an individual. Now only in *MEDICINE*, abnormal individual sensitivity to a food or drug. E17.
2 A mental constitution, view, feeling, or mode of behaviour peculiar to a person, nation, etc.; something highly individualized or eccentric. M17.

C. BEATON The surprised eyebrows . . the bold gestures . . all of these idiosyncrasies are derived from Lina Cavalieri. C. RYCROFT The absence of imagery accompanying thought seems to be an idiosyncrasy common among scientists. R. STRANGE My intentions have been orthodox. Idiosyncrasy would be misplaced here.

3 A mode of expression peculiar to an author. M19.

idiosyncratic /ˌɪdɪə(ʊ)sɪnˈkratɪk/ *adjective.* L18.
[ORIGIN from IDIOSYNCRASY (after Greek *sugkratikos* mixed together): see -ATIC.]
Of, pertaining to, or of the nature of idiosyncrasy; characteristic of an individual.

M. N. COX Her idiosyncratic, peculiarly unrepeatable personal qualities. *Do-It-Yourself* An idiosyncratic choice, such as a black or scarlet suite.

■ **idiosyncratical** *adjective* (now *rare*) idiosyncratic L17. **idiosyncratically** *adverb* in an idiosyncratic manner M17.

idiot /ˈɪdɪət/ *noun & adjective.* ME.
[ORIGIN Old French & mod. French from Latin *idiota* ignorant person from Greek *idiōtēs* private person, plebeian, layman, ignorant person, from *idios* private, peculiar. See also EEJIT.]
▸**A** *noun.* **1** A person with extremely low intelligence. *obsolete* in *MEDICINE*. ME. ▸**b** A stupid person, a fool, a blockhead. *colloq.* LME. ▸†**c** A person of weak intellect maintained as an amusement; a jester, a fool. E16–E18.

J. R. ACKERLEY The small blank eyes mooned stolidly at me . . it was like being gaped at by the village idiot. **b** E. M. FORSTER Charles clenched his fist and cried, 'The idiot, the idiot, the little fool!' P. G. WODEHOUSE She was incensed with this idiot who had flung himself before her car.

†**2** An uneducated or ignorant person; a simple person. LME–E18. ▸**b** A layman. LME–M17.
– COMB.: **idiot board** a board displaying a television script to a speaker as an aid to memory; **idiot box** *colloq.* a television set; **idiot card** = *idiot board* above; **idiot light** *colloq.* a warning light that goes on when a fault occurs in a device; **idiot-proof** *adjective* (*colloq.*) foolproof; **idiot savant** (*a*) a person who has a mental disability or learning difficulties but displays brilliance in a specific area, esp. one involving memory; (*b*) a person who is extremely unworldly but displays natural wisdom and insight.
▸**B** *attrib.* or as *adjective.* Of, pertaining to, or characteristic of an idiot or idiocy; idiotic. LME.

J. WAINWRIGHT The idiot woman rode her horse directly into my path. A. SILLITOE Baxter was whistling some idiot song.

■ **idiotish** *adjective* (now *rare*) somewhat idiotic M16. **idiotize** *verb* (*a*) *verb intrans.* become idiotic; (*b*) *verb trans.* make idiotic or into an idiot; make a fool of: L16. **idiotry** *noun* (*a*) *SCOTS LAW* idiocy; (*b*) idiotic behaviour: L15.

idiotic /ɪdɪˈɒtɪk/ *adjective.* E18.
[ORIGIN from IDIOT, after Greek *idiōtikos* or Latin *idioticus* uneducated, ignorant, unskilful: see -IC.]
Characteristic of an idiot or idiots; unintelligent; stupid, foolish.

V. WOOLF She was completely reckless; did the most idiotic things out of bravado. H. L. MENCKEN The army is so stupid as to be virtually idiotic.

idiotical /ɪdɪˈɒtɪk(ə)l/ *adjective.* Now *rare.* M17.
[ORIGIN formed as IDIOTIC: see -ICAL.]
†**1** Uneducated, plain, ignorant. M17–E18.
2 Idiotic. M17.

idiotically /ɪdɪˈɒtɪk(ə)li/ *adverb.* M17.
[ORIGIN from (the same root as) IDIOTICAL: see -LY[2].]
In an idiotic manner.

idioticon /ɪdɪˈəʊtɪk(ə)n/ *noun.* M19.
[ORIGIN German from Greek *idiōtikon* use as noun of neut. sing. of *idiōtikos* uneducated. Cf. IDIOT.]
A dictionary, word list, etc., of words and phrases peculiar to a dialect, a particular group of people, etc.

idiotism /ˈɪdɪətɪz(ə)m/ *noun.* L16.
[ORIGIN French *idiotisme* idiom, idiocy, from Latin *idiotismus* common or vulgar manner of speaking from Greek *idiōtismos*. In branch II partly from IDIOT + -ISM.]
▸**I** †**1** = IDIOM 1. L16–L17.
†**2** = IDIOM 2. E17–M18.
3 = IDIOM 3. Now *rare* or *obsolete*. E17.
▸**II 4** = IDIOCY. L16.

idiotope /ˈɪdɪə(ʊ)təʊp/ *noun.* M20.
[ORIGIN from IDIO- + Greek *topos* place.]
IMMUNOLOGY. An antigenic determinant acting as (part of) an idiotype.

idiotype /ˈɪdɪə(ʊ)tʌɪp/ *noun.* M19.
[ORIGIN from IDIO- + -TYPE.]
†**1** *CHEMISTRY.* A substance of the same type as another. M–L19.
2 *BIOLOGY.* The set of all hereditary determinants of an individual. Formerly also, the genotype only. E20.
3 *IMMUNOLOGY.* A set of one or more antigenic determinants associated usu. with the binding region of an immunoglobulin and characteristic of a particular clone of antibody-producing cells. M20.
■ **idiotypic** /-ˈtɪp-/ *adjective* of or pertaining to an idiotype M19.

-idium /ˈɪdɪəm/ *suffix.* Pl. **-idia** /ˈɪdɪə/, **-idiums**.
[ORIGIN mod. Latin dim. ending corresp. to -IUM (cf. Greek *-idion*).]
BIOLOGY. Forming nouns denoting small structures, as ***gonidium***, ***nephridium***, etc.

idle /ˈʌɪd(ə)l/ *noun.* OE.
[ORIGIN from the adjective In branch II from the verb.]
▸**I** †**1** Something useless, vain, or frivolous. Freq. in ***in idle***, in vain, without cause. OE–L15.
†**2** Idleness. OE–L17.
3 An idle person. *rare.* M17.
▸**II 4** An act of idling. L19.
5 Idling (of an engine); idling speed. Freq. *attrib.* M20.

idle /ˈʌɪd(ə)l/ *adjective.*
[ORIGIN Old English *īdel* = Old Frisian *īdel*, Old Saxon *īdal* empty, worthless (Dutch *ijdel* vain, useless, frivolous, trifling, conceited), Old High German *ītal* empty, useless (German *eitel* bare, mere, worthless, vain), from West Germanic: ult. origin unknown.]
†**1** Empty, vacant; void (*of*). OE–LME.
2 Of an action, thought, word, etc.: lacking worth or significance, useless; ineffective, vain, trifling. OE. ▸**b** Baseless, groundless. L16.

SWIFT It is idle to propose remedies, before we are assured of the disease. A. TREW I'm sorry. It was just idle curiosity. **b** E. BOWEN Robert would never listen to idle gossip.

3 Of a thing: useless. Now *rare*. OE.

SHAKES. *Com. Err.* Usurping ivy, brier, or idle moss.

4 a Of a person: not working, doing nothing. OE. ▸**b** Of time etc.: unoccupied; characterized by inaction or lack of occupation. ME.

a R. BURN They are idle for want of such work as they are able to do. M. ARGYLE There has been a decline of the old 'idle rich' . . living partly on unearned income. **b** T. BROWN Persons . . that have a great deal of Idle Time lying upon their Hands.

5 Having a dislike for work or activity; lazy, indolent. ME.

S. LEACOCK 'Well, of all the idle creatures!' she exclaimed. 'Loafing here in the sand.'

6 Of a thing: inactive, unoccupied; not moving or in operation. LME. ▸**b** Of money: out of circulation. M20.

I. WATTS Satan finds some mischief still For idle hands to do. JO GRIMOND If they are used for a month . . they must stand idle for eleven. U. BENTLEY The forces of convention . . had lain so idle for so long.

run idle (of machinery) run without doing work or transmitting power.
– SPECIAL COLLOCATIONS & COMB.: **idle and disorderly person** *LAW* (now *hist.*) an unlicensed pedlar; a common prostitute or beggar when walking the streets. **idleman** *rare* a man without occupation. **idle wheel** an intermediate wheel between two geared wheels, esp. to allow them to rotate in the same direction.
■ †**idleby** *noun* [-BY] an idle person. L16–E18. **idlehood** *noun* (*arch.*) idleness M16.

idle /ˈʌɪd(ə)l/ *verb.* LME.
[ORIGIN from the adjective.]
†**1** *verb trans.* Make vain or worthless. Only in LME.
2 *verb intrans.* Move idly. L16.

W. D. HOWELLS A clear brown brook idles through the pastures.

3 *verb intrans.* Be idle; pass the time in idleness. M17. ▸**b** *verb trans.* Pass (time) in idleness. M17.

J. FOWLES It seemed to him to explain all his previous idling through life. *New Yorker* The drugstore . . . where one could idle respectably. **b** R. HAYMAN Idling away the evenings on the hotel terrace.

4 *verb trans.* Cause to be idle. L18.

O. WILDE I had better not come . . . You should be reading and I would idle you.

5 *verb intrans.* Of an engine: run while disconnected from a load or out of gear, so as to perform no external or useful work; run very slowly. Freq. as ***idling verbal noun***. E20. ▸**b** *verb trans.* Cause (an engine) to idle. E20.

W. GOLDING Waiting at the traffic lights, the engine idling. **b** M. ATWOOD At the dock he idled the motor and practically threw her onto the shore.

idling speed: at which an engine idles.

idleness /ˈʌɪd(ə)lnɪs/ *noun*. OE.
[ORIGIN from IDLE *adjective* + -NESS.]
†**1** Vanity, emptiness. Esp. in ***in idleness***, in vain. OE–LME.
2 The state or condition of being idle or unoccupied; lack of occupation; habitual avoidance of work; inactivity, indolence; an instance of this. OE.

S. JOHNSON Unable to support any of his children . . in the hereditary dignity of idleness.

bread of idleness: see BREAD *noun*[1].
3 Groundlessness, worthlessness, triviality, futility. M17.

idler /ˈʌɪdlə/ *noun*. M16.
[ORIGIN from IDLE *verb* + -ER[1].]
1 A person who idles or is idle; a lazy indolent person. M16.

A. MASON A crowd of rich young idlers . . gathered in a corner.

2 NAUTICAL. A person on a ship who is on constant day duty and so not liable for the night watch. L18.
3 A wheel or roller which transmits no power when in contact with a moving belt etc., but serves as a support or guide. L19. ▸**b** = ***idle wheel*** s.v. IDLE *adjective*. L19.

idlesse /ˈʌɪdlɛs/ *noun*. *pseudo-arch*. L16.
[ORIGIN from IDLE *adjective* + -ESS[2].]
Idleness.

idli /ˈɪdli/ *noun*. M20.
[ORIGIN Malayalam, Kannada *iḍḍali*.]
A steamed cake of rice and black gram, popular in the southern part of the Indian subcontinent.

idly /ˈʌɪdli/ *adverb*. OE.
[ORIGIN from IDLE *adjective* + -LY[2].]
1 Vainly, uselessly; frivolously, carelessly, ineffectively. OE.

C. PHILLIPS He kicked idly at a ball of dust.

2 In an idle or lazy way; inactively; indolently. LME.

L. URIS British troops stood by idly.

Ido /ˈiːdəʊ/ *noun & adjective*. E20.
[ORIGIN Ido = offspring.]
(Of) an artificial language based on Esperanto.

idocrase /ˈʌɪdəkreɪz, -s/ *noun*. E19.
[ORIGIN from Greek *eidos* form + *krasis* mixture.]
MINERALOGY. = VESUVIANITE.

idol /ˈʌɪd(ə)l/ *noun, adjective, & verb*. ME.
[ORIGIN Old French & mod. French †*id(e)le*, *idole* from Latin *idolum* image, form, apparition, (ecclesiastical Latin) idol, from Greek *eidōlon*, from *eidos* form, shape.]
▸ **A** *noun*. **I** From Jewish and Christian use.
1 An image or representation of a god or divinity used as an object of worship; a false god; *arch. derog.* a material object of worship in a Christian church. ME.

E. H. GOMBRICH Idols of which the Bible speaks: that people prayed before them.

Moorish idol: see MOORISH *adjective*[2].
2 A person or thing which is the object of extreme or excessive devotion. M16.

S. BERINGTON Money, the Idol of other People, was the least of his Care. A. MCCOWEN My early idols were Jack Hulbert and Cicely Courtneidge.

matinée idol.
▸ **II** From classical Greek and Latin use.
†**3** An image or representation of a person or thing; *esp.* a statue. M16–E17. ▸**b** A likeness, an imitation. L16–M17. ▸**c** A counterfeit, a sham; an impostor, a pretender. L16–M17.
4 An image without substance; a reflection, a phantom. Now *rare*. M16.
5 A fantasy, a fancy. Now *rare*. L16. ▸**b** PHILOSOPHY (now *hist.*). A false mental image or conception; a false or misleading notion; a fallacy. L17.
b idols of the tribe, **idols of the cave**, **idols of the market**, **idols of the theatre** four classes of fallacies referred by Bacon (1620) respectively to limitations of human mind, prejudices of idiosyncrasy, influence of words, philosophical and logical prepossessions.
▸ **B** *attrib.* or as *adjective*. Of, pertaining to, or resembling an idol. M16.
▸ **C** *verb trans.* Idolize. Now only *poet.* L16.

idola *noun* pl. of IDOLUM.

idolater /ʌɪˈdɒlətə/ *noun*. Also **-tor**. LME.
[ORIGIN from Old French & mod. French *idolâtre* (from Proto-Romance (medieval Latin) *idolatra* for *idololatra*, *-tres* from Greek *eidōlolatrēs*: see -LATER; cf. IDOLATRY) + -ER[1], or from IDOLATRY after *astronomer*, *astronomy*.]
1 A person who worships idols or images of deities or divinities. LME.

J. NORRIS Idolaters . . pay that Religious Worship . . to something else that is not God.

2 A person who idolizes or adores a person or thing. M16.

A. C. SWINBURNE The idolators of either [author] insisted . . on the superior claims of their respective favorite.

■ **idolatress** *noun* (now *rare*) a female idolater E17.

idolatric /ʌɪˈdɒlətrɪk/ *adjective*. *rare*. M17.
[ORIGIN medieval Latin *idolatricus*, from *idolatria* IDOLATRY: see -IC.]
Idolatrous.

†**idolatrical** *adjective*. M16–L18.
[ORIGIN formed as IDOLATRIC + -AL[1].]
Idolatrous.

idolatrize /ʌɪˈdɒlətrʌɪz/ *verb*. Also **-ise**. L16.
[ORIGIN from IDOLATRY + -IZE.]
†**1** *verb intrans.* Worship an idol or idols; practise idolatry. L16–E18.
2 *verb trans.* Make an idol of, worship idolatrously; idolize. E17.

A. B. GROSART We are so used to idolatrize Shakespeare because of his simply incomparable genius.

idolatrous /ʌɪˈdɒlətrəs/ *adjective*. M16.
[ORIGIN from IDOLATER + -OUS.]
1 Of, pertaining to, or characteristic of idolatry; devoted to idolatry. M16.

T. FULLER He saw an idolatrous altar at Damascus.

2 Of a person: worshipping an idol or idols, worshipping false gods. E17.

MILTON The Philistines Idolatrous, uncircumcised, unclean.

■ **idolatrously** *adverb* L16. **idolatrousness** *noun* L16.

idolatry /ʌɪˈdɒlətri/ *noun*. ME.
[ORIGIN Old French & mod. French *idolâtrie* from Proto-Romance (medieval Latin) *idolatria* for ecclesiastical Latin *idololatria* from Greek *eidōlolatreia*, from *eidōlon* IDOL *noun*: see -LATRY.]
1 The worship of idols; the offering of divine honours to a created object. ME.
2 Excessive devotion to or veneration for a person or thing; adoration. LME.

ROSEMARY MANNING I borrowed an idea from Dickens, whom I love this side of idolatry.

idolise *verb* var. of IDOLIZE.

idolism /ˈʌɪd(ə)lɪz(ə)m/ *noun*. E17.
[ORIGIN from IDOL *noun* + -ISM.]
1 Idolatry. E17.
2 = IDOL *noun* 5b. L17.
■ **idolist** *noun* a worshipper of idols, an idolater E17.

idolize /ˈʌɪd(ə)lʌɪz/ *verb*. Also **-ise**. L16.
[ORIGIN from IDOL *noun* + -IZE.]
1 *verb trans.* Make an idol of, worship idolatrously; adore or love to excess. L16.

T. GALE The Moon is the same . . with Diana, which the Gauls greatly idolized. E. O'BRIEN The mother came to idolize the child, because it was quiet.

2 *verb intrans.* Practise idolatry. *rare*. M17.
■ **idolizer** *noun* M17.

idoloclast /ʌɪˈdɒləklast/ *noun*. E19.
[ORIGIN from IDOL *noun* after *iconoclast*.]
A destroyer of idols; an iconoclast.

idolothyte /ʌɪˈdɒləθʌɪt/ *adjective & noun*. Now *rare* or *obsolete*. M16.
[ORIGIN ecclesiastical Latin *idolothytus* from Greek *eidōlothutos* offered to idols, from *eidōlon* IDOL *noun* + *thutos* sacrificed.]
(A thing) offered to an idol.

idolum /ʌɪˈdəʊləm/ *noun*. Pl. **-la** /-lə/. E17.
[ORIGIN Latin *idolum* from Greek *eidōlon* IDOL *noun*.]
1 An image without substance; a phantom; a mental image, an idea. E17.
2 = IDOL *noun* 5b. M17.

idoneous /ʌɪˈdəʊnɪəs/ *adjective*. Now *rare*. M16.
[ORIGIN from Latin *idoneus* fit, suitable + -OUS.]
Apt, fit, suitable.
■ **idoneity** /ʌɪdəˈniːɪti, -ˈneɪɪti/ *noun* [late Latin *idoneitas*] fitness, suitability, aptness E17. **idoneousness** *noun* E18.

IDP *abbreviation*.
Internally displaced person.

idrialin /ˈɪdrɪəlɪn/ *noun*. Now *rare*. Also **-ine** /-iːn/. M19.
[ORIGIN formed as IDRIALITE: see -IN[1], -INE[5].]
CHEMISTRY & MINERALOGY. Idrialite.

idrialite /ˈɪdrɪəlʌɪt/ *noun*. M19.
[ORIGIN from *Idria* (now Idrija) in Slovenia, SE Europe + -LITE.]
CHEMISTRY & MINERALOGY. A colourless crystalline aromatic hydrocarbon, $C_{22}H_{11}$, which occurs naturally as a combustible mineral coloured brownish black by admixture with cinnabar, clays, etc.

idryl /ˈɪdrʌɪl, -rɪl/ *noun*. M19.
[ORIGIN formed as IDRIALITE + -YL.]
CHEMISTRY. A naturally occurring mixture of hydrocarbons including fluoranthene; fluoranthene.

Idumean /ɪdjʊˈmiːən, ʌɪd-/ *noun & adjective*. *hist.* Also **-maean**. OE.
[ORIGIN from Latin *Idumaea* from Greek *Idoumaia* from Hebrew *'ĕdōm* Edom (see below) + -AN, -EAN.]
▸**A** *noun*. A member of a people inhabiting Idumaea or Edom, an ancient kingdom situated between Egypt and Palestine. OE.
▸ **B** *adjective*. Of or pertaining to Idumaea or Edom. L17.

idyll /ˈɪdɪl, ˈʌɪd-/ *noun*. Also **-yl**, in Latin form (earlier) †**idyllium**, pl. **-ia**. L16.
[ORIGIN Latin *idyllium*, from Greek *eidullion* dim. of *eidos* form, picture.]
1 A short description in verse or (freq. more fully ***prose idyll***) in prose of a picturesque scene or incident, esp. in rustic life. L16.
2 An episode suitable for treatment in such verse or prose, *esp.* a love story. M19.

L. STRACHEY If the . . elements of an idyll are happiness, love and simplicity, an idyll it was.

3 MUSIC. An instrumental composition on a pastoral or sentimental subject. L19.
■ **iˈdyllian** *adjective* (*rare*) idyllic E18. **iˈdyllic** *adjective* of, pertaining to, or resembling an idyll; making a suitable subject for an idyll: M19. **iˈdyllically** *adverb* L19. **idyllist** *noun* a writer of idylls L18. **idyllize** *verb trans.* make into an idyll L19.

IE *abbreviation*.
Indo-European.

i.e. *abbreviation*.
Latin *Id est* that is to say.

-ie /i/ *suffix*.
Var. (esp. *Scot.*, *Austral.*, & *NZ*) of -Y[6], as in ***birdie***, ***doggie***, ***roughie***, ***sickie***; used also in independent formations, as ***bookie***, ***movie***.

iechyd da /jɛxiːd ˈdɑː/ *interjection*. *Welsh*. L20.
[ORIGIN Welsh, lit. 'good health'.]
Expr. good wishes before drinking: cheers! good health!

IED *abbreviation*.
Improvised explosive device.

IEE *abbreviation*.
Institution of Electrical Engineers.

IEEE *abbreviation*. *US*.
Institute of Electrical and Electronics Engineers.

I.Eng. *abbreviation*.
Incorporated Engineer.

-ier /ɪə/ *suffix*. See also -YER.
[ORIGIN Of varied origin in native words; in words from French repr. French *-ier* from Latin *-arius*: see -ARY[1]. Cf. -EER.]
Forming nouns from nouns, denoting a person whose employment, profession, etc., is concerned with a thing, also (rarely) agent nouns from verbs in (i) Middle English words based chiefly on native words, in which the suffix is unstressed, as ***clothier***, ***collier***, ***furrier***; (ii) later words of French origin, in which the suffix is stressed, as ***bombardier***, ***cashier***.

ier-oe /ɪərˈəʊ/ *noun*. *Scot*. E18.
[ORIGIN Gaelic *iar-ogha*, from *iar* after + *ogha* grandchild.]
A great-grandchild.

IF *abbreviation*.
Intermediate frequency.

if /ɪf/ *conjunction & noun*.
[ORIGIN Old English *gif*, *gyf*, corresp. to Old Frisian *jef*, *ef*, *jof*, *of*, Old Saxon *ef*, *of* (Dutch *of*), Old High German *ibu*, *oba*, *ube*, also *niba*, *noba*, *nube* if not (German *ob* whether, if), Old Norse *ef* if, Gothic *ibai*, *iba* whether, lest, *niba(i)* if not, *jabai* if, although: ult. origin unknown.]
▸ **A** *conjunction* **I 1** Introducing a condition where the question of fulfilment or non-fulfilment is left open: given the hypothesis or proviso that, in the event that. (In *arch.* & *formal* lang. verb of *if* clause may be in pres. subjunct.) OE. ▸**b** With clause reduced to *if* and a word or phr. Also (often after *few*, *seldom*, etc.; introducing a more extreme term), or perhaps not even; *if not* (often after *many*, *most*, etc.; introducing a more extreme term), or perhaps even. ME. ▸**c** In rhetorical use, the main clause expressing a proposition which is implied to be as true as that contained in the *if* clause manifestly or self-evidently is: as truly as. Also, in comparing two situations: whereas. ME.

J. CARLYLE I'll be hanged if I ever give you anything. F. W. CROFTS I'm blessed if I know. C. CLAIBORNE If the fish smells clean . . chances are it is fresh. O. NORTON I wasn't to worry if I found his tablets in the bathroom. **b** T. HERBERT Frogs are of great vertue, if physically used. *Bookman* [He] labours . . little, if at all, over the newspaper proofs. V. WOOLF I really must catch the first post if possible. M. KEANE Her reason if not now her life was in some danger. **c** P. LIVELY Dirty beggar . . , sixty if he was a day. V. S. PRITCHETT If a minute before he was drunkish, he was now sober. *Independent* It's a white poppy play if ever there was one.

2 With past subjunct. both in *if* clause and principal clause, implying that the condition was not, is not, or will not be fulfilled: on the supposition that, supposing. OE.

R. MACAULAY I should get on better if I saw everything in black and white. G. B. SHAW Would you mind if I shewed him your draft?

3 With principal clause suppressed and *if* clause standing on its own, expr.: (***a***) a wish (now always ***if only*** —***!***); (***b***) an exclamation of surprise (the verb being qualified by *not*). OE.

V. WOOLF A fortnight already gone . . . If only one could sip slowly . . every grain of every hour! T. DREISER Well, by jing, if it ain't Tom.

4 Introducing a concession (the clause often reduced to *if* and a word or phr.): while it is true that, though admittedly. Also, at the risk that, even if. **ME.**

F. W. CROFTS If he was not greatly liked in a personal capacity, he was respected as a sound business man. F. MUIR It foamed happily, if a bit glutinously. *Bodleian Library Record* Three interesting, if repetitious, publications.

▸ **II 5** Introducing a noun clause, chiefly as obj. of verbs such as *ask*, *doubt*, *know*, etc.: whether. **OE.**

Law Times He asked if his wife was there. SCOTT FITZGERALD It was doubtful if he knew who Andrew Jackson was. B. KEATON I went to New York, to see if I could get work there. A. BROOKNER Mummy was wondering if you would like to join us.

6 In the hope or on the off chance that, to see whether. *arch.* **ME.**

AV *Mark* 11:13 And seeing a figtree . . hee came, if haply hee might find any thing thereon.

– PHRASES: ***and if***: see AND *conjunction*[1] 11. ***as if***: see AS *adverb* etc. ***be nothing if not***: see NOTHING *pronoun & noun*. **if and only if**: introducing a condition which is necessary as well as sufficient. **if and when** at the future time (if any) that. ***if anything***: see ANYTHING *pronoun*. **if I were you** (in proffering advice) in your place. ***if not***: see sense 1b above. ***if only***: see sense 3 above. **if so be (that)** *arch. & dial.* if it should happen that, supposing. **if that** *arch.* supposing, if. ***if you*** PLEASE.

▸ **B** *noun*. An expression or condition of uncertainty; a proviso. **E16.**

ifs and ands: see AND *noun*. ***ifs and ans***: see AN *noun*. ***ifs and buts***: see BUT *noun*.

IFC *abbreviation*.

International Finance Corporation.

Ife /ˈiːfi/ *noun*. **M20.**

[ORIGIN A town in western Nigeria, the religious centre of the Yoruba people.]

Used ***attrib.*** to designate the art of the Yoruba people, esp. their bronzes and terracottas, the first examples of which were found at Ife.

-ifer *suffix* see -FER.

-iferous *suffix* see -FEROUS.

iff /ɪf ənd ˈəʊnlɪ ɪf/ *conjunction*. **M20.**

[ORIGIN Written abbreviation.]

MATH. & LOGIC. If and only if.

iffy /ˈɪfi/ *adjective*. *colloq.* **M20.**

[ORIGIN from IF *conjunction* + -Y[1].]

Full of or subject to conditions; doubtful, uncertain.

J. HEGLAND We can't afford to waste any more gas driving around—the trip home is iffy enough as it is. JO-ANN GOODWIN There's something iffy about smooching with your mother.

■ Also **iffish** *adjective* **L20.**

-ific, -ification *suffixes* see -FIC, -FICATION.

-iform *suffix* see -FORM.

IFR *abbreviation*.

Instrument flight rules, used to regulate the flying and navigating of an aircraft using instruments alone.

Iftar /ˈɪftɑː/ *noun*. **L19.**

[ORIGIN Arabic *ifṭār* fast breaking, breakfast, from *faṭara* split, cleave, break apart.]

The meal eaten by Muslims after sunset during Ramadan.

-ify *suffix* see -FY.

Ig *abbreviation*.

BIOCHEMISTRY. Immunoglobulin.

I.GasE. *abbreviation*.

Institution of Gas Engineers.

Igbo /ˈiːɡbəʊ/ *noun & adjective*. Also **Ebo**, **Ibo**, /ˈiːbəʊ/. **M18.**

[ORIGIN African name.]

▸ **A** *noun*. Pl. same, **-os**.

1 A member of a people of SE Nigeria. **M18.**

2 The Kwa language of this people. **E19.**

▸ **B** *adjective*. Of or pertaining to this people or their language. **M18.**

IgG *abbreviation*.

BIOCHEMISTRY. Gamma globulin, immunoglobulin G.

iggerant *adjective* see IGNORANT.

igloo /ˈɪɡluː/ *noun*. In sense 2 also **agloo**, **aglu**, /ˈaɡluː/. **M19.**

[ORIGIN Inupiaq *iglu* house.]

1 An Eskimo dome-shaped hut, usu. one built from blocks of snow. **M19.** ▸**b** *transf.* Any similarly shaped building or structure used for storage, shelter, etc. **M20.**

2 A cavity in the snow above a seal's breathing hole. **M19.**

Ignatian /ɪɡˈneɪʃ(ə)n/ *adjective & noun*. **E17.**

[ORIGIN from *Ignatius* (see below) + -AN.]

▸ **A** *adjective*. **1** Of or pertaining to St Ignatius Loyola (1491–1556) or the Society of Jesus, of which he was a founder. **E17.**

2 Of or pertaining to St Ignatius, bishop of Antioch, martyred at Rome *c* 107, or the letters attributed to him. **M19.**

▸ **B** *noun*. A follower of St Ignatius Loyola; a Jesuit. **E17.**

Ignatius's bean /ɪɡˈneɪʃəsɪz biːn/ *noun phr.* Also **Ignatius' bean** /ɪɡˈneɪʃəs/. **M18.**

[ORIGIN St *Ignatius* Loyola (see IGNATIAN).]

The highly poisonous seed of a climbing tropical shrub, *Strychnos ignatii* (family Loganiaceae). Also more fully ***St Ignatius's bean***, ***St Ignatius' bean***.

igneous /ˈɪɡnɪəs/ *adjective*. **M17.**

[ORIGIN from Latin *igneus* from *ignis* fire, + -OUS: see -EOUS.]

1 Pertaining to or of the nature of fire; fiery; produced by the action of fire. **M17.**

2 GEOLOGY. Produced by volcanic or magmatic agency; (of rock) that has solidified from lava or magma. **L18.**

ignes fatui *noun phr.* pl. of IGNIS FATUUS.

ignicolist /ɪɡˈnɪkəlɪst/ *noun*. **E19.**

[ORIGIN from Latin *ignis* fire + *-cola* (from *colere* to worship) + -IST.]

A fire worshipper.

igniferous /ɪɡˈnɪf(ə)rəs/ *adjective*. **E17.**

[ORIGIN from Latin *ignifer* fire-bearing, from *ignis* fire: see -FEROUS.]

Producing fire.

ignify /ˈɪɡnɪfʌɪ/ *verb trans. rare.* **L16.**

[ORIGIN from Latin *ignis* fire + -FY.]

Cause to burn; set on fire.

ignimbrite /ˈɪɡnɪmbrʌɪt/ *noun*. **M20.**

[ORIGIN from Latin *ignis* fire + *imbris*, *imber* shower of rain, storm cloud + -ITE[1].]

GEOLOGY. Any pyroclastic rock, typically a welded tuff, deposited from or formed by the settling of a *nuée ardente*.

ignipotent /ɪɡˈnɪpət(ə)nt/ *adjective*. **M17.**

[ORIGIN from Latin *ignipotent-* (Virgilian epithet of Vulcan), from *ignis* fire + *potent-* POTENT *adjective*[2].]

Ruling or having power over fire.

ignis fatuus /ˌɪɡnɪs ˈfatjʊəs/ *noun phr.* Pl. **ignes fatui** /ˌɪɡniːz ˈfatjʊʌɪ, ˌɪɡneɪz ˈfatjʊiː/. **M16.**

[ORIGIN mod. Latin = foolish fire, so called from its erratic flitting from place to place.]

1 A phosphorescent light seen hovering or floating over marshy ground, perh. due to the combustion of methane; a will-o'-the-wisp. **M16.**

2 *fig.* A delusive guiding principle, hope, or aim. **L16.**

Y. MENUHIN I don't fear indolence, confident . . that the gift is not an ignis fatuus, there one minute and gone the next.

†**ignite** *adjective*. **LME–E18.**

[ORIGIN Latin *ignitus* pa. pple of *ignire*: see IGNITE *verb*.]

Glowing with heat, white-hot or red-hot; *fig.* hot, ardent.

ignite /ɪɡˈnʌɪt/ *verb*. **M17.**

[ORIGIN Latin *ignit-* pa. ppl stem of *ignire* set on fire, from *ignis* fire.]

1 *verb trans.* Make intensely hot; *spec.* (CHEMISTRY) heat to the point of combustion or chemical change. **M17.**

2 *verb trans.* Set fire to, kindle. **E19.**

D. M. THOMAS The stokers set the fire going by igniting the people's hair. *fig.*: *Company* She felt no-one could match Alan or ignite the special feelings she'd had with him.

3 *verb intrans.* Catch fire, begin to burn. **E19.**

L. DEIGHTON Bombcases stuffed full of benzol, rubber and phosphorus that ignited on impact.

4 *verb trans.* Bring (an electric arc) into being. **E20.**

■ **ignitaˈbility** *noun* ignitibility **E19.** **ignitable** *adjective* ignitible **M19.** **ignitiˈbility** *noun* ability to be ignited **E20.** **ignitible** *adjective* able to be ignited **M17.**

igniter /ɪɡˈnʌɪtə/ *noun*. In sense 2 also **-tor**. **L19.**

[ORIGIN from IGNITE *verb* + -ER[1].]

1 A device which or a person who ignites something; *esp.* a device to set fire to an explosive or combustible. **L19.**

2 ELECTRONICS. In an ignitron, a small auxiliary anode that serves to restrike the arc in each cycle. **M20.**

ignition /ɪɡˈnɪʃ(ə)n/ *noun*. **E17.**

[ORIGIN (French from) medieval Latin *ignitio(n-)*, formed as IGNITE *verb*: see -ION.]

1 The action of subjecting something to the full action of fire; *spec.* (CHEMISTRY) heating to the point of combustion or chemical change. **E17.**

2 The action of setting fire to something; the process of catching fire or beginning to burn. **E19.**

3 The action of starting the combustion of the mixture in the cylinder of an internal-combustion engine; the mechanism for starting this process. **E20.**

4 The striking of an electric arc. **E20.**

– COMB.: **ignition key**: to operate the ignition mechanism of a motor vehicle engine; **ignition tube** CHEMISTRY a small test tube of heat-resistant glass.

ignitor *noun* see IGNITER.

ignitron /ɪɡˈnʌɪtrɒn/ *noun*. **M20.**

[ORIGIN from IGNITE *verb*, IGNITION + -TRON.]

ELECTRONICS. A mercury-arc rectifier of a kind having a pool cathode, a single anode, and an igniter, the timing of the igniter being used to control the rectifier output. Cf. EXCITRON.

ignivomous /ɪɡˈnɪvəməs/ *adjective*. **E17.**

[ORIGIN from late Latin *ignivomus* (from *ignis* fire + *-vomus* -vomiting) + -OUS.]

Vomiting or discharging fire.

ignoble /ɪɡˈnəʊb(ə)l/ *adjective, verb, & noun*. **LME.**

[ORIGIN (French from) Latin *ignobilis*, formed as I-[2] + *(g)nobilis* NOBLE *adjective*.]

▸ **A** *adjective*. **1** Not noble in birth or rank; of humble origin or social status. **LME.**

E. A. FREEMAN A West-Saxon house which, two generations back, had been undistinguished, perhaps ignoble.

ignoble hawk FALCONRY any of the short-winged hawks (e.g. the goshawk and sparrowhawk) which chase or rake after their prey instead of swooping down on it.

2 Not noble in character or quality; dishonourable, mean-spirited. **L16.**

MILTON Counsel'd ignoble ease, and peaceful sloath.

▸ **B** *verb trans.* Make ignoble; give a bad reputation to. *rare.* **L16.**

▸ **C** *noun*. A person of ignoble rank or character. Usu. in *pl.* Now *rare.* **E17.**

■ **ignoˈbility** *noun* ignoble quality **LME.** **ignobleness** *noun* **LME.** **ignobly** *adverb* **L16.**

ignominious /ɪɡnəˈmɪnɪəs/ *adjective*. **LME.**

[ORIGIN (Old French & mod. French *ignominieux* from) Latin *ignominiosus*, from *ignominia*: see IGNOMINY, -OUS.]

1 Causing ignominy or (public) disgrace; humiliating. **LME.**

A. MASON The lamentable gulf between the prophesied glory and the ignominious fact.

2 Of a person: covered with or deserving ignominy; infamous. **L16.**

D. H. LAWRENCE Hermione appeared . . to ridicule him and make him look ignominious in the eyes of everybody.

■ **ignominiously** *adverb* **E17.** **ignominiousness** *noun* **E18.**

ignominy /ˈɪɡnəmɪni/ *noun*. **M16.**

[ORIGIN (French *ignominie* from) Latin *ignominia*, formed as I-[2] + (var. of) *nomen* name, reputation: see -Y[3].]

1 Public disgrace or dishonour; infamy. **M16.**

Gentleman (Mumbai) He had to suffer the ignominy of being dropped from the team.

2 Infamous quality or conduct. *arch.* **M16.**

LD MACAULAY He then repays by ingratitude the benefits which he has purchased by ignominy.

ignomy /ˈɪɡnəmi/ *noun*. Now *arch. rare.* **M16.**

[ORIGIN Contr.]

= IGNOMINY.

ignoramus /ɪɡnəˈreɪməs/ *noun*. **L16.**

[ORIGIN Latin = we do not know, (in legal use) we take no notice of (it). In sense 2 perh. from *Ignoramus*, a comedy by George Ruggle (1615) satirizing lawyers.]

1 The endorsement formerly made by a grand jury on an indictment which they rejected as not being backed by sufficient evidence to bring before a petty jury. Chiefly in ***find an ignoramus***, ***return an ignoramus***, ***bring in an ignoramus***. *obsolete* exc. *hist.* **L16.**

2 An ignorant person. **E17.**

F. MCCOURT We are the laziest gang of ignoramuses it has ever been his misfortune to teach.

ignorance /ˈɪɡn(ə)r(ə)ns/ *noun*. **ME.**

[ORIGIN Old French & mod. French from Latin *ignorantia*, from *ignorant-*: see IGNORANT, -ANCE.]

1 The fact or condition of being ignorant; lack of knowledge (general or particular). **ME.** ▸**b** In full ***time of ignorance***. The period of Arab history prior to the teaching of Muhammad. **L18.**

W. SOYINKA Every care was taken to ensure that he was kept in ignorance of what had occurred. P. BARKER She didn't know what an ovary was but she wasn't going to admit ignorance.

invincible ignorance: see INVINCIBLE 1b.

†**2** An offence or sin caused by lack of knowledge. **LME–E17.**

■ **ignorancy** *noun* (long *rare*) **E16.**

ignorant /ˈɪɡn(ə)r(ə)nt/ *adjective & noun*. In sense A.3 also (*non-standard & joc.*) **iggerant** /ˈɪɡ(ə)r(ə)nt/. **LME.**

[ORIGIN Old French & mod. French from Latin *ignorant-* pres. ppl stem of *ignorare*: see IGNORE, -ANT[1].]

▸ **A** *adjective*. **1** Lacking knowledge (general or particular); not versed *in* a subject, unaware *of* a fact, *that*. **LME.** ▸**b** Marked by or resulting from ignorance. Also *poet.*, that keeps one in ignorance. **LME.**

A. RADCLIFFE I am ignorant that till now I ever made you this offer. G. STEIN Melanctha with all her . . wisdom was really very ignorant of evil. I. MURDOCH But I'm so stupid and ignorant . . . I know nothing. A. FRASER The trooper who was supposed to know the district proved alarmingly ignorant. **b** SHAKES. *Wint. T.* If you know aught which does behove my knowledge . . imprison't not In ignorant concealment.

†**2** Of a thing: unknown. **LME–M17.**

3 Ill-mannered, uncouth. *dial. & colloq.* **L19.**

▸ **B** *noun*. An ignorant person. Now *rare.* **LME.**

■ **ignorantly** *adverb* **LME.**

ignoratio elenchi /ɪgnəˌreɪʃɪəʊ ɪˈlɛŋkʌɪ/ *noun phr.* Pl. **ignorationes elenchi** /ˌɪgnəreɪʃɪˈəʊniːz/. L16.
[ORIGIN medieval Latin, translating Greek *hē tou elegkou agnoia* ignorance of the conditions of valid proof.]
A logical fallacy which consists in apparently refuting an opponent while actually disproving something not asserted; *gen.* any argument which is irrelevant to its professed purpose.

ignoration /ɪgnəˈreɪʃ(ə)n/ *noun.* E17.
[ORIGIN Latin *ignoratio(n-)*, from *ignorat-* pa. ppl stem of *ignorare*: see IGNORE, -ATION.]
1 The fact or condition of being ignorant. *rare.* E17.
2 The action of ignoring or disregarding someone or something; the fact of being ignored. M19.

ignore /ɪgˈnɔː/ *verb trans.* L15.
[ORIGIN (Old French & mod. French *ignorer* from) Latin *ignorare*, formed as I-² + base *gno-* know.]
1 Be ignorant of. Now *arch. rare.* L15.
R. BOYLE Others . . desirous to be taught by me, the little that I know, and they ignore.
2 Refuse to recognize or take notice of; disregard intentionally. E19.
D. H. LAWRENCE Was he going to ignore her, was he going to take no further notice of her? R. K. NARAYAN She ignored her surroundings . . , her attention being concentrated upon her movements. L. GORDON She followed natural paths which ignored artificial boundaries.
3 Of a grand jury: reject (an indictment) on the grounds of insufficient evidence (cf. IGNORAMUS 1). *obsolete* exc. *hist.* M19.
■ **ignorable** *adjective* M19.

ignotum per ignotius /ɪgˌnəʊtəm pər ɪgˈnəʊtɪəs/ *noun phr.* LME.
[ORIGIN Late Latin, lit. 'the unknown by means of the more unknown'.]
An explanation which is harder to understand than what it is meant to explain.

iguana /ɪˈgwɑːnə/ *noun.* M16.
[ORIGIN Spanish from Arawak *iwana*.]
1 A large arboreal lizard, *Iguana iguana*, of Central and S. America. Also, any of various similar or related lizards of the same family, Iguanidae. M16.
marine iguana: see MARINE *adjective*.
2 In Africa: a large monitor lizard of the genus *Varanus*; *esp.* the Nile monitor, *V. niloticus*. Cf. GOANNA. M18.
■ **iguanian** *noun & adjective* (*a*) *noun* an iguanid or related lizard; *spec.* an iguanid, agamid, or chameleon; (*b*) *adjective* of, pertaining to, or designating such lizards: M19. **iguanid** *noun & adjective* (*a*) *noun* any lizard of the family Iguanidae, typified by the genus *Iguana* and largely confined to the New World; (*b*) of, pertaining to, or characteristic of this family: L19. **iguanoid** *noun & adjective* = IGUANID M19.

iguanodon /ɪˈgwɑːnədɒn/ *noun.* E19.
[ORIGIN from IGUANA + -ODON, from its teeth being similar to an iguana's.]
Any of various large extinct ornithischian dinosaurs of the genus *Iguanodon*, of late Jurassic and early Cretaceous times, with well-developed hind limbs and a long thick tail.

i.h.p. *abbreviation.*
Indicated horsepower.

ihram /ɪxˈrɑːm, ɪˈrɑːm/ *noun.* E18.
[ORIGIN Arabic *'iḥrām*, ult. from *ḥarama* forbid. Cf. HAREM.]
1 The sacred state into which a Muslim must enter before performing a pilgrimage, during which sexual intercourse, shaving, cutting one's nails, and several other actions are forbidden. E18.
2 The costume worn by a Muslim in this state, consisting of two lengths of seamless usu. white fabric, one worn about the hips, the other over the shoulders or sometimes only over the left shoulder. E18.

IHS *abbreviation.*
[ORIGIN Late Latin repr. Greek IH(ΣΟΥ)Σ or *Iē(sou)s*.]
Jesus.

IHT *abbreviation.*
In the UK: inheritance tax.

iimbongi *noun pl.* see IMBONGI.

iiwi /iˈiːwi/ *noun.* L18.
[ORIGIN Hawaiian.]
A Hawaiian honeycreeper, *Vestiaria coccinea*, whose red feathers were formerly used to make the cloaks of Hawaiian chiefs.

Ijo /ˈiːdʒəʊ/ *noun & adjective.* Also **Ijaw** /ˈiːdʒɔː/. M19.
[ORIGIN Ijo *ịjọ*.]
► **A** *noun.* Pl. same. A member of a people inhabiting the Niger delta; the Niger-Congo language of this people. M19.
► **B** *attrib.* or as *adjective.* Of or pertaining to the Ijo or their language. M20.

ijolite /ˈiːdʒə(ʊ)lʌɪt/ *noun.* L19.
[ORIGIN from Swedish *Ijo* (= Finnish *Ii*) a village and district on the Finnish coast + -LITE.]
PETROGRAPHY. A plutonic rock consisting essentially of nepheline and pyroxene, without feldspar.
■ **ijoˈlitic** *adjective* M20.

ijtihad /ɪdʒtiːˈhɑːd/ *noun.* L19.
[ORIGIN Arabic *ijtihād* struggle, effort, from *ijtahada* strive.]
ISLAM. The exercising of discretionary judgement (esp. by a mujtahid) in order to deduce a law or rule of conduct which is not self-evident in the scriptural sources; the right to exercise this judgement.

ikat /ˈiːkɑːt/ *noun.* M20.
[ORIGIN Malay, lit. 'tie, fasten'.]
(A fabric made using) an Indonesian technique of textile decoration in which warp or weft threads, or both, are tied at intervals and dyed before weaving.

ikbal /ˈɪkbɑːl/ *noun.* E20.
[ORIGIN Turkish, lit. 'good fortune', from Arabic *'iqbāl*.]
hist. A favoured member of the harem of an Ottoman Sultan.

ike *noun* see IKEY.

ikebana /ɪkɪˈbɑːnə/ *noun.* E20.
[ORIGIN Japanese, from *ike* make live + *bana* flower.]
The art of Japanese flower arrangement, with formal display according to strict rules.

ikey /ˈʌɪki/ *noun & adjective. slang. derog.* (*offensive*). As noun also **ike** /ʌɪk/. M19.
[ORIGIN Colloq. abbreviation of Jewish male forename *Isaac*.]
► **A** *noun.* (A person resembling) a Jew; a moneylender. M19.
► **B** *adjective.* Artful, knowing; having a good opinion of oneself. L19.

ikon *noun* var. of ICON.

IL *abbreviation.*
1 Illinois.
2 Institute of Linguists.

il- /ɪl/ *prefix*¹.
Var. of Latin IN-² before *l*. Cf. IM-², IR-².

il- /ɪl/ *prefix*².
Var. of Latin IN-³ before *l*. Cf. I-², IM-², IR-².

-il /əl, ɪl/ *suffix.*
[ORIGIN Repr. Latin *-ilis*.]
Forming adjectives and occas. nouns, some adopted through French, as ***civil***, ***fossil***, ***utensil***. Cf. -ILE.

Ila /ˈiːlə/ *noun & adjective.* Pl. **Ba-ila** /bəˈiːlə/, (of noun) same. E20.
[ORIGIN Bantu.]
► **A** *noun.* **1** A member of a people inhabiting Zambia. E20.
2 The Bantu language of this people. E20.
► **B** *attrib.* or as *adjective.* Of or pertaining to the Ila or their language. E20.

Ilamba *noun & adjective* var. of LAMBA *noun*².

ilang-ilang *noun* var. of YLANG-YLANG.

Ilanun *noun* var. of ILLANUN.

Ilchester /ˈɪltʃɪstə/ *noun & adjective.* M20.
[ORIGIN A town in Somerset, SW England.]
(Designating) a variety of cheese made from Cheddar, beer, garlic, and spices.

†**ile** *noun* var. of AISLE.

-ile /ʌɪl/ *suffix.*
Var. of -IL, esp. in adoptions through French, as ***agile***, ***erectile***, ***fragile***; *spec.* in STATISTICS (on the model of Latin ordinal numerals of the type *sextilis* etc.), forming nouns denoting those values of a variate that divide a population into the indicated number of equal groups, or the groups themselves (***decile***, ***percentile***).

ILEA /ˈɪlɪə/ *abbreviation.*
hist. Inner London Education Authority.

ileal /ˈɪlɪəl/ *adjective.* L19.
[ORIGIN from ILEUM + -AL¹.]
ANATOMY & ZOOLOGY. Of, within, or supplying the ileum.

ileectomy /ɪlɪˈɛktəmi/ *noun.* L19.
[ORIGIN from ILEO- + -ECTOMY.]
Surgical removal of all or part of the ileum; an instance of this.

ileitis /ɪlɪˈʌɪtɪs/ *noun.* M19.
[ORIGIN from ILEUM + -ITIS.]
MEDICINE. Inflammation of the ileum.

ileo- /ˈɪlɪəʊ/ *combining form.* Before a vowel also **ile-**.
[ORIGIN from ILEUM + -O-.]
Chiefly MEDICINE. Of, pertaining to, or involving the ileum.
■ **ileoˈcaecal** *adjective* related to or (esp.) connecting the ileum and the caecum L19. **ileocoˈlitis** *noun* inflammation of the ileum and the colon L19. **ileocoˈlostomy** *noun* (an instance of) surgical connection of the ileum with the colon; the passage so formed: L19. **ileˈostomy** *noun* [Greek *stoma* mouth] (an instance of) surgical attachment of the ileum to the abdominal wall to form an artificial anus; the opening so formed: L19.

†**ileon** *noun.* LME–M18.
[ORIGIN medieval Latin (in Greek form). Cf. Old French & mod. French *iléon*.]
= ILEUM.

ileum /ˈɪlɪəm/ *noun.* L17.
[ORIGIN medieval Latin, var. of ILIUM app. by confusion with *ileus* (see ILEUS).]
ANATOMY & ZOOLOGY. The third portion of the small intestine, between the jejunum and the caecum. Also, the homologous or analogous part in lower vertebrates, insects, etc.

ileus /ˈɪlɪəs/ *noun.* L17.
[ORIGIN Latin *ileus*, *ileos* from Greek *ileos*, *eileos* colic, app. from *eilein* to roll.]
MEDICINE. (Painful) obstruction of the intestine, esp. the ileum, due to mechanical obstruction or (more fully ***paralytic ileus***) failure of peristalsis.

ilex /ˈʌɪlɛks/ *noun.* LME.
[ORIGIN Latin = holm oak.]
1 = HOLM *noun*² 2. LME.
2 Any of various trees of the genus *Ilex* (family Aquifoliaceae); = HOLLY *noun* 1. M16.

ilia *noun pl.* see ILIUM.

iliac /ˈɪlɪak/ *adjective & noun.* E16.
[ORIGIN Late Latin *iliacus*, from *ilia*: see ILEUM, ILIUM, -AC.]
► **A** *adjective.* **1** Of the nature of or pertaining to ileus; pertaining to or affecting the ileum. Chiefly in ***iliac passion*** below. Now *rare* or *obsolete.* E16.
2 Of or pertaining to the flank, or to the ilium or hip bone. M16.
– SPECIAL COLLOCATIONS: **iliac artery**: branching from the abdominal aorta and supplying the legs and pelvis. **iliac passion** (now *rare* or *obsolete*) = ILEUS. **iliac vein** any of several major veins draining blood from the lower body to the inferior vena cava.
► **B** *noun.* †**1** = ILEUS. Only in M16.
2 An iliac artery, vein, etc. L18.

iliacus /ɪˈlʌɪəkəs/ *noun.* E17.
[ORIGIN Late Latin: see ILIAC.]
ANATOMY. A muscle in the groin region which, with the psoas, flexes the hip. Also †***iliacus internus***, ***iliacus muscle***.

Iliad /ˈɪlɪad/ *noun.* E17.
[ORIGIN Title of an epic poem attributed to Homer, describing the climax of the siege of Troy, from Latin *Iliad-*, *Ilias* from Greek *Iliados*, *Ilias*, (*poiēsis*) (poem) of Troy, from *Ilion* Troy (whence Latin *Ilium*): see -AD¹.]
1 A long story or Homeric epic, *esp.* one dealing with martial feats. E17.
2 A long series or account of events, esp. disasters. E17.
■ **Iliadic** /ɪlɪˈadɪk/ *adjective* of, pertaining to, or of the nature of an Iliad L19. **Iliadist** *noun* a writer of Iliads E18.

Ilian /ˈɪlɪən/ *adjective & noun.* L16.
[ORIGIN from Latin *Ilium*: see ILIAD, -AN.]
► **A** *adjective.* Of or pertaining to any of the successive towns of Ilium in the Trojan plain. L16.
► **B** *noun.* A native or inhabitant of Ilium. M19.

Iliat /ˈɪlɪɑːt/ *noun.* E19.
[ORIGIN Turkish *ilāt* pl. of *il* country, wandering pastoral tribe.]
Any of several nomadic tribes scattered throughout Iran.

iligant /ˈɪlɪg(ə)nt/ *adjective.* Chiefly *Irish.* Also **ill-**. E19.
[ORIGIN Repr. a pronunc.]
Elegant.

ilio- /ˈɪlɪəʊ/ *combining form*¹. E19.
[ORIGIN from ILIUM 3: see -O-.]
Chiefly ANATOMY. Relating to or involving the ilium, as ***iliofemoral***, ***iliolumbar***, ***iliosacral***. Also, involving or including the iliacus, as ***iliopsoas***.

†**ilio-** *combining form*². Only in M19.
[ORIGIN from ILIUM 1: see -O-.]
= ILEO-.

†**ilion** *noun* see ILIUM.

-ility /ˈɪlɪti/ *suffix.*
[ORIGIN French *-ilité* or its source Latin *-ilitas*: see -ITY.]
In or forming nouns from adjectives ending in *-il*, *-ile*, or *-le*, with senses as -ITY, as ***civility***, ***servility***, ***ability***.

ilium /ˈɪlɪəm/ *noun.* Also (earlier) in Greek form †**ilion**. Pl. **ilia** /ˈɪlɪə/, †**ilions**. LME.
[ORIGIN Latin: in classical Latin only in pl. *ilia* flanks, sides, (also) entrails. See also ILEUM.]
†**1** = ILEUM. LME–E19.
2 The anterior or superior bone of the pelvis, the hip bone, usu. (as in humans) articulating with the sacrum, and fused with the ischium and pubis to form the innominate bone. L16.
†**3** In *pl.* The flanks. L16–E18.

ilk /ɪlk/ *adjective*¹, *pronoun*¹, & *noun.*
[ORIGIN Old English *ilca* masc., *ilce* fem. & neut., from Germanic pronominal stem repr. also in Gothic *is*, Old High German *ir*, (also mod.) *er* he, Latin *is* that, *idem* same, + base of ALIKE *adjective*: cf. SUCH *adjective & pronoun*, WHICH. See also THILK.]
► **A** *adjective.* Same, very same. *obsolete* exc. *Scot. arch.* OE.
► **B** *pronoun & noun.* **1** *The* or *that* same person or thing. *obsolete* exc. *Scot. arch.* OE.
2 *spec.* *The* or *that* same place, estate, or name. Only in ***of that ilk***. *Scot.* L15.
SIR W. SCOTT Knockwinnocks of that Ilk.
3 A class, a sort, a kind. L18.

I

> M. LOWRY Were not Bolowski and his ilk the enemies of their own race. *London Review of Books* Pronouncements of this ilk seem mainly designed to leave one's readers breathless and sputtering.

– NOTE: Sense 3 arose out of a misunderstanding of the earlier Scottish use of *of that ilk* (sense 2).

ilk /ɪlk/ *adjective*[2] & *pronoun*[2]. *Scot.* (formerly also *N. English*) Now *rare*. ME.
[ORIGIN formed as EACH.]
Each.

ilka /ˈɪlkə/ *adjective* (in mod. usage also classed as a *determiner*). Now only *Scot.* ME.
[ORIGIN from ILK *adjective*[2] & *pronoun*[2] + A *adjective*.]
Each, every.

ill /ɪl/ *noun*. ME.
[ORIGIN from the adjective.]
1 Evil; the opposite of good. ME. ▸**b** Wickedness, depravity. Formerly also, an instance or act of this. *arch.* ME.

> TENNYSON Oh yet we trust that somehow good Will be the final goal of ill.

2 Hostility, malevolence, unfriendly feeling. Now only, something unfriendly, unfavourable, or harmful. ME.

> W. TREVOR Mrs Maylam . . . would hear no ill of Studdy and was clearly on his side.

speak ill of: see SPEAK *verb*.
3 (A) misfortune, disaster, trouble. ME.

> T. GRAY No sense have they of ills to come.

4 Harm, injury. LME.
5 A disease, a sickness. Now chiefly *dial.* LME.
louping ill, ***tail ill***, etc.

ill /ɪl/ *adjective* & *adverb*. Compar. WORSE *adjective*, superl. WORST *adjective*. ME.
[ORIGIN Old Norse *illr* adjective, *illa* adverb, *ilt* use as noun of neut. of adjective: ult. origin unknown.]
▸ **A** *adjective*. **1** Of a person (*obsolete* exc. *dial.*), conduct, or actions: morally evil, wicked, depraved, immoral. *arch.* ME. ▸**b** Of opinion, reputation, etc.: attributing or implying wickedness or immorality. L15.

> T. HARDY The roads were dotted with roving characters of possibly ill intent.

2 Malevolent; hostile, unkind; harsh. ME. ▸**b** Of an animal: savage, vicious. Now *dial.* L15.

> SHELLEY Ill tongues shall wound me.

3 Doing or tending to do harm; hurtful, detrimental; prejudicial; disagreeable, objectionable. ME. ▸**b** Of an omen, conditions, etc.: unlucky, unpropitious, disastrous; miserable, wretched. ME. ▸†**c** Of food: unwholesome, harmful to health. L15–E18.

> J. BUCHAN 'Ill weather,' said Jaikie. 'Hellish,' was the answer. **b** POPE Ill fortune led Ulysses to our isle. *Proverb*: It's an ill wind that blows nobody good.

4 Difficult, hard, (*to do*). *arch.* ME.

> E. NESBIT And if a lad is ill to bind, Or some young maid is hard to lead.

5 Inferior in quality or condition; not good; defective; unsatisfactory; unskilful; inefficient. ME. ▸**b** Of manners or conduct: impolite, unseemly, rude. L16.

> J. RUSKIN The first shoots of it enfeebled by ill gardening.

6 Not in good health, sick, (chiefly *pred.*); (of health) unsound. (The predominant mod. sense.) LME.

> J. AUSTEN Lady Bertram, in consequence of a little ill-health, . . gave up the house in town. V. BRITTAIN Soon after we returned from Italy I became ill with jaundice. J. GATHORNE-HARDY Children . . . can look very well one moment, and an hour . . later be extremely ill.

▸ **B** *adverb*. **1** Wickedly, evilly, immorally. *obsolete* exc. as passing into other senses. ME.
2 Malevolently, unkindly; with hostility; unfavourably. ME.

> G. GREENE Even Burnet found it hard to speak ill of her at that time.

3 Painfully, harmfully; unpleasantly. *obsolete* exc. *dial.* ME.
4 Unpropitiously; unhappily. ME.

> B. JONES This urge to be away/ . . bodes ill both for your life and art.

5 Not well, badly, defectively, faultily; improperly; unskilfully, inefficiently; with difficulty. ME.

> E. WAUGH Some books I have sent to be bound in Bristol came back very ill done. N. FREELING Well, my dear, it would ill become me to complain. P. LIVELY There were demobbed soldiers everywhere, conspicuous in their ill-fitting new suits.

– SPECIAL COLLOCATIONS, PHRASES, & COMB.: ***be taken ill***: see TAKE *verb*. **do an ill turn to** harm (a person or his or her interests). ***ill-advised***: see ADVISED. **ill-affected** *adjective* (*a*) not well-disposed, unfriendly; †(*b*) affected with illness. **ill-assorted** *adjective* not well matched. **ill at ease** embarrassed, uneasy. **ill-behaved** *adjective* badly brought up, rude. **ill-beloved** *adjective* (*arch.*) not loved, disliked. ***ill blood***: see BLOOD *noun*. **ill-boding** *adjective* boding evil, of ill omen. **ill-bred** *adjective* badly brought up, rude. **ill breeding** bad manners, rudeness. **ill-concealed** *adjective* that one does not feel the need to conceal. **ill-conditioned** *adjective* (*a*) of evil disposition; (*b*) in bad condition. **ill-deedy** *adjective* (now *Scot. arch.*) given to evil deeds, mischievous. **ill-defined** *adjective* not clearly defined. **ill-disposed** *adjective* (*a*) disposed to evil; malevolent; (*b*) unfavourably disposed, disinclined. **ill effect** a harmful effect, an unpleasant consequence, (freq. in *pl.*). **ill-equipped** *adjective* not adequately equipped or qualified. **ill fame** disrepute (***house of ill fame***: see HOUSE *noun*[1]). **ill-fated** *adjective* (*a*) having or destined to an evil or unhappy fate; (*b*) bringing bad fortune. ***ill feeling***: see FEELING *noun*. **ill-formed** *adjective* badly formed; *spec.* in LINGUISTICS, incorrectly formed or derived from stated grammatical rules, grammatically incorrect. **ill-formedness** *noun* the state or condition of being ill-formed. **ill-founded** *adjective* (of an idea etc.) not well founded, groundless. **ill-got** *adjective* (*arch.*), **ill-gotten** *adjective* gained by wicked or unlawful means. **ill-judged** *adjective* unwise; badly considered. **ill-looking** *adjective* unattractive, ugly. **ill luck** bad luck, misfortune. **ill-mannered** *adjective* having bad manners, rude. **ill-matched** *adjective* unsuited; not fit to be a pair, be adversaries, etc. **ill-omened** *adjective* having a bad omen, inauspicious. **ill-placed** *adjective* badly placed; inopportune. **ill repute** disrepute (***house of ill repute***: see HOUSE *noun*[1]). **ill-starred** *adjective* born under an evil star; ill-fated, unlucky, destined to failure. **ill success** partial or complete failure. **ill temper** bad temper. ***ill THIEF***. **ill-timed** *adjective* done or occurring at an inappropriate time. **ill-treat** *verb trans.* treat badly or cruelly, abuse. **ill treatment**, **ill usage**, **ill use** [USE *noun*] bad or cruel treatment, abuse. **ill-use** *verb trans.* [USE *verb*] = ***ill-treat*** above. **ill will** = ***ill feeling*** above. **ill-willer** a person who harbours ill will towards another. **ill-willing** *adjective* harbouring ill will, malevolent. **ill-wisher** = ***ill-willer*** above. ***in ill part***: see PART *noun*. ***take a thing ill***: see TAKE *verb*. ***with an ill grace***: see GRACE *noun*.

Ill. *abbreviation*.
Illinois.

illachrymable /ɪˈlakrɪməb(ə)l/ *adjective*. *rare*. E17.
[ORIGIN Latin *illacrimabilis*, formed as IL-[2] + *lacrimare* weep: see -ABLE. Cf. LACHRYMAL.]
Incapable of weeping.

Illanun /ɪˈljɑːnən/ *noun* & *adjective*. Also **Ila-** /ɪˈlɑː-/. Pl. of noun same. L19.
[ORIGIN Illanun, lit. 'lake people'.]
A member of, of or pertaining to, a Moro people in the Philippines; (of) the language of this people.
■ Earlier **Illano** /ɪˈljɑːnəʊ/ *noun* (now *rare*), pl. **-os** L18.

illapse /ɪˈlaps/ *noun*. Now *rare*. E17.
[ORIGIN Latin *illapsus*, formed as ILLAPSE *verb*.]
The action of slipping or falling in or of gently permeating something.

illapse /ɪˈlaps/ *verb intrans.* Now *rare*. M17.
[ORIGIN Latin *illaps-* pa. ppl stem of *illabi* slip or fall in: see IL-[1], LAPSE *verb*.]
Slip or fall in, gently permeate.

illaqueate /ɪˈlakwɪeɪt/ *verb trans.* Now *rare*. M16.
[ORIGIN Latin *illaqueat-* pa. ppl stem of *illaqueare*, formed as IL-[1] + *laqueare* to snare, from *laqueus* noose, snare: see -ATE[3].]
Catch (as) in a noose; ensnare, entrap.
■ **illaqueable** *adjective* (*rare*) able to be ensnared L17.

illatinate /ɪˈlatɪnət/ *adjective*. *rare*. E20.
[ORIGIN from IL-[2] + LATIN *adjective* & *noun* + -ATE[2], after ILLITERATE *adjective*.]
Having no knowledge of Latin.

illation /ɪˈleɪʃ(ə)n/ *noun*. M16.
[ORIGIN Latin *illatio(n-)*, from *illat-*: see ILLATIVE, -ATION.]
The action of inferring or drawing a conclusion from premisses; an inference, a conclusion.

illative /ɪˈleɪtɪv/ *noun* & *adjective*. L16.
[ORIGIN Latin *illativus*, from *illat-* ppl stem of *inferre* INFER.]
▸ **A** *noun*. **1** A word or phrase introducing or stating an inference, as English *so*, *therefore*, etc. L16.
2 GRAMMAR. *The* illative case; a word, form, etc., in the illative case. M20.
▸ **B** *adjective*. **1** Of a word or phrase: introducing or stating an inference. E17.
2 Inferential. M17.
3 GRAMMAR. Designating, being in, or pertaining to a case in some inflected languages expressing motion into. L19.
■ **illatively** *adverb* M17.

illaudable /ɪˈlɔːdəb(ə)l/ *adjective*. L16.
[ORIGIN Latin *illaudabilis*, formed as IL-[2] + LAUDABLE.]
Not laudable, unworthy of praise.
■ **illaudably** *adverb* (*rare*) M18.

Illawarra /ɪləˈwɒrə/ *noun*. L19.
[ORIGIN See below.]
1 Used *attrib.* to designate trees native to Illawarra, a district in New South Wales, Australia. L19.
Illawarra pine, **Illawarra mountain pine** an Australian cypress pine, *Callitris rhomboidea*.
2 In full ***Illawarra shorthorn***, ***Illawarra dairy shorthorn***. (An animal of) a breed of usu. red or roan dairy cattle. E20.

illegal /ɪˈliːg(ə)l/ *adjective* & *noun*. E17.
[ORIGIN Old French & mod. French *illégal* or medieval Latin *illegalis*, from Latin IL-[2] + *legalis* LEGAL *adjective*.]
▸ **A** *adjective*. Not legal; contrary to or forbidden by law. E17.

> C. HILL All taxation without consent of Parliament was declared illegal. *Sunday (Kolkata)* The party has also asked the government to . . evict all illegal migrants.

illegal operation *spec.* an abortion performed illegally.
▸ **B** *noun*. **1** An illegal immigrant. M20.

> *Times* The 'illegals' . . will be deported back to the homelands. P. THEROUX Half the people who worked there were illegals.

2 *hist.* A Soviet secret agent working in a foreign country. M20.
■ **illegalize** *verb trans.* make illegal E19. **illegally** *adverb* E17.

illegality /ɪliːˈgalɪti, ɪlɪ-/ *noun*. M17.
[ORIGIN Old French & mod. French *illégalité* or medieval Latin *illegalitas*, formed as ILLEGAL: see -ITY.]
1 The quality or condition of being illegal. M17.
2 An illegal act. L19.

illegible /ɪˈlɛdʒɪb(ə)l/ *adjective*. M17.
[ORIGIN from IL-[2] + LEGIBLE.]
1 Not legible. M17.

> D. LEAVITT Her illegible messages zigzagging off the page in a pencil-breaking scrawl.

†**2** Incomprehensible to read. M18–E19.
■ **illegiˈbility** *noun* the quality of being illegible E19. **illegibly** *adverb* E19.

illegit /ɪlɪˈdʒɪt/ *noun*. *colloq.* E20.
[ORIGIN Abbreviation.]
= ILLEGITIMATE *noun* 1.

illegitimacy /ɪlɪˈdʒɪtɪməsi/ *noun*. M17.
[ORIGIN from ILLEGITIMATE *adjective* & *noun*: see -ACY.]
The quality or state of being illegitimate.

illegitimate /ɪlɪˈdʒɪtɪmət/ *adjective* & *noun*. M16.
[ORIGIN from late Latin *illegitimus* after LEGITIMATE *adjective*: see IL-[2], -ATE[2].]
▸ **A** *adjective*. **1** Born to parents who are not lawfully married, not entitled in law to full filial rights. M16.

> A. FRASER He was an illegitimate son, born before her marriage.

2 *gen.* Not legitimate; not in accordance with or authorized by law; not in accordance with a rule; irregular, abnormal. L16.

> A. J. AYER Physical symbols . . fail to satisfy this condition, and some positivists . . regard . . them as illegitimate.

3 Of drama: concerned with spectacle rather than literary quality. E19.
▸ **B** *noun*. **1** An illegitimate person; a person who does something illegitimate or irregular. L17.
2 A free settler in Australia. *obsolete* exc. *hist.* E19.
– NOTE: By the civil and canon laws, and since 1926 by the law of England, a child born out of wedlock is legitimated by the subsequent marriage of the parents.
■ **illegitimately** *adverb* M17. **illegitimatize** *verb trans.* = ILLEGITIMATE *verb* E19.

illegitimate /ɪlɪˈdʒɪtɪmeɪt/ *verb trans.* E17.
[ORIGIN from the adjective: see -ATE[3]. Cf. LEGITIMATE *verb*.]
Declare illegitimate.

illegitimation /ˌɪlɪdʒɪtɪˈmeɪʃ(ə)n/ *noun*. L15.
[ORIGIN medieval Latin *illegitimatio(n-)*, formed as ILLEGITIMATE *adjective*: see -ATION.]
1 The action of declaring someone or something to be illegitimate; a declaration of illegitimacy. L15.
†**2** Illegitimacy. L16–E18.

illfare /ˈɪlfɛː/ *noun*. Now chiefly *joc.* ME.
[ORIGIN from ILL *adjective* + FARE *noun*[1].]
The condition of faring badly, mishap, unsatisfactoriness.

ill-favoured /ɪlˈfeɪvəd/ *adjective*. Also ***-favored**. M16.
[ORIGIN from ILL *adjective* + FAVOUR *noun* + -ED[2].]
Having a displeasing appearance, unattractive; disagreeable, objectionable.
■ **ill-favouredly** *adverb* M16. **ill-favouredness** *noun* M16.

ill humour /ɪl ˈhjuːmə/ *noun phr.* Also ***-or**. M16.
[ORIGIN from ILL *adjective* + HUMOUR *noun*.]
†**1** A disordered or diseased bodily humour. M16–M17.
2 A bad mood; bad temper, irritability; sullenness, moroseness. L17.

> E. B. BROWNING In a childish fit of ill humour, I took refuge . . in a *hat* box.

■ **ill-humoured** *adjective* bad-tempered, sullen L17. **ill-humouredly** *adverb* L18.

illiberal /ɪˈlɪb(ə)r(ə)l/ *adjective*. M16.
[ORIGIN Old French & mod. French *illibéral* from Latin *illiberalis* mean, sordid, formed as IL-[2] + *liberalis* LIBERAL *adjective*.]
1 Not suitable to or characteristic of a free person; not relating to or acquainted with the liberal arts; ill-bred, unrefined; mean, vulgar, rude. M16.

> R. HAKLUYT Mechanicall & illiberall crafts.

2 Not generous; mean, stingy. E17.
3 Narrow-minded, bigoted; opposed to liberal principles. M17.

> G. S. FRASER His illiberal prejudice against the Germans no doubt helped.

■ **illiberalism** *noun* illiberality, absence of liberal principles M19. **illiberalize** *verb trans.* make illiberal E19. **illiberally** *adverb* E17.

illiberality /ɪˌlɪbəˈralɪti/ *noun*. L16.
[ORIGIN French *illibéralité*, formed as ILLIBERAL: see -ITY.]
The quality of being illiberal.

illicit /ɪˈlɪsɪt/ *adjective*. E16.
[ORIGIN Old French & mod. French *illicite* or Latin *illicitus*, formed as IL-^{2} + LICIT.]
Not allowed; improper, irregular; unlawful; *esp.* not sanctioned by law, rule, or custom.

D. L. SAYERS My unhappy son had formed an illicit connection with a young woman. E. WAUGH The . . trout . . were taken by . . illicit means without respect for season or ownership.

illicit process LOGIC a syllogistic fallacy in which a term not distributed in the premisses is distributed in the conclusion.
■ **illicitly** *adverb* E19. **illicitness** *noun* E19. †**illicitous** *adjective* illicit: only in 17.

illigant *adjective* var. of ILIGANT.

illimitable /ɪˈlɪmɪtəb(ə)l/ *adjective*. L16.
[ORIGIN from IL-^{2} + LIMITABLE.]
Unable to be limited or bounded; limitless, boundless.

D. H. LAWRENCE The great dark, illimitable kingdom of death, there humanity was put to scorn.

■ **illimitaˈbility** *noun* M19. **illimitableness** *noun* M19. **illimitably** *adverb* M18.

illimitation /ɪˌlɪmɪˈteɪʃ(ə)n/ *noun*. *rare*. E17.
[ORIGIN from IL-^{2} + LIMITATION.]
Freedom from or lack of limitation.

illimited /ɪˈlɪmɪtɪd/ *adjective*. E17.
[ORIGIN from IL-^{2} + LIMITED.]
Unlimited, unrestricted, unrestrained.
■ **illimitedly** *adverb* E17. **illimitedness** *noun* M17.

illinition /ɪlɪˈnɪʃ(ə)n/ *noun*. Now *rare* or *obsolete*. L17.
[ORIGIN Late Latin *illinitio(n-)* from *illinit-* pa. ppl stem of *illinire* var. of Latin *illinere*, formed as IL-^{1} + *linere* smear: see -ION.]
1 The smearing on or rubbing in of ointment etc. L17.
†**2 a** A process for calcining metals by rubbing with salt solutions. Only in L17. ▸**b** A thin crust or coating on a metal, cloth, etc. L18–E19.

illinium /ɪˈlɪnɪəm/ *noun*. E20.
[ORIGIN from *Illinois* University, USA, where the element was mistakenly reported to have been identified: see -IUM.]
HISTORY OF SCIENCE. The element of atomic no. 61, later named ***promethium***.

Illinoian /ɪlɪˈnɔɪ(j)ən/ *noun & adjective*. M19.
[ORIGIN from *Illinois* (see ILLINOIS) + -AN.]
▸ **A** *noun*. **1** = ILLINOISAN. M19.
2 GEOLOGY. A Pleistocene glaciation in N. America, preceding the Wisconsin and approximating to the Saale of northern Europe, or its deposits. L19.
▸ **B** *adjective*. GEOLOGY. Designating or pertaining to the Illinoian. L19.

Illinois /ɪlɪˈnɔɪ(z)/ *noun & adjective*. E18.
[ORIGIN French from Algonquian, in some uses repr. the name of the state.]
▸ **A** *noun*. Pl. same.
1 A member of a confederation of Algonquian peoples formerly inhabiting an area in and around the present Midwestern state of Illinois in the US. E18.
2 The language of the Illinois. E18.
▸ **B** *adjective*. Of or pertaining to the Illinois or the state of Illinois. E18.

Illinoisan /ɪlɪˈnɔɪ(j)ən, -ɔɪz(ə)n/ *noun*. M19.
[ORIGIN from *Illinois* (see ILLINOIS) + -AN.]
A native or inhabitant of the Midwestern state of Illinois, USA. Cf. ILLINOIAN *noun*.

illipe /ˈɪlɪpi/ *noun*. Also **illupi** /ˈɪlʊpi/ & other vars. M19.
[ORIGIN Tamil *iluppai*, *ir-*, Malayalam *iruppa*.]
An evergreen tree of southern India, *Madhuca longifolia* (family Sapotaceae), the seeds of which yield a fat used for candles and soap, and as a substitute for butter.

illiquid /ɪˈlɪkwɪd/ *adjective*. L17.
[ORIGIN from (the same root as) IL-^{2} + LIQUID *adjective*.]
1 LAW (now only *Scot.*). Of a right, debt, or claim: not clear or manifest; not ascertained and constituted by a written obligation or a decree of a court. L17.
2 Of an asset, investment, etc.: not easily or readily realizable. E20.
■ **illiˈquidity** *noun* the character of being illiquid E20.

illish /ˈɪlɪʃ/ *adjective*. *rare*. M17.
[ORIGIN from ILL *adjective* + -ISH^{1}.]
Somewhat unwell.

D. WELCH She had been half asleep and was still illish from 'flu.

illite /ˈɪlʌɪt/ *noun*. M20.
[ORIGIN from ILLINOIS a state of the US + -ITE^{1}.]
MINERALOGY. Any of a group of clay minerals resembling micas whose lattice does not expand on absorption of water.
■ **illitic** /ɪˈlɪtɪk/ *adjective* composed of or containing illite M20.

illiteracy /ɪˈlɪt(ə)rəsi/ *noun*. M17.
[ORIGIN from ILLITERATE *adjective* + -ACY.]
1 The quality or state of being illiterate; lack of education; *esp.* inability to read and write. Also *gen.*, ignorance, lack of understanding (of any activity etc.). M17.

R. DAVIES Money illiteracy is as restrictive as any other illiteracy. A. BURGESS She . . had left school at ten, and this explained her illiteracy.

2 A manifestation of illiteracy, an error due to illiteracy. E18.

J. K. TOOLE The illiteracies and misconceptions burbling from the dark minds of these students.

illiterate /ɪˈlɪt(ə)rət/ *adjective & noun*. LME.
[ORIGIN Latin *illitteratus*, formed as IL-^{2} + LITERATE *adjective*.]
▸ **A** *adjective*. **1** Of a person: uneducated, *esp.* unable to read and write; (of a thing) characterized by or showing ignorance of reading or writing; uneducated, unlearned, unpolished. LME. ▸**b** *gen.* Characterized by ignorance or lack of education or subtlety (in any activity etc.). M20.

CONAN DOYLE Certain letters . . . were in an illiterate handwriting. R. GITTINGS He married an illiterate girl—she could not write her own name. A. BURGESS My grandmother was illiterate and had to have the evening newspaper read out to her. **b** A. J. P. TAYLOR I am musically illiterate. I cannot follow sonata form, let alone a fugue.

2 Unwritten; inarticulate. *rare*. M17.
▸ **B** *noun*. An illiterate person; *esp.* a person unable to read and write. E17.

A. TATE Impressionistic education . . is . . making us a nation of illiterates: a nation of people without letters. G. BORDMAN Berlin, a musical illiterate, undoubtedly understood that composing an opera . . required more.

■ **illiterately** *adverb* L17. **illiterateness** *noun* M17. **illiterati** /ɪˈlɪtərɑːtiː/ *noun pl.* [Latin, pl. of *illitteratus*] illiterate, unlearned, or uneducated people L18. **illiterature** *noun* [after LITERATURE] (*a*) illiteracy, lack of education; (*b*) literature of poor quality: L16.

ill nature /ɪl ˈneɪtʃə/ *noun phr.* M17.
[ORIGIN from ILL *adjective* + NATURE *noun*.]
Malevolent or unkind character; spitefulness, churlishness.

ill-natured /ɪlˈneɪtʃəd/ *adjective*. E17.
[ORIGIN from (the same root as) ILL NATURE + -ED^{2}.]
Having an ill nature; spiteful, churlish.
■ **ill-naturedly** *adverb* L17.

illness /ɪlnɪs/ *noun*. E16.
[ORIGIN from ILL *adjective* + -NESS.]
†**1** Wickedness, depravity, immorality. E16–E18.
†**2** Unpleasantness, disagreeableness; hurtfulness; difficulty. L16–E18.
3 Ill health; the state of being ill; (a) disease, (a) sickness, (an) ailment. L17.

J. GATHORNE-HARDY Personal conflicts, stress and problems are a common cause of physical illness. N. MAILER I was like a man who is told he has a mortal illness. P. ROTH Not until she'd phoned . . had he . . been aware of his brother's illness.

illocal /ɪˈləʊk(ə)l/ *adjective*. Now *rare*. E17.
[ORIGIN Late Latin *illocalis*, formed as IL-^{2} + *localis* LOCAL *adjective*.]
Not local; having no location in space.
■ **illoˈcality** *noun* the quality or condition of being illocal L17.

illocution /ɪləˈkjuːʃ(ə)n/ *noun*. M20.
[ORIGIN from IL-^{1} + LOCUTION.]
PHILOSOPHY & LINGUISTICS. An action performed by saying or writing something, e.g. ordering, warning, promising. Cf. PERLOCUTION 2.
■ **illocutionary** *adjective* of, pertaining to, or of the nature of an illocution (cf. LOCUTIONARY, PERLOCUTIONARY) M20.

illogic /ɪˈlɒdʒɪk/ *noun*. M19.
[ORIGIN from IL-^{2} + LOGIC, after ILLOGICAL.]
Illogicality; lack of or opposition to logic.

Nature With the same illogic with which the Englishman will eat cow but not dog.

illogical /ɪˈlɒdʒɪk(ə)l/ *adjective*. L16.
[ORIGIN from IL-^{2} + LOGICAL *adjective*.]
Not logical; devoid of or contrary to logic; lacking the principles of sound reasoning.
■ **illogiˈcality** *noun* illogical quality or character; lack of logic; unreasonableness; an instance of this: M19. **illogically** *adverb* M17. **illogicalness** *noun* M17.

illoyal /ɪˈlɔɪəl/ *adjective*. *rare*. E17.
[ORIGIN from IL-^{2} + LOYAL *adjective*.]
Not loyal; disloyal.

ill-tempered /ɪlˈtɛmpəd/ *adjective*. E17.
[ORIGIN Partly from ILL *adverb* + TEMPERED; partly from ILL *adjective* + TEMPER *noun* + -ED^{2}.]
†**1** In an unhealthy or disordered condition. Only in 17.
2 Having a bad temper; irritable. E17.
■ **ill-temperedly** *adverb* L19.

illth /ɪlθ/ *noun*. *rare*. M19.
[ORIGIN from ILL *adjective* + -TH^{1}.]
Being ill; the opposite of health or wealth.

illucidate /ɪˈluːsɪdeɪt, ɪˈljuː-/ *verb trans.* *rare*. M16.
[ORIGIN Late Latin *illucidat-* pa. ppl stem of *illucidare* after Latin *elucidare* ELUCIDATE with substitution of IL-^{1}.]
Shed light on; explain, make clear, elucidate.

illude /ɪˈluːd, ɪˈljuːd/ *verb trans.* Now *literary*. LME.
[ORIGIN Latin *illudere*: see ILLUSION.]
†**1** Make fun of; deride. LME–E17.
2 Trick, impose upon, deceive with false hopes, delude. LME.

MORTIMER COLLINS They had allowed their imaginations to illude them.

illuk /ˈɪlʊk/ *noun*. M19.
[ORIGIN Sinhalese *iluk*.]
The lalang grass.

illume /ɪˈluːm, ɪˈljuːm/ *verb & noun*. Chiefly *poet.* LME.
[ORIGIN Contr. of ILLUMINE.]
▸ **A** *verb trans.* **1** Light up; make bright or shining; illumine; illuminate (*lit.* & *fig.*). LME.
†**2** Set alight, kindle. *rare*. E–M18.
▸ **B** *noun*. Illumination. M19.

illuminance /ɪˈluːmɪn(ə)ns, ɪˈljuː-/ *noun*. M20.
[ORIGIN from ILLUMINATE *verb* + -ANCE.]
PHYSICS. The amount of luminous flux per unit area; = ILLUMINATION 2C.

illuminant /ɪˈluːmɪnənt, ɪˈljuː-/ *noun & adjective*. Now *rare*. M17.
[ORIGIN Latin *illuminant-* pres. ppl stem of *illuminare*: see ILLUMINATE *verb*, -ANT^{1}.]
▸ **A** *noun*. A thing which illumines or illuminates; a source of illumination. M17.
▸ **B** *adjective*. Illuminating, enlightening. L17.

illuminate /ɪˈluːmɪnət, ɪˈljuː-/ *noun*. *arch.* E17.
[ORIGIN formed as ILLUMINATE *verb*: see -ATE^{1}.]
A spiritually or intellectually enlightened person; a person claiming special enlightenment or knowledge.

illuminate /ɪˈluːmɪneɪt, ɪˈljuː-/ *verb*. Pa. pple & ppl adjective (*arch.*, earlier) **-ate** /-ət/, **-ated**. LME.
[ORIGIN Earliest as pa. pple, from Latin *illuminatus*, from *illuminat-* pa. ppl stem of *illuminare*, formed as IL-^{1} + *lumin-*, *lumen* light: see -ATE^{2}, -ATE^{3}. Cf. ILLUMINE *verb*.]
▸ **I** *verb trans.* **1** Light up, give light to, make bright by light; decorate with lights, esp. in celebration. LME. ▸**b** Direct a beam of microwaves or other radiation at (an object, area, etc.). M20.

CONAN DOYLE Striking a match, he illuminated the melancholy place. J. C. POWYS Philip produced an electric flashlight . . to illuminate their way. E. BOWEN The Waterloo victory, for which Dublin illuminated herself. *fig.*: G. VIDAL For an instant a look of pure delight illuminated that lean, sombre face.

2 Shed spiritual light on; enlighten spiritually. Now only as *fig.* use of sense 1 above. L15.

DEFOE That He . . would further illuminate them with a beam of his heavenly grace.

3 Enlighten intellectually; give knowledge or understanding to. M16.

M. RULE They have confused rather than illuminated scholars.

4 Throw light on (a subject); explain, make clear; elucidate. L16.

L. DURRELL I . . do not feel that they explain Justine, but . . they do illuminate her actions.

5 Decorate (an initial letter etc. in a manuscript, a manuscript) with elaborate tracery or designs in gold, silver, and colours. L16.
6 Make splendid or illustrious; shed a lustre on. E17.

DISRAELI Hampden was to have illuminated with his genius this new order of government.

7 Set alight, kindle. *rare*. M17.
▸ **II** *verb intrans.* **8** Light up; be decorated with lights, esp. in celebration. E18.
■ **illuminated** *adjective* (*a*) that has been or is being illuminated; (*b*) *spec.* of or pertaining to illuminati: E17. **illuminatingly** *adverb* in an illuminating manner L19.

illuminati *noun pl.* see ILLUMINATO.

illumination /ɪˌluːmɪˈneɪʃ(ə)n, ɪˌljuː-/ *noun*. ME.
[ORIGIN Old French & mod. French from late Latin *illuminatio(n-)*, from *illuminat-*: see ILLUMINATE *verb*, -ATION.]
1 a An instance of spiritual enlightenment; an inspiration, a revelation. Freq. in *pl.* ME. ▸**b** Spiritual enlightenment, divine inspiration. LME.

Ashmolean Buddha . . reached what is known as the illumination, i.e. grasped the fundamental of his . . doctrine.

2 The action of illuminating with light; the fact or condition of being illuminated with light; a lighting up, a supplying of light; light. M16. ▸**b** The lighting up of a building, street, town, etc., esp. with coloured lights arranged in designs, as part of a celebration or as an attraction, an instance of this; in *pl.*, lights used in such a decoration. L17. ▸**c** PHYSICS. = ILLUMINANCE. M19.

P. SCOTT A naked electric bulb provided illumination. J. HIGGINS It was a place of shadows, the only illumination coming from the candles.

3 Intellectual enlightenment; information, learning. Formerly also in *pl.*, intellectual gifts. M17.

R. S. BALL The illumination which mathematics alone can afford.

4 The decoration of (an initial letter etc. in) a manuscript with elaborate tracery or designs in gold, silver, and colours; a design or illustration used in such decoration, an illuminated page. Formerly also, the colouring of maps or prints. L17.

K. CLARK Many of them were printed on vellum and had illuminations, like manuscripts.

illuminatism /ɪˈluːmɪnətɪz(ə)m, ɪˈljuː-/ *noun*. Now *rare*. L18.
[ORIGIN from ILLUMINATO or German *Illuminaten* + -ISM.]
= ILLUMINISM.
■ **illuminatist** *noun* = ILLUMINIST M19.

illuminative /ɪˈluːmɪnətɪv, ɪˈljuː-/ *adjective*. M17.
[ORIGIN French *illuminatif*, *-ive* or medieval Latin *illuminativus*, from Latin *illuminat-*: see ILLUMINATE *verb*, -ATIVE.]
1 Capable of illuminating, lighting up, or giving light. M17.

K. DIGBY The illuminative action of fire.

2 Capable of enlightening spiritually or intellectually. M17.

SOUTHEY The purgative, illuminative, and unitive stages of devotion.

illuminato /ɪˌluːmɪˈnɑːtəʊ, ɪˌljuː-/ *noun*. Also **I-**. Usu. in pl. **-ti** /-tiː/. L16.
[ORIGIN Italian = enlightened; pl. partly from Latin *illuminati* pl. of *illuminatus*: see ILLUMINATE *verb*. In German context translating German *Illuminaten*.]
A member of any of various sects or societies claiming special enlightenment, *spec*. (*a*) a sect of 16th-cent. Spanish heretics, (*b*) a secret society founded by Adam Weishaupt in Bavaria in 1776, holding deistic and republican principles and organized like the Freemasons. Also *gen*., a person claiming special knowledge on any subject.

illuminator /ɪˈluːmɪneɪtə, ɪˈljuː-/ *noun*. L15.
[ORIGIN ecclesiastical Latin, from Latin *illuminat-*: see ILLUMINATE *verb*, -OR.]
1 A shedder of spiritual light, a spiritual enlightener. Now only as *fig*. use of sense 2 below. L15. **2** A person or thing which lights up something; an illuminating agent. L16. **3** A person who illuminates manuscripts. L17.

J. BACKHOUSE The great nunneries must have supported their own scribes and illuminators.

4 An intellectual enlightener; a giver of knowledge or understanding. L18.

J. WAIN The greatness of Coghill as an illuminator of Shakespeare.

■ **illuminatory** *adjective* (*rare*) illuminative, explanatory M18.

illumine /ɪˈluːmɪn, ɪˈljuː-/ *verb*. Chiefly *literary*. ME.
[ORIGIN Old French & mod. French *illuminer* from Latin *illuminare* ILLUMINATE *verb*.]
▸ **I** *verb trans*. **1** = ILLUMINATE *verb* 2. ME.
2 = ILLUMINATE *verb* 1. LME. ▸**b** Brighten as with light, make radiant. E16.

J. STEINBECK Then he lighted another cigarette, and the match illumined his dark face. E. BOWEN Gas-lighting came to Dublin in 1825, in time to illumine the new premises. **b** SHAKES. *Ven. & Ad.* And as the bright sun glorifies the sky, So is her face illumined with her eye. R. DAVIES Sort of tribute from play-goers whose life he had illumined.

3 = ILLUMINATE *verb* 3. E16.

LYTTON This benighted mind, only illumined by a kind of miserable astuteness.

4 = ILLUMINATE *verb* 5. E16.
▸ **II** *verb intrans*. **5** = ILLUMINATE *verb* 8. E16.
■ **illuminable** *adjective* M18. **illuminer** *noun* LME.

illuminé /ilymine (*pl. same*); ɪˈluːmɪneɪ, ɪˈljuː-/ *noun*. Also **I-**. L18.
[ORIGIN French = enlightened.]
= ILLUMINATO.

illuminise *verb* var. of ILLUMINIZE.

illuminism /ɪˈluːmɪnɪz(ə)m, ɪˈljuː-/ *noun*. Also **I-**. L18.
[ORIGIN French *illuminisme*, formed as ILLUMINE *verb*: see -ISM.]
The doctrine or principles of any illuminati; (a doctrine involving) belief in or a claim to intellectual or spiritual enlightenment.
■ **illuminist** *noun* an adherent of illuminism, a person who claims spiritual or intellectual enlightenment E19. **illumiˈnistic** *adjective* pertaining to or of the nature of illuminism M19.

illuminize /ɪˈluːmɪnʌɪz, ɪˈljuː-/ *verb*. *rare*. Also **-ise**. E19.
[ORIGIN from ILLUMINE *verb* + -IZE.]
1 *verb intrans*. Be an illuminist. E19.
2 *verb trans*. Initiate into illuminism or a body of illuminati. E19.

illuminometer /ɪˌluːmɪˈnɒmɪtə, ɪˌljuː-/ *noun*. L19.
[ORIGIN from ILLUMINATION + -OMETER.]
A photometer, *esp*. one for measuring illuminance.

†**illuminous** *adjective*[1]. L15–M18.
[ORIGIN from IL-[2] + LUMINOUS.]
Bright, illuminatory.

illuminous /ɪˈluːmɪnəs, ɪˈljuː-/ *adjective*[2]. *rare*. M17.
[ORIGIN from IL-[2] + LUMINOUS.]
Not luminous, dark, opaque.

illupi *noun* var. of ILLIPE.

illusion /ɪˈluːʒ(ə)n, ɪˈljuː-/ *noun*. ME.
[ORIGIN Old French & mod. French from Latin *illusio(n-)*, from *illus-* pa. ppl stem of *illudere* mock, jest at, formed as IL-[1] + *ludere* play: see -ION.]
▸ **I** †**1** The action of deceiving, esp. by appearances; an act of deception. ME–L17.
2 A thing that deceives or deludes by giving a false impression. In early use sometimes *spec*. an apparition. LME.

New York Times The current notion that token integration will satisfy his people . . is an illusion. Y. MENUHIN Each of us had married an illusion, she as well as I.

3 The fact or condition of being deceived or deluded by appearances; a deception, a delusion; (an instance of) misapprehension of the true state of affairs. L16.

E. FROMM Most people are . . unaware that most of what they hold to be true . . is illusion. J. BRODSKY A communal apartment . . strips off any illusions about human nature.

be under the illusion believe wrongly (*that*).
4 (An instance of) the sense perception of an external object suggesting a false belief as to its nature. L18.

G. ORWELL When you said it to yourself you had the illusion of actually hearing bells.

argument from illusion PHILOSOPHY the argument that the objects of sense experience, usu. called ideas, appearances, or sense data, cannot be objects in a physical world independent of the perceiver since they vary with his or her condition and environment. ***optical illusion***: see OPTICAL *adjective*.
5 A thin and transparent kind of tulle. M19.
▸ †**II 6** (An instance of) derision or mockery. LME–M17.
■ **illusional** *adjective* pertaining to, characterized by, or subject to illusions E20. **illusionary** *adjective* characterized by illusions; resembling an illusion; illusory: L19.

illusionism /ɪˈluːʒ(ə)nɪz(ə)m, ɪˈljuː-/ *noun*. M19.
[ORIGIN from ILLUSION + -ISM.]
1 The theory that the material world is an illusion; disbelief in objective existence; theory dealing with illusions. M19.
2 The use of illusionary effects, esp. in art. M20.

illusionist /ɪˈluːʒ(ə)nɪst, ɪˈljuː-/ *noun*. M19.
[ORIGIN formed as ILLUSIONISM + -IST.]
1 An adherent of illusionism. M19.
2 A person who produces illusions; *spec*. a conjuror, a magician. M19.
■ **illusioˈnistic** *adjective* of or pertaining to illusionism or illusionists E20.

illusive /ɪˈluːsɪv, ɪˈljuː-/ *adjective*. Now *rare*. E17.
[ORIGIN medieval Latin *illusivus*, from *illus-*: see ILLUSION, -IVE.]
Tending to illude or deceive by false appearances; deceptive, illusory.
■ **illusively** *adverb* E19. **illusiveness** *noun* E18.

illusor /ɪˈluːsə, ɪˈljuː-/ *noun*. *rare*. LME.
[ORIGIN ecclesiastical Latin, from *illus-*: see ILLUSION, -OR.]
A deceiver, a deluder.

illusory /ɪˈluːs(ə)ri, ɪˈljuː-/ *adjective*. L16.
[ORIGIN ecclesiastical Latin *illusorius*, formed as ILLUSOR: see -ORY[2].]
Tending to deceive or delude by false appearances; having the character of an illusion; deceptive.

B. UNSWORTH He was haunted by small sounds and movements, most of them illusory. J. MCDOUGALL His illusory paradise was brutally destroyed by the arrival of his first little brother. A. ARONSON The Elizabethan preoccupation with faulty visual perception and with the illusory nature of eyesight.

■ **illusorily** *adverb* M17. **illusoriness** *noun* E18.

illustratable /ɪləˈstreɪtəb(ə)l, ˈɪləstreɪt-/ *adjective*. M19.
[ORIGIN from ILLUSTRATE *verb* + -ABLE.]
Able to be illustrated; suitable for illustration.

†**illustrate** *adjective*. M16–E18.
[ORIGIN Latin *illustratus* pa. pple, formed as ILLUSTRATE *verb*: see -ATE[2].]
Illuminated, resplendent, clear.

illustrate /ˈɪləstreɪt/ *verb trans*. Pa. pple †**-ate** (earlier), **-ated**. E16.
[ORIGIN Latin *illustrat-* pa. ppl stem of *illustrare*, formed as IL-[1] + *lustrare* illuminate: see -ATE[3].]
▸ **I** †**1** Shed light on, light up, illumine. E16–L19.

C. COTTON The Windows . . Illustrating the noble Room. *fig*.: R. BOYLE The Mind of Man . . Illustrated by the Beams of Heavenly Light, and Joy.

2 Shed lustre on; make illustrious or famous; confer distinction on. Now *rare*. M16.

GIBBON Mr. Wedderburne . . who now illustrates the title of Lord Loughborough.

†**3** Make lustrous or bright; adorn. L16–M18.
4 Set in a good light; display to advantage. Now *rare* or *obsolete*. E17.

H. CROSSE The deformitie of the one doth much illustrate and beautifie the other.

▸ **II 5** Make clear, elucidate, explain; *esp*. clarify or support using examples, give an example or illustration of, exemplify. M16.

T. BEDDOES Many experiments . . tending to illustrate this important subject. R. KIPLING Kim illustrated the motion and stood like a stork. C. CONNOLLY He chose his quotations to illustrate how . . the present can always be illuminated by the past.

6 Support or clarify (a description, account, etc.) using drawings, photographs, or other pictures; *esp*. provide (a book, magazine article, etc.) with pictorial illustrations. M17.

R. MACAULAY Painting water-colour sketches to illustrate travel books. *Soldier* The route is not without its hazards as the picture . . illustrates.

illustrated /ˈɪləstreɪtɪd/ *adjective & noun*. M19.
[ORIGIN from ILLUSTRATE *verb* + -ED[2].]
▸ **A** *adjective*. Having illustrations. M19.

J. BRODSKY This was a copiously illustrated encyclopedia.

▸ **B** *noun*. An illustrated newspaper or magazine. L19.

illustration /ɪləˈstreɪʃ(ə)n/ *noun*. LME.
[ORIGIN Old French & mod. French from Latin *illustratio(n-)*, formed as ILLUSTRATE *verb*: see -ATION.]
▸ **I** †**1** Lighting up, illumination; spiritual or intellectual enlightenment. LME–M18.

DONNE Such an illustration, such an irradiation, . . that by that light . . he could have read in the night. E. VAUX A divine illustration cleared his understanding.

2 The action of making someone or something illustrious or famous; the fact of being made illustrious or famous; distinction; an instance of this. Now *rare*. E17.

THACKERAY My maxim is, that genius is an illustration, and merit is better than any pedigree.

▸ **II 3** The action or fact of making something clear or evident; setting out clearly or with supporting examples; elucidation; explanation; exemplification. M16. ▸**b** A thing which makes something clear or evident; an explanation, a clarification; an example, an instance. L16.

b P. BROOK *Sergeant Musgrave's Dance* can be taken . . as an illustration of how true theatre comes into being.

4 The illustrating of a subject pictorially; the provision of a book, magazine article, etc., with drawings, photographs, or other pictures. E19. ▸**b** A picture illustrating a description, account, reference, etc.; a drawing, photograph, or other picture in a book, magazine article, etc. E19.

b R. JARRELL Have you ever thought of doing illustrations for *The Jungle Book*?

■ **illustrational** *adjective* of or pertaining to illustration; illustrative: L19.

illustrative /ˈɪləstrətɪv, ɪˈlʌst-/ *adjective*. M17.
[ORIGIN from ILLUSTRATE *verb* + -IVE.]
Serving or tending to illustrate or make clear; providing an illustration or example (*of*); explanatory.

J. TYNDALL Taking, as an illustrative case, the passage from air into water. *Southern Rag* Essential information . . of which the films would be illustrative.

■ **illustratively** *adverb* M17.

illustrator /ˈɪləstreɪtə/ *noun*. L16.
[ORIGIN ecclesiastical Latin, formed as ILLUSTRATE *verb*: see -OR. Later directly from ILLUSTRATE *verb*.]
A person who or thing which illustrates something; *esp*. a person who illustrates a book etc.

illustratory /ˈɪləstreɪt(ə)ri, ɪˈlʌstrə-/ *adjective*. Now *rare*. M18.
[ORIGIN from ILLUSTRATE *verb* + -ORY[2].]
Illustrative.

†**illustricity** *noun*. M17.
[ORIGIN Irreg. from Latin *illustris* + -ITY: see ILLUSTRIOUS, -ICITY.]
1 An illustrious person. Only in M17.
2 Illustriousness. M–L18.

illustrious /ɪˈlʌstrɪəs/ *adjective*. M16.
[ORIGIN from Latin *illustris* clear, bright, evident, distinguished, famous + -OUS.]
1 Having the lustre of high rank, fame, or eminence; distinguished, renowned. M16.

C. LAMB She traced her descent . . to the illustrious, but unfortunate, house of Derwentwater. CONAN DOYLE When . . a client is sufficiently illustrious, even the rigid British law becomes human and elastic.

†**2** Lit up; lustrous, bright, shining. E17–L19. ▸**b** Not lustrous, dull. *rare* (Shakes.). Only in E17.
†**3** Clearly evident, obvious. M17–L18.
■ **illustriously** *adverb* M17. **illustriousness** *noun* M17.

illustrissimo /ɪlʌˈstrɪsɪməʊ/ *noun & adjective*. Now *rare*. Pl. of noun **-mos**, **-mi** /-miː/. E17.
[ORIGIN Italian from Latin *illustrissimus* superl. of *illustris* ILLUSTRIOUS.]
(A person who is) most illustrious, esp. as belonging to the Italian aristocracy.

illuvial /ɪˈluːvɪəl, ɪˈljuː-/ *adjective*. E20.
[ORIGIN from IL-[1] + *-luvial*, after ALLUVIAL, ELUVIAL.]
SOIL SCIENCE. Pertaining to or resulting from illuviation; illuviated.

illuviation /ɪˌluːvɪˈeɪʃ(ə)n, ɪˌljuː-/ *noun*. E20.
[ORIGIN formed as ILLUVIAL + -ATION.]
SOIL SCIENCE. The introduction of salts or colloids into one soil horizon from another by percolating water.
■ **iˈlluviated** *ppl adjective* having received material by illuviation E20.

illy /ˈɪlli/ *adverb*. Now chiefly *US*. LME.
[ORIGIN from ILL *adjective* + -LY².]
Badly, ill.

Illyrian /ɪˈlɪrɪən/ *adjective & noun*. M16.
[ORIGIN from Latin *Illyrius* (= Greek *Illurios*), from *Illyria* (see below) + -AN.]
▸ **A** *adjective*. **1** Of or pertaining to a region of varying extent primarily on the east coast of the Adriatic known as Illyria, in ancient times a country extending northwards to the Danube, conquered by the Romans in the 3rd and 2nd cents. BC, for much of the 19th cent. and until 1918 a division of the Austro-Hungarian empire, and now part of Slovenia and Croatia. M16.
2 Designating or pertaining to the group of ancient dialects represented by modern Albanian. Formerly also, designating or pertaining to a division of the S. Slavonic languages. E17.
▸ **B** *noun*. **1** A native or inhabitant of Illyria; *esp.* a member of an Indo-European people inhabiting ancient Illyria. L16.
2 The language of Illyria; the group of ancient dialects represented by modern Albanian. Formerly also, a division of the S. Slavonic languages. L19.

Illyrism /ˈɪlɪrɪz(ə)m/ *noun*. M19.
[ORIGIN formed as ILLYRIAN + -ISM.]
Advocacy of Slovene, Croatian, and Serb nationalism.
■ **Illyrist** *adjective & noun* (*a*) *adjective* of or pertaining to Illyrism, supporting Illyrism; (*b*) *noun* a supporter of Illyrism: E20.

illywhacker /ˈɪlɪwakə/ *noun*. *Austral. slang*. Also **-wacker** /-w-/. M20.
[ORIGIN Unknown.]
A confidence trickster.

ilmenite /ˈɪlmənʌɪt/ *noun*. E19.
[ORIGIN from the *Ilmen* Mountains (in the southern Urals) + -ITE¹.]
MINERALOGY. A common trigonal oxide of ferrous iron and titanium, occurring in massive form or as opaque black crystals, often as an accessory mineral in basic igneous rocks, and a source of titanium.

ilmenorutile /ˌɪlmənəʊˈruːtʌɪl/ *noun*. M19.
[ORIGIN from ILMENITE + -O- + RUTILE.]
MINERALOGY. A black variety of rutile containing iron, niobium, and tantalum.

ILO *abbreviation*.
International Labour Organization.

Ilocano /ɪləˈkɑːnəʊ/ *noun & adjective*. L19.
[ORIGIN Filipino Spanish, from *Ilocos*, name of two provinces in the Philippines.]
▸ **A** *noun*. Pl. **-os**. A member of a people inhabiting NW Luzon in the Philippines; the Austronesian language of this people. L19.
▸ **B** *adjective*. Of or pertaining to the Ilocanos or their language. E20.
■ Also **Iloco** *noun & adjective* M19.

ilot *noun* var. of ISLOT.

ILR *abbreviation*.
Independent local radio.

ILS *abbreviation*.
Instrument landing system.

ilsemannite /ˈɪlsəmənʌɪt/ *noun*. L19.
[ORIGIN from J. C. *Ilsemann* (1727–1822), German chemist, + -ITE¹.]
MINERALOGY. A blue molybdenum-containing mineral, probably a hydrated oxide, which forms as a soluble crust or earthy deposit.

ilvaite /ˈɪlvʌɪt/ *noun*. E19.
[ORIGIN from Latin *Ilva* Elba + -ITE¹.]
MINERALOGY. A basic silicate of calcium and iron, crystallizing in either the monoclinic or the orthorhombic system.

IM *abbreviation*.
Intramuscular.

im- /ɪm/ *prefix*¹.
Var. of Latin IN-² before *b, m, p*. Cf. IL-¹, IR-¹.

im- /ɪm/ *prefix*².
Var. of Latin IN-³ before *b, m, p*. Cf. I-², IL-², IR-².

image /ˈɪmɪdʒ/ *noun*. ME.
[ORIGIN Old French & mod. French from Latin *imago*, *imagin-* rel. to *imitari* IMITATE.]
1 A representation of the external form of a person or thing in sculpture, painting, etc.; *esp.* a statue or figurine of a saint etc. as an object of veneration. ME. ▸†**b** A constellation considered as the figure or delineation of a person etc. LME–L17. ▸**c** A person who in manner, look, etc., resembles an artificial representation of the human form; *colloq.* someone as an object of amusement or contempt. M16.

AV *Matt.* 22:20 And he sayth unto them, Whose is this image and superscription? S. SPENDER The floor of the vault was covered with images removed from buildings. **c** S. RICHARDSON Can the pretty image speak, Mrs Jervis? I vow she has speaking eyes! J. CONRAD How goes it, you old image?

graven image, ***waxen image***.
2 An optical appearance or counterpart produced by light or other radiation from an object reflected in a mirror, refracted in a lens, etc. ME.

K. CLARK The *camera obscura* which projects an image onto a white sheet.

after-image: see AFTER-. ***double image***: see DOUBLE *adjective & adverb*. ***latent image***: see LATENT *adjective & noun*. ***mirror image***: see MIRROR *noun*. ***multiple image***: see MULTIPLE *adjective*.
3 Aspect, appearance, form; semblance, likeness. (Now chiefly in ref. to *Genesis* 1:26, 27.) ME. ▸**b** A visible appearance; a figure; an apparition. Long *arch. rare*. M16.

E. H. SEARS We grow into the image of what we love. M. L. KING We fail to think of them as fellow human beings . . moulded in the same divine image. **b** TENNYSON An image seem'd to pass the door, To look at her.

4 A person or thing in which the appearance etc. of another is reproduced; a counterpart, a copy. ME. ▸**b** A symbol, an emblem. M16. ▸**c** An embodiment (esp. *of* a particular quality); a type; a typical example. M16.

T. GRANGER Sleepe is the image of death. OED He is the very image of his father. **b** W. TENNANT This noisome dungeon . . affords . . an image of the gate of Tartarus, rather than the porch of Paradise. **c** M. E. BRADDON Mr. Sampson dropped his cigar, and sat transfixed, an image of half amused astonishment.

living image of a person with a striking resemblance to (another). ***spit and image***, ***spit image***: see SPIT *noun*². ***spitting image***: see SPIT *verb*².
5 A mental representation of something; an idea, a conception. LME. ▸**b** The character of a person, organization, product, etc., as perceived by the public; *esp.* a cultivated favourable reputation. E20.

A. RADCLIFFE She endeavoured to dismiss his image from her mind. W. JAMES We . . saw no need of optical and auditory images to interpret optical and auditory sensations by. L. HUDSON Snakes are a remarkably common image in . . dreams. **b** K. AMIS It was time to improve the paper's image, give it a touch of quality.

b ***brand image***, ***corporate image***, etc.
6 A spoken or written description, *esp.* a vivid or graphic one. E16.

M. W. MONTAGU Theocritus . . has only given a plain image of the way of life amongst the peasants.

7 A simile, a metaphor, a figure of speech. M16.

R. C. TRENCH To speak of death as a sleep, is an image common to all languages.

8 MATH. The element or set into which a given element or set is mapped by a particular function or transformation. (Foll. by *of* the given thing; *by* or *under* the function etc.) L19.
9 RADIO. An undesired signal whose frequency is as much above that of the local oscillator of a superheterodyne receiver as the signal sought is below it, and which therefore may cause interference. M20.
– COMB.: **image-breaker** a breaker of images, an iconoclast; **image converter** an electronic device for converting an invisible image (formed by infrared radiation, X-rays, etc.) into a visible image; an image tube; **image dissector** a form of television camera in which the current emitted by the photoemissive surface is directly amplified to form the video signal; **image intensifier** an image tube or similar device used to produce a brighter version of an image incident on a photoelectric screen; **image-maker** (*a*) a carver, sculptor, etc., of images; (*b*) a person concerned with creating a public image of a politician, product, etc.; ***image*** ORTHICON; **image processing** the analysis and manipulation of a digitized image, esp. in order to improve its quality; **image tube** an electron tube in which an image, formed by light or other radiation on a photoemissive surface, produces a flow of electrons which can be used to reproduce the image in a different form; **image-worship** the worship of images; idolatry.
■ **imageless** *adjective* E19.

image /ˈɪmɪdʒ/ *verb trans*. LME.
[ORIGIN Partly from Old French & mod. French *imager*, partly from the noun.]
1 a Form a mental image of (something to be executed); devise, plan. Now *rare* or *obsolete* exc. as in sense b. LME. ▸**b** Imagine, picture (*to oneself*). E18.

b J. MOORE We image to ourselves the Tarpeian Rock as a tremendous precipice.

2 Describe, esp. vividly or graphically. E17.

ADDISON Satan's Approach to the Confines of the Creation, is finely imaged in the beginning of the Speech.

3 Copy, imitate; resemble. *rare*. E17.

G. CHAPMAN They his clear virtues emulate, In truth and justice imaging his state. POPE None imag'd e'er like thee my master lost.

4 Reflect, mirror. L18.

S. ROGERS Hail, noblest structures imaged in the wave.

5 Make a representation of the external form of (someone or something) in sculpture, painting, etc.; represent by an image (*lit. & fig.*); obtain a representation of by television, radar, or other technique. E19.

J. A. FROUDE Traces of the fair beauty of the monastic spirit we may yet see imaged in the sculptured figures. A. C. CLARKE The familiar rocky terrain was imaged on TV and sonar screen.

magnetic resonance imaging: see MAGNETIC *adjective*. ***thermal imaging***: see THERMAL *adjective*.
6 Symbolize, typify. E19.

SHELLEY O stream! . . Thou imagest my life.

■ **imageable** *adjective* L17.

imaged /ˈɪmɪdʒd/ *adjective*. L16.
[ORIGIN from IMAGE *noun, verb*: see -ED², -ED¹.]
1 Represented by an image (*lit. & fig.*). L16.
2 Decorated with an image or images. *rare*. L18.

imager /ˈɪmɪdʒə/ *noun*. LME.
[ORIGIN Old French *image(u)r* (mod. *imagier*), formed as IMAGE *noun*: see -ER².]
1 a *hist.* A maker of images; a sculptor, a carver. LME. ▸**b** A device which reproduces an image of something. L20.
2 A person who describes something vividly or graphically. L19.
3 A person who forms a mental image or images. M20.

imagery /ˈɪmɪdʒ(ə)ri/ *noun*. ME.
[ORIGIN Old French *imagerie*, from *image(u)r*: see IMAGER, -ERY.]
1 Images collectively; statuary, carving. Formerly also, an image. ME. ▸†**b** Figured work on a textile fabric; embroidery. LME–L18.

W. HALLIFAX A Statue, which the Turks, zealous enemies of all Imagery, have thrown down. *transf.*: WORDSWORTH The visible scene . . With all its solemn imagery, its rocks, Its woods.

†**2** The use of images as objects of veneration; idolatry. LME–E17.
†**3** The art of painting; the art of carving or statuary. M16–E17.
†**4** Workmanship, make; fashion. L16–M17.

JER. TAYLOR Dress your people unto the imagery of Christ.

†**5** The embodiment of a quality etc. L16–M17.
6 The use of rhetorical images; such images collectively. Also, ornate figurative illustration, esp. as used for a particular effect. L16.

J. H. NEWMAN The glowing imagery of prophets. M. FORSTER We were told, in that quaint hospital imagery, that Em had 'turned the corner'.

7 Orig., the formation of mental images; imagination, groundless belief. Later, mental images collectively. E17.

J. SPEED Nor is she to be condemned vpon the imagerie of his suspicious head. SHELLEY Like a dream's dim imagery.

imagic /ˈɪmɪdʒɪk/ *adjective*. M20.
[ORIGIN from IMAGE *noun* + -IC.]
Like an image.

imaginable /ɪˈmadʒɪnəb(ə)l/ *adjective*. LME.
[ORIGIN Late Latin *imaginabilis*, from *imaginare*: see IMAGINE, -ABLE.]
That can be imagined; conceivable.

F. HOWERD I managed to stammer that it was the most exciting prospect imaginable.

■ **imaginaˈbility** *noun* (*rare*) M19. **imaginableness** *noun* E18. **imaginably** *adverb* M17.

imaginal /ɪˈmadʒɪn(ə)l/ *adjective*¹. M17.
[ORIGIN App. from IMAGINE + -AL¹.]
Of or pertaining to the imagination; *rare* imaginary. Also, of or pertaining to a mental image or images.
■ **imaginally** *adverb* (*rare*) E20.

imaginal /ɪˈmadʒɪn(ə)l/ *adjective*². L19.
[ORIGIN from Latin *imagin-* (see IMAGE *noun*) + -AL¹.]
ENTOMOLOGY. Of or pertaining to an insect imago; of the nature of an imago.
imaginal disc any of a number of thickenings of the epidermis in the larvae of holometabolous insects, which on pupation develop into organs of the imago.

imaginary /ɪˈmadʒɪn(ə)ri/ *adjective & noun*. LME.
[ORIGIN Latin *imaginarius*, from *imagin-*, *imago*: see IMAGE *noun*, -ARY¹.]
▸ **A** *adjective*. **1** Existing only in the imagination; not real or actual. LME. ▸**b** Of a line etc.: thought of as being drawn through or between specified points. E17. ▸**c** MATH. That is, or that relates to or involves, the square root of a negative quantity. E18.

J. M. MURRY I do not believe it is imaginary; I have based my narrative squarely on the facts.

†**2** Relating to the imagination; imaginative. LME–L17.

SHAKES. *Sonn.* My soul's imaginary sight Presents thy shadow to my sightless view.

†**3** Of the nature of an image or representation. L16–M17.

SHAKES. *Lucr.* Much imaginary work was there . . A hand, a foot, a face, . . Stood for the whole to be imagined.

†**4** Supposed; putative. *rare*. Only in M17.

DONNE His Imaginary father Joseph.

†**5** Imaginable. M–L17.

A. LOVELL All imaginary enquiry was made after them, but . . there was no news to be had.

▸ **B** *noun*. †**1** The standard-bearer in a Roman legion who carried the image of the emperor. Only in LME.

†**2** An imagination; a fancy. E–M18.

3 *MATH*. An imaginary quantity or expression. M19.

■ **imaginarily** *adverb* L16. **imaginariness** *noun* (*rare*) E18.

imagination /ɪˌmadʒɪˈneɪʃ(ə)n/ *noun*. ME.

[ORIGIN Old French & mod. French from Latin *imaginatio(n-)*, from *imaginat-* pa. ppl stem of *imaginari* IMAGINE: see -ATION.]

1 The action of imagining or forming mental images or concepts of external objects not present to the senses; the result of this process. ME.

J. FORTESCUE We nede in this case to vse coniecture and ymaginacion. C. S. LEWIS I never mistook imagination for reality.

2 The mental faculty which forms images or concepts of external objects not present to the senses, and of their relations (to each other or to the subject). ME.

SHAKES. *All's Well* I have forgot him; my imagination Carries no favour in't but Bertram's. K. GERSHON Like every living Jew I have in imagination seen the gas-chamber the mass-grave.

†**3** **a** Scheming or devising; a device, a plan, a plot; a fanciful project. LME–M18. ▸**b** Expectation, anticipation. E–M17.

a AV *Lam.* 3:60 Thou hast seene all their vengeance; and all their imaginations against me. **b** MARVELL To tell you truly mine owne imagination, I thought he would not open it while I was there.

4 **a** The faculty of fanciful thought; fancy. LME. ▸**b** The creative faculty of the mind; the ability to frame new and striking concepts. E16.

a C. JACKSON It's that over-active imagination of yours . . that sees things that aren't there. **b** SHAKES. *Mids. N. D.* And as imagination bodies forth The forms of things unknown.

5 The mind; thinking; thought, opinion. Long *rare* or *obsolete*. LME.

J. DAVIES Upon the first sight thereof, it run into our imagination, that they were the Cosaques.

imaginative /ɪˈmadʒɪnətɪv/ *adjective*. LME.

[ORIGIN Old French & mod. French *imaginatif*, *-ative* from medieval Latin *imaginativus*, from Latin *imaginat-*: see IMAGINATION, -ATIVE.]

1 Given to using, or having, the faculty of imagination. LME.

DAY LEWIS Had I been an imaginative child, I should have looked for the Sleeping Beauty there. L. BLUE All the best cooks tell you to be imaginative with offal.

2 Of or pertaining to the faculty of imagination or its use. LME.

M. TIPPETT Schönberg's imaginative life was unusually rich and powerful.

3 Existing only in the imagination; unreal, imaginary. Long *rare* or *obsolete*. L15.

T. CARTWRIGHT His righteousnesse imputed unto us, is not an imaginative, but a true righteousnesse.

4 Characterized by, resulting from, or showing in a high degree, the faculty of imagination. E19.

J. F. LEHMANN It seemed to me to have a quite extraordinary imaginative power.

■ **imaginatively** *adverb* LME. **imaginativeness** *noun* M17.

imagine /ɪˈmadʒɪn/ *verb*. ME.

[ORIGIN Old French & mod. French *imaginer* from Latin *imaginare* form an image of, represent, *imaginari* picture to oneself, fancy, from *imagin-*, *imago*: see IMAGE *noun*.]

▸ **I** *verb trans.* **1** Form a mental image or concept of, picture to oneself (something non-existent or not present to the senses). ME.

W. WHARTON These are really show birds. We can't imagine where they come from. J. LE CARRÉ In his mind's eye, Smiley now imagined the scene that was playing inside the bank.

2 Create as a mental conception, conceive; assume. LME.

R. GRAFTON Imagine you see before your eyes your wyves, and daughters in daunger.

3 Devise, plot, plan. *arch.* LME.

T. KEIGHTLEY Fisher . . also was arraigned for imagining to deprive the King of his title and dignity.

†**4** Consider, ponder. LME–L16.

LD BERNERS Euer he imagined, how to do plesure to the peple.

5 Conjecture, guess, suspect, suppose; *colloq.* suppose, be of the opinion (*that*). LME.

W. ROBERTS You might imagine him in the full prime and mettle of his years. E. BOWEN I imagine she meant it kindly.

6 Form an idea with regard to (something not known with certainty); form the idea (*that*). M16.

M. EDGEWORTH He did not imagine that he could reform every abuse.

▸ **II** *verb intrans.* †**7** Consider, meditate; plan. LME–L16.

T. COGAN Divines that imagine and study upon high and subtile matters.

8 Form mental images or ideas (†*of*); exercise the faculty of imagination. L16.

SYD. SMITH If it can be shown that women may be trained to reason and imagine as well as men.

■ **imaginator** *noun* (*rare*) = IMAGINER LME. **imaginer** *noun* a person who imagines L15. **imagining** *noun* the action of the verb; (freq. in *pl.*) something imagined, a fantasy: ME. **imaginist** *noun* (*rare*) an imaginative person E19.

imagineer /ɪˌmadʒɪˈnɪə(r)/ *noun & verb*. M20.

[ORIGIN from IMAGINE + -EER after *engineer*.]

▸ **A** *noun*. A person who devises and implements a wholly new or apparently fantastic technology, concept, etc.; *spec.* a person responsible for creating roller coaster rides or other attractions in theme parks. M20.

▸ **B** *verb trans.* Devise and implement (such a technology, concept, etc.). L20.

■ **imagineering** *noun* M20.

imagines *noun pl.* see IMAGO.

imagist /ˈɪmɪdʒɪst/ *noun & adjective*. Also **I-**. E20.

[ORIGIN from IMAGE *noun* + -IST.]

▸ **A** *noun*. **1** A member of a group of early 20th-cent. poets who, in revolt against romanticism, sought clarity of expression through the use of precise images. E20.

2 *PHILOSOPHY*. A conceptualist who believes that universals exist as mental images as opp. to mental concepts. M20.

▸ **B** *attrib.* or as *adjective*. Of or pertaining to imagists or imagism. E20.

■ **imagism** *noun* the doctrine or practice of imagists E20. **imaˈgistic** *adjective* of or pertaining to imagism E20. **imaˈgistically** *adverb* M20.

imago /ɪˈmeɪɡəʊ/ *noun*. Pl. **imagines** /ɪˈmeɪdʒɪniːz/, **imagos**. L18.

[ORIGIN Latin: see IMAGE *noun*.]

1 *ENTOMOLOGY*. The final, fully developed form of an insect after passing through all stages of metamorphosis. L18.

2 *PSYCHOANALYSIS*. An unconscious image of an archetype or of someone (esp. a parent) which influences a person's behaviour etc. E20.

imam /ɪˈmɑːm/ *noun*. E17.

[ORIGIN Arabic *'imām* leader, from *'amma* lead the way.]

1 The leader of prayers in a mosque. E17.

2 (**I-**.) (A title of) any of various Muslim leaders, esp. one succeeding Muhammad as the leader of Shiite Islam. M17.

■ **imamate** *noun* the office or dignity of an imam E18.

imambara /ɪmɑːmˈbɑːrə/ *noun*. M19.

[ORIGIN Urdu, formed as IMAM + Hindi *bārā* enclosure.]

In the Indian subcontinent: (the gardens, courtyards, etc., surrounding) a building in which Shiite Muslims assemble at the time of Muharram; *transf.* a large tomb.

Imam Bayildi /ɪˌmɑːm ˈbɑːjɪldi/ *noun phr.* M20.

[ORIGIN Turkish *imam bayıldı*, lit. 'the imam fainted' (from pleasure at, or because of the cost of, the dish).]

A dish, originating in Turkey, consisting of aubergines stuffed with a garlic-flavoured onion-and-tomato mixture and cooked in oil.

IMAP *abbreviation*.

COMPUTING. Internet Mail Access Protocol.

I.Mar.E. *abbreviation*.

Institute of Marine Engineers.

imaret /ɪˈmɑːrɛt, ˈɪmərɛt/ *noun*. E17.

[ORIGIN Turkish *imaret* from Arabic *'imāra* building, edifice.]

In Turkey: a hospice for pilgrims and travellers; now usu., a soup kitchen.

Imari /ɪˈmɑːri/ *noun*. L19.

[ORIGIN A town in NW Kyushu, Japan.]

Used *attrib.* to designate (articles of) a type of Hizen porcelain.

IMAX /ˈʌɪmaks/ *noun*. M20.

[ORIGIN from I(MAGE *noun* + MAX(IMUM *noun*.]

(Proprietary name for) a technique of widescreen cinematography which produces an image approximately ten times larger than that from standard 35 mm film.

imbalance /ɪmˈbaləns/ *noun*. L19.

[ORIGIN from IM-[2] + BALANCE *noun*.]

An unbalanced condition; a lack of proportion or relation between corresponding things.

†**imbalm** *verb* var. of EMBALM.

imbalsamation /ɪmˌbɔːlsəˈmeɪʃ(ə)n/ *noun*. *rare*. E19.

[ORIGIN from IM-[1] + BALSAM *noun* + -ATION.]

Embalming. Chiefly *fig.*

†**imbank** *verb*, †**imbar** *verb* vars. of EMBANK, EMBAR.

†**imbarcation** *noun* var. of EMBARKATION.

†**imbarge** *noun & verb*, †**imbargo** *noun & verb* vars. of EMBARGE, EMBARGO.

imbark /ɪmˈbɑːk/ *verb*[1] *trans.* Also †**em-**. M17.

[ORIGIN from IM-[1], EM-[1] + BARK *noun*[2].]

Enclose in or cover with bark.

†**imbark** *verb*[2], †**imbarkation** *noun* vars. of EMBARK *verb*[1], EMBARKATION.

†**imbarn** *verb trans.* Also **em-**. E17–L18.

[ORIGIN from IM-[1], EM-[1] + BARN *noun*[1].]

Gather into a barn or barns.

†**imbarque** *verb* var. of EMBARK *verb*[1].

†**imbase** *verb* var. of EMBASE.

†**imbathe** *verb*, †**imbattle** *verb* vars. of EMBATHE, EMBATTLE *verb*[1].

imbauba /ɪmˈbɔːbə, ɪmbəˈuːbə/ *noun*. M19.

[ORIGIN Portuguese *imbaúba*, *imbaíba* from Tupi *ãbai'ïb* hollow tree.]

(The timber of) any of several tropical American trees of the genus *Cecropia*, of the mulberry family, *esp.* the trumpet tree, *C. peltata*.

imbecile /ˈɪmbɪsiːl/ *adjective & noun*. M16.

[ORIGIN French †*imbécille* (now *-ile*) from Latin *imbecillus*, *-is* lit. 'without support', from *in-* IM-[2] + var. of *baculum* stick, staff.]

▸ **A** *adjective*. **1** Weak, feeble; *esp.* physically weak, impotent. Now *rare* or *obsolete*. M16.

2 Mentally weak; stupid, idiotic. E19.

▸ **B** *noun*. A person of extremely low intelligence; a stupid person, a fool. E19.

■ **imbecilely** *adverb* M19.

imbecilic /ɪmbɪˈsɪlɪk/ *adjective*. E20.

[ORIGIN from IMBECILE + -IC.]

Characteristic of an imbecile; idiotic.

imbecilitate /ɪmbɪˈsɪlɪteɪt/ *verb trans.* Now *rare* or *obsolete*. M17.

[ORIGIN from IMBECILITY after *debilitate*, *facilitate*, etc.: see -ATE[3].]

Make imbecile, weak, or feeble; enfeeble.

imbecility /ɪmbɪˈsɪlɪti/ *noun*. LME.

[ORIGIN Old French & mod. French *imbécillité* from Latin *imbecillitat-* from *imbecillus*: see IMBECILE, -ITY.]

1 Weakness, debility, feebleness, impotence; incapacity (*to do*). Now *rare* or *obsolete*. LME.

2 Extremely low intelligence; stupidity, foolishness. Also, an imbecilic act. E17.

imbed *verb* var. of EMBED.

†**imbellish** *verb*, †**imbellishment** *noun* vars. of EMBELLISH, EMBELLISHMENT.

†**imbetter** *verb* var. of EMBETTER.

imbibe /ɪmˈbʌɪb/ *verb trans.* LME.

[ORIGIN Latin *imbibere*, from *in-* IM-[1] + *bibere* drink.]

†**1** Cause to absorb moisture or liquid; soak, imbue, or saturate with moisture; steep. LME–E19.

2 Of a thing: suck up, drink in, absorb (moisture). LME.

W. COWPER So barren sands imbibe the shower.

3 Take up, absorb, assimilate (gas, rays, heat, etc.). Also, take into solution or suspension. LME.

4 *fig.* Drink in, absorb, assimilate (knowledge, ideas, etc.); take into one's mind or moral system. M16. ▸†**b** Instil *into*. M18–E19.

E. WAUGH The poor fellow had come . . from the United States to imbibe European culture.

5 Drink (a liquid, esp. alcoholic liquor). Also, inhale. M17. ▸†**b** *transf.* & *fig.* Swallow up. M17–E18.

P. ROTH They dizzily imbibed sweet chocolate drinks.

■ **imbiber** *noun* M18.

imbibition /ɪmbɪˈbɪʃ(ə)n/ *noun*. L15.

[ORIGIN medieval Latin *imbibitio(n-)* absorption, infusion, from *imbibit-* pa. ppl stem of *imbibere*: see IMBIBE, -ITION.]

†**1** Soaking or saturation with liquid; steeping, solution; an instance of this. L15–L17.

2 The taking up of liquid etc.; absorption; *fig.* assimilation of ideas etc. E17.

3 Drinking. M19.

■ **imbibitional** *adjective* of, pertaining to, or resulting from imbibition E20.

†**imbind** *verb*, †**imbitter** *verb*, †**imblaze** *verb* vars. of EMBIND, EMBITTER, EMBLAZE *verb*[1].

imblossom *verb* var. of EMBLOSSOM.

imbodiment *noun*, **imbody** *verb* see EMBODIMENT, EMBODY.

†**imbog** *verb*, †**imbold** *verb* vars. of EMBOG, EMBOLD.

imbolden *verb* var. of EMBOLDEN.

imbongi /ɪmˈbɒŋɡi/ *noun*. *S. Afr.* Pl. **izimbongi** /ɪz-/, **iimbongi** /iː-/. M19.

[ORIGIN Xhosa, Zulu.]

A (composer and) reciter of poems praising a chief etc.

†**imborder** *verb* var. of EMBORDER.

imbosom *verb* var. of EMBOSOM.

†**imboss** *verb*[1], *verb*[2], †**imbossed** *adjective*, †**imbossment** *noun* vars. of EMBOSS *verb*[1], *verb*[2], EMBOSSED, EMBOSSMENT.

†**imbosture** *noun* var. of EMBOSTURE

imbound *verb* var. of EMBOUND.

†**imbow** *verb*, **imbowed** *adjective* vars. of EMBOW, EMBOWED.

†**imbowel** *verb* var. of EMBOWEL.

imbower *verb* see EMBOWER.

†**imbrace** *verb & noun*, †**imbracement** *noun*, †**imbracer** *noun* vars. of EMBRACE *verb*[1] & *noun*, EMBRACEMENT, EMBRACER *noun*[1].

imbrangle *verb* var. of EMBRANGLE.

imbreathe /ɪm'briːð/ *verb trans.* Also **em-** /ɪm-, ɛm-/. LME.
[ORIGIN from IM-[1], EM-[1] + BREATHE *verb*. Cf. INBREATHE.]
1 Breathe in, inhale. LME.
2 Inspire (*with*); instil. LME.

†**imbred** *adjective*, **imbreed** *verb* vars. of INBRED, INBREED.

imbreviate /ɪm'briːvɪeɪt/ *verb trans.* E17.
[ORIGIN medieval Latin *imbreviat-* pa. ppl stem of *imbreviare*, from *in-* IM-[1] + late Latin *brevis*, *breve* summary, (medieval Latin) writ, letter: see -ATE[3].]
Put into the form of a brief; enrol, register.

imbrex /'ɪmbrɛks/ *noun*. Pl. **imbrices**. /'ɪmbrɪsiːz/. M19.
[ORIGIN Latin, from *imber* rain shower.]
ARCHAEOLOGY. A curved roof tile used to cover joints in a Roman tiled roof. Cf. TEGULA 2.

imbricate /'ɪmbrɪkət, -keɪt/ *adjective*. E17.
[ORIGIN Latin *imbricatus* pa. pple of *imbricare* cover with rain-tiles, from *imbrex*, *imbric-* roof tile: see IMBREX, -ATE[2].]
†**1** Formed like a gutter tile or pantile. E–M17.
2 Chiefly *BOTANY & ZOOLOGY*. Covered with or composed of scales or scalelike parts overlapping like roof tiles. M17. ▸**b** Overlapping like tiles. L18.
3 = IMBRICATED 4. L19.

imbricate /'ɪmbrɪkeɪt/ *verb*. L18.
[ORIGIN Latin *imbricat-* pa. ppl stem of *imbricare*: see IMBRICATE *adjective*, -ATE[3].]
1 *verb trans.* Place so as to overlap like roof tiles. L18.
2 *verb trans. & intrans.* Overlap like roof tiles. E19.
■ **imbricative** *adjective* = IMBRICATE *adjective* 2.

imbricated /'ɪmbrɪkeɪtɪd/ *adjective*. E18.
[ORIGIN formed as IMBRICATE *verb* + -ED[1].]
†**1** Of a leaf: curved like a gutter tile. Only in E18.
2 Composed of parts which overlap like roof tiles; covered by overlapping leaves, scales, tiles, etc. M18.
3 Of leaves, scales, etc.: arranged so as to overlap each other like roof tiles. M18.
4 Resembling in pattern a surface of overlapping roof tiles. L19.

imbrication /ɪmbrɪ'keɪʃ(ə)n/ *noun*. M17.
[ORIGIN from IMBRICATE *verb* or *adjective* + -ION.]
†**1** Covering with tiles. Only in M17.
2 An overlapping as of roof tiles; a decorative pattern or arrangement of scales etc. resembling overlapping tiles. E18.

imbrices *noun* pl. of IMBREX.

imbroccata /ɪmbrə'kɑːtə/ *noun*. Also †**em-**; †**-ocado**, pl. **-os**. L16.
[ORIGIN Italian, from *imbroccare* give a thrust over the opponent's weapon in fencing, from *brocco*, †*brocca* stud, nail.]
hist. A downward pass or thrust in fencing.

imbroglio /ɪm'brəʊlɪəʊ/ *noun*. Also †**em-**. Pl. **-os**. M18.
[ORIGIN Italian, from *imbrogliare* confuse, corresp. to French *embrouiller* EMBROIL *verb*[1].]
1 A confused heap. *arch.* M18.
2 A state of great confusion; a complicated or difficult (esp. political or dramatic) situation; a confused misunderstanding. E19.

J. CAREY A misty imbroglio of past loves and losses. S. KNIGHT This imbroglio of corruption, blackmail and murder brought down the coalition government.

†**imbroil** *verb & noun*, **imbrown** *verb* vars. of EMBROIL *verb*[1] *& noun*, EMBROWN.

imbrue /ɪm'bruː/ *verb trans.* Also **em-** /ɪm-, ɛm-/. LME.
[ORIGIN Old French *embruer*, *embrouer* bedaub, bedabble, from *en-* IM-[1] + Old French *breu*, *bro* (ult. from Germanic base of BROTH).]
▸ **I** †**1** Stain, dirty, defile. LME–L16.
2 Stain (one's hands, sword, etc.) *in* or *with* (blood etc.). E16. ▸**b** Cover with blood from bleeding wounds. L16.
†**3** Soak; steep *in*; saturate *with*. M16–M17.
†**4** *fig.* Steep *in*, imbue *with* (ideas, opinions, etc.); infect. M16–L17.
†**5** Make bloody; wound; pierce, cut. L16–M19.
▸ †**II 6** Pour (liquid). *rare* (Spenser). Only in L16.
■ **imbruement** *noun* (*rare*) tincture, infusion, imbuing L16.

imbrute /ɪm'bruːt/ *verb*. Also **em-** /ɪm-, ɛm-/. M17.
[ORIGIN from IM-[1], EM-[1] + BRUTE *noun*.]
1 *verb trans.* Degrade to the level of a brute; make bestial; brutalize. M17.
2 *verb intrans.* Sink or lapse to the level of a brute; become bestial or degraded. M17.
■ **imbrutement** *noun* E19.

imbue /ɪm'bjuː/ *verb trans.* LME.
[ORIGIN French *imbu*, †*imbu(i)t* pa. pple from Latin *imbutus* pa. pple of *imbuere* moisten, stain, imbue.]
1 Saturate, wet through; dye, tinge, impregnate (*with*). LME. ▸**b** = IMBRUE *verb* 2. M19.

WORDSWORTH Beamy radiance, that imbues Whate'er it strikes with gem-like hues.

2 Permeate, pervade, inspire (*with* an opinion, habit, feeling, etc.). M16.

D. CARNEGIE This experience imbued him with a confidence that was invaluable.

■ **imbuement** *noun* (*rare*) L17.

imburse /ɪm'bəːs/ *verb trans.* Now *rare* or *obsolete*. M16.
[ORIGIN medieval Latin *imbursare* put in one's purse, appropriate, from *in-* IM-[1] + late Latin *bursa* purse.]
1 Put into a purse; stow away, store up. M16.
2 Pay, reimburse. Formerly also, enrich. M17.
■ **imbursement** *noun* (*rare*) M17.

imbuya /ɪm'bwiːə/ *noun*. E20.
[ORIGIN Portuguese *imbuia* from Guarani.]
(The timber of) a Brazilian tree, *Phoebe porosa*, of the laurel family.

IMCO *abbreviation*.
Intergovernmental Maritime Consultative Organization.

I.Mech.E. *abbreviation*.
Institution of Mechanical Engineers.

IMEI *abbreviation*.
International mobile equipment identity.

-imeter /ɪmɪtə/ *suffix*.
Form of -METER with *-i-* provided by first element or merely connective (***calorimeter***, ***evaporimeter***). Cf. -OMETER.

IMF *abbreviation*.
International Monetary Fund.

imfe *noun* var. of IMPHEE.

IMHO *abbreviation*.
In my humble opinion.

imidazole /ɪmɪ'deɪzəʊl, ɪ'mɪdəzəʊl/ *noun*. L19.
[ORIGIN from IMIDE + AZO- + -OLE[2].]
CHEMISTRY. A colourless crystalline azole, $C_3H_4N_2$. Also called ***glyoxaline***.

imide /'ɪmʌɪd/ *noun*. M19.
[ORIGIN French, arbitrary alt. of AMIDE.]
CHEMISTRY. Any of a class of compounds containing the divalent group ·NH· or ·NR· (R = alkyl), esp. where this is bonded to acid groups (i.e. occurs as ·CONHCO·). Cf. IMINE.
■ **imidic** *adjective* pertaining to or of the nature of an imide; (of an acid) having the formula R·C(NH)OH: L19.

imido- /ɪ'mʌɪdəʊ/ *combining form*.
[ORIGIN from IMIDE + -O-.]
CHEMISTRY. Forming nouns with the senses 'of an imide', 'that is an imide'.

imine /'ɪmiːn/ *noun*. L19.
[ORIGIN from AMINE on the analogy of *imide*, *amide*.]
CHEMISTRY. Any of a class of organic compounds containing the divalent group ·NH· or ·NR· (R = alkyl) bonded to one or two non-acidic carbon atoms. Cf. IMIDE.

I.Min.E. *abbreviation*.
Institution of Mining Engineers.

imino- /ɪ'miːnəʊ/ *combining form*. Also as attrib. adjective **imino**.
[ORIGIN from I.MIN.E. + -O-.]
CHEMISTRY. Designating or containing the group characteristic of imines.
■ **imino acid** *noun* an organic acid containing both an imino and a carboxyl group E20.

imipramine /ɪ'mɪprəmiːn/ *noun*. M20.
[ORIGIN from IMI(NE + PR(OPYL + AMINE.]
PHARMACOLOGY. A tricyclic tertiary amine, $C_{19}H_{24}N_2$, used to treat depression.
– NOTE: A proprietary name for this drug is TOFRANIL.

imitable /'ɪmɪtəb(ə)l/ *adjective*. M16.
[ORIGIN French, or late Latin *imitabilis*, from *imitari* IMITATE: see -ABLE. Cf. earlier INIMITABLE.]
†**1** Deserving of imitation. M16–L18.
2 Able to be imitated. L16.
■ **imita'bility** *noun* L17. **imitableness** *noun* M17.

imitate /'ɪmɪteɪt/ *verb trans.* M16.
[ORIGIN Latin *imitat-* pa. ppl stem of *imitari* copy, rel. to *imago* image: see -ATE[3].]
1 Do or try to do after the manner of; follow the example of; copy in action. M16. ▸**b** Mimic, counterfeit. E17. ▸†**c** Endeavour *to do* something. E17–E19.

GIBBON In the form and disposition of his . . epistles, he imitated the younger Pliny. E. M. FORSTER Isn't it intolerable that a person whom we're told to imitate should go round spreading slander. **b** J. C. POWYS Sam answered the owl's cry, imitating it exactly.

2 Make or produce a copy or representation of. L16. ▸**b** Use (a literary composition etc.) as a model. E18.

b DRYDEN The adventures of Ulysses . . are imitated in the first six books of Virgil's Æneis.

3 Be, become, or make oneself like, simulate (intentionally or unintentionally). L16.

OED A lath painted to imitate iron.

imitation /ɪmɪ'teɪʃ(ə)n/ *noun & adjective*. LME.
[ORIGIN Old French & mod. French from Latin *imitatio(n-)*, formed as IMITATE: see -ATION.]
▸ **A** *noun*. **1** The action or practice of imitating or copying. LME.

Proverb Imitation is the sincerest form of flattery.

2 The result or product of imitating; a copy, an artificial likeness; a thing made to look like something else; a counterfeit. E17.

Esquire It was the most uncanny imitation of an elephant they'd ever heard.

3 A method of translation looser than paraphrase in which modern examples and illustrations are used for old, and domestic for foreign; a composition of this nature. M17.
4 *MUSIC*. The repetition of a phrase or melody, usually at a different pitch, in another part or voice, with or without other modifications. E18.
▸ **B** *adjective*. Made in imitation of a real or genuine article or substance. M19.

R. M. PEARL An imitation gem is a substance which is wholly manufactured.

■ **imitational** *adjective* M19.

imitative /'ɪmɪtətɪv/ *adjective*. L16.
[ORIGIN Late Latin *imitativus*, formed as IMITATE: see -ATIVE.]
1 Characterized by or consisting in imitation. L16.
imitative arts: see ART *noun*[1]. **imitative word** a word that reproduces a natural sound (e.g. *fizz*) or whose sound is felt to correspond to the appearance etc. of the object or action described (e.g. *blob*, *jag*, *jam*, *jerk*).
2 Given to imitation; prone to imitate, copy, or mimic. M18.
3 That imitates the appearance of something else; simulative, fictitious, counterfeit. M19.
■ **imitatively** *adverb* L19. **imitativeness** *noun* M19.

imitator /'ɪmɪteɪtə/ *noun*. E16.
[ORIGIN Latin (orig. partly through French *imitateur*), formed as IMITATE: see -OR.]
A person who or thing which imitates, copies, or follows another; a person who produces an imitation of something.
■ **imitatress** *noun* = IMITATRIX M19.

imitatrix /ɪmɪ'teɪtrɪks/ *noun*. Pl. **-trices** /-trɪsiːz/, **-trixes**. E17.
[ORIGIN Latin, fem. of IMITATOR: see -TRIX.]
A female imitator.

IMM *abbreviation*.
Institution of Mining and Metallurgy.

immaculacy /ɪ'makjʊləsi/ *noun*. L18.
[ORIGIN from IMMACULATE + -ACY.]
Immaculate condition or quality.

immaculate /ɪ'makjʊlət/ *adjective*. LME.
[ORIGIN Latin *immaculatus*, formed as IM-[2] + MACULATE *adjective*.]
1 Free from moral stain; pure, spotless, unblemished. LME.

A. B. JAMESON Convinced of his wife's immaculate purity.

Immaculate Conception *THEOLOGY* the doctrine that the Virgin Mary was from the moment of her conception free from original sin. **Immaculate Lamb** Jesus Christ (after 1 *Peter* 1:19).
2 Spotlessly clean or neat; perfectly tidy, in perfect condition. L16. ▸**b** Chiefly *BOTANY & ZOOLOGY*. Without spots. E19.

C. MCCULLERS He was always immaculate and . . soberly dressed. *Times* An immaculate mill house beautifully situated in the country. **b** T. BEWICK He describes the male bird to be of an immaculate white.

3 Free from fault or error. M19.

G. GORDON Adding his wild squiggle to her immaculate typing. M. RULE The Deanes took pains to record the guns with immaculate watercolour sketches.

■ **immaculately** *adverb* E18. **immaculateness** *noun* M17.

immalleable /ɪ'malɪəb(ə)l/ *adjective*. *rare*. L17.
[ORIGIN from IM-[2] + MALLEABLE.]
Not malleable.

immanacle /ɪ'manək(ə)l/ *verb trans.* *rare*. M17.
[ORIGIN from IM-[1] + MANACLE *noun*.]
Bind with manacles; fetter.

immane /ɪ'meɪn/ *adjective*. *arch.* E17.
[ORIGIN Latin *immanis* monstrous, huge, savage, (earlier) wicked, cruel, formed as IM-[2] + *manis*, *manus* good.]
1 Monstrous in size or strength. E17.
2 Monstrous in character; inhumanly cruel. E17.
■ **immanely** *adverb* E17. †**immanity** *noun* (*a*) monstrous cruelty; (*b*) hugeness: M16–L17.

immanence /ˈɪmənəns/ *noun*. E19.
[ORIGIN from IMMANENT + -ENCE.]
The fact or condition of being immanent.
– COMB.: **immanence philosophy** a theory developed in Germany in the late 19th cent. that reality exists only through being immanent in conscious minds.
■ **immanency** *noun* the quality of being immanent M17.

immanent /ˈɪmənənt/ *adjective*. M16.
[ORIGIN Late Latin *immanent-* pres. ppl stem of *immanere*, formed as IM-^{1} + Latin *manere* remain, dwell: see -ENT.]
1 Indwelling, inherent (*in*); (of God) permanently pervading and sustaining the universe. Cf. TRANSCENDENT. M16.
W. J. BATE This sense of process is immanent throughout all of Johnson's writing.
2 PHILOSOPHY. Of an action: that is performed entirely within the mind of the subject, and produces no external effect. Opp. ***transient*** or ***transitive***. Now *rare*. E17.
■ **immaˈnental** *adjective* of or pertaining to immanence L19. **immanently** *adverb* E18.

immanentism /ˈɪmənəntɪz(ə)m/ *noun*. E20.
[ORIGIN from IMMANENT + -ISM.]
Belief in immanence, esp. the immanence of God.
■ **immanentist** *adjective & noun* (**a**) *adjective* holding or characterized by the doctrine of immanentism; (**b**) *noun* a believer in the immanence of God: E20.

immanifest /ɪˈmanɪfɛst/ *adjective*. *rare*. M17.
[ORIGIN Late Latin *immanifestus* obscure, formed as IM-^{2} + Latin *manifestus* MANIFEST *adjective*.]
Not manifest or evident.

immantation /ɪmanˈteɪʃ(ə)n/ *noun*. L19.
[ORIGIN medieval Latin *immantatio(n-)*, from *immantat-* pa. ppl stem of *immantare* clothe with a mantle, from *mantum* MANTLE *noun*: see -ATION.]
The investiture of a newly elected pope with the ceremonial mantle.

immantle /ɪˈmant(ə)l/ *verb trans*. E17.
[ORIGIN from IM-^{1} + MANTLE *noun*.]
Cover with, or as with, a mantle.

immarble /ɪˈmɑːb(ə)l/ *verb trans*. *rare*. M17.
[ORIGIN from IM-^{1} + MARBLE *noun*. Cf. ENMARBLE.]
Make into marble; make as cold, hard, or immovable, as marble.

immarcescible /ɪmɑːˈsɛsɪb(ə)l/ *adjective*. Now *rare*. Also **-essible**. LME.
[ORIGIN Late Latin *immarcescibilis*, formed as IM-^{2} + *marcescere*, *marcere* fade: see -IBLE.]
Unfading; imperishable.

immarginate /ɪˈmɑːdʒɪnət/ *adjective*. E19.
[ORIGIN from IM-^{2} + MARGINATE *adjective*.]
BOTANY & ENTOMOLOGY. Having no distinct margin.

†**immask** *verb trans*. *rare* (Shakes.). Only in L16.
[ORIGIN from IM-^{1} + MASK *noun*^{2} or *verb*^{2}.]
Disguise.

immaterial /ɪməˈtɪərɪəl/ *adjective & noun*. LME.
[ORIGIN Late Latin *immaterialis*, formed as IM-^{2} + *materialis* MATERIAL.]
▸ **A** *adjective*. **1** Not material; not consisting of matter; spiritual. LME. ▸**b** Having little substance, flimsy. *rare*. E17.
J. BRODSKY We sensed a strange intensity in the air, something immaterial.
†**2** Not pertinent to the matter in hand. L16–M17.
3 Of an abstract thing: of no consequence, unimportant. L17.
CONAN DOYLE You will be given a perfectly free hand. Surely the actual name of your client is immaterial. P. G. WODEHOUSE Whether Wilfred Slingsby was crushed or defiant was immaterial.
▸ **B** *noun*. In *pl*. Non-material things. M17.
■ **immateriˈality** *noun* (**a**) the quality or character of being immaterial; (**b**) *rare* an immaterial thing: L16. **immaterialize** *verb trans*. make immaterial or incorporeal M17. **immaterially** *adverb* M17.

immaterialism /ɪməˈtɪərɪəlɪz(ə)m/ *noun*. E18.
[ORIGIN from IMMATERIAL + -ISM, after *materialism*.]
The doctrine that all things exist only as the ideas or perceptions of a mind.
■ **immaterialist** *noun* E18.

immatriculate /ɪməˈtrɪkjʊleɪt/ *verb trans*. *rare*. E18.
[ORIGIN from IM-^{1} + MATRICULATE *verb*. Cf. French *immatriculer*.]
Matriculate.
■ **immatricuˈlation** *noun* L19.

immature /ɪməˈtjʊə/ *adjective*. M16.
[ORIGIN Latin *immaturus* untimely, unripe, formed as IM-^{2} + *maturus* MATURE *adjective*.]
†**1** Of death: premature. M16–M19.
2 Not mature; not yet fully developed; unripe; lacking emotional or intellectual development. L16.
ANTHONY HUXLEY A 'June drop' of immature fruits. V. WOOLF She was extremely immature, like a child still, attached to dolls, to old slippers.
immature cataract OPHTHALMOLOGY: markedly but not yet fully opaque, with the lens usu. swollen and its superficial layers largely transparent. **immature soil** SOIL SCIENCE: not having a fully developed profile.
■ **immaturely** *adverb* M17.

immaturity /ɪməˈtjʊərɪti/ *noun*. M16.
[ORIGIN from IMMATURE + -ITY.]
†**1** Prematureness, untimeliness. M16–L17.
2 Immature condition or state; unripeness; lack of maturity of character etc. E17.
3 An immature thing; an action etc. which shows the person who does it to be immature. M17.

immeasurable /ɪˈmɛʒ(ə)rəb(ə)l/ *adjective*. LME.
[ORIGIN from IM-^{2} + MEASURABLE.]
Not measurable; immense.
■ **immeasuraˈbility** *noun* E19. **immeasurableness** *noun* M16. **immeasurably** *adverb* LME.

immeasured /ɪˈmɛʒəd/ *adjective*. L16.
[ORIGIN from UNMEASURED, with prefix-substitution. Cf. French †*immesuré*.]
Unmeasured; immense.

†**immechanical** *adjective*. E18.
[ORIGIN from UNMECHANICAL, with prefix-substitution.]
1 Not of a physical or material nature or origin. Only in 18.
2 Of a person: not practical. Only in M18.

immediacy /ɪˈmiːdɪəsi/ *noun*. E17.
[ORIGIN from IMMEDIATE + -ACY.]
The quality or condition of being immediate; direct relation; directness.
H. JAMES Questions . . bearing with varying degrees of immediacy on the subject. K. VONNEGUT The bone-rattling immediacy of front-line journalism.

immediate /ɪˈmiːdɪət/ *adjective & adverb*. LME.
[ORIGIN Old French & mod. French *immédiat* or late Latin *immediatus*, formed as IM-^{2} + *mediatus* MEDIATE *adjective*.]
▸ **A** *adjective*. **1** Of a person or thing in relation to another: not separated by any intervening agent or medium. LME. ▸**b** *spec*. (*hist*.) Designating the feudal relation between two people, one of whom derives the right of possession from the other directly. M16.
R. HOOKER The true immediate cause why baptisme . . is necessary. L. DEIGHTON My immediate boss is working on one of those interminable reports.
2 Nearest, next, or close, in space or order. LME.
P. LEVI We did at least get to know our immediate district.
3 Of relation or action between two things: direct, without any intervening medium or agency. M16.
J. ROSENBERG The painting has all the freshness of an immediate study from life.
4 Present or nearest in time; most urgent, occurring or taking effect without delay; done at once, instant. M16.
A. TREW We must ask him to take immediate steps to keep sightseers away. R. WEST The immediate preludes . . were not auspicious. J. MORTIMER She forgot about the past, and thought of her immediate future. J. A. MICHENER The exiled dictator faced immediate death if he returned to Mexico.
5 That directly concerns a person etc.; having a direct bearing. E18.
P. DRISCOLL I had one immediate concern: the British consulate. BOSW. SMITH She allowed her colonies to trade only so far as suited her own immediate interests.
– SPECIAL COLLOCATIONS: **immediate access store** COMPUTING a store whose access time is negligible. **immediate constituent** LINGUISTICS any of the main grammatical or morphological subdivisions of a sentence, phrase, or word. **immediate inference**: drawn from a single premiss, without the intervention of a middle term. **immediate knowledge**: gained without reasoning.
▸ **B** *adverb*. [Partly from medieval Latin *immediate*.] Immediately. Long *obsolete* exc. *rare*. *non-standard*. LME.
W. OWEN If it were not so,—I should hop it, immejit.
■ **immediateness** *noun* M17.

immediately /ɪˈmiːdɪətli/ *adverb & conjunction*. LME.
[ORIGIN from IMMEDIATE + -LY^{2}, rendering medieval Latin *immediate*.]
▸ **A** *adverb*. **1** Without intermediary agency; in direct connection or relation; so as to affect directly. LME.
2 With no person, thing, or distance intervening; next (before or after); closely. LME.
3 Without delay, at once, instantly. LME.
▸ **B** *conjunction*. At the moment that, as soon as. M19.

immediatism /ɪˈmiːdɪətɪz(ə)m/ *noun*. E19.
[ORIGIN from IMMEDIATE *adjective* + -ISM.]
1 Immediacy. *rare*. E19.
2 The principle or practice of immediate action; US HISTORY the policy of the immediate abolition of slavery. M19.
■ **immediatist** *noun* M19.

immedicable /ɪˈmɛdɪkəb(ə)l/ *adjective*. M16.
[ORIGIN Latin *immedicabilis*, formed as IM-^{2} + *medicabilis* curable, MEDICABLE.]
Incurable; irremediable.
■ **immedicableness** *noun* (*rare*) E18. **immedicably** *adverb* M19.

Immelmann /ˈɪm(ə)lmən/ *noun*. Also **-man**. E20.
[ORIGIN Max *Immelmann* (1890–1916), German fighter pilot.]
In full ***Immelmann turn***. An aerobatic manoeuvre consisting of a half loop followed by a half roll, resulting in reversal of direction and increased height.

immelodious /ɪmɪˈləʊdɪəs/ *adjective*. E17.
[ORIGIN from IM-^{2} + MELODIOUS.]
Unmelodious.

immember /ɪˈmɛmbə/ *verb trans*. *rare*. M17.
[ORIGIN from IM-^{1} + MEMBER *noun*.]
Incorporate as a member.

immemorable /ɪˈmɛm(ə)rəb(ə)l/ *adjective*. M16.
[ORIGIN Latin *immemorabilis*, formed as IM-^{2} + *memorabilis* MEMORABLE.]
1 Not memorable; not worth remembering. M16.
†**2** = IMMEMORIAL. M17–L18.

immemorial /ɪmɪˈmɔːrɪəl/ *adjective*. E17.
[ORIGIN medieval Latin *immemorialis*, formed as IM-^{2} + Latin *memorialis* MEMORIAL *adjective*.]
Ancient beyond memory or record; very old; long established. Freq. *postpositive* in ***time immemorial*** s.v. TIME *noun*.
TENNYSON The moan of doves in immemorial elms.
■ **immemorially** *adverb* E17. **immemorialness** *noun* E18.

immense /ɪˈmɛns/ *adjective & noun*. LME.
[ORIGIN Old French & mod. French from Latin *immensus* immeasurable, formed as IM-^{2} + *mensus* pa. pple of *metiri* measure (after Greek *ametros*).]
▸ **A** *adjective*. **1** Extraordinarily or immeasurably large or great; vast, boundless. LME.
W. BOYD The immense mock-Tudor Government House. G. GREENE She felt an immense relief because nothing . . had been required.
2 Extremely good, splendid. *slang*. M18.
▸ **B** *noun*. Immense extent; immensity. L18.
■ **immensely** *adverb* in an immense degree; *colloq*. very much: M17. **immenseness** *noun* E17.

immensikoff /ɪˈmɛnsɪkɒf/ *noun*. *slang*. Now *rare* or *obsolete*. L19.
[ORIGIN Fanciful elaboration of *immense* to rhyme with *toff*, in a music hall song (*c* 1868) by Arthur Lloyd, who wore a fur-trimmed overcoat.]
A heavy overcoat.

immensity /ɪˈmɛnsɪti/ *noun*. LME.
[ORIGIN Old French & mod. French *immensité* or Latin *immensitas*, from *immensus* IMMENSE: see -ITY.]
1 Immeasurableness, boundlessness; vastness; vast magnitude. LME.
2 Infinite being; infinity; infinite space. M17.
3 An immense quantity or extent (*of*); a thing, being, etc., of immense scale. L18.

immensurable /ɪˈmɛnʃ(ə)rəb(ə)l, -sjə-/ *adjective*. L15.
[ORIGIN French, or late Latin *immensurabilis*, formed as IM-^{2} + *mensurabilis* MENSURABLE.]
Immeasurable.

†**immensurate** *adjective*. M17–M18.
[ORIGIN Late Latin *immensuratus*, formed as IM-^{2} + Latin *mensuratus* pa. pple of *mensurare* MEASURE *verb*: see -ATE^{2}.]
Immense, unmeasured.

immer *noun* var. of EMBER *noun*^{2}.

immerd /ɪˈməːd/ *verb trans*. *rare*. M17.
[ORIGIN from medieval Latin (whence Old French & mod. French *emmerder*), formed as IM-^{1} + Latin *merda* dung, ordure.]
Bury in or cover with dung.

immerge /ɪˈməːdʒ/ *verb*. Now *rare*. Also **emerge**. E17.
[ORIGIN Latin *immergere*: see IMMERSE.]
1 *verb trans*. Dip or plunge in a liquid; immerse. E17.
2 *verb trans*. *fig*. = IMMERSE 2. E17.
3 *verb intrans*. Plunge or dip oneself in a liquid; sink. E18. ▸†**b** Of a celestial object: enter into the shadow of another in an eclipse; disappear in an occultation; sink below the horizon. Cf. IMMERSION 2. Only in 18.
■ **immergence** *noun* M19.

†**immerit** *noun*. E17–M18.
[ORIGIN from IM-^{2} + MERIT *noun*.]
Lack of merit; (a) demerit.

†**immerited** *adjective*. E17–L18.
[ORIGIN from IM-^{2} + *merited* pa. pple of MERIT *verb*.]
Undeserved.

†**immeritorious** *adjective*. M17–L18.
[ORIGIN from IM-^{2} + MERITORIOUS.]
Undeserving.

immerse /ɪˈməːs/ *verb*. E17.
[ORIGIN Latin *immers-* pa. ppl stem of *immergere*, formed as IM-^{1} + *mergere* dip, MERGE.]
1 *verb trans*. Dip, plunge, or submerge in a liquid; *spec*. baptize by immersion. E17. ▸†**b** *fig*. Include; merge. E17–M18.
R. P. JHABVALA Some buffaloes were bathing, immersed so deeply that only their heads were visible above water. *transf*.: J. TYNDALL A traveller immersed to the waist in the jaws of a fissure. **b** I. WATTS We ought . . to immerse our private in the public safety.

2 *verb trans. fig.* Involve deeply, absorb in a particular activity or condition. Usu. in *pass.* or *refl.* M17.

J. KRANTZ Fauve immersed herself in the world of modeling. B. EMECHETA You're immersed in your work.

3 *verb intrans.* Plunge oneself, become absorbed. Now *rare* or *obsolete*. M17.

■ **immersible** *adjective* M19. **immersive** *adjective* †(**a**) characterized by or involving immersion; (**b**) (of a computer display or system) generating a three-dimensional image which appears to surround the user: M17.

immersed /ɪˈməːst/ *adjective*. LME.

[ORIGIN from IMMERSE + -ED[1].]

1 That has been immersed; submerged. LME.

†**2** ASTRONOMY. In darkness, eclipsed. M17–M19.

3 BOTANY & ZOOLOGY. Embedded, sunken. E19.

immersion /ɪˈməːʃ(ə)n/ *noun*. Also (now *rare*) **emersion**. L15.

[ORIGIN Late Latin *immersio(n-)*, from Latin *immers-*: see IMMERSE, -ION.]

1 Immersing or being immersed; *fig.* absorption in an activity or condition. L15. ▸**b** The administration of Christian baptism by plunging the whole person in water. M17.

ADDISON The Doctor.. gives her Two or Three total Emersions in the Cold Bath. M. IGNATIEFF Our dull and patient immersion in the records of the past.

2 ASTRONOMY. The disappearance of a celestial object behind another or into its shadow, as in an eclipse or occultation. L17.

3 A method of teaching a foreign language by the exclusive use of that language, usu. at a special school. Chiefly *N. Amer.* M20.

attrib.: *Time* I've been taking immersion courses in French.

– COMB.: **immersion foot** MEDICINE trench foot; **immersion heater** an electric heater designed for direct immersion in a liquid to be heated, esp. as a fixture in a hot-water tank; **immersion suit**: designed to give the wearer buoyancy and insulation when in the water.

■ **immersionism** *noun* the doctrine or practice of immersion in baptism M19. **immersionist** *noun* an adherent of immersionism M19.

immesh /ɪˈmɛʃ/ *verb trans.* L18.

[ORIGIN from IM-[1] + MESH *noun*.]

= ENMESH.

immethodical /ɪmɪˈθɒdɪk(ə)l/ *adjective*. L16.

[ORIGIN from IM-[2] + METHODICAL.]

Having no method; unmethodical.

■ **immethodically** *adverb* E17.

immetrical /ɪˈmɛtrɪk(ə)l/ *adjective*. L16.

[ORIGIN from IM-[2] + METRICAL *adjective*[1].]

Not metrical; unmetrical.

■ **immetrically** *adverb* L19. **immetricalness** *noun* M19.

immie *noun* var. of IMMY.

immigrant /ˈɪmɪgr(ə)nt/ *noun & adjective*. L18.

[ORIGIN Latin *immigrant-* pres. ppl stem of *immigrare*, after EMIGRANT: see IMMIGRATE.]

▸ **A** *noun*. **1** A person who settles as a permanent resident in a different country. Also (esp. in Britain), a descendant of such a person. L18.

E. WILSON The immigrants from feudalism and famine in Europe were finding in the crowded American cities new misery.

LANDED *immigrant*.

2 BIOLOGY etc. An animal or plant living or growing in a region to which it has migrated; a cell growing in tissue into which it has moved. L19.

▸ **B** *attrib.* or as *adjective*. Of or pertaining to immigrants; that is an immigrant. E19.

Times There was some criticism.. at this high proportion of immigrant children. P. ROTH My immigrant grandparents ...coming, at the turn of the century, to America.

immigrate /ˈɪmɪgreɪt/ *verb*. E17.

[ORIGIN Latin *immigrat-* pa. ppl stem of *immigrare*, formed as IM-[1] + *migrare* MIGRATE: see -ATE[3].]

1 *verb intrans.* Come to settle as a permanent resident in a different country. Foll. by *into*. E17. ▸**b** BIOLOGY etc. (Of a cell) move into different tissue; (of an animal or plant) migrate to a different geographical region. L19.

2 *verb trans.* Bring (a person) into a country as a settler. L19.

immigration /ɪmɪˈgreɪʃ(ə)n/ *noun*. M17.

[ORIGIN from IMMIGRATE + -ATION.]

1 The action of immigrating; the process of authorizing this (freq. *attrib.*). M17. ▸**b** A department at a frontier, airport, etc., where the documentation of (potential) immigrants is scrutinized on their arrival. *colloq.* M20.

T. WARTON The Saracens.. at their immigration into Spain. *attrib.*: C. PHILLIPS Bertram concentrated on the signs.. behind the desk of the immigration officer. **b** F. HOYLE Quickly we were into the reception hall and through immigration [at London Airport].

2 A group of immigrants. *US*. M19.

Saturday Review A far vaster immigration.. began pouring through the city portals.

imminence /ˈɪmɪnəns/ *noun*. E17.

[ORIGIN Latin *imminentia*, formed as IMMINENT: see -ENCE.]

1 A thing that is imminent; *esp.* impending evil. Now *rare*. E17.

SHAKES. *Tr. & Cr.* I.. dare all imminence that gods and men Address their dangers in.

2 The quality or fact of being imminent. M17.

R. COBB She appeared to carry the imminence of death in every part of her. L. WHISTLER Report came of the imminence of war over Czechoslovakia.

■ **imminency** *noun* = IMMINENCE 2 M17.

imminent /ˈɪmɪnənt/ *adjective*. LME.

[ORIGIN Latin *imminent-* pres. ppl stem of *imminere* project, be impending, formed as IM-[1] + *minere* project: see -ENT.]

1 Of an event, esp. danger or disaster: impending, soon to happen. LME.

E. WAUGH The prospect of action, for a few days imminent, now postponed. B. BAINBRIDGE He wondered what Meyer had meant by danger. Was it imminent or to come later? C. PHILLIPS He displayed no signs of imminent departure.

†**2** Immanent. E17–M19.

3 Projecting, overhanging. *arch.* E18.

■ **imminently** *adverb* M16.

immingle /ɪˈmɪŋg(ə)l/ *verb trans.* E17.

[ORIGIN from IM-[1] + MINGLE *verb*.]

Mingle, blend.

†**imminution** *noun*. L16–L18.

[ORIGIN Latin *imminutio(n-)*, from *imminut-* pa. ppl stem of *imminuere* lessen, formed as IM-[1] + *minuere* lessen: see -ION.]

Lessening, decrease.

immiscible /ɪˈmɪsɪb(ə)l/ *adjective*. L17.

[ORIGIN Late Latin *immiscibilis*, formed as IM-[2] + MISCIBLE.]

Unable to be mixed; *spec.* (of a liquid) incapable of forming a true solution *with* or *in* another liquid.

T. CHALMERS Like water and oil, they are immiscible.

■ **immisciˈbility** *noun* M18.

immiseration /ɪˌmɪzəˈreɪʃ(ə)n/ *noun*. M20.

[ORIGIN from IM-[1] + MISER(ABLE + -ATION, translating German *Verelendung*.]

Impoverishment.

J. K. GALBRAITH The prospect of the progressive immiseration of the masses, worsening economic crises and.. bloody revolution.

■ **iˈmmiserate** *verb trans.* [back-form.] impoverish L20. **immiseriˈzation** *noun* = IMMISERATION M20.

immission /ɪˈmɪʃ(ə)n/ *noun*. Now *rare*. E16.

[ORIGIN Latin *immissio(n-)*, from *immiss-* pa. ppl stem of *immittere*: see IMMIT, -ION.]

1 A thing that is immitted. E16.

2 The action of immitting; insertion, injection. L16.

immit /ɪˈmɪt/ *verb trans.* Now *rare*. Infl. **-tt-**. LME.

[ORIGIN Latin *immittere* send in, introduce, formed as IM-[1] + *mittere* send.]

Put in, insert, introduce.

immitigable /ɪˈmɪtɪgəb(ə)l/ *adjective*. L16.

[ORIGIN Late Latin *immitigabilis*, formed as IM-[2] + MITIGABLE.]

Unable to be mitigated.

■ **immitigably** *adverb* E19.

immittance /ɪˈmɪt(ə)ns/ *noun*. M20.

[ORIGIN Blend of IMPEDANCE and ADMITTANCE.]

ELECTRICITY. Admittance and impedance (as a combined concept).

immix /ɪˈmɪks/ *verb trans.* Now *rare*. Orig. & chiefly as pa. pple †**immixt**, **immixed** /ɪˈmɪkst/. LME.

[ORIGIN Orig. pa. pple, from Latin *immixtus* pa. pple of *immiscere*, formed as IM-[1] + *miscere* mix; verb (E16) as back-form. or from IM-[1] + MIX *verb*.]

Mix in, mix up; involve (*in*).

immixture /ɪˈmɪkstʃə/ *noun*. M19.

[ORIGIN from IM-[1] + MIXTURE.]

The action of mixing up or mingling; the fact of being involved (*in*).

immobile /ɪˈməʊbʌɪl/ *adjective*. ME.

[ORIGIN Old French & mod. French from Latin *immobilis*, formed as IM-[2] + *mobilis* MOBILE *adjective*.]

Incapable of moving or being moved, immovable; motionless, stationary.

P. G. WODEHOUSE There was something.. immobile about the boy's attitude.. to suggest that nothing could shift him. A. S. BYATT The man watched him, expecting him to move again, but he sat, immobile.

immobilise *verb* var. of IMMOBILIZE.

immobilism /ɪˈməʊbɪlɪz(ə)m/ *noun*. M20.

[ORIGIN French *immobilisme*, formed as IMMOBILE: see -ISM.]

A policy or attitude of extreme conservatism or opposition to change.

immobility /ɪmə(ʊ)ˈbɪlɪti/ *noun*. LME.

[ORIGIN Old French & mod. French *immobilité* or late Latin *immobilitas*, from *immobilis*: see IMMOBILE, -ITY.]

The quality or condition of being immobile.

immobilize /ɪˈməʊbɪlʌɪz/ *verb trans.* Also **-ise**. L19.

[ORIGIN French *immobiliser*, formed as IMMOBILE: see -IZE. Cf. MOBILIZE.]

1 Make or keep immobile; restrict the free movement of; *spec.* keep (a limb, a patient) restricted in movement for healing purposes. L19. ▸**b** Withdraw (coin) from circulation to support banknotes. L19.

R. MACAULAY She stood still, immobilized by shock. M. RULE The English carracks were immobilised with scarcely a breath of wind. *Times* Use wheel clamps to immobilize offending vehicles.

2 BIOLOGY. Esp. of an organism: convert (a plant nutrient or other substance) into a form in which it is unavailable to (other) organisms. M20.

■ **immobiliˈzation** *noun* L19. **immobilizer** *noun* someone or something which immobilizes something, *spec.* a device for immobilizing a motor vehicle in order to prevent theft M20.

immoderacy /ɪˈmɒd(ə)rəsi/ *noun*. *rare*. L17.

[ORIGIN from IMMODERATE + -ACY.]

Immoderateness.

immoderate /ɪˈmɒd(ə)rət/ *adjective*. LME.

[ORIGIN Latin *immoderatus*, formed as IM-[2] + *moderatus* MODERATE *adjective*.]

Not moderate; lacking in moderation; unrestrained, excessive; extreme. Formerly also (*rare*), boundless.

LD MACAULAY His immoderate zeal against the unfortunate clan. E. JOHNSON A rather short, plump.. youngster, jolly-looking and given to immoderate laughter.

■ **immoderately** *adverb* LME. **immoderateness** *noun* M16.

immoderation /ɪˌmɒdəˈreɪʃ(ə)n/ *noun*. LME.

[ORIGIN French *immodération* or Latin *immoderatio(n-)*, formed as IM-[2] + *moderatio(n-)* MODERATION.]

Immoderateness, excess. Formerly also, an extreme; an immoderate act.

immodest /ɪˈmɒdɪst/ *adjective*. L16.

[ORIGIN French *immodeste* or Latin *immodestus*, formed as IM-[2] + MODEST.]

Lacking modesty or decency; forward, impudent, boastful; indelicate, improper.

R. MACAULAY Female bathing was thought extremely immodest. P. LIVELY I was by far the best looking.. and the most immodest.

■ **immodestly** *adverb* L16.

immodesty /ɪˈmɒdɪsti/ *noun*. L16.

[ORIGIN French *immodestie* or Latin *immodestia*, formed as IM-[2] + MODESTY.]

Lack of modesty or decency; forwardness, impudence; indelicacy, impropriety; an instance of this.

immodulated /ɪˈmɒdjʊleɪtɪd/ *adjective*. *rare*. M18.

[ORIGIN from IM-[2] + *modulated* pa. pple of MODULATE.]

Without (vocal) modulation.

immolate /ˈɪmə(ʊ)lət/ *adjective*. *arch.* M16.

[ORIGIN Latin *immolatus* pa. pple, formed as IMMOLATE *verb*: see -ATE[2].]

Immolated.

immolate /ˈɪmə(ʊ)leɪt/ *verb trans.* M16.

[ORIGIN Latin *immolat-* pa. ppl stem of *immolare* (orig.) sprinkle with sacrificial meal, formed as IM-[1] + *mola* meal: see -ATE[3].]

1 Offer in sacrifice; kill (a victim) in sacrifice. M16.

D. WILSON Human victims were immolated to the Thunderer. M. M. KAYE The old Rani, immolating herself in the flames that consumed the body of her husband.

2 Give up to destruction, loss, etc., for the sake of something else; sacrifice (*to*). M17.

E. BOWEN Railings.. had been immolated to a forgotten war. CLIVE JAMES In him there is no element of the self-immolating drudge.

immolation /ɪmə(ʊ)ˈleɪʃ(ə)n/ *noun*. LME.

[ORIGIN Latin *immolatio(n-)*, formed as IMMOLATE *verb*: see -ATION.]

1 Sacrificial slaughter of a victim. LME. ▸**b** A sacrificial victim. Long *rare*. L16.

2 Deliberate destruction or loss for the sake of something else. L17.

immolator /ˈɪmə(ʊ)leɪtə/ *noun*. M17.

[ORIGIN Latin, formed as IMMOLATE *verb*: see -OR.]

A person who kills a victim in sacrifice.

†**immoment** *adjective*. *rare* (Shakes.). Only in E17.

[ORIGIN from IM-[2] + MOMENT *noun*.]

Of no moment; trifling.

immomentous /ɪmə(ʊ)ˈmɛntəs/ *adjective*. *rare*. E18.

[ORIGIN from IM-[2] + MOMENTOUS.]

Not momentous; unimportant.

immoral /ɪˈmɒr(ə)l/ *adjective*. M17.

[ORIGIN from IM-[2] + MORAL *adjective*.]

Not consistent with or not conforming to accepted moral principles; *esp.* dissolute, depraved. Cf. AMORAL.

G. GREENE They form the immoral background to that extraordinary period of haphazard violence.

immoral earnings: see EARNING *noun*[1] 3.

■ **immoralism** *noun* [after German *Immoralismus*] a system of thought or behaviour which rejects accepted moral principles

E20. **immoralist** *noun* an advocate of immorality L17. **immoralize** *verb trans.* make immoral M18. **immorally** *adverb* E18.

immorality /ɪməˈralɪti/ *noun.* M16.
[ORIGIN medieval Latin *immoralitas*, formed as IM-[2] + late Latin *moralitas* MORALITY.]
1 Disregard for moral principles; immoral character or conduct; dissoluteness, depravity. M16.
2 An immoral act or practice; a vice. M17.

†immorigerous *adjective.* E17–M18.
[ORIGIN from IM-[2] + MORIGEROUS.]
Obstinate; disobedient, rebellious.

immortal /ɪˈmɔːt(ə)l/ *adjective & noun.* LME.
[ORIGIN Latin *immortalis* undying (also as noun pl., the gods), formed as IM-[2] + *mortalis* MORTAL *adjective.*]
► **A** *adjective.* **1** Not mortal; undying, living for ever. LME. ▸**b** Of or pertaining to immortal beings or immortality; divine. M16.

F. HOYLE Such 'primitive' cells are potentially immortal, dying only in adverse conditions.

2 Everlasting, eternal, unfading, imperishable; *spec.* (of fame or someone or something famous) remembered or celebrated forever. L15.

E. BOWEN Everything. . . would stay sealed up, immortal, in an inner room in his consciousness.

the Immortal Memory: see MEMORY.
► **B** *noun.* **1** An immortal being; *esp.* in *pl.*, the gods of classical antiquity. M17.
2 (**I-**.) In *pl.* The royal bodyguard of ancient Persia. E19.
3 A person of enduring fame; *spec.* (**I-**) a member of the Académie Française. L19.
■ **immortalism** *noun* (*rare*) belief in immortality L18. **immortalist** *noun* a person who believes in immortality M17. **immortally** *adverb* L15.

immortalise *verb* var. of IMMORTALIZE.

immortality /ɪmɔːˈtalɪti/ *noun.* ME.
[ORIGIN Latin *immortalitas*, formed as IMMORTAL: see -ITY.]
1 Endless life or existence; exemption from death; perpetuity. ME.
2 Enduring fame or remembrance. M16.

immortalize /ɪˈmɔːt(ə)lʌɪz/ *verb trans.* Also **-ise**. M16.
[ORIGIN from IMMORTAL *adjective* + -IZE.]
1 Make everlasting; perpetuate; confer enduring fame upon. M16.

H. T. COCKBURN A genius . . who has immortalized Edinburgh,— Walter Scott.

2 Endow with eternal life. M17.
■ **immortaliˈzation** *noun* E17. **immortalizer** *noun* E18.

immortelle /ɪmɔːˈtɛl/ *noun.* M19.
[ORIGIN French, from *fleur immortelle* everlasting flower.]
= EVERLASTING *noun* 4; esp. *Xeranthemum annuum* (see XERANTHEMUM).

immortification /ɪˌmɔːtɪfɪˈkeɪʃ(ə)n/ *noun.* E17.
[ORIGIN medieval Latin *immortificatio(n-)*, formed as IM-[2] + ecclesiastical Latin *mortificatio(n-)* MORTIFICATION.]
Lack of mortification of the soul or passions.
■ **immortified** *adjective* [repr. medieval Latin *immortificatus*] not mortified M19.

immote /ɪˈməʊt/ *adjective.* Long *rare.* E17.
[ORIGIN Latin *immotus*, formed as IM-[2] + *motus* pa. pple of *movere* MOVE *verb.*]
Unmoved.

immotile /ɪˈməʊtʌɪl/ *adjective.* L19.
[ORIGIN from IM-[2] + MOTILE.]
Not motile; incapable of movement.

immotive /ɪˈməʊtɪv/ *adjective.* E17.
[ORIGIN from IM-[2] + MOTIVE *adjective.*]
Unmoving; incapable of movement.

immovable /ɪˈmuːvəb(ə)l/ *adjective & noun.* Also (now the usual form in LAW) **-veable**. LME.
[ORIGIN from IM-[2] + MOVABLE.]
► **A** *adjective.* **1** Unable to be moved; incapable of movement; motionless, stationary. LME.

D. BREWSTER The sun stood immovable in the centre of the universe.

2 *fig.* Unalterable, fixed; (of a person) steadfast, unyielding; emotionless, impassive. LME.

H. BELLOC The young man . . lives in a static world. For him things are immovable. J. BUCHAN There was a mild and immovable fanaticism in his pale eyes.

immovable feast: see FEAST *noun.*
3 LAW. Of property: not liable to be removed, permanent (as land, buildings, etc.). LME.
► **B** *noun.* LAW. Immovable property. Usu. in *pl.* L16.
■ **immovaˈbility** *noun* LME. **immovableness** *noun* E17. **immovably** *adverb* LME.

immram /ˈɪmrɑːm/ *noun.* Also **imram**. Pl. **-a** /-ə/. L19.
[ORIGIN Old Irish *imram* (mod. *iomramh*), from *imm-rá* row around.]
Any of various stories of fabulous sea voyages written in Ireland between the late 8th and 11th cents.

immund /ɪˈmʌnd/ *adjective. rare.* E17.
[ORIGIN Latin *immundus*, formed as IM-[2] + *mundus* clean, pure.]
Dirty; impure.
■ **immundity** *noun* dirtiness; impurity: M18.

immune /ɪˈmjuːn/ *adjective & noun.* LME.
[ORIGIN Latin *immunis* exempt from a service or charge, formed as IM-[2] + *munis* ready for service.]
► **A** *adjective.* **1** Exempt; free (*from* some liability). Now only in LAW. LME.

W. S. CHURCHILL The officials pleaded that they were immune because they were acting under Government orders.

2 BIOLOGY. (Partially or wholly) invulnerable to (an) infection, poison, etc., esp. owing to the inherited or (naturally or artificially) induced presence of antibodies specific to the agent. Foll. by *against*, *from*, *to*. L19. ▸**b** Of, pertaining to, or producing immunity. E20.

b K. LANDSTEINER The immune antibodies . . react . . with the antigens that were used for immunizing. *Times* A deficiency disease of the body's immune defence system.

3 *fig.* Wholly protected (*from* something harmful or distasteful); not susceptible (*to*). L19. ▸**b** Of a computer system: protected against damage by hackers and viruses. L20.

New York Times Golden ages when these who governed . . have been immune from acts of rage and insanity. B. CHATWIN She failed to charm him: he was immune to her kind of charm.

– SPECIAL COLLOCATIONS: †**immune body** an antibody. **immune globulin** (*a*) a preparation containing antibodies, suitable for use as an antiserum; (*b*) = IMMUNOGLOBULIN. **immune response** the reaction of the body to the introduction of an antigen. **immune system** those structures and functions of an organism responsible for maintaining immunity.
► **B** *noun.* An immune person or thing. L19.

immune /ɪˈmjuːn/ *verb trans. rare.* M19.
[ORIGIN from the adjective.]
Make immune.

immunise *verb* var. of IMMUNIZE.

immunity /ɪˈmjuːnɪti/ *noun.* LME.
[ORIGIN Latin *immunitas*, formed as IMMUNE *adjective & noun*: see -ITY.]
1 LAW. Exemption *from* taxation, jurisdiction, an obligation or duty, etc.; *gen.* privilege. LME. ▸**b** An exemption or privilege; *spec.* (ECCLESIASTICAL) (an) exemption from a secular or civil liability, duty, etc. LME.
diplomatic immunity: see DIPLOMATIC *adjective.*
†**2** Undue freedom, licence. L16–L17.
3 Freedom or protection from or *from* anything harmful or distasteful; lack of susceptibility (*to*). L16.

P. ACKROYD He was offered immunity from prosecution if he would testify.

4 BIOLOGY. The ability to resist a specific infection, poison, etc., esp. owing to lymphocytes and phagocytes and (in vertebrates) antibodies. Cf. IMMUNE *adjective* 2. L19.

BETTY SMITH Vaccination was a giving of the harmless form of smallpox to work up immunity.

immunize /ˈɪmjʊnʌɪz/ *verb.* Also **-ise**. L19.
[ORIGIN from IMMUNE *adjective* + -IZE.]
1 *verb trans.* Make immune, esp. by inoculation. L19.
2 *verb intrans.* Of an antigen: produce immunity *against* an agent. M20.
■ **immuniˈzation** *noun* L19. **immunizer** *noun* E20.

immuno- /ˈɪmjʊnəʊ, ɪˈmjuːnəʊ/ *combining form* of IMMUNE *adjective*, IMMUNITY, IMMUNOLOGY: see -O-.
■ **immunoˈassay** *noun* (a) determination of the presence or quantity of a substance, esp. a protein, through its properties as an antigen M20. **immunoˈblotting** *noun* a technique for analysing or identifying proteins in a mixture, involving separation by electrophoresis followed by staining with antibodies L20. **immunoˈcompetent** *adjective* having a normal immune response M20. **immunoˈcompromised** *adjective* having an impaired immune system L20. **immunocytoˈchemistry** *noun* the cytochemistry of the immune system M20. **immunodeˈficiency** *noun* a reduction in the normal immune defences of the body M20. **immunodeˈficient** *adjective* (partly) lacking in immunity L20. **immunodeˈpressant** *adjective & noun* = IMMUNOSUPPRESSANT M20. **immunodeˈpressed** *adjective* = IMMUNOSUPPRESSED L20. **immunodeˈpression** *noun* = IMMUNOSUPPRESSION M20. **immunodeˈpressive** *adjective* = IMMUNOSUPPRESSIVE *adjective* M20. **immunodiˈffusion** *noun* a technique for detecting or measuring antibodies and antigens by their precipitation when diffused together through a gel or other medium M20. **immunofluoˈrescence** *noun* a technique for determining the location of an antigen (or antibody) in tissues by reaction with an antibody (or antigen) labelled with a fluorescent dye M20. **immunofluoˈrescent** *adjective* of, pertaining to, or involving immunofluorescence M20. **iˈmmunogen** *noun* any substance that elicits an immune response or produces immunity in the recipient E20. **immunoˈgenic** *adjective* of, pertaining to, or possessing the ability to elicit an immune response M20. **immunosuˈppressant** *adjective & noun* = IMMUNOSUPPRESSIVE M20. **immunosuˈppressed** *adjective* (of an individual) rendered incapable of an effective immune response M20. **immunosuˈppression** *noun* suppression of the immune response in an individual, esp. to prevent rejection of transplanted tissue M20. **immunosuˈppressive** *adjective & noun* (*a*) *adjective* suppressing the function of the immune system; (*b*) *noun* a drug which promotes immunosuppression: M20. **immunoˈtherapy** *noun* the prevention or treatment of disease by modification of the immune response E20.

immunochemistry /ˌɪmjʊnəʊˈkɛmɪstri, ɪˌmjuːnəʊ-/ *noun.* E20.
[ORIGIN from IMMUNO- + CHEMISTRY.]
The chemical study of immunity; biochemical study or investigation of or using immunoglobulins.
■ **immunochemical** *adjective* E20. **immunochemically** *adverb* M20. **immunochemist** *noun* an expert in or student of immunochemistry M20.

immunoelectrophoresis /ˌɪmjʊnəʊɪˌlɛktrəfəˈriːsɪs, ɪˌmjuːnəʊ-/ *noun.* M20.
[ORIGIN from IMMUNO- + ELECTROPHORESIS.]
A technique for identification of proteins in a mixture (as serum) by electrophoresis and subsequent immunodiffusion.
■ **immunoelectrophoretic** *adjective* M20. **immunoelectrophoretically** *adverb* M20.

immunogenetics /ˌɪmjʊnəʊdʒɪˈnɛtɪks, ɪˌmjuːnəʊ-/ *noun.* M20.
[ORIGIN from IMMUNO- + GENETICS.]
Genetics studied by means of immunological techniques; the branch of medicine that deals with the genetic aspects of immunity.
■ **immunogenetic** *adjective* of or pertaining to immunogenetics M20. **immunogenetically** *adverb* L20.

immunoglobulin /ˌɪmjʊnəʊˈglɒbjʊlɪn, ɪˌmjuːnəʊ-/ *noun.* M20.
[ORIGIN from IMMUNO- + GLOBULIN.]
BIOCHEMISTRY & MEDICINE. Any of a group of proteins present in vertebrates in the serum and cells of the immune system, which have a characteristic arrangement of subunits in their molecular structure, and function as antibodies.

immunology /ɪmjʊˈnɒlədʒi/ *noun.* E20.
[ORIGIN from IMMUN(ITY + -OLOGY.]
The branch of science which studies resistance to infection in humans and animals.
■ **immunoˈlogic**, **immunoˈlogical** *adjectives* of or pertaining to immunology or immunity E20. **immunoˈlogically** *adverb* E20. **immunologist** *noun* E20.

immure /ɪˈmjʊə/ *verb & noun.* L16.
[ORIGIN French *emmurer* or medieval Latin *immurare*, formed as IM-[1] + *murus* wall.]
► **A** *verb trans.* †**1** Surround with a wall or walls; fortify. L16–M18.
2 Enclose within walls; confine (as) in a prison; *fig.* enclose, surround, confine. L16.

I. MURDOCH Otto was still immured in the summer-house. K. LINES You shall be immured in a vault . . until you are released by death. JO GRIMOND The increasing volume of legislation which keeps Members . . immured together and isolated from the world.

3 Build into or entomb in a wall. L17.

G. G. SCOTT The end of the tomb has been immured in the lower part of the chapel.

► †**B** *noun.* A wall. *rare* (Shakes.). Only in E17.
■ **immuˈration** *noun* imprisonment, confinement L19. **immurement** *noun* = IMMURATION M18.

immusical /ɪˈmjuːzɪk(ə)l/ *adjective.* Now *rare.* E17.
[ORIGIN from IM-[2] + MUSICAL *adjective.*]
Unmusical.

immutable /ɪˈmjuːtəb(ə)l/ *adjective.* LME.
[ORIGIN Latin *immutabilis*, formed as IM-[2] + *mutabilis* MUTABLE.]
1 Not mutable; not subject or liable to change; unalterable. LME.

P. USTINOV Those for whom the . . law is immutable, instead of being as changeable as the seasons.

2 Not varying in different cases; invariable. E17.
■ **immutaˈbility** *noun* L15. **immutably** *adverb* E17.

immy /ˈɪmi/ *noun.* Also **immie**. M20.
[ORIGIN Prob. from IMITATION: see -Y[6].]
A kind of glass marble made to imitate one of another material.

IMO *abbreviation.*
International Maritime Organization.

i-mode /ˈʌɪməʊd/ *noun.* E21.
[ORIGIN from I *pronoun* + MODE *noun.*]
A technology that allows data to be transferred to and from Internet sites via mobile phones.

imp /ɪmp/ *noun.* OE.
[ORIGIN Rel. to IMP *verb.*]
1 A young shoot of a plant; a sapling; a sucker, a scion. *obsolete* exc. *Scot.* OE. ▸†**b** A young person; a youth, a boy. LME–L19.
†**2** A shoot or slip used in grafting; a graft. LME–E18.
3 A scion or descendant, esp. of a noble family; an offspring, a child. *arch.* LME. ▸**b** A follower, an adherent, esp. of glory, chivalry, etc. *arch.* LME.
4 A (person regarded as a) child of the Devil; a little devil. E16. ▸**b** A mischievous child. M17.
LINCOLN imp.

5 A piece added on to eke out or enlarge something. *obsolete* exc. *dial.* L16.

imp /ɪmp/ *verb trans.*
[ORIGIN Old English *impian* corresp. to Old High German *impfōn* (German *impfen*), shortened analogues of *impitōn* (Middle High German *impfeten*), from Proto-Romance, from medieval Latin *impotus* graft, from Greek *emphutos* implanted, engrafted, verbal adjective of *emphuein*, from *en-* IM-¹ + *phuein* plant.]
†**1** Graft, engraft. OE–M18.
2 *fig.* Implant, set or fix in. *arch.* ME.
3 FALCONRY. †**a** Add (feathers) to the wing of a bird to improve the power of flight. Also foll. by *in*. L15–E18. ▸**b** Add feathers to (the wing of a bird) to improve the power of flight. Also foll. by *with*. L16.
b imp the wings of strengthen or improve the flight or power of.
4 Enlarge, add to, (as) by grafting. *arch.* L16.

impack /ɪm'pak/ *verb trans. rare.* L16.
[ORIGIN Anglo-Latin *impaccare* pack, formed as IM-¹ + *paccare* pack wool etc.: see PACK *verb*¹.]
Pack (up); press together into a mass.

impact /'ɪmpakt/ *noun.* L18.
[ORIGIN from Latin *impact-* pa. ppl stem of *impingere* IMPINGE.]
1 The striking of one body on or against another; a collision. L18.

A. TREW The impact was softened by the sand. *Manchester Evening News* The car . . careered . . into the path of the wagon. She was killed on impact.

2 The (strong) effect of one thing, person, action, etc., on another; an influence; an impression. E19.

L. WOOLF To describe the impact of illness or insanity upon such a remarkable mind. *Independent on Sunday* The prospect of German monetary union has already had a dramatic impact on financial markets.

– COMB.: **impact crater** a crater or hollow supposedly produced by the impact of a meteorite; **impact printer**: that depends on mechanical pressure to transfer ink from a ribbon to the paper; **impact strength** the ability of a material to resist breaking when struck; **impact test** any of various tests which measure an object's resistance to breaking under sudden stress, usu. by applying a blow; **impact wrench** an electric or pneumatic power wrench used for inserting and removing nuts, bolts, screws, etc.
■ **impactful** *adjective* having a major impact or effect M20.

impact /ɪm'pakt/ *verb.* E17.
[ORIGIN Partly from Latin *impactus* pa. pple of *impingere* IMPINGE, partly back-form. from IMPACTED.]
1 *verb trans.* Press closely or fix firmly (*in, into*). E17.
2 *verb trans.* Stamp or impress *on*. *rare.* L17.
3 *verb intrans.* Come forcibly into contact with a (larger) body or surface. (Foll. by *against, on*, etc.) E20. ▸**b** Have a pronounced effect *on*. E20.

b *Independent* A treatment aimed at impacting on the disease itself rather than the symptoms.

4 *verb trans.* Cause to impinge *on, against*, etc. M20.

impacted /ɪm'paktɪd/ *adjective.* E17.
[ORIGIN from Latin *impactus* (see IMPACT *verb*) + -ED¹.]
1 Pressed closely in, firmly fixed. E17. ▸**b** MEDICINE. Of faeces: wedged in the intestine. Of the intestine: blocked by hardened faeces. M19. ▸**c** MEDICINE. Of a bone fracture: having the broken parts driven firmly together. M19. ▸**d** Of a tooth: prevented from erupting by bone or another tooth. L19.

d *Practical Health* The shock of having impacted wisdom teeth removed.

2 That has been struck by an impacting body; (of an impacting body) that has struck something. E20.
3 *fig.* Of an area: overcrowded, esp. so as to put severe pressure on public services etc. *US.* M20.

impaction /ɪm'pakʃ(ə)n/ *noun.* M18.
[ORIGIN from IMPACT *verb* + -ION.]
1 The action of becoming or condition of being impacted. M18.
2 *spec.* in MEDICINE. The lodging of a mass of (usu. hardened) faeces in the intestine so that defecation is prevented or impeded; the obstruction so caused. M19. ▸**b** An impacted mass of faeces. E20.
3 The action or process of causing a body to impact on a surface etc. M20.

impactite /ɪm'paktʌɪt/ *noun.* M20.
[ORIGIN from IMPACT *noun* + -ITE¹, after TEKTITE.]
GEOLOGY. Any piece of glassy material formed in or around a meteorite crater by the heat of impact.

impactive /ɪm'paktɪv/ *adjective.* M20.
[ORIGIN from IMPACT *noun* + -IVE.]
Of, pertaining to, or characterized by impact; having an impact.

impactor /ɪm'paktə/ *noun.* E20.
[ORIGIN from IMPACT *verb* + -OR.]
1 A device etc. that delivers impacts or blows. E20.
2 An impinger, *esp.* one in which particles are deposited on a dry surface rather than in a liquid. M20.

impaint /ɪm'peɪnt/ *verb trans.* Long *rare.* L16.
[ORIGIN from IM-¹ + PAINT *verb*.]
Depict by painting on something.

impair /ɪm'pɛː/ *noun*¹. *arch.* M16.
[ORIGIN from IMPAIR *verb*.]
An act of impairing; the fact of being impaired; impairment.

impair /'ɪmpɛː; *in senses A.3, B.1 foreign* ɛ̃pɛr (*pl. same*)/ *adjective & noun*². E17.
[ORIGIN French = unequal, formed as IM-² + PAIR *noun*² & *adjective*.]
▸ **A** *adjective.* †**1** Unfit, inferior. *rare* (Shakes.). Only in E17.
2 Not paired; not forming one of a pair. M19.
3 ROULETTE. Of or pertaining to an odd number or the odd numbers collectively. M20.
▸ **B** *noun.* **1** ROULETTE. An odd number; the odd numbers collectively. M19.
2 An unpaired individual thing; an odd one. *rare.* L19.

impair /ɪm'pɛː/ *verb.* Orig. †**app-**; also †**em-**. ME.
[ORIGIN Old French *empeirier* from Proto-Romance, formed as IM-¹ + late Latin *pejorare*, from Latin *pejor* worse.]
1 *verb trans.* Make less effective or weaker; devalue; damage, injure. ME.

A. BURGESS Being toothless did not impair one's capacity to eat army food. *Which?* Corneal ulcers . . can permanently impair vision.

2 *verb intrans.* Become less effective or weaker; deteriorate; suffer injury or loss. Now *rare* or *obsolete*. ME.

SOUTHEY His own health and faculties impairing day by day.

■ **impairer** *noun* L16. **impairment** *noun* the action of impairing, the fact of being impaired ME.

impaired /ɪm'pɛːd/ *ppl adjective.* E17.
[ORIGIN from IMPAIR *verb* + -ED¹.]
1 *gen.* That has been impaired. E17.

F. SPALDING An attack of rheumatic fever . . left his health permanently impaired. J. GATHORNE-HARDY They become anxious, their performance impaired.

2 Of the driver of a vehicle, or driving: adversely affected by alcohol or narcotics. *Canad.* M20.

Toronto Daily Star Ange Gardien . . was charged with impaired driving.

impala /ɪm'pɑːlə, -'palə/ *noun.* Also **-lla**. L19.
[ORIGIN Zulu *i-mpala*: cf. PALLAH.]
A medium-sized reddish-brown grazing antelope, *Aepyceros melampus*, of southern and eastern African savannah, the male of which has lyre-shaped horns.

impalace /ɪm'palɪs/ *verb trans. arch.* L18.
[ORIGIN from IM-¹ + PALACE.]
Place or install in a palace. Usu. in *pass.*

impale /ɪm'peɪl/ *verb trans.* Also **em-** /ɪm-, ɛm-/. M16.
[ORIGIN French *empaler* or medieval Latin *impalare*, formed as IM-¹ + *palus* stake, PALE *noun*¹.]
1 Enclose with pales, stakes, etc.; surround (as) with a palisade; fence in (*lit. & fig.*). Now *rare.* M16. ▸†**b** MILITARY. Enclose or surround (troops) for defence. M16–M17.

T. HOOD So he might impale a strip of soil.

2 Surround for adornment; encircle as with a crown or garland; border, edge. *arch.* M16.

LYTTON All the laurels that ever with praise Impaled human brows.

3 HERALDRY. Combine (two coats of arms, or one coat *with* another) by placing them side by side on one shield, separated by a vertical line down the middle. E17.

T. H. WHITE It was charged with the impaled arms of her husband and of her father.

4 Transfix (a body etc. *on* or *with* a stake etc.), esp. (*hist.*) as a form of torture or capital punishment. E17.

R. GRAVES He would hang or impale any man found guilty of rape. B. COTTLE The cruel shrike . . impales his little victims on thorns. *fig.*: P. ACKROYD Impaled upon his own lacerating self-consciousness he has fantasies of suicide.

■ **impaler** *noun* L17. **impaling** *noun* (*a*) the action of the verb; (*b*) = IMPALEMENT 2: L16.

impalement /ɪm'peɪlm(ə)nt/ *noun.* Also **em-** /ɪm-, ɛm-/. L16.
[ORIGIN French *empalement*, from *empaler*: see IMPALE, -MENT. Later from the verb.]
1 The action or an act of enclosing with pales, stakes, etc.; an enclosing fence or palisade. L16.
2 HERALDRY. The combining of two coats of arms placed side by side on one shield and separated by a vertical line down the middle; the arms so combined. E17.
3 The action or an act of transfixing a body etc. on, *on*, or *with* a stake etc., esp. (*hist.*) as a form of torture or capital punishment; the fact of being so impaled. M17.
†**4** BOTANY. The calyx of a flower; (in a plant of the composite family) the involucre. L17–L18.

impall /ɪm'pɔːl/ *verb trans. rare.* M17.
[ORIGIN from IM-¹ + PALL *noun*¹.]
Enfold or wrap (as) in a pall.

impalla *noun* var. of IMPALA.

impalpable /ɪm'palpəb(ə)l/ *adjective.* E16.
[ORIGIN French, or late Latin *impalpabilis*, formed as IM-² + PALPABLE.]
1 Imperceptible to the touch; intangible; *esp.* (of powder) very fine, not containing grains that can be felt. E16.
2 Not easily grasped or understood by the mind; producing no definite mental impression. L18.

H. STURGIS Sainty was aware of the slightest, most impalpable change in his friend's manner.

■ **impalpa'bility** *noun* E17. **impalpably** *adverb* L18.

impalsy /ɪm'pɔːlzi, -'pɒl-/ *verb trans. rare.* L16.
[ORIGIN from IM-¹ + PALSY *noun*¹.]
Affect (as) with palsy; paralyse.

impanate /ɪm'peɪnət/ *adjective.* M16.
[ORIGIN medieval Latin *impanatus* pa. pple of *impanare*, formed as IM-¹ + *panis* bread: see -ATE².]
CHRISTIAN CHURCH. Of the body and blood of Christ: present in the bread (and wine) after consecration.

impanated /ɪm'peɪnətɪd/ *adjective.* Long *rare.* L16.
[ORIGIN from medieval Latin *impanat-* (see IMPANATION) + -ED¹.]
= IMPANATE.

impanation /ɪmpə'neɪʃ(ə)n/ *noun.* M16.
[ORIGIN medieval Latin *impanatio(n-)*, from *impanat-* pa. ppl stem of *impanare*: see IMPANATE, -ATION.]
CHRISTIAN CHURCH. In Eucharistic doctrine: the presence of the body and blood of Christ in the bread (and wine) after consecration.

impanator /'ɪmpəneɪtə/ *noun.* M19.
[ORIGIN medieval Latin, formed as IMPANATION: see -OR, -ATOR.]
CHRISTIAN CHURCH. A person who holds the doctrine of impanation.

impanel /ɪm'pan(ə)l/ *verb*¹ *trans. rare.* Infl. **-ll-**, ***-l-**. L16.
[ORIGIN from IM-¹ + PANEL *noun*¹.]
1 Fit (as) with a panel or panels. L16.
2 Insert as a panel or panels. M19.

impanel *verb*² & *noun* var. of EMPANEL.

imparadise /ɪm'parədʌɪs/ *verb trans.* Also **em-** /ɪm-, ɛm-/. L16.
[ORIGIN from IM-¹, EM-¹ + PARADISE. Cf. French *emparadiser*, Italian *imparadisare*.]
1 Place (as) in paradise; bring into a state of supreme happiness; enrapture. L16.
2 Make a paradise of (a state or place). M17.

†**impardonable** *adjective.* E16–L18.
[ORIGIN from IM-² + PARDONABLE.]
Not to be pardoned, unpardonable.

imparipinnate /ɪm,parɪ'pɪnət/ *adjective.* M19.
[ORIGIN from Latin *impar* uneven after PARIPINNATE.]
BOTANY. Pinnate with a terminal leaflet and an odd number of leaflets in all.

imparisyllabic /ɪm,parɪsɪ'labɪk/ *adjective & noun.* M18.
[ORIGIN from Latin *impar* unequal after PARISYLLABIC.]
GRAMMAR. ▸**A** *adjective.* Of a Greek or Latin noun: not having the same number of syllables in all cases of the singular. M18.
▸ **B** *noun.* An imparisyllabic noun. L19.

imparity /ɪm'parɪti/ *noun.* Now *rare* or *obsolete*. M16.
[ORIGIN Late Latin *imparitas*, from Latin *impar* unequal, uneven, formed as IM-² + *par* equal. Cf. PARITY *noun*¹.]
1 The quality or condition of being unequal: inequality. M16.
†**2** The quality of being unlike; dissimilarity in nature or character. Only in 17.
†**3** The quality, in a whole number, of not being divisible into two equal integral parts; an odd number. Only in M17.

impark /ɪm'pɑːk/ *verb trans.* LME.
[ORIGIN Anglo-Norman *enparker*, Old French *emparquer* (Anglo-Latin *imparcare*), formed as EM-¹, IM-¹ + *parc* PARK *noun*.]
1 Enclose (animals) in a park. LME.
2 Enclose (land) for a park; fence in. LME.

imparl /ɪm'pɑːl/ *verb. obsolete* exc. *hist.* Also †**em-**. LME.
[ORIGIN Anglo-Norman *enparler*, Old French *emparler* speak, plead, formed as EM-¹, IM-¹ + *parler* speak: see PARLE.]
1 *verb intrans.* LAW. (Obtain time to) confer in order to settle a dispute amicably. LME.
†**2** *verb intrans.* Consult *together* or *with* another on a matter; confer. LME–E17.
†**3** *verb trans.* Talk over; discuss. *rare.* E17–E19.

imparlance /ɪm'pɑːləns/ *noun. obsolete* exc. *hist.* Also †**em-**. L16.
[ORIGIN Old French *emparlance*, from *emparler*: see IMPARL, -ANCE.]
†**1** The action of consulting together on a matter, esp. before taking action; conference, discussion. L16–E19.
2 LAW. An extension of the time allowed for a response in pleading a case, so that the two parties can confer and negotiate an amicable settlement; a petition for, or the granting of, this time. E17.

imparsonee /ɪm,pɑːsə'niː/ *adjective.* E17.
[ORIGIN Repr. medieval Latin (*persona*) *impersonata*, from Latin *im-* IN-² + Anglo-Latin *personata* fem. pa. pple of *personare* indict, institute, from Latin *persona*: see PARSON, PERSON *noun*, -EE¹.]

I

ECCLESIASTICAL HISTORY. Presented, instituted, and inducted into a parsonage or rectory. Only in ***parson imparsonee***.

impart /ɪmˈpɑːt/ *verb*. LME.
[ORIGIN Old French *impartir* from Latin *impartire*, formed as IM-¹ + *part-*, *pars* PART *noun*.]
1 *verb trans.* Give a part or share of (a thing *to* a person etc.); bestow, give. LME.

J. GALSWORTHY The moustache . . imparted a somewhat military look to his face. R. C. HUTCHINSON A particular countryside imparts a special character to the men it breeds.

†**2** *verb intrans.* Share, partake *in*. L15–E17. ▸**b** *verb trans.* Have or get a share of; share, partake. (Foll. by *of*.) M16–M17.
3 *verb trans.* Communicate (information, news, etc., *to*); tell, relate, (a story, an account, etc.). M16.

J. AGATE The first object in writing is to impart information.

†**4** *verb trans.* Give a share of (something) to each of a number of people; distribute. M16–E17.
■ **impartable** *adjective* (long *rare*) LME. **imparˈtation** *noun* the action of imparting, impartment, communication E19. **imparter** *noun* L16. **impartment** *noun* the action or fact of imparting; something imparted, *esp.* a communication: E17.

impartial /ɪmˈpɑːʃ(ə)l/ *adjective*. L16.
[ORIGIN from IM-² + PARTIAL *adjective*.]
1 Not partial; not favouring one party or side more than another; unprejudiced, unbiased; fair. L16.

J. G. FARRELL An impartial and objective justice was abandoned. P. NORMAN Mrs Durham made no distinction, treating Anthony and him with impartial severity.

†**2** Partial. L16–E17.
†**3** Not partial or fragmentary; entire, complete. *rare*. Only in E18.
■ **impartialist** *noun* a person who is or professes to be impartial M17. **impartially** *adverb* E17.

impartiality /ɪm,pɑːʃɪˈalɪti/ *noun*. E17.
[ORIGIN from IMPARTIAL + -ITY.]
1 The quality or character of being impartial; freedom from prejudice or bias; fairness. E17.
†**2** Completeness. *rare*. Only in E18.

impartible /ɪmˈpɑːtɪb(ə)l/ *adjective & noun*. L16.
[ORIGIN Late Latin *impartibilis*, formed as IM-² + *partibilis* PARTIBLE.]
▸ **A** *adjective*. Incapable of being divided or parted; indivisible L16.
▸ **B** *noun*. A thing that is indivisible. L18.
■ **impartiˈbility** *noun* M17. **impartibly** *adverb* M17.

imparticipable /ɪmpɑːˈtɪsɪpəb(ə)l/ *adjective & noun*. L18.
[ORIGIN from IM-² + PARTICIPABLE.]
(A thing that is) unable to be shared or participated in.

impartite /ɪmˈpɑːtʌɪt/ *adjective*. *rare*. M19.
[ORIGIN from IM-² + PARTITE.]
Not divided into parts, undivided.

impassable /ɪmˈpɑːsəb(ə)l/ *adjective*. M16.
[ORIGIN from IM-² + PASSABLE, perh. through French *impassable*.]
1 Impossible to traverse or travel through. M16.

M. KEANE Now, most of the paths were choked and impassable.

†**2** That cannot pass (away or through). L18–M19.

Examiner As impassable through Heaven's gates, as is a camel through the needle's eye.

3 Unable to be passed or made to pass. *rare*. M19.

Pall Mall Gazette When half a million gilt sixpences in circulation make half-sovereigns practically impassable.

■ **impassaˈbility** *noun* L18. **impassableness** *noun* E18. **impassably** *adverb* E19.

impasse /amˈpɑːs, ˈampɑːs, *foreign* ɛ̃pɑːs/ *noun*. M19.
[ORIGIN French, formed as IM-² + stem of *passer* PASS *verb*.]
1 A position from which there is no escape, a deadlock. M19.

F. ASTAIRE I find myself blocked by a sort of mental impasse. E. M. BRENT-DYER Margot . . scribbled in the details . . thankful to be out of the impasse so easily.

2 *lit.* A road etc. without an outlet, a blind alley. L19.

impassible /ɪmˈpasɪb(ə)l/ *adjective*. ME.
[ORIGIN Old French & mod. French from ecclesiastical Latin *impassibilis*, formed as IM-² + PASSIBLE.]
1 Chiefly THEOLOGY. Incapable of suffering or feeling pain. ME.
2 Incapable of suffering injury or damage. L15.
†**3** Not to be endured; insufferable. E16–M17.
4 Incapable of feeling or emotion. L16.
■ **impassiˈbility** *noun* ME. **impassibleness** *noun* M17. **impassibly** *adverb* L17.

impassion /ɪmˈpaʃ(ə)n/ *verb trans.* Also †**em-**. L16.
[ORIGIN Italian †*impassionare* (now *-nn-*), formed as IM-¹ + *passione* PASSION *noun*.]
Fill with passion; arouse the feelings of; excite.
■ **impassionment** *noun* (*rare*) the action of impassioning; the state of being impassioned: L16.

impassionate /ɪmˈpaʃ(ə)nət/ *adjective*¹. Now *rare*. L16.
[ORIGIN Italian †*impassionato* pa. pple of †*impassionare*: see IMPASSION, -ATE².]
= IMPASSIONED.
■ **impassionately** *adverb* E19.

impassionate /ɪmˈpaʃ(ə)nət/ *adjective*². Now *rare*. E17.
[ORIGIN from IM-² + PASSIONATE *adjective*.]
Free from passion; calm, dispassionate.

impassionate /ɪmˈpaʃ(ə)neɪt/ *verb*. Now *rare* or *obsolete*. L16.
[ORIGIN from IMPASSIONATE *adjective*¹: see -ATE³.]
1 *verb trans.* = IMPASSION. L16.
†**2** *verb intrans.* Be or become impassioned. Only in M17.

impassioned /ɪmˈpaʃ(ə)nd/ *adjective*. Also †**em-**. E17.
[ORIGIN from IMPASSION + -ED¹.]
Filled with passion; deeply moved or excited; passionate, ardent.

M. BARING An ardent naturalist and an impassioned bird's egg collector. P. GAY Erikson's book . . generated some impassioned debates.

■ **impassionedly** *adverb* M19. **impassionedness** *noun* L19.

impassive /ɪmˈpasɪv/ *adjective*. E17.
[ORIGIN from IM-² + PASSIVE *adjective*.]
1 Not subject or liable to suffering. E17.

J. WESLEY He was impassive, incapable of suffering.

2 Without sensation; impervious to injury; invulnerable. L17. ▸**b** Deprived of sensation; unconscious. M19.

POPE On the impassive Ice the light'nings play. **b** DICKENS The two medical students seemed to look on the impassive form with . . so little hope.

3 Unmoved by or not displaying emotion; calm. L17.

F. POHL Knefhausen kept his face impassive, although his heart was filled with glee. S. HAZZARD Nicholas Cartledge was impassive, neither patient nor impatient.

■ **impassively** *adverb* E19. **impassiveness** *noun* M17. **impaˈssivity** *noun* L18.

impaste /ɪmˈpeɪst/ *verb trans.* M16.
[ORIGIN Italian *impastare*, from *im-* IM-¹ + *pasta* PASTE *noun*.]
1 Enclose in or encrust (as) with a paste. M16.
2 Make or form into a paste or crust. L16.
3 Paint by laying colour on thickly. E18.

impasto /ɪmˈpastəʊ/ *noun*. L18.
[ORIGIN Italian, formed as IMPASTE.]
1 The action of painting by laying colour on thickly; this manner of painting. L18.
2 CERAMICS. Enamel etc. colours standing out in relief on a surface. E20.

impatience /ɪmˈpeɪʃ(ə)ns/ *noun*. LME.
[ORIGIN Old French & mod. French from Latin *impatientia*, formed as IM-² + PATIENCE *noun*.]
1 Failure to bear suffering, annoyance, etc., with equanimity; irascibility; intolerance *of*. Also foll. by *at*, *with*. LME.
2 Intolerance of delay; restless longing or eagerness (*for*, *to do*). L16.

M. KEANE His good manners hardly hid his impatience to be alone.

impatiency /ɪmˈpeɪʃ(ə)nsi/ *noun*. Now *rare* or *obsolete*. M16.
[ORIGIN Latin *impatientia*: see IMPATIENCE, -ENCY.]
The quality or condition of being impatient; impatience; an instance of this.

impatiens /ɪmˈpatɪɛnz/ *noun*. Pl. same. L18.
[ORIGIN mod. Latin (see below) from Latin = IMPATIENT, with ref. to the readiness of the capsules to burst open when touched.]
Any plant of the genus *Impatiens* (family Balsaminaceae), the members of which bear irregular spurred usu. showy flowers and include the garden balsam, *I. balsamina*, and the busy Lizzie, *I. walleriana*. Also called ***balsam***, ***touch-me-not***.

impatient /ɪmˈpeɪʃ(ə)nt/ *adjective & noun*. LME.
[ORIGIN Old French & mod. French from Latin *impatient-*, *-ens*, formed as IM-² + PATIENT *adjective*.]
▸ **A** *adjective*. †**1** Intolerable, unbearable. LME–M17.
2 Lacking patience; irritable, intolerant, easily provoked. LME. ▸**b** Unable or unwilling to endure or put up with something; intolerant *of*. Also foll. by *at*, *with*. L15.

SHAKES. *Mids. N. D.* Will you tear Impatient answers from my gentle tongue? C. G. WOLFF She certainly perceived her mother as remote, disapproving, impatient and unloving. **b** U. S. GRANT They were growing impatient at lying idle so long. L. GORDON He was impatient of the kind of research that seemed incapable of fruitful conclusions.

3 Unwilling to endure delay; in a hurry *for*, *to do*. L16.

JANET MORGAN He was impatient for more authority.

4 Characterized by or expressive of impatience. E18.

M. SHADBOLT There was an impatient knock on the glass . . : someone else was waiting.

▸ **B** *noun*. An impatient person. E16.
■ **impatiently** *adverb* LME. **impatientness** *noun* (long *rare* or *obsolete*) M16.

†**impatronize** *verb*. Also **-ise**. L16.
[ORIGIN French *impatroniser* alt. of Old French *empatroner*, *-ir*, from or after Italian *impatronire*, *impadronire*, formed as IM-¹ + Old French & mod. French *patron*, Italian *padrone* PATRON *noun*: see -IZE.]
1 *verb trans.* Put (oneself, another) in possession *of*. L16–L17.
2 *verb trans.* Take possession of. E17–L18.
■ †**impatronization** *noun* the action or an act of putting in possession *of* or taking possession of; mastery, possession: E17–M19.

impave /ɪmˈpeɪv/ *verb trans.* *rare*. M17.
[ORIGIN from IM-¹ + PAVE *verb*.]
Set in a pavement, pave.

impavid /ɪmˈpavɪd/ *adjective*. *rare*. M19.
[ORIGIN Latin *impavidus*, formed as IM-², PAVID.]
Unafraid, undaunted.

impawn /ɪmˈpɔːn/ *verb trans.* L16.
[ORIGIN from IM-¹ + PAWN *noun*³ & *verb*.]
1 Put in pawn, pledge as security; pawn. L16.

SHAKES. *1 Hen. IV* Let there be impawn'd Some surety for a safe return again. J. WEST She offered to impawn the family jewels.

2 Pledge (*lit.* & *fig.*). E17.

impayable /ɪmˈpeɪəb(ə)l; *in sense 3 foreign* ɛ̃pɛjabl/ *adjective*. ME.
[ORIGIN French, formed as IM-² + *payer* PAY *verb*¹: see -ABLE.]
†**1** Implacable, unappeasable. Only in ME.
2 Impossible to pay or discharge. L18.
3 Priceless, invaluable; extraordinary, absurd. E19.

G. ALLEN I shrieked with laughter, 'Elsie,' I cried . . . 'you are *impayable*'.

impeach /ɪmˈpiːtʃ/ *noun*. Also †**em-**. M16.
[ORIGIN from the verb.]
†**1** Hindrance, impediment, prevention. M16–E17.
†**2** Injury, damage, detriment. L16–E17.
3 Calling in question; (an) accusation. L16.

impeach /ɪmˈpiːtʃ/ *verb*. Also †**em-**. LME.
[ORIGIN Old French *empe(s)cher* (mod. *empêcher* prevent) from late Latin *impedicare* catch, entangle, formed as IM-¹ + *pedica* FETTER *noun*.]
†**1** *verb trans.* Impede, hinder, prevent. LME–L17. ▸**b** Prevent access to, blockade. LME–L16. ▸**c** Embarrass or trouble *oneself*. L15–M16.
†**2** *verb trans.* Affect detrimentally; hurt, damage, impair. LME–L17.
3 *verb trans.* Challenge, call in question; disparage. LME.

A. K. GREEN My daughter's happiness is threatened and her character impeached.

4 *verb trans.* Make an accusation against (a person); accuse *of*, charge *with*. LME. ▸**b** Give evidence against (esp. an accomplice); inform against. E17. ▸**c** Find fault with (a thing). E19.

W. GODWIN Go to the next justice of the peace and impeach us. **b** W. WYCHERLEY Because you know your self most guilty, you impeach your Fellow Criminals first.

5 *verb trans.* Accuse of treason or other high crime (esp. against the state) before a competent tribunal. LME.

H. COX Latimer was impeached and accused by the voice of the Commons. P. F. BOLLER The only President ever to be impeached, he behaved with dignity . . during the . . trial.

■ **impeachable** *adjective* able to be impeached; liable to accusation or charge: LME. **impeacher** *noun* M16.

impeachment /ɪmˈpiːtʃm(ə)nt/ *noun*. Also †**em-**. LME.
[ORIGIN Old French *empe(s)chement* (mod. *empêchement*), formed as IMPEACH *verb* + -MENT.]
†**1** Hindrance, prevention, obstruction. LME–L17.
2 Challenge, calling in question; disparagement, deprecation. LME.
3 **a** An accusation, a charge. Now *obsolete* exc. (with ref. to Sheridan's *The Rivals*) in ***the soft impeachment***. LME. ▸**b** LAW. ***impeachment of waste***, the liability of a tenant to make compensation for any damage to the rented property. LME. ▸**c** The accusation and prosecution of a person for treason or other high crime (esp. against the state) before a competent tribunal. M17.
†**4** Detriment, impairment, injury, damage. M16–M17.

impearl /ɪmˈpɔːl/ *verb trans.* *poet.* Also **em-** /ɪm-, ɛm-/. L16.
[ORIGIN French *emperler* or Italian *impelare*, formed as EM-¹, IM-¹ + PEARL *noun*¹.]
1 Deck with pearls or pearl-like drops. L16.
2 Form into pearl-like drops. L16.

MILTON Dew-drops, which the Sun Impearls on every leaf and every flouer.

3 Make pearly or pearl-like. M17.

impeccable /ɪmˈpɛkəb(ə)l/ *adjective & noun*. M16.
[ORIGIN Latin *impeccabilis*, formed as IM-² + *peccare* to sin: see -ABLE.]
▸ **A** *adjective*. **1** Incapable of sin or error. M16.

H. LATIMER Though she never sinned, yet she was not so impeccable, but she might have sinned. A. SILLITOE It wouldn't do for the old folks to see him less than impeccable.

2 Faultless, unblemished; unerring. E17.

I. MURDOCH She had observed an impeccable discretion . . , so that hardly anyone knew her for a sympathizer. A. J. P. TAYLOR Thompson, a man of impeccable orthodoxy, had been appointed Dean of Divinity.

▸ **B** *noun*. An impeccable person. M18.
■ **impeccaˈbility** *noun* E17. **impeccableness** *noun* L17. **impeccably** *adverb* L19.

impeccancy /ɪmˈpɛk(ə)nsi/ *noun*. **E17.**
[**ORIGIN** ecclesiastical Latin *impeccantia*, formed as **IM-**² + *peccantia* **PECCANCY**.]
The quality of being without sin or error.

impeccant /ɪmˈpɛk(ə)nt/ *adjective*. **M18.**
[**ORIGIN** from **IM-**² + Latin *peccare* to sin + **-ANT**¹, or from earlier **PECCANT**.]
Without sin or error; blameless.

impecuniary /ɪmpɪˈkjuːnɪəri/ *adjective*. **E19.**
[**ORIGIN** from **IM-**² + **PECUNIARY**.]
1 = **IMPECUNIOUS**. **E19.**
2 Not having to do with money. **M19.**

impecunious /ɪmpɪˈkjuːnɪəs/ *adjective*. **L16.**
[**ORIGIN** from **IM-**² + **PECUNIOUS**.]
In need of money; poor, penniless.

E. JOHNSON An impecunious youth making a precarious living.

■ **impecuniˈosity** *noun* lack of money, poverty **E19.** **impecuniousness** *noun* **L20.**

impedance /ɪmˈpiːd(ə)ns/ *noun*. **L19.**
[**ORIGIN** from **IMPEDE** *verb* + **-ANCE**.]
1 *ELECTRICITY*. The combined opposition to the passage of an (alternating) electric current exerted by the resistance (R) and the reactance (X), measured as the ratio of the electromotive force to the resulting current, and representable as $Z = \sqrt{(R^2 + X^2)}$ or as a complex number $R + jX$. **L19.**
2 *MECHANICS & ACOUSTICS*. Any of several analogous properties of oscillatory mechanical systems that represent the force, pressure, etc., necessary to produce a given speed, rate of flow, etc. **E20.**
acoustic impedance the ratio of the pressure over an imaginary surface in a sound wave to the rate of flow across it. **mechanical impedance** the ratio of the force in the direction of motion to the velocity of the vibration. **specific acoustic impedance** the ratio of the pressure at any point in a sound wave to the resulting particle velocity.

impede /ɪmˈpiːd/ *verb trans*. **L16.**
[**ORIGIN** Latin *impedire* lit. 'shackle the feet', formed as **IM-**¹ + *ped-*, *pes* foot.]
Stand in the way of; obstruct, hinder.

W. GERHARDIE Our progress had been impeded by a car that blocked the road. A. S. NEILL He is holding back the work, and they may throw him out for impeding progress.

impedient /ɪmˈpiːdɪənt/ *adjective*. **LME.**
[**ORIGIN** from **IMPEDE** *verb* + **-ENT**, after **EXPEDIENT** *adjective*.]
That impedes or hinders; obstructive.

impediment /ɪmˈpɛdɪm(ə)nt/ *noun*. **LME.**
[**ORIGIN** Latin *impedimentum* hindrance, pl. *-menta* baggage, from *impedire* **IMPEDE**: see **-I-**, **-MENT**.]
1 The fact of impeding someone or something, the condition of being impeded; a hindrance, an obstruction. **LME.**

SHAKES. *Rich. III* Thus far . . Have we march'd on without impediment. P. LIVELY My gender was never an impediment.

2 A physical defect, now esp. in one's speech, as a stammer, a stutter. **L15.**

A. FRASER His stiff manner, to which a speech impediment contributed. M. DRABBLE He had stammered atrociously . . . but he had learned to turn his impediment to advantage.

3 *sing.* & (usu.) in *pl.* Travelling equipment, esp. of an army etc.; impedimenta. **M16.**
■ **impediˈmental** *adjective* constituting an impediment; obstructive: **L16.**

impedimenta /ɪmˌpɛdɪˈmɛntə/ *noun pl.* **E17.**
[**ORIGIN** Latin: see **IMPEDIMENT**.]
Travelling equipment, esp. of an army etc.; encumbrances.

G. GISSING Having stowed away certain impedimenta . . , he took his travelling-bag in his hand. HARPER LEE There was no sign of piano, organ, hymn-books, church programmes—the familiar ecclesiastical impedimenta.

impedite /ˈɪmpɪdʌɪt/ *verb trans*. Now *rare* or *obsolete*. Pa. pple & ppl adjective **-ited**, †**-ite**. **M16.**
[**ORIGIN** Latin *impedit-* pa. ppl stem of *impedire* **IMPEDE**: see **-ITE**².]
†**1** = **IMPEDE**. **M16–L17.**
2 *ASTROLOGY*. In *pass.* Of a planet: have its influence hindered by the position of another. **M17.**

impeditive /ɪmˈpɛdɪtɪv/ *adjective*. **M17.**
[**ORIGIN** from **IMPEDITE** *verb* + **-IVE**.]
Tending to impede or obstruct; obstructive.

impel /ɪmˈpɛl/ *verb trans*. Infl. **-ll-**. **LME.**
[**ORIGIN** Latin *impellere*, formed as **IM-**¹ + *pellere* drive.]
1 Drive or cause to move onward; propel. **LME.**

J. IMISON A ship impelled by the wind and tide.

2 Drive, force, or constrain (a person) *to* or *into* an action, *to do* something; urge, incite. **L15.**

M. IGNATIEFF Man's . . . needs impel him forward on the path to their satisfaction.

■ **impellent** *adjective* & *noun* (**a**) *adjective* driving or urging on, impelling; (**b**) *noun* an impelling force or agent: **E17.** **impeller** *noun* (**a**) *gen.* a person or thing which impels; (**b**) *esp.* (the rotating part of) a machine designed to move a fluid by rotation, as a centrifugal pump or a compressor: **L17.** **impellor** *noun* = **IMPELLER** (b) **E20.**

impend /ɪmˈpɛnd/ *verb*. **L16.**
[**ORIGIN** Latin *impendere*, formed as **IM-**¹ + *pendere* hang.]
1 *verb intrans.* Of evil or danger: hang threateningly (*over*); loom. Also *gen.*, be about to happen; be imminent. **L16.**

E. BOWEN A trough of low pressure, a negative feeling of bother, impended over her. G. PATTEN The strange thrill . . that invariably came upon him when danger threatened or battle impended.

2 *verb trans.* Hover or loom over; be imminent or near to. *rare*. **M17.**

W. PENN The dreadful Judgments that now impend the Nation.

3 *verb intrans.* Hang or be suspended *over*; overhang. **L18.**

K. WHITE Mournful larches o'er the wave impend.

impendent /ɪmˈpɛnd(ə)nt/ *adjective*. Now *rare*. **L16.**
[**ORIGIN** Latin *impendent-* pres. ppl stem of *impendere*, or from **IMPEND**: see **IMPEND**, **-ENT**.]
1 = **IMPENDING** 1. **L16.**
2 = **IMPENDING** 2. **E17.**
■ **impendence** *noun* imminence **M17.** **impendency** *noun* imminent or threatening character; an impending circumstance: **M17.**

impending /ɪmˈpɛndɪŋ/ *adjective*. **L17.**
[**ORIGIN** from **IMPEND** + **-ING**².]
1 Of evil, danger, etc.: threatening, imminent. **L17.**

R. COBB She had an annoying habit of being able to spot impending disaster well ahead. R. V. JONES It was brought about by the impending collapse of France—now only five days away.

2 Overhanging. Now *rare*. **M18.**

W. COWPER Terribly arch'd and aquiline his nose, And overbuilt with most impending brows.

impenetrability /ɪmˌpɛnɪtrəˈbɪlɪti/ *noun*. **M17.**
[**ORIGIN** from **IMPENETRABLE**: see **-ABILITY**.]
1 That property of matter in virtue of which two bodies cannot occupy the same space at the same time. **M17.**
2 The quality or condition of being impenetrable; imperviousness, inscrutability. **E18.**

impenetrable /ɪmˈpɛnɪtrəb(ə)l/ *adjective*. **LME.**
[**ORIGIN** Old French & mod. French *impénétrable* from Latin *impenetrabilis*, formed as **IM-**² + *penetrabilis* **PENETRABLE**.]
1 Impossible to penetrate, pierce, or enter. **LME.**

TOLKIEN Coats of mail gilded and silvered and impenetrable. J. JOHNSTON Impenetrable banks of rhododendrons bordered the avenue.

2 Impossible to understand; inscrutable, unfathomable. **M16.**

A. POWELL Features at once expressive and impenetrable, concealing as much as they revealed. *Times* Passages of rhapsodic flimflam recalling Marie Corelli at her most impenetrable.

3 Impervious to intellectual or moral influences, impressions, or ideas. **L16.**

E. WHARTON Minds impenetrable to reason have generally some crack through which suspicion filters.

4 Of matter: having impenetrability. **M17.**
■ **impenetrableness** *noun* **L17.** **impenetrably** *adverb* **M17.**

impenetrate /ɪmˈpɛnɪtreɪt/ *verb trans*. **M19.**
[**ORIGIN** from **IM-**¹ + **PENETRATE**.]
Penetrate deeply, permeate.
■ **impeneˈtration** *noun* **M19.**

impenetrative /ɪmˈpɛnɪtrətɪv/ *adjective*. *rare*. **L17.**
[**ORIGIN** from **IM-**² + **PENETRATIVE**.]
Not penetrating or incisive.

impenitence /ɪmˈpɛnɪt(ə)ns/ *noun*. **E17.**
[**ORIGIN** Late (eccl.) Latin *impaenitentia*, formed as **IM-**² + *paenitentia* **PENITENCE**. Cf. French *impénitence*.]
The fact or condition of being impenitent; hardness of heart, obduracy.
■ **impenitency** *noun* the quality or state of being impenitent **M16.**

impenitent /ɪmˈpɛnɪt(ə)nt/ *adjective* & *noun*. **LME.**
[**ORIGIN** ecclesiastical Latin *impaenitent-*, formed as **IM-**² + *paenitent-*: see **PENITENT** *adjective*. Cf. French *impénitent*.]
► **A** *adjective*. Not penitent; having no contrition for sin; obdurate, unrepentant. **LME.**

J. CAIRD To forgive an impenitent man and to continue to punish a penitent are equally impossible.

► **B** *noun*. An impenitent person. **M16.**
■ **impenitently** *adverb* **M17.**

†**impeople** *verb* var. of **EMPEOPLE**.

†**imperate** *verb trans*. Pa. pple & ppl adjective **-ate** (earlier), **-ated**. **LME–E18.**
[**ORIGIN** Orig. pa. pple, from Latin *imperatus* pa. pple of *imperare* command, rule: see **-ATE**², **-ATE**³.]
Command, rule.
■ †**imperation** *noun* (*rare*) the action of commanding: only in **L18.**

imperatival /ɪmˌpɛrəˈtʌɪv(ə)l/ *adjective*. **L19.**
[**ORIGIN** from **IMPERATIVE** + **-AL**¹.]
GRAMMAR. Of or pertaining to the imperative mood.

imperative /ɪmˈpɛrətɪv/ *adjective* & *noun*. **LME.**
[**ORIGIN** Late Latin *imperativus* lit. 'specially ordered' translating Greek *prostaktikē* (*egklisis* mood), from Latin *imperat-* pa. ppl stem of *imperare* command, rule: see **EMPEROR**, **-ATIVE**.]
► **A** *adjective*. **1** *GRAMMAR*. Designating or pertaining to a grammatical mood expressing a command, request, or exhortation. **LME.**
imperative logic *PHILOSOPHY* a system of formal logic based on the commands and obligations contained in the imperative mood.
2 Having the quality or property of commanding; characterized by or expressing a command; peremptory. **L16.**

M. KEANE She gave these orders in an imperative, hot rush of words.

3 Demanding obedience, action, etc.; that must be done or performed; urgent; obligatory. **E19.**

T. COLLINS It was absolutely imperative that I should go thirty miles.

► **B** *noun*. **1** *GRAMMAR*. The imperative mood; a word, form, etc., in the imperative mood. **M16.**
2 An imperative action, speech, condition, etc.; an action etc. involving or expressing a command. **E17.**

C. G. WOLFF Edith Wharton . . had rejected the social imperative of feminine passivity.

CATEGORICAL **imperative**. **territorial imperative**: see **TERRITORIAL** *adjective*.
■ **imperatively** *adverb* **E17.** **imperativeness** *noun* **M19.** **imperativism** *noun* (*PHILOSOPHY*) a form of reasoning based on the concept of obligation contained in the imperative mood **E20.** **imperativist** *noun* & *adjective* (*PHILOSOPHY*) (**a**) *noun* a person who bases his or her reasoning on a concept of obligation; (**b**) *adjective* of or pertaining to reasoning based on a concept of obligation: **M20.**

imperator /ɪmpəˈrɑːtɔː/ *noun*. Also (as a title) **I-**. **M16.**
[**ORIGIN** Latin, from *imperat-*: see **IMPERATIVE**, **-OR**. Cf. **PRINCEPS**.]
1 *ROMAN HISTORY*. Orig., commander (a title conferred by the salutation of soldiers on a victorious general under the Republic). Later, head of the state (in whose name all victories were won), emperor. Cf. **PRINCEPS**. **M16.**
2 *gen.* An absolute ruler, an emperor; a commander. Long *rare* or *obsolete*. **L16.**
■ **imperatorship** *noun* the rank or position of imperator **M19.**

imperatorial /ɪmˌpɛrəˈtɔːrɪəl/ *adjective*. **M17.**
[**ORIGIN** from Latin *imperatorius*, formed as **IMPERATOR**, + **-AL**¹.]
Of or pertaining to an imperator, emperor, or commander; imperial.
■ **imperaˈtorially** *adverb* (*rare*) **M19.**

imperatrix /ɪmpəˈrɑːtrɪks/ *noun*. Also (as a title) **I-**. Pl. **-trices** /-trɪsiːz/. **E17.**
[**ORIGIN** Latin, fem. of **IMPERATOR**: see **-TRIX**.]
An empress.

imperceivable /ɪmpəˈsiːvəb(ə)l/ *adjective*. *rare*. **E17.**
[**ORIGIN** from **IM-**² + **PERCEIVABLE**.]
Imperceptible.
■ **imperceivableness** *noun* **E18.** **imperceivably** *adverb* **E17.**

†**imperceiverant** *adjective*. *rare* (Shakes.). Only in **E17.**
[**ORIGIN** from **IM-**² + alt. (with insertion of *-er-*) of French *percevant* pres. pple of *percevoir* **PERCEIVE**: see **-ANT**¹.]
Not perceiving; undiscerning.

imperceptibility /ˌɪmpəsɛptɪˈbɪlɪti/ *noun*. **E17.**
[**ORIGIN** from **IMPERCEPTIBLE** + **-ILITY**.]
The quality or condition of being imperceptible; inability to be perceived.

imperceptible /ɪmpəˈsɛptɪb(ə)l/ *adjective* & *noun*. **LME.**
[**ORIGIN** French, or from medieval Latin *imperceptibilis*, formed as **IM-**² + late Latin *perceptibilis* **PERCEPTIBLE**.]
► **A** *adjective*. **1** Unable by its nature to be perceived. **LME.**

A. TUCKER Some diseases . . proceeding from an imperceptible vermin within us.

2 So slight, gradual, or subtle, as to be hardly perceptible. **M17.**

P. CAREY A series of moves as imperceptible as the hands of a clock.

► **B** *noun*. An imperceptible thing. **E18.**
■ **imperceptibleness** *noun* **L17.** **imperceptibly** *adverb* **E17.**

imperception /ɪmpəˈsɛpʃ(ə)n/ *noun*. **M17.**
[**ORIGIN** from **IM-**² + **PERCEPTION**.]
Absence or lack of perception.

imperceptive /ɪmpəˈsɛptɪv/ *adjective*. **M17.**
[**ORIGIN** from **IM-**² + **PERCEPTIVE** *adjective*.]
Not perceptive or perceiving; lacking perception.

impercipient /ɪmpəˈsɪpɪənt/ *adjective* & *noun*. **E19.**
[**ORIGIN** from **IM-**² + **PERCIPIENT** *adjective*.]
► **A** *adjective*. Not perceiving; lacking perception. **E19.**
► **B** *noun*. A person who lacks perception. **L19.**
■ **impercipience** *noun* **L19.**

imperfect /ɪmˈpəːfɪkt/ *adjective* & *noun*. **ME.**
[**ORIGIN** Old French & mod. French *imparfait* from Latin *imperfectus*, formed as **IM-**² + *perfectus* **PERFECT** *adjective*.]
► **A** *adjective* **I 1** Lacking some quality or attribute necessary for full efficiency or normality; substandard; faulty. **ME.**

B. DUFFY A man with an imperfect command of English.

2 Lacking some usual or necessary part; not fully formed or done; incomplete. **LME.**

J. A. FROUDE The history of the time is too imperfect to justify a positive conclusion.

†3 Committing a fault, bad, evil. LME–M17.
4 Of a person: not fully accomplished or instructed *in*. L16.
▸II 5 *GRAMMAR*. Designating, being in, or pertaining to a verbal aspect or a tense denoting a (usu. past) action going on but not completed. LME.
6 *MUSIC*. Orig. (of a note), that is twice rather than three times the length of a note of the next lower denomination. Later (of an interval), that is other than a fourth, fifth, or octave. LME.
†7 *MATH*. (Of a number) not equal to the sum of its factors; (of a square, cube, etc.) having an irrational root. M16–E18.
8 *BOTANY*. Of a flower: lacking some normal part; now *esp*. lacking functional stamens or pistils. E18. ▸b *MYCOLOGY*. (Of a state or stage in the fungal life cycle) characterized by asexual spores, or by absence of spores; (of a fungus) in the asexual state, *esp*. having no (known) sexual state. L19.
9 *LAW*. Not legally binding. M19.
– SPECIAL COLLOCATIONS: **imperfect cadence** *MUSIC* a cadence ending on a chord other than the direct chord of the tonic. **imperfect competition** *ECONOMICS* a commercial situation in which elements of monopoly allow individual producers or consumers to exercise some control over a market price. **imperfect induction** *PHILOSOPHY* induction from an incomplete set of instances. **imperfect rhyme** a rhyme that only partly satisfies the usual criteria (e.g. English *love* and *move*).
▸B *noun*. 1 *GRAMMAR*. The imperfect aspect or tense; a word, form, etc., in an imperfect aspect or tense. L19.
2 In *pl*. Goods of imperfect quality that must be sold at a reduced price. M20.
■ **imperfectly** *adverb* LME. **imperfectness** *noun* LME.

imperfect /ɪmˈpəːfɪkt, ɪmpəˈfɛkt/ *verb trans*. M16.
[ORIGIN from IMPERFECT *adjective* or from IM-[2] + PERFECT *verb*.]
1 Make imperfect; destroy the perfection of. Long *rare*. M16.
2 Not make perfect; not complete. Chiefly as ***imperfected*** *ppl adjective*. M16.

imperfectible /ɪmpəˈfɛktɪb(ə)l/ *adjective*. *rare*. M19.
[ORIGIN from IM-[2] + PERFECTIBLE.]
Unable to be made perfect.
■ **imperfectiˈbility** *noun* M19.

imperfection /ɪmpəˈfɛkʃ(ə)n/ *noun*. LME.
[ORIGIN Old French & mod. French from late Latin *imperfectio(n-)*, from *imperfectus* IMPERFECT *adjective*: see -ION.]
1 The condition or quality of being imperfect; incompleteness; faultiness. Also, an instance of this; a fault, a blemish. LME.

A. MASON He must be free from any imperfection of body, any frailty of mind. J. VIORST With all its imperfections, the psychoanalytic perspective offers the most profound insights.

2 *MUSIC*. The action of causing a note to be twice rather than three times the length of a note of the next lower denomination. Also, the condition of such a note. Now *rare* or *obsolete*. L16.
3 a *PRINTING*. In *pl*. Letters that are lacking in a font; types cast or supplied to make up a deficiency in a font. *obsolete* exc. *hist*. L17. ▸b *BOOKBINDING*. A surplus or missing sheet. L17.

imperfective /ɪmpəˈfɛktɪv/ *noun & adjective*. E17.
[ORIGIN from IMPERFECT *adjective* + -IVE.]
▸A *noun*. †1 An imperfection. *rare*. Only in E17.
2 *GRAMMAR*. An imperfective aspect or form of a verb. M20.
▸B *adjective*. †1 Characterized by imperfection; imperfect. Only in L17.
2 *GRAMMAR*. Designating, being in, or pertaining to a verbal aspect expressing action without reference to its completion. M19.

imperforable /ɪmˈpəːf(ə)rəb(ə)l/ *adjective*. M17.
[ORIGIN medieval Latin *imperforabilis*, formed as IM-[2] + *perforare* PERFORATE *verb* + -ABLE.]
Unable to be perforated.

imperforate /ɪmˈpəːfərət/ *adjective*. L17.
[ORIGIN from IM-[2] + PERFORATE *adjective*.]
1 Chiefly *ANATOMY & ZOOLOGY*. Not perforated; having no perforation, opening, or foramen; (of the anus etc.) not having the opening normally present. L17.
2 Of a sheet of postage stamps or a single stamp: not provided with rows of perforations. L19.

imperforated /ɪmˈpəːfəreɪtɪd/ *adjective*. M17.
[ORIGIN from IM-[2] + PERFORATED.]
Not perforated, imperforate.

imperforation /ˌɪmpəːfəˈreɪʃ(ə)n/ *noun*. M17.
[ORIGIN from IM-[2] + PERFORATION.]
The condition of being imperforate; an instance of this.

imperformable /ɪmpəˈfɔːməb(ə)l/ *adjective*. *rare*. L17.
[ORIGIN from IM-[2] + PERFORMABLE.]
Unable to be performed.

imperial /ɪmˈpɪərɪəl/ *adjective & noun*. Also †**em-**. LME.
[ORIGIN Old French & mod. French *impérial* from Latin *imperialis*, from *imperium* rule, EMPIRE: see -AL[1], -IAL.]
▸A *adjective* I 1 Of or pertaining to an empire or a sovereign state ranking with an empire; *spec*. (*hist*.) of or pertaining to the British Empire. LME.

A. GHOSH A drive by the imperial government to recruit Indians for an expeditionary force.

2 Of or pertaining to an emperor (also in honorific titles). LME.

J. BRODSKY Tsarskoe Selo . . was the summer residence of the imperial family.

Her Imperial Highness, ***Your Imperial Majesty***, etc.
3 Of the nature or rank of an emperor or supreme ruler; supreme in authority. LME.
4 Having a commanding quality or aspect; majestic; august. LME. ▸b Assuming or affecting a commanding manner; domineering; imperious. L16.
5 Appropriate to an emperor or supreme ruler; magnificent. M18.
▸II 6 Designating any of various products or commodities of a certain (esp. a great) size or quality. M17. ▸b *spec*. Chiefly *hist*. Designating a size of paper, 30 × 22 inches (762 × 559 mm) or (*US*) 31 × 23 inches (787 × 584 mm). M17.
7 Of non-metric weights and measures: used or formerly used by statute in Britain. M19.
– SPECIAL COLLOCATIONS: **imperial eagle** a large eagle, *Aquila heliaca*, of southern Europe and central Asia, having dark plumage with white on the head and neck. **imperial elephant**, **imperial mammoth**: of the extinct species *Mammuthus imperator*, of the Pleistocene of N. America. **imperial** GALLON. ***imperial mammoth***: see ***imperial elephant*** above. ***imperial pint***: see PINT *noun*[1] 1. **imperial preference** a system of tariff concessions granted by members of the British Empire or Commonwealth to one another.
▸B *noun*. †1 A kind of silk cloth. L15–L19.
2 A follower or adherent of an emperor; a member of a body of imperial troops. E16. ▸b An emperor; an imperial personage. L16.
3 A kind of card game combining features of écarté and piquet. Now *rare* or *obsolete*. L16.
4 a A former Flemish coin. *obsolete* exc. *hist*. L17. ▸b A gold coin formerly in use in Russia. *obsolete* exc. *hist*. M19.
5 A former size of paper, 30 × 22 inches (762 × 559 mm) or (*US*) 31 × 23 inches (787 × 584 mm). E18.
6 Chiefly *hist*. A trunk for luggage fitted on to or adapted for the roof of a coach. L18.
7 [Chiefly associated with Emperor Napoleon III of France.] A small part of a beard left growing beneath the lower lip. M19.
■ **imperially** *adverb* M16. **imperialness** *noun* E18.

imperialise *verb* var. of IMPERIALIZE.

imperialism /ɪmˈpɪərɪəlɪz(ə)m/ *noun*. M19.
[ORIGIN from IMPERIAL + -ISM.]
1 An imperial system of government; the (esp. despotic or arbitrary) rule of an emperor. M19.

fig.: D. H. LAWRENCE Let us have done with the ugly imperialism of any absolute.

2 The principle or spirit of empire; *spec*. (*hist*.) the extending of the British Empire where trade required the protection given by imperial rule, the union of different parts of the British Empire for purposes of warlike defence, internal commerce, etc. L19.
3 (The belief in the desirability of) the acquisition of colonies and dependencies, or the extension of a country's influence through trade, diplomacy, etc. Usu. *derog*. E20.

N. GORDIMER South Africa is an advanced capitalist state in the last stage of imperialism.

imperialist /ɪmˈpɪərɪəlɪst/ *noun & adjective*. E17.
[ORIGIN from IMPERIAL + -IST, after French *impérialiste*.]
▸A *noun*. 1 A follower or adherent of an emperor, esp. (1600–1800) of the Holy Roman Emperor. E17.
2 An advocate of imperial rule or of an imperial form of government. E19.
3 An advocate or agent of (esp. British or American) imperialism. L19.
▸B *attrib*. or as *adjective*. Adhering, pertaining to, or characteristic of imperialism. M19.
■ **imperiaˈlistic** *adjective* of, pertaining to, or characteristic of an imperialist or imperialism L19. **imperiaˈlistically** *adverb* L19.

imperiality /ˌɪmpɪərɪˈalɪti/ *noun*. LME.
[ORIGIN from IMPERIAL + -ITY.]
†1 Imperial rank, power, or authority. LME–E17.
2 An emperor; an imperial personage, such personages collectively. *joc*. L19.

imperialize /ɪmˈpɪərɪəlʌɪz/ *verb*. Also **-ise**. M17.
[ORIGIN formed as IMPERIALITY + -IZE.]
†1 *verb intrans*. Behave as an emperor or absolute ruler. *rare*. Only in M17.
2 *verb trans*. †a Attach to the cause of an emperor. *rare*. Only in M17. ▸b Cause to be or adhere to an empire or imperial policy. E19.

imperil /ɪmˈpɛrɪl, -r(ə)l/ *verb trans*. Also †**em-**. Infl. **-ll-**, ***-l-**. LME.
[ORIGIN from IM-[1], EM-[1] + PERIL, prob. after *endanger*.]
Bring or put into danger, risk.

J. BERMAN The mother's life was also imperilled.

imperious /ɪmˈpɪərɪəs/ *adjective*. M16.
[ORIGIN Latin *imperiosus*, from *imperium* rule, EMPIRE + -OUS.]
1 Overbearing, domineering, dictatorial. M16.

L. STRACHEY There were signs of an imperious, a peremptory temper, an egotism that was strong and hard.

†2 Having imperial rank; belonging or appropriate to an emperor or supreme ruler. L16–E18.
†3 Exercising a commanding influence; ruling, sovereign; having a commanding position, demeanour, etc.; majestic. L16–E19.
4 That conveys an absolute command or demand; urgent, imperative. (Earlier in IMPERIOUSLY 2.) E17.

O. MANNING Gibbon held up an imperious hand and Beaker's apology limped to a halt.

imperiously /ɪmˈpɪərɪəsli/ *adverb*. M16.
[ORIGIN from IMPERIOUS + -LY[2].]
1 In a domineering manner; overbearingly, dictatorially. M16.
2 In the manner of an absolute command or demand; urgently, imperatively. M16.
†3 In the manner of supreme or absolute rule, imperially, majestically. L16–M17.

imperiousness /ɪmˈpɪərɪəsnɪs/ *noun*. L16.
[ORIGIN formed as IMPERIOUSLY + -NESS.]
†1 Imperial character or dignity; absolute rule or sovereignty; empire. L16–L17.
2 Overbearing character, disposition, or manner. E17.
3 Overmastering or imperative quality; urgency. M17.

imperishable /ɪmˈpɛrɪʃəb(ə)l/ *adjective & noun*. M17.
[ORIGIN from IM-[2] + PERISHABLE *adjective*.]
▸A *adjective*. That cannot perish; not subject to decay; indestructible, immortal, enduring. M17.
▸B *noun*. An imperishable person or thing. E20.
■ **imperishaˈbility** *noun* E19. **imperishableness** *noun* E19. **imperishably** *adverb* E19.

†**imperite** *adjective*. E17–E18.
[ORIGIN Latin *imperitus* inexperienced, unskilled, formed as IM-[2] + *peritus* experienced.]
Unskilled, ignorant.

imperium /ɪmˈpɪərɪəm/ *noun*. M17.
[ORIGIN Latin.]
Command; absolute power; supreme or imperial power; empire.
imperium in imperio /ɪn ɪmˈpɪərɪəʊ/ a supreme authority within the jurisdiction of another authority.

impermanent /ɪmˈpəːmənənt/ *adjective*. M17.
[ORIGIN from IM-[2] + PERMANENT *adjective*.]
Not permanent or lasting; unenduring; transient.
■ **impermanence** *noun* the fact or condition of being impermanent; lack of permanence: L18. **impermanency** *noun* the quality or state of being impermanent, impermanence M17.

impermeable /ɪmˈpəːmɪəb(ə)l/ *adjective*. L17.
[ORIGIN French *imperméable* from late Latin *impermeabilis*, formed as IM-[2] + *permeabilis* PERMEABLE.]
1 Unable to be penetrated through. L17.
2 *spec*. Not permitting the passage of water, or of other liquids or gases. M18.
■ **impermeaˈbility** *noun* M18.

impermeated /ɪmˈpəːmɪeɪtɪd/ *adjective*. E19.
[ORIGIN from IM-[2] + PERMEATE *verb* + -ED[1].]
Not permeated, not penetrated.

impermissible /ɪmpəˈmɪsɪb(ə)l/ *adjective*. M19.
[ORIGIN from IM-[2] + PERMISSIBLE.]
Not permissible; not to be allowed.
■ **impermissiˈbility** *noun* M20.

imperscriptible /ɪmpəˈskrɪptɪb(ə)l/ *adjective*. *rare*. M19.
[ORIGIN from IM-[2] + Latin *perscript-* pa. ppl stem of *perscribere* write at length, register, formed as PER-[1] + *scribere* write, + -IBLE.]
Not backed by a written authority.

impersistent /ɪmpəˈsɪst(ə)nt/ *adjective*. M19.
[ORIGIN from IM-[2] + PERSISTENT *adjective*.]
Not persistent or enduring.

impersonal /ɪmˈpəːs(ə)n(ə)l/ *adjective & noun*. LME.
[ORIGIN Late Latin *impersonalis*, formed as IM-[2] + *personalis* PERSONAL *adjective*.]
▸A *adjective*. 1 *GRAMMAR*. Of a verb: used only in the 3rd person sing. without a definite subject, as English *it snows*, *methinks*. Of a pronoun: used to designate an unspecified referent, as English *any*, *some*, *anyone*, *something*. LME.
2 Having no personal feeling, reference, or tone. M17.

E. GLASGOW An economic disaster was as impersonal as an earthquake. J. BRODSKY Even the most ardent anti-Semitic remarks bore an air of impersonal inertia.

3 Having no personality; not existing as a person. M19.
▸B *noun*. *GRAMMAR*. An impersonal verb. E17.
■ **impersoˈnality** *noun* (*a*) impersonal quality; (*b*) an impersonal being or creation: M18. **impersonally** *adverb* L16. **impersonalness** *noun* L19.

impersonate /ɪmˈpəːs(ə)nət/ *adjective*. *arch*. E19.
[ORIGIN formed as IMPERSONATE *verb*: see -ATE[2].]
Embodied in a person; invested with personality; impersonated.

impersonate /ɪmˈpəːs(ə)neɪt/ *verb trans.* E17.
[ORIGIN from IM-[1] + Latin *persona* PERSON *noun* + -ATE[3], after *incorporate*.]
1 Represent in a personal or bodily form; personify. E17. ▸**b** Manifest in one's own person; typify. M19.
W. WARBURTON The Jews and Christians, as well as the Heathens, impersonated Chance under the name of Fortune. H. H. MILMAN His age acknowledged Benedict as the perfect type of.. religion, and Benedict impersonated his age.
2 Pretend to be (another person) for the purpose of entertainment or fraud; act (a character). E18.
CONAN DOYLE He would have to dispose of the body.. and.. find a substitute who would impersonate her. K. TYNAN The plot requires all three of its women to impersonate beardless boys.

impersonation /ɪmˌpəːsəˈneɪʃ(ə)n/ *noun.* E19.
[ORIGIN from IMPERSONATE *verb*: see -ATION.]
1 The action of impersonating someone; the fact of being impersonated; personification. E19. ▸**b** An instance of this; a person or thing representing a principle, idea, etc. M19.
R. TRAVERS Had McHattie spoken to.. 'Lee Weller'.. Frank Butler would have been arrested.. for impersonation. **b** C. MERIVALE He proclaimed himself.. the supreme impersonation of the laws.
2 The dramatic or comic representation of a character; an instance of this. E19.
W. H. AUDEN Started to joke about their time at St Edmund's and.. do impersonations of the staff.

impersonator /ɪmˈpəːs(ə)neɪtə/ *noun.* M19.
[ORIGIN from IMPERSONATE *verb* + -OR.]
A person who impersonates others.
FEMALE ***impersonator***. ***male impersonator***: see MALE *adjective* & *noun*.

impersonify /ɪmpəˈsɒnɪfʌɪ/ *verb trans. arch.* E19.
[ORIGIN from IM-[1] + PERSONIFY, after *impersonate*.]
Personify.
■ **impersonifiˈcation** *noun* L18.

imperspirable /ɪmpəˈspʌɪrəb(ə)l/ *adjective.* Now *rare.* L17.
[ORIGIN from IM-[2] + PERSPIRABLE.]
Not capable of perspiring.

impersuadable /ɪmpəˈsweɪdəb(ə)l/ *adjective.* E18.
[ORIGIN from IM-[2] + PERSUADABLE.]
Not persuadable.

impertinence /ɪmˈpəːtɪnəns/ *noun.* E17.
[ORIGIN Old French & mod. French, or from IMPERTINENT *adjective*: see -ENCE. Cf. IMPERTINENCY.]
1 Lack of pertinence; irrelevance. Also, an instance of this; an irrelevance. E17.
MILTON Of like impertinence is that Example of Jacob.. who.. vow'd the Tenth of all that God should give him.
2 The fact or character of being out of place; inappropriateness; absurdity. Also, an instance of this; an incongruity; an absurdity. E17.
R. SOUTH A Petition, fraught with Nonsense and Incoherence, Confusion and Impertinence.
3 Impertinent interference; presumption; insolence in speech or behaviour, esp. to a superior; lack of proper respect. Also, an instance of this. E18.
HAZLITT We resent wholesome counsel as an impertinence. C. S. FORESTER Your impertinence in presenting yourself.. in your present state of ignorance.

impertinency /ɪmˈpəːtɪnənsi/ *noun.* Now *rare.* L16.
[ORIGIN formed as IMPERTINENCE: see -ENCY.]
1 = IMPERTINENCE 2. L16.
2 = IMPERTINENCE 1. E17.
3 = IMPERTINENCE 3. E17.

impertinent /ɪmˈpəːtɪnənt/ *adjective & noun.* LME.
[ORIGIN Old French & mod. French, or late Latin *impertinent-*, *-ens* not pertinent: see IM-[2], PERTINENT *adjective*.]
▸ **A** *adjective.* 1 Not belonging (*to*); unconnected, unrelated. Long *rare* or *obsolete*. LME.
COLERIDGE The more distant, disjointed and impertinent to.. any common purpose, will they appear.
2 Not pertaining to the matter in hand; irrelevant. Now *rare* exc. *LAW*. LME.
J. S. WHARTON The costs occasioned by any impertinent matter.. to be paid by the party introducing it.
3 Out of place; inappropriate, incongruous; absurd. L16. ▸†**b** Of a person: absurd, silly. M17–E18.
P. BARROUGH Many ignorant practitioners.. have endeavoured to cure this infirmity with many impertinent medicines.
4 Interfering in what does not concern one; presumptuous; insolent in speech or behaviour, esp. to a superior; lacking in proper respect. E17.
I. MURDOCH People will ask questions, including impertinent ones about your sex life. A. MUNRO He would think it impertinent, for anybody to assume he is sad.
▸ **B** *noun.* †1 An impertinent or irrelevant matter. Only in E17.
2 An impertinent person. *arch.* M17.
W. P. SCARGILL Henry St. John.. rebuked the young impertinents.
■ **impertinently** *adverb* LME. **impertinentness** *noun* (long *rare* or *obsolete*) L17.

imperturbable /ɪmpəˈtəːbəb(ə)l/ *adjective.* LME.
[ORIGIN Late Latin *imperturbabilis*, formed as IM-[2] + *perturbare* PERTURB: see -ABLE.]
Not perturbable or excitable; (habitually) calm.
A. LEWIS Weston looked at her, surprised at the emotion.. this normally imperturbable woman was showing.
■ **imperturbaˈbility** *noun* M19. **imperturbableness** *noun* M19. **imperturbably** *adverb* M19.

imperturbation /ˌɪmpəːtəˈbeɪʃ(ə)n/ *noun.* M17.
[ORIGIN Late (eccl.) Latin *imperturbatio(n-)*, formed as IM-[2] + PERTURBATION.]
Freedom from perturbation; calmness.

imperturbed /ɪmpəˈtəːbd/ *adjective.* E18.
[ORIGIN from IM-[2] + PERTURBED.]
Not perturbed; undisturbed, unmoved.

imperviable /ɪmˈpəːvɪəb(ə)l/ *adjective.* E19.
[ORIGIN Alt. of IMPERVIOUS: see -ABLE.]
Impervious; impermeable.

impervious /ɪmˈpəːvɪəs/ *adjective.* M17.
[ORIGIN from Latin *impervius*, formed as IM-[2] + PERVIOUS: see -OUS.]
1 Not affording passage (*to* water etc.); impenetrable. M17.
N. CALDER The overlying rocks must be impervious, otherwise the oil simply escapes.
2 *fig.* Not responsive (*to* argument, feeling, etc.). M17.
H. GUNTRIP There is something wrong.. if our theoretical ideas remain.. impervious to change for too long. M. DRABBLE They were impervious both to his charm and to his aggression.
■ **imperviously** *adverb* L18. **imperviousness** *noun* E18.

impest /ɪmˈpɛst/ *verb trans.* Also **em-** /ɛm-, ɪm-/. L16.
[ORIGIN French *empester*, formed as EM-[1], IM-[1] + PEST.]
Infect with a plague or pestilence.

impetigo /ɪmpɪˈtʌɪgəʊ/ *noun.* Pl. **-tigos**, **-tigines** /-ˈtɪdʒɪniːz/. LME.
[ORIGIN Latin, from *impetere* assail, attack: see IMPETUS.]
MEDICINE. Any of various pustular skin diseases. Now *esp.* a contagious acute superficial skin infection (esp. of children) usu. caused by staphylococci and producing vesicles and crusted inflammation.
■ **impetiginous** /ɪmpɪˈtɪdʒɪnəs/ *adjective* pertaining to, resembling, or of the nature of impetigo E17.

impetrate /ˈɪmpətrət/ *adjective.* Long *obsolete* exc. *Scot.* L15.
[ORIGIN Latin *impetratus* pa. pple, formed as IMPETRATE *verb*: see -ATE[2].]
Obtained by request; impetrated.

impetrate /ˈɪmpətreɪt/ *verb trans.* Pa. t. & pple **-ated**, (long *obsolete* exc. *Scot.*) **-ate** /-ət/. L15.
[ORIGIN Latin *impetrat-* pa. ppl stem of *impetrare*, formed as IM-[1] + *patrare* bring to pass: see -ATE[3]. Cf. PERPETRATE.]
1 Chiefly *THEOLOGY*. Obtain by request or entreaty; procure. L15.
2 Entreat, beseech; ask for. Now *rare*. M16.
■ **impetrative** *adjective* (*rare*) impetratory E17. **impetratory** *adjective* (chiefly *THEOLOGY*) having the quality of obtaining something (as) by request E17.

impetration /ɪmpəˈtreɪʃ(ə)n/ *noun.* L15.
[ORIGIN Anglo-Norman *impetracioun* or Latin *impetratio(n-)*, formed as IMPETRATE *verb*: see -ATION.]
1 Chiefly *THEOLOGY*. The action or an act of obtaining something by request. L15. ▸**b** *ECCLESIASTICAL HISTORY*. The obtaining from the court of Rome of English church benefices in the gift of the king etc. L15. ▸**c** *LAW* (now *hist.*). The obtaining of a writ. M17.
2 Entreaty, request. E17.

impetuosity /ɪmˌpɛtjʊˈɒsɪti/ *noun.* LME.
[ORIGIN Old French & mod. French *impétuosité* from late Latin *impetuositas*, from *impetuosus*: see IMPETUOUS, -ITY.]
The quality or character of being impetuous; vehemence; an instance of this.
J. PINKERTON Flames.. issued forth with great impetuosity. S. T. WARNER I have always regretted the impetuosity with which I have given books and letters away.

impetuous /ɪmˈpɛtjʊəs/ *adjective.* LME.
[ORIGIN from Old French & mod. French *impétueux* from late Latin *impetuosus*, formed as IMPETUS: see -OUS, -UOUS.]
1 Moving violently or rapidly. LME.
S. WILLIAMS Strength to resist the most impetuous winds.
2 Acting with or done with rash or sudden energy; vehement; ardent. LME.
S. HAZZARD After the impetuous beginning, he would puzzle them by turning out staid and cautious. J. BARNES An ardent, impetuous nature which fretted at any wanton infliction of disappointment or boredom.
■ **impetuously** *adverb* L15. **impetuousness** *noun* LME.

impetus /ˈɪmpɪtəs/ *noun.* M17.
[ORIGIN Latin = assault, force, from *impetere* assail, formed as IM-[1] + *petere* seek.]
1 The force or energy with which a body moves; impulsion. M17.
A. THWAITE The current.. takes its impetus and gathers speed Only beyond the sluice-gate.
2 *fig.* Moving force, (an) impulse, a stimulus. M17.
H. ARENDT Only in Austria did the revolutionary impetus find its natural outlet. M. MUGGERIDGE A visit.. by Gandhi.. gave a great impetus to Swarajist sentiment among the students.

Impeyan /ˈɪmpɪən/ *adjective.* L19.
[ORIGIN from Sir Elijah *Impey* (1732–1809), English jurist, and his wife Mary (d. 1818) + -AN.]
Impeyan pheasant, a stocky pheasant, *Lophophorus impeyanus*, of the Himalayas, the male of which has brilliant iridescent plumage. Also called ***monal***, ***Himalayan monal***.

imphee /ˈɪmfi/ *noun.* Also **imfe**. M19.
[ORIGIN Zulu *imfe* sweet cane.]
Any of several southern African varieties of sorghum.

impi /ˈɪmpi/ *noun.* M19.
[ORIGIN Zulu.]
Chiefly *hist.* A body of Zulu warriors or armed men.

impicture /ɪmˈpɪktʃə/ *verb trans.* Also **em-** /ɪm-, ɛm-/. E16.
[ORIGIN from IM-[1], EM-[1] + PICTURE *noun*.]
Represent (as) in a picture; portray.

impierce *verb* var. of EMPIERCE.

†**impierceable** *adjective.* LME–L17.
[ORIGIN from IM-[2] + PIERCEABLE.]
Not pierceable; unable to be pierced.

impiety /ɪmˈpʌɪɪti/ *noun.* ME.
[ORIGIN Old French & mod. French *impiété* or Latin *impietas*, from *impius*: see IMPIOUS, -TY[1].]
1 Lack of reverence for God or a god; ungodliness; an instance of this. ME.
AV *2 Esd.* 3:29 When I came thither, and had seen impieties without number. H. WILLIAMSON Phidias eventually was accused of impiety.. what in a later age would be called blasphemy.
2 Lack of respect or dutifulness; an instance of this. M16.
W. LAW Can you think it a less impiety to contemn and vilify a brother? R. SCRUTON To neglect my parents in old age is.. an act of impiety.

†**impight** *verb* var. of EMPIGHT.

impignorate /ɪmˈpɪgnəreɪt/ *verb trans.* Chiefly *Scot.* Pa. pple **-ate** (earlier), **-ated**. M16.
[ORIGIN Orig. pa. pple, from medieval Latin *impignoratus* pa. pple of *impignorare* pledge, mortgage, formed as IM-[1] + *pignor-*, *-nus* a pledge: see -ATE[2], -ATE[3].]
Pledge, pawn, mortgage.
■ **impignoˈration** *noun* L15.

impinge /ɪmˈpɪn(d)ʒ/ *verb.* M16.
[ORIGIN Latin *impingere*, formed as IM-[1] + *pangere* drive in.]
1 *verb trans.* Fasten or fix on forcibly (*lit.* & *fig.*). M16.
SYD. SMITH Appealing to the absurdities of a past age, and impinging them upon the present.
2 *verb intrans.* Strike; come into forcible contact; collide. (Foll. by *on*, *upon*.) E17.
JOYCE Through one of the broken panes I heard the rain impinge upon the earth.
3 *verb trans.* Strike or throw (a thing) forcibly on or *on* something else. *rare.* M17.
T. L. PEACOCK He impinged his foot with a force that overbalanced himself.
4 *verb intrans.* Encroach, have an effect, *on* or *upon*. M18.
Illustrated London News I should be impinging on the province of the reviewers. R. DAHL Still the same habit of thrusting his face forward at you, impinging on you.
5 *verb trans.* Strike; come into forcible contact with; collide with. L18.
Practitioner The striker's thumb.. impinges the skull of his opponent.
■ **impingement** *noun* L17. **impinger** *noun* any of various instruments used for collecting samples of particles suspended in air etc. E20.

impious /ˈɪmpɪəs, ɪmˈpʌɪəs/ *adjective.* M16.
[ORIGIN from Latin *impius*, formed as IM-[2] + PIOUS: see -OUS.]
1 Not pious; lacking in reverence for God or a god; wicked, profane. M16.
S. K. PENMAN Those impious knaves even robbed the archbishop of a silver cross.
2 Lacking in respect or dutifulness. *rare.* E17.
■ **impiously** *adverb* L16. **impiousness** *noun* (long *rare*) L16.

impish /ˈɪmpɪʃ/ *adjective.* E17.
[ORIGIN from IMP *noun* + -ISH[1].]
Of or like an imp; mischievous.
E. FEINSTEIN A series of practical jokes that recall her impish treatment of Nina. I. MCEWAN She was pretty, impish and freckled, with a pointed chin.
■ **impishly** *adverb* M19. **impishness** *noun* L19.

impiteous /ɪmˈpɪtɪəs/ *adjective. rare.* L15.
[ORIGIN from IM-[2] + PITEOUS.]
Ruthless, pitiless.

I

implacable /ɪmˈplakəb(ə)l/ *adjective*. LME.
[ORIGIN Latin *implacabilis*, formed as IM-[2] + *placabilis* PLACABLE.]
1 Unable to be appeased; irreconcilable; inexorable. LME.
C. G. WOLFF A.. lonely child, convinced of the world's implacable hostility. J. CHEEVER The.. Duke was an implacable anti-Fascist.
2 Unable to be assuaged or mitigated. Now *rare* or *obsolete*. L15.
SPENSER O how I burne with implacable fire.
■ **implacaˈbility** *noun* M16. **implacableness** *noun* M17. **implacably** *adverb* M17.

implacental /ɪmpləˈsɛnt(ə)l/ *adjective & noun*. M19.
[ORIGIN from IM-[2] + PLACENTAL.]
ZOOLOGY. (A mammal) that develops no placenta, as a monotreme marsupial.

implant /ˈɪmplɑːnt/ *noun*. L19.
[ORIGIN from the verb.]
1 A thing that has been implanted, esp. in the body, as a piece of tissue, a capsule containing radioactive material, etc. L19.
New Scientist In recent years surgeons have been fitting an increasing number of implants.
2 The action or an act of implanting a thing, esp. in the body. M20.
Times French doctors today made the world's first implant of an atomic powered heart simulator.

implant /ɪmˈplɑːnt/ *verb*. LME.
[ORIGIN Late Latin *implantare* engraft, formed as IM-[1] + *plantare* PLANT *verb*.]
1 *verb trans.* Embed, insert, or fix *in* something. Usu. in *pass.* LME. ▸**b** SURGERY. Place or insert (tissue, or some artificial object) in the body. L19. ▸**c** Chiefly MEDICINE. Provide *with* by implantation. E20. ▸**d** PHYSICS. Introduce (atoms, ions, etc.) into a substance by bombardment. M20.
J. PINKERTON Patrinite sometimes occurs in globular masses, implanted in other rocks.
2 *verb trans.* Instil, establish, (a principle, idea, etc., *in* a mind etc.). Freq. in *pass.* M16.
E. HEMINGWAY We are making a huge conscript army without the time to implant the discipline. E. AMADI Tam Jaja.. stared at her intensely as if trying to implant his.. view in her mind.
3 *verb trans.* Set in the ground, plant. Also, plant (ground etc.) *with*. E17.
H. J. STEPHEN Trees, while still implanted in the ground, are parcel of the freehold.
4 *verb intrans.* EMBRYOLOGY. Of an ovum: undergo implantation. M20.
■ **implantable** *adjective* M20. **implanter** *noun* M17.

implantation /ɪmplɑːnˈteɪʃ(ə)n, -plan-/ *noun*. L16.
[ORIGIN French, from *implanter*, formed as IMPLANT *verb*: see -ATION.]
1 ANATOMY. The (manner or place of) insertion of a tooth, a muscle, etc. L16.
2 The action or an act of planting something in the ground. E17.
3 The instilling or establishing of a principle, idea, etc., in the mind etc. M17.
4 SURGERY. The process or an act of implanting something in the body. L19.
5 EMBRYOLOGY. The attachment of a fertilized ovum (blastocyst) to the wall of the uterus. E20.
6 PHYSICS. The introduction of atoms or other particles into a substance by bombardment. M20.

implausible /ɪmˈplɔːzɪb(ə)l/ *adjective*. E17.
[ORIGIN from IM-[2] + PLAUSIBLE *adjective*.]
†**1** Not worthy or desirous of applause. Only in E17.
2 Not having the appearance of truth, probability, or acceptability; not plausible. L17.
R. SCRUTON It is most implausible that the Church should retain political while losing its spiritual authority. H. JACOBSON She had invented a number of transparently implausible domestic tasks for herself.
■ **implausiˈbility** *noun* L16. **implausibly** *adverb* E19.

impleach /ɪmˈpliːtʃ/ *verb trans. poet.* Also †**em-**. L16.
[ORIGIN from IM-[1], EM-[1] + PLEACH *verb*.]
Entwine, interweave. Usu. in *pass.*

implead /ɪmˈpliːd/ *verb trans.* Also †**em-**. LME.
[ORIGIN Anglo-Norman *empleder* = Old French *empleidier, emplaidier*, formed as IM-[1], EM-[1] + *plaidier* PLEAD.]
1 Prosecute or take proceedings against (a person, organization, etc.); involve in a lawsuit. LME.
†**2** Arraign, accuse, impeach. L16–M19.
3 Plead (*with*). *rare*. M17.
■ †**impleadable** *adjective* (*a*) (of a person) that may be sued, (of a suit) that may be prosecuted; (*b*) able to be pleaded or made a plea: L16–E19. †**impleader** *noun* L16–L18.

impledge /ɪmˈplɛdʒ/ *verb trans.* Now chiefly *literary*. Also †**em-**. M16.
[ORIGIN from IM-[1], EM-[1] + PLEDGE *noun*.]
Pledge, give as security; pawn.

implement /ˈɪmplɪm(ə)nt/ *noun*. LME.
[ORIGIN Partly from medieval Latin *implementa* pl., from *implere* employ, spend, extended use (by assoc. with *implicare* EMPLOY *verb*) of Latin *implere*; partly from late Latin *implementum* filling up, from Latin *implere* fill up, fulfil, formed as IM-[1] + *plere* fill: see -MENT.]
1 A piece of equipment; an article of furniture, dress, etc. Now only in *pl.* LME. ▸†**b** *gen.* In *pl.* Requisites. E17–M18.
A. B. JAMESON They wear the stole and alba.. and bear the implements of the mass.
2 A tool, instrument, or utensil, employed in a particular trade, activity, etc.; ARCHAEOLOGY a weapon or tool, usu. deliberately shaped (freq. with specifying word denoting association with a particular period or culture). M16.
W. TREVOR Spades we need.. and forks and secateurs and all garden implements.
3 SCOTS LAW. Fulfilment, full performance. M17.
■ **impleˈmental** *adjective* L17.

implement /ˈɪmplɪmɛnt, -m(ə)nt/ *verb trans.* E18.
[ORIGIN from the noun.]
1 Complete or execute (a contract etc.); fulfil (an undertaking); put (a decision or plan) into effect. E18. ▸**b** Satisfy or fulfil (a condition). *rare*. M19.
E. CRANKSHAW It was left to Arakcheyev to implement the system. ANTHONY SMITH A regulation.. was issued.. but was never implemented. R. HOLE The NHS reforms, uncosted and untried anywhere and implemented at speed against much opposition.
2 Fill up, supplement. M19.
3 Provide or fit with an implement or implements. *rare*. L19.
■ **implemenˈtation** *noun* E20.

implementiferous /ˌɪmplɪmɛnˈtɪf(ə)rəs/ *adjective*. L19.
[ORIGIN formed as IMPLEMENT *verb* + -I- + -FEROUS.]
GEOLOGY. Of a deposit: containing (stone) implements of human origin.

impletion /ɪmˈpliːʃ(ə)n/ *noun*. *arch.* L15.
[ORIGIN Late Latin *impletio(n-)*, from Latin *implet-* pa. ppl stem of *implere* (see IMPLEMENT *noun*) + -ION.]
The action of filling; the condition of being filled; fullness. Formerly also, fulfilment.

†**implex** *adjective*. Only in 18.
[ORIGIN Latin *implexus* pa. pple, formed as IMPLEX *verb*.]
Involved, complicated.

†**implex** *verb trans.* E17–M19.
[ORIGIN Latin *implex-* pa. ppl stem of *implectere* entwine, formed as IM-[1] + *plectere* twist, plait.]
Entwine; complicate. Chiefly as ***implexed*** *ppl adjective*.

impliable /ɪmˈplʌɪəb(ə)l/ *adjective*. *rare*. E17.
[ORIGIN from IM-[2] + PLIABLE.]
Not pliable; inflexible.

implicans /ˈɪmplɪkanz/ *noun*. Pl. **-cants** /-kants/. E20.
[ORIGIN Latin, pres. pple of *implicare*: see IMPLICATE *verb*.]
LOGIC. In implication, the proposition that implies another.

implicate /ˈɪmplɪkət/ *adjective & noun*. LME.
[ORIGIN Latin *implicatus* pa. pple, formed as IMPLICATE *verb*: see -ATE[2], -ATE[1].]
▸ **A** *adjective*. **1** Intertwined, twisted together; wrapped up *with*, involved or entangled *in*. Now *rare*. LME.
†**2** Involved, intricate. M16–M17.
▸ **B** *noun*. †**1** Entanglement, confusion. Only in M17.
2 That which is implied or involved. L19.
A. M. FAIRBAIRN The doctrine and its implicates must simply be stated.

implicate /ˈɪmplɪkeɪt/ *verb trans.* LME.
[ORIGIN Latin *implicat-* pa. ppl stem of *implicare*, formed as IM-[1] + *plicare* fold: see -ATE[3].]
▸ **I 1** Intertwine; entwine, entangle. Now *rare*. LME.
fig.: H. ROGERS Christianity was not designed to be.. implicated with the fortunes of any earthly polity.
▸ **II 2** Involve in its nature or meaning; lead to as a consequence or inference; imply. E17.
E. PARSONS So much reserve and mystery.. assuredly implicated something wrong. P. ACKROYD The demands of 'social utility' are implicated in the idea of the poet as dramatist.
3 Show or purport to show (a person) to be concerned or involved (*in* a crime, charge, etc.). L18.
W. SOYINKA He has implicated you in his statement.
4 In *pass.* Be affected or involved in the operation of something. Freq. foll. by *in*. L18.
Scientific American Strings were originally implicated in the formation of galaxies.
■ **implicature** *noun* (LINGUISTICS) the action of implying a meaning beyond the literal sense of what is explicitly stated; a meaning so implied: M20.

implication /ɪmplɪˈkeɪʃ(ə)n/ *noun*. LME.
[ORIGIN Latin *implicatio(n-)*, formed as IMPLICATE *verb*: see -ATION.]
1 The action or an act of intertwining, entwining, or entangling; the condition of being intertwined, entwined, or entangled. Now *rare*. LME.
J. MARTINEAU The mystic implication of his nature with ours.
2 The action of implying; the fact of being implied or involved, without being plainly expressed; a thing implied or involved in something else. M16. ▸**b** LOGIC. A relationship between propositions such that the one implies the other. Also, a proposition asserting such a relationship. E20.
B. BETTELHEIM To different persons the same symbol could have entirely different implications. M. GORDON She hadn't known exactly what he'd meant, but the implications hadn't pleased her.
by implication by what is implied; as a natural inference. **b** ***logical implication***: see LOGICAL *adjective*. ***material implication***: see MATERIAL *adjective*. STRICT ***implication***.

implicational /ɪmplɪˈkeɪʃ(ə)n(ə)l/ *adjective*. L19.
[ORIGIN from IMPLICATION + -AL[1].]
LOGIC. Of, concerned with, or using implication.
■ **implicationally** *adverb* E20.

implicative /ɪmˈplɪkətɪv/ *adjective*. E17.
[ORIGIN from IMPLICATE *verb* + -IVE.]
1 Having the quality of implying; tending to imply or implicate. E17.
2 LOGIC. Designating or pertaining to a relationship between propositions such that the one implies the other. Also, designating or pertaining to a proposition asserting such a relationship. E20.
■ **implicatively** *adverb* L16. **implicativeness** *noun* M20.

implicit /ɪmˈplɪsɪt/ *adjective*. L16.
[ORIGIN French *implicite* or Latin *implicitus* entangled, entwined, later form of *implicatus*: see IMPLICATE *adjective & noun*.]
1 Implied though not plainly expressed; necessarily or naturally involved (*in*); able to be inferred. L16. ▸**b** Of an idea or feeling: not clearly formulated, vague, indefinite. Now *rare*. M17. ▸**c** Virtually or potentially contained *in*. M17.
M. BRADBURY I was offering a paraphrase of its implicit as opposed to its surface meaning. C. PRIEST It was nothing she said, it was just implicit in her every glance. **b** D. HUME Views and sentiments.. so implicit and obscure that they often escape our strictest attention. **c** J. M. MURRY The reference to Shakespeare is implicit in every page.
2 Of faith, obedience, etc.: not independently reached by the individual but resting on the authority of the Church etc.; absolute, unquestioning. E17. ▸**b** Of a person: characterized by implicit faith, obedience, etc. Now *rare* or *obsolete*. L17.
E. ROOSEVELT I had implicit confidence in his ability to help the country in a crisis.
†**3** Entangled, entwined, twisted together; involved. E17–E19.
J. BEATTIE No hand had wove the implicit maze.
■ **implicitly** *adverb* E17. **implicitness** *noun* the quality of being implicit; implicit belief or obedience: L17. **implicity** *noun* (long *rare* or *obsolete*) implicitness E17.

impling /ˈɪmplɪŋ/ *noun*. *rare*. L18.
[ORIGIN from IMP *noun* + -LING[1].]
A little imp.

implode /ɪmˈpləʊd/ *verb intrans. & trans.* L19.
[ORIGIN from IM-[1] + Latin *plodere, plaudere* clap, after *explode*.]
(Cause to) burst or collapse inwards.

imploration /ɪmpləˈreɪʃ(ə)n/ *noun*. Now *rare*. L16.
[ORIGIN French †*imploration* or Latin *imploratio(n-)*, from *implorat-* pa. ppl stem of *implorare*: see IMPLORE *verb*, -ATION.]
The action or an act of imploring; supplication, beseeching.
G. CATLIN Their earnest implorations for divine forgiveness and mercy.

†**implorator** *noun*. *rare* (Shakes.). Only in E17.
[ORIGIN medieval Latin, from Latin *implorat-*: see IMPLORATION, -OR.]
A person who implores.

†**implore** *noun*. *rare*. L16–E17.
[ORIGIN from the verb.]
An act of imploring; imploration.

implore /ɪmˈplɔː/ *verb*. E16.
[ORIGIN French *implorer* or Latin *implorare* invoke with tears, formed as IM-[1] + *plorare* weep.]
1 *verb trans.* Beg earnestly for (help, forgiveness, etc.); entreat (a person *to do*). E16. ▸**b** Utter as a supplication or entreaty. M19.
A. RADCLIFFE He threw himself at her feet to implore forgiveness. W. STYRON 'Nathan, don't go!' she implored him desperately. **b** G. GREENE He simply implored, 'Stop it, please stop it.'
2 *verb intrans.* Utter entreaties, supplicate. E16.
W. LITHGOW Holding up my hand, and imploring for our lives.
■ **imploringly** *adverb* in an imploring manner E19. **imploringness** *noun* (an) imploring quality M19.

implosion /ɪmˈpləʊʒ(ə)n/ *noun*. **L19.**
[ORIGIN from IMPLODE after *explosion*.]
1 A bursting or collapsing inward. **L19.**

J. NARLIKAR When the core of a star collapses . . the inner part . . undergoes an implosion, while the outer part undergoes an explosion. *fig.*: *Listener* There was an implosion, as firms rushed together from great financial conglomerates.

2 *PHONETICS*. The sharp intake of air in the pronunciation of some consonants. **L19.**

implosive /ɪmˈpləʊsɪv/ *adjective & noun*. **L19.**
[ORIGIN formed as IMPLOSION after *explosive*.]
▸ **A** *adjective*. Formed by implosion; tending to implode. **L19.**
▸ **B** *noun*. *PHONETICS*. A sound formed by implosion. **L19.**
■ **implosively** *adverb* **L19.** **implosiveness** *noun* **M20.**

†**imploy** *noun*, *verb*, †**imployer** *noun*, †**imployment** *noun* vars. of EMPLOY *noun*, *verb*, etc.

implume *verb* var. of EMPLUME.

implunge /ɪmˈplʌn(d)ʒ/ *verb trans*. Now *rare*. Also †**em-**. **L16.**
[ORIGIN from IM-[1], EM-[1] + PLUNGE *verb*.]
Plunge *in* or *into*.

impluvium /ɪmˈpluːvɪəm/ *noun*. Pl. **-ia** /-ɪə/. **E19.**
[ORIGIN Latin, from *impluere* rain into.]
ROMAN ANTIQUITIES. The square basin in the centre of the atrium of a Roman house, which received rainwater from an opening in the roof.

imply /ɪmˈplʌɪ/ *verb trans*. Also †**em-**. **LME.**
[ORIGIN Old French *emplier* from Latin *implicare*: see IMPLICATE *verb*. Cf. EMPLOY *verb*.]
†**1** Enfold, entangle, (*lit. & fig.*). **LME–E19.**

C. LAMB If it be egotism to imply and twine with his . . identity the griefs . . of another.

2 Involve as a necessary consequence; involve the truth or existence of (a thing not expressly asserted). **E16.** ▸**b** Of a word etc.: mean, signify. **E17.**

I. WALTON In Job . . mention is made of fish-hooks, which must imply Anglers in those times. J. MCDOUGALL The wish for nirvana . . does not necessarily imply a wish to die.

†**3** Employ. **M16–M17.**
4 Express indirectly; insinuate, suggest, hint (at). **L16.**

D. H. LAWRENCE Her voice seemed to imply that she was glad to get back to Shortlands. B. BETTELHEIM Translators need to be very sensitive not only to what is written but also to what is implied.

impocket /ɪmˈpɒkɪt/ *verb trans*. Also **em-** /ɪm-, ɛm-/. **E18.**
[ORIGIN from IM-[1], EM-[1] + POCKET *noun*.]
Pocket; put into one's pocket.

†**impoison** *verb* var. of EMPOISON.

impolder /ɪmˈpəʊldə/ *verb trans*. Also **em-** /ɪm-, ɛm-/. **L19.**
[ORIGIN Dutch *impolderen*, formed as IM-[1] + POLDER.]
Reclaim from the sea; make a polder of.

impolicy /ɪmˈpɒlɪsi/ *noun*. **M18.**
[ORIGIN from IM-[2] + POLICY *noun*[1], after IMPOLITIC.]
Bad policy; inexpediency.

impolite /ɪmpəˈlʌɪt/ *adjective*. **E17.**
[ORIGIN Latin *impolitus*, formed as IM-[2] + *politus* POLITE.]
†**1** Not polished; *fig.* unrefined. Only in **17.**
2 Not courteous; uncivil, ill-mannered, rude. **M18.**

K. VONNEGUT She imagined that I used certain impolite words . . to cause a sensation. A. S. BYATT Celia felt it would be impolite to ask how old he was.

■ **impolitely** *adverb* **M18.** **impoliteness** *noun* **L18.**

impolitic /ɪmˈpɒlɪtɪk/ *adjective*. **L16.**
[ORIGIN from IM-[2] + POLITIC *adjective*.]
Not politic; not according to good policy; inexpedient.

T. CLANCY He decided it would be impolitic to ask any family questions of his own.

■ **impolitical** *adjective* (now *rare*) = IMPOLITIC **M18.** **impolitically** *adverb* **M18.** **impoliticly** *adverb* **E17.** **impoliticness** *noun* (now *rare*) **L18.**

imponderabilia /ɪm,pɒnd(ə)rəˈbɪlɪə/ *noun pl*. **E20.**
[ORIGIN mod. Latin, neut. pl. of *imponderabilis* that cannot be weighed: see -IA[2].]
Imponderables, imponderable factors.

imponderable /ɪmˈpɒnd(ə)rəb(ə)l/ *adjective & noun*. **L18.**
[ORIGIN from IM-[2] + PONDERABLE.]
▸ **A** *adjective*. **1** Chiefly *PHYSICS*. Having no weight. **L18.** ▸**b** Of extremely small weight or amount. **M19.**
2 *fig.* Unable to be assessed or calculated. **E19.**

Guardian It is not so much the calculable cost but the possible, imponderable one.

▸ **B** *noun*. An imponderable thing; *esp.* a thing that cannot be assessed or calculated. **M19.**

A. BURGESS A faith of blood and instinct and somatic consciousness and other imponderables.

■ **imponderableness** *noun* **M19.** **imponderably** *adverb* **L19.**

imponderous /ɪmˈpɒnd(ə)rəs/ *adjective*. *rare*. **M17.**
[ORIGIN from IM-[2] + PONDEROUS.]
Imponderable.

†**impone** *verb trans*. **E16.**
[ORIGIN Latin *imponere*, formed as IM-[1] + *ponere* to place.]
1 Place upon something; impose. **E16–E18.**
2 Stake, wager. *rare* (Shakes.). Only in **E17.**

imponent /ɪmˈpəʊnənt/ *noun*. **M19.**
[ORIGIN Alt. of IMPOSER after OPPONENT, OPPOSER.]
A person who imposes something.

imporous /ɪmˈpɔːrəs/ *adjective*. Long *rare*. **M17.**
[ORIGIN from IM-[2] + POROUS *adjective*.]
Not porous.

import /ˈɪmpɔːt/ *noun*. **L16.**
[ORIGIN from the verb.]
1 Something implied or signified by a word, document, etc.; meaning; great significance, importance. **L16.**

H. KELLER She grasps the import of whole sentences, catching . . the meaning of words she doesn't know. V. SACKVILLE-WEST His visit had not been without import to him. B. BETTELHEIM A word that, because of its ancient religious associations, suggests something of deepest import.

existential import: see EXISTENTIAL *adjective* 2.
2 Something imported or brought in, the amount or value of what is imported; an imported article or commodity. Usu. in *pl.* **L17.**

Sunday (Kolkata) Not much progress has been made in reducing imports of . . , fertilisers, and iron and steel. *attrib.*: *Soldier* There are strict import regulations about bringing such animals into the United Kingdom.

invisible imports: see INVISIBLE *adjective & noun*.
3 The action of importing, importation. **L18.**

G. J. GOSCHEN It is an error . . to look on the balance of trade as a mere question of import and export.

import /ɪmˈpɔːt, ˈɪmpɔːt/ *verb*. **LME.**
[ORIGIN Latin *importare* carry or bring in, (in medieval Latin) imply, mean, be of consequence, formed as IM-[1] + *portare* carry.]
▸ **I** Convey; signify; matter; cause.
1 *verb trans*. Signify, denote, mean; involve, imply, indicate. **LME.** ▸**b** Convey as information; express, state. **LME.** ▸**c** Portend. Cf. IMPORTUNE *verb* 4. Long *rare*. **L15.**

R. SOUTH Having thus seen, what is imported in a Man's trusting his Heart. **b** LD MACAULAY They . . passed a resolution importing that they relied . . on His Majesty's gracious promise.

2 *verb trans*. Be of consequence or importance to; relate to, concern; be incumbent on. Only in 3rd person (freq. impers.). *arch.* **M16.** ▸**b** *verb intrans*. Be of consequence or significance; be important, matter. Only in 3rd person. *arch.* **M16.**

SIR W. SCOTT Let me say . . what it imports thee to know. JAS. MILL There is nothing which more vitally imports the American people.

†**3** *verb trans*. Bring about, cause; involve as a consequence. **M16–E18.**
▸ **II** Bring in, introduce; communicate.
4 *verb trans*. Bring or introduce from an external source or from one use etc. to another; *spec.* bring in (goods etc.) from another country. **E16.**

F. L. WRIGHT America has always assumed that culture . . had to come from European sources—be imported. W. WHARTON Most canaries in the United States are imported from Germany and Japan.

5 *verb trans*. Bring or communicate (information etc.). *obsolete* exc. as passing into senses 1b, 4. **M16.**
■ **importable** *adjective* able to be imported or introduced **M16.**

importance /ɪmˈpɔːt(ə)ns/ *noun*. **E16.**
[ORIGIN French from medieval Latin *importantia* significance, consequence, from *important-*: see IMPORTANT, -ANCE.]
▸ **I 1** The fact or quality of being important; significance, consequence. **E16.** ▸**b** An important person or thing. **L16.** ▸**c** Personal consequence, dignity. **L17.**

D. H. LAWRENCE It's of no importance . . . it doesn't matter in the least. N. MAILER The importance of the journey must be estimated by my dread of doing it. **b** R. GRAVES Old importances came swimming back—Wine, meat, log-fires, a roof over the head. **c** R. INGALLS His only importance comes through her. M. DRABBLE He thinks he is enjoying his work, his new importance, his power, his eminence.

†**2** Urgency; importunity. **L16–L18.**
▸ †**II 3** Meaning, import. **M16–E18.**
■ **importancy** *noun* (*a*) = IMPORTANCE 1; †(*b*) = IMPORTANCE 2: **M16.**

important /ɪmˈpɔːt(ə)nt/ *adjective*. **LME.**
[ORIGIN medieval Latin *important-*, *-ans* pres. pple of *importare* be of consequence: see IMPORT *verb*, -ANT[1].]
1 Having great significance; carrying with it great or serious consequences; weighty, momentous. **LME.** ▸**b** Of a person: having high rank; consequential; pompous, pretentious. **E18.** ▸**c** Of an antique etc.: very valuable. **E20.** ▸**d** Preceded by an adverb of degree and modifying a sentence or complete phrase (passing into *adverb*): what is *more*, *most*, etc., important; *more*, *most*, etc., significantly. Cf. IMPORTANTLY 2. **M20.**

A. J. CRONIN His work was the important thing, beside it all else was trivial. N. MOSLEY It becomes so important to me that I see a whole stretch of days ruined if I do not get it. **b** R. P. WARREN People from Washington . . began to come, . . important people whose names were in the papers. A. SCHLEE Charlotte, important with the burden of her guilt, was not to be restrained. **d** R. H. W. BROWN One must wait until the soil is damp enough and, more important, warm enough. *Physics Bulletin* Most important of all, the foreign guests must be assured that the hosts will ease all problems of entry into their country.

†**2** Urgent, importunate. **L16–M17.**

importantly /ɪmˈpɔːt(ə)ntli/ *adverb*. **E17.**
[ORIGIN from IMPORTANT + -LY[2].]
1 In an important manner; to an important degree. **E17.**

D. WELCH He glided in and out of Mr Butler's room, carrying papers importantly. M. SPARK Ruth assumed Barbara to be someone importantly on her side.

2 Modifying a sentence or complete phrase, usu. preceded by an adverb of degree: what is (*more*, *most*, etc.) important; (*more*, *most*, etc.) significantly. (Considered *erron.* by some.) Cf. IMPORTANT 1d. **M20.**

C. WILLIAMS The first outrage against *pietas*, and (more importantly) the first imagined proclamation of *pietas* from the heavens. *Daily Telegraph* But, importantly in this case, there is a well-built girl attendant who is chased about the stage.

importation /ɪmpɔːˈteɪʃ(ə)n/ *noun*. **E17.**
[ORIGIN from IMPORT *verb* + -ATION.]
1 The action of importing or bringing in something, *spec.* goods from another country. **E17.**
2 A thing which is imported. **M17.**
3 *LOGIC*. The inference that if a proposition implies that a second proposition implies a third, then the first and second together imply the third. **E20.**

importee /ɪmpɔːˈtiː/ *noun*. **M19.**
[ORIGIN from IMPORT *verb* + -EE[1].]
A person imported from another country.

importer /ɪmˈpɔːtə/ *noun*. **E18.**
[ORIGIN from IMPORT *verb* + -ER[1].]
A person who or thing which imports something, *esp.* a merchant who imports goods from other countries.

†**importless** *adjective*. *rare* (Shakes.). Only in **E17.**
[ORIGIN from IMPORT *noun* + -LESS.]
Without import; trivial.

importunacy /ɪmˈpɔːtjʊnəsi/ *noun*. **M16.**
[ORIGIN from IMPORTUNATE *adjective* + -ACY.]
= IMPORTUNITY 3.

importunate /ɪmˈpɔːtjʊnət/ *adjective*. **E16.**
[ORIGIN from Latin *importunus* (see IMPORTUNE *adjective*) + -ATE[2], perh. after OBSTINATE *adjective*.]
1 Persistently demanding, pressing. **E16.** ▸**b** Urgent; busy. *arch.* **M16.**

V. SACKVILLE-WEST They were accosted by importunate women. K. HULME I apologise for being importunate. **b** W. C. BRYANT This maze of dusty streets, Forever shaken by the importunate jar Of commerce.

†**2** Inopportune, untimely. **E16–M17.**
†**3** Grievous; troublesome. **M16–E19.**
■ **importunately** *adverb* **L15.** **importunateness** *noun* **M16.**

importunate /ɪmˈpɔːtjʊneɪt/ *verb trans*. Long *rare*. **L16.**
[ORIGIN from IMPORTUNATE *adjective*: see -ATE[3].]
= IMPORTUNE *verb* 1.
■ **importunator** *noun* **E17.**

importune /ɪmpɔːˈtjuːn/ *adjective & noun*. **LME.**
[ORIGIN French *importun*, *-une* or Latin *importunus* inconvenient, unsuitable, unseasonable, formed as IM-[2] + *Portunus* the protecting god of harbours (opp. *opportunus* OPPORTUNE).]
▸ **A** *adjective*. **1** = IMPORTUNATE *adjective* 1. **LME.**
†**2** = IMPORTUNATE *adjective* 3. **LME–M19.**
†**3** = IMPORTUNATE *adjective* 1b. **LME–M17.**
†**4** = IMPORTUNATE *adjective* 2. **LME–E18.**
▸ †**B** *noun*. An importunate person. **L16–M18.**
■ **importunely** *adverb* (now *rare*) **LME.**

importune /ɪmpɔːˈtjuːn/ *verb*. **M16.**
[ORIGIN French *importuner* or medieval Latin *importunari*, from Latin *importunus*: see IMPORTUNE *adjective & noun*.]
1 *verb trans. & intrans*. Ask or request of (a person) persistently or pressingly. **M16.** ▸†**b** Urge or impel (a person or thing). Only in **E17.** ▸**c** Solicit for purposes of prostitution. **M19.**

P. S. BUCK His uncle . . came importuning to his door. B. CHATWIN She importuned them for money.

2 *verb trans*. Ask or beg for (a thing) persistently and pressingly. **L16.**

SHAKES. *L.L.L.* The daughter of the King of France . . Importunes personal conference with his Grace.

†**3** *verb trans*. Burden, trouble, pester. **L16–L18.**
†**4** *verb trans*. Portend. Cf. IMPORT *verb* 1c. Only in **L16.**
■ **importuner** *noun* **M17.**

importunity /ɪmpɔːˈtjuːnɪti/ *noun.* LME.
[ORIGIN Old French & mod. French *importunité* from Latin *importunitas*, from *importunus*: see IMPORTUNE *adjective*, -ITY.]
1 Persistency or insistency in requesting or demanding. LME.
D. WELCH I began to hate his wheedling importunity.
†**2** Trouble, grievousness. LME–M18.
†**3** Inopportunity; untimeliness. L15–L16.

†**impose** *noun. rare.* L16–E17.
[ORIGIN from the verb.]
Imposition.

impose /ɪmˈpəʊz/ *verb.* Also †**em-**. L15.
[ORIGIN Old French & mod. French *imposer*, †*em-*, based on Latin *imponere* place on or into, inflict, deceive (see IM-[1]), but re-formed on Latin pa. pple *impositus* and Old French & mod. French *poser*: see POSE *verb*[1].]
▸ **I** *verb trans.* †**1** Lay (a crime etc.) to the account of; impute to. Foll. by *on*, *upon*. L15–M17.
SHAKES. *Hen. V* The imputation of his wickedness . . should be imposed upon his father that sent him.
2 Put, apply, or bestow authoritatively. *obsolete* exc. as passing into sense 4. E16.
J. BRYANT The name was imposed antecedent to his birth.
3 Subject *to*. Long *rare*. M16.
4 Lay or inflict (a tax, duty, charge, obligation, etc.) (*on* or *upon*), esp. forcibly; compel compliance with; force (oneself) *on* or *upon* the attention etc. of. L16.
R. GRAVES A new tax was imposed . . to provide money for the German wars. N. BLAKE He was more accustomed to imposing discipline than to being disciplined. A. FRASER Not one single condition was suggested, let alone imposed on the king. K. MOORE The present imposed itself once more upon her consciousness.
5 Lay, place, or put, on (*arch.*); *spec.* in PRINTING, arrange (pages of type) in order so as to form the correct sequence after printing and folding. L16. ▸**b** Place in command or office; appoint. *obsolete* exc. as passing into sense 4. E17.
6 Palm or pass off (a thing) *upon* (a person). E17.
▸ **II** *verb intrans.* †**7** Levy a tax (*upon* persons or goods). E17–L19.
8 Exert influence (*on* or *upon*) by impressive character or appearance; presume *on* or *upon*, force oneself *on* or *upon*, take advantage. E17.
J. LUBBOCK Mechanism that imposes through its extreme simplicity. C. ISHERWOOD Most rich people, . . can be imposed upon to almost any extent. T. HEGGEN The crew members imposed on him outrageously with their demands for . . his time.
9 Practise deception *on* or *upon*. M17.
■ **imposable** *adjective* (*rare*) M17. **imposement** *noun* (*rare*) the action of imposing, an imposition M17. **imposer** *noun* L16.

imposing /ɪmˈpəʊzɪŋ/ *adjective.* M17.
[ORIGIN from IMPOSE *verb* + -ING[2].]
1 Dictatorial; exacting. Now *rare*. M17.
2 Deceptive. Now *rare*. M18.
3 Impressive or daunting in appearance or manner. L18.
A. DAVIS There was something imposing about him which evoked total silence and attention. R. DAHL An imposing country mansion . . . a mighty house with turrets on its roof.
■ **imposingly** *adverb* E19. **imposingness** *noun* E19.

imposition /ɪmpəˈzɪʃ(ə)n/ *noun.* LME.
[ORIGIN Old French & mod. French, or Latin *impositio(n-)*, formed as IM-[1] + *positio(n-)* POSITION *noun*.]
1 The action of putting or laying something on; *spec.* (**a**) ECCLESIASTICAL the laying on of hands in blessing, ordination, etc.; (**b**) PRINTING the imposing of pages. LME.
2 The action of applying, bestowing, or ascribing. LME. ▸†**b** Imputation, accusation. *rare* (Shakes.). Only in E17.
3 The action of imposing a charge, obligation, duty, etc.; the action of imposing oneself. Formerly also, taxation. LME.
C. HAMPTON The imposition of blanket censorship and the silencing of all opposition newspapers.
4 A thing imposed or inflicted; an unfair or inconvenient demand or burden. Formerly also, a command or charge laid on a person. LME. ▸**b** A piece of work imposed as punishment at school. M18.
E. WAUGH There is a woeful imposition called 'a week on duty'. D. DELILLO Is this an imposition, James? Just say so.
5 The action or an act of deceiving or being deceived; deception. M17.

impossibilism /ɪmˈpɒsɪbɪlɪz(ə)m/ *noun.* L19.
[ORIGIN from IMPOSSIBLE *adjective* + -ISM.]
Belief in ideas or policy, esp. on social reform, that are held to be unrealizable or impractical.
■ **impossibilist** *noun* M19.

impossibilitate /ɪmˌpɒsɪˈbɪlɪteɪt/ *verb trans. rare.* E17.
[ORIGIN medieval Latin *impossibilitat-* pa. ppl stem of *impossibilitare*, from Latin *impossibilitas*: see IMPOSSIBILITY, -ATE[3]. Cf. Spanish *imposibilitar*, Italian *impossibilitare*.]
Make impossible.

impossibility /ɪmˌpɒsɪˈbɪlɪti/ *noun.* LME.
[ORIGIN Old French & mod. French *impossibilité* or Latin *impossibilitas*, from *impossibilis*: see IMPOSSIBLE, -ITY.]
1 The quality of being impossible; an impossible thing. LME.
R. CAMPBELL It was a sheer impossibility for any doctor, . . to make rain. E. H. JONES The impossibility of reconciling the Church with modern civilization.
†**2** Inability, impotence. LME–L18.

impossible /ɪmˈpɒsɪb(ə)l/ *adjective & noun.* ME.
[ORIGIN Old French & mod. French, or Latin *impossibilis*, formed as IM-[2] + *possibilis* POSSIBLE *adjective*.]
▸ **A** *adjective.* **1** Not possible; unable to be done or exist; extremely difficult, inconvenient, or implausible. ME. ▸**b** MATH. = IMAGINARY *adjective* 1c. Opp. POSSIBLE *adjective* 5. Now *rare*. L17.
B. EMECHETA He had made it impossible for Ezekiel to know the whereabouts of his son. I. MCEWAN It's . . difficult for me to walk down stairs, and completely impossible to walk up them. N. SAHGAL The voyage was a quest, . . and Cythera a paradise, an impossible dream.
mission impossible: see MISSION *noun*.
2 Outrageous, unsuitable, intolerable. Opp. POSSIBLE *adjective* 4. *colloq.* E19.
H. JAMES Grace is impossible—I don't know what's the matter with her. A. BURGESS Without a car life in Malaya was impossible. Life in Malaya was impossible anyway.
▸ **B** *noun.* **1** An impossible thing, an impossibility. Usu. in *pl.* ME.
2 With *the*: that which is or seems impossible. L18.
F. NANSEN The difficult . . takes a little time; the impossible . . takes a little longer.
■ **impossibleness** *noun* (*rare*) LME. **impossibly** *adverb* L16.

impost /ˈɪmpəʊst/ *noun*[1]. L15.
[ORIGIN Italian *imposta* use as noun of fem. pa. pple of *imporre*, from Latin *imponere* IMPOSE *verb*.]
1 The upper course of a pillar, often in the form of a projecting ornamental moulding, on which the foot of an arch rests. L15.
2 A horizontal block supported by upright stones, as in a dolmen. M18.

impost /ˈɪmpəʊst/ *noun*[2]. M16.
[ORIGIN French (now *impôt*) from medieval Latin *impostus*, *-um* use as noun of masc. or neut. of Latin *impostus*, *impositus* pa. pple of *imponere* IMPOSE *verb*.]
1 A tribute, a tax, a duty; *spec.* a customs duty. M16.
G. GORER Very high imposts on alcoholic drinks have had a greater influence on national sobriety.
2 The weight carried by a horse in a handicap race. *slang.* L19.

imposter *noun* var. of IMPOSTOR.

†**imposthumate** *verb*, **imposthumation** *noun*, **imposthume** *noun* vars. of IMPOSTUMATE, IMPOSTUMATION, IMPOSTUME.

impostor /ɪmˈpɒstə/ *noun.* Also **-er**, (earliest) †**-ure**. L16.
[ORIGIN French *imposteur* from late Latin contr. of *impositor*, from Latin *imposit-* pa. ppl stem of *imponere* IMPOSE *verb*: see -OR. In earliest use confused with IMPOSTURE.]
A deceiver, a cheat; *esp.* a person who assumes a false identity in order to deceive others.
E. H. GOMBRICH An artist was little better than an impostor who demanded ridiculous prices for something that could hardly be called honest work. J. BARNES Her parrot was clearly authentic, and . . the Hôtel-Dieu bird was definitely an impostor.
■ **impostorship** *noun* E17. **impostress** *noun* (now *rare*) a female impostor E17.

impostorous /ɪmˈpɒst(ə)rəs/ *adjective.* M16.
[ORIGIN In sense 1 from IMPOSTURE; in sense 2 from IMPOSTOR: see -OUS. Cf. IMPOSTROUS.]
†**1** Of the nature of an imposture. M16–M17.
2 Having the character of an impostor, practising as an impostor. E17.

impostrous /ɪmˈpɒstrəs/ *adjective.* E17.
[ORIGIN Contr.]
1 = IMPOSTOROUS 2. E17.
2 = IMPOSTOROUS 1. M17.

†**impostumate** *verb trans. & intrans.* Also **-sthum-**. Pa. pple & ppl adjective **-ate**, **-ated**. L16–L18.
[ORIGIN Alt. of APOSTUMATE after IMPOSTUME.]
Form an abscess (in).

impostumation /ɪmˌpɒstjʊˈmeɪʃ(ə)n/ *noun.* Now *rare*. Also **-sthum-**. E16.
[ORIGIN Alt. of APOSTUMATION after IMPOSTUME.]
1 An abscess, a cyst. E16.
2 The formation of an abscess; suppuration. M16.

impostume /ɪmˈpɒstjuːm/ *noun.* Now *rare*. Also **-sthume**. LME.
[ORIGIN Old French *empostume* alt. of *apostume*: see APOSTUME.]
An abscess, a cyst.
fig.: BROWNING The imposthume I prick to relieve thee of,—Vanity.

imposture /ɪmˈpɒstʃə/ *noun.* M16.
[ORIGIN French from late Latin *impostura*, from Latin *impost-* pa. ppl stem of *imponere* IMPOSE *verb*: see -URE.]
1 (An act of) wilful and fraudulent deception. M16.
†**2** Var. of IMPOSTOR. L16–M17.
■ **imposturous** *adjective* (now *rare*) †(**a**) given to practising imposture; (**b**) deceptive, fraudulent: E17.

imposure /ɪmˈpəʊʒə/ *noun. rare.* L17.
[ORIGIN from IMPOSE *verb* + -URE.]
An imposition.

impotable /ɪmˈpəʊtəb(ə)l/ *adjective.* E17.
[ORIGIN from IM-[2] + POTABLE *adjective*.]
Undrinkable.

impotence /ˈɪmpət(ə)ns/ *noun.* LME.
[ORIGIN Old French & mod. French from Latin *impotentia*, formed as IM-[2] + *potentia*: see POTENCE *noun*[1].]
1 Lack of strength or power; helplessness; weakness; feebleness. LME.
F. W. H. MYERS A feeling of terrible impotence burdens me—I am so powerless.
2 Inability to achieve erection of the penis; (esp. of a male) inability to have sexual intercourse or to reach orgasm or *popularly* to procreate. L15.
P. GAY Don Juan is afraid of impotence, perhaps of being a repressed homosexual.
†**3** Lack of self-restraint. E16–E18.

impotency /ˈɪmpət(ə)nsi/ *noun.* LME.
[ORIGIN Latin *impotentia*: see IMPOTENCE, -ENCY.]
1 = IMPOTENCE 1. LME.
†**2** = IMPOTENCE 3. M16–E18.
3 = IMPOTENCE 2. L16.

impotent /ˈɪmpət(ə)nt/ *adjective & noun.* LME.
[ORIGIN Old French & mod. French from Latin *impotent-*, *-ens*, formed as IM-[2] + POTENT *adjective*[2].]
▸ **A** *adjective.* **1** Powerless, helpless, ineffective; physically weak, decrepit. LME.
ISAIAH BERLIN Individual wills may not be all-powerful, but neither are they totally impotent.
2 Unable to achieve erection of the penis; (esp. of a male) unable to have sexual intercourse or to reach orgasm or *popularly* to procreate. L15.
W. WHARTON An . . artificial-insemination business for wives of sterile or impotent men.
†**3** Unrestrained, passionate. L16–E18.
▸ **B** *noun.* **1** An impotent person. L15.
2 *collect. pl.* *The* class of impotent people. M18.
R. H. TAWNEY The Council . . insists on regular reports as to the . . relief of the impotent.
■ **impotently** *adverb* (**a**) powerlessly, feebly; †(**b**) unrestrainedly: E17. †**impotentness** *noun* (*rare*) M16–E18.

impound /ɪmˈpaʊnd/ *verb trans.* Also †**em-**. LME.
[ORIGIN from IM-[1], EM-[1] + POUND *noun*[2].]
1 Shut up (esp. seized cattle) in a pound. LME.
2 Shut in or enclose (a person or thing) as in a pound. M16. ▸**b** *spec.* Confine and store (water) in a reservoir; confine water so as to form (a reservoir). M19.
3 Take legal possession of, confiscate. M17.
■ **impoundable** *adjective* L17. **impoundage** *noun* = IMPOUNDMENT E17. **impounder** *noun* E19. **impoundment** *noun* (**a**) the action of impounding, the condition of being impounded; (**b**) a body of water confined to form a reservoir: M17.

impoverish /ɪmˈpɒv(ə)rɪʃ/ *verb trans.* Also †**em-**. LME.
[ORIGIN Old French *empoveriss-* lengthened stem of *empov(e)rir* (mod. *empauvrir*), formed as EM-[1], IM-[1] + *povre* POOR *adjective*: see -ISH[2].]
1 Make poor, reduce to poverty. LME. ▸†**b** Strip *of* some form of wealth. E17–E18.
J. GATHORNE-HARDY I found no evidence of over-high rents—why should councils wish to impoverish their local practices? M. PIERCY She would end up homeless and impoverished.
2 *fig.* Weaken or reduce the quality of; deprive of some quality; affect adversely. M17.
E. WAUGH Endowed with the most splendid language . . young writers seem intent to debase and impoverish it.
■ **impoverisher** *noun* E17.

impoverishment /ɪmˈpɒv(ə)rɪʃm(ə)nt/ *noun.* Also †**em-**. LME.
[ORIGIN Anglo-Norman *empoverissement*, from Old French *empov(e)rir*: see IMPOVERISH, -MENT.]
The action of impoverishing someone or something; the condition of being impoverished; an instance of this.

†**impower** *verb* var. of EMPOWER.

impracticable /ɪmˈpraktɪkəb(ə)l/ *adjective & noun.* M17.
[ORIGIN from IM-[2] + PRACTICABLE.]
▸ **A** *adjective.* **1** Not practicable; unable to be carried out or done; impossible in practice. M17.
J. F. LEHMANN In the end the scheme was abandoned as impracticable.
2 a Of a road etc.: impassable. M17. ▸**b** Of a person or thing: unmanageable, intractable. E18.

a G. GROTE The pass appeared impracticable. **b** B. H. MALKIN One of those impracticable beings, on whom good example, good advice . . are equally thrown away.

▸ **B** *noun*. An impracticable person. *rare*. E19.

■ **impractica'bility** *noun* (**a**) the quality or condition of being impracticable; (**b**) an impracticable thing: M18. **impracticableness** *noun* M17. **impracticably** *adverb* L18.

impractical /ɪmˈpraktɪk(ə)l/ *adjective*. M19.
[ORIGIN from IM-² + PRACTICAL *adjective*.]
Not practical; not sensible or realistic; not skilled at manual tasks.

M. RULE The idea had to be abandoned as impractical on our site. M. SCAMMELL She was . . naive and impractical and unsuited to the tough, scheming world of the young Soviet republic.

■ **impracti'cality** *noun* E20. **impractically** *adverb* M20. **impracticalness** *noun* (*rare*) E20.

imprecate /ˈɪmprɪkeɪt/ *verb*. E17.
[ORIGIN Latin *imprecat-* pa. ppl stem of *imprecari*, formed as IM-¹ + *precari* PRAY *verb*: see -ATE³.]
1 *verb trans.* **a** Invoke or call down (evil *on* a person etc.). E17. ▸**b** Beg for; entreat (something good). *rare*. M17.

a SMOLLETT She . . imprecated a thousand curses upon his head.

2 *verb trans.* Invoke evil on (a person); curse. Now *rare* or *obsolete*. E17.

W. MINTO His co-religionists were imprecating him as the man who had brought this persecution upon them.

3 *verb trans.* Pray to, call on, (a god etc.). Long *rare* or *obsolete*. M17.

W. PRYNNE Which I shall dayly imprecate the God of Peace speedily to accomplish.

†**4** *verb intrans.* Pray; invoke evil. M–L17.

imprecation /ɪmprɪˈkeɪʃ(ə)n/ *noun*. LME.
[ORIGIN Latin *imprecatio(n-)*, formed as IMPRECATE: see -ATION.]
1 The action or an act of imprecating, *spec.* of invoking or calling down evil on a person etc.; cursing. LME.
2 A prayer, an entreaty. Now *rare*. L16.
3 An invocation of evil; *esp.* a spoken curse or other expression of hostility. E17.

T. MO An immense crowd of Chinese, howling imprecations and with offensive weapons in their hands.

imprecatory /ˈɪmprɪkeɪt(ə)ri, ɪmˈprɛkət(ə)ri/ *adjective*. L16.
[ORIGIN medieval Latin *imprecatorius*, formed as IMPRECATE *verb*: see -ORY².]
Expressing or involving imprecation; maledictory.
■ **imprecatorily** *adverb* L19.

imprecise /ɪmprɪˈsʌɪs/ *adjective*. E19.
[ORIGIN from IM-² + PRECISE *adjective*.]
Not precise; lacking precision.
■ **imprecisely** *adverb* M20. **impreciseness** *noun* E20.

imprecision /ɪmprɪˈsɪʒ(ə)n/ *noun*. E19.
[ORIGIN from IM-² + PRECISION *noun*.]
Lack of precision; an instance of this.

impredicable /ɪmˈprɛdɪkəb(ə)l/ *adjective*. E17.
[ORIGIN from IM-² + PREDICABLE.]
Unable to be predicated.
■ **impredica'bility** *noun* E20.

impredicative /ɪmˈprɛdɪkətɪv/ *adjective*. M20.
[ORIGIN from IM-² + PREDICATIVE *adjective*.]
LOGIC. Of a proposition, thing, etc.: not definable except in terms of a totality of which it is itself a part.

impregn /ɪmˈpriːn/ *verb trans.* Now only *poet*. LME.
[ORIGIN Late Latin *impregnare*: see IMPREGNATE *verb*.]
1 Make (a female) pregnant; fertilize (*lit.* & *fig.*). LME.
2 Fill *with*; imbue, permeate, (*with*). M17.

impregnable /ɪmˈprɛgnəb(ə)l/ *adjective*¹. LME.
[ORIGIN Old French *imprenable*, formed as IM-² + *prenable* takeable, from *pren-* stem of *prendre* take from Latin *prehendere*: see -ABLE; -*g*- perh. after *reign*, and Old French vars.]
(Of a fortress etc.) unable to be taken by force; *fig.* proof against attack, unassailable.

A. MACLEAN The Schloss Adler is inaccessible and impregnable. It would require a battalion of paratroops to take it. A. STORR She carries within an impregnable conviction of being lovable.

■ **impregna'bility** *noun* M19. **impregnableness** *noun* (long *rare*) E17. **impregnably** *adverb* E17.

impregnable /ɪmˈprɛgnəb(ə)l/ *adjective*². L19.
[ORIGIN from IMPREGNATE *verb* + -ABLE.]
Able to be impregnated.

impregnant /ɪmˈprɛgnənt/ *adjective* & *noun*. L15.
[ORIGIN Partly from IM-¹ + PREGNANT *adjective*¹, partly from late Latin *impregnant-* pres. ppl stem of *impregnare*: see IMPREGNATE *verb*, -ANT¹.]
▸ **A** *adjective*. †**1** Impregnated, pregnant. L15–E18.
2 That impregnates, impregnating. *arch. rare*. E19.
▸ **B** *noun*. A thing which impregnates; *spec.* a substance used for the impregnation of something else. M17.

impregnate /ɪmˈprɛgnət/ *adjective*. L15.
[ORIGIN Late Latin *impregnatus* pa. pple, formed as IMPREGNATE *verb*: see -ATE².]
1 Pregnant, fruitful, (*lit.* & *fig.*). L15.
2 Imbued, permeated, *with*. M17.

impregnate /ˈɪmprɛgneɪt, ɪmˈprɛgneɪt/ *verb*. E17.
[ORIGIN Late Latin *impregnat-* pa. ppl stem of *impregnare*, formed as IM-¹ + *pregnare* be pregnant: see -ATE³.]
1 *verb trans.* Orig., fill. Later, fill (something) *with* a substance etc. diffused through it; imbue, saturate. Usu. in *pass.* E17. ▸**b** *fig.* Imbue or fill (*with* feelings, moral qualities, etc.). M17.

J. ARBUTHNOT Water impregnated with some penetrating Salt. **b** LYTTON He had sought to impregnate his colleagues with the same loftiness of principle. L. DURRELL Seek an atmosphere less impregnated with the sense of deracination and failure.

2 *verb trans.* Be diffused through (something); permeate, fill, saturate. M17.
3 *verb trans.* Make (a female) pregnant; BIOLOGY fertilize (a female reproductive cell or ovum). M17. ▸**b** *verb intrans.* Become pregnant, conceive. *rare*. E18.
4 *verb trans. fig.* Make fruitful or productive. M17.
■ **impregnatable** *adjective* E20. **impregnator** *noun* a person who or thing which impregnates E18.

impregnation /ɪmprɛgˈneɪʃ(ə)n/ *noun*. LME.
[ORIGIN Old French & mod. French, or formed as IMPREGNATE *verb*: see -ATION.]
1 The action or process of making a female pregnant; fertilization. LME.
2 The action of imbuing or the fact of being imbued with something; diffusion through a substance; saturation. M17. ▸**b** *spec.* The saturation of wood with a preservative. L19.
3 That with which something is impregnated; an impregnating element etc. E18.

impreparation /ɪmˌprɛpəˈreɪʃ(ə)n/ *noun*. Long *rare*. L16.
[ORIGIN from IM-² + PREPARATION.]
Lack of preparation; unpreparedness.

impresa /ɪmˈpreɪzə/ *noun*. L16.
[ORIGIN Italian = undertaking, device, from Proto-Romance verb, whence also EMPRISE. Cf. IMPRESE.]
1 An emblem, a device; *esp.* one accompanied by a motto. L16.
2 A sentence accompanying an emblem; a motto, a maxim, a proverb. Long *rare*. E17.

impresario /ɪmprɪˈsɑːrɪəʊ/ *noun*. Pl. **-os**. M18.
[ORIGIN Italian, formed as IMPRESA + -*ario* -ARY¹.]
An organizer or sponsor of public entertainments; a manager of an operatic or a concert company.

imprescriptible /ɪmprɪˈskrɪptɪb(ə)l/ *adjective*. L16.
[ORIGIN medieval Latin *imprescriptibilis*, formed as IM-² + PRESCRIPTIBLE.]
Not subject to prescription; unable to be legally taken away or abandoned.

T. PAINE The natural and imprescriptible rights of man . . are liberty, property, security, and resistance of oppression.

imprese /ɪmˈpreɪz/ *noun*. Long *rare*. L16.
[ORIGIN Obsolete French from Italian IMPRESA. See also IMPRESS *noun*³.]
1 = IMPRESA 1. L16.
†**2** = IMPRESA 2. E17–E19.

impress /ˈɪmprɛs/ *noun*¹. L16.
[ORIGIN from IMPRESS *verb*¹.]
1 The act of impressing or stamping; a mark made by pressure of a seal, stamp, etc. (Foll. by *of*.) L16.

T. MEDWIN Bluish marks . . as if made by the impress of the fingers. H. N. HUMPHREYS The reverse is incused with the impress of an amphora.

2 *fig.* A characteristic or distinctive mark or quality; a lasting effect or influence. L16. ▸**b** An impression on the mind or senses. Now *rare*. L16.

E. A. POE His obscurity . . bore the impress of his genius. H. JAMES She would . . have left a deeper impress upon her time. **b** E. K. KANE Some painful impress of solitary danger . . kept them closing up continually.

impress /ˈɪmprɛs/ *noun*². *obsolete* exc. *hist.* Now *rare*. E17.
[ORIGIN from IMPRESS *verb*².]
Impressment; enforced service in the army or navy.

impress /ˈɪmprɛs/ *noun*³. *obsolete* exc. *hist.* E17.
[ORIGIN Var. of IMPRESE, assoc. with IMPRESS *noun*¹.]
1 = IMPRESA 1. E17.
†**2** = IMPRESA 2. Only in 17.

†**impress** *noun*⁴. E17.
[ORIGIN Var. of IMPREST *noun*.]
1 = IMPREST *noun* 1. E17–E18.
2 A charge made on the pay of a naval officer who had not accounted satisfactorily for public money advanced to him. Only in E19.

impress /ɪmˈprɛs/ *verb*¹. Pa. t. & pple **impressed**, †**imprest**. LME.
[ORIGIN Old French & mod. French *empresser*, formed as EM-¹, IM-¹ + PRESS *verb*¹ after Latin *imprimere* (see IMPRESSION).]
▸ **I** *verb trans.* **1** Apply with pressure; press (a thing) *on* another so as to leave a mark; imprint or stamp (a character or quality) *on*, as if by pressure. LME. ▸**b** Produce or communicate (motion), exert (force), by pressure. (Foll. by *on*.) E18. ▸**c** ELECTRICITY. Apply (a voltage) to a device or circuit. L19.

SHELLEY He did impress On the green moss his tremulous step. **b** C. LYELL Movements . . impressed on a wide expanse of ocean.

2 *fig.* Cause to have a lasting effect or influence or to make an impression *on* or *upon* a person, the mind, etc., (foll. by simple obj., *that*, *what*, etc.); enforce or urge (a rule of conduct etc.) *on* or *upon*. LME.

R. G. COLLINGWOOD My work in archeology . . impressed upon me the importance of the 'questioning activity'. S. UNWIN He . . impressed upon me that I must walk there.

†**3** Print; make a typographical impression of. E16–L18.
4 Exert pressure on; mark (something) *with* the pressure of a stamp, seal, etc. L16. ▸**b** *fig.* Stamp or imprint *with* a particular character, quality, etc. E19.

A. RADCLIFFE The Marquis seizing her hand, impressed it with kisses. L. STEPHEN The ring . . was impressed with the seal of the Prophet. **b** LYTTON The words were impressed with a wild and melancholy depth of feeling.

5 Produce a lasting effect or influence on the mind or feelings of; affect or influence deeply; make a favourable impression on; strike. (Foll. by *with*.) M18.

J. GALSWORTHY The fellow had impressed him—great range, real genius! J. BUCHAN How did he impress you, Dick, when you knew him? D. PLANTE I wondered if she was trying to impress me with what she knew.

▸ **II** *verb intrans.* †**6** Press in; press or throng *about*. LME–L15.
7 Appear impressive; make a favourable impression. M20.
■ **impressed** *adjective* (**a**) *gen.* that has been impressed (*lit.* & *fig.*); deeply and favourably affected or influenced; (**b**) ZOOLOGY & BOTANY sunk in, depressed, marked by surface depressions: LME.

impress /ɪmˈprɛs/ *verb*² *trans.* Pa. t & pple **impressed**, †**imprest**. L16.
[ORIGIN from IM-¹ + PRESS *verb*².]
1 Chiefly *hist.* Levy or provide (a force) for military or naval service, enlist; *spec.* compel (men) to serve in the army or esp. the navy. Also, seize (goods etc.) for royal or public service. L16.

A. DUGGAN A travel-warrant . . authorising them to impress transport and requisition billets. C. RYAN A number of Poles, impressed into the German Army.

2 Enlist or make use of in an argument etc. *arch.* M17.

F. W. FARRAR Hypotheses into the service of which Philology was impressed.

†**impress** *verb*³ *trans.* *rare*. Pa. t. & pple **impressed**, **imprest**. M17.
[ORIGIN Var. of IMPREST *verb*¹. Cf. IMPRESS *noun*⁴.]
1 = IMPREST *verb*¹ 1. M17–E19.
2 Levy a charge on (the pay of a naval officer) because of unsatisfactory accounting for public money advanced. Only in E19.

impressible /ɪmˈprɛsɪb(ə)l/ *adjective*. Also (earlier) †**-able**. LME.
[ORIGIN from IMPRESS *verb*¹ + -ABLE, -IBLE.]
Able to be impressed (*lit.* & *fig.*); susceptible, impressionable.
■ **impressi'bility** *noun* M18.

impression /ɪmˈprɛʃ(ə)n/ *noun* & *verb*. LME.
[ORIGIN Old French & mod. French from Latin *impressio(n-)*, from *impress-* pa. ppl stem of *imprimere*, formed as IM-¹ + *premere* PRESS *verb*¹: see -ION.]
▸ **A** *noun* **1** **a** Pressure applied by one thing on or into the surface of another; an instance or effect of such pressure; the stamping of a character or quality *on*. LME. ▸†**b** A charge, an attack, an assault. LME–L18. ▸†**c** PROSODY & RHETORIC. A stress, an emphasis. M17–E19. ▸**d** An impact or shock of an atmospheric or physical force. Now *rare* or *obsolete*. L17.

a B. JOWETT The creation of the world is the impression of order on a previously existing chaos. **b** S. JOHNSON Elephants . . by the violence of their impression . . often threw the enemy into disorder.

2 A mark produced on a surface by pressure, esp. by the application of a stamp, seal, etc. Also, a cast, a copy. LME. ▸**b** DENTISTRY. A mould (from which a positive cast may be made) formed by the imprint of the teeth, gums, etc., in a soft material. M19.

G. BERKELEY As . . a seal [is said] to make an impression upon wax. D. L. DINELEY Moulds or impressions are left in any soft mud or sand. *fig.*: W. COWPER If it bear The stamp and clear impression of good sense.

3 The effective action of one thing on another; influence; a change produced in a passive subject by the operation of an external cause. LME. ▸†**b** *spec.* An atmospheric influence, condition, or phenomenon. LME–L17.

J. IMISON One of the hardest metals; a file can scarcely make any impression on it. W. S. CHURCHILL Rupert's cavalry . . could make no impression on the London pikemen and musketeers.

4 a An effect produced on the mind, conscience, or feelings. LME. ▸**b** An effect produced on the senses; a sensation. E17. ▸**c** A (vague or mistaken) notion or belief impressed on the mind. E17.

a E. A. FREEMAN A deep impression had been made on the minds of Englishmen. P. ROTH Strong first impressions had of course been formed. **b** B. JOWETT Our impressions of hearing may be affected by those of sight. **c** OED It is a mere impression, and I may easily be mistaken. R. TRAVERS Burgess . . dug his own grave under the impression he was opening a mining shaft.

5 a The process of printing. Now *rare*. E16. ▸**b** The result of printing; a print taken from type or other surfaces. M16. ▸**c** (The printing of) the number of copies of a book, newspaper, etc., issued at one time. L16. ▸**d** An essentially unaltered reprint of a book etc. from standing type, plates, film, etc., as opp. to a new edition. E20.

a GIBBON The impression of the fourth volume had consumed three months. **b** M. M. HEATON Very early impressions of Dürer's engravings are seldom now to be met with. **c** J. COLLINGES 6000 of his books being sold, if 1500 be allowed to an Impression. **d** J. GROSS The book . . quickly ran through half-a-dozen impressions, and Birrell . . found himself a minor celebrity.

6 A representation of a person or thing by an artist, a mimic, etc.; a brief impersonation of a well-known personality. M20.

D. NATHAN Peter would come in and do a few impressions of Kenneth Horne and others.

▸ **B** *verb*. *rare*.
†**1** *verb intrans.* Stamp; make an impression. Only in E17.
2 *verb trans.* Make an impression on, affect. M19.

– COMB.: **impression compound** an impression material manufactured from a number of different ingredients, *esp.* one that is a non-elastic thermoplastic solid; **impression material** a substance used in taking dental impressions.

■ **impressional** *adjective* (*a*) impressionable; (*b*) of or pertaining to an impression or impressions: M19. **impressionless** *adjective* (*rare*) M19.

impressionable /ɪmˈprɛʃ(ə)nəb(ə)l/ *adjective*. M19.
[ORIGIN French, from *impressionner*, formed as IMPRESSION: see -ABLE.]

1 Susceptible to impressions; easily influenced. M19.

J. MORTIMER How impressionable he was—he had been speaking French when they came out of *Hiroshima Mon Amour*.

2 Able to be impressed. *rare*. L19.

Life Tinfoil thin enough to be impressionable by the metal style.

■ **impressionaˈbility** *noun* M19. **impressionableness** *noun* M19.

impressionary /ɪmˈprɛʃ(ə)n(ə)ri/ *adjective*. L19.
[ORIGIN from IMPRESSION *noun* + -ARY¹.]
Impressionistic.

impressionism /ɪmˈprɛʃ(ə)nɪz(ə)m/ *noun*. In branch II usu. **I-**. M19.
[ORIGIN In branch I directly from IMPRESSION *noun*, in branch II from French *impressionnisme*, formed as IMPRESSIONIST: see -ISM.]

▸ †**I 1** The philosophy of David Hume (1711–76) regarding sensations. *rare*. Only in M19.

▸ **II 2** A school or style of painting, originating in France in the late 19th cent., aiming at representation of the visual impression or overall effect of a subject, scene, etc., rather than of its detail; *transf.* an analogous literary style. L19.

3 A style of musical composition in which clarity of structure and theme is subordinate to harmonic effects, characteristically using the whole-tone scale. L19.

impressionist /ɪmˈprɛʃ(ə)nɪst/ *noun & adjective*. L19.
[ORIGIN French *impressionniste* (orig. applied unfavourably in 1874 with ref. to Claude Monet's painting *Impression: soleil levant*), formed as IMPRESSION *noun*: see -IST.]

▸ **A** *noun*. **1** (Usu. **I-**.) An adherent or practitioner of Impressionism in painting, literature, or music. Also, a painting by an Impressionist. L19.

2 An entertainer whose act consists of imitations or impersonations of well-known personalities etc. M20.

▸ **B** *attrib.* or as *adjective*. Of or pertaining to impressionists or (usu. **I-**) Impressionism. L19.

impressionistic /ɪmˌprɛʃəˈnɪstɪk/ *adjective*. L19.
[ORIGIN Partly from IMPRESSIONIST, partly from IMPRESSION *noun*: see -ISTIC.]
Of, pertaining to, or characteristic of impressionism or impressionists; subjective, unsystematic.

■ **impressionistically** *adverb* E20.

impressive /ɪmˈprɛsɪv/ *adjective*. L16.
[ORIGIN from IMPRESS *verb*¹ + -IVE.]

†**1** Able to be easily impressed; susceptible (*to*); impressible. L16–M17.

J. SPENCER The multitude . . cannot but be greatly impressive to any great and religious Perswasions concerning Prodigies.

2 Making a deep impression on the mind or senses, esp. so as to cause approval or admiration; (of language, a scene, etc.) capable of exciting deep feeling. L16.

D. W. GOODWIN There is now impressive evidence that drinking and pregnancy do not mix. B. LOPEZ What was so impressive about the bear we saw . . was how robust he seemed.

■ **impressively** *adverb* E19. **impressiveness** *noun* M17.

impressment /ɪmˈprɛsm(ə)nt/ *noun*¹. L18.
[ORIGIN from IMPRESS *verb*² + -MENT.]
The action or practice of impressing someone or something for public service; enlistment or use in an argument etc.

impressment /ɪmˈprɛsm(ə)nt/ *noun*². *rare*. M19.
[ORIGIN French *empressement*, formed as IMPRESS *verb*¹ + -MENT.]
Earnestness, ardour.

impressure /ɪmˈprɛʃə/ *noun*. Now *rare*. L15.
[ORIGIN from IMPRESS *verb*¹ + -URE, after *pressure*.]
1 The action of impressing or exerting pressure. L15.
2 A mark made by pressure; an impression; an indentation. E17.
3 An impression on the mind or senses. E17.

imprest /ˈɪmprɛst/ *noun & adjective*. M16.
[ORIGIN from IM-¹ + PREST *noun*¹, prob. partly after *in prest* (see PREST *noun*¹), though *im-* appears in medieval Latin cognates (cf. IMPREST *verb*¹). See also IMPRESS *noun*⁴.]

▸ **A** *noun*. **1** Money advanced to a person for use in state business. Formerly also, advance pay for those in military and naval service. M16.

2 *gen.* An advance, a loan. L17.

J. LE CARRÉ He . . lavished a sizable part of our secret imprest on encouraging more breeds of trout.

– COMB.: **imprest system** COMMERCE a system under which a person is advanced a fixed sum of money to meet expenses and at the end of a definite period is advanced a further sum equal to the amount spent, so as to restore the float to the original amount.

▸ †**B** *adjective*. Of money: lent or paid in advance, esp. to those in military, naval, or public service. L16–M18.

†**imprest** *verb*¹ *trans.* M16.
[ORIGIN from Italian & medieval Latin *imprestare* lend, advance as an imprest, formed as IM-¹ + Latin *praestare* furnish, (in medieval Latin) lend, rel. to *praesto* at hand, within reach.]
1 Advance or lend (money). M16–E19.
2 Draw (a bill etc.) *upon* an account or a person. E–M17.

†**imprest** *verb*² *trans.* M17–E18.
[ORIGIN from pa. pple of IMPRESS *verb*², perh. also confused with IMPREST *verb*¹.]
Impress for the army or navy.

†**imprest** *verb*³, *verb*⁴, *verb*⁵ *pa. t. & pple*: see IMPRESS *verb*¹, *verb*², *verb*³.

imprevisible /ɪmprɪˈvɪzɪb(ə)l/ *adjective*. *rare*. L19.
[ORIGIN from IM-² + PREVISE + -IBLE.]
Unable to be foreseen.

imprévu /ɛ̃prevy/ *noun*. M19.
[ORIGIN French, formed as IM-² + *prévu* pa. pple of *prévoir* foresee.]
The unexpected, *the* unforeseen.

imprimatur /ɪmprɪˈmeɪtə, -ˈmɑːtə, -ˈmɑːtʊə/ *noun*. M17.
[ORIGIN Latin = let it be printed, 3rd person sing. pres. subjunct. pass. of *imprimere* IMPRINT *verb*.]
In the Roman Catholic Church, an official licence authorizing the printing of an ecclesiastical or religious work etc.; *gen.* official approval, an official sanction.

J. BRONOWSKI Galileo collected . . four imprimaturs, and early in 1632 the book was published. P. GAY The psychological function of this partially unconscious fiction is to give the imprimatur to the child's aggressive impulses.

imprimatura /ˌɪmpriːməˈtʊərə/ *noun*. M20.
[ORIGIN Italian *imprimitura*.]
A usu. coloured transparent primer or glaze applied to an artist's canvas or panel.

†**imprime** *verb & noun*. Also **em-**. L16.
[ORIGIN from IM-¹, EM-¹ + PRIME *adjective* or *noun*¹ or Latin *primus* first.]
HUNTING. ▸**A** *verb trans.* Separate (a deer) from the rest of the herd. L16–L18.
▸ **B** *noun*. An act of separating a deer from the rest of the herd. L16–M18.

imprimis /ɪmˈprʌɪmɪs/ *adverb*. *arch.* LME.
[ORIGIN Latin, assim. form of *in primis* among the first things, from *in* IN *preposition* + *primis* abl. pl. of *primus* first.]
In the first place.

imprimitive /ɪmˈprɪmɪtɪv/ *adjective*. E18.
[ORIGIN from IM-² + PRIMITIVE *adjective*.]
†**1** Not following primitive usage or tradition. *rare*. Only in E18.
2 MATH. Of a group: not primitive. L19.

imprint /ˈɪmprɪnt/ *noun*. Also (earlier) †**em-**. LME.
[ORIGIN Old French & mod. French *empreinte* use as noun of fem. pa. pple of *empreindre*: see IMPRINT *verb*, PRINT *noun*.]

1 A mark produced by pressure on a surface; an impression, a stamp. LME. ▸**b** *fig.* A lasting impression or sign of some emotion, experience, action, etc.; an influence; an effect. E17.

H. MOORE Clay is wonderful stuff to punch and feel that the imprint of your fist is left in it. J. T. STORY He put coal dust on the blotter and read the imprint of my letter. **b** C. G. WOLFF Edith Wharton had to contend with the part of herself that carried Mother's imprint. P. D. JAMES His face, his clothes, the confident gaze, all bore the unmistakable imprint of success.

2 A publisher's or printer's name, often with an address, date, and other details of publication, printed in a book etc., usu. on the title page, or at the foot of a single sheet; any of various names used as imprints by a publishing house; *loosely* a publishing house. L18.

P. ACKROYD The Woolfs had agreed to print Eliot's . . work under the imprint of the Hogarth Press. A. BLOND The New English Library (. . an imprint of Hodder and Stoughton).

3 Something printed; *spec.* a postage stamp printed on the paper to be used. L19.

Library The Library now has an almost complete collection of Norwegian imprints.

4 (**I-**.) A typeface derived from Caslon [named after the periodical for which it was designed]. E20.

imprint /ɪmˈprɪnt/ *verb trans.* Also (earlier) †**em-**. LME.
[ORIGIN Old French *empreinter*, from *empreint* pa. pple of *empreindre*, ult. from Latin *imprimere*, formed as IM-¹ + *premere* PRESS *verb*¹. Cf. PRINT *verb*.]

1 Mark by pressure; make an imprint or impression of (a figure etc.) *on*; impress *with* a figure etc. LME. ▸†**b** Print (a book etc.) by means of a press and type. L15–E19.

M. SHELLEY A land never before imprinted by the foot of man. DICKENS Each sometimes stops and slowly imprints a deeper footstep in the fallen leaves.

2 *fig.* Impress *on* or fix *in* the mind, memory, etc.; impart, impress (a quality, character, etc.) *on* or *in* a person or thing. LME.

C. BLACKWOOD She had remained for ever imprinted on his memory. C. PHILLIPS He would pick out a spot, . . and try and imprint it on his mind.

3 PSYCHOLOGY. Cause (esp. a young animal) to accept or recognize a person, animal, or thing as the proper object of an innate response, esp. as a parent; cause (an animal etc.) to be so accepted or recognized. Foll. by *on*, *to*. Freq. in *pass.* and as ***imprinting*** *verbal noun*. M20.

B. THORPE The parent . . fish may become imprinted to the young as well as the young to the parent.

■ **imprinter** *noun* M16.

imprison /ɪmˈprɪz(ə)n/ *verb trans.* Also (earlier) †**em-**. ME.
[ORIGIN Old French *emprisoner* (mod. *-onner*), formed as EM-¹, IM-¹ + PRISON *noun*.]
Put or keep in a prison or other place of confinement; confine, shut up, (*lit.* & *fig.*).

G. K. CHESTERTON A desperate thing imprisoned in this box of thin wood. V. GLENDINNING She was imprisoned for her political activities and for her advocacy of birth control. KARL MILLER The inscrutable child who appears . . both excluded and imprisoned, locked out and locked in. P. LIVELY I . . am as imprisoned by my time as you were by yours.

■ **imprisonable** *adjective* able to be imprisoned, liable to imprisonment; (of an offence) for which a person can be imprisoned: E17. **imprisoner** *noun* M17.

imprisonment /ɪmˈprɪz(ə)nm(ə)nt/ *noun*. LME.
[ORIGIN Anglo-Norman *enprisounement*, Old French *-one-*, formed as IMPRISON: see -MENT.]
The action or an act of imprisoning someone or (*transf.* & *fig.*) something; the fact or condition of being imprisoned.

E. CRANKSHAW Imprisonment was not enough. They must receive six thousand lashes.

false imprisonment: see FALSE *adjective*.

impro /ˈɪmprəʊ/ *noun*. *slang*. L20.
[ORIGIN Abbreviation: cf. IMPROV.]
Improvisation in performance.

improbability /ɪmˌprɒbəˈbɪlɪti/ *noun*. L16.
[ORIGIN from IMPROBABLE: see -ITY.]
1 The quality of being improbable. L16.
2 An improbable circumstance or thing. E17.

improbable /ɪmˈprɒbəb(ə)l/ *adjective*. L16.
[ORIGIN French, or Latin *improbabilis* hard to prove, formed as IM-² + *probabilis* PROBABLE *adjective*.]
Not probable; not likely to be true or to happen; unlikely; difficult to believe, though true or existent.

ISAIAH BERLIN These alternatives may be improbable; but they must at least be conceivable. E. J. HOWARD Listing . . a number of improbable things which could not possibly have happened to it. J. S. HUXLEY The improbable plumage and glorious brightness of some exotic birds. N. MAILER It seemed not improbable that Pangborn could be the maniac who did it.

■ **improbableness** *noun* E18. **improbably** *adverb* M17.

improbation /ɪmprəˈbeɪʃ(ə)n/ *noun*. M16.
[ORIGIN Latin *improbatio(n-)* disproof, refutation, from *improbat-* pa. ppl stem of *improbare* disapprove, reject, formed as IM-² + *probare* PROVE *verb*: see -ATION. In sense 2 from French.]
1 Disproof. Long only *spec.* (SCOTS LAW), disproof of a writ as invalid or forged; *esp.* an action brought to disprove a writ on these grounds. M16.
†**2** Disapproval. M17–L18.

improbative /ɪmˈprəʊbətɪv/ *adjective*. M18.
[ORIGIN Anglo-Latin *improbativus* tending to refute, from Latin *improbat-*: see IMPROBATION, -ATIVE. Cf. PROBATIVE.]
Liable to disproof; not proved to be genuine.

improbity /ɪmˈprəʊbɪti, -ˈprɒb-/ *noun*. LME.
[ORIGIN Latin *improbitas*, formed as IM-[2] + *probitas* PROBITY.]
†**1** Audacity. Only in LME.
2 Wickedness, lack of moral integrity; dishonesty. L16.

improficiency /ɪmprəˈfɪʃ(ə)nsi/ *noun*. Now *rare*. M17.
[ORIGIN from IM-[2] + PROFICIENCY.]
Lack of proficiency.

†**improfitable** *adjective*. ME–E18.
[ORIGIN from IM-[2] + PROFITABLE.]
Unprofitable.

improgressive /ɪmprəˈɡrɛsɪv/ *adjective*. Now *rare*. E19.
[ORIGIN from IM-[2] + PROGRESSIVE *adjective*.]
Not progressive.
■ **improgressively** *adverb* M19. **improgressiveness** *noun* E19.

improlific /ɪmprəˈlɪfɪk/ *adjective*. *rare*. M17.
[ORIGIN from IM-[2] + PROLIFIC.]
Not prolific.

†**imprompt** *adjective*. L16–M18.
[ORIGIN from IM-[2] + PROMPT *adjective*.]
Unready.

impromptu /ɪmˈprɒm(p)tjuː/ *adverb, noun, adjective, & verb*. M17.
[ORIGIN French from Latin *in promptu* at hand, in readiness, from *promptus* readiness: see PROMPT *noun*.]
▸ **A** *adverb*. Without preparation; on the spur of the moment; extempore. M17.

G. GREENE The actor had been ready to play impromptu the part of Chavel.

▸ **B** *noun*. Something composed, uttered, or done impromptu; an improvisation; *spec.* a musical composition having the character of an improvisation. L17.

B. EARNSHAW The music that he played, Furious and subtle with an impromptu that might be art. G. GREENE 'I still don't know how you came here.' 'Just an impromptu. I was in an inn about sixty miles from here.'

▸ **C** *adjective*. Composed, uttered, or done impromptu; improvised; makeshift. M18.

J. CAREY He threw away brilliant impromptu things in conversation. N. MAILER Dennis had an impromptu press conference right on the steps of the prison. D. M. THOMAS Some were making impromptu labels out of bits of string and torn-off paper.

▸ **D** *verb trans. & intrans.* Improvise; extemporize. E19.

improper /ɪmˈprɒpə/ *adjective*. LME.
[ORIGIN Old French & mod. French *impropre* or Latin *improprius*, formed as IM-[2] + *proprius* PROPER *adjective*.]
1 Incorrect, inaccurate, irregular, wrong. LME.

I. MURDOCH These would make terrible wounds, and Pat felt . . it would be improper to use them. H. WILSON To provide . . contact with the party machine, which it would be unprocedural, if not improper, to attempt through the Civil Service.

improper fraction MATH. a fraction whose value is greater than one, with the numerator greater than the denominator.

2 Unsuitable, inappropriate. L16.

R. BOYLE A Plain being a very improper place for such a purpose.

3 Unbecoming, unseemly, indecorous. E17.

G. SANTAYANA This deportment, undignified . . on weekdays, was positively improper on Sundays. A. CARTER Melanie felt improper, like a chorus girl taking Holy Communion in fishnet tights.

■ **improperly** *adverb* LME. **improperness** *noun* (*rare*) E17.

†**improper** *verb trans*. LME–M17.
[ORIGIN Anglo-Latin *impropriare*: see IMPROPRIATE.]
= IMPROPRIATE.

improperium /ɪmprəˈpɪərɪəm/ *noun*. Pl. **-ria** /-rɪə/. L19.
[ORIGIN Late Latin = reproach.]
ROMAN CATHOLIC CHURCH. Each of a series of antiphons with responses forming part of the liturgical service for Good Friday, purported to echo Christ's reproach of the Jewish people (as representing all humanity). Usu. in *pl.*

†**improportional** *adjective*. E17–L18.
[ORIGIN from IM-[2] + PROPORTIONAL *adjective*.]
Disproportionate.

impropriate /ɪmˈprəʊprɪeɪt/ *verb trans*. Pa. pple & ppl adjective **-ate** /-ət/, **-ated**. E16.
[ORIGIN Anglo-Latin *impropriat-* pa. ppl stem of *impropriare*, from Latin IM-[1] + *proprius* PROPER *adjective*: see -ATE[3]. Cf. earlier IMPROPER *verb*.]
Appropriate. Now only *spec.*, annex (an ecclesiastical benefice) to a corporation or person as corporate or private property; *esp.* place (tithes or ecclesiastical property) in lay hands.

impropriation /ɪmˌprəʊprɪˈeɪʃ(ə)n/ *noun*. M16.
[ORIGIN Anglo-Latin *impropriatio(n-)*, formed as IMPROPRIATE: see -ATION.]
1 The action of impropriating a benefice etc.; the proprietorship conveyed by this action. M16.
2 An impropriated benefice; property, tithes, etc., held by an ecclesiastical or lay organization. M16.
†**3** *gen.* Appropriation; a thing appropriated. E17–E18.

impropriator /ɪmˈprəʊprɪeɪtə/ *noun*. E17.
[ORIGIN from IMPROPRIATE + -OR.]
A person to whom a benefice is impropriated.
■ **impropriˈatrix** *noun* a female impropriator L18.

impropriety /ɪmprəˈprʌɪəti/ *noun*. E17.
[ORIGIN French *impropriété* or Latin *improprietas*, from *improprius* IMPROPER *adjective*: see -ITY.]
1 Incorrectness; inaccuracy. E17.

J. S. MILL We may therefore say, without impropriety, that the quality forms part of its signification.

2 Unbecomingness, unseemliness, indecency; improper conduct. E17.

G. S. HAIGHT There was undeniable impropriety in a young girl's going about alone.

3 Unsuitableness, inappropriateness. L17.
4 An instance of improper conduct, language, etc. L17.

A. N. WILSON His name could not be mentioned; it was on a level with the coarsest impropriety or profanity.

†**improsperity** *noun*. E16–E18.
[ORIGIN from IM-[2] + PROSPERITY.]
The state or condition of being unprosperous, absence of prosperity.

improsperous /ɪmˈprɒsp(ə)rəs/ *adjective*. Now *rare* or *obsolete*. L16.
[ORIGIN from IM-[2] + PROSPEROUS.]
†**1** Of luck etc.: unpropitious. L16–M17.
2 Unprosperous; unlucky. E17.
■ †**improsperously** *adverb* L16–L17.

improv /ˈɪmprɒv/ *noun*. *slang*. L20.
[ORIGIN Abbreviation: cf. IMPRO.]
An improvisation in performance.

†**improvable** *adjective*[1]. *rare*. Also **improve-**. E17–E18.
[ORIGIN from IMPROVE *verb*[1] + -ABLE.]
Able to be disproved or condemned.

improvable /ɪmˈpruːvəb(ə)l/ *adjective*[2]. Also **improve-**. M17.
[ORIGIN from IMPROVE *verb*[2] + -ABLE.]
1 That may be taken advantage of or used profitably; serviceable. Now *rare* or *obsolete*. M17.
2 Orig. (of land), able to be profitably cultivated; able to be made more productive by cultivation. Now chiefly *gen.*, able to be made better. M17.

New Yorker Bill saw the world as . . quite bad; Gina saw it as improvable.

■ **improvaˈbility** *noun* L18. **improvableness** *noun* M17. **improvably** *adverb* M18.

improve /ɪmˈpruːv/ *noun*. *Austral. slang*. M20.
[ORIGIN from IMPROVE *verb*[2].]
A course of improvement. Only in ***on the improve***, improving, getting better in health etc.

†**improve** *verb*[1] *trans*. LME.
[ORIGIN Old French *improver* (mod. *improuver*) from Latin *improbare* condemn, disapprove, formed as IM-[2] + *probare* approve.]
1 Disprove, refute. LME–E17.
2 Disapprove, disallow; censure, condemn. E16–M18.

improve /ɪmˈpruːv/ *verb*[2]. Also (earlier) †**em-**, †**improw**. E16.
[ORIGIN Anglo-Norman *emprower*, *emprouer* (in Anglo-Latin *appro(w)are*, *appruare*), from Old French *em-* EM-[1], IM-[1] + *prou* profit (from late Latin *prode*, evolved from Latin *prodest* is of advantage), later infl. by PROVE *verb*. Cf. APPROVE *verb*[1].]
▸ **I** *verb trans*. **1** †**a** *refl.* Make a profit for (oneself), avail (oneself) *of* profitably. E16–M17. ▸†**b** Increase the price or value of (esp. land). M16–M18. ▸**c** Turn (land) to profit; cultivate or make more productive or valuable by cultivation. *obsolete* exc. as passing into sense 4. M17. ▸†**d** Invest or lay out (money) profitably. M17–M19.
2 **a** Avail oneself of, utilize, (a person or thing). Now only *spec.* (*US*), make use of or occupy (a place). E16. ▸**b** Make good use of, take advantage of, (an occasion, event, etc.); *arch.* make use of for spiritual edification. M16.

b BOSW. SMITH The Roman army improved the victory of their fleet by . . marching to Egesta. E. P. THOMPSON He . . had been improving the time in prison by collecting examples . . of other parodists.

b improve the* SHINING *hour.

3 Make greater in amount or degree; increase, develop, intensify. *obsolete* exc. as passing into sense 4. E16.
4 Increase the quality or value of; bring into a better or more desirable condition or state; make better; *arch.* make better or more advantageous by converting *into*. E17.

H. JAMES The purpose of improving one's mind by foreign travel. S. J. PERELMAN Flowers . . studied the *Harvard Classics*, with which he was improving himself. R. DAVIES Ismay was abroad, staying with a French family to improve her accent. *Dumfries Courier* Union Members . . in search of an improved pay offer.

5 Lose or cause to disappear in the process of making better or more profitable. Foll. by *away*, *off*, etc. L18.
▸ **II** *verb intrans*. **6** Increase, advance, develop. Now *dial.* exc. as passing into sense 8. M17.
7 Foll. by *on*, *upon*: make or produce something better than. L17.

J. B. PRIESTLEY We all know this England, which at its best cannot be improved upon. G. GREENE Ford's apprenticeship with Conrad had borne its fruit, but he had improved on the Master.

8 Increase in value or excellence; become better. E18.

E. WAUGH Some of the characters improve with age, they grow wiser and kinder. B. PYM She began to plan a visit, after the New Year, when the weather improved.

improveable *adjective*[1], *adjective*[2] vars. of IMPROVABLE *adjective*[1], *adjective*[2].

improvement /ɪmˈpruːvm(ə)nt/ *noun*. Also (earlier) †**em-**, †**improwement**. LME.
[ORIGIN Anglo-Norman *emprowement*, formed as IMPROVE *verb*[2]: see -MENT.]
†**1** Profitable management or use; the realization of the profits of something; profit. LME–E16. ▸**b** Profitable investment of money. M17–E18.
2 The turning of land to profit; the cultivation of land, or now *esp.* the erection of buildings, fences, etc., on land, to improve the condition and value. Also, a piece of land improved by cultivation, building, etc.; now *esp.* buildings, fences, etc., by which a piece of land is improved. Now *N. Amer. & NZ* and passing into senses 5 and 6. L15.
†**3** The action or process of making or becoming greater; (an) increase, (a) growth, development, intensification. M16–L18.
4 The utilization of a person or thing. Now only, the making good use or taking advantage of an occasion, event, etc.; *arch.* the profitable use of something for spiritual edification. E17.
5 The action or process of making or becoming better or more valuable; the state of being better. M17.

H. BLAIR Exercise is the chief source of improvement in all our faculties. D. W. GOODWIN The goal is not so much a . . cure . . as it is to bring about improvement.

6 An act of making or becoming better; an addition or alteration which increases the quality or value of something. L17.

H. JAMES It's a great advantage to have a new house; you get all the latest improvements. GEORGE MOORE Better to retain his . . mistakes than to accept any suggestions, even if they were improvements.

7 The production of something better than something else; a result of this. Foll. by *on*, *upon*. E18.

A. EDEN The appearance and manner of the boys . . seemed to be an improvement on my generation. R. ELLMANN 'I suffer, therefore I may be,' was his improvement upon Descartes.

improver /ɪmˈpruːvə/ *noun*. M17.
[ORIGIN from IMPROVE *verb*[2] + -ER[1].]
1 A person who improves something; *esp.* a person who makes improvements to increase the quality or value of a thing. M17. ▸**b** A person who works for a low wage or none to improve his or her skill. M19.

b J. FOWLES His apprentices, improvers and the rest were atrociously lodged.

2 Something that improves; *spec.* (**a**) = ***dress-improver*** s.v. DRESS *noun*; (**b**) a chemical substance added to a foodstuff by a manufacturer to improve it in some way. M17.

Scotsman Recent . . proposals recommended banning the use of all flour 'improvers' which included preservatives.

■ **improvership** *noun* the position of an improver (IMPROVER 1b) L19.

improvidence /ɪmˈprɒvɪd(ə)ns/ *noun*. LME.
[ORIGIN Late Latin *improvidentia*, formed as IM-[2] + *providentia* PROVIDENCE.]
The fact or quality of being improvident.

R. NIEBUHR The poverty of the workers was due to their laziness and their improvidence.

improvident /ɪmˈprɒvɪd(ə)nt/ *adjective*. L15.
[ORIGIN from IM-[2] + PROVIDENT *adjective*, or from late Latin *improvident-*, formed as IM-[2] + *provident-* pres. ppl stem of *providere* PROVIDE *verb*: see -ENT.]
1 Unforeseeing. L15.

W. S. CHURCHILL Parliament . . was eager for war, improvident in preparation, and resentful in paying for it.

2 Incautious, unwary; heedless. L16.

J. C. OATES She was to be accused of reckless, improvident thinking.

3 Lacking foresight; spendthrift; failing to provide for the future. E17.

H. KELLER I am improvident enough to prefer present joy to hoarding riches against a rainy day.

■ **improvidently** *adverb* LME. **improvidentness** *noun* (*rare*) E18.

improving /ɪmˈpruːvɪŋ/ *ppl adjective*. M17.
[ORIGIN from IMPROVE *verb*[2] + -ING[2].]
That makes or becomes better; *spec.* that improves the mind, understanding, or character.

A. J. P. TAYLOR No Sexton Blake, no comics, nothing but improving works.

■ **improvingly** *adverb* M19.

improvisation /ˌɪmprəvʌɪˈzeɪʃ(ə)n, -prɒvɪ-/ *noun*. L18.
[ORIGIN from IMPROVISATOR or IMPROVISATORE: see -ATION.]
The action of improvising; something done or produced on the spur of the moment; *spec.* a piece of improvised music or verse.

Q. CRISP Matters would . . have been even worse if my entire programme had been an improvisation. *Photographer* Equipment was 'very basic' so he discovered a lot about improvisation.

■ **improvisational** *adjective* of or pertaining to improvisation, of the nature of an improvisation E20. **improvisationally** *adverb* M20.

improvisator /ɪmˈprɒvɪzeɪtə/ *noun*. L18.
[ORIGIN Anglicized from IMPROVISATORE.]
An improviser.

improvisatore /improvizaˈtoːre; ˌɪmprəviːzəˈtɔːri/ *noun*. Also **-vv-** /-vv-/. Pl. **-ri** /-ri/, **-res** /-rɪz/. M18.
[ORIGIN Italian *improvvisatore*, from *improvvisare* IMPROVISE. See also IMPROVISATOR.]
An (Italian) improviser; an improviser in an Italian manner.

improvisatorial /ˌɪmprəvʌɪzəˈtɔːrɪəl, -prɒvɪz-/ *adjective*. E19.
[ORIGIN from IMPROVISATOR + -IAL.]
Of, pertaining to, or of the nature of an improviser; improvisatory.

improvisatory /ɪmprəvʌɪˈzeɪt(ə)ri, -prɒvɪ-, -ˈvʌɪzə-/ *adjective*. E19.
[ORIGIN formed as IMPROVISATORIAL: see -ORY[2].]
Of or pertaining to improvisation; of the nature of (an) improvisation.

Times Lit. Suppl. His way of writing, his pouncing, wiredrawn, improvisatory eloquence, amounts to a classic style.

improvisatrice /improvizaˈtriːtʃe, ˌɪmprəviːzəˈtriːtʃi/ *noun*. Also **-vv-**. Pl. **-ci** /-tʃi/. E19.
[ORIGIN Italian, fem. of *improvvisatore*: see IMPROVISATORE, -TRICE.]
A female *improvisatore*.

improvise /ˈɪmprəvʌɪz/ *verb trans. & intrans.* E19.
[ORIGIN French *improviser* or its source Italian *improvvisare*, from *improvviso* extempore from Latin *improvisus* unforeseen, formed as IM-[2] + *provisus* pa. pple of *providere* PROVIDE.]
1 Compose (music or verse) or utter or do (anything) on the spur of the moment. E19.

J. B. PRIESTLEY He was able to improvise the most amusing little tunes. R. G. COLLINGWOOD No rule can tell you how to act . . . you must improvise as best you can.

2 Provide or construct (something) as a makeshift. M19.

K. GRAHAME Knotting the sheets . . together and tying . . the improvised rope round the central mullion. P. ROTH Each appeared to have improvised a uniform from a heap of old clothes.

improviser /ˈɪmprəvʌɪzə/ *noun*. E19.
[ORIGIN from IMPROVISE + -ER[1].]
A person who improvises or composes extempore.

improvvisatore, ***improvvisatrice*** *nouns* vars. of IMPROVISATORE, IMPROVISATRICE.

†**improw** *verb*, †**improwement** *noun* see IMPROVE *verb*[2], IMPROVEMENT.

imprudence /ɪmˈpruːd(ə)ns/ *noun*. LME.
[ORIGIN Old French & mod. French, or Latin *imprudentia*, formed as IMPRUDENT: see -ENCE.]
1 The quality or fact of being imprudent; lack of prudence; indiscretion; rashness. LME.
2 An instance of this; an imprudent act. LME.
■ Also †**imprudency** *noun* L16–E19.

imprudent /ɪmˈpruːd(ə)nt/ *adjective*. LME.
[ORIGIN Latin *imprudent-*, formed as IM-[2] + *prudent-* PRUDENT.]
Not prudent, lacking in discretion; rash, incautious.
■ **imprudently** *adverb* M16. **imprudentness** *noun* (*rare*) E18.

impsonite /ˈɪmps(ə)nʌɪt/ *noun*. E20.
[ORIGIN from *Impson* Valley in Oklahoma, USA + -ITE[1].]
An asphaltic mineral similar to albertite.

impudence /ˈɪmpjʊd(ə)ns/ *noun*. LME.
[ORIGIN Latin *impudentia*, formed as IMPUDENT: see -ENCE.]
1 Shamelessness; immodesty, indelicacy; an instance of this. *obsolete* exc. *dial.* LME.
2 Shameless effrontery; insolent disrespect; insolence, presumption; an instance of this. E17.
3 Freedom from diffidence, cool confidence; an instance of this. E17.

impudency /ˈɪmpjʊd(ə)nsi/ *noun*. Now *rare*. E16.
[ORIGIN formed as IMPUDENCE: see -ENCY.]
1 = IMPUDENCE 2. E16.
2 = IMPUDENCE 1. M16.
†**3** = IMPUDENCE 3. Only in E17.

impudent /ˈɪmpjʊd(ə)nt/ *adjective & noun*. LME.
[ORIGIN Latin *impudent-*, *-ens*, formed as IM-[2] + *pudent-*, *-ens* ashamed, modest, orig. pres. pple of *pudere* feel ashamed: see -ENT.]
▸ **A** *adjective*. †**1** Lacking in shame or modesty; indelicate. LME–M18.
2 Presumptuous, shamelessly forward; insolently disrespectful. M16.

N. MONSARRAT The remark had been injudicious and . . undeniably impudent.

▸ **B** *noun*. An impudent person. Now *rare* or *obsolete*. L16.
■ **impudently** *adverb* M16. **impudentness** *noun* (*rare*) L16.

impudicity /ɪmpjʊˈdɪsɪti/ *noun*. E16.
[ORIGIN French *impudicité* from Latin *impudicitia*, from *impudicus* shameless, formed as IM-[2] + *pudicus*, from *pudere* feel ashamed: see -ICITY.]
Shamelessness, immodesty.

impugn /ɪmˈpjuːn/ *verb trans.* LME.
[ORIGIN Latin *impugnare*, formed as IM-[1] + *pugnare* to fight.]
†**1** Fight against; attack, assail, assault (a person, city, etc.). LME–E17. ▸**b** Fight in resistance against; withstand, oppose. L16–M17.
2 Assail (an opinion, action, etc.) by argument; call into question; dispute the truth or validity of; oppose as erroneous. LME. ▸**b** Assail the actions of, question the statements etc. of; find fault with; accuse. Now *rare*. LME.

R. PORTER To speak of quackery is not automatically to impugn the motives of unqualified practitioners.

■ **impugnable** *adjective* liable to be impugned LME. **impugner** *noun* LME. **impugnment** *noun* the action or fact of impugning something or (now *rare*) someone M19.

impugnation /ɪmpʌɡˈneɪʃ(ə)n/ *noun*. Now *rare* or *obsolete*. LME.
[ORIGIN Latin *impugnatio(n-)*, from *impugnat-* pa. ppl stem of *impugnare* IMPUGN: see -ATION.]
†**1** The action of attacking or assaulting a person; spiritual assault, temptation. LME–M17.
2 The action of impugning something or someone; calling into question, disputing. LME.

impuissance /ɪmˈpjuːɪs(ə)ns, -ˈpwɪs-/ *noun*. L15.
[ORIGIN Old French & mod. French, formed as IM-[2] + PUISSANCE.]
Impotence, powerlessness, weakness.

impuissant /ɪmˈpjuːɪs(ə)nt, -ˈpwɪs-/ *adjective*. E17.
[ORIGIN French, formed as IM-[2] + PUISSANT.]
Impotent, powerless, weak.

impulse /ˈɪmpʌls/ *noun*. M17.
[ORIGIN from Latin *impulsus* noun, from *impuls-* pa. ppl stem of *impellere* IMPEL.]
▸**I 1** A physical act of impelling; an application of (sudden) force causing motion; a thrust, a push. M17.
2 The effect of impulsion; motion caused by (sudden) application of force; momentum, impetus. M17.
3 *PHYSICS*. An indefinitely large force of brief duration, producing a finite momentum. L18. ▸**b** The average value of a force multiplied by its time of action, equal to the change of momentum of a body acted on by the force. L19.
b specific impulse the ratio of the thrust produced in a rocket engine to the rate of consumption of propellant.
4 *PHYSICS*. Each of the oscillations making up a wave; a sudden momentary change in amplitude, a pulse. E19.
5 *PHYSIOLOGY*. The wave of electrical excitation that passes along a nerve during conduction of a signal. M19.
6 *MEDICINE*. The pulse; *esp.* the beat of the heart felt on the wall of the chest. Now *rare*. M19.
▸**II 7** Incitement or stimulus to action arising from a state of mind or feeling; an instance of this. M17.

B. WEBB Haldane has one overpowering impulse: he likes to be . . behind the scenes at the seat of power.

8 Force or influence exerted on the mind by an external stimulus; an instance of this; (a) suggestion, incitement, instigation. M17.

WORDSWORTH One impulse from a vernal wood May teach you more . . Than all the sages can.

9 Sudden or involuntary inclination to act, without premeditation; an instance of this. M18.

A. DAVIS I had a sudden impulse to turn around. M. M. KAYE He had . . acted on impulse and without giving due thought to the possible consequences of the action. T. MALLON What made him purchase the book was more impulse than focused intention.

– ATTRIB. & COMB.: In the sense 'done, made, or acting on impulse', as ***impulse buy***, ***impulse buyer***, ***impulse buying***. Special combs., as **impulse clock** a secondary clock operated by regular electrical impulses transmitted from a master clock; **impulse turbine**: in which the rotor is driven by the change of momentum of the working fluid without a drop in pressure.

impulse /ˈɪmpʌls/ *verb trans.* E17.
[ORIGIN from the noun, or from Latin *impuls-*: see IMPULSE *noun*.]
Give an impulse to; impel; instigate.

impulsion /ɪmˈpʌlʃ(ə)n/ *noun*. LME.
[ORIGIN Old French & mod. French, or Latin *impulsio(n-)*, from *impuls-*: see IMPULSE *noun*, -ION.]
1 The action or an act of impelling or imparting motion; thrusting, pushing, pressing against something; the condition of being pushed or thrust. LME.
2 An external influence exerted on the mind or conduct; instigation. M16.
3 Determination to action resulting from natural tendency or excitement; an impulse. M16.
4 A tendency to onward movement imparted by a force or influence; impetus. L18.

impulsive /ɪmˈpʌlsɪv/ *adjective & noun*. LME.
[ORIGIN Old French & mod. French *impulsif*, *-ive* or late Latin *impulsivus*, from *impuls-*: see IMPULSE *noun*, -IVE.]
▸ **A** *adjective*. **1** Having the property of impelling or imparting motion; characterized by onward movement or impetus. LME. ▸**b** *PHYSICS*. Of a force, current, etc.: consisting of, or of the nature of, an impulse or impulses. E19.
2 Impelling or determining to action. M16.
3 Actuated or characterized by impulse; apt to be moved by sudden impulse or emotion; prompted by sudden impulse. M18.

D. H. LAWRENCE A quick, careless, impulsive boy. S. MORLEY I wish David would think rather more carefully before he does these impulsive things.

▸ †**B** *noun*. An impelling agent or cause. E–M17.
■ **impulsively** *adverb* M18. **impulsiveness** *noun* M17. **impulˈsivity** *noun* impulsiveness L19.

†**impulsor** *noun*. M17–E18.
[ORIGIN Latin, from *impuls-*: see IMPULSE *noun*, -OR.]
A person who or thing which impels something.

impulsory /ɪmˈpʌls(ə)ri/ *adjective*. *rare*. M17.
[ORIGIN from Latin *impuls-* (see IMPULSE *noun*) + -ORY[2].]
Tending to impel or force forward.

impunctate /ɪmˈpʌŋkteɪt/ *adjective*. E19.
[ORIGIN from IM-[2] + PUNCTATE *adjective*.]
BIOLOGY & MEDICINE. Not punctate; not marked or studded with points, dots, or spots.

†**impune** *adjective*. E17–M18.
[ORIGIN Latin *impunis*: see IMPUNITY.]
Having impunity, unpunished.
■ †**impunely** *adverb* with impunity, without punishment E17–M18.

impunible /ɪmˈpjuːnɪb(ə)l/ *adjective*. *rare*. M17.
[ORIGIN from IM-[2] + medieval Latin *punibilis*, from *punire* punish: see -IBLE.]
Not punishable.
■ **impunibly** *adverb* without punishment; with impunity: M18.

impunitive /ɪmˈpjuːnɪtɪv/ *adjective*. M20.
[ORIGIN from IM-[2] + PUNITIVE *adjective*.]
PSYCHOLOGY. Adopting or characterized by an attitude of acceptance of frustration without anger or any attempt to blame someone.
■ **impunitively** *adverb* M20.

impunity /ɪmˈpjuːnɪti/ *noun*. M16.
[ORIGIN Latin *impunitas*, from *impunis* unpunished, formed as IM-[2] + *poena* penalty, punishment, *punire* punish: see -ITY.]
Exemption from punishment; exemption from injury or loss as a consequence of action, security. Freq. in ***with impunity***, in such a way as to be exempt(ed) from punishment or from injury or loss.

impure /ɪmˈpjʊə/ *adjective & noun*. LME.
[ORIGIN Latin *impurus*, formed as IM-[2] + *purus* pure.]
▸ **A** *adjective*. **1** Containing some offensive matter; dirty. LME. ▸**b** Not ceremonially pure; unhallowed. E17.
2 Not morally pure; immoral, licentious. M16.
3 Mixed with or containing some foreign matter, esp. of an inferior kind; contaminated, adulterated. E17. ▸**b** Mixed in style; (of a language etc.) containing foreign idioms, grammatical blemishes, or imprecise terminology. E17. ▸**c** Of a colour: containing a mixture of another colour. M19.
▸ **B** *noun*. An immoral or licentious person. Now *rare*. L18.
■ **impurely** *adverb* E17. **impureness** *noun* M16.

impurify /ɪmˈpjʊərɪfʌɪ/ *verb trans.* L17.
[ORIGIN from IMPURE *adjective* after *purify*.]
Make impure.

impurist /ɪmˈpjʊərɪst/ *noun*. M20.
[ORIGIN from IMPURE *adjective* after *purist*.]
A person who is not a purist; an opponent of purism.

impuritan /ɪmˈpjʊərɪt(ə)n/ *noun*. E17.
[ORIGIN from IMPURE *adjective* after *puritan*.]
A person who is impure; a person who is not a puritan; (also **I-**) *hist.* a person who is not a Puritan, an opponent of Puritanism.
■ **impuritanism** *noun* E19.

impurity /ɪmˈpjʊərɪti/ *noun*. LME.
[ORIGIN French †*impurité* (now *impureté*) or Latin *impuritas*, formed as IMPURE *adjective*: see -ITY.]
1 The quality or condition of being morally impure; moral corruption; sexual immorality, unchastity; a morally impure thing. LME.
2 The quality or condition of containing some offensive matter; dirtiness; foul matter, dirt. L16.
3 The quality or condition of containing foreign matter, esp. of an inferior kind, or of being impure in style; contamination, adulteration; a constituent or element which detracts from purity. E17. ▸**b** An impurity atom; *esp.* an atom of dopant in the lattice of a semiconductor. M20.

– COMB.: **impurity atom**: of an element different from the bulk of the substance in which it is present; **impurity level** an energy level in a semiconductor due to an impurity atom; **impurity semiconductor**: in which most of the carriers of electric current are electrons and holes from impurity atoms.

†**impurple** *verb* var. of EMPURPLE.

imputable /ɪmˈpjuːtəb(ə)l/ *adjective*. E17.
[ORIGIN medieval Latin *imputabilis*, from Latin *imputare*: see IMPUTE, -ABLE.]
1 That may be imputed *to*; chargeable, attributable, *to*. E17.
†**2** Liable to imputation; culpable. M17–L18.
■ **imputaˈbility** *noun* L18.

imputation /ɪmpjʊˈteɪʃ(ə)n/ *noun*. M16.
[ORIGIN French, or late Latin *imputatio(n-)*, from Latin *imputat-* pa. ppl stem of *imputare* IMPUTE: see -ATION.]
1 The action of imputing or attributing something, esp. a fault or crime, to a person; the fact of being charged with a fault, crime, etc.; *spec*. (***a***) CHRISTIAN THEOLOGY attribution to believers of the righteousness of Christ and to Christ of human sin; (***b***) ECONOMICS attribution of value to resources in accordance with the value of the products to which they contribute. M16.
2 An instance of imputing a fault, crime, etc., to a person; an accusation, a charge. L16.
A. JOHN I was absolved from all blame: all charges, all imputations were withdrawn.
– COMB.: **imputation tax**: levied according to the total profits of a company.

imputative /ɪmˈpjuːtətɪv/ *adjective*. L16.
[ORIGIN Late Latin *imputativus*, from *imputat-*: see IMPUTATION, -ATIVE.]
Characterized by being imputed; existing or arising by imputation.
■ **imputatively** *adverb* by imputation L16.

impute /ɪmˈpjuːt/ *verb trans*. LME.
[ORIGIN Old French & mod. French *imputer* from Latin *imputare* bring into the reckoning or charge, formed as IM-[1] + *putare* reckon.]
1 Foll. by *to*: regard (esp. a fault or crime) as being done or caused or possessed by; attribute or ascribe to the discredit (less commonly, the credit) of; *spec*. (***a***) CHRISTIAN THEOLOGY attribute (righteousness or guilt) to by vicarious substitution; (***b***) ECONOMICS attribute or assign (value) to a product or process by inference from the value of the products or processes to which it contributes. LME.
R. WELLEK I do not believe there . . was a single reputable 'New' critic who has taken the position imputed to him. E. WAUGH We must not impute damnation to a human soul. C. G. WOLFF Lily is . . not guilty of the transgression he imputes to her.
†**2** Reckon, take into account; consider. M16–L18.
3 Charge or arraign *with* a fault, etc.; accuse. Long *rare*. L16.
†**4** Impart. L16–L17.
■ **imputer** *noun* (*rare*) E17.

imputrescence /ɪmpjuːˈtrɛs(ə)ns/ *noun*. M17.
[ORIGIN from IM-[2] + PUTRESCENCE.]
Absence of putrescence or decomposition.

imputrescible /ɪmpjuːˈtrɛsɪb(ə)l/ *adjective*. M17.
[ORIGIN from IM-[2] + PUTRESCIBLE.]
Not subject to putrefaction or decomposition; incorruptible.
■ **imputresciˈbility** *noun* E18.

imram, **imrama** *nouns* see IMMRAM.

IMRO *abbreviation*.
Investment Management Regulatory Organization.

IMS *abbreviation*.
hist. Indian Medical Service.

imshi /ˈɪmʃi/ *verb intrans*. (*imper*.). *military slang*. Also **-shee**. E20.
[ORIGIN from colloq. Arabic *'mšī* imper. of *mišī* go.]
Go away!

I.Mun.E. *abbreviation*.
Institution of Municipal Engineers.

IN *abbreviation*.
Indiana.

In *symbol*.
CHEMISTRY. Indium.

in /ɪn/ *noun*. M17.
[ORIGIN from IN *adverb*.]
1 ***ins and outs***, (less commonly) ***outs and ins***: ▸**a** All the details or ramifications of a matter; devious turns to and fro in a course of action, a road, etc. M17. ▸**b** *hist*. People who were constantly being admitted to and discharged from the workhouse. L19.
2 POLITICS. A member of the party that is in office. Usu. in *pl*., contrasted with **outs**. M18.
3 In some games: a member of the side whose turn it is to play. E19.
4 An entrance; permission to enter. *Scot*. L19.
5 An introduction to, or influence with, a person of power or authority or a famous person. (Foll. by *with*.) *colloq*. E20.

in /ɪn/ *attrib. adjective*. L16.
[ORIGIN IN *adverb* used attrib., or as positive of *inner*, *inmost*.]
1 That is in; internal; that lies, remains, lives, is situated, or is used in or within. L16.
2 Fashionable; confined to or common to a particular group. M20.
A. HAILEY The bar of Jim's Garage . . was currently an 'in' place in downtown Detroit.

in /ɪn/ *verb*. Also †**inn**. Infl. **-nn-**.
[ORIGIN Old English *(ge)innian* (cf. Old High German *(ge)innōn* take up), partly from Germanic base of IN *adverb*, partly from INN *noun*.]
▸**I** *verb trans*. **1** Take in, include; enclose (esp. waste land). Formerly also, give or put in. Now *dial*. OE.
2 Gather into a barn or stockyard; harvest; get in, collect. LME.
▸†**II** *verb intrans*. **3** Go in; make a beginning. OE–M17.

in /ɪn/ *adverb*.
[ORIGIN Old English (i) *in(n)*, used with verbs of motion (= Old Frisian, Old Saxon, Dutch *in*, Old High German *in* (with secondary lengthening), German *ein*, Old Norse, Gothic *inn*); (ii) *inne*, used with verbs of position (= Old Frisian, Old Saxon *inna*, Old High German *inna*, -*i*, -*e*, Old Norse *inni*, Gothic *inna*), orig. locative.]
▸**I** Of motion.
1 a Expr. motion from a point outside a space to a point inside it; so as to pass into a place or medium, esp. a building or a room. OE. ▸**b** Expr. motion in the direction of some point, specified or implied; to a position attained by coming from outside; near to some point or limit. E18.
a J. CONRAD I went in and sat down. G. HOUSEHOLD He must have a boat to take him . . to the rock face where he plunged in. **b** W. BLACK The swans were sailing close in by the reeds.
b join in, ***muck in***, ***pitch in***, etc.
2 In addition to the due amount or number; into the bargain. M17.
throw in: see THROW *verb*.
▸**II** Of position.
3 Within a certain space or medium, esp. a building or a room; inside one's usual place of abode or work; so as to be enclosed or confined. ME.
HOR. WALPOLE A dame over the way, that has just locked in her boarders. J. N. MCILWRAITH A number of soldiers were in swimming at the foot of the bluff. J. P. DONLEAVY 'May I please speak to Mr. MacDoon?' 'I'll see if he's in.'
4 On the inside. ME.
H. B. TRISTRAM A sheepskin coat with the woolly side in.
▸**III** *spec*.
5 In prison. L16.
6 Engaged or implicated in a matter, esp. an unlawful one; included among those chosen, published, etc. L16.
7 Of a politician or party: in or into office, in or into power. E17.
8 Of a fire or flame: burning, continuing to burn. M17.
9 Of the tide: with the water higher and nearer. L17.
10 In fashion; in season. L17.
Time Mass communication is out, personal communication is in.
11 In some games: having the turn to play, esp. (CRICKET) to bat. M18.
C. CAUSLEY He might have been last man in for England.
12 Of a school: in session, in progress. *Scot*. & *NZ*. E19.
13 Of a train, ship, etc.: at the platform, dock, etc. Of a harvest, order, etc.: having arrived or been received. L19.
New Yorker Verdicts on our attempts to ransom hostages with arms sales . . are not in yet.
14 Of a person's fortune or luck: exerting favourable action or influence. E20.
– PHRASES: ***be in at the finish***: see FINISH *noun*. **day in, day out** throughout a long succession of days. **in at** present at; contributing to. **in between** = BETWEEN *adverb*. **in for** (*a*) about to undergo (esp. something unpleasant) (***have it in for***, seek revenge on); (*b*) competing in or for; (*c*) involved in; committed to. **in on** sharing in; privy to (a secret etc.). **in with** on friendly or good terms with; NAUTICAL close in to, near, (land). **week in, week out**, **year in, year out** throughout a long succession of weeks (years).

in /ɪn/ *preposition*. Before a consonant also (now *arch*. & *dial*.) **i'**.
[ORIGIN Old English *in* = Old Frisian, Old Saxon, Old High German (Dutch, German), Gothic *in*, Old Norse *í* rel. to Latin *in* (older *en*), Greek *en*, *eni*, Old Irish *i n-*, Welsh *yn*, Lithuanian *ĩ*, Old Prussian *en*, Old Church Slavonic *vŭ(n-)*, Russian *v* (*vo*, *vn-*), from Indo-European.]
▸**I** Of position and location.
1 Within the limits or bounds of; within. OE. ▸**b** With names of towns having public or private importance. Cf. AT 1b. OE.
M. KEANE Jane was sitting up in bed drinking . . tea. I. MURDOCH Sarah was in Australia with her husband. L. BRUCE He talked exactly like the balloons in comic strips. **b** SOUTHEY A day in London is more wearying to me than a walk up Scawfell.
2 Referring to non-physical things treated as having extension or content. OE.
J. AUSTEN To see such an undersized . . man, set up for a fine actor, is very ridiculous in my opinion. K. GERSHON Like every living Jew I have in imagination seen the gas-chamber.
3 In relation to; in the context of; as a member of. OE.
LD MACAULAY The place of the clergyman in society. B. WEBB In opinion, Snowden is now a collectivist liberal. *Belfast Telegraph* It is up to us in local government to press ahead with our plans.
4 Expr. relation to a garment, covering, etc., which envelops or is worn. OE.
LONGFELLOW A huge tome, bound In brass and wild-boar's hide. G. GREENE A little old man in a black cassock.
5 On (with ref. to position). Long *rare* exc. *Scot*. OE.
T. HARDY No other boy in the heath has had such a bonfire.
†**6** Among. OE–M16.
7 Defining the part of something affected. ME.
G. B. SHAW The prima donna was deaf in the left ear.
8 With numbers, nouns of quantity, etc.: as a proportionate part of. L16.
Law Times A debtor . . offered 6s. 8d. in the pound. E. COURSE From Redhill to Tonbridge the maximum gradient was 1 in 250.
▸**II** Of situation, manner, etc.
9 a Expr. situation as determined by location, environment, or a material thing. OE. ▸**b** Expr. situation within the range of one of the senses or within a sphere of action. LME.
a J. A. FROUDE Brought in chains to Rome. J. TYNDALL His guides had lost their way in the fog. M. ROBERTS They sit in silence for the rest of the journey. *New Yorker* Walking in the dark . . we felt . . vulnerable. **b** MILTON Spirits that stand In sight of God's high Throne. A. TROLLOPE The living of Framley was in the gift of the Lufton family.
10 Expr. manner, degree, or means. OE. ▸**b** Expr. the material of construction or execution. M17. ▸**c** Following a phr. specifying a superl.: within the category of things mentioned. M19.
HENRY FIELDING He was drinking her ladyship's health . . in a cup of her ale. M. PATTISON Bede is writing in a dead language. F. HALL Drift-wood was lying about in large quantities. G. B. SHAW His success with Mozart's symphony in E flat. *Television Today* Half the first night audience were seated in two arcs behind the stage. D. ABSE He spoke in his special booming voice. **b** DICKENS Half-length portraits, in crayons. **c** *Radio Times* The most dazzling cruises in holiday history.
in confidence, ***in fun***, ***in jest***, ***in part***, ***in the same way***, etc.
11 Having the condition of; in a state of. OE. ▸**b** With ref. to animals: pregnant with. L16.
LD MACAULAY Leaving their castles in ruins. I. MURDOCH He woke in horror to the sound of a howling dog.
in cash, ***in flower***, ***in love***, ***in print***, ***in tears***, etc. **b *in calf***, ***in foal***, etc.
12 Expr. occupation in an activity: in the process of, in the act of. Chiefly with nouns of action & verbal nouns ME. ▸†**b** Used before a verbal noun expr. either occupation or an action to which a thing or person is subjected, = A *preposition*[1] 8, and now omitted, the verbal noun functioning as pres. pple. LME–M19.
H. JAMES A young lady seated on a bench in deep and lonely meditation. R. HARDY The Warden lifted his stick in salute. **b** W. WHISTON He went on in worshipping them. W. HONE This carriage . . had been three years in building.
13 Expr. aim or purpose: with abstract nouns ME.
MILTON She thus in answer spake. J. F. COOPER He went in quest of his new applicant. J. CONRAD In memory of her eldest brother.
▸**III** Of time.
14 In contexts where another preposition or no preposition is now usual. OE.
SWIFT This engine . . set out in four hours after my landing. G. CRABBE No Sunday shower Kept him at home in that important hour. J. BERESFORD In a chilling evening . . after you have carefully stirred a very ticklish fire.
15 Within the limits of (a specified period of time); during (a process occupying time); in the course of. OE. ▸**b** Preceding a noun denoting a period of time during which something has not happened, must not happen, etc., or has not been exceeded; for. L15.
G. BERKELEY I never saw a first-rate picture in my life. T. JEFFERSON I think our acquaintance commenced in 1764. JAMES WHITE All the gentlemen's houses you see in a railway excursion. *New Yorker* Elevators were in their infancy. **b** R. A. HEINLEIN The place smelled like a vault that has not been opened in years. *Scientific American* The greatest dust storm in more than a century.
16 Before or at the end of (a specified length of time). ME.
G. B. SHAW You'll be fast asleep in ten minutes.
▸**IV** Of motion and direction.
17 Into. Now only with verbs implying motion or change. OE.
R. HARDY I'm going to put all this in my next bulletin. W. GOLDING He . . looked in the window of the bookshop. B. BAINBRIDGE Tell them to jump in the lake.
†**18** Against, towards; to. ME–M16.
19 On, upon; along. Long *obsolete* exc. *Scot*. ME.
▸**V** Pregnant & ellipt. uses.
20 With refl. pronoun: apart from any relation to others; in a person's or thing's own essence or nature. ME.

I

J. S. MILL Of things absolutely or in themselves.

in itself.

21 In spiritual union with. ME.

AV *1 Cor.* 15:22 As in Adam all die, euen so in Christ shall all be made aliue.

22 Inherent in; within the capacity of. ME.

Nature Anyone who has it in him to do heroic deeds.

23 In the person of, with the identity of; in the case of. LME.

E. A. FREEMAN How great a captain England possessed in her future King.

24 In the hands of; legally vested in. LME.

25 Partaking or sharing in; implicated in; engaged in. E18. ▸**b** Engaged in dealing with, as a trade or business. M20.

E. WRIGHT He and Brady might have been in this from the start. **b** E. BOWEN Her father is rich, he is in tea.

▸ **VI** Constructional uses.

26 Expr. the relation which a verb has to an indirect obj. OE.

S. AUSTIN A regular war with France was not to be engaged in without negotiations. B. JOWETT The wise and mighty one who is to be held in honour. F. M. PEARD She spent a fortune in shoes and gloves. J. CONRAD The inhabitants delight in describing it as the 'Pearl of the Ocean'.

27 Expr. the relation of an adjective or noun to a certain sphere to which its qualification, attribute, etc., is limited. OE.

BOSWELL We talked of belief in ghosts. W. C. SMITH Let nothing shake your trust in her. T. H. HUXLEY The river-water . . is usually rich in organic impurities. I. MURDOCH Ann was reading for a degree in English. *New Yorker* He . . took deep pleasure in his friendship with the . . peasants.

28 Expr. the relation of a quantitative statement or measurement to the thing measured. ME.

MILTON Equal in number to that Godless crew. W. SHARP A man six feet two inches in height. *Daily Telegraph* £380 million in grants and loans.

29 In adverbial & prepositional phrs. where *in* precedes a noun (or an adjective). ME.

in common, ***in conclusion***, ***in fact***, ***in general***, ***in truth***, etc.; ***in case of***, ***in common with***, ***in favour of***, ***in honour of***, ***in regard to***, etc.

– PHRASES: ***have it in one***: see HAVE *verb*. **in it** (*a*) in a matter and of an advantageous or beneficial nature (chiefly in ***what is in it for X?*** & similar phrs.); (*b*) in a matter and of significance. **in so far as** to the extent or degree that. **in that** in the fact that; seeing that; because. **not be in it** *colloq.* be nothing in comparison; not count for anything. **nothing in it**, **not much in it**, **little in it** no or little difference between things being compared; no or little advantage to be seen in one possibility rather than another.

in- /ɪn/ *prefix*[1] (*combining form*).
[ORIGIN from IN *adverb*, IN *preposition* & (later) IN *adjective*.]

1 In Old English IN *adverb* was freely used in collocation with verbs of motion or change of state; in the inf. it usu. preceded the verb, in derived verbal nouns & adjectives it always did. In this position it came at length to be written in comb. with the verb: so ***income***, ***incomer***, ***incoming***, beside ***come in***. Also in other (Old English & later) formations with the sense 'in, within, internal', as ***inborn***, ***inland***; ***inpatient***; with the sense of IN *adjective* 2, as ***in-group***, ***in-joke***.

2 Prepositional phrs. composed of IN *preposition* + noun give rise to (usu. hyphenated) attrib. adjectives, as ***in-calf***, ***in-car***.

3 GEOMETRY. Repr. ***inscribed***, as ***incentre***, ***in-circle***.

■ **in-basket** *noun* (a basket used as) an in-tray M20. **in-box** *noun* (*a*) *N. Amer.* an in-tray; (*b*) COMPUTING the window in which a user's received emails are displayed: M20. **in-car** *adjective* occurring, situated, or carried in a car M20. **in-ˈcollege** *adjective* living in a college; designating or pertaining to teaching, administration, etc., carried out within college precincts: L19. **in-ground** *adjective* (of a swimming pool) embedded in the ground L20. **in-hand** *adjective* held in the hand; immediately available; (of a horse) led by hand, not ridden: M20. **in-joke** *noun* a joke which can be appreciated by only a limited group of people M20. **in-ˈmilk** *adjective* (of a cow etc.) producing milk M20. **in-ˈservice** *adjective* (esp. of training) given or received while the person concerned is in an occupation; (of reliability etc.) during the period of use of an object: M20. **in-side** *noun* (CRICKET) the side which is batting M19. **insourcing** *noun* the reallocation of work previously done by an outside supplier to in-house staff L20. **in-spawn** *adjective* that is about to spawn E20. **in-thing** *noun* a fashionable thing (*to do*) M20. **in-transit** *adjective* that is being transported or in transit E20. **in-tray** *noun* a tray for incoming documents in an office M20.

in- /ɪn/ *prefix*[2]. Before *l* **il-** /ɪl/; before *b*, *m*, or *p* **im-** /ɪm/; before *r* **ir-** /ɪr/.

Repr. Latin *in-* from *in* preposition, used esp. with verbs & their derivs. with the senses 'into, in, within', 'on, upon', 'towards, against', sometimes expr. onward motion or continuance, sometimes intensive, sometimes trans., & in other cases with no appreciable force. Often with parallel forms in EN-[1] (EM-[1]).

in- /ɪn/ *prefix*[3]. Before *l* **il-** /ɪl/; before *b*, *m* or *p* **im-** /ɪm/; before *r* **ir-** /ɪr/; before *gn* **i-** /ɪ/ (not productive).

Repr. Latin *in-* = Greek *a-*, *an-*, Germanic *un-*, prefixed chiefly to adjectives & their derivs. to express negation or privation. The modern tendency is to restrict *in-* to words answering to Latin types and to use *un-* in other cases.

in. *abbreviation*.
Inch(es).

-in /ɪn/ *suffix*[1]. See also **-EIN**.
[ORIGIN Alt. of -INE[5].]
CHEMISTRY. **1** Forming nouns denoting (*a*) neutral organic compounds, esp. proteins, glycerides, and glycosides, as ***albumin***, ***alizarin***, ***haematin***, ***insulin***, ***pepsin***; (*b*) some pharmaceutical products, as ***niacin***, ***penicillin***.
2 Forming nouns denoting heterocyclic compounds with a single unsaturated ring of six atoms, none of which is nitrogen, as ***dioxin***.

-in /ɪn/ *suffix*[2].
[ORIGIN from IN *adverb*.]
Appended to verbs & derived agent nouns (occas. to adjectives) to form nouns denoting an event at which many people publicly and collectively perform some action together, usu. as a form of protest, as ***sing-in***, ***sit-in***, ***sleep-in***, ***teach-in***.

-ina /ˈiːnə/ *suffix*[1].
[ORIGIN Repr. Latin fem. suffix found in *regina* queen, extended in Italian or Spanish, and thence in English.]
Forming feminine titles, as ***tsarina***, and female forenames, as ***Christina***. Also forming names of musical instruments, as ***concertina***.

-ina /ˈʌɪnə/ *suffix*[2].
[ORIGIN Repr. Latin neut. pl. of adjectives in *-inus*: see -INE[1].]
Forming names of some plant and animal groups, as ***globigerina***.

inability /ɪnəˈbɪlɪti/ *noun*. L15.
[ORIGIN from IN-[3] + ABILITY. Cf. Old French & mod. French *inhabilité*, medieval Latin *inhabilitas*.]
1 The condition of being unable; lack of ability, power, or means. (Foll. by *to do*; (arch.) *for*, *of doing*.) L15.

R. SOUTH Their Inability for, and frequent contrariety to the bringing about such designs. A. MASON He could not even—the inability distressed him out of all proportion—read people's minds. N. SYMINGTON A central difficulty in her life was an inability to say directly . . what she felt.

†**2** *spec.* Physical infirmity. M17–M19.

†**inable** *verb* var. of ENABLE *verb*.

in absentia /ɪn abˈsɛntɪə, -ʃɪə/ *adverbial phr.* L19.
[ORIGIN Latin.]
In his, her, or their absence.

inabstinence /ɪnˈabstɪnəns/ *noun*. M17.
[ORIGIN from IN-[3] + ABSTINENCE.]
Lack of abstinence; failure to abstain.

in abstracto /ɪn abˈstraktəʊ/ *adverbial phr.* E17.
[ORIGIN Latin = in the abstract.]
As an abstract thing.

inaccentuation /ˌɪnəksɛntjʊˈeɪʃ(ə)n/ *noun*. M19.
[ORIGIN from IN-[3] + ACCENTUATION.]
The condition of being unaccented.

inacceptable /ɪnəkˈsɛptəb(ə)l/ *adjective*. L19.
[ORIGIN from IN-[3] + ACCEPTABLE.]
Unacceptable.
■ ˌ**inacceptaˈbility** *noun* E20.

inaccessible /ɪnəkˈsɛsɪb(ə)l/ *adjective*. LME.
[ORIGIN Old French & mod. French, or late Latin *inaccessibilis*, formed as IN-[3] + ACCESSIBLE.]
Not accessible; that cannot be reached or entered; (of a person) not open to friendly approaches or influence.

GIBBON This savage hero was not inaccessible to pity. D. DELILLO A few rocky beaches, the best of them inaccessible except by boat. P. GAY The inaccessible regions of the mind are more sizable, and doubtless more important.

■ ˌ**inaccessiˈbility** *noun* M17. **inaccessibleness** *noun* E17. **inaccessibly** *adverb* E18.

inaccordant /ɪnəˈkɔːd(ə)nt/ *adjective*. E19.
[ORIGIN from IN-[3] + ACCORDANT.]
Not in agreement or harmony; inharmonious.

inaccuracy /ɪnˈakjʊrəsi/ *noun*. M18.
[ORIGIN from INACCURATE: see -ACY.]
The quality or condition of being inaccurate; imprecision; an instance of this.

inaccurate /ɪnˈakjʊrət/ *adjective*. M18.
[ORIGIN from IN-[3] + ACCURATE.]
Not accurate; inexact, imprecise, incorrect.
■ **inaccurately** *adverb* M17. **inaccurateness** *noun* L17.

inacquaintance /ɪnəˈkweɪnt(ə)ns/ *noun*. E17.
[ORIGIN from IN-[3] + ACQUAINTANCE.]
The state of being unacquainted; lack of acquaintance.

inact /ɪnˈakt/ *verb*. M17.
[ORIGIN from IN-[2] + ACT *verb*.]
†**1** *verb trans.* Actuate. Only in M17.
2 *verb intrans.* Act *in*, *within*. *rare*. M19.

inaction /ɪnˈakʃ(ə)n/ *noun*. M17.
[ORIGIN from IN-[3] + ACTION *noun*.]
Absence of action; inertness, sluggishness.

inactivate /ɪnˈaktɪveɪt/ *verb trans.* E20.
[ORIGIN from INACTIVE + -ATE[3].]
Make inactive.
■ **inactiˈvation** *noun* E20.

inactivator /ɪnˈaktɪveɪtə/ *noun*. M20.
[ORIGIN from INACTIVATE + -OR.]
A person who or thing which inactivates something; *spec.* in PHARMACOLOGY & PHYSIOLOGY, a person considered in respect of his or her speed of metabolizing and hence inactivating a drug.

inactive /ɪnˈaktɪv/ *adjective*. E18.
[ORIGIN from IN-[3] + ACTIVE *adjective*.]
1 Not active; disinclined to act; indolent; passive. E18.
2 CHEMISTRY. Not rotating the plane of polarization of polarized light. Freq. qualified by ***optically***. M19.
■ **inactively** *adverb* M18.

inactivity /ɪnakˈtɪvɪti/ *noun*. M17.
[ORIGIN from IN-[3] + ACTIVITY.]
The quality or condition of being inactive; lack of activity; sluggishness; passiveness.

J. C. CALHOUN The highest wisdom of a state is a wise and masterly inactivity. C. G. WOLFF She did not write . . . They were not, however, months of total inactivity.

inactuate /ɪnˈaktjʊeɪt, -tʃʊ-/ *verb trans. arch.* M17.
[ORIGIN from IN-[2] + ACTUATE.]
Make active; stir into activity.

inadaptability /ˌɪnədaptəˈbɪlɪti/ *noun*. M19.
[ORIGIN from IN-[3] + ADAPTABILITY.]
Lack of adaptability; inability to be adapted.

inadaptable /ɪnəˈdaptəb(ə)l/ *adjective*. E20.
[ORIGIN from IN-[3] + ADAPTABLE.]
Unable to be adapted.

inadaptive /ɪnəˈdaptɪv/ *adjective*. L19.
[ORIGIN from IN-[3] + ADAPTIVE.]
Not adaptive.

inadept /ɪnəˈdɛpt, ɪnˈadɛpt/ *adjective*. *rare*. L19.
[ORIGIN from IN-[3] + ADEPT *adjective*.]
Not adept.

inadequacy /ɪnˈadɪkwəsi/ *noun*. L18.
[ORIGIN from INADEQUATE: see -ACY.]
The condition or quality of being inadequate; an instance of this.

V. BRITTAIN Lives were being thrown away through the inadequacy of the medical services in the Mediterranean. R. BUSH A perpetual feeling of unworthiness—a sense of inadequacy attendant on a life of self-examination. *Maledicta* People . . who confess their inadequacies or even villainies.

inadequate /ɪnˈadɪkwət/ *adjective* & *noun*. L17.
[ORIGIN from IN-[3] + ADEQUATE *adjective*.]
▸ **A** *adjective*. Not adequate; insufficient; (of a person) incompetent, unable to deal with a situation. (Foll. by *to*, *for*, *to do*.) L17.

J. R. GREEN The ordinary resources of the Crown . . were inadequate to meet the expenses of war. C. PHILLIPS Leslie Carter's shop stood alone, its wooden walls thin with age, its roof inadequate.

▸ **B** *noun*. A person whose character or abilities are insufficient to meet the expectations of society. M20.
■ **inadequately** *adverb* L17. **inadequateness** *noun* L17.

inadequation /ˌɪnadɪˈkweɪʃ(ə)n, -ʒ(ə)n/ *noun*. M17.
[ORIGIN from IN-[3] + ADEQUATION.]
Lack of equivalence or exact correspondence.

inadhesive /ɪnədˈhiːsɪv, -zɪv/ *adjective*. E19.
[ORIGIN from IN-[3] + ADHESIVE *adjective*.]
Not adhesive.

inadmissible /ɪnədˈmɪsɪb(ə)l/ *adjective*. L18.
[ORIGIN from IN-[3] + ADMISSIBLE.]
Unable to be admitted or allowed.
■ ˌ**inadmissiˈbility** *noun* E19. **inadmissibly** *adverb* M19.

in-a-door /ˈɪnədɔː/ *adverb*. *arch.* E17.
[ORIGIN from IN *adverb* + A *adjective* + DOOR.]
Indoors; at home.

inadventurous /ɪnədˈvɛntʃ(ə)rəs/ *adjective*. *rare*. M19.
[ORIGIN from IN-[3] + ADVENTUROUS.]
= UNADVENTUROUS.
■ **inadventurousness** *noun* M19.

inadvertence /ɪnədˈvəːt(ə)ns/ *noun*. LME.
[ORIGIN medieval Latin *inadvertentia*, formed as IN-[3] + ADVERTENCE.]
The quality or character of being inadvertent; inattention; carelessness; an instance of this.

O. WILDE Whether by inadvertence or direction . . the Duchess left out some essential words.

■ Also **inadvertency** *noun* L16.

inadvertent /ɪnədˈvəːt(ə)nt/ *adjective*. M17.
[ORIGIN from IN-[3] + Latin *advertent-* pres. ppl stem of *advertere* ADVERT *verb*: see -ENT.]
1 Of a person: not properly attentive or observant. M17.
2 Of an action: unintentional. E18.

V. GLENDINNING The pregnancy was inadvertent and unwanted by Rebecca.

■ **inadvertently** *adverb* L17.

inadvisable /ɪnəd'vʌɪzəb(ə)l/ *adjective*. L19.
[ORIGIN from IN-[3] + ADVISABLE.]
Not expedient; imprudent.
■ ˌinadvisaˈbility *noun* M19.

inadvisedly /ɪnəd'vʌɪzɪdli/ *adverb*. *rare*. M17.
[ORIGIN from IN-[3] + ADVISEDLY.]
Without proper consideration; imprudently, rashly.

inaesthetic /ɪniːs'θɛtɪk, -ɛs-/ *adjective*. Also ***ines-**. M19.
[ORIGIN from IN-[3] + AESTHETIC *adjective*.]
Unaesthetic.

inagglutinable /ɪnə'gluːtɪnəb(ə)l/ *adjective*. E20.
[ORIGIN from IN-[3] + AGGLUTINABLE.]
BIOLOGY & MEDICINE. Unable to be agglutinated.
■ ˌinagglutinaˈbility *noun* E20.

†**inaidable** *adjective*. *rare* (Shakes.). Only in E17.
[ORIGIN from IN-[3] + AIDABLE.]
Unable to be aided.

inajá /ɪnə'dʒɑː/ *noun*. M19.
[ORIGIN Portuguese from Tupi *inaiá*.]
A palm tree of the Amazon region and Trinidad, *Maximiliana maripa*, with very long leaves.

inaka *noun* var. of INANGA.

inalienable /ɪn'eɪlɪənəb(ə)l/ *adjective*. M17.
[ORIGIN from IN-[3] + ALIENABLE.]
Not alienable; that cannot be transferred from its present ownership or relation.

R. NIEBUHR Defeating the experiment in feudalism . . and giving each family inalienable rights in the soil.

■ inalienaˈbility *noun* L18. **inalienably** *adverb* M18.

inalterable /ɪn'ɔːlt(ə)rəb(ə)l, -'ɒl-/ *adjective*. M16.
[ORIGIN from IN-[3] + ALTERABLE.]
Unalterable; not subject to change.
■ inalteraˈbility *noun* E18. **inalterably** *adverb* M17.

inambitious /ɪnam'bɪʃəs/ *adjective*. *rare*. E17.
[ORIGIN from IN-[3] + AMBITIOUS *adjective*.]
Not ambitious.

†**inamel** *noun*, *verb* vars. of ENAMEL *noun*, *verb*.

†**inamelled** *adjective* var. of ENAMELLED.

inamissible /ɪnə'mɪsɪb(ə)l/ *adjective*. Now *rare*. M17.
[ORIGIN French, or medieval Latin *inamissibilis*, formed as IN-[3] + AMISSIBLE.]
Not liable to be lost.
■ ˌinamissiˈbility *noun* M18. **inamissibleness** *noun* E18.

inamorata /ɪˌnamə'rɑːtə/ *noun*. Also †**en-**. M17.
[ORIGIN Italian (now *innam-*), fem. of INAMORATO.]
A female lover.

K. LETTE A plethora of female inamoratas awaits me. Oh, it's such a bore being perfect.

inamorate /ɪ'nam(ə)rət/ *adjective & noun*. L16.
[ORIGIN Anglicized from Italian †*inamorato*, *-ta* (now *innam-*) pa. pple of *inamorare*: see INAMORATE *verb*, -ATE[2].]
▸ **A** *adjective*. Enamoured, in love. L16.
▸ †**B** *noun*. A lover. Only in E17.

†**inamorate** *verb trans*. Also (earlier) **en-**. L16–E18.
[ORIGIN Italian *inamorare* (now *innam-*) fall in love, from *in-* IN-[2] + *amore* love: see -ATE[3].]
Inspire with love, enamour.

inamoration /ɪˌnamə'reɪʃ(ə)n/ *noun*. *rare*. M17.
[ORIGIN from INAMORATE *verb* + -ATION.]
Enamourment.

inamorato /ɪˌnamə'rɑːtəʊ/ *noun*. Also †**en-**. Pl. **-os**. L16.
[ORIGIN Italian (now *innam-*), pa. pple of *inamorare*: see INAMORATE *verb*.]
A male lover.

†**inamour** *verb* var. of ENAMOUR.

in and in /ɪn (ə)nd 'ɪn/ *adverbial, noun, & adjectival phr*. Also (the usual form as adjective) **in-and-in**. M17.
[ORIGIN from IN *adverb* + AND *conjunction*[1] + IN *adverb*.]
▸ **A** *adverbial phr*. Further and further in; continually inwards. M17.
breed in and in: see BREED *verb*.
▸ **B** *noun phr*. †**1** A throw with four dice, falling all alike or as two doublets; a gambling game based on this. M–L17.
2 A space which opens up and reveals continually something yet further in. L19.
3 The stage in a swindle at which the swindler risks his or her own money with that of the dupe. *slang*. M20.
▸ **C** *adjectival phr*. Designating breeding within a limited stock; *fig*. intimate and exclusive. M19.

in and out /ɪn (ə)nd 'aʊt/ *adverbial & adjectival phr*. Also (the usual form as adjective) **in-and-out**. ME.
[ORIGIN from IN *adverb* + AND *conjunction*[1] + OUT *adverb*.]
▸ **A** *adverbial phr*. **1** Alternately in and out; now in, now out. ME.
2 Inside and outside. L19.
▸ **B** *adjectival phr*. Designating a person who or thing which is alternately in and out of something. M17.
in-and-out boy, **in-and-out man** *slang* a man who is in and out of prison; a burglar. **in-and-out work** discontinuous work; irregular or illegal practice.
■ **in-and-outer** *noun* a person who is only moderately skilled, or erratic in performance; a person who holds office intermittently: E20.

inane /ɪ'neɪn/ *adjective & noun*. M16.
[ORIGIN Latin *inanis* empty, vain.]
▸ **A** *adjective*. Empty, void; silly, senseless, pointless. M16.

C. KINGSLEY Dilating into vast inane infinities. A. HIGGINS They had stared at her before making inane suggestions. Hopeless, she thought, they know nothing.

▸ **B** *noun*. A void or empty thing; empty space; emptiness. *arch*. L17.
■ **inanely** *adverb* L19. **inaneness** *noun* L20.

inanga /'iːnaŋə/ *noun*. *NZ*. Also **inaka** /'iːnakə/. M19.
[ORIGIN Maori.]
1 A small migratory Australasian fish, *Galaxias maculatus*, the young of which are eaten as whitebait. Also called ***jollytail***. M19.
2 An evergreen shrub or small tree, *Dracophyllum longifolium*, of the family Epacridaceae, native to New Zealand. L19.

inanimate /ɪn'anɪmət/ *adjective & noun*. LME.
[ORIGIN Late Latin *inanimatus* lifeless, formed as IN-[3] + ANIMATE *adjective*.]
▸ **A** *adjective*. **1** Without life, lifeless; *spec*. not endowed with animal life. LME.

N. SYMINGTON As human beings we share certain essential features with the inanimate world as a whole.

inanimate nature all of nature other than the animal world.
2 Without the activity of life; spiritless, dull. E18.

D. PAE His arms grasped the girl's inanimate form.

▸ **B** *noun*. An inanimate thing; inanimate nature. M17.
■ †**inanimated** *adjective* = INANIMATE *adjective* M17–E19. **inanimately** *adverb* L19. **inanimateness** *noun* M17.

inanimate /ɪn'anɪmeɪt/ *verb trans*. Now *rare*. L16.
[ORIGIN Late Latin *inanimat-* pa. ppl stem of *inanimare* inspire, fire, formed as IN-[2] + ANIMATE *verb*.]
Animate, infuse life into; encourage, enliven.

inanimation /ˌɪnanɪ'meɪʃ(ə)n/ *noun*. L18.
[ORIGIN from IN-[3] + ANIMATION.]
Absence of life or liveliness.

inanition /ɪnə'nɪʃ(ə)n/ *noun*. LME.
[ORIGIN Late Latin *inanitio(n-)*, from Latin *inanit-* pa. ppl stem of *inanire* make empty, formed as INANE: see -ITION.]
The action or process of emptying; the condition of being empty; a condition of exhaustion resulting from lack of nourishment.

inanity /ɪ'nanɪti/ *noun*. E16.
[ORIGIN Latin *inanitas*, formed as INANE: see -ITY.]
1 Lack of substance or solidity; unsatisfactoriness; lack of ideas; senselessness, silliness; the quality of being devoid of interest. E16. ▸**b** An inane remark or practice. M17. ▸**c** Lack of active interest in life; idleness. L18.

P. CAREY I return my eyes to the inanity of the television. **b** P. LIVELY I corrected the inanities encouraged by her grandmothers.

2 The quality or condition of being void or empty; emptiness. E17.

in antis /ɪn 'antɪs/ *adjectival phr*. M19.
[ORIGIN Latin.]
CLASSICAL ARCHITECTURE. (Of columns) positioned between two antas; (of a building) having walls prolonged beyond the front, with terminating pilasters in line with columns of a facade.

inapparent /ɪnə'par(ə)nt/ *adjective*. E17.
[ORIGIN from IN-[3] + APPARENT.]
Not apparent or manifest.

inappeasable /ɪnə'piːzəb(ə)l/ *adjective*. M19.
[ORIGIN from IN-[3] + APPEASABLE.]
Unable to be appeased.

inappellable /ɪnə'pɛləb(ə)l/ *adjective*. E19.
[ORIGIN French †*inappelable*, from *appeler* APPEAL *verb*: see IN-[3], -ABLE.]
Unable to be appealed against.

inappetence /ɪn'apɪt(ə)ns/ *noun*. L17.
[ORIGIN from IN-[3] + APPETENCE.]
Lack of appetite, desire, or longing.
■ Also **inappetency** *noun* E17.

inappetent /ɪn'apɪt(ə)nt/ *adjective*. L18.
[ORIGIN from IN-[3] + APPETENT.]
Without appetite, desire, or longing.

inapplicable /ɪn'aplɪkəb(ə)l, ɪnə'plɪk-/ *adjective*. M17.
[ORIGIN from IN-[3] + APPLICABLE.]
Not applicable; unsuitable.
■ **inapplicaˈbility** *noun* the quality or condition of being inapplicable; an instance of this: L17. **inapplicably** *adverb* M19.

inapplication /ˌɪnaplɪ'keɪʃ(ə)n/ *noun*. E18.
[ORIGIN from IN-[3] + APPLICATION.]
1 Lack of application; failure to apply oneself to duties, negligence. E18.
2 Inapplicability. L18.

inapposite /ɪn'apəzɪt/ *adjective*. M17.
[ORIGIN from IN-[3] + APPOSITE *adjective*.]
Not apposite.
■ **inappositely** *adverb* M17. **inappositeness** *noun* L19.

inappreciable /ɪnə'priːʃəb(ə)l, -ʃɪə-/ *adjective*. L18.
[ORIGIN from IN-[3] + APPRECIABLE.]
†**1** Unable to be sufficiently appreciated; priceless. L18–M19.
2 Imperceptible; insignificant. E19.
3 Unable to be appreciated. M19.
■ **inappreciably** *adverb* M19.

inappreciation /ˌɪnəpriːʃɪ'eɪʃ(ə)n, -sɪ-/ *noun*. M19.
[ORIGIN from IN-[3] + APPRECIATION.]
Lack of appreciation; failure to appreciate someone or something sufficiently.

inappreciative /ɪnə'priːʃ(ɪ)ətɪv/ *adjective*. M19.
[ORIGIN from IN-[3] + APPRECIATIVE.]
Not appreciative.
■ **inappreciatively** *adverb* L19. **inappreciativeness** *noun* M19.

inapprehensible /ˌɪnaprɪ'hɛnsɪb(ə)l/ *adjective*. M17.
[ORIGIN Late Latin *inapprehensibilis*, formed as IN-[3] + APPREHENSIBLE.]
Not apprehensible; unable to be grasped by the senses or intellect.

inapprehension /ˌɪnaprɪ'hɛnʃ(ə)n/ *noun*. M18.
[ORIGIN from IN-[3] + APPREHENSION.]
Lack of apprehension; failure to grasp by the senses or intellect.

inapprehensive /ˌɪnaprɪ'hɛnsɪv/ *adjective*. M17.
[ORIGIN from IN-[3] + APPREHENSIVE.]
Not grasping with the senses or intellect; not anxious.
■ **inapprehensiveness** *noun* M17.

inapproachable /ɪnə'prəʊtʃəb(ə)l/ *adjective*. E19.
[ORIGIN from IN-[3] + APPROACHABLE.]
Not approachable; inaccessible.

inappropriate /ɪnə'prəʊprɪət/ *adjective*. E19.
[ORIGIN from IN-[3] + APPROPRIATE *adjective*.]
Not appropriate; unsuitable.

R. D. LAING Responsiveness adequate to the infant will be inappropriate to an older child.

■ **inappropriately** *adverb* M19. **inappropriateness** *noun* M19.

inapt /ɪn'apt/ *adjective*. L17.
[ORIGIN from IN-[3] + APT. Cf. INEPT.]
1 Not suitable; inappropriate. L17.
2 Unskilful, awkward. E19.
■ **inaptly** *adverb* M19. **inaptness** *noun* E19.

inaptitude /ɪn'aptɪtjuːd/ *noun*. E17.
[ORIGIN from IN-[3] + APTITUDE. Cf. INEPTITUDE.]
Unsuitableness; unskilfulness.

inarable /ɪn'arəb(ə)l/ *adjective*. M17.
[ORIGIN medieval Latin *inarabilis*; later from IN-[3] + ARABLE *adjective*.]
Not arable; impossible to plough.

inarch /ɪn'ɑːtʃ/ *verb*[1] *trans*. Also †**en-**. E17.
[ORIGIN from IN-[2], EN-[1] + ARCH *verb*[1].]
HORTICULTURE. Graft by connecting a growing branch without separation from the parent stock.

inarch *verb*[2] var. of ENARCH *verb*[1].

inarguable /ɪn'ɑːgjʊəb(ə)l/ *adjective*. L19.
[ORIGIN from IN-[3] + ARGUABLE.]
Not open to argument; irrefutable.

Washington Post Generally, they said there was no inarguable reasoning to support either course of action.

■ **inarguably** *adverb* M20.

inarm /ɪn'ɑːm/ *verb trans*. *poet*. Also **en-** /ɪn-, ɛn-/. E17.
[ORIGIN from IN-[1] or IN-[2], EN-[1] + ARM *noun*[1]. Cf. French *embrasser*.]
Clasp within or as with the arms; embrace.

BROWNING Gallant and lady . . Enarming each the other. F. W. H. MYERS Norway's inarming melancholy sea.

inarticulacy /ɪnɑː'tɪkjʊləsi/ *noun*. E20.
[ORIGIN from INARTICULATE: see -ACY.]
The quality or condition of being inarticulate; lack of clarity or fluency in expressing oneself.

Daily Telegraph 'Y' know' and 'I mean' and other apologies for inarticulacy.

inarticulate /ɪnɑː'tɪkjʊlət/ *adjective*. E17.
[ORIGIN from IN-[3] + ARTICULATE *adjective*; in sense 2 corresp. to late Latin *inarticulatus*.]
1 Not jointed or hinged; *spec*. in *ZOOLOGY & BOTANY*, not having joints or articulations. E17. ▸**b** *ZOOLOGY*. Designating or pertaining to (an animal of) the division Inarticulata of brachiopods having valves not joined by a hinge. L19.
2 Of sound or speech: not articulate. Also, indistinctly pronounced. E17.

J. BEATTIE Inarticulate sounds may be divided into musical sound and noise. G. SWIFT Inarticulate sounds—coughs, grunts, clearings of the throat.

3 Unable to speak distinctly; unable to express oneself clearly and fluently. M18. ▸**b** Not expressed, unspoken. E20.

R. CHURCH He was . . gentle and inarticulate. He never spoke. A. S. BYATT He could give an inarticulate woman the right hints about . . her clumsy sentences. **b** P. H. GIBBS Nobody cheered as the President passed, but there was the deep silence of inarticulate emotion.

4 Having no distinct meaning; unintelligible. **M19.**

G. BRIMLEY Inarticulate gibberish.

■ **inarticulated** *adjective* = INARTICULATE 1, 2 **E19.** **inarticulately** *adverb* **M17.** **inarticulateness** *noun* **M18.**

inarticulation /ˌɪnɑːtɪkjʊˈleɪʃ(ə)n/ *noun. rare.* **M18.**
[ORIGIN from IN-³ + ARTICULATION.]
Absence of distinct articulation; inarticulate utterance.

CHESTERFIELD It was by the ambiguity of the expression . . not by the inarticulation of the words.

in articulo mortis /ɪn ɑːˌtɪkjʊləʊ ˈmɔːtɪs/ *adverbial phr.* **L16.**
[ORIGIN Latin = in the article of death.]
At the point or moment of death.

inartificial /ˌɪnɑːtɪˈfɪʃ(ə)l/ *adjective. arch.* **L16.**
[ORIGIN from IN-³ + ARTIFICIAL *adjective*; in sense 1 from Latin *inartificialis* (translating Greek *atekhnos*) not according to the rules of logic (lit. 'art').]
†**1** Of an argument: not deduced by logic from accepted premisses but derived from authority or testimony. **L16–E18.**
2 Not in accordance with artistic principles; rude, clumsy, inartistic. *arch.* **E17.**
†**3** Not produced by artifice or constructive skill; natural. **M–L17.**
4 Not pretending or pretended; artless, unaffected, natural. **M17.**
5 Without complexity or elaboration; plain, simple, straightforward. **E19.**
■ **inartificially** *adverb* **E17.**

inartistic /ɪnɑːˈtɪstɪk/ *adjective.* **M19.**
[ORIGIN from IN-³ + ARTISTIC.]
1 Not in accordance with artistic principles. **M19.**

GEO. ELIOT Inartistic figures crowding the canvass of life without adequate effect.

2 Without artistic skill, talent, or appreciation. **L19.**

E. C. STEDMAN An inartistic nature and a dull or commonplace mind.

■ **inartistically** *adverb* **M19.**

inasmuch /ɪnəzˈmʌtʃ/ *adverb.* **ME.**
[ORIGIN Orig. 3 words, from IN *preposition* + AS *adverb* + MUCH *adjective* or *noun*, translating Old French *en tant (que)*, Latin *in tantum (ut)*.]
1 Foll. by *as*: in so far as, to such a degree as. **ME.**

C. BLACKWOOD Inasmuch as she could be pleased, the idea of this marriage pleased her.

2 Foll. by *as*: in that; seeing or considering that; since, because. **LME.**

B. GUEST Inasmuch as Gray was Perdita's father, he was to be treated with . . respect.

inattention /ɪnəˈtɛnʃ(ə)n/ *noun.* **L17.**
[ORIGIN from IN-³ + ATTENTION.]
1 Failure to pay attention or take notice; heedlessness, negligence. **L17.**
2 Lack of courteous personal attention. **L18.**

inattentive /ɪnəˈtɛntɪv/ *adjective.* **L17.**
[ORIGIN from IN-³ + ATTENTIVE.]
1 Not paying attention; heedless, negligent. **L17.**
2 Neglecting to show courtesy. **L18.**
■ **inattentively** *adverb* **M18.** **inattentiveness** *noun* **M18.**

inaudible /ɪnˈɔːdɪb(ə)l/ *adjective.* **LME.**
[ORIGIN Late Latin *inaudibilis*, from (the same root as) IN-³ + AUDIBLE.]
Not audible; imperceptible to the ear.

SHAKES. *All's Well* Th' inaudible and noiseless foot of Time. V. BRITTAIN He was so shy that his few remarks were almost inaudible.

■ **inaudiˈbility** *noun* **E19.** **inaudibly** *adverb* **L18.**

inaugur /ɪˈnɔːɡə/ *verb trans.* Now *rare* or *obsolete.* **M16.**
[ORIGIN Old French & mod. French *inaugurer* or Latin *inaugurare*: see INAUGURATE.]
†**1** = INAUGURATE 1. **M16–E18.**
2 = INAUGURATE 4. **L19.**

inaugural /ɪˈnɔːɡjʊr(ə)l/ *adjective & noun.* **L17.**
[ORIGIN French, from *inaugurer* inaugurate from Latin *inaugurare* INAUGURATE: see -AL¹.]
▸ **A** *adjective.* Of or pertaining to inauguration; forming part of an inauguration ceremony. Of a lecture, meeting, etc.: first in a series or course. **L17.**

Vanity Fair The promise of recovery offered in President Franklin Roosevelt's inaugural address.

▸ **B** *noun.* An inaugural speech, address, or lecture. **M19.**

inaugurate /ɪˈnɔːɡjʊreɪt/ *verb trans.* **L16.**
[ORIGIN Latin *inaugurat-* pa. ppl stem of *inaugurare* take omens from the flight of birds, formed as IN-¹ + *augurari* AUGUR *verb*: see -ATE³.]
1 Admit to office (*US* esp. the presidency) by a formal ceremony. **L16.**
2 Make auspicious; confer solemnity or sanctity upon. *rare.* **E17.**
3 Enter into (an undertaking or course of action, a significant period of time) formally or ceremoniously; initiate, introduce, begin. **M18.**

E. F. BENSON She said that we . . must inaugurate an intellectual regeneration in London. P. ACKROYD His return to Harvard also inaugurated a period in which he was beset by worries.

4 Open or dedicate to public use by a formal ceremony. **M19.**
■ **inauguratory** *adjective* pertaining to inauguration; inaugural: **L18.** **inaugurative** *adjective* having the function of inaugurating; inaugural: **M19.**

inauguration /ɪˌnɔːɡjʊˈreɪʃ(ə)n/ *noun.* **M16.**
[ORIGIN Old French & mod. French, or late Latin *inauguratio(n-)*, formed as INAUGURATE: see -ATION.]
1 Formal or ceremonial admission to an office (*US* esp. the presidency); an inaugural occasion or ceremony. **M16.**

J. S. MILL I . . always dated from these conversations my own . . inauguration as an original and independent thinker.

2 The formal or definite beginning of or introduction to a course of action, a significant period of time, etc. **M19.**

J. A. FROUDE To the one . . the advent of Antichrist, to the other the inauguration of the millennium.

3 The formal or ceremonious introduction of something into public use. **M19.**
– COMB.: **Inauguration Day** *US* the day (currently 20 January following the presidential election) on which the president is inaugurated.

†**inaunter** *conjunction* var. of ENAUNTER.

inauspicious /ɪnɔːˈspɪʃəs/ *adjective.* **L16.**
[ORIGIN from IN-³ + AUSPICIOUS.]
Portending evil; ill-omened, unlucky.

A. COWLEY On that Trees Top an inauspicious Crow Foretold some ill to happen. SHAFTESBURY I begin this inauspicious Work, which my ill Stars and you have assign'd me.

■ **inauspiciously** *adverb* **L17.** **inauspiciousness** *noun* **M17.**

inauthentic /ɪnɔːˈθɛntɪk/ *adjective.* **L16.**
[ORIGIN from IN-³ + AUTHENTIC *adjective.*]
Not authentic; not genuine; unreliable, unreal.
■ ˌ**inauthenˈticity** *noun* **L19.**

inauthoritative /ɪnɔːˈθɒrɪtətɪv, -teɪtɪv/ *adjective.* **M17.**
[ORIGIN from IN-³ + AUTHORITATIVE.]
Not authoritative; having no authority.

in banco /ɪn ˈbaŋkəʊ/ *adverbial phr.* **M19.**
[ORIGIN Latin = on the bench.]
hist. Of a law court: sitting as a full bench of judges.

in-being /ˈɪnbiːɪŋ/ *noun.* **L16.**
[ORIGIN from IN *adverb* + BEING *noun.*]
†**1** *THEOLOGY.* Each of the constituents of the Trinity. **L16–M17.**

A. GOLDING In the same most single essence are three Persons or In-beings.

2 The fact of being within; existence in something else. **E17.**

T. WARREN 'Tis such an union and in-being in Christ. J. NEILL Believing . . gives them a real subsistence and in-being in the Soul.

3 Inward or essential nature. **M17.**

J. RUSKIN Men get to know . . their inbeing—to know themselves . . what is in them.

inbent /ˈɪnbɛnt/ *adjective.* Long *rare.* **L16.**
[ORIGIN from IN *adverb* + BENT *adjective.*]
Bent or curved inwards; directed inwards.

in-between /ɪnbɪˈtwiːn/ *noun & adjective.* **E19.**
[ORIGIN from *in between* s.v. IN *adverb.*]
▸ **A** *noun.* **1** An interval. **E19.**
2 A person who intervenes. **E19.**
▸ **B** *adjective.* Intermediate, placed between. **L19.**

in-betweener /ɪnbɪˈtwiːnə/ *noun.* **E20.**
[ORIGIN formed as IN-BETWEEN + -ER¹.]
A person who occupies or takes up an intermediate (esp. mental) position or attitude.

inbind /ɪnˈbʌɪnd/ *verb trans.* Pa. t. & pple **inbound** /ɪnˈbaʊnd/. **L18.**
[ORIGIN from IN-¹ + BIND *verb.*]
Bind within; *spec.* bind within a book or manuscript. Usu. in *pass.*

Ampleforth Journal A transcription of the fragment inbound in the Sarum Missal in the monastery library. *fig.*: D. H. LAWRENCE He had never been very closely inbound into the family.

inboard /ˈɪnbɔːd/ *adverb, preposition, adjective, & noun.* Orig. *NAUTICAL.* **M19.**
[ORIGIN from IN *preposition* + BOARD *noun.*]
▸ **A** *adverb.* Within the sides or towards the centre of a boat, aircraft, vehicle, etc. **M19.**

E. K. KANE It passes inboard through a block. *Times* Inboard-mounted disc brakes.

▸ **B** *preposition.* Within (a boat etc.), inside. **M19.**
▸ **C** *adjective.* Situated within or towards the centre of a boat, aircraft, vehicle, etc.; interior. **M19.**

Rudder Even in large sailing boats the use of an inboard engine is sometimes not advisable.

▸ **D** *noun.* (A boat equipped with) a motor mounted within the hull. *N. Amer.* **E20.**

inborn /ˈɪnbɔːn, ɪnˈbɔːn/ *adjective.* **OE.**
[ORIGIN from IN-¹ + BORN *adjective*, after late Latin *innatus* INNATE.]
†**1** Born in the place or country specified or in question; native. **OE–L19.**

MILTON Those old and inborn names of successive Kings.

2 (Of a quality etc.) existing in a person from birth, innate; *MEDICINE* (esp. of a metabolic disorder) congenital and hereditary. **E16.**

L. DURRELL A native and inborn scepticism kept me free from the toils of any denominational religion.

3 Of a person: born such, such by nature. **E19.**

Westminster Gazette Every in-born artist has a natural method, like the song-birds of the air.

inbound /ˈɪnbaʊnd/ *adjective.* **L19.**
[ORIGIN from IN *adverb* + BOUND *adjective*¹.]
Bound or headed inward, homeward-bound.

inbound *verb pa. t. & pple* of INBIND.

inbread /ˈɪnbrɛd/ *noun.* Now *rare.* **M17.**
[ORIGIN from IN *adverb* + BREAD *noun*¹.]
The extra loaf in a baker's dozen.

inbreak /ˈɪnbreɪk/ *noun. rare.* **L17.**
[ORIGIN from IN *adverb* + BREAK *noun*¹, after *outbreak.*]
An invasion, a forcible entry.
■ Also **inbreaking** *noun* **M17.**

inbreath /ˈɪnbrɛθ/ *noun.* **E20.**
[ORIGIN from IN *adverb* + BREATH.]
A drawing in of the breath, an inhalation.

inbreathe /ɪnˈbriːð/ *verb trans.* **LME.**
[ORIGIN from IN-¹ + BREATHE *verb*, after Latin *inspirare*. Cf. IMBREATHE.]
1 Introduce or instil by breathing. (Foll. by *into.*) **LME.**

fig.: T. GATAKER They cannot inbreath into us such knowledg that shal quiet and allay our . . hearts. J. A. SYMONDS So true and delicate a spirit is inbreathed into the old forms.

2 Give inspiration to. **E19.**
3 Draw in as breath; inhale. **L19.**

J. R. ILLINGWORTH He felt himself inbreathing power from on high.

inbred /ɪnˈbrɛd, ˈɪnbrɛd/ *adjective.* Also †**im-**. **L16.**
[ORIGIN from IN *adverb* + BRED *adjective.*]
1 Inborn, innate, inherent. **L16.**

R. BOYLE Your inbred Curiosity, and love of Experimental Learning.

†**2** Bred in the place specified or in question; native. **E–M17.**
3 Characterized or produced by inbreeding. **L19.**

R. L. STEVENSON Sore-eyed, short-lived, inbred fishermen.

inbreed /ɪnˈbriːd/ *verb.* Also **im-** /ɪm-/. Pa. t. & pple **-bred** /-ˈbrɛd/. **M16.**
[ORIGIN from IN-¹ + BREED *verb*. In sense 3, prob. back-form. from INBREEDING.]
†**1** *verb intrans.* Come into being, originate. Only in **M16.**
2 *verb trans.* Breed, engender, or produce internally. **L16.**

M. SULLIVAN Stressing positive attributes creates or inbreeds these values, which become the . . guiding beliefs of employees.

3 *verb trans. & intrans.* Breed from closely related members of a species, esp. over several generations. Cf. earlier INBREEDING. **M20.** ▸**b** *verb intrans.* (Marry and) produce offspring from within a family or small social group, for successive generations. **M20.**

inbreeding /ˈɪnbriːdɪŋ/ *verbal noun.* **M19.**
[ORIGIN from IN *adverb* + BREEDING.]
Breeding from closely related members of a species (as siblings, parent and offspring, etc.). Also, (marriage and) the production of offspring from within a closed community.

inbring /ɪnˈbrɪŋ/ *verb trans.* Long *obsolete* exc. *Scot.* Infl. as BRING; pa. t. & pple usu. **-brought** /-ˈbrɔːt/. **OE.**
[ORIGIN from IN-¹ + BRING, translating Latin *offerre.*]
Bring in, introduce; *esp.* in *SCOTS LAW*, bring in by legal authority, produce in court, confiscate.
■ **inbringer** *noun* a person who introduces or imports something **E16.**

in-build /ɪnˈbɪld/ *verb trans.* Pa. t. & pple **-built** /-ˈbɪlt/. **E20.**
[ORIGIN from IN-¹ + BUILD *verb*. Cf. INBUILT.]
Build in; incorporate as part of a structure.

Press & Journal (Aberdeen) Timber-frame has to be well supervised to make sure that you don't in-build problems.

inbuilt /ˈɪnbɪlt/ *ppl adjective.* **E20.**
[ORIGIN from IN *adverb* + *built* pa. pple of BUILD *verb.*]
Incorporated in a structure; already part of or (naturally) present in something.

Catholic Herald Any nation has an in-built resistance to immigrants. *Daily Telegraph* They . . contain an in-built device to ensure that no dazzle occurs.

†**inburning** *ppl adjective. rare* (Spenser). Only in L16.
[ORIGIN from IN *adverb* + BURNING *adjective*.]
Burning inwardly.

inburst /ˈɪnbəːst/ *noun. rare.* M19.
[ORIGIN from IN *adverb* + BURST *noun*: cf. *outburst*.]
An irruption; a sudden entry or incursion.

inburst /ɪnˈbəːst/ *verb intrans. rare.* Infl. as BURST *verb*; pa. t. & pple usu. **-burst**. M16.
[ORIGIN from IN-[1] + BURST *verb*.]
Burst in; come in suddenly or violently.

in-bye /ɪnˈbʌɪ/ *adverb & adjective.* Chiefly *Scot. & N. English.* Also **in-by**. E18.
[ORIGIN from IN *adverb* + BY *adverb*.]
▸ **A** *adverb.* In an inward direction; closer or further towards the centre or interior. E18.
▸ **B** *adjective.* Inner, in the interior; *spec.* designating or pertaining to a farm's land lying nearest to the farm buildings. E19.

Inc. /ɪŋk/ *ppl adjective. N. Amer.* E20.
[ORIGIN Abbreviation.]
In names of companies: incorporated, constituted as a legal corporation.

H. L. MENCKEN An Englishman writes *Ltd.* after the name of a limited liability bank . . as we write *Inc.*

Inca /ˈɪŋkə/ *noun & adjective.* Also ***Inka**, (earlier) †**Ing(u)a**. L16.
[ORIGIN Quechua = lord, king, royal person. Earlier form is Spanish corruption.]
▸ **A** *noun.* Pl. **-s**, same.
1 A member of a S. American Indian people of the central Andes before the Spanish conquest in the early 16th cent.; *spec.* their king or emperor, a member of the royal family. L16.

J. BRONOWSKI From 1438 onwards, the Incas had conquered three thousand miles of coastline.

2 (Usu. **i-**.) Any of several hummingbirds of the genus *Coeligena*. M20.
▸ **B** *attrib.* or as *adjective.* Of or pertaining to the Incas. E17.
Inca dove a small dove of Central America and the south-western US, *Scardafella inca*. **Inca tern** a dark grey tern, *Larosterna inca*, of Peru and Chile.

†**incage** *verb* var. of ENCAGE.

Incaic /ɪŋˈkeɪɪk/ *adjective.* E20.
[ORIGIN from INCA + -IC.]
= INCAN.

incalculable /ɪnˈkalkjʊləb(ə)l/ *adjective.* L18.
[ORIGIN from IN-[3] + CALCULABLE.]
1 Of an amount or number too great for calculation. L18.

LYTTON They say his wealth is incalculable. S. MORLEY His influence on David was incalculable.

2 Unable to be estimated or forecast. L18.

G. F. CHAMBERS The incalculable number of meteor-streams that must exist in the solar system. *Pall Mall Gazette* The incalculable dangers of the 'narcotic' remedies.

3 Of a person, disposition, etc.: unpredictable. L19.

GEO. ELIOT Anxiety about the beloved but incalculable son.

▪ **incalcula'bility** *noun* L19. **incalculableness** *noun* M19. **incalculably** *adverb* E19.

incalescent /ɪnkəˈlɛs(ə)nt/ *adjective.* Now *rare* or *obsolete*. L17.
[ORIGIN Latin *incalescent-* pres. ppl stem of *incalescere*, formed as IN-[2] + *calescere* grow warm: see -ENT.]
Becoming hot or warm; increasing in warmth.
▪ **incalescence** *noun* the action or process of becoming hot or warm; a rise in temperature: M17.

in-calf /ɪnˈkɑːf, ˈɪnkɑːf/ *adjective.* M16.
[ORIGIN from IN-[1] + CALF *noun*[1].]
Of a cow: that is in calf, pregnant.
▪ **in'calver** *noun* an in-calf cow M19.

incall /ɪnˈkɔːl/ *verb.* Long *obsolete* exc. *Scot.* ME.
[ORIGIN from IN-[1] + CALL *verb*, after Latin *invocare* INVOKE.]
1 *verb trans.* Call in, call upon, invoke. ME.
2 *verb intrans.* Call *on* or *upon*; pray *for*, *that*. L16.

incame *verb pa. t.* of INCOME *verb*

in camera /ɪn ˈkam(ə)rə/ *adverbial phr.* E19.
[ORIGIN Late Latin = in the chamber: see CAMERA.]
In a judge's private chambers, not in open court; *gen.* in secret or private session, not in public.

†**incameration** *noun.* L17–E18.
[ORIGIN French *incamération*, from *incamérer* from Italian *incamerare*, from *in-* IN-[2] + *camera* chamber, the papal treasury: see -ATION.]
Annexation to the papal domain.

†**incamp** *verb*, †**incampment**, vars. of ENCAMP, ENCAMPMENT.

Incan /ˈɪŋk(ə)n/ *adjective.* L19.
[ORIGIN from INCA + -AN.]
Of or pertaining to the Incas.

incandesce /ɪnkanˈdɛs/ *verb.* L19.
[ORIGIN Back-form. from INCANDESCENT.]
1 *verb intrans.* Be or become incandescent; glow with heat. L19.
2 *verb trans.* Make incandescent; cause to glow. *rare.* L19.

incandescence /ɪnkanˈdɛs(ə)ns/ *noun.* M17.
[ORIGIN formed as INCANDESCENT: see -ENCE.]
1 The state of being inflamed with anger, passion, etc.; ardency, fervour. M17.

D. LESSING Now she sounded listless, flat, all the incandescence of fury gone.

2 The state of being incandescent; the emission of light by a heated object or body. L18. ▸**b** Glowing or intense heat. *rare.* M19. ▸**c** Glowing or incandescent matter. M19.

J. TYNDALL Meteorites . . brought to incandescence by friction against the earth's atmosphere. W. SPOTTISWOODE The light is due to the incandescence of a fine thread of carbon.

incandescent /ɪnkanˈdɛs(ə)nt/ *adjective & noun.* L18.
[ORIGIN French from Latin *incandescent-* pres. ppl stem of *incandescere* glow, formed as IN-[2] + *candescere* become white, from *candidus* white: see CANDID, -ESCENT.]
▸ **A** *adjective.* **1** Glowing with heat. L18. ▸**b** Of a lamp etc.: producing light by means of a white-hot glowing filament. L19.

J. IMISON If the heated body is not luminous or incandescent, as hot water, for instance. J. TYNDALL The spectrum of incandescent sodium-vapour consists of a brilliant band.

2 Glowing, brightly shining, luminous. M19.

W. GOLDING It was incandescent daylight . . an atmosphere with a luminescence in it.

3 (Becoming) warm or intense in feeling, expression, etc.; ardent, fiery. M19.

P. LIVELY She feels incandescent, aflame with private triumphs.

▸ **B** *noun.* An incandescent lamp or burner. E20.
▪ **incandescently** *adverb* E19.

incant /ɪnˈkant/ *verb.* M16.
[ORIGIN Latin *incantare* chant, charm, formed as IN-[2] + *cantare* sing.]
1 †**a** *verb trans. & intrans.* Use incantation or enchantment (on). M16–M17. ▸**b** *verb trans.* Raise (a spirit) by a charm or incantation. *rare.* E20.
2 *verb trans.* Chant, intone. M20.

M. SPARK They sat in the twilight . . incanting witches' spells.

incantation /ɪnkanˈteɪʃ(ə)n/ *noun.* LME.
[ORIGIN Old French & mod. French from late Latin *incantatio(n-)*, from Latin *incantat-* pa. ppl stem of *incantare*: see INCANT, -ATION.]
A magical formula chanted or spoken; an utterance of such a formula, the use of such a formula in magic; *gen.* (the use of) any magical act or ceremony.

J. JONES He is using words as incantation, magically.

▪ **incantational** *adjective* incantatory M20. **'incantator** *noun* (*rare*) a person who uses incantations, an enchanter LME. **in'cantatory** *adjective* using or of the nature of (an) incantation M17.

incapable /ɪnˈkeɪpəb(ə)l/ *adjective & noun.* L16.
[ORIGIN French, or late Latin *incapabilis*, formed as IN-[3] + *capabilis* CAPABLE.]
▸ **A** *adjective.* **1** Lacking or deficient in ordinary powers or natural ability; incompetent; not capable of rational conduct. L16.

LD MACAULAY That the finances might not be ruined by incapable and inexperienced Papists. C. MACKENZIE He's utterly drunk and incapable.

†**2** Foll. by *of*: unable to receive, contain, or keep something. E17–M19. ▸**b** Impatient or intolerant *of*. M17–E18.

LEIGH HUNT This dandy would be incapable of his own wealth. **b** STEELE Your Temper is Wanton, and incapable of the least Pain.

3 Foll. by *of*: unable to be affected or influenced by; insensible to. Now *rare* or *obsolete*. E17.

SHAKES. *Haml.* As one incapable of her own distress.

4 Not having the capacity or fitness for a specified purpose, action, etc.; unable. Foll. by *of*, †*to do*. E17. ▸**b** *spec.* Too honest etc. to be capable *of*. M18.

A. T. ELLIS Something in me . . was arid and incapable of desire. L. GORDON The madman, living in mental isolation, is incapable of judging the quality of his ideas. **b** E. YOUNG The world . . was incapable of so great a guilt. SIR W. SCOTT My foes . . have laid things to my charge whereof I am incapable.

5 Not (esp. legally) qualified or entitled; disqualified. Foll. by *of*, †*to do*. M17.

ADDISON The Jews . . are in most, if not all, Places incapable of either Lands or Offices.

6 Of a nature or in a condition not allowing or admitting of a specified thing; not susceptible *of* (improvement etc.). Foll. by *of*, †*to do*. L17.

B. STEWART Unavoidable loss of heat which is incapable of accurate measurement.

▸ **B** *noun.* An incompetent or incapable person. E19.
▪ **incapa'bility** *noun* M17. **incapableness** *noun* M17. **incapably** *adverb* M19.

incapacious /ɪnkəˈpeɪʃəs/ *adjective.* Now *rare.* E17.
[ORIGIN from late Latin *incapac-*, *-ax*, formed as IN-[3] + CAPACIOUS.]
1 Lacking mental ability or capacity for something; unable to comprehend or apprehend; incapable. E17.
†**2** Not sufficiently capacious; not spacious; *fig.* narrow, limited. M17–E18.

incapacitant /ɪnkəˈpasɪt(ə)nt/ *noun.* M20.
[ORIGIN from INCAPACIT(ATE + -ANT[1].]
A substance capable of temporarily incapacitating a person etc. without wounding or killing.

incapacitate /ɪnkəˈpasɪteɪt/ *verb trans.* M17.
[ORIGIN from INCAPACIT(Y + -ATE[3].]
Make incapable or unfit; disqualify, *spec.* in law.

M. MEYER The fear that he might find himself incapacitated by illness. S. HAZZARD By undertaking to raise them, Dora had incapacitated herself for earning a livelihood.

▪ **incapaci'tation** *noun* L18.

incapacity /ɪnkəˈpasɪti/ *noun.* E17.
[ORIGIN French *incapacité* or late Latin *incapacitas*, formed as IN-[3] + *capacitas* CAPACITY.]
1 Lack of capacity; inability, powerlessness; an instance of this. (Foll. by *for*, *of*, *to do*.) E17. ▸**b** Inability to take, receive, or deal with something in some way. Foll. by *for*, *of*. M17.

G. A. BIRMINGHAM A man who might make a wreck of a boat through incapacity to manage her. E. CRANKSHAW Inhibited by . . ignorance and intellectual incapacity, he failed to think of anything effective to do.

2 Legal disqualification; an instance of this. M17.

C. MERIVALE The laws . . inflicted upon him civil incapacity to the fullest extent.

Incaparina /ɪŋkapəˈriːnə/ *noun.* M20.
[ORIGIN from Institute of Nutrition of Central America and Panama + Amer. Spanish *f)ariña* powdered manioc (from Latin *farina* flour, meal).]
A preparation of vegetable protein, used as a dietary supplement.

in capite /ɪn ˈkapɪteɪ/ *adverbial phr.* M16.
[ORIGIN Latin.]
= ***in chief*** (a) s.v. CHIEF *noun*.

incapsulate *verb* var. of ENCAPSULATE.

†**incaptivate** *verb* var. of ENCAPTIVATE.

incarcerate /ɪnˈkɑːs(ə)rət/ *ppl adjective. arch.* E16.
[ORIGIN medieval Latin *incarceratus* pa. pple, formed as INCARCERATE *verb*: see -ATE[2].]
Imprisoned; confined, shut in.

incarcerate /ɪnˈkɑːsəreɪt/ *verb trans.* M16.
[ORIGIN medieval Latin *incarcerat-* pa. ppl stem of *incarcerare*, formed as IN-[2] + *carcer* prison: see -ATE[3].]
Imprison, confine, shut in.

E. CRANKSHAW They were incarcerated in the damp and gloomy cells of the Peter and Paul Fortress.

▪ **incarcerated** *ppl adjective* (**a**) MEDICINE (esp. of a hernia) confined or constricted so as to be immovable or irreducible; (**b**) *gen.* that has been incarcerated: L18. **incarcerator** *noun* E19.

incarceration /ɪnˌkɑːsəˈreɪʃ(ə)n/ *noun.* LME.
[ORIGIN Old French & mod. French from medieval Latin *incarceratio(n-)* imprisonment, formed as INCARCERATE *verb*: see -ATION.]
1 MEDICINE. †**a** Retention of pus in a wound. Only in LME. ▸**b** Obstruction or strangulation of a hernia. E19.
2 *gen.* The action of incarcerating; the fact of being incarcerated. M16.

incardinate /ɪnˈkɑːdɪneɪt/ *verb trans.* E17.
[ORIGIN Late Latin *incardinat-* pa. ppl stem of *incardinare* ordain to the first rank in a church, formed as IN-[2] + *cardin-*, *cardo* hinge, *cardinalis* chief presbyter: see CARDINAL *noun*, -ATE[3].]
CHRISTIAN CHURCH. Institute as principal priest, deacon, etc., at a particular church or place; institute to a cardinalship; place under the jurisdiction of an ordinary.

incarn /ɪnˈkɑːn/ *verb. arch.* LME.
[ORIGIN Late Latin *incarnare*: see INCARNATE *verb*.]
1 *verb trans.* Cover with flesh, heal over (a wound etc.). LME. ▸**b** *verb intrans.* Cause flesh to grow, induce healing. M16. ▸**c** *verb intrans.* Become covered with flesh; heal. L17.
2 *verb trans.* Embody in flesh; incarnate. *rare.* M16.

incarnadine /ɪnˈkɑːnədʌɪn/ *adjective, verb, & noun.* Now *arch. & poet.* As verb also **en-** /ɪn-, ɛn-/. L16.
[ORIGIN French *incarnadin(e)* from Italian *incarnadino* var. of *incarnatino* carnation, flesh colour, from *incarnato* formed as INCARNATE *adjective*: see -INE[1].]
▸ **A** *adjective.* Flesh-coloured, crimson; occas. (in allus. to Shakes.: see sense B. below), bloodstained. L16.
▸ **B** *verb trans.* Dye flesh-coloured or crimson; (in allus. to Shakes. *Macb.*) stain with blood. E17.

SHAKES. *Macb.* This my hand will rather The multitudinous seas incarnadine, Making the green one red.

▸ **C** *noun.* Flesh colour, crimson; blood-red. M17.

BYRON No Barbaric blood can reconcile us now Unto that horrible incarnadine.

incarnalize *verb* var. of ENCARNALIZE.

I

incarnate /ɪnˈkɑːneɪt, -ət/ *adjective*. LME.
[ORIGIN ecclesiastical Latin *incarnatus* pa. pple of *incarnari* be made flesh, formed as IN-[2] + *carn-*, *caro* flesh; in sense 2 from French *incarnat* or mod. Latin *incarnatus*: see -ATE[2].]
1 Of a person, spirit, quality, etc.: embodied in flesh, in human form; embodied in a recognizable or the most perfect form. Freq. ***postpositive***. LME.

> SIR W. SCOTT Whether there be a devil incarnate in you or no. E. O'BRIEN Phrases such as 'how are you' . . or 'dear one' were mockery incarnate.

2 Flesh-coloured; light rosy pink or crimson. *obsolete* exc. *BOTANY*. M16.

> C. DARWIN The common red and incarnate clovers.

incarnate /ˈɪnkɑːneɪt, ɪnˈkɑː-/ *verb*. M16.
[ORIGIN ecclesiastical Latin *incarnat-* pa. ppl stem of *incarnare*, *-ari* make, be made, flesh: see INCARNATE *adjective*, -ATE[3].]
▸ †**I 1** *verb trans.* = INCARN 1. M16–E18. ▸**b** *verb intrans.* = INCARN 1C. L17–M18.
2 *verb trans.* Make carnal, degrade from spiritual nature. M–L17.
▸ **II 3** *verb trans.* Embody in flesh or (esp.) in a human form. M16.
4 *verb trans.* **a** Put (an idea etc.) into concrete form; realize. L16. ▸**b** Be the living embodiment or type of; embody (a quality etc.). E19.

> E. CLODD The ennobling qualities incarnated in some hero . . meet with admiring response. **b** D. CECIL Chosen less for herself than because she seemed momentarily to incarnate a boyish ideal.

incarnation /ɪnkɑːˈneɪʃ(ə)n/ *noun & adjective*. ME.
[ORIGIN Old French & mod. French from ecclesiastical Latin *incarnatio(n-)*, formed as INCARNATE *verb*: see -ATION.]
▸ **A** *noun* **I 1 a** *CHRISTIAN THEOLOGY*. (Freq. **I-**.) The embodiment of God in human form as Jesus. ME. ▸**b** *gen.* The action of incarnating or fact of being incarnated in flesh or (esp.) in human form. E17.

> G. PRIESTLAND He picked the form of a young Galilean Jew. Christians call it 'The Incarnation'. **b** R. W. EMERSON The thoughts he delights to utter are the reason of his incarnation.

2 a A body etc. in which a soul or spirit is incarnated; an incarnate form (of something); the form or appearance assumed by a thing at a particular time; the period of time spent in such an incarnation. M18. ▸**b** A living type or embodiment (*of* a quality etc.). E19.

> **a** E. YOUNG When shall my soul her incarnation quit? L. MACNEICE There are few bodies which I should prefer for my next incarnation. L. ALTHER In its current incarnation, the town hosted tourists and skiers. A. BROOKNER In some future incarnation they would reap the reward promised in the Bible. **b** W. GERHARDIE I leaned forward, the incarnation of attention.

▸ **II 3** (A dye or pigment of) flesh colour, light rosy pink, or crimson. *arch.* LME.
4 The growth of new flesh on or in a wound etc.; healing up. Also, a growth of new flesh. Now *rare*. LME.
†**5** Conception (in the womb). *rare*. M16–L17.
▸ **B** *attrib.* or as *adjective*. Flesh-coloured; of a light rosy pink or crimson. ME.
■ **incarnational** *adjective* of or pertaining to the theological doctrine of the incarnation E20. **incarnationist** *noun* a believer in an incarnation M19.

†**incarnative** *adjective & noun*. LME–E18.
[ORIGIN French *incarnatif*, *-ive* or medieval Latin *incarnativus*, formed as INCARN: see -ATIVE.]
(A medicine or application intended for) promoting healing and causing flesh to grow on or in a wound etc.

†**incase** *verb* var. of ENCASE.

incasement *noun* see ENCASEMENT.

incatenation /ˌɪnkatɪˈneɪʃ(ə)n/ *noun*. *arch.* M18.
[ORIGIN medieval Latin *incatenatio(n-)*, from *incatenat-* pa. ppl stem of *incatenare* enchain, formed as IN-[2] + *catenare* bind with chains: see CATENATE, -ATION.]
Putting or fastening in chains; harnessing; linking, being linked.

†**incauteious** *adjective*. E17–M18.
[ORIGIN from IN-[3] + CAUTELOUS.]
Incautious.

incaution /ɪnˈkɔːʃ(ə)n/ *noun*. E18.
[ORIGIN from IN-[3] + CAUTION *noun*.]
Lack of caution; heedlessness, rashness.

incautious /ɪnˈkɔːʃəs/ *adjective*. M17.
[ORIGIN from IN-[3] + CAUTIOUS, after Latin *incautus*.]
Not cautious; heedless, rash.

> A. BURGESS His rage and nausea made Lawrence incautious in talking against the war. R. ELLMANN He was incautious enough to form a friendship with Lord Ronald Gower.

■ **incautiously** *adverb* E18. **incautiousness** *noun* L18.

incavation /ɪnkəˈveɪʃ(ə)n/ *noun*. L18.
[ORIGIN Alt. of EXCAVATION: see IN-[2].]
The action of hollowing or bending inwards. Also, a hollow depression, a hollowed place.

†**incave** *verb* var. of ENCAVE.

incede /ɪnˈsiːd/ *verb intrans. rare*. LME.
[ORIGIN Latin *incedere*, formed as IN-[2] + *cedere* go.]
Move on, advance, esp. with a measured or stately pace.

incend /ɪnˈsɛnd/ *verb trans.* Long *rare*. E16.
[ORIGIN Latin *incendere*: see INCENSE *noun*, *verb*[2].]
†**1** Inflame (the mind, feelings, etc.); incite to action. E16–L17.
†**2** Engender (bodily heat); heat (the body or a part of the body). M16–E17.
3 Set on fire, kindle. L16.

incendiary /ɪnˈsɛndjəri/ *adjective & noun*. LME.
[ORIGIN Latin *incendiarius*, from *incendium* conflagration, from *incendere* set fire to: see INCENSE *noun*, -ARY[1].]
▸ **A** *adjective* **1 a** Combustible; *spec.* (*MILITARY*) adapted or used for setting on fire an enemy's buildings, ships, etc. LME. ▸**b** Of or pertaining to the malicious setting on fire of property. E17.

> **b** D. M. MULOCK The glare of some incendiary fire.

a incendiary bomb: filled with a substance for causing a fire at the point of impact.
2 *fig.* Tending to stir up strife; inflammatory. E17.

> J. REED Their newspapers . . publish incendiary and crime-inciting appeals to mob violence.

▸ **B** *noun*. **1** A person who maliciously sets property on fire; an arsonist. LME. ▸**b** = ***incendiary bomb*** above. M20.
2 *fig.* A person who stirs up strife; an inflammatory agitator. L16. ▸†**b** A thing which stirs up passion, strife, etc.; an incentive to evil. E17–E18.
■ **incendiarism** *noun* (**a**) inflammatory agitation; (**b**) the practice or commission of arson: L17.

incendiate /ɪnˈsɛndɪeɪt/ *verb trans. rare*. E18.
[ORIGIN formed as INCENDIUM + -ATE[3].]
Set on fire.
■ †**incendiator** *noun*: only in M17.

†**incendium** *noun*. M17–M18.
[ORIGIN Latin: see INCENDIARY.]
A conflagration; a volcanic eruption.

incendivity /ɪnsɛnˈdɪvɪti/ *noun*. E20.
[ORIGIN from Latin *incendere* (see INCENSE *noun*) + -IVITY.]
The ability to effect ignition or set something on fire.
■ **inˈcendive** *adjective* of or pertaining to incendivity; capable of effecting ignition: M20.

incensation /ɪnsɛnˈseɪʃ(ə)n/ *noun*. M19.
[ORIGIN from INCENSE *verb*[1] + -ATION.]
The action or an act of censing.

incense /ˈɪnsɛns/ *noun*. Also (earlier) †**en-**. ME.
[ORIGIN Old French & mod. French *encens* from ecclesiastical Latin *incensum* use as noun of neut. of *incensus* pa. pple of *incendere* set fire to, formed as IN-[2] + root of *candere* to glow.]
1 a An aromatic gum or spice used for producing a sweet smell when burned. ME. ▸**b** The smoke or perfume of this, esp. when burned as part of religious ceremonial. LME.

> **a** P. S. BUCK He burned a little incense before them. **b** M. COX Palm Sunday found Monty . . in Milan Cathedral—all banners and incense.

b ***male incense***: see MALE *adjective & noun*.
2 Orig., the smoke or odour of a burnt sacrifice. Later, a pleasant perfume or fragrance. ME.

> SHELLEY The matin winds from the expanded flowers Scatter their hoarded incense.

3 *fig.* Something offered in homage; prayer, praise, flattery. LME.

> H. REED The incense of flattery which his satellites were forever burning beneath his nostrils.

– COMB.: **incense cedar** a cedar of western N. America, *Calocedrus decurrens*, whose leaves smell of turpentine when bruised; **incense tree** any of various tropical trees yielding fragrant gum; esp. *Protium heptaphyllum*, of the torchwood family, of S. America; **incense wood** the wood of *Protium heptaphyllum* (see ***incense tree*** above).

incense /ˈɪnsɛns/ *verb*[1]. Also (earlier) †**en-**. ME.
[ORIGIN Old French & mod. French *encenser*, from *encens*, or ecclesiastical Latin *incensare*, from *incensum*: see INCENSE *noun*.]
1 *verb trans.* Waft incense towards, esp. as part of religious ceremonial; burn incense to (a god etc.); cense. ME.

> *Toronto Life* At the end of Mass Father Walsh incenses the casket.

2 *verb intrans.* Burn or offer incense. Long *rare*. LME.
3 *verb trans.* Suffuse with fragrance, scent. Formerly, drive *out* by diffusing fragrance. E16.

> L. L. NOBLE Wild roses incensed the fresh air.

4 *verb trans.* Burn or offer as incense (*lit.* & *fig.*). E17.
5 *verb trans.* Offer homage or adulation to, flatter. Now *rare* or *obsolete*. M18.

incense /ɪnˈsɛns/ *verb*[2] *trans.* Also (earlier) †**en-**. LME.
[ORIGIN Old French *incenser*, from Latin *incens-* pa. ppl stem of *incendere*: see INCENSE *noun*.]
†**1 a** Inflame, excite, (a person *with* ardent feeling etc.). LME–M17. ▸**b** Inflame, excite, (ardent feeling). L16–E19.
2 *spec.* Make angry, enrage; exasperate. L15.

> P. ROTH It put our Portnoy into a rage, incensed The Temper Tantrum Kid.

†**3** Set on fire, kindle; consume with fire, burn. L15–E18.
†**4** Incite to some action; urge, instigate. (Foll. by *to*, *to do*.) M16–M17.

> T. FULLER By which speech he incensed the English to go on with him.

■ **incensement** *noun* (now *rare*) the fact of being incensed; anger, exasperation: L16.

incensed /ɪnˈsɛnst/ *adjective*. M16.
[ORIGIN from INCENSE *verb*[2] + -ED[1].]
†**1** Set on fire, kindled; *fig.* aroused, excited. M16–L17.
2 Angry, enraged; exasperated. L16.
3 *HERALDRY*. Of an animal: having flames coming out of its mouth and ears. L16.

incenser /ˈɪnsɛnsə/ *noun*. M16.
[ORIGIN French *encenseur*, formed as INCENSE *verb*[1]: see -ER[2].]
A person who burns or offers incense.

†**incension** *noun*. LME.
[ORIGIN Latin *incensio(n-)* burning, from *incens-* pa. ppl stem of *incendere*: see INCENSE *noun*, -ION.]
1 Burning; conflagration. LME–M17.
2 Bodily heating or inflammation. L16–M18.

†**incensive** *adjective & noun*. *rare*. L16.
[ORIGIN French †*incensif*, *-ive* or medieval Latin *incensivus*, from Latin *incens-*: see INCENSION, -IVE.]
▸ **A** *adjective*. **1** Angry. Only in L16.
2 Tending to excite angry feelings. M–L17.
▸ **B** *noun*. = INCENTIVE *noun* 1. Only in E17.

incensory /ˈɪnsɛns(ə)ri/ *noun*. E17.
[ORIGIN medieval Latin *incensorium*, from *incensum* INCENSE *noun*: see -ORY[1].]
†**1** (An altar of) a burnt offering. *rare*. Only in E17.
2 A censer, a thurible. M17.

incenter *noun* see INCENTRE.

incentive /ɪnˈsɛntɪv/ *noun*. LME.
[ORIGIN Latin *incentivum* use as noun of neut. of *incentivus*: see INCENTIVE *adjective*.]
1 Something that arouses feeling or incites to action; an incitement *to*; a provocation; a motive. LME.

> H. ARENDT Behind these obvious . . incentives to anti-Jewish attitudes there was a deeper cause. I. MURDOCH Her visit was an incentive to tidy the flat.

2 A payment, concession, etc., made to stimulate greater productivity by workers. M20.
■ **incentivize** *verb trans.* give an incentive to M20.

incentive /ɪnˈsɛntɪv/ *adjective*. E17.
[ORIGIN In branch I from Latin *incentivus* setting the tune, inciting, from *incent-* var. of *incant-* (see INCANTATION): see -IVE. In branch II also infl. by INCENSIVE.]
▸ **I 1** Tending to arouse feeling or incite to action; provocative. E17.

> R. NORTH The Lord Shaftesbury . . made an incentive speech in the House of Lords.

2 Serving as an incentive to productivity; involving such incentives. M20.

> J. UPDIKE It shows up in the books and affects everybody's end-of-the-month incentive bonus. *Sydney Morning Herald* We offer our top performers overseas incentive travel.

▸ †**II 3** Having the property of setting on fire or kindling. M17–E18.

incentor /ɪnˈsɛntə/ *noun*. Now *rare*. L16.
[ORIGIN Late Latin = setter of a tune, inciter, from Latin *incent-*: see INCENTIVE *adjective*, -OR.]
A person who stirs up strife etc.; a person who incites *to* action.

incentre /ˈɪnsɛntə/ *noun*. Also ***-ter**. E20.
[ORIGIN from IN-[1] + CENTRE *noun*.]
GEOMETRY. The centre of the inscribed circle of a figure, esp. of a triangle.

incept /ɪnˈsɛpt/ *verb*. M16.
[ORIGIN Latin *incept-*: see INCEPTION.]
1 *verb trans.* Undertake, begin, enter upon. Now *rare* or *obsolete*. M16.
2 *hist. verb intrans.* = COMMENCE *verb* 3. M19.
3 *verb trans. BIOLOGY*. Take in (food etc.), ingest. M19.

inception /ɪnˈsɛpʃ(ə)n/ *noun*. LME.
[ORIGIN (Old French & mod. French from) Latin *inceptio(n-)*, from *incept-* pa. ppl stem of *incipere* begin: see INCIPIENT.]
1 The action of entering upon some undertaking, process, or stage of existence; beginning, commencement. LME.

> R. G. COLLINGWOOD He feels it not only after his work is completed, but from its inception.

2 The action of incepting, esp. (*hist.*) commencement at a university. L17.

inceptisol /ɪnˈsɛptɪsɒl/ *noun*. M20.
[ORIGIN from Latin *inceptum* a beginning, from *incipere* begin (see INCIPIENT), + -I- + -SOL.]
SOIL SCIENCE. A soil of an order in which the formation of distinct horizons is not far advanced, and which shows little severe weathering.

inceptive /ɪnˈsɛptɪv/ *noun & adjective*. E17.
[ORIGIN Late Latin *inceptivus*, formed as INCEPT: see -IVE.]
▸ **A** *noun*. GRAMMAR. An inceptive verb. E17.
▸ **B** *adjective*. **1** Commencing, incipient; marking the beginning of something, initial. M17.
2 GRAMMAR & LOGIC. Expressing the beginning of (an) action; esp. in ***inceptive verb***. M17.

inceptor /ɪnˈsɛptə/ *noun*. L15.
[ORIGIN medieval Latin (in classical Latin = beginner), formed as INCEPT: see -OR.]
hist. A person who incepts or is about to incept at a university.

†**incertain** *adjective*. LME–M18.
[ORIGIN Old French & mod. French, formed as IN-[3], CERTAIN.]
Uncertain.
■ †**incertainly** *adverb* M16–E18.

†**incertainty** *noun*. L15–L18.
[ORIGIN Old French *incertaineté*, formed as INCERTAIN after *certaineté* CERTAINTY.]
(An) uncertainty.

incertitude /ɪnˈsəːtɪtjuːd/ *noun*. LME.
[ORIGIN (Old French & mod. French from) late Latin *incertitudo*, formed as IN-[3], CERTITUDE.]
1 Subjective uncertainty; doubt, hesitation. LME.
A. ALISON The King was distracted by the most cruel incertitude.
2 (An) objective uncertainty; unpredictability. E17.
A. G. GARDINER He knows nothing . . of the incertitudes of life.

incessable /ɪnˈsɛsəb(ə)l/ *adjective*. *arch. rare*. LME.
[ORIGIN (French †*incessable* from) late Latin *incessabilis*, from *cessare* CEASE *verb*: see IN-[3], -ABLE.]
Incessant.
■ **incessably** *adverb* E16.

incessant /ɪnˈsɛs(ə)nt/ *adjective & adverb*. LME.
[ORIGIN (Old French & mod. French from) late Latin *incessant-*, formed as IN-[3] + Latin *cessant-* pres. ppl stem of *cessare* CEASE *verb*: see -ANT[1].]
▸ **A** *adjective*. **1** Ceaseless, continual, unremitting. LME.
D. LESSING The noise of the wind was an incessant metallic whispering. W. SOYINKA Daodu was an incessant conversationalist.
†**2** Never-ending, perpetual. M16–M17.
▸ **B** *adverb*. Without pause, unceasingly. *poet*. M16.
■ **incessancy** *noun* the quality of being incessant E17. **incessantly** *adverb* (*a*) unceasingly; †(*b*) without pause, immediately: LME. **incessantness** *noun* E18.

†**incession** *noun*. *rare*. M16–M19.
[ORIGIN Late Latin *incessio(n-)*, from *incess-* pa. ppl stem of *incedere*: see INCEDE, -ION.]
Onward motion, progression (*lit.* & *fig.*).

incest /ˈɪnsɛst/ *noun*. ME.
[ORIGIN Latin *incestus* noun (or *incestum* use as noun of neut. of *incestus* adjective, unchaste), formed as IN-[3] + *castus* chaste.]
Sexual intercourse between close relatives, *spec.* (in law and formerly in ecclesiastical law) between any persons related within the prohibited degrees as regards marriage.

incestuous /ɪnˈsɛstjʊəs/ *adjective*. E16.
[ORIGIN Late Latin *incestuosus*, from Latin *incestus*: see INCEST, -OUS.]
1 Of the nature of, involving, or guilty of incest. E16. ▸†**b** Adulterous. M–L17.
N. SYMINGTON He was beginning to become aware of his incestuous wishes towards his mother.
†**2** Begotten by incest. L16–E17.
3 *fig.* Of a relationship etc.: unwholesomely close; operating within an excessively restricted circle. M20.
Washington Post The incestuous old-boy network.
■ **incestuously** *adverb* E16. **incestuousness** *noun* M17.

inch /ɪn(t)ʃ/ *noun*[1].
[ORIGIN Late Old English *ynće*, corresp. to Old High German *unza*, Gothic *unkja*, from Latin *uncia* twelfth part: see OUNCE *noun*[1].]
1 As a measure of length: the twelfth part of a foot; 2.54 cm. Also, an area or volume equal to that of a square or cube whose edges are one inch long. LOE. ▸**b** As a unit of rainfall: the quantity sufficient to cover a horizontal surface to the depth of one inch, equivalent to 3630 cubic feet on an acre (approx. 253.7 cu. metres on a hectare). M19. ▸**c** As a unit of measurement of the flow of water (more fully ***miner's inch***, ***inch of water***): the amount of water that will pass in 24 hours through an opening of 1 square inch under a constant head of 6 inches (about 14,000 gallons, 64,000 litres). M19. ▸**d** As a unit of atmospheric or hydrostatic pressure: a pressure equal to that exerted by a column of mercury 1 inch high; 33.86 mb. L19.
G. CRABBE Jonas Kindred . . Was six feet high, and look'd six inches higher. L. D. STAMP A useful map . . on the scale of 25 miles to one inch.
2 *transf.* & *fig.* A very small distance, measure, amount, or degree; the least amount or part (of space, time, etc.). ME.
W. COWPER That I may avail myself of every inch of time. H. NISBET He could not see an inch before him. A. J. CRONIN There isn't an inch of space.
3 In *pl.* (Considerable) height, stature. E17.
Graphic To make the most of her inches she had . . the habit of holding her head thrown back.
– PHRASES: **by inches** = *inch by inch* below. *every inch*: see EVERY *adjective* 1. **inch by inch** by small or imperceptible degrees, little by little. **within an inch of** *fig.* very close to. **within an inch of one's life** almost to death; *hyperbol.* extremely severely.
– ATTRIB. & COMB.: With a numeral etc. prefixed, = INCHED, as *six-inch*. **inchworm** = GEOMETER *noun* 3.

inch /ɪn(t)ʃ/ *noun*[2]. ME.
[ORIGIN Gaelic *innis* /ˈɪnɪʃ/ island = Old Irish & mod. Irish *inis*, Welsh *ynys*, prob. rel. (obscurely) to Latin *insula* island.]
1 A small island. Freq. in Scottish place names. *Scot.* & *Irish*. ME.
2 *transf.* A meadow on the bank of a river. Also, a piece of rising ground in the middle of a plain. *Scot.* E16.

inch /ɪn(t)ʃ/ *verb*. L16.
[ORIGIN from INCH *noun*[1].]
1 *verb intrans.* & *trans.* Make (one's way) by inches or by small degrees. L16.
W. GOLDING He inched along the path, with shuffling steps. M. SHADBOLT The man inched his way across the face of the building.
2 *verb trans.* Eke *out* by inches or small amounts. Now *rare*. L16.
3 *verb trans.* Drive or push by inches or small degrees. M17.
E. BOWEN Inching open the door, he took a dekko into the outer office.
4 *verb trans.* Measure the number of inches in. Now *rare* or *obsolete*. L17.

†**inchangeable** *adjective*. *rare*. L16–L18.
[ORIGIN from IN-[3] + CHANGEABLE.]
Unchangeable.

†**inchant** *verb*, †**inchanter** *noun*, etc., vars. of ENCHANT etc.

†**incharitable** *adjective*. L15–L17.
[ORIGIN from IN-[3] + CHARITABLE *adjective*.]
Not charitable.

inchastity /ɪnˈtʃastɪti/ *noun*. Now *rare*. L16.
[ORIGIN from IN-[3] + CHASTITY.]
Lack of chastity.

inched /ɪn(t)ʃt/ *adjective*. E17.
[ORIGIN from INCH *noun*[1], *verb*: see -ED[2], -ED[1].]
With a numeral etc. prefixed: that is (so many) inches in length, diameter, etc.

†**incheer** *verb* var. of ENCHEER.

incher /ˈɪn(t)ʃə/ *noun*. L19.
[ORIGIN from INCH *noun*[1] + -ER[1].]
With a numeral prefixed: a thing having a length, diameter, etc., of the number of inches specified.

inchmeal /ˈɪn(t)ʃmiːl/ *adverb & noun*. M16.
[ORIGIN from INCH *noun*[1] + -MEAL.]
▸ **A** *adverb*. By inches; little by little. M16.
▸ **B** *noun*. ***by inchmeal*** = sense A. above. M16.

inchoate /ɪnˈkəʊeɪt, ˈɪnk-, -ət/ *adjective*. M16.
[ORIGIN Latin *inchoatus* pa. pple of *inchoare* var. of *incohare* begin: see -ATE[2].]
1 Just begun, incipient, rudimentary; not yet fully formed or developed; LAW (of an offence) anticipating or preparatory to a further criminal act. M16.
R. HUNTFORD All three were now troubled by inchoate doubts about survival. SYD. SMITH Many inchoate acts are innocent, the consummation of which is a capital offence.
2 Chaotic, confused; (of thought or language) incoherent. E20.
G. GREENE I have seldom listened to more inchoate rubbish. *Times Lit. Suppl.* The inchoate welter of recent published poetry.
■ **inchoately** *adverb* E17. **inchoateness** *noun* M19.

inchoate /ˈɪnkəʊeɪt/ *verb*. Now *rare*. E17.
[ORIGIN Latin *inchoat-* pa. ppl stem of *inchoare*: see INCHOATE *adjective*, -ATE[3].]
1 *verb trans.* Produce the first stages of, commence. Also, cause to begin, bring about. E17.
2 *verb intrans.* Make a beginning, commence. E17.

inchoation /ɪnkəʊˈeɪʃ(ə)n/ *noun*. LME.
[ORIGIN Late Latin *inchoatio(n-)*, formed as INCHOATE *verb*: see -ATION.]
†**1** Elementary knowledge, first principles. Only in LME.
2 Beginning, commencement; an initial stage. M16.

inchoative /ɪnˈkəʊətɪv, ˈɪnkəʊ-/ *noun & adjective*. M16.
[ORIGIN Late Latin *inchoativus*, formed as INCHOATE *verb*: see -IVE.]
▸ **A** *noun*. An inchoative or inceptive verb. M16.
▸ **B** *adjective*. **1** That is in an initial stage; rudimentary, inchoate. M17.
2 Of a verb: denoting the beginning of an action; inceptive. M17.

†**incicurable** *adjective*. *rare*. M17–L18.
[ORIGIN from IN-[3] + Latin *cicurare* CICURATE + -ABLE.]
Of a plant: that cannot be naturalized.

incide /ɪnˈsʌɪd/ *verb*. Now *rare* or *obsolete*. L16.
[ORIGIN Latin *incidere* INCISE.]
1 *verb trans.* & *intrans.* In surgery: make an incision (in). L16.
2 *verb trans.* Of an internal remedy: loosen, disperse, (phlegm etc.). E17.

incidence /ˈɪnsɪd(ə)ns/ *noun*. LME.
[ORIGIN Old French & mod. French, from *incident*, or medieval Latin *incidentia*, from *incident-*: see INCIDENT *adjective*, -ENCE.]
†**1** A casual or subordinate occurrence or matter. LME–M17.
2 **a** PHYSICS. The falling of a line, or of something (esp. light) moving in a line, upon a surface. E17. ▸**b** *gen.* The fact or action of falling upon or affecting something. M17.
a R. W. DITCHBURN The direction of reflection is on the side of the normal opposite to the direction of incidence. F. HOYLE The normal rate of incidence of cosmic rays on the Earth.
a angle of incidence the angle between a ray etc. incident on a surface and the normal to the surface at the point of incidence.
3 The range or scope of a thing; the extent of a thing's influence; *esp.* the rate or frequency of occurrence *of* a phenomenon among a group of people. E19.
D. W. GOODWIN Studies have shown a high incidence of alcoholism in a parent of women alcoholics. N. SYMINGTON He . . noted the frequent incidence of religious imagery in their utterances. A. BRIGGS Battles in Parliament about the incidence of taxation on different sections of the community.

†**incidency** *noun*. E17.
[ORIGIN formed as INCIDENCE + -ENCY.]
1 A casual or subordinate occurrence or circumstance. E17–E18.
SHAKES. *Wint. T.* Declare What incidency thou dost guess of harm Is creeping toward me.
2 The quality of being liable to fall or happen (*to* a person); a thing liable to befall (someone). Only in 17.
3 PHYSICS. = INCIDENCE *noun* 2a. M17–E18.

incident /ˈɪnsɪd(ə)nt/ *noun*. LME.
[ORIGIN Old French & mod. French, use as noun of adjective: see INCIDENT *adjective*.]
1 Something that occurs casually in connection with something of which it forms no essential part; a subordinate or accessory event. LME.
2 *gen.* A distinct occurrence or event, *esp.* one that attracts general attention or is noteworthy in some way. LME. ▸†**b** A matter, an affair. *rare*. L15–M18. ▸**c** An event which increases international tension or may precipitate open warfare; a particular episode in a war; a fracas; a public disturbance. E20.
E. H. JONES Apart from one or two incidents, she . . recalled hardly anything of these years. **c** M. SPARK It would be . . unfair . . to involve the British Consulate in an incident of that kind. *Clitheroe Advertiser & Times* Young vandals were probably responsible for two incidents in the town.
3 A natural or characteristic accompaniment. Now chiefly (LAW), a privilege, burden, custom, etc., commonly attaching to an office, an estate, etc. E17.
R. H. TAWNEY They entrusted to bureaucracies work which . . had formerly been done as an incident of tenure.
4 **a** A distinct piece of action in a play or poem, orig. one subordinate to the main plot. L17. ▸**b** A single feature in a picture, *esp.* one that does not form part of the main design. *rare*. E18.
5 An incidental charge or expense. Usu. in *pl.* Now chiefly *Scot.* M18.
– COMB.: **incident room** a centre set up by the police (freq. near the scene of the occurrence) to coordinate operations connected with a particular crime, accident, etc.

incident /ˈɪnsɪd(ə)nt/ *adjective*. LME.
[ORIGIN (Old French & mod. French from) Latin *incident-* pres. ppl stem of *incidere* fall upon, happen to, formed as IN-[2] + *cadere* to fall: see -ENT.]
▸ **I** †**1** = INCIDENTAL *adjective* 2, 2b. LME–M18.
†**2** **a** Relevant or pertinent *to*. LME–E17. ▸**b** LAW. Attaching itself as a privilege, burden, etc., *to* an office, estate, etc. L15.
3 Apt or liable to happen (*to*); naturally attaching (*to*) or consequent (*on*, *upon*). L15.
T. REID The fallacies incident to categorical syllogisms. J. LANG The noise . . incident on . . the breaking up of the little camp.
†**4** Liable or subject *to*. E17–M18.
▸ **II** **5** Esp. of light or other radiation: falling on or striking against a surface. M17.
F. HOYLE Clean ice absorbs about two-thirds of the sunlight incident upon it.
■ **incidently** *adverb* (now *rare*) incidentally E16.

incidental /ɪnsɪˈdɛnt(ə)l/ *adjective & noun*. E17.
[ORIGIN Orig. from medieval Latin *incidentalis* (cf. *angulus incidentalis* angle of incidence), from Latin *incident-*: see INCIDENT *adjective*, -AL[1]. In mod. use from INCIDENT *noun* + -AL[1].]
▸ **A** *adjective*. **1** Liable to happen *to*; naturally attaching *to*. E17.
J. INGLIS The dangers incidental to pigsticking.
2 Occurring as something casual or of secondary importance; not directly relevant *to*; following (*up*)*on* as a subordinate circumstance. M17. ▸**b** Of an expense or charge:

I

incurred apart from the main sum disbursed. **M18.** ▸**c** Casually met with. *rare.* **M19.**

H. SPENCER With the . . moral man, correct conduct . . is merely incidental upon the fulfilment of his own nature. O. W. HOLMES Writing verse should be an incidental occupation only, not interfering with the hoe . . or the ledger.

incidental music: used as a background to the action of a play, film, broadcast, etc.

▸**B** *noun.* An incidental circumstance, event, etc.; in *pl.*, incidental expenses. **E18.**

■ **incidentalist** *noun* a person who describes or insists on what is merely incidental **E20.** **incidentally** *adverb* in an incidental manner, as a casual or subordinate circumstance; (introducing a remark not strictly relevant) as a further thought: **M17.**

†**incider** *noun.* **L16–M18.**

[ORIGIN from INCIDE + -ER[1].]

A medicine for loosening or dispersing phlegm etc.; an instrument for making surgical incisions.

incinerate /ɪnˈsɪnəreɪt/ *verb.* Pa. pple **-ated**, †**-ate**. **L15.**

[ORIGIN medieval Latin *incinerat-* pa. ppl stem of *incinerare*, formed as IN-[2] + *ciner-*, *cinis* ashes: see -ATE[3].]

1 *verb trans.* Burn to ashes; *spec.* (esp. *US*) cremate (a body). **L15.**

2 *verb intrans.* Be burnt to ashes. **E19.**

■ **inciˈneration** *noun* **E16.** **incinerator** *noun* an apparatus for incinerating refuse etc. **L19.**

†**incipher** *verb* see ENCIPHER.

incipient /ɪnˈsɪpɪənt/ *noun & adjective.* **L16.**

[ORIGIN Latin *incipient-* pres. ppl stem of *incipere* undertake, begin, formed as IN-[2] + *capere* take: see -ENT.]

▸**A** *noun.* †**1** A beginner. Only in **L16.**

2 HEBREW GRAMMAR. The verbal form denoting an uncompleted action. Now usu. called ***imperfect***. **M19.**

▸**B** *adjective.* In an initial or early stage; beginning to develop. **M17.**

A. S. BYATT She examined herself hopefully for signs of incipient nervous breakdown.

incipient species a group of plants or animals in the process of evolving and not yet sufficiently distinct to be described as a full species.

■ **incipience** *noun* beginning, commencement; an initial or early stage: **M19.** **incipiency** *noun* incipience **E19.** **incipiently** *adverb* **M19.**

incipit /ˈɪnsɪpɪt/ *noun.* **L19.**

[ORIGIN Latin, 3rd person sing. pres. indic. of *incipere* (see INCIPIENT), used by medieval scribes to indicate the beginning of a new treatise, poem, division, etc.]

The opening words of a manuscript, a printed book (usu. an early one), a chanted liturgical text, etc. Cf. EXPLICIT *noun*.

†**incircle** *verb* var. of ENCIRCLE.

in-circle /ˈɪnsəːk(ə)l/ *noun.* **L19.**

[ORIGIN from IN-[1] + CIRCLE *noun*.]

GEOMETRY. A circle inscribed in a figure so as to touch its sides.

incircumscription /ɪnˌsəːkəmˈskrɪpʃ(ə)n/ *noun.* Now *rare.* **M17.**

[ORIGIN Late Latin *incircumscriptio(n-)*, formed as IN-[3], CIRCUMSCRIPTION.]

The condition of not being limited; boundlessness; infinitude.

incircumspect /ɪnˈsəːkəmspɛkt/ *adjective.* Now *rare.* **M16.**

[ORIGIN from IN-[3] + CIRCUMSPECT.]

Not circumspect.

incisal /ɪnˈsʌɪz(ə)l/ *adjective.* **E20.**

[ORIGIN from INCIS(OR + -AL[1].]

DENTISTRY. Designating or pertaining to the cutting edge of an incisor or a canine tooth.

incise /ɪnˈsʌɪz/ *verb.* **M16.**

[ORIGIN French *inciser*, from Latin *incis-* pa. ppl stem of *incidere*, formed as IN-[2] + *caedere* to cut.]

1 *verb trans.* Cut into, make a cut in; cut marks upon; engrave *with* figures. **M16.**

2 *verb trans.* Produce, form, or trace by cutting; carve or engrave (a figure, inscription, etc.). **M17.** ▸**b** *verb trans. & intrans.* GEOLOGY. Of a river: cut (a channel or valley) in a landform. **L19.**

■ **incised** *adjective* (**a**) that has been incised; (**b**) BOTANY & ZOOLOGY having notches in the edge: **LME.**

incisiform /ɪnˈsʌɪzɪfɔːm/ *adjective.* **L19.**

[ORIGIN from INCIS(OR + -I- + -FORM.]

ZOOLOGY. Having the form of an incisor, esp. a mouse's incisor.

incision /ɪnˈsɪʒ(ə)n/ *noun.* **LME.**

[ORIGIN Old French & mod. French, or late Latin *incisio(n-)*, from Latin *incis-*: see INCISE, -ION.]

1 A division made by cutting, as one made in soft tissue during surgery; *esp.* (SURGERY) the initial opening through the surface of the body. **LME.** ▸**b** BOTANY & ZOOLOGY. A sharp and deep indentation, as in a leaf or an insect's wing. **L16.**

2 The action or an act of cutting into something, esp. in the course of a surgical operation. **LME.** ▸**b** *fig.* Incisiveness, keenness of action or apprehension. **M19.**

b Y. MENUHIN The incision and drive of a Toscanini performance were unmistakeable.

†**3** = INSITION. Only in **17.**

4 The cutting and deepening of its channel by a river; the channel so formed. **E20.**

■ **incisional** *adjective* of, pertaining to, or resulting from a surgical incision **E20.**

incisive /ɪnˈsʌɪsɪv/ *adjective & noun.* **LME.**

[ORIGIN medieval Latin *incisivus*, from Latin *incis-*: see INCISE, -IVE.]

▸**A** *adjective.* **1** Having the quality of cutting into something; cutting, penetrating. **LME.**

†**2** Sharp or keen in physical qualities or activities; piercing; (of medicine) that loosens phlegm etc. **LME–L17.**

3 DENTISTRY. Designating or pertaining to an incisor. **E19.**

4 Mentally sharp; producing a very clear and impressive mental effect; trenchant. **M19.**

CONAN DOYLE A faint but incisive scent was apparent. P. GROSSKURTH Joan Riviere had one of the most brilliant and incisive minds.

▸†**B** *noun.* A drug for loosening phlegm etc. **LME–E18.**

■ **incisively** *adverb* **L19.** **incisiveness** *noun* **M19.**

inciso- /ɪnˈsʌɪzəʊ/ *combining form.* **M19.**

[ORIGIN from Latin *incisus* pa. pple of *incidere*: see INCISE, -O-.]

BOTANY & ZOOLOGY. Forming chiefly adjectives describing shapes of leaves etc., with the sense 'incised and —', as ***inciso-dentate***, ***inciso-serrate***, etc.

incisor /ɪnˈsʌɪzə/ *noun.* **L17.**

[ORIGIN medieval Latin, in *dens incisor* incisor tooth, from Latin, lit. 'cutter', from *incis-*: see INCISE, -OR.]

A narrow-edged tooth adapted for cutting; in humans, any of the front four teeth in each jaw. Also ***incisor tooth***.

incisure /ɪnˈsɪʒə/ *noun.* Also in Latin form **incisura** /ɪnsɪˈʒʊərə/, pl. **-rae** /-riː/. **L16.**

[ORIGIN Latin *incisura*, from *incis-*: see INCISE, -URE.]

A deep indentation in an edge or surface; a notch.

incitation /ɪnsʌɪˈteɪʃ(ə)n, -sɪ-/ *noun.* **LME.**

[ORIGIN Old French & mod. French, or Latin *incitatio(n-)*, from *incitat-* pa. ppl stem of *incitare*: see INCITE, -ATION.]

1 The action of inciting; incitement, stimulation. **LME.**

†**2** = INCITEMENT 2. **M16–E18.**

†**3** Power of inciting. **M–L17.**

incite /ɪnˈsʌɪt/ *verb trans.* **L15.**

[ORIGIN Old French & mod. French *inciter* from Latin *incitare*, formed as IN-[2] + *citare* set in rapid motion, raise: see CITE.]

1 Urge, spur on, (a person); stir up, animate; stimulate *to do* something. Also foll. by *to*, *against*. **L15.**

R. G. COLLINGWOOD Young people . . read these stories, and . . are thereby incited to a career of crime. J. BERGER The anarchist leaders are inciting the workers to attack the centre.

2 Provoke, prompt, (an action). **E17.**

N. GORDIMER He went on trial . . for inciting the strike.

■ **inciteful** *adjective* offering incitement; provocative: **L20.** **inciter** *noun* **L16.**

incitement /ɪnˈsʌɪtm(ə)nt/ *noun.* **L15.**

[ORIGIN from INCITE + -MENT.]

1 The action or an act of inciting to action. **L15.**

A. J. AYER He and his wife were arrested and charged with incitement to civil disobedience.

2 A thing which incites a person or provokes an action; a stimulus, an incentive. **L16.**

incitive /ɪnˈsʌɪtɪv/ *noun & adjective.* *rare.* **M18.**

[ORIGIN from INCITE + -IVE.]

▸**A** *noun.* An incitement, an incentive. **M18.**

▸**B** *adjective.* Having the quality of inciting. **L19.**

incitory /ɪnˈsʌɪtəri/ *adjective.* *rare.* **M20.**

[ORIGIN from INCITE + -ORY[2].]

= INCITIVE *adjective*.

†**incivil** *adjective.* **M16.**

[ORIGIN Old French & mod. French, or Latin *incivilis*, formed as IN-[3] + *civilis* CIVIL *adjective*.]

1 Not of the rank of a free citizen. Only in **M16.**

2 Savage, barbarous. Only in **L16.**

3 Not according to civil law. Only in **E17.**

4 Unmannerly, uncivil. Only in **17.**

incivility /ɪnsɪˈvɪlɪti/ *noun.* **M16.**

[ORIGIN French *incivilité* or late Latin *incivilitas*, from Latin *incivilis*: see INCIVIL, -ITY.]

1 a Uncivil or impolite behaviour; discourtesy, rudeness. **M16.** ▸†**b** Lack of good manners or good breeding. **L16–L17.**

†**2** Lack of civilization; uncivilized condition, barbarism. **L16–E19.**

3 An act of rudeness. **M17.**

incivilization /ɪnˌsɪvɪlʌɪˈzeɪʃ(ə)n/ *noun.* Also **-isation**. **E19.**

[ORIGIN from IN-[3] + CIVILIZATION.]

Uncivilized condition; lack of civilization.

incivism /ˈɪnsɪvɪz(ə)m/ *noun.* Also in French form ***incivisme*** /ɛ̃sivism/. **L18.**

[ORIGIN French *incivisme*, from *in-* IN-[3] + *civisme* CIVISM.]

Lack of loyalty to the state, esp. (*hist.*) to the French Republic after the Revolution.

†**inclasp** *verb* var. of ENCLASP.

inclave *adjective* see ENCLAVÉ.

inclemency /ɪnˈklɛm(ə)nsi/ *noun.* **M16.**

[ORIGIN Latin *inclementia*, from *inclement-*: see INCLEMENT, -ENCY.]

1 Severity of weather or climate; (an instance of) severe, esp. cold or stormy, weather. **M16.**

†**2** Lack of clemency of disposition; pitilessness. **L16–M17.**

inclement /ɪnˈklɛm(ə)nt/ *adjective.* **E17.**

[ORIGIN French *inclément* or Latin *inclement-*, formed as IN-[3], CLEMENT.]

1 Of climate or weather: not mild or temperate; severe, *esp.* cold or stormy. **E17.**

I. EDWARDS-JONES They're . . sporting funky ski jackets to keep them chicly snug in the inclement weather.

†**2** Not merciful or kind; pitiless, severe, cruel. **E17–M19.**

■ **inclemently** *adverb* **L18.**

inclinable /ɪnˈklʌɪnəb(ə)l/ *adjective.* Also †**en-**. **LME.**

[ORIGIN Old French *enclinable*, formed as INCLINE *verb*: see -ABLE.]

1 Favourably disposed; willing to assent or submit *to*; amenable. **LME.**

2 Mentally inclined or disposed *to do* something. Formerly also ***absol.*** & foll. by *to*, *for*, *that*. **LME.**

3 Having an inclination or tendency *to* some physical quality, condition, or action. **E17.**

B. LOPEZ The kind of wind nineteenth-century sailors called 'inclinable to calm'.

4 Able to be inclined or sloped. *rare.* **L18.**

■ †**inclinableness** *noun* **E17–E18.**

inclination /ɪnklɪˈneɪʃ(ə)n/ *noun.* **LME.**

[ORIGIN Old French & mod. French, or Latin *inclinatio(n-)*, from *inclinat-* pa. ppl stem of *inclinare*: see INCLINE *verb*, -ATION.]

▸**I 1** The condition of being mentally inclined *to do* something; an instance of this; a tendency of the mind, will, or desires towards a particular thing; a propensity *for*. Also foll. by *to*, *toward*, †*of*. **LME.** ▸†**b** A person's natural disposition or character. **LME–E18.** ▸**c** Liking, affection. **M17.**

C. G. WOLFF Although Edith was clearly intellectual by inclination she never attended school. E. AMADI She had neither the strength nor the inclination to do so. H. JACOBSON He had never . . shown the slightest inclination towards music or the theatre.

†**2** The action of inclining or directing the mind to something. **E16–E17.**

3 An action or practice to which a person is inclined. **E16.** ▸†**b** A person for whom one has a (special) liking. **L17–E18.**

4 A tendency or propensity in a thing to a physical condition or quality. Formerly, the general character of a thing. **L16.**

▸**II 5** The action or an act of bending towards something; *spec.* a bending of the body or head in a bow. **L15.** ▸†**b** The action of tilting a container in order to pour out liquid without disturbing the sediment. **M17–M18.**

6 The fact or condition of sloping; deviation from the normal horizontal or vertical position; slope, slant. Also, the amount of this. **L15.** ▸**b** PHYSICS. The (amount of) dip or deviation from the horizontal of a magnetic needle or a magnetic field, esp. the earth's. **L17.**

7 The angle between the orbital plane of a planet, comet, etc., and the plane of the ecliptic, or (for a satellite) that of the equator of the primary (ASTRONOMY); *gen.* (the amount of) the deviation of one line or plane relative to another, usu. measured by the angle between them. **M16.**

■ **inclinational** *adjective* (*rare*) **E19.**

inclinatory /ɪnˈklʌɪnət(ə)ri/ *adjective.* **E17.**

[ORIGIN from Latin *inclinat-* INCLINATION + -ORY[2].]

Pertaining to or characterized by inclination or dip. Chiefly in ***inclinatory needle***, a dipping needle.

incline /ˈɪnklʌɪn/ *noun.* **E17.**

[ORIGIN from the verb.]

†**1** Mental tendency; disposition. Only in **E17.**

2 An inclined plane or surface; a slope, esp. on a road or railway. **M19.**

incline /ɪnˈklʌɪn/ *verb.* Also †**en-**. **ME.**

[ORIGIN Old French *encliner* from Latin *inclinare*, formed as IN-[2] + *clinare* bend.]

▸**I** *verb trans.* **1** Bend or bow (the head, the body, oneself) towards a thing, or forward and downward. **ME.**

P. LIVELY The young man inclines his head graciously.

incline one's ear listen favourably (*to*).

†**2** *fig.* Cause to obey or be subject *to* a person or thing; subject. **LME–L15.**

3 Bend (the mind, the will, etc.) towards a course of action; make willing or favourably disposed (*to do*, *to* a thing). **LME.** ▸**b** Desire. **M18.**

J. WESLEY To hear them speak . . might incline one to think they were not far from the kingdom of God. BURKE I hope . . your good-nature will incline you to some degree of indulgence towards human frailty. JANET MORGAN It is easy to understand why she started to write; character, skills and circumstance all inclined her in that direction.

†**4** Direct (something abstract) towards a particular object; apply, bestow. **M16–E17.**

5 Cause to depart from a given direction, esp. the vertical or horizontal; bend, slope, tilt. **L16.**

A. R. AMMONS The wind inclines the cedars.

▸ **II** *verb intrans.* **6** Bend the head or body forward, esp. in a bow. Now *rare.* **ME.** ▸**b** *fig.* Submit, yield, (*to*); accede (*to*). **LME.**

7 Have a mental leaning *towards*; be predisposed or have an inclination *to* or *to do*; turn in mind or feeling in a given direction; take sides with a particular party, cause, etc. **ME.**

D. H. LAWRENCE If she inclined towards self-indulgence in any direction, it was in the direction of food. J. HILTON When it comes to believing things without actual evidence, we all incline to what we find most attractive. V. WOOLF She would not push her way. She inclined to be passive. H. J. LASKI The upper house of Convocation . . naturally inclined to his side.

8 Have or take a direction or position which departs from a given direction, esp. from the vertical or horizontal; slope, slant; have or take an oblique position; deviate. **E16.** ▸**b** *MILITARY.* Move in a direction at angles with the front of the formation in order to gain ground to the flank whilst advancing. **L18.**

T. HARDY The clock slowly inclined forward and fell. M. LOWRY His steps teetered to the left, he could not make them incline to the right.

9 Tend, esp. towards a specified quality or condition; have an attribute in an incipient degree. Foll. by *to*, *towards*. **M16.**

GIBBON Victory inclined to the side of the allies. T. BEWICK The top of the head . . dark brown, inclining to black. C. BEATON She was . . short . . , inclining towards the petite and the plump.

■ **inclining** *noun* (*a*) the action of the verb; the state of being inclined; (*b*) *arch.* a following, a party: **LME.**

inclined /ɪnˈklʌɪnd/ *ppl adjective.* Also (earlier) †**en-**. **LME.**
[ORIGIN from INCLINE *verb* + -ED[1].]
1 Having a mental tendency or propensity towards a particular thing; favourably disposed (*to do*; *to*, *for*). **LME.**

J. MARQUAND I was inclined to agree with him. E. WAUGH Do come with her whenever you feel inclined. B. MALAMUD My father was criminally inclined. B. T. BRADFORD He was inclined to shyness. P. GROSSKURTH Arthur . . had plenty of opportunities for illicit amours if so inclined.

2 Having a physical tendency *to* or *to do* something. **LME.**
3 Having a direction or position that departs from the vertical or horizontal, or makes an angle with something else; sloping. **M16.**
inclined plane a sloping plane, esp. as a means of reducing the force needed to raise a load.

incliner /ɪnˈklʌɪnə/ *noun.* **E17.**
[ORIGIN from INCLINE *verb* + -ER[1].]
A person who or thing which inclines; *spec.* a chair in which a person can lie back with legs supported.

inclinometer /ɪnklɪˈnɒmɪtə/ *noun.* **M19.**
[ORIGIN from Latin *inclinare* (as etymon of *inclination*) + -OMETER.]
1 An instrument for measuring the angle between the earth's magnetic field and the horizontal. **M19.**
2 An instrument for measuring the inclination of a slope. **M19.**
3 An instrument for measuring the inclination of a ship or aircraft to the horizontal. **E20.**

inclip /ɪnˈklɪp/ *verb trans. arch. rare.* Infl. **-pp-**. **E17.**
[ORIGIN from IN-[1] + CLIP *verb*[1].]
Clasp, enclose, embrace.

†**incloistered** *adjective* see ENCLOISTERED.

inclose *verb*, **inclosure** *noun*, vars. of ENCLOSE, ENCLOSURE.

†**incloud** *verb* var. of ENCLOUD.

include /ɪnˈkluːd/ *verb trans.* **LME.**
[ORIGIN Latin *includere*, formed as IN-[2] + *claudere* to shut.]
1 Shut in; enclose. *obsolete* exc. in *pass.* **LME.**
2 Contain as part of a whole or as a subordinate element; contain by implication, involve. **LME.**

W. CRUISE A power of appointment . . includes a right to appoint . . absolutely. V. WOOLF Nor is it true that bananas include moisture as well as sustenance. G. ORWELL An underground organization which had included almost every human being he had ever known.

3 Place in a class or category; treat or regard as part of a whole; allow to share in a right, privilege, or activity. **M16.**

D. WELCH She . . did not seem to mind when Li . . did not include her in the invitation. A. BRIGGS Harrington included the gentry in his 'nobility', but historians . . distinguished between the two.

include in *joc. & colloq.* specifically include. **include out** *joc. & colloq.* specifically exclude.

†**4** Bring to a close, conclude. *rare* (Shakes.). Only in **L16.**
■ **includable** *adjective* **L18.** **includible** *adjective* **E19.**

included /ɪnˈkluːdɪd/ *adjective.* **M16.**
[ORIGIN from INCLUDE + -ED[1].]
1 That is included. **M16.**
2 *spec.* ▸**a** *BOTANY.* Of a stamen or style: not protruding beyond the corolla. **M19.** ▸**b** *BOTANY.* (Of phloem) embedded in secondary xylem; (of sapwood) embedded in heartwood. **M20.** ▸**c** *LINGUISTICS.* Forming part of a sentence; not constituting a sentence. **M20.**

including /ɪnˈkluːdɪŋ/ *preposition.* **M19.**
[ORIGIN Use of pres. pple of INCLUDE *verb*: see -ING[2].]
If one takes into account; inclusive of.

J. RUSKIN A large body of . . landscapists comes into this class, including most clever sketchers from nature. *Times* There were five females among the passengers, including the stewardess.

includingly /ɪnˈkluːdɪŋli/ *adverb. rare.* **LME.**
[ORIGIN from *including* pres. pple of INCLUDE: see -ING[2], -LY[2].]
In a manner that includes.

incluse /ɪnˈkluːs/ *adjective & noun. obsolete* exc. *hist.* Also †**en-**. **LME.**
[ORIGIN Latin *inclusus* pa. pple of *includere* INCLUDE.]
▸ †**A** *adjective.* Confined, shut in. Only in **LME.**
▸ **B** *noun.* A hermit, a recluse. **LME.**

inclusion /ɪnˈkluːʒ(ə)n/ *noun.* **E17.**
[ORIGIN Latin *inclusio(n-)*, from *inclus-* pa. ppl stem of *includere* INCLUDE: see -ION.]
1 The action or an act of including; the fact or condition of being included; an instance of this. **E17.**

A. BROOKNER The idea of being Heather's best friend seemed to guarantee my inclusion in any future festivities. *Financial Times* The British and Irish governments have rejected the inclusion of Sinn Fein in political discussions.

2 A thing which is included; *spec.* (*GEOLOGY*), a solid fragment or a globule of liquid or gas enclosed within a rock or mineral; (*METALLURGY, CYTOLOGY*, etc.) a discrete body or particle recognizably distinct from the substance in which it is embedded. **M19.**
3 *MATH.* In full ***inclusion function***, ***inclusion map***, ***inclusion mapping***. A mapping of a set A into a set B containing A which maps each element of A on to itself. **M20.**
– COMB.: **inclusion body** a protein capsule enclosing infective particles in a virus; ***inclusion function***, ***inclusion map***, ***inclusion mapping***: see sense 3 above.
■ **inclusionary** *adjective* aiming not to exclude people from any section of society, esp. those previously or usually excluded **M20.**

inclusive /ɪnˈkluːsɪv/ *adjective.* **L16.**
[ORIGIN medieval Latin *inclusivus*, from Latin *inclus-*: see INCLUSION, -IVE.]
1 That includes, encloses, or contains. **L16.** ▸**b** Including much or all, esp. all incidental or accessory items; comprehensive, all-embracing. **E17.** ▸**c** Foll. by *of*: containing (a specified element) as part of a whole. **E18.**

WORDSWORTH Altar and image, and the inclusive walls. **b** G. GORER The categories . . were . . too inclusive, lumping together answers which could usefully have been analysed separately. *Times* Inclusive holidays offered by various tour operators. *Daily Express* A wide choice of tariffs, all with inclusive talktime every month. **c** H. BASCOM The police patrol launch . . registered to carry fifty policemen inclusive of her small crew. J. LEES-MILNE A cheap ticket, amounting to £154 inclusive of flight and hotel.

inclusive fitness *GENETICS* the ability of an individual organism to pass on its genes to the next generation, taking into account the shared genes passed on by the organism's close relatives. ***inclusive OR***: see OR *noun*[2].

†**2** That is included. **L16–M18.**
3 Not excluding any section of society; (of language) deliberately non-sexist, esp. in avoiding the use of masculine words such as *he* and *man* to cover both men and women. **L20.**
■ **inclusiveness** *noun* **M18.** **inclusivism** *noun* the principle or practice of being inclusive **L20.** **inclusivist** *noun* **L20.** **incluˈsivity** *noun* (*rare*) inclusiveness **M20.**

inclusive /ɪnˈkluːsɪv/ *adverb.* **LME.**
[ORIGIN medieval Latin, from *inclusivus* (see INCLUSIVE *adjective*) + adverbial ending *-e*.]
So as to include the stated limits or extremes in a series. Opp. ***exclusive***.

P. G. HAMERTON From Monday till Saturday inclusive.

inclusively /ɪnˈkluːsɪvli/ *adverb.* **LME.**
[ORIGIN In sense 1 from INCLUSIVE *adverb*; in sense 2 formed as INCLUSIVE *adjective*: see -LY[2].]
1 = INCLUSIVE *adverb* **LME.**
2 So as to include; by including a part or parts of a whole. **L15.**

inclusory /ɪnˈkluːs(ə)ri/ *adjective. rare.* **L18.**
[ORIGIN from Latin *inclus-* (see INCLUSION) + -ORY[2].]
Inclusive.

incoagulable /ɪnkəʊˈagjʊləb(ə)l/ *adjective.* **M17.**
[ORIGIN medieval Latin *incoagulabilis*, formed as IN-[3] + *coagulabilis* COAGULABLE.]
Not coagulable.
■ **incoagulaˈbility** *noun* **E20.**

incoctible /ɪnˈkɒktɪb(ə)l/ *adjective. rare.* **L17.**
[ORIGIN from Latin *incoctus* uncooked, formed as IN-[3] + *coctus*, from *coct-* pa. ppl stem of *coquere* to cook, + -IBLE.]
Indigestible.

incoercible /ɪnkəʊˈəːsɪb(ə)l/ *adjective.* **E18.**
[ORIGIN from IN-[3] + COERCIBLE.]
1 Of a substance: volatile; incapable of being liquefied. Now *rare* or *obsolete.* **E18.**
2 That cannot be coerced or restrained; irrepressible. **M18.**

†**incoffin** *verb* var. of ENCOFFIN.

incog /ɪnˈkɒg/ *noun, adjective, & adverb. colloq.* **L17.**
[ORIGIN Abbreviation.]
= INCOGNITO.

incogitable /ɪnˈkɒdʒɪtəb(ə)l/ *adjective.* **E16.**
[ORIGIN Latin *incogitabilis*, formed as IN-[3] + COGITABLE.]
Unthinkable, inconceivable.

†**incogitancy** *noun.* **E17.**
[ORIGIN Latin *incogitantia*, from *incogitant-*: see INCOGITANT, -ANCY.]
1 Thoughtlessness, negligence. **E17–M18.**
2 Lack of the faculty of thought. **M–L17.**

incogitant /ɪnˈkɒdʒɪt(ə)nt/ *adjective.* **E17.**
[ORIGIN Latin *incogitant-*, formed as IN-[3] + *cogitant-* pres. ppl stem of *cogitare* think: see -ANT[1].]
1 Thoughtless; inconsiderate. **E17.**
2 Lacking the faculty of thought. **E18.**
■ **incogitantly** *adverb* **M17.**

incogitative /ɪnˈkɒdʒɪtətɪv/ *adjective. rare.* **L17.**
[ORIGIN from IN-[3] + COGITATIVE.]
= INCOGITANT.

incognisable *adjective* var. of INCOGNIZABLE.

incognita /ɪnˈkɒgnɪtə/ *noun*[1] *pl.* **M19.**
[ORIGIN Latin, neut. pl. of *incognitus* unknown: see INCOGNITO.]
Unknown things or places.

incognita /ɪnkɒgˈniːtə, *foreign* inˈkoːɲita/ *adjective & noun*[2]. **L17.**
[ORIGIN Italian, fem. of *incognito* unknown: see INCOGNITO.]
▸ **A** *adjective.* Of a woman: disguised; unknown. **L17.**
▸ **B** *noun.* Pl. **-tas**, **-te** /-te/. A disguised or unknown woman, esp. one's lover. **E18.**

incognito /ɪnkɒgˈniːtəʊ, ɪnˈkɒgnɪtəʊ/ *adjective, adverb, & noun.* **M17.**
[ORIGIN Italian from Latin *incognitus* unknown, formed as IN-[3] + *cognitus* pa. pple of *cognoscere* know.]
▸ **A** *adjective.* Of a person: concealed under a disguised or assumed identity; unknown. **M17.**

K. TYNAN The disguise . . renders him about as effectively incognito as a walrus in a ballet-skirt.

▸ **B** *adverb.* Under a disguised or assumed identity. **M17.**

A. FRASER Brother and sister travelled incognito.

▸ **C** *noun.* Pl. **-os**.
1 A person who conceals his or her identity; an anonymous or unknown person. **M17.**
2 The condition of being unknown, anonymity; assumed or pretended identity. **E19.**

S. LEACOCK He had appeared . . in the costume of a Unitarian Clergyman, under the incognito of the Bishop of Bongee.

incognizable /ɪnˈkɒ(g)nɪzəb(ə)l/ *adjective.* Also **-isable**. **M18.**
[ORIGIN from IN-[3] + COGNIZABLE.]
Not cognizable; unable to be known, recognized, or understood.
■ **incognizaˈbility** *noun* **M19.**

incognizance /ɪnˈkɒ(g)nɪz(ə)ns/ *noun.* **M19.**
[ORIGIN from IN-[3] + COGNIZANCE.]
The quality or condition of being incognizant.

incognizant /ɪnˈkɒ(g)nɪz(ə)nt/ *adjective.* **M19.**
[ORIGIN from IN-[3] + COGNIZANT.]
Not cognizant; without knowledge or understanding *of*; unconscious, unaware, *of*.

incognoscible /ɪnkɒgˈnɒsɪb(ə)l/ *adjective.* **L17.**
[ORIGIN Late Latin *incognoscibilis*, formed as IN-[3], COGNOSCIBLE.]
Unknowable; unable to be learned.
■ **incognosciˈbility** *noun* **E19.**

incoherence /ɪnkə(ʊ)ˈhɪər(ə)ns/ *noun.* **E17.**
[ORIGIN from IN-[3] + COHERENCE.]
1 Lack of coherence or connection, esp. in thought or language; incongruity, inconsistency; an instance of this, an incoherent or disconnected statement. **E17.**
2 Lack of cohesion. **L17.**
3 *PHYSICS.* The property (of waves or wave phenomena) of being incoherent; lack of a definite or stable phase relationship between waves at different points (in space or in time). **M20.**
■ **incoherency** *noun* = INCOHERENCE 1 **L17.**

incoherent /ɪnkə(ʊ)ˈhɪər(ə)nt/ *adjective.* **E17.**
[ORIGIN from IN-[3] + COHERENT.]
1 Consisting of or forming a group of incongruous parts; not unified in any way; uncoordinated. **E17.**

G. BERKELEY An incoherent fortuitous system, governed by chance.

2 (Of thought, language, etc.) without logical connection; disconnected, disjointed; inconsistent; (of a person etc.) characterized or marked by such thought or language. **M17.**

I

ALDOUS HUXLEY Abject and agitated, he moved among the guests, stammering incoherent apologies.

3 Without physical coherence or cohesion; unconnected, loose; incongruous, incompatible. **M17.**
4 *PHYSICS.* Producing, involving, or consisting of waves that lack any definite or stable phase relationship with each other. **E20.**

Nature If light from two incoherent sources . . enters the holes, each source will produce its own fringes.

■ **incoherently** *adverb* **M17.**

incohesion /ɪnkə(ʊ)ˈhiːʒ(ə)n/ *noun.* **L19.**
[ORIGIN from IN-[3] + COHESION.]
Lack of cohesion.

incohesive /ɪnkə(ʊ)ˈhiːsɪv/ *adjective.* **E19.**
[ORIGIN from IN-[3] + COHESIVE.]
Not cohesive.

incoincidence /ɪnkəʊˈɪnsɪd(ə)ns/ *noun.* **L18.**
[ORIGIN from IN-[3] + COINCIDENCE.]
(A) lack of coincidence or agreement.

incoincident /ɪnkəʊˈɪnsɪd(ə)nt/ *adjective.* **M17.**
[ORIGIN from IN-[3] + COINCIDENT.]
Not coincident; not identical.

incombustible /ɪnkəmˈbʌstɪb(ə)l/ *adjective & noun.* **L15.**
[ORIGIN medieval Latin *incombustibilis*, formed as IN-[3] + *combustibilis* COMBUSTIBLE.]
▸ **A** *adjective.* Not combustible. **L15.**
▸ **B** *noun.* An incombustible substance or constituent. **E19.**
■ **incombustiˈbility** *noun* **L17.** **incombustibleness** *noun* **E18.**

income /ˈɪnkʌm/ *noun*[1]. **ME.**
[ORIGIN In early use from Old Norse *innkoma* arrival; later from IN *adverb* + COME *verb*.]
1 Entrance, arrival; beginning. Now *rare* exc. *Scot.* **ME.** ▸**b** *spec.* The coming of divine influence into the soul. Now *rare* or *obsolete.* **M17.**
†**2** A fee paid on entering, an entrance fee. **M16–E18.**
3 A newcomer, a new arrival. Now chiefly *Scot.* **M16.**
4 The (amount of) money or other assets received or due to be received from employment, business, investments, etc., esp. periodically or in the course of a year. Formerly also in *pl.*, receipts, emoluments. **L16.**

J. K. GALBRAITH Men who are without work *do* miss the income they no longer earn. G. ORWELL His total income was fifteen shillings a week. C. G. WOLFF The couple managed to live very well on the income from their combined inheritances.

– COMB. & PHRASES: ***fixed income***; **income group** a section of the population graded by income; **incomes policy** a Government policy aimed at controlling inflation by restricting increases in wages, dividends, etc.; **income support** a system by which people on low incomes can, according to their circumstances, claim a payment from the state; **income tax**: levied on personal income; ***negative income tax*** (a scheme entailing) a state payment to an individual based on the extent to which his or her income is below a prescribed level; ***national income***: see NATIONAL *adjective*; ***psychic income***: see PSYCHIC *adjective*; ***unearned income***: see UNEARNED *adjective*.
■ **incomeless** *adjective* **E19.**

income /ˈɪnkʌm, ˈɪŋkʌm/ *noun*[2]. *Scot. & N. English.* **E19.**
[ORIGIN from IN *adverb* + COME *verb*. Cf. ANCOME, ONCOME, UNCOME.]
A swelling such as a boil, abscess, or tumour.

income /ɪnˈkʌm/ *verb intrans.* Long *obsolete* exc. *Scot.* Pa. t. **-came** /-ˈkeɪm/; pa. pple **-come.** **OE.**
[ORIGIN from IN-[1] + COME *verb*. Now chiefly repl. by *come in*.]
Come in, enter. Now chiefly as ***income ppl adjective***.

incomer /ˈɪnkʌmə/ *noun*[1]. **LME.**
[ORIGIN from IN-[1] + COMER.]
A person who enters or comes in; a visitor; a newcomer; an immigrant; a successor to a position vacated by another; *SHOOTING* a bird which flies towards the gun.

incomer /ˈɪnkʌmə/ *noun*[2]. **L20.**
[ORIGIN from INCOME *noun*[1] + -ER[1].]
A person who earns a specified kind or level of income. Usu. with specifying word.
high incomer, ***low incomer***, etc.

incoming /ˈɪnkʌmɪŋ/ *noun.* **ME.**
[ORIGIN from IN-[1] + COMING *noun*.]
1 The action or fact of coming in; arrival, entrance. **ME.**
†**2** A place of entrance. **LME–E16.**
3 = INCOME *noun*[1] 4. Usu. in *pl.* **L16.**

incoming /ˈɪnkʌmɪŋ/ *adjective.* **M18.**
[ORIGIN from IN-[1] + COMING *adjective*.]
That comes in, enters, or arrives; (of a person) succeeding another; (of profit) accruing.

S. BELLOW I was about to board a plane and he was on the incoming flight. E. FEINSTEIN The flat . . was soon to be occupied by incoming tenants.

in commendam /ɪn kɒˈmɛndam/ *adverbial phr.* **M17.**
[ORIGIN Latin *dare in commendam* give (a benefice) in charge or trust, from *commendare* COMMEND *verb*.]
ECCLESIASTICAL HISTORY. With the revenues of a benefice accruing to the holder (orig., temporarily, pending the arrival of a new incumbent, later, for life, esp. when a former incumbent was allowed to retain his benefice and its revenues following preferment).

incommensurable /ɪnkəˈmɛnʃ(ə)rəb(ə)l, -sjə-/ *adjective & noun.* **M16.**
[ORIGIN Late Latin *incommensurabilis*, formed as IN-[3] + COMMENSURABLE.]
▸ **A** *adjective.* **1** *MATH.* Having no common measure, integral or fractional (*with* another quantity); irrational. **M16.**
2 Having no common standard of measurement; not comparable in respect of magnitude or value. **M17.**

D. H. LAWRENCE The vision on the canvas is for ever incommensurable with the canvas, or the paint.

3 Foll. by *with*: not worthy to be compared with; utterly disproportionate to; falling short of. **M19.**

S. TURNER The forces of either were so incommensurable with the numbers and bravery of the people they attacked.

▸ **B** *noun.* An incommensurable quantity. Usu. in *pl.* **M18.**
■ **incommensuraˈbility** *noun* **L16.** **incommensurableness** *noun* (*rare*) **L17.** **incommensurably** *adverb* incomparably **M17.**

incommensurate /ɪnkəˈmɛnʃ(ə)rət, -sjə-/ *adjective.* **M17.**
[ORIGIN from IN-[3] + COMMENSURATE *adjective*.]
†**1** Having parts out of proportion; disproportioned. Only in **M17.**
2 Not of equal or corresponding measure or degree; out of proportion; inadequate. Foll. by *with, to.* **L17.**

D. MELTZER They find the responsibilities incommensurate with the powers to implement their judgements.

3 = INCOMMENSURABLE *adjective* 2. **L17.**
■ **incommensurately** *adverb* **E19.** **incommensurateness** *noun* **E18.**

incommiscible /ɪnkəˈmɪsɪb(ə)l/ *adjective.* *rare.* **E17.**
[ORIGIN Late Latin *incommiscibilis*, formed as IN-[3] + *commiscibilis*, from *commiscere* mix together, formed as COM- + *miscere* MIX *verb*: see -IBLE.]
Unable to be mixed together.

incommodate /ɪnˈkɒmədeɪt/ *verb trans.* Long *rare.* Pa. pple †**-ate, -ated.** **E17.**
[ORIGIN formed as INCOMMODATION: see -ATE[3].]
Inconvenience, incommode.

incommodation /ˌɪnkɒməˈdeɪʃ(ə)n/ *noun.* Now *rare* or *obsolete.* **M17.**
[ORIGIN from Latin *incommodat-* pa. ppl stem of *incommodare* INCOMMODE *verb* + -ATION.]
The action of incommoding; the fact of being incommoded; (an) inconvenience.

†**incommode** *noun & adjective.* **E16.**
[ORIGIN French from Latin *incommodus*: see INCOMMODITY.]
▸ **A** *noun.* An inconvenience. Only in **E16.**
▸ **B** *adjective.* = INCOMMODIOUS 1, 4. **L17–M18.**

incommode /ɪnkəˈməʊd/ *verb trans.* **L16.**
[ORIGIN French *incommoder* or Latin *incommodare*, formed as IN-[3] + *commodus* convenient: see COMMODIOUS.]
1 Subject to inconvenience or discomfort; put to trouble; annoy. **L16.**

E. BOWEN In order that they might not incommode the patients, the pupils came and went by a basement door. Y. MENUHIN We were not the only travelers to be incommoded by the flood.

2 Hinder, impede, obstruct, (an action etc.). **E18.**

incommodious /ɪnkəˈməʊdɪəs/ *adjective.* **M16.**
[ORIGIN from IN-[3] + COMMODIOUS.]
1 Causing inconvenience or discomfort; troublesome, annoying. **M16.** ▸†**b** Of a person, a person's character: troublesome, difficult to get on with. **L16–L18.**
†**2** Unprofitable; unsuitable; inappropriate. **M16–E18.**
†**3** Damaging, harmful. **L16–M17.**
4 Of a place, room, etc.: not convenient for the purpose; not affording good accommodation. **E17.**
■ **incommodiously** *adverb* **M16.** **incommodiousness** *noun* the quality of being incommodious; (an) inconvenience: **E17.**

incommodity /ɪnkəˈmɒdɪti/ *noun.* **LME.**
[ORIGIN Old French & mod. French *incommodité* from Latin *incommoditas*, from *incommodus*, formed as IN-[3] + *commodus* convenient: see IN-[3], COMMODIOUS, -ITY.]
An incommodious quality, condition, or state; (an) inconvenience, (a) disadvantage, (a) discomfort.

incommunicable /ɪnkəˈmjuːnɪkəb(ə)l/ *adjective.* **M16.**
[ORIGIN Late Latin *incommunicabilis* not to be imparted, formed as IN-[3] + *communicabilis*: see COMMUNICABLE.]
1 = INCOMMUNICATIVE. **M16.**
2 Unable to be imparted or shared. **L16.**

C. JOHNSTON To wrest from the sovereign an essential part of the incommunicable power of the crown.

3 Unable to be communicated by speech; unspeakable, unutterable; ineffable. **M17.**

J. F. FERRIER Its true meaning is utterly incommunicable by one being to another.

4 Not in communication; lacking communication. **M17.**
■ ˌ**incommunicaˈbility** *noun* **M17.** **incommunicableness** *noun* **E17.** **incommunicably** *adverb* **E17.**

incommunicado /ˌɪnkəmjuːnɪˈkɑːdəʊ/ *adjective & adverb.* Also in Spanish form **incomunicado** /*also foreign* inkomuniˈkaðo/. **M19.**
[ORIGIN Spanish *incomunicado* pa. pple of *incomunicar* deprive of communication.]
▸ **A** *adjective.* Having no means of communication with others; *esp.* (of a prisoner) held in solitary confinement. **M19.**

R. HUNTFORD He would be incommunicado for a year at least.

▸ **B** *adverb.* Without means of communication with others. **M20.**

Independent He was held incommunicado for 48 hours clad only in underpants.

incommunicating /ɪnkəˈmjuːnɪkeɪtɪŋ/ *adjective.* **L17.**
[ORIGIN from IN-[3] + COMMUNICATE *verb* + -ING[2].]
Not communicating; lacking communication.

incommunicative /ɪnkəˈmjuːnɪkətɪv/ *adjective.* **L17.**
[ORIGIN from IN-[3] + COMMUNICATIVE.]
Uncommunicative.
■ **incommunicatively** *adverb* **M19.** **incommunicativeness** *noun* **L18.**

incommutable /ɪnkəˈmjuːtəb(ə)l/ *adjective.* **LME.**
[ORIGIN Sense 1 from Latin *incommutabilis*, formed as IN-[3], COMMUTABLE; sense 2 from IN-[3] + COMMUTABLE.]
1 Not changeable; not liable to alteration; immutable. **LME.**
2 Unable to be commuted or exchanged. **L18.**
■ **incommutaˈbility** *noun* **L17.**

incompact /ɪnkəmˈpakt, ɪnˈkɒmpakt/ *adjective.* **E17.**
[ORIGIN from IN-[3] + COMPACT *adjective*.]
Not compact; lacking cohesion (*lit. & fig.*).
■ **incompactly** *adverb* **E18.** **incompactness** *noun* **E18.**

in-company /ɪnˈkʌmp(ə)ni/ *adjective.* **M20.**
[ORIGIN from IN-[1] + COMPANY *noun*.]
Occurring or existing within a company; *esp.* designating training received by a person while employed by a company.

incomparable /ɪnˈkɒmp(ə)rəb(ə)l/ *adjective, adverb, & noun.* **LME.**
[ORIGIN Old French & mod. French from Latin *incomparabilis*, formed as IN-[3] + *comparabilis* COMPARABLE.]
▸ **A** *adjective.* **1** With which there is no comparison, esp. for excellence; unequalled in manner, kind, or degree; matchless, peerless. **LME.**

H. G. WELLS Almost every man . . finds it necessary to believe that he is . . incomparable as a lover.

2 Unable to be compared (*with, to*). **E17.**

Scientific American Two rectangles are called incomparable if neither one can be placed inside the other and aligned.

▸ †**B** *adverb.* Incomparably. **L15–M17.**
▸ **C** *noun.* An incomparable person or thing. **E18.**
■ **incomparaˈbility** *noun* **L15.** **incomparableness** *noun* **M17.** **incomparably** *adverb* in an incomparable manner or degree; in a way that does not admit of comparison: **LME.**

†**incompass** *verb* var. of ENCOMPASS.

incompatibility /ˌɪnkəmpatɪˈbɪlɪti/ *noun.* **E17.**
[ORIGIN French *incompatibilité*, from *incompatible*, formed as INCOMPATIBLE: see -ITY.]
1 The property or condition of being incompatible. **E17.** ▸**b** *BIOLOGY & MEDICINE.* The incapacity of cells or tissues of one individual to tolerate those of another when a union between them is attempted, esp. in grafting and transplantation, in blood transfusion, and in parasitism. **E20.** ▸**c** *BIOLOGY.* Inability to produce viable offspring despite the bringing together of fertile gametes; now *esp.* such inability occurring among conspecific individuals (as in many fungi and angiosperms). **E20.**

b *Woman's Own* The Rhesus incompatibility which can affect their babies.

2 An incompatible thing or quality; an instance of being incompatible. **L17.**

New Yorker Divorce for trivial incompatibilities continues to offend.

incompatible /ɪnkəmˈpatɪb(ə)l/ *adjective & noun.* **LME.**
[ORIGIN medieval Latin *incompatibilis*, formed as IN-[3] + *compatibilis* COMPATIBLE.]
▸ **A** *adjective.* **1** Incapable of existing together in the same person; opposed in character; discordant. (Foll. by *with,* †*to.*) **LME.** ▸†**b** Of a person: intolerant *of.* **E–M17.** ▸**c** Of an item of equipment: unable to be used in conjunction with some other item. **M20.**

I. MURDOCH Taman's state of mind . . became a dark battlefield of incompatible emotions. M. T. TSUANG Complete recovery was not incompatible with a diagnosis of dementia praecox.

2 Unable to agree or be in harmony together; at variance. **M16.**

M. HOLROYD They were fond of each other, but incompatible.

3 *ECCLESIASTICAL.* Of benefices etc.: unable to be held together. **L16.**
†**4** Irreconcilable. *rare.* **E–M17.**

5 Of a drug or drugs: reacting (*with* another substance) in such a way that the two should not be administered together. **E19.**
6 *BIOLOGY & MEDICINE.* Exhibiting or causing immunological or reproductive incompatibility. **E20.**
► **B** *noun.* An incompatible person or thing. **E18.**
■ **incompatibleness** *noun* **E17.** **incompatibly** *adverb* **E18.**

incompetence /ɪnˈkɒmpɪt(ə)ns/ *noun.* **M17.**
[**ORIGIN** French *incompétence* after *incompétent* **INCOMPETENT**: see **-ENCE**.]
The property, quality, or fact of being incompetent.

R. HUNTFORD Allowing *Discovery* to be frozen in so that she could not escape was considered professional incompetence.

■ **incompetency** *noun* (an instance of) incompetence **E17.**

incompetent /ɪnˈkɒmpɪt(ə)nt/ *adjective & noun.* **L16.**
[**ORIGIN** (French *incompétent* from) late Latin *incompetent-*, formed as **IN-**^{3} + *competent-* **COMPETENT** *adjective*.]
► **A** *adjective.* **1** Not legally competent. **L16.**
2 †**a** Insufficient, inadequate. **E17–E19.** ►**b** *MEDICINE.* Esp. of a valve or sphincter: unable to function properly, thus causing reflux or incontinence. **M19.**

b G. BOURNE An incompetent cervix will cause miscarriage at about the 20th week of pregnancy.

3 Chiefly of a person: of inadequate ability or fitness; lacking the requisite capacity or qualification; incapable. **M17.**
4 Logically inadmissible or illegitimate. **M19.**
5 *GEOLOGY.* Of a rock or stratum: apt to undergo plastic deformation when compressed. Of a structure or process: largely involving incompetent rocks. **L19.**
► **B** *noun.* An incompetent person. **M19.**
■ **incompetently** *adverb* **M17.**

incompletable /ɪnkəmˈpliːtəb(ə)l/ *adjective.* **E20.**
[**ORIGIN** from **IN-**^{3} + **COMPLETABLE**.]
Unable to be completed.
■ **incompletableness** *noun* **L19.** **incompleta'bility** *noun* **E19.**

incomplete /ɪnkəmˈpliːt/ *adjective.* **LME.**
[**ORIGIN** Late Latin *incompletus*, formed as **IN-**^{3} + Latin *completus* **COMPLETE** *adjective*.]
1 Not complete; not fully formed; unfinished; not whole or thorough; lacking something, imperfect. **LME.**
incomplete symbol *PHILOSOPHY* a symbol that does not designate something having independent reality. ***verb of incomplete predication***: see **PREDICATION** 2.
2 *MATH. & LOGIC.* Of a formal system: containing true propositions for which no proof of validity is possible using only the formal rules of the system. **M20.**
■ **incompletely** *adverb* **LME.** **incompleteness** *noun* **M17.**

incompleted /ɪnkəmˈpliːtɪd/ *adjective.* **M19.**
[**ORIGIN** from **IN-**^{3} + *completed* pa. pple of **COMPLETE** *verb*.]
= **UNCOMPLETED.**

incompletion /ɪnkəmˈpliːʃ(ə)n/ *noun.* **E19.**
[**ORIGIN** from **IN-**^{3} + **COMPLETION**.]
The property of not having been completed or of not having completed something.

incompletive /ɪnkəmˈpliːtɪv/ *adjective & noun.* **M20.**
[**ORIGIN** from **INCOMPLETE** + **-IVE**.]
GRAMMAR. (Designating) an aspect of verbs in some languages that indicates the incompletion of an action or process.

incomplex /ɪnˈkɒmplɛks/ *adjective.* **M17.**
[**ORIGIN** Late Latin *incomplexus*, formed as **IN-**^{3} + Latin *complexus* **COMPLEX** *adjective*.]
Not complex; simple, not complicated.

incompliance /ɪnkəmˈplʌɪəns/ *noun.* Now *rare.* **M17.**
[**ORIGIN** from **IN-**^{3} + **COMPLIANCE**.]
†**1** Lack of conformity. Only in **M17.**
†**2** Unaccommodating disposition; lack of complaisance. **L17–E19.**
3 Failure to comply, non-compliance. **E18.**
■ **incompliancy** *noun* (*rare*) **M17.** **incompliant** *adjective* (now *rare*) **M17.**

†**incomplicate** *adjective.* *rare.* **L17–E19.**
[**ORIGIN** from **IN-**^{3} + **COMPLICATE** *adjective*.]
Not complicated; simple.

†**incomplying** *adjective.* *rare.* **M17–M18.**
[**ORIGIN** from **IN-**^{3} + **COMPLY** + **-ING**^{2}.]
Unaccommodating; not compliant.

†**incomposed** *adjective.* **E17.**
[**ORIGIN** from **IN-**^{3} + **COMPOSED**.]
1 Discomposed, agitated; disordered. **E17–M18.**
2 Not composite or compound. **M–L17.**
■ †**incomposedly** *adverb* **E–M17.** †**incomposedness** *noun* **M17–E18.**

incomposite /ɪnˈkɒmpəzɪt/ *adjective.* **L17.**
[**ORIGIN** Latin *incompositus*, formed as **IN-**^{3} + *compositus* **COMPOSITE** *adjective*.]
Not composite.

incompossible /ɪnkəmˈpɒsɪb(ə)l/ *adjective.* **E17.**
[**ORIGIN** medieval Latin *incompossibilis*, formed as **IN-**^{3} + *compossibilis* **COMPOSSIBLE**.]
Not possible together; incompatible.
■ ˌ**incompossi'bility** *noun* **E17.**

†**incompounded** *adjective.* **E17–M18.**
[**ORIGIN** from **IN-**^{3} + **COMPOUNDED**.]
Not compounded, not compound.

incomprehended /ˌɪnkɒmprɪˈhɛndɪd/ *adjective.* *rare.* **M17.**
[**ORIGIN** from **IN-**^{3} + *comprehended* pa. pple of **COMPREHEND**.]
Not comprehended; beyond understanding.
■ **incomprehending** *adjective* (*rare*) lacking understanding **L19.**

incomprehensible /ˌɪnkɒmprɪˈhɛnsɪb(ə)l/ *adjective & noun.* **LME.**
[**ORIGIN** Latin *incomprehensibilis*, formed as **IN-**^{3} + *comprehensibilis* **COMPREHENSIBLE**.]
► **A** *adjective.* **1** Chiefly *THEOLOGY.* Unable to be contained or circumscribed within limits; boundless. *arch.* **LME.**
2 Unable to be understood, unintelligible; *arch.* beyond the reach of intellect or research, unfathomable. **LME.**

D. ACHESON The papers were long, tremendously complex, and totally incomprehensible.

†**3** Unable to be physically grasped or taken hold of; impalpable. *rare.* **E17–M18.**
► **B** *noun.* An incomprehensible thing or being. **M16.**
■ **in,comprehensi'bility** *noun* the property or attribute of being incomprehensible; an inconceivable or unintelligible thing: **L16.** **incomprehensibleness** *noun* **E17.** **incomprehensibly** *adverb* **LME.**

incomprehension /ˌɪnkɒmprɪˈhɛnʃ(ə)n/ *noun.* **E17.**
[**ORIGIN** from **IN-**^{3} + **COMPREHENSION**.]
The fact of not understanding; failure to understand.

incomprehensive /ˌɪnkɒmprɪˈhɛnsɪv/ *adjective.* **M17.**
[**ORIGIN** from **IN-**^{3} + **COMPREHENSIVE**.]
1 Deficient in understanding. **M17.**
2 Incomprehensible. Now *rare.* **M17.**
3 Not inclusive. **L18.**

incompressible /ɪnkəmˈprɛsɪb(ə)l/ *adjective.* **M18.**
[**ORIGIN** from **IN-**^{3} + **COMPRESSIBLE**.]
Unable to be compressed into a smaller volume.
■ ˌ**incompressi'bility** *noun* **M18.**

incomputable /ɪnkəmˈpjuːtəb(ə)l/ *adjective.* **E17.**
[**ORIGIN** from **IN-**^{3} + Latin *computabilis* **COMPUTABLE**.]
Unable to be computed; incalculable.

incomunicado *adjective & adverb* see **INCOMMUNICADO.**

inconceivable /ɪnkənˈsiːvəb(ə)l/ *adjective & noun.* **E17.**
[**ORIGIN** from **IN-**^{3} + **CONCEIVABLE**.]
► **A** *adjective.* Unable to be mentally conceived of; unthinkable, unimaginable; *colloq.* very remarkable, extraordinary. **E17.**

B. JOWETT Even these inconceivable qualities of space . . may be made the subject of reasoning. H. JAMES A domain of immeasurable extent and almost inconceivable splendour. R. RENDELL It was inconceivable to him that anyone would give three hundred pounds for such a thing.

► **B** *noun.* An inconceivable thing. **E18.**
■ ˌ**inconceiva'bility** *noun* **M19.** **inconceivableness** *noun* **M17.** **inconceivably** *adverb* in an inconceivable manner; to an inconceivable degree, unimaginably; *colloq.* remarkably, exceedingly: **M17.**

inconcinnity /ɪnkənˈsɪnɪti/ *noun.* *arch.* **E17.**
[**ORIGIN** Latin *inconcinnitas*, formed as **IN-**^{3} + **CONCINNITY**, or from **IN-**^{3} + **CONCINNITY**.]
Lack of proportion; awkwardness, inelegance; impropriety, unsuitableness; an instance of this.

†**inconcinnous** *adjective.* **M17.**
[**ORIGIN** Latin *inconcinnus*, formed as **IN-**^{3} + **CONCINNOUS**, or from **IN-**^{3} + **CONCINNOUS**.]
1 Incongruous. Only in **M17.**
2 *MUSIC.* Inharmonious, contrary to the principles of harmony. **E18–E19.**

inconcludent /ɪnkənˈkluːd(ə)nt/ *adjective.* *rare.* **L17.**
[**ORIGIN** from **IN-**^{3} + **CONCLUDENT**.]
Inconclusive.

inconclusible /ɪnkənˈkluːsɪb(ə)l/ *adjective.* *rare.* **M17.**
[**ORIGIN** from **IN-**^{3} + **CONCLUSIBLE**.]
Unable to be concluded.

inconclusion /ɪnkənˈkluːʒ(ə)n/ *noun.* **M19.**
[**ORIGIN** from **IN-**^{3} + **CONCLUSION**.]
Inconclusiveness; an inconclusive result.

inconclusive /ɪnkənˈkluːsɪv/ *adjective.* **L17.**
[**ORIGIN** from **IN-**^{3} + **CONCLUSIVE**.]
1 Not conclusive in argument or evidence; not convincing or decisive. **L17.**
2 Not conclusive in action; reaching no final result, producing no conclusive effect. **M19.**
■ **inconclusively** *adverb* **M18.** **inconclusiveness** *noun* **L17.**

inconcrete /ɪnˈkɒnkriːt/ *adjective.* Now *rare.* **E17.**
[**ORIGIN** Late Latin *inconcretus* incorporeal, formed as **IN-**^{3} + Latin *concretus* **CONCRETE** *adjective*.]
Not concrete; abstract.

in concreto /ɪn kɒnˈkriːtəʊ/ *adverbial phr.* **E17.**
[**ORIGIN** Latin.]
As a concrete thing.

†**inconcussible** *adjective.* Also **-able.** **L16–E18.**
[**ORIGIN** French †*inconcussible*, formed as **IN-**^{3} + Latin *concuss-* (see **CONCUSS** *verb*): see **-IBLE**.]
Unable to be shaken; firmly fixed; stable.

incondensable /ɪnkənˈdɛnsəb(ə)l/ *adjective.* **E19.**
[**ORIGIN** from **IN-**^{3} + **CONDENSABLE**.]
Unable to be condensed; *esp.* unable to be reduced from gas or vapour to a liquid condition.
■ Also **incondensible** *adjective* **M18.**

incondite /ɪnˈkɒndɪt/ *adjective.* **M16.**
[**ORIGIN** Latin *inconditus*, formed as **IN-**^{3} + *conditus* pa. pple of *condere* put together.]
Crude, unpolished, unrefined; (esp. of literary or artistic works) badly constructed or composed.
■ **inconditely** *adverb* **E19.**

inconditionate /ɪnkənˈdɪʃ(ə)nət/ *adjective & noun.* **M17.**
[**ORIGIN** from **IN-**^{3} + **CONDITIONATE** *adjective & noun*.]
► **A** *adjective.* Not subject to or limited by conditions; unconditioned. Now *rare.* **M17.**
► **B** *noun.* *PHILOSOPHY.* An unconditioned entity; a form under which the unconditioned is conceived. **E19.**

Inconel /ˈɪnkənɛl/ *noun.* **M20.**
[**ORIGIN** App. from International Nickel Company + (*n*)*el* (after *nickel*).]
(Proprietary name for) any of various alloys of nickel containing chromium and iron, and resistant to corrosion at high temperatures.

inconfidence /ɪnˈkɒnfɪd(ə)ns/ *noun.* *rare.* **E17.**
[**ORIGIN** from **IN-**^{3} + **CONFIDENCE** *noun*.]
Lack of confidence, distrust.

inconfident /ɪnˈkɒnfɪd(ə)nt/ *adjective.* *rare.* **E17.**
[**ORIGIN** from **IN-**^{3} + **CONFIDENT** *adjective*.]
1 Breaking a trust or confidence; untrustworthy, indiscreet. **E17.**

Church Times It would be commercially inconfident and improper to go into details.

†**2** Not confident, distrustful. Only in **M17.**

inconformable /ɪnkənˈfɔːməb(ə)l/ *adjective.* **E17.**
[**ORIGIN** from **IN-**^{3} + **CONFORMABLE** *adjective*.]
1 Inconsistent *with*, not according in form or character *to*. **E17.**
2 Of a person: refusing or omitting to conform; *esp.* (*ENGLISH HISTORY*) not conforming to the practices of the Established Church. **M17.**

inconformity /ɪnkənˈfɔːmɪti/ *noun.* *arch.* **L16.**
[**ORIGIN** from **IN-**^{3} + **CONFORMITY**.]
1 Refusal or omission to conform (*to*, *with*); nonconformity. **L16.**
2 Dissimilarity, incongruity; lack of conformity (*to*, *with*). **E17.**

incongenial /ɪnkənˈdʒiːnɪəl/ *adjective.* Now *rare* or *obsolete.* **L18.**
[**ORIGIN** from **IN-**^{3} + **CONGENIAL**.]
Not congenial, uncongenial.

incongruence /ɪnˈkɒŋgrʊəns/ *noun.* **E17.**
[**ORIGIN** Latin *incongruentia*, formed as **INCONGRUENT**: see **-ENCE**.]
Lack of congruence; disagreement, incongruity.

incongruent /ɪnˈkɒŋgrʊənt/ *adjective.* **LME.**
[**ORIGIN** Latin *incongruent-*, formed as **IN-**^{3} + **CONGRUENT**.]
Not congruent; incompatible, unsuitable, incongruous.
incongruent melting point *CHEMISTRY* the dissociation temperature of a solid compound which is not stable as a liquid.
■ **incongruently** *adverb* in an incongruent manner; incongruously; *CHEMISTRY* as independent components (with ref. to phase changes, as melting of alloys, etc.): **M16.**

incongruity /ɪnkənˈgruːɪti/ *noun.* **M16.**
[**ORIGIN** Late Latin *incongruitas*, formed as **IN-**^{3} + *congruitas* **CONGRUITY**.]
1 Lack of harmony or consistency of parts or elements; incoherence; an instance of this. **M16.**

J. BUTLER Hence arises that amazing incongruity, and seeming inconsistency of character. SIR W. SCOTT He must have smiled at the incongruity of the clerk's apparel.

†**2** *GRAMMAR.* Violation of rules of concord; solecism. **M16–E17.**
3 Lack of appropriateness or suitability; absurdity; an instance of this. **L16.**

B. JOWETT He felt no incongruity in the veteran . . correcting the youthful Socrates.

4 Disagreement in character or qualities; discrepancy, inconsistency; an instance of this. **E17.**

J. F. W. HERSCHEL There we find no contradictions, no incongruities, but all is harmony. C. KINGSLEY The quaint incongruity of the priestly and the lay elements in his speech.

incongruous /ɪnˈkɒŋgrʊəs/ *adjective.* **E17.**
[**ORIGIN** from Latin *incongruus*, formed as **IN-**^{3} + **CONGRUOUS**: see **-OUS**.]
†**1** *GRAMMAR.* Violating the rules of concord; incorrect. Only in **17.**
2 Not appropriate; unsuitable, out of place, absurd. **E17.**

R. WARNER To be thinking of . . love while dressing for a funeral may seem an incongruous thing. D. ATHILL His hands—broad peasant hands . . look incongruous because the rest of him is finely made.

3 Disagreeing in character or qualities; out of keeping, discordant, inconsistent. (Foll. by *with*, †*to*.) (Passing into sense 2.) E17.

W. HOLTBY The cats were the only incongruous occupants of that precise impersonal room. D. CECIL A.. mixture of incongruous characteristics as to bewilder anyone who came into contact with him.

4 Having disparate or inharmonious parts or elements; incoherent. M17.

BURKE We are not at all embarrassed.. by any incongruous mixture of coercion and restraint.

■ **incongruously** *adverb* M17. **incongruousness** *noun* E18.

inconjunct /ɪnkən'dʒʌŋkt/ *adjective*. E17.
[ORIGIN from IN-[3] + CONJUNCT *adjective*.]
Not in conjunction; *spec.* in *ASTROLOGY* (of two planets or their positions) so placed that neither affects the other.

inconnected /ɪnkə'nɛktɪd/ *adjective*. *rare*. M18.
[ORIGIN from IN-[3] + CONNECTED.]
Not connected, disconnected.
■ **inconnectedness** *noun* L19.

†**inconnection** *noun*. Also **-exion**. E17–E19.
[ORIGIN from IN-[3] + CONNECTION.]
Lack of connection; unconnectedness.

inconnu /'ɪŋkənuː; *foreign* ɛ̃kɔny (*pl. same*)/ *noun*. In sense 1 fem. **-ue**. Pl. (in sense 1) **-s**, (in sense 2) same. E19.
[ORIGIN French = unknown.]
1 An unknown person, a stranger. E19.
2 A predatory freshwater salmonid game fish, *Stenodus leucichthys*, of the Eurasian and N. American Arctic. Orig. *Canad.* E19.

inconquerable /ɪn'kɒŋk(ə)rəb(ə)l/ *adjective*. M17.
[ORIGIN from IN-[3] + CONQUERABLE.]
Unconquerable.

inconscience /ɪn'kɒnʃ(ə)ns/ *noun*. L19.
[ORIGIN from IN-[3] + CONSCIENCE.]
Lack of conscience or consciousness.

inconscient /ɪn'kɒnʃɪənt/ *adjective*. L19.
[ORIGIN from IN-[3] + CONSCIENT.]
Unconscious, unwitting.
■ **inconsciently** *adverb* E20.

inconscious /ɪn'kɒnʃəs/ *adjective*. Now *rare*. L17.
[ORIGIN from late Latin *inconscius* unaware, ignorant + -OUS; later from IN-[3] + CONSCIOUS *adjective*.]
Unconscious; unaware (*of*).
■ **inconsciously** *adverb* M19.

inconsecutive /ɪnkən'sɛkjʊtɪv/ *adjective*. M19.
[ORIGIN from IN-[3] + CONSECUTIVE.]
Not consecutive, not in order or sequence; inconsequent.

Times They follow one another in an absolutely inconsecutive and irrelevant manner. V. WOOLF Odd little gusts of inconsecutive conversations reached her.

■ **inconsecutively** *adverb* M19. **inconsecutiveness** *noun* M19.

inconsequence /ɪn'kɒnsɪkw(ə)ns/ *noun*. L16.
[ORIGIN Latin *inconsequentia*, formed as INCONSEQUENT: see -ENCE.]
▸**I 1** Lack of logical sequence; illogicality, inconclusiveness. Also, an instance of this; an illogical conclusion or argument. L16.

T. GATAKER Mr. S. himself could not but see the inconsequence of his own argument.

2 The practice or habit of thinking, speaking, or acting disconnectedly or illogically. E19.

W. J. LOCKE Her inconsequence and flapperish immaturity.

3 Lack of natural connection of ideas, action, or events; irrelevance, disconnection. Also, an instance of this; an irrelevant action or circumstance. M19.

E. A. POE The whole of this paragraph must now appear a tissue of inconsequence and incoherence.

▸**II 4** The condition or fact of being of no consequence or importance. M18.

inconsequent /ɪn'kɒnsɪkw(ə)nt/ *adjective*. L16.
[ORIGIN Latin *inconsequent-*, not logically consequent, formed as IN-[3] + *consequent-* CONSEQUENT *adjective*.]
▸**I 1** Involving illogical reasoning or fallacious argument. L16. ▸**b** Not following naturally, having no rational connection, irrelevant. L19.
2 Not following logically, erroneously inferred. E17. ▸**b** Of ideas or subjects: disconnected, haphazard. M19.
3 Of a person: characterized by inconsequence in thought, speech, or action. L18.
▸†**II 4** Of no consequence, unimportant, trivial. *rare*. Only in M18.
■ **inconsequently** *adverb* E17. **inconsequentness** *noun* (*rare*) E18.

inconsequential /ˌɪnkɒnsɪ'kwɛnʃ(ə)l/ *adjective & noun*. E17.
[ORIGIN from IN-[3] + CONSEQUENTIAL.]
▸**A** *adjective*. **1** Characterized by inconsequence of reasoning, thought, or speech; inconsequent. E17.

O. CROMWELL I cannot let such gross mistakes and inconsequential reasonings pass. J. NORRIS The loose and inconsequential Reasoner.. in his wild ramble may happen to light upon Truth.

2 Of no consequence, unimportant, trivial. L18.
▸**B** *noun*. A thing of little importance; a triviality. E20.

Economist News never buried under frothy inconsequentials.

■ **inconsequentiˈality** *noun* M19. **inconsequentially** *adverb* M18. **inconsequentialness** *noun* M20.

inconsiderable /ɪnkən'sɪd(ə)rəb(ə)l/ *adjective*. L16.
[ORIGIN French †*inconsidérable* or late Latin *inconsiderabilis*, formed as IN-[3] + CONSIDERABLE *adjective*.]
†**1** Impossible to reckon or imagine; incalculable. L16–M17.
2 Not worth considering; unimportant, insignificant, trifling. M17. ▸**b** Of very small value, amount, or size. M17.

STEELE A trifling inconsiderable Circumstance. **b** A. GHOSH It was a large head, with a not inconsiderable cranial capacity.

†**3** Inconsiderate, thoughtless. M17–E18.
■ **inconsiderableness** *noun* M17. **inconsiderably** *adverb* M17.

†**inconsideracy** *noun*. *rare*. M18–M19.
[ORIGIN from INCONSIDERATE: see -ACY.]
Inconsiderateness.

inconsiderate /ɪnkən'sɪd(ə)rət/ *adjective & noun*. LME.
[ORIGIN Latin *inconsideratus*, formed as IN-[3] + CONSIDERATE *adjective*.]
▸**A** *adjective* **I 1** Done, made, or acting thoughtlessly; unadvised, precipitate, rash. LME.

POPE Inconsiderate authors wou'd rather be admir'd than understood. ISAAC TAYLOR An inconsiderate application of genuine principles to particular instances.

†**2** Careless or regardless *of*. Only in 17.
3 Lacking or showing lack of consideration or regard for the feelings of others. M19.

P. ANGADI He is too lazy and inconsiderate to put himself out for anybody. B. T. BRADFORD How inconsiderate of me, I haven't even asked you about your health.

▸†**II 4** Of no importance; inconsiderable, trifling. M17–E18.
▸**B** *noun*. An inconsiderate or thoughtless person. L16.
■ **inconsiderately** *adverb* LME. **inconsiderateness** *noun* L16.

inconsideration /ˌɪnkənsɪdə'reɪʃ(ə)n/ *noun*. E16.
[ORIGIN French *inconsidération* or late Latin *inconsideratio(n-)*, formed as IN-[3] + Latin *consideratio(n-)* CONSIDERATION.]
1 Failure or refusal to consider; thoughtlessness, rashness. E16. ▸†**b** An instance of this; a thoughtless act. L16–M17.
2 Lack of consideration or regard for the feelings of others. L19.

inconsidered /ɪnkən'sɪdəd/ *adjective*. *rare*. L16.
[ORIGIN from IN-[3] + CONSIDERED, after Latin *inconsideratus*, French *inconsidéré*.]
Not thought about or considered.

DONNE God will scarce hearken to sudden inconsidered irreverent Prayers.

inconsistence /ɪnkən'sɪst(ə)ns/ *noun*. Now *rare* or *obsolete*. M17.
[ORIGIN from INCONSISTENT after *consistence*: see -ENCE.]
1 = INCONSISTENCY 1. M17.
2 = INCONSISTENCY 2. M17.

inconsistency /ɪnkən'sɪst(ə)nsi/ *noun*. M17.
[ORIGIN from INCONSISTENT after *consistency*: see -ENCY.]
1 Lack of consistency; incompatibility, discrepancy. (Foll. by *between*, *with*.) M17.

ADDISON An eminent instance of the inconsistency of our Religion with Magic. B. JOWETT Nor is there any inconsistency in wise and good fathers having foolish and worthless sons. C. THUBRON In nothing is the inconsistency of Soviet Communism greater than in the emperors it reveres or forgets.

2 An inconsistent thing or act; a discrepancy. M17.

S. JOHNSON The many inconsistencies which folly produces, or infirmity suffers in the human mind. N. CHOMSKY It is a simple matter.. to discover inconsistencies and even absurdities in their answers.

inconsistent /ɪnkən'sɪst(ə)nt/ *adjective & noun*. M17.
[ORIGIN from IN-[3] + CONSISTENT *adjective*.]
▸**A** *adjective* **I 1** Not in keeping, discordant, at variance. Foll. by *with*, †*to*. M17. ▸**b** Of two or more things: incompatible, incongruous. M17.

H. A. L. FISHER Privileges are freely granted.., which are inconsistent with the exercise of state authority. **b** P. F. BOLLER I always thought that the sword and the gospel were utterly inconsistent.

2 Lacking harmony between different parts or elements; self-contradictory. M17.

J. GALSWORTHY His feelings were too mixed, too inconsistent for expression.

3 Of a person: not consistent in thought or action; acting at variance with principles or former conduct. E18.

E. YOUNG Ah! how unjust to nature, and himself, Is thoughtless, thankless, inconsistent man!

▸†**II 4** Of a substance: not solid or firm, fluid. L17–M19.
▸**B** *noun*. In *pl.* Inconsistent things, acts, or statements. M17.

F. BOWEN Two Inconsistents.. cannot both be true.

■ **inconsistently** *adverb* M17.

inconsolable /ɪnkən'səʊləb(ə)l/ *adjective*. L16.
[ORIGIN French, or Latin *inconsolabilis*, formed as IN-[3] + *consolabilis*, from *consolari* CONSOLE *verb*: see -ABLE.]
1 Of grief, trouble, etc.: unable to be alleviated or assuaged. L16.

T. BLACKLOCK Impell'd by deep inconsolable grief, She breathes her soft, her melancholy strain.

2 Of a person: unable to be consoled or comforted; disconsolate. L17.

M. BARING Lady Hengrave promised Marjorie a new doll, but Marjorie was inconsolable.

■ ˌ**inconsolaˈbility** *noun* M19. **inconsolableness** *noun* E18. **inconsolably** *adverb* E18.

inconsonance /ɪn'kɒns(ə)nəns/ *noun*. E19.
[ORIGIN from INCONSONANT after *consonance*: see -ANCE.]
Lack of agreement or harmony.
■ **inconsonancy** *noun* (*rare*) M17.

inconsonant /ɪn'kɒns(ə)nənt/ *adjective*. M17.
[ORIGIN from IN-[3] + CONSONANT *adjective*.]
Not consonant or agreeable *to*; not agreeing or harmonizing *with*.
■ **inconsonantly** *adverb* M19.

inconspicuous /ɪnkən'spɪkjʊəs/ *adjective*. E17.
[ORIGIN from Latin *inconspicuus* (formed as IN-[3] + CONSPICUOUS) + -OUS.]
†**1** Unable to be seen or perceived; invisible, indiscernible. E17–L18.
2 Not easily seen or noticed; not prominent or striking; *spec.* in *BOTANY* (of flowers) small, and green or pale. E19.

H. W. BATES The majority of forest-trees in equatorial Brazil have small and inconspicuous flowers. M. AMSTERDAM He started looking around for a place to throw it, that would be inconspicuous.

■ **inconspicuously** *adverb* M17. **inconspicuousness** *noun* E17.

†**inconstance** *noun*. LME.
[ORIGIN Old French & mod. French, formed as INCONSTANCY: see -ANCE.]
1 a = INCONSTANCY 1a. LME–E18. ▸**b** = INCONSTANCY 1b. E16–E17.
2 = INCONSTANCY 2. Only in E16.

inconstancy /ɪn'kɒnst(ə)nsi/ *noun*. E16.
[ORIGIN Latin *inconstantia*, from *inconstant-*: see INCONSTANT, -ANCY. Cf. INCONSTANCE.]
1 a Lack of stability or steadfastness of character or purpose; fickleness. E16. ▸**b** Of things or events: lack of uniformity, variability, irregularity. E17.

a H. JAMES You are contrasting my inconstancy with your own fidelity. **b** J. COWELL The inconstancy of mans estate, and the mutability of time.

†**2** Inconsistency (of statements etc.); an instance of this. M16–E17.
†**3** [Alt. of INCONTINENCY.] Incontinence. L16–E17.

inconstant /ɪn'kɒnst(ə)nt/ *adjective & noun*. LME.
[ORIGIN Old French, or Latin *inconstant-*, formed as IN-[3] + *constant-* CONSTANT *adjective*.]
▸**A** *adjective*. **1** Not steadfast or faithful; fickle, changeable. LME.

H. P. BROUGHAM The fickle, inconstant, volatile temper of the people. M. SEYMOUR-SMITH Woman as deceiver and inconstant lover.

2 Of things: variable, irregular. E16.

SHAKES. *Rom. & Jul.* O, swear not by.. th' inconstant moon, That monthly changes in her circled orb. E. POSTE The orthography of the Veronese MS. is extremely inconstant.

†**3** Inconsistent *with*. Only in M17.
▸**B** *noun*. An inconstant person or thing. M17.
■ **inconstantly** *adverb* M16.

inconstruable /ɪnkən'struːəb(ə)l/ *adjective*. L19.
[ORIGIN from IN-[3] + CONSTRUABLE.]
Unable to be construed.

inconsumable /ɪnkən'sjuːməb(ə)l/ *adjective*. M17.
[ORIGIN from IN-[3] + CONSUMABLE *adjective*.]
1 Unable to be consumed (by fire etc.). M17.

SHELLEY Ever still Burning, yet ever inconsumable.

2 *ECONOMICS*. Intended for repeated use and not for consumption. L18.

L. GRONLUND The inconsumable things, like machinery, leather, coin.

†**inconsumptible** *adjective*. L16–E18.
[ORIGIN French †*inconsomptible*, *-sumpt-*, or late Latin *inconsumptibilis*, formed as IN-[3] + *consumptibilis*, from *consumpt-* pa. ppl stem of *consumere* CONSUME *verb*: see -IBLE.]
= INCONSUMABLE 1.

incontaminate /ɪnkən'tamɪnət/ *adjective*. Long *rare*. LME.
[ORIGIN Latin *incontaminatus*, formed as IN-[3] + *contaminatus* pa. pple of *contaminare*: see CONTAMINATE *verb*.]
Uncontaminated, undefiled.

incontestable /ɪnkən'tɛstəb(ə)l/ *adjective*. Also **-ible**. L17.
[ORIGIN French, or medieval Latin *incontestabilis*, formed as IN-[3] + *contestabilis*, from *contestari* CONTEST *verb*: see -ABLE, -IBLE.]
Not open to question or argument; unquestionable, indisputable.

B. WEBB He is disliked and distrusted . . , but his cleverness . . as an after-dinner speaker is incontestable.

■ **incontesta'bility** *noun* (*rare*) M19. **incontestableness** *noun* (*rare*) E18. **incontestably** *adverb* E18.

†**incontested** *adjective*. Only in 18.
[ORIGIN from IN-[3] + CONTEST *verb* + -ED[1].]
Uncontested, undisputed.

incontestible *adjective* var. of INCONTESTABLE.

incontinence /ɪn'kɒntɪnəns/ *noun*. LME.
[ORIGIN Old French & mod. French, or Latin *incontinentia*, formed as IN-[3] + *continentia* CONTINENCE. Cf. INCONTINENCY.]
1 Lack of self-restraint with regard to sexual desire; promiscuity. LME.

J. A. SYMONDS Handsome youths are admonished by Pindar to beware of lawlessness and shun incontinence.

2 MEDICINE. Lack of voluntary control over the passing of urine or faeces. (Foll. by *of*.) M18.

P. PARISH This makes the patient empty his bladder more frequently, and . . this often leads to incontinence.

3 *gen*. Lack of constraint; inability to contain or restrain. (Foll. by *of*.) M19.

CARLYLE [They] do not waste themselves by incontinence of tongue.

incontinency /ɪn'kɒntɪnənsi/ *noun*. Now *rare*. LME.
[ORIGIN formed as INCONTINENCE: see -ENCY.]
1 = INCONTINENCE 1. LME.
2 = INCONTINENCE 3. E18.
3 = INCONTINENCE 2. L18.

incontinent /ɪn'kɒntɪnənt/ *adjective*. LME.
[ORIGIN Old French & mod. French, or Latin *incontinent-*, formed as IN-[3] + CONTINENT *adjective*.]
1 Lacking self-restraint, esp. with regard to sexual desire; promiscuous. LME.
2 *gen*. Unable to contain or restrain. Usu. foll. by *of*. M17.
3 MEDICINE. Lacking voluntary control over the passing of urine or faeces. E19.
doubly incontinent: see DOUBLY 1.

incontinent /ɪn'kɒntɪnənt/ *adverb*. Now *arch*. *rare*. LME.
[ORIGIN Old French *incontenant*, *en-* = Spanish, Italian *incontinente*, from late Latin *in continenti* (sc. *tempore*) 'in continuous time', without an interval. Cf. CONTINENT *adjective*.]
= INCONTINENTLY *adverb*[1].

incontinently /ɪn'kɒntɪnəntli/ *adverb*[1]. *arch*. LME.
[ORIGIN from INCONTINENT *adverb* + -LY[2].]
At once, immediately, without delay.

incontinently /ɪn'kɒntɪnəntli/ *adverb*[2]. M16.
[ORIGIN from INCONTINENT *adjective* + -LY[2].]
In an incontinent manner; with lack of (esp. sexual) self-restraint.

incontinuity /ˌɪnkɒntɪ'njuːɪti/ *noun*. *rare*. M19.
[ORIGIN from IN-[3] + CONTINUITY.]
(A) lack of continuity, (a) discontinuity.

incontinuous /ɪnkən'tɪnjʊəs/ *adjective*. *rare*. M19.
[ORIGIN from IN-[3] + CONTINUOUS.]
Not continuous, discontinuous.

incontrollable /ɪnkən'trəʊləb(ə)l/ *adjective*. Now *rare*. L16.
[ORIGIN from IN-[3] + CONTROLLABLE.]
1 Impossible to restrain or regulate; uncontrollable. L16.
†**2** Fixed, unalterable, unchangeable. E–M17.
†**3** Incontrovertible, unquestionable. Only in M17.
■ **incontrollably** *adverb* M17.

incontrovertible /ˌɪnkɒntrə'vəːtɪb(ə)l/ *adjective*. M17.
[ORIGIN from IN-[3] + CONTROVERTIBLE.]
Indisputable, indubitable.

M. RENAULT Laurie . . . had had this explained to him many times and accepted it as incontrovertible fact.

■ **ˌincontroverti'bility** *noun* L18. **incontrovertibly** *adverb* M17.

in contumaciam /ɪn kɒntjʊ'meɪsɪəm/ *adverbial phr*. L19.
[ORIGIN Latin.]
While in contempt of court.

inconvenience /ɪnkən'viːnɪəns/ *noun & verb*. LME.
[ORIGIN Old French (mod. *inconvenance*) from Latin *inconvenientia* incongruity, inconsistency, formed as IN-[3] + CONVENIENCE *noun*. Cf. INCONVENIENCY.]
► **A** *noun*. †**1** (An) incongruity, (an) inconsistency, (an) absurdity. LME–E18.
†**2** Unsuitableness, unfitness. LME–L17.
†**3** Unbecoming or unseemly behaviour, (an) impropriety. LME–M16.
4 (A) mischief, (an) injury, (a) misfortune. *obsolete* exc. as passing into sense 5. LME.
5 Lack of adaptation to personal requirements or ease; (a) disadvantage, (a) discomfort. L15.

E. M. FORSTER I really came . . to thank you for so kindly giving us your rooms last night. I hope that you have not been put to any great inconvenience. J. GATHORNE-HARDY As we get older we begin to suffer from an increasing amount of major and minor illnesses, diseases and inconveniences.

► **B** *verb trans*. Put to inconvenience, cause inconvenience to. E17.

E. WAUGH An umbrella under his left arm further inconvenienced him. A. T. ELLIS I believe in God . . but on the whole this belief inconveniences rather than supports me.

inconveniency /ɪnkən'viːnɪənsi/ *noun*. Now *rare*. LME.
[ORIGIN Latin *inconvenientia*: see INCONVENIENCE, -ENCY.]
†**1** = INCONVENIENCE *noun* 4. LME–E18.
†**2** = INCONVENIENCE *noun* 1. M16–L17.
3 = INCONVENIENCE *noun* 5. M16.
†**4** = INCONVENIENCE *noun* 3. E17–M18.

inconvenient /ɪnkən'viːnɪənt/ *adjective & noun*. LME.
[ORIGIN Old French from Latin *inconvenient-*, formed as IN-[3] + CONVENIENT *adjective*.]
► **A** *adjective*. †**1** Incongruous, inconsistent, absurd. LME–L17.
†**2** Unsuitable, unfitting, (*for*, *to*). LME–M19.
†**3** Unbecoming, unseemly, improper. L15–L17.
4 Causing trouble, difficulties, or discomfort; awkward, troublesome, disadvantageous. M17.

T. S. ELIOT If I went away it would be very inconvenient for them. L. P. HARTLEY Always popping off to church at inconvenient times.

► †**B** *noun*. **1** An incongruity, an inconsistency, an absurdity. Only in LME.
2 An unbecoming act, an impropriety. LME–M16.
3 An inconvenience. LME–M19.
■ **inconveniently** *adverb* E16.

†**inconversable** *adjective*. Also **-ible**. L16–E18.
[ORIGIN from IN-[3] + CONVERSABLE.]
Not conversable; unsociable; uncommunicative.

inconvertible /ɪnkən'vəːtɪb(ə)l/ *adjective*. M17.
[ORIGIN French, or late Latin *inconvertibilis*, formed as IN-[3] + Latin *convertibilis* CONVERTIBLE *adjective*; later from IN-[3] + CONVERTIBLE *adjective*.]
1 Unable to be changed into something else. M17.
2 Not interchangeable; not equivalent or synonymous. E18.
3 Unable to be exchanged for something else; *spec*. (of currency) that cannot be converted into another form on demand. M19.
■ **inconverti'bility** *noun* E19. **inconvertibleness** *noun* E18. **inconvertibly** *adverb* L19.

inconvincible /ɪnkən'vɪnsɪb(ə)l/ *adjective*. M17.
[ORIGIN from IN-[3] + CONVINCIBLE.]
Not convincible; not open to conviction.

†**incony** *adjective*. *slang*. L16–M17.
[ORIGIN Unknown.]
Rare, fine, delicate.

incoordination /ˌɪnkəʊɔːdɪ'neɪʃ(ə)n/ *noun*. Also **inco-or-**, ***incoör-**. L19.
[ORIGIN from IN-[3] + COORDINATION.]
Lack of coordination, esp. of muscular action.

incoronate /ɪn'kɒrənət/ *adjective*. M19.
[ORIGIN Italian *incoronato* or medieval Latin *incoronatus* pa. pple of *incoronare* to crown, formed as IN-[2] + Latin *corona* CROWN *noun*: see -ATE[2].]
Wearing or having a crown; crowned.

incoronation /ˌɪnkɒrə'neɪʃ(ə)n/ *noun*. Now *rare*. L15.
[ORIGIN from medieval Latin *incoronat-* pa. ppl stem of *incoronare* (see INCORONATE), + -ATION. Partly from Italian *incoronazione*.]
A coronation, a crowning.

incorporable /ɪn'kɔːp(ə)rəb(ə)l/ *adjective*. *rare*. E17.
[ORIGIN from INCORPORATE *verb* + -ABLE.]
Able to be incorporated.

†**incorporal** *adjective*. M16–M18.
[ORIGIN Latin *incorporalis*, formed as IN-[3] + *corporalis* CORPORAL *adjective*.]
Immaterial, incorporeal.

†**incorporality** *noun*. E17–L18.
[ORIGIN Late Latin *incorporalitas*, formed as INCORPORAL: see -ITY.]
The state or quality of being incorporeal.

incorporate /ɪn'kɔːp(ə)rət/ *adjective*[1]. *rare*. LME.
[ORIGIN Late Latin *incorporatus* not embodied, from *in-* IN-[3] + *corporatus* CORPORATE *adjective*.]
Without body or material substance; incorporeal.

incorporate /ɪn'kɔːp(ə)rət/ *adjective*[2]. LME.
[ORIGIN Late Latin *incorporatus* pa. pple of *incorporare*: see INCORPORATE *verb*, -ATE[2].]
1 United in or *in*, *into* one body; combined (*with* another thing). Now *rare*. LME.
2 a Of a company etc.: formally constituted as a corporation. LME. ›†**b** Of a person: admitted to fellowship with others, as a member of the same corporation. L16–L17. ›†**c** That constitutes a close connection. L16–M18.
3 Having a bodily form; embodied. LME.

incorporate /ɪn'kɔːpəreɪt/ *verb*. LME.
[ORIGIN Late Latin *incorporat-* pa. ppl stem of *incorporare*, formed as IN-[2] + *corporare* CORPORATE *verb*: see -ATE[3].]
► **I** *verb trans*. **1** Combine or unite into one body or uniform substance; mix together. LME.

CAPT. COOK Stirring up the several ingredients, till they were perfectly incorporated.

2 Put (one thing) *in* or *into* another to form one whole; include, absorb. LME.

ALDOUS HUXLEY The amoeba, when it finds a prey, flows round it, incorporates it, and oozes on. M. GIROUARD Often an orchard, or a vegetable garden . . , was incorporated into the layout.

3 a Combine or form into an organization; *esp*. constitute as a legal corporation. Usu. in *pass*. LME. ›**b** Admit, enrol (a person) *into*, *in* an organization; *spec*. admit as a graduate of another university *ad eundem*. M16.

a T. LUNDBERG When a company is incorporated, the initial subscribing shareholders . . enter into a form of contract.

4 Provide with a body; embody. *rare*. E17.
► **II** *verb intrans*. **5** Of one thing: combine *with* to form one body. L16.

D. BREWSTER The Water will gradually incorporate with the Syrup.

6 Of two or more things: unite so as to form one body; form a close union. Now *rare* or *obsolete*. E17.
7 Become constituted as a legal corporation. M20.
■ **incorporating** *adjective* (*a*) that incorporates; (*b*) LINGUISTICS employing or formed by incorporation; polysynthetic: E17.

incorporation /ɪnˌkɔːpə'reɪʃ(ə)n/ *noun*. LME.
[ORIGIN Late Latin *incorporatio(n-)*, formed as INCORPORATE *verb*: see -ATION.]
1 The action of incorporating two or more things, or one thing with another; the process or condition of being incorporated. LME. ›**b** LINGUISTICS. The combination of two or more different parts of speech in one word, as when the object of a verb is inserted between its stem and termination. L19.
2 a The action or process of forming into a community or corporation. LME. ›†**b** A document which gives legal status to a corporation. L15–E17. ›**c** The action of incorporating a graduate of one university into another. M20.
3 An incorporated society or company; a corporation. M16.
4 (An) embodiment. *rare*. M17.

incorporative /ɪn'kɔːp(ə)rətɪv/ *adjective*. L16.
[ORIGIN from INCORPORATE *verb* + -IVE.]
Characterized by or tending to incorporation.

incorporator /ɪn'kɔːpəreɪtə/ *noun*. E19.
[ORIGIN from INCORPORATE *verb* + -OR.]
1 A person who incorporates or combines things into one body or substance. E19.
2 A person who takes part in the formation of an incorporated company. L19.
3 A member of one university who is incorporated into another. L19.

in corpore /ɪn 'kɔːpəreɪ/ *adjectival & adverbial phr*. E20.
[ORIGIN Latin, lit. 'in the body'.]
BIOLOGY. = IN VIVO.

incorporeal /ɪnkɔː'pɔːrɪəl/ *adjective & noun*. LME.
[ORIGIN from Latin *incorporeus* (formed as IN-[3] + *corporeus*, from *corpor-*, *corpus* body) + -AL[1].]
► **A** *adjective*. **1** Not composed of matter; of or pertaining to immaterial beings. LME.
2 LAW. Having no material existence in itself, but connected as a right to some actual thing. E17.
incorporeal hereditament.
► **B** *noun*. In *pl*. Incorporeal things. E17.
■ **ˌincorpore'ality** *noun* M19. **incorporeally** *adverb* E17.

incorporeity /ˌɪnkɔːpə'riːɪti, -'reɪɪti/ *noun*. E17.
[ORIGIN medieval Latin *incorporeitas*, formed as INCORPOREAL: see -ITY.]
The quality or state of being incorporeal; an incorporeal attribute.

incorpsed /ɪn'kɔːpst/ *adjective*. *rare*. E17.
[ORIGIN from IN-[2] + CORPSE *noun* + -ED[2].]
Made into one body (*with*).

incorrect /ɪnkə'rɛkt/ *adjective*. LME.
[ORIGIN French, or Latin *incorrectus*, formed as IN-[3] + CORRECT *adjective*.]
†**1** *gen*. Uncorrected. LME–E17.
2 Of a book: not corrected for the press; containing many errors. L15.
3 Of style, behaviour, etc.: improper, faulty. L17.

T. MEDWIN According to . . Brummel, it is highly incorrect to be helped a second time to soup.

4 Of a statement, description, etc.: erroneous, inaccurate. E19.

J. H. SHORTHOUSE That lazy facility which always gives a meaning, though often an incorrect one. N. SYMINGTON It is incorrect to think that Freud was the first to challenge the notion.

■ **incorrectitude** *noun* (*rare*) the state of being incorrect; incorrectness: L19. **incorrectly** *adverb* E17. **incorrectness** *noun* the quality of being incorrect; an instance of this, an error: L17.

incorrespondence /ˌɪnkɒrɪˈspɒnd(ə)ns/ *noun. rare.* M17.
[ORIGIN from IN-[3] + CORRESPONDENCE.]
Lack of correspondence or harmony.
■ Also **incorrespondency** *noun* E19.

incorrigible /ɪnˈkɒrɪdʒɪb(ə)l/ *adjective & noun.* ME.
[ORIGIN Old French & mod. French, or Latin *incorrigibilis*, formed as IN-[3] + *corrigibilis* CORRIGIBLE.]
▸ **A** *adjective.* **1** Of a person, a habit, etc.: incurably bad or depraved. ME.
L. STRACHEY Within a few weeks the incorrigible reprobate was at his tricks again.
†**2** Of something defective: that cannot be set right. Of disease: incurable. M16–E19.
3 †**a** So good that it cannot be improved. *rare.* Only in E17. ▸**b** That cannot be verified or proved false. *rare.* M20.
▸ **B** *noun.* **1** An incorrigible person. M18.
2 A thing not open to verification. *rare.* M20.
■ **incorrigi'bility** *noun* L15. **incorrigibleness** *noun* M17. **incorrigibly** *adverb* E17.

incorrodible /ɪnkəˈrəʊdɪb(ə)l/ *adjective.* M19.
[ORIGIN from IN-[3] + CORRODIBLE.]
Unable to be corroded.

incorrupt /ɪnkəˈrʌpt/ *adjective.* LME.
[ORIGIN Latin *incorruptus*, formed as IN-[3] + *corruptus* CORRUPT *adjective.*]
1 Of a dead human body, or other organic matter: free from decomposition. LME.
2 Morally uncorrupted; honourable. Now *rare.* LME.
3 Not debased or perverted; *spec.* (of a text etc.) not affected by error or corruption. Now *rare.* M16.
■ †**incorrupted** *adjective* = INCORRUPT E16–M18. **incorruptly** *adverb* (now *rare*) L16. **incorruptness** *noun* L17.

incorruptible /ɪnkəˈrʌptɪb(ə)l/ *adjective & noun.* ME.
[ORIGIN Old French & mod. French, or ecclesiastical Latin *incorruptibilis*, formed as IN-[3] + CORRUPTIBLE.]
▸ **A** *adjective.* **1** Unable to decay or decompose; everlasting. ME.
AV *1 Cor.* 15:52 The trumpet shall sound, and the dead shall be raised incorruptible.
2 Unable to be morally corrupted, *esp.* unable to be bribed. M17.
DICKENS A man of incorruptible integrity.
▸ **B** *noun.* **1** ECCLESIASTICAL HISTORY. A member of an early Christian sect who maintained the incorruptibility of the body of Jesus. Usu. in *pl.* E18.
2 An incorruptible person, a person of rigid honesty or uncompromising idealism. Only in ***sea-green incorruptible*** (after Carlyle's *French Revolution*, where applied to Robespierre). M19.
■ **incorrupti'bility** *noun* L15. **incorruptibleness** *noun* (now *rare* or *obsolete*) LME. **incorruptibly** *adverb* L16.

incorruption /ɪnkəˈrʌpʃ(ə)n/ *noun.* LME.
[ORIGIN Old French & mod. French, or ecclesiastical Latin *incorruptio(n-)*, formed as IN-[3] + *corruptio(n-)* CORRUPTION.]
1 Freedom from physical decomposition. Freq. in biblical allusions. LME.
AV *1 Cor.* 15:42 It is sowen in corruption, it is raised in incorruption.
2 Freedom from corrupt conduct. E17.

†**incounter** *noun, verb* vars. of ENCOUNTER *noun, verb.*

in-country /ˈɪnkʌntri/ *noun & adjective.* M16.
[ORIGIN from IN-[1] + COUNTRY *noun.*]
▸ **A** *noun.* The inland or central part of a country; the mainland. *Scot.* Now *rare.* M16.
▸ **B** *adjective.* In the country; in a country understood contextually. M20.

†**incourage** *verb*, †**incouragement** vars. of ENCOURAGE, ENCOURAGEMENT.

incourse /ˈɪnkɔːs/ *noun. arch. rare.* LME.
[ORIGIN Latin *incursus*, from *incurs-* (see INCURSION), assim. to *concourse* etc.]
An inflow, an inrush, an incursion.

incover *verb* var. of ENCOVER.

incrassate /ɪnˈkrasət/ *adjective.* L15.
[ORIGIN Late Latin *incrassatus* pa. pple, formed as INCRASSATE *verb*: see -ATE[2].]
†**1** Thickened in consistency. L15–L17.
2 BOTANY & ZOOLOGY. Of thick or swollen form. M18.

incrassate /ɪnˈkraseɪt/ *verb trans. & intrans.* Now *rare.* E17.
[ORIGIN Late Latin *incrassat-* pa. ppl stem of *incrassare*, formed as IN-[2] + *crassare* make thick, from *crassus* thick: see -ATE[3].]
Thicken in consistency or form.
■ **incrassated** *adjective* thickened; *esp.* (BOTANY & ZOOLOGY) = INCRASSATE *adjective* 2: M17. **incra'ssation** *noun* M17.

increase /ˈɪŋkriːs, ɪnˈkriːs/ *noun.* Also †**en-**. LME.
[ORIGIN from the verb.]
1 The action, process, or fact of becoming greater; growth, enlargement, extension. LME. ▸†**b** *spec.* The rising of the tide; the waxing of the moon. M16–M17. ▸**c** The action or a method of increasing in knitting. L19.
2 Growth in number or frequency; multiplication; *spec.* the multiplication of humans, animals, or plants; reproduction. LME.
SHAKES. *Lear* Dry up in her the organs of increase.
†**3** Growth in some specified quality or respect, esp. wealth or power. LME–E19.
4 The result of increasing; the amount by which something is increased, an addition. LME.
W. S. JEVONS When their wages are raised, the increase comes out of the pockets of their employers.
5 Offspring (of humans or animals); *arch.* crops; *fig.* the product or result of any action. M16.
AV *1 Sam.* 2:33 And all the increase of thine house shall die in the floure of their age.
– PHRASES: **on the increase** increasing, becoming greater or more frequent.
■ †**increaseful** *adjective* (*rare*) productive, fruitful: only in L16.

increase /ɪnˈkriːs, ˈɪŋkriːs/ *verb.* Also †**en-**. ME.
[ORIGIN Anglo-Norman *encres-* = Old French *encreis-* stem of *encreistre* from Latin *increscere*, formed as IN-[2] + *crescere* grow.]
1 *verb trans. & intrans.* Make or become greater in size, amount, duration, or degree; enlarge, extend, intensify. ME. ▸**b** *spec.* in KNITTING. Add (a specified number of stitches) to the number of stitches in a row so as to widen the piece. M19.
S. PLATH I could sense the boy's interest dwindle as the pull of his mother increased. *Economist* Wage rates have increased by 10 per cent. D. W. GOODWIN Whether increasing the price of alcohol results in a decrease of alcoholism is not known.
2 *verb intrans. & trans.* Become or make more numerous, multiply, esp. by propagation. ME.
TENNYSON And watch her harvest ripen, her herd increase.
3 *verb intrans.* & (now *rare* or *obsolete*) *trans.* Become or make greater or more advanced *in* some specified quality or respect. LME.
SLOAN WILSON Diamonds had increased in value a great deal since the war.
4 *verb intrans. & trans.* Become or make richer or more powerful; (cause to) thrive. *arch.* LME.
5 *verb intrans.* Of a Latin noun or adjective: have one syllable more in the genitive than in the nominative. *arch.* E17.
■ **increasable** *adjective* capable of or liable to increase M16. **increasableness** *noun* L17. **increaser** *noun* (**a**) a person who or thing which makes something greater; (**b**) *arch.* a person who promotes or advances something; (**c**) an animal or plant which multiplies to a specified extent: LME. **increasingly** *adverb* to an increasing degree, at an increasing rate; more and more: L16.

increasement /ɪnˈkriːsm(ə)nt/ *noun.* Now *rare.* Also †**en-**. LME.
[ORIGIN from INCREASE *verb* + -MENT.]
1 The action or process of increasing; growth, extension, multiplication. LME.
2 The result of increasing; progeny, produce; an addition. LME.

increate /ɪnkriːˈeɪt/ *adjective.* LME.
[ORIGIN ecclesiastical Latin *increatus*, formed as IN-[3] + Latin *creatus* pa. pple of *creare* CREATE *verb*: see -ATE[2].]
Of a divine being or attribute: not created.
■ Also †**increated** *adjective* M16–E18.

incredibility /ɪnˌkrɛdɪˈbɪlɪti/ *noun.* E17.
[ORIGIN Latin *incredibilitas*, formed as INCREDIBLE: see -ITY.]
The quality or fact of being incredible; an incredible thing.

incredible /ɪnˈkrɛdɪb(ə)l/ *adjective.* LME.
[ORIGIN Latin *incredibilis*, formed as IN-[3] + CREDIBLE.]
1 Not credible; that cannot be believed. LME. ▸**b** Hard to believe; of exceedingly great quantity, quality, etc.; surprising. Now *colloq.* L15.
F. FERGUSSON Wishes to reveal this figment of the Greek imagination as, literally, incredible. **b** T. MORRISON The fury she created in the women of the town was incredible. R. INGALLS He was possessed of incredible strength.
†**2** Unbelieving. LME–M18.
■ **incredibleness** *noun* E17. **incredibly** *adverb* L15.

increditable /ɪnˈkrɛdɪtəb(ə)l/ *adjective. rare.* L17.
[ORIGIN from IN-[3] + CREDITABLE.]
Not creditable.

incredulity /ɪnkrɪˈdjuːlɪti/ *noun.* LME.
[ORIGIN Old French & mod. French *incrédulité* from Latin *incredulitas*, formed as INCREDULOUS: see -ITY.]
1 Unwillingness to believe; disbelief. LME.
A. T. ELLIS She believed him, her native incredulity powerless against the force of her affection. A. MASON These were so bizarre that Simon listened at first out of sheer incredulity.
†**2** *spec.* Religious disbelief. M16–M17.

incredulous /ɪnˈkrɛdjʊləs/ *adjective.* L16.
[ORIGIN from Latin *incredulus* (formed as IN-[3] + CREDULOUS) + -OUS: see -ULOUS.]
1 Unwilling to believe; sceptical; (of an action) marked or prompted by incredulity. Formerly also *spec.*, lacking religious belief. L16.
P. G. WODEHOUSE At first he was blankly incredulous. It could not be Judson. A. MACLEAN Earth's first visitor from outer space . . couldn't . . have been the object of more incredulous consternation.
†**2** Not to be believed; incredible. E17–M18.
■ **incredulously** *adverb* E19. **incredulousness** *noun* E18.

incremation /ɪŋkrɪˈmeɪʃ(ə)n/ *noun.* Now *rare* or *obsolete.* E19.
[ORIGIN from IN-[2] + CREMATION.]
Cremation.

increment /ˈɪŋkrɪm(ə)nt/ *noun & verb.* LME.
[ORIGIN Latin *incrementum*, from stem of *increscere* INCREASE *verb*: see -MENT.]
▸ **A** *noun.* **1** The action or process of (esp. gradually) increasing or becoming greater; an increase, a growth, *esp.* a uniform or regular one. LME. ▸**b** HERALDRY. The waxing of the moon. Now only in ***in increment***, ***in her increment***, increscent. E17. ▸**c** RHETORIC. = AUXESIS 1. M18.
2 The amount of increase; an addition; an amount gained, a profit, *esp.* a uniform or regular one. LME. ▸**b** MATH. & PHYSICS. A small (or infinitesimal) positive or negative change in a variable quantity or function. E18. ▸**c** FORESTRY. (The value of) the increase in the quantity of wood produced by a tree or group of trees during a limited period. L19.
J. GATHORNE-HARDY £650 a year. And that went on, you got minuscule increments I think.
UNEARNED ***increment***.
†**3** Something that promotes growth in a plant. *rare.* LME–E18.
▸ **B** *verb trans. & intrans.* Increase by an increment or increments. M19.

incremental /ɪŋkrɪˈmɛnt(ə)l/ *adjective.* E18.
[ORIGIN from INCREMENT *noun* + -AL[1].]
Of or pertaining to an increment or increments; advancing by increments.
Times The increases for the district nurses amount to £40 a year at the lower end of the incremental scale and £60 at the upper end. M. IGNATIEFF The slow, incremental liberalization of restrictions on Jews.
■ **incrementalism** *noun* belief in change by degrees, gradualism M20. **incrementalist** *noun & adjective* (**a**) *noun* an adherent of incrementalism; (**b**) *adjective* of or pertaining to incrementalism or incrementalists: L20. **incrementally** *adverb* in an incremental manner, by increments M20.

increpation /ɪŋkrɪˈpeɪʃ(ə)n/ *noun. arch.* E16.
[ORIGIN Latin *increpatio(n-)*, from *increpat-* pa. ppl stem of *increpare* scold, chide, formed as IN-[2] + *crepare* make a noise, creak: see -ATION.]
(A) reproof, (a) rebuke.

increscent /ɪnˈkrɛs(ə)nt/ *noun & adjective.* L16.
[ORIGIN Latin *increscent-* pres. ppl stem of *increscere* INCREASE *verb*: see -ENT.]
▸ **A** *noun.* Chiefly HERALDRY. The waxing moon. L16.
▸ **B** *adjective.* Increasing; *esp.* (of the moon) waxing (in HERALDRY depicted with the horns directed to the dexter side). Cf. DECRESCENT *adjective.* M17.

incriminate /ɪnˈkrɪmɪneɪt/ *verb trans.* M18.
[ORIGIN Late Latin *incriminat-* pa. ppl stem of *incriminare* accuse, formed as IN-[2] + *criminare* CRIMINATE: see -ATE[3].]
Charge with a crime; involve in an accusation or charge; tend to prove the guilt of.
E. WILSON An incriminating manifesto, which would have cost . . Michelet his head, was lying . . on the table. D. MAY She managed to say nothing that would incriminate herself or the organisation.
■ **incriminating** *ppl adjective* incriminatory M19. **incrimi'nation** *noun* M17. **incriminator** *noun* (*rare*) M19. **incriminatory** *adjective* tending to incriminate someone M19.

incrimson *verb* var. of ENCRIMSON.

incrispated /ɪnˈkrɪspeɪtɪd/ *adjective. rare.* M18.
[ORIGIN from late Latin *incrispat-* pa. ppl stem of *incrispare* curl, formed as IN-[2] + *crispare* curl, wrinkle: see -ED[1].]
Stiffly curled.

†**incroach** *verb & noun* var. of ENCROACH.

incroyable /ɛ̃krwajabl/ *noun.* Pl. pronounced same. L18.
[ORIGIN French = incredible.]
hist. A French fop or dandy of the period 1795–9.

incrust *verb* see ENCRUST.

incrustate /ɪnˈkrʌsteɪt/ *adjective.* E17.
[ORIGIN Latin *incrustatus* pa. pple of *incrustare*, formed as IN-[2] + *crustare* form a crust (from *crusta* crust): see -ATE[2].]
†**1** Formed or hardened into a crust. E17–M18.
2 Enveloped (as) with a crust. *obsolete* exc. BOTANY. L17.

incrustate /ˈɪnkrʌsteɪt/ *verb trans.* Now *rare.* Also **en-** /ɪn-, ɛn-/. L16.
[ORIGIN Latin *incrustat-* pa. ppl stem of *incrustare*: see INCRUSTATE *adjective*, -ATE[3].]
Cover with a crust or hardened coating or layer.

incubate /ˈɪŋkjʊbeɪt/ *noun*. **M20**.
[ORIGIN from INCUBATE *verb* after *filtrate, precipitate* etc.: see -ATE[1].]
A preparation or material that has been incubated.

incubate /ˈɪŋkjʊbeɪt/ *verb*. **M17**.
[ORIGIN Latin *incubat-* pa. ppl stem of *incubare* lie on, formed as IN-[2] + *cubare* lie: see -ATE[3].]
1 *verb trans.* Hatch or aid the development of (eggs) by maintaining warmth, either (as with most birds) by sitting upon, or by other natural or artificial means. **M17**. ▸**b** *verb trans. gen.* Maintain (esp. cells or micro-organisms) in a controlled environment suitable for growth and development; maintain at a constant temperature. **E20**. ▸**c** *verb intrans.* Undergo incubation; develop, grow. **E20**.

J. A. MICHENER In time the other eggs, incubated solely by action of the sun, hatched. R. DAWKINS Gannets and guillemots incubate one egg at a time. **b** *Science Journal* The inoculated samples were incubated for up to 27 days at various temperatures. **c** J. BRONOWSKI The full moon . . gives the time needed for the eggs to incubate undisturbed. *fig.*: N. ANNAN His grouches incubate in the heat of his devotion.

2 *verb intrans.* (Chiefly of a bird) sit on eggs; *fig.* brood. **M17**.

incubation /ɪŋkjʊˈbeɪʃ(ə)n/ *noun*. **E17**.
[ORIGIN Latin *incubatio(n-)* brooding, formed as INCUBATE *verb*: see -ATION.]
1 The action of incubating eggs; the embryonic development of an animal within an egg. **E17**. ▸**b** The process or an instance of incubating something in a controlled environment. **E20**.
2 MEDICINE. (The process occurring during) the period elapsing between exposure to an infection or disease and the appearance of the first symptoms. **M19**.
3 GREEK HISTORY. The practice of sleeping in a temple in the hope of experiencing a vision etc. **L19**.
■ **incubational** *adjective* **M19**.

incubative /ˈɪŋkjʊbeɪtɪv/ *adjective*. **M19**.
[ORIGIN from INCUBATE *verb* + -IVE.]
Of, pertaining to, or characterized by incubation, esp. of a disease.

incubator /ˈɪŋkjʊbeɪtə/ *noun*. **M19**.
[ORIGIN from INCUBATE *verb* + -OR.]
1 An animal, esp. a bird, which incubates its eggs. **M19**.
2 An apparatus for hatching eggs under artificial conditions. **M19**. ▸**b** An apparatus in which a constant temperature is maintained, esp. for rearing premature babies or for culturing micro-organisms. **L19**.
– COMB.: **incubator bird** = MEGAPODE *noun*.

incubatory /ɪŋkjʊˈbeɪt(ə)ri/ *adjective*. **L19**.
[ORIGIN from INCUBATE *verb* + -ORY[2].]
= INCUBATIVE.

incubi *noun pl.* see INCUBUS.

†**incubiture** *noun*. **M17–M18**.
[ORIGIN from Latin *incubit-* pa. ppl stem of *incubare* lie on, INCUBATE *verb* + -URE.]
= INCUBATION 1.

incubous /ˈɪŋkjʊbəs/ *adjective*. **M19**.
[ORIGIN from Latin *incubare* lie on, INCUBATE *verb* + -OUS.]
BOTANY. (Of a leaf, esp. in a foliose liverwort) pointing forward so that its upper edge overlaps the lower edge of the leaf above; (of a plant) having its leaves so arranged. Opp. SUCCUBOUS.

incubus /ˈɪŋkjʊbəs/ *noun*. Pl. **-buses**, **-bi** /-bʌɪ/. **ME**.
[ORIGIN Late Latin = Latin *incubo* nightmare, from *incubare*: see INCUBATE *verb*.]
1 An evil spirit supposed to descend upon sleeping people and esp. to have sexual intercourse with sleeping women. **ME**.
2 An oppressive nightmare; a person who or thing which oppresses or troubles like a nightmare. **M16**.

M. L. KING The incubus of racial injustice. P. ACKROYD What an incubus my aesthetic personality might become if I were . . trapped within it.

incud- *combining form* see INCUDO-.

incudes *noun* pl. of INCUS.

incudo- /ɪnˈkjuːdəʊ/ *combining form*. Before a vowel **incud-**. **L19**.
[ORIGIN from Latin *incud-* INCUS: see -O-.]
ANATOMY. Forming adjectives & nouns with the sense 'of the incus of the ear and —', as *incudo-stapedial*.

†**in cuerpo** *adverbial phr.* **E17–E20**.
[ORIGIN from IN *preposition* + Spanish *cuerpo* body from Latin *corpus*.]
Without a cloak or upper garment to conceal the shape of the body; in unsuitable dress; undressed.

inculcate /ˈɪnkʌlkeɪt/ *verb trans.* **M16**.
[ORIGIN Latin *inculcat-* pa. ppl stem of *inculcare* stamp in with the heel, press in, formed as IN-[2] + *calcare* tread, from *calc-*, *calx* heel: see -ATE[3].]
Instil (an idea, habit, etc.) into a person or a person's mind by forceful admonition or persistent repetition. (Foll. by *in*, *on*, etc.)

M. MITCHELL Mammy . . laboured to inculcate in her the qualities that would make her . . desirable as a wife. A. STORR Military training is designed to inculcate the notion that men are by no means equal. ISAIAH BERLIN They would at least inculcate into the barbarous Scythians the Latin language.

■ **inculcator** *noun* **L17**. **inculcatory** *adjective* (*rare*) **L19**.

inculcation /ɪnkʌlˈkeɪʃ(ə)n/ *noun*. **M16**.
[ORIGIN Late Latin *inculcatio(n-)*, formed as INCULCATE: see -ATION.]
The action or an act of inculcating something.

A. J. TOYNBEE Indoctrination . . counteracted by the inculcation of some less narrow loyalty.

inculpable /ɪnˈkʌlpəb(ə)l/ *adjective*. Now *rare*. **L15**.
[ORIGIN Late Latin *inculpabilis*, formed as IN-[3] + Latin *culpabilis* CULPABLE.]
Not culpable; blameless.
■ **inculpa'bility** *noun* **M18**. **inculpableness** *noun* **M16**. **inculpably** *adverb* **M16**.

†**inculpate** *adjective*. *rare*. **E–M17**.
[ORIGIN Late Latin *inculpatus* pa. pple, formed as INCULPATE *verb*: see -ATE[2].]
Unblamed, blameless.

inculpate /ˈɪnkʌlpeɪt/ *verb trans.* **L18**.
[ORIGIN Late Latin *inculpat-* pa. ppl stem of *inculpare*, formed as IN-[2] + Latin *culpare* to blame, from *culpa* fault: see -ATE[3]. Cf. INCULPATE *adjective*.]
1 Accuse; blame. **L18**.

E. JONES He blamed himself, but also inculpated his fiancée.

2 Involve in a charge, incriminate. **M19**.

CONAN DOYLE Someone came into your room and placed the pistol there in order to inculpate you.

■ **incul'pation** *noun* the action or an act of inculpating someone **L18**. **in'culpative** *adjective* = INCULPATORY **E19**. **in'culpatory** *adjective* attributing fault or blame **M19**.

incult /ɪnˈkʌlt/ *adjective*. Now *rare*. **L16**.
[ORIGIN Latin *incultus*, formed as IN-[3] + *cultus* pa. pple of *colere* cultivate.]
1 Of a person, manners, style, etc.: unpolished, unrefined; inelegant. **L16**.
2 Of land etc.: uncultivated. **M17**.

†**incultivate** *adjective*. **M17–E19**.
[ORIGIN from IN-[3] + Latin *cultivatus* pa. pple of *cultivare* CULTIVATE: see -ATE[2].]
= INCULTIVATED.

†**incultivated** *adjective*. **M17–E18**.
[ORIGIN from IN-[3] + CULTIVATE + -ED[1].]
Uncultivated, unpolished.

inculturation /ɪnˌkʌltʃəˈreɪʃ(ə)n/ *noun*. **M20**.
[ORIGIN from IN-[2] + CULTURE *noun* + -ATION.]
1 = ENCULTURATION. **M20**.
2 CHRISTIAN CHURCH. The adaptation of Christian liturgy to a non-Christian cultural background. **L20**.

†**inculture** *noun*. *rare*. **M17–M19**.
[ORIGIN from IN-[3] + CULTURE *noun*.]
Absence of culture or cultivation.

incumbence /ɪnˈkʌmbəns/ *noun*. Now *rare*. **E17**.
[ORIGIN formed as INCUMBENCY: see -ENCE.]
A matter that is incumbent; a duty, an obligation. Also, the fact of being incumbent.

incumbency /ɪnˈkʌmb(ə)nsi/ *noun*. **E17**.
[ORIGIN from INCUMBENT *noun*: see -ENCY. Cf. Anglo-Latin *incumbentia*.]
1 The quality of being incumbent as a duty; an incumbent duty or obligation. Now *rare*. **E17**.

DONNE The duties of a man, of a friend . . and all the incumbencies of a family. BROWNING Speaks or keeps silence . . Without the least incumbency to lie.

2 The condition of lying or pressing on something; brooding (*lit.* & *fig.*). Also, an incumbent weight or mass. Now *rare* or *obsolete*. **M17**.

WORDSWORTH Felt Incumbencies more awful, visitings Of the Upholder of the tranquil soul. *Cornhill Magazine* The stream is choked with its compact incumbency of snow.

3 The position, tenure, or sphere of an incumbent. **M17**.

R. MACAULAY The living of St. Anne's, . . one of those incumbencies with what is known as scope.

incumbent /ɪnˈkʌmbənt/ *noun*. **LME**.
[ORIGIN Anglo-Latin *incumbent-*, *-ens* use as noun of pres. pple of Latin *incumbere*: see INCUMBENT *adjective*, -ENT.]
1 The holder of an ecclesiastical benefice. **LME**.

K. AMIS The post of private chaplain . . had had half a dozen incumbents.

2 *gen.* The holder of any post or position. **L17**.

J. C. RANSOM The principal resistance . . will come from the present incumbents of the professorial chairs.

incumbent /ɪnˈkʌmbənt/ *adjective*. **L15**.
[ORIGIN Latin *incumbent-* pres. ppl stem of *incumbere* lie on, lean on, apply oneself to, formed as IN-[2] + *-cumbere*: see CUMBENT.]
†**1** **a** Impending, imminent, threatening. **L15–L18**. ▸**b** Weighing on the mind or feelings. **M–L17**.

a G. MORRIS The proselytes will return to their original sentiments as soon as the incumbent terror is removed. **b** HOBBES Ambition, and Covetousnesse are Passions . . that are perpetually incumbent, and pressing.

†**2** Bending or applying one's energies to some work; closely occupied with something. (Foll. by *on*, *over*, *to*.) **M16–E19**.

CLARENDON The multiplicity of business the king was incumbent to at that time.

3 Resting or falling on a person as a duty or obligation. Freq. foll. by *on*, *upon*. **M16**. ▸†**b** Falling as a charge or pecuniary liability. **L17–L18**.

E. CRANKSHAW Responsibility towards his own people which it was incumbent upon a Russian autocrat to shoulder. J. I. M. STEWART It was incumbent on me to follow where he led.

4 †**a** In occupation of an ecclesiastical benefice. (Foll. by *on*.) **E–M17**. ▸**b** *gen.* In occupation or having the tenure of any post or position. **M20**.

a T. FULLER He was never incumbent on any living with cure of souls. **b** E. ROOSEVELT I never fooled myself about the difficulties of defeating the incumbent administration.

5 That lies or presses with its weight *on* something else. Also (*poet.*), overhanging, leaning *over*; GEOLOGY (of a stratum etc.) overlying. **E17**. ▸**b** BOTANY & ZOOLOGY. Lying close along a surface, as an anther along a filament, or an insect's wing laid flat. **M18**.

incumber *noun*, *verb*, **incumberment** *noun*, **incumbrance** *noun* vars. of ENCUMBER *noun*, *verb*, ENCUMBERMENT, ENCUMBRANCE.

incunable /ɪnˈkjuːnəb(ə)l/ *noun*. **L19**.
[ORIGIN French, formed as INCUNABULUM.]
= INCUNABULUM 2.

incunabulum /ɪnkjʊˈnabjʊləm/ *noun*. Pl. (earlier) **-la** /-lə/. **E19**.
[ORIGIN Latin *incunabula* neut. pl. swaddling clothes, cradle, formed as IN-[2] + *cunae* cradle.]
1 In *pl.* The early stages of development of a thing. **E19**.
2 A book printed at an early date; *spec.* one printed before 1501. **M19**.
■ **incunabular** *adjective* of or pertaining to an incunabulum or incunabula **L19**. **incunabulist** *noun* a person who collects or is interested in incunabula **E20**.

incur /ɪnˈkəː/ *verb*. Infl. **-rr-**. **LME**.
[ORIGIN Latin *incurrere*, formed as IN-[2] + *currere* run.]
▸ **I** *verb trans.* **1** Find, or make, oneself subject to (danger, displeasure, etc.); bring on oneself (expense, obligation, etc.). **LME**.

H. JAMES The responsibility Olive had incurred in undertaking to form this generous young mind. R. G. COLLINGWOOD I did not even neglect my work to the extent of incurring punishment for idleness. G. CLARE The medical fees incurred during his illness.

†**2** Run into; come upon, meet with. **L16–L17**.
†**3** Cause to be incurred; bring (something) *on* someone; entail. **E17–L18**.

G. HAKEWILL Not naming it expressely, lest . . he should incurre hatred against the Christian . . Religion.

▸ **II** *verb intrans.* **4** †**a** Fall or come *to* or *into*; fall, occur, (within a given period of time etc.). **M16–L17**. ▸†**b** Become apparent to the eye etc.; occur. Only in **17**. ▸**c** Devolve, accrue; supervene. Long *rare* or *obsolete*. **L18**.

a M. HALE Kircherus . . supposeth the first 15 Dynasties to have incurred before the Flood. **c** T. JEFFERSON The principal, with the interest incurring.

†**5** Run *into* (danger etc.); make oneself liable *to*. **M16–E17**.
■ **incurrable** *adjective* (*rare*) **E19**.

incurable /ɪnˈkjʊərəb(ə)l/ *adjective* & *noun*. **ME**.
[ORIGIN Old French & mod. French, or late Latin *incurabilis*, formed as IN-[3] + *curabilis* CURABLE.]
▸ **A** *adjective*. Unable to be cured (*lit.* & *fig.*). **ME**.

LD MACAULAY The faults of James's head and heart were incurable. R. LOWELL He was dying of the incurable Hodgkin's disease.

▸ **B** *noun*. A person who cannot be cured. **M17**.

R. KIPLING Heatherlegh, the Doctor, kept . . a hospital . . for Incurables.

■ **incura'bility** *noun* **M17**. **incurableness** *noun* **E17**. **incurably** *adverb* **E16**.

incuriosity /ɪnˌkjʊərɪˈɒsɪti/ *noun*. **E17**.
[ORIGIN from INCURIOUS after CURIOSITY.]
The quality of being (subjectively) incurious; lack of curiosity about things.

incurious /ɪnˈkjʊərɪəs/ *adjective*. **L16**.
[ORIGIN Partly from Latin *incuriosus* careless, formed as IN-[3] + *curiosus* careful (see CURIOUS), + -OUS; partly from IN-[3] + CURIOUS *adjective*.]
▸ **I** Subjectively.
1 Careless, heedless; untroubled. (Foll. by *of*.) *arch.* **L16**.

CLARENDON In his Cloaths . . , he was not only incurious, but too negligent.

2 Uninquiring; devoid of curiosity. **E17**.

DAY LEWIS Too lazy now to conduct . . research, and too incurious.

†**3** Not precise or particular; uncritical; undiscriminating. M17–M18.

R. HERRICK Base in action as in clothes; Yet . . they will please The incurious villages.

4 Not careful in observation; inattentive. L17.

J. HENRY Resembles the latter, in the bark and leaf so much, that an incurious eye might be deceived.

▶ **II** Objectively.

†**5** Not carefully or exquisitely prepared, made, or done; plain, coarse. E17–E19.

†**6** Not elaborate or abstruse; simple. *rare*. E–M17.

7 Not remarkable; deficient in interest, not arousing curiosity. M18.

■ **incuriously** *adverb* E17. **incuriousness** *noun* E17.

incurrence /ɪnˈkʌr(ə)ns/ *noun*. M17.
[ORIGIN formed as INCURRENT: see -ENCE.]
The action or fact of incurring liabilities etc.

incurrent /ɪnˈkʌr(ə)nt/ *adjective*. L16.
[ORIGIN Latin *incurrent-* pres. ppl stem of *incurrere* INCUR: see -ENT.]
1 Orig., falling within (a period). Later, running in; penetrating into the interior. L16.
2 Serving as or providing an entrance. M19.

incursion /ɪnˈkəːʃ(ə)n/ *noun*. Also †**en-**. LME.
[ORIGIN Latin *incursio(n-)*, from *incurs-* pa. ppl stem of *incurrere* INCUR: see -ION.]
1 A hostile invasion; a sudden attack; a raid. LME.

N. CHOMSKY Thailand blockaded the Cambodian coast and carried out border incursions. *fig*.: W. PALEY The sudden and critical incursion of the disease.

2 The action of running in or running against. E17.

S. JOHNSON The inevitable incursion of new images.

incursive /ɪnˈkəːsɪv/ *adjective*. L16.
[ORIGIN medieval Latin *incursivus*, from Latin *incurs-*: see INCURSION, -IVE.]
Given to making incursions; aggressive; invasive.

incurvate /ɪnˈkəːvət/ *adjective*. LME.
[ORIGIN Latin *incurvatus* pa. pple, formed as INCURVATE *verb*: see -ATE[2].]
Incurved.

incurvate /ˈɪnkəːveɪt/ *verb*. L16.
[ORIGIN Latin *incurvat-* pa. ppl stem of *incurvare* INCURVE *verb*: see -ATE[3]. Cf. INCURVATE *adjective*.]
1 *verb trans*. Bring into a curved shape; bend; crook; *spec*. bend or curve inwards. L16.
†**2** *verb intrans*. Curve; bend, bow. M–L17.

incurvation /ɪnkəːˈveɪʃ(ə)n/ *noun*. E17.
[ORIGIN Latin *incurvatio(n-)*, formed as INCURVATE *verb*: see -ATION.]
1 The action or process of bending or curving; an instance of this. E17. ▸†**b** Bowing in reverence or worship. E17–E18.
2 The condition of being bent; curved formation, curvature; an instance of this. M17.
3 A curving inwards; the condition of being curved inwards. E19.

incurvature /ɪnˈkəːvətʃə/ *noun*. *rare*. E19.
[ORIGIN formed as INCURVATE *verb*: see -URE.]
A curving inwards; an inward curvature or bend.

incurve /ˈɪnkəːv/ *noun*. L19.
[ORIGIN from the verb.]
An inward curve; *spec*. in BASEBALL & SOFTBALL, the curving of a pitched ball inwards (towards the batter), (the course of) a ball pitched so as to curve in this way.

incurve /ɪnˈkəːv/ *verb*. LME.
[ORIGIN Latin *incurvare*, formed as IN-[2] + *curvare* CURVE *verb*.]
1 *verb trans*. Bend into a curve; bend (something) inwards. Freq. as ***incurved*** *ppl adjective*. LME.
2 *verb intrans*. Curve or bend (inwards). E18.

incus /ˈɪŋkəs/ *noun*. Pl. **incudes** /ˈɪŋkjʊdiːz, ɪnˈkjuːdiːz/. M17.
[ORIGIN Latin *incus*, *incud-* anvil (from its shape).]
1 ANATOMY & ZOOLOGY. The middle of the three small bones which conduct sound through the mammalian ear, homologous with the quadrate of reptiles. Cf. MALLEUS, STAPES. M17.
2 ZOOLOGY. In rotifers, a part of the chitinous mouth apparatus, upon which the mallei work. M19.

incuse /ɪnˈkjuːz/ *adjective & noun*. E19.
[ORIGIN Latin *incusus* pa. pple of *incudere*: see INCUSE *verb*.]
(A figure or an impression on a coin etc.) that has been hammered or stamped in.

incuse /ɪnˈkjuːz/ *verb trans*. M19.
[ORIGIN Latin *incus-* pa. ppl stem of *incudere* forge.]
Impress (a figure etc.) by stamping; mark (a coin etc.) with an impressed figure.

incut /ˈɪnkʌt/ *adjective*. L19.
[ORIGIN from IN-[1] + CUT *ppl adjective*.]
Set in (as if) by cutting.

incyst *verb* var. of ENCYST.

Ind. *abbreviation*.
1 Independent.
2 India.
3 Indian.
4 Indiana.

indaba /ɪnˈdɑːbə/ *noun*. E19.
[ORIGIN Zulu *indaba* discussion.]
1 A conference between or with members of southern African black peoples. E19.
2 A person's business, problem, or concern. *S. Afr. colloq*. L20.

indagate /ˈɪndəgeɪt/ *verb trans*. Now *rare* or *obsolete*. E17.
[ORIGIN Latin *indagat-* pa. ppl stem of *indagare* investigate: see -ATE[3].]
Search into; investigate.
■ **indaˈgation** *noun* (an) investigation L16. **indagator** *noun* an investigator E17.

indamine /ˈɪndəmiːn/ *noun*. L19.
[ORIGIN from INDO-[2] + AMINE.]
CHEMISTRY. A blue dye, $NH_2C_6H_4$ $N{=}C_6H_4{=}NH$; any of various blue and green derivatives of this, used to make safranines.

†**indanger** *verb* var. of ENDANGER.

Indanthrene /ˈɪndanθriːn/ *noun*. Also **-en** /-ɛn/, **i-**. L19.
[ORIGIN from INDO-[2] + ANTHR(ACENE + -ENE.]
CHEMISTRY. (Proprietary name for) any of a large class of vat dyes derived from or containing indanthrone or other anthraquinone compounds. Also (**i-**), indanthrone.

indanthrone /ˈɪndanθrəʊn/ *noun*. E20.
[ORIGIN from INDANTHRENE + -ONE.]
CHEMISTRY. (Any of numerous dyes derived from) a blue aromatic compound, $C_{28}H_{14}N_2O_4$, the molecule of which consists of two anthraquinone nuclei linked by imino groups.

indart /ɪnˈdɑːt/ *verb trans*. Also †**en-**. L16.
[ORIGIN from IN-[1], EN-[1] + DART *verb*.]
Cause to dart in.

indazole /ˈɪndəzəʊl/ *noun*. L19.
[ORIGIN from INDO-[2] + AZ(O- + -OLE[2].]
CHEMISTRY. (Any derivative of) a crystalline compound, $C_7H_6N_2$, in which a benzene ring is fused to a pyrazole ring.

†**indear** *verb*, †**indearment** *noun* vars. of ENDEAR, ENDEARMENT.

†**indeavour** *verb & noun* var. of ENDEAVOUR.

indebt /ɪnˈdɛt/ *verb trans*. L16.
[ORIGIN Back-form. from INDEBTED, perh. after French *endetter*.]
1 Involve in debt. Chiefly *refl*. L16.
2 Bring under an obligation. E17.

indebted /ɪnˈdɛtɪd/ *adjective*. Also †**en-**. ME.
[ORIGIN from Old French *endetté* pa. pple of *endetter* involve in debt, refashioned after Latin (medieval Latin *indebitare*): see IN-[2], DEBT *noun*, -ED[1].]
1 Under obligation to another on account of some liability incurred or claim unsatisfied; liable for some omission of duty etc.; bound. Long *arch. rare*. ME.

JOSEPH HALL When I have promised, I am indebted; and debts may be claimed, must be paid.

2 Under obligation on account of money borrowed; owing money, in debt (*to*). LME.
†**be indebted** owe (a specified sum).
3 Under obligation for favours etc. received; owing gratitude *to* (someone or something) *for* a benefit. LME.

F. MARRYAT They were indebted to him for the situation they hold now in the forest.

■ **indebtedness** *noun* (**a**) the condition of being under obligation for services etc. rendered; (**b**) the condition of being in debt; the sum owed: M17. **indebtment** *noun* (*rare*) indebtedness M17.

†**indecence** *noun*. *rare*. Only in 18.
[ORIGIN from INDECENT (perh. after French *indécence*): see -ENCE.]
= INDECENCY 1.

indecency /ɪnˈdiːs(ə)nsi/ *noun*. L16.
[ORIGIN Latin *indecentia*, from *indecent-*: see INDECENT, -ENCY.]
1 Unseemliness; unbecoming or outrageous conduct; an instance of this. L16.

H. SPENCER The indecency of excluding . . the English at the same time that other strangers are received.

†**2** Unseemliness of form; an instance of this. L16–M17.

J. SYLVESTER Th'unpleasing blemish of deformed marks; As lips too great, . . Or sinking nose, or such indecencies.

3 A quality or condition which offends against recognized standards of decency. Also, an indecent act, an offence against decency. L17.

C. DARWIN The hatred of indecency . . is a modern virtue.

indecent /ɪnˈdiːs(ə)nt/ *adjective*. L16.
[ORIGIN Old French & mod. French *indécent* or Latin *indecent-*, formed as IN-[3] + DECENT.]
1 Unbecoming; in extremely bad taste; highly unsuitable. L16.

J. A. FROUDE It is indecent to owe money to a political antagonist. *Sunday (Kolkata)* Most such foundation stones were laid in indecent haste.

†**2** Uncomely, inelegant. L16–M18.

J. BLAGRAVE His thighs lean, his feet and knees indecent.

3 Offending against recognized standards of decency, esp. in relation to sexual matters; immodest; suggesting or tending to obscenity. E17.

E. TEMPLETON The nightgown was not made of transparent stuff; this would have been indecent. R. ELLMANN Yeats circulated a testimonial of support for Wilde at the time of the prosecution for indecent behaviour.

indecent assault a sexual attack not involving rape. ***indecent exposure***.
■ **indecently** *adverb* L16. **indecentness** *noun* (*rare*) E18.

indeciduous /ɪndɪˈsɪdjʊəs/ *adjective*. M17.
[ORIGIN from IN-[3] + DECIDUOUS.]
†**1** Not liable to be shed; permanently attached. Only in M17.
2 BOTANY. Not deciduous; evergreen. M18.

indecipherable /ɪndɪˈsʌɪf(ə)rəb(ə)l/ *adjective*. E19.
[ORIGIN from IN-[3] + DECIPHERABLE.]
Unable to be deciphered.
■ **indecipheraˈbility** *noun* L19. **indecipherableness** *noun* E19. **indecipherably** *adverb* E20.

indecision /ɪndɪˈsɪʒ(ə)n/ *noun*. M18.
[ORIGIN French *indécision*, formed as IN-[3] + DECISION.]
Lack of decision; inability to make up one's mind; hesitation. Also (*rare*), an instance of this.

indecisive /ɪndɪˈsʌɪsɪv/ *adjective*. E18.
[ORIGIN from IN-[3] + DECISIVE. Cf. UNDECISIVE.]
1 Not such as to decide a matter; inconclusive. E18.

LD MACAULAY On the Upper Rhine . . an indecisive predatory war was carried on. E. DOWDEN In place of truth he found only a conflict of indecisive reasonings.

2 Characterized by indecision; undecided; hesitating. L18.

C. BLACKWOOD Always an indecisive man, he was incapable of either rejecting or accepting their advice.

3 Uncertain; not definite, indistinct. E19.

T. HARDY A contrasting prospect eastward, in the shape of indecisive and palpitating stars.

■ **indecisively** *adverb* E19. **indecisiveness** *noun* L18.

indeclinable /ɪndɪˈklʌɪnəb(ə)l/ *adjective & noun*. LME.
[ORIGIN French *indéclinable* from Latin *indeclinabilis*, formed as IN-[3] + *declinare* DECLINE *verb*: see -ABLE.]
▶ **A** *adjective*. †**1** Undeviating, unchangeable, constant. LME–M17.
2 GRAMMAR. Unable to be declined; having no inflections. LME.
▶ **B** *noun*. GRAMMAR. An indeclinable word. M16.
■ **indeclinableness** *noun* M17. **indeclinably** *adverb* E17.

indecomposable /ˌɪndiːkəmˈpəʊzəb(ə)l/ *adjective*. E19.
[ORIGIN from IN-[3] + DECOMPOSABLE.]
Unable to be decomposed.
■ **indecomposaˈbility** *noun* M20.

indecorous /ɪnˈdɛk(ə)rəs/ *adjective*. L17.
[ORIGIN from Latin *indecorus*, formed as IN-[3] + DECOROUS, + -OUS.]
†**1** Unbecoming, inappropriate. Only in L17.
2 Lacking decorum or propriety; improper; in bad taste. Also (*rare*), immodest, indecent. L17.

M. SINCLAIR Quietly, and with no indecorous haste, she went . . into the drawing-room to receive Rawcliffe. W. S. CHURCHILL Stories of keyholes, of indecorous costumes and gestures, regaled the public ear.

■ **indecorously** *adverb* E19. **indecorousness** *noun* L17.

indecorum /ɪndɪˈkɔːrəm/ *noun*. L16.
[ORIGIN Latin, use as noun of neut. sing. of *indecorus* adjective: see INDECOROUS.]
1 An indecorous action or proceeding; an offence against recognized standards of behaviour. L16.

G. GROTE This was a flagrant indecorum, and known violation of the order of the festival.

2 The quality of being indecorous; lack of decorum; improper behaviour. M17.

A. BELL A general improvement in public behaviour helped to prevent any further general indecorum.

indeed /ɪnˈdiːd/ *adverb*. Orig. two words. ME.
[ORIGIN from IN *preposition* + DEED *noun*. See also ***in deed*** s.v. DEED *noun*.]
▶ **I** **1** In truth, really; *postpositive* definitely, without doubt. ME.

L. MORRIS Amid the crowd of youths He showed a Prince indeed. D. H. LAWRENCE He was indeed a brave man. S. BEDFORD Melanie's sister was very ill indeed.

indeed and indeed *arch. colloq.* really and truly.
2 In reality; in real nature etc. as opp. to what is merely apparent. LME.

L. MORRIS The Muses' Eyes, who were indeed Women, though god-like.

3 In point of fact, as a matter of fact. M16.

D. du Maurier John . . might leave the cups till morning to be washed, as indeed he had.

4 Admittedly. **M16.**

J. T. Fowler Latin, not classical indeed, but good of its kind.

5 In speech, expr. an emphasized (affirmative or negative) reply or response. **L16.** ▸**b** With approving or ironic echo. **M18.**

R. Lehmann 'Poor fellow. You give him my greetings.' . . 'I will indeed'. **b** Disraeli 'Who is this Mr. Grey?' 'Who, indeed!'

6 (*interrog.*) Really? Is it so? **L16.**

Dickens 'That's Jarsper's.' 'Indeed?' said Mr Datchery.

▸**II 7** As *interjection*. Expr. irony, contempt, incredulity, etc. **M19.**

J. Ruskin Damask curtains indeed! That's all very fine. B. Jowett 'O, indeed,' I said, 'what a wonderful thing, and what a great blessing!'

▪ **indeedy** *adverb* (*colloq.*, chiefly *N. Amer.*) = INDEED *adverb* 5 **M19.**

indefatigable /ɪndɪˈfatɪɡəb(ə)l/ *adjective*. **E17.**
[ORIGIN French †*indéfatigable* (now *infatigable*) or Latin *indefatigabilis*, formed as IN-³ + DE- + *fatigare* exhaust: see -ABLE.]
Unable to be wearied or tired out; untiring; unremitting in effort.

C. Chaplin The American is . . an indefatigable tryer. P. Gay His indefatigable efforts to secure the guardianship.

▪ **indefatigaˈbility** *noun* **M17.** **indefatigableness** *noun* **M17.** **indefatigably** *adverb* **L16.**

indefeasible /ɪndɪˈfiːzɪb(ə)l/ *adjective*. **M16.**
[ORIGIN from IN-³ + DEFEASIBLE.]
(Esp. of a claim, right, etc.) not liable to be made void; unable to be forfeited or annulled.
▪ **indefeasiˈbility** *noun* **E19.** **indefeasibleness** *noun* (*rare*) **M18.** **indefeasibly** *adverb* **M16.**

indefectible /ɪndɪˈfɛktɪb(ə)l/ *adjective*. **M17.**
[ORIGIN from IN-³ + DEFECTIBLE.]
1 Not liable to failure or decay; that cannot fall short or be destroyed. **M17.**
2 Not subject to defect; faultless. **M19.**
▪ **indefectiˈbility** *noun* **E17.** **indefectibly** *adverb* (*rare*) **M19.**

†**indefective** *adjective*. **M17–E18.**
[ORIGIN medieval Latin *indefectivus*, formed as IN-³ + late Latin *defectivus* DEFECTIVE.]
Free from defect; faultless, flawless.

indefensible /ɪndɪˈfɛnsɪb(ə)l/ *adjective*. **E16.**
[ORIGIN from IN-³ + DEFENSIBLE.]
1 Unable to be defended or maintained in argument; unjustifiable. **E16.**

A. Lurie To do that would be both morally and practically indefensible.

2 Incapable of being defended by armed force. **M16.**

J. A. Michener Barbarians were free to come storming across their indefensible eastern frontier.

▪ **indefensiˈbility** *noun* **E19.** **indefensibleness** *noun* **L17.** **indefensibly** *adverb* **L18.**

†**indeficient** *adjective*. **L15–M19.**
[ORIGIN French †*indéficient* or late Latin *indeficient-*, formed as IN-³ + DEFICIENT.]
Unfailing, unceasing.
▪ †**indeficiency** *noun* **E17–M18.** †**indeficiently** *adverb* **LME–E17.**

indefinable /ɪndɪˈfʌɪnəb(ə)l/ *adjective & noun*. **L17.**
[ORIGIN from IN-³ + DEFINABLE.]
▸**A** *adjective*. Unable to be defined or exactly described; not susceptible of definition. **L17.**

H. Sturgis There was that indefinable sense of spring in the air.

▸**B** *noun*. An indefinable person or thing. **E19.**
▪ **indefinaˈbility** *noun* **E20.** **indefinableness** *noun* **L19.** **indefinably** *adverb* **M19.**

indefinite /ɪnˈdɛfɪnɪt/ *adjective & noun*. **M16.**
[ORIGIN Latin *indefinitus*, formed as IN-³ + DEFINITE *adjective*.]
▸**A** *adjective* **I 1** Having no clearly determined being or character; indeterminate, vague, undefined. **M16.**

O. Manning The smudge, pale and indefinite at first, deepened in colour. B. Emecheta He had to be satisfied with that indefinite answer.

2 Of undetermined extent, amount, or number; unlimited. **L16.** ▸†**b** Boundless, infinite. **M17–M18.**

U. Bentley She had been taken into a nursing home for an indefinite period.

▸**II** *spec.* **3** GRAMMAR. Of a word or tense: not defining or determining the thing, place, time, or manner to which it refers. **M16.**
4 LOGIC. Of a proposition: having no mark of quantity, not distinguishing between some and all. **M16.**
5 BOTANY. **a** Of stamens or other floral parts: too numerous to be easily counted. **M19.** ▸**b** Of an inflorescence etc.: racemose and capable of continued (axial) growth. **M19.**
– SPECIAL COLLOCATIONS: **indefinite article** the individualizing adjective *a*, *an*, or its equivalents in other languages. **indefinite integral** MATH. an integral expressed without limits and hence containing an indeterminate additive constant.

▸**B** *noun*. An indefinite thing, word, statement, etc.; a thing of indefinite nature or meaning, or which cannot be classed, specified, or defined. **L16.**
▪ **indefinitely** *adverb* (*a*) to an indefinite extent, for an indefinite period; (*b*) in an indefinite manner, without specification, vaguely: **LME.** **indefiniteness** *noun* **L16.**

indefinition /ˌɪndɛfɪˈnɪʃ(ə)n/ *noun*. **L19.**
[ORIGIN from IN-³ + DEFINITION.]
A condition of being indefinite.

indefinitive /ɪndɪˈfɪnɪtɪv/ *adjective*. *rare*. **L16.**
[ORIGIN from IN-³ + DEFINITIVE *adjective*.]
Not definitive; indeterminate.

indefinitude /ɪndɪˈfɪnɪtjuːd/ *noun*. **L17.**
[ORIGIN from INDEFINITE after *infinite*, *infinitude*.]
†**1** The condition of having no known limit; indefinable number or amount. Only in **L17.**
2 Lack of definiteness or precision; undefined state. **E19.**

indefinity /ɪndɪˈfɪnɪti/ *noun*. *rare*. **E17.**
[ORIGIN from INDEFINITE after *infinite*, *infinity*.]
†**1** = INDEFINITUDE 1. Only in **17.**
2 = INDEFINITUDE 2. **M18.**

indeformable /ɪndɪˈfɔːməb(ə)l/ *adjective*. **L19.**
[ORIGIN from IN-³ + DEFORMABLE.]
Not deformable; unable to be put out of shape.

indehiscent /ɪndɪˈhɪs(ə)nt/ *adjective*. **E19.**
[ORIGIN from IN-³ + DEHISCENT.]
BOTANY. Of a fruit: not dehiscent, not splitting open to release the seed.
▪ **indehiscence** *noun* **M19.**

indelectable /ɪndɪˈlɛktəb(ə)l/ *adjective*. *rare*. **M18.**
[ORIGIN from IN-³ + DELECTABLE.]
Unpleasant, disagreeable.

indeliberate /ɪndɪˈlɪb(ə)rət/ *adjective*. Now *rare*. **E17.**
[ORIGIN from IN-³ + DELIBERATE *adjective*.]
†**1** Of a person, quality, etc.: lacking in deliberation; rash. Only in **17.**
2 Of an action: done without deliberation or forethought; hasty; spontaneous. **M17.**
▪ **indeliberately** *adverb* **L17.** **indelibeˈration** *noun* **E17.**

indelible /ɪnˈdɛlɪb(ə)l/ *adjective*. **L15.**
[ORIGIN French *indélébile* or Latin *indelebilis*, formed as IN-³ + DELIBLE.]
Unable to be deleted, blotted out, or effaced (*lit.* & *fig.*); permanent; (of ink, a pencil, etc.) that makes permanent marks.

C. Darwin Man still bears in his bodily frame the indelible stamp of his lowly origin. J. C. Powys The striking originality . . of the young servant had made an indelible impression upon the peer's mind. W. S. Churchill The King . . bears the indelible shame of the deed. G. Priestland A priest has private and indelible powers to celebrate the Mass.

▪ **indeliˈbility** *noun* (*rare*) **E19.** **indelibly** *adverb* **E17.**

indelicate /ɪnˈdɛlɪkət/ *adjective*. **M18.**
[ORIGIN from IN-³ + DELICATE.]
1 Lacking in or offensive to a sense of delicacy or propriety; coarse; indecent. **M18.**
†**2** Of food: coarse. **M–L18.**
3 Lacking in tact or regard for the feelings of others. **E19.**
▪ **indelicacy** *noun* **E18.** **indelicately** *adverb* **E19.**

indemnify /ɪnˈdɛmnɪfʌɪ/ *verb trans.* **E17.**
[ORIGIN from Latin *indemnis* unhurt + -FY. Cf. medieval Latin *indemnificare*.]
1 Preserve, protect, or keep free *from*, secure *against* (harm or loss); secure against legal responsibility for events; give an indemnity to. **E17.**

W. Blackstone The fact indemnified the peace officers . . if they killed any of the mob in endeavouring to suppress such riot.

2 Compensate *for* loss suffered, expenses incurred, disadvantages, annoyances, hardships, etc. **L17.**

H. L. Mencken The man who has been injured should be indemnified for all his expenses.

†**3** Make up for. Only in **M18.**
▪ **indemnifiˈcation** *noun* (*a*) the action or fact of being indemnified; (*b*) a payment or other recompense so made: **M17.** **indemnifier** *noun* **L19.**

indemnity /ɪnˈdɛmnɪti/ *noun*. **LME.**
[ORIGIN Old French & mod. French *indemnité* from late Latin *indemnitas*, from *indemnis* free from loss or hurt, formed as IN-³ + *damnum*: see DAMAGE *noun*, -ITY.]
1 (An undertaking to provide) security or protection against hurt, damage, or loss. **LME.**
2 Compensation for loss or damage incurred; indemnification. **LME.** ▸**b** A sum paid as compensation, orig. & formerly *spec.* to a bishop or archdeacon for losses incurred when a church was impropriated to an abbey etc. Now *esp.*, a payment exacted by a victorious belligerent as a condition of peace. **M16.**
3 A legal exemption from the penalties or liabilities incurred by a course of action. **L17.**
– PHRASES: **act of indemnity** a parliamentary etc. act granting exemption from the penalties attached to any unconstitutional or illegal proceeding. ***double indemnity***: see DOUBLE *adjective* & *adverb*.

indemonstrable /ɪndɪˈmɒnstrəb(ə)l, ɪnˈdɛmən-/ *adjective*. **L16.**
[ORIGIN from IN-³ + DEMONSTRABLE.]
Unable to be demonstrated or proved; *esp.* primary, axiomatic.
▪ **indemonstraˈbility** *noun* **L18.** **indemonstrably** *adverb* **M17.**

indene /ˈɪndiːn/ *noun*. **L19.**
[ORIGIN from IND(OLE + -ENE.]
CHEMISTRY. A colourless liquid bicyclic aromatic hydrocarbon, C_9H_8, which is obtained from coal tar and is an intermediate in the manufacture of synthetic resins etc.; any derivative of this.

indent /ɪnˈdɛnt, ˈɪndɛnt/ *noun*[1]. **L15.**
[ORIGIN from INDENT *verb*[1].]
1 = INDENTURE *noun* 2. **L15.** ▸**b** A certificate of a money claim; *spec.* an indented certificate issued by a government for the principal or interest due on the public debt. *obsolete* exc. *hist.* **L18.**
2 An incision in the edge of a thing; a deep angular recess. **L16.**
3 An official requisition for stores. **L18.**
4 An order for goods, *esp.* (*hist.*) one sent to Britain from abroad. **E19.**
5 An indention in printing or writing; an indented line. **L19.**

indent /ˈɪndɛnt/ *noun*[2]. **L17.**
[ORIGIN from INDENT *verb*[2].]
A dent or depression in a surface.

indent /ɪnˈdɛnt/ *verb*[1]. **LME.**
[ORIGIN Anglo-Norman *endenter*, medieval Latin *indentare*, formed as IN-² + Latin *dent-*, *dens* tooth.]
▸**I 1 a** *verb trans.* Make a toothlike incision or incisions in the edge of; notch; give a zigzag outline to. **LME.** ▸**b** *verb trans.* Form a deep recess or recesses in (a coastline etc.); penetrate deeply. **M16.** ▸**c** *verb intrans.* Recede, form a recess. **L18.**

R. Tate Five longitudinal ribs which indent the edges of the plate. **b** A. Trew The southern side was heavily indented by the bay at Uklarvik, and by Kolfjord. **c** G. Grote At the spot here mentioned, the gulf indents eastward.

†**2** *verb intrans.* Move in a zigzag or serrated line; turn from side to side in one's course. **M16–M17.**

Shakes. *Ven. & Ad.* See the dew-bedabbled wretch Turn, and return, indenting with the way.

3 *verb trans.* Set inward from the margin of the column the beginning of (one or more lines of writing or type); begin (a line etc.) with a blank space. **L17.**

J. Moxon You must indent your Line four Spaces at least. S. Curran Outline tabs let you indent the first line of paragraphs automatically.

4 *verb trans.* Make an incision in (a board, etc.) for the purpose of mortising or dovetailing; join together by this method. **M18.**
▸**II 5** *verb trans.* Cut (a document drawn up in duplicate) with a zigzag, wavy, or other line, so that the two parts exactly tally; draw up (a document) in two or more corresponding copies. *hist.* **LME.**
†**6** *verb intrans.* Enter into an engagement by indentures; make a formal agreement; covenant (*with* a person *for* a thing). **L15–L18.**

Goldsmith I fire with indignation when I see persons wholly destitute of . . genius indent to the press.

†**7** *verb trans.* Contract for, bind oneself to, or promise (as) by making indentures; stipulate, promise. **M16–L18.** ▸†**b** Engage (a person) as a servant etc. (as) by indentures. **L18–E19.**

P. Holland He would not indent ought for his owne securitie.

8 *verb intrans.* Make out a written order with a duplicate or counterfoil; make a requisition (*up*)*on* a person *for* a thing. **E19.**

A. Burgess You will indent for further supplies . . through Dr. Hazard.

9 *verb trans.* Order by an indent; order a supply of (a commodity). **L19.**
▪ †**indentment** *noun* **L16–E18.**

indent /ɪnˈdɛnt/ *verb*[2]. **LME.**
[ORIGIN from IN-² + DENT *verb*.]
†**1** *verb trans.* Inlay, set, emboss. **LME–M18.**
2 *verb trans.* Form as a dent or depression; strike or force inwards so as to form a dent or hollow; imprint by pressure. **LME.**

Dryden Deep Scars were seen indented on his Breast. Pope Deep in the neck his fangs indent their hold.

3 *verb trans.* Make a dent in the surface of (a thing); mark with a surface hollow. **L16.**

Dickens Mr. Pickwick . . indenting his pillow with a tremendous blow. E. Bowen His nose poked slyly out between two of the rails and the same two rails indented his forehead.

4 *verb intrans.* Receive or take an indentation; become indented. **M17.**

indentation /ɪndɛnˈteɪʃ(ə)n/ *noun*. E18.
[ORIGIN from INDENT *verb*¹, *verb*² + -ATION.]
▸ **I** from INDENT *verb*¹.
1 A cut, notch, or angular incision in an edge; a deep recess in a coastline; a series of incisions. E18.

H. T. BUCKLE The Greek coast is full of indentations. H. JACOBSON A faint fetching indentation in her left nostril which intrigued me.

2 The action of indenting; the condition of being indented. M19.

F. HEATH The indentation assuming various shapes, often being deeply incised.

3 = INDENTION 2. M19.
hanging indentation: see HANGING *adjective*.
▸ **II** from INDENT *verb*².
4 The action of impressing so as to form a dent; a depression thus formed; a deep depression in a surface. M19.

Times Injurious compression of . . soil, by the indentation of its wheels. E. O'BRIEN The . . goblets . . have beautiful indentations to fit exactly the print of a thumb or a finger.

– COMB.: **indentation hardness**: as determined by an indentation test; **indentation test**: for determining the hardness of a solid by making an indentation in a sample under standard conditions and measuring its size or the distance moved by the indenter.

indented /ɪnˈdɛntɪd/ *ppl adjective*. LME.
[ORIGIN from INDENT *verb*¹, *verb*² + -ED¹.]
▸ **I** from INDENT *verb*¹.
1 Having the edge or margin cut with angular incisions; deeply or strongly serrated. LME. ▸**b** Having a serrated or zigzag figure, direction, or course; constructed with salient and re-entrant angles. L16.
2 HERALDRY. Of an ordinary etc.: having a series of toothlike indentations or notches. LME.
3 Of a legal document: cut zigzag or wavy at the top or edge; cut into counterparts by a zigzag line. LME.
4 Bound or engaged by an indenture or formal covenant. M18.
5 (Of type or writing) set inward so as to break the line of the margin. M19.
▸ **II** from INDENT *verb*².
6 Impressed, forced in so as to make a hollow in a surface. Also, marked with depressions or dents. M17.

indenter /ɪnˈdɛntə/ *noun*. Also **-or**. M17.
[ORIGIN from INDENT *verb*¹, *verb*² + -ER¹, -OR.]
▸ **I** from INDENT *verb*¹.
1 A person who orders something by indent. M17.
▸ **II** from INDENT *verb*².
2 A thing which produces indentations; *spec.* a small hard object used for producing an indentation in a solid (as in an indentation test). E20.

indenting /ɪnˈdɛntɪŋ/ *noun*. LME.
[ORIGIN from INDENT *verb*¹, *verb*² + -ING¹.]
▸ **I** from INDENT *verb*¹.
1 = INDENTATION 1, 2. LME.
2 The making of an indenture or indent. LME.
▸ **II** from INDENT *verb*².
3 = INDENTATION 4. L16.
†**4** Inlaying or embossing; inlaid work. Only in M18.

indention /ɪnˈdɛnʃ(ə)n/ *noun*. M18.
[ORIGIN Irreg. from INDENT *verb*¹, *verb*² + -ION.]
▸ **I** from INDENT *verb*¹.
1 = INDENTATION 1, 2. M18.
2 The indenting of a line etc. in printing or writing; the leaving of a blank space at the beginning of a line at the commencement of a new paragraph. E19.
hanging indention: see HANGING *adjective*.
▸ **II** from INDENT *verb*².
3 = INDENTATION 4. *rare*. M19.

indentor *noun* var. of INDENTER.

indenture /ɪnˈdɛntʃə/ *noun*. LME.
[ORIGIN Branch I from Anglo-Norman *endenture* from medieval Latin *indentura*, from *indentatus* pa. pple of *indentare*: see INDENT *verb*¹, -URE; branch II from INDENT *verb*².]
▸ **I 1** †**a** Jointing by means of notches or indentations. Only in LME. ▸**b** The action of indenting or notching an edge; an incision, indentation, or notch on the edge of a thing. L17.
2 A deed between two or more parties with mutual covenants executed in copies which all have their edges indented for identification; a sealed agreement or contract. LME. ▸**b** A contract by which an apprentice is bound to a master. Formerly also, a contract by which a person was bound to service in the British colonies. LME. ▸**c** An official or formal list, inventory, certificate, voucher, etc., orig. one prepared in duplicate. LME. ▸**d** *fig.* A contract; (a) mutual agreement. M16.
b take up one's indentures receive one's indentures back on completion of apprenticeship.
†**3** A zigzag line or course; a doubling back. L16–L18.
▸ **II** †**4** An inlaying or embossing. Only in M17.
5 A hollow or depression in a surface. L18.
■ **indentureship** *noun* the position of being indentured as an apprentice, servant, etc. L19.

indenture /ɪnˈdɛntʃə/ *verb*. M17.
[ORIGIN from the noun.]
†**1** *verb intrans.* Move in a zigzag line. Only in M17.
†**2** *verb intrans.* Enter into an indenture; covenant. Only in M17.
3 *verb trans.* Bind by indentures, esp. as an apprentice. Freq. as ***indentured*** *ppl adjective*. M17.
4 *verb trans.* Make an indentation in; indent. L18.

independable /ɪndɪˈpɛndəb(ə)l/ *adjective*. E19.
[ORIGIN from IN-³ + DEPENDABLE.]
Not dependable; untrustworthy.

independence /ɪndɪˈpɛnd(ə)ns/ *noun*. M17.
[ORIGIN from INDEPENDENT *adjective*, partly after French *indépendance*: see -ENCE.]
1 The condition or quality of being independent. M17.

W. STUBBS The proud independence of the Percies was becoming . . a source of danger. C. IVES Americans . . still have enough independence of thought . . to work out their own way of progress. LYNDON B. JOHNSON The new West African republic of Senegal was celebrating its independence.

Declaration of Independence: see DECLARATION 4.
2 An income sufficient to relieve one from the need to earn one's living. E19.

THACKERAY You are heir to a little independence.

– COMB.: **Independence Day** a day celebrating the anniversary of national independence; *esp.* 4 July in the US, commemorating the making of the Declaration of Independence in 1776.

independency /ɪndɪˈpɛnd(ə)nsi/ *noun*. E17.
[ORIGIN formed as INDEPENDENCE + -ENCY.]
1 = INDEPENDENCE 1. Now *rare*. E17.
2 CHRISTIAN CHURCH (**I-**.) The principle that each local congregation is autonomous and responsible to God alone; *spec.* Congregationalism. Now *hist.* M17.
3 = INDEPENDENCE 2. M18.
4 An autonomous state. E19.

independent /ɪndɪˈpɛnd(ə)nt/ *adjective*, *noun*, & *adverb*. E17.
[ORIGIN from IN-³ + DEPENDENT *noun*, *adjective*, partly after French *indépendant*.]
▸ **A** *adjective*. **1** Not subject to the authority or control of any person, country, etc.; free to act as one pleases, autonomous. (Foll. by *of*.) E17.

ADAM SMITH An independent workman, such as a weaver or shoe-maker. E. R. PITMAN In 1829, Greece was acknowledged as an independent state, having its own king. H. J. LASKI The Church is independent of all civil institution.

2 a Not dependent or contingent on something else for its existence, validity, effectiveness, etc. Foll. by *of*, †*on*. E17. ▸**b** Not influenced or affected by others; (of an inquiry, audit, investigator, observer, etc.) (carried out by people) outside the organization concerned. L18.

a STEELE Beauty and Merit are Things real, and independent on Taste and Opinion. H. MOORE It has a life of its own, independent of the object it represents. **b** J. A. H. MURRAY Here four independent witnesses . . confirm each other.

3 CHRISTIAN CHURCH (**I-**.) Believing in or practising Independency; *spec.* Congregational. Now *hist.* M17.
4 Not dependent on another for financial support; *spec.* rich enough not to need to earn one's living. L17. ▸**b** Of income: sufficient to make one financially independent. Esp. in ***independent means***. L18.

G. GISSING What I inherited . . makes me independent; there is no need of any arrangements about money.

5 Not influenced by others in one's opinions or conduct; thinking or acting for oneself. M18. ▸**b** That is an independent in politics; not attached to any particular party. L19. ▸**c** Refusing to become indebted to others for help. L19.

R. COBDEN An independent and energetic man who will vote as he pleases. **c** OED The widow . . is very independent, and refuses all pecuniary aid.

6 MATH. **a** (Of one of a set of axioms, equations, or quantities) incapable of being expressed in terms of, or derived or deduced from, the others; (of a set) consisting of such axioms etc. M18. ▸**b** Not depending on another quantity for its value. M19.
– SPECIAL COLLOCATIONS: **Independent Broadcasting Authority** a former UK corporation which superseded the Independent Television Authority in 1972 and also took responsibility for commercial sound broadcasting. **independent float** in critical path analysis, the amount of leeway which can occur in any one activity without affecting the overall timing. **Independent Labour Party**: founded by Keir Hardie in 1893, orig. to coordinate efforts to secure parliamentary representation for labour unions, independent of Liberal support. **independent school**: that receives no grant from the Government and is not subject to the control of a local authority. **independent suspension** (in motor vehicles etc.) a form of suspension in which each wheel is supported independently of the others. **independent television** the television service controlled by the Independent Television (or Broadcasting) Authority; ***Independent Television (Authority)***, a corporation, free of direct government control and not financed by licence fees, which until 1972 supervised commercial television broadcasting in Britain. **independent variable** MATH.: whose variation does not depend on that of another.
▸ **B** *noun*. **1** CHRISTIAN CHURCH (**I-**.) A member of an Independent church; *spec.* a Congregationalist. Now *hist.* M17.
2 A person who or thing which is independent; *esp.* a retailer whose shop is not part of a chain. L17. ▸**b** A politician etc. who is not attached to any particular party. Also in names of newspapers. E19.
▸ **C** *adverb*. Independently or irrespective *of*. Formerly also, apart *from*. L17.

G. GROTE Quite independent of regard to the feelings of others.

■ **independentism** *noun* the principles of a person independent in politics or religion; *spec.* (**I-**) = INDEPENDENCY 2: M17. **independently** *adverb* M17.

indeprivable /ɪndɪˈpraɪvəb(ə)l/ *adjective*. Now *rare*. M18.
[ORIGIN from IN-³ + DEPRIVABLE.]
Of which one cannot be deprived; that cannot be taken away.

indescribable /ɪndɪˈskraɪbəb(ə)l/ *adjective* & *noun*. L18.
[ORIGIN from IN-³ + DESCRIBABLE.]
▸ **A** *adjective*. **1** That cannot be described; indefinite, vague. L18.

QUILLER-COUCH A bald-headed man with hairy hands . . and the indescribable air of a matrimonial agent.

2 That is beyond description; too beautiful, terrible, etc., to be adequately described. L18.

A. J. P. TAYLOR It gave me a decade of intense, almost indescribable misery.

▸ **B** *noun*. Something that cannot be described; formerly *spec.* in *pl.* (*slang*), trousers. L18.
■ **indescribaˈbility** *noun* (*a*) the quality of being indescribable; (*b*) an indescribable thing: E19. **indescribableness** *noun* (*rare*) L19. **indescribably** *adverb* L18.

indesert /ɪndɪˈzəːt/ *noun*. Now *rare*. E17.
[ORIGIN from IN-³ + DESERT *noun*¹.]
1 In *pl.* Faults. E17.
2 Lack of merit. M17.

indesignate /ɪnˈdɛzɪɡnət/ *adjective*. *arch.* M19.
[ORIGIN from IN-³ + DESIGNATE *adjective*.]
LOGIC. Not quantified; indefinite.

†**indesinent** *adjective*. E17–L18.
[ORIGIN from IN-³ + Latin *desinent-* pres. ppl stem of *desinere* leave off: see -ENT.]
Unceasing, perpetual.
■ †**indesinently** *adverb* L16–M18.

indestructible /ɪndɪˈstrʌktɪb(ə)l/ *adjective* & *noun*. L17.
[ORIGIN from IN-³ + DESTRUCTIBLE.]
▸ **A** *adjective*. Impossible to destroy. L17.
▸ **B** *noun*. An indestructible thing. M19.
■ **indestructiˈbility** *noun* L17. **indestructibleness** *noun* M19. **indestructibly** *adverb* M19.

indetectable /ɪndɪˈtɛktəb(ə)l/ *adjective*. M19.
[ORIGIN from IN-³ + DETECTABLE.]
Impossible to detect; too slight to be detected.
■ Also **indetectible** *adjective* M19.

indeterminable /ɪndɪˈtəːmɪnəb(ə)l/ *adjective*. L15.
[ORIGIN Late Latin *indeterminabilis*, formed as IN-³ + *determinabilis* finite: see DETERMINABLE.]
†**1** Unable to be limited in respect of range, number, etc. *rare*. L15–L17.
2 Of a dispute, difficulty, etc.: unable to be decided. E17.
3 Unable to be established or ascertained definitely. M17. ▸**b** BIOLOGY. Of which the species etc. cannot be determined. M19.
■ **indeterminableness** *noun* (*rare*) L19. **indeterminably** *adverb* in an indeterminable or (formerly) indefinite manner L15.

indeterminacy /ɪndɪˈtəːmɪnəsi/ *noun*. M17.
[ORIGIN from INDETERMINATE + -ACY.]
The quality of being indeterminate; lack of definiteness.
indeterminacy principle, **principle of indeterminacy** PHYSICS = UNCERTAINTY ***principle***.

indeterminate /ɪndɪˈtəːmɪnət/ *adjective*. LME.
[ORIGIN Late Latin *indeterminatus*, formed as IN-³ + DETERMINATE *adjective*.]
†**1** Not marked or specified. Only in LME.
2 Not fixed in extent, amount, character, etc.; of uncertain size etc.; indefinite. E17. ▸**b** MATH. Of an equation: having an unlimited number of solutions. Of a quantity: having no definite value; having no definable value (as 0/0, ∞ – ∞, etc.). E18. ▸**c** Of a statement, word, etc.: vague, lacking in precision. L18. ▸**d** ENGINEERING. = HYPERSTATIC. Usu. with ***statically***. E20.

V. WOOLF All were dressed in indeterminate shades of grey and brown. A. BROOKNER A lady of indeterminate age, her hair radiantly ash blonde, her nails scarlet. **c** H. WILSON The evidence is scrappy and indeterminate, partly because of the informal nature of Cabinet proceedings.

3 Not fixed or established; uncertain. E17.

W. H. PRESCOTT The place of its sittings, before indeterminate . . was fixed at Valladolid.

4 Not settled or decided. M17.
5 Not determined by motives; acting freely. M19.
– SPECIAL COLLOCATIONS: **indeterminate sentence**: that leaves the date of a prisoner's release dependent on his or her conduct and progress. **indeterminate vowel** the obscure vowel /ə/ heard in 'a moment ago'; = SCHWA.

■ **indeterminately** *adverb* (*a*) vaguely, indefinitely; †(*b*) without distinction, indifferently: L16. **indeterminateness** *noun* M17.

indetermination /ˌɪndɪtəːmɪˈneɪʃ(ə)n/ *noun*. E17.
[ORIGIN from INDETERMINATE + -ATION.]
†**1** An indeterminate number or quantity. Only in E17.
2 Undetermined or unsettled quality or condition; uncertainty. M17.

indetermined /ɪndɪˈtəːmɪnd/ *adjective*. Now *rare*. E17.
[ORIGIN from IN-³ + DETERMINED *adjective*.]
Not determined, fixed, or decided; indeterminate.

indeterminism /ɪndɪˈtəːmɪnɪz(ə)m/ *noun*. L19.
[ORIGIN from IN-³ + DETERMINISM.]
1 The theory that human action is not wholly determined by motives. L19.
2 = INDETERMINACY. E20.
■ **indeterminist** *noun & adjective* (*a*) *noun* a holder of the doctrine of indeterminism; (*b*) *adjective* of, pertaining to, or holding the doctrine of indeterminism: L19. **indetermiˈnistic** *adjective* E20.

†**indevirginate** *adjective*. *rare*. E17–E19.
[ORIGIN from IN-³ + obsolete pa. pple of DEVIRGINATE.]
Virgin; unsullied.

†**indevoted** *adjective*. M17–M18.
[ORIGIN from IN-³ + DEVOTED *adjective*.]
Disloyal (*to*), disaffected.

indevotion /ɪndɪˈvəʊʃ(ə)n/ *noun*. E16.
[ORIGIN from IN-³ + DEVOTION.]
Lack of (religious) devotion; indevout feeling or conduct.

indevout /ɪndɪˈvaʊt/ *adjective*. LME.
[ORIGIN from IN-³ + DEVOUT: orig. translating late Latin *indevotus*, formed as IN-³ + Latin *devotus*: see DEVOUT.]
Lacking in religious spirit; not devout.
■ **indevoutly** *adverb* L17. **indevoutness** *noun* M19.

index /ˈɪndɛks/ *noun*. Pl. **indexes**, (esp. *techn.*) **indices** /ˈɪndɪsiːz/. LME.
[ORIGIN Latin *index*, *indic-* forefinger, informer, etc., formed as IN-² + *-dex*, *-dic-*, from base repr. by *dicere* say, Greek *deiknunai* show.]
1 The finger used in pointing, the forefinger. Now usu. ***index finger***. LME. ▸**b** ORNITHOLOGY. The second (occas. the first) digit of the manus in a bird's wing. L19.
2 A piece of wood, metal, etc., which serves as a pointer; *spec.* (in a scientific instrument) a pointer which moves along a graduated scale so as to show movements or amounts. L16. ▸**b** The arm of a surveying instrument; an alidade. L16. ▸**c** A hand of a clock or watch; the gnomon of a sundial. Now *rare*. L16.
3 A thing which serves to point *to* a fact or conclusion; a sign or indication *of*. L16.

M. HOLROYD Her letters . . are a good index to her state of mind. CLIVE JAMES A town where the index of all achievement is to have your name in lights.

card index: see CARD *noun*². **Expurgatory Index** = ***Index Expurgatorius*** below. **Index Expurgatorius** /ˌɛkspəːgəˈtɔːrɪəs/ [Latin = expurgatory] ROMAN CATHOLIC CHURCH (now *hist.*) a list of passages to be deleted from a book before it was considered fit for reading; a list of authors considered fit to read only after the removal of objectionable matter from their works, later included in the *Index Librorum Prohibitorum*. ***Index Librorum Prohibitorum*** /lɪˈbrɔːrəm ˌprəʊhɪbɪˈtɔːrəm/ [Latin = of forbidden books] ROMAN CATHOLIC CHURCH (now *hist.*) an official list of heretical or otherwise undesirable books forbidden to the faithful or sanctioned only after the removal of objectionable passages. **the Index** = ***Index Librorum Prohibitorum*** above.

4 A list of things in (usu. alphabetical) order; *esp.* a list, usu. at the end of a book, giving the names, topics, etc., mentioned in the book and the places where they occur. Formerly also, a table of contents. L16.
5 †**a** MUSIC. = DIRECT *noun* 2. L16–M19. ▸**b** TYPOGRAPHY. A hand-shaped symbol with a pointing finger used to draw attention to a note etc. Also called ***fist***. E18.
6 MATH. **a** A subscript or superscript symbol denoting some characteristic of a quantity or function, as the exponent in x^2, etc. L17. ▸†**b** The integral part of a logarithm. L17–E19. ▸**c** COMPUTING. A quantity which is fixed in relation to the operations laid down by a program, but which takes a prescribed sequence of values as the program is run. M20. ▸**d** COMPUTING. Any of a sequence of numbers, each specifying one of an ordered set of items. M20.
7 A number or formula expressing a specific property, esp. a ratio; *esp.* in ANATOMY, a formula expressing the ratio between two dimensions (esp. of the skull). E19.
cephalic index: see CEPHALIC *adjective*. ***refractive index***: see REFRACTIVE 4. ***wind-chill index***: see WIND *noun*¹.
8 ECONOMICS. (A number in) a scale relating (usu. in the form of a percentage) the level of prices, wages, etc., at a particular time to those at a date taken as a base. L19.
cost-of-living index, ***retail price index***, etc.
9 ENGINEERING. Each of the predetermined movements during indexing. M20.
– COMB.: **index case** MEDICINE the first identified case in a group of related cases of a particular communicable or heritable disease; ***index finger***: see sense 1 above; **index fossil** a fossil that is useful for dating and correlating the strata in which it is found; also called ***guide fossil***; **index-link** *verb trans.* adjust the value of (a pension etc.) to the level of the cost-of-living index; **index-linked** *adjective* (of a pension, bond, etc.) of which the value is adjusted in line with the cost-of-living index, to offset the effects of inflation; **index number** (*a*) = sense 8 above; (*b*) a number in an index; *esp.* a vehicle registration number; **index register** COMPUTING a register whose contents may be added to or subtracted from the address portion of an instruction before execution, which is thus increased or decreased by a prescribed amount, enabling the instruction to be used repeatedly on different operands.
■ **indexless** *adjective* (of a book etc.) lacking an index M19.

index /ˈɪndɛks/ *verb*. E18.
[ORIGIN from the noun.]
1 *verb trans.* Provide (a book etc.) with an index; enter (an item) in an index. E18.
2 *verb trans.* Serve as an index to; indicate. L18.
3 *verb trans.* ROMAN CATHOLIC CHURCH (now *hist.*). Place (a book) on the *Index Librorum Prohibitorum*. E19.
4 *verb trans.* & *intrans.* ENGINEERING. Move (esp. by partial rotation) from one predetermined position to another, in order that an operation may be repeated at different locations, or different operations performed; obtain (a desired number of divisions or operations) thus. E20.
5 *verb trans.* COMPUTING. Modify (an instruction or its address) by causing the addition of the contents of an index register to the address before execution; carry out (a series of operations) by this means. M20.
■ **indexable** *adjective* M20. **indeˈxation** *noun* adjustment in rates of payment etc. to reflect variations in the cost-of-living index or other economic indicator M20. **indexer** *noun* a person who compiles an index to a book etc. M19. **indexible** *adjective* M20.

indexical /ɪnˈdɛksɪk(ə)l/ *adjective*. E19.
[ORIGIN Irreg. from INDEX *noun* + -ICAL.]
Arranged like or relating to the index of a book etc.
■ **indexically** *adverb* in the manner of an index, alphabetically E18.

indi- /ˈɪndi/ *combining form*.
[ORIGIN from INDIGO.]
CHEMISTRY. Derived from or related to indigo.
■ **indiˈrubin** *noun* a red crystalline substance, $C_{16}H_{10}O_2N_2$, resembling indigotin but with oxidized indolyl rather than indoxyl nuclei M19.

India /ˈɪndɪə/ *noun*. M17.
[ORIGIN A subcontinent, and a country occupying much of that subcontinent, in southern Asia.]
1 Used *attrib.* to designate things made in, associated with, or imported from the subcontinent of India, or the present Republic of India, or (*hist.*) pertaining to the East India Company or the government of India under British rule (1858–1947). Cf. INDIAN *adjective* 1. M17.
India House *hist.* the office of the East India Company in London. **India ink** (now *N. Amer.*) = ***Indian ink*** s.v. INDIAN *adjective*. **India Office** *hist.* the department of the British Government dealing with Indian affairs. **India paper** (*a*) a thin paper orig. imported from China, used for high quality prints and illustrations; (*b*) a thin tough opaque printing paper, used esp. for bibles. **India proof** an artist's or engraver's proof specially printed on India paper. See also INDIARUBBER.
2 *ellipt.* India paper, India silk, etc. E18.

indialite /ˈɪndɪəlʌɪt/ *noun*. M20.
[ORIGIN from INDIA + -LITE.]
MINERALOGY. The hexagonal dimorphous form of cordierite.

Indiaman /ˈɪndɪəmən/ *noun*. Pl. **-men**. E18.
[ORIGIN from INDIA + MAN *noun* as in *man of war*, etc.]
hist. A ship engaged in trade with the Indian subcontinent; *spec.* (also ***East Indiaman***) a ship of large tonnage belonging to the East India Company.

Indian /ˈɪndɪən/ *noun & adjective*. ME.
[ORIGIN from INDIA + -AN.]
▸ **A** *noun*. **1** A native or inhabitant of the subcontinent of India or the Republic of India. ME. ▸**b** *hist.* A European, esp. a Briton, (formerly) resident in the Indian subcontinent. Chiefly in ***old Indian***, ***returned Indian***. M18.
2 A member of any of the aboriginal peoples of America. Also more fully ***American Indian***. See note below. M16. ▸**b** Any of the hunted players in the children's game of cowboys and Indians. L19.
Apache Indian, ***Sioux Indian***, etc. ***North American Indian***, ***South American Indian***, etc. ***Red Indian***: see RED *adjective*.
3 The language spoken by any American Indian people or (*rare*) any of the Indian peoples of Asia. M16.
4 *ellipt.* **a** Indian corn, tea, etc. M17. ▸**b** An Indian meal; an Indian restaurant. *colloq.* L20.
5 a An indigenous inhabitant of the Philippines, *esp.* one who has converted to Christianity. L17. ▸†**b** An indigenous inhabitant of Australia or New Zealand. M18–M19.
6 *The* southern constellation Indus. L17.
▸ **B** *adjective*. **1** Belonging to, made in, or originating from the subcontinent of India or the present Republic of India. Formerly also, Asian. LME.

MILTON Toward the Springs Of Ganges or Hydaspes, Indian streams. W. ROBERTS Of China . . the Emperor and other Indian monarchs.

2 Of, belonging to, or characteristic of the aboriginal peoples of America. L16.

WORDSWORTH The shrouded Body . . Answering with more than Indian fortitude.

– SPECIAL COLLOCATIONS: **Indian almond** (the edible kernel of) a Malayan terminalia, *Terminalia catappa*, widely planted in the tropics. **Indian bean tree** a North American tree, *Catalpa bignonioides* (family Bignoniaceae), widely planted in urban parks in Europe. ***Indian cedar***: see CEDAR 1. **Indian clubs** (a pair of) bottle-shaped clubs swung to exercise the arms in gymnastics. ***Indian corn***: see CORN *noun*¹ 3b. **Indian cress** the nasturtium, *Tropaeolum majus*, formerly used as a salad plant. **Indian cup** the pitcher plant, *Sarracenia purpurea*. **Indian currant** = ***coralberry*** s.v. CORAL *noun*. **Indian defence** CHESS any of various defences in which Black opens by moving the king's knight, usu. following with a fianchetto. ***Indian devil***: see DEVIL *noun* 5. ***Indian* ELEPHANT**. **Indian English**: spoken by an inhabitant of the Indian subcontinent whose native language is not English. **Indian fig** = ***prickly pear*** s.v. PRICKLY *adjective*. **Indian fig tree** = ***banyan tree*** s.v. BANYAN 4. **Indian file** (in) single file, the order usu. adopted by N. American Indians in moving through woods. **Indian giver** *N. Amer.* a person who asks back a present he or she has given or expects an exact equivalent in return. **Indian grass** *N. Amer.* a tall perennial prairie grass, *Sorghastrum nutans*, often grown as fodder. **Indian hemp** (*a*) a tropical race of hemp, *Cannabis sativa* subsp. *indica*, the source of marijuana; (*b*) a N. American plant, *Apocynum cannabinum* (family Apocynaceae), the bark of which yields a fibre formerly used to make ropes etc. **Indian ink** (*a*) a black pigment made orig. in China and Japan; (*b*) a dark ink made from this, used esp. in drawing and technical graphics. **Indian lake** a crimson pigment made from stick-lac treated with alum and alkali. **Indian liquorice** (the root of) the jequirity, *Abrus precatorius*. ***Indian madder***: see MADDER *noun* 1. **Indian mallow** a yellow-flowered mallow, *Abutilon theophrasti*, of warmer parts of Eurasia, which yields a fibre like jute and is widely naturalized; also called ***American jute***, ***Chinese jute***, ***velvetleaf***. **Indian meal**: ground from maize. **Indian millet** (*a*) = BULRUSH ***millet***; (*b*) = DURRA. ***Indian Mutiny***: see MUTINY *noun* 2. **Indian Ocean** the ocean south of India, extending from the east coast of Africa to Malaya. **Indian paint** a N. American boraginaceous plant, *Lithospermum canescens*, whose root yields a red dye. ***Indian paintbrush***: see ***paintbrush*** (b) s.v. PAINT *noun*. **Indian path** *N. Amer.* a narrow path through the woods, such as is made by Indians moving in single file. **Indian** PEAFOWL. **Indian pear** = ***juneberry*** s.v. JUNE. **Indian physic** any of several N. American plants with medicinal properties, esp. *Gillenia trifoliata*, of the rose family. **Indian pink** = CAROLINA ***pink***. **Indian pipe** a N. American saprophytic plant, *Monotropa uniflora* (family Pyrolaceae), with a solitary drooping flower. **Indian plantain** any of several N. American plants of the genus *Arnoglossum*, of the composite family. ***Indian poke***: see POKE *noun*² 2b. **Indian potato** any of several plants with tubers eaten by American Indians, *esp.* the potato bean, *Apios americana*. **Indian problem** CHESS: based on the theme of combining two pieces to allow an opponent to escape from stalemate, while using them to prepare a trap in the form of discovered checkmate. **Indian pudding** a New England dish made of maize, molasses, and suet. **Indian red** orig., a yellow-red earth containing ferric oxide; now chiefly, (the colour of) any of various red pigments prepared by oxidation of ferrous salts. **Indian restaurant**: operated by people from the Indian subcontinent, serving Indian food. ***Indian rhinoceros***: see RHINOCEROS 1. ***Indian rice***: see RICE *noun*² 2. **Indian rope trick** the supposed feat, by natives of the Indian subcontinent, of climbing an upright unsupported length of rope. ***Indian* ROSEWOOD**. †**Indian rubber** = INDIARUBBER. ***Indian runner***: see RUNNER 5d. ***Indian saffron***: see SAFFRON *noun*. ***Indian* SARSAPARILLA**. **Indian shot** the plant *Canna indica*, from its round hard black seeds. **Indian sign** *N. Amer.* (*a*) a track revealing the presence of Indians; (*b*) *colloq.* a magic spell; a curse, a jinx. ***Indian silk-cotton tree***: see SILK *noun & adjective*. **Indian summer** a period of calm dry warm weather in late autumn in the northern US or elsewhere; *fig.* a tranquil late period of life etc. **Indian tea** (*a*) tea grown in India or Sri Lanka, considered stronger than China tea; (*b*) any of several N. American plants whose leaves are used to make an infusion. ***Indian teak***: see TEAK *noun* 1. **Indian tobacco** a N. American medicinal plant, *Lobelia inflata* (family Lobeliaceae), which tastes like tobacco when chewed. ***Indian* TRAGACANTH**. **Indian turnip** (the edible corm of) a N. American aroid plant, *Arisaema triphyllum*. **Indian weed** *arch.* (*US*) tobacco. **Indian yellow** an orange-yellow pigment orig. obtained from the urine of cows fed on mango leaves.
– NOTE: *Indian* and *Red Indian* are regarded as old-fashioned and inappropriate when referring to the native peoples of America. Since the 1970s *American Indian* has been steadily replaced in the US, esp. in official contexts, by *Native American*, but it remains acceptable, although it is preferable to refer to specific peoples where possible.

Indianan /ɪndɪˈɑːnən/ *noun*. M20.
[ORIGIN from *Indiana* (see INDIANIAN) + -AN.]
= INDIANIAN.

Indianesque /ɪndɪəˈnɛsk/ *adjective*. M19.
[ORIGIN from INDIAN + -ESQUE.]
Of N. American Indian type.

Indianian /ɪndɪˈanɪən/ *noun*. L18.
[ORIGIN from *Indiana* (see below) + -IAN.]
A native or inhabitant of Indiana, a north central state of the US.

Indianise *verb* var. of INDIANIZE.

Indianism /ˈɪndɪənɪz(ə)m/ *noun*. M17.
[ORIGIN from INDIAN + -ISM.]
1 (Devotion to) the customs and culture of N. American Indians. M17.
2 A word or idiom characteristic of Indian English or N. American Indians. M19.
■ **Indianist** *noun* a student of or expert in the languages, customs, etc., of the Indian subcontinent M19.

Indianize /ˈɪndɪənʌɪz/ *verb*. Also **-ise**. L17.
[ORIGIN from INDIAN + -IZE.]
†**1** *verb intrans.* Live like a N. American Indian. *rare*. L17–E18.
2 *verb trans.* Make Indian or N. American Indian in character, form, habits, etc. E18.

I

■ **Indiani'zation** *noun* E20.

Indianness /ˈɪndɪənnɪs/ *noun*. M20.
[ORIGIN from INDIAN + -NESS.]
The quality of being Indian or displaying Indian characteristics.

Indianologist /ɪndɪəˈnɒlədʒɪst/ *noun*. L19.
[ORIGIN from INDIAN + -OLOGIST.]
An expert on or student of American Indians.

indiarubber /ˈɪndɪəˌrʌbə, ˌɪndɪəˈrʌbə/ *noun & adjective*. Also **I-**, and (earlier) as two words. L18.
[ORIGIN from INDIA + RUBBER *noun*[1].]
▸ **A** *noun*. **1** Rubber, caoutchouc. L18.
2 An eraser made of rubber. L18.
3 In *pl.* Rubber overshoes. *US*. M19.
– COMB.: **indiarubber plant** = *rubber plant* s.v. RUBBER *noun*[1].
▸ **B** *adjective*. Made of indiarubber; flexible or elastic like indiarubber. M19.

Indic /ˈɪndɪk/ *adjective*. M19.
[ORIGIN Latin *Indicus* from Greek *Indikos*, from INDIA: see -IC.]
Of or pertaining to India; *esp.* designating or pertaining to the Indian branch of the Indo-Iranian languages (cf. INDO-ARYAN).

indican /ˈɪndɪkan/ *noun*. M19.
[ORIGIN from Latin *indicum* INDIGO + -AN.]
CHEMISTRY. **1** An indoxyl glucoside occurring in the leaves of woad and indigo plants and yielding indigo on hydrolysis and oxidation. M19.
2 A substance (orig. thought similar to the above) found in urine, in which it occurs as a product of amino-acid metabolism: (the potassium salt of) indoxylsulphuric acid, $C_8H_6NOSO_2OH$. M19.
■ **indica'nuria** *noun* (*MEDICINE*) the presence of excessive amounts of indican in the urine L19.

indicant /ˈɪndɪk(ə)nt/ *adjective & noun*. E17.
[ORIGIN Latin *indicant-* pres. ppl stem of *indicare* INDICATE: see -ANT[1].]
▸ **A** *adjective*. That indicates; indicative. *rare*. E17.
▸ **B** *noun*. A thing which indicates. E17.

indicate /ˈɪndɪkeɪt/ *verb trans*. Pa. pple **-ated**, (earlier) †**-ate**. E17.
[ORIGIN Latin *indicat-* pa. ppl stem of *indicare*, formed as IN-[2] + *dicare* proclaim: see -ATE[3].]
1 Point out or to, make known, show; (of a meter etc.) register a reading of; (esp. *MEDICINE*) suggest as a desirable or necessary course of action (usu. in *pass.*). E17. ▸**b** Of a person: direct attention to (by speech or writing, occas. by gesture). E19.

> *British Medical Journal* Recourse to this method is . . indicated when the teeth to be replaced are front teeth. P. G. WODEHOUSE Strategy, rather than force, seemed to the curate to be indicated. J. MARQUAND The rather battered silver travelling clock . . indicated that the hour was a quarter past six. N. MAILER I mention this as a way of indicating how hard it was to locate his place. **b** C. HAMPTON He indicates a pile of books on a table by the bed.

2 Point to the presence, existence, or reality of; be a sign or symptom of; imply. E18.

> N. SYMINGTON Then she said something which indicated a powerful resentment of me. D. W. GOODWIN Studies indicate that most of the drinking drivers are . . serious problem drinkers.

3 State or express briefly; give an indication of. M18.

> A. BAIN My last argument . . can only be indicated here; the full illustration belongs to a more advanced stage of the exposition. O. MANNING Quintin indicated he could find his own way up to the drawing-room.

indication /ɪndɪˈkeɪʃ(ə)n/ *noun*. LME.
[ORIGIN Latin *indicatio(n-)*, formed as INDICATE: see -ATION.]
1 The action or an instance of indicating; something that indicates or suggests; a sign, a symptom, a hint; *MEDICINE* a symptom which suggests a particular disease, syndrome, or remedial course of action. LME. ▸**b** A reading registered by a meter or other instrument. M18. ▸**c** *MINING*. Something that indicates the presence of ore, oil, etc. *US*. M19.

> J. B. PRIESTLEY There was every indication now that the fine autumn weather . . had at last come to an end. K. CLARK A great artist whose early work gives no indication of the character of his genius. G. HUNTINGTON He would have liked to hear whether she was going. She gave no indication either way. W. GOLDING Day after day a complex of tiny indications had added up and now presented me with a picture.

2 Something indicated or suggested; *MEDICINE* a remedy or treatment which is indicated by the symptoms as desirable. LME.

indicative /ɪnˈdɪkətɪv/ *adjective & noun*. LME.
[ORIGIN Old French & mod. French *indicatif*, *-ive* from late Latin *indicativus* (translating Greek *horistikē* (sc. *egklisis* mood)), formed as INDICATE: see -ATIVE.]
▸ **A** *adjective*. **1** *GRAMMAR*. Designating the mood of a verb of which the essential function is to state an objective fact (as opp. to something wished, thought of, etc., by the speaker). LME. ▸**b** Of a statement etc.: having the verb in the indicative mood. M17.

> **b** A. J. AYER Every indicative sentence, whether it is literally meaningful or not, shall be regarded as expressing a statement.

2 That indicates or points out; that hints or suggests. LME.

> RICHARD SAUNDERS The next is called Index, the indicative or demonstrative finger.

3 Giving indications *of*; suggestive *of*. M17.

> P. G. WODEHOUSE Percy gave a languid gesture indicative of the man of affairs whose time was not his own.

▸ **B** *noun*. *GRAMMAR*. (An instance of) the indicative mood; a verb in the indicative mood. M16.
■ **indicatively** *adverb* E17.

indicator /ˈɪndɪkeɪtə/ *noun*. M17.
[ORIGIN from INDICATE + -OR. In branch II translating Latin *indicator*, (sense 7) French *indicateur*.]
▸ **I 1** A thing that serves to give an indication or suggestion (*of* something else); an indication. M17. ▸**b** A geological clue to the presence of gold. L19. ▸**c** *ECOLOGY*. A group or species of plants or animals whose presence acts as a sign of particular environmental conditions. E20.

> J. A. FROUDE They [clothes] were the outward indicators of the inward and spiritual nature. A. LURIE The sack suit is a middle-class indicator.

2 A person who or thing which points out or indicates. E19. ▸**b** *PHILOSOPHY*. A word which is the only one usable as a means of reference to something. M20.

> J. A. FROUDE Birds . . were celestial indicators of the gods' commands. **b** *attrib.*: W. V. QUINE The indicator words: 'this', 'that', 'I', 'you', 'he', 'now', 'here', 'then', 'there', 'today', 'tomorrow'.

3 A device which indicates the condition of a machine etc.; a recording instrument attached to a piece of apparatus; a pointer, light, etc., which draws attention or gives warning. M19. ▸**b** A display board giving current information, e.g. for train or aircraft departures. E20. ▸**c** A device (now usu. a flashing light) on a motor vehicle for indicating an intended change of direction. M20.

> *attrib.*: *Which?* For most cookers, . . the indicator light going out gave a satisfactory indication that the oven was nearly at its steady temperature.

4 Something used in a scientific experiment to indicate some quality, change, etc.; *esp.* in *CHEMISTRY*, a substance which may be used to indicate whether the concentration of some ion (esp. hydrogen) is above or below a particular value, usu. by a characteristic colour. M19. ▸**b** An isotope used as a (radioactive) tracer. E20.
▸ **II** †**5** *ANATOMY*. The muscle which extends the index finger. *rare*. L17–E20.
6 = ***honeyguide*** (a) s.v. HONEY *noun*. L18.
7 *MATH*. = TOTIENT. E20.
– COMB.: **indicator diagram**: of the variation of pressure and volume within the cylinder of a reciprocating engine; **indicator lamp**: which lights up to show that a machine etc. is in a certain condition.

indicatory /ɪnˈdɪkət(ə)ri, ˈɪndɪkeɪt(ə)ri/ *adjective*. L16.
[ORIGIN from INDICATE + -ORY[2].]
†**1** *MEDICINE*. Indicating the nature or tendency of a disease; symptomatic. L16–E17.
2 Serving to indicate; indicative *of* something. M18.

> C. W. THOMSON The box which covers the coil and indicatory part of the thermometer. W. BELSHAM Great preparations . . indicatory of an approaching siege.

indicatrix /ɪndɪˈkeɪtrɪks, ɪnˈdɪkətrɪks/ *noun*. Pl. **-trices** /-trɪsiːz/. M19.
[ORIGIN mod. Latin, fem. of Latin INDICATOR: see -TRIX.]
1 *GEOMETRY*. The curve in which a surface is cut by a plane close and parallel to the tangent plane at a point, indicating the nature of the curvature at that point. *rare*. M19.
2 *CRYSTALLOGRAPHY*. An imaginary ellipsoidal surface whose axes represent the refractive indices of a crystal. Also ***optical indicatrix***. L19.

indicavit /ɪndɪˈkeɪvɪt/ *noun*. *obsolete* exc. *hist*. L16.
[ORIGIN Latin = he has pointed out, 3 sing. perf. indic. used as noun.]
LAW. A writ of prohibition by which a suit raised by one ecclesiastic against another for tithes amounting to at least a fourth part of the profits of an advowson might be removed from the ecclesiastical court to the king's court.

indices *noun pl.* see INDEX *noun*.

indicia *noun* pl. of INDICIUM.

indicial /ɪnˈdɪʃ(ə)l/ *adjective*. M19.
[ORIGIN from INDICIUM + -AL[1].]
Of, pertaining to, or of the nature of an index or indicium; indicative.

indicible /ɪnˈdɪsɪb(ə)l/ *adjective*. Long *rare*. L15.
[ORIGIN French, or late Latin *indicibilis* formed as IN-[3] + Latin *dicere* say + *-ibilis* -IBLE.]
Unspeakable, inexpressible.

indicium /ɪnˈdɪsɪəm/ *noun*. Pl. **-cia** /-sɪə/. E17.
[ORIGIN Latin, formed as INDEX *noun*.]
An indication, a sign; a distinguishing mark. Usu. in *pl.*

> SIR W. SCOTT The corpse afforded no other *indicia* respecting the fate of Kennedy.

†**indico** *noun & adjective* var. of INDIGO.

indicolite /ɪnˈdɪkəlʌɪt/ *noun*. Also **-g-** /-g-/. E19.
[ORIGIN from Latin *indicum* INDIGO + -O- + -LITE.]
An indigo-blue variety of tourmaline, used as a gemstone.

indict /ɪnˈdʌɪt/ *verb*[1] *trans*. Also (earlier) †**endite**, †**indite**. ME.
[ORIGIN Legal Anglo-Norman *enditer* corresp. in form but not in sense to Old French *enditier* (= INDITE *verb*[2]), from Proto-Romance, from Latin *indict-* pa. ppl stem of *indicere* proclaim, appoint, impose, formed as IN-[2] + *dicere* pronounce, utter.]
1 Bring a charge against; accuse (a person) of a crime or *as* a culprit by legal process. ME.

> L. STEFFENS The son of a former mayor was indicted for misconduct in office. *Orlando (Florida) Sentinel* Brown was indicted . . on a charge of giving a gun to a felon.

2 Make a subject of indictment *against*. *rare*. M17.

> SIR W. SCOTT It is indited against Simon Glover . . that he hath spoken irreverent discourses.

■ **indic'tee** *noun* a person indicted for a crime L16. **indicter** *noun* LME.

†**indict** *verb*[2] *trans*. M16–E18.
[ORIGIN Latin *indict-*: see INDICT *verb*[1].]
Declare authoritatively, announce, proclaim.

indictable /ɪnˈdʌɪtəb(ə)l/ *adjective*. LME.
[ORIGIN from INDICT *verb*[1] + -ABLE.]
1 Liable to be indicted for an offence. LME.
2 Of an offence: that makes a person liable to indictment, with trial by jury. Opp. ***summary***. E18.
■ **indictably** *adverb* E19.

indiction /ɪnˈdɪkʃ(ə)n/ *noun*. LME.
[ORIGIN Latin *indictio(n-)*, from *indict-*: see INDICT *verb*[1], -ION.]
1 *hist*. The fiscal period of fifteen years, instituted by the Emperor Constantine in AD 313, which became a means of dating ordinary events and transactions. LME. ▸**b** A specified year in the indiction, indicated by number. LME. ▸**c** The decree of the Roman Emperors fixing the valuation on which the property tax was assessed at the beginning of each indiction; the tax paid on the basis of this assessment. L16.
2 The action of ordaining or announcing authoritatively and publicly; an appointment, a declaration, a proclamation. *arch*. M16.

> H. L'ESTRANGE According to the Kings indiction, the Assembly met . . at Edenburgh.

■ **indictional** *adjective* (*rare*) E18.

in dictione /ˌɪn dɪktɪˈəʊni/ *adjectival phr*. E19.
[ORIGIN Latin, translating Greek *para tēn lexin* in relation to the wording (Aristotle).]
Of a logical fallacy: arising from the wording used to express it. Cf. EXTRA DICTIONEM.

†**indictive** *adjective*. M17.
[ORIGIN Sense 1 from Latin *indictivus*, from *indict-*; sense 2 from INDICT *verb*[1]: see -IVE.]
1 Proclaimed or appointed by authority. M17–E18.
2 Containing an indictment, accusatory. *rare*. Only in L19.

indictment /ɪnˈdʌɪtm(ə)nt/ *noun*. Also (earlier) †**endite-**, †**indite-**. ME.
[ORIGIN Anglo-Norman *enditement*, formed as INDICT *verb*[1]: see -MENT.]
1 The action of indicting or accusing, a formal accusation; the legal process (in English Law *hist.*) in which a formal accusation is preferred to and presented by a grand jury. ME. ▸**b** The legal document containing a written accusation of a serious crime to be tried by jury or (in English Law *hist.*) grand jury. E16.

> BUNYAN How sayest thou? Art thou guilty of this indictment or not?

bill of indictment (*a*) (in English Law *hist.*) a written accusation as preferred to a grand jury. (*b*) = sense 1b above.
2 *SCOTS LAW*. A form of process by which a person is brought to trial at the instance of the Lord Advocate; the corresponding formal written charge. M18.
3 *transf.* & *fig.* Censure, condemnation; a writing, a circumstance, etc., that serves to censure or condemn. L19.

> M. IGNATIEFF A speech whose indictment of the Cabinet rang at the end of every paragraph. M. MEYER He composed this poem . . as an indictment of his countrymen for their lassitude.

indie /ˈɪndi/ *noun & adjective*. *colloq.* Also **indy**. E20.
[ORIGIN Abbreviation of INDEPENDENT *noun & adjective*: see -IE.]
▸ **A** *noun*. **1** An independent producer of films, broadcast programmes, records, etc. E20.
2 A musician or band whose music is recorded by an independent company. L20.
3 Deliberately spontaneous and independent music as produced by such bands. L20. ▸**b** A person fond of such music. L20.
▸ **B** *adjective*. Independent; *spec.* of or pertaining to an indie or indies. M20.

Indies /ˈɪndɪz/ *noun pl.* **M16.**
[**ORIGIN** Pl. of *Indy* obsolete & dial. var. of **INDIA**.]
1 (Usu. with *the*.) India and adjacent regions of SE Asia. Also (now *rare*), the West Indies. *arch.* **M16.**
†**2** A region of great wealth, esp. one to which profitable voyages may be made. **L16–M18.**

indifference /ɪnˈdɪf(ə)r(ə)ns/ *noun.* **LME.**
[**ORIGIN** formed as **INDIFFERENCY**: see **-ENCE**.]
1 The quality of being indifferent or neutral, neither good nor bad. Now only, mediocrity. *rare.* **LME.**
†**2** Absence of bias or favour for one side or another; impartiality. **L15–M18.**

HENRY FIELDING Gentlemen.. to be seated with.. seeming indifference.. unless there be any.. whose degrees claim.. precedence.

3 Absence of active feeling for or against; *esp.* absence of care or concern for, or interest in, a person or thing; unconcern, apathy. (Foll. by *to*.) **M17.**

W. C. WILLIAMS She.. fascinated me, not for her beauty.., but for a provocative indifference to rule and order. E. O'BRIEN 'I really don't care'. It was a thing he said often.. to assure himself of his indifference.

4 Lack of difference or distinction between things. Now *rare.* **M17.**
5 The fact of not mattering, or making no difference; unimportance; an instance or thing of unimportance. **M17.**

C. FREEMAN That brief meeting was of complete indifference to him; she was only one of the many people who had inquired about the apartments.

6 Freedom of thought or choice; equal power to take either of two courses. Now *rare.* **E18.**

W. CUNNINGHAM The indifference of the human will, its perfect ability to choose this or that.

– **COMB.**: **indifference curve** *ECONOMICS* a curve on a graph (the axes of which represent quantities of two commodities), which links those combinations of quantities which the consumer regards as of equal value; **indifference map** *ECONOMICS* a graph displaying a family of indifference curves; **indifference point** (*a*) the midpoint of a magnet where the attractions of both poles are equal; (*b*) *PSYCHOLOGY* a position on a scale at which there is apparent subjective equality of two contrasted sensations (as warmth and coolness) or tendencies (as underestimation or overestimation of magnitude).

indifferency /ɪnˈdɪf(ə)r(ə)nsi/ *noun.* Now *rare* or *obsolete.* **LME.**
[**ORIGIN** Latin *indifferentia*, from *indifferent-*: see **INDIFFERENT**, **-ENCY**.]
1 = **INDIFFERENCE** 2. **LME.**
†**2** = **INDIFFERENCE** 6. **M16–L17.**
3 Lack of difference in nature or character; substantial equivalence. **M16.**
4 = **INDIFFERENCE** 5. **M16.**
5 Ambiguity, equivocality. **L16.**
6 = **INDIFFERENCE** 3. **E17.**

indifferent /ɪnˈdɪf(ə)r(ə)nt/ *adjective, noun, & adverb.* **LME.**
[**ORIGIN** Old French & mod. French *indifférent* or Latin *indifferent-* formed as **IN-**[3] + **DIFFERENT** *adjective*.]
▸ **A** *adjective.* **1** Not inclined to prefer one person or thing to another; unbiased, impartial, disinterested; fair, just, even-handed. Now *rare.* **LME.**

H. P. BROUGHAM They dare not go before an impartial judge and indifferent jury.

2 Having no inclination or feeling for or against a person or thing; lacking interest in or feeling for something; unconcerned, unmoved, uninterested. (Foll. by *to*.) **LME.**

E. BOWEN Max seemed indifferent to the rain; though he certainly would not seek it. J. AGEE Richard tried to be sure whether this was said in affection or dislike,.. it was neither, just an indifferent statement of fact. E. JOHNSON Dickens liked and disliked people; he was never merely indifferent.

†**3** Not different; equal, even; identical. **LME–E18.**

R. SCOT It is indifferent to saie in the English toong; She is a witch; or, She is a wise woman.

4 Regarded as not mattering either way; unimportant, immaterial; non-essential. *arch.* **E16.**

DRYDEN Whigs, 'Tis indifferent to your humble servant, whatever your party says or thinks of him.

†**5** Having a neutral relation to (two or more things); impartially applicable; (of a word) equivocal, ambiguous. **E16–L17.**
†**6** Not extreme; moderate; of medium quality, character, size, etc. **E16–E18.**

G. MARKHAM Make not your career too long.. or too short.. but competent and indifferent.

†**7** Having freedom of thought or choice; having equal power to take either of two courses. **M16–L17.**

J. LOCKE A man is at Liberty to lift up his Hand.. or to let it rest quiet: He is perfectly indifferent to either.

†**8** Not more advantageous to one person or party than to another. **M16–M17.**

T. FULLER An indifferent Place, for mutual Ease, in mid-way betwixt both.

9 Not definitely possessing either of two opposite qualities; *esp.* neither good nor bad. **M16.** ▸**b** Not very good; poor, inferior, quite bad. **M16.** ▸**c** In poor health, ailing. *obsolete* exc. *dial.* **M18.**

P. F. STRAWSON The finding of reasons, good, bad or indifferent, for what we believe on instinct. **b** A. S. NEILL Indifferent scholars who, under discipline, scrape through college.. and become.. mediocre doctors, and incompetent lawyers. I. COLEGATE He was an indifferent shot, though not a positively bad one. **c** H. NELSON I have been but very indifferent, but I am much recovered.

10 Neutral in some physical property, as chemically, magnetically, or electrically. Also *BIOLOGY* (*arch.*) (of tissue etc.) undifferentiated. **M19.**
▸ **B** *noun.* **1** A person who is neutral or not partisan; an apathetic person. **M16.**

THACKERAY The indifferents might be counted on to cry King George or King James, according as either should prevail.

2 In *pl.* Immaterial or unimportant things; non-essentials. Now *rare* or *obsolete.* **E17.**
▸ **C** *adverb.* = **INDIFFERENTLY** 4. *arch.* **L16.**

SIR W. SCOTT You have seen me act my part indifferent well.

indifferentism /ɪnˈdɪf(ə)r(ə)ntɪz(ə)m/ *noun.* **L18.**
[**ORIGIN** from **INDIFFERENT** + **-ISM**.]
A spirit of indifference professed and practised; *esp.* the principle that differences of religious belief are of no importance; absence of interest in religious matters.

R. A. VAUGHAN The signs of a growing toleration or indifferentism meet him on every side. R. BOLDREWOOD These people either did not know.. or, with the absurd indifferentism of Englishmen, did not care.

■ **indifferentist** *noun & adjective* (*a*) *noun* an adherent or advocate of indifferentism; (*b*) *adjective* of or pertaining to indifferentism or indifferentists: **L18.**

indifferently /ɪnˈdɪf(ə)r(ə)ntli/ *adverb.* **LME.**
[**ORIGIN** formed as **INDIFFERENTISM** + **-LY**[2].]
1 Equally, alike, indiscriminately. **LME.**
†**2** Impartially. **LME–M19.**
3 Unconcernedly. **LME.**
4 To some extent, moderately, fairly (*well* etc.). Now *rare.* **M16.**
†**5** Neutrally. **E17–E18.**
6 Not very well; poorly, badly. **L17.**

indigena /ɪnˈdɪdʒɪnə/ *noun. arch.* Pl. **-nae** /-niː/. **L16.**
[**ORIGIN** Latin: see **INDIGENOUS**.]
A native, an aboriginal.
■ **indigenal** *adjective & noun* **E18.**

indigence /ˈɪndɪdʒ(ə)ns/ *noun.* **LME.**
[**ORIGIN** Old French & mod. French, or Latin *indigentia*, from *indigent-*: see **INDIGENT**, **-ENCE**.]
†**1** The fact or condition of needing; lack or need *of* a thing; lack, deficiency; requirement. **LME–L18.**
2 Lack of the means of subsistence; poverty, destitution. **LME.**
†**3** An instance of want; a need. **LME–L17.**
■ Also **indigency** *noun* **E17.**

indigene /ˈɪndɪdʒiːn/ *adjective & noun.* **L16.**
[**ORIGIN** French *indigène* from Latin **INDIGENA**.]
▸ †**A** *adjective.* Native, indigenous. **L16–L17.**
▸ **B** *noun.* A native, an aboriginal; *Austral.* a native of Papua or New Guinea. **M17.**

indigenisation *noun* var. of **INDIGENIZATION**.

indigenity /ɪndɪˈdʒɛnɪti/ *noun.* **L19.**
[**ORIGIN** from **INDIGENOUS** + **-ITY**.]
The quality of being indigenous.

indigenization /ɪnˌdɪdʒɪnʌɪˈzeɪʃ(ə)n/ *noun.* Also **-isation**. **M20.**
[**ORIGIN** from **INDIGENOUS** + **-IZATION**.]
The act or process of making predominantly indigenous; adaptation or subjection to indigenous influence or dominance; *spec.* the increased use of indigenous people in government, employment, etc.
■ **inˈdigenist** *noun & adjective* (*a*) *noun* a supporter of indigenization; (*b*) *adjective* pertaining to or favouring indigenization: **M20.** **inˈdigenize** *verb trans.* **M20.**

indigenous /ɪnˈdɪdʒɪnəs/ *adjective.* **M17.**
[**ORIGIN** from Latin *indigena* (a) native from *indi-* strengthened form of *in-* **IN-**[2] + *-gena* from base of *gignere* beget: see **-OUS**.]
1 Born or produced in a particular land or region; (esp. of flora and fauna) native or belonging naturally *to* (a region, a soil, etc.), not introduced. **M17.** ▸**b** *transf.* & *fig.* Inborn, innate. **M19.**

RIDER HAGGARD The indigenous flora and fauna of Kukuanaland. C. STEAD He could tell the indigenous Malays from the new imports from India. C. FRANCIS My.. garden turned out to have only four plants which are indigenous to Britain. **b** L. TRILLING Poetry is indigenous to the very constitution of the mind.

2 Of, pertaining to, or concerned with the native inhabitants of a region. **M19.**

H. READ Objects made by uncultured peoples in accordance with a native and indigenous tradition. N. CHOMSKY What is remarkable about the Indochina war is the inability of the American invaders to establish indigenous governments that can rule effectively.

■ **indigenously** *adverb* **M19.** **indigenousness** *noun* **L19.**

indigent /ˈɪndɪdʒ(ə)nt/ *adjective & noun.* **LME.**
[**ORIGIN** Old French & mod. French from Latin *indigent-*, pres. ppl stem of *indigere* lack, from *indi-* (see **INDIGENOUS**) + *egere* be in want, need: see **-ENT**.]
▸ **A** *adjective.* **1** Lacking in what is necessary; falling short of the proper standard; deficient. **LME.** ▸**b** Destitute *of*, void *of*. *arch.* **L15.** ▸†**c** In need *of*; requiring the aid of. **L16–E18.**
2 Lacking the necessities of life; characterized by poverty; poor, needy. **LME.**
▸ **B** *noun.* An indigent or poor person. **LME.**

†**indigest** *adjective & noun.* **LME.**
[**ORIGIN** Latin *indigestus* unarranged, formed as **IN-**[3] + *digestus* pa. pple of *digerere* **DIGEST** *verb*.]
▸ **A** *adjective.* Undigested; crude, immature, confused; unarranged. **LME–E19.**
▸ **B** *noun.* A shapeless mass. *rare* (Shakes.). Only in **L16.**

indigest /ɪndɪˈdʒɛst, -dʌɪ-/ *verb.* Chiefly *joc.* **E19.**
[**ORIGIN** from **IN-**[3] + **DIGEST** *verb*, after **INDIGESTION**.]
1 *verb trans.* Fail to digest. **E19.**
2 *verb intrans.* Fail to be digested; cause or suffer indigestion. **M19.**

indigested /ɪndɪˈdʒɛstɪd, -dʌɪ-/ *adjective.* **L16.**
[**ORIGIN** from **IN-**[3] + *digested* pa. pple of **DIGEST** *verb*.]
1 Not ordered or arranged; shapeless, unformed, chaotic. **L16.** ▸**b** Not ordered in the mind; not thought out; ill-considered. **L16.**
2 That has not undergone digestion in the stomach. **E17.**

indigestible /ɪndɪˈdʒɛstɪb(ə)l, -dʌɪ-/ *adjective.* **L15.**
[**ORIGIN** French, or late Latin *indigestibilis*, formed as **IN-**[3] + *digestibilis* **DIGESTIBLE**.]
Incapable of being digested, difficult to digest; not easily assimilated as food.

F. KING She felt heavy and sick, as though sated from an indigestible meal. *fig.*: T. SHARPE The contents of Sir Godber's speech were wholly indigestible.

■ **indigestiˈbility** *noun* **E19.** **indigestibleness** *noun* (*rare*) **E17.** **indigestibly** *adverb* **M19.**

indigestion /ɪndɪˈdʒɛstʃ(ə)n, -dʌɪ-/ *noun.* **LME.**
[**ORIGIN** Old French & mod. French, or late Latin *indigestio(n-)*, formed as **IN-**[3] + **DIGESTION**.]
1 Difficulty in digesting; pain or discomfort in the abdomen after eating, often (mistakenly) thought due to a failure to digest food. **LME.** ▸**b** A case or attack of indigestion. **E18.**
2 Undigested condition; (an instance of) disorder, imperfection. *rare.* **M17.**

indigestive /ɪndɪˈdʒɛstɪv, -dʌɪ-/ *adjective.* **M17.**
[**ORIGIN** from **IN-**[3] + **DIGESTIVE**.]
Characterized by, suffering from, or liable to indigestion.

indigitate /ɪnˈdɪdʒɪteɪt/ *verb.* **E17.**
[**ORIGIN** Latin *indigitat-* pa. ppl stem of *indigitare* call upon, invoke. Erron. assoc. with Latin *digitus* finger.]
†**1** *verb trans.* Call; indicate by name; proclaim; declare. Only in **17.**
†**2** *verb trans.* Point out (as) with a finger; show, indicate. **E17–E18.**
3 *verb intrans. ANATOMY* = **INTERDIGITATE** 1. **M19.**

indigitation /ɪnˌdɪdʒɪˈteɪʃ(ə)n/ *noun.* **M17.**
[**ORIGIN** formed as **INDIGITATE** + **-ATION**.]
†**1** The action of pointing out or indicating; an indication; a declaration. **M17–E18.**
2 Computing or conversing by means of the fingers. **E19.**
3 *ANATOMY.* (An) interdigitation (esp. of muscle and tendon). Now *rare.* **M19.**

indign /ɪnˈdʌɪn/ *adjective.* Now only *poet.* **ME.**
[**ORIGIN** Old French & mod. French *indigne* or Latin *indignus*, formed as **IN-**[3] + *dignus* worthy.]
1 Unworthy, undeserving. (Foll. by *of*, *to*.) **ME.**
2 Unworthy of a person or circumstance; unbecoming; shameful, disgraceful. **M16.** ▸**b** Of punishment or suffering: undeserved. **M18.**

indignant /ɪnˈdɪɡnənt/ *adjective.* **L16.**
[**ORIGIN** Latin *indignant-* pres. ppl stem of *indignari* regard as unworthy, from *indignus*: see **INDIGN**, **-ANT**[1].]
Affected with indignation; provoked to anger by something regarded as unworthy or unjust; moved by a mixture of anger, scorn, and contempt. (Foll. by *at*, *with*, *that*.)

DICKENS He feels indignant that Helena's brother should dispose of him so coolly. C. R. MARKHAM He published an indignant pamphlet on the subject of his wrongs.

■ **indignance** *noun* (*rare*) **L16.** **indignancy** *noun* (*rare*) **L18.** **indignantly** *adverb* †(*a*) *rare* with indignity; (*b*) in an indignant manner: **E17.**

I

indignation /ɪndɪɡˈneɪʃ(ə)n/ *noun*. LME.
[ORIGIN Old French & mod. French, or Latin *indignatio(n-)*, from *indignat-* pa. ppl stem of *indignari*: see INDIGNANT, -ATION.]
†**1 a** The action of treating as unworthy of notice; disdain, contempt; contemptuous behaviour. LME–M16. ▸**b** Treating with indignity; an indignity. Long *rare*. E16.
2 Anger excited by a sense of wrong, or by injustice, wickedness, or misconduct; righteous anger. Foll. by *against, at, with,* †*of,* †*upon*. LME.
†**3** Discomfort of the stomach; nauseated condition. *rare*. LME–M17.
– COMB.: **indignation meeting** a meeting to express collective indignation.

indignatory /ɪnˈdɪɡnət(ə)ri/ *adjective*. *rare*. E17.
[ORIGIN from Latin *indignat-* (see INDIGNATION) + -ORY².]
Expressive of indignation.

†**indignify** *verb trans*. L16–M18.
[ORIGIN from IN-³ + DIGNIFY.]
Treat with indignity; dishonour; represent as unworthy.

indignity /ɪnˈdɪɡnɪti/ *noun*. L16.
[ORIGIN French *indignité* or Latin *indignitas*, from *indignus* INDIGN: see -ITY.]
†**1** The quality or condition of being unworthy; unworthiness; in *pl.*, undeserving traits. L16–L17.
2 Unbecoming or dishonourable condition; loss or lack of dignity; humiliating quality. Also, a shameful or undignified action. L16.

GOLDSMITH A mind too proud to stoop to such indignities. A. T. ELLIS The indignity of peering into other people's intimacies had appalled me.

3 Scornful, contemptuous, or humiliating treatment; injury accompanied by insult; an act which causes humiliation, a slight, an affront. L16.

SHAKES. *Temp.* The poor monster's my subject, and he shall not suffer indignity. A. S. BYATT She was afraid . . . of peripheral indignities inflicted by hospitals.

†**4** Anger excited by a wrong; indignation. L16–L18.

indigo /ˈɪndɪɡəʊ/ *noun & adjective*. Also †**-ico**. M16.
[ORIGIN Spanish *índico* from Latin *indicum* from Greek *indikon*, from *indikos*: see INDIC.]
▸ **A** *noun*. Pl. **-os**.
1 A dark blue powder used as a vat dye, orig. obtained from certain plants but now mainly made synthetically. Also, the chief chemical constituent of this, indigotin. M16. ▸**b** A kind or sample of this dye. E17.
2 Any of various plants, esp. of the tropical leguminous genus *Indigofera*, from which indigo or a similar dye is obtainable. E17.
bastard indigo *US* a leguminous plant of the genus *Amorpha*, esp. *A. fruticosa*. **false indigo** (*a*) a leguminous plant of the genus *Baptisia*, esp. *B. tinctoria*; (*b*) = *bastard indigo* above.
3 A deep violet-blue, located in the spectrum between blue and violet. E17.
– COMB.: **indigo bird** (*a*) a N. American bunting, *Passerina cyanea*, the male of which has bright blue plumage; (*b*) any of several parasitic African weaver birds of the genus *Vidua* and the subfamily Viduinae, the males of which have glossy plumage of a blue- or purplish-black colour; **indigo bunting** = *indigo bird* (a) above; **indigo finch** = *indigo bird* above; **indigo plant** = sense 2 above; **indigo snake** a large blue-black, brown, or particoloured colubrid snake, *Drymarchon corais*, found in the south-eastern US and tropical America; also called *cribo*, *gopher snake*; **indigo white** a white soluble crystalline compound, $C_{16}H_{12}N_2O_2$, obtained by reduction of indigotin.
▸ **B** *attrib.* or as *adjective*. Of a deep violet-blue colour. M19.

indigo blue /ˌɪndɪɡəʊ ˈbluː/ *noun & adjectival phr*. E18.
[ORIGIN from INDIGO + BLUE *noun*, *adjective*.]
▸ **A** *noun phr*. **1** The violet-blue colour of indigo. E18.
2 = INDIGOTIN. M19.
▸ **B** *adjectival phr*. Of the blue colour of indigo. M19.

indigoferous /ɪndɪˈɡɒf(ə)rəs/ *adjective*. E19.
[ORIGIN from INDIGO + -FEROUS.]
Bearing or producing indigo.

indigoid /ˈɪndɪɡɔɪd/ *adjective & noun*. E20.
[ORIGIN from INDIGO + -OID.]
CHEMISTRY. ▸**A** *adjective*. Related to indigotin in molecular structure. E20.
▸ **B** *noun*. An indigoid compound, esp. a dye. M20.

indigolite *noun* var. of INDICOLITE.

indigotic /ɪndɪˈɡɒtɪk/ *adjective*. M19.
[ORIGIN formed as INDIGOTIN + -IC.]
Of, pertaining to, or produced from indigo.

indigotin /ɪnˈdɪɡətɪn, ɪndɪˈɡəʊtɪn/ *noun*. M19.
[ORIGIN from INDIGO + euphonic *-t-* + -IN¹.]
CHEMISTRY. A dark-blue crystalline compound, $C_{16}H_{10}N_2O_2$, which is the essential constituent of indigo and has a molecule consisting of two linked indoxyl molecules.

†**indiligent** *adjective*. M16–M18.
[ORIGIN Latin *indiligent-*, formed as IN-³ + *diligent-* attentive, careful: see DILIGENT.]
Inattentive, heedless, careless; idle, slothful.
■ †**indiligence** *noun* L15–M17. †**indiligently** *adverb* M17–L18.

†**indiminishable** *adjective*. *rare*. M17–L18.
[ORIGIN from IN-³ + DIMINISH + -ABLE.]
That cannot be diminished.

Indio /ˈɪndɪəʊ/ *noun*. Pl. **-os**. M19.
[ORIGIN Spanish *indio*, Portuguese *índio* Indian.]
A member of any of the indigenous peoples of America or eastern Asia in areas formerly subject to Spain or Portugal.

indirect /ɪndɪˈrɛkt, ɪndʌɪ-/ *adjective*. LME.
[ORIGIN Old French & mod. French, or medieval Latin *indirectus*, formed as IN-³ + DIRECT *adjective*.]
1 GRAMMAR. †**a** Not in full grammatical concord. Only in LME. ▸**b** Of speech or narration: put in a reported form, not in the speaker's own words; oblique. M19.
2 Of a route, path, etc.: not straight, crooked, devious. Also, of a movement: oblique. L15. ▸**b** Of an action or feeling: not straightforward and honest; not open; deceitful, corrupt. Now *rare* or *obsolete*. M16. ▸**c** Of a succession, title, etc.: not derived by direct descent. L16.
3 Not taking the shortest course to the desired objective; not going straight to the point; not acting or exercised with direct force; roundabout. L16. ▸**b** LOGIC. Of a proof, method, etc.: proceeding by consideration of the proposition contradictory to that in question. M17. ▸**c** Of taxation: levied on goods and services (and hence paid by the consumer in the form of increased prices) rather than on income or profits. E19. ▸**d** Of a scientific technique, process, etc.: involving intermediate stages, not effecting a simple conversion. M19.
4 Not directly aimed at or attained; not immediately resulting from an action or cause. E19.

B. JOWETT Happiness is not the direct aim, but the indirect consequence of the good government.

5 Of or pertaining to work and expenses which cannot be apportioned to any particular job or undertaking; pertaining to overhead charges or subsidiary work. E20.
– SPECIAL COLLOCATIONS: **indirect address** COMPUTING: specifying the location of information about the address of the operand, rather than the location of the operand itself. **indirect aggression** aggression against another nation by other than military means. **indirect evidence** = CIRCUMSTANTIAL *evidence*. **indirect fire** gunfire aimed at a target which cannot be seen. **indirect lighting**: that makes use of light diffused by reflection from the ceiling, walls, or other surface(s). **indirect object** GRAMMAR: denoting a person or thing affected by a verbal action but not primarily acted on (e.g. *him* in *give him the book*). **indirect passive** GRAMMAR: having for its subject the indirect or prepositional object of the active (e.g. *he* in *he was given the book*, *he was laughed at*). **indirect question** GRAMMAR a question in indirect speech (e.g. *they asked who I was*). **indirect rule** a system of government in which the governed people retain certain administrative and legal etc. powers.
■ **indirectness** *noun* E17.

†**indirected** *adjective*. *rare*. E17–E19.
[ORIGIN from IN-³ + *directed* pa. pple of DIRECT *verb*.]
Not directed or guided.

indirection /ɪndɪˈrɛkʃ(ə)n, ɪndʌɪ-/ *noun*. L16.
[ORIGIN from INDIRECT after *direction*.]
1 Lack of straightforwardness in action; an act or practice which is not straightforward and honest; deceit, malpractice. L16.
2 Indirect movement or action; a devious or circuitous course; roundabout means or method. E17.

indirectly /ɪndɪˈrɛktli, ɪndʌɪ-/ *adverb*. LME.
[ORIGIN from INDIRECT + -LY².]
1 By indirect action, means, or connection; through an intervening person or thing. LME. ▸**b** Not in express terms; by suggestion or implication. L16.
2 Not in a straight line or with a straight course; circuitously, obliquely. L15. ▸†**b** By crooked methods; wrongfully, unfairly. L16–E17. ▸†**c** Not to the point; evasively. L16–E18.
3 GRAMMAR. In or by indirect speech. L19.

indiscernible /ɪndɪˈsəːnɪb(ə)l/ *adjective & noun*. M17.
[ORIGIN from IN-³ + DISCERNIBLE.]
▸ **A** *adjective*. **1** Unable to be discerned; imperceptible, undiscoverable. M17.
2 Unable to be distinguished (*from* something else); indistinguishable. M17.
▸ **B** *noun*. A thing that cannot be discerned; a thing that cannot be distinguished from some other thing. E18.
■ **indiscerniˈbility** *noun* L19. **indiscernibleness** *noun* M17. **indiscernibly** *adverb* M17.

†**indiscerpible** *adjective*. M17–M19.
[ORIGIN from IN-³ + DISCERPIBLE.]
= INDISCERPTIBLE.

indiscerptible /ɪndɪˈsəːptɪb(ə)l/ *adjective*. M18.
[ORIGIN from IN-³ + DISCERPTIBLE.]
Unable to be divided into parts; not destructible by dissolution of parts.
■ **indiscerptibility** *noun* M18.

indisciplinable /ɪnˈdɪsɪplɪnəb(ə)l, ˌɪndɪsɪˈplɪn-/ *adjective*. Now *rare*. E17.
[ORIGIN from IN-³ + DISCIPLINABLE.]
Unable to be disciplined; not amenable to discipline; intractable.

indiscipline /ɪnˈdɪsɪplɪn/ *noun*. L18.
[ORIGIN from IN-³ + DISCIPLINE *noun*.]
Absence or lack of discipline; lack of order or control by authority.

indiscoverable /ɪndɪˈskʌv(ə)rəb(ə)l/ *adjective*. E17.
[ORIGIN from IN-³ + DISCOVERABLE.]
Not discoverable, undiscoverable.

indiscreet /ɪndɪˈskriːt/ *adjective*¹. Also (earlier) †**-crete**. LME.
[ORIGIN Latin *indiscretus* (see INDISCRETE *adjective*¹) in medieval Latin sense 'careless, indiscreet'.]
†**1** Lacking discernment or sound judgement. LME–L17.
2 Injudicious or imprudent in speech or action; unwary, unthinking; not discreet, esp. about other people's secrets. L16.
■ **indiscreetly** *adverb* LME. **indiscreetness** *noun* M17.

†**indiscreet** *adjective*² see INDISCRETE.

indiscrete /ɪndɪˈskriːt/ *adjective*¹. Also (earlier) †**-creet**. E17.
[ORIGIN Latin *indiscretus* unseparated, undistinguished, formed as IN-³ + DISCRETE *adjective*.]
†**1** Not separate or distinguishable from contiguous objects or parts. E–M17.
2 Not divided or divisible into distinct parts. L18.

M. MONIER-WILLIAMS Next all was water, all a chaos indiscrete.

†**indiscrete** *adjective*² see INDISCREET *adjective*¹.

indiscretion /ɪndɪˈskrɛʃ(ə)n/ *noun*. ME.
[ORIGIN Old French & mod. French *indiscrétion* or late Latin *indiscretio(n-)*, formed as IN-³ + *discretio(n-)*: see DISCRETION.]
1 Lack of discretion, the fact or quality of being indiscreet. Orig. chiefly, lack of discernment or discrimination. Now, lack of sound judgement in speech or action; injudicious or unwary conduct; imprudence; *euphem.* a transgression of social morality. ME.

S. CHITTY That his mistress should sleep naked . . he regarded as the height of indiscretion.

2 An indiscreet or imprudent act; *euphem.* a transgression of social morality. E17.

Q. CRISP His indiscretion in telling so many people of what . . was a private matter between them.

indiscriminate /ɪndɪˈskrɪmɪnət/ *adjective*. L16.
[ORIGIN formed as IN-³ + Latin *discriminatus* DISCRIMINATE *adjective*.]
1 Not distinguished by discernment or discrimination; done without making distinctions; haphazard; not selective. L16.

Birds Magazine Hedges, too many of which are being destroyed by indiscriminate stubble burning.

2 Of a person: not using or exercising discrimination; making no distinctions. L18.

M. R. MITFORD Without being one of his indiscriminate admirers, I like parts of his books.

■ **indiscriminately** *adverb* M17. **indiscriminateness** *noun* L19.

indiscriminating /ɪndɪˈskrɪmɪneɪtɪŋ/ *adjective*. M18.
[ORIGIN from IN-³ + DISCRIMINATING.]
Not discriminating; that does not make or recognize distinctions.
■ **indiscriminatingly** *adverb* E19.

indiscrimination /ˌɪndɪskrɪmɪˈneɪʃ(ə)n/ *noun*. M17.
[ORIGIN from IN-³ + DISCRIMINATION.]
The fact of not discriminating; lack of distinction; lack of discrimination or discernment.

indiscriminative /ɪndɪˈskrɪmɪnətɪv/ *adjective*. M19.
[ORIGIN from IN-³ + DISCRIMINATIVE.]
Not discriminative; not characterized by or inclined to discrimination.
■ †**indiscriminatively** *adverb* L17–E18.

indispensable /ɪndɪˈspɛnsəb(ə)l/ *adjective & noun*. Also (now *rare*) **-ible**. M16.
[ORIGIN medieval Latin *indispensabilis*, *-ibilis* formed as IN-³ + DISPENSABLE.]
▸ **A** *adjective*. †**1** Unable to be allowed or provided for by ecclesiastical dispensation. M16–M17.
2 Of an obligation, duty, etc.: unable to be dispensed with, disregarded, or neglected. Now *rare*. M17.

GIBBON The citizens . . had purchased an exemption from the indispensable duty of defending their country.

3 Unable to be dispensed with or done without; absolutely necessary or vital. L17.

E. JOHNSON A knowledge of shorthand was almost indispensable for a career in journalism. H. BAILEY Winifred was indispensable to Vera, who could not go . . unless she left a responsible adult in the house.

▸ **B** *noun*. An indispensable person or thing; in *pl.* (*arch. colloq.*), trousers. L17.
■ **indispensaˈbility** *noun* M17. **indispensableness** *noun* M17. **indispensably** *adverb* E17.

indispose /ɪndɪˈspəʊz/ *verb trans*. M17.
[ORIGIN from IN-³ + DISPOSE *verb*.]
1 Make unfit or incapable (*to do*, *for*). Now *spec.* affect with illness or injury, incapacitate. Cf. INDISPOSED 4. M17.

J. WILKINS That prejudice.. did indispose them for an equal judgment of things. DEFOE He was a little indisposed by a Fall that he had received.

2 Make averse or unwilling; disincline. **L17.**

J. SCOTT The miseries of the revolution.. had totally indisposed the people towards any interference with politics.

3 Cause to be unfavourably disposed; make unfriendly. Now *rare*. **M18.**

J. H. HARRIS She has long indisposed the whole kingdom against her.

4 Remove or avoid a physical tendency or inclination *to*; make not liable or subject *to*. **E19.**

COLERIDGE Inoculation.. has so entered into the constitution, as to indispose it to infection.

indisposed /ɪndɪˈspəʊzd/ *adjective*. **LME.**
[ORIGIN Partly from French *indisposé* or Latin *indispositus*; partly from IN-[3] + DISPOSED.]
†**1** Not properly arranged or organized; disordered, disorganized, unprepared. **LME–L17.**
†**2** Not properly fitted, unqualified. *rare*. **LME–M17.**
†**3** Of evil disposition or inclination. **LME–L16.**
4 Suffering from a (usu. slight) physical disorder; unwell. **LME.**

HENRY FIELDING Mr. Allworthy had been for some days indisposed with a cold.

5 Disinclined, unwilling, averse (*to* or *to do* something). **LME.**

G. CRABBE Unfit to rule and indisposed to please.

6 Not favourably disposed or inclined (*towards*); unfriendly, unfavourable. Now *rare*. **M17.**

CLARENDON The king.. was sufficiently indisposed towards the persons or the principles of Mr. Calvin's disciples.

7 Not having a physical inclination or tendency; not liable or subject (*to*). **M17.**

J. WEDGWOOD The saturated marine solution is indisposed to crystallize.

indisposition /ˌɪndɪspəˈzɪʃ(ə)n/ *noun*. **LME.**
[ORIGIN French, or from IN-[3] + DISPOSITION, after INDISPOSED.]
†**1** Lack of adaptation to some purpose or circumstances; unfitness, incapacity. **LME–M18.**

R. BOYLE We examine other plants.. and observe.. their disposedness or indisposition to yield spirits or oyls.

2 Physical disorder; ill health, (esp. slight) illness. **LME.**

G. GISSING A trifling indisposition kept her to her room.

3 The state of not being mentally disposed (*to* or *to do* something); disinclination, unwillingness. **LME.**

CASTLEREAGH He declined the proposal evidently from indisposition to receive a British force within his dominions.

4 The state of being unfavourably disposed *to* or *towards*; aversion. Now *rare*. **LME.**

CLARENDON This Indisposition of the King towards the Duke was exceedingly encreased and aggravated.

†**5** Lack of arrangement or order; disorder. **L16–L17.**
6 Lack of physical inclination or tendency; the condition of not being liable or subject *to* something. **E20.**

indisputable /ɪndɪˈspjuːtəb(ə)l, ɪnˈdɪspjʊtəb(ə)l/ *adjective*. **M16.**
[ORIGIN Late Latin *indisputabilis*, formed as IN-[3] + *disputabilis* DISPUTABLE.]
Unable to be disputed; unquestionable.

P. G. WODEHOUSE They.. did not deny his great talents, which were.. indisputable. A. THWAITE An indisputable fact, which didn't seem to offer any matter for discussion.

■ **indisputaˈbility** *noun* **L19.** **indisputableness** *noun* **E18.** **indisputably** *adverb* **M17.**

indisputed /ɪndɪˈspjuːtɪd/ *adjective*. Now *rare* or *obsolete*. **M17.**
[ORIGIN from IN-[3] + *disputed* pa. pple of DISPUTE *verb*.]
Not disputed, unquestioned.

indisseverable /ɪndɪ(s)ˈsɛv(ə)rəb(ə)l/ *adjective*. *rare*. **M17.**
[ORIGIN from IN-[3] + DISSEVER + -ABLE.]
Indivisible; unable to be dissevered.
■ **indisseverably** *adverb* **L16.**

indissociable /ɪndɪˈsəʊʃ(ɪ)əb(ə)l, -sɪə-/ *adjective*. **M17.**
[ORIGIN IN-[3] + DISSOCIABLE.]
Unable to be dissociated.

H. WOTTON Your tender and generous heart (for these attributes are indissociable).

indissoluble /ɪndɪˈsɒljʊb(ə)l/ *adjective*. **L15.**
[ORIGIN Latin *indissolubilis*, formed as IN-[3] + *dissolubilis* DISSOLUBLE.]
1 Of a bond or connection: unable to be dissolved, undone, or broken; perpetually binding, firm. Chiefly *fig*. **L15.**

L. GORDON The indissoluble link that made Virginia closer to her father.. was his profession as man of letters. R. STRANGE A pledge which binds them in an indissoluble union for the rest of their lives.

2 Unable to be dissolved into its elements; unable to be decomposed, disintegrated, or destroyed; indestructible. **M16.**
†**3** *CHEMISTRY*. = INSOLUBLE 3. Also, infusible. **M17–E19.**
■ **indissolublist**, **-bilist** *noun & adjective* (**a**) *noun* a person who believes that marriage is indissoluble and that divorced people should not remarry in church; (**b**) *adjective* of or holding this belief: **M20.** **indissoluˈbility** *noun* **L17.** **indissolubleness** *noun* **M17.** **indissolubly** *adverb* **M16.**

†**indissolvable** *adjective*. **M16–L18.**
[ORIGIN from IN-[3] + DISSOLVABLE.]
= INDISSOLUBLE.

indissuadable /ɪndɪˈsweɪdəb(ə)l/ *adjective*. *rare*. **E20.**
[ORIGIN from IN-[3] + DISSUADE + -ABLE.]
That cannot be dissuaded; inexorable.
■ **indissuadably** *adverb* **L19.**

†**indistant** *adjective*. **M17–L18.**
[ORIGIN medieval Latin *indistant-*, formed as IN-[3] + *distant-* DISTANT.]
Not distant, not separated by a gap; without gap or interval, continuous.

indistinct /ɪndɪˈstɪŋkt/ *adjective*. **M16.**
[ORIGIN Latin *indistinctus*, formed as IN-[3] + DISTINCT.]
1 Not apprehended by the senses or mental faculties so as to be clearly distinguished or discerned, or to present a clear distinction of parts; confused, blurred; faint, dim, obscure. **M16.**

B. EMECHETA Any warning voices she might hear in herself were too indistinct to be effective. A. MACLEAN Captain Bower's words were blurred and indistinct. C. GEBLER Night began to fall. The elm tree became a dark indistinct shape. B. T. BRADFORD He had died in 1909.. and her memories of him were smudged and indistinct.

2 Not distinct or distinguished from each other or from something else; not clearly defined or delimited. Now *rare*. **E17.**

T. WRIGHT Three sacred persons in Trinitie, distinguished really, and yet indistinct essentially.

3 Not distinguishing between different things; undiscriminating. Now *rare*. **M17.**
■ **indistinctly** *adverb* **LME.** **indistinctness** *noun* **E18.**

indistinction /ɪndɪˈstɪŋkʃ(ə)n/ *noun*. Now *rare*. **E17.**
[ORIGIN from IN-[3] + DISTINCTION, after *indistinct*.]
1 The fact of not distinguishing or making distinctions; (a) failure to perceive or make a difference. **E17.**
2 The condition or fact of not being distinct or different; lack of distinguishing characteristics. **M17.**
†**3** Indistinctness, obscurity, dimness. **M17–L18.**
4 Lack of distinction or eminence. *joc. rare*. **M19.**

Athenaeum Persons of distinction or in-distinction.

indistinctive /ɪndɪˈstɪŋktɪv/ *adjective*. Now *rare*. **M19.**
[ORIGIN from IN-[3] + DISTINCTIVE.]
Without distinctive character or features; not markedly different.
■ **indistinctively** *adverb* without distinction; without discriminating: **L17.** **indistinctiveness** *noun* **M19.**

indistinguishable /ɪndɪˈstɪŋgwɪʃəb(ə)l/ *adjective*. **E17.**
[ORIGIN from IN-[3] + DISTINGUISHABLE.]
1 Unable to be distinguished as different *from* something else, or from each other; of which the parts are not distinguishable. **E17.**

R. W. CLARK In the unconscious, fact was indistinguishable from emotionally charged fiction. J. WINTERSON The woman forced wire and flower into an indistinguishable whole.

2 Unable to be clearly perceived (by the senses or the mind); imperceptible. **M17.**

D. L. SAYERS The symptoms of arsenical poisoning and of acute gastritis are really indistinguishable.

■ **indistinguishaˈbility** *noun* **L19.** **indistinguishableness** *noun* **M18.** **indistinguishably** *adverb* **L17.**

indistinguished /ɪndɪˈstɪŋgwɪʃt/ *adjective*. Now *rare*. **E17.**
[ORIGIN from IN-[3] + DISTINGUISHED.]
Not distinguished; undistinguished.

indistributable /ɪndɪˈstrɪbjʊtəb(ə)l, ˌɪndɪstrɪˈbjuːtəb(ə)l/ *adjective*. *rare*. **M19.**
[ORIGIN from IN-[3] + DISTRIBUTABLE.]
Unable to be distributed.

indisturbable /ɪndɪˈstəːbəb(ə)l/ *adjective*. *rare*. **M17.**
[ORIGIN from IN-[3] + DISTURB *verb* + -ABLE.]
Unable to be disturbed.

indisturbance /ɪndɪˈstəːb(ə)ns/ *noun*. Now *rare*. **M17.**
[ORIGIN from IN-[3] + DISTURBANCE.]
Absence of disturbance; undisturbed condition; quietness, peace.

indite /ɪnˈdʌɪt/ *verb*[1] *trans*. Now *rare*. Also (earlier) †**en-**. **ME.**
[ORIGIN Old French *enditier*: see INDICT *verb*[1].]
1 Put into words, compose (a poem, story, speech, etc.); give a literary form to; express or describe in a literary composition. **ME.** ▸**b** Put into writing; write (a letter etc.). **LME.**

AV *Ps.* 45:1 My heart is inditing a good matter. DISRAELI Men far too well acquainted with their subject to indite such tales. **b** P. G. WODEHOUSE A writer should surely find.. golden sentences bubbling up.. when he is inditing a letter to the girl he loves.

†**2** Speak, suggest, or inspire (a form of words to be repeated or written down); = DICTATE *verb* 1. **LME–E19.**
†**3** Enjoin as a law or precept; = DICTATE *verb* 2. Also, dictate to (a person). **LME–E18.**
■ **inditer** *noun* **LME.** **inditing** *noun* the action of the verb; something indited, a letter, speech, etc.: **LME.**

†**indite** *verb*[2] see INDICT *verb*[1].

inditement /ɪnˈdʌɪtm(ə)nt/ *noun*[1]. Now *rare*. **M16.**
[ORIGIN from INDITE *verb*[1] + -MENT.]
The action of composing in prose or verse; (a) composition.

†**inditement** *noun*[2] see INDICTMENT *noun*.

indium /ˈɪndɪəm/ *noun*. **M19.**
[ORIGIN from INDI(GO + -IUM, from two characteristic indigo lines in its spectrum.]
A soft silvery-white metallic chemical element, atomic no. 49, occurring esp. in zinc ores (symbol In).

indivertible /ɪndʌɪˈvəːtɪb(ə)l, ɪndɪ-/ *adjective*. *rare*. **E19.**
[ORIGIN from IN-[3] + DIVERTIBLE.]
Unable to be diverted or turned aside.

†**individable** *adjective*. **E–M17.**
[ORIGIN from IN-[3] + DIVIDABLE.]
Unable to be divided; indivisible.

individua *noun pl*. see INDIVIDUUM.

individual /ɪndɪˈvɪdjʊ(ə)l/ *adjective & noun*. **LME.**
[ORIGIN medieval Latin *individualis*, from Latin *individuus*, from *in-* IN-[3] + *dividuus* divisible (formed as DIVIDE *verb*): see -UAL.]
▸ **A** *adjective*. †**1** One in substance or essence; indivisible. **LME–L17.**
†**2** That cannot be separated; inseparable. **L16–M17.**
3 Existing as a separate indivisible identity; numerically one; single, as distinct from others of the same kind; particular. **E17.** ▸†**b** Identical, selfsame. **M17–E19.**

BURKE All powers delegated from the board to any individual servant of the company. T. HARDY So familiar with the spot that he knew.. individual cows by their names.

4 Of, pertaining, or peculiar to a single person or thing, rather than a group; characteristic of an individual. **E17.** ▸**b** Intended to serve one person; designed to contain one portion. **L19.**

M. MITCHELL No public protest could be raised..., and individual protests were silenced with jail sentences. R. INGALLS He had died after an ordinary anaesthetic.. all anyone could say in explanation was 'individual reaction'. B. BETTELHEIM All rules are based on generalizations, they disregard what is individual. **b** *Listener* We then took six individual dariole moulds, the kind used for baking little castle cakes.

individual variable *LOGIC* a variable that denotes various individuals.

5 Distinguished from others by qualities of its own; marked by a peculiar or striking character. **M17.**

G. GREENE The writing seemed to him, after the copper-plate of the office, very individual.

▸ **B** *noun*. **1** A single thing or a group of things regarded as a unit; a single member of a class or group. **E17.** ▸**b** A thing which is determined by properties peculiar to itself and cannot be subdivided into others of the same kind. **E17.** ▸**c** *BIOLOGY*. An organism regarded as having a separate existence; a single member of a species, or of a colonial or compound organism. **L18.**
2 A single human being, as opp. to a group. **E17.** ▸**b** A human being, a person. **M18.**

A. S. NEILL Individuals composing the crowd may be unanimous in hating the rules. **b** F. HUME He appeared to be an exceedingly unpleasant individual. C. HOPE Individuals arrived there in their private cars.

†**3** *ellipt*. One's individual person, self. **M17–E19.**

individualise *verb* var. of INDIVIDUALIZE.

individualism /ɪndɪˈvɪdjʊ(ə)lɪz(ə)m/ *noun*. **E19.**
[ORIGIN from INDIVIDUAL + -ISM, after French *individualisme*.]
1 Self-centred feeling or conduct as a principle; a way of life in which an individual pursues his or her own ends or ideas; free and independent individual action or thought; egoism. **E19.**

W. HOLTBY Sarah could hardly forbear to cheer this triumph of co-operation over individualism. *Sunday Times* It is as though our youth do not have any individualism—they just follow the mob.

2 The social theory which advocates the free and independent action of the individual; laissez-faire. **M19.**
3 = INDIVIDUALITY 2, 3. **M19.**

Blackwood's Magazine Their ideas of God did not possess that individualism and personality. P. GAY He is bound to be committed to individualism, to seek out what is unique.

4 *PHILOSOPHY*. The doctrine that reality is constituted of individual entities. Also, the doctrine that the self is the only knowable existence. *rare*. **L19.**

I

5 A characteristic or peculiarity of one person or thing. L19.

6 *BIOLOGY.* Symbiosis in which the product of the association appears to be a distinct organism, as in lichen. L19.

■ **individualist** *noun & adjective* (*a*) *noun* a person who takes an independent or egoistic course in thought or action; an adherent of individualism; (*b*) *adjective* = INDIVIDUALISTIC: M19. **individua'listic** *adjective* of or pertaining to individualism or individualists; characterized by individualism: L19. **individua'listically** *adverb* L19.

individuality /ˌɪndɪvɪdjʊˈalɪti/ *noun.* E17.

[ORIGIN from INDIVIDUAL + -ITY. In early use from medieval Latin *individualitas*.]

1 The sum of the attributes which distinguish one person or thing from others of the same kind; strongly marked individual character; in *pl.*, individual characteristics. E17.

> J. McDOUGALL It is parents who give their children a sense of self, enjoyment in their individuality.

2 Indivisibility, inseparability; an indivisible or inseparable thing. Now *rare* or *obsolete*. M17.

3 The fact or condition of existing as an individual; separate and continuous existence; the action or position of individual members of a society. M17.

> BURKE Individuality is left out of their scheme of government. The state is all in all. W. PALEY Consciousness carries identity and individuality along with it.

4 An individual thing or personality. L18.

individualize /ɪndɪˈvɪdjʊ(ə)lʌɪz/ *verb trans.* Also **-ise**. M17.

[ORIGIN from INDIVIDUAL + -IZE.]

1 Make individual or give an individual character to; characterize, distinguish by distinctive qualities, esp. from other persons or things. M17.

2 Point out or notice individually; specify, particularize. Now *rare*. M17.

■ **individualizer** *noun* M19. **individuali'zation** *noun* the action of individualizing; the fact or condition of being individualized: M18.

individually /ɪndɪˈvɪdjʊ(ə)li/ *adverb.* L16.

[ORIGIN from INDIVIDUAL + -LY².]

†**1** Indivisibly; inseparably. L16–E17.

2 Personally; in an individual capacity. M17.

> M. R. MITFORD To me individually it would be a great release to be quit . . of the garden.

3 In an individual or distinctive manner; as individuals; singly, one by one. M17.

> D. ROWE Individually we are very weak, but as part of a group we can be . . strong.

– PHRASES: †**individually the same** identically the same. **individually different** different as individuals though perhaps identical in species.

†**individuate** *adjective.* E17.

[ORIGIN medieval Latin *individuatus* pa. pple, formed as INDIVIDUATE *verb*: see -ATE².]

1 Undivided, indivisible, inseparable. E17–M18.

2 = INDIVIDUATED 2. Only in 17.

individuate /ɪndɪˈvɪdjʊeɪt/ *verb trans.* E17.

[ORIGIN medieval Latin *individuat-* pa. ppl stem of *individuare*, from Latin *individuus*: see INDIVIDUAL, -ATE³.]

1 Give an individual character to; distinguish from others of the same kind; individualize; single out. E17.

> P. L. COURTIER The heart, that loves its object to select, To individuate.

2 Form into an individual or distinct entity; give individual organization or form to. M17.

> J. SCOTT That which individuates any Society, or makes it a distinct Body . . , is the Charter or Law.

■ **individuative** *adjective* (*rare*) individualizing M19.

individuated /ɪndɪˈvɪdjʊeɪtɪd/ *ppl adjective.* M17.

[ORIGIN from INDIVIDUATE *verb* + -ED¹.]

†**1** Undivided, indivisible, inseparable. M–L17.

2 Made individual; individualized. L17. ▸**b** *PSYCHOLOGY.* Of a person: that has been through the process of individuation. M20.

individuation /ˌɪndɪvɪdjʊˈeɪʃ(ə)n/ *noun.* E17.

[ORIGIN medieval Latin *individuatio(n-)*, formed as INDIVIDUATE *verb*: see -ATION.]

1 The action or process of individuating, or of distinguishing as individual; *SCHOLASTIC PHILOSOPHY* the means to individual existence, as distinct from that of the species. E17. ▸**b** *JUNGIAN PSYCHOLOGY.* The process of establishing the wholeness and autonomy of the individual self by the integration of consciousness and the collective unconscious. E20.

2 The condition of being an individual; individuality, personal identity. M17.

3 *BIOLOGY.* The development or maintenance of a functional organic unity; in colonial organisms, the development of separate but interdependent units. M19.

†**individuity** *noun.* E17–E19.

[ORIGIN medieval Latin *individuitas*, from Latin *individuus*: see INDIVIDUAL, -ITY.]

Individuality.

individuum /ɪndɪˈvɪdjʊəm/ *noun.* Now *rare*. Pl. **-dua** /-djʊə/ (chiefly in senses 1, 2), **-duums** (chiefly in sense 3). M16.

[ORIGIN Latin = indivisible particle, atom, (in late Latin) an individual, use as noun of neut. of *individuus*: see INDIVIDUAL.]

1 Esp. in *SCHOLASTIC LOGIC*. A member of a species; = INDIVIDUAL *noun* 1b. M16.

2 Something which cannot be divided; an indivisible entity. L16.

3 An individual person or thing. L16.

indivisible /ɪndɪˈvɪzɪb(ə)l/ *adjective & noun.* LME.

[ORIGIN Late Latin *indivisibilis*, formed as IN-³ + *divisibilis* DIVISIBLE.]

▸ **A** *adjective.* Not divisible; that cannot be divided; incapable of being distributed among a number. LME.

> C. THUBRON So flat and brown were both land and water they seemed indivisible.

▸ **B** *noun.* Something which cannot be divided; an indivisible entity. M17.

■ **indivisi'bility** *noun* M17. **indivisibleness** *noun* (now *rare*) M17. **indivisibly** *adverb* M16.

indivision /ɪndɪˈvɪʒ(ə)n/ *noun.* Now *rare*. E17.

[ORIGIN Late Latin *indivisio(n-)*, from Latin IN-³ + *divisio(n-)* DIVISION.]

Lack of division; undivided condition.

Indo- /ˈɪndəʊ/ *combining form*¹.

[ORIGIN from Latin *Indus*, Greek *Indos* Indian: see -O-.]

Forming nouns and adjectives with the sense 'Indian and —', chiefly denoting the combination of Indian with some other (ethnological or linguistic) characteristic.

■ **Indo-Aby'ssinian** *adjective* of or pertaining to both the Dravidians of India and the Hamites of NE Africa L19. **Indo-'African** *adjective* (*a*) of or pertaining to both India and Africa; (*b*) pertaining to Indians and Africans in South Africa: M19. **Indo-'Anglian** *adjective & noun* (*a*) *adjective* of or pertaining to literature in English written by Indian authors; (*b*) *noun* a writer of such literature: L19. **Indo-'British** *adjective* of or pertaining to both India and Great Britain, or Indo-Britons, or British rule in India; Anglo-Indian: E20. **Indo-'Briton** *noun* = ANGLO-INDIAN *noun* M19. **Indo-Chi'nese** *adjective & noun* (*a*) *adjective* of or pertaining to Indo-China, the SE Asian peninsula containing Myanmar (Burma), Thailand, Malaya, Laos, Cambodia, and Vietnam, or (*hist.*) French Indo-China, the French colonies of Laos, Cambodia, and Vietnam; (*b*) *noun* (pl. same) a native or inhabitant of (French) Indo-China: E19. **Indo-Ger'manic** *noun & adjective* = INDO-EUROPEAN *noun* 1 & *adjective* E19. **Indo-'Germanist** *noun* = INDO-EUROPEANIST L19. **Indo-'Hittite** *noun* a hypothetical language believed to be the common ancestor of Indo-European and Hittite E20. **Indo-Ma'layan** *adjective* of or pertaining to both India and Malaya; *spec.* designating an ethnological region comprising Sri Lanka, the Malay peninsula, and the Malayan islands: M19. **Indo-Pa'cific** *adjective & noun* (*a*) *adjective* of or pertaining to the Indian Ocean and the adjacent parts of the Pacific; of or pertaining to the group of languages (usu. called ***Austronesian***) spoken in the islands of this region; (*b*) *noun* the Indo-Pacific seas or ocean: L19. **Indo-Pak** *adjective* (*colloq.*) = INDO-PAKISTANI *adjective* M20. **Indo-Paki'stan, Indo-Paki'stani** *adjectives* pertaining to both India and Pakistan, or their inhabitants M20. **Indo-Portu'guese** *noun & adjective* (of or pertaining to) modified Portuguese as used in parts of India L19. **Indo-Sara'cenic** *adjective* designating or pertaining to an architectural style combining Indian and Muslim features L19. **Indo-'Scythian** *noun & adjective* (*a*) *noun* a member of an ancient central Asian people of Scythian origin, dominant in northern India and Bactria *c* 128 BC–C AD 450; (*b*) *adjective* of or pertaining to the Indo-Scythians: L18.

indo- /ˈɪndəʊ/ *combining form*².

[ORIGIN from IND(IGO + -O-.]

CHEMISTRY. Used in names of compounds related to or derived from indigo, esp. derivatives of indole.

■ **indo'aniline** *noun* a violet aniline dye, $O{=}C_6H_4{=}N{\cdot}C_6H_4NH_2$; any derivative of this: L19.

Indo- /ˈɪndəʊ/ *combining form*³.

[ORIGIN from *Indus* (see below) + -O-.]

Of or pertaining to the River Indus in the northern part of the Indian subcontinent.

■ **Indo-Gan'getic** *adjective* of the Rivers Indus and Ganges; *spec.* designating the plain through which they flow, occupying much of the northern part of the Indian subcontinent: L19.

Indo-Aryan /ɪndəʊˈɛːrɪən/ *adjective & noun.* M19.

[ORIGIN from INDO-¹ + ARYAN.]

(Designating or pertaining to) the Indian branch of the Indo-Iranian language family, including Sanskrit, Prakrit, and Pali, and the modern languages Hindi, Bengali, Marathi, Nepalese, Sinhalese, etc., and often also including the Dard languages (in this wider sense also called *Indic*).

indochinite /ɪndəʊˈtʃʌɪnʌɪt/ *noun.* M20.

[ORIGIN from *Indo-China* (see INDO-CHINESE + -ITE¹.]

GEOLOGY. A tektite from the strewn field of Indo-China.

†**indocible** *adjective.* M16–L18.

[ORIGIN French, or late Latin *indocibilis* from *docibilis* DOCIBLE, or from IN-³ + DOCIBLE.]

Incapable of being taught or instructed; unteachable.

■ †**indocibility** *noun* E17–M19.

indocile /ɪnˈdəʊsʌɪl/ *adjective.* E17.

[ORIGIN French, or Latin *indocilis* from *docilis* DOCILE, or from IN-³ + DOCILE.]

Not docile; not teachable or submissive, intractable.

■ **indo'cility** *noun* M17.

indoctrinate /ɪnˈdɒktrɪneɪt/ *verb trans.* Also (*rare*) †**en-**. E17.

[ORIGIN from INDOCTRINE + -ATE³, or from IN-², EN-¹ + DOCTRINATE.]

1 Teach (a person); instruct *in* a subject, bring *into* the knowledge of something. E17. ▸**b** Teach (a subject etc.) *rare*. E19.

> D. LIVINGSTONE No pains whatever are taken to indoctrinate the adults of the tribe. C. GEIKIE He rather trained their spiritual character than indoctrinated them in systematic theology.

2 Imbue with an idea or doctrine; *spec.* teach systematically to accept (esp. partisan or tendentious) ideas uncritically; brainwash. M19.

> W. LIPPMANN With the instruments of the terror, censorship and propaganda, the fascist leaders indoctrinated the mass. D. LODGE They had been indoctrinated since adolescence with the idea . . that contraception was a grave sin.

■ **indoctri'nation** *noun* the action or process of indoctrinating; formal instruction; (an instance of) brainwashing: M17. **indoctrinator** *noun* L19. **indoctrinatory** *adjective* that indoctrinates; relating or pertaining to indoctrination: M20.

†**indoctrine** *verb trans.* Also (earlier) **en-**. LME–E19.

[ORIGIN Old French *endoctriner*, formed as EN-¹, IN-² + DOCTRINE.]

Teach, instruct.

Indo-European /ˌɪndəʊjʊərəˈpiːən/ *noun & adjective.* E19.

[ORIGIN from INDO-¹ + EUROPEAN.]

▸ **A** *noun* **1** **a** The group of cognate languages which includes most European and many Asian ones; the hypothetical parent language of this group (also called ***primitive Indo-European***, ***Proto-Indo-European***). E19. ▸**b** A speaker of an Indo-European language; *spec.* a speaker of Proto-Indo-European. M19.

2 †**a** An Indianized European. *rare*. Only in E19. ▸**b** A native or inhabitant of SE Asia who is wholly or partly of European descent. M20.

▸ **B** *adjective.* Of, pertaining to, or characteristic of Indo-European or Indo-Europeans. E19.

■ **Indo-Europeanist** *noun* an expert in or student of the Indo-European languages E20.

Indo-Iranian /ˌɪndəʊɪˈreɪnɪən, -ˈrɑː-/ *adjective & noun.* L19.

[ORIGIN from INDO-¹ + IRANIAN.]

▸ **A** *adjective.* Of or pertaining to both India and Iran; *spec.* designating a branch of Indo-European comprising the Indo-Aryan (Indic) and Iranian languages. L19.

▸ **B** *noun.* The Indo-Iranian languages collectively; a speaker of (any of) these. L19.

indole /ˈɪndəʊl/ *noun.* Also (now *rare*) **-ol** /-ɒl/. M19.

[ORIGIN from INDO-² + -OLE².]

CHEMISTRY. A crystalline heteroaromatic compound, C_8H_7N, which has a molecule consisting of fused benzene and pyrrole rings, has an unpleasant odour, and occurs in coal tar, in faeces, and (as derivatives) in plants.

– COMB.: **indoleacetic** *adjective*: ***indoleacetic acid***, each of seven isomeric acetic acid derivatives of indole; *esp.* one of these (***indole-3-acetic acid***), which is an important plant growth hormone.

■ **in'dolic** *adjective* containing, derived from, characteristic of, or characterized by indole E20. **'indolyl** *noun* the radical $\cdot C_8H_6N$, of which seven isomers exist, derived from indole (***indolylacetic acid*** = ***indoleacetic acid*** above) E20.

indolence /ˈɪnd(ə)l(ə)ns/ *noun.* E17.

[ORIGIN French, or Latin *indolentia* freedom from pain, formed as IN-³ + *dolent-* pres. ppl stem of *dolere* suffer or give pain: see -ENCE.]

†**1** Insensibility or indifference to pain. E17–E18.

†**2** Freedom from pain; a neutral state in which neither pain nor pleasure is felt. M17–M18.

3 The inclination to avoid exertion or trouble; love of ease, laziness; idleness. E18.

> A. MUNRO Tahiti to her means palm trees . . and the sort of . . indolence that has never interested her. C. PETERS Her indolence—she habitually stayed in bed all morning.

■ Also †**indolency** *noun* E17–M18.

indolent /ˈɪnd(ə)l(ə)nt/ *adjective.* M17.

[ORIGIN Late Latin *indolent-*, *-ens*, formed as IN-³ + *dolent-*: see INDOLENCE, -ENT.]

1 *MEDICINE.* Of an ulcer, tumour, etc.: causing no pain, painless. Also, slow to heal, (of a disease or condition) slow to develop. M17.

2 Averse to work or exertion; self-indulgent, lazy, idle. E18.

> HOR. WALPOLE I am naturally indolent and without application to any kind of business. R. P. WARREN An appearance of swiftness and great competence despite the indolent posture. E. TEMPLETON She wandered from one dusky room into the other, too indolent to put the light on.

■ **indolently** *adverb* E18.

indoles /ˈɪndɒliːz/ *noun.* *rare*. L17.

[ORIGIN Latin, from *indu-* in, within, + root of *alescere* grow up: see ADOLESCENT.]

Innate quality or character.

Indology /ɪnˈdɒlədʒi/ *noun.* L19.

[ORIGIN from INDO-¹ + -LOGY.]

The branch of knowledge that deals with the history, literature, philosophy, etc., of India.

■ **Indo'logical** *adjective* M20. **Indologist** *noun* E20.

†**indomable** *adjective*. L15–E18.
[ORIGIN French, or Latin *indomabilis*, formed as IN-[3] + *domabilis* tameable, from *domare* to tame: see -ABLE.]
Untameable.

indomethacin /ɪndəʊˈmɛθəsɪn/ *noun*. M20.
[ORIGIN from INDO(LE + METH(YL + AC(ETIC, elems. of the systematic name + -IN[1].]
PHARMACOLOGY. A yellowish-white powdery indole derivative, $C_{19}H_{16}NO_4Cl$, which has anti-inflammatory, antipyretic, and analgesic properties and is used to treat rheumatoid arthritis, gout, etc.

indomitable /ɪnˈdɒmɪtəb(ə)l/ *adjective*. M17.
[ORIGIN Late Latin *indomitabilis*, formed as IN-[3] + *domitare*: see DAUNT *verb*, -ABLE.]
†**1** Intractable, untameable. Only in M17.
2 Difficult or impossible to subdue; resolute against adversity or opposition; stubbornly persistent. E19.
J. COLVILLE Reynaud is as indomitable as Pétain is defeatist. A. BROOKNER The will was there, the indomitable will, the refusal to give up.
■ **indomitaˈbility** *noun* M19. **indomitableness** *noun* M19. **indomitably** *adverb* M19.

Indonesian /ɪndəˈniːzjən, -ʒ(ə)n/ *noun & adjective*. M19.
[ORIGIN from *Indonesia* (see below), from INDO-[1] + Greek *nēsos* island + -IA[1]: see -AN.]
▸ **A** *noun*. **1** A native or inhabitant of Indonesia, a large island group in SE Asia, and now esp. of the federal republic of Indonesia, comprising Java, Sumatra, southern Borneo, western New Guinea, the Moluccas, Sulawesi, and many other smaller islands. M19. ▸**b** A member of the chief pre-Malay population of the island group Indonesia. L19.
2 The western branch of the Austronesian language family; *spec.* the national language of the republic of Indonesia (= BAHASA ***Indonesia***). M20.
▸ **B** *adjective*. **1** Of or pertaining to Indonesia or Indonesians. M19.
2 Of, pertaining to, or designating the language(s) of Indonesia. M19.

indoor /ˈɪndɔː/ *adjective*. E18.
[ORIGIN from IN *preposition* + DOOR *noun*, replacing earlier *within-door*.]
1 Situated, done, carried on, or used within a building or under cover; designed or adapted to be so used etc. E18.
THACKERAY I don't care for indoor games . . but I . . long to see a good English hunting-field. L. GORDON Mrs Dalloway paid for the luxury of an indoor lavatory. S. MORLEY Promoters whose plan it was to start . . an indoor pony-racing track in Atlantic City.
indoor cricket: see CRICKET *noun*[2].
2 *hist.* Within the workhouse or poorhouse. M19.
H. FAWCETT The indoor relief given in London is a charge upon the whole metropolis.

indoors /ɪnˈdɔːz/ *adverb*. L18.
[ORIGIN formed as INDOOR + -S[1], replacing earlier *within doors*.]
Within or into a house or other building; under cover.
J. BUCHAN If I spoke to a child its mother would snatch it . . and race indoors with it. G. ORWELL The light indoors was too dull to read by.
her indoors: see HER *pers. pronoun*[1] 1.

Indophile /ˈɪndəʊfʌɪl/ *noun*. M19.
[ORIGIN from INDO-[1] + -PHILE.]
A lover or admirer of India or Indian things.

indorsation /ɪndɔːseɪʃ(ə)n/ *noun*. Chiefly *Scot.* Also (earlier) **en-** /ɪn-, ɛn-/. L15.
[ORIGIN from *indorse* var. of ENDORSE *verb* + -ATION.]
= ENDORSEMENT.

indorse *verb*, **indorsement** *noun* vars. of ENDORSE *verb*, ENDORSEMENT.

†**indow** *verb* see ENDOW.

†**indowment** *noun* var. of ENDOWMENT.

indoxyl /ɪnˈdɒksʌɪl, -sɪl/ *noun*. L19.
[ORIGIN from INDO-[2] + OXY- + -YL.]
CHEMISTRY. A bright yellow soluble crystalline compound, C_8H_7NO, 3-hydroxyindole, which oxidizes in air to give indigotin; a radical derived from this by loss of the hydroxyl proton.

indraft *noun* see INDRAUGHT.

†**indrape** *verb trans.* E17–M19.
[ORIGIN from IN-[2] + DRAPE *verb*.]
Make into cloth; weave.

indraught /ˈɪndrɑːft/ *noun*. Also ***indraft**. L16.
[ORIGIN from IN-[1] + DRAUGHT *noun*.]
1 An inward flow or stream, as of air or water. L16.
G. ADAMS The larger the fire, the sharper is the indraught of the air.
2 An opening into land from the sea; an inlet, an inward passage. *obsolete* exc. *dial.* L16.
3 The act of drawing in; inward attraction. L17.
Daily News The indraft of the towns is irresistible, . . the capable young men abandon country labour.

indraw /ɪnˈdrɔː/ *verb trans.* Pa. t. **indrew** /ɪnˈdruː/; pa. pple **indrawn** /ɪnˈdrɔːn/. LME.
[ORIGIN from IN-[1] + DRAW *verb*.]
Draw in. Chiefly as ***indrawing*** *ppl adjective & verbal noun*, ***indrawn*** *ppl adjective*.
■ **indrawal** *noun* (*rare*) the action of drawing in; an indraught: M19.

†**indrench** *verb trans.* Also (earlier) **en-**. L16–E17.
[ORIGIN from IN-[2], EN-[1] + DRENCH *verb*.]
Immerse, soak, drown.

indrew *verb pa. t.* of INDRAW.

indri /ˈɪndri/ *noun*. Also **indris** /ˈɪndrɪs/. M19.
[ORIGIN from Malagasy *indry!* lo! behold!, or *indry izy!* there he is!, mistaken for the name of the animal, which in Malagasy is *babakoto* (see BABACOOTE).]
A large woolly black and white lemur of Madagascar, *Indri indri*, having long hind legs and a short tail and progressing by long leaps between trees. Also, any lemur of the family Indriidae, as the sifaka.
woolly indri: see WOOLLY *adjective*.

indricothere /ɪndrɪkəˈθɪə/ *noun*. M20.
[ORIGIN mod. Latin *Indricotherium*, from Russian *indrik* giant animal of folklore + Greek *thērion* wild animal.]
PALAEONTOLOGY. Any of a group of very tall extinct herbivorous ungulate mammals, found as fossils of the Oligocene epoch.

†**indubious** *adjective*. E17–M19.
[ORIGIN from Latin *indubius* + -OUS, or from IN-[3] + DUBIOUS.]
Not open to doubt or question; certain, indubitable.

indubitable /ɪnˈdjuːbɪtəb(ə)l/ *adjective*. LME.
[ORIGIN Latin *indubitabilis* from *dubitabilis* DUBITABLE, or from IN-[3] + DUBITABLE.]
Impossible to doubt; certain, evident.
■ **indubitaˈbility** *noun* M20. **indubitableness** *noun* E18. **indubitably** *adverb* unquestionably, without doubt L15.

indubitatively /ɪnˈdjuːbɪtətɪvli/ *adverb*. *rare*. M19.
[ORIGIN from IN-[3] + DUBITATIVELY.]
= INDUBITABLY.

induce /ɪnˈdjuːs/ *verb trans.* Also †**en-**. LME.
[ORIGIN Latin *inducere*, formed as IN-[2] + *ducere* lead, or from French *enduire* (cf. ENDUE).]
1 Lead, persuade, influence (a person). Foll. by *to do* something, (now *rare*) *to* an action, condition, etc. LME.
BURKE To induce us to this, Mr. Fox laboured hard. G. GREENE The twist in Dr Downman's character which induced him to put into blank verse his advice. K. M. E. MURRAY I am tired and am trying to induce someone to carry me.
nothing will induce me to — I will never be persuaded to —.
†**2** Introduce (a practice, law, condition, etc.). Foll. by *into*. LME–M19. ▸**b** Introduce by way of argument or illustration; adduce, quote. LME–M17. ▸**c** Introduce or present (a person); bring in as a character in a literary work. L15–M18.
3 Bring about, produce, give rise to. LME. ▸**b** PHYSICS. Produce (an electric current, a magnetic state) by induction. L18. ▸**c** MEDICINE. Initiate (labour) artificially; bring on labour in (a mother), accelerate the birth of (a child). M19. ▸**d** MICROBIOLOGY. Cause (a bacterium containing a prophage) to begin the lytic cycle. M20.
Nature [224]Ra with a short . . half life induces in man chiefly osteosarcomas. D. DU MAURIER Endeavoured to induce in me his passion for the planting of rare shrubs. J. HALIFAX Shamanistic trance, frequently induced by powerful hallucinogens. **c** *absol.*: S. KITZINGER Some hospitals induce if the baby is as much as a week 'overdue'.
†**4** Introduce (a person) *to* a subject; initiate (*into*), accustom *to*; instruct, teach. L15–M16.
†**5** Lead to as a conclusion; suggest, imply. L15–M17.
6 Infer; derive by reasoning from particular facts. M16.
Science From a sufficient number of results a proposition or law is induced.
†**7** Put (*up*)*on* or *over* as a covering. M16–L18.
■ **inducer** *noun* a person who or thing which induces; *esp.* an agent that brings about induction: M16.

induced /ɪnˈdjuːst/ *ppl adjective*. E17.
[ORIGIN from INDUCE + -ED[1].]
Brought on, caused, produced, by attraction, persuasion, etc.; caused or brought into being artificially, or by some external agent or process; not spontaneous; having been produced or affected by induction.
induced drag AERONAUTICS that part of the drag on an aerofoil due to trailing vortices; also called ***vortex drag***. **induced radioactivity**: produced in normally non-radioactive material by irradiation. **induced reaction** CHEMISTRY a reaction that is accelerated by the presence of an inductor.

inducement /ɪnˈdjuːsm(ə)nt/ *noun*. L16.
[ORIGIN from INDUCE + -MENT.]
1 A thing which induces someone *to do* something; an attraction, an incentive. L16. ▸†**b** A ground or reason which inclines one to a belief or course of action. L16–L17.
J. A. FROUDE He resisted the inducements which . . were urged upon him to come forward in the world. A. FRASER He had no personal inducement to linger in a country which had treated him so ill.
†**2** The action of inducing; persuasion, influence. E–M17.
3 †**a** A preamble or introduction to a book or subject. Only in E17. ▸**b** LAW. Introduction; introductory matter. Chiefly in ***matters of inducement***, introductory statements in a pleading explaining the matter in dispute. L18.

inducible /ɪnˈdjuːsɪb(ə)l/ *adjective*. M17.
[ORIGIN from INDUCE + -IBLE.]
†**1** Able to be inferred. Only in M17.
2 Able to be brought on, brought about, or caused. L17. ▸**b** BIOCHEMISTRY. Of an enzyme system: activated in the presence of an appropriate inducer. M20.
■ **induciˈbility** *noun* (esp. BIOCHEMISTRY) the property or state of being inducible M20.

inducive /ɪnˈdjuːsɪv/ *adjective*. *rare*. E17.
[ORIGIN from INDUCE + -IVE.]
Tending to induce or give rise to something. (Foll. by *of*, *to*.)

induct /ɪnˈdʌkt/ *verb trans.* LME.
[ORIGIN Latin *induct-* pa. ppl stem of *inducere* INDUCE.]
1 **a** ECCLESIASTICAL. Introduce formally into possession of a benefice or living. LME. ▸**b** Introduce formally into office; install. M16. ▸**c** Place or install in a seat, a room, etc. E18.
N. HAWTHORNE Lately he has taken orders, and been inducted to a small country living. **c** DICKENS Received with signal marks of approbation, and inducted into the most honourable seats.
2 Lead, conduct *into*. *rare*. E17.
3 Introduce *to*; initiate *into*. E17.
THACKERAY The pleasures to which the footman inducted him. J. S. HUXLEY I was inducted into the mysteries of Eton football.
4 Enrol or conscript for military service. *US*. M20.
■ **inducˈtee** *noun* (*US*) a person inducted into military service M20.

inductance /ɪnˈdʌkt(ə)ns/ *noun*. L19.
[ORIGIN from INDUCTION + -ANCE.]
ELECTRICITY. **1** That property of a circuit or device by virtue of which any variation in the current flowing through it induces an electromotive force in the circuit itself or in another conductor; the magnitude of this. L19.
mutual inductance: see MUTUAL *adjective*. SELF-INDUCTANCE.
2 = INDUCTOR 3C. E20.

inductile /ɪnˈdʌktʌɪl/ *adjective*. M18.
[ORIGIN from IN-[3] + DUCTILE.]
Not ductile or pliable; unyielding, stubborn.

induction /ɪnˈdʌkʃ(ə)n/ *noun*. LME.
[ORIGIN Old French & mod. French, or Latin *inductio(n-)*, formed as INDUCT: see -ION.]
1 **a** LOGIC. The process of inferring or verifying a general law or principle from the observation of particular instances; an instance of this; a conclusion thus reached. Cf. DEDUCTION 3. LME. ▸**b** The citing or enumerating *of* a number of separate facts etc. esp. in order to prove a general statement. M16. ▸**c** MATH. The process of proving the truth of a theorem by showing that if it is true of any one case in a series then it is true of the next case, and that it is true in a particular case. Freq. more fully ***mathematical induction***. M19.
a T. FOWLER Induction . . is the inference from the particular to the general, from the known to the unknown. R. FRY I . . put forward my system as . . a provisional induction from my own aesthetic experiences. **b** H. ROGERS Rather as a most extensive induction of facts, than as an instance of their successful application.
a *imperfect induction*: see IMPERFECT *adjective*.
2 ECCLESIASTICAL. The action or ceremony of formally placing an incumbent in possession of a church and its revenues. LME. ▸**b** In Presbyterian Churches: the placing of a minister already ordained into a new pastoral charge. L19.
3 Formal introduction to an office or position; installation. LME. ▸**b** Enlistment into military service. *US*. M20.
b *attrib.*: *Times Lit. Suppl.* One summer the dreaded Induction Notice comes and he goes to war.
†**4** The action of inducing by persuasion; inducement. L15–L16.
5 Introduction to or initiation into the knowledge of something. Freq. *attrib.* E16.
B. MASON Oh, I knew it was The Test, our puberty rite, our induction into manly ways.
6 That which leads on or in *to* something; an introduction. Now *rare*. M16. ▸**b** An introductory statement; a preface (to a book etc.). *arch.* M16. ▸†**c** The initial step in an undertaking. *rare* (Shakes.). Only in L16.
G. BUCK An induction to those succeeding evils which pursued that inconsiderate marriage.
7 The action of introducing or bringing in (a person, a custom, etc.). *rare*. E17.
8 The action of bringing on, producing, or causing something. M17. ▸**b** MEDICINE. The artificial initiation of labour. M19. ▸**c** EMBRYOLOGY. The determination of the pattern of development or differentiation of a region or group of cells by the influence of another. E20. ▸**d** BIOCHEMISTRY. Initiation or acceleration of synthesis of an enzyme as a result of the introduction of a specific substance (the

inducer). **M20.** ▸**e** *MICROBIOLOGY.* The initiation of the lytic cycle in a bacterium containing a prophage. **M20.**
d *SEQUENTIAL* ***induction.***

9 *PHYSICS.* The action or process of producing an electrical or magnetic state in a body by proximity to an electrified or magnetized body, without physical contact. **E19.** ▸**b** Magnetic or electric flux or flux density. Usu. with specifying word. **M19.**
UNIPOLAR ***induction.***

– **COMB.:** **induction coil**: in which an electric current is induced; *esp.* a transformer in which a current in a primary coil induces a current (esp. as high-voltage pulses) in a (concentric) secondary coil; **induction furnace**: for melting metals by induction heating; **induction hardening**: of steel surfaces by induction heating followed by quenching; **induction heating**: of a material by inducing an electric current within it; **induction loop** a wiring circuit installed in a public building which carries amplified sound (usually speech) in the form of electromagnetic signals which can be received by the hearing aid of a partially deaf person; **induction motor** an AC electric motor in which the force results from the interaction of a magnetic field in the stationary windings with the currents induced in the rotor.

▪ **inductional** *adjective* **E19.**

inductive /ɪnˈdʌktɪv/ *adjective.* **LME.**
[**ORIGIN** Old French *inductif, -ive*, or late Latin *inductivus* hypothetical, (in medieval Latin) inducing, leading to, formed as **INDUCT**: see **-IVE.**]
1 Leading on (*to* an action etc.); inducing. **LME.**
†**2** Productive *of*, giving rise *to*. **E17–L18.**
3 *LOGIC.* Of, based on, or characterized by induction; using a method of induction. Cf. **DEDUCTIVE. M18.**
4 *PHYSICS.* Of the nature of, pertaining to, or due to electric or magnetic induction; possessing inductance. **M19.**
5 Introductory. **M19.**
6 *EMBRYOLOGY.* Of, pertaining to, or producing induction of development or differentiation. **M20.**
▪ **inductively** *adverb* **E18.** **inductiveness** *noun* **M19.** **inducˈtivity** *noun* (*rare*) power of or capacity for (esp. magnetic) induction **L19.**

inductivism /ɪnˈdʌktɪvɪz(ə)m/ *noun.* **M19.**
[**ORIGIN** from **INDUCTIVE** + **-ISM.**]
The use of or preference for inductive methods; the belief that scientific laws can be inferred from observational evidence. Opp. **DEDUCTIVISM.**
▪ **inductivist** *noun & adjective* (***a***) *noun* a person who advocates inductivism or inductive methods; (***b***) *adjective* of, pertaining to, or employing inductivism or inductive methods: **M20.**

inductomeric /ɪnˌdʌktə(ʊ)ˈmɛrɪk/ *adjective.* **M20.**
[**ORIGIN** from **INDUCTION** after **ELECTROMERIC.**]
CHEMISTRY. Of, pertaining to, or designating the polarizing effect exerted along a saturated chemical bond by an external electric field.

inductor /ɪnˈdʌktə/ *noun.* **M17.**
[**ORIGIN** Late Latin, or from **INDUCT** + **-OR.**]
1 A person who inducts or initiates. *rare.* **M17.**
2 A person who inducts a member of the clergy to a benefice. **E18.**
3 A part of an electrical apparatus which acts inductively on another, esp. to produce an electromotive force or a current. **M19.** ▸**b** A conductor or device in which an electromotive force or current is induced. **M19.** ▸**c** A device (usu. a coil) possessing inductance or used on account of its inductance. **E20.**
4 *CHEMISTRY.* A substance which accelerates a reaction by reacting with one of the substances involved, so differing from a catalyst by being consumed. **E20.**
5 *EMBRYOLOGY.* (A substance produced by) a region of an embryo capable of causing induction of development or differentiation. **E20.**

inductory /ɪnˈdʌkt(ə)ri/ *adjective. rare.* **M17.**
[**ORIGIN** from **INDUCTIVE** by suffix-substitution, or from **INDUCT**: see **-ORY**[2].]
Introductory.

indue *verb* var. of **ENDUE.**

indulge /ɪnˈdʌldʒ/ *verb.* **E17.**
[**ORIGIN** Latin *indulgere* allow space or time for, give rein to.]
▸ **I** *verb trans.* **1** Treat (a person) with excessive kindness; gratify by compliance or absence of restraint; humour by yielding to the wishes of. (Foll. by *in.*) **E17.** ▸**b** *refl.* Give free course to one's inclination or liking; gratify oneself. (Foll. by *in.*) **M17.** ▸**c** Favour or gratify (a person) *with* something given or granted. **L18.**

> HARPER LEE She's never let them get away with anything, she never indulged them. **b** L. BRUCE I would indulge myself in bizarre melodramatic fantasies.

2 Grant an indulgence, privilege, or dispensation to. **M17.**
3 Gratify (a desire or inclination); give free course to, yield to, give oneself up to; cherish, foster. **M17.**

> E. F. BENSON She was quite willing to indulge any foolish prejudices of her husband. L. NAMIER He . . retires to his closet . . . to indulge the melancholy enjoyment of his own ill humour.

4 Bestow, grant as a favour; allow or concede as an indulgence. Now *rare.* **M17.**

> S. HALLIFAX A Valuable privilege is likewise indulged to Graduates in this faculty.

5 *COMMERCE.* Grant an indulgence on (a bill), or to (a person) on a bill. **M18.**

▸ **II** *verb intrans.* †**6** Grant indulgence *to* (a propensity etc., *rare* a person); give free course *to*, give way *to*. **M17–L18.**
7 Foll. by *in*: give rein to one's inclination for; gratify one's desire or appetite for; take one's pleasure in. **E18.**

> H. T. LANE We believe that children develop bad habits by indulging in them. T. SHARPE Observing his fellow travellers and indulging in British Rail's high tea.

8 Gratify a desire, appetite, etc.; take one's pleasure; *spec.* (*colloq.*) partake (freely) of intoxicants. **E18.**

> P. O'DONNELL Tarrant . . took out his cigar case. He had not indulged all night.

▪ **indulged** *ppl adjective* (***a***) that has received and accepted an indulgence; *esp.* (*SCOTTISH HISTORY*) (of a Presbyterian minister) licensed to hold services; (***b***) gratified or favoured by compliance; humoured: **L17.** **indulger** *noun* **M17.** **indulging** *ppl adjective* that indulges; indulgent: **M18.** **indulgingly** *adverb* **L18.**

indulgence /ɪnˈdʌldʒ(ə)ns/ *noun.* **LME.**
[**ORIGIN** Old French & mod. French from Latin *indulgentia*, from *indulgent-*: see **INDULGENT, -ENCE.**]
▸ **I 1** The act of indulging a person; the fact of being indulgent; gratification of another's desire or humour; overly lenient treatment. **LME.** ▸**b** An instance of this; a favour or privilege granted. **L16.**

> H. MARTINEAU Indulgence is given her as a substitute for justice. H. JAMES I had not been properly introduced and could only throw myself upon her indulgence. **b** LD MACAULAY He ordered them to be . . supplied with every indulgence.

2 The action of indulging an inclination etc.; yielding to or gratification of a propensity (foll. by *of, to*); the action of indulging *in* a practice. **M17.** ▸**b** The practice of indulging one's own inclinations; self-gratification, self-indulgence. Also, an indulgent habit, a luxury. **M17.**

> J. MORTIMER Overcome with . . the indulgence of grief, he sank to his knees. P. GAY The indulgence in heedless pleasure entails later pain. **b** M. SHELLEY The time . . arrives, when grief is rather an indulgence than a necessity. R. W. EMERSON Human nature is prone to indulgence.

▸ **II 3** *ROMAN CATHOLIC CHURCH.* A grant of remission of the temporal punishment still due to sin after sacramental absolution. **LME.** ▸†**b** Remission of sin. Only in **LME.**

> D. LODGE An indulgence was a kind of spiritual voucher obtained by performing some devotional exercise.

4 *hist.* A grant of religious liberties, as special favours rather than legal rights, to Nonconformists. **M17.** ▸**b** A licence offered during the reigns of Charles II and James II (VII) to Presbyterian ministers in Scotland to hold services on various conditions. **L17.**
Declaration of Indulgence a proclamation of religious liberties; *esp.* either of those made in Scotland under Charles II in 1672 and James II (VII) in 1687. ***plenary indulgence***: see **PLENARY** *adjective.*
5 *COMMERCE.* An extension, made as a favour, of the time within which a bill of exchange or a debt is to be paid. **E19.**

indulgence /ɪnˈdʌldʒ(ə)ns/ *verb trans.* **L16.**
[**ORIGIN** from the noun.]
†**1** Grant or permit as an indulgence or favour. Only in **L16.**
2 *ROMAN CATHOLIC CHURCH.* Attach an indulgence to (a particular act or object). Freq. as ***indulgenced*** *ppl adjective*, conveying an indulgence. **M19.**

indulgency /ɪnˈdʌldʒ(ə)nsi/ *noun.* Now *rare.* **M16.**
[**ORIGIN** Latin *indulgentia*: see **INDULGENCE** *noun*, **-ENCY.**]
1 The quality or practice of being indulgent; indulgent disposition or action. **M16.** ▸**b** An indulgence; a favour. **M18.**
2 = **INDULGENCE** *noun* 2. **L17.**
†**3** = **INDULGENCE** *noun* 3. **L17–M19.**

indulgent /ɪnˈdʌldʒ(ə)nt/ *adjective.* **E16.**
[**ORIGIN** French, or Latin *indulgent-* pres. ppl stem of *indulgere*: see **INDULGE, -ENT.**]
1 That indulges; disposed to gratify by compliance or humour, or to overlook failings; ready to show favour or leniency; (overly) lenient, not exercising (due) restraint. (Foll. by *to.*) **E16.**

> E. CALDWELL He came along in a generation that was fed so much sugar and cream by indulgent parents. D. H. LAWRENCE He followed her look, and laughed quietly, with indulgent resignation.

2 Indulging or disposed to indulge oneself; self-indulgent. **L17.**

> E. O'BRIEN Soon she would be indulgent and order a champagne cocktail.

▪ **indulgently** *adverb* **L16.**

induline /ˈɪndjʊliːn/ *noun.* Also **-in** /-ɪn/. **L19.**
[**ORIGIN** from **INDO-**[2] + **-ULE** + **-INE**[5], **-IN**[1].]
CHEMISTRY. Any of a group of insoluble blue azine dyes.

indult /ɪnˈdʌlt/ *noun.* **L15.**
[**ORIGIN** French from late Latin *indultum* grant, concession, use as noun of neut. of Latin *indultus* pa. pple of *indulgere* **INDULGE.**]
1 *ROMAN CATHOLIC CHURCH.* A licence granted by the Pope authorizing an act that the common law of the Church does not sanction. **L15.**
†**2** A special privilege granted by authority; a licence or permission. **M16–E17.**

indulto /ɪnˈdʌltəʊ, *foreign* ɪnˈdulto/ *noun.* Pl. **-os** /-əʊz, *foreign* -ɔs/. **M17.**
[**ORIGIN** Spanish & Portuguese = exemption, privilege, licence, from late Latin *indultum*: see **INDULT.**]
†**1** = **INDULT M17–E19.**
2 *hist.* A duty paid to the King of Spain or Portugal, *spec.* on imported goods. **L17.**

indument /ˈɪndjʊm(ə)nt/ *noun.* Now *rare.* **L15.**
[**ORIGIN** Latin *indumentum* garment, from *induere* put on: see **-MENT.**]
†**1** Clothing, apparel; a garment, a vesture. **L15–L17.** ▸**b** *fig.* A material body. **L16–L17.**
2 A covering of hairs, feathers, etc.; an integument; an indumentum. **L16.**

indumentum /ɪndjʊˈmɛntəm/ *noun.* Pl. **-ta** /-tə/. **M19.**
[**ORIGIN** formed as **INDUMENT.**]
BOTANY. The covering of hairs, scales, etc., on (part of) a plant, esp. when dense.

induna /ɪnˈduːnə/ *noun. S. Afr.* **M19.**
[**ORIGIN** Zulu, from nominal prefix *in-* + *duna* councillor, headman, overseer, captain.]
1 A tribal councillor or headman. **M19.**
2 *transf.* A person, esp. a black person, in authority; a foreman. **M20.**

induplicate /ɪnˈdjuːplɪkət/ *adjective.* **E19.**
[**ORIGIN** from **IN-**[2] + **DUPLICATE** *adjective.*]
BOTANY. Of leaves, petals (when in the bud): folded or rolled in at the edges without overlapping.
▪ **indupliˈcation** *noun* (*BOTANY & ZOOLOGY*) (an instance of) folding or doubling in **L19.**

indurable /ɪnˈdjʊərəb(ə)l/ *adjective. rare.* **LME.**
[**ORIGIN** medieval Latin *indurabilis*, formed as **IN-**[3] + *durabilis* **DURABLE.**]
Not durable; not lasting.

†**indurance** *noun* var. of **ENDURANCE.**

indurate /ˈɪndjʊrət/ *ppl adjective.* Now *rare.* **LME.**
[**ORIGIN** Latin *induratus* pa. pple, formed as **INDURATE** *verb*: see **-ATE**[2].]
1 Made hard, hardened. **LME.**
2 Morally hardened, made callous; obstinate. **LME.**

indurate /ˈɪndjʊreɪt/ *verb.* **M16.**
[**ORIGIN** Latin *indurat-* pa. ppl stem of *indurare* make hard, formed as **IN-**[2] + *durus* hard: see **-ATE**[3].]
1 *verb trans.* Harden (the heart); make callous or unfeeling; make obstinate. **M16.**

> H. M. WILLIAMS It is the curse of revolutionary calamities to indurate the heart.

2 *verb trans.* Make (a substance) hard; harden, solidify. **L16.**

> R. KIRWAN Two beds of indurated clay. O. SACKS The superficial temporal artery may become exquisitely tender . . and visibly indurated.

3 *verb trans.* Make hardy; inure. **L16.**
4 *verb intrans.* Become or grow hard. **M17.** ▸**b** Of a custom: become fixed or established. **M19.**

> J. BARNES Soft cheeses collapse; firm cheeses indurate.

induration /ɪndjʊˈreɪʃ(ə)n/ *noun.* **LME.**
[**ORIGIN** Old French & mod. French, or late Latin *induratio(n-)*, formed as **INDURATE** *verb*: see **-ATION.**]
1 The action of hardening; the process of being hardened or becoming hard; hardened condition; *esp.* (***a***) consolidation or hardening of a rock or soil by heat, pressure, chemical action, etc.; (***b***) *MEDICINE* abnormal hardening of an organ or tissue. **LME.**
2 A hardening of character or feeling; obstinacy, stubbornness; callousness. **L15.**

indurative /ˈɪndjʊərətɪv/ *adjective.* **L16.**
[**ORIGIN** formed as **INDURATE** *verb*: see **-ATIVE.**]
Having a hardening tendency or quality.

†**indure** *verb* var. of **ENDURE.**

Indus /ˈɪndəs/ *noun.* **E18.**
[**ORIGIN** Latin = an Indian.]
(The name of) a constellation of the southern hemisphere between Capricorn and Pavo; the Indian.

indusium /ɪnˈdjuːzɪəm/ *noun.* Pl. **-ia** /-ɪə/. **E18.**
[**ORIGIN** Latin = tunic, from *induere* put on (a garment).]
BIOLOGY & ANATOMY. Any of various thin membranous coverings, as (***a***) (now *rare*) the amnion; (***b***) the larval case of some insects; (***c***) a collection of hairs enclosing the stigma of some flowers; (***d***) a flap of tissue covering a sorus on a fern leaf; (***e***) the thin layer of grey matter on the upper surface of the corpus callosum.
▪ **indusial** *adjective* **E19.** **indusiate** *adjective* having an indusium **M19.**

industrial /ɪnˈdʌstrɪəl/ *adjective & noun.* **L15.**
[**ORIGIN** from (the same root as) **INDUSTRY** + **-AL**[1]; later after French *industriel.*]
▸ **A** *adjective.* **1** Pertaining to or of the nature of industry or productive labour; resulting from industry; engaged in or connected with industry, esp. with manufacturing. **L15.**

> J. L. Motley Such of the industrial classes as could leave . . had wandered away to Holland and England. U. Bentley The city's buildings were still charred with two hundred years of industrial soot.

2 Of a substance or material: of a quality suitable for industrial use. **E20.**
3 Characterized by highly developed industries. **E20.**

> J. D. Bernal Only the industrial countries of Europe . . contributed to modern science.

– SPECIAL COLLOCATIONS: **industrial action** action such as a strike or working to rule taken by employees. **industrial archaeology** the branch of archaeology that deals with the equipment and workings of industry in former times. **industrial disease** a disease contracted in the course of employment, esp. in a factory. **industrial dispute** a dispute between employers and employees. **industrial espionage** spying directed towards discovering the secrets of a rival manufacturer or other industrial company. **industrial estate** an area of land devoted to industrial use, usu. with an integrated plan. **industrial injury**: sustained in the course of employment, esp. in a factory. **industrial language** *colloq.* bad language, swearing. ***industrial* MELANISM. industrial park** = *industrial estate* above. **industrial relations**: between employers and employees. **industrial revolution** the rapid development of a nation's industry through the introduction of machines, esp. (freq. with cap. initials) in Britain in the late 18th and early 19th cents. **industrial school** *hist.* a school established in Britain in the 19th cent. to enable needy children to learn a trade. ***industrial tribunal***: see TRIBUNAL *noun*.

► **B** *noun*. **1** A person engaged in industrial activities. **M19.**
2 (A share in) a joint-stock industrial enterprise. **L19.**
■ **industrialism** *noun* a social or economic system arising from the existence of great industries; the organization of industrial occupations: **M19. industrialist** *noun* a person engaged in or connected with (the management or ownership of) industry; a manufacturer: **M19. industrially** *adverb* **M19.**

industrialize /ɪnˈdʌstrɪəlʌɪz/ *verb*. Also **-ise**. **L19.**
[ORIGIN from INDUSTRIAL + -IZE.]
1 *verb trans.* Affect with or devote to industrialism; occupy or organize industrially. Freq. as ***industrialized*** *ppl adjective*. **L19.**
industrialized building a form of construction in which industrial methods are used (esp. prefabrication, mechanization, standardization); a building erected by such methods.
2 *verb intrans.* Become industrial. **M20.**
■ **industriaLiˈzation** *noun* the process of industrializing; the fact of being industrialized; the conversion of an organization into an industry: **E20.**

industrious /ɪnˈdʌstrɪəs/ *adjective*. **L15.**
[ORIGIN French *industrieux* or late Latin *industriosus*, from *industria*: see INDUSTRY, -OUS.]
†**1** Showing intelligent or skilful work; skilful, clever, ingenious. **L15–L17.**
2 Showing application, endeavour, or effort; painstaking, zealous, attentive. (Foll. by *in*, *to do*.) **M16.**
3 Showing assiduous or steady work; diligent, hard-working. **L16.**

> *Esquire* The sober, industrious citizens of the upper-middle class.

†**4** Showing design or purpose; intentional, designed, voluntary. **E17–E19.**
5 = INDUSTRIAL *adjective*. *rare*. **E19.**
■ **industriously** *adverb* **L15. industriousness** *noun* **L16.**

industry /ˈɪndəstri/ *noun*. **LME.**
[ORIGIN Old French & mod. French *industrie* or Latin *industria* diligence: see -Y[3].]
1 Diligence or assiduity in the performance of a task or effort; close and steady application to a task; exertion. **LME.**

> K. Tynan A climax towards which she has climbed, with unflourished industry.

2 Systematic work or labour; habitual employment in useful work. Now *esp.* work in manufacturing and production; trade and manufacture collectively. **LME.**

> R. Burns A man that has been bred up in the trade of begging, will never . . fall to industry. Carlyle The Leaders of Industry . . are virtually the Captains of the World. R. Ingalls She had started out with the introduction of agriculture, the coming of industry.

†**3** Intelligent working; skill, ingenuity, cleverness. **L15–E17.**
†**4** An application of skill, cleverness, or craft; a device; a crafty expedient. **L15–E17.**
5 A particular form or branch of productive labour; a trade, a manufacture. **M16.**

> S. O'Faoláin The founder of an industry—glass-making. *Studio Week* The most . . . productive tool in the music industry today.

6 ARCHAEOLOGY. A collection of prehistoric implements of the same age found at an archaeological site, generally with typical debris from their manufacture, and used as evidence of the original technique of working; the technique so revealed. **E20.**
7 A particular (profitable) activity; *esp.* diligent work devoted to the study of a particular person or other subject. *colloq.* **M20.**

> *Daily Telegraph* The brisk pick-up of business in the abortion industry. C. Osborne I did not want to become involved in the Eliot industry.

– PHRASES: ***basic industry***: see BASIC *adjective* 1. ***cottage industry***. ***growth industry***: see GROWTH *adjective*. ***heavy industry***: see HEAVY *adjective*. ***light industry***: see LIGHT *adjective*[1]. ***primary industry***: see PRIMARY *adjective*. ***secondary industry***: see SECONDARY *adjective*. ***tertiary industry***: see TERTIARY *adjective*.
– COMB.: **industry-wide** *adjective* extending or prevalent throughout a particular industry.

indwell /ɪnˈdwɛl/ *verb*. Pa. t. & pple **-dwelt** /-dwɛlt/. **LME.**
[ORIGIN from IN-[1] + DWELL *verb*, orig. rendering Latin *inhabitare* inhabit.]
1 *verb trans.* Dwell in, inhabit, occupy as a dwelling. Now chiefly *fig.*, (esp. of God, the Holy Spirit) be permanently present in, possess (the heart, soul, mind, etc.). **LME.**
2 *verb intrans.* Dwell, abide, live (*in*). **LME.**
■ **ˈindweller** *noun* (*a*) a person who lives in a place, an inhabitant; (*b*) a mere resident, a sojourner: **LME. ˈindwelling** *adjective* (*a*) that dwells within, inhabits, or possesses; (*b*) MEDICINE (of a catheter, electrode, etc.) left more or less permanently fixed in the body: **LME.**

indy *noun & adjective* var. of INDIE.

-ine /ʌɪn, ɪn, iːn/ *suffix*[1].
[ORIGIN Repr. French *-in*, *-ine* or Latin *-inus*, *-ina*, *-inum*. Cf. -INE[3], -INE[4].]
Forming adjectives with the sense 'of, pertaining to, of the nature of'. Orig. & chiefly with Latin noun stems, as ***Alpine***, ***aquiline***, ***canine***, ***supine***; freq. in BIOLOGY, forming adjectives from the names of genera, as ***bovine***, ***equine***, ***feline***, or of subfamilies (in Latin *-inae*) or tribes (in Latin *-ini*).

-ine /ʌɪn/ *suffix*[2].
[ORIGIN Repr. Latin *-inus*, from Greek *-inos*.]
Forming adjectives with the sense 'of the nature of, resembling', esp. from names of minerals, plants, etc., as ***adamantine***, ***crystalline***, ***hyacinthine***.

-ine /ɪn, iːn/ *suffix*[3].
[ORIGIN Repr. or after French *-ine*, Latin *-ina*, Greek *-inē*: see -INE[1].]
Forming fem. nouns, as ***heroine***, ***margravine***, ***Trappistine***.

-ine /ɪn, iːn, ʌɪn/ *suffix*[4].
[ORIGIN Repr. French *-ine*, Latin *-ina* in uses as nouns of adjectives: see -INE[1].]
Forming (esp. abstract) nouns, as ***concubine***, ***doctrine***, ***fascine***, ***medicine***, ***rapine***. Now freq. forming names of derived substances, similative appellations, diminutives, etc., as ***brilliantine***, ***dentine***, ***figurine***, ***nectarine***, ***tambourine***.

-ine /iːn, ɪn/ *suffix*[5]. See also -EINE.
[ORIGIN from -INE[4].]
1 Used in CHEMISTRY to form names of substances (orig. & chiefly with stems representing the sources of the substances), esp. alkaloids (***cocaine***, ***strychnine***), amino acids (***glycine***, ***thymine***), amines (***aniline***, ***hydrazine***), and halogens (***chlorine***), and formerly also in MINERALOGY (***olivine***).
2 CHEMISTRY. Forming nouns denoting compounds with a single ring of six atoms, one at least of which is nitrogen, as ***azine***.

inearth /ɪˈnəːθ/ *verb trans.* Chiefly *poet.* **E19.**
[ORIGIN from IN-[1] + EARTH *noun*[1].]
Bury, inter.

inebriant /ɪˈniːbrɪənt/ *noun*. **E19.**
[ORIGIN from INEBRIATE *verb* after *intoxicant*: see -ANT[1].]
An inebriating substance or agent; an intoxicant.

inebriate /ɪˈniːbrɪət/ *noun*. **L18.**
[ORIGIN from (the same root as) INEBRIATE *verb*: see -ATE[1].]
An intoxicated person; *esp.* a habitual drunkard.

inebriate /ɪˈniːbrɪeɪt/ *verb trans.* Pa. pple & ppl adjective **-ated**, (*arch.*) **-ate** /-ət/. **LME.**
[ORIGIN Orig. pa. pple, from Latin *inebriatus* pa. pple of *inebriare*, formed as IN-[2] + *ebriare* intoxicate, from *ebrius* drunk: see -ATE[2], -ATE[3].]
1 Make drunk; intoxicate. **LME.**

> W. Cowper While . . the cups That cheer but not inebriate, wait on each. *fig.*: Disraeli A sophisticated rhetorician, inebriated with the exuberance of his own verbosity.

†**2** Water, moisten; refresh (as) with drink. **E–M17.**

inebriation /ɪˌniːbrɪˈeɪʃ(ə)n/ *noun*. **E16.**
[ORIGIN Late Latin *inebriatio(n-)*, from Latin *inebriat-* pa. ppl stem of *inebriare*: see INEBRIATE *verb*, -ATION.]
The action of inebriating someone; the condition of being inebriated; intoxication.

inebriety /ɪnɪˈbrʌɪəti/ *noun*. **L18.**
[ORIGIN from IN-[2] + EBRIETY.]
The state or habit of being inebriated; (habitual) drunkenness.

inebrious /ɪˈniːbrɪəs/ *adjective*. *rare*. **LME.**
[ORIGIN from IN-[2] + Latin *ebriosus* + -OUS, perh. after Old French or medieval Latin; later directly from IN-[2] + EBRIOUS.]
†**1** Inebriating, intoxicating. **LME–E18.**
2 Inebriated, (habitually) drunken. **M19.**

inedible /ɪnˈɛdɪb(ə)l/ *adjective*. **E19.**
[ORIGIN from IN-[3] + EDIBLE *adjective*.]
Not edible, unfit to be eaten; *colloq.* unpalatable.

> P. Bowles It would not be amusing . . to sleep in dirty beds, eat inedible meals.

■ **inediˈbility** *noun* **L19.**

inédit /inedi/ *noun*. Pl. pronounced same. **E20.**
[ORIGIN French: cf. INEDITA.]
An unpublished work; *fig.* something secret or unrevealed.

inedita /ɪnˈɛdɪtə/ *noun pl.* **L19.**
[ORIGIN mod. Latin, use as noun of neut. pl. of Latin *ineditus*, formed as IN-[3] + *editus* pa. pple of *edere* give out, EDIT *verb*.]
Unpublished writings.

inedited /ɪnˈɛdɪtɪd/ *adjective*. **M18.**
[ORIGIN from IN-[3] + EDIT *verb* + -ED[1].]
1 Not edited, not published; not described in any published work. **M18.**
2 Published without editorial alterations or additions. **M19.**

ineducable /ɪnˈɛdjʊkəb(ə)l, -dʒʊ-/ *adjective & noun*. **L19.**
[ORIGIN from IN-[3] + EDUCABLE.]
► **A** *adjective*. Unable to be educated, esp. as a result of mental disability. **L19.**
► **B** *noun*. An ineducable person. **M20.**
■ **ineducaˈbility** *noun* **E20.**

ineffable /ɪnˈɛfəb(ə)l/ *adjective & noun*. **LME.**
[ORIGIN Old French & mod. French, or Latin *ineffabilis*, formed as IN-[3] + *effabilis*, from *effari* speak out, formed as EF- + *fari* speak: see -ABLE.]
► **A** *adjective*. **1** Too great to be expressed in words; unutterable, indefinable, indescribable. **LME.**

> R. Rendell The three coffins were borne up the aisle with ineffable slowness.

2 Not to be uttered. Formerly also, not to be disclosed. **L16.**
†**3** Unpronounceable. *rare*. **M–L17.**
► **B** *noun*. **1** A person or thing not to be mentioned or named; *spec.* (*arch.*) in *pl.*, trousers. **E19.**
2 A person, thing, or condition which is beyond description or expression. **M20.**

> *Library* A flight of spiritual stairs leading the contemplator ever closer to the ineffable.

■ **ineffaˈbility** *noun* **E17. ineffableness** *noun* **L17. ineffably** *adverb* **L15.**

ineffaceable /ɪnɪˈfeɪsəb(ə)l/ *adjective*. **E19.**
[ORIGIN from IN-[3] + EFFACE + -ABLE.]
Impossible to efface or obliterate; indelible.

> Southey The everlasting and ineffaceable infamy of bombarding Copenhagen.

■ **ineffaceaˈbility** *noun* **L19. ineffaceably** *adverb* **E19.**

ineffective /ɪnɪˈfɛktɪv/ *adjective & noun*. **M17.**
[ORIGIN from IN-[3] + EFFECTIVE.]
► **A** *adjective*. **1** Not producing any, or the desired, effect; ineffectual, inoperative, inefficient. **M17.**

> J. R. Ackerley Since her hostile attitude was seen to be as inconvenient as it was ineffective, she relented. W. Wharton I also feel ineffective, helpless; Vron could do these things ten times better than I can.

2 Lacking in artistic effect. **M19.**
► **B** *noun*. An ineffective person or thing. **M19.**
■ **ineffectively** *adverb* **M17. ineffectiveness** *noun* **M19.**

ineffectual /ɪnɪˈfɛktʃʊəl/ *adjective*. **LME.**
[ORIGIN medieval Latin *ineffectualis*; later from IN-[3] + EFFECTUAL.]
1 Having no effect; unavailing, unsuccessful, fruitless. **LME.**

> D. Brewster When he found his reasoning ineffectual, he appealed to direct experience.

2 Not producing the desired effect; not fulfilling expectations; tame. **L18.**

> E. K. Kane The phosphorescence was not unlike the ineffectual fire of the glow-worm.

3 Failing in one's purpose or role; inadequate. **M19.**

> S. Morley We spent a year . . in a science class taken by an absurd and ineffectual master.

■ **ineffectuˈality** *noun* **L17. ineffectually** *adverb* **E17. ineffectualness** *noun* **M17.**

inefficacious /ˌɪnɛfɪˈkeɪʃəs/ *adjective*. **M17.**
[ORIGIN from IN-[3] + EFFICACIOUS.]
Not efficacious; ineffective.
■ **inefficaciously** *adverb* **E18. inefficaciousness** *noun* **M17.**

inefficacy /ɪnˈɛfɪkəsi/ *noun*. **E17.**
[ORIGIN Late Latin *inefficacia*; later from IN-[3] + EFFICACY.]
Lack of efficacy; inability to produce the desired effect.

> R. L. Stevenson The usual inefficacy of the lamps, which . . shed but a dying glimmer even while they burned.

■ Also **ineffiˈcacity** *noun* (*rare*) **E18.**

inefficiency /ɪnɪˈfɪʃ(ə)nsi/ *noun*. **M18.**
[ORIGIN from IN-[3] + EFFICIENCY.]
Lack of efficiency; ineffectiveness, incompetence; an instance of this.

inefficient /ɪnɪˈfɪʃ(ə)nt/ *adjective & noun*. **M18.**
[ORIGIN from IN-[3] + EFFICIENT.]
▸ **A** *adjective*. Not efficient; unable to work effectively; incompetent; wasteful. **M18.**
▸ **B** *noun*. An inefficient person. **L19.**
■ **inefficiently** *adverb* **E19.**

inegalitarian /ˌɪnɪɡalɪˈtɛːrɪən/ *adjective & noun*. **M20.**
[ORIGIN from IN-[3] + EGALITARIAN.]
▸ **A** *adjective*. Of or pertaining to inequality; favouring or marked by inequality. **M20.**
▸ **B** *noun*. A person who denies or opposes equality between people. **M20.**
■ **inegalitarianism** *noun* **M20.**

inelaborate /ɪnɪˈlab(ə)rət/ *adjective*. **E17.**
[ORIGIN from IN-[3] + ELABORATE *adjective*.]
Not elaborate; simple in design or workmanship; not complicated or ornate.
■ **inelaborately** *adverb* **E19.**

inelastic /ɪnɪˈlastɪk/ *adjective*. **M18.**
[ORIGIN from IN-[3] + ELASTIC *adjective*.]
1 Not elastic or resilient, either rigid or plastic. **M18.** ▸**b** PHYSICS. Of a collision or scattering (esp. of subatomic particles): involving a reduction in total translational kinetic energy of the bodies or particles colliding. **M19.**
2 *fig.* Not adaptable; inflexible, unyielding. **M19.** ▸**b** ECONOMICS. Of demand or supply: unresponsive to, or varying less than in proportion to, changes in price. **L19.**

Spectator The House of Lords show not firmness . . but inelastic obstinacy and obstructiveness. G. S. FRASER Jonson with his strong . . but inelastic mind would shy away from Donne's agility in paradox. **b** *Lancet* Demand for cigarettes is inelastic . . . If prices rise by 1% demand falls, but by . . less than 1%.

■ **inelastically** *adverb* **M20.** **inelasticity** /ˌɪnɪlaˈstɪsɪti/ *noun* the quality or condition of being inelastic; an instance of this: **E19.**

inelegance /ɪnˈɛlɪɡ(ə)ns/ *noun*. **E18.**
[ORIGIN from INELEGANT: see -ANCE.]
The quality or fact of being inelegant; lack of refinement; clumsiness; an instance of this.
■ Also **inelegancy** *noun* (now *rare*) **E18.**

inelegant /ɪnˈɛlɪɡ(ə)nt/ *adjective*. **E16.**
[ORIGIN French *inélégant* from Latin *inelegant-*, formed as IN-[3] + *elegant-*: see ELEGANT.]
1 Lacking elegance or refinement; ungraceful, clumsy; coarse, crude; (of language or style) unpolished. **E16.**
2 Lacking in aesthetic refinement or delicacy. **M17.**
■ **inelegantly** *adverb* **L17.**

ineligible /ɪnˈɛlɪdʒɪb(ə)l/ *adjective & noun*. **L18.**
[ORIGIN from IN-[3] + ELIGIBLE.]
▸ **A** *adjective*. †**1** Of an action: inexpedient, unsuitable, undesirable. Only in **L18.**
2 Legally or officially disqualified for election to an office or position. **L18.**

T. JEFFERSON My wish . . was that the President should be elected for seven years, and be ineligible afterwards.

3 Not suitable or desirable, esp. as a partner in marriage. **E19.**
▸ **B** *noun*. An ineligible person; *spec.* an undesirable marriage partner. **L19.**

Westminster Gazette Eligible men as a class are so much less agreeable than the ineligibles.

■ **ineligiˈbility** *noun* **L18.** **ineligibly** *adverb* **M19.**

ineliminable /ɪnɪˈlɪmɪnəb(ə)l/ *adjective*. **L19.**
[ORIGIN from IN-[3] + ELIMINABLE.]
Unable to be eliminated.

ineloquent /ɪnˈɛləkwənt/ *adjective*. **M16.**
[ORIGIN from IN-[3] + ELOQUENT.]
Not eloquent; lacking eloquence.
■ **ineloquence** *noun* **M19.** **ineloquently** *adverb* **E19.**

ineluctable /ɪnɪˈlʌktəb(ə)l/ *adjective*. **E17.**
[ORIGIN Latin *ineluctabilis*, formed as IN-[3] + *eluctari* struggle out: see -ABLE.]
Unable to be resisted or avoided; inescapable.

M. BEERBOHM 'There', he said, 'is the ineluctable hard fact you wake to . . . The gods have spoken.' I. MURDOCH He felt himself confronted with an ineluctable choice between an evident truth and a fable.

■ **ineluctaˈbility** *noun* **M20.** **ineluctably** *adverb* **M17.**

ineludible /ɪnɪˈluːdɪb(ə)l, -ˈljuː-/ *adjective*. **L17.**
[ORIGIN from IN-[3] + ELUDE + -IBLE.]
Unavoidable, inescapable.
■ Earlier **ineludable** *adjective* (*rare*) **M17.**

inenarrable /ɪnɪˈnarəb(ə)l/ *adjective*. **LME.**
[ORIGIN Old French & mod. French *inénarrable* from Latin *inenarrabilis*, formed as IN-[3] + *enarrare* narrate: see E-, NARRATE, -ABLE.]
Unable to be narrated or told; indescribable, unspeakable.

M. DAVIES That sacred . . Mystery of the Holy Trinity is ineffable and inenarrable by any Creature. *Listener* The music has an inenarrable greatness which quite transcends the occasion of its composition.

inenubilable /ɪnɪˈnjuːbɪləb(ə)l/ *adjective*. *rare*. **E20.**
[ORIGIN from IN-[3] + Latin *enubilare* make clear (see ENUBILATE) + -ABLE.]
Unable to be cleared of clouds or mist; *fig.* inexplicable.

M. BEERBOHM There is nothing in England to be matched with . . that mysterious inenubilable spirit, spirit of Oxford.

inept /ɪˈnɛpt/ *adjective*. **M16.**
[ORIGIN Latin *ineptus*, formed as IN-[3] + *aptus* APT. Cf. INAPT.]
1 Unsuitable *for* (or †*to*) a purpose, unfit (*arch.*). In SCOTS LAW, invalid, void. **M16.**

J. RAY The Air . . would contain but few nitrous Particles, and so be inept to maintain the Fire. SIR W. SCOTT Extrajudicial confession . . was totally inept, and void of all strength and effect from the beginning.

2 Lacking in judgement or skill; foolish, clumsy, incompetent. **E17.**

W. HARDING Alcott, inept as ever, dreamily felled a tree without looking where it was going. A. ALVAREZ The young graduate student, too shy and inept to make conversation.

3 Not suited to the occasion; out of place, inappropriate. **L17.**

J. MARTINEAU If the doctrine were true, could anything be more inept than an allusion to it?

■ **ineptly** *adverb* **E16.** **ineptness** *noun* **E17.**

ineptitude /ɪˈnɛptɪtjuːd/ *noun*. **M16.**
[ORIGIN Latin *ineptitudo*, from *ineptus* INEPT: see -TUDE and cf. INAPTITUDE.]
1 Lack of aptitude or fitness *for* (or †*to*) something; unsuitability, invalidity. **M16.**

STEELE That Ineptitude for Society, which is frequently the Fault of us Scholars.

2 Lack of judgement or ability; incompetence, clumsiness; an instance of this, an inept action. **M17.**

C. BLACKWOOD His farm, which he ran with an amateurish ineptitude that resulted in an . . annual loss. A. POWELL The complaints . . were in connection with some ineptitude committed in regard to the luggage.

inequable /ɪnˈɛkwəb(ə)l/ *adjective*. **E18.**
[ORIGIN Latin *inaequabilis*, formed as IN-[3] + EQUABLE.]
Not uniform; uneven, unequal.

inequal /ɪnˈiːkw(ə)l/ *adjective*. Now *rare*. **LME.**
[ORIGIN Latin *inaequalis*, formed as IN-[3] + EQUAL *adjective*.]
Unequal; (of a surface) uneven.
inequal hours *hist.*: formed by dividing daytime and night-time each into twelve equal parts, and so varying in length according to the season.

inequalitarian /ˌɪnɪkwɒlɪˈtɛːrɪən/ *noun & adjective*. **L19.**
[ORIGIN from INEQUALITY after EQUALITARIAN: see -ARIAN.]
= INEGALITARIAN.

inequality /ɪnɪˈkwɒlɪti/ *noun*. **LME.**
[ORIGIN Old French *inequalité* (mod. *inégalité*) or Latin *inaequalitas*, formed as INEQUAL: see -ITY.]
1 Lack of equality between persons or things; disparity in size, number, quality, etc. **LME.** ▸**b** Difference of rank or circumstances; social or economic disparity. **L15.** ▸**c** Superiority or inferiority in relation to something; *esp.* the condition of being unequal *to* a task, inadequacy. **M16.**

New York Review of Books Inequality of opportunity is no longer a concern of federal government. **b** M. EDGEWORTH The inequality between the rich and the poor shocked him.

2 Lack of uniformity; unevenness, irregularity, fluctuation; an instance of this. **LME.**
3 Inconsistency in treatment of people or distribution of things; unfairness, inequity. **M16.**
4 ASTRONOMY. A deviation from uniformity in the motion of a planet or satellite. **L17.**
5 MATH. An expression of the relation between quantities that are not of equal value or magnitude, employing a sign such as $\neq$ 'not equal to', $>$ 'greater than', $<$ 'less than'. **L19.**
– PHRASES: ***Schwarz's inequality***, ***the Schwarz inequality***: see SCHWARZ.

inequilateral /ˌiːnɪːkwɪˈlat(ə)r(ə)l, ˌɪnɛ-/ *adjective*. **M17.**
[ORIGIN from IN-[3] + EQUILATERAL.]
Having unequal sides.

inequitable /ɪnˈɛkwɪtəb(ə)l/ *adjective*. **M17.**
[ORIGIN from IN-[3] + EQUITABLE.]
Not equitable, unfair.
■ **inequitably** *adverb* **M19.**

inequity /ɪnˈɛkwɪti/ *noun*. **M16.**
[ORIGIN from IN-[3] + EQUITY.]
Lack of equity or justice; unfairness, bias; an instance of this.

H. KISSINGER Allende . . blamed the capitalist system for social and economic inequities. E. FEINSTEIN The inequity of their mother's demands on them.

inequivalent /ɪnɪˈkwɪv(ə)l(ə)nt/ *adjective*. *rare*. **M16.**
[ORIGIN from IN-[3] + EQUIVALENT *adjective*.]
Chiefly MATH. Not equivalent, not of equal value.
■ **inequivalence** *noun* **L19.**

inequivalve /ɪnˈiːkwɪvalv/ *adjective*. **L18.**
[ORIGIN from IN-[3] + EQUI- + VALVE *noun*.]
CONCHOLOGY. Having the valves of the shell of different sizes.
■ Also **inequivalved**, **inequiˈvalvular** *adjectives* **E19.**

ineradicable /ɪnɪˈradɪkəb(ə)l/ *adjective*. **E19.**
[ORIGIN from IN-[3] + ERADICATE + -ABLE.]
Unable to be eradicated or rooted out.

inerasable /ɪnɪˈreɪzəb(ə)l/ *adjective*. **E19.**
[ORIGIN from IN-[3] + ERASE + -ABLE.]
Unable to be erased or effaced.

†**inergetical** *adjective*. *rare*. **L17–E18.**
[ORIGIN from IN-[3] + EN)ERGETICAL.]
Without energy; sluggish, inactive.
■ Also †**inergetic** *adjective* (*rare*) **E–M19.**

inerrable /ɪnˈɛrəb(ə)l, -ˈəːr-/ *adjective*. **M16.**
[ORIGIN Latin *inerrabilis*, formed as IN-[3] + *errare* err, wander: see -ABLE.]
Incapable of erring; not liable to err; infallible.
■ **inerraˈbility** *noun* **E17.**

inerrant /ɪnˈɛr(ə)nt/ *adjective*. **M17.**
[ORIGIN Latin *inerrant-* fixed, formed as IN-[3] + *errant-*: see ERRANT.]
†**1** ASTRONOMY. Of a star: fixed. Only in **M17.**
2 That does not err; unerring. **M19.**
■ **inerrancy** *noun* **M19.**

inerratic /ɪnɪˈratɪk/ *adjective*. **M17.**
[ORIGIN from IN-[3] + ERRATIC *adjective*.]
Not erratic or wandering; fixed; following a fixed course.

inert /ɪˈnəːt/ *adjective & noun*. **M17.**
[ORIGIN Latin *inert-*, *iners* unskilled, inactive, formed as IN-[3] + *art-*, *ars* skill, ART *noun*[1].]
▸ **A** *adjective*. **1** Of matter or a material thing: having no inherent power of action, motion, or resistance; inanimate; having the property of inertia. **M17.** ▸**b** Without active chemical or physiological properties; unreactive. **E19.**

F. BOWEN If matter is essentially inert, every change in it must be produced by the mind.

2 Of a person, an animal, etc.: inactive, slow; not inclined for or capable of action or movement; motionless. **L18.**

R. P. WARREN He lay beneath the high carved headboard of his bed, inert as a log. A. BROOKNER With their curiously inert attitude to life, I doubt that they would even notice my absence.

– SPECIAL COLLOCATIONS: **inert gas** (*a*) a (relatively) unreactive gas; (*b*) *spec.* = ***noble gas*** s.v. NOBLE *adjective* (usu. in *pl.*).
▸ **B** *noun*. An inert or unreactive substance. **M20.**
■ **inertly** *adverb* **M18.** **inertness** *noun* **M17.**

inertia /ɪˈnəːʃə/ *noun*. **E18.**
[ORIGIN Latin = inactivity, formed as INERT: see -IA[1].]
1 PHYSICS. The property of a body, proportional to its mass, by virtue of which it continues in a state of rest or uniform straight motion in the absence of an external force. **E18.** ▸**b** In other physical properties: the tendency to continue in some state, to resist change. **L19.**

J. F. LAMB Blood has a high inertia and so a prolonged force must be applied to it.

centre of inertia: see CENTRE *noun*. ***MOMENT of inertia***. ***product of inertia***: see PRODUCT *noun*. **b *thermal inertia***.
2 *transf.* Inactivity; disinclination to act or exert oneself; sloth; apathy. **E19.**

L. GORDON Her diary admits to terrible rage followed by inertia and depression. E. MANNIN It was a landscape of total inertia to which only the river gave life.

3 PHOTOGRAPHY. The notional exposure for zero density, used to calculate the speed of emulsions and obtained by extrapolation of the straight portion of the characteristic curve. **L19.**
– COMB.: **inertia reel**: allowing the automatic adjustment and esp. locking during rapid deceleration of a safety belt rolled round it; **inertia selling** the sending of goods not ordered, in the hope that the recipient will not take action to refuse them and will later make payment.
■ **inertialess** *adjective* having no inertia; responding instantaneously to a change in the action of a force: **E20.**

inertial /ɪˈnəːʃ(ə)l/ *adjective*. **M19.**
[ORIGIN from INERTIA + -AL[1].]
1 Of, pertaining to, or of the nature of inertia. **M19.**
2 PHYSICS. Designating a frame of reference in which bodies continue at rest or in uniform straight motion unless acted on by a force. **M19.**
– SPECIAL COLLOCATIONS: **inertial guidance**: of a vehicle or vessel by an inertial navigation system. **inertial homeothermy**: achieved by virtue of thermal inertia in a massive animal. **inertial navigation**: in which the course is computed from measurements of acceleration, without external observations. **inertial system** (*a*) PHYSICS an inertial frame of reference; (*b*) a system for carrying out inertial guidance.
■ **inertially** *adverb* by means of or as a result of inertia or inertial forces **M20.**

inertion /ɪˈnəːʃ(ə)n/ *noun*. **M16.**
[ORIGIN from INERT after EXERTION: see -ION.]
Inert condition; inertness, inactivity, sloth.

inerudite /ɪnˈɛrʊdʌɪt/ *adjective*. E19.
[ORIGIN Latin *ineruditus*, formed as IN-[3] + ERUDITE.]
Unlearned; uninstructed.

inescapable /ɪnɪˈskeɪpəb(ə)l, ɪnɛ-/ *adjective*. L18.
[ORIGIN from IN-[3] + ESCAPE *verb* + -ABLE.]
Unable to be escaped or avoided; inevitable.
■ **inescapaˈbility** *noun* M20. **inescapably** *adverb* L19.

inescutcheon /ɪnɪˈskʌtʃ(ə)n, ɪnɛ-/ *noun*. E17.
[ORIGIN from IN-[1] + ESCUTCHEON.]
HERALDRY. A small shield or coat of arms placed within a larger shield.

inesite /ˈɪnɪzʌɪt, ˈʌɪnəzʌɪt/ *noun*. L19.
[ORIGIN from Greek *ines* fibres + -ITE[1].]
MINERALOGY. A triclinic hydrated calcium manganese silicate occurring as pink fibrous masses.

in esse /ɪn ˈɛsi/ *adjectival phr*. L16.
[ORIGIN Latin.]
In actual existence. Opp. IN POSSE.

inessential /ɪnɪˈsɛnʃ(ə)l/ *adjective & noun*. L17.
[ORIGIN from IN-[3] + ESSENTIAL *adjective*.]
▸ **A** *adjective*. **1** Devoid of essence; insubstantial, abstract. L17.

SHELLEY His inessential figure cast no shade Upon the golden floor.

2 Not necessary to the constitution of a thing; not essential. M19.

A. STORR A number of what appear inessential details are in fact important.

▸ **B** *noun*. An inessential thing. L18.

D. M. DAVIN I am . . going to cut out inessentials.

■ **inessentiality** /-ʃɪˈal-/ *noun* M19.

inessive /ɪnˈɛsɪv/ *adjective & noun*. L19.
[ORIGIN from Latin *inesse* be in or at, formed as IN-[2] + *esse* be: see -IVE.]
GRAMMAR. ▸**A** *adjective*. Designating, being in, or pertaining to a case (esp. in Finnish) indicating location or position in or within. L19.
▸ **B** *noun*. *The* inessive case; a word, form, etc., in the inessive case. L19.

inesthetic *adjective* see INAESTHETIC.

inestimable /ɪnˈɛstɪməb(ə)l/ *adjective & adverb*. LME.
[ORIGIN Old French & mod. French from Latin *inaestimabilis*, formed as IN-[3] + *aestimabilis* ESTIMABLE.]
▸ **A** *adjective*. **1** Unable to be estimated, reckoned, or computed; too great or profound to be assessed or calculated. LME.
2 Too precious to be estimated, of surpassing value; priceless, invaluable. L16.
▸ †**B** *adverb*. Inestimably. LME–L16.
■ **inestimably** *adverb* in an inestimable manner, to an inestimable degree LME.

ineuphonious /ɪnjuːˈfəʊnɪəs/ *adjective*. L19.
[ORIGIN from IN-[3] + EUPHONIOUS.]
Not euphonious.

inevasible /ɪnɪˈveɪsɪb(ə)l/ *adjective*. M19.
[ORIGIN from IN-[3] + Latin *evas-* (see EVASION) + -IBLE.]
Unable to be evaded.

inevictable /ɪnɪˈvɪktəb(ə)l/ *adjective*. *rare*. L19.
[ORIGIN from IN-[3] + EVICT + -ABLE.]
Unable to be evicted.

inevidence /ɪnˈɛvɪd(ə)ns/ *noun*. Now *rare*. M17.
[ORIGIN medieval Latin *inevidentia*, formed as INEVIDENT: see -ENCE.]
†**1** Lack of evidence or manifestation (*of* something). M–L17.
†**2** Uncertainty. M–L17.
3 The condition of not being evident or clearly discernible; lack of clearness, obscurity. L17.

inevident /ɪnˈɛvɪd(ə)nt/ *adjective*. Now *rare*. E17.
[ORIGIN Late Latin *inevident-*, formed as IN-[3] + *evident-*: see EVIDENT.]
Not evident or manifest; not clear, obscure.

inevitable /ɪnˈɛvɪtəb(ə)l/ *adjective & noun*. LME.
[ORIGIN Latin *inevitabilis*, formed as IN-[3] + *evitabilis* EVITABLE.]
▸ **A** *adjective*. **1** Unable to be avoided; unavoidable. LME.

G. GREENE For the first time he realised the pain inevitable in any human relationship. B. EMECHETA She would delay the hearing of it until it became inevitable.

2 Bound or sure to occur or appear; *colloq*. tiresomely familiar. L19. ▸**b** Of character-building, plot development, etc.: so true to nature etc. as to preclude alternative treatment or solution. E20.

D. JACOBSON A large china vase, containing the inevitable pair of dead flies. L. GORDON She tended to dramatize the inevitable disappointments that attend high aspiration. **b** *Notes & Queries* The 'inevitable' phrase, that gift to the world past all praise.

▸ **B** *noun*. A thing which cannot be escaped or avoided; an inevitable fact, event, truth, etc.; a person who or thing which is bound to be used, employed, etc. M19.
■ **inevitaˈbility** *noun* M17. **inevitableness** *noun* E17. **inevitably** *adverb* LME.

inexact /ɪnɪɡˈzakt, ɪnɛɡ-/ *adjective*. E19.
[ORIGIN from IN-[3] + EXACT *adjective*.]
Not exact; not strictly correct or precise; not strict or rigorous.
■ **inexactly** *adverb* M19. **inexactness** *noun* E19.

inexactitude /ɪnɪɡˈzaktɪtjuːd, ɪnɛɡ-/ *noun*. L18.
[ORIGIN from IN-[3] + EXACTITUDE.]
The quality or character of being inexact; lack of exactitude, accuracy, or precision; an inaccuracy.
TERMINOLOGICAL ***inexactitude***.

in excelsis /ɪn ɛkˈsɛlsɪs/ *adverbial phr*. LME.
[ORIGIN Latin = in the highest (places): cf. EXCELSIOR.]
= ***in the highest*** s.v. HIGH *adjective, adverb, & noun*.

inexcitable /ɪnɪkˈsʌɪtəb(ə)l, ɪnɛk-/ *adjective*. *rare*. E17.
[ORIGIN Latin *inexcitabilis*, formed as IN-[3] + *excitare* EXCITE + -ABLE; in sense 2 from IN-[3] + EXCITABLE.]
†**1** From which one cannot be roused. E–M17.
2 Not excitable. E19.
■ **inexcitaˈbility** *noun* (*rare*) M19.

inexclusively /ɪnɪkˈskluːsɪvli, ɪnɛk-/ *adverb*. L18.
[ORIGIN from IN-[3] + EXCLUSIVELY.]
Not exclusively; so as not to exclude others.

inexcusable /ɪnɪkˈskjuːzəb(ə)l, ɪnɛk-/ *adjective*. LME.
[ORIGIN Latin *inexcusabilis*, formed as IN-[3] + *excusabilis* EXCUSABLE.]
Not excusable; unable to be excused or justified.
■ **inexcusableness** *noun* E17. **inexcusably** *adverb* L16.

†**inexecrable** *adjective*. *rare* (Shakes.). Only in L16.
[ORIGIN from IN-[2] + EXECRABLE.]
Most execrable or abhorred.

SHAKES. *Merch. V.* O, be thou damn'd, inexecrable dog!

— NOTE: By many editors thought to be an error for ***inexorable***.

inexecutable /ɪnˈɛksɪkjuːtəb(ə)l/ *adjective*. E19.
[ORIGIN from IN-[3] + EXECUTABLE.]
Unable to be executed or carried into effect.

inexecution /ˌɪnɛksɪˈkjuːʃ(ə)n/ *noun*. L17.
[ORIGIN from IN-[3] + EXECUTION.]
Lack or neglect of execution or performance; the fact or condition of not being carried into effect.

inexertion /ɪnɪɡˈzəːʃ(ə)n/ *noun*. L18.
[ORIGIN from IN-[3] + EXERTION.]
Lack of exertion; failure to exert oneself or exercise a power or faculty.

inexhausted /ɪnɪɡˈzɔːstɪd/ *adjective*. E17.
[ORIGIN from IN-[3] + EXHAUST *verb* + -ED[1].]
Not exhausted.

inexhaustible /ɪnɪɡˈzɔːstɪb(ə)l/ *adjective*. E17.
[ORIGIN from IN-[3] + EXHAUSTIBLE.]
1 Unable to be exhausted, consumed, or used up; (of a receptacle or vessel) unable to be exhausted or emptied. E17.

R. LINDNER From a literally inexhaustible storehouse of material I have chosen a handful of stories.

2 Of a person or personal attribute: unable to be exhausted or worn out. M18.

Times He was an inexhaustible participant in the International Union of Crystallography.

■ **inexhaustiˈbility** *noun* M19. **inexhaustibleness** *noun* E19. **inexhaustibly** *adverb* L17.

inexhaustive /ɪnɪɡˈzɔːstɪv/ *adjective*. E18.
[ORIGIN from IN-[3] + EXHAUST *verb* + -IVE.]
= INEXHAUSTIBLE 1.
■ **inexhaustively** *adverb* L19.

inexist /ɪnɪɡˈzɪst, ɪnɛɡ-/ *verb intrans*. L17.
[ORIGIN from IN-[1] + EXIST. Cf. INEXISTENT *adjective*[1].]
Exist in something; be inherent *in*.

inexistence /ɪnɪɡˈzɪst(ə)ns, ɪnɛɡ-/ *noun*[1]. Now *rare*. E17.
[ORIGIN from IN-[3] + EXISTENCE.]
The fact or condition of not existing; non-existence.
■ Also †**inexistency** *noun* L17–M18.

inexistence /ɪnɪɡˈzɪst(ə)ns, ɪnɛɡ-/ *noun*[2]. M17.
[ORIGIN from IN-[2] + EXISTENCE.]
The fact or condition of existing in something; inherence.

inexistent /ɪnɪɡˈzɪst(ə)nt, ɪnɛɡ-/ *adjective*[1]. M16.
[ORIGIN Late Latin *inexistent-* pres. ppl stem of *inexistere*, formed as IN-[2] + *existere*: see EXIST, and cf. INEXIST *verb*.]
Existing in something; inherent.

†**inexistent** *adjective*[2]. M17–E18.
[ORIGIN from IN-[3] + EXISTENT.]
Not existing; non-existent.

inexorable /ɪnˈɛks(ə)rəb(ə)l/ *adjective & noun*. M16.
[ORIGIN French, or Latin *inexorabilis*, formed as IN-[3] + EXORABLE.]
▸ **A** *adjective*. Unable to be moved or persuaded by entreaty or request (esp. for mercy), rigidly severe; immovable, relentless (*lit. & fig.*). M16.

H. JAMES He was therefore dismissed with gracious but inexorable firmness. O. MANNING The train, slow and inexorable as time, slid on.

▸ **B** *noun*. A person who is inexorable. M18.
■ **inexoraˈbility** *noun* E17. **inexorableness** *noun* E17. **inexorably** *adverb* E17.

inexpectancy /ɪnɪkˈspɛkt(ə)nsi, ɪnɛk-/ *noun*. *rare*. M17.
[ORIGIN from IN-[3] + EXPECTANCY.]
Absence of expectancy; the condition of not being expectant.

inexpectant /ɪnɪkˈspɛkt(ə)nt, ɪnɛk-/ *adjective*. M19.
[ORIGIN from IN-[3] + EXPECTANT *adjective*.]
Not expectant; devoid of expectation.

inexpedience /ɪnɪkˈspiːdɪəns, ɪnɛk-/ *noun*. Now *rare*. L16.
[ORIGIN formed as INEXPEDIENCY: see -ENCE.]
= INEXPEDIENCY.

inexpediency /ɪnɪkˈspiːdɪənsi, ɪnɛk-/ *noun*. M17.
[ORIGIN from IN-[3] + EXPEDIENCY, or from INEXPEDIENT: see -ENCY.]
The quality of being inexpedient; disadvantageousness; unadvisableness.

inexpedient /ɪnɪkˈspiːdɪənt, ɪnɛk-/ *adjective*. L16.
[ORIGIN from IN-[3] + EXPEDIENT *adjective*.]
Not expedient; not advantageous, useful, or suitable; inadvisable.

inexpensive /ɪnɪkˈspɛnsɪv, ɪnɛk-/ *adjective*. M19.
[ORIGIN from IN-[3] + EXPENSIVE.]
1 Not expensive or costly; cheap. M19.
2 Not extravagant; not spending a great deal. M19.
■ **inexpensively** *adverb* M19. **inexpensiveness** *noun* M19.

inexperience /ɪnɪkˈspɪərɪəns, ɪnɛk-/ *noun*. L16.
[ORIGIN French *inexpérience* from late Latin *inexperientia*, formed as IN-[3] + *experientia* EXPERIENCE *noun*.]
Lack of experience; the condition of not having practical acquaintance with some work, activity, etc.; the lack of knowledge or skills resulting from this.

C. G. WOLFF She . . begged to be forgiven for her inexperience and ignorance. A. T. ELLIS My mother . . changed the subject out of deference to my youth and inexperience.

inexperienced /ɪnɪkˈspɪərɪənst, ɪnɛk-/ *adjective*. E17.
[ORIGIN from IN-[3] + EXPERIENCED.]
Not experienced (*in*); lacking the knowledge or skill resulting from experience.

T. HARDY Like an inexperienced actress who, having at last . . spoken her speeches, does not know how to move off.

inexpert /ɪnˈɛkspəːt/ *adjective & noun*. LME.
[ORIGIN Old French from Latin *inexpertus* untried, inexperienced, formed as IN-[3] + *expertus* EXPERT *adjective*.]
▸ **A** *adjective*. †**1** Without experience, inexperienced. Foll. by *in*, *of*. LME–M19.
2 Lacking the readiness, aptitude, or dexterity derived from experience; not expert. L16.
▸ **B** *noun*. An unskilled person; a person who is not an expert. L19.

inexpertise /ˌɪnɛkspəːˈtiːz/ *noun*. E20.
[ORIGIN from IN-[3] + EXPERTISE.]
Lack of expertise.

inexpiable /ɪnˈɛkspɪəb(ə)l/ *adjective*. LME.
[ORIGIN Latin *inexpiabilis*, formed as IN-[3] + *expiabilis* EXPIABLE.]
1 Of an offence: unable to be expiated or atoned for. LME.

R. MACAULAY They appear conscious of some immense and inexpiable sin.

2 Of a feeling: unable to be appeased by expiation; irreconcilable. L16.

J. WAIN But in Shakespeare guilt is not inexpiable; the self-inflicted wound can heal.

inexpiate /ɪnˈɛkspɪət/ *adjective*. E17.
[ORIGIN Latin *inexpiatus*, formed as IN-[3] + EXPIATE *adjective*.]
†**1** Unappeased. Only in E17.
2 Not expiated or atoned for. E19.

inexplainable /ɪnɪkˈspleɪnəb(ə)l, ɪnɛk-/ *adjective*. *rare*. E17.
[ORIGIN from IN-[3] + EXPLAINABLE.]
Unable to be explained; inexplicable.

†**inexpleble** *adjective*. M16–L18.
[ORIGIN Latin *inexplebilis*, formed as IN-[3] + *explere* fill up: see -BLE.]
Unable to be filled or satisfied; insatiable.

inexplicable /ɪnɪkˈsplɪkəb(ə)l, ɪnɛk-, ɪnˈɛksplɪ-/ *adjective & noun*. LME.
[ORIGIN French, or Latin *inexplicabilis* that cannot be unfolded or loosened, formed as IN-[3] + *explicabilis* EXPLICABLE.]
▸ **A** *adjective*. **1** Unable to be explained or accounted for; inscrutable; unintelligible. LME.
†**2** Unable to be expressed in words; indescribable. E16–L17.
†**3** Unable to be unfolded, untwisted, or disentangled; very intricate or complex. M16–E18.
▸ **B** *noun*. An inexplicable thing. M18.
■ **inexplicaˈbility** *noun* the quality of being inexplicable; an inexplicable thing: L18. **inexplicableness** *noun* M17. **inexplicably** *adverb* M17.

inexplicit /ɪnɪkˈsplɪsɪt, ɪnɛk-/ *adjective*. E19.
[ORIGIN from IN-[3] + EXPLICIT *adjective*.]
Not explicit; not definitely or clearly expressed.

inexplorable /ɪnɪk'splɔːrəb(ə)l, ɪnɛk-/ *adjective*. M17.
[ORIGIN from IN-³ + EXPLORE + -ABLE.]
Unable to be explored.

inexplosive /ɪnɪk'spləʊsɪv, ɪnɛk-/ *adjective*. M19.
[ORIGIN from IN-³ + EXPLOSIVE *adjective*.]
Not explosive; not liable to or capable of explosion.

inexpressible /ɪnɪk'sprɛsɪb(ə)l, ɪnɛk-/ *adjective & noun*. E17.
[ORIGIN from IN-³ + EXPRESSIBLE.]
▸ **A** *adjective*. Unable to be expressed in words; unutterable, indescribable. E17.
▸ **B** *noun*. **1** An inexpressible thing. M17.
2 *spec.* In *pl.* Trousers. *arch. colloq.* L18.
■ **inexpressibly** *adverb* M17.

inexpressive /ɪnɪk'sprɛsɪv, ɪnɛk-/ *adjective*. M17.
[ORIGIN from IN-³ + EXPRESSIVE.]
1 = INEXPRESSIBLE *adjective*. *arch.* M17.
2 Not expressive; not expressing (a) meaning, feeling, character, etc. M18.
■ **inexpressively** *adverb* E19. **inexpressiveness** *noun* E19.

inexpugnable /ɪnɪk'spʌgnəb(ə)l, ɪnɛk-/ *adjective*. LME.
[ORIGIN Old French & mod. French from Latin *inexpugnabilis*, formed as IN-³ + *expugnabilis* EXPUGNABLE.]
(Of a fortress, army, country, etc.) unable to be taken by assault or overthrown by force; impregnable; invincible.

fig.: MRS H. WARD A certain inexpugnable dignity surrounded him.

■ **inexpugnably** *adverb* M17. **inexpugnableness** *noun* E18.

inexpungible /ɪnɪk'spʌndʒɪb(ə)l, ɪnɛk-/ *adjective*. Also **-geable** /-dʒəb(ə)l/. L19.
[ORIGIN from IN-³ + EXPUNGE + -IBLE.]
Unable to be expunged or obliterated.

inextended /ɪnɪk'stɛndɪd, ɪnɛk-/ *adjective*. *rare*. M18.
[ORIGIN from IN-³ + EXTENDED.]
Unextended; without extension.

inextensible /ɪnɪk'stɛnsɪb(ə)l, ɪnɛk-/ *adjective*. M19.
[ORIGIN from IN-³ + EXTENSIBLE.]
Not extensible; unable to be stretched or drawn out in length.
■ **inextensiˈbility** *noun* (*rare*) E19.

in extenso /ɪn ɪk'stɛnsəʊ, ɛk-/ *adverbial phr*. E19.
[ORIGIN Latin, from *in* in + *extenso* ablative of *extensus*: see EXTENSE.]
In full, at length.

M. MEYER A wonderfully mature assessment which repays quoting *in extenso*.

inextinct /ɪnɪk'stɪnkt, ɪnɛk-/ *adjective*. *rare*. E17.
[ORIGIN Latin *inex(s)tinctus*, or from IN-³ + EXTINCT *adjective*.]
Unextinguished. Chiefly *fig.*

J. WILSON He had not supposed such a capacity of love had yet remained inextinct.

inextinguishable /ɪnɪk'stɪŋgwɪʃəb(ə)l, ɪnɛk-/ *adjective*. L15.
[ORIGIN from IN-³ + EXTINGUISH + -ABLE.]
Unable to be extinguished; unquenchable; indestructible.
■ **inextinguishably** *adverb* E19.

inextinguished /ɪnɪk'stɪŋgwɪʃt, ɪnɛk-/ *adjective*. Now *rare*. M18.
[ORIGIN from IN-³ + EXTINGUISH + -ED¹.]
Not extinguished; still burning.

inextirpable /ɪnɪk'stəːpəb(ə)l, ɪnɛk-/ *adjective*. E17.
[ORIGIN Latin *inex(s)tirpabilis*, formed as IN-³ + *ex(s)tirpare* EXTIRPATE: see -ABLE.]
Unable to be extirpated or rooted out.

in extremis /ɪn ɛk'striːmɪs, ɪk-/ *adverbial phr*. M16.
[ORIGIN Latin, from *in* in + *extremis* ablative pl. of *extremus*: see EXTREME.]
At the point of death; in great difficulty.

inextricable /ɪn'ɛkstrɪkəb(ə)l, ɪnɪk'strɪk-/ *adjective*. M16.
[ORIGIN Latin *inextricabilis*, formed as IN-³ + *extricare* EXTRICATE: see -ABLE.]
1 (Of a circumstance) unable to be escaped from; (of a place, esp. a maze) so complicated or confusing that no means of exit can be found (now *rare*). M16.

E. COOKE That he should run himself into inextricable Danger by going on.

2 (Of a knot, coil, etc.) unable to be disentangled or untied; (of a problem, difficulty, argument, etc.) unable to be solved or resolved, intricately involved or confused. E17. ▸**b** Of a grasp: unable to be loosened or detached. M19.

S. SPENDER They know inextricable knots which bind each to himself. L. DURRELL For those of us . . who are at all conscious of the inextricable tangle of human thoughts.

3 Intricate, elaborate, exquisitely wrought. *rare*. L17.

HANNAH MORE A net of such exquisite art and inextricable workmanship.

■ **inextricaˈbility** *noun* M19. **inextricably** *adverb* L16.

†**ineye** *verb trans*. *rare*. LME–E18.
[ORIGIN from IN-² + EYE *noun*, after Latin *inoculare*.]
HORTICULTURE. Engraft.

INF *abbreviation*.
Intermediate-range nuclear force(s).

inf /ɪnf/ *noun*. M20.
[ORIGIN Abbreviation.]
MATH. Infimum (of).

inface /'ɪnfeɪs/ *noun*. L19.
[ORIGIN Contr. of *inward facing escarpment*.]
PHYSICAL GEOGRAPHY. The steep scarp face of a cuesta.

infall /'ɪnfɔːl/ *noun*. M17.
[ORIGIN from IN-¹ + FALL *noun*², after Dutch *inval*.]
1 An attack, inroad, or incursion *upon* an army, town, etc., or *into* a country. Now *rare*. M17.
2 The place where water enters a reservoir, canal, etc. M17.
3 Chiefly ASTRONOMY. (An instance of) falling into or upon a body (esp. a planet) from an outside source; material which falls or has fallen (e.g. cosmic dust). L19.

infallibility /ɪnˌfalɪ'bɪlɪti/ *noun*. E17.
[ORIGIN French †*infallibilité* or medieval Latin *infallibilitas*, formed as IN-³ + FALLIBLE: see -ITY.]
The quality or fact of being infallible.

N. MOSLEY Goering . . likened what he saw as Hitler's infallibility to that of the Pope.

infallible /ɪn'falɪb(ə)l/ *adjective*. L15.
[ORIGIN French *infaillible* or late Latin *infallibilis*, formed as IN-³ + Latin *fallere* deceive: see -IBLE.]
1 Of a person, judgement, etc.: not liable to err or be deceived; *spec.* (ROMAN CATHOLIC CHURCH) (of the Pope) incapable of erring in pronouncing dogma as doctrinally defined. L15.

P. HOWARD It would be nice to pretend that *The Times* is infallible.

2 Of a thing: not liable to prove false or erroneous; not liable to fail in action or operation; *rare* that cannot fail to be or come, certain. L15.

W. SOYINKA And it barely managed to be sweet, thus failing the infallible test of a real fruit. P. FERGUSON There's always an infallible way to be popular with nurses.

■ **infallibilism** *noun* the principle of the infallibility of a person or thing, esp. of the Pope L19. **infallibilist** *noun* a person who believes in or upholds the infallibility of a person or thing, esp. of the Pope L19. **infallibleness** *noun* (*rare*) infallibility L16. **infallibly** *adverb* L15.

infalling /'ɪnfɔːlɪŋ/ *noun*. Now *rare* or *obsolete*. M16.
[ORIGIN from IN-¹ + FALLING *noun*.]
A falling in. Formerly also, an invasion.

infalling /'ɪnfɔːlɪŋ/ *adjective*. M20.
[ORIGIN from IN-¹ + FALLING *ppl adjective*.]
Falling into or towards something.

infamatory /ɪn'famət(ə)ri/ *adjective*. *rare*. E17.
[ORIGIN medieval Latin *infamatorius*, from *infamat-* pa. ppl stem of *infamare* INFAME *verb*: see -ORY².]
Bringing infamy. Formerly also, defamatory.

infame /ɪn'feɪm/ *noun*. Long *arch. rare*. LME.
[ORIGIN Old French (also *en-*) from late Latin *infamium* for classical Latin *infamia* INFAMY.]
= INFAMY.

†**infame** *adjective*. E16–M18.
[ORIGIN French *infâme* from Latin *infamis*: see INFAMY.]
= INFAMOUS.

infame /ɪn'feɪm/ *verb trans*. Now *arch.* or *joc.* LME.
[ORIGIN Old French *enfamer* from Latin *infamare*, from *infamis*: see INFAMY.]
1 Make infamous; hold up to infamy. LME.

W. PENN This inhuman Practice will infame your Government.

†**2** Defame, speak ill of; accuse of something infamous. L15–L18.

infamize /'ɪnfəmʌɪz/ *verb trans*. Now *rare* or *obsolete*. Also **-ise**. L16.
[ORIGIN from Latin *infamis* (see INFAMY) + -IZE.]
= INFAME *verb*.

†**infamonize** *verb trans*. *rare* (Shakes.). Only in L16.
[ORIGIN Alt.]
= INFAMIZE.

infamous /'ɪnfəməs/ *adjective*. LME.
[ORIGIN medieval Latin *infamosus* for Latin *infamis*: see INFAMY, -OUS.]
1 Of ill fame or repute; notorious, esp. for wickedness, evil, etc. LME.

C. THIRLWALL He appears to have been more infamous for sacrilege than for bloodshed. C. FRANCIS The vessels packed with Irish emigrants were infamous for overcrowding, disease and frequency of shipwrecks.

2 Deserving of infamy, shamefully wicked or vile; abominable. L15.

H. MAUNDRELL Detest the very ground on which was acted such an infamous Treachery.

3 LAW (now *hist.*). (Of a person) deprived of all or certain citizen's rights as a consequence of conviction for a serious crime such as forgery, perjury, etc.; (of a crime or punishment) involving or entailing such loss of rights. M16.
– SPECIAL COLLOCATIONS: **infamous crime** *spec.* (LAW, now *hist.*) buggery.
■ **infamously** *adverb* E17. **infamousness** *noun* (*rare*) M17.

infamy /'ɪnfəmi/ *noun*. L15.
[ORIGIN Old French & mod. French *infamie* from Latin *infamia*, from *infamis*, formed as IN-³ + *fama* FAME *noun*: see -Y³.]
1 Bad reputation; scandalous repute; public shame or disgrace; an instance of this. L15.

R. GRENEWEY Now was the time to blot out the infamies of their former conspiracies. E. A. FREEMAN Two caitiffs . . whose names are handed down to infamy.

2 The quality of being shamefully vile; a disgraceful act. L15.

Q. BELL He . . realised the infamy of slavery when he saw how monstrously a Negro might be treated. P. ACKROYD At the time of my greatest success, I was suspected of the greatest infamies.

3 LAW (now *hist.*). The loss of all or certain citizen's rights resulting from conviction for a serious crime such as forgery, perjury, etc. E17.

infancy /'ɪnf(ə)nsi/ *noun*. LME.
[ORIGIN Latin *infantia* inability to speak, childhood, from *infant-*, *infans*: see INFANT *noun*¹, -ANCY.]
1 The condition of being an infant; the earliest period of human life, early childhood, babyhood. Also (chiefly *literary*), infants collectively. LME.

P. THOMPSON When tender infancy evinces needless terror at cow, or dog, or shaggy goat. N. MOSLEY This move from prep school to public school was traditionally held to be a release from infancy. M. SCAMMELL There had been twins, but they had been born prematurely and had died in infancy.

2 The earliest period in the history of a thing capable of development; the initial and rudimentary stage in any process of growth. M16.

R. HUNTFORD The science of nutrition was then in its infancy.

3 LAW (now *hist.*). The condition of not yet being of full age, minority. M17.

†**infand** *adjective*. E17–L19.
[ORIGIN Latin *infandus*, formed as IN-³ + *fandus* gerundive of *fari* speak: see -AND.]
Unspeakable; nefarious.
■ Also †**infandous** *adjective* M17–L19.

†**infang** *noun*. *Scot. rare*. M16–E19.
[ORIGIN Abbreviation.]
= INFANGTHIEF.

infangthief /'ɪnfaŋθiːf/ *noun*. OE.
[ORIGIN from IN *adverb* + pa. pple of FANG *verb*¹ + THIEF.]
LAW (now *hist.*). The right of the lord of a manor to try and to punish a thief caught within the limits of his demesne.

infant /'ɪnf(ə)nt/ *noun*¹ *& adjective*. LME.
[ORIGIN Old French & mod. French *enfant* from Latin *infant-*, *infans* use as noun of *infans* unable to speak, formed as IN-³ + pres. pple of *fari* speak: see -ANT¹.]
▸ **A** *noun*. **1** A child during the earliest period of life after birth or (now *rare*) in the womb; a baby, a young child. LME. ▸**b** A beginner in or newcomer to an activity etc.; something in an early stage of development. E16.

D. W. GOODWIN If the mother is intoxicated while breast feeding, the infant will be intoxicated. J. CRACE I slept, glad to be free of squalling infants and the attentions of the Professor. **b** *New Brunswick Daily Mail* As every political infant cannot fail to recognise, the . . question was . . unconnected with party politics.

TERRIBLE *infant*.

2 a LAW (now *hist.*). A person not yet of full age, a minor. E16. ▸**b** A ruler who has not yet attained the age at which he or she is constitutionally capable of exercising sovereignty. L18.
†**3** A youth of noble birth. *rare*. L16–E17.
4 A thing of exceptional size, strength, etc. *joc.* M19.
▸ **B** *attrib.* or as *adjective*. **1** That is or is like an infant; in the earliest stage of development; undeveloped, nascent, incipient. L16.

K. AMIS The sheep clustered by the infant oak-tree looked up suddenly and turned their heads. T. MO A girl of seven carries her infant brother in a gay cloth sling.

2 Of, belonging to, or suitable for an infant or infants; childlike; childish, infantile. L16.

D. WALCOTT Like the sound Of infant voices from the Mission School.

– SPECIAL COLLOCATIONS & COMB.: **infant mistress** a female infant teacher. **infant mortality** the death of infants, *spec.* of those less than a year old. **infant prodigy** a very precocious or talented child. **infant school** (chiefly *hist.*) a primary school intended for children between the ages of 5 and 7. **infant teacher** a teacher of young children; *spec.* a teacher in an infant school.
■ **infanthood** *noun* infancy M19. †**infantical** *adjective* (*rare*) of or pertaining to infants E17–M18. **infantize** *verb trans.* (*rare*) †(*a*) give birth to; (*b*) make childlike: E17.

infant /ˈɪnf(ə)nt/ *noun*[2]. Now *rare* or *obsolete*. **M16.**
[ORIGIN formed as INFANTE.]
= INFANTA, INFANTE.

infanta /ɪnˈfantə/ *noun*. **L16.**
[ORIGIN Spanish, Portuguese fem. of INFANTE.]
hist. A daughter of the King and Queen of Spain or Portugal; *spec.* the eldest daughter who is not heir to the throne. Formerly also *gen.*, a girl, a princess.

infante /ɪnˈfanteɪ/ *noun*. **M16.**
[ORIGIN Spanish & Portuguese from Latin *infant-, infans*: see INFANT *noun*[1].]
hist. A son of the King and Queen of Spain or Portugal other than the heir to the throne; *spec.* the second son.

infanteer /ɪnf(ə)nˈtɪə/ *noun*. *slang*. **M20.**
[ORIGIN from INFANT(RY + -EER.]
An infantryman.

infanticide /ɪnˈfantɪsʌɪd/ *noun*. **M17.**
[ORIGIN French from late Latin *infanticidium, -da*, from Latin *infant-*: see INFANT *noun*[1], -CIDE.]
1 The killing of infants; *esp.* (chiefly *hist.*), the custom of killing newborn infants. **M17.** ▸**b** The killing of an infant by one or both of the parents or with parental consent; *spec.* in ENGLISH LAW, the killing of a child under a year old by its mother during postnatal depression. **L18.**
2 A person who kills an infant, esp. his or her own child. **L17.**
■ **infantiˈcidal** *adjective* of, pertaining to, or practising infanticide **M19.**

infanticipate /ɪnf(ə)nˈtɪsɪpeɪt/ *verb intrans.* Chiefly *US & joc.* **M20.**
[ORIGIN from INFANT *noun*[1] + ANT)ICIPATE *verb*.]
Be expecting the birth of one's child.
■ **infanticiˈpation** *noun* the state of expecting the birth of one's child **M20.**

infantile /ˈɪnf(ə)ntʌɪl/ *adjective*. **LME.**
[ORIGIN French, or Latin *infantilis*, from *infant-*: see INFANT *noun*[1], -ILE.]
1 Of, pertaining to, or characteristic of an infant or infancy; being in infancy or the earliest stage of development; childish, immature. **LME.**

H. JOLLY Infantile eczema is commoner in babies fed on cow's milk. M. GORDON It was infantile to cry like this, at thirty-eight, because she wanted her parents.

infantile paralysis poliomyelitis (esp. in children).
2 *PHYSICAL GEOGRAPHY.* Of, pertaining to, or characteristic of the earliest stages of erosion. **L19.**

infantilise *verb* var. of INFANTILIZE.

infantilism /ɪnˈfantɪlɪz(ə)m/ *noun*. **L19.**
[ORIGIN from INFANTILE + -ISM.]
MEDICINE & PSYCHOLOGY. Persistence or recurrence, in adult life, of an infantile or childish condition or behaviour pattern; abnormal physical, sexual, or psychological immaturity.
■ **infantiˈlistic** *adjective* **M20.**

infantility /ɪnf(ə)nˈtɪlɪti/ *noun*. **M17.**
[ORIGIN from INFANTILE + -ITY.]
The quality or fact of being infantile; an instance of infantile behaviour.
– NOTE: Rare before **20.**

infantilize /ɪnˈfantɪlʌɪz/ *verb trans.* Also **-ise**. **M20.**
[ORIGIN from INFANTILE + -IZE.]
Prolong or inculcate a state of infancy or infantile behaviour in; treat (a person) as infantile.

C. G. WOLFF Take care of your complexion, my dear ... Such injunctions toward women are ultimately infantilizing.

■ **infantiliˈzation** *noun* **M20.**

infantine /ˈɪnf(ə)ntʌɪn/ *adjective*. Chiefly *literary*. **E17.**
[ORIGIN French †*infantin* var. of Old French & mod. French *enfantin*, formed as INFANT *noun*[1]: see -INE[1].]
= INFANTILE 1.

infantry /ˈɪnf(ə)ntri/ *noun*. **L16.**
[ORIGIN French *infanterie* from Italian *infanteria*, from *infante* youth, foot soldier, from Latin *infant-*: see INFANT *noun*[1], -ERY.]
1 Soldiers marching or fighting on foot; the body of foot soldiers. **L16.**

C. V. WEDGWOOD Two hundred infantry and forty horsemen crossed from the mainland to the Isle of Wight.

light infantry: see LIGHT *adjective*[1]. **mounted infantry** soldiers who are mounted for transit but who fight on foot.
2 *collect.* Infants. *joc.* **E17.**

M. NEEDHAM The little dirty Infantry, which swarms up and down in Alleys and Lanes.

– COMB.: **infantryman** a soldier of an infantry regiment.

infarct /ɪnˈfɑːkt/ *noun*. **L19.**
[ORIGIN mod. Latin *infarctus*, from *infarct-* pa. ppl stem of *infarcire* stuff into or with, formed as IN-[2] + *farcire* stuff.]
MEDICINE. An area of tissue affected by infarction; a region of dead tissue caused by the blocking of an artery or other vessel. Also, an instance of (esp. myocardial) infarction.
■ **infarcted** *adjective* affected by infarction **E19.**

infarction /ɪnˈfɑːkʃ(ə)n/ *noun*. **L17.**
[ORIGIN formed as INFARCT + -ION.]
MEDICINE. Orig., congestion or (vascular) obstruction. Now, the death of tissues due to the blocking of (esp. the arterial) blood supply. Also, an infarct.

infare /ˈɪnfɛː/ *noun*. **OE.**
[ORIGIN from IN-[1] + FARE *noun*[1].]
†**1** The action of entering; an entrance, a way in. **OE–ME.**
2 A feast or entertainment given on entering a new house; *esp.* a reception for a bride in her new home. *Scot., N. English, & US.* **LME.**

†**infatigable** *adjective*. **E16–E18.**
[ORIGIN French from Latin *infatigabilis*, formed as IN-[3] + *fatigare* FATIGUE *verb* + -ABLE.]
= INDEFATIGABLE.

infatuate /ɪnˈfatjʊət, -tʃʊ-/ *adjective & noun*. **L15.**
[ORIGIN Latin *infatuatus* pa. pple, formed as INFATUATE *verb*: see -ATE[2], -ATE[1].]
▸ **A** *adjective*. Infatuated. Now *rare*. **L15.**

M. BEERBOHM The young man, .. at once thrifty and infatuate, had planned a luncheon *à deux*.

▸ **B** *noun*. An infatuated person. **M20.**

infatuate /ɪnˈfatjʊeɪt, -tʃʊ-/ *verb trans.* **M16.**
[ORIGIN Latin *infatuat-* pa. ppl stem of *infatuare*, formed as IN-[2] + FATUOUS: see -ATE[3].]
†**1** Reduce to foolishness, show the foolishness of; frustrate, bring to nothing. **M16–E18.**

R. YOUNGE That I have unmasked their faces, is to infatuate their purpose.

2 Orig., make foolish or fatuous, inspire with folly. Now chiefly, inspire with an intense esp. amorous and usu. transitory passion. **M16.**

R. WARNER He was, it was said, quite ridiculously infatuated with the lady. I. MURDOCH You're just infatuated with Oxford, you think it's all so impressive and grand.

■ **infatuatedly** *adverb* in an infatuated manner **M19.**

infatuation /ɪnˌfatjʊˈeɪʃ(ə)n, -tʃʊ-/ *noun*. **M17.**
[ORIGIN from INFATUATE *verb* + -ATION.]
The action of infatuating someone; the condition of being infatuated; an instance of this.

J. AUSTEN Your infatuation about that girl blinds you. E. FEINSTEIN To her, love was felt for 'what is akin' and infatuation only for what is alien.

infauna /ˈɪnfɔːnə/ *noun*. **E20.**
[ORIGIN from IN-[1] + FAUNA.]
ZOOLOGY. The animal life found within a marine sediment.
■ **infaunal** *adjective* **L20.**

infaust /ɪnˈfɔːst/ *adjective*. Now *rare* or *obsolete*. **E17.**
[ORIGIN Latin *infaustus*, perh. through French †*infauste*.]
Unlucky, unfortunate.

infeasible /ɪnˈfiːzɪb(ə)l/ *adjective*. **M16.**
[ORIGIN from IN-[3] + FEASIBLE.]
Not feasible, impracticable; impossible.

Nineteenth Century They pronounced it not only infeasible, but of very doubtful benefit.

■ **infeasiˈbility** *noun* **M17.**

†**infect** *adjective*. **LME.**
[ORIGIN Latin *infectus* pa. pple, formed as INFECT *verb*.]
1 Affected detrimentally. Only in **LME.**
2 Tainted *with* disease, infected. **LME–M16.**
3 Tainted or contaminated *with* a fault, defect, or vice; morally corrupted (*rare* after **E17**). **LME–L19.**

infect /ɪnˈfɛkt/ *verb trans.* **LME.**
[ORIGIN Latin *infect-* pa. ppl stem of *inficere* dip in, stain, taint, spoil, formed as IN-[2] + *facere* put, do.]
1 Affect (a person, animal, or organ) with disease; introduce a disease-causing micro-organism into. **LME.** ▸**b** Affect (a computer) with a computer virus. **L20.**

P. THEROUX Every cut became infected and had to be scrubbed with hot water. E. FEINSTEIN The tuberculosis that infected, and finally killed, all of his children.

2 Contaminate (air, water, etc.) with harmful organisms or noxious matter; make harmful to health. **LME.**
3 Taint or contaminate with moral corruption; deprave; exert a bad influence upon. **LME.**

S. JOHNSON Indolence is .. one of the vices from which those whom it infects are seldom reformed.

†**4** Affect detrimentally or unpleasantly; spoil or corrupt with some addition; adulterate. **LME–L17.** ▸**b** Infest, beset. **M16–E18.**
5 Affect or impregnate with a (freq. noxious) substance; taint. Formerly also, dye, colour, stain. **L15.**

E. K. KANE Our snow-water has been infected .. by a very perceptible flavor and odor of musk.

6 Instil a (now only bad or harmful) belief or opinion into. **L15.**

J. WHYTE Books .. full of pestilent doctrines, blasphemy and heresy, to infect the people.

7 Affect (esp. a person) *with* some quality, esp. a feeling, communicate a feeling to (a person); (of a feeling) take hold of. **L16.** ▸**b** *CELTIC PHILOLOGY.* Of a sound: affect and alter the quality of (a sound in a syllable) by proximity. **L19.**

N. ALGREN The very heat that enervates men infects women with restlessness.

8 Taint with crime; involve in crime. Now *rare*. **L16.** ▸**b** *LAW* (now *hist.*). Involve (a ship or cargo) in the seizure to which contraband etc. is liable. **M18.**
– NOTE: Senses 3–7 are now usually interpreted as fig. uses of sense 1.
■ **infectible** *adjective* able to be infected **E17.** †**infecter** *noun* **E16–M18.** **infector** *noun* **L16.**

infection /ɪnˈfɛkʃ(ə)n/ *noun*. **LME.**
[ORIGIN Old French & mod. French, or late Latin *infectio(n-)*, formed as INFECT *verb*: see -ION.]
▸ **I 1 a** The contamination of air, water, etc., by disease-causing agents. Now *rare* or *obsolete*. **LME.** ▸**b** The agency by which disease is caused or transmitted. **LME.** ▸**c** The transmission of disease (formerly esp. without direct contact); the introduction into the body of disease-causing micro-organisms; the process of infecting; the state of being infected. **M16.** ▸**d** (An) infectious disease; an epidemic. **M16.** ▸**e** The entry of a virus into, or the presence of a virus in, a computer. **L20.**

d H. BAILEY She was often very ill with .. streptococcal infections.

2 Moral or spiritual contamination; (a) depravity. **LME.**
†**3** The action or process of affecting detrimentally; the fact of being spoilt or corrupted. **LME–E17.**
4 Instillation of bad or harmful beliefs or opinions. **E16.**
5 The communication of a feeling or quality from one person to another. **E17.** ▸**b** *CELTIC PHILOLOGY.* Alteration of a sound under the influence of a sound in a neighbouring syllable. **L19.**

R. DAVIES It was impossible that he should love Ismay so much without her loving him by infection.

6 *LAW* (now *hist.*). The communication to the rest of a cargo or to a ship of liability to seizure from association with contraband etc. **L19.**
▸ †**II 7** Affection, liking. *joc. rare* (Shakes.). Only in **L16.**

infectious /ɪnˈfɛkʃəs/ *adjective*. **M16.**
[ORIGIN from INFECTION + -OUS. Cf. INFECTUOUS.]
1 Able to cause disease, unhealthy, infecting. **M16.**
infectious hepatitis, ***infectious mononucleosis***, ***infectious parotitis***, etc.
2 Of (a) disease: communicable; liable to be transmitted from one person to another by transfer of micro-organisms. Also, (of a person) infected, liable to infect others. **M16.**
†**3** Affected with disease. **M16–E18.**
4 Tending or liable to contaminate character, morals, etc. Now *rare*. **M16.**
5 Of an action, emotion, etc.: having the quality of spreading from one to another; easily communicable. **E17.**

E. PHILLPOTTS Her volubility was infectious. D. BROWN Langdon felt himself caught up in the man's infectious enthusiasm.

6 *LAW* (now *hist.*). Of contraband etc.: rendering the rest of a cargo or the ship liable to seizure. **L19.**
■ **infectiously** *adverb* **E17.** **infectiousness** *noun* **E17.**

infective /ɪnˈfɛktɪv/ *adjective*. **LME.**
[ORIGIN medieval Latin *infectivus*, formed as INFECT *verb*: see -IVE. In recent medical use from INFECT *verb* + -IVE.]
Capable of infecting (with disease); pathogenic. Also, morally infectious.
■ **infectiveness** *noun* **L19.** **infecˈtivity** *noun* the quality of being infective; the degree of infectiousness or virulence: **L19.**

infectum /ɪnˈfɛktəm/ *noun*. **M20.**
[ORIGIN Latin, use as noun of neut. of *infectus* unfinished, formed as IN-[3] + *factus* pa. pple of *facere* make imperfect.]
In Latin, the category including the present, imperfect, and simple future tenses.

†**infectuous** *adjective*. **L15–M18.**
[ORIGIN from late Latin *infectus* dyeing + -OUS.]
= INFECTIOUS.

infecund /ɪnˈfɛk(ə)nd, ɪnˈfiːk-/ *adjective*. **LME.**
[ORIGIN Latin *infecundus*, formed as IN-[3] + *fecundus* FECUND.]
Not fecund; barren, unproductive.

infecundity /ɪnfɪˈkʌndɪti/ *noun*. **E17.**
[ORIGIN Latin *infecunditas*, formed as INFECUND: see -ITY.]
The quality of being infecund; barrenness, unproductiveness.

infeed /ˈɪnfiːd/ *noun*. **E20.**
[ORIGIN from IN-[1] + FEED *noun*.]
The action or process of supplying a machine with work; a mechanism which carries out this process.

infeft /ɪnˈfɛft/ *verb trans.* Pa. t. & pple **infeft**. **LME.**
[ORIGIN Scot. var. of ENFEOFF.]
SCOTS LAW (now *hist.*). Invest with heritable property; = ENFEOFF 1.
■ **infeftment** *noun* **LME.**

infelicitous /ɪnfɪˈlɪsɪtəs/ *adjective.* M19.
[ORIGIN from IN-³ + FELICITOUS.]
Not felicitous; unhappy, unfortunate; *esp.* not appropriate.
■ **infelicitously** *adverb* M19.

infelicity /ɪnfɪˈlɪsɪti/ *noun.* LME.
[ORIGIN Latin *infelicitas*, from *infelic-*, *-ix* unhappy, formed as IN-³ + *felix* happy: see -ITY.]
1 The state of being unhappy or unfortunate; unhappiness, misery; bad luck, misfortune. Also, an instance of misfortune; a cause of unhappiness. LME.
> P. HEYLIN By the unhappiness of my Destiny, or the infelicity of the Times, deprived of my Preferments. *Spectator* These infelicities of travel were of frequent occurrence, and endured with cheerfulness.

2 The quality of not being appropriate to an occasion or circumstance; inappropriateness, inaptness; an inappropriate expression or detail of style. E17.
> P. LIVELY He used to write back . . correcting what he considered infelicities of style.

†**infeoff** *verb* var. of ENFEOFF.

infer /ɪnˈfəː/ *verb.* Infl. **-rr-**. L15.
[ORIGIN Latin *inferre* bear or bring in, inflict, make (war), cause, (in medieval Latin) deduce, formed as IN-² + *ferre* BEAR *verb*¹.]
†**1** *verb trans.* Bring about; inflict; wage (war). L15–M18. ▸**b** Confer, bestow. L15–E17. ▸**c** Make, cause to be. W. adjective compl. *rare*. Only in M17.
†**2** *verb trans.* Bring in, introduce in conversation or writing; mention, relate; adduce. L15–E18.
3 *verb trans.* Deduce or draw as a conclusion from or *from* facts or reasoning. E16. ▸**b** *verb intrans.* Draw a conclusion or inference. L16.
> D. M. DAVIN You would have been able to infer from the room alone the nature of those who lived in it. H. GREEN She inferred from this last remark that she had his blessing. *New York Review of Books* We cannot penetrate Bach's mind, but we can infer something about how it developed.

4 *verb trans.* Involve as a consequence; imply. (This use is widely considered incorrect, esp. with a person as the subject.) M16.
> SIR W. SCOTT They are . . more benign in demeanour than their physiognomy or aspect might infer. B. RUSSELL I do not wish to infer that they should have been allowed to go on hunting heads. *Private Eye* I can't stand fellers who infer things about good clean-living Australian Sheilahs.

inferable /ɪnˈfəːrəb(ə)l/ *adjective.* Also **-rr-**. L18.
[ORIGIN from INFER + -ABLE.]
Able to be inferred; deducible.
■ **infera'bility** *noun* E20. **inferably** *adverb* by inference E20.

inference /ˈɪnf(ə)r(ə)ns/ *noun.* L16.
[ORIGIN medieval Latin *inferentia*, from Latin *inferent-* pres. ppl stem of *inferre*: see INFER, -ENCE.]
1 The action or process of inferring; LOGIC the drawing of a conclusion from data or premisses; illation. L16.
> W. STUBBS This . . is not a matter of inference It is a recorded fact of history.

2 A conclusion drawn from data or premisses; an implication; the conclusion that is intended to be drawn. E17.
> R. MACAULAY You draw no inference from your facts. P. H. KOCHER These four are named 'first', with the inference that they deserve priority.

inferential /ɪnfəˈrɛnʃ(ə)l/ *adjective.* M17.
[ORIGIN formed as INFERENCE + -AL¹.]
Of, pertaining to, or depending on inference; of the nature of (an) inference.
■ **inferentially** *adverb* in an inferential manner; in the way of or by means of inference: L17.

inferible *adjective* var. of INFERRIBLE.

inferior /ɪnˈfɪərɪə/ *adjective & noun.* LME.
[ORIGIN Latin, compar. of *inferus* low: see -IOR.]
▸ **A** *adjective.* **1** Lower in position. Now chiefly *techn.* LME. ▸**b** ANATOMY & BIOLOGY. Designating a part or organ situated below another (esp. of the same kind), or in a relatively low position. M16. ▸**c** ASTRONOMY. Of a planet: having its orbit within that of the earth (as Mercury, Venus). M17. ▸**d** Of a letter, figure, or symbol: written or printed below the line L19.
> J. D. DANA The old Glacial drift . . being observed in several places as an inferior deposit.

2 Lower in degree, rank, quality, importance, etc.; subordinate; LAW (of a court) subordinate to another in the judicial hierarchy and able to have its decisions overturned by a higher court. (Foll. by *to*.) Cf. earlier B.1 below. L15.
> J. C. POWYS Barter had been so humiliated . . that . . he felt himself to be inferior to every educated man he met. B. BETTELHEIM Not an inferior copy of his parents but a person in his own right.

3 Low in rank, quality, etc.; comparatively bad. M16.
> GLADSTONE The country with which he shows so inferior an acquaintance.

4 Later. *rare*. M17.

– SPECIAL COLLOCATIONS: ***inferior conjunction***: see CONJUNCTION 2. **inferior meridian** the part of the celestial meridian which lies below the pole. **inferior ovary** BOTANY: positioned below the calyx, enclosed in the receptacle. †**inferior stone** = LUNAR *caustic*.

▸ **B** *noun.* **1** A person inferior to another, esp. in rank; a subordinate. LME.
> H. L. MENCKEN Never let your inferiors do you a favor.

2 A thing inferior to another, esp. in importance. L16.
3 TYPOGRAPHY. An inferior letter, figure, or symbol. L19.
■ **inferiorly** *adverb* M16.

inferiority /ɪnˌfɪərɪˈɒrɪti/ *noun.* L16.
[ORIGIN Prob. from medieval Latin *inferioritas*, formed as INFERIOR + -ITY.]
The quality or condition of being inferior; lower rank, position, or state.
– COMB.: **inferiority complex** in Adlerian psychology, an unrealistic feeling of general inadequacy caused by actual or supposed inferiority in one sphere, sometimes with aggressive behaviour in compensation; *colloq.* an exaggerated feeling of personal inadequacy.

infernal /ɪnˈfəːn(ə)l/ *adjective & noun.* LME.
[ORIGIN Old French & mod. French from Christian Latin *infernalis*, from *infernus* below, subterranean, later used as noun = hell, after masc. pl. *inferni* the shades, neut. pl. *inferna* the lower regions; parallel to Latin *inferus* (see INFERIOR) as *supernus* SUPERNAL to *superus* (see SUPERIOR): see -AL¹.]
▸ **A** *adjective.* **1** Of, pertaining to, or characteristic of the underworld of ancient mythology, or hell in Jewish and Christian belief. LME.
> MILTON The flocking shadows pale Troop to the infernal jail. C. KINGSLEY The infernal hiss and crackle of the flame.

2 Devilish, fiendish. LME.
> W. K. KELLY An infernal plot . . had been formed; . . miscreants went about, poisoning food.

3 Detestable, tiresome. *colloq.* M18.
> E. WAUGH What's all this infernal nonsense about boots?

– SPECIAL COLLOCATIONS: **infernal machine** *arch.* an apparatus (usu. disguised) for producing an explosion to destroy life or property.
▸ **B** *noun.* **1** An inhabitant of the underworld or hell; a devil. Usu. in *pl.* L16. ▸**b** A person or thing of infernal character. Formerly *spec.* an infernal machine. Now *rare*. L16.
2 In *pl.* The infernal regions. Long *rare*. E17.
■ **infer'nality** *noun* †(*a*) *rare* the infernal world and its occupants; (*b*) the quality of being infernal; an instance of this: L16. **infernalize** *verb trans.* give a fiendish or infernal character to E19. **infernally** *adverb* M17.

inferno /ɪnˈfəːnəʊ/ *noun.* Pl. **-os**. M19.
[ORIGIN Italian from Christian Latin *infernus*: see INFERNAL.]
Hell, esp. (***the inferno***) with ref. to Dante's *Divine Comedy*; a scene of horror or distress; *esp.* a raging fire.

infero- /ˈɪnf(ə)rəʊ/ *combining form.* M19.
[ORIGIN from Latin *inferus* low: see -O-.]
Chiefly ZOOLOGY. Forming mainly adjectives with the sense 'in or towards the lower part and —', as ***infero-anterior***, ***infero-lateral***, ***infero-posterior***.

inferrable *adjective* var. of INFERABLE.

inferrible /ɪnˈfəːrɪb(ə)l/ *adjective.* Also **inferible**. M17.
[ORIGIN medieval Latin *inferibilis*, formed as INFER + -IBLE.]
= INFERABLE.
■ **inferri'bility** *noun* M19. **inferribly** *adverb* (*rare*) E20.

infertile /ɪnˈfəːtʌɪl/ *adjective.* L16.
[ORIGIN French, or late Latin *infertilis*, formed as IN-³ + *fertilis* FERTILE.]
Not fertile; unproductive; incapable of producing offspring.
> C. DARWIN Animals and plants, when removed from their natural conditions, are often rendered . . infertile or completely barren. P. THEROUX Littered with rocks and sand, the soil could not have looked more infertile.

infertility /ɪnfəˈtɪlɪti/ *noun.* M16.
[ORIGIN Late Latin *infertilitas*, from *infertilis*: see INFERTILE, -ITY.]
The quality or condition of being infertile; unproductiveness; incapability of producing offspring.

infest /ɪnˈfɛst/ *verb trans.* LME.
[ORIGIN Old French & mod. French *infester* or Latin *infestare*, from *infestus* hostile, unsafe.]
1 Attack or annoy persistently; harass. Now *rare*. LME.
2 Attack, trouble, be present, in large numbers or persistently; overrun. M16.
> J. C. OATES His mattress was filthy and infested with bedbugs. A. T. ELLIS She wished that Finn's caique might sink in waters infested with small sharks. *fig.*: V. GLENDINNING Her essay . . was infested with 'mere, irresponsible silliness.'

infestation /ɪnfɛˈsteɪʃ(ə)n/ *noun.* LME.
[ORIGIN Old French & mod. French, or late Latin *infestatio(n-)*, from Latin *infestat-* pa. ppl stem of *infestare*: see INFEST, -ATION.]
The action of infesting someone or something; an attack of infesting insects etc.; the state or condition of being infested.

†**infestious** *adjective.* L16–E18.
[ORIGIN Irreg. from Latin *infestus* or INFEST, after *infectious*: see -OUS.]
Hostile; troublesome.
■ Also †**infestuous** *adjective* L16–E18.

†**infestive** *adjective*¹. *rare*. L16–E18.
[ORIGIN from INFEST + -IVE.]
Tending to infest someone or something; troublesome.

infestive /ɪnˈfɛstɪv/ *adjective*². *rare*. E17.
[ORIGIN Latin *infestivus*, formed as IN-³ + FESTIVE.]
Not festive; without mirth.
■ **infe'stivity** *noun* absence of festivity; dullness: E18.

infeudation /ɪnfjuːˈdeɪʃ(ə)n/ *noun.* L15.
[ORIGIN medieval Latin *infeudatio(n-)*, *infeod-*, from *infeudat-* pa. ppl stem of *infeudare*, *infeodare* enfeoff, from *feudum*, *feodum*: see FEE *noun*², -ATION.]
LAW (now *hist.*). Enfeoffment; a deed of enfeoffment.
infeudation of tithes the granting of tithes to laymen.

infibulate /ɪnˈfɪbjʊleɪt/ *verb trans.* E17.
[ORIGIN Latin *infibulat-* pa. ppl stem of *infibulare*, formed as IN-² + FIBULA: see -ATE³.]
Fasten with a clasp or buckle (*rare*). Now *spec.* perform infibulation on (a girl or woman). Chiefly as ***infibulated*** *ppl adjective.*

infibulation /ɪnˌfɪbjʊˈleɪʃ(ə)n/ *noun.* M17.
[ORIGIN from INFIBULATE + -ATION.]
The action of fastening something, esp. the human sexual organs with a clasp. Now *spec.* the partial stitching together of the labia, freq. after excision of the clitoris, to prevent sexual intercourse.

infidel /ˈɪnfɪd(ə)l/ *noun & adjective.* L15.
[ORIGIN French *infidèle* or Latin *infidelis* unfaithful, unbelieving, formed as IN-³ + *fidelis* faithful, from *fides* FAITH.]
▸ **A** *noun.* **1** Chiefly *hist.* An adherent of a religion other than one's own; *spec.* (*a*) (from a Christian point of view) a Muslim; (*b*) (from a Muslim point of view) a Christian; (*c*) (from a Jewish point of view) a Gentile. L15.
> DEFOE Propagating the Christian faith among infidels. A. HALEY Their wares of . . beer were for infidels only, since the Moslem Mandinkas never drank.

†**2** A person who is unfaithful to a duty. E16–M17.
3 A person who does not believe in religion, or in a particular religion; *esp.* (*hist.*) a person who does not believe in the traditional (Christian) religion of a country. *derog.* M16.
> D. CUPITT Religious doctrines and rituals stress the distinction between believers and infidels.

4 A person who does not believe in a specified (non-religious) thing. Foll. by *in*, †*to*, †*against*. E17.
▸ **B** *adjective.* **1** Chiefly *hist.* Of a person: unbelieving; adhering to a religion other than one's own; pagan, heathen. L15. ▸†**b** Incredulous, sceptical. *rare*. E17–E18.
> J. CLAVELL This victory had saved . . Christendom from being ravaged . . by the infidel hordes.

2 Of an action, a view, etc.: of, pertaining to, or characteristic of an infidel or infidels. M18.
> *Times Lit. Suppl.* Carlile's dogged commitment to the freedom of the press and to infidel ideas.

■ **infi'delic** *adjective* (*rare*) E17. **infidelism** *noun* (*rare*) M19.

infidelise *verb* var. of INFIDELIZE.

infidelity /ɪnfɪˈdɛlɪti/ *noun.* LME.
[ORIGIN Old French & mod. French *infidélité* or Latin *infidelitas*, from *infidelis*: see INFIDEL, -ITY.]
1 Lack of faith; disbelief in religious matters or a particular religion, esp. Christianity. LME. ▸†**b** An infidel opinion or practice. *rare*. M16–M17.
2 Unfaithfulness or disloyalty to a friend, superior, etc. Now *esp.* lack of sexual faithfulness to a partner. LME. ▸**b** An unfaithful act. E18.
3 *gen.* Disbelief, incredulity. L16.

infidelize /ˈɪnfɪd(ə)lʌɪz/ *verb. rare*. Also **-ise**. M19.
[ORIGIN from INFIDEL + -IZE.]
1 *verb trans.* Make infidel or heathen. M19.
2 *verb intrans.* Profess infidelity. L19.

infield /ˈɪnfiːld/ *noun & adverb.* L15.
[ORIGIN from IN-¹ + FIELD *noun*.]
▸ **A** *noun.* **1** The (usu. arable) farmland lying near a farmstead; *transf.* arable land as opp. to pasture; land regularly manured and cropped. L15.
infield and outfield *hist.* a system of husbandry confining manuring and tillage to the infield land.
2 BASEBALL. The area enclosed within the base lines, the diamond; each of the four fielders stationed on its boundaries. M19.
3 CRICKET. The part of the playing area near the wicket; any fielder(s) stationed in this area. L19.
4 The area enclosed by a racetrack. *US*. E20.
▸ **B** *adverb.* In or towards the centre of a playing field. M19.

infielder /ˈɪnfiːldə/ *noun.* M19.
[ORIGIN from INFIELD *noun* + -ER¹.]
CRICKET & BASEBALL. A fielder stationed in the infield.

infieldsman /ˈɪnfiːldzmən/ *noun*. Pl. **-men**. E20.
[ORIGIN from IN-[1] + FIELDSMAN.]
CRICKET. An infielder.

in fieri /ɪn ˈfʌɪərʌɪ/ *adjectival phr*. M17.
[ORIGIN medieval Latin, from Latin IN *preposition* + *fieri* be made, come into being.]
In the process of being made or coming into being.

infight /ˈɪnfʌɪt/ *verb*. ME.
[ORIGIN from IN-[1] + FIGHT *verb*.]
†**1** *verb trans*. Fight against, attack. Only in ME.
2 *verb intrans*. Fight or box at close quarters. E20.

infighting /ˈɪnfʌɪtɪŋ/ *noun*. E19.
[ORIGIN from IN-[1] + FIGHTING *noun*.]
1 Fighting or boxing at closer quarters than arm's length. E19.

L. WOOLLEY Two [spears] have plain butts and are intended for in-fighting.

2 *fig*. Hidden conflict or competitiveness within a group or organization. E20.

WILBUR SMITH She would use even the dirtiest in-fighting to see that Rod was not overlooked.

■ **infighter** *noun* E19.

infigured /ɪnˈfɪgəd/ *adjective*. E17.
[ORIGIN from IN-[2] + FIGURED.]
Marked or adorned with figures.

infill /ˈɪnfɪl/ *noun*. M20.
[ORIGIN from the verb.]
1 The filling in of a cavity, space, etc.; *spec*. in town planning, the filling of vacant gaps between houses. M20.
2 Something used to fill up a hole or cavity. M20.

infill /ɪnˈfɪl/ *verb trans*. & *intrans*. M19.
[ORIGIN from IN-[1] + FILL *verb*.]
Fill up or in (a cavity, space, etc.).
■ **ˈinfilling** *noun* = INFILL *noun* L19.

infilter /ɪnˈfɪltə/ *verb trans*. M19.
[ORIGIN from IN-[1] + FILTER *verb*.]
= INFILTRATE *verb* 1.

infiltrate /ˈɪnfɪltreɪt, ɪnˈfɪl-/ *noun*. L19.
[ORIGIN from the verb.]
Chiefly *MEDICINE*. An infiltrated substance; an infiltration.

infiltrate /ˈɪnfɪltreɪt/ *verb*. M18.
[ORIGIN from IN-[2] + FILTRATE *verb*.]
1 *verb trans*. Introduce (a fluid) by filtration. (Foll. by *into*, *through*.) M18.

British Medical Journal 2% plain lignocaine was infiltrated into the wound.

2 *verb trans*. & *intrans*. Permeate (*into*, *through*) by filtration. M18.

Scientific American To collect floodwater that infiltrates the gravel beds of desert streams.

3 *verb trans*. & *intrans*. Penetrate, gain entrance or access to, (enemy lines, an opposing political organization, etc.) surreptitiously and by degrees. M20. ▸**b** *verb trans*. Introduce (troops, a spy, etc.) into enemy lines, an opposing political organization, etc., in this way. M20.

I. WALLACE The Reds might infiltrate every free nation of Africa, and control the continent in a year. J. A. MICHENER Six thousand mounted troops . . started cautiously infiltrating toward the western edge. *fig*.: S. NAIPAUL He was . . resentful of her for thus infiltrating his consciousness. **b** R. DEACON Any spies who might have been infiltrated into the ranks of prisoners-of-war.

■ **inˈfiltrative** *adjective* (*rare*) of the nature of or productive of infiltration M19. **infiltrator** *noun* M20.

infiltration /ɪnfɪlˈtreɪʃ(ə)n/ *noun*. LME.
[ORIGIN from INFILTRATE *verb* + -ION.]
1 The action or process of infiltrating (something); the process or condition of being infiltrated. LME.

J. L. MYRES The southward infiltration of Albanian and Slav into districts formerly Romanized. *Times* Alleged Communist infiltration into the Oxford branch of the National Union of Railwaymen. A. POWELL The only hint of human infiltration of these pastures came from distant sheep.

2 An infiltrated deposit. E19.
– COMB.: **infiltration anaesthesia** local anaesthesia; **infiltration capacity** the maximum rate at which soil in a given condition can absorb water.

infiltrometer /ɪnfɪlˈtrɒmɪtə/ *noun*. M20.
[ORIGIN from INFILTR(ATION + -OMETER.]
An apparatus for measuring the rate at which soil absorbs water.

infimum /ɪnˈfʌɪməm/ *noun*. M20.
[ORIGIN Latin = lowest part, use as noun of neut. of *infimus* lowest.]
MATH. The largest number that is less than or equal to each of a given set of real numbers; an analogous quantity for a subset of any other ordered set. Opp. ***supremum***.

in fine /ɪn ˈfʌɪni, ˈfiːni/ *adverbial phr*. M16.
[ORIGIN Latin.]
Finally, in short, to sum up.

infinitation /ˌɪnfɪnɪˈteɪʃ(ə)n/ *noun*. M17.
[ORIGIN Latin *infinitatio(n-)*, from *infinitat-* pa. ppl stem of *infinitare* make infinite, formed as INFINITE: see -ATION.]
LOGIC. The action of making infinite; the condition of being made infinite.

infinite /ˈɪnfɪnɪt/ *adjective*, *adverb*, & *noun*. LME.
[ORIGIN Latin *infinitus* unbounded, unlimited, formed as IN-[3] + FINITE *adjective* & *noun*.]
▸ **A** *adjective*. **1** Having no limit or end; boundless, endless; immeasurably great in extent, duration, degree, etc. LME. ▸†**b** Occupying an indefinitely long time; tedious, endless. L16–M17.

J. BUCHAN For the humble and unfortunate he had infinite charity. B. BETTELHEIM What goes on in the infinite (or possibly finite, but nevertheless unimaginably vast) outer space.

infinite regress a sequence of reasoning, argument, justification, etc., which can never come to an end.
2 Innumerable, very many. LME.
†**3** Indefinite in nature, meaning, etc.; indeterminate. E16–M17.
4 *GRAMMAR*. Of a verb part or form: not limited by person or number. M16.
5 *MATH*. Having no limit; greater than any assignable number or magnitude; having an uncountable number of elements, digits, terms, etc. L17.
6 *MUSIC*. Of a musical structure: that can be repeated infinitely. E19.
▸ †**B** *adverb*. Infinitely. E16–L17.
▸ **C** *noun*. **1** That which is infinite or has no limit; an infinite being, thing, quantity, etc.; *spec*. (***a***) ***the infinite***, infinite space; (***b***) ***the Infinite***, God. M16.

P. DAVIES Measuring the infinite must rank as one of the great-est enterprises of the human intellect.

2 *An* exceedingly large number or (formerly) amount. Foll. by *of*. *arch*. M16.

J. RUSKIN That Calais tower has an infinite of symbolism in it.

3 *MATH*. An infinite quantity. M17.
■ **infinitely** *adverb* LME. **infiniteness** *noun* LME.

infinitesimal /ˌɪnfɪnɪˈtɛsɪm(ə)l/ *noun* & *adjective*. M17.
[ORIGIN mod. Latin *infinitesimus*, formed as INFINITE (cf. CENTESIMAL): see -AL[1].]
▸ **A** *noun*. †**1** *MATH*. The member of a series corresponding to infinity. Only in M17.
2 *MATH*. An infinitesimal quantity; a fraction which approaches zero. E18.
3 An extremely small or insignificant quantity, amount, etc. M19.
▸ **B** *adjective*. **1** (Of a quantity) infinitely or indefinitely small; relating to or involving quantities which approach zero. E18.
infinitesimal calculus: see CALCULUS 1.
2 *gen*. Extremely minute or insignificant. M18.
■ **infinitesimally** *adverb* E19.

infinitise *verb* var. of INFINITIZE.

infinitist /ɪnˈfɪnɪtɪst/ *noun*. L19
[ORIGIN from INFINITE + -IST.]
A person who believes that God or the world is infinite.
■ **infinitism** *noun* the views or belief of an infinitist E20.

infinitival /ˌɪnfɪnɪˈtʌɪv(ə)l/ *adjective*. M19.
[ORIGIN formed as INFINITIVE + -AL[1].]
GRAMMAR. Of or pertaining to the infinitive.
■ **infinitivally** *adverb* L19.

infinitive /ɪnˈfɪnɪtɪv/ *adjective* & *noun*. LME.
[ORIGIN Latin *infinitivus* unlimited, indefinite, infinitive, formed as IN-[3] + *finitivus* definite, formed as FINITE *adjective*: see -IVE.]
GRAMMAR. ▸ **A** *adjective*. Designating or pertaining to a form of a verb expressing the verbal notion without relation to a particular subject (traditionally classed as a mood). LME.
▸ **B** *noun*. The infinitive form of a verb; a verb in this. M16.
split infinitive: see SPLIT *ppl adjective*.
■ **infinitively** *adverb* in the infinitive form E18.

infinitize /ˈɪnfɪnɪtʌɪz/ *verb trans*. *rare*. Also **-ise**. E20.
[ORIGIN from INFINITE + -IZE.]
Make infinite.

infinitude /ɪnˈfɪnɪtjuːd/ *noun*. M17.
[ORIGIN formed as INFINITE after *magnitude*: see -TUDE.]
1 = INFINITY 1. M17.
2 = INFINITY 2. M17.

infinitum /ɪnfɪˈnʌɪtəm/ *noun*. L16.
[ORIGIN Latin, formed as INFINITE.]
Infinity; an infinitude, an endless amount or number. Cf. AD INFINITUM.

infinity /ɪnˈfɪnɪti/ *noun*. LME.
[ORIGIN Old French & mod. French *infinité* from Latin *infinitas*, formed as INFINITE: see -ITY.]
1 The quality or attribute of being infinite or having no limit; boundlessness. LME.

M. IGNATIEFF What we have in common with each other beneath the infinity of our differences.

2 An infinite thing; infinite extent, amount, duration, etc.; a boundless expanse; an unlimited time. LME.

T. ROETHKE I learned not to fear infinity, The far field, the windy cliffs of forever. L. NIVEN It seemed to go out forever . . to a point at infinity.

infinity pool a swimming pool constructed to give the impression that it merges into the surrounding landscape.
3 Immensity, vastness; an indefinitely great amount or number. Foll. by *of*. LME.

ALDOUS HUXLEY Every object and event contains within itself an infinity of depths within depths.

to infinity endlessly, without limit.
4 *MATH*. Infinite quantity (denoted by ∞); an infinite number (*of* something). L17. ▸**b** Infinite distance; a point which is (effectively) infinitely distant; *esp*. in *OPTICS*, any distance from which an image can be focused with a lens set for maximum distance, i.e. from which light rays arrive effectively parallel. M19.

infirm /ɪnˈfəːm/ *adjective*. LME.
[ORIGIN Latin *infirmus*, formed as IN-[3] + *firmus* FIRM *adjective*.]
1 Weak, unsound; unable to resist pressure or weight, frail, feeble. Now *rare*. LME. ▸**b** *transf*. Of an argument, title, etc.: weak; invalid. Now *rare*. M16.
2 Of the mind, a decision, etc.: not firm or strong in character or purpose; weak, irresolute. E16.
3 Not physically strong or healthy; weak or feeble, esp. through old age. L16.
■ **infirmly** *adverb* E17. **infirmness** *noun* L16.

infirm /ɪnˈfəːm/ *verb trans*. Now *rare*. LME.
[ORIGIN Latin *infirmare* weaken, invalidate, formed as INFIRM *adjective*.]
†**1** Weaken the hold of (belief) over the mind; impair the force of (an argument, reason, etc.); make doubtful or less certain. LME–L17.
†**2** Make physically infirm or frail; weaken, impair the strength of. M16–M17.
3 Invalidate (a law, custom, evidence, etc.); declare invalid, call into question. M16.

infirmarer /ɪnˈfəːm(ə)rə/ *noun*. LME.
[ORIGIN Old French *enfermerier*, from *enfermerie* infirmary, formed as INFIRMARY: see -ER[2].]
hist. A person in charge of (the patients in) an infirmary in a medieval monastery.

infirmary /ɪnˈfəːm(ə)ri/ *noun*. LME.
[ORIGIN medieval Latin *infirmaria*, formed as INFIRM *adjective*: see -ARY[1].]
(A part of) a building for the treatment of the sick or wounded, orig. in a religious establishment, school, etc.; a hospital.
■ **infirˈmarian** *noun* (*hist*.) = INFIRMARER M17.

infirmation /ɪnfəːˈmeɪʃ(ə)n/ *noun*. *rare*. E19.
[ORIGIN Latin *infirmatio(n-)*, from *infirmat-* pa. ppl stem of *infirmare*: see INFIRM *verb*, -ATION.]
The action of weakening or invalidating evidence etc.

infirmative /ɪnˈfəːmətɪv/ *adjective*. *rare*. E17.
[ORIGIN from INFIRM *verb* + -ATIVE.]
Tending to weaken or invalidate.

infirmity /ɪnˈfəːmɪti/ *noun*. LME.
[ORIGIN Latin *infirmitas*, formed as INFIRM *adjective*: see -ITY.]
1 Weakness or lack of strength; lack of power to do something; an instance of this. LME. ▸**b** Lack of validity in an argument or title. E17.
2 Physical weakness, debility, frailty of body, etc., resulting from some defect, disease, or (esp.) old age; a specific physical weakness; *esp*. a failing in one of the faculties. Formerly also, an illness. LME.

Gentleman's Magazine A gentleman . . who felt the infirmities of age at an earlier period than most do. *Countryman* His increasing infirmity meant that he only grew plants able to fend for themselves.

3 (A) weakness or defect of character; (a) moral weakness or frailty. LME.
†**4** A noxious vegetative growth. *rare*. L16–M18.

infix /ˈɪnfɪks/ *noun*. E17.
[ORIGIN from (the same root as) INFIX *verb*; in sense 2 after *prefix*, *suffix*.]
†**1** A fixing in; fixed position. Only in E17.
2 *GRAMMAR*. An affix inserted into a word. L19.

infix /ɪnˈfɪks/ *verb trans*. E16.
[ORIGIN Partly from Latin *infix-* pa. ppl stem of *infigere* fix in formed as IN-[2] + *figere* fasten; partly from IN-[1] or IN-[2] + FIX *verb*.]
1 Fix or fasten (a thing) in or *in*; implant or insert firmly. E16. ▸**b** Fix or fasten on something. E17.

fig.: EDWARD WHITE So deeply is this habit of thought infixed in modern readers.

2 Fix or impress (a fact etc.) *in* the mind or memory. M16.
3 *GRAMMAR*. Insert (an affix) into a word. M19.
■ **infixation** *noun* (*GRAMMAR*) the action of infixing; the state of being infixed: E20. **infixion** *noun* (*rare*) = INFIXATION M17.

in flagrante /ɪn fləˈgranti/ *adverbial phr*. *colloq*. E17.
[ORIGIN Abbreviation of IN FLAGRANTE DELICTO or similar Latin phr.]
= IN FLAGRANTE DELICTO.
– NOTE: Rare before 20.

in flagrante delicto /ɪn flə,grantɪ dɪˈlɪktəʊ/ *adverbial phr.* L18.
[ORIGIN Latin = in the heat of the crime: cf. IN FLAGRANTE, FLAGRANT, DELICT.]
In the very act of committing an offence; *spec.* in the act of adultery or other sexual misconduct.
E. PAUL His cringing wife and the imaginary lover he had always sworn to catch *in flagrante delicto*.

inflame /ɪnˈfleɪm/ *verb*. Also (now *rare*) **en-** /ɪn-, ɛn-/. ME.
[ORIGIN Old French & mod. French *enflammer* from Latin *inflammare*, formed as IN-[2] + *flamma* FLAME *noun*.]
▸ **I** *verb trans.* **1** Excite with strong feeling or passion; rouse to anger or animosity. ME. ▸**b** Rouse (a passion). ME.
W. ROBERTSON Stimulants like wine inflame the senses. S. T. WARNER A dance wanton enough to inflame a maypole. P. HOWARD The gruesome horror stories that had inflamed public opinion.
2 Set on fire, kindle. Now *rare*. LME. ▸**b** Light up as with flame. L15.
W. FALCONER The fuse . . inflames the powder. **b** SHELLEY The torches Inflame the night to the eastward.
3 Heat, make hot; *esp.* raise (the body or blood) to a feverish temperature. LME. ▸**b** Induce inflammation or painful swelling in. M17.
R. CHANDLER We had . . lattices to admit the air, while cool; and shutters to exclude it, when inflamed. **b** M. SPARK Freddy had arrived with an arm swollen and inflamed from a new vaccination.
4 Make worse or more intense; aggravate. Formerly also, increase (a price or charge). E17.
V. GLENDINNING Lettie inflamed Rebecca's raw self-doubt and was never forgiven for it.
▸ **II** *verb intrans.* **5** Catch fire. Formerly also, become very hot. LME.
J. TYNDALL It first smokes and then violently inflames.
6 Become passionately excited. M16.
CARLYLE I know how soon your noble heart inflames when sympathy and humanity appeal to it.
7 Become heated by disease or stimulants; be affected by inflammation or painful swelling. L16.
▪ †**inflameable** *adjective* = INFLAMMABLE *adjective* E17–E18. **inflamer** *noun* a person or thing which inflames; *esp.* an instigator: E17.

inflammable /ɪnˈflaməb(ə)l/ *adjective & noun*. LME.
[ORIGIN medieval Latin *inflammabilis*, from *inflammare*: see INFLAME, -ABLE.]
▸ **A** *adjective*. †**1** Of a part of the body: liable to become inflamed. Only in LME.
2 Liable to catch fire; readily ignited. E17.
†**inflammable air** hydrogen.
3 Easily roused or excited; passionate, excitable. E19.
D. H. LAWRENCE The Englishman was in a strange, inflammable state, the German was excited.
▸ **B** *noun*. An inflammable substance. Usu. in *pl.* L18.
– NOTE: With reference to fire freq. repl. in official use by *flammable*, to avoid possible misunderstanding as 'not flammable', with interpretation of the prefix as IN-[3].
▪ **inflammaˈbility** *noun* M17. **inflammableness** *noun* L17. **inflammably** *adverb* M19.

inflammation /ɪnfləˈmeɪʃ(ə)n/ *noun*. LME.
[ORIGIN Latin *inflammatio(n-)*, from *inflammat-* pa. ppl stem of *inflammare*: see INFLAME, -ATION. Perh. partly from Old French & mod. French *inflammation*.]
1 MEDICINE. The condition, usu. involving redness, warmth, swelling, and pain, produced locally in the tissues as a reaction to injury, infection, etc.; an instance of this. LME.
2 The action of setting on fire or catching fire; the condition of being in flames. E16. ▸†**b** A blazing object or phenomenon. M16–M18.
3 The action of exciting or rousing to strong emotion; the condition of being so roused. L16.
†**4** Increase in cost. *rare*. Only in E19.

inflammatory /ɪnˈflamət(ə)ri/ *noun & adjective*. L17.
[ORIGIN from INFLAMMAT(ION + -ORY[2].]
▸ **A** *noun*. A thing that inflames or excites strong feeling or passions. Now *rare* or *obsolete*. L17.
▸ **B** *adjective*. **1** Tending to excite with strong feeling or passion. Now usu., tending to rouse anger or animosity. E18.
D. WIGODER We . . attacked each other, with vicious inflammatory verbal threats.
2 Tending to heat the blood or excite the senses; stimulating. Now *rare*. M18.
3 Of the nature of, resulting from, or characterized by inflammation of the tissues. M18.
†**4** Characterized by or causing a blazing condition. M–L18.
▪ **inflammatorily** *adverb* M19.

inflate /ɪnˈfleɪt/ *ppl adjective*. Now *rare* or *obsolete*. LME.
[ORIGIN Latin *inflatus* pa. pple, formed as INFLATE *verb*: see -ATE[2].]
= INFLATED.

inflate /ɪnˈfleɪt/ *verb*. LME.
[ORIGIN Latin *inflat-* pa. ppl stem of *inflare*, formed as IN-[2] + *flare* to blow: see -ATE[3].]
1 *verb trans.* Distend by filling with air or gas; *gen.* swell, distend. LME.
S. BELLOW A beach ball you inflated with your breath.
2 *verb trans.* Puff up with or *with* pride, vanity, satisfaction, etc.; elate. M16.
J. PORTER Character that prosperity could not inflate, nor adversity depress.
3 *verb trans.* Increase greatly or beyond accepted limits; *spec.* (ECONOMICS) bring about inflation in relation to (a currency, an economy), raise (prices) artificially. M19. ▸**b** *verb intrans.* Resort to (monetary) inflation; undergo (excessive) increase or monetary inflation. M20.
W. S. JEVONS Prices and credit mutually inflate each other. C. HOPE The enemies of our country like nothing better than to inflate the figures of those killed. **b** *Daily Telegraph* In these days of rapidly inflating house prices. *Weekend Australian* A permanent population of 25,000 which inflates to 100,000 during holiday periods.
▪ **inflatable** *adjective & noun* (*a*) *adjective* able to be blown up or filled with air or gas; (*b*) *noun* an inflatable dinghy, toy, etc.: L19. **inflated** *adjective* (*a*) that has been distended or inflated; *esp.* (of language) turgid, bombastic; (*b*) ZOOLOGY & BOTANY having a bulging form and hollow interior, as if filled with air: L16. **inflatedness** *noun* M19. **inflater**, **inflator** *nouns* a person or thing which inflates something; *spec.* an air pump for inflating tyres etc.: L19.

inflation /ɪnˈfleɪʃ(ə)n/ *noun*. ME.
[ORIGIN Latin *inflatio(n-)*, from *inflat-*, formed as INFLATE *verb*: see -ATION.]
1 The action of inflating with air or gas; the condition of being inflated with air or gas or of being distended as if with air. ME.
2 The condition of being puffed up with pride, vanity, satisfaction, etc. E16.
3 Turgidity of style; bombast. E17.
K. ALLOTT She can express an apocalyptic element in feeling without inflation.
4 (Unduly) great expansion or increase; *spec.* (*a*) ECONOMICS (undue) increase in the quantity of money circulating, in relation to the goods available for purchase; (*b*) *popularly* inordinate general rise in prices leading to a fall in the value of money. Opp. ***deflation***. M19.
Dumfries & Galloway Standard A major part of our economic policy is to keep inflation as low as possible.
– COMB.: **inflation-proof** *verb trans. & adjective* protect(ed) from the effects of economic inflation.
▪ **inflationary** *adjective* of, characterized by, or leading to monetary inflation (***inflationary spiral***, a vicious circle caused by higher wages leading to higher prices, which in turn force up wages) E20. **inflationism** *noun* (ECONOMICS) the policy of inflating a currency; the condition of being inflated: E20. **inflationist** *noun* an advocate of inflation, esp. as being beneficial to trade L19.

inflect /ɪnˈflɛkt/ *verb*. LME.
[ORIGIN Latin *inflectere*, formed as IN-[2] + *flectere* to bend.]
1 *verb trans.* Bend inwards; bend into a curve or angle; *gen.* bend, curve. LME.
fig.: O. SACKS Most of Miss H's hating and blaming was inflected inwards upon herself.
†**2** *verb trans.* OPTICS. Diffract. M17–M19.
3 GRAMMAR. **a** *verb trans.* Modify the form of (a word) to express a particular grammatical function or attribute: see INFLECTION 2. M17. ▸**b** *verb intrans.* Undergo inflection. L19.
4 *verb trans.* Vary the intonation of (the voice); MUSIC flatten or sharpen (a note) by a chromatic semitone. E19.
A. S. BYATT His voice was . . a southern industrial Yorkshire, less inflected and singing than Winifred's northern one.
▪ **inflectable** *adjective* (GRAMMAR) able to be inflected M20. **inflected** *adjective* (*a*) that has been inflected; (*b*) *spec.* (of a language) characterized by inflection: M17. **inflectedness** *noun* E19.

inflection /ɪnˈflɛkʃ(ə)n/ *noun*. Also **-exion**. LME.
[ORIGIN Old French & mod. French *inflexion* or Latin *inflexio(n-)*, from *inflex-* pa. ppl stem of *inflectere*: see INFLECT, -ION.]
1 The action of bending (inwards). Formerly, ability to bend. LME. ▸**b** The condition of being inflected or bent; a bend, a curvature. M17.
fig.: J. BRYANT The allusion will not be . . obtained by undue inflexions or distortions. **b** D. STOREY Ellipses . . drawn . . with scarcely an inflection that broke the line.
2 GRAMMAR. Modification in the form of a word by means of affixation, vowel change, etc., to express a particular grammatical function or attribute, as number, case, gender, tense, mood, etc. L16. ▸**b** An inflected form of a word. Also, an affix used to inflect a word. M17.
3 Change of intonation of the voice; (in speaking or singing) a change in tone or pitch. L16.
E. CALDWELL She whispered quietly with a cautious inflection of her voice that sounded . . wistful and apprehensive. *fig.*: C. CONNOLLY Sentences which were able to express the subtlest inflections of sensibility and meaning.
†**4** OPTICS. Diffraction. E18–M19.
5 GEOMETRY. Change in the direction of curvature. E18.
point of inflection a point on a curve at which inflection occurs.
– COMB.: **inflection point** (*a*) = *point of inflection* above; (*b*) (chiefly *US*) a time of significant change in a situation (esp. in business), a turning point.
▪ **inflectionless** *adjective* without modulation or grammatical inflection L19.

inflectional /ɪnˈflɛkʃ(ə)n(ə)l/ *adjective*. Also **-flex-**. M19.
[ORIGIN from INFLECTION + -AL[1].]
1 Of, pertaining to, or characterized by grammatical inflection. M19.
2 GEOMETRY. Of or pertaining to a point of inflection. M19.
▪ **inflectionally** *adverb* L19.

inflective /ɪnˈflɛktɪv/ *adjective*. M17.
[ORIGIN from INFLECT + -IVE.]
†**1** Of the air: tending to diffract rays of light. M17–E18.
2 Of, pertaining to, or characterized by grammatical inflection. L18.

inflexed /ɪnˈflɛkst/ *adjective*. M17.
[ORIGIN from Latin *inflex-* pa. ppl stem of *inflectere* INFLECT + -ED[1].]
Bent or curved inwards.

inflexible /ɪnˈflɛksɪb(ə)l/ *adjective*. LME.
[ORIGIN Latin *inflexibilis*, formed as IN-[3] + *flexibilis* FLEXIBLE.]
1 Unable to be bent; rigid, not pliant. LME.
2 Adhering unswervingly to a purpose or opinion; obstinate, uncompromising. LME.
D. PRATER He remained inflexible against any form of compromise.
3 Unalterable, rigidly fixed. L17.
G. H. NAPHEYS Nature's laws are more inflexible than iron.
▪ **inflexiˈbility** *noun* E17. **inflexibly** *adverb* M16.

inflexion *noun*, **inflexional** *adjective* vars. of INFLECTION, INFLECTIONAL.

inflict /ɪnˈflɪkt/ *verb trans.* M16.
[ORIGIN Latin *inflict-* pa. ppl stem of *infligere*, formed as IN-[2] + *fligere* strike down.]
1 Afflict (a person) *with* something painful or disagreeable. Now *joc. rare*. M16.
Macmillan's Magazine We should be inflicted with less . . twaddle and useless verbosity.
2 Impose or lay (a wound, blow, penalty, defeat, etc.) on a person or thing as something painful or unpleasant to be endured. (Foll. by *on*, *upon*.) L16. ▸**b** Force (an unwelcome person or thing) *on*, *upon*. Freq. *joc.* E19.
E. WAUGH Punitive expeditions suffered more harm than they inflicted. N. ANNAN The oppressive regime which Leslie inflicted on his daughter. **b** R. BOLT I was commanded into office; it was inflicted on me. *Southern Rag* People who want to *share* the music, not have it inflicted on them.
▪ **inflictable** *adjective* that may be imposed or inflicted E19. **inflicter** *noun* E17. **inflictor** *noun* M18.

infliction /ɪnˈflɪkʃ(ə)n/ *noun*. M16.
[ORIGIN Late Latin *inflictio(n-)*, formed as INFLICT: see -ION.]
1 The action of inflicting pain, punishment, annoyance, etc. Formerly also, the fact of being inflicted. M16.
R. J. SULLIVAN The infliction of such exemplary punishment.
2 An instance of pain, punishment, etc., inflicted; *colloq.* a nuisance. L16.
R. BOYLE Distress'd by such Persecutions, as seem to be Divine Inflictions. M. BRIDGMAN What an infliction he must be!

inflictive /ɪnˈflɪktɪv/ *adjective*. E17.
[ORIGIN formed as INFLICT + -IVE.]
Inflicting or tending to inflict pain or suffering; of or pertaining to infliction.

in-flight /ˈɪnflʌɪt/ *adjective*. M20.
[ORIGIN from IN-[1] + FLIGHT *noun*[1].]
Occurring, supplied, etc., during an aircraft's flight.

inflorescence /ɪnflɔːˈrɛs(ə)ns, -flə-/ *noun*. M18.
[ORIGIN mod. Latin *inflorescentia*, from late Latin *inflorescere* come into flower: see IN-[2], FLORESCENCE.]
BOTANY. **1** The mode in which the flowers of a plant are arranged in relation to the axis and to each other. M18. ▸**b** The flowers of a plant collectively. M19.
DEFINITE ***inflorescence***.
2 The process of flowering or coming into flower. E19.

inflow /ˈɪnfləʊ/ *noun*. M19.
[ORIGIN from IN-[1] + FLOW *noun*[1].]
The action of flowing in, influx; that which flows in.
Daily Telegraph The inflow of money from savers had picked up.

inflow /ɪnˈfləʊ/ *verb intrans.* LME.
[ORIGIN from IN-[1] + FLOW *verb*.]
1 Flow in. LME.
†**2** Esp. of a star: exert influence. LME–M17.

influence /ˈɪnflʊəns/ *noun*. LME.
[ORIGIN Old French & mod. French, or medieval Latin *influentia* (whence also Provençal, Spanish *influencia*, Italian *influenza*), from Latin *influent-* pres. ppl stem of *influere* flow in, formed as IN-[2] + *fluere* flow: see -ENCE.]
†**1** The action of flowing in, influx; flowing matter. LME–E18.

I

2 *ASTROLOGY.* A supposed emanation of ethereal fluid or (in later theories) occult force from the stars affecting human character, destiny, etc. **LME.** ▸†**b** Inherent nature or disposition, ascribed to astral influence. **LME–M17.**

SPENSER What euill starre On you hath frown'd, and pourd his influence bad? J. RUSKIN One of the leaden influences on me of the planet Saturn. *transf.*: MILTON Store of ladies, whose bright eyes Rain influence.

†**3** The inflow of a divine or secret force or principle; the force etc. flowing in thus. **LME–M17.**

AV *Wisd.* 7:25 A pure influence flowing from the glory of the Almighty.

4 An action exerted, imperceptibly or by indirect means, by one person or thing on another so as to cause changes in conduct, development, conditions, etc. (Foll. by *in*, *on*, *upon*.) **L16.** ▸**b** Ascendancy, moral or political power (*over* or *with* a person or group). **M17.**

J. ROSENBERG No traces of this first teacher's influence appear in Rembrandt's work. B. T. BRADFORD In England she might conceivably be able to exercise some influence over him. **b** M. MOORCOCK My uncle's influence must be considerable. He had pulled strings in every department.

sphere of influence: see SPHERE *noun* 6. **under the influence** *colloq.* drunk. UNDUE ***influence***.

5 A person or thing exercising such action or power. **M18.**

P. G. HAMERTON Musical studies, the most powerful of softening influences. C. HOPE Looper would act as a moderating influence on her daughter when she was gone.

6 *ELECTRICITY.* Induction. *arch.* **L19.**

– COMB.: **influence line** *ENGINEERING* a graph showing how, at a given point in a structure, the stress, moment, etc., varies with the position of the load; **influence peddler** *N. Amer.* a person who uses his or her position or political influence in exchange for money or favours.

influence /ˈɪnflʊəns/ *verb.* **M17.**
[ORIGIN from the noun.]

1 *verb trans.* **a** Affect (sometimes improperly or corruptly) the mind or actions of. **M17.** ▸**b** Affect the condition of, have an effect on. **M17.**

a E. W. BEMIS Expenditures to 'influence' city council. *Femina* Bhindranwale was a magnetic speaker and he influenced a lot of local people. **b** G. R. PORTER Specific gravity of glass is influenced by the degree of heat to which it has been exposed. D. HALBERSTAM He wanted to influence events, to be a mover.

†**2** *verb trans.* Cause to flow in; infuse, instil. **M17–E18.**

3 *verb intrans.* Exert influence. Orig. foll. by †*on*, †*upon*. **L17.**

■ **influenceable** *adjective* **M19.** **influencer** *noun* **M17.** **influencive** *adjective* (*rare*) influential **E18.**

influent /ˈɪnflʊənt/ *adjective & noun.* **LME.**
[ORIGIN Latin *influent-*: see INFLUENCE *noun*, -ENT.]

▸**A** *adjective.* **1** Flowing in. **LME.**

2 Exercising astral influence or occult power. Long *arch.* **LME.**

3 *ECOLOGY.* That is an influent (see B.2 below). **LME.**

▸**B** *noun.* **1** A stream (esp. a tributary) which flows into another stream or a lake. **M19.**

2 *ECOLOGY.* An organism having a major effect on the balance of a plant or animal community. *arch.* **E20.**

influential /ɪnflʊˈɛnʃ(ə)l/ *adjective & noun.* **L16.**
[ORIGIN from medieval Latin *influentia* INFLUENCE *noun* + -AL[1].]

▸**A** *adjective.* †**1** *ASTROLOGY.* Pertaining to, of the nature of, or exercising astral influence. **L16–M17.** ▸**b** *transf.* Exercising or caused by divine or supernatural influence. **M17–M18.**

2 Exerting a powerful influence or effect *on*. **M17.**

I. BARROW Hurtful errours, influential on practice.

3 Having or marked by great power or influence. **M18.**

J. BERMAN Her influential books helped to transform the condition of women in early twentieth century America. N. GORDIMER Carole . . became influential in the debating society.

▸**B** *noun.* An influential person. **M19.**

■ **influentially** *adverb* (*a*) by or in the way of influence; †(*b*) *ELECTRICITY* by induction: **M17.**

influenza /ɪnflʊˈɛnzə/ *noun.* **M18.**
[ORIGIN Italian, lit. 'influence', from medieval Latin *influentia* INFLUENCE *noun*: the Italian word *influenza* has, in addition to the various senses of English *influence*, that of 'outbreak of an epidemic', hence 'an epidemic'; its specific application to the 1743 influenza epidemic which began in Italy led to its adoption as the standard English term for the disease. Cf. FLU.]

A highly contagious viral infection of the lining of the trachea and bronchi, often epidemic, and usu. marked by fever, weakness, muscular aches, coughing, and watery catarrh. Freq. loosely, any acute respiratory infection accompanied by fever.

gastric influenza: see GASTRIC *adjective*. ***Spanish influenza***: see SPANISH *adjective*.

■ **influenzal** *adjective* **E19.**

influx /ˈɪnflʌks/ *noun.* **L16.**
[ORIGIN (French from) late Latin *influxus*, from Latin *influere* to flow in: see IN-[2], FLUX *noun*.]

1 An inflow of liquid, air, light, etc. **L16.** ▸**b** The point at which a stream or river flows into a larger stream, a lake, etc. **M17.**

2 *transf.* A continuous entry of people (esp. visitors or immigrants) or things into a place. **M17.**

I. COLEGATE The influx of tourists and foreign residents has made my local villagers richer. A. BROOKNER This sudden influx of money might seem to promise them a different life.

†**3** = INFLUENCE *noun* 3, 4, 4b. **M17–E18.**

influxion /ɪnˈflʌkʃ(ə)n/ *noun.* Now *rare.* **E17.**
[ORIGIN Late Latin *influxio(n-)*, from *influx-* pa. ppl stem of *influere*: see IN-[2], FLUXION.]

Inflow, (an) influx.

info /ˈɪnfəʊ/ *noun. colloq.* **E20.**
[ORIGIN Abbreviation.]

Information.

L. CODY Look, what's the info on this kidnapping? *Woman's Realm* Big, colourful pictures and info about today's pop stars.

■ **info'mania** *noun* excessive enthusiasm for the accumulation and dissemination of information **L20.** **infowar** *noun* = ***cyberwar*** s.v. CYBER- **L20.**

in-foal /ˈɪnfəʊl/ *adjective.* **E20.**
[ORIGIN from IN-[1] + FOAL *noun*.]

Of a mare: that is in foal, pregnant.

infobahn /ˈɪnfəʊbɑːn/ *noun. colloq.* **L20.**
[ORIGIN Blend of INFORMATION and AUTOBAHN.]

A high-speed computer network, esp. the Internet.

infold /ˈɪnfəʊld/ *noun.* Also (earlier) †**en-**. **L16.**
[ORIGIN from IN-[2], EN-[1] + FOLD *noun*[2].]

A convolution; a fold.

infold *verb*[1], *verb*[2] see ENFOLD *verb*[1], *verb*[2].

infolded /ɪnˈfəʊldɪd/ *ppl adjective.* **L19.**
[ORIGIN from IN-[1] + FOLD *verb*[1] + -ED[1].]

Turned or folded in.

infolding /ˈɪnfəʊldɪŋ/ *noun.* **L19.**
[ORIGIN from IN-[1] + FOLDING *noun*.]

A folding or turning in; an inward fold.

infolio /ɪnˈfəʊlɪəʊ/ *noun. rare.* Pl. **-os**. **M19.**
[ORIGIN from IN-[1] + FOLIO *noun*.]

A folio volume.

infomediary /ɪnfəˈmiːdjəri/ *noun.* **L20.**
[ORIGIN Blend of INFORMATION and INTERMEDIARY.]

A commercial organization which acts as a broker for the transmission of information between consumers and businesses (esp. in Internet commerce), supplying such functions as market and customer satisfaction research, etc., and providing data security.

infomercial /ɪnfəˈməːʃ(ə)l/ *noun.* Chiefly *US.* Also **inform-**. **L20.**
[ORIGIN Blend of INFORMATION and COMMERCIAL: cf. INFO.]

An advertising film, esp. on television, which promotes a product etc. in an informative and purportedly objective style.

inforce *verb* see ENFORCE *verb*.

†**inforcible** *adjective* var. of ENFORCIBLE.

inform /ɪnˈfɔːm/ *adjective.* Now *rare* or *obsolete*. **M16.**
[ORIGIN French *informe* or Latin *informis*, formed as IN-[3] + *forma* FORM *noun*.]

1 Having no definite or regular form; shapeless, misshapen, deformed. **M16.**

C. COTTON Bleak Crags, and naked Hills, And the whole Prospect so inform and rude.

2 Without form; having no shaping or actuating principle. **M17.**

R. VILVAIN An inform lump . . without a Soul is neither Man nor Beast. J. NORRIS In the old creation we read of a void and inform mass.

inform /ɪnˈfɔːm/ *verb.* Also (earlier) †**en-**. **ME.**
[ORIGIN Old French *enfo(u)rmer* (mod. *informer*) from Latin *informare* shape, form an idea of, describe, formed as IN-[2] + *forma* FORM *noun*.]

▸**I** Give form to; shape.

†**1** *verb trans.* Give form or shape to; arrange, compose, fashion. **ME–L17.** ▸**b** *verb intrans.* Take form or shape; materialize. **L16–M17.**

2 *verb trans.* Give a formative principle or vital quality to; imbue *with* a feeling, principle, or quality. **LME.** ▸**b** Be the essential quality or principle of; permeate, inspire. **LME.**

TENNYSON Her constant beauty doth inform Stillness with love, and day with light. H. BELLOC As a poem is informed by a . . scheme of rhythm. **b** B. MAGEE The depth of passion which informs this defence of liberty.

3 *verb trans.* Of a soul or life-giving source: impart life or spirit to; inspire, animate. **E17.**

M. PRIOR Long as Breath informs this fleeting Frame.

▸**II** Impart knowledge to; tell, instruct, teach.

4 *verb trans.* Form (the mind or character); impart knowledge or instruction to; teach. Now *rare* or *obsolete*. **ME.** ▸†**b** Instruct (a person) in a subject or course of action. Foll. by *how*, *in*, *of*, *to*, *to do*. **ME–M18.** ▸†**c** Give instructions or directions, direct or bid *to do*. **LME–M18.** ▸†**d** Direct, guide. **M17–M19.**

ROBERT BURTON That leaves his son to a covetous Schoolemaster to be informed. W. GIFFORD So may thy varied verse, from age to age Inform the simple, and delight the sage.

†**5** *verb trans.* Give instruction in (a subject); teach or spread (a faith etc.). **ME–E17.**

6 *verb trans.* Give (a person) knowledge of a particular fact, occurrence, etc. Foll. by *about*, *of*, (arch.) *on*, *that*. **LME.**

T. HARDY When Somerset reached the hotel he was informed that somebody was waiting to see him. B. EMECHETA To make sure that all the arrangements were made before he informed her. P. ACKROYD Neither of them had informed their parents in advance about their intentions. R. ELLMANN 'I was ploughed, of course,' Wilde informed a friend afterwards.

†**7** *verb trans.* Make (a fact or occurrence) known; tell (a thing) to (a person). **LME–E19.**

W. LAUD The bishop informs that that county is very full of impropriations. SOUTHEY My mother will inform you my town direction as soon as I have one.

†**8** **a** *verb trans.* Give (a magistrate etc.) accusatory information *against* a person. Only in **E16.** ▸**b** *verb intrans.* Give accusatory information *on* or *against* a person. **L16.**

b M. SCAMMELL Someone who knew Taissa's background informed on her, and she was soon dismissed.

9 *verb refl.* Get instruction or information *on* or *about*; get to know, learn, *of*, *that*. **E17.**

W. DAMPIER They came purposely to view our Ship, and . . to inform themselves what we were. C. JOHNSTON The motive . . was to inform myself particularly in the laws.

†**10** *verb intrans.* Give information, report. Only in **17.**

informal /ɪnˈfɔːm(ə)l/ *adjective.* **LME.**
[ORIGIN from IN-[3] + FORMAL *adjective*.]

▸**I** **1** Not done or made according to a recognized form; irregular, unofficial, unconventional. **LME.**

M. RULE An informal alliance was formed between the Barbers' Company and the Fellowship of Surgeons. *Sunday Express* This garden is . . very informal I don't think you could find a straight edge anywhere!

informal ballot paper, **informal vote** *Austral. & NZ* a spoilt or invalid ballot paper. **informal patient**: admitted to a psychiatric hospital on a non-compulsory basis.

2 Without formality or ceremony; unceremonious. Of language, clothing, etc.: everyday, casual. **E19.**

R. JARRELL He was a nice-looking and informal and unassuming man, a very human one. N. PODHORETZ Everything . . was easy and informal . . and no one seemed to care whether my tie was on or off. A. THWAITE A few . . guests were encouraged to stay on for a cold informal supper.

▸†**II** **3** Deranged, insane. *rare* (Shakes.). Only in **E17.**

■ **infor'mality** *noun* absence of formality; an instance of this, an informal act: **L16.** **informally** *adverb* **E19.**

informant /ɪnˈfɔːm(ə)nt/ *noun.* **M17.**
[ORIGIN from INFORM *verb* + -ANT[1].]

▸†**I** **1** Something which inspires, animates, or actuates. Only in **M17.**

▸**II** **2** *gen.* A person who gives information. **L17.**

E. F. BENSON I don't care whether your informants are correct or not in what they tell you.

3 *LAW.* A person who informs against another; an informer. **L18.**

4 A person from whom a linguist, anthropologist, etc., obtains information about language, dialect, or culture. **L19.**

Language The language must be learnt from the lips of a native informant.

informatics /ɪnfəˈmatɪks/ *noun.* **M20.**
[ORIGIN from INFORMAT(ION + -ICS, translating Russian *informatika*.]

Information science and technology.

information /ɪnfəˈmeɪʃ(ə)n/ *noun.* **LME.**
[ORIGIN Old French & mod. French from Latin *informatio(n-)*, from *informat-* pa. ppl stem of *informare* INFORM *verb*: see -ATION.]

▸**I** **1** Formation or moulding of the mind or character; training, instruction, teaching. Now *rare* or *obsolete*. **LME.** ▸†**b** An instruction. **LME–M18.** ▸†**c** Divine instruction; inspiration. **LME–M16.**

2 Communication of the knowledge of some fact or occurrence. **LME.**

G. BORROW For your information, however, I will tell you that it is not.

3 Knowledge or facts communicated about a particular subject, event, etc.; intelligence, news. **LME.** ▸†**b** An item of news; (in early use) an account (*of* something). **E16–M19.** ▸**c** Without necessary relation to a recipient: that which inheres in or is represented by a particular arrangement, sequence, or set, that may be stored in, transferred by, and responded to by inanimate things; *MATH.* a statistically defined quantity representing the probability of occurrence of a symbol, sequence, message, etc., as against a number of possible alternatives. **E20.**

C. G. WOLFF Edith Wharton began to collect background information for an historical novel. W. WHARTON Can you give me any information about the patient? You were close to him. B. EMECHETA Missy screamed in excitement at this piece of information. **c** *Nature* The precise sequence of the bases is the code which carries the genetical information.

inside information: see INSIDE *adjective*. *white information*: see WHITE *adjective*.

4 *LAW*. **a** A formal (written) statement or accusation presented to a court or magistrate in order to institute criminal proceedings. LME. ▸**b** A statement of the facts of a civil claim presented by the Attorney General or other officer on behalf of the Crown. E17. ▸**c** *SCOTS LAW* (now *hist.*). A written argument on a criminal case ordered by the High Court of Justiciary if the case raises difficult points of law or (formerly) by a Lord Ordinary in the Court of Session when reporting to the Inner House. Now *rare*. L17. **5** The action of informing against, charging, or accusing a person. *obsolete* exc. as a transf. use of sense 4a. L15.

▸†**II 6** The giving of a form or essential character to something; inspiration (as of the body by the soul). M17–L19.

– COMB.: **information booth**, **information bureau**, **information centre**, **information desk**: where information is given and questions answered; **information officer** a person engaged in the provision of specialized information; **information processing** the processing of information so as to yield new or more useful information; **information retrieval** the tracing of information stored in books, computers, etc.; **information revolution** (the economic and industrial impact of) the increase in the availability of information and the changes in its storage and dissemination owing to the use of computers; **information room** a communications centre within a police station where information is collected and disseminated; **information science** (the branch of knowledge that deals with) the storage, retrieval, and dissemination of (esp. scientific or technical) information; **information scientist** a person employed to provide an information service; a person who studies the methods used to do so; an expert in or student of information science; ***information superhighway***: see SUPERHIGHWAY 2; **information technologist** an expert in or student of information technology; **information technology** technology that deals with the storage, processing, and dissemination of information esp. using computers; **information theory** the quantitative theory, based on a precise definition of information and the theory of probability, of the coding and transmission of signals and information.

■ **informational** *adjective* of or pertaining to information; conveying information: E19. **informationally** *adverb* M20.

informative /ɪnˈfɔːmətɪv/ *adjective*. LME.
[ORIGIN medieval Latin *informativus*, from Latin *informat-*: see INFORMATION, -IVE.]
1 Formative; giving life, shape, or an essential quality. LME. **2** Of the nature of or pertaining to legal information. E17. **3** Giving information; instructive. M17.

T. FULLER The most informative Histories to Posterity . . are such as were written by the Eye-witnesses thereof. P. LIVELY One of those busy informative paintings full of detail.

informative double = *INFORMATORY double*.
■ **informatively** *adverb* M16. **informativeness** *noun* E20.

informator /ɪnˈfɔːmətə/ *noun*. *obsolete* exc. *hist.* M16.
[ORIGIN Late Latin, from Latin *informat-*: see INFORMATION, -OR.]
An instructor, a teacher.

informatory /ɪnˈfɔːmət(ə)ri/ *adjective*. LME.
[ORIGIN from Latin *informat-* (see INFORMATION) + -ORY².]
Instructive, informative.
informatory double *BRIDGE* a double intended to give information to one's partner rather than to score a penalty.
■ **informatorily** *adverb* (*BRIDGE*) informatively, in order to inform E20.

informed /ɪnˈfɔːmd/ *adjective*. LME.
[ORIGIN from INFORM *verb* + -ED¹.]
Knowing or acquainted with the facts; educated, knowledgeable. Now freq. in ***well-informed***, ***ill-informed***.

Daily Express Lights . . to keep the driver informed when anything goes wrong with the lubrication. W. K. HANCOCK Informed opinion was ready to welcome the report. M. SEYMOUR-SMITH It is essential to view his beliefs from an anthropologically informed point of view. R. C. A. WHITE In such cases the consent is illusory because it is not informed.

informed consent permission granted in the knowledge of the possible consequences, esp. that given by a patient to a doctor for treatment with full knowledge of the possible risks and benefits.
■ **informedly** /-mɪdli/ *adverb* M17. **informedness** /-mɪdnɪs/ *noun* M20.

informer /ɪnˈfɔːmə/ *noun*. LME.
[ORIGIN from INFORM *verb* + -ER¹.]
▸**I** †**1** An instructor, a teacher. LME–M17.

R. MATHEWS Experience which is the truest informer, speaks aloud in this matter also.

2 A person who gives information or intelligence, an informant. LME.

SIR W. SCOTT He talks no Gaelic, nor had his informer much English.

3 A person who informs against another, *spec.* for reward. E16.

R. MACAULAY She's an informer. She set the police on us. C. HOPE Their campus spy, usually an overworked informer.

common informer: see COMMON *adjective*.

▸**II 4** A person or thing which gives form, life, or inspiration. *poet.* LME.

POPE Nature! informer of the Poet's art, Whose force alone can raise or melt the heart.

informercial *noun* var. of INFOMERCIAL.

informidable /ɪnˈfɔːmɪdəb(ə)l, ɪnfɔːˈmɪd-/ *adjective*. *rare*. L17.
[ORIGIN from IN-³ + FORMIDABLE.]
Not formidable, not to be feared.

informity /ɪnˈfɔːmɪti/ *noun*. Long *rare*. L16.
[ORIGIN Late Latin *informitas*, from Latin *informis*: see INFORM *adjective*, -ITY.]
The condition of being unformed, shapeless, or misshapen.

informosome /ɪnˈfɔːməsəʊm/ *noun*. M20.
[ORIGIN from INFORM(ATION + -O- + -SOME³.]
CYTOLOGY. A type of ribonucleoprotein in which the messenger RNA may be undetectable until later in development, found in the eggs of certain fishes and echinoderms.

†**infortunate** *verb trans.* L16–L18.
[ORIGIN medieval Latin *infortunat-* pa. ppl stem of *infortunare*, formed as IN-³ + FORTUNATE *verb*.]
Subject to evil or unlucky influence; make unfortunate.

infortune /ɪnˈfɔːtʃuːn, -tʃ(ə)n/ *noun*. LME.
[ORIGIN Old French & mod. French, formed as IN-³ + FORTUNE *noun*.]
†**1** Lack of good fortune, ill luck; a misfortune, a mishap. LME–M17. **2** *ASTROLOGY*. An inauspicious or malevolent planet or aspect, *esp.* Saturn or Mars. LME.

†**infortunity** *noun*. LME–E18.
[ORIGIN Old French *infortunité*, formed as INFORTUNE: see -ITY.]
Unfortunate condition, ill luck, adversity; an instance of this, a misfortune.

infotainment /ɪnfəˈteɪnm(ə)nt/ *noun*. L20.
[ORIGIN from INFO(RMATION + ENTER)TAINMENT.]
Broadcast matter that seeks both to inform and to entertain.

infra /ˈɪnfrə/ *adverb*. L19.
[ORIGIN Latin.]
Later, further on (in a book or article); = BELOW *adverb* 1c.

infra- /ˈɪnfrə/ *prefix*.
[ORIGIN Latin *infra* below, underneath, beneath, (in medieval Latin also) within.]
Forming mainly adjectives with the senses 'below, beneath' (in situation or position), 'lower, inferior' (in status or quality).

– NOTE: Opp. SUPRA-. Freq. also treated as opp. SUPER- (cf. SUB-).
■ **infraclass** *noun* (*TAXONOMY*) a taxonomic grouping ranking next below a subclass M20. **infraˈcostal** *adjective* (*ANATOMY*) situated beneath the ribs L19. **infraˈhuman** *adjective* that is below the human level L19. **infraˈlittoral** *adjective* (*ECOLOGY*) (**a**) = SUBLITTORAL *adjective*; (**b**) designating or pertaining to the region of a lake containing rooted vegetation: M19. **infraˈmarginal** *adjective & noun* (a structure, organ, etc.) situated below the margin or border M19. **inframaˈxillary** *adjective* (**a**) = SUBMANDIBULAR; (**b**) of or pertaining to the lower jawbone: M19. **infra-ˈorbital** *adjective* (*ANATOMY*) situated below the orbit of the eye E19. **infraorder** *noun* (*TAXONOMY*) a taxonomic grouping ranking next below a suborder M20. **infraˈrenal** *adjective* (*ANATOMY*) situated below the kidneys L19. **infraspeˈcific** *adjective* (*TAXONOMY*) at a level lower than that of the species M20.

infract /ɪnˈfrakt/ *adjective*. Long *rare*. M16.
[ORIGIN Latin *infractus*, formed as IN-³ + *fractus* broken.]
Unbroken, unimpaired; sound, whole.

infract /ɪnˈfrakt/ *verb trans.* Chiefly *US*. L18.
[ORIGIN Latin *infract-* pa. ppl stem of *infringere* INFRINGE.]
Break (a rule, an agreement, etc.); violate, infringe.
■ **infractor** *noun* E16.

infraction /ɪnˈfrakʃ(ə)n/ *noun*. LME.
[ORIGIN Latin *infractio(n-)*, formed as INFRACT *verb*: see -ION.]
1 The action or an act of breaking an agreement; (a) violation, (an) infringement. LME.

A. S. NEILL These and other infractions of rules carry automatic fines. A. BROOKNER Any infraction of the liberty of such simple people would be a form of assault.

2 The action of breaking or fracturing; a fracture. E17.

infradian /ɪnˈfreɪdɪən/ *adjective*. M20.
[ORIGIN from INFRA- + *-dian*, after CIRCADIAN.]
PHYSIOLOGY. Of a rhythm or cycle: having a frequency lower than circadian, i.e. a period longer than a day. Cf. ULTRADIAN.

infra dig /ɪnfrə ˈdɪg/ *adjectival phr. colloq.* E19.
[ORIGIN Abbreviation of Latin *infra dignitatem* beneath (one's) dignity.]
Beneath the dignity of one's position; undignified.

Scouting A bit infra dig . . touting for reader-support like this? S. BELLOW Doing the floors on his knees, didn't bother him . . . It never occurred to him that it was infra dig.

infragrant /ɪnˈfreɪgr(ə)nt/ *adjective*. E19.
[ORIGIN from IN-³ + FRAGRANT.]
Lacking fragrance; malodorous.

SYD. SMITH We shall both be a brown infragrant powder in thirty or forty years. M. WEBB Sparsely in the hedges grew the pale, infragrant flowers of early autumn.

infralapsarian /ɪnfrəlapˈsɛːrɪən/ *noun & adjective*. Also **I-**. M18.
[ORIGIN formed as INFRA- + Latin *lapsus* fall, LAPSE *noun* + -ARIAN. Cf. SUPRALAPSARIAN.]
THEOLOGY. ▸**A** *noun*. A Calvinist holding the view that God's election of only some to everlasting life was not originally part of the divine plan, but a consequence of the Fall of Man. M18.
▸**B** *adjective*. Of or pertaining to the infralapsarians or their doctrine. L18.
■ **infralapsarianism** *noun* the doctrine of the infralapsarians M19.

inframe *verb* var. of ENFRAME.

†**infranchise** *verb* var. of ENFRANCHISE.

infrangible /ɪnˈfrandʒɪb(ə)l/ *adjective*. L16.
[ORIGIN French, or medieval Latin *infrangibilis*, formed as IN-³ + *frangibilis* FRANGIBLE.]
1 Unbreakable. L16.

F. W. ROBERTSON No iron bar is absolutely infrangible. *fig.*: J. UPDIKE That heaping measure of maternal love which makes for an infrangible soundness of spirit.

2 Unable to be infringed; inviolable. M19.
■ **infrangiˈbility** *noun* E19. **infrangibly** *adverb* E19.

infrared /ɪnfrəˈrɛd/ *adjective & noun*. L19.
[ORIGIN from INFRA- + RED *adjective*, *noun*.]
▸**A** *adjective*. **1** Of electromagnetic radiation: lying beyond the red end of the visible spectrum, having a wavelength between that of red light and that of microwaves (about 800 nm to 1 mm). L19. **2** Involving, producing, or pertaining to (the use of) infrared radiation, esp. as emitted by heated bodies; sensitive to infrared radiation. E20.
▸**B** *noun*. (Usu. with *the*.) The infrared part of the spectrum. L19.
the far infrared, **the near infrared** the part of the infrared far from, close to, the visible spectrum.

infrasonic /ɪnfrəˈsɒnɪk/ *adjective*. E20.
[ORIGIN from INFRA- + SONIC.]
Of, pertaining to, or designating sound waves or vibrations having a frequency below the audible range (i.e. less than 15–30 Hz).

infrasound /ˈɪnfrəsaʊnd/ *noun*. M20.
[ORIGIN from INFRA- + SOUND *noun*².]
(A) sound of infrasonic frequency.

infrastructure /ˈɪnfrəstrʌktʃə/ *noun*. E20.
[ORIGIN French, formed as INFRA- + STRUCTURE *noun*.]
The foundation or basic structure of an undertaking; *spec.* (**a**) the collective permanent installations (airfields, naval bases, etc.) forming a basis for military activity; (**b**) the installations and services (power stations, sewers, roads, housing, etc.) regarded as the economic foundation of a country.

Broadcast The best laid plans . . come to nothing unless there is a sound and properly considered infrastructure. *Guardian* Britain needs to invest an extra £3.5 billion . . in its basic infrastructure of housing, roads, and sewers.

■ **infrastructural** *adjective* M20.

infrequency /ɪnˈfriːkw(ə)nsi/ *noun*. E17.
[ORIGIN Latin *infrequentia*, formed as INFREQUENT: see -ENCY.]
†**1** The fact or condition of being deserted or seldom visited. Also, fewness. Only in 17.

P. HOLLAND It was the solitude and infrequency of the place that brought the dragon thither.

2 The fact or condition of being infrequent or occasional; rarity. L17.

C. LAMB The relish of such exhibitions must be in proportion to the infrequency of going. A. FLINT The infrequency of gangrene is shown by its having occurred in but one of 133 cases.

■ Also **infrequence** *noun* (*rare*) M17.

infrequent /ɪnˈfriːkwənt/ *adjective*. M16.
[ORIGIN Latin *infrequent-*, formed as IN-³ + *frequent-* FREQUENT *adjective*.]
†**1** Little used or practised; unaccustomed, uncommon. Only in M16. **2** Not occurring often; happening rarely; (qualifying an agent noun) seldom doing the action indicated. E17.

W. WOLLASTON A sparing and infrequent worshiper of the Deity. H. JACOBSON Our meetings became more and more infrequent and then stopped altogether.

3 Seldom met with, not plentiful, uncommon. L17.
■ **infrequently** *adverb* L17.

infrigidate /ɪnˈfrɪdʒɪdeɪt/ *verb trans.* Long *rare*. M16.
[ORIGIN Late Latin *infrigidat-* pa. ppl stem of *infrigidare*, formed as IN-² + *frigidus* cold, FRIGID: see -ATE³.]
Make cold; chill, cool.

infrigidation /ˌɪnfrɪdʒɪˈdeɪʃ(ə)n/ *noun*. Now *rare*. LME.
[ORIGIN Late Latin *infrigidatio(n-)*, formed as INFRIGIDATE: see -ATION.]
The action of cooling; the condition of being cooled.

infringe /ɪnˈfrɪn(d)ʒ/ *verb*. M16.
[ORIGIN Latin *infringere*, formed as IN-² + *frangere* to break.]
†**1** *verb trans.* Break (down), destroy; foil, defeat, frustrate. M16–E18.
2 *verb trans.* Break (a law), violate (an oath, treaty, etc.); contravene. M16.

> CLARENDON The undoubted Fundamental priviledge of the Commons in Parliament, . . had never been infringed, or violated. A. TREW By taking his submarine within 15 kilometres of Krakoy, Yenev would be infringing Norwegian territorial rights.

†**3** *verb trans.* Refute, contradict, deny. L16–M17.
†**4** *verb trans.* Break the force of, diminish the strength of; enfeeble, impair. Only in 17.
5 *verb intrans.* Break in or encroach *on* or *upon*. M18.

> B. GUEST Jealousy toward a rival who had infringed upon his former domain.

■ **infringer** *noun* M16.

infringement /ɪnˈfrɪn(d)ʒm(ə)nt/ *noun*. L16.
[ORIGIN from INFRINGE + -MENT.]
†**1** Refutation, contradiction. L16–M17.
2 (A) breaking or breach of a law, obligation, right, etc. E17.

> E. CRANKSHAW The least infringement of the rules was savagely punished. A. BRINK Minor infringements like staying out after ten at night.

3 A breaking in, an encroachment, an intrusion. L17.

> N. SHUTE Designers . . , energetic in fighting the least infringement upon . . their own sphere of action.

infructescence /ɪnfrʌkˈtɛs(ə)ns/ *noun*. L19.
[ORIGIN from IN-² + Latin *fructus* fruit, after INFLORESCENCE.]
BOTANY. An aggregate fruit.

infructuous /ɪnˈfrʌktjʊəs/ *adjective*. E17.
[ORIGIN from Latin *infructuosus*, formed as IN-³ + *fructuosus* FRUCTUOUS: see -OUS.]
Not bearing fruit; unfruitful, barren; *fig.* unprofitable, ineffective.
■ **infructuose** *adjective* = INFRUCTUOUS E18. **infructuously** *adverb* E19.

infrustrable /ɪnˈfrʌstrəb(ə)l/ *adjective*. *rare*. L17.
[ORIGIN from IN-³ + FRUSTRABLE.]
Unable to be frustrated or foiled.
■ **infrustrably** *adverb* M18.

infula /ˈɪnfjʊlə/ *noun*. Pl. **-lae** /-liː/. E17.
[ORIGIN Latin.]
1 *ECCLESIASTICAL.* Either of the two ribbons of a bishop's mitre. E17.
2 *ROMAN ANTIQUITIES.* A woollen headband worn by a priest etc. or placed on a sacrificial victim. E18.

infundibulum /ɪnfʌnˈdɪbjʊləm/ *noun*. Pl. **-la** /-lə/. M16.
[ORIGIN Latin = funnel, from *infundere* pour in: see INFUSE.]
ANATOMY & ZOOLOGY. Any of various funnel-shaped cavities and structures of the body; *esp.* the hollow stalk which connects the hypothalamus and the posterior pituitary gland.
■ **infundibular** *adjective* (*ANATOMY*) funnel-shaped; of or pertaining to an infundibulum: E18. **infundibuliform** *adjective* (*BOTANY & ZOOLOGY*) funnel-shaped M18.

infuriant /ɪnˈfjʊərɪənt/ *noun*. M20.
[ORIGIN medieval Latin *infuriant-* pres. ppl stem of *infuriare*: see INFURIATE *verb*, -ANT¹.]
A fact, condition, etc., which provokes a person to anger.

infuriate /ɪnˈfjʊərɪət/ *adjective*. Now *literary*. M17.
[ORIGIN medieval Latin *infuriatus* pa. pple, formed as INFURIATE *verb*: see -ATE².]
Provoked to fury; mad with rage, frantic.
■ **infuriately** *adverb* L19.

infuriate /ɪnˈfjʊərɪeɪt/ *verb trans.* M17.
[ORIGIN medieval Latin *infuriat-* pa. ppl stem of *infuriare*, formed as IN-² + *furiare* madden, from *furia* FURY: see -ATE³.]
Provoke to fury; make extremely angry.

> B. T. BRADFORD Audra was so infuriated by his attitude . . she could barely contain herself.

■ **infuriating** *adjective* provoking, maddeningly vexatious L19. **infuriatingly** *adverb* L19. **infuriˈation** *noun* M19.

infuse /ɪnˈfjuːz/ *verb*. LME.
[ORIGIN Latin *infus-* pa. ppl stem of *infundere*, formed as IN-² + *fundere* pour.]
1 *verb trans.* Introduce (a liquid ingredient) by pouring; pour in; *MEDICINE* perform infusion of. (Foll. by *into*.) LME. ▸**b** *transf.* & *fig.* Instil (grace, life, spirit, etc.) into the mind, heart, etc. Formerly also, insinuate. E16.

> SWIFT By the force of that soporiferous medicine infused into my liquor. *American Journal of Physiology* Saline was infused into a vein. **b** W. S. CHURCHILL Lanfranc . . rapidly infused new life into the English Church. M. COX An educational institution can infuse ideals and mould . . a personality.

†**2** *verb trans.* Pour, shed, *on*, *upon*. LME–L17.
3 *verb trans.* Steep (a herb, tea, etc.) in a liquid so as to extract the soluble constituents; macerate. LME. ▸**b** *verb intrans.* Undergo the process of infusion. E17.

> C. LUCAS They infuse the ashes of burned vegetables in their water.

4 *verb trans.* Affect, esp. flavour, (a liquid) *with* some substance, as a herb steeped in it; *fig.* imbue or pervade with or *with* a quality etc. Usu. in *pass.* M16.

> R. HOGGART Very banal verses [may be] infused with decent emotion. P. V. PRICE Hippocrates . . used wine infused with cinnamon. C. THUBRON The intemperance of a Vesuvius infuses his whole frame.

■ **infuser** *noun* (*a*) a person who infuses or instils some quality; (*b*) a device for infusing tea leaves in a cup of water: L16. **infusive** *adjective* †(*a*) divinely infused, innate; (*b*) having the quality of infusing or instilling something: M17.

infusible /ɪnˈfjuːzɪb(ə)l/ *adjective*. M16.
[ORIGIN from IN-³ + FUSIBLE.]
Unable to be fused or melted.
■ **infusiˈbility** *noun* L18.

infusion /ɪnˈfjuːʒ(ə)n/ *noun*. LME.
[ORIGIN Old French & mod. French, or Latin *infusio(n-)*, formed as INFUSE: see -ION.]
1 The pouring in of a liquid, the fact of being poured in; a liquid that is poured in. LME. ▸**b** *MEDICINE.* Continuous injection into a vein or tissue, esp. of large volumes of fluid over a long period. E17.
2 a An extract obtained by steeping a substance in water. Formerly also, (a small body of) water containing dissolved organic matter. LME. ▸**b** The steeping of a substance in a liquid in order to impregnate it with the soluble constituents. L16.

> **a** S. RUSHDIE Infusions of herbs in well-boiled water were constantly administered.

3 The infusing or instilling into the mind, heart, etc., of a principle, quality, etc. LME. ▸†**b** Character infused into a person at birth; innate quality. *rare* (Shakes.). Only in E17. ▸†**c** (An) insidious suggestion. M17–M18.

> P. ROTH Carried along by an exciting infusion of Wild West bravado.

4 The introduction of a modifying element; an infused element, an admixture. E17.

> A. J. TOYNBEE The present population is mainly native American in race, with a . . small infusion of European . . blood.

5 The pouring of water over a person in baptism (opp. *immersion*); = AFFUSION. M18.

infusoriform /ɪnfjʊˈsɔːrɪfɔːm/ *adjective*. L19.
[ORIGIN from INFUSORIUM + -FORM.]
ZOOLOGY. Having the form of an infusorium; *spec.* designating a dispersive larva or larval stage in some mesozoan cephalopod parasites.

infusorium /ɪnfjʊˈsɔːrɪəm/ *noun*. Also **I-**. Pl. **-ia** /-ɪə/. L18.
[ORIGIN Use as noun of neut. of mod. Latin *infusorius*, formed as INFUSE.]
ZOOLOGY (now *hist.*). A member of the former class Infusoria of sessile and free-swimming protozoans first found in infusions of decaying organic matter. Usu. in *pl.*
■ **infusorial** *adjective* of or pertaining to (a member of) the Infusoria M19. **infusorian** *adjective & noun* (*a*) *adjective* infusorial; (*b*) *noun* = INFUSORIUM: M19.

infusory /ɪnˈfjuːs(ə)ri, -z-/ *adjective & noun*. *arch.* E19.
[ORIGIN from INFUSORIUM + -ORY².]
ZOOLOGY. ▸**A** *adjective.* = INFUSORIAL. E19.
▸**B** *noun.* = INFUSORIUM. M19.

†**Ing** *noun & adjective* see YIN *noun*² & *adjective*².

-ing /ɪŋ/ *suffix*¹.
[ORIGIN Old English *-ung*, *-ing* = Old Saxon *-unga* (Middle Low German, Middle Dutch *-inge*, Dutch *-ing*), Old High German *-unga*, *-ung* (Middle High German *-unge*, German *-ung*), Old Norse *-ung*, *-ing*.]
1 Forming nouns usu. from verbs, occas. by analogy from nouns or adverbs, denoting (*a*) verbal action, as ***fighting***, ***swearing***, ***blackberrying***, or an instance of it, an act (with pl. *-ings*), as ***wedding***, ***outing***; also, an occupation or skill, as ***banking***, ***fencing***, ***glassblowing***; (*b*) (sometimes usu. in *pl.*) a thing resulting from or produced by an action or process, as ***building***, ***carving***, ***earnings***; also, a thing involved in an action or process, as ***covering***; (*c*) the material, substance, or things involved in an action or process, as ***bedding***, ***clothing***, ***flooring***, ***washing***; freq. from nouns without any corresp. verb, as ***sacking***, ***scaffolding***.
2 Forming the gerund of verbs, i.e. a noun which is a distinct part of the verb and retains certain of its functions, esp. those of governing an obj. and being qualified by an adverb instead of by an adjective, as ***I love reading poetry*** (= the reading of poetry); ***after having written a letter*** (= after the completion of writing a letter); ***the habit of speaking loosely*** (= loose speaking). Developed from 1, initially perh. partly in imit. of the Latin gerund, in the late 14th cent.; not found in other Germanic langs.

-ing /ɪŋ/ *suffix*².
[ORIGIN Alt. of Old English *-ende* = Latin *-ent-*, Greek *-ont-*, Sanskrit *-ant-*.]
Forming the pres. pple of verbs; freq. in adjectives of ppl origin or force, as ***charming***, ***cunning***, ***willing*** (and occas. in adjectives formed from nouns in imitation of these, as ***hulking***); also in prepositions and adverbs of ppl origin, as ***during***, ***notwithstanding***.

-ing /ɪŋ/ *suffix*³.
[ORIGIN Old English from Germanic: cf. -LING¹.]
Forming derivative masc. nouns with the sense 'one belonging to or of the kind of', hence as patronymics or diminutives, as ***atheling***, ***farthing***, ***gelding***, ***sweeting***.

†**Inga** *noun & adjective* see INCA.

†**ingage** *noun*, *verb*, †**ingagement** *noun* see ENGAGE *noun*, *verb*, ENGAGEMENT.

ingan /ˈɪŋən/ *noun*. *dial.* (chiefly *Scot.*). E18.
[ORIGIN Repr. a pronunc.]
= ONION *noun*.

ingaol *verb* var. of ENJAIL.

†**ingarrison** *verb* var. of ENGARRISON.

ingate /ˈɪngeɪt/ *noun*. *N. English*. LME.
[ORIGIN from IN-¹ + GATE *noun*².]
1 The action or faculty of entering. Also, entry upon a period of life. LME.
2 A way in, an entrance. L16.
3 *sing.* & (usu.) in *pl.* Goods coming into a town or port; duty on these. Cf. OUTGATE 3. *obsolete* exc. *hist.* E17.

ingather /ɪnˈɡaðə/ *verb trans.* M16.
[ORIGIN from IN-¹ + GATHER *verb*.]
Gather in (esp. a harvest).
■ **ingatherer** *noun* L15. **ingathering** *noun* (*a*) the gathering in of crops etc.; *Scot.* the collecting of money due; (*b*) the congregating of Jews in (modern) Israel: E16.

ingem *verb* var. of ENGEM.

ingeminate /ɪnˈdʒɛmɪneɪt/ *verb trans.* Also (earlier) †**en-**. L16.
[ORIGIN Latin *ingeminat-* pa. ppl stem of *ingeminare*, formed as IN-² + GEMINATE *verb*.]
1 Utter two or more times; reiterate. Now chiefly in ***ingeminate peace***, call repeatedly for peace. L16.
†**2** Double (a thing); repeat (an action). *rare*. Only in 17.

ingemination /ɪnˌdʒɛmɪˈneɪʃ(ə)n/ *noun*. Now *rare*. L16.
[ORIGIN formed as INGEMINATE: see -ATION.]
1 Repeated utterance, reiteration. L16.
2 The action or process of doubling, duplication. M17.

†**ingender** *verb* var. of ENGENDER.

†**ingendrure** *noun* var. of ENGENDRURE.

ingenerable /ɪnˈdʒɛn(ə)rəb(ə)l/ *adjective*. Now *rare*. LME.
[ORIGIN Late Latin *ingenerabilis*, formed as IN-³ + GENERABLE.]
Unable to be generated. Chiefly in ***ingenerable and incorruptible***.
■ **ingeneraˈbility** *noun* L16.

ingenerate /ɪnˈdʒɛn(ə)rət/ *adjective*¹. Now *rare*. L16.
[ORIGIN Latin *ingeneratus* pa. pple of *ingenerare*: see INGENERATE *verb*.]
Inborn, innate. Formerly also, congenital.

ingenerate /ɪnˈdʒɛn(ə)rət/ *adjective*². M17.
[ORIGIN ecclesiastical Latin *ingeneratus*, formed as IN-³ + GENERATE *ppl adjective*.]
Not generated; self-existent.
■ **ingenerateness** *noun* L17.

ingenerate /ɪnˈdʒɛnəreɪt/ *verb trans.* Now *rare*. Pa. pple **-ated**, †**-ate**. E16.
[ORIGIN Latin *ingenerat-* pa. ppl stem of *ingenerare*, formed as IN-² + GENERATE *verb*.]
Generate within; engender, produce.
■ **ingeneˈration** *noun* M17.

†**ingenia** *noun* pl. of INGENIUM.

ingenio /ɪnˈdʒiːnɪəʊ/ *noun*. *obsolete* exc. *hist.* Pl. **-os**. E17.
[ORIGIN Spanish = engine, mill.]
In the W. Indies: a sugar mill, a sugar-works.

ingeniosity /ɪnˌdʒiːnɪˈɒsɪti/ *noun*. Now *rare*. LME.
[ORIGIN (French *ingéniosité* from) medieval Latin *ingeniositas*, from Latin *ingeniosus*: see INGENIOUS, -ITY.]
The quality of being ingenious; ingenuity.

ingenious /ɪnˈdʒiːnɪəs/ *adjective*. LME.
[ORIGIN (French *ingénieux* from) Latin *ingeniosus*, from INGENIUM: see -OUS.]
▸**I 1** Orig., possessing high mental ability, talented, intelligent, discerning. Now *spec.* clever at making, inventing, or contriving things, esp. of a curious or unexpected nature. LME.

> T. BROWN Wine . . makes the dull ingenious. T. GENT Travels of Cyrus . . worthy the Perusal of every ingenious Person. J. BARZUN To be ingenious about devising activities is the mark of the 'imaginative' teacher.

2 Exemplifying high mental ability, showing intelligence. Now *spec.* cleverly contrived or made. L15.

T. HEARNE 'Twas a good ingenious Sermon, about Praise. H. JACOBSON He was a great advocate for electricity and ingenious electrical gadgets.

▸ †**II** Used by confusion for INGENUOUS or Latin *ingenuus*. **3** Having a noble disposition; *spec.* honourably candid or straightforward. L16–L18. **4** Well-born. Of education etc.: befitting a well-born person. L16–L18.

■ **ingeniously** *adverb* LME. **ingeniousness** *noun* M16.

†**ingenit** *adjective*. Also **-ite**. E17–E18.
[ORIGIN Latin *ingenitus* pa. pple of *ingignere* engender, formed as IN-[2] + *gignere* beget.]
Inborn, innate. Also, native.

ingenium /ɪnˈdʒiːnɪəm/ *noun*. Pl. ***-ia*** /-ɪə/. L19.
[ORIGIN Latin = mind, intellect.]
Mental ability, talent; a person possessing this. Also, mental inclination, disposition.

†**ingenteel** *adjective*. M17–L18.
[ORIGIN from IN-[3] + GENTEEL *adjective*.]
Ungenteel.

ingénue /ˈanʒeɪnjuː; *foreign* ɛ̃ʒeny (*pl. same*)/ *noun*. Also **-gen-**. M19.
[ORIGIN French, fem. of *ingénu* INGENUOUS.]
An artless innocent young woman, esp. as a stage role; an actress playing such a role.

I. SINCLAIR A parade of jailbait ingénues and crooning models.

ingenuity /ɪndʒɪˈnjuːɪti/ *noun*. L16.
[ORIGIN Latin *ingenuitas*, formed as INGENUOUS: see -ITY.]
▸ **I** Senses connected with INGENUOUS.
†**1** Freeborn status. L16–M17.
†**2** Nobility of character; high-mindedness. L16–E18.
3 Candour, ingenuousness. Now *rare*. L16.

W. GODWIN An expression of frankness, ingenuity, and unreserve.

▸ **II** Senses connected with INGENIOUS.
4 Orig., high mental ability, talent, intelligence, discernment. Now *spec.* cleverness at making, inventing, or contriving things, esp. of a curious or unexpected nature; skilfulness of contrivance or design. L16.

A. S. BYATT She had supposed human ingenuity would find ways round food shortages and overpopulation.

5 An ingenious device, an artifice. M17.

ingenuous /ɪnˈdʒɛnjʊəs/ *adjective*. L16.
[ORIGIN from Latin *ingenuus* lit. 'native, inborn', formed as IN-[2] + base of *gignere* beget: see -OUS, -UOUS.]
▸ **I 1** Noble in character; generous, high-minded. Now *rare* or *obsolete*. L16. ▸†**b** Of an animal or thing: of high quality or character. E–M17.
†**2** Of education, studies: liberal, befitting a freeborn person. E17–M18.
3 Honourably straightforward; frank, candid. E17. ▸**b** Innocently frank or open; artless. L17.

W. HOGARTH I will be ingenuous enough to confess something of this may be true. **b** J. CONRAD A young civilian . . with an ingenuous young countenance.

4 Chiefly ROMAN HISTORY. Freeborn. M17.
▸ †**II 5** = INGENIOUS I. L16–L18.

■ **ingenuously** *adverb* L16. **ingenuousness** *noun* the quality of being ingenuous; *esp.* (innocent) frankness, openness: E17.

ingest /ɪnˈdʒɛst/ *verb trans*. E17.
[ORIGIN Latin *ingest-* pa. ppl stem of *ingerere* carry in, bring in, thrust in, formed as IN-[2] + *gerere* bear, carry.]
Take (food or drink) into the body by swallowing or absorbing.

P. ROTH The child refuses to ingest any food—takes it and holds it in his mouth for hours, but refuses to swallow. R. F. CHAPMAN In some insects . . digestion may begin before the food is ingested. *fig.*: C. THUBRON The machine ingested our money but gave back no apple juice.

ingesta /ɪnˈdʒɛstə/ *noun pl*. E18.
[ORIGIN Latin, neut. pl. of *ingestus* pa. pple of *ingerere*: see INGEST.]
Substances introduced into the body as nourishment; food and drink.

ingestion /ɪnˈdʒɛstʃ(ə)n/ *noun*. E17.
[ORIGIN Late Latin *ingestio(n-)*, formed as INGEST: see -ION.]
The taking of food or drink into the body by swallowing or absorption.

ingestive /ɪnˈdʒɛstɪv/ *adjective*. M19.
[ORIGIN from INGEST + -IVE.]
Having the function of taking in nourishment.

Ingin *noun & adjective* see INJUN.

ingine *noun*, †**ingined** *adjective* see ENGINE *noun*, ENGINED.

†**ingineer** *noun* var. of ENGINEER *noun*.

ingle /ˈɪŋg(ə)l/ *noun*[1]. Orig. *Scot*. E16.
[ORIGIN Perh. from Gaelic *aingeal* fire, light, Irish *aingeal* live ember.]
1 A domestic fire; a fire burning on a hearth. E16.
2 An open fireplace, an inglenook. M19.
– COMB.: **ingle-bench** a bench beside a fire; **ingle-cheek** *Scot*. the jamb of a fireplace; **inglenook** a chimney corner; **ingleside** a fireside.

ingle /ˈɪŋg(ə)l/ *noun*[2] *& verb*. L16.
[ORIGIN Unknown.]
▸ **A** *noun*. **1** A catamite. L16.
2 An intimate friend. *rare*. M17.
▸ †**B** *verb trans*. Fondle, caress; coax. L16–L19.

ingliding /ˈɪnglʌɪdɪŋ/ *ppl adjective*. M20.
[ORIGIN from IN *adverb* + GLIDE *verb* + -ING[2].]
PHONETICS. Having a glide towards a central vowel sound (as /ə/).

American Speech The low-country ingliding diphthongs in *date*, *boat*.

inglorious /ɪnˈglɔːrɪəs/ *adjective*. M16.
[ORIGIN from Latin *inglorius* (from *gloria* GLORY *noun*) + -OUS, or from IN-[3] + GLORIOUS.]
1 Bringing no glory or honour (to a person); shameful, ignominious. M16.

LD MACAULAY It involved the country in an inglorious, unprofitable, and interminable war.

2 Not glorious or famous. Now *rare*. L16.

T. GRAY Some mute inglorious Milton here may rest.

■ **ingloriously** *adverb* L16. **ingloriousness** *noun* M17.

†**inglut** *verb* var. of ENGLUT.

ingluvies /ɪnˈgluːviiːz/ *noun*. Pl. same. E18.
[ORIGIN Latin = crop, maw.]
ZOOLOGY. The crop of a bird, insect, etc.
■ **ingluvial** *adjective* M19.

in-goal /ˈɪngəʊl/ *noun & adjective*. L19.
[ORIGIN from IN-[1] + GOAL *noun*.]
RUGBY. (Designating) the part of a rugby ground at either end of the field of play, between the goal line and the dead ball line.

ingoing /ɪnˈgəʊɪŋ/ *noun*. Now *rare*. ME.
[ORIGIN from IN-[1] + GOING *noun*.]
1 The action or an act of going in or entering. ME.
2 A sum paid by a tenant or purchaser for fixtures etc. on taking over premises. E20.

ingoing /ˈɪngəʊɪŋ/ *adjective*. E19.
[ORIGIN from IN-[1] + GOING *adjective*.]
1 That goes in or inwards; that enters. E19.
2 Penetrating, thorough. E20.

ingorge *verb* see ENGORGE.

ingot /ˈɪŋgət/ *noun*. LME.
[ORIGIN Perh. from IN-[1] + Old English *goten* pa. pple of *ġēotan* pour, cast in metal.]
†**1** A mould in which metal is cast. LME–L18.
2 A block (usu. oblong) of cast metal, esp. of gold, silver, or (now) steel. L16.
– COMB.: **ingot iron**: containing too little carbon to temper, and nearly pure by industrial standards.
■ **ingoted** *adjective* wealthy, rich M19.

Ingoush *noun & adjective* var. of INGUSH.

†**ingrace** *verb* var. of ENGRACE.

†**ingraff** *verb* var. of ENGRAFF.

†**ingraft** *verb* var. of ENGRAFT.

ingrain /ˈɪngreɪn, ɪnˈgreɪn/ *adjective & noun*. M16.
[ORIGIN from *in grain* s.v. GRAIN *noun*[1].]
▸ **A** *adjective*. **1** Dyed in grain; dyed with fast colours before manufacture; thoroughly dyed. M16. ▸**b** Of a carpet: reversible, with different colours interwoven. M19.
2 Of a quality, disposition, habit, etc.: inborn, inherent, firmly fixed. M19.
▸ **B** *noun*. **1** (A) material dyed in grain. *rare*. M19.
2 A thing which is ingrained or inherent. L19.

ingrain /ɪnˈgreɪn/ *verb trans*. Also (earlier) **en-** /ɛn-, ɪn-/. LME.
[ORIGIN from IN-[1], EN-[1] + GRAIN *verb*[1].]
†**1** Dye with cochineal; dye in fast colours, dye in grain. LME–M19.
2 Cause (a dye) to sink deeply into the texture of a fabric; work into a substance's fibre or *fig.* into a person's character etc. M17.

ingrained /ɪnˈgreɪnd/ *adjective*. E16.
[ORIGIN Orig. from INGRAIN *verb* + -ED[1]; later from IN *adverb* + GRAINED *adjective*[2].]
1 In the inmost texture; deeply rooted, inveterate. E16.

G. K. CHESTERTON It was an ingrained simplicity and arrogance. P. ROTH Out of the oldest and most ingrained of habits, I wanted to please them.

2 Of a person: thorough. M17.
■ **ingrainedly** /-nɪdli/ *adverb* M19.

ingram /ˈɪŋgrəm/ *adjective & noun*. Long *obsolete* exc. *dial*. M16.
[ORIGIN Alt. of IGNORANT.]
▸ **A** *adjective*. Ignorant; stupid. M16.
▸ **B** *noun*. An ignorant person. M17.

†**ingrandize** *verb* var. of ENGRANDIZE.

ingrate /ˈɪngreɪt, ɪnˈgreɪt/ *adjective & noun*. LME.
[ORIGIN Latin *ingratus* unpleasant, ungrateful, formed as IN-[3] + *gratus* pleasing, grateful.]
▸ **A** *adjective*. †**1** Not of a pleasant or friendly disposition; unfriendly. LME–M16.
2 Not feeling or showing gratitude; ungrateful. LME.
†**3** Not pleasing or acceptable to the mind or senses; disagreeable, unwelcome. E16–E18.
▸ **B** *noun*. An ungrateful person. E17.

ingrateful /ɪnˈgreɪtfʊl, -f(ə)l/ *adjective*. Now *rare*. M16.
[ORIGIN from IN-[3] + GRATEFUL.]
†**1** = INGRATE *adjective* 1. M16–M18.
2 = INGRATE *adjective* 2. M16.
■ †**ingratefully** *adverb* M16–E18. †**ingratefulness** *noun* L16–M17.

ingratiate /ɪnˈgreɪʃɪeɪt/ *verb*. E17.
[ORIGIN from Latin *in gratiam* into favour + -ATE[3], after Italian †*ingratiare*, *ingraziare*.]
1 *verb refl*. Get oneself into favour; gain grace or favour (*with*); make oneself agreeable (*to*). E17.

D. H. LAWRENCE He never ingratiated himself anywhere, . . but kept to himself. M. M. KAYE Courtiers who had once flattered and fawned on him hastened to ingratiate themselves with the new power behind the throne.

†**2** *verb trans*. Bring (a person or thing) into favour (*with* someone); make (a person or thing) agreeable (*to*). M17–M18.
3 *verb intrans*. Gain grace or favour (†*with*). M17.

A. STORR 'Good' behaviour designed to placate and to ingratiate.

■ **ingratiating** *adjective* that ingratiates, intended to gain grace or favour M17. **ingratiatingly** *adverb* L19. **ingratiˈation** *noun* E19. **ingratiatory** *adjective* tending to ingratiate, ingratiating M19.

ingratitude /ɪnˈgratɪtjuːd/ *noun*. ME.
[ORIGIN Old French & mod. French, or late Latin *ingratitudo*, formed as INGRATE: see -TUDE.]
1 Lack or absence of gratitude, ungratefulness. ME.
†**2** Unpleasant feeling, unfriendliness. L15–M16.

†**ingrave** *verb*[1], *verb*[2] vars. of ENGRAVE *verb*[1], *verb*[2].

†**ingraven** *verb* var. of ENGRAVEN *verb*[1]

†**ingraver** *noun* var. of ENGRAVER.

ingravescent /ɪngrəˈvɛs(ə)nt/ *adjective*. E19.
[ORIGIN Latin *ingravescent-* pres. ppl stem of *ingravescere* grow heavy or worse, formed as IN-[2] + *gravescere*, from *gravis* heavy, severe: see -ESCENT.]
MEDICINE. (Gradually) increasing in severity.
■ **ingravescence** *noun* E19.

ingravidate /ɪnˈgravɪdeɪt/ *verb trans*. Now *rare*. M17.
[ORIGIN Late Latin *ingravidat-* pa. ppl stem of *ingravidare* make heavy or pregnant, formed as IN-[2] + *gravidus*: see GRAVID, -ATE[3].]
Load, weigh; make heavy; impregnate.
■ **ingraviˈdation** *noun* the action of ingravidating; the state of being ingravidated; pregnancy: E17.

ingredience /ɪnˈgriːdɪəns/ *noun & verb*. Now *rare*. E16.
[ORIGIN Orig. a respelling of *ingredients*; sense 2 formed as INGREDIENT (see -ENCE).]
▸ **A** *noun*. †**1** *pl. & sing*. The ingredients in or content of a medicine, potion, etc.; a mixture containing various ingredients. E16–M17. ▸**b** A single ingredient or element. L16–M17.
2 The fact or process of entering in as an ingredient or by physical movement. M16.
▸ †**B** *verb trans*. Introduce as an ingredient; provide with ingredients. M17–E19.
■ †**ingrediency** *noun* M17–M19.

ingredient /ɪnˈgriːdɪənt/ *adjective & noun*. LME.
[ORIGIN Latin *ingredient-* pres. ppl stem of *ingredi* enter, formed as IN-[2] + *gradi* proceed, walk: see -ENT.]
▸ **A** *adjective*. **1** Entering into a thing as a constituent element. *arch*. LME.
†**2** Entering into a thing by moving or running in. E–M17.
▸ **B** *noun*. **1** A component part or constituent element in a mixture or combination. LME.

J. T. STORY I began to appreciate that Felix was the homicidal ingredient in all this madness. R. INGALLS She had all the salad ingredients out.

†**2** The chief or main constituent. E–M17.

Ingres paper /ˈaŋgrə peɪpə/ *noun phr*. E20.
[ORIGIN J. A. D. *Ingres* (1780–1867), French painter.]
A French mould-made paper for drawing; thick and mottled paper.

ingress /ˈɪngrɛs/ *noun*. LME.
[ORIGIN Latin *ingressus*, from *ingress-* pa. ppl stem of *ingredi*: see INGREDIENT.]
1 a A place or means of entrance; an entrance. LME. ▸**b** The action or fact of going in or entering; capacity or right of entrance. L15.

b T. S. ELIOT We have been forced to allow ingress to innumerable dull and tedious books.

2 The action of beginning a thing; a beginning, an attempt; the commencement of something. *arch.* LME.
3 *ASTROLOGY & ASTRONOMY.* The arrival of the sun or a planet in a certain part of the sky; the beginning of a transit. M17.

ingress /ɪnˈɡrɛs/ *verb trans. & intrans. rare.* ME.
[ORIGIN Latin *ingress-*: see INGRESS *noun*.]
Enter, go in(to), invade.

ingression /ɪnˈɡrɛʃ(ə)n/ *noun.* L15.
[ORIGIN French †*ingression* or Latin *ingressio(n-)*, formed as INGRESS *verb*: see -ION.]
The action of going in or entering; entrance; invasion.

ingressive /ɪnˈɡrɛsɪv/ *adjective & noun.* M17.
[ORIGIN from Latin *ingress-* (see INGRESS *noun*) + -IVE.]
▸ **A** *adjective.* **1** Having the quality or character of entering; *spec.* (*GRAMMAR*) denoting entering upon action, inceptive. M17.
2 *PHONETICS.* Of a speech sound: made with intake of air. Of an airflow: inward. M20.
▸ **B** *noun.* An ingressive verb; an ingressive sound. M20.
■ **ingressively** *adverb* E20.

Ingrian /ˈɪŋɡrɪən/ *noun & adjective.* E18.
[ORIGIN from *Ingria* (see below) + -AN.]
▸ **A** *noun.* **1** A native or inhabitant of Ingria, a region at the eastern end of the Gulf of Finland. E18.
2 An almost extinct Finno-Ugric language of Ingria. M20.
▸ **B** *adjective.* Of or pertaining to Ingria or the Ingrians. L18.

ingroove *verb* var. of ENGROOVE.

†**ingross** *verb* var. of ENGROSS.

in-group /ˈɪŋɡruːp/ *noun.* E20.
[ORIGIN from IN-[1] + GROUP *noun*.]
A small group of people whose common interest tends to exclude others.

ingrowing /ˈɪŋɡrəʊɪŋ/ *adjective.* M19.
[ORIGIN from IN *adverb* + GROW *verb* + -ING[2].]
Growing inwards or within something; *spec.* (of a toenail) growing so as to press into the flesh.

ingrown /ˈɪŋɡrəʊn/ *adjective.* L17.
[ORIGIN from IN-[1] + GROWN.]
1 That has or is grown within a thing; native, innate. L17.
2 Of a toenail: that has grown into the flesh. L19.
3 *PHYSICAL GEOGRAPHY.* Of a meander: asymmetric due to lateral erosion during formation. E20.

ingrowth /ˈɪŋɡrəʊθ/ *noun.* M19.
[ORIGIN from IN-[1] + GROWTH.]
1 The action of growing inwards. M19.
2 A thing which has grown inwards or within something. M19.

†**Ingua** *noun & adjective* see INCA.

Inguaeonic *noun & adjective* var. of INGVAEONIC.

ingubu /ɪŋˈɡuːbuː/ *noun. S. Afr.* M19.
[ORIGIN Zulu *ingubo* blanket, cloak.]
Orig., a skin blanket or garment. Later, any article of clothing.

inguinal /ˈɪŋɡwɪn(ə)l/ *adjective.* LME.
[ORIGIN Latin *inguinalis*, from *inguin-*, *inguen* groin: see -AL[1].]
ANATOMY. Of, belonging to, or situated in the groin.
■ **inguinally** *adverb* E20.

ingulf *verb* see ENGULF.

ingurgitate /ɪnˈɡəːdʒɪteɪt/ *verb.* L16.
[ORIGIN Latin *ingurgitat-* pa. ppl stem of *ingurgitare*, formed as IN-[2] + *gurgit-*, *gurges* whirlpool, gulf: see -ATE[3].]
1 *verb trans.* Swallow greedily or immoderately. L16. ▸**b** Cram with food. L16.
2 *verb intrans.* Eat or drink to excess, guzzle. L16.
3 *verb trans.* Swallow up as a gulf or whirlpool; engulf. E17.
■ **ingurgiˈtation** *noun* M16.

Ingush /ˈɪŋɡʊʃ, ɪnˈɡʊʃ/ *noun & adjective.* Also **-goush**. E20.
[ORIGIN Russian.]
▸ **A** *noun.* Pl. same, **-es**.
1 A member of a Caucasian people living chiefly in the Ingush republic in the central Caucasus, between Chechnya and North Ossetia. E20.
2 The N. Caucasian language of this people. M20.
▸ **B** *attrib.* or as *adjective.* Of or pertaining to the Ingush or their language. E20.

ingustable /ɪnˈɡʌstəb(ə)l/ *adjective.* Now *rare.* E17.
[ORIGIN from IN-[3] + GUSTABLE.]
Unable to be tasted; not perceptible by the sense of taste.

Ingvaeonic /ɪŋvɪˈɒnɪk/ *noun & adjective.* Also **Inguae-** /ɪŋwɪ-/. M20.
[ORIGIN from Latin *Ingaevones* a Germanic tribe + -IC.]
PHILOLOGY. (Of or pertaining to) the hypothetical language from which the earliest recorded dialects of West Germanic (except Old High German) descended.

†**ingyre** *verb trans.* E16–M18.
[ORIGIN French *ingérer* or Latin *ingerere*: see INGEST. The *y* is unexpl.]
Introduce forcibly or violently. Chiefly *refl.*, intrude.

†**inhabile** *adjective.* E16–M19.
[ORIGIN Old French & mod. French, or Latin *inhabilis*, formed as IN-[3] + *habilis*: see ABLE *adjective*, HABILE *adjective*.]
Unfit, unable; unqualified.
■ †**inhability** *noun* LME–M18.

inhabit /ɪnˈhabɪt/ *verb.* Also †**en-**. LME.
[ORIGIN Old French *enhabiter* or Latin *inhabitare*, formed as IN-[2] + *habitare*: see HABIT *verb*.]
1 *verb trans.* Dwell in, occupy as an abode; live permanently or habitually in (a region, element, etc.). LME.

> E. BOWEN He and she could inhabit one house in intact solitude. D. ABSE I inhabited a serious suit; black tie, armband. M. SARTON The spirit that inhabited this house was unique.

2 *verb intrans.* Dwell, live; have one's abode; lodge. LME.
†**3** *verb trans.* Settle or people (a place). (Foll. by *with*.) LME–M17.
†**4** *verb trans.* Establish or settle (a person, etc.) in a place; provide with a habitation; house. L15–E17. ▸**b** *verb intrans.* Take up one's abode, settle. M–L16.
■ **inhabited** *adjective* (**a**) that is inhabited, lived-in, having inhabitants; (**b**) storiated: L16. **inhabiter** *noun* (*arch.*) (**a**) an inhabitant; †(**b**) a colonist: LME. **inhabitress** *noun* a female inhabitant E17.

†**inhabitable** *adjective*[1]. LME.
[ORIGIN Old French & mod. French from Latin *inhabitabilis*, formed as IN-[3] + *habitabilis* HABITABLE.]
1 Not habitable, not adapted to human habitation. LME–M18.
2 Uninhabited. E16–E17.

inhabitable /ɪnˈhabɪtəb(ə)l/ *adjective*[2]. L16.
[ORIGIN from INHABIT + -ABLE. Earlier in UNINHABITABLE.]
Able to be inhabited, suitable for habitation.
■ **inhabitaˈbility** *noun* M19.

inhabitance /ɪnˈhabɪt(ə)ns/ *noun.* Now *rare.* L15.
[ORIGIN formed as INHABITANT: see -ANCE.]
†**1** A habitation, an abode, a dwelling. L15–E17.
2 Residence, inhabitation. L16.

inhabitancy /ɪnˈhabɪt(ə)nsi/ *noun.* L17.
[ORIGIN formed as INHABITANT: see -ANCY.]
The fact of inhabiting; residence as an inhabitant, esp. for a specified period so as to become entitled to the rights and privileges of a regular inhabitant.

inhabitant /ɪnˈhabɪt(ə)nt/ *adjective & noun.* LME.
[ORIGIN Anglo-Norman, Old French *enhabitant*, *in-*, formed as INHABIT: see -ANT[1].]
▸ **A** *adjective.* Inhabiting, dwelling, resident. Now *rare* or *obsolete* exc. in ***inhabitant householder***, ***inhabitant occupier***. LME.
▸ **B** *noun.* **1** A person who or animal which inhabits a place; a permanent resident. (Foll. by *of*, †*in*.) LME.
2 A person who fulfils the residential or legal requirements for being a member of a state or parish. *US.* L18.

†**inhabitate** *verb trans.* E17–L18.
[ORIGIN Latin *inhabitat-* pa. ppl stem of *inhabitare*: see INHABIT, -ATE[3].]
= INHABIT 1.

inhabitation /ɪnˌhabɪˈteɪʃ(ə)n/ *noun.* LME.
[ORIGIN Late Latin *inhabitatio(n-)*, formed as INHABITATE: see -ATION.]
1 The action of inhabiting; the fact or condition of being or becoming inhabited. LME. ▸**b** *fig.* Spiritual indwelling. E17.
†**2** An inhabited region or building; a dwelling. LME–M17.
†**3** A collection of inhabitants; inhabitants collectively; population. *rare.* L16–E19.

inhabitiveness /ɪnˈhabɪtɪvnɪs/ *noun.* E19.
[ORIGIN from INHABIT + -IVE + -NESS.]
PHRENOLOGY. The disposition always to live in the same place; attachment to country and home.

inhalant /ɪnˈheɪl(ə)nt/ *adjective & noun.* Also **-ent**. E19.
[ORIGIN from INHALE *verb* + -ANT[1].]
▸ **A** *adjective.* Of or pertaining to inhalation; serving for inhalation. E19.
▸ **B** *noun.* **1** An inhalant opening or pore. *rare.* E19.
2 A device for inhaling; a preparation for inhaling. L19.

inhalation /ɪnhəˈleɪʃ(ə)n/ *noun.* E17.
[ORIGIN medieval Latin *inhalatio(n-)*, from *inhalat-* pa. ppl stem of *inhalare*: see INHALE *verb*, -ATION.]
1 The action or an act of inhaling or breathing in; *spec.* the inhaling of medicines or anaesthetics in the form of a gas or vapour. E17.
2 *MEDICINE.* A preparation to be inhaled in the form of a vapour or spray. L19.
■ **inhalational** *adjective* M20.

inhalator /ˈɪnhəleɪtə/ *noun.* E20.
[ORIGIN from INHALE *verb* + -ATOR.]
A device for inhaling (esp. oxygen); a respirator.

inhalatorium /ɪnˌheɪləˈtɔːrɪəm/ *noun.* Pl. **-ria** /-rɪə/, **-riums**. E20.
[ORIGIN from INHALE *verb* after *sanatorium*.]
MEDICINE (now *hist.*). A building or room used for the treatment of respiratory complaints with vaporized medicaments.

inhale /ɪnˈheɪl/ *verb & noun.* E18.
[ORIGIN Latin *inhalare*, formed as IN-[2] + *halare* breathe.]
▸ **A** *verb trans. & intrans.* Breathe in; draw in by breathing; take (esp. tobacco smoke) into the lungs. E18.

> L. DURRELL I inhaled the warm summer perfume of her dress and skin. J. HELLER I do smoke . . . I even inhale. A. BRINK He inhaled the smoke, savouring it. B. T. BRADFORD She . . took several deep breaths, inhaling and exhaling for a few seconds.

▸ **B** *noun.* An act of inhaling, esp. of inhaling tobacco smoke. M20.

> *New Yorker* I had just finished my inhale and was about to blow out.

inhalent *adjective & noun* var. of INHALANT.

inhaler /ɪnˈheɪlə/ *noun.* L18.
[ORIGIN from INHALE *verb* + -ER[1].]
1 A device for administering a medicinal or anaesthetic gas or vapour, esp. to relieve nasal or bronchial congestion. Formerly also, a respirator. L18.
2 A person who inhales. M19.

†**inhance** *verb* var. of ENHANCE.

inharmonic /ɪnhɑːˈmɒnɪk/ *adjective.* L19.
[ORIGIN from IN-[3] + HARMONIC *adjective*.]
Chiefly *MUSIC.* Not harmonic; dissonant.
■ †**inharmonical** *adjective* L17–L19.

inharmonious /ɪnhɑːˈməʊnɪəs/ *adjective.* E18.
[ORIGIN from IN-[3] + HARMONIOUS.]
1 Of sound: not in harmony; sounding disagreeably; discordant. E18.
2 Not harmonious in relation, action, or sentiment; disagreeing; not in accordance. M18.
■ **inharmoniously** *adverb* E19. **inharmoniousness** *noun* M18.

inharmony /ɪnˈhɑːməni/ *noun. rare.* L18.
[ORIGIN from IN-[3] + HARMONY.]
Lack of harmony; discord.

inhaul /ˈɪnhɔːl/ *noun.* M19.
[ORIGIN from IN-[1] + HAUL *noun*.]
NAUTICAL. An appliance for hauling in; *spec.* a rope used to haul in the clew of a sail.
■ Also **inhauler** *noun* L18.

inhaust /ɪnˈhɔːst/ *verb trans. rare.* M16.
[ORIGIN from IN-[2] + Latin *haust-* pa. pple of *haurire* draw.]
Draw or suck in; inhale; imbibe.

inhearse /ɪnˈhəːs/ *verb trans.* Also **en-** /ɪn-, ɛn-/. L16.
[ORIGIN from IN-[1], EN-[1] + HEARSE *noun*[1].]
Put into a hearse.

inheaven /ɪnˈhɛv(ə)n/ *verb trans.* Also **en-** /ɪn-, ɛn-/. E17.
[ORIGIN from IN-[1], EN-[1] + HEAVEN *noun*.]
Place in or raise to heaven; delight.

†**inheld** *verb pa. t. & pple*: see INHOLD.

inhell /ɪnˈhɛl/ *verb trans. rare.* E17.
[ORIGIN from IN-[1] + HELL *noun*.]
Put or confine in hell.

inhere /ɪnˈhɪə/ *verb intrans.* M16.
[ORIGIN Latin *inhaerere*, formed as IN-[2] + *haerere* to stick.]
†**1** Adhere, cling *to*. *rare.* Only in M16.
2 Exist as an essential, permanent, or characteristic attribute, quality, etc., of a thing; form an element of something; belong to the intrinsic nature of something. Foll. by *in*. L16. ▸**b** Of a right, power, function, etc.: be vested *in*. M19.

> D. HUME The particular qualities, which form a substance, are commonly refer'd to an unknown something, in which they are supposed to inhere. H. READ From what has already been said of the nature of beauty, it will be evident that this quality inheres in any work of art. R. NIEBUHR The significant social power is the power which inheres in the ownership of the means of production.

†**3** Stick *in*, be or remain fixed or lodged *in*, (*lit. & fig.*). E17–M19.

inherence /ɪnˈhɪər(ə)ns, -ˈhɛr-/ *noun.* L16.
[ORIGIN medieval Latin *inherentia*, from *inherent-* var. of Latin *inhaerent-*: see INHERENT, -ENCE.]
The fact or condition of inhering; the state or quality of being inherent; permanent existence *in* something.
■ Also **inherency** *noun* E17.

inherent /ɪnˈhɪər(ə)nt, -ˈhɛr-/ *adjective.* L16.
[ORIGIN Latin *inhaerent-* pres. ppl stem of *inhaerere*: see INHERE, -ENT.]
†**1** Fixed, situated, or contained in or *in* something (*lit. & fig.*). L16–E19.
2 Existing in something as an essential, permanent, or characteristic attribute or quality; forming an element of something; intrinsic, essential. (Foll. by *in*.) L16. ▸**b** Of a right, power, or function: vested *in* or attached to a person, office, etc. E17.

> J. A. MICHENER The little building has an inherent poetry that could not have sprung entirely from the hands of an architect. A. TOFFLER There is nothing inherent in the evolutionary process to guarantee man's own survival. E. FROMM Change and growth are inherent qualities of the life process.

■ **inherently** *adverb* E17.

inherit /ɪnˈhɛrɪt/ *verb*. Orig. †**en-**. ME.
[ORIGIN Old French *enheriter* make heir from late Latin *inhereditare* appoint as heir, formed as IN-² + *hered-*, *heres* heir.]
1 *verb trans.* Come into possession of, as a right; receive or hold as one's portion. Chiefly in biblical translations and allusions. ME.

AV *Luke* 18:18 Good master, what shall I doe to inherit eternall life?

2 *verb trans.* Take or receive (property, a privilege, title, etc.) as an heir at the death of a former possessor; get or come into possession of by legal descent or succession. LME. ▸**b** Derive or possess (a quality or character, physical or mental) by transmission from a progenitor or progenitors. L16. ▸**c** Receive or have from a predecessor or predecessors in office etc. M19.

b JO GRIMOND His children . . inherited the exemplary character and looks of their parents. **c** G. K. CHESTERTON It is the rule, inherited from the old régime. *Southern Rag* The musical culture which we inherit in this country is frequently . . sexist.

†**3** *verb trans.* Make heir, put in possession. LME–L16.
4 *verb trans.* Be heir to (a person); succeed as heir. LME.
5 *verb intrans.* Come into or take possession of an inheritance. M16. ▸**b** Derive being or a quality *from*. L19.

E. H. JONES He has presumably inherited, his parents being dead.

inheritable /ɪnˈhɛrɪtəb(ə)l/ *adjective*. Also †**en-**. LME.
[ORIGIN Anglo-Norman *enheritable* able to be made heir, formed as INHERIT: see -ABLE.]
1 Capable of inheriting; entitled to succeed (to property etc.) by legal right. LME.
2 Able to be inherited; that may or can descend by law to an heir. L15.
■ **inheritaˈbility** *noun* L18. **inheritableness** *noun* L18. **inheritably** *adverb* M16.

I

inheritage /ɪnˈhɛrɪtɪdʒ/ *noun*. *rare*. M16.
[ORIGIN from INHERIT + -AGE.]
That which is inherited; an inheritance, a heritage.

inheritance /ɪnˈhɛrɪt(ə)ns/ *noun*. Also †**en-**. LME.
[ORIGIN Anglo-Norman *enheritaunce* being admitted as heir, formed as INHERIT: see -ANCE.]
▸**I 1** Hereditary succession to a property, title, office, etc.; a continual right to an estate invested in a person and his or her heirs. LME.

C. G. SELIGMAN The eldest son is the chief heir; women have no right of inheritance.

2 The fact or property of inheriting or having inherited something. LME.

H. CARE English Liberties, or the free-born Subject's Inheritance. R. DAWKINS Inheritance of many genetic characters such as human height.

▸**II 3** Property, or an estate, which passes by law to an heir or heirs on the death of the possessor. LME. ▸**b** A property, quality, characteristic, etc., inherited from a progenitor or progenitors. E17.

R. HOLMES His maternal grandmother died, leaving him a considerable inheritance of . . thirty thousand francs. **b** L. M. MONTGOMERY The merry expression which was her inheritance from her father.

4 A thing that one obtains or comes into possession of by right or divine grant; *esp.* (in biblical use) the blessings received by God's chosen people. M16.
– COMB.: **inheritance tax** a tax on inherited property levied on individual beneficiaries, *spec.* one varying according to their degrees of relationship to the testator.

inheritor /ɪnˈhɛrɪtə/ *noun*. LME.
[ORIGIN from INHERIT + -OR.]
A person who inherits something; an heir. (Foll. by *of*.)

inheritress /ɪnˈhɛrɪtrɪs/ *noun*. E16.
[ORIGIN from INHERITOR: see -ESS¹.]
= INHERITRIX.

inheritrix /ɪnˈhɛrɪtrɪks/ *noun*. Pl. **-trices** /-trɪsiːz/, **-trixes**. M16.
[ORIGIN formed as INHERITRESS: see -TRIX.]
A female inheritor, an heiress.
■ Also †**inheritrice** *noun* E16–L17.

inhesion /ɪnˈhiːʒ(ə)n/ *noun*. M17.
[ORIGIN Late Latin *inhaesio(n-)*, from Latin *inhaes-* pa. ppl stem of *inhaerere*: see INHERE, -ION.]
The action or fact of inhering, esp. as a quality or attribute; inherence.

inhiate /ˈɪnhʌɪeɪt/ *verb intrans*. Now *rare*. M16.
[ORIGIN Latin *inhiat-* pa. ppl stem of *inhiare* gape at, formed as IN-² + *hiare* gape: see -ATE³.]
Open the mouth wide, gape.

inhibin /ɪnˈhɪbɪn/ *noun*¹. M20.
[ORIGIN from Latin *inhibere* INHIBIT: see -IN¹.]
PHYSIOLOGY. A gonadal hormone which inhibits the secretion of follicle-stimulating hormone.

inhibin *noun*² var. of next.

inhibine /ˈɪnhɪbiːn/ *noun*. Also **-in** /-ɪn/. M20.
[ORIGIN from INHIBIT + -INE⁵.]
Any of a group of natural antibacterial substances found mainly in honey and saliva.

inhibit /ɪnˈhɪbɪt/ *verb trans.* LME.
[ORIGIN Latin *inhibit-* pa. ppl stem of *inhibere* hold in, hinder, formed as IN-² + *habere* hold.]
1 Forbid (a person) to do something, prohibit from doing something; *spec.* forbid (an ecclesiastic) to exercise clerical functions. (Foll. by *from doing*, †*from* a thing, †*to do*.) LME.

LD MACAULAY A clause was . . inserted which inhibited the Bank from advancing money.

†**2** Forbid or prohibit the doing of or engaging in (a thing, action, or practice). L15–E19.

C. LAMB At school all play-going was inhibited.

3 Restrain, prevent. M16.

DAY LEWIS A kind of near-neurotic inertia or negativism which inhibited me from pressing my love upon her. P. GOODMAN Certain aims are forbidden and punishable . . ; so we inhibit them and put them out of our mind. B. PYM Her presence inhibited any attempt at that kind of conversation. I. MURDOCH I had the satisfaction of seeing her inhibit her impulse to ask me where I was going. *Flex* The zinc ion has been shown to inhibit viral duplication.

■ **inhibited** *adjective* (**a**) that has been inhibited; forbidden, restrained; (**b**) subject to inhibition, unable to express feelings or impulses: E17. **inhibitedness** *noun* M20. **inhibiter** *noun* = INHIBITOR 1 E17. **inhibiting** *adjective* (**a**) forbidding, prohibitive; (**b**) causing restraint or inhibition: E17. **inhibitingly** *adverb* M20. **inhibitive** *adjective* serving or tending to inhibit someone or something M19.

inhibition /ɪn(h)ɪˈbɪʃ(ə)n/ *noun*. LME.
[ORIGIN Old French & mod. French, or Latin *inhibitio(n-)*, formed as INHIBIT: see -ION.]
1 Chiefly ECCLESIASTICAL & LAW. The action or an act of forbidding; a (formal) prohibition. LME. ▸**b** *spec.* Formerly in ENGLISH LAW, an order prohibiting dealing with a specified piece of land for a given period or until further notice; also, a writ forbidding a court to proceed in a suit on the grounds that it is beyond the cognizance of that court, a prohibition. In ECCLESIASTICAL LAW, an order suspending the jurisdiction of an inferior court during an episcopal visitation; an order suspending a member of the clergy from ministerial duty. In SCOTS LAW, a writ prohibiting a person from contracting a possible charge on or selling heritable property; formerly also, a writ obtained by a husband to prevent his wife from obtaining credit. M16.
2 The action or an act of preventing, hindering, or checking. E17. ▸**b** PHYSIOLOGY. The checking or repression of an organ or function, esp. in the nervous system, by the action of another or of a drug. L19. ▸**c** CHEMISTRY & BIOCHEMISTRY. The slowing or prevention of a reaction or process by a specific substance. E20.

S. JOHNSON It is said that no torture is equal to the inhibition of sleep, long continued. E. P. THOMPSON A 'religion of the heart' . . notorious for the inhibition of all spontaneity.

3 (A) scrupulous or emotional resistance to thought, action, etc. In PSYCHOLOGY, (a) voluntary or involuntary restraint on the direct expression of a natural impulse; the process whereby a learned response is weakened in the absence of reinforcement. L19.

C. HILL Cromwell . . had no inhibitions about using the loyalty and enthusiasm of the lower-class radicals. E. H. JONES She tried out her half-formed ideas in her circle without inhibition. *Hairdo Ideas* Answers all your questions and helps free you of inhibitions.

reactive inhibition: see REACTIVE *adjective* 3. ***retroactive inhibition***: see RETROACTIVE 3.

inhibitor /ɪnˈhɪbɪtə/ *noun*. M19.
[ORIGIN from INHIBIT + -OR. Cf. earlier INHIBITER.]
1 A person who inhibits something; *spec.* in SCOTS LAW, a person who takes out an inhibition. M19.
2 A thing which inhibits someone or something. E20. ▸**b** GENETICS. A gene whose presence prevents the expression of some other gene at a different locus. E20. ▸**c** CHEMISTRY & BIOCHEMISTRY. A substance which slows down or prevents a particular reaction or process, or diminishes the activity of some reactant or catalyst. E20.

W. JAMES Danger is for most men the great inhibitor of action.

inhibitory /ɪnˈhɪbɪt(ə)ri/ *adjective*. L15.
[ORIGIN medieval Latin *inhibitorius*, formed as INHIBIT + -ORY².]
1 Prohibitory. L15.

J. LINGARD An inhibitory breve, forbidding all archbishops . . to give judgment in the . . cause of Henry against Catharine.

2 That restrains or prevents something; causing inhibition. M19.

P. GROSSKURTH Anxiety, if excessive, can be inhibitory to development.

†**inhold** *verb trans.* Infl. as HOLD *verb*; pa. t. & pple usu. **inheld**. L15.
[ORIGIN from IN-¹ + HOLD *verb*.]
1 Keep in, retain, withhold. L15–E18.
2 Contain, enclose. Only in E17.

■ †**inholder** *noun* (**a**) a tenant; (**b**) a thing which holds or contains something: L16–L17.

inhomogeneity /ɪnˌhɒmə(ʊ)dʒɪˈniːɪti, -ˈneɪɪti; ɪnˌhəʊm-/ *noun*. L19.
[ORIGIN from IN-³ + HOMOGENEITY.]
1 A thing which is not homogeneous with its surroundings; a local irregularity. L19.
2 The property of being inhomogeneous; lack of homogeneity. E20.

inhomogeneous /ˌɪnhɒmə(ʊ)ˈdʒiːnɪəs, -ˈdʒɛn-; ˌɪnhəʊm-/ *adjective*. E20.
[ORIGIN from IN-³ + HOMOGENEOUS.]
1 Not uniform throughout; composed of diverse constituents; heterogeneous. E20.
2 MATH. Consisting of terms that are not all of the same degree or dimensions. M20.
■ **inhomogeneously** *adverb* E20.

†**inhoop** *verb trans.* *rare* (Shakes.). Only in E17.
[ORIGIN from IN-¹ + HOOP *noun*¹ or *verb*¹.]
Place in a hoop; surround by a hoop.

inhospitable /ɪnhɒˈspɪtəb(ə)l, ɪnˈhɒspɪt-/ *adjective*. L16.
[ORIGIN French, formed as IN-³ + HOSPITABLE.]
1 Not welcoming to strangers; not showing hospitality to guests. L16.

G. B. SHAW Hector: I'm sorry to be inhospitable; but will you kindly leave the house?

2 Of a region: not offering shelter or sustenance; bleak, hostile. E17.

B. LOPEZ The tree line, where one first encounters the inhospitable soils of the tundra.

■ **inˌhospitaˈbility**, **inhospitableness** *nouns* M17. **inhospitably** *adverb* M17.

†**inhospital** *adjective*. L16–E18.
[ORIGIN Latin *inhospitalis*, formed as IN-³ + *hospitalis* hospitable: see HOSPITAL *adjective*.]
= INHOSPITABLE.

inhospitality /ˌɪnhɒspɪˈtalɪti/ *noun*. L16.
[ORIGIN Latin *inhospitalitas*, formed as INHOSPITAL: see -ITY.]
The quality or practice of being inhospitable; lack of hospitality.

in-house /*as adjective* ˈɪnhaʊs, *as adverb* ɪnˈhaʊs/ *adjective & adverb*. M20.
[ORIGIN from IN-¹ + HOUSE *noun*¹.]
▸**A** *adjective*. Of or pertaining to the internal affairs of an institution or organization; existing within an institution or organization. M20.

Lebende Sprachen Microcircuits . . made by outside suppliers or by . . in-house facilities. S. I. LANDAU Will it be written entirely by an in-house staff of dictionary editors?

▸**B** *adverb*. Internally; without outside assistance. M20.

Flight International Avoid carrying out tasks in-house which can be executed by subcontractors. *Bookcase* Gary felt it was time to keep a good idea and develop it in-house.

inhuman /ɪnˈhjuːmən/ *adjective & noun*. Also (earlier) †**-ane**. LME.
[ORIGIN Latin *inhumanus*, formed as IN-³ + *humanus* HUMAN *adjective*.]
▸**A** *adjective*. **1** Of a person: callous, unfeeling, merciless. Of conduct, an action, etc.: brutal, barbarous, cruel. Cf. INHUMANE 2. LME.

SHAKES. *Tit. A.* Her spotless chastity, Inhuman traitors, you constrain'd and forc'd. C. G. WOLFF Having been dehumanized, they act with inhuman indifference to the feelings of others.

2 Not human; not of the normal human type. M16.

J. B. CABELL Planet-stricken folk, who had spied . . upon an inhuman loveliness, and so, must pine away.

▸†**B** *noun*. A brutal or subhuman person. M17–M18.
■ **inhumanly** *adverb* L15. **inhumanness** /-n-n-/ *noun* (*rare*) M17.

inhumane /ɪnhjʊˈmeɪn/ *adjective*. LME.
[ORIGIN Orig. var. of INHUMAN *adjective*; later from IN-³ + HUMANE.]
†**1** See INHUMAN *adjective*. LME.
2 Not humane; without compassion for misery or suffering. Cf. INHUMAN *adjective* 1. E19.

inhumanely /ɪnhjʊˈmeɪnli/ *adverb*. L16.
[ORIGIN from INHUMANE + -LY².]
Orig., inhumanly, cruelly. Now, not humanely; without compassion (though not with intentional cruelty).

D. ROWE The 'mentally ill' . . are often treated inhumanely and sometimes very cruelly.

inhumanism /ɪnˈhjuːmənɪz(ə)m/ *noun*. E20.
[ORIGIN from IN-³ + HUMANISM.]
Lack of humanism; inhumanity.

inhumanitarian /ˌɪnhjʊmanɪˈtɛːrɪən/ *noun & adjective*. M20.
[ORIGIN from IN-³ + HUMANITARIAN.]
▸ **A** *noun*. A person who does not accept the views and practices of humanitarianism. M20.
▸ **B** *adjective*. Rejecting or disregarding humanitarian views or practices. M20.

inhumanity /ɪnhjʊˈmanɪti/ *noun*. L15.
[ORIGIN Old French & mod. French *inhumanité*, or Latin *inhumanitas*, from *inhumanus* INHUMAN *adjective*: see -ITY.]
1 The quality of being inhuman or inhumane; lack of compassion, cruelty. L15. ▸**b** An instance of this; a cruel act. M17.
†**2** Lack of politeness; incivility. M16–M17.

inhumate /ɪnˈhjuːmeɪt, ˈɪnhjʊmeɪt/ *verb trans. rare*. E17.
[ORIGIN Latin *inhumat-* pa. ppl stem of *inhumare* INHUME: see -ATE³.]
Bury, inter; = INHUME 1.

inhumation /ɪnhjʊˈmeɪʃ(ə)n/ *noun*. L16.
[ORIGIN from INHUMATE or INHUME: see -ATION.]
†**1** A method of distillation in which vessels were buried in earth within a circular fire. L16–M17.
2 The action or practice of burying the dead; the fact of being buried; interment. M17.

> F. SMYTH Any corpse dug up after a period of inhumation in the area.. would contain.. arsenic. *Scientific American* Inhumation of the bones.. was the last stage in the treatment of the deceased.

3 The burying of something in or under the ground. M17.

inhume /ɪnˈhjuːm/ *verb trans*. E17.
[ORIGIN Latin *inhumare*, formed as IN-² + *humus* ground.]
1 Bury (a corpse); place in the grave, inter. E17. ▸†**b** Of the earth or a tomb: cover (the dead). E17–L18.
2 *gen*. Bury in the ground; cover with soil. Now *rare* or *obsolete*. E17.

inhumorous /ɪnˈhjuːm(ə)rəs/ *adjective*. E20.
[ORIGIN from IN-³ + HUMOROUS.]
Not humorous; without humour.
■ **inhumorously** *adverb* L19.

iniencephalus /ˌɪnɪɛnˈkɛf(ə)ləs, -ˈsɛf-/ *noun*. M19.
[ORIGIN from INION + Greek *egkephalos* brain.]
MEDICINE. (A deformed fetus exhibiting) iniencephaly.
■ **iniencephalic** *adjective* L19. **iniencephaly** *noun* a developmental abnormality of the skull and upper spine, in which the brain and spinal cord protrude through an opening in the occiput and upper spinal canal E20.

inimic /ɪˈnɪmɪk/ *adjective. arch. rare*. L17.
[ORIGIN Latin *inimicus*: see ENEMY.]
Adverse, hostile.

inimicable /ɪˈnɪmɪkəb(ə)l/ *adjective. rare*. E19.
[ORIGIN from IN-³ + AMICABLE, after *inimical*.]
= INIMICAL.

inimical /ɪˈnɪmɪk(ə)l/ *adjective*. E16.
[ORIGIN Late Latin *inimicalis*, from *inimicus*: see ENEMY, -AL¹.]
1 Unfriendly, hostile, (*to*). E16.

> H. A. L. FISHER The only organized and educated body of men, .. instead of being inimical, was an ally. H. CARPENTER He was firmly convinced.. that the female psychology was.. different from—and largely inimical to—that of the male.

2 Adverse, detrimental, harmful, (*to*). M17.

> P. F. BOLLER A dangerous monopoly inimical to the interests of the majority.

■ **inimiˈcality** *noun* L18. **inimically** *adverb* M19. **inimicalness** *noun* M17.

†**inimicitious** *adjective*. M17–M18.
[ORIGIN from Latin *inimicitia* enmity, from *inimicus* ENEMY, + -OUS.]
= INIMICAL.

†**inimicous** *adjective*. L16–E18.
[ORIGIN from Latin *inimicus* ENEMY + -OUS.]
= INIMICAL.

inimitable /ɪˈnɪmɪtəb(ə)l/ *adjective & noun*. L15.
[ORIGIN French, or Latin *inimitabilis*, formed as IN-³ + *imitabilis* IMITABLE.]
▸ **A** *adjective*. Surpassing or defying imitation; without compare, peerless. L15.

> *Sunday Express* In his own inimitable way he tells us what to drink.

▸ **B** *noun*. An inimitable person or thing. M18.

> *Times* A creditable and exuberant expression of one of the great inimitables of jazz.

■ **inimitaˈbility** *noun* E18. **inimitableness** *noun* M17. **inimitably** *adverb* M17.

in infinitum /ɪn ɪnfɪˈnʌɪtəm/ *adverbial phr*. M16.
[ORIGIN Latin.]
To infinity, without end. Cf. AD INFINITUM.

inion /ˈɪnɪɒn/ *noun*. E19.
[ORIGIN Greek = nape of the neck.]
ANATOMY. The projecting part of the occipital bone at the base of the skull.

†**inique** *adjective*. E16–M18.
[ORIGIN Latin *iniquus*, formed as IN-³ + *aequus* equal, just.]
Unjust, iniquitous.

iniquitous /ɪˈnɪkwɪtəs/ *adjective*. E18.
[ORIGIN from INIQUITY + -OUS.]
Characterized by or full of iniquity; grossly unjust, wicked.
■ **iniquitously** *adverb* L18. **iniquitousness** *noun* L19.

iniquity /ɪˈnɪkwɪti/ *noun*. ME.
[ORIGIN Old French *iniquité* from Latin *iniquitas*, from *iniquus*: see INIQUE, -ITY.]
▸ **I 1** Immoral, unrighteous, or harmful action or conduct; gross injustice, wickedness, sin. Also, the quality of being wicked or sinful. ME. ▸**b** In *pl*. Wrongful acts; sins, injuries, injustices. L15.

> ROBERT WATSON The iniquity and unrelenting cruelty exercised. A. J. P. TAYLOR My father regarded Oxford as a sink of iniquity. **b** A. BRINK To.. expose the iniquities of the Security Police. M. SCAMMELL A feudal system whose iniquities were to provide much of the fuel for the Revolution.

2 (**I-**.) A (comic) character in morality plays, representing a particular vice or vice in general. L16.
3 Inequality, inequity, unfairness. *obsolete* exc. as passing into sense 1. L16.
▸ †**II 4** Unfavourable or adverse influence or operation. M16–E17.

†**iniquous** *adjective*. M17–L18.
[ORIGIN from Latin *iniquus* (see INIQUE) + -OUS.]
Unjust, wicked, iniquitous.

inirritable /ɪnˈɪrɪtəb(ə)l/ *adjective*. Now *rare* or *obsolete*. L18.
[ORIGIN from IN-³ + IRRITABLE.]
Chiefly PHYSIOLOGY. Not irritable, unresponsive to stimulus.
■ **inirritaˈbility** *noun* L18.

inisle *verb* var. of ENISLE.

initial /ɪˈnɪʃ(ə)l/ *noun*. E17.
[ORIGIN from the adjective.]
1 An initial letter; *esp*. (in *pl*.) the initial letters of two or more names of a person, or of words forming any name or phrase. E17.

> A. UTTLEY A big blue handkerchief with his initials embroidered in the corner. J. HUTCHINSON The earliest books left spaces for initials.. which were completed by illuminators. *New Scientist* The commands are based on initials such as CV for 'centre vertically'.

2 An initial stage or element *of* something; a beginning. Now *rare*. M17.
3 MUSIC. More fully ***absolute initial***. Each of the prescribed notes on which a plainsong melody may begin in any given mode. L19.
4 BOTANY. An initial cell. E20.

initial /ɪˈnɪʃ(ə)l/ *adjective*. E16.
[ORIGIN Latin *initialis*, from *initium* beginning: see -AL¹.]
1 Of or pertaining to the beginning; existing at, constituting, or occurring at the beginning; first, primary. E16. ▸**b** BOTANY. Of a plant cell: dividing into two daughter cells, one of which develops into the tissues and organs of the plant while the other remains within the meristem. L19.

> J. GALSWORTHY From this initial mistake of hers all the subsequent trouble, sorrow and tragedy have come. *Gentleman (Mumbai)* The trade protocol.. was valid for an initial period of five years. C. PETERS After a while the initial euphoria of having a place of his own wore off.

initial line MATH. (in a system of polar coordinates) the line from which an angle is measured. **initial public offering** (chiefly *US*) a company's flotation on the stock exchange (abbreviation *IPO*). **initial teaching alphabet** a 44-letter phonetic alphabet used to help those beginning to read and write English, esp. in British primary schools in the 1960s.
2 Standing at the beginning of a word, of a division in a book or piece of writing, or of the alphabet. E17.

> G. BURNET The initial letters of his name.., as W. E... for Will. Exon.

■ **initially** *adverb* E17.

initial /ɪˈnɪʃ(ə)l/ *verb trans*. Infl. **-ll-**, ***-l-**. M19.
[ORIGIN from the noun.]
Mark or sign with initials; put one's initials to or on; *spec*. signify thus the intention of later formal ratification.

> *Time* The signing of a Panama Canal treaty that was initialed last month.

initialese /ɪˌnɪʃəˈliːz/ *noun*. M20.
[ORIGIN from INITIAL *noun* + -ESE.]
The use of abbreviations formed by using the initial letters of the words to be shortened.

initialise *verb* var. of INITIALIZE.

initialism /ɪˈnɪʃ(ə)lɪz(ə)m/ *noun*. L19.
[ORIGIN from INITIAL *noun* + -ISM.]
A group of initial letters used as an abbreviation, *esp*. one in which each letter is pronounced separately (cf. ACRONYM); the use of such initials.

initialize /ɪˈnɪʃ(ə)lʌɪz/ *verb trans. & intrans*. Also **-ise**. M19.
[ORIGIN from INITIAL *noun* + -IZE.]
1 Designate by or use an initial or initials instead of the full name. *rare*. M19.
2 COMPUTING. Set or become set to a value or in a state suitable for the start of an operation. M20.

> *Personal Software* There is a substantial amount of code to be entered to initialise the program. *Television* The ROM and the CPU were.. faulty, but the machine still wouldn't initialise when these had been replaced.

■ **initialiˈzation** *noun* (COMPUTING) the action or process of initializing; the computer operations involved in this: M20.

initiand /ɪˈnɪʃɪand/ *noun*. M20.
[ORIGIN Latin *initiandus* gerundive of *initiare* INITIATE *verb*: see -AND.]
A person about to be initiated.

initiate /ɪˈnɪʃɪət/ *adjective & noun*. E17.
[ORIGIN Latin *initiatus* pa. pple, formed as INITIATE *verb*: see -ATE².]
▸ **A** *adjective*. **1** Admitted into some society or position; instructed in some (secret) knowledge. E17. ▸†**b** Of or belonging to a newly initiated person. *rare* (Shakes.). Only in E17.

> M. AYRTON Lycus was deeply religious and initiate in the mysteries of the Mother.. Demeter.

2 Begun, commenced, introduced. M18.
▸ **B** *noun*. †**1** Something initiated or newly introduced. *rare*. Only in E17.
2 A person who has been initiated; a beginner, a novice. E19.

> J. BAYLEY It is hinted that only initiates, those really in the know, can understand. W. STYRON For the initiate ours is a cruel language.

initiate /ɪˈnɪʃɪeɪt/ *verb*. M16.
[ORIGIN Latin *initiat-* pa. ppl stem of *initiare* begin, from *initium* beginning: see -ATE³.]
1 *verb trans*. Introduce (a person) with due ceremonies or rites into a society or position, or into the knowledge of some (esp. secret or occult) principle or practice; *gen*. acquaint with or instruct in the elements of anything. (Foll. by *in*, *into*.) M16. ▸**b** *verb intrans*. Perform or undergo an initiation. E18.

> I. MCEWAN It was Raymond who initiated me into the secrets of adult life.

2 *verb trans*. Begin, introduce, set going, originate. E17. ▸**b** *verb intrans*. Have its beginning; commence. E17.

> E. F. BENSON Whether it was customary for unmarried ladies to initiate a call on an unmarried man. J. K. TOOLE I have succeeded in initiating several work-saving methods. **b** S. TOLANSKY If pure deuterium gas can be raised to a temperature.. of 500 million degrees C., then a thermo-nuclear reaction should initiate.

initiated /ɪˈnɪʃɪeɪtɪd/ *ppl adjective & noun*. L16.
[ORIGIN from INITIATE *verb* + -ED¹.]
▸ **A** *ppl adjective*. That has been initiated. L16.
▸ **B** *noun*. **1** An initiate. M18.
2 *collect. pl*. *The* people who have been initiated. M19.

> A. EDEN A catch was concealed which the initiated could press to open a door.

initiation /ɪˌnɪʃɪˈeɪʃ(ə)n/ *noun*. L16.
[ORIGIN Latin *initiatio(n-)* (in sense 2 in medieval Latin), formed as INITIATE *verb*: see -ATION.]
1 Formal introduction with due ceremonies or rites into a society, position, or (secret) knowledge; instruction in the elements of a subject or practice; an instance of this. L16.

> L. VAN DER POST The long night of the initiation of the Esquire into Knighthood. J. VIORST The recognition that others have .. claims upon her love is our initiation into jealousy.

initiation ceremony, ***initiation rite***, etc.
2 The action or an act of beginning or originating something; the fact of being begun; commencement, origination. M17.

initiative /ɪˈnɪʃətɪv, -ʃə-/ *noun*. L18.
[ORIGIN French, formed as INITIATE *verb* + -IVE.]
1 The action of initiating something or of taking the first step or the lead; an act setting a process or chain of events in motion; an independent or enterprising act. L18. ▸**b** *spec*. A proposal made by one nation or group of nations to another, with a view to improving relations between them. M20.

> W. SOYINKA Did he contact you or did the initiative come from you? H. KISSINGER The most important diplomatic initiative .. was toward Hanoi. *Dance Theatre Journal* These companies were set up as purely regional initiatives.

2 The power or right to begin something. L18. ▸**b** *spec*. The right of (a specified number of) citizens outside the legislature to propose legislation (as in Switzerland and parts of the US). L19.

> C. G. WOLFF The outside world and all that went with it: autonomy and initiative.

3 Mental power to initiate things; enterprise, self-motivation to action. E20.

> S. LEACOCK The peculiar quality that is called initiative—the ability to act promptly on one's own judgment.

– PHRASES: **have the initiative** have the first choice of action; *esp*. (MILITARY) be able to influence or control the enemy's movements. **on one's own initiative** without being prompted by others. ***Strategic Defense Initiative***: see STRATEGIC *adjective*. **take the initiative** be the first to take action.

I

initiative /ɪˈnɪʃɪətɪv, -ʃə-/ *adjective*. M17.
[ORIGIN from INITIATE *verb* + -IVE.]
Characterized by initiating something; of or pertaining to initiation.

> *Times* Bowater . . will take the first initiative step . . next week.

■ **initiatively** *adverb* M17.

initiator /ɪˈnɪʃɪeɪtə/ *noun*. L17.
[ORIGIN from INITIATE *verb* + -OR.]
1 A person who or thing which initiates someone or something. L17.
2 An explosive or device used to detonate the main charge. E20.
3 *CHEMISTRY*. Any substance which starts a chain reaction. M20.
■ **initiatress** *noun* (*rare*) a female initiator M19. **initiˈatrix** *noun*, pl. **-trices** /-trɪsiːz/, **-trixes**, a female initiator M19.

initiatory /ɪˈnɪʃɪət(ə)ri, ˌɪnɪʃɪˈeɪt(ə)ri/ *adjective*. E17.
[ORIGIN from INITIATE *verb* + -ORY[2].]
1 Pertaining to or constituting a beginning; initial, introductory, preliminary. E17.

> T. HARDY Those automatic initiatory acts and touches which represent among housewives the installation of another day.

2 Pertaining to initiation; serving to initiate into some society, position, or special knowledge. M17.

> W. WARBURTON Which he did by the initiatory Rite of water-baptism.

inition /ɪˈnɪʃ(ə)n/ *noun*. *rare*. LME.
[ORIGIN Old French & mod. French from medieval Latin *initio(n-)*, from Latin *init-* pa. ppl stem of *inire* go into, enter: see -ION.]
Entrance, beginning, initiation.

injail *verb* var. of ENJAIL.

†**injealous** *verb* see ENJEALOUS.

inject /ɪnˈdʒɛkt/ *verb trans*. L16.
[ORIGIN Latin *inject-* pa. ppl stem of *inicere* throw in, formed as IN-[2] + *jacere* throw.]
†**1** Throw or cast *on* a thing. L16–E18.
2 Drive or force (esp. a fluid, medicine, etc.) into a passage, cavity, or solid material under pressure; introduce by injection. E17. ▸**b** Introduce or feed (a current, beam of particles, charge carriers, etc.) into a substance or device. M20. ▸**c** *ASTRONAUTICS*. Put *into* (*an*) *orbit*. M20.

> A. DAVIS They had begun to inject the drug into the veins in their necks. J. S. FOSTER Cavity fills may be blown or injected into the cavity wall after construction.

3 *fig.* Introduce suddenly or with force or by way of interruption; insert; suggest, interject. M17.

> J. BARZUN A delivers an opinion while B thinks of the one he will inject as soon as he decently can. M. RULE Full of new ideas and injecting new enthusiasm into the project.

4 Fill or charge (a cavity etc.) by injection; administer a medicine etc. to (a person or animal) by injection. (Foll. by *with*.) M18.

> C. LYELL Such rents must be injected with melted matter. R. INGALLS They injected me a lot . . so I fell asleep.

■ **injected** *adjective* that has been injected; *spec.* (**a**) *MEDICINE* bloodshot, congested; (**b**) (more fully ***fuel-injected***) having fuel injection: M18.

injectable /ɪnˈdʒɛktəb(ə)l/ *adjective & noun*. M19.
[ORIGIN from INJECT + -ABLE.]
▸ **A** *adjective*. Able to be injected, esp. into the body; suitable for injection. M19.
▸ **B** *noun*. A substance suitable for injection; *esp.* a drug or medicine suitable for injection directly into the bloodstream. M20.

injection /ɪnˈdʒɛkʃ(ə)n/ *noun*. LME.
[ORIGIN French, or Latin *injectio(n-)*, formed as INJECT: see -ION.]
1 The action of or an act of driving or forcing (a fluid) into a passage, cavity, or solid material under pressure; *esp.* in *MEDICINE*, introduction of a medicine, preservative, etc., by means of a (hypodermic) syringe. LME. ▸**b** In full ***fuel injection***. The direct introduction of fuel under pressure into the combustion unit of an internal-combustion engine. E20. ▸**c** The act of introducing a current, beam of particles, etc., into a substance or device. M20. ▸**d** *ASTRONAUTICS*. The (time of) entry or placing (of a spacecraft, satellite, etc.) into an orbit or trajectory. M20.

> A. BROOKNER I . . summoned the doctor, demanded vitamin injections.

b ***solid injection***: see SOLID *adjective & adverb*.
2 A substance which is injected. LME.
3 *fig.* The sudden or forceful introduction of a thing from outside; the suggestion of an idea into the mind; the interjection of a statement into an argument etc.; a suggestion, a hint. E17.

> A. BEVAN The injection of several million pounds here would refresh the Service.

4 *MEDICINE*. Congestion with blood; bloodshot condition. E19.
5 *MATH*. A one-to-one mapping. M20.
– COMB.: **injection moulding** the making of moulded articles from rubber or plastic by injecting heat-softened material into a mould; **injection well**: into which gas, air, or water is forced so as to increase the yield from interconnected wells.

injective /ɪnˈdʒɛktɪv/ *adjective*. M20.
[ORIGIN from INJECT + -IVE.]
MATH. Of the nature of or pertaining to an injection or one-to-one mapping.

injector /ɪnˈdʒɛktə/ *noun*. M18.
[ORIGIN from INJECT + -OR.]
A thing which or (occas.) person who injects something; *esp.* (**a**) a device for injecting water into a steam engine; (**b**) (more fully ***fuel injector***) the nozzle and valve through which fuel is sprayed into a combustion chamber.

injera /ˈɪndʒərə/ *noun*. M20.
[ORIGIN Amharic.]
A white leavened Ethiopian bread made from teff flour, similar to a crêpe.

†**injewel** *verb* var. of ENJEWEL.

†**injoin** *verb* var. of ENJOIN.

†**injoint** *verb intrans*. *rare* (Shakes.). Only in E17.
[ORIGIN from IN-[1] + JOINT *verb*.]
Unite, join.

injucundity /ɪndʒʊˈkʌndɪti/ *noun*. *rare*. E17.
[ORIGIN Latin *injucunditas*, from *injucundus* unpleasant, formed as IN-[3] + *jucundus* JOCUND + -ITY. Partly from IN-[3] + JUCUNDITY.]
Unpleasantness, disagreeableness.

injudicial /ɪndʒʊˈdɪʃ(ə)l/ *adjective*. *rare*. E17.
[ORIGIN from IN-[3] + JUDICIAL *adjective*.]
Not judicial. Formerly also, injudicious.
■ **injudicially** *adverb* M17.

injudicious /ɪndʒʊˈdɪʃəs/ *adjective*. E17.
[ORIGIN from IN-[3] + JUDICIOUS.]
1 Not displaying judgement or discretion; showing lack of judgement; unwise, ill-judged. E17.
†**2** Of a person: lacking sound judgement. M17–M18.
■ **injudiciously** *adverb* E17. **injudiciousness** *noun* M17.

Injun /ˈɪndʒ(ə)n/ *noun & adjective*. *colloq.*, *offensive* (chiefly *N. Amer.*). Also (earlier, now *rare*) **Ingin**. L17.
[ORIGIN Repr. colloq. & dial. pronunc. of INDIAN.]
▸ **A** *noun*. A N. American Indian. L17.
honest Injun honestly, really, genuinely.
▸ **B** *adjective*. Of or pertaining to N. American Indians. M19.

injunct /ɪnˈdʒʌŋ(k)t/ *verb trans*. L19.
[ORIGIN Latin *injunct-* pa. ppl stem of *injungere* ENJOIN, after INJUNCTION.]
Prohibit or restrain by injunction.

injunction /ɪnˈdʒʌŋ(k)ʃ(ə)n/ *noun*. LME.
[ORIGIN Late Latin *injunctio(n-)*, formed as INJUNCT: see -ION.]
▸ **I 1** The action of enjoining or authoritatively directing someone; an authoritative or emphatic admonition or order. LME.

> E. JONES He sent her a sum of money with strict injunctions that she was to spend it . . on a holiday.

2 *LAW*. A judicial process whereby a person is restrained from beginning or continuing an action threatening or invading the legal right of another, or is compelled to carry out a certain act, e.g. to make restitution to an injured party. M16.

> H. EVANS I had taken the decision to publish in great secrecy, fearing an injunction to stop us.

▸ †**II 3** Conjunction; union. L15–M17.

injunctive /ɪnˈdʒʌŋ(k)tɪv/ *adjective & noun*. E17.
[ORIGIN formed as INJUNCT + -IVE.]
▸ **A** *adjective*. **1** Having the character or quality of directing or ordering. E17.
2 *GRAMMAR*. Designating or pertaining to a form of a verb in some Indo-European languages that has secondary personal endings and expresses injunction. E20.
▸ **B** *noun*. *GRAMMAR*. An injunctive verb. E20.
■ **injunctively** *adverb* E17.

injure /ˈɪndʒə/ *verb*. LME.
[ORIGIN Back-form. from INJURY *noun*.]
1 *verb trans*. Do injustice or wrong to (a person); wrong. LME.
2 *verb trans*. Do harm to; inflict damage on, esp. on the body of; hurt, harm, impair. LME. ▸**b** *verb intrans*. Become injured, receive injury. M19.

> W. S. CHURCHILL Peel fell from his horse . . and was fatally injured. R. MACAULAY Anything was right that might injure the authorities. M. SCAMMELL Kopelev . . . was aware of the colonel's ire when his pride was injured.

†**3** *verb trans*. Insult, abuse, slander. M16–M17.
■ **injurer** *noun* L16.

injured /ˈɪndʒəd/ *adjective*. M17.
[ORIGIN from INJURE + -ED[1].]
That has been injured; wronged; offended; hurt. Also, expressing a feeling of offendedness.

> J. K. TOOLE 'Where do you think up excuses like that?' 'Well, it's true,' Darlene answered in an injured voice. R. INGALLS His parents . . were in the hospital, were badly injured. *absol.*: A. TREW 'How are the injured?' . . 'There are seven receiving treatment. Three for burns.'

injured innocence (freq. *iron.*) the offended attitude of a person who is undeservedly accused of something.

injuria /ɪnˈdʒʊərɪə/ *noun*. Pl. **-iae** /-ɪiː/. L19.
[ORIGIN Latin: see INJURY.]
LAW. An invasion of another's rights; an actionable wrong.

injurious /ɪnˈdʒʊərɪəs/ *adjective*. LME.
[ORIGIN from French *injurieux* or Latin *injuriosus*, from *injuria* INJURY: see -OUS.]
Hurtful, harmful, wrongful; (of language or, formerly, a person) insulting, calumnious.

> SHAKES. *Coriol.* Call me their traitor! Thou injurious tribune! SIR W. SCOTT He holds a late royal master of mine in deep hate for some injurious treatment . . which he received at his hand. O. MANNING Only his diplomat's charm had remained untouched by this injurious climate. B. BETTELHEIM We worry that his actions are harmful at the moment or may be injurious to his future.

injurious affection *LAW* a situation in which part of a person's land is acquired compulsorily under statutory powers and the remaining part is consequently reduced in value. **injurious falsehood** *LAW* the tort consisting of a maliciously false statement intended to cause damage to another person as regards property.
■ **injuriously** *adverb* L15. **injuriousness** *noun* M17.

injury /ˈɪn(d)ʒ(ə)ri/ *noun*. LME.
[ORIGIN Anglo-Norman *injurie* (mod. French *injure* insult) from Latin *injuria* use as noun of fem. of *injurius* unjust, wrongful, formed as IN-[3] + *jur-*, *jus* right: see -Y[3].]
1 Wrongful action or treatment; violation or infringement of another's rights; suffering wilfully inflicted; a wrongful act, a wrong inflicted or suffered. LME.
†**2** Intentionally hurtful or offensive speech or words; an insult, an affront, a taunt. LME–E18.
3 Hurt or loss caused to or sustained by a person or thing; harm, detriment; damage, esp. to the body; an instance of this. LME.

> J. BARNES William the Conqueror fell from his horse and received the injury from which he later died. *Which?* A good shoe will lessen the risk of injury.

do oneself an injury hurt oneself. ***personal injury***: see PERSONAL *adjective*.
– COMB.: **injury time** *FOOTBALL* extra playing time allowed by a referee to compensate for time lost in dealing with injuries.

†**injust** *adjective*. LME–E18.
[ORIGIN Old French & mod. French *injuste* from Latin *injustus*, formed as IN-[3] + *justus* JUST *adjective*.]
Not just; opposed to justice.
■ †**injustly** *adverb* LME–E18.

injustice /ɪnˈdʒʌstɪs/ *noun*. LME.
[ORIGIN Old French & mod. French from Latin *injustitia*, from *injustus*: see INJUST, -ICE[1].]
Unjust action; wrong; unfairness; an unjust act.
do a person an injustice judge a person unfairly.

†**injustifiable** *adjective*. *rare*. M17–E18.
[ORIGIN from IN-[3] + JUSTIFIABLE.]
Unjustifiable.

ink /ɪŋk/ *noun*[1]. ME.
[ORIGIN Old French *enque* (mod. *encre*) from late Latin *encau(s)tum* from Greek *egkauston* purple ink, from *egkaiein* burn in.]
1 Coloured fluid used in writing with a pen on paper etc.; coloured viscous paste used to mark paper etc. in printing, duplicating, writing with a ballpoint pen, etc.; an example of this. ME.

> M. MILNER I . . made a fairly accurate drawing of them in ink and oil chalks. J. CRACE He sits with clean parchment, newly mixed inks.

black ink, ***blue ink***, ***invisible ink***, etc. ***marking ink***, ***printer's ink***, ***printing ink***, ***sympathetic ink***, ***writing ink***, etc. ***Indian ink***: see INDIAN *adjective*. ***Japan ink***: see JAPAN *noun*. ***red ink***: see RED *adjective*.
2 The black liquid ejected by cuttlefish and other cephalopods to assist in escaping predators, etc., and from which sepia is obtainable. L16.

> G. DURRELL Fishermen . . with . . dark stains of octopus ink on their shirts.

3 Cheap wine, esp. red wine (*US & Austral.*); *NZ* liquor in general. Cf. INKED 2. *slang*. E20.
– COMB.: **ink ball** *PRINTING HISTORY* a hand-held rounded pad used for inking type; **inkberry** a low-growing N. American holly, *Ilex glabra*, with black berries and nearly thornless leaves; **ink block** *PRINTING HISTORY* a block or table on which ink was spread before being taken up by rollers or ink balls; **ink-blot test** (an example of) the Rorschach test; **ink cap** any of several fungi of the genus *Coprinus*, of which the gills dissolve into a black liquid after maturation; *SHAGGY* ***ink cap***; **ink-fish** a cuttlefish or squid; **inkjet printer** a printer in which characters and other marks are formed by a jet of ink projected on to the paper; **ink pad** an ink-soaked pad used for inking a rubber stamp; **inkpot** a small pot for holding writing ink; **inkshed** *joc.* [after *bloodshed*] the shedding or spilling of ink; consumption or waste of ink in writing; **ink-slinger** *derog.* a professional writer; **inkstand** a stand for one or more bottles to hold ink, often with a pen tray etc.; **inkweed** *Austral. & NZ* a tropical American pokeweed, *Phytolacca octandra*, naturalized in Australasia, so called from its small black berries, which contain a reddish juice; **inkwell** a pot for ink fitted into a hole in a desk.
■ **inkless** *adjective* E19.

ink /ɪŋk/ *noun*[2]. L16.
[ORIGIN Unknown.]
†**1** A mill rind. L16–E18.
2 A socket in which a vertical shaft or spindle rests. *rare*. L19.

ink /ɪŋk/ *verb trans*. M16.
[ORIGIN from INK *noun*[1].]
1 Mark, stain, or smear with or as with ink. M16. ▸**b** Cover (types etc.) with ink in order to print from them. E18.
2 Go or cover *over* with ink; trace *in* with ink (lines previously drawn in pencil); blot *out* with ink; cover *up* with ink. E19.
3 Sign, put one's signature to, (a contract etc.); engage by contract. *colloq*. (chiefly *N. Amer.*). M20.

G. VIDAL He promptly inked a multiple nonexclusive contract with Universal.

Inka *noun & adjective* see INCA.

inked /ɪŋ(k)t/ *adjective*. L18.
[ORIGIN from INK *verb*, *noun*[1]: see -ED[1], -ED[2].]
1 Covered or smeared with ink; coloured with ink. Also ***inked-in*** etc. L18.
2 Intoxicated, drunk. *Austral. & NZ slang*. L19.

inken /ˈɪŋk(ə)n/ *adjective*. Now *rare*. E17.
[ORIGIN from INK *noun*[1] + -EN[4].]
Of ink; written in ink.

inker /ˈɪŋkə/ *noun*. L19.
[ORIGIN from INK *verb* + -ER[1].]
A person or thing which uses or applies ink; *spec*. (***a***) *hist*. a telegraph instrument which recorded messages in ink; (***b***) PRINTING any of a set of rollers which coat a printing surface with ink.

inkhorn /ˈɪŋkhɔːn/ *noun & adjective*. LME.
[ORIGIN from INK *noun*[1] + HORN *noun*.]
▸**A** *noun*. *hist*. A small portable vessel for holding writing ink. LME.
▸**B** *attrib*. or as *adjective*. Of a term, word, language, etc.: literary, bookish, learned. M16.
▪ **inkhornism** *noun* (*rare*) use of inkhorn terms, pedantry L16.

†**inkindle** *verb* var. of ENKINDLE.

inkish /ˈɪŋkɪʃ/ *adjective*. *rare*. L17.
[ORIGIN from INK *noun*[1] + -ISH[1].]
Inky, black.

inkle /ˈɪŋk(ə)l/ *noun*. M16.
[ORIGIN Unknown.]
hist. **1** A kind of linen tape formerly much used, as to make laces; a piece of this tape. M16.
2 The linen thread or yarn from which this tape was manufactured. M16.

inkle /ˈɪŋk(ə)l/ *verb*. *rare*. LME.
[ORIGIN Unknown. In later use back-form. from INKLING.]
1 *verb trans*. Give a hint of, communicate in an undertone or whisper. LME.
2 *verb trans. & intrans*. Get an inkling or a notion of or *of*. M19.

inkling /ˈɪŋklɪŋ/ *noun*. LME.
[ORIGIN from INKLE *verb* + -ING[1].]
1 The action of mentioning in an undertone; a faint or slight mention or rumour. *obsolete* exc. *dial*. LME.
2 A hint or slight intimation given or received; a suggestion; a vague knowledge or notion; a suspicion. (Foll. by *of*.) E16. ▸†**b** A suspicion *of* or *against* a person. E17–E18.

E. ROOSEVELT The admiral refused to give me the slightest inkling of what he had decided to do. P. FERGUSON She had had no inkling of his identity. V. SETH If Jan's surprised, she shows no inkling Of it at all.

3 An inclination, a slight desire. *dial*. L18.

in-kneed /ˈɪn-niːd, ɪnˈniːd/ *adjective*. Now *rare*. E18.
[ORIGIN from IN *adverb* + KNEE *noun* + -ED[2].]
Having the legs bent inwards at the knees.

inknot /ɪnˈnɒt/ *verb trans*. *rare*. Also **en-** /ɪn-, ɛn-/. Infl. **-tt-**. E17.
[ORIGIN from IN-[1], EN-[1] + KNOT *verb*.]
Include in or with a knot; tie in.

inkosi /ɪŋˈkəʊsi/ *noun*. *S. Afr*. M19.
[ORIGIN Nguni.]
(The title of) a Zulu ruler, chief, or high official.
▪ **inkosikazi** /ɪŋkəʊsɪˈkɑːzi/ *noun* [Nguni -*kazi* wife of] (***a***) the wife of a Zulu chief; (***b***) (a respectful name for) a married woman: M19.

inky /ˈɪŋki/ *adjective*. L16.
[ORIGIN from INK *noun*[1] + -Y[1].]
1 Of or pertaining to ink; written in ink; using ink; literary. L16.

Listener It had started off as a music magazine to rival the weekly inky press.

2 Full of ink. L16.
3 Black, dark. L16.

W. GERHARDIE The inky blackness of the night. J. BUCHAN Long pools of inky water filled the ruts.

inky cap = ***ink cap*** s.v. INK *noun*[1].
4 Stained with ink. E17.
▪ **inkiness** *noun* (*rare*) E17.

INLA *abbreviation*.
Irish National Liberation Army.

inlaid *verb pa. t. & pple* of INLAY *verb*.

in-lamb /ɪnˈlam, ˈɪnlam/ *adjective*. M16.
[ORIGIN from IN-[1] + LAMB *noun*.]
Of a ewe: pregnant.

inland /ˈɪnlənd, -land; *as adverb also* ɪnˈland/ *noun, adjective, & adverb*. OE.
[ORIGIN from IN-[1] + LAND *noun*[1].]
▸**A** *noun*. **1** *hist*. The inner part of an estate, feudal manor, or farm cultivated by the owner. Opp. OUTLAND *noun* 1. OE.
2 *sing*. & (now *rare*) in *pl*. The interior part of a country or region, remote from the sea or frontiers. Formerly also, the part of a country near to the capital and centres of population. M16.

A. GARVE Our inland is still very empty country, and a lot of it isn't easily accessible.

▸**B** *adjective*. **1** Of or pertaining to the interior part of the country or region; remote from the sea or frontiers. M16. ▸†**b** Having the sophistication characteristic of the capital or population centres of a country. Only in E17.

P. HEYLIN All the In-land Towns in this large Estate.

2 Carried on or operating within the limits of a country. M16.

SWIFT A pamphlet printed in England for a general excise or inland duty.

– SPECIAL COLLOCATIONS: **inland duty** a tax payable on inland trade. **inland ice (sheet)** an extensive thick sheet of ice underlain by rock; *spec*. the ice cap over the interior of Greenland. ***inland navigation***. ***inland port***: see PORT *noun*[1] 2. **inland revenue** in the UK, the revenue consisting of taxes and inland duties; (with cap. initials) the government department responsible for assessing and collecting these. **inland sea** an entirely landlocked large body of salt or fresh water.
▸**C** *adverb*. In or towards the interior part of a country; away from the sea or frontiers. L16.

T. MO Where the river rises thousands of miles inland. V. S. NAIPAUL On the coast there would have been . . descendants of the slave mahogany log-cutters. Inland, there was a Mayan population.

▪ **inlander** *noun* a native or inhabitant of the inland of a country E17. **inlandish** *adjective* of or pertaining to the interior of a country or region L16.

†**inlarge** *verb*, †**inlargement** *noun* vars. of ENLARGE, ENLARGEMENT.

inlaut /ˈɪnlaʊt/ *noun*. L19.
[ORIGIN German, from *in* in + *Laut* sound.]
PHILOLOGY. A medial or internal sound; a sound which occurs in the middle of a word.

inlaw /ˈɪnlɔː/ *verb & noun*. *obsolete* exc. *hist*. LOE.
[ORIGIN from IN *adverb* + LAW *noun*[1], after *outlaw*.]
▸**A** *verb trans*. Bring within the authority and protection of the law; reverse the outlawry of (a person). LOE.
▸**B** *noun*. A person who is within the domain and protection of the law. ME.

in-law /ˈɪnlɔː/ *noun & adjective*. *colloq*. L19.
[ORIGIN from -IN-LAW.]
▸**A** *noun*. A relative by marriage. Usu. in *pl*. L19.
▸**B** *attrib*. or as *adjective*. Of or pertaining to relatives by marriage. L19.

-in-law /ɪnˈlɔː/ *suffix*.
[ORIGIN from IN *preposition* + LAW *noun*[1], after Anglo-Norman *en ley*, Old French *en loi* (*de mariage*) in law (of marriage).]
Appended to nouns of personal relationship with the sense 'by marriage, in the eye of canon law', as ***father-in-law***, ***sister-in-law***.

inlay /ˈɪnleɪ, ɪnˈleɪ/ *noun*. E17.
[ORIGIN from the verb.]
1 The process or art of inlaying. *rare*. E17.
2 A piece of material inlaid or prepared for inlaying; inlaid work. L17. ▸**b** DENTISTRY. A filling of gold, porcelain, etc., which is preformed in the required shape before being cemented into a cavity. L19.

inlay /ɪnˈleɪ/ *verb trans*. Pa. t. & pple **inlaid**. M16.
[ORIGIN from IN-[1] + LAY *verb*[1].]
†**1** Lay (as) in a place of concealment or preservation M16–M17.
2 Lay (a thing) in the substance of something else so that their surfaces are flush. L16. ▸**b** Insert (a page of a book, an illustration, etc.) in a space cut in a page that is larger and thicker. E19.
3 Fit (a thing) with a substance of a different kind embedded in its surface; diversify by the insertion of another material in a decorative design. L16.
▪ **inlayer** *noun* M17.

inleague *verb* see ENLEAGUE.

inleak /ˈɪnliːk/ *noun*. E20.
[ORIGIN from IN-[1] + LEAK *noun*.]
Leakage into the inside of a thing.

in-leakage /ˈɪnliːkɪdʒ/ *noun*. E20.
[ORIGIN from IN-[1] + LEAKAGE.]
= INLEAK.

inlet /ˈɪnlɛt, -lɪt/ *noun*. ME.
[ORIGIN from IN-[1] + LET *verb*[1].]
1 Letting in; admission. Now *rare*. ME.
2 A small arm of the sea, a narrow indentation of a sea coast or the bank of a lake or river. L16.
3 A way of admission; an entrance. E17.
attrib.: ***inlet pipe***, ***inlet valve***, etc. ***inlet manifold***: see MANIFOLD *noun* 5.
4 A piece inserted or inlaid. L18.
5 ANATOMY. An aperture giving entrance to a cavity; the upper opening into the pelvic, thoracic, etc., cavities. Cf. OUTLET *noun* 1C. E19.

inlet /ˈɪnlɛt/ *verb trans*. Infl. **-tt-**. Pa. t. & pple **inlet**. ME.
[ORIGIN from IN-[1] + LET *verb*[1].]
†**1** Allow to enter; admit. ME–L17.
2 Insert, inlay. M19.

inlier /ˈɪnlʌɪə/ *noun*. M19.
[ORIGIN from IN-[1] after OUTLIER.]
An area or outcrop of rock surrounded by rocks younger in age. Cf. OUTLIER.

†**inlight** *verb*, †**inlighten** *verb* vars. of ENLIGHT, ENLIGHTEN.

in limine /ɪn ˈlɪmɪni/ *adverbial phr*. E19.
[ORIGIN Latin.]
On the threshold; at the outset.

in-line /ˈɪnlʌɪn/ *noun & adjective*. E20.
[ORIGIN from IN-[1] + LINE *noun*[2].]
▸**A** *noun*. **1** TYPOGRAPHY. A typeface with a white line running through the thick strokes of the letters. E20.
2 An in-line engine. M20.
▸**B** *adjective*. **1** (Composed of parts) arranged or situated in a line; *esp*. (of an internal-combustion engine) having (usu. vertical) cylinders arranged in one or more rows. E20.
2 Chiefly ENGINEERING. Involving, employing, or forming part of a continuous, usu. linear, sequence of operations or machines (as in an assembly line). M20.
3 COMPUTING. **a** Designating data processing which does not require input data to be sorted into batches. M20. ▸**b** = ONLINE *adjective* 1. M20.
4 TYPOGRAPHY. Designating or pertaining to a typeface with a white line running through the thick strokes of the letters. M20.
– SPECIAL COLLOCATIONS: **in-line skates** a pair of roller skates in which the wheels on each boot are fixed in a single line along its sole.

†**inlink** *verb*, †**inlist** *verb*, †**inlive** *verb*, vars. of ENLINK etc.

†**inliven** *verb* var. of ENLIVEN.

†**inlock** *verb* var. of ENLOCK.

in loco /ɪn ˈləʊkəʊ/ *adverbial & prepositional phr*. L17.
[ORIGIN Latin.]
▸**A** *adverbial phr*. In a place; in the place, locally. *rare*. L17.
▸**B** *prepositional phr*. In place of. Chiefly in ***in loco parentis*** /pəˈrɛntɪs/, in place of a parent. E18.

inlook /ˈɪnlʊk/ *noun*. M19.
[ORIGIN from IN-[1] + LOOK *noun*.]
Looking within; introspection.

inlooker /ˈɪnlʊkə/ *noun*. *rare*. L16.
[ORIGIN from IN-[1] + LOOKER.]
A person who looks into a thing, an inspector.

in-lot /ˈɪnlɒt/ *noun*. *obsolete* exc. *N. Amer*. M17.
[ORIGIN from IN-[1] + LOT *noun*.]
1 A plot of land or allotment that is part of a larger plot. M17.
2 N. AMER. HISTORY. A plot of land for settlement, large enough for a house, garden, and outbuildings. L18.

†**inly** *adjective*. OE–E17.
[ORIGIN from IN *adverb* + -LY[1]; later prob. from INLY *adverb*.]
Inward, internal; heartfelt.

inly /ˈɪnli/ *adverb*. Now *literary*. OE.
[ORIGIN from IN *adverb* + -LY[2].]
Inwardly; within, internally, in the inner nature; in a way that goes to the heart; intimately, closely; thoroughly.

inlying /ˈɪnlʌɪɪŋ/ *adjective*. M19.
[ORIGIN from IN-[1] + LYING *adjective*[1].]
Lying inside; placed or situated in the interior.

in-maintenance /ˈɪnmeɪnt(ə)nəns, -tɪn-/ *noun*. M19.
[ORIGIN from IN-[1] + MAINTENANCE.]
Chiefly *hist*. Maintenance for a person living in a workhouse etc.

inmate /ˈɪnmeɪt/ *noun & adjective*. L16.
[ORIGIN Prob. orig. from INN *noun* (later assoc. with IN *adverb*) + MATE *noun*[2].]
▸**A** *noun*. **1** A person who shares a house with another or others. In early use *spec*. a lodger, a subtenant. Now *rare*. L16.

H. JAMES We have never had a lodger or any kind of inmate.

2 An inhabitant or occupier *of* a house, esp. along with others. Now chiefly, an inhabitant *of* an institution, as an asylum or a prison. L16.

M. AMSTERDAM The warden, . . at the asylum, noticed one of the inmates sitting on a small stool.

3 A person not native to the place where he or she lives; a stranger, a foreigner. Now *rare* or *obsolete*. L16.
▸ †**B** *attrib.* or as *adjective*. That is an inmate. E17–E19.

inmeat /ˈɪnmiːt/ *noun*. *obsolete* exc. *dial.* LME.
[ORIGIN from IN-¹ + MEAT *noun*.]
sing. & (usu.) in *pl.* The edible viscera of an animal; entrails.

in medias res /ɪn ˌmɛdɪɑːs ˈreɪz, ˌmiːdɪɑːs ˈriːz/ *adverbial phr.* L18.
[ORIGIN Latin.]
Into the midst of things; *esp.* into the middle of a narrative, without preamble.

in medio /ɪn ˈmiːdɪəʊ/ *adverbial phr.* E17.
[ORIGIN Latin.]
In the middle; in an undecided state.

in memoriam /ɪn mɪˈmɔːrɪam/ *prepositional & noun phr.* M19.
[ORIGIN Latin.]
▸ **A** *prepositional phr.* To the memory of, in memory of. M19.
▸ **B** *noun phr.* A poem, notice, etc., in memory of a dead person. L19.

in-migrant /ˈɪnmʌɪɡr(ə)nt/ *noun & adjective*. Orig. *US*. M20.
[ORIGIN from IN-¹ + MIGRANT.]
(Designating) a person who has migrated from one place to another in the same country.

in-migration /ˈɪnmʌɪɡreɪʃ(ə)n/ *noun*. Orig. *US*. M20.
[ORIGIN from IN-¹ + MIGRATION.]
The action of migrating from one place to another within the same country.

inmix /ɪnˈmɪks/ *verb trans.* & *intrans.* L19.
[ORIGIN from IN-¹ + MIX *verb*.]
Mix in, blend.

inmost /ˈɪnməʊst/ *adjective, noun, & adverb*. OE.
[ORIGIN from IN *adverb* + -MOST.]
▸ **A** *adjective*. Situated furthest within, most inward; *spec.* (of thoughts, feelings etc.) most intimate, deepest, closest. OE.

SHELLEY From the inmost depths of its green glen. O. SACKS To know about a man, we ask 'What is his story—his real, inmost story?' W. RAEPER It was to Helen that he confided many of his inmost thoughts.

▸ **B** *noun*. The inmost part. OE.

J. FORD Be sure To lodge it in the inmost of thy bosom.

▸ **C** *adverb*. Most inwardly. *rare*. OE.
■ **inmostly** *adverb* (*rare*) M19.

inn /ɪn/ *noun*.
[ORIGIN Old English *inn* (corresp. to Old Norse *inni*) from Germanic, from base of IN *adverb*.]
1 *sing.* & in *pl.* A dwelling place, an abode, a lodging; a house. Long *obsolete* exc. *Scot.* OE.

fig.: COVERDALE *Isa.* 32:18 The soule is the Inne of God.

2 [translating Latin *hospitium*.] A house of residence for students. *obsolete* exc. as preserved in names of buildings (orig.) so used, esp. ***Inns of Chancery***, ***Inn of Court*** below. ME.
3 A public house providing accommodation, refreshments, etc., for payment, esp. for travellers. Now also, a public house serving alcoholic liquor for consumption on the premises, whether providing accommodation or not. LME.

E. H. JONES The inns where the family stayed on . . the journey. *fig.*: SIR W. SCOTT That dark inn, the grave!

– PHRASES: **Inns of Chancery** *hist.* buildings in London formerly used as hostels for law students. **Inn of Court** (*a*) any of the sets of buildings in London belonging to the four legal societies having the exclusive right of admitting people to the English bar; any of these societies; (*b*) a similar society in Ireland. ***motor inn***: see MOTOR *noun & adjective*.
– COMB.: **innholder** (now *rare* or *obsolete*), **innkeeper** a person who manages or owns an inn. **innkeeping** *noun & adjective* (*a*) *noun* the owning or managing of an inn; (*b*) *adjective* that owns or manages an inn.

inn /ɪn/ *verb*¹. Now *rare*. OE.
[ORIGIN from the noun.]
1 *verb trans.* Lodge, house, find accommodation for. OE.
2 *verb intrans.* Lodge, find accommodation, stay. LME. ▸**b** Of a coach etc.: stop at an inn. M18.

†**inn** *verb*² var. of IN *verb*.

innards /ˈɪnədz/ *noun pl.* *colloq.* E19.
[ORIGIN Repr. a pronunc. of *inwards* pl. of INWARD *noun*.]
Entrails; bowels; *fig.* the inside or internal parts.

R. KIPLING 'E feels 'is innards 'eavin', 'is bowels givin' way. R. H. MORRIESON I saw her . . curious and scornful expression that wrung out my innards. E. BLISHEN He . . stared into the piano, as if making an inventory of its innards.

innascibility /ɪ(n),nasɪˈbɪlɪti/ *noun*. Now *rare*. E17.
[ORIGIN ecclesiastical Latin *innascibilitas*, from *innascibilis* incapable of being born, formed as IN-³ + *nascibilis* who can be born, from *nasci* be born: see -IBLE, -ITY.]
CHRISTIAN THEOLOGY. The attribute of being independent of birth.

R. CUDWORTH God is the only . . Unmade Being . . his very essence is Ingenerability or Innascibility.

innate /ɪˈneɪt, ˈɪneɪt/ *adjective*. LME.
[ORIGIN Latin *innatus* pa. pple of *innasci*, formed as IN-² + *nasci* be born.]
1 Inborn, natural, inherent. LME.

T. COLLINS The horse has not half the innate sagacity of the ox. J. F. KENNEDY As believers in a democratic system, we have always had faith in its innate powers of resistance. A. STORR The disagreement between biologists as to what is learned and what is innate.

2 BOTANY. Of a part or organ: attached at the apex of another, not adnate. M19.
■ **innately** *adverb* M17. **innateness** *noun* E18. **innatism** *noun* (belief in) the innateness of a quality, aptitude, etc. E20. †**innative** *adjective* [after NATIVE *adjective*] innate; native: E16–M19.

innavigable /ɪˈnavɪɡəb(ə)l, ɪnˈna-/ *adjective*. E16.
[ORIGIN French, or Latin *innavigabilis*, formed as IN-³ + NAVIGABLE.]
Not navigable; impassable by boat or ship.

inner /ˈɪnə/ *adjective & noun*.
[ORIGIN Old English *inner(r)a*, *in(n)ra* (compar. of IN *adverb*) = Old Frisian *inra*, Old High German *innaro*, *-ero* (German *innere*), Old Norse *innri*, *iðri*: see -ER³.]
▸ **A** *adjective*. **1** Situated (more) within or inside; (more or further) inward; internal; *fig.* more secret, central, or essential. Opp. ***outer***. OE.

U. BENTLEY From the entrance hall . . , glassy corridors led away into the inner reaches of the school. M. PIERCY He was a widely social man with inner and outer circles of pals.

2 Designating the mind or soul; mental; spiritual. OE.

A. STORR Dreams are dramatizations of situations existing in the patient's inner world. C. G. WOLFF The difficulties . . of her life—the sense of inner desolation and loneliness.

– SPECIAL COLLOCATIONS & COMB.: **inner Bar** LAW. King's or Queen's Counsel collectively. **inner Cabinet** a group of decision-makers within a ministerial Cabinet etc. **inner child** a person's supposed original or authentic self, esp. when regarded as damaged or repressed by childhood traumas; that part of one's personality which manifests itself in childish activities. **inner circle** an exclusive group of friends or associates within a larger group. **inner city** the central area of a city, esp. if dilapidated or characterized by overcrowding, poverty, etc. **inner-directed** *adjective* (PSYCHOLOGY) governed by one's own standards formed in childhood and not by external pressures. ***inner ear***: see EAR *noun*¹. **inner forme** PRINTING the printing surface (orig. type) containing the pages from which the inner side of a sheet is printed, including matter for the second page of the printed sheet. **inner light** in the Society of Friends, direct spiritual contact with God. **inner man**, **inner woman** (*a*) the soul or mind (of a man or woman); (*b*) *joc.* the stomach (of a man or woman). **inner planet**: with an orbit inside the asteroid belt. **inner reserve** FINANCE a secret reserve not disclosed in a balance sheet and due to an understatement of certain capital assets. **inner space** (*a*) the region between the earth and outer space, or below the surface of the sea; (*b*) the part of the mind not normally accessible to consciousness. **inner speech** the mental or internal system or structure which lies behind language. **inner-spring** *adjective & noun* (*N. Amer.*) (*a*) *adjective* = ***INTERIOR-sprung***; (*b*) *noun* an interior-sprung mattress. ***Inner Temple***: see TEMPLE *noun*¹ 6. **inner tube** a separate inflatable tube inside the cover of a pneumatic tyre. ***inner woman***: see ***inner man*** above.
▸ **B** *noun*. The inner part of something; an inner position; *spec.* (a shot which hits) the division of a target next outside the bull's-eye. L19.
■ **innermore** *adverb & adjective* (*obsolete* exc. *dial.*) †(*a*) more inward or within; (*b*) situated more within, inner: ME. **innerness** *noun* L19.

innerly /ˈɪnəli/ *adjective*. Long *obsolete* exc. *Scot.* LME.
[ORIGIN from INNER *adjective* + -LY¹.]
1 Inner, interior. LME.
2 Kindly, affectionate. *Scot.* E19.

innerly /ˈɪnəli/ *adverb*. Now *literary*. ME.
[ORIGIN from INNER *adjective* + -LY².]
Inwardly, internally. Formerly also, more within.

innermost /ˈɪnəməʊst/ *adjective & noun*. LME.
[ORIGIN from INNER *adjective* + -MOST.]
▸ **A** *adjective*. Most or furthest within; inmost, deepest, most secret. LME.

B. BETTELHEIM Asking a child to reveal his . . innermost thoughts to us is a questionable procedure.

▸ **B** *noun*. The or an innermost part. Now *rare*. L17.

innervate /ˈɪnəveɪt, ɪˈnəːveɪt/ *verb trans.* L19.
[ORIGIN from IN-² + NERVE *noun* + -ATE³.]
ANATOMY & PHYSIOLOGY. Supply (an organ or part) with nerves, or with nervous stimulation. Chiefly as ***innervated ppl adjective***.

innervation /ɪnəˈveɪʃ(ə)n, ɪnəː-/ *noun*. M19.
[ORIGIN formed as INNERVATE + -ATION.]
1 ANATOMY & PHYSIOLOGY. The action or process of innervating; nervous stimulation. Also, the condition of being innervated; the supply of nerve fibres to, or disposition of nerve fibres within, an organ or part. M19.
2 PSYCHOLOGY. = KINAESTHESIS. L19.

innerve /ɪˈnəːv/ *verb trans.* E19.
[ORIGIN from IN-² + NERVE *verb* or *noun*.]
Animate, invigorate.

inness /ˈɪn-nɪs/ *noun*. M19.
[ORIGIN from IN *adverb* or *attrib. adjective* + -NESS.]
The quality or state of being in.

†**innew** *verb* var. of ENNEW.

inning /ˈɪnɪŋ/ *noun*¹. OE.
[ORIGIN from IN *verb* + -ING¹. See also INNINGS.]
†**1** A putting or getting in; contents; income. Only in OE.
2 The action of getting in, esp. of crops; harvesting. Now *rare* or *obsolete*. LME.
3 The action of taking in, inclosing, etc.; *esp.* the reclaiming of marsh or flooded land. M16. ▸**b** In *pl.* Land taken in or reclaimed (from the sea etc.). E18.
4 BASEBALL. Each division of a game during which both sides have a turn at batting. M19.

inning /ˈɪnɪŋ/ *noun*². Now *rare* or *obsolete*. OE.
[ORIGIN from INN *verb*¹ + -ING¹.]
The action of INN *verb*¹; lodging, housing; a lodging.

innings /ˈɪnɪŋz/ *noun*. Pl. same, (*colloq.*) **-es**. M18.
[ORIGIN from INNING *noun*¹ + -S¹.]
1 In cricket and similar games: a portion of a game during which a side or a player is in, e.g. batting, hitting, etc.; the play or score of one player during one spell of being in. M18.

M. COX Mr. White-Thomson's side owed their victory to the splendid innings of A. C. Benson, Esq.

2 The time during which a person, party, principle, etc., is in power or possession; a term of or opportunity for an activity; a turn. M19.

W. R. GREG The new ideas . . got their innings, and . . have ruled the national policy from 1830 till 1875.

a good innings, **a long innings** *colloq.* a long life.

Inniskilling /ɪnɪˈskɪlɪŋ/ *noun*. E18.
[ORIGIN The county town of Fermanagh, N. Ireland (now *Enniskillen*).]
hist. A soldier of a regiment originally raised for the defence of Enniskillen in 1689, later the 5th Royal Inniskilling Dragoon Guards (cf. ***the Skins*** s.v. SKIN *noun*).
■ **Inniskilliner** *noun* L18.

innit /ˈɪnɪt/ *interjection*. *colloq.* M20.
[ORIGIN Repr. a pronunc.]
Isn't it. Cf. ENNIT.

†**innoble** *verb* var. of ENNOBLE.

innocence /ˈɪnəs(ə)ns/ *noun*. ME.
[ORIGIN Old French & mod. French from Latin *innocentia*, from *innocent-*: see INNOCENT, -ENCE. Cf. INNOCENCY.]
1 a Freedom from sin or guilt in general; the state of being untouched by evil; moral purity. ME. ▸**b** Freedom from specific guilt; the fact of not being guilty of a charge; guiltlessness. M16.

a R. SOUTH How came our first Parents to sin, and to lose their Primitive Innocence?

2 Freedom from cunning or artifice; guilelessness, artlessness, simplicity, lack of suspicion; lack of knowledge or sense, naivety. LME.

ADDISON My little Daughter . . asked me with a great deal of innocence, why I never told them. B. EMECHETA None of them wished to display their innocence . . by asking any more questions.

3 An innocent person or thing. Now *rare*. LME.
4 Harmlessness, innocuousness. *rare*. E19.
5 BOTANY. = BLUET (b). *US*. E19.
– PHRASES: ***INJURED innocence***.

innocency /ˈɪnəs(ə)nsi/ *noun*. LME.
[ORIGIN Latin *innocentia*: see INNOCENCE, -ENCY.]
1 a = INNOCENCE 1a. LME. ▸**b** = INNOCENCE 1b. E16.
2 = INNOCENCE 2. L15.
3 = INNOCENCE 4. M17.
4 = INNOCENCE 3. E18.

innocent /ˈɪnəs(ə)nt/ *adjective & noun*. ME.
[ORIGIN Old French & mod. French, or Latin *innocent-*, formed as IN-³ + *nocent-* pres. ppl stem of *nocere* hurt, injure: see -ENT.]
▸ **A** *adjective*. **1** Free from sin or guilt in general; morally pure; untouched by evil. ME.

M. LEITCH Changing from the innocent slip of a young thing . . to the ugly old whore.

2 Free from specific guilt; that has not committed the offence in question; not deserving the punishment etc. inflicted; not guilty. (Foll. by *of*.) LME. ▸**b** Foll. by *of*: Free or devoid of; without. *colloq.* E18. ▸**c** Entirely free of responsibility for or involvement in an event, while suffering circumstantially from it. E19.

H. ARENDT Trying to save an innocent man they employed the . . methods . . adopted in the case of a guilty one. P. H. JOHNSON He was innocent of the particular badness with which F. had charged him. Z. MEDVEDEV Grishin was possibly not entirely innocent of corruption. **b** J. COLBORNE The windows are small apertures . . innocent of glass. G. DURRELL His skull-cap was innocent of decoration.

innocent party the innocent person in a particular situation; formerly *spec.* in LAW, the party who successfully obtained a divorce decree under the old system of matrimonial offence. **c innocent bystander** etc.

3 Devoid of cunning or artifice; guileless, artless, simple; unsuspecting; naive, inexperienced, ingenuous; (now *dial.*) lacking intelligence or sense, half-witted, imbecile. LME.

G. GREENE Milly felt inexperienced and stupidly innocent in front of Kay. K. A. PORTER I *was* innocent.. as a calf;.. a simple soul without a care.

4 Not arising from or involving evil intent or motive; producing no ill effect or result; harmless, innocuous; MEDICINE not malignant, benign. E16. ▸**b** That does not break the law; lawful, permitted. E19.

W. DAMPIER Calabash.. is of a sharp and pleasing Taste, and is very innocent. B. FRANKLIN I think no pleasure innocent, that is to man hurtful.

innocent conveyance LAW a conveyance which does not have any tortious operation, and does not create a discontinuance or result in forfeiture.

▸**B** *noun*. **1** A person free from sin, not disposed to do harm, or unacquainted with evil, *esp.* a young child; the class of innocent people. ME.

ADDISON The pretty Innocent walks blindfold among burning Plough-shares, without being scorched.. by them.

the Holy Innocents, **the Innocents** the young children murdered by Herod after the birth of Jesus (*Matthew* 2:16); ***Holy Innocents' Day***, ***Innocents' Day***, 28 December, on which the massacre of the Holy Innocents is commemorated.

2 A person innocent of a charge or undeserving of punishment; a guiltless person. Now *rare* or *obsolete*. ME.

J. CHAMBERLAYNE Those who shall conspire to indict an Innocent falsely and maliciously of Felony.

3 A guileless, simple, naive, or unsuspecting person; a person lacking knowledge or intelligence, a simpleton, an idiot. LME.

4 BOTANY. Usu. in *pl.* (treated as *sing.*) = INNOCENCE 5. US. M19.

■ **innocently** *adverb* LME. †**innocentness** *noun* (*rare*) L15–E18.

innocuity /ɪnɒˈkjuːɪti/ *noun*. M19.
[ORIGIN formed as INNOCUOUS + -ITY.]
Innocuousness.

innocuous /ɪˈnɒkjʊəs/ *adjective*. L16.
[ORIGIN from Latin *innocuus*, formed as IN-[3] + *nocuus*, from *nocere* hurt, + -OUS.]
Not harmful or hurtful; harmless; inoffensive.

R. L. STEVENSON A tumblerful of the playful, innocuous American cocktail. I. MURDOCH These 'relationships' which Millie cultivated remained at a level of innocuous flirtation.

■ **innocuously** *adverb* M17. **innocuousness** *noun* M17.

innominable /ɪˈnɒmɪnəb(ə)l/ *adjective*. *arch.* LME.
[ORIGIN Latin *innominabilis*, formed as IN-[3] + *nominabilis* NOMINABLE.]
Impossible to name; not fit to be named.

Fraser's Magazine Those innominable garments, the mere allusion to which is sufficient to shock ears polite.

innominate /ɪˈnɒmɪnət/ *adjective*. M17.
[ORIGIN Late Latin *innominatus*, formed as IN-[3] + NOMINATE *adjective*.]
1 Not named; anonymous. Now *rare* exc. ANATOMY (see below). M17.

innominate artery ANATOMY a large artery which branches from the aortic arch and divides into the right common carotid and right subclavian arteries. **innominate bone** ANATOMY either of the two hip bones formed by the fusion of the ilium, ischium, and pubis. **innominate vein** ANATOMY either of two large veins of the neck formed by the junction of the external jugular and subclavian veins.

2 LAW. Of a contract: not belonging to any of the recognized categories. L18.

in nomine /ɪn ˈnəʊmɪneɪ, ˈnɒm-/ *noun phr.* M17.
[ORIGIN Latin = in the name (of).]
An instrumental composition in fugal style (prob. orig. one set to a Latin text including the words *in nomine*); a free fugue in which the answer does not exactly correspond with the subject.

innovate /ˈɪnəveɪt/ *verb*. M16.
[ORIGIN Latin *innovat-* pa. ppl stem of *innovare* renew, alter, formed as IN-[2] + *novare* make new, from *novus* new: see -ATE[3].]
†**1** *verb trans.* Change (a thing) into something new; alter; renew. M16–E19.

SIR W. SCOTT The dictates of my father were.. not to be altered, innovated, or even discussed.

2 *verb trans.* Introduce (something) for the first time; introduce as new; COMMERCE introduce on to the market. M16.

Times Review of Industry Nylon.. was first invented in 1928, but not innovated until 1939.

3 *verb intrans.* Bring in or introduce something new; make a change or changes in something established. L16.

BURKE To innovate is not to reform. *Physics Bulletin* The very large firms,.. do not truly innovate and.. may hinder innovation because they are so inflexible.

innovation /ɪnəˈveɪʃ(ə)n/ *noun*. LME.
[ORIGIN Latin *innovatio(n-)*, formed as INNOVATE: see -ATION.]
1 The action of innovating; the introduction of a new thing; the alteration of something established; *spec.* †(*a*) (political) revolution; (*b*) SCOTS LAW = NOVATION 2; (*c*) COMMERCE the introduction of a new product on to the market. LME.

Dumfries & Galloway Standard The Government place considerable emphasis on promoting innovation and enterprise.

2 A result or product of innovating; a thing newly introduced; a change made in something; a new practice, method, etc.; *spec.* †(*a*) a (political) revolution; (*b*) COMMERCE a product newly introduced on to the market. LME.

ROBERT JOHNSON Neither doth he willingly arme them for feare of sedition and innovations. L. M. MONTGOMERY They've never had a female teacher.. before and she thinks it is a dangerous innovation. E. M. ROGERS It matters little whether or not an innovation has.. advantage over the idea it is replacing.

3 BOTANY. A newly formed shoot which has not completed its growth; *spec.* (in a moss) a shoot formed at or near the apex of the thallus, the older parts dying off behind. M19.

■ **innovational** *adjective* E19. **innovationist** *noun* (*rare*) a person who favours innovations E19.

innovative /ˈɪnəveɪtɪv, -vət-/ *adjective*. E17.
[ORIGIN from INNOVATE + -IVE.]
Having the character or quality of innovating; characterized by innovation.
■ **innovatively** *adverb* L20. **innovativeness** *noun* M20.

innovator /ˈɪnəveɪtə/ *noun*. L16.
[ORIGIN Late Latin, formed as INNOVATE: see -OR.]
A person who innovates, an introducer of innovations. Formerly also *spec.*, a revolutionary.

innovatory /ɪnəˈveɪt(ə)ri, ˈɪnəvət-/ *adjective*. M19.
[ORIGIN from INNOVATE + -ORY[2].]
Of innovating character or tendency.

innoxious /ɪˈnɒkʃəs/ *adjective*. Now *rare*. E17.
[ORIGIN from Latin *innoxius*, formed as IN-[3] + NOXIOUS, + -OUS.]
†**1** Innocent, guiltless, blameless. *rare*. E17–L18.
2 Not noxious; harmless, innocuous. M17.
■ **innoxiously** *adverb* M17. **innoxiousness** *noun* M17.

in nubibus /ɪn ˈnjuːbɪbəs/ *adverbial & adjectival phr.* L16.
[ORIGIN Latin.]
In the clouds; as yet unsettled; undecided; incapable of being carried out.

in nuce /ɪn ˈnuːkeɪ/ *adverbial phr.* M19.
[ORIGIN Latin.]
In a nutshell; in a condensed form.

innuendo /ɪnjʊˈɛndəʊ/ *verb*. E18.
[ORIGIN from the noun.]
1 *verb intrans.* Make innuendoes. E18.
2 *verb trans.* Imply or convey by innuendo; attack (a person) by making an innuendo. M18.
3 *verb trans.* Chiefly LAW. Interpret or construe by attaching an innuendo. M19.

innuendo /ɪnjʊˈɛndəʊ/ *adverb & noun*. M16.
[ORIGIN Latin = by nodding at, pointing to, intimating, abl. gerund of *innuere* nod to, signify, formed as IN-[2] + *nuere* nod.]
▸**A** *adverb*. Meaning, that is to say, to wit, (esp. in legal documents, introducing a parenthetical explanation of the precise reference of a preceding noun or pronoun). M16.
▸**B** *noun*. Pl. **-o(e)s**.
1 A parenthetical explanation of, or construction put upon, a word or expression; *esp.* in an action for libel or slander, the harmful meaning alleged to be conveyed by a word or expression not in itself actionable. L17. ▸**b** A word or expression parenthetically explained; a blank to be filled with the name of the person to whom it is alleged to refer. *arch.* M18.
2 An allusive or oblique remark, hint, or suggestion, usu. disparaging; a remark with a (usu. suggestive) double meaning; allusion, hinting, suggestion. L17.

A. WILSON Innuendo, direct attack, or friendly teasing, she had had enough.. criticism for today. L. DEIGHTON Her ears were attuned to chance remarks and she never missed an innuendo. Y. MENUHIN The Kreisler sound was all subtle emphasis, innuendo, dropped hints.

Inuit *noun & adjective* var. of INUIT.

†**innumberable** *adjective*. LME–E18.
[ORIGIN Old French & mod. French *innombrable* formed as INNUMERABLE, assim. to *number*.]
= INNUMERABLE.

innumerable /ɪˈnjuːm(ə)rəb(ə)l/ *adjective & noun*. ME.
[ORIGIN Latin *innumerabilis*, formed as IN-[3] + NUMERABLE.]
▸**A** *adjective*. Too many to be counted; numberless, countless. Freq. ***postpositive***. ME.

I. WATTS Behold the innumerable host Of Angels cloth'd in light! J. A. MICHENER The Saracens.. would borrow from them concepts innumerable. A. GHOSH The light was filtered through the innumerable.. coconut palms which grew around the house.

▸**B** *absol.* as *noun*. Countless numbers, many, (†*of*). M16.
■ **innumeraˈbility** *noun* E17. **innumerableness** *noun* L16. **innumerably** *adverb* L16.

innumeracy /ɪˈnjuːm(ə)rəsi/ *noun*. M20.
[ORIGIN from IN-[3] + NUMERACY.]
The quality or state of being innumerate.

innumerate /ɪˈnjuːm(ə)rət/ *adjective & noun*. M20.
[ORIGIN from IN-[3] + NUMERATE *adjective*.]
▸**A** *adjective*. Unacquainted with the basic principles of mathematics and science; not numerate. M20.
▸**B** *noun*. An innumerate person. L20.

innumerous /ɪˈnjuːm(ə)rəs/ *adjective*. Now *literary*. M16.
[ORIGIN Late Latin *innumerosus*, formed as IN-[3] + NUMEROUS.]
Innumerable.

innutrition /ɪnjʊˈtrɪʃ(ə)n/ *noun*. L18.
[ORIGIN from IN-[3] + NUTRITION.]
Lack of nutrition or nourishment.

innutritious /ɪnjʊˈtrɪʃəs/ *adjective*. L18.
[ORIGIN from IN-[3] + NUTRITIOUS.]
Not nutritious; providing no nourishment.

innutritive /ɪˈnjuːtrɪtɪv/ *adjective*. M19.
[ORIGIN from IN-[3] + NUTRITIVE.]
= INNUTRITIOUS.

ino- /ˈɪnəʊ/ *combining form* of Greek *is* (genit. *inos*) fibre, muscle: see **-O-**.
Forming mostly nouns in PHYSIOLOGY & BIOCHEMISTRY.
■ **inogen** *noun* (*obsolete* exc. *hist.*) the supposed energy-yielding substance of muscle L19. **inolith** *noun* (MEDICINE) a fibrous concretion L19.

-ino /ˈiːnəʊ/ *suffix*. Pl. **-inos**.
[ORIGIN Extracted from NEUTRINO.]
PARTICLE PHYSICS. Forming names of particles and quanta from the names of bosons of which they are supersymmetric counterparts, as ***gravitino***.

†**inobedience** *noun*. ME–L19.
[ORIGIN Old French *inobediance* from late Latin *inoboedientia*, formed as IN-[3] + Latin *obedientia* OBEDIENCE.]
= DISOBEDIENCE.

†**inobedient** *adjective*. ME–E19.
[ORIGIN Old French *inobedient* or late Latin *inobedient-*, formed as IN-[3] + Latin *oboedient-* OBEDIENT.]
= DISOBEDIENT.

inobnoxious /ɪnəbˈnɒkʃəs/ *adjective*. *rare*. M17.
[ORIGIN from IN-[3] + OBNOXIOUS.]
Not obnoxious; not exposed *to*.

inobservable /ɪnəbˈzəːvəb(ə)l/ *adjective*. Long *rare*. E17.
[ORIGIN Latin *inobservabilis*, formed as IN-[3] + *observabilis* OBSERVABLE *adjective*.]
Unable to be observed, not noticeable.

inobservance /ɪnəbˈzəːv(ə)ns/ *noun*. E17.
[ORIGIN French, or Latin *inobservantia*, formed as IN-[3] + *observantia* OBSERVANCE.]
1 Failure to observe or notice; inattention. E17.
2 Failure to keep or observe a law, custom, promise, etc. E17.
■ Also **inobservancy** *noun* (*rare*) L17.

inobservant /ɪnəbˈzəːv(ə)nt/ *adjective*. M17.
[ORIGIN Late Latin *inobservant-*, formed as IN-[3] + OBSERVE + -ANT[1].]
That does not observe or notice; unobserving.

inobservation /ˌɪnɒbzəˈveɪʃ(ə)n/ *noun*. *rare*. L16.
[ORIGIN from IN-[3] + OBSERVATION.]
†**1** = INOBSERVANCE 2. L16–E18.
2 = INOBSERVANCE 1. E18.

inobtrusive /ɪnəbˈtruːsɪv/ *adjective*. *rare*. L18.
[ORIGIN from IN-[3] + OBTRUSIVE.]
Unobtrusive; modest, retiring.

inoccupation /ˌɪnɒkjʊˈpeɪʃ(ə)n/ *noun*. L18.
[ORIGIN from IN-[3] + OCCUPATION.]
Lack of occupation; unoccupied condition.

inocula *noun* pl. of INOCULUM.

inoculable /ɪˈnɒkjʊləb(ə)l/ *adjective*. M19.
[ORIGIN from INOCULATE + -ABLE.]
Able to be infected or transmitted by inoculation.
■ **inoculaˈbility** *noun* M19.

inoculant /ɪˈnɒkjʊl(ə)nt/ *noun*. E20.
[ORIGIN from INOCULATE + -ANT[1].]
A substance suitable for inoculating, esp. (METALLURGY) into molten metal.

inoculate /ɪˈnɒkjʊleɪt/ *verb*. LME.
[ORIGIN Latin *inoculat-* pa. ppl stem of *inoculare* engraft, implant, formed as IN-[2] + *oculus* eye, bud: see -ATE[3].]
1 *verb trans.* HORTICULTURE. Graft (a bud, a shoot) into a plant of a different type; subject (a plant) to budding. Now *rare* or *obsolete*. LME.

fig.: SHAKES. *Haml.* Virtue cannot so inoculate our old stock but we shall relish of it.

2 MEDICINE & BIOLOGY. **a** *verb trans.* Introduce (an infective agent) into an organism. Also, introduce (cells or organisms) into a culture medium. E18. ▸**b** *verb trans.* Introduce an infective agent into (an organism), esp. so as to immunize against a disease; vaccinate. Also, introduce cells or organisms into (a culture medium). E18. ▸**c** *verb intrans.* Perform inoculation. M18. ▸**d** *verb trans.* *fig.* Imbue (a person, community, etc.) *with* a feeling, habit, etc. E19.

3 *verb trans.* METALLURGY. Add a substance to (a molten metal) in order to modify the microstructure of the cast metal. M20.
■ **inoculative** *adjective* characterized by or pertaining to inoculation E18. **inoculator** *noun* E17.

inoculation /ɪˌnɒkjʊˈleɪʃ(ə)n/ *noun.* LME.
[ORIGIN Latin *inoculatio(n-)* grafting, formed as INOCULATE: see -ATION.]
†**1** HORTICULTURE. Grafting, esp. of a bud into a plant of a different type. LME–L18.
2 **a** MEDICINE & VETERINARY MEDICINE. The deliberate introduction into the body of a micro-organism (orig. *spec.*, of smallpox virus), esp. in order to induce immunity to a disease; vaccination. Also occas., accidental infection through a wound. E18. ▸**b** MICROBIOLOGY. The (usu. deliberate) introduction of a micro-organism into a plant, or into a culture medium. L19.
3 METALLURGY. The addition of an inoculant to molten metal. M20.

inoculist /ɪˈnɒkjʊlɪst/ *noun. rare.* L18.
[ORIGIN from INOCULATION + -IST. Cf. French *inoculiste.*]
A person who practises or advocates inoculation.

inoculum /ɪˈnɒkjʊləm/ *noun.* Pl. **-la** /-lə/. E20.
[ORIGIN from Latin *inoculare* INOCULATE after *coagulum.*]
(A quantity of) infective material used for or capable of inoculating an organism or culture medium.

†**inodiate** *verb trans.* M17–E18.
[ORIGIN Late Latin *inodiat-* pa. ppl stem of *inodiare*, ult. from Latin *in odio*: see ANNOY *noun*, -ATE[3].]
Make odious.

inodorous /ɪnˈəʊd(ə)rəs/ *adjective.* M17.
[ORIGIN from Latin *inodorus* (formed as IN-[3] + *odorus* ODOROUS) + -OUS, or from IN-[3] + ODOROUS.]
1 Without odour, smell, or scent. M17.
2 Having an unpleasant smell; malodorous. E19.
■ **inodorously** *adverb* M19.

in-off /ɪnˈɒf/ *noun.* M20.
[ORIGIN from IN *adverb* + OFF *preposition.*]
BILLIARDS & SNOOKER. = ***losing hazard*** s.v. HAZARD *noun.*

inoffensive /ɪnəˈfɛnsɪv/ *adjective.* E17.
[ORIGIN from IN-[3] + OFFENSIVE *adjective.*]
1 Not objectionable or offensive; not causing offence. E17.
J. HELLER He laughed in the friendliest, most inoffensive fashion.
2 Doing or causing no harm; innocuous, unoffending. M17.
R. DAVIES Sherry is not the inoffensive drink innocent people suppose.
■ **inoffensively** *adverb* L16. **inoffensiveness** *noun* M17.

inofficial /ɪnəˈfɪʃ(ə)l/ *adjective. rare.* M17.
[ORIGIN from IN-[3] + OFFICIAL *adjective.*]
Not official, unofficial.

inofficious /ɪnəˈfɪʃəs/ *adjective.* E17.
[ORIGIN Latin *inofficiosus*, formed as IN-[3] + *officiosus* OFFICIOUS, or from IN-[3] + OFFICIOUS.]
†**1** Not ready to do one's duty; not inclined to oblige. E17–M19.
2 LAW. Not in accordance with moral duty. M17. **inofficious testament**: making no legacy to relatives or others who have a moral claim on the testator.
3 Without purpose, function, or operation. L19.

inoperable /ɪnˈɒp(ə)rəb(ə)l/ *adjective.* L19.
[ORIGIN from IN-[3] + OPERABLE.]
1 Unable to be operated on successfully, unsuitable for a surgical operation. L19.
I. MURDOCH She developed a quick inoperable tumour and passed away.
2 Unable to be operated or used; unfit for use; unworkable, impractical. M20.
Daily Telegraph Eight of the fire extinguishers were inoperable. V. S. NAIPAUL That gift of fantasy became inoperable as soon as I came to England.
■ **inoperaˈbility** *noun* M20. **inoperably** *adverb* L20.

inoperative /ɪnˈɒp(ə)rətɪv/ *adjective.* M17.
[ORIGIN from IN-[3] + OPERATIVE *adjective.*]
Not operative; not working; LAW without practical force, invalid.
■ **inoperativeness** *noun* L19.

inoperculate /ɪnəˈpəːkjʊlət/ *adjective & noun.* M19.
[ORIGIN from IN-[3] + OPERCULATE *adjective.*]
BOTANY & ZOOLOGY. ▸**A** *adjective.* Lacking an operculum (as certain snails, fungal asci, etc.). M19.
▸**B** *noun.* An inoperculate organism (esp. a fungus). M20.

†**inopinate** *adjective.* L16–E19.
[ORIGIN Latin *inopinatus*, formed as IN-[3] + *opinatus* pa. pple of *opinari* suppose, believe, think: see -ATE[2].]
Not thought of; unexpected.

inopportune /ɪnˈɒpətjuːn, ˌɪnɒpəˈtjuːn/ *adjective.* E16.
[ORIGIN Late Latin *inopportunus* unfitting, formed as IN-[3] + *opportunus* OPPORTUNE.]
Not opportune; inappropriate, inconvenient; unsuited to the moment or occasion; untimely.
■ **inopportunely** *adverb* M16. **inopportuneness** *noun* M19. **inopportunism** *noun* the habit of acting inopportunely; the state or fact of being inopportune: L19.

inopportunist /ˌɪnɒpəˈtjuːnɪst/ *noun & adjective.* L19.
[ORIGIN from INOPPORTUNE + -IST, after *opportunist.*]
▸**A** *noun.* A person who believes a policy or action to be inopportune; *esp.* (*hist.*) a person who in 1870 opposed the doctrine of papal infallibility as inopportune. L19.
▸**B** *adjective.* Of or belonging to inopportunists. L19.

inopportunity /ˌɪnɒpəˈtjuːnɪti/ *noun.* E16.
[ORIGIN Late Latin *inopportunitas*, formed as INOPPORTUNE, or from INOPPORTUNE: see -ITY.]
The quality or fact of being inopportune.

inoppressive /ɪnəˈprɛsɪv/ *adjective. rare.* M17.
[ORIGIN from IN-[3] + OPPRESSIVE *adjective.*]
Not oppressive.

inoppugnable /ɪnəˈpʌgnəb(ə)l/ *adjective. rare.* L19.
[ORIGIN from IN-[3] + OPPUGN + -ABLE.]
Unassailable.

inorb /ɪˈnɔːb/ *verb trans.* M19.
[ORIGIN from IN-[2] + ORB *noun*[1].]
Place in an orb; enclose or surround with an orb; encircle.

inorderly /ɪnˈɔːdəli/ *adverb & adjective.* Chiefly *Scot.* Now *rare.* L15.
[ORIGIN from IN-[3] + ORDERLY *adverb, adjective.*]
▸**A** *adverb.* In a disorderly manner, irregularly. L15.
▸**B** *adjective.* Disorderly, irregular. L16.

inordinacy /ɪˈnɔːdɪnəsi/ *noun.* E17.
[ORIGIN from INORDINATE: see -ACY.]
The quality or condition of being inordinate; immoderation.

†**inordinance** *noun.* LME–L18.
[ORIGIN from IN-[3] + ORDINANCE, assoc. with INORDINATE.]
An inordinate action or practice; an excess.

inordinancy /ɪˈnɔːdɪnənsi/ *noun.* Now *rare.* E17.
[ORIGIN formed as INORDINANCE: see -ANCY.]
Inordinacy.

inordinate /ɪˈnɔːdɪnət/ *adjective.* LME.
[ORIGIN Latin *inordinatus*, formed as IN-[3] + *ordinatus* pa. pple of *ordinare* ORDAIN: see -ATE[2].]
1 Devoid of order; deviating from the rule; irregular; not controlled or restrained. LME.
J. R. ILLINGWORTH To restore this inordinate state of humanity to order.
2 Not kept within orderly limits; immoderate, excessive. LME.
A. S. BYATT There are faces in history that have attracted an inordinate share of devotion.
3 Of a person: not conforming or subject to law or order; disorderly, unrestrained in feelings or conduct. LME.
K. TYNAN Shakespeare is dealing with the problem of inordinate men.
†**4** MATH. Irregular; not in regular order; not equilateral. L16–E19.
■ **inordinately** *adverb* LME. **inordinateness** *noun* L16.

inordination /ɪˌnɔːdɪˈneɪʃ(ə)n/ *noun.* Now *rare.* E17.
[ORIGIN Latin *inordinatio(n-)* disorder, formed as IN-[3] + *ordinatio(n-)* ORDINATION.]
Inordinacy.

inorganic /ɪnɔːˈganɪk/ *adjective & noun.* L18.
[ORIGIN from IN-[3] + ORGANIC.]
▸**A** *adjective* **1** **a** Not having the characteristics of living organisms; inanimate; not composed of or derived from living matter. L18. ▸**b** CHEMISTRY. Orig., of, pertaining to, or designating substances not derived from or found in living organisms. Now, of, pertaining to, or designating substances which do not contain carbon (except in some simple cases: see note below). Cf. ORGANIC *adjective* 4b. M19.
b inorganic chemistry the branch of chemistry that deals with the properties and reactions of inorganic substances.
2 Not provided with or acting by bodily organs. E19.
SHELLEY Speak Spirit! from thine inorganic voice I only know that thou art moving near.
3 Not arising or growing naturally from an organization or structure; artificial; extraneous. M19.
4 Without organization or systematic arrangement. M19.
▸**B** *noun.* CHEMISTRY. An inorganic chemical. M20.
– NOTE: Simple compounds of carbon, as oxides, carbonates, carbides, and forms of the pure element, as diamond and graphite, are classed as inorganic.
■ †**inorganical** *adjective* (**a**) = INORGANIC *adjective* 2; (**b**) = INORGANIC *adjective* 1: only in 17. **inorganically** *adverb* (**a**) without (reference to) organization; (**b**) not by the action of living organisms: L17.

inorganisation *noun,* **inorganised** *adjective* vars. of INORGANIZATION, INORGANIZED.

inorganization /ˌɪnɔːg(ə)nʌɪˈzeɪʃ(ə)n/ *noun.* Also **-isation**. M19.
[ORIGIN from IN-[3] + ORGANIZATION.]
Absence of organization; unorganized condition.

inorganized /ɪnˈɔːg(ə)nʌɪzd/ *adjective.* Also **-ised**. M17.
[ORIGIN from IN-[3] + ORGANIZE *verb* + -ED[1].]
Not organized; lacking organization.

inornate /ɪnˈɔːnɪt, ɪnɔːˈneɪt/ *adjective.* E16.
[ORIGIN Latin *inornatus*, formed as IN-[3] + *ornatus* ORNATE, or from IN-[3] + ORNATE *adjective.*]
Not ornate; unadorned, plain; simple.

inosculate /ɪˈnɒskjʊleɪt/ *verb intrans. & trans.* L17.
[ORIGIN from IN-[2] + Latin *osculare* provide with a mouth or outlet, from *osculum* dim. of *os* mouth, after Greek *anastomoun* (see ANASTOMOSIS): see -ATE[3].]
1 Chiefly ANATOMY. (Cause to) be united by interpenetrating or fitting closely together; intertwine. (Foll. by *with.*) *arch.* L17.
2 ANATOMY. Connect or be connected by anastomosis; anastomose. *arch.* L17.
3 *transf. & fig.* (Cause to) grow together, pass into, or unite closely. E19.
■ **inoscuˈlation** *noun* L17.

inosic /ɪˈnəʊsɪk/ *adjective.* M19.
[ORIGIN from INO- + -OSE[2] + -IC.]
= INOSINIC.
■ **inosate** *noun* = INOSINATE M19.

inosine /ˈɪnə(ʊ)siːn/ *noun.* Also †**-in**. E20.
[ORIGIN formed as INOSIC + -INE[5], -IN[1].]
BIOCHEMISTRY. A naturally occurring nucleoside composed of hypoxanthine linked to ribose, which is an important intermediate in the metabolism of purine and is used in kidney transplantation to provide a temporary source of sugar.

inosinic /ɪnə(ʊ)ˈsɪnɪk/ *adjective.* M19.
[ORIGIN formed as INOSIC + -IC.]
BIOCHEMISTRY. ***inosinic acid***, a colourless crystalline organic acid, the phosphate of inosine, which is important in nucleic acid synthesis.
■ **inosinate** /ɪˈnəʊsɪneɪt/ *noun* a salt or ester of inosinic acid M19.

†**inosite** *noun.* M–L19.
[ORIGIN formed as INOSIC + -ITE[1].]
CHEMISTRY. = INOSITOL.

inositol /ʌɪˈnəʊsɪtɒl/ *noun.* L19.
[ORIGIN from INOSITE + -OL.]
BIOCHEMISTRY. Each of the nine stereoisomers of hexahydroxycyclohexane, $(\cdot CHOH \cdot)_6$; *spec.* = MYO-INOSITOL.

inostensible /ɪnɒˈstɛnsɪb(ə)l/ *adjective.* L18.
[ORIGIN from IN-[3] + OSTENSIBLE.]
Not ostensible; unavowed.
■ **inostensibly** *adverb* L18.

inotropism /ɪnə(ʊ)ˈtrəʊpɪz(ə)m/ *noun.* E20.
[ORIGIN from INO- + TROPISM.]
PHYSIOLOGY. Modification of the force or speed of contraction of muscle.
■ **inotropic** /-ˈtrəʊpɪk, -ˈtrɒpɪk/ *adjective* E20.

in ovo /ɪn ˈəʊvəʊ/ *adverbial phr.* M19.
[ORIGIN Latin.]
In the egg; in embryo (*lit. & fig.*).

inower /ɪnˈaʊə, ɪnˈəʊə/ *adverb. Scot.* M16.
[ORIGIN from IN *adverb* + Scot. form of OVER *adverb.*]
In towards some point; *esp.* nearer a fire.

inoxidable /ɪnˈɒksɪdəb(ə)l/ *adjective. rare.* M19.
[ORIGIN from IN-[3] + OXIDABLE.]
= INOXIDIZABLE.

inoxidizable /ɪnˈɒksɪdʌɪzəb(ə)l/ *adjective.* Also **-isable**. M19.
[ORIGIN from IN-[3] + OXIDIZABLE.]
Not (readily) oxidizable; not susceptible to rusting.

in pari materia /ɪn ˌpɑːri məˈtɛːrɪə, ɪn ˌpɛːri məˈtɪərɪə/ *adverbial phr.* M19.
[ORIGIN Latin.]
In an equivalent case or position.

in partibus /ɪn ˈpɑːtɪbəs/ *adverbial phr.* L17.
[ORIGIN Latin *in partibus (infidelium)* in the regions (of the infidels).]
ROMAN CATHOLIC CHURCH. In full ***in partibus infidelium*** /ɪnfɪˈdeɪlɪəm, -ˈdiːlɪ-/. In heretical territory (with ref. to a titular bishop etc., esp. in a Muslim country).

in parvo /ɪn ˈpɑːvəʊ, -wəʊ/ *adverbial phr.* E20.
[ORIGIN Latin.]
In little, in miniature, on a small scale.

inpatient /ˈɪnpeɪʃ(ə)nt/ *noun.* M18.
[ORIGIN from IN-[1] + PATIENT *noun.*]
A patient who stays overnight in a hospital where he or she receives medical attention. Opp. ***outpatient***.

in pectore /ɪn ˈpɛktəri/ *adverbial phr.* M19.
[ORIGIN Latin = in one's breast.]
= IN PETTO 1.

in perpetuum /ɪn pəˈpɛtjʊəm/ *adverbial phr.* M17.
[ORIGIN Latin.]
For all time, in perpetuity.

in personam /ɪn pəˈsəʊnam/ *adjectival phr.* L18.
[ORIGIN Latin = against a person.]
LAW. Made or availing against or affecting a specific person only; imposing a personal liability. Freq. *postpositive*. Cf. IN REM.

in petto /ɪn ˈpɛtəʊ/ *adverbial phr.* L17.
[ORIGIN Italian = in the breast.]
1 In contemplation; undisclosed, secretly, (esp. of the appointment of cardinals not named as such). L17.
2 [By confusion with PETTY *adjective*.] In miniature, on a small scale; in short. M19.

in-phase /ˈɪnfeɪz, ɪnˈfeɪz/ *adjective.* E20.
[ORIGIN from IN-[1] + PHASE *noun*.]
Of, pertaining to, or designating electrical signals that are in phase.

in-pig /ɪnˈpɪɡ, ˈɪnpɪɡ/ *adjective.* M20.
[ORIGIN from IN-[1] + PIG *noun*[1].]
Of a sow: that is in pig; pregnant.

in pontificalibus /ɪn ˌpɒntɪfɪˈkeɪlɪbəs, -ˈkɑːl-/ *adverbial phr.* LME.
[ORIGIN Latin: see also PONTIFICALIBUS.]
In the full vestments of a cardinal, archbishop, etc.; in pontificals.

in posse /ɪn ˈpɒsi/ *adjectival phr.* L16.
[ORIGIN Latin.]
In the condition of being possible. Opp. IN ESSE.

in potentia /ɪn pəˈtɛnʃɪə/ *adverbial phr.* E17.
[ORIGIN Latin.]
In potentiality.

inpouring /ˈɪnpɔːrɪŋ/ *noun.* E18.
[ORIGIN from IN-[1] + POURING *noun*.]
The action or an act of pouring something in; (an) infusion. Also, (an) inflow, (an) inrush.

in propria persona /ɪn ˌprəʊprɪə pəˈsəʊnə, pəː-/ *adverbial phr.* M17.
[ORIGIN Latin.]
In one's own person.

in puris naturalibus /ɪn ˌpjʊərɪs natjʊˈrɑːlɪbəs, -ˈreɪl-/ *adverbial phr.* E17.
[ORIGIN Latin: cf. PURIS NATURALIBUS.]
In one's natural state; stark naked.

input /ˈɪnpʊt/ *noun.* E16.
[ORIGIN from IN-[1] + PUT *noun*[1].]
†**1** An insertion. *Scot.* Only in E16.
2 A sum put in; a contribution. *Scot.* M17.
3 What is put into or utilized by any process or system; something contributed to a whole. L19. ▸**b** The energy supplied to a machine; *spec.* an electrical signal entering an electronic device. E20. ▸**c** ECONOMICS. The total resources (including raw materials, manpower, etc.) necessary to production, which are deducted from output in calculating profits. E20. ▸**d** Data or program instructions fed into or processed by a computer. M20.

C. HOPE We weren't connected to the structures of Government power, we had no input there. **c** *Ecologist* The poor . . never will be able to pay for . . the inputs required for technological agriculture.

4 A place where or a device through which an input (esp. an electrical signal) may enter a system. E20.

Hi-Fi Sound This recorder has inputs for microphone, radio and magnetic and/or ceramic pickup cartridges.

5 The process of putting in or feeding in; *esp.* the feeding of data etc. into a computer. M20.

H. M. ROSENBERG A counter . . enables the data to be recorded automatically in digital form for computer input.

input /ˈɪnpʊt/ *verb trans.* Infl. **-tt-**. Pa. t. & pple **-put**, (sense 3 also) **-putted**. LME.
[ORIGIN from IN-[1] + PUT *verb*[1]: in earliest use after Latin *imponere*, in mod. use after the noun.]
†**1** Put on, impose. Only in LME.
†**2** Install as a tenant; appoint to an office. *Scot.* L15–M18.
3 Feed (data, a program) into a computer. (Foll. by *to*, *into*.) M20.

inquartation /ɪnkwɔːˈteɪʃ(ə)n/ *noun.* L19.
[ORIGIN French, or from IN-[2] + QUARTATION.]
The addition of silver to gold so as to make the proportions at least three to one prior to purification of the gold using nitric acid.

inquest /ˈɪnkwɛst/ *noun.* Also †**en-**. ME.
[ORIGIN Old French *enqueste* (mod. *enquête*) from Proto-Romance & medieval Latin *inquesta* use as noun of fem. pa. pple of Proto-Romance var. of Latin *inquirere* INQUIRE.]
1 A judicial inquiry by means of a jury to decide a matter of fact; *spec.* an inquiry by a coroner's court into the cause of a sudden, unexplained, or suspicious death. Formerly, any official inquiry into a matter of public interest. ME.

W. STUBBS The great inquest of all, the Domesday survey. S. COX The searching inquest of the Judge eternal.

inquest of office an inquiry held by a jury and an officer of the Crown to decide cases of escheat, forfeiture, etc., that would entitle the Crown to the possession of land.

2 A jury appointed to decide a matter of fact; *spec.* a coroner's jury. ME.
grand inquest, **great inquest** *hist.* a grand jury (***grand inquest of the nation***, ***great inquest of the nation***, the House of Commons).
3 *gen.* & *transf.* †**a** A question, a query. LME–M19. ▸†**b** A search for something; orig. *esp.* a knight's quest for adventure. L15–L17. ▸**c** An investigation into a matter. Now chiefly (*colloq.*) a discussion, after the event, of a (poor) performance in a game, an examination, etc. E17.

inquiet /ɪnˈkwʌɪət/ *adjective.* Now *rare*. LME.
[ORIGIN Latin *inquietus*, formed as IN-[3] + QUIET *adjective*.]
†**1** Restless, turbulent. LME–M16.
2 Anxious, uneasy in mind. E16.
■ **inquietly** *adverb* (*rare*) LME.

inquiet /ɪnˈkwʌɪət/ *verb trans.* Now *rare*. LME.
[ORIGIN Old French & mod. French *inquiéter* from Latin *inquietare*, formed as INQUIET *adjective*.]
1 Disturb the peace or repose of (a person); harass, molest. LME.
2 Make uneasy, disquiet. L15.
■ **inquieˈtation** *noun* the action of disturbing or molesting; the condition of being disturbed: LME.

inquietude /ɪnˈkwʌɪətjuːd/ *noun.* LME.
[ORIGIN Old French & mod. French *inquiétude* or late Latin *inquietudo*, formed as INQUIET *adjective*: see -TUDE.]
†**1** Disturbance of one's peace or repose; molestation. LME–L18.
2 MEDICINE. Restlessness of the body caused by pain, discomfort, etc. Now *rare*. L16.
3 Uneasiness of mind, disquietude; in *pl.*, disquieting thoughts. M17.

inquilab /ˈɪŋkɪlɑːb/ *noun.* M20.
[ORIGIN Urdu *inqalāb*, *inqilāb* change, turn, revolution.]
In the Indian subcontinent: a revolution or uprising.

inquiline /ˈɪnkwɪlʌɪn/ *noun.* M17.
[ORIGIN Latin *inquilinus* sojourner, from *incolere* inhabit, formed as IN-[2] + *colere* dwell: see -INE[1].]
1 A person who sojourns or lodges in a place. *rare.* M17.
2 An animal which lives in the abode of another which tolerates its presence; *spec.* in ENTOMOLOGY, an insect which lodges in a gall produced by another species. L19.
■ **inquilinism** /ˈɪnkwɪlɪnɪz(ə)m/ *noun* the habit or condition of being an inquiline L20. **inquiˈlinous** *adjective* living in the nest or gall of another animal L19.

inquinate /ˈɪnkwɪneɪt/ *verb trans.* Now *rare*. M16.
[ORIGIN Latin *inquinat-* pa. ppl stem of *inquinare* pollute: see -ATE[3].]
Pollute, taint, corrupt.
■ **inquiˈnation** *noun* (***a***) the action of polluting; polluted condition; (***b***) a defilement, a polluting agent: LME.

inquirable /ɪnˈkwʌɪərəb(ə)l/ *adjective.* Now *rare* or *obsolete*. Also **en-** /ɪn-, ɛn-/. L15.
[ORIGIN from INQUIRE + -ABLE.]
Chiefly LAW. That admits or calls for inquiry.

inquiration /ɪnkwʌɪˈreɪʃ(ə)n/ *noun. dial.* & *colloq.* Also **en-** /ɪn-, ɛn-/. L18.
[ORIGIN Irreg. from INQUIRE + -ATION.]
Enquiry; an enquiry.

inquire /ɪnˈkwʌɪə/ *verb.* Also **en-** /ɪn-, ɛn-/ (see note below). ME.
[ORIGIN Old French *enquerre* (mod. new formation *enquérir*) from Proto-Romance var. of Latin *inquirere*, formed as IN-[2] + *quaerere* ask.]
1 †**a** *verb trans.* Examine, investigate. ME–L18. ▸**b** *verb intrans.* Make investigation (*into*). ME.

a J. WOODALL The use of a Probe . . sometimes to enquire the depth of a wound. **b** B. BETTELHEIM He felt no need to inquire into my motives.

2 *verb trans.* Seek knowledge of (a thing) by asking a question; ask to be told. (Foll. by subord. clause (& direct speech) or (now less usu.) simple obj., *of* or (*Scot.*) *at* the person asked.) ME.

R. BURNS The wily mother . . inquires his name. S. LEWIS Club members . . stopped him to inquire, 'How's your good lady getting on?' W. TREVOR She enquired of me if I knew . . Lady Lord-Blood.

3 *verb intrans.* Put a question or questions; ask. (Foll. by *about* or *after* a matter, *of* or (*Scot.*) *at* the person asked.) ME. ▸**b** Foll. by *for*, (arch.) *after*: make request for (a thing); ask to see (a person). E16.

H. JAMES She enquired scrupulously about her husband's health. M. COX He had been encouraged to inquire freely of his parents on religious matters. **b** AV *Acts* 9:11 Inquire in the house of Judas, for one called Saul of Tarsus. *Harper's Magazine* I enquired at house after house for board.

inquire after *spec.* make inquiries about the health etc. of.
†**4** *verb trans.* Question, interrogate, (a person). ME–L17.
†**5** *verb trans.* Search for, try to find; *esp.* search *out*. ME–L18.
†**6** *verb trans.* Call for, require. *rare.* E16–M17.
†**7** *verb trans.* Name, call. *rare* (Spenser). Only in L16.
– NOTE: British English tends to distinguish *enquire* meaning 'ask' from *inquire* meaning 'make investigation'; the distinction is not made in North America, where *inquire* is generally the form used.
■ **inquirer** *noun* L16. **inquiring** *ppl adjective* that inquires; seeking or disposed to seek information, answers, etc.: L16. **inquiringly** *adverb* M17.

inquirendo /ɪnkwʌɪˈrɛndəʊ/ *noun.* Pl. **-os**. E17.
[ORIGIN Latin (= by inquiring), ablative gerund of *inquirere* INQUIRE.]
1 LAW (now *hist.*). An authorization to an official to make investigation on behalf of the Crown or government. E17.
2 *gen.* An investigation. M19.

inquiry /ɪnˈkwʌɪri/ *noun.* Also **en-** /ɪn-, ɛn-/ (see note below). LME.
[ORIGIN from INQUIRE + -Y[3].]
▸ **I 1** Investigation, examination. LME.
2 An investigation, an examination, *esp.* an official one; *spec.* (in full ***public inquiry***) a judicial investigation, held under the auspices of a Government department, into a matter of public concern. E16.

J. BARTH A special . . inquiry into the circumstances surrounding his death.

▸ **II 3** The putting of a question, asking, interrogation; COMMERCE demand for a commodity. LME.

A. GOLDING We coulde learne nothinge therof by enquiry. *Stock & Land* (*Melbourne*) Inquiry for good cattle from northern N.S.W. had strengthened considerably since the rain.

4 A question, a query. M16.

N. MAILER Leonard . . had already made his inquiries about who owned the estate.

– PHRASES: ***court of inquiry***: see COURT *noun*[1]. ***directory enquiries***: see DIRECTORY *noun*. ***help the police in their enquiries***, ***help the police with their enquiries***: see HELP *verb* 5c. ***jury of inquiry***: see JURY *noun*. ***public inquiry***: see sense 2 above. ***tribunal of inquiry***: see TRIBUNAL *noun* 3. ***writ of inquiry***: see WRIT *noun* 2.
– COMB.: **inquiry agent** a private detective; **inquiry office** an office answering questions from callers etc.
– NOTE: In British English freq. spelled *in-* in branch I, *en-* in branch II; cf. INQUIRE *verb*.

I

†**inquisite** *verb trans.* M17–M18.
[ORIGIN from Latin *inquisit-* (see INQUISITION *noun*) or back-form. from INQUISITION *noun*.]
1 Proceed against (a person) by the methods of the Inquisition. M17–M18.
2 Make inquiry into, investigate. M17–M18.

inquisition /ɪŋkwɪˈzɪʃ(ə)n/ *noun.* In sense 3 usu. **I-**. LME.
[ORIGIN Old French & mod. French from Latin *inquisitio(n-)*, from *inquisit-* pa. ppl stem of *inquirere* INQUIRE: see -ION.]
1 (An instance of) the action or process of inquiring deeply into a matter in order to discover the facts; (a) searching examination or investigation. LME.
2 A judicial inquiry, an inquest. Also, a document recording the results of such an inquiry. LME.
3 *hist.*. *The* judicial institution set up by the papacy in 1232 for the persecution of heresy by special ecclesiastical courts. Also (in full ***Spanish Inquisition***), *the* organization with similar functions established under the Spanish crown in 1479, which became notorious for its severity. E16.
4 A relentless questioning of a person. M19.

K. WILLIAMS An interview which she described as 'a 1½ hour inquisition'.

■ **inquisitional** *adjective* pertaining to the Inquisition or to (esp. harsh or relentless) inquiry M17.

inquisition /ɪŋkwɪˈzɪʃ(ə)n/ *verb trans.* M17.
[ORIGIN from the noun.]
hist. Proceed against by the Inquisition.

inquisitive /ɪnˈkwɪzɪtɪv/ *adjective.* LME.
[ORIGIN Old French *inquisitif*, *-tive* from late Latin *inquisitivus*, from Latin *inquisit-*: see INQUISITION *noun*, -IVE.]
Given to or desirous of inquiring; of an inquiring turn of mind; intellectually curious; *spec.* unduly curious about the affairs of others, prying.

CONAN DOYLE The garbage papers which cater for an inquisitive public. A. F. DOUGLAS-HOME Man is incurably inquisitive, and always trying to discover the origin of things. J. MORTIMER A pale man with inquisitive, almost colourless eyes. A. BROOKNER They were not inquisitive about my habits or relationships.

■ **inquisitively** *adverb* L16. **inquisitiveness** *noun* L16.

inquisitor /ɪnˈkwɪzɪtə/ *noun.* In sense 2 also **I-**. LME.
[ORIGIN French *inquisiteur* (Anglo-Norman *-tour*) from Latin *inquisitor*, from *inquisit-*: see INQUISITION *noun*, -OR.]
1 A person whose official duty is to inquire or examine (in matters of crime, taxation, etc.); *gen.* a curious inquirer, an investigator. LME. ▸†**b** An informer, a spy. L16–L18.
2 *hist.* An officer of the Inquisition, esp. the Spanish Inquisition. M16.
Grand Inquisitor the director of the court of the Inquisition in some countries. **Inquisitor General** the head of the Spanish Inquisition.
■ **inquisitorship** *noun* M19. **inquisitress** *noun* a female inquisitor E18.

inquisitorial /ɪnˌkwɪzɪˈtɔːrɪəl/ *adjective.* M18.
[ORIGIN formed as INQUISITORY + -AL[1].]
1 Of, relating to, or functioning as an (official) inquisitor. M18. ▸**b** Offensively or impertinently curious; prying. L18.
2 LAW. Of a system of criminal procedure: in which the judge has the duty to investigate the facts. Opp. ***accusatorial***. M19.
■ **inquisitorially** *adverb* M19. **inquisitorialness** *noun* M19.

inquisitory /ɪnˈkwɪzɪt(ə)ri/ *adjective*. Now *rare* or *obsolete*. M17.
[ORIGIN medieval Latin *inquisitorius*, from Latin INQUISITOR: see -ORY[2].]
= INQUISITORIAL 1.

inquorate /ɪnˈkwɔːrət, -eɪt/ *adjective*. L20.
[ORIGIN from IN-[3] + QUORATE.]
Of a meeting: not quorate, not having a quorum.

†**inrage** *verb* var. of ENRAGE.

†**inrail** *verb trans*. Also (earlier) **en-**. E16–E18.
[ORIGIN from IN-[1], EN-[1] + RAIL *verb*[2].]
Enclose (as) with rails; rail in.

†**inrapture** *verb* var. of ENRAPTURE.

in re /ɪn ˈreɪ, ɪn ˈriː/ *adverbial, adjectival, & prepositional phr*. E17.
[ORIGIN Latin.]
▸ **A** *adverbial phr*. In reality. E17.
▸ **B** *adjectival phr*. **1** LOGIC. = EXTRA DICTIONEM. M19.
2 PHILOSOPHY. Of a universal: existing only in the particulars that instantiate it. Cf. ANTE REM, POST REM. L19.
▸ **C** *prepositional phr*. In the (legal) case of; with regard to. Cf. RE *preposition*. L19.

†**inregister** *verb* see ENREGISTER.

in rem /ɪn ˈrɛm/ *adjectival phr*. M18.
[ORIGIN Latin = against a thing.]
LAW. Made or availing against or affecting a thing, and therefore other people generally; imposing a general liability. Freq. *postpositive*. Cf. IN PERSONAM.

in rerum natura /ɪn ˌreɪrəm nəˈtjʊərə, ˌriːrəm/ *adverbial phr*. L16.
[ORIGIN Latin.]
In nature, in the physical world.

INRI *abbreviation*.
Latin *Iesus Nazarenus Rex Iudaeorum* Jesus of Nazareth, King of the Jews.

†**inrich** *verb* var. of ENRICH.

inro /ˈɪnrəʊ/ *noun*. Pl. **-os**, same. E17.
[ORIGIN Japanese *inrō*, from *in* seal + *rō* basket.]
An ornamental box with compartments for seals, medicines, etc., formerly worn by Japanese on a girdle.

inroad /ˈɪnrəʊd/ *noun*. M16.
[ORIGIN from IN *adverb* + ROAD *noun*, in sense 'riding'.]
1 A hostile incursion; a raid, a foray. M16.
2 *transf*. & *fig*. A serious or significant encroachment (*on*, *upon*) or intrusion (*into*). Now usu. in *pl*. M17.

J. R. GREEN They protested against . . Papal inroads on the liberties of the Church. B. T. BRADFORD The Ninth Earl . . had . . made considerable inroads into their immense wealth. *Atlantic Monthly* Democrats have made substantial inroads among affluent upper-middle-class voters.

inroad /ˈɪnrəʊd/ *verb*. E17.
[ORIGIN from the noun.]
†**1** *verb trans*. Make an inroad into, invade. E–M17.
2 *verb intrans*. Make inroads. *rare*. M19.

†**inrol** *verb* var. of ENROL.

inrolled /ˈɪnrəʊld, ɪnˈrəʊld/ *adjective*. L19.
[ORIGIN from IN-[1] + ROLL *verb* + -ED[1].]
BOTANY. Having the margins rolled inwards; involute.

inrolling /ˈɪnrəʊlɪŋ/ *ppl adjective*. L19.
[ORIGIN from IN-[1] + ROLLING *adjective*.]
Of a wave etc.: that rolls in.

inroot *verb* var. of ENROOT.

inrun /ˈɪnrʌn/ *noun*. L19.
[ORIGIN from IN-[1] + RUN *noun*. In sense 2 translating German *Anlauf*.]
1 An act of running in; an inrush. L19.
2 In ski-jumping: an approach run. M20.

inrunning /ˈɪnrʌnɪŋ/ *ppl adjective*. M19.
[ORIGIN from IN-[1] + RUNNING *ppl adjective*.]
Of a bay etc.: extending far inland. Of a stream: flowing into a larger stream, the sea, etc.

inruption /ɪnˈrʌpʃ(ə)n/ *noun*. E19.
[ORIGIN Refashioning of IRRUPTION, emphasizing *in-*.]
A violent bursting in.

inrush /ˈɪnrʌʃ/ *noun*. E19.
[ORIGIN from IN-[1] + RUSH *noun*[2].]
A rushing in, an influx.

inrush /ɪnˈrʌʃ/ *verb intrans*. Now *rare*. E17.
[ORIGIN from IN-[1] + RUSH *verb*[2].]
Enter with force or speed; rush in.

inrushing /ˈɪnrʌʃɪŋ/ *ppl adjective*. M19.
[ORIGIN from IN-[1] + RUSH *verb*[2] + -ING[2].]
Entering with speed or force; rushing in.

ins *abbreviation*.
1 Inches.
2 Insurance.

†**insabbatist** *noun*. *rare*. M17–E19.
[ORIGIN from French *insabbaté* or medieval Latin *insabbatus*, *-sab(b)atatus*, + -IST.]
A member of the sect of the Waldenses.

in saecula saeculorum /ɪn ˈsʌɪkjʊlə sʌɪkjʊˈlɔːrəm/ *adverbial phr*. L16.
[ORIGIN Late Latin = to the ages of ages.]
To all eternity; for ever.

insalata /ɪnsəˈlɑːtə/ *noun*. M20.
[ORIGIN Italian, formed as SALAD.]
A salad (in Italian cookery).

insalivate /ɪnˈsalɪveɪt/ *verb trans*. M19.
[ORIGIN from IN-[2] + SALIVATE.]
1 Mix or impregnate (food) with saliva. M19.
2 Moisten with saliva. L19.
■ **insaliˈvation** *noun* M19.

insalubrious /ɪnsəˈl(j)uːbrɪəs/ *adjective*. M17.
[ORIGIN from Latin *insalubris*, formed as IN-[3] + *salubris* SALUBRIOUS: see -OUS.]
Esp. of a climate or locality: not salubrious, unhealthy.

insalubrity /ɪnsəˈl(j)uːbrɪti/ *noun*. M17.
[ORIGIN French *insalubrité* or from IN-[3] + SALUBRITY.]
Unhealthy character (esp. of a climate or locality); unwholesomeness.

insalutary /ɪnˈsaljʊt(ə)ri/ *adjective*. L17.
[ORIGIN from IN-[3] + SALUTARY *adjective*.]
1 Harmful to health; insalubrious. L17.
2 Not having a healthy mental or social influence. *rare*. M19.

insane /ɪnˈseɪn/ *adjective & noun*. M16.
[ORIGIN Latin *insanus*, formed as IN-[3] + SANE.]
▸ **A** *adjective*. **1** In a state of mind that precludes normal perception and behaviour, and ordinary social interaction; mad; psychotic. M16. ▸**b** Reserved or intended for the use of mentally ill people. E19.

P. THEROUX She lost her mind and died insane. **b** D. WIGODER I didn't need to be locked up in an insane asylum.

†**2** Causing insanity. Only in E17.

SHAKES. *Macb*. Have we eaten on the insane root That takes the reason prisoner?

3 Of an action: extremely foolish, irrational. M19.

D. DELILLO 'When are you off?' 'A seven o'clock flight . . . Isn't it insane?'

▸ **B** *noun*. **1** An insane person. *arch*. L18.
2 *collect. pl. The* class of insane people. E19.
general paralysis of the insane: see PARALYSIS 1.
■ **insanely** *adverb* M19. **insaneness** *noun* L19.

†**insanguine** *verb* see ENSANGUINE.

†**insanie** *noun*. Only in L16.
[ORIGIN French †*insanie* from Latin *insania*, formed as INSANE.]
Insanity, madness.

insanify /ɪnˈsanɪfʌɪ/ *verb*. *rare*. E19.
[ORIGIN from INSANE *adjective* + -I- + -FY.]
1 *verb trans*. Make insane. E19.
2 *verb intrans*. Cause insanity. L19.

insanitary /ɪnˈsanɪt(ə)ri/ *adjective*. L19.
[ORIGIN from IN-[3] + SANITARY.]
Not sanitary; harmful to health.
■ **insanitariness** *noun* L19.

insanitation /ɪnˌsanɪˈteɪʃ(ə)n/ *noun*. L19.
[ORIGIN from IN-[3] + SANITATION.]
Lack of sanitation; insanitary condition.

insanity /ɪnˈsanɪti/ *noun*. L16.
[ORIGIN Latin *insanitas*, formed as INSANE: see -ITY.]
1 The state or condition of being insane; mental derangement. L16.

A. G. GARDINER The mother . . whom she slew in one of her fits of insanity. A. CLARE He was . . found not guilty by reason of insanity.

2 Extreme folly or irrationality; an instance of this. M19.

insatiable /ɪnˈseɪʃəb(ə)l/ *adjective*. LME.
[ORIGIN Old French *insaciable* or Latin *insatiabilis*, formed as IN-[3] + SATIATE *verb*: see -ABLE.]
Not satiable; unable to be satisfied; inordinately greedy.

R. LINDNER You call me insatiable; you're the one who's never satisfied. J. CAREY A man with an insatiable appetite for shellfish.

■ **insatiaˈbility** *noun* M17. **insatiableness** *noun* M16. **insatiably** *adverb* L16.

insatiate /ɪnˈseɪʃɪət/ *adjective*. LME.
[ORIGIN Latin *insatiatus*, formed as IN-[3] + *satiatus* pa. pple of *satiare* SATIATE *verb*.]
That is not satiated; never satisfied. (Foll. by *of*, *for*.)

O. WILDE He has already had an enormous sum . . but is insatiate for money.

insatiated /ɪnˈseɪʃɪeɪtɪd/ *adjective*. *rare*. E18.
[ORIGIN from IN-[3] + SATIATE *verb* + -ED[1].]
Not satiated.

insatiety /ɪnsəˈtʌɪɪti/ *noun*. Now *rare*. L16.
[ORIGIN Old French *insacieté* from Latin *insatietas*, formed as IN-[3] + *satietas* SATIETY.]
The condition of being insatiate; unsatisfied desire or demand.

insaturable /ɪnˈsatʃʊrəb(ə)l, -tjʊr-/ *adjective*. LME.
[ORIGIN Latin *insaturabilis*, formed as IN-[3] + *saturare* SATURATE *verb*: see -ABLE.]
†**1** Insatiable. LME–M17.
2 Unable to be saturated. M19.

inscape /ˈɪnskeɪp/ *noun*. M19.
[ORIGIN Perh. from IN *adverb* + SCAPE *noun*[3]. Cf. SCAPE *noun*[4].]
The inward essential unique quality of an observed object as embodied in literary, artistic, etc., expression. Cf. INSTRESS.
– NOTE: Orig. in the poetic theory of the English poet Gerard Manley Hopkins (1844–89).

inscenation /ɪnsɪˈneɪʃ(ə)n/ *noun*. L19.
[ORIGIN from IN-[2] + SCENE *noun* + -ATION, prob. after German *Inszenierung*.]
(A) theatrical representation.

inscience /ˈɪnsɪəns/ *noun*. Now *rare*. L16.
[ORIGIN Latin *inscientia* ignorance, formed as IN-[3] + *scientia* knowledge: see SCIENCE.]
The condition of not knowing; ignorance.

inscient /ˈɪnsɪənt/ *adjective*. Now *rare*. L16.
[ORIGIN Latin *inscient-*, *-ens* ignorant, formed as IN-[3] + *scient-* having knowledge: see SCIENCE.]
Not knowing; ignorant.

†**insconce** *verb* var. of ENSCONCE.

inscribe /ɪnˈskrʌɪb/ *verb trans*. LME.
[ORIGIN Latin *inscribere*, formed as IN-[2] + *scribere* write.]
1 Write (a letter, word, sentence, etc., *in* or *on* stone, metal, paper, etc.), esp. so as to be conspicuous or durable. LME. ▸**b** Enter the name of (a person) on an official document or list; enrol. E17. ▸**c** Issue (stock etc.) in the form of shares with registered holders. Chiefly as ***inscribed*** *ppl adjective*. L19.

SAKI Francesca . . inscribed the figure 4 on the margin of her theatre programme. V. MEYNELL The names inscribed on the small brass tablet . . were Skeat and Wylie.

2 GEOMETRY. Draw (a figure) within another so that their boundaries touch but do not intersect. L16.

C. HUTTON To inscribe a circle in a regular polygon.

3 Mark (a sheet, tablet, etc.) with characters etc., esp. so as to be conspicuous or durable. M17. ▸**b** Place an informal dedication (*to* a person) in or on (a book etc.). M17.

V. WOOLF A disc inscribed with a name. **b** P. ROTH It was the night I received the little dictionary inscribed 'From me to you'.

■ **inscribable** *adjective* (chiefly GEOMETRY) able to be inscribed M19. **inscriber** *noun* L18.

inscript /ˈɪnskrɪpt/ *noun*. E17.
[ORIGIN Latin *inscriptum* use as noun of neut. of *inscriptus* pa. pple, formed as INSCRIPTIBLE.]
Something inscribed; an inscription.

inscriptible /ɪnˈskrɪptɪb(ə)l/ *adjective*. *rare*. L17.
[ORIGIN from Latin *inscript-* pa. ppl stem of *inscribere* INSCRIBE + -IBLE.]
GEOMETRY. Inscribable.

inscription /ɪnˈskrɪpʃ(ə)n/ *noun*. LME.
[ORIGIN Latin *inscriptio(n-)*, from *inscript-*: see INSCRIPTIBLE, -ION.]
1 Orig., a short descriptive or dedicatory passage placed at the beginning of a book; a title, a heading. Later, an informal dedication of a book etc. LME.
†**2** CIVIL & SCOTS LAW. An accusation or challenge made with the condition that proof of its falsity would render the accuser liable to penalty for calumny. L15–E18.
3 A letter, word, sentence, etc., that is inscribed on stone, metal, paper, etc., esp. so as to be conspicuous or durable. M16.

W. TREVOR An inscription on a brass plaque that read: *To Charles Edward Burrows*. M. COX Monty composed a memorial inscription.

4 ANATOMY. A marking on some organ produced by contact with another, esp. where a tendon crosses a muscle. L16.
5 GEOMETRY. The action of inscribing one figure within another. L16.
6 *gen*. The action of inscribing. Chiefly *fig*. M17.
7 The action of issuing stock etc. in the form of shares with registered holders; inscribed stock. L18.
■ **inscriptional** *adjective* L18. **inscriptionless** *adjective* M17.

inscriptive /ɪnˈskrɪptɪv/ *adjective*. M18.
[ORIGIN from Latin *inscript-* (see INSCRIPTIBLE) + -IVE.]
Of the nature of an inscription; belonging to or used in inscriptions.

inscroll /ɪnˈskrəʊl/ *verb trans*. *arch*. L17.
[ORIGIN from IN-[1], IN-[2] + SCROLL *noun*.]
Inscribe or enter on a scroll.

inscrutable /ɪnˈskruːtəb(ə)l/ *adjective & noun*. LME.
[ORIGIN ecclesiastical Latin *inscrutabilis*, formed as IN-[3] + *scrutari* to search: see SCRUTINY, -ABLE.]
▸ **A** *adjective*. **1** That cannot be understood by investigation; wholly mysterious. LME.

R. CHRISTIANSEN A supreme being of infinite power, inscrutable to human reason.

2 Impenetrable, unfathomable. *rare*. E19.

N. HAWTHORNE The guide . . held his torch down into an inscrutable pit beneath our feet.

▶ **B** *noun.* An inscrutable thing. M17.

■ **inscruta'bility** *noun* M17. **inscrutableness** *noun* E18. **inscrutably** *adverb* L16.

insculp /ɪn'skʌlp/ *verb trans.* Now *rare* or *obsolete.* Pa. pple **-sculpt**, **-sculped**. LME.
[ORIGIN Latin *insculpere*, formed as IN-[2] + *sculpere* carve.]
1 Carve or sculpt (a figure, inscription, etc.). LME.
2 Shape by cutting; ornament with carved figures or inscriptions. L16.

insculptor /ɪn'skʌlptə/ *noun. rare.* L16.
[ORIGIN from Latin *insculpt-* pa. ppl stem of *insculpere*: see INSCULP, -OR.]
A person who carves or sculpts a figure, inscription, etc.; a sculptor.

†**insculpture** *noun.* E–M17.
[ORIGIN French, formed as IN-[2] + SCULPTURE *noun.*]
A carved or sculpted figure, inscription, etc.

insculpture /ɪn'skʌlptʃə/ *verb trans. arch.* L18.
[ORIGIN from IN-[2] + SCULPTURE *verb.*]
Carve or sculpt (a figure, inscription, etc.).

in se /ɪn 'siː, 'seɪ/ *adverbial phr.* M19.
[ORIGIN Latin.]
PHILOSOPHY. In itself.

†**insearch** *verb* var. of ENSEARCH.

insecable /ɪn'sɛkəb(ə)l/ *adjective. rare.* E17.
[ORIGIN Latin *insecabilis*, formed as IN-[3] + *secabilis*, from *secare* cut: see -ABLE.]
Unable to be cut.

insect /'ɪnsɛkt/ *noun.* Pl. **insects**, **insecta** /ɪn'sɛktə/ (now only as mod. Latin taxonomic name). E17.
[ORIGIN Latin (sc. *animal*) *insectum*, pl. *insecta*, from *insect-* pa. ppl stem of *insecare* cut up or into, from *in-* IN-[2] + *secare* cut; translating Greek (sc. *zōion*) *entomon*: see ENTOMO-.]
1 Orig., any small invertebrate or (occas.) other cold-blooded animal, esp. with a segmented body and several pairs of legs. Now only as a loose extension of sense 2, any terrestrial arthropod. E17.

R. LOVELL Of Insects, few are used as meat, except snailes. MILTON At once came forth whatever creeps the ground, Insect or Worme.

2 Any member of the class Insecta of small arthropods which have the body divided into head, thorax, and abdomen, the thorax bearing three pairs of legs and usu. one or two pairs of wings. E17.
3 *fig.* An insignificant, contemptible, or annoying person. L17.

T. HEARNE He, the little Insect, was recommended to King William.

– COMB.: **insect powder**: for killing or driving away insects.
– NOTE: The modern scientific sense 2 was only gradually distinguished from the classical and popular sense 1.
■ **in'sectan** *adjective* of, belonging to, or characterizing an insect, or the class Insecta L19. **insec'tarium** *noun*, pl. **-ia** /-ɪə/, **-iums**, a place for keeping and breeding insects L19. **insectary** *noun* = INSECTARIUM L19. **insec'tiferous** *adjective* producing or containing insects E19. **insect-like** *adjective* like an insect L18. **in'sectual** *adjective* resembling an insect or insects; insignificant: E20. **insecty** *adjective* full of or containing many insects M19.

insect /ɪn'sɛkt/ *verb trans.* M17.
[ORIGIN Latin *insect-*: see INSECT *noun.*]
Cut into. Chiefly as ***insected*** *ppl adjective.*

insecta *noun pl.* see INSECT *noun.*

insecticide /ɪn'sɛktɪsʌɪd/ *noun & adjective.* M19.
[ORIGIN from INSECT *noun* + -CIDE.]
▶ **A** *noun.* **1** A person who or thing which kills insects; *spec.* a substance used to kill insects. M19.
2 The killing of insects. *rare.* M19.
▶ **B** *adjective.* Insecticidal. M19.
■ **insecti'cidal** *adjective* of, pertaining to, or of the nature of an insecticide; tending to kill insects: M19.

insectile /ɪn'sɛktʌɪl/ *adjective.* E17.
[ORIGIN from INSECT *noun* + -ILE.]
Resembling, characteristic of, or of the nature of an insect or insects; insectan; insecty.

insection /ɪn'sɛkʃ(ə)n/ *noun.* M17.
[ORIGIN Late Latin *insectio(n-)*, from *insect-*: see INSECT *noun*, -ION.]
The action of cutting into something; incision; division into sections; an incision, a division.

insectivore /ɪn'sɛktɪvɔː/ *noun.* M19.
[ORIGIN from mod. Latin *Insectivora* pl. (see below), from *insectivorus*: see INSECTIVOROUS.]
An insectivorous animal or plant; *spec.* any animal of the order Insectivora of small, short-legged, mostly nocturnal mammals, having simple teeth and often a mobile sensitive snout, including moles, hedgehogs, shrews, etc.

insectivorous /ɪnsɛk'tɪv(ə)rəs/ *adjective.* M17.
[ORIGIN from mod. Latin *insectivorus* (after Latin *carnivorus* CARNIVOROUS) + -OUS: see INSECT *noun*, -VOROUS.]
Feeding on insects; (of a plant) able to capture and digest insects (as the sundew, the Venus flytrap, etc.).

■ **insectivory** *noun* the habit of feeding on insects L20.

insectology /ɪnsɛk'tɒlədʒi/ *noun.* Now *rare.* M18.
[ORIGIN from INSECT *noun* + -OLOGY.]
Entomology, esp. as it deals with insects in relation to human economics.

insecure /ɪnsɪ'kjʊə/ *adjective.* M17.
[ORIGIN medieval Latin *insecurus* unsafe, or from IN-[3] + SECURE *adjective.*]
1 Lacking assurance or confidence, uncertain. M17.

B. BETTELHEIM How anxious and insecure we were behind our show of defiance. C. THUBRON Like an insecure child, I began to crave for any kind of contact, even abuse.

2 Unsafe; not firm; (of ice, ground, etc.) liable to give way. M17.

J. TYNDALL The ice on the edge . . was loose and insecure. T. TANNER There *was* social order and stability, but it was always precarious and insecure.

■ **insecurely** *adverb* E18. **insecureness** *noun* (*rare*) E18.

insecurity /ɪnsɪ'kjʊərɪti/ *noun.* M17.
[ORIGIN medieval Latin *insecuritas* or from IN-[3] + SECURITY.]
1 The quality or state of lacking assurance or confidence, uncertainty. M17.

D. DELILLO There was a deep restlessness in him, an insecurity. L. VAN DER POST He found at the core of their neurosis a sense of insecurity.

2 The quality or condition of being unsafe; lack of firmness; liability of ice, ground, etc., to give way. Also, an insecure or dangerous state of affairs. M17. ▸**b** An instance or case of insecurity; an insecure thing. M17.

J. H. NEWMAN The insecurity of great prosperity has been the theme of poets and philosophers.

inseeing /'ɪnsiːɪŋ/ *adjective. rare.* L16.
[ORIGIN from IN-[1] + SEEING *ppl adjective.*]
Seeing into something; having insight.

inseity /ɪn'siːɪti, -'seɪɪti/ *noun.* L19.
[ORIGIN from IN SE + -ITY.]
PHILOSOPHY. The quality or state of being in itself.

inselberg /'ɪns(ə)lbəːɡ, -z-/ *noun.* Pl. **-s**, **-e** /-ə/. E20.
[ORIGIN German, from *Insel* island + *Berg* mountain.]
PHYSICAL GEOGRAPHY. An isolated hill or mountain which rises abruptly from the surrounding landscape, esp. from an arid plain.

inseminate /ɪn'sɛmɪneɪt/ *verb trans.* E17.
[ORIGIN Latin *inseminat-* pa. ppl stem of *inseminare*, formed as IN-[2] + *seminare* sow: see -ATE[3].]
1 Sow (*lit. & fig.*). (Foll. by *in.*) E17.
2 *spec.* Introduce semen into (a female) by natural or (esp.) by artificial means. E20.
■ **inseminator** *noun* M20.

insemination /ɪn,sɛmɪ'neɪʃ(ə)n/ *noun.* M17.
[ORIGIN from INSEMINATE: see -ATION.]
1 The action or an act of inseminating, the fact of being inseminated. M17.
2 *spec.* The introduction of semen into a female by natural or (esp.) by artificial means. M19.
artificial insemination: see ARTIFICIAL *adjective* 1.

insensate /ɪn'sɛnseɪt, -sət/ *adjective.* L15.
[ORIGIN ecclesiastical Latin *insensatus*, formed as IN-[3] + *sensatus* SENSATE *adjective.*]
1 Without sense or understanding; stupid, foolish. L15.

N. MOSLEY His insensate silly . . chaff . . makes Viv rude and on the defensive.

2 Without physical sensation or feeling; inanimate. E16.

J. R. MACDUFF Dull, pulseless, unresponsive as the insensate stone. *fig.*: I. MURDOCH Conrad Lomas appeared . . , making his way across the dance floor, thrusting the insensate couples aside.

3 Without sensibility, unfeeling. M16.

N. MONSARRAT The worst characteristics of a Norman baron: insensate cruelty, consuming greed.

■ **insensately** *adverb* M19. **insensateness** *noun* (*rare*) M17.

insense /ɪn'sɛns/ *verb trans. obsolete* exc. *dial.* Also (earlier) †**en-**. LME.
[ORIGIN Old French *ensenser*, formed as EN-[1] + SENSE *noun*: see IN-[2]]
Cause (a person) to understand or know something; inform, enlighten.

insensibility /ɪn,sɛnsɪ'bɪlɪti/ *noun.* LME.
[ORIGIN Partly from Old French & mod. French *insensibilité* or late Latin *insensibilitas*, partly from IN-[3] + SENSIBILITY.]
1 Incapability or deprivation of physical feeling or sensation; unconsciousness. LME. ▸**b** Physical insensitiveness (*to* something). E19.

E. W. LANE I fell from my horse in a state of insensibility. **b** W. IRVING Perfect hardihood and insensibility to the changes of the seasons.

2 The quality of being imperceptible. *rare.* M17.
3 Lack of or incapacity for mental feeling or emotion; indifference. L17.

R. SOUTH An utter insensibility of any good or kindness done him by others. L. HELLMAN The insensibility that forced Arthur to make fun of what had harmed me.

insensible /ɪn'sɛnsɪb(ə)l/ *adjective.* LME.
[ORIGIN Partly from Old French & mod. French, or Latin *insensibilis*, partly from IN-[3] + SENSIBLE *adjective.*]
1 Unable to be perceived by the senses; non-material. Now *rare.* LME. ▸**b** Too small or gradual to be perceived; inappreciable. L16.

b OED Passing by insensible gradations into the next sense.

2 a Incapable of physical sensation. Now *rare.* LME. ▸**b** Deprived of physical sensation; unconscious. LME. ▸**c** Incapable of physically feeling or perceiving (something specified). Foll. by *of, to.* E16.

a M. FOTHERBY Fire, Haile, and Snow, meere insensible things. **b** C. THUBRON Two or three more vodkas . . and I'd be insensible. **c** GEO. ELIOT The martial fury by which men became insensible to wounds.

3 Chiefly LAW. Unable to be understood; unintelligible. M16.

T. HUTCHINSON Several inaccuracies and insensible expressions in the New England Bill.

4 Lacking sense or intelligence. Now *rare* or *obsolete.* M16.

G. ADAMS People stupid and insensible, illiterate and incapable of learning.

5 Incapable of mentally feeling or perceiving (something specified); unaware; indifferent. (Foll. by *of, to*, or subord. clause) E17. ▸**b** Incapable of feeling or emotion; callous, apathetic. E17.

C. MERIVALE Not insensible how much he owed to their faithful services. J. CONRAD I had to appear insensible to her distress. **b** A. G. GARDINER It would be an insensible heart that did not feel the surge of this strong music.

■ †**insensibleness** *noun* M16–E18. **insensibly** *adverb* LME.

insensitive /ɪn'sɛnsɪtɪv/ *adjective.* L16.
[ORIGIN from IN-[3] + SENSITIVE *adjective.*]
1 Lacking mental or moral sensitivity; not susceptible; indifferent; unsympathetic. L16.
†**2** Lacking physical feeling or consciousness; inanimate. E17–E18.
3 Of an organ, limb, etc.: lacking in feeling or sensation. M19. ▸**b** Of a substance, device, etc.: not susceptible or responsive to some physical influence, as that of light. L19. ▸**c** MATH. & PHYSICS. Of a quantity: (relatively) unaffected by variation in some related quantity. M20.
■ **insensitively** *adverb* M20. **insensitiveness** *noun* M19. **insensi'tivity** *noun* lack of sensitivity M20.

insentient /ɪn'sɛnʃ(ə)nt/ *adjective.* M18.
[ORIGIN from IN-[3] + SENTIENT *adjective.*]
Not sentient; lacking physical feeling or consciousness; inanimate.
■ **insentience** *noun* the fact or condition of being insentient M19.

inseparable /ɪn'sɛp(ə)rəb(ə)l/ *adjective & noun.* LME.
[ORIGIN Latin *inseparabilis*, formed as IN-[3] + SEPARABLE.]
▶ **A** *adjective.* Not separable; unable to be separated or disjoined (*from*); GRAMMAR (of a prefix, or a verb in respect of a prefix) that cannot be used as a separate word. LME.

T. CAPOTE For seven years the two friends had been inseparable, each . . irreplaceable to the other. *Femina* Pain is . . an inseparable part of my life.

▶ **B** *noun.* An inseparable person, esp. a friend, or thing. Usu. in *pl.* E16.

R. DAVIES Off the stage they were inseparables.

■ **insepara'bility** *noun* E17. **inseparableness** *noun* L16. **inseparably** *adverb* LME.

inseparate /ɪn'sɛp(ə)rət/ *adjective.* Now *rare.* L16.
[ORIGIN from IN-[3] + SEPARATE *adjective.*]
Not separate (*from*); united, undivided; inseparable.
■ **inseparately** *adverb* M16.

insequent /'ɪnsɪkwənt, ɪn'siːk-/ *adjective.* L19.
[ORIGIN from IN-[3] + *-sequent* as in CONSEQUENT *adjective*, SUBSEQUENT.]
PHYSICAL GEOGRAPHY. Of a stream, valley, or drainage pattern: apparently haphazard in form, not determined by underlying structures.

insert /'ɪnsəːt/ *noun.* L19.
[ORIGIN from INSERT *verb*, or abbreviation of INSERTION.]
A thing (to be) inserted, as a loose page of advertisements etc. in a magazine, a piece of material in a garment, a shot in a cinema film, etc.

Gramophone I did not read the insert before playing the cassette. *Broadcast* The . . magazine will . . carry a couple of pages of advertising and some inserts.

insert /ɪn'səːt/ *verb trans.* Pa. pple **-serted**, †**-sert**. L15.
[ORIGIN Latin *insert-* pa. ppl stem of *inserere*, formed as IN-[2] + *serere* plant, join, put into.]
1 Introduce (a word, paragraph, etc.) into a piece of text; interpolate; put as an advertisement, article, etc., into a newspaper or magazine; include. L15.

P. G. WODEHOUSE Insert that advertisement in the *Daily Mail.*

I

2 Put or place in or between; fit or thrust in. (Foll. by *in*, *into*, *between*.) **E16.**

A. NIN I inserted the key in the lock. M. DRABBLE She raised a small forkful to her mouth, inserted it, chewed.

3 *ANATOMY, ZOOLOGY, & BOTANY.* Attach (an organ, esp. a muscle) at a specified point. Chiefly as ***inserted** ppl adjective.* **E19.**

■ **insertable** *adjective* **L19. inserting** *noun* (*a*) the action of the verb; (*b*) something inserted: **E17. inserter** *noun* **E17. insertor** *noun* **L16.**

insertion /ɪnˈsəːʃ(ə)n/ *noun.* **M16.**
[ORIGIN Late Latin *insertio(n-)*, formed as INSERT *verb*: see -ION.]
1 Something which is inserted; a word, paragraph, etc., inserted in a piece of text; each appearance of an advertisement etc. in different issues of a newspaper or magazine. **M16.** ▸**b** A piece of embroidery or needlework made to be inserted in plain material as a decoration. **M19.**

E. W. LANE When I find trifling insertions of this kind . . in my translation.

great insertion: see GREAT *adjective*.
2 The action of inserting; introduction into or between something. **L16.** ▸**b** *ASTRONAUTICS.* = INJECTION 1d. **M20.**

OED Trade notices are charged at the rate of 1/6 per insertion. A. MASON The gap between the shutters was wide enough for the insertion of a knife blade.

3 *ANATOMY, ZOOLOGY, & BOTANY.* The (place or manner of) attachment of an organ, esp. a muscle. **L16.**
— COMB.: **insertion gain**, **insertion loss** *ELECTRICITY* the increase, or decrease, in power, voltage, or current resulting from insertion of a device or network between a load and the power source.
■ **insertional** *adjective* **M19. insertioned** *adjective* (*NEEDLEWORK*) decorated with an insertion **L19.**

insertive /ɪnˈsəːtɪv/ *adjective.* **M17.**
[ORIGIN Latin *insertivus*, formed as INSERT *verb* + -IVE.]
Characterized by insertion.

†**insertment** *noun. rare.* **L17–E19.**
[ORIGIN from INSERT *verb* + -MENT.]
BOTANY. sing. & in *pl.* The medullary rays.

†**inservient** *adjective.* **M17–E19.**
[ORIGIN Latin *inservient-* pres. ppl stem of *inservire* be serviceable, formed as IN-[2] + *servire* SERVE *verb*[1]: see -ENT.]
Serving or subservient *to* some purpose; serviceable, useful.

inessorial /ɪnsɛˈsɔːrɪəl/ *adjective.* **M19.**
[ORIGIN from mod. Latin *Insessores* perchers pl. of late Latin *insessor*, agent noun of *insidere* sit upon, formed as IN-[2] + *sedere* sit: see -IAL.]
ORNITHOLOGY. Adapted for perching.

INSET /ˈɪnsɛt/ *abbreviation.*
In-service education and training.

inset /ˈɪnsɛt/ *noun.* **M16.**
[ORIGIN from IN-[1] + SET *noun*[1].]
1 Orig., a place where water flows in, a channel. Later, an inflow of water. **M16.**

C. LYELL There are tidal influences combined with the general insets from the Atlantic.

2 Something set in or inserted; *esp.* an extra page or pages inserted in a book etc.; a small map, photograph, etc., inserted within the border of a larger one; a piece of cloth etc. let into a garment. **L16.**

J. S. FOSTER Simple plan shapes with the minimum of insets and projections. I. MCEWAN A boxed inset at the foot of the page.

inset /ɪnˈsɛt/ *verb trans.* Infl. **-tt-**. Pa. pple **-set**, **-setted**. **OE.**
[ORIGIN from IN-[1] + SET *verb*[1].]
†**1** Institute, initiate. Only in **OE.**
†**2** Set (a person) in office; appoint. **ME–L16.**
3 Set (a jewel) in or *in* precious metal or jewellery. *rare.* **M17.**
4 Set in, insert, make flush; *spec.* insert as an inset, decorate with an inset. **L19.**

Times The map . . now includes inset maps. *Which?* If you want to move close to walls, . . choose a model with inset wheels.

■ **insetter** *noun* a person who or thing which inserts pages etc. **L19. insetting** *noun* (*a*) *TYPOGRAPHY* indention; (*b*) insertion, fixing: **E16.**

inseverable /ɪnˈsɛv(ə)rəb(ə)l/ *adjective.* **M16.**
[ORIGIN from IN-[3] + SEVERABLE.]
Unable to be severed or divided; inseparable.

G. CATLIN The offence is lost in the inseverable iniquity in which all join.

■ **inseverably** *adverb* **M17.**

inshallah /ɪnˈʃalə/ *interjection.* **M19.**
[ORIGIN Arabic *in šāʾ Allāh*.]
If God wills it; *Deo volente*.

inshell /ɪnˈʃɛl/ *verb trans.* Also **en-** /ɪn-, ɛn-/. *rare.* **E17.**
[ORIGIN from IN-[1], EN-[1] + SHELL *noun*.]
Withdraw within a shell.

inshining /ˈɪnʃʌɪnɪŋ/ *noun.* **E18.**
[ORIGIN from IN *adverb* + SHINE *verb* + -ING[1].]
A shining in; illumination.

inshining /ˈɪnʃʌɪnɪŋ/ *adjective.* **M19.**
[ORIGIN from IN *adverb* + SHINING *adjective*.]
That shines in.

†**inship** *verb trans.* Infl. **-pp-**. **L16–E17.**
[ORIGIN from IN-[1] + SHIP *noun*.]
Put into a ship; embark.

inshoot /ˈɪnʃuːt/ *noun.* **L19.**
[ORIGIN from IN-[1] + SHOOT *noun*[1].]
BASEBALL. The act of causing the ball to move rapidly by pitching with a curve; a ball which moves in this way.

inshore /ɪnˈʃɔː, ˈɪnʃɔː/ *adjective & adverb.* **E18.**
[ORIGIN from IN-[1] + SHORE *noun*[1].]
▸ **A** *adjective.* Situated or carried on close to a shore. **E18.**
▸ **B** *adverb.* Towards a shore; close(r) to a shore. **M18.**
inshore of nearer to the shore than.

†**inshrine** *verb* var. of ENSHRINE.

inside /ɪnˈsʌɪd/, *as adjective* ˈɪnsʌɪd/ *noun, adverb, adjective, & preposition.* **LME.**
[ORIGIN from IN-[1] + SIDE *noun*.]
▸ **A** *noun* **1** **a** *sing.* & in *pl.* The interior of the body; the stomach and bowels. Chiefly *colloq.* **LME.** ▸**b** *gen.* The inner part of something; the interior. **M16.** ▸**c** Inward nature, thought, or meaning. **L16.** ▸**d** *The* middle part *of* a week etc. **L19.** ▸**e** Private information on a specified topic; a position affording such information. **E20.**

a R. LINDNER Her insides contracted in a spasm of disgust. **b** M. ATWOOD She's been sick of the taste of the inside of her own mouth. C. ISHERWOOD He sucked the insides out of the eggs. **d** C. ISHERWOOD I can't even keep a man faithful to me for the inside of a month.

b ***patent insides***: see PATENT *adjective*.
2 The inner side or surface; the side of a path etc. that is next to a wall or away from a road. **E16.** ▸**b** *FENCING.* The right-hand side of a sword. Now *rare.* **L17.**

M. FORSTER There was ice on the inside of the window.

inside out with the inner surface turned out; ***know inside out***, know thoroughly; ***turn inside out***, turn the inner side outwards; *colloq.* cause confusion or a mess in.
3 Chiefly *hist.* (The place of) a passenger travelling inside a coach etc. **L18.**

R. BOLDREWOOD I picked myself up and went to help out the insides.

4 *FOOTBALL, HOCKEY*, etc. A position towards the centre of the field; a player in that position. **L19.**

J. POTTER George and Boozy moved up on the German insides like a pair of avenging demons.

▸ **B** *adverb.* **1** Into or in the inner part; within; internally. **LME.** ▸**b** In a position affording private information on a specified topic. *rare.* **L19.** ▸**c** In prison. *slang.* **L19.**

G. GREENE He mistook the house . . for a quiet inn and walked inside. C. GEBLER The little mustard dish that had blue glass inside. H. BASCOM He . . is strangely calm inside Over-confident? **c** C. HOPE During his years inside there had circulated copies of his speech from the dock.

2 On the inner side. **E19.**
3 Foll. by *of*: within the space of, less than, a specified period. **M19.**
▸ **C** *adjective.* **1** Situated on, or in, the inside; interior; internal. **E17.** ▸**b** Derived from the inside, involving private information on a specified topic. **L19.**

A. MUNRO He reaches quickly into his inside pocket. **b** A. BULLOCK Bevin's position in the Government gave them . . inside knowledge of what was happening.

2 Of a person: travelling inside a coach etc. (chiefly *hist.*); employed within a house etc., working indoors. **E19.**
3 *FOOTBALL, HOCKEY*, etc. Designating (a player in) a position towards the centre of the field. **L19.**
inside forward, ***inside left***, ***inside right***, etc.
▸ **D** *preposition.* Inside of; on or to the inner side of, in or into the inner part of; within. **L18.**

M. B. KEATINGE All must hurry inside the gates. D. DELILLO A mule was standing just inside the olive grove. *Running* Who would be the first man inside the magic 12 hours?

— SPECIAL COLLOCATIONS & COMB.: **inside country** *Austral.* settled areas near the coast. **inside information**: not accessible to outsiders. **inside job** *colloq.* a crime etc. involving a person living or working on the premises burgled etc. **inside leg** the length of one's leg from crotch to ankle, or of the equivalent part of a pair of trousers. ***inside straight***: see STRAIGHT *noun*[1]. **inside track** the track of a racecourse etc. which is shorter because of a curve; *fig.* a position of advantage.

insider /ɪnˈsʌɪdə/ *noun.* **E19.**
[ORIGIN from INSIDE + -ER[1].]
1 Chiefly *hist.* An inside passenger in a coach etc. **E19.**
2 A person who is within some society, organization, etc.; a person who is party to a secret, esp. so as to gain an unfair advantage. **M19.**

Independent Insiders cashed in on their knowledge. I. MCEWAN Charles . . brought back an insider's tales of drunkenness . . in the House of Commons.

3 A pocket, a pocketbook. *US slang.* **M19.**
— COMB.: **insider dealing** *STOCK EXCHANGE* trading to one's own advantage through having inside knowledge.

insidious /ɪnˈsɪdɪəs/ *adjective.* **M16.**
[ORIGIN from Latin *insidiosus* cunning, deceitful, from *insidiae* ambush, trick: see -OUS.]
Full of wiles or plots; proceeding or progressing secretly or subtly; treacherous; crafty.

R. L. STEVENSON They assailed me with artful questions and insidious offers of correspondence in the future. M. T. TSUANG The insidious course of the disease.

■ **insidiously** *adverb* **M16. insidiousness** *noun* **L17.**

insight /ˈɪnsʌɪt/ *noun*[1]. **ME.**
[ORIGIN Prob. of Scandinavian & Low German origin: cf. Swedish *insikt*, Danish *insigt*, Dutch *inzicht*, German *Einsicht*. See IN-[1], SIGHT *noun*.]
†**1** Internal sight, mental vision. Also, understanding, wisdom. **ME–M17.** ▸**b** Knowledge *of* or skill *in* (a particular subject or area). **ME–M17.**
†**2** A mental looking *to* or *upon* something; consideration; respect. **ME–L15.**
†**3** Physical sight; inspection; a look. **LME–M17.**
4 Penetration (into character, circumstances, etc.) with the understanding; an instance of this. **L16.** ▸**b** *PSYCHOLOGY.* (A) sudden perception of the solution to a problem or difficulty (in animals, indicative of ideation and reasoning); *esp.* in *PSYCHOANALYSIS*, perception of one's repressed drives and their origin. **E20.**

A. BULLOCK With greater historical insight . . he compared Attlee to Campbell-Bannerman. C. PHILLIPS His thoughts did contain astute insights into the current state of the island.

■ **insighted** *adjective* having insight, insightful **L16. insightful** *adjective* full of insight **E20. insightfully** *adverb* **M20. insightfulness** *noun* **L20.**

†**insight** *noun*[2]. *Scot. & N. English.* **LME–L19.**
[ORIGIN Perh. same word as INSIGHT *noun*[1].]
Goods; *esp.* household furniture. Opp. OUTSIGHT *noun*[1].

insigne /ɪnˈsɪgni/ *noun sing.* Pl. (earlier) INSIGNIA. **L18.**
[ORIGIN Latin: see INSIGNIA.]
A badge, an ensign, an emblem.

†**insigne** *adjective.* **LME–E18.**
[ORIGIN French from Latin *insignis*: see INSIGNIA.]
Distinguished; eminent; remarkable.

insignia /ɪnˈsɪgnɪə/ *noun.* **M17.**
[ORIGIN Latin, pl. of *insigne* mark, sign, badge of office, use as noun of neut. of *insignis* distinguished (as by a mark), formed as IN-[2] + *signum* sign: see -IA[2]. Cf. ENSIGN *noun*.]
1 *pl.* Badges or distinguishing marks (*of* office, honour, etc.); emblems (*of* a nation, person, etc.). **M17.**

J. G. BALLARD The squadron insignia were still legible.

2 *sing.* (Pl. **-ias**.) A badge or distinguishing mark (*of* office, honour, etc.); an emblem (*of* a nation, person, etc.). **L18.**

Times I saw not a single racer . . bearing an insignia that seemed out of place.

3 Usu. as *pl.* Marks or tokens indicative of something. **L18.**

P. ROTH His deeply furrowed face bore all the insignia of his lifelong exertion.

insignificance /ɪnsɪgˈnɪfɪk(ə)ns/ *noun.* **L17.**
[ORIGIN from INSIGNIFICANT *adjective* (see -ANCE), or from IN-[3] + SIGNIFICANCE.]
1 The state or quality of being insignificant; lack of significance or force; unimportance; triviality. **L17.**

B. BETTELHEIM Her own wounded feelings receded into insignificance.

pale into insignificance: see PALE *verb*[2].
2 Lack of meaning. *rare.* **M18.**

insignificancy /ɪnsɪgˈnɪfɪk(ə)nsi/ *noun.* **M17.**
[ORIGIN formed as INSIGNIFICANCE (see -ANCY), or from IN-[3] + SIGNIFICANCY.]
†**1** Lack of meaning; an instance of this. **M–L17.**
2 Lack of significance or force; unimportance, triviality. Also, an instance of this; an insignificant thing or person. **M17.**

insignificant /ɪnsɪgˈnɪfɪk(ə)nt/ *adjective & noun.* **M17.**
[ORIGIN from IN-[3] + SIGNIFICANT.]
▸ **A** *adjective.* **1** Lacking signification; meaningless. **M17.**
†**2** Devoid of weight or force; ineffective, ineffectual. **M17–M18.**
3 Of no importance; trivial, trifling; contemptible. **M17.**

R. LYND He would never be anything more than an insignificant doctrinaire with a gift for saying bitter things. L. GORDON A document which her male descendants assumed to be insignificant.

4 Small in size; petty, mean. **M18.**
▸ **B** *noun.* A meaningless thing; an unimportant or contemptible person. **E18.**
■ **insignificantly** *adverb* **M17.**

†**insignificative** *adjective.* **M17–M18.**
[ORIGIN from IN-[3] + SIGNIFICATIVE.]
Not significative.

insignis /ɪnˈsɪgnɪs/ *noun.* **M19.**
[ORIGIN mod. Latin (from former taxonomic name *Pinus insignis*) from Latin = remarkable.]
The Monterey pine, *Pinus radiata*.

insimplicity /ɪnsɪmˈplɪsɪti/ *noun. rare.* L19.
[ORIGIN from IN-[3] + SIMPLICITY.]
Lack of simplicity.

insincere /ɪnsɪnˈsɪə/ *adjective.* M17.
[ORIGIN Latin *insincerus*, formed as IN-[3] + *sincerus* SINCERE.]
Not sincere; disingenuous; not candid.

M. SCAMMELL A reaction against excessive and often insincere adulation.

■ **insincerely** *adverb* E17.

insincerity /ɪnsɪnˈsɛrɪti/ *noun.* M16.
[ORIGIN Late Latin *insinceritas*, formed as IN-[3] + *sinceritas* SINCERITY.]
†1 Lack of purity; corruption. Only in M16.
2 The quality of being insincere; an instance of this. L17.

†**insinew** *verb trans.* Also **en-**. L16–E17.
[ORIGIN from IN-[2], EN-[1] + SINEW.]
Provide with sinews; *fig.* inspire with strength.

insinking /ˈɪnsɪŋkɪŋ/ *noun.* L19.
[ORIGIN from IN-[1] + SINKING *noun*.]
A sinking in; a depression.

insinuant /ɪnˈsɪnjʊənt/ *adjective. rare.* M17.
[ORIGIN from INSINUATE *verb* + -ANT[1].]
Insinuating, wheedling, ingratiating.

insinuate /ɪnˈsɪnjʊeɪt/ *verb.* E16.
[ORIGIN Latin *insinuat-* pa. ppl stem of *insinuare*, formed as IN-[2] + *sinuare* to curve: see -ATE[3].]
1 *verb trans. LAW.* Enter (a deed or document) on the official register; lodge (a deed or document) for registration. Now *rare* or *obsolete* exc. in the Commissions issued by the Bishop of Winchester to the Deans of Jersey and Guernsey as his Commissaries. E16.
2 *verb trans.* Introduce or impart to the mind indirectly or covertly; instil subtly and imperceptibly. E16.

F. D. MAURICE In which wisdom was to be insinuated not enforced.

3 *verb trans.* Convey (a statement etc.) indirectly or obliquely, hint (*that*). M16.

A. ARONSON Iago . . poisons Othello's mind by insinuating what Desdemona must have 'seen'. M. SCAMMELL She insinuated that he had neglected his mother.

4 *verb trans.* Express indirectly; suggest, imply. *arch.* M16.

SIR W. SCOTT Our metropolis . . whereby I insinuate Glasgow.

5 *verb trans.* Introduce (oneself, another, etc.) into favour, office, etc., by subtle manipulation. Freq. foll. by *into*. M16. ▸†**b** *verb intrans.* Work or wheedle oneself *into*, ingratiate oneself *with*. L16–M18.

T. MORRISON An idea insinuated itself. P. D. JAMES Insinuating himself into the family.

6 *verb trans.* Introduce (a thing, oneself) subtly and deviously into a place; cause (a thing) to enter gradually. L16. ▸†**b** *verb intrans.* Be introduced subtly and deviously into a place; penetrate gradually. E17–L18.

M. BEERBOHM Into the lobe of her left ear he insinuated the hook of the black pearl. P. G. WODEHOUSE A head insinuated itself into the room furtively. E. LINKLATER Juan was able to squeeze and insinuate himself among the other sight-seers.

†7 *verb trans.* Draw, attract, (a person etc.) subtly or covertly *to* something. L16–L17.
■ **insinuatingly** *adverb* in an insinuating manner E19. **insinuatingness** *noun (rare)* the state of being insinuating E18. **insinuator** *noun* L16. **insinuatory** *adjective* insinuative L19.

insinuation /ɪnˌsɪnjʊˈeɪʃ(ə)n/ *noun.* L15.
[ORIGIN Latin *insinuatio(n-)*, formed as INSINUATE: see -ATION.]
†1 Notification, publication. *Scot.* Only in L15.
†2 *LAW.* The production or delivery of a will for official registration. E16–E18.
3 The action or an act of introducing something to the mind indirectly or covertly. M16.
4 The action or an act of conveying a derogatory suggestion or implication indirectly or obliquely; an oblique hint. M16. ▸†**b** *RHETORIC.* A speech designed to win over its hearers. M16–E17.

V. NABOKOV The biography . . teems with factual errors, snide insinuations, and blunders. *Daily Mirror* There was the continual insinuation that another driver could have done a better job than me.

5 The action of introducing oneself or another into favour, office, etc., by subtle manipulation; an instance of this. M16.
6 The action or an act of introducing a thing or oneself subtly and deviously into a place; covert entrance. E17.

J. KINGDOM Spencer had written two books deploring the insinuation of state tentacles into economic life.

7 A winding, a twisting. *rare.* E17.

insinuative /ɪnˈsɪnjʊətɪv/ *adjective.* E17.
[ORIGIN formed as INSINUATE + -IVE.]
1 Tending to insinuate; having the property of insinuating. E17.
2 Characterized by or involving insinuation; given to making insinuations. M17.
■ **insinuatively** *adverb* E17. **insinuativeness** *noun (rare)* E18.

insinuendo /ɪnˌsɪnjʊˈɛndəʊ/ *noun.* Pl. **-os**. L19.
[ORIGIN Blend of INSINUATION and INNUENDO *noun*.]
(An) insinuation.

insipid /ɪnˈsɪpɪd/ *adjective & noun.* E17.
[ORIGIN French *insipide* or late Latin *insipidus*, formed as IN-[3] + *sapidus* SAPID.]
▸ **A** *adjective.* **1** Tasteless; having only a slight taste; lacking flavour. E17.

C. GEBLER Horn-shaped pastries filled with insipid-tasting custard.

2 *fig.* Lacking liveliness; dull, uninteresting. E17.

W. SOYINKA His assistants . . appeared insipid, starved parodies of himself.

†3 Devoid of intelligence or judgement; stupid, foolish. E17–L18.
▸ **B** *noun.* An insipid person or thing; a person who is deficient in sense, spirit, etc. E18.
■ **insipidly** *adverb* M17. **insipidness** *noun* E17.

insipidity /ɪnsɪˈpɪdɪti/ *noun.* E17.
[ORIGIN from INSIPID + -ITY.]
1 Lack of taste or flavour. E17.
†2 Lack of intelligence or judgement; stupidity, folly. E17–M18.
3 Lack of life or interest, dullness. E18.
4 An insipid remark, person, etc. E19.

insipience /ɪnˈsɪpɪəns/ *noun.* Now *rare* or *obsolete.* LME.
[ORIGIN formed as INSIPIENT: see -ENCE.]
The quality of being insipient.

insipient /ɪnˈsɪpɪənt/ *adjective & noun.* Now *rare* or *obsolete.* LME.
[ORIGIN Latin *insipient-*, *-ens*, formed as IN-[3] + *sapient-*: see SAPIENT *adjective*.]
▸ **A** *adjective.* Lacking in wisdom; foolish. LME.
▸ †**B** *noun.* An unwise or foolish person. L15–M17.

insist /ɪnˈsɪst/ *verb.* LME.
[ORIGIN Latin *insistere*, formed as IN-[2] + *sistere* stand.]
1 *verb intrans.* Dwell at length or emphatically *on* or †*in*, †*to* a matter; (foll. by *on*) maintain positively. LME. ▸**b** *verb trans.* Maintain positively *that*. E18.

B. JOWETT Socrates is not prepared to insist on the literal accuracy of this description. **b** J. P. HENNESSY Henry Trollope insisted that he was well enough to join his parents.

2 *verb intrans.* Stand or rest *on*. Now *rare* or *obsolete.* L16.
3 *verb intrans.* Persist *in* a course of action; follow steadfastly *in* a person's steps; persevere. *arch.* L16.
4 *verb intrans.* Make a persistent demand for something. (Foll. by *on*.) E17. ▸**b** *verb trans.* Demand persistently *that*. L17.

C. HILL The Short Parliament . . insisted on peace with the Scots. D. CUSACK You are not to upset yourself, I insist. R. HUNTFORD Scott nonetheless insisted on pushing blindly on. **b** J. HELLER I . . insisted they let her go. J. C. OATES Della insisted . . that the wedding party be held at her house.

5 *verb trans.* Utter insistently. L19.

D. H. LAWRENCE 'But which village do the bandits come from?' she insisted.

— NOTE: In isolated use before L16.
■ **insister** *noun* E17. **insistingly** *adverb* with insistence, insistently M19. **insistive** *adjective* having the character or quality of insisting M17.

insistence /ɪnˈsɪst(ə)ns/ *noun.* LME.
[ORIGIN from INSIST: see -ENCE.]
The action of insisting; the fact or quality of being insistent.

A. W. KINGLAKE A . . tone of insistence bordering at times on intimidation. J. RATHBONE On the insistence of the girls we . . joined them.

insistency /ɪnˈsɪst(ə)nsi/ *noun.* M19.
[ORIGIN from INSISTENT: see -ENCY.]
Insistence; an instance of this.

insistent /ɪnˈsɪst(ə)nt/ *adjective & noun.* E17.
[ORIGIN from INSIST + -ENT.]
▸ **A** *adjective.* **1** Standing or resting on something. *rare.* E17.
2 That dwells emphatically on something maintained or demanded; persistent; obtruding itself on one's attention. M19.

J. AGATE John Gielgud was anxious, even insistent, that I should not write about . . last night's performance. P. BOWLES An insistent electric bell shrilled without respite.

▸ **B** *noun.* An insistent person. *rare.* M19.
■ **insistently** *adverb* L19.

†**insisture** *noun. rare* (Shakes.). Only in E17.
[ORIGIN from INSIST *verb* + -URE.]
Constancy, persistency, continuance.

†**insition** *noun.* LME–M19.
[ORIGIN Latin *insitio(n-)*, from *insit-* pa. ppl stem of *inserere* engraft, formed as IN-[2] + *serere* sow, plant: see -ITION.]
The action of engrafting, engraftment, a graft, (*lit.* & *fig.*).

insititious /ɪnsɪˈtɪʃəs/ *adjective.* M17.
[ORIGIN Latin *insiticius*, from *insit-*: see INSITION, -ITIOUS[1].]
Of engrafted or inserted nature, introduced from outside, (*lit.* & *fig.*).

in situ /ɪn ˈsɪtjuː/ *adverbial phr.* M18.
[ORIGIN Latin.]
In its (original) place; in position.

†**inslave** *verb*, †**insnare** *verb* vars. of ENSLAVE, ENSNARE.

†**insnarl** *verb* see ENSNARL.

insobriety /ɪnsəˈbrʌɪəti/ *noun.* E17.
[ORIGIN from IN-[3] + SOBRIETY.]
Lack of sobriety; intemperance, esp. in drinking.

insociable /ɪnˈsəʊʃəb(ə)l/ *adjective.* Now *rare.* L16.
[ORIGIN Latin *insociabilis*, formed as IN-[3] + *sociabilis* SOCIABLE.]
†1 That cannot be associated; incompatible. L16–L17.
2 Not disposed to mix with others; unsociable. L16.
■ **insociaˈbility** *noun* unsociableness M18.

insolate /ˈɪnsəleɪt/ *verb trans.* E17.
[ORIGIN Latin *insolat-* pa. ppl stem of *insolare*, formed as IN-[2] + *sol* sun: see -ATE[3].]
Expose to the sun's rays, esp. in order to dry.

insolation /ɪnsəˈleɪʃ(ə)n/ *noun.* E17.
[ORIGIN Latin *insolatio(n-)*, formed as INSOLATE + -ATION.]
Exposure to the sun's rays, esp. for drying or bleaching or as medical treatment; harmful exposure to the sun's rays; *spec.* sunstroke.

insole /ˈɪnsəʊl/ *noun.* M19.
[ORIGIN from IN *adjective* + SOLE *noun*[2].]
The inner sole of a shoe or boot. Also, a detachable piece of material worn inside a shoe or boot for warmth etc.

insolence /ˈɪns(ə)l(ə)ns/ *noun.* LME.
[ORIGIN Latin *insolentia*, formed as INSOLENT: see -ENCE.]
1 Orig., arrogant or overbearing conduct or disposition. Later, impertinently insulting behaviour. Also (now *rare*), an instance of this, an insolent act. LME.

MILTON The Sons of Belial, flown with insolence and wine. E. M. FORSTER 'May me and Lucy get down from our chairs?' he asked, with scarcely veiled insolence.

†2 The condition of being unused to a thing. Also, unusualness. LME–M17.

insolency /ˈɪns(ə)l(ə)nsi/ *noun.* Now *arch. rare.* L15.
[ORIGIN formed as INSOLENCE: see -ENCY.]
1 = INSOLENCE 1. L15.
†2 Unusualness; an unusual act or occurrence. E–M17.

insolent /ˈɪns(ə)l(ə)nt/ *adjective & noun.* LME.
[ORIGIN Latin *insolent-*, formed as IN-[3] + *solent-* pres. ppl stem of *solere* be accustomed: see -ENT.]
▸ **A** *adjective* **I 1** Orig., arrogant or overbearing in conduct or behaviour. Later, offensively contemptuous; impertinently insulting. LME.

J. GAY 'What arrogance!' the snail replied; 'How insolent is upstart pride!' R. WEST Cook's face was bland, but her tone was unmistakably insolent.

†2 Going beyond the bounds of propriety; extravagant, immoderate. LME–E18.

STEELE All the Extremities of Household Expence, Furniture and insolent Equipage.

▸ †**II 3** Unaccustomed to a thing; inexperienced. L15–L16.
4 Unusual, strange. L16–M17.

J. BRINSLEY Words which are insolent, hard and out of use, are to be as warily avoided.

▸ **B** *noun.* An insolent person. L16.
■ **insolently** *adverb* LME.

insolidity /ɪnsəˈlɪdɪti/ *noun.* Now *rare* or *obsolete.* L16.
[ORIGIN from IN-[3] + SOLIDITY.]
Lack of firmness or substantialness; flimsiness.

insolubilize /ɪnˈsɒljʊbɪlʌɪz/ *verb trans.* Also **-ise**. L19.
[ORIGIN from Latin *insolubilis* INSOLUBLE *adjective* + -IZE.]
Make incapable of dissolving.
■ **insolubiliˈzation** *noun* E20.

insoluble /ɪnˈsɒljʊb(ə)l/ *adjective & noun.* LME.
[ORIGIN Old French & mod. French, or Latin *insolubilis*, formed as IN-[3] + *solubilis* SOLUBLE *adjective*.]
▸ **A** *adjective.* **1** Impossible to loosen or untie; indissoluble. Now *rare.* LME. ▸†**b** Of an argument: irrefutable. M16–L17.
2 Of a difficulty, problem, etc.: impossible to solve. LME.

P. FERGUSON They were a problem, annoying but not insoluble. M. RULE The difficulties appeared to be insoluble.

3 Unable to be dissolved in a liquid. E18.

F. SMYTH Arsenious oxide is practically insoluble in cold water.

4 Of a debt: impossible to discharge. M19.
▸ **B** *noun.* An insoluble difficulty or problem. LME.
■ **insoluˈbility** *noun* E17. **insolubleness** *noun* L17. **insolubly** *adverb* L19.

insolvable /ɪnˈsɒlvəb(ə)l/ *adjective.* M17.
[ORIGIN from IN-[3] + SOLVABLE.]
†1 = INSOLUBLE *adjective* 1. M17–E18.
2 = INSOLUBLE *adjective* 2. L17.
3 = INSOLUBLE *adjective* 3. E19.
4 Unable to be cashed. *rare.* M19.
■ **insolvaˈbility** *noun* M19. **insolvably** *adverb* L18.

insolvent /ɪnˈsɒlv(ə)nt/ *adjective & noun*. **L16**.
[**ORIGIN** from **IN-**[3] + **SOLVENT** *adjective*.]
▸ **A** *adjective*. **1** Unable to pay one's debts or meet one's liabilities; bankrupt. **L16**. ▸**b** Of a law etc.: relating to insolvents or insolvency. **M19**.

E. **FERBER** Gifts . . from insolvent patients who proffered them in lieu of cash.

†**2** Unable to be cashed. **M17–E18**.
▸ **B** *noun*. An insolvent person. **E18**.
▪ **insolvency** *noun* **M17**.

insomnia /ɪnˈsɒmnɪə/ *noun*. Also (earlier) †**-nie**, **-nium** /-nɪəm/. **E17**.
[**ORIGIN** Latin, from *insomnis* sleepless (formed as **IN-**[3] + *somnus* sleep) + **-IA**[1].]
Chronic inability to sleep; sleeplessness.
▪ **insomniac** *noun & adjective* (**a**) *noun* a person who suffers from insomnia; (**b**) *adjective* affected with or exhibiting insomnia: **E20**.

insomnolent /ɪnˈsɒmnələnt/ *adjective & noun*. *rare*. **M19**.
[**ORIGIN** from **IN-**[3] + **SOMNOLENT**.]
(A person) affected with insomnia.
▪ **insomnolence** *noun* **E19**. **insomnolency** *noun* **E19**.

insomuch /ɪnsə(ʊ)ˈmʌtʃ/ *adverb*. **LME**.
[**ORIGIN** Orig. 3 words, from **IN** *preposition* + **SO** *adverb* + **MUCH** *adjective* or *noun*, translating Old French *en tant (que)*: at first alternative to **INASMUCH**, later differentiated.]
1 To such an extent; so much. *rare*. **LME**.

J. **BADCOCK** If one fact . . has lost a particle of its interest . . insomuch is the Editor's design frustrated.

2 Foll. by *as*: ▸**a** Inasmuch as, seeing that. **LME**. ▸†**b** To such an extent that, so that. **L16–M17**. ▸**c** To such an extent as, so as. **M17**.

a *Westminster Review* The present law is inoperative; insomuch as the Universities . . contain teachers who have never subscribed this . . confession.

3 Foll. by *that*: to such an extent that, so that. **LME**.

A. **ALISON** The rain fell in torrents, insomuch that . . the soldiers were often ankle-deep in water.

†**4** Inasmuch as, in that. **LME–E17**.

insouciance /ɪnˈsuːsɪəns, *foreign* ɛ̃susjɑ̃ːs/ *noun*. **L18**.
[**ORIGIN** French, formed as **INSOUCIANT**: see **-ANCE**.]
Carefreeness, lack of concern.

N. **PEVSNER** His landscapes have . . the happiest insouciance of handling. *Observer* 'Size is no problem, I promise you,' he says with refreshing insouciance.

insouciant /ɪnˈsuːsɪənt, *foreign* ɛ̃susjɑ̃/ *adjective*. **E19**.
[**ORIGIN** French, formed as **IN-**[3] + *souciant* pres. pple of *soucier* to care, from Latin *sollicitare* disturb: see **-ANT**[1].]
Carefree, undisturbed.

J. **UPDIKE** Norma . . he had last seen wandering in insouciant nudity.

▪ **insouciantly** *adverb* **L19**.

insoul *verb* see **ENSOUL**.

Insp. *abbreviation*.
Inspector (as a police rank).

inspan /ɪnˈspan/ *verb trans*. *S. Afr*. Infl. **-nn-**. **E19**.
[**ORIGIN** Afrikaans from Dutch *inspannen*, from *in-* **IN-**[1] + *spannen* **SPAN** *verb*[2].]
1 Yoke (oxen, horses, etc.) in a team to a vehicle; harness (a wagon). **E19**.
2 *fig*. Persuade (a person) to give assistance or service; use as a makeshift. **E20**.

Rand Daily Mail Mrs Barton often gets on the telephone and inspans private householders to help out.

inspeak /ɪnˈspiːk/ *verb trans*. Infl. as **SPEAK** *verb*; pa. t. usu. **-spoke** /-ˈspəʊk/, pa. pple usu. **-spoken** /-ˈspəʊk(ə)n/. **L17**.
[**ORIGIN** from **IN-**[1] + **SPEAK** *verb*: cf. German *einsprechen*.]
In devotional language: produce in the soul by speech.

†**inspect** *noun*. **L15–M18**.
[**ORIGIN** App. from Latin *inspectus*, formed as **INSPECT** *verb*.]
Inspection, examination.

inspect /ɪnˈspɛkt/ *verb*. **E17**.
[**ORIGIN** Latin *inspect-* pa. ppl stem of *inspicere*, formed as **IN-**[2] + *specere* look, or Latin *inspectare* frequentative of *inspicere*.]
1 *verb trans*. View or examine closely and critically, esp. in order to assess quality or to check for shortcomings; *spec*. examine officially (documents, military personnel, etc.). **E17**.

J. **STEINBECK** He leaned over and inspected the sacking closely. M. **SCAMMELL** Prisoners were obliged to stand by their beds while they were inspected by two officers. *Which?* Planning applications . . are kept by the council, and you have the right to inspect them.

†**2** *verb intrans*. Make an examination *into*, *among*. Only in **18**.

inspection /ɪnˈspɛkʃ(ə)n/ *noun*. **LME**.
[**ORIGIN** Old French & mod. French from Latin *inspectio(n-)*, formed as **INSPECT** *verb*: see **-ION**.]
1 Careful examination or scrutiny; *spec*. official examination; an instance of this. (Foll. by *of*, †*into*, †*over*, †*upon*.) **LME**.

V. **BRITTAIN** Our Matron came round . . on a tour of inspection of our cubicles. J. A. **MICHENER** An inspection of the man's work forced him to recognize it as a superior job.

2 Insight, perception. Now *rare* or *obsolete*. **E16**.
†**3** A plan of a piece of ground etc. which has been inspected; a survey. **L17–L18**.
– **COMB.**: **inspection-car** (chiefly *US*): used in inspecting a railway track; **inspection chamber** a manhole; **inspection cover** a manhole cover.
▪ **inspectional** *adjective* of or relating to inspection; *spec*. able to be understood at sight: **E18**.

inspective /ɪnˈspɛktɪv/ *adjective*. **E17**.
[**ORIGIN** Late Latin *inspectivus*, formed as **INSPECT** *verb*: see **-IVE**.]
†**1** Concerned with investigation; theoretical. **E–M17**.
2 Watchful, attentive. **L17**.

inspector /ɪnˈspɛktə/ *noun*. Also (as a title) **I-**. **E17**.
[**ORIGIN** Latin, formed as **INSPECT** *verb*: see **-OR**.]
1 A person who examines or looks carefully at something; *spec*. an official appointed to report on the workings of a service etc., esp. with regard to the observance of regulations or standards, or to conduct a public inquiry. **E17**. ▸**b** A person who looks *into* a thing from curiosity, for information, etc. Now *rare*. **M17**.
inspector of factories, ***inspector of mines and quarries***, ***inspector of nuclear installations***, ***inspector of schools***, etc. **inspector-general** the head of an inspectorate. **inspector of taxes** an official who assesses income tax payable. ***SANITARY inspector***.
2 A police officer ranking below a superintendent and above a sergeant. **M19**.
▪ **inspectoral** *adjective* = **INSPECTORIAL** **M19**.

inspectorate /ɪnˈspɛkt(ə)rət/ *noun*. **M18**.
[**ORIGIN** from **INSPECTOR** + **-ATE**[1].]
1 The office or function of an inspector; a body of official inspectors. **M18**.
2 A district under official inspection. **M19**.

inspectorial /ɪnspɛkˈtɔːrɪəl/ *adjective*. **M18**.
[**ORIGIN** formed as **INSPECTORATE** + **-IAL**.]
Of or relating to an inspector; having the rank of an inspector.

inspectorship /ɪnˈspɛktəʃɪp/ *noun*. **M18**.
[**ORIGIN** formed as **INSPECTORATE** + **-SHIP**.]
The rank or position of an inspector.

inspectress /ɪnˈspɛktrɪs/ *noun*. Now *rare*. **L18**.
[**ORIGIN** formed as **INSPECTORATE** + **-ESS**[1].]
A female inspector.

†**inspersion** *noun*. **M16–M18**.
[**ORIGIN** Latin *inspersio(n-)*, from *inspers-* pa. ppl stem of *inspergere*, formed as **IN-**[2] + *spargere* scatter, sprinkle: see **-ION**.]
The action or an act of sprinkling something on.

inspeximus /ɪnˈspɛksɪməs/ *noun*. **E17**.
[**ORIGIN** Latin, lit. 'we have inspected': the first word in recital of the inspection of charters etc.]
hist. A charter in which the grantor vouched for having inspected an earlier charter which was recited and confirmed.

insphere *verb* var. of **ENSPHERE**.

in-sphere /ˈɪnsfɪə/ *noun*. **L19**.
[**ORIGIN** from **IN-**[1] + **SPHERE** *noun*.]
MATH. A sphere which touches all the faces of a given polyhedron.

inspirate /ˈɪnspɪreɪt/ *verb trans*. **E17**.
[**ORIGIN** Latin *inspirat-* pa. ppl stem of *inspirare*: see **INSPIRE**, **-ATE**[3].]
Orig., = **INSPIRE**. Now only (*PHONETICS*), utter during inhalation.

inspiration /ɪnspəˈreɪʃ(ə)n/ *noun*. **ME**.
[**ORIGIN** Old French & mod. French from late Latin *inspiratio(n-)*, formed as **INSPIRATE**: see **-ATION**.]
▸ **I 1 a** *spec*. Divine prompting or guidance; *esp*. that under which the books of Scripture are believed by some to have been written. **ME**. ▸**b** *gen*. The prompting of the mind to exalted thoughts, to creative activity, etc. Also, a quality of a thing that shows creative activity. **M17**. ▸**c** Undisclosed prompting from an influential source to express a particular viewpoint. **L19**.

a B. F. **WESTCOTT** The early Fathers teach us that Inspiration is an operation of the Holy Spirit acting through men. **b** M. **GIROUARD** The swags in the deep plasterwork frieze were of late eighteenth-century inspiration. A. **MUNRO** The importance of Prince Henry the Navigator was in the inspiration . . of other explorers.

a moral inspiration: according to which the inspiration of Scripture is confined to moral and religious teaching. **plenary inspiration**: according to which the inspiration of Scripture extends to all subjects treated. **verbal inspiration**: according to which every word of Scripture is dictated by God.
2 A thought, utterance, etc., that is inspired; a sudden brilliant or timely idea. **L16**.

Time Downey had an inspiration to do something on behalf of . . 'our senior citizens'. M. **SCAMMELL** Among his many inspirations was a device for deflecting radar beams.

3 An inspiring influence; a source of inspiration. **M19**.

Church Times The 'elders' or spiritual fathers, whose counsel and prayer is an inspiration to many.

▸ **II 4** The action or an act of drawing in breath. **LME**.
†**5** The action of blowing on or into something. **E16–E18**.

inspirational /ɪnspəˈreɪʃ(ə)n(ə)l/ *adjective*. **M19**.
[**ORIGIN** from **INSPIRATION** + **-AL**[1].]
1 Deriving character or substance from inspiration, that is under the influence of inspiration. **M19**.
2 Of or relating to inspiration. **L19**.
3 Inspiring. **L19**.
▪ **inspirationally** *adverb* under the influence of inspiration; as regards inspiration: **L19**.

inspirationist /ɪnspəˈreɪʃ(ə)nɪst/ *noun*. **M19**.
[**ORIGIN** formed as **INSPIRATIONAL** + **-IST**.]
A believer in inspiration. Usu. with specifying word, as ***plenary inspirationist***, a believer in plenary inspiration.

inspirator /ˈɪnspəreɪtə/ *noun*. **E17**.
[**ORIGIN** Late Latin, formed as **INSPIRATE**: see **-OR**. In sense 2, from **INSPIRE** + **-ATOR**: cf. *respirator*.]
1 A person who or thing which provides inspiration. Now *rare*. **E17**.
2 An apparatus for drawing in air or vapour. **L19**.

inspiratory /ɪnˈspʌɪrət(ə)ri/ *adjective*. **L18**.
[**ORIGIN** from **INSPIRATE** + **-ORY**[2].]
Serving to draw in the air in respiration.

inspire /ɪnˈspʌɪə/ *verb*. Also (earlier) †**en-**. **ME**.
[**ORIGIN** Old French & mod. French *inspirer* from Latin *inspirare*, formed as **IN-**[2] + *spirare* breathe.]
▸ **I 1 a** *verb trans*. Of a divine or supernatural agency: impart a truth, impulse, idea, etc., to. **ME**. ▸**b** *verb trans*. *gen*. Animate *with* a (noble or exalted) feeling, *to do* something (noble or exalted). **LME**. ▸**c** *verb intrans*. Provide inspiration; elevate or exalt the mind. **LME**.

a L. **STRACHEY** He mused, and was inspired: the Great Exhibition came into his head. C. **HOPE** Church and Regime believed themselves divinely inspired. **b** OED Romanus was inspired to compose these hymns. W. S. **CHURCHILL** The American republic had . . inspired the mass of Frenchmen with a new taste for liberty. Z. **MEDVEDEV** A leader who is capable of inspiring people to work harder.

2 *verb trans*. **a** Of a divine or supernatural agency: impart, suggest, (a revelation, idea, etc.). **LME**. ▸**b** *gen*. Arouse in the mind, instil, (a feeling, impulse, etc.). **L16**.

b R. **NIEBUHR** The symbols . . which inspire awe and reverence in the citizen. R. **WARNER** There was much in him that inspired confidence. D. **ACHESON** The General's retirement inspired sincere regret.

3 *verb trans*. Of an influential source: secretly prompt (a person etc.); suggest the expression of (a viewpoint). **L19**.
▸ **II 4 a** *verb trans*. Breathe upon or into. Now *rare* or *obsolete*. **LME**. ▸†**b** *verb intrans*. Breathe, blow. Only in **16**.

a **POPE** Descend, ye Nine! . . The breathing instruments inspire.

5 *verb trans*. **a** Breathe (life, a soul, etc.) *in*, *into*. Now chiefly *fig*. **LME**. ▸†**b** Blow, breathe (a vapour etc.) into or on something. **M16–L17**.

b J. **SYLVESTER** The wily Snake A poysoned air inspired . . In Eve's frail breast.

6 *verb trans. & intrans*. Take (air) into the lungs in breathing; inhale. Opp. ***expire***. **LME**.
▪ **inspired** *adjective* that is inspired; *esp*. (**a**) as though prompted by divine inspiration; (of a guess) intuitive but correct; (**b**) secretly prompted by an influential source: **LME**. **inspiredly** /-rɪdli/ *adverb* **L16**. **inspirer** *noun* a person who or thing which inspires **LME**. **inspiring** *ppl adjective* that inspires; *esp*. that elevates or exalts the mind: **M17**. **inspiringly** *adverb* **E19**.

inspirit /ɪnˈspɪrɪt/ *verb trans*. **E17**.
[**ORIGIN** from **IN-**[1] + **SPIRIT** *noun*.]
Put life or spirit into; encourage, incite (*to* action, *to do*).

H. T. **BUCKLE** Those great men, who, by their writings, inspirited the people to resistance.

▪ **inspiritingly** *adverb* in a manner that inspirits someone **E19**.

inspissate /ɪnˈspɪsət/ *ppl adjective*. Now *rare*. **E17**.
[**ORIGIN** Late Latin *inspissatus* pa. pple, formed as **INSPISSATE** *verb*: see **-ATE**[2].]
Made thick or dense.

inspissate /ɪnˈspɪseɪt/ *verb*. **E17**.
[**ORIGIN** Late Latin *inspissat-* pa. ppl stem of *inspissare*, formed as **IN-**[2] + *spissus* thick, dense: see **-ATE**[3].]
1 *verb trans*. Make thick or dense; *esp*. reduce (a liquid) to a semi-solid consistency. **E17**.

G. **BERKELEY** Pitch is tar inspissated.

2 *verb intrans*. Become thick or dense. **M18**.
▪ **inspiˈssation** *noun* **E17**. **ˈinspissator** *noun* an apparatus for thickening serum etc. by heat **L19**.

inspoke, **inspoken** *verbs* see **INSPEAK**.

inst. *abbreviation*.
1 Institute.
2 Institution.

inst. /ɪnst/ *adjective*. **L18**.
[**ORIGIN** Abbreviation.]
COMMERCE. = **INSTANT** *adjective* 2b. Now usu. with 'day' understood, following an ordinal numeral.

instability /ɪnstəˈbɪlɪti/ *noun*. LME.
[ORIGIN French *instabilité* from Latin *instabilitas*, from *instabilis*: see INSTABLE, -ITY.]
The quality of being unstable; lack of stability. Also, an instance of this.

L. NKOSI The constant.. flights of fancy.. create an impression of emotional instability.

instable /ɪnˈsteɪb(ə)l/ *adjective*. Now *rare*. LME.
[ORIGIN Old French & mod. French, or from Latin *instabilis*, formed as IN-[3] + *stabilis* STABLE *adjective*, or from IN-[3] + STABLE *adjective*.]
Not stable; characterized by instability; unstable.

install /ɪnˈstɔːl/ *verb trans*. Also **-stal**, infl. **-ll-**. LME.
[ORIGIN medieval Latin *installare*, formed as IN-[2] + *stallum* STALL *noun*[1].]
1 Invest (a person) with an office or rank by seating in a stall or official seat, or by some other ceremonial procedure. Freq. foll. by *in*. LME. ▸**b** Establish (a person etc.) in a place, condition, etc. Freq. foll. by *in*. L16.

G. PEELE Amurath's soldiers have by this install'd Good Abdelmelec in his royal seat. D. HUME Cromwell was declared protector; and with great solemnity installed in that high office. **b** J. KRANTZ Two other permanent house guests were immediately installed in the house. R. HUNTFORD To cope with workaday detail, Shackleton installed a business manager.

2 Place (an apparatus, system, etc.) in position for service or use. M19.

S. BELLOW I arranged to have the garbage-disposal unit installed in the sink. I. MURDOCH The new art nouveau lantern which Pat had installed illuminated the steps.

■ **installer** *noun* E17.

installation /ɪnstəˈleɪʃ(ə)n/ *noun*. LME.
[ORIGIN medieval Latin *installatio(n-)*, from *installat-* pa. ppl stem of *installare*: see INSTALL, -ATION.]
1 The action or an act of installing something or someone; the fact of being installed. LME.

J. LINGARD The cardinal had invited the nobility.. to assist at his installation. H. BAILEY With the.. installation of Winifred's old nanny as housekeeper. R. LARDNER The thirty-four-dollar synthetic radio had done nothing but croak since.. its installation. *attrib*.: *Which?* British Telecom can supply home pay-phones .. but.. there are installation costs to consider.

2 An apparatus, system, etc., that has been installed for service or use. L19.

F. FITZGERALD A thousand Vietnamese Marines.. seized the radio station, the corps headquarters, and other key installations.

3 An art exhibit constructed within a gallery as part of an exhibition. M20.

installment *noun*[1], *noun*[2] see INSTALMENT *noun*[1], *noun*[2].

instalment /ɪnˈstɔːlm(ə)nt/ *noun*[1]. Now *rare*. Also **-ll-**. L16.
[ORIGIN from INSTALL + -MENT.]
1 The action of installing something or someone; the fact of being installed; installation. L16.
†**2** A place or seat in which a person is installed. *rare*. L16–E17.

instalment /ɪnˈstɔːlm(ə)nt/ *noun*[2]. Also ***-ll-**. M18.
[ORIGIN Alt. (prob. by assoc. with INSTALMENT *noun*[1]) of ESTALMENT.]
†**1** The arrangement of the payment of a sum of money in fixed portions at fixed times. M–L18.
2 Each of the several parts, successively falling due, of a sum payable. L18.

R. DAHL What about the monthly installments on the television set? E. FROMM Buying all that he can afford to buy either for cash or on instalments.

3 Any of several parts (esp. of a serial story etc.) supplied, published, etc., at different times. E19.

C. RYCROFT Freud's *The Psychopathology of Everyday Life* first appeared in two instalments.. as articles. B. WEBB Five instalments of news at 10, 1, 4, 7 and 9.30 break up the day.

– COMB.: **instalment plan** *N. Amer.* hire purchase.

Instamatic /ɪnstəˈmatɪk/ *noun*. Also **i-**. M20.
[ORIGIN from INSTA(NT *adjective* + AUTO)MATIC.]
(Proprietary name for) a type of small fixed-focus camera for taking snapshots.

†**instamp** *verb* see ENSTAMP.

instance /ˈɪnst(ə)ns/ *noun*. ME.
[ORIGIN Old French & mod. French from Latin *instantia*, in medieval Latin objection, example to the contrary (translating Greek *enstasis* objection), from *instant-*: see INSTANT *adjective*, -ANCE.]
▸**I 1** Urgency in speech or action; urgent entreaty; earnestness, persistence. Now chiefly in ***at the instance of*** below. ME. ▸†**b** In *pl*. Urgent or repeated entreaties. M17–M19.

H. JAMES He had asked her, with much instance, to come out and take charge of their friend.

†**2** An impelling motive or cause. L16–M17.
▸†**II 3** Presence; the present time. LME–L16.
4 An instant, a moment. M–L17.
▸**III** †**5** *SCHOLASTIC LOGIC*. A case adduced in objection to or disproof of a universal assertion. L16–L17.
6 A fact or example illustrating a general truth; a person or thing for which an assertion is valid; a particular case. L16. ▸†**b** A particular or point characteristic of or included in something general or abstract; a detail. M17–M18.

J. THURBER There are dozens of.. instances of the dwindling of the male in the animal kingdom. H. J. LASKI The signs of change are in each instance slight, though collectively they acquire significance.

†**7** A thing which proves or indicates something; a sign, a token; evidence. L16–L18.

HENRY FIELDING I beg you to accept a guinea as a small instance of my gratitude.

▸**IV 8** *SCOTS LAW*. An indictment which must be pursued at the appointed time, failing which no further action can be taken. E17.
9 A process in a court of justice; a suit. M17.
– PHRASES: **at the instance of** at the request or suggestion of. **court of first instance** *LAW* a court of primary jurisdiction. **for instance** (*a*) as an example; (*b*) *colloq*. an example. **in the first instance**, **in the second instance**, etc., in the first (or second etc.) place; at the first (or second etc.) stage of a proceeding. **in this instance** in this case, on this occasion.
– COMB.: **Instance Court** *hist*. a branch of the Admiralty Court dealing with private maritime matters.

instance /ˈɪnst(ə)ns/ *verb*. LME.
[ORIGIN from the noun.]
▸†**I 1** *verb trans*. Urge, entreat earnestly, importune. LME–M18.
▸**II 2** *verb intrans*. Cite an instance; adduce an example in illustration or proof. (Foll. by *in*.) Now *rare*. E17.

G. WHITE It would be needless to instance in sheep, which frequently flock together.

3 *verb trans*. Illustrate or prove by means of an example etc.; exemplify. E17.

F. SPALDING Bloomsbury's interest in the affairs.. instanced their radicalism.

4 *verb trans*. Cite (a fact, a case) as an example or instance. E17.

P. GAY I instance only the amazing papers on technique dating from before World War I.

instancy /ˈɪnst(ə)nsi/ *noun*. E16.
[ORIGIN Latin *instantia*: see INSTANCE *noun*, -ANCY.]
1 The quality of being pressing; urgency; solicitation; pressing nature. E16.
2 Closeness, imminence. *rare*. M17.
3 Immediacy, instantaneity. *rare*. M19.

instant /ˈɪnst(ə)nt/ *noun*. LME.
[ORIGIN from INSTANT *adjective* & *adverb* after medieval Latin *instans* (sc. *tempus*) present moment of time.]
1 An extremely short space of time; a moment. LME.

G. ORWELL He did see them, for a fleeting instant.

2 A precise (esp. the present) point of time; a particular moment; *COMMERCE* the current month. E16.

P. BROOK These were only fragmentary impressions that .. came into being at the instant they were required.

3 An instant beverage, *spec*. instant coffee. M20.

Punch One of those dispensers which trickle hot water onto a tiny measure of dusty instant.

4 (Also **I-**.) (Proprietary name for) a lottery ticket that may be scratched or opened to reveal immediately whether a prize has been won. L20.
– PHRASES: **in an instant**, **on the instant** immediately. **the instant** *adverbial* as soon as, the very moment that. **this instant!** now, at once!

instant /ˈɪnst(ə)nt/ *adjective* & *adverb*. LME.
[ORIGIN Old French & mod. French from Latin *instant-* pres. ppl stem of *instare* be present or at hand, apply oneself to, formed as IN-[2] + *stare* stand: see -ANT[1].]
▸**A** *adjective* **1 a** Pressing, urgent. LME. ▸**b** Of a person, an action: urgent, importunate. *arch*. L15.

a J. H. NEWMAN He has instant need of you. **b** J. TYRRELL The Bishops were instant with the King to make Peace.

2 a Present now or at the time in question; current. *arch*. LME. ▸**b** *COMMERCE*. Of the current month. Now usu. with 'day' understood, following an ordinal numeral. Freq. abbreviated to INST. LME.
3 Close at hand, impending, imminent. Now *rare*. E16.

STEELE The evil which.. may seem distant, to him is instant and ever before his eyes.

4 Occurring immediately or without delay. L16.

A. THWAITE Gosse took an instant dislike to him. A. BROOKNER She .. had obtained instant relief from acupuncture.

instant camera: of a type with internal processing which produces a finished print rapidly after each exposure. **instant messaging** the exchange of typed messages between computer users in real time. **instant replay** *TELEVISION* the immediate repetition of a sequence in a filmed (sports) event, often in slow motion.
5 Of food: that can be prepared easily for immediate use. E20. ▸**b** *fig*. Hurriedly produced. M20.

News Chronicle Instant bread comes as small frozen pebble shapes which fluff up to fresh crisp rolls. **b** A. TOFFLER No product is more swiftly fabricated or more ruthlessly destroyed than the instant celebrity.

▸**B** *adverb*. Immediately, at once. *poet*. E16.

instantaneous /ɪnst(ə)nˈteɪnɪəs/ *adjective*. M17.
[ORIGIN from medieval Latin *instantaneus*, from Latin *instant-* (see INSTANT *adjective* & *adverb*) after medieval Latin *momentaneus*: see -ANEOUS.]
1 Occurring or done within an instant or instantly. M17. ▸**b** *PHOTOGRAPHY* (now chiefly *hist*.). Of, pertaining to, or designating an exposure of brief duration controlled by a rapid shutter mechanism (in contrast to a time exposure). M19.

W. GOLDING The applause was instantaneous and overwhelming.

2 *MATH*. & *PHYSICS*. Of a variable value, axis of rotation, etc.: existing at or pertaining to a particular instant. E19.
■ **instantaˈneity** *noun* the quality of being instantaneous M18. **instantaneously** *adverb* M17. **instantaneousness** *noun* E18.

instanter /ɪnˈstantə/ *adverb*. Now *arch*. or *joc*. L17.
[ORIGIN Latin.]
Immediately, at once.

instantial /ɪnˈstanʃ(ə)l/ *adjective*. M17.
[ORIGIN from Latin *instantia* INSTANCE *noun* + -AL[1].]
Of or pertaining to an instance or instances; providing an instance.
instantial premiss *LOGIC* a premiss concerned with or arising from a particular case.

instantiate /ɪnˈstanʃɪeɪt/ *verb trans*. M20.
[ORIGIN formed as INSTANTIAL + -ATE[3].]
Represent by an instance.

J. HOLLOWAY Two apples.. both instantiate the single universal redness. D. R. HOFSTADTER Our intelligence is not disembodied, but is instantiated in physical objects: our brains.

■ **instantiˈation** *noun* M20.

instantize /ˈɪnstəntʌɪz/ *verb trans*. Also **-ise**. M20.
[ORIGIN from INSTANT *adjective* + -IZE.]
Make (food) available in an instant form. Chiefly as ***instantized*** *ppl adjective*.

New Scientist The formulated, instantised, convenience foods will no longer look like meat, milk, cereal or vegetable.

instantly /ˈɪnst(ə)ntli/ *adverb* & *conjunction*. LME.
[ORIGIN from INSTANT *adjective* + -LY[2].]
▸**A** *adverb*. **1** Urgently, persistently, with importunity. *arch*. LME.
†**2** Just at this or that moment; just, now. L15–M17.
3 Immediately, at once. E16.

F. CHICHESTER Though I closed the throttle instantly, it seemed an age before the engine stopped.

▸**B** *conjunction*. The moment that, as soon as. L18.

THACKERAY He ran across the grass instantly he perceived his mother.

instar /ˈɪnstɑː/ *noun*. L19.
[ORIGIN Latin = form, figure, likeness.]
ZOOLOGY. (An individual animal at) any of the stages in the life of an insect or other arthropod, between successive ecdyses.

instar /ɪnˈstɑː/ *verb trans*. *poet*. Infl. **-rr-**. L16.
[ORIGIN from IN-[1] + STAR *noun*[1].]
1 Set among the stars; make a star of. L16.

J. FORD Our heart is high instarr'd in brighter spheres.

2 Adorn (as) with a star or stars. M17.

POPE The shining circlets of his golden hair.. Instarr'd with gems and gold.

instate /ɪnˈsteɪt/ *verb trans*. Also †**en-**. E17.
[ORIGIN from IN-[2], EN-[1] + STATE *noun*. Cf. earlier REINSTATE.]
1 Put (a person etc.) into a certain position or condition; install, establish, (*in* office etc.). E17.

E. BOWEN What seemed a provisional measure worked so well as to instate yet another tradition.

†**2** Endow or invest (a person) *with*. E–M17.
■ **instatement** *noun* (now *rare*) L17.

in statu nascendi /ɪn ˌstatjuː naˈsɛndiː/ *adjectival phr*. L19.
[ORIGIN Latin.]
In the process of creation, formation, or construction.

in statu pupillari /ɪn ˌstatjuː pjuːpɪˈlɑːriː/ *adjectival phr*. M19.
[ORIGIN Latin.]
Under guardianship; of junior status at a university; not having a master's degree.

in statu quo /ɪn ˌstatjuː ˈkwəʊ/ *adjectival phr*. E17.
[ORIGIN Latin.]
More fully ***in statu quo ante*** /ˈanti/, (rare) ***prius*** /ˈprʌɪəs/. In the same state as formerly.

instauration /ɪnstɔːˈreɪʃ(ə)n/ *noun*. E17.
[ORIGIN Latin *instauratio(n-)*, from *instaurat-* pa. ppl stem of *instaurare* restore, formed as IN-[2] + stem also of *restaurare* RESTORE *verb*: see -ATION.]
1 The action of restoring or repairing something; renovation, renewal. E17.
2 Institution, founding, establishment. Now *rare*. E17.

I

instaurator /ˈɪnstɔːreɪtə/ *noun*. E17.
[ORIGIN Late Latin, from *instaurat-*: see INSTAURATION, -OR.]
A person who repairs or renews something. Also, a person who establishes something, a founder.

instead /ɪnˈstɛd/ *adverb*. ME.
[ORIGIN Orig. two words, from IN *preposition* + STEAD *noun*. Cf. *in a person's stead* s.v. STEAD *noun*.]
1 *instead of*, in place of, in lieu of, for; rather than. ME.
OED I found it on the floor instead of in the drawer. D. ABSE He had whisky instead of blood running through his body. J. KRANTZ Instead of taking you to the station, I should have driven you straight home.
2 As a substitute or alternative. M17.
Newsweek Not to put their petro-billions into U.S. Treasury bonds, but to invest in American industry instead. *Soldier* He failed to find a single 'tough old bird' but instead returned with pictures of three charming young ladies.

†**insteep** *verb trans.* Also **en-**. L16–L18.
[ORIGIN from IN-[1], EN-[1] + STEEP *verb*[1].]
Immerse; steep or soak *in*.

instep /ˈɪnstɛp/ *noun*. LME.
[ORIGIN Unknown: cf. West Frisian *ynstap* opening in a shoe for insertion of the foot.]
1 The portion of the human foot comprising the arch between the toes and the ankle. LME.
2 The part of a shoe, stocking, etc., fitting over or under the instep. E17.
3 A thing resembling an instep in shape. L17.
4 ZOOLOGY. A part of an animal's foot corresponding to the human instep. *rare*. E18.

instigate /ˈɪnstɪgeɪt/ *verb trans.* M16.
[ORIGIN Latin *instigat-* pa. ppl stem of *instigare*, formed as IN-[2] + *stigare* prick, incite: see -ATE[3].]
1 Urge on, incite, (a person *to* an action, *to do* esp. something evil). M16.
B. JOWETT You must not instigate your elders to a breach of faith.
2 Bring about, initiate, provoke. M19.
E. FEINSTEIN He instigated the relationship himself by calling upon Marina at home.
■ **instigative** *adjective* (*rare*) tending to instigate; stimulative, provoking: M17. **instigator** *noun* a person who instigates something; an inciter: L16. **instiˈgatrix** *noun* (*rare*), pl. **-trices** /-trɪsiːz/, a female instigator E17.

instigation /ɪnstɪˈgeɪʃ(ə)n/ *noun*. LME.
[ORIGIN Old French & mod. French, or Latin *instigatio(n-)*, formed as INSTIGATE: see -ATION.]
1 The action or an act of instigating someone or something; urging, incitement. LME.
S. UNWIN At my instigation work was started on a Guide to Royalty.
2 An incentive, a stimulus, a spur. E16.

instil /ɪnˈstɪl/ *verb trans.* Also *-**ll**. Infl. **-ll-**. LME.
[ORIGIN Latin *instillare*, formed as IN-[2] + *stillare*, from *stilla* a drop.]
1 Put (liquid) *into* a thing by drops or in small quantities. LME.
2 Introduce (a feeling, idea, or principle) *in* or *into*, esp. gradually or covertly. M16.
C. HAMPTON We have to instil in them a work ethic tied to a reward system. M. MOORCOCK I. . could easily instil my own confidence into those seeking my help.
3 Imbue *with*. M17.
Sunday Express I went to Norfolk, and there I was instilled with a love of the countryside.
■ **instiˈllation** *noun* the action of instilling; that which is instilled: M16. **instiller** *noun* E17.

instinct /ˈɪnstɪŋ(k)t/ *noun*. LME.
[ORIGIN Latin *instinctus* instigation, impulse, from *instinct-* pa. ppl stem of *instinguere* incite, impel, formed as IN-[2] + *stinguere* prick.]
†**1** Instigation, impulse, prompting. LME–M18.
2 Orig., intuitive power. Later, innate impulsion; a natural propensity to act without conscious intention; *spec.* an innate usu. fixed pattern of behaviour in most animals in response to certain stimuli. LME. ▸**b** Unconscious skill; intuition; an instance of this. L16.
OED The instinct to suck as possessed by the young of all mammals. A. P. HERBERT By instinct she ran first towards the wharf gate. D. NOBBS His first wild instinct was to accelerate. **b** C. CHAPLIN Her instinct was unfailing in recognising those that had genuine talent. K. CORNELL As an actress, what I've had has been an instinct for being somebody else.
the herd instinct: see HERD *noun*[1].
■ **instinctless** *adjective* L19.

instinct /ɪnˈstɪŋ(k)t/ *adjective*. M16.
[ORIGIN Latin *instinctus* pa. pple of *instinguere*: see INSTINCT *noun*.]
†**1** Naturally present; innate. M16–E17.
†**2** Impelled, excited, animated. (Foll. by *with*.) M16–E18.
3 Imbued or inspired *with*. L18.
B. CORNWALL Through all the palace . . Instinct with light, a living splendour ran. M. BRADBURY He looks at these people, instinct with the times.

†**instinct** *verb trans.* M16.
[ORIGIN Latin *instinct-*: see INSTINCT *noun*.]
1 Instigate, prompt. M16–L17.
2 Implant naturally or as an instinct. M16–M18.

†**instinction** *noun*. LME.
[ORIGIN French, or late Latin *instinctio(n-)*, formed as INSTINCT *verb*: see -ION.]
1 Instigation, prompting, inspiration. LME–L17.
2 (A) natural impulse, (an) instinct. M16–M18.

instinctive /ɪnˈstɪŋ(k)tɪv/ *adjective & adverb*. L15.
[ORIGIN from INSTINCT *noun* + -IVE.]
▸ **A** *adjective*. Of or pertaining to instinct; (as if) resulting from instinct. L15.
J. DEWEY The human being is born with a greater number of instinctive tendencies than other animals. N. MOSLEY Women's knowledge was instinctive while men's had to be learned. J. LEHANE The break is usually automatic and . . becomes instinctive, but . . a verbal signal may be given.
▸ **B** *adverb*. Instinctively. *poet. rare*. E18.
■ **instinctively** *adverb* in an instinctive manner, by instinct E17.

instinctual /ɪnˈstɪŋ(k)tjʊ(ə)l/ *adjective*. E20.
[ORIGIN from INSTINCT *noun* + -UAL.]
Of or pertaining to instinct; involving or dependent on instinct.
■ **instinctually** *adverb* M20.

institor /ˈɪnstɪtə/ *noun*. M17.
[ORIGIN Latin, from *instit-* pa. ppl stem of *insistere* step on, follow, pursue, begin work on: see INSIST, -OR.]
Chiefly ROMAN & SCOTS LAW (now *hist.*). A factor, an agent; a broker, a retailer.
■ **instiˈtorial** *adjective* of or pertaining to an institor M19. **institorian** *adjective* institorial M19.

institute /ˈɪnstɪtjuːt/ *noun*[1]. L15.
[ORIGIN Latin *institutum* design, precept, use as noun of neut. pa. pple of *instituere*: see INSTITUTE *verb*.]
†**1** Purpose, design. L15–L17.
2 Something instituted; an established law, custom, etc.; an institution. L15.
MILTON Teaching and promoting . . the institutes and customs of civil life.
3 A principle or element of instruction; in *pl.*, a digest of the elements of a subject, esp. of jurisprudence. M16.
R. H. TAWNEY The edition of the *Institutes [of Justinian]* which appeared in 1559.
4 A society or organization for the promotion of a scientific, educational, etc., object; the building used by such a society or organization. E19.
J. MASTERS When we got to the Institute, Victoria went off to play whist. *Medway Extra* Participation is open to all . . research institutes and universities within the community.
Rural Institute: see RURAL *adjective*. *Women's Institute*: see WOMAN *noun*.

institute /ˈɪnstɪtjuːt/ *noun*[2]. L17.
[ORIGIN Latin *institutus* pa. pple, formed as INSTITUTE *verb*.]
ROMAN, CIVIL, & SCOTS LAW. The person to whom an estate is first given in a testament or destination.

institute /ˈɪnstɪtjuːt/ *verb trans.* Pa. pple & ppl adjective †**-tute** (earlier), **-tuted**. ME.
[ORIGIN Latin *institut-* pa. ppl stem of *instituere* establish, arrange, teach, formed as IN-[2] + *statuere* set up.]
1 Establish (a person) in a position; appoint (a person *to* or *into* a position) now only to a cure of souls. ME. ▸**b** ROMAN & CIVIL LAW. Appoint as heir. L16.
D. MASSON Young . . was instituted to the united vicarages of St. Peter and St. Mary. **b** S. HALLIFAX All children . . were to be instituted or disinherited by name.
2 Set up, establish, found; bring into use or practice. LME. ▸†**b** Ordain *that*. L15–M17. ▸†**c** Order, arrange. M16–M18. ▸**d** Set in operation; initiate, start. L18.
ISAIAH BERLIN Adequate safeguards were instituted against too reckless a trampling upon the . . past. **d** A. BRINK Ben . . instituted inquiries. I. MURDOCH Do you imagine that you can institute a revolution by propounding theory?
†**3** Ground or establish in principles; train, instruct. M16–M19.
■ **instituter** *noun* M16. **institutive** *adjective* having the character or quality of instituting something; tending to the institution of something: E17.

institution /ɪnstɪˈtjuːʃ(ə)n/ *noun & adjective*. LME.
[ORIGIN Old French & mod. French from Latin *institutio(n-)*, from *institut-*: see INSTITUTE *verb*, -ION.]
▸ **A** *noun*. **1** The action or an act of instituting something; the fact of being instituted. LME. ▸**b** CHRISTIAN CHURCH. The establishment of a sacrament, esp. the Eucharist, by Christ. Also, a passage (e.g. *this is my body, this is my blood*) of the prayer used in consecrating the Eucharist. M16.
ADAM SMITH Before the Institution of coined money . . people must always have been liable to the grossest frauds.
2 a CHRISTIAN CHURCH. The appointment of a person to a cure of souls. LME. ▸**b** ROMAN & CIVIL LAW. The appointment of an heir. M17.
3 An established law, custom, or practice. LME. ▸**b** A well-established or familiar practice or object. *colloq.* M19.
W. S. CHURCHILL The institution of Negro slavery had long reigned almost unquestioned. **b** R. MACAULAY The British Sunday was an institution.
peculiar institution: see PECULIAR *adjective*.
†**4** The giving of form or order to a thing; orderly arrangement; the established order by which a thing is regulated. E16–E19.
†**5** Training, instruction, education. M16–L18.
†**6** = INSTITUTE *noun*[1] 3. M16–E19.
7 A society or organization, *esp.* one founded for charitable or social purposes and freq. providing residential care; the building used by such a society or organization. E18.
D. WIGODER I would not be here, in a mental institution.
▸ **B** *attrib.* or as *adjective*. In, of, or pertaining to an institution. E19.

institutional /ɪnstɪˈtjuːʃ(ə)n(ə)l/ *adjective*. E17.
[ORIGIN from INSTITUTION + -AL[1].]
1 Of, pertaining to, or originated by institution; organized. E17. ▸**b** Of a religion: expressed or organized through institutions. E20. ▸**c** LINGUISTICS. Institutionalized. M20.
R. C. A. WHITE Necessary institutional and procedural background is given. **b** A. E. J. RAWLINSON The Christianity of history is a sacramental and institutional religion.
2 Of, pertaining to, or concerned with (a digest of) the elements of a subject, esp. of jurisprudence. M18.
3 Of or pertaining to a society or organization for the promotion of a purpose, esp. a charitable or social one. Also, supposedly characteristic of such an institution; lacking individuality; routine, uniform. L19. ▸**b** Of advertising: that lays stress on a firm rather than on its product. E20.
J. MORTIMER The only institutional buildings left unchanged are the church . . and the Rectory. G. SWIFT He pours into pale blue institutional teacups.
■ **institutionally** *adverb* M19.

institutionalise *verb* var. of INSTITUTIONALIZE.

institutionalism /ɪnstɪˈtjuːʃ(ə)n(ə)lɪz(ə)m/ *noun*. M19.
[ORIGIN from INSTITUTIONAL + -ISM.]
The system of institutions; belief in such a system. Also *spec.*, the principles of institutional religion; the characteristics of institutional life.

institutionalist /ɪnstɪˈtuːʃ(ə)n(ə)lɪst/ *noun*. E19.
[ORIGIN formed as INSTITUTIONALISM + -IST.]
A person who writes on the elements of a subject. Also, an adherent of institutionalism.

institutionalize /ɪnstɪˈtjuːʃ(ə)n(ə)lʌɪz/ *verb trans.* Also **-ise**. M19.
[ORIGIN from INSTITUTIONAL + -IZE.]
1 Make institutional; convert into or treat as an institution. Freq. as ***institutionalized*** *ppl adjective*. M19. ▸**b** LINGUISTICS. Of a speech community: recognize or accept (a word, phrase, etc.). Usu. in *pass.* M20.
C. FRANCIS The Spaniards . . had institutionalised torture under the guise of the Inquisition. M. SEYMOUR-SMITH A marvellous satirist . . who had sold out to institutionalized religion.
institutionalized racism unequal treatment of people from different ethnic backgrounds that is established in practice or by custom and usage, e.g. in the workings of a police force or other body.
2 Place or keep (a person needing care) in an institution; subject to institutional life, esp. for a period of time resulting in unfitness for life outside an institution. Freq. as ***institutionalized*** *ppl adjective*. E20.
Daily Telegraph Because he was hopelessly institutionalised he was unable to look after himself when free. G. PALEY You're a handicapped person mentally . . . You should have been institutionalized years ago.
■ **institutionaliˈzation** *noun* M20.

institutionary /ɪnstɪˈtjuːʃ(ə)n(ə)ri/ *adjective*. M17.
[ORIGIN from INSTITUTION + -ARY[1].]
†**1** Of or pertaining to (elements of) instruction; educational. M17–M18.
2 Of or pertaining to institution or an institution or institutions. E19.

institutor /ˈɪnstɪtjuːtə/ *noun*. M16.
[ORIGIN Latin, formed as INSTITUTE *verb* + -OR.]
1 A person who institutes or establishes something; a founder, an organizer. M16.
†**2** A person who teaches. E17–E19.
3 In the American Episcopal Church: a bishop or presbyter who institutes a minister into a parish or church. E19.
■ **institutress** *noun* a female institutor L18. **instiˈtutrix** *noun*, pl. **-trices** /-trɪsiːz/, an institutress E18.

†**instore** *verb trans.* LME.
[ORIGIN Latin *instaurare*: see INSTAURATION.]
1 Restore, repair, renew. LME–M16.
2 Erect, establish, commence. Only in LME.
3 Provide, supply; store *with*. LME–M19.

in-store /ˈɪnstɔː/ *adjective*. M20.
[ORIGIN from IN-[1] + STORE *noun*.]
Of or relating to goods etc. held in store; situated or taking place in a store.

Inst. P. *abbreviation*.
Institute of Physics.

instreaming /ˈɪnstriːmɪŋ/ *noun*. M19.
[ORIGIN from IN-[1] + STREAMING *noun*.]
The action or an act of streaming in; inflow.

instreaming /ˈɪnstriːmɪŋ/ *ppl adjective*. M19.
[ORIGIN from IN-[1] + STREAMING *ppl adjective*.]
That streams in; inflowing.

instress /ˈɪnstrɛs/ *noun*. M19.
[ORIGIN from IN-[1] + STRESS *noun*.]
The force of the individual or essential quality of an observed object on the mind of the observer. Cf. INSCAPE.
– NOTE: In the poetic theory of the English poet Gerard Manley Hopkins (1844–89).

in-stroke /ˈɪnstrəʊk/ *noun*. *rare*. L19.
[ORIGIN from IN-[1] + STROKE *noun*[1].]
A stroke directed inwards; a striking inwards; *esp.* the action which carries a piston further into the cylinder of an engine.

instruct /ɪnˈstrʌkt/ *verb trans*. Pa. pple & ppl adjective †**instruct** (earlier), **-ed**. LME.
[ORIGIN Latin *instruct-* pa. ppl stem of *instruere* set up, furnish, fit out, teach, formed as IN-[2] + *struere* pile up, build.]
▸ **I 1** Provide with knowledge or information; teach, educate. (Foll. by *in* a subject, a religious belief, etc., †*to*, †*to do*.) LME.
SHAKES. *Tit. A.* I was their Tutor to instruct them. J. C. OATES Vernon instructed them .. in composition, literature, and 'elocution'.
2 Give information to (a person) about a particular fact etc.; inform *that*. L15. ▸**b** LAW. Give information as a client to (a solicitor) or as a solicitor to (a counsel); authorize (a solicitor, a counsel) to act for one. M19.
T. KENEALLY The journal was at pains to instruct citizens on their rights. **b** DICKENS Having been instructed by Mrs. Martha Bardell, to commence an action against you. M. GILBERT Our client .. instructs us most emphatically that she dispatched three undervests.
3 Provide with authoritative directions as to action; direct, command, (a person *to do*). E16.
G. BOYCOTT We were instructed not to leave the hotel.
▸ **II** †**4** Provide *with*; put in order; prepare, equip. Chiefly *poet.* L15–L18.
5 SCOTS LAW. Provide (a statement) with evidence or proof; confirm by evidence; prove. L16.
PATRICK WALKER It was also a day of very astonishing apparitions .. which I can instruct the truth of.
■ **instructer** *noun* (now *rare*) an instructor M16. **instructible** *adjective* (*rare*) E17.

instruction /ɪnˈstrʌkʃ(ə)n/ *noun*. LME.
[ORIGIN Old French & mod. French from Latin *instructio(n-)*, formed as INSTRUCT: see -ION.]
1 The action or an act of instructing; teaching, education. Freq. foll. by *in*. LME.
J. C. OATES Hiram gave instructions .. in arithmetic, classical mythology, and world geography.
2 (An item of) the knowledge etc. taught; an instructive rule; a precept. LME.
†**3** (An item of) information given to a person about a particular fact etc. LME–M17.
4 A direction, an order, (*to* a person). Freq. in *pl.* LME. ▸**b** LAW. In *pl.* Directions given to a solicitor or a counsel. M18. ▸**c** COMPUTING. A direction in a computer program defining and effecting an operation. M20.
R. INGALLS Suzanne had given them four different sets of detailed instructions. J. WAIN I gave very careful instructions that they were to be kept away from you. **b** M. GILBERT My instructions are quite clear ... He is prepared to plead guilty to the offence as charged.
■ **instructional** *adjective* E19.

instructive /ɪnˈstrʌktɪv/ *adjective & noun*. E17.
[ORIGIN from INSTRUCT *verb* + -IVE.]
▸ **A** *adjective*. **1** Having the character or quality of instructing; conveying instruction; enlightening. E17.
2 GRAMMAR. Designating, being in, or pertaining to the case used in the Finno-Ugric and other language groups to express means. M19.
▸ **B** *noun*. GRAMMAR. *The* instructive case; a word, form, etc., in the instructive case. L19.
■ **instructively** *adverb* M17. **instructiveness** *noun* M17.

instructor /ɪnˈstrʌktə/ *noun*. LME.
[ORIGIN Latin, formed as INSTRUCT *verb* + -OR.]
1 A person who instructs; a teacher, a demonstrator. LME.
A. BURGESS I was a map-reading instructor in the army.
2 A teacher in higher education ranking below a professor. *N. Amer.* E18.
Partisan Review The academic hierarchy, from instructor up to full professor.
■ **instructorship** *noun* the rank or position of an instructor L19. **instructress** *noun* a female instructor M17.

instrument /ˈɪnstrʊm(ə)nt/ *noun*. ME.
[ORIGIN Old French & mod. French from Latin *instrumentum*, from *instruere*: see INSTRUCT *verb*, -MENT.]
1 A thing used in or for performing an action; a means. ME. ▸**b** *transf.* A person so made use of. ME.
H. J. LASKI The Cabinet .. had already become the fundamental administrative instrument. D. M. FRAME For self-study the material is experience, the instrument judgment. **b** *New York Times* The accused assassin must be an instrument of the radical right.
2 More fully ***musical instrument***. A contrivance or device for producing musical sounds by vibration, wind, percussion, etc. ME.
B. EMECHETA They heard stringed instruments like guitars.
original instrument: see ORIGINAL *adjective*.
3 LAW. A formal legal document. LME. ▸**b** SCOTS LAW. A formal and duly authenticated record, drawn up by a notary public, of any transaction. M16.
I. MURDOCH A sort of informal document, not .. a legal instrument, was drawn up. G. F. KENNAN It would be wrong to attribute excessive importance to the instruments signed at Brest-Litovsk.
†**4** A part of the body having a special function; an organ. LME–E18.
5 A tool, an implement, *esp.* one used for delicate or scientific work. LME. ▸**b** A device whose function is to register and measure; *spec.* a measuring device in an aeroplane etc. serving to determine the position or speed. L17. ▸†**c** Apparatus. Only in L17.
P. GALLICO The chattering sound of printing machines, stock tickers and telegraph instruments. P. O'BRIAN The surgeons were putting a final razor edge on their instruments. **b** C. A. LINDBERGH It was often necessary to fly through them, navigating by instruments only. D. BAGLEY All instruments would be working, recording air pressure, humidity, temperature.
– COMB.: **instrument board**, **instrument panel** a surface, esp. in a car or aeroplane, containing the dials etc. of measuring instruments.

instrument /ˈɪnstrʊm(ə)nt/ *verb*. E18.
[ORIGIN from the noun.]
1 LAW. **a** *verb intrans.* Draw up an instrument. E18. ▸**b** *verb trans.* Address an instrument to, petition by means of an instrument. M18.
2 *verb trans.* MUSIC. Make an instrumental arrangement or score of (a piece of music). E19.
3 *verb trans.* Equip or provide with instruments (for measuring, recording, etc.). M20.

instrumental /ɪnstrʊˈmɛnt(ə)l/ *adjective & noun*. LME.
[ORIGIN Old French & mod. French from medieval Latin *instrumentalis*, formed as INSTRUMENT *noun*: see -AL[1].]
▸ **A** *adjective*. **1** Serving as an instrument or means to achieve a particular end or purpose. (Foll. by *to*, *in*.) LME. ▸**b** Serving well for a particular purpose; useful, efficient. Now *rare* or *obsolete*. E17.
P. GAY The passion for power may be instrumental in the acquisition of money. R. ELLMANN She .. was instrumental in arranging for a series of English productions of his plays. **b** SWIFT It would be very instrumental to have a law made.
2 Of music: performed on or composed for an instrument or instruments, *spec.* not accompanying a vocal part. E16. ▸**b** Of the nature of or belonging to a musical instrument. *rare*. L17.
M. TIPPETT When the music is to be instrumental only, more is left to our imagination.
3 Of, pertaining to, or arising from an instrument. M16.
J. F. W. HERSCHEL We are obliged to have recourse to instrumental aids.
†**4** (Of a part of the body) having a special function; organic. M16–E17.
5 GRAMMAR. Expressing the means used; *spec.* designating, being in, or pertaining to a case (in Russian etc.) indicating a means or instrument. E19.
6 PSYCHOLOGY. Of or designating a form of conditioning in which the reinforcing stimulus is applied only after a particular response of the organism. M20.
▸ **B** *noun*. †**1** A part of the body having a special function; an organ. Only in M16.
†**2** A thing which serves as an instrument or means to achieve a particular end or purpose. L16–M17.
3 GRAMMAR. *The* instrumental case; a word, form, etc., in the instrumental case. E19.
4 A piece of music (to be) performed by an instrument or instruments, not by the voice. M20.
■ **instrumentally** *adverb* L16. **instrumentalness** *noun* M17.

instrumentalism /ɪnstrʊˈmɛnt(ə)lɪz(ə)m/ *noun*. E20.
[ORIGIN from INSTRUMENTAL + -ISM.]
The pragmatic philosophy of the American philosopher John Dewey (1859–1952), holding that thought is an instrument designed to solve practical problems over a wide range and that truth is not final and static but changes as these problems change.

instrumentalist /ɪnstrʊˈmɛnt(ə)lɪst/ *noun*. E19.
[ORIGIN from INSTRUMENTAL *adjective* + -IST.]
1 A person who plays a musical instrument; a performer of instrumental music. E19.
2 An adherent of instrumentalism. E20.

instrumentality /ˌɪnstrʊmɛnˈtalɪti/ *noun*. M17.
[ORIGIN from INSTRUMENTAL *adjective* + -ITY.]
1 The quality or condition of being instrumental; the fact or function of serving as an instrument or means to achieve a particular end or purpose. M17.
2 A thing which is employed for a purpose or end; a means. L17.

instrumentary /ɪnstrʊˈmɛnt(ə)ri/ *adjective*. M16.
[ORIGIN from INSTRUMENT *noun* + -ARY[1].]
†**1** Serving for a particular vital function; organic. M16–M17.
†**2** Of the nature of or serving as an instrument or means. E–M17.
3 SCOTS LAW. Of or relating to a deed or legal instrument. E18.

instrumentation /ˌɪnstrʊmɛnˈteɪʃ(ə)n/ *noun*. M19.
[ORIGIN French, formed as INSTRUMENT *verb* + -ATION.]
1 The arrangement or composition of music for particular musical instruments; the instruments used in any one piece of music. Also (*rare*), playing on musical instruments. M19.
2 Operation or provision of means; instrumental agency. M19.
3 The use of an instrument, esp. for delicate or scientific work; operation with an instrument. L19.
4 The design and provision of instruments for measurement, control, etc.; such instruments collectively. M20.

instyle /ɪnˈstʌɪl/ *verb trans*. Also **en-** /ɪn-, ɛn-/. L16.
[ORIGIN from IN-[2], EN-[1] + STYLE *noun* or *verb*.]
Call by the style or name of.

insuavity /ɪnˈswɑːvɪti/ *noun*. Now *rare* or *obsolete*. E17.
[ORIGIN Latin *insuavitas*, formed as IN-[3] + SUAVITY.]
Lack of suavity; unpleasantness.

insubjection /ɪnsəbˈdʒɛkʃ(ə)n/ *noun*. *rare*. E19.
[ORIGIN from IN-[3] + SUBJECTION.]
Lack of subjection; the state of not being subject to authority or control.

insubmergible /ɪnsəbˈməːdʒɪb(ə)l/ *adjective*. Now *rare*. E19.
[ORIGIN from IN-[3] + SUBMERGIBLE *adjective*.]
Unable to be submerged, = INSUBMERSIBLE.

insubmersible /ɪnsəbˈməːsɪb(ə)l/ *adjective*. *rare*. M19.
[ORIGIN from IN-[3] + SUBMERSIBLE *adjective*.]
Unable to be submerged, = INSUBMERGIBLE.

insubmissive /ɪnsəbˈmɪsɪv/ *adjective*. *rare*. M19.
[ORIGIN from IN-[3] + SUBMISSIVE.]
Not submissive; not disposed to submit.

insubordinate /ɪnsəˈbɔːdɪnət/ *adjective & noun*. M19.
[ORIGIN from IN-[3] + SUBORDINATE *adjective*.]
▸ **A** *adjective*. Not obedient to orders; defiant of authority; rebellious, disobedient. M19.
▸ **B** *noun*. An insubordinate person. L19.
■ **insubordinately** *adverb* L19.

insubordination /ˌɪnsəbɔːdɪˈneɪʃ(ə)n/ *noun*. L18.
[ORIGIN from (the same root as) INSUBORDINATE + -ATION.]
The fact or condition of being insubordinate; disobedience to orders; defiance of authority; rebelliousness; an act or instance of this.

insubstantial /ɪnsəbˈstanʃ(ə)l/ *adjective*. E17.
[ORIGIN Late Latin *insubstantialis*, formed as IN-[3] + *substantialis* SUBSTANTIAL.]
1 Not existing in substance or reality; not real, imaginary, illusory. E17.
J. R. SEELEY It was no insubstantial city, such as we fancy in the clouds.
2 Lacking solidity or substance; not substantial. E17.
E. B. BROWNING A common cough striking on an insubstantial frame began my bodily troubles. F. DONALDSON A novel of a purely popular kind, with an insubstantial plot.
■ **insubstantiˈality** *noun* M19. **insubstantially** *adverb* L20.

insuccess /ɪnsəkˈsɛs/ *noun*. M17.
[ORIGIN from IN-[3] + SUCCESS.]
Lack of success.

insudation /ɪnsʊˈdeɪʃ(ə)n/ *noun*. M17.
[ORIGIN from Latin *insudat-* pa. ppl stem of *insudare*, formed as IN-[2] + *sudare* sweat: see -ATION. Cf. EXUDATION.]
†**1** Sweating; *fig.* heavy labour. *rare*. Only in M17.
2 MEDICINE. Seepage of plasma or other constituents of blood into or through the walls of a blood vessel. M20.

†**insue** *verb* var. of ENSUE.

insufferable /ɪnˈsʌf(ə)rəb(ə)l/ *adjective*. LME.
[ORIGIN from IN-³ + SUFFERABLE, perh. through French *insouffrable* (now dial.).]
Unable to be borne or endured; intolerable, unbearable. Now *esp.* unbearably arrogant or conceited.

P. G. WODEHOUSE There was an insufferable suggestion of . . fatherliness in his attitude which she found irritating. N. COWARD You're quite insufferable; I expect it's because you're drunk.

■ **insufferableness** *noun* L16. **insufferably** *adverb* E17.

insuffice /ɪnsəˈfʌɪs/ *verb intrans. rare*. M19.
[ORIGIN from IN-³ + SUFFICE *verb*.]
Be insufficient.

insufficience /ɪnsəˈfɪʃ(ə)ns/ *noun*. Now *rare* or *obsolete*. LME.
[ORIGIN Old French, formed as INSUFFICIENCY: see -ENCE.]
1 = INSUFFICIENCY 1. LME.
2 = INSUFFICIENCY 2. L15.

insufficiency /ɪnsəˈfɪʃ(ə)nsi/ *noun*. E16.
[ORIGIN Late Latin *insufficientia*, from *insufficient-*: see INSUFFICIENT, -ENCY.]
1 Inability of a person to fulfil requirements; unfitness, incompetence; an instance of this. *arch.* E16.
2 Deficiency in the force, quality, or amount of something; inadequacy. M16.

C. G. WOLFF She is limited . . by the insufficiency of her experience in the actual world. J. BRODSKY I am far from accusing the English language of insufficiency.

3 MEDICINE. Physical incapacity or impotence; impaired ability of an organ or system to do its natural work. E18.

Lancet Limbs with chronic venous insufficiency.

insufficient /ɪnsəˈfɪʃ(ə)nt/ *adjective*. LME.
[ORIGIN Old French from late Latin *insufficient-* formed as IN-³ + *sufficient-* SUFFICIENT.]
†**1** Of a person: not capable of fulfilling requirements; unfit; incompetent. LME–L17. ▸**b** Not having enough of a thing; inadequately provided with money etc. LME–E17.

SPENSER Soe as the bishop . . may justly rejecte them as incapable and insufficient.

2 Of a thing: deficient in force, quality, or amount; inadequate. LME.

R. ELLMANN The staples were weak gruel, suet and water . . . Such food was revolting and insufficient.

■ **insufficiently** *adverb* LME. **insufficientness** *noun* (long *rare* or *obsolete*) LME.

insufflate /ˈɪnsəfleɪt/ *verb trans*. L17.
[ORIGIN Late Latin *insufflat-* pa. ppl stem of *insufflare*, formed as IN-² + Latin *sufflare* SUFFLATE.]
1 THEOLOGY. †**a** Blow or breathe (a spirit etc.) into a person. Only in L17. ▸**b** Blow or breathe on (a person) to symbolize spiritual influence. E20.
2 MEDICINE. Blow (air, gas, powder, etc.) into an opening or cavity of the body. L17.
■ **insufflator** *noun* (chiefly MEDICINE) an instrument for insufflating air, powder, etc., esp. into the lungs L19.

insufflation /ɪnsəˈfleɪʃ(ə)n/ *noun*. LME.
[ORIGIN Late Latin *insufflatio(n-)*, formed as INSUFFLATE: see -ATION.]
1 THEOLOGY. **a** The action or an act of blowing on a person to symbolize spiritual influence. LME. ▸**b** The action or an act of blowing or breathing a spirit etc. into a person. E17.
2 Chiefly MEDICINE. The blowing or breathing (of a gas, powder, etc.) into an opening or cavity (of the body). E19.
3 MEDICINE. Distension with air. L19.

insula /ˈɪnsjʊlə/ *noun*. Pl. **-lae** /-liː/. M19.
[ORIGIN Latin = island.]
1 ROMAN HISTORY. A block of buildings; a square or space mapped out or divided off. M19.
2 ANATOMY. A region of the brain deep in the cerebral cortex. Also called ***island of Reil***. L19.

insular /ˈɪnsjʊlə/ *noun & adjective*. M16.
[ORIGIN Late Latin *insularis*, formed as INSULA: see -AR¹.]
▸ **A** *noun*. A native or inhabitant of an island; an islander. Now *rare*. M16.
▸ **B** *adjective*. **1** Of or pertaining to an island; inhabiting or situated on an island. E17. ▸**b** PHYSICAL GEOGRAPHY. Of climate: equable because of the influence of the sea (as that of islands and sheltered coasts). M19.
2 Of the nature of an island; forming an island. M17.

A. R. WALLACE A description of the great insular land—Australia.

3 Of, pertaining to, or characteristic of islanders; ignorant of or indifferent to cultures, peoples, etc., outside one's own experience; narrow-minded. L18. ▸**b** PALAEOGRAPHY. Designating or pertaining to a development of Latin script current in the British Isles in the early Middle Ages. E20.

G. SANTAYANA He felt how incredibly insular it was to suppose that England meant home for everybody. B. GUEST The magazine would not be insular, but international in intent.

4 Detached, separated, isolated; MEDICINE of or pertaining to the insula, or the islets of Langerhans; *spec.* (of sclerosis) disseminated. L19.
■ **insularism** *noun* the quality of being insular; narrow-mindedness: L19. **insularize** *verb trans.* (*rare*) make insular; represent as an island: L19. **insularly** *adverb* M19. **insulary** *adjective* & *noun* (now *rare* or *obsolete*) (**a**) *adjective* insular; (**b**) *noun* an inhabitant of an island; an islander: L16.

insularity /ɪnsjʊˈlarɪti/ *noun*. M18.
[ORIGIN formed as INSULA + -ITY.]
1 The state or condition of being an islander; ignorance of or indifference to cultures, peoples, etc., outside one's own experience; narrow-mindedness. M18.

BARONESS ORCZY When our prejudiced insularity was at its height, when to an Englishman . . the whole of . . Europe was a den of immorality.

2 The state or condition of being an island. L18.

J. PINKERTON The insularity of Britain was first shown by Agricola, who sent his fleet round it.

insulate /ˈɪnsjʊlət/ *adjective*. Now *rare*. E18.
[ORIGIN Latin *insulatus*, formed as INSULA: see -ATE².]
Detached, isolated; insulated.

insulate /ˈɪnsjʊleɪt/ *verb trans*. M16.
[ORIGIN from Latin INSULA or as INSULATE *adjective*: see -ATE³.]
1 Make (land) into an island. *arch.* M16.

D. WILSON Ere Britain had been insulated from the continent.

2 Cause (a thing etc.) to stand detached from its surroundings; isolate. E18.

M. M. KAYE Insulated by distance and the slower pace of life . . Ash had soon lost interest in . . political wrangling.

3 Isolate by the interposition of non-conductive materials, to prevent the passage of electricity, heat, or sound. M18.

Pall Mall Gazette Two coils of insulated copper wire. *Home Plumbing* Insulating jackets are available to lag hot water cylinders.

insulating tape: impregnated with an insulating compound and used to cover exposed electrical wires etc.
■ **insulant** *adjective* & *noun* †(**a**) *adjective* insulating (electrically); (**b**) *noun* an insulating material: E19. **insulative** *adjective* of or pertaining to insulation; providing insulation: M20.

insulation /ɪnsjʊˈleɪʃ(ə)n/ *noun*. M18.
[ORIGIN from INSULATE *verb* + -ATION.]
1 The action of insulating or the condition of being insulated against the passage of electricity, heat, or sound; the degree to which something is insulated. M18. ▸**b** Insulating or non-conductive material. L19.

Electrical Review Higher Voltage demands better insulation. **b** J. S. FOSTER Practical ways of incorporating insulation in wall construction.

2 The action or an act of detaching or separating a thing etc. from its surroundings; the state or condition of being isolated. L18.

G. WAKEFIELD An absolute insulation . . from the reasonable benefits of society.

3 The action of making land into an island; the fact of being made into an island; an island. M19.

insulator /ˈɪnsjʊleɪtə/ *noun*. E19.
[ORIGIN formed as INSULATION + -OR.]
A substance or device which resists or prevents the passage of electricity, heat, or sound.

insulin /ˈɪnsjʊlɪn/ *noun*. Also †**-ine**. E20.
[ORIGIN from Latin INSULA (with ref. to the islets of Langerhans: see below) + -IN¹, -INE⁵.]
A polypeptide hormone (whose composition varies slightly between species) which is produced by the islets of Langerhans and is involved in carbohydrate metabolism in humans and some other vertebrates, and whose deficiency causes diabetes mellitus.
– COMB.: **insulin coma**: caused by insulin shock; **insulin shock** (**a**) hypoglycaemia, with weakness and sweating, resulting from excess blood insulin; (**b**) = ***insulin treatment*** below; **insulin treatment** treatment of mental illness by inducing insulin coma.

insulse /ɪnˈsʌls/ *adjective*. Now *rare* or *obsolete*. E17.
[ORIGIN Latin *insulsus*, formed as IN-³ + *salsus* witty, lit. 'salted', pa. pple of *salere* to salt, from *sal* salt.]
1 Lacking wit or sense; dull, stupid; senseless. E17.
2 Tasteless, insipid. L17.
■ **insulsity** *noun* E17.

insult /ˈɪnsʌlt/ *noun*. E17.
[ORIGIN French *insulte* or ecclesiastical Latin *insultus*, formed as IN-² + Latin *saltus* leap, after *insultare*: see INSULT *verb*.]
1 An act or the action of attacking; (an) attack, (an) assault. Formerly *spec.* (MILITARY), an open and sudden attack without formal preparations. *arch.* E17. ▸**b** MEDICINE. An action or process causing injury to the body or disturbance of its normal functions; the injury or disturbance so caused; trauma. E20.

H. H. WILSON The . . pirate . . by whom the trade of the Company was subjected to repeated insult. **b** D. W. GOODWIN The body adapts rapidly to chemical insults.

2 The action or an act of insulting a person etc.; an instance of this; an insulting remark or action. Also (*colloq.*), a thing so worthless or contemptible as to be offensive. L17.

W. S. CHURCHILL Many are the insults and slanders which we have allowed to pass . . unanswered. W. WHARTON Vegas, plumb smack in the middle of a desert, is an insult to nature.

add insult to injury behave offensively as well as harmfully.

insult /ɪnˈsʌlt/ *verb*. M16.
[ORIGIN Latin *insultare*, formed as IN-² + *saltare* iterative-intensive of *salire* leap, jump.]
1 *verb intrans.* Show arrogance or scorn; boast, exult, esp. insolently or contemptuously. Also foll. by *over*, *on*, the person or thing scorned; *in*, *of*, the cause of boasting. *arch.* M16.

S. DANIEL They know how, The Lyon being dead euen Hares insult. S. PEPYS The Dutch do mightily insult of their victory, and they have great reason. DE QUINCEY We all know that it was not in his nature to insult over the fallen.

2 *verb trans.* Treat with scornful abuse; subject to indignity; (of a person or thing) offend the modesty or self-respect of. E17.

J. UPDIKE This stranger should be told that insulting local people was not the way to win friends. I. MURDOCH You insult us by implying that we don't care.

†**3** *verb intrans.* Make an attack or assault. M–L17.
4 *verb trans.* Attack, assault, (now only *fig.*). Formerly *spec.* (MILITARY), attack openly and suddenly without formal preparations. L17.

G. P. R. JAMES A group of night-ramblers walked along insulting the ear of night with cries.

■ **insultable** *adjective* (*rare*) able to be insulted M19. **insultant** *adjective* (*rare*) insulting E17. **insulter** *noun* L16. **insultingly** *adverb* in an insulting manner E17. †**insultment** *noun* (*rare*, Shakes.) the action of insulting, insult: only in E17.

insultation /ɪnsʌlˈteɪʃ(ə)n/ *noun*. Now *rare* or *obsolete*. E16.
[ORIGIN Old French, or Latin *insultatio(n-)*, from *insultat-* pa. ppl stem of *insultare*: see INSULT *verb*, -ATION.]
1 The action or an act of insulting; contemptuous speech or behaviour; insult. E16.
†**2** Attack, assault. L16–M17.

†**insume** *verb trans*. L16–M17.
[ORIGIN Alt. by substitution of IN-² of ASSUME *verb*.]
Take in, absorb.

insuperable /ɪnˈsuːp(ə)rəb(ə)l, -ˈsjuː-/ *adjective*. ME.
[ORIGIN Old French, or Latin *insuperabilis*, formed as IN-³ + SUPERABLE.]
1 Unable to be overcome or vanquished; unconquerable, invincible. Now *rare* or *obsolete* exc. as passing into sense 3. ME.

P. HOLLAND Three hundred thousand fighting men . . all invincible soldiers, and appointed with armes insuperable.

2 Of a barrier, gulf, etc.: unable to be surmounted or passed over. Now chiefly as passing into sense 3. M17.

HENRY MORE Whether we . . admire the height of some insuperable and inaccessible Rock or Mountain.

3 *fig.* Of a difficulty, problem, etc.: unable to be surmounted or overcome. M17.

E. WAUGH At first the difficulties of imitation appeared to be insuperable. I. MURDOCH The absence of any insuperable barrier to their advance to higher levels of income. D. ADAMS He had finally won through against what had seemed to be insuperable odds.

4 Unable to be surpassed. *rare*. M19.

A. BURGESS A crystal set, a miracle . . for music and speech of insuperable clarity.

■ **insuperaˈbility** *noun* E18. **insuperably** *adverb* L17.

insupportable /ɪnsəˈpɔːtəb(ə)l/ *adjective*. M16.
[ORIGIN Old French & mod. French, formed as IN-³ + SUPPORT *verb*: see -ABLE.]
1 Unable to be endured or borne; insufferable; unbearable. M16.

G. K. CHESTERTON He . . became that elegant and rather insupportable person whom Gregory had first encountered. M. MEYER The combination of overwork, poverty and literary failure became almost insupportable.

†**2** Unable to be resisted; irresistible. L16–L17.
3 Unable to be supported or sustained by reasons; unjustifiable, indefensible. M17.

M. GORDON He was always making large insupportable statements like, 'London was nothing after the eighteenth century.'

■ **insupportableness** *noun* L16. **insupportably** *adverb* L17.

insupposable /ɪnsəˈpəʊzəb(ə)l/ *adjective. rare*. M17.
[ORIGIN from IN-³ + SUPPOSABLE.]
Unable to be supposed.

insuppressible /ɪnsəˈprɛsɪb(ə)l/ *adjective*. E17.
[ORIGIN from IN-³ + SUPPRESS + -IBLE.]
Unable to be suppressed; irrepressible.

SMOLLETT Seized with insuppressible sorrow at the prospect of my misery he burst into tears.

insuppressive /ɪnsəˈprɛsɪv/ *adjective. rare*. E17.
[ORIGIN from IN-³ + SUPPRESSIVE.]
Insuppressible.

insurance /ɪnˈʃʊər(ə)ns/ *noun*. Also (earlier) †**en-**. LME.
[ORIGIN Old French *enseürance*, formed as ENSURE, INSURE: see -ANCE.]
1 The action or a means of ensuring or making certain; assurance, guarantee. Now chiefly as passing into sense 2. LME.

W. J. MICKLE An offering grateful to their gods, as the most acceptable insurance of the divine protection. E. CRANKSHAW The British were . . thinking . . , only of insurance against possible German aggression.

2 The act or process of insuring property, life, etc.; a contract by which one party undertakes on receipt of a premium to secure another against financial loss by a payment in the event of loss, damage, injury, etc. Cf. ASSURANCE 6. M17. ▸**b** The sum paid for insuring something; a premium. M17. ▸**c** A sum (to be) paid out as compensation; the amount for which property or life is insured. M19. ▸**d** In full ***National Insurance***. A system of compulsory contribution from employed adults below pension age and from employers to provide state assistance in sickness, unemployment, retirement, etc. L19.

Dumfries & Galloway Standard The insurance cannot stop the motor car going wrong but it can take care of the expense. *Society (Mumbai)* Here we have good health insurance and that takes care of many of our problems. **b** *London Gazette* The Insurance upon our Convoy to the Levant is very high. OED His Insurance falls due this month.

social insurance: see SOCIAL *adjective*.
3 Something which provides safety (*against*). E20.
– COMB.: **insurance agent**: employed to collect premiums from door to door; **insurance company**: engaged in insuring lives, property, etc.; **insurance policy** (*a*) a contract of insurance; (*b*) a document detailing such a policy and constituting a contract; (*c*) *fig.* a measure taken as a precaution; **insurance premium** = sense 2c above; **insurance stamp** a stamp certifying the payment of a sum, usu. paid weekly, for National Insurance.
■ †**insurancer** *noun* a person who provides insurance or assurance M17–E19.

insurant /ɪnˈʃʊər(ə)nt/ *noun*. M19.
[ORIGIN from INSURE + -ANT[1].]
The person to whom an insurance policy is issued.

insure /ɪnˈʃʊə/ *verb*. LME.
[ORIGIN Alt. by substitution of IN-[2] of ENSURE.]
†**1** *verb trans.* Make (a person) sure (*of* a thing); assure. LME–L17.

T. PRESTON I insure you he is a king most vile and pernicious. J. SCOTT The most effectual Care . . to insure us of God's performing his Part.

2 *verb trans.* Secure the payment of a sum of money in the event of loss of, damage to, or injury to (property, life, a limb, etc.) by the payment of a premium; secure the payment of (a sum of money) in the event of or *against* such a loss etc. by the payment of a premium. M17. ▸**b** *verb intrans.* Issue an insurance policy; take out insurance. M17.
the insured the person in respect of whom an insurance payment is secured, or on whose death, illness, or injury insurance becomes due.
3 *verb trans.* Make certain, guarantee; ensure. L17.

J. RUSKIN Want of care in the points which insure the building's endurance.

4 *verb trans.* Make safe, secure (*against*, *from*). E18.

J. D. BURNS The evidence of trials past does not insure them against trials that may come.

– NOTE: See note at ENSURE.
■ **insuraˈbility** *noun* the quality of being insurable L19. **insurable** *adjective* able to be insured, suitable for insuring; sufficient to make a ground for insurance: E19. **insurer** *noun* M16.

insurge /ɪnˈsəːdʒ/ *verb*. Now *rare* or *obsolete*. E16.
[ORIGIN Latin *insurgere*: see INSURGENT.]
†**1** *verb intrans.* Arise, spring up. Only in 16.
†**2** *verb intrans.* Rise in opposition or rebellion *against*; revolt. M16–E17.
3 *verb trans.* Stir up; raise in rebellion. L18.

insurgence /ɪnˈsəːdʒ(ə)ns/ *noun*. M19.
[ORIGIN formed as INSURGENT: see -ENCE.]
Insurgency.

insurgency /ɪnˈsəːdʒ(ə)nsi/ *noun*. E19.
[ORIGIN formed as INSURGENCE: see -ENCY.]
The quality or state of being insurgent; the tendency to be insurgent; a rising, a revolt.

F. FITZGERALD Fortified villages such as the British had used against the Communist insurgency in Malaya.

insurgent /ɪnˈsəːdʒ(ə)nt/ *noun & adjective*. M18.
[ORIGIN French †*insurgent* from Latin *insurgent-* pres. ppl stem of *insurgere*, formed as IN-[2] + *surgere* rise: see -ENT.]
▸ **A** *noun*. A person who rebels or rises in active revolt against authority; a rebel, a revolutionary. M18.

DAY LEWIS The unexpectedness of an ultimatum delivered by insurgents who have achieved a revolution.

▸ **B** *adjective*. **1** Of the sea etc.: surging up, rushing in. L18.

fig.: D. H. LAWRENCE Her voice was full of insurgent tenderness.

2 Rising in active revolt, rebelling; rebellious. E19.

R. WHELAN Insurgent planes swooped down over the road to machine-gun the helpless refugees.

insurmountable /ɪnsəˈmaʊntəb(ə)l, -səː-/ *adjective*. L17.
[ORIGIN from IN-[3] + SURMOUNTABLE.]
Unable to be surmounted or overcome.

C. HOPE The problem seemed insurmountable.

■ **insurmountably** *adverb* M18.

insurpassable /ɪnsəˈpɑːsəb(ə)l, -səː-/ *adjective*. *rare*. M19.
[ORIGIN from IN-[3] + SURPASSABLE.]
Unable to be surpassed.

insurrect /ɪnsəˈrɛkt/ *verb intrans*. Now *rare* or *obsolete*. M17.
[ORIGIN Latin *insurrect-* pa. ppl stem of *insurgere*: see INSURGENT.]
†**1** Arise. Only in M17.
2 Rise in insurrection or revolt. E19.

insurrection /ɪnsəˈrɛkʃ(ə)n/ *noun*. LME.
[ORIGIN Old French & mod. French from late Latin *insurrectio(n-)*, formed as INSURRECT: see -ION.]
The action or an act of rising against authority or government; a rebellion, a revolt, an uprising.

E. WILSON Driven underground, they now plotted an insurrection. *fig.*: P. ROTH Your escapade, your risk, your daily insurrection against all your overwhelming virtues.

■ **insurrectional** *adjective* (now *rare*) E19. **insurrectionary** *adjective & noun* (*a*) *adjective* of, pertaining to, or resembling insurrection; given to insurrection; (*b*) *noun* a person who takes part in or encourages insurrection: L18. **insurrectionist** *noun* an insurrectionary M19.

insurrecto /ɪnsəˈrɛktəʊ/ *noun*. Pl. **-os**. E20.
[ORIGIN Spanish, from Latin *insurrectus* pa. pple of *insurgere*: see INSURGENT.]
Esp. in Spain and Spanish-speaking countries: an insurgent, a rebel; an insurrectionist.

insusceptible /ɪnsəˈsɛptɪb(ə)l/ *adjective*. E17.
[ORIGIN from IN-[3] + SUSCEPTIBLE *adjective*.]
Not susceptible; not able to receive impressions; not liable to be affected or influenced.

R. H. CHARLES Souls in Sheol were conceived as insusceptible of ethical progress. L. P. BROCKETT Insusceptible to all those influences . . which so powerfully affect most peoples.

■ **insusceptiˈbility** *noun* E19.

inswinger /ˈɪnswɪŋə/ *noun*. E20.
[ORIGIN from IN-[1] + SWINGER *noun*[1].]
1 CRICKET. A ball bowled with a swerve or swing from off to leg; a bowler who bowls such balls. E20.
2 FOOTBALL. A pass or kick that sends the ball curving towards the goal. L20.
■ **inswing** *noun* [back-form.] CRICKET the swerve or swing imparted to an inswinger E20.

int. *abbreviation*.
1 Interior.
2 Internal.
3 International.

i'nt *verb* see BE.

†**intablature** *noun* var. of ENTABLATURE.

intabulate /ɪnˈtabjʊleɪt/ *verb trans*. M17.
[ORIGIN medieval Latin *intabulat-* pa. ppl stem of *intabulare*, from Latin IN-[2] + *tabula* table: see -ATE[3]. In sense 2 back-form. from INTABULATION.]
1 Enter or inscribe in a table or list. *rare*. M17.
2 MUSIC. Make an intabulation of. L20.

intabulation /ɪnˌtabjʊˈleɪʃ(ə)n/ *noun*. M17.
[ORIGIN formed as INTABULATE: see -ATION. In sense 2 translating Italian *intavolatura* writing in tablature, formed as IN-[2] + *tavolatura* TABLATURE.]
†**1** The laying down of boards or planks. *rare*. Only in M17.
2 MUSIC. An arrangement for lute or keyboard. M20.

intact /ɪnˈtakt/ *adjective*. LME.
[ORIGIN Latin *intactus*, formed as IN-[3] + *tactus* pa. pple of *tangere* to touch.]
Untouched; not affected by anything that causes injury, damage, or loss; unblemished; unimpaired.

M. RULE A wooden warship had been recovered almost intact. B. T. BRADFORD Her love for Vincent remained intact and unchanged.

■ **intactness** *noun* L19.

intacta /ɪnˈtaktə/ *adjective*. M20.
[ORIGIN Latin, fem. of *intactus* (see INTACT), extracted from VIRGO INTACTA.]
Inviolate, unaffected; not spoiled or sullied.

†**intaglia** *noun* var. of INTAGLIO *noun*.

intagliated /ɪnˈtalɪeɪtɪd/ *adjective*. L18.
[ORIGIN from Italian *intagliato* pa. pple of *intagliare*: see INTAGLIO, -ED[1].]
Carved on the surface; engraved in or as in intaglio; incised.

intaglio /ɪnˈtalɪəʊ, -ˈtɑːl-/ *noun & verb*. Also †**-ia**. M17.
[ORIGIN Italian, from *intagliare* engrave, formed as IN-[2] + *tagliare* to cut.]
▸ **A** *noun*. Pl. **-os**.
1 A figure or design incised or engraved; a cutting or engraving in a hard material. M17.
2 A thing ornamented with incised work; *esp.* a precious stone having a figure or design cut on its surface. M17. ▸**b** A mould of something to be cast or struck in relief. E19.
3 The process or art of engraving or carving in a hard material; printing in which the image is engraved or etched into a metal plate or cylinder so that it lies below the non-printing areas. Also, the condition of being incised. M18.

Ashmolean Men of the Renaissance shared . . a passion for precious . . stones carved in relief or intaglio. *attrib.*: H. ALLEN He began to indent rapidly a deft little intaglio design of vines and flowers.

▸ **B** *verb trans.* Engrave with a sunken pattern; execute in intaglio. M19.

†**intail** *noun*, *verb* vars. of ENTAIL *n*, *verb*[2].

intake /ˈɪnteɪk/ *noun & adjective*. Orig. *Scot.* & *N. English*. ME.
[ORIGIN from phr. *take in*: see IN *adverb*, TAKE *verb*.]
▸ **A** *noun*. **1** A piece of land taken in from a moorland, common, etc.; an enclosure. Chiefly *N. English*. ME.
2 The place where water is channelled from a body of water to drive a mill, supply a canal, etc. LME.
3 A narrowing or abrupt contraction made in the width of a tube, stocking, etc.; the point at which this is made. M18.
4 The act of taking in or receiving from outside; a thing which is taken in, a quantity received. E19. ▸**b** (A member of) a group of entrants to the army, a school, a trade, etc. M20.

N. BAWDEN Sara heard her quick intake of breath. *Decanter* A moderate daily intake is beneficial to health. **b** *Nature* The school should be functioning by 1975, with an intake of 100 students.

5 An imposition; a cheat. *Scot.* E19.
6 MINING. A passage by which a current of air is introduced into a mine. M19.
7 A duct or passage by which air etc. is introduced into a machine. M20.
▸ **B** *attrib.* or as *adjective*. That takes in; of the nature of or pertaining to an intake. E20.
intake manifold: see MANIFOLD *noun* 5.

intaking /ɪnˈteɪkɪŋ/ *noun*. L16.
[ORIGIN from IN-[1] + TAKING *noun*.]
1 The action of capturing or taking by force. *Scot.* Long *arch.* L16.
2 The taking of moorland into cultivation. *Scot.* E19.
3 A taking in from the outside. E20.

intangible /ɪnˈtandʒɪb(ə)l/ *adjective & noun*. E17.
[ORIGIN French, or medieval Latin *intangibilis*, or from IN-[3] + TANGIBLE.]
▸ **A** *adjective*. **1** Not tangible; unable to be touched; impalpable. E17.

J. TYNDALL The assumption of this wonderful intangible aether. P. GAY It was that intangible thing, morale, . . that gave Britain her victories.

2 *fig.* Unable to be mentally grasped. L19.
▸ **B** *noun*. An intangible thing; an asset which cannot be precisely measured. E20.

Economist Net tangible assets may be defined as total assets less 'intangibles' (goodwill, patents, etc.), current liabilities, and funded debt. H. ROBBINS That was the intangible in the back of Johnny's mind.

■ **intangiˈbility** *noun* (*a*) inviolability; (*b*) intangible quality: L18. **intangibleness** *noun* (*rare*) E19. **intangibly** *adverb* L17.

†**intangle** *verb*, †**intanglement** *noun* vars. of ENTANGLE, ENTANGLEMENT.

intarissable /ɪnˈtarɪsəb(ə)l/ *adjective*. *rare*. M17.
[ORIGIN French, formed as IN-[3] + *tarissable*, from *tariss-*, *tarir* dry up: see -ABLE.]
Unable to be dried up; inexhaustible.

intarsia /ɪnˈtɑːsɪə/ *noun*. In sense 1, 2 also **-io** /-ɪəʊ/, pl. **-os**. M19.
[ORIGIN Italian *intarsio*.]
1 (A piece of) mosaic woodwork, esp. made in 15th-cent. Italy; the art of making this. Also called ***tarsia***. M19.

attrib.: H. F. JONES The seats of the stalls . . ornamented with intarsia work. *fig.*: *Listener* Poems, with their tesselated intarsia of natural scenery, natural passion and liturgical imagery.

2 (A piece of) similar inlaid work in stone, metal, or glass. M19.
3 A method of knitting with a number of colours in which a separate length or ball of yarn is used for each area of colour (as opp. to the different yarns being carried at the back of the work). Freq. *attrib.* M20.

integer /ˈɪntɪdʒə/ *adjective & noun*. E16.
[ORIGIN Latin = intact, formed as IN-[3] + *tag-*, *teg-* base of *tangere* to touch.]
▸ **A** *adjective*. †**1** Having no part lacking; entire. Only in E16.
†**2** Marked by moral integrity; honest. Only in M17.
3 MATH. That is a whole number; integral. *obsolete* exc. as attrib. use of the noun M17.

▸ **B** *noun*. **1** *MATH*. A whole number. **L16**.
†**2** A unit of measurement or reckoning. **E–M19**.
3 A whole or entire thing or entity; a thing complete in itself. **M19**.

integrable /ˈɪntɪɡrəb(ə)l/ *adjective*. **E18**.
[ORIGIN from INTEGRATE *verb* + -ABLE.]
Chiefly *MATH*. Able to be integrated.
■ **integraˈbility** *noun* **E19**.

integral /ˈɪntɪɡr(ə)l, *as adjective also* ɪnˈtɛɡr(ə)l/ *adjective* & *noun*. **M16**.
[ORIGIN Late Latin *integralis*, formed as INTEGER: see -AL¹.]
▸ **A** *adjective*. **1** Belonging to or making up a whole; constituent, component; necessary to the completeness or integrity of the whole, not merely attached. **M16**.

> E. M. GOULBURN Recreation must form an integral part of human life. R. T. GLAZEBROOK This cylinder has an open-ended steel barrel with integral fins. *Motor Trend* Its front air dam has integral foglights.

2 Made up of component parts which together constitute a unity; *esp*. in *LOGIC*, consisting of or divisible into parts external to each other. **L16**.

> *Which?* An integral washer/drier which washes and tumble dries in one drum.

3 Having no part or element separated or lacking; whole, complete. **E17**.

> A. STORR Their novels are attempts to make some kind of coherent, integral whole.

4 *MATH*. **a** That is, or is denoted by, a whole number; involving only whole numbers, not fractional. **M17**. ▸**b** Relating to or involving integrals (see sense B.4 below) or integration. **E18**.
b *integral calculus*: see CALCULUS 1. **integral sign** the sign ∫ placed before the integrand, denoting an integral.
▸ **B** *noun*. **1** An entire or undivided thing; a whole. Now only as a *fig*. use of sense 4, a total sum. **E17**.

> *Nature* What is seen in a sun-spot is the integral . . of all that is taking place . . in many thousand miles of solar atmosphere.

†**2** An integral part or element; a constituent, a component. **M–L17**.
†**3** *GRAMMAR*. A word or part of speech that expresses a distinct notion rather than a relation between notions. **L17–M19**.
4 *MATH*. An expression of which a given function is a derivative, and which expresses the area under the curve of the graph of the given function. Also, a function which satisfies a given differential equation. **E18**.
definite integral: see DEFINITE *adjective*. *indefinite integral*: see INDEFINITE *adjective*. *particular integral*: see PARTICULAR *adjective*.
■ **inteˈgrality** *noun* **E17**. **integrally** *adverb* **L15**.

integralism /ɪnˈtɛɡr(ə)lɪz(ə)m/ *noun*. **L19**.
[ORIGIN from INTEGRAL + -ISM.]
A doctrine or theory that involves the concept of an integral whole.
■ **integralist** *noun* & *adjective* (*a*) *noun* an adherent of integralism; (*b*) *adjective* of or pertaining to integralism or integralists: **E20**.

integrand /ˈɪntɪɡrand/ *noun*. **L19**.
[ORIGIN Latin *integrandus* gerundive of *integrare* INTEGRATE *verb*: see -AND.]
MATH. A function that is to be integrated.

integrant /ˈɪntɪɡr(ə)nt/ *adjective* & *noun*. **M17**.
[ORIGIN French *intégrant*, from *intégrer* from Latin *integrare*: see INTEGRATE *verb*, -ANT¹.]
▸ **A** *adjective*. Of parts: making up or contributing to a whole; constituent; essential to the completeness of the whole. **M17**.
▸ **B** *noun*. A thing which integrates; a component. **E19**.

integraph /ˈɪntɪɡrɑːf/ *noun*. **L19**.
[ORIGIN French *intégraphe*, from *intégral* (formed as INTEGRAL) or *intégrer* (see INTEGRANT) + *-graphe* -GRAPH.]
A device which automatically plots a curve expressing the variation in the integral of a given function as a parameter is varied.

integrate /ˈɪntɪɡrət/ *adjective*. **LME**.
[ORIGIN Latin *integratus* pa. pple of *integrare*: see INTEGRATE *verb*, -ATE².]
1 Made up of separate parts, composite; belonging to a whole; complete, perfect. **LME**.
2 *PSYCHOLOGY*. In E.R. Jaensch's theory: of, pertaining to, or designating people with strong eidetic imagery. **M20**.

integrate /ˈɪntɪɡreɪt/ *verb*. **M17**.
[ORIGIN Latin *integrat-* pa. ppl stem of *integrare*, formed as INTEGER: see -ATE³.]
1 *verb trans*. Make entire or complete; make up, compose, constitute (a whole). **M17**. ▸**b** Complete or perfect by the addition of the necessary parts. **L17**.

> W. CHILLINGWORTH The particular doctrines which integrate Christianity.

2 *verb trans*. *MATH*. Obtain the integral of. **E18**. ▸**b** *gen*. Indicate or register the mean value or total sum of (a physical quantity, as area, temperature, etc.). Freq. as ***integrating** ppl adjective* (of instruments). **M19**.
3 *verb trans*. Put or bring together (parts) to form a whole; combine into a whole. **E19**.

> J. UPDIKE Bech's books still waited to be integrated with the books already there.

4 *verb trans*. Bring (racially or culturally differentiated peoples) into equal membership of a society or system. Also, desegregate. Cf. SEGREGATE *verb* 1b. **M20**. ▸**b** *verb intrans*. Become (racially or culturally) integrated. **M20**.

> C. HOPE Father Lynch . . insisted on integrating the two dozen black servants . . into the white congregation. **b** V. GLENDINNING Johnny integrated happily enough in the coarse goldrush life.

■ **integrator** *noun* (*a*) an instrument for performing integration, esp. for indicating or registering the total amount or mean value of some physical quantity; (*b*) ***system integrator***: see SYSTEM: **L19**.

integrated /ˈɪntɪɡreɪtɪd/ *ppl adjective*. **L16**.
[ORIGIN from INTEGRATE *verb* + -ED¹.]
1 Combined into a whole; united; undivided. **L16**. ▸**b** Designating or characterized by a personality in which the component elements combine harmoniously. **M20**. ▸**c** Uniting several components previously regarded as separate. **M20**.

> **b** *Lancet* The plaintiff was well integrated and had learned to live with the problem. **c** *Business Education Today* An integrated course is one in which separate aspects of the curriculum . . are subordinate to an overall unifying factor.

c integrated circuit *ELECTRONICS* a single chip etc. of material replacing a conventional electric circuit.
2 Of an institution, group, etc.: not divided by considerations of race or culture; not segregated. **M20**.

integration /ɪntɪˈɡreɪʃ(ə)n/ *noun*. **E17**.
[ORIGIN Latin *integratio(n-)*, from *integrat-*: see INTEGRATE *verb*, -ATION.]
1 The making up or composition of a whole by adding together or combining separate parts; combination into a whole. **E17**. ▸**b** The harmonious combination of the different elements in a personality. **M20**.
2 *MATH*. The process or an instance of obtaining the integral of a function (the reverse of ***differentiation***). **E18**.
constant of integration the indeterminate additive constant which arises when any function is integrated (the derivative of any constant being zero). ***integration by parts***: see PART *noun*.
3 The process of bringing about or achieving equal membership of a population or social group; removal or absence of discrimination against groups or people on racial or cultural grounds; desegregation. Cf. SEGREGATION 1(f). **M20**.
■ **integrational** *adjective* **M20**. **integrationist** *noun* & *adjective* (*a*) *noun* an advocate of (racial or cultural) integration; (*b*) *adjective* of or pertaining to people or policies favouring integration: **M20**.

integrative /ˈɪntɪɡrətɪv/ *adjective*. **M19**.
[ORIGIN from INTEGRATE *verb* + -IVE.]
Having the quality of integrating; tending to integrate.

integrin /ˈɪntəɡrɪn, ɪnˈtɛɡrɪn/ *noun*. **L20**.
[ORIGIN from *integr-* in INTEGRAL + -IN¹.]
BIOCHEMISTRY. Any of a class of animal transmembrane proteins involved in the adhesion of cells to each other and to their substrate.

integrism /ˈɪntɪɡrɪz(ə)m/ *noun*. **M20**.
[ORIGIN French *intégrisme*, from *intégrer*: see INTEGRANT, -ISM.]
= INTEGRALISM.
■ **integrist** *noun* & *adjective* = INTEGRALIST *noun* & *adjective* **E20**.

integrity /ɪnˈtɛɡrɪti/ *noun*. **LME**.
[ORIGIN French *intégrité* or Latin *integritas*, formed as INTEGER: see -ITY.]
1 The condition of having no part or element taken away or lacking; undivided state; completeness. **LME**.

> C. LYELL The integrity of the cones . . shows that the country has not been agitated by violent earthquakes. H. MACMILLAN To preserve the integrity and independence of Jordan.

2 The condition of not being marred or violated; unimpaired or uncorrupted condition; original state; soundness. **LME**.

> S. JOHNSON This prayer, that I might try the integrity of my faculties, I made in Latin verse.

3 †**a** Freedom from moral corruption; innocence, sinlessness. **M16–L17**. ▸**b** Soundness of moral principle; the character of uncorrupted virtue; uprightness, honesty, sincerity. **M16**.

> **b** W. SOYINKA Old comrades . . divest themselves of reason and integrity and plunge greedily into . . exploitation. C. HOPE Their aim was personal sanctity combined with financial integrity.

integro-differential /ˌɪntɪɡrəʊdɪfəˈrɛnʃ(ə)l/ *adjective*. **E20**.
[ORIGIN from INTEGRAL *adjective* + -O- + DIFFERENTIAL *adjective*.]
MATH. Involving both integral and differential quantities.

integument /ɪnˈtɛɡjʊm(ə)nt/ *noun*. **E17**.
[ORIGIN Latin *integumentum*, from *integere* cover in, formed as IN-² + *tegere* to cover: see -MENT.]
1 Something with which an object is covered, enclosed, or clothed; a covering, a coating. **E17**.
2 A natural outside covering of (part of) an animal or plant body, as a skin, husk, rind, shell, etc. **M17**.
■ **integuˈmental** *adjective* **M19**. **integuˈmentary** *adjective* **M19**.

intein /ˈɪntiːn/ *noun*. **L20**.
[ORIGIN from INTERNAL + PROTEIN.]
BIOCHEMISTRY. An internal segment of amino acids that is excised from a protein precursor to generate a new protein.

intel /ˈɪntɛl/ *noun*. *military slang*. **L20**.
[ORIGIN Abbreviation.]
Military intelligence; information.

intellect /ˈɪntɪlɛkt/ *noun*. **LME**.
[ORIGIN Old French & mod. French, or Latin *intellectus* perception, discernment, meaning, sense, from *intellect-* pa. ppl stem of *intellegere*: see INTELLIGENT.]
1 The faculty of knowing and reasoning; power of thought; understanding; analytic intelligence. **LME**.

> M. L. KING The mind's faith, wherein the intellect assents to a belief that God exists.

†**2** The meaning or purport (of a word or passage). Only in **16**.
3 A person of (usu. great) intelligence, an intellectual; *collect*. intellectual people. Formerly also, a rational being. **E17**.

> CARLYLE Where . . nearly all the Intellect of the place assembled of an evening. A. J. P. TAYLOR A cleverer man than his son. . . one of the most formidable intellects I have encountered.

4 In *pl*. Intellectual powers, mental faculties; wits, senses. *arch*. *colloq*. **L17**.

> S. JOHNSON My judgment embarrassed, and my intellects distorted.

■ **intellected** *adjective* (*rare*) endowed with intellect (of specified kind or quality) **L18**.

intellectible /ɪntɪˈlɛktɪb(ə)l/ *adjective*. **M16**.
[ORIGIN Late Latin *intellectibilis*, from Latin *intellect-*: see INTELLECT, -IBLE.]
PHILOSOPHY. †**1** Capable of understanding. **M–L16**.
2 Able to be apprehended by the intellect alone. **M19**.

intellection /ɪntɪˈlɛkʃ(ə)n/ *noun*. **LME**.
[ORIGIN Late Latin *intellectio(n-)* sense, understanding, from Latin *intellect-*: see INTELLECT, -ION.]
†**1** The faculty of understanding; intellect. **LME–L18**. ▸**b** The immediate knowledge or intelligence ascribed to divine beings. **E17–M18**.
2 (The result of) a particular act of understanding; a notion, an idea. Freq. in *pl*. Now *rare*. **L16**.

> B. H. SMART An intellection having once occurred, remains with us as a notion or something known.

3 The action or process of understanding; the exercise or activity of the intellect; *spec*. understanding, as distinct from imagination. **E17**.

> J. NORRIS They . . seem to leave no room for any distinction between intellection and imagination.

intellective /ɪntɪˈlɛktɪv/ *adjective*. **LME**.
[ORIGIN Late Latin *intellectivus*, from Latin *intellect-*: see INTELLECT, -IVE.]
1 Having the faculty of understanding; having intellect. **LME**.
2 Of or pertaining to (the) understanding or intellect. **LME**.
3 Characterized by a high degree of understanding; intelligent. **E16**.
†**4** = INTELLECTIBLE 2; *GRAMMAR* abstract. **M17–E19**.
■ **intellectively** *adverb* †(*a*) intelligibly; (*b*) in relation to the intellect: **L16**.

intellectual /ɪntɪˈlɛktjʊəl/ *adjective* & *noun*. **LME**.
[ORIGIN Latin *intellectualis*, from *intellectus* INTELLECT: see -UAL.]
▸ **A** *adjective*. **1** Of or pertaining to the intellect or understanding; that is describable as such in relation to the intellect. **LME**. ▸**b** That appeals to, engages, or requires the exercise of the intellect. **M19**.

> L. MACNEICE Spiritually bankrupt Intellectual snobs. A. J. AYER The moment of his greatest intellectual awakening was his discovery of the geometry of Euclid. F. WELDON They applied their intellectual energies . . to the practical details of domestic life. **b** E. A. FREEMAN Skill in the more intellectual branches of warfare.

intellectual property *LAW* property that is the product of creativity and does not exist in tangible form (as patents, copyright, etc.).
†**2** (Able to be) apprehended only by the intellect; non-material, spiritual. **LME–E18**.

> BACON To descend from spirits and intellectual forms to sensible and material forms.

3 a Characterized by or possessing understanding or intelligence. *obsolete* exc. as in sense b. **L15**. ▸**b** Possessing a high degree of understanding or (esp. analytic) intelligence; given to the exercise of the intellect. Also, of, pertaining to, or characteristic of an intellectual or intellectuals. **E19**.

> **a** MILTON Who would loose . . this intellectual being? **b** J. TYNDALL The interest which the intellectual public of England take in the question. E. F. BENSON I thought you would have spectacles . . . large kind hands . . . an intellectual expression.

▸ **B** *noun*. †**1** The intellect, the mind. **L16–M17**.

2 In *pl.* ▸**a** Intellectual powers, mental faculties; wits, senses. *arch. colloq.* **E17.** ▸**b** Things pertaining to the intellect. Now *rare* or *obsolete*. **M17.**
3 A person of superior (or supposedly superior) intellect, *esp.* one having an analytic mind; an enlightened person. **M17.**

C. HILL Cromwell was no intellectual: the cast of his mind was practical, pragmatic, never doctrinaire. P. HOWARD Delane was not an intellectual. He had little taste for literature or learning.

■ **intellectu'ality** *noun* [late Latin *intellectualitas*] the quality or state of being intellectual; intellectual power or ability: **LME.** **intellectually** *adverb* **LME.** **intellectualness** *noun* (*rare*) **M19.**

intellectualise *verb* var. of **INTELLECTUALIZE.**

intellectualism /ɪntɪˈlɛktjʊəlɪz(ə)m/ *noun.* **E19.**
[**ORIGIN** from **INTELLECTUAL** + **-ISM**, after German *Intellektualismus*.]
1 *PHILOSOPHY.* The doctrine that knowledge is derived from the action of the intellect or pure reason. **E19.**
2 Devotion to intellectual pursuits; (excessive) exercise of the intellect rather than the emotions. **M19.**

intellectualist /ɪntɪˈlɛktjʊəlɪst/ *noun & adjective.* **E17.**
[**ORIGIN** formed as **INTELLECTUALISM** + **-IST.**]
▸ **A** *noun.* A devotee of the intellect; *PHILOSOPHY* an adherent of intellectualism. **E17.**
▸ **B** *adjective.* Of or pertaining to intellectualism or intellectualists; of the nature of an intellectualist. **M19.**
■ **intellectua'listic** *adjective* pertaining to or characteristic of intellectualists or intellectualism **L19.** **intellectua'listically** *adverb* **E20.**

intellectualize /ɪntɪˈlɛktjʊəlʌɪz/ *verb.* Also **-ise.** **E19.**
[**ORIGIN** formed as **INTELLECTUALISM** + **-IZE.**]
1 *verb trans.* Make intellectual; give an intellectual character to. **E19.**

A. LORDE Black women writers . . don't seem to need to intellectualize this capacity to feel.

2 *verb intrans.* Exercise the intellect; talk or write intellectually. **E19.**

Blackwood's Magazine Yet could I sit and moralize, and intellectualize, for hours.

■ **intellectuali'zation** *noun* **E19.**

intelligence /ɪnˈtɛlɪdʒ(ə)ns/ *noun & verb.* **LME.**
[**ORIGIN** Old French & mod. French from Latin *intelligentia*, formed as **INTELLIGENT**: see **-ENCE.**]
▸ **A** *noun.* **1** The faculty of understanding; intellect. **LME.**

S. SASSOON Was it a mistake . . to try and keep intelligence alive when I could no longer call my life my own?

artificial intelligence: see **ARTIFICIAL** *adjective* 2.
2 Quickness or superiority of understanding, sagacity. **LME.**

C. G. WOLFF He was a man of considerable intelligence and intellectual promise. *Atlantic Monthly* Nothing so gives the illusion of intelligence as personal association with large sums of money.

3 The action or fact of understanding something; knowledge, comprehension (*of* something). Now *rare* or *obsolete*. **LME.**

JOHN HAMILTON It helpis us to the trew intelligence of the scripture.

4 An intelligent or rational being, esp. a spiritual one; a spirit. **LME.**

B. MAGEE History is being directed by some outside intelligence (usually God) in accordance with its own purposes. C. SAGAN There may be a time . . when contact will be made with another intelligence on a planet of some far-distant star.

5 Knowledge communicated by or obtained from another; news; information, *spec.* of military value. Formerly also in *pl.*, items of information. **LME.** ▸**b** Exchange of knowledge, information, opinion, etc.; communication, esp. of secret information. Now *rare* or *obsolete*. **M16.** ▸†**c** A relation or basis of communication between people or parties; an understanding *between* or *with*. **L16–E19.**

R. V. JONES I had the ultimate responsibility for providing Intelligence, . . pictures of what the Germans were doing. R. DAHL We were enthralled by this piece of intelligence. **b** G. ORWELL They had confessed to intelligence with the enemy. **c** BACON That ill intelligence that we many times see between great personages.

6 (People employed in) the obtaining of information, esp. of military or political value; the secret service, espionage. **E17.**
– **ATTRIB.** & **COMB.**: In the sense 'of or concerned with the gathering of information', as ***intelligence agency***, ***intelligence department***, ***intelligence officer***, ***intelligence service***, etc. Special combs., as **intelligence quotient** a number arrived at by intelligence tests and intended to denote the ratio of a person's intelligence to the normal or average; **intelligence test**: designed to measure intelligence rather than acquired knowledge.
▸ †**B** *verb.* **1** *verb trans.* Bring news of; bring news to, inform. **L16–M17.**
2 *verb intrans.* Convey intelligence; tell tales; act as a spy. Freq. as ***intelligencing*** *ppl adjective.* **E17–E18.**
■ **intelligenced** *adjective* (*rare*) having intelligence (of a specified kind or quality) **E17.**

intelligencer /ɪnˈtɛlɪdʒ(ə)nsə/ *noun.* **M16.**
[**ORIGIN** from **INTELLIGENCE** + **-ER**[1], perh. after French †*intelligencier*.]
1 A person who conveys intelligence or information; *spec.* an informer, a spy, a secret agent. *arch.* **M16.**
2 A bringer of news, a messenger, an informant. *arch.* exc. (**I-**) in titles of newspapers. **L16.**

intelligency /ɪnˈtɛlɪdʒ(ə)nsi/ *noun.* Now *rare.* **L16.**
[**ORIGIN** Latin *intelligentia*: see **INTELLIGENCE**, **-ENCY.**]
†**1** = **INTELLIGENCE** *noun* 5b. **L16–E18.**
2 = **INTELLIGENCE** *noun* 4. **M17.**
†**3** = **INTELLIGENCE** *noun* 5. **L17–M18.**
4 = **INTELLIGENCE** *noun* 1. **L19.**

intelligent /ɪnˈtɛlɪdʒ(ə)nt/ *adjective & noun.* **E16.**
[**ORIGIN** from Latin *intelligent-*, earlier *intellegent-* pres. ppl stem of *intellegere* lit. 'choose among', formed as **INTER-** + *legere* pick up, gather, choose, read: see **-ENT.**]
▸ **A** *adjective.* **1** Having the faculty of understanding, possessing intelligence; *spec.* having or showing a high degree of understanding, quick to comprehend, sagacious. **E16.**

C. SAGAN Those planets in which intelligent forms have arisen. A. BURGESS Unit officers were considered intelligent enough to be able to take in the facts.

intelligent design a theory which states that life, or the universe, cannot have arisen by chance, and instead has been designed and created by some intelligent entity; the process of creation by such an entity.
2 Cognizant *of*, acquainted *with*, well-versed *in*. **M16.**
†**3** Giving information, communicative. *rare* (Shakes.). Only in **E17.**
4 Of a device, system, or machine: able to vary its behaviour in response to varying situations, requirements, and past experience; *spec.* (esp. of a computer terminal) having its own data-processing capability, incorporating a microprocessor. **M20.**
▸ **B** *noun.* †**1** A recipient of information. *rare.* Only in **E16.**
2 An intelligent or rational being. Now *rare.* **E17.**
†**3** A person who conveys intelligence or information; an informant, a spy. **E17–M18.**
■ **intelligently** *adverb* **L17.**

intelligential /ɪnˌtɛlɪˈdʒɛnʃ(ə)l/ *adjective.* **E17.**
[**ORIGIN** from Latin *intelligentia* **INTELLIGENCE** + **-AL**[1].]
1 = **INTELLECTUAL** *adjective* 1. **E17.**
2 = **INTELLECTUAL** *adjective* 3. **M17.**

intelligentsia /ɪnˌtɛlɪˈdʒɛntsɪə/ *noun.* **E20.**
[**ORIGIN** Russian *intelligentsiya* from Polish *inteligencja* from Latin *intelligentia* **INTELLIGENCE.**]
The part of a nation (orig. in pre-revolutionary Russia) having aspirations to intellectual activity, a section of society regarded as possessing culture and political initiative; *pl.* the members of this section of a nation or society, intellectuals.

G. STEINER As Stalinism turned to nationalism and technocracy . . the revolutionary intelligentsia went to the wall.

intelligible /ɪnˈtɛlɪdʒɪb(ə)l/ *adjective & noun.* **LME.**
[**ORIGIN** Latin *intellegibilis*, *intelli-*, from *intellegere*: see **INTELLIGENT**, **-IBLE.**]
▸ **A** *adjective.* †**1** Capable of understanding; intelligent. **LME–L18.**

T. GALE Plato supposeth the Universe . . a living intelligible creature.

2 *PHILOSOPHY.* Able to be apprehended only by the understanding, not by the senses. Opp. **SENSIBLE** *adjective* 1. **LME.**

J. NORRIS The Intelligible world, . . of a nature purely spiritual and intellectual, . . not sensible, but intelligible only.

3 Able to be understood; comprehensible. **E16.**

H. JAMES I can give no intelligible account of how I fought out the interval. I. A. RICHARDS Most of the difficult and obscure points about the structures of the arts . . become easily intelligible.

▸ **B** *noun.* That which is intelligible; an object of understanding. **E17.**
■ **intelligi'bility** *noun* **L17.** **intelligibleness** *noun* **E17.** **intelligibly** *adverb* **E17.**

intelligize /ɪnˈtɛlɪdʒʌɪz/ *verb.* Also **-ise.** **E19.**
[**ORIGIN** Irreg. from Latin *intellegere* (see **INTELLIGENT**) + **-IZE.**]
1 *verb intrans.* Exercise the intelligence. *rare.* **E19.**
2 *verb trans.* Make intelligent or intellectual; take into the intellect. **L19.**

Intelpost /ˈɪntɛlpəʊst/ *noun.* **L20.**
[**ORIGIN** from *Int*ernational *El*ectronic *Post*.]
The electronic transmission of messages and graphics internationally by fax, telex, or microcomputer.

Intelsat /ˈɪntɛlsat/ *noun.* Also **INTELSAT.** **M20.**
[**ORIGIN** from *Int*ernational *Tel*ecommunications *Sat*ellite (Consortium).]
An international organization operating a system of commercial communications satellites; a satellite owned by this organization.

intemerate /ɪnˈtɛm(ə)rət/ *adjective.* Now *rare.* **LME.**
[**ORIGIN** Latin *intemeratus*, formed as **IN-**[3] + *temeratus* pa. pple of *temerare* violate: see **-ATE**[2].]
Inviolate; unblemished.

intemperance /ɪnˈtɛmp(ə)r(ə)ns/ *noun.* **LME.**
[**ORIGIN** Old French & mod. French *intempérance* or Latin *intemperantia*, formed as **IN-**[3] + *temperantia* **TEMPERANCE.**]
†**1** Intemperateness, inclemency, severity of weather or climate. **LME–E18.**
2 Lack of moderation or restraint; excess, immoderation; (an act of) overindulgence. **LME.**
3 Overindulgence in or addiction to alcohol. **E17.**
■ Also †**intemperancy** *noun* **M16–L17.**

intemperate /ɪnˈtɛmp(ə)rət/ *adjective.* **LME.**
[**ORIGIN** Latin *intemperatus*, formed as **IN-**[3] + **TEMPERATE** *adjective*.]
1 Not temperate; (esp. of climate or weather) inclement, severe. Now *rare.* **LME.**

W. LEYBOURN The Zones are either Temperate or Intemperate, and the Intemperate are either Cold or Hot.

2 Characterized by or given to overindulgence in a passion or appetite. **LME.** ▸**b** *spec.* Immoderate in the use of alcoholic drink; addicted to alcohol. **L17.**

SHAKES. *Meas. for M.* His concupiscible intemperate lust. **b** H. WILLIAMSON Was it the rum in the trenches that had started him off on his intemperate habits?

3 Lacking temperance or moderation in conduct, action, etc.; exceeding normal restrictions; immoderate; violent. **E16.**

ROBERT WATSON The intemperate zeal of the reformers.

■ **intemperately** *adverb* **LME.** **intemperateness** *noun* **M16.**

†**intemperature** *noun.* **M16.**
[**ORIGIN** from **IN-**[3] + **TEMPERATURE.**]
1 An abnormal or distempered condition of the body. **M16–L18.**
2 Inclemency, severity of weather or climate. **L16–E19.**

intempestive /ɪntɛmˈpɛstɪv/ *adjective.* **E17.**
[**ORIGIN** Latin *intempestivus*, formed as **IN-**[3] + **TEMPESTIVE.**]
Untimely, unseasonable, inopportune.
■ **intempestively** *adverb* (*rare*) **M16.**

intemporal /ɪnˈtɛmp(ə)r(ə)l/ *adjective.* **M17.**
[**ORIGIN** from **IN-**[3] + **TEMPORAL** *adjective*[1].]
Not temporal; eternal, everlasting.

intend /ɪnˈtɛnd/ *verb.* Also (earlier) †**en-**. **ME.**
[**ORIGIN** Old French & mod. French *entendre*, †*intendre* from Latin *intendere* extend, direct, intend, promote, formed as **IN-**[2] + *tendere* to stretch.]
▸ †**I** Direct the attention to.
1 a *verb intrans.* Direct the mind, pay heed, *to*, *unto*. **ME–E17.** ▸**b** *verb refl.* Devote oneself; in *pass.*, be devoted. **E16–E17.**
2 *verb intrans.* Endeavour, strive, *to do*. **LME–L17.**
3 *verb intrans.* & *trans.* Listen, give ear (to). **LME–M16.**
4 *verb intrans.* & *trans.* Give personal service or attendance (to). **LME–M17.**
5 *verb trans.* Occupy oneself with, look after. **LME–L18.** ▸**b** Superintend, direct. Cf. **INTENDANT** *noun.* **L18–M19.**

J. COLLIER The Priest is supposed only to intend the Affairs of Religion.

▸ †**II** Apprehend mentally.
6 *verb trans.* Understand. **ME–E17.**
7 *verb intrans.* Have or come to an understanding; agree together. **LME–E16.**
8 *verb intrans.* Have an opinion; think, judge. **L16–M17.**
9 *verb trans.* Understand as being, in law; interpret legally. Cf. **INTENDMENT** *noun* 3b. **E17–L18.**
▸ **III** Direct the mind to something to be done.
†**10** *verb intrans.* Be minded or resolved. Chiefly with *adverb.* **LME–M17.**

M. GROVE Let me heare from you, how that you doe entend.

11 *verb trans.* Have as one's purpose (an action etc.); plan *to do*, contemplate *doing*. **LME.**

G. GREENE Mr Smith asked me to stop the car . . and I thought he intended to take a photograph. T. MO Atkins is the last man to take umbrage where offence was not intended. B. T. BRADFORD He brought his fist down on the table much harder than he had intended. *Soldier* I . . intend staying to the end of my time.

12 *verb trans.* Design or destine for or *for* a purpose or use, *as* a thing; have the desire for (a person or thing) *to be*, *to do*. Foll. by *for* a person: have the desire that (a person) shall have or enjoy, or be depicted by. **L16.**

R. MONTAGU The regales that are intended for him not being yet at an end. DICKENS A degree of familiarity which he . . intended for a . . compliment. E. O'NEILL In a welcoming . . grimace, intended as a smile. J. BUCHAN I was not intended by Providence for a philologist. I. MURDOCH He had . . informed her that he intended their liaison to be lasting. K. AMIS I think we were intended to meet.

13 *verb trans.* Mean or refer to by one's words. Also (now *rare*), of a word, phrase, etc.: signify, denote. **L16.** ▸†**b** Designate as something; call. *rare.* **L16–E17.**

HENRY FIELDING This word . . intends persons without virtue or sense. N. MOSLEY They rewrote some of his books to say the opposite of what he had intended. **b** SPENSER Vesper, whom we the Euening-starre intend.

▸ **IV** Fix in a course, direct.
14 *verb trans.* Direct (the eyes, thoughts, etc.) *to* or *towards* an object. Now *rare*. LME.

> C. PATMORE Intend thine eye Into the dim and undiscovered sky.

15 *verb intrans. & trans.* Direct (one's course), make (one's way). *arch.* LME. ▸†**b** *verb intrans.* Set out for or *for* a destination. Sometimes as ellipt. use of sense 11, plan to go or start. M17–E19.

> JAS. HARRIS As if . . a company of travellers, in some wide forest, were all intending for one city. G. CRABBE Guide him to Fairy-land, who now intends That way his flight. **b** J. WESLEY Pray let us know when you or your brother intend for this Kingdom.

†**16** *verb intrans.* Incline or tend in a given direction. LME–M17.

> A. GOLDING The wil intendeth rather to commaund than to obey, and vnto freedom rather than bondage.

†**17** *verb trans.* Institute (legal proceedings). *Scot.* L16–M18.
†**18** *verb trans.* Assert, claim; pretend. (Foll. by *that*.) L16–M17.

> SHAKES. *Rich. III* Tremble and start at wagging of a straw, Intending deep suspicion.

▸ †**V** Stretch, extend.
19 *verb trans.* Stretch (out), esp. to the maximum limit; strain, make tense. L16–M19.

> T. MOORE One of the wings of the Swan has been . . intended . . to cover . . Leda. W. HAMILTON When we intend the vital powers above the suitable degree we occasion a hindrance, a pain.

20 *verb trans.* Increase the intensity of. L16–E18.

> C. PURSHALL A small quantity of *Aqua Vitae* sprinkled upon the Freezing Mixture, wonderfully intends its Force.

▪ **intended** *ppl adjective & noun* (*a*) *ppl adjective* that has been intended; *esp.* designed to be what is denoted by the noun; formerly also, (of a person) resolved *to do*; (*b*) *noun* (*colloq.*) one's intended husband or wife: L15. **intendedly** *adverb* by design, on purpose M17.

intendance /ɪnˈtɛnd(ə)ns/ *noun*. M18.
[ORIGIN French, formed as INTENDANT: see -ANCE.]
1 The function of an intendant; superintendence, direction. Also *spec.*, a department of the French public service, e.g. the war commissariat; the officials conducting it. M18.
2 The official quarters of an intendant. L19.

intendancy /ɪnˈtɛnd(ə)nsi/ *noun*. Also **-ency**. L16.
[ORIGIN from INTENDANT: see -ANCY. In sense 2 from Spanish *intendencia*.]
1 The position, function, or period of office of an intendant; a body of intendants. L16.
2 In S. America: a district under the control of an intendant. E19.

intendant /ɪnˈtɛnd(ə)nt/ *noun*. Also †**-ent**. M17.
[ORIGIN French, from Latin *intendent-* pres. ppl stem of *intendere*: see INTEND, -ANT¹.]
1 Chiefly as the title of certain officials: a superintendent, a director; *esp.* (in 17th- and 18th-cent. France) any of certain agents of the King appointed to supervise the administration of justice, finance, etc., in the provinces on behalf of central government. M17.

> EVELYN Sir Christopher Wren, his Majesties Surveyor and Intendent of his Buildings.

intendant-general a chief intendant.
2 The administrator of an opera house or theatre. Also, a musical director, a conductor. L19.

intendence /ɪnˈtɛnd(ə)ns/ *noun*. LME.
[ORIGIN from INTEND *verb* + -ENCE.]
The paying of attention; attendance. Now only (*hist.*) in ***writ of intendence and respondence***, a writ issued under the Great Seal in the 13th to 15th cents. in favour of a person who had received an appointment from the King, ordering all concerned to attend him and respond to his requests.

intendency *noun* var. of INTENDANCY.

†**intendent** *noun* var. of INTENDANT.

intender /ɪnˈtɛndə/ *noun*. E16.
[ORIGIN from INTEND + -ER¹.]
A person who intends or purposes.

†**intender** *verb* var. of ENTENDER.

†**intendiment** *noun*. E16.
[ORIGIN medieval Latin *intendimentum*: cf. INTENDMENT.]
1 Knowledge, understanding. Only in 16.
2 Purpose, (an) intention. L16–E17.
3 Attentive consideration. *rare* (Spenser). Only in L16.

intending /ɪnˈtɛndɪŋ/ *ppl adjective*. M17.
[ORIGIN from INTEND + -ING².]
That intends; *esp.* (with agent noun) who intends to be.

> *Times* I have to warn intending visitors that they will find the exhibition plunged in . . gloom.

intendment /ɪnˈtɛndm(ə)nt/ *noun*. Also (earlier) †**en-**. LME.
[ORIGIN Old French & mod. French *entendement*, from *entendre*: see INTEND, -MENT. Cf. INTENDIMENT.]
†**1** The faculty or action of understanding. LME–E17.
†**2** Way of understanding something; interpretation. LME–M17.
3 a Meaning intended; signification, import. Now *rare*. LME. ▸**b** LAW. The sense in which the law understands a thing. L16.

> **a** *Notes & Queries* A phrase of sinister and odious intendment. **b** *Times* Doubts whether the use of such powers . . was within the intendment of the legislation.

†**4** What a person aims at; purpose, intention. Also, the purpose of a thing. LME–E19.
†**5** Tendency, inclination. E16–E17.

intenerate /ɪnˈtɛnəreɪt/ *verb trans.* Now *rare*. L16.
[ORIGIN mod. Latin *intenerat-* pa. ppl stem of *intenerare*, formed as IN-² + Latin *tener* tender: see -ATE³.]
Make soft or tender.
▪ **inteneˈration** *noun* E17.

†**intenible** *adjective*. *rare* (Shakes.). Only in E17.
[ORIGIN Perh. from IN-³ + var. of TENABLE *adjective*, with active force as in INCAPABLE *adjective* 2 unable to contain.]
Incapable of holding or containing something.

> SHAKES. *All's Well* This captious and intenible sieve.

intensate /ɪnˈtɛnseɪt/ *verb trans.* *rare*. M19.
[ORIGIN from INTENSE + -ATE³.]
Make intense, intensify.
▪ **intenˈsation** *noun* E19.

intensative /ɪnˈtɛnsətɪv/ *noun & adjective*. M19.
[ORIGIN Extension of INTENSIVE.]
= INTENSITIVE.

intense /ɪnˈtɛns/ *adjective*. LME.
[ORIGIN Old French & mod. French *intens(e)* or Latin *intensus* stretched tight, strained, pa. pple of *intendere* INTEND.]
1 Of a condition, quality, feeling, etc.: existing in a very high degree; extremely strong, keen, or pronounced. Of a colour: very deep. LME. ▸**b** Of a thing: having a quality in a very high degree; intensely bright, hot, etc.; PHOTOGRAPHY dense. M17.

> E. BOWEN She felt an intense morbid solicitude. R. SILVERBERG Though it was not yet noon, the heat was intense. *Atlantic Monthly* The pressure of human crowding is most intense in the cities. **b** P. BOWLES The intense sky, too blue to be real.

2 Of personal, esp. mental, action: strenuously directed to an end; highly concentrated. M17.

> A. SILLITOE The afternoon visit was preceded by a few hours of intense preparation. C. HOPE Feeling uncomfortable beneath her cool, intense scrutiny.

3 Possessing, exhibiting, or marked by intensity of feeling. Formerly, intent *upon* or *about*. M17.

> T. MORRISON Their friendship was as intense as it was sudden. M. PIERCY Tracy was intense Enthusiastic. All the way on or all the way off. *Wisden Cricket Monthly* David does have a tendency to get intense about the game. *transf.*: R. LEHMANN A short but very intense song.

▪ **intensely** *adverb* †(*a*) with concentrated effort or attention; (*b*) in a very high degree, very strongly or greatly; (*c*) with intensity of feeling: E17. **intenseness** *noun* E17.

intensification /ɪnˌtɛnsɪfɪˈkeɪʃ(ə)n/ *noun*. M19.
[ORIGIN from INTENSIFY + -FICATION.]
1 The action of intensifying; intensified condition. M19. ***RITE of intensification***.
2 PHOTOGRAPHY. The process of increasing the opacity of a negative. L19.

intensify /ɪnˈtɛnsɪfʌɪ/ *verb*. E19.
[ORIGIN from INTENSE + -I- + -FY: app. coined by Coleridge.]
1 *verb trans.* Make intense; augment, strengthen, heighten, deepen. E19. ▸**b** PHOTOGRAPHY. Increase the opacity of (a negative), so as to produce a stronger contrast of light and shade. M19.

> J. RABAN The oil boom has simply intensified Dubai's traditional buzz of water traffic. N. SYMINGTON In psychosis all the emotions are enormously intensified.

2 *verb intrans.* Grow in intensity. M19.

> I. MCEWAN As the morning heat had intensified, the crowds had diminished.

▪ **intensifier** *noun* a thing which intensifies; *spec.* (*a*) PHOTOGRAPHY a chemical used to intensify a negative; (*b*) = ***hydraulic intensifier*** s.v. HYDRAULIC *adjective*; (*c*) GRAMMAR a word or prefix giving force or emphasis; (*d*) = ***image intensifier*** s.v. IMAGE *noun*: M19.

intension /ɪnˈtɛnʃ(ə)n/ *noun*. E17.
[ORIGIN Latin *intensio(n-)*, from *intens-* pa. ppl stem of *intendere*: see INTEND, -ION. A doublet of INTENTION.]
1 The action of stretching or straining. Now *rare* or *obsolete*. E17.

> T. HOGG His voice . . was intolerably shrill, harsh . . of the most cruel intension.

2 Strenuous exertion of the mind or will; earnest attention, intentness. E17.

> *Cornhill Magazine* Suddenly I found myself springing to my feet, and listening with an agony of intension.

3 Increase in degree or force; intensification. E17.

> W. SANDERSON Brightness is the Intension of Light.

4 (Notable) degree of a quality; strength, force, intensity. Freq. opp. EXTENSION 3. E17.

> *Nineteenth Century* The essence of farming on virgin soils is extension; on old land it is intension.

5 LOGIC. The internal content of a concept; the sum of the attributes contained in it. Opp. EXTENSION 4b. M19.
▪ **intensional** *adjective* (PHILOSOPHY) relating to the attributes contained in a concept L19. **intensionalist** *noun & adjective* (PHILOSOPHY) (*a*) *noun* a person who considers a concept from the standpoint of its inner attributes; (*b*) *adjective* relating to the attributes contained in a concept: M20. **intensioˈnality** *noun* (PHILOSOPHY) the state or fact of being intensional M20. **intensionally** *adverb* (PHILOSOPHY) by way of intension L19.

intensitive /ɪnˈtɛnsɪtɪv/ *adjective & noun*. E19.
[ORIGIN Irreg. from INTENSITY + -IVE.]
(A word, prefix, etc.) that serves to intensify or emphasize.

intensity /ɪnˈtɛnsɪti/ *noun*. M17.
[ORIGIN from INTENSE + -ITY.]
1 The quality of being intense; extreme degree of or *of* a quality, condition, etc. M17. ▸**b** Concentrated quality of an action, emotion, etc. M19.

> H. E. BATES Momentarily the intensity of his anger blinded him. J. RULE The sun . . seemed robbed of its intensity by a cool wind. B. EMECHETA The intensity of the knocks progressed from the first mild knock to a final thunderous one. **b** J. WAIN She . . stared into his face with an intensity that scorched him. R. HOLMES Shelley was writing with a creative intensity he had never before achieved.

2 PHYSICS etc. A (measurable) amount of energy, brightness, magnetic field, etc. L18.

> E. RUTHERFORD A magnetic field of only moderate intensity. N. TINBERGEN Powers of adaptation to low light intensities.

intensive /ɪnˈtɛnsɪv/ *adjective & noun*. LME.
[ORIGIN Old French & mod. French *intensif*, *-ive* or medieval Latin *intensivus*, formed as INTENSE: see -IVE.]
▸ **A** *adjective*. †**1** Of a very high degree; vehement, intense. LME–L17.
2 Of an activity: assiduously directed towards an object; highly concentrated. E17.

> L. VAN DER POST His intensive reading of philosophy . . had provided him with a knowledge in depth. R. INGALLS The creature . . appears from intensive analysis to be a giant lizard-like animal.

intensive care special medical treatment, with constant monitoring, of a dangerously ill patient; ***intensive care unit***, the part of a hospital where this is performed.
3 Of or relating to intensity or logical intension as opp. to extent; having the quality of intensity. E17.

> *Educational Review* In visiting the schools . . one comes to learn that the knowledge acquired is more intensive than extensive.

4 Having the property of intensifying; *esp.* (GRAMMAR) giving force or emphasis. E17.
5 ECONOMICS. Of a method of farming etc.: designed to increase productiveness within a limited area (rather than enlarging the area of production). M19.
6 As 2nd elem. of comb.; making much use of the thing specified. Esp. in ***capital-intensive***, ***labour-intensive***. M20.
▸ **B** *noun*. A thing which intensifies; *spec.* (GRAMMAR) an intensifier. E19.
▪ **intensively** *adverb* L15. **intensiveness** *noun* M17.

intent /ɪnˈtɛnt/ *noun*. Also (earlier) †**en-**. ME.
[ORIGIN Old French *entent* from Latin *intentus* verbal noun from *intendere* INTEND, and Old French & mod. French *entente* from Proto-Romance, also from Latin *intendere*.]
1 Chiefly LAW: the act or fact of intending; intention, purpose. Formerly also, inclination, will; what is willed, one's desire. ME. ▸†**b** A design, a project. ME–M19.

> T. KENEALLY The intent of the . . prisoners from Brinnlitz was to deliver the Schindlers . . across the Swiss border. **b** G. P. R. JAMES The nobles joining in his intent, showered their largess upon their retainers.

letter of intent: see LETTER *noun*¹. **with intent** with the intention of committing a crime.
†**2** Attention, heed; intent observation. ME–E18.
†**3** Assiduous effort. ME–L15.
†**4** Mind, understanding; opinion, judgement. ME–E17.
†**5** Meaning, import; LAW intendment. ME–M18.

> W. BLACKSTONE Merchandize, within the intent of the statute, by which a profit may be fairly made.

6 The object of an action etc.; an aim, a purpose. Now *rare* exc. in ***for all intents and purposes***, ***to all intents*** (***and purposes***), for all practical purposes, in effect. ME.

> N. SYMINGTON When a story is used to convey a conscious intent the result is poor literature.

†**to the intent** (**that**) in order that.
†**7** The subject of a discourse etc. LME–L17.

intent /ɪnˈtɛnt/ *adjective*. LME.
[ORIGIN Latin *intentus* pa. pple of *intendere*: see INTENT *noun*.]
1 Having the mind concentrated on something; engrossed in an activity etc., firmly resolved on a purpose. (Foll. by *on*, †*to do*, *upon*.) LME.
J. LONDON It would have been easier to go on the train, but.. he was intent on saving money. E. BUSHEN A fleet of planes, murderously intent. G. SWIFT Your head was lowered and you were intent on your reading.
2 Of the faculties, a look, etc.: directed with strained attention; intense. LME.
K. AMIS His face.. wore a small intent frown, as if he were hard of hearing.
■ **intently** *adverb* LME. **intentness** *noun* M17.

†**intent** *verb*. Also **en-**. ME.
[ORIGIN Old French *ententer*, (in sense 3) French *intenter*, both from Latin *intentare* frequentative of *intendere* INTEND.]
1 *verb trans.* Purpose, intend (an action, *to do*). ME–L16.
2 *verb intrans. & trans.* Direct the mind (to a thing). LME–E17.
3 *verb trans.* Institute (legal proceedings). *Scot.* E16–E19.

intention /ɪnˈtɛnʃ(ə)n/ *noun*. Also †**en-**. LME.
[ORIGIN Old French *entencion* (mod. *intention*) from Latin *intentio(n-)*, from *intent-* pa. ppl stem of *intendere*: see INTEND, -ION. A doublet of INTENSION.]
▸ **I** *gen.* **1 a** (Intense or concentrated) direction of or *of* the mind, attention, eyes, etc., to an object. *arch.* LME. ▸†**b** The action of stretching or making something tense. L16–M17.
a JONSON My soule.. Is hurt with mere intention on their follies. M. HALE When thou prayest do it considerately, advisedly, with the whole Intention of thy Soul.
†**2** The mind, the understanding; one's judgement or opinion. LME–E16.
3 Meaning, import. *arch.* LME.
4 The action or fact of intending to do a thing; what one intends to do, one's aim or design. Also, the purpose of an action etc. LME. ▸**b** In *pl.* Intended mode of behaviour, esp. (*colloq.*) towards a woman in respect of marriage. L18. ▸**c** An author's aim or intended meaning in a literary work. M20.
M. KEANE None of them showed the smallest intention of getting out of the car. A. SCHLEE Absently or with some intention, he had let his hand fall on the back of it. *Which?* Overall, the intention is to leave pensioners' benefit entitlement broadly unchanged. **b** T. CAPOTE Mr. Bell, entirely unaware of his guests' intentions, which included throttling him with a belt.., was glad to have company. A. BROOKNER So delicate a suitor is Lautner that Mimi has no idea of his intentions.
†**5** Intensification. E17–M18.
▸ **II** *spec.* **6** MEDICINE. An aim in a healing process; a method of treatment. *arch.* exc. in ***first intention*** (a), ***second intention*** (a) below. LME.
7 SCHOLASTIC LOGIC. A concept formed by directing the mind towards an object. Usually in ***first intention*** (b), ***second intention*** (b) below. M16.
8 ROMAN CATHOLIC CHURCH. **a** The special object for which a mass is celebrated, an intercession offered, etc. L16. ▸**b** The serious purpose, on the part of the celebrant, to perform the rites prescribed by the Church (regarded as essential to the validity of the sacrament). M19.
– PHRASES: **first intention** (*a*) MEDICINE the healing of a wound by natural union of the parts without granulation; (*b*) SCHOLASTIC LOGIC a primary concept, formed by the direct application of the mind to the thing itself, e.g. the concepts of *a tree*, *an oak*. ***honourable intentions***: see HONOURABLE *adjective*. **particular intention** ROMAN CATHOLIC CHURCH = sense 8a above. **second intention** (*a*) MEDICINE the healing of a wound by granulation after suppuration; (*b*) SCHOLASTIC LOGIC a secondary concept, formed by the application of the mind to first intentions in their relations to each other, e.g. the concepts of *genus*, *species*, *difference*, *identity*. **special intention** ROMAN CATHOLIC CHURCH = sense 8a above.
– COMB.: **intention movement** a movement by an animal serving simply to signal that a further movement will follow; **intention tremor**: manifested whenever a movement is attempted, freq. a consequence of brain damage.

intentional /ɪnˈtɛnʃ(ə)n(ə)l/ *adjective*. M16.
[ORIGIN French *intentionnel* or medieval Latin *intentionalis*, from Latin *intentio(n-)*: see INTENTION, -AL¹.]
1 Of or pertaining to intention; existing (only) in intention. M16.
W. CRUISE The second will never operated, it was only intentional.
intentional fallacy: that consists in confusing an author's intended meaning in a work with its actual meaning.
2 In scholastic logic and (later) phenomenology: of or pertaining to the operations of the mind; existing in or for the mind. M16.
intentional concept: denoting a mental state whose object may or may not exist. **intentional object** (in phenomenology) the object (real or imaginary) to which each act of consciousness is directed.
3 Done on purpose; deliberate. E18.
SYD. SMITH We accuse nobody of intentional misrepresentation.
■ **intentioˈnality** *noun* the quality or fact of being intentional; *esp.* (in phenomenology) the fact of being directed at an object (as a supposed quality of every act of consciousness): E17. **intentionally** *adverb* in an intentional manner or relation; *esp.* deliberately, on purpose: E17.

intentionalism /ɪnˈtɛnʃ(ə)n(ə)lɪz(ə)m/ *noun*. L19.
[ORIGIN from INTENTIONAL + -ISM.]
1 The theory that the world is the result of conscious design. *rare*. L19.
2 The theory that a literary work should be judged in terms of the author's intentions: see ***intentional fallacy*** s.v. INTENTIONAL *adjective* 1. L19.
■ **intentionalist** *noun & adjective* (*a*) *noun* a person who advocates intentionalism; (*b*) *adjective* of or pertaining to intentionalism: M20.

intentioned /ɪnˈtɛnʃ(ə)nd/ *adjective*. M17.
[ORIGIN from INTENTION + -ED².]
Having intentions (of a specified kind). Usu. with qualifying adverb, esp. *well*.

intentive /ɪnˈtɛntɪv/ *adjective*. Now *rare* or *obsolete*. Also (earlier) †**en-**. LME.
[ORIGIN Old French *ententif*, *intentif*, *-ive*, from *entent*: see INTENT *noun*, -IVE.]
1 Of a person: attentive, assiduous. LME.
2 Of the faculties or thoughts, an action, a look, etc.: intently directed. LME.
ALBERT SMITH Many.. were at breakfast.. with such intentive appetites, that they took no notice of the courteous salute.
■ **intentively** *adverb* ME. **intentiveness** *noun* M16.

inter /ˈɪntə/ *adjective & noun*. *colloq.* Also **inter.** (point). L19.
[ORIGIN Abbreviation of INTERMEDIATE *adjective & noun*.]
▸ **A** *adjective*. Intermediate. L19.
▸ **B** *noun*. An intermediate examination in a degree course etc. M20.

inter /ɪnˈtəː/ *verb trans.* Infl. **-rr-**. ME.
[ORIGIN Old French & mod. French *enterrer* from Proto-Romance, formed as IN-² + Latin *terra* earth.]
1 Deposit (a corpse) in the earth, or in a grave or tomb; bury. ME. ▸**b** *fig.* Cover, hide, or imprison (esp. oneself) in something. E17.
†**2** Place in the ground; cover with soil. E17–E18.

inter- /ˈɪntə/ *combining form*.
[ORIGIN Repr. Old French & mod. French *inter-*, *entre-* (cf. ENTER-¹) or its source Latin *inter-*, from *inter* (preposition & adverb) between, among, amid, in between, in the midst.]
1 In adverbial relation to verbs (or their derivs.) or adjectives, or in adjectival relation to nouns, with sense '(situated, occurring, etc.) between or among persons or things', often expr. mutual or reciprocal action or relation, as ***inter-agent***, ***interbreed***, ***interchange***, ***interlace***, ***interlocution***. In words adopted from French and Latin and in English words modelled on these, and as a freely productive prefix.
2 In prepositional relation to nouns expressed or implied, with the sense 'situated, occurring, etc. between (things of the kind indicated)', often in contrast to words in INTRA-, as ***intercity***, ***intercontinental***, ***intermolecular***.
■ **inter-ˈallied** *adjective* existing or constituted between allies or allied forces E20. **interalˈveolar** *adjective* (ANATOMY & ZOOLOGY) situated or existing between alveoli M19. **inter-Aˈmerican** *adjective* existing between the countries of N. and S. America; of or pertaining to relationships between such countries: M20. **interˈanimate** *verb trans.* (*rare*) animate mutually M17. **interaniˈmation** *noun* mutual animation E20. **interˈannual** *adjective* existing between (that of) different years L20. **interarˈterial** *adjective* existing between or connecting arteries E20. **interarˈticular** *adjective* situated or occurring between contiguous surfaces of a joint E19. **interaˈtomic** *adjective* situated, existing, or occurring between atoms M19. **interavailaˈbility** *noun* the fact of being interavailable E20. **interaˈvailable** *adjective* (of train tickets etc.) equally available from and valid on different transport undertakings L20. **interbank** *adjective* agreed, arranged, or operating between banks M20. **interbrain** *noun* (ANATOMY) the diencephalon L19. **intercaˈpillary** *adjective* (ANATOMY) existing or occurring between the capillaries M19. **interˈcellular** *adjective* occurring between the cells of one or more organisms M19. **interˈcellularly** *adverb* between cells M20. **interˈcensal** *adjective* occurring between two censuses; of or pertaining to a period between censuses: L19. **interchapter** *noun* a passage of text placed between chapters M19. **interˈchurch** *adjective* concerning (members of) several Christian denominations E20. **interˈcity** *adjective & noun* (*a*) *adjective* occurring or travelling between cities; *spec.* designating a fast train or train service between main towns; (*b*) *noun* an intercity train: E20. **inter-class** *adjective* occurring or carried on between social classes E20. **interˈclavicle** *noun* (ZOOLOGY) a membrane bone between the two clavicles in many amphibians and reptiles and in monotremes L19. **interclaˈvicular** *adjective & noun* (ZOOLOGY & ANATOMY) (a bone) situated between the clavicles M19. **interˈcoastal** *adjective* existing, carried on between, or connecting different coasts E20. **intercollege** *adjective* intercollegiate E20. **intercoˈllegiate** *adjective* occurring or conducted between colleges; involving (members of) different colleges: L19. **intercoˈlonial** *adjective* connecting, occurring between, or concerning different colonies M19. **intercombiˈnation** *noun* mutual combination; *spec.* (PHYSICS) an electronic transition between atomic states of different multiplicities; (in full ***intercombination line***) a spectral line produced by such a transition: M19. **intercoˈmmunal** *adjective* existing or occurring between communities or races E20. **intercoˈmmunity** *noun* the quality of being common to various things; the condition of having things in common or taking part in the same things: L16. **interˈcompany** *adjective* made or occurring between different companies E20. **intercomˈparison** *noun* (a) comparison of each of a number of things with one another M19. **interconˈversion** *noun* the process of converting each of two or more things into the other(s) M19. **interconˈvert** *verb trans.* convert into one another M20. **interconvertiˈbility** *noun* the quality of being interconvertible M19. **interconˈvertible** *adjective* mutually convertible E19. **interˈcorrelate** *verb trans. & intrans.* correlate with one another E20. **intercorreˈlation** *noun* statistical correlation that relates each of a number of variates with the others E20. **inter-county** *adjective* occurring or carried on between counties L19. **interˈcranial** *adjective* situated or occurring within the skull E20. **interˈcrural** *adjective* situated or occurring between the legs L17. **interˈcrystalline** *adjective* situated or occurring between crystals, esp. those which form a metal E20. **interˈcultural** *adjective* (*a*) (of tillage) carried out while a crop is still growing; (*b*) taking place or forming a communication between cultures, belonging to or derived from different cultures: L19. **interdefinaˈbility** *noun* (LOGIC) the quality of being interdefinable M20. **interdeˈfinable** *adjective* (LOGIC) able to be defined by each other M20. **interdenomiˈnational** *adjective* pertaining to different Christian denominations; involving or composed of members of different denominations: L19. **interdenomiˈnationally** *adverb* between or as regards different Christian denominations L20. **interdepartˈmental** *adjective* occurring between or pertaining to different departments L19. **interdepartˈmentally** *adverb* between departments E20. **interdiaˈlectal** *adjective* taking place or existing between dialects; belonging in common to or derived from different dialects: M20. **interdiˈffuse** *verb trans. & intrans.* diffuse among other things or in another substance, esp. a gas L19. **interdiˈffusion** *noun* mutual diffusion M19. **interˈdine** *verb intrans.* (of members of different castes or tribal groups) eat a meal together E20. **interdoˈminion** *adjective* occurring or carried on between (former) dominions of the British Commonwealth M20. **inter-eˈlectrode** *adjective* (of the interval) that exists between two or more electrodes E20. **inter-ˈethnic** *adjective* occurring or existing between ethnic groups; belonging to or used by different ethnic groups: E20. **interfaith** *adjective* pertaining to different religions; involving or composed of members of different religions: M20. **interfaˈmilial**, **interˈfamily** *adjectives* existing or occurring between (members of) different families M20. **interfaˈscicular** *adjective* (ANATOMY & BOTANY) situated between fascicles M19. **interˈfemoral** *adjective* (chiefly ZOOLOGY) situated between the thighs E19. **interfenesˈtration** *noun* the spacing of the windows of a building E19. **interˈfertile** *adjective* capable of producing seed or offspring when crossed with an individual of another variety, race, etc. E20. **interferˈtility** *noun* the property of being interfertile E20. **interˈfibrillar** *adjective* existing or occurring between fibrils L19. **interˈfile** *verb trans.* file among each other or among other items M20. **interˈfinger** *verb intrans.* (GEOLOGY) = INTERDIGITATE 1 E20. **inter-firm** *adjective* carried on between two or more business firms M20. **interfoliˈaceous** *adjective* (BOTANY) situated between two opposite leaves M18. **interˈfoliar** *adjective* (BOTANY) interfoliaceous M19. **intergaˈlactic** *adjective* of, pertaining to, or occurring in the regions between galaxies; involving more than one galaxy: E20. **intergaˈlactically** *adverb* by means of or as regards intergalactic travel L20. **intergeneˈrational** *adjective* existing or occurring between different generations of people; involving more than just one generation: M20. **intergeneˈrationally** *adverb* between generations; from one generation to another: L20. **intergeˈneric** *adjective* (BIOLOGY) formed or obtained from (individuals of) different genera E20. **intergenic** /-ˈdʒɛn-/ *adjective* occurring or existing between neighbouring genes M20. **interˈglandular** *adjective* (ANATOMY) situated or occurring between glands L19. **intergovernˈmental** *adjective* involving (representatives of) more than one government E20. **intergovernˈmentally** *adverb* by (representatives of) more than one government L20. **interˈgranular** *adjective* situated or occurring between granules or grains L19. **intergroup** *adjective* existing or occurring between (members of) different groups, esp. different social or political groups M20. **interˈhalogen** *adjective* (of a chemical compound) composed of two different halogens M20. **interhemiˈspheric** *adjective* situated or existing between the two hemispheres of the brain E20. **interˈictal** *adjective* (MEDICINE) occurring during or characteristic of a period between one ictus and another M20. **interindiˈvidual** *adjective* existing or occurring between individuals L19. **interindustry** *adjective* (ECONOMICS) existing or occurring between industries; based on more than one industry: M20. **interˈinfluence** *noun* influence of a number of things on each other M20. **interˈinfluencing** *noun* the fact of influencing each other E20. **interˈinsular** *adjective* existing or occurring between islands M19. **interiˈonic** *adjective* existing or occurring between ions E20. **inter-island** *adjective* existing or occurring between islands; pertaining to travel or communication between islands; involving (representatives of) more than one island: M19. †**interjoin** *verb trans.* (*rare*, Shakes.) join reciprocally: only in E17. **interˈknit** *verb trans. & intrans.* intertwine, interweave L16. **interˈknot** *verb trans.* knot together E17. **interlaˈboratory** *adjective* occurring between or involving different laboratories: M20. **interlaˈcustrine** *adjective* situated between lakes E20. **interlaˈmellar** *adjective* (ZOOLOGY) situated between or among lamellae (esp. of the gills) M19. **interlevel** *noun* a level of language serving to relate other linguistic levels M20. **interˈlibrary** *adjective* (esp. of book lending) between libraries L19. **interˈlobate** *adjective* (PHYSICAL GEOGRAPHY) situated or deposited between the lobes of a glacier L19. **interˈlobular** *adjective* (ANATOMY & MEDICINE) situated or occurring between lobes or lobules M19. **interloˈcation** *noun* (*rare*) (*a*) an interposition; something interposed; (*b*) an intermediate location: E17. **interˈlucent** *adjective* (*rare*) shining between things E18. **interˈmetallic** *adjective & noun* (designating) a compound formed from two or more metallic elements E20. **intermiˈgration** *noun* interchange of abode or habitat L17. **interˈmine** *verb trans.* (*rare*) intersect with mines or veins E17. **intermiˈtotic** *noun & adjective* (CYTOLOGY) (a cell) capable of further division; existing or occurring between mitoses: M20. **intermoduˈlation** *noun* (ELECTRONICS) mutual distortion of two sinusoidal signals M20. **intermoˈlecular** *adjective* situated, existing, or occurring between molecules M19. **intermoˈlecularly** *adverb* between molecules M20. **intermont** *adjective* intermontane E20. **interˈmontane** *adjective* situated between mountains E19. **interˈmountain** *adjective* intermontane E20. **interˈneural** *adjective & noun* (ZOOLOGY) (a spine, ray, etc.) situated between neural spines or arches M19. **interˈnuclear** *adjective* situated, occurring,

or existing between nuclei L19. **inter'nuptial** *adjective* (**a**) of or pertaining to intermarriage; (**b**) occurring between two marriages: M19. **inter'orbital** *adjective* (ANATOMY) situated between the eye sockets M19. **inter'osculate** *verb intrans.* inosculate, interpenetrate; (esp. of biological species) intergrade, overlap in characteristics: L19. **interoscu'lation** *noun* the action or fact of interosculating L19. **inter'osseous** *adjective* (ANATOMY) situated between bones M18. **inter'page** *verb trans.* print or insert on intermediate pages M19. **inter'palpebral** *adjective* situated between the eyelids L19. **interpa'rietal** *adjective & noun* (ANATOMY) (the bone) situated at the back of the skull, between the parietal bones M19. **interpha'langeal** *adjective* (ANATOMY) situated between two adjacent phalanges L19. **inter'plait** *verb trans. & intrans.* plait together E19. **inter'planar** *adjective* (CRYSTALLOGRAPHY) existing between the planes of a crystal lattice M20. **interplane** *adjective* (AERONAUTICS) situated between or connecting the upper and lower wings of a biplane E20. **inter'planetary** *adjective* situated or existing between planets; of or pertaining to travel between planets: L17. **in'terplicate** *verb trans.* (*rare*) fold between or together E17. **inter'pluvial** *adjective & noun* (of, pertaining to, or designating) any period of relatively dry conditions in equatorial regions during the geological past, esp. in the Pleistocene (cf. INTERGLACIAL) E20. **inter'point** *verb trans. & intrans.* insert a point or points in (a thing) or between (things) L16. **inter'polar** *adjective* situated between the poles (of a battery, etc.) L19. **interpole** *noun* an auxiliary pole placed between the main poles to increase the efficiency of a commutator E20. **interpro'vincial** *adjective* situated or carried on between provinces M19. **inter'proximal** *adjective* (DENTISTRY) of, situated in, or relating to the region between adjacent teeth L19. **inter'pubic** *adjective* situated between the right and left pubic bones M19. **interpulse** *adjective & noun* (**a**) *adjective* existing or occurring between one pulse and the next; (**b**) *noun* (ASTRONOMY) a weaker pulse occurring between the main pulses of radiation from some pulsars: M20. **inter'pupillary** *adjective* existing between the pupils of the eyes E20. **inter'quartile** *adjective* (STATISTICS) situated between the first and third quartiles of a distribution L19. **inter'radial** *adjective & noun* (ZOOLOGY) (a part or structure) situated between rays or radii, as of an echinoderm L19. **inter'radius** *noun* (ZOOLOGY) an interradial part or axis L19. **inter'renal** *adjective* situated between the kidneys; *spec.* (ZOOLOGY) designating the steroid-producing tissue of fish: L19. **inter'scapular** *adjective* (ANATOMY & ZOOLOGY) situated between the scapulae E18. **interscho'lastic** *adjective* occurring between schools E20. **inter'segment** *noun* †(**a**) MATH. an intercept; (**b**) ZOOLOGY in certain segmented animals, the part of the body between two segments: L17. **inter'sensory** *adjective* registered by two or more senses M20. **intersen'tential** *adjective* (LINGUISTICS) existing, or pertaining to the relationship, between sentences M20. **inter'septal** *adjective* (ANATOMY & ZOOLOGY) situated between septa M19. **inter-'service** *adjective* existing between, formed from, or common to the armed services M20. **intersession** *noun* (**a**) *US* a short period between university terms, sometimes used by students to engage in projects outside the normal academic programme; (**b**) *Canad.* a short university term in which thirteen weeks of course material is covered in five or six weeks of intensive study: E20. **inter'shoot** *verb trans. & intrans.* (*arch.*) shoot or dart between or among (things) M19. **intersi'dereal** *adjective* situated or occurring between the stars M17. **inter'social** *adjective* existing between associates M19. **inter'sow** *verb trans.* (now *rare*) intersperse E17. **interspe'cific** *adjective* formed or obtained from (individuals of) different species; occurring among individuals of different species: L19. **inter'sphere** *verb trans.* (*arch.*) bring within another's sphere L19. **inter'spinal**, **inter'spinous** *adjectives* (ANATOMY) situated between the spines or spinous processes of the vertebrae M19. **inter'stadial** *adjective & noun* (GEOLOGY) (pertaining to, characteristic of, or designating) a minor period of ice retreat during a glacial period E20. **interstage** *adjective* situated or occurring between successive stages of an apparatus E20. **inter-'station** *adjective* occurring between two stations or tuning positions on a radio M20. **inter'stellar** *adjective* situated between stars; of or relating to the regions of space between the stars: E17. **inter-strain** *adjective* (BIOLOGY) existing or occurring between (genetic) strains; formed by crossing two strains: M20. **intersy'llabic** *adjective* occurring between syllables M20. **intersystem** *adjective* existing or occurring between systems; ***intersystem crossing*** (Physics), radiationless transition of an excited molecule to a state of different multiplicity: E20. **interterri'torial** *adjective* existing between or involving different territories L19. **intertesta'mental** *adjective* designating or pertaining to Jewish writings composed approximately between 200 BC and AD 100 (after the latest Old Testament book and before the beginning (or the end) of the New Testament period), and regarded as non-canonical M20. **inter'tidal** *adjective* occurring or living between the limits of low and high tides L19. **inter'tillage** *noun* (*US*) intercropping E20. **inter'tilled** *adjective* (*US*) that has been intercropped E20. **inter'tonic** *adjective* (LINGUISTICS) occurring between tones or stresses E20. **intertranslata'bility** *noun* the property of being intertranslatable M20. **intertrans'latable** *adjective* able to be translated from one language to another and vice versa M19. **intertrans'verse** *adjective* (ANATOMY) situated between the transverse processes of the vertebrae M19. **inter'trochlear** *adjective* (ANATOMY) situated in the trochlear surface of a joint L19. **intertu'bercular** *adjective* (ANATOMY) situated or existing between tubercles L19. **inter'tubular** *adjective* situated between tubes or tubules M19. **inter'union** *noun & adjective* (**a**) *noun* mutual or reciprocal union; interblending; (**b**) *adjective* occurring between trade unions: E19. **inter-uni'versity** *adjective* existing or occurring between universities; involving (members of) different universities: L19. **interva'rietal** *adjective* formed from or occurring between (members of) different plant varieties E20. **inter'veinal** *adjective* situated or occurring between the veins of a leaf M20. **inter'vertebral** *adjective* situated or existing between vertebrae L18. **interven'tricular** *adjective* (ANATOMY) situated between the ventricles (of the heart or brain) M19. **inter'vital** *adjective* (*rare*) existing between two lives or two stages of existence M19. **inter'war** *adjective* existing in the period between two wars, *spec.* the period 1919–39 M20. **interweft** *noun* (*rare*) interweaving; interwoven work: E20. **inter'xylary** *adjective* (BOTANY) (of phloem) situated within the secondary xylem L19. **inter'zonal** *adjective* existing or carried on between zones L19.

inter. *abbreviation.*
Intermediate.

interact /ˈɪntərakt/ *noun.* M18.
[ORIGIN from INTER- 2 + ACT *noun*, after French ENTR'ACTE.]
= ENTR'ACTE.

interact /ɪntərˈakt/ *verb intrans.* M19.
[ORIGIN from INTER- 1 + ACT *verb*.]
Act reciprocally, act on each other; behave in a way that influences and responds to another. (Foll. by *with*.)

D. ATTENBOROUGH The molecules began to interact with one another to form even more complex compounds. R. BUSH Two streams of modernism grew, interacted and diverged in Eliot's poetry.

■ **interactant** *noun* a person who or thing which interacts M20. **interactor** *noun* a person who interacts with others M20.

interaction /ɪntərˈakʃ(ə)n/ *noun.* M19.
[ORIGIN from INTERACT *verb* + -ION.]
1 Reciprocal action; action or influence of persons or things on each other. M19.
2 PHYSICS. A particular way in which matter, particles, and fields affect one another, e.g. through gravitation or electromagnetism. M20.
strong interaction, ***weak interaction***, etc.
■ **interactional** *adjective* L19. **interactionally** *adverb* M20.

interactionism /ɪntərˈakʃ(ə)nɪz(ə)m/ *noun.* E20.
[ORIGIN from INTERACTION + -ISM.]
PHILOSOPHY. The theory that there are two entities, mind and body, each of which can have an effect on the other. See also SYMBOLIC ***interactionism***.

interactionist /ɪntərˈakʃ(ə)nɪst/ *noun & adjective.* E20.
[ORIGIN formed as INTERACTIONISM + -IST.]
▸ **A** *noun.* A person who advocates interactionism or interaction, esp. as an explanation of something. E20.
▸ **B** *adjective.* Of or pertaining to interactionism or interactionists. E20.

Nature Piaget rejects both extremes of the heredity–environment controversy without lapsing into an interactionist stance.

interactive /ɪntərˈaktɪv/ *adjective.* M19.
[ORIGIN from INTERACT *verb* + -IVE.]
1 Reciprocally active; acting upon or influencing each other. M19.
2 Designating or pertaining to a computer terminal or system that allows a two-way flow of information between it and a user; responding to input from a user. M20.
■ **interactively** *adverb* L20. **interac'tivity** *noun* (**a**) an activity that involves interaction; (**b**) the property of being interactive: M20.

inter-agency /ɪntərˈeɪdʒ(ə)nsi/ *noun & adjective.* M18.
[ORIGIN from INTER- 1,2 + AGENCY.]
▸ **A** *noun.* The fact of being an inter-agent. M18.
▸ **B** *adjective.* Occurring between different agencies; constituted from more than one agency. M20.

inter-agent /ɪntərˈeɪdʒ(ə)nt/ *noun.* M18.
[ORIGIN from INTER- 1 + AGENT.]
An intermediate agent; an intermediary.

inter alia /ɪntər ˈeɪlɪə, ˈal-/ *adverbial phr.* M17.
[ORIGIN Latin, from *inter* among + *alia* accus. neut. pl. of *alius* another.]
Among other things.

inter alios /ɪntər ˈeɪlɪəʊs, ˈal-/ *adverbial phr.* M17.
[ORIGIN Latin, from *inter* among + *alios* accus. masc. pl. of *alius* another.]
Among other people.

interamnian /ɪntərˈamnɪən/ *adjective.* L18.
[ORIGIN from Latin *interamnus*, formed as INTER- + *amnis* river, + -IAN.]
Lying between two rivers; enclosed by rivers.

interbed /ɪntəˈbɛd/ *verb trans.* Infl. **-dd-**. E19.
[ORIGIN from INTER- 1 + BED *verb*.]
GEOLOGY. Embed (esp. a stratum) among others; interstratify. Chiefly as ***interbedded*** *ppl adjective.*

interblend /ɪntəˈblɛnd/ *verb.* L16.
[ORIGIN from INTER- 1 + BLEND *verb*[2].]
†**1** *verb trans.* Interpose. *rare.* Only in L16.
2 *verb trans. & intrans.* Blend intimately; intermingle. L16.

interbreed /ɪntəˈbriːd/ *verb.* Pa. t. & pple **-bred** /-ˈbrɛd/. M19.
[ORIGIN from INTER- 1 + BREED *verb*.]
1 *verb intrans.* Of animals of different races or stocks, or of a single population: breed with each other. M19.
2 *verb intrans.* Cause animals to interbreed; practise breeding between the members of two stocks. M19.
3 *verb trans.* Breed (offspring) from individuals of different races or species; produce by crossbreeding. M19.

intercalarium /ɪntəkəˈlɛːrɪəm/ *noun.* Pl. **-ia** /-ɪə/. L19.
[ORIGIN mod. Latin *intercalarium* neut. sing. of *intercalarius* INTERCALARY *adjective*.]
ZOOLOGY. **1** An element between adjacent neural arches in the vertebral column of elasmobranchs and some other fishes. L19.
2 In cyprinoid fishes, an ossicle forming part of the Weberian apparatus linking the inner ear with the swim bladder. L19.

intercalary /ɪnˈtəːkəl(ə)ri, ɪntəˈkal(ə)ri/ *adjective & noun.* E17.
[ORIGIN Latin *intercalari(u)s*, from *intercalare*: see INTERCALATE, -Y[3].]
▸ **A** *adjective.* **1** Of a day or month: inserted at intervals in a calendar in order to harmonize with the solar year. E17.
2 Of a year: having an intercalated day or month. M17.
†**3** Of a line or stanza: inserted at intervals in a composition; of the nature of a refrain. M17–E19.
4 Of the nature of an insertion between the members of a series or the parts of a whole; intervening. M18.
▸ **B** *noun.* = INTERCALARIUM 1. E20.

intercalate /ɪnˈtəːkəleɪt/; *as noun also* ɪntəˈkaleɪt/ *verb & noun.* E17.
[ORIGIN Latin *intercalat-* pa. ppl stem of *intercalare* proclaim the insertion of a day etc. in the calendar, formed as INTER- + *calare* proclaim solemnly: see -ATE[3].]
▸ **A** *verb.* **1** *verb trans.* Insert into the calendar as an intercalary day or month. E17.
2 *verb trans.* Insert or interpose as an additional or extraneous item; GEOLOGY interbed; CHEMISTRY introduce an extraneous atom, molecule, etc., between the layers of a crystal lattice. Chiefly as ***intercalated*** *ppl adjective.* E19.
3 *verb intrans.* Become part of a sequence etc. as an extraneous item; become intercalated *in* or inserted *into*. M20.
▸ **B** *noun.* CHEMISTRY. An atom, molecule, etc., that enters between the layers of a crystal lattice; a compound formed in this way. M20.
■ **intercalative** *adjective* characterized by intercalation L19. **intercalator** *noun* a molecule which is inserted into another, larger molecule, esp. of a nucleic acid L20. **intercalatory** *adjective* (*rare*) = INTERCALARY E17.

intercalation /ɪntəkəˈleɪʃ(ə)n/ *noun.* L16.
[ORIGIN French, or Latin *intercalatio(n-)*, formed as INTERCALATE: see -ATION.]
1 The insertion of an additional day or month into the calendar in a particular year; an intercalated day or space of time. L16.
2 *gen.* The action of intercalating something; (an) interpolation. M17.

†**intercale** *verb trans.* E17–E19.
[ORIGIN French *intercaler* or its source Latin *intercalare*: see INTERCALATE.]
= INTERCALATE *verb* 1, 2.

intercameral /ɪntəˈkam(ə)r(ə)l/ *adjective.* E20.
[ORIGIN from INTER- 2 + Latin CAMERA chamber + -AL[1].]
Involving or occurring between the two chambers of a legislature; situated between or separating two chambers of an organism.

intercede /ɪntəˈsiːd/ *verb.* L16.
[ORIGIN Old French & mod. French *intercéder* or Latin *intercedere*, formed as INTER- + *cedere* go.]
1 *verb intrans.* ROMAN HISTORY. Interpose a veto. L16.
2 *verb intrans.* Interpose on behalf of another; plead (*with* a person, *for, on behalf of* another). L16.

N. MONSARRAT He prayed to the saint to intercede on his behalf.

†**3** *verb trans. & intrans.* Come between or *between*; intervene (between). L16–L18.
†**4** *verb intrans.* Intervene by obstruction or prevention. Only in M17.
■ **interceder** *noun* M17.

intercept /ˈɪntəsɛpt/ *noun.* E19.
[ORIGIN from the verb.]
1 An interception, esp. of a ball passed or thrown towards an opponent. E19.
2 MATH. The part of a coordinate axis between the origin and the point where a line etc. cuts the axis. M19.
3 A message, signal, etc., intended for someone else and obtained by covert means, esp. in espionage or warfare. E20.
4 The difference between the observed altitude of a celestial object and the calculated one. E20.

intercept /ɪntəˈsɛpt/ *verb.* LME.
[ORIGIN Latin *intercept-* pa. ppl stem of *intercipere*, formed as INTER- + *capere* take, seize.]
1 *verb trans.* Mark off or include (a certain length or line) between two points or lines; contain between limits. LME.
2 *verb trans.* Put an end to, check, (an action, effect, etc.). LME. ▸†**b** Prevent, hinder, (a person or thing). L16–L18.
3 *verb trans.* Obstruct so as to prevent from continuing to a destination; stop in the course of a journey; obtain covertly (a message etc. meant for another); obstruct the passage of (light, heat, etc.). M16. ▸**b** Stop (passage, motion through space). L16.

M. MEYER A shortage of letters led him to suspect . . that his mail was being intercepted. R. V. JONES They were detected by our radar, and intercepted by two Spitfires. M. DRABBLE Hilda intercepted her gaze. F. NOLAN Are you suggesting . . that the Russian messages intercepted at Bletchley are not genuine?

†**4** *verb trans.* Interrupt, break in on, (esp. a narrative or a person speaking). L16–M18.
†**5** *verb intrans.* Intervene. Only in 17.

6 *verb trans.* Cut off (a thing) *from* another thing; cut off from sight, access, etc. M17.
■ **interceptable** *adjective* L20. †**intercepter** *noun* (rare) E17–L19. **interceptible** *adjective* L20.

interception /ɪntəˈsɛpʃ(ə)n/ *noun*. LME.
[ORIGIN Latin *interceptio(n-)*, formed as INTERCEPT *verb*: see -ION.]
†1 MEDICINE. The interruption of the motion or passage of bodily humours. LME–M17.
2 The action or an act of intercepting; the fact of being intercepted. L16. ▸b *spec.* The action of closing in on and trying to destroy an enemy aircraft or missile. M20.
3 The fact of containing or enclosing between points, lines, or boundaries. *rare*. M17.

interceptive /ɪntəˈsɛptɪv/ *adjective*. LME.
[ORIGIN from Latin *intercept-* (see INTERCEPT *verb*) + -IVE.]
Having the quality of intercepting.

interceptor /ɪntəˈsɛptə/ *noun*. L16.
[ORIGIN Latin, formed as INTERCEPT *verb*: see -OR.]
1 A person who or thing which intercepts. L16.
2 *spec.* A fast aircraft designed for intercepting hostile aircraft. Also more fully ***interceptor fighter***, ***interceptor plane***. M20.

intercession /ɪntəˈsɛʃ(ə)n/ *noun*. LME.
[ORIGIN Old French & mod. French, or Latin *intercessio(n-)*, from *intercess-* pa. ppl stem of *intercedere*: see INTERCEDE, -ION.]
1 The action of interceding or pleading on behalf of another, esp. by prayer; a prayer on behalf of another; in *pl.*, the part of a church service at which such prayers are said. LME. ▸†b A petition or pleading on one's own behalf. L15–M18.

Times A service of thanksgiving and intercession at 2.45 pm on Wednesday.

2 ROMAN HISTORY. The action of interposing a veto. L16.
†3 Cessation, intermission. L16–L17.
†4 Interposition, intervention. E–M17.
■ **intercessional** *adjective* M19. **intercessionary** *adjective* employed in intercession; intercessional: M19.

intercessive /ɪntəˈsɛsɪv/ *adjective*. E17.
[ORIGIN Late Latin *intercessivus*, from *intercess-*: see INTERCESSION, -IVE.]
Characterized by intercession; intercessory.

intercessor /ɪntəˈsɛsə/ *noun*. L15.
[ORIGIN Old French or Latin, from *intercess-*: see INTERCESSION, -OR.]
1 A person who intercedes on behalf of another, esp. by prayer. L15.
†2 An intermediary, a go-between. M16–E17.
■ **interceˈssorial** *adjective* L18.

intercessory /ɪntəˈsɛs(ə)ri/ *adjective*. L16.
[ORIGIN medieval Latin *intercessorius*, from Latin *intercessor*: see INTERCESSOR, -ORY[2].]
Having the function or purpose of intercession; that intercedes for others.

interchain /ˈɪntətʃeɪn/ *adjective*. L20.
[ORIGIN from INTER- 2 + CHAIN *noun*.]
CHEMISTRY. Existing between different polymer chains.

interchain /ɪntəˈtʃeɪn/ *verb trans. rare*. L16.
[ORIGIN from INTER- 1 + CHAIN *verb*.]
Chain or link to one another.

interchange /ˈɪntətʃeɪn(d)ʒ/ *noun*. Also †**enter-**. LME.
[ORIGIN Partly from the verb, partly from Old French *entrechange*, formed as ENTER-[1], INTER- + CHANGE *noun*.]
1 a The action or an act of giving and receiving reciprocally; reciprocal exchange between two parties; *spec.* an exchange of words. LME. ▸b The change of either of two things for the other, or of one thing for another; the taking by each of the place or nature of the other. L16.

a J. MCDOUGALL His daily interchange with colleagues. b E. CLODD Lower races still ascribe power of interchange to man and brute.

2 Alternate or varied succession; alternation. M16.

A. STORR Sometimes our will prevails, and sometimes that of the other . . and we accept this interchange as a normal part of life.

3 a In full ***interchange station***. A station where passengers can change from one railway line, bus service, etc., to another. L19. ▸b A junction of two or more roads designed on several levels to allow vehicles to go from one road to another without crossing a flow of traffic. M20.

interchange /ɪntəˈtʃeɪn(d)ʒ/ *verb*. Also †**enter-**. LME.
[ORIGIN Old French *entrechangier*, formed as ENTER-[1], INTER- + *chang(i)er* CHANGE *verb*.]
1 *verb trans.* a Of two parties: exchange with each other; give and receive reciprocally. LME. ▸b Of one party: exchange *with* another. M16.

W. IRVING There were repeated cheerings and salutations interchanged between the shore and the ship. b H. MACMILLAN I interchanged some useful messages with Menzies.

2 *verb trans.* Put each of (two things) in the place of the other; transpose. Formerly also, to exchange (one thing) *for* another. LME.

T. WRIGHT *L* and *r* were constantly interchanged in the languages of the middle ages.

3 *verb trans.* Cause (things) to follow each other alternately or in succession. LME. ▸b *verb intrans.* Alternate *with*. L15.
4 *verb intrans.* (Of two parties or things) take one another's place; (of one) change places (*with*). E20.

Journal of Genetics One-half of chromosome IX had interchanged . . with an end-piece of the long chromosome. A. CAMPBELL An important principle of Old English word-formation is that etymologically related suffixes can interchange.

■ **interchanger** *noun* (*a*) a person who interchanges something; (*b*) a heat exchanger: M19.

interchangeable /ɪntəˈtʃeɪn(d)ʒəb(ə)l/ *adjective & adverb*. LME.
[ORIGIN Old French *entrechangeable*, formed as INTERCHANGE *verb*: see -ABLE.]
▸ **A** *adjective*. †1 Mutual, reciprocal. LME–M17.
2 Of two things: able to be interchanged; allowing an exchange of place or function. Of one thing: able to be exchanged *with* another. L15.

J. S. FOSTER Progress in the manufacture of interchangeable components . . is still slow. C. THUBRON The peasant women looked interchangeable with their men, unsexed by the same shapeless trousers and jackets.

†3 Alternating. M16–L18.
†4 Subject to change, changeable. L16–M18.
▸ †**B** *adverb*. Mutually. LME–M17.
■ **interchangeaˈbility** *noun* E19. **interchangeableness** *noun* M16. **interchangeably** *adverb* (*a*) (now *rare*) mutually, respectively; †(*b*) alternately; (*c*) by way of interchange; (of the use of words) synonymously, with equal meaning or force: LME.

†**interchangement** *noun*. *rare*. E17–L18.
[ORIGIN Old French *entrechangement*, formed as INTERCHANGE *verb*: see -MENT.]
= INTERCHANGE *noun* 1a.

†**intercision** *noun*. L16.
[ORIGIN French †*intercision* or Latin *intercisio(n-)*, from *intercis-* pa. ppl stem of *intercidere* cut through, formed as INTER- + *caedere* to cut: see -ION.]
1 The action or an act of cutting through something; a cross-section. L16–E18.
2 The action or an act of stopping or interrupting something, esp. temporarily. E17–E19.

†**interclose** *noun* var. of ENTERCLOSE.

†**interclude** *verb trans*. E16.
[ORIGIN Latin *intercludere* formed as INTER- + *claudere* shut.]
1 Close or block (a passage); prevent the passage of. E16–L17.
2 Shut up, confine. E16–E19.
3 Shut off or cut off *from*. M16–E17.
■ †**interclusion** *noun* L16–L18.

intercolumn /ˈɪntəkɒləm/ *noun*. M17.
[ORIGIN Latin *intercolumnium*, formed as INTER- + *columna* pillar.]
ARCHITECTURE. = INTERCOLUMNIATION 1.

intercolumnar /ɪntəkəˈlʌmnə/ *adjective*. M19.
[ORIGIN from INTER- 2 + COLUMNAR.]
Situated or placed between two columns.

intercolumniation /ˌɪntəkəlʌmnɪˈeɪʃ(ə)n/ *noun*. Also **-columnation** /-kɒləmˈneɪʃ(ə)n/. E17.
[ORIGIN formed as INTERCOLUMN + -ATION.]
ARCHITECTURE. 1 The space between two adjacent columns. E17.
2 The spacing of the columns of a building. M19.
■ **intercoˈlumniary** *adjective* (*rare*) = INTERCOLUMNAR M17.

intercom /ˈɪntəkɒm/ *noun*. *colloq*. M20.
[ORIGIN Abbreviation of INTERCOMMUNICATION.]
A system of internal communication by telephone, radio, etc., between or within units of an organization, e.g. aircraft, security patrols.

D. LODGE The captain came on the intercom to inform the passengers that the plane had burst a . . tyre.

intercommon /ɪntəˈkɒmən/ *verb & noun*. Also (earlier) †**enter-**. LME.
[ORIGIN Anglo-Norman *entrecomuner*, formed as ENTER-[1], INTER- + *comuner*: see COMMUNE *verb*.]
▸ **A** *verb intrans*. †1 Have communication or dealings with each other or with another; associate. (Foll. by *with*.) LME–L17.

W. PENN The Brittains and Saxons began to grow tame to each other, and intercommon amicably.

†2 Share or participate *with* others, or mutually. L16–M17.
3 Share in the use of the same common land. M17.
▸ **B** *noun*. The action, practice, or right of intercommoning. Now *rare*. LME.
■ **intercommonage** *noun* the practice of sharing something, esp. common pasture E17. **intercommoner** *noun* M16.

intercommune /ɪntəkəˈmjuːn, ɪntəˈkɒmjuːn/ *verb*. Also (earlier) †**enter-**. LME.
[ORIGIN formed as INTERCOMMON: cf. COMMUNE *verb*.]
1 *verb intrans.* Have communication or conversation with each other or with another. Now *rare* or *obsolete*. LME.
2 *verb intrans.* Have dealings or relations, esp. with rebels or denounced people. *obsolete* exc. SCOTS LAW (now *hist.*). LME.
letter of intercommuning, **writ of intercommuning**: issued by the Privy Council and prohibiting communication with person(s) named.
3 *verb trans.* SCOTS LAW (now *hist.*). Denounce by writ of intercommuning; prohibit communication with. L17.
■ **intercommuner** *noun* (SCOTS LAW, now *hist.*) a person who has dealings with a person denounced by law E17.

intercommunicate /ɪntəkəˈmjuːnɪkeɪt/ *verb*. Also (earlier) †**enter-**. L16.
[ORIGIN Anglo-Latin *intercommunicat-* pa. ppl stem of *intercommunicare*, formed as INTER-, COMMUNICATE *verb*.]
1 *verb intrans.* Communicate with each other; (of rooms etc.) have access from each into the other. L16.
2 *verb trans.* Communicate, impart, or transmit to and from each other. Long *rare* or *obsolete*. E17.
■ **intercommunicaˈbility** *noun* the quality of being intercommunicable L19. **intercommunicable** *adjective* capable of or suitable for intercommunication E19. **intercommunicative** *adjective* (*rare*) characterized by or designed for intercommunication M17.

intercommunication /ˌɪntəkəmjuːnɪˈkeɪʃ(ə)n/ *noun*. Also (earlier) †**enter-**. LME.
[ORIGIN Anglo-Latin *intercommunicatio(n-)*, formed as INTERCOMMUNICATE: see -ATION.]
1 The action or fact of intercommunicating; *esp.* the mutual exchange of ideas, information, etc. LME.
2 (A means of) passage to and fro by connecting routes or lines of communication. M19.

intercommunion /ɪntəkəˈmjuːnjən/ *noun*. M18.
[ORIGIN from INTER- 1 + COMMUNION.]
1 Mutual fellowship, esp. between members of different religions or denominations. M18. ▸b Participation in each others' Eucharists, to the extent of receiving Communion, by members of different Christian denominations. E20.
2 Mutual action or relation between things with regard to their functions. E19.

B. JOWETT When all these studies reach the point of intercommunion and connection with one another.

interconnect /ɪntəkəˈnɛkt/ *verb trans. & intrans*. M19.
[ORIGIN from INTER- 1 + CONNECT.]
Connect with each other.

Scientific American The human brain is composed of . . nerve cells, each of which projects . . fibres that . . interconnect. T. MO A maze of interconnected waterways.

■ **interconnectedness** *noun* the property or state of being interconnected E20. **interconnection**, **-connexion** *noun* mutual connection M19. **interconnector** *noun* something that interconnects things, esp. electrically M20.

intercontinental /ˌɪntəkɒntɪˈnɛnt(ə)l/ *adjective*. M19.
[ORIGIN from INTER- 2 + CONTINENTAL.]
Situated or existing between, or connecting, different continents; (capable of) travelling from one continent to another.
intercontinental ballistic missile a ballistic missile able to be sent from one continent to another.
■ **intercontinentally** *adverb* between continents M20.

intercooler /ˈɪntəkuːlə/ *noun*. E20.
[ORIGIN from INTER- 1 + COOLER.]
An apparatus for cooling gas heated by compression, esp. before it is compressed a second time (e.g. in a supercharged engine).
■ **intercool** *verb trans.* equip or provide with an intercooler E20.

intercostal /ɪntəˈkɒst(ə)l/ *adjective & noun*. L16.
[ORIGIN from INTER- 2 + Latin *costa* rib + -AL[1].]
▸ **A** *adjective*. Situated or occurring between the ribs (of the body or of a ship). L16.
▸ **B** *noun*. In *pl.* Intercostal muscles, nerves, arteries, etc. L17.
■ **intercostally** *adverb* between the ribs L19.

intercourse /ˈɪntəkɔːs/ *noun & verb*. Also (earlier) †**enter-**. LME.
[ORIGIN Old French & mod. French *entrecours* exchange, commerce, from Latin *intercursus*, from *intercurs-* pa. ppl stem of *intercurrere* intervene, formed as INTER- + *currere* to run.]
▸ **A** *noun* **I** 1 Communication or dealings (orig. *spec.* of a mercantile kind) between countries, localities, etc. LME.

W. LIPPMANN An increasing freedom of trade and intercourse within a state makes for an increasing participation in the common life of mankind.

2 a *sing.* & (now *rare* or *obsolete*) in *pl.* Social communication between individuals; habitual contact in conversation, correspondence, or action. M16. ▸b = ***SEXUAL intercourse***. L18.

a H. JAMES The intercourse between these two ladies had been neither frequent nor intimate. R. HUGHES Mrs Thornton thought it good for them to have some intercourse with other children outside their own family. b JOYCE He . . did not scruple . . to attempt illicit intercourse with a female domestic. *Boston Globe* The ailment can be transmitted by male homosexual intercourse.

3 Communion between a human being and God or other spiritual being. M16.

†**4** Exchange of ideas; discussion. L16–L17.
†**5** Intercommunication between things or parts; a means of intercommunication; an entrance. L16–L18.
6 Continuous interchange *of* letters, looks, etc. Now *rare* or *obsolete*. L16.

I. D'ISRAELI These letters were afterwards followed by an intercourse of civilities.

†**7** Interchange of one thing with another, alternation. L16–M17.
▸ †**II 8** Intervention; an intervening course or space, an interval. M16–M18.
▸ †**B** *verb*. **1** *verb trans. & intrans.* Run (through or across). *rare*. L16–E17.
2 *verb intrans.* Have social intercourse (*with*). *rare*. L16–L18.

intercrop /*as verb* ɪntəˈkrɒp, *as noun* ˈɪntəkrɒp/ *verb & noun*. L19.
[ORIGIN from INTER- 1 + CROP *verb*.]
▸ **A** *verb intrans. & trans.* Infl. **-pp-**. Raise (a crop) among plants of a different kind, usu. in the space between rows; cultivate (land) in this way. L19.
▸ **B** *noun*. A crop raised by intercropping. M20.

intercross /*as verb* ɪntəˈkrɒs, *as noun* ˈɪntəkrɒs/ *verb & noun*. E18.
[ORIGIN from INTER- 1 + CROSS *verb*, *noun*.]
▸ **A** *verb trans. & intrans.* **1** Cross (each other); place across each other. E18.
2 Of animals or plants of different breeds, varieties, etc.: (cause to) breed or propagate with each other. M19.
▸ **B** *noun*. An instance or result of intercrossing animals or plants. M19.

intercurrent /ɪntəˈkʌr(ə)nt/ *adjective*. E17.
[ORIGIN Latin *intercurrent-* pres. ppl stem of *intercurrere*: see INTERCOURSE, -ENT.]
1 a Of time or events: intervening. E17. ▸†**b** Of objects: intervening; situated between others. M–L17.
2 Of a disease, esp. an infection: occurring by chance during the course of another more chronic disease; recurring. Formerly also (of a fever), apt to occur at any time of year. L17.
3 Of the pulse: having an extra beat. E18.
■ **intercurrence** *noun* the fact or state of being intercurrent E17.

intercut /ɪntəˈkʌt/ *verb*. Infl. **-tt-**. Pa. t. & pple **intercut**. E17.
[ORIGIN from INTER- 1 + CUT *verb*.]
†**1** *verb trans.* Cut into; divide (as) by cutting; intersect. *rare*. E17–E18.
2 CINEMATOGRAPHY. Insert a scene or shot into (an existing scene); alternate (shots from different scenes). (Foll. by *with*.) M20.

I. C. JARVIE Resnais . . intercuts scenes from the heroine's memories . . with her present *affaire*. T. BARR He will be intercutting from you standing, to you sitting, and back to you standing.

interdeal /ɪntəˈdiːl/ *verb intrans.* Pa. t. & pple **-dealt** /-dɛlt/. L16.
[ORIGIN from INTER- 1 + DEAL *verb*.]
Deal or negotiate mutually.

interdealer /ɪntəˈdiːlə/ *adjective*. M20.
[ORIGIN from INTER- 2 + DEALER.]
STOCK EXCHANGE. Made or occurring between dealers; (of a broker) trading chiefly with dealers or market-makers.

interdental /ɪntəˈdɛnt(ə)l/ *adjective & noun*. L19.
[ORIGIN from INTER- 2 + DENTAL.]
▸ **A** *adjective*. **1** Situated or placed between teeth or the teeth. L19.
2 PHONETICS. Pronounced by placing the tip of the tongue between the teeth. L19.
▸ **B** *noun*. PHONETICS. An interdental sound. M20.
■ **interdentally** *adverb* E20.

interdepend /ɪntədɪˈpɛnd/ *verb intrans.* M19.
[ORIGIN from INTER- 1 + DEPEND.]
Depend on each other.

interdependent /ɪntədɪˈpɛnd(ə)nt/ *adjective*. M18.
[ORIGIN from INTER- 1 + DEPENDENT *adjective*.]
Dependent on each other.
■ **interdependence** *noun* E19. **interdependency** *noun* M19. **interdependently** *adverb* L19.

†**interdice** *noun*. E17–E18.
[ORIGIN Unknown. Cf. INTERTIE.]
= INTERTIE.

interdict /ˈɪntədɪkt/ *noun*. Also (earlier) †**entredit(e)**. ME.
[ORIGIN Old French *entredit* from Latin *interdictum* (to which the English word was later assim.), use as noun of neut. pa. pple of *interdicere* interpose by speech, forbid by decree, formed as INTER- + *dicere* say.]
1 ROMAN CATHOLIC CHURCH. An authoritative sentence debarring a designated person, group, or place from ecclesiastical functions and privileges. ME.

M. ELPHINSTONE He . . suspended all the ceremonies of religion, as if the country were under an interdict.

2 a ROMAN LAW. A decree of the magistrate, commanding or forbidding something. E17. ▸**b** *Scots & CIVIL LAW*. A court order forbidding an act or proceedings complained of as illegal or wrongful; an injunction. M18.

b *Oban Times* Mr. Muir went to the Court of Session . . . An interdict was granted.

3 *gen*. An authoritative or peremptory prohibition. E17.

interdict /ɪntəˈdɪkt/ *verb trans.* Also (earlier) †**entredite**. Pa. t. & pple **-dicted**, (now *literary*) **-dict**. ME.
[ORIGIN from INTERDICT *noun* after Old French *entredire* from Latin *interdicere*: see INTERDICT *noun*]
1 ROMAN CATHOLIC CHURCH. Cut off authoritatively from ecclesiastical functions and privileges; lay under an interdict. ME.
2 Forbid, prohibit, esp. (LAW) by interdiction; debar or preclude (as) by a command; restrain (oneself) *from* an action. (Foll. by *from*; with double obj.) LME.

G. SANDYS Who . . will . . interdict thee his tabernacle. H. COGAN They interdicted that great Court from proceeding any further against them.

3 Impede (an enemy, supplies) by aerial bombing. M20.
■ **interdictive** *adjective* interdictory E17. **interdictory** *adjective* having the effect of interdicting something or someone; conveying interdiction, prohibitory: M18.

interdiction /ɪntəˈdɪkʃ(ə)n/ *noun*. Also (earlier) †**enter-**. LME.
[ORIGIN Latin *interdictio(n-)*, from *interdict-*: see INTERDICTOR, -ION.]
1 The issuing of an interdict; the action of interdicting a person etc.; the condition of being interdicted. LME.
2 SCOTS LAW (now *hist.*). A restraint imposed on a person judged incapable of managing his or her own affairs owing to mental weakness or instability. L16.
3 The interruption of supply operations by aerial bombing. M20.

interdictor /ɪntəˈdɪktə/ *noun*. M17.
[ORIGIN Late (eccl.) Latin, from *interdict-* pa. ppl stem of *interdicere*: see INTERDICT *noun*, -OR.]
1 A person who issues an interdict; SCOTS LAW (now *hist.*) a person responsible for consent to heritable transactions by someone under an interdiction. M17.
2 An aircraft designed for interdiction. M20.

interdigital /ɪntəˈdɪdʒɪt(ə)l/ *adjective*. M20.
[ORIGIN from INTER- 2 + DIGIT + -AL[1].]
1 Situated between or connecting fingers or toes. M20.
2 ELECTRONICS. Esp. of a transducer: having the form of two interdigitating series of parallel strips. M20.
■ **interdigitally** *adverb* L20.

interdigitate /ɪntəˈdɪdʒɪteɪt/ *verb*. M19.
[ORIGIN from INTER- 1 + DIGIT + -ATE[3].]
1 *verb intrans.* Interlock like the fingers of two clasped hands; project or be inserted alternately. (Foll. by *with*.) M19.
2 *verb trans.* Cause to interdigitate. Chiefly as ***interdigitated*** *ppl adjective*. M19.

J. OSBORNE Normal interdigitated relationship of the upper and lower posterior teeth.

■ **interdigiˈtation** *noun* the action or condition of interdigitating; an interdigitating process etc.: M19.

interdisciplinary /ɪntəˈdɪsɪplɪn(ə)ri, ˌɪntədɪsɪˈplɪn(ə)ri/ *adjective*. E20.
[ORIGIN from INTER- 2 + DISCIPLINE *noun* + -ARY[1].]
Of or pertaining to two or more branches of learning; contributing to or derived from two or more disciplines.
■ **ˌinterdiscipliˈnarity** *noun* interdisciplinary quality L20. **ˈinterdiscipline** *noun* an interdisciplinary subject L20. **interˈdiscipline** *adjective* = INTERDISCIPLINARY M20.

†**interess** *noun*. LME.
[ORIGIN Anglo-Norman *interesse* from medieval Latin *interesse*, use as noun of Latin inf.: see INTEREST *noun*.]
1 = INTEREST *noun* 1. LME–M17.
2 = INTEREST *noun* 2, 3. LME–E18.
3 = INTEREST *noun* 11. LME–L15.
4 = INTEREST *noun* 10. E16–E18.

†**interess** *verb trans.* Pa. pple **-ed**, **-rest**. L16.
[ORIGIN French *intéresser* concern, (formerly) damage, from Latin *interesse*: see INTEREST *noun*.]
1 = INTEREST *verb* 1. L16–L17.
2 = INTEREST *verb* 2. Usu. in *pass.* L16–M17.
3 Injure; damage. L16–M17.
4 Cause to take an active part (*in*); = INTEREST *verb* 4. E17–E18.
5 = INTEREST *verb* 5. M–L17.
■ †**interessee** *noun* (*rare*) an interested party E17–E19.

interesse termini /ɪntərˌɛsi ˈtəːmɪnʌɪ/ *noun phr.* M17.
[ORIGIN medieval Latin, lit. 'interest of term or end'.]
LAW (now *hist.*). A right of entry on a leasehold estate, acquired through a demise.

interest /ˈɪnt(ə)rɪst/ *noun*. LME.
[ORIGIN from INTERESS *noun*, partly by addition of parasitic *t*, partly by assoc. with Old French *interest* damage, loss (mod. *intérêt*), app. use as noun of Latin *interest* it makes a difference, it concerns, it matters, 3rd person sing. pres. indic. of *interesse* differ, be of importance, formed as INTER- + *esse* be.]
▸ **I 1** The fact or relation of having a share or concern in, or a right to, something, esp. by law; a right or title, esp. to (a share in) property or a use or benefit relating to property; (a) share *in* something. LME. ▸†**b** Participation in doing or causing something. M17–M18. ▸**c** A financial share or stake in something; the relation of being one of the owners or beneficiaries of an asset, company, etc. L17.

c J. MORTIMER Has someone else got an interest in the film rights?

2 A thing which is to the advantage of someone; (a) benefit, (an) advantage. Freq. in *pl.* LME.

R. HUNTFORD He always had the interests of his protégés at heart.

3 The relation of being involved or concerned as regards potential detriment or (esp.) advantage. M16.
4 = SELF-INTEREST. E17.
5 Personal influence (*with* a person etc.). E17.
6 A thing that is of some importance to a person, company, state, etc. Freq. in *pl.* E17.

J. MORTIMER Simeon pursued his political interests more doggedly. M. PIERCY He would suggest she take up some new interest or hobby.

7 A business, cause, or principle that is of some importance to a number of people; a party or group having such a thing in common, esp. in matters of politics or business. L17.

J. GALSWORTHY Mrs. Smeech, . . an aged person, connected with the charring interest. C. V. WEDGWOOD Cooke . . was now wholly in the King's interest. P. GAY Institutions can be captured by special interests.

8 A state of feeling in which one wishes to pay particular attention to a thing or person; (a feeling of) curiosity or concern. L18.

J. RUSKIN He who can take no interest in what is small. K. AMIS I seem to have failed to hold your interest. E. H. JONES They had no interest in field-sports.

9 The quality or power of arousing such a feeling; the quality of being interesting. E19.

C. G. WOLFF It is not . . a novel whose interest lies in plot.

▸ **II** Senses rel. to medieval Latin *interesse* compensation for a debtor's defaulting.
10 Money charged for the use of money lent or for not having to repay a debt, according to a specified ratio. M16.

E. NESBIT You shall pay me back the pound, and sixty per cent interest.

†**11** Injury, detriment; compensation for injury. L16–E17.
– PHRASES: **at interest** (of money borrowed or lent) on the condition that interest is to be charged. **compound interest**: reckoned on the principal together with the accumulated unpaid interest. ***controlling interest***: see CONTROL *verb*. **declare an interest**, **declare one's interest** make known one's financial etc. interest in an undertaking before the discussion of it. ***human interest***: see HUMAN *adjective*. **in the best interest of**, **in the best interests of** to the greatest advantage or benefit of. **in the interest of**, **in the interests of** (*a*) *arch.* on the side of; (*b*) out of consideration for, to the advantage or benefit of. LANDED ***interest***. **lose interest (in)** (of a person) become bored (with); (of a thing) become boring. ***open interest***: see OPEN *adjective*. ***outside interest***: see OUTSIDE *adjective*. ***public interest***: see PUBLIC *adjective*. **simple interest**: reckoned on the principal only and paid at fixed intervals. ***Site of Special Scientific Interest***: see SITE *noun*. ***special interest***: see SPECIAL *adjective*. ***vested interest***: see VESTED *ppl adjective*[1] 2. **with interest** with interest charged or paid; *fig.* with increase or augmentation.
– COMB.: **interest group** a group of people sharing a common identifying interest.

interest /ˈɪnt(ə)rɪst/ *verb trans.* E17.
[ORIGIN Alt. of INTERESS *verb* after INTEREST *noun*.]
1 Invest (a person) with a share in or title to something, esp. a spiritual privilege. E17.
2 Cause (a person) to have an interest or concern *in* (a matter); involve. Usu. in *pass.* E17.
3 Of a thing: concern, affect, relate to. Now *rare* or *obsolete*. M17.
4 Cause (a person) to take a personal interest or share *in* a scheme, business, etc.; cause to become interested (*in*); *refl.* take an active part *in*. M17.

M. ATWOOD He'd tried to interest Alma in chess and mathematics.

5 Affect with a feeling of interest; arouse the curiosity or concern of. E18.

B. WEBB Human nature and its problems interest me.

interested /ˈɪnt(ə)rɪstɪd/ *adjective*. E17.
[ORIGIN from INTEREST *verb* + -ED[1].]
1 Characterized by a feeling of interest (*in*). Also foll. by *to learn*, *see*, etc. E17.

Lady's Pictorial I shall be interested to know how the wedding goes off. J. HELLER They don't seem interested in doing much more.

2 Influenced by considerations of personal advantage or self-interest. E18.

LD MACAULAY He was generally thought interested and grasping.

3 Having an interest, share, or concern, in something; affected, involved. E19.

New York Law Journal The witness.. was an interested witness. P. HOWARD The Times is steered by all these and other interested parties.

■ **interestedly** *adverb* M18. **interestedness** *noun* E18.

interesterification /ˌɪntərɪstɛrɪfɪˈkeɪʃ(ə)n, -rɛs-/ *noun*. M20.
[ORIGIN from INTER- 1 + ESTERIFICATION.]
CHEMISTRY. The exchange of alkoxy or acyl groups between an ester and another compound.
■ **interesˈterify** *verb trans. & intrans.* subject to or undergo this process M20.

interesting /ˈɪnt(ə)rɪstɪŋ/ *adjective*. E18.
[ORIGIN from INTEREST *verb* + -ING².]
†**1** That concerns or is relevant (*to*); important. E18–E19.
2 That affects a person with a feeling of interest; having qualities which arouse interest. E18.
in an interesting condition: see CONDITION *noun* 8.
■ **interestingly** *adverb* in an interesting manner, so as to arouse interest; (modifying a sentence) it is interesting that; (earlier in UNINTERESTINGLY *adverb*): E19. **interestingness** *noun* M18.

interface /ˈɪntəfeɪs/ *noun & verb*. L19.
[ORIGIN from INTER- 1 + FACE *noun*.]
▸ **A** *noun*. **1** A surface at which two portions of matter or space meet. L19.

Science Journal Ways of reducing drag at the interface between ski and snow. A. C. CLARKE The sharply defined plane which marked the water–air interface on the sonar screen.

2 A means or place of interaction between two systems, organizations, etc.; a meeting point or common ground between two parties, disciplines, etc. M20.

New Scientist Estuaries occupy an interface which is administrative as well as topographical. *Globe & Mail (Toronto)* The successful candidate will.. function as a prime interface to development and manufacturing.

3 An apparatus for connecting two electrical or electronic devices or systems so that they can be operated jointly or communicate with each other; an apparatus enabling a user to communicate with a computer. M20.

S. CURRAN A few modern typewriters.. are specifically designed with an optional computer communications interface.

▸ **B** *verb*. **1** *verb trans.* Connect (scientific equipment) *with* or *to* so as to make joint operation possible. M20.

Which Micro? It can be interfaced with virtually any micro on the market.

2 *verb intrans.* Be operated jointly (*with*). M20.

Offshore Engineer The responder.. can interface with most existing vehicle tether systems.

3 *verb intrans.* Of a person, organization, etc.: come into interaction, interact, *with*. M20.

New York Times Business has to interface with government increasingly.

interfacial /ɪntəˈfeɪʃ(ə)l/ *adjective*¹. M19.
[ORIGIN from INTER- 2 + Latin *facies* face + -AL¹.]
Included between two faces of a crystal.

interfacial /ˈɪntəfeɪʃ(ə)l/ *adjective*². E20.
[ORIGIN from INTERFACE *noun* + -IAL.]
Existing or occurring at an interface.
■ **interfacially** *adverb* M20.

interfacing /ˈɪntəfeɪsɪŋ/ *noun*. M20.
[ORIGIN from INTER- 1 + FACING.]
(A piece of) stiffish material, esp. buckram, between two layers of fabric in collars etc.

interfere /ɪntəˈfɪə/ *verb*. Also †**enter-**. LME.
[ORIGIN Branch I from Old French *entreferir*; branch II from Old French *s'entreferir* strike each other; both formed as ENTER-¹, INTER- + *ferir* (mod. *férir*) from Latin *ferire* to strike.]
▸ †**I** *verb trans.* **1** Intermingle; intersperse *with*; interpose. LME–L15.
▸ **II** *verb intrans.* **2** Of a person or persons: enter into something without right or invitation, or intending to hinder or obstruct (foll. by *with*). Of a thing: come into conflict or collision (*with*). Of things: strike against each other (now *rare*). LME. ▸**b** Foll. by *with*: molest or assault sexually. M20.

B. T. BRADFORD I wouldn't want her to think he was interfering, queering her pitch. A. STORR The primary instinct was being blocked or interfered with. J. JOHNSTON Her nails.. were .. short, so as not to interfere with her piano playing.

3 Of a horse: = CUT *verb* 30. Of a hoof or foot: strike the inside of the fetlock of another leg. M16.
†**4** *verb intrans.* Clash in opinions, tendencies, etc.; conflict. M17–M19.
†**5** Intersect, cross each other. M17–E18.
6 Intervene so as to affect an action. (Foll. by *in*, *between*.) M18.

P. G. WODEHOUSE It is better for a third party to quarrel with a buzz-saw than to interfere between husband and wife. N. COWARD I'm not going to interfere Let them fight if they want to. *Times* Nato should not seek to interfere in Italy's internal affairs.

7 Of light or other waves: mutually act upon each other and produce interference. (Foll. by *with*.) E19.
8 CHESS. Of a piece: obstruct the line of action of another piece. (Foll. by *with*.) E20.
9 BROADCASTING. Transmit a signal which is received simultaneously *with* the signal sought by the receiver; cause or emit interference. E20.
10 BASEBALL & AMER. FOOTBALL. Interpose so as to obstruct an opposing player. E20.
■ **interferer** *noun* E19. **interfering** *ppl adjective* that interferes; *esp.* (of a person) having a propensity to interfere in other people's affairs: L16. **interferingly** *adverb* M19. **interferingness** *noun* L19.

interference /ɪntəˈfɪər(ə)ns/ *noun*. M18.
[ORIGIN from INTERFERE + -ENCE, after *difference* etc.]
1 The action or fact of interfering or meddling (*with* a person, *in* a thing, etc.). M18.

M. IGNATIEFF He sought to defend the autonomy of the universities from government interference.

2 SCIENCE. The mutual action of two waves of similar wavelength when they combine and form a resultant wave in which the amplitude is increased or reduced. M19.
3 Disturbance of the transmission or reception of radio waves by extraneous signals or phenomena; signals etc. causing such disturbance; unwanted effects arising from such disturbance. L19.

A. MCCOWEN When his car came down the drive, electrical interference could be seen on our new television set.

4 MECHANICS. **a** The collision of the tips of the teeth of a gearwheel with the flanks of those of the mating wheel. E20. ▸**b** The amount by which the external dimension of a part exceeds the internal dimension of the part into which it has to fit. M20.
5 LINGUISTICS. The influence of the pronunciation or other features of a person's native language on a later acquired language. M20.
– COMB.: **interference fit** MECHANICS a fit between two mating parts for which, within the tolerances, there is always an interference between them; **interference fringe** each of a series of light and dark bands, or bands of different colours, produced by the interference of light (e.g. from two point sources); usu. in *pl.*; **interference pattern**: of interference fringes.

interferential /ɪntəfəˈrɛnʃ(ə)l/ *adjective*. L19.
[ORIGIN from INTERFERENCE + -IAL, after *differential* etc.]
Involving or employing interference, esp. of light.

interferogram /ɪntəˈfɪərəgram/ *noun*. E20.
[ORIGIN formed as INTERFEROMETER + -O- + -GRAM.]
A pattern formed by wave interference, *esp.* one represented in a photograph or diagram.

interferometer /ɪntəfəˈrɒmɪtə/ *noun*. L19.
[ORIGIN from INTERFERE + -OMETER.]
An instrument in which wave interference is employed to make precise measurements of length or displacement in terms of the wavelength.
■ ˌ**interferoˈmetric** *adjective* of or pertaining to interferometry; employing or of the nature of an interferometer: M20. ˌ**interferoˈmetrically** *adverb* by means of interferometry M20. **interferometry** *noun* the action of measuring interference phenomena; (the branch of science that deals with) the use of interferometers: E20.

interferon /ɪntəˈfɪərɒn/ *noun*. M20.
[ORIGIN formed as INTERFEROMETER + *-on*.]
Any of several proteins which are produced by and released from animal cells in response to the entry of a virus, and inhibit virus replication in other cells.

interflow /ˈɪntəfləʊ/ *noun*. E17.
[ORIGIN from INTER- 1 + FLOW *noun*¹.]
†**1** A flow between things; a channel, a strait. Only in E17.
2 An instance of interflowing, an intermingling. M19.

interflow /ɪntəˈfləʊ/ *verb*. L16.
[ORIGIN from INTER- 1 + FLOW *verb*.]
1 *verb intrans. & †trans.* Flow between (things). L16.
2 *verb intrans.* Flow into each other, intermingle. M19.

interfluent /ɪntəˈfluːənt/ *adjective*. M17.
[ORIGIN from Latin *interfluent-* pres. ppl stem of *interfluere*: see INTERFLUOUS, -ENT.]
1 Flowing between things, interflowing. Now *rare*. M17.
2 Flowing into each other, intermingling. L19.
■ **interfluence** *noun* (*rare*) E19.

interfluous /ɪnˈtəːflʊəs/ *adjective*. M17.
[ORIGIN from Latin *interfluus* (from *interfluere* interflow formed as INTER- + *fluere* to flow) + -OUS.]
= INTERFLUENT.

interfluve /ˈɪntəfluːv/ *noun*. E20.
[ORIGIN from INTERFLUVIAL.]
GEOLOGY. An interfluvial region, *esp.* one between the valleys of a dissected upland.

interfluvial /ɪntəˈfluːvɪəl/ *adjective*. M19.
[ORIGIN from INTER- 2 + FLUVIAL.]
Situated between (the valleys of) adjacent watercourses.

interfold /ɪntəˈfəʊld/ *verb trans.* Also †**enter-**. L16.
[ORIGIN from INTER- 1, ENTER-¹ + FOLD *verb*¹.]
Fold together or within each other.

interfulgent /ɪntəˈfʌldʒ(ə)nt/ *adjective*. *rare*. E18.
[ORIGIN from INTER- 1 + FULGENT.]
Shining among or between things.

interfuse /ɪntəˈfjuːz/ *verb*. L16.
[ORIGIN Latin *interfus-* pa. ppl stem of *interfundere*, formed as INTER- + *fundere* pour.]
1 *verb trans.* Permeate (a thing) *with* an infusion or mixture of something else. Usu. in *pass.* L16.

W. BLACK The wonderful light greens of the Spring foliage seemed to be interfused with a lambent sunshine.

2 *verb trans.* Pour in among something. Usu. in *pass.* M17.

WORDSWORTH A sense sublime Of something far more deeply interfused, Whose dwelling is the light.

3 *verb trans.* In *pass.* Be fused or blended together. M19.

J. R. LOWELL The character and its intellectual product are inextricably interfused.

4 *verb intrans.* Of two things: fuse or blend with each other. M19.

R. FIRBANK Moon-lit lawns and.. trees stretched away, interfusing far off into soft deeps of velvet.

5 *verb trans.* Of one thing: permeate and blend with. L19.
■ **interfusion** *noun* the action of interfusing; the fact of being interfused: E19.

interglacial /ɪntəˈgleɪsɪəl, -ʃ(ə)l/ *adjective & noun*. M19.
[ORIGIN from INTER- 2 + GLACIAL.]
GEOLOGY. ▸**A** *adjective*. Occurring or formed between glacial periods. M19.
▸ **B** *noun*. An interglacial period. E20.

interglaciation /ˌɪntəgleɪsɪˈeɪʃ(ə)n/ *noun*. M20.
[ORIGIN from INTER- 2 + GLACIATION.]
GEOLOGY. = INTERGLACIAL *noun*.

intergrade /ˈɪntəgreɪd/ *noun*. L19.
[ORIGIN from INTER- 2 + GRADE *noun*.]
Chiefly BIOLOGY. An intermediate form.

intergrade /ɪntəˈgreɪd/ *verb intrans.* L19.
[ORIGIN from INTER- 1 + GRADE *verb*.]
Chiefly BIOLOGY. Pass into another form by a series of intervening forms.
■ **intergraˈdation** *noun* the action or fact of intergrading L19.

intergrow /ɪntəˈgrəʊ/ *verb*. Infl. as GROW *verb*; pa. t. usu. **-grew** /-ˈgruː/, pa. pple usu. **-grown** /-ˈgrəʊn/. L19.
[ORIGIN from INTER- 1 + GROW *verb*.]
1 *verb intrans.* Esp. (MINERALOGY) of crystals: grow into each other. L19.
2 *verb trans.* Intersperse with something growing. Only as ***intergrown*** *ppl adjective*. *rare*. L19.

intergrowth /ˈɪntəgrəʊθ/ *noun*. M19.
[ORIGIN from INTER- 1 + GROWTH.]
The growing (of things) into each other; a thing produced by intergrowing.

interim /ˈɪnt(ə)rɪm/ *noun, adverb, & adjective*. M16.
[ORIGIN Latin (adverb), from *inter* between + adverbial ending *-im*.]
▸ **A** *noun*. **1** ECCLESIASTICAL HISTORY. (Usu. **I-**.) A provisional arrangement for the adjustment of religious differences between the German Protestants and the Roman Catholic Church in the mid 16th cent. M16. ▸**b** *gen.* A temporary or provisional arrangement. M16.
†**2** A thing done in an interval; an interlude. L16–M17.
3 An intervening time; *the* meantime. E17.

SIR W. SCOTT How we shall prevent the guilty person from escaping in the interim.

4 An interim dividend. M20.
▸ **B** *adverb*. In the meantime; meanwhile. Now *rare*. L16.
▸ **C** *adjective*. Done, made, provided, etc., in or for the meantime; provisional, temporary. Formerly (of time), intervening. E17.
interim dividend: announced on the basis of a company's financial results for a period less than a full financial year (usu. six months).
■ **interiˈmistic** *adjective* = INTERIM *adjective* M19. †**interimistical** *adjective* = INTERIM *adjective*: only in M17.

Interimsethik /ˈɪntərɪmsˌeːtɪk/ *noun*. Also anglicized as ***interim-ethic*** /ˈɪntərɪmˌɛθɪk/. E20.
[ORIGIN German, formed as INTERIM + *Ethik* ethics.]
THEOLOGY. The moral principles of Jesus interpreted as meant for people expecting the imminent end of the world; *transf.* a code of behaviour for use in a specific temporary situation.

interior /ɪnˈtɪərɪə/ *adjective & noun*. L15.
[ORIGIN Latin = inner, compar. adjective from *inter* between: see -IOR.]
▸ **A** *adjective*. **1** Situated (more) within or inside; belonging to or concerned with the inside. Opp. ***exterior***. L15.
interior to on the inner side or inside of.
2 Mental; spiritual; pious, devout. E16.

M. SCHAPIRO Little or no interior life, at most a charming appearance.

3 Concerned with or pertaining to the domestic (as opp. to foreign) affairs of a state. M18.
4 Situated within a country or region and at a distance from the coast or frontier, inland; belonging to interior regions. L18.
– SPECIAL COLLOCATIONS: **interior angle** GEOMETRY: between adjacent sides of a rectilinear figure. ***interior ballistics***. **interior decoration** the planned coordination for artistic effect of

I

colours and furniture, etc., in a room or building. **interior design** the design of the interior of a building according to artistic and architectural criteria. **interior monologue** a form of writing in which the inner thoughts of a person are presented. **interior spring mattress**: having coiled springs inside it. **interior-sprung** *adjective* (of a mattress) having coiled springs inside.

▸ **B** *noun*. **1** The interior part of something; the inside. **L16.** ▸**b** The interior part of a country or region. **L18.** ▸**c** (A picture or representation of) the inside of a room or building. **E19.** ▸**d** The internal organs of the body, *esp.* the digestive system. *colloq.* **M19.**
c *Dutch interior*: see DUTCH *adjective*.
2 Inner nature or being; inward mind; soul, character. Now usu. with *of*. **L16.**
3 The internal affairs of a state; the department of Government concerned with these. **M19.**
■ **interiorly** *adverb* (**a**) in or on the inside, internally; (**b**) inwardly, intimately; (**c**) mentally, spiritually: **E17.**

interiorise *verb* var. of INTERIORIZE.

interiority /ɪnˌtɪərɪˈɒrɪti/ *noun*. **E18.**
[ORIGIN medieval Latin *interioritas*, formed as INTERIOR: see -ITY.]
The quality of being interior or inward; inner character or nature; depth of feeling, subjectivity.

interiorize /ɪnˈtɪərɪərʌɪz/ *verb trans.* Also **-ise**. **E20.**
[ORIGIN from INTERIOR + -IZE.]
= INTERNALIZE 1, 2; connect with the soul.
■ **interioriˈzation** *noun* **M20.**

interjacent /ɪntəˈdʒeɪs(ə)nt/ *adjective*. **M16.**
[ORIGIN Latin *interjacent-* pres. ppl stem of *interjacere*, formed as INTER- + *jacere* to lie: see -ENT.]
Situated or existing between things; intervening.
■ **interjacency** *noun* **M17.**

interject /ɪntəˈdʒɛkt/ *verb*. **L16.**
[ORIGIN Latin *interject-* pa. ppl stem of *interjicere* interpose, formed as INTER- + *jacere* to throw, cast.]
1 *verb trans.* Introduce abruptly, esp. into a conversation; remark parenthetically or as an interruption. **L16.** ▸**b** In *pass.* Lie or be situated *between*. Long *rare*. **L16.**

B. T. BRADFORD 'We'll get to that later,' Estelle interjected . . brusquely. B. UNSWORTH He was reading from a script but interjecting his own remarks from time to time.

†**2** *verb intrans.* Intersect; intervene. *rare*. **L16–L17.**
■ **interjector** *noun* a person who makes an interjection **L19.** **interjectory** *adjective* characterized by interjections; of the nature of an interjection: **M19.**

interjection /ɪntəˈdʒɛkʃ(ə)n/ *noun*. **LME.**
[ORIGIN Old French & mod. French from Latin *interjectio(n-)*, formed as INTERJECT: see -ION.]
1 The utterance of an exclamation expressing emotion; an exclamation; an interjected remark. **LME.**

R. GITTINGS His excited interjections of 'By God!' when anything moved him.

2 An exclamation regarded as a part of speech. **LME.**

SHAKES. *Much Ado* How now! interjections? Why then, some be of laughing, as ha, ha, he.

3 The action of interjecting or interposing something. **L16.**
■ **interjectionary** *adjective* interjectory **L19.**

interjectional /ɪntəˈdʒɛkʃ(ə)n(ə)l/ *adjective*. **M18.**
[ORIGIN from INTERJECTION + -AL[1].]
Of, pertaining to, or of the nature of an interjection.
■ **interjectionally** *adverb* **M19.**

interjectural /ɪntəˈdʒɛktʃ(ə)r(ə)l/ *adjective*. **L18.**
[ORIGIN Alt. of INTERJECTIONAL after *conjectural*.]
= INTERJECTIONAL.

interkinesis /ɪntəkɪˈniːsɪs, -kʌɪ-/ *noun*. **E20.**
[ORIGIN from INTER- 1 + KINESIS.]
CYTOLOGY. A stage in cell division sometimes occurring between the first and second divisions of meiosis.

interlace /ˈɪntəleɪs/ *noun*. **E20.**
[ORIGIN from the verb.]
1 The action or result of interlacing. **E20.**

Daily Mail The upturned brim has fancy straw interlace, giving a ribbon effect. *attrib.*: E. H. GOMBRICH He was obviously trained in the intricate interlace work of eleventh-century ornament.

2 TELEVISION. The system, process, or result of scanning with interlaced lines or dots. **M20.**

interlace /ɪntəˈleɪs/ *verb*. Also (earlier) †**enter-**. **LME.**
[ORIGIN Old French *entrelacier*, from *entre-* ENTER-[1], INTER- + *lacier* LACE *verb*.]
▸ **I** *verb trans.* **1** Unite (two or more things) by interweaving strands. Chiefly *fig.*, bind together intricately, entangle, involve. **LME.**

W. COWPER Close interlaced with purple cordage strong.

2 Cross alternately over and under each other; *fig.* mix by alternation. **E16.**

F. W. FARRAR The two are inextricably interlaced. A righteous life is the result of faith, and faith is deepened by a righteous life. I. MCEWAN He was holding Stephen's hand, their fingers were interlaced.

†**3** Weave (a thing) into another; insert, interpolate. **M16–L17.**
4 Intersperse, vary, mix *with*. **L16.**

fig.: W. BLACK Beautiful green meadows interlaced with streams.

5 TELEVISION. Scan so that alternate lines or other sets of picture elements form one sequence which is followed by the other lines etc. in a second sequence; build up (a picture) in this way. **E20.**
▸ **II** *verb intrans.* †**6** Become entangled or involved. **LME–E17.**
7 Cross and recross as if woven together; lie in alternate directions as the fingers of clasped hands. **L16.**
■ **interlacedly** *adverb* in an interlaced manner **M17.** **interlacement** *noun* interweaving, intermingling; an interlaced arrangement or structure: **E17.**

interlaid *verb pa. t. & pple* of INTERLAY *verb*.

interlaminar /ɪntəˈlamɪnə/ *adjective*. **M19.**
[ORIGIN from INTER- 2 + LAMINA + -AR[1].]
1 ANATOMY. Situated between laminae or plates. **M19.**
2 Situated or occurring between the layers of a laminate or composite. **M20.**

interlaminate /ɪntəˈlamɪneɪt/ *verb trans.* **E19.**
[ORIGIN from INTER- 1 + LAMINATE *verb*.]
Insert in or between alternate laminae or plates.
■ **interlamiˈnation** *noun* the action of interlaminating; an interlaminated formation: **M19.**

interlanguage /ˈɪntəlaŋgwɪdʒ/ *noun*. **E20.**
[ORIGIN from INTER- 1 + LANGUAGE *noun*[1].]
An auxiliary language; a blend of languages, as (**a**) a pidgin; (**b**) a language student's idiom deriving from his or her native language and the language being learned.

interlanguage /ɪntəˈlaŋgwɪdʒ/ *adjective*. **M20.**
[ORIGIN from INTER- 2 + LANGUAGE *noun*[1].]
Occurring between or pertaining to two or more languages.

interlard /ɪntəˈlɑːd/ *verb trans.* Also (earlier) †**enter-**. **LME.**
[ORIGIN Old French & mod. French *entrelarder*, from *entre-* ENTER-[1], INTER- + *larder* LARD *verb*.]
†**1** Mix with alternate layers of fat; thread (lean meat) with strips of fat before cooking. **LME–L18.**

transf.: W. LITHGOW Grey Marble, interlarded with white Alabaster.

2 Interpolate, interpose. Now *rare*. **M16.**

T. CARTE Boyish speeches in which he often interlarded the words O tempora, O mores.

3 *fig.* = LARD *verb* 4. **L16.** ▸**b** Become intermingled with; run through. **M17.**

C. CONNOLLY My jokes, a combination of puns and personal remarks interlarded with . . wisecracks. D. PRATER He also began to write a history . . interlarding his prose text with verse.
b W. CONGREVE Lying is a figure of speech that interlards the greatest part of my conversation.

■ **interlardment** *noun* the action of interlarding; something interlarded: **M18.**

interlay /ˈɪntəleɪ/ *noun*. **E20.**
[ORIGIN from the verb.]
An inserted layer; *spec.* in PRINTING (now *hist.*), a sheet of (cut out) paper placed between a letterpress printing plate and its base to give increased pressure on certain areas.

interlay /ɪntəˈleɪ/ *verb trans.* Pa. t. & pple **-laid** /-ˈleɪd/. **E17.**
[ORIGIN from INTER- 1 + LAY *verb*[1].]
Lay between or among, interpose; provide with inserted material.

interlayer /ˈɪntəleɪə/ *noun & adjective*. **M20.**
[ORIGIN from INTER- 1, 2 + LAYER *noun*.]
▸ **A** *noun*. A layer sandwiched between two others. **M20.**
▸ **B** *adjective*. Situated or occurring between two layers. **M20.**

interleaf /ˈɪntəliːf/ *noun*. Pl. **-leaves** /-liːvz/. **M18.**
[ORIGIN from INTER- 2 + LEAF *noun*[1].]
An extra leaf to prevent set-off or for additional notes etc., inserted between the ordinary leaves of a book.

interleave /ˈɪntəliːv/ *noun*. **M20.**
[ORIGIN from the verb.]
COMPUTING. The action or process of interleaving digits etc.

interleave /ɪntəˈliːv/ *verb trans.* **M17.**
[ORIGIN from INTER- 2 + LEAF *noun*[1] (pl. *leaves*).]
1 Insert (blank) leaves between the ordinary leaves of (a book). **M17.**

J. G. LOCKHART He is going to interleave his copy and annotate largely.

2 *transf.* & *fig.* Foll. by *with*: insert something at regular intervals between (the parts of). **M19.**

DE QUINCEY Any feasible plan for interleaving days of hardship with days of ease. A. BROOKNER She would start . . laying cups and plates, interleaved with tiny napkins of écru linen.

3 COMPUTING. Combine (sequences of digits, addresses, etc.) by successively taking one item from each of a number of groups. **M20.**

interleukin /ɪntəˈluːkɪn/ *noun*. **L20.**
[ORIGIN from INTER- 2 + LEUK(OCYTE + -IN[1].]
PHYSIOLOGY. Any of several glycoproteins which are produced by leucocytes and are involved in lymphocyte formation and the immune response.

interline /ˈɪntəlʌɪn/ *adjective*. **M20.**
[ORIGIN from INTER- 2 + LINE *noun*[2].]
Designating or pertaining to transport using more than one route, service, etc.

Aviation News The motorway link between the airports is sufficient for interline traffic.

interline /ɪntəˈlʌɪn/ *verb*[1]. Also (earlier) †**enter-**. **LME.**
[ORIGIN medieval Latin *interlineare*, formed as INTER- + Latin *linea* LINE *noun*[2].]
1 *verb trans.* Insert additional words between the lines of (a document). Usu. in *pass.* (Foll. by *with*.) **LME.**

G. SHELVOCKE Written by several hands, and interlin'd in a great many places.

2 *verb trans.* Insert (a word or words) between the lines of a document. **L16.**

W. STUBBS These words were found interlined in Richard's grant.

3 *verb intrans.* Make interlinear insertions. **L16.**

SWIFT Blot out, correct, insert, refine, Enlarge, diminish, interline.

†**4** *verb trans.* Mark with lines, esp. of various colours. **L16–M17.**
†**5** *verb trans.* Intersperse with lines of something else; insert as lines in something. **E17–M18.**

T. WATSON Mercy interlined with judgment. DEFOE I saw the foot . . interlined among the horse.

interline /ɪntəˈlʌɪn/ *verb*[2] *trans.* **L15.**
[ORIGIN from INTER- 1 + LINE *verb*[1].]
Put an extra layer of (stiffened) material between the lining and the outer material of (the whole or part of a garment).

interline /ɪntəˈlʌɪn/ *verb*[3]. **L20.**
[ORIGIN from INTER- 2 + LINE *noun*[2].]
1 *verb intrans.* **a** Use transport by more than one route, service, etc. **L20.** ▸**b** Provide interconnections with another service. **L20.**
2 *verb trans.* Provide interconnecting transport for. **L20.**

interlineal /ɪntəˈlɪnɪəl/ *adjective*. **E16.**
[ORIGIN French *interlinéal* or medieval Latin *interlinealis*, formed as INTER- + late Latin *linealis* LINEAL.]
= INTERLINEAR 1.

interlinear /ɪntəˈlɪnɪə/ *adjective*. **LME.**
[ORIGIN medieval Latin *interlinearis*, formed as INTER- + Latin *linearis* LINEAR.]
1 Written or printed between the lines of a text. **LME.**
Interlinear Gloss *spec.* Anselm's gloss on the Vulgate, written in manuscripts between the lines of the Latin text.
2 Of a book: having the same text in different languages printed on alternate lines. **E17.**
■ **interlinearly** *adverb* **M19.** **interlineary** *adjective* interlinear **E17.**

interlineate /ɪntəˈlɪnɪeɪt/ *verb trans. & intrans.* **L17.**
[ORIGIN medieval Latin *interlineat-* pa. ppl stem of *interlineare*: see INTERLINE *verb*[1], -ATE[3]. In mod. use perh. back-form. from INTERLINEATION.]
= INTERLINE *verb*[1]. Chiefly as ***interlineated*** *ppl adjective*.

interlineation /ˌɪntəlɪnɪˈeɪʃ(ə)n/ *noun*. **E16.**
[ORIGIN medieval Latin *interlineatio(n-)*, formed as INTERLINEATE: see -ATION.]
The insertion of a word or words between the lines of a document or text; a word, phrase, etc., so inserted.

Notes & Queries This manuscript shows late additions in the form of interlineations and marginal balloons.

interlingua /ɪntəˈlɪŋgwə/ *noun*. **E20.**
[ORIGIN from INTER- 1 + Latin *lingua* tongue.]
An artificially devised international language; *spec.* (**I-**) one formerly promoted by the International Auxiliary Language Association of New York, formed of elements common to the Romance languages.

interlingual /ɪntəˈlɪŋgw(ə)l/ *adjective*. **M19.**
[ORIGIN from INTER- 1, 2 + LINGUAL *adjective*.]
Between or relating to two languages; of or relating to an artificial interlanguage.

interlinguist /ɪntəˈlɪŋgwɪst/ *noun*. **E20.**
[ORIGIN from INTER- 1 + LINGUIST.]
A scholar or an advocate of an interlanguage or interlanguages.

interlinguistic /ɪntəlɪŋˈgwɪstɪk/ *adjective*. **L19.**
[ORIGIN from INTER- 1 + LINGUISTIC.]
†**1** Intermingling in speech. *rare*. Only in **L19.**
2 Of or relating to an interlanguage; between or relating to two languages. **M20.**

interlinguistics /ɪntəlɪŋˈgwɪstɪks/ *noun*. **M20.**
[ORIGIN from INTER- 1 + LINGUISTICS.]
The branch of knowledge that deals with the relationships between languages; the study of interlingual relationships in order to devise an interlanguage.

interlining /ɪntəˈlʌɪnɪŋ/ *noun*[1]. LME.
[ORIGIN from INTERLINE *verb*[1] + -ING[1].]
= INTERLINEATION.

interlining /ˈɪntəlʌɪnɪŋ/ *noun*[2]. L19.
[ORIGIN from INTER- 1 + LINING *noun*[1]. Cf. INTERLINE *verb*[2].]
An extra layer placed between the outer material and the lining of a garment or quilt for added stiffness or warmth; the material for this.

interlink /ɪntəˈlɪŋk/ *verb trans. & intrans.* L16.
[ORIGIN from INTER- 1 + LINK *verb*[1].]
Link or be linked together (*with*).
■ **interlinkage** *noun* the action of interlinking, the state of being interlinked; an interlinked system: E20.

interlock /ˈɪntəlɒk/ *noun & adjective*. L19.
[ORIGIN from the verb.]
▸ **A** *noun*. **1** The fact or condition of being interlocked. *rare*. L19.
2 a CINEMATOGRAPHY. Synchronism between two or more electric motors in separate pieces of equipment; the mechanism by which this is effected. E20. ▸**b** A mechanism for preventing a set of operations being performed other than in the prescribed sequence. M20.
▸ **B** *adjective*. Designating a fabric knitted with closely interlocking stitches. E20.

interlock /ɪntəˈlɒk/ *verb*. M17.
[ORIGIN from INTER- 1 + LOCK *verb*[1].]
1 *verb intrans*. Engage with each other or fit together by partial overlapping or interpenetration of parts. M17. ▸**b** Of headwaters of different rivers: lie in an alternating sequence, although flowing in different directions. *US*. M18.

R. S. R. FITTER There were still large patches of green country interlocking with the tongues of buildings. J. A. MICHENER Powerful thorns that interlocked with those of other plants to make the globe impenetrable.

2 *verb trans*. Lock or clasp within each other. Usu. in *pass*. E19.

R. WARNER The ailerons of the two planes were almost interlocked as they climbed together. S. BRETT In a state of high nervous tension, constantly interlocking and unwinding his fingers.

3 *verb trans*. Chiefly RAILWAYS. Connect (switches, controls, etc.) so that they cannot be operated independently or unsafely. L19.
4 *verb trans*. CINEMATOGRAPHY. Connect (the electric motors in separate pieces of equipment) so as to ensure synchronous operation. E20.
■ **interlocker** *noun* a device for interlocking switches etc. L19.

interlocution /ɪntələˈkjuːʃ(ə)n/ *noun*. M16.
[ORIGIN Latin *interlocutio(n-)*, from *interlocut-* pa. ppl stem of *interloqui*, formed as INTER- + *loqui* speak: see -ION.]
1 The action of persons speaking and replying; dialogue, discourse, conversation. M16. ▸†**b** Alternate reading or speaking, as in making responses or reading alternate verses. L16–M17.
†**2** The action of replying; a reply, a response. L16–L18.
†**3** The action of interrupting (one's own or another's) speech; an interruption, an interpolation. L16–L17.
†**4** LAW. A judgement deciding a point within a case, but not the whole case. Cf. INTERLOCUTOR *noun*[2] Only in E18.

interlocutor /ɪntəˈlɒkjʊtə/ *noun*[1]. E16.
[ORIGIN mod. Latin, from Latin *interlocut-*: see INTERLOCUTION, -OR.]
1 A person who takes part in a conversation, dialogue, or discussion. E16. ▸**b** With possess.: the person with whom one is in conversation. M19.

R. BENTLEY The Interlocutors in this Dialogue, are Socrates and one Minos an Athenian. **b** H. JAMES He looked at his interlocutor as if the question might have a double meaning.

2 The middleman of a minstrel troupe, who questions the end-men and acts as compère. *US*. L19.
■ **interlocutress**, **interlocutrice**, **interlocutrix** *nouns* a female interlocutor M19.

interlocutor /ɪntəˈlɒkjʊtə/ *noun*[2]. E16.
[ORIGIN from medieval Latin *interlocutorius*, from Latin *interlocut-* pa. ppl stem of *interloqui* (in late Latin = pronounce an interlocutory sentence): see INTERLOCUTION, -OR.]
SCOTS LAW. A judgement deciding a point within a case, but not necessarily the whole case; any order of a civil court.

interlocutory /ɪntəˈlɒkjʊt(ə)ri/ *adjective & noun*. L15.
[ORIGIN medieval Latin *interlocutorius*, from Latin *interlocut-*: see INTERLOCUTOR *noun*[2], -ORY[2].]
▸ **A** *adjective*. **1** LAW. Of a decree or judgement: given in the course of an action or as a preliminary to coming to trial; preliminary, provisional, interim. L15.
2 Of, pertaining to, or occurring in dialogue or conversation. L16.
3 Interpolated into a conversation or narrative. E19.
▸ †**B** *noun*. LAW. An interlocutory decree. E17–L18.

interlope /ɪntəˈləʊp/ *verb*. E17.
[ORIGIN Back-form. from INTERLOPER.]
1 *verb intrans*. Orig. (*obsolete* exc. *hist*.), trade without authorization, interfere with another's trade or privileges. Now, intrude, meddle in another's affairs. E17.
†**2** *verb trans*. **a** Introduce without authorization. Only in M17. ▸**b** Intrude on. *rare*. Only in E18.
■ **interloˈpation** *noun* (*rare*) an act of interloping, an intrusion E19.

interloper /ˈɪntələʊpə/ *noun*. L16.
[ORIGIN from INTER- 1 + *-loper* as in LAND-LOPER.]
1 An unauthorized trader; one who trespasses on the rights of a trade monopoly. Also, a vessel engaged in unauthorized trading. *obsolete* exc. *hist*. L16.
2 A person who meddles in another's business (esp. for profit); an intruder. M17.

interlucation /ɪntəluːˈkeɪʃ(ə)n/ *noun*. *rare*. M17.
[ORIGIN Latin *interlucatio(n-)*, from *interlucat-* pa. ppl stem of *interlucare* lop or thin a tree, formed as INTER- + *luc-*, *lux* light: see -ATION.]
The action or an instance of thinning a tree or wood.

interlude /ˈɪntəluːd, -ljuːd/ *noun & verb*. Also (earlier) †**enter-**. ME.
[ORIGIN medieval Latin *interludium*, formed as INTER- + *ludus* play.]
▸ **A** *noun*. **1** A short, usu. light, dramatic piece, orig. one performed between acts of the miracle plays, later one performed separately. ME. ▸†**b** Any performance or action considered as drama. LME–M17.
2 An interval, as between acts of a play or between broadcast programmes; something performed or done during this. M17. ▸**b** MUSIC. An instrumental piece played between verses of a psalm or hymn, or in the interval of a church service. M19.

G. BERKELEY We went to see a play, with interludes of music.

3 An intervening time, space, or event which contrasts with what goes before or after; *spec*. a temporary amusement; an entertaining episode. M18.

H. A. L. FISHER The reign of Canute was but an interlude, more important for Scandinavian than for British history. A. C. BOULT On our way to Munich we had an amusing interlude. P. ABRAHAMS Harriet was a beautiful and painful interlude in his young life.

▸ **B** *verb*. †**1** *verb intrans*. Write or perform a dramatic interlude. L16–E17.
2 *verb trans. & intrans*. Interrupt or come between as an interlude. *rare*. M19.
■ **interˈludial** *adjective* L19.

interlunar /ɪntəˈluːnə/ *adjective*. L16.
[ORIGIN App. from French †*interlunaire* from Latin *interlunium* after *lunaire* (formed as LUNAR): see INTER-.]
Designating or pertaining to the period between the disappearance of the old and the appearance of the new moon.
■ **interluˈnation** *noun* (now *rare*) an interlunar period; *fig*. a dark interval: E19. ˈ**interlune** *noun* (*rare*) an interlunar period M19.

intermarriage /ɪntəˈmarɪdʒ/ *noun*. Also †**enter-**. L16.
[ORIGIN from INTER- 1, ENTER-[1] + MARRIAGE.]
1 The action or an act of marrying; marriage. *obsolete* in *gen*. sense. L16.
2 Marriage between people of different ethnic groups, castes, religions, etc. E17.
3 Marriage between near relations. L19.
■ **intermarriageable** *adjective* capable of intermarrying L19.

intermarry /ɪntəˈmari/ *verb intrans*. Also †**enter-**. L16.
[ORIGIN from INTER- 1, ENTER-[1] + MARRY *verb*.]
1 Enter into marriage, marry. *obsolete* in *gen*. sense. L16.
2 Of the members of an ethnic group, caste, religion, etc.: become connected by marriage to one another or to members of a different ethnic group, caste, religion, etc. (Foll. by *with*.) E17.

J. RABAN They intermarried. They mixed Persian and Indian culture with their own Arabian stock.

3 Of near relations: marry each other. M19.

intermaxillary /ɪntəmakˈsɪləri/ *adjective & noun*. Now *rare*. E19.
[ORIGIN from INTER- 2 + MAXILLA + -ARY[2].]
ANATOMY & ZOOLOGY. ▸ **A** *adjective*. Situated between the maxillae (of the vertebrate upper jaw). Also, premaxillary. E19.
▸ **B** *noun*. An intermaxillary bone. M19.

intermeddle /ɪntəˈmɛd(ə)l/ *verb*. *arch*. Also †**enter-**. LME.
[ORIGIN Anglo-Norman *entremedler* = Old French *entremesler*, formed as ENTER-[1], INTER- + *mesler* MEDDLE.]
†**1** *verb trans*. Mix together, intermingle, *with*. LME–M18.
2 *verb intrans. &* †*refl*. Concern or occupy oneself *with* or *in*; *esp*. interfere. L15.
■ **intermeddler** *noun* †(**a**) a person who is concerned or occupied with something; (**b**) a person who interferes, a meddler: L16.

intermède /ɛ̃tɛrmɛd/ *noun*. Pl. pronounced same. L18.
[ORIGIN French formed as INTERMEDIO.]
†**1** = INTERMEDIUM 3. Only in L18.
2 = INTERMEDIO. E19.
– NOTE: Formerly fully naturalized.

intermedi *noun pl.* see INTERMEDIO.

intermedia *noun pl.* see INTERMEDIUM.

intermediacy /ɪntəˈmiːdɪəsi/ *noun*. E18.
[ORIGIN from INTERMEDIATE *adjective*: see -ACY.]
The state or fact of being intermediate.

intermedial /ɪntəˈmiːdɪəl/ *adjective & noun*. L16.
[ORIGIN from INTER- 1 + MEDIAL.]
▸ **A** *adjective*. **1** Intermediate. L16.
†**2** = INTERMEDIARY *adjective* 2. M17–M19.
▸ **B** *noun*. An intermediate. Long *rare*. E17.

intermediary /ɪntəˈmiːdjəri/ *adjective & noun*. L18.
[ORIGIN French *intermédiaire* from Italian *intermediario*, from Latin *intermedius*: see INTERMEDIATE *adjective & noun*, -ARY[2].]
▸ **A** *adjective*. **1** Situated or occurring between two things; intermediate. L18.

J. HAWTHORNE During this intermediary stage of her life.

2 Mediatory; serving as a means of mediation or interaction. E19.
▸ **B** *noun*. **1** A person who acts between others, a mediator, a go-between. L18.

H. KISSINGER We approached the North Vietnamese directly without a foreign intermediary.

2 Something acting between persons or things; a medium, a means. M19.
3 An intermediate form or stage. M19.

intermediate /ɪntəˈmiːdɪət/ *adjective & noun*. LME.
[ORIGIN medieval Latin *intermediatus*, from Latin *intermedius*, formed as INTER- + *medius* middle: see -ATE[2].]
▸ **A** *adjective*. **1** Coming or occurring between two things in time, place, order, character, etc. LME. ▸**b** *spec*. Designating (a nuclear missile of) a range less than intercontinental. M20.

A. S. BYATT Facing them . . were several rows of little girls, intermediate girls, larger girls. R. SCRUTON *Tristan* seems to mark . . an intermediate step between Mozart and Schoenberg. **b** *Sunday Post (Glasgow)* An agreement on longer range intermediate missiles.

2 PETROGRAPHY. Of a rock: having a silicate content between that of acidic and that of basic rocks. L19.
3 NUCLEAR PHYSICS. (Of a neutron) having less energy than a fast neutron but more than a thermal neutron; (of a reactor) utilizing such neutrons. M20.
– SPECIAL COLLOCATIONS: **intermediate host** ZOOLOGY an organism infected by a juvenile or asexual stage of a parasitic animal. **intermediate frequency**: to which a radio signal is converted during heterodyne reception. **intermediate school** *NZ* a school for children aged between about eleven and thirteen.
▸ **B** *noun*. **1** An intermediate person or thing. M17. ▸**b** CHEMISTRY & BIOCHEMISTRY. A compound which after being produced in one reaction participates in another; *spec*. a substance manufactured from naturally occurring materials for use in the synthesis of dyes, plastics, etc. E20.

A. S. NEILL The youngest range from five to seven, the intermediates from eight to ten, and the oldest from eleven to fifteen.

2 An intermediary, a go-between. L19.
■ **intermediately** *adverb* M18. **intermediateness** *noun* M19.

intermediate /ɪntəˈmiːdɪeɪt/ *verb intrans*. E17.
[ORIGIN from INTER- 1 + MEDIATE *verb*. Cf. INTERMEDIATOR.]
1 Act as an intermediary, mediate. E17.
†**2** Interfere. E17–E18.
■ ˌ**intermediˈation** *noun* E17.

intermediator /ɪntəˈmiːdɪeɪtə/ *noun*. E16.
[ORIGIN medieval Latin, formed as INTERMEDIATE *adjective & noun*: see -OR.]
A person who or thing which intermediates; a mediator.

intermedii *noun pl.* see INTERMEDIO.

intermedin /ɪntəˈmiːdɪn/ *noun*. M20.
[ORIGIN from mod. Latin (*pars*) *intermedia* intermediate part (of the pituitary) + -IN[1].]
PHYSIOLOGY. = MELANOCYTE-***stimulating hormone***.

intermedio /interˈmɛːdjo, ɪntəˈmɛdɪəʊ/ *noun*. Pl. **-*d*(*i*)*i*** /-d(j)i/. L19.
[ORIGIN Italian, formed as INTERMEDIUM. Cf. INTERMÈDE.]
A musical interlude between the acts of a play or an opera. Cf. INTERMEZZO.

intermedium /ɪntəˈmiːdɪəm/ *noun*. Pl. **-ia** /-ɪə/, **-iums**. L16.
[ORIGIN Late Latin, use as noun of neut. sing. of Latin *intermedius*: see INTERMEDIATE *adjective & noun*.]
1 An intervening action or performance. Now only *spec*. (MUSIC), = INTERMEDIO. L16.
2 An interval of time or space. Now *rare* or *obsolete*. E17.
3 An intermediate agent, an intermediary. M17. ▸**b** PHYSICS. A medium through which energy is transmitted. Now *rare* or *obsolete*. E19.
4 ZOOLOGY. [mod. Latin *os intermedium*.] In tetrapods: a carpal in the centre of the wrist joint; a tarsal in the centre of the ankle joint. L19.

†**intermell** *verb*. LME.
[ORIGIN Old French *entremeller*, *-mesler* (mod. *-mêler*), formed as ENTER-[1], INTER- + MELL *verb*.]
1 *verb trans*. Mix together, intermingle. LME–M19.
2 *verb intrans*. Meddle, interfere *with*. L15–L16.

interment /ɪnˈtəːm(ə)nt/ *noun*. ME.
[ORIGIN from INTER *verb* + -MENT.]
The action or an act of interring or burying; (a) burial, esp. with ceremony.

J. CRACE Nowadays, one selects either cremation or interment.

I

intermesh /ɪntəˈmɛʃ/ *verb intrans.* E20.
[ORIGIN from INTER- 1 + MESH *verb*.]
Mesh or interlock with one another.

R. D. LAING To see how interpersonal and neurological recovery intermeshed to generate . . a new personality.

†**intermess** *noun* var. of ENTREMESS.

intermewed /ɪntəˈmjuːd/ *adjective*. Now *rare*. L16.
[ORIGIN from Old French *entremué* half-moulted + -ED[2].]
Of a hawk: that has moulted in captivity but not reached full adult plumage.

intermezzo /ɪntəˈmɛtsəʊ/ *noun*. Pl. **-zzi** /-tsi/, **-zzos**. L18.
[ORIGIN Italian, formed as INTERMEDIUM. Cf. MEZZO *adverb*.]
1 A short light dramatic, musical, or other performance inserted between the acts of a play or (formerly) an opera. L18.
2 A short connecting instrumental movement in an opera or other musical work; a similar piece performed independently; a short piece for a solo instrument. M19.

interminable /ɪnˈtəːmɪnəb(ə)l/ *adjective*. LME.
[ORIGIN Old French & mod. French, or late Latin *interminabilis*, formed as IN-[3] + *terminare*: see TERMINATE *verb*, -ABLE.]
1 Endless. LME.

J. CONRAD The sea-reach . . stretched before us like the beginning of an interminable waterway.

2 With no prospect of an end; tediously long or habitual. M19.

B. TARKINGTON He went back to the library, waited an interminable half hour, then returned. A. J. P. TAYLOR Mrs Jones . . was already studying the interminable committees. P. LIVELY Malcolm . . turned a rich coffee brown during that interminable languid Dorset summer.

■ **interminaˈbility** *noun* L17. **interminableness** *noun* L17. **interminably** *adverb* LME.

interminate /ɪnˈtəːmɪnət/ *adjective*. Now *rare*. L15.
[ORIGIN Latin *interminatus*, formed as IN-[3] + TERMINATE *adjective*: see -ATE[2].]
Endless; infinite.
interminate decimal MATH.: recurring or infinite.

intermingle /ɪntəˈmɪŋg(ə)l/ *verb*. L15.
[ORIGIN from INTER- 1 + MINGLE *verb*.]
1 *verb trans. & intrans.* Mix or mingle together. Freq. foll. by *with*. L15.

R. STRANGE These three themes emerge and intermingle constantly in what follows.

2 *verb trans.* Intersperse (a thing) *with* some other thing. M16.

H. A. L. FISHER The intermingling of manual labour with study and devotional exercises.

■ **interminglement** *noun* (*rare*) L19.

interministerial /ˌɪntəmɪnɪˈstɪərɪəl/ *adjective*. M19.
[ORIGIN from INTER- 2 + MINISTERIAL. Cf. INTERMINISTERIUM.]
1 Of or pertaining to a period between two ministries. M19.
2 Involving or constituted from the ministers, representatives, or members of different departments of state. M20.

interministerium /ˌɪntəmɪnɪˈstɪərɪəm/ *noun*. *rare*. M18.
[ORIGIN from INTER- 2 + Latin *ministerium* MINISTRY.]
The period between two ministries.

†**intermise** *noun* var. of ENTERMISE.

intermission /ɪntəˈmɪʃ(ə)n/ *noun*. LME.
[ORIGIN Old French & mod. French, or Latin *intermissio(n-)*, from *intermiss-* pa. ppl stem of *intermittere*: see INTERMIT, -ION.]
1 The fact of ceasing for a time; a temporary pause or cessation. LME. ▸**b** Temporary rest or respite (*from*). Now *rare* or *obsolete*. L16.

JOHN PHILLIPS This eruption lasted two nights and two days without intermission.

2 A space of time between events or periods of action; *spec.* the interval between the parts of a play, film, concert, etc. M16.

N. GORDIMER She was struggling back through the crowded foyer at intermission.

intermissive /ɪntəˈmɪsɪv/ *adjective*. L15.
[ORIGIN from INTERMISSION + -IVE.]
Of the nature of or pertaining to (an) intermission; intermittent.

intermit /ɪntəˈmɪt/ *verb*. Infl. **-tt-**. M16.
[ORIGIN Latin *intermittere*, formed as INTER- + *mittere* let go.]
1 *verb trans.* Cease, suspend, (an action, practice, etc.) for a time. Formerly also, interrupt (a person, an action, etc.). M16. ▸**b** Omit, leave out. L16.

b A. S. BYATT Marcus should intermit a year of his education, in order to recuperate.

2 *verb intrans.* Esp. MEDICINE. Cease or stop for a time. L16.
■ **intermittedly** *adverb* in an intermitted manner E19. **intermittingly** *adverb* in an intermitting manner, intermittently M17.

intermittence /ɪntəˈmɪt(ə)ns/ *noun*. L18.
[ORIGIN French, from *intermittent*, formed as INTERMITTENT: see -ENCE.]
The quality or fact of being intermittent; (a) cessation or suspension for a time.

J. UPDIKE Intermittences of peace . . . afford glimpses of what might be a better world.

intermittency /ɪntəˈmɪt(ə)nsi/ *noun*. M17.
[ORIGIN from INTERMITTENT: see -ENCY.]
= INTERMITTENCE.
– COMB.: **intermittency effect** PHOTOGRAPHY the difference in the density of an emulsion when exposed to a given amount of light in short bursts, and as a continuous exposure.

intermittent /ɪntəˈmɪt(ə)nt/ *adjective & noun*. M16.
[ORIGIN Latin *intermittent-* pres. ppl stem of *intermittere*: see INTERMIT, -ENT.]
▸ **A** *adjective*. That ceases for a time; occurring at intervals; not continuous. M16.

D. DELILLO As the terrain rises and drops, you get intermittent views of those rock masses. D. WIGODER I must have relapsed into intermittent sleep and restlessness.

intermittent CLAUDICATION. **intermittent sterilization** MICROBIOLOGY: by alternately allowing heat-resistant spores to germinate and raising the temperature to kill the resulting vegetative cells.
▸ **B** *noun*. An intermittent fever. L17.
■ **intermittently** *adverb* M19.

intermix /ɪntəˈmɪks/ *verb trans. & intrans.* M16.
[ORIGIN Orig. pa. pple, from Latin *intermixtus* pa. pple of *intermiscere*, formed as INTER- + *miscere* mix.]
Mix or blend together.
■ **intermixable** *adjective* M20. **intermixedly** *adverb* (long *rare*) with intermixture L16.

intermixture /ɪntəˈmɪkstʃə/ *noun*. L16.
[ORIGIN from Latin *intermixt-* pa. ppl stem of *intermiscere* (see INTERMIX) + -URE, after MIXTURE.]
1 The action of intermixing; the fact of being intermixed. L16.
2 (A quantity of) something intermixed with or added to something else. L16.

intermodal /ɪntəˈməʊd(ə)l/ *adjective*. M20.
[ORIGIN from INTER- 2 + MODE *noun* + -AL[1].]
Designating the conveyance of goods by more than one method of transport.
■ **intermodalism** *noun* the use of more than one method of transport in conveying goods L20.

intern /ɪnˈtəːn/; *as noun also* ˈɪntəːn/ *adjective & noun*. As noun also **interne**. E16.
[ORIGIN Old French & mod. French *interne* from Latin *internus* inward, internal, from *in* adverb + *-ternus* suffix.]
▸ **A** *adjective*. **1** = INTERNAL *adjective* 2. E16.
2 = INTERNAL *adjective* 1, 3. E17.
▸ **B** *noun*. **1** A recent medical graduate, resident and working under supervision in a hospital as part of his or her training. Chiefly *N. Amer.* L19.
2 A person in any profession gaining practical experience under supervision. Chiefly *N. Amer.* E20.
■ **internship** *noun* (chiefly *N. Amer.*) the position of an intern; the period of such a position: E20.

intern /ɪnˈtəːn/; *in sense 3 usu.* ˈɪntəːn/ *verb*. E17.
[ORIGIN French *interner*, formed as INTERN *adjective & noun*.]
†**1** *verb intrans.* Become incorporated or united with another being. Only in E17.
2 *verb trans.* Confine as a prisoner; oblige to reside within prescribed limits of a country etc. without permission to leave them. M19.

S. SPENDER At the outbreak of war, they were in France where Franz was interned as an enemy alien. B. MALAMUD When they caught me peddling I was interned for six months in a work camp.

3 *verb intrans.* Act as an intern. Chiefly *N. Amer.* M20.

M. FRENCH Norm finished med school . . but then he was interning.

■ **interˈnee** *noun* a person who is interned E20.

internal /ɪnˈtəːn(ə)l/ *adjective & noun*. E16.
[ORIGIN mod. Latin *internalis*, from Latin *internus*: see INTERN *noun & adjective*, -AL[1].]
▸ **A** *adjective*. **1** Of or pertaining to the mind or soul, mental or spiritual; of or pertaining to the inner nature of a thing, intrinsic. E16.

P. BARKER Those who were compelled to talk to themselves, thrashing out some unending internal feud.

2 Of or pertaining to the inside or interior of something; within the limits of something; *spec.* of or affecting the inside of a body. L17. ▸**b** ANATOMY. Situated further from the surface of the body, or nearer the median line. Opp. ***external***. M19.

B. BAINBRIDGE The Connolly woman has internal bleeding from a boot in her belly. M. RULE The whole of the internal structure was unstable and inherently dangerous.

3 Of or pertaining to the domestic affairs of a nation. L18.

R. NIEBUHR Social inequality leads not only to internal strife but to conflict between various national communities.

4 Designating a student or examiner who is in residence at a university as well as taking or marking its examinations. L19.
5 Used or applying within an organization. M20.

M. FRAYN He put down the outside phone and picked up the internal one.

– SPECIAL COLLOCATIONS: **internal clock** a person's innate sense of time; BIOLOGY = *BIOLOGICAL clock*. **internal-combustion engine**: with its motive power generated by the explosion of gases or vapour with air in a cylinder. **internal conversion** PHYSICS (**a**) transfer of the whole energy of a gamma-ray photon emitted by a nucleus to an orbital electron; (**b**) radiationless transition of an excited molecule from one electronic energy state to another of the same multiplicity. ***internal ear***: see EAR *noun*[1]. **internal energy** PHYSICS the energy possessed by a system in consequence of the positions, relative motions, and interactions of its components. **internal evidence**: derived from the content of the thing discussed. **internal exile** penal banishment from a part of one's own country. **internal friction** resistance to the deformation or flow of a substance, arising from the interaction of component molecules etc. **internal medicine** the branch of medicine that deals with the diagnosis and treatment of disease by medical as opp. to surgical means. **internal object** PSYCHOANALYSIS a fantasized subjective image of an object as the target of emotions otherwise directed at the object itself. **internal pressure**: arising in a liquid from intermolecular attraction. **internal property** PHILOSOPHY a property belonging essentially to an object or proposition. ***internal*** RELATION. **internal rhyme**: involving a word in the middle of a line and another at the end of the line or in the middle of the next. **internal revenue** US inland revenue. **internal secretion** PHYSIOLOGY the secretion of substances into the blood; a substance secreted into the blood, *esp.* a hormone. **internal stress**: arising within a substance (e.g. through differential heating), not imposed from without.
▸ **B** *noun*. **1** An intrinsic or essential attribute, quality, etc. Now only in *pl.* M17.
†**2** The inner nature or soul. M17–L18.
†**3** A medicine or remedy to be taken internally. L17–E18.
■ **interˈnality** *noun* the quality or fact of being internal E19. **internally** *adverb* L16.

internalize /ɪnˈtəːn(ə)lʌɪz/ *verb trans.* Also **-ise**. L19.
[ORIGIN from INTERNAL *adjective* + -IZE.]
1 Make internal; give an internal or subjective character to. L19.
2 Adopt or incorporate as one's own (the attitudes, values, etc., of another person or social group). M20. ▸**b** Transfer emotions felt for an object to (a fantasized subjective image of that object); redirect (an emotion) away from its target towards oneself. M20.

M. FRENCH It would never have occurred to *me* to have an affair . . . God, how I'd internalized sexual morality.

3 LINGUISTICS. Acquire knowledge of and the ability to apply (a set of rules) as part of native-speaker competence. M20.
■ **internaliˈzation** *noun* L19.

internat. *abbreviation*.
International.

international /ɪntəˈnaʃ(ə)n(ə)l/ *adjective & noun*. L18.
[ORIGIN from INTER- 2 + NATIONAL.]
▸ **A** *adjective*. **1** Existing, occurring, or carried on between nations; pertaining to relations, communications, travel, etc., between nations. L18.

A. BULLOCK From this in turn followed the rejection of force in settling international disputes. *Sunday Express* The two rushed off to an international phone box in Leicester Square.

2 Agreed on by many nations; used by, or able to be used by, (the people of) many nations. L19.

R. P. JHABVALA It was an international hotel and was largely filled with foreign travellers.

3 Of or pertaining to the First International (see sense B.3 below). L19.
– SPECIAL COLLOCATIONS: ***International Baccalaureate***: see BACCALAUREATE 3. **International Brigade** *hist.* a body of volunteers raised internationally by foreign Communist Parties, which fought for the Republic in the Spanish Civil War of 1936–9. ***international candle***: see CANDLE *noun* 3. **international code** a code of signals by which sailors of all nations can hold communication at sea. ***international comity***: see COMITY 2a. **International Court of Justice** a judicial court of the United Nations. **International Date Line** = *date line* (a) s.v. DATE *noun*[2]. **international driving licence**, **international driving permit**: allowing the holder to drive a specified class of vehicle in various countries. **international Gothic** a style in painting, sculpture, and the decorative arts that spread across western Europe in the late 14th and early 15th cents., characterized by secular themes and delicate naturalistic detail. **international law** a body of rules established by custom or treaty and agreed as binding in the relations between one nation and another. **International Monetary Fund** an organization with a monetary pool on which member nations can draw, established in 1945 to promote international trade and stabilization of currencies. **international orange** *adjective & noun* (of) a bright orange colour, visible from a great distance. **International Phonetic Alphabet** a set of phonetic symbols for international use, based on the Roman and Greek alphabets with the addition of some special symbols and diacritical marks. **international standard book number** an identification number allocated internationally to each (edition or format of a) book published; abbreviation *ISBN*; (cf. ***standard book number*** s.v. STANDARD *adjective*). **international style** (**a**) a naturalistic functional style of 20th-cent. architecture; (**b**) = ***international Gothic*** above. **International System of Units** a system of physical units (with a set of scaling prefixes) derived without multiplying factors

I

from the basic independent units of the metre, kilogram, second, ampere, kelvin, candela, and mole. **international unit** *BIOLOGY & MEDICINE* any of various units of activity or potency defined for vitamins, sera, hormones, etc.

▸ **B** *noun.* **1** A person having relations with two different nations, esp. as native of one and resident in another. **L19.**

S. MORLEY They were internationals who just happened to live in California and came from England.

2 A contest, usu. in sports, between representatives or teams from different nations; a person taking part in such a contest. **L19.**

Gentleman (Mumbai) He is the best Indian bat for Tests as well as one-day internationals.

3 (**I-**.) Any of various socialist organizations founded for the worldwide promotion of socialism or Communism; *spec.* = ***First International***, ***Second International***, ***Third International***, ***Fourth International*** below. Also, a member of any of these organizations. **L19.**

First International an international workers' association founded in 1864 by Karl Marx to promote the joint political action of the working classes in all countries and dissolved in 1876. **Second International** a socialist organization founded in Paris in 1889 to celebrate the 100th anniversary of the French Revolution, now a loose association of social democrats. **Third International** an organization founded in Moscow in 1919 by delegates from twelve countries to promote Communism and support the Russian Revolution and dissolved in 1943; also called ***Comintern***. **Fourth International** a body of Trotskyist organizations formed in 1938 in opposition to the Stalin-dominated Third International.

4 ***the International***, = INTERNATIONALE 2. **E20.**

■ **internatioˈnality** *noun* international quality, condition, or character **M19.** **internationally** *adverb* **M19.**

Internationale /ˌɪntənaʃjəˈnɑːl/ *noun.* **L19.**
[ORIGIN French, use as noun (in sense 2 sc. *chanson* song) of fem. of *international* international.]
1 = INTERNATIONAL *noun* 3. **L19.**
2 ***the Internationale***, a revolutionary song composed by Eugène Pottier in 1871 and adopted by (orig. French) socialists. **E20.**

internationalise *verb* var. of INTERNATIONALIZE.

internationalism /ɪntəˈnaʃ(ə)n(ə)lɪz(ə)m/ *noun.* **M19.**
[ORIGIN from INTERNATIONAL + -ISM.]
1 International character or spirit; the advocacy of a community of interests among nations. **M19.**
2 (**I-**.) The principles of or support for any of the Internationals. **L19.**
■ **internationalist** *noun* **M19.**

internationalize /ɪntəˈnaʃ(ə)n(ə)lʌɪz/ *verb trans.* Also **-ise**. **M19.**
[ORIGIN formed as INTERNATIONALISM + -IZE.]
Make international in character or use; *spec.* bring a country, territory, etc. under the protection or control of two or more nations.
■ **internationaliˈzation** *noun* **L19.**

interne *noun* see INTERN *adjective & noun.*

internecinal /ɪntəˈnɛsɪn(ə)l/ *adjective. rare.* **M19.**
[ORIGIN formed as INTERNECINE + -AL¹.]
Destructive, deadly.

internecine /ɪntəˈniːsʌɪn/ *adjective.* **M17.**
[ORIGIN Latin *internecinus*, from *internecio(n-)* general slaughter, extermination, from *internecare* slaughter, exterminate, formed as INTER- + *necare* kill: see -INE¹.]
1 Deadly; characterized by great slaughter. **M17.**
2 Mutually destructive. Now also, of or pertaining to internal conflict in a group or organization. **M18.**

T. C. BOYLE The root of his troubles lay in internecine squabbling between the various tribes under his leadership. *Observer* The Tories, plunged into internecine warfare over Europe, are deeply pessimistic over their prospects.

internecive /ɪntəˈniːsɪv/ *adjective. rare.* **E19.**
[ORIGIN Latin *internecivus* var. of *internecinus* INTERNECINE: see -IVE.]
Mutually destructive.

internet /ˈɪntənɛt/ *verb & noun.* As noun now usu. **I-**. **M20.**
[ORIGIN from INTER- 1 + NET(WORK.]
▸ **A** *verb trans. & intrans.* Infl. **-tt-**. Connect or be connected to a computer network (now esp. the Internet). **M20.**
▸ **B** *noun.* Orig. (in form ***internet***), a computer network consisting of or connecting a number of smaller networks, such as two or more local area networks connected by a shared communications protocol. Now (usu. ***the Internet***), a global computer network providing a variety of information and communication facilities to its users, and consisting of a loose confederation of interconnected networks which use standardized communication protocols. **L20.**
– COMB.: **Internet appliance** a small computer designed esp. to provide easy access to the Internet; **Internet cafe** a simple cafe where customers pay to access the Internet; **Internet Protocol** a standard that specifies the format and addressing scheme of packets of data sent over the Internet or other network.

interneuron /ɪntəˈnjʊərɒn/ *noun.* Also **-rone** /-rəʊn/. **M20.**
[ORIGIN from INTER(NUNCIAL + NEURON.]
PHYSIOLOGY. Any neuron which transmits impulses between other neurons, esp. as part of a reflex arc.

interneuronal /ɪntənjʊˈrəʊn(ə)l/ *adjective.* **M20.**
[ORIGIN Partly from INTERNEURON + -AL¹, partly from INTER- 2 + NEURONAL.]
PHYSIOLOGY. Occurring or existing between neurons; of, pertaining to, or affecting an interneuron.

internist /ɪnˈtəːnɪst/ *noun. N. Amer.* **E20.**
[ORIGIN from INTERN(AL + -IST.]
A general physician. Also, a specialist in internal medicine.

internment /ɪnˈtəːnm(ə)nt/ *noun.* **L19.**
[ORIGIN from INTERN *verb* + -MENT.]
The action of interning someone; confinement within the limits of a country etc.
– COMB.: **internment camp** a detention camp for prisoners of war and aliens.

internode /ˈɪntənəʊd/ *noun.* Also (now *rare*) in Latin form **-nodium** /-ˈnəʊdɪəm/, pl. **-dia** /-dɪə/. **M17.**
[ORIGIN Latin *internodium*, formed as INTER- 2 + NODE.]
1 *BOTANY.* The part of a plant stem between adjacent nodes. **M17.**
2 *ANATOMY & ZOOLOGY.* A slender part between two nodes or joints, as a finger bone; *spec.* a myelinated length of nerve fibre between two nodes of Ranvier. **E18.**
■ **interˈnodal** *adjective* **M19.**

†**internunce** *noun.* Also **-nonce**. **M17–M19.**
[ORIGIN French formed as INTERNUNCIAL.]
= INTERNUNCIO.

internuncial /ɪntəˈnʌnʃ(ə)l/ *adjective.* **M19.**
[ORIGIN from Latin *internuntius* (see INTERNUNCIO) + -AL¹.]
1 *PHYSIOLOGY.* Conveying signals between parts of the (nervous) system; of the nature of an interneuron. **M19.**
2 Of or pertaining to an internuncio; having the function of conveying messages between parties etc. **L19.**

internuncio /ɪntəˈnʌnsɪəʊ/ *noun.* Pl. **-os**. **M17.**
[ORIGIN Italian *internunzio* from Latin *internuntius*, formed as INTER- + *nuntius* messenger.]
1 A messenger between two parties; a go-between. **M17.**
2 An official papal representative or ambassador at a foreign court, ranking below a nuncio. **L17.**
3 *hist.* A minister representing a government (esp. of Austria) at Constantinople (Istanbul). **E18.**

internuncius /ɪntəˈnʌnsɪəs/ *noun.* **L17.**
[ORIGIN medieval Latin var. of Latin *internuntius*: see INTERNUNCIO.]
= INTERNUNCIO 1.

interocean /ɪntərˈəʊʃ(ə)n/ *adjective.* **E20.**
[ORIGIN from INTER- 2 + OCEAN.]
= INTEROCEANIC.

interoceanic /ˌɪntərəʊʃɪˈanɪk, -sɪ-/ *adjective.* **M19.**
[ORIGIN from INTER- 2 + OCEANIC.]
Situated between oceans; connecting two oceans.

interoceptor /ɪntərəʊˈsɛptə/ *noun.* **E20.**
[ORIGIN from INTER(IOR + -O- + RE)CEPTOR: cf. EXTEROCEPTOR.]
PHYSIOLOGY. A sensory receptor which receives stimuli from within the body, esp. from the gut.
■ **interoˈceptive** *adjective* **E20.**

interoperable /ɪntərˈɒp(ə)rəb(ə)l/ *adjective.* **M20.**
[ORIGIN from INTER- 1 + OPERABLE.]
Able to operate in conjunction.
■ **interoperaˈbility** *noun* **L20.** **interoperate** *verb intrans.* operate in conjunction **L20.**

inter partes /ɪntə ˈpɑːtiːz/ *adjectival phr.* **E19.**
[ORIGIN Latin.]
LAW. (Of an action) relevant only to the two parties in a particular case; (of a deed etc.) made between two parties.

†**interpel** *verb trans.* Infl. **-ll-**. **LME.**
[ORIGIN Latin *interpellare* interrupt by speaking, formed as INTER- + *-pellare* thrust or direct oneself.]
1 Appeal to, petition. **LME–L16.**
2 Interrupt (a person) in speaking. **M16–M17.**
3 *SCOTS LAW.* Prohibit, prevent. **E18–M19.**

interpellant /ɪntəˈpɛl(ə)nt/ *noun.* **M19.**
[ORIGIN French, pres. pple of *interpeller* from Latin *interpellare*: see INTERPEL, -ANT¹.]
A person who addresses an interpellation in a foreign parliament.

interpellate /ɪnˈtəːpɪleɪt/ *verb trans.* **L16.**
[ORIGIN Latin *interpellat-* pa. ppl stem of *interpellare*: see INTERPEL, -ATE³.]
†**1** Interrupt. Only in **L16.**
2 In a parliament: interrupt the order of the day by questioning (a minister) on a point of government policy. **L19.**
■ **interpellator** *noun* **E17.**

interpellation /ɪnˌtəːpɪˈleɪʃ(ə)n/ *noun.* **E16.**
[ORIGIN Latin *interpellatio(n-)*, formed as INTERPELLATE: see -ATION.]
†**1** The action of appealing to or entreating someone; intercession. **E16–M17.**
†**2** A summons. **L16–E18.**
†**3** Interruption. **E17–M19.**
4 The action of interpellating a minister in a parliament. **M19.**

interpenetrate /ɪntəˈpɛnɪtreɪt/ *verb.* **E19.**
[ORIGIN from INTER- 1 + PENETRATE *verb*.]
1 *verb trans.* Penetrate thoroughly; permeate, pervade. **E19.**
2 *verb intrans. & trans.* Of two or more things: penetrate (each other). **E19.**
3 *verb trans. & intrans.* (with *with*). *ARCHITECTURE.* Appear to penetrate (a moulding etc.). **M19.**
■ **interpeneˈtration** *noun* (**a**) the action of interpenetrating; (**b**) *ARCHITECTURE* the intersection and (*spec.*) the continuation beyond the intersection of two or more mouldings etc.: **E19.** **interpenetrative** *adjective* **M19.**

interpersonal /ɪntəˈpəːs(ə)n(ə)l/ *adjective.* **M19.**
[ORIGIN from INTER- 2 + PERSONAL.]
(Of a relationship, behaviour, etc.) that is between people; pertaining to or involving a relationship between people.

C. LASCH Reforms designed to improve the quality of communication . . and promote interpersonal skills. *New Internationalist* Greater scope for individual initiative and better interpersonal relationships.

■ ˌ**interpersoˈnality** *noun* **M20.** **interpersonally** *adverb* **M20.**

interphase /ˈɪntəfeɪz/ *noun & adjective.* **E20.**
[ORIGIN from INTER- 2 + PHASE *noun*.]
▸ **A** *noun.* **1** *CYTOLOGY.* In cell division: the stage between successive mitoses, or between the first and second divisions of meiosis. **E20.**
2 *PHYSICAL CHEMISTRY.* The region between two phases in which properties differ from the bulk properties of either phase. **M20.**
▸ **B** *adjective.* Occurring or existing between two phases or states of matter; of or pertaining to (an) interphase. **M20.**

I

interplant /ɪntəˈplɑːnt/ *verb trans.* **E20.**
[ORIGIN from INTER- 1 + PLANT *verb*.]
Plant (a specified crop or plant) together *with* another crop or plant; plant (land) with a mixture of crops or plants.

G. WRIGLEY On the fertile soils of East Africa bananas are interplanted with coffee. *Anthropology Today* Most of the plots are small and interplanted.

interplay /ˈɪntəpleɪ/ *noun.* **M19.**
[ORIGIN from INTER- 1 + PLAY *noun*.]
Reciprocal or free interaction; the operation or influence of two or more things on each other.

E. CRANKSHAW The state of Russia . . is the outcome of the interplay between the subject people . . and the autocracy.

interplay /ˈɪntəpleɪ/ *verb intrans.* **L19.**
[ORIGIN from INTER- 1 + PLAY *verb*.]
Exert mutual influence.

interplead /ɪntəˈpliːd/ *verb.* Also †**enterplede**. **M16.**
[ORIGIN Anglo-Norman *enterpleder*, formed as INTER- + PLEAD.]
1 *verb intrans. LAW.* Of people: litigate with each other to determine a matter for the assistance of a third party. **M16.**
†**2** *verb trans.* Plead in excuse or defence. **L16–E18.**

interpleader /ɪntəˈpliːdə/ *noun.* **M16.**
[ORIGIN Anglo-Norman *enterpleder* use as noun of inf.: see INTERPLEAD, -ER⁴.]
LAW. A suit pleaded between two parties to determine a matter of claim or right to property held by a third party and esp. to determine to which claimant delivery or payment should be made.

Interpol /ˈɪntəpɒl/ *noun.* **M20.**
[ORIGIN Abbreviation of *International police*.]
The International Criminal Police Commission founded in 1923 and based in Paris.

interpolable /ɪnˈtəːpələb(ə)l/ *adjective.* **L19.**
[ORIGIN from INTERPOLATE *verb* + -ABLE.]
Able to be interpolated.
■ **interpolaˈbility** *noun* **M20.**

interpolate /ɪnˈtəːpələt/ *noun.* **E20.**
[ORIGIN formed as INTERPOLATE *verb* + -ATE¹.]
MATH. A value arrived at by interpolation.

†**interpolate** *adjective.* **LME–M17.**
[ORIGIN Latin *interpolatus* pa. pple, formed as INTERPOLATE *verb*: see -ATE².]
Esp. of a fever: intermittent, interrupted. Cf. INTERPOLATE *verb* 6.

interpolate /ɪnˈtəːpəleɪt/ *verb.* **E17.**
[ORIGIN Latin *interpolat-* pa. ppl stem of *interpolare* refurbish, alter, formed as INTER- + *-polare* rel. to *polire* POLISH *verb*.]
▸ **I** †**1** *verb trans.* Polish; refurbish. *rare.* **E17–E18.**
2 *verb trans.* Alter (a book) by the insertion of new material, esp. in order to mislead as to date of composition etc. **E17.** ▸**b** Modify by new additions. **M19.**

T. WRIGHT The poem of Beowulf . . has been much interpolated by Christian transcribers.

3 *verb trans.* Insert (esp. misleading words or passages) in a book etc. **M17.** ▸**b** *transf.* Insert as something additional or different; *esp.* interject (a remark etc.) in conversation. **E19.**

R. GITTINGS He interpolated an extra stanza into his own poem. **b** E. F. BENSON 'You don't really mean that?' interpolated the other.

4 *verb intrans.* Make insertions or interpolations. E18.
5 *verb trans.* MATH. Insert (a term, a value) into a series by interpolation. L18. ▸**b** *verb intrans.* Perform or use interpolation. L19.
▸ †**II 6** *verb trans.* Interrupt with a pause. Cf. INTERPOLATE *adjective* Only in L17.
■ **interpolant** *noun* (MATH.) a value or expression used in finding another by interpolation E20. **interpolative** *adjective* having the effect of interpolation E19. **interpolatory** *adjective* serving to interpolate M20.

interpolation /ɪnˌtəːpəˈleɪʃ(ə)n/ *noun.* E17.
[ORIGIN French, or Latin *interpolatio(n-)*, formed as INTERPOLATE *verb*: see -ATION.]
†**1** The action of polishing or refurbishing. Only in 17.
2 The action of inserting words into or altering a book etc., esp. in order to mislead; an interpolated word or passage. E17.

N. FREELING There are heaps of interpolations and irrelevancies in different coloured inks.

3 (An) insertion of something additional or different; *spec.* (MATH.) insertion of an intermediate term or value into a series by estimation or calculation from the known values. M18.

interpolator /ɪnˈtəːpəleɪtə/ *noun.* M17.
[ORIGIN from INTERPOLATE *verb* + -OR.]
1 A person who interpolates something. M17.
2 ENGINEERING. A device or apparatus which guides a tool through a smooth curve when provided with a set of points defining the curve. M20.

interpolymer /ˈɪntəpɒlɪmə/ *noun.* M20.
[ORIGIN from INTER- 1 + POLYMER.]
CHEMISTRY. A copolymer, *esp.* one having the units in completely random order.
■ **interpolymeriˈzation** *noun* the action or process of interpolymerizing M20. **interpoˈlymerize** *verb trans. & intrans.* combine to form an interpolymer M20.

†**interpone** *verb trans.* E16–L19.
[ORIGIN Latin *interponere* place between, formed as INTER- + *ponere* to place.]
Chiefly SCOTS LAW. Interpose. Freq. in ***interpone one's authority***, intervene to prevent something.

interposal /ɪntəˈpəʊz(ə)l/ *noun.* E17.
[ORIGIN from INTERPOSE + -AL[1].]
= INTERPOSITION.

interpose /ɪntəˈpəʊz/ *verb.* L16.
[ORIGIN Old French & mod. French *interposer*, based on Latin *interponere* (see INTERPONE) but re-formed on Latin pa. pple *interpositus* and Old French & mod. French *poser*: see POSE *verb*[1].]
1 *verb trans.* Place *between* (in space or time), put in an intermediate position, esp. to obstruct or delay. L16. ▸**b** *verb intrans.* Come between in position, stand in the way. E17. ▸†**c** *verb trans.* Place in alternation, cause to alternate. Only in 17. ▸**d** *verb trans. & intrans.* CHESS. Move (a piece) so as to obstruct another piece, esp. when this is giving check. M18.

G. SANTAYANA His champagne glass had been filled . . before he could interpose a deprecating hand. A. BURGESS Growing impatient with art, he seems to . . interpose nothing between the reader and the vision. **b** H. H. WILSON Three columns . . moved to the right, as if intending to interpose between the lines and the town.

†**2** *verb trans.* Obstruct, intercept, (a person or thing). Only in 17.
3 *verb trans.* Exercise or advance (a veto or objection) by way of interference. E17.
4 *verb intrans.* & †*refl.* Interfere in a matter, intervene between parties or on a person's behalf. (Foll. by *between*.) E17.

W. COWPER None interposed To avert his woeful doom. J. R. GREEN The Archbishop interposed between the rival claimants to the crown.

5 *verb trans. & intrans.* Introduce (an opinion, an aside, etc.) as a digression; *esp.* say (words) as an interruption. E17.

S. BRETT 'I don't think you've met my wife, Frances,' Charles interposed hastily.

■ **interposer** *noun* L16. †**interposure** *noun* (an) interposition E17–M18.

interposition /ɪntəpəˈzɪʃ(ə)n/ *noun.* LME.
[ORIGIN Old French & mod. French, or Latin *interpositio(n-)*, from *interposit-* pa. ppl stem of *interponere*: see INTERPONE, -ION.]
1 The action or an act of placing oneself or something between; the fact or condition of being placed between. LME.
2 The action or an act of interfering in a matter; (an) intervention. LME.

interpret /ɪnˈtəːprɪt/ *verb.* LME.
[ORIGIN Old French & mod. French *interpréter* or Latin *interpretari* explain, translate, from *interpret-*, *-pres* agent, broker, translator, interpreter, formed as INTER- + base corresp. to Sanskrit *prath-* spread about.]
1 *verb trans.* Explain the meaning of (something mysterious or abstruse, foreign words, a dream, etc.). Formerly also, translate. LME. ▸**b** Explain to oneself, understand. L18. ▸**c** Obtain significant information from (a photograph), esp. for military purposes. M20.

C. HOPE Father Lynch would interpret this . . saying that by that 'place' Kruger undoubtedly meant a physical location. **b** GEO. ELIOT Her knowledge of the youth of nineteen might help . . in interpreting the man of thirty-four.

2 *verb trans.* Give a particular explanation of; explain or construe (an action etc.) in a specified manner. LME. ▸†**b** Explain or translate by a specified term. M16–L17.

I. MURDOCH He gave a jerky gesture which was interpreted by Donald as a gesture of dismissal. K. CLARK The medieval mind, which was adept at interpreting everything symbolically. D. DELILLO I wanted a sign, something to interpret as favorable.

3 *verb intrans.* Give the meaning or explanation of something; *spec.* act as an interpreter, esp. of a foreign language. LME.
4 *verb trans.* Bring out or represent stylistically the meaning of (a creative work, a dramatic role, etc.) according to one's understanding of the creator's ideas. M19.
5 *verb trans.* COMPUTING. Execute (a source language statement or program) as an interpreter. M20.

interpretable /ɪnˈtəːprɪtəb(ə)l/ *adjective.* E17.
[ORIGIN Late Latin *interpretabilis*, from *interpretari*: see INTERPRET, -ABLE.]
Able to be interpreted or explained.
■ **interpretaˈbility** *noun* M19.

interpretant /ɪnˈtəːprɪt(ə)nt/ *noun.* E20.
[ORIGIN from INTERPRET + -ANT[1].]
PHILOSOPHY. The effect of a proposition or sign-series on the person who interprets it.

interpretate /ɪnˈtəːprɪteɪt/ *verb trans. & intrans.* Now *rare* or *obsolete*. E17.
[ORIGIN Latin *interpretat-* pa. ppl stem of *interpretari*: see INTERPRET, -ATE[3].]
Interpret.

interpretation /ɪnˌtəːprɪˈteɪʃ(ə)n/ *noun.* LME.
[ORIGIN Old French & mod. French *interprétation* or Latin *interpretatio(n-)*, formed as INTERPRETATE: see -ATION.]
1 The action of explaining the meaning of something; *spec.* the proper explanation or signification of something. Formerly also, (a) translation of a book etc. LME. ▸**b** The technique of obtaining significant information from a photograph. M20.
2 An explanation given; a way of explaining; (a) construction put upon an action etc. Formerly also, a commentary on a book etc. LME.
3 (A) stylistic representation of a creative work, dramatic role, etc., according to one's understanding of the creator's ideas. L19.
■ **interpretational** *adjective* M19.

interpretative /ɪnˈtəːprɪtətɪv/ *adjective.* M16.
[ORIGIN medieval Latin *interpretativus*, formed as INTERPRETATE: see -IVE.]
1 Having the quality or function of interpreting; explanatory. M16.
2 Deduced or deducible by interpretation; inferential. Now *rare* or *obsolete*. E17.
■ **interpretatively** *adverb* E17. **interpretativeness** *noun* M20.

interpreter /ɪnˈtəːprɪtə/ *noun.* LME.
[ORIGIN Anglo-Norman *enterpretour*, *inter-* = Old French *interprete(ë)ur*, *entre-* from late Latin *interpretator*, formed as INTERPRETATE: see -ER[2].]
1 †**a** A person who interprets laws, texts, etc., in an official capacity; a commentator. LME–L17. ▸**b** A person who interprets a (particular) thing (in a particular way); a person who construes an action etc. in a specified manner. M16.

b *Times* Beecham's gifts tend to typecast him as an interpreter of even-numbered Beethoven.

2 A person, esp. an official, who translates orally the words of people speaking different languages. Formerly also, a translator of books etc. LME.
†**3** A messenger of the gods; *spec.* Mercury. L15–L17.
4 COMPUTING. **a** A machine which prints on to a punched card the characters equivalent to the pattern of holes. M20. ▸**b** A program which executes a source program one statement at a time. M20.
■ **interpretership** *noun* the position of an (esp. official) interpreter M19.

†**interpretess** *noun.* E18–L19.
[ORIGIN from INTERPRET(ER + -ESS[1].]
= INTERPRETRESS.

interpretive /ɪnˈtəːprɪtɪv/ *adjective.* M17.
[ORIGIN from INTERPRET + -IVE.]
1 = INTERPRETATIVE. M17.
2 COMPUTING. Of a routine or program: functioning as an interpreter. M20.

interpretress /ɪnˈtəːprɪtrɪs/ *noun.* Now *rare*. L18.
[ORIGIN from INTERPRETER + -ESS[1].]
A female interpreter.

interpunction /ɪntəˈpʌŋ(k)ʃ(ə)n/ *noun.* Now *rare* or *obsolete*. E17.
[ORIGIN Latin *interpunctio(n-)*, from *interpunct-* pa. ppl stem of *interpungere*, formed as INTER- + *pungere* to prick: see -ION.]
Punctuation.

interpunctuation /ˌɪntəpʌŋ(k)tʃʊˈeɪʃ(ə)n, -tjʊ-/ *noun.* Now *rare*. E18.
[ORIGIN from INTER- 1 + PUNCTUATION.]
Punctuation.
■ **interˈpunctuate** *verb trans. & intrans.* punctuate; use punctuation: M19.

interracial /ɪntəˈreɪʃ(ə)l/ *adjective.* L19.
[ORIGIN from INTER- 2 + RACIAL *adjective*.]
Of, involving, or existing between different races.
■ **interracially** *adverb* M20.

interreges *noun* pl. of INTERREX.

interregnum /ɪntəˈrɛgnəm/ *noun.* Pl. **-nums**, **-na** /-nə/. L16.
[ORIGIN Latin, formed as INTER- 2 + *regnum* REIGN *noun*. Cf. INTERREIGN.]
†**1** Temporary authority or rule exercised during a vacancy of the throne or a suspension of the normal government. L16–L18.
2 An interval during which the normal government is suspended, esp. during the period between the end of a monarch's rule and the accession of his or her successor; any period of cessation or suspension of rule, authority, etc. L16.

fig.: J. R. ACKERLEY His courtship . . persisted through all her marriages, becoming articulate again in the interregnums.

3 An interval, a pause, a break. M17.
■ **interregnal** *adjective* pertaining to or of the nature of an interregnum M17.

interreign /ˈɪntəreɪn/ *noun.* Now *rare*. M16.
[ORIGIN from INTER- 2 + REIGN *noun*, after INTERREGNUM Cf. Old French & mod. French *interrègne*.]
†**1** = INTERREGNUM 1. M16–E17.
2 = INTERREGNUM 2. L16.

interrelate /ɪntərɪˈleɪt/ *verb trans. & intrans.* E19.
[ORIGIN from INTER- 1 + RELATE *verb*.]
Relate mutually or one to another.
■ **interrelatedness** *noun* the quality or condition of being interrelated M19.

interrelation /ɪntərɪˈleɪʃ(ə)n/ *noun.* M19.
[ORIGIN from INTER- 1 + RELATION.]
(A) mutual or reciprocal relation.
■ **interrelationship** *noun* M19.

interrer /ɪnˈtəːrə/ *noun.* E17.
[ORIGIN from INTER *verb* + -ER[1].]
A person who inters or buries someone or something.

interrex /ˈɪntərɛks/ *noun.* Pl. **interreges** /ɪntəˈriːdʒiːz/. L16.
[ORIGIN Latin, formed as INTER- + *rex* king.]
A person holding the supreme authority in a state during an interregnum.

interrogant /ɪnˈtɛrəg(ə)nt/ *noun. arch.* M17.
[ORIGIN Latin *interrogant-* pres. ppl stem of *interrogare*: see INTERROGATE, -ANT[1].]
= INTERROGATOR.

interrogate /ɪnˈtɛrəgeɪt/ *verb.* Also †**enter-**. L15.
[ORIGIN Latin *interrogat-* pa. ppl stem of *interrogare*, formed as INTER- + *rogare* ask: see -ATE[3].]
1 *verb trans.* Question (a person), esp. closely, thoroughly, or formally. Also, ask or utter as a question. L15. ▸†**b** Ask about (something). Only in 17.

H. SPURLING I sat between the two ladies and was amiably interrogated by both. E. FEINSTEIN The French police interrogated him extensively and released him for lack of evidence.

2 *verb intrans.* Chiefly LAW. Ask questions. E17.
3 *verb trans.* Transmit a signal to (a transponder, or a vehicle etc. fitted with one) to elicit a response, usu. as a coded signal giving information about identity, condition, etc. M20. ▸**b** Elicit information from (a computer file etc.) by electronic means. M20.
■ **interrogaˈtee** *noun* a person who is interrogated E19. **interrogatingly** *adverb* in an interrogating manner L19.

interrogation /ɪnˌtɛrəˈgeɪʃ(ə)n/ *noun.* LME.
[ORIGIN Old French & mod. French, or Latin *interrogatio(n-)*, formed as INTERROGATE: see -ATION.]
1 The action or process of interrogating someone or asking questions; an instance of this, a questioning. LME.

A. BRIEN Being held without interrogation or charge . . is definitely a breach of the law. I. MURDOCH Jean . . sat staring at Rose, waiting for the next question, as in an interrogation.

2 A question, an enquiry. LME.
3 RHETORIC. Questioning, or a question, as a form of speech. M16.
4 (A) transmission of a signal to a transponder etc. to elicit a response, usu. as a coded signal; a signal so transmitted. M20.
– COMB.: **interrogation mark**, **interrogation point** a question mark.
■ **interrogational** *adjective* interrogative L19.

interrogative /ɪntəˈrɒɡətɪv/ *adjective & noun.* E16.
[ORIGIN Late Latin *interrogativus*, formed as INTERROGATE: see -IVE.]
▸ **A** *adjective.* **1** Pertaining to or of the nature of questioning; having the form or force of a question; (of a word, particle, etc.) used in formulating questions. E16. ***interrogative pronoun*** etc.
2 Given to asking questions, inquisitive. *rare.* E18.
▸ **B** *noun.* **1** A word or form used in formulating questions; *esp.* an interrogative pronoun. E16.
2 A question. *rare.* L16.
■ **interrogatively** *adverb* L16.

interrogator /ɪnˈtɛrəɡeɪtə/ *noun.* M18.
[ORIGIN Late Latin, formed as INTERROGATE: see -OR.]
1 A person who interrogates someone. M18.
2 A radio or radar transmitter designed to interrogate a transponder etc. M20.

interrogatory /ɪntəˈrɒɡət(ə)ri/ *noun & adjective.* M16.
[ORIGIN As noun from medieval Latin *interrogatoria* pl. of *interrogatorium*; as adjective from late Latin *interrogatorius*, formed as INTERROGATE: see -ORY[1], -ORY[2].]
▸ **A** *noun.* **1** A question; *spec.* (LAW) a formal, esp. written, question put to a party or witness and required to be answered on oath. M16.
2 LAW. Questioning of an accused person. *rare.* E19.
▸ **B** *adjective.* = INTERROGATIVE *adjective.* L16.

interrogee /ɪnˌtɛrəˈɡiː/ *noun.* M20.
[ORIGIN from INTERROG(ATE + -EE[1].]
A person who is interrogated.

in terrorem /ɪn tɛˈrɔːrɛm/ *adverbial & adjectival phr.* E17.
[ORIGIN Latin = into a state of terror.]
(Done) as a warning or to deter.

interrupt /ɪntəˈrʌpt/ *noun.* M20.
[ORIGIN from the verb.]
COMPUTING. (A signal causing) an interruption of the execution of a program, e.g. to allow immediate execution of another program.

†**interrupt** *adjective.* LME–M17.
[ORIGIN Old French from Latin *interruptus* pa. pple, formed as INTERRUPT *verb.*]
Interrupted; *rare* forming a breach or gap.

MILTON Our adversarie, whom no bounds Prescrib'd . . nor yet the main abyss Wide interrupt, can hold.

interrupt /ɪntəˈrʌpt/ *verb.* LME.
[ORIGIN Latin *interrupt-* pa. ppl stem of *interrumpere*, formed as INTER- + *rumpere* to break.]
†**1** *verb trans.* Stop or prevent (an action); thwart (a person) in some action (foll. by *of*, *to do*). LME–M17. ▸**b** Put an end to, destroy. L16–E17.
2 *verb trans. & intrans.* Act so as to break (usu. temporarily) the continuous progress of (an action, condition, etc.); break in on the activity, esp. speech, of (a person). LME. ▸†**b** *verb trans.* Suspend (a law). LME–L16. ▸**c** *verb trans.* Say in interruption. E19.

R. GRAVES This condition would interrupt his right over her as a permanent chattel. G. VIDAL 'I was not aware . . .' I began, but she interrupted me with an airy wave of her hand. P. HOWARD The First World War interrupted these pioneering experiments. **c** C. HOPE 'The trouble was . . .'. Blashford interrupted angrily, 'The trouble was Lynch was mad.'

3 *verb trans.* Break the continuity of, make a gap or space in; obstruct (a view etc.). M17.

K. ISHIGURO An expanse of paved concrete interrupted occasionally by thin young trees.

■ **interruptable** *adjective* = INTERRUPTIBLE M20. **interrupter** *noun* (**a**) a person who interrupts; (**b**) a device for interrupting an electric current: L16. **interruptible** *adjective* able to be interrupted E17. **interruptingly** *adverb* in the way of interruption M17. **interruptive** *adjective* having the quality of interrupting M17. **interruptor** *noun* [Latin] = INTERRUPTER E16. **interruptory** *adjective* = INTERRUPTIVE M19.

interrupted /ɪntəˈrʌptɪd/ *adjective.* M16.
[ORIGIN from INTERRUPT *verb* + -ED[1].]
1 That has been interrupted. M16.
2 BOTANY. Of an inflorescence etc.: divided by intervals of bare axis; discontinuous. Of a pinnate leaf: having smaller leaflets interposed between the main leaflets. M19.
– SPECIAL COLLOCATIONS: **interrupted cadence** MUSIC: where the penultimate dominant chord is followed not by the expected chord of the tonic but by another, usu. that of the submediant. **interrupted screw**: with part of its thread cut away.
■ **interruptedly** *adverb* M17.

interruption /ɪntəˈrʌpʃ(ə)n/ *noun.* LME.
[ORIGIN Old French & mod. French, or Latin *interruptio(n-)*, formed as INTERRUPT *verb*: see -ION.]
†**1** The action or an act of preventing something or thwarting someone; obstruction. LME–L16.
2 A break (usu. temporary) in the continuous progress of an action, condition, etc., esp. speech; (a) hindrance of the course or continuance of something. LME. ▸**b** Temporary cessation, suspension. E17.

BURKE I still go on with the work I have in hand, but with terrible interruptions. L. CHARTERIS The two men listened without interruption.

3 A breach of continuity in space or order; the formation or existence of a gap or space. LME.

J. WOODWARD The Interruptions of the Strata.

4 LAW. (A) legal action to prevent the exercise of a right or privilege. Long only *spec.* (*Scot.*) (a) legal action taken to lengthen the period of time during which a prescriptive right is established. LME.

inter se /ɪntə ˈseɪ/ *adverbial phr.* M19.
[ORIGIN Latin.]
Between or among themselves.

interseam /ɪntəˈsiːm/ *verb trans.* Long *rare.* L16.
[ORIGIN French *entresemer* sow among, formed as ENTER-[1], INTER- + *semer* from Latin *seminare* sow. Freq. assoc. with SEAM *verb.*]
Adorn *with* something sprinkled or scattered between. Usu. in *pass.*

intersect /ˈɪntəsɛkt/ *noun.* M17.
[ORIGIN from (the same root as) INTERSECT *verb.*]
†**1** = INSECT *noun.* Only in M17.
2 GEOMETRY. A point of intersection. L19.

intersect /ɪntəˈsɛkt/ *verb.* E17.
[ORIGIN Latin *intersect-* pa. ppl stem of *intersecare* cut asunder, intersect, formed as INTER- + *secare* cut.]
1 *verb trans.* Divide by passing through or lying across; cross. Freq. in *pass.* (foll. by *by*, *with*). E17. ▸**b** GEOMETRY. Of a line, surface, etc.: cross (a line or surface) so as to have at least one point in common. M17. ▸**c** Of a person: come across (a person, a path); intercept. *rare.* M19.

P. CAREY That perfect green landscape of his imagination, intersected with streams and redolent of orange blossom. A. MUNRO The street crossed the railway tracks. At the foot of the hill, it intersected the main street.

2 *verb intrans.* Of lines, surfaces, roads, etc.: cross or cut each other or *with* another. M19.

B. TARKINGTON He set up fountains . . where the streets intersected. *fig.*: M. L. KING The crisis of Negro aspirations intersects with the urban crisis.

■ **intersectant** *adjective* (*rare*) intersecting M19.

intersection /ɪntəˈsɛkʃ(ə)n/ *noun.* M16.
[ORIGIN Latin *intersectio(n-)*, formed as INTERSECT *verb*: see -ION.]
1 The action or fact of intersecting. M16.
2 The place where two or more things intersect; *spec.* (GEOMETRY) the point at which a line intersects a line or surface, or the line common to two intersecting surfaces. M16. ▸**b** A place where two or more roads intersect or form a junction. Chiefly *N. Amer.* M19.
3 MATH. & LOGIC. The relation of two classes each of which includes part of the other; the resulting set of elements common to both. E20.

intersectional /ɪntəˈsɛkʃ(ə)n(ə)l/ *adjective*[1]. M19.
[ORIGIN from INTERSECTION + -AL[1].]
Of, pertaining to, or characterized by intersection.

intersectional /ɪntəˈsɛkʃ(ə)n(ə)l/ *adjective*[2]. M19.
[ORIGIN from INTER- 2 + SECTION *noun* + -AL[1].]
Existing or prevailing between sections.

intersegmental /ɪntəsɛɡˈmɛnt(ə)l/ *adjective.* L19.
[ORIGIN from INTER- 2 + SEGMENT *noun* + -AL[1].]
Esp. ZOOLOGY & LINGUISTICS. Situated or occurring between segments.
■ **intersegmentally** *adverb* between segments E20.

†**intersert** *verb trans.* Also **enter-**. L16–M18.
[ORIGIN Latin *intersert-* pa. ppl stem of *interserere* formed as INTER- + *serere* put, place, insert.]
Insert between other things; *rare* supply with insertions.
■ †**intersertion** *noun* (**a**) the action of inserting; (**b**) something which is inserted: E17–L18.

intersertal /ɪntəˈsəːt(ə)l/ *adjective.* L19.
[ORIGIN formed as INTERSERT + -AL[1].]
PETROGRAPHY. Of or designating the texture of igneous rocks consisting largely of feldspar laths, with granular augite or other minerals occupying the spaces between them.

intersex /ˈɪntəsɛks/ *noun.* E20.
[ORIGIN from INTER- 1 + SEX *noun.*]
BIOLOGY. (The condition of being) an abnormal form or individual of a dioecious species, having characteristics of both sexes.

intersexual /ɪntəˈsɛkʃʊəl/ *adjective & noun.* M19.
[ORIGIN from INTER- 1, 2 + SEXUAL.]
▸ **A** *adjective.* **1** Existing between the sexes. M19.
2 BIOLOGY. Having characteristics of both sexes. E20.
▸ **B** *noun.* BIOLOGY. An intersexual individual. E20.
■ **intersexuˈality** *noun* E20.

intershock /ɪntəˈʃɒk/ *verb. rare.* E17.
[ORIGIN In sense 1 from French *s'entrechoquer*. In sense 2 from INTER- 1 + SHOCK *verb*[2].]
†**1** *verb trans.* Strike or attack mutually. Only in E17.
2 *verb intrans.* Strike together, collide. M17.

intersole *noun* see ENTRESOL.

interspace /ˈɪntəspeɪs/ *noun.* LME.
[ORIGIN from INTER- 1 + SPACE *noun.*]
1 A space between two things. LME.
2 A space of time between two events etc. E17.

interspace /ɪntəˈspeɪs/ *verb trans.* L17.
[ORIGIN from INTER- 1 + SPACE *verb.*]
Put or occupy a space between.

intersperse /ɪntəˈspəːs/ *verb trans.* Also †**entersparse**. M16.
[ORIGIN Latin *interspers-* pa. ppl stem of *interspergere*, formed as INTER- + *spargere* scatter, sprinkle.]
1 Diversify, adorn, or provide (a thing) *with* things scattered or placed at intervals. M16.

R. P. JHABVALA He interspersed his recitation with commentaries and sometimes broke into song. I. MURDOCH Waltzes, tangos and slow foxtrots, interspersed with eightsome reels.

2 Scatter among or between other things; place here and there in the course of something. M17.

C. LYELL Large heaps of oysters . . with interspersed stone implements.

■ **interspersal** *noun* (*rare*) interspersion L19. **interspersedly** *adverb* in an interspersed manner M17.

interstate /ˈɪntəsteɪt/ *adjective, adverb, & noun.* Chiefly *US & Austral.* M19.
[ORIGIN from INTER- 2 + STATE *noun.*]
▸ **A** *adjective.* Existing or carried on between states, esp. of the US or Australia. M19.
▸ **B** *adverb.* To, in, or into another state. *Austral.* E20.
▸ **C** *noun.* A road, esp. a motorway, between states. L20.

interstice /ɪnˈtəːstɪs/ *noun.* LME.
[ORIGIN Latin *interstitium*, from *intersistere* stand between, formed as INTER- + *sistere* stand.]
1 An intervening (usu. empty) space; *esp.* a relatively small or narrow space, a chink, a crevice. LME. ▸**b** PHYSICS. The space between adjacent atoms or ions in a crystal lattice. M20.

N. GORDIMER She oiled herself, spreading her toes to get at the interstices.

2 An intervening space of time. Now chiefly CHRISTIAN CHURCH in *pl.*, the intervals required between the reception of the various degrees of holy orders. M17.

interstitia *noun pl.* see INTERSTITIUM.

interstitial /ɪntəˈstɪʃ(ə)l/ *adjective & noun.* M17.
[ORIGIN from (the same root as) INTERSTITIA + -AL[1].]
▸ **A** *adjective.* **1** Pertaining to, forming, or occupying interstices. M17. ▸**b** ANATOMY & MEDICINE. (Of tissue) situated between the cells of other tissue; (of a condition or process) occurring in the interstices of an organ, or in interstitial tissue. E19. ▸**c** PHYSICS. Situated between the normally occupied points of a crystal lattice. M20. ▸**d** CRYSTALLOGRAPHY. Containing ions or atoms in interstitial positions (see sense 1c above). M20.
2 Occupying an interval in time or order. M19.
– SPECIAL COLLOCATIONS: **interstitial cell** ANATOMY a Leydig cell in the testis.
▸ **B** *noun.* PHYSICS. An interstitial atom or ion. M20.
■ **interstitialcy** *noun* (CRYSTALLOGRAPHY) an imperfection in a crystal lattice, associated with the displacement of lattice atoms by interstitial atoms M20. **interstitially** *adverb* in or through interstices L18.

interstitium /ɪntəˈstɪʃɪəm/ *noun.* Pl. **-iums**, **-ia** /-ɪə/. L16.
[ORIGIN formed as INTERSTICE.]
†**1** = INTERSTICE 1. L16–E18. ▸**b** = INTERSTICE 2. L16–E18.
2 ANATOMY & ZOOLOGY. The tissue or region lying between the principal cells, tissues, etc., of a part of the body. M20.

interstratify /ɪntəˈstratɪfʌɪ/ *verb trans.* E19.
[ORIGIN from INTER- 1 + STRATIFY.]
GEOLOGY. In *pass.*, (of strata) be alternated or interspersed *with* other strata.
■ **interstratifiˈcation** *noun* the condition of being interstratified; an interstratified layer or deposit: M19.

intersubjective /ɪntəsəbˈdʒɛktɪv/ *adjective.* L19.
[ORIGIN from INTER- 1 + SUBJECTIVE *adjective.*]
PHILOSOPHY. Existing between conscious minds; shared by more than one conscious mind.
■ **intersubjectively** *adverb* M20. ˌ**intersubjecˈtivity** *noun* M20.

intertangle /ɪntəˈtaŋɡ(ə)l/ *verb trans.* Also †**enter-**. L16.
[ORIGIN from INTER- 1, ENTER-[1] + TANGLE *verb.*]
Tangle together; intertwine confusedly and inextricably.
■ **intertanglement** *noun* intertangled state or condition; something intertangled: E19.

intertex /ɪntəˈtɛks/ *verb trans.* Long *rare* or *obsolete.* L16.
[ORIGIN Latin *intertexere*, formed as INTER- 1 + *texere* weave.]
Weave together, intertwine.

intertextuality /ˌɪntətɛkstjʊˈalɪti/ *noun.* L20.
[ORIGIN French *intertextualité*: see INTER-, TEXTUALITY.]
The relationship between (literary) texts; the fact or an instance of relating or alluding to other texts.
■ **interˈtextual** *adjective* L20. **interˈtextually** *adverb* L20.

intertexture /ɪntəˈtɛkstʃə/ *noun.* M17.
[ORIGIN from Latin *intertext-* pa. ppl stem of *intertexere* (see INTERTEX) + -URE.]
1 The action of interweaving; the fact or condition of being interwoven. M17.
2 An intertwined or interwoven structure. M17.

I

intertie /ˈɪntətʌɪ/ *noun*. E18.
[ORIGIN Orig., alt. of INTERDICE interpreted as pl. Later, from INTER- 1 + TIE *noun*[1].]
A horizontal piece of timber etc. connecting two vertical pieces.

intertissued /ɪntəˈtɪʃuːd, -sjuːd/ *adjective*. Also †**enter-**. L16.
[ORIGIN from Old French *entretissu*, formed as ENTER-[1], INTER- + TISSUE *noun*, + -ED[1].]
Interwoven.

intertribal /ɪntəˈtrʌɪb(ə)l/ *adjective*. M19.
[ORIGIN from INTER- 2 + TRIBAL *adjective*.]
Existing or carried on between different tribes.

intertrigo /ɪntəˈtrʌɪgəʊ/ *noun*. E18.
[ORIGIN Latin = a sore place caused by chafing.]
MEDICINE. Inflammation caused by the rubbing of one skin surface against another.

intertropical /ɪntəˈtrɒpɪk(ə)l/ *adjective*. L18.
[ORIGIN from INTER- 2 + TROPICAL *adjective*.]
Of or pertaining to regions between the tropics; tropical.

intertwine /ˈɪntətwʌɪn/ *noun*. *rare*. E19.
[ORIGIN from the verb.]
Intertwinement; something intertwined.

intertwine /ɪntəˈtwʌɪn/ *verb*. M17.
[ORIGIN from INTER- 1 + TWINE *verb*[1].]
1 *verb trans*. Twine (things) together; entwine (one thing *with* another). M17.

> M. SCAMMELL The history of the Church was inextricably intertwined with the history of the nation.

2 *verb trans*. Twine round. *rare*. E18.
3 *verb intrans*. Become entwined. L18.
■ **intertwinement** *noun* the fact of intertwining; intertwined state or condition; an intertwined formation: M19. **intertwiningly** *adverb* so as to intertwine E19.

intertwist /ɪntəˈtwɪst/ *verb trans*. M17.
[ORIGIN from INTER- 1 + TWIST *verb*.]
Twist together; intertwine; intertangle.

Intertype /ˈɪntətʌɪp/ *noun*. E20.
[ORIGIN from *Inter*national *Type*setting Machine Company, which manufactured machines of this type.]
PRINTING. (Proprietary name for) a composing machine which produces type in whole lines rather than individual letters.

interurban /ɪntərˈəːb(ə)n/ *adjective & noun*. L19.
[ORIGIN from INTER- 2 + URBAN *adjective*.]
▸ **A** *adjective*. Carried on between, or connecting, different cities or towns. L19.
▸ **B** *ellipt*. as *noun*. An interurban railway or train. *US*. E20.

interval /ˈɪntəv(ə)l/ *noun*. Also (in sense 5) *-**vale** /-veɪl/. ME.
[ORIGIN Old French *entreval(e)*, *-valle* (mod. *intervalle*) ult. from Latin *intervallum* orig. = space between ramparts, formed as INTER- 2 + *vallum* rampart. Var. in sense 5 by assoc. with VALE *noun*[2].]
1 The period of time between two events, actions, parts of an action, etc.; a pause; *spec*. a break in a theatre etc. performance. ME. ▸**b** *spec*. The period between recurrences of a disease or condition, esp. an intermittent fever. Now *rare* or *obsolete*. M17.

> R. ELLMANN He was bored at times, during intervals between visits of friends.

2 An open space between two things or two parts of the same thing; a gap, an opening. LME.
3 The space of time intervening between two points of time; an intervening time. Orig. in ***by intervals*** below. L16. ▸**b** PHYSICS. A quantity, invariant under the Lorentz transformation, that represents the separation of two events in space-time. E20.

> W. S. CHURCHILL The interval of twelve years had been filled by events without name or sanction.

4 MUSIC. The difference of pitch between two sounds, in melody or harmony. E17.

> A. KOESTLER Attunement of the strings to the intervals in the scale.

5 A low-level tract of land, esp. along a river. M17.
6 The distance between persons or things in respect of position, qualities, etc. M19.

> A. BAIN From turtle to stale oat-cakes, or a piece of black bread, what a mighty interval!

7 MATH. A range between one numerical value and another; *spec*. a set composed of all the numbers between two given numbers, or an analogously defined subset of any partially ordered set. M19.
– PHRASES: **at intervals** (*a*) now and again, not continuously; (*b*) here and there. ***at short intervals***: see SHORT *adjective*. †**by intervals** (*a*) = ***at intervals*** (a) above; (*b*) alternately. **closed interval** MATH.: including the terminal numbers. ***compound interval***: see COMPOUND *adjective*. **open interval** MATH.: excluding the terminal numbers. ***simple interval***: see SIMPLE *adjective*.
– COMB.: **interval signal**: indicating continuity of transmission during a short break in a broadcast programme; **interval training** ATHLETICS: in which a runner alternately runs and jogs over set distances (cf. REPETITION ***training***).
■ **interˈvallary** *adjective* (*rare*) = INTERVALLIC M19. **interˈvallic** *adjective* of or pertaining to an interval or intervals M19.

interval /ˈɪntəv(ə)l/ *verb*. *rare*. Infl. **-ll-**, *** -l-**. M17.
[ORIGIN from the noun.]
†**1** *verb intrans*. Come between or in an interval; form an interval. Only in M17.
2 *verb trans*. Orig., separate by an interval; administer at intervals. Later, break or interrupt at intervals. M17.

intervale *noun* see INTERVAL *noun*.

†**intervallum** *noun*. Pl. **-lla**, **-llums**. L16–M17.
[ORIGIN Latin: see INTERVAL *noun*.]
= INTERVAL *noun* 1, 3.

intervalometer /ɪntəvəˈlɒmɪtə/ *noun*. M20.
[ORIGIN from INTERVAL *noun* + -OMETER.]
PHOTOGRAPHY. An attachment for a camera that enables photographs to be taken regularly at set intervals.

intervein /ɪntəˈveɪn/ *verb trans*. E17.
[ORIGIN from INTER- 1 + VEIN *noun* or *verb*.]
1 Intersect (as) with veins. E17.
2 Place in alternate veins. Usu. in *pass*. E19.

intervene /ɪntəˈviːn/ *verb*. L16.
[ORIGIN Latin *intervenire*, formed as INTER- + *venire* come.]
†**1** *verb trans*. Come between, interfere with; prevent, hinder. L16–M19.

> DE QUINCEY Woodlands of birch . . intervening the different estates with natural sylvan marches.

2 *verb intrans*. Come in as something extraneous. L16.

> WORDSWORTH In his worst pursuits . . sometimes there did intervene Pure hopes of high intent.

3 *verb intrans*. Happen or take place between other events; occur in the meantime. E17.

> CARLYLE If some cleaning of the Augis stable have not intervened for a long while.

4 *verb intrans*. (Of space or time) extend or lie *between* places or events; (of a thing) lie, be situated, *between*. E17.

> J. BUCHAN The long ridge which intervenes between the Chilterns and Cotswold. T. PYNCHON In the years intervening Oedipa had remembered Jesus.

5 *verb intrans*. Come between, esp. so as to modify or prevent a result etc.; interfere; LAW (formerly esp. of the King's or Queen's Proctor in a divorce case) interpose in a lawsuit to which one was not an original party. M17.

> W. S. CHURCHILL Britain . . had refused to intervene in the internal affairs of Italy. R. CHURCH Before Mother could intervene, Jack accepted the situation.

intervener /ɪntəˈviːnə/ *noun*[1]. E17.
[ORIGIN from INTERVENE + -ER[1].]
A person who intervenes; LAW a person who intervenes in a lawsuit to which he or she was not an original party.
■ Also **intervenor** *noun* M19.

intervener /ɪntəˈviːnə/ *noun*[2]. M19.
[ORIGIN formed as INTERVENER *noun*[1] after *interpleader* etc.: see -ER[4].]
LAW. The intervention of a person in a lawsuit.

intervenient /ɪntəˈviːnɪənt/ *adjective & noun*. L16.
[ORIGIN Latin *intervenient-* pres. ppl stem of *intervenire*: see INTERVENE, -ENT.]
▸ **A** *adjective*. **1** That comes in between; that comes in as something extraneous. L16.
2 That lies or is situated between other things or points in space. E17.
3 Occurring between certain points of time or events. E17.
4 Intervening in action; intermediary. M17.
▸ **B** *noun*. A person who intervenes, an intervener. E17.
■ †**intervenience** *noun* the fact of intervening; (an) intervention: E17–E19.

intervent /ɪntəˈvɛnt/ *verb trans*. Long *rare*. L16.
[ORIGIN Latin *intervent-*: see INTERVENTION.]
Come between, obstruct, thwart.

intervention /ɪntəˈvɛnʃ(ə)n/ *noun*. LME.
[ORIGIN French, or Latin *interventio(n-)*, from *intervent-* pa. ppl stem of *intervenire*: see INTERVENE, -ION.]
1 The action or an act of coming between or interfering, esp. so as to modify or prevent a result etc.; LAW the action or an act of one, not originally a party to a suit, who intervenes. LME.

> N. CHOMSKY A massive American intervention in the internal affairs of Laos in an effort to defeat the . . insurgents. G. WINOKUR Depression is a clinical state often requiring intervention.

2 Intermediate agency; the fact of coming in or being employed as an intermediary. M17.

> A. BROOKNER A world from which Oscar had been miraculously freed by the intervention of chance.

3 The fact of coming or being situated between in place, time, or order. M17. ▸**b** An intervening thing, event, or period of time. L17.

> ADAM SMITH Notwithstanding the intervention of one or two dear years.

■ **interventional** *adjective* of or pertaining to intervention E19. **interventionism** *noun* the principle or practice of intervention E20. **interventionist** *noun* a person who favours intervention M19.

interventor /ɪntəˈvɛntə/ *noun*. E18.
[ORIGIN Latin, in late Latin = mediator, formed as INTERVENTION: see -OR.]
A person who intervenes.

interversion /ɪntəˈvəːʃ(ə)n/ *noun*. M18.
[ORIGIN Late Latin *interversio(n-)*, from Latin *intervers-* pa. ppl stem of *intervertere*: see INTERVERT, -ION.]
†**1** Embezzlement. Only in M18.
2 The action or an act of giving a different turn to; changing, inverting. M20.

intervert /ɪntəˈvəːt/ *verb trans*. Now *rare*. L16.
[ORIGIN Latin *intervertere*, formed as INTER- + *vertere* to turn.]
†**1** Put to a use other than that intended; misapply, misuse. L16–M17. ▸**b** Divert to one's own use, embezzle. E17–M19.
2 Give a different turn to; change, invert. M17.

interview /ˈɪntəvjuː/ *noun*. Also †**enter-**. E16.
[ORIGIN French †*entreveue*, *-vue*, from *entrevoir* have a glimpse of, *s'entrevoir* see each other (formed as ENTER-[1], INTER- + *voir* see), after *vue* VIEW *noun*.]
1 A meeting of people face to face, esp. for the purpose of consultation. E16. ▸**b** A meeting or conversation between a journalist or radio or television presenter and a person whose views are sought for publication or broadcasting; the published or broadcast result of this. M19. ▸**c** An oral examination of a candidate for employment, a place in higher education, etc. Also, an interrogation of a person by the police etc. about a specific event. E20.

> M. M. KAYE The interview had been a short one . . both had confined themselves to a few words. **b** C. ACHEBE I read an interview he gave to a popular magazine. W. SOYINKA My picture appeared in the New York Times as the result of a press interview. **c** T. CAPOTE Young Rupp . . had already undergone one extensive interrogation, and . . was scheduled for a second interview. R. INGALLS She looked through the want ads and wrote for interviews.

†**2** **a** Looking into, inspection. M–L16. ▸**b** A view, a glance, a glimpse, (*of* a thing). E17–E18.
†**3** Mutual view (*of* each other). *rare*. E–M17.

interview /ˈɪntəvjuː/ *verb*. Also †**enter-**. M16.
[ORIGIN Partly from French *entrevu* pa. pple of *(s')entrevoir* (see INTERVIEW *noun*) on the analogy of INTERVIEW *noun*, partly from INTERVIEW *noun*.]
†**1** *verb intrans. & trans*. Have a personal meeting (with). Only in M16.
†**2** *verb trans*. Catch a glimpse of, glance at, view. L16–E17.
3 *verb trans*. Conduct an interview with (a person), esp. (of a journalist or radio or television presenter) with someone whose views are sought for publication or broadcasting. Also, conduct an oral examination of (a candidate for employment, a place in higher education, etc.); (of the police etc.) interrogate (a person) about a specific event. M19. ▸**b** *verb intrans*. Conduct an interview or interviews. M20.

> B. MOORE The reporters tried to interview him. *Sunday Post (Glasgow)* The police chief issued a description of a man they want to interview.

4 *verb intrans*. Of a candidate for employment, a place in higher education, etc.: undergo an interview; perform *well*, *badly*, etc., when being interviewed. L20.
■ **interviewˈee** *noun* a person who is interviewed L19. **interviewer** *noun* M19.

intervisit /ɪntəˈvɪzɪt/ *verb intrans*. E17.
[ORIGIN French *entrevisiter*, formed as ENTER-[1], INTER- + *visiter* to visit.]
Exchange visits.

inter vivos /ɪntə ˈviːvəʊs/ *adverbial & adjectival phr*. M19.
[ORIGIN Latin.]
(Made) between living people (esp. of a gift as opp. to a legacy).

intervocal /ɪntəˈvəʊk(ə)l/ *adjective*. *rare*. L19.
[ORIGIN from INTER- 2 + Latin *vocalis* vocal, a vowel.]
Intervocalic.

intervocalic /ˌɪntəvə(ʊ)ˈkalɪk/ *adjective*. L19.
[ORIGIN formed as INTERVOCAL + -IC.]
Occurring between vowels.
■ **intervocalically** *adverb* M20.

intervolution /ɪntəvəˈluːʃ(ə)n/ *noun*. M19.
[ORIGIN from INTERVOLVE after *involve*, *involution*.]
Intervolved condition; a winding.

intervolve /ɪntəˈvɒlv/ *verb*. M17.
[ORIGIN from INTER- 1 + Latin *volvere* to roll, after *involve* etc.]
1 *verb trans*. Wind or roll up (things) within each other; wind or involve (a thing) within the coils of something else. M17.
2 *verb intrans*. Wind within each other. *rare*. L19.

interweave /ɪntəˈwiːv/ *verb*. Also †**enter-**. Pa. t. **-wove** /-ˈwəʊv/; pa. pple **-woven** /-ˈwəʊv(ə)n/, **-wove**. L16.
[ORIGIN from INTER- 1 + WEAVE *verb*[1].]
1 *verb trans*. Weave together, interlace, (things, one thing *with* another). L16.

Scotsman The interweaving of delicately-coloured silk threads on a grey ground.

2 *verb trans.* Blend (things) intimately. L16.

D. W. GOODWIN Drinking became interwoven with everything pleasurable.

3 *verb intrans.* Be or become interwoven. E19.

interwind /ɪntəˈwʌɪnd/ *verb.* Pa. t. & pple **-wound** /-ˈwaʊnd/. L17.
[ORIGIN from INTER- 1 + WIND *verb*[1].]
1 *verb trans.* Wind together (things, one thing *with* another); intertwine. L17.
2 *verb intrans.* Be or become interwound. L19.

interwork /ɪntəˈwəːk/ *verb.* Pa. t. & pple **interworked**, (earlier, now *arch. & literary*) **interwrought** /ɪntəˈrɔːt/. E17.
[ORIGIN from INTER- 1 + WORK *verb.*]
1 *verb trans.* Work (a thing) into and through another; combine (things) by interpenetration. E17.
2 *verb intrans.* Work upon each other; interact. M19.

interwound *verb pa. t. & pple* of INTERWIND.

interwove *verb pa. t. & pple*: see INTERWEAVE.

interwoven /ɪntəˈwəʊv(ə)n/ *adjective.* M17.
[ORIGIN pa. pple of INTERWEAVE.]
Woven together, interlaced; intimately blended together.
■ **interwovenly** *adverb* (*rare*) L17.

interwoven *verb pa. pple*: see INTERWEAVE.

interwreathe /ɪntəˈriːð/ *verb trans.* M17.
[ORIGIN from INTER- 1 + WREATHE *verb.*]
Wreathe together; intertwine (as) in a wreath.

interwrought *verb* see INTERWORK.

†**intestable** *adjective.* L16.
[ORIGIN Late Latin *intestabilis*, formed as IN-[3] + *testabilis*, from *testari*: see INTESTATE.]
1 Legally incapable of making, or of benefiting by, a will. L16–M18.
2 Disqualified from being a witness or giving evidence. Only in M17.

intestacy /ɪnˈtɛstəsi/ *noun.* M18.
[ORIGIN from INTESTATE *adjective* + -ACY.]
LAW. The condition or fact of dying without having made a will.

intestate /ɪnˈtɛsteɪt/ *adjective & noun.* LME.
[ORIGIN Latin *intestatus*, formed as IN-[3] + TESTATE *adjective*[1]: see -ATE[2].]
▸ **A** *adjective.* **1** Not having made a will. LME.

R. GITTINGS Her husband had died intestate, and she . . took a year to obtain administration of his estate.

2 Not disposed of by will; belonging to the estate of an intestate; of or pertaining to an intestate. M16.

S. HALLIFAX The Roman Law concerning Intestate Succession.

▸ **B** *noun.* A person who dies without making a will. M17.

intestation /ɪntɛˈsteɪʃ(ə)n/ *noun. rare.* M19.
[ORIGIN from IN-[3] + TESTATION, after *intestate.*]
Deprivation of the right of making a will.

intestinal /ɪnˈtɛstɪn(ə)l/ *adjective.* LME.
[ORIGIN from INTESTINE *noun* + -AL[1].]
Of or pertaining to the intestines; found in or affecting the intestines.
intestinal flora symbiotic bacteria normally present in the gut. ***vasoactive intestinal polypeptide***, ***vasoactive intestinal peptide***: see VASOACTIVE.

intestine /ɪnˈtɛstɪn/ *noun.* LME.
[ORIGIN Latin *intestinum*, use as noun of neut. of *intestinus*: see INTESTINE *adjective.*]
sing. & (usu.) in *pl.* The lower part of the alimentary canal, from the pyloric end of the stomach to the anus. In *sing.* also the whole alimentary canal from the mouth downward, esp. in invertebrate animals. Cf. BOWEL *noun*, GUT *noun*
large intestine the caecum, colon, and rectum collectively. **small intestine** the duodenum, jejunum, and ileum collectively.

intestine /ɪnˈtɛstɪn/ *adjective.* LME.
[ORIGIN Latin *intestinus*, from *intus* within: see -INE[1].]
1 Taking place within a nation; internal, domestic, civil. LME.
†**2** Inborn, inward, innate. L16–L17.
†**3** Taking place within the body; seated in the bowels; intestinal. E17–E18.
4 Taking place within any thing or place; internal, interior. Now *rare.* E17.

†**inthral(l)** *verbs* vars. of ENTHRAL.

†**inthrone** *verb* var. of ENTHRONE.

inthronize *verb* var. of ENTHRONIZE.

inthrust /ɪnˈθrʌst/ *adjective. rare.* M17.
[ORIGIN from IN-[1] + pa. pple of THRUST *verb.*]
That is or has been thrust in.

inti /ˈɪnti/ *noun.* Pl. same. L20.
[ORIGIN Spanish from Quechua *ynti* sun, the Inca sun god.]
A former monetary unit of Peru, equal to 100 céntimos.

†**intice** *verb*, †**inticement** *noun*, vars. of ENTICE, ENTICEMENT.

intichiuma /ˌɪntɪtʃɪˈuːmə/ *noun pl.* L19.
[ORIGIN Arrernte.]
Sacred ceremonies performed by some Central Australian Aborigines with the purpose of increasing the totemic plants or animals, and thus ensuring a good food supply.

intifada /ɪntɪˈfɑːdə/ *noun.* L20.
[ORIGIN Arabic *intifāda* shaking off.]
An uprising by Arabs; *spec.* that begun by Palestinians in 1987 against Israelis.

intill /ɪnˈtɪl/ *preposition.* Also **intil.** ME.
[ORIGIN from IN *adverb* + TILL *preposition.*]
1 Of motion, direction, change of condition: into. *Scot. & N. English.* ME.
2 Of place, position, condition, state, time: in. *Scot.* LME.

intilted /ˈɪntɪltɪd/ *ppl adjective.* M20.
[ORIGIN from IN-[1] + TILT *verb*[1] + -ED[1].]
Tilted inwards.

intima /ˈɪntɪmə/ *noun.* Pl. **-mae** /-miː/. L19.
[ORIGIN Abbreviation of TUNICA *intima.*]
ANATOMY & ZOOLOGY. The innermost coating or membrane of a part or organ, esp. of a vein or artery.

intimacy /ˈɪntɪməsi/ *noun.* M17.
[ORIGIN from INTIMATE *adjective* + -ACY.]
1 Intimate friendship or acquaintance; close familiarity; an instance of this. M17. ▸**b** *euphem.* Sexual intercourse. L17.

A. FRASER So great was their intimacy that rumours of a stronger tie—amorous, even marital—persisted. **b** *Westminster Gazette* She stayed the night . . at his father's house . . . Intimacy took place on that occasion.

†**2** Inner or inmost nature; an inward quality or feature. M17–L18.
3 Intimate or close connection or union. *rare.* E18.
4 Closeness of observation or knowledge. E18.

†**intimado** *noun.* Pl. **-os.** L17–E19.
[ORIGIN Alt. of INTIMATE *noun* after Spanish words in -ADO.]
= INTIMATE *noun* 2.

intimal /ˈɪntɪm(ə)l/ *adjective.* E20.
[ORIGIN from INTIMA + -AL[1].]
ANATOMY & ZOOLOGY. Of the intima.

intimate /ˈɪntɪmət/ *noun & adjective.* E17.
[ORIGIN Late Latin *intimatus* pa. pple of *intimare*, from *intimus* (noun) a close friend, (adjective) innermost: see -ATE[2].]
▸ **A** *noun.* †**1** A characteristic example of a human type. Only in E17.
2 A very close friend or associate. E17.
▸ **B** *adjective.* **1** Of or pertaining to the inmost nature or fundamental character of a thing; essential; intrinsic. Now chiefly in scientific use. M17. ▸**b** Entering deeply or closely into a matter. E19.
2 Proceeding from, concerning, or relating to one's deepest thoughts or feelings; closely personal, private. M17.
3 Involving very close connection or union; thoroughly mixed, united. M17.

R. W. EMERSON There is an intimate interdependence of intellect and morals.

4 Of knowledge: resulting from close familiarity; deep, extensive. M17.
5 United by friendship or other personal relationship; familiar, close. Also, pertaining to or dealing with close personal relations. M17. ▸**b** Familiarly associated; closely personal. L19. ▸**c** Having or seeking to create an informal, warm, friendly atmosphere. E20.

L. M. MONTGOMERY An intimate friend, . . a really kindred spirit to whom I can confide my inmost soul. A. N. WILSON Having children in common . . they had something more . . intimate than could ever be shared by friends and lovers. J. KRANTZ Waking up with someone seemed more intimate than making love in some ways. **b** H. JAMES These diminutive intimate things bring one near to the Old Roman life. **c** W. BOYD The armchairs had been arranged in intimate groups.

6 *euphem.* Having sexual intercourse (*with, together*). L19. ▸**b** Pertaining to or involving the sexual organs or bodily orifices. E20.

R. MACAULAY Some of them were . . what newspapers call intimate together, without having undergone marriage. **b** K. AMIS There was a long, fairly passionate embrace with a certain amount of intimate caressing. *Times* Intimate searches (of body orifices) will be conducted by police officers.

■ **intimately** *adverb* M17.

intimate /ˈɪntɪmeɪt/ *verb trans.* E16.
[ORIGIN Late Latin *intimat-* pa. ppl stem of *intimare* announce: see INTIMATE *noun & adjective*, -ATE[3].]
1 Make known formally; announce, state. E16.

Manchester Examiner A notice . . intimating a reduction of ten per cent in the wages of miners.

2 *gen.* Make known; indicate; imply, hint at. M16. ▸**b** Mention indirectly or in passing. M17.

B. T. BRADFORD He had gently intimated that he thought the committee members were panicking unnecessarily. A. ARONSON Those areas of human conflict that the stage could only intimate but not portray.

†**3** Make intimate, familiarize. E–M17.

intimation /ɪntɪˈmeɪʃ(ə)n/ *noun.* LME.
[ORIGIN Old French & mod. French, or late Latin *intimatio(n-)*, formed as INTIMATE *verb*: see -ATION.]
1 The action or an act of making known or announcing something; (a) formal notification or announcement. LME. ▸**b** LAW. Notification of a requirement made by law, coupled with an announcement of the penalty that will be incurred in case of default. Now *rare* or *obsolete.* M17.
2 The action or an act of making known informally or indirectly; an indication; a suggestion, a hint. M16.

intime /ɛ̃tim/ *adjective.* E17.
[ORIGIN French, from Latin *intimus* innermost.]
Intimate. Now only *spec.* friendly, familiar, cosy.
– NOTE: Formerly fully naturalized.

intimidate /ɪnˈtɪmɪdeɪt/ *verb trans.* M17.
[ORIGIN medieval Latin *intimidat-* pa. ppl stem of *intimidare*, from Latin IN-[2] + *timidus* TIMID: see -ATE[3].]
Terrify, overawe, cow. Now *esp.* force to or deter from some action by threats or violence.

M. MEAD They permit themselves to be . . bullied and intimidated and bribed by their more aggressive neighbours. L. GORDON She was intimidated by the achievements of Austen, Meredith, and Hardy.

■ **intimiˈdation** *noun* the action of intimidating someone, now *esp.* in order to interfere with the free exercise of political or social rights; the fact or condition of being intimidated: M17. **intimidator** *noun* a person who intimidates someone or employs intimidation M19. **intimiˈdatory** *adjective* tending, or intended, to intimidate M19.

intimism /ˈɪntɪmɪz(ə)m/ *noun.* Also ***intimisme*** /ɛ̃timism/. E20.
[ORIGIN French *intimisme*, formed as INTIME, -ISM.]
A style of intimate domestic genre painting using impressionist techniques.

intimist /ˈɪntɪmɪst/ *noun & adjective.* Also ***intimiste*** /ɛ̃timist (*pl. same*)/ E20.
[ORIGIN from (the same root as) INTIMISM: see -IST.]
▸ **A** *noun.* A painter following the principles of intimism. E20.
▸ **B** *adjective.* Of or pertaining to intimism. M20.

intimity /ɪnˈtɪmɪti/ *noun.* E17.
[ORIGIN from INTIME + -ITY. In sense 2 app. from French *intimité.*]
1 Close friendship, intimacy. *rare.* E17.

W. OWEN I . . suffer a hunger for Intimity . . I ought to be in love and am not.

2 Intimate quality or nature; inwardness; privacy. L19.

Saturday Review One of the very best pictures of . . a Court 'in intimity' that exists.

intinction /ɪnˈtɪŋ(k)ʃ(ə)n/ *noun.* M16.
[ORIGIN Late Latin *intinctio(n-)*, from Latin *intinct-* pa. ppl stem of *intingere* dip in: see -ION.]
†**1** *gen.* The action of dipping in, esp. in something coloured; the liquid in which something has been dipped. M16–M17.
2 ECCLESIASTICAL. The action or practice of dipping the bread of the Eucharist in the wine so that the communicant may receive both together. L19.

intine /ˈɪntɪn, -ʌɪn/ *noun.* M19.
[ORIGIN from Latin *intimus* innermost, after EXTINE.]
BOTANY. The inner wall of a pollen grain. Opp. EXINE.

†**intire** *adjective, adverb, & noun* var. of ENTIRE *adjective, adverb, & noun.*

†**intitle** *verb* var. of ENTITLE.

intitulation /ɪnˌtɪtjʊˈleɪʃ(ə)n/ *noun.* LME.
[ORIGIN Old French, or medieval Latin *intitulatio(n-)* from late Latin *intitulat-* pa. ppl stem of *intitulare*: see INTITULE, -ATION.]
1 The action of entitling or providing something with a title or superscription; a superscription, a title. LME.
2 The action of bestowing a title; a designation. L16.

intitule /ɪnˈtɪtjuːl/ *verb trans.* Also †**en-.** L15.
[ORIGIN Old French & mod. French *intituler* ENTITLE.]
1 Provide (a book or document) with a heading or superscription; entitle (a book etc.). L15. ▸†**b** Ascribe (a book) *to* a person as its author. M–L16. ▸†**c** Prefix *to* a book the name of a person to whom it is dedicated. M–L17.
†**2** Dedicate *to* by name or title; name after someone. L15–E18.
3 Give a (specified) title or designation to. *arch.* M16.
†**4** Provide (a person) with a title *to* an estate; *gen.* give (a person or thing) a rightful claim *to* a possession, privilege, designation, etc., or *to be, have,* or *do* something. L16–L18. ▸†**b** Invest with a rank, function, etc. L16–E17.
†**5** Represent (something) as the cause of a particular action or effect. (Foll. by *to.*) M17–E18.

into /ˈɪntʊ, ˈɪntə/ *preposition & adjective.*
[ORIGIN Old English *in(n)tō* from IN *adverb* + TO *preposition*, where the adverb expresses general direction, and the preposition refers to a particular point or place.]

▸ **A** *preposition.* **I** Of motion or direction: ordinary uses.

1 After words expr. or implying motion: to a position within a space or thing having material extension; to the interior of; so as to enter. **OE.** ▸**b** With the verb understood by ellipsis, or expressed in a verbal noun or other word. **L15.**

J. BUCHAN I got into the train at Victoria. J. STEINBECK He slipped his feet into his sandals. A. CARTER A cold misery was seeping into her bones. V. S. PRITCHETT Sheep . . loaded into lorries. **b** R. KIPLING At dusk he harries the Abazai—at dawn he is into Bonair.

2 Pregnant uses. ▸**a** So as to be possessed by. **OE.** ▸**b** Before a collective noun: expr. admission to membership or participation. **M16.**

a *Law Times* Alternative modes of getting the legal estate into the same person. **b** J. BARNES She had been born into the Norman nobility. P. BOOTH She had been . . the first to buy into the Polo Club.

3 Introducing a new condition, state, or activity entered upon or begun. **OE.**

V. WOOLF What awful fix had they got themselves into? G. GREENE We would launch into literary criticism. I. MURDOCH She went into . . infectious fits of laughter.

4 a Introducing the substance or form which anything becomes or takes up. **ME.** ▸**b** Introducing the condition or result brought about by some action. **M16.**

a T. HARDY A yew bush cut into a quaint . . shape. R. HARDY The sound seemed . . first sibilant, then deepening into menace. W. BRONK To . . translate what someone said / in one language into another. **b** *Argosy* Only too glad . . to drink themselves into a stupor. W. GOLDING Plato's Golden Children are bred and trained into fitness.

5 Introducing the parts produced by division, breaking, folding, etc. **LME.**

THOMAS HUGHES Tearing up old newspapers . . into small pieces. R. MACAULAY Jane went . . , her world tumbling into bits about her.

6 In reference to a non-physical thing, esp. a realm of thought or department of the mind, treated as having extension or content. **E16.**

R. MACAULAY Things Katherine . . just took into consideration. I. MURDOCH Sidney . . offered to initiate me into the pleasures of . . wine.

7 *MATH.* **a** Expr. the relationship of a multiplier to a multiplicand. *arch.* **M16.** ▸**b** Expr. the relationship of a divisor to a dividend. **M20.** ▸**c** Expr. the relationship of a set to its image under a mapping when not every element of the image set has an inverse image in the first set. Cf. sense B. below and **ONTO.** **M20.**

a J. PLAYFAIR The weight multiplied into the height to which it is raised.

8 To a (freq. far advanced) point in (a period of time). **L16.**

A. S. BYATT After parties, he worked into the small hours. R. COBB My mother . . could walk quite fast well on into her seventies.

9 Expr. direction without actual motion of the agent after such verbs as *turn, look, search.* **E17.**

D. ABSE Then he stared into the fire. R. HARDY He . . removed his shirt, facing into the faint wind.

10 As an addition to. Now only in ***into the bargain*** s.v. **BARGAIN** *noun* 2. **M17.**

11 So as to collide with or come in forcible contact with. **E19.**

Cape Times The delivery van ran into a flock of sheep, killing 25. G. HOUSEHOLD I nearly walked slap into a sentry.

tear into: see **TEAR** *verb*[1].

▸ **II 12** Of position: = **IN** *preposition.* Long chiefly *Scot.* **OE.**

J. KNOX Devouring woulves into sheip skynnes.

13 Interested or involved in; knowledgeable about. *colloq.* **M20.**

Listener Margaret is 'into' astrology and consults the *I-Ching.* M. ATWOOD They could be violent, into whips.

▸ †**III 14** Even to (a place or point); to the very —. **ME–M16.**

15 Towards, in the direction of. Cf. sense 9 above. **ME–M17.**

16 Until, on to, up to (a time or date). **LME–M16.**

17 Unto, to (a thing or person). **LME–E17.**

SHAKES. *Cymb.* That he enchants societies into him.

18 Unto (a purpose or result); in order to, with a view to. **LME–E16.**

19 Defining the particular part of anything in which it is penetrated, pierced, etc. **E16–L18.**

DEFOE I . . fired again, and shot him into the head.

▸ **B** *adjective. MATH.* Designating a mapping of one set on a subset of another. **M20.**

in-toed /ˈɪntəʊd/ *adjective.* **L18.**
[**ORIGIN** from **IN** *adverb* + **TOED.**]
Having the toes turned inwards.

intolerable /ɪnˈtɒl(ə)rəb(ə)l/ *adjective & adverb.* **LME.**
[**ORIGIN** Old French & mod. French *intolérable* or Latin *intolerabilis*, from **IN-**[3] + *tolerabilis* **TOLERABLE.**]

▸ **A** *adjective.* **1** That cannot be tolerated or put up with; unbearable, insupportable. **LME.** ▸†**b** Excessive, extreme, exceedingly great. Cf. **AWFUL** *adjective* 4. **M16–E18.**

A. MACLEAN The strain on the . . arm was intolerable, . . as if the shoulder sinews were being torn apart. J. KRANTZ He was intolerable, she loathed the very sound of his voice. **b** SHAKES. *1 Hen. IV* O monstrous but one halfpenny-worth of bread to this intolerable deal of sack!

2 That cannot be withstood, irresistible. *rare.* **LME.**

Harper's Magazine To . . scourge away . . Hassan's men with intolerable musketry.

▸ †**B** *adverb.* Intolerably, insufferably; exceedingly, extremely. **L16–E18.**

M. COWPER Dr. Dunster preached an intolerable dull Sermon.

■ **intoleraˈbility** *noun* the quality of being intolerable; intolerableness: **L16.** **intolerableness** *noun* **L16.** **intolerably** *adverb* (*a*) in an intolerable manner or degree; unbearably; †(*b*) excessively, extremely: **LME.**

intolerant /ɪnˈtɒl(ə)r(ə)nt/ *adjective & noun.* **M18.**
[**ORIGIN** Latin *intolerant-*, from **IN-**[3] + *tolerant-* pres. ppl stem of *tolerare* **TOLERATE**: see **-ANT**[1].]

▸ **A** *adjective* **1 a** Not having the capacity to tolerate or endure a specified thing. Foll. by *of.* **M18.** ▸**b** *ECOLOGY.* Unable to flourish under certain conditions; *spec.* (of trees or other plants) unable to flourish in deep shade. **L19.**

a D. W. GOODWIN More women than men are physiologically intolerant of alcohol.

2 *spec.* Not tolerating opinions or practices different from one's own, esp. in religious matters; denying or refusing to others the right to dissent. **M18.**

H. MORLEY One or other of the rival creeds in its most . . intolerant form.

▸ **B** *noun.* An intolerant person. **M18.**

■ **intolerance** *noun* (*a*) the fact or quality of being intolerant of something; (*b*) *spec.* absence of tolerance for difference of opinion or practice, esp. in religious matters; narrow-minded or bigoted opposition to dissent: **M18.** †**intolerancy** *noun* (*rare*) = **INTOLERANCE** **E17–L18.** **intolerantly** *adverb* **M18.**

†**intolerating** *adjective.* **E18–M19.**
[**ORIGIN** from **IN-**[3] + *tolerating* pres. pple of **TOLERATE.**]
= **INTOLERANT.**

intoleration /ˌɪntɒləˈreɪʃ(ə)n/ *noun. rare.* **M16.**
[**ORIGIN** from **IN-**[3] + **TOLERATION.**]
Lack of toleration; intolerance. Formerly also, impatience.

†**intomb** *verb* var. of **ENTOMB.**

intombi /ɪnˈtɒmbi/ *noun.* **E19.**
[**ORIGIN** Xhosa, Zulu.]
In southern Africa: a young black woman who has been ritually prepared for marriage.

intonable /ɪnˈtəʊnəb(ə)l/ *adjective.* **M19.**
[**ORIGIN** from **INTONE** *verb* + **-ABLE.**]
Able to be intoned.

intonaco /ɪnˈtəʊnəkəʊ/ *noun.* Also **-ico** /-ɪkəʊ/. Pl. **-os.** **E19.**
[**ORIGIN** Italian *intonico*, †*-aco*, from *intonicare* cover with plaster, ult. from Latin *tunica* coat, **TUNIC.**]
The final coating of plaster spread upon a wall or other surface, esp. for fresco painting.

intonate /ˈɪntəneɪt/ *verb*[1] *trans.* Now *rare.* **E17.**
[**ORIGIN** Latin *intonat-* pa. ppl stem of *intonare*, from **IN-**[2] + *tonare* to thunder: see **-ATE**[3].]
Utter with a loud voice like thunder.

intonate /ˈɪntəneɪt/ *verb*[2] *trans.* **L18.**
[**ORIGIN** medieval Latin *intonat-* pa. ppl stem of *intonare* **INTONE** *verb*: see **-ATE**[3].]

1 Recite in a singing voice; intone. **L18.**

2 Utter or pronounce with a particular tone; give a specified intonation to. **E19.**

3 *PHONETICS.* Voice (a consonant). *rare.* **M19.**

intonation /ɪntəˈneɪʃ(ə)n/ *noun.* **E17.**
[**ORIGIN** medieval Latin *intonatio(n-)*, formed as **INTONATE** *verb*[2]: see **-ATION.**]

1 *ECCLESIASTICAL.* The opening phrase of a plainsong melody, preceding the reciting note, and usu. sung either by the priest alone, or by one or a few of the choristers; the recitation of this. **E17.**

2 The action of intoning, or reciting in a singing voice; *esp.* the musical recitation of psalms, prayers, etc., in a liturgy, usu. in monotone. **L18.**

3 The utterance or production (by the voice, an instrument, etc.) of musical tones, with ref. to manner or style, esp. to exactitude of pitch or relation to the key or harmony. **L18.**

J. A. SYMONDS A . . soprano . . true to the least shade in intonation.

4 Manner of utterance of the tones of the voice in speaking; modulation of the voice; accent. **L18.**

J. WAIN The . . voice went on, in a . . sub-Cockney intonation.

– COMB.: **intonation contour** a succession of levels of pitch extending over an utterance; **intonation curve** the rising and falling of pitch within an utterance; **intonation pattern** a pattern of variations in pitch; **intonation phoneme** = **INTONEME.**

■ **intonational** *adjective* of or pertaining to intonation **L19.** **intonationally** *adverb* **M20.**

intonator /ˈɪntə(ʊ)neɪtə/ *noun.* **M18.**
[**ORIGIN** from **INTONE** *verb* + **-ATOR.**]

1 A monochord for the study of musical intervals, with a diagram indicating the divisions of the string necessary for the production of the notes of the scale in exact intonation. Formerly, a tuning fork. **M18.**

2 A person who intones. *rare.* **M19.**

intone /ɪnˈtəʊn/ *noun.* **M16.**
[**ORIGIN** from the verb.]

†**1** Something intoned; a song or chant. Only in **M16.**

2 The action of intoning; the tone of voice used in intoning. **L19.**

intone /ɪnˈtəʊn/ *verb.* Also (earlier, now *rare*) **en-.** **L15.**
[**ORIGIN** medieval Latin *intonare*, formed as **IN-**[2] + *tonus* **TONE** *noun*; *en-* from Old French *entoner* (mod. *entonner*).]

1 *verb trans. & intrans.* Utter in musical tones, chant; *spec.* recite in a singing voice (esp. a psalm, prayer, etc. in a liturgy), usu. in a monotone. **L15.**

A. BURGESS An age-old Hindu prayer was intoned. B. EMECHETA The priest . . kept mumbling and intoning.

2 *verb trans.* Utter with a particular tone or intonation. **M19.**

G. P. MARSH A clear . . and properly intoned . . pronunciation.

■ **intonement** *noun* (*rare*) the action of intoning or chanting **M19.** **intoner** *noun* **M19.**

intoneme /ɪnˈtəʊniːm/ *noun.* **M20.**
[**ORIGIN** Contr. of ***INTONATION phoneme***: see **-EME.**]
An intonation pattern that contributes to the meaning of an utterance.

intonico *noun* var. of **INTONACO.**

intorsion /ɪnˈtɔːʃ(ə)n/ *noun.* **M18.**
[**ORIGIN** French from late Latin *intorsio(n-)*, *intortio(n-)*, from **IN-**[2] + *torsio(n-)* **TORSION.**]
The action of twisting; *spec.* (*a*) *BOTANY* the spiral twisting of the stem of a plant; (*b*) *OPHTHALMOLOGY* rotation of the eyeballs in which the tops approach each other and the bottoms move away from each other.

intorted /ɪnˈtɔːtɪd/ *adjective.* Now *rare.* **E17.**
[**ORIGIN** from Latin *intort-* pa. ppl stem of *intorquere*, from **IN-**[2] + *torquere* to twist: see **-ED**[1].]
Twisted or curled inwards; twisted, wreathed, involved (*lit. & fig.*).

in toto /ɪn ˈtəʊtəʊ/ *adverbial phr.* **L18.**
[**ORIGIN** Latin.]
Completely, without exception; altogether, in all.

Intourist /ˈɪntʊərɪst/ *noun.* **M20.**
[**ORIGIN** Russian *Inturist* abbreviation of *inostrannyĭ turist* foreign tourist.]
(The name of) the State Travel Bureau of the former USSR, dealing with tourists from abroad.

in-town /ˈɪntaʊn; *as adverb* ɪnˈtaʊn/ *noun, adjective, & adverb.* **M16.**
[**ORIGIN** from **IN** *adverb* + **TOWN** *noun.*]

▸ **A** *noun.* = **INFIELD** *noun* 1. *Scot.* **M16.**

▸ **B** *adjective.* Situated or taking place within the centre of a town. **E19.**

▸ **C** *adverb.* Into the centre of a town. **M20.**

intoxicant /ɪnˈtɒksɪk(ə)nt/ *adjective & noun.* **M19.**
[**ORIGIN** from **INTOXICATE** *verb*: see **-ANT**[1]. See also **TOXICANT.**]

▸ **A** *noun.* An intoxicating substance or liquor. **M19.**

▸ **B** *adjective.* Intoxicating. **L19.**

intoxicate /ɪnˈtɒksɪkət/ *ppl adjective.* Now *rare.* **LME.**
[**ORIGIN** medieval Latin *intoxicatus* pa. pple, formed as **INTOXICATE** *verb*: see **-ATE**[2].]

†**1 a** Impregnated in or smeared with poison; rendered poisonous. **LME–M17.** ▸**b** Killed by poison. **L15–E17.**

2 Inebriated, intoxicated (*lit. & fig.*). **L15.**

J. TODHUNTER Such sun and air make me intoxicate With a strange passion.

intoxicate /ɪnˈtɒksɪkeɪt/ *verb.* **LME.**
[**ORIGIN** medieval Latin *intoxicat-* pa. ppl stem of *intoxicare*, from **IN-**[2] + Latin *toxicum* poison: see **TOXIC** *adjective*, **-ATE**[3].]

†**1** *verb trans.* Poison; *fig.* corrupt morally or spiritually. **LME–M19.**

2 *verb trans.* Stupefy, madden or deprive of the ordinary use of the senses or reason with a drug or alcoholic liquor; inebriate, make drunk. **L16.** ▸**b** *fig.* Make unsteady or delirious in mind or feelings; excite or exhilarate beyond self-control. **L16.**

P. PARISH The double scotch . . makes a novice drinker feel unpleasantly intoxicated. **b** J. BUCHAN After . . confinement in London the . . countryside intoxicated me. V. WOOLF Round they whirled, intoxicated by the music.

3 *verb intrans.* Cause intoxication. **L17.**

■ **intoxicatedly** *adverb* like a person who is intoxicated **L19.** **intoxicating** *ppl adjective* causing intoxication (freq. *fig.*) **M17.**

intoxicatingly *adverb* L19. **intoxicative** *adjective* (*rare*) (*a*) tending to intoxicate; †(*b*) poisonous; (*c*) pertaining to or characteristic of intoxication: M17. **intoxicator** *noun* (*rare*) a person who intoxicates; formerly, a poisoner: M18.

intoxication /ɪnˌtɒksɪˈkeɪʃ(ə)n/ *noun*. LME.
[ORIGIN French, or medieval Latin *intoxicatio(n-)*, formed as INTOXICATE *verb*: see -ATION. See also TOXICATION.]
1 The action of poisoning; (an instance of) the state of being poisoned. *obsolete* exc. MEDICINE (now *rare*). LME. ▸†**b** *fig.* The corruption of the moral or mental faculties; a cause or occasion of this. L15–E18.

P. MANSON A class of intoxication diseases which depend on toxins generated by germs.

2 The action of inebriating or making someone stupid, insensible, or disordered in intellect, with a drug or alcoholic liquor; the condition of being so stupefied or disordered. M17. ▸**b** *fig.* The action or power of exhilarating or highly exciting the mind; elation or excitement beyond the bounds of sobriety. E18.

b ALDOUS HUXLEY The intoxication of success had evaporated.

intoximeter /ɪnˈtɒksɪmiːtə/ *noun*. Orig. *US*. Also **I-**. M20.
[ORIGIN from INTOXI(CATION + -METER.]
A device for measuring the alcohol content of a person's breath, esp. in cases of suspected drunken driving.

intra- /ˈɪntrə/ *combining form*.
[ORIGIN Latin (esp. mod. Latin) *intra* on the inside, within. This use of *intra-* does not occur in classical Latin, and is rare in late Latin.]
Forming adjectives (usu. from adjectives) with the sense 'situated, occurring, or carried on within'. Opp. EXTRA-.
– NOTE: Sometimes confused with INTER-.
■ **intra-abˈdominal** *adjective* situated or occurring within the abdomen L19. **intra-arˈterial** *adjective* occurring within or administered into an artery L19. **intra-aˈtomic** *adjective* occurring or existing within an, or the, atom E20. **intraˈcapsular** *adjective* (ANATOMY) situated or occurring within a capsule L19. **intraˈcardiac**, **intraˈcardial** *adjectives* situated or occurring within the heart L19. **intraˈcardially** *adverb* into the heart E20. **intraˈcellular** *adjective* (BIOLOGY) situated or occurring within a, or the, cell or cells L19. **intraˈcellularly** *adverb* (BIOLOGY) within a cell or cells L19. **intraˈcerebral** *adjective* situated or occurring within the cerebrum of the brain L19. **intraˈcerebrally** *adverb* in or into the cerebrum E20. **intraciˈsternal** *adjective* (MEDICINE) occurring within or administered into a cistern of the body, esp. of the brain M20. **intraciˈsternally** *adverb* (by injection) into a cistern M20. **intraˈcoastal** *adjective* situated close to the coast E20. **intracontiˈnental** *adjective* situated or occurring entirely within a continent E20. **intraˈcranial** *adjective* situated or occurring within the cranium or skull M19. **intraˈcranially** *adverb* within or into the cranium E20. **intraˈcultural** *adjective* occurring within a particular culture M20. **intraˈculturally** *adverb* within a culture M20. **intracuˈtaneous** *adjective* = INTRADERMAL L19. **intracuˈtaneously** *adverb* = INTRADERMALLY E20. **intraday** *adjective* occurring within one day L20. **intraˈdermal** *adjective* situated or applied within the skin E20. **intraˈdermally** *adverb* in or into the skin E20. **intraˈdermic** *adjective* = INTRADERMAL L19. **intra-epiˈthelial** *adjective* situated within the epithelium L19. **intra-Euroˈpean** *adjective* occurring or carried on within Europe M20. **intrafaˈllopian** *adjective* (MEDICINE) situated or occurring within a Fallopian tube; ZYGOTE *intrafallopian transfer*: L20. **intrafaˈscicular** *adjective* (BOTANY) situated within a vascular bundle. **intrafoliˈaceous** *adjective* (BOTANY) situated on the inner side of a leaf M18. **intraforˈmational** *adjective* (GEOLOGY) formed or occurring within a geological formation L19. **intraˈgastric** *adjective* applied or situated within the stomach E20. **intraˈgastrically** *adverb* into the stomach M20. **intraˈgenic** *adjective* (BIOLOGY) situated or occurring within a gene L20. **intragroup** *adjective* existing or occurring within a group or between members of a group E20. **intraheˈpatic** *adjective* situated or occurring within the liver E20. **intraˈlingual** *adjective* (*a*) MEDICINE situated or occurring within the tongue; (*b*) = INTRA-LINGUISTIC: L19. **intra-linˈguistic** *adjective* within a given language; within the bounds of language M20. **intraˈlobular** *adjective* (ANATOMY) (esp. of vessels) situated or occurring within the lobules of an organ or structure M19. **intrameˈdullary** *adjective* situated or performed within the medulla of an organ or structure, as of the spinal cord, a bone, etc. L19. **intraˈmembranous** *adjective* (BIOLOGY) situated within or between the layers of a membrane, esp. a cell membrane L19. **intramerˈcurial** *adjective* (ASTRONOMY) situated within the orbit of Mercury L19. **intraˈmontane** *adjective* situated in a mountainous area M19. **intramunˈdane** *adjective* situated or existing within the (material) world M19. **intraˈmuscular** *adjective* situated or taking place within, or administered into a muscle L19. **intraˈmuscularly** *adverb* (by injection) into a muscle E20. **intraˈnational** *adjective* occurring or carried on within a nation state E20. **intraˈnuclear** *adjective* situated within a nucleus (esp. of a cell) L19. **intra-ˈocular** *adjective* situated or occurring within the eyeball E19. **intra-ˈoral** *adjective* situated within the mouth L19. **intraperiˈcardial** *adjective* situated within or administered into the pericardium L19. **intraperitoˈneal** *adjective* situated or taking place within (the cavity of) the peritoneum M19. **intraperitoˈneally** *adverb* within or (esp. by injection) into (the cavity of) the peritoneum L19. **intraˈpersonal** *adjective* taking place or existing within the mind M20. **intraˈpetiolar** *adjective* (BOTANY) (*a*) (of an axillary bud) formed immediately under the base of the petiole and surrounded by it so as not to appear until the leaf has fallen; (*b*) (of a stipule or pair of confluent stipules) situated between the petiole and the axis: M19. **intraˈpsychic**, **intraˈpsychical** *adjectives* (PSYCHOLOGY) occurring or existing within the psyche or self E20. **intraˈpulmonary** *adjective* occurring or administered within the lungs L19. **intraˈracial** *adjective* within, or occurring within, a biological race E20. **intraˈregional** *adjective* occurring or carried on within a region M20. **intraˈspinal** *adjective* occurring within or administered into the spinal cord M19. **intra-subˈjective** *adjective* (PSYCHOLOGY) (of a reaction, response, etc.) occurring within a person E20. **intrathoˈracic** *adjective* situated or occurring within the thorax M19. **intraˈtropical** *adjective* situated or occurring within the tropics E19. **intra-ˈurban** *adjective* carried on within an urban area L19. **intravaˈginal** *adjective* (*a*) ANATOMY situated within the vagina; (*b*) BOTANY within the sheath of a leaf: M19. **intravaˈrietal** *adjective* (BIOLOGY) occurring or existing between individuals of the same variety E20. **intravenˈtricular** *adjective* (ANATOMY) situated or contained within a ventricle of the brain or heart L19. **intravenˈtricularly** *adverb* (ANATOMY) into or within a ventricle M20. **intraˈverbal** *adjective* within a word M20.

intractable /ɪnˈtraktəb(ə)l/ *adjective*. L15.
[ORIGIN Latin *intractabilis*, formed as IN-[3] + TRACTABLE.]
1 Of a thing: difficult to shape or work; not easily treated or dealt with. L15.

J. KRANTZ His hair still jumped up in that intractable cowlick. *Scientific American* Cancer and such intractable viral diseases as AIDS.

2 Of a person or animal: not manageable or docile; uncontrollable; refractory, stubborn. M16.

H. READ The young schoolmaster who had struggled for two years with an intractable group of . . boys.

■ **intractaˈbility** *noun* L16. **intractableness** *noun* M17. **intractably** *adverb* E19.

intractile /ɪnˈtraktɪl, -ʌɪl/ *adjective*. *rare*. E17.
[ORIGIN from IN-[3] + TRACTILE.]
†**1** Incapable of being drawn out in length; not ductile. Only in E17.
2 = INTRACTABLE *adjective* 1. L19.

intrada /ɪnˈtrɑːdə/ *noun*. M18.
[ORIGIN Italian *intrata*, older form of *entrata* entry, prelude.]
MUSIC. An introduction, a prelude.

intrados /ɪnˈtreɪdɒs/ *noun*. L18.
[ORIGIN French, formed as INTRA- + *dos* back.]
ARCHITECTURE. The lower or inner curve of an arch; *esp.* the lower curve of the voussoirs which form the arch. Cf. EXTRADOS.

intraglacial /ɪntrəˈgleɪʃ(ə)l, -sɪəl/ *adjective*. L19.
[ORIGIN from INTRA- + GLACIAL.]
GEOLOGY. **1** Embedded within a glacier; = ENGLACIAL *adjective*. L19.
2 Designating or pertaining to the terrain formerly occupied by a glacier or ice sheet. L19.

†**intrail** *noun* var. of ENTRAIL *noun*[1].

intramolecular /ɪntrəməˈlɛkjʊlə/ *adjective*. L19.
[ORIGIN from INTRA- + MOLECULAR.]
Situated, existing, or occurring within a molecule or the molecules of a body or substance.
■ **intramolecularly** *adverb* within a molecule M20.

intramural /ɪntrəˈmjʊər(ə)l/ *adjective*. M19.
[ORIGIN from INTRA- + Latin *murus* wall + -AL[1].]
1 Situated, existing, or performed within the walls of a city or building or within a community, institution, etc. M19. ▸**b** Forming part of normal university or college studies. E20. ▸**c** Taking place within one educational establishment only. Chiefly *N. Amer.* M20.
2 ANATOMY & BIOLOGY. Situated within the wall of a hollow organ, or of a cell. L19.
■ **intramurally** *adverb* E20.

†**intrance** *verb* var. of ENTRANCE *verb*.

intraneous /ɪnˈtreɪnɪəs/ *adjective*. *rare*. LME.
[ORIGIN from late Latin *intraneus* inner + -OUS.]
Inner, internal; domestic.

Intranet /ˈɪntrənɛt/ *noun*. Also **i-**. L20.
[ORIGIN from INTRA- + NET *noun*[1] after INTERNET.]
TELECOMMUNICATIONS & COMPUTING. A local or restricted communications network; *spec.* a private network created using World Wide Web software.

intransferable /ɪntransˈfəːrəb(ə)l, ɪnˈtransf(ə)r-; -trɑː-, -nz-/ *adjective*. L18.
[ORIGIN from IN-[3] + TRANSFERABLE.]
Not transferable; unable to be transferred.

intransgressible /ɪntranzˈgrɛsɪb(ə)l, -trɑː-, -ns-/ *adjective*. E17.
[ORIGIN from IN-[3] + TRANSGRESS *verb* + -IBLE.]
That cannot or may not be transgressed.

intransient /ɪnˈtransɪənt, -ˈtrɑː-, -nz-/ *adjective*. Now *rare*. M17.
[ORIGIN from IN-[3] + TRANSIENT *adjective*.]
Permanent, unchanging: not passing away or to another.

intransigeance *noun*, **intransigeant** *adjective & noun* vars. of INTRANSIGENCE, INTRANSIGENT.

intransigence /ɪnˈtransɪdʒ(ə)ns, -ˈtrɑː-, -nz-/ *noun*. Also **-geance**. L19.
[ORIGIN from INTRANSIGENT + -ENCE.]
The quality of being intransigent; uncompromising hostility; irreconcilability.
■ Also **intransigency** *noun* L19.

intransigent /ɪnˈtransɪdʒ(ə)nt, -ˈtrɑː-, -nz-/ *adjective & noun*. Also **-geant**. L19.
[ORIGIN French, from Spanish *los intransigentes* the party of the extreme left in the Spanish Cortes (1873–4); ult. formed as IN-[3] + pres. pple of Latin *transigere* come to an understanding: see TRANSACT, -ENT.]
▸ **A** *adjective*. Unwilling to negotiate or make any concession; obdurate, uncompromising. L19.

A. MACLEAN The Lieutenant . . is uncooperative, intransigent and downright disobedient. C. PETERS The Duke of Wellington's intransigent stand against reform might block the passage of the bill.

▸ **B** *noun*. An uncompromising holder of (orig. republican) principles. L19.
■ **intransigentism** *noun* the republican principles of the early intransigents L19. **intransigently** *adverb* E20.

intransitable /ɪnˈtransɪtəb(ə)l, -ˈtrɑː-, -nz-/ *adjective*. *rare*. M19.
[ORIGIN from IN-[3] + TRANSITABLE.]
Intraversable; not offering any means of transit.

intransitive /ɪnˈtransɪtɪv, -ˈtrɑː-, -nz-/ *adjective & noun*. E17.
[ORIGIN Late Latin *intransitivus* not passing over, formed as IN-[3] + TRANSITIVE.]
▸ **A** *adjective*. **1** GRAMMAR. Of a verb, the construction of a verb: expressing action which is limited to the subject; not taking a direct object. Cf. TRANSITIVE *adjective* 2, NEUTER *adjective* 1b. E17.
2 That does not pass on to another person, or beyond certain limits (specified or implied). *rare*. M17.
3 MATH. & LOGIC. Of a relation: of a kind which can exist between a first thing or person and a second, and between the second and a third, but need not exist between the first and the third. Of a group: containing elements in intransitive relation. L19.

B. RUSSELL *Spouse* is symmetrical but intransitive; . . *father* is both asymmetrical and intransitive.

▸ **B** *noun*. An intransitive verb. E19.
■ **intransitively** *adverb* M17. **intransiˈtivity** *noun* the property or quality of being intransitive L19. **intransitivize** *verb trans.* (GRAMMAR) make intransitive; chiefly as ***intransitivizing*** *ppl adjective*: M20.

intransparency /ɪntranˈspar(ə)nsi, -trɑː-; -ˈspɛː-/ *noun*. E20.
[ORIGIN from IN-[3] + TRANSPARENCY.]
The quality of being opaque; an instance of this.

intransparent /ɪntranˈspar(ə)nt, -trɑː-; -ˈspɛː-/ *adjective*. M19.
[ORIGIN from IN-[3] + TRANSPARENT.]
Not transparent; unable to be seen through.

intrant /ˈɪntr(ə)nt/ *noun & adjective*. Chiefly *Scot.* E16.
[ORIGIN Latin *intrant-* pres. ppl stem of *intrare* enter, in medieval Latin senses: see -ANT[1].]
▸ **A** *noun*. **1** A person who takes legal possession of land etc. Now *rare*. E16.
2 A person who enters a college, institution, association, etc. M16.
3 A person who enters a room, building, etc. *rare*. M17.
4 A person who enters into holy orders. M17.
▸ **B** *adjective*. Entering (an office, profession, etc.); newly appointed. L16.

†**intrap** *verb* var. of ENTRAP.

intrapluvial /ɪntrəˈpluːvɪəl/ *adjective & noun*. M20.
[ORIGIN from INTRA- + PLUVIAL *adjective*.]
GEOLOGY. ▸**A** *adjective*. Of, pertaining to, or designating relatively short, drier periods (less marked than interpluvials) that may have occurred during pluvials. M20.
▸ **B** *noun*. An intrapluvial period. M20.

intrapolation /ɪnˌtrapəˈleɪʃ(ə)n/ *noun*. E20.
[ORIGIN from INTRA- + INTER)POLATION.]
= INTERPOLATION 3. Also more widely, (an) inference within the scope or framework of what is known.
■ **inˈtrapolate** *verb trans. & intrans.* = INTERPOLATE *verb* 5, 5b M20.

intraspecies /ˈɪntrəspiːʃiːz/ *adjective*. E20.
[ORIGIN from INTRA- + SPECIES.]
= INTRASPECIFIC.

intraspecific /ɪntrəspəˈsɪfɪk/ *adjective*. E20.
[ORIGIN from INTRA- + SPECIFIC.]
Produced, occurring, or existing within a (taxonomic) species or between individuals of a single species.

intratelluric /ɪntrətɛˈljʊərɪk/ *adjective*. L19.
[ORIGIN from INTRA- + TELLURIC *adjective*[2].]
GEOLOGY. Situated, occurring, or originating in the interior of the earth.

intrathecal /ɪntrəˈθiːk(ə)l/ *adjective*. L19.
[ORIGIN from INTRA- + THECAL.]
1 ZOOLOGY. Contained or enclosed within the theca (e.g. of a polyp). L19.
2 MEDICINE. Occurring within or administered into the spinal theca. E20.
■ **intrathecally** *adverb* E20.

intrauterine /ɪntrəˈjuːtərʌɪn, -rɪn/ *adjective*. M19.
[ORIGIN from INTRA- + UTERINE.]
Situated, occurring, or passed within the uterus.
intrauterine device a contraceptive device to be placed in the uterus.

intravasation /ɪnˌtravəˈseɪʃ(ə)n/ *noun*. L17.
[ORIGIN from INTRA- after EXTRAVASATION.]
MEDICINE. The entrance into a vessel of matter (e.g. pus) formed in the surrounding tissues.

I

intravascular /ɪntrəˈvaskjʊlə/ *adjective*. L19.
[ORIGIN from INTRA- + VASCULAR.]
Chiefly ANATOMY. Situated or occurring within a vessel of an animal or plant, esp. within a blood vessel.
■ **intravascularly** *adverb* within the vascular system E20.

intravenous /ɪntrəˈviːnəs/ *adjective & noun*. M19.
[ORIGIN from INTRA- + VENOUS.]
▸ **A** *adjective*. Existing or taking place within a vein or the veins. M19.
▸ **B** *noun*. An intravenous injection or feeding. M20.
■ **intravenously** *adverb* L19.

intraversable /ɪntrəˈvəːsəb(ə)l/ *adjective*. E19.
[ORIGIN from IN-³ + TRAVERSABLE.]
That cannot be traversed or crossed.

intra vires /ɪntrə ˈvʌɪriːz/ *adverbial phr*. L19.
[ORIGIN Latin = within the powers.]
Chiefly LAW. Within the powers or legal authority (*of* a corporation or person). Opp. ULTRA VIRES.

intravital /ɪntrəˈvʌɪt(ə)l/ *adjective*. L19.
[ORIGIN from INTRA- + VITAL *adjective*, perh. infl. by INTRA VITAM.]
BIOLOGY. Performed on, applied to, or occurring in something alive; in vivo.
■ **intravitally** *adverb* during life, in a living organism M20.

intra vitam /ɪntrə ˈviːtam/ *adjectival phr*. L19.
[ORIGIN Latin.]
BIOLOGY. Taking place during life; while still living. Cf. IN VIVO.

I

intrazonal /ɪntrəˈzəʊn(ə)l/ *adjective*. E20.
[ORIGIN from INTRA- + ZONAL.]
SOIL SCIENCE. Designating any soil which differs from the soil characteristic of its climatic and vegetational zone owing to the overriding influence of relief, parent material, or other local factor.

intreat *verb* see ENTREAT.

†**intreaty** *noun* var. of ENTREATY.

intrench /ɪnˈtrɛn(t)ʃ/ *verb*. M16.
[ORIGIN from IN-² + TRENCH *noun & verb*. See also ENTRENCH.]
1 *verb trans. & intrans.* Var. of ENTRENCH. M16.
2 *verb trans.* Make a trench in; furrow. M18.

†**intrenchant** *adjective*. *rare*. Only in E17.
[ORIGIN from IN-³ + TRENCHANT *adjective*.]
Unable to be cut.

intrenched *ppl adjective*, **intrenchment** *noun* vars. of ENTRENCHED, ENTRENCHMENT.

intrepid /ɪnˈtrɛpɪd/ *adjective*. L17.
[ORIGIN French *intrépide* or Latin *intrepidus*, formed as IN-³ + *trepidus* agitated, alarmed.]
Fearless; undaunted; daring; brave.

H. MARTINEAU Is there to be no pride in intrepid patriotism? E. H. JONES Others remembered her as an intrepid slider on frozen ponds.

■ **intreˈpidity** *noun* the quality of being intrepid; fearlessness, courage, boldness: E18. **intrepidly** *adverb* E18. **intrepidness** *noun* intrepidity E17.

intricacy /ˈɪntrɪkəsi/ *noun*. E17.
[ORIGIN from INTRICATE *adjective* + -ACY.]
1 The quality or state of being intricate; complexity; complicated or involved condition. E17.

DRYDEN It often puzzles the reader with the Intricacy of its Notions. J. E. T. ROGERS The lock must have varied in value, according to . . the intricacy of its workmanship.

2 A complication; an entangled or involved state of affairs; a perplexing difficulty. In *pl.*, the fine detail and complexities of a subject or practice. E17.

D. WELCH It isn't easy, even for a doctor, to understand all the intricacies of nursing.

intricate /ˈɪntrɪkət/ *adjective*. LME.
[ORIGIN Latin *intricatus* pa. pple of *intricare* entangle, perplex formed as IN-² + *tricae* trifles, tricks, perplexities, from *tricari* make difficulties: see -ATE².]
1 Perplexingly entangled or involved; interwinding in a complicated manner. LME.

D. DELILLO Along the intricate and twisting paths. J. CRACE Every beast is woven an intricate necklace of straw.

2 Of ideas, statements, etc.: perplexingly involved or complicated in meaning; entangled; obscure. LME.

L. EDEL Winston was impatient, irritable; he could not wait for the end of such long and intricate sentences.

■ **intricately** *adverb* M16. **intricateness** *noun* intricacy L16.

intricate /ˈɪntrɪkeɪt/ *verb trans*. Now *rare*. M16.
[ORIGIN Latin *intricat-* pa. ppl stem of *intricare*: see INTRICATE *adjective*, -ATE³.]
1 Make (a thing) involved or obscure; complicate. M16.
2 Entangle or ensnare (an animal or person); involve, embarrass, perplex. M16.
■ †**intrication** *noun* the action of intricating; the condition of being intricated; (a) complication, (an) entanglement: LME–L18.

intrigant *noun & adjective* var. of INTRIGUANT.

intrigante *noun* var. of INTRIGUANTE.

intriguant /ˈɪntrɪɡ(ə)nt; *foreign* ɛ̃triɡɑ̃ (*pl. same*)/ *noun & adjective*. Also **-gant**. L18.
[ORIGIN French, pres. pple of *intriguer*: see INTRIGUE *verb*, -ANT¹.]
▸ **A** *noun*. An intriguer. L18.
▸ **B** *adjective*. Intriguing; scheming. E19.

intriguante /ɛ̃triɡɑ̃ːt/ *noun*. Also **-gante**. Pl. pronounced same. E19.
[ORIGIN French, fem. of *intriguant*: see INTRIGUANT.]
A woman who intrigues.

intrigue /ɪnˈtriːɡ, ˈɪntriːɡ/ *noun*. M17.
[ORIGIN French from Italian *intrigo*, *-ico*, from *intrigare* entangle, from Latin *intricare*: see INTRICATE *adjective*.]
†**1** Intricacy, complexity; a complicated contrivance, state of affairs, or mode of action. M–L17.
2 Underhand plotting or scheming; an instance of this, a plot. M17.

B. BAINBRIDGE Unknowingly enmeshed in a tangle of shady dealings and secret intrigues. *Country Quest* Power and political intrigue were very much the matters of the day in thirteenth century Britain.

†**3** The plot of a play, poem, or romance. M17–E18.
4 A clandestine love affair. M17. ▸**b** *transf.* The combination of queen and jack in certain card games. M19.

STEELE Taken in an Intrigue with another Man's wife.

intrigue /ɪnˈtriːɡ/ *verb*. E17.
[ORIGIN French *intriguer* from Italian *intrigare*: see INTRIGUE *noun*.]
1 *verb trans.* Trick, deceive, cheat; embarrass, puzzle, perplex. Now *rare* or *obsolete*. E17.

S. WILLIAMS To intrigue and baffle a brave and meritorious people out of their rights and liberties.

2 *verb intrans.* Carry on a secret or illicit love affair. M17.

S. PEPYS The people . . make no scruple of saying that the king do intrigue with Mrs. Stewart.

3 *verb intrans.* Use influence secretly to achieve one's ends; plot *with* a person; scheme. L17. ▸**b** *verb trans.* Accomplish by underhand scheming. Now *rare*. L17.

L. MACNEICE Donald, Lord of the Isles, intrigued with Henry of England and crossed the Minch as a rebel.

4 *verb trans.* Entangle, involve; complicate. Now *rare* or *obsolete*. L17.

J. CHILD The way . . is not . . hidden from us in the dark, or intrigued with difficulties.

5 *verb trans.* Arouse the curiosity or interest of; puzzle, fascinate. Usu. in *pass.* L19.

C. SAGAN Something puzzles him, intrigues him, has implications that excite him.

■ **intriguer** *noun* a person who carries on an intrigue M17. **intriguess** *noun* (*rare*) a female intriguer M18. **intriguing** *adjective* (*a*) forming secret plots or schemes; (*b*) arousing interest, or curiosity, curious, fascinating: L17. **intriguingly** *adverb* M18.

intrinse /ɪnˈtrɪns/ *adjective*. *rare*. E17.
[ORIGIN Perh. abbreviation of INTRINSICATE.]
Intricate, entangled, involved.

intrinsic /ɪnˈtrɪnsɪk/ *adjective & noun*. L15.
[ORIGIN Old French & mod. French *intrinsèque* from late Latin *intrinsecus*, from Latin *intrinsecus* adverb inwardly, inwards: see -IC.]
▸ **A** *adjective* **1** **a** Situated within; interior, inner. *obsolete* in *gen.* sense. L15. ▸**b** ANATOMY. Of a muscle: contained wholly within the organ on which it acts. Also, (of a tumour) arising in the part or tissue in which it is found. M19.
†**2** Inward, secret, private. L15–L17. ▸**b** Intimate. E–M17.
3 Belonging to a thing in itself, or by its very nature; inherent, essential, natural (*to*). Of worth: real, not illusory or superficial. M17. ▸**b** MATH. Not involving reference to external coordinates. M19. ▸**c** PHYSICS. Of a semiconductor: owing its electrical conductivity to thermally excited electrons from the principal substance present, rather than to electrons from impurity atoms. Also, designating or pertaining to such conduction. M20.

M. SEYMOUR-SMITH These, whatever their intrinsic interest, are the letters of a famous poet. D. CAUTE Measuring the intrinsic value of a course by the size of its audience. A. ARONSON Their compassionate realisation of the existence of evil as an intrinsic part of the human condition. **b** W. WHEWELL The intrinsic equation to the circle is $s = a\theta$, a being the radius.

intrinsic factor BIOCHEMISTRY a glycoprotein secreted by the stomach which enables the body to absorb vitamin B_{12}.
▸ **B** *noun*. An intrinsic part or quality. Long *rare*. M17.

intrinsical /ɪnˈtrɪnsɪk(ə)l/ *adjective*. Now *rare*. M16.
[ORIGIN from late Latin *intrinsecus* (see INTRINSIC) + -ICAL.]
†**1** = INTRINSIC *adjective* 2. M16–M17. ▸**b** = INTRINSIC *adjective* 2b. E17–L19.
2 = INTRINSIC *adjective* 3. M16.
†**3** = INTRINSIC *adjective* 1. L16–L17.
■ **intrinsiˈcality** *noun* (an instance of) intrinsicalness M19. **intrinsicalness** *noun* the state or quality of being intrinsic L17.

intrinsically /ɪnˈtrɪnsɪk(ə)li/ *adverb*. L16.
[ORIGIN from INTRINSIC *adjective* or INTRINSICAL: see -ICALLY.]
†**1** Internally, inwardly, within (*lit. & fig.*). L16–M17.
2 By, or in relation to, the inner nature of the thing: in itself; inherently, essentially. E17.

†**intrinsicate** *adjective*. M16–E17.
[ORIGIN App. from Italian *intrinsecato*, *-sicato* familiar, confused in meaning with *intricato* intricate.]
Intricate, involved, entangled.

intro /ˈɪntrəʊ/ *noun*. *colloq.* Also **intro.** (point). Pl. **-os**. E19.
[ORIGIN Abbreviation.]
= INTRODUCTION.

intro- /ˈɪntrəʊ/ *prefix*.
[ORIGIN Latin *intro* adverb 'to the inside'.]
In words adopted from Latin and in English formations modelled on these, and as a freely productive prefix, with the senses 'within', 'inwards'.
■ **intro-ˈactive** *adjective* having the property of acting within; mutually active: M19. **introˈessive** *adjective & noun* (GRAMMAR) (designating, being in, or pertaining to) the case which expresses 'motion into' E20. **introˈflexed** *ppl adjective* bent or curved inwards M19. **introˈflexion** *noun* an inward bending or curvature M19. **intromoˈlecular** *adjective* (*rare*) intramolecular L19. **introˈpulsive** *adjective* having the quality of driving inwards E19. **introˈsuction** *noun* (long *rare*) the action of sucking inwards M17.

introduce /ɪntrəˈdjuːs/ *verb trans*. LME.
[ORIGIN Latin *introducere*, formed as INTRO- + *ducere* lead, bring.]
1 **a** Bring (a person) into a place, society, or group. LME. ▸**b** Bring, put, or lead into or in; insert. LME.

a G. GREENE The fourth member was . . Liz, . . introduced for reasons of utility. **b** I. MURDOCH He took a piece of . . paper and . . introduced it carefully underneath the little curled up thing. R. DAWKINS They introduced a baby swallow into a magpie's nest.

†**2** Bring about, induce. LME–L17.
†**3** Bring (a person) into the knowledge of something; initiate; instruct. Cf. INTRODUCTION 3. L15–E16.
4 Add or incorporate, esp. as a new feature or element. (Foll. by *into*.) L15.

A. BRIGGS Spenser introduced many allegorical devices into his . . *Epithalamion*.

5 Bring into use or practice; institute (a law, custom, etc.). E17.

J. A. MICHENER Thus chewing gum was introduced to the States. *Clitheroe Advertiser & Times* A suggestion to relieve traffic congestion . . by introducing a parking restriction.

6 Usher in, bring forward with preliminary or preparatory matter; announce; begin, come immediately before the start of. M17.

A. HAMILTON Rain introduced with much Thunder and Lightning. SIR W. SCOTT This discussion served to introduce the young soldier's experiences. T. MORRISON Unless Eva . . introduced the subject, no one ever spoke of her disability.

7 Bring into personal acquaintance; make known to or *to* a person or group. Orig. ***introduce into the acquaintance of***. M17. ▸**b** Present formally, as at court, in an assembly such as the House of Lords or Commons, to society, etc. L17. ▸**c** Acquaint (a person) with an idea or thing. Foll. by *to*. M18.

T. S. ELIOT Let me introduce you to my wife. P. ACKROYD Eliot and Verdenal were introduced and did not simply meet by chance. **b** *Law Times* A new . . Peer of Ireland . . is not introduced, but simply takes and subscribes the oath. F. HUME Curtis introduced her to society. **c** L. GORDON Janet Case . . introduced her to the feminist cause.

8 Bring to the notice or cognizance of a person or group; bring a bill or proposal before Parliament etc. M18.

LYNDON B. JOHNSON Mills . . introduced the new bill to the House.

■ **introduceable** *adjective* L17. **introduced** *ppl adjective* (*a*) brought in, inserted, made known; (*b*) BOTANY & ZOOLOGY (of a species) not native to the area in which it occurs: M17. †**introducement** *noun* the action of introducing; an introduction: M16–L18. **introducer** *noun* E17. **introducible** *adjective* able to be introduced or brought in L17.

introduction /ɪntrəˈdʌkʃ(ə)n/ *noun*. LME.
[ORIGIN Old French & mod. French, or Latin *introductio(n-)*, from *introduct-* pa. ppl stem of *introducere*: see INTRODUCE, -ION.]
†**1** The action or process of leading to or preparing for something; a preliminary or initiatory step or stage. LME–M17.
2 **a** The action or an act of introducing a person or thing. LME. ▸**b** A practice or thing newly introduced; a plant or animal species brought into a region in which it is not native. E17. ▸**c** The issuing of new shares by a company through the medium of a stock exchange. E20.

a *Times* The divisions . . in Protestant . . circles, since the introduction of direct rule.

†**3** Initiation in the knowledge of a subject; instruction in rudiments; a first lesson; in *pl.*, rudiments, elements. Cf. INTRODUCE 3. LME–E18.
4 **a** A preliminary explanation of an author's or speaker's design or purpose; the part of a book, lecture, speech, etc., which leads up to the subject treated. E16. ▸**b** A text explaining the elementary principles of a subject. M16. ▸**c** A preliminary course of study; matter introductory to the special study of a subject. L19.

b A. J. BALFOUR By an Introduction to a subject is meant a brief survey. **c** J. FERGUSSON The study of Etruscan art is a necessary introduction to that of Roman.

5 a The action of personally introducing a person; *esp.* the formal presentation of one person to another. E18. ▸**b** The process of becoming acquainted with a thing; a means of this. E19. ▸**c** A letter of introduction. E19.

a W. IRVING Boswell was made happy by an introduction to Johnson. D. PARKER No introductions, . . for each guest wore a card with his . . name . . on it. **c** *Radio Times* The BBC's New York office has given me introductions to the broadcasting people in Montreal.

a letter of introduction: see LETTER *noun*[1].

6 MUSIC. The preliminary passage or movement of a piece of music, often thematically different from the main section. L19.

introductive /ɪntrəˈdʌktɪv/ *adjective*. L15.
[ORIGIN medieval Latin *introductivus*, from Latin *introduct-*: see INTRODUCTION, -IVE.]
1 Causing or promoting the introduction *of* something. L15.
2 Leading on to something that follows. M17.

introductor /ɪntrəˈdʌktə/ *noun*. *arch.* M17.
[ORIGIN Late Latin, from Latin *introduct-*: see INTRODUCTION, -OR.]
An introducer; *spec.* an official who introduces people at a royal court.

introductory /ɪntrəˈdʌkt(ə)ri/ *adjective & noun*. LME.
[ORIGIN Late Latin *introductorius*, from Latin *introduct-*: see INTRODUCTION, -ORY[2].]
▸ **A** *noun*. †**1** An introductory text. LME–M16.
2 A preliminary step. M17.
▸ **B** *adjective*. †**1** Serving to introduce something. Foll. by *of*. E17–E19.
2 Leading up or on to something; preliminary. M17.

R. INGALLS There were even introductory drum-rolls. *NATFHE Journal* The book is intended as an introductory textbook.

3 Serving to introduce someone personally. L18.
■ **introductorily** *adverb* in an introductory manner; by way of introduction: M19.

introductress /ɪntrəˈdʌktrɪs/ *noun*. M17.
[ORIGIN from INTRODUCTOR + -ESS[1].]
A female introducer.

introgression /ɪntrəˈgrɛʃ(ə)n/ *noun*. M17.
[ORIGIN from Latin *introgredi* step in, formed as INTRO- + *gradi* proceed, walk, after *egress, egression, ingress, ingression*: see -ION.]
1 A going or coming in. M17.
2 BIOLOGY. The transfer of genetic information from one (usu. plant) species to another as a result of hybridization between them and repeated back crossing. M20.
■ **introgress** *verb intrans.* (BIOLOGY) (of a species, or of a gene) undergo introgression M20. **introgressed** *ppl adjective* transferred by or resulting from introgression M20.

introgressive /ɪntrəˈgrɛsɪv/ *adjective*. M20.
[ORIGIN from INTROGRESSION + -IVE.]
BIOLOGY. Characterized by, bringing about, or resulting from introgression.
introgressive hybridization = INTROGRESSION 2.

introit /ˈɪntrɔɪt, ɪnˈtrəʊɪt/ *noun*. LME.
[ORIGIN Old French & mod. French *introït* from Latin *introitus* entrance, from *introire* enter, formed as INTRO- + *ire* go.]
1 The action or an act of going in; (an) entrance. Long *rare*. LME.
2 ECCLESIASTICAL. An antiphon or psalm sung while the priest approaches the altar to celebrate the Eucharist. Also, the first two or three words of the office of a particular day. L15.

introjection /ɪntrə(ʊ)ˈdʒɛkʃ(ə)n/ *noun*. M19.
[ORIGIN from INTRO- after *projection*.]
1 The action of throwing oneself into, or eagerly beginning, some course or pursuit. M19.
2 PHILOSOPHY. A theory according to which external objects are images of elements within the consciousness of the individual. L19.
3 a PSYCHOANALYSIS. The transfer of emotional energy from an object to a subjective image of it; internalization. E20. ▸**b** PSYCHOLOGY. The inward adoption of the attitudes, values, and expectations of one's parents or others by whom one is anxious to be accepted; identification. M20.
■ **introject** *verb trans.* (PSYCHOLOGY) incorporate an inward image of (an external object, or the values and attitudes of others) into oneself E20. **introjectionism** *noun* belief in a theory of introjection E20. **introjectionist** *adjective* pertaining to introjection E20. **introjective** *adjective* (PSYCHOLOGY) that is introjected; characterized by introjection: M20.

intromission /ɪntrə(ʊ)ˈmɪʃ(ə)n/ *noun*. M16.
[ORIGIN French, or Latin *intromissio(n-)*, formed as INTRO- + *missio(n-)* MISSION *noun*.]
1 Interference; *esp.* (chiefly SCOTS LAW) the action of assuming the possession and management of another's property, either with or without legal authority. Also, the transactions of an agent or subordinate with the money of his or her employer or principal. M16.
vicious intromission intromission without legal authority.
2 The action of sending, letting, or putting something in; *spec.* the insertion of the penis into the vagina in sexual intercourse. E17.

intromit /ɪntrə(ʊ)ˈmɪt/ *verb*. Infl. **-tt-**. LME.
[ORIGIN Latin *intromittere* introduce, formed as INTRO- + *mittere* send.]
1 *verb intrans.* Interfere, meddle. Also foll. by *with*. Now *Scot.* LME. ▸**b** SCOTS LAW. Have monetary dealings; *esp.* deal with property or effects, either as administrator, agent, etc., or without legal right. Usu. foll. by *with*. E16.
2 *verb refl.* Interfere (*with* or *in* something). Now *rare*. L15.
3 *verb trans.* Cause or allow to enter; put, send, or let in. Now *rare*. L16.
■ **intromitter** *noun* a person who intromits, *spec.* (SCOTS LAW) with the property of another L15.

intromittent /ɪntrə(ʊ)ˈmɪt(ə)nt/ *adjective*. M19.
[ORIGIN Latin *intromittent-* pres. ppl stem of *intromittere*: see INTROMIT, -ENT.]
Chiefly ZOOLOGY. Having the function of intromission; usu. designating the male copulatory organ.

intron /ˈɪntrɒn/ *noun*. L20.
[ORIGIN from INTR(AGENIC + -ON.]
GENETICS. A segment of an RNA molecule which does not code for proteins, is excised during or soon after transcription, and takes no part in forming the eventual gene product; a section of DNA which codes for this. Cf. EXON *noun*[2]
■ **inˈtronic** *adjective* L20.

intropunitive /ɪntrə(ʊ)ˈpjuːnɪtɪv/ *adjective*. M20.
[ORIGIN from INTRO- + PUNITIVE *adjective*.]
PSYCHOLOGY. Blaming oneself rather than other people or events; of or pertaining to an unreasonable feeling of responsibility or guilt.
■ **intropunitiveness** *noun* M20.

introrse /ɪnˈtrɔːs/ *adjective*. M19.
[ORIGIN Latin *introrsus*, from *introversus* (turned) inwards, from INTRO- + *versus* pa. pple of *vertere* turn.]
BOTANY & ENTOMOLOGY. (Of a part) turned or directed inwards; *spec.* (of an anther) releasing its pollen towards the centre of the flower.

introscope /ˈɪntrəskəʊp/ *noun*. M20.
[ORIGIN from INTRO- + -SCOPE.]
ENGINEERING. A long narrow instrument incorporating a light source and designed to permit visual examination of the interior of tubes, narrow-mouthed vessels, etc.

introspect /ɪntrə(ʊ)ˈspɛkt/ *verb*. L17.
[ORIGIN Latin *introspect-* pa. ppl stem of *introspicere* look into, or from *introspectare* frequentative of this, from INTRO- + *specere* look.]
1 *verb trans.* Look into, esp. intellectually; examine in detail. Now *rare*. L17.
2 *verb intrans.* Examine one's own thoughts or feelings. L19.
■ **introspectable** *adjective* = INTROSPECTIBLE M20. **introspectible** *adjective* able to be examined by introspection E20.

introspection /ɪntrə(ʊ)ˈspɛkʃ(ə)n/ *noun*. L17.
[ORIGIN from INTROSPECT + -ION.]
Close inspection, intellectual examination, esp. of one's own mind; observation of one's own thoughts, feelings, or mental state.

G. S. HAIGHT The habit of introspection, which led to . . psychological analysis.

■ **introspectionism** *noun* (PSYCHOLOGY) (**a**) = *INTROSPECTIVE psychology*; (**b**) = INTROSPECTION: E20. **introspectionist** *noun* a person who practises introspection, esp. as a method in psychological inquiry L19.

introspective /ɪntrə(ʊ)ˈspɛktɪv/ *adjective*. E19.
[ORIGIN from INTROSPECT or INTROSPECTION + -IVE.]
Of, pertaining to, or characterized by introspection; given to introspection.

W. C. WILLIAMS A silent, introspective sort of chap. S. NAIPAUL Education . . will be . . introspective, . . coming to terms with the inner motions of mind body and soul.

introspective psychology psychology based on the direct observation of one's own mental states.
■ **introspectively** *adverb* M19. **introspectiveness** *noun* L19.

†**introsume** *verb trans.* M17–E18.
[ORIGIN from INTRO- + Latin *suere* take, as a var. of INSUME, after *assume, consume*.]
Take (medicine) internally; absorb (nutriment).

introsusception /ɪntrə(ʊ)səˈsɛpʃ(ə)n/ *noun*. Now *rare* or *obsolete*. L18.
[ORIGIN from INTRO- after *intussusception*.]
= INTUSSUSCEPTION.
■ **introsuscepted** *adjective* = INTUSSUSCEPTED M19.

introuvable /ɛ̃truvabl/ *adjective*. E19.
[ORIGIN French, formed as IN-[3] + *trouver* find + -ABLE.]
Unfindable, undiscoverable.

introversible /ɪntrə(ʊ)ˈvəːsɪb(ə)l/ *adjective*. L19.
[ORIGIN from INTRO- as the opposite of EVERSIBLE.]
Able to be introverted or drawn inwards, as the finger of a glove.

introversion /ɪntrə(ʊ)ˈvəːʃ(ə)n/ *noun*. M17.
[ORIGIN from INTROVERT *verb* after *evert, eversion*, etc.: see -ION.]
1 a The action or an act of turning the thoughts inwards to the contemplation of one's own thoughts or feelings or of inward or spiritual things. M17. ▸**b** The fact or tendency of having one's thoughts and interests directed chiefly inwards and withdrawing from the external world. Opp. EXTROVERSION 3. E20.

a J. WESLEY The attending to the voice of Christ within you is . . Introversion. **b** V. BROME Jung characterized introversion as 'a hesitant, reflective, retiring nature'.

2 The action of physically turning inwards, esp. of drawing an outer part into the interior; the condition of being turned inwards. L18.
■ **introversive** *adjective* characterized by or having the quality or effect of introversion E19.

introvert /ˈɪntrəvəːt/ *noun & adjective*. L19.
[ORIGIN from INTROVERSION Cf. CONVERT *noun*.]
▸ **A** *noun*. †**1** ZOOLOGY. A part or organ that is or can be introverted. Only in L19.
2 A person characterized by introversion; a withdrawn or reserved person. Opp. EXTROVERT *noun*. E20.

A. S. NEILL The introvert sits in a corner and dreams of what should be.

▸ **B** *adjective*. Given to or characterized by introversion; introverted. Opp. EXTROVERT *adjective*. E20.

introvert /ɪntrə(ʊ)ˈvəːt/ *verb trans.* M17.
[ORIGIN mod. Latin *introvertere*, formed as INTRO- + *vertere* to turn.]
1 Turn (the mind, one's thinking, etc.) inwards upon itself; direct (one's interest or effort) to that which is internal or spiritual. M17.
2 Turn or bend inwards (physically); *esp.* in ZOOLOGY turn (a part or organ) inside out within its own tube or base (cf. EVERT). L18.
■ **introvertive** *adjective* introversive M19.

intrude /ɪnˈtruːd/ *verb*. Also (earlier) †**en-**. M16.
[ORIGIN Latin *intrudere*, from *in-* IN-[2] + *trudere* to thrust.]
1 *verb intrans. & refl.* †**a** Usurp an office, a right, etc., without legitimate title or claim. Also foll. by *on, upon*. Cf. INTRUSION 1. M16–L17. ▸**b** Enter forcibly or encroach, without consent, invitation, or welcome. Foll. by *into*, †*in* (a place, company, etc.), *on, upon* (a person or group, a person's privacy, etc.). L16.

b Q. CRISP The telephone . . enables people to barge into our homes . . and . . they intrude upon us. I. MURDOCH If you intrude on someone's grief, you're like a spectator. M. MILNER Into such reflections intruded the image of the . . stone.

2 *verb trans.* Introduce (a thing) forcibly or without consent (foll. by *between, into*, †*in*). Also, force (something unwelcome) *on* or *upon* a person. M16.

J. BRYCE The tendency which intruded earthly Madonnas . . between the worshipper and the . . Deity. R. BUCHANAN Prepared to intrude ministers . . at the point of the bayonet.

3 *verb trans.* †**a** Enter forcibly. *rare*. Only in L16. ▸**b** GEOLOGY. Be forced or thrust into. E20.
■ **intruder** *noun* (**a**) a person who or thing which intrudes; (**b**) *spec.* a housebreaker, a trespasser: M16. **intrudingly** *adverb* in an intruding manner E18.

intruded /ɪnˈtruːdɪd/ *adjective*. M16.
[ORIGIN from INTRUDE + -ED[1].]
1 Brought, crowded, or thrust in, esp. forcibly or without consent. M16.
2 GEOLOGY. = INTRUSIVE *adjective* 2b. M19.

intruse /ɪnˈtruːs/ *verb trans. & intrans.* *obsolete* exc. *Scot.* LME.
[ORIGIN Latin *intrus-* pa. ppl stem of *intrudere* INTRUDE.]
= INTRUDE.

intrusion /ɪnˈtruːʒ(ə)n/ *noun*. LME.
[ORIGIN Old French & mod. French, or medieval Latin *intrusio(n-)*, from Latin *intrus-* pa. ppl stem of *intrudere*: see INTRUDE, -ION.]
1 Orig., invasion; usurpation. Now, the action or an act of usurping a vacant estate or office without legitimate title or claim; *spec.* (LAW) the entry of a stranger after the determination of a particular estate of freehold (as a life tenancy) before the remainder man or reversioner; also, a trespass on the lands of the crown. LME. ▸**b** The settlement of a minister of the Church of Scotland without the consent of the congregation. E18.
2 The action or an act of entering forcibly or without invitation or welcome, or of introducing something inappropriately; uninvited or unwelcome entrance or appearance; encroachment on a person's property or rights. L16.

N. GORDIMER There was an intrusion. The telephone rang. D. PRATER The intrusion of visitors who arrived with letters of introduction. D. WIGODER I resented the intrusion into my private world.

3 The action or an act of introducing or forcing a thing in; the fact of being so introduced. Also, something thrust in, a forcible or unwelcome addition. M17. ▸**b** *spec.* in GEOLOGY. The influx of (molten) rock into fissures or between strata; a portion of intruded rock. M19.

A. G. GARDINER Word-magic belongs to poetry. In prose it is an intrusion. E. O'BRIEN Whether his presence was welcome or an intrusion. **b** F. HOYLE Ailsa Craig, a small intrusion of granite in the Firth of Clyde.

intrusive /ɪnˈtruːsɪv/ *adjective & noun*. M17.
[ORIGIN from Latin *intrus-* (see INTRUSION) + -IVE.]
▸ **A** *adjective*. **1** Characterized by intruding; done or carried out with intrusion. M17.

R. ELLMANN The biographer is necessarily intrusive, a trespasser. V. GLENDINNING There had been some upsettingly intrusive interviews.

intrusive growth the growth of some plant cells by intrusion between others (opp. *symplastic growth*).

2 That has been introduced or thrust in. M19. ▸b GEOLOGY. Of an igneous rock: forced, while molten, into fissures or between strata of other rocks. M19.

b *Naturalist* Intrusive igneous rocks in sills and dykes.

intrusive r an *r* pronounced in hiatus, as in the phr. *the idea(r) of*.

▸ B *noun*. GEOLOGY. An intrusive rock or rock mass. L19.

■ **intrusively** *adverb* M19. **intrusiveness** *noun* M19.

intrust *verb* var. of ENTRUST.

intubate /ˈɪntjʊbeɪt/ *verb trans.* E17.
[ORIGIN from IN-[2] + Latin *tuba* tube + -ATE[3].]
†1 Form into tubes. Only in E17.
2 MEDICINE. Insert a tube into an aperture of the body of (a patient), subject to intubation. L19.

intubation /ɪntjʊˈbeɪʃ(ə)n/ *noun*. L19.
[ORIGIN from INTUBATE + -ATION.]
Chiefly MEDICINE. The insertion of a tube into (a part of) the body, esp. the trachea or oesophagus, for the purpose of diagnosis, treatment, force-feeding, etc.

intue /ɪnˈtjuː/ *verb trans. rare*. M19.
[ORIGIN Latin *intueri*: see INTUITION.]
Know or perceive by intuition; intuit.

intuent /ˈɪntjʊənt/ *adjective. rare*. M19.
[ORIGIN Latin *intuent-* pres. ppl stem of *intueri*: see INTUITION, -ENT.]
That knows by intuition.

intuit /ɪnˈtjuːɪt/ *verb*. L18.
[ORIGIN Latin *intuit-*: see INTUITION.]
†1 *verb trans.* Tutor, instruct. *rare*. Only in L18.
2 a *verb intrans.* Receive or assimilate knowledge by direct perception. M19. ▸b *verb trans.* Know immediately without reasoning; know by intuition. M19.

b *Notes & Queries* Objects can be intuited as existing without us. D. MELTZER We intuit rather than observe the emotional atmosphere in the consulting room.

■ **intuitable** *adjective* L19. **intuiter** *noun* L19.

intuition /ɪntjʊˈɪʃ(ə)n/ *noun*. LME.
[ORIGIN Late Latin *intuitio(n-)*, from Latin *intuit-* pa. ppl stem of *intueri* look upon, consider, contemplate, formed as IN-[2] + *tueri* look: see -ION. Cf. French *intuition*.]
1 SCHOLASTIC PHILOSOPHY. Spiritual insight or perception; instantaneous spiritual communication. LME.

ADDISON Our Superiors are guided by Intuition, and our Inferiors by Instinct.

†2 The action of looking at or into; an inspection, a look. L15–M17.
3 Immediate apprehension by the mind without the intervention of reasoning, direct or immediate insight; an instance of this. Also, the faculty of apprehending in this way. L16. ▸b PHILOSOPHY. Immediate apprehension by the intellect alone; an instance of this. M17. ▸c KANTIAN PHILOSOPHY. Immediate apprehension by a sense or senses; an instance of this. L18.

P. BOWLES Her intuition generally let her know when Port was up to something. D. BAGLEY Wyatt didn't have any real facts—merely vague intuitions. A. GRAY A flash of intuition separate from logic or evidence made him sure this man was the thief. b J. S. MILL The truths known by intuition are the original premises from which all others are inferred.

†4 The action of mentally examining; contemplation, consideration; perception, recognition. E17–M18.
†5 Purpose, intention; reference, respect. E17–E18.

intuitional /ɪntjʊˈɪʃ(ə)n(ə)l/ *adjective*. M19.
[ORIGIN from INTUITION + -AL[1].]
1 Of, pertaining to, or derived from intuition; of the nature of intuition. M19.
2 Of or pertaining to a theory or philosophical school which holds that certain elements of knowledge are perceived directly by the intellect alone. M19.
3 Having intuition. L19.
■ **intuitionally** *adverb* by intuition, intuitively L19.

intuitionalism /ɪntjʊˈɪʃ(ə)n(ə)lɪz(ə)m/ *noun. rare*. M19.
[ORIGIN from INTUITIONAL + -ISM.]
PHILOSOPHY. The doctrine or theory of the intuitional school; = INTUITIONISM 1, 2.
■ **intuitionalist** *noun* = INTUITIONIST M19.

intuitionism /ɪntjʊˈɪʃ(ə)nɪz(ə)m/ *noun*. M19.
[ORIGIN from INTUITION + -ISM.]
1 PHILOSOPHY. The doctrine that in perception external objects are known immediately by intuition. M19.
2 PHILOSOPHY. The doctrine that certain basic truths are perceived directly by intuition. Now also, any ethical theory that is founded in intuition. L19.
3 MATH. The theory that mathematics is founded on extra-linguistic constructs based on pure intuition, and in particular that the law of the excluded middle might not be valid for infinite classes. E20.

intuitionist /ɪntjʊˈɪʃ(ə)nɪst/ *noun & adjective*. M19.
[ORIGIN formed as INTUITIONISM + -IST.]
PHILOSOPHY. ▸A *noun*. A person who holds a theory of intuitionism. M19.
▸ B *adjective*. Of or pertaining to a theory or school of intuitionism. L19.
■ **intuitioˈnistic** *adjective* holding a theory of intuitionism L19. **intuitioˈnistically** *adverb* M20.

intuitive /ɪnˈtjuːɪtɪv/ *adjective & noun*. L15.
[ORIGIN medieval Latin *intuitivus*, from *intuit-*: see INTUITION, -IVE. Cf. French *intuitif, -ive*.]
▸ A *adjective*. †1 (Of sight or vision) clear, accurate, unerring; (of spiritual perception) instant, all-encompassing. L15–M17.
2 a Of a faculty or gift: innate, not acquired by learning. E17. ▸b Of knowledge or mental perception: known or apprehended immediately and fully without reasoning. M17.

b J. GATHORNE-HARDY Diagnosis is intuitive sometimes. You simply know.

3 Of the mind or a mental process: acting or comprehending immediately and without reasoning, operating through intuition. Opp. ***discursive***. M17.

J. ROSENBERG A contrast between the intellectual approach of the great French artist and Rembrandt's more intuitive one. *Atlantic Monthly* People perceive themselves to be immune and . . possessed of an intuitive power . . to choose safe partners.

4 Of a person: possessing intuition. M17.
5 PHILOSOPHY. Of or pertaining to the theory or school which holds that certain basic truths are apprehended by intuition; intuitionist. M19.

B. RUSSELL Our immediate knowledge of truths may be called intuitive knowledge.

▸ B *noun*. A person who works by intuition. E20.
■ **intuitively** *adverb* L16. **intuitiveness** *noun* M19.

intuitivism /ɪnˈtjuːɪtɪvɪz(ə)m/ *noun*. M19.
[ORIGIN from INTUITIVE + -ISM.]
1 The doctrine that certain basic truths can be established by intuition. M19.
2 The faculty of intuition; insight. L19.

intuitivist /ɪnˈtjuːɪtɪvɪst/ *adjective*. M19.
[ORIGIN formed as INTUITIVISM + -IST.]
Of or pertaining to the theory or school of intuitivism.

intumesce /ɪntjʊˈmɛs/ *verb intrans*. L18.
[ORIGIN from Latin *intumescere* swell up, formed as IN-[2] + *tumescere* inceptive of *tumere* be swollen: see -ESCE.]
Swell up, bubble up.

intumescence /ɪntjʊˈmɛs(ə)ns/ *noun*. M17.
[ORIGIN French, from Latin *intumescere*: see INTUMESCE, -ENCE.]
1 The process of swelling up. M17.
2 The bubbling up of a fluid or molten mass. M17.
3 MEDICINE & BOTANY. A swelling of any part of the body or of a plant. E19.

intumescent /ɪntjʊˈmɛs(ə)nt/ *adjective*. L19.
[ORIGIN from INTUMESCE, INTUMESCENCE + -ENT.]
Swelling up; bubbling, foaming.

†**inturbidate** *verb trans. rare*. L17–M19.
[ORIGIN from IN-[2] + TURBID + -ATE[3].]
Make turbid, cloud; disturb, confuse.

inturn /ˈɪntəːn/ *noun*. L16.
[ORIGIN from IN *adverb* + TURN *noun*.]
1 An inward turn or curve; *spec.* a turning in of the toes. L16.
†2 WRESTLING. The act of putting a leg between the thighs of an opponent and lifting him up. Only in 17.
3 CURLING. An inward turn of the elbow and an outward turn of the hand made in delivering a stone. L19.
■ **inturned** *ppl adjective* turned inward M19. **inturning** *verbal noun* a turning in LME.

†**intuse** *noun. rare* (Spenser). Only in L16.
[ORIGIN Latin *intusum* use as noun of neut. pa. pple of *intundere* bruise.]
A bruise.

intussusception /ɪntəsəˈsɛpʃ(ə)n/ *noun*. E18.
[ORIGIN French, or mod. Latin *intussusceptio(n-)*, from Latin *intus* within + *susceptio(n-)* SUSCEPTION. In sense 1 formed on SUSCEPTION.]
1 Absorption, taking in. E18.
2 BIOLOGY. Growth by the intercalation or insertion of new material into an existing structure. M18.
3 a MEDICINE. The inversion or telescoping of one portion of intestine within the next; an instance of this. Also, the mass of intestine involved in this. E19. ▸b An insertion in the manner of intestinal intussusception. E19.
■ **intussuscepted** *adjective* having undergone intussusception E19. **intussusceptum** /ɪntəsəˈsɛptəm/ *noun* [mod. Latin, neut. pa. pple of *intussuscipere* take within] MEDICINE the inner, enveloped portion of intestine in an intussusception M19. **intussuscipiens** /ɪntəsəˈsɪpɪɛnz/ *noun* [mod. Latin, pres. pple of *intussuscipere* take within] MEDICINE the outermost portion of intestine in an intussusception M19.

†**intwine** *verb* var. of ENTWINE *verb*.

intwist *verb* var. of ENTWIST.

Inuit /ˈɪnjʊɪt, ˈɪnʊɪt/ *noun & adjective*. Also **Innuit**. M18.
[ORIGIN Inupiaq, pl. of *inuk* person. Cf. INUK.]
▸ A *noun*. Pl. same, **-s**. (A member of) an indigenous people of northern Canada and parts of Greenland and Alaska. Also, their language, Inupiaq. Cf. YUPIK. M18.
▸ B *adjective*. Of or pertaining to the Inuit or their language. M19.
– NOTE: *Inuit* is preferred to *Eskimo* by the peoples of NW Canada to western Greenland, and the term has official status in Canada. It is not accurate for speakers of Aleut and Yupik.

Inuk /ˈɪnʊk/ *noun & adjective*. E19.
[ORIGIN Inupiaq, lit. 'person'. Cf. INUIT.]
▸ A *noun*. Pl. same, **-s**. A member of the Inuit people. E19.
▸ B *adjective*. Of or pertaining to the Inuk or their language. M20.

Inuktitut /ɪˈnʊktɪtʊt/ *noun & adjective*. Also **-tituk** /-tɪtʊk/. L20.
[ORIGIN Inupiaq, lit. 'the Eskimo way', title of a periodical.]
In Canada: (of) the Inupiaq language.

inula /ˈɪnjʊlə/ *noun*. E19.
[ORIGIN Latin: see ELECAMPANE.]
Any of various showy yellow-rayed composite plants of the genus *Inula*; *esp.* elecampane, *I. helenium*.

inulase /ˈɪnjʊleɪz/ *noun*. L19.
[ORIGIN from INUL(IN + -ASE.]
BIOCHEMISTRY. An enzyme which hydrolyses inulin to fructose, found esp. in some fungi.

inulin /ˈɪnjʊlɪn/ *noun*. E19.
[ORIGIN formed as INULA + -IN[1].]
CHEMISTRY. A fructan present in the roots of various composite plants.

†**inumbrate** *verb trans*. LME–E19.
[ORIGIN Latin *inumbrat-* pa. ppl stem of *inumbrare*, formed as IN-[2] + *umbra* shade, shadow: see -ATE[3].]
Cast a shadow on; shade; overshadow.

inunct /ɪˈnʌŋkt/ *verb trans. rare*. E16.
[ORIGIN Latin *inunct-* pa. ppl stem of *inunguere*, formed as IN-[2] + *unguere* smear, anoint.]
Apply ointment to, smear.

inunction /ɪˈnʌŋ(k)ʃ(ə)n/ *noun*. L15.
[ORIGIN Latin *inunctio(n-)*, formed as INUNCT: see -ION.]
†1 The anointing with oil in consecration and other religious rites. Cf. UNCTION. L15–L17.
2 The action or an act of anointing or rubbing in oil or ointment. E17.

inundant /ɪˈnʌnd(ə)nt/ *adjective*. E17.
[ORIGIN Latin *inundant-* pres. ppl stem of *inundare*: see INUNDATE, -ANT[1].]
Overflowing, inundating, flooding.

inundatal /ˈɪnʌndeɪt(ə)l/ *adjective*. Now *rare*. M19.
[ORIGIN Irreg. from INUNDATE + -AL[1].]
ECOLOGY. Of a plant: growing in areas subject to flooding.

inundate /ˈɪnʌndeɪt/ *verb trans*. L16.
[ORIGIN Latin *inundat-* pa. ppl stem of *inundare*, formed as IN-[2] + *undare* flow: see -ATE[3].]
1 Flood, submerge, cover with water etc. L16.

J. BARNES Rain fell heavily; the plain they were crossing became inundated.

2 *transf.* & *fig.* Overwhelm, cover, provide *with* in abundance. E17.

G. WASHINGTON I was inundated with letters.

inundation /ɪnʌnˈdeɪʃ(ə)n/ *noun*. LME.
[ORIGIN Old French *inondacion* (mod. *-tion*) or Latin *inundatio(n-)*, formed as INUNDATE: see -ATION.]
1 The action of inundating; the fact of being inundated; a flood. LME.

S. HAUGHTON Rich plains . . fertilized by their periodic inundations.

2 *transf.* & *fig.* Overwhelming abundance; an overflowing, a superabundance, an invasion. M16.

A. TOFFLER In every conceivable field . . we face an inundation of innovation.

Inupiaq /ɪˈnuːpɪak/ *noun & adjective*. Also **Inupiat** /ɪˈnuːpɪat/, **Inupik** /ɪˈnuːpɪk/. M20.
[ORIGIN Inupiaq, from *inuk* person + *piaq* genuine.]
(Of) the language of the Inuit, a major division of the Eskimo-Aleut family. Also called INUKTITUT. Cf. YUPIK.

Inupik *noun & adjective* see INUPIAQ.

inurbane /ɪnəːˈbeɪn/ *adjective*. E17.
[ORIGIN Latin *inurbanus*, formed as IN-[3] + *urbanus* URBANE.]
Uncouth, unpolished; *esp.* uncivil, rude.
■ **inurbanely** *adverb* E17.

inurbanity /ɪnəːˈbanɪti/ *noun*. L16.
[ORIGIN French *inurbanité* or medieval Latin *inurbanitas*, from IN-[3] + Latin *urbanitas* URBANITY.]
Lack of urbanity; uncouthness; *esp.* rudeness, impoliteness.

inure /ɪˈnjʊə/ *verb*[1]. Also **enure** /ɛˈnjʊə, ɪˈnjʊə/. LME.
[ORIGIN Anglo-Norman, from phr. meaning 'in use, in practice'; cf. IN-[2], EN-[1], URE *noun*[1].]
1 *verb trans.* Accustom or habituate *to*, harden or render impervious *to*. LME.
R. MAY We have become . . inured to living in a state of quasi-anxiety. R. MCALMON We . . must inure ourselves to the sight of grim reality. M. FORSTER The hospital staff were sad, inured though they were to such tragedies.
†**2** *verb trans.* Put into effect or operation, practise, perform. L15–L16.
3 *verb intrans.* Chiefly LAW. Take effect, come into operation; accrue. L16.
GLADSTONE A relation . . that might virtually inure by usage only. *National Observer (US)* Showing that the public at large derives benefits approaching those that inure directly to mail users.
■ **inurement** *noun* the action of inuring; the state of being inured: L16.

†**inure** *verb*[2] *trans.* L16.
[ORIGIN Latin *inurere* burn in, formed as IN-[2] + *urere* burn.]
1 Brand in, impress by burning. L16–L17.
2 Burn in a flame. Only in E18.

inurn /ɪˈnəːn/ *verb trans.* Also **enurn** /ɪˈnəːn, ɛˈnəːn/. E17.
[ORIGIN from IN-[2], EN-[1] + URN *noun* & *verb*[1].]
Put (ashes) in an urn after cremation; bury, inter.
■ **inurnment** *noun* M20.

inusitate /ɪˈnjuːzɪteɪt/ *adjective*. Now *rare*. M16.
[ORIGIN Latin *inusitatus*, formed as IN-[3] + *usitatus* pa. pple of *usitari* use often: see -ATE[2].]
Unusual, little-used, out of use.
■ **inusitateness** *noun* (*rare*) L19. **inusiˈtation** *noun* (*rare*) E19.

†**inustion** *noun*. E17.
[ORIGIN Late Latin *inustio(n-)* branding, from *inust-* pa. ppl stem of *inurere* INURE *verb*[2]: see -ION.]
1 Burning. Only in E17.
2 Burning in, branding. Only in M17.
3 Cauterization. L17–E19.

in utero /ɪn ˈjuːtərəʊ/ *adverbial & adjectival phr.* E18.
[ORIGIN Latin.]
In the womb; before birth.

inutile /ɪnˈjuːtɪl/ *adjective*. LME.
[ORIGIN Old French & mod. French from Latin *inutilis*, formed as IN-[3] + *utilis* useful. Cf. UTILE *adjective*.]
Useless, pointless, unprofitable.

inutility /ɪnjuːˈtɪlɪti/ *noun*. L16.
[ORIGIN French *inutilité* from Latin *inutilitas*, formed as IN-[3] + *utilitas*: see INUTILE, -ITY.]
1 Uselessness, pointlessness, unprofitableness. L16.
2 An instance of uselessness; a useless thing or person. E19.

inutterable /ɪnˈʌt(ə)rəb(ə)l/ *adjective*. Now *rare*. E17.
[ORIGIN from IN-[3] + UTTERABLE.]
That cannot be uttered; unutterable.

invaccinate /ɪnˈvaksɪneɪt/ *verb trans. rare*. L19.
[ORIGIN from IN-[2] + VACCINATE.]
Introduce into the system by vaccination.
■ **invacciˈnation** *noun* L19.

in vacuo /ɪn ˈvakjʊəʊ/ *adverbial phr.* M17.
[ORIGIN Latin.]
In a vacuum.

invade /ɪnˈveɪd/ *verb*. LME.
[ORIGIN Latin *invadere*, from *in-* IN-[2] + *vadere* go.]
1 *verb trans.* Attack, assault (a person, a group, etc.). *obsolete* exc. *dial.* LME.
2 *verb trans.* & *intrans.* Enter or make an incursion into (a place, a country, etc.), esp. in a hostile manner, in large numbers, or with armed force; attack; MEDICINE & ECOLOGY spread into. Also foll. by *into*, *on*, *upon*. L15.
S. CHITTY On 23 August 1914 the Germans invaded. *British Medical Journal* These tumours . . may directly invade into the mandible. *transf.*: C. PHILLIPS It disturbed him that these memories should invade his mind.
3 *verb trans.* Intrude on, infringe, or violate (property, rights, liberties, etc.). E16. ▸†**b** Usurp, take possession of. E17–E18.
W. TREVOR She had invaded his greatest privacy.
■ **invadable** *adjective* M18. **invader** *noun* E16.

invaginate /ɪnˈvadʒɪneɪt/ *verb*. M17.
[ORIGIN from INVAGINATION: see -ATE[3].]
1 *verb trans.* Put in a sheath. Long *rare*. M17.
2 *verb trans.* ANATOMY & MEDICINE. Turn or double (a tubular sheath) back within itself. M19.
3 *verb intrans.* Become invaginated. L19.

invaginated /ɪnˈvadʒɪneɪtɪd/ *ppl adjective*. M19.
[ORIGIN from INVAGINATE + -ED[1].]
Orig., inserted or received into a sheath or opening; *esp.* intussuscepted. Now usu., having undergone invagination, folded or pushed inwards to form a hollow.

invagination /ɪnˌvadʒɪˈneɪʃ(ə)n/ *noun*. M17.
[ORIGIN mod. Latin *invaginatio(n-)*, formed as IN-[2] + VAGINA: see -ATION.]
Orig., the action of sheathing something; *esp.* intussusception. Now usu., the folding in of a surface or membrane to form a hollow cavity or pouch; the cavity so formed.

invalid /ɪnˈvalɪd/ *adjective*[1]. M16.
[ORIGIN Latin *invalidus*, from IN-[3] + *validus* VALID. See also INVALID *adjective*[2] & *noun*.]
1 Having no force, efficacy, or cogency, esp. in law; void. M16.
R. GRAVES He declared the wills technically invalid because of some legal flaw.
†**2** Without power or strength; weak, feeble. M17–E19.
■ **invalidly** *adverb* so as to be invalid, without validity *adverb* E18. **invalidness** *noun* M17.

invalid /ˈɪnvəliːd, -ɪd/ *adjective*[2] & *noun*. M17.
[ORIGIN Use of INVALID *adjective*[1].]
▸ **A** *adjective*. Infirm or disabled from sickness, disease, or injury. M17.
J. BARNES His invalid son, who had just suffered his first attack of epilepsy.
▸ **B** *noun*. **1** An infirm or sickly person. E18.
J. WAIN My wife's a hopeless invalid, completely bedridden.
invalid car, ***invalid chair***, ***invalid diet***, ***invalid table***, etc.
2 A person, esp. a member of the armed forces, disabled by illness or injury. E18.
■ **invalidish** *adjective* E19. **invalidism** *noun* the state or condition of being an invalid; chronic infirmity or ill health that prevents activity: L18. **invalidy** *adjective* (*colloq.*, *rare*) L19.

invalid /ɪnˈvalɪd/ *verb*[1] *trans.* Now *rare*. M17.
[ORIGIN from INVALID *adjective*[1]: cf. INVALIDATE.]
Make invalid; invalidate.

invalid /ˈɪnvəliːd, -ɪd/ *verb*[2]. L18.
[ORIGIN from INVALID *adjective*[2].]
1 *verb trans.* Treat as an invalid; remove or discharge from employment or active service on account of illness or injury. L18.
M. SCAMMELL Wounded in the lung and . . invalided out of the army with TB.
2 *verb trans.* Make an invalid; disable by illness or injury. Usu. in *pass.* E19.
H. CARPENTER His mother, invalided for many years with tuberculosis, died when he was eight.
3 *verb intrans.* Become an invalid, become unfit for active work through illness. E19.

invalidate /ɪnˈvalɪdeɪt/ *verb trans.* M17.
[ORIGIN medieval Latin *invalidat-* pa. ppl stem of *invalidare* invalidate, annul, formed as INVALID *adjective*[1]: see -ATE[3]. Perh. partly after French *invalider*.]
Make (an argument, contract, etc.) invalid; *esp.* deprive of legal efficacy.
J. BERMAN Freud's neurotic symptoms do not invalidate his psychological theories.
■ **invaliˈdation** *noun* L18.

invalidity /ɪnvəˈlɪdɪti/ *noun*. M16.
[ORIGIN French *invalidité* or medieval Latin *invaliditas*, formed as INVALID *adjective*[1]: see -ITY. In sense 3 partly from INVALID *adjective*[2].]
1 The quality of being (esp. legally) invalid. M16.
F. MYERS Suspicion of the invalidity of the evidence.
†**2** Weakness, incapacity. L16–L17.
3 The condition of being an invalid; bodily infirmity. L17.
invalidity allowance, ***invalidity benefit***, ***invalidity pension***, etc.

invaluable /ɪnˈvaljʊ(ə)b(ə)l/ *adjective*. L16.
[ORIGIN from IN-[3] + VALUABLE.]
1 Above and beyond valuation; of surpassing or transcendent worth or merit, priceless; inestimable. L16.
A. TREW As Vrakoy's only . . teleprinter operator, she was . . an invaluable source of information.
2 Without value. M17.
■ **invaluableness** *noun* M17. **invaluably** *adverb* E17.

†**invalued** *adjective*. *rare*. *poet.* E17–E19.
[ORIGIN from IN-[3] + VALUED.]
Of which the value has not been reckoned; invaluable.

Invar /ˈɪnvɑː/ *noun*. E20.
[ORIGIN Abbreviation of INVARIABLE.]
(Proprietary name for) an alloy of iron or steel (*c* 64 per cent) and nickel (*c* 36 per cent), which has a very small coefficient of expansion.

invariable /ɪnˈvɛːrɪəb(ə)l/ *adjective* & *noun*. LME.
[ORIGIN Old French & mod. French, or late Latin *invariabilis*, from IN-[3] + *variabilis* VARIABLE *adjective*.]
▸ **A** *adjective*. **1** Unchangeable, unalterable; unchanging, constant; unvarying. LME.
J. GALSWORTHY She had asked Phil to dinner many times; his invariable answer had been 'Too busy'.
2 MATH. (Of a quantity) constant; (of a point, line, etc.) fixed. E18.
▸ **B** *noun*. MATH. An invariable quantity, a constant. M19.
■ **invariaˈbility** *noun* M17. **invariableness** *noun* M17. **invariably** *adverb* without change; without exception: M17.

invariance /ɪnˈvɛːrɪəns/ *noun*. L19.
[ORIGIN from INVARIANT: see -ANCE.]
1 MATH. The character of remaining unaltered after an operation or (esp. linear) transformation. (Foll. by *under*.) L19.
2 *gen.* The property of remaining unaltered or of being the same in different circumstances; an instance of this, an invariant. M20.
■ Also **invariancy** *noun* L19.

invariant /ɪnˈvɛːrɪənt/ *noun* & *adjective*. M19.
[ORIGIN from IN-[3] + VARIANT.]
▸ **A** *noun*. **1** MATH. ▸**a** A function of the coefficients in an expression such that, if that expression is linearly transformed, the same function of the new coefficients is equal to the first function multiplied by some power of a constant pertaining to the transformation. M19. ▸**b** Any quantity or expression which is invariant under a specified transformation or operation. E20.
2 *gen.* An invariant property or feature. M20.
▸ **B** *attrib.* or as *adjective*. **1** Unvarying, invariable. L19.
2 PHYSICAL CHEMISTRY. Having no degrees of freedom. L19.
3 MATH. & PHYSICS. Unchanged by a specified transformation or operation. (Foll. by *under*.) E20.

invaried /ɪnˈvɛːrɪd/ *adjective*. *rare*. L17.
[ORIGIN from IN-[3] + VARIED.]
Not varied; unvaried.

invasion /ɪnˈveɪʒ(ə)n/ *noun*. LME.
[ORIGIN Old French & mod. French, or late Latin *invasio(n-)*, from Latin *invas-* pa. ppl stem of *invadere*: see INVADE, -ION.]
1 **a** The action of invading a country or territory, esp. with armed force; a hostile incursion. LME. ▸**b** *fig.* A harmful incursion of any kind, e.g. of the sea, disease, moral evil, etc. E16. ▸**c** MEDICINE. The spreading of pathogenic micro-organisms or malignant cells that are already in the body to new sites. L19.
a J. M. ROBERTS A whole world . . going under in a chaos of barbarian invasions.
†**2** An assault or attack on a person, a building, etc. LME–M18.
3 Intrusion; encroachment upon a person's property, rights, privacy, etc. LME.
D. C. PEATTIE Being spanked by a parent never struck me as an invasion of the soul's dignity.
4 ECOLOGY. The spread of a plant or animal population into an area formerly free of that species. E20.
■ **invasionist** *noun* a person who advocates or believes in an invasion M19.

invasive /ɪnˈveɪsɪv/ *adjective*. LME.
[ORIGIN French †*invasif*, *-ive* or medieval Latin *invasivus*, from Latin *invas-*: see INVASION, -IVE.]
1 Of, pertaining to, or of the nature of invasion or attack; offensive. LME.
A. FORBES What course of invasive action did it behove Lord Chelmsford to pursue?
2 Characterized by invasion; invading. L16. ▸**b** MEDICINE. Of, exhibiting, or characterized by invasiveness. E20. ▸**c** MEDICINE. Of a diagnostic procedure: involving the entry of an instrument into the body. L20.
C. TOMALIN She sensed the evident hostility many . . felt for the invasive white people.
3 Tending to intrude upon the domain or rights of another. L17.
H. J. S. MAINE A proceeding invasive of tribal rights and calculated to enfeeble them.
■ **invasiveness** *noun* (MEDICINE) the ability of pathogenic micro-organisms or malignant cells that are already in the body to spread to new sites M20.

invecked /ɪnˈvɛkt/ *adjective*. Now *rare*. L15.
[ORIGIN Anglicized from Latin *invect-*: see INVECTIVE.]
Chiefly HERALDRY. Bordered by or (of an edge) consisting of a series of small convex lobes; scalloped.

†**invect** *verb*. M16.
[ORIGIN from Latin *invect-*: see INVECTIVE.]
1 *verb trans.* Bring in, import, introduce. Only in M16.
2 *verb intrans.* Inveigh, utter invectives. Only in E17.

invected /ɪnˈvɛktɪd/ *adjective*. M17.
[ORIGIN formed as INVECT + -ED[1].]
†**1** Brought in, introduced. Only in M17.
2 HERALDRY. = INVECKED. M17.

invective /ɪnˈvɛktɪv/ *adjective* & *noun*. LME.
[ORIGIN Old French & mod. French *invectif*, *-ive* adjective, *invective* noun, from late Latin *invectivus*, as noun *invectiva* (*oratio*), from *invect-* pa. ppl stem of *invehere*: see INVEIGH, -IVE.]
▸ **A** *adjective*. Using or characterized by denunciatory language; vituperative, abusive. Now *rare*. LME.
Weekend Magazine (Montreal) He became invective, insisted he be served a coffee.

▶ **B** *noun.* **1** A violent verbal attack or denunciation. E16.

> C. HOPE The . . tirade of Father Lynch's invective as he briskly cursed the scrambling altar boys.

2 Denunciatory or opprobrious language; vehement denunciation; vituperation. L16.

> V. BROME His invective against his enemies included phrases like 'slimy bastard'.

■ **invectively** *adverb* (now *rare*) M16. **invectiveness** *noun* (*rare*) M17.

inveigh /ɪnˈveɪ/ *verb.* Also †**en-**. L15.
[ORIGIN Latin *invehere* carry in, mediopassive *invehi* be borne into, attack, assail with words, from *in-* IN-[2] + *vehere* carry.]
†**1** *verb trans.* Orig., carry in, introduce (*rare*). Later, entice, inveigle. L15–L17.
2 *verb intrans.* Speak in order to denounce, reproach, or censure; speak vehemently. Foll. by *against*, †*upon*. E16.

> R. OWEN In language which recalled Stalinist socialist realism he inveighed against 'alien' Western influences.

■ **inveigher** *noun* (*rare*) L16.

inveigle /ɪnˈviːɡ(ə)l, ɪnˈveɪɡ(ə)l/ *verb trans.* Also †**en-**. L15.
[ORIGIN Anglo-Norman *envegler* alt. (cf. ENSAMPLE *noun*) of Old French & mod. French *aveugler* to blind, from *aveugle* blind, prob. from Proto-Romance. Cf. VEIGLE.]
†**1** Beguile, deceive. L15–E18.
2 **a** Win over or captivate by deceitful allurement; entice, seduce. M16. ▸†**b** Entrap, ensnare, entangle. M16–E18. ▸**c** Guilefully draw (a person), *into*, *to*, *from*, etc., an action, conduct, a place, etc. M16.

> **a** J. L. MOTLEY An organized system of harlotry, by which the soldiers and politicians of France were inveigled. **c** R. HAYMAN He blamed his son for inveigling him into the investment.

■ **inveiglement** *noun* M16. **inveigler** *noun* M16.

†**inveil** *verb* var. of ENVEIL.

invein /ɪnˈveɪn/ *verb trans. rare.* Also (earlier) †**en-**. E16.
[ORIGIN from IN-[2] (EN-[1]) + VEIN *verb*.]
Streak or diversify with or as with veins.

†**invelop** *verb* var. of ENVELOP.

†**invenom** *verb* var. of ENVENOM.

invent /ɪnˈvɛnt/ *verb trans.* L15.
[ORIGIN Latin *invent-* pa. ppl stem of *invenire* come upon, discover, from *in-* IN-[2] + *venire* come.]
1 Find out, discover, esp. by search or endeavour. Now *rare* or *obsolete*. L15.
2 †**a** Devise, contrive; plan, plot. Also with inf. M16–E19. ▸**b** Devise as an untruth (a statement or story, or an element of one). M16. ▸†**c** Devise (a subject, idea, or method of treatment for a work of art or literature) by means of the intellect or imagination. L16–L17.

> **b** J. VAN DRUTEN She's an imaginary character I invented.

3 Create, produce, or construct by original thought or ingenuity; devise or originate (a new art, instrument, process, etc.). Formerly also with inf. M16.

> H. L. MENCKEN There was no . . progress in the cure of disease until man began inventing remedies.

†**4** Found, establish, institute, appoint. M16–L17.
■ **inventable**, **inventible** *adjectives* M17. **inventor** *noun* E16. **inventress** *noun* E16. **inventrix** *noun* (long *rare*) E17.

inventar /ˈɪnvɪntə/ *noun & verb. obsolete* exc. *Scot.* As noun also **-er**. LME.
[ORIGIN Old French *inventaire* from late Latin *inventarium*: see INVENTORY.]
▶ **A** *noun.* = INVENTORY *noun*. LME.
▶ **B** *verb trans.* Make an inventory of, catalogue. M17.

†**inventary** *noun & verb* var. of INVENTORY.

†**inventer** *noun*[1]. M16–E19.
[ORIGIN from INVENT + -ER[1].]
An inventor.

inventer *noun*[2] var. of INVENTAR *noun*.

invention /ɪnˈvɛnʃ(ə)n/ *noun.* ME.
[ORIGIN Latin *inventio(n-)*, formed as INVENT: see -ION.]
▶ **I** **1** An act or the action of finding or finding out; discovery. *arch.* ME. ▸**b** RHETORIC. The selecting of topics to be treated, or of arguments to be used. LME. ▸†**c** The solving of a problem. L15–M17.
2 The faculty of inventing or devising; creativity, inventiveness. L15.

> W. H. PRESCOTT His invention was ever busy devising intrigues.

3 An act or the action of devising, contriving, or fabricating something. L15. ▸**b** The devising of a subject, idea, or method of treatment for a work of art or literature, by means of the intellect or imagination. L15.

> R. W. SOUTHERN Inventions of new words are important historical events. **b** J. BRODSKY Neither in invention nor in . . world view does . . Russian prose of today offer anything . . new.

†**4** The manner in which a thing is devised or constructed; design. E16–E18.
5 The contrivance or production of a new art, instrument, process, etc.; origination, introduction. M16.

> P. GOODMAN The essence of invention is to be hitherto-unthought-of.

▶ **II** **6** Something devised; a contrivance, a design, a plan. Formerly also, a discovery. LME. ▸**b** A fictitious statement or story; a fabrication. E16.

> **b** T. S. ELIOT The aunt was a pure invention On the spur of the moment.

†**7** A work of art or literature as produced by means of the intellect or imagination. L15–E17.
8 A new art, instrument, process, etc., originated by the ingenuity of some person. L15.

> M. MEAD It is no longer possible . . to keep inventions like gunpowder to use in firecrackers.

– PHRASES: **Invention of the Cross** (a festival held on 3 May commemorating) the reputed finding of the Cross by Helena, mother of the Emperor Constantine, in AD 326.

inventive /ɪnˈvɛntɪv/ *adjective.* LME.
[ORIGIN French *inventif*, *-ive* or medieval Latin *inventivus*, formed as INVENT: see -IVE.]
1 Having the faculty of invention; original, apt, or quick in contriving or devising. Also foll. by *of*. LME.

> G. GREENE He had been too inventive; he had to draw the line . . between what was real . . and unreal.

2 Characterized by invention; produced by or showing original contrivance. E17.

> J. RUSKIN Great art . . must be inventive, that is, be produced by the imagination.

■ **inventively** *adverb* M19. **inventiveness** *noun* M17.

inventory /ˈɪnv(ə)nt(ə)ri/ *noun & verb.* Also †**-ary**, (*rare*) †**invitory**. LME.
[ORIGIN medieval Latin *inventorium* alt. of late Latin *inventarium* lit. 'list of what is found', formed as INVENT: see -ORY[1]. Cf. INVENTAR.]
▶ **A** *noun.* **1** A detailed list of items such as goods in stock, a person's property, the contents of a storage box, room, building, etc., occas. with a statement giving the nature and value of each item. LME.

> S. BELLOW She . . made an inventory of all the objects on the desk. E. HARDWICK Alex was making an inventory of Sarah's Philadelphia house.

2 *gen.* A list, a catalogue; a detailed account. E16. ▸**b** *spec.* (LINGUISTICS) A list of a specified type of linguistic features in a language. M20.

> J. G. BALLARD Scanning the timber store, making an inventory of its possibilities.

3 *transf.* The quantity or stock of goods etc. which are or may be made the subject of an inventory. L17.

> *High Times* Buying out local inventories endlessly, because the shelves could . . be restocked by smugglers.

▶ **B** *verb trans.* & (*rare*) *intrans.* Make an inventory or descriptive list of goods, a person's characteristics, etc.; enter in an inventory, catalogue; amount (to) in an inventory. E16.

> G. H. LORIMER She inventoried about $10,000 as she stood. D. L. SAYERS He had the air of inventorying its contents with a view to assessing their value.

■ **invenˈtorial** *adjective* L20. **invenˈtorially** *adverb* (*rare*, Shakes.): only in 17. **inˈventorize** *verb trans. & intrans.* make an inventory (of) E17.

inveracious /ɪnvəˈreɪʃəs/ *adjective.* L19.
[ORIGIN from IN-[3] + VERACIOUS.]
Untruthful, untrue.

inveracity /ɪnvəˈrasɪti/ *noun.* M19.
[ORIGIN from IN-[3] + VERACITY.]
Untruthfulness; an untruth, a false statement.

inverecund /ɪnˈvɛrɪkʌnd/ *adjective. rare.* M17.
[ORIGIN Latin *inverecundus* shameless, formed as IN-[3] + *verecundus* reverent, modest, from *vereri* revere.]
Unabashed, shameless.

inverisimilitude /ɪnˌvɛrɪsɪˈmɪlɪtjuːd/ *noun.* E19.
[ORIGIN from IN-[3] + VERISIMILITUDE.]
Lack of verisimilitude; unlikelihood; improbability.

invermination /ɪnˌvəːmɪˈneɪʃ(ə)n/ *noun.* E19.
[ORIGIN from IN-[2] + VERMINATION.]
The condition of being infested with (intestinal) worms or other vermin.

Inverness /ɪnvəˈnɛs/ *noun.* M19.
[ORIGIN A city in the Highland region of Scotland.]
1 ***Inverness cape***, the cape from an Inverness cloak. M19.
2 ***Inverness cloak***, ***Inverness coat***, ***Inverness overcoat***, a man's sleeveless cloak with a removable cape. L19.

inverse /ˈɪnvəːs, ɪnˈvəːs/ *adjective & noun.* LME.
[ORIGIN from Latin *inversus* pa. pple of *invertere* INVERT *verb*.]
▶ **A** *adjective.* **1** Turned upside down; inverted. LME.

> T. HOOD A tower builded on a lake, Mock'd by its inverse shadow.

2 MATH. **a** Of two operations, relations, etc.: such that the starting point or antecedent of the one is the result or conclusion of the other, and vice versa; (of one such operation, relation, etc.) opposite in nature or effect (to the other). Opp. ***direct***. M17. ▸**b** GEOMETRY. Of a point, line, curve, etc.: related to another point, line, curve, etc. by a geometrical inversion. L19.
3 Inverted in position, order, or relations; proceeding in the opposite or reverse direction or order. M19.

> B. MAGEE Such fascinated detestation is a kind of inverse love.

4 CRYSTALLOGRAPHY. Having the reverse of some usual relation. Now only *spec.* (of a spinel structure) having half the trivalent cations in the tetrahedral holes normally occupied by the divalent cations. L19.
– SPECIAL COLLOCATIONS: **inverse proportion** = ***inverse ratio*** (b) below. **inverse ratio** (***a***) a ratio in which the terms are reversed with respect to a given ratio; (***b***) the relationship of two quantities, one of which increases (esp. in exact proportion) as the other decreases, and vice versa. **inverse spelling** an unetymological spelling based on the spelling of another word containing an element that is no longer pronounced, as *limb* from Old English *lim* after *lamb* (from Old English *lamb*). **inverse square** the relation of two quantities one of which varies inversely as the square of the other; ***inverse square law***, by which the intensity of an effect, as gravitational attraction, illumination, etc., decreases in inverse proportion to the square of the distance from the source of the effect.
▶ **B** *noun.* **1** An inverted state or condition. Also, a thing which is in reverse order to something else. L17.
2 MATH. & LOGIC. A ratio, process, curve, proposition, etc., which is the result of inversion; an inverse ratio; an inverse function. L17. ▸**b** *spec.* in MATH. An element which, when combined with a given element by a given operation, produces the identity element for that operation. E20.

> **b** OED The inverse of any number with respect to multiplication is the reciprocal.

3 In rouge-et-noir: the section of the table in which are placed bets that the colour of the first card dealt will not be the same as that of the winning row. Also, the game of rouge-et-noir. M19.

inverse /ɪnˈvəːs/ *verb trans.* Now *rare*. E17.
[ORIGIN from INVERSE *adjective & noun*.]
Turn upside down; invert; reverse in order or direction.
■ **inversed** *ppl adjective* (long *rare*) reversed; turned upside down; turned inward: LME.

inversely /ɪnˈvəːsli/ *adverb.* M17.
[ORIGIN from INVERSE *adjective* + -LY[2].]
1 In an inverse manner or order; by inversion; in inverse proportion. M17.
2 Invertedly; upside down. L18.
inversely conical, **inversely pyramidal**: with the vertex downward.

inversion /ɪnˈvəːʃ(ə)n/ *noun.* M16.
[ORIGIN Latin *inversio(n-)*, from *invers-* pa. ppl stem of *invertere*: see INVERT *verb*, -ION.]
▶ **I** Reversal, transposition.
†**1** RHETORIC. The turning of an argument against the person who advances it. M16–M17.
2 A reversal of position, order, sequence, or relation. L16.
3 RHETORIC. = ANASTROPHE. L16.
4 MILITARY. A drill movement by which the relative positions of the troops are changed; *spec.* one by which a rank becomes a file. M17.
5 MATH. **a** The reversal of a ratio by interchanging the antecedent and consequent. M17. ▸**b** GEOMETRY. A transformation in which each point of a given figure is replaced by another point on the same straight line from a fixed point, esp. in such a way that the product of the distances of the two points from the centre of inversion is constant. Also, any similar transformation involving a more complex relation of corresponding points or lines. L19. ▸**c** MATH. The process of finding a function $g(y)$ which either yields a variable x when its argument is a given function $y = f(x)$ of that variable, or else yields a given function under a given transformation. L19.
6 MUSIC. The action of inverting an interval, chord, phrase, or subject. Also, the interval, chord, etc., so produced (in relation to the original one). E19.
7 CHEMISTRY. **a** Decomposition of an optically active carbohydrate (esp. sucrose) by which the direction of the optical rotatory power is reversed. M19. ▸**b** Orig., the reversal of the direction of optical rotation observed in certain substitution reactions. Now, the change of configuration which occurs when a reactant enters along the axis of the bond between a central atom and the leaving group, causing the other substituents on the central atom to pass through a plane perpendicular to this axis (regardless of any effect on optical activity). Also more fully WALDEN INVERSION. L19.
8 LOGIC. A form of immediate inference in which a new proposition is formed whose subject is the negative of that of the original proposition. L19.
9 In full ***sexual inversion***. Homosexuality. Also, the adoption of dress, behaviour, or a role, typical of the opposite sex. L19.
10 METEOROLOGY. In full ***temperature inversion***. An increase of air temperature with height (the reverse of the usual decrease); a layer of air having such a reversed gradient.

Also, an increase of temperature with depth of water. **E20.**

11 *BIOLOGY.* A (chromosome segment exhibiting) reversal of the order of the genes as compared with the normal order on the chromosome. **E20.**

12 *ELECTRICITY.* The conversion of direct current into alternating current. Opp. ***rectification***. **E20.**

13 *PHYSICAL CHEMISTRY.* A transformation of a substance, esp. an enantiotropic one, from one solid form to another. **E20.**

14 *TELECOMMUNICATIONS.* Reversal of the order of the component frequencies of a signal. **M20.**

15 *COMPUTING.* The conversion of either of the two binary digits or signals into the other; negation. **M20.**

16 *PHYSICS.* In full ***population inversion***. A transposition of the relative numbers of atoms or molecules occupying certain energy levels. **M20.**

▸ **II** Alteration in use.

†**17** = METAPHOR 1. **M–L16.**

†**18** Diversion to an improper use; perversion. **E–M18.**

▸ **III** The action of turning, or state of being turned, vertically.

19 A turning upside down. **L16.**

20 *GEOLOGY.* The folding back of stratified rocks upon each other, so that older strata overlie newer. **M19.**

▸ **IV** The action of turning, or state of being turned, in or inwards.

21 Chiefly *MEDICINE.* Introversion; a turning inside out (esp. of the uterus). **L16.**

22 *MEDICINE.* A twisting of the foot so that the sole faces inwards. **M19.**

– COMB.: **inversion compound** a place name in which the second element is a name, title, etc., in the genitive case or otherwise showing ownership of the first element; **inversion temperature** (*a*) *PHYSICS* the temperature (for any particular gas) at which the Joule–Thomson effect changes sign, so that the gas is neither heated nor cooled when allowed to expand without doing any work; (*b*) *PHYSICAL CHEMISTRY* the temperature at which two solid forms of a substance can coexist in equilibrium.

inversive /ɪnˈvəːsɪv/ *adjective.* **L19.**
[ORIGIN from Latin *invers-* (see INVERSION) + -IVE.]
Characterized by inversion.

†**inversor** *noun. rare.* Only in **M19.**
[ORIGIN from INVERSE *verb* + -OR.]
= INVERTOR 1.

invert /ˈɪnvəːt/ *noun & adjective.* **M19.**
[ORIGIN from the verb.]

▸ **A** *noun.* **1** An inverted arch, as at the bottom of a canal or sewer. **M19.**

2 *PSYCHOLOGY.* A person who exhibits instincts or behaviour characteristic of the opposite sex. **L19.**

3 Sugar formed by the breaking up of sucrose into dextrose and laevulose. **E20.**

▸ **B** *attrib.* or as *adjective.* Inverted. **L19.**

invert soap: whose surface-active ion is a cation (rather than the more usual anion); a cationic detergent. **invert sugar** = sense A.3 above.

invert /ɪnˈvəːt/ *verb.* **M16.**
[ORIGIN Latin *invertere*, formed as IN-² + *vertere* turn (lit. 'turn inside-out').]

▸ **I** Reverse, transpose.

1 *verb trans.* Turn back to front, reverse; change the relations of so as to produce the opposite. **M16.** ▸**b** *verb intrans.* Change to the opposite. Now *rare* or *obsolete.* **E17.**

†**2** *verb trans. RHETORIC.* Turn an argument against the person who advances it. **M17–L18.**

3 *verb trans. MUSIC.* Change the relative position of the notes of (an interval or chord) by raising the lowest note (usu. by an octave). Also, modify (a phrase or subject) by reversing the direction of its movement in pitch. **M19.**

4 a *verb intrans. GEOMETRY.* Be transformed by inversion *into.* Now *rare* or *obsolete.* **M19.** ▸**b** *verb trans. MATH.* Transform by inversion; find the inverse of. **M20.**

5 *verb trans. CHEMISTRY.* Subject (a compound) to inversion; *esp.* break up (sucrose) into dextrose and laevulose. **M19.**

6 *verb intrans. CHEMISTRY.* Of a substance: undergo inversion. **L19.**

7 *verb trans. LOGIC.* Obtain the inverse of (a proposition). **L19.**

8 *verb trans. TELECOMMUNICATIONS.* Subject (a signal) to a heterodyne process that reverses the order of the component frequencies. **M20.**

▸ **II** Change the use of.

†**9** *verb trans.* Use (a word) metaphorically rather than literally. Only in **L16.**

†**10** *verb trans.* Divert from its proper purpose; pervert to another use. **L16–L17.**

▸ **III** Turn upside down.

11 *verb trans.* Turn upside down. Formerly also *fig.*, overthrow, upset. **L16.**

▸ **IV 12** *verb trans.* Chiefly *MEDICINE.* Turn inside out. **E17.**

†**13** *verb trans.* Turn in or inward. Only in **M17.**

invertant /ɪnˈvəːt(ə)nt/ *adjective. rare.* **E19.**
[ORIGIN from INVERT *verb* + -ANT¹.]
HERALDRY. = INVERTED 2.

invertase /ˈɪnvəːteɪz, ɪnˈvəːt-/ *noun.* **L19.**
[ORIGIN from INVERT *verb* + -ASE.]
BIOCHEMISTRY. An enzyme, extractable from yeast, which catalyses the inversion of sucrose. Also called ***saccharase***, ***sucrase***.

invertebracy /ɪnˈvəːtɪbrəsi/ *noun. joc.* **L19.**
[ORIGIN from INVERTEBRATE *adjective* 2: see -ACY.]
Spinelessness; lack of firmness or conviction.

invertebral /ɪnˈvəːtɪbr(ə)l/ *adjective. rare.* **E19.**
[ORIGIN from IN-³ + VERTEBRAL.]
= INVERTEBRATE *adjective.*

Invertebrata /ɪnˌvəːtɪˈbrɑːtə/ *noun pl.* **E19.**
[ORIGIN mod. Latin, from French *invertébrés*, from *in-* IN-³ + VERTEBRA.]
ZOOLOGY. (Members of) a group which includes all animals except vertebrates.
– NOTE: No longer in use in formal taxonomy.

invertebrate /ɪnˈvəːtɪbrət/ *adjective & noun.* **E19.**
[ORIGIN from INVERTEBRATA: see -ATE¹, -ATE².]

▸ **A** *noun.* **1** An animal without a backbone or spinal column; an animal not belonging to the subphylum Vertebrata. **E19.**

2 *fig.* A person without strength of character or principles. **M19.**

▸ **B** *adjective.* **1** (Of an animal) not having a backbone or spinal column; of or pertaining to invertebrates. **M19.**

2 *fig.* Without moral courage, firmness, or consistency. **L19.**

inverted /ɪnˈvəːtɪd/ *adjective.* **L16.**
[ORIGIN from INVERT *verb* + -ED¹.]

1 Reversed in position, relation, or order; turned upside down or back to front; turned inwards or inside out. **L16.**

2 *HERALDRY.* Of a charge: used upside down. Of a bird's wings: with the tips pointed downwards. Of two animals: facing each other across the middle of the field. **E17.**

3 *MUSIC.* Of a chord or interval: having the lowest note raised (usu. by an octave). **E19.**

4 *PHONETICS.* Produced with the tip of the tongue turned upwards towards the hard palate. **L19.**

5 *PSYCHOLOGY.* Of the sex instincts: turned towards one's own sex; homosexual. **L19.**

– SPECIAL COLLOCATIONS: ***inverted comma***: see COMMA 4. ***inverted pendulum***: see PENDULUM *noun.* **inverted pleat**: with two parallel contrary pleats forming a recessed band. **inverted snob** a person who likes or takes pride in what a snob normally disapproves of. **inverted snobbery** the practices or attitudes of an inverted snob. **inverted spelling** = ***inverse spelling*** s.v. INVERSE *adjective.*

■ **invertedly** *adverb* in an inverted manner; upside down; with inversion of order: **L17.**

invertend /ˈɪnvətɛnd/ *noun.* **L19.**
[ORIGIN Latin *invertendus*, from *invertere* INVERT *verb*: see -END.]
LOGIC. The proposition from which another proposition is obtained by inversion.

inverter /ɪnˈvəːtə/ *noun.* **E17.**
[ORIGIN from INVERT *verb* + -ER¹.]

1 *gen.* A person who or thing which inverts or produces inversion. *rare.* **E17.**

2 *ELECTRICITY.* An apparatus which converts direct current into alternating current. Cf. INVERTOR 1. **E20.** ▸**b** *TELECOMMUNICATIONS.* A device that inverts a signal. **M20.** ▸**c** *COMPUTING.* A device that converts either of the two binary digits or signals into the other. **M20.**

invertible /ɪnˈvəːtɪb(ə)l/ *adjective.* **L19.**
[ORIGIN from INVERT *verb* + -IBLE.]

1 Able to be inverted. **L19.** ▸**b** That tends to invert the usual order. *rare.* **L19.**

2 *MATH.* Of an element of a set: having an inverse (*spec.* an inverse for multiplication) in the set. **M20.**

■ **invertiˈbility** *noun* **M20.**

invertor /ɪnˈvəːtə/ *noun.* **E20.**
[ORIGIN from INVERT *verb* + -OR.]

1 *ELECTRICITY.* An instrument for reversing an electric current; a commutator. Also occas., = INVERTER 2. **E20.**

2 *ANATOMY.* A muscle which turns a part (as the foot) inwards. **E20.**

invest /ɪnˈvɛst/ *verb.* **M16.**
[ORIGIN Old French & mod. French *investir* or Latin *investire* clothe, surround, formed as IN-² + *vestis* clothing. In branch II after Italian *investire.*]

▸ **I 1** *verb trans.* **a** Clothe; envelop, or surround *in, with,* or as with, a garment. Of a garment etc.: clothe, cover, adorn. **M16.** ▸**b** Put on as clothes or ornaments; don. **L16.** ▸**c** Embed in or surround *with* hardened heat-resistant material. **L19.**

2 *verb trans.* Clothe *with* or *in* the insignia of a position or rank; install *in* a position or rank with the customary rites or ceremonies. **M16.**

3 *verb trans.* Establish (a person) *in* any rank, position, property, etc.; endow *with* power, authority, or privilege. **M16.** ▸**b** Settle (a right or power) *in* (a person). **L16.**

> J. GILBERT The innocent being is by law invested with the right to enjoy security. **b** R. D. LAING I was frightened by the power invested in me as a psychiatrist.

4 *verb trans.* Provide or endow with attributes, qualities, or a character. Foll. by *with*, †*in.* **E17.**

> P. BOWLES Her superstitious fancy had invested them with magical importance. M. PIERCY She tried to invest her tone with some of the bitter irony she felt.

5 *verb trans. MILITARY.* Surround with a hostile force; besiege, beleaguer. **E17.**

▸ **II 6** *verb trans.* Expend (money, effort) in something from which a return or profit is expected, now esp. in the purchase of property, shares, etc., for the sake of the interest, dividends, or profits accruing from them. **E17.** ▸**b** *verb intrans.* Make an investment, invest capital; *colloq.* lay out money *in* a (useful) purchase. **M19.** ▸**c** *verb trans.* & *intrans.* Lay out (money) in betting on a horse race, or in football pools, etc. **M20.**

> P. H. JOHNSON She had inherited money from an aunt—enough, invested, to bring in five hundred a year. J. A. MICHENER A new life where we can invest our money and our energy and build our own paradise. **b** *Sugar* Chucked out all my scuzzy make-up and invested in a new make-up bag. **c** H. CECIL He went to the £5 tote windows and invested . . £100 on Maiden Aunt.

■ **inˈvestable**, **-ible** *adjective* able to be invested **L19.** †**investient** *adjective* coating, enveloping, enfolding **L17–M18.** **investor** *noun* a person who invests or makes an investment **L16.**

†**investigable** *adjective*¹. **LME–E18.**
[ORIGIN ecclesiastical Latin *investigabilis*, formed as IN-³ + *vestigare* track, trace: see -ABLE.]
Incapable of being traced; undiscoverable, unsearchable.

investigable /ɪnˈvɛstɪgəb(ə)l/ *adjective*². **L16.**
[ORIGIN Late Latin *investigabilis*, from *investigare*: see INVESTIGATE, -ABLE.]
Able to be investigated, traced out, or searched into; open to investigation, inquiry, or research.

investigate /ɪnˈvɛstɪgeɪt/ *verb.* **E16.**
[ORIGIN Latin *investigat-* pa. ppl stem of *investigare*, formed as IN-² + *vestigare* track, trace out: see -ATE³.]

1 *verb trans.* Search or inquire into; examine (a matter) systematically or in detail; make an (official) inquiry into. **E16.**

> *Dumfries Courier* Police and fire brigade officials are investigating the cause of the fire. R. ELLMANN R. B. Haldane . . as a member of the Home Office committee investigating prisons had access to any prison.

2 *verb intrans.* Make a search or systematic inquiry. **E16.**

> R. BRADBURY They'll never come and investigate to see what happened to us.

■ **investigator** *noun* a person who investigates; a researcher, a detective: **M16.** **investigaˈtorial** *adjective* pertaining to or characteristic of an investigator or investigation **E19.** **investigatory** *adjective* of an investigating nature or character **M19.**

investigation /ɪnˌvɛstɪˈgeɪʃ(ə)n/ *noun.* **LME.**
[ORIGIN Old French & mod. French, or Latin *investigatio(n-)*, formed as INVESTIGATE: see -ATION.]

1 The action or process of investigating; systematic examination; careful research. **LME.**

> G. CHEYNE There is scarce a Geometer, but has his own Method of Investigation.

2 An instance of this; a systematic inquiry; a careful study of a particular subject. **L18.**

> J. THURBER A recent investigation of the worries and concerns of five thousand selected Americans. N. SYMINGTON The central area of Freud's investigations was the unconscious.

■ **investiˈgational** *adjective* **E20.**

investigative /ɪnˈvɛstɪgətɪv, -geɪtɪv/ *adjective.* **E19.**
[ORIGIN from Latin *investigat-* (see INVESTIGATE) + -IVE.]

1 Characterized by or inclined to investigation. **E19.**

> *Time* The laws . . put heavy restraints on the investigative and prosecutorial powers of the state.

2 Of journalism or broadcasting: investigating and seeking to expose malpractice, miscarriage of justice, etc. Of a journalist etc.: engaged in this. Orig. *US.* **M20.**

> *Daily Telegraph* Mr Lewis's classic piece of investigative reporting into the plight of the Indians in the Brazilian rainforest.

investitive /ɪnˈvɛstɪtɪv/ *adjective.* **L18.**
[ORIGIN from Latin *investit-* (see INVESTITURE) + -IVE.]
Having the property or function of investing.

investiture /ɪnˈvɛstɪtjə, -tʃə/ *noun.* **LME.**
[ORIGIN medieval Latin *investitura*, from Latin *investit-* pa. ppl stem of *investire* INVEST: see -URE.]

1 The action or ceremony of clothing someone in the insignia of a position or rank; the ceremonial or formal investing of a person with a position, rank, or benefice. **LME.**

2 Endowment with an attribute or quality; establishment in any state of privilege or honour. **E17.**

3 The action of clothing or robing; a thing which clothes or covers. Chiefly *fig.* **M17.**

4 = INVESTMENT 4. Now *rare.* **M17.**

†**5** = INVESTMENT 5. **M18–M19.**

investment /ɪnˈvɛs(t)m(ə)nt/ *noun*. L16.
[ORIGIN from INVEST + -MENT.]
▸ **I 1** The act of putting on clothes or vestments; clothing; robes, vestments. Now *rare* or *obsolete*. L16.
2 a An outer covering of any kind; an envelope; a coating. M17. ▸**b** Heat-resistant material used to embed or surround an object and allowed to harden, to allow soldering (in DENTISTRY), or to form a mould for investment casting. L19.
3 The action of investing or fact of being invested with a position, rank, right, or attribute; endowment. M17.
4 MILITARY. The surrounding or blockading *of* a place by a hostile force. E19.
▸ **II 5** The investing of money (now also time or effort); an instance of this. E17.

W. HUTTON Private saving . . would boost investment and growth. *New Yorker* The investment of thirty years and billions of dollars in cancer research.

6 An amount of money invested. Also, anything in which money etc. is or may be invested. M19.

Investors Chronicle People who need to live off their investments.

– COMB.: **investment bank** (chiefly in the US) a bank (similar to a UK merchant bank) that purchases large holdings of newly issued shares and resells them to investors; **investment bond** a single-premium investment in a life-insurance policy; **investment casting** a lost-wax technique for making small, accurate castings in heat-resistant alloys using a mould formed around a pattern of wax or similar material which is then removed by melting; **investment currency** the currency used in the buying and selling of foreign securities through a market separate from a controlled market in foreign exchange; **investment grade** a level of credit rating for stocks regarded as carrying a minimal risk to investors; **investment material** = sense 2b above; **investment trust** a limited company whose business is the investment of shareholders' funds, the shares being traded like those of any other public company.

investure /ɪnˈvɛstʃə, -tjə/ *noun*. L16.
[ORIGIN from INVEST + -URE.]
Investiture into a position, rank, or benefice. Also, the military investment of a city etc.

inveteracy /ɪnˈvɛt(ə)rəsi/ *noun*. L17.
[ORIGIN from INVETERATE *adjective & noun*: see -ACY.]
The quality of being inveterate; the state of being entrenched or of long standing. Also, an instance of this; deep-rooted or long-lasting prejudice or hostility.

inveterate /ɪnˈvɛt(ə)rət/ *adjective & noun*. LME.
[ORIGIN Latin *inveteratus* pa. pple of *inveterare* make old, formed as IN-[2] + *veter-*, *vetus* old: see -ATE[2].]
▸ **A** *adjective*. **1** Of disease: of long standing, chronic; resisting treatment. LME. ▸**b** Long established, ancient, old. Now chiefly of a (bad) habit, prejudice, etc.: deep-rooted, obstinate, ingrained E16. ▸**c** Persistent, lasting. L18.

H. LYTE Medicines against an old inueterate cough. **b** EVELYN Rotten wood, . . especially that which is taken out of an Inveterate willow tree. J. A. FROUDE His relations with Francis . . were those of inveterate hostility. **c** E. MANNIN A big part of Ahmad's charm was his inveterate desire to please.

2 Settled or confirmed in a habit or practice; habitual, hardened, obstinate. L15.

H. T. LANE She had been made a hard liar by hard treatment, and was . . an inveterate mischief-maker. D. M. THOMAS She . . enjoyed writing—she was, for example, an inveterate letter-writer.

3 Full of obstinate prejudice or hatred; embittered, malignant; virulent. Now *rare* or *obsolete*. E16.
▸ **B** *noun*. A person who is confirmed in some (bad) habit; a confirmed or hardened offender. E18.
■ **inveterately** *adverb* M17. **inveterateness** *noun* M17.

†**inveterate** *verb trans*. L16–M19.
[ORIGIN from INVETERATE *adjective & noun* or from Latin *inveterat-* pa. ppl stem of *inveterare*: see INVETERATE *adjective & noun*, -ATE[3].]
Make inveterate; establish by long usage or custom; harden, confirm.
■ †**inveteration** *noun* (*rare*) the action of making something inveterate; the process of becoming inveterate: M17–E18.

inviable /ɪnˈvʌɪəb(ə)l/ *adjective*. E20.
[ORIGIN from IN-[3] + VIABLE *adjective*[1].]
BIOLOGY. Unable to survive; unable to germinate, grow, or develop; unable to perform its proper biological role.
■ **inviaˈbility** *noun* the state or condition of being inviable E20.

invidious /ɪnˈvɪdɪəs/ *adjective*. E17.
[ORIGIN Latin *invidiosus*, from *invidia* ill will: see ENVY *noun*, -IOUS.]
1 Giving or likely to give offence or arouse ill feeling. E17. ▸†**b** Viewed with ill will or dislike; odious *to* a person. *rare*. Only in E18.

DRYDEN He rose, and took th'advantage of the times, To load young Turnus with invidious crimes. D. ADAMS It's none of my business and it puts me in an invidious position.

2 Of a thing: likely to arouse ill feeling or envy against the possessor. M17.

LD MACAULAY Catharine saw all the peril of such a step, and declined the invidious honor.

3 Envious, grudging, jealous. Now *rare* or *obsolete*. M17.
4 Of a comparison or distinction: unjust, unfairly discriminating. E18.

E. JOHNSON Amid the . . plenty of Dickens's creation it is almost invidious to single out individual novels.

■ **invidiously** *adverb* M17. **invidiousness** *noun* L17.

†**invigilancy** *noun*. *rare*. E17–E18.
[ORIGIN from IN-[3] + VIGILANCY.]
Absence of vigilance or watchfulness.

invigilate /ɪnˈvɪdʒɪleɪt/ *verb*. M16.
[ORIGIN Latin *invigilat-* pa. ppl stem of *invigilare*, formed as IN-[2] + *vigilare* watch, from *vigil* watchful: see -ATE[3].]
1 *verb intrans. & trans.* Keep watch; watch carefully. Now *spec.* watch over students at (an examination). M16.
†**2** *verb trans.* Arouse; make watchful. *rare*. Only in E17.
■ **invigiˈlation** *noun* L19. **invigilator** *noun* a person who watches over students at an examination L19.

invigor *verb* see INVIGOUR.

invigorate /ɪnˈvɪg(ə)rət/ *ppl adjective*. *rare*. E18.
[ORIGIN formed as INVIGORATE *verb*.]
Filled with vigour; invigorated.

invigorate /ɪnˈvɪgəreɪt/ *verb trans*. M17.
[ORIGIN medieval Latin *invigorat-* pa. ppl stem, formed as IN-[2] + Latin *vigorare* make strong, from *vigor*: see VIGOUR *noun*, -ATE[3].]
Make vigorous; fill with life and energy; strengthen, animate. Freq. as ***invigorating*** *ppl adjective*.

B. T. BRADFORD The quick walk from the evening performance had been invigorating. D. ADAMS I find your scepticism rewarding and invigorating.

■ **invigorant** *noun* something that invigorates; an invigorating drink or medicine, a tonic: E19. **invigoratingly** *adverb* so as to invigorate someone or something L19. **invigoˈration** *noun* M17. **invigorative** *adjective* (*rare*) that tends to invigorate; invigorating: M19. **invigorator** *noun* M19.

invigour /ɪnˈvɪgə/ *verb trans*. Also *-**or**; (earlier) †**en-**. E17.
[ORIGIN Old French & mod. French *envigo(u)rer* formed as EN-[1], IN-[2] + Latin *vigorare* (see INVIGORATE *verb*); later from IN-[2] + VIGOUR.]
Fill with vigour; invigorate.

†**invinate** *ppl adjective*. *rare*. M16.
[ORIGIN medieval Latin *invinatus* pa. pple of *invinare*: see INVINATION.]
Embodied or included in wine.

invination /ɪnvɪˈneɪʃ(ə)n/ *noun*. M18.
[ORIGIN from Latin *invinare*, formed as IN-[2] + *vinum* wine: see -ATION.]
CHRISTIAN CHURCH. In Eucharistic doctrine: the presence of the blood (and, according to most holders of the doctrine, also the body) of Christ in the wine after consecration.

invincible /ɪnˈvɪnsɪb(ə)l/ *adjective & noun*. LME.
[ORIGIN Old French & mod. French from Latin *invincibilis*, formed as IN-[3] + *vincibilis*, from *vincere* conquer: see -IBLE.]
▸ **A** *adjective*. **1** Unable to be vanquished, overcome, or subdued; unconquerable. LME. ▸**b** Insurmountable, insuperable. LME.

Sunday Express Honeyghan . . surprised everyone by ripping the . . title off the previously invincible Don Curry.

b invincible ignorance (orig. THEOLOGY): which the ignorant person does not have the means to overcome.
†**2** Unable to be excelled; unsurpassable. E16–E17.
▸ **B** *noun*. A person who is invincible. M17.
■ **invinciˈbility** *noun* invincibleness L17. **invincibleness** *noun* E17. **invincibly** *adverb* M16.

in vino veritas /ɪn ˌviːnəʊ ˈverɪtas/ *interjection*. L16.
[ORIGIN Latin, lit. 'there is truth in wine'.]
Truth comes out under the influence of alcohol; a drunken person tells the truth.

inviolable /ɪnˈvʌɪələb(ə)l/ *adjective*. LME.
[ORIGIN Old French & mod. French, or Latin *inviolabilis*, formed as IN-[3] + VIOLABLE.]
1 To be kept sacred or free from attack; not to be infringed or dishonoured. LME.
†**2** Not yielding to force or violence; unable to be broken, forced, or injured. L15–E18.
■ **inviolaˈbility** *noun* the quality or fact of being inviolable L18. **inviolableness** *noun* (now *rare*) inviolability E17. **inviolably** *adverb* L15.

inviolate /ɪnˈvʌɪələt/ *adjective*. LME.
[ORIGIN Latin *inviolatus*, formed as IN-[3] + *violat-* pa. ppl stem of *violare* VIOLATE *verb*: see -ATE[2].]
Free or exempt from violation; uninjured, unimpaired, unbroken; not profaned or debased.

JOHN BROOKE He took with him assurances of the King's inviolate attachment. B. MAGEE The truth is to be kept inviolate, and handed on unsullied.

■ **inviolacy** *noun* inviolateness M19. **inviolately** *adverb* L15. **inviolateness** *noun* the quality of being inviolate M19.

inviolated /ɪnˈvʌɪəleɪtɪd/ *adjective*. M16.
[ORIGIN from IN-[3] + *violated* pa. pple of VIOLATE *verb*.]
Not violated, inviolate.

†**invious** *adjective*. E17–E18.
[ORIGIN from Latin *invius*, formed as IN-[3] + *via* way, road: see -OUS.]
Having no roads or ways; pathless, trackless.

†**inviron** *verb* var. of ENVIRON.

invirtuate /ɪnˈvəːtjʊeɪt/ *verb trans*. *rare*. M17.
[ORIGIN from IN-[2] + VIRTUE + -ATE[3].]
Make virtuous; endow with virtue or power.

inviscate /ɪnˈvɪskeɪt/ *verb trans*. LME.
[ORIGIN Late Latin *inviscat-* pa. ppl stem of *inviscare* smear with or snare with birdlime, formed as IN-[2] + *viscum* birdlime: see -ATE[3].]
1 Make viscid or sticky; mix or cover with a sticky substance. LME.
2 Catch in some sticky substance. *rare*. M17.
■ **inviˈscation** *noun* LME.

inviscid /ɪnˈvɪsɪd/ *adjective*. E20.
[ORIGIN from IN-[3] + VISCID *adjective*.]
1 Not viscid or sticky. E20.
2 PHYSICS. Having no or negligible viscosity. E20.

†**invised** *adjective*. *rare* (Shakes.). Only in L16.
[ORIGIN from Latin *invisus* unseen + -ED[1].]
Unseen, invisible.

invisible /ɪnˈvɪzɪb(ə)l/ *adjective & noun*. ME.
[ORIGIN Old French & mod. French, or Latin *invisibilis* formed as IN-[3] + *visibilis* VISIBLE.]
▸ **A** *adjective*. **1** Unable to be seen; that by its nature is not perceivable by the eye. ME. ▸**b** Of an association: covert, not having a visible, open organization. M17.

N. TINBERGEN Ultraviolet light, which is entirely invisible to us. R. WEST She moved past me . . , holding her hands in front of her as though she bore invisible gifts. *transf.*: *Observer* Its . . absorbent surfaces and special metals are designed to make it almost invisible to radar.

the Church Invisible: see CHURCH *noun* 3.
2 Not in sight; hidden, obscured. Also, kept hidden, secret. M16.

F. FORSYTH The president's palace was invisible, hidden behind the warehouse. J. HELLER He remains invisible and anonymous.

3 Too small or inconspicuous to be easily discerned; imperceptible. M17.

J. BALDWIN He sank far down in his seat, as though crouching might make him invisible. J. CAIRD Mabel . . had worn her . . hair in a bun, over which she put a fine 'invisible' net.

– SPECIAL COLLOCATIONS: **invisible earnings**: from invisible exports. **invisible export**, **invisible import** any of the items such as shipping services, insurance, profits on foreign investment, money spent by foreign visitors, etc., which are not tangible commodities but which involve payment between countries (usu. in *pl.*). **invisible green** a very dark shade of green, almost black. ***invisible import***: see ***invisible export*** above. **invisible ink**: for writing words etc. which cannot be seen until the paper is heated or otherwise treated. **invisible man** (*a*) (with direct or implied allusion to H. G. Wells's novel *The Invisible Man*) a man who cannot be seen; (*b*) a man who is (deliberately) inconspicuous. **invisible mending** repair of material, clothing, etc., so carefully done as to be undetectable. **invisible mender** a person who or business which undertakes invisible mending.
▸ **B** *noun*. **1** An invisible thing, person, or being. M17. **the invisible** the unseen world; God.
2 In *pl.* Invisible exports and imports. M20.

Daily Mirror America . . is now beginning to record deficits on the invisibles, which add to its basic trade deficit.

■ **invisiˈbility** *noun* (*a*) the quality or condition of being invisible; (*b*) an invisible entity: M16. **invisibleness** *noun* M16. **invisibly** *adverb* LME.

invita Minerva /ɪnˌvʌɪtɑː mɪˈnəːvɑː/ *adverbial phr*. L16.
[ORIGIN Latin = Minerva (the goddess of wisdom) unwilling.]
When one is not in the mood; without inspiration.

invitation /ɪnvɪˈteɪʃ(ə)n/ *noun*. LME.
[ORIGIN French, or Latin *invitatio(n-)*, from *invitat-* pa. ppl stem of *invitare* invite.]
▸ **A** *noun*. **1** The action of inviting someone to come, attend, or take part. LME. ▸**b** The spoken or written form in which a person is invited. E17.
2 The action or an act of enticing or attracting; attraction, inducement, allurement. L16. ▸**b** BRIDGE. A bid which encourages, but does not compel, the bidder's partner to continue to game or slam. E20.
▸ **B** *attrib.* or as *adjective*. **1** Containing or constituting an invitation. E19.
invitation card, ***invitation letter***, ***invitation list***.
2 Of an event, contest, etc.: open only to those who have received an invitation. E19.

Press & Journal (Aberdeen) The top sprinters . . have all enjoyed a diet of invitation races on the . . circuits.

invitational /ɪnvɪˈteɪʃ(ə)n(ə)l/ *adjective & noun*[1]. Chiefly *N. Amer.* E20.
[ORIGIN from INVITATION + -AL[1].]
▸ **A** *adjective*. Characterized by invitation. Of a contest etc.: open only to those invited. E20.

Chambers's Journal Philip walked the room's length with invitational pauses.

▸ **B** *absol.* as *noun*. An invitational contest etc. E20.

Evening Telegram (Newfoundland) John Hamilton won the June Invitational on his first try Monday.

invitatory /ɪnˈvʌɪtət(ə)ri/ *adjective & noun*. ME.
[ORIGIN Late Latin *invitatorius*, from Latin *invitare* invite: see -ORY[2].]
▸ **A** *adjective*. **1** Eccl. ***invitatory psalm***, the *Venite*, Psalm 95 (94 in the Vulgate), with its antiphon, which begins the first office of the day. ME.
2 That invites or tends to invite; containing or conveying an invitation. M17.
▸ **B** *noun*. **1** Any of various forms of invitation used in religious worship; *spec*. the invitatory psalm. LME. ▸**b** ROMAN CATHOLIC CHURCH (now *hist.*). The introit. LME.
2 An invitation. M17.

invite /ˈɪnvʌɪt/ *noun*. *colloq*. E17.
[ORIGIN from INVITE *verb*.]
†**1** An attraction, a bait. Only in E17.
2 The act of inviting; an invitation. M17.

F. BURNEY Everybody bowed and accepted the invite but me. W. H. AUDEN An invite with gilded edges.

invite /ɪnˈvʌɪt/ *verb trans*. M16.
[ORIGIN French *inviter* or Latin *invitare*.]
1 Ask (a person) to come with one's permission *to* or *into* a place or *to* an event. Foll. by *in*: ask (a person) to come into one's house. M16. ▸**b** *refl*. Announce one's intention or desire to come; impose oneself. M16.

T. HARDY He . . invited Margery and her father to his house. R. LARDNER Ada was invited to a party. **b** P. FERGUSON He'll have to take us as he finds us, inviting himself round here.

2 Ask (a person) *to do* something assumed to be agreeable or advantageous. M16. ▸**b** Politely request (something) from a person. M19.

T. HARDY They were also invited to dine. DAY LEWIS A small girl called Violet who . . invited me to kiss her. **b** A. S. NEILL After the lecture, I invited questions.

3 Entice or encourage (a person) *to do* something or *to go* somewhere. Now only of a thing. M16.

D. M. THOMAS The dining room was . . so large . . that it invited people to eat in silence.

4 Tend to bring on; encourage unintentionally. L16.

F. MORYSON One looke invites another. C. S. FORESTER In war as in the jungle, to fly is to invite pursuit and attack.

†**5** Attract physically, draw. L17–E19.
■ **invitant** /ˈɪnvɪt(ə)nt/ *noun* (*a*) a person who gives an invitation; (*b*) a person who is invited: L16. **invited** *adjective* that has received an invitation M17. **inviˈtee** *noun* a person who is invited; *spec*. (LAW) a person who is invited on to the premises by the owner or occupier for some business or material object: M19. **invitement** *noun* (now *rare* or *obsolete*) (*a*) (an) invitation; (*b*) (an) inducement; allurement; encouragement to come: L16. **inviter** *noun* L16. **inviting** *adjective* (*a*) that invites or gives an invitation; (*b*) attractive; alluring; tempting: L16. **invitingly** *adverb* M17. **invitingness** *noun* the quality of being alluring; attractiveness: M17. **invitress** *noun* a female inviter E17.

†**invitory** *noun & verb* see INVENTORY.

in vitro /ɪn ˈviːtrəʊ/ *adjectival & adverbial phr*. L19.
[ORIGIN Latin, lit. 'in glass'.]
BIOLOGY. (Performed, obtained, or occurring) in a test tube or elsewhere outside a living organism.

in vivo /ɪn ˈviːvəʊ/ *adjectival & adverbial phr*. E20.
[ORIGIN Latin.]
BIOLOGY. (Performed, obtained, or occurring) within a living organism. Cf. INTRA VITAM.

invocable /ˈɪnvəkəb(ə)l/ *adjective*. M19.
[ORIGIN from INVOKE + -ABLE.]
Able to be invoked or called upon.

invocant /ˈɪnvək(ə)nt, ɪnˈvəʊk(ə)nt/ *noun*. M18.
[ORIGIN from INVOKE + -ANT[1].]
A person who invokes someone or something.

invocate /ˈɪnvəkeɪt/ *verb*. Now *rare*. M16.
[ORIGIN Latin *invocat-* pa. ppl stem of *invocare* INVOKE: see -ATE[3].]
1 *verb trans*. Invoke, call upon, appeal to. M16.
†**2** *verb intrans*. Make an invocation; call in prayer (*on* or *upon*). L16–E19.

invocation /ɪnvə(ʊ)ˈkeɪʃ(ə)n/ *noun*. LME.
[ORIGIN Old French & mod. French from Latin *invocatio(n-)*, formed as INVOCATE: see -ATION.]
1 The action or an act of invoking or calling upon God, a deity, etc., in prayer (an act or form of supplication). LME. ▸**b** ECCLESIASTICAL. A form of invocatory prayer as part of a public religious service; a petition. Also, the name or appellation used in invoking a divinity, etc. E19.
2 The action or an act of summoning a devil, spirit, etc., by incantation; an incantation used for this; a charm, a spell. LME.
3 LAW. The calling in of papers or evidence from another case. E19.

invocative /ɪnˈvɒkətɪv/ *adjective*. E19.
[ORIGIN from INVOCATION: see -IVE.]
Characterized by invocation.

invocatory /ɪnˈvɒkət(ə)ri, ˈɪnvəkeɪt(ə)ri/ *adjective*. L17.
[ORIGIN from INVOCATION: see -ORY[2].]
Of the nature of, characterized by, or used in, invocation.

invoice /ˈɪnvɔɪs/ *noun & verb*. M16.
[ORIGIN Orig. pl. of †*invoy*, from French †*envoy*, ENVOI.]
▸ **A** *noun*. **1** A list of items of goods sent or services performed, with a statement of the sum due. M16.
2 A consignment of invoiced goods. *rare*. L19.
▸ **B** *verb trans*. Send an invoice to (a person, a company). Also, list (goods etc.) on an invoice. L17.

invoke /ɪnˈvəʊk/ *verb trans*. L15.
[ORIGIN Old French & mod. French *invoquer* from Latin *invocare*, formed as IN-[2] + *vocare* call.]
1 Call on (God, a deity, etc.) in prayer or as a witness. L15.

A. ALVAREZ A broken necklace or a cold in the nose, and they'd be weeping and invoking heaven.

2 Summon (a spirit) by charms or incantation; conjure; *fig*. give rise to, evoke. E17. ▸**b** Utter (a sacred *name*) in invocation. L17.

LYTTON Thou shalt stand by my side while I invoke the phantom. R. BUSH He wrote a dramatic lyric that invokes the romance of Italy. **b** T. BROWN Wrinkled witches, when they truck with hell, Invoke thy name, and use it for a spell.

3 Call for earnestly; beg for, implore. E17.

E. MANNIN Linton invoked God's blessing on his house. V. WOOLF She invoked his help against this attack upon the jolly human heart.

4 Appeal to or call upon to come or to do something. L17.

J. MICHIE A criminal invokes conscience to his aid To support an individual withdrawal from a communal crusade.

5 LAW. Call in papers or evidence from another case. E19.
6 Appeal to in support or confirmation; cite as authority; postulate as an explanation. M19.

A. DAVIS The argument he had invoked when he rejected our bail motion. J. BERMAN Eliot invokes a clinical authority to confirm his intuition.

7 Put into operation or into effect; call for the observance or performance of. M19.

K. M. E. MURRAY There was a dismissal clause to be invoked if the Editor should not proceed as fast as the Delegates considered reasonable. *Which Computer?* The GD command invokes the graphics drawing language.

■ **invoker** *noun* M17.

involatile /ɪnˈvɒlətʌɪl/ *adjective*. M17.
[ORIGIN from IN-[3] + VOLATILE.]
†**1** Not flying, wingless. *rare*. Only in M17.
2 Not volatile; unable to be vaporized. M19.

involucel /ɪnˈvɒljʊsɛl/ *noun*. Also (earlier) in Latin form **involucellum** /ɪnˌvɒljʊˈsɛləm/, pl. **-lla** /-lə/. M18.
[ORIGIN mod. Latin *involucellum* dim. of INVOLUCRUM: cf. French *involucelle*.]
BOTANY. A whorl of bracts surrounding one of the divisions in an inflorescence, a partial or secondary involucre; *spec*. the epicalyx of one of the flowers in the capitulum of a scabious or allied plant.
■ **involuˈcellate** *adjective* having an involucel or involucels E19.

involucra *noun* pl. of INVOLUCRUM.

involucre /ˈɪnvəl(j)uːkə/ *noun*. L16.
[ORIGIN French, or from Latin INVOLUCRUM.]
1 Something which envelops or enwraps; a case, a covering, an envelope; *esp*. formerly in ANATOMY, an envelope of (membranous) tissue. L16.
2 BOTANY. A whorl or rosette of bracts surrounding an inflorescence (esp. a capitulum), or at the base of an umbel. L18. ▸**b** A sheath of tissue surrounding the male or female sexual organs of some liverworts. L19.
partial involucre: see PARTIAL *adjective*.
■ **invoˈlucral** *adjective* (BOTANY) of or pertaining to an involucre E19. **invoˈlucrate** *adjective* (BOTANY) having an involucre M19.

involucrum /ɪnvəˈl(j)uːkrəm/ *noun*. Pl. **-cra** /-krə/. L17.
[ORIGIN Latin, from *involvere* INVOLVE.]
1 An outer covering, an envelope; a covering membrane; = INVOLUCRE 1. L17.
2 BOTANY. = INVOLUCRE 2. M18.

involuntary /ɪnˈvɒlənt(ə)ri/ *adjective*. M16.
[ORIGIN from IN-[3] + VOLUNTARY *adjective*.]
1 Not done willingly or by choice; independent of volition, unintentional. M16. ▸**b** PHYSIOLOGY. Of a nerve, muscle, etc.: concerned in bodily actions or processes which are independent of the will. M19.

D. LESSING Our experiences, some chosen, some involuntary, mature us differently. M. SCAMMELL He experienced that involuntary sense of guilt we all seem to feel when a loved one dies.

†**2** Unwilling; not exercising the will. L16–M18.
■ **involuntarily** *adverb* in an involuntary manner; without exercise or cooperation of the will: M16. **involuntariness** *noun* M17.

involute /ˈɪnvəl(j)uːt/ *adjective & noun*. M17.
[ORIGIN Latin *involutus* pa. pple of *involvere* INVOLVE.]
▸ **A** *adjective*. **1** Involved; entangled; intricate. Formerly also, hidden, obscure. M17.
2 Chiefly ZOOLOGY. Rolled up in a spiral; *esp*. (of a shell) having the whorls wound closely round the axis. M17.
3 MATH. In the form of an involute. E18.
4 BOTANY. Of a leaf etc.: rolled inwards at the edges. M18.
▸ **B** *noun*. MATH. A curve such as is traced out by a point on a taut string unwound from a given curve in the plane of that curve. Cf. EVOLUTE *noun & adjective*. L18.

involute /ˈɪnvəl(j)uːt/ *verb intrans*. E20.
[ORIGIN Back-form. from INVOLUTED.]
Chiefly PHYSIOLOGY. Shrink, fold in upon itself; undergo involution.

involuted /ˈɪnvəl(j)uːtɪd/ *adjective*. E19.
[ORIGIN from INVOLUTE *adjective & noun* + -ED[1].]
1 Chiefly BIOLOGY. Folded in upon itself; involute; convoluted. E19.
2 *fig*. Convoluted; involved. E20.
■ **invoˈlutedly** *adverb* L19.

involution /ɪnvəˈluːʃ(ə)n/ *noun*. LME.
[ORIGIN Latin *involutio(n-)*, from *involut-* pa. ppl stem of *involvere* INVOLVE: see -ION.]
1 ANATOMY. A folding, curling, or turning inwards; (a part of) a structure so formed. LME.
2 a A thing that enfolds; an envelope, a covering. L16. ▸**b** The action of involving or fact of being involved; implicit inclusion; implication. E17.
3 Entanglement, complication; intricacy of (literary) construction or style. Also, something complicated; an intricate movement, a tangle. E17.
4 MATH. **a** The raising of a quantity to any (orig., a positive) power. *arch*. E18. ▸**b** GEOMETRY. A projective correspondence between pairs of points on a line, such that the product of the distances of each pair from a certain fixed point on the line is constant. M19. ▸**c** A function or transformation that is equal to its inverse. E20.
5 PHYSIOLOGY. Shrinkage, regression, or atrophy of a part or organ (esp. the uterus) when inactive, or in old age. M19.
■ **involutional** *adjective* (chiefly PSYCHOLOGY) of or pertaining to physiological involution or mental disturbances associated with this change; ***involutional depression***, ***involutional melancholia***, prolonged depression beginning late in life: E20. **involutionary** *adjective* characterized by involution; retrograde E20. **involutory** *adjective* (MATH.) that is an involution M20.

I

involve /ɪnˈvɒlv/ *verb trans*. Also †**en-**. LME.
[ORIGIN Latin *involvere*, formed as IN-[2] + *volvere* roll.]
1 Wrap, surround, enfold, envelop. Foll. by *in*, †*with*. LME.

E. B. BROWNING I saw Fog only, the great tawny weltering fog, Involve the passive city.

2 Make obscure or difficult to understand; complicate, entangle. LME.

E. PAGITT This doctrine . . is involved with absurdities, and inexplicable contradictions. OED We must not further involve the statement; it is intricate enough already.

3 Bring (a person) into a matter; embroil (a person) *in* trouble, difficulties, perplexity, etc. Freq. in *pass*. LME. ▸**b** Commit emotionally; concern closely *with* another, *in* a matter. Freq. in *pass*. M20.

A. MILLER If you want to commit suicide do it alone, don't involve others. J. HELLER I dislike getting involved in long conversations. **b** M. PIERCY I thought you'd be involved with some guy. J. GATHORNE-HARDY I don't think you can help people unless you're prepared to be involved.

4 Wind spirally; wreathe, coil. M16. ▸**b** *fig*. Join as by winding together; intertwine *with*. M17.

MILTON Some of the Serpent kinde, . . involv'd Thir Snakie foulds. **b** L. STERNE Our misfortunes were involved together.

5 †**a** Include covertly *in* or *under* something; wrap up. E17–E18. ▸**b** Include, contain, comprehend. M17. ▸**c** Contain implicitly; include as essential; imply, call for, entail. M17. ▸**d** Affect, concern directly. M19.

c P. ROTH I didn't realise that there was so much psychology involved in dentistry. G. PRIESTLAND Being a Christian involves constant growth. **d** U. S. GRANT The safety of the nation was involved. I. COMPTON-BURNETT You, . . are virtually of the family and involved in its changes. H. WILSON There have been twenty-one changes of prime minister this century, involving fifteen men.

6 Absorb completely; envelop, overwhelm. E17. ▸**b** Engross; occupy (a person) fully. M20.

TENNYSON My love involves the love before; My love is vaster passion now. **b** R. P. JHABVALA He was completely involved in the work of the movement.

7 Implicate in a charge or crime; cause or prove (a person) to be concerned. M17.
8 MATH. Raise (a quantity) to a power. Now *rare* or *obsolete*. L17.
■ **involver** *noun* M19.

involved /ɪnˈvɒlvd/ *adjective*. E17.
[ORIGIN from INVOLVE + -ED[1].]
1 Curved spirally; entwined, enwrapped, entangled. E17.
†**2** Not straightforward and open; underhand, covert. E17–E18.
3 Intricate, complicated. M17. ▸**b** Contained by implication, implicit. *rare*. M19.

G. GREENE The involved beautiful unintelligible handwriting.

4 Concerned, caring, committed. L20.

Observer The involved and caring father . . eases up on his career just as his wife does when their baby is born.

■ **involvedly** /-vɪdli/ *adverb* in a way that is involved implicitly E17. **involvedness** /-vɪdnɪs/ *noun* M17.

involvement /ɪnˈvɒlvm(ə)nt/ *noun*. M17.
[ORIGIN from INVOLVE + -MENT.]
†**1** An enveloping structure; a wrapping; an envelope, a case, a covering. Only in M17.
2 The action or process of involving something or someone; the fact or condition of being involved. E18. ▸**b** An involved condition, manner, or style; an entanglement, a confused or complicated state of affairs. E19.

P. BOWLES He hoped to avoid involvement in the affair. J. BERMAN The dangers of emotional involvement with his patient. *Sunday (Kolkata)* A sense of belonging and involvement. **b** *Fraser's Magazine* The plot . . depended . . on the 'involvement' consequent on the fact that every one . . is in love with . . Celeste. V. GLENDINNING A brief and trivial involvement with the Austrian girl.

3 What is involved or implied in something; a necessary consequence or condition. L19.

invulnerable /ɪnˈvʌln(ə)rəb(ə)l/ *adjective*. L16.
[ORIGIN Latin *invulnerabilis*, from IN-[3] + *vulnerare* wound: see -ABLE.]
Not liable to damage or harm, esp. from attack; unassailable. Of a person: unable to be physically or emotionally hurt.

I. BANKS Invulnerable, uncaring, the silver planes fly on through the furious hail of exploding shells. R. ELLMANN His role of invulnerable and detached profligate is challenged by love.

■ **invulneraˈbility** *noun* the quality or state of being invulnerable L18. **invulnerableness** *noun* M17. **invulnerably** *adverb* so as to be invulnerable M19.

invultuation /ɪnˌvʌltjʊˈeɪʃ(ə)n/ *noun*. *rare*. Also **invultation** /ɪnvʌlˈteɪʃ(ə)n/. M19.
[ORIGIN medieval Latin *invultuatio(n-)* from *invultuare* make a likeness, formed as IN-[2] + *vultus* visage, likeness: see -ATION.]
The making of a likeness, esp. a waxen effigy of a person for purposes of witchcraft.

inwale /ˈɪnweɪl/ *noun*. L19.
[ORIGIN from IN *adverb* + WALE *noun*[1].]
A horizontal timber on the inside of a boat.

inwall /ˈɪnwɔːl/ *noun*. E17.
[ORIGIN from IN *adverb* + WALL *noun*[1].]
An inner or inside wall.

inwall *verb* var. of ENWALL.

inward /ˈɪnwəd/ *adjective & noun*.
[ORIGIN Old English *innanweard*, *inneweard*, *inweard*, from inflected forms or base of IN *adverb*, *preposition* + *-weard* -WARD.]
▸ **A** *adjective*. **1** Situated within; that is the inner or innermost part; that is on the inside. OE. ▸**b** Situated in or belonging to the interior of a country or region; inland. Now *rare*. M17. ▸**c** Of speech etc.: not clearly enunciated; muffled, indistinct. L18.
2 Within or of the mind, soul, or spirit; mental, spiritual. ME. ▸†**b** Deeply felt, earnest, heartfelt. LME–E17. ▸**c** Spiritually minded, pious; contemplative; introverted, reserved. LME.

J. M. MURRY The most intimate motion of Keats' inward life. J. STEINBECK What he said . . made her give a small inward start.

3 Close, intimate; familiar, well acquainted. Now *rare*. L15.

F. QUARLES Friendly to all men, inward but with few.

†**4** Existing in or pertaining to a country or place; domestic, civil. E16–E19.
†**5** Secret, private; confidential. M16–E17.
6 Directed or proceeding towards the inside; coming in from outside. M19.

Independent In order to help China modernise . . the Government has encouraged foreign inward investment.

▸ **B** *noun*. **1** In *pl.* & (now *rare*) *sing.* The inner part, the inside. Usu. *spec.* the internal parts or organs of the body, the entrails. OE.
2 The inner nature or essence of a thing or person; thoughts, mental processes. *rare*. OE.
†**3** An intimate or familiar acquaintance. *rare*. Only in E17.
4 In *pl.* Articles coming in or imported; dues on such articles. M18.

inward /ˈɪnwəd/ *adverb*.
[ORIGIN Old English *innanweard* etc.: see INWARD *adjective & noun*.]
1 Towards the inside or interior; into a country or place. OE. ▸†**b** On the inside, within, internally. LME–L17.
2 *fig.* †**a** Within the mind or soul, mentally, inwardly. OE–M17. ▸**b** Into the mind or soul; into one's own thoughts. ME.

b C. WILSON Yeats's reaction . . was to turn inward, into a world of fantasy.

– COMB.: **inward-looking** *adjective* introverted, self-absorbed; parochial, insular.

inwardly /ˈɪnwədli/ *adverb*. OE.
[ORIGIN from INWARD *adjective & noun* + -LY[2].]
1 †**a** In or from the inmost heart; with deep emotion or feeling; heartily, fervently, earnestly. OE–M17. ▸**b** In mind or thought, mentally; at heart; in reality; secretly. ME.

b J. UPDIKE Harry calculates inwardly that he has made a thousand a month on his gold. L. WHISTLER He was inwardly apprehensive as well as outwardly adventurous.

b *groan inwardly*: see GROAN *verb*.
†**2** Intimately, thoroughly; closely. ME–E18.
3 On the inside, in the inner part; within, internally. L15. ▸**b** In words to oneself, not aloud. M16.
4 Towards the inside or inner part; towards that which is within, into the mind or soul. Now *rare* or *obsolete*. M17.

inwardness /ˈɪnwədnɪs/ *noun*. LME.
[ORIGIN from INWARD *adjective* + -NESS.]
†**1** The inner part or region; in *pl.*, inner parts, entrails. Only in LME.
2 Intimacy, familiarity; close friendship. Now *rare*. L16.
3 Intrinsic character; inner nature, essence, or meaning. E17.
4 The quality or condition of being inward or inside something else. *lit.* & *fig.* E17.
5 **a** Depth or intensity of feeling or thought. M19. ▸**b** Preoccupation with one's inner self, self-absorption; concern with spiritual or philosophical matters rather than externalities; spirituality. M19.

a *Gramophone* Arrau plays with sublime inwardness and a flow of rhythm and tone which is uniquely fine. **b** D. PRATER One whose gift was to be the expression of inwardness and the visionary. A. BROOKNER The sight of those whom he loved . . lifted the veil of inwardness from Oscar's face.

inwards /ˈɪnwədz/ *adverb & adjective*. ME.
[ORIGIN from INWARD *adverb* + -S[3].]
▸ **A** *adverb*. = INWARD *adverb*. ME.
▸ **B** *adjective*. = INWARD *adjective* 6. *rare*. M16.

inwarp /ɪnˈwɔːp/ *verb trans.* *rare*. E19.
[ORIGIN from IN-[1] + WARP *verb*.]
Weave in, interweave.

inweave /ɪnˈwiːv/ *verb trans.* Also **en-**. Pa. t. **-wove** /-ˈwəʊv/; pa. pple **-woven** /-ˈwəʊv(ə)n/, **-wove**. LME.
[ORIGIN from IN-[1], or IN-[2], EN-[1] + WEAVE *verb*[1].]
1 Combine or decorate *with* something inserted or entwined. LME.
2 Weave in; weave (things) together; interweave. L16.

fig.: J. RUSKIN Our moral feelings are . . inwoven with our intellectual powers.

3 Insert or depict by weaving or entwining. Foll. by *in*, *into*, *on*. L16.

D. ROCK A vast number of figures and animals inwoven into its fabric. *fig.*: COLERIDGE To inweave in a poem of the loftiest style . . such minute matters of fact.

4 Form by weaving or plaiting. *rare*. M17.

inwick /ˈɪnwɪk/ *noun & verb*. E19.
[ORIGIN from IN *adverb* + WICK *verb*[1].]
CURLING. ▸ **A** *noun*. A shot made so as to strike the inside of another stone and glance off it to the tee. E19.
▸ **B** *verb intrans.* Make an inwick. E19.

inwind *verb* var. of ENWIND.

inwinter /ˈɪnwɪntə/ *verb trans.* M20.
[ORIGIN from IN-[1] + WINTER *verb*.]
Protect (animals, esp. sheep) by providing food and shelter during severe weather.

inwit /ˈɪnwɪt/ *noun*. *arch.* ME.
[ORIGIN from IN *adverb* + WIT *noun*.]
1 Conscience; inward sense of right and wrong. ME.
2 Reason, understanding; wisdom. ME.
†**3** Courage; heart, soul, mind. *rare*. Only in LME.

inwith /ɪnˈwɪð/ *preposition & adverb*. *obsolete* exc. *Scot.* ME.
[ORIGIN from IN *adverb* + WITH *preposition*. Cf. WITHIN.]
▸ †**A** *preposition*. **1** Of place: within, inside of. ME–E16.
2 Of time: within the period of. Only in ME.
▸ **B** *adverb*. †**1** Of position: within, inside. ME–M16.
2 Of direction: inwards. M18.

†**inwomb** *verb* var. of ENWOMB.

inwork /ɪnˈwəːk/ *verb*. *rare*. Pa. t. & pple **-worked**, (*arch.* & *literary*) **-wrought** /-ˈrɔːt/. L16.
[ORIGIN from IN-[1] or IN *adverb* + WORK *verb*. See also INWROUGHT.]
1 *verb intrans.* Work within or inside. L16.
2 *verb trans.* Work, embroider, or weave (something) *in* or *on*. L17.
3 *verb trans.* Work or produce (some effect) *in*. M19.
■ **ˈinworker** *noun* a person who works within; now *esp.* a person who works on the employer's premises: L16. **ˈinworking** *noun* †(**a**) action, energy; (**b**) (an) internal operation, (a) working within: L16.

inwove, **inwoven** *verbs* see INWEAVE.

inwrap *verb* var. of ENWRAP.

inwreathe *verb* var. of ENWREATHE.

inwrought /ɪnˈrɔːt, *attrib.* ˈɪnrɔːt/ *ppl adjective*. Also **en-** /ɪn-, ɛn-/. M17.
[ORIGIN from IN *adverb* + *wrought* pa. pple of WORK *verb*.]
1 Of a fabric etc.: decorated *with*, having something worked in. *lit.* & *fig.* M17.

G. BIRDWOOD Sumptuously inwrought apparel.

2 Of a pattern, figure, etc.: worked into or embroidered on a fabric. M18.

WORDSWORTH Flowers enwrought On silken tissue.

3 **a** Worked into something as a constituent. M18. ▸**b** Worked together or blended *with* something; combined, intermingled, entangled. E19.

inwrought *verb pa. t. & pple*: see INWORK *verb*.

inyala *noun* see NYALA.

inyanga /ɪnˈjɑːŋə/ *noun*. *S. Afr.* M19.
[ORIGIN Zulu.]
A traditional herbalist and medicine man, sometimes acting as diviner or magician.

inyoke /ɪnˈjəʊk/ *verb trans.* *rare*. L16.
[ORIGIN from IN-[1] + YOKE *verb*.]
Yoke or join (*to*, *unto*, etc.).

Io /ˈʌɪəʊ/ *noun*[1] *& interjection*. *arch.* L16.
[ORIGIN Latin *io*, Greek *iō*.]
(An exclamation) expr. joy or triumph.
– COMB.: *Io paean*: see PAEAN 1.

io /ˈʌɪəʊ/ *noun*[2]. Pl. **ios**. L19.
[ORIGIN mod. Latin, from Greek *Iō*, the daughter of the river god Inachus.]
In full ***io moth***. A large, mainly yellow N. American moth, *Automeris io*, having prominent eyespots on the hindwings.

I/O *abbreviation*.
COMPUTING. Input/output.

IOC *abbreviation*.
International Olympic Committee.

iod- *prefix* see IODO-.

iodargyrite /ʌɪəˈdɑːdʒɪrʌɪt/ *noun*. M19.
[ORIGIN from IODO- + CER)ARGYRITE.]
Native silver iodide, AgI, a yellow or greenish mineral crystallizing in the hexagonal system.

iodate /ˈʌɪədeɪt/ *noun*. E19.
[ORIGIN from IODIC + -ATE[1].]
CHEMISTRY. A salt of iodic acid; *spec.* a salt of iodic(V) acid. Cf. PERIODATE.

iodated /ˈʌɪə(ʊ)deɪtɪd/ *adjective*. M19.
[ORIGIN from IOD(INE *noun* + -ATE[3] + -ED[1].]
Impregnated or treated with iodine; iodinated.

iodic /ʌɪˈɒdɪk/ *adjective*. E19.
[ORIGIN from IODO- + -IC. Cf. French *iodique*.]
1 CHEMISTRY. Of or pertaining to iodine. Chiefly in ***iodic acid***, any of several oxo acids of iodine, *esp.* that of its pentavalent oxidation state (HIO_3). Cf. PERIODIC *adjective*[2]. E19.
2 MEDICINE. Caused by administration of iodine. *arch.* *rare*. L19.

iodide /ˈʌɪədʌɪd/ *noun*. E19.
[ORIGIN from IODINE *noun* + -IDE.]
CHEMISTRY. A compound of iodine with a less electronegative element or radical; a salt or ester of hydriodic acid.

iodimetry /ʌɪəˈdɪmɪtri/ *noun*. L19.
[ORIGIN from IODI(NE *noun* + -METRY.]
CHEMISTRY. Redox titration using iodine; *spec.* the quantitative analysis of a solution of a reducing agent by titration with a standard solution of iodine. Cf. IODOMETRY.
■ **iodiˈmetric** *adjective* of or pertaining to iodimetry L19. **iodiˈmetrically** *adverb* by means of iodimetry L19.

iodinate /ˈʌɪədɪneɪt, ʌɪˈɒdɪneɪt/ *verb trans.* E20.
[ORIGIN from IODINE *noun* + -ATE[3].]
Treat with iodine; CHEMISTRY introduce one or more iodine atoms into (a compound or molecule), usu. in place of hydrogen. Freq. as ***iodinated*** *ppl adjective*.
■ **iodinatable** *adjective* (chiefly of a protein) able to be iodinated L20. **iodiˈnation** *noun* L19.

iodine /ˈʌɪədiːn, -ʌɪn, -ɪn/ *noun & verb*. E19.
[ORIGIN from French *iode* from Greek *iōdēs* violet-coloured, from *ion* violet + *-eidēs* like: see -OID, -INE[5].]
▸ **A** *noun*. A chemical element of the halogen group, atomic no. 53, which is a greyish-black solid that forms a dense violet vapour (symbol I). E19.
▸ **B** *verb trans.* Treat with iodine. M19.
– COMB.: **iodine number** the degree of unsaturation of a hydrocarbon chain, etc., as measured by the number of grams of iodine absorbed by 100 grams of the substance; **iodine scarlet** mercuric iodide, HgI_2, a brilliant red toxic powder; **iodine value** = ***iodine number*** above.
■ **iˈodinized** *adjective* (of a material) treated or impregnated with iodine E20.

iodise *verb* var. of IODIZE.

iodism /ˈʌɪədɪz(ə)m/ *noun*. M19.
[ORIGIN from IODO- + -ISM.]
MEDICINE. Chronic poisoning by iodine (or its compounds).

iodize /ˈʌɪədʌɪz/ *verb trans.* Also **-ise**. M19.
[ORIGIN from IODO- + -IZE.]
Orig. (in PHOTOGRAPHY), treat or impregnate with silver iodide. Now usu., add iodine or an iodide to (a substance, e.g. table salt). Chiefly as ***iodized*** *ppl adjective*.
■ **iodiˈzation** *noun* the process or practice of iodizing something; the addition of iodine or an iodine compound to a substance: E20.

iodo- /ˈʌɪədəʊ, ʌɪˈəʊdəʊ/ *combining form*. Before a vowel also **iod-**. E20.
[ORIGIN from mod. Latin *iodum* IODINE: see -O-.]
1 CHEMISTRY. Denoting compounds formed by replacement of one or more hydrogen atoms by iodine, as ***iodobenzene***, ***iodoform***, ***iodophenol***, or other compounds or mixture containing iodine.
2 Of or pertaining to iodine.
■ **iodomethane** *noun* a sweet-smelling liquid, CH_3I (methyl iodide), used as a methylating agent L19. **iˈodophil(e)** *adjective* (esp. of bacteria which contain compounds similar to starch) readily stained by iodine E20. **iodoˈphilic** *adjective* = IODOPHIL(E) M20. **iodoˈprotein** *noun* any protein containing iodine E20.

iodoform /ʌɪˈəʊdə(ʊ)fɔːm, ˈʌɪədə(ʊ)fɔːm/ *noun*. M19.
[ORIGIN from IODO- + FORM(YL, after *chloroform*.]
A yellow crystalline compound of iodine, CHI_3, analogous to chloroform, having a strong sweetish odour and used in tests for alcohols, and as an external antiseptic; triiodomethane.

iodometry /ʌɪəˈdɒmɪtri/ *noun*. L19.
[ORIGIN from IODO- + -METRY.]
CHEMISTRY. Redox titration using iodine; *spec.* the quantitative analysis of a solution of an oxidizing agent by addition of excess iodide to liberate iodine which is then titrated, usu. with thiosulphate using starch as indicator. Cf. IODIMETRY.
■ **iodoˈmetric** *adjective* of or pertaining to iodometry M19. **iodoˈmetrically** *adverb* by means of iodometry E20.

iodophor /ʌɪˈəʊdə(ʊ)fɔː, ˈʌɪəd-/ *noun*. M20.
[ORIGIN from IODO- + -PHOR(E.]
CHEMISTRY. Any compound which complexes with iodine; *spec.* any substance in which iodine is stabilized and solubilized by combination with a surfactant for use as a disinfectant.

†**ioduret** *noun*. E–M19.
[ORIGIN from IODO- + -URET.]
CHEMISTRY. = IODIDE.
■ †**iodu̇retted** *adjective* = IODATED M–L19.

iodyrite /ʌɪˈɒdɪrʌɪt/ *noun*. M19.
[ORIGIN from IODO- after CERARGYRITE.]
MINERALOGY. = IODARGYRITE.

iolite /ˈʌɪə(ʊ)lʌɪt/ *noun*. E19.
[ORIGIN German *Iolit(h)*, from Greek *ion* violet + *lithos* stone: see -LITE.]
MINERALOGY. = CORDIERITE.

IOM *abbreviation*.
Isle of Man.

ion /ˈʌɪən/ *noun*. M19.
[ORIGIN Greek, neut. pres. pple of *ienai* go.]
PHYSICS & CHEMISTRY. Orig., either of the constituents which pass to the electrodes during electrolysis. Now *gen.*, any individual atom, molecule, or group having a net electric charge (either positive or negative) due to loss or gain of one or more electrons. Cf. ANION, CATION.
– COMB.: **ion burn** the damaging of the phosphor of a cathode-ray tube by negative ions focused on the screen; an ion spot so produced; **ion chamber** an ionization chamber; **ion drive** (*a*) = *ion propulsion* below; (*b*) = *ion engine* below; **ion engine**: that employs ion propulsion; **ion etching** the controlled removal of extremely thin layers of material from a surface with a beam of ions; **ion exchange**: of ions of like charge between an insoluble solid and a solution in contact with it; ***ion-exchange resin***, any synthetic polymer suitable for use as an ion exchanger, usu. having a porous cross-linked molecular network with ionized or ionizable groups weakly attached; **ion exchanger** a solid involved or used in ion exchange; an apparatus for effecting ion exchange; **ion gun** a device which produces a beam of ions; **ion implantation**: of ions in a substance to make a semiconductor; **ion pair** (*a*) a pair of oppositely charged ions held together in a solution by electrostatic attraction; (*b*) a negative ion (or an electron) and a positive ion formed from a neutral atom or molecule by the action of radiation; **ion propulsion** rocket propulsion in which thrust is produced by the electrically accelerated ejection of ions formed inside the engine; **ion rocket** a rocket (engine) that employs ion propulsion; **ion source** a device for producing ions, *spec.* an ion gun; **ion spot** (*a*) a dark spot on a screen caused by ion burn; (*b*) a white spot in a television picture produced by ionized gas molecules striking the target of the camera; **ion trap** a device designed to catch ions to prevent them from causing an ion spot on a screen.

-ion /(ə)n, ɪən, jən/ *suffix*.
[ORIGIN Repr. French *-ion*, Latin *-ion-*, *-io*.]
Forming nouns denoting (***a***) verbal action, as ***excision***, ***damnation***, ***pollution***; (***b***) an instance of this, as ***a suggestion***, ***a notion***, ***an action***; (***c***) a resulting state or product, as ***vexation***, ***concoction***, ***completion***. Usu. appears in *-tion*, *-sion*, *-xion*, esp. -ATION.

Ionian /ʌɪˈəʊnɪən/ *noun & adjective*. M16.
[ORIGIN from Latin *Ionius* from Greek *Iōnios* (from *Iōnia* Ionia) + -AN.]
► **A** *noun*. A member of the Hellenic people who occupied Attica and colonized western Asia Minor (part of which was named Ionia after them), the islands of the Aegean and those off the west coast of Greece, etc.; a native or inhabitant of Ionia. M16.
► **B** *adjective*. Of or pertaining to Ionia or the Ionians; Ionic. M16.
Ionian mode MUSIC (*a*) an ancient Greek mode, characterized as soft and light; (*b*) the last of the church modes (with C as final and G as dominant), corresponding to the modern major key of C.

Ionic /ʌɪˈɒnɪk/ *adjective*[1] & *noun*. L16.
[ORIGIN Latin *Ionicus* from Greek *Iōnikos*, from *Iōnia* Ionia: see -IC.]
► **A** *adjective*. **1** ARCHITECTURE. Designating one of the three Greek orders, characterized by a column with scroll shapes on either side of the capital. L16.
†**2** MUSIC. In the ancient Ionian mode. L16–E19.
3 Of or pertaining to Ionia or the Ionians; Ionian. L16.
Ionic dialect the most important of the three main branches of ancient Greek. **Ionic school** (**of philosophy**), **Ionic sect** (**of philosophy**): founded by Thales of Miletus in Asiatic Ionia.
4 CLASSICAL PROSODY. Designating a foot consisting of two long syllables followed by two short or two short followed by two long; pertaining to or consisting of such feet. M17.
► **B** *noun*. †**1** An Ionian; a member of the Ionic school of philosophy. L16–E17.
2 CLASSICAL PROSODY. An Ionic foot or verse; Ionic metre. E17.
3 The Ionic dialect of ancient Greek. M17.
4 TYPOGRAPHY. A typeface distinguished by prominent serifs and a high degree of legibility. M19.
■ **Ionicism** /-sɪz(ə)m/ *noun* something characteristic of Ionians or the Ionic dialect; Ionic character: E19. **Ionicize** /-sʌɪz/ *verb* (*a*) *verb intrans.* use the Ionic dialect; (*b*) *verb trans.* make Ionic: M19. **Ionism** /ˈʌɪənɪz(ə)m/ *noun* = IONICISM L18.

ionic /ʌɪˈɒnɪk/ *adjective*[2]. L19.
[ORIGIN from ION + -IC.]
PHYSICS & CHEMISTRY. **1** Of or pertaining to ions; composed of or containing ions; that is an ion. L19.
2 Involving or employing ions; *spec.* (of a bond) electrovalent. E20.
– SPECIAL COLLOCATIONS: **ionic strength** CHEMISTRY a quantity representing the strength of the electric field in a solution of ions, equal to the sum of the molalities of each type of ion present multiplied by the square of their charges.
■ **ionically** *adverb* by means of ions or an ionic bond; as regards or in terms of ions: E20.

ionicity /ʌɪəˈnɪsɪti/ *noun*. M20.
[ORIGIN from IONIC *adjective*[2]: see -ICITY.]
CHEMISTRY. Ionic character (in a chemical bond or a crystal).

ionisation *noun*, **Ionise** *verb*[1], **ionise** *verb*[2] vars. of IONIZATION etc.

ionium /ʌɪˈəʊnɪəm/ *noun*. E20.
[ORIGIN from ION + -IUM.]
CHEMISTRY. A radioactive isotope of thorium with atomic mass 230, produced by the α -decay of uranium-234. (Symbol ^{230}Th.)

ionization /ʌɪənʌɪˈzeɪʃ(ə)n/ *noun*. Also **-isation**. L19.
[ORIGIN from ION + -IZATION.]
1 The state of being ionized; the process of ionizing. L19.
specific ionization: see SPECIFIC *adjective*.
2 MEDICINE. = CATAPHORESIS 1. E20.
– COMB.: **ionization chamber** an instrument for measuring radiation intensity by measuring the charge on the ions produced by the radiation in a volume of gas; **ionization constant** PHYSICAL CHEMISTRY = *DISSOCIATION constant*; **ionization current**: arising out of the movement in an electric field of the ions and electrons in an ionized gas; **ionization energy** = ***ionization potential*** below; **ionization gauge** an instrument for measuring the degree of vacuum in a vessel from the ionization current produced in the residual gas; **ionization potential** the energy required to remove an electron in its lowest energy state from an atom.

Ionize /ˈʌɪənʌɪz/ *verb*[1] *intrans. & trans.* Also **-ise**. E19.
[ORIGIN Greek *iōnizein*, from *Iōnia* Ionia: see -IZE.]
Ionicize.

ionize /ˈʌɪənʌɪz/ *verb*[2]. Also **-ise**. L19.
[ORIGIN from ION + -IZE.]
1 *verb trans. & intrans.* PHYSICS. Convert (an atom) into an ion by loss or gain of one or more electrons; produce ions in (a substance). L19.
2 *verb intrans.* PHYSICS. Dissociate into ions; become converted into an ion or ions. E20.
3 *verb trans.* MEDICINE. ►**a** Introduce (a substance) into tissue by means of cataphoresis. (Foll. by *into*.) E20. ►**b** Treat by cataphoresis. E20.
■ **ionizable** *adjective* E20. **ionizer** *noun* an agent which produces ionization, *spec.* with the purpose of improving the quality of air in a room E20. **ionizing** *ppl adjective* that ionizes; chiefly in ***ionizing radiation***, radiation of sufficient energy to cause ionization in matter through which it passes: L19.

ionogen /ˈʌɪənədʒ(ə)n, ʌɪˈɒnədʒ(ə)n/ *noun*. Now *rare*. E20.
[ORIGIN from ION + -O- + -GEN.]
PHYSICAL CHEMISTRY. Any compound which exists as ions when dissolved in a solvent.

ionogenic /ʌɪˌɒnə(ʊ)ˈdʒɛnɪk/ *adjective*. E20.
[ORIGIN formed as IONOGEN + -IC.]
CHEMISTRY. †**1** Of an atom or radical: promoting ionization elsewhere in the molecule of which it forms part. Only in E20.
2 Able to be ionized chemically. E20.

ionogram /ʌɪˈɒnə(ʊ)gram/ *noun*. M20.
[ORIGIN from ION (in sense 1 extracted from IONOSPHERE) + -O- + -GRAM.]
1 A record of reflected radio pulses produced by an ionosonde. M20.
2 CHEMISTRY. The result of an ionographic separation, usu. a series of spots or bands on the support medium. M20.

ionography /ʌɪəˈnɒgrəfi/ *noun*. M20.
[ORIGIN from ION + -OGRAPHY.]
CHEMISTRY. The migration in an electric field of ions or charged colloidal particles in a buffer solution held on a support (usu. filter paper), esp. as used to separate components of a mixture.
■ **ionoˈgraphic** *adjective* of or pertaining to ionography M20.

ionomer /ʌɪˈɒnəmə/ *noun*. M20.
[ORIGIN from ION + -O- + -MER.]
Any of a class of thermoplastic resins in which there is ionic bonding between the polymer chains.

ionone /ˈʌɪənəʊn/ *noun*. L19.
[ORIGIN Greek *ion* violet + -ONE.]
CHEMISTRY. (Proprietary name in the US for) either of two isomeric liquid aromatic ketones (α-***ionone*** and β-***ionone***), $(CH_3)_3C_6H_6CH{=}CHCOCH_3$, used esp. in perfumery for their strong odour of violets.

ionophore /ʌɪˈɒnə(ʊ)fɔː/ *noun*. M20.
[ORIGIN from ION + -O- + -PHORE.]
BIOLOGY. An agent which is able to transport ions across a lipid membrane in a cell.
■ **ionophorous** /ʌɪəˈnɒf(ə)rəs/ *adjective* M20.

ionophoresis /ʌɪˌɒnə(ʊ)fəˈriːsɪs/ *noun*. M20.
[ORIGIN from ION after *electrophoresis*.]
BIOCHEMISTRY. The migration in an electric field of ions in solution, esp. as used to separate the components of a mixture.
■ **ionophoretic** /-ˈrɛtɪk/ *adjective* M20.

ionosonde /ʌɪˈɒnə(ʊ)sɒnd/ *noun*. M20.
[ORIGIN from IONO(SPHERE + SONDE.]
An instrument sent aloft to investigate the ionosphere by transmitting radio pulses into it and recording their echoes.

ionosphere /ʌɪˈɒnəsfɪə/ *noun*. E20.
[ORIGIN from ION + -O- + -SPHERE.]
A region of the outer atmosphere, upwards of 50–80 km (30–50 miles), which contains many ions and free electrons and is able to reflect radio waves, allowing long-range transmission; also, a corresponding region above the surfaces of other planets.
■ **ionospheric** /ʌɪˌɒnə(ʊ)ˈsfɛrɪk/ *adjective* of, pertaining to, or involving the ionosphere M20. **ionoˈspherically** *adverb* by the ionosphere M20. **ionoˈsphericist** *noun* (*rare*) = IONOSPHERIST L20. **ionoˈspherist** *noun* (*rare*) a person who studies the ionosphere M20.

ionotropy /ʌɪəˈnɒtrəpi/ *noun*. E20.
[ORIGIN from ION + -O- + Greek *tropia* turning (from *trepein* turn) + -Y[3].]
CHEMISTRY. **1** Tautomerism occurring through the migration of part of the molecule as an ion. E20.
2 The ordering of particles in a gel that results when an electrolyte is added to a colloidal suspension. M20.
■ **ionotropic** /-ˈtrəʊpɪk, -ˈtrɒpɪk/ *adjective* pertaining to or exhibiting ionotropy M20.

iontophoresis /ʌɪˌɒntə(ʊ)fəˈriːsɪs/ *noun*. E20.
[ORIGIN from Greek *iont-*, ION pres. pple of *ienai* go + -O- + -PHORESIS.]
MEDICINE. = CATAPHORESIS 1, *spec.* for the passage of ions into the body.
■ **iontophoretic** /-ˈrɛtɪk/ *adjective* of, pertaining to, or employing iontophoresis M20. **iontophoretically** *adverb* by means of iontophoresis M20.

IOP *abbreviation*.
Institute of Physics.

-ior /ɪə, jə/ *suffix*.
[ORIGIN Latin.]
Forming adjectives of comparison, as ***inferior***, ***superior***, ***ulterior***, ***junior***, ***senior***.

iota /ʌɪˈəʊtə/ *noun*. LME.
[ORIGIN Greek *iōta*, of Phoenician origin: cf. YOD.]
1 The ninth (and smallest) letter (Ι, ι) of the Greek alphabet). LME.
iota subscript a small iota written beneath a long vowel, forming the second element of a diphthong but not pronounced.
2 *fig.* The smallest or a very small part or quantity. Cf. JOD, JOT *noun*[1]. M17.

> E. LEWIS You have not changed one iota since you left me at college. N. SYMINGTON I could not remember an iota more than that.

iotacism /ʌɪˈəʊtəsɪz(ə)m/ *noun*. M16.
[ORIGIN Late Latin *iotacismus* from late Greek *iōtakismos*, formed as IOTA + -ISM with hiatus-filling *k*.]
Excessive use or repetition of the letter iota or I; *spec.* the pronunciation of other Greek vowels like iota. Cf. ITACISM.

IOU /ʌɪəʊˈjuː/ *noun*. L18.
[ORIGIN Repr. pronunc. of 'I owe you'.]
A document constituting a formal acknowledgement of a debt, usu. bearing the three letters 'IOU', a specified sum, and a signature.
– NOTE: Repr. the statement 'I owe you' the letters *IOU* occur E17.

I

-ious /ɪəs, əs/ *suffix*.
[ORIGIN from -*i* (cf. -I-) + -OUS, repr. Latin -*iosus*, French -*ieux*.]
Forming adjectives with the sense 'characterized by, full of', as ***cautious***, ***curious***, ***spacious***. Often corresp. to nouns in -*ion*, esp. those in -*tion*, -*cion*, -*sion*, as ***rebellion***, ***rebellious***, ***infection***, ***infectious***. See -ITIOUS[2], -OUS.

IOW *abbreviation*.
Isle of Wight.

Iowan /ˈʌɪəwən/ *noun & adjective*. M19.
[ORIGIN from *Iowa* (see below) + -AN.]
▸ **A** *noun*. A native or inhabitant of Iowa, a state of the US. M19.
▸ **B** *adjective*. Of or pertaining to Iowa; *spec.* in GEOLOGY of, pertaining to or designating one of the glacial episodes in the Pleistocene of N. America. L19.

IP *abbreviation*.
COMPUTING. Internet Protocol.

IPA *abbreviation*.
1 International Phonetic Alphabet.
2 International Phonetic Association.
3 India pale ale.

IPCS *abbreviation*.
Institution of Professional Civil Servants.

ipecac /ˈɪpɪkak/ *noun*. *colloq*. L18.
[ORIGIN Abbreviation.]
= IPECACUANHA.

I

ipecacuanha /ˌɪpɪkakjʊˈanə/ *noun*. E17.
[ORIGIN Portuguese from Tupi-Guarani *ipekaaguéne*, from *ipe* small + *kaa* leaves + *guéne* vomit.]
1 The root of *Cephaelis ipecacuanha*, a Brazilian plant of the madder family; an extract or preparation of this, formerly much used as an emetic and expectorant. Also, the plant itself. E17.
2 Any of various other plants with emetic roots; a preparation of such a root. E18.
American ipecacuanha a plant of the rose family, *Gillenia trifoliata*, of the US. **bastard ipecacuanha** a S. American plant, *Asclepias curassavica* (family Asclepiadaceae). **black ipecacuanha**, **Peruvian ipecacuanha** a S. American plant of the madder family, *Psychotria emetica*, used as an inferior substitute for ipecacuanha. **white ipecacuanha** a S. American plant of the violet family, *Hybanthus calceolaria*.
– COMB.: **ipecacuanha wine** the filtered infusion of ipecacuanha root in wine.

ipiti /ɪˈpiːti/ *noun*. *S. Afr.* M19.
[ORIGIN Zulu *i-phithi*.]
The blue duiker, *Cephalophus monticola*, a very small antelope of southern and central African forests.

IPO *abbreviation*.
Initial public offering.

iPod /ˈʌɪpɒd/ *noun*. E21.
[ORIGIN from *i* (orig. in *iMac*, proprietary name for a type of personal computer made by the company Apple, where it stood for *Internet*) + POD noun[2].]
(Proprietary name for) a type of small portable MP3 player.

ipoh /ˈiːpəʊ/ *noun*. L18.
[ORIGIN Malay.]
The upas tree, *Antiaris toxicaria*, of the mulberry family, or a creeping shrub, *Strychnos ignatii* (family Loganiaceae), both native to SE Asia and having a poisonous sap. Also, the poison itself.

ipomoea /ɪpəˈmiːə/ *noun*. L18.
[ORIGIN mod. Latin (see below), from Greek *ip-*, *ips* woodworm + *homoios* like.]
BOTANY. Any of various mostly tropical twining or creeping plants of the genus *Ipomoea*, of the bindweed family, which includes the morning glory, *I. purpurea*, and many other ornamentals, and the sweet potato, *I. batatas*.

ippon /ˈɪpɒn/ *noun*. M20.
[ORIGIN Japanese.]
A score of one full point in judo, karate, etc.

iproniazid /ʌɪprə(ʊ)ˈnʌɪəzɪd/ *noun*. M20.
[ORIGIN from *isopropyl* (see ISO-) + ISO)NIAZID.]
PHARMACOLOGY. A derivative of isoniazid, $(CH_3)_2CH{\cdot}NH{\cdot}NH{\cdot}CO{\cdot}C_5H_4N$, used, usu. as the crystalline phosphate, in the treatment of depression and (formerly) tuberculosis.

ips *abbreviation*.
1 Inches per second.
2 COMPUTING. Instructions per second.

ipse dixit /ɪpsiː ˈdɪksɪt, ɪpseɪ/ *noun phr.* *pl.* ***ipse dixits***. L16.
[ORIGIN Latin, lit. 'he himself said (it)', translating Greek *autos epha*, phr. used of Pythagoras by his followers.]
An unproven assertion resting only on the authority of a speaker; a dogmatic statement; a dictum.

ipseity /ɪpˈseɪɪti, ɪpˈsiːɪti/ *noun*. M17.
[ORIGIN from Latin *ipse* self + -ITY, after EGOITY.]
Personal identity; selfhood; self-centredness.

ipsilateral /ɪpsɪˈlat(ə)r(ə)l/ *adjective*. E20.
[ORIGIN from Latin *ipse* self + LATERAL *adjective*.]
MEDICINE. Belonging to or occurring on the same or on one side of the body; connecting two parts on the same side. Opp. ***contralateral***.
■ **ipsilaterally** *adverb* on the same or on one side of the body M20.

ipsissima verba /ɪpˌsɪsɪmə ˈvəːbə/ *noun phr.* *pl.* E19.
[ORIGIN Latin.]
The precise words used by a writer or speaker.

ipso facto /ɪpsəʊ ˈfaktəʊ/ *adverbial phr.* M16.
[ORIGIN Latin.]
By that very fact or act; by the fact itself; thereby. Cf. EO IPSO.

ipso jure /ɪpsəʊ ˈdʒʊəreɪ, ˈdʒʊəri/ *adverbial phr.* L16.
[ORIGIN Latin.]
By the operation of the law itself.

Ipswichian /ɪpˈswɪtʃɪən/ *adjective & noun*. M20.
[ORIGIN from *Ipswich*, a town in Suffolk, East Anglia + -IAN.]
GEOLOGY. ▸**A** *adjective*. Designating or pertaining to the most recent interglacial of the Pleistocene in Britain, and the corresponding stratigraphic stage. M20.
▸ **B** *noun*. The Ipswichian interglacial or stage. M20.

IQ *abbreviation*.
Intelligence quotient.

†**-ique** *suffix* var. of -IC.

IR *abbreviation*.
Infrared.

Ir *symbol*.
CHEMISTRY. Iridium.

ir- /ɪ/ *prefix*[1].
Var. of Latin IN-[2] before *r*. Cf. IL-[1], IM-[1].

ir- /ɪ/ *prefix*[2].
Var. of Latin IN-[3] before *r*. Cf. I-[2], IL-[2], IM-[2].

IRA *abbreviation*.
1 Irish Republican Army.
2 Individual retirement account. *US*.

iracund /ˈʌɪrəkʌnd/ *adjective*. *rare*. E19.
[ORIGIN Latin *iracundus*, from *ira* anger + -*cundus* inclining to.]
Inclined to anger; choleric, irascible.
■ **iraˈcundity** *noun* M19.

irade /ɪˈrɑːdi/ *noun*. L19.
[ORIGIN Turkish *ırade* from Arabic *ʾirāda* will, decree, from *ʾarāda* intend.]
hist. A written decree issued in the name of a Sultan of Turkey during the Ottoman period.

†**Iraki** *noun & adjective* see IRAQI.

Iranian /ɪˈreɪnɪən, ɪˈrɑː-/ *noun & adjective*. L18.
[ORIGIN from *Iran* (see below) + -IAN.]
▸ **A** *noun*. **1** A native or inhabitant of Iran (formerly Persia), a country in the Middle East; a speaker of an Iranian language. L18.
2 LINGUISTICS. One of the two groups of languages in the Indo-Iranian branch of Indo-European, comprising Old Persian and Avestan and their modern descendants or cognates; the language of the Iranians. E19.
▸ **B** *adjective*. Of or pertaining to Iran (formerly Persia) or Iranian. M19.
■ **Iranianist** *noun* a student of Iran or Iranian L20. **Iranic** /ɪˈranɪk/ *adjective* M19. **Iranize** /ɪˈranʌɪz/ *verb trans.* make Iranian in character etc. L19.

Iraqi /ɪˈrɑːki/ *noun & adjective*. Also **-qui**, (earlier) †**-ki**. E19.
[ORIGIN from *Iraq* (see below) + -I[2].]
▸ **A** *noun*. A native or inhabitant of Iraq, a country in the Middle East. E19.
▸ **B** *adjective*. Of or pertaining to Iraq or its inhabitants. E20.
■ **Iraqiˈzation** *noun* making Iraqi in character etc. M20. **Iraqize** *verb trans.* make Iraqi in character etc. M20.

irascible /ɪˈrasɪb(ə)l/ *adjective*. LME.
[ORIGIN Old French & mod. French from late Latin *irascibilis*, from Latin *irasci* grow angry, from *ira* anger: see -IBLE.]
1 Easily provoked to anger or resentment; prone to anger; irritable, hot-tempered. LME.

> C. BLACKWOOD These irascible old figures started to make their habitual peevish fuss.

irascible principle (in Platonic philosophy) one of the two parts of irrational human nature (the other being the *concupiscible*), the seat of courage, anger, etc.
2 Of an emotion, action, etc.: characterized by, arising from, or exhibiting anger. M17.

> P. GROSSKURTH A domestic tyrant, Jakob oppressed his family with his irascible temper.

■ **irasciˈbility** *noun* LME.

irate /ʌɪˈreɪt/ *adjective*. M19.
[ORIGIN Latin *iratus*, from *ira* anger: see -ATE[2].]
Angry, incensed, enraged.
■ **irately** *adverb* L19. **irateness** *noun* L20.

IRBM *abbreviation*.
Intermediate-range ballistic missile.

IRC *abbreviation*.
COMPUTING. Internet Relay Chat, an area of the network where users can communicate interactively with each other.

ire /ʌɪə/ *noun*. Now chiefly *rhet.* ME.
[ORIGIN Old French & mod. French from Latin *ira* anger.]
Anger; wrath.
■ **ireful** *adjective* (**a**) angry; (**b**) irascible: ME. **irefully** *adverb* angrily L15. **irefulness** *noun* (*rare*) wrathfulness LME. **ireless** *adjective* E19.

irenarch /ˈʌɪrɪnɑːk/ *noun*. *rare*. E18.
[ORIGIN Late Latin *irenarcha* from Greek *eirēnarkhēs*, from *eirēnē* peace + -*arkhēs* -ARCH.]
hist. An Eastern provincial governor or keeper of the peace, under the Roman and Byzantine Empires.

irenic /ʌɪˈrɛnɪk, -ˈriː-/ *adjective*. Also **ei-**. M19.
[ORIGIN Greek *eirēnikos*, from *eirēnē* peace: see -IC. Cf. French *irénique*.]
Pacific; conciliatory, non-polemical; irenical.

irenical /ʌɪˈrɛnɪk(ə)l, -ˈriː-/ *adjective*. Also **ei-**. M17.
[ORIGIN formed as IRENIC + -AL[1].]
Peaceful; conciliatory, tending to promote peace, esp. in theological or ecclesiastical disputes.
■ **irenically** *adverb* L19.

irenicon *noun* see EIRENICON.

irenics /ʌɪˈrɛnɪks, -ˈriː-/ *noun*. L19.
[ORIGIN from IRENIC: see -ICS.]
Irenical theology. Opp. ***polemics***.

Irgun /ɪəˈgʊn/ *noun*. M20.
[ORIGIN mod. Hebrew *ʾirgūn* (*ṣĕḇāʾī lĕʾummī*) (national military) organization.]
A militant right-wing Zionist organization founded in 1931 and disbanded after the creation of Israel in 1948.
■ **Irgunist** *noun* a member of this organization M20.

Irianese /ɪrɪəˈniːz/ *noun & adjective*. M20.
[ORIGIN from *Irian* Jaya (see below) + -ESE.]
▸ **A** *noun*. Pl. same. A native or inhabitant of Irian Jaya (formerly Dutch New Guinea or Netherlands New Guinea), since 1963 a province of Indonesia. M20.
▸ **B** *adjective*. Of or pertaining to Irian Jaya. L20.

Iricism /ˈʌɪrɪsɪz(ə)m/ *noun*. M18.
[ORIGIN Irreg. from IRISH after *Scotticism*.]
An Irish expression, characteristic, etc.

irid /ˈʌɪrɪd/ *noun*. E19.
[ORIGIN Greek *irid-* IRIS: see -ID[2].]
1 The iris of the eye. *rare*. E19.
2 BOTANY. Any plant of the iris family. M19.

irid- *combining form* see IRIDO-.

iridaceous /ʌɪrɪˈdeɪʃəs, ɪr-/ *adjective*. M19.
[ORIGIN from mod. Latin *iridaceus*, from Latin *irid-*, IRIS: see -ACEOUS.]
BOTANY. Of or pertaining to the family Iridaceae, which includes the genus *Iris*.

iridal /ˈʌɪrɪd(ə)l/ *adjective*. M19.
[ORIGIN from Latin *irid-*, IRIS + -AL[1].]
1 Of or pertaining to the rainbow. *rare*. M19.
2 ANATOMY & MEDICINE. Of or pertaining to the iris of the eye; = IRIDIC *adjective*[2]. M19.

iridectomy /ʌɪrɪˈdɛktəmi, ɪr-/ *noun*. Also (earlier) †**-omia**. E19.
[ORIGIN formed as IRIDAL + -ECTOMY.]
Surgical removal of a part of the iris; an instance of this.
■ **iridectomize** *verb trans.* perform iridectomy on L19.

iridencleisis /ˌʌɪrɪdɛnˈklʌɪsɪs, ˌɪr-/ *noun*. M19.
[ORIGIN from IRID- + Greek *egkleiein* shut up, after Greek nouns of action in -*isis*.]
MEDICINE. Surgical trapping of a portion of the iris in an incision of the cornea, usu. to relieve glaucoma; an instance of this.

irideremia /ˌʌɪrɪdəˈriːmɪə, ˌɪr-/ *noun*. M19.
[ORIGIN formed as IRIDENCLEISIS + Greek *erēmia* lack, absence.]
MEDICINE. Congenital absence of the iris.

irides *noun pl.* see IRIS *noun*.

iridescent /ɪrɪˈdɛs(ə)nt/ *adjective*. L18.
[ORIGIN from Latin *irid-*, IRIS + -ESCENT.]
Displaying colours like those of the rainbow, or those reflected from soap bubbles etc.; glittering or flashing with an array of colours which changes as the observer moves.

> E. WAUGH The brook . . broke into innumerable iridescent cascades as it fell. *fig.*: J. S. BLACKIE The best fictions, without a deep moral significance beneath, are only iridescent froth.

■ **iridesce** *verb intrans.* (*rare*) shine in an iridescent manner L19. **iridescence** *noun* the quality of being iridescent; a glittering play of changing colours: E19. **iridescently** *adverb* L18.

iridial /ʌɪˈrɪdɪəl/ *adjective*. E20.
[ORIGIN Irreg. formed as IRIDIAN + -IAL.]
ANATOMY & MEDICINE. = IRIDAL *adjective* 2, IRIDIC *adjective*[2].

iridian /ʌɪˈrɪdɪən/ *adjective*. *rare*. M19.
[ORIGIN from Latin *irid-*, IRIS + -IAN.]
1 = IRIDAL *adjective* 2, IRIDIC *adjective*[2]. M19.
2 Rainbow-like; brilliantly coloured. L19.

iridic /ɪˈrɪdɪk, ʌɪ-/ *adjective*[1]. *rare*. **M19.**
[**ORIGIN** from **IRIDIUM** + **-IC.**]
CHEMISTRY. Of or containing iridium; *esp*. of iridium in the tetravalent state (cf. **IRIDIOUS**).

iridic /ʌɪˈrɪdɪk/ *adjective*[2]. **L19.**
[**ORIGIN** from Latin *irid-*, **IRIS** + **-IC.**]
ANATOMY & MEDICINE. Of or pertaining to the iris of the eye.

iridious /ɪˈrɪdɪəs, ʌɪ-/ *adjective*. *rare*. **M19.**
[**ORIGIN** from **IRIDIUM** + **-OUS.**]
CHEMISTRY. Containing iridium; *esp*. of iridium in the trivalent state (cf. **IRIDIC** *adjective*[1]).

iridium /ɪˈrɪdɪəm, ʌɪ-/ *noun*. **E19.**
[**ORIGIN** from Latin *irid-*, *iris* rainbow (on account of its forming compounds of various colours) + **-IUM.**]
A white metallic chemical element, atomic no. 77, belonging to the platinum group and used in certain hard alloys (symbol Ir).

irido- /ˈʌɪrɪdəʊ, ˈɪr-/ *combining form* of Greek *irid-*, **IRIS**: see **-O-**. Before a vowel also **irid-**. Chiefly *MEDICINE*, in the sense 'of the iris of the eye'; occas. in other senses of *iris*.
■ **iridocyˈclitis** *noun* inflammation of the iris and the ciliary body **L19.** **iridocyte** *noun* (*ZOOLOGY*) a refractive cell which causes iridescence in the skin of certain fishes, cephalopods, etc. **L19.** **iridodiˈalysis** *noun* (surgical or traumatic) separation of the iris from the ciliary ring **L19.** **iriˈdodesis** *noun* [Greek *desis* binding] a surgical operation in which the iris is secured in a certain position by a ligature **M19.** **iridodonesis** /-dəʊˈniːsɪs/ *noun* [Greek *doneein* shake] tremulousness of the iris **L19.** **iridoˈplegia** *noun* paralysis of the iris **L19.** **iriˈdotomy** *noun* (an instance of) surgical incision of the iris **M19.**

iridology /ʌɪrɪˈdɒlədʒi, ɪr-/ *noun*. **E20.**
[**ORIGIN** from **IRIDO-** + **-LOGY.**]
The study of the iris of the eye, esp. as a diagnostic method in alternative medicine.
■ **iridologist** *noun* **L20.**

iridosmine /ɪrɪˈdɒsmʌɪn, ʌɪr-/ *noun*. **E19.**
[**ORIGIN** from **IRIDIUM** + **OSMIUM** + **-INE**[5].]
A native alloy of iridium and osmium, *spec*. with about two-thirds iridium, crystallizing in the hexagonal system. Cf. **OSMIRIDIUM.**

iris /ˈʌɪrɪs/ *noun & verb*. **LME.**
[**ORIGIN** Latin from Greek *iris*, *irid-* rainbow, iris.]
▸ **A** *noun*. Pl. **irises**, (esp. sense 4a) **irides** /ˈʌɪrɪdiːz/.
1 A variety of quartz (formerly, any mineral) producing iridescent reflections. **LME.**
2 Any plant of the large genus *Iris* (family Iridaceae), widespread in the northern hemisphere, members of which are characteristically tuberous or bulbous with sword-shaped equitant leaves and showy blooms; a plant of any of several related genera. Also, a flower of such a plant. **LME.**
bearded iris, Florentine iris, Japanese iris, mourning iris, peacock iris, snake's head iris, stinking iris, etc.
3 A rainbow, esp. (freq. **I-**) personified; a many-coloured refraction of light from drops of water; a rainbow-like or iridescent appearance; a coloured halo; a combination of brilliant colours. *poet*. **L15.** ▸**b** (**I-**.) *GREEK MYTHOLOGY*. The goddess of the rainbow, who acted as the messenger of the gods; *fig*. a messenger. **L16.**

> SHAKES. *Tr. & Cr.* His crest, that prouder than blue Iris bends. *fig.*: SHELLEY If Liberty Lent not life its soul of light, Hope its iris of delight.

4 a *ANATOMY & ZOOLOGY*. A flat circular coloured membrane suspended vertically in the aqueous humour of the eye, and separating the anterior from the posterior chamber, having within its centre an opening (the pupil) which varies so as to control the amount of light reaching the retina. **E16.** ▸**b** *PHOTOGRAPHY & CINEMATOGRAPHY*. In full ***iris diaphragm***. An adjustable diaphragm of thin overlapping plates for regulating the size of a control hole, esp. for admitting light to a lens or lens system. Also, the action or an act of irising. **M19.**

> **b** K. REISZ An iris may . . introduce . . a shot in a more telling way than a fade. *Scientific American* The lens was too fast . . , and so he stopped it down to *f*9 with a cardboard iris.

▸ **B** *verb intrans*. *PHOTOGRAPHY & CINEMATOGRAPHY*. Operate or act (in the manner of) an iris diaphragm. Chiefly foll. by *in* (or *out*): fade in a picture from the centre of the frame outwards (or from the edges inwards). **M20.**
■ **irisate** *verb trans*. (*rare*) make iridescent **E19.** **iriˈsation** *noun* the process of making iridescent; iridescence: **M19.**

irised /ˈʌɪrɪst/ *adjective*. **E19.**
[**ORIGIN** from **IRIS** *noun* + **-ED**[2].]
1 Coloured like a rainbow; iridescent. **E19.**
2 With qualifying adjective: having an iris (of the eye) of a specified kind. **L19.**

Irish /ˈʌɪrɪʃ/ *adjective & noun*. **ME.**
[**ORIGIN** from Old English *Īr*(*as* inhabitants of *Īrland* Ireland (obscurely based on Old Irish *Ériu*: see **HIBERNIAN**) + **-ISH**[1]. Cf. Old Norse *Írskr*. See also **ERSE.**]
▸ **A** *adjective*. **1** Of, pertaining to, or native to Ireland, an island lying west of Great Britain, now divided into the Republic of Ireland and Northern Ireland. **ME.** ▸†**b** Of or belonging to (the Gaelic inhabitants of) the Scottish Highlands. **M16–M18.**
Northern Irish: see **NORTHERN** *adjective*. ***Southern Irish***: see **SOUTHERN** *adjective*.
2 In, of, or pertaining to the language Irish. **M16.**
3 Having a nature or quality (regarded as) characteristic of Ireland or its people; (of a statement) paradoxical, (apparently) illogical, self-contradictory. *offensive*. **L16.**

> R. HILL 'Marcus wouldn't dare to tell a lie . . unless it was true!' 'Irish,' said Pascoe.

— **SPECIAL COLLOCATIONS & COMB.**: **Irish American** an American of Irish origin. **Irish-American** *adjective* of or pertaining to an Irish American or the Irish community in the US. **Irish apricot** *joc*. a potato. **Irish Australian** an Australian of Irish origin. **Irish-Australian** *adjective* of or pertaining to an Australian of Irish origin or the Irish community in Australia. ***Irish blackguard***: see **BLACKGUARD** *noun* 5. **Irish bridge** an open stone drain carrying water across a road. ***Irish bull***: see **BULL** *noun*[4] 1. ***Irish coffee***: see **COFFEE** *noun*. **Irish deer**, **Irish elk** a large extinct deer, *Megaceros giganteus*, remains of which have been found in Ireland and other parts of Europe. **Irish Gaelic** = sense B.2 below. **Irish green** = **CONNEMARA** *marble*. **Irish harp** = **CLAIRSCHACH. Irish horse** *nautical slang* (now *hist*.) tough salt beef. **Irish hurricane** = ***Irishman's hurricane*** s.v. **IRISHMAN. Irish lace** any of a variety of laces made in Ireland, esp. crochet. ***Irish mantle***: see **MANTLE** *noun*. **Irish martingale** (in riding) a short leather strap connecting two rings through which the reins of a horse are passed. **Irish moss** = **CARRAGEEN. Irish pennant** *nautical slang* an untidy end of rope flying loose in the wind. **Irish point** a kind of needlepoint lace made in Ireland. ***Irish potato***: see **POTATO** *noun* 2. ***Irish pound***: see **POUND** *noun*[1]. **Irish promotion**, **Irish rise** = ***Irishman's promotion*** s.v. **IRISHMAN. Irish Sea** the sea separating Ireland from England and Wales. **Irish setter** (an animal of) a breed of setter with a long silky dark red coat and a long feathered tail. **Irish stew**: of mutton, potato and onion. **Irish Sweep**, **Irish Sweepstake**: organized by Irish hospitals on the results of English horse races, esp. the Derby and the Grand National. **Irish terrier** (an animal of) a breed of large wire-haired terrier, with a sandy or reddish-coloured coat. **Irish whiskey**: distilled in Ireland, esp. from malted barley. **Irish wolfhound** (an animal of) a breed of large, rough-coated hound, often grey in colour. **Irish yew** a fastigiate variety of yew, *Taxus baccata*, freq. cultivated.
▸ **B** *noun*. Pl. same, (in sense 1b) †**Irishes**.
1 *collect. pl*. *The* people of Ireland, or their immediate descendants in other countries, *esp*. those of Celtic origin. **ME.** ▸†**b** An Irishman. Chiefly *Scot*. **L16–E19.**
black Irish: see **BLACK** *adjective*. ***the luck of the Irish***: see **LUCK** *noun*. **wild Irish** *hist*. those people of Ireland not subject to English rule.
2 The form of Gaelic used in Ireland. **LME.** ▸†**b** Scottish Gaelic. **E16–E18.**
Old Irish: see **OLD** *adjective*.
3 *ellipt*. Irish linen, whiskey, etc. **L18.**

> J. K. JEROME He had found a place . . where you could really get a drop of Irish worth drinking.

4 Temper; passion. *colloq*. **M19.**

> *Islander* (*Victoria, BC*) I'm afraid she'd really get her 'Irish' up.

■ **Irisher** *noun* (*colloq*.) a person of Irish origin **E19.** **Iˈrishian** *noun* a person familiar with the Celtic language or antiquities of Ireland **E19.** **Irishism** *noun* an Irish expression, statement, etc. (see **IRISH** *adjective* 3) **E18.** **Irishize** *verb trans*. make Irish in character **M19.** **Irishly** *adverb* **L16.** **Irishness** *noun* **E19.** **Irishy** *adjective* like the Irish, somewhat Irish **L19.**

Irishman /ˈʌɪrɪʃmən/ *noun*. Pl. **-men**. **ME.**
[**ORIGIN** from **IRISH** *adjective* + **MAN** *noun*.]
1 A man of Irish birth or descent. **ME.**
2 In full ***wild Irishman*** = **MATAGOURI.** *NZ*. **M19.**
— **PHRASES**: **Irishman's hurricane** *nautical slang* a dead calm. **Irishman's promotion**, **Irishman's rise** *colloq*. a reduction in wages. **wild Irishman** (*a*) *hist*. any of the wild Irish; (*b*) see sense 2 above.

Irishry /ˈʌɪrɪʃri/ *noun*. **LME.**
[**ORIGIN** from **IRISH** *adjective* + **-RY.**]
1 *collect*. (*hist*.) The native Irish, as opp. to English settlers in Ireland. **LME.**
2 Irish character or nationality; an Irish trait. **M19.**

Irishwoman /ˈʌɪrɪʃwʊmən/ *noun*. Pl. **-women** /-wɪmɪn/. **LME.**
[**ORIGIN** from **IRISH** *adjective* + **WOMAN** *noun*.]
A woman of Irish birth or descent.

iritis /ʌɪˈrʌɪtɪs/ *noun*. **E19.**
[**ORIGIN** Irreg. from Latin **IRIS** + **-ITIS.**]
MEDICINE. Inflammation of the iris.
■ **iritic** /ʌɪˈrɪtɪk/ *adjective* pertaining to or affected with iritis; affecting the iris: **M19.**

irk *noun*[1] var. of **ERK.**

irk /əːk/ *verb & noun*[2]. **ME.**
[**ORIGIN** Perh. from Old Norse *yrkja* **WORK** *verb*, Swedish *yrka* claim, demand, insist.]
▸ **A** *verb*. **1** *verb intrans*. Grow weary (*of*); feel vexed, annoyed, or disgusted (*with*, *at*); be reluctant, find it tiresome, *to do*. Now *rare*. **ME.**
†**2** *verb trans*. Be weary of or disgusted with; loathe. **LME–E17.**
3 *verb trans*. Make weary, bore; irritate, annoy; disgust. **LME.**
▸ **B** *noun*. Irksomeness, annoyance. *rare*. **L16.**

irksome /ˈəːks(ə)m/ *adjective*. **LME.**
[**ORIGIN** from **IRK** *verb* + **-SOME**[1].]
†**1** Weary; disgusted; bored. Foll. by *of*. **LME–M19.**
2 Tedious, tiresome; troublesome, annoying. Formerly also, painful, disgusting, loathsome. **LME.**

> ISAIAH BERLIN Laws . . will only seem irksome to those whose reason is dormant.

■ **irksomely** *adverb* †(*a*) painfully; (*b*) in a tiring, annoying, or troublesome way: **M16.** **irksomeness** *noun* **LME.**

†**irnen** *adjective* var. of **IRONEN.**

IRO *abbreviation*.
1 Inland Revenue Office.
2 International Refugee Organization.

iroha /iˈroha, ɪˈrəʊhɑː/ *noun*. *arch*. Also †***-fa***. **M19.**
[**ORIGIN** Japanese, from the opening syllables *i, ro, ha* or (formerly) *fa* in one method of listing.]
The Japanese kana or syllabary.

iroko /ɪˈrəʊkəʊ, iː-/ *noun*. Pl. **-os**. **L19.**
[**ORIGIN** Yoruba.]
Any of various African trees of the genus *Chlorophora*, of the mulberry family, esp. *C. excelsa* and *C. regia* (in full ***iroko tree***). Also, the timber of such a tree. Also called ***West African teak***, ***Nigerian teak***, ***yellow-wood***.

iron /ˈʌɪən/ *noun & adjective*.
[**ORIGIN** Old English *īren*, perh. alt. of *īse(r)n* = Old Saxon, Old High German *īsarn* (Dutch *ijzen*, German *Eisen*), Old Norse *ísarn*, Gothic *eisarn*, from Germanic, prob. from Celtic and rel. to Latin *aes*, *ais* bronze, Old English *ār* **ORE** *noun*[1], Sanskrit *ayas*.]
▸ **A** *noun* **I 1** A malleable, magnetic, readily oxidizable metal which is a chemical element of the transition series (atomic no. 26), occurs abundantly in certain ores and in meteorites, and is widely used, chiefly in alloys such as steel, for tools, implements, structures, machinery, etc. (symbol Fe). **OE.** ▸**b** A variety or sort of iron or ferrous alloy. Freq. with specifying word. **M17.**
b *bog iron*, ***cast iron***, ***ingot iron***, ***pig iron***, ***red iron***, ***white iron***, ***wrought iron***, etc.
2 *MEDICINE*. A preparation of a compound of iron, used chiefly to treat anaemia. **E19.**
3 *GEOLOGY*. A meteorite which contains a high proportion of iron. **E19.**
▸ **II** A thing made of iron.
4 Any of various instruments, appliances, tools, or utensils, now or formerly made of the metal. Freq. preceded by specifying word. **OE.**
climbing iron, ***curling iron***, ***fire iron***, ***grappling iron***, ***pinking iron***, ***soldering iron***, etc.
5 An iron weapon; a sword. Also, iron weapons collectively. *obsolete* exc. *dial*. **OE.**

> SHAKES. *Twel. N.* Meddle you must, that's certain, or forswear to wear iron about you.

6 An iron shackle or fetter. Usu. in *pl*. *arch*. **OE.**

> LD MACAULAY When the Earl reached the Castle his legs were put in irons.

7 An instrument heated and used for branding or cauterizing. **LME.**

> J. A. MICHENER I'll get the smithy to make us some irons.

8 In *pl*. Dies used in striking coins. *obsolete* exc. *hist*. **L15.**
9 Any of various devices used when heated to press fabrics. In mod. use *spec*. an (electrical) appliance with a heavy flat base which uses dry heat or steam. **E17.**

> E. HARDWICK The scent of a hot iron on a shirt collar.

flat iron, ***goffering iron***, ***steam iron***, etc.
10 *WHALING* etc. A harpoon (= **HARPING-IRON**). **L17.**
11 Money. Cf. **IRON MAN** 2, **BRASS** *noun* 3. *slang*. **L18.**
12 *GOLF*. A club having an iron or steel head which is angled in order to loft the ball. Now freq. with a number prefixed indicating the degree of angle. **E19.**

> *Golf World* Better to practise . . with the same club—something like a 6-iron.

13 A gun; *spec*. a pistol. Also, firearms collectively. *slang*. **M19.**

> R. BOLDREWOOD Put down your irons . . or . . we'll drop ye where ye stand. J. CARROLL I never carry iron. This ain't Chicago.

shooting iron.
14 In *pl*. Leg supports to correct malformations. **M19.**
15 *HORSEMANSHIP*. A stirrup (usu. in *pl*.); *esp*. a stirrup iron. **L19.**

> E. BAIRD The toe is well into the iron. *Horse & Hound* Cold Blood's rider lost both irons.

16 In *pl*. More fully ***eating irons***. Eating utensils. *dial*. & *slang*. **E20.**

> JOCELYN BROOKE I thought some tea would be nice, only I hadn't any eating-irons.

17 = ***corrugated iron*** s.v. **CORRUGATE.** Chiefly *Austral*. & *NZ*. **E20.**
18 An old motor vehicle. *slang*. **M20.**
19 A jemmy, a crowbar. *criminals' slang*. **M20.**
20 = ***iron hoof*** below. *slang*. *derog*. **M20.**
21 [Ellipt. for ***iron curtain*** below.] A fire curtain in a theatre. *theatrical slang*. **M20.**
▸ **III** *transf*. & *fig*. **22** As an allusion to warfare or slaughter. **OE.**

> *Daily News* Great questions . . are decided, not by speeches and majorities, but by iron and blood.

23 As a type of extreme hardness or strength. **E17.**

P. GALLICO She was no longer a woman of ice, iron and whalebone.

– PHRASES: **Clerk of the Irons** (*obsolete* exc. *hist.*) an officer of the Royal Mint who had charge of the manufacture and use of the dies. ***corrugated iron***: see CORRUGATE 1. **fresh off the irons**, **new off the irons** fresh from school or studies; newly made or prepared; brand-new. ***have nerves of iron***: see NERVE *noun*. **have many irons in the fire**, **have too many irons in the fire** (***a***) be engaged in (too) many occupations or undertakings; (***b***) use several expedients or alternatives to attain a purpose. **in irons** (***a***) having the feet or hands fettered, *fig.* in bondage, in captivity; (***b***) (of a sailing vessel) head to wind and unable to come about or tack either way. ***new off the irons***: see ***fresh off the irons*** above. ***standing iron***: see STANDING *adjective*. **strike while the iron is hot** act promptly; seize an opportunity. **the iron entered into his soul** [*Psalms* 105:18, from Latin mistranslation of Hebrew for 'his person entered into the iron', i.e. fetters] he became deeply and permanently affected by captivity or ill treatment.

▸ **B** *adjective*. **I** Of iron.

1 Consisting or made of iron. **OE.**

I. MURDOCH The iron side-pieces had long ago rusted into the head and foot boards. G. GREENE The window was guarded by iron bars.

▸ **II** Resembling or held to resemble iron.

2 Physically hard or strong; robust, tough, enduring. **LME.**

BYRON Though aged, he was so iron of limb, Few of our youth could cope with him. J. STEINBECK She tapped his arm with an iron finger.

3 Cruel, merciless, implacable, stern, severe. **L16.** ▸**b** Firm, inflexible; stubborn, obstinate, unyielding. **E17.**

BURKE The first Republick in the world . . is under her iron yoke. **b** J. STEINBECK He . . held back in his impatience with an iron control. C. G. WOLFF The daughter developed into a woman of iron determination.

4 Base, debased; wicked. **L16.**

HENRY SMITH Look not for a golden life in an iron world.

5 Resembling iron in appearance; iron-coloured. Also (*rare*), resembling iron oxide; rust-coloured. **E17.**

6 Of metallic tone, harsh, dull, unmusical. **L19.**

– COMB. & SPECIAL COLLOCATIONS: **iron age** (***a***) the last and worst age of the world according to Greek and Roman mythology; a time of wickedness or oppression; (***b***) (with cap. initials) ARCHAEOLOGY a period when weapons and implements were first made of iron; ***iron*** ALUM; **iron bacterium** any of various chiefly freshwater bacteria which are capable of oxidizing ferrous salts (some obtaining energy thereby) and storing the resulting ferric hydroxide; **ironbark** *Austral.* (the wood of) any of several eucalypts with very hard bark; esp. *Eucalyptus paniculata* (more fully ***grey ironbark***), and *E. sideroxylon* (more fully ***red ironbark***); **iron-binding** *adjective & noun* (CHEMISTRY) (***a***) *adjective* able to combine with iron atoms; (***b***) *noun* combination with iron; **iron blue** (***a***) (of) a blue colour like some kinds of iron or steel; (***b***) the pigment Prussian blue; **iron-blue** (more fully ***iron-blue dun***, ***iron-blue fly***, ***iron-blue spinner***) ANGLING (an artificial fly imitating) a mayfly of the genus *Baetis*; **iron-bound** *adjective* bound with or as with iron; (of a coast) rock-bound; rigorous, hard and fast; **Iron Chancellor** Bismarck (see BISMARCKIAN); **iron chink** a machine for cleaning and gutting fish; **iron-clay** *noun & adjective* (***a***) *noun* = ***clay ironstone*** s.v. CLAY *noun*; (***b***) *adjective* of mixed iron and clay; **Iron Cross** a German (orig. Prussian) decoration awarded for distinguished services in war; **iron curtain** an impenetrable barrier (orig. a fire curtain in a theatre); *spec.* (*hist.*) (with cap. initials) a notional barrier to the passage of people and information between the Soviet bloc and the West; **Iron Duke** the first Duke of Wellington (1769–1852); **iron gang** *Austral.* a gang of prisoners working in irons; **iron-glance** specular haematite; **Iron Guard** an anti-Semitic, Fascist, terrorist Romanian political party; **iron hand** firmness or inflexibility in controlling; ***iron hand in a velvet glove***, firmness or inflexibility masked by a gentle or urbane manner. **iron-handed** *adjective* inflexible; severe, rigorous; despotic; **iron-hard** *adjective* as hard as iron; extremely hard; **iron-headed** *adjective* capped or tipped with iron; *fig.* hard-headed, determined; **iron-hearted** *adjective* extremely hard-hearted; cruel, pitiless; **iron hoof** *slang*, *derog.* [rhyming slang for *poof*] a homosexual man; **iron horse** (***a***) a steam locomotive; (***b***) a bicycle or motorcycle; **iron jubilee** the seventieth anniversary of an event; **iron lace** *Austral.* decorative cast ironwork; **iron lady** a brave, tough, or intransigent woman; **iron law** ECONOMICS: stating that wages tend to sink to mere subsistence level; **iron loss** ELECTRICITY = ***core loss*** s.v. CORE *noun*[1]; **iron lung** a rigid airtight metal case fitted over a patient's body, used for giving prolonged artificial respiration by means of mechanical pumps; **iron maiden** an instrument of torture consisting of a box lined with iron spikes, into which the victim is shut; **iron mask** a mask, supposedly made of iron, worn by a political prisoner who died in the Bastille in 1703 and whose identity is disputed; the prisoner himself; **ironmaster** the proprietor of an iron foundry or ironworks; **iron mike** *slang* an automatic steering device on a ship; **iron mountain** a mountain rich in iron ore; **iron ore** any rock or mineral from which iron is or may be extracted; **iron pan** SOIL SCIENCE a hardpan in which iron oxides are the chief cementing agents; **iron paper** extremely thin sheet iron; ***iron pyrites***: see PYRITES 2; **iron rations** (esp. a soldier's) emergency rations of preserved food, biscuits, etc.; **iron-sand** GEOLOGY: containing particles of iron ore; **iron-shot** *adjective* (MINERALOGY) containing streaks or markings of iron; **ironsmith** (now *rare* or *obsolete*) a person who works in iron, a blacksmith; **iron-sponge** iron, or iron oxide, in a spongy form having a large surface area; **iron tree** any of various trees and shrubs with very hard wood; *esp.* the Malaysian *Metrosideros vera*, of the myrtle family; **ironware** small ware or goods made of iron; **ironweed** (***a***) *dial.* hard-head, *Centaurea nigra*; (***b***) *N. Amer.* any of various plants of the genus *Vernonia*, of the composite family, related to hemp agrimony; **ironwood** the extremely hard wood of various trees of many different families and countries; any of the trees producing such wood.

■ **ironless** *adjective* without iron; not containing iron: **LME. iron-like** *adjective* resembling (that of) iron (*lit.* & *fig.*) **L16.**

iron /ˈʌɪən/ *verb*. **LME.**

[ORIGIN from the noun.]

1 *verb trans.* Fit, cover, or arm with iron. Chiefly as pa. pple: see IRONED *adjective* 2. **LME.**

R. W. EMERSON What if Trade . . thatch with towns the prairie broad With railways ironed o'er. *Lancashire Life* We had to take our clogs to be 'ironed'.

2 *verb trans.* Shackle; put in irons. **M17.**

P. F. TYTLER Wallace was cast into a dungeon and heavily ironed.

3 *verb trans. & intrans.* Smooth or press (cloth etc.) with a heated iron. Also *transf.* & *fig.*, (foll. by *out*) smooth, flatten; resolve (a problem). **L17.** ▸**b** *verb intrans.* Of a garment, material, etc.: become smooth by being pressed with an iron. **M20.**

P. ROTH Dressed in a light, freshly laundered shirt whose lapels were ironed flat. *Headlight* The car is independently sprung and irons out the road very well. *Ring* He connected with the jab . . , followed with a right. That . . ironed Mike to the canvas. **b** *Modern Language Notes* The 'potential intransitive', . . as . . 'this dress *washes* and *irons* . . easily'.

4 [back-form. from IRONY *noun*.] ▸**a** *verb trans.* Treat with irony, speak ironically to. Chiefly *joc.* **M18.** ▸**b** *verb intrans.* Use irony, speak ironically. Chiefly *joc.* **E19.**

– COMB.: **iron-on** *adjective* that can be attached to a fabric by ironing.

■ **ironer** *noun* a person who irons; *spec.* a person whose occupation is ironing clothes etc.: **L18.**

ironclad /ˈʌɪənklad/ *adjective & noun*. **M19.**

[ORIGIN from IRON *noun & adjective* + *clad* pa. pple of CLOTHE.]

▸ **A** *adjective*. **1** Protected or covered with iron; *esp.* (of a naval vessel) armour-plated. **M19.**

2 *fig.* Strict, rigorous, hard and fast. **M19.**

M. PUZO You know you got an ironclad contract . . and I can't fire you.

3 Of a plant: able to withstand cold and frost. *US*. **L19.**

▸ **B** *noun*. **1** An ironclad ship. **M19.**

2 *transf.* & *fig.* Something resembling an armoured ship; something tough or impregnable. **M19.**

ironed /ˈʌɪənd/ *adjective*. **ME.**

[ORIGIN from IRON *noun*, *verb*: see -ED[2], -ED[1].]

†**1** Made of iron. Only in **ME.**

2 That has been ironed; *spec.* (***a***) fitted, covered, armed, or strengthened with iron; (***b***) put in irons; fettered. **LME.**

ironen /ˈʌɪənən/ *adjective*. *obsolete* exc. *dial.* Also †**irnen**. **ME.**

[ORIGIN from IRON *noun* + -EN[4].]

Made (solely) of iron.

iron-grey /ʌɪənˈɡreɪ/ *adjective & noun*. Also ***-gray**. **OE.**

[ORIGIN from IRON *noun* + GREY *adjective*.]

▸ **A** *adjective*. Of the dark grey colour of freshly broken iron, or of dark hair when turning grey. **OE.**

▸ **B** *noun*. **1** An iron-grey horse or dog; a person whose dark hair is grizzled. **E16.**

2 A dark grey colour resembling that of freshly broken iron. **M16.**

ironic /ʌɪˈrɒnɪk/ *adjective*. **M17.**

[ORIGIN French *ironique* or late Latin *ironicus* from Greek *eirōnikos* dissembling, feigning ignorance, formed as IRONY *noun*: see -IC.]

Pertaining to irony; uttering or given to irony; of the nature of or containing irony; happening in a way contrary to what is expected, ironical.

P. LARKIN All these honours seem ironic; when I was really doing good stuff, no one knew or cared. P. MATTHIESSEN He tends to communicate with wry laconic comments and ironic gestures.

ironical /ʌɪˈrɒnɪk(ə)l/ *adjective*. **L16.**

[ORIGIN formed as IRONIC: see -ICAL.]

1 Of the nature of irony; wry, sarcastic; happening in a way contrary to what is expected, ironic. **L16.**

2 That (habitually) uses irony. **L16.**

†**3** Dissembling; feigned, pretended. *rare*. **M17–E18.**

■ **ironically** *adverb* **L16. ironicalness** *noun* **L18.**

ironing /ˈʌɪənɪŋ/ *noun*. **E18.**

[ORIGIN from IRON *verb* + -ING[1].]

The pressing and smoothing of clothes, household linen, etc., with a heated iron; the clothes etc. which are to be or have been ironed.

– COMB.: **ironing blanket** a thick blanket folded and used to protect a surface on which clothes etc. are ironed; **ironing board** a long narrow padded board, on adjustable legs, on which clothes etc. are ironed; **ironing cloth**: (dampened and) put between an iron and fabric being ironed.

ironise *verb* var. of IRONIZE.

ironist /ˈʌɪr(ə)nɪst/ *noun*. **E18.**

[ORIGIN from Greek *eirōn* dissembler, user of irony + -IST.]

A person who uses irony; an ironical speaker or writer.

ironize /ˈʌɪr(ə)nʌɪz/ *verb*. Also **-ise**. **E17.**

[ORIGIN formed as IRONIST: see -IZE.]

1 *verb trans.* Make ironical, use ironically. **E17.**

2 *verb intrans.* Use irony, speak ironically. **M17.**

iron man /ˈʌɪən man/ *noun phr.* Pl. **iron men**. **E17.**

[ORIGIN from IRON *noun & adjective* + MAN *noun*.]

1 A man of iron; a brave, tough, or intransigent man; *esp.* a robust sportsman. **E17.** ▸**b** A multi-event sporting contest demanding stamina; *spec.* a triathlon involving consecutively a 2.4 mile (3.9 km) swim, a 112 mile (180 km) cycle ride, and a 26.2 mile (42.2 km) run. **L20.**

2 A dollar; *Austral.* formerly also, a pound. Cf. IRON *noun* 11. *slang* (chiefly *US*). **E20.**

iron mold, †**iron-mole** *nouns* see IRON MOULD.

ironmonger /ˈʌɪənmʌŋɡə/ *noun*. **ME.**

[ORIGIN from IRON *noun* + MONGER.]

A dealer in metal utensils, tools, etc.; a hardware merchant.

ironmongery /ˈʌɪənmʌŋɡ(ə)ri/ *noun*. **E18.**

[ORIGIN from IRONMONGER: see -ERY.]

1 The goods dealt in by an ironmonger; hardware. **E18.** ▸**b** *transf.* Paraphernalia; machinery, tackle. **L19.** ▸**c** Firearms. *slang*. **E20.**

2 An ironmonger's shop or place of business. **M19.**

3 The craft or business of the ironmonger; smith's work. **L19.**

iron mould /ˈʌɪənməʊld/ *noun & verb*. Also **-mold**, (earlier) †**-mole**. **E17.**

[ORIGIN from IRON *noun* + MOLE *noun*[1], MOULD *noun*[5], perh. by assoc. with MOULD *noun*[4].]

▸ **A** *noun*. A spot or discoloration on cloth etc. caused by rust or an ink stain. **E17.**

▸ **B** *verb trans. & intrans.* Stain or become stained with iron mould. **E18.**

Ironside /ˈʌɪənsʌɪd/ *noun*. **ME.**

[ORIGIN from IRON *adjective* + SIDE *noun*.]

1 (A name for) a man of great bravery; *spec.* (***a***) Edmund II, king of England (1016); (***b***) (also ***Ironsides***) Oliver Cromwell. **ME.**

2 In *pl.* Cromwell's troopers in the English Civil War. Also occas. in *sing.* a Puritan soldier; a devout warrior. **M17.**

ironstone /ˈʌɪənstəʊn/ *noun*. **E16.**

[ORIGIN from IRON *noun* + STONE *noun*.]

Any of various freq. hard rocks which contain a high proportion of iron minerals; iron ore; *esp.* any iron-rich, coarsely banded or unbanded sedimentary rock.

clay ironstone: see CLAY *noun*. ***red ironstone***: see RED *adjective*.

– COMB.: **ironstone china** a hard, white, opaque type of stone china.

ironwork /ˈʌɪənwəːk/ *noun*. **LME.**

[ORIGIN from IRON *noun* + WORK *noun*.]

1 Work in iron; that part of anything which is made of iron, iron goods collectively. **LME.**

2 In *pl.*, freq. treated as *sing.* An establishment where iron is smelted, or where heavy iron goods are made. **L16.**

■ **ironworker** *noun* a person who works in iron; a person employed in an ironworks: **LME.**

irony /ˈʌɪrəni/ *noun*. **E16.**

[ORIGIN Latin *ironia*, Greek *eirōneia* simulated ignorance, from *eirōn* dissembler: see -Y[3].]

1 Dissimulation, pretence; *esp.* (also ***Socratic irony***), a pose of ignorance assumed in order to entice others into making statements that can then be challenged. **E16.**

2 The expression of meaning using language that normally expresses the opposite; *esp.* the humorous or sarcastic use of praise to imply condemnation or contempt. **E16.** ▸**b** An instance of this; an ironical utterance or expression. **M16.**

Face A Bradford-based duo with a neat line in irony.

3 Discrepancy between the expected and the actual state of affairs; a state of affairs that seems deliberately contrary to what is expected and is often wryly amusing. **M17.**

R. CRITCHFIELD Thatcherism, with some irony, had made Britain's leading socialist very rich. *Time* Winchester is alert to . . history's ironies.

4 A literary technique, orig. in Greek tragedy, by which the full significance of a character's words or actions is clear to the audience or reader but unknown to the character. Also ***dramatic irony***, ***tragic irony***. **E20.**

irony /ˈʌɪəni/ *adjective*. **LME.**

[ORIGIN from IRON *noun* + -Y[1].]

Consisting of or containing iron; of the nature of or resembling iron.

Iroquoian /ɪrəˈkwɔɪən, -ˈkɔɪ-/ *adjective & noun*. **L17.**

[ORIGIN from IROQUOIS + -AN.]

▸ **A** *adjective*. Of or pertaining to the Iroquois or the language family Iroquoian (see B.1 below). **L17.**

▸ **B** *noun*. **1** A language family which includes Iroquois, Huron, Cherokee, and several other N. American Indian languages. **L19.**

2 An Iroquois. **M20.**

Iroquois /ˈɪrəkwɔɪ, -kɔɪ/ *adjective & noun*. **M17.**

[ORIGIN French, from Algonquian.]

▸ **A** *adjective*. Of or pertaining to a group of N. American Indian peoples comprising the Mohawks, Oneidas,

Senecas, Onondagas, Tuscaroras, and Cayugas; of or pertaining to (any of) the languages of this group. M17.
▸ **B** *noun*. Pl. same.
1 A member of this group. L17.
2 The language of (any of) the Iroquois. M18.

irradiance /ɪˈreɪdɪəns/ *noun*. M17.
[ORIGIN from IRRADIANT + -ANCE.]
1 The fact of irradiating; the emission of rays of light, emitted radiance. Also (*fig.*), the shedding of spiritual or intellectual radiance. M17.
2 The flux of radiant energy per unit area (normal to the direction of flow of radiant energy through a medium). M20.
■ **irradiancy** *noun* = IRRADIANCE 1 M17.

irradiant /ɪˈreɪdɪənt/ *adjective*. E16.
[ORIGIN Latin *irradiant-* pres. ppl stem of *irradiare* IRRADIATE *verb*: see -ANT¹.]
Emitting rays of light; shining brightly. Also (*fig.*), shedding spiritual or intellectual radiance.

irradiate /ɪˈreɪdɪət/ *adjective*. L15.
[ORIGIN Latin *irradiatus* pa. pple, formed as IRRADIATE *verb*: see -ATE².]
Illuminated, made bright or brilliant. (Foll. by *with*.)

POPE The Theban Bard, depriv'd of sight, Within, irradiate with prophetic light.

irradiate /ɪˈreɪdɪeɪt/ *verb*. L16.
[ORIGIN Latin *irradiat-* pa. ppl stem of *irradiare*, formed as IR-¹ + *radiare* shine, from *radius* ray: see -ATE³.]
1 *verb intrans.* Emit rays, shine (*on*, *upon*). L16.

G. HORNE Day was the state of the hemisphere, on which light irradiated.

2 *verb trans.* Direct rays of light on; make bright by causing light to fall on, illuminate. L16. ▸**b** ASTROLOGY. Cast influence on. E17. ▸**c** Expose to the action of some kind of radiation other than visible light, as X-rays, ultraviolet radiation, or neutrons. E20.

W. GOLDING The candles of the saloon irradiated her face. **c** *Technology* Food can be preserved for long periods if irradiated.

3 *verb trans. transf.* & *fig.* ▸**a** Illuminate with spiritual, intellectual, etc., light; *esp.* throw light on (something intellectually obscure). E17. ▸**b** Brighten as with light; light up (the face) with beauty, gladness, animation, etc. M17. ▸**c** Adorn with splendour. *poet.* E18.

a P. V. PRICE The great wine will irradiate all the others . . chosen to accompany it. **b** H. ALLEN A smile of vivid brightness irradiated the face of the stranger.

4 *verb trans.* Radiate, send out (as) in rays. E17.

G. ADAMS Their powers decay according to their distances from the centres from which they irradiated.

†**5** *verb intrans.* Radiate, diverge in the form of rays. L17–L18.
6 *verb intrans.* Become radiant; light up. Now *rare* or *obsolete*. E19.

W. IRVING The eye is taught to brighten, the lip to smile, and the whole countenance to irradiate.

■ **irradiated** *adjective* (**a**) that has been irradiated; (**b**) HERALDRY represented as surrounded by rays: L18.

irradiation /ɪˌreɪdɪˈeɪʃ(ə)n/ *noun*. L16.
[ORIGIN Old French & mod. French, or late Latin *irradiatio(n-)*, formed as IRRADIATE *verb*: see -ATION.]
1 The action of irradiating; subjection to or emission of rays of light. L16. ▸**b** A ray of light, a beam. M17.
2 *fig.* **a** Intellectual enlightenment; illumination of the mind. L16. ▸**b** A diffusion of spiritual light. M17.
3 The (real or supposed) emission or emanation of a fluid, influence, principle, or virtue, from an active centre. Orig. chiefly PHYSIOLOGY. E17.

BACON There seemeth . . in the Act of Enuy, an Eiaculation, or Irradiation of the Eye. G. DANIEL Metallurgy and megalith building in Europe before any irradiation from the Aegean or the ancient East.

4 a OPTICS. The apparent extension of the edges of a strongly illuminated object when seen against a dark ground. M19. ▸**b** PHOTOGRAPHY. The scattering of light by silver halide crystals in the emulsion, causing diffuseness of the image. E20.
5 Exposure to the action of some kind of radiation other than visible light (esp. ionizing radiation); (an instance of) the action or process of irradiating something in this way. E20.

Nature Human diploid cells can be transformed *in vitro* into tumorogenic cells by x-ray irradiation. *Super Marketing* Many microbiologists favoured irradiation because it was practically the only . . safeguard against food poisoning bacteria.

irradiative /ɪˈreɪdɪətɪv/ *adjective*. M19.
[ORIGIN from IRRADIATE *verb* + -IVE.]
Tending to irradiate; illuminative.

irradiator /ɪˈreɪdɪeɪtə/ *noun*. M18.
[ORIGIN from IRRADIATE *verb* + -OR.]
A person who or thing which irradiates (now usu. with invisible radiation).

irradicable /ɪˈradɪkəb(ə)l/ *adjective*. *rare*. E18.
[ORIGIN from IR-² + Latin *radicare* take root (taken as if = uproot) + -ABLE.]
Unable to be rooted out; = INERADICABLE.

†**irrased** *ppl adjective*. L15–L19.
[ORIGIN from IR-¹ + *rased* pa. pple of RASE *verb*¹. Cf. medieval Latin *irrasus* scraped in.]
HERALDRY. = INDENTED 2. Cf. ERASE *verb* 1.

irrationable /ɪˈraʃ(ə)nəb(ə)l/ *adjective*. Now *rare* or *obsolete*. L16.
[ORIGIN Latin *irrationabilis*, from IR-² *rationabilis*, formed as RATIO *noun* + -ABLE.]
1 Not endowed with reason; = IRRATIONAL *adjective* 2. L16.
2 Not in accordance with reason; unreasonable; = IRRATIONAL *adjective* 3. M17.
■ **irrationa'bility** *noun* unreasonableness, irrationality M17.

irrational /ɪˈraʃ(ə)n(ə)l/ *adjective* & *noun*. LME.
[ORIGIN Latin *irrationalis*, formed as IR-² + *rationalis* RATIONAL *adjective*, *noun*¹.]
▸ **A** *adjective*. **1** MATH. Of a number, quantity, or magnitude: not rational, not commensurable with the natural numbers, not expressible by an ordinary (finite) fraction but only by an infinite continued fraction or an infinite series (e.g. a non-terminating decimal). LME.

P. DAVIES All irrational numbers, such as π, need infinite decimals.

2 Not endowed with reason. L15.

C. G. WOLFF The irrational component of man's nature—the element that he shares with all other animals.

3 Contrary to or not in accordance with reason; unreasonable, utterly illogical, absurd. M17.

M. PIERCY Maybe all husbands acted in irrational rage sometimes.

4 GREEK PROSODY. (Of a syllable) having a metrical value not corresponding to its actual time value; (of a metrical foot) containing such a syllable. M19.
▸ **B** *noun*. **1** A being not endowed with or guided by reason. M17.
2 MATH. An irrational number or quantity; a surd. L17.
■ **irrationalize** *verb trans.* make irrational L19. **irrationally** *adverb* M17.

irrationalism /ɪˈraʃ(ə)n(ə)lɪz(ə)m/ *noun*. E19.
[ORIGIN from IRRATIONAL + -ISM.]
A system of belief or action that disregards or contradicts rational principles.
■ **irrationalist** *noun* & *adjective* (**a**) *noun* a person who practises or advocates irrationalism; (**b**) *adjective* marked by or advocating irrationalism: M19. **irrationa'listic** *adjective* characterized by irrationalism; contrary to reason, illogical: E20.

irrationality /ɪˌraʃəˈnalɪti/ *noun*. L16.
[ORIGIN from IRRATIONAL *adjective* + -ITY.]
1 MATH. The quality of being irrational. L16.
2 The quality of not being guided by, or not being in accordance with, reason; absurdity of thought or action. M17. ▸**b** An irrational thing, action, or thought; an absurdity. L17.
3 OPTICS. The inequality of the ratios of the dispersion of the various colours in spectra produced by refraction through different substances. L18.
4 The quality of being devoid of reason. E19.
5 GREEK PROSODY. The quality of being an irrational syllable or foot. M19.

irrealisable *adjective* var. of IRREALIZABLE.

irreality /ɪrɪˈalɪti/ *noun*. *rare*. E19.
[ORIGIN from IR-² + REALITY.]
Unreality.

irrealizable /ɪˈrɪəlʌɪzəb(ə)l/ *adjective*. Also **-isable**. M19.
[ORIGIN from IR-² + REALIZABLE.]
Unable to be realized; unrealizable.

irrebuttable /ɪrɪˈbʌtəb(ə)l/ *adjective*. M19.
[ORIGIN from IR-² + REBUTTABLE.]
Unable to be rebutted.

irreceptive /ɪrɪˈsɛptɪv/ *adjective*. M19.
[ORIGIN from IR-² + RECEPTIVE.]
Not capable of receiving; unreceptive.

irreciprocal /ɪrɪˈsɪprək(ə)l/ *adjective*. L19.
[ORIGIN from IR-² + RECIPROCAL *adjective*.]
Not reciprocal.

irreciprocity /ɪˌrɛsɪˈprɒsɪti/ *noun*. L19.
[ORIGIN from IR-² + RECIPROCITY.]
Absence of reciprocity.

irreclaimable /ɪrɪˈkleɪməb(ə)l/ *adjective*. E17.
[ORIGIN from IR-² + RECLAIMABLE.]
†**1** Uncontrollable, implacable. *rare*. Only in E17.
2 Unable to be reformed or redeemed. M17.
3 Of land: unable to be brought under cultivation. L18.
4 Unable to be called back or revoked; irrevocable. M19.
■ **irreclaima'bility** *noun* L19. **irreclaimableness** *noun* L18. **irreclaimably** *adverb* without the possibility of being reclaimed M17.

irreclaimed /ɪrɪˈkleɪmd/ *adjective*. *rare*. E19.
[ORIGIN from IR-² + RECLAIM *verb* + -ED¹.]
Not brought under civilization or cultivation; unreclaimed.

irrecognisable *adjective* var. of IRRECOGNIZABLE.

irrecognition /ɪˌrɛkəgˈnɪʃ(ə)n/ *noun*. E19.
[ORIGIN from IR-² + RECOGNITION.]
Absence of recognition; non-recognition.

irrecognizable /ɪˈrɛkəgnʌɪzəb(ə)l/ *adjective*. Also **-isable**. M19.
[ORIGIN from IR-² + RECOGNIZABLE.]
Unable to be recognized; unrecognizable.
■ **irrecogniza'bility** *noun* M19. **irrecognizably** *adverb* M19.

irrecollection /ɪˌrɛkəˈlɛkʃ(ə)n/ *noun*. Now *rare*. M18.
[ORIGIN from IR-² + RECOLLECTION.]
Absence of recollection; forgetfulness.

irreconcilable /ɪˌrɛk(ə)nˈsʌɪləb(ə)l, ɪˈrɛk(ə)nsʌɪləb(ə)l/ *adjective* & *noun*. Also **-ileable**. L16.
[ORIGIN from IR-² + RECONCILABLE.]
▸ **A** *adjective*. **1** Of people, their feelings, etc.: unable to be reconciled or brought into friendly relations; implacably hostile. (Foll. by *to*.) L16.

H. JAMES They belonged by temperament to irreconcilable camps.

2 Of statements, ideas, etc.: unable to be brought into harmony or made consistent; incompatible. (Foll. by *to*, *with*.) E17.

N. SYMINGTON How characteristics, seemingly irreconcilable, can exist in the same person.

▸ **B** *noun*. **1** A person who refuses to be reconciled; *esp.* a politician who refuses to compromise. M18.
2 In *pl.* Principles, ideas, etc., that cannot be harmonized with each other. L19.
■ **irreconcila'bility** *noun* M19. **irreconcilableness** *noun* E17. **irreconcilably** *adverb* E17.

†**irreconciled** *adjective*. L16–M18.
[ORIGIN from IR-² + RECONCILE + -ED¹.]
Not reconciled; *spec.* in a state at variance with God.

irreconcilement /ɪˈrɛk(ə)nsʌɪlm(ə)nt/ *noun*. M18.
[ORIGIN from IR-² + RECONCILEMENT.]
The state or fact of being unreconciled.

irreconciliable /ɪˌrɛk(ə)nˈsɪlɪəb(ə)l/ *adjective*. Now *rare*. E17.
[ORIGIN French *irréconciliable* from late Latin *irreconciliabilis*, from IR-² + *reconciliare* RECONCILE: see -ABLE.]
= IRRECONCILABLE *adjective*.
■ **irreconcilia'bility** *noun* M19. **irreconciliableness** *noun* M17. **irreconciliably** *adverb* E17.

irreconciliation /ɪˌrɛk(ə)nsɪlɪˈeɪʃ(ə)n/ *noun*. M17.
[ORIGIN from IR-² + RECONCILIATION.]
The fact or condition of being unreconciled.

irrecoverable /ɪrɪˈkʌv(ə)rəb(ə)l/ *adjective*. LME.
[ORIGIN from IR-² + RECOVERABLE. Cf. French *irrécouvrable*.]
1 Chiefly of something lost: that cannot be recovered or retrieved. LME.

L. GORDON The childhood summers at St Ives were marked in memory as the irrecoverable paradise.

2 a *fig.* Unable to be remedied or rectified; irretrievable. LME. ▸**b** Unable to be restored to health; incurable; that cannot be restored to life, as after drowning, suffocation, etc. *arch.* L16.

a C. NESS A final and irrecoverable fall.

†**3** Unable to be recalled or revoked; irrevocable. M16–E19.

A. TUCKER Persons lying under an irrecoverable sentence of death.

†**4** Unable to be recovered from. Only in 17.
■ **irrecoverableness** *noun* E17. **irrecoverably** *adverb* L16.

irrecuperable /ɪrɪˈkuːp(ə)rəb(ə)l/ *adjective*. Long *arch*. LME.
[ORIGIN Old French from late Latin *irrecuperabilis*, formed as IR-² + Latin *recuperare* RECUPERATE: see -ABLE.]
Unable to be recovered from, incurable. Formerly also, that cannot be regained.

irrecusable /ɪrɪˈkjuːzəb(ə)l/ *adjective*. *arch.* L18.
[ORIGIN French *irrécusable* or late Latin *irrecusabilis*, formed as IR-² + *recusabilis*, from *recusare* to refuse: see RECUSANT, -ABLE.]
Of a statement etc.: unable to be refused acceptance.

HOR. WALPOLE I will give him an irrecusable proof.

■ **irrecusably** *adverb* M19.

irredeemable /ɪrɪˈdiːməb(ə)l/ *adjective* & *noun*. E17.
[ORIGIN from IR-² + REDEEMABLE.]
▸ **A** *adjective*. **1** Unable to be redeemed or bought back. Of a Government annuity: not terminable by repayment of the sum originally paid by the annuitant. E17. ▸**b** Of paper currency: not convertible into cash. M19.
irredeemable debenture: which contains no provision for repayment of the principal money.
2 *fig.* That admits of no release or change of state; absolute, fixed, hopeless; beyond redemption; thoroughly depraved. M19.

E. A. POE An air of stern, deep, and irredeemable gloom hung over and pervaded all. W. SOYINKA The smell of irredeemable corruption that travels with you.

▸ **B** *noun.* Something irredeemable; *spec.* †(*a*) an irredeemable annuity; (*b*) an irredeemable debenture. E18.

▪ **ˌirredeemaˈbility** *noun* (*rare*) L18. **irredeemably** *adverb* in an irredeemable manner; *esp.* so as to be past redemption, hopelessly, utterly: L16.

irredenta /irreˈdenta, ɪrɪˈdɛntə/ *noun.* Pl. ***-te*** /-te/, ***-tas*** /-təz/. E20.

[ORIGIN Italian: see IRREDENTIST.]

A region containing people ethnically related to the inhabitants of one state but politically subject to another.

ALDOUS HUXLEY British Honduras still is regarded by the Guatemalans as an *irredenta*.

irredentist /ɪrɪˈdɛntɪst/ *noun & adjective.* Also **I-**. L19.

[ORIGIN Italian *irredentista*, from (*Italia*) *irredenta* unredeemed or unrecovered (Italy) + *-ista* -IST.]

▸ **A** *noun.* In Italian politics (after 1878): an advocate of the return to Italy of all Italian-speaking districts subject to other countries. Also, an advocate of a policy of reuniting to one country a territory for the moment subject to another country. L19.

▸ **B** *adjective.* Of or pertaining to irredentists or irredentism; advocating irredentism. L19.

Belfast Telegraph The Irish Government is . . frightened of being seen to betray its irredentist claim to Northern Ireland.

▪ **irredentism** *noun* the policy or programme of irredentists, in Italy or elsewhere L19.

irreducible /ɪrɪˈdjuːsɪb(ə)l/ *adjective.* M17.

[ORIGIN from IR-² + REDUCIBLE.]

1 Unable to be brought to or *to* a desired form, state, condition, etc. M17. ▸**b** *spec.* Unable to be reduced to a simpler or more intelligible form; unable to be resolved into elements or brought under any recognized principle. M19.

H. HALLAM The fashions of dress and amusements are generally capricious and irreducible to rule.

2 MEDICINE. Esp. of a hernia: whose contents cannot be returned to the normal position by other than surgical treatment. M19.

3 Unable to be reduced to a smaller number or amount; the fewest or smallest possible. M19.

R. D. LAING The irreducible elements of psychotherapy are a therapist, a patient, and a regular . . time and place.

4 Unable to be reduced to submission; invincible, insuperable. M19.

▪ **ˌirreduciˈbility** *noun* L18. **irreducibleness** *noun* E19. **irreducibly** *adverb* M19.

irreductible /ɪrɪˈdʌktɪb(ə)l/ *adjective. rare.* M18.

[ORIGIN French *irréductible*, from IR-² + *réductible*, from Latin *reduct-* pa. ppl stem of *reducere* REDUCE: see -IBLE.]

= IRREDUCIBLE.

▪ **ˌirreductiˈbility** *noun* M19.

irredundant /ɪrɪˈdʌnd(ə)nt/ *adjective.* E20.

[ORIGIN from IR-² + REDUNDANT.]

MATH. Containing no redundant elements.

▪ **irredundance** *noun* E20. **irredundancy** *noun* M20.

irreferable /ɪˈrɛf(ə)rəb(ə)l, ɪrɪˈfəː-/ *adjective. rare.* E19.

[ORIGIN from IR-² + REFERABLE.]

Not referable; unable to be referred *to* something.

irreflection /ɪrɪˈflɛkʃ(ə)n/ *noun.* Also **-flexion**. M19.

[ORIGIN from IR-² + REFLECTION, perh. after French *irréflexion*.]

Lack of reflection in action or conduct.

irreflective /ɪrɪˈflɛktɪv/ *adjective.* M19.

[ORIGIN from IR-² + REFLECTIVE, perh. after French *irréfléchi*.]

Unreflecting, unthinking.

▪ **irreflectively** *adverb* M19. **irreflectiveness** *noun* M19.

irreflexion *noun* var. of IRREFLECTION.

irreflexive /ɪrɪˈflɛksɪv/ *adjective.* L19.

[ORIGIN from IR-² + REFLEXIVE.]

Not reflexive. Chiefly MATH. & LOGIC, (of a relation) which never holds between a term and itself. Cf. REFLEXIVE *adjective* 6.

▪ **irreflexiveness** *noun* M20. **irreflexˈivity** *noun* M20.

irreformable /ɪrɪˈfɔːməb(ə)l/ *adjective.* E17.

[ORIGIN from IR-² + REFORMABLE. Sense 2 prob. after French *irréformable*.]

1 Unable to be reformed. E17.

2 Chiefly of papal dogma: incapable of revision or alteration. E19.

▪ **ˌirreformaˈbility** *noun* L19.

irrefragable /ɪˈrɛfrəgəb(ə)l/ *adjective.* M16.

[ORIGIN Late Latin *irrefragabilis*, formed as IR-² + *refragari* oppose, contest, opp. *suffragari* (cf. SUFFRAGE): see -ABLE.]

1 Unable to be refuted or disproved; incontrovertible, incontestable, undeniable. M16.

J. C. OATES In deference to . . the irrefragable nature of her decision, they were absolutely silent.

2 Unable or not allowed to be broken; indestructible; inviolable; irresistible. Now *rare*. M16.

▪ **irrefragaˈbility** *noun* the quality of being irrefragable; *rare* an irrefragable statement: E17. **irrefragably** *adverb* L16.

irrefrangible /ɪrɪˈfrandʒɪb(ə)l/ *adjective.* E18.

[ORIGIN from IR-² + REFRANGIBLE.]

1 Unable to or not allowed to be broken or violated; inviolable. E18.

2 OPTICS. Not refrangible; unable to be refracted. E20.

▪ **irrefrangibly** *adverb* L19.

irrefutable /ɪˈrɛfjʊtəb(ə)l, ɪrɪˈfjuː-/ *adjective.* E17.

[ORIGIN Late Latin *irrefutabilis*, from IR-² + *refutabilis*, from *refutare* REFUTE: see -ABLE.]

Unable to be refuted or disproved; incontrovertible.

▪ **ˌirrefutaˈbility** *noun* M19. **irrefutably** *adverb* L17.

irregardless /ɪrɪˈgɑːdlɪs/ *adjective & adverb.* Chiefly *non-standard* or *joc.* E20.

[ORIGIN Prob. blend of IRRESPECTIVE and REGARDLESS.]

= REGARDLESS.

irregenerate /ɪrɪˈdʒɛn(ə)rət/ *adjective. rare.* M17.

[ORIGIN from IR-² + REGENERATE *adjective*.]

Not regenerate; unregenerate.

irregular /ɪˈrɛgjʊlə/ *adjective & noun.* LME.

[ORIGIN Old French *irreguler* (later and mod. *irrégulier*) from late and (esp.) medieval Latin *irregularis*: see IR-², REGULAR.]

▸ **A** *adjective.* **I** *gen.* **1** Not conforming to rule, law, or moral principle; lawless, disorderly. LME.

2 Of a thing: not in conformity with rule, principle, accepted convention, customary procedure, etc.; not in accordance with what is usual, normal, or prescribed; anomalous, abnormal. L15.

LD MACAULAY The Declaration of Right, an instrument which was indeed revolutionary and irregular. E. BOWEN His frequent presence about a house where young girls were could have been thought irregular. V. GLENDINNING There had been complaints . . about her irregular private life.

3 Not of regular or symmetrical form or arrangement; (of a surface) uneven. L16.

E. WAUGH They could see the irregular roofs of the palace buildings. A. GHOSH His only irregular features are his eyebrows, which are slightly out of alignment.

4 Not uniform in continuance, occurrence, or succession; occurring at unequal rates or intervals. Also, of an agent: doing something at irregular intervals. E17.

E. TEMPLETON Taking a deep breath to steady the irregular beating of her heart. C. CHAPLIN His theatrical engagements became irregular.

▸ **II** *spec.* **5** ECCLESIASTICAL (chiefly ROMAN CATHOLIC CHURCH). Not in conformity with the rule of the Church or of some ecclesiastical order; disqualified for ordination or exercise of clerical functions. LME.

6 GRAMMAR. Of a part of speech, esp. a verb: not following the usual or normal mode of inflection or conjugation. Of an inflection: formed in this way. L16.

7 BOTANY. Of a flower: having the parts of one of its whorls (esp. the petals) differing in form, size, etc.; *esp.* = ZYGOMORPHIC. L18.

8 ASTRONOMY. **a** Of a galaxy: having an irregular shape, lacking any apparent axis of symmetry or central nucleus. E19. ▸**b** Of a variable star: fluctuating in brightness with no regular cycle. E20.

9 MILITARY. Of forces, troops: not belonging to the regular or established army organization; not forming an organized military body. M19.

E. A. FREEMAN The Danes . . put the irregular English levies to flight.

▸ **B** *noun.* **1** A person not belonging to the regular body or doing something irregularly; an irregular or occasional practitioner, attendant, member of the clergy, etc. LME. ▸**b** MILITARY. A soldier not of the regular army. Usu. in *pl.*, irregular troops. M18.

b M. MOORCOCK They had no identifiable uniforms at all. I guessed they were irregulars.

2 An imperfect piece of merchandise, esp. cloth, sold at a reduced price. Usu. in *pl. N. Amer.* M20.

▪ **irregularly** *adverb* L16.

irregularity /ɪˌrɛgjʊˈlarɪti/ *noun.* ME.

[ORIGIN Old French & mod. French *irrégularité* from late Latin *irregularitas*, from *irregularis*: see IRREGULAR, -ITY.]

1 ECCLESIASTICAL (chiefly ROMAN CATHOLIC CHURCH). Infraction of the rules as to entrance into or exercise of holy orders; an impediment or disqualification by which a person is debarred from normal clerical functions or advancement. ME.

2 *gen.* **a** A breach of rule or principle; an irregular, lawless, or disorderly act. L15. ▸**b** Lack of conformity to rule, law, or principle; deviation from what is usual or normal; abnormality, anomalousness. L16.

a W. TENNANT In a rude age . . crimes and irregularities are more frequent. *Sunday (Kolkata)* There were a lot of irregularities like non-payment to teachers.

3 Lack of regularity, symmetry, evenness, or uniformity, in shape, arrangement, succession, etc.; inequality of form, position, rate, etc.; *spec.* in BOTANY, unlikeness of the petals etc. of a flower (see IRREGULAR *adjective* 7). M17. ▸**b** An instance of this; *esp.* a part not uniform or symmetrical with the rest, as an unevenness of a surface etc. M17.

b V. S. NAIPAUL They intended to turn all the irregularities of nature into straight lines or graded curves.

irregulate /ɪˈrɛgjʊleɪt/ *verb trans.* Now *rare.* E17.

[ORIGIN Prob. from IR-² + REGULATE *verb*, after *irregular*.]

Make irregular; disorder.

irregulated /ɪˈrɛgjʊleɪtɪd/ *adjective. rare.* M17.

[ORIGIN from IR-² + REGULATE *verb* + -ED¹: cf. medieval Latin *irregulatus*.]

Unregulated.

†**irregulous** *adjective. rare* (Shakes.). Only in E17.

[ORIGIN from IRREGULAR, by substitution of -OUS (cf. -ULOUS).]

Unruly, disorderly, lawless.

irrelate /ɪrɪˈleɪt/ *adjective. rare.* M19.

[ORIGIN from IR-² + Latin *relatus* pa. pple: see RELATE *verb*, -ATE².]

Not related, unrelated.

irrelation /ɪrɪˈleɪʃ(ə)n/ *noun.* M19.

[ORIGIN from IR-² + RELATION.]

Absence of relation, lack of connection.

irrelative /ɪˈrɛlətɪv/ *adjective.* M17.

[ORIGIN from IR-² + RELATIVE *adjective*.]

1 Not having relations to each other, or *to* something else; unrelated, unconnected. Also *spec.* (METAPHYSICS), having no relations, absolute. M17.

2 Having no bearing on the matter in hand; irrelevant. M17.

▪ **irrelatively** *adverb* M17. **irrelativeness** *noun* M17.

irrelevance /ɪˈrɛlɪv(ə)ns/ *noun.* Orig. *Scot.* M16.

[ORIGIN from IRRELEVANT: see -ANCE.]

The fact or quality of being irrelevant, lack of pertinence; an irrelevant remark, circumstance, etc.

▪ Also **irrelevancy** *noun* L16.

irrelevant /ɪˈrɛlɪv(ə)nt/ *adjective.* Orig. *Scot.* M16.

[ORIGIN from IR-² + RELEVANT. Cf. French †*irrelevant*.]

Not relevant or pertinent to the case; that does not apply. (Foll. by *to*.)

D. WELCH He would treat my remark as an irrelevant interruption. D. W. GOODWIN Why alcoholics drink is irrelevant to the diagnosis of alcoholism.

▪ **irrelevantly** *adverb* E19.

irrelievable /ɪrɪˈliːvəb(ə)l/ *adjective.* L17.

[ORIGIN from IR-² + RELIEVABLE.]

Not relievable, unable to be relieved.

irreligion /ɪrɪˈlɪdʒ(ə)n/ *noun.* L16.

[ORIGIN French *irréligion* or late Latin *irreligio(n-)*, formed as IR-² + Latin *religio(n-)*: see RELIGION.]

1 Lack of religion; hostility to or disregard of religious principles; irreligious conduct. L16.

†**2** A false or perverted religion. L16–M17.

▪ **irreligionism** *noun* a system of irreligion; irreligious theory: M19. **irreligionist** *noun* a person who supports or practises irreligion; a professed opponent of religion: L18.

irreligious /ɪrɪˈlɪdʒəs/ *adjective.* LME.

[ORIGIN Latin *irreligiosus*, formed as IR-² + *religiosus*: see RELIGIOUS. Cf. French *irréligieux*.]

1 Not religious; hostile to or showing disregard for religion; ungodly; godless. LME.

H. ROGERS The irreligious monarch . . slept during the greater part of the sermon.

†**2** Believing in, practising, or pertaining to a false religion. L16–M17.

▪ **irreligiously** *adverb* L16. **irreligiousness** *noun* L16.

irreluctant /ɪrɪˈlʌkt(ə)nt/ *adjective. rare.* L17.

[ORIGIN from IR-² + RELUCTANT.]

Not reluctant; willing.

irremeable /ɪˈrɛmɪəb(ə)l, ɪˈriːmɪəb(ə)l/ *adjective.* Now chiefly *poet.* M16.

[ORIGIN Latin *irremeabilis*, from IR-² + *remeare* go back, from RE- + *meare* go, pass: see -ABLE.]

Admitting of no return; from, by, or through which there is no return.

J. HAWKESWORTH The irremeable waters of Styx.

▪ **irremeably** *adverb* E19.

irremediable /ɪrɪˈmiːdɪəb(ə)l/ *adjective.* LME.

[ORIGIN Latin *irremediabilis*, formed as IR-² + *remediabilis*: see REMEDIABLE. Cf. French *irrémédiable*.]

Not remediable; that does not admit of remedy, cure, or correction; incurable, irreparable.

▪ **irremediableness** *noun* E17. **irremediably** *adverb* LME.

irrememberable /ɪrɪˈmɛmb(ə)rəb(ə)l/ *adjective. rare.* M19.

[ORIGIN from IR-² + REMEMBERABLE.]

Unable to be remembered.

irremissible /ɪrɪˈmɪsɪb(ə)l/ *adjective.* LME.

[ORIGIN Old French & mod. French *irrémissible* or ecclesiastical Latin *irremissibilis*, formed as IR-² + Latin *remissibilis*: see REMISSIBLE.]

1 Unable to be forgiven; unpardonable. LME.

2 Unable to be remitted as an obligation or duty; unalterably binding. **M17.**
■ **irremissibly** *adverb* **L15.**

irremissive /ɪrɪˈmɪsɪv/ *adjective. rare.* **L16.**
[ORIGIN from IR-[2] + REMISSIVE.]
Continuous, unremitting.

irremovable /ɪrɪˈmuːvəb(ə)l/ *adjective & noun.* **L16.**
[ORIGIN from IR-[2] + REMOVABLE.]
▸ **A** *adjective.* **1** Not removable; unable to be removed or displaced; not subject to removal. **L16.** ▸**b** Unable to be displaced from office or position; permanent. **M17.**
†**2** Unable to be moved; immovable, inflexible (*lit. & fig.*). **L16–E19.**
▸ **B** *noun.* A person who cannot be removed, a person whose position is permanent. **M19.**
■ **irremovaˈbility** *noun* **E19.** **irremovableness** *noun* **E17.** **irremovably** *adverb* **M17.**

irremunerable /ɪrɪˈmjuːn(ə)rəb(ə)l/ *adjective. rare.* **E17.**
[ORIGIN from IR-[2] + REMUNERABLE. Cf. medieval Latin *irremunerabilis.*]
Unable to be remunerated, rewarded, or repaid.

†**irrenowned** *adjective. rare* (Spenser). Only in **L16.**
[ORIGIN from IR-[2] + RENOWNED.]
Without renown or fame; unrenowned.

irrepairable /ɪrɪˈpɛːrəb(ə)l/ *adjective.* Now *rare.* **L16.**
[ORIGIN from IR-[2] + REPAIRABLE.]
1 = IRREPARABLE 1. **L16.**

> *Car Mechanics* Irrepairable damage to you might be a . . welding job to someone else.

2 Too far decayed or damaged to be repaired. **E18.**

irreparable /ɪˈrɛp(ə)rəb(ə)l/ *adjective.* **LME.**
[ORIGIN Old French & mod. French *irréparable* from Latin *irreparabilis*, from IR-[2] + *reparabilis* REPARABLE.]
1 Not reparable; unable to be rectified, remedied, or made good. **LME.**

> *New York Times* These inhuman crimes do irreparable damage to the good name of Ireland. J. C. OATES She wept with the pain of it: the sense of irreparable loss.

2 Unable to be repaired; = IRREPAIRABLE 2. *rare.* **L18.**
■ **irreparaˈbility** *noun* **M18.** **irreparableness** *noun* **E18.** **irreparably** *adverb* in an irreparable manner; so as to be beyond reparation or remedy: **LME.**

irrepassable /ɪrɪˈpɑːsəb(ə)l/ *adjective. rare.* **L16.**
[ORIGIN from IR-[2] + RE- + PASSABLE.]
Unable to be passed again.

irrepealable /ɪrɪˈpiːləb(ə)l/ *adjective.* **M17.**
[ORIGIN from IR-[2] + REPEALABLE.]
Unable to be repealed or annulled; irrevocable.
■ **irrepealaˈbility** *noun* **E19.** **irrepealably** *adverb* **M17.**

irrepentance /ɪrɪˈpɛnt(ə)ns/ *noun. rare.* **E17.**
[ORIGIN from IR-[2] + REPENTANCE.]
Absence of repentance.

irreplaceable /ɪrɪˈpleɪsəb(ə)l/ *adjective.* **E19.**
[ORIGIN from IR-[2] + REPLACEABLE.]
Not liable to be restored or repaid, irredeemable; of which the loss cannot be made good or the place filled by an equivalent.

> B. T. BRADFORD She was fully convinced that no one was irreplaceable. M. FLANAGAN They're mortal—irreplaceable as a life.

■ **irreplaceably** *adverb* **M20.**

irrepleviable /ɪrɪˈplɛvɪəb(ə)l/ *adjective.* Now *rare.* **M16.**
[ORIGIN medieval Latin *irreplegiabilis*, from IR-[2] + *repliviabilis*, from *repleviare* formed as REPLEVY *verb*: see -ABLE.]
LAW. = IRREPLEVISABLE.

irreplevisable /ɪrɪˈplɛvɪsəb(ə)l/ *adjective.* Now *rare.* **E17.**
[ORIGIN from IR-[2] + REPLEVISABLE.]
LAW. Unable to be replevied or delivered on sureties.

irreprehensible /ˌɪrɛprɪˈhɛnsɪb(ə)l/ *adjective.* Now *rare.* **LME.**
[ORIGIN Late Latin *irreprehensibilis*, from IR-[2] + *reprehensibilis* REPREHENSIBLE.]
Not reprehensible or blameworthy; irreproachable.

irrepresentable /ˌɪrɛprɪˈzɛntəb(ə)l/ *adjective.* **L17.**
[ORIGIN from IR-[2] + REPRESENTABLE.]
Not representable.

irrepressible /ɪrɪˈprɛsɪb(ə)l/ *adjective.* **E19.**
[ORIGIN from IR-[2] + REPRESS + -IBLE.]
Unable to be repressed, restrained, or put down.

> J. P. HENNESSY She was by nature gay and vivacious, with an irrepressible sense of humour.

■ **irrepressiˈbility** *noun* **M19.** **irrepressibly** *adverb* **M19.**

irreproachable /ɪrɪˈprəʊtʃəb(ə)l/ *adjective.* **M17.**
[ORIGIN French *irréprochable*, from IR-[2] + *réprochable* REPROACHABLE.]
Not reproachable; free from blame, faultless.

> H. JAMES Harold's irreproachable—hasn't a vice.

■ **irreproachaˈbility** *noun* **M19.** **irreproachableness** *noun* **E19.** **irreproachably** *adverb* **E18.**

irreproducible /ˌɪriːprəˈdjuːsɪb(ə)l/ *adjective.* **M19.**
[ORIGIN from IR-[2] + REPRODUCIBLE.]
Not reproducible.
■ **irreproduciˈbility** *noun* **L20.**

irreprovable /ɪrɪˈpruːvəb(ə)l/ *adjective.* Now *rare.* **LME.**
[ORIGIN from IR-[2] + REPROVABLE.]
1 Undeserving of reproof; blameless, irreproachable. **LME.**
†**2** Unable to be disproved or confuted; irrefutable. **L16–M17.**

irreption /ɪˈrɛpʃ(ə)n/ *noun.* **L16.**
[ORIGIN Late Latin *irreptio(n-)*, from *irrept-* pa. ppl stem of *irrepere* creep in, from IR-[1] + *repere* creep: see -ION.]
Creeping in, stealthy entrance; a thing which has crept in, esp. into a text.

> *Encounter* Protection against casual and deplorable irreptions creeping into the language. G. W. S. FRIEDRICHSEN There had been casual but continued irreptions from the old Latin.

■ **irreptitious** /ɪrɛpˈtɪʃəs/ *adjective* characterized by (an) irreption **L17.**

†**irreputable** *adjective.* **E–M18.**
[ORIGIN from IR-[2] + REPUTABLE.]
Not reputable, not of good repute; disreputable.

irresistable /ɪrɪˈzɪstəb(ə)l/ *adjective.* Now *rare.* **E17.**
[ORIGIN from IR-[2] + RESIST *verb* + -ABLE.]
= IRRESISTIBLE.

> P. GREENHALGH They were by no means irresistable by Pompey's army. R. DAVIES Ismay had a coarse streak . . part of her irresistable allurement.

■ **irresistaˈbility** *noun* **M17.** **irresistableness** *noun* **L17.** **irresistably** *adverb* **M17.**

irresistance /ɪrɪˈzɪst(ə)ns/ *noun.* **M17.**
[ORIGIN from IR-[2] + RESISTANCE.]
Absence of resistance; non-resistance.

irresistible /ɪrɪˈzɪstɪb(ə)l/ *adjective.* **L16.**
[ORIGIN medieval Latin *irresistibilis* or from IR-[2] + RESISTIBLE.]
Unable to be withstood; too strong, weighty, or fascinating to be resisted.
■ **irresistiˈbility** *noun* **E17.** **irresistibleness** *noun* **E17.** **irresistibly** *adverb* in a irresistible manner; so as to be irresistible: **M17.**

†**irresistless** *adjective.* **M17–L18.**
[ORIGIN Blend of IRRESISTIBLE and RESISTLESS.]
Resistless, irresistible.

irresoluble /ɪrɪˈzɒljʊb(ə)l/ *adjective.* **M17.**
[ORIGIN Latin *irresolubilis* indissoluble, formed as IR-[2] + RE- + SOLUBLE.]
1 Unable to be decomposed, dissolved, or liquefied **M17.**
2 Unable to be solved or explained. **M17.**

> *Times* Mr Foot's irresoluble leadership dilemma is obvious.

irresolute /ɪˈrɛzəluːt/ *adjective.* **L16.**
[ORIGIN Latin *irresolutus* not loosened, or from IR-[2] + RESOLUTE *adjective.*]
†**1** Unexplained; left ambiguous or obscure. **L16–E17.**
2 Uncertain or undecided as to a course of action. **L16.**

> I. D'ISRAELI Buckingham was irresolute, and scarcely knew what to decide on.

3 Lacking in resolution or decisiveness. **E17.**

> J. H. NEWMAN Cicero . . was irresolute, timid and inconsistent.

■ **irresolutely** *adverb* **E17.** **irresoluteness** *noun* **L17.** **irresoˈlution** *noun* **L16.**

irresolvable /ɪrɪˈzɒlvəb(ə)l/ *adjective.* **M17.**
[ORIGIN from IR-[2] + RESOLVABLE.]
1 Of a problem, dilemma, etc.: unable to be resolved or solved. **M17.**
2 Unable to be resolved into elements or parts; that cannot be analysed. **L18.**

irresolved /ɪrɪˈzɒlvd/ *adjective.* Long *rare.* **L16.**
[ORIGIN from IR-[2] + RESOLVED.]
Not resolved; undecided, uncertain; irresolute.

irrespectful /ɪrɪˈspɛktfʊl, -f(ə)l/ *adjective. rare.* **L17.**
[ORIGIN from IR-[2] + RESPECTFUL.]
Disrespectful.

irrespective /ɪrɪˈspɛktɪv/ *adjective & adverb.* **M17.**
[ORIGIN from IR-[2] + RESPECTIVE *adjective.*]
▸ **A** *adjective.* †**1** Disrespectful. Only in **M17.**
2 Characterized by disregard of particular persons, circumstances, or conditions. Now *rare.* **M17.**
3 Existing or considered without respect or regard to something else. Also foll. by *of.* **L17.**
▸ **B** *adverb.* Without regard to or consideration of something else; independently. Foll. by *of.* **M17.**

> A. J. AYER People sometimes judge actions to be right irrespective of their consequences.

irrespectively /ɪrɪˈspɛktɪvli/ *adverb.* **E17.**
[ORIGIN from IRRESPECTIVE + -LY[2].]
†**1** In a manner showing disregard of particular persons or circumstances. Also, disrespectfully. **E17–E18.**
2 = IRRESPECTIVE *adverb.* Also foll. by *of*, †*to.* **M17.**

irrespirable /ɪˈrɛsp(ə)rəb(ə)l, ɪrɪˈspʌɪ-/ *adjective.* **E19.**
[ORIGIN from IR-[2] + RESPIRABLE or from French *irrespirable.*]
Not breathable; unfit for respiration.

irresponsible /ɪrɪˈspɒnsɪb(ə)l/ *adjective & noun.* **M17.**
[ORIGIN from IR-[2] + RESPONSIBLE.]
▸ **A** *adjective.* Not answerable for conduct or actions; exempt from or incapable of legal responsibility. Also lacking, or done without, a sense of responsibility. **M17.**

> T. DE W. TALMAGE The prisoner was idiotic and irresponsible. D. H. LAWRENCE I'm irresponsible as a puff of wind. *Listener* We are not dealing . . with an irresponsible, politically-motivated organization in trade unions.

▸ **B** *noun.* An irresponsible person. **L19.**

> L. MUMFORD His adolescent years found him one of the . . irresponsibles of his little town.

■ **irresponsiˈbility** *noun* **E19.** **irresponsibleness** *noun* **M17.** **irresponsibly** *adverb* **M19.**

irresponsive /ɪrɪˈspɒnsɪv/ *adjective.* **M19.**
[ORIGIN from IR-[2] + RESPONSIVE.]
Not responding to a force or stimulus; giving no answer to a question or inquiry.
■ **irresponsively** *adverb* **L20.** **irresponsiveness** *noun* **M19.**

irrestrainable /ɪrɪˈstreɪnəb(ə)l/ *adjective.* **M17.**
[ORIGIN from IR-[2] + RESTRAINABLE.]
Not restrainable.
■ **irrestrainably** *adverb* **L17.**

irrestrictive /ɪrɪˈstrɪktɪv/ *adjective.* **E18.**
[ORIGIN from IR-[2] + RESTRICTIVE.]
Not restrictive; without restriction.

irretention /ɪrɪˈtɛnʃ(ə)n/ *noun.* **E19.**
[ORIGIN from IR-[2] + RETENTION.]
Lack of retention; failure to retain something.

irretentive /ɪrɪˈtɛntɪv/ *adjective.* **M18.**
[ORIGIN from IR-[2] + RETENTIVE *adjective.*]
Not retentive.
■ **irretentiveness** *noun* **M19.**

irreticence /ɪˈrɛtɪs(ə)ns/ *noun.* **E20.**
[ORIGIN from IR-[2] + RETICENCE.]
The condition of being irreticent; an instance of this.

irreticent /ɪˈrɛtɪs(ə)nt/ *adjective.* **M19.**
[ORIGIN from IR-[2] + RETICENT.]
Not reticent.

irretraceable /ɪrɪˈtreɪsəb(ə)l/ *adjective.* **M19.**
[ORIGIN from IR-[2] + RETRACE + -ABLE.]
Unable to be retraced.

irretractable /ɪrɪˈtraktəb(ə)l/ *adjective. rare.* **L16.**
[ORIGIN from IR-[2] + RETRACTABLE.]
Unable to be retracted or taken back.

irretrievable /ɪrɪˈtriːvəb(ə)l/ *adjective.* **L17.**
[ORIGIN from IR-[2] + RETRIEVABLE.]
Unable to be retrieved; irrecoverable; irreparable.

> A. BROOKNER All wrongs were righted; nothing was irretrievable.

■ **irretrievaˈbility** *noun* **M19.** **irretrievably** *adverb* in an irretrievable manner; so as to be irretrievable: **L17.**

irreverence /ɪˈrɛv(ə)r(ə)ns/ *noun.* **ME.**
[ORIGIN Latin *irreverentia*, from *irreverent-*: see IRREVERENT, -ENCE.]
1 The fact or quality of being irreverent; absence or violation of reverence. **ME.**
2 An irreverent act or utterance. **M18.**
■ **irreveˈrential** *adjective* irreverent **M17.** **ˌirreveˈrentially** *adverb* **L17.**

irreverend /ɪˈrɛv(ə)r(ə)nd/ *adjective.* **L16.**
[ORIGIN from IR-[2] + REVEREND *adjective.*]
1 = IRREVERENT 1. **L16.**
2 Not reverend; unworthy of veneration. **M18.**

irreverent /ɪˈrɛv(ə)r(ə)nt/ *adjective.* **LME.**
[ORIGIN Latin *irreverent-*, from IR-[2] + *reverent-* pres. ppl stem of *revereri* REVERE: see -ENT.]
1 Not reverent; showing disrespect to a sacred or venerable person or thing. **LME.**

> H. JAMES She . . became . . in impatience and the expression of contempt, very free and absolutely irreverent. I. MURDOCH I don't like seeing the gods portrayed on the stage. It's irreverent.

†**2** = IRREVEREND 2. Only in **L15.**
■ **irreverently** *adverb* **LME.**

irreversible /ɪrɪˈvəːsɪb(ə)l/ *adjective.* **M17.**
[ORIGIN from IR-[2] + REVERSIBLE.]
1 Unable to be undone, repealed, or annulled; unalterable, irrevocable; unable to be turned in the opposite direction or overturned. **M17.**

> E. SHOWALTER Lobotomy is the most extreme and irreversible form of medical intervention in schizophrenia. J. HELLER I began to perceive the first signs of irreversible physical decay.

2 *PHYSICAL CHEMISTRY.* Of a colloid or colloidal system: unable to be changed from a gelatinous state into a sol by a reversal of the treatment which turns the sol into a gel or gelatinous precipitate. **E20.**
■ **ˌirreversiˈbility** *noun* **E19.** **irreversibleness** *noun* (now *rare* or *obsolete*) **E17.** **irreversibly** *adverb* in an irreversible manner; so as not to be reversed: **E17.**

irrevocable /ɪˈrɛvəkəb(ə)l/ *adjective*. LME.
[ORIGIN (Old French & mod. French *irrévocable* from) Latin *irrevocabilis*, from IR-² + *revocabilis* REVOCABLE.]
1 Unable to be recalled or recovered. LME.
I. MURDOCH It's gone, .. the past, it is irrevocable.
2 Unable to be annulled or undone; unalterable, irreversible. LME.
D. ADAMS There is nothing you can do ... It was done. It was irrevocable.
■ **irrevocaˈbility** *noun* E17. **irrevocableness** *noun* M17. **irrevocably** *adverb* beyond recall or recovery; unalterably, irreversibly: L15.

irrevoluble /ɪˈrɛvəljʊb(ə)l/ *adjective*. *rare*. M17.
[ORIGIN from IR-² + REVOLUBLE.]
Having no finite period of revolution, whose revolution is never completed.

irrigable /ˈɪrɪgəb(ə)l/ *adjective*. M19.
[ORIGIN from IRRIGATE + -ABLE.]
Able to be irrigated.

irrigate /ˈɪrɪgeɪt/ *verb*. E17.
[ORIGIN Latin *irrigat-* pa. ppl stem of *irrigare*, from IR-¹ + *rigare* wet, water: see -ATE³.]
1 *verb trans.* Supply with moisture; moisten, wet. Now *rare*. E17.
2 **a** *verb trans. & intrans.* Water (land) by means of channels or streams passing through, or with a sprinkler system; (of a stream etc.) supply (land) with water. E17. ▸**b** *verb trans.* MEDICINE. Supply (a part, a wound, etc.) with a constant flow of liquid, for the purpose of cooling, cleansing, disinfection, etc. L19.
a J. YEATS The country was .. artificially irrigated by a network of canals. *New Yorker* If you want anything growing besides native things, you have to irrigate. G. S. FRASER The green Nile irrigates a barren region.
3 *verb trans. fig.* Refresh or make fruitful as with water. L17.
4 *verb intrans.* Drink; take a drink. *slang* (chiefly *US*). M19.
■ **irrigative** *adjective* serving to irrigate; of or pertaining to irrigation: M19. **irrigator** *noun* E19. **irrigatory** *adjective* of or pertaining to irrigation L19.

irrigation /ɪrɪˈgeɪʃ(ə)n/ *noun*. E17.
[ORIGIN Latin *irrigatio(n-)*, formed as IRRIGATE: see -ATION.]
1 The action or fact of supplying or being supplied with moisture; a moistening or wetting. Now *rare*. E17.
2 **a** The action of supplying land with water by means of channels or streams, or by sprinkling water over the surface of the ground. E17. ▸**b** MEDICINE. The application of a constant stream or shower of liquid to a part of the body, in order to cool, cleanse, disinfect, etc. E17.
a E. HEATH The occasional green square where crops were being grown under irrigation.
a *attrib.*: ***irrigation canal***, ***irrigation ditch***, etc.
3 *fig.* Refreshment; fertilization. M17.
■ **irrigational** *adjective* L19. **irrigationist** *noun* a person interested in irrigation L19.

irriguous /ɪˈrɪgjʊəs/ *adjective*. Now *rare*. L15.
[ORIGIN from Latin *irriguus* supplied with water, from IR-¹ + *riguus* watered, from *rigare*: see IRRIGATE, -OUS.]
1 Supplying water or moisture. L15.
2 Irrigated; moistened, wet; (esp. of land) well-watered, watery. M17.

irrision /ɪˈrɪʒ(ə)n/ *noun*. *arch*. E16.
[ORIGIN Latin *irrisio(n-)*, from *irris-* pa. ppl stem of *irridere* laugh at, from IR-¹ + *ridere* laugh: see -ION.]
Derision, mockery.

irritable /ˈɪrɪtəb(ə)l/ *adjective*. M17.
[ORIGIN Latin *irritabilis*, from *irritare*: see IRRITATE *verb*¹, -ABLE.]
1 Readily excited to anger or impatience; easily annoyed. M17.
P. H. GIBBS He was not always in a good humour. Sometimes he was irritable and nervy.
2 (Of a thing) readily excited to action; highly responsive to stimulus; (of a bodily organ or part) excessively or abnormally sensitive. L18.
irritable bowel (syndrome) a stress-related condition with recurrent abdominal pain and bowel dysfunction.
3 BIOLOGY. Capable of actively responding to physical stimulus of some kind. L18.
■ **irritaˈbility** *noun* the quality or state of being irritable M18. **irritably** *adverb* M19.

irritament /ˈɪrɪtəm(ə)nt/ *noun*. Now *rare* or *obsolete*. M17.
[ORIGIN Latin *irritamentum*, from *irritare* IRRITATE *verb*¹: see -MENT.]
A thing that excites or provokes an action, feeling, or state; an irritant.

irritant /ˈɪrɪt(ə)nt/ *adjective*¹ & *noun*. E17.
[ORIGIN from IRRITATE *verb*¹ + -ANT¹.]
▸ **A** *adjective*. †**1** Exciting, provocative, rousing. E–M17.
2 Causing physical (or occas. mental) irritation; irritating. E19.
R. ADAMS Buckthorn had been bitten .. and the wound .. was irritant and painful. P. PARISH Potassium salts are irritant when taken by mouth; they may cause ulceration of the stomach.
▸ **B** *noun*. An irritant substance, body, or agency; a poison etc. which produces irritation; *fig.* something which is (mentally) irritating. E19.
JONATHAN MILLER Any irritant which succeeds in entering the windpipe .. excites the .. cough reflex.
■ **irritancy** *noun*¹ irritating quality or character; irritation, annoyance: M19.

irritant /ˈɪrɪt(ə)nt/ *adjective*². E16.
[ORIGIN Late Latin *irritant-* pres. ppl stem of *irritare*: see IRRITATE *verb*², -ANT¹.]
ROMAN, CIVIL, & SCOTS LAW. Making null and void.
■ **irritancy** *noun*² the fact of making, or condition of being made, null and void L17.

irritate /ˈɪrɪteɪt/ *verb*¹ *trans*. M16.
[ORIGIN Latin *irritat-* pa. ppl stem of *irritare*: see -ATE³.]
†**1** Excite, provoke, rouse (a person etc.). Foll. by *to*, *into*, *to do*. M16–M19. ▸**b** Aggravate, excite, provoke (an action, emotion, etc.). E17–E19.
2 Excite to impatient or angry feeling; annoy, exasperate, provoke. L16.
J. C. POWYS These things irritated her so much that she could have boxed his ears. V. GLENDINNING These domestic crises bored and irritated Wells. R. INGALLS So boring, and actually sometimes irritating.
3 MEDICINE. Excite (a bodily organ or part) to abnormal action or an abnormal condition; produce an uneasy sensation in, inflame mildly. L17.
G. NAYLOR Too much coffee would irritate his ulcer.
4 BIOLOGY. Produce an active response in (an organ etc.) by the application of a stimulus; stimulate to vital action. E19.
C. DARWIN The central glands of a leaf were irritated with a small .. brush.
■ **irritated** *adjective* that has been irritated or provoked; impatient, angry, (foll. by *at*, *by*, *with*, *that*) L16. **irritatedly** *adverb* in an irritated manner L19. **irritatingly** *adverb* in a irritating manner M19. **irritative** *adjective* causing irritation M17. **irritator** *noun* (*rare*) M19.

irritate /ˈɪrɪteɪt/ *verb*² *trans*. E17.
[ORIGIN Late Latin *irritat-* pa. ppl stem of *irritare* make void, from Latin *irritus* invalid: see -ATE³.]
ROMAN, CIVIL, & SCOTS LAW. Make null and void; annul.

irritation /ɪrɪˈteɪʃ(ə)n/ *noun*. LME.
[ORIGIN Latin *irritatio(n-)*, formed as IRRITATE *verb*¹: see -ATION.]
1 The action of provoking to activity; incitement. Now *rare*. LME.
DE QUINCEY Arts and sciences .. vast machinery for the irritation and development of the human intellect.
2 MEDICINE. Production of abnormal sensitiveness or action in a bodily part or organ; production of mild inflammation. L17.
3 Anger, impatience, provocation; a cause of this. E18.
J. GARDNER It was not frightening .. but acutely annoying, one more irritation among a thousand. D. WIGODER 'Can't you get here on time?' he asked, covering his irritation with .. casualness.
4 BIOLOGY. The production of some active response (as motion, contraction, nervous impulse) in an organ, tissue, etc., by the application of a stimulus. L18.

†**irrite** *adjective*. LME–M18.
[ORIGIN Anglo-Norman, Old French *irrit* or Latin *irritus*, from IR-² + *ratus* established, valid.]
Void, of no effect.

irrorate /ˈɪrərət/ *adjective*. *rare*. E19.
[ORIGIN Latin *irroratus* pa. pple, formed as IRRORATE *verb*: see -ATE².]
ENTOMOLOGY. Irrorated.

irrorate /ˈɪrəreɪt/ *verb trans*. E17.
[ORIGIN Latin *irrorat-* pa. ppl stem of *irrorare* bedew, from IR-¹ + *rorare* drop dew, from *ror-*, *ros* dew: see -ATE³.]
†**1** Wet or sprinkle as with dew; moisten. Only in 17.
2 ENTOMOLOGY. As ***irrorated*** pa. pple: sprinkled minutely (*with* dots). M19.

irroration /ɪrəˈreɪʃ(ə)n/ *noun*. E17.
[ORIGIN Late Latin *irroratio(n-)*, formed as IRRORATE *verb*: see -ATION.]
†**1** (A) sprinkling or wetting as with dew; (a) moistening. E17–L18.
2 ENTOMOLOGY. A sprinkling of minute dots or spots of colour. M19.

irrotational /ɪrəʊˈteɪʃ(ə)n(ə)l/ *adjective*. L19.
[ORIGIN from IR-² + ROTATIONAL.]
PHYSICS. Esp. of fluid motion: not rotational, having no rotation.
■ **ˌirrotatioˈnality** *noun* M20. **irrotationally** *adverb* L19.

irruent /ˈɪrʊənt/ *adjective*. *rare*. M17.
[ORIGIN Latin *irruent-* pres. ppl stem of *irruere* rush in or upon: see -ENT.]
Rushing (in); running rapidly.

irrumate /ˈɪrʊmeɪt/ *verb trans*. M17.
[ORIGIN Latin *irrumat-* pa. ppl stem of *irrumare* give suck, from IR-¹ + *ruma* teat: see -ATE³.]
†**1** Suck in. Only in M17.
2 Perform irrumation on (a person). L19.
■ **irrumator** *noun* L19.

irrumation /ɪrʊˈmeɪʃ(ə)n/ *noun*. L19.
[ORIGIN Latin *irrumatio(n-)*, formed as IRRUMATE: see -ATION.]
Insertion of the penis into a sexual partner's mouth.

irrupt /ɪˈrʌpt/ *verb*. *rare*. M19.
[ORIGIN Latin *irrupt-* pa. ppl stem of *irrumpere* break in, from IR-¹ + *rumpere* break.]
1 *verb trans.* Break into. M19.
2 *verb intrans.* Burst or break in, enter forcibly; *spec.* (of birds or other animals) migrate into an area in abnormally large numbers. L19.
S. NAIPAUL Its roots were .. threatening to irrupt through the floor.
■ **irruptive** *adjective* having the quality or character of bursting in; making, or tending to, irruption: L16.

irruption /ɪˈrʌpʃ(ə)n/ *noun*. M16.
[ORIGIN Latin *irruptio(n-)*, formed as IRRUPT: see -ION.]
▸ **I** **1** The action of bursting or breaking in; a violent entry or invasion, esp. of a hostile force or people. M16.
M. IGNATIEFF This sudden irruption of riot into the little frame of Natasha's existence.
2 *spec.* An abrupt local increase in the numbers of a migrant bird or other animal. E20.
Bird Watching Immigrations or irruptions of Continental birds looking for 'open ground'.
▸ **II** **3** [By confusion.] = ERUPTION. E17.

IRS *abbreviation*. *US*.
Internal Revenue Service.

Irvingite /ˈəːvɪŋʌɪt/ *noun & adjective*. M19.
[ORIGIN from *Irving* (see below) + -ITE¹.]
▸ **A** *noun*. A member of the Catholic Apostolic Church, which followed the teachings of Edward Irving (1792–1834), orig. a minister of the Church of Scotland. M19.
▸ **B** *attrib.* or as *adjective*. Of or pertaining to the Irvingites. L19.
■ **Irvingism** *noun* the doctrines and principles of the Irvingites M19.

is /ɪz/ *noun*. *rare*. L19.
[ORIGIN from the verb.]
That which exists, that which is; the fact or quality of existence.

is *verb* see BE *verb*.

is- *combining form* see ISO-.

Is. *abbreviation*.
1 Isaiah (in the Bible).
2 Island(s).
3 Isle(s).

ISA *abbreviation*.
1 /ˈʌɪsə/ Individual savings account (held under a UK scheme allowing individuals to hold shares, unit trusts, and cash free of tax on dividends, interest, and capital gains).
2 COMPUTING. Industry standard architecture.

Isa. *abbreviation*.
Isaiah (in the Bible).

Isabel /ˈɪzəbɛl/ *noun*. E19.
[ORIGIN French *Isabelle* = ISABELLA.]
1 = ISABELLA 1. E19.
2 A kind of fancy pigeon, a small variety of the pouter so called from its colour. M19.
3 A variety of N. American grape; = ISABELLA 2b. M19.

Isabella /ɪzəˈbɛlə/ *noun*. E17.
[ORIGIN A female forename, French *Isabelle*, but the immediate ref. is unkn.]
1 In full ***Isabella colour***. (A) greyish yellow; a light buff. E17.
2 **a** A kind of peach. M17. ▸**b** In full ***Isabella grape***. A N. American vine *Vitis labrusca*, with large fruit, sometimes purple, often green and red; the fruit of this vine. M17.

isabelline /ɪzəˈbɛlɪn, -ʌɪn/ *adjective*. M19.
[ORIGIN from ISABELLA + -INE¹.]
Of an Isabella colour, greyish-yellow.

isadelphous /ʌɪsəˈdɛlfəs/ *adjective*. M19.
[ORIGIN from *is-* var. of ISO- + Greek *adelphos* brother + -OUS.]
BOTANY. Of a flower: having diadelphous stamens with the same number in each bundle.

isagoge /ʌɪsəˈgəʊdʒiː, -giː/ *noun*. M16.
[ORIGIN Latin from Greek *eisagōgē*, from *eis* into + *agein* to lead.]
An introduction.

isagogic /ʌɪsəˈgɒdʒɪk/ *adjective & noun*. E19.
[ORIGIN Latin *isagogicus* from Greek *eisagōgikos*, from *eisagōgē*: see ISAGOGE, -IC.]
▸ **A** *adjective*. Of or pertaining to an isagoge; introductory to any branch of study. E19.
▸ **B** *noun*. Usu. in *pl.* (treated as *sing.*). Introductory studies; *esp.* the branch of theology which is introductory to exegesis and deals with the literary and external history of the books of the Bible. M19.

Isaian /ʌɪˈzʌɪən, ʌɪˈzeɪən/ *adjective.* L19.
[ORIGIN from *Isaiah* (see below) + -AN.]
Of or belonging to the prophet Isaiah or the book of the Old Testament and Hebrew Scriptures that bears his name.
■ Also **Isaiˈanic** *adjective* E19.

isallobar /ʌɪsˈaləʊbɑː/ *noun.* E20.
[ORIGIN from IS(O)- + ALLO- + BAR *noun*⁴.]
METEOROLOGY. A line (imaginary or on a map) connecting points at which the barometric pressure has changed by an equal amount during a specified time.
■ **isalloˈbaric** *adjective* E20.

isangoma *noun* var. of SANGOMA.

isapostolic /ˌʌɪsapəˈstɒlɪk/ *adjective.* M19.
[ORIGIN from ecclesiastical Greek *isapostolos* equal to an apostle: see IS-, APOSTLE, -IC.]
Equal to, or contemporary with, the apostles: an epithet given in the Orthodox Church to a notable associate of the apostles, or to the evangelist of a non-Christian people.

isatin /ˈʌɪsətɪn/ *noun.* M19.
[ORIGIN from Latin *isatis* woad from Greek: see -IN¹.]
CHEMISTRY. A reddish-orange crystalline heterocyclic compound, $C_8H_5NO_2$, related to indole and indigo.
■ **isatoˈgenic** *adjective*: *isatogenic acid*, an unstable crystalline acid, $C_8H_4NO_2{\cdot}COOH$, related to isatin L19.

-isation *suffix* var. of -IZATION.

isatoic /ʌɪsəˈtəʊɪk/ *adjective.* L19.
[ORIGIN from ISATIN + -OIC.]
CHEMISTRY. **1** ***isatoic acid***, *N*-carboxyanthranilic acid, $C_6H_4(COOH)(NHCOOH)$, known only as its derivatives; formerly also, isatoic anhydride. L19.
2 ***isatoic anhydride***, the bicyclic anhydride, $C_8H_5NO_3$, of isatoic acid, obtained by oxidation of isatin. L19.

Isaurian /ʌɪˈsɔːrɪən/ *noun & adjective.* L18.
[ORIGIN from *Isauria* (see below) + -AN.]
▸ **A** *noun.* A native or inhabitant of Isauria, an ancient country in Asia Minor, between Cilicia and Phrygia; *spec.* any of a line of emperors of the Eastern Roman Empire. L18.
▸ **B** *adjective.* Of or pertaining to Isauria or the emperors called after it. M19.

isba /izˈba/ *noun.* Also ***izba***. L18.
[ORIGIN Russian *izba* (rel. to STOVE *noun*).]
A Russian hut or log house.

isblink /ˈiːsblɪŋk/ *noun.* L18.
[ORIGIN Swedish, or from corresp. words in Danish, German, Dutch.]
= ***iceblink*** s.v. BLINK *noun* 5a.

ISBN *abbreviation.*
International standard book number.

Iscariot /ɪˈskarɪət/ *noun.* M17.
[ORIGIN Latin *Iscariota* from Greek *Iskariōtēs*, surname of Judas, the disciple who betrayed Jesus; perh. from Hebrew *ʾīš qĕriyyōṯ* man of Qerioth (a place in ancient Palestine).]
A traitor or betrayer of the worst kind; = JUDAS 1.
■ **Iscariotic** /ˌɪskarɪˈɒtɪk/ *adjective* of or pertaining to Judas Iscariot L19. **Iscariˈotical** *adjective* characteristic of or resembling Judas Iscariot; wickedly treacherous: E17. **Iscariotism** *noun* a practice characteristic of Judas Iscariot, *esp.* parsimonious employment of church funds (cf. *John* 12:5) L19.

ischaemia /ɪˈskiːmɪə/ *noun.* Also ***ischemia**. L19.
[ORIGIN mod. Latin, from Greek *iskhaimos* stopping blood, from *iskhein* hold + *haima* blood: see -IA¹.]
MEDICINE. Orig., the staunching of bleeding. Now only, local anaemia; deficiency of blood supply to (part of) an organ.
■ **ischaemic** *adjective* pertaining to or characterized by ischaemia (***transient ischaemic attack***: see TRANSIENT *adjective* 1) L19. **ischaemically** *adverb* by, or as a result of, ischaemia M20.

ischia *noun* pl. of ISCHIUM.

ischiadic /ɪskɪˈadɪk/ *adjective.* Now *rare.* E18.
[ORIGIN Latin *ischiadicus* from Greek *iskhiadikos*, from *iskhiad-*, *iskhias* pain in the hip, from *iskhion* hip joint: see -IC.]
Of or pertaining to the ischium; ischiatic.

ischial /ˈɪskɪəl/ *adjective.* M19.
[ORIGIN from ISCHIUM + -AL¹.]
Of or pertaining to the ischium; ischiadic.
ischial tuberosity the projection of the ischium into the middle of the buttock, which takes the weight when sitting.

ischiatic /ɪskɪˈatɪk/ *adjective.* M17.
[ORIGIN medieval Latin *ischiaticus* (after adjectives in *-aticus*), for Latin *ischiadicus*: see ISCHIADIC.]
1 Troubled or affected with sciatica. Now *rare* or *obsolete.* M17.
2 ANATOMY. Of or near the ischium or hip. M18.
ischiatic notch = ***sciatic notch*** s.v. SCIATIC *adjective* 1.

ischio- /ˈɪskɪəʊ/ *combining form.*
[ORIGIN from ISCHIUM: see -O-.]
Chiefly ANATOMY. Relating to or involving the ischium and —, as ***ischioanal***, ***ischioiliac***, ***ischiorectal***.

ischiorrhogic /ˌɪskɪə(ʊ)ˈrɒdʒɪk/ *adjective.* M19.
[ORIGIN Greek *iskhiorrhōgikos*, orig. = having broken hips, limping, from *iskhion* hip joint + *rhōg-* *rhōx* broken.]
CLASSICAL PROSODY. Of an iambic line: having a spondee in the second, fourth, or sixth place.

ischium /ˈɪskɪəm/ *noun.* Pl. **-ia** /-ɪə/. E17.
[ORIGIN Latin from Greek *iskhion* hip joint, (later) ischium.]
The posterior or inferior bone of the pelvis, on which the body rests when sitting, fused with the ilium and the pubis to form the innominate bone.

ischuria /ɪˈskjʊərɪə/ *noun.* Now *rare* or *obsolete.* Also anglicized as **ischury** /ˈɪskjʊri/. E17.
[ORIGIN Late Latin from Greek *iskhouria*, from *iskhein* hold + *ouron* urine: see -IA¹.]
Difficulty in passing urine, due either to suppression or to retention.

ISDN *abbreviation.*
TELECOMMUNICATIONS. Integrated services digital network, a telecommunications network through which sound, images, and data can be transmitted as digitized signals.

-ise /ʌɪz, iːz/ *suffix*¹.
Forming (usu. abstract) nouns and repr. Old & mod. French *-ise*, Old French *-ice*, either from Latin *-itia*, *-itium* or of independent formation; as ***exercise***, ***franchise***, ***merchandise***, ***expertise***. Cf. -ICE¹.

-ise *suffix*² var. of -IZE.

isel /ˈʌɪz(ə)l/ *noun.* Now *dial.* Also **izle**.
[ORIGIN Old English *ysel*, *ysle*, cogn. with Middle High German *usele*, *usel*, mod. German dial. *Üsel*, *Ussel*, *Issel* spark, Old Norse *usli* fire, from same base as Latin *ust-*, *urere* burn.]
A spark; an ember; usu. in *pl.*, sparks, embers; ashes. Also, floating sparks from a conflagration; extinct sparks, particles of soot, smuts.

isentropic /ʌɪsɛnˈtrɒpɪk/ *adjective & noun.* L19.
[ORIGIN from ISO- + ENTROPIC.]
PHYSICS. ▸**A** *adjective.* Of equal entropy; (of a line in a diagram) joining points representing successive states of a system in which the entropy remains constant; (of a process) involving no change in entropy. L19.
▸ **B** *noun.* An isentropic line. L19.
■ **isentropically** *adverb* without change in entropy M20.

-iser *suffix* var. of -IZER.

isethionic /ʌɪˌsiːθɪˈɒnɪk/ *adjective.* M19.
[ORIGIN from *is-* var. of ISO- + ETHIONIC.]
CHEMISTRY. ***isethionic acid***, a monobasic acid, $HO{\cdot}CH_2{\cdot}CH_2{\cdot}SO_3H$, used as a detergent and surfactant; 2-hydroxyethanesulphonic acid.
■ **iseˈthionate** *noun* a salt of isethionic acid M19.

Isfahan /ɪsfəˈhɑːn, ˈɪsfəhɑːn/ *adjective & noun.* Also **Isp-** /ɪsp-/. M20.
[ORIGIN A province and town in west central Iran.]
▸ **A** *adjective.* Designating a type of handwoven rug, the most distinguished examples of which were produced in Isfahan in the 16th cent. M20.
▸ **B** *noun.* An Isfahan rug. M20.

-ish /ɪʃ/ *suffix*¹.
[ORIGIN Old English *-isc* corresp. to Gothic *-isks*, Old Norse *-iskr*, Old High German, Old Saxon, Old Frisian *-isc*, German, Dutch *-isch*, from Germanic: cogn. with Greek *-iskos* dim. suffix of nouns.]
Forming adjectives: (***a***) from national or other class names, as ***English***, ***Jewish***, ***Scottish***, ***Turkish***; (***b***) from other nouns, with the sense 'of the nature or character of (a person, animal, etc.)', now chiefly *derog.*, 'having the (bad or objectionable) qualities of', as ***boorish***, ***boyish***, ***foolish***, ***sluggish***, ***waspish***, ***womanish***; also from names of things, with the sense 'of the nature of, tending to', as ***bookish***, ***feverish***; or from other parts of speech, as ***snappish***, ***uppish***; (***c***) from adjectives, with the sense 'approaching the quality of, somewhat', app. first with words of colour, as ***bluish***, ***reddish***, etc.; later also with other adjectives, and now, in colloq. use, possible with nearly all monosyllabic adjectives, and some others, e.g. ***brightish***, ***coldish***, ***narrowish***, ***oldish***; (***d***) *colloq.* from names of hours of the day or numbers of years, with the sense 'round about, somewhere near (the time or period of)', as ***elevenish***, ***fortyish***.

-ish /ɪʃ/ *suffix*².
Forming verbs repr. French *-iss-* lengthened stem of verbs in *-ir* from Latin *-isc-* inceptive suffix, as ***abolish***, ***establish***, ***finish***, ***punish***; sometimes repr. other French endings, as ***astonish***, ***distinguish***.

ishan /ˈiːʃɑːn/ *noun.* E20.
[ORIGIN Perh. from Arabic dial. *īšān* from Persian *nīšān* mark.]
A prehistoric mound in Iraq.

Ishihara /ɪʃɪˈhɑːrə/ *noun.* E20.
[ORIGIN Shinobu *Ishihara* (1879–1963), Japanese ophthalmologist.]
OPHTHALMOLOGY. Used *attrib.* with ref. to a test for colour blindness (the ***Ishihara test***) devised by Ishihara, in which the subject is asked to distinguish numbers or pathways printed in coloured spots on a background of spots of a different colour or colours.

Ishmael /ˈɪʃmeɪl/ *noun.* M17.
[ORIGIN The son of Abraham and Hagar: see *Genesis* 16 and 25.]
A person resembling Ishmael, *esp.* an outcast, a person at war with society.
■ **Ishmaelite** *noun* (***a***) a descendant of Ishmael, as some Arabs claim to be; (***b***) = ISHMAEL: L16. **Ishmaelitish** *adjective* of, pertaining to, of the nature of an Ishmaelite L17. **Ishmaelitism** *noun* the character and action of an Ishmaelite L19.

Isiac /ˈʌɪsɪak, ˈɪs-/ *noun & adjective.* E18.
[ORIGIN Latin *Isiacus* from Greek *Isiakos*, from *Isis* (see below): see -AC.]
▸ **A** *noun.* A priest or worshipper of Isis. E18.
▸ **B** *adjective.* Of or relating to Isis, the principal goddess of ancient Egyptian mythology. M18.
■ **Iˈsiacal** *adjective* = ISIAC *adjective* E17.

isidium /ʌɪˈsɪdɪəm/ *noun.* Pl. **-dia** /-dɪə/. M19.
[ORIGIN mod. Latin genus name formerly used to include all genera bearing isidia, from *Isis Isidis* the goddess Isis (with ref. to her disc and horns).]
BOTANY. A coral-like or wartlike excrescence of the thallus in certain lichens, having the function of vegetative propagation after detachment.
■ **isidial** *adjective* of or pertaining to an isidium E20. **isidiate** *adjective* bearing isidia M20. **isiˈdiferous** *adjective* = ISIDIATE L19. **isidioid** *adjective* resembling or of the nature of an isidium; bearing isidia: M19.

Isidorian /ɪzɪˈdɔːrɪən/ *adjective.* L19.
[ORIGIN from *Isidorus* (see below) + -IAN.]
Of or pertaining to Isidorus or Isidore, esp. St Isidore, archbishop of Seville 600–36, author of several historical and ecclesiastical works, and of twenty books of *Origines* (Etymologies), of value for the history of Latin.

Isindebele *noun & adjective* var. of SINDEBELE.

isinglass /ˈʌɪzɪŋglɑːs/ *noun.* M16.
[ORIGIN Alt. (with assim. to *glass*) of early Dutch †*huysenblas*, from †*huysen*, †*huys* sturgeon + †*blas* (now *blaas*) bladder (cf. German *Hausenblase*).]
1 A firm whitish semi-transparent substance, a comparatively pure form of gelatin, obtained from the swim bladders of some freshwater fishes, esp. the sturgeon, and used in cookery for making jellies etc., for clarifying liquors, in the manufacture of glue, and for other purposes. Also, any of several similar substances made from hides, hoofs, etc. M16.
2 Mica (from its resembling in appearance some kinds of isinglass). M17.

Islam /ˈɪzlɑːm, ˈɪs-; ɪsˈlɑːm, ɪz-/ *noun.* E17.
[ORIGIN Arabic *ʾislām*, from *ʾaslama* submit, surrender (spec. to God). Cf. MUSLIM.]
1 The religious system established through the prophet Muhammad; the Muslim religion; the body of Muslims, the Muslim world. E17.
†**2** A Muslim. E17–E19.
■ **Islamiˈzation** *noun* = ISLAMICIZATION M20. **Islamize** *verb trans. & intrans.* convert to or practise Islam M19.

Islamic /ɪzˈlamɪk, ɪzˈlɑːmɪk, ɪs-/ *adjective.* L18.
[ORIGIN from ISLAM + -IC.]
Of or pertaining to Islam; Muslim.
■ **Islamicization** /-sʌɪˈzeɪʃ(ə)n/ *noun* the process of Islamicizing a country, institution, etc. L20. **Islamicize** /-sʌɪz/ *verb trans.* convert (a country, institution, etc.) to Islamic principles L20.

Islamism /ˈɪzləmɪz(ə)m, ˈɪs-/ *noun.* M18.
[ORIGIN formed as ISLAMIC + -ISM.]
= ISLAM 1.
■ **Islamist** *noun* (***a***) an orthodox Muslim; (***b***) an expert in or student of Islam: M19.

Islamite /ˈɪzləmʌɪt, ɪs-/ *noun & adjective. arch.* L18.
[ORIGIN from ISLAM + -ITE¹.]
▸ **A** *noun.* A Muslim. L18.
▸ **B** *adjective.* Islamic, Muslim. M19.
■ **Islaˈmitic** *adjective* Muslim L18.

Islamophobia /ɪzˈlaməˌfəʊbɪə/ *noun.* L20.
[ORIGIN from ISLAM +-PHOBIA.]
Hatred or fear of Islam or Muslims.
■ **Islamophobe**, **Islamophobic** *nouns & adjectives* L20.

island /ˈʌɪlənd/ *noun*¹.
[ORIGIN Old English (Anglian) *ēgland*, (West Saxon) *īeġland*, *īġland*, later *īland* (= Old Frisian *eiland*, Middle Dutch, Middle Low German *eilant*, Old Norse *eyland*), from *īeġ*, *īġ* island, (in compounds) water, sea + LAND *noun*¹.]
1 A piece of land completely surrounded by water; *spec.* one not large enough to constitute a continent. Formerly also (and still in certain place names, as ***Thorney Island***), a peninsula; a place cut off at high water or during floods. OE. ▸**b** In *pl.* In biblical translations: the lands beyond the sea, the coasts of the Mediterranean. Cf. ISLE *noun*¹ 2. M16. ▸**c** *spec.* (*ellipt.*) Any of certain specific islands (the Isle of Wight, the Hebrides, certain Pacific islands, etc.). Also, a specific prison on an island. E19.

R. INGALLS Dense pinewoods . . covered all the islands of the archipelago.

2 *transf.* An elevated piece of land surrounded by marsh or river plain; a piece of woodland surrounded by prairie or flat open country; a detached block of buildings. Also, an individual or a people, detached or standing out alone.

E17. ▸**b** More fully *traffic island*, (US) *safety island*. A raised or marked area in the road to direct traffic and provide a refuge for pedestrians. M19. ▸**c** ANATOMY. = ISLET 2b. L19. ▸**d** A small isolated ridge or structure between the lines in fingerprints. L19. ▸**e** More fully *speech island*. A small area inhabited by speakers of a language or dialect other than that spoken in the surrounding areas. L19. ▸**f** A piece of furniture in a private house or in a museum, library, etc., surrounded by unoccupied floor space. Freq. *attrib.* M20. ▸**g** The superstructure of a ship, esp. of an aircraft carrier. M20.

J. LEONI This House . . stands in an Island, being surrounded by four streets. J. CHEEVER Sheep surrounded the bus, isolated this little island of elderly Americans.

– PHRASES: †**island of ice** an iceberg; a large mass of floating ice. *island of* REIL. THOUSAND *island*. *Vulcanian Islands*: see VULCANIAN *adjective*.

– COMB.: **island arc** GEOGRAPHY any curved chain of (freq. volcanic) islands typically located at a tectonic plate margin and having a deep trench on the convex side; **island area** each of three administrative areas in Scotland (Orkney, Shetland, Western Isles), consisting of groups of islands; **Island Carib** (*a*) the Carib people of the Lesser Antilles; (*b*) the language of this people; **island continent** a continent completely surrounded by water; **island-hill** a hill or mountain rising directly out of a plain; **island-hop** *verb intrans.* move from one island to another; *spec.* (of the US army in the Pacific during the war of 1941–45) recapture Japanese-occupied islands one after another; **islandman** (now *dial.*) an islander; **island-mountain** = *island-hill* above; **island platform** a platform at a railway station, with through lines on each side of it; *island universe*: see UNIVERSE 2c.

■ **islandless** *adjective* devoid of islands M19.

†**Island** *noun*² var. of ICELAND.

island /ˈʌɪlənd/ *verb trans.* M17.

[ORIGIN from ISLAND *noun*¹.]

1 Make into or like an island; place or enclose (as) on an island; insulate, isolate. M17.

M. LOWRY The narrow sloping lawn, islanded by rose beds.

2 Set or dot with or as with islands. E19.

islander /ˈʌɪləndə/ *noun*. M16.

[ORIGIN from ISLAND *noun*¹ + -ER¹.]

A native or inhabitant of an island.

Andaman Islander, *Channel Islander*, *Falkland Islander*, *South Islander*, *South Sea Islander*, *Virgin Islander*, etc.

isle /ʌɪl/ *noun*¹. Now chiefly *literary* & in place names. ME.

[ORIGIN Old French *ile* (mod. *île*), (Latinized) †*isle* from Latin *insula*.]

1 = ISLAND *noun*¹ 1. Now usu., a small island. ME.

Ecologist The early Phoenician traders . . called Britain the Isle of Honey.

British Isles, *Isle of Purbeck*, *Isle of Man*, *Isle of Wight*, *Western Isles*, etc.

2 In biblical translations: a land beyond the sea (esp. in *the isles of the Gentiles*). Cf. ISLAND *noun*¹ 1b. LME.

– COMB.: **isleman** *rare* = ISLESMAN.

■ **isleless** /-l-l-/ *adjective* devoid of islands L16.

†**isle** *noun*² var. of AISLE.

isle /ʌɪl/ *verb trans.* L16.

[ORIGIN from ISLE *noun*¹.]

Make an isle of; place or set as or in an isle; insulate; = ISLAND *verb* 1.

Isle of Wight disease /ʌɪl əv ˈwʌɪt dɪˌziːz/ *noun phr.* E20.

[ORIGIN *Isle of Wight*, an island off the coast of Hampshire, England.]

A disease of bees first found in the Isle of Wight in 1904, caused by the parasitic mite *Acarapis woodi*.

islesman /ˈʌɪlzmən/ *noun*. Pl. **-men**. E19.

[ORIGIN from ISLE *noun*¹ + -'S¹ + MAN *noun*.]

A native or inhabitant of any group of islands, esp. of the Hebrides, Orkneys, or Shetland.

islet /ˈʌɪlɪt/ *noun*. M16.

[ORIGIN Old French *islet*, *-ete* (mod. *îlette*) dim. of ISLE *noun*¹: see -ET¹.]

1 A little island, an ait. M16.

2 *transf.* **a** Something resembling a small island; a small piece of land markedly differing in character from its surroundings; an isolated tract or spot. Cf. ISLAND *noun*¹ 2. M17. ▸**b** ANATOMY. An isolated portion of tissue or group of cells, surrounded by parts of a different structure; *esp.* = *islet of Langerhans* s.v. LANGERHANS 1. M19.

■ **isleted** *adjective* placed like an islet; studded with islets: L19.

islomania /ʌɪlə(ʊ)ˈmeɪnɪə/ *noun*. M20.

[ORIGIN from ISLE *noun*¹ + -O- + -MANIA.]

A passion or craze for islands.

islot /ˈʌɪlət/ *noun*. Now *rare*. Also **ilot**. L18.

[ORIGIN Old French (later *îlot*) dim. of ISLE *noun*¹: see -OT¹.]

An islet.

ism /ˈɪz(ə)m/ *noun*. Chiefly *derog.* L17.

[ORIGIN -ISM used generically. Cf. WASM.]

A form of doctrine, theory, or practice having, or claiming to have, a distinctive character or relationship.

Kendal Mercury Irrespective of isms and creeds. G. B. SHAW The proletarian Isms are very much alike.

-ism /ɪz(ə)m/ *suffix*.

[ORIGIN French *-isme*, chiefly from Latin *-ismus* from Greek *-ismos* forming nouns of action from verbs in *-izein*, in part also from Latin *-isma* from Greek, forming nouns expr. something done.]

Forming usu. abstract nouns expr. (*a*) a process or practice or its result, as *baptism*, *criticism*, *organism*, freq. with corresp. verbs in -IZE; (*b*) the conduct characteristic of a class of people, as *heroism*, *patriotism*; a (sometimes abnormal) condition of a person or thing, as *alcoholism*, *barbarism*, *dwarfism*, *parallelism*; (*c*) (adherence to) a system of theory, belief, or practice (religious, philosophical, political, scientific, etc.), as *atheism*, *Buddhism*, *Darwinism*, *feminism*, *hedonism*, *Marxism*, *socialism*, *Wesleyism*; also, a system of discrimination based on a particular criterion, as *racism*, *sexism*: usu. with corresp. personal nouns and adjectives in -IST; (*d*) a peculiarity or characteristic of a nation, individual, etc., esp. in language, as *Americanism*, *colloquialism*, *Spoonerism*.

Ismaeli *noun & adjective* var. of ISMAILI.

Ismaelite /ˈɪzmeɪəlʌɪt, ˈɪs-/ *noun*. Now *rare*. In sense 2 also **Ismailite**. LME.

[ORIGIN from French, Latin, & Greek *Ismael* Ishmael (see ISHMAEL) or (in sense 2) formed as ISMAILI + -ITE¹.]

1 A descendant of Ishmael. Formerly also, an Arab regarded as a descendant of Ishmael; *gen.* a Muslim. LME.

2 An Ismaili. M19.

■ **Ismaelism** *noun* (*a*) the doctrinal system of the Ismailis; †(*b*) Islam: L18. **Ismaelitic** *adjective* of or belonging to the Ismailis L19.

Ismaili /ɪsˈmʌɪli, -ˈmɑːli/ *noun & adjective*. Also **Ismaeli**. M19.

[ORIGIN from Arabic *ʾIsmāʿīl* (see below) + -I².]

(A person) belonging to the branch of Shiite Islam which holds that at the death in 765 of the sixth Shiite imam the imamate ought to have descended to the posterity of his deceased eldest son ʾIsmāʿīl.

■ **Ismailian** *noun & adjective* M19.

Ismailite *noun* see ISMAELITE.

Isnik *adjective* var. of IZNIK.

ISO *abbreviation*.

1 (Companion of the) Imperial Service Order.

2 International Organization for Standardization.

iso- /ˈʌɪsəʊ/ *combining form*. Also occas. before a vowel **is-**. Also (CHEMISTRY) as attrib. adjective **iso**.

[ORIGIN Greek *isos* equal.]

1 Used in words adopted from Greek and in English words modelled on these, and as a freely productive prefix, mainly in scientific and technical use, with the sense 'equal'.

2 [Extracted from ISOMER.] CHEMISTRY. Forming names of compounds and radicals which are isomers of those whose names follow, as *isoborneol*, *isomaltose*, *isophthalate*, etc.; *spec.* designating hydrocarbons containing a $(CH_3)_2CH\cdot$ group at the end of a chain, as *isobutyl*, *isopentane*, etc. (Formerly regarded as a separable prefix and printed in italics (often with a hyphen). The IUPAC recommendation is that it should always be directly attached to the remainder of the parent name (and be printed in ordinary type).)

■ **isenˈthalpic** *adjective* of or relating to equal enthalpy E20. **isoˈallele** *noun* (GENETICS) an allele indistinguishable from another allele in its effect on the phenotype except when special techniques are employed M20. **isoaˈllelic** *adjective* of (the nature of) an isoallele M20. **isoˈantibody** *noun* (IMMUNOLOGY) an antibody elicited by an isoantigen E20. **isoˈantigen** *noun* (IMMUNOLOGY) a natural antigen in one individual which is capable of eliciting antibody formation only in other, genetically different, individuals of the same species M20. **isoantiˈgenic** *adjective* of, pertaining to, or being an isoantigen M20. **isobath** /-baθ/ *noun* [Greek *bathos* depth] a line (imaginary or on a map) joining places where water has equal depth; an underwater contour: L19. **isoˈbathic** *adjective* of the nature of an isobath; depicting isobaths: L19. **isoˈbathytherm** *noun* = ISOTHERMOBATH L19. **isobiˈlateral** *adjective* having the same structure on both sides; *esp.* (of leaves) having no evident distinction of upper and under surface: L19. **isoˈcaloric** *adjective* of equal calorific value E20. **isocaˈlorically** *adverb* in a way that leaves the calorific value unchanged M20. **isoˈcephaly** *noun* the convention, in Greek reliefs, of representing the heads of all the figures at nearly the same level E20. **isoˈcercal** *adjective* [Greek *kerkos* tail] ICHTHYOLOGY having equal lobes in the tail, with the vertebral column straight, not bent up (cf. HOMOCERCAL) L19. **isochore** /-kɔː/ *noun* [Greek *khōra* space] a curve on a diagram that represents a physical system at constant volume E20. **isochroous** /ʌɪˈsɒkrəʊəs/ *adjective* [Greek *khroa* colour] of a uniform colour M19. **isoˈcitrate** *noun* an ester or salt of isocitric acid E20. **isoˈcitric** *adjective*: *isocitric acid*, a tribasic carboxylic acid, $C_6H_8O_7$, isomeric with citric acid, which is an intermediate in the Krebs cycle M19. **isoˈcrymal** *adjective & noun* [Greek *krumos* cold] (a line, imaginary or on a map) connecting places at which the temperature is the same during a specified coldest part of the year M19. **isocryme** *noun* = ISOCRYMAL *noun* M19. **isoˈdiaphere** *noun* [Greek *diapherein* differ] each of two or more nuclides in which the difference between the numbers of protons and neutrons is the same, as a nucleus and its α-decay product L20. **isodiˈmorphism** *noun* (CRYSTALLOGRAPHY) isomorphism between two dimorphous substances in both of their forms M19. **isodiˈmorphous** *adjective* (CRYSTALLOGRAPHY) having or exhibiting isodimorphism M19. **isoˈeugenol** *noun* an aromatic liquid phenol that occurs in essential oils, esp. ylang-ylang; 2-methoxy-4-propenylphenol: L19. **isoˈflavone** *noun* (CHEMISTRY) a crystalline compound whose derivatives occur in many plants (esp. pulses), freq. as glycosides M20. **isogeˈneic** *adjective* (IMMUNOLOGY) = SYNGENEIC *adjective* M20. **isograft** *noun & verb trans.* (*a*) graft between individuals of the same species (cf. HOMOTRANSPLANT), esp. between genetically identical individuals E20. **ˌisohaemaggluˈtiˈnation** *noun* (IMMUNOLOGY) isoagglutination of red blood cells E20. **ˌisohaemaˈgglutinin** *noun* (IMMUNOLOGY) an isoagglutinin which is an antibody to a blood group antigen E20. **isoˈhalsine** *noun* [irreg. from Greek *hals* salt] = ISOHALINE *noun* E20. **isohel** *noun* [Greek *hēlios* sun] a line (imaginary or on a map) connecting points having the same amount or duration of sunshine E20. **isohelic** /-ˈhiːlɪk/ *adjective* of the nature of an isohel L19. **isohyet** /-hʌɪt/ *noun* [Greek *huetos* rain] = ISOHYETAL *noun* L19. **isohyetal** /-ˈhʌɪt(ə)l/ *adjective & noun* (a line on a map etc.) connecting places having equal annual or seasonal precipitation L19. **isoiˈmmune** *adjective* of, producing, or exhibiting isoimmunization M20. **isoimmuniˈzation** *noun* (an instance of) the development of an isoantibody in an individual against an antigen derived from another individual of the same species M20. **isokiˈnetic** *adjective* characterized by a constant or equal speed; *esp.* (*a*) (of sampling methods for moving fluids) not disturbing the flow; (*b*) (of a machine) producing a constant speed irrespective of power input; (*c*) PHYSIOLOGY of or pertaining to muscular action with a constant rate of movement: M20. **isokiˈnetically** *adverb* at a constant or equal speed M20. **isoˈlecithal** *adjective* [Greek *lekithos* yolk] = HOMOLECITHAL E20. **isoˈlectic** *adjective* (LINGUISTICS) = ISOLEXIC E20. **isolex** *noun* (LINGUISTICS) a line (imaginary or on a map) bounding an area in which some item of vocabulary occurs; a lexical isogloss: E20. **isoˈlexic** *adjective* (LINGUISTICS) pertaining to or of the nature of an isolex E20. **isoline** = ISOPLETH 1 M20. **isolux** *adjective* = ISOPHOTAL *adjective* E20. **isomagˈnetic** *noun & adjective* (*a*) *noun* a line (imaginary or on a map) connecting places which have the same value of a particular parameter of the earth's magnetic field; (*b*) *adjective* designating or (of a chart) depicting such lines: L19. **isomeˈtropia** *noun* [after *isometric*, *hypermetropia*] equal refractive power in both eyes (opp. ANISOMETROPIA) E20. **isoˈnitrile** *noun* = ISOCYANIDE L19. **isoosˈmotic** *adjective* = ISOSMOTIC E20. **isopheˈnomenal** *adjective* (of a line on a map etc.) connecting places at which phenomena of any kind are equal M19. **isopiestic** /-pʌɪˈɛstɪk/ *adjective & noun* [Greek *piestos* compressible] (*a*) *adjective* = ISOBARIC *adjective* 1; (*b*) *noun* = ISOBAR *noun* 1: L19. **isoˈplastic** *adjective* = HOMOPLASTIC 2 E20. **isoˈplasty** *noun* = HOMOPLASTY E20. **isoˈpropanol** *noun* a liquid secondary alcohol, $CH_3CHOH\cdot CH_3$, used as a solvent and in the production of acetone; propan-2-ol: M20. **isoˈpropyl** *noun* the radical $(CH_3)_2CH-$ (*isopropyl alcohol* = ISOPROPANOL) M19. **isosmotic** /ʌɪsɒzˈmɒtɪk/ *adjective* (PHYSIOLOGY) of or having the same osmotic pressure (foll. by *with*) L19. **isospore** *noun* (BOTANY) an undifferentiated spore L19. **isosporous** /ʌɪˈsɒsp(ə)rəs/ *adjective* (BOTANY) = HOMOSPOROUS L19. **isoˈstructural** *adjective* (MINERALOGY) having the same or similar crystal structure (foll. by *with*) E20. **isoˈthermobath** *noun* a line (imaginary or on a map) connecting points of equal temperature at various depths in a vertical section of the sea L19. **isothioˈcyanate** *noun* (CHEMISTRY) a compound containing the group $-N{=}C{=}S$ as a substituent or ligand L19. **isotone** *noun* [from ISOTOPE, with *n* for *neutron* replacing *p* for *proton*] PHYSICS each of two or more different nuclides having the same number of neutrons M20. **isoˈzooid** *noun* (BIOLOGY) a zooid, or individual of a colonial animal, not differentiated from the rest M19.

isoagglutination /ˌʌɪsəʊəgluːtɪˈneɪʃ(ə)n/ *noun*. E20.

[ORIGIN from ISO- + AGGLUTINATION.]

IMMUNOLOGY. Agglutination of cells (esp. sperms or erythrocytes) of an individual by a substance from a (genetically different) conspecific individual.

■ **isoaˈgglutinate** *verb trans. & intrans.* cause isoagglutination (of) E20. **isoaˈgglutinative** *adjective* pertaining to or causing isoagglutination E20. **isoaˈgglutinin** *noun* an agglutinin from an individual that agglutinates cells of (genetically different) conspecific individuals; *esp.* an isohaemagglutinin: E20. **isoaggluˈtinogen** *noun* (IMMUNOLOGY) a substance (esp. a blood group antigen) that elicits or reacts with an isoagglutinin E20.

isobar /ˈʌɪsə(ʊ)bɑː/ *noun*. In sense 2 orig. †**isobare**. M19.

[ORIGIN from Greek *isobaros* of equal weight, from *iso-* ISO- + *bare-*, *baros* weight, *barus* heavy.]

1 PHYSICAL GEOGRAPHY & METEOROLOGY. A line (on a map or chart, or imaginary) connecting places at which the atmospheric pressure is the same (at a given time, or on average). M19.

2 PHYSICS. A line or formula that represents a physical system at constant pressure. L19.

3 PHYSICS. Each of two or more nuclides which have the same mass number but different atomic numbers (and so belong to different elements). E20.

isobaric /ʌɪsə(ʊ)ˈbarɪk/ *adjective & noun*. L19.

[ORIGIN from ISOBAR + -IC.]

▸ **A** *adjective* **1 a** Indicating equal atmospheric pressure; containing or relating to isobars. L19. ▸**b** Occurring at or pertaining to a constant pressure. E20.

2 PHYSICS. Of, pertaining to, or being nuclides that are isobars. (Foll. by *with*.) E20.

isobaric spin = ISOSPIN.

3 MEDICINE. Of, pertaining to, or designating a solution for spinal anaesthesia having the same density as the cerebrospinal fluid. M20.

▸ **B** *noun*. = ISOBAR 2. E20.

■ **isobarically** *adverb* at constant pressure, without a change in pressure M20. **isobaroˈmetric** *adjective* (*rare*) = ISOBARIC *adjective* 1a M19.

isocarboxazid /ˌʌɪsə(ʊ)kɑːˈbɒksəzɪd/ *noun*. M20.

[ORIGIN from ISO- + CARB(ONYL + OX- + HYDR)AZID(E, elems. of the chemical name.]

PHARMACOLOGY. A hydrazine derivative used in the form of a white powder as an antidepressant.

– NOTE: A proprietary name for this drug is MARPLAN.

isocheim /ˈʌɪsə(ʊ)kʌɪm/ *noun*. M19.
[ORIGIN from ISO- + Greek *kheima* winter weather.]
PHYSICAL GEOGRAPHY. A line (imaginary or on a map) connecting places having the same mean winter temperature; an isotherm of mean winter temperature.
■ **isoˈcheimal** *adjective & noun* (of or pertaining to) an isocheim M19.

isochimenal /ʌɪsə(ʊ)ˈkʌɪmɪn(ə)l/ *adjective & noun*. M19.
[ORIGIN from French *isochimène*, formed as ISO- + Greek *kheimainein* be stormy, be wintry, from *kheima* winter weather, + -AL[1].]
▸ **A** *adjective*. = ISOCHEIMAL *adjective*. M19.
▸ **B** *noun*. = ISOCHEIM. M19.

isochromatic /ˌʌɪsə(ʊ)krə(ʊ)ˈmatɪk/ *adjective & noun*. E19.
[ORIGIN from ISO- + CHROMATIC *adjective*.]
▸ **A** *adjective*. **1** *OPTICS*. Of a single colour or tint; *spec.* designating a fringe in an interference pattern obtained with birefringent material (as a biaxial crystal) which in photoelastic testing indicates points where the difference between the principal stresses is the same. Also, representing or depicting such fringes. E19.
2 *PHOTOGRAPHY*. = ORTHOCHROMATIC. *obsolete* exc. *hist.* L19.
▸ **B** *noun*. An isochromatic fringe or line. E20.

isochron /ˈʌɪsə(ʊ)krɒn/ *adjective & noun*. Also (earlier, & in senses A., B.1 always) **-chrone** /-krəʊn/. L17.
[ORIGIN Greek *isokhronos* (see ISOCHRONAL).]
▸ **A** *adjective*. = ISOCHRONOUS *adjective* 1. L17.
▸ **B** *noun*. †**1** A curve in which a body descends through equal spaces in equal times. Only in L18.
2 A line (imaginary or on a map) connecting points at which a particular event occurs or occurred at the same time. L19.
3 A line (imaginary or on a map or diagram) connecting points at which some chosen time interval has the same value. M20.
4 *GEOLOGY*. In the isotopic dating of rock, a straight line whose gradient represents the time since the isotopic content of a sample was fixed (e.g. by crystallization), obtained by plotting against each other the ratios of the amounts of two radioisotopes to that of a single stable isotope, in two or more samples having the same history but different ratios. M20.
5 *GEOLOGY*. A line (imaginary or on a map) connecting points on the sea floor formed at the same time. M20.

isochronal /ʌɪˈsɒkrən(ə)l/ *adjective & noun*. L17.
[ORIGIN from mod. Latin *isochronus*, from Greek *isokhronos* (formed as ISO- + *khronos* time): see -AL[1].]
▸ **A** *adjective*. **1** = ISOCHRONOUS *adjective* 1. L17.
2 Of a line: connecting points at which a particular event occurs or occurred at the same time. Of a diagram: depicting such lines. E20.
▸ **B** *noun*. = ISOCHRON *noun* 2. M20.
■ **isochronally** *adverb* = ISOCHRONOUSLY L19.

isochronic /ʌɪsə(ʊ)ˈkrɒnɪk/ *adjective*. L18.
[ORIGIN formed as ISOCHRONAL + -IC.]
1 = ISOCHRONOUS *adjective* 1. L18.
2 = ISOCHRONAL *adjective* 2; *spec.* in *GEOGRAPHY* (of a line on a map etc.) connecting points which can be reached in a specified time from a given starting point. L19.
■ **isochronical** *adjective* (*rare*) = ISOCHRONIC L18.

isochronism /ʌɪˈsɒkrənɪz(ə)m/ *noun*. L18.
[ORIGIN formed as ISOCHRONAL + -ISM.]
1 The character or property of being isochronous, or of oscillating or taking place in equal spaces of time. L18.
2 *PROSODY*. The character or property of being isochronous. M20.

isochronous /ʌɪˈsɒkrənəs/ *adjective*. E18.
[ORIGIN formed as ISOCHRONAL + -OUS.]
1 a Equal in duration, or in frequency, as the motions of a pendulum; characterized by or relating to (repetitive) motions of equal duration; *spec.* in *PROSODY*, equal in metrical length. E18. ▸**b** Equal in duration, frequency, etc., *to* or *with* something. L18.
2 *PALAEONTOLOGY*. Originating or formed at the same period. L19.
■ **isochronously** *adverb* M18.

isochrony /ʌɪˈsɒkrəni/ *noun*. M20.
[ORIGIN formed as ISOCHRONISM after *synchrony* etc.]
= ISOCHRONISM.

isoclinal /ʌɪsə(ʊ)ˈklʌɪn(ə)l/ *adjective & noun*. M19.
[ORIGIN from ISO- + Greek *klinein* to lean, slope + -AL[1].]
▸ **A** *adjective*. **1** Of lines: having equal slope; *spec.* in *PHYSICAL GEOGRAPHY*, indicating or connecting points on the earth's surface at which the magnetic inclination is the same. M19.
2 *GEOLOGY*. Designating a fold so acute that the two limbs are parallel, or strata so folded. L19.
▸ **B** *noun*. Chiefly *PHYSICAL GEOGRAPHY*. An isoclinal line. L19.
■ **isoclinally** *adverb* M20.

isocline /ˈʌɪsə(ʊ)klʌɪn/ *noun*. L19.
[ORIGIN from Greek *isoklinēs* equally balanced, formed as ISOCLINAL.]
1 An isoclinal line or fold. L19.
2 a *SURVEYING*. A line (imaginary or on a map) connecting points of equal gradient. M20. ▸**b** *gen.* A line connecting points where the rate of change of some quantity is the same. M20.

isoclinic /ʌɪsə(ʊ)ˈklɪnɪk/ *adjective & noun*. M19.
[ORIGIN formed as ISOCLINAL + -IC.]
▸ **A** *adjective*. **1** = ISOCLINAL *adjective* 1. M19.
2 Corresponding to or depicting the locus of points in a body where each of the principal stresses is in some fixed direction. E20.
▸ **B** *noun*. **1** Each of two or more lines of equal slope. Freq. in *pl.* L19.
2 An isoclinic line or curve. E20.

isocolon /ʌɪsə(ʊ)ˈkəʊlən/ *noun*. *rare*. M16.
[ORIGIN formed as ISO- + COLON *noun*[2].]
CLASSICAL PROSODY & RHETORIC. (The use of) a succession of phrases of equal (syllabic) length or structure.

isocracy /ʌɪˈsɒkrəsi/ *noun*. M17.
[ORIGIN Greek *isokratia* equality of power or political rights, formed as ISO- + *kratos*, *krate-* strength, power: see -CRACY.]
Equality of power or rule; a system of government in which all the people possess equal political power.

isocratic /ʌɪsə(ʊ)ˈkratɪk/ *adjective*. E19.
[ORIGIN formed as ISOCRACY: see -IC.]
1 Of, pertaining to, or advocating isocracy. E19.
2 *CHEMISTRY*. Of or involving a mobile chromatographic phase whose composition is kept constant and uniform. L20.
■ **ˈisocrat** *noun* an advocate of isocracy L19.

isocyanate /ʌɪsə(ʊ)ˈsʌɪəneɪt/ *noun*. L19.
[ORIGIN from ISO- + CYANATE.]
CHEMISTRY. The radical ·N=C=O; any of the class of compounds containing this, some of which are used in making polyurethane.
■ **isocyˈanic** *adjective*: ***isocyanic acid***, an isomeric form of cyanic acid, HN=C=O L19.

isocyanide /ʌɪsə(ʊ)ˈsʌɪənʌɪd/ *noun*. L19.
[ORIGIN formed as ISO- + CYANIDE.]
CHEMISTRY. Any of the class of toxic, malodorous, usu. liquid compounds having the formula RNC (where R is an alkyl, aryl, etc., radical). Also called ***carbylamine***, ***isonitrile***.

isodiabatic /ˌʌɪsə(ʊ)dʌɪəˈbatɪk/ *adjective*. M19.
[ORIGIN from ISO- + Greek *diabatikos* able to pass through. Cf. ADIABATIC.]
PHYSICS. Relating to or indicating the transmission of equal amounts of heat to and from a body or substance.

isodiametric /ˌʌɪsə(ʊ)dʌɪəˈmɛtrɪk/ *adjective*. L19.
[ORIGIN from ISO- + DIAMETRIC.]
Having equal diameters; *spec.* (***a***) *BOTANY* (of a cell) roughly spherical or polyhedral; (***b***) *CRYSTALLOGRAPHY* (of a crystal) having three equal axes.

isodose /ˈʌɪsə(ʊ)dəʊs/ *noun*. E20.
[ORIGIN from ISO- + DOSE *noun*.]
An imaginary line or surface, or a graphical representation of one, connecting points (esp., in the human body) that receive equal doses of radiation. Now usu. *attrib.*, as ***isodose chart***, ***isodose contour***, ***isodose surface***, etc.

isodynamic /ˌʌɪsə(ʊ)dʌɪˈnamɪk/ *adjective*. M19.
[ORIGIN from Greek *isodunamos* equal in power, formed as ISO- + *dunamis* power, + -IC.]
1 Of equal force, value, or efficacy. *rare*. M19.
2 Chiefly *PHYSICAL GEOGRAPHY*. Indicating or connecting points (on the earth's surface, etc.) at which the intensity of the magnetic force is the same. Cf. ISOGAM 2. M19.
■ **isodynamical** *adjective* M19.

isoelectric /ˌʌɪsəʊɪˈlɛktrɪk/ *adjective*. L19.
[ORIGIN from ISO- + ELECTRIC.]
1 Equal in electrical potential; containing or indicating no potential difference. L19.
2 (Composed of particles) having no net electric charge; equal as regards electric charge. Chiefly in ***isoelectric point***, the point (usually pH value) at which an amphoteric molecule or a colloidal particle is electrically neutral in a solution. E20. ▸**b** Carried out or occurring at the isoelectric point. Esp. in ***isoelectric focusing***, electrophoresis in which the resolution is improved by maintaining a pH gradient between the electrodes. M20.
■ **isoelectrically** *adverb* (*BIOCHEMISTRY*) by making use of the different isoelectric points of the components of a mixture (in order to separate them) M20.

isoelectronic /ˌʌɪsəʊɪlɛkˈtrɒnɪk, -ɛl-/ *adjective*. E20.
[ORIGIN from ISO- + ELECTRON *noun*[2] + -IC.]
CHEMISTRY & PHYSICS. (Composed of atoms or molecules) having the same number of (valence) electrons. (Foll. by *with*.)

isoenzyme /ˈʌɪsəʊˌɛnzʌɪm/ *noun*. M20.
[ORIGIN from ISO- + ENZYME.]
BIOCHEMISTRY. Each of two or more chemically different forms of an enzyme.
■ **isoenˈzymic** *adjective* M20.

isoflor /ˈʌɪsə(ʊ)flɔː/ *noun*. M20.
[ORIGIN from ISO- + FLOR(A.]
A line (imaginary or on a map) linking areas containing equal numbers of plant species.

isogam /ˈʌɪsə(ʊ)gam/ *noun*. E20.
[ORIGIN App. from ISO- + GAMMA *noun*.]
1 A line (imaginary or on a map) connecting points where the acceleration due to gravity has the same value. Freq. *attrib.* E20.
2 An isodynamic line. M20.

isogamy /ʌɪˈsɒgəmi/ *noun*. L19.
[ORIGIN from ISO- + -GAMY.]
BIOLOGY. The reproductive union of two equal and similar gametes or cells. Opp. ANISOGAMY, HETEROGAMY.
■ **isogamete** /ʌɪsə(ʊ)ˈgamiːt/ *noun* either of two similar uniting cells L19. **isogamous** *adjective* characterized by isogamy L19.

isogenic /ʌɪsə(ʊ)ˈdʒɛnɪk, -ˈdʒiːnɪk/ *adjective*. M20.
[ORIGIN from ISO- + GENE + -IC.]
BIOLOGY. Having the same or a closely similar genotype.

isogenous /ʌɪˈsɒdʒɪnəs/ *adjective*. L19.
[ORIGIN from ISO- + -GENOUS. Cf. ecclesiastical Greek *isogenēs* equal in kind or nature.]
BIOLOGY. Chiefly of organs or parts: having the same or a similar (esp. embryological) origin.
■ **isogeny** *noun* the condition of being isogenous L19.

isogeotherm /ʌɪsə(ʊ)ˈdʒiːə(ʊ)θəːm/ *noun*. M19.
[ORIGIN from ISO- + GEO- + Greek *thermē* heat, *thermos* hot.]
GEOLOGY. A line or surface (imaginary or on a diagram) connecting points in the interior of the earth having the same temperature.
■ **isogeoˈthermal** *adjective* of the nature of an isogeotherm M19.

isogloss /ˈʌɪsə(ʊ)glɒs/ *noun*. E20.
[ORIGIN from ISO- + Greek *glōssa* tongue, word.]
LINGUISTICS. (A line on a map indicating) the boundary of an area of occurrence of a significant linguistic feature (as of vocabulary or pronunciation).
■ **isoˈglossic** *adjective* E20.

isoglottal /ʌɪsə(ʊ)ˈglɒt(ə)l/ *adjective*. M20.
[ORIGIN from ISO- + Greek *glōtta*, *glōssa* tongue + -AL[1].]
= ISOGLOSSIC.
■ Also **isoglottic** *adjective* M20.

isogon /ˈʌɪsəg(ə)n, -gɒn/ *noun*. L17.
[ORIGIN from Greek *isogōnios* equiangular: see ISO-, -GON.]
1 *GEOMETRY*. An isogonal figure. Now *rare* or *obsolete*. L17.
2 An isogonic line. E20.

isogonal /ʌɪˈsɒg(ə)n(ə)l/ *adjective*. M19.
[ORIGIN from ISOGON + -AL[1].]
1 = ISOGONIC *adjective*[1]. M19.
2 Having equal angles, equiangular. L19.

isogonic /ʌɪsə(ʊ)ˈgɒnɪk/ *adjective*[1] *& noun*. M19.
[ORIGIN formed as ISOGONAL + -IC.]
▸ **A** *adjective*. Indicating equal angles; *spec.* in *PHYSICAL GEOGRAPHY* (chiefly of lines on a map etc.) indicating or connecting points of the earth's surface at which the magnetic declination, wind direction, etc., is the same. M19.
▸ **B** *noun*. An isogonic line. L19.

isogonic /ʌɪsə(ʊ)ˈgɒnɪk/ *adjective*[2]. E20.
[ORIGIN French *isogonique*, perh. formed as ISOGONAL.]
BIOLOGY. Of an organ: growing in proportion (with its parent body).
■ **isogony** /ʌɪˈsɒgəni/ *noun* = ISOMETRY 2 M20.

isogram /ˈʌɪsə(ʊ)gram/ *noun*. L19.
[ORIGIN from ISO- + -GRAM.]
= ISOPLETH 1.

isograph /ˈʌɪsə(ʊ)grɑːf/ *noun*. M19.
[ORIGIN from ISO- + -GRAPH.]
1 A drawing instrument consisting of two (or more) short rulers joined in parallel or by a hinge. M19.
2 *LINGUISTICS*. = ISOGLOSS. M20.

isohaline /ʌɪsə(ʊ)ˈheɪlʌɪn/ *adjective & noun*. E20.
[ORIGIN from ISO- + Greek *hal-*, *hals* salt + -INE[1].]
OCEANOGRAPHY. ▸**A** *adjective*. Of a constant salinity throughout; (of a line or surface) connecting points which have the same salinity. E20.
▸ **B** *noun*. An isohaline line or surface. M20.

isohydric /ʌɪsə(ʊ)ˈhʌɪdrɪk/ *adjective*. L19.
[ORIGIN from ISO- + HYDRIC *adjective*[1].]
1 *PHYSICAL CHEMISTRY*. Of solutions: having the same (hydrogen) ion concentration; that mix without change of ionization. L19.
2 *PHYSIOLOGY*. Occurring without causing any change in pH, as the removal of carbon dioxide from the tissues by the blood. E20.

isoionic /ʌɪsəʊʌɪˈɒnɪk/ *adjective*. E20.
[ORIGIN from ISO- + IONIC *adjective*[2].]
CHEMISTRY. Of a solute or solution: giving rise to or containing no non-colloidal ions other than those formed by dissociation of the solvent.
isoionic point the point (usu. pH value) at which the average number of protons attached to the basic groups of solute molecules is equal to the average number dissociated from the acidic groups.

isolable /ˈʌɪs(ə)ləb(ə)l/ *adjective*. **M19**.
[ORIGIN from ISOLATE *verb* + -ABLE.]
Able to be isolated.
■ **isolaˈbility** *noun* **L20**.

isolatable /ˈʌɪsəleɪtəb(ə)l, ʌɪsə(ʊ)ˈleɪ-/ *adjective*. **M20**.
[ORIGIN formed as ISOLABLE.]
= ISOLABLE.
■ **isolataˈbility** *noun* **M20**.

isolate /ˈʌɪs(ə)lət/ *adjective & noun*. **E19**.
[ORIGIN from (the same root as) ISOLATED.]
▸ **A** *adjective*. = ISOLATED. **E19**.
▸ **B** *noun*. **1** An isolated thing; *esp.* a thing abstracted from its normal context for study. **L19**.
2 In perfumery, a compound purified from a natural oil. **E20**.
3 MICROBIOLOGY. A group, esp. a pure culture, of similar micro-organisms isolated for study. **M20**.
4 SOCIOLOGY & PSYCHOLOGY. A person, community, group, or (occas.) an animal isolated from normal social interaction, from choice or through separation or rejection. **M20**.
5 BIOLOGY. A population which has become distinct from the parent species through the operation of an isolating mechanism. **M20**.

isolate /ˈʌɪsəleɪt/ *verb trans*. **E19**.
[ORIGIN Back-form. from ISOLATED (now regarded as the pa. pple of the verb); partly after French *isoler*: see -ATE[3].]
1 Place or set apart or alone; cause to stand alone or detached, separated from or unconnected with other things or persons. Also, distinguish, identify. **E19**.

W. S. CHURCHILL Until agrarian problems could be isolated from other political issues, there was little hope. M. MEYER Strindberg withdrew into himself and isolated himself. . from his colleagues. A. MUNRO Blizzards still isolate the towns and villages. J. M. COETZEE I isolated over four hundred different characters in the script.

2 CHEMISTRY. Obtain or extract (a substance) in a pure form. **M19**.

M. PYKE A few milligrams of vitamin B12 had been isolated and the nature of its complex molecule established.

3 ELECTRICITY. Insulate, esp. by a physical gap; disconnect. **M19**.
4 Subject (an infected person or place) to strict quarantine. **L19**.

isolated /ˈʌɪsəleɪtɪd/ *adjective*. **M18**.
[ORIGIN from French *isolé* from Italian *isolato* from late Latin *insulatus* made an island, from Latin *insula* island: see -ATE[2], -ED[1]. Cf. ISOLATE *verb*.]
Placed or standing apart or alone; detached or separate from other things or persons; unconnected with anything else; solitary.

J. REED There were still isolated cases of defiance towards the new Government, but they were rare. B. EMECHETA An isolated place, hidden. . by the surrounding desert and hills. L. NKOSI A bitter man, secretive and isolated.

isolated pawn CHESS: without other pawns of the same colour in adjacent files.

isolati *noun pl.* see ISOLATO.

isolating /ˈʌɪsəleɪtɪŋ/ *ppl adjective*. **M19**.
[ORIGIN from ISOLATE *verb* + -ING[2].]
That isolates; LINGUISTICS (of a language) in which words tend not to vary in form (by either agglutination or inflection) according to grammatical function; = ANALYTIC *adjective* 3.
isolating barrier, **isolating mechanism** a geographical, ecological, seasonal, physiological, or other factor which limits or prevents interbreeding between groups of plants or animals.

isolation /ʌɪsəˈleɪʃ(ə)n/ *noun & adjective*. **M19**.
[ORIGIN from ISOLATE *verb* + -ATION, partly after French *isolation*.]
▸ **A** *noun*. **1** The action of isolating something or someone; the fact or condition of being or having been isolated; separation from other things or persons; solitariness. **M19**. ▸**b** The separation of a chemical substance in a pure state. **M19**. ▸**c** The complete separation of patients with a contagious or infectious disease from contact with other people; the prevention of access to a place so infected. **L19**.

Daily Telegraph The loneliness and sense of isolation from ordinary life that fame brings. *Ecologist* The growing isolation of the US in the global food market.

in isolation considered singly and not relative to something else. SPLENDID ***isolation***.
2 a PSYCHOLOGY & SOCIOLOGY. The separation of a person or thing from the normal (social) environment or context, either deliberately for study, or as a result of some inherent tendency. **L19**. ▸**b** PSYCHOANALYSIS. A defence mechanism whereby a particular wish or thought loses emotional significance by being isolated from its normal context. **E20**.
3 BIOLOGY. The limitation or prevention of interbreeding between groups of plants or animals by some isolating mechanism, leading to the development of new species or varieties. **E20**.
▸ **B** *attrib*. or as *adjective*. Designating a procedure, place of confinement, etc., by which isolation is effected. **M19**.
isolation camp, ***isolation hospital***, ***isolation ward***, etc.

isolationism /ʌɪsəˈleɪʃ(ə)nɪz(ə)m/ *noun*. **E20**.
[ORIGIN from ISOLATION + -ISM.]
The policy of seeking (political or national) isolation.

isolationist /ʌɪsəˈleɪʃ(ə)nɪst/ *noun & adjective*. **L19**.
[ORIGIN formed as ISOLATIONISM + -IST.]
▸ **A** *noun*. A person who favours or advocates (political or national) isolationism. **L19**.
▸ **B** *adjective*. Characteristic of or being an isolationist. **L19**.

isolative /ˈʌɪsələtɪv/ *adjective*. **L19**.
[ORIGIN from ISOLATE *verb* + -ATIVE.]
1 PHILOLOGY. Of a sound change: taking place independently of adjacent sounds. Opp. COMBINATIVE 2. **L19**.
2 *gen*. Tending to isolate something or someone. **M20**.

isolato /iːsəˈlɑːtəʊ/ *noun*. Pl. **-ti** /-ti/, **-tos**. **M19**.
[ORIGIN Italian.]
An isolated person, an outcast.

isolator /ˈʌɪsəleɪtə/ *noun*. **M19**.
[ORIGIN from ISOLATE *verb* + -OR.]
A person who or thing which isolates something or someone; a contrivance for isolating something; an insulator.

isoleucine /ʌɪsə(ʊ)ˈluːsiːn/ *noun*. **E20**.
[ORIGIN from ISO- + LEUCINE.]
BIOCHEMISTRY. A hydrophobic amino acid, $CH_3CH_2CH(CH_3)CH(NH_2)COOH$, which occurs in proteins and is essential in the human diet; 2-amino-3-methylpentanoic acid.

isolog *noun* see ISOLOGUE.

isologous /ʌɪˈsɒləɡəs/ *adjective*. **M19**.
[ORIGIN from ISO- + Greek *logos* relation, ratio (see LOGOS) + -OUS, after *homologous*.]
1 CHEMISTRY. Of two or more (series of) compounds: having comparable or related molecular structures; now usu. *spec*., (of compounds) having identical molecular structure but different atoms of the same valency at some position(s) in the molecule. Cf. HOMOLOGOUS *adjective* 4. **M19**.
2 MEDICINE & BIOLOGY. Genetically identical, esp. as regards immunological factors; involving such individuals. **M20**.

isologue /ˈʌɪsə(ʊ)lɒɡ/ *noun*. Also ***-log**. **L19**.
[ORIGIN from ISO- + -LOGUE.]
CHEMISTRY. Each of two or more isologous compounds.

isomer /ˈʌɪsəmə/ *noun*. **M19**.
[ORIGIN from Greek *isomerēs* sharing equally, formed as ISO- + *meros* part, share.]
1 CHEMISTRY. A substance isomeric with another; any of a number of isomeric compounds or forms of a compound. **M19**.
geometrical isomer, ***optical isomer***, ***structural isomer***, etc.
2 PHYSICS. Each of two or more nuclei having the same atomic number and mass number but different radioactive properties, as a result of being in different energy states; *esp*. a nucleus in a metastable excited state rather than the ground state. Also ***nuclear isomer***. **M20**.

isomerase /ʌɪˈsɒməreɪz/ *noun*. **M20**.
[ORIGIN from ISOMER + -ASE.]
BIOCHEMISTRY. Any of various enzymes which bring about an isomerization reaction.

isomeric /ʌɪsə(ʊ)ˈmɛrɪk/ *adjective*. **M19**.
[ORIGIN formed as ISOMER + -IC.]
1 CHEMISTRY. Of two or more compounds, or of one compound in relation to another: composed of the same elements in the same proportions, and having the same molecular weight, but forming substances with different properties owing to the different grouping or arrangement of the constituent atoms. (Foll. by *with*.) **M19**.
2 PHYSICS. Of, pertaining to, or designating nuclear isomers. **M20**.
– NOTE: In sense 1, formerly extended to include compounds in which the number of atoms in one is a multiple of those in the other, or restricted to those with similar functional groups and hence similar properties.
■ **isomerically** *adverb* as regards isomers; by isomerization: **L19**.

isomeride /ʌɪˈsɒmərʌɪd/ *noun*. *rare*. **M19**.
[ORIGIN formed as ISOMER + -IDE.]
CHEMISTRY. = ISOMER 1.

isomerise *verb* var. of ISOMERIZE.

isomerism /ʌɪˈsɒmərɪz(ə)m/ *noun*. **M19**.
[ORIGIN from ISOMER + -ISM.]
1 CHEMISTRY. The fact or condition of being isomeric; identity of percentage composition in compounds differing in properties. **M19**.
geometrical isomerism: in which compounds differ in the spatial arrangement of atoms relative to a (rigid) double bond. **optical isomerism**: in which compounds differ in the spatial arrangement of atoms around one or more asymmetric carbon atoms, and hence usu. in optical activity. STEREOISOMERISM. **structural isomerism**: in which molecules having the same constituent atoms have different structures, the atoms being joined in different sequences.
2 PHYSICS. The fact or condition of being nuclear isomers. **M20**.

isomerize /ʌɪˈsɒmərʌɪz/ *verb trans. & intrans*. Also **-ise**. **L19**.
[ORIGIN from ISOMER + -IZE.]
CHEMISTRY. Change into an isomer (of the original substance). Usu. foll. by *into*, *to*.
■ **isomeriˈzation** *noun* (CHEMISTRY) the conversion of a compound into an isomer of itself **L19**.

isomerous /ʌɪˈsɒm(ə)rəs/ *adjective*. **M19**.
[ORIGIN from Greek *isomerēs* (see ISOMER) + -OUS.]
BIOLOGY. Having the same number of (similar) parts; *spec*. in BOTANY (of a flower) having the same number of parts in each whorl (opp. HETEROMEROUS 2b).

isometric /ʌɪsə(ʊ)ˈmɛtrɪk/ *adjective & noun*. **M19**.
[ORIGIN from Greek *isometria* equality of measure, formed as ISO- + -METRY: see -IC.]
▸ **A** *adjective*. **1** Of equal measure or dimensions. **M19**.
2 DRAWING. Designating a method of projection or perspective in which the three principal dimensions are represented by three axes 120° apart, with all measurements on the same scale, used in technical and architectural drawing. **M19**.
3 CRYSTALLOGRAPHY. = CUBIC *adjective* 2b. **M19**.
4 PHYSIOLOGY. Of, pertaining to, or designating muscular action in which tension is developed without contraction of the muscle. **L19**.
5 PHYSICS. Relating to, or taking place under, conditions of constant volume. **L19**.
6 BIOLOGY. Of growth: maintaining constant proportions with increase in size. **M20**.
7 MATH. That is an isometry; related by an isometry. Foll. by *to*. **M20**.
▸ **B** *noun*. **1** PHYSICS. A line in a diagram that corresponds to or represents states of equal volume. **L19**.
2 In *pl*. A system of stationary physical exercises in which muscles are caused to act isometrically against one another or against an unyielding object. **M20**.

isometrical /ʌɪsə(ʊ)ˈmɛtrɪk(ə)l/ *adjective*. **M19**.
[ORIGIN formed as ISOMETRIC + -AL[1].]
= ISOMETRIC *adjective* 2, 3.

isometrically /ʌɪsə(ʊ)ˈmɛtrɪk(ə)li/ *adverb*. **M19**.
[ORIGIN from ISOMETRIC *adjective* or ISOMETRICAL: see -ICALLY.]
1 DRAWING. In the manner of isometric projection. **M19**.
2 PHYSIOLOGY. Under isometric conditions. **E20**.
3 MATH. By means of or in the manner of an isometry. **M20**.

isometry /ʌɪˈsɒmɪtri/ *noun*. **M20**.
[ORIGIN formed as ISOMETRIC: see -Y[3].]
1 MATH. A one-to-one transformation of one metric space into another that preserves the distances or metrics between each pair of points. **M20**.
2 BIOLOGY. (Growth exhibiting) constancy of proportion with increase in size. Cf. ALLOMETRY. **M20**.

isomorph /ˈʌɪsə(ʊ)mɔːf/ *noun*. **M19**.
[ORIGIN from ISO- + -MORPH.]
1 A substance or organism isomorphic with another. **M19**.
2 LINGUISTICS. A line (imaginary or on a map) bounding an area in which a particular morphological form occurs; a morphological isogloss. *rare*. **E20**.

isomorphic /ʌɪsə(ʊ)ˈmɔːfɪk/ *adjective*. **M19**.
[ORIGIN formed as ISOMORPH + -IC.]
1 CHEMISTRY & MINERALOGY. Isomorphous; pertaining to or involving isomorphism. **M19**.
2 MATH. & PHILOSOPHY. Of groups or other sets: corresponding to each other in form, and in the nature and product of their operations; related by or being an isomorphism. Foll. by *to*, *with*. **L19**.
3 BIOLOGY. Of closely similar form but independent origin. *rare*. **L19**.
4 BOTANY. In algae and certain fungi: designating a type of alternation of generations in which the two forms are morphologically similar. **M20**.
5 LINGUISTICS. Similar in morphological structure, having similar morphological forms. **M20**.
■ **isomorphically** *adverb* (*a*) MATH. & PHILOSOPHY by an isomorphism; (*b*) in an isomorphic manner: **M20**.

isomorphism /ʌɪsə(ʊ)ˈmɔːfɪz(ə)m/ *noun*. **E19**.
[ORIGIN formed as ISOMORPH + -ISM.]
1 CHEMISTRY & MINERALOGY. The property of crystallizing in the same or closely related forms, esp. as exhibited by substances of analogous composition. **E19**.
2 MATH. & PHILOSOPHY. Identity of form and operations between two or more groups or other sets; an exact correspondence as regards the number of constituent elements and the relations between them; *spec*. a one-to-one homomorphism. **L19**.
3 BIOLOGY. A similarity of appearance displayed by organisms having different genotypes. **E20**.
4 PSYCHOLOGY. A correspondence assumed to exist between the structure of mental events and that of the underlying neural events. **M20**.

isomorphous /ʌɪsə(ʊ)ˈmɔːfəs/ *adjective*. **E19.**
[ORIGIN formed as ISOMORPH + -OUS.]
1 *CHEMISTRY & MINERALOGY*. Having the property of crystallizing in the same or closely related geometric forms, esp. owing to analogous composition. Cf. HOMOEOMORPHOUS. **E19.**
2 *MATH*. = ISOMORPHIC 2. *rare*. **L19.**
■ **isomorphously** *adverb* (*MINERALOGY*) in such a way as to produce isomorphous substances **E20.**

-ison /ɪs(ə)n/ *suffix*.
Repr. Old French *-aison*, *-eison*, *-eson*, *-ison*, Latin *-atio(n-)* (later adopted in the learned form -ATION), *-etio(n-)*, *-itio(n-)*, in nouns, as ***comparison***, ***jettison***, ***orison***, ***venison***.

isoniazid /ʌɪsə(ʊ)ˈnʌɪəzɪd/ *noun*. **M20.**
[ORIGIN from ISO- + NI(COTINIC + HYDR)AZID(E.]
PHARMACOLOGY. A soluble colourless crystalline compound, $C_5H_5N{\cdot}CO{\cdot}NH{\cdot}NH_2$, which is used as a bacteriostatic drug esp. in the treatment of tuberculosis.

isonomy /ʌɪˈsɒnəmi/ *noun*. **E17.**
[ORIGIN Italian *isonomia* from Greek, ult. formed as ISO- + *nomos* law: see -Y[3].]
Equality of people before the law; equality of political rights among the citizens of a state.
■ **isonomic** /ʌɪsə(ʊ)ˈnɒmɪk/ *adjective* (***a***) characterized by isonomy; (***b***) *rare* having equal laws or rights: **M19.**

isooctane /ʌɪsəʊˈɒkteɪn/ *noun*. **E20.**
[ORIGIN from ISO- + OCTANE.]
†**1** A liquid hydrocarbon, $CH_3{\cdot}(CH_2)_4{\cdot}CH(CH_3){\cdot}CH_3$, that occurs in petroleum; 2-methylheptane. Only in **E20.**
2 A colourless liquid hydrocarbon, $(CH_3)_3C\,CH_2{\cdot}CH(CH_3){\cdot}CH_3$, used in aviation fuels, as a solvent and anti-knock, and as a standard in the determination of octane numbers; 2,2,4-trimethylpentane. **M20.**

isopach /ˈʌɪsə(ʊ)pak/ *noun*. **E20.**
[ORIGIN from ISO- + Greek *pakhus* thick.]
1 *GEOLOGY*. = ISOPACHYTE. **E20.**
2 = ISOPACHIC *noun*. **M20.**

isopachic /ʌɪsə(ʊ)ˈpakɪk/ *adjective & noun*. **M20.**
[ORIGIN formed as ISOPACH + -IC.]
▸ **A** *adjective*. Corresponding to or depicting the locus of points in a body where the sum of the principal stresses has the same value. **M20.**
▸ **B** *noun*. An isopachic line or curve. **M20.**

isopachous /ʌɪsə(ʊ)ˈpakəs, ʌɪˈsɒpəkəs/ *adjective*. **E20.**
[ORIGIN formed as ISOPACH + -OUS.]
GEOLOGY. Depicting or pertaining to isopachytes; of the nature of an isopachyte.

isopachyte /ʌɪsə(ʊ)ˈpakʌɪt/ *noun*. **E20.**
[ORIGIN from ISO- + Greek *pakhutēs* thickness.]
GEOLOGY. A line (on a map or diagram) joining points below which a particular stratum or group of strata has the same thickness.

isoperimeter /ˌʌɪsəʊpəˈrɪmɪtə/ *noun*. **M16.**
[ORIGIN Greek *isoperimetros*, formed as ISO- + PERIMETER.]
GEOMETRY. Each of two or more figures having equal perimeters. Usu. in *pl.*
■ **isoperimetrical** /ˌʌɪsə(ʊ)pɛrɪˈmɛtrɪk(ə)l/ *adjective* of or pertaining to isoperimeters, having equal perimeters **E18.** **isoperimetry** *noun* (*rare*) the branch of mathematics that deals with (problems concerning) isoperimetrical figures **E19.**

isophane *noun*[1] var. of ISOPHENE.

isophane /ˈʌɪsə(ʊ)feɪn/ *adjective & noun*[2]. **M20.**
[ORIGIN from ISO- + Greek *-phanēs* showing, appearing, from *phainein* show.]
PHARMACOLOGY. ▸**A** *adjective*. Designating the ratio of the amounts of protamine and insulin which are respectively necessary to precipitate all the insulin and all the protamine in solutions of these, such that the resulting mixed solutions have equal turbidity. **M20.**
isophane insulin = sense B. below.
▸ **B** *noun*. A crystalline mixture of insulin and protamine in the isophane ratio with zinc, which has longer lasting effects than pure insulin. **M20.**

isophene /ˈʌɪsə(ʊ)fiːn/ *noun*. Also **-phane** /-feɪn/. **E20.**
[ORIGIN formed as ISOPHANE *adjective & noun*[2]: cf. PHENO- 2.]
A line (imaginary or on a map) linking places in which seasonal biological phenomena (the flowering of plants etc.) occur at the same time.
■ **isoˈphenal** *adjective* **E20.**

isophone /ˈʌɪsə(ʊ)fəʊn/ *noun*. *rare*. **E20.**
[ORIGIN from ISO- + PHONE *noun*[1].]
LINGUISTICS. A line (imaginary or on a map) bounding an area in which some feature of pronunciation occurs; a phonetic isogloss.
■ **isoˈphonic** *adjective* **E20.**

isophote /ˈʌɪsə(ʊ)fəʊt/ *noun*. Also **-phot** /-fɒt/. **E20.**
[ORIGIN from ISO- + Greek *phōt-*, *phōs* light.]
A line (imaginary or in a diagram) connecting points where the intensity of light or other radiation is the same.
■ **isoˈphotal** *adjective & noun* (depicting or of the nature of) an isophote **E20.** **isoˈphotic** *adjective* = ISOPHOTAL *adjective* **M20.**

isopleth /ˈʌɪsə(ʊ)plɛθ/ *noun*. **E20.**
[ORIGIN from Greek *isoplēthēs* equal in quantity, formed as ISO- + *plēthos* multitude, quantity.]
1 A line (imaginary or on a map or diagram) connecting points for which some chosen quantity has the same value. **E20.**
2 *PHYSICAL CHEMISTRY*. A line or surface (in a diagram) joining points that represent mixtures having the same composition. **E20.**
■ **isoplethal** /-ˈpliːθ(ə)l/ *adjective* carried out or occurring at constant composition **E20.**

isopod /ˈʌɪsəpɒd/ *noun*. **M19.**
[ORIGIN from mod. Latin *Isopoda* (see below), from Greek *iso-* ISO- + *pod-*, *pous* foot.]
ZOOLOGY. Any crustacean of the order Isopoda, characterized by a dorsoventrally flattened body, and seven similar pairs of thoracic legs equal in length, and comprising the terrestrial woodlice and allied marine and freshwater species, some being parasitic. Cf. AMPHIPOD.
■ **isopodan** /ʌɪˈsɒpəd(ə)n/ *adjective & noun* (***a***) *adjective* = ISOPODOUS; (***b***) *noun* = ISOPOD: **M19.**

isopodous /ʌɪˈsɒpədəs/ *adjective*. **E19.**
[ORIGIN formed as ISOPOD + -OUS.]
ZOOLOGY. Belonging to or having the characteristics of the order Isopoda (see ISOPOD).

isopolity /ʌɪsə(ʊ)ˈpɒlɪti/ *noun*. **M19.**
[ORIGIN Greek *isopoliteia*, formed as ISO- + POLITY.]
Chiefly *hist*. Equality of rights of citizenship between different communities or states; mutual recognition of civic rights.

isoprenaline /ʌɪsə(ʊ)ˈprɛnəliːn/ *noun*. **M20.**
[ORIGIN from elems. of the systematic name N-*isopro*pylnor*adrenaline*.]
PHARMACOLOGY. A sympathomimetic amine, $C_6H_3(OH)_2CH(OH)CH_2NHCH(CH_3)_2$, a derivative of adrenalin used, freq. in aerosol form, for the relief of bronchial asthma and pulmonary emphysema. Also called (in US) ***isoproterenol***.

isoprene /ˈʌɪsə(ʊ)priːn/ *noun*. **M19.**
[ORIGIN App. from ISO- + PR(OPYL)ENE.]
A volatile, flammable, colourless liquid, $CH_2{=}C(CH_3)CH{=}CH_2$, obtainable from petroleum and forming the structural unit of natural and synthetic rubbers; 2-methyl-1,3-butadiene.
– COMB.: **isoprene rule**: that the carbon skeleton of a terpene is made up of linked isoprene units; **isoprene unit** the arrangement of five carbon atoms found in (polymers of) the isoprene molecule (the single or double nature of the bonds being disregarded).
■ **isoprenoid** /ˈʌɪsə(ʊ)prɪnɔɪd, ʌɪsə(ʊ)ˈpriːnɔɪd/ *adjective & noun* (***a***) *adjective* containing or designating the isoprene unit; composed of such units; (***b***) *noun* an isoprenoid compound: **M20.**

isoproterenol /ˌʌɪsə(ʊ)prəʊtəˈriːnɒl/ *noun*. *US*. **M20.**
[ORIGIN from elems. of the semi-systematic name N-*isopro*pylar*terenol*.]
PHARMACOLOGY. = ISOPRENALINE.

Isoptera /ʌɪˈsɒptərə/ *noun pl*. **L19.**
[ORIGIN mod. Latin, from ISO- + Greek *pteron* wing: see -A[3].]
(Members of) an order of insects that comprises the termites.
■ **isopteran** *noun & adjective* **E20.**

isopycnal /ʌɪsə(ʊ)ˈpɪkn(ə)l/ *noun & adjective*. **E20.**
[ORIGIN from ISO- + Greek *puknos* dense + -AL[1].]
OCEANOGRAPHY. ▸**A** *noun*. A line (imaginary or on a map or chart) or an imaginary surface connecting points which have the same density. **E20.**
▸ **B** *adjective*. That is an isopycnal. **M20.**

isopycnic /ʌɪsə(ʊ)ˈpɪknɪk/ *adjective & noun*. **L19.**
[ORIGIN formed as ISOPYCNAL + -IC.]
▸ **A** *adjective*. (Connecting points) of the same density or of constant density. Also (*BIOCHEMISTRY*), pertaining to or designating ultracentrifugal separative techniques which rely on differences in density between the components of a mixture. **L19.**
▸ **B** *noun*. *METEOROLOGY*. A line (imaginary or on a map or chart) or an imaginary surface connecting points at which the density (esp. of the atmosphere) is the same. Cf. ISOSTERE 1a. **L19.**

isorhythm /ˈʌɪsə(ʊ)rɪð(ə)m/ *noun*. Also **-rrh-**. **M20.**
[ORIGIN from ISO- + RHYTHM.]
The rhythmic structure of isorhythmic music.

isorhythmic /ʌɪsə(ʊ)ˈrɪðmɪk/ *adjective*. Also **-rrh-**. **L19.**
[ORIGIN from ISO- + RHYTHMIC.]
1 Of a poem etc.: constructed in the same rhythm or metre (as another). **L19.**
2 *MUSIC*. Of, characterized by, or designating a line or part, esp. a canto fermo, in which the rhythm is often repeated but the pitch of the notes is varied each time. **M20.**

isorrhythm *noun*, **isorrhythmic** *adjective* vars. of ISORHYTHM, ISORHYTHMIC.

isosbestic /ʌɪsə(ʊ)sˈbɛstɪk/ *adjective*. **E20.**
[ORIGIN from ISO- + Greek *sbestos* extinguished (from *sbennunai* quench) + -IC.]
PHYSICAL CHEMISTRY. ***isosbestic point***, a wavelength at which absorption of light by a liquid remains constant as the equilibrium between its component substances is shifted.

isosceles /ʌɪˈsɒsɪliːz/ *adjective & noun*. **M16.**
[ORIGIN Late Latin from Greek *isoskelēs*, formed as ISO- + *skelos* leg.]
GEOMETRY. ▸**A** *adjective*. Of a triangle: having two of its sides equal. Of a trapezoid: having the two non-parallel sides equal. **M16.**
▸ **B** *noun*. An isosceles triangle. *rare*. **L16.**

isoseismal /ʌɪsə(ʊ)ˈsʌɪzm(ə)l/ *adjective & noun*. **M19.**
[ORIGIN from ISO- + SEISMAL.]
▸ **A** *adjective*. Of a line (imaginary or on a map): connecting points at which the intensity of an earthquake shock is the same. **M19.**
▸ **B** *noun*. An isoseismal line. **M19.**
■ **isoseismic** *adjective* = ISOSEISMAL *adjective* **M19.**

isospin /ˈʌɪsə(ʊ)spɪn/ *noun*. **M20.**
[ORIGIN Contr. of *isotopic spin*, *isobaric spin*.]
PHYSICS. A vector quantity associated with subatomic particles and atomic nuclei, expressing that the strong interaction does not depend on the electric charge, its quantum number (symbol *T* or *I*) being so assigned that similar particles differing only in charge-related properties can be treated as different states of a single particle.

isostasy /ʌɪˈsɒstəsi/ *noun*. **L19.**
[ORIGIN from ISO- + Greek *stasis* station + -Y[3].]
Chiefly *GEOLOGY*. Equilibrium or stability due to equality of (hydrostatic) pressure; *spec*. the general state of equilibrium thought to exist within the earth's crust, portions of the lithosphere beneath the oceans and continents being supported by underlying denser material that yields or flows under their weight.

isostatic /ʌɪsə(ʊ)ˈstatɪk/ *adjective*. **L19.**
[ORIGIN from ISOSTASY: see -STATIC.]
1 *GEOLOGY*. Pertaining to, produced by, or characterized by isostasy. **L19.**

B. W. SPARKS Large ice sheets caused an isostatic depression of the areas they occupied.

2 Performed under or involving conditions in which equal pressure is applied from all directions. **M20.**
■ **isostatically** *adverb* (***a***) *GEOLOGY* as regards isostasy; by, or as a result of, isostatic forces; (***b***) by pressure applied equally from all directions: **E20.**

isostere /ˈʌɪsə(ʊ)stɪə/ *noun*. In sense 2 also **-ster**. **E20.**
[ORIGIN from ISO- + Greek *stereos* solid.]
1 **a** Chiefly *METEOROLOGY*. A line (imaginary or on a map or diagram) or an imaginary surface connecting points where something (e.g. a body of water, the atmosphere) has equal specific volumes. Cf. ISOPYCNIC *noun*. **E20.** ▸**b** *PHYSICAL CHEMISTRY*. A line on a graph showing the pressure of a gas required to produce a given amount of adsorption at different temperatures. **E20.**
2 *CHEMISTRY*. Each of two or more isosteric molecules or ions (see ISOSTERIC 4). **E20.**

isosteric /ʌɪsə(ʊ)ˈstɛrɪk/ *adjective*. **M19.**
[ORIGIN formed as ISOSTERE + -IC.]
†**1** Having equal atomic volumes. **M–L19.**
2 Relating to equal specific volume. **E20.**
3 *PHYSICAL CHEMISTRY*. Of a heat of adsorption: corresponding to a constant amount of adsorbed material as the pressure and temperature vary (equilibrium being maintained). **E20.**
4 *CHEMISTRY*. Having the same number of valence electrons arranged in a similar manner. **E20.**
■ **isosterism** /-ˈstɪər-/ *noun* (*CHEMISTRY*) the condition of being isosteric **M19.**

isotactic /ʌɪsə(ʊ)ˈtaktɪk/ *adjective*. **M20.**
[ORIGIN from ISO- + Greek *taktos* arranged, ordered + -IC.]
CHEMISTRY. Having or designating a polymeric structure in which all the repeating units have the same stereochemical configuration.
■ **isotacˈticity** *noun* **M20.**

isoteles /ʌɪˈsɒtɪliːz/ *noun*. Pl. same. **M19.**
[ORIGIN from Greek *isotelēs* adjective = paying equal taxes, formed as ISO- + *telos* tax.]
GREEK HISTORY. Any of a favoured class of resident aliens at Athens, who were given civic though not political rights.
■ **isotely** *noun* the condition of an isoteles **M19.**

isotheral /ʌɪˈsɒθ(ə)r(ə)l, ˈʌɪsə(ʊ)θɪər(ə)l/ *adjective & noun*. **M19.**
[ORIGIN formed as ISOTHERE + -AL[1].]
PHYSICAL GEOGRAPHY. ▸**A** *adjective*. Of a line (imaginary or on a map): connecting places having the same mean summer temperature. **M19.**
▸ **B** *noun*. = ISOTHERE. **M19.**

isothere /ˈʌɪsə(ʊ)θɪə/ *noun*. **M19.**
[ORIGIN French *isothère*, formed as ISO- + Greek *there-*, *theros* summer.]
PHYSICAL GEOGRAPHY. An isotheral line; an isotherm of mean summer temperature.

isotherm /ˈʌɪsə(ʊ)θəːm/ *noun.* M19.
[ORIGIN French *isotherme*, formed as ISO- + Greek *thermē* heat, *thermos* hot.]
1 PHYSICAL GEOGRAPHY. A line (imaginary or on a map) passing through points (esp. on the earth's surface) having the same mean temperature; an isothermal line. M19.
2 An isothermal line in a diagram. L19.
Langmuir adsorption isotherm, ***Langmuir isotherm***: see LANGMUIR.
■ **iso'thermic** *adjective* = ISOTHERMAL *adjective* L19.

isothermal /ʌɪsə(ʊ)ˈθəːm(ə)l/ *adjective & noun.* E19.
[ORIGIN formed as ISOTHERM + -AL[1].]
▸ **A** *adjective* **1 a** PHYSICAL GEOGRAPHY. Of a line (imaginary or on a map or chart): connecting places on the earth's surface at which the temperature for a particular period, or the mean annual temperature, is the same. E19. ▸**b** PHYSICS. Designating (imaginary) lines or surfaces of equal temperature in a heated body, as a crystal. M19. ▸**c** PHYSICS. Of a line in a diagram: joining points representing states or conditions of equal temperature. L19.
2 Occurring at a constant temperature; pertaining to or involving constancy of temperature with time. L19.
3 Having the same temperature throughout. E20.
▸ **B** *noun.* An isothermal line, *spec.* in a diagram; an isothermal surface. M19.
■ **isothermally** *adverb* at a constant temperature, without change in temperature L19.

isotonic /ʌɪsə(ʊ)ˈtɒnɪk/ *adjective.* E19.
[ORIGIN from Greek *isotonos* of equal tension or tone, formed as ISO- + *tonos* TONE *noun*: see -IC.]
1 MUSIC. Of a system of tuning: characterized by equal intervals, as equal temperament (see TEMPERAMENT *noun* 9). E19.
2 PHYSIOLOGY. Designating or pertaining to a solution having the same osmotic pressure as some particular solution (esp. that in a cell, or a body fluid). (Foll. by *with*.) L19.
3 PHYSIOLOGY. Of, pertaining to, or designating muscular action in which the muscle contracts more or less freely. L19.
■ **isotonically** *adverb* (PHYSIOLOGY) under isotonic conditions M20. **isotonicity** /-ˈnɪsɪti/ *noun* (*a*) the property or state of being equal in osmotic pressure; (*b*) the osmotic pressure (of the blood): L19.

isotope /ˈʌɪsətəʊp/ *noun.* E20.
[ORIGIN from ISO- + Greek *topos* place (with ref. to occupying the same place in the periodic table).]
1 Each of two or more varieties of a particular chemical element which have different numbers of neutrons in the nucleus, and therefore different relative atomic masses and different nuclear (but the same chemical) properties. Also freq., any distinct kind of atom or nucleus (= NUCLIDE). E20.
2 *spec.* BIOLOGY & BIOCHEMISTRY. A less common, usu. radioactive, isotope of an element as used in tracer or other studies. M20.

Science Mice were labeled . . by injection with 10 μc of isotope.

– COMB.: **isotope dilution** diminution of the concentration of one isotope (or isotopically labelled compound) by the addition of another isotope of the same element (or of the unlabelled compound), esp. as a technique for measuring the amount of an element or compound in a system by introducing a known amount of a different isotope (or a labelled compound) and then measuring its concentration in a sample of the mixture; **isotope effect** a variation in some physical or chemical characteristic between one isotope of an element and another; **isotope shift** a small difference in the wavelength of corresponding spectral lines of different isotopes of an element owing to the different masses and charge distributions of their nuclei.
■ **isotopism** *noun* = ISOTOPY E20.

isotopic /ʌɪsəˈtɒpɪk/ *adjective.* E20.
[ORIGIN from ISOTOPE + -IC.]
1 Of, pertaining to, or being an isotope or isotopes of an element. E20.
isotopic number the number of neutrons in a nucleus minus the number of protons.
2 Of or pertaining to isospin. Orig. & chiefly in ***isotopic spin*** = ISOSPIN. M20.
3 Containing or being a less common or special isotope, e.g. as a label. Cf. ISOTOPE 2. M20.
4 (Of a method) employing or depending on isotopes; obtained by such a method. M20.
■ **isotopically** *adverb* as regards isotopes or isotopic constitution; by means of isotopes or isotopic methods: M20.

isotopy /ʌɪˈsɒtəpi/ *noun.* E20.
[ORIGIN from ISOTOPIC + -Y[3].]
The fact or condition of being isotopic, or of having isotopes.

isotransplantation /ˌʌɪsə(ʊ)transplɑːnˈteɪʃ(ə)n, -trɑː-/ *noun.* E20.
[ORIGIN from ISO- + TRANSPLANTATION.]
MEDICINE & BIOLOGY. †**1** = HOMOTRANSPLANTATION. Only in E20.
2 The operation of transplanting tissue from one individual to another of the same inbred strain. M20.
■ **iso'transplant** *noun* a piece of tissue transplanted from one individual to another of the same inbred strain (cf. ISOGRAFT) M20. **isotrans'planted** *adjective* that is an isotransplant M20.

isotron /ˈʌɪsə(ʊ)trɒn/ *noun.* M20.
[ORIGIN from ISO(TOPE + -TRON.]
PHYSICS. A machine for separating isotopes in the form of ions, by differential deflection in an electric field.

isotropic /ʌɪsə(ʊ)ˈtrɒpɪk/ *adjective.* M19.
[ORIGIN from ISO- + Greek *tropos* turn + -IC.]
Of a material or a body: having the same physical properties in all directions. Of a property: not varying with direction. Opp. ANISOTROPIC.
■ **isotropically** *adverb* equally in all directions L19. **isotropous** /ʌɪsə(ʊ)ˈtrəʊpəs/ *adjective* = ISOTROPIC L19. **isotropy** /ʌɪˈsɒtrəpi/ *noun* the condition or quality of being isotropic L19.

isotype /ˈʌɪsə(ʊ)tʌɪp/ *noun*[1]. L19.
[ORIGIN from ISO- + -TYPE. Cf. Greek *isotupos* shaped alike.]
†**1** BIOLOGY. A type or form of animal or plant common to different countries or regions. L19–E20.
2 MINERALOGY. A mineral which is isotypic with another; an assemblage of isotypic minerals. E20.
3 BOTANY. A duplicate of the holotype. E20.

isotype /ˈʌɪsə(ʊ)tʌɪp/ *noun*[2]. Also **I-**. M20.
[ORIGIN Acronym, from International system of typographic picture education.]
An international picture language devised by the Austrian sociologist Otto Neurath (1882–1945), used esp. to display statistical information in a visual form. Also, an individual pictographic symbol.

isotypic /ʌɪsə(ʊ)ˈtɪpɪk/ *adjective.* E20.
[ORIGIN from ISOTYPE *noun*[1] + -IC.]
MINERALOGY. Having analogous crystal structure and (usu.) chemical composition; exhibiting such similarity. Foll. by *with*.
■ **isotypism** /ʌɪsə(ʊ)ˈtʌɪpɪz(ə)m/, **isotypy** /ˈʌɪsə(ʊ)tʌɪpi/ *nouns* the character or state of being isotypic; isotypic relationship: M20.

isoxazole /ʌɪˈsɒksəzəʊl/ *noun.* L19.
[ORIGIN from ISO- + OXAZOLE.]
CHEMISTRY. An isomer of oxazole, with similar properties; any substituted derivative of this.

isozyme /ˈʌɪsə(ʊ)zʌɪm/ *noun.* M20.
[ORIGIN from ISO- + EN)ZYME.]
BIOCHEMISTRY. = ISOENZYME.
■ **iso'zymic** *adjective* M20.

ISP *abbreviation.*
Internet service provider.

ispaghula /ˌɪspəˈguːlə/ *noun.* Also **ispaghul** /ˈɪspəguːl/. E19.
[ORIGIN Persian, Urdu *ispaġol* from *asp* horse + Urdu *ġol* ear, with allus. to the shape of the leaves.]
A plantain, esp. *Plantago ovata*, native to southern Asia, the dried seeds of which are used medicinally.

Ispahan *adjective & noun* var. of ISFAHAN.

ispravnik /isˈpravɲik, ɪsˈprɑːvnɪk/ *noun.* Pl. **-i** /-i/, **-s**. M19.
[ORIGIN Russian, lit. 'executor'.]
hist. A chief of police in a rural district in tsarist Russia.

I-spy /ʌɪˈspʌɪ/ *noun.* Also (now *rare*) **hi-**, **Hy-** /hʌɪ-/. L18.
[ORIGIN from I *pronoun* + SPY *verb*.]
Any of various children's games involving looking or seeing: orig., a form of hide-and-seek in which the hiders, when discovered (with a cry of 'I spy'), chased the seekers back to a den; now usu., a verbal guessing game in which one participant gives the initial letter of a visible object which the others have to identify.

Israel /ˈɪzreɪl/ *noun.* OE.
[ORIGIN Latin from Greek from Hebrew *Yiśrā'ēl* lit. 'he that strives with God', name conferred on Jacob (*Genesis* 32:29).]
1 The Hebrew nation or people whose descent is traditionally traced from the patriarch Jacob (also called Israel), each of whose twelve sons became the founder of a tribe. Cf. ***children of Israel*** s.v. CHILD *noun*. OE.
2 CHRISTIAN CHURCH. The Christian Church, or true Christians collectively, regarded as the chosen people of God. LME.

Israeli /ɪzˈreɪli/ *adjective & noun.* M20.
[ORIGIN from *Israel* (see below, also the northern kingdom of the ancient Hebrew nation) + -I[2].]
▸ **A** *adjective.* Of or pertaining to Israel, a country in SW Asia with the River Jordan forming part of its eastern border and with a coastline on the Mediterranean Sea. M20.
▸ **B** *noun.* A native or inhabitant of Israel. M20.

Israelite /ˈɪzrəlʌɪt/ *noun & adjective.* LME.
[ORIGIN Late Latin (Vulgate) *Israelita* from Greek *Israēlitēs*, Hebrew *yiśrē'ēlī*, from *Yiśrā'ēl*: see ISRAELI, -ITE[1].]
▸ **A** *noun.* **1** A member of the people of ancient Israel; a member of the Hebrew people; a Jew. LME.
2 CHRISTIAN CHURCH. A Christian regarded as one of the chosen people of God; a true Christian. *arch.* LME.
▸ **B** *adjective.* Of or pertaining to ancient Israel; Jewish. M19.
■ **Israelitic** *adjective* (*rare*) = ISRAELITISH E17. **Israelitish** *adjective* of or pertaining to the Israelites or ancient Israel; Jewish: M16.

issei /ˈiːseɪ/ *noun.* *N. Amer.* Pl. same. M20.
[ORIGIN Japanese, from *ichi* one + *sei* generation.]
A Japanese immigrant to North America. Cf. NISEI, SANSEI.

ISSN *abbreviation.*
International standard serial number.

issuable /ˈɪʃ(j)ʊəb(ə)l, ˈɪsjʊ-/ *adjective.* M16.
[ORIGIN from ISSUE *noun*, *verb* + -ABLE.]
1 LAW. That admits of an issue being taken; with regard to which or during which issue may be joined. M16.
2 Of a writ, summons, etc.: that may be issued; liable or authorized to be issued. M17.
3 Liable to issue as the proceeds of any property, investment, or source of revenue. L17.
■ **issuably** *adverb* in an issuable manner; so as to raise an issue: L18.

issuance /ˈɪʃ(j)ʊəns, ˈɪsjʊ-/ *noun.* *US.* M19.
[ORIGIN from ISSUANT: see -ANCE.]
The action of issuing, putting out, or giving out.

issuant /ˈɪʃ(j)ʊənt, ˈɪsjʊ-/ *adjective.* E17.
[ORIGIN from ISSUE *verb* + -ANT[1], after French pres. pples in *-ant*.]
1 HERALDRY. Esp. of an animal of which the upper half alone is visible: rising from the base of a chief, or (less usually) from another bearing or from the base of an escutcheon. E17.
2 Issuing or proceeding from a place or source. Now *rare*. M17.

issue /ˈɪʃuː, ˈɪsjuː/ *noun.* ME.
[ORIGIN Old French & mod. French *issue*, †*eissue* from Proto-Romance, ult. from Latin EXITUS. In branch VI from the verb.]
▸ **I 1** The action of going, passing, or flowing out; (power of) egress or exit; outgoing, outflow. ME. ▸†**b** A sally, a sortie. L15–L17.

J. TYNDALL The whole volume . . escaped from beneath the ice . . forming a fine arch at its place of issue.

2 MEDICINE. A discharge of blood or other matter from the body, either due to disease or produced surgically by counterirritation; an incision or artificial ulcer made for the purpose of causing such a discharge. Now *rare* or *obsolete*. LME.
3 The termination or close of an action or proceeding or (formerly) a period of time. Now *rare*. L15.

W. ROBERTSON Before the negotiations at Crespy were brought to an issue.

▸ **II 4** A place or means of egress; a way out, an outlet. ME. ▸**b** The point where a body of water flows out; the mouth of a river, the outlet of an inland sea, etc. Also, an outflowing stream. LME.

THACKERAY As my Lady . . passed through one door . . my Lord . . departed by another issue.

▸ **III 5** Produce, proceeds; the profits arising from lands or tenements, amercements, or fines. *obsolete* exc. in LAW. ME. ▸†**b** A fine; an order for levying this. LME–M18.
6 a Offspring, progeny; a child, children; a descendant, descendants. Now chiefly in LAW exc. with ref. to legal succession. LME. ▸†**b** A race, a stock, a breed. Only in 17. ▸**c** A young animal. *rare*. L18.

a E. LINKLATER He married a Miss Harriet Dormer, by whom he had issue Hildebrand, . . Cuthbert, and Anne.

7 The outcome or product *of* a practice or condition. E17. ▸†**b** An action, a deed (in relation to the doer). *rare* (Shakes.). Only in E17.

W. SANDERSON From an Artizan's excellencies, proceed those extravagant varieties . . which are not the issues of an idle brain. **b** SHAKES. *Jul. Caes.* There shall I try, In my oration, how the people take The cruel issue of these bloody men.

▸ **IV 8** The way an action or course of proceedings turns out; the event, a result, a consequence. LME. ▸†**b** The event or fortune happening to a person; luck in an undertaking. LME–M17. ▸†**c** The result of a discussion or examination of a question; a decision, a conclusion. LME–E18. ▸**d** The outcome of an argument, evidence, etc. E17.

R. GRAVES Pharas . . doubted the issue of the day and wished to be in a neutral position. **b** SHAKES. *Ant. & Cl.* Jointing their force 'gainst Caesar, Whose better issue in the war from Italy Upon the first encounter drave them.

▸ **V 9** LAW. The point in question, between contending parties in an action, when one side affirms and the other denies. LME.
10 An important topic or problem for debate or discussion. LME. ▸**b** Personal problems or difficulties. *colloq.* (orig. *US*). L20.

G. F. KENNAN In Britain, the question of relations with Russia was a hotly contested issue. M. SCAMMELL The main issue between them was still whether or not to have children. M. FOOT Their pusillanimity in tackling the great issue of mass unemployment. *Studio Week* On an issue as vital as this there is no room for complacency. **b** S. RUSHDIE We dealt with some issues. We confronted the anger that needed to be faced.

▸ **VI 11** The action of issuing or giving or sending out officially or publicly banknotes, bonds, shares, postage stamps, certificates, etc. M19. ▸**b** The set number or amount of coins, shares, copies of a publication, etc., issued at one time, or distinguished in design, content, or numbers from those issued at another time. M19.

▸**c** An item or amount of something given out or distributed, esp. in the army. **M19.**

Leeds Mercury Larger powers of control should be given to the local authorities over the issue of the licenses. **b** P. HOWARD *The Times* maintained publication and never lost an issue. *What Investment* The City Letter will tell you how . . to invest, which issues to apply for. **c** C. MCCULLOUGH They were dressed in a new issue of jungle green. *attrib.*: *Royal Air Force Journal* I put on a pair of R.A.F. issue shoes. *Guns & Weapons* Whatever they bought had to fire issue ammunition.

12 *BIBLIOGRAPHY.* A subdivision of an edition or of an impression constituting a distinct form of the edition (or impression) sheets, normally indicated by the provision of a new title page, with or without other changes. **E20.**
13 A book issued in a library. Usu. in *pl.*, as an item in statistics of books issued to borrowers. **M20.**

– PHRASES: **at issue** (*a*) *LAW* in the position of parties of which one affirms and the other denies a point; *gen.* (of people or parties) taking opposite sides of a case or contrary views of a matter; (*b*) (of a matter or question) in dispute. ***bank of issue***: see BANK *noun*[3] 3. ***collateral issue***: see COLLATERAL *adjective*. ***false issue***: see FALSE *adjective*. ***force the issue***: see FORCE *verb*[1]. **in the issue** as things turn or turned out; in the event. **issue of fact** *LAW* an issue raised by denying something alleged as a fact. **issue of law** *LAW* an issue about the application of the law to facts assumed or admitted to exist. **join issue** (*a*) *LAW* (chiefly *hist.*)(of the parties) submit an issue jointly for decision; (of one party) accept the issue tendered by the opposite party; (*b*) *transf.* accept or adopt a disputed point as the basis of argument in a controversy; proceed to argument *with* a person *on* a particular point, offered or selected; (*c*) take up a contrary view on or *on* a question. **make an issue of** make a fuss about, turn into a subject of contention. ***rights issue***: see RIGHT *noun*[1]. ***side issue***: see SIDE *noun*. **take issue** = ***join issue*** (b), (c) above. **the issue**, **the whole issue** *slang* everything, the lot.

■ **issueless** *adjective* without issue; *esp.* having no offspring: **LME.**

issue /ˈɪʃuː, ˈɪsjuː/ *verb*. **ME.**
[ORIGIN from the noun.]

▸ **I** *verb intrans.* **1 a** Go or come out; flow out. Freq. foll. by *out*, *forth*, *from*. **ME.** ▸**b** *transf. & fig.* Go or come out of a state or condition; emerge. **L15.** ▸**c** Come out as a branch, branch out. Formerly also, stand or stick out, protrude. **M16.**

G. SANTAYANA Mr. Alden might be seen at church time issuing from his mansion. P. BROOK Words issuing as sounds from people's mouths. C. PETERS An English family nervously issuing forth to see the show. **b** T. BRUGIS He had had many quarrels, and had issued out of them advantagiously. **c** T. HERBERT From his head issue foure great hornes.

2 Proceed as offspring; be born or descended. *obsolete* exc. in *LAW*. **ME.**

AV *2 Kings* 20:18 Thy sonnes that shall issue from thee, which thou shalt beget.

3 Come as proceeds or revenue; accrue. Chiefly in ***issuing out of*** (lands etc.). **ME.**
4 Proceed as from a source; take one's or its origin, be derived, spring. **L15.** ▸**b** Proceed or arise as a result or consequence; result. **L16.**

T. S. ELIOT The kind of faith that issues from despair. **b** G. ORWELL All wisdom, all happiness, all virtue, are held to issue directly from his leadership and inspiration.

5 Come to a result (in a specified way); end or result *in*. **M17.**

DEFOE We have had a hard day's work, but I hope it will issue well. J. A. FROUDE A philosophy which issues in such conclusions.

6 Be sent out officially or publicly; be published. **M17.**

A. CRUMP The number of coins issuing from the mint each year varies considerably.

▸ **II** *verb trans.* **7** Of a containing thing or (formerly) a means of exit or operative force: allow to pass out; let out, emit, discharge. **LME.**

W. TOOKE A mountain . . is continually issuing smoke. R. S. BALL Agents which stored up heat in summer and issued it in winter. *absol.*: SHAKES. *Hen. V* I must perforce compound With mistful eyes, or they will issue too.

†**8** Give birth to; bear (offspring). Usu. in *pass.*, be born, spring. **LME–L17.**
9 Give or send out authoritatively or officially; publish, emit, put into circulation (coins, banknotes, etc.). Formerly freq. foll. by *out*, *forth*. **E17.**

G. VIDAL After the directors' meeting he'll issue a statement. R. L. FOX He issued orders that his army should not plunder the native land. P. ACKROYD A reader's ticket was issued to him.

when-issued: see WHEN *adverb & conjunction*.

10 †**a** Bring to an issue or settlement; settle (a dispute etc.); terminate. Chiefly *US*. **M17–E18.** ▸**b** Give a certain issue or result to; cause to end *in* something. Now *rare*. **L17.**

b H. BUSHNELL The child is sure to be issued finally in a feeling of confirmed disrespect.

11 Give (something) out officially to (a person); supply (a person) officially *with*. **E20.**

J. LE CARRÉ A machine took his money and issued him with a ticket. A. BURGESS We were issued with pint mugs.

■ **issuer** *noun* **L15.** **issuing** *noun* (*a*) the action of the verb; †(*b*) a place of issue, an outlet: **LME.**

ist /ɪst/ *noun*. Chiefly *joc.* & *derog.* **E19.**
[ORIGIN -IST used generically.]
A follower of an ism; a holder of some special doctrine or system of belief; an expert in a particular science, art, or pursuit. Chiefly used in a context suggesting some group of words in *-ist*.

L. MANN He himself wasn't a Socialist or any other ist.

-ist /ɪst/ *suffix*.
[ORIGIN French *-iste*, Latin *-ista*, Greek *-istēs* forming agent nouns from verbs in *-izein*: see -IZE.]
Forming personal nouns, sometimes agent nouns corresp. to verbs in -IZE, as ***antagonist***; more freq. denoting (*a*) a person who makes a systematic study of a particular art or science or who is occupied with something professionally or on a large scale: orig. corresp. to Greek abstract nouns in *-ia*, *-mat-*, etc., as ***chemist***, ***dramatist***, ***economist***, ***geologist***; later formed from nouns of other origins, as ***dentist***, ***pianist***, ***tobacconist***; (*b*) an adherent of a particular system of beliefs, principles, discrimination, etc., corresp. to nouns in -ISM, and often used also as adjectives, as ***Buddhist***, ***Darwinist***, ***idealist***, ***Marxist***, ***positivist***, ***racist***.

-ista /ˈɪstə/ *suffix*. *colloq.* **M20.**
[ORIGIN from the Spanish ending *-ista*, as in SANDINISTA.]
Forming nouns with the sense 'a person associated with a particular activity', freq. with a derogatory force, as ***fashionista***.

istana /ɪˈstɑːnə/ *noun*. **M19.**
[ORIGIN Malay from Sanskrit *āsthāna* place of audience.]
In Malay kingdoms: a ruler's palace.

isthmi *noun pl.* see ISTHMUS.

isthmian /ˈɪsθmɪən, ˈɪstm-, ˈɪsm-/ *adjective*. **E17.**
[ORIGIN from Latin *isthmius* from Greek *isthmios*, + -AN.]
Of or pertaining to an isthmus, *spec.* (**I-**) the Isthmus of Corinth in southern Greece.
■ **isthmic** *adjective* = ISTHMIAN **L16.**

isthmus /ˈɪsθməs, ˈɪstməs, ˈɪsməs/ *noun*. Pl. **-muses**, (*rare*) **-mi** /-mʌɪ/. **M16.**
[ORIGIN Latin from Greek *isthmos*.]
1 *GEOGRAPHY.* A narrow portion of land, enclosed on each side by water and connecting two larger bodies of land; a neck of land. **M16.**
2 *ANATOMY & ZOOLOGY.* A narrow part or organ connecting two larger parts, as the fauces between the mouth and the pharynx, or the band of tissue between the two lobes of the thyroid gland. **E18.**

-istic /ɪstɪk/ *suffix*.
[ORIGIN French *-istique* orig. from Latin *-isticus*, Greek *-istikos*, from *-ikos* -IC added to noun stems in *-istēs* -IST.]
Forming adjectives from nouns in -IST or -ISM, as ***antagonistic***, ***realistic***, or occas. corresp. to verbs in -IZE in the absence of a noun in -IST, as ***characteristic***.

istle *noun* var. of IXTLE.

Istrian /ˈɪstrɪən/ *adjective & noun*. **E17.**
[ORIGIN from *Istria* (see below) + -AN.]
▸ **A** *adjective*. Of or pertaining to Istria, a peninsula near the head of the Adriatic Sea. **E17.**
Istrian marble, **Istrian stone** a fine limestone resembling marble.
▸ **B** *noun*. A native or inhabitant of Istria. **E17.**

ISV *abbreviation*.
COMPUTING. Independent software vendor.

IT *abbreviation*.
Information technology.

it /ɪt/ *noun*. *colloq.* Also **It**. **M20.**
[ORIGIN Abbreviation of ITALIAN *adjective*.]
Italian vermouth. Only in ***gin and it***.

it /ɪt/ *pers. pronoun, 3 sing. neut. subjective (nom.) & objective (dat. & accus.), & possess. adjective*. Orig. †**hit**. Also (before or after certain words, *arch.*) **'t**.
[ORIGIN Old English *hit* neut. nom. & accus. of Germanic demonstr. stem repr. also in HE *pronoun*.]
▸ **A** *pronoun*. **I** Subjective uses.
1 The inanimate or abstract thing or (where sex is not particularized) the animal or young child or (*derog.*) the person previously mentioned, implied, or easily identified. **OE.**

B. NILSON Heat the milk until it is just lukewarm. D. LESSING Rosemary began sobbing, as a child does when it finds a refuge. I. MCEWAN When people shake their heads, . . it can mean all sorts of things. C. DALE I take each day as it comes.

2 The subject of thought, attention, enquiry, etc.; the person or thing in question. (As subj. of BE *verb*, with a noun or pers. pronoun as pred., freq. followed by a rel. clause (often used to emphasize the pred.: cf. sense 4c below) or with such a clause implied, in statements or questions regarding identity.) **OE.** ▸†**b** There *is* etc. **ME–E17.** ▸**c** Introducing a ballad etc.: the subject of the song or tale. *arch.* **E17.**

SCOTT FITZGERALD Some one was walking in the kitchen, and he knew by the light footfall that it was not his wife. T. ALLBEURY What is it you want? **b** C. MARLOWE Cousin, it is no dealing with him now. **c** COLERIDGE It is an ancient mariner.

3 As subj. of an impers. verb or impers. statement, without ref. to any agent, in statements of weather, the time of day, the season of the year, a state of affairs, a physical or mental sensation, etc. **OE.** ▸**b** In statements as to amount of space, distance, or length of time. **L16.**

T. HARDY It being summer time the miller was much occupied with business. OED It is all over with poor Jack. E. TAYLOR It's not yet ten o'clock. J. HIGGINS It was suddenly very quiet in the preparation room. **b** *News Chronicle* It is a long way from 1937.

it blows hard, ***it rains***, ***it thunders***, etc.

4 Placed before the verb as anticipatory subj., when the logical subj. of the verb is an inf. phr., a clause (esp. after a verb in *pass.*), or a sentence. **OE.** ▸**b** As anticipatory subj., repr. the topic of a sentence, when the logical subj. is a noun, esp. with attributes. Now *poet.*, *rhet.*, & *colloq.* **OE.** ▸**c** In a periphrastic introductory clause with *be*, bringing into prominence an adverbial adjunct or the subj. of a clause. **ME.**

TENNYSON We die—does it matter when? SCOTT FITZGERALD It disturbed him that her smile could have no root in mirth. D. LESSING It's the landlord's business to fix the rent. I. MURDOCH Mrs. Witcher, it was said, had once been a shorthand typist. R. P. JHABVALA It may be due to the ghostly light that she looks like a ghost. J. SIMMS It is not easy to live with a genius. **b** J. L. HERLIHY It was a disturbing spectacle, this crazy-eyed searcher flailing his arms. **c** OED It is not everybody who can afford to take a holiday. *Proverb*: It's an ill wind that blows nobody any good.

▸ **II** Objective uses.
5 As obj. (direct, indirect, or after prepositions): the thing etc. (see sense 1 above) previously mentioned, implied, or easily identified. **OE.** ▸**b** Used as anticipatory obj. when the logical obj. is an inf. phr. or a clause. Cf. sense 4 above. **L16.** ▸**c** Itself: direct & indirect objective. *arch.* exc. after prepositions. **L16.**

D. H. LAWRENCE He folded his rain-coat and laid it along the . . ledge. J. STEINBECK He bought a gallon of red wine and drank most of it himself. D. WELCH He kissed the puppy's nose and cuddled it in his arms. J. D. SALINGER I can't always pray when I feel like it. C. LASSALLE Now come on . . give it a go! C. DALE He called her 'love' as if he meant it. **b** T. HARDY She thought it best to secure a protector of some kind. M. DICKENS I take it your mother has gone to America. **c** SHAKES. *John* My heart hath one poor string to stay it by. OED The tree draws to it all the moisture from the adjacent ground.

6 As a vague or indefinite obj. of a trans. verb, after a preposition, etc. Also as obj. of a verb which is predominantly intrans., giving the same meaning as the intrans. use, and as obj. of many verbs formed (freq. as nonce words) from nouns meaning 'act the character, use the thing, indicated'. **M16.**

MILTON Trip it as ye go On the light fantastick toe. J. K. JEROME We decided that we would . . inn it, and pub it when it was wet. J. MASTERS We . . lord it over the country entirely by the good will of the average native. J. I. M. STEWART Make it snappy. Taxi's waiting. M. GEE Watch it, Mum. You'll knock off all the needles.

In imprecations: ***damn it***, ***hang it***, etc.

▸ **III 7** As antecedent to a relative expressed or understood: that (which), the one (that). *rare*. **ME.**

AV *Isa.* 51:9 Art thou not it that hath cut Rahab?

▸ **IV 8** Sexual intercourse. Cf. ***do it*** (a) s.v. DO *verb*. Now *colloq.* **E17.**
9 In emphatic *pred.* use: the actual thing required or expected; the acme. **M19.**

H. M. SMITH I have some new plus-fours which are 'it'.

10 In *pred.* use: in children's games, the player who has to catch others. **M19.**
11 Sex appeal. *colloq.* **E20.**

Bystander A film star who has proved to producers . . that she is blessed with that undefinable quality called 'It'.

– PHRASES ETC.: (A selection of cross-refs. only is included.) ***at it***: see AT *preposition*. ***be for it***: see FOR *preposition*. ***get it***: see GET *verb*. ***go for it***: see GO *verb*. ***have it in for***: see HAVE *verb*. ***hit it off***: see HIT *verb*. ***in it***: see IN *preposition*. ***it is said*** etc.: see SAY *verb*[1]. ***it is told*** etc.: see TELL *verb*. ***it says*** etc.: see SAY *verb*[1]. ***it tells*** etc.: see TELL *verb*. **'taint** *non-standard* it ain't, it isn't. **that's it** *colloq.* (*a*) there is no more to it than that; (*b*) = ***this is it*** below. **this is it** *colloq.* (*a*) the event previously spoken about or feared is about to happen; (*b*) that is the difficulty. **'tis** it is. **'twas** it was. **'twere** it were. **'twill** it will. **'twould** it would. ***watch it***: see WATCH *verb*. ***with it***: see WITH *preposition*. ***worth it***: see WORTH *adjective*.

▸ **B** *possess. adjective*. = ITS *possess. adjective*. Now *dial.* **LME.**

A. GOLDING It hath no forme of it owne.

It. *abbreviation*.
Italian.

ITA *abbreviation*.
1 Independent Television Authority.
2 Initial teaching alphabet.

ita /ˈɪtə/ *noun*. Also **eta** /ˈiːtə/. **M19**.
[ORIGIN Arawak *ite*.]
(More fully ***ita palm***) a tropical American fan palm, *Mauritia flexuosa*; a drink made from its fermented sap.

itabirite /ɪˈtabɪrʌɪt/ *noun*. **M19**.
[ORIGIN from *Itabira*, a town in Minas Gerais, Brazil + -ITE[1].]
PETROGRAPHY. An iron-rich slate consisting chiefly of layers of quartz and iron oxides.

itacism /ˈiːtəsɪz(ə)m/ *noun*. **M19**.
[ORIGIN mod. Latin *itacismus*, from Greek *ēta* ETA *noun*[1], prob. after Latin *iotacismus*: see IOTACISM.]
LINGUISTICS. In Greek, the pronunciation of the vowel eta as, or the reduction of various vowels and diphthongs to, the sound /iː/ (represented in classical Greek by the letter iota); (an instance of) the erroneous substitution in Greek manuscripts of iota for another vowel or diphthong. Cf. IOTACISM.
■ **itacist** /-sɪst/ *noun* a person who practises or favours itacism **M19**. **itacistic** /-ˈsɪstɪk/ *adjective* characterized by itacism **L19**.

itacolumite /ɪtəˈkɒljʊmʌɪt/ *noun*. **M19**.
[ORIGIN from *Itacolumi*, a mountain in Minas Gerais, Brazil + -ITE[1].]
PETROGRAPHY. A schistose quartzite, usu. containing mica, chlorite, and talc, sometimes forming flexible slabs.

itaconic /ɪtəˈkɒnɪk/ *adjective*. **M19**.
[ORIGIN from partial anagram of ACONITINE (involved in its orig. preparation) + -IC.]
CHEMISTRY. ***itaconic acid***, a crystalline acid, $CH_2{=}C(COOH)CH_2COOH$, obtained in fermentation of sugar by the mould *Aspergillus terreus*; methylenesuccinic acid.
■ **itaconate** /ɪˈta-/ *noun* a salt or ester of itaconic acid **M19**.

I

ital. *abbreviation*.
Italic (type).

Italian /ɪˈtaljən/ *noun & adjective*. **LME**.
[ORIGIN Italian *italiano*, from *Italia* Italy: see -AN.]
▸ **A** *noun*. **1** A native or inhabitant of Italy, a country in southern Europe comprising a peninsula jutting into, and offshore islands in, the Mediterranean Sea. **LME**.
2 The Romance language of Italy. **L15**.
3 *ellipt*. A thing or (kind of) article originating in Italy; *spec*. (***a***) Italian cloth; (***b***) Italian vermouth. **L19**.
▸ **B** *adjective*. Of or pertaining to Italy, its people, or its modern Romance language; native to or originating or produced in Italy. **E16**.
Italian cypress: see CYPRESS *noun*[1] 1. **Italian earth** the colour sienna. **Italian garden**: characterized by clipped trees, box-edged beds of flowers, paved paths, statues, fountains, etc., and often arranged in terraces. **Italian hand**, **Italian handwriting** *arch*. the kind of handwriting first developed in Italy and now current in almost all countries using the Roman alphabet. **Italian iron** (*obsolete* exc. *hist*.) a cylindrical iron used for fluting or crimping lace, frills, etc. **Italian millet** foxtail millet. **Italian opening** *CHESS*: in which each player moves successively the king's pawn, the knight on a dark square, and the king's bishop to the fourth rank; also called ***Giuoco Piano***. **Italian paste** the dough from which macaroni and vermicelli are made. **Italian pink** = ***Dutch pink*** s.v. DUTCH *adjective*. **Italian quilting**: manufactured in a design composed of parallel lines of stitching. **Italian roof** a hip roof. ***Italian* RYEGRASS**. **Italian stitch** a form of cross stitch. **Italian vermouth** a sweet kind of vermouth. **Italian warehouse** a shop etc. supplying Italian groceries, fruits, olive oil, etc.
■ **Italiaˈnesque** *adjective* Italian in style or character **M19**. **Italianity** /ɪtalɪˈanɪti/ *noun* Italian quality or character **L19**. **Italianly** *adverb* (*rare*) **L16**.

Italianate /ɪˈtaljəneɪt, -nət/ *adjective*. **L16**.
[ORIGIN Italian *italianato*, formed as ITALIAN: see -ATE[2].]
Made Italian; (that has become or been made) Italian in character or appearance.

Italianate /ɪˈtaljəneɪt/ *verb trans*. Long *rare*. **M16**.
[ORIGIN formed as ITALIAN: see -ATE[3].]
Make Italian; Italianize. Orig. & chiefly as ***Italianated*** *ppl adjective*.

Italianise *verb* var. of ITALIANIZE.

Italianism /ɪˈtaljənɪz(ə)m/ *noun*. **L16**.
[ORIGIN from ITALIAN + -ISM.]
1 An Italian practice or characteristic; an Italian expression or idiom. **L16**.
2 Italian spirit or taste; attachment to Italian ideas; sympathy with Italy. **E19**.

Italianist /ɪˈtaljənɪst/ *noun & adjective*. **L16**.
[ORIGIN from ITALIAN + -IST.]
▸ **A** *noun*. **1** An Italianate person. *rare*. **L16**.
2 An expert in or student of Italian language, literature, and culture. **M20**.
▸ **B** *adjective*. Of, pertaining to, or characterized by Italianism. **L19**.

Italianize /ɪˈtaljənʌɪz/ *verb*. Also **-ise**. **L16**.
[ORIGIN French *italianiser*, formed as ITALIAN: see -IZE.]
1 *verb trans*. Make Italian in character or style. **L16**.
2 *verb intrans*. Practise Italian styles or habits; become Italian in character, tastes, etc. **M17**.
■ **Italianiˈzation** *noun* **M19**. **Italianizer** *noun* **M19**.

Italic /ɪˈtalɪk/ *adjective & noun*. **LME**.
[ORIGIN Latin *Italicus* from Greek *Italikos*, from *Italia* Italy from Latin: see -IC.]
▸ **A** *adjective*. †**1** = ITALIAN *adjective*. **LME–M18**.
2 a *ARCHITECTURE*. = COMPOSITE *adjective* 2. **M16**. ▸**b** *CLASSICAL HISTORY*. Of or pertaining to the Greek colonies in southern Italy, *esp*. of or pertaining to the Pythagorean and Eleatic schools of philosophy founded there in the 6th cent. BC. **M17**. ▸**c** *hist*. Of or pertaining to ancient Italy or its peoples; *spec*. of or pertaining to parts of ancient Italy other than Rome. **L17**.
3 (Usu. **i-**.) Of printed or handwritten characters: generally cursive and sloping to the right. Also, of type, printing, or handwriting: composed of such characters. **E17**. ▸**b** Of handwriting: modelled on the style used by professional scribes in 16th-cent. Italy. **M20**.
4 *LINGUISTICS*. Of, pertaining to, or characteristic of Italic (see sense B.3 below). **M19**.
▸ **B** *noun*. **1** A member of an Italic school of philosophy (see sense A.2b above). **L16**.
2 (Usu. **i-**.) In *pl*. & *sing*. Italic characters (in printing now usu. employed for emphasis, in titles of works, or to distinguish a word or phrase, esp. a foreign one). **L17**.
3 A branch of the Indo-European language family including Osco-Umbrian, Latin, and the Romance languages; *spec*. (***a***) the ancient languages of this group; (***b***) Osco-Umbrian. **L19**.
■ **Italicism** /-sɪz(ə)m/ *noun* (*rare*) an Italian expression or idiom **L18**.

italicize /ɪˈtalɪsʌɪz/ *verb trans*. Also **-ise**. **L18**.
[ORIGIN from ITALIC + -IZE.]
Print in italics; (in writing) underscore with a single line, to indicate characters to be printed in italic. Now also *fig*., pronounce with emphasis.

> COLERIDGE The italicized words *if I can*. C. BEATON Ordinarily unpretentious men and women . . started to italicize certain phrases by their inflections.

■ **italiciˈzation** *noun* **L19**.

Italiot /ɪˈtalɪət/ *noun & adjective*. **M17**.
[ORIGIN Greek *Italiōtēs*, from *Italia* Italy: see -OT[2].]
▸ **A** *noun*. A person of Greek descent living in ancient Italy. **M17**.
▸ **B** *adjective*. Of or pertaining to the Greek colonies in ancient southern Italy. **M17**.

Italo- /ˈɪtələʊ, ɪˈtaləʊ/ *combining form*.
[ORIGIN from ITAL(IAN + -O-.]
Forming adjective and noun combs. with the meaning 'Italian (and) —' as ***Italo-Byzantine***, ***Italo-Grecian***.
■ **Italo-ˈCeltic** *adjective & noun* (of or pertaining to) a postulated common parent language of Italian and Celtic **L19**. **Italophil(e)** *adjective & noun* (a person who is) friendly to Italy or fond of Italy and Italian things **E20**. **Italoˈphobia** *noun* dread or dislike of Italy and Italian things **E20**.

itatartaric /ɪtətɑːˈtarɪk/ *adjective*. **L19**.
[ORIGIN from ITA(CONIC + TARTARIC.]
CHEMISTRY. ***itatartaric acid***, a crystalline acid, dihydroxyitaconic acid, $CH_2OH{\cdot}C(OH)(COOH){\cdot}CH_2\,COOH$, obtained as a by-product in the production of itaconic acid by fermentation.
■ **itaˈtartrate** *noun* a salt or ester of itatartaric acid **L19**.

ITC *abbreviation*. *hist*.
Independent Television Commission.

itch /ɪtʃ/ *noun*. **OE**.
[ORIGIN from the verb.]
1 A sensation of irritation in the skin, causing a desire to scratch or rub it; *spec*. (now *rare*) the skin disease scabies. Also (with specifying words), any of various skin diseases of which itching is a symptom. **OE**.

> M. PIERCY I feel a cumulative dissatisfaction like an itch between my shoulder blades.

barber's itch, ***dhobi itch***, ***grocer's itch***, ***ground itch***, ***swimmer's itch***, etc.
2 *fig*. A restless or urgent desire (*for*, *to do*); a hankering (*after*). **M16**.

> G. M. TREVELYAN Leaders of the Eighteenth Century were not harassed by the perpetual itch to make money.

SEVEN YEAR ***itch***.
– COMB.: **itch mite** a parasitic acarid mite, *Sarcoptes scabiei*, which burrows in the human skin, causing scabies; **itchweed** *N. Amer*. false hellebore, *Veratrum viride*.

itch /ɪtʃ/ *verb*.
[ORIGIN Old English *ġiċċan*, *gyċċan*, corresp. to Old Saxon *jukkian*, Middle Dutch & mod. Dutch *jeuken*, Old High German *jucchen* (German *jucken*), from West Germanic.]
1 *verb intrans*. Experience an itch of the skin; (of a part of the body) be the site of an itch, cause a desire to scratch or rub. **OE**.

> H. G. WELLS You scratch the tip of your nose because it itches.

2 *verb intrans*. Have a restless or urgent desire (*to do*, *for*). **ME**.

> E. NESBIT Young wives come in, a-smiling, grave, With secrets that they itch to tell.

itching ears (people with) a restless desire to hear something new. **itching palm** avarice.

3 *verb trans*. Cause to itch. **L16**.

> R. CAMPBELL The thick super-salty water of the Mediterranean, which tires and itches the naked eye.

itching /ˈɪtʃɪŋ/ *noun*. **ME**.
[ORIGIN from ITCH *verb* + -ING[1].]
1 A feeling of irritation in the skin, causing a desire to scratch or rub. **ME**.
2 *fig*. A restless desire or hankering, = ITCH *noun* 2. **ME**.

itchy /ˈɪtʃi/ *adjective*. Now *colloq*. **M16**.
[ORIGIN from ITCH *noun* + -Y[1].]
Affected by itching or an itch; *fig*. restless.
■ **itchiness** *noun* **L19**.

ite /ʌɪt/ *noun*. **M19**.
[ORIGIN Use as independent word of -ITE[1]. Cf. ISM.]
A person or thing that is or may be designated by a noun in *-ite*.

-ite /ʌɪt/ *suffix*[1].
[ORIGIN Corresp. to French *-ite*, Latin *-ita* (*-ites*), from Greek *-itēs*.]
1 Forming nouns and adjectives denoting (***a***) a native of a place, a member of a people, etc., as ***Gibeonite***, ***Levite***, ***Stagirite***, etc.; (***b***) (freq. *derog*.) a follower of a person, doctrine, or school, as ***Irvingite***, ***Luddite***, ***Pre-Raphaelite***, ***Trotskyite***, etc.
2 a *PALAEONTOLOGY*. Forming names of fossil organisms, as ***ammonite***, ***belemnite***, ***echinite***, etc. ▸**b** Forming names of minerals and rocks, comprising names of ancient origin, as ***anthracite***, ***chlorite***, ***haematite***, etc., and many mod. formations, as ***andesite***, ***brewsterite***, ***cobaltite***, ***carbonatite***, ***labradorite***, etc. (often superseding names in *-ine* etc.). ▸**c** Forming names of tektites from different regions, as ***australite***, ***indochinite***, etc.
3 *ANATOMY & ZOOLOGY*. Forming names of constituent parts, segments, or joints of a body or organ, as ***coxopodite***, ***somite***, etc.
4 *CHEMISTRY*. **a** Forming names of substances, esp. explosives and other commercial products, as ***cordite***, ***dynamite***, ***ebonite***, ***vulcanite***, etc., and (formerly) sugars and other polyhydric compounds, as ***dulcite***, ***inosite***, ***mannite***, etc. (often superseded by names in *-itol*). ▸**b** Forming names of salts or esters of acids ending in *-ous*, as ***nitrite***, ***sulphite***, etc.

-ite /ʌɪt/ *suffix*[2].
[ORIGIN from Latin *-itus*, pa. ppl ending of verbs in *-ire*, *-ere*, or from corresp. Proto-Romance *-ito*.]
In adjectives, nouns, and verbs derived from Latin or Romance, as ***erudite***, ***composite***, ***favourite***; ***appetite***; ***expedite***, ***unite***.

item /ˈʌɪtəm/ *adverb*, *noun*, & *verb*. **LME**.
[ORIGIN Latin = just so, similarly, moreover, from *ita* thus, so.]
▸ **A** *adverb*. Likewise, also. Chiefly used to introduce and draw attention to a new statement, particular, or entry, esp. in a list or formal document. **LME**.

> A. PRICE Item, one emerald-and-diamond necklace, . . item one diamond tiara.

▸ **B** *noun*. **1** Formerly, a statement, maxim, or warning, orig. such as was introduced by the word 'item' (see sense A. above). Now (*US dial*.), an intimation, a hint. **M16**.
2 An individual thing, article, or unit included in a set, list, computation, or total, as (***a***) an entry or thing entered in an account or register; (***b***) a detail or category of expenditure; (***c***) a news story; (***d***) a member of a set of linguistic units. **L16**. ▸**b** *COMPUTING*. Any quantity of data treated as a unit, e.g. a field, a group of fields, or a record. **M20**.

> R. INGALLS On a news programme . . that item had not been heard by other people. M. SCAMMELL A few items of warm clothing could make all the difference. M. MEYER He missed Swedish food, asking friends to send him such items as split peas and dill. D. ADAMS I think you will find an item in the bill to that effect.

▸ **C** *verb trans*. Itemize. Now *rare*. **E17**.

itemize /ˈʌɪtəmʌɪz/ *verb trans*. Also **-ise**. **M19**.
[ORIGIN from ITEM *noun* + -IZE.]
Set down by items; enter as an item; specify the items of (a bill etc.).

> J. KRANTZ She knew there were other expenses . . but couldn't itemize them off-hand. B. BETTELHEIM The idea that if you . . adhere to certain itemized instructions, certain results will automatically follow.

■ **itemiˈzation** *noun* the action of itemizing something; an instance of this: **L19**. **itemizer** *noun* **L19**.

iter /ˈɪtə, ˈʌɪtə/ *noun*. Pl. **iters**, **itinera** /ʌɪˈtɪn(ə)rə/. **L16**.
[ORIGIN Latin = journey, way, road.]
1 *hist*. A circuit of an itinerant judge, esp. a justice in eyre. Formerly also, a record of proceedings during a circuit. **L16**.
2 A Roman road or line of travel. **M18**.
3 *ANATOMY*. A narrow passage; *spec*. the cerebral aqueduct. *arch*. **L19**.

iterant /ˈɪtər(ə)nt/ *adjective*. **E17**.
[ORIGIN Latin *iterant-* pres. ppl stem of *iterare*: see ITERATE *verb*, -ANT[1].]
That iterates or repeats something; repeating, echoing.

■ **iterance** *noun* iteration, repetition E17. **iterancy** *noun* the condition of being iterant; iterance: L19.

iterate /ˈɪtərət/ *noun*. E20.
[ORIGIN from the verb, or from Latin *iteratus* pa. pple of *iterare*: see ITERATE *verb*, -ATE[1].]
MATH. A quantity arrived at by iteration.

iterate /ˈɪtəreɪt/ *verb*. M16.
[ORIGIN Latin *iterat-* pa. ppl stem of *iterare* repeat, from *iterum* again: see -ATE[3].]
1 *verb trans.* Do (something) over again; repeat (an action). Now *rare*. M16.
2 *verb trans.* Say again, state repeatedly. M16.
3 *verb intrans. MATH.* Employ iteration; make repeated use of a formula by substituting in it each time the result of the previous application. M20.

iteration /ɪtəˈreɪʃ(ə)n/ *noun*. LME.
[ORIGIN Latin *iteratio(n-)*, formed as ITERATE *verb*: see -ATION.]
1 a (A) repetition of an action, process, or performance. LME. ▸**b** *MATH.* The repetition of an operation on its product; *esp.* the repeated use of a formula which provides a closer approximation to the solution of a given equation when an approximate solution is substituted in the formula, so that a series of successively closer approximations is obtained; (a single application of) such a formula. E20.
2 The repetition of something said. M16.

iterative /ˈɪtərətɪv/ *adjective & noun*. L15.
[ORIGIN French *itératif*, *-ive* (in sense 1) and late Latin *iterativus* (in sense 2), formed as ITERATE *verb*: see -IVE.]
▸ **A** *adjective* **1 a** Characterized by repeating or being repeated. L15. ▸**b** *MATH.* Of the nature of, employing, or resulting from iteration. E20.
2 *GRAMMAR.* Denoting repetition of action; frequentative. E19.
▸ **B** *noun. LINGUISTICS.*
1 An iterative verb or aspect. M19.
2 A word expressing repetition of an action, sound, etc. M20.
■ **iteratively** *adverb* M19. **iterativeness** *noun* M19.

iteroparous /ɪtərə(ʊ)parəs/ *adjective*. M20.
[ORIGIN from Latin *iterum* again + -O- + -PAROUS.]
BIOLOGY. Of or designating a species or organism which reproduces more than once during its lifetime. Cf. SEMELPAROUS.
■ **iteroparity** /-ˈparɪti/ *noun* the state or condition of being iteroparous M20.

It girl /ˈɪt gəːl/ *noun. colloq.* E20.
[ORIGIN from IT *pers. pronoun* + GIRL *noun*: coined by the US screenwriter Elinor Glyn with ref. to the actress Clara Bow and her roles in such films as *It* (1927).]
A glamorous, successful young woman, now *spec.* one who has achieved celebrity because of her socialite lifestyle.

I-Thou /ʌɪˈðaʊ/ *adjective*. M20.
[ORIGIN German *ich-du*, from *ich* I + *du* you (sing.).]
Of a personal relationship (esp. with God): formed by direct encounter.

ithyphallic /ɪθɪˈfalɪk/ *noun & adjective*. E17.
[ORIGIN Late Latin *ithyphallicus* from Greek *ithuphallikos*, from *ithuphallos*, from *ithus* straight + *phallos* PHALLUS: see -IC.]
▸ **A** *noun*. A poem in ithyphallic metre. Also, an obscene or sexually explicit poem. E17.
▸ **B** *adjective*. **1** Of a cult, ceremony, carved figure, etc.: associated with or characterized by (the symbol of) a phallus, esp. in the context of Bacchic festivals in ancient Greece; *spec.* composed in the metre of the Bacchic hymns (the trochaic dimeter brachycatalectic). L18.
2 Grossly indecent, obscene. M19.

ithyphallus /ɪθɪˈfaləs/ *noun*. L19.
[ORIGIN Greek *ithuphallos*: see ITHYPHALLIC.]
A phallus.

Iti /ˈʌɪtʌɪ/ *noun & adjective. slang. derog.* Also **Itie**, **Ity**. M20.
[ORIGIN Dim. of ITALIAN or alt. of EYETIE.]
(An) Italian. Cf. EYETIE.

-itic /ɪtɪk/ *suffix*.
[ORIGIN Corresp. to French *-itique*, Latin *-iticus*, Greek *-itikos*: see -IC.]
1 Forming adjectives from nouns in -ITE[1], as ***Capernaitic***, ***dendritic***, ***Semitic***.
2 Forming adjectives and nouns from nouns esp. in -ITIS, or from other bases, as ***arthritic***, ***diphtheritic***, ***gabbroitic***, ***Nigritic***.

Itie *noun & adjective* var. of ITI.

itinera *noun pl.* see ITER.

itineracy /ɪˈtɪn(ə)rəsi, ʌɪ-/ *noun*. E19.
[ORIGIN from ITINER(ATE *adjective* + -ACY.]
= ITINERANCY.

itinerancy /ɪˈtɪn(ə)r(ə)nsi, ʌɪ-/ *noun*. L18.
[ORIGIN from ITINERANT: see -ANCY.]
1 Itinerant preaching or ministry, esp. as practised on Methodist circuits. L18.
2 The state or condition of being itinerant; a journey from place to place. E19.

itinerant /ɪˈtɪn(ə)r(ə)nt, ʌɪ-/ *adjective & noun*. L16.
[ORIGIN Late Latin *itinerant-* pres. ppl stem of *itinerari*, from Latin *itiner-*, *iter*: see ITINERARY *adjective*, -ANT[1].]
▸ **A** *adjective*. **1** Of a judge: travelling from place to place on circuit. L16.
2 Journeying; travelling or pertaining to travel, esp. in the course of selling or other work; (of a Methodist etc. minister) preaching in a circuit. M17.

A. THWAITE He decided to make his living as an itinerant painter . . and travelled England on foot.

3 Movable from place to place. L17.
▸ **B** *noun*. A person who travels from place to place, esp. as a preacher, actor, etc. M17.

itinerarium /ɪˌtɪnəˈrɛːrɪəm/ *noun*. Pl. **-ria** /-rɪə/. E18.
[ORIGIN Late Latin: see ITINERARY *noun*.]
1 *SURGERY.* A rod used in lithotomy. *rare*. (Dicts.). E18.
2 = ITINERARY *noun* 2, 3. M18.

itinerary /ʌɪˈtɪn(ə)rəri, ɪ-/ *noun*. LME.
[ORIGIN Late Latin *itinerarium* use as noun of neut. of *itinerarius*: see ITINERARY *adjective*, -ARY[1].]
1 A line or course of travel; a route. LME.

B. LOPEZ They moved nomadically . . according to the itineraries of the animals they pursued.

2 A record or account of a journey. L15.
3 a A book describing a route or routes and providing detailed information for travellers; a guidebook. M16. ▸**b** A sketch of a proposed route; a travel plan. M19.

b *Sunday Express* If you've plenty of time and a flexible itinerary, do as the locals do, risk standby.

4 An itinerant. *rare*. E18.

itinerary /ʌɪˈtɪn(ə)rəri, ɪ-/ *adjective*. M16.
[ORIGIN Late Latin *itinerarius*, from Latin *itiner-*, *iter* journey, way, road: see -ARY[1].]
1 Of or pertaining to a journey, travelling, or (the description) of roads. M16.
2 = ITINERANT *adjective*. E17.

†**itinerate** *adjective*. E17–M18.
[ORIGIN formed as ITINERATE *verb*: see -ATE[2].]
= ITINERANT *adjective*.

itinerate /ɪˈtɪn(ə)reɪt, ʌɪ-/ *verb*. E17.
[ORIGIN Late Latin *itinerat-* pa. ppl stem of *itinerari*: see ITINERANT, -ATE[3].]
1 *verb intrans.* Travel from place to place. E17. ▸**b** Travel from place to place preaching, esp. on a Methodist circuit. L18.
2 *verb trans.* Journey through. *rare*. M19.

itineration /ɪˌtɪnəˈreɪʃ(ə)n, ʌɪ-/ *noun*. E17.
[ORIGIN from ITINERATE *verb* + -ATION.]
The action of itinerating; a preaching or lecturing tour.

-ition /ˈɪʃ(ə)n/ *suffix*.
[ORIGIN Repr. French *-ition*, Latin *-itio(n-)* suffix forming nouns from verbs with pa. ppl stem in *-it-*: cf. -ION.]
Forming nouns, chiefly with the senses of -ATION, as ***audition***, ***disposition***, ***rendition***, ***volition***, etc.

-itious /ˈɪʃəs/ *suffix*[1].
[ORIGIN Late Latin *-itius* alt. of Latin *-icius*: cf. -OUS.]
Forming adjectives, as ***adventitious***, ***factitious***, ***fictitious***, ***supposititious***, etc.

-itious /ˈɪʃəs/ *suffix*[2].
[ORIGIN Repr. Latin *-itiosus*, from *-itio(n-)* -ITION + *-osus* -OUS: cf. -IOUS.]
Forming adjectives corresp. chiefly to nouns in *-ition*, as ***ambitious***, ***nutritious***, ***superstitious***, etc.

itis /ˈʌɪtɪs/ *noun*. E20.
[ORIGIN Use as independent word of -ITIS.]
A condition or disease (that may be) designated by a word ending in *-itis*.

Canadian Magazine He was home in six months with . . 'every kind of "itis" you could think of.'

-itis /ˈʌɪtɪs/ *suffix*.
[ORIGIN Greek suffix forming the fem. of adjectives ending in *-itēs*, combined with (expressed or implied) *nosos* disease, to form names of diseases affecting a specified part of the body.]
Forming nouns denoting diseased states or symptoms, esp. involving inflammation, affecting particular parts of the body, as ***appendicitis***, ***bronchitis***, ***peritonitis***, ***tonsillitis***, etc. Now also occas. (*colloq.*) forming nouns denoting a state of mind or tendency that is compared to a disease, as ***telephonitis***.

ITN *abbreviation*.
Independent Television News.

ITO *abbreviation*.
International Trade Organization.

-itol /ɪtɒl/ *suffix*.
[ORIGIN from -ITE[1] + -OL.]
CHEMISTRY. Forming the names of polyhydric alcohols, as ***hexitol***.

-itous /ɪtəs/ *suffix*.
[ORIGIN from -IT(Y + -OUS, from or after French *-iteux*, Latin *-itosus*.]
Forming adjectives corresp. to nouns ending in *-ity*, as ***calamitous***, ***felicitous***, ***gratuitous***, ***iniquitous***, etc.

its /ɪts/ *possess. pronoun. rare*. E17.
[ORIGIN Absol. use of ITS *adjective* (in mod. usage also classed as a.]
Its one(s), that or those belonging or pertaining to it.

its /ɪts/ *possess. adjective* (in mod. usage also classed as a *determiner*), *3 sing. neut.* Also **it's** (now considered *erron.*). L16.
[ORIGIN from IT *pronoun* + -'S[1].]
Of it; of itself; which belongs or pertains to it(self).

G. M. TREVELYAN Country house life, with its hunting and shooting. I. MURDOCH The question had arisen of its being sold. G. VIDAL Henry appeared with the telephone on its extension cord.

itself /ɪtˈsɛlf/ *pronoun*. OE.
[ORIGIN from IT *pronoun* + SELF *adjective* (but long interpreted as SELF *noun*).]
▸ **I** *refl.* **1** Refl. form (indirect, direct, & after prepositions) of IT *pronoun*: (to, for, etc.) the thing in question. OE.

I. MURDOCH A sturdy foot, which had begun to insert itself in the crack of the door. J. C. POWYS His family had completely ruined itself in its service of the king. E. H. GOMBRICH If something is only designed to fit its purpose we can let beauty look after itself.

by itself apart from its surroundings; automatically, spontaneously. **in itself** considered separately from other things. ***speak for itself***: see SPEAK *verb*. ***thing in itself***: see THING *noun*[1].
▸ **II** *emphatic*. **2** In apposition to a noun (subjective or objective): that particular thing, the very thing, that thing alone. OE.

I. MURDOCH The Abbey itself is quite hidden in trees. C. RAYNER The big table upon which was spread a white cloth, itself covered with an array of instruments. H. JAMES She was kindness itself to me.

3 (Not appositional.) It; not something else. L16.

OED The dear old place looked just itself.

itsy-bitsy /ɪtsɪˈbɪtsi/ *adjective. colloq.* M20.
[ORIGIN from childish form of LITTLE *adjective* + BITSY *adjective*: see -SY.]
Small, (charmingly) insubstantial, tiny. Also (*derog.*) fiddly, arty-crafty, twee. Cf. ITTY-BITTY *adjective*.

Observer The rather sentimental and itsy-bitsy patterns . . for wear by the young. H. HOWARD If Frankie was here he'd break you into itsy-bitsy pieces.

■ **itsy-bitsiness** *noun* M20.

itty /ˈɪti/ *adjective. colloq.* L18.
[ORIGIN from childish form of LITTLE *adjective* + -Y[6].]
Little (chiefly of or in speaking to babies or small domestic animals).

D. RUNYON He . . starts whispering, 'There, there, there, my itty oddleums'.

itty-bitty /ɪtɪˈbɪti/ *adjective. colloq.* M20.
[ORIGIN from ITTY + BITTY *adjective*.]
= ITSY-BITSY *adjective*.

ITU *abbreviation*.
1 Intensive therapy unit.
2 International Telecommunication Union.

-itude *suffix* see -TUDE.

ITV *abbreviation*.
Independent television.

Ity *noun & adjective* var. of ITI.

-ity /ɪti/ *suffix*. After *i* **-ety**.
[ORIGIN from or after Old French & mod. French *-ité* from Latin *-itas*, *-itatis*. Cf. -TY[1].]
Forming nouns expressing state or condition, as ***purity***, ***authority***, ***dubiety***, ***majority***, ***superiority***, etc., an instance of this as ***a profanity***, ***a monstrosity***, etc., or a quantity measuring the degree of a condition as ***porosity***, ***humidity***, etc.

itzebu /ɪtsɪˈbuː/ *noun*. Also **-boo**. E17.
[ORIGIN Japanese *ichi*, †*itze* one + *bu* division, quarter.]
A gold or silver coin worth a quarter of a ryo, formerly used in Japan. In later use, a quarter of a dollar or yen.

IU *abbreviation*.
International unit.

IUCD *abbreviation*.
Intrauterine contraceptive device.

IUCN *abbreviation*.
International Union for the Conservation of Nature.

IUD *abbreviation*.
1 Intrauterine (contraceptive) device.
2 Intrauterine death (of a fetus).

iulidan /ʌɪˈjuːlɪd(ə)n/ *noun*. L19.
[ORIGIN from mod. Latin *Iulidae* (see below), formed as IULUS: see -AN.]
ZOOLOGY. A millipede of the family Iulidae.

iulus /ʌɪˈjuːləs/ *noun*. Now *rare*. Also **julus** /ˈjuːləs, ˈdʒuː-/. Pl. **-li** /-lʌɪ, -liː/. **M17**.
[**ORIGIN** Latin from Greek *ioulos* down, catkin, millipede.]
†**1** A catkin. **M17–M18**.
2 A millipede; *spec.* one of the genus *Julus*. **M17**.

-ium /ɪəm/ *suffix*.
[**ORIGIN** mod. Latin from Latin, repr. Greek *-ion*.]
1 *gen.* In various nouns derived from or modelled on Latin or Greek words, as ***alluvium***, ***auditorium***, ***euphonium***, ***geranium***, ***proscenium***, etc.
2 *CHEMISTRY.* **a** Forming the names of most metallic elements, as ***cadmium***, ***iridium***, ***lithium***, ***magnesium***, ***osmium***, ***palladium***, ***potassium***, ***rhodium***, ***sodium***, ***titanium***, ***uranium***, etc., and occas. other cationic species, as ***ammonium***. ▸**b** Used (after ***ammonium***) to form the names of various protonated, mostly organic, bases, as ***ethidium***, ***hydrazinium***, etc. Cf. **-ONIUM**.
3 *ANATOMY & BOTANY.* Forming the names of anatomical structures, esp. receptacles, as ***archegonium***, ***epithelium***, ***gametangium***, ***mycelium***, ***pericardium***, etc. Cf. **-IDIUM**.

IUPAC *abbreviation*.
International Union of Pure and Applied Chemistry.

IUPAP *abbreviation*.
International Union of Pure and Applied Physics.

IV *abbreviation*.
Intravenous(ly).

Ivan /ˈʌɪv(ə)n, iːˈvan/ *noun*. *slang*. **L19**.
[**ORIGIN** Russian male forename, corresp. to *John*.]
A Russian, *esp.* a Russian soldier. Orig. ***Ivan Ivanovitch*** /ʌɪˈvanəvɪtʃ/ [with added patronymic = son of Ivan], a typical Russian, a personification of the Russian people.

-ive /ɪv/ *suffix*.
[**ORIGIN** Old French & mod. French *-if*, *-ive* (= Italian, Spanish *-ivo*), from Latin *-ivus*.]
Forming adjectives with the sense 'tending to, having the nature or quality of', as ***active***, ***descriptive***. Also forming derived nouns, as ***adjective***, ***locomotive***. Cf. **-ATIVE**.

ivermectin /ʌɪvəˈmɛktɪn/ *noun*. **L20**.
[**ORIGIN** from *i* + A)VERMECTIN.]
PHARMACOLOGY. A synthetic compound of the avermectin group used as an anthelmintic, esp. in the treatment of river blindness in humans and worm infestation in domestic animals.

IVF *abbreviation*.
In vitro fertilization.

ivi /ˈiːviː/ *noun*. **M19**.
[**ORIGIN** Fijian *ivi*, Samoan *ifi*.]
The Tahiti chestnut, *Inocarpus fagifer*, a leguminous evergreen tree bearing spikes of white or yellow flowers and dark edible fruit.

Ivicene /ˈɪvɪsiːn/ *noun & adjective*. **E20**.
[**ORIGIN** from French *Iviça* Ibiza (see below) + Spanish *-eño* **-ENE**.]
(An animal of) a breed of hound from the Balearic Island of Ibiza, characterized by large, pointed, pricked ears and white, fawn, or reddish-brown colouring. Also called ***Ibicencan hound***, ***Ibizan hound***.

ivied /ˈʌɪvɪd/ *adjective*. Also **ivyed**. **L18**.
[**ORIGIN** from **IVY** *noun* + **-ED**[2].]
Overgrown or covered with ivy. Also *fig.* (*US*), (academically) distinguished, prestigious, (cf. ***Ivy League*** s.v. **IVY** *noun*).

> H. JACOBSON I loved the ivied cloisters. *New Yorker* An ivied golf club might set a new member back . . ten thousand dollars.

-ivity /ˈɪvɪti/ *suffix*.
[**ORIGIN** from **-IVE** + **-ITY**.]
Forming nouns from adjectives in *-ive* expressing a state or condition, as ***captivity***, ***sensivity***, etc., an instance of this, as ***activity***, ***festivity***, etc., or a quantity measuring the degree of a condition, as ***conductivity*** etc.

-ivore *suffix* see **-VORE**.

Ivorian /ʌɪˈvɔːrɪən/ *adjective & noun*. **M20**.
[**ORIGIN** from **IVORY** + **-IAN**, after French *ivoirien*.]
▸ **A** *adjective*. Of or pertaining to the Ivory Coast, a republic (formerly a French protectorate) on the Gulf of Guinea in W. Africa. **M20**.
▸ **B** *noun*. A native or inhabitant of the Ivory Coast; *spec.* a member of any of the indigenous peoples, as opp. to one of French descent. **L20**.

ivoride /ˈʌɪvərʌɪd/ *noun & adjective*. **L19**.
[**ORIGIN** from **IVORY** + **-IDE**.]
(Made of) a kind of artificial ivory.

ivoried /ˈʌɪvərɪd/ *adjective*. **ME**.
[**ORIGIN** from **IVORY** + **-ED**[2].]
Made of ivory; made like ivory; provided or adorned with ivory.

> *Nineteenth Century* On thy bare and ivoried shoulder.
> W. DE LA MARE Tipped arrow, ivoried bow, and rain-soaked quiver.

ivorine /ˈʌɪvəriːn, -ʌɪn/ *noun*. **L19**.
[**ORIGIN** from **IVORY** + **-INE**[4].]
(Proprietary name for) any of various products, either imitating ivory or (as cosmetics, dentifrices, etc.) producing a colour or smoothness resembling that of ivory.

ivorine /ˈʌɪvəriːn, -ʌɪn/ *adjective*. *rare*. **LME**.
[**ORIGIN** from **IVORY** + **-INE**[1].]
†**1** Consisting or made of ivory. Only in **LME**.
2 White and smooth like ivory. **L19**.

-ivorous *suffix* see **-VOROUS**.

ivory /ˈʌɪv(ə)ri/ *noun & adjective*. **ME**.
[**ORIGIN** Old French *yvoire* from Proto-Romance, from Latin *ebor-*, *ebur* ivory, rel. to Egyptian *āb*, *ābu*, Coptic *ebou*, *ebu* elephant.]
▸ **A** *noun* **1** **a** The hard creamy-white substance composing the main part of the tusks of the elephant, mammoth, hippopotamus, walrus, and narwhal, highly valued as a material for articles of use or ornament. **ME**. ▸**b** A tusk or tooth made of this. **L19**.
2 The colour of ivory; ivory white. **L16**.

> *Daily News* Nearly all recent brides have worn ivory.

3 A substance resembling ivory, or made in imitation of it. **M18**.
4 *collect. sing.* & in *pl.* The teeth. *slang*. **L18**.

> *Guardian* I gets his head in a leg scissors and he sinks his ivories into my thigh.

5 *collect. sing.* & in *pl.* The keys of a piano or similar instrument. *colloq.* **E19**.

> THACKERAY It's a wonder how any fingers can move over the jingling ivory so quickly as Miss Cann's.

6 Any of various objects formerly made of ivory, as †(***a***) a season ticket; (***b***) (*collect. sing.* & *in pl.*) dice; (***c***) in *pl.*, billiard balls. *colloq.* **M19**.
7 An ornament, carving, etc., made of ivory. **L19**.

> W. MASKELL The famous Assyrian ivories . . preserved in the British Museum.

– **PHRASES**: †**black ivory** *slang*. African slaves as a commodity. **fossil ivory**: obtained from the tusks of mammoths. **tickle the ivories**, **tinkle the ivories** *colloq.* play the piano. **vegetable ivory** the hard albumen of the nut or seed of certain palms, esp. the tropical American *Phytelephas macrocarpa*, which resembles ivory in hardness, colour, and texture, and is used for ornamental work, buttons, etc.

▸ **B** *adjective*. **1** Made or consisting of ivory. **LME**.

> A. S. BYATT Little butter knives with blunt ends and ivory handles.

2 Resembling ivory; of the colour or texture of ivory. **L16**.

> OUIDA She turned her ivory shoulder on him. A. MUNRO Beryl was dressed up in a satiny ivory dress.

– **COMB. & SPECIAL COLLOCATIONS**: **ivory-bill** a rare N. American woodpecker, *Campephilus principalis*; **ivory-billed** *adjective* having a bill resembling ivory; ***ivory-billed woodpecker*** = ***ivory-bill*** above; **ivory black** a black pigment from calcined ivory; **ivory board** a kind of pasteboard with both surfaces smooth; **ivory gull** an all-white circumpolar gull, *Pagophila eburnea*; **ivory nut** the seed of *Phytelephas macrocarpa*, the albumen of which hardens into vegetable ivory; **ivory nut palm**, **ivory palm** any of various tropical American palms of the genus *Phytelephas*, or Micronesian ones of the genus *Metroxylon*, which bear nuts yielding vegetable ivory; **ivory-paper** art paper or thin card with a polished surface; **ivory plum** *US* (the fruit of) the checkerberry, *Gaultheria procumbens*, or its ally the creeping snowberry, *G. hispidula*; **ivory tower** a state of seclusion from the ordinary world and protection from the harsh realities of life; **ivorytype** *PHOTOGRAPHY* a hand-coloured print produced by various processes, intended to resemble a painting on ivory; **ivory-white** *noun & adjective* (of) the colour of ivory; **ivorywood** the Australian tree *Siphonodon australe* (family Siphonodontaceae), or its timber, which is used for drawing instruments etc.
■ **ivory-like** *adjective* resembling (that of) ivory **M19**.

ivy /ˈʌɪvi/ *noun*.
[**ORIGIN** Old English *ifiġ*, rel. to Old High German *ebah* (German dial. *Efa(i)*, *Ewich*) and 1st elem. of Middle Low German *iflōf*, *iwlōf*, Low German, Dutch *eiloof* (with **LEAF** *noun*[1]), Middle High German *ebehöu*, *ephöu*, German *Efeu* (with **HAY** *noun*[1]).]
1 An evergreen woody climber, *Hedera helix* (family Araliaceae), covering old walls, tree trunks, shady banks, etc., of which the western European form has dark green shining leaves, palmately lobed on the non-flowering shoots, and umbels of greenish-yellow flowers, succeeded by dark berries. Also (usu. with specifying word), any plant of the genus *Hedera*. **OE**. ▸†**b** [With ref. to the ivy's having formerly been sacred to Bacchus.] Ivy used outside a building as a sign that wine was sold inside. Cf. ***ivy bush***, ***ivy garland*** below. **LME–E17**. ▸**c** = ***poison ivy*** s.v. **POISON** *noun, adjective, & adverb*. *US*. **L18**.
2 With specifying word. Any of various (usu. climbing or creeping) plants of other genera. **LME**.
Boston ivy: see **BOSTON** *noun* 5. ***German ivy***: see **GERMAN** *noun*[1] & *adjective*[1]. ***ground ivy***: see **GROUND** *noun*. **KENILWORTH IVY**. ***SWEDISH ivy***.
– **COMB.**: **ivy berry** *US* the wintergreen, *Gaultheria procumbens*; **ivy bush** a bushy branch of ivy; formerly, (a representation of) such a branch displayed outside an inn as a sign that wine was sold there; **ivy garland** a garland of ivy, formerly the sign of a house where wine was sold; **ivy geranium** a pelargonium with five-angled leaves, *Pelargonium peltatum*; **ivy leaf** (***a***) a leaf of ivy; †(***b***) *fig.* a thing of little value, a trifle; **Ivy League** a group of long-established eastern US universities of high academic and social prestige; **Ivy Leaguer** a (former) member of one of the universities of the Ivy League; **ivy-leaved** *adjective* having palmately lobed leaves like those of the ivy; ***ivy-leaved bellflower***, a creeping plant of the bellflower family, *Wahlenbergia hederacea*, bearing nodding blue flowers and found in boggy places in western Europe; ***ivy-leaved speedwell***, a Eurasian speedwell of cultivated ground, *Veronica hederifolia*; ***ivy-leaved toadflax***, a trailing plant of the figwort family, *Cymbalaria muralis*, with mauve and yellow flowers, native on rocky ground in southern Europe and widely naturalized on old walls; **ivy-tod** *arch.* an ivy-bush; **ivy tree** (***a***) *NZ* any of several evergreen trees of the genus *Pseudopanax*, related to the ivy; (***b***) *N. Amer.* mountain laurel, *Kalmia latifolia*.

ivy /ˈʌɪvi/ *verb trans.* **M19**.
[**ORIGIN** from the noun, or back-form. from **IVIED**.]
Cover with or as with ivy.

ivyed *adjective* var. of **IVIED**.

IWC *abbreviation*.
International Whaling Commission.

iwi /ˈiːwiː/ *noun*. *NZ*. Pl. same. **M19**.
[**ORIGIN** Maori.]
A Maori tribe.

iwis /ɪˈwɪs/ *adjective, noun, & adverb*. Long *arch.* Also **ywis**.
[**ORIGIN** Old English *ġewis* = Old High German *giwis* (German *gewiss*) from Germanic, from base also of **WISE** *adjective*, **WIT** *verb*. Cf. **WIS** *verb*[1], *verb*[2].]
▸ †**A** *adjective*. Certain. Only in **OE**.
▸ †**B** *noun*. Certainty: in ***mid iwis*** [**MID** *preposition*[1].], with certainty, certainly. **OE–ME**.
▸ **C** *adverb*. Certainly, assuredly, indeed, truly. **ME**.
– **NOTE**: In later use freq. written *I wis* and taken erron. as = *I wot* (I know), as if from **WIT** *verb*: see also **WIS** *verb*[2]

IWW *abbreviation*.
Industrial Workers of the World.

ixia /ˈɪksɪə/ *noun*. **M16**.
[**ORIGIN** Latin from Greek.]
†**1** = **CHAMELEON** 2. **M16–E17**.
2 *BOTANY.* Any of various southern African plants of the genus *Ixia*, of the iris family, with large showy flowers of various colours. Also called ***corn lily***. **L18**.

Ixionian /ɪksɪˈəʊnɪən/ *adjective*. **L17**.
[**ORIGIN** from *Ixion* (see below) + **-IAN**.]
Of or pertaining to Ixion, in Greek mythology a king of Thessaly punished by being bound to an eternally revolving wheel in Hades.
the Ixionian wheel endless torment.

ixnay /ˈɪksneɪ/ *interjection & verb*. *US slang*. **M20**.
[**ORIGIN** Pig Latin for **NIX** *interjection*, *verb*.]
▸ **A** *interjection*. ***ixnay on***, ***ixnay to***, expr. rejection of something. **M20**.
▸ **B** *verb trans.* Cancel or stop. **M20**.

ixodid /ɪkˈsəʊdɪd/ *noun & adjective*. **E20**.
[**ORIGIN** mod. Latin *Ixodidae* (see below), from *Ixodes* genus name, from Greek *ixōdēs* sticky.]
▸ **A** *noun*. Pl. **-ids**, **-ides** /-ɪdiːz/. A tick of the family Ixodidae. **E20**.
▸ **B** *attrib.* or as *adjective*. Designating or pertaining to a tick of the family Ixodidae. **E20**.

ixora /ɪkˈsɔːrə/ *noun*. **E19**.
[**ORIGIN** mod. Latin (see below), from Portuguese *Iswara* from Sanskrit *īśvara* lord, master, epithet of Hindu deities, the flowers of certain species being used as votive offerings.]
Any of various evergreen shrubs or small trees of the genus *Ixora*, of the madder family, mostly native to tropical Africa and Asia, which bear compact corymbs of white or brightly coloured flowers.

ixtle /ˈɪkstli/ *noun*. Also **istle** /ˈɪstli, ˈɪst(ə)l/. **M19**.
[**ORIGIN** Amer. Spanish, from Nahuatl *ixtli*.]
A fibre obtained (in Mexico and Central America) from *Bromelia sylvestris* and species of *Agave*, esp. *A. funkiana* and *A. lecheguilla*, and used for cordage, nets, carpets, etc.

Iyengar /ɪˈjɛŋgɑː/ *noun*. **L20**.
[**ORIGIN** named after B. K. S. *Iyengar* (b. 1918), the Indian yoga teacher who devised it.]
A type of hatha yoga focusing on the correct alignment of the body.

Iyyar /ˈiːjɑː/ *noun*. **M18**.
[**ORIGIN** Hebrew *ʼiyyār*.]
In the Jewish calendar, the eighth month of the civil and second of the religious year, usu. coinciding with parts of April and May. Formerly called ***Ziv***.

izakaya /ɪzəˈkʌɪə/ *noun*. Pl. same, **-s**. **L20**.
[**ORIGIN** Japanese, based on *iru* be in a place, stay + *sakaya* liquor shop.]
A Japanese cafe or bar that serves alcoholic drinks and a variety of small dishes or snacks.

izar /ɪˈzɑː/ *noun*. **M19**.
[**ORIGIN** Arabic *ʼizār*.]
An enveloping outer garment worn by Muslim women (and, in some countries, Muslim men). Also, the lower garment of the *ihram*.

izard /ˈɪzəd/ *noun*. L18.
[ORIGIN French *isard*, Gascon *isart*, perh. of Iberian origin.]
The Pyrenean variety of the chamois.

Izarra /iːˈzɑːrə/ *noun*. Also **Izzara**. E20.
[ORIGIN Basque, lit. 'star'.]
A brandy-based liqueur from the Pyrenees, flavoured with herbs.

-ization /ʌɪˈzeɪʃ(ə)n/ *suffix*. Also **-isation**.
[ORIGIN from or after French *-isation* (Italian *-izzazione*, Spanish *-ización*): see -IZE, -ATION.]
Forming nouns of action from verbs in -IZE, or by analogy where no verb exists, as ***metrization***.

izba *noun* var. of ISBA.

-ize /ʌɪz/ *suffix*. Also **-ise**.
[ORIGIN from or after French *-iser* (Italian *-izzare*, Spanish *-izar*) from late Latin *-izare*, from Greek *-izein*.]
1 Forming trans. verbs with the sense 'make or treat in a specified way', as ***anatomize***, ***characterize***, ***idolize***, ***tantalize***, etc.
2 Forming intrans. verbs with the sense 'do in a specified way, follow a specified practice', as ***agonize***, ***apologize***, ***botanize***, ***sympathize***, ***theorize***, etc.
3 Forming trans. and intrans. verbs with the sense 'bring or come into some specified state', as ***authorize***, ***extemporize***, ***fertilize***, ***fossilize***, ***jeopardize***, ***moralize***, ***pedestrianize***, ***temporize***, etc.
4 Forming trans. and intrans. verbs from ethnic adjectives with the sense 'make or become like the country, people, language, etc. in character, naturalize as', as ***Americanize***, ***anglicize***, ***gallicize***, ***Latinize***, ***Russianize***, etc.
5 Forming trans. and intrans. verbs from personal names, with the sense 'treat or act like or according to the method of', as ***bowdlerize***, ***galvanize***, ***mesmerize***, etc.
6 Forming trans. verbs from names of substances, with the sense 'impregnate, treat, combine, affect, or influence with', as ***alkalize***, ***carbonize***, ***oxidize***, etc.

-izer /ˈʌɪzə/ *suffix*. Also **-iser**.
[ORIGIN formed as -IZE + -ER[1].]
Forming agent nouns from verbs in -IZE.

izimbongi *noun pl.* see IMBONGI.

izle *noun* var. of ISEL.

Iznik /ˈɪznɪk/ *adjective*. Also **Isnik**. M20.
[ORIGIN A town in Asian Turkey, the classical Nicaea. Cf. NICENE *adjective*.]
Designating a type of pottery or tiles made at Iznik, or imitations of it, from the 15th to the 17th cents., characterized by the use of brilliant pigments.

Izod /ˈʌɪzɒd/ *noun*. Also **i-**. E20.
[ORIGIN E. G. *Izod* (fl. 1903), Brit. engineer, who devised the test.]
Used ***attrib.*** with ref. to an impact test (***Izod test***) in which a notched specimen is broken by a blow from a pendulum, the energy absorbed (***Izod value***) being determined from the decrease in the swing of the pendulum.

Izzara *noun* var. of IZARRA.

izzard /ˈɪzəd/ *noun*. *arch. & dial.* M18.
[ORIGIN Alt. of ZED.]
The letter Z.

izzat /ˈɪzʌt/ *noun*. Also ***izzut***. M19.
[ORIGIN Persian, Urdu *ʿizzat*, from Arabic *ʿizza* glory.]
Honour, reputation, credit, prestige.

> E. M. FORSTER Trying to increase his izzat—in plain Anglo-Saxon, to score.

I

Jj

J, j /dʒeɪ/.
The tenth letter of the modern English alphabet, orig. a modification of the letter I. From the 11th to the 17th cent. the letter I, i represented both the vowel sound of *i*, and the sound /dʒ/. To keep the inconspicuous small ı distinct various scribal expedients were used: an initial ı was often prolonged above or below the line, or both; a final ı was generally prolonged below the line; and in both cases the tail in cursive writing at length became a curve. The 'dot' was also used with the tailed form, giving rise to the mod. letter j. This was at first merely a final form of i, used in Latin in such forms as 'filij', and in roman numerals, as j, ij, iij, vj, viij, xij. In the 17th cent. the two forms of the letter came to be differentiated, i remaining for the vowel and j being used for the consonant, with the capital form of the latter, J, being introduced. The sound normally represented by the letter in English is the palato-alveolar affricate /dʒ/. In certain words, esp. in proper names or alien terms from German and other languages, j retains the Roman value /j/. In a few French words, distinctly recognized as alien, j retains the French sound /ʒ/. Pl. **J's, Js**.
▸ **I 1** The letter and its sound.
2 The shape of the letter.
J-curve *STATISTICS* a J-shaped graph or distribution. **J-shaped** *adjective* having a shape or a cross-section like the capital letter J (without a right-angled crosspiece).
▸ **II** Symbolical uses.
3 Used to denote serial order; applied e.g. to the tenth group or section, sheet of a book, etc. Formerly *rare* (the old order of the Roman alphabet, H, I, K, being retained).
J acid *CHEMISTRY.* 2-amino-5-naphthol-7-sulphonic acid, $C_{10}H_9NO_4S$, an intermediate in the production of azo dyes by coupling reactions. **JK flip-flop** *ELECTRONICS* a flip-flop with two inputs and two outputs which changes to the complementary state when both triggering pulses are one.
4 Used to replace the roman numeral i in final position, as in j, ij, vj, etc. Now *rare*.
5 *PHYSICS.* **a** [abbreviation of **JOULE**] The mechanical equivalent of heat. ▸**b** Quantized angular momentum, *esp.* the total angular momentum of an electron (j) or assemblage of electrons (J).
6 *ELECTRICITY.* (Italic *j*.) ▸**a** Electric current. ▸**b** The imaginary quantity $\sqrt{-1}$, the square root of minus one. Cf. **I**, I 7.
▸ **III 7** Abbrevs.: **J** = joule(s).

JA *abbreviation.*
1 Jamaica.
2 Judge Advocate.
3 Justice of Appeal.

jab /dʒab/ *verb & noun. colloq.* **E19.**
[ORIGIN Var., orig. Scot., of **JOB** *verb*[1].]
▸ **A** *verb.* Infl. **-bb-**.
1 *verb trans.* Pierce or poke with the end or point of something; stab. **E19.** ▸**b** Give (a person) a quick short blow with the fist, hit with a straight punch. **E20.**
B. BAINBRIDGE A broken bough . . jabbed Adolf in the ribs.
2 *verb trans.* Thrust (something) with a quick sharp blow (*in, into*). **E19.**
I. MCEWAN He kept talking, jabbing his forefinger in the air.
3 *verb intrans.* Stab a person or thing; throw quick short punches. **E19.**
H. BASCOM The combatants circle each other, feinting and jabbing.
4 *verb trans. & intrans.* Inject or inoculate (a person, a vein) with a hypodermic needle. **M20.**
▸ **B** *noun.* **1** An act of jabbing; a quick short blow with something pointed, or with the fist; a straight punch. **L19.**
fig.: E. AMADI He winced with . . a particularly searing jab of pain.
2 A hypodermic injection, *esp.* a vaccination. *colloq.* **E20.**
Holiday Which? Typhoid and polio jabs are recommended by the DHSS for all the islands.
3 A radio signal of momentary duration. **M20.**

jabber /ˈdʒabə/ *verb & noun.* **L15.**
[ORIGIN Imit.: cf. **GABBER** *verb*, **JABBLE** *verb*[1], **JAVVER**.]
▸ **A** *verb.* **1** *verb intrans.* Talk rapidly and indistinctly; speak fluently but with little sense; chatter, gabble, prattle; *derog.* talk in a language the hearer does not understand. **L15.** ▸**b** Utter inarticulate sounds rapidly and volubly; chatter like a monkey, bird, etc. **E19.**
H. ALLEN She jabbered at him in a dialect he could not understand. W. STYRON I began jabbering at Sophie with brainless unrestraint. *New Yorker* Friends would come over . . to jabber and gossip about all the excitement.
2 *verb trans.* Utter or say rapidly and indistinctly; express by jabbering; *derog.* speak (a language) without being understood. **M16.**
HUGH MILLER Poor idiot, . . come every day to the churchyard, to . . jabber in broken expressions his grief.
▸ **B** *noun.* The action of jabbering; rapid and indistinct or unintelligible talk; gabble, chatter; gibberish. **E18.**
■ **jabberer** *noun* **L17.**

jabbers /ˈdʒabəz/ *noun.* Also **jabers** /ˈdʒeɪbəz/. **E19.**
[ORIGIN Alt. of *Jesus*: cf. **BEJABERS**.]
Jesus: chiefly as interjection, expr. amazement or emphasis.

jabberwocky /ˈdʒabəwɒki/ *adjective & noun.* **E20.**
[ORIGIN Title of a poem in Lewis Carroll's *Through the Looking Glass*.]
▸ **A** *adjective.* Nonsensical, meaningless; reversed in order. **E20.**
▸ **B** *noun.* Invented or meaningless language; nonsensical behaviour. Also, a piece of nonsensical writing or speech, esp. for comic effect. **E20.**
V. VINGE The translation was slow and full of alternative meanings and jabberwocky.

jabble /ˈdʒab(ə)l/ *noun.* Chiefly *Scot.* **L18.**
[ORIGIN from **JABBLE** *verb*[2].]
A slight agitated movement of water etc.; a splashing in small waves or ripples.

jabble /ˈdʒab(ə)l/ *verb*[1] *trans. & intrans.* **L16.**
[ORIGIN Imit.: cf. **GABBLE** *verb*, **JABBER** *verb*.]
= **JABBER** *verb*.

jabble /ˈdʒab(ə)l/ *verb*[2]. *Scot.* **M18.**
[ORIGIN App. imit.: see **-LE**[3].]
1 *verb trans.* Shake up or agitate (esp. a liquid); cause to splash. **M18.**
2 *verb intrans.* Splash in small waves or ripples. **E19.**

jabers *noun* var. of **JABBERS**.

jabiru /ˈdʒabɪruː/ *noun.* **L18.**
[ORIGIN Tupi-Guarani *jabirú*, from *j* (demonstr.) that which has + *abirú* swollen (with ref. to the large neck of the jabiru (sense 1)): cf. Portuguese *jaburu*.]
1 A large white stork, *Jabiru mycteria*, of tropical and subtropical America. Also ***jabiru stork***. **L18.**
2 Either of two storks of the genus *Ephippiorhynchus*, (*a*) the black-necked stork, *E. asiaticus*, of SE Asia and Australia, and (*b*) the saddlebill stork, *E. senegalensis*, of Africa. **L18.**

jaborandi /dʒabəˈrandi/ *noun.* Also (earlier) †**jaburandiba**. **E17.**
[ORIGIN Portuguese from Tupi-Guarani *jaburandi* lit. 'person who makes saliva, one who spits'; also *jaburandiba* (*iba* plant, tree).]
A drug made from the dried leaves of any of several S. American plants of the genus *Pilocarpus*, of the rue family, which contain the alkaloid pilocarpine and promote salivation when chewed. Also, any of these plants or other S. American plants with similar properties.

jabot /ˈʒabəʊ/ *noun.* Pl. pronounced same. **E19.**
[ORIGIN French = bird's crop, shirt-frill, prob. from a Proto-Romance base meaning 'crop, maw, gullet'.]
1 A frill on the front of a man's shirt, edging the opening. Now chiefly *hist.* **E19.**
2 An ornamental frill on a woman's bodice. **L19.**

jaboticaba /ˌdʒabɒtɪˈkɑːbə/ *noun.* Also **-but-**. **E17.**
[ORIGIN Portuguese from Tupi *iauotiʼkaua*.]
A Brazilian evergreen tree, *Myrciaria cauliflora*, of the myrtle family, which bears clusters of white flowers and purple fruits directly on the trunk and branches. Also, the fruit of this tree.

†**jaburandiba** *noun* see **JABORANDI**.

jacal /həˈkɑːl/ *noun.* **M19.**
[ORIGIN Mexican Spanish from Nahuatl *xacalli* contr. of *xamitl calli* adobe house.]
A hut built of erect stakes filled in with wattle and mud, common in Mexico and the south-western US; an adobe house. Also, the material or method used in building such a hut.

jacamar /ˈdʒakəmɑː/ *noun.* **E19.**
[ORIGIN French, app. from Tupi.]
Any of various small insectivorous birds of tropical S. America of the family Galbulidae, with partly iridescent plumage.

jacana /ˈdʒakənə/ *noun.* Also **jaçana** /dʒasəˈnɑː/. **M18.**
[ORIGIN Portuguese *jaçanã* from Tupi-Guarani *jasanã*.]
Any of various small tropical wading birds of the family Jacanidae, which have greatly elongated toes and claws, enabling them to walk on floating vegetation.
wattled jacana: see **WATTLED** 2.

jacaranda /dʒakəˈrandə/ *noun.* **M18.**
[ORIGIN Portuguese from Tupi-Guarani *jakaraʼna*.]
1 Any of various tropical American trees with fragrant and ornamental wood. Now chiefly, any tree of the genus *Jacaranda* (family Bignoniaceae), with showy tubular blue or purple flowers and usu. pinnate leaves; esp. *J. mimosifolia*, native to Brazil, much grown as a street tree in warm climates. **M18.**
2 The wood of any of these trees. **M19.**

jacent /ˈdʒeɪs(ə)nt/ *adjective.* Long *rare.* **M16.**
[ORIGIN Latin *jacent-* pres. ppl stem of *jacere* lie: see **-ENT**.]
Lying, recumbent; *fig.* sluggish.

jacinth /ˈdʒasɪnθ, ˈdʒeɪ-/ *noun & adjective.* **ME.**
[ORIGIN Old French *iacinte* (mod. *jacinthe*) or medieval Latin *iacintus*, alt. of Latin *hyacinthus* **HYACINTH**.]
▸ **A** *noun.* **1** A kind of precious stone; = **HYACINTH** 1. **ME.** ▸**b** The colour of jacinth, blue or occas. reddish orange; *HERALDRY* the colour tenné, reddish orange, in blazoning by precious stones. **LME.**
†**2** A dyed fabric of a blue or violet colour. Only in **LME.**
3 = **HYACINTH** 2, 3. Now *rare.* **M16.**
4 = **HYACINTH** 4. **M19.**
▸ **B** *attrib.* or as *adjective.* Of the colour of jacinth. **E16.**

jacitara /dʒasɪˈtɑːrə/ *noun.* **M19.**
[ORIGIN Portuguese from Tupi *yasítara*.]
In full ***jacitara palm***. Any of various tropical American prickly climbing palms of the genus *Desmoncus*, esp. *D. orthacanthos*, native to the Amazon region.

Jack /dʒak/ *noun*[1]. Also **j-**. Pl. **-s**, (in sense 22, also) same. **LME.**
[ORIGIN Pet form of male forename *John*, perh. through dim. *Jankin*; the resemblance to French *Jacques* (from Proto-Romance from Latin *Jacobus* **JACOB**) is unexpl.]
▸ **I** (A figure of) a man.
1 a (A name for) a (male) representative of the common people, (a name for) an ordinary man. **LME.** ▸**b** A lad, a chap; *esp.* a rough or low-born man. *obsolete* exc. *dial.* **M16.** ▸**c** Used as a form of address to an unknown person. *colloq.* (orig. *US*). **L19.**
a J. WAINWRIGHT He had that world-weary look of the working Jack who'd seen everything.
2 A figure of a man which strikes the bell on the outside of a clock. Also ***Jack of the clock***. Cf. branch II below. **L15.**
quarter-Jack.
3 a A sailor. Now more fully ***Jack tar***. **M17.** ▸**b** A serving man; a labourer; an odd-job man. **E18.** ▸**c** A lumberjack. *N. Amer. colloq.* **L19.** ▸**d** A (military) policeman; a detective. Cf. **JOHN** 3. *slang.* **L19.**
4 *CARDS.* Orig., the knave of trumps in the game of all fours. Later (formerly considered *slang*), any of the lowest court cards bearing the representation of a male youth, a knave. **L17.**
Field His partner had an equally important card—the Jack of diamonds.
▸ **II** A thing which saves human labour; a device, a tool.
5 A machine for turning the spit when roasting meat, either wound up like a clock or operated by the current of heated air up a chimney. Also ***roasting Jack***. **LME.**
6 Any of various contrivances consisting (solely or essentially) of a roller or winch. **LME.**
7 A frame on which to saw wood. **L16.**
8 A part of the mechanism in a spinet, harpsichord, etc., connecting a key to its corresponding string, and causing the string to be plucked when the key is pressed down; a key of a spinet etc. **L16.**
9 A bootjack. Now *rare* or *obsolete.* **L17.**
10 A device, usually portable, for lifting or moving heavy objects by a force acting from below; *spec.* one placed under a vehicle to raise it off the ground so that a wheel can be changed or the underneath examined. **E18.**
Rally Sport They then had to change two punctures, during which the car fell off the Jack.
11 a An oscillating lever, such as those in a stocking frame or knitting machine. **M18.** ▸**b** = **HECK** *noun*[1] 6. **M19.**
12 a *hist.* A counter made to resemble a sovereign. **M19.** ▸**b** Money. *slang* (orig. *US*). **L19.** ▸**c** *sing.* & (occas.) in *pl.* Five pounds; a five-pound note. Also ***Jack's alive***. *slang.* **M20.**

b J. Dos Passos I thought I better come up here and see the folks before I spent all my Jack.

13 ELECTRICITY. More fully *jack socket*. A socket with two or more pairs of terminals, for the rapid introduction of a device into a circuit by means of a suitable plug. L19.

▶ **III** A thing of smaller than normal size.

†**14** A very small amount; the least bit; a whit. Only in M16.

15 a BOWLS. A smaller bowl placed as a mark for the players to aim at. Also (now *rare*) *jack-bowl*. E17. ▸**b** In *pl.* & (occas.) *sing.*, a game played by tossing and catching small round pebbles or star-shaped pieces of metal; *sing.* a pebble or piece of metal used for this. Also more fully *jackstone(s)*. Cf. DIBS *noun*[1]. E19.

16 BUILDING. A small brick used as a closer at the end of a course. Long *rare* or *obsolete*. E18.

17 A quarter of a pint; an imperial gill. *dial.* M18.

18 NAUTICAL. Either of a pair of iron bars at the head of the topgallant mast, supporting the royal and skysail masts. Also *Jack crosstree*. M19.

19 A portable cresset or fire basket used in hunting or fishing at night. *US.* M19.

20 A small schooner-rigged vessel used in the Newfoundland fisheries. Also *jack boat*. M19.

21 A tablet of heroin. *slang.* M20.

▶ **IV** In names of animals.

22 a Orig., a pike, *Esox lucius*, esp. when young or small. Now also, any of various similar fishes, as the pikeperch. Also *jackfish*. L16. ▸**b** Any of numerous marine fishes of the family Carangidae, many of which are used as food. Also *jackfish*. Cf. SCAD *noun*[2]. Orig. *W. Indian*. L17.

23 The male of various animals; *spec.* (*a*) a male hawk, *esp.* a male merlin (in full †*Jack-merlin*; (*b*) *US* a male ass, *esp.* one kept for breeding mules (= JACKASS 1). E17.

24 a = *jacksnipe* below. L19. ▸**b** A laughing jackass, a kookaburra. Cf. JACKO, JACKY 4. *Austral.* L19. ▸**c** = JACKRABBIT. L19.

– PHRASES & COMB.: *a roll Jack Rice couldn't jump over*: see ROLL *noun*[1]. **before one can say Jack Robinson** very quickly or suddenly. **California Jack** a card game resembling all fours. *Cousin Jack*: see COUSIN *noun*. **every man jack** *colloq.* each and every person. *goggle-eye Jack*: see GOGGLE-EYE 2(b). **I'm all right, Jack** *colloq.*: expr. selfish complacency. **Jack-a-Lent** *arch.* (*a*) *rare* a character in a mummers' play; (*b*) a figure of a man, set up to be pelted, in a game played during Lent; (*c*) a contemptible or insignificant person or thing; (*d*) a puppet. **Jack and Jill** boy and girl, man and woman. **jack arch** a small arch only one brick in thickness, esp. as used in numbers to support a floor. **Jack ashore** *noun & adjectival phr.* (*slang*) (the condition or state of being) excited, elated, etc. **jack bean** a subtropical climbing leguminous plant of the genus *Canavalia*, esp. *C. ensiformis*. **Jack-block** NAUTICAL a large wooden block used to raise and lower a topgallant mast. *jack boat*: see sense 20 above. *Jack-bowl*: see sense 15a above. †**Jack-boy** a boy employed in menial work; *spec.* a stable boy, a groom, a postillion. **Jack-by-the-hedge** garlic mustard, *Alliaria petiolata*. *Jack crosstree*: see sense 18 above. **Jack curlew** a whimbrel, *Numenius phaeopus*. *jackfish*: see sense 22 above. **Jack-fishing** (*a*) fishing for jack; (*b*) *US* fishing at night by means of a jack or cresset. *Jack Frost*: see FROST *noun*. **Jack-go-to-bed-at-noon** the yellow goat's beard, *Tragopogon pratensis*, whose flowers close about midday. **jackhammer** a portable rock-drill worked by compressed air. **Jack-hunting** *US* hunting by means of a jack light. **Jack-in-a-bottle** *dial.* a long-tailed tit (from the shape of its nest). **Jack-in-office** a self-important minor official. **Jack in the basket** NAUTICAL a kind of warning beacon. **Jack-in-the-bush** (*a*) *local* = GARLIC-*mustard*; (*b*) = *Jack-in-the-green* (*a*) below. **Jack-in-the-green** (*a*) a man or boy enclosed in a pyramid of wood or wicker and leaves as part of May-Day celebrations; (*b*) a variety of the primrose in which the calyx is transformed into leaves. **jack-in-the-hedge** = *jack-by-the-hedge* above. **jack-in-the-pulpit** any of various plants of the arum family with an erect spadix overarched by the enfolding spathe, *esp.* (*a*) *dial.* cuckoo pint, *Arum maculatum*; (*b*) *N. Amer.* any of several woodland plants of the genus *Arisaema*. **Jack-jump-about** *dial.* any of several spreading plants, *esp.* ground elder, *Aegopodium podagraria*. **Jack Ketch** [an executioner, 1663–86] *hist.* an executioner, a hangman. **Jack-ladder** NAUTICAL (*a*) = JACOB'S LADDER 2; (*b*) = JACK CHAIN 2. **jack light** *US* a light carried in a jack or cresset for hunting or fishing at night. **jack mackerel** a carangid game fish, *Trachurus symmetricus*, of the eastern Pacific. *Jack-merlin*: see sense 23(a) above. **Jack Mormon** *US* (*a*) a non-Mormon on friendly terms with Mormons; (*b*) a nominal or backsliding Mormon. *Jack Napes*: see JACKANAPES. **Jack oak** = *blackjack* (*d*) s.v. BLACK *adjective*. **jack of all trades** a person who can do many different kinds of work. **Jack of both sides** (now *rare*) a person who shifts his or her support. *Jack of the clock*: see sense 2 above. †**Jack out of office** a person who has been dismissed from office, or whose official role has gone. **Jack-pin** NAUTICAL a belaying pin. **jack pine** a small N. American pine, *Pinus banksiana*, with short needles. **jack plane** a long heavy plane used for rough work. **jack plug**: for use with a jack or jack socket. **Jack-pudding** a buffoon, a clown. **jack-roll** *noun & verb* (*a*) *noun* a winch or windlass turned directly by handles; (*b*) *verb trans.* steal from (a drunken person). *Jack's alive*: see sense 12c above. **jack salmon** *US* the pikeperch, *Stizostedion vitreum*. †**Jack-sauce** a cheeky or impudent man. **jack screw** a jack (see sense 10 above) having a rack and a pinion wheel or screw and a handle turned by hand, used esp. to move heavy cargo in a ship's hold. **jack shaft** ENGINEERING any of various kinds of auxiliary or intermediate shaft driven by another shaft or by a set of gears. **Jack-sharp** *N. English* a stickleback. †**jacksmith** a maker of roasting jacks. **jacksnipe** a small dark snipe, *Lymnocryptes minimus*; any of various similar birds, *esp.* (*US*) the pectoral sandpiper. *jack socket*: see sense 13 above. **Jack-spaniard** a large Caribbean wasp of the genus *Polistes*. **jackstay** NAUTICAL (*a*) a rope, metal bar, or batten placed along a yard to bend the head of a square sail to; (*b*) a line secured at both ends to serve as a support for an awning etc. *jackstone*: see sense 15b above. *Jack tar*: see sense 3a above. **Jack the Lad** [nickname of Jack Sheppard, an 18th-cent. thief] (*a*) a young troublemaker; (*b*) a working-class hero; (*c*) a wanted criminal. *Jack the Ripper*: see RIPPER 1b. **Jack-towel** a roller towel. †**Jack-weight**: forming part of the mechanism in an early form of the roasting jack. *lazy jack*: see LAZY *adjective*. **on one's Jack (Jones)** *slang* alone. **play the Jack** do a mean trick. *three-cornered Jack*. *yellow Jack*: see YELLOW *adjective*. See also JACK-A-DANDY, JACK-O'-LANTERN, JACKRABBIT, etc.

jack /dʒak/ *noun*[2]. *arch.* LME.

[ORIGIN Old French & mod. French *jaque*, perh. immed. from Spanish, Portuguese *jaco*, perh. from Arabic]

1 A sleeveless tunic or jacket, usu. of quilted leather and later freq. plated with iron for protection in battle; a coat of mail. In early use also, any jacket. LME.

2 A vessel for holding liquor or for drinking from, usu. of waxed leather coated outside with tar or pitch (cf. *blackjack* s.v. BLACK *adjective*); a (leather) jug or tankard. L16.

jack /dʒak/ *noun*[3]. Also **jak**. L16.

[ORIGIN Portuguese *jaca* from Malayalam *chakka*.]

A tree of tropical Asia, *Artocarpus heterophyllus*, related to the breadfruit, but with a larger and coarser fruit; the fruit of this tree.

jack /dʒak/ *noun*[4]. M17.

[ORIGIN Prob. use of JACK *noun*[1], as if short for 'jack flag', i.e. a small flag (as distinguished from the ensign).]

A small version of a national flag flown at the bow of a vessel in harbour to indicate its nationality. See also *Union Jack* s.v. UNION *noun*[2].

– COMB.: **jackstaff** (*a*) a short staff, usu. set at the bow of a ship, on which a jack is hoisted; (*b*) a staff carrying the flag that is to show above the masthead.

†**Jack** *noun*[5]. *colloq.* L17–M18.

[ORIGIN Abbreviation.]

= JACOBITE *noun*[2].

jack /dʒak/ *adjective*. *Austral. slang.* E20.

[ORIGIN from JACK *verb*.]

Tired *of* something or someone; bored.

jack /dʒak/ *verb*[1]. M19.

[ORIGIN from JACK *noun*[1].]

1 *verb intrans.* Hunt or fish at night with a jack (JACK *noun*[1] 19). *US.* M19.

2 *verb trans.* Foll. by *up*: ▸**a** Lift up with a jack (JACK *noun*[1] 10). M19. ▸**b** Increase; force or bolster up. *colloq.* E20. ▸**c** Arrange, organize. *NZ slang.* M20.

a *Practical Motorist* In order to lift the car high enough . . we had to jack up the body. **b** A. Tyler Her son's an old skinflint. Always wanting to jack up the price. **c** D. M. Davin There'll be some cold meat in the safe . . . I'll jack up a feed.

3 a *verb trans.* Ruin; abandon. Usu. foll. by *up*. M19. ▸**b** *verb intrans.* Give *up* suddenly or promptly. *colloq.* M19.

4 *verb trans.* Foll. by *in*: abandon, leave; give up, stop. M20.

B. Trapido She jacked in Oxford after knowing Jacob . . and went to live with him instead.

5 *verb intrans.* Foll. by *off*: ▸**a** Go away, depart. M20. ▸**b** Masturbate. *slang.* M20.

■ **jacker** *noun* L19.

jack /dʒak/ *verb*[2] *trans. slang.* M20.

[ORIGIN from HIJACK.]

Take (something) illicitly; steal. Also, rob (someone).

Guardian Two of our backpacks had been 'jacked' from the bus along with our return plane tickets. *Washington Post* I tried to jack this kid for his lunch.

jack-a-dandy /dʒakəˈdandi/ *noun*. M17.

[ORIGIN from JACK *noun*[1] + *dandy*: see DANDY *noun*[2].]

An arrogant or conceited man; a dandy.

jackal /ˈdʒakɔːl, -k(ə)l/ *noun & verb*. E17.

[ORIGIN from (with assim. to JACK *noun*[1]) Turkish *çakal* from Persian *šagāl* rel. to Sanskrit *śṛgāla*.]

▶ **A** *noun*. **1** Any of several wild omnivorous doglike mammals of the genus *Canis*, of Africa and S. Eurasia, which have erect ears and a bushy tail and hunt in packs as foragers; *spec.* (more fully ***golden jackal***, ***common jackal***) *C. aureus*. E17.

saddleback jackal: see SADDLEBACK *noun* 2.

2 *fig.* A person who acts like a jackal, *esp.* one who serves or does subordinate preparatory work or drudgery for another. L17.

M. C. Clarke [Richard's] . . ingratitude towards his jackal, Buckingham, who wrought hard to help him to his bad eminence.

▶ **B** *verb intrans.* Do subordinate work or drudgery. E20.

jack-a-lantern *noun* var. of JACK-O'-LANTERN.

jackanapes /ˈdʒakəneɪps/ *noun*. Orig. †**Jack Napes**. Pl. same, **-napeses**. E16.

[ORIGIN Perh. from a playful name for a tame ape, with *n-* as in *newt*, *nickname*, etc., and *-s* as in *Hobbs* and other surnames.]

1 A tame ape or monkey. *arch.* E16.

2 A person displaying qualities or behaviour associated with apes; a ridiculous upstart; an impertinent person; *joc.* a cheeky, forward child. M16.

T. Mo Nor will I be judged by a pair of young jackanapes with . . time on their hands.

jackaroo /dʒakəˈruː/ *noun & verb*. *Austral. colloq.* Also ... M19.

[ORIGIN from JACK *noun*[1] + KANG)AROO *noun*.]

▶ **A** *noun*. †**1** A white man living outside the areas of settlement. M–L19.

2 Orig., a new colonist working to gain experience in the bush. Now, a novice on a sheep station or cattle station. L19.

▶ **B** *verb intrans.* Lead the life of a jackaroo; gain experience of bush farming. L19.

jackass /ˈdʒakas/ *noun*. E18.

[ORIGIN from JACK *noun*[1] + ASS *noun*[1].]

1 A male ass or donkey. E18.

2 The kookaburra, *Dacelo novaeguineae*, so called from its loud discordant cry. Also more fully ***laughing jackass***. L18. ▸**b** In Tasmania: the grey butcher-bird, *Cracticus torquatus*. L19.

3 A stupid or foolish person; = ASS *noun*[1] 2. *derog.* E19.

I. Asimov He's an undiplomatic young jackass.

4 NAUTICAL. **a** A kind of heavy rough boat used in Newfoundland, *esp.* a two-masted vessel with square sails on the mainmast, formerly used in seal hunting. E19. ▸**b** A tapering canvas bag stuffed with oakum etc., used to block the hawseholes of a seagoing vessel. *US.* L19.

– COMB.: **jackass barque** a ship with the same sails as a barquentine but rigged differently; **jackass brig**: having a square topsail and topgallant sail instead of a gaff topsail; **jackass-fish** an Australian marine food fish, *Nemadactylus macropterus*, with an elongated pectoral fin ray; also called ***morwong***; **jackass frigate** a small frigate; **jackass penguin** a penguin, *Spheniscus demersus*, with a harsh braying cry; †**jackass-rabbit** = JACKRABBIT; **jackass-rigged** *adjective* (of a schooner) having three masts with square sails set on the foremast and having no maintopmast; **jackass schooner** a jackass-rigged schooner.

■ **jaˈckassery** *noun* stupidity; a piece of folly: M19.

jackboot /ˈdʒakbuːt/ *noun*. Also **jack-boot**. L17.

[ORIGIN from JACK *noun*[1] or JACK *noun*[2] + BOOT *noun*[2].]

1 A large strong leather boot, the top of which covers the knee, worn esp. by cavalry soldiers in the 17th and 18th cents. and by German soldiers under the Nazi regime. L17.

Sun (Baltimore) The . . master race types are still swaggering through the streets in their polished jack-boots.

2 *fig.* Military oppression; rough bullying tactics. M18.

Listener A county about to be obliterated under the casual jackboot of a boundaries commission.

■ **jackbooted** *adjective* wearing jackboots M19.

jack chain /ˈdʒaktʃeɪn/ *noun*. M17.

[ORIGIN from JACK *noun*[1] + CHAIN *noun*.]

1 A chain of unwelded links each consisting of a double loop of wire resembling a figure of 8, but with the loops in planes at right angles to each other. M17.

2 FORESTRY. A continuous spiked chain used to move logs as if on a conveyor belt. E20.

jackdaw /ˈdʒakdɔː/ *noun*. M16.

[ORIGIN from JACK *noun*[1] + DAW *noun*.]

1 A small, gregarious, grey and black Eurasian crow, *Corvus monedula*, which often nests in old buildings, and may hoard small objects or food. M16.

2 = *boat-tail* s.v. BOAT *noun*. *US.* E18.

jacked /dʒakt/ *adjective*. LME.

[ORIGIN from JACK *noun*[2] + -ED[2].]

†**1** Wearing a jack (JACK *noun*[2] 1). Only in LME.

2 Hardened and thickened as leather for jackboots. E18.

jackeen /dʒaˈkiːn/ *noun*. *Irish.* M19.

[ORIGIN Dim. of JACK *noun*[1]: see -EEN[2].]

A self-assertive worthless person; *spec.* a city-dweller.

jackeroo *noun & verb* var. of JACKAROO.

jacket /ˈdʒakɪt/ *noun*. LME.

[ORIGIN Old French *ja(c)quet* dim. of *jaque*: see JACK *noun*[2], -ET[1].]

▶ **I 1** An outer garment for the upper part of the body, now usu. with sleeves. Also, a short coat without tails worn in shooting, riding, cycling, etc. LME. ▸**b** A waistcoat. *US.* E18. ▸**c** A jockey's loose-fitting blouse of silk or satin (orig. a jacket) in a racehorse-owner's distinctive colours. M19. ▸**d** A thing worn or fastened round the torso for protection, support, etc. E20.

C. Gebler Soldiers in their shirt sleeves, their jackets thrown over their shoulders.

bedjacket, ***bomber jacket***, ***dinner jacket***, ***Eton jacket***, ***Nehru jacket***, ***reefer jacket***, ***smoking jacket***, ***tuxedo jacket***, ***waxed jacket***, ***Zouave jacket***, etc. ***dust a person's jacket***: see DUST *verb*. **d** ***flak jacket***, ***life jacket***, ***straitjacket***, etc.

2 *transf.* With qualifying colour adjective: a person wearing a jacket of the specified colour, esp. as a uniform. E19.

bluejacket etc.

▶ **II 3 a** The natural (usu. hairy) covering or coat of various animals; the skin of a seal, fish, etc. E17. ▸**b** The skin of a cooked potato. M19.

a *Stock & Land (Melbourne)* Breeding first cross ewes . . carrying a good jacket of fine wool is the aim.

4 a An outer covering or casing, *esp.* one placed round a pipe, a steam cylinder, a boiler, etc., to insulate or

...E19. ▸**b** More fully ***dust jacket***. A protective (a... usu. decorative) paper cover placed round a bound book, usu. with the title and author's name printed on it. L19. ▸**c** A folder or envelope containing an official document, and displaying a list of its contents, instructions for its disposition, etc. *US.* L19. ▸**d** *MILITARY.* A coil or cylinder of wrought iron or steel placed round the barrel of a gun to strengthen or protect it. L19.

> **a** M. FARADAY A jacket of sheet caoutchouc was put over the saddle.

– COMB.: **jacket crown** *DENTISTRY* an artificial crown fitted over a natural crown, which is usually ground down to receive it; **jacket potato** a potato cooked in its skin.
▪ **jacketless** *adjective* M19.

jacket /ˈdʒakɪt/ *verb trans.* E19.
[ORIGIN from the noun.]
1 Eject (a person) from a rightful place. *slang.* E19.
2 Cover with or enclose in a jacket, esp. a straitjacket. M19.
3 Beat, thrash. *dial. & colloq.* L19.

Jackey *noun* var. of JACKY.

jack-in-the-box /ˈdʒakɪnðəbɒks/ *noun.* Also **jack-in-a-box** /-ɪnəbɒks/. M16.
[ORIGIN from JACK *noun*[1] + IN *preposition* + THE + BOX *noun*[2].]
†**1** *CHRISTIAN CHURCH.* The consecrated host (alluding to its reservation in a pyx). *derog.* Only in M16.
†**2** A cheat; *spec.* a thief giving tradesmen empty boxes instead of ones containing payment. L16–E18.
3 A kind of firework; *spec.* one that glows for a period before suddenly erupting with a loud bang into a shower of sparks. M17.
4 A toy consisting of a box containing a figure on a spring, which leaps up when the lid is raised. E18.
5 Any of various mechanical devices consisting essentially of a screw and a box or frame. E18.
6 a A West Indian tree, *Hernandia sonora* (family Hernandiaceae), bearing large nuts that rattle in their pericarps when shaken. M18. ▸**b** Wild arum, *Arum maculatum*. *dial.* L19.

jackknife /ˈdʒaknʌɪf/ *noun & verb.* Pl. **-knives** /-nʌɪvz/. E18.
[ORIGIN from *jack* (perh. JACK *noun*[1]) + KNIFE *noun*.]
▸ **A** *noun.* **1** A large clasp knife carried in the pocket. E18.
2 *SWIMMING.* A kind of dive executed by first doubling up and then straightening the body before entering the water. More fully ***jackknife dive***. E20.
3 A case of jackknifing by an articulated lorry (see sense B.2 below). M20.
4 *STATISTICS.* A method of assessing the variability of data by repeating a calculation on the sets of data obtained by removing one value from the complete set. M20.
▸ **B** *verb.* **1** *verb trans.* Cut with a jackknife. E19.
2 *verb intrans.* Double up like a jackknife; *spec.* of (the sections of) an articulated lorry: fold against (themselves or) itself, e.g. when skidding or reversing. L19.
3 *verb intrans.* Do a jackknife dive. E20.

jackleg /ˈdʒaklɛg/ *noun*[1] *& adjective.* *US colloq. & dial.* M19.
[ORIGIN from JACK *noun*[1] + LEG *noun*.]
(A person who is) incompetent, unskilled, unscrupulous, or dishonest.

> S. KING Even a jackleg carpenter like Vic Palfrey could . . build better than that.

▪ **jacklegged** *adjective* incompetent, unskilled, unscrupulous, dishonest M19.

jackleg *noun*[2] var. of JOCKTELEG.

jack-line /ˈdʒaklʌɪn/ *noun.* E17.
[ORIGIN from JACK *noun*[1] + LINE *noun*[2].]
A kind of thin three-stranded rope or line used esp. in sailing.

jackman /ˈdʒakmən/ *noun.* *Scot. obsolete* exc. *hist.* Pl. **-men**. M16.
[ORIGIN App. from JACK *noun*[1] 3b + MAN *noun*. Referred by Sir W. Scott to JACK *noun*[2].]
An attendant or retainer of a nobleman or landowner.

Jacko /ˈdʒakəʊ/ *noun.* *Austral. slang.* Pl. **-os**. E20.
[ORIGIN from JACK(ASS + -O.]
A kookaburra. Cf. JACK *noun*[1] 24b, JACKY 4.

jack-o'-lantern /ˈdʒakəlantən/ *noun.* Also **jack-a-lantern**, (in sense 1 and 2, earlier) **jack-with-the-lantern**. M17.
[ORIGIN from JACK *noun*[1] + O' *preposition*[2] + LANTERN *noun*.]
†**1** A man with a lantern; a night watchman. M17–E18.
2 An ignis fatuus, a will-o'-the-wisp; *fig.* something misleading or elusive. Also (chiefly *NAUTICAL*), corposant, St Elmo's fire. L17.
3 A lantern made of the rind of a large turnip or a pumpkin, in which holes are cut to represent eyes, nose, and mouth. *Scot., N. English, & N. Amer.* M19.

jackpot /ˈdʒakpɒt/ *noun.* L19.
[ORIGIN from JACK *noun*[1] + POT *noun*[1].]
1 *CARDS.* In draw poker, a pot or pool that accumulates until one of the players can open the betting with a pair of jacks or better; *fig.* any large prize, as from a lottery or gambling machine, *esp.* one that accumulates until it is won. L19.

> J. DIDION I won two twenty-five-dollar jackpots. F. DONALDSON Others get the jackpots and the girls.

hit the jackpot: see HIT *verb*.
2 A dilemma; trouble, esp. with the law; an arrest. *slang.* E20.

jackrabbit /ˈdʒakrabɪt/ *noun.* *N. Amer.* M19.
[ORIGIN Abbreviation of ***JACKASS-rabbit*** (so called from its long ears).]
Any of several large N. American hares of the genus *Lepus*, with very long ears and legs.

Jack Russell /dʒak ˈrʌs(ə)l/ *noun.* E20.
[ORIGIN from Revd John (*Jack*) *Russell* (1795–1883), English clergyman and dog-breeder.]
A small working terrier with short legs and a rough or smooth coat, usu. white with dark black or brown markings. Also ***Jack Russell terrier***.

jacks /dʒaks/ *noun.* Now *Irish.* E17.
[ORIGIN Var. of JAKES.]
A lavatory.

jackshay /ˈdʒakʃeɪ/ *noun.* *Austral.* Also **-shea**. L19.
[ORIGIN Unknown.]
A tin quart-pot.

jackshit /dʒakˈʃɪt/ *noun.* *N. Amer. coarse slang.* M20.
[ORIGIN from JACK *noun*[1] + SHIT *noun*.]
Anything at all; nothing.

> D. ALLISON I don't need no man to tell me jackshit about my child.

jacksie /ˈdʒaksi/ *noun.* *slang.* Also **-sy**. L19.
[ORIGIN from JACK *noun*[1] + -SY.]
The buttocks.

Jacksonian /dʒakˈsəʊnɪən/ *adjective*[1] *& noun.* E19.
[ORIGIN from *Jackson* (see below) + -IAN.]
▸ **A** *adjective.* Pertaining to or characteristic of Andrew Jackson (1767–1845), seventh president of the United States of America, a prominent Democrat. E19.
▸ **B** *noun.* A follower of Jackson. E19.
▪ **Jacksonianism** *noun* the political convictions of Jacksonians E20.

Jacksonian /dʒakˈsəʊnɪən/ *adjective*[2]. L19.
[ORIGIN from John Hughlings *Jackson* (1835–1911), English physician and neurologist + -IAN.]
MEDICINE. Designating or characteristic of a form of epilepsy in which seizures begin at one site (usu. a digit or the angle of the mouth); designating a seizure of this kind.

jackstraw /ˈdʒakstrɔː/ *noun.* Also **jack-straw**. L16.
[ORIGIN from JACK *noun*[1] + STRAW *noun*. Partly from *Jack Straw*, a leader in the rising of the Commons in 1381.]
1 A person of no substance, worth, or consideration. L16.
2 In *pl.* A set of straws or other thin strips, used in a game in which they are thrown in a heap, and each must be picked up singly without disturbing any other; (treated as *sing.*) this game. E19.
3 A jot, a whit. E19.

jacksy *noun* var. of JACKSIE.

jack-up /ˈdʒakʌp/ *noun.* M20.
[ORIGIN from JACK *verb* + UP *adverb*[1].]
A type of offshore oil-drilling rig, the legs of which are lowered to the seabed from the operating platform. Also ***jack-up rig***.

jack-with-the-lantern *noun* see JACK-O'-LANTERN.

Jacky /ˈdʒaki/ *noun.* Also **-ey**, **j-**. L18.
[ORIGIN Dim. of JACK *noun*[1]: see -Y[6].]
1 Gin. *slang.* L18.
2 In full ***Jacky Jacky***. An Australian Aborigine. *Austral. slang (offensive).* M19.
3 A sailor. *slang.* L19.
4 A kookaburra. Cf. JACK *noun*[1] 24b, JACKO. *Austral. colloq.* L19.
– COMB.: **Jacky Winter** *Austral.* the brown flycatcher, *Microeca leucophaea* (family Eopsaltridae); also called ***post-boy***, ***spinks***.

jackyard /ˈdʒakjɑːd/ *noun.* L19.
[ORIGIN from JACK *noun*[1] + YARD *noun*[2].]
NAUTICAL. A spar used in fore-and-aft rigged craft, chiefly yachts, to spread the foot of a large gaff topsail out beyond the peak of the mainsail.
▪ **jackyarder** *noun* a jackyard topsail L19.

Jacob /ˈdʒeɪkəb/ *noun.* M17.
[ORIGIN Male forename, from ecclesiastical Latin *Jacobus*, Greek *Iakōbos*, from Hebrew *Yaʿăqōḇ*: sense 4 with ref. to *Genesis* 30:39–42. Cf. JAMES.]
†**1** = JACOBUS. Only in M17.
2 A ladder. *slang.* Now *rare* or *obsolete.* E18.
†**3** A foolish person. *slang.* Only in E19.
4 (An animal of) a piebald breed of sheep, usu. two- or four-horned, kept since the 18th cent. as an ornamental park breed and, esp. in the Hebrides, for wool. Also ***Jacob sheep***, ***Jacob's sheep***. E20.

Jacobaea /dʒakəˈbiːə/ *noun.* M18.
[ORIGIN mod. Latin, perh. from German *S. Jacobs Kraut*.]
1 ***Jacobaea lily***, = ***Jacobean lily*** s.v. JACOBEAN *adjective*. M18.
2 Orig., ragwort, *Senecio jacobaea* (formerly called ***St James's wort***). Now, a related purple-flowered southern African plant, *S. elegans*, grown for ornament. L18.

Jacobean /dʒakəˈbiːən/ *adjective & noun.* L18.
[ORIGIN from mod. Latin *Jacobaeus* from ecclesiastical Latin *Jacobus* James: see JACOB, -EAN.]
▸ **A** *adjective.* **1** Of or pertaining to the apostle St James or the Epistle of St James. L18.
2 Of, pertaining to, or characteristic of the reign or times of James I, king of England 1603–25 (the later part of his reign as James VI of Scotland, 1567–1625). M19. ▸**b** *spec.* Designating the architectural style prevalent in England around this time, consisting of very late Gothic combined with many classical features. L19. ▸**c** Of furniture: made in the style of the Jacobean period; of the colour of dark oak. E20.
3 Of or pertaining to the American novelist and critic Henry James (1843–1916), = JAMESIAN *adjective* 2. E20.
– SPECIAL COLLOCATIONS: **Jacobean lily** a Mexican ornamental bulbous plant, *Sprekelia formosissima* (family Amaryllidaceae), with crimson funnel-shaped flowers.
▸ **B** *noun.* **1** A person, esp. a statesman or writer, of the time of James I. L19.
2 = JACOBITE *noun*[2] 2. E20.

Jacobethan /dʒakəˈbiːθ(ə)n/ *adjective.* M20.
[ORIGIN Blend of JACOBEAN and ELIZABETHAN.]
Of design: displaying a combination of the Elizabethan and Jacobean styles.

Jacob Evertsen /dʒeɪkəb ˈɛvəts(ə)n, *foreign* jakɒp ˈɪəvəts(ə)n/ *noun.* *S. Afr.* E18.
[ORIGIN Said to be a 17th-cent. Dutch sea captain.]
= JACOPEVER.

Jacobi /ˈdzakəbi/ *noun.* L19.
[ORIGIN See JACOBIAN.]
MATH. **1** ***Jacobi equation***, ***Jacobi's equation***, ***Jacobi identity***, an identity of the form $a(bc) + b(ca) + c(ab) = 0$, where *a*, *b*, *c* are operators or functions. L19.
2 ***Jacobi polynomial***, ***Jacobi's polynomial***, any of a set of polynomial functions of three variables, $J_n(p,\ q;\ x)$, equivalent to the hypergeometric functions $F(-n,\ p + n;\ q;\ x)$. L19.

Jacobian /dʒəˈkəʊbɪən/ *adjective & noun.* M19.
[ORIGIN from *Jacobi* (see below) + -AN.]
MATH. ▸**A** *adjective.* Designating or pertaining to any of various concepts discovered, introduced, or investigated by the German mathematician K. G. J. Jacobi (1804–51). M19.
Jacobian function = ***theta function*** (a) s.v. THETA.
▸ **B** *noun.* A determinant whose constituents are the derivatives of a number of functions $(u, v, w, \ldots)$ with respect to each of the same number of variables $(x, y, z, \ldots)$. L19.

Jacobin /ˈdʒakəbɪn/ *noun*[1] *& adjective*[1]. ME.
[ORIGIN Old French & mod. French from medieval Latin *Jacobinus* from ecclesiastical Latin *Jacobus*: see JACOB, -IN[2]. Sense 1 from assoc. with the church of S. Jacques in Paris.]
▸ **A** *noun.* **1** A friar of the order of St Dominic; a Dominican. ME.
2 *hist.* A member of a French political society established in 1789 at the old Dominican convent in Paris to maintain and propagate the principles of democracy and equality. L18.
3 A sympathizer with the principles of the Jacobins of the French Revolution; a radical or revolutionary in politics or social organization. L18.

> M. J. LASKY The Black Jacobins of Africa.

▸ **B** *adjective.* **1** Of or pertaining to the Dominican friars. M16.
2 Of or pertaining to the Jacobins of the French Revolution (*hist.*); radical, revolutionary. L18.

> E. P. THOMPSON The Jacobin tradition . . of self-education and of rational criticism of political and religious institutions.

▪ **Jacoˈbinic**, **Jacoˈbinical** *adjectives* of, pertaining to, or characteristic of the Jacobins of the French Revolution; radical: L18. **Jacobinize** *verb trans.* imbue with radical or revolutionary ideas L18.

†**Jacobin** *noun*[2] *& adjective*[2]. E16–M18.
[ORIGIN Old French from medieval Latin *Jacobinus* alt. of *Jacobita* JACOBITE *noun*[1] *& adjective*[1].]
= JACOBITE *noun*[1] *& adjective*[1].

jacobin /ˈdʒakəbɪn/ *noun*[3]. L17.
[ORIGIN French *jacobine* fem. of JACOBIN *noun*[1].]
1 A breed of fancy pigeon with reversed feathers on the back of the neck like a cowl or hood; a pigeon of this breed. L17.
2 Either of two hummingbirds with neck feathers resembling a hood, *Florisuga mellivora* and *Melanotrochilus fuscus*. M19.

Jacobinism /ˈdʒakəbɪnɪz(ə)m/ *noun*. **L18**.
[ORIGIN French *Jacobinisme*, formed as JACOBIN *noun*[1] & *adjective*[1]: see -ISM.]
The doctrine or practice of the Jacobins of the French Revolution; radical or revolutionary principles.

Jacobite /ˈdʒakəbʌɪt/ *noun*[1] & *adjective*[1]. **LME**.
[ORIGIN medieval Latin *Jacobita*, from *Jacobus*: see JACOB, -ITE[1].]
▸ **A** *noun*. **1** ECCLESIASTICAL HISTORY. A member of a Monophysite Christian Church taking its name from Jacobus Baradaeus of Edessa, a Syrian monk who revived the Eutychian doctrine in the 6th cent. **LME**.
†**2** = JACOBIN *noun*[1] 1. **M16–E19**.
▸ **B** *adjective*. ECCLESIASTICAL HISTORY. Of or pertaining to the Jacobites. **M17**.

Jacobite /ˈdʒakəbʌɪt/ *noun*[2] & *adjective*[2]. **E17**.
[ORIGIN from ecclesiastical Latin *Jacobus* (see JACOB) + -ITE[1].]
▸ **A** *adjective*. †**1** Of or pertaining to James I, king of England; Jacobean. Only in **E17**.
2 *hist.* Designating, of, or pertaining to a Jacobite or the Jacobites. **L17**. ▸**b** Of glass or pottery: bearing inscriptions and emblems which indicate Jacobite sympathies. **M20**.
▸ **B** *noun*. **1** *hist.* A supporter of James II, King of England (reigned 1685–8), after his removal from the throne in 1688, or of his descendants or the Stuarts. Cf. WILLIAMITE *noun* 2. **L17**.
2 An admirer of Henry James (see JACOBEAN *adjective* 3). **E20**.
■ **Jacobitical** /-ˈbɪt-/ *adjective* of or pertaining to the Jacobites, holding Jacobite principles **L18**. **Jacobitish** *adjective* (*rare*) = Jacobitical **E18**. **Jacobitishly** *adverb* (*rare*) **L19**. **Jacobitism** *noun* (*hist.*) the principles of the Jacobites; adherence to or sympathy with the Stuart cause: **E18**.

Jacob's ladder /dʒeɪkəbz ˈladə/ *noun phr.* **M18**.
[ORIGIN W. allus. to Jacob's dream of a ladder reaching to heaven, as described in *Genesis* 28:12.]
1 A common garden plant and rare British native of limestone scree, *Polemonium caeruleum* (family Polemoniaceae), with corymbs of blue (or white) flowers, so called from its long pinnate leaves with closely spaced leaflets. **M18**.
2 NAUTICAL. A rope or chain ladder. **M19**.
3 An elevator consisting of a series of bucket-shaped receptacles attached to an endless chain. **M19**.

Jacob's membrane /ˈdʒeɪkəbz ˈmɛmbreɪn/ *noun phr.* **M19**.
[ORIGIN Arthur *Jacob* (d. 1874), Irish ophthalmic surgeon.]
ANATOMY. The layer of rods and cones in the retina of the eye.

Jacobson /ˈdʒeɪkəbs(ə)n/ *noun*. **M19**.
[ORIGIN Ludwig Levin *Jacobson* (1783–1843), Danish anatomist and physician.]
1 ANATOMY. ***Jacobson's nerve***, the tympanic nerve, a branch of the glossopharyngeal (ninth cranial) nerve. **M19**.
2 ZOOLOGY. ***Jacobson's organ***, an olfactory organ well-developed in many vertebrates, notably snakes and lizards, occurring as (one of) a pair of sacs or tubes usu. in the roof of the mouth. **L19**.

Jacob's staff /dʒeɪkəbz ˈstɑːf/ *noun phr.* **M16**.
[ORIGIN W. allus. to St James (ecclesiastical Latin *Jacobus*), whose symbols are a pilgrim's staff and a scallop shell, or *Genesis* 30:37–43, 32:10.]
†**1** A pilgrim's staff. **M16–M17**.
2 **a** *hist.* An instrument for taking the altitude of a celestial object. **M16**. ▸**b** An instrument for measuring distances and heights, consisting of a rod fitted with a cursor. **L18**.

Jacobus /dʒəˈkəʊbəs/ *noun*. **E17**.
[ORIGIN ecclesiastical Latin: see JACOB.]
hist. (An unofficial name for) an English gold coin, the sovereign or unite, struck in the reign of James I and equivalent to 20, 22, or 24 shillings.

jaconet /ˈdʒakənɪt/ *noun*. **M18**.
[ORIGIN Urdu *Jagannāth(purī)* (now Puri) in India, its place of origin: see JUGGERNAUT.]
A cotton cloth resembling cambric, *esp.* a dyed waterproof variety used for poulticing etc.

jacopever /ˈjakəpiːvə/ *noun*. Chiefly *S. Afr.* Pl. same. **E20**.
[ORIGIN from JACOB EVER(TSEN).]
Any of several edible marine fishes distinguished by reddish skin and large eyes; *esp.* the S. Atlantic scorpaenid *Sebastichthys capensis*.

jacquard /ˈdʒakɑːd, -kəd/ *adjective & noun*. Also **J-**. **M19**.
[ORIGIN J. M. *Jacquard*, French inventor (1752–1834).]
▸ **A** *adjective*. **1** Designating an attachment to a loom which enables the pattern in the cloth to be produced automatically by means of punched cards; designating a loom fitted with this. **M19**.
2 Designating a fabric, article, or pattern made with the aid of this; of an intricate variegated design. **M19**.
> A. LURIE A lavender jacquard sweater.

▸ **B** *noun*. **1** A jacquard fabric, pattern, or article. **M19**.
> *Radio Times* Many other quality fabrics . . including plains, florals and jacquards.

2 A jacquard attachment or loom. **L19**.

jacqueminot /ˈʒakmɪnəʊ, *foreign* ʒakmino (*pl. same*)/ *noun*. **L19**.
[ORIGIN Vicomte J. F. *Jacqueminot* (1787–1865), French general. Earlier as GÉNÉRAL JACQUEMINOT.]
A hybrid perpetual rose with deep crimson flowers. Also ***Jacqueminot rose***.

jacquerie /ˈʒeɪk(ə)ri, *foreign* ʒakri (*pl. same*)/ *noun*. **E16**.
[ORIGIN Old French & mod. French, from male forename *Jacques*. Cf. JACK *noun*[1] 1.]
The revolt of the peasants of northern France against the nobles in 1357–8; any popular rising of the peasantry.

jactance /ˈdʒakt(ə)ns/ *noun*. *rare*. **LME**.
[ORIGIN Old French & mod. French, or Latin *jactantia* boasting, from *jactant-* pres. ppl stem of *jactare*: see JACTATION, -ANCE.]
Boasting, bragging.
■ **jactancy** *noun* boastfulness, boasting **LME**.

jactation /dʒakˈteɪʃ(ə)n/ *noun*. **L16**.
[ORIGIN Latin *jactatio(n-)*, from *jactat-* pa. ppl stem of *jactare*, frequentative of *jacere* to throw: see -ATION.]
1 Boasting, bragging, ostentatious display. **L16**.
2 (A) restless tossing and turning of the body. **L17**.

jactitation /dʒaktɪˈteɪʃ(ə)n/ *noun*. **M17**.
[ORIGIN medieval Latin *jactitatio(n-)* false declaration tending to someone's detriment, from Latin *jactitare* bring forward in public, utter, (later) boast, frequentative of *jactare*: see JACTATION, -ATION. In sense 2 app. an expressive extension of JACTATION 2.]
1 Public display or declaration, esp. of a boastful nature; boasting, bragging. Now *rare* or *obsolete* exc. in ***jactitation of marriage*** below. **M17**.
jactitation of marriage LAW (now *hist.*) false declaration that one is married to a specified person.
2 MEDICINE. Orig., = JACTATION 2. Now, convulsive movement of a limb, muscle, or muscle group. **M17**.

jacu /dʒəˈkuː/ *noun*. **E19**.
[ORIGIN Portuguese from Tupi *jacú*.]
Any of various guans of the genus *Penelope*, esp. *P. marail* or *P. jacquacu*.

jaculate /ˈdʒakjʊleɪt/ *verb*. *rare*. **E17**.
[ORIGIN Latin *jaculat-* pa. ppl stem of *jaculari* dart, hurl, from *jaculum* a dart, from *jacere* to throw: see -ATE[3].]
1 *verb trans.* Dart, hurl. **E17**.
2 *verb intrans.* Dart forward. **E17**.
■ **jacuˈlation** *noun* the action of hurling or throwing; a throw: **E17**. **jaculator** *noun* (**a**) a person who hurls or throws; †(**b**) (in full ***jaculator fish***) = ARCHER 4: **M18**.

jacutinga /dʒakjʊˈtɪŋgə/ *noun*. **M19**.
[ORIGIN Portuguese from Tupi = a guan (whose plumage the ore is said to resemble), from *jacú* JACU + *tinga* white.]
Any of various kinds of soft gold-bearing iron ore found in Brazil.

Jacuzzi /dʒəˈkuːzi/ *noun*. Also **j-**. **M20**.
[ORIGIN Candido *Jacuzzi* (c 1903–86), US inventor.]
(Proprietary name for) a kind of large bath which uses underwater jets of warm water to massage the body.

jadam /ˈdʒadam/ *noun*. **E20**.
[ORIGIN Malay.]
A type of silver or brass niello ware from the Malay peninsula and Sumatra, used esp. for decorating belt buckles.

jade /dʒeɪd/ *noun*[1]. **LME**.
[ORIGIN Unknown.]
1 An inferior or worn-out horse, a nag. Now *rare*. **LME**.
2 A woman, *esp.* a headstrong or disreputable one. *arch.* or *joc.* **M16**.
> *fig.*: CLIVE JAMES Grand Central Station was saved by public outcry but public outcry is a fickle jade.

■ **jadish** *adjective* (now *rare*) **L16**. **jady** *adjective* (*rare*) **L19**.

jade /dʒeɪd/ *noun*[2] & *adjective*. **L16**.
[ORIGIN French (*le jade* for earlier *l'ejade*) from Spanish *ijada* (in *piedra de ijada* lit. 'colic stone') from Proto-Romance, from Latin *ilia* flanks.]
▸ **A** *noun*. **1** Either of two hard minerals used for implements and ornaments, *esp.* a pale green variety of gem quality, (**a**) = NEPHRITE; (**b**) = JADEITE. Also, any of various other ornamental green minerals. **L16**.
serpentine jade: see SERPENTINE *noun*.
2 A colour resembling that of jade; a light bluish-green. **E20**.
– COMB.: **jade-green** *noun & adjective* (of) the colour jade; **jade-stone** = sense A.1 above.
▸ **B** *adjective*. Made of or resembling jade; of the colour of jade. **M19**.

jade /dʒeɪd/ *verb*. **E17**.
[ORIGIN from JADE *noun*[1].]
1 *verb trans.* Exhaust, wear out; fatigue, tire; sate, dull. **E17**.
2 *verb intrans.* Become tired or worn out; flag. **E17**.
†**3** *verb trans.* Fool, trick. Only in **17**.

jaded /ˈdʒeɪdɪd/ *adjective*. **L16**.
[ORIGIN from JADE *noun*[1], *verb*: see -ED[2], -ED[1].]
†**1** Disreputable. Only in **L16**.
2 Dulled or sated by continual experience or indulgence. **M17**.
> *Sunday Express* I'm not cynical though—just a little jaded perhaps. *Sunday Times* Jaded fashion editors and blasé buyers.

3 Tired, worn out. **L17**.
> T. HARDY A little rest for the jaded animal being desirable, he did not hasten. M. S. POWER He was too jaded, too drunk to do anything about it.

■ **jadedly** *adverb* **L19**. **jadedness** *noun* **L19**.

jadeite /ˈdʒeɪdʌɪt/ *noun*. **M19**.
[ORIGIN from JADE *noun*[2] + -ITE[1].]
MINERALOGY. A monoclinic silicate of sodium, aluminium, and ferric iron, of the pyroxene group, resembling nephrite and prized as jade.
■ **jadeitic** /dʒeɪˈdɪtɪk/ *adjective* approximating to jadeite in composition **M20**.

j'adoube /ʒadub/ *interjection*. **E19**.
[ORIGIN French, from *je, j'* I + 1st person sing. of *adouber*: see DUB *verb*[1].]
CHESS. Indicating that a player wishes to touch a piece without making a move.

Jaeger /ˈjeɪgə/ *noun*[1]. **M19**.
[ORIGIN E. R. *Jaeger* von Jasthal (1818–84), Austrian ophthalmologist.]
Used in *possess.* and *attrib.* to designate a series of short passages printed in typefaces of different sizes and used for testing sharpness of vision.

jaeger /ˈdʒeɪgə/ *noun*[2]. Also (earlier) **jager**, †**jäger**. **M19**.
[ORIGIN Anglicized from JÄGER.]
▸ **I** **1** Formerly, any predatory seabird. Now *spec.* each of three Arctic-breeding skuas, *Stercorarius pomarinus*, *S. parasiticus*, and *S. longicaudus*. **M19**.
long-tailed jaeger the long-tailed skua, *Stercorarius longicaudus*. **parasitic jaeger** = ***Arctic*** SKUA. POMARINE ***jaeger***.
▸ **II** **2** See JÄGER.

Jaffa /ˈdʒafə/ *noun*. **L19**.
[ORIGIN A port in Israel (biblical *Joppa*), where the fruit was first grown.]
In full ***Jaffa orange***. (Proprietary name for) a large, oval, thick-skinned variety of orange.
Jaffa cake a sponge biscuit with an orange-flavoured jelly filling and chocolate topping.

jaffle /ˈdʒaf(ə)l/ *noun*. *Austral.* **M20**.
[ORIGIN Proprietary name for a kind of toaster.]
A toasted sandwich.

JAG *abbreviation*.
Judge Advocate General.

jag /dʒag/ *noun*[1]. **LME**.
[ORIGIN from JAG *verb*.]
1 *hist.* An ornamental point or projection made by cutting the edge of a garment; a slash or cut made in the surface of a garment to show a different colour underneath. **LME**.
2 A projecting tendril, branch, bristle, or thread; *Scot.* a prickle, a thorn. **LME**.
3 A shred of cloth, a scrap, a fragment; in *pl.*, rags, tatters. *obsolete* exc. *dial.* **M16**.
4 A sharp projection or point; a pointed division of a wing or leaf; a sharp or rugged point of rock etc. **L16**.
> H. N. HUTCHINSON Clutching an outstanding jag of the rock. *fig.*: *Time* Tinkering with numbers . . could cause a sharp downward jag in an earnings report.

5 A prick with something sharp; *spec.* an injection. Chiefly *Scot.* **L17**.
6 A jagged piece of metal fitted to the end of a ramrod, fastened to a rag and used to clean a rifle barrel. **M19**.
■ **jaggy** *adjective* jagged; *Scot.* prickly: **E18**.

jag /dʒag/ *noun*[2]. **L16**.
[ORIGIN Unknown.]
1 A small load of hay, wood, etc. *dial.* & *US.* **L16**. ▸**b** A bag, a bundle. *dial.* & *US.* **L18**. ▸**c** A portion, a quantity. *US.* **M19**.
2 **a** As much alcoholic drink as a person can take. Also, a drinking bout; the state or a period of being drunk. *dial.* & *colloq.* **L17**. ▸**b** An intense period of indulgence in a particular activity, emotion, interest, etc. *colloq.* (orig. *US*). **E20**.
> **a** J. T. FARRELL But it wasn't like a jag, for that could be slept off. **b** M. BINCHY Starting a crying jag that was going to last two hours. *New York Times* An amphetamine-powered talking jag.

jag /dʒag/ *verb trans.* Infl. **-gg-**. **LME**.
[ORIGIN Rel. to JOG *verb*: cf. RAG *verb*[1], TAG *noun*[1].]
1 Stab, pierce. Now only (*Scot.*, *N. English*, & *US dial.*) prick (as) with a thorn, needle, etc. **LME**.
2 *hist.* Slash or pink (a garment etc.) for ornamentation. **LME**.
3 Make indentations in the edge or surface of; cut or tear unevenly. **M16**.

†**Jagannath** *noun* see JUGGERNAUT.

Jagatai *noun & adjective* see CHAGATAI.

jagati /ˈdʒʌgətiː/ *noun*. **M19**.
[ORIGIN Sanskrit.]
A Vedic metre of four twelve-syllable lines.

jäger /ˈjeɪgə/ *noun*. Also **jaeger**. See also JAEGER. **L18**.
[ORIGIN German, from *jagen* hunt, pursue. See also YAGER *noun*[1].]
▸ **I** **1** Orig., a marksman in the German or Austrian infantry. Later, a member of a battalion of riflemen in these armies. Now, a member of a regiment using the name as an official title. **L18**.

2 A (Ge...an or Swiss) huntsman or hunter. **E19.**
3 A... attendant wearing a huntsman's costume. Cf. CHASSEUR 2a. **E19.**
▸ **II** See JAEGER *noun*[2].

jagged /ˈdʒagɪd, *in sense 2 also* dʒagd/ ***adjective***[1]. **LME.**
[ORIGIN from JAG *noun*[1], *verb*: see -ED[2], -ED[1].]
1 Edged with sharp projections and deep indentations; having a ragged or uneven edge; irregularly and sharply pointed. **LME.**

> A. J. CRONIN The jagged edge of broken glass. C. FRANCIS The jagged teeth of the Scilly rocks. C. HOPE Jagged dark blue stripes.

2 *hist.* Of a garment etc.: cut into jags for ornamentation; pinked, slashed. **LME.**
3 Of a leaf, petal, etc.: having sharp projections and deeply and irregularly indented edges. Of a plant: having jagged leaves or flowers. **LME.**
jagged chickweed a small weed of the pink family, *Holosteum umbellatum*, with toothed or jagged white petals.
■ **jaggedly** *adverb* **L17.** **jaggedness** *noun* **E16.**

jagged /dʒagd/ ***adjective***[2]. *colloq.* (chiefly *US*). **M18.**
[ORIGIN from JAG *noun*[2] + -ED[2].]
1 Drunk, intoxicated by alcohol. **M18.**
2 Intoxicated by or under the influence of drugs. **M20.**

jagger /ˈdʒagə/ ***noun***[1]. *dial.* **E16.**
[ORIGIN from JAG *noun*[2], *verb* + -ER[1].]
1 A pedlar, a hawker. Also, a carrier, a carter. **E16.**
2 *MINING* (now *hist.*). A driver of packhorses, a person in charge of trains of trucks. **M18.**

jagger /ˈdʒagə/ ***noun***[2]. *obsolete* exc. *hist.* Also **yager**, **yagger**, /ˈjag-/. **E17.**
[ORIGIN Dutch *jager*, abbreviation of *haringjager*, from *haring* herring + *jager* hunter (cf. JÄGER), from *jagen* hunt, pursue.]
A vessel taking supplies to deep-sea fishing boats and bringing back their catches.

jagger /ˈdʒagə/ ***noun***[3]. **E19.**
[ORIGIN from JAG *verb* + -ER[1].]
A person who or thing which jags something.

jaggery /ˈdʒag(ə)ri/ ***noun***. **L16.**
[ORIGIN Portuguese *xagara*, *jag(a)ra*, *jagre* from Malayalam *cakkarā* from Sanskrit *śarkarā* sugar.]
A coarse dark brown sugar made in India by evaporation of the sap of various palms.
– COMB.: **jaggery palm** any of several palms that yield jaggery, esp. *Caryota urens*.

jagir /ˈdʒɑːgɪə/ ***noun***. Also **jaghir**. **E17.**
[ORIGIN Persian & Urdu *jāgīr*, from Persian *jā* place + *gīr* holding.]
In parts of the Indian subcontinent: a grant of the public revenues or produce of a district to an individual or group, for either private use or public benefit; a district subject to such a grant; the income derived from such a grant.
■ **jagirdar** /ˈdʒɑːgɪədɑː/ *noun* a holder of a jagir **L18.**

jagt /jakt/ ***noun***. **M19.**
[ORIGIN Danish = YACHT *noun*: cf. Norwegian, Swedish *jakt*.]
In Scandinavia, a small single-masted coastal vessel, rigged either with square sails or as a cutter or sloop.

jaguar /ˈdʒagjʊə/ ***noun***. **E17.**
[ORIGIN Portuguese from Tupi-Guarani *yaguára* carnivorous animal, jaguar (cf. JAGUARETE).]
A large carnivorous feline, *Panthera onca*, of Central and S. America, mainly yellowish-brown with dark spots grouped in rosettes.

jaguarete /dʒagjʊəˈrɛteɪ/ ***noun***. **M18.**
[ORIGIN Tupi-Guarani *yaguareté* jaguar, formed as JAGUAR + *-eté* true.]
A supposed variety of the jaguar.
– NOTE: The Guarani name for the jaguar (as opp. to carnivores in general), mistaken by European writers for a distinct variety.

jaguarundi /dʒagwəˈrʌndi, jagwɑː-/ ***noun***. Also **-rondi** /-ˈrɒndi/. **M19.**
[ORIGIN Portuguese from Tupi-Guarani, formed as JAGUAR + *undi* dark.]
An American wild cat, *Felis yagouaroundi*, larger than the domestic cat, with a long body and tail and inhabiting forest and scrub from Arizona to Argentina.

Jah /dʒɑː, jɑː/ ***noun***. **M16.**
[ORIGIN Repr. (orig. in the Bible) Hebrew *Yāh*, abbreviation of *Yahweh* JEHOVAH.]
God.
– NOTE: Rare before **M20** when it was popularized by the Rastafarian movement.

Jahveh *noun* var. of YAHWEH.

Jahvism *noun* var. of YAHWISM.

jai alai /hʌɪ əˈlʌɪ/ ***noun phr.*** **E20.**
[ORIGIN Spanish, from Basque *jai* festival + *alai* merry.]
= PELOTA 1.

Jai Hind /dʒʌɪ ˈhɪnd/ ***interjection***. **M20.**
[ORIGIN Hindi, from *jai* long live! + *Hind* India.]
In India: a salutation used in exchange of greetings, at a public meeting, etc.

jail /dʒeɪl/ ***noun & verb***. Also **gaol**. **ME.**
[ORIGIN Old Northern French *gaiole*, *gayolle*, *gaole* or Old French *jaiole*, *geole*, etc. (mod. *geôle*) prison, from Proto-Romance and popular Latin dim. of Latin *cavea* CAGE *noun*.]
▸ **A** *noun*. **1** A place or building for the confinement of people accused or convicted of a crime or offence. Now *spec.* a public prison for the detention of people committed by process of law. **ME.**

> JOSEPH HALL He was committed to the gayle of Newgate.

deliver a jail: see DELIVER *verb* 2.
2 Imprisonment. **LME.**

> *Radio Times* Campaigning to free her husband . . from jail in the USSR.

3 *transf.* & *fig.* A place of confinement. **LME.**

> SPENSER His happie soule to heaven went Out of this fleshlie gaole.

– COMB.: **jailbait** *slang* a girl under the age of consent; **jailbird** a prisoner, *esp.* a long-term prisoner; a habitual criminal; **jailbreak** an escape from a jail; ***jail-delivery***: see DELIVERY *noun* 1; **jail fever** typhus, formerly endemic in jails and other crowded places; **jailhouse** (chiefly *US*) a prison.
▸ **B** *verb trans.* Imprison; put in jail. **E17.**

> *Times* He was jailed for 12 years for a series of 'shocking and disturbing offences'.

– NOTE: In Britain *gaol* is used in some official contexts, but otherwise is restricted to literary use, *jail* being the usual form. In American English *jail* is the usual spelling.

jailer /ˈdʒeɪlə/ ***noun***. Also **gaoler**, **jailor**. **ME.**
[ORIGIN from (the same root as) JAIL + -ER[2].]
A person in charge of a jail or the prisoners in a jail.
■ **jaileress** *noun* a female jailer **M18.** **jailership** *noun* the position or office of a jailer **L15.**

Jain /dʒʌɪn, dʒeɪn/ ***noun & adjective***. Also **Jaina** /ˈdʒʌɪnə, ˈdʒeɪnə/. **L18.**
[ORIGIN Hindi from Sanskrit *jaina* of or pertaining to a Jina, from *jina* (see JINA), lit. 'victor, overcomer', from *ji-* conquer or *jyā-* overcome.]
▸ **A** *noun*. An adherent of a non-brahminical religion established about the 6th cent. BC, characterized by its stress on non-violence and strict asceticism as means to liberation. **L18.**
▸ **B** *adjective*. Of or pertaining to the Jains or their religion. **E19.**
■ **Jainism** *noun* the Jain religion **M19.** **Jainist** *noun & adjective* (now *rare*) = JAIN **E19.**

Jaipur /dʒʌɪˈpʊə/ ***adjective***. **L19.**
[ORIGIN See below.]
Of, pertaining to, or made in Jaipur, capital of the Indian state of Rajasthan, or the former Indian state of Jaipur.
■ **Jaipuri** /dʒʌɪˈpʊəri/ *noun* the Rajasthani dialect of the Jaipur area **E20.**

jak *noun* var. of JACK *noun*[3].

jake /dʒeɪk/ ***noun***[1]. *US colloq.* **M19.**
[ORIGIN Prob. the male forename *Jake*, abbreviation of *Jacob*.]
In full ***country jake***. A rustic lout or simpleton.

jake /dʒeɪk/ ***noun***[2]. *slang* (orig. *US*). **E20.**
[ORIGIN Abbreviation of *Jamaica*.]
An alcoholic drink made from Jamaica ginger. Also, methylated spirits used as an alcoholic drink.

jake /dʒeɪk/ ***adjective***. *slang* (chiefly *Austral.* & *NZ*). **E20.**
[ORIGIN Unknown.]
Excellent, admirable, fine.

> S. KING Everything seemed jake until he found the dope.

■ Also **jakea'loo**, **jaker'loo** *adjective* **E20.**

jakes /dʒeɪks/ ***noun***. **M16.**
[ORIGIN Perh. from male forename *Jacques* or the genit. of *Jack*: see JACK *noun*[1].]
1 A privy, a lavatory. **M16.**
2 Excrement; filth. **L16.**

jakkalsbessie /ˈjak(ə)lsˌbɛsi, *foreign* ˈjakals-/ ***noun***. *S. Afr.* **M19.**
[ORIGIN Afrikaans, from *jakkals* jackal + *bessie* berry.]
(The fruit of) either of two tropical African trees, an ebony, *Diospyros mespiliformis*, and *Sideroxylon inerme* (family Sapotaceae).

Jakun /dʒɑːˈkuːn/ ***noun & adjective***. **M19.**
[ORIGIN Jakun.]
▸ **A** *noun*. Pl. **-s**, same. A member of an aboriginal people of the southern part of the Malay peninsula; the language of this people. **M19.**
▸ **B** *attrib.* or as *adjective*. Of or pertaining to the Jakuns or their language. **M20.**

jalap /ˈdʒaləp, ˈdʒɒləp/ ***noun & verb***. **M17.**
[ORIGIN French from Spanish *jalapa*, in full *purga de Jalapa*, from *Jalapa*, *Xalapa* a Mexican city. Cf. JOLLOP *noun*[2].]
▸ **A** *noun*. **1** A purgative drug obtained from the tuberous roots of a Mexican climbing plant, *Ipomoea purga*, and from certain other plants of the bindweed family. **M17.**
2 The plant yielding this drug; (with specifying word) any of certain other plants yielding a similar drug. **L17.**
false jalap = ***marvel of Peru*** s.v. MARVEL *noun*[1].
▸ **B** *verb trans.* Dose or purge with jalap. *rare.* **M18.**

jalapeño /haləˈpeɪnjəʊ, -ˈpiːnəʊ/ ***noun***. Pl. **-os**. **M20.**
[ORIGIN Mexican Spanish.]
A very hot green chilli pepper. Also ***jalapeño pepper***.

jalebi /dʒəˈleɪbiː/ ***noun***. **M19.**
[ORIGIN Hindi, Urdu *jalebī*.]
An Indian sweet made by frying a coil of batter and then soaking it in syrup.

jaleo /xaˈleo/ ***noun***. **M19.**
[ORIGIN Spanish, lit. 'halloo'.]
Clapping to accompany Andalusian dancing; a lively Andalusian dance.

jalfrezi /dʒalˈfreɪzi/ ***noun***. **L20.**
[ORIGIN Bengali, from *jal* hot.]
A medium-hot Indian dish consisting typically of chicken or lamb with fresh chillies, tomatoes, and onions.

jali /ˈdʒɑːliː/ ***noun***. **L20.**
[ORIGIN Urdu, from *jaal* a net.]
Indian ornamental openwork in wood, metal, stone, etc.

jalopy /dʒəˈlɒpi/ ***noun***. *colloq.* **E20.**
[ORIGIN Unknown.]
A battered old motor vehicle or aeroplane.

jalouse /dʒəˈluːz/ ***verb trans.*** **L17.**
[ORIGIN French *jalouser* regard with jealousy, from *jaloux*, *-ouse* JEALOUS.]
1 Have a suspicion of; surmise, guess. *Scot.* **L17.**
2 Suspect; be suspicious about. *Scot.* **E18.**
3 Regard with jealousy. Also, begrudge jealously. **L19.**

jalousie /ˈdʒaluziː/ ***noun***. **M18.**
[ORIGIN French, lit. 'jealousy'; also, a type of blind or shutter.]
A blind or shutter made from a row of angled slats to exclude sun and rain and control the entry of air and light.
■ **jalousied** *adjective* provided with a jalousie **M19.**

Jam /dʒɑːm/ ***noun***[1]. **E18.**
[ORIGIN Unknown.]
hist. (A hereditary title of) any of certain princes and noblemen in Sind, Kutch, and Saurashtra in the Indian subcontinent.

jam /dʒam/ ***noun***[2]. **M18.**
[ORIGIN Perh. from JAM *verb*[1].]
1 A conserve of fruit and sugar boiled to a thick consistency. **M18.**

> E. ACTON To preserve . . the true flavour and the colour of fruit in jams . . boil them rapidly.

2 Something easy, good, or pleasant. **L19.**

> T. A. GUTHRIE Ah! . . I thought you wouldn't find it all jam.

3 Affected manners; self-importance. *Austral. slang.* **L19.**
– PHRASES: **jam on it** some additional pleasure, ease, advantage, etc. (in ***have jam on it***, ***like jam on it***, ***want jam on it*** etc.). **jam tomorrow** a pleasant thing continually promised but usu. never produced. ***money for jam***: see MONEY *noun*.
– COMB.: **jam jar** (***a***) a jar designed for holding jam; (***b***) *rhyming slang* a car.

jam /dʒɑːm/ ***noun***[3]. *obsolete* exc. *hist.* **L18.**
[ORIGIN from JAMA *noun*[1].]
A kind of dress for a child.

jam /dʒam/ ***noun***[4]. **E19.**
[ORIGIN from JAM *verb*[1].]
1 The action of jamming; the fact or condition of being jammed; a crush, a squeeze; a mass of things or persons crowded together or interlocked so as to prevent individual movement; *spec.* such an accumulation of logs in a river or traffic in a street. **E19.** ▸**b** *fig.* An awkward or difficult situation. **E20.**

> **b** P. H. GIBBS 'I'm in the devil of a jam,' said Robin gloomily.

log jam, ***traffic jam***, etc.
2 The action or an act of jamming radio, radar, etc., signals. **E20.**
3 Jazz or popular music simultaneously improvised by a number of performers; a period of playing such music, an informal gathering of musicians improvising together (also ***jam session***). *colloq.* **E20.**

> *Southern Rag* Meadowcroft fetched his instrument and joined in an impromptu jam session.

– COMB.: **jam-proof** *adjective* protected against jamming; ***jam session***: see sense 3 above; **jam-up** *colloq.* = sense 1 above.

jam /dʒam/ ***verb***[1]. Infl. **-mm-**. **E18.**
[ORIGIN Prob. symbolic.]
1 *verb trans.* Press or squeeze (an object) tightly between two converging bodies or surfaces; wedge or fix immovably in a space. **E18.** ▸**b** Bruise or crush by pressure. **M19.** ▸**c** Block (a passage etc.) by crowding in. **M19.**

> M. PIERCY Our three chairs are jammed between chimney and basement door. **c** E. AMADI Adults jammed their doorways to watch.

2 *verb intrans.* Become fixed, wedged, or held immovably; stick fast. **E18.**

> C. RYCROFT She had to use a public telephone but the coins jammed and she had to loosen them.

3 *verb trans.* Press, squeeze, crowd, or force (a number of objects) together in a compact mass. **M18.**

J. G. BALLARD They . . floated in the canals, jammed together around the pillars of the bridges.

4 *verb trans.* Thrust, drive, or force, esp. violently. Usu. foll. by *against, in, into, on*, etc. **L18.**

W. WHARTON I jam the brakes but they don't grab straight and we almost flip. P. FERGUSON Gareth wordlessly jammed his scraper . . into the cupboard's edge.

5 *verb trans.* Cause (a component of a machine) to become wedged or immovable; make (a machine, gun, etc.) unworkable in this way. **M19.** ▸**b** *verb intrans.* Of a machine, gun, etc.: become wedged or immovable and so unworkable. **L19.** ▸**c** *verb trans.* Interfere, esp. deliberately, with (radio or radar signals) so as to make them unintelligible or useless; prevent reception of (a signal) by doing this. **E20.**

J. DIDION A Garuda 727 that had jammed its landing gear. **b** C. HOPE A comparatively new weapon . . inclined to jam when fired in haste. **c** *Daily Telegraph* The Post Office is jamming broadcasts by the pirate radio ship.

6 **a** *verb intrans.* Play in a jam or jam session (see JAM *noun*[4] 3). *colloq.* **M20.** ▸**b** *verb trans.* Improvise (a tune etc.). **M20.**

jam /dʒam/ *verb*[2] *trans. colloq.* Infl. **-mm-**. **M19.**
[ORIGIN from JAM *noun*[2].]
1 Spread with jam. **M19.**
2 Make into jam. **M19.**

jam /dʒam/ *adverb & adjective. Orig. US.* **E19.**
[ORIGIN from JAM *verb*[1].]
▸**A** *adverb.* Closely; in close contact, with firm pressure. Foll. by *against, up.* **E19.**
– COMB.: **jam-full** *adjective* packed full, completely filled; **jam-pack** *verb trans.* pack tightly, fill; **jam-packed** *adjective* tightly packed, closely crowded or squeezed together.
▸**B** *adjective.* Excellent, perfect; thorough. Usu. foll. by *up. colloq.* **M19.**

Jam. *abbreviation.*
1 Jamaica.
2 James (New Testament).

jama /ˈdʒɑːmə/ *noun*[1]. Also **jamah**. **L18.**
[ORIGIN Urdu from Persian *jāma* clothing. Cf. PYJAMAS.]
A long cotton gown worn in the Indian subcontinent.

jama /ˈdʒʌmə/ *noun*[2]. Also **jumma**. **L18.**
[ORIGIN Urdu *jam(a)'* collection, amount, account from Arabic *jama'* addition, total, aggregate.]
During British rule in India, the assessment for land revenue from an estate or division of country.
jamabundi /-bʌndi/ [Persian & Urdu *-bandī* a tie, a band, from Sanskrit *bandh* settlement] (a document recording) the settlement of revenues.

jama /ˈdʒɑːmə/ *noun*[3]. *colloq.* **M20.**
[ORIGIN Abbreviation.]
Pyjama. Usu. in *pl.*

jamadar /ˈdʒʌmədɑː/ *noun.* Also **jem-** /ˈdʒɛm-/. **M18.**
[ORIGIN Urdu *jam(a)'dār* from Persian, from Arabic *jama'*, *jamā'a(t)* muster + Persian *-dār* holding, holder.]
In the Indian subcontinent: a junior army or police officer; a minor official; the head of a body of servants; *hist.* an Indian officer in a sepoy regiment.

jamah *noun* var. of JAMA *noun*[1].

Jamaica /dʒəˈmeɪkə/ *noun.* **M18.**
[ORIGIN A large W. Indian island.]
1 Used *attrib.* to designate things native to or imported from Jamaica. **M18.**
Jamaica ebony = COCUS; the tree yielding cocus. **Jamaica ginger** = *white ginger* s.v. GINGER *noun*. ***Jamaica satinwood***: see SATIN *noun*. **Jamaica pepper** allspice. ***Jamaica sorrel***: see SORREL *noun*[1] 2.
2 *ellipt.* Jamaica coffee, rum, etc. **L18.**

Jamaican /dʒəˈmeɪk(ə)n/ *noun & adjective.* **L17.**
[ORIGIN from JAMAICA + -AN.]
▸**A** *noun.* **1** A native or inhabitant of the W. Indian island of Jamaica. **L17.**
2 The variety of English spoken in Jamaica. **M20.**
▸**B** *adjective.* Of or pertaining to Jamaica or the Jamaicans. **L19.**
■ **Jamaicanism** *noun* a Jamaican word or idiom **M20.**

jaman /ˈdʒɑːmən/ *noun.* Also **jamoon** /ˈdʒɑːmuːn/. **E19.**
[ORIGIN Hindi *jāmun, jāman*, Punjabi *jammūṇ*, from Sanskrit *jambula, jambūla*.]
= JAMBOLAN.

jamb /dʒam/ *noun.* Also **jambe**. **ME.**
[ORIGIN Old French & mod. French *jambe* leg, vertical support, from Proto-Romance (whence late Latin *gamba* hoof) from Greek *kampē* flexure, joint.]
1 ARCHITECTURE. Either of the side posts of a doorway, window, or mantelpiece, on which the lintel rests; in *pl.*, the stone sides of a fireplace. Cf. CHEEK *noun* 5. **ME.**

M. PIERCY She slid a dinner knife between jamb and frame and popped the bolt of the lock.

2 Either of any two side pieces. *rare.* **LME.**
3 **a** A piece of leg armour made of metal or hardened leather. Cf. JAMBEAU, JAMBER. **LME.** ▸**b** HERALDRY. = GAMB. **L15.**
4 A projecting wing of a building. *Scot.* **M16.**
5 A column; a columnar mass or pillar in a quarry or mine. **L17.**
6 MINING. A bed of clay or stone running across a mineral vein or seam. **E18.**

jambalaya /dʒambəˈleɪə/ *noun. Orig. US.* **L19.**
[ORIGIN Louisiana French from Provençal *jambalaia*.]
A dish composed of rice mixed with shrimps, ham, chicken, turkey, etc.; *fig.* a mixture, a jumble.

jambe *noun* var. of JAMB.

†**jambeau** *noun.* Pl. **-s**, **-x**. **LME–E18.**
[ORIGIN App. Anglo-Norman deriv. of French *jambe*: see JAMB *noun*.]
A piece of leg armour; a leg. Cf. JAMB 3a, next.

†**jamber** *noun.* Also **-bier**. **ME–E18.**
[ORIGIN Anglo-Norman *jamber*, Old French & mod. French *jambière* leg armour, from *jambe* leg.]
A piece of leg armour, *esp.* a greave. Cf. JAMB 3a, prec.

jambo /ˈdʒambəʊ/ *noun.* Pl. **-os**. Also **-bu** /-buː/. **L16.**
[ORIGIN Sanskrit *jambu, -bū*, and its derivs., as *jambula, jambūla*: cf. JAMBOLAN.]
In the Indian subcontinent: any of various trees of the genera *Syzygium* and *Eugenia* (family Myrtaceae), or their fruit; *esp.* (**a**) the roseapple, *S. jambos*; (**b**) the jambolan, *S. cumini*; (**c**) the Malay apple, *S. malaccense*.

jambolan /ˈdʒambəlan/ *noun.* **E17.**
[ORIGIN Sanskrit *jambula, jambūla*, formed as JAMBO.]
An Indian and SE Asian tree, *Syzygium cumini* (family Myrtaceae); the fruit of this tree, an edible purplish-red berry. Also called ***jaman***.

jamboree /dʒambəˈriː/ *noun. Orig. US slang.* **M19.**
[ORIGIN Unknown.]
A period of unrestrained celebration or enjoyment; an occasion when a lot of people meet for a pleasurable or frivolous common purpose.

Observer The Institute of Directors' annual jamboree.

jambu *noun* var. of JAMBO.

jamdani /dʒɑːmˈdɑːni/ *noun.* **M19.**
[ORIGIN Persian & Urdu *jāmdānī*.]
In the Indian subcontinent: a kind of brocaded muslin, usu. with a floral pattern.

James /dʒeɪmz/ *noun.* **M16.**
[ORIGIN Male forename, from Old French = Provençal, Catalan *Jaume, Jacme*, Spanish *Jaime*, Italian *Giacomo*, from Proto-Romance alt. of Latin *Jacobus* JACOB.]
1 †**a** ***James Royal***, a silver coin of James VI of Scotland. Only in **M16.** ▸**b** A sovereign (the coin). Cf. JACOBUS. *arch. slang.* **M19.**
b half-James a half sovereign.
2 = JEMMY 3. **E19.**
3 = JEMMY 4. **E19.**

Jamesian /ˈdʒeɪmzɪən/ *adjective & noun.* **L19.**
[ORIGIN from the surname *James* (see below) + -IAN.]
▸**A** *adjective.* **1** Of or pertaining to the American philosopher and psychologist William James (1842–1910) or his work. **L19.**
2 Of or pertaining to his brother, the American (later naturalized British) novelist and critic Henry James (1843–1916) or his work. Cf. JACOBEAN *adjective* 3. **E20.**
▸**B** *noun.* A follower or admirer of William James or Henry James or their work. **M20.**

jamesonite /ˈdʒeɪms(ə)nʌɪt/ *noun.* **E19.**
[ORIGIN from Robert *Jameson* (1774–1854), Scot. mineralogist + -ITE[1].]
MINERALOGY. A grey monoclinic sulphide of lead, antimony, and iron, usu. occurring as fibrous masses. Also called ***feather-ore***.

James's powder /ˈdʒeɪmzɪz ˈpaʊdə/ *noun phr. obsolete* exc. *hist.* **M18.**
[ORIGIN from Robert *James* (1703–76), English physician.]
An antimonial preparation formerly much used as a febrifuge.

†**Jamestown weed** *noun phr.* see JIMSON.

Jamie Green /dʒeɪmɪ ˈɡriːn/ *noun.* **M19.**
[ORIGIN Personal name, of unknown origin.]
NAUTICAL. A type of sail found on tea clippers. Cf. ***Jimmy Green*** s.v. JIMMY *noun*[2].

jamma *noun* var. of JUMMA.

jammer /ˈdʒamə/ *noun.* **M20.**
[ORIGIN from JAM *verb*[1] + -ER[1].]
A person who or thing which jams; *spec.* a transmitter used for jamming.

jammies /ˈjamiːz/ *noun pl. colloq.* **E20.**
[ORIGIN Abbreviation.]
Pyjamas.

jammy /ˈdʒami/ *adjective.* **M19.**
[ORIGIN from JAM *noun*[2] + -Y[1].]
Covered with jam, sticky; *colloq.* excellent; very lucky; easy.

jamoon *noun* var. of JAMAN.

jampan /ˈdʒɑːmpɑːn/ *noun.* **M19.**
[ORIGIN Bengali *jhāmpān*, Hindi *jhappān*.]
A kind of sedan chair carried by four people, used in hill country in the Indian subcontinent.

jams /dʒamz/ *noun pl.* **M20.**
[ORIGIN from PYJAMAS.]
(Proprietary name for) loose knee-length shorts or swimming trunks.

Jan. *abbreviation.*
January.

jandal /ˈdʒand(ə)l/ *noun. NZ.* **M20.**
[ORIGIN Prob. from *J(apanese) (s)andal*.]
(Proprietary name for) a light sandal with a thong between the big and second toe; a flip-flop.

†**jane** *noun*[1]. **LME–L17.**
[ORIGIN Old French *Janne(s*: see JEAN.]
A small silver Genoan coin introduced into England towards the end of the 14th cent.

Jane /dʒeɪn/ *noun*[2]. Also **j-**. **E20.**
[ORIGIN Female forename.]
1 ***plain Jane***, a plain or unattractive girl or woman. **E20.**
2 A woman, a girl; a girlfriend. *slang* (orig. *US*). **E20.**

S. KING There had been . . occasions when he had simply awakened next to some anonymous jane.

3 ***Jane Doe***, the female counterpart of John Doe: an anonymous female; (*colloq.*) an ordinary or typical female. Chiefly *US.* **M20.**

Janeite /ˈdʒeɪnʌɪt/ *noun.* **L19.**
[ORIGIN from *Jane* (see below) + -ITE[1].]
An admirer of the writings of the English novelist Jane Austen (1775–1817).

jangada /dʒəŋˈɡɑːdə/ *noun.* **L16.**
[ORIGIN Portuguese from Malayalam *caṅṅāḍam* from Sanskrit *saṃghāṭa* joining together.]
A log raft with a seat and lateen sail, used as a fishing boat in the north of Brazil and Peru. Formerly also, a type of catamaran used in southern India.

jangle /ˈdʒaŋɡ(ə)l/ *noun.* **ME.**
[ORIGIN Orig. from Anglo-Norman or Old French *jangler* (see JANGLE *verb*); later from JANGLE *verb*.]
1 Idle talk, chatter, jabber; an idle word. Long *obsolete* exc. *dial.* **ME.**
2 Contention, altercation, bickering. Now *rare*. **ME.**
3 A discordant sound, ring, or clang. **L18.**

C. MCCULLERS The sharp jangle of the doorbell.

4 Confused and noisy talk; the mingled din of voices. **M19.**

jangle /ˈdʒaŋɡ(ə)l/ *verb.* **ME.**
[ORIGIN Old French *jangler, gengler* = Provençal *janglar*, prob. from Germanic form repr. by Middle Dutch & mod. Dutch *jangelen*.]
▸**I** *verb intrans.* **1** Talk excessively or noisily; chatter, babble. *obsolete* exc. *dial.* **ME.**
2 Speak angrily, harshly, or discordantly; grumble; dispute, squabble. *arch.* **ME.**
3 Make a discordant or unmusical noise. **L15.**

N. SHUTE Morris dancing . . with flying ribbons and little bells that jangled at the knee.

▸**II** *verb trans.* **4** Say or utter in a noisy, babbling, discordant, or contentious manner; produce (a sound that is harsh and discordant). **LME.**
5 Cause (a bell etc.) to make a harsh discordant sound; *transf.* irritate (the nerves etc.). **E17.**

F. KING A gust of wind jangled a metal shop sign. B. CASTLE Getting up in a rush always jangles my nerves.

■ **jangler** *noun* †(**a**) a chatterer; a storyteller, a jester; (**b**) a noisy disputant: **ME. jangly** *adjective* harsh-sounding, discordant; irritating; irritable: **L19.**

Janglish /ˈdʒaŋɡlɪʃ/ *noun. colloq.* **L20.**
[ORIGIN Blend of JAPANESE and ENGLISH *noun*: see -LISH.]
= JAPLISH.

janissary /ˈdʒanɪs(ə)ri/ *noun.* Also **-iz-** /-ɪz-/. **E16.**
[ORIGIN French *janissaire*, ult. from Turkish *yeniçeri*, from *yeni* new + *çeri* troops.]
1 A member of a body of Turkish infantry, orig. composed mainly of tributary children of Christians, forming the Sultan's guard and the main part of the standing army from the 14th to the 18th cents. **E16.**
2 A devoted follower, supporter, or guard. **M16.**
3 *hist.* A member of a Turkish armed escort for travellers in the East. **E17.**
– COMB.: **janissary music** = ***Turkish music*** s.v. TURKISH *adjective*.

janitor /ˈdʒanɪtə/ *noun.* **M16.**
[ORIGIN Latin, from *janua* door, entrance: see -OR.]
1 A doorkeeper, a porter; *hist.* an ostler. **M16.**
2 A caretaker of a building, esp. a school, responsible for its cleaning, heating, etc. **E18.**
■ **jani'torial** *adjective* **L19. janitress** *noun* a female janitor **E19. janitrix** *noun* (*rare*) = JANITRESS **M19.**

…zary *noun* var. of **JANISSARY**.

janken /ˈdʒaŋk(ə)n/ *noun*. **M20.**
[**ORIGIN** Japanese.]
A children's game played by using the hands to represent one of three things, paper, scissors, or stone.

janker /ˈdʒaŋkə/ *noun*. *Scot.* See also **JINKER** *noun*². **E19.**
[**ORIGIN** Unknown.]
A long pole on wheels for carrying logs, casks, etc.

jankers /ˈdʒaŋkəz/ *noun*. *military slang*. **E20.**
[**ORIGIN** Unknown.]
Punishment for a defaulter; the cells used for this.
> J. GASH The sergeant put me on jankers a fortnight for cheating.

jann /dʒɑːn/ *noun*. **L18.**
[**ORIGIN** Arabic *jānn* jinn.]
= **JINN**.

jannock /ˈdʒanək/ *noun*. *N. English*. **L15.**
[**ORIGIN** Unknown.]
A loaf of leavened oaten bread.

jannock /ˈdʒanək/ *adjective & adverb*. *dial.* See also **JONICK**. **E19.**
[**ORIGIN** Uncertain: perh. from **JANNOCK** *noun*.]
▸ **A** *adjective*. Fair, straightforward; genuine. **E19.**
▸ **B** *adverb*. In a fair, genuine, or straightforward manner. **M19.**

Jansenist /ˈdʒans(ə)nɪst/ *noun*. **M17.**
[**ORIGIN** from Cornelis *Jansen* (1585–1638), Bishop of Ypres, Flanders + **-IST**.]
ECCLESIASTICAL HISTORY. An adherent of the Roman Catholic school of thought holding the doctrines of Jansen, who maintained (claiming the support of St Augustine) the perverseness and inability for good of the natural human will.
■ **Jansenism** *noun* **M17.** **Janseˈnistic** *adjective* of, pertaining to, or holding the doctrines of Jansenism or the Jansenists **M18.** **Janseˈnistical** *adjective* = **JANSENISTIC** **M18.**

J

jansky /ˈdʒanski/ *noun*. **M20.**
[**ORIGIN** Karl C. *Jansky* (1905–50), US radio engineer.]
A unit used in radio astronomy to express the strength of radio sources, equal to 10^{-26} watt per sq. metre per hertz. (Symbol Jy.)

janty *adjective* see **JAUNTY** *adjective*.

January /ˈdʒanjʊ(ə)ri/ *noun*. **OE.**
[**ORIGIN** Latin *Januarius* use as noun (sc. *mensis* month) of adjective from *Janus*: see **JANUS**.]
The first month of the year in the Gregorian calendar.
May and January: see **MAY** *noun*².

Janus /ˈdʒeɪnəs/ *attrib. adjective*. **M17.**
[**ORIGIN** Latin, name of a god who in Roman mythology was the guardian of doors and gates and presided over beginnings, being represented with two faces, one on the front and another on the back of his head.]
1 Having a dual function, purpose, attitude, etc. Also ***Janus-faced***. **M17.**
> A. STORR Aggression seems . . both necessary and undesirable . . —a Janus aspect.

2 (Of a material) having a double facing; (of a device) having a two-way action. **M19.**
3 *CHEMISTRY*. Designating any of a group of basic azo dyes containing a quaternary ammonium group, often with safranine as the diazo component. **L19.**
Janus green either of two basic azo dyes derived from safranine, used as biological stains.

Jap /dʒap/ *noun & adjective*. *colloq.* (*derog. & offensive*). **L19.**
[**ORIGIN** Abbreviation.]
= **JAPANESE**.
Jap silk *arch.* = ***Japanese silk*** s.v. **JAPANESE** *adjective*.

Japan /dʒəˈpan/ *noun*. Also †**-on**. **L16.**
[**ORIGIN** See below.]
▸ **I** **1** Used *attrib.* to designate things native to or brought from Japan, a country off the east coast of the Asian land mass. (Now largely superseded by **JAPANESE** *adjective*.) **L16.**
Japan cedar = **CRYPTOMERIA**. **Japan clover** = **LESPEDEZA**. **Japan current** *the* Kuroshio. **Japan earth** = **CATECHU**. **Japan ink** a high-quality black ink, glossy when dry. ***Japan lacquer***: see **LACQUER** *noun* 3. **Japan laurel** = **AUCUBA**. **Japan paper** = ***Japanese paper*** s.v. **JAPANESE** *adjective*. ***Japan pepper***: see **PEPPER** *noun*. ***Japan quince***: see **QUINCE** 2. **Japan rose** (***a***) = ***Japanese rose*** (a) s.v. **JAPANESE** *adjective*; †(***b***) the camellia. **Japan varnish** = ***Japanese lacquer*** s.v. **LACQUER** *noun* 3. **Japan wax** = ***Japanese wax*** s.v. **JAPANESE** *adjective*.
▸ **II** †**2** A native of Japan; a Japanese person. Only in **E17.**
3 (Usu. **j-**.) A varnish of exceptional hardness which originally came from Japan. Also, any of several similar varnishes, *esp.* (***a***) a black varnish obtained by cooking asphalt with linseed oil, used for producing a black gloss on metal and other materials; (***b***) a varnish-like liquid made from shellac, linseed oil, and turpentine, used as a medium in which to grind colours and for drying pigments. **L17.** ▸**b** *fig.* Deceptive outward appearance, veneer. **M19.**
4 (Also **j-**.) ▸**a** Japanese porcelain. **E18.** ▸†**b** Japanese silk. **E18–E19.**
5 (Also **j-**.) Japanese work, work in the Japanese style; *esp.* work that is varnished and adorned with painted or raised figures. **E18.**

japan /dʒəˈpan/ *verb trans.* Also **J-**. Infl. **-nn-**. **L17.**
[**ORIGIN** from the noun.]
1 Lacquer with japan; varnish with a material that gives a hard black gloss. **L17.**
2 Make black and glossy. **E18.**
3 [With ref. to the black clerical coat.] = **ORDAIN** *verb* 9. *slang*. **M18.**

Japanese /dʒapəˈniːz/ *noun & adjective*. **E17.**
[**ORIGIN** from **JAPAN** *noun* + **-ESE**.]
▸ **A** *noun*. Pl. same, †**-eses**.
1 A native of Japan; a person of Japanese descent. **E17.**
2 The Japanese language. **E19.**
▸ **B** *adjective*. Of or pertaining to Japan, its people, or its language. **E18.**
– **SPECIAL COLLOCATIONS**: **Japanese anemone** any of several autumn-flowering cultivated varieties or hybrids of *Anemone hupehensis*, bearing large pink or white flowers. ***Japanese anise***: see **ANISE** 2. **Japanese ape** = ***Japanese macaque*** below. ***Japanese artichoke***: see **ARTICHOKE** 3. **Japanese beetle** a scarabaeid beetle, *Popillia japonica*, which has become a pest of foliage and grasses in eastern N. America. **Japanese cedar** = **CRYPTOMERIA**. **Japanese cherry** any of several ornamental flowering cherries, the Japanese *Prunus serrulata* and hybrids of it. **Japanese current** = **KUROSHIO**. **Japanese deer** = **SIKA** *noun*¹. **Japanese flower** a piece of coloured paper which unfolds like a flower when placed in water. **Japanese garden**: in which clipped shrubs, water, bridges, rocks, gravel, stone lanterns, etc., are used in a formal design, without masses of bright colour. **Japanese iris** a variety of the irises *Iris kaempferi* or *I. laevigata*. **Japanese knotweed** a tall rhizomatous Japanese plant, *Fallopia japonica* (family Polygonaceae), grown for ornament and now widely naturalized, with broad cuspidate leaves and axillary panicles of small white flowers. ***Japanese lacquer***: see **LACQUER** *noun* 3. **Japanese lantern** = ***Chinese lantern*** (a) s.v. **CHINESE** *adjective*. **Japanese laurel** a Far Eastern aucuba, *Aucuba japonica*, much grown for ornament in the west. **Japanese macaque** a pink-faced macaque of Japan, *Macaca fuscata*. **Japanese maple** any of several maples native to Japan, esp. *Acer palmatum* and *A. japonicum*, cultivated for their decorative foliage. **Japanese medlar** = **LOQUAT**. **Japanese monkey** = ***Japanese macaque*** above. ***Japanese oyster***: see **OYSTER** *noun* 1. **Japanese paper**: made by hand, originally and chiefly in Japan, from the bark of the mulberry tree. ***Japanese privet***. ***Japanese quince***: see **QUINCE** 2. ***Japanese raisin tree***. **Japanese rose** (***a***) any of several roses native to Japan; esp. = **RUGOSA**; (***b***) = **KERRIA**. **Japanese screen** an embroidered screen made in Japan. **Japanese silk** fine soft silk of a type orig. made in Japan, = **HABUTAI**. **Japanese spaniel** (an animal of) a breed of small, black and white or brown and white, long-coated dog. **Japanese tissue (paper)** a type of strong thin transparent paper. **Japanese vellum** a costly paper handmade in Japan from the inner bark of the paper mulberry tree, *Broussonetia papyrifera*. **Japanese waltzing mouse**, **Japanese waltzer** a mutant of *Mus musculus bactrianus*, a house mouse native to central and eastern Asia (cf. **WALTZER** 2). **Japanese wax** a yellow wax obtained from the berries of certain sumacs (***Japanese wax tree***: see **WAX** *noun*¹). ***Japanese wineberry***: see ***wineberry*** s.v. **WINE** *noun*. ***Japanese wisteria***: see **WISTERIA** 1.

Japanesery /dʒapəˈniːz(ə)ri/ *noun*. **L19.**
[**ORIGIN** from **JAPANESE**, after French **JAPONAISERIE**.]
Japanese characteristics or fashion; in *pl.*, Japanese ornaments, knick-knacks, etc.

Japanesey /dʒapəˈniːzi/ *adjective*. *colloq.* Also **-sy**. **L19.**
[**ORIGIN** from **JAPANESE** *adjective* + **-Y**¹.]
Having or inclining to a Japanese character.

Japanesque /dʒapəˈnɛsk/ *adjective & noun*. **L19.**
[**ORIGIN** from **JAPAN** *noun* + **-ESQUE**.]
▸ **A** *adjective*. Japanese in style or manner. **L19.**
▸ **B** *noun*. A design or ornament in Japanese style. **L19.**

Japanesy *adjective* var. of **JAPANESEY**.

Japanimation /dʒəˌpanɪˈmeɪʃ(ə)n/ *noun*. **L20.**
[**ORIGIN** Blend of *Japan* and **ANIMATION**.]
= **ANIME**.

Japanise *verb* var. of **JAPANIZE**.

Japanism /dʒəˈpanɪz(ə)m/ *noun*. **L19.**
[**ORIGIN** from **JAPAN** *noun* + **-ISM**.]
The branch of knowledge that deals with Japanese things; devotion to Japanese things; a thing characteristic of Japan.

Japanize /ˈdʒapənʌɪz/ *verb trans.* Also **-ise**. **L19.**
[**ORIGIN** formed as **JAPANISM** + **-IZE**.]
Make Japanese.
■ **Japaniˈzation** *noun* **L19.**

japanned /dʒəˈpand/ *adjective*. **L17.**
[**ORIGIN** from **JAPAN** *verb*, **JAPAN** *noun*: see **-ED**¹, **-ED**².]
1 That has been japanned. **L17.**
japanned leather: treated with Japan lacquer and dried by heat.
2 (**J-**.) Made or become Japanese. *rare*. **M19.**

Japanner /dʒəˈpanə/ *noun*. **E17.**
[**ORIGIN** from **JAPAN** *noun*, **JAPAN** *verb* + **-ER**¹.]
†**1** A Japanese person. **E17–M18.**
2 (**j-**.) A person who japans things. **L17.** ▸†**b** A shoeblack. *joc.* **E–M18.**

japanning /dʒəˈpanɪŋ/ *noun*. **L17.**
[**ORIGIN** from **JAPAN** *verb* + **-ING**¹.]
The action of japanning things; material used in japanning.

Japano- /ˈdʒapənəʊ/ *combining form*.
[**ORIGIN** from **JAPAN** *noun* + **-O-**.]
Forming adjectives with the sense 'of Japan or the Japanese (and) —', as ***Japano-Chinese***, ***Japano-Korean***.
■ **Japaˈnolatry** *noun* excessive devotion to Japanese art and customs **L19.** **Japaˈnologist** *noun* an expert in or student of Japanese matters **L19.** **Japanophile** *noun* a lover of Japan or the Japanese people **E20.**

jape /dʒeɪp/ *noun*. **ME.**
[**ORIGIN** Rel. to **JAPE** *verb*.]
†**1** A trick, a device to deceive or cheat; a deception, a fraud. **ME–E19.**
2 A device to amuse; a merry or idle tale; a jest, a joke, a jibe. **ME.**
> *Sunday Express* For Nik . . the hardships of army life are a jolly jape.

†**3** A trifle, a toy, a trinket, a plaything. **LME–L16.**
– **NOTE**: Obsolete generally by **E17**, but revived in literary use in **19**.

jape /dʒeɪp/ *verb*. **LME.**
[**ORIGIN** App. combining the form of Old French *japer* (mod. *japper*) to yelp, yap, with the sense of Old French *gaber* mock, deride.]
†**1** *verb trans.* Trick, beguile, deceive. Only in **LME.**
†**2** *verb trans. & intrans.* Seduce or have sexual intercourse with (a woman). **LME–L16.**
†**3** *verb trans.* Mock, deride, insult. **LME–E19.**
4 *verb intrans.* Say or do something in jest or mockery; jest, joke, jeer. **LME.**
– **NOTE**: Obsolete generally by **E17**, but revived in literary use in **19**.

japer /ˈdʒeɪpə/ *noun*. **LME.**
[**ORIGIN** from **JAPE** *verb* + **-ER**¹.]
†**1** A trickster, an impostor; a seducer. **LME–L15.**
2 A person who jests or plays jokes; *esp.* a professional jester. **LME.**
– **NOTE**: In sense 2 obsolete by **L16**, but revived in **19**.

japery /ˈdʒeɪp(ə)ri/ *noun*. Long *rare*. **ME.**
[**ORIGIN** from **JAPE** *noun*, *verb* + **-ERY**.]
Jesting speech, ribaldry; a joke, a jest.

Japhetic /dʒəˈfɛtɪk/ *adjective*. **E19.**
[**ORIGIN** from *Japheth* (Latin *Japhetus*) (see below) + **-IC**.]
Of or (supposedly) descended from Japheth, one of the sons of Noah; *arch.* Indo-European.
■ **Japhethite** /ˈdʒeɪfəθʌɪt/, **-tite** /-tʌɪt/ *noun* a (supposed) descendant of Japheth **M19.**

japish /ˈdʒeɪpɪʃ/ *adjective*. **E20.**
[**ORIGIN** from **JAPE** *noun* + **-ISH**¹.]
Of the nature of a jape; inclined to jest.
■ **japishly** *adverb* **L19.** **japishness** *noun* **L19.**

Japlish /ˈdʒaplɪʃ/ *noun*. *colloq.* **M20.**
[**ORIGIN** Blend of **JAPANESE** and **ENGLISH** *noun*: see **-LISH**.]
A blend of Japanese and English spoken by Japanese, either the Japanese language freely interlarded with English expressions or unidiomatic English spoken by a Japanese person. Cf. **JANGLISH**.

†**Japon** *noun* var. of **JAPAN**.

japonaiserie /ʒapɔnezri/ *noun*. Pl. pronounced same. **L19.**
[**ORIGIN** French: cf. **CHINOISERIE**.]
= **JAPANESERY**.

†**Japonian** *noun & adjective*. **L16.**
[**ORIGIN** from **JAPON** + **-IAN**.]
▸ **A** *noun*. A Japanese person. **L16–L17.**
▸ **B** *adjective*. Japanese. **E17–L18.**

japonic /dʒəˈpɒnɪk/ *adjective*. Also †**J-**. **L17.**
[**ORIGIN** formed as **JAPONIAN** + **-IC**.]
Japanese. *obsolete* exc. in ***japonic acid***, an acid said to occur in catechu.

japonica /dʒəˈpɒnɪkə/ *noun*. **E19.**
[**ORIGIN** mod. Latin, fem. of *Japonicus* pertaining to Japan.]
Any of several plants (thought to be) native to Japan; esp. *Chaenomeles speciosa*, the Japanese quince, a spring-flowering pink flowered ornamental shrub of the rose family, native to China and Myanmar (Burma) and widely cultivated in Japan; the round white, green, or yellow edible fruit of this. Formerly also, the camellia, *Camellia japonica*.

jar /dʒɑː/ *noun*¹. **L15.**
[**ORIGIN** Rel. to **JAR** *verb*¹.]
1 Disagreement; (a) divergence or conflict of opinions; dissension, quarrelling; a dispute, a quarrel, *esp.* one of a petty or domestic nature. Now *rare*. **L15.**
> W. COWPER Thy senate is a scene of civil jar. A. JESSOPP Once . . a family jar put two households at war.

at a jar, **at jar** at discord, in a state of dissension or variance.
2 A harsh inharmonious or grating sound or combination of sounds; a quivering or tremulous sound. Formerly *spec.* in *MUSIC*, a discord. **L15.**
> SIR W. SCOTT Bolt and bar Resumed their place with sullen jar. I. D'ISRAELI The critic's fastidious ear listens to . . the jar of rude rhymes.

†**3** A vibration or tick of the clock. *rare* (Shakes.). Only in **E17.**

> SHAKES. *Wint. T.* I love thee not a jar o' th' clock behind What lady she her lord.

4 A vibration or tremulous movement resulting from concussion, *esp.* one felt in the body; a thrill of the nerves, mind, or feelings caused by, or resembling the effect of, a physical shock. **E19.**

> K. AMIS The train . . stopped without the slightest jar.

5 *OIL INDUSTRY. sing.* & in *pl.* A tool used to produce a heavy upward blow in a drill hole, e.g. on a bit that has become stuck. **M19.**

– **COMB.:** **jar ramming** *FOUNDING* = ***jolt ramming*** s.v. JOLT *noun*.

jar /dʒɑː/ *noun*[2]. **L16.**
[**ORIGIN** French *jarre* from Arabic *jarra*.]
1 A usu. cylindrical container of glass, earthenware, or stoneware with no spout or handle (or with two handles). Orig., a large earthenware vessel for holding water, oil, wine, etc. **L16.**
LEYDEN jar.
2 Such a container and its contents; as much as a jar will hold (formerly a measure of capacity varying according to the commodity). **L16.** ▸**b** A glass of beer or other alcoholic drink. *colloq.* **E20.**

> A. MUNRO I've made about five million jars of jam. **b** *Air Gunner* We called into the pub for a quick jar.

†**3** *ELECTRICITY.* A unit of capacity equal to 1111 picofarads. **E–M20.**

jar /dʒɑː/ *noun*[3]. *arch.* **L17.**
[**ORIGIN** Later form of CHAR *noun*[1]: see AJAR *adverb*[1] & *pred. adjective*[1].]
on the jar, †***at jar***, †***on a jar***, †***on jar***, (of a door) partly open, ajar.

jar /dʒɑː/ *verb*[1]. Infl. **-rr-**. **E16.**
[**ORIGIN** Prob. imit.]
▸ **I 1** *verb intrans.* Make a harsh grating sound or a musical discord; sound in discord with other sounds. **E16.**

> BYRON My heart and harp have lost a string, And both may jar.

2 *verb intrans.* Fall harshly *on*, or (formerly) sound harshly *in*, the ear. Freq. *fig.*, strike with a discordant or painful effect *on* the nerves, feelings, mind, conscience, etc. **M16.**

> THACKERAY His laugh jars on one's ear. R. CROMPTON Her voice . . began to jar upon his nerves. G. S. FRASER The rhymes that jar on me.

3 *verb trans.* Shake into vibration; trill. Formerly, grind (one's teeth). **M16.** ▸**b** Give a jar or shock to (the nerves, mind, or feelings). **L18.**

> O. W. HOLMES A sudden gust . . jars all the windows. **b** G. GREENE She was jarred . . by the heave of the train. J. BAYLEY It is a comment which jars me in the reading.

†**4 a** *verb intrans.* (Of a clock) tick; (of minutes) tick by. **L16–E17.** ▸**b** *verb trans.* Cause to tick. *rare* (Shakes.). Only in **L16.**
5 *verb intrans.* Strike against something (or each other) with a grating sound or so as to cause vibration; clash. Foll. by *(up)on*, *with*, *against*. **M17.**

> M. O. W. OLIPHANT His boat of life had . . jarred upon the . . shores of the eternal land.

6 *verb trans.* Cause to sound discordantly. **M17.**

> DE QUINCEY Every impulse of bad health jars . . some string in the . . harp of human volition.

7 *verb intrans.* Vibrate audibly, esp. with a grating or grinding sound; vibrate or shake from an impact or shock. **M18.**

> J. WESLEY The ship shook and jarred with so . . grating a motion. D. WELCH The truck was jarring to a standstill.

8 *verb trans.* Drive into a position or condition by a jarring sound or vibration. **E19.**

> J. HERSEY The siren jarred her awake. P. DE VRIES Words seemed to have been jarred out of him by a bump in the road.

9 *verb trans.* Injure by concussion or impact. **L19.**
▸ **II 10** *verb intrans.* Of opinions, statements, systems, etc., or (formerly) persons: be at discord in character or effect; be at variance, disagree, conflict. **M16.** ▸**b** Come into conflict, clash. **E17.**

> P. BROOK Blending . . so that contradictory styles do not jar. M. GIROUARD Unity of colour prevented one room . . jarring with the next. **b** G. BRIMLEY Clashing sympathies jarred . . harshly within him.

11 *verb intrans.* Be at strife; dispute, bicker, wrangle. **M16.**

> C. BURY We were . . jarring and saying disagreeable things.

jar /dʒɑː/ *verb*[2] *trans.* Infl. **-rr-**. **M18.**
[**ORIGIN** from JAR *noun*[2].]
Preserve (fruit) in a jar; bottle.

jarabe /xaˈraβe/ *noun*. Also **-ve**. **M19.**
[**ORIGIN** Amer. Spanish from Spanish = syrup.]
A Mexican pair dance in which the man dances the zapateado steps, performed esp. as an exhibition dance in national costume.

jararaca /dʒɑːrəˈrɑːkə/ *noun*. **E17.**
[**ORIGIN** Portuguese from Tupi-Guarani *yararáka*.]
Any of several S. American pit vipers of the genus *Bothrops*, esp. *B. jararaca* of Brazil.

jarave *noun* var. of JARABE.

jardinière /ʒɑːdɪˈnjɛː/ *noun*. **M19.**
[**ORIGIN** French, lit. 'female gardener'.]
1 An ornamental receptacle, pot, or stand for the display of growing or cut flowers. **M19.**
2 *COOKERY.* A garnish made with cooked vegetables. **M19.**

jarful /ˈdʒɑːfʊl, -f(ə)l/ *noun*. **M19.**
[**ORIGIN** from JAR *noun*[2] + -FUL.]
As much or as many as a jar will hold.

jargle /ˈdʒɑːɡ(ə)l/ *verb intrans.* Long *obsolete* exc. *dial.* **M16.**
[**ORIGIN** Old French *jargoillier*, *garg-* warble as a bird, murmur as a brook, prob. from an imit. base: cf. JARGON *noun*[1].]
Utter a harsh or shrill sound; chatter, jar.

jargon /ˈdʒɑːɡ(ə)n/ *noun*[1]. **LME.**
[**ORIGIN** Old French *jargoun*, *gergon*, *gargon*: ult. origin unknown.]
1 (A vocal sound resembling) the inarticulate utterance of birds, twittering, chattering. *arch.* **LME.**
2 Unintelligible or meaningless talk or writing; nonsense, gibberish. **LME.**
3 A jingle or assonance of rhymes. *rare.* **L16.**
†**4** A conventional method of writing or conversing by means of otherwise meaningless symbols; a cipher, a code. **L16–E18.**
5 A barbarous or debased language or variety of speech; *esp.* a hybrid speech arising from a mixture of languages. Also (*derog.*), a language one does not understand. **M17.**

> H. C. BAILEY Proclaimed her wrongs in a jargon of several languages.

Chinook Jargon: see CHINOOK *noun* 2.
6 (A form of) speech or writing having many unfamiliar terms or restricted to a particular category of people or occupation. **M17.**

> L. DEIGHTON He . . avoided jargon, as much as one can . . when dealing with . . new techniques. E. AMADI The coup . . was bloodless, in the jargon of journalists.

7 A medley or babel of sounds. **E18.**

> R. FIRBANK There uprose a jargon of voices.

■ **jargonaut** *noun* [after ARGONAUT] a person who uses jargon **M20.** **jargoˈneer** *noun* a person who uses jargon **E20.** **jargoˈnesque** *adjective* characterized by the use of jargon, composed in jargon **L19.** **jarˈgonic** *adjective* (*rare*) pertaining to or of the nature of jargon **E19.** **jargonish** *adjective* resembling or characteristic of jargon **M19.** **jargonist** *noun* a person who uses jargon **M19.** **jargoˈnistic** *adjective* of the nature of jargon, characterized by jargon **M20.**

jargon /ˈdʒɑːɡ(ə)n/ *noun*[2]. Also **-goon** /-ˈɡuːn/. **M18.**
[**ORIGIN** French from Italian *giargone*, usu. identified (ult.) with ZIRCON.]
A colourless, yellowish, or smoky variety of the mineral zircon found in Sri Lanka. Also called ***Matara diamond***.

jargon /ˈdʒɑːɡ(ə)n/ *verb*. **LME.**
[**ORIGIN** Old French *jargonner*, formed as JARGON *noun*[1].]
1 *verb intrans.* Warble, twitter, chatter. *arch.* **LME.**
2 *verb intrans.* Utter jargon; talk unintelligibly. **L16.**
■ **jargoner** *noun* a person who uses jargon **L19.**

jargonelle /dʒɑːɡəˈnɛl/ *noun*. Also **-el**. **L17.**
[**ORIGIN** French, dim. of JARGON *noun*[2]: see -EL[2].]
An early-ripening (orig. inferior) variety of pear.

jargonize /ˈdʒɑːɡ(ə)nʌɪz/ *verb*. Also **-ise**. **E19.**
[**ORIGIN** from JARGON *noun*[1] + -IZE.]
1 *verb intrans.* Talk or use jargon. **E19.**
2 *verb trans.* Bring into or *into* a condition by means of jargon; translate into jargon. **E19.**
■ **jargoniˈzation** *noun* **E19.**

jargoon *noun* var. of JARGON *noun*[2].

jarhead /ˈdʒɑːhɛd/ *noun*. *US slang.* **E20.**
[**ORIGIN** from JAR *noun*[2] + HEAD *noun*.]
1 A mule. **E20.** ▸**b** A foolish or stupid person. **M20.**
2 [alluding to the mule mascot of the Army football teams] Orig., a member of the US Army. Now usu., a member of the US Marine Corps. **M20.**

†**jark** *noun*. *criminals' slang.* **M16–E19.**
[**ORIGIN** Unknown.]
A seal, a certificate.
– **COMB.:** **jarkman** an educated beggar who fabricated counterfeit passes, licences, and certificates for others.

jarl /jɑːl/ *noun*. **E19.**
[**ORIGIN** Old Norse: see EARL.]
hist. A Norse or Danish chieftain or under-king.
■ **jarldom** *noun* the territory governed by a jarl **E19.** **jarlship** *noun* the function or office of a jarl **M19.**

jarless /ˈdʒɑːlɪs/ *adjective*. **L19.**
[**ORIGIN** from JAR *noun*[1] + -LESS.]
Free from jars or jolts; causing no jar.

Jarlsberg /ˈjɑːlzbəːɡ/ *noun*. **L20.**
[**ORIGIN** Named after the town of *Jarlsberg*, Norway.]
(Proprietary name for) a kind of hard yellow Norwegian cheese with many small holes and a mild, nutty flavour.

jarool *noun* var. of JARUL.

jarosite /ˈdʒarəsʌɪt/ *noun*. **M19.**
[**ORIGIN** from the *Jaroso* ravine in Almeria, S. Spain + -ITE[1].]
MINERALOGY. A hexagonal basic sulphate of potassium and iron that is a secondary mineral occurring as yellow or brown crusts on ferruginous ores.

jarovization /jarəvʌɪˈzeɪʃ(ə)n/ *noun*. Also **-isation**. **M20.**
[**ORIGIN** from Russian *yarovizatsiya*, from *yarovoĭ* spring-sown: see -IZATION.]
= VERNALIZATION.

jarrah /ˈdʒarə/ *noun*. **M19.**
[**ORIGIN** Nyungar *jarril*.]
The mahogany gum tree, *Eucalyptus marginata*, of western Australia; its reddish-brown timber, noted for durability.

jarring /ˈdʒɑːrɪŋ/ *adjective*. **M16.**
[**ORIGIN** from JAR *verb*[1] + -ING[2].]
That jars; *esp.* grating on the ear or on the feelings or nerves; discordant, conflicting, clashing.

> F. DONALDSON Life continued, with not a jarring incident to mar the serenity.

■ **jarringly** *adverb* **L16.** **jarringness** *noun* **M19.**

jarul /dʒəˈruːl/ *noun*. Also **jarool**. **M19.**
[**ORIGIN** Hindi *jārul*, Bengali *jārul*, from Sanskrit *jāṭali*.]
A deciduous tree, *Lagerstroemia speciosa*, of the purple loosestrife family, native to tropical Asia and bearing large panicles of purple or white flowers; the wood of this tree. Also called ***pride of India***, ***queen's flower***.

jarvey /ˈdʒɑːvi/ *noun*. *colloq.* Now *rare.* **E19.**
[**ORIGIN** By-form of *Jarvis*, *Jervis*, male forename.]
1 A hackney coachman; *Irish*, the driver of a jaunting car. **E19.**
2 A hackney coach. **E19.**
– **COMB.:** **jarvey-car** *Irish* a jaunting car.

Jas. *abbreviation*.
James.

jasey /ˈdʒeɪzi/ *noun*. *arch.*, *joc.*, & *colloq.* **L18.**
[**ORIGIN** Perh. alt. of JERSEY *noun*[2], so called because made of Jersey yarn.]
A wig, *esp.* one made of worsted.

jasmine /ˈdʒasmɪn, ˈdʒaz-/ *noun*. Also **-in**, (chiefly *arch.*) **jessamin(e)** /ˈdʒɛsəmɪn/. **M16.**
[**ORIGIN** French *jasmin*, †*jessemin* from Arabic *yāsamīn* (Hispano- & N. African Arabic *yasmīn*, whence Spanish *jazmín*, Portuguese *jasmin*) from Persian *yāsaman*. See also JESSAMY.]
1 Any of various ornamental and climbing shrubs of the genus *Jasminum* of the olive family, cultivated for their fragrant white or yellow salver-shaped flowers; *esp.* one of the common species *J. officinale*, with white flowers, and the yellow-flowered *J. humile* and *J. mesnyi*. Also (with specifying word), any of various fragrant plants of other genera and families. **M16.**
Arabian jasmine an evergreen climbing jasmine, *Jasminum sambac*, with fragrant clusters of white flowers that are used to flavour tea; also called *mogra*. ***Cape jasmine***: see CAPE *noun*[1]. **Carolina jasmine** = GELSEMIUM. **Chilean jasmine** a S. American woody liana, *Mandevilla laxa* (family Apocynaceae), with fragrant white flowers. ***MADAGASCAR jasmine***. **night jasmine** a shrub or small tree of southern Asia, *Nyctanthes arbor-tristis*, allied to the jasmine, with fragrant night-blooming flowers. **red jasmine** = FRANGIPANI 2. **winter jasmine** a winter-flowering jasmine, *Jasminum nudiflorum*, bearing yellow flowers on leafless branches.
2 A perfume derived from the flowers of the jasmine. **L17.**
– **COMB.:** **jasmine tea**: perfumed with jasmine.
■ **jasmined** *adjective* adorned with jasmine **E19.**

jasp /dʒɑːsp, dʒasp/ *noun*. Now *rare* or *obsolete*. **ME.**
[**ORIGIN** Old French & mod. French *jaspe*: see JASPER *noun*[1].]
= JASPER *noun*[1] 1.

jaspé /ˈdʒaspeɪ, *foreign* ʒaspe/ *adjective*. **M19.**
[**ORIGIN** French, pa. pple of *jasper* to marble.]
Marbled, mottled, variegated.

jasper /ˈdʒaspə/ *noun*[1] & *adjective*. **ME.**
[**ORIGIN** Old French *jaspre* var. of *jaspe* (also mod.) from Latin *iaspis* from Greek, of oriental origin.]
▸ **A** *noun*. **1** Formerly, any bright-coloured chalcedony other than carnelian, the most valued being of a green colour. Now, an opaque cryptocrystalline variety of quartz, usu. red, yellow, or brown, owing to the presence of haematite. **ME.**
2 A kind of hard fine porcelain invented by Josiah Wedgwood and used for Wedgwood cameos and other delicate work. Also ***jasperware***. **E19.**
– **COMB.:** **jasper-opal** an impure opal containing haematite and having the colour of yellow jasper; ***jasperware***: see sense 2 above.
▸ **B** *adjective*. Made or consisting of jasper. **E18.**
■ **jaspered** *adjective* = JASPER *adjective* **E17.** **jasperize** *verb trans.* convert by petrifaction into jasper or a form of silica resembling jasper **M19.** **jaspery** *adjective* of the nature of, resembling, or containing jasper **L18.**

jasper /ˈdʒaspə/ *noun*[2]. *US colloq.* (usu. *derog.*). **L19.**
[**ORIGIN** *Jasper*, male forename.]
A person, a fellow; *spec.* a rustic simpleton.

jasperoid /ˈdʒaspərɔɪd/ *adjective & noun.* L19.
[ORIGIN from JASPER *noun*[1] + -OID.]
▶ **A** *adjective.* Like jasper in appearance or structure. L19.
▶ **B** *noun.* GEOLOGY. A rock in which silica, in the form of fine-grained quartz or chalcedony, has replaced some of the original constituents (usually the carbonate of limestone). L19.

jaspis /ˈdʒaspɪs/ *noun.* Long *rare* or *obsolete.* LME.
[ORIGIN Latin *iaspis*: see JASPER *noun*[1].]
= JASPER *noun*[1] 1.

jasponyx /dʒasˈpɒnɪks/ *noun.* Long *rare* or *obsolete.* E17.
[ORIGIN Latin *iaspонyx* from Greek *iasponux*, from *iaspis* JASPER *noun*[1] + *onux* ONYX.]
(An) onyx partaking of the character of jasper or containing bands of jasper.

jassid /ˈdʒasɪd/ *adjective & noun.* L19.
[ORIGIN mod. Latin *Jassidae* (see below), from *Iassus* genus name from Latin name of a former town in Asia Minor: see -ID[3].]
ZOOLOGY. ▶**A** *adjective.* Of, pertaining to, or designating the homopteran family Cicadellidae of leafhoppers, which includes several pests of cereals, fodder crops, etc. L19.
▶ **B** *noun.* A leafhopper of this family. L19.

Jat /dʒɑːt/ *noun*[1] *& adjective.* E17.
[ORIGIN Hindi *Jāṭ*.]
▶ **A** *noun.* A member of a population group settled in the north-west of the Indian subcontinent, present also by immigration in Afghanistan and Iran, and identified with the Gypsies of Syria. E17.
▶ **B** *attrib.* or as *adjective.* Of or pertaining to the Jats. M19.

jat *noun*[2] var. of JATI.

jat' /jatj/ *noun.* Also (earlier) †**yat** & other vars. M18.
[ORIGIN Old Church Slavonic *jatĭ*.]
The Slavonic character written ѣ in the Glagolitic alphabet and ѣ in the Cyrillic alphabet, generally transliterated from both alphabets as *ě*; the sound represented by these characters; the Common Slavonic sound from which it developed.

Jataka /ˈdʒɑːtəkə/ *noun.* E19.
[ORIGIN Pali *jātaka* birth, nativity (story) from Sanskrit, from *jan-* be born.]
In Buddhist literature, a story of one or other of the former incarnations of the Buddha; a collection of such stories.

jatha /dʒəˈtɑː/ *noun.* E20.
[ORIGIN Punjabi, Hindi *jăthā*.]
In the Indian subcontinent: an armed or organized band of Sikhs.

jati /ˈdʒɑːti/ *noun.* Also **jat** /dʒɑːt/. L19.
[ORIGIN Hindi *jāt*, *jāti* from Sanskrit *jāti* birth.]
In the Indian subcontinent: a caste, a tribe, a class.

JATO /ˈdʒeɪtəʊ/ *abbreviation.*
Jet-assisted take-off.

jauk /dʒɔːk/ *verb intrans. Scot.* L15.
[ORIGIN Unknown.]
Trifle, delay, dawdle.

jaunce /dʒɔːns/ *verb & noun.* L16.
[ORIGIN Perh. from Old French: cf. JAUNT *verb*.]
▶ **A** *verb trans. & intrans.* (Cause to) prance; traipse. *arch.* L16.
▶ **B** *noun.* A tiring journey. Long *obsolete* exc. *dial.* L16.

jaundice /ˈdʒɔːndɪs/ *noun.* ME.
[ORIGIN Old French *jaunice* (mod. *-isse*) yellowness, from *jaune* yellow: see -ICE[1]. For the intrusive *d* cf. *sound*.]
1 MEDICINE. A condition characterized by yellowness of the skin, conjunctiva, and tissues, and occas. disordered vision, often due to obstruction of the bile duct or disease of the liver. ME.
obstructive jaundice: see OBSTRUCTIVE *adjective* 2.
2 *fig.* A jaundiced condition or viewpoint; envy, jealousy, resentment. L16.

DRYDEN Jealousie, the jaundice of the soul. D. FRANCIS 'It sounds dry,' I said with jaundice.

†**3** = ICTERUS 2. E–M17.

jaundice /ˈdʒɔːndɪs/ *verb trans.* L18.
[ORIGIN App. back-form. from JAUNDICED.]
1 Affect with jaundice. Chiefly *fig.*, tinge with envy, jealousy, or resentment. L18.
2 Tinge with yellow, make yellow. L19.

jaundiced /ˈdʒɔːndɪst/ *adjective.* M17.
[ORIGIN from JAUNDICE *noun* + -ED[2].]
1 Affected with jaundice. Of the complexion: unnaturally yellow. M17.
2 *gen.* Yellow-coloured. Now *rare.* M17.

LYTTON A comely matron .. in a jaundiced satinet gown.

3 Affected or tinged with envy, jealousy, or resentment. L17.

W. WHEWELL He was naturally querulous and jaundiced in his views. M. EDWARDES The 'tea break strike' .. reinforced the jaundiced view of Britain from overseas.

jaune /ʒoːn/ *adjective.* LME.
[ORIGIN French from Latin *galbinum* greenish-yellow.]
Yellow. *obsolete* exc. in names of pigments.
jaune brilliant cadmium yellow.
– NOTE: Formerly fully naturalized.

jaunt /dʒɔːnt/ *noun.* L16.
[ORIGIN Rel. to the verb.]
1 A tiring or troublesome journey. Now only as an *iron.* use of sense 2. L16.
2 An excursion, a journey; *esp.* a pleasure trip. L17.

P. THEROUX A tourist on a ten-day jaunt through ruins and cathedrals. C. WILLIAMS My jaunts to the Law Courts .. had ceased.

3 Jaunty manner or bearing. *rare.* E18.

K. LAING A second-division clerk with an outrageous jaunt in his walk.

jaunt /dʒɔːnt/ *verb.* L16.
[ORIGIN Unknown: cf. JAUNCE.]
†**1** *verb trans.* Exercise or tire (a horse) by riding it up and down. L16–E17.
†**2** *verb trans.* Carry about on a prancing horse or in a vehicle. *rare.* L16–E19.
3 *verb intrans.* Traipse about; run to and fro. L16.
4 *verb intrans.* Make a short journey, trip, or excursion, esp. for pleasure; take a jaunt. M17.

D. LESSING I've rushed around London, .. jaunted off to Somerset and Dorset.

5 *verb intrans.* Move jauntily. *rare.* L19.
– COMB.: **jaunting car** in Ireland, a light, two-wheeled horse-drawn vehicle for carrying four passengers seated either back to back or facing inwards, with a seat in front for the driver.

jaunty /ˈdʒɔːnti/ *noun. nautical slang.* Also **jonty** /ˈdʒɒnti/. E20.
[ORIGIN Perh. alt. of GENDARME.]
The master-at-arms on a ship.

jaunty /ˈdʒɔːnti/ *adjective.* Also (earlier) †**janty**. M17.
[ORIGIN French *gentil*: see GENTLE *adjective*, GENTEEL.]
†**1** (Of a person, manner, etc.) well-bred, gentlemanly, genteel; (of a thing) elegant, stylish, smart. M17–M19.
2 Having or expressing a sprightly confident manner; perky, carefree, debonair. L17. ▸**b** Lively, brisk. E18.

S. RUSHDIE He leaned round corners on his bicycle, taking them at a jaunty angle. P. FERGUSON Downstairs the doorbell gave out its jaunty chimes. I. MURDOCH His jaunty roguish teasing air of a spoilt boy. **b** K. MANSFIELD He couldn't .. stride off, jaunty as a young man.

■ **jauntily** *adverb* E19. **jauntiness** *noun* E18.

jaup /dʒɔːp/ *noun & verb. Scot. & N. English.* Also **jawp**. E16.
[ORIGIN Prob. imit.]
▶ **A** *noun.* **1** The splash of liquid against a surface; a spot of water, mud, etc., resulting from splashing. E16.
2 The sound made by liquid sloshing around in a container. E19.
▶ **B** *verb.* **1** *verb intrans.* Splash, slosh around; make a splashing sound. E16.
2 *verb trans.* Cause (liquid) to splash or slosh around; splash with water, mud, etc. E16.

Java /ˈdʒɑːvə/ *noun.* M19.
[ORIGIN A large island in the Malay archipelago, now part of Indonesia.]
1 Used *attrib.* to designate things from or associated with Java. M19.
Java almond a SE Asian tree, *Canarium luzonicum* (cf. KANARI). **Java canvas** open-weave canvas for embroidery etc. **Java man** a fossil hominid, *Homo* (formerly *Pithecanthropus*) *erectus*, remains of which were first found in Java in 1891. ***Java pepper***: see PEPPER *noun*. **Java plum** = JAMBOLAN. **Java sparrow** a bird of the waxbill family, *Padda oryzivora*, native to Java and Bali and often kept as an aviary bird.
2 Coffee from Java; *gen.* (*N. Amer. slang*) coffee. M19.
3 COMPUTING. (Proprietary name for) a general-purpose computer programming language used esp. for creating applications for the Internet and other networks. L20.

javaite /ˈdʒɑːvəʌɪt/ *noun.* M20.
[ORIGIN from JAVA + -ITE[1].]
GEOLOGY. A tektite from the strewn field of Java.

Javan /ˈdʒɑːv(ə)n/ *adjective & noun.* E17.
[ORIGIN formed as JAVAITE + -AN.]
▶ **A** *adjective.* Of or pertaining to Java or its people. E17.
▶ **B** *noun.* A native or inhabitant of Java. E17.

Javanese /dʒɑːvəˈniːz/ *noun & adjective.* E18.
[ORIGIN from JAVAN + *-n-* + -ESE.]
▶ **A** *noun.* Pl. same, †**-eses**.
1 A native or inhabitant of Java. E18.
2 The Austronesian language of central Java. M19.
▶ **B** *adjective.* Of or pertaining to Java, its people, or their language; Javan. E18.

javanite /ˈdʒɑːv(ə)nʌɪt/ *noun.* M20.
[ORIGIN formed as JAVANESE + -ITE[1].]
GEOLOGY. = JAVAITE.

javel /ˈdʒav(ə)l/ *noun.* Long *rare.* LME.
[ORIGIN Unknown.]
A low-born dishonest person or criminal.

javelin /ˈdʒav(ə)lɪn/ *noun & verb.* LME.
[ORIGIN Old French & mod. French *javeline* alt. of JAVELOT.]
▶ **A** *noun.* **1** A light throwing spear used as a weapon or in field athletics; the sporting event in which this is thrown. LME.

Dumfries Courier Ian had to settle for 3rd place in the javelin. *fig.*: J. G. WHITTIER Piercing the waves .. With the slant javelins of rain.

†**2** A pike; a lance. E16–M19.
3 HERALDRY. A charge consisting of a short spear with a barbed head. L19.
– COMB.: **javelin fish** an Indo-Pacific food fish, *Pomadasys hasta*, of the grunt family; **javelin man** *hist.* (*a*) a member of a sheriff's retinue armed with a pike who escorted the judges at assizes; (*b*) a javelineer; **javelin-snake** a dart-snake, *esp.* a snakelike lizard of the genus *Acontias*.
▶ **B** *verb trans.* Strike or pierce with or as with a javelin. M19.
■ **javeliˈneer** *noun* a soldier armed with a javelin E17.

javelina /havəˈliːnə/ *noun. N. Amer.* E19.
[ORIGIN Spanish *jabalina*, from fem. form of *jabalí* wild boar, from Arabic *jabalī* mountaineer.]
= PECCARY.

Javelle water /ʒaˈvɛl ˌwɔːtə/ *noun phr.* Also **Javel water**, †**Javel(le)'s water**. E19.
[ORIGIN *Javel*, a village, now a suburb of Paris, where the solution was first used.]
A solution of sodium or potassium hypochlorite, used as a bleach or disinfectant. Also called ***eau de Javelle***.

†**javelot** *noun.* ME–E18.
[ORIGIN Old French & mod. French from Proto-Gallo-Romance *gabalottus*.]
A small spear or javelin thrown with the hand or from a catapult.

Javel water *noun phr.* var. of JAVELLE WATER.

javver /ˈdʒavə/ *verb intrans.* Long *obsolete* exc. *dial.* LME.
[ORIGIN Imit.: cf. JABBER.]
= JABBER *verb* 1.

jaw /dʒɔː/ *noun*[1]. LME.
[ORIGIN Old French *joe* cheek, jaw, Anglo-Norman *jowe* cheek, jaw, of unknown origin.]
1 Either of the bony structures forming the framework of the mouth, and the seizing, biting, or masticating apparatus of vertebrates; *sing.* usu. the mandible (the ***lower jaw***), less commonly the maxilla (the ***upper jaw***); the part of the head containing these. LME. ▸**b** Any of various parts or organs associated with the mouth in certain invertebrates and used for grasping, piercing, or grinding during feeding etc. L19.

M. MOORCOCK He had a clean-shaven jaw. J. A. MICHENER He did see some jaws drop in fear. **b** T. H. HUXLEY In the Arthropoda, what are usually termed jaws are modified limbs.

locked jaw: see LOCKED *adjective*[2]. *LUMPY jaw*.
2 In *pl.* The bones and associated structures of the mouth including the teeth, regarded as instruments of biting, gripping, crushing, and devouring; the cavity formed by these parts; the mouth, the throat. LME.

SPENSER The hungry Spaniells .. With greedy iawes her ready foe to teare. M. MILNER A girl acrobat hanging onto the rope with only her jaws.

jaws wag: see WAG *verb*.
3 A side of a narrow pass or channel (usu. in *pl.*); in *pl.*, the narrow entrance into something. LME.

J. A. SYMONDS The torrent, foaming down between black jaws of rain-stained granite. *Snooker Scene* The cue-ball striking the jaw of the middle pocket.

4 *fig.* In *pl.* The grip of any devouring agency, as death, time, etc. M16.

TENNYSON Into the jaws of Death, Into the mouth of Hell Rode the six hundred. *Guardian* Watch for the moment that snatches defeat from the jaws of victory.

5 Talkativeness; idle or impudent talk; a (long) talk, a speech; a chat, incessant chatter. Cf. JAW-JAW *noun. colloq.* M18.

G. B. SHAW Lets have a jaw over some supper. *Times Lit. Suppl.* Committee work is just endless jaw.

6 In *pl.* The seizing or holding parts of a machine etc., arranged in pairs and usu. able to open and close; *spec.* (NAUTICAL) the end of a boom or gaff which clasps the mast with its projecting ends. L18.

DIY Success! Grip the upright piece in a vice or the jaws of a portable work-bench.

Jaws of Life *N. Amer.* (proprietary name for) a hydraulic apparatus used to pry apart the wreckage of crashed vehicles in order to free people trapped inside.
– COMB.: **jawbreaker** *colloq.* (*a*) a word with many syllables or difficult to pronounce; (*b*) a large, hard, or sticky sweet; **jaw-breaking** *adjective* (*colloq.*) difficult to pronounce; **jaw clutch** a dog clutch or other form of clutch in which one part engages in the jaws of the other; **jaw-crusher** a machine with jaws for crushing ore etc.; **jaw-dropping** *adjective* such as causes one's jaw to drop; astonishing, amazing, awe-inspiring; **jaw-fallen** *adjective* having the lower jaw fallen or hanging loose; dejected; **jaw rope** NAUTICAL the rope which fastens the jaws of a boom or

gaff round a mast; **jawsmith** *US slang* a talkative person; *esp.* a loud-mouthed demagogue; **jaw tooth** a molar tooth.
■ **jawed** *adjective* having jaws (of a specified kind) E16. **jawless** *adjective* lacking jaws; ZOOLOGY (of a fish) agnathan: E18. **jawy** *adjective* (*rare*) (**a**) of or pertaining to the jaw; (**b**) forceful in language: M17.

jaw /dʒɔː/ *noun*². *Scot. & N. English.* E16.
[ORIGIN Unknown. Cf. JAW *verb*¹.]
1 The rush of a wave; a surging wave, a billow. E16.
2 A quantity of water or other liquid dashed, splashed, or poured out. E19.

jaw /dʒɔː/ *verb*¹. *Scot.* E16.
[ORIGIN Unknown. Cf. JAW *noun*².]
1 *verb intrans.* Rush in waves; dash, pour, splash; surge. E16.
2 *verb trans.* Pour or dash (water) in waves; throw (liquid) in quantity. L17.

jaw /dʒɔː/ *verb*². E17.
[ORIGIN from JAW *noun*¹.]
†**1** *verb trans.* Seize or devour with the jaws; use the jaws on. Only in E17.
2 *verb intrans.* Speak, talk, esp. at length; chatter. Cf. JAW-JAW *verb*. *colloq.* M18.

G. BENFORD They've been jawing about the new hydro plant for ten hours.

3 *verb trans.* Admonish, lecture, scold. *colloq.* E19.

F. NORRIS She jawed him for making an exhibition of himself.

jawan /dʒəˈwɑːn/ *noun*. Also **ji-** /dʒɪ-/. M19.
[ORIGIN Urdu *jawān* from Persian = young man: ult. rel. to YOUNG *adjective*.]
In the Indian subcontinent, a male police constable or private soldier.

jawar, jawari *nouns* vars. of JOWAR, JOWARI.

jawbone /ˈdʒɔːbəʊn/ *noun & verb*. L15.
[ORIGIN from JAW *noun*¹ + BONE *noun*.]
▸ **A** *noun*. **1** A bone of the jaws; *spec.* the bone of the lower jaw, the mandible; either (left or right) half of this. L15.
2 An animal's jawbone used as a musical instrument; also (in *pl.*), castanets. M19.
3 = CREDIT *noun* 6. *N. Amer. slang.* M19.
▸ **B** *verb trans. & intrans.* Seek to restrain (a trade union or other body in a dispute) by persuasion. Chiefly as ***jawboning*** *verbal noun*. *US slang.* M20.

jaw-hole /ˈdʒɔːhəʊl/ *noun*. M18.
[ORIGIN Partly from JAW *noun*¹, partly from JAW *noun*², *verb*¹, + HOLE *noun*¹.]
1 A hole into which dirty water etc. is thrown, a drain. *Scot. & N. English.* M18.
2 An opening, an abyss. M19.

Jawi /ˈdʒɑːwi/ *noun & adjective*. E19.
[ORIGIN Malay.]
▸ **A** *noun*. Orig., the Malay vernacular. Now, the Malay language written in Arabic script. E19.
▸ **B** *attrib.* or as *adjective*. Of or pertaining to Jawi. E20.

jaw-jaw /ˈdʒɔːdʒɔː/ *verb & noun*. M19.
[ORIGIN Redupl. of JAW *verb*², *noun*¹.]
▸ **A** *verb intrans.* Talk, esp. at length or to no purpose. M19.
▸ **B** *noun*. Talking; *esp.* lengthy and pointless discussion. M20.
– NOTE: Rare until popularized by Winston Churchill's remark, 'To jaw-jaw is always better than to war-war' (1954).

jawp *noun & verb* var. of JAUP.

jaws harp /dʒɔːz ˈhɑːp/ *noun phr.* Also **jaw's harp**. L19.
[ORIGIN Alt.]
= ***Jew's harp*** s.v. JEW *noun*.

jay /dʒeɪ/ *noun & adjective*. L15.
[ORIGIN Old French (mod. *geai*) from late Latin *gaius*, *gaia*, perh. from male praenomen *Gaius*.]
▸ **A** *noun*. **1** Any of various medium-sized birds of the crow family, with varied, often colourful, plumage; *spec.* the Eurasian *Garrulus glandarius*, a raucous, woodland bird with pinkish-brown plumage marked with black, white, and blue. L15.
blue jay: see BLUE *adjective*. ***CANADA jay***. ***Siberian jay***: see SIBERIAN *adjective*. ***Steller jay***, ***Steller's jay***: see STELLER.
2 Any of various other birds; *esp.* a jackdaw; a chough. *obsolete* exc. *dial.* L15.
3 An impertinent chatterer. Also, a flashy or absurdly dressed person; a stupid or silly person. *colloq.* E16.
– COMB.: **jay-bird** *colloq.* = sense A.1 above (***naked as a jay-bird***: see NAKED *adjective*); **jay-hawker** (chiefly *US*), a raiding guerrilla or irregular soldier (orig. in and around eastern Kansas).
▸ **B** *attrib.* or as *adjective*. Dull, unsophisticated, inferior, poor. *US colloq.* L19.

Jaycee /dʒeɪˈsiː/ *noun*. *colloq.* M20.
[ORIGIN from initial letters of *Junior Chamber*.]
A member of a Junior Chamber of Commerce.
■ **Jaycette** /dʒeɪsiːˈɛt/ *noun* a female Jaycee M20.

jaywalker /ˈdʒeɪwɔːkə/ *noun*. Orig. *US.* E20.
[ORIGIN from JAY + WALKER *noun*².]
A pedestrian who crosses or walks in a street without regard for traffic.
■ **jaywalk** *verb intrans.* behave as a jaywalker (chiefly as ***jaywalking*** *verbal noun*) E20.

jazerant /ˈdʒaz(ə)r(ə)nt/ *noun*. *obsolete* exc. *hist.* Also (earlier) †**jesserant**. LME.
[ORIGIN Old French *jaseran(t)*, *-enc* orig. an adjective, in *osberc* (*hauberc*) *jazerant*, = Spanish *cota jacerina*, of unknown origin.]
A light coat of armour made of small metal plates riveted to each other or attached to a tunic of leather or stout cloth.

jazz /dʒaz/ *noun & adjective*. E20.
[ORIGIN Unknown.]
▸ **A** *noun*. **1** A type of music of US black origin, characterized by its use of improvisation, syncopated phrasing, and a regular or forceful rhythm; *loosely* syncopated dance music. E20.

D. BRUBECK When there is not complete freedom of the soloist, it ceases to be jazz.

MODERN jazz. ***symphonic jazz***: see SYMPHONIC 3.
2 Energy, excitement, excitability. *colloq.* E20.

J. GALSWORTHY With all the jazz there is about, she'd appreciate somebody restful.

3 Meaningless or empty talk, nonsense; pretentious behaviour; unnecessary ornamentation; nonsensical stuff. *colloq.* E20.

E. MCBAIN 'How was school today, darling?' 'Oh, the same old jazz'.

and all that jazz and all that sort of thing, et cetera.
4 Sexual intercourse. *slang.* E20.
▸ **B** *attrib.* or as *adjective*. **1** Of or pertaining to jazz; involved in, featuring, or based on jazz. E20.

B. SCHULBERG How true jazz music was, how it echoed everything .. churning inside me.

2 Of fantastic design; gaudy, vivid; jazzy. E20.
– SPECIAL COLLOCATIONS & COMB.: **jazz age** the era of jazz; *spec.* the early nineteen twenties; **jazz funk** popular dance music incorporating elements of jazz and funk; **jazzman** a (male) jazz musician; **jazz rock** popular music having the characteristics of both jazz and rock.

jazz /dʒaz/ *verb*. *colloq.* E20.
[ORIGIN from the noun.]
1 *verb trans.* Play (music) in the style of jazz; give a jazz style to; enliven, brighten up; make more colourful or exciting; excite. Freq. foll. by *up*. E20.

L. OLIVIER A hideously jazzed-up version of 'God Save the Queen'. *Sunday Express* Jazz it up with fruity olive oil, paprika and fresh parsley.

2 *verb intrans.* Play jazz; dance to jazz music; move in a bizarre or fantastic manner. E20.

P. SCOTT Water reflections are jazzing on the undersurface of the shade.

3 *verb trans. & intrans.* Have sexual intercourse (with). *slang.* E20.

J. T. FARRELL She was a woman now, who got regular jazzing and knew what it was all about.

■ **jazzer** *noun* (*colloq.*) a person who plays or dances to jazz; a jazz enthusiast: E20.

jazzbo /ˈdʒazbəʊ/ *noun*. *arch. US slang.* Pl **-os**. E20.
[ORIGIN Unknown: perh. rel. to JAZZ *noun*.]
1 Poor variety theatre, vulgar comedy. E20.
2 A person, *esp.* a black person; *spec.* (**a**) a (black) performer in variety theatre; (**b**) an old or dissolute (black) person. E20.

Jazzercise /ˈdʒazəsʌɪz/ *noun*. Also **j-**. L20.
[ORIGIN from JAZZ *noun* + EXERCISE *noun*. Cf. DANCERCISE.]
(Proprietary name for) a form of physical exercise in the form of dancing to the accompaniment of jazz music.

jazzify /ˈdʒazɪfʌɪ/ *verb trans.* E20.
[ORIGIN from JAZZ *noun* + -I- + -FY.]
Make jazzy; jazz up.
■ **jazzifiˈcation** *noun* M20.

jazzy /ˈdʒazi/ *adjective*. E20.
[ORIGIN from JAZZ *noun* + -Y¹.]
Pertaining to or resembling jazz; characterized by jazz; spirited, lively, exciting; vivid, gaudy; *derog.* pretentiously showy, unrestrained.

Chambers's Journal To sing some jazzy stuff called 'Alexander's Rag Time Band'. B. BROADFOOT He bought a new car, the jazziest in Calgary. W. ALLEN A couple dressed like American tourists, wearing jazzy Hawaiian shirts.

■ **jazzily** *adverb* E20. **jazziness** *noun* E20.

JCL *abbreviation*.
COMPUTING. Job control language.

JCR *abbreviation*.
Junior Common (or Combination) Room.

JCS *abbreviation*. *US.*
Joint Chiefs of Staff.

jealous /ˈdʒɛləs/ *adjective*. ME.
[ORIGIN Old French *gelos* (mod. *jaloux*) from medieval Latin *zelosus*, from Christian Latin *zelus* from Greek *zēlos* ZEAL: see -OUS.]
1 **a** Troubled by the fear, suspicion, or belief that one is being or might be displaced in someone's affections; (disposed to be) distrustful of the fidelity of a spouse or lover; overly possessive of a friend, lover, or spouse. (Foll. by *of*.) ME. ▸**b** Of God: demanding absolute faithfulness and exclusive worship. ME. ▸**c** *gen.* Resentful or envious of another person or of his or her possible or actual success, advantage, or superiority; disposed to rivalry. LME.

a H. E. BATES A person of possessive and jealous desire. J. BARTH Some guys would get jealous if their wife played tennis with another man. N. MAILER He was so insanely jealous Couldn't stand the thought of her meeting another man. **c** R. K. NARAYAN He is very jealous, won't tolerate a pinch of original work. M. WEST I was jealous because she was getting something I never had. M. SEYMOUR-SMITH The poet .. was jealous of Riding's poetic accomplishments.

†**2** Devoted, zealous; *rare* angry. LME–M17.
†**3** Amorous; fond; lustful. LME–E17.
4 Foll. by *of*: protective of; careful in guarding; watchful over. LME.

SIR W. SCOTT The chief is young, and jealous of his rank.

5 Suspicious; apprehensive, worried, fearful. (Foll. by *of* or subord. clause.) *obsolete* exc. *dial.* LME. ▸†**b** Doubtful, mistrustful. Only in 17.
6 Vigilant, watchful, careful. L18.

H. KELLER I guarded both doll and cradle with the most jealous care.

■ **jealously** *adverb* LME. **jealousness** *noun* (now *rare*) LME.

jealousy /ˈdʒɛləsi/ *noun*. ME.
[ORIGIN Old French *gelosie* (mod. *jalousie*), from *gelos*: see JEALOUS, -Y³.]
1 **a** The consuming fear, suspicion, or belief that one is being or might be displaced in someone's affections; distrust of the fidelity of a spouse or lover. ME. ▸**b** Of God: intolerance of the worship of other gods. ME. ▸**c** Resentment or envy of another person or of his or her possible or actual success, advantage, or superiority; rivalry. LME.

a AV *S. of S.* 8:6 Iealousie is cruel as the graue: the coales thereof are coales of fire. A. S. NEILL Jealousy arises from the combination of love with possessiveness about the loved object. **c** L. GORDON Malice .. arose from her jealousy of her sister-in-law, who managed to publish stories. R. INGALLS Their quarrels, misunderstandings and jealousies were .. like those of other families.

†**2** **a** Anger, wrath. LME–M17. ▸**b** Devotion, eagerness. LME–M16.
3 Concern or anxiety for the preservation or well-being of something or someone; vigilance or care in guarding something or someone. LME.
4 Suspicion; apprehension of evil; mistrust. *obsolete* exc. *dial.* LME.
5 = JALOUSIE. Chiefly *Jamaican.* L18.

jean /dʒiːn/ *adjective & noun*. L15.
[ORIGIN Old French *Janne* (mod. *Gênes*) from medieval Latin *Janua* Genoa, city in Italy.]
▸ **A** *adjective*. †**1** Originating from Genoa, Genoese. L15–E17.
2 Designating a heavy twilled cotton fabric, now usu. denim; made of this. L18.

City Limits Paul's in his late 20's, wears a jean jacket.

▸ **B** *noun*. **1** Orig. †***jean fustian***. A heavy twilled cotton fabric, now usu. denim. L16.
2 In *pl.* Garments of this material. Now usu. hard-wearing trousers of this (or other) material, worn esp. for leisure or for physical work (also ***pair of jeans***). M19.

N. GORDIMER He was barefoot and in white canvas jeans and a checked shirt. P. BOOTH The faded blue jeans were immaculately pressed. *attrib.*: M. ATWOOD He wears crumbling jeans suits.

■ **jeaned** *adjective* wearing jeans M20.

jeannette /dʒəˈnɛt/ *noun*. Also **jeanette**. L18.
[ORIGIN from JEAN + -ETTE.]
Any of various types of material resembling jean.

jebel /ˈdʒɛbɛl/ *noun*. M19.
[ORIGIN Arabic *jabal*, (colloq.) *jebel*, pl. *jibāl*, mountain.]
In the Middle East and N. Africa: a mountain, a range of hills. Freq. in specific names.

Jedi /ˈdʒɛdʌɪ/ *noun*. Pl. same, **-is**. L20.
[ORIGIN Invented name.]
A member of the mystical knightly order in the *Star Wars* films, trained to use the Force in guarding peace and justice in the Universe. Also ***Jedi knight***.

jee /dʒiː/ *verb, interjection, & noun*. Chiefly *Scot.* Pa. t. & pple **jeed**. E18.
[ORIGIN Unknown. Cf. GEE *verb*², *interjection*¹.]
▸ **A** *verb*. **1** *verb intrans.* Move, stir; move to one side. E18.
2 *verb trans.* Cause to move; move aside, shift. E18.
▸ **B** *interjection*. = GEE *interjection*¹; instructing a horse pulling a plough etc. to move or turn. E19.
▸ **C** *noun*. A move, a motion, a sideways turn. Also, an instruction to a horse pulling a plough etc. to move or turn. E19.

J

Jeep /dʒiːp/ *noun & verb*. Orig. *US*. Also **j-**. **M20.**
[**ORIGIN** from GP *general purpose*, prob. infl. by 'Eugene the Jeep', a shape-changing character of great resourcefulness and power introduced into the cartoon strip *Popeye* in 1936.]
▸ **A** *noun*. (Proprietary name for) a small sturdy motor vehicle having emergency four-wheel drive, orig. and esp. one used for military purposes. **M20.**
▸ **B** *verb intrans. & trans.* (Usu. **j-**.) Travel by Jeep. **M20.**
■ **jeepable** *adjective* negotiable by Jeep **M20.**

jeepers /ˈdʒiːpəz/ *interjection. slang* (orig. *US*). Also **jeepers creepers** /ˈdʒiːpəz ˈkriːpəz/. **E20.**
[**ORIGIN** Alt. of **JESUS**.]
= **JEEZ** *interjection*.

DENNIS POTTER Jeepers, Joanie. What lovely, lovely little rose-buds!

jeepney /ˈdʒiːpni/ *noun*. **M20.**
[**ORIGIN** from **JEEP** + **JIT**)**NEY**.]
In the Philippines: a jitney bus converted from a Jeep; a small bus, a minibus.

jeer /dʒɪə/ *noun*[1]. **L15.**
[**ORIGIN** Perh. var. of **GEAR**.]
NAUTICAL. *sing.* & (usu.) in *pl.* Tackle for hoisting and lowering the lower yards.

jeer /dʒɪə/ *verb & noun*[2]. **M16.**
[**ORIGIN** Unknown.]
▸ **A** *verb*. **1** *verb intrans.* Speak or call out in derision or mockery; scoff derisively. (Foll. by *at*.) **M16.** ▸**b** *verb trans.* Say or call out in derision or mockery. **E20.**

D. M. THOMAS Some looked sorry for them, but others laughed and jeered. P. ANGADI I jeer at her uneducated, brainless approach to life and laugh openly at her. **b** A. MCCOWEN When passing a waiting bus queue, he would often jeer, 'Look at the poor!'

J

2 *verb trans.* Address or treat with scornful derision; mock, taunt. **L16.**

C. M. YONGE The mob pelted him and jeered him by his assumed name of King Arthur.

3 *verb trans.* Drive or force (*into*, *out of*, etc.) by jeering. **M17.**

H. MARTINEAU They would jeer me off the stand.

▸ **B** *noun*. †**1** A huff, a bad temper. *rare*. Only in **L16.**
2 An act of jeering; a scoff, a jibe, a taunt. **E17.**

C. H. SPURGEON A blow is much sooner forgotten than a jeer.

†**3** The action of jeering; mockery, scoffing, derision. **M17–M18.**
■ **jeerer** *noun* **M16.** **jeeringly** *adverb* in a jeering manner **M17.**

jeera /ˈdʒiːrə/ *noun*. Also **zeera** /ˈziːrə/. **L20.**
[**ORIGIN** Hindi *jīrā*.]
In Indian cookery: the spice cumin.

jeerga *noun* see **JIRGA**.

jeet kune do /ˈdʒiːt kuːn duː/ *noun phr.* **L20.**
[**ORIGIN** Chinese (Cantonese), lit. 'the way of the intercepting fist'.]
A modern martial art incorporating elements of kung fu, fencing, and boxing, devised by the US film actor Bruce Lee (1941–73).

Jeeves /dʒiːvz/ *noun*. **M20.**
[**ORIGIN** A character in the novels of P. G. Wodehouse.]
A valet, a personal attendant, *esp.* one who is resourceful and omniscient.

Jeez /dʒiːz/ *interjection. slang*. Also **G-**, **-ze**. **E20.**
[**ORIGIN** Abbreviation of **JESUS**.]
Expr. discovery, enthusiasm, annoyance, surprise, or emphasis; = **GEE** *interjection*[2].

†**jeezy** *noun* see **GIZZ**.

jefe /ˈhɛfeɪ/ *noun*. *US colloq.* **L19.**
[**ORIGIN** Spanish, from French *chef* **CHIEF** *noun*.]
A boss, a leader, a person in charge of something. Often as a form of address.

POUL ANDERSON I *am* their jefe, the founder of this whole shebang. T. CLANCY But such handsome grandsons you will have, *jefe*.

jeff /dʒɛf/ *noun*. *US slang. derog.* **L19.**
[**ORIGIN** from *Jefferson* Davis (1808–89), president of the Confederate States 1861–5.]
A tedious man, a bore; a rustic, a hick, *esp.* a Southerner; (among black people) a white man. Also ***Jeff Davis*** /ˈdeɪvɪs/.
Mutt and Jeff: see **MUTT**.

jeff /dʒɛf/ *verb intrans. Printers' slang* (now *hist.*). **M19.**
[**ORIGIN** Unknown.]
Throw or gamble with quadrats used as dice.

Jeffersonian /dʒɛfəˈsəʊnɪən/ *noun & adjective*. **L18.**
[**ORIGIN** from *Jefferson* (see below) + **-IAN**.]
US HISTORY. ▸ **A** *noun*. A supporter or follower of Thomas Jefferson, president of the US 1801–9; an adherent of the political doctrines held by or attributed to Jefferson; a Democrat. **L18.**
▸ **B** *adjective*. Of or pertaining to President Jefferson; supporting the doctrines of Jefferson or his followers; Democratic. **L18.**
■ **Jeffersonianism** *noun* **L19.**

Jeffrey pine /ˈdʒɛfrɪ pʌɪn/ *noun phr.* Also **Jeffrey's pine**. **M19.**
[**ORIGIN** from John *Jeffrey*, Scot. plant-collector.]
A large pine of California and Oregon, *Pinus jeffreyi*, with a spreading head of drooping branches.

jehad *noun* var. of **JIHAD**.

Jehoshaphat /dʒɪˈhɒʃəfat/ *interjection*. Orig. *US*. Also **-sa-** /-sə-/. **M19.**
[**ORIGIN** A king of Judah (*1 Kings* 15:22 etc.).]
A mild expletive, expr. surprise, alarm, etc. Freq. in ***jumping Jehoshaphat***.

Jehovah /dʒɪˈhəʊvə/ *noun*. **M16.**
[**ORIGIN** medieval Latin *Iehoua(h)* from Hebrew *YHWH*, *JHVH* repr. the Tetragrammaton or divine name (too sacred for utterance), with insertion of the vowels of *ʼădōnāy* my lord. Cf. **ADONAI**, **YAHWEH**.]
(The principal and personal name of) God in the Old Testament; the Lord.
Jehovah's Witness, **Jehovah Witness** a member of a fundamentalist millenary sect, the Watchtower Bible and Tract Society, which rejects institutional religion and gives precedence to the claims of the sect when these conflict with those of the state.
– **NOTE**: Popularized in Christian usage at the Renaissance and occurring in Tindale's translation of the Bible.

Jehovist /dʒɪˈhəʊvɪst/ *noun*. **M18.**
[**ORIGIN** from **JEHOVAH** + **-IST**.]
†**1** An adherent of the view that the Hebrew word YHWH or JHVH in the Old Testament and Hebrew Scriptures was originally pronounced 'Jehovah'. Only in **M18.**
2 *The* author(s) of those parts of the Pentateuch in which the name for God is Jehovah. Cf. **ELOHIST**, **YAHWIST**. **M19.**
■ **Jehoˈvistic** *adjective* of or pertaining to the Jehovist or Jehovists; characterized by the use of the name Jehovah: **M19.**

Jehu /ˈdʒiːhjuː/ *noun & verb*. *joc.* **E17.**
[**ORIGIN** A king of Israel, who drove his chariot furiously (*2 Kings* 9:20).]
▸ **A** *noun*. A coach or cab driver, *esp.* one who drives fast or recklessly. **E17.**
▸ **B** *verb intrans. & trans.* Drive. *rare*. **E19.**

jejunal /dʒɪˈdʒuːn(ə)l/ *adjective*. **L19.**
[**ORIGIN** from **JEJUNUM** + **-AL**[1].]
Of or pertaining to the jejunum.

jejune /dʒɪˈdʒuːn/ *adjective*. **E17.**
[**ORIGIN** Latin *jejunus* fasting, barren, unproductive, meagre. Sense 2b perh. from idea that word is from Latin *juvenis* young (compar. *junior*) or French *jeune* young.]
†**1** Without food, fasting; undernourished, hungry. **E17–M18.**
2 Intellectually unsatisfying, lacking substance, shallow, simplistic; dull, dry, insipid, vapid. **E17.** ▸**b** Puerile, childish; naive. **L19.**

A. TROLLOPE Jejune words and useless empty phrases. C. I. GLICKSBERG Such methods were jejune and spurious, unproductive of genuine critical insight. **b** G. B. SHAW His jejune credulity as to the absolute value of his concepts.

3 Not nourishing or substantial; scanty; meagre, frugal; (of land) poor, barren. **M17.**

W. SALMON The Cider is impoverished and made thin, Jejune, hard and ill-tasted.

■ **jejunely** *adverb* **E17.** **jejuneness**, **jejunity** *nouns* **E17.**

jejuno- /dʒɪˈdʒuːnəʊ/ *combining form* of next: see **-O-**.
■ **jejuno-duoˈdenal** *adjective* related to or (esp.) connecting the jejunum and duodenum **L19.** **jejunoˈileum** *noun* the small intestine excluding the duodenum; the jejunum and ileum considered together: **L19.** **jeˌjunojejuˈnostomy** *noun* (the making of) a connection between two parts of the jejunum, bypassing the intervening part **E20.** **jejunostomy** /dʒɛdʒʊˈnɒstəmi/ *noun* (an instance of) surgical opening of the jejunum through the abdominal wall, usu. for the purpose of introducing food **L19.**

jejunum /dʒɪˈdʒuːnəm/ *noun*. **M16.**
[**ORIGIN** medieval Latin, from Latin adjective (sc. *intestinum*) neut. of *jejunus* fasting: so called because usu. found to be empty after death.]
ANATOMY. The second part of the small intestine, connecting the duodenum and ileum.

Jekyll /ˈdʒɛkɪl, ˈdʒiː-/ *noun*. **L19.**
[**ORIGIN** The hero of R. L. Stevenson's story 'Strange Case of Dr Jekyll and Mr Hyde' (1886).]
The good side to a person's or thing's character; an apparently good and respectable person or thing. Cf. **HYDE**.

I. HAY We encountered surprisingly few Hydes. Nearly all were Jekylls . . of the most competent and courteous type.

Jekyll and Hyde (a person or thing) having two opposed aspects.

jelab *noun* var. of **DJELLABA**.

Jelalaean *adjective* var. of **GELALAEAN**.

jelick /ˈdʒɛlɪk, ˈjɛlɪk/ *noun*. Also **yelek**. **E19.**
[**ORIGIN** Turkish *yelek*.]
A waistcoat or bodice worn by Turkish women.

jell /dʒɛl/ *verb & noun*. *colloq.* **M18.**
[**ORIGIN** Back-form. from **JELLY** *noun*[1] *& verb*. Cf. **GEL** *noun*[1].]
▸ **A** *verb*. **1** *verb intrans.* Become a jelly; congeal, jelly. **M18.** ▸**b** *fig.* Take or hold a definite or satisfactory shape, cohere, crystallize. Cf. **GEL** *verb*. **E20.**

L. M. ALCOTT The jelly won't jell. **b** K. TYNAN The three plots simply do not jell. *Times* The present Parliament . . will jell in time.

2 *verb trans.* Turn into jelly, jellify. Also (*fig.*), give shape to, make clear and definite. **E20.**
▸ **B** *noun*. A jelly, a gel. **L19.**

jellaba *noun* var. of **DJELLABA**.

jellied /ˈdʒɛlɪd/ *adjective*. **LME.**
[**ORIGIN** from **JELLY** *noun*[1] *& verb*: see **-ED**[1], **-ED**[2].]
1 Coated with jelly; set in jelly. **LME.**
jellied eels: see **EEL** *noun* 1.
2 Turned into jelly; brought to or having the consistency of jelly; congealed, coagulated. **L16.**

jellify /ˈdʒɛlɪfʌɪ/ *verb*. **E19.**
[**ORIGIN** from **JELLY** *noun*[1] + **-FY**.]
1 *verb trans.* Convert into jelly; reduce to the consistency of jelly. **E19.**
2 *verb intrans.* Become or turn into a jelly. **L19.**
■ **jellifiˈcation** *noun* **L19.**

jello /ˈdʒɛləʊ/ *noun*. Chiefly *N. Amer.* Also **J-**, (proprietary) **Jell-O**. **E20.**
[**ORIGIN** from **JELLY** *noun*[1] + **-O**.]
(The powder used to make) a fruit-flavoured gelatin dessert; jelly.

Black Scholar Her firm young breasts quivering like a dish of molded jello.

jelloped /ˈdʒɛləpt/ *adjective*. Also **joll-** /ˈdʒɒl-/, **jowl-** /ˈdʒaʊl-/, **-pp-**. **E17.**
[**ORIGIN** from alt. of **JOLLOP** *noun*[1] + **-ED**[2].]
HERALDRY. Having wattles of a specified tincture distinct from that of the body, wattled.

jelly /ˈdʒɛli/ *noun*[1] *& verb*. **LME.**
[**ORIGIN** Old French & mod. French *gelée* frost, jelly, from use as noun of Latin *gelata* fem. pa. pple of *gelare* freeze, from *gelu* frost.]
▸ **A** *noun*. **1** An item of food having the form of a soft, firm, somewhat elastic, usu. semi-transparent material made by cooling (in a mould or dish) a liquid preparation containing gelatin etc. and (orig.) meat or fish stock, (now more commonly) sweetened fruit juice, etc.; a flavoured and coloured product from which a similar substance can be made; a dessert made of this. Also, a conserve of fruit boiled with sugar and strained. **LME.** ▸†**b** Gelatin. **E–M19.**

Punch He shook all over like a badly-set jelly. T. STERLING The lamb was tender . . . She ate the mint jelly separately. R. GODDEN My favourite, a pink fruit jelly . . I ate it all.

blackcurrant jelly, ***redcurrant jelly***, etc. ***table jelly***: see **TABLE** *noun*.
2 Matter with the consistency of a jelly; a gelatinous substance or object of any kind. **E17.** ▸**b** A gelatinous mass formed by the alga *Nostoc* on soil, formerly supposed to be the remains of a fallen meteor. **M17.** ▸**c** With specifying word (esp. *sea*): a jellyfish or similar animal. **L17.** ▸**d** A tablet of the drug Temazepam. *slang*. **L20.**

V. NABOKOV A brain of a different brand than that of the synthetic jellies preserved in the skulls around him. *Guardian* Her doctor . . prescribed a diaphragm and a contraceptive jelly. B. BYARS Normally this would have turned his knees to jelly.

mineral jelly: see **MINERAL** *adjective*. ***PETROLEUM jelly***. ***royal jelly*** the secretion produced by honey bees to feed the larvae of the colony, esp. those that will become queens. ***WHARTON'S jelly***. **c** ***comb jelly***: see **COMB** *noun*[1].
– **COMB.**: **jelly baby** a soft gelatinous sweet in the shape of a baby; **jelly bag**: through which fruit pulp is strained in the making of jelly; **jelly bean** (orig. *US*) (**a**) a bean-shaped sweet with a gelatinous centre and a hard sugar coating; (**b**) *slang* an unpleasant, weak, or dishonest person; *spec.* a pimp; **jelly-bellied** *adjective* (*slang*) fat; **jelly-belly** *slang* a fat person; **jelly paint** a non-drip paint with the consistency of jelly; **jelly plant** any of various Australian seaweeds from which commercial gelling agents are extracted; **jelly powder** a crystalline powder used in the preparation of jellies; **jelly roll** *N. Amer.* (**a**) a cylindrical cake containing jelly or jam; (**b**) *slang* a lover; sexual intercourse; the vagina; **jelly sandal**, **jelly shoe** a sandal made from brightly coloured or translucent moulded plastic.
▸ **B** *verb*. Cf. earlier **JELLIED** *adjective*.
1 *verb intrans.* Come to the consistency of jelly; set as a jelly; congeal, solidify, coagulate. **E17.**
2 *verb trans.* Convert into jelly; cause to set or coagulate; reduce to the consistency of jelly. **E17.**
■ **jellygraph** *noun & verb* (*obsolete* exc. *hist.*) (**a**) *noun* an appliance used for copying documents etc., of which the essential part is a sheet of jelly; (**b**) *verb trans.* copy with a jellygraph: **E20.** **jelly-like** *adjective* resembling (that of) jelly, *esp.* having the consistency of jelly **L18.**

jelly *noun*[2] var. of **GELLY**.

jellyfish /ˈdʒɛlɪfɪʃ/ *noun*. Pl. **-es** /-ɪz/, (usu.) same. **E18.**
[**ORIGIN** from **JELLY** *noun*[1] + **FISH** *noun*[1].]
†**1** A kind of oceanic fish (perh. = ***lancetfish*** (b) s.v. **LANCET** *noun*). *rare*. Only in **E18.**

2 Any marine coelenterate invertebrate of medusoid form, having a dome-shaped gelatinous body with hanging tentacles; *esp.* a member of the class Scyphozoa in which this form is dominant. Cf. earlier **JELLY** *noun*[1] 2c. **M19.** ▸**b** *fig.* A feeble, irresolute, spineless, or sluggish person. *colloq.* **L19.**

jelutong /dʒɛˈluːtɒŋ/ *noun.* **M19.**
[**ORIGIN** Malay.]
Any of several Malaysian trees of the genus *Dyera* (family Apocynaceae), esp. *D. costulata*, which produces a latex when tapped; this latex; the light-coloured wood of such a tree.

jemadar *noun* var. of **JAMADAR.**

Jemima /dʒɪˈmʌɪmə/ *noun. colloq.* Also **j-**. **L19.**
[**ORIGIN** Female forename.]
1 A made-up tie. **L19.**
2 In *pl.* Elastic-sided ankle boots. **E20.**

jemmy /ˈdʒɛmi/ *noun & verb.* **M18.**
[**ORIGIN** Pet form of male forename *James*: see **-Y**[6].]
▸ **A** *noun.* †1 A dandy, a fop. Also ***Jemmy Jessamy*** *adjective*, dandified, foppish. *slang.* **M18–E19.**
†2 A kind of riding boot. Also ***jemmy boot***. *slang.* **M–L18.**
3 A short crowbar used by burglars to force open windows and doors, freq. one made in sections that screw together. Cf. **JAMES** 2, **JIMMY** *noun*[1]. **E19.**
4 A sheep's head as a culinary dish. Cf. **JAMES** 3. *arch. slang.* **M19.**
▸ **B** *verb trans.* Force open (a lock, window, etc.) with a jemmy or similar implement. *colloq.* **M20.**

J. TORRINGTON The meter's cashbox had been jemmied and its contents returned to general circulation.

je ne sais quoi /ʒənsɛkwa, dʒə nə seɪ ˈkwɑː/ *noun phr.* **M17.**
[**ORIGIN** French, lit. 'I do not know what'.]
An indefinable quality, something indescribable or inexpressible.

Smash Hits She positively oozes style. She has that certain *je ne sais quoi*.

jenever *noun* var. of **GENEVER.**

Jennerian /dʒɛˈnɪərɪən/ *adjective.* **E19.**
[**ORIGIN** from *Jenner* (see below) + **-IAN.**]
Of, pertaining to, or commemorating the English physician Edward Jenner (1749–1823), who pioneered the principles of vaccination; made by or following the methods of Jenner.

jennet /ˈdʒɛnɪt/ *noun.* Also **gen(n)et**. **LME.**
[**ORIGIN** French *genet* from Spanish †*ginete* (now *jinete*) light horseman from Hispano-Arabic *Zenēti* (Arabic *Zanātī*) from *Zanāta* Berber tribe famed for horsemanship.]
A small Spanish horse, esp. a pacer.

jenneting /ˈdʒɛnɪtɪŋ/ *noun.* **E17.**
[**ORIGIN** from French *Jeannet* pet form of *Jean* **JOHN**, as in Norman French *pomme de Jeannet* (John's apple, as usu. ripe by St John's Day, 24 June): see **-ING**[3].]
An early-ripening variety of apple.

jenny /ˈdʒɛni/ *noun.* **E17.**
[**ORIGIN** Pet form of female forenames *Janet*, *Jennifer*, or *Jane*, serving as a fem. of *Jack*.]
1 Used **attrib.** to designate a female animal, esp. a bird, or a small one. **E17.** ▸**b** A female ass or donkey. **L18.**
2 *hist.* = ***spinning jenny*** s.v. **SPINNING** *noun.* **L18.**
3 A large locomotive crane. **M19.**
4 **BILLIARDS.** A losing hazard made with the object ball close to a cushion. **M19.**
– **COMB. & PHRASES:** ***creeping Jenny***; **jenny-long-legs** *Scot.* a crane fly; **jenny spinner** (***a***) *Scot. & N. English* a crane fly; (***b***) **ANGLING** (an artificial fly imitating) a male mayfly of the genus *Baetis*; **jenny wren** (***a***) (popular and child's name for) the wren; (***b***) *US* = ***HERB Robert***.

jeofail /ˈdʒɛfeɪl/ *noun.* **M16.**
[**ORIGIN** Anglo-Norman *jeo fail* I am at fault, i.e. *jeo* (French *je*) I, *fail* 1st person sing. pres. indic. of *faillir* **FAIL** *verb*.]
1 **LAW.** A mistake or oversight in pleading or other legal proceeding: an acknowledgement of such error. *obsolete* exc. *hist.* **M16.**
†2 A mistake, an error. **M16–E19.**

jeon *noun* see **JUN.**

jeopard /ˈdʒɛpəd/ *verb. arch.* **LME.**
[**ORIGIN** Back-form. from **JEOPARDY.**]
1 *verb trans.* Jeopardize, endanger, put at risk. **LME.** ▸†**b** *verb intrans.* Risk oneself, run a risk; venture, adventure. **LME–L16.**
†2 *verb trans.* Stake, bet. **LME–L16.**

jeopardize /ˈdʒɛpədʌɪz/ *verb trans.* Also **-ise**. **M17.**
[**ORIGIN** from **JEOPARD** or **JEOPARDY** + **-IZE.**]
Put into jeopardy, endanger, put at risk.

K. VONNEGUT The drunk and vicious people, who jeopardize all life on earth. M. COX This . . behaviour could jeopardize Monty's chance of gaining a scholarship.

jeopardy /ˈdʒɛpədi/ *noun.* **ME.**
[**ORIGIN** Old French *iu parti*, later *ieu* (*geu*) *parti* divided play, even game, uncertain chance: in medieval Latin *jocus partitus*. For the change of *t* to *d* cf. **CARD** *noun*[2], **DIAMOND** *noun & adjective*; for the spelling *-eo-* cf. **PEOPLE** *noun*.]
†1 **CHESS** etc. A puzzle, a problem. **ME–L15.** ▸†**b** A device, a trick, a stratagem. **ME–M16.**
†2 A deed involving peril; a daring exploit. **ME–E19.**
3 Risk of loss, harm, or death; peril, danger; **LAW** danger arising from being on trial for a criminal offence. Freq. in ***in jeopardy***. **ME.**

Times The chances of an important . . match at Twickenham are put in jeopardy by the weather. E. KUZWAYO This would place me in jeopardy with the authorities, who already saw me as a troublemaker.

double jeopardy: see **DOUBLE** *adjective & adverb*.
†4 A state of uncertainty as to the outcome of a game, undertaking, etc. **ME–L16.**

jequirity /dʒɪˈkwɪrɪti/ *noun.* Also **-quer-**. **L19.**
[**ORIGIN** French *jéquirity* from Tupi-Guarani *jekiriti*.]
A leguminous vine, *Abrus precatorius*, native to the Indian subcontinent and widely naturalized in the tropics, whose roots are used as a substitute for liquorice; its red-and-black seeds, used in India etc. as beads or weights. Also called ***Indian liquorice***, ***crab's eyes***, etc.

jer /jɛː/ *noun.* **M18.**
[**ORIGIN** Old Church Slavonic *jerŭ*, *jerĭ*, Russian *er* (pl. *ery*), *er'*.]
Either of the pairs of Slavonic characters written ⱏ, ⱐ in the Glagolitic alphabet and ъ, ь in the Cyrillic alphabet; (an example of) any of the forms of these characters; either or both of the sounds represented by these characters or the Common Slavonic sounds from which they developed.

Jer. *abbreviation.*
Jeremiah (Old Testament).

jerbil *noun* var. of **GERBIL.**

jerboa /dʒəːˈbəʊə, ˈdʒəːbəʊə/ *noun.* **M17.**
[**ORIGIN** mod. Latin *jerboa*, *gerboa* from Arabic *yarbū'(a)*, dial. *jarbū'*.]
Any of various small chiefly nocturnal rodents of the family Dipodidae, of arid regions in Africa and Eurasia, which have very long hind legs and short forelegs, a long tufted tail, and great powers of jumping.
– **COMB.:** **jerboa kangaroo** = **BETTONG**; **jerboa mouse** an American kangaroo rat; **jerboa rat** *Austral.* any of various jumping rodents of the Australian genera *Notomys* and *Conilurus*.

jereed *noun* var. of **JERID.**

jeremejevite /jɛrɪˈmeɪəvʌɪt/ *noun.* Also **ere-**. **L19.**
[**ORIGIN** from P. V. *Eremeev* (1830–99), Russian mineralogist + **-ITE**[1].]
MINERALOGY. A hexagonal aluminium borate mineral, usu. occurring as colourless prisms.

jeremiad /dʒɛrɪˈmʌɪad/ *noun.* **L18.**
[**ORIGIN** French *jérémiade*, from *Jérémie* from ecclesiastical Latin *Jeremias* Jeremiah (see **JEREMIAH**), with allus. to the Lamentations of Jeremiah in the Bible: see **-AD**[2].]
A lamentation; a list of woes or complaints; a doleful tirade.

D. J. ENRIGHT Jeremiads about poor sick England. J. BERMAN The author . . is ready to denounce his own colleagues in a single jeremiad.

Jeremiah /dʒɛrɪˈmʌɪə/ *noun.* **L18.**
[**ORIGIN** A Hebrew prophet (see **JEREMIAD**), Hebrew *Yirmĕyāhū* app. lit. 'Yahweh loosens (the womb)'.]
A person given to lamentation or woeful complaining, a denouncer of the times, a dismal prophet.

E. H. GOMBRICH The Jeremiahs of his time who decried contemporary styles.

Jeremianic /ˌdʒɛrɪmʌɪˈanɪk/ *adjective.* **L19.**
[**ORIGIN** from **JEREMIAH** after *messianic*.]
Of or pertaining to the prophet Jeremiah or the book of the Old Testament and Hebrew Scriptures which bears his name.

jerepigo /dʒɛrɪˈpiːgəʊ/ *noun. S. Afr.* Also **-pico**. **M19.**
[**ORIGIN** Alt. of **GEROPIGA.**]
A sweet fortified wine.

†**jerfalcon** *noun* var. of **GYRFALCON.**

Jericho /ˈdʒɛrɪkəʊ/ *noun. colloq.* **E16.**
[**ORIGIN** A town in the Jordan Valley, where King David told his servants to stay until their beards were grown (*2 Samuel* 10:5).]
(The name of) a place of retreat or concealment; a remote place.

THACKERAY She may go to Bath, or she may go to Jericho for me.

jerid /dʒəˈriːd/ *noun.* Also **jereed**. **M17.**
[**ORIGIN** Arabic *jarīd* palm branch stripped of its leaves, lance, javelin.]
hist. A wooden javelin used in equestrian games in Muslim countries, esp. in the Ottoman Empire; a game in which this was used.

jerk /dʒəːk/ *noun*[1]. **M16.**
[**ORIGIN** Prob. imit.: cf. **JERT** *noun & verb*, **YERK** *verb & noun*.]
†1 A stroke with a whip, a lash; *fig.* a lash of sarcasm, a cutting remark. **M16–L18.**
2 A quick suddenly arrested movement; a sharp sudden pull, throw, push, thrust, or twist. **L16.** ▸**b** In *pl.* (usu. with *the*). Involuntary spasms of the limbs or features, esp. due to religious excitement. **E19.** ▸**c** **PHYSIOLOGY.** An involuntary muscular contraction caused by, and used to test, a spinal motor reflex; an involuntary contraction of a group of muscles, myoclonus. **L19.** ▸**d** A dance characterized by jerking movements. **M20.** ▸**e** **WEIGHTLIFTING.** The rapid lifting of a weight from shoulder level to above the head by straightening the arms (and legs). **M20.**

B. TARKINGTON The contrivance stopped with a heart-shaking jerk before Isabel's house. P. BARKER The minute hand moved, not smoothly, but in a series of jerks.

e clean and jerk.
3 *fig.* A short sharp witty speech; a sally. Now *rare* or *obsolete*. **L16.**
4 An insignificant, contemptible, stupid, or unpleasant person. Cf. **JERKWATER**. *slang* (orig. *US*). **M20.**

Melody Maker I think he's a jerk . . I hate all loud, ignorant people of whatever political persuasion. M. FORSTER He was just a dull, boring, harmless jerk.

5 **PHYSICS.** Rate of change of acceleration (with respect to time). **M20.**
– **PHRASES:** **physical jerks** *colloq.* physical or gymnastic exercises. **put a jerk in it** *colloq.* act vigorously, smartly, or quickly.

jerk /dʒəːk/ *noun*[2]. **L18.**
[**ORIGIN** from **JERK** *verb*[2]: see also **JERKY** *noun*[1].]
Jerked meat, charqui.

jerk /dʒəːk/ *verb*[1]. **M16.**
[**ORIGIN** from (the same root as) **JERK** *noun*[1].]
†1 *verb trans.* Strike with or as with a whip, lash; *fig.* lash with satire or ridicule. **M16–E18.**
2 *verb trans.* Move by a sharp suddenly arrested motion; give a sudden thrust, push, pull, or twist to. **L16.** ▸**b** Throw or toss with a quick sharp motion. **L18.**

J. R. LOWELL We poor puppets, jerked by unseen wires. J. STEINBECK The little man jerked down the brim of his hat. A. TREW 'Resume normal scanning,' echoed Krasnov, jerking his chin outwards. **b** *fig.*: J. LONDON The alarm clock went off, jerking Martin out of sleep.

3 *verb intrans.* Give a jerk; bow or nod with a jerk; move with a jerk. **L16.**

D. ABSE The trams . . jerked to a halt. F. TUOHY She did not answer but jerked away. A. HIGGINS The rabbit jerked once or twice, involuntary muscular spasms, then was still.

4 *verb trans.* Utter (words or sounds) abruptly or sharply. Usu. foll. by *out*. **E17.**
†5 *verb intrans.* Aim satire, sneer, carp (*at*). **M17–E18.**
6 *verb trans.* Serve up (soda, beer, etc.) at a soda fountain, bar, etc. Cf. ***SODA jerk***. *US colloq.* **L19.**
7 *verb intrans. & trans.* Foll. by *off*: masturbate. *coarse slang.* **E20.**
8 *verb trans.* **WEIGHTLIFTING.** Raise (a weight) from shoulder level to above the head by straightening the arms (and legs). **M20.**
clean and jerk.
– **COMB.:** **jerk-line** *N. Amer.* a rope used instead of reins to guide a team of mules etc.; **jerk-off** *adjective & noun* (*coarse slang*, orig. *US*) (***a***) *adjective* pornographic; contemptible, pathetic; (***b***) *noun* = **JERK** *noun*[1] 4.
■ **jerker** *noun* a person who or thing which jerks (***tear-jerker***: see **TEAR** *noun*[1]) **L16.** **jerkingly** *adverb* jerkily **L19.**

jerk /dʒəːk/ *verb*[2] *trans.* **E18.**
[**ORIGIN** Amer. Spanish *charquear*, from *charqui* from Quechua *echarqui* dried flesh in long strips, *echarquini* prepare dried meat: cf. **CHARQUI.**]
Cure (meat, esp. beef) by cutting it into pieces and drying it, orig. in the sun.

jerk *verb*[3] var. of **JERQUE.**

jerkin /ˈdʒəːkɪn/ *noun.* **E16.**
[**ORIGIN** Unknown.]
Orig. (now *hist.*), a man's close-fitting jacket or doublet, often of leather, with or without sleeves and having a short skirt. Now, a sleeveless jacket, a long waistcoat.

jerkin head /ˈdʒəːkɪnhɛd/ *noun.* **M19.**
[**ORIGIN** Perh. from alt. of *jerking* pres. ppl adjective of **JERK** *verb*[1] + **HEAD** *noun*, but cf. earlier **KIRKIN HEAD.**]
ARCHITECTURE. The end of a roof that is hipped for only part of its height, leaving a truncated gable.

jerkwater /ˈdʒəːkwɔːtə/ *adjective. US colloq.* **M19.**
[**ORIGIN** from **JERK** *verb*[1] + **WATER** *noun*: from the need of early railway engines in remote locations to be supplied with water from streams using a bucket on a rope.]
(Of a train) serving small and remote settlements, running on a branch line; *gen.* small and remote, insignificant, inferior, hick.

J. DOS PASSOS A little jerkwater town back in South Dakota.

jerky /ˈdʒəːki/ *noun*[1]. *N. Amer.* **M19.**
[**ORIGIN** Amer. Spanish *charqui*, *charque*: see **CHARQUI**. Cf. **JERK** *noun*[2], *verb*[2].]
Jerked meat, esp. beef.

jerky /ˈdʒəːki/ *adjective & noun*[2]. M19.
[ORIGIN from JERK *noun*[1] + -Y[1].]
▸ **A** *adjective*. Characterized by jerks or sudden abrupt or twitching movements; *fig.* spasmodic. M19.

G. GREENE The rather jerky succession of short stage scenes is given smoothness and continuity in the cinema. R. DAHL He kept making quick jerky little movements with his head.

▸ **B** *noun*. A springless wagon; a shaky, jolting vehicle. *US*. M19.
■ **jerkily** *adverb* in a jerky manner; by fits and starts: L19. **jerkiness** *noun* M19.

jeroboam /dʒɛrəˈbəʊəm/ *noun*. E19.
[ORIGIN A king of Israel (*1 Kings* 11:28, 14:16).]
Orig., a large measure, bowl, or cup of wine etc. Now, a large wine bottle, equivalent to four ordinary bottles.

jerque /dʒəːk/ *verb trans*. Now *rare*. Also **jerk**. E19.
[ORIGIN Perh. from Italian *cercare* to search.]
Search or check (a vessel) to make sure that all the cargo has been duly delivered and declared.
■ **jerquer** *noun* an official who searches or checks a vessel in this way E18.

jerrican *noun* var. of JERRYCAN.

jerry /ˈdʒɛri/ *noun*[1]. *arch. colloq.* E18.
[ORIGIN Pet form of male forenames *Jeremy, Jeremiah, Gerald*, or *Gerard*.]
†**1** ***jerry-cum-mumble***, ***jerry-mumble***, (***a***) *verb trans.* shake or tumble (someone) about; (***b***) a person who tumbles or shakes. E18–L19.
2 In full ***jerry-shop***. A tavern, a rough public house. See also TOM-AND-JERRY *noun* 2. M19.
3 More fully ***jerry hat***. A round felt hat. M19.
4 A machine for shearing cloth. L19.

jerry /ˈdʒɛri/ *noun*[2]. *slang*. M19.
[ORIGIN Prob. dim. of JEROBOAM: see -Y[6].]
A chamber pot.

Jerry /ˈdʒɛri/ *noun*[3]. *colloq.* (orig. *military slang*). E20.
[ORIGIN Alt. of GERMAN *noun*[1] & *adjective*[1], perh. infl. by JERRY *noun*[1]: see -Y[6].]
(A name for) a German, *spec.* a German soldier; a German aircraft. Also, the Germans or German soldiers collectively. Cf. FRITZ *noun*[1].

jerry /ˈdʒɛri/ *noun*[4]. *Austral. & NZ slang*. E20.
[ORIGIN Unknown: cf. JERRY *adjective*[2], *verb*.]
take a jerry (to), investigate and understand (something or someone).

jerry /ˈdʒɛri/ *adjective*[1]. *colloq.* L19.
[ORIGIN Abbreviation.]
Jerry-built; constructed insubstantially and hurriedly from inferior materials.
■ **jerryism** *noun* jerry-building L19.

jerry /ˈdʒɛri/ *adjective*[2]. *US slang*. E20.
[ORIGIN Unknown: cf. JERRY *verb*, *noun*[4].]
be jerry (foll. by *on, on to, to*), be aware (of), understand.

Jerry /ˈdʒɛri/ *adjective*[3]. *colloq.* M20.
[ORIGIN from JERRY *noun*[3].]
German.

jerry /ˈdʒɛri/ *verb intrans. slang* (chiefly *Austral. & NZ*). L19.
[ORIGIN Unknown: cf. JERRY *adjective*[2], *noun*[4].]
Foll. by *to*: understand, realize, get wise to.

jerry-build /ˈdʒɛrɪbɪld/ *verb trans. colloq.* Pa. t. & pple **-built** /-bɪlt/. M19.
[ORIGIN Unknown.]
Build insubstantially from inferior materials; build to sell but not to last. Chiefly as ***jerry-built*** *ppl adjective*.

F. KING The flat's so tiny and so jerry-built that every sound can be heard from one room to another.

■ **jerry-builder** *noun* a person who builds houses etc. hurriedly and insubstantially from inferior materials L19.

jerrycan /ˈdʒɛrɪkan/ *noun*. Also **jerrican**. M20.
[ORIGIN from JERRY *adjective*[3] + CAN *noun*.]
A container for petrol, water, etc., orig. five-gallon and metal, of a type first used in Germany and later adopted by the Allied forces in the Second World War.

Jersey /ˈdʒəːzi/ *noun*[1]. E18.
[ORIGIN New *Jersey*, a state of the US: see NEW JERSEY.]
Used ***attrib.*** to designate people or things coming from or associated with New Jersey.
Jersey blue (***a***) *hist.* a colonial New Jersey soldier (so called from the blue uniform); (***b***) a native or inhabitant of New Jersey; (***c***) a breed of chicken. **Jersey justice** strict or severe justice. **Jersey lightning** *colloq.* a strong kind of applejack, peach brandy, or whisky. **Jersey pine** the scrub pine, *Pinus virginiana*. **Jersey tea** a small US shrub, *Ceanothus americanus*, of the buckthorn family, the leaves of which have been used as a substitute for tea; also called ***New Jersey tea***. **Jersey wagon** a light carriage formerly used in New Jersey.

jersey /ˈdʒəːzi/ *adjective & noun*[2]. In senses A.2, B.3 also **J-**. L16.
[ORIGIN *Jersey*, the largest of the Channel Islands.]
▸ **A** *adjective*. **1** Of or from Jersey; *spec.* designating or made of the fabric jersey (see sense B.1 below). L16.

N. FREELING A nearly new jersey cocktail dress.

2 Designating, of, or pertaining to a breed of usu. fawn dairy cattle orig. bred in Jersey and producing milk of high fat content. M19.
▸ **B** *noun*. **1** Orig., a fine woollen worsted fabric made in Jersey. Now, any machine-knitted slightly elastic plain fabric. L16. ▸†**b** Combed wool ready for spinning. M17–L19.

Observer Short evening dresses . . in silk jersey.

2 A knitted usu. woollen pullover or similar garment. Also, a distinguishing upper garment or shirt worn by a football etc. team. M19.

P. BOWLES Do you mind bringing me my jersey? . . With this rain and wind I feel cold. D. STOREY Occasionally they changed sides, swapping jerseys.

yellow jersey: see YELLOW *adjective*.
3 (An animal of) the Jersey breed of cattle. M19.
■ **jerseyed** *adjective* wearing a jersey M19.

Jerseyman /ˈdʒəːzɪmən/ *noun*. Pl. **-men**. L17.
[ORIGIN from *Jersey* (see below) + MAN *noun*.]
1 A (male) native or inhabitant of the state of New Jersey, USA. Now *rare*. L17.
2 A (male) native or inhabitant of Jersey in the Channel Islands. E19.

jert /dʒəːt/ *noun & verb*. *obsolete* exc. *dial.* M16.
[ORIGIN Prob. imit.: cf. JERK *noun*[1], *verb*[1].]
▸ **A** *noun*. = JERK *noun*[1]. M16.
▸ **B** *verb trans. & intrans.* = JERK *verb*[1]. M16.

jerupiga *noun* var. of GEROPIGA.

Jerusalem /dʒəˈruːs(ə)ləm/ *noun & interjection*. LME.
[ORIGIN A city in Israel, sacred to Jews, Christians, and Muslims.]
▸ **A** *noun*. **1** Used ***attrib.*** and after *of* in names of things from or associated with Jerusalem. LME.
Jerusalem artichoke: see ARTICHOKE. **Jerusalem cherry** a kind of nightshade, *Solanum pseudocapsicum*, grown for its decorative red berries in winter. **Jerusalem cross** HERALDRY: having a bar across the end of each limb and a cross potent. **Jerusalem letters** letters or symbols tattooed on the arm or body, such as pilgrims or visitors to Jerusalem sometimes bore in testimony or memory of their visit. **Jerusalem pony** a donkey (so called in reference to Jesus's riding into Jerusalem on an ass). **Jerusalem sage** a Mediterranean labiate plant, *Phlomis fruticosa*, with large yellow flowers, grown for ornament. **Jerusalem thorn** a thorny leguminous tree, *Parkinsonia aculeata*, native to tropical America and grown for ornament. ***oak of Jerusalem***: see OAK *noun*.
2 *fig.* An ideal or heavenly city, place, or situation. Freq. in ***the new Jerusalem***. LME.

W. BLAKE I will not cease from Mental Fight . . till we have built Jerusalem In England's green & pleasant Land. *Listener* Both . . looked forward to the same new Jerusalem . . in which . . bureaucracy would be no more.

▸ **B** *interjection*. Expr. mild alarm or surprise. M19.

jes /dʒɛs/ *adverb. colloq. & dial.* (chiefly *US*, esp. *black English*). Also **jes'**. M19.
[ORIGIN Repr. a pronunc. Cf. JEST *adverb*.]
= JUST *adverb*.

jess /dʒɛs/ *noun & verb*. ME.
[ORIGIN Old French *ges* nom. sing. & accus. pl. of *get* (mod. *jet* cast) from Proto-Romance var. of Latin *jactus* a throw, from *jacere* to throw.]
▸ **A** *noun*. A short strap of leather, silk, or other material fastened round each of the legs of a hawk used in falconry, usu. having a small ring to which a leash may be attached. Usu. in *pl.* ME.
▸ **B** *verb trans.* Put jesses on (a hawk). M19.
■ **jessed** /dʒɛst/ *adjective* (of a hawk) wearing jesses; HERALDRY having jesses of a specified tincture: E17.

jessamin(e) *noun* see JASMINE.

jessamy /ˈdʒɛsəmi/ *noun*. *obsolete* exc. *dial. & W. Indian*. M17.
[ORIGIN Alt. of *jessamine* var. of JASMINE.]
1 = JASMINE 1. M17.
†**2** A man who scents himself with perfume or who wears a sprig of jessamine; a dandy, a fop. Cf. ***Jemmy Jessamy*** s.v. JEMMY *noun* 1. M18–M19.

jessant /ˈdʒɛs(ə)nt/ *adjective*. L16.
[ORIGIN In sense 2 from Old French *gesant* (later *gisant*) lying, pres. pple of *gésir* from Latin *jacere* to lie: see -ANT[1]. In sense 1 perh. a different word.]
HERALDRY. **1** Of a charge (as a branch or flower): represented as held in or issuing from the mouth of an animal etc. L16.
2 Of a charge: represented as lying over and partly covering another. *rare*. E17.

Jesse /ˈdʒɛsi/ *noun*[1]. *obsolete* exc. *hist.* LME.
[ORIGIN The father of David and ancestor of Jesus (*1 Samuel* 16:12, *Isaiah* 11:1).]
More fully ***tree of Jesse***. A genealogical tree representing the lineage of Jesus, used in medieval churches as a decoration for a wall, window, vestment, etc., or in the form of a large branched candlestick.
■ **Jessean** /dʒɛˈsiːən/ *adjective* (long *rare* or *obsolete*) belonging to Jesse or to his son King David E17.

Jesse /ˈdʒɛsi/ *noun*[2]. *US slang* (now *rare*). Also **Jessy**. M19.
[ORIGIN Perh. formed as JESSE *noun*[1], from a joc. interpretation of 'There shall come a rod out of the stem of Jesse' (*Isaiah* 11:1).]
Severe treatment or handling.

†**jesserant** *noun* var. of JAZERANT.

jessie /ˈdʒɛsi/ *noun*. *colloq.* Also **jessy**. E20.
[ORIGIN Female forename.]
A cowardly or effeminate man. Also, a male homosexual.

Jessy *noun*[1] var. of JESSE *noun*[2].

jessy *noun*[2] var. of JESSIE.

jest /dʒɛst/ *noun*. Also †**g-**. See also GEST *noun*[1]. LME.
[ORIGIN Later spelling of GEST *noun*[1].]
▸ **I 1** See GEST *noun*[1] I. LME.
▸ **II** †**2** A satirical utterance, a lampoon; an idle tale. LME–E17.

T. WASHINGTON Alexander taking it for a iest would not beleeve it.

3 A mocking or jeering speech; a taunt, a jeer. Also, a piece of raillery or banter. M16.

W. COWPER Might he but set the rabble in a roar, He cared not with what jest.

4 A saying intended to excite laughter; a witticism, a joke. M16. ▸**b** Something funny to relate; a ludicrous event or circumstance. L16.

I. MURDOCH Edward giggled feebly at this jest. **b** POPE To complete the Jest, Old Edward's Armour beams on Cibber's breast.

5 a The opposite of earnest or seriousness; trifling sport, fun. Chiefly in ***in jest***, not seriously, in fun. M16. ▸**b** Jesting, joking, merriment; ridicule. L16. ▸**c** A thing that is not serious or earnest; a jocular affair. M18.

b SHAKES. *Haml.* Alas, poor Yorick! . . : a fellow of infinite jest. **c** R. S. THOMAS Life's bitter jest is hollow.

6 A prank, a frolic; a trick played in sport, a practical joke. Now *rare*. L16.

W. IRVING Students famous for their love of a jest—set the college on fire.

7 An object of or matter for jesting or derision; a laughing stock. L16.

B. TAYLOR Lowly virtue is the jest of fools.

– COMB.: **jest-book** a book of jests or amusing stories.
■ **jestful** *adjective* full of jesting, jocular M19.

jest /dʒɛst/ *verb*. Also †**g-**. E16.
[ORIGIN Var. of GEST *verb*.]
1 *verb intrans.* Utter jibes or taunts; jeer, mock. Usu. foll. by *at*. E16. ▸**b** *verb trans.* Jeer at; ridicule. E18.

F. BROOKE He . . made an oath he would never jest at spirits again. **b** G. P. R. JAMES He jested his companion upon his gravity.

2 *verb intrans.* Speak or act in a trifling manner or not seriously; trifle. M16.

LYTTON Jest not, Pausanius; you will find me in earnest.

3 *verb intrans.* Say something amusing or facetious; make witty or humorous remarks; joke. M16. ▸**b** *verb trans.* Usu. with adverb or phr. expr. result: bring into a given condition by jesting. M16. ▸†**c** *verb intrans.* Disport or amuse oneself; make merry. L16–M17.

R. C. HUTCHINSON Grown-ups jesting to hide their troubles from children. *Sunday Express* He has jested that divorce lawyers will soon be extinct. **b** C. LAMB That freak . . jested me out of a good three hundred pounds a year. **c** SHAKES. *Rich. II* As gentle and as jocund as to jest Go I to fight.

■ **jestingly** *adverb* in the manner of a person who jests; by way of a joke: M16.

jest /dʒɛst/ *adverb. colloq. & dial.* E19.
[ORIGIN Repr. a pronunc.: cf. JES.]
= JUST *adverb*.

jester /ˈdʒɛstə/ *noun*. Also †**g-**. ME.
[ORIGIN from JEST *verb*, GEST *verb* + -ER[1].]
1 A professional reciter of romances. *arch.* ME.
2 A mimic, a buffoon; a person whose profession is to amuse; *esp.* a professional joker or clown maintained in a medieval court etc., a fool. E16.
3 A person who jests, or speaks or acts in jest; a person given to uttering jests or witticisms, a joker. E16.
■ **jestership** *noun* the position of a jester M19.

Jesu *noun* see JESUS.

Jesuist /ˈdʒɛzjʊɪst/ *noun & adjective*. Long *rare*. L16.
[ORIGIN French †*Jésuiste*, formed as JESUIT + -IST.]
= JESUIT.

Jesuit /ˈdʒɛzjʊɪt/ *noun & adjective*. M16.
[ORIGIN French *jésuite* or mod. Latin *Jesuita*, from JESUS + *-ita* -ITE[1].]
▸ **A** *noun*. **1** A member of the Society of Jesus, a Roman Catholic order which was founded by Ignatius Loyola and others in 1534 to propagate the faith among unbelievers, and was prominent in the Church's struggle against the Reformation. M16.
Jesuits' bark the medicinal bark of species of *Cinchona*, introduced into Europe from the Jesuit Missions in S. America as a source of quinine; **Jesuits' nut** the seed of the water chestnut *Trapa natans*; **Jesuits' tea** an infusion of the leaves of *Psoralea glandulosa*, a S. American leguminous shrub.
2 *transf.* A dissembling person; a prevaricator. *derog.* M17.

D. SHUB Lenin is a political Jesuit who . . has molded Marxism to his aims of the moment.

3 A kind of lady's dress buttoning up to the neck. Long *obsolete* exc. *hist.* **M18.**

▸ **B** *attrib.* or as ***adjective***. That is a Jesuit; of or belonging to the Society of Jesus; Jesuitical. **M16.**

– **NOTE:** By their enemies the Jesuits were accused of teaching that the end justifies the means, and the style of argument adopted by a few of their moralists was ascribed to the order as a whole, thus giving rise to sense A.2 and the corresponding opprobrious uses of *Jesuitical*, *Jesuitry*, and other derivs. These uses give offence to some Roman Catholics.

■ **†Jesuited** *adjective* made or become a Jesuit; imbued with the principles or character of the Jesuits: **E17–M19. Jesuitess** *noun* (*hist.*) a nun of an order established on the principles of the Jesuits, but not recognized by papal authority and suppressed by Pope Urban VIII in 1631 **E17.**

Jesuitical /dʒɛzjʊˈɪtɪk(ə)l/ *adjective*. In sense 2 also **j-**. **E17.**
[**ORIGIN** from **JESUIT** + **-ICAL**.]
1 Of or pertaining to the Jesuits. **E17.**
2 Having the character once ascribed to the Jesuits; deceitful, dissembling; practising equivocation. Also, hair-splitting, oversubtle. **E17.**

M. HASTINGS People only call a man Jesuitical when they are beaten in an argument.

– **NOTE:** See note s.v. **JESUIT.**

■ **Jesuitic** *adjective* (now *rare*) = **JESUITICAL M17. Jesuitically** *adverb* **E17.**

Jesuitise *verb* var. of **JESUITIZE.**

Jesuitism /ˈdʒɛzjʊɪtɪz(ə)m/ *noun*. **E17.**
[**ORIGIN** from **JESUIT** *noun* + **-ISM**.]
1 The system, doctrine, principles, or practice of the Jesuits. **E17.**
2 Principles or practice such as those once ascribed to the Jesuits; Jesuitry. **E17.**
3 A Jesuitical quibble or equivocation. *rare.* **M18.**

Jesuitize /ˈdʒɛzjʊɪtʌɪz/ *verb*. Also **-ise**. **E17.**
[**ORIGIN** from **JESUIT** *noun* + **-IZE**.]
1 *verb trans.* Imbue with Jesuit principles; make Jesuitical. **E17.**
2 *verb intrans.* Behave like a Jesuit; propound Jesuitical doctrines. **E17.**

Jesuitry /ˈdʒɛzjʊɪtri/ *noun*. **M19.**
[**ORIGIN** from **JESUIT** *noun* + **-RY**.]
The principles, doctrine, or practices of the Jesuits. Chiefly *derog.*, subtle casuistry or prevarication; the doctrine that the end justifies the means.
– **NOTE:** See note s.v. **JESUIT.**

Jesus /ˈdʒiːzəs/ *noun & interjection*. Also (*arch.*) **Jesu** /ˈdʒiːzjuː/ (now chiefly *voc.*). **ME.**
[**ORIGIN** Christian Latin *Iesus* (in oblique cases *Iesu*) from Greek *Iēsous* (in oblique cases *Iēsou*) from late Hebrew or Aramaic *Yēšūaʿ* var. of earlier *Yĕhōšūaʿ* Joshua.]
▸ **A** *noun*. **1** (The name of) the central figure of the Christian faith, a Jewish preacher (*c* 5 BC–*c* AD 30) regarded by his followers as the Son of God and God incarnate. More fully ***Jesus Christ*** (see **CHRIST** *noun* 2). **ME.**
CREEPING Jesus. ***find Jesus***: see **FIND** *verb*. **Jesus wept!** *interjection* expr. strong exasperation. **Society of Jesus** the Jesuit order. ***sweet Jesus***: see **SWEET** *adjective & adverb*.
2 A figure or representation of Jesus. **L15.**
– **COMB.:** **Jesus freak** a (usu. young) person combining a lifestyle like that of a hippy with fervent evangelical Christianity; ***Jesus PSALTER***.
▸ **B** *interjection*. Expr. surprise, dismay, disbelief, relief, etc. Also ***Jesus Christ***. **L16.**

P. BOWLES 'Jesus!' he cried. 'I'm glad to be here!'

jet /dʒɛt/ *noun*[1] & *adjective*. **ME.**
[**ORIGIN** Anglo-Norman *geet*, Old French *jaiet*, *jayet* (mod. *jais*) from Latin *gagates* **GAGATE**.]
▸ **A** *noun*. **1** A hard compact black form of lignite, capable of receiving a brilliant polish, which has the property of attracting light bodies when electrified by rubbing and was formerly much used in making ornaments. Formerly also, a black colouring matter. **ME.**
2 The colour of jet; a deep glossy black. **LME.**
†3 Black marble. **LME–M17.**
– **COMB.:** **jet-black** *adjective* black like jet; glossy black.
▸ **B** *attrib.* or as ***adjective***. **1** Made or consisting of jet. **LME.**
2 Of the colour of jet, jet-black. **E17.**

jet /dʒɛt/ *noun*[2]. **E17.**
[**ORIGIN** Partly from **JET** *verb*[2] (and *verb*[1]), partly from senses of French *jet*, from *jeter* to throw. See also **JUT** *noun*[2].]
†1 A projecting part of a building; a pier, a jetty. *rare.* **E17–L18.**
†2 An affected movement or jerk of the body; a swagger. **L17–E18.**
3 A stream of liquid, gas, or (more rarely) solid particles shot forward or thrown upwards (either in a spurt or continuously), esp. by pressure from a small opening. **L17.** ▸**b** *ASTRONOMY*. A thin elongated structure extending from or emitted by a cometary or galactic nucleus, the solar chromosphere, or other body. **M19.** ▸**c** In full ***jet stream***. A fast narrow current in the atmosphere or ocean; *spec.* one in the upper troposphere at middle latitudes that blows horizontally from west to east. **M20.**

S. SPENDER I directed the jet of water from the nozzle of the hose. A. WEST My father blew out a thin jet of cobalt-blue cigar smoke.

4 A large ladle. **E18.**
5 A spout or nozzle for emitting water, gas, etc. **E19.**
6 A projection at the end of a type in casting, and subsequently broken off. **L19.**
7 A jet plane; a jet engine. *colloq.* **M20.**

J. WYNDHAM More planes went over . . travelling very fast, with their jets shrieking.

jumbo jet: see **JUMBO** *adjective*.
– **ATTRIB. & COMB.:** In the sense 'of, pertaining to, or powered by a jet engine', as ***jet aircraft***, ***jet fighter***, ***jet plane***, etc. Special combs., as **jet age** the era of travel by jet aircraft; **jetboat** a motor boat propelled by a jet of water pumped out from below the stern; **jet engine** an engine in which jet propulsion is used to provide forward thrust; *esp.* an aircraft engine that takes in air and ejects hot compressed air and exhaust gases; **Jetfoil** (US proprietary name for) a type of passenger-carrying hydrofoil with a stabilization and control system based on that of an aircraft; **jet lag** tiredness, temporal disorientation, and other effects suffered by a person after a flight involving marked differences in local time; **jet-lagged** *adjective* suffering from jet lag; **jet pipe** the exhaust duct of a jet engine; **jet-propelled** *adjective* having or employing a means of jet propulsion; *fig.* very fast, frenzied; **jet propulsion** the ejection of a usu. high-speed jet of gas (or liquid) as a source of propulsive power, esp. for aircraft; **jet set** *colloq.* a (or *the*) set of wealthy and fashionable people who frequently travel by air; **jet-setter** *colloq.* a member of the jet set; **jet ski** *noun & verb* (**a**) *noun* (proprietary name for) a small jet-propelled vehicle which skims across the surface of water and is ridden in a similar way to a motorcycle; (**b**) *verb intrans.* ride on such a vehicle; ***jet stream***: see sense 3c above; **jet turbine** a turbojet engine; **Jetway** (proprietary name for) an air bridge.

jet /dʒɛt/ *noun*[3]. *arch.* **M18.**
[**ORIGIN** By-form of **GIST** *noun*[3].]
= **GIST** *noun*[3].

†jet *noun*[4] see **GET** *noun*[2].

†jet *verb*[1]. Infl. **-tt-**. **LME.**
[**ORIGIN** App. from Anglo-Norman *gettre*, Old French *getter*, *jetter*, mod. *jeter* to throw, cast, etc., but the senses are those of Latin *jactare se*, *jactari* vaunt oneself, boast.]
▸ **I** Of gait and motion.
1 *verb intrans. & trans.* (with *it*). ▸**a** Assume a pompous gait in walking; strut, swagger. Also (of an animal), prance. **LME–L17.** ▸**b** Move along jauntily, caper, trip. **M16–L17.**
2 *verb intrans.* Stroll; walk, go. **M16–L18.**
3 *verb trans.* Traverse ostentatiously, parade (the streets). **M–L16.**
▸ **II** Of behaviour.
4 *verb intrans.* Act or behave boastfully, brag. **E16–M17.**
5 *verb intrans.* Revel, run riot; indulge in riotous living. **E16–M17.**

jet /dʒɛt/ *verb*[2]. Infl. **-tt-**. **L16.**
[**ORIGIN** Old French & mod. French *jeter* throw, cast, from Proto-Romance var. of Latin *jactare*: cf. **JUT** *verb*[2].]
†1 *verb intrans.* **a** Project, protrude, jut. Freq. foll. by *out*. **L16–M18.** ▸**b** *transf.* Encroach *on*, *upon*. **L16–M17.**

L. EVANS Little Ridges jetting out from the principal Chains of Mountains. **b** SHAKES. *Tit. A.* Think you not how dangerous It is to jet upon a prince's right?

†2 *verb trans.* Build *out* (part of a house, etc.); cause to project. **M17–E18.**
3 *verb trans.* Throw, cast, toss. *obsolete* exc. *dial.* **M17.**
†4 *verb intrans.* Spring, hop, bound, dart. **M17–E19.**

J. MONTGOMERY He hoped to see . . The wingless squirrel jet from tree to tree.

†5 *verb intrans.* Move or be moved with a jerk or jerks; jolt, jog. **M–L17.**
6 *verb intrans.* Of a bird: move the tail up and down jerkily. Now *rare.* **M17.**
7 *verb intrans.* Spout or spurt forth; issue in a (curved) jet or jets. **L17.**

V. WOOLF Fountains jet; drops descend. *Trucking International* He opened the tank's main hatches so the petrol jetted out.

8 *verb trans.* Emit in a jet or jets. **E18.**

P. BARKER A tram rattled past and jetted sparks.

9 *verb trans. BUILDING*. Loosen and remove (sand, gravel, etc.) by directing jets of water or compressed air on to it, esp. so as to make a hole for pile-driving; sink (a pile) by this means. Chiefly as ***jetting*** *verbal noun*. **E20.**

jet /dʒɛt/ *verb*[3] *intrans. & trans. colloq.* Infl. **-tt-**. **M20.**
[**ORIGIN** from **JET** *noun*[2] 7.]
Travel or convey by jet plane.

P. FULLER Art bureaucrats are jetting around the capitals of the world.

jetavator /ˈdʒɛtəveɪtə/ *noun*. **M20.**
[**ORIGIN** from **JET** *noun*[2] + **ELEVATOR**.]
A ring-shaped deflector surrounding the exit nozzle of a rocket engine which can be swivelled into the exhaust gases to alter the direction of thrust.

jet d'eau /ʒedo/ *noun*. Pl. ***jets d'eau*** (pronounced same). **L17.**
[**ORIGIN** French = jet of water.]
An ornamental jet of water rising from a fountain or pipe; a fountain or pipe from which such a jet rises.

jeté /ʒɛˈteɪ, *foreign* ʒəte (*pl. same*)/ *noun*. **M19.**
[**ORIGIN** French, pa. pple (sc. *pas* step) of *jeter* throw.]
BALLET. A step in which a spring is made from one foot to land on the other, esp. with one leg extended forwards and the other backwards.
grand jeté /grɑ̃/: achieving a high elevation. **jeté en tournant** /ɒ̃ ˈtʊənɒ̃ː, *foreign* ɑ̃ turnɑ̃/: executed with a turning movement; also called ***tour jeté***. **split jeté**: in which both legs are raised in a horizontal line.

jetliner /ˈdʒɛtlʌɪnə/ *noun*. **M20.**
[**ORIGIN** Blend of **JET** *noun*[2] and **AIRLINER**.]
A large jet aircraft carrying passengers.

jeton /ˈdʒɛtən, *in sense 2 foreign* ʒətɔ̃ (*pl. same*)/ *noun*. **M20.**
[**ORIGIN** Old French & mod. French, from *jeter* cast up (accounts), calculate: see **JET** *verb*[2].]
1 = **JETTON**. **M20.**
2 A metal disc used instead of a coin for insertion in a public telephone box, esp. in France. **M20.**

jetsam /ˈdʒɛts(ə)m/ *noun*. Also (*arch.*) **jetson** /ˈdʒɛts(ə)n/. **L16.**
[**ORIGIN** Contr. of **JETTISON** *noun*.]
LAW. **1** Goods discarded from a ship and washed ashore; *spec.* such material thrown overboard in order to lighten a vessel (also called ***waveson***). Usu. assoc. with **FLOTSAM**; cf. also **LAGAN**. **L16.**
†2 The throwing of goods overboard; = **JETTISON** *noun*. **M17–L19.**

jets d'eau *noun* pl. of **JET D'EAU**.

†jetteau *noun*. **E–M18.**
[**ORIGIN** Confusion of Italian *getto* (*d'acqua*) & French **JET D'EAU**.]
= **JET D'EAU.**

jetted /ˈdʒɛtɪd/ *adjective*[1]. **L19.**
[**ORIGIN** from **JET** *noun*[1] + **-ED**[2].]
Ornamented with jet; trimmed with jet beads.

jetted /ˈdʒɛtɪd/ *adjective*[2]. **E20.**
[**ORIGIN** App. from **JET** *verb*[2] + **-ED**[1].]
Of a pocket: having no flap, but an outside seam on either edge.

†jettee *noun* var. of **JETTY** *noun*.

jettison /ˈdʒɛtɪs(ə)n, -z(ə)n/ *noun*. **LME.**
[**ORIGIN** Anglo-Norman *getteson*, Old French *getaison* from Latin *jactatio(n-)*, from *jactare*: see **-ISON**.]
1 The action of throwing goods overboard, esp. in order to lighten a ship in distress. **LME.**
2 *fig.* Abandonment, disregard. **L19.**

jettison /ˈdʒɛtɪs(ə)n, -z(ə)n/ *verb trans.* **M19.**
[**ORIGIN** from the noun.]
1 Throw overboard (cargo, articles of merchandise, etc.), esp. in order to lighten a ship in distress. **M19.** ▸**b** Release or drop from an aircraft or spacecraft in flight; *spec.* drop (a bomb) intentionally from an aircraft elsewhere than over an assigned target. **M20.**
2 *fig.* Discard, abandon, get rid of, (something no longer wanted). **L19.**

Daedalus He jettisoned much of what we think of as Victorianism.

■ **jettisonable** *adjective* able to be jettisoned; *esp.* designed to be readily detachable from an aircraft etc. in flight: **M20.**

jetton /ˈdʒɛt(ə)n/ *noun*. **M18.**
[**ORIGIN** French **JETON**.]
A counter or token used to operate slot machines, as a gambling chip, and (formerly) in accounting.

jetty /ˈdʒɛti/ *noun*. Also **†jettee**. **LME.**
[**ORIGIN** Old French *jetee*, *getee*, use as noun of fem. pa. pple of *jeter* throw: see **JET** *noun*[2], **-Y**[5]. Cf. **JUTTY** *noun*.]
1 A mole, pier, breakwater, etc., constructed at a harbour entrance or running out into the sea, a lake, a river, etc., esp. for protective or defensive purposes. Also, an outwork protecting a pier. **LME.** ▸**b** A projecting part of a wharf; a landing pier. **LME.**
2 A projecting part of a building; *esp.* an overhanging upper storey. *obsolete* exc. *hist.* **LME.**
3 A bulwark, a bastion. *obsolete* exc. *hist.* **M16.**

jetty /ˈdʒɛti/ *adjective*. **L15.**
[**ORIGIN** from **JET** *noun*[1] + **-Y**[1].]
1 Of the colour of jet; jet-black. Also ***jetty-black***. **L15.**
2 Of the nature or composition of jet. **L19.**

jetty /ˈdʒɛti/ *verb trans.* **LME.**
[**ORIGIN** from the noun.]
1 Chiefly *hist.* Cause (the upper storey of a building) to project; provide (a building) with a projecting upper storey. Usu. in *pass.* **LME.**
2 Provide with a jetty or pier. *rare.* **L19.**

jeu /ʒø/ *noun*. Pl. **jeux** /ʒøː/. **E18.**
[**ORIGIN** French from Latin *jocus* **JOKE** *noun*.]
The French for 'play', 'game', occurring in various phrases used in English
■ ***jeu de mots*** /də mo/ [lit. 'of words'] a play on words, a pun **M18.** ***jeu de paume*** /də pom/ [lit. 'of the palm (of the hand)'] real tennis;

J

a court where this is played: L18. ***jeu de société*** /də sɔsjete/ [lit. 'of society'] a party game or amusement (esp. in *pl.*) E19. ***jeu d'esprit*** /dɛspri/ [lit. 'of wit'] a playful action in which some cleverness is displayed; (now usu.) a humorous literary trifle: E18.

jeune fille /ʒœn fij/ *noun & adjectival phr.* M19.
[ORIGIN French.]
▸ **A** *noun phr.* Pl. **-s -s** (pronounced same). A young girl, an ingénue. M19.
▸ **B** *attrib.* or as *adjectival phr.* Characteristic of an ingénue. L19.

jeune premier /ʒœn prəmje/ *noun phr.* Also (fem.) ***jeune première*** /prəmjɛːr/. Pl. **-s -s** (pronounced same). M19.
[ORIGIN French, lit. 'first young man (woman)'.]
An actor who plays the part of a principal lover or young hero (or heroine).

jeunes filles, jeunes premiers *noun phrs.* pls. of JEUNE FILLE, JEUNE PREMIER.

jeunesse /ʒœnɛs/ *noun.* L18.
[ORIGIN French.]
Young people; the young.

jeunesse dorée /ʒœnɛs dɔre/ *noun phr.* M19.
[ORIGIN French, lit. 'gilded youth'.]
Orig., in France, a group of fashionable counter-revolutionaries formed after the fall of Robespierre. Now (*gen.*), young people of wealth and fashion.

jeux *noun* pl. of JEU *noun.*

Jew /dʒuː/ *noun.* ME.
[ORIGIN Old French *giu*, earlier *juiu* (mod. *juif*) from Latin *Judaeus* from Greek *Ioudaios* from Aramaic *yĕhūḏāy*, Hebrew *yĕhūḏī*, from *yĕhūḏāh* Judah, a son of the Hebrew patriarch Jacob, the tribe descended from Judah.]
1 A Jewish person; a person whose religion is Judaism; *hist.* an Israelite. ME.
Ashkenazic Jew, German Jew, Oriental Jew, Portuguese Jew, Russian Jew, Sephardic Jew, etc. ***Conservative Jew***: see CONSERVATIVE *adjective.* **Black Jew** (*a*) an Indian or black person of Jewish descent; (*b*) = FALASHA. ***wandering Jew***: see WANDERING *ppl adjective.*
2 A person who behaves in a manner formerly attributed to Jews; *spec.* a grasping or extortionate person, one who drives hard bargains. *derog.* & considered *offensive.* E16.
3 A pedlar. *colloq.* Now *rare.* E19.
4 A ship's tailor. *nautical slang.* E20.
– ATTRIB. & COMB.: In the sense 'Jewish', as ***Jew boy, Jew girl, Jew man*** (now usu. *derog. & offensive*). Special combs., as **Jew-baiter** a person who practises Jew-baiting; **Jew-baiting** systematic harrying or persecution of Jews; **Jew-lizard** a large Australian lizard, *Amphibolurus barbatus*, with spiny scales round the throat; **Jew plum** = OTAHEITE ***apple***; **Jew's apple** (the fruit of) the egg-plant, *Solanum melongena*; **Jew's ear** [mistranslation of medieval Latin *auricula Judae* Judas's ear: so called from its shape and its frequent occurrence on the elder, the tree from which Judas Iscariot reputedly hanged himself] an edible cup-shaped fungus, *Auricularia auricula-Judae*, growing on the roots and trunks of trees; **Jew's eye** (a proverbial expression for) something valued highly; **Jew's harp** a musical instrument consisting of an elastic steel tongue, usu. of metal, fixed at one end to a small lyre-shaped frame, and bent at the other end at right angles, which is played by holding the frame between the teeth and striking the free end of the tongue with the finger; **Jew's mallow** (*a*) a jute-yielding plant, *Corchorus olitorius*, of the linden family, used as a pot-herb in Egypt, Syria, etc.; (*b*) a double-flowered ornamental shrub, *Kerria japonica*, of the rose family; **Jews' stone, Jewstone** [translating medieval Latin *lapis Judaicus*] (*a*) (now *rare* or *obsolete*) marcasite; (*b*) (now *rare* or *obsolete*) fossil sea urchin spines found in Syria, formerly used in medicine; (*c*) *local* a hard rock of uneven or difficult fracture; **Jew's trump** (now *rare*) = ***Jew's harp*** above.
– NOTE: In medieval England Jews, though engaged in many pursuits, were particularly familiar as moneylenders, a profession debarred to Christians at this time. Thus the name 'Jew' came to be associated in the popular mind with the usury and extortionate practices associated with the medieval system of moneylending, and gave rise to the opprobrious sense 2 above.
■ **Jewism** *noun* †(*a*) Judaism; (*b*) *rare* an idiom or characteristic of Jews: L16. **Jewy** *adjective* (*derog.*) resembling or typical of a Jew or Jews; having characteristics attributed to Jewish people: E20.

Jew /dʒuː/ *verb trans. slang, offensive.* Also **j-**. E19.
[ORIGIN from the noun.]
Drive a hard bargain with, get a financial advantage over, cheat; beat *down* in price.
> W. G. HAMMOND We were unmercifully jewed for all the refreshments.

jewel /ˈdʒuːəl/ *noun.* ME.
[ORIGIN Anglo-Norman *juel, jeuel*, Old French *joel* (nom. sing. *joyaus*, mod. *joyau*), ult. based on Latin *jocus* jest.]
1 An article of value used for (personal) adornment, *esp.* one made of gold, silver, or precious stones. Now usu., a small ornament containing a precious stone or stones, worn for personal adornment. ME. ▸**b** An ornament worn as the badge of an order of honour, or as a mark of distinction. L17.
2 *fig.* A thing or person highly prized; something of great beauty or worth. ME.
> J. CARLYLE She is quite a jewel of a servant.

jewel in the crown the best in a particular class of assets.
3 A precious stone, a gem; *esp.* one worn as an ornament. L16. ▸**b** A precious stone, usu. a ruby, used for a pivot hole in a watch (on account of its hardness and resistance to wear). E19. ▸**c** An imitation of a real gem, esp. as a piece of costume jewellery. L19.
– COMB.: **jewel-block** *NAUTICAL* either of two small blocks suspended at the ends of main and fore- topsail yards, through which the halyards of studdingsails are passed; **jewel box, jewel case** (*a*) a box or case containing jewels or for jewellery; (*b*) a plastic storage box for a compact disc; **jewelfish** a scarlet and green cichlid fish, *Hemichromis bimaculatus*, kept in aquaria; **jewelweed** either of two N. American balsams, the orange-flowered *Impatiens capensis* (naturalized in Britain) and the yellow-flowered *I. pallida*.

jewel /ˈdʒuːəl/ *verb trans.* Infl. **-ll-**, ***-l-**. L16.
[ORIGIN from the noun.]
Chiefly as ***jewelled*** *ppl adjective.*
1 Provide, adorn, or set with jewels. L16. ▸**b** Fit (a watch) with jewels for the pivot holes. E19.
2 *fig.* Bedeck or adorn as with jewels. E19.
> P. LIVELY The Nile, at night, is jewelled. The bridges wear necklaces of coloured lights.

■ **jewelling** *noun* (*a*) the action of the verb; (*b*) jewels used for pivot holes in a watch; (*c*) a trimming on a dress consisting of (imitation) jewels: E17.

jeweller /ˈdʒuːələ/ *noun.* Also ***-eler**. ME.
[ORIGIN Anglo-Norman *jueler*, Old French *juelier* (mod. *joaillier*), formed as JEWEL *noun*: see -ER[2].]
A person who works with precious stones etc.; a dealer in jewellery.
jeweller's putty: see PUTTY *noun* 1. ***jeweller's rouge***: see ROUGE *noun*[1] 5.

jewellery /ˈdʒuːəlri/ *noun.* Also **jewelry**. LME.
[ORIGIN Old French *juelerie* (mod. *joaillerie*) from *juelier*: see JEWELLER In mod. use a new formation from JEWEL *noun*, JEWELLER: see -ERY.]
Gems or ornaments made or sold by jewellers, *esp.* precious stones in mountings; jewels collectively or as a form of adornment.

jewelly /ˈdʒuːəli/ *adjective.* M18.
[ORIGIN from JEWEL *noun* + -Y[1].]
1 Having many jewels; adorned with or wearing jewels. M18.
2 Resembling a jewel; having the brilliance of a jewel. M19.

jewelry *noun* var. of JEWELLERY.

Jewess /ˈdʒuːɛs, -ɪs/ *noun.* ME.
[ORIGIN from JEW *noun* + -ESS[1].]
A female Jew; a Jewish woman.

jewfish /ˈdʒuːfɪʃ/ *noun.* Pl. **-es** /-ɪz/, (usu.) same. L17.
[ORIGIN App. from JEW *noun* + FISH *noun*[1].]
Any of various fishes, esp. of the percoid families Serranidae and Sciaenidae; *spec.* (*a*) a grouper, *Epinephelus itajara*, that is a sporting and food fish of the Atlantic and Pacific coasts of N. America; (*b*) = MULLOWAY; (*c*) a drum, *Otolithes ruber*, of the tropical Pacific and Indian Oceans.

Jewish /ˈdʒuːɪʃ/ *adjective.* M16.
[ORIGIN from JEW *noun* + -ISH[1].]
1 Of, belonging to, or characteristic of, the Jews; of or relating to Judaism; Israelitish, Hebrew. M16.
2 Marked by the extortion or sharp practices formerly attributed to Jewish moneylenders. *derog.* & considered *offensive.* E17.
■ **Jewishly** *adverb* M16. **Jewishness** *noun* †(*a*) Judaism; (*b*) Jewish character or quality: L16.

Jewry /ˈdʒʊəri/ *noun.* ME.
[ORIGIN Anglo-Norman *juerie*, Old French *juierie* (mod. *juiferie*), formed as JEW *noun*: see -ERY.]
1 The ancient land of the Jews, Judea; biblical Palestine. *arch.* ME.
2 *hist.* The district inhabited by Jews in a town or city; a Jews' quarter, a ghetto. ME.
†**3** Judaism. ME–M16.
4 The Jewish people, nation, or community; Jews collectively. ME.

jezail /dʒəˈzʌɪl, -ˈzeɪl/ *noun.* M19.
[ORIGIN Urdu *jazā'il*.]
A long heavy Afghan musket.

Jezebel /ˈdʒɛzəbɛl/ *noun.* M16.
[ORIGIN The wife of Ahab king of Israel (*1 Kings* 21:5–15, *2 Kings* 9:30–37).]
A wicked or shameless woman. Also, a woman who wears heavy make-up.

jezia *noun* var. of JIZYA.

JFET *abbreviation.*
ELECTRONICS. Junction field-effect transistor.

JG *abbreviation.*
Junior grade (esp. of naval rank).

Jheri curl /ˈdʒɛri ˌkəːl/ *noun.* L20.
[ORIGIN from *Jheri*, the nickname of R. W. Redding (1907–98), the US developer of the product used to create the hairstyle + CURL *noun*]
A black male hairstyle in which the hair is styled into tight ringlets with a glossy finish.

jhil /dʒiːl/ *noun.* Also **jheel**. E19.
[ORIGIN Hindi *jhīl*.]
In the Indian subcontinent: a (large) pool or lake left after a flood.

jhula /ˈdʒuːlə/ *noun.* M19.
[ORIGIN Hindi *jhūlā* swing, swing rope.]
A simple rope suspension bridge in the Himalayas.

jhum /dʒuːm/ *noun.* Also †***joom***. M19.
[ORIGIN Local name in SE Bangladesh.]
A system of shifting cultivation practised in the hill forests of the Indian subcontinent and SE Asia; a tract of land cultivated using this system.
■ ***jhuming*** *noun* cultivation using this system L19.

jiao /dʒaʊ/ *noun.* Pl. same. M20.
[ORIGIN Chinese *jiǎo*.]
A monetary unit of China, equal to one-tenth of a yuan.

jib /dʒɪb/ *noun*[1]. M17.
[ORIGIN Unknown.]
1 On a sailing vessel, a triangular staysail stretching from the outer end of the jib boom to the foretopmast head or from the bowsprit to the masthead. M17.
flying jib, slave jib, Yankee jib, etc.
2 The lower lip. Also, the mouth; the face; the nose. *dial.* & *colloq.* E19.
the cut of a person's jib *colloq.* the appearance or look of a person.
– COMB.: **jib boom** a spar run out from the end of the bowsprit; **jib guy** a stout rope supporting a jib boom; **jib-headed** *adjective* (of a topsail) shaped like a jib; **jib-header** a topsail shaped like a jib; **jib sheet** any of the ropes by which a jib is trimmed; **jib topsail** a light triangular sail set above a gaff mainsail.

jib /dʒɪb/ *noun*[2]. M18.
[ORIGIN Perh. abbreviation of GIBBET *noun*[1].]
The projecting arm of a crane; the boom of a derrick.

jib /dʒɪb/ *noun*[3]. M19.
[ORIGIN from JIB *verb*[2].]
A horse that jibs.

jib /dʒɪb/ *verb*[1] *trans. & intrans.* Infl. **-bb-**. L17.
[ORIGIN Unknown.]
NAUTICAL. = GYBE *verb* 1.

jib /dʒɪb/ *verb*[2] *intrans.* Also **gib**. Infl. **-bb-**. E19.
[ORIGIN Perh. formed as GIBE *verb*[1].]
1 Of a horse or other animal in harness: stop and refuse to go on; move restively backwards or sideways instead of going on. E19.
> A. POWELL Jerking aside his head like a horse jibbing at a proffered apple.

2 Of a person: refuse to proceed or advance; draw back, turn aside; (foll. by *at*) show aversion to or distaste for. L19.
> J. CAREY Orwell . . jibbed at Auden's mention of 'necessary murder' in his poem 'Spain'.

jibba /ˈdʒɪbə/ *noun.* Also **-ah**, **dj-**. M19.
[ORIGIN Repr. a pronunc.]
= JUBBA.

jibber /ˈdʒɪbə/ *noun.* M19.
[ORIGIN from JIB *verb*[2] + -ER[1].]
1 An animal that jibs. M19.
2 A person who jibs. M20.

jibber /ˈdʒɪbə/ *verb intrans.* E19.
[ORIGIN Imit.: cf. GIBBER *verb*.]
= GIBBER *verb*.
– COMB.: **jibber-jabber** *v intrans. & noun* (indulge in) senseless talk.

jib-door /ˈdʒɪbdɔː/ *noun.* E19.
[ORIGIN from unexpl. 1st elem. + DOOR.]
A door set flush in a wall and decorated so as to be indistinguishable.

jibe /dʒʌɪb/ *noun*[1]. Also **g-**. L16.
[ORIGIN from GIBE *verb*[1].]
A scoffing or sneering speech; a taunt, a jeer.
> ISAIAH BERLIN Almost all Herzen's gibes and insults are directed against the hated Germans.

jibe *noun*[2] see GYBE *noun*[2].

jibe /dʒʌɪb/ *verb*[1]. Also **g-**.
[ORIGIN Uncertain: perh. from Old French *giber* handle roughly, (mod. dial.) kick (repr. in mod. French by *regimber* buck, rear, cf. JIB *verb*[2]).]
1 *verb intrans.* Speak sneeringly or tauntingly; jeer, scoff. Usu. foll. by *at*. M16.
2 *verb trans.* Speak scoffingly or sneeringly to; flout, taunt. L16.
■ **jiber** *noun* M16. **jibingly** *adverb* in a jibing manner E17.

jibe /dʒʌɪb/ *verb*[2] *intrans.* Chiefly *N. Amer.* Also **g-**. E19.
[ORIGIN Unknown.]
Agree; be in harmony or accord. Usu. foll. by *with*.

jibe *verb*[3] see GYBE *verb*.

jicama /ˈhiːkəmə/ *noun.* E17.
[ORIGIN Mexican Spanish *jícama* from Nahuatl *xicama*.]
The tuberous root of the yam bean, *Pachyrhizus erosus*, as a vegetable eaten cooked or raw, esp. in salads; the plant itself, a leguminous vine cultivated esp. in Central America.

jicara /ˈhikara/ *noun*. Also **-ro** /-rəʊ/, pl. **-os** /-əʊs/. M19.
[ORIGIN Amer. Spanish *jícara* (the fruit), *jícaro* (the tree) from Nahuatl *xicalli* container made from the fruit.]
In Central America: (the fruit of) the calabash tree, *Crescentia cujete*.

Jicarilla /hɪkəˈriːljə/ *noun & adjective*. M19.
[ORIGIN Mexican Spanish, dim. of JICARA.]
▸ **A** *noun*. Pl. same, **-s**. A member of an Apache group in New Mexico and nearby states; the dialect of this group. M19.
▸ **B** *attrib*. or as *adjective*. Of or pertaining to the Jicarilla or their dialect. L19.

jicaro *noun* var. of JICARA.

JICTAR /ˈdʒɪktɑː/ *abbreviation*.
Joint Industry Committee for Television Advertising Research.

jiff /dʒɪf/ *noun*. *colloq*. L18.
[ORIGIN Abbreviation.]
= JIFFY 1.

jiffle /ˈdʒɪf(ə)l/ *verb intrans*. L17.
[ORIGIN Unknown.]
Shuffle, fidget.

jiffy /ˈdʒɪfi/ *noun*. *colloq*. L18.
[ORIGIN Unknown.]
1 A very short space of time. Freq. in ***in a jiffy***. L18.
W. S. MAUGHAM I can explain that to you in half a jiffy. DENNIS POTTER It won't take a jiffy.
2 (**J-**.) In full ***Jiffy bag***. (Proprietary name for) a type of padded envelope. M20.
– COMB.: ***Jiffy bag***: see sense 2 above; **Jiffy pot** (proprietary name for) a type of plant pot made from wood pulp and peat, used for growing plants from seed, cuttings, etc.

jig /dʒɪɡ/ *noun*[1]. M16.
[ORIGIN Unknown.]
1 A lively folk dance usu. in triple time, with jumping movements. M16. ▸**b** A piece of music for such a dance; *spec*. a gigue. L16.
†**2** A lively, comic, often scurrilous song; *derog*. a metrical version of a psalm. L16–L17.
3 A comic sketch put on at the end or in an interval of a play. *obsolete* exc. *hist*. L16.
4 A trick, a practical joke; a jest, an object of amusement. Now only in ***the jig is up***, the game is up, it is all over. *slang*. L16.
5 Any of various devices or machines for performing operations which involve movements up and down or to and fro; *esp*. (**a**) for catching fish (cf. GIG *noun*[2] 2); (**b**) for dressing ore; (**c**) for holding a piece of work in position and guiding the drills or other tools that operate on it; (**d**) = JIGGER *noun*[1] 7f. M18.
– PHRASES: **in jig time** *colloq*. (chiefly *US*) extremely quickly, in a very short time.
– COMB.: **jig-bore** *verb trans*. drill (a hole) with a jig borer; **jig borer** (a person who operates) a machine for drilling holes in or machining the surfaces of a component, usu. having a vertical spindle mounted above an adjustable table; **jig button** a steel bush for positioning a jig plate accurately on a lathe; **jigman** a man who works an ore-dressing jigger; **jig plate** (a part of) a jig consisting of a steel plate which carries bushes which guide the drill.

jig /dʒɪɡ/ *noun*[2]. *US slang*. *derog*. & *offensive*. E20.
[ORIGIN Unknown.]
A black person.

jig /dʒɪɡ/ *verb*. Infl. **-gg-**. L16.
[ORIGIN from JIG *noun*[1]; partly also back-form. from JIGGER *noun*[1].]
1 a *verb trans*. Sing or play as a jig or in the style of a jig. L16. ▸**b** *verb trans*. & *intrans*. Dance (a jig or similar lively dance). Also ***jig it***. L17.
2 *verb trans*. & *intrans*. (Cause to) move up and down or to and fro with a rapid jerky motion. Cf. JIGGER *verb*. E17.
3 *verb trans*. & *intrans*. Fish (for) or catch with a jig. M18.
4 *verb trans*. Separate coarser and finer portions of (ore) using a jigger. L18.
5 *verb trans*. & *intrans*. Provide or equip (a factory etc.) with jigs. Cf. REJIG *verb*. E20.

jigaboo /ˈdʒɪɡəbuː/ *noun*. *US slang*. *derog*. & *offensive*. E20.
[ORIGIN Rel. to JIG *noun*[2]. Cf. *bug*, *bugaboo*.]
A black person.

jig-a-jig /dʒɪɡəˈdʒɪɡ, ˈdʒɪɡədʒɪɡ/ *adverb*, *adjective*, *noun*, & *verb*. Also **jig-jig** /dʒɪɡˈdʒɪɡ, ˈdʒɪɡdʒɪɡ/, **-jog** /-dʒɒɡ/. E17.
[ORIGIN Imit.: cf. JIG *verb*, JOG *verb*.]
▸ **A** *adverb & adjective*. With or having a jigging or jogging motion. E17.
▸ **B** *noun*. **1** A jigging or jogging motion. E17.
2 Sexual intercourse. *slang* (esp. *Pidgin English*). M20.
G. GREENE Captain want jig jig, my sister pretty girl school-teacher.
▸ **C** *verb intrans*. Infl. **-gg-**.
1 Move with a jigging or jogging motion. M17.
2 Have sexual intercourse. *slang* (esp. *Pidgin English*). L19.

jigamaree /dʒɪɡəməˈriː/ *noun*. *dial*. & *colloq*. E19.
[ORIGIN Arbitrary expansion of JIG *noun*[1].]
A trick, a manoeuvre; (usu. *derog*.) fanciful contrivance; a thingummy.

jigger /ˈdʒɪɡə/ *noun*[1]. M16.
[ORIGIN Chiefly from (the same root as) JIG *verb* + -ER[1]; the relationship of some senses is obscure.]
▸ **I 1 a** A door. *slang*. M16. ▸**b** A passage between or at the back of houses; a back entry or alley. *local*. E20.
2 a An illicit distillery. *slang*. E19. ▸**b** A drink of spirits, a dram. Also, a measure used in mixing cocktails etc.; a small glass holding this quantity. *N. Amer. slang*. M19.
▸ **II 3** A person who dances a jig. L17.
4 In full ***jigger coat***. A woman's short loosely fitting jacket. M20.
5 FORESTRY. A short plank, set into a tree trunk, on which a feller stands to work. *NZ*. M20.
▸ **III 6** NAUTICAL. ▸**a** A small tackle consisting of a double and a single block with a rope. E18. ▸**b** A small sail at the stern; a fishing vessel with such a sail. M19.
7 a A contrivance for catching fish which is operated by jerking up and down. M18. ▸**b** MINING. A kind of sieve for dressing ore by shaking with water; a person who uses this. L18. ▸**c** = JOLLEY. E19. ▸**d** BILLIARDS & SNOOKER. A rest for a cue. Chiefly *Scot*. M19. ▸**e** GOLF. A short iron with a narrow face, used for approach shots. L19. ▸**f** A device for dyeing by passing pieces of fabric back and forth through a dye bath over a set of rollers. L19.
8 Any small mechanical device; a gadget. *colloq*. (orig. *US*). L19.
9 A light vehicle; a handcar; a bicycle. *colloq*. L19.
– COMB.: ***jigger coat***: see sense 4 above; **jigger-mast** NAUTICAL (**a**) a small mast at the stern, on which a jigger is hoisted; (**b**) the aftermost mast of a four-masted sailing vessel; **jigger-tackle** NAUTICAL = sense 6a above.
■ **jiggerer** *noun* a person who uses or works with a jigger L19.

jigger /ˈdʒɪɡə/ *noun*[2]. Also **ch-** /tʃ-/. M18.
[ORIGIN Alt. of CHIGOE.]
1 A tropical flea, *Tunga penetrans*, native to the Americas and introduced elsewhere, the female of which burrows beneath human skin causing painful sores. Also ***jigger flea***. Also called ***chigoe***, ***pique***, ***sand flea***. M18.
2 A harvest mite. Also called ***red bug***. *US*. E20.

jigger /ˈdʒɪɡə/ *verb*. M19.
[ORIGIN from JIG *verb*, JIGGER *noun*[1]: in senses 2, 3 prob. euphem. for BUGGER *verb*.]
1 *verb intrans*. Of a fish: jerk or tug repeatedly at a fishing line. M19.
2 *verb trans*. Confound, damn, curse. Freq. in imprecations. *slang*. M19.
DICKENS 'Well then', said he, 'I'm jiggered if I don't see you home'. X. HERBERT 'The law demands co-operation.' 'Jigger the law.'
3 *verb trans*. Tire out, exhaust; damage, spoil, break. Also foll. by *up*. Freq. in *pass*. *slang*. M19.
Telegraph (Brisbane) The firing pin's jiggered and the sights are sloppy. B. T. BRADFORD I'm looking forward to a nice cup of tea. I suddenly feel jiggered.
4 *verb trans*. BOOKBINDING. Rub (a tool) to and fro along an impressed line etc. in a binding, in order to impart a polish. L19.
5 *verb trans*. POTTERY. Shape with a jigger or jolley. M20.
6 *verb trans*. Manipulate or rearrange (figures etc.), esp. so as to mislead; tamper with. *colloq*. (chiefly *US*). M20.

jiggery-pokery /ˌdʒɪɡ(ə)rɪˈpəʊk(ə)ri/ *noun*. *colloq*. L19.
[ORIGIN Prob. alt. of earlier (Scot.) *joukery-pawkery* s.v. JOUKERY *noun*.]
Deceitful or dishonest dealing; trickery.

jigget /ˈdʒɪɡɪt/ *verb intrans*. *colloq*. L17.
[ORIGIN from JIG *verb*.]
Jig; hop or jerk about; shake up and down.
■ **jiggety** *adjective* characterized by jiggeting, inclined to jigget L19.

jiggish /ˈdʒɪɡɪʃ/ *adjective*. M17.
[ORIGIN from JIG *noun*[1] + -ISH[1].]
1 Inclined to jigging or dancing; frivolous. M17.
2 Resembling a jig; suitable for a jig. E18.

jiggle /ˈdʒɪɡ(ə)l/ *verb & noun*. M19.
[ORIGIN Partly from JIG *verb* + -LE[3]; partly alt. of JOGGLE *verb*[1] to express smaller movements.]
▸ **A** *verb trans*. & *intrans*. Move up and down or to and fro jerkily, rock or shake lightly. M19.
▸ **B** *noun*. A jiggling movement; a light rapid rocking. L19.

jiggy /ˈdʒɪɡi/ *adjective*. *US slang*. M20.
[ORIGIN from JIG *verb* + -Y[1].]
1 Jittery, fidgety; trembling, especially as the result of drug withdrawal. M20. ▸**b** Mentally agitated or disturbed; crazy. M20. ▸**c** Excitedly energetic; uninhibited, often in a sexual manner. L20.
2 Attractive; stylish; wonderful. L20.

jig-jig, **jig-jog** *adverb*, *adjective*, *noun*, & *verb* vars. of JIG-A-JIG.

jigotai /dʒɪɡəˈtʌɪ/ *noun*. M20.
[ORIGIN Japanese, from *ji* self + *go* defence + *tai* posture.]
A defensive posture in judo.

jigsaw /ˈdʒɪɡsɔː/ *noun*, *adjective*, & *verb*. L19.
[ORIGIN from JIG *verb* + SAW *noun*[1].]
▸ **A** *noun*. **1** A saw with a narrow vertically reciprocating blade, used for cutting curved lines or patterns. L19.
2 In full ***jigsaw puzzle***. A puzzle consisting of a picture mounted on wood, board, etc., and cut into irregular interlocking pieces to be reassembled. E20.
fig.: *Oxford Times* As the excavation proceeds more . . pieces of the archaeological jigsaw puzzle will be discovered.
▸ **B** *attrib*. or as *adjective*. ARCHITECTURE. Characterized by the use of fretwork patterns. L19.
▸ **C** *verb trans*. **1** Cut or shape with a jigsaw. L19.
2 (Re)assemble in the manner of a jigsaw puzzle. M20.

jihad /dʒɪˈhɑːd, -ˈhad/ *noun*. Also **jehad**. M19.
[ORIGIN Arabic *jihād* lit. 'effort'.]
1 Among Muslims: a war or struggle against unbelievers; *transf*. a campaign or crusade in some cause. M19.
Sunday Herald The TV presenter who wages consumer jihad on unscrupulous companies.
2 ***greater jihad***, (in Muslim use) the spiritual struggle within oneself against sin. M20.
■ **jihadi** *noun*, pl. **jihadis** a person involved in a jihad, an Islamic militant E20. **jihadist** *noun* = JIHADI M20.

jilbab /dʒɪlˈbɑːb/ *noun*. L20.
[ORIGIN Persian *jilbāb* from Arabic = garment, dress, veil.]
A full-length outer garment, traditionally covering the head and hands, worn in public by some Muslim women.

jildi /ˈdʒɪldi/ *noun*, *adverb*, & *verb*. *military slang* (orig. *Indian*). Also **juldy** /ˈdʒʊldi/ & other vars. L19.
[ORIGIN Hindi *jaldī* quickness.]
▸ **A** *noun*. Haste; ***on the jildi***, in a hurry. L19.
▸ **B** *adverb*. Quickly. E20.
▸ **C** *verb trans*. & *intrans*. Hurry. E20.

jill *noun*[1], *noun*[2] vars. of GILL *noun*[4], *noun*[5].

jill /dʒɪl/ *verb intrans*. *colloq*. M20.
[ORIGIN Unknown.]
Of a boat: move idly (*about*, *around*).

jillaroo /dʒɪləˈruː/ *noun*. *Austral*. *colloq*. Also **jilleroo**. M20.
[ORIGIN from female forename *Jill* after JACKAROO.]
A female novice on a sheep station or cattle station.

jillet /ˈdʒɪlɪt/ *noun*. *Scot*. M18.
[ORIGIN Dim. of female forename *Jill*, or from GILL *noun*[4]: see -ET[1].]
A frivolous or irresponsible young woman.

jill-flirt *noun* var. of GILL-FLIRT.

jillion /ˈdʒɪljən/ *noun*. *colloq*. (chiefly *N. Amer*.). M20.
[ORIGIN Fanciful formation after BILLION, MILLION.]
A great many, an extremely large quantity.

jilt /dʒɪlt/ *noun*. L17.
[ORIGIN Uncertain: sense 2 prob. from the verb.]
†**1** An immoral woman; a kept mistress. Also (*Scot*.), = JILLET. L17–E19.
2 A person (orig. and esp. a woman) who jilts a lover. L17.
■ **jiltish** *adjective* L17.

jilt /dʒɪlt/ *verb trans*. M17.
[ORIGIN Unknown.]
1 Deceive, cheat, trick, break faith with. Long *rare* (as transf. use of 2). M17.
THACKERAY But Fortune shook her swift wings and jilted him too.
2 Abruptly reject or abandon (a lover, fiancé, etc.); be faithless to. L17.
J. C. POWYS The youthful Vicar . . had jilted her to marry a maid-servant.

jimber-jawed /ˈdʒɪmbədʒɔːd/ *adjective*. *US colloq*. M19.
[ORIGIN Prob. from alt. of GIMBAL + JAWED.]
Having a protruding lower jaw.

Jim Crow /dʒɪm ˈkrəʊ/ *noun*, *adjective*, & *verb*. Chiefly *US*. M19.
[ORIGIN See below.]
▸ **A** *noun* **1 a** The eponymous black character in the early 19th-cent. plantation song 'Jim Crow'; a performer of this song; the dance involved in its performance. M19. ▸**b** A black person. *slang* (*derog*. & *offensive*). M19. ▸**c** Racial discrimination, esp. against black people in the US. M20.
C R. OTTLEY Negro soldiers had suffered all forms of Jim Crow.
a jump Jim Crow (**a**) perform the dance involved in the performance of 'Jim Crow'; (**b**) *fig*. change one's political principles or party.
2 An implement for bending or straightening iron rails by the pressure of a screw. L19.
▸ **B** *attrib*. or as *adjective*. Characteristic of or set apart for black people; racially segregated. M19.
Time Southern newspapers . . relegated announcements of black births, deaths and marriages to special Jim Crow pages. K. BOYLE It was the Jim Crow gallery. Colored people goes upstairs, other people goes down.
▸ **C** *verb trans*. Segregate racially; discriminate against (black or other non-white people). E20.
■ **Jim Crowism** *noun* (**a**) a system or the practice of racial discrimination or segregation; (**b**) the action of changing one's political party. M19.

J

jim-dandy /dʒɪmˈdandi/ *noun & adjective*. *N. Amer. colloq.* **L19.**
[ORIGIN from *Jim* pet form of male forename *James* + DANDY *noun*[2], *adjective*.]
▶ **A** *noun*. An excellent person or thing. **L19.**
▶ **B** *adjective*. Remarkably fine, outstanding. **L19.**

jiminy /ˈdʒɪmɪni/ *interjection*. Also **-mm-**. **E19.**
[ORIGIN Alt. of GEMINI *interjection*: euphem. for *Jesus (Christ)*.]
Expr. surprise. Chiefly in ***by Jiminy***, ***Jiminy Christmas***, ***Jiminy cricket***.

jimjam /ˈdʒɪmdʒam/ *noun*. *colloq.* **M16.**
[ORIGIN Fanciful redupl. with vowel variation: cf. FLIMFLAM, WHIM-WHAM.]
1 A fanciful or trivial article, a knick-knack. Long *rare*. **M16.**
2 ***the jimjams***, a state of nervous agitation or apprehension, the jitters; (*spec.*) *slang* delirium tremens. **L19.**

jimminy *interjection* var. of JIMINY.

jimmy /ˈdʒɪmi/ *noun*[1] & *verb*. *colloq.* (chiefly *N. Amer.*). **M19.**
[ORIGIN Alt. of JEMMY *noun*.]
▶ **A** *noun*. A crowbar used by a burglar; = JEMMY *noun* 3. **M19.**
▶ **B** *verb trans*. Force (*open*) with a jemmy. **L19.**

Jimmy /ˈdʒɪmi/ *noun*[2]. Also **Jimmie**. **M19.**
[ORIGIN Pet form of male forename *James*: see -Y[6].]
1 In full ***Jimmy Grant***. An immigrant; an emigrant. *Austral. & NZ slang*. **M19.**
2 In full ***Jimmy O'Goblin***. A sovereign; = GOBLIN *noun*[2]. *rhyming slang*. *obsolete* exc. *hist.* **L19.**
3 In full ***Jimmy the One***. First Lieutenant. *nautical slang*. **E20.**
4 ***the Jimmies***, = JIMJAM 2. *slang*. **E20.**
5 In full ***Jimmy Riddle***. = PIDDLE *noun*. *rhyming slang*. **M20.**
6 Used as a form of address to a male stranger. *colloq.* (chiefly *Scot.*). **L20.**
– PHRASES: ***dismal Jimmy***: see DISMAL *adjective* 4. **Jimmy Ducks** *nautical slang* (*obsolete* exc. *hist.*) a sailor in charge of the livestock carried to serve as food on long voyages. ***Jimmy Grant***: see sense 1 above. **Jimmy Green** = JAMIE GREEN. ***Jimmy O'Goblin***: see sense 2 above. **Jimmy Skinner** *rhyming slang* dinner. ***Jimmy the One***: see sense 3 above. **Jimmy Woodser** *Austral. & NZ slang* (a drink taken by) a solitary drinker.

jimp /dʒɪmp/ *adjective & adverb*. *Scot. & N. English*. Also **g-**. **E16.**
[ORIGIN Unknown: cf. GIM.]
▶ **A** *adjective*. **1** Slender, graceful, neat. **E16.**
2 Of measure or quantity: barely sufficient, scanty. **E17.**
▶ **B** *adverb*. Barely, scarcely. **E19.**
■ **jimply** *adverb* slenderly, scantily **L18.**

jimson /ˈdʒɪms(ə)n/ *noun*. *US*. Orig. †**Jamestown weed**. Also **jimpson** /dʒɪmps(ə)n/. **L17.**
[ORIGIN Alt. of *Jamestown*, a town in Virginia, USA.]
In full ***jimson weed***. Thorn apple, *Datura stramonium*.

jimswinger /ˈdʒɪmswɪŋə/ *noun*. *Southern US*. **L19.**
[ORIGIN Unknown.]
A swallow-tailed coat, *esp.* a frock coat. Also ***jimswinger coat***.

Jina /ˈdʒɪnə/ *noun*. **E19.**
[ORIGIN Sanskrit *jina*: see JAIN.]
JAINISM. A great Jain teacher who has attained liberation from karma; a sculptured representation of such a teacher.

Jindyworobak /dʒɪndɪˈwɒrəbak/ *noun & adjective*. *Austral.* **M20.**
[ORIGIN Wuywurung *jindi worabak* to annex, join.]
▶ **A** *noun*. A member or supporter of a group founded in Australia in 1938 to promote Australianness in literature, art, etc. **M20.**
▶ **B** *attrib*. or as *adjective*. Of or pertaining to this group. **M20.**

jing /dʒɪŋ/ *noun & interjection*. Also **jings** /-z/. Orig. *Scot.* **L18.**
[ORIGIN Alt.]
More fully ***by jing(s)***. = JINGO *interjection & noun* 2.

jingall *noun* var. of GINGALL.

jingbang /dʒɪŋˈbaŋ/ *noun*. *slang*. **M19.**
[ORIGIN Unknown.]
the whole jingbang, the lot, everyone, the whole company or affair.

jingle /ˈdʒɪŋg(ə)l/ *verb & noun*. Also †**g-**. **LME.**
[ORIGIN Imit.: cf. JANGLE *verb*, *noun*.]
▶ **A** *verb*. **1** *verb intrans*. Make a noise as of small metallic objects being shaken together; make a light ringing sound more prolonged and continuous than clinking. **LME.** ▸**b** Proceed or move with such a sound. **M18.**

> W. McCay I hear Christmas bells jingling!

2 *verb trans*. Cause to make such a sound. **LME.**

> J. Barth Oliver laughed and jingled his three guineas.

3 *verb intrans*. **a** Play with (the sounds of) words; *derog.* versify. **M17.** ▸**b** Of prose or verse: be characterized by alliteration or other features suggesting a jingle. **L17.**
▶ **B** *noun*. **1** A jingling noise; a sound intermediate between clinking and ringing. **L16.**
2 A thing that jingles, esp. a small bell. **E17.**
3 a The affected repetition of the same sound or similar sounds, as in alliteration, rhyme, or assonance; (usu. *derog.*) any arrangement of words achieving its effect by sound rather than by sense. **M17.** ▸**b** A short tune, verse, or slogan played or sung in a radio or television commercial. **M20.**
4 A two-wheeled one-horse cart with seats, formerly used esp. in Ireland, Cornwall, and Australia; a governess cart. **E19.**
5 (The shell of) a bivalve mollusc of the family Anomidae, having an asymmetric shell with a hole or notch for the siphon; a saddle oyster. Also ***jingle shell***. Orig. *US*. **L19.**
– PHRASES & COMB.: †**jingle-boy** *slang* (**a**) a coin; (**b**) a man with plenty of money in his pockets. ***jingle shell***: see sense B.5 above. **jingling Johnny** (**a**) *slang* a Turkish crescent or *pavillon chinois* (percussion instruments with jingling bells); (**b**) *Austral. & NZ slang* a person who shears sheep by hand; in *pl.*, hand shears. **jingling match** a game in which one player keeps ringing a bell while the others, all blindfolded, try to catch him or her.
■ **jingly** *adjective* characterized by jingling, resembling a jingle **E19.**

jingle-jangle /ˈdʒɪŋg(ə)lˌdʒaŋg(ə)l/ *noun & verb*. **L16.**
[ORIGIN Redupl. of JINGLE with vowel variation: see JANGLE *noun*, *verb*. Cf. TWINGLE-TWANGLE.]
▶ **A** *noun*. An alternating jingle of sounds; a thing that makes, or an utterance marked by, such a sound. **L16.**
▶ **B** *verb intrans*. Make or move with an alternating jingle of sounds. **L19.**

jingler /ˈdʒɪŋglə/ *noun*. Also †**g-**. **L16.**
[ORIGIN from JINGLE *verb* + -ER[1].]
1 A person who or thing which jingles. **L16.**
†**2** A dealer, esp. in horses, at a country fair. *slang*. *rare*. **L17–M19.**

jingo /ˈdʒɪŋgəʊ/ *interjection*, *noun*, & *adjective*. Also **J-**. **L17.**
[ORIGIN Unknown. Sense A.3 orig. from a use of *by jingo* in a popular song.]
▶ **A** *interjection & noun*. †**1** In full ***hey jingo!***, ***high jingo!*** A conjuror's call for, or an exclamation of surprise at, the appearance of something. **L17–E18.**
2 ***by jingo!***, (rare) ***by the living jingo!***, expr. surprise or affirmation. *colloq.* **L17.**
3 Pl. **-oes**. An advocate of a bellicose foreign policy; a loud and blustering patriot, a chauvinist, a jingoist. Orig., one who supported the sending of a British fleet into Turkish waters to resist Russia in 1878. **L19.**
▶ **B** *attrib*. or as *adjective*. Of or pertaining to jingoists; characterized by jingoism. **L19.**
■ **jingoish** *adjective* = JINGO *adjective* **L19.**

jingoism /ˈdʒɪŋgəʊɪz(ə)m/ *noun*. **L19.**
[ORIGIN from JINGO + -ISM.]
The advocacy or practice of a bellicose foreign policy; loud and blustering patriotism.
■ **jingoist** *noun & adjective* (**a**) *noun* a supporter of jingoism; (**b**) *adjective* jingoistic: **L19.** **jingo'istic** *adjective* characterized by jingoism **L19.**

jings *noun & interjection* var. of JING.

jink /dʒɪŋk/ *noun*. Orig. *Scot.* **L17.**
[ORIGIN Rel. to JINK *verb*[1].]
1 †**a** ***high jinks***, antics indulged in at drinking parties, usu. involving the throwing of dice to decide who should perform some frivolous act. **L17–L19.** ▸**b** In *pl.* Usu. more fully ***high jinks***. Boisterous or exuberant play; unrestrained merrymaking. **M19.**
2 An act of eluding someone or something; a quick turn, *esp.* one made so as to elude a pursuer, a tackler, etc. **L18.**

jink /dʒɪŋk/ *verb*[1]. Orig. *Scot.* **E18.**
[ORIGIN Uncertain: perh. imit.]
1 *verb intrans*. **a** Wheel about in dancing; dance. *Scot.* **E18.** ▸**b** Move with quick sudden action or turns; change direction nimbly; dart; dodge, move elusively. **L18.**

> **b** R. Jefferies A rabbit . . jinked away under a rhododendron bush. I. Fleming Jinking occasionally to spoil the men's aim.

2 *verb trans*. Elude by dodging, evade. **L18.**
3 *verb trans*. Trick, cheat, swindle. **L18.**

jink /dʒɪŋk/ *verb*[2] *trans*. & *intrans*. **E19.**
[ORIGIN Imit.: cf. CHINK *verb*[1].]
(Cause to) make a short metallic sound.

jinker /ˈdʒɪŋkə/ *noun*[1]. Chiefly *Scot.* **E18.**
[ORIGIN from JINK *verb*[1] + -ER[1].]
A person, animal, or thing that jinks or dodges.

jinker /ˈdʒɪŋkə/ *noun*[2]. *Austral.* Also **jun-** /ˈdʒʌŋ-/. **L19.**
[ORIGIN Var. of JANKER.]
A contrivance consisting of two pairs of wheels joined by chains, for carrying tree trunks etc. Also, a two-wheeled vehicle resembling a gig, sometimes with a single seat, used in trotting.

jinker /ˈdʒɪnkə/ *noun*[3]. **M20.**
[ORIGIN from alt. of JINX *verb* + -ER[1].]
A person who brings bad luck or who puts a jinx on someone or something.

jinn /ˈdʒɪn/ *noun*. Also **djinn**, **jinnee** /dʒɪniː/. **E19.**
[ORIGIN Arabic *jinnī* masc. sing., pl. *jinn*. Cf. GENIE.]
In Arabian stories and Muslim mythology: a spirit of an order lower than the angels, able to appear in human or animal form and to exercise supernatural influence.

jinny /ˈdʒɪni/ *noun*. **L19.**
[ORIGIN Pet form of female forename *Jane*.]
MINING. A stationary engine used to draw trucks up or down an inclined plane. Also (in full ***jinny-road***), an underground inclined plane worked by gravity.

jinricksha /dʒɪnˈrɪkʃə/ *noun*. Also **-rikisha** /-ˈrɪkɪʃə/. **L19.**
[ORIGIN Japanese *jin-riki-sha*, from *jin* person + *riki* strength, power + *sha* carriage.]
A rickshaw.

jinx /dʒɪŋks/ *noun & verb*. Orig. *US*. **E20.**
[ORIGIN Prob. from JYNX.]
▶ **A** *noun*. A person who or thing which seems to bring bad luck or exercise evil influence; a hoodoo. **E20.**
▶ **B** *verb trans*. Cast a spell on, bring bad luck on. Freq. in *pass.* **E20.**

jipijapa /hiːpɪˈhɑːpə/ *noun*. **M19.**
[ORIGIN *Jipijapa*, a town in Ecuador.]
1 An almost stemless palmlike plant, *Carludovica palmata* (family Cyclanthaceae), native to tropical America; the fibre produced from its leaves. Also called ***Panama hat palm***, ***Panama hat plant***. **M19.**
2 In full ***jipijapa hat***. A Panama hat. **L19.**

jipper /ˈdʒɪpə/ *verb & noun*. *dial. & slang*. **E19.**
[ORIGIN Unknown.]
▶ **A** *verb trans*. = BASTE *verb*[2] 1. **E19.**
▶ **B** *noun*. Gravy; dripping; stew. **L19.**

jippo /ˈdʒɪpəʊ/ *noun*. *dial. & slang*. **E20.**
[ORIGIN from JIPPER + -O.]
= JIPPER *noun*.

jird /dʒəːd/ *noun*. **M18.**
[ORIGIN Berber *(a)gherda*.]
Any of several long-tailed burrowing rodents of the genera *Meriones* and *Sekeetamys* (family Muridae), found in deserts and steppes from North Africa to China and including *M. unguiculatus*, the species usu. kept as the pet gerbil.

jirene *noun* var. of GYRENE.

jirga /ˈdʒɪəgə/ *noun*. Also †**jeerga**. **E19.**
[ORIGIN Pashto.]
An assembly or council of Pathan or Baluchi headmen.

jirine *noun* var. of GYRENE.

jism /ˈdʒɪz(ə)m/ *noun*. *slang* (orig. *US*). Also **gism** & other vars. **M19.**
[ORIGIN Unknown.]
Energy, strength; semen, sperm.

jist /dʒɪst/ *adverb*. *colloq. & dial.* **E19.**
[ORIGIN Repr. a pronunc.]
= JUST *adverb*.

jit /dʒɪt/ *noun*[1]. *arch. US slang*. **E20.**
[ORIGIN Abbreviation.]
= JITNEY 1.

jit /dʒɪt/ *noun*[2]. **L20.**
[ORIGIN Shona, from *jit* to dance.]
A style of dance music popular in Zimbabwe.

jitney /ˈdʒɪtni/ *noun & adjective*. *N. Amer.* **E20.**
[ORIGIN Unknown.]
▶ **A** *noun*. **1** A five-cent piece, a nickel. *arch. slang*. **E20.**
2 A bus or other vehicle carrying passengers for a low fare (orig. five cents). **E20.**
▶ **B** *attrib*. or as *adjective*. Cheap, improvised, ramshackle. *arch. slang*. **E20.**

jitter /ˈdʒɪtə/ *noun & verb*. *colloq.* **E20.**
[ORIGIN Unknown.]
▶ **A** *noun*. **1** In *pl.* Extreme nervousness; a state of emotional (and physical) tension; agitation. Usu. with *the*. **E20.**

> F. M. Ford The publishers here have the jitters so badly . . they won't look at anything new. *Economist* Recession jitters now afflicting . . economists.

2 Chiefly ELECTRONICS. Slight random or irregular variation, esp. in the shape or timing of a regular pulse; unsteadiness of an image etc. due to this. **M20.**
▶ **B** *verb*. **1** *verb intrans*. Move or act nervously; exhibit nervousness. **E20.**
2 *verb trans*. Chiefly ELECTRONICS. Subject to slight random or irregular variation. **M20.**

jitterbug /ˈdʒɪtəbʌg/ *noun & verb*. Orig. *US*. **M20.**
[ORIGIN from JITTER *verb* + BUG *noun*[2].]
▶ **A** *noun*. **1** A jittery or nervous person; an alarmist. Also, an attack of the jitters. **M20.**
2 A jazz musician; a devotee of swing; a person who dances the jitterbug. **M20.**
3 An energetic dance, popular in the 1940s, performed chiefly to swing music. **M20.**
▶ **B** *verb intrans*. Infl. **-gg-**. Dance the jitterbug. **M20.**

jittery /ˈdʒɪtəri/ *adjective*. *colloq.* **M20.**
[ORIGIN from JITTER + -Y[1].]
Nervy, jumpy, on edge.

> S. S. Tepper Certainly he was on a high, jittery, strung-up, unable to relax. G. Rawlins Governments . . get jittery whenever their populations make it hard to know what's going on.

■ **jitteriness** *noun* M20.

jiu-jitsu, **jiu-jutsu** *nouns & verbs* see JU-JITSU.

jiva /ˈdʒiːvə/ *noun*. E19.
[ORIGIN Sanskrit *jīva*.]
HINDUISM & JAINISM. The soul; the embodied self; the vital principle.

Jivaro /ˈhiːvərəʊ/ *noun & adjective*. M19.
[ORIGIN Spanish *jíbaro* prob. from Jivaro *Shuara*, *Shiwora* (their name for themselves).]
▸ **A** *noun*. Pl. same, **-os**. A member of a S. American Indian people of Ecuador and Peru; the language of this people. M19.
▸ **B** *attrib.* or as *adjective*. Of or pertaining to the Jivaro or their language. M19.

jive /dʒʌɪv/ *noun, verb, & adjective*. Orig. *US*. E20.
[ORIGIN Unknown.]
▸ **A** *noun*. **1** Talk, conversation; *spec.* misleading, empty, or pretentious talk. Now also, something worthless, phoney, or unpleasant; = JAZZ *noun* 3. *slang*. E20.
2 a Jazz, *esp.* swing. E20. ▸**b** Lively and uninhibited dancing to jazz or other popular music. M20.
3 A variety of American black English associated esp. with jazz musicians and enthusiasts. Also ***jive talk***. M20.
4 Marijuana. *slang*. M20.
▸ **B** *verb*. **1** *slang*. ▸**a** *verb trans.* Mislead, fool; taunt, sneer at. E20. ▸**b** *verb intrans.* Talk nonsense, jest; fool around. M20.
2 *verb intrans.* Make sense; fit in. *N. Amer. colloq.* M20.
3 *verb intrans.* **a** Play jive music. M20. ▸**b** Dance energetically to jive or other popular music. M20.
▸ **C** *adjective*. Acting wrongly; pretentious, phoney, deceitful. *US slang*. L20.
– COMB.: **jive-ass** *US slang* a person who loves fun or excitement; a deceitful or pretentious person.
■ **jiver** *noun* a person who jives M20. **jivey** *adjective* (*slang*, chiefly *US*) of, pertaining to, or characterized by jive; misleading, phoney, pretentious: M20.

jiwan *noun* var. of JAWAN.

jizya /ˈdʒɪzjə/ *noun*. *obsolete* exc. *hist.* Also **jezia** /ˈdʒɛzɪə/. L17.
[ORIGIN Persian *jezya(t)* from Arabic *jizya*.]
A poll tax imposed by Islamic law on non-Muslim subjects in Muslim countries; *spec.* that exacted by the Mughal emperors in India.

jizz /dʒɪz/ *noun*[1]. *colloq.* E20.
[ORIGIN Unknown.]
The indefinable combination of characters by which a given bird, plant, etc., can be quickly recognized in the field.

jizz /dʒɪz/ *noun*[2]. *slang*. M20.
[ORIGIN Abbreviation.]
= JISM.

jnana /dʒ(ə)ˈnɑːnə, -ˈɲɑːnə/ *noun*. E19.
[ORIGIN Sanskrit *jñāna*, from *jñā-* know.]
HINDUISM. Spiritual knowledge, as a means of salvation.
– COMB.: ***jnana-marga*** /-mɑːɡə/ [*mārga* path] the way to salvation through spiritual knowledge or asceticism.
■ ***jnani*** /-niː/ *noun* a worshipper or devotee of *jnana-marga* L19.

j.n.d. *abbreviation*.
SCIENCE. Just noticeable difference.

Jnr *abbreviation*.
Junior.

jo /dʒəʊ/ *noun*. *Scot.* Also **joe**. Pl. **joes**. E16.
[ORIGIN Scot. form of JOY *noun*.]
A sweetheart, one's beloved. Freq. as a form of address.

Joachimite /ˈdʒəʊəkɪmʌɪt/ *noun*. L18.
[ORIGIN from *Joachim* (see below) + -ITE[1].]
ECCLESIASTICAL HISTORY. A heretical follower of Joachim of Fiore (*c* 1132–1202), abbot of Fiore in Calabria and Italian mystic.
■ **Joachimism** *noun* the doctrines of Joachim of Fiore E20. **Joachimist** *noun* = JOACHIMITE E20. **Joachism** *noun* = JOACHIMISM E20. **Joachist**, **Joachite** *nouns* = JOACHIMITE E20.

Joan /dʒəʊn/ *noun*. L16.
[ORIGIN Female forename, orig. (Latin) *Jo(h)anna* fem. of *Jo(h)annes*: see JOHN.]
1 (A name for) a female rustic. L16.
2 *hist.* A close-fitting cap worn by women in the latter half of the 18th cent. M18.

joanna /dʒəʊˈanə/ *noun*. *rhyming slang*. M19.
[ORIGIN *Joanna*, female forename: see JOAN.]
= PIANO *noun*[2] 1.

Joannes *noun* var. of JOHANNES.

job /dʒɒb/ *noun*[1]. M16.
[ORIGIN Unknown.]
1 A piece of work, *esp.* one done for hire or profit; *spec.* a small distinct piece of work done as part of one's occupation or profession or as a separate operation. Also ***job of work***. M16. ▸**b** A theft, robbery, or other criminal act, *esp.* one arranged beforehand. *criminals' slang*. E18. ▸**c** PRINTING. A small piece of miscellaneous work, as the printing of posters, cards, or anything on a single sheet. L18.
M. ATWOOD I did this grudgingly, as I did most jobs around the house. **b** *Public Opinion* Stolen property sufficient to connect the thief with several 'jobs'.
2 A public service or position of trust turned to private or party advantage; a transaction in which duty or public interest is sacrificed for private or party advantage. M17. ▸†**b** Personal profit; private interest. M17–L18.
POPE Who makes a Trust or Charity a Job.
3 Something that has to be done, a transaction, a task; *colloq.* a difficult task. L17. ▸**b** A paid position of employment; *transf.* a person's particular task or responsibility. M19. ▸**c** = ***job lot*** below. M19. ▸**d** A commission to back a racehorse; a horse on which such bets are placed. L19. ▸**e** Of a manufactured item, esp. a motor vehicle or aircraft, or (*joc.*) a person, esp. a pretty girl: an (excellent) example of its type. *slang*. E20.
BROWNING 'Tis an ugly job: but soldiers obey commands. R. BADEN-POWELL My wounds sewn up and dressed, a job which took nearly four hours. *Ulverston (Cumbria) News* A complete re-roofing and paint job on South Lakeland district council's offices. *Sunday (Kolkata)* The Bombay Hospital did a commendable job in saving Dada's life. **b** D. LESSING Young women who had left £7 a week typing jobs in London. *Evening Telegraph (Grimsby)* It is not our job to call off the Test. **e** S. BELLOW He drove a dairy truck, one of those electric jobs. *Glasgow Herald* She hung towels over the . . mirrors when she took a bath, convinced they were two-way jobs.
4 A state of affairs, an occurrence, a business. Chiefly in ***bad job***, ***good job*** below. *colloq.* L17.
5 An operation involving plastic surgery. Usu. with specifying word. *colloq.* M20.
breast job, ***face job***, ***nose job***, etc.
– PHRASES ETC.: **bad job** (*a*) an unfavourable circumstance (***make the best of a bad job***: see BEST *adjective*); (*b*) a thing on which labour is spent in vain (esp. in ***give a thing up as a bad job***). ***bob a job***: see BOB *noun*[6]. ***brown job***: see BROWN *adjective*. **get on with the job** proceed with one's work, continue with one's affairs. **good job** a fortunate fact or circumstance (*that*). **have a job** be hard put to it (*to do*). ***inside job***: see INSIDE *adjective*. ***jobs for the boys***: see BOY *noun*. **just the job** *colloq.* exactly what is wanted, the very thing. ***make a clean job of***: see CLEAN *adjective*. **make a good job of**, **make a job of** transact or manage successfully. ***odd job***: see ODD *adjective*. **on the job** (*a*) hard at work, busy; committing a crime; *euphem.* engaged in sexual intercourse; (*b*) (of a racehorse) out to win and well backed. **on-the-job** *adjective* done or occurring while a person is at work. ***outside job***: see OUTSIDE *adjective*. ***straight job***: see STRAIGHT *adjective*[1] & *adverb*[1]. **the Devil's job**, **the Devil's own job** something extremely difficult.
– ATTRIB. & COMB.: In the sense 'hired by the job or for a limited time', as ***job-coach***, ***job-gardener***, ***job horse***, etc. Special combs., as **job analysis** analysis of the essential factors of a particular task or piece of work and the necessary qualifications of the person who is to perform it; **job analyst** a person who practises job analysis; **jobcentre** an employment exchange displaying information about available jobs; **job club** an organization providing support and practical help for the long-term unemployed in seeking work; **job-control** *adjective* (COMPUTING) designating a language which enables a user to determine the tasks to be undertaken by the operating system; **job creation** the provision of new opportunities for paid employment, esp. as part of a policy to provide work for the unemployed; **job description** a formal account of an employee's responsibilities; **jobholder** a person who holds a particular job; **job-hopper** a person who practises job-hopping; **job-hopping** the act or practice of changing from one job to another in quick succession; **job horse** *hist.* a horse hired out by a jobmaster; **job house** a printing house specializing in jobwork; **job-hunt** *verb intrans.* (*colloq.*) seek employment; **job-hunter** *colloq.* a person who seeks employment; **job lot** a miscellaneous group of articles bought together; *derog.* any miscellaneous group of things, persons, etc.; **jobmaster** *hist.* a person who keeps a livery stable and hires out horses, harnesses, and carriages for any job; **job-office** = ***job-house*** above; **job press** a small press designed for job-printing; **job-print**, **job-printing** the printing of jobwork; **job rotation** the practice of moving employees between different tasks to promote experience and variety; **job-share** *verb & noun* (*a*) *verb intrans.* be employed or work under a job-sharing arrangement; (*b*) *noun* (an instance of) job-sharing; **job-sharer** a person who job-shares; **job sharing** a working arrangement by which a full-time job is done jointly by several part-time employees, who share the remuneration etc.; **jobsheet** a sheet on which are recorded details of a job that has been done; **job shop** (*a*) a workshop where small pieces of work are done; (*b*) = ***job-house*** above; **job-type** (special or ornamental) type used in jobwork; **jobwork** (*a*) work done and paid for by the job; piecework; (*b*) the printing of posters, cards, or other miscellaneous items.
■ **jobbish** *adjective* of the nature of a job; characterized by jobbery: L18. **jobster** *noun* = JOBBER L19.

job /dʒɒb/ *noun*[2]. M16.
[ORIGIN from JOB *verb*[1].]
An act of jobbing; an abrupt stab with the point or sharp end of something; a peck, a thrust; a jerk or wrench of the bit in a horse's mouth.

Job /dʒəʊb/ *noun*[3]. L16.
[ORIGIN A biblical patriarch, whose story forms a book in the Old Testament and Hebrew Scriptures.]
1 ***Job's tears***, a grass of eastern Asia, *Coix lacryma-jobi*, having round shining grains resembling tears, which are used as beads. L16.
2 ***Job's comforter***, a person who aggravates distress under the guise of administering comfort. M18.

job /dʒɒb/ *verb*[1]. Infl. **-bb-**. LME.
[ORIGIN Imit., app. expr. the sound of a brief forcible action: cf. BOB *verb*[2], DAB *verb*, STAB *verb*. See also JAB *verb*.]
1 *verb trans.* Pierce to a small depth with a forcible but abruptly arrested action; peck, stab, prod, punch; jerk (a horse's mouth) with the bit; strike with a sharp or cutting stroke. LME.
S. BARING-GOULD Let the horse go, but don't job his mouth in that way.
2 *verb intrans.* Thrust *at* so as to stab or pierce; (of a bird) peck *at*; penetrate *into*. LME.
3 *verb trans.* Thrust (a pointed thing) abruptly into something else. L16.

job /dʒɒb/ *verb*[2]. Infl. **-bb-**. L17.
[ORIGIN from JOB *noun*[1].]
1 *verb intrans.* Do jobs or odd pieces of work; do piecework. L17.
2 a *verb trans.* Buy and sell (stock or goods) as a middleman or broker. L17. ▸**b** *verb intrans.* Buy and sell stock; deal or speculate in stocks. E18.
a *Observer* His game plan is to . . buy in, . . then . . job the shares on at a profit.
3 *verb trans.* Let or deal with for profit. Now usu. foll. by *out*. E18.
G. KEILLOR Why the state jobbed out the survey to drunks is a puzzle.
4 *verb trans.* Give *away* by jobbery; get (a person) *into* some position by jobbery. E18.
5 a *verb intrans.* Turn a public service or a position of trust to private or party advantage; practise jobbery. M18. ▸**b** *verb trans.* Deal with corruptly for or turn to private or party advantage. E19.
b H. H. ASQUITH The duties of the trierarchy, . . are habitually evaded or jobbed.
6 *verb trans. & intrans.* Hire or (*rare*) hire out (a horse, carriage, etc.) for a particular job or period of time. L18.
H. MAYHEW Very few noblemen . . bring their carriage-horses to town; . . they nearly all job.
7 *verb trans.* Complete (a task). Chiefly in ***that job's jobbed***. *colloq.* M19.
8 *verb trans.* Put *off* by artifice. Cf. ***fob off*** (FOB *verb*[1] 2). L19.
9 *verb trans.* Cheat; betray. Cf. FRAME *verb* 10. *slang* (orig. *US*). E20.
– WITH ADVERBS IN SPECIALIZED SENSES: **job backwards** make calculations retrospectively, esp. on Stock Exchange transactions, with the knowledge of subsequent events; *fig.* use hindsight. **job off** sell (goods) at very low prices.

†**job** *verb*[3] var. of JOBE.

jobation /dʒəʊˈbeɪʃ(ə)n/ *noun*. *colloq.* L17.
[ORIGIN from JOBE *verb* + -ATION.]
The action of JOBE *verb*; a reproof, esp. of a lengthy and tedious character; a talking to. Also, a long discussion.

jobber /ˈdʒɒbə/ *noun*. L17.
[ORIGIN from JOB *verb*[2] + -ER[1].]
1 A person who buys goods etc. in bulk from a producer or importer, and sells them to a retailer or consumer; a broker, a middleman. L17.
2 A person who does odd jobs; a person employed by the job, as opp. to one in continuous employment; a pieceworker. E18.
3 A member of a stock exchange who deals in stocks or shares on his or her own account; a stockjobber, a dealer. Also, a middleman who acts between holders of stocks or shares and brokers, a broker-dealer. (Not now in official use on the British Stock Exchange.) E18.
4 A person who uses a public office or position of trust for private or party advantage. M18.
5 A person who hires out horses etc. for a particular job or period of time; a jobmaster. M19.
■ **jobbery** *noun* the turning of a public office, position of trust, etc., to private gain or advantage: M19.

jobbernowl /ˈdʒɒbənəʊl/ *noun*. *colloq.* L16.
[ORIGIN from French *jobard*, from Old French *jobe* stupid, silly + NOLL.]
1 The head, esp. of a stupid person. L16.
2 A stupid person, a blockhead. L16.

jobbie /ˈdʒɒbi/ *noun*. *colloq.* Also **-y**. E20.
[ORIGIN from JOB *noun*[1] + -IE.]
1 A person. *US*. E20.
2 An object or thing, esp. of a specified type. M20.
3 (A lump or piece of) excrement; an act of defecation. *euphem.* L20.

jobbing /ˈdʒɒbɪŋ/ *verbal noun*. M18.
[ORIGIN from JOB *verb*[2] + -ING[1].]
The action of JOB *verb*[2]; *esp.* the printing of small miscellaneous items.

jobbing /ˈdʒɒbɪŋ/ *ppl adjective*. E18.
[ORIGIN from JOB *verb*[2] + -ING[2].]
That jobs; *spec.* (*a*) employed in odd or occasional pieces of work; (*b*) using a public office etc. for private or party advantage, given to jobbery.
jobbing builder, ***jobbing gardener***, ***jobbing printer***, etc.

jobble /ˈdʒɒb(ə)l/ *noun*. M19.
[ORIGIN Imit.: cf. JABBLE *noun*.]
= JABBLE *noun*.

jobby *noun* var. of JOBBIE.

†jobe *verb trans. colloq.* Also **job**. L17–L18.
[ORIGIN from JOB *noun*[3], with allus. to the lengthy reproofs administered to Job.]
Rebuke in a long and tedious harangue.

jobless /ˈdʒɒblɪs/ *adjective & noun.* E19.
[ORIGIN from JOB *noun*[1] + -LESS.]
▸ **A** *adjective.* **1** Free from jobbery. *rare.* E19.
2 Out of work, unemployed. E20.
▸ **B** *noun collect. pl. The* class of unemployed people. L20.
■ **joblessness** *noun* the state of being out of work E20.

Jo block /ˈdʒəʊ blɒk/ *noun phr. colloq.* M20.
[ORIGIN Abbreviation of JOHANSSON.]
A Johansson block.

Jocism /ˈdʒəʊsɪz(ə)m/ *noun.* M20.
[ORIGIN French *Jocisme* acronym, from *Jeunesse Ouvrière Chrétienne* 'Christian working youth': see -ISM.]
An organization aimed at spreading Christianity amongst working people, set up by Joseph Cardijn in Belgium in 1924 and later extended to other parts of Europe.
■ **Jocist** *noun* M20.

Jock /dʒɒk/ *noun*[1]. E16.
[ORIGIN Scot. form of JACK *noun*[1].]
1 a (A name for) a representative male of the common people. *Scot.* E16. ▸**b** A Scottish or (formerly) northern English sailor; a Scottish soldier; a member of a Scottish regiment. More widely, (a form of address to) a Scotsman. Freq. as a nickname. *slang.* L18.

> **a** *Daily News* The proverb says..'there is a silly Jock for every silly Jenny'. **b** *Scottish Field* Kilts, trews, bonnets, pipe bands ..have helped enormously to make the Jock the man he is.

2 A countryman, a rustic, a clown. *Scot.* M16.

jock /dʒɒk/ *noun*[2]. *colloq.* L18.
[ORIGIN Abbreviation.]
1 = JOCKEY *noun* 5. L18.
2 = JOCKEY *noun* 5C. L20.
3 A pilot or astronaut. Also, an enthusiast for or participant in any specified activity, as ***computer jock***. *N. Amer.* M20.

> T. CLANCY The best fighter jock in the Air Force or Navy.

jock /dʒɒk/ *noun*[3]. *coarse slang.* L18.
[ORIGIN Unknown.]
The genitals of a man or (formerly) a woman.

jock /dʒɒk/ *noun*[4]. *dial. & slang.* L19.
[ORIGIN Unknown.]
Food.

jock /dʒɒk/ *noun*[5]. *N. Amer. slang.* E20.
[ORIGIN from JOCK(STRAP.]
1 = JOCKSTRAP 1. E20.
2 = JOCKSTRAP 2. Chiefly *derog.* M20.

> R. JAFFE I was a big jock at prep school. Football and all that.

jocker /ˈdʒɒkə/ *noun. N. Amer. slang.* L19.
[ORIGIN Perh. from JOCK *noun*[3] + -ER[1].]
1 A tramp who is accompanied by a youth who begs for him and may act as his catamite. Cf. PRUSHUN. L19.
2 An active male homosexual. E20.

jockette /dʒɒˈkɛt/ *noun. rare.* M20.
[ORIGIN from JOCK *noun*[2] + -ETTE.]
A female jockey.

jockey /ˈdʒɒki/ *noun.* L16.
[ORIGIN Dim. or pet form of JOCK *noun*[1]: see -Y[6].]
1 (Also **J-**.) = JOCK *noun*[1] 1a (chiefly *Scot.*). Also, a lad; an underling. L16.
2 A horse-dealer. *obsolete* exc. *dial.* M17. ▸**b** A person having the supposed character of a horse-dealer; a fraudulent bargainer, a cheat. *rare.* L17.
†3 A person who rides or drives a horse; a postillion, a courier. M17–M19.
4 A strolling minstrel or beggar. *Scot. obsolete* exc. *hist.* L17.
5 A rider in horse races, *esp.* a professional one. L17. ▸**b** *transf.* A driver of a motor vehicle. Chiefly *N. Amer.* E20. ▸**c** = ***disc jockey*** s.v. DISC *noun.* M20.
jump jockey: see JUMP *verb.*
6 FASHION. A flat trimming on the shoulder of a close-fitting sleeve. L19.
7 More fully ***jockey spider***. A venomous black Australian spider, *Latrodectus hasseltii*, the female of which has a red stripe on the upper side of its abdomen. Also = KATIPO. *Austral.* E20.
8 (Also **J-**.) (Proprietary name for) a man's briefs or shorts. M20.

> J. UPDIKE He takes clean Jockey pants, T-shirts, ..and a sports shirt from the closet.

– COMB.: **jockey boot** a top boot of a type formerly worn by jockeys; **jockey box** (**a**) *hist.* a box in a wagon, under the driver's seat, for carrying small articles; (**b**) *US* a glove compartment; **jockey cap** a peaked cap of the style worn by jockeys; **jockey club** (**a**) a club or association for the promotion and regulation of horse-racing; *spec.* (with cap. initials) that established at Newmarket, the supreme UK authority on all matters connected with horse-racing; (**b**) a toilet water with a scent esp. of rose and jasmine; **jockey coat** (chiefly *Scot.*) a kind of greatcoat, *esp.* one made of broadcloth with wide sleeves; **jockey pulley** a small wheel which rides either on top of a larger one, esp. to obtain a higher speed of rotation, or on top of a belt or chain between two working pulleys or gears to keep the belt or chain taut; **jockey shorts** (proprietary name for) men's close-fitting underpants with a short leg; **jockey sleeve** a wide sleeve like that of a jockey coat; ***jockey spider***: see sense 7 above; **jockey wheel** (**a**) = ***jockey pulley*** above; (**b**) a small adjustable wheel at the nose of a caravan or trailer.

jockey /ˈdʒɒki/ *verb.* E18.
[ORIGIN from the noun.]
1 *verb trans.* Behave towards in the manner attributed to horse-dealers; gain the advantage of or manipulate by trickery; outwit, overreach. E18. ▸**b** Get (a person or thing) *out, into, away*, etc., by trickery; cheat or do *out of.* E18.

> **b** F. L. ALLEN He adroitly jockeyed.. Dougherty out of the Cabinet.

2 *verb intrans. & trans.* Ride (a horse) as a jockey. M18.
3 *verb intrans.* Struggle to secure an advantage, esp. by skilful manoeuvres or artifice. Usu. foll. by *for.* E19.

> W. IRVING To get a good seat.. a vast deal of jockeying and unfair play was shown. M. PIERCY Everybody was jockeying for telephone time.

jockeyship /ˈdʒɒkɪʃɪp/ *noun.* M18.
[ORIGIN from JOCKEY *noun, verb* + -SHIP.]
The art of a jockey; skill in horse-racing. Also, the practice of jockeying; trickery, artifice.

Jocko /ˈdʒɒkəʊ/ *noun.* Pl. **-os**. L18.
[ORIGIN Bantu: cf. *còkò* kind of monkey.]
(A personal name for) a chimpanzee or other ape.

jockstrap /ˈdʒɒkstrap/ *noun.* L19.
[ORIGIN from JOCK *noun*[3] + STRAP *noun.*]
1 A support or protector for a man's genitals, worn esp. by sportsmen. Also (*rare*), a cache-sexe. L19.
2 An athletic (as opp. to an aesthetic or intellectual) man, esp. at a university. *N. Amer. slang.* M20.

jockteleg /ˈdʒɒktəlɛg/ *noun. Scot. & N. English.* Also **jackleg** /ˈdʒaklɛg/, **†joctaleg**, & other vars. Orig. **†Jock the leg**. M17.
[ORIGIN Perh. from JOCK *noun*[1] + *the* + LEG *noun*, with ref. to the leg-shape of some early knives.]
A (large) clasp knife.

jocose /dʒəˈkəʊs/ *adjective.* L17.
[ORIGIN Latin *jocosus*, from *jocus* JOKE *noun*: see -OSE[1].]
1 Of a person, a person's disposition, etc.: fond of joking; playful, waggish, jocular. L17.
2 Of speech, writing, or action: of the nature of or containing a joke; said or done jokingly; playful, jocular. L17.
■ **jocosely** *adverb* E18. **jocoseness** *noun* E18.

jocoserious /dʒəʊkəʊˈsɪərɪəs, dʒɒk-/ *adjective.* M17.
[ORIGIN from Latin *joco-* combining form of *jocus* JOKE *noun* (see -O-) + SERIOUS.]
Half jocular, half serious; blending jokes and serious matters.

jocosity /dʒəˈkɒsɪti/ *noun.* E16.
[ORIGIN formed as JOCOSE + -ITY.]
1 Jocose quality or disposition, esp. in speech or action; mirth, merriment. E16.
2 A jocose saying or act; a piece of jesting. M19.

joctaleg *noun* var. of JOCKTELEG.

†jocular *noun.* LME–E19.
[ORIGIN Old French *joculer* alt. (after Latin) of *jougler(e)*, *-leur*: see JUGGLER.]
A professional jester or minstrel.

jocular /ˈdʒɒkjʊlə/ *adjective.* E17.
[ORIGIN Latin *jocularis*, from *joculus* dim. of *jocus* JOKE *noun*: see -AR[1].]
1 Of a person or a person's disposition: fond of joking; speaking or acting in jest or merriment. E17.

> B. T. BRADFORD Trying to be jocular and making a bad joke about tragic heroines.

2 Of speech or action: of the nature of or containing a joke; said or done jokingly. L17.

> S. MORLEY Letters couched.. in jocular self-deprecation.

■ **jocuˈlarity** *noun* the quality or an instance of being jocular; mirthfulness, jocundity: M17. **jocularly** *adverb* M17.

joculator /ˈdʒɒkjʊleɪtə/ *noun. obsolete* exc. *hist.* LME.
[ORIGIN Latin, from *joculat-* pa. ppl stem of *joculari* to jest: see -ATOR. Cf. JONGLEUR, JUGGLER.]
A professional jester, minstrel, or jongleur.

jocund /ˈdʒɒk(ə)nd, ˈdʒəʊk-/ *adjective.* Now only *literary.* LME.
[ORIGIN Old French *jocond*, *jocund* from Latin *jocundus* late var. of *jucundus* pleasant, agreeable (from *juvare* to help, to delight) by assoc. with *jocus* JOKE *noun.*]
Feeling or expressing cheerfulness; mirthful, merry, light-hearted; pleasant, cheering, delightful.

> H. WOUK A jocund crowd poured into the canopied entrance for the wedding brunch.

■ **jocundly** *adverb* LME.

jocundity /dʒəˈkʌndɪti/ *noun.* LME.
[ORIGIN Late Latin *jucunditas*, from *jucundus*: see JOCUND, -ITY.]
1 Jocund quality or condition; mirth, gaiety. LME.
†2 Spiritual joy or delight. LME–E17.

jod /dʒɒd, jəʊd/ *noun.* Long *rare.* L16.
[ORIGIN medieval Latin formed as YOD: cf. IOTA, JOT *noun*[1].]
A jot, an iota.

jodel *verb & noun* see YODEL.

jodhpurs /ˈdʒɒdpəz/ *noun pl.* Also **J-**, **-pors** /-pɔːz/. In attrib. use & in comb. usu. in sing. **jodhpur**. L19.
[ORIGIN *Jodhpur*, a town and district in Rajasthan, NW India.]
1 Long riding breeches, wide around the hips but close-fitting from knee to ankle. Also ***jodhpur riding breeches***. L19.
2 Indian trousers cut loosely at the top but close-fitting below the knee. E20.
– COMB.: **jodhpur boot** an ankle-high boot, orig. worn with jodhpurs.
■ **jodhpured** *adjective* wearing jodhpurs M20.

Jodo /ˈdʒəʊdəʊ/ *noun & adjective.* Also **Jo-do**. E18.
[ORIGIN Japanese *jōdo* lit. 'pure land'.]
(Designating or pertaining to) a Japanese Buddhist sect which teaches salvation through absolute faith in their Buddha, the Buddha Amida, and constant repetition of a prayer invoking his name.

jods /dʒɒdz/ *noun pl. colloq.* M20.
[ORIGIN Abbreviation.]
Jodhpurs.

joe /dʒəʊ/ *noun*[1]. M18.
[ORIGIN Abbreviation.]
hist. = JOHANNES.

Joe /dʒəʊ/ *noun*[2] *& verb. slang.* L18.
[ORIGIN Familiar abbreviation of the male forename *Joseph.*]
▸ **A** *noun.* **1** = In full ***Joe Miller*** [English comedian (1684–1738), whose name was attached to a popular joke book after his death]. A book of jokes. Also, a joke, *esp.* a stale joke. L18.
2 A fellow, a chap; an average man. Also, an American. M19.

> J. OSBORNE While everyone else is sitting on their hands you're the Joe at the back cheering.

3 *hist.* [from Charles *Joseph* La Trobe (1801–75), Lieutenant Governor of Victoria.] A taunt to, or warning of the approach of, a policeman. Also as *interjection. Austral. & NZ.* M19.
4 A French Canadian. *Canad.* M20.
– COMB. & PHRASES: ***GI Joe***; ***Holy Joe***: see HOLY *adjective*; **Joe Blake** *Austral. rhyming slang* a snake; **Joe Bloggs** (a nickname for) a hypothetical average man; **Joe Blow** (chiefly *N. Amer.*) = ***Joe Bloggs*** above; ***Joe* MANTON**; ***Joe Miller***: see sense 1 above; **Joe Public** (a member of) an audience; (a nickname for) an average member of the public; ***Joe Sixpack***: see SIX-PACK; **Joe Soap** (a nickname for) a slow-witted or ordinary person; ***little Joe***: see LITTLE *adjective*; SLOPPY ***Joe***.
▸ **B** *verb trans.* Taunt (esp. a policeman) with a cry of 'Joe': see sense A.3 above. *Austral. & NZ.* M19.

joe /dʒəʊ/ *noun*[3]. *N. Amer. slang.* M20.
[ORIGIN Unknown.]
Coffee.

joe *noun*[4] var. of JO.

joe-pye weed /ˈdʒəʊpʌɪ wiːd/ *noun phr. N. Amer.* E19.
[ORIGIN Unknown.]
Either of two tall perennial plants, *Eupatorium purpureum* and *E. maculatum*, of the composite family, bearing clusters of tubular purplish flowers.

joes /dʒəʊz/ *noun pl. Austral. slang.* E20.
[ORIGIN Unknown.]
Depression, the blues.

Joey /ˈdʒəʊi/ *noun*[1]. M19.
[ORIGIN Familiar abbreviation of male forename *Joseph* (see JOE *noun*[2], -Y[6]), in branch I from Joseph Hume (1777–1855), politician and financial expert, in branch II from the clown Joseph Grimaldi (1779–1837).]
▸ **I** **†1** A fourpenny piece. *slang.* M–L19.
2 A threepenny bit. *slang. obsolete* exc. *hist.* M20.
▸ **II** **3** A clown. *colloq.* L19.

joey /ˈdʒəʊi/ *noun*[2]. *Austral. & NZ.* E19.
[ORIGIN Unknown.]
A young kangaroo or wallaby; a young possum; any young animal or child.

jog /dʒɒg/ *noun*[1]. E17.
[ORIGIN from JOG *verb.*]
1 a An act of jogging or moving mechanically up and down. E17. ▸**b** An act of jogging along; a slow measured walk or trot. M17. ▸**c** A gentle run taken as a form of exercise. M20.

> **b** R. BOLDREWOOD The slow, hopeless, leg-weary jog to which ..the horses.. had long been reduced. **c** *Sun* Your bedroom curtains were still drawn when I passed on my morning jog.

2 An act of jogging a thing or person; a shake; a slight push, a nudge. M17.

> *fig.*: B. REID I have no memory of things past until I'm given a little jog.

jog /dʒɒg/ *noun*². E18.
[ORIGIN In sense 1 var. of JAG *noun*¹. With senses 2 and 3 cf. JOGGLE *noun*².]
†**1** A projecting point on an edge or surface (cf. JAG *noun*¹ 4); a protuberance, a swelling. *rare*. E–M18.
2 A right-angled notch or step in a surface or straight line; the space cut out by such a notch. *US*. M19.

Scientific American Following a road northward, there are abrupt jogs to the east or west.

3 *CRYSTALLOGRAPHY*. A step in a dislocation where it passes from one atomic plane to another. M20.
■ **jogged** *adjective* having a jog or jogs M18.

jog /dʒɒg/ *verb*. Infl. **-gg-**. LME.
[ORIGIN Var. of JAG *verb*: cf. SHOG *verb*.]
†**1** *verb trans*. = JAG *verb* 1. Only in LME.
2 *verb trans*. Shake, move, or throw *up* (esp. a heavy body) with a push or jerk; shake *up*. M16.

W. C. RUSSELL Masses of this froth.. were jogged clean off the water, and struck the deck.

3 *verb intrans*. Walk or ride with a jolting pace; move on at a heavy pace; trudge (*on, along*). Also, move on, be off. M16. ▸**b** Run at a gentle pace, esp. for physical exercise. M20.

R. CHURCH Once an hour a horse-bus jogged along. *fig.*: E. M. FORSTER We live and let live, and assume that things are jogging on fairly well elsewhere. **b** *Disability Now* People suddenly out jogging in their brand new trainers and kit.

4 *verb trans*. **a** Give a slight push to, so as to shake; nudge, esp. so as to arouse to attention. L16. ▸**b** *fig*. Give a gentle reminder to (esp. one's memory). E17.

G. SWIFT He looked into his.. glass and jogged the sliver of lemon at the bottom.

5 *verb intrans*. Move up and down or to and fro with a heavy unsteady motion; move about as if shaken. L16.

B. BAINBRIDGE He was jogging up and down.. on the tips of his toes.

— NOTE: Rare before 16.

joget /ˈdʒɒgət/ *noun*. L19.
[ORIGIN Malay.]
A popular Malay dance in which the dancers improvise to music; a place where such dancing occurs.

jogger /ˈdʒɒgə/ *noun*. L17.
[ORIGIN from JOG *verb* + -ER¹.]
A person who or thing which jogs; *spec*. (***a***) a person who runs at a gentle pace for physical exercise; (***b***) a device for giving a slight push to some part of a mechanism.

joggle /ˈdʒɒg(ə)l/ *noun*¹. E18.
[ORIGIN from JOGGLE *verb*¹.]
An act or the action of joggling; a jog, a jolt; a shaking loosely from side to side.

joggle /ˈdʒɒg(ə)l/ *noun*². E18.
[ORIGIN Perh. from JOG *noun*² + -LE¹.]
A joint between two pieces of stone, concrete, etc., in which a projection on one fits into a recess in the other, or both have a recess holding a piece of stone or other masonry, so as to prevent their being pulled apart; a piece of stone etc. in such a joint.

joggle /ˈdʒɒg(ə)l/ *verb*¹ *trans. & intrans*. E16.
[ORIGIN Dim. or frequentative of JOG *verb*: see -LE³.]
(Cause to) move to and fro with a succession of short jerky movements; shake or rock about, as if loose or unsteady.

H. B. STOWE My grandmother's broad shoulders joggling with a secret laugh. A. MUNRO Both parents busy themselves.. with the children.. joggling them, singing to them.

■ **joggly** *adjective* (*dial. & colloq.*) shaky, unsteady E19.

joggle /ˈdʒɒg(ə)l/ *verb*² *trans*. E19.
[ORIGIN from JOGGLE *noun*².]
Join (stone etc.) by means of a joggle; fasten with a joggle.

jog-jog /ˈdʒɒgdʒɒg/ *adverb & adjective*. L18.
[ORIGIN Redupl. of JOG *verb*.]
▸ **A** *adverb*. With a jogging motion or pace. L18.
▸ **B** *adjective*. Characterized by jogging; = JOG-TROT *adjective*. L18.

jog-trot /ˈdʒɒgtrɒt/ *adjective, noun, adverb, & verb*. M17.
[ORIGIN from JOG *verb, noun*¹ + TROT *noun*¹.]
▸ **A** *adjective* **1 a** Of action: steady unhurried; routine; monotonous, humdrum. M17. ▸**b** Of a person: acting in a steady, unhurried way; easy-going; keeping up a monotonous routine. M18.

b GOLDSMITH Honest jog-trot men, who go on smoothly and dully.

2 Of the nature of or suitable for a jog-trot. L18.
▸ **B** *noun*. A jogging trot; a slow, dull, or easy-going pace; *fig*. a steady, unhurried, but persistent way of doing something. M18.

C. J. LEVER There was nothing to break the monotonous jog-trot of daily life.

▸ **C** *adverb*. At a jog-trot pace. M19.
▸ **D** *verb intrans. & trans*. (with *it*). Infl. **-tt-**. Go or move at a jog-trot. M19.

Johannean /dʒə(ʊ)ˈhanɪən/ *adjective*. M19.
[ORIGIN from medieval Latin *Johannes* (see JOHN) + -AN.]
= JOHANNINE.

Johannes /dʒə(ʊ)ˈhaniːz/ *noun*. Also **Joannes**. M18.
[ORIGIN Late Latin *Joannes*, medieval Latin *Johannes* (see JOHN) in the legend of the coin: see below.]
hist. A Portuguese gold coin minted by Joannes or João V (1703–50), current in New England and later also Ireland.

Johannine /dʒə(ʊ)ˈhanʌɪn/ *adjective*. M19.
[ORIGIN formed as JOHANNES + -INE¹.]
CHRISTIAN CHURCH. Of, belonging to, or characteristic of, the apostle John or his gospel.

Johannisberger /dʒə(ʊ)ˈhanɪsbəːgə/ *noun*. E19.
[ORIGIN German, from *Johannisberg*: see below.]
A fine white wine produced at Johannisberg in the Rheingau, Germany.

Johannite /dʒə(ʊ)ˈhanʌɪt/ *noun*. M16.
[ORIGIN medieval Latin *Jo(h)annitae* pl. from Greek *Iōannitai*, *Iōannēs* JOHN: see -ITE¹.]
†**1** A knight of an order called the Knights of St John. M16–E18.
2 A follower or adherent of John Chrysostom (*c* 347–407), bishop of Constantinople, after his deposition from the patriarchate in 404. *obsolete* exc. *hist*. L17.

Johansson /jə(ʊ)ˈhans(ə)n/ *adjective*. E20.
[ORIGIN Carl E. *Johansson*, 20th-cent. Swedish armaments inspector.]
Designating a steel block made with flat parallel faces to a highly accurate prescribed length, used with others of different sizes to make up standard lengths.

johar /ˈdʒəʊhə/ *noun*. E19.
[ORIGIN Hindi *jauhar*, *johar* from Sanskrit *jatu-gṛha* a house built of combustible materials.]
hist. The sacrificial burning of Rajput women to avoid their being captured by an enemy.

John /dʒɒn/ *noun*. LME.
[ORIGIN Male forename from late Latin *Joannes*, medieval Latin *Johannes* from Greek *Iōannēs* from Hebrew *Yōḥānān* for *Yĕhōḥānān* lit. 'God (Yahweh) is gracious'.]
1 (A form of address to) a man, esp. a male servant. *colloq*. LME.

THACKERAY Crimson footmen,.. came in. It was pitiable to see the other poor Johns slink off.

†**2** A priest. Chiefly in ***Sir John***. *derog*. LME–M17.
3 (Also **j-**.) A policeman. Also [after French *gendarme*] ***Johndarm***. Cf. JACK *noun*¹ 3d. *slang*. M17.

V. PALMER The police came... and it was me that was nabbed. But the Johns let me off.

4 (Also **j-**.) The client of a prostitute. *slang* (orig. *US*). E20.
5 In full ***John Thomas***. The penis. *slang*. M20.
6 (**j-**.) A lavatory. *colloq*. (chiefly *N. Amer.*). M20.

L. DUNCAN I'm going to.. cut up Griffin's credit cards and flush them down the John.

— COMB. & PHRASES: ***Dear John (letter)***: see DEAR *adjective*¹; **John-a-dreams** a dreamy or idle fellow; †**John-a-nokes** [*John* (who dwells) *at the oak*] an anonymous party, usu. the plaintiff, in a legal action; an ordinary person; **John-apple** = *APPLE-john*; †**John-a-stiles** an anonymous party, usu. the defendant, in a legal action; ***John Barleycorn***: see BARLEYCORN 1b; **johnboat** *US* a small, flat-bottomed boat chiefly for use on inland waterways; **John Citizen** an ordinary man, esp. as a member of the community; ***John Collins***: see COLLINS *noun*¹; **John Company** *joc.* (*hist.*) the East India Company; ***Johndarm***: see sense 3 above; **John Doe** (***a***) *US LAW* an anonymous party, usu. the plaintiff, in a legal action, formerly *spec*. (*ENGLISH LAW*) in the now obsolete action of ejectment (cf. RICHARD *Roe*); (***b***) *N. Amer. colloq*. an ordinary or typical citizen; (***c***) *US colloq*. a signature; **John-go-to-bed-at-noon** *dial*. any of several plants with flowers which close about midday; *esp*. yellow goat's beard, *Tragopogon pratensis*; **John Hancock**, (*local*) **John Henry** *US colloq*. a signature; **John hop** *Austral. & NZ slang* = sense 3 above; **John Innes (compost)** any of a group of composts prepared according to formulae developed at the John Innes Horticultural Institution in the late 1930s; **John Q. Public** *N. Amer. colloq*. (a member of) the general public; ***John Roscoe***: see ROSCOE; ***John Thomas***: see sense 5 above; ***long John***: see LONG *adjective*¹; ***Sir John***: see sense 2 above; ***square John***: see SQUARE *adjective*; ***sweet John***: see SWEET *adjective & adverb*.

John Bull /dʒɒn ˈbʊl/ *noun*. L18.
[ORIGIN A character repr. the English nation in J. Arbuthnot's satire *Law is a Bottomless Pit* (1712).]
1 The English nation personified; the English collectively. L18.
2 An individual Englishman exemplifying the supposedly typical national character. L18.
■ **John-ˈBullish** *adjective* typically English L18. **John-ˈBullishness** *noun* L19. **John-ˈBullism** *noun* the typical English character; a typically English act, utterance, or characteristic: L18.

John Canoe /dʒɒn kəˈnuː/ *noun*. *W. Indian*. Also **Jonkanoo**. L18.
[ORIGIN Prob. from Ewe.]
An elaborately masked dancer in a celebration held at Christmas; this celebration.

John Crow /dʒɒn ˈkrəʊ/ *noun*. *W. Indian*. E19.
[ORIGIN Alt. of ***carrion crow*** s.v. CROW *noun*¹ 1.]
1 The turkey buzzard, *Cathartes aura*. E19.
2 ***John Crow nose***, ***John Crow's nose***, a bright red plant, *Scybalium jamaicense* (family Balanophoraceae), resembling a fungus and parasitic on trees. M19.

John Dory /dʒɒn ˈdɔːri/ *noun*. M18.
[ORIGIN from JOHN + DORY *noun*¹.]
A dory, *Zeus faber*, found in inshore waters of the eastern Atlantic and the Mediterranean.
American John Dory a dory, *Zenopsis ocellata*, of the Atlantic coast of N. America.

Johne /ˈjəʊnə/ *noun*. E20.
[ORIGIN H. A. *Johne* (1839–1910), German veterinary surgeon.]
VETERINARY MEDICINE. ***Johne's disease***, an infectious enteritis of cattle and sheep, characterized by diarrhoea and progressive emaciation. Hence ***Johne's bacillus***, the bacterium that causes it, *Mycobacterium johnei*.

Johnny /ˈdʒɒni/ *noun*. Also **Johnnie**. L17.
[ORIGIN Dim. of JOHN: see -Y⁶, -IE.]
1 A fellow, a chap. Freq. as a derog. form of address to a man regarded as inferior, *esp*. a soldier of a colonized country in the army of the colonizing power. *colloq*. L17. ▸**b** = JOHN 3. *slang*. M19.

G. A. BIRMINGHAM That's the sort of way those scientific Johnnies talk. L. DEIGHTON This is the Johnny who interrogated Bernard.

2 A gentoo penguin. Also ***Johnny penguin***. M19.
3 (**j-**.) = JOHN 6. *colloq*. (chiefly *US*). M20.
4 (**j-**.) A condom. Also ***rubber Johnny***. *slang*. M20.
— PHRASES: ***jingling Johnny***: see JINGLE. ***rubber Johnny***: see sense 4 above.
— COMB.: **Johnny-come-lately** (***a***) a newcomer; (***b***) = ***Johnny Raw*** below; **Johnny Crapaud**, **Johnny Crapeau** *arch. colloq*. (***a***) a Frenchman, a French Canadian; †(***b***) the French nation personified; **Johnny Head-in-Air**, **Johnny Head-in-the-Air** *colloq*. a dreamy fellow; **Johnny-jump-up** *N. Amer.* any of several kinds of wild or cultivated pansy or violet; **Johnny Newcome** (***a***) = ***Johnny Raw*** below; (***b***) a newcomer of any kind; ***Johnny penguin***: see sense 2 above; **Johnny Raw** an inexperienced youngster; a novice; **Johnny Reb** *US* (a northern name for) a Confederate soldier during the American Civil War.

johnnycake /ˈdʒɒnɪkeɪk/ *noun*. Also **johnny cake**. M18.
[ORIGIN from unkn. 1st elem. + CAKE *noun*.]
A maize-meal cake usu. baked or toasted (*US*); a wheatmeal cake usu. baked or fried (*Austral. & NZ*); a type of scone (*W. Indian*).

Johnson /ˈdʒɒns(ə)n/ *noun*. *US*. M19.
[ORIGIN A surname.]
1 (Also **j-**.) The penis. *coarse slang*. M19.

M. AMIS You're naked and shielding your Johnson in a cataract of breaking glass.

2 ***Johnson bar***, a long heavy lever used to reverse the motion of a steam locomotive. M20.

Johnsonese /dʒɒnsəˈniːz/ *noun*. M19.
[ORIGIN formed as JOHNSONIAN + -ESE.]
(Language imitative of) the style of Dr Johnson (see JOHNSONIAN).

Johnsonian /dʒɒnˈsəʊnɪən/ *adjective*. L18.
[ORIGIN from Dr Samuel *Johnson* (see below) + -IAN.]
Of or pertaining to Dr Samuel Johnson (1709–84), a celebrated English man of letters and lexicographer; *esp*. characteristic, typical, or reminiscent of Johnson's style of English, having many words derived or formed from Latin.
■ **Johnsoniˈana** *noun pl*. sayings, writings, etc., of or about Dr Johnson, or matters connected with him L18. **Johnsonianism** *noun* Johnsonian style; a Johnsonian phrase: E19. **ˈJohnsonism** *noun* = JOHNSONIANISM M19.

Johnson noise /ˈdʒɒns(ə)n nɔɪz/ *noun phr*. M20.
[ORIGIN J. B. *Johnson* (1887–1970), naturalized US physicist.]
ELECTRONICS. Electrical noise caused by the random thermal motion of conduction electrons.

Johnswort /ˈdʒɒnzwəːt/ *noun*. *US*. M18.
[ORIGIN Abbreviation.]
= ***St John's wort*** s.v. SAINT *noun & adjective*.

joie de vivre /ʒwadəvivr, ʒwɑː də ˈviːvrə/ *noun phr*. L19.
[ORIGIN French = joy of living.]
A feeling of healthy enjoyment of life; exuberance, high spirits.

join /dʒɔɪn/ *noun*. E17.
[ORIGIN from the verb.]
1 An act of joining; the fact of being joined; a point, line, or surface at which two or more things are joined. E17.

P. LIVELY The paving was worn smooth by feet, the joins between the stones almost obliterated.

2 *MATH*. = UNION *noun*² 12. M20.

J

join /dʒɔɪn/ *verb*. ME.
[ORIGIN Old French & mod. French *joign-* pres. stem of *joindre* from Latin *jungere*, from Indo-European base repr. also by YOKE *noun*[1].]
▸ **I** Put together.
1 *verb trans.* Put together, so as to unite or make continuous; fasten, attach, connect, unite, (one thing to another, or several together); (freq. foll. by *to*, *together*). Formerly also, combine in a mixture. ME. ▸†**b** *spec.* Harness; yoke. LME–E18. ▸**c** GEOMETRY. Connect (points) by a straight line. M17.

I. MURDOCH Donald seemed to attach himself directly to Tim as if invisible threads joined their bodies. B. EMECHETA A bridge joining the village to the mainland. J. MCDOUGALL The threads of discourse, broken off in.. childhood, can now be joined once more.

2 *verb trans.* Construct or form (a whole, wooden furniture, etc.) by putting parts together. *obsolete* exc. in ***join company***. ME.
3 *verb trans.* Bring or combine (troops etc.) into one body or company. Formerly also *refl.*, attach (oneself) to a company etc. ME.
4 *verb trans.* Link or unite (people etc. together, or one *with* or *to* another) in marriage, friendship, or any kind of alliance; unite, ally. ME.

Book of Common Prayer We are gathered together.. to joyn together this man and this woman in holy matrimony. E. YOUNG Life is the.. solitude; Death joins us to the great majority.

5 *verb trans.* Put (a female animal, as a cow) to mate with a male. Now *Austral. & NZ*. LME.

Stock & Land (Melbourne) Mr Wyllie joined several heifers last year and one of them is barren.

6 *verb trans.* Put or bring into close contact, cause to touch each other. Chiefly *arch.* LME.

POPE O'er the pale marble shall they join their heads. I. MURDOCH Join his two hands palm to palm.

†**7** *verb trans.* Add so as to increase the amount or number. LME–E18.
▸ **II** Come or be put together.
8 *verb intrans.* Come or be brought into contact; become connected or fastened together; be in contact; be adjacent, adjoin (foll. by †*to*, †*with*). ME.

I. D'ISRAELI Parallel lines can no more join together in politics than in geometry. OED On the side where the two gardens join.

9 *verb intrans.* **a** Combine in action or purpose, enter into association, *with*. LME. ▸**b** Take part *in* an action etc. (specified or *absol.* understood). M16.

a W. CRUISE His co-trustees.. refused to join with him in the execution of the trust. R. HUGHES Sickening giddiness joined with the shock and pain to give.. poignancy to her crying. **b** N. MOSLEY I tried to get these two to join in some of the activities. J. K. TOOLE On the second chorus the entire ensemble joined in the song. P. BOWLES He laughed good-naturedly and she joined in.

10 *verb intrans.* Come together or meet in conflict. Now *rare* or *obsolete*. LME.
11 *verb intrans.* Of qualities etc.: come or exist together in operation. LME.

TENNYSON Tho' truths in manhood darkly join.

†**12** *verb intrans.* ASTRONOMY & ASTROLOGY. Come into conjunction; be in conjunction. LME–L17.
▸ **III** Come into contact, contiguity, company, or union with.
13 *verb trans.* Come or go into the company of (a person); accompany; take part with (a person or persons) *in* an action etc.; take one's place with or in (a group, procession, etc.). E18.

R. K. NARAYAN You joined Gandhi and lost all sense of caste. P. ROTH He should join the revolution. J. MORTIMER He.. had joined an old doctor on his rounds. C. PHILLIPS They.. joined the thin line of traffic streaming away from the capital. I. MURDOCH Duncan.. waved to her, beckoning her to join him.

14 *verb trans. & intrans.* Become a member of (a society, organization, etc.). E18.

OED Is he a member of our society? When did he join? M. S. POWER He.. joined the police force. *Dumfries Courier* He stayed on.. for an extra year then joined the Worthing firm.

15 *verb trans.* Be or become connected or continuous with; be adjacent to, adjoin. Also, go to and follow (a path, a road, etc.) esp. at a specified point; get on (a train, bus, etc.) at a specific point or time. E18.

G. GREENE He joined the Orient Express at Ostend. E. H. JONES A little stream ran down through the plot to join the.. river.

– PHRASES: **join action** enter into a debate or dispute. ***join battle***: see BATTLE *noun*. ***joined patent***: see PATENT *adjective* 2. ***join forces***: see FORCE *noun*[1]. ***join hands***: see HAND *noun*. ***join issue***: see ISSUE *noun*. ***join the majority***: see MAJORITY.
– WITH ADVERBS IN SPECIALIZED SENSES: **join up** (*a*) enlist in one of the armed forces; (*b*) unite, connect, (*with*). (*c*) ***joined-up***, (of handwriting) written with the characters joined, cursive; (esp. of a policy) characterized by coordination and coherence of thought, integrated.
■ **joinable** *adjective* (*rare*) LME. **joining** *noun* (*a*) the action or an act of the verb; the fact of being joined; (*b*) a place where things join or are joined; a thing which joins or connects: LME.

joinant /ˈdʒɔɪnənt/ *adjective*. Now *rare* or *obsolete*. LME.
[ORIGIN Old French & mod. French *joignant* pres. pple of *joindre*: see JOIN *verb*, -ANT[1].]
Adjoining, adjacent. Long only in HERALDRY, conjoined.

joinder /ˈdʒɔɪndə/ *noun*. LME.
[ORIGIN Anglo-Norman, use as noun of Old French & mod. French *joindre*: see JOIN *verb*, -ER[4].]
Chiefly LAW. The act of joining; union.

†**joined-stool** *noun* see JOINT-STOOL.

joiner /ˈdʒɔɪnə/ *noun & verb*. ME.
[ORIGIN Anglo-Norman *joignour*, Old French *joigneor*, from *joindre*: see JOIN *verb*, -ER[2].]
▸ **A** *noun*. **1** A person who (as a profession) does light woodwork and esp. constructs furniture, fittings, etc., by joining pieces of wood. ME.

J. YEATS The workshops.. of joiners and cabinet-makers.

2 *gen.* A person who joins, connects, or unites people or things. Now *rare* or *obsolete*. L15.
3 A person who readily joins societies etc. *colloq.* L19.

S. NAIPAUL Steve was.. a joiner of societies.

– COMB.: **joiner-work**, **joiner's-work** woodwork made by a joiner.
▸ **B** *verb intrans.* Do the work of a joiner. Chiefly as ***joinering*** *verbal noun*. M19.

joinery /ˈdʒɔɪnəri/ *noun*. L17.
[ORIGIN from JOINER *noun* + -Y[3]: see -ERY.]
The art of a joiner; the construction of wooden furniture etc.; *collect.* articles made by a joiner.

Do-It-Yourself Their sheds have.. cedar as exterior cladding, while joinery, such as windows, is in softwood.

joint /dʒɔɪnt/ *noun*. ME.
[ORIGIN Old French & mod. French (also †*jointe*) use as noun of *joint(e)* pa. pple of *joindre*: see JOIN *verb*.]
▸ **I** The place at which things or parts join.
1 An anatomical structure or mechanism by which two bones are fitted and held together, usu. so that relative movement is possible; the place of connection of two movable parts in an invertebrate, esp. an arthropod. ME.

P. ROTH The tissue of my muscles and the joints between my bones. W. SOYINKA The fingers have become.. stiff at the joints. K. WILLIAMS Every bone and joint ached.

2 A point at which, or a contrivance by which, two parts of an artificial structure are joined, either rigidly (as with bricks, timbers, etc.), or so as to allow movement (as in a hinge etc.). LME. ▸**b** BOOKBINDING. A piece of flexible material forming the hinge of a book cover. M19.
dovetail joint, ***mitre joint***, ***scarf joint***, etc.
3 The part of a plant stem from which a leaf or branch grows; a node. E16.
4 GEOLOGY. A crack or fissure intersecting a mass of rock, usually occurring in sets of parallel planes. E17.
▸ **II** Any of the parts or sections whose connection makes up a body or structure.
†**5** *gen.* A portion, an item. *rare*. Only in ME.
6 A part of an animal, plant, or other structure connected by a joint or joints to an adjacent part or parts; *esp.* such a part of a digit or limb; a phalanx; BOTANY an internode. LME.

SHAKES. *Tr. & Cr.* I have with exact view perus'd thee, Hector, And quoted joint by joint. J. WILCOX The pipe has twelve separate joints. *Garden News* This will keep the leaf joints short and.. increase the number of flowers.

7 *spec.* Any of the parts into which an animal carcass is divided for food. L16.

R. CROMPTON They ate.. a joint of cold beef. *Courier (N. Kent)* The fresh meat department.. giving shoppers a wider choice of joints for any occasion.

▸ **III** †**8** = JOINTURE 2. Only in E16.
9 A place of meeting for drinking or (formerly) *spec.*, for illicit drinking, opium-smoking, etc.; *gen.* a place, a house. *colloq.* (chiefly *N. Amer.*). E19. ▸**b** A stall or tent at a circus or fair. *slang* (orig. *US*). E20. ▸**c** Prison. *US slang*. M20.

D. HEWETT No one's got any manners in this joint. E. TROOP A beachside hamburger joint used by the college surfing trade. F. DONALDSON The above address.. is a joint belonging to a friend of mine.

juke joint: see JUKE *noun*.
10 A marijuana cigarette. *slang*. M20.
11 A piece of creative work, *esp.* a film or piece of music. Chiefly *black slang*. L20.
– PHRASES: **out of joint** (*a*) (of a bone or bodily part) dislocated; ***put a person's nose out of joint***: see NOSE *noun*; (*b*) *fig.* disordered, out of order. ***SYNOVIAL joint***. ***universal joint***: see UNIVERSAL *adjective*.
– COMB.: **joint bolt**: threaded at both ends for holding together the two parts of a joint; **joint box** a junction box; **joint-grass** *US* a creeping grass, *Paspalum distichum*, which roots at the nodes; **joint mouse** a loose fragment of cartilage, bone, etc., floating in the cavity of a joint (usu. in *pl.*); **joint-plane** GEOLOGY a plane in rock in which a joint exists or is liable to form; an exposed surface that was once such a plane; **joint-rule** a folding rule made of jointed or hinged pieces; **joint-saw**: with a curved working face for making compass joints etc.; **joint-snake** = ***glass snake*** s.v. GLASS *noun & adjective*; **jointweed** *US* a small jointed plant, *Polygonella articulata*, related to and resembling knotgrass.

joint /dʒɔɪnt/ *adjective* (orig. *pa. pple*). ME.
[ORIGIN Old French & mod. French *joint(e)* pa. pple of *joindre*: see JOIN *verb*.]
1 Joined, combined, united; *spec.* (of the lives of two or more people) contemporaneous, concurrent. Now only *attrib.* ME. ▸†**b** Made up of parts joined or fastened together. LME–E18.

J. H. NEWMAN Civilized by the joint influences of religion and of chivalry. E. E. KAY During the joint lives of the trustees.

2 Of a person or persons: sharing *with* another or others in some possession, action, state, etc.; *esp.* being or doing (what is expressed by the noun) together or in common. LME.

SHAKES. *Coriol.* I.. Made him joint-servant with me. C. G. WOLFF Aunt Eliza and Evelina are the joint proprietors of a little notions shop. M. IGNATIEFF Paul was named joint heir of the Maltser industrial empire.

3 Of a single thing, action, etc.: held, done, made, etc., by two or more people etc. in conjunction; of or belonging to more than one at once. LME.

J. RULE All of their joint property. A. THWAITE He wrote a.. letter to Gosse, encouraging him in their joint aim. *Which?* If built after 1937, the drain is the joint responsibility of all the householders.

joint and several (of an obligation etc.) undertaken and signed by two or more people, of whom each is liable for the whole obligation etc.
– SPECIAL COLLOCATIONS & COMB.: ***joint account***: see ACCOUNT *noun* 2. **joint adventure** SCOTS LAW a partnership entered into only for a particular enterprise and not constituting a firm for continuing business. **joint committee**: composed of members nominated by two or more distinct bodies. **joint denial** LOGIC the negation of each of two or more propositions. **joint family** an extended family in which married children share the family home, living under the authority of the head of the family. ***joint patent***: see PATENT *adjective* 2. †**joint-ring** a finger ring made of two separable halves. **joint stock** capital held jointly; a common fund. **joint-stock bank**, **joint-stock company**: formed on the basis of a joint stock. **joint tenancy** the holding of an estate by two or more joint tenants (cf. ***TENANCY in common***). **joint tenant** a person holding an undivided estate jointly with another or others and whose interest, on death, passes to the survivor or survivors. **joint venture** a commercial enterprise undertaken jointly by two or more parties otherwise retaining their separate identities.

joint /dʒɔɪnt/ *verb*. M16.
[ORIGIN from JOINT *noun*.]
1 *verb trans.* Connect or fasten together by a joint or joints. M16. ▸**b** Fill up the joints of (masonry) with mortar etc., point. E18. ▸**c** Prepare (a board etc.) for being joined to another by planing the edge. E19.

Practical Woodworking Those old chairmakers knew exactly how to joint these components to one another.

2 *verb trans.* Divide (a body or member) at a joint or into joints. M16.

R. GRAVES He himself skinned and jointed the hare.

3 *verb intrans.* Fit exactly *into* as a joint. Long *rare*. L17.
4 *verb intrans.* Of a growing plant: form joints. L18.

jointed /ˈdʒɔɪntɪd/ *adjective*. LME.
[ORIGIN from JOINT *noun* + -ED[2].]
1 Provided with, constructed with, or having joints. LME. ▸**b** *spec.* (BOTANY) Having or appearing to have joints; separating readily at the joints. L16.
2 Having joints of a specified kind. L16.
■ **jointedly** *adverb* M19. **jointedness** *noun* L19.

†**jointer** *noun*[1]. M–L16.
[ORIGIN from JOINT *adjective* or *joint-* in JOINTURE: see -ER[1]. Cf. JOINTRESS.]
A joint possessor; a person who holds a jointure.

jointer /ˈdʒɔɪntə/ *noun*[2]. M17.
[ORIGIN from JOINT *verb* + -ER[1].]
1 CARPENTRY. A long plane used in jointing. Also ***jointer plane***. M17.
2 A tool for jointing masonry. E18.
3 Any of several shrubs of the genus *Piper* having prominent nodes on the stem. *W. Indian*. M19.
4 A person employed in jointing wires, pipes, etc. M19.

jointing /ˈdʒɔɪntɪŋ/ *noun*. LME.
[ORIGIN from JOINT *verb* + -ING[1].]
1 A joint; a junction. LME.
2 The action of JOINT *verb*. L16.
3 The formation of joints or fissures in rock etc.; the nature or arrangement of these. L17.

jointless /ˈdʒɔɪntlɪs/ *adjective*. M16.
[ORIGIN from JOINT *noun* + -LESS.]
Without a joint or joints; stiff, rigid. Also, in one piece.

jointly /ˈdʒɔɪntli/ *adverb*. ME.
[ORIGIN from JOINT *adjective* + -LY[2].]
1 In conjunction, in combination; unitedly; not severally or separately. ME.
†**2** So as to be spatially joined; in contact; adjacently. LME–E18. ▸†**b** Continuously in space or time. LME–M16.
†**3** At the same time, simultaneously. LME–L17.

jointress /ˈdʒɔɪntrɪs/ *noun*. E17.
[ORIGIN from JOINTER *noun*[1] + -ESS[1].]
A widow who holds a jointure; a dowager.

joint-stool /ˈdʒɔɪntstuːl/ *noun*. *obsolete* exc. *hist*. Earlier †**joined-stool**. LME.
[ORIGIN Orig. from pa. pple of JOIN *verb* + STOOL *noun*; later alt. after JOINT *noun*.]
A stool made of parts skilfully joined or fitted together by a joiner.
– NOTE: Freq. mentioned in 16–18 as an article of furniture; also (for some unknown reason) in allusive or proverbial phrs. expr. disparagement or ridicule.

jointure /ˈdʒɔɪntjʊə/ *noun & verb*. ME.
[ORIGIN Old French & mod. French from Latin *junctura* JUNCTURE.]
▸ **A** *noun*. **1** A joining, a junction, a joint. Formerly also, the action of joining, union. Now *rare*. ME.
2 Orig., the joint holding of property by a husband and wife for life, or in tail as a provision for the latter in the event of her widowhood. Now, an estate settled on a wife for the period during which she survives her husband. LME. ▸†**b** A dowry. L15–E17.
†**3** A joint tenancy. L16–M18.
▸ **B** *verb trans*. Settle a jointure on; provide with a jointure. M17.
■ **jointured** *adjective* provided with a jointure M18.

jointuress /ˈdʒɔɪntjʊərɪs/ *noun*. L17.
[ORIGIN Alt. of JOINTRESS after JOINTURE.]
= JOINTRESS.

jointworm /ˈdʒɔɪntwəːm/ *noun*. E18.
[ORIGIN from JOINT *noun* + WORM *noun*.]
†**1** A tapeworm. Only in E18.
2 (The larval form of) any of several chalcid flies of the genus *Harmolita* (or *Tetramesa*) which form galls near joints on grain stems, causing them to bend. *US*. M19.

jointy /ˈdʒɔɪnti/ *adjective*. L16.
[ORIGIN from JOINT *noun* + -Y[1].]
Having numerous joints.

joist /dʒɔɪst/ *noun & verb*. Earlier †**gist**. LME.
[ORIGIN Old French *giste* beam supporting a bridge (mod. *gîte*), from use as noun of Proto-Romance neut. pa. pple of Latin *jacere* lie down.]
▸ **A** *noun*. Each of a series of parallel supporting beams of timber, steel, etc., to which floorboards, ceiling laths, etc., are attached. LME.
▸ **B** *verb trans*. Provide with or fix on joists. M16.
■ **joisting** *noun* the structure or arrangement of joists; joists collectively: L16. **joistless** *adjective* M19.

jojoba /həˈhəʊbə, həʊ-/ *noun*. E20.
[ORIGIN Mexican Spanish.]
An evergreen desert shrub, *Simmondsia chinensis* (family Simmondsiaceae), of Mexico and the south-western US, whose seeds yield an oil used as a lubricant and in cosmetics.

Jokari /dʒəˈkɑːri/ *noun*. M20.
[ORIGIN Unknown.]
(Proprietary name for) any of various games played with bat and ball.

joke /dʒəʊk/ *noun*. L17.
[ORIGIN Orig. slang, perh. from Latin *jocus* jest, wordplay: cf. German *Jucks*, *Jux* joke, spree, Dutch *jok* jest.]
1 A thing said or done to excite laughter or amusement, freq. in the form of a short anecdote or a question and answer; a witticism, a jest. Also, a ridiculous person, thing, or circumstance. L17. ▸**b** A laughing stock. L18.

K. MANSFIELD He looked like a little comic picture waiting for the joke to be written underneath. J. MORTIMER Fred had made a joke and Henry hadn't laughed. *attrib.*: C. PHILLIPS The taxi was .. popular when he first arrived .. but had rapidly become a joke car. **b** J. F. COOPER I shall be the standing joke of the mess-table. J. CAREY He was .. a flop at gaining support. As a Labour MP he was a joke.

2 Something not serious or true; a matter to be dismissed lightly. E18.

J. WAIN Bad luck, superstition, fear, they aren't jokes.

– PHRASES: ***beyond a joke***: see BEYOND *preposition* 6. **no joke** *colloq*. a serious matter. **practical joke** a trick played on a person to have a laugh at his or her expense. ***standing joke***: see STANDING *adjective*. ***take a joke***: see TAKE *verb*.
– COMB.: **jokesmith** a maker or inventor of jokes.
■ **jokeless** *adjective* devoid of jokes, lacking humour or wit M19. **jokelet** *noun* a little joke M19. **jokesome** *adjective* characterized by jokes, facetious E19.

joke /dʒəʊk/ *verb*. L17.
[ORIGIN from the noun or from Latin *jocari* to jest.]
1 *verb intrans*. Make a joke or jokes, jest. L17. ▸**b** *verb trans*. Utter as a joke. E20.

M. STEWART You've got to be joking. *Star & Style* Even from his sick bed he laughed and joked with everyone. P. ROTH It's too awful even to joke about. **b** M. GEE 'Things of beauty should be kept together,' he had joked, .. though Less hadn't noticed the humour.

joking relationship ANTHROPOLOGY: in which one individual or group is permitted or obliged to make fun of another.
2 *verb trans*. Make the object of a joke or jokes; poke fun at. M18.

SMOLLETT Miss Snapper .. pretended to joke me upon my passion for Narcissa.

3 *verb trans*. Obtain by joking. Foll. by *out*. M19.

C. CLARKE A fellow who will joke and laugh the money out of your pocket.

■ **joˈkee** *noun* (*colloq*.) a person on whom a joke is played M19. **jokingly** *adverb* in a joking manner E18.

joker /ˈdʒəʊkə/ *noun*. E18.
[ORIGIN from JOKE *verb* + -ER[1].]
1 A person who jokes. E18.

T. S. ELIOT Are you a devil Or merely a lunatic practical joker? W. WHARTON In our family my role is the joker, the comedian.

practical joker a person who plays practical jokes.
2 A man, a fellow. *slang* (esp. *Austral. & NZ*). E19.

M. SHADBOLT I like the looks of you. You look a clean living young joker.

3 A playing card usu. ornamented with the figure of a jester, used orig. as the top trump in euchre and later in poker as a wild card, now esp. in rummy games. Also, a device used in playing a trick. L19.
joker in the pack *fig*. an unpredictable factor or participant.
4 A clause unobtrusively inserted in a bill or document which affects its operation in a way not immediately apparent, esp. by frustrating its intention or disadvantaging one of the concerned parties; *fig*. a drawback, a snag. *US*. E20.
■ **jokery** *noun* jesting, raillery M18.

jokester /ˈdʒəʊkstə/ *noun*. L19.
[ORIGIN from JOKE *verb* + -STER.]
A person who makes (esp. petty) jokes.

jokey /ˈdʒəʊki/ *adjective*. Also **joky**. E19.
[ORIGIN from JOKE *noun* + -Y[1].]
Inclined to joke; having the quality of a joke; subject to jokes, ridiculous.

N. GORDIMER She wrapped both serious and jokey presents elaborately. I. MCEWAN The conversation was joky and mock-cynical, but embodied some truth.

■ **jokily** *adverb* L20. **jokiness** *noun* M19.

jokist /ˈdʒəʊkɪst/ *noun*. E19.
[ORIGIN from JOKE *noun* + -IST.]
A professed or habitual joker.

jokul /ˈjœkʊl/ *noun*. L18.
[ORIGIN Icelandic *jökull* icicle, ice, glacier, from Old Norse *jǫkull*: see ICKLE *noun*. Cf. ICICLE.]
In Iceland, a mountain permanently covered with snow and ice; (in proper names) a glacier.

jole *noun*[1], *noun*[2], *noun*[3] vars. of JOWL *noun*[1], *noun*[2], *noun*[3].

jolie laide /ʒɔli lɛd/ *noun phr*. Pl. **-s -s** (pronounced same). L19.
[ORIGIN French, from *jolie* pretty + *laide* ugly (fem. adjectives).]
An attractively or fascinatingly ugly woman.

jolley /ˈdʒɒli/ *noun*. Also **jolly**. L19.
[ORIGIN Unknown.]
A horizontal lathe used in pottery-making; a jigger.
■ **jolleying** *noun* the practice of using a jolley E20.

jollier /ˈdʒɒlɪə/ *noun*[1]. Also **jollyer**. L19.
[ORIGIN from JOLLEY + -ER[1].]
A person who makes pottery using a jolley.

jollier /ˈdʒɒlɪə/ *noun*[2]. *US*. L19.
[ORIGIN from JOLLY *verb* + -ER[1].]
A jovial or sociable person.

jollification /ˌdʒɒlɪfɪˈkeɪʃ(ə)n/ *noun*. *colloq*. E19.
[ORIGIN from JOLLY *adjective* + -FICATION.]
Jollity; (a) merrymaking; *spec*. a party.

H. GREEN I'm too old for that sort of idiot jollification. K. WATERHOUSE Various functions, .. leaving parties and other jollifications.

jollify /ˈdʒɒlɪfʌɪ/ *verb*. *colloq*. E19.
[ORIGIN formed as JOLLIFICATION + -FY.]
1 *verb trans*. Make jolly or merry; *esp*. make slightly tipsy. E19.
2 *verb intrans*. Make merry; *esp*. indulge in alcoholic drink. M19.

jollily /ˈdʒɒlɪli/ *adverb*. ME.
[ORIGIN from JOLLY *adjective* + -LY[2].]
In a jolly manner.

jolliment /ˈdʒɒlɪm(ə)nt/ *noun*. Long *obsolete* exc. *dial*. L16.
[ORIGIN from JOLLY *adjective* + -MENT.]
Mirth, merriment.

jolliness /ˈdʒɒlɪnɪs/ *noun*. LME.
[ORIGIN from JOLLY *adjective* + -NESS.]
The state or quality of being jolly.

†**jollitry** *noun*. L17–M18.
[ORIGIN from JOLLITY after *gallantry*, *pleasantry*, etc.]
= JOLLITY 1, 2.

jollity /ˈdʒɒlɪti/ *noun*. ME.
[ORIGIN Old French *jolité*, from *joli*: see JOLLY *adjective & adverb*, -TY[1].]
1 The quality or condition of being jolly, cheerful, or festive; exuberant mirth or cheerfulness. ME. ▸†**b** A joke, a jest. L16–E17.

R. CROMPTON He dreamed of .. a life of untrammelled joy and jollity. P. FERGUSON She sang .. music-hall songs .. defused of all jollity.

2 Merrymaking, revelry; in *pl*., festivities. ME. ▸†**b** Splendour, magnificence. M16–L17.

J. CAREY Children weren't encouraged in Happy Valley, since they interfered with the jollity. P. THEROUX Years ago, when we ran around painted with woad, those jollities turned into orgies.

†**3** Pleasure; *esp*. sexual pleasure, lust. ME–E17.
†**4** Insolence, presumption. ME–E17.

jollo /ˈdʒɒləʊ/ *noun*. *Austral. slang*. Pl. **-os**. E20.
[ORIGIN from JOLL(ITY + -O.]
A party, a celebration; a binge.

Jollof /ˈdʒɒləf/ *noun & adjective*. Also **Jolof** /ˈdʒəʊlɒf/, (earlier) †**Jolloif**. Pl. of noun **-s**, same. M18.
[ORIGIN Wolof.]
= WOLOF.
jollof rice a W. African stew made with fish, meat, rice, chilli peppers, etc.

jollop /ˈdʒɒləp/ *noun*[1]. M17.
[ORIGIN Prob. alt. of JOWL *noun*[2] + LAP *noun*[1]. Cf. DEWLAP. Earlier in *jolloped* var. of JELLOPED.]
The wattle of a cock or turkey.

jollop /ˈdʒɒləp/ *noun*[2]. *slang*. E20.
[ORIGIN Alt. of JALAP.]
1 (A drink of) strong liquor. E20.
2 A purgative, a medicine. M20.

jollop(p)ed *adjective* var. of JELLOPED.

jolly /ˈdʒɒli/ *noun*[1]. *slang*. E19.
[ORIGIN Absol. use of JOLLY *adjective*.]
1 A Royal Marine. E19.
2 A cheer, a shout. M19.

jolly /ˈdʒɒli/ *noun*[2]. E19.
[ORIGIN Abbreviation.]
= JOLLY BOAT.

Jolly /ˈdʒɒli, ˈjɒli/ *noun*[3]. L19.
[ORIGIN P. von *Jolly* (1809–84), German physicist.]
Jolly balance, †***Jolly's balance***, a balance in which the elongation of a helical spring indicates the weight of the body hanging on it, used esp. in determining the specific gravities of minerals.

jolly /ˈdʒɒli/ *noun*[4]. *colloq*. L19.
[ORIGIN Abbreviation of JOLLIFICATION.]
1 A party, a celebration; an enjoyable trip. Also ***jolly-up***. L19.

W. HAGGARD A splendid wedding, the sort of big jolly Charles Russell enjoyed.

2 ***get one's jollies***, enjoy oneself, get pleasure or excitement. M20.

Daily Telegraph The kind of people who get their jollies from military history and guns.

jolly *noun*[5] var. of JOLLEY.

jolly /ˈdʒɒli/ *adjective & adverb*. ME.
[ORIGIN Old French *jolif* (later and mod. *joli*) †merry, †pleasant, pretty, perh. from Old Norse *jól* midwinter festival, feast, YULE: see -Y[7].]
▸ **A** *adjective* **I 1** Of cheerful disposition or character; good-humoured; merry, bright, lively. ME. ▸†**b** *spec*. Lively on account of youth or good health. ME–L16.

D. H. LAWRENCE A big jolly fellow, with a touch of the bounder about him. E. FEINSTEIN The jolly peasant nannies who looked after her.

2 In high spirits; exhilarated. Chiefly *pred*. ME. ▸**b** *spec*. Exhilarated with drink, tipsy. M17.

J. NAGENDA Monkey, as befitted a guest, .. was endeavouring to look jolly. **b** Z. TOMIN The locals .. were in various—mostly jolly—stages of inebriation.

3 Characterized by conviviality and merriment; festive. LME.

THACKERAY He became a viveur and jolly dog about town. B. PYM To make our Christmas a particularly jolly one.

▸ †**II 4** Of cheerful courage, gallant, brave; *derog*. excessively self-confident, defiantly bold. ME–M17.
▸ **III** †**5** Bright or colourful in appearance; showy, splendid; finely dressed; *fig*. (of words etc.) specious. LME–L17.
6 Good-looking; handsome; pretty. Now *dial*. LME.
7 Well-built, plump. Now chiefly with connotations of cheerfulness. *colloq*. M17.
▸ **IV 8** †**a** Amorous; wanton, lustful. LME–M17. ▸**b** Of an animal: in heat. *obsolete* exc. *dial*. E16.
▸ **V 9** *gen*. Splendid, excellent. *arch*. M16.

DRYDEN Graze not too near the Banks, my jolly Sheep. F. W. FARRAR For he's a jolly good fe-el-low, Which nobody can deny.

10 Very pleasant or agreeable. Now *colloq*. M16.

J. UPDIKE Getting old could be jolly if you stayed strong.

11 Used with intensive force: great, fine. Now *colloq*. M16.

C. DARWIN Are not these a jolly lot of assumptions?

J

– SPECIAL COLLOCATIONS & COMB.: **Jolly Roger** a pirates' flag, usu. black with a white skull and crossbones. **jollytail** *Austral.* any small freshwater fish of the genus *Galaxias*, *esp.* the inanga, *G. maculatus*.

▸ **B** *adverb*. **1** Extremely, very. Now *colloq.* M16.

J. GRENFELL Jolly well played! Absolutely smashing! H. SECOMBE It's all jolly exciting, isn't it?

2 In a jolly manner; merrily; pleasantly. E17.

jolly /ˈdʒɒli/ *verb*. E17.
[ORIGIN from JOLLY *adjective*.]
1 *verb intrans.* Make merry, enjoy oneself. *rare*. E17.
2 *verb trans.* Keep or make jolly or cheerful by friendly behaviour etc. Foll. by *along*, *up*, etc. *colloq.* M19.

J. B. PRIESTLEY Arranging . . entertainments . . and generally jollying everybody along. J. T. STORY Trying to jolly each other up with anecdotes.

3 *verb trans.* Ridicule, poke fun at, tease. L19.

R. ELLMANN Wilde . . jollies us for being so much harsher that he is.

jolly boat /ˈdʒɒlɪbəʊt/ *noun*. L17.
[ORIGIN Origin of 1st elem. uncertain: perh. rel. to YAWL *noun*[1].]
A clinker-built ship's boat, smaller than a cutter, with a bluff bow and very wide transom.

jollyer *noun* var. of JOLLIER *noun*[1].

†**jollyhead** *noun*. *rare* (Spenser). Only in L16.
[ORIGIN from JOLLY *adjective* + -HEAD[1].]
Jollity.

jolt /dʒəʊlt, dʒɒlt/ *noun*. L16.
[ORIGIN Rel. to JOLT *verb*.]
†**1** A knock of the head etc. against something. *rare*. L16–E17.
2 An abrupt movement or jerk (esp. in a moving vehicle) causing a person or thing to alter position briefly and violently. M17. ▸**b** *fig.* A mental shock, a surprise. L19. ▸**c** A blow in boxing. E20.

J

P. BOWLES A cigarette which, after awakening with a jolt, he accepted automatically. D. A. DYE The solid jolt of the weapon against his shoulder was reassuring. T. O. ECHEWA He . . braked suddenly, . . giving everyone an uncomfortable jolt. **b** *Scotsman* Labour is only just recovering from the jolt in the . . by-election.

3 A drink or small quantity of spirits. *slang* (chiefly *US*). E20. ▸**b** A prison sentence. *slang* (orig. *US*). E20. ▸**c** A quantity of a drug, esp. as an injection. *slang* (chiefly *US*). E20.

R. THOMAS She took two . . glasses . . . I poured a generous jolt into both of them.

– COMB.: **jolt ramming** *FOUNDING* repeated lifting and dropping of a moulding box, containing a pattern and sand, so as to pack the sand around the pattern (freq. *attrib.*); **jolt-squeeze** *FOUNDING* simultaneous or successive jolting and squeezing of a box containing a pattern and sand so as to pack the sand around the pattern (usu. *attrib.*).

▪ **joltless** *adjective* free from jolts E19.

jolt /dʒəʊlt, dʒɒlt/ *verb*. L16.
[ORIGIN Perh. rel. to JOT *verb*[1]: cf. JOLT *noun*, JOLT-HEAD.]
1 *verb trans.* Shake or disturb from one's seat or position (esp. in a moving vehicle) with a jolt or succession of jolts; transport or convey with a jolt or jolts. L16. ▸**b** *fig.* Startle, shock. L19.

T. HOOD My scanty breath was jolted out with many a sudden groan. W. BLACK We were once more jolted over the unmade roads. **b** J. S. HUXLEY The dropping of the first atomic bomb on Hiroshima . . deeply jolted our moral conscience. M. AMIS Obstacles intended to jolt and scare me awake with sudden noise. D. PRATER He was to be jolted into a harsher reality.

†**2** *verb trans.* Butt or push with the head, elbow, etc.; knock; nudge. E17–L18.
3 *verb intrans.* Move with a jolt; (of a vehicle etc.) move along with a succession of jolts, as on a rough uneven road; (of a passenger) be transported in this way. E18.

A. G. GARDINER A carriage . . jolting noisily through the night. D. H. LAWRENCE A blinding flash went over his brain, his body jolted. I. MURDOCH She jolted against the side of the passenger seat.

▪ **jolter** *noun* E17. **jolter** *verb trans.* & *intrans.* (*rare*) [-ER[5]] jolt continuously E19. **joltingly** *adverb* in a jolting manner M19.

jolter-head /ˈdʒəʊltəhɛd/ *noun*. Now *rare*. E17.
[ORIGIN Extension of JOLT-HEAD.]
= JOLT-HEAD 2.
▪ **jolter-headed** *adjective* thickheaded M18. **jolter-ˈheadedness** *noun* M19.

jolt-head /ˈdʒəʊlthɛd/ *noun*. Now *rare* or *obsolete*. M16.
[ORIGIN Rel. to JOLT *verb*.]
†**1** A large clumsy head; a stupid head. M16–E18.
2 A thickheaded person; a blockhead. L16.
▪ **jolt-headed** *adjective* (now *rare* or *obsolete*) thickheaded M16.

jolty /ˈdʒəʊlti, ˈdʒɒlti/ *adjective*. M19.
[ORIGIN from JOLT *noun* + -Y[1].]
Characterized by jolting; having or causing jolts.
▪ **joltiness** *noun* L19.

Joly /ˈdʒɒli/ *noun*. L19.
[ORIGIN John *Joly* (1857–1933), Irish physicist.]
Joly's steam calorimeter, a device for determining the specific heat of a substance by measuring the weight of steam that condenses on a known mass of the substance in raising its temperature to that of the steam.

Jomon /ˈdʒəʊmən/ *adjective*. M20.
[ORIGIN Japanese *jōmon* cord mark.]
Designating an early handmade earthenware pottery found in Japan and freq. decorated with impressed rope patterns. Also, designating the early Neolithic or pre-Neolithic culture characterized by this pottery.

Jon. *abbreviation*.
Jonah (in the Bible).

Jonagold /ˈdʒɒnəgəʊld/ *noun*. M20.
[ORIGIN Blend of JONATHAN *noun* and ***Golden Delicious***.]
A dessert apple of a variety with greenish-gold skin and crisp flesh.

Jonah /ˈdʒəʊnə/ *noun* & *verb*. As noun also †**Jonas**, pl. **-sses**. L16.
[ORIGIN A Hebrew prophet (Hebrew *yōnāh* lit. 'dove'), the subject of a book in the Old Testament and Hebrew Scriptures.]
▸ **A** *noun*. **1** A person who seems to bring bad luck. L16.
2 ***Jonah crab***, a large deep-water crab, *Cancer borealis*, of the east coast of N. America. L19.
▸ **B** *verb trans.* Bring bad luck to. L19.

Jonathan /ˈdʒɒnəθ(ə)n/ *noun*. L18.
[ORIGIN Male forename.]
1 The United States of America personified; the people of the US collectively; a supposedly typical US citizen. Also ***Brother Jonathan***. L18.
2 A variety of red-skinned autumn eating apple, first introduced in the US. M19.
▪ **Jonathaniˈzation** *noun* Americanization M19.

Jones /dʒəʊnz/ *noun*. L19.
[ORIGIN A common Brit. surname. Sense 2 is said to come from *Jones* Alley in Manhattan, assoc. with drug addicts.]
1 In *pl.* A person's neighbours or social equals. Chiefly in ***keep up with the Joneses***, try to emulate or not to be outdone by one's neighbours. L19.
2 (**j-**.) A drug addict's habit. *US slang*. M20.

jong /jɒŋ/ *noun*[1]. *S. Afr. colloq. offensive*. E17.
[ORIGIN Afrikaans.]
Orig. (*hist.*), a Coloured male slave or servant. Later, a form of address to a young man or woman, used esp. among young people.

jong /dʒɒŋ/ *noun*[2]. Also **dzong**. E20.
[ORIGIN Tibetan *rdzoṅ* fortress.]
In Tibet: a building constituting a prefecture, freq. also used as a fortress or monastery; also, a territorial and administrative division.

jonga /ˈdʒɒŋgə/ *noun*. L19.
[ORIGIN Bantu (NW) *njaŋga*.]
In Jamaica, a small freshwater prawn, *Macrobrachium jamaicensis*.

jonglery /ˈdʒɒŋgləri/ *noun*. E17.
[ORIGIN French *jonglerie*, formed as JONGLEUR: see -ERY.]
The performance of a *jongleur*.

jongleur /ʒɔ̃glœːr/ *noun*. Pl. pronounced same. L18.
[ORIGIN French, alt. of *jougleur* (Old French *jogleor* accus. of *joglere*) from Latin *joculator* jester: see JUGGLER.]
hist. An itinerant minstrel.

jonick /ˈdʒɒnɪk/ *adjective* & *adverb*. *Austral. colloq.* Also **-nn-**. L19.
[ORIGIN Var. of JANNOCK *adjective* & *adverb*.]
Fair(ly); genuine(ly); right.

Jonkanoo *noun* var. of JOHN CANOE.

jonnick *adjective* & *adverb* var. of JONICK.

jonnop /ˈdʒɒnɒp/ *noun*. *Austral. slang*. M20.
[ORIGIN Contr. of ***JOHN hop***.]
A policeman.

jonquil /ˈdʒʌŋkwɪl, ˈdʒɒn-/ *noun* & *adjective*. E17.
[ORIGIN mod. Latin *jonquilla* or French *jonquille* from Spanish *junquillo* dim. of *junco* from Latin *juncus* rush, reed.]
▸ **A** *noun*. **1** A kind of narcissus, *Narcissus jonquilla*, with rushlike leaves and fragrant yellow flowers, used in perfumery. E17.
Queen Anne's jonquil: see QUEEN ANNE.
2 The colour of a jonquil; a pale yellow. L18.
▸ **B** *adjective*. Of the colour of a jonquil; pale yellow. E19.

Jonsonian /dʒɒnˈsəʊnɪən/ *adjective*. L19.
[ORIGIN from *Jonson* (see below) + -IAN.]
Of, pertaining to, or characteristic of the English dramatist Ben Jonson (*c* 1573–1637) or his works.

jonty *noun* var. of JAUNTY *noun*.

jook *verb*, **jookery** *noun* vars. of JOUK *verb*[2], JOUKERY.

†**joom** *noun* & *verb* var. of JHUM.

jordan /ˈdʒɔːd(ə)n/ *noun*[1]. LME.
[ORIGIN medieval Latin *jurdanus*, of unknown origin.]
†**1** A bulbous pot or vessel formerly used by physicians and alchemists. Only in LME.
2 A chamber pot; *fig.* a stupid person. Now *dial.* LME.

Jordan /ˈdʒɔːd(ə)n/ *noun*[2]. E20.
[ORIGIN M. E. C. *Jordan* (1838–1922), French mathematician.]
MATH. **1** ***Jordan curve***, any curve that is topologically equivalent to a circle, i.e. is closed and does not cross itself. E20.
2 ***Jordan curve theorem***, ***Jordan theorem***, ***Jordan's curve theorem***, ***Jordan's theorem***, the theorem that any Jordan curve in a plane divides the plane into just two distinct regions having the curve as their common boundary. E20.

jordan almond /ˈdʒɔːd(ə)n ˈɑːmənd/ *noun phr*. LME.
[ORIGIN App. from French or Spanish *jardin* garden + ALMOND: in later times assoc. with the River Jordan.]
A fine variety of almond, now coming chiefly from Malaga. Also, a sugar-coated almond.

Jordanian /dʒɔːˈdeɪnɪən/ *adjective* & *noun*. M20.
[ORIGIN from *Jordan* (see below), also a river running into the Dead Sea -IAN.]
▸ **A** *adjective*. Of or pertaining to the kingdom of Jordan in the Middle East. M20.
▸ **B** *noun*. A native or inhabitant of Jordan. M20.

Jordanite /ˈdʒɔːd(ə)nʌɪt/ *noun*. M20.
[ORIGIN from *Jordan* (see below) + -ITE[1].]
A believer in the doctrines of Jordan, a 20th-cent. Jamaican preacher with followers in Guyana.

joree /dʒəˈriː/ *noun*. *US*. L19.
[ORIGIN Imit. of the bird's call.]
= CHEWINK.

jornada /xɔrˈnaða, hɔːˈnɑːdə/ *noun*. Pl. **-as** /-as, -əz/. M17.
[ORIGIN Spanish = Italian *giornata*, French *journée* JOURNEY.]
†**1** An act of a play; a book or canto of a poem. M17–M19.
2 In Mexico etc.: a day's journey; *spec.* one across a waterless desert tract with no place to halt. E19.

joro /ˈdʒɔːrəʊ/ *noun*. Pl. **-os**. L19.
[ORIGIN Japanese *jorō*.]
In Japan, a prostitute.

jorram /ˈjɒərəm/ *noun*. *Scot.* L18.
[ORIGIN Gaelic *iorram*, *iurram*.]
A Gaelic boat song; *loosely* any Scottish song.

jorum /ˈdʒɔːrəm/ *noun*. M18.
[ORIGIN Perh. from *Joram* (*2 Samuel* 8:10).]
A large drinking bowl; the contents of this; *esp.* a bowl of punch.

joruri /ˈdʒɔːruri/ *noun*. L19.
[ORIGIN Japanese *jōruri*, from the name of a character in a popular recitation.]
1 A dramatic recitation to music, accompanying a Japanese puppet performance. L19.
2 Japanese puppet drama. M20.

Jos. *abbreviation*.
Joseph.

Joseph /ˈdʒəʊzɪf/ *noun*. L16.
[ORIGIN Male forename (Hebrew *yōsēp* lit. 'may he (God) increase'), esp. of various biblical characters, spec. one of the twelve sons of Jacob and of the husband of Mary the mother of Jesus.]
1 In plant names: (***a***) ***Joseph's flower*** (now *dial.*), yellow goat's beard, *Tragopogon pratensis*, so called in allus. to the bearded figure of St Joseph in art; (***b***) ***Joseph and Mary*** (*dial.*), lungwort, either native, *Pulmonaria longifolia*, or of gardens, *P. officinalis*, so called from the flowers being pink and blue at different stages. L16.
2 *hist.* A long cloak with a small cape and buttons down the front, worn chiefly by women when riding. M17.
3 A violin made by Joseph Guarnieri del Gesù (1698–1744), Italian violin-maker. Cf. GUARNERIUS. L19.
▪ **Josephism** *noun* = JOSEPHINISM M19.

Josephine /ˈdʒəʊzɪfɪn, -ʌɪn/ *adjective*. M19.
[ORIGIN from *Joseph* (see below) + -INE[1].]
Of or pertaining to Emperor Joseph II of Austria (1741–90) or the ecclesiastical measures introduced by him.
▪ **Josephinism** *noun* the ecclesiastical policy of the Emperor Joseph II L19.

josephinite /ˈdʒəʊzɪfɪnʌɪt, dʒəʊzɪˈfiːnʌɪt/ *noun*. L19.
[ORIGIN from *Josephine* county in Oregon, USA + -ITE[1].]
MINERALOGY. The terrestrial (as opp. to meteoric) alloy of nickel and iron, having about 67 to 77 per cent of nickel.

Josephite /ˈdʒəʊzɪfʌɪt/ *noun*[1]. M16.
[ORIGIN from St *Joseph* (1439–1515), Abbot of Volokolamsk, Russian reformer + -ITE[1].]
hist. A member of a party formed among Russian Orthodox monks in the 16th cent., who defended the holding of property by monastic communities.

Josephite /ˈdʒəʊzɪfʌɪt/ *noun*[2] & *adjective*. M19.
[ORIGIN from *Joseph* (see below) + -ITE[1].]
▸ **A** *noun*. A member of any of various religious societies of St Joseph. M19.
▸ **B** *adjective*. Designating or pertaining to the Josephites. L20.

Josephson /ˈdʒəʊzɪfs(ə)n/ *noun*. L20.
[ORIGIN Brian David *Josephson* (b. 1940), Brit. physicist.]
PHYSICS. Used ***attrib.*** with ref. to an effect whereby an electric current can flow from one superconducting metal to another with no potential difference between them if

they are separated by a sufficiently thin layer of an insulator, the application of a potential difference causing the current to oscillate with a frequency proportional to the voltage.

Scientific American The Josephson junction is the fastest switch known. *Observer* Other computer companies are much less active in Josephson technology.

josh /dʒɒʃ/ *verb & noun. slang.* M19.
[ORIGIN Unknown.]
▸ **A** *verb.* **1** *verb trans.* Make fun of, tease. M19.

B. T. BRADFORD They joshed him unmercifully about being late.

2 *verb intrans.* Indulge in banter. M19.

E. FERBER This is very pleasant, sitting here gabbing and joshing in the hot of the day. A. HAILEY Brett dropped into the kitchen where he joshed with the cooks.

▸ **B** *noun.* A good-natured or teasing joke; banter. L19.

Saturday Review We found him tired-eyed and peaked, .. not a man for josh and chatter.

■ **josher** *noun* L19. **joshingly** *adverb* in a joshing manner M20.

Josh. *abbreviation.*
Joshua (in the Bible).

Joshua /ˈdʒɒʃjʊə/ *noun. US.* M19.
[ORIGIN Prob. from *Joshua*, leader of the ancient Israelites, whose story forms a book in the Old Testament and Hebrew Scriptures, with allus. to the branching shape of the tree resembling that of Joshua brandishing a spear: see *Joshua* 8:18.]
More fully ***Joshua palm***, ***Joshua tree***, ***Joshua yucca***. A small evergreen tree, *Yucca brevifolia*, of the agave family, bearing clustered white flowers and found in western desert regions.

joskin /ˈdʒɒskɪn/ *noun. slang.* L18.
[ORIGIN Unknown: cf. BUMPKIN *noun*[1].]
A country bumpkin; a foolish person.

joss /dʒɒs/ *noun*[1]. E18.
[ORIGIN Perh. ult. from Portuguese †*deos*, *deus* from Latin *deus* god, through Javanese *dejos*: cf. Dutch *joosje*, *josie*.]
A Chinese figure of a god, an idol.
– COMB.: **joss house** a Chinese temple; **joss man** a Chinese priest or holy man; a missionary; **joss stick** a thin stick of fragrant tinder mixed with clay, burnt as incense.

joss /dʒɒs/ *noun*[2]. *dial.* or *Austral. slang.* M19.
[ORIGIN Unknown.]
= BOSS *noun*[4] 1.

josser /ˈdʒɒsə/ *noun. slang.* L19.
[ORIGIN from JOSS *noun*[1] + -ER[1].]
1 A clergyman. *Austral.* L19.
2 A man, esp. an old or contemptible one. L19.

jostle /ˈdʒɒs(ə)l/ *noun.* Also **justle** /ˈdʒʌs(ə)l/. E17.
[ORIGIN from JOSTLE *verb*.]
†**1** A struggle, a tussle. Only in E17.
2 The action or an act of jostling; a collision; a rough push or thrust. E17.

jostle /ˈdʒɒs(ə)l/ *verb.* Also (earlier) **justle** /ˈdʒʌs(ə)l/. LME.
[ORIGIN from JUST *verb*[2] + -LE[3].]
†**1** *verb intrans.* Have sexual intercourse *with*. *rare.* Only in LME.
2 *verb intrans.* Knock or push *against*, come into collision *with*; push and shove, esp. in a crowd; make one's way by pushing or shoving. M16. ▸**b** Vie or struggle *for* something. (Foll. by *with* another.) E17.

M. DE LA ROCHE Piers jostled against him in the doorway. A. WEST They would jostle round him covering him with wet kisses. R. DAHL People were pushing and jostling and trying to get .. closer to the famous girl. D. WIGODER I .. jostled with tens of thousands of young people crammed into Trafalgar Square. **b** A. TREW The .. locals had now to jostle with each other for tables, food and drink. M. RULE In Europe two major powers, France and Spain, jostled for control.

†**3** *verb intrans.* Come into collision in a tournament; joust. L16–M18.
4 *verb trans.* Come into rough collision with, knock or push against, elbow. L16. ▸**b** *verb trans. & intrans. spec.* Push against (another competitor) during a horse race so as to obstruct or delay. E18.

V. WOOLF The pavement was crowded with people; jostling each other. *fig.*: F. RAPHAEL All the practical questions .. jostled pettier and grander ones.

5 *verb trans.* Push, drive, or force, roughly or unceremoniously, *from*, *into*, *out of*, etc. L16.

G. SWIFT The guard jostled me back towards the double doors.

6 *verb trans.* Bring (things) into collision. M17.

J. G. BALLARD The vendors .. jostled their carts against each other.

■ **jostlement** *noun* the action of jostling M19.

jot /dʒɒt/ *noun*[1]. L15.
[ORIGIN Latin *iota* from Greek *iōta* IOTA. Cf. JOD.]
The smallest letter or written part of any writing; *gen.* (usu. in neg. contexts) the very least or a very little part or amount, a whit.

H. JACOBSON She was not a jot more lucid than I was. B. NEIL Goodness me, you haven't changed one jot.

jot /dʒɒt/ *noun*[2]. Long *dial.* M17.
[ORIGIN from JOT *verb*[1].]
A jolt, a bump.

jot /dʒɒt/ *verb*[1] *trans. & intrans. obsolete* exc. *dial.* Infl. **-tt-**. M16.
[ORIGIN Cf. JOLT *verb*.]
Jolt, bump.

jot /dʒɒt/ *verb*[2] *trans.* Infl. **-tt-**. E18.
[ORIGIN from JOT *noun*[1].]
Write down briefly or hastily; make a short note of. Usu. foll. by *down*.

G. VIDAL I tend to mislay the notes I jot down as reminders. K. WATERHOUSE I brandished the envelope .. on which Douglas had jotted the address.

■ **jotting** *noun* (*a*) the action of the verb; (*b*) a brief hasty note: E19. **jotty** *adjective* of the nature of fragmentary notes M19.

jota /ˈxota/ *noun.* M19.
[ORIGIN Spanish.]
A northern Spanish folk dance performed by one or more couples in rapid triple time; a piece of music for this dance.

jotter /ˈdʒɒtə/ *noun.* E19.
[ORIGIN from JOT *verb*[2] + -ER[1].]
1 A person who jots down something. E19.
2 A small pad or exercise book used for making notes etc. L19.

Jotun /ˈjəʊt(ə)n/ *noun.* M19.
[ORIGIN Old Norse *jǫtunn* = Old English *eoten*, from Germanic.]
A member of a supernatural race of giants in Scandinavian mythology.

joual /ʒwal, ʒuːˈɑːl/ *noun.* M20.
[ORIGIN Canad. French dial. from French *cheval* horse.]
Demotic Canadian French characterized by non-standard pronunciations and grammar, and influenced by English vocabulary and syntax.

joub *noun* var. of JUBE *noun*[2].

jougs /dʒuːɡz/ *noun pl.* L16.
[ORIGIN French *joug* or Latin *jugum* yoke. The pl. form refers to the device's hinged halves.]
SCOTTISH HISTORY. An instrument of punishment consisting of a hinged iron collar locked round an offender's neck and attached by a chain to a wall or post.

jouissance /ʒwisɑ̃ːs/ *noun.* Also †**-isance**. L15.
[ORIGIN French, from *jouir* enjoy: see -ANCE.]
†**1** The possession and use *of* something advantageous or pleasing. L15–E17.
2 Pleasure, delight; mirth, festivity. L16.

R. SCRUTON His eyes were alight with sudden jouissance.

– NOTE: Formerly fully naturalized.

jouk /dʒuːk/ *verb*[1] *intrans. obsolete* exc. *dial.* LME.
[ORIGIN Old Northern French *joquier*, *jochier* (mod. *jucher*) be at rest.]
†**1** Lie asleep or at rest; lie close. Also, remain. Only in LME.
2 Of a bird: perch, roost, sit (on a branch, perch, etc.). LME.

jouk /dʒuːk/ *verb*[2]. *Scot. & N. English.* Also **jook**. LME.
[ORIGIN Uncertain: perh. rel. to DUCK *verb*.]
1 *verb intrans.* †**a** Bend like a tumbler or acrobat. Only in LME. ▸**b** Bow quickly or jerkily in salutation or deference. M16.
2 *verb intrans.* Bend or turn the body quickly and neatly downwards or sideways to avoid a missile, blow, etc.; dodge; duck. E16. ▸**b** Dart or spring neatly out of the way or out of sight; hide, skulk. E16.

b R. L. STEVENSON Jouk in here among the trees.

3 *verb trans.* Evade or dodge by ducking, bending, or springing aside. L18.

joukery /ˈdʒuːkəri/ *noun. Scot. & N. English.* Also **jookery**. LME.
[ORIGIN from JOUK *verb*[2] + -ERY.]
Dodging; trickery, deceit.
– COMB.: **joukery-pawkery** [cf. PAWK *noun*] clever trickery, legerdemain.

joule /dʒuːl/ *noun.* Also **J-**. Pl. **-s**, same. L19.
[ORIGIN James Prescott *Joule* (1818–89), English physicist.]
PHYSICS. **1** Orig., a unit of electrical energy equal to the amount of work done (or heat generated) by a current of one ampere acting for one second against a resistance of one ohm. Now (equivalently), the SI unit of energy and work equal to the work done by a force of one newton when its point of application moves one metre in the direction of the force; 10^7 ergs. (Symbol J.) L19.
2 (Usu. **J-**.) Used *attrib.* and in *possess.* to designate principles, phenomena, etc., discovered by Joule or arising out of his work. L19.
Joule effect (*a*) = ***Joule heating*** below; (*b*) a change in the linear dimensions of a body in a magnetic field. **Joule heating**: that occurs when an electric current flows through a resistance. **Joule's equivalent** = ***mechanical equivalent of heat*** s.v. EQUIVALENT *noun*. **Joule's law**: (*a*) that the heat produced by an electric current i flowing through a resistance R for a time t is proportional to i^2Rt; (*b*) that the internal energy of a given mass of an ideal gas depends only on its temperature.

■ **joulean** /ˈdʒuːlɪən/ *adjective* (chiefly *US*) of or pertaining to Joule heating L19.

Joule–Thomson /dʒuːlˈtɒms(ə)n/ *noun.* L19.
[ORIGIN from J. P. *Joule* (see JOULE) + Sir William *Thomson*, Lord Kelvin (see KELVIN).]
Used *attrib.* with ref. to an effect whereby a change of temperature occurs in a gas when it expands through a porous plug or throttle without doing external work, the gas being cooled if initially below its inversion temperature, or heated if above it.
■ Also **Joule–Kelvin** *noun* E20.

jounce /dʒaʊns/ *verb & noun.* LME.
[ORIGIN Prob. imit.: cf. FLOUNCE *verb*[1].]
▸ **A** *verb.* **1** *verb intrans.* Move violently up and down; bump, bounce, jolt *along*. LME.

A. TYLER Every time the car jounced, something rattled on the back seat. K. LETTE We jounced over the cobbled country lanes.

2 *verb trans.* Jolt, bump; shake up and down; give (a person) a shaking. L16.
▸ **B** *noun.* A bump, a jolt; a jolting pace. L18.

joundy *verb & noun* see JUNDY.

jour /ʒuːr/ *noun*[1]. Pl. pronounced same. LME.
[ORIGIN Old French & mod. French from Latin *diurnum* neut. sing. (used as noun in popular Latin) of *diurnus* DIURNAL.]
†**1** A day. LME–M16.
2 A kind of open stitch used in lace-making. Usu. in *pl.* M19.
– PHRASES: BONHEUR DU JOUR. ***plat du jour***: see PLAT *noun*[4].

jour /dʒəː/ *noun*[2]. *US colloq.* E19.
[ORIGIN Abbreviation.]
= JOURNEYMAN.

journal /ˈdʒəːn(ə)l/ *noun & adjective.* LME.
[ORIGIN Old French *jurnal*, *jornal* (mod. *journal*), use as noun of *journal* adjective, for earlier *jornel* from late Latin *diurnalis* DIURNAL.]
▸ **A** *noun.* **I** A book, a record.
†**1** ECCLESIASTICAL. = DIURNAL *noun* 1. LME–M16.
†**2** **a** A book containing information for travellers, esp. concerning the daily stages of a route; an itinerary. LME–E17. ▸**b** A record of travel. Long *obsolete* exc. as in senses 6, 7 below. E17.
3 BOOKKEEPING. A daily record of commercial transactions entered as they occur, esp. with statements of the accounts to which each is to be debited and credited. L15.
†**4** A record of public events or public transactions noted down as they occur. M16–L17.
5 ***the Journals***, a record of the daily proceedings in the Houses of Parliament, kept by the Clerk of the House. M16.
6 A personal record of events or matters of interest, written up every day or as events occur, usu. in more detail than a diary. E17.

R. P. JHABVALA During my first few months here, I kept a journal so I have some record of my early impressions. C. ACHEBE 'Do you keep a detailed diary of what is happening day to day?' 'I do keep a journal'.

7 NAUTICAL. A log, a logbook. L17.
8 A daily newspaper; any daily publication. Also, a periodical. E18.

B. PYM An article Rupert had .. just written for a journal of which he was editor. E. FEINSTEIN Marina's poetry .. was published in a literary journal.

▸ **II** †**9** A day's travel; a journey. E–M17.
10 *hist.* As much land as can be ploughed in a day. M17.
▸ **III** **11** *techn.* The part of a shaft or axle which rests on the bearings. Also, the bearing itself. E19.
– COMB.: **journal bearing** *techn.* the support at each end of a horizontal shaft or axle; **journal book** a diary; a daybook; **journal box** *techn.* the metal housing of a journal and its bearings; **journal letter** a letter written as a diary.
▸ †**B** *adjective.* **1** Performed, happening, or recurring every day; daily. L16–M17.
2 Of or belonging to a single day; ephemeral. *rare.* Only in L17.
■ **journalet** *noun* (*rare*) a little journal L18.

journal /ˈdʒəːn(ə)l/ *verb trans.* E19.
[ORIGIN from JOURNAL *noun & adjective*.]
1 Record in a journal. E19.
2 *techn.* Provide with or fix as a journal (JOURNAL *noun* 11). L19.

journalese /dʒəːnəˈliːz/ *noun. colloq.* L19.
[ORIGIN from JOURNAL *noun* + -ESE.]
The hackneyed style of language supposedly characteristic of some newspaper writing.

Sunday Express You don't write your essays in journalese—your teachers will correct you.

journalier /ʒurnalje (*pl. same*), dʒəːnəˈlɪə/ *adjective & noun.* As fem. adjective also ***-ière*** /-jɛːr/. E18.
[ORIGIN French, from JOURNAL *noun & adjective*.]
▸ **A** *adjective.* †**1** Of a newspaper: published daily. Only in E18.
2 Changeable, variable. M18.

A. BROOKNER 'She looks very pretty when .. animated and rather plain when she is not.' '*Journalière*, that used to be called.'

▸ **B** *noun*. A newspaper writer, a journalist. **E18.**

journalise *verb* var. of **JOURNALIZE.**

journalism /ˈdʒəːn(ə)lɪz(ə)m/ *noun*. **M19.**
[**ORIGIN** French *journalisme*, formed as **JOURNAL** *noun & adjective*: see **-ISM.**]
The occupation or profession of a journalist; journalistic writing; newspapers and periodicals collectively. See also **PHOTOJOURNALISM.**

Listener For newspapermen throughout the world Washington has always been the Mecca of journalism.

New Journalism: see **NEW** *adjective*.

journalist /ˈdʒəːn(ə)lɪst/ *noun*. **L17.**
[**ORIGIN** formed as **JOURNALISM**: see **-IST.**]
1 A person who earns a living by writing for or editing a newspaper or periodical. Also, a reporter for radio or television. See also **PHOTOJOURNALIST. L17.**

V. GLENDINNING Charles . . had become a staff journalist, contributing under the pen-name of 'Iran'.

2 A person who keeps a journal. Now *rare*. **E18.**
■ **journaˈlistic** *adjective* of, pertaining to, or characteristic of journalists or journalism **E19. journaˈlistically** *adverb* in a journalistic manner; by means or through the medium of newspapers or periodicals: **L19.**

journalize /ˈdʒəːn(ə)lʌɪz/ *verb*. Also **-ise. M18.**
[**ORIGIN** from **JOURNAL** *noun* + **-IZE.**]
1 *verb trans.* Enter in a journal or book for daily accounts; *spec.* in **BOOKKEEPING**, make a journal entry for (a transaction, an account) in which the debit and credit accounts are specified. **M18.**
2 *verb trans. & intrans.* Enter, record, or describe (a thing or an event) in or as in a personal journal. **L18.**

N. HAWTHORNE I would gladly journalize some of my proceedings, and describe things and people. G. GISSING A man who can't journalize . . nowadays inevitably turns to fiction.

■ **journalizer** *noun* **M19.**

J

journey /ˈdʒəːni/ *noun & verb*. **ME.**
[**ORIGIN** Old French *jornee* (mod. *journée* day, day's work or travel) from Proto-Romance var. of Latin *diurnum* daily portion, (in late Latin) day, use as noun of neut. of *diurnus* **DIURNAL.**]
▸ **A** *noun* †**I 1** A day. **ME–M17.**
▸ **II 2** †**a** The distance that can be travelled in a day (as a specific measure usu. estimated at 20 miles, approx. 32 km). **ME–M16.** ▸**b** The portion of a march or expedition actually done in a day. Now *rare* or *obsolete*. **L15.**
3 An act of going from one place to another or of travelling for a specified distance or period of time; a march, a ride, a drive, etc., or a combination of these; an excursion or expedition, esp. to some distance. (Not usu. applied to sea travel: cf. ***voyage***). **ME.** ▸**b** *fig.* The passage through life. **ME.** ▸**c** The travelling of a vehicle along a certain route between two fixed points at a stated time. **M19.**

O. HENRY Ninety miles it was; a six days' journey. E. R. BURROUGHS Within a short journey of the stamping-ground of his tribe. A. BULLOCK His first journey out of the United Kingdom. *Nature* Four journeys to the moon. M. MILNER The journey would be too expensive and I thought I had done enough travelling. **b** DICKENS A quicker journey to the old man, and a swift inheritance to the young one.

†**4** A military expedition, a campaign; occas., any military enterprise, as a siege. **LME–E17.**
▸ **III** A day's work.
5 A day's labour; a certain fixed amount of daily labour; a daily spell of work. *obsolete* exc. *dial.* **ME.**
†**6** A day's fighting; (the day of) a battle. Cf. **DAY** *noun* 10. **ME–E17.**
†**7** A day's activity or business; *gen.* activity, business. **LME–L17.**
8 *techn.* An amount of work done at one time, as in a day. **LME.** ▸**b** The coinage of a certain weight of gold or silver, orig. the amount which could be coined in a day (180.0321 troy ounces of gold or 720 oz of silver). **L16.** ▸**c** **GLASS-MAKING.** A spell of work in which a certain quantity of raw material is converted into glass. **L19.**
9 A set of trams in a colliery. **L19.**
– **COMB.:** **journey-pride** *dial.* excitement or alarm at the prospect of travelling; **journey-proud** *adjective* (*dial.*) excited or alarmed at the prospect of travelling; **journeys accounts** *LAW* (now *hist.*) the number of days (usu. fifteen) after the abatement of a writ within which a new writ might be obtained; **journey-weight** = sense 8b above.
▸ **B** *verb* **I 1** *verb intrans.* Go on or make a journey; travel. **ME.**

J. SYMONS Stanley journeyed up and down between London and Brighton every day. TOLKIEN I have journeyed in this land.

2 *verb trans.* Travel over, traverse. Now *rare*. **M16.**
▸ †**II 3** *verb trans.* *SCOTS LAW*. Remand (a person); postpone (a matter in litigation); adjourn. **L15–E17.**
■ **journeyer** *noun* a person who journeys, a traveller **LME.**

journeyman /ˈdʒəːnɪmən/ *noun*. Pl. **-men. LME.**
[**ORIGIN** from **JOURNEY** *noun* + **MAN** *noun*.]
1 A person who, having served an apprenticeship, is qualified to work in an art, craft, or trade, for daily wages or as the assistant or employee of another; a qualified artisan or mechanic who works for another. **LME.**

Times A number of sugar barges are idle . . because of a strike of 100 journeymen.

2 A person who is not a master of his or her trade or business; a person hired to work for another. Usu. *derog.* **M16.**

HOR. WALPOLE The colouring was worse . . than that of the most errant journeymen to the profession.

3 *ASTRONOMY*. More fully ***journeyman clock***. A secondary clock in an observatory, used in the comparison of primary or standard clocks. **M18.** ▸**b** = ***impulse clock*** s.v. **IMPULSE** *noun*. **E20.**

journeywoman /ˈdʒəːnɪwʊmən/ *noun*. Pl. **-women** /-wɪmɪn/. **M18.**
[**ORIGIN** formed as **JOURNEYMAN** + **WOMAN** *noun*.]
A woman working at a trade for daily wages.

journey-work /ˈdʒəːnɪwəːk/ *noun*. **E17.**
[**ORIGIN** formed as **JOURNEYMAN** + **WORK** *noun*.]
1 Work done for daily wages or for hire; the work of a journeyman. **E17.**
2 Work delegated to a subordinate or done for hire; servile, inferior, or inefficient work. Usu. *derog.* **E17.**

A. C. SWINBURNE The swift impatient journey-work of a rough and ready hand.

journo /ˈdʒəːnəʊ/ *noun*. *slang* (orig. *Austral.*). Pl. **-os. M20.**
[**ORIGIN** Abbreviation of **JOURN(ALIST** + **-O.**]
= **JOURNALIST** 1.

joust /dʒaʊst/ *noun*. Also **just** /dʒʌst/, †**giust. ME.**
[**ORIGIN** Old French *juste*, *jouste* (mod. *joute*), from *juster*: see **JOUST** *verb*.]
hist. A combat between two knights or men-at-arms on horseback with lances; *spec.* such a combat for exercise or sport; a tilt. Also (in *pl.*), a series of such encounters, a tournament.

joust /dʒaʊst/ *verb intrans.* Also **just** /dʒʌst/. **ME.**
[**ORIGIN** Old French *juster*, *jouster* (mod. *jouter*) bring together, unite, engage on horseback from Proto-Romance verb meaning 'approach, come together, meet', from Latin *juxta* near together.]
†**1** Join battle, encounter, engage; *esp.* fight on horseback as a knight or man-at-arms. **ME–M17.**
2 *hist.* Engage in a joust or tournament; run at tilt with lances on horseback. **ME.**
■ **jouster** *noun* **ME. jousting** *noun* fighting or tilting on horseback with a lance; *spec.* a tournament: **ME.**

J'Ouvert /dʒuːˈveɪ/ *noun*. **L20.**
[**ORIGIN** French Creole, from French *jour ouvert* day opened.]
In the Caribbean: the official start of carnival, at dawn on the Monday preceding Lent.

Jove /ˈdʒəʊv/ *noun*. *poet.* **LME.**
[**ORIGIN** Latin *Jovis*, *Jovem*, etc., oblique cases of Old Latin *Jovis*. Cf. **JUPITER.**]
1 The chief of the gods of the ancient Romans. **LME.**
bird of Jove: see **BIRD** *noun*. **by Jove** *colloq.* expr. surprise or approval. ***flower of Jove***: see **FLOWER** *noun*.
2 The planet Jupiter. **LME.**

jovial /ˈdʒəʊvɪəl, -vj(ə)l/ *adjective*. **L16.**
[**ORIGIN** French, from late Latin *jovialis*, formed as **JOVE**: see **-AL**[1].]
†**1** *ASTROLOGY*. Under the influence of Jupiter, said as a natal planet to impart joy and happiness. **L16–M19.**
2 Characterized by mirth, humour, or festivity; convivial. **L16.**

C. MACKENZIE Dr. Maclaren's usually jovial florid face was lined with bad temper. H. WOUK Something infectiously jovial about him, a spark of devilish amusement in his lively blue eyes.

3 Of or pertaining to the planet Jupiter. Now *rare*. **M17.**
■ **joviˈality** *noun* the quality of being jovial; mirth, festivity, conviviality: **E17. jovialize** *verb trans.* make jovial; cause to be jolly: **E17. jovially** *adverb* in a jovial manner; with jollity or mirth: **E17. jovialness** *noun* **M17. jovialty** *noun* (now *rare*) = **JOVIALITY E17.**

Jovian /ˈdʒəʊvɪən/ *adjective & noun*. **M16.**
[**ORIGIN** formed as **JOVE** + **-IAN.**]
▸ **A** *adjective*. **1** Of, pertaining to, or resembling (that of) Jove. **M16.**

V. SACKVILLE-WEST She hated him for his Jovian detachment and superiority. Y. MENUHIN A Jovian figure, . . so immense that a viola in his arms . . seemed no bigger than a violin.

2 *ASTRONOMY*. Of or pertaining to the planet Jupiter; (of a planet) resembling Jupiter, esp. in mass and density; *spec.* designating the four planets Jupiter, Saturn, Uranus, and Neptune in the solar system. **L18.**
▸ **B** *noun*. **1** A person who resembles or imitates Jove. Long *rare*. **L16.**
2 An (imagined) inhabitant of the planet Jupiter. **E20.**

R. BRADBURY The blue-skinned Jovian . . said nothing.

jovicentric /dʒəʊvɪˈsɛntrɪk/ *adjective*. **M19.**
[**ORIGIN** from **JOVE** + **-I-** + **-CENTRIC.**]
ASTRONOMY. Having Jupiter as the centre. Cf. **GEOCENTRIC** *adjective* 2.

Jovinianist /dʒəʊˈvɪnɪənɪst/ *noun*. **M19.**
[**ORIGIN** from medieval Latin *Jovinianus* Jovinian (see below) + **-IST.**]
ECCLESIASTICAL HISTORY. A follower or adherent of Jovinian, a 4th-cent. Milanese monk who denied the superiority of virginity over marriage and the particular merit of abstinence, holding that all forms of Christian living are equally rewarded in heaven.

jow /dʒaʊ/ *noun*. *Scot. & N. English*. **E16.**
[**ORIGIN** Perh. a form of **JOWL** *noun*[4].]
1 A single stroke or pull in the ringing of a bell; the ringing, tolling, or sound of a bell. *Scot.* **E16.**
2 A knock, push. **L18.**

jow /dʒaʊ/ *verb*. *Scot. & N. English*. **E16.**
[**ORIGIN** Perh. a form of **JOWL** *verb*.]
1 *verb trans.* Ring or toll (a bell), esp. without giving a full swing. *Scot.* **E16.** ▸**b** *verb intrans.* Of a bell: toll, ring. **L18.**
2 *verb trans.* Knock, strike, (esp. the head). **E19.**

jowar /dʒaʊˈɑː/ *noun*. Also **jawar. E19.**
[**ORIGIN** Hindi *jauār*, *joār*.]
In the Indian subcontinent: a kind of sorghum, = **DURRA.**

jowari /dʒaʊˈɑːriː/ *noun*. Also **jawari. E19.**
[**ORIGIN** Hindi *jauārī*, *joārī*.]
= **JOWAR.**

jowel /ˈdʒaʊəl/ *noun*. Chiefly *dial.* **E16.**
[**ORIGIN** Uncertain: perh. rel. to French *joualle* yoke, arch, space.]
Orig., a pier of a wooden bridge. Now, the arch or space between adjacent piers of a bridge.

jower /ˈdʒaʊə/ *verb intrans.* *dial. & US local*. **E17.**
[**ORIGIN** Imit.]
Growl; scold; mutter or grumble quietly or unintelligibly.

jowl /dʒaʊl/ *noun*[1]. Also (now *rare*) **jole** /dʒəʊl/, (earlier) †**chavel** & other vars.
[**ORIGIN** Old English *ċeafl* corresp. to Old Saxon *kaflun* (dat. pl.), Flemish *kavel* gum, rel. to Middle High German *kivel*, Dutch *kevel*.]
1 A jawbone; a jaw; *esp.* the lower jaw; in *pl.*, the jaws. **OE.**
†**2** Idle or malicious talk; = **JAW** *noun*[1] 5. **ME–L16.**
3 Either of the cheeks of the face. **M17.**
cheek by jowl: see **CHEEK** *noun*.
– **NOTE:** Forms with *j-* recorded from 16th cent., perh. after **JOWL** *noun*[3]. Cf. **JOWL** *noun*[2].

jowl /dʒaʊl/ *noun*[2]. Also (now *rare*) **jole** /dʒəʊl/ (earlier) †**cholle** & other vars.
[**ORIGIN** Old English *ċeole*, *-u* = Old Saxon, Old High German *kela* (German *Kehle*), throat, gullet.]
The external throat or neck of a person when pendulous or fleshy; the dewlap of a bovine animal; the crop or the wattle of a bird etc.

F. NORRIS His cheek and . . thick neck ran together to form a great, tremulous jowl.

– **NOTE:** Forms with *j-* recorded from 16th cent., perh. after **JOWL** *noun*[3]. Cf. **JOWL** *noun*[1].

jowl /dʒaʊl/ *noun*[3]. Also (now *rare*) **jole** /dʒəʊl/, †**cholle** & other vars. **LME.**
[**ORIGIN** Unknown.]
1 The head of a person or an animal. *obsolete* exc. *dial.* **LME.**
2 *spec.* The head of a fish; the head and shoulders of certain fishes, as the salmon, sturgeon, and ling, as food. **LME.**

jowl /dʒaʊl/ *noun*[4]. Now *dial.* **E16.**
[**ORIGIN** from **JOWL** *verb*.]
1 A bump; a blow, esp. on the head; a knock. **E16.**
2 A single stroke of a bell; the tolling, ringing, or clang of a bell. Cf. **JOW** *noun*. **E19.**

jowl /dʒəʊl/ *verb*. Now *dial.* **LME.**
[**ORIGIN** Perh. from **JOWL** *noun*[3].]
1 *verb trans.* Bump, strike, knock; push. **LME.** ▸**b** Strike (a ball) with a stick. **LME.**
2 *verb trans. & intrans.* (Cause to) toll, knell, or ring slowly. Cf. **JOW** *verb* 1. **L19.**

jowled /dʒaʊld/ *adjective*. **M19.**
[**ORIGIN** from **JOWL** *noun*[1] + **-ED**[2].]
Having jowls or jaws, esp. of a specified kind. Chiefly as 2nd elem. of comb.
fat-jowled, ***grey-jowled***, ***heavy-jowled***, etc.

jowler /ˈdʒaʊlə/ *noun*. *obsolete* exc. *dial.* **L17.**
[**ORIGIN** from **JOWL** *noun*[1] + **-ER**[1].]
A heavy-jawed dog, *esp.* a beagle.

jowlop(p)ed *adjective* var. of **JELLOPED.**

jowly /ˈdʒaʊli/ *adjective*. **L19.**
[**ORIGIN** from **JOWL** *noun*[1] + **-Y**[1].]
Having large or prominent jowls.

P. LIVELY A fattish, jowly face, pointed nose, sharp eyes, grey wig.

joy /dʒɔɪ/ *noun*. **ME.**
[**ORIGIN** Old French *joie*, *joye* (mod. *joie*), from Proto-Romance fem. from Latin *gaudia* pl. of *gaudium* joy, from *gaudere* rejoice.]
1 Vivid pleasure arising from a sense of well-being or satisfaction; exultation; gladness, delight; an instance of this. Also as *interjection*, expr. pleasure, delight, etc. **ME.** ▸**b** The expression of glad feeling; outward rejoicing; mirth. **ME.** ▸**c** Result, satisfaction, success. Usu. in neg. contexts and freq. *iron. colloq.* **M20.**

DAY LEWIS I was . . flooded with incredulous joy like a prisoner . . released after years of solitary confinement. MERLE COLLINS She felt all the joy of the season of spring. **b** WORDSWORTH The valley rings with mirth and joy. **c** P. D. JAMES The lab will get the . . tissue under the microscope, but I don't think you'll get any joy.

2 A pleasurable, happy, or felicitous state or condition; *esp.* the bliss or blessedness of heaven. Also, paradise, heaven. Long *arch. rare.* **ME.**

3 a A source, object, or cause of happiness; a delight. **ME.** ▸**b** A sweetheart, a loved child; darling, beloved. Cf. **JO.** Chiefly *dial.* **E16.**

a *Daily Telegraph* A joy to look at and a great pleasure to use. B. T. BRADFORD Her darling little baby, . . who was the joy of her life.

†**4** Joyful adoring praise and thanksgiving; = **GLORY** *noun* 2. **ME–L15.**

†**5** A jewel. **L16–E19.**

– PHRASES: ***give a person joy (of)***, ***give a person the joy (of)***: see ***wish a person joy (of)*** below. ***joy of a planet*** ASTROLOGY the fact or condition of a planet being in the house where it is most powerful. ***jump for joy***: see **JUMP** *verb*. ***pride and joy***: see **PRIDE** *noun*[1]. STRENGTH ***through joy***. TRAVELLER'S ***joy***. ***wish a person joy (of)***, (*arch.*) ***give a person joy (of)***, †***wish a person the joy (of)***, †***give a person the joy (of)*** (freq. *iron.*) express one's good wishes to a person (on a happy occasion); congratulate (on).

– COMB.: **joy-bells**: rung on a festive occasion; **joy-flight** an aerial joyride; **joy-house** *slang* a brothel; **joy juice** *N. Amer. slang* alcoholic drink; **joypad** an input device for a computer games console which uses buttons to control the motion of an image on the screen; **joy-pop** *slang* (an inhalation or injection of) an illegal drug; **joy-pop** *verb intrans.* (*slang*) inhale or inject an illegal drug; **joy-popper** *slang* an occasional taker of illegal drugs; **joyride** *noun & verb intrans.* (*colloq.*) (go for) a pleasure trip in a car, aeroplane, etc., esp. without the owner's permission; **joyrider** a person who goes on a joyride; **joystick** (**a**) *slang* the control lever of an aeroplane; the controls of a vehicle; (**b**) a small lever that can be moved in either of two dimensions to control a moving image on a television or VDU screen; **joy-wheel** a Ferris wheel.

■ **joyless** *adjective* without joy, cheerless; having or causing no joy: **LME. joylessly** *adverb* **M18. joylessness** *noun* **E17. joysome** *adjective* (*rare*) joyous **E17.**

joy /dʒɔɪ/ *verb*. **ME.**

[ORIGIN Old French *joïr* (mod. *jouir*) from Proto-Romance var. of Latin *gaudere* rejoice.]

†**1** *verb refl.* Experience joy; enjoy oneself; rejoice. **ME–E18.**

2 *verb intrans.* Feel or show joy; be glad; delight, exult. Also foll. by *in*, *to do*. **ME.** ▸**b** ASTROLOGY. Of a planet: be in the house where it is most powerful. Cf. ***joy of a planet*** s.v. **JOY** *noun*. **M17.**

3 *verb trans.* Fill with joy; gladden, give delight to. *arch.* **ME.** ▸†**b** In *pass.* Be delighted; be made joyous. **LME–E18.**

4 *verb trans.* Derive enjoyment from; possess or use with enjoyment; enjoy. Formerly also, have the use or benefit of. *arch.* **ME.**

†**5** *verb trans.* Salute or greet with expressions of joy, welcome, or honour. Formerly also, glorify, extol. **LME–E18.** ▸**b** Give or wish (a person) joy of something; congratulate. (Foll. by *in*, *of*). **L15–E18.**

joyance /ˈdʒɔɪəns/ *noun*. Chiefly *poet.* **L16.**

[ORIGIN from **JOY** *verb* + **-ANCE**.]

1 The feeling or showing of joy; rejoicing; delight; enjoyment. **L16.**

2 Enjoying oneself; (a) festivity, (a) merrymaking. **L16.**

3 Joyous character or quality; delight, charm. **M19.**

■ **joyancy** *noun* the quality or state of being joyous; joyousness: **M19. joyant** *adjective* (*rare*) feeling or showing joy; joyous: **M19.**

Joycean /ˈdʒɔɪsɪən/ *adjective & noun*. **E20.**

[ORIGIN from *Joyce* (see below) + **-AN**.]

▸ **A** *adjective*. Of, pertaining to, or characteristic of the Irish writer James Joyce (1882–1941) or his works. **E20.**

▸ **B** *noun*. An admirer or student of Joyce or his work. **M20.**

joyful /ˈdʒɔɪfʊl, -f(ə)l/ *adjective*. **ME.**

[ORIGIN from **JOY** *noun* + **-FUL**.]

1 Full of joy; having, showing, or expressing joy; elated, glad, delighted. **ME.**

A. ARONSON A medley of emotions, joyful anticipation, fear that the lover may fail to come. D. PRATER She admired . . his uncomplicated manliness and joyful acceptance of all that life had to offer.

O be joyful, **oh be joyful** *slang* alcoholic drink.

2 Causing joy; delightful. **ME.**

JULIETTE HUXLEY The words I heard inspired by the joyful gift of divine love.

■ **joyfully** *adverb* **ME. joyfulness** *noun* **L15.**

joyous /ˈdʒɔɪəs/ *adjective*. **ME.**

[ORIGIN Anglo-Norman, or Old French *joios* (mod. *joyeux*), from *joie* **JOY** *noun*: see **-OUS**.]

1 Having a joyful nature or mood; full of glad feeling; expressive of joy. **ME.**

B. T. BRADFORD She had a joyous, carefree disposition, and laughter sprang readily to her lips.

2 Causing joy; gladdening. **LME.**

■ †**joyousity** *noun* the quality or state of being joyous: **LME–E19. joyously** *adverb* **L15. joyousness** *noun* **M16.**

JP *abbreviation*.

Justice of the Peace.

JPEG /ˈdʒeɪpɛg/ *abbreviation*.

COMPUTING. Joint Photographic Experts Group, a standard format for compressing image files.

Jr *abbreviation*.

Junior.

jt *abbreviation*.

Joint.

Ju /dʒuː/ *adjective*. **E20.**

[ORIGIN Chinese (Wade-Giles) *Ju Chou* Ruzhou: see below.]

Designating a type of Chinese pottery with buff body and blue-green glaze produced in Ruzhou, in Henan province, in the 12th cent.

jua kali /dʒʊə ˈkali/ *noun phr.* **L20.**

[ORIGIN Kiswahili, lit. 'hot sun', referring to the outdoor nature of the work.]

In Kenya: small-scale craft or artisanal work, such as making textiles, bicycle repair, etc.

juba /ˈdʒuːbə/ *noun*. *US.* **M19.**

[ORIGIN Unknown.]

A kind of dance originating among plantation slaves of the southern US, accompanied by clapping of the hands, patting of the knees and thighs, striking of the feet on the floor, and a refrain in which the word *juba* is frequently repeated.

jubba /ˈdʒʌbə, ˈdʒʊbə/ *noun*. Also **-ah**. **M16.**

[ORIGIN Arabic, whence also French **JUPE**: see also **JIBBA**.]

A type of long open cloth coat with wide sleeves, worn esp. by Muslims.

jube /ˈdʒuːbi/ *noun*[1]. **E18.**

[ORIGIN French *jubé* from Latin *jube* imper. of *jubere* bid, order, first word of the formula *Jube, domine, benedicere* Sir, bid a blessing, addressed by a deacon to a celebrant before the reading of the Gospel, which in some places was done from a church's rood loft.]

ECCLESIASTICAL. †**1** A chair in a church for the preacher. Only in **E18.**

2 A rood loft or screen and gallery dividing the choir of a church from the nave. **M18.**

jube /dʒuːb/ *noun*[2]. Also **joub**. **E18.**

[ORIGIN Persian *jūb*.]

In Iranian cities, an open watercourse.

jube /dʒuːb/ *noun*[3]. *colloq.* (esp. *Austral. & NZ*). **M20.**

[ORIGIN Abbreviation.]

= **JUJUBE** 2.

jubilance /ˈjuːbɪl(ə)ns/ *noun*. **M19.**

[ORIGIN from **JUBILANT** + **-ANCE**.]

Great joy, exulting gladness.

■ **jubilancy** *noun* **L19.**

jubilant /ˈdʒuːbɪl(ə)nt/ *adjective*. **M17.**

[ORIGIN Latin *jubilant-* pres. ppl stem of *jubilare* **JUBILATE** *verb*: see **-ANT**[1].]

Making a joyful noise, rejoicing with songs and acclamations. Now usu., making demonstrations of joy, exultingly glad; expressing or manifesting joy.

E. JONES He . . wrote a jubilant letter as if all the difficulties in his career had now been overcome. J. G. FARRELL Mrs. Rice . . was still flushed and jubilant over her victory.

■ **jubilantly** *adverb* **M19.**

jubilarian /dʒuːbɪˈlɛːrɪən/ *noun*. **L18.**

[ORIGIN from medieval Latin *jubilarius* pertaining to a jubilee + **-AN**.]

A person who celebrates his or her jubilee; *spec.* (ROMAN CATHOLIC CHURCH), a priest, monk, or nun who has been such for fifty years.

jubilate /dʒuːbɪˈleɪti, juːbɪˈlaːteɪ/ *noun*. **ME.**

[ORIGIN from Latin = shout for joy!, imper. of *jubilare*: see **JUBILATE** *verb*.]

1 More fully ***jubilate deo*** /ˈdiːəʊ, ˈdeɪəʊ/. Psalm 100 (99 in the Vulgate), used as a canticle in the Anglican service of matins; a musical setting of this. **ME.**

2 A call to rejoice; an outburst of joyous triumph. **M18.**

3 ROMAN CATHOLIC CHURCH. The third Sunday after Easter, so called because Psalm 66 (65 in the Vulgate), which in Latin begins with *Jubilate*, was formerly used as the introit on that day. **E20.**

jubilate /ˈdʒuːbɪleɪt/ *verb*. **E17.**

[ORIGIN Latin *jubilat-* pa. ppl stem of *jubilare* (rustic word) call, halloo, (in Chr. writers) shout for joy: see **-ATE**[3].]

†**1** *verb trans.* Make glad. Only in **E17.**

2 *verb intrans.* Utter sounds of joy or exultation; make demonstrations of joy; rejoice, exult. **M17.**

M. MEAD We jubilate over birth and dance at weddings.

jubilation /dʒuːbɪˈleɪʃ(ə)n/ *noun*. **LME.**

[ORIGIN Latin *jubilatio(n-)*, formed as **JUBILATE** *verb*: see **-ATION**.]

Loud utterance of joy, exultation, (public) rejoicing; an expression of exultant joy.

C. R. LOW The jubilations of the garrison were short-lived. R. K. NARAYAN At the Harvest Festival the usual jubilation was absent.

jubilean /dʒuːbɪˈliːən/ *adjective*. **E17.**

[ORIGIN from **JUBILEE** + **-AN**.]

Of or pertaining to a jubilee.

jubilee /ˈdʒuːbɪliː/ *noun*. **LME.**

[ORIGIN Old French & mod. French *jubilé* from ecclesiastical Latin *jubilaeus* (sc. *annus* year) (with assim. to *jubilare* **JUBILATE** *verb*) from ecclesiastical Greek *iōbēlaios*, from *iōbēlos* from Hebrew *yōḇēl* jubilee, orig. ram, (hence) ram's horn, with which the jubilee year was proclaimed.]

1 More fully ***year of jubilee***. A year of emancipation and restoration, according to Mosaic law (*Leviticus* 25) to be kept every 50 years, during which Hebrew slaves were to be set free, and lands and houses were to revert to their former owners. **LME.** ▸**b** *transf. & fig.* A time of restitution, remission, or release. **L16.**

2 ROMAN CATHOLIC CHURCH. A period of remission from the penal consequences of sin, granted under certain conditions for a year, usu. at intervals of 25 years. **LME.**

3 Orig., the fiftieth anniversary of an event; the celebration of the completion of 50 years of reign, activity, or continuance in a particular condition etc.; = ***golden jubilee*** s.v. **GOLDEN** *adjective*. Now (freq. with specifying word), a similar anniversary of any round number of years (*rare* before **19**). **LME.** ▸†**b** A period of 50 years. **M17–E18.**

diamond jubilee: see **DIAMOND** *noun & adjective*. ***iron jubilee***: see **IRON** *noun & adjective*. ***silver jubilee***: see **SILVER** *noun & adjective*.

4 A season or occasion of joyful celebration or general rejoicing. **LME.**

5 Exultant joy, general or public rejoicing, jubilation. **E16.** ▸**b** Shouting; joyful shouting; sound of jubilation. **M16.** ▸**c** A black American folk song of an optimistic and joyful kind, often having a religious basis. **L19.**

jubilize /ˈdʒuːbɪlʌɪz/ *verb intrans.* Now *rare*. Also **-ise**. **M17.**

[ORIGIN from Latin *jubilare* **JUBILATE** *verb* + **-IZE**.]

= **JUBILATE** *verb* 2.

juck /dʒʌk/ *verb intrans.* Also **juke** /dʒuːk/. **E17.**

[ORIGIN Imit. (cf. **CHUCK** *verb*[1]), but perh. orig. transf. use of **JUG** *verb*[3].]

Of a partridge: make its characteristic sound or call.

jucundity /dʒəˈkʌndɪti/ *noun*. Now *rare* or *obsolete*. **M16.**

[ORIGIN Latin *jucunditat-*, from *jucundus* **JOCUND**: see **-ITY**.]

= **JOCUNDITY**.

Jud. *abbreviation*.

Judith (Apocrypha).

Judaean /dʒuːˈdiːən/ *noun & adjective*. Also ***Judean**. **M17.**

[ORIGIN from Latin *Judaeus* from Greek *Ioudaios*, from *Ioudaia* Judaea (see below): see **-AN**.]

▸ **A** *noun*. A native or inhabitant of Judaea, the southernmost district of ancient Palestine. **M17.**

▸ **B** *adjective*. Of or pertaining to Judaea. **M19.**

Judaeo- /dʒuːˈdiːəʊ/ *combining form*. Also ***Judeo-**.

[ORIGIN from Latin *Judaeus* Judaean, Jewish: see **JEW** *noun*, **-O-**.]

Forming adjective & noun combs. with the senses 'pertaining to the Jews or Judaism', 'Jewish and —', as ***Judaeo-Arabic***, ***Judaeo-Christian***.

■ **Judaeo-German** *noun & adjective* Yiddish **M19. Judaeophobe** *noun* a person who has a dread or strong dislike of Jews **L19. Judaeo'phobia** *noun* dread or strong dislike of Jews **L19. Judaeo-Spanish** *noun & adjective* Ladino **M19.**

Judahite /ˈdʒuːdəʌɪt/ *adjective & noun*. *hist.* **L19.**

[ORIGIN from *Judah* (see below) + **-ITE**[1].]

▸ **A** *adjective*. Of or pertaining to Judah, an ancient Hebrew tribe and kingdom. **L19.**

▸ **B** *noun*. A member of the tribe, or an inhabitant of the kingdom, of Judah. **E20.**

Judaic /dʒuːˈdeɪɪk/ *adjective*. **E17.**

[ORIGIN Latin *Judaicus* from Greek *Ioudaïkos*, from *Ioudaios* **JEW** *noun*.]

Of or pertaining to the Jews, Jewish; of a Jewish character, characteristic of the Jews.

■ **Judaical** *adjective* = **JUDAIC L15. Judaically** *adverb* **L16.**

Judaise *verb* var. of **JUDAIZE**.

Judaism /ˈdʒuːdeɪɪz(ə)m/ *noun*. **LME.**

[ORIGIN Christian Latin *Judaismus* from Greek *Ioudaïsmos*, from *Ioudaios* **JEW** *noun*: see **-ISM**.]

1 The profession or practice of the Jewish religion; the religion of the Jews, with a belief in one God and a basis in Mosaic and rabbinical teachings. **LME.**

Conservative Judaism: see **CONSERVATIVE** *adjective*. ***Liberal Judaism***: see **LIBERAL** *adjective*.

2 Adoption of Jewish practices on the part of Christians; a practice or cast of thought associated with Jews. **M17.**

3 *hist.* = **JEWRY** 2. Also, in official documents, the revenue derived by the Crown from Jews; the treasury which received this money. **M19.**

■ **Judaist** *noun* a person who follows Jewish practice or ritual; *esp.* (in ECCLESIASTICAL HISTORY) a Jewish Christian of the apostolic age: **M19. Juda'istic** *adjective* of, pertaining to, or characteristic of Judaists **M19.**

Judaize /ˈdʒuːdeɪʌɪz/ *verb*. Also **-ise**. **L16.**

[ORIGIN Christian Latin *judaizare* from Greek *ioudaïzein*, from *Ioudaios* **JEW** *noun*: see **-IZE**.]

1 *verb intrans.* Behave like a Jew; follow Jewish customs or religious rites. **L16.**

2 *verb trans.* Make Jewish; imbue with Jewish doctrines or principles. **M17.**

■ **Judai'zation** *noun* **E19. Judaizer** *noun* a person who Judaizes; *spec.* an early Christian who observed the Mosaic law: **M17.**

J

Judas /ˈdʒuːdəs/ *noun*. In sense 3 now usu. **j-**. **LME**.
[**ORIGIN** *Judas* Iscariot, the disciple who betrayed Jesus: see **JESUS** *noun*.]
1 A person who treacherously betrays another under the semblance of friendship; a traitor or betrayer of the worst kind. Cf. **ISCARIOT**. **LME**.
2 More fully ***Judas of the paschal***. A tall piece of wood, painted like a candle, which rose from the central branch of the seven-branched paschal candlestick and at Easter was surmounted by the paschal candle of wax. *obsolete* exc. *hist*. **LME**.
3 More fully ***judas hole***, ***judas window***. A small aperture in a door (in some old houses, or in prison cells), through which a person can look without being noticed from the other side; a peephole. **M19**.
– **COMB.**: **Judas-colour**, **Judas-coloured** *adjective* (of the hair or beard) red (from the medieval belief that Judas Iscariot had red hair and beard); **Judas goat** an animal used to lead others to destruction; ***judas hole***: see sense 3 above; **Judas kiss** an act of betrayal (*Matthew* 26:48); **Judas priest** *interjection* alt. of *Jesus Christ* in an oath; **Judas tree** a leguminous tree of southern Europe, *Cercis siliquastrum*, with abundant purple flowers which appear in spring before the leaves; any of several other trees of this genus; ***judas window***: see sense 3 above.

judcock /ˈdʒʌdkɒk/ *noun*. **E17**.
[**ORIGIN** App. from *judge-cock*, with allus. to its black crown.]
= ***jacksnipe*** s.v. **JACK** *noun*[1].

judder /ˈdʒʌdə/ *verb & noun*. **M20**.
[**ORIGIN** Imit.: cf. **SHUDDER** *verb*.]
▸ **A** *verb intrans*. (Esp. of a mechanism) shake or vibrate violently; (of the voice in singing) oscillate between greater and less intensity. **M20**.

> G. **JOSIPOVICI** When one turns the hot water off the whole house jars and judders.

▸ **B** *noun*. An instance of juddering; the condition of juddering. **M20**.

Judean *noun & adjective* see **JUDAEAN**.

Judenrat /ˈjuːd(ə)nraːt/ *noun*. Pl. ***-e*** /-ə/. **M20**.
[**ORIGIN** German = Jewish council.]
A council representing a Jewish community in a locality controlled by the Germans during the Second World War.

judenrein /ˈjuːd(ə)nrʌɪn/ *adjective*. **M20**.
[**ORIGIN** German = free from Jews.]
Of a society, organization, etc., *spec*. in Nazi Germany: without Jewish members, out of which Jews have been expelled.

> C. **ROTH** The survivors . . were . . sent to the death camps, Warsaw being now *judenrein*.

Judeo- *combining form* see **JUDAEO-**.

Judg. *abbreviation*.
Judges (in the Bible).

judge /dʒʌdʒ/ *noun*. **ME**.
[**ORIGIN** Old French & mod. French *juge* from Latin *judic-*, *judex*, from *jus* right, law + *-dicus* saying, speaking.]
1 A public officer appointed to administer the law; a person (now only a qualified lawyer) who has authority to hear and try cases in a court of justice. **ME**.

> C. **ISHERWOOD** It is the voice of a judge, summing up and charging the jury.

2 God or Christ regarded as the supreme arbiter at the Last Judgement. **ME**.
3 In ancient Israel in the period between Joshua and the kings: an officer (usu. a leader in war) invested with temporary authority. In *pl*. (treated as *sing*.) (**J-**), the Book of Judges, a book of the Old Testament and Hebrew Scriptures, containing the history of the period of the judges. **LME**.
4 A person appointed to decide in any contest, competition, or dispute; an arbiter, an umpire. **LME**.

> **JOSEPH PARKER** No blind man will be appointed as a judge of pictures in the Academy.

5 A person who or thing which judges of or decides anything in question. Freq. in ***be judge***, form an opinion, give a decision. **LME**.

> C. **MACKENZIE** He must be the judge of the best moment to make his announcement.

6 A person qualified to form or pronounce an opinion; one capable of judging or estimating. **M16**.

> J. A. **MICHENER** My daughter was a better judge of men than I was.

7 *ANGLING*. A kind of artificial fly. **M19**.
– **PHRASES**: **as God is my judge**: emphasizing the truth of one's assertion. ***be judge***: see sense 5 above. ***circuit judge***: see **CIRCUIT** *noun*. **judge advocate** a barrister who advises a court martial on points of law and sums up the case. **Judge Advocate General** a civil officer in supreme control of courts martial in the army or air force. ***judge and warrant***: see **WARRANT** *noun*[1]. ***Judge Ordinary***: see **ORDINARY** *adjective*. ***Judges' lodgings***: see **LODGING** 4c. ***judge's marshal***: see **MARSHAL** *noun*[1] 4b. **Judges' Rules** *ENGLISH LAW* (now *hist*.) rules drawn up by the Queen's Bench regarding the admissibility of the accused's statements as evidence. ***red judge***: see **RED** *adjective*. ***salute the judge***: see **SALUTE** *verb*. ***sober as a judge***: see **SOBER** *adjective*.
– **COMB.**: **judge-made** *adjective* (of law) constituted by judicial decisions.
▪ **judgelike** *adjective & adverb* (***a***) *adjective* resembling a judge, appropriate to a judge; (***b***) *adverb* in the manner of a judge: **M17**.

judge /dʒʌdʒ/ *verb*. **ME**.
[**ORIGIN** Old French *jugier*, later & mod. *juger*, from Latin *judicare*, from *judex*: see **JUDGE** *noun*.]
▸ **I** *verb trans*. **1** Try, or pronounce sentence on (a person) in a court of justice; sit in judgement on. **ME**.

> M. **WEST** Christ will come a second time, in glory, to judge the living and the dead.

†**2** *spec*. Pronounce sentence against (a person); sentence, condemn. Foll. by *to* a penalty, *to do*, *to suffer*. **ME–L17**.

> **BACON** Some whose offences are pilfring . . they judge to be whipped.

3 Decide judicially or authoritatively *that*, *who*, etc.; order judicially (a person) *to do*. **ME**.

> *Grimsby Gazette* The referee judged that Palace goalkeeper George Wood had carried the ball beyond the line.

4 Form an opinion about (a thing) so as to arrive at a correct notion of it; estimate, appraise. **ME**.

> E. **WELTY** Bowman, who . . judged a woman's age on sight, set her age at fifty. E. **AMADI** You can only judge people by what they say and do.

5 a Foll. by obj. clause: form the opinion, hold as an opinion; come to a conclusion, infer; think, consider, suppose. **ME**. ▸**b** Infer, conclude, or suppose (a person or thing) to be or *to be*. **ME**.

> **a** P. **BOWLES** Madame . . judged that the right moment for intervention had arrived. G. **GREENE** I played the scene . . over again in my mind trying to judge whether any irrevocable words had been spoken. **b** B. **MARTIN** They judge the Moon to be a Globe like our Earth. J. **KRANTZ** Vito judged the time ripe to break the silence.

6 Govern or rule (a country), esp. (*hist*.) as a judge in ancient Israel. **LME**.
7 Assign or award by judgement; adjudge. Now *rare* or *obsolete*. **LME**.
8 Declare or pronounce authoritatively (a person) to be or *to be*. Also foll. by *for*. Now *rare*. **LME**.

> *Stock & Land (Melbourne)* A two-year-old red bull . . was judged champion.

9 Pronounce an opinion on, criticize; *esp*. pronounce an adverse opinion on, condemn, censure. **LME**.

> J. M. **ROBERTS** He judged it in terms very like those of a Jewish prophet.

10 Give sentence concerning (a matter); try (a case); determine, decide, (a question). **E16**.
▸ **II** *verb intrans*. **11** *hist*. In ancient Israel: exercise the functions of a judge. **ME**.
12 Act as judge; try a case and pronounce a sentence in a court of justice. Also, pronounce a critical opinion. **LME**.

> A. **MUNRO** People are dead now . . . It isn't up to us to judge.

13 Give a decision or opinion on any matter, esp. between contending parties; arbitrate. **LME**.

> **BROWNING** God must judge 'twixt man and me.

14 Form an (esp. correct) opinion of or *of* a thing (*from* or *by* data); make up one's mind as to the truth of a matter. Also (*LOGIC*), make a mental assertion or statement. **LME**.

> J. **TYNDALL** From its form and colour he could . . judge of its condition. L. **DURRELL** The others are already asleep to judge by the heavy snoring. M. **COX** Judging from his letters home, Monty was in good spirits.

judgematic /dʒʌdʒˈmatɪk/ *adjective*. *colloq*. Now *rare*. Also **judgmatic**. **M19**.
[**ORIGIN** formed as **JUDGEMATICAL**.]
= **JUDGEMATICAL**.

judgematical /dʒʌdʒˈmatɪk(ə)l/ *adjective*. *colloq*. Now *rare*. Also **judgmat-**. **L18**.
[**ORIGIN** Irreg. from **JUDGE** *noun*, *verb* + *-matic* after *dogmatic*: see **-ICAL**, **-AL**[1].]
Characterized by good practical judgement; judicious, discerning. Also, behaving like a judge, judicial.
▪ **judgematically** *adverb* **E19**.

judgement /ˈdʒʌdʒm(ə)nt/ *noun*. Also (esp. *LAW* & *N. Amer*.) **judgment**. **ME**.
[**ORIGIN** Old French & mod. French *jugement*, from *juger*: see **JUDGE** *verb*, **-MENT**.]
1 The action of trying a cause in a court of justice; trial. Now *rare*. **ME**.

> B. **GELDOF** Adult men making stern accusations stood in judgement of a frightened 11-year-old boy.

2 In full ***Last Judgement***. In some faiths: the judgement of humankind by God expected to take place at the end of the world, when each is rewarded or punished according to his or her merits. **ME**.

> G. **GORER** The soul survives after the death of the body and comes to Judgment.

3 The sentence of a court of justice; a judicial decision or order in court. **ME**. ▸**b** *LAW*. An assignment of chattels or chattel interests made by judgement or decree of court; the certificate of such judgement as a security or form of property. Cf. ***judgement-debt*** below. **L17**.

> *Holiday Which?* This judgment will be used as a guideline in future claims for holiday compensation.

4 A divine sentence or decision; *spec*. (now freq. *joc*.) a misfortune or calamity regarded as a divine punishment or as a token of divine displeasure. **ME**.

> J. **WAIN** The 'plane crash had been a judgement on the parents for wickedness.

5 Any formal or authoritative pronouncement, as of an umpire or arbiter. Now *rare*. **ME**.

> J. **RULE** David accepted the teacher's judgement that being left-handed was babyish!

6 The pronouncing of a deliberate (esp. adverse or critical) opinion on a person or thing; an opinion so pronounced. **ME**.

> A. J. **CRONIN** Her sense of justice . . detected in the review . . a note of prejudice, a judgment of the man rather than the artist.

7 In biblical translations: (***a***) justice, righteousness (= **DOOM** *noun*[1] 4); (***b***) a divine decree or ordinance; (***c***) a sentence or decision in a person's favour; (one's) right. **LME**.

> **COVERDALE** *Ps*. 119:30 I have chosen the way of treuth, thy iudgmentes haue I layed before me. AV *Isa*. 61:8 For I the Lord loue Iudgement, I hate robbery for burnt offering. AV *Deut*. 10:18 He doeth execute the iudgement of the fatherlesse, and widow.

8 The formation of an opinion or notion concerning something by exercising the mind on it; an opinion, an estimate. **LME**.

> *Times* In his judgment they . . had no occasion to bow down to any one. *Southern Rag* This is a much more difficult judgement to make.

9 The function of the mind by which it arrives at a notion of a thing; the critical faculty. **M16**. ▸**b** Good judgement; discernment. **L16**. ▸†**c** A person having (good) judgement. Only in **17**. ▸**d** Reason, senses, wits. *Scot*. **E19**.

> D. **FRANCIS** Take the horses . . and use your own judgement about whether to canter. J. **HELLER** He shows poor judgment in colors and styles. R. **DAVIES** He was a man whose enthusiasms sometimes outran his judgement. **b** *Sunday Times* The biographer's gifts—balance, judgement, accuracy—are just the ones Wilde . . ridiculed. **c** **SIR** T. **BROWNE** To undervalue a solid Judgment, because he knows not the genealogy of Hector.

10 *LOGIC*. The action of predicating or mentally apprehending the relation between two objects of thought; a proposition, as formed in the mind. **E18**.
– **PHRASES**: **against one's better judgement** contrary to what one knows to be wiser or more desirable. ***arrest of judgement***: see **ARREST** *noun*. **Day of Judgement** the day on which the Last Judgement is believed to take place, doomsday. ***judgement by default***: see **DEFAULT** *noun*. ***Last Judgement***: see sense 2 above. **private judgement** the formation of personal or individual opinion (esp. in religious matters), as opp. to the acceptance of a statement or doctrine on authority. **sit in judgement** preside as a judge at a trial; pass judgement (*up*)*on* a person (with an assumption of superiority).
– **COMB.**: **judgement creditor** a creditor in whose favour a judgement has been given ordering the payment of the debt due; **Judgement Day** = ***Day of Judgement*** above; **judgement debt** a debt for the payment of which a judgement has been given; **judgement debtor**: against whom a judgement ordering payment has been given; **judgement hall** (chiefly *hist*.) a public building in which trials at law are held; **judgement note** *US* a promissory note containing a power of attorney to enter judgement and take out execution ex parte if the debtor defaults; **judgement seat** a seat on which a judge sits when trying a cause or pronouncing judgement; a tribunal; **judgement summons**: issued in a County Court against a person who has failed to pay a judgement debt.
– **NOTE**: The spelling *judgment* is conventional in legal contexts and in North American English.
▪ **judgemented** *adjective* (as 2nd elem. of comb. or with preceding adverb) having judgement or discernment of a specified kind **M16**.

judgemental /dʒʌdʒˈmɛnt(ə)l/ *adjective*. Also **judgmental**. **E20**.
[**ORIGIN** from **JUDGEMENT** + **-AL**[1].]
Involving the exercise of judgement; inclined to make moral judgements.
▪ **judgementally** *adverb* **L20**.

judger /ˈdʒʌdʒə/ *noun*. **LME**.
[**ORIGIN** from **JUDGE** *verb* + **-ER**[1].]
A person who or thing which judges, a judge; *esp*. a person who forms, or who is (well or ill) qualified to form, an opinion.

judgeship /ˈdʒʌdʒʃɪp/ *noun*. **L17**.
[**ORIGIN** from **JUDGE** *noun* + **-SHIP**.]
The office of judge, the function of a judge.

judgess /ˈdʒʌdʒɪs/ *noun*. Now *rare*. **M16**.
[**ORIGIN** from **JUDGE** *noun* + **-ESS**[1].]
A female judge; a woman who judges.

judging /ˈdʒʌdʒɪŋ/ *ppl adjective*. **L16**.
[**ORIGIN** from **JUDGE** *verb* + **-ING**[2].]
That has the function of judging, judicial; *spec*. able to judge, judicious, discerning. Also, censorious.

■ **judgingly** *adverb* M17.

judgmatic, **judgmatical** *adjectives* vars. of JUDGEMATIC, JUDGEMATICAL.

judgment *noun* see JUDGEMENT.

judgmental *adjective* var. of JUDGEMENTAL.

judication /dʒuːdɪˈkeɪʃ(ə)n/ *noun.* E17.
[ORIGIN Latin *judicatio(n-)*, from *judicat-* pa. ppl stem of *judicare* JUDGE *verb*: see -ATION.]
The action of judging; judgement.

judicative /ˈdʒuːdɪkətɪv/ *adjective.* LME.
[ORIGIN medieval Latin *judicativus*, from Latin *judicat-*: see JUDICATION, -ATIVE.]
Having the function of trying causes or passing sentences; judicial, juridical.

judicator /ˈdʒuːdɪkeɪtə/ *noun.* M18.
[ORIGIN Late Latin, from Latin *judicat-*: see JUDICATION, -ATOR.]
A person who judges, a person who acts as a judge.

judicatory /ˈdʒuːdɪkət(ə)ri, dʒʊˈdɪkət(ə)ri/ *noun.* L16.
[ORIGIN Late Latin *judicatorium* (glossing Greek *dikastērion*), formed as JUDICATOR: see -ORY[1]. In sense 2 from medieval Latin *judicatorium* in same sense (cf. French †*judicatoire* noun).]
1 A court of judicature; a body having judicial authority; a tribunal. Now chiefly *Scot.* (esp. in *ECCLESIASTICAL LAW*). L16.
2 Judicature; a system of judicature. L16.

judicatory /ˈdʒuːdɪkət(ə)ri, dʒʊˈdɪkət(ə)ri/ *adjective.* Now *rare* or *obsolete.* E17.
[ORIGIN Late (eccl.) Latin *judicatorius*, formed as JUDICATOR: see -ORY[2].]
Having the function of judging or passing sentence; of or pertaining to judgement.

judicature /ˈdʒuːdɪkətʃə, dʒʊˈdɪk-/ *noun.* M16.
[ORIGIN medieval Latin *judicatura*, from Latin *judicat-*: see JUDICATION, -URE.]
1 The action of judging; administration of justice by duly constituted courts; judicial process. Freq. in ***court of judicature***. M16.
Supreme Court of Judicature the court constituted by Acts of Parliament in 1873 and 1875, which united the former separate Courts of Chancery, King's or Queen's Bench, Common Pleas, Exchequer, Admiralty, etc. (since 2005 officially called the ***Senior Courts of England and Wales***).
2 The office, function, or authority of a judge. M16.
3 = JUDICIARY *noun* 2. L16.

RICHARD WATSON If the witnesses of the resurrection had been examined before any judicature.

†**4** *fig.* Mental judgement; formation or authoritative expression of opinion; criticism. M17–M18.
– COMB.: **Judicature Acts** the statutes establishing the Supreme Court of Judicature, and regulating its practice.

judicial /dʒʊˈdɪʃ(ə)l/ *adjective & noun.* LME.
[ORIGIN Latin *judicialis*, from *judicium* legal proceedings, tribunal, judgement, from *judic-*, *judex* JUDGE *noun*: see -IAL.]
► **A** *adjective.* **1** Of or pertaining to proceedings in a court of law; of or pertaining to the administration of justice; resulting from or fixed by a judgement in court. LME. ►**b** Of law: enforced by secular judges and tribunals. Opp. ***ceremonial***, ***moral***. M16. ►**c** *THEOLOGY.* Inflicted by God as a judgement or punishment; of the nature of a divine judgement. E17.

G. M. TREVELYAN Administrative and judicial authority still rested with the gentlemen Justices of the Peace. **c** LD MACAULAY An infatuation such as, in a more simple age, would have been called judicial.

2 a Pertaining to the judgement of the reputed influence of the celestial objects on human affairs. Chiefly in ***judicial astrology*** s.v. ASTROLOGY 2. LME. ►†**b** *MEDICINE.* = CRITICAL 1. M16–M17. ►**c** Giving judgement or a decision on a matter; disposed to pass judgement, critical. L16.

c R. W. EMERSON The intercourse of society . . is one wide, judicial investigation of character.

3 That has or shows sound judgement; judicious. Now *rare.* L15.

C. C. TRENCH Many a country gentleman restored his depleted fortunes by a judicial alliance.

4 Having the function of judgement; invested with authority to judge causes. M16.

H. COX Parliaments were originally judicial as well as legislative assemblies.

5 Of a judge; proper to a judge. E19.
– PHRASES & SPECIAL COLLOCATIONS: **judicial combat** *hist.* a combat engaged in to decide a controversy. **Judicial Committee of the Privy Council**: established in 1832 for the disposal of appeals made to the King or Queen in Council, chiefly from courts in dependent countries. **judicial duel** *hist.* a duel engaged in to decide a controversy. **judicial factor** *SCOTS LAW* a factor appointed by the Court of Session or the sheriff court to administer the estate of another. **judicial murder** an unjust, though legal, death sentence or execution. **judicial review** a procedure by which a judicial body may pronounce on the validity of an act of legislature (in the US) or a decision of an inferior court or public authority (in the UK). ***judicial separation***: see SEPARATION 5. ***judicial torture***: see TORTURE *noun.*
► †**B** *noun.* **1** A judicial law or ordinance. LME–E18.
2 A determination, a decision, a judgement. LME–M17. ►**b** *ASTROLOGY.* A determination as to a future event from the positions of celestial objects; the system of such determinations. L15–M17.
3 A legal judgement. M16–M17.
■ **judiciˈality** *noun* the quality or character of being judicial M19. **judicialize** *verb trans.* make judicial; treat judicially, arrive at a judgement or decision on: L19. **judicially** *adverb* LME.

judiciary /dʒʊˈdɪʃ(ə)ri/ *adjective & noun.* LME.
[ORIGIN Latin *judiciarius*, from *judicium*: see JUDICIAL, -ARY[1].]
► **A** *adjective.* **1** = JUDICIAL *adjective* 1. Now *rare.* LME.
†**2** = JUDICIAL *adjective* 2a. Also, pertaining to the giving of judgements or decisions by any kind of divination, as physiognomy. L16–M18.
†**3** = JUDICIAL *adjective* 4. L17–E19.
judiciary combat *hist.* = ***judicial combat*** s.v. JUDICIAL *adjective.*
► **B** *noun.* †**1** Divination as an art; judicial astrology. Also, a judicial astrologer. L16–M17.
2 A body of judges or people having judicial power; a court of justice; a legal tribunal; judges or legal tribunals collectively. E19.

Daily Telegraph Separation of powers between the legislature, the executive and the judiciary.

judicious /dʒʊˈdɪʃəs/ *adjective.* L16.
[ORIGIN from French *judicieux*, from Latin *judicium* (whence French †*judice*): see JUDICIAL, -OUS.]
1 Of a person, the faculties etc.: having or exercising sound judgement; discreet, wise, sensible. Now *esp.* (***a***) sensible in relation to practical matters; wise in adapting means to ends; capable and careful in action, prudent; (***b***) sensible in intellectual matters; sound in discernment. L16.

A. COLLINS One of the most Judicious of Interpreters, the great Grotius. J. A. MICHENER A judicious administrator who found personal pleasure when his fields produced more wheat.

2 Of action, thought, etc.: proceeding from or showing sound judgement (esp. in practical matters); marked by discretion, wisdom, or good sense. L16.

M. DRABBLE Popularity had been cheaply purchased by the judicious distribution of . . jelly cubes. A. GHOSH A judicious mixture of practical and theoretical knowledge.

†**3** = JUDICIAL *adjective* 1. E–M17.
■ **judiciously** *adverb* E17. **judiciousness** *noun* M17.

judo /ˈdʒuːdəʊ/ *noun.* L19.
[ORIGIN Japanese, from *jū* gentle + *dō* way.]
A refined form of ju-jitsu using principles of movement and balance, practised as a sport or a form of physical exercise.
■ **judoist** *noun* a person who practises or is expert in judo M20. **judoka** /ˈdʒuːdəʊkə/ *noun*, pl. **-s**, same, = JUDOIST M20.

Judy /ˈdʒuːdi/ *noun. slang.* E19.
[ORIGIN Pet form of female forename *Judith*, orig. with ref. to the wife of Punch in Punch-and-Judy shows.]
A woman, a girl. Formerly also *spec.*, a woman of ridiculous appearance.
Punch-and-Judy show: see PUNCH *noun*[4] 3.

†**juffer** *noun.* L17–E19.
[ORIGIN Dutch, lit. 'young woman': see YUFFROUW.]
A piece of timber about 12 cm (4¾ inches) square.

jug /dʒʌg/ *noun*[1]. Now *rare.* M16.
[ORIGIN Pet form of female forenames *Joan*, *Joanna*, *Jenny*.]
1 A plain woman; a maidservant; a mistress or girlfriend; a prostitute. M16.
2 In local names of small birds: ***bank-jug***, the chiffchaff; ***hedge-jug***, the long-tailed tit. L19.

jug /dʒʌg/ *noun*[2]. M16.
[ORIGIN Prob. spec. use of JUG *noun*[1].]
1 A deep vessel for holding liquids, usu. with a cylindrical, tapering, or swelling body, having a handle and often a spout or lip for pouring. Also *US*, a large jar with a narrow mouth. M16. ►**b** A jug used as a wind or rhythm instrument in a jazz or folk group. M20.

L. MACNEICE Poured water from the jug into the cup.

beer jug, ***milk jug***, ***toby jug***, etc.
2 A jug with its contents; the liquid in a jug. M17.

H. ALLEN Debrülle now opened small brown jugs of Asti Spumante.

3 (A) prison, (a) jail. Also more fully ***stone-jug***. *slang.* L18.

D. FRANCIS Just out of jug, he is.

4 A bank. *slang.* M19.
5 In *pl.* A woman's breasts. *slang* (chiefly *N. Amer.*). M20.
– COMB.: **jug-and-bottle** *adjective* (*arch.*) designating a bar of a public house at which alcoholic liquors are sold for consumption off the premises; **jug band** a jazz or folk band in which jugs are used as instruments; **jug handle** (***a***) the handle of a jug; (***b***) a secure hold for climbing, cut into rock; **jug-handle** *adjective* shaped like a jug handle; **jug-handled** *adjective* (***a***) placed on one side, as the handle of a jug; (***b***) *fig.* (*US*) one-sided, unbalanced. **jughead** *slang* (chiefly *US*), *derog.* a foolish or stupid person or animal (esp. a horse, a mule, etc.); **jug kettle** a tall kettle resembling a jug with a lid.
■ **juglet** *noun* a small jug-shaped vessel M20.

jug /dʒʌg/ *noun*[3]. *slang.* E20.
[ORIGIN Abbreviation.]
= JUGGINS.

jug /dʒʌg/ *noun*[4]. Also **jug-jug**. M20.
[ORIGIN Unknown.]
A savoury Barbadian dish made with pork and beef, served esp. at Christmas.

Jug /juːg/ *adjective & noun*[5]. *colloq.* (freq. *derog.*). M20.
[ORIGIN Abbreviation of *Jugoslav*, *Jugoslavian* vars. of YUGOSLAV, YUGOSLAVIAN.]
= YUGOSLAVIAN.

jug /dʒʌg/ *verb*[1]. Infl. **-gg-**. L16.
[ORIGIN from JUG *noun*[2].]
†**1** *verb intrans.* Use a jug; drink. L16–L17.
2 *verb trans.* Stew or boil (esp. a hare or rabbit), orig. in a jug or jar. M18.
jugged hare.
3 *verb trans.* Shut up in jail; imprison; *transf.* confine. *slang.* M19.

S. BELLOW The hotel could jug him for trespassin'.

4 *verb intrans.* Fish with a bait attached to a floating jug. *US.* L19.

jug /dʒʌg/ *verb*[2] *intrans.* Infl. **-gg-**. L16.
[ORIGIN Imit.: cf. JUG *interjection & noun*[6].]
Of a nightingale or (less commonly) other bird: make its characteristic sound or note (resembling 'jug').

jug /dʒʌg/ *verb*[3] *intrans.* Infl. **-gg-**. L16.
[ORIGIN App. a by-form of JOUK *verb*[1] with specialized application. Cf. JUCK *verb*.]
Of partridges etc.: crowd or nestle together on the ground; collect in a covey.

Shooting They fly . . to where they are going to jug for the night.

jug /dʒʌg/ *interjection & noun*[6]. Freq. redupl. **jug-jug**. E16.
[ORIGIN Imit.]
(Repr.) the sound or note made by the nightingale or (less commonly) some other bird.

J

juga *noun* pl. of JUGUM.

jugal /ˈdʒuːg(ə)l/ *adjective & noun.* Now *rare* or *obsolete.* L16.
[ORIGIN Latin *jugalis*, from *jugum* YOKE *noun*[1]: see -AL[1].]
► **A** *adjective.* **1** *ANATOMY.* Of or pertaining to the zygoma or bony arch of the cheek; malar, zygomatic. L16.
2 *ZOOLOGY* (chiefly *ENTOMOLOGY*). Of or pertaining to a jugum. M20.
► **B** *noun. ANATOMY.* The zygomatic bone. M19.

jugate /ˈdʒuːgət/ *adjective.* L19.
[ORIGIN Latin *jugatus* pa. pple of *jugare* join together: see -ATE[2].]
1 *NUMISMATICS.* Placed side by side. L19.
2 *ENTOMOLOGY.* Pertaining to or possessing wings linked by a jugum. L19.

juge d'instruction /ʒyʒ dɛ̃stryksjɔ̃/ *noun phr.* Pl. ***juges d'instruction*** (pronounced same). L19.
[ORIGIN French.]
In France: an examining magistrate, a police magistrate.

Jugendstil /ˈjuːgənt-ʃtiːl/ *noun & adjective.* E20.
[ORIGIN German, from *Jugend* youth (the name of a German magazine started in 1896) + *Stil* style.]
(Of, pertaining to, or designating) German art nouveau.

juger /ˈdʒuːdʒə/ *noun.* Also (earlier) in Latin form †**-erum**, pl. †**-era**. LME.
[ORIGIN Latin *jugerum*.]
An ancient Roman measure of land containing 28,800 (Roman) square feet, equivalent to about a quarter of a hectare (three-fifths of an acre).

juges d'instruction *noun phr.* pl. of JUGE D'INSTRUCTION.

jugful /ˈdʒʌgfʊl, -f(ə)l/ *noun.* M19.
[ORIGIN from JUG *noun*[2] + -FUL.]
As much as a jug will hold.
by a jugful *US slang* by a great deal, by a long way (usu. in neg. contexts).

Juggernaut /ˈdʒʌgənɔːt/ *noun.* In sense 1 also **Jagannath** /ˈjagənɑːθ, ˈjʌ-/. M17.
[ORIGIN Sanskrit *Jagannātha*, from *jagat* world + *nātha* lord, protector.]
1 *HINDU MYTHOLOGY.* A title of Krishna, a pre-eminent avatar of Vishnu; *spec.* the image of this god at Puri in Orissa, annually carried in procession on an enormous cart, under the wheels of which many devotees are said to have formerly thrown themselves to be crushed. M17.
2 *fig.* An institution, practice, or idea to which a person is blindly devoted or ruthlessly sacrificed. M19.

Sailplane & Gliding Misplaced conceptions of national pride, and the whole Olympic bureaucratic Juggernaut.

3 (**j-**.) A large heavy vehicle; *spec.* a large heavy lorry. M19.

D. LODGE Huge concrete highways, vibrating with the thunder of passing juggernauts.

■ **Juggernautish** *adjective* E19.

juggins /ˈdʒʌgɪnz/ *noun. slang.* L19.
[ORIGIN Perh. a use of the surname *Juggins*, from JUG *noun*[1]. Cf. MUGGINS.]
A simpleton, a person easily taken in or imposed upon.

juggle /ˈdʒʌg(ə)l/ *verb & noun*. LME.
[ORIGIN Back-form. from JUGGLER, or from Old French *jogler*, *jug-* from Latin *joculari* to jest, from *joculus* dim. of *jocus* JOKE *noun*.]
▸ **A** *verb*. †**1** *verb intrans*. Amuse or entertain with jesting, buffoonery, tricks, etc. LME–E17.
2 *verb trans*. Deceive, trick, cheat, beguile (*out of*). LME. ▸**b** Bring, convey, or change by magic, conjuring, trickery, or deceit. L16.

J. S. BLACKIE The Spirit of Error . . juggles the plain understandings of men that they become the sport of every quibble. JOHN BRIGHT They have no system of compounding which would juggle men out of their franchise. **b** T. JEFFERSON Our debt was juggled from forty-three up to eighty millions.

3 *verb intrans*. Practise magic or legerdemain; conjure. LME. ▸**b** *verb intrans. & trans*. Perform feats of dexterity (with); *esp*. continuously toss and catch (several objects) so as to keep at least one in the air while handling the others; *fig*. adroitly balance, handle, or manipulate (a thing or several things simultaneously). (Foll. by *with*.) L19.

R. DAVIES He can't juggle and he can't walk rope. J. UPDIKE Van Horne juggled . . five tangerines, his hands a frantic blur. **b** T. C. WOLFE Pearl juggled carefully with the proposals of several young men. A. TYLER She'd been so preoccupied with paying the rent and juggling the budget.

4 *verb intrans. transf. & fig*. Play tricks *with* so as to cheat or deceive. E16.

Lancashire Evening Telegraph Whatever way Mr. Trippier wants to juggle with figures, he is now a member for 869 more people.

▸ **B** *noun*. A conjuror's trick, *esp*. one claimed to be done by magic or occult influence; an act of deception, an imposture, a fraud. M17.
■ **jugglement** *noun* (*rare*) the process or a piece of juggling; a juggler's trick: LME.

J

juggler /ˈdʒʌglə/ *noun*. LOE.
[ORIGIN Old French *joglere*, *jug-*, *joug-* (cf. JONGLEUR) from Latin *joculator*, from *joculari*: see JUGGLE, -ER[1], and cf. Old French *jogler* from medieval Latin *jocularis* buffoon, use as noun of the adjective (see JOCULAR *adjective*).]
1 Orig., a person who practises magic or witchcraft, a magician, a wizard, a sorcerer. Now, a conjuror, a performer of feats of dexterity, a person who juggles with several objects. LOE.

R. DAHL It said there would be jugglers and conjurers and acrobats.

†**2** A jester, a buffoon. Freq. *derog*. ME–L16.
3 *transf. & fig*. A deceiver, a trickster. ME.
■ **juggleress** *noun* (now *rare*) a female juggler LME.

jugglery /ˈdʒʌgləri/ *noun*. ME.
[ORIGIN Old French *joglerie*, *jug-*, from *jogler*, *jug-*: see JUGGLE *verb*, -ERY.]
1 Pretended magic or witchcraft; conjuring, legerdemain. Formerly also, minstrelsy, buffoonery. ME.
2 *transf*. Trickery, deception. L17.

jug-jug *noun*[1] var. of JUG *noun*[4].

jug-jug *interjection & noun*[2] see JUG *interjection & noun*[6].

juglone /ˈdʒuːgləʊn, ˈdʒʌg-/ *noun*. L19.
[ORIGIN from Latin *juglans* walnut + -ONE.]
CHEMISTRY. A compound obtained from walnuts and acting as a mild herbicide and fungicide; 5-hydroxy-1,4-naphthoquinone, $C_{10}H_6O_3$.

Jugoslav, **Jugoslavian** *nouns & adjectives* vars. of YUGOSLAV, YUGOSLAVIAN.

jugular /ˈdʒʌgjʊlə, ˈdʒuːg-/ *adjective & noun*. L16.
[ORIGIN Late Latin *jugularis*, from Latin JUGULUM: see -AR[1].]
▸ **A** *adjective*. **1** ANATOMY. Of or pertaining to the neck or throat; *spec*. designating or pertaining to any of several large veins of the neck, as the paired ***external jugular vein***, which conveys blood from the face and scalp, and the paired ***internal jugular vein*** (also simply ***jugular vein***), which conveys blood from the face, neck, and brain. L16.
2 ICHTHYOLOGY. (Of a fish) having the ventral fins anterior to the pectoral, in the throat region; (of a ventral fin) so situated. M18.
▸ **B** *noun*. ANATOMY. A jugular vein, *esp*. the internal jugular vein. E17.
go for the jugular, **go for a person's jugular** attack violently; subject to a strong attack, usu. in speech or writing.

jugulate /ˈdʒʌgjʊleɪt, ˈdʒuːg-/ *verb trans*. E17.
[ORIGIN Latin *jugulat-* pa. ppl stem of *jugulare* cut the throat of, slay, formed as JUGULUM: see -ATE[3].]
1 Kill, esp. by cutting the throat. E17.
2 *fig*. Stop (a thing or process, esp. a disease) by powerful restrictive action. L19.
■ **juguˈlation** *noun* E17.

jugulo- /ˈdʒuːgjʊləʊ, ˈdʒʌg-/ *combining form* of JUGULAR *adjective & noun*, or of JUGULUM: see -O-.

jugulum /ˈdʒuːgjʊləm/ *noun*. E18.
[ORIGIN Latin = collarbone, throat, dim. of *jugum* YOKE *noun*[1].]
ANATOMY & ZOOLOGY. Orig., the collarbone. Now, the throat, or (esp. in birds) the lower front part of the neck; ENTOMOLOGY any of various corresponding parts in insects.

jugum /ˈdʒuːgəm/ *noun*. Pl. **-ga** /-gə/. M19.
[ORIGIN Latin = YOKE *noun*[1].]
1 BOTANY. **a** A pair of leaflets in a pinnate leaf. M19. ▸**b** Each of the ridges on the carpels of an umbelliferous plant. L19.
2 a ZOOLOGY. A process of the dorsal valve of some articulate brachiopods. L19. ▸**b** ENTOMOLOGY. A lobe on the forewing or some moths, serving to interlock with the hindwing in flight. L19.
3 ANATOMY. A connecting ridge of bone. Freq. with mod. Latin adjectives. L19.

juice /dʒuːs/ *noun*. ME.
[ORIGIN Old French & mod. French *jus* from Latin *jus* broth, sauce, vegetable juice.]
1 The extractable liquid part of a vegetable or fruit, commonly containing its characteristic flavour and other properties. ME. ▸**b** *spec*. The juice of the grape, made into wine. Now also *gen*. (*N. Amer. slang*), alcoholic drink. LME. ▸**c** The liquor from the sugar cane, esp. made ready for evaporation. L17. ▸**d** Electricity, electric current. *slang*. L19. ▸**e** Petrol. *slang*. E20. ▸**f** A drug; drugs. *slang*. M20.

J. JOHNSTON Juice from the berries stained her fingers purple. A. CARTER The maid squeezed the aromatic juice from an orange into a chilled goblet. **e** *Road Racer* He ran out of juice on the last lap.

b ***torpedo juice***: see TORPEDO *noun*.
2 The fluid part of animal or human tissue; *arch*. a body fluid or humour (usu. in *pl*.); *spec*. (with specifying word) a digestive secretion. LME.

C. CONRAN Baste the roast with the juices which have already collected in the tin. J. H. BURN Juices capable of digesting food enter the small intestine from the pancreas.

leave to stew in one's own juice, ***let stew in one's own juice***: see JUICE *noun*.
3 *gen*. The fluid naturally contained in or coming from anything. LME.
4 *fig*. The essence of a thing, in which its characteristic (esp. positive) qualities are found. Now also (in *pl*.), a person's vitality or creative, expressive, etc., faculties. LME. ▸†**b** The emoluments or profits of a profession or office. *colloq*. E16–E17. ▸**c** Influence or money obtained by or used in corrupt or criminal activities. Also, money lent at a usurious rate of interest, or the interest extorted usuriously. *US slang*. M20.

QUILLER-COUCH So stimulating to the creative juices of our . . writers.

– COMB.: **juice harp** *slang*. [alt.] = ***Jew's harp*** s.v. JEW *noun*; **juice-joint** *N. Amer. slang* a bar, club, or stall serving either alcoholic or non-alcoholic liquor.
■ **juiceless** *adjective* E17.

juice /dʒuːs/ *verb trans*. E17.
[ORIGIN from the noun.]
1 Moisten or suffuse with juice or some other liquid. *rare*. E17.
2 Extract the juice from (a fruit, vegetable, etc.). E17.
3 Inspire; animate, liven *up*. *slang*. M20.
– NOTE: Rare before 20.

juiced /dʒuːst/ *adjective*. L16.
[ORIGIN from JUICE *noun*, *verb*: see -ED[2], -ED[1].]
1 Having juice, esp. of a specified kind or quality. Usu. as 2nd elem. of comb. L16.
2 That has been juiced, having had the juice extracted. M20.
3 Intoxicated. Also foll. by *up*. *slang*. M20.

juicer /ˈdʒuːsə/ *noun*. E20.
[ORIGIN formed as JUICED + -ER[1].]
1 An electrician. *slang*. E20.
2 An appliance used to extract juice from fruit and vegetables. M20.
3 An alcoholic. *US slang*. M20.

juicy /ˈdʒuːsi/ *adjective*. LME.
[ORIGIN from JUICE *noun* + -Y[1].]
1 Full of or having much juice; succulent. LME.

R. CROMPTON The oranges . . were very yellow and juicy and rather overripe.

2 Of weather: rainy, wet. *colloq*. M19.
3 Interesting, intellectually stimulating. *colloq*. M19.
4 Suggestive, esp. sexually; piquant, sensational. *colloq*. L19.

R. KENAN These and other bits of juicy gossip were well known among the cast and crew.

5 *gen*. Excellent, first-rate. E20.

Melody Maker We anticipate a juicy new contract.

■ **juicily** *adverb* (*slang*) (*a*) excellently, well; (*b*) suggestively, scandalously: E20. **juiciness** *noun* E17.

ju-jitsu /dʒuːˈdʒɪtsuː/ *noun & verb*. Also **jiu-** /dʒuː-/, **-jutsu** /-ˈdʒʌtsuː/. L19.
[ORIGIN Japanese *jūjutsu*, from *jū* gentle + *jutsu* skill.]
▸ **A** *noun*. A Japanese system of unarmed combat using an opponent's strength and weight to his or her disadvantage, now also practised as physical training. Cf. JUDO. L19.
▸ **B** *verb trans*. Overcome by means of ju-jitsu. E20.

juju /ˈdʒuːdʒuː/ *noun*[1]. Also **ju-ju**. E17.
[ORIGIN W. African, prob. from French *joujou* plaything, redupl. formation from *jouer* to play from Latin *jocare*.]
A charm, amulet, fetish, or idol of some W. African peoples; the supernatural or magical power believed to be associated with such an object; a ban or interdiction effected by this (cf. TABOO *noun*). Also, the system of observances connected with such objects.

W. SOYINKA He arrested somebody for using bad juju against another man. That man nearly died. R. WEST She was a ju-ju, she controlled the natural forces which permit us to live.

■ **jujuism** *noun* the system of beliefs and observances connected with jujus L19.

juju /ˈdʒuːdʒuː/ *noun*[2]. M20.
[ORIGIN Uncertain; perh. from JUJU *noun*[1] or from Yoruba *jo jo* dance.]
A style of music popular among the Yoruba in Nigeria and characterized by the use of guitars and variable-pitch drums.

ju-ju /ˈdʒuːdʒuː/ *noun*[1]. *slang*. M20.
[ORIGIN Redupl. of *-ju-* in MARIJUANA.]
A marijuana cigarette.

ju-ju *noun*[2] var. of JUJU *noun*.

jujube /ˈdʒuːdʒuːb/ *noun*. LME.
[ORIGIN French, or medieval Latin *jujuba* ult. from Latin *zizyphum* from Greek *zizuphos*, *-on*. Cf. ZIZYPHUS.]
1 An edible berry-like drupe, the fruit of various trees of the genus *Ziziphus*, of the buckthorn family. LME. ▸**b** Any of the trees which produce this fruit, esp. *Ziziphus jujuba*, extending from the Mediterranean to China, and *Z. lotus* of N. Africa. Also ***jujube tree***. M16.
2 A sweet or confection made of gum arabic, gelatin, etc., orig. one flavoured with or tasting like this fruit. M19.

R. DAHL Mint jujubes for the boy next door—they'll give him green teeth for a month.

juke /dʒuːk/ *noun & verb*[1]. *slang* (orig. *US*). M20.
[ORIGIN Prob. from Gullah *juke*, *joog* disorderly, wicked, of W. African origin: cf. Mande *dyougou* wicked.]
▸ **A** *noun*. More fully ***juke house***, ***juke joint***. A roadhouse, a brothel; *spec*. one providing food, drinks, and music for dancing. M20.
▸ **B** *verb intrans*. Dance, esp. at a juke joint or to the music of a jukebox. M20.

juke *verb*[2] var. of JUCK.

jukebox /ˈdʒuːkbɒks/ *noun*. Also **juke-box**. M20.
[ORIGIN from JUKE *noun* + BOX *noun*[2].]
1 A machine that automatically plays selected gramophone records or compact discs on insertion of a coin or coins. M20.
2 COMPUTING. A device for holding a number of CD-ROMs in such a way that any of them can be played or accessed. L20.

jukskei /ˈjœkskeɪ/ *noun*. *S. Afr.* E19.
[ORIGIN Afrikaans, from *juk* YOKE *noun*[1] + *skei* pin, SKEY *noun*.]
1 = SKEY *noun*. E19.
2 A game resembling quoits, orig. played with yoke pins; the bottle-shaped peg used in this game. M20.

juku /ˈdʒʊkuː/ *noun*. M20.
[ORIGIN Japanese.]
In Japan: a private school or college attended in addition to an ordinary educational institution; *esp*. one that offers intensive preparation for an examination.

Jul. *abbreviation*.
July.

juldy *noun*, *adverb*, *& verb* var. of JILDI.

julep /ˈdʒuːlɛp/ *noun*. LME.
[ORIGIN Old French, or medieval Latin *julapium* from Arabic *julāb* from Persian *gulāb* rose water, from *gul* rose + *āb* water.]
1 A sweet drink, esp. as a vehicle for medicine; a medicated drink used as a demulcent or mild stimulant. LME.
2 A mixture of brandy, whisky, or other spirit with sugar, ice, and some flavouring, usu. mint. Chiefly *US*. L18.

Julian /ˈdʒuːlɪən/ *adjective*. L16.
[ORIGIN Latin *Julianus*, from *Julius* (see below): see -AN.]
Of or pertaining to the Roman statesman Gaius Julius Caesar (d. 44 BC); *spec*. of or pertaining to the reform of the calendar instituted by him in 46 BC.
Julian Alps the Alps in NE Italy and Slovenia, SE Europe. **Julian calendar** the calendar based on a solar year of 365¼ days and with an intercalary day every fourth year, including every centenary year (cf. ***Gregorian calendar*** s.v. GREGORIAN *adjective* 1). **Julian year** (the average length of) a year of the Julian calendar.

Julianist /ˈdʒuːlɪənɪst/ *noun*. L17.
[ORIGIN from *Julian* (see below) + -IST.]
ECCLESIASTICAL HISTORY. A member of a sect of Monophysites led by Julian, bishop of Halicarnassus early in the 6th cent.

Julia set /ˈdʒuːlɪə sɛt/ *noun phr.* L20.
[ORIGIN G. M. *Julia* (1893–1978), Algerian-born French mathematician.]
MATH. The set of complex numbers which do not stay within a bounded region of the complex plane when a given mapping, esp. one of the form $z \to z^2 + c$ (where *c* is a constant complex number), is repeatedly applied to them.

julienne /dʒuːlɪˈɛn, *foreign* ʒyljen (*pl. same*)/ *adjective & noun.* E18.
[ORIGIN French, from male forename *Jules* or *Julien*.]
▸ **A** *adjective.* **1** Designating soup made of various vegetables (esp. carrots), chopped and cooked in meat stock. E18.
2 Designating a small thin strip of a vegetable etc.; (of a vegetable etc.) cut into such strips; (of a dish or garnish) consisting of or containing such strips. L19.
▸ **B** *noun.* **1** Julienne soup. M19.
2 A julienne strip; a dish of julienne vegetables etc. E20.

C. CONRAN Sprinkle the salad with the juliennes of mushroom and lemon peel.

■ **julienned** *adjective* cut into julienne strips M20.

Juliet cap /ˈdʒuːlɪət ˈkap/ *noun phr.* E20.
[ORIGIN The heroine of Shakespeare's *Romeo & Juliet* (as worn as part of the usual costume).]
A small network ornamental cap worn by brides etc.

julio /ˈdʒuːlɪəʊ/ *noun.* Pl. **-os**. Also (earlier) †**july**. M16.
[ORIGIN Italian *giulio* from Latin *Julius* (see below).]
hist. An Italian silver coin of small denomination, struck by Pope Julius II (1503–13).

julus *noun* var. of IULUS.

July /dʒʊˈlʌɪ/ *noun*[1]. Pl. **-ies**, **-ys**. ME.
[ORIGIN Anglo-Norman *julie* from Latin *Julius* (sc. *mensis* month): see JULIAN *adjective*.]
The seventh month of the year in the Gregorian calendar.
Fourth of July: see FOURTH *noun* 1.
– COMB.: **July highflyer** a day-flying Palaearctic geometrid moth, *Hydriomena furcata*, of variable grey-brown colour.

†**july** *noun*[2] see JULIO.

jumar /ˈdʒuːmə/ *noun & verb.* M20.
[ORIGIN Unknown: orig. Swiss.]
MOUNTAINEERING. ▸**A** *noun.* A clamp which when attached to a fixed rope automatically tightens when weight is applied and relaxes when it is removed, thus facilitating the climbing of the rope; a climb using such clips. M20.
▸ **B** *verb intrans.* Climb with the aid of jumars. M20.

jumart /ˈdʒuːmɑːt/ *noun.* Also †**gimar**. L17.
[ORIGIN French, formerly *jumare* from Provençal *gemerre*, *gemarre*.]
A fictitious hybrid animal, said to be born of a mating between a bull and a mare or she-ass, or between a horse or ass and a cow.

jumbal /ˈdʒʌmb(ə)l/ *noun.* Also **jumble**. E17.
[ORIGIN Perh. var. of GIMBAL.]
Orig. a kind of fine sweet cake or biscuit, freq. made in the form of a ring or roll. Now also (*US*), a thin crisp sweet cake, flavoured with lemon peel or almonds.

jumbie /ˈdʒʌmbi/ *noun.* Chiefly *W. Indian.* Also **jumby**. E19.
[ORIGIN Kikongo *zumbi* fetish. Cf. ZOMBIE.]
A ghost, an evil spirit.
– COMB.: **jumbie bead** the hard seed of any of several W. Indian leguminous trees and shrubs; a jumble-bead; **jumbie bean** (*a*) = ***jumbie bead*** above; (*b*) = ***jumbie tree*** below; **jumbie bird** a bird of ill omen, *esp.* an ani or an owl; **jumbie tree** any of several W. Indian leguminous trees, *esp.* the lead tree, *Leucaena latisiliqua*.

jumble /ˈdʒʌmb(ə)l/ *noun*[1]. M17.
[ORIGIN from JUMBLE *verb*.]
▸ **I 1** A confused or disorderly mixture or collection, a medley. Also, disorder, muddle. M17.

R. K. NARAYAN All the dolls and toys were . . all in a jumble. D. WIGODER What a crazy jumble of agitated chaos!

2 *collect.* Miscellaneous cheap or second-hand articles to be sold at a charitable sale etc. L19. ▸**b** *ellipt.* A jumble sale. M20.

b DYLAN THOMAS A pair of postman's trousers from Bethesda Jumble.

▸ **II 3** A shock, a shaking, a jolting; *colloq.* a ride in a carriage. *arch.* L17.
– COMB.: **jumble sale** a sale of jumble to raise money for charity etc.
■ **jumbly** *adjective* confused, chaotic, in a jumble M19.

Jumble /ˈdʒʌmb(ə)l/ *noun*[2]. *slang.* M20.
[ORIGIN Alt. of *John Bull*.]
A white person.

jumble *noun*[3] var. of JUMBAL.

jumble /ˈdʒʌmb(ə)l/ *verb.* E16.
[ORIGIN App. from imit. base + -LE[3].]
1 *verb intrans.* Move about in mingled disorder; flounder about in confusion. E16. ▸**b** *fig.* Be or become mixed up *with*; come *together*. *rare.* M16.
2 *verb trans.* **a** Mingle in disorder; muddle up, confuse. Usu. foll. by *together*, *up*. M16. ▸**b** Make (*up*) in a confused or random manner. L16. ▸**c** Confuse mentally, bewilder. M17. ▸**d** Put, bring, or cast in confusion or disorder. Foll. by *in*, *out*, *down*, etc. Now *rare* or *obsolete*. L17.

a R. INGALLS She was repeating a lot of misinformation, jumbling thoughts.

3 *verb trans.* Stir up or mix the ingredients of (a liquid etc.); shake up or jolt (esp. a person). Now *rare*. M16. ▸**b** *verb intrans.* Bounce, shake, or jolt about, esp. in travel. Now *rare*. M18.

M. UNDERWOOD As though infants must . . be jumbled in a cradle like travellers in a mail-coach. **b** J. WINTERSON Our coach jumbles over the Alps.

4 *verb intrans.* Make a noise, esp. a rumbling or thumping one; play discordantly or noisily on an instrument, strum. Now *rare*. M16.
†**5** *verb trans. & intrans.* Copulate (with). L16–L17.
■ **jumblement** *noun* (*a*) the action or an act of jumbling; (*b*) a confused mixture: L17.

jumble-bead /ˈdʒʌmb(ə)lbiːd/ *noun.* M19.
[ORIGIN Alt. of JUMBIE *bead*, prob. after *mumble*.]
A jequirity seed, esp. as used in charms etc.

jumbo /ˈdʒʌmbəʊ/ *noun & adjective.* E19.
[ORIGIN Prob. the 2nd elem. of MUMBO-JUMBO. Popularized as the name of an elephant, famous for its size, orig. at London Zoo and in 1882 sold to a circus.]
▸ **A** *noun.* Pl. **-os**.
1 A big (occas. big and clumsy) person, animal, or thing, esp. an elephant; a thing which is very large of its kind. Also, a very skilful or successful person or thing. E19.

J. MAY There were bracket fungi . . stiff jumbos . . capable of bearing a man's weight. A. BLOND He published *The Thorn Birds*, a classic jumbo.

2 ENGINEERING. Any of various large types of equipment used in drilling, lifting, dumping, etc. E20.
3 NAUTICAL. The fore staysail in a fore-and-aft rigged vessel; the largest foresail, corresponding to the Genoa jib of the modern yacht rig. E20.
4 = ***jumbo jet*** below. M20.
▸ **B** *attrib.* or as *adjective.* Very large of its kind; unusually large. L19.

Miami Herald Jumbo bluefish, some up to 15 pounds.

– SPECIAL COLLOCATIONS & COMB.: **jumbo jet** a large jet aeroplane with a seating capacity of several hundred passengers. **jumbo-size**, **jumbo-sized** *adjectives* of a very large size.
■ **jumboism** *noun* preference for largeness E20. **jumboˈmania** *noun* idolization of largeness L19.

jumboize /ˈdʒʌmbəʊʌɪz/ *verb trans.* Also **-ise**. M20.
[ORIGIN from JUMBO + -IZE.]
Enlarge (a ship, esp. a tanker) by inserting a new middle section between the bow and stern.
■ **jumboizer** *noun* M20.

jumbuck /ˈdʒʌmbʌk/ *noun.* *Austral. & NZ colloq.* E19.
[ORIGIN Unknown.]
A sheep.

jumby *noun* var. of JUMBIE.

jume /dʒuːm/ *noun.* L19.
[ORIGIN S. Amer. name.]
A glasswort, *Salicornia bergii*, of southern S. America, which yields much soda when burnt.

jumelle /ʒuːˈmɛl/ *adjective.* L15.
[ORIGIN French, fem. (masc. *jumeau*), from Latin *gemellus* dim. of *geminus* twin.]
Twinned, paired; made or shaped in couples or pairs, double.

jument /ˈdʒuːm(ə)nt/ *noun.* Now *rare* or *obsolete.* LME.
[ORIGIN Latin *jumentum* (contr. of *jugimentum*) yoke-beast, from *jug-* base of *jungere* join, *jugum* YOKE *noun*[1].]
A beast of burden; any beast.
■ **juˈmentous** *adjective* (MEDICINE) (of urine) like that of a horse; highly coloured, rank, and turbid: M19.

jumma *noun* var. of JAMA *noun*[2].

jump /dʒʌmp/ *noun*[1]. M16.
[ORIGIN from JUMP *verb*.]
1 An act of jumping; a spring from the ground or other base; a leap, a bound; *spec.* an act or type of jumping, as an athletic performance. M16. ▸**b** A distance jumped. Also, a place to be jumped across or (in ski-jumping etc.) from; an obstacle to be cleared by jumping, in hurdle-racing, hunting, etc. M19. ▸**c** A descent on a parachute. E20. ▸**d** A journey, a trip. *slang.* E20. ▸**e** An act of copulation. *slang.* M20.

G. B. L. WILSON The dancer holds a particular pose, . . and progresses in a series of hops or small jumps. **b** *Daily Telegraph* Riding . . jumps. **c** I. MCEWAN He made a parachute jump for charity and cracked his shin.

loop jump, ***salchow jump***, ***ski jump***, etc.
†**2** *fig.* The moment of deciding to act, esp. without knowing the result; a dangerous or critical moment, a crisis. L16–M17. ▸**b** A venture, a hazard, a risk. Only in E17.

b SHAKES. *Ant. & Cl.* Our fortune lies Upon this jump.

3 A movement in which a thing is abruptly thrown up or forward; *spec.* (the angle which measures) the vertical movement of the muzzle of a gun at the moment of discharge. E17.
4 *fig.* A sudden and abrupt rise in position, amount, price, value, etc.; an abrupt change of level either upward or downward; an abrupt rise of level in building; a fault in geological stratification. M17.

Daily News Canary seed exhibits a sudden upward jump of several shillings. G. BORDMAN This encouraging jump in numbers coincided with a . . slump in quality.

5 *fig.* A sudden and abrupt transition from one thing, idea, stage, etc. to another, omitting intermediate stages; an interval or gap involving such sudden transition, in argument, technological development, etc. L17. ▸**b** CONTRACT BRIDGE. A bid higher than is necessary in the suit concerned. E20.

C. WESTON From paperhanging to murder—that's a pretty big jump.

6 A robbery, orig. one involving a jump from a window etc. *arch. slang.* L18.
7 A sudden involuntary movement caused by a shock or excitement; a start. In *pl.*, nervous starts; an affliction characterized by this, *spec.* (*a*) chorea; (*b*) *slang* delirium tremens. L19.

H. JAMES You came up and touched Gordon on the shoulder, and he gave a little jump. T. O'BRIEN At first you get the jumps . . . You feel like J. Edgar Hoover's on your tail.

8 Jazz music with a strong rhythm. M20.

Melody Maker A 1940's jump band.

– PHRASES ETC.: ***broadjump***: see BROAD *adjective*. **for the jump** = ***for the high jump*** s.v. HIGH *adjective, adverb, & noun*. **get the jump on**, **have the jump on** gain, have, a lead over, have an advantage over by prompt action. ***high jump***: see HIGH *adjective, adverb, & noun*. ***hop, skip, and jump***, ***hop, step, and jump***: see HOP *noun*[2] 1. ***long-jump***: see LONG *adjective*[1]. **one jump ahead** one step or stage ahead (of or *of* a rival etc.); just avoiding a pursuer etc. (*lit.* & *fig.*). **on the jump** *colloq.* (chiefly *N. Amer.*) (*a*) moving quickly; (*b*) abruptly; swiftly. ***running jump***: see RUNNING *adjective*. ***split jump***: see SPLIT *ppl adjective*. ***triple jump***: see TRIPLE *adjective & adverb*. **two jumps ahead** two steps or stages ahead (of or *of* a rival, pursuer, etc.); also with other numbers.
– COMB.: **jump bid** = sense 5b above; **jump blues** a style of black popular music which combined elements of swing and blues; **jump boot** a parachutist's boot; **jump master** a person in charge of parachutists; **jumpstation** COMPUTING a site on the World Wide Web containing a collection of hypertext links, usu. to pages on a particular topic; **jumpsuit** a one-piece garment covering the whole body, of a kind orig. worn by parachutists. (See also combs. of JUMP *verb*.)

jump /dʒʌmp/ *noun*[2]. *obsolete* exc. *hist.* M17.
[ORIGIN Alt. of JUPE.]
1 A man's short coat of the 17th and 18th cents., fitted to the upper torso, and having long sleeves, buttons down the front, and a vented skirt extending to the thighs. Also ***jump-coat***. M17.
2 *sing.* & (usu.) in *pl.* A kind of woman's underbodice, usu. fitted to the bust, and worn instead of stays, esp. in the 18th cent. M17.

jump /dʒʌmp/ *verb.* E16.
[ORIGIN Prob. imit. of the sound of feet coming to the ground: cf. BUMP *verb*[1], THUMP *verb*.]
1 *verb intrans.* Of an inanimate object: be moved or thrown up with a sudden jerk. E16.

H. CAINE The sea was beginning to jump. C. PHILLIPS The car jumped forward, the man obviously having some trouble with the clutch.

2 *verb intrans.* **a** Spring from the ground or another base by flexion and sudden muscular extension of the legs or (in some animals) some other part of the body; throw oneself upward, forward, backward, or downward, from a base; leap, bound; *spec.* leap with both feet, as opp. to hopping. M16. ▸**b** Move suddenly and quickly, as with a leap, bound, spring, etc. E18. ▸**c** Move with an involuntary jerk as the result of excitement, shock, etc.; start. E18. ▸**d** (Of jazz or similar music) have a strong or exciting rhythm; (of a place, esp. a place of entertainment) be full of activity, excitement, or enjoyment. *colloq.* (orig. *US*). M20.

a R. K. NARAYAN Perhaps I can jump into the sea. SLOAN WILSON They had jumped from the planes . . at nightfall . . dropped behind the German lines. W. WHARTON I jump up and down, keep the heart muscles pumping. MERLE COLLINS She jumped across the drain. **b** E. WELTY He jumped nimbly to his feet and ran out of the garden. JAN MORRIS Hastily Yasar . . jumped out of the car to open the back door. R. INGALLS Joe jumped up from his seat. **c** J. MCDOUGALL He often jumped with fright when his wife came up behind him.

3 *verb intrans.* Agree completely, coincide, tally. (Foll. by *together*, *with*.) M16.

Guardian One passage in Mr. Morley's speech jumps with a letter we print today.

4 *verb intrans.* **a** Pass abruptly from one thing, idea, state, etc., to another, omitting intermediate stages; rise suddenly in position, amount, price, value, etc. **L16.** ▸**b** Come *to* or arrive *at* (a conclusion etc.) precipitately, without examining the premisses. **E18.**

> **a** TOLKIEN Treebeard often went back to some earlier point, or jumped forward asking questions about later events. *London Daily News* Profits jumped from £737,000 to £1 million in 1986. *Medway Extra* The waiting list . . has jumped . . from 2,187 to 3,202. **b** P. KAVANAGH He was inclined to jump to conclusions sometimes, to act on impulse.

5 a *verb trans.* Leap or spring over or across (an obstacle etc.). **L16.** ▸**b** Get on (a ship, a train, etc.), esp. dangerously or illegally by jumping (*US*). Also, leave (a place or thing) suddenly. **L19.** ▸**c** Of a thing: spring off, leave (the course, track, rail, etc.). **L19.** ▸**d** *verb intrans. & trans.* CONTRACT BRIDGE. Raise (a bid) higher than necessary in the suit concerned. **E20.**

> **a** J. DICKEY Lewis went forward from me and jumped the gully. M. CHABON An enormous BMW Motorcycle . . jumped the curb. **b** *Video for You* Desperate escaped prisoners jump passing train. M. MOORCOCK Patsy jumped the first bus he saw going East. *City Limits* Sylvan planned to jump camp and slope off into New York.

†**6** *verb trans.* Hastily agree upon or effect (a marriage). **L16–E17.**
7 *verb trans.* Effect or do as with a jump. Now *rare*. **E17.**
†**8** *verb trans.* Hazard, risk. *rare* (Shakes.). Only in **E17.**
9 *verb trans.* Skip over, ignore, pass by, evade. **M18.** ▸**b** Fail to stop at (a red traffic light); *gen.* anticipate permission or a signal to act. **M20.**

> G. BORDMAN Sam and Steve jump their . . bill. **b** J. PORTER She jumped a red light . . it was a damned silly place to have traffic lights. *Motor Cycle News* I was left at the beginning because they jumped the start but I went well.

10 *verb trans.* **a** Pounce on or attack (a person) unexpectedly; rob, cheat. **L18.** ▸**b** Take summary possession of (a piece of land) after alleged abandonment or forfeiture by the former occupant. Chiefly *N. Amer.* **M19.**

> **a** J. W. SCHULTZ I was always expecting the war party to jump us. M. PIERCY 'Whose dog was it?' 'I was just minding my own business and the damn thing jumped me.'

11 *verb trans.* **a** Cause to jump; drive suddenly forward; startle. **E19.** ▸**b** Cause (game) to start from cover; spring. **M19.** ▸**c** Sauté. Chiefly as ***jumped*** *ppl adjective*. **L19.**

> **a** J. KELMAN He messed a shot badly . . actually jumped the cueball off the table.

12 *verb trans.* Flatten, or shorten and thicken the end of (an iron rail or bar) by endwise blows. **M19.** ▸**b** Join (rails etc.) end on end, *spec.* by welding the flattened ends together. **M19.**
13 *verb trans.* QUARRYING. Drill by means of a jumper. **M19.**

– PHRASES, & WITH ADVERBS & PREPOSITIONS IN SPECIALIZED SENSES: **go and jump in the lake**, **go jump in the lake** *colloq.* = ***jump in the lake*** below. **jump at** *colloq.* spring as a predator; *fig.* eagerly accept or take advantage of. ***jump bail***: see BAIL *noun*[1]. **jump down a person's throat** *colloq.* berate, reprimand, or contradict a person fiercely. **jump for joy** *fig.* be joyfully excited. **jump in the lake** *colloq.* (usu. in *imper.*) go away and stop being a nuisance. ***jump Jim Crow***: see JIM CROW *noun* 1a. **jump on** *colloq.* attack or criticize severely and without warning. ***jump on the bandwagon***: see ***bandwagon*** s.v. BAND *noun*[2]. **jump out of one's skin** be extremely startled. **jump rope** *N. Amer.* skip with a skipping rope. ***jump salty***: see SALTY *adjective*[1] 5. **jump ship** (of a seaman) leave his ship before the expiry of his contract; *gen.* desert. ***jump the gun***: see GUN *noun*. **jump the queue** move ahead of one's place in a queue of people; *fig.* take unfair precedence over others. **jump the shark** *US colloq.* (of a television series) reach a point when far-fetched events are included merely for the sake of novelty. ***jump through the hoops***: see HOOP *noun*[1]. **jump to** *colloq.* accept or obey readily. **jump to it** take prompt and energetic action. **jump to the eyes** be noticed or noticeable. **jump up** (*a*) rise quickly to a standing position; (*b*) dance the jump-up.

– COMB.: **jump-about** = ***Jack-jump-about*** s.v. JACK *noun*[1]; **jump ball** BASKETBALL a ball thrown vertically between two opposing players by the referee; **jump-cut** CINEMATOGRAPHY & TELEVISION (*a*) the excision of part of a shot in order to break its continuity of action and time; (*b*) the abrupt transition from one scene to another which is discontinuous in time; **jumped-up** *adjective* (*colloq.*) newly or suddenly risen in status or importance, upstart; conceited, presumptuously arrogant; **jump jet** a jet aircraft which can take off and land vertically; **jump jockey** a jockey who rides in steeplechases; **jump lead** either of a pair of leads for conveying electric charge from one car battery to another during a jump-start; **jump-off** (*a*) *US colloq.* a place from which a person must jump; (*b*) *US slang* the start of a military operation; (*c*) SHOW-JUMPING an additional round to resolve a tie; **jump ring** a wire ring made by bringing the two ends together without soldering or welding; **jump-rock** any of several freshwater sucker fishes of the genus *Moxostoma*, of the southern US; **jump rope** (chiefly *N. Amer.*) a skipping rope; **jump seat** (*a*) (a carriage equipped with) a movable carriage seat; (*b*) a folding seat in a car; **jump shot** (*a*) (BILLIARDS & SNOOKER etc.) a shot which causes the cue ball to jump over another ball; (*b*) BASKETBALL a throw at the net taken with both feet off the ground; **jump spark** a spark produced by a potential difference applied to two electrical conductors separated by a narrow gap; usu. *attrib.*, designating devices or methods employing this; **jump-start** *verb & noun* (*a*) *verb trans.* start (a vehicle) using the charge from another vehicle's battery by means of jump leads; (*b*) *noun* an act of jump-starting a vehicle; **jump take-off** AERONAUTICS a vertical take-off; **jump turn** SKIING a turn made while jumping; **jump-up** (*a*) a jump in an upward direction; (*b*) *Austral.* an escarpment; (*c*) an informal West Indian dance; **jump-weld** a weld effected by hammering together the heated ends of two pieces of metal.
▪ **jumpable** *adjective* **E19.**

jump /dʒʌmp/ *adverb & adjective*. Now *rare* or *obsolete*. **M16.**
[ORIGIN Rel. to JUMP *verb*.]
▸ †**A** *adverb*. With exact coincidence or agreement; exactly, precisely. **M16–M17.**
▸ **B** *adjective*. Coinciding, exactly agreeing; even; exact, precise. **L16.**

jumped /dʒʌmpt/ *ppl adjective*. **M19.**
[ORIGIN from JUMP *verb* + -ED[1].]
1 That has jumped; (of food) sautéed.
2 Foll. by *up*: newly or suddenly risen in status or importance; conceited, presumptuously arrogant.

> A. BURGESS He was wealthy but in the manner of the jumped-up working class, unhealthily frugal. M. FLANAGAN He was clearly pleased with himself and very jumped-up about the show.

jumper /ˈdʒʌmpə/ *noun*[1]. **E17.**
[ORIGIN from JUMP *verb* + -ER[1].]
1 A person who or animal, fish, etc., which jumps or leaps. **E17.** ▸**b** A ticket inspector, a ticket-collector. *slang*. **E20.** ▸**c** BASKETBALL. (A player of) a jump ball or jump shot. **M20.**
high jumper, ***long jumper***, etc.
2 a QUARRYING. A heavy drill worked either by hand or by means of a hammer, used to make blasting holes in rock etc. **M18.** ▸**b** A mechanism controlling the star-wheel of a repeating clock. **M18.** ▸**c** ELECTRICITY. A wire used to cut out an instrument or part of a circuit, or to temporarily close a gap in a circuit. **M18.**
3 *hist.* (**J-.**) A member of a Methodist sect found in Wales in the 18th cent. whose religious worship was characterized by jumping and dancing. **L18.**
4 An adult or larval insect characterized by jumping. **L18.** ▸**b** In full ***jumper ant***. An Australian stinging ant of the genus *Myrmecia*. **M19.**
5 A rough sledge for use on broken or difficult ground. *N. Amer.* **E19.**
6 A person who summarily takes possession of a piece of land (see JUMP *verb* 10b). Chiefly *N. Amer.* **M19.**
7 NAUTICAL. A chain or wire stay from the outer end of the jib boom to the dolphin-striker in a square-rigged ship. **L19.**

– COMB.: ***jumper ant***: see sense 4b above; **jumper cable** a jump lead; **jumper stay** NAUTICAL a truss stay from the root of the lower cross-stress to the fore side of the masthead; **jumper strut** a short metal or wooden strut canted forward to add support to the long mast of a Bermuda-rigged yacht; **jumper-wire** = ***jumping-wire*** s.v. JUMPING *verbal noun*.
▪ **jumperism** *noun* (*hist.*) the principles of the Methodist Jumpers **E19.**

jumper /ˈdʒʌmpə/ *noun*[2]. **M19.**
[ORIGIN Prob. from JUMP *noun*[2] + -ER[1].]
1 *hist.* A loose outer jacket or shirt reaching to the hips, made of canvas, serge, coarse linen, etc., and worn esp. by sailors etc. **M19.**
2 A knitted pullover, a jersey. Also, a loose-fitting blouse worn over a skirt. **E20.**
3 In *pl.* A one-piece garment, worn esp. by children; rompers. **E20.**
4 A pinafore dress. Also ***jumper dress***. *N. Amer.* **M20.**

– COMB.: ***jumper dress***: see sense 4 above; **jumper suit** (*a*) a pinafore dress; (*b*) a woman's suit consisting of a jumper and skirt made of the same material, usu. wool.

jumper /ˈdʒʌmpə/ *verb trans.* **E19.**
[ORIGIN from JUMPER *noun*[1].]
1 QUARRYING. Blast or bore (a hole) with a jumper. **E19.**
2 ELECTRICITY. Connect by means of a jumper. **E20.**

jumping /ˈdʒʌmpɪŋ/ *verbal noun*. **M16.**
[ORIGIN from JUMP *verb* + -ING[1].]
The action of JUMP *verb*.
high-jumping, ***long-jumping***, etc.

– COMB. & PHRASES: **jumping board**, **jumping-off board** a springboard; **jumping-off ground**, **jumping-off place** (*a*) *colloq.* a place at which a person alights at the end of a journey, *spec.* (*N. Amer.*) a place regarded as being the furthest limit of civilization or settlement; (*b*) a place from which a person moves into a region beyond; **jumping pole** a pole used in jumping long distances or in pole-vaulting; **jumping wire** a serrated wire running from the stemhead of a submarine to the forward edge of the bridge casing and from the after edge to the stern, for cutting a way through defensive nets when submerged.

jumping /ˈdʒʌmpɪŋ/ *ppl adjective*. **M16.**
[ORIGIN formed as JUMPING *noun* + -ING[2].]
That jumps.
jumping bean (*a*) a tropical American plant seed (esp. of *Sebastiania pavoniana*, family Euphorbiaceae) containing a moth larva whose movements cause the seed to jump about; (*b*) a toy consisting of a small bean-shaped capsule containing a weight which causes it to move unaided down a sloping surface. **jumping deer** *N. Amer.* (*a*) a pronghorn; (*b*) a mule deer. **jumping gene** (*colloq.*) = TRANSPOSON. **jumping hare** = ***spring hare*** s.v. SPRING *noun*[1]. **jumping jack** (*a*) a toy figure of a man, esp. with movable limbs attached to strings; (*b*) a small firework producing repeated explosions. **jumping louse** = ***flea-louse*** s.v. FLEA *noun*. **jumping mouse** (*a*) any of several mouselike rodents of the Palaearctic family Zapodidae, having long hind feet; (*b*) = ***jumping rat*** below. **jumping rat** any rodent of the jerboa family Dipodidae. **jumping seed** = ***jumping bean*** (a) above. **jumping shrew** = ***ELEPHANT shrew***. **jumping spider** any of various small hairy spiders (*spec.* of the family Salticidae) which do not spin webs but catch their prey by leaping on it.
▪ **jumpingly** *adverb* **M16.**

jumpy /ˈdʒʌmpi/ *adjective*. **M19.**
[ORIGIN from JUMP *noun*[1] + -Y[1].]
1 Characterized by sudden movements from one thing or state to another. **M19.**

> J. O'FAOLAIN She wanted to see what happened next but the image had gone jumpy. J. C. OATES His mind is too jumpy for sleep.

2 Characterized by sudden involuntary movements caused by nervous excitement; nervous, easily startled. **L19.**

> R. P. JHABVALA She got more nervous, positively jumpy and crazy. M. ANGELOU We left for the elevators . . jumpy with excitement.

▪ **jumpily** *adverb* **L20.** **jumpiness** *noun* **L19.**

jun /dʒʌn/ *noun*. Also **jeon** (see below), (*hist.*) **chon** /tʃɒn/. Pl. same. **M20.**
[ORIGIN Korean.]
A monetary unit of Korea (now the jun in North Korea, the jeon in South Korea), equal to one-hundredth of a won.

Jun. *abbreviation*.
1 June.
2 Junior.

junco /ˈdʒʌŋkəʊ/ *noun*. Pl. **-o(e)s**. **E18.**
[ORIGIN Spanish from Latin *juncus* rush.]
†**1** The reed bunting, *Emberiza schoeniclus*. Only in **E18.**
2 Any of several buntings of N. and Central America of the genus *Junco*; a snow sparrow. **L19.**

junction /ˈdʒʌŋ(k)ʃ(ə)n/ *noun & verb*. **E18.**
[ORIGIN Latin *junctio(n-)*, from *junct-* pa. ppl stem of *jungere* JOIN *verb*: see -ION.]
▸ **A** *noun*. **1** The action of joining; the fact of being joined; union, combination. **E18.**

> T. JEFFERSON The latter effected a junction . . with another part of their fleet. M. ARNOLD The junction of a talent for abstruse reasoning with much literary inexperience.

2 In full ***junction canal***, ***junction line***, ***junction railway***. A canal or railway forming a connection between two other lines or with a centre of commerce. Chiefly in proper names. Now *rare*. **L18.**
Grand Junction Canal, ***Lancaster and Preston Junction***, etc.
3 The point or place at which two things join or are joined, a meeting place; *spec.* the place or station on a railway where lines meet and unite (freq. in proper names). **M19.** ▸**b** ELECTRONICS. A transition zone in a semiconductor between two regions of different conductivity type (usually *n*-type and *p*-type). **M20.**

> SLOAN WILSON He took a wrong turn at a junction of corridors. D. ATTENBOROUGH The builders . . move these living tubes of glue . . across the leaf junction until the two edges are joined. P. THEROUX At . . a convenient railway junction . . I changed for the Bournemouth train.

Clapham Junction, ***Willesden Junction***, etc. ***T-junction*** etc.

– COMB.: **junction box** a closed rigid box or casing used to enclose and protect junctions of electric wires or cables; **junction diode**, **junction rectifier** ELECTRONICS a diode consisting essentially of a piece of semiconductor containing a rectifying junction between differently doped regions; **junction transistor** ELECTRONICS a transistor consisting essentially of a piece of semiconductor containing two (or more) junctions that divide it into three (or more) differently doped regions.

▸ **B** *verb intrans.* Form a junction, join. Foll. by *with*, *on to*. Chiefly *Austral. & NZ*. **E20.**
▪ **junctional** *adjective* **L19.**

juncture /ˈdʒʌŋ(k)tʃə/ *noun*. **LME.**
[ORIGIN Latin *junctura* joint, from *junct-*: see JUNCTION, -URE.]
1 The place at which, or structure by which, two things are joined; a joint, a junction. **LME.** ▸†**b** A joint of the body. **LME–E18.** ▸**c** LINGUISTICS. The transition between two speech segments or between an utterance and (potential) preceding or following silence; the phonetic feature that marks such a transition. **M20.**

> B. T. BRADFORD The Blackamoor Inn, which was the juncture of several roads.

c ***open juncture***: see OPEN *adjective*. ***terminal juncture***: see TERMINAL *adjective*.
2 The action of joining together; the condition of being joined together; joining, junction. **LME.**

> F. W. L. ADAMS This . . Khalif . . anticipated the Suez Canal by his juncture of the Nile and the Red Sea.

3 A convergence or concurrence of events or circumstances; a particular (esp. critical) posture of affairs or point in time. **M17.**

> H. GREEN How idiotic to start an illness at this juncture when she would get small help. F. FITZGERALD The United States came to Vietnam at a critical juncture of Vietnamese history.

4 Something that connects two things; a connecting link; a means of connection or union. *rare*. L17.
■ **junctural** *adjective* (chiefly LINGUISTICS) M20. **juncturally** *adverb* (chiefly LINGUISTICS) M20.

jundy /ˈdʒʌndi/ *verb & noun*. *Scot.* Also (earlier) †**joundy**. L17.
[ORIGIN Unknown.]
▸ **A** *verb trans. & intrans.* Push with the elbow or shoulder; jog, jostle. L17.
▸ **B** *noun*. **1** A push with the elbow; a jog, a shove. M18.
2 *fig.* A steady course, a jog-trot. L19.

June /dʒuːn/ *noun*. ME.
[ORIGIN Old French & mod. French *juin* from Latin *Junius* (sc. *mensis* month) var. of *Junonius* sacred to the goddess Juno.]
The sixth month of the year in the Gregorian calendar, in which the summer solstice occurs in the northern hemisphere.
– COMB.: **juneberry** (the fruit of) any of several N. American shrubs of the genus *Amelanchier*, of the rose family, with showy white flowers; **June bug** any of various beetles which appear in June, as (*a*) a scarab of the genus *Phyllophaga*, of the northern US, (*b*) (more fully ***green June bug***) a scarab, *Cotinus nitida*, of the southern US; **June grass** *N. Amer.* common meadow grass, *Poa pratensis*.

june /dʒuːn/ *verb intrans. US colloq. & dial.* M19.
[ORIGIN App. from the noun.]
Move in a lively fashion, hurry; be restless or aimless; wander *around*.

Juneteenth /dʒuːnˈtiːnθ/ *noun*. M20.
[ORIGIN Blend of JUNE and NINETEENTH.]
In the US: a festival held annually on the nineteenth of June by African Americans (esp. in the southern states), to commemorate emancipation from slavery in Texas on that day in 1865.

Junggrammatiker /ˈjʊŋgramatɪkə/ *noun pl.* E20.
[ORIGIN German = young grammarians.]
LINGUISTICS. The members of a late 19th-cent. school of historical linguists who held that phonetic changes (sound laws) operate without exceptions.

Jungian /ˈjʊŋɪən/ *adjective & noun*. M20.
[ORIGIN from *Jung* (see below) + -IAN.]
▸ **A** *adjective*. Of or pertaining to Carl Gustav Jung (1875–1961), the Swiss leader of the school of analytic psychology, or his beliefs, as in the collective unconscious. M20.
▸ **B** *noun*. A follower or adherent of Jung. M20.
■ **Jungianism** *noun* the beliefs or psychological system of Jung M20.

jungle /ˈdʒʌŋg(ə)l/ *noun*. L18.
[ORIGIN Hindi *jaṅgal*, from Sanskrit *jāṅgala* rough and arid (of terrain).]
1 Orig. in the Indian subcontinent, later in other (esp. tropical) regions: (an area of) uncultivated land overgrown with underwood, long grass, or tangled vegetation, esp. as the home of wild animals; the luxuriant and often almost impenetrable vegetation covering such a tract. L18.

W. BRONK They slashed / the jungle and burned it and planted . . corn.

law of the jungle: see LAW *noun*[1].
2 *transf. & fig.* A wild tangled mass; a place of bewildering complexity or confusion. Now freq., a place where the 'law of the jungle' prevails, a scene of ruthless competition, struggle, or exploitation, (freq. with specifying word). M19. ▸**b** A camp for hoboes etc. *N. Amer. slang*. E20.

S. LEACOCK Our potatoes are buried in a jungle of autumn burdocks. *Sunday Times* Namier . . fitted especially ill in the academic jungle.

3 A style of dance music incorporating elements of ragga, hip hop, and hard core and featuring very fast electronic drum tracks and slower synthesized bass lines. L20.
– COMB.: **jungle-bashing** *slang* movement through a jungle, esp. by soldiers; **jungle bunny** *slang* (*derog. & offensive*) a black person; **jungle cat** a small wild cat, *Felis chaus*, of forest and scrubland in Indo-china and Sri Lanka; **jungle cock** a male jungle fowl; **jungle fever** malaria; **jungle fowl** (*a*) any of several birds of the Far Eastern genus *Gallus*, closely related to pheasants (***red jungle fowl***: see RED *adjective*); (*b*) *Austral.* a megapode; **jungle green** (of) a dark green colour; **jungle gym** a climbing frame for a children's playground; **jungle hen** a female jungle fowl; **jungle juice** *slang* alcoholic liquor, esp. when very powerful or prepared illicitly or under primitive conditions; **jungle law** = ***law of the jungle*** s.v. LAW *noun*[1]; **jungle rice** a kind of millet, *Echinochloa colona*, found as a weed of rice fields in tropical countries; **jungle rot** *slang* any skin disorder acquired in humid tropical regions.

jungle /ˈdʒʌŋg(ə)l/ *verb*. M19.
[ORIGIN from the noun.]
1 *verb trans.* Drive *out* by the influence of the jungle. *rare*. M19.
2 *verb intrans.* Prepare a meal at or live together in a hoboes' camp. Usu. foll. by *up*. *US slang*. E20.

jungled /ˈdʒʌŋg(ə)ld/ *adjective*. M19.
[ORIGIN from JUNGLE *noun* + -ED[2].]
Covered with jungle or wild undergrowth.

jungly /ˈdʒʌŋgli/ *adjective*. In sense 2 also **jungli**. E19.
[ORIGIN from JUNGLE *noun* + -Y[1]. Var. after -I[2]: cf. also Hindi *jaṅglī*, formed as JUNGLE *noun*.]
1 Of the nature of, characterized by, or resembling jungle; having much jungle. E19.
2 Inhabiting a jungle. Now *rare*. L19.

Junian /ˈdʒuːnɪən/ *adjective*. E19.
[ORIGIN from *Junius* (see below) + -AN.]
1 Of or pertaining to the philologist and antiquary Francis Junius (1589–1677). E19.
2 Of or pertaining to the 'Letters of Junius', a series of vituperative letters which appeared in the *Public Advertiser*, 1768–72, attacking various prominent Tory politicians. L19.

junior /ˈdʒuːnɪə/ *adjective & noun*. ME.
[ORIGIN Latin (for *juvenior*) compar. of *juvenis* young: see -IOR. Cf. SENIOR.]
▸ **A** *adjective*. **1** After a person's name: that is the younger of two bearing the same name in a family, esp. a son of the same name as his father. Also (now *rare*) = MINOR *adjective* 1b. ME.

DICKENS Snawley junior . . I'll warm you with a severe thrashing.

2 Of a thing or (now *rare*) a person: of later rise or appearance in history, of later date; more modern. (Foll. by *to*). L16.

R. BENTLEY The Cretan civilization was apparently junior to that of the Nile valley.

3 †**a** Belonging to youth or earlier life; youthful, juvenile. E17–L18. ▸**b** Intended for children or young people. Also, smaller than the normal size. M19.

b *Practical Motorist* A 'junior' frame saw is a useful back-up.

4 Of lesser age or standing or more recent appointment, of lower position on a scale, (foll. by *to*). In N. American colleges and schools and Scottish universities: belonging to the second last year of a course (in Scotland *spec.* of an honours degree course). M18.

G. GREENE I had published a first novel, and I found myself a junior guest . . at a great publisher's do. *Sunday Express* The most junior boy in the house had to do a solo spot.

– SPECIAL COLLOCATIONS: **junior barrister** = sense B.2 below. **junior college** *US*: offering a two-year course, esp. in preparation for completion at a senior college. **junior combination room** a junior common room at Cambridge University. **junior common room** (at certain universities) a common room for undergraduates, the undergraduates entitled to use a common room. **junior high school** *N. Amer.*: intermediate between elementary school and high school. ***junior*** LIGHTWEIGHT. ***junior*** MIDDLEWEIGHT. **junior miss** (orig. *US*) a young teenage girl. ***junior*** OPTIME. **junior school** the lower forms in some fee-paying schools; *hist.* a state school for children in the younger age range, roughly between 7 and 11. ***junior*** WELTERWEIGHT.
▸ **B** *noun*. **1** A person who is younger than or junior to another (freq. after possess.). More generally (chiefly *US*), a child, *esp.* a young boy (freq. as a form of address). M16.

B. NEIL His mother had run off with a man nine years her junior. *Which?* Be prepared to pay more for . . the top stylist than . . for the less experienced junior.

2 A barrister who has not taken silk. M19.
■ **juniorate** *noun* in the Society of Jesus, a two-year course for junior members preparatory to entering the priesthood, a seminary for those taking this course M19. **juniorship** *noun* the condition of a junior, juniority L18.

juniority /dʒuːnɪˈɒrɪti/ *noun*. L16.
[ORIGIN from JUNIOR *adjective* + -ITY, after earlier *seniority*.]
The state or condition of being junior (in age, appointment, rank, etc.).

juniper /ˈdʒuːnɪpə/ *noun*. LME.
[ORIGIN Latin *juniperus*.]
1 Any of various coniferous evergreen shrubs and trees of the genus *Juniperus*, *esp.* one of the common European species *J. communis*, a hardy spreading shrub or low tree, which has bluish-black or purple pungent-tasting berries and yields juniper oil. Also ***juniper tree***. LME. ▸**b** Any of various coniferous trees of other genera, *esp.* the American larch or hackmatack, *Larix laricina*, and the white cedar, *Chamaecyparis thyoides*, of the southern US. M18.
2 In biblical translations: a desert plant, *Retama raetam*, a leguminous shrub with rushlike branches. LME.
– COMB. & PHRASES: **juniper oil**, **oil of juniper** a volatile oil from juniper cones, used medicinally and in flavouring gin.

junk /dʒʌŋk/ *noun*[1]. LME.
[ORIGIN Old French *junc*, (also mod.) *jonc*, from Latin *juncus*.]
†**1** A rush (plant). LME–E16.
2 SURGERY. An old form of splint consisting of rigid material (orig. rushes or reeds) inside a cloth wrapping. E17.

junk /dʒʌŋk/ *noun*[2]. LME.
[ORIGIN Unknown.]
1 Chiefly NAUTICAL. ▸†**a** An old or inferior cable or rope. Usu. ***old junk***. LME–M18. ▸**b** Old cable or rope, cut up into short lengths and used for making oakum etc. M17. ▸**c** Salt meat (formerly used as food on long voyages), compared to pieces of old rope. Also ***salt junk***. M18.
2 A piece or lump of something, a chunk. E18.

H. LAWSON The remains—a meal of junk of badly-hacked bread, a basin of dripping.

3 The mass of thick oily cellular tissue beneath the case and nostrils of a sperm whale, containing spermaceti. M19.
4 Any discarded or waste material that can be put to some use. Now usu., second-hand or discarded articles of little or no use or value; rubbish. M19.

BETTY SMITH She and her brother, . . like other Brooklyn kids, collected rags, paper, metal, rubber, and other junk. D. FRANCIS The junk I sold to secondhand shops and the best bits to dealers.

5 A narcotic drug, *esp.* heroin; narcotic drugs collectively. *slang* (orig. *US*). E20.
6 = ***junk food*** below. L20.

P. THEROUX Eating junk, Guppy Cola and jelly sandwiches.

– COMB.: **junk art** three-dimensional art made from discarded material; **junk bond** FINANCE a high-yielding high-risk security, *esp.* one issued to finance a takeover; **junk-bottle** *US* a thick strong bottle of green or black glass; **junk-dealer** *US* a marine-store dealer; **junk DNA** GENETICS DNA that does not code for a protein and does not seem to serve any useful purpose, usu. occurring in repetitive sequences of nucleotides; **junk food** food that appeals to popular (esp. juvenile) taste but has little nutritional value; **junk jewellery** = COSTUME ***jewellery***; **junk mail** circulars, advertisements, etc., sent by post to a large number of addresses; **junkman** *noun*[1] a dealer in marine stores or second-hand goods; **junk playground** an adventure playground using waste materials; **junk science** untested or unproven theories when presented as scientific fact (esp. in a court of law); **junk sculpture** = ***junk art*** above; **junk shop** (*a*) a marine store; (*b*) a shop dealing in miscellaneous cheap second-hand goods or (*derog.*) antiques.

junk /dʒʌŋk/ *noun*[3]. M16.
[ORIGIN Portuguese *junco* or French †*juncque* (now *jonque*), from Malay *jong*, partly also from Dutch *jonk*.]
A flat-bottomed type of sailing vessel used in the China seas, with a square prow, prominent stem, full stern, suspended rudder, and lugsails.
– COMB.: **junkman** *noun*[2] a member of the crew of a junk.

junk /dʒʌŋk/ *verb trans.* L18.
[ORIGIN from JUNK *noun*[2].]
1 Cut into chunks; cut *off* in a lump. L18.
2 Treat as junk or rubbish; discard, abandon. E20.

F. FORSYTH He . . junked the can in the trash basket. R. COOVER It's time we junked the whole beastly business. *Combat Handguns* It . . had enough shortcomings to warrant junking the whole idea.

Junker /ˈjʊŋkə/ *noun*[1]. *obsolete* exc. *hist.* M16.
[ORIGIN German, earlier *Junkher(r*, from Middle High German *junc* YOUNG *adjective* + *herre* (mod. *Herr*) lord, HERR: cf. YOUNKER.]
A young German noble; *spec.* a member of the reactionary party of the Prussian aristocracy who aimed to maintain the exclusive privileges of their class; a narrow-minded, overbearing (younger) member of the German aristocracy.
■ ***junkerdom*** *noun* the body or world of Junkers; the condition or character of a Junker: L19.

junker /ˈdʒʌŋkə/ *noun*[2]. *US slang*. E20.
[ORIGIN from JUNK *noun*[2] + -ER[1].]
A drug addict; a drug peddler.

junker *noun*[3] var. of JINKER *noun*[2].

junket /ˈdʒʌŋkɪt/ *noun & verb*. LME.
[ORIGIN Old French & mod. French *jonquette*, from *jonc* rush from Latin *juncus*.]
▸ **A** *noun*. **1** A basket (orig. made of rushes); *esp.* one for fish. Long *obsolete* exc. *dial.* LME.
2 A cream cheese or other preparation of cream (orig. made in a rush basket or served on a rush mat). Now *spec.* a dish consisting of curds sweetened and flavoured, freq. served with fruit or cream. LME.
3 Any dainty sweet, cake, or confection. *obsolete* exc. *dial.* M16.
4 A feast, a banquet; a festive gathering. Now also, a picnic party, a pleasure excursion with eating and drinking; *spec.* (*N. Amer.*) an official's tour at public expense. M16.

T. ROETHKE I . . was there last month, as part of a lecture-reading junket.

▸ **B** *verb intrans.* Hold or take part in a banquet, feast, or other festive gathering; (chiefly *N. Amer.*) join in a picnic, go on a pleasure excursion. M16.
■ **junkeˈteer** *noun* (orig. *US*) = JUNKETER M20. **junketer** *noun* a person who feasts or takes part in a junketing E19. **junketing** *noun* (*a*) the action of the verb; (*b*) a feast, a banquet, a festive gathering; a picnic: M16.

junkie /ˈdʒʌŋki/ *noun & adjective*. *slang* (orig. *US*). Also (esp. as adjective) **junky**. E20.
[ORIGIN from JUNK *noun*[2] + -IE, -Y[6].]
▸ **A** *noun*. A drug addict; *occas.* a drug peddler. E20.
▸ **B** *attrib.* or as *adjective*. That is a drug addict; of a drug addict. M20.

W. S. BURROUGHS He spoke in his dead, junkie whisper.

junky *noun & adjective*[1] see JUNKIE.

J

junky /ˈdʒʌŋki/ *adjective*². M20.
[ORIGIN from JUNK *noun*² + -Y¹.]
Worthless, valueless, rubbishy.

Juno /ˈdʒuːnəʊ/ *noun*. Pl. **-os**. E17.
[ORIGIN Latin *Juno(n-)*, a Roman god, wife of Jupiter and goddess of marriage and childbirth.]
1 A woman of stately beauty. E17.
2 A jealous wife. Now *rare*. E17.
■ **Juˈnonian** *adjective* of or pertaining to Juno; Junoesque: L18.

Junoesque /dʒuːnəʊˈɛsk/ *adjective*. M19.
[ORIGIN formed as JUNO + -ESQUE.]
Of a woman: beautiful and stately.

Junr *abbreviation*.
Junior.

junta /ˈdʒʌntə, ˈhʊ-/ *noun*. E17.
[ORIGIN Spanish, Portuguese *junta* (whence French *junte*) from Italian *giunta* from Proto-Romance use as noun of Latin *juncta* fem. pa. pple of *jungere* JOIN *verb*.]
1 A Spanish or Italian deliberative or administrative council or committee. E17.
2 *gen.* A body of people combined for a common (esp. political) purpose; a self-elected committee or council, a cabal. Now freq. *spec.*, a political or military clique or faction taking power after a revolution or *coup d'état*. E18.

junto /ˈdʒʌntəʊ/ *noun*. Pl. **-os**. E17.
[ORIGIN Alt. of JUNTA after Spanish nouns in -o.]
1 = JUNTA 2. E17.
†**2** = JUNTA 1. E–M18.

jupati /ˈdʒuːpəti/ *noun*. M19.
[ORIGIN Portuguese from Tupi *yupáti*.]
A Brazilian palm, *Raphia taedigera*, with large leaves whose long stalks are used locally as a building material.

J

jupe /dʒuːp; *foreign* ʒyp (*pl. same*)/ *noun*. ME.
[ORIGIN Old French & mod. French from Arabic JUBBA.]
1 A man's loose jacket, tunic, or jerkin. Now only *Scot.* ME.
†**2** A woman's jacket, gown, or bodice. In *pl.* also, a kind of bodice or stays. *Scot.* E18–E20.
3 A woman's skirt. E19.

Jupiter /ˈdʒuːpɪtə/ *noun*. ME.
[ORIGIN Latin *Juppiter*, *Jupiter*, from *Jovis-pater* lit. 'Jove Father', corresp. to Sanskrit *dyauṣ pitṛ* lit. 'heaven father': see JOVE.]
1 The chief of the gods of the ancient Romans, corresponding to the Greek Zeus, orig. a sky god, associated with lightning and the thunderbolt. ME.
by Jupiter *literary*: used as an oath, or expr. surprise or approval. **Jupiter's beard** (**a**) a southern European evergreen leguminous shrub, *Anthyllis barba-jovis*; (**b**) the houseleek, *Sempervivum tectorum*. **Jupiter's distaff** a yellow-flowered sage, *Salvia glutinosa*.
2 The fifth planet in order of distance from the sun, and the largest planet in the solar system, whose orbit lies between those of Mars and Saturn. ME.
†**3** ALCHEMY. The metal tin. LME–M18.
4 HERALDRY. The tincture azure in the fanciful blazon of arms of sovereign princes. *obsolete* exc. *hist.* L16.

jupon /ˈdʒuːpɒn, dʒuːˈpɒn/ *noun*. LME.
[ORIGIN Old French *juppon*, (also mod.) *jupon*, from JUPE: see -OON. Cf. GIPON.]
hist. A close-fitting tunic or doublet; *esp.* one worn under a hauberk, sometimes of thick material and padded Also, a sleeveless surcoat worn outside armour, of rich material and emblazoned with arms.

Jura /ˈdʒʊərə/ *noun & adjective*. E19.
[ORIGIN A range of mountains on the border between France and Switzerland.]
GEOLOGY. ▶**A** *noun*. Jurassic rocks or strata; the Jurassic system. E19.
▶**B** *attrib.* or as *adjective*. = JURASSIC *adjective*. M19.

jural /ˈdʒʊər(ə)l/ *adjective*. M17.
[ORIGIN from Latin *jur-*, *jus* right, law + -AL¹.]
1 Of or relating to law or its administration; legal. M17.
2 PHILOSOPHY. Of or pertaining to rights and obligations. M19.
■ **jurally** *adverb* with reference to law, or to rights and obligations L19.

jurament /ˈdʒʊərəm(ə)nt/ *noun*. L15.
[ORIGIN Late Latin *juramentum*, from *jurare* swear: see -MENT.]
1 An oath. Long *rare*. L15.
2 At Oxford University, a logical disputation. Chiefly in ***do juraments***, attend one logical disputation a term, as part of the prescribed BA course. *obsolete* exc. *hist.* L15.

jurant /ˈdʒʊər(ə)nt/ *noun & adjective*. L16.
[ORIGIN Latin *jurant-* pres. ppl stem of *jurare* swear: see -ANT¹.]
▶**A** *noun*. A person who takes an oath; *spec.* (SCOTTISH HISTORY) a person who took the oath of allegiance to William and Mary or their successors (opp. NONJURANT *noun*). L16.
▶**B** *adjective*. Taking an oath; *spec.* (SCOTTISH HISTORY) taking the oath of allegiance to William and Mary or their successors (opp. NONJURANT *adjective*). E18.

Jurassic /dʒʊˈrasɪk/ *adjective & noun*. M19.
[ORIGIN French *Jurassique*, from JURA: see -IC. Cf. *Liassic*, *Triassic*.]
GEOLOGY. ▶**A** *adjective*. Designating or pertaining to the second period of the Mesozoic era, following the Triassic and preceding the Cretaceous, characterized by the prevalence of oolitic limestone, the predominance of reptiles, and evidence of the first birds. M19.
▶**B** *noun*. The Jurassic period; the system of rocks dating from this time. M19.

jurat /ˈdʒʊərat/ *noun*¹. LME.
[ORIGIN medieval Latin *juratus* lit. 'sworn man', use as noun of masc. pa. pple of Latin *jurare* swear: see -AT¹.]
1 A person who has taken an oath or who performs some duty on oath; *spec.* one sworn to give information and in other ways assist the administration of justice. *obsolete* exc. *hist.* LME.
2 A municipal officer (esp. of the Cinque Ports) holding a position similar to that of an alderman. LME.
3 A municipal magistrate in certain French towns. LME.
4 In the Channel Islands: each of a body of magistrates, elected for life, who in conjunction with the Bailiff form the Royal Court for administration of justice. M16.

jurat /ˈdʒʊərat/ *noun*². L18.
[ORIGIN Latin *juratum* use as noun of neut. pa. pple of *jurare* swear: see -AT¹.]
LAW. A memorandum as to where, when, and before whom an affidavit is sworn.

jurator /dʒʊˈreɪtə/ *noun*. *rare*. E17.
[ORIGIN Latin, from *jurat-*: see JURATORY, -ATOR.]
= JURAT *noun*¹ 1.

juratory /ˈdʒʊərət(ə)ri/ *adjective*. Now *rare*. M16.
[ORIGIN Late Latin *juratorius* confirmed by oath, from *jurat-* pa. ppl stem of *jurare* swear: see -ORY².]
Of or pertaining to an oath or oaths; expressed or contained in an oath.

†**jure** *verb trans. rare* (Shakes.). Only in L16.
[ORIGIN Back-form. from JUROR.]
Make a juror of (a person).

†**jurediction** *noun* see JURISDICTION.

jure divino /ˌdʒʊərɪ dɪˈviːnəʊ/ *adverbial phr.* L16.
[ORIGIN Latin.]
By divine right or authority.

juriballi /jʊərɪˈbali/ *noun*. Also **euri-**, **-bali**. M19.
[ORIGIN Arawak.]
Any of several S. American trees belonging to the family Meliaceae, esp. *Trichilia moschata*; the bark of this tree, formerly used as a febrifuge.

juridic /dʒʊˈrɪdɪk/ *adjective*. E16.
[ORIGIN Latin *juridicus*, from *jur-*, *jus* right, law + *-dicus* saying, speaking, from *dicere* say: see -IC.]
1 Of or pertaining to law, legal. E16.
2 = JURIDICAL 2. L19.

juridical /dʒʊˈrɪdɪk(ə)l/ *adjective*. E16.
[ORIGIN formed as JURIDIC + -AL¹.]
1 Of, pertaining to, or connected with the administration of law or judicial proceedings; legal. E16.
2 Assumed by law to exist. M19.
■ **juridically** *adverb* E17.

jurimetrics /dʒʊərɪˈmɛtrɪks/ *noun*. M20.
[ORIGIN from Latin *jur-*, *jus* right, law + -I- + *-metrics*, after *biometrics*, *econometrics*.]
The use of scientific methods in the study of legal matters.
■ **jurimetrician** /-ˈtrɪʃ(ə)n/, **jurimetricist** *nouns* an expert in or student of jurimetrics M20.

juring /ˈdʒʊərɪŋ/ *adjective*. *rare*. E18.
[ORIGIN from JUR(OR + -ING².]
hist. Taking the oath of allegiance to William and Mary or their successors. Opp. NONJURING.

jurisconsult /ˌdʒʊərɪskənˈsʌlt/ *noun*. E17.
[ORIGIN Latin *jurisconsultus*, from *juris* genit. of *jus* right, law + *consultus* skilled, from *consult-*: see CONSULT *verb*.]
A person learned in law, esp. in civil or international law; an expert in jurisprudence.

jurisdiction /dʒʊərɪsˈdɪkʃ(ə)n/ *noun*. Also (earlier) †**juredíction**. ME.
[ORIGIN Old French *juredíction*, (also mod.) *jurid-* from Latin *jurisdictio(n-)*, from *juris* genit. of *jus* right, law + *dictio(n-)*: see DICTION. Later assim. to Latin.]
1 Exercise of judicial authority, or of the functions of a judge or legal tribunal; power of administering law or justice. Also, power or authority in general; administration, control. ME.

> M. IGNATIEFF The Cabinet had no jurisdiction over military matters.

contentious jurisdiction: see CONTENTIOUS 2. ***summary jurisdiction***: see SUMMARY *adjective* 1C.
2 The extent or range of judicial or administrative power; the territory over which such power extends. LME.

> H. MARTINEAU Whether he should not send on this procession, and keep the next . . within his jurisdiction.

peculiar jurisdiction: see PECULIAR *adjective*.
3 A judicature; a court, or series of courts, of justice. L17.

> J. Q. ADAMS The jurisdictions to which resort must be had . . are those of municipal police.

■ **jurisdictional** *adjective* M17. **jurisdictionally** *adverb* in the way of a judicial decision; with regard to jurisdiction: L17.

jurisdictive /dʒʊərɪsˈdɪktɪv/ *adjective*. *rare*. M17.
[ORIGIN from JURISDICTION, on the analogy of *administration*, *administrative*, etc.]
Of or pertaining to jurisdiction.

jurisprude /ˈdʒʊərɪspruːd/ *noun*. M20.
[ORIGIN Back-form from JURISPRUDENCE, after PRUDE *noun*.]
A jurisprudent, *spec.* one who makes a display of learning or who is overly serious.

jurisprudence /dʒʊərɪsˈpruːd(ə)ns/ *noun*. E17.
[ORIGIN Late Latin *jurisprudentia*, from *juris* genit. of *jus* right, law + *prudentia* skill, proficiency.]
1 a Knowledge of or skill in law. Now *rare*. E17. ▸**b** The science which treats of human laws (written or unwritten) in general; the philosophy of law. M18.
2 A system or body of law; a legal system. Also, the decision of a court. M17.
– PHRASES: ***medical jurisprudence***.

jurisprudent /dʒʊərɪsˈpruːd(ə)nt/ *noun & adjective*. E17.
[ORIGIN French †*jurisprudent*, from *jurisprudence*, formed as JURISPRUDENCE: see -ENT.]
▶**A** *noun*. An expert in or student of jurisprudence; a person learned in law; a jurist. E17.
▶**B** *adjective*. Skilled in jurisprudence; having knowledge of the principles of law. M18.

jurisprudential /ˌdʒʊərɪsprʊˈdɛnʃ(ə)l/ *adjective*. L18.
[ORIGIN from JURISPRUDENCE after *prudence*, *prudential*.]
Of or pertaining to jurisprudence.
■ **jurisprudentialist** *noun* a writer on or expert in jurisprudence E19. **jurisprudentially** *adverb* with regard to jurisprudence E19.

jurist /ˈdʒʊərɪst/ *noun*. L15.
[ORIGIN French *juriste* or medieval Latin *jurista*, from Latin *jur-*, *jus* right, law: see -IST.]
1 A person who practises in law; a lawyer; a judge. Now *US*. L15.
2 An expert in law; a legal writer. E17.
3 In the ancient British universities: a person studying or taking a degree in law. L17.
■ **juˈristic**, **juˈristical** *adjectives* of or belonging to a jurist; pertaining to the study of law: M19. **juˈristically** *adverb* L19.

juror /ˈdʒʊərə/ *noun*. LME.
[ORIGIN Anglo-Norman *jurour*, Old French *jureor* (mod. *jureur*) from Latin *jurator*, from *jurat-* pa. ppl stem of *jurare* swear, from *jur-*, *jus* right, law: see -OR.]
1 A member of a jury in a court of justice or at a coroner's inquest. LME.
common juror, ***grand juror***, ***special juror***, etc.
†**2** [From the corrupt conduct formerly attributed to jurors.] A person who makes a false statement about an accused person; a slanderer, an oppressor; a covetous man. LME–M16.
3 Chiefly *hist.* A person who takes or has taken an oath; a person who swears allegiance to some body or cause. Cf. NONJUROR. L16.
4 Each of a body of people appointed to judge and award prizes in a competition. M19.

jury /ˈdʒʊəri/ *noun*. LME.
[ORIGIN Anglo-Norman *juree* jury from Old French *juree* oath, juridical inquiry from Anglo-Latin *jurata* use as noun of fem. pa. pple of Latin *jurare* swear, from *jur-*, *jus* right, law.]
1 A group of people (orig. all men), usu. twelve in number, sworn to give a verdict on some question or questions submitted to them in a court of justice or at a coroner's inquest, usu. on evidence presented to them, but orig. from their own knowledge. LME.

> S. BUTLER The barrister who is trying to persuade a jury to acquit a prisoner. J. BUCHAN The jury found it a case of suicide while of unsound mind.

common jury: see COMMON *adjective*. ***coroner's jury***: see CORONER 1. ***grand jury***: see GRAND *adjective*¹. ***hang a jury***: see HANG *verb*. **jury de medietate linguae** /diː mɛdɪəˌteɪti ˈlɪŋgwiː, deɪ mɛdɪəˌtɑːti ˈlɪŋgwʌɪ/ [medieval Latin = of a moiety of language] *hist.* a jury composed half of Englishmen and half of foreigners, for the trial of some aliens. **the jury is (still) out on** a decision or conclusion has not yet been reached on (a controversial subject). **jury of matrons** *hist.* a jury of women empanelled to inquire into a case of alleged pregnancy, *esp.* one involving a woman sentenced to death. ***petit jury***: see PETIT *adjective*¹. ***petty jury***: see PETTY *adjective*. ***special jury***: see SPECIAL *adjective*. ***traverse jury***: see TRAVERSE *noun*. ***trial jury***: see TRIAL *noun*.
†**2** *transf.* A group of twelve; a dozen. L16–M17.

> T. FULLER All the Jurie of the Apostles.

3 *hist.* Any of several bodies whose functions corresponded in part to those of a British jury. M19.
4 A body of people appointed to judge and award prizes in a competition. M19.
– COMB.: **jury box** an enclosed space in which the jury sits in court; **jury fixer** *US* a person who bribes or otherwise illegally influences a jury or juror; **jury-fixing** *US* bribery of a jury or jurors; **jury list**: of people liable to be summoned to act as jurors; **juryman** a man serving on a jury, a male juror; **jurywoman** a woman serving on a jury, a female juror.

jury- /ˈdʒʊəri/ *combining form*. Also as adjective **jury**. **E17.**
[ORIGIN Perh. ult. from Old French *ajurie* aid, from *aju-* pres. stem of *aidier* AID *verb* + *-rie* -RY.]
NAUTICAL. (Serving) as a temporary expedient, makeshift.
jury-leg *joc.* a wooden leg. **jury-mast** a mast put up in place of one that has been broken or carried away. **jury-rig** *verb trans.* supply with temporary rigging. **jury-rudder** a contrivance taking the place of a damaged rudder.

jus /ʒy, ʒuː/ *noun*. **M20.**
[ORIGIN French.]
A thin gravy made from the pan juices of roast meat; a sauce.

jus /dʒʌs/ *adverb. colloq. & dial.* Also **jus'**. **E19.**
[ORIGIN Repr. a pronunc.]
= JUST *adverb*.

jus cogens /dʒʌs ˈkəʊdʒɛnz/ *noun phr.* **L19.**
[ORIGIN Latin = compelling law.]
A principle of international law which cannot be set aside by agreement or acquiescence; a peremptory norm of general international law.

jus gentium /dʒʌs ˈdʒɛnʃɪəm/ *noun phr.* **M16.**
[ORIGIN Latin = law of nations.]
= ***international law*** s.v. INTERNATIONAL *adjective*.

jus primae noctis /dʒʌs ˌprʌɪmiː ˈnɒktɪs/ *noun phr.* **L19.**
[ORIGIN Latin = right of the first night.]
= ***droit du seigneur*** s.v. DROIT *noun*[1].

jusqu'au bout /ʒysko bu/ *adverbial phr.* **E20.**
[ORIGIN French = up to the end.]
To the bitter end; until a conclusive victory has been gained.

†**jussel** *noun*. **LME–E19.**
[ORIGIN Old French = juice, broth, from Latin *juscellum* dim. of *jusculum* dim. of *jus* broth, soup: see -EL[2].]
COOKERY. (A) mixed meat stew or mince.

Jussiaean /dʒʌsɪˈiːən/ *adjective*. Also **Jussieu(e)an** /dʒʌsɪˈjuːən/. **E19.**
[ORIGIN from Latinized form of *Jussiaeus*, *Jussieu* (see below) + -AN.]
BOTANY (now *hist.*). Designating or pertaining to the natural system of plant classification devised by the French botanists Bernard de Jussieu (1699–1777) and his nephew Antoine Laurent de Jussieu (1748–1836).

jussion /ˈdʒʌʃ(ə)n/ *noun*. *rare*. **L18.**
[ORIGIN French from Latin *jussio(n-)* order, command, formed as JUSSIVE: see -ION.]
Order, command.

jussive /ˈdʒʌsɪv/ *adjective & noun*. **M19.**
[ORIGIN from Latin *juss-* pa. ppl stem of *jubere* to command + -IVE.]
▸ **A** *adjective*. Esp. of a form of a verb: expressing a command or order. **M19.**
▸ **B** *noun*. A verbal form expressing a command. **E20.**

†**just** *noun* var. of JOUST *noun*.

just /dʒʌst/ *adjective*. **LME.**
[ORIGIN Old French & mod. French *juste* from Latin *justus*, from *jus* right, law.]
1 That does what is morally right, righteous; THEOLOGY considered or made righteous, esp. by God. *arch.* **LME.**
the sleep of the just: see SLEEP *noun*.
2 Impartial in one's dealings; giving every one his or her due; fair, unbiased. **LME.** ▸†**b** Faithful or honourable in one's social relations. Foll. by *of*, *to*. **E17–E19.**

> D. FRANCIS He had decided, as he was a just and logical person, that her sex was immaterial. J. C. OATES Twelve jurors who had seemed.. to be just and upright and unprejudiced men.

3 a In accordance with the principles of moral right or of equity; equitable, fair; (of a reward, punishment, etc.) deserved, merited. **LME.** ▸**b** In accordance with the law, lawful, rightful. **LME.**

> **a** P. B. HINCHLIFF The just cause must be made to succeed. R. DAVIES The destruction of the existing order was the inevitable preamble to any beginning of the just society. R. C. A. WHITE The criminal process.. will bring them their just deserts. *Sunday Times* A lower starting rate would be socially just (by cutting the tax burden of the poor). **b** *Liverpool Mercury* Any wrongful act, done intentionally, without just cause or excuse, was a malicious act.

a just war: deemed to be morally or theologically justifiable.
4 Having reasonable or adequate grounds; well-founded. **LME.**

> ELIZABETH HAMILTON Alas! My fears were just.

5 Conforming to a particular standard; proper; correct, appropriate. **LME.** ▸**b** MUSIC. Set or tuned according to the exact vibration intervals of the notes; non-tempered, natural. Esp. in ***just intonation***. **M19.**
†**6** Of a measurement, amount, number, etc.: exact, precise; (of an instrument or action) uniform in operation, regular, even. **LME–E19.**
7 Of an idea, opinion, etc.: right, true, correct. **LME.** ▸†**b** Of a copy, description, etc.: exact, accurate. **M16–L18.**
†**8** Corresponding exactly, equal; even, level. **M16–E19.**
†**9** Full, proper, complete. **L16–L18.**

just /dʒʌst/ *verb*[1] *trans. rare*. **M16.**
[ORIGIN Aphet. from ADJUST.]
Adjust.

†**just** *verb*[2] var. of JOUST *verb*.

just /dʒʌst/ *adverb*. **LME.**
[ORIGIN from the adjective: cf. adverbial use of French *juste*. See also JES, JEST *adverb*, JIST, JUS.]
1 Exactly, precisely; actually; closely, close. **LME.**

> T. HARDY They had been standing just by the drawing-room door. T. S. ELIOT It is impossible to say just what I mean! C. P. SNOW Someone dropped a ruler just then. R. K. NARAYAN You are just the person I was looking for. G. GREENE He remembered now: it was just three years ago. J. SIMMS He looked just like an ordinary boy.

†**2 a** So as to fit exactly, in a close-fitting way. **L15–L17.** ▸**b** With precision, accurately; punctually; correctly. **M16–M18.**
3 a Exactly at the moment spoken of; precisely now or then. **L15.** ▸**b** A very little before; with little preceding interval; within a brief preceding period; very recently. **M17.** ▸**c** A very little after, very soon. **L17.**

> **a** E. NESBIT Alice was just asking Noel how he would deal with the robber.. when we heard a noise downstairs. **b** I. MURDOCH Gosh, I believe I've just swallowed a furry caterpillar! **c** DEFOE Tell his excellency I am just a coming.

†**4** In expressions of assent: exactly so, just so, right, quite. **M16–L17.**
5 No more than; only, merely; barely. **M17.**

> B. PYM I'm just getting the place ready. J. B. MORTON Using my telescope, I could just make out the name on her bows. *Observer* It is ridiculous to think you can spend your entire life with just one person. M. KEANE Expensive ideas which he felt just young enough to develop. W. WHARTON I get scared just going around Paris.

6 a Neither more nor less than, simply; absolutely; actually, really. **E18.** ▸**b** Truly, indeed. *colloq.* **M19.**

> **a** E. BOWEN After all these years, Diana just walking in! A. S. BYATT I just can't settle to any work. JACQUELINE WILSON They're just morons, though they think they're dead original. **b** J. B. PRIESTLEY She let herself go all right, didn't she just!

– PHRASES: †**even just** = senses 1, 3 above. **just about** almost (exactly); almost completely. ***just a minute***: see MINUTE *noun*. **just as** precisely in the way that, to the same degree as. ***just as well***: see WELL *adverb*. ***just in case***: see CASE *noun*[1]. **just in time** narrowly avoiding lateness, at the last possible moment; COMMERCE (relating to or designating) a factory system whereby materials are delivered immediately before they are required. **just it** precisely the thing or point in question. ***just my luck***, ***just his luck***, ***just our luck***, etc.: see LUCK *noun*. **just now** (*a*) only a very short time ago; (*b*) at this exact moment; (*c*) (chiefly *S. Afr.*) very soon, in a little while. ***just* QUIETLY**. **just so** (*a*) exactly as has been said; (*b*) in the required or appropriate manner; (*c*) very close or friendly; (*d*) very neatly and carefully; (*e*) neat and tidy, fastidious. **just-so story** a story which purports to explain the origin of something, a myth. ***just the job***: see JOB *noun*[1]. ***just the same***: see SAME *adverb*. **just too bad** unfortunate but inevitable. ***not just a pretty face***: see PRETTY *adjective* 3a. **only just** by a very narrow margin, barely.

justaucorps /ʒystokɔːr/ *noun*. Pl. same. **M17.**
[ORIGIN French, from *juste* close-fitting + *au corps* to the body.]
hist. A close-fitting outer garment; *spec.* (*a*) a man's coat, usu. worn over a waistcoat, with a skirt flaring out to the knees; (*b*) a woman's riding jacket resembling a frock coat.

juste milieu /ʒystə miljø/ *noun phr.* **M19.**
[ORIGIN French, lit. 'the right mean'.]
A happy medium, the golden mean; judicious moderation, esp. in politics.

> A. J. P. TAYLOR One looks in vain in their history for a *juste milieu*, for common sense.

justice /ˈdʒʌstɪs/ *noun*. **LOE.**
[ORIGIN Old French & mod. French from Latin *justitia*, from *justus* JUST *adjective*: see -ICE[1].]
▸ **I** Judicial administration of law or equity.
1 Maintenance of legal, social, or moral principles by the exercise of authority or power; assignment of deserved reward or punishment; giving of due deserts. **LOE.** ▸**b** Justice personified, *spec.* as a goddess holding balanced scales and a sword. **L16.**

> *Observer* I am glad that justice was done. P. ROTH They should have cut my head off. That would have been justice. *Which?* Who could possibly defend the idea of someone being deprived of legal support to get justice. **b** A. F. DOUGLAS-HOME A picture.. showing.. Justice holding the scales with her foot on the Duke of Hamilton's neck.

2 The administration of law or of legal processes; judicial proceedings. **ME.** ▸†**b** The people administering the law; a judicial assembly, a court of justice. **ME–M17.**

> *New York Times* We will do everything possible to see that those responsible are brought to justice.

†**3** Infliction of punishment on an offender, *esp.* capital punishment; execution. **LME–E17.**
▸ **II** The quality of being just.
4 The quality or fact of being just; (the principle of) just dealing or conduct; integrity, impartiality, fairness. **ME.**

> T. O. ECHEWA The elders.. in spite of their long-winded orations about justice were prone to deviousness and chicanery.

†**5** THEOLOGY. The state of being righteous, righteousness. **M16–E17.**
6 Conformity (of an action or thing) to moral right or to reason, truth, or fact; = JUSTNESS 2, 3. **L16.**

> J. UPDIKE Bech.. was enraptured by what seemed the beautiful justice of the remark. P. HOWARD The paper that had thundered for reform.. could see the justice of the case for women's suffrage.

▸ **III** An administrator of justice.
7 *gen.* A judicial officer, a judge, a magistrate. **ME.**
8 a A judge presiding over or belonging to one of the superior courts; *spec.* in England, a member of the Supreme Court of Judicature. **ME.** ▸**b** A Justice of the Peace (see below); (occas.) any inferior magistrate. Chiefly in ***the Justices***. **L16.**
– PHRASES: ***bed of justice***: see BED *noun*. **Chief Justice** (*a*) *hist.* (the title of) the judge presiding over the court of King's or Queen's Bench or of Common Pleas; (*b*) *US* (the title of) the presiding judge in the Supreme Court or in the supreme court of a state. ***College of Justice***: see COLLEGE 1. ***COMMUTATIVE justice***. **Department of Justice** *US* a government department headed by the Attorney General. ***DISTRIBUTIVE justice***. **do justice to** (*a*) give (a person) his or her due, treat fairly by acknowledging the merits etc. of (someone); (*b*) treat (a subject or thing) in a manner showing due appreciation, deal with as is right or fitting; †(*c*) pledge with a drink. **do oneself justice** perform something one has to do in a manner worthy of one's abilities. **in justice to** in fairness to. ***Jersey justice***: see JERSEY *noun*[1]. **Justice Clerk** = ***Lord Justice Clerk*** below. **Justice General** = ***Lord Justice General*** below. ***justice in eyre***: see EYRE 1. **Justice of the Peace** a lay magistrate appointed to preserve the peace in a county, town, etc., and discharge other local magisterial functions, as hearing minor cases and granting licences; a subordinate magistrate in a specific district; abbreviation *JP*. **Lord Chief Justice** (*a*) *hist.* = ***Chief Justice*** (a) above; (*b*) (the title of) the judge presiding over the King's or Queen's Bench Division of the High Court. **Lord Justice, Lord Justice of Appeal** (pl. **Lords Justices**) a judge in the Court of Appeal. **Lord Justice Clerk** *Scot.* (the title of) the vice-president of the High Court of Justiciary. **Lord Justice General** *Scot.* (the title of) the president of the High Court of Justiciary. ***Lord Justice of Appeal***: see ***Lord Justice*** above. **Mr Justice —, Mrs Justice —**: a form of address or mode of reference to a High Court judge. ***miscarriage of justice***: see MISCARRIAGE 2. ***myrmidon of justice***: see MYRMIDON 3. **poetical justice, poetic justice** the ideal justice in distribution of rewards and punishments supposed to befit a poem or other work of imagination; well-deserved unforeseen retribution or reward. ***rough justice***: see ROUGH *adjective*. **with justice** with justification, reasonably.
– COMB.: **justice-seat** a court of justice, a place where justice is dispensed; a sitting of a court.
■ **justiceship** *noun* the office or position of a justice or judge **M16.**

justice /ˈdʒʌstɪs/ *verb*. Now *rare*. **ME.**
[ORIGIN Anglo-Norman *justicer* = Old French *justicier* from medieval Latin *justitiare* exercise justice over, from Latin *justitia*: see JUSTICE *noun*.]
†**1** *verb trans.* Administer justice to; rule, govern. **ME–L15.**
†**2** *verb trans.* Try in a court of law; bring to trial; punish judicially. **ME–M18.**
3 *verb intrans.* Administer justice. Chiefly as ***justicing*** *verbal noun*. **E17.**

justicer /ˈdʒʌstɪsə/ *noun*. *arch.* **ME.**
[ORIGIN Anglo-Norman, Old French *justicier* formed as JUSTICIARY *noun*[1]: see -ER[2].]
1 A person who maintains or carries out justice; a supporter or defender of right. **ME.**
2 Orig., a ruler or governor invested with judicial authority. Later, a judge, a magistrate. **LME.**
3 *spec.* = JUSTICE *noun* 8a. **M16.**

justiciable /dʒʌˈstɪʃəb(ə)l/ *adjective & noun*. **LME.**
[ORIGIN Anglo-Norman & Old French & mod. French = (a person) amenable to a jurisdiction, formed as JUSTICE *verb*: see -ABLE.]
▸ **A** *adjective*. Liable to be tried in a court of justice; subject to jurisdiction. **LME.**
▸ **B** *noun*. A person subject to the jurisdiction of another. *rare*. **L19.**
■ **justiciaˈbility** *noun* **E19.**

justicial /dʒʌˈstɪʃ(ə)l/ *adjective*. *rare*. **LME.**
[ORIGIN medieval Latin *justitialis*, from *justitia* JUSTICE *noun*: see -AL[1].]
Of or pertaining to justice or the administration of justice.

Justicialism /dʒʌˈstɪʃ(ə)lɪz(ə)m/ *noun*. Also in Spanish form **Justicialismo** /dʒʌˌstɪʃəˈlɪzməʊ/; **j-**. **M20.**
[ORIGIN Spanish *justicialismo*, from *justicia* justice + *-al* -AL[1] + *-ismo* -ISM.]
The political doctrine claimed by Juan Domingo Perón (1895–1974), president of Argentina (1946–55 and 1973–4), a combination of Fascism and socialism. Cf. PERONISM.
■ **Justicialist** *adjective* **M20.**

justiciar /dʒʌˈstɪʃə/ *noun*. **L15.**
[ORIGIN medieval Latin *justitiarius*: see JUSTICIARY *noun*[1], -AR[2].]
1 *hist.* **a** = JUSTICE *noun* 8a. **L15.** ▸**b** Either of two supreme judges under early Scottish kings. **E17.**
2 *hist.* More fully ***Chief Justiciar***. The regent and deputy of the Norman and early Plantagenet kings, who presided over the king's court; = JUSTICIARY *noun*[1] 3. **L16.**
3 *gen.* An administrator of justice; a person who maintains or carries out justice. *arch.* **E17.**
4 Chiefly *hist.* Any of various Continental officials or functionaries. **M19.**
■ **justiciarship** *noun* the office of justiciar **L17.**

justiciary /dʒʌˈstɪʃ(ə)ri/ *noun*[1]. **M16.**
[**ORIGIN** medieval Latin *justitiarius*, *-ciarius* judge, from Latin *justitia* **JUSTICE** *noun*: see **-ARY**[1].]
1 A person who maintains or carries out justice; an administrator of justice. **M16.**
†**2** *CHRISTIAN THEOLOGY*. A believer in the ability to attain righteousness by one's own efforts. **M16–E18.**
3 *hist.* More fully ***Chief Justiciary*** = **JUSTICIAR** 2. **E18.**
4 *hist.* = **JUSTICE** *noun* 8a. **M18.**
5 Any of various Continental officials or functionaries. **M18.**
■ **justiciaryship** *noun* the office of justiciary **E18.**

justiciary /dʒʌˈstɪʃ(ə)ri/ *noun*[2]. *Scot.* **LME.**
[**ORIGIN** medieval Latin *justitiaria* office of a judge or justiciar, formed as **JUSTICIARY** *noun*[1] + **-ARY**[1].]
The jurisdiction or office of a justiciar or justiciary.
High Court of Justiciary the supreme criminal court of Scotland.

justiciary /dʒʌˈstɪʃ(ə)ri/ *adjective*. **L16.**
[**ORIGIN** medieval Latin *justitiarius* judicial, from Latin *justitia* **JUSTICE** *noun* + *-arius* **-ARY**[1].]
Pertaining to or connected with the administration of justice or the office of a justice.

justicies /dʒʌˈstɪʃiːz/ *noun*. **M16.**
[**ORIGIN** Anglo-Latin, first word of the writ, 2nd person sing. pres. subjunct. of medieval Latin *justiciare* **JUSTICE** *verb*.]
LAW (now *hist.*). A writ directed to a sheriff, allowing him to hold plea of debt in his county court for sums exceeding the usual limit of forty shillings.

justifiable /ˈdʒʌstɪfʌɪəb(ə)l/ *adjective*. **E16.**
[**ORIGIN** Old French & mod. French, from *justifier* **JUSTIFY**: see **-ABLE**.]
†**1** = **JUSTICIABLE** *adjective*. **E16–M17.**
2 Able to be legally or morally justified; able to be shown to be just, reasonable, or correct; defensible. **M16.** ▸†**b** Of an assertion etc.: able to be maintained or defended. **E–M17.**

R. CROMPTON In a moment of justifiable exasperation, he threw a beer bottle at her head. J. GATHORNE-HARDY It's quite justifiable to give a massive dose of drugs to sedate them.

justifiable HOMICIDE.
■ **justifiaˈbility** *noun* **L19.** **justifiableness** *noun* **M17.** **justifiably** *adverb* **LME.**

justification /ˌdʒʌstɪfɪˈkeɪʃ(ə)n/ *noun*. **LME.**
[**ORIGIN** Old French & mod. French, or Christian Latin *justificatio(n-)*, from *justificat-* pa. ppl stem of *justificare*: see **JUSTIFY**, **-FICATION**.]
†**1** Administration of justice or the law; execution of sentence; capital punishment. Long *Scot. rare*. **LME–L19.**
2 *THEOLOGY*. The action whereby humankind is justified or made righteous by God; the fact or condition of being so justified. **LME.**
†**3** An ordinance; an ordained form. **LME–E17.**
4 a The action of justifying or of showing something to be just, right, or proper. **L15.** ▸**b** That which justifies; a defence; a good reason or cause. **L15.**

a J. BUTLER Nothing can with reason be urged in justification of revenge. **b** M. L. KING The curse of poverty has no justification in our age. R. INGALLS Reading Xenophon's explanation and justification of his conduct.

5 *LAW*. **a** The showing or maintaining in court that one had sufficient reason for doing the thing with which one is charged; a circumstance giving grounds for such a plea. **E16.** ▸**b** The justifying of bail. **L18.**
6 The action of adjusting or arranging something exactly. Now *spec.* the action, process, or result of justifying print or lines of text. **L17.**

justificative /ˈdʒʌstɪfɪkeɪtɪv/ *adjective*. *rare*. **E17.**
[**ORIGIN** French *justificatif*, *-ive*, from Christian Latin *justificat-*: see **JUSTIFICATION**, **-IVE**.]
Serving to justify; justificatory.

justificatory /ˈdʒʌstɪfɪkeɪt(ə)ri, ˌdʒʌstɪfɪˈkeɪt(ə)ri/ *adjective*. **L16.**
[**ORIGIN** medieval Latin *justificatorius*, from Christian Latin *justificat-*: see **JUSTIFICATION**, **-ORY**[2].]
Tending to justify something; serving or intended to support a statement.

justified /ˈdʒʌstɪfʌɪd/ *adjective*. **M16.**
[**ORIGIN** from **JUSTIFY** + **-ED**[1]. Earlier in **UNJUSTIFIED**.]
Just, right, righteous; warranted; having good cause or reason, correct; supported by evidence; (in printing etc.) that has been justified.

M. BARING What Burstall told him cheered him, and he felt justified in continuing. A. J. CRONIN He would repay it, he would show her . . that her faith in him was justified. B. GELDOF I thought we were justified and therefore any risk was acceptable.

justify /ˈdʒʌstɪfʌɪ/ *verb*. **ME.**
[**ORIGIN** Old French & mod. French *justifier* from Christian Latin *justificare* do justice to, vindicate, from Latin *justus* **JUST** *adjective*: see **-FY**.]
†**1** *verb trans.* Administer justice to, rule; keep or bring under the rule of law; treat justly. **ME–E17.**
†**2** *verb trans.* Inflict a judicial penalty on, punish; sentence, condemn; *esp.* (*Scot.*) punish with death, execute. **ME–L19.**
3 *verb trans.* Prove or maintain the rightness, worth, or innocence of; vindicate. **LME.**

M. PATTISON The difficult task of justifying science in the eyes of the nation. M. WEST History . . is always written to justify the survivors. M. PIERCY I don't have to justify myself to you.

4 *verb trans.* Absolve, acquit; *spec.* in *THEOLOGY*, declare righteous on the grounds of Christ's merit, or make inherently righteous by the infusion of grace. **LME.**
5 *verb trans.* Support or back up (an assertion, opinion, etc.) by evidence or testimony; confirm, prove, verify. **LME.** ▸†**b** Maintain as true, affirm, assert. **L16–L18.** ▸†**c** Acknowledge as true or genuine. Only in **E17.**

GIBBON The narratives of antiquity are justified by the experience of modern times.

6 *verb intrans. & trans.* *LAW*. Show adequate grounds for (doing the thing with which one is charged). **E16.**
justify bail show by oath when providing bail that one has sufficient funds to do so.
7 *verb trans.* **a** Show or maintain the justice or reasonableness of (an action, claim, etc.); defend as right or proper. **M16.** ▸**b** Make right, proper, or reasonable; give adequate grounds for, warrant. **M17.**

a MILTON I may assert th' eternal Providence, And justifie the wayes of God to men. J. A. MICHENER We've gathered here . . to hear a great man try to justify his mistakes. M. FOOT No socialist . . would ever have justified the resort to these perverted means to secure his ends. **b** M. PRIOR The end must justifie the means; He only sins who ill intends. A. MILLER Life is God's most precious gift; no principle . . may justify the taking of it. G. GREENE To justify these payments he had to compose a regular supply of reports.

8 *verb trans.* Orig., make exact, adjust to exact shape, size, or position. Now *spec.* in *TYPOGRAPHY* etc., adjust spacing along (a line of text) to a prescribed measure so that adjacent lines are of equal length; arrange (a body of text) into lines of equal length. **M16.**
■ **justifier** *noun* a person who or thing which justifies someone or something **E16.** **justifyingly** *adverb* in a justifying manner **E18.**

justing *verbal noun* var. of **JOUSTING**.

Justinianian /dʒʌˌstɪnɪˈeɪnɪən/ *adjective*. **E19.**
[**ORIGIN** from *Justinian* (see below) + **-IAN**.]
Of or pertaining to Justinian I, emperor of the Eastern Roman or Byzantine Empire 527–65.
Justinianian code a compilation of Roman law made by order of Justinian I.
■ **Juˈstinianist** *noun* a person learned in the Justinianian code, a student of civil law **M17.**

justle *noun*, *verb* vars. of **JOSTLE** *noun*, *verb*.

justly /ˈdʒʌs(t)li/ *adverb*. **ME.**
[**ORIGIN** from **JUST** *adjective* + **-LY**[2].]
1 Exactly, precisely, accurately, closely. *obsolete* exc. *dial.* **ME.**
2 Uprightly, righteously. *arch.* **LME.**
3 In accordance with justice or equity, deservedly; with good reason; rightly, properly. **LME.**

J. BUCHAN Your family was unpopular—I understand, justly unpopular. R. LEHMANN He was a beautiful swimmer, and justly proud of his torso.

justness /ˈdʒʌs(t)nɪs/ *noun*. **LME.**
[**ORIGIN** from **JUST** *adjective* + **-NESS**.]
†**1** The quality of being righteous or upright, righteousness. **LME–E18.**
2 The quality or fact of being morally right or equitable or of having reasonable grounds; rightfulness; fairness; validity. **LME.**
3 Conformity to truth or to a standard; correctness; propriety. **M17.**

jut /dʒʌt/ *noun*[1]. *obsolete* exc. *dial.* **M16.**
[**ORIGIN** from (the same root as) **JUT** *verb*[1].]
A push, thrust, or knock against a resisting body; the shock of collision.

jut /dʒʌt/ *noun*[2]. **E18.**
[**ORIGIN** Var. of **JET** *noun*[2]: cf. **JUT** *verb*[2].]
†**1** = **JET** *noun*[2] 2. Only in **E18.**
2 A jutting out; a projection, a protruding point. Cf. **JET** *noun*[2] 1. **L18.**

M. GRAY The jut of the porch sheltered this window.

– **COMB.**: **jut-jawed** *adjective* having a jutting jaw.

jut /dʒʌt/ *verb*[1]. *obsolete* exc. *dial.* Infl. **-tt-**. **M16.**
[**ORIGIN** App. imit.]
1 *verb intrans.* Strike, knock, or push *against*. **M16.**
2 *verb trans.* Push, shove, jolt; knock against. **M16.**

jut /dʒʌt/ *verb*[2]. Infl. **-tt-**. **M16.**
[**ORIGIN** Var. of **JET** *verb*[2], by assim. to **JUTTY** *verb*, *noun*.]
1 *verb intrans.* Project, protrude; stick *out*. **M16.**

K. MANSFIELD Into the middle of the room a black stove jutted. J. C. POWYS A small landing-stage which jutted out into the river.

2 *verb trans.* Cause to jut (*out*). **M20.**

A. S. BYATT She put up her head and jutted out her chin with . . determination.

■ **juttingly** *adverb* in a jutting manner **M19.**

Jute /dʒuːt/ *noun*[1].
[**ORIGIN** Old English *Eotas*, *Iotas* pl. (cf. Icelandic *Jótar* people of Jutland (Old Norse *Jótland*) in Denmark), alt. in late Middle English after medieval Latin *Jutae*, *Juti*.]
A member of a Low German tribe which invaded and settled in parts of southern Britain in the 5th and 6th cents.
■ **Jutish** *adjective* of or pertaining to the Jutes **M19.**

jute /dʒuːt/ *noun*[2] & *adjective*. **M18.**
[**ORIGIN** Bengali *jhuṭo* from Prakrit (of central Asia) *j(h)uṣṭi*.]
▸ **A** *noun*. A fibre obtained from the phloem of the plants *Corchorus capsularis* and *C. olitorius*, of the linden family, which is imported chiefly from Bangladesh and West Bengal, and used in the manufacture of coarse sacking, canvas, twine, rope, etc.; either of the plants which provide this fibre. **M18.**
American jute, **Chinese jute** Indian mallow, *Abutilon theophrasti*, used as a substitute for jute.
▸ **B** *adjective*. Made of jute. **M18.**

jutka /ˈdʒʌtkə/ *noun*. **L19.**
[**ORIGIN** Hindi *jhaṭkā* a jerk, jolt, lurch.]
In southern India, a light two-wheeled vehicle drawn by a horse.

†**jutty** *noun*. **L15.**
[**ORIGIN** Var. of **JETTY** *noun*: cf. **JUT** *verb*[2].]
1 A pier, a breakwater, an embankment; = **JETTY** *noun* 1. **L15–E19.**
2 A projecting part of a wall or building; = **JETTY** *noun* 2. **E16–E18.**

jutty /ˈdʒʌti/ *adjective*. **E19.**
[**ORIGIN** from **JUT** *noun*[2] + **-Y**[1].]
Characterized by jutting out; projecting.

†**jutty** *verb*. **LME.**
[**ORIGIN** Rel. to **JUTTY** *noun*: cf. also **JETTY** *verb*.]
1 *verb intrans.* Project, jut. **LME–M19.**
2 *verb trans.* Project beyond, overhang. Only in **L16.**

juve /dʒuːv/ *noun*. *slang*. **M20.**
[**ORIGIN** Abbreviation. Cf. **JUVIE**.]
A juvenile, a young person; *spec.* (***a***) a juvenile lead; (***b***) a juvenile delinquent.

juvenal /ˈdʒuːvən(ə)l/ *noun*[1] & *adjective*. **L16.**
[**ORIGIN** Latin *juvenalis* (= *juvenilis*), from *juvenis* young person: see **-AL**[1].]
▸ †**A** *noun*. A youth; a juvenile. **L16–M19.**
▸ **B** *adjective*. Juvenile. Now *ORNITHOLOGY* (chiefly *US*). **M17.**

Juvenal /ˈdʒuːvən(ə)l/ *noun*[2]. **L16.**
[**ORIGIN** Decimus Junius *Juvenalis* (see below).]
A writer whose work can be likened to that of the Roman satirist Juvenal (**AD** *c* 60–*c* 130); a satirist.
■ **Juveˈnalian** *adjective* resembling or characteristic of Juvenal **M19.**

juvenescence /dʒuːvəˈnɛs(ə)ns/ *noun*. **E19.**
[**ORIGIN** formed as **JUVENESCENT**: see **-ESCENT**.]
Youth, youthfulness; the process of becoming young or youthful; the transition from infancy to youth.

juvenescent /dʒuːvəˈnɛs(ə)nt/ *adjective*. **E19.**
[**ORIGIN** Latin *juvenescent-* pres. ppl stem of *juvenescere* reach the age of youth: see **-ESCENT**.]
Becoming young or youthful; in the process of ageing from infancy to youth.

juvenile /ˈdʒuːvənʌɪl/ *adjective* & *noun*. **E17.**
[**ORIGIN** Latin *juvenilis*, from *juvenis* (a) young (person): see **-ILE**.]
▸ **A** *adjective*. **1** Young, youthful. **E17.**

H. B. STOWE The order was . . carried to Aunt Chloe by . . half a dozen juvenile messengers. V. NABOKOV She seemed to have grown less juvenile, more of a woman overnight.

2 Belonging to, characteristic of, suited to, or intended for youth or young people; (freq. *derog.*) immature, childish. **M17.**

R. CROMPTON A book of ghost stories from the juvenile library at school. M. FITZHERBERT Aubrey's views were often juvenile and always muddled.

3 *GEOLOGY*. Of water, gases, etc.: originating from magma and newly brought to the surface; not meteoric. **E20.**
– **SPECIAL COLLOCATIONS**: **juvenile court** a court of law for the trial of young offenders. **juvenile delinquency** the (habitual) committing of offences against the law by a minor or minors. **juvenile delinquent** a person engaged in juvenile delinquency. **juvenile hormone** *ENTOMOLOGY* each of a number of hormones that control larval development in insects and inhibit metamorphosis. **juvenile lead** = sense B.1b below; *spec.* an actor who plays the leading youthful part in a play etc.; the role so played. **juvenile leaf** a distinct kind of leaf characteristic of the immature stages of certain trees, shrubs, or woody climbers. **juvenile offender** a person below a specific age (18 in most countries, in *ENGLISH LAW* between the ages of 10 and 17) who has committed a crime.
▸ **B** *noun*. **1** A young person, a youth; a young creature, *esp.* a bird in its first full plumage. **M18.** ▸**b** *THEATRICAL*. An actor who plays a youthful part. **L19.**

M. Cox His new book was 'for juveniles'. *Bird Watching* Juveniles look similar to winter adults and can lack the yellow tip to the bill.

2 A book written for children. M19.
■ **juvenilely** *adverb* E18. **juvenileness** *noun* E18. **juvenilize** *verb trans.* make or keep young or youthful; ENTOMOLOGY arrest the normal development of: M19.

juvenilia /dʒuːvəˈnɪlɪə/ *noun pl.* E17.
[ORIGIN Latin, neut. pl. of *juvenilis* JUVENILE *adjective*.]
Literary or artistic works produced in an author's or artist's youth.

juvenility /dʒuːvəˈnɪlɪti/ *noun.* E17.
[ORIGIN Latin *juvenilitas*, formed as JUVENILE *adjective*: see -ITY.]
1 Youthfulness; juvenile manner, quality, or character. E17.
2 In *pl.* Juvenile characteristics, acts, or ideas. M17.
3 Young people collectively, youth. E19.

juventude /ˈdʒuːv(ə)ntjuːd/ *noun. rare.* LME.
[ORIGIN from Latin *juventut-*, *juventus*, from *juvenis*: see JUVENILE, -TUDE Cf. medieval Latin *juventitudo*.]
Youth.

juvescence /dʒuːˈvɛs(ə)ns/ *noun. rare.* E20.
[ORIGIN Irreg. contr. of JUVENESCENCE.]
The process of becoming young, juvenescence.

juvia /ˈdʒuːvɪə, ˈhuː-/ *noun.* M19.
[ORIGIN Amer. Spanish from Arawak.]
The Brazil nut; (also ***juvia tree***) the tree, *Bertholletia excelsa*, bearing Brazil nuts.

juvie /ˈdʒuːvi/ *noun. US slang.* M20.
[ORIGIN Abbreviation Cf. JUVE.]
A juvenile, a juvenile delinquent. Also, a detention centre or a court for juvenile delinquents.

juxta- /ˈdʒʌkstə/ *prefix.*
[ORIGIN Repr. Latin *juxta* adverb & preposition.]
Near to, by the side of, according to.
■ **juxta-arˈticular** *adjective* (ANATOMY) situated near a joint E20. **juxta-maˈrine** *adjective* situated by the sea L19. **juxta-ˈspinal** *adjective* situated by the side of the (or a) spine L19.

juxtaglomerular /ˌdʒʌkstəɡlɒˈmɛrʊlə/ *adjective.* M20.
[ORIGIN from JUXTA- + GLOMERULAR.]
ANATOMY. Situated next to a glomerulus of the kidney; *spec.* designating a body or complex of bodies associated with the afferent arteriole of a glomerulus and containing secretory cells with a regulatory function.

juxtapose /dʒʌkstəˈpəʊz/ *verb trans.* M19.
[ORIGIN French *juxtaposer*, formed as JUXTA- + POSE *verb*[1].]
Place (two or more things) side by side or close to one another; place (one thing) beside another.

R. Ellmann The self only comes to exist when juxtaposed with other people. E. Wilson Juxtaposing . . hues in a rainbow. J. Brodsky By juxtaposing one faith with another we . . take them out of their context.

juxtaposit /dʒʌkstəˈpɒzɪt/ *verb trans. rare.* L17.
[ORIGIN from JUXTA- + Latin *posit-* pa. ppl stem of *pōnere* put, place.]
= JUXTAPOSE.

juxtaposition /dʒʌkstəpəˈzɪʃ(ə)n/ *noun.* M17.
[ORIGIN French, formed as JUXTAPOSE: see POSITION *noun*.]
The action of juxtaposing two or more things; the fact or condition of being juxtaposed.
■ **juxtapositional** *adjective* relating to or characterized by juxtaposition M19.

juxtapositive /dʒʌkstəˈpɒzɪtɪv/ *adjective.* L19.
[ORIGIN from JUXTAPOSITION + -IVE.]
GRAMMAR. Designating, being in, or pertaining to a case expressing juxtaposition.

Jy *abbreviation.*
ASTRONOMY. Jansky.

jynx /dʒɪŋks/ *noun.* Now *rare*. Pl. **jynxes**, †**jynges**. M17.
[ORIGIN mod. Latin from Latin *iynx* from Greek *iugx*, pl. *iugges*.]
The wryneck, *Jynx torquilla*.

jyrene, **jyrine** *nouns* vars. of GYRENE.

J

Kk

K, k /keɪ/.
The eleventh letter of the modern English alphabet and the tenth of the ancient Roman one, corresp. to Greek *kappa*, Phoenician and general Semitic *kaph*. The sound denoted by the letter in English, as in Greek and Latin, is the voiceless velar plosive consonant /k/. At an early period of Latin orthography, the letter C (orig. repr. Greek *gamma*) was used for the k sound, and the letter K itself fell into disuse, except in a few archaic spellings. In Old English, K was merely a supplemental symbol occasionally used instead of C for the velar sound. After the Norman Conquest, in accordance with Norman usage, C was retained for the velar only before *a, o, u, l,* and *r*, and K was substituted for the same sound before *e, i, y,* and (later) *n*. Hence, in native words, initial K now appears only before *e, i, y,* and before *n* (= Old English *cn-*), where it is no longer pronounced in standard English. Medially and finally, K is used after a consonant (***ask, twinkle***), or long vowel (***make, like, week***); after a short vowel, *ck* is used instead of *cc* or *kk*, but the unstressed suffix, formerly *-ick* (***musick***), is now *-ic*, though, when a suffix in *e* or *i* follows, K reappears (***traffic, trafficker, trafficking***). Beside native K words, largely confined to *ke-, ki-,* and *kn-*, there are now many foreign words of recent adoption, in which K may also precede *a, o, u, l, r,* and *h*. In words from Greek K is also usu. retained rather than Latinized to C, and in some cases, notably words in *kilo-*, K represents Greek *chi*. Pl. **K's, Ks**.
▸ **I 1** The letter and its sound.
the five K's the five distinguishing signs of the Sikh Khalsa: kesh (uncut hair, covered by a turban, and beard), kangha (comb), kara (steel bangle), kirpan (short sword), and kaccha (short trousers, originally for riding).
▸ **II** Symbolical uses.
2 Used to denote serial order; applied e.g. to the eleventh (also freq. the tenth, either I or J being omitted) group or section, sheet of a book, etc.
3 PHYSICS etc. ▸**a** (Italic *k*.) Thermal conductivity. ▸**b** (Italic *k*.) Boltzmann's constant. ▸**c** (Cap. K.) Used to designate a series of short-wavelength X-ray emission lines of an excited atom, arising from electron transitions to the innermost, lowest-energy atomic orbit, of principal quantum number 1; hence ***K-shell***, this orbit; ***K-electrons***, electrons in this shell; ***K-capture***, the capture by an atomic nucleus of one of the K-electrons. Cf. **L**, **L** 5b, **M**, **M** 6a. ▸**d** ***K-meson***, ***K-particle***, = KAON; ***K-mesic***, kaonic.
4 [from abbreviation of KILO-: cf. branch III below.] (Usu. *k*.) In COMPUTING, 1,000 (bytes) or, strictly, 1,024 (2^{10}); in BIOCHEMISTRY, 1,000 (in expr. molecular weights of proteins); *gen*. (esp. in specifying salaries in job advertisements) a thousand (pounds etc.).
▸ **III 5** Abbrevs.: **K** = (CHEMISTRY) [Latin] *kalium* potassium; kelvin; the drug ketamine; King; King's; Knight; (NAUTICAL) knot(s); Köchel (preceding the number of a composition by Mozart in the catalogue made by Ludwig von Köchel). **k** = (as prefix) kilo-.

ka /kɑː/ *noun*. L19.
[ORIGIN Egyptian.]
The spiritual part of a human being or a god which, according to the ancient Egyptians, survived after death and could reside in a statue of the dead person.

Kaaba /ˈkɑːəbə/ *noun*. Also (earlier) **Al-kaaba** /al-/, **C-**. E17.
[ORIGIN Arabic *(al-)kaʿba* lit. '(the) square house'.]
The square-shaped building in the centre of the Great Mosque in Mecca, Saudi Arabia, in the direction of which Muslims must face in doing the obligatory prayer.

kaama /ˈkɑːmə/ *noun*. Also **k(h)ama**. E19.
[ORIGIN Nama.]
= HARTEBEEST.

Kaapenaar /ˈkɑːpənɑː/ *noun*. *S. Afr.* Also **Kap-**, (in sense 2) **k-**. M19.
[ORIGIN Afrikaans, from *kaap* Cape + *-enaar* pers. suffix.]
1 A native or inhabitant of Cape Town, South Africa, or of the Cape peninsula and its environs. M19.
2 An edible silver sea bream, *Argyrozona argyrozona*. E20.

kab /kab/ *noun*. Also †**c-**. M16.
[ORIGIN Hebrew *qab* hollow or concave vessel. Cf. *2 Kings* 6:25.]
An ancient Hebrew unit of capacity equal to approx. 2 litres, or 3½ pints.

Kababish /kəˈbɑːbɪʃ/ *noun pl. & adjective*. L18.
[ORIGIN Arabic *kabābīš* pl.]
▸ **A** *noun pl*. A nomadic Arab people of the northern Kordofan and Dongola areas of Sudan. L18.
▸ **B** *attrib*. or as *adjective*. Of or pertaining to the Kababish. M19.

kabaddi /kəˈbadi/ *noun*. Also **kabadi**. M20.
[ORIGIN Uncertain: cf. Kurukh *kavada* mouthful, Kannada *kabalisu* to gulp. Sanskrit *kavaḍa*, Hindi *kabaḍḍī* cry at kabaddi.]
A team pursuit game popular in the north of the Indian subcontinent in which the two teams alternately send a player into the opposing team's court to try to touch one of the opponents while repeating the word 'kabaddi' (to show that the breath is being held as the rules require).

Kabaka /kəˈbɑːkə/ *noun*. L19.
[ORIGIN Bantu.]
(The title of) the ruler of the former province of Buganda in Uganda, or of the Baganda.

kabane /kəˈbɑːneɪ/ *noun*. L19.
[ORIGIN Japanese.]
In ancient Japan, a series or system of titles of rank.

kabaragoya /kəbɑːrəˈgəʊjə/ *noun*. L17.
[ORIGIN Unknown.]
A large monitor lizard, *Varanus salvator*, of SE Asia.

Kabardian /kəˈbɑːdɪən/ *adjective & noun*. L19.
[ORIGIN from *Kabarda* (Russian place name) + -IAN.]
▸ **A** *adjective*. Of or pertaining to a people of the Kabardino-Balkarian Republic of Russia, in the northern Caucasus. L19.
▸ **B** *noun*. **1** A member of this people. M20.
2 The NW Caucasian language of this people. M20.
■ **Kabardine** *noun* (*rare*) = KABARDIAN *noun* 1 E19. **Kabarˈdinian** *adjective & noun* = KABARDIAN L19.

kabassou /kəˈbasuː/ *noun*. L18.
[ORIGIN French from Galibi *capaçou*.]
Any of several naked-tailed armadillos of the genus *Cabassous*.

Kabbalah /kəˈbɑːlə, ˈkabələ/ *noun*. Also **Cabala**, **Cabbala**, **Kabbala**, **Qabalah**, & (in sense 2) with lower-case initial. E16.
[ORIGIN medieval Latin *cab(b)ala* from rabbinical Hebrew *qabbālāh* tradition, from *qibbēl* receive, accept.]
1 An ancient Jewish tradition of mystical interpretation of the Bible, using esoteric methods (including ciphers) and significant esp. in Hasidism, of which the Zohar is the basic text. E16.
2 †**a** (An) oral tradition. M–L17. ▸**b** (An) esoteric doctrine; (a) mystic interpretation; occult lore. M17.
■ **Kabbalism** *noun* the system of the Kabbalah; (an) esoteric doctrine, occult lore: L16. **Kabbalist** *noun* a person versed in the Kabbalah or in mystic arts M16. **Kabbaˈlistic** *adjective* pertaining to or of the nature of the Kabbalah or Kabbalists; having a private or mystic sense: E17. **Kabbaˈlistical** *adjective* L16. **Kabbaˈlistically** *adverb* M17.

kabeljou /ˈkɑːb(ə)ljəʊ, kɑːb(ə)lˈjəʊ/ *noun*. *S. Afr.* Also **-jauw**, **-jouw**, & other vars. Pl. same. M18.
[ORIGIN Afrikaans from Dutch *kabeljauw*, cogn. with French *cabillaud* cod.]
= MEAGRE *noun*¹. Also called ***kob***, ***salmon bass***.

Kabinett /kabɪˈnɛt, *foreign* -bi-/ *noun*. E20.
[ORIGIN German *Kabinettwein* lit. 'cabinet or chamber wine', from its orig. being kept in a special cellar.]
Wine, esp. German wine, of exceptional quality; *spec*. one made in Germany from grapes that can ferment without added sugar. Also ***Kabinett wine***.

Kabistan /kabɪˈstɑːn/ *noun & adjective*. Also **C-**. E20.
[ORIGIN For *Kubistan* (see below): cf. KUBA.]
(Designating) a finely woven, short-napped rug or carpet with intricate geometric design made in Kubistan, a district in NE Azerbaijan.

kablooey /kəˈbluːi/ *adjective & interjection*. *N. Amer. colloq*. L20.
[ORIGIN Imit.]
▸ **A** *adjective*. Destroyed, ruined. L20.
▸ **B** *interjection*. Repr. the sound of a hard blow or an explosion. L20.

kabloona /kəˈbluːnə/ *noun*. L18.
[ORIGIN Inupiaq (Inuit) *kabluna* big eyebrow.]
Among Inuit people: a person who is not an Inuit; a white person.

kabob *noun* see KEBAB.

kaboodle *noun* var. of CABOODLE.

kaboom /kəˈbuːm/ *interjection & noun*. *colloq*. L20.
[ORIGIN Imit.]
(Repr. the sound of) a loud explosion.

kaboura /kəˈbʊərə/ *noun*. Also **-ri** /-ri/. L19.
[ORIGIN Unknown.]
In Guyana: a bloodsucking fly of the genus *Simulium*.

kabuki /kəˈbuːki/ *noun & adjective*. L19.
[ORIGIN Japanese, orig. (as verb) act dissolutely; later interpreted as from *ka* song + *bu* dance + *ki* art, skill.]
(Of, pertaining to, or characteristic of) a traditional and popular form of Japanese drama with highly stylized song, mime, and dance, performed by male actors only.

Kabuli /kəˈbuːli/ *adjective & noun*. Also †**C-**. L19.
[ORIGIN from *Kabul* (see below) + -I².]
▸ **A** *adjective*. Of or pertaining to the city or province of Kabul in Afghanistan. L19.
▸ **B** *noun*. **1** A native or inhabitant of Kabul; a Kabuli horse. L19.
2 The dialect of Tajik used in Kabul. M20.

Kabyle /kəˈbʌɪl/ *noun & adjective*. M18.
[ORIGIN Prob. from Arabic *qabāʾil* pl. of *qabīla* tribe.]
▸ **A** *noun*. **1** An individual or people belonging to a group of Berber peoples inhabiting northern Algeria. M18.
2 The Berber dialect of these peoples. L19.
▸ **B** *attrib*. or as *adjective*. Of or pertaining to the Kabyles or their language. M19.

kaccha /ˈkʌtʃʌ/ *noun*. Also **kuccha**. L20.
[ORIGIN Punjabi.]
Short trousers ending above the knee, worn as one of the five distinguishing signs of the Sikh Khalsa, symbolizing loyalty and discipline.

kacha *adjective & noun* var. of KUTCHA.

Kachin /kəˈtʃɪn/ *noun & adjective*. L19.
[ORIGIN Burmese.]
▸ **A** *noun*. Pl. **-s**, same. A member of a group of Tibeto-Burman peoples inhabiting the mountainous regions in the north-east of Myanmar (Burma); the language of these peoples, having various dialects. L19.
▸ **B** *attrib*. or as *adjective*. Of or pertaining to the Kachins or their language. L19.

kachina /kəˈtʃiːnə/ *noun*. L19.
[ORIGIN Hopi *kacina* supernatural from Keresan.]
A deified ancestral spirit in N. American Pueblo Indian mythology.
– COMB.: **kachina dance** a ceremonial dance performed by men in masks and elaborate costumes impersonating the kachinas whom they seek to invoke; **kachina doll** a wooden doll representing a kachina.

ka-ching /kəˈtʃɪŋ/ *noun & interjection*. Also **ker-ching**. L20.
[ORIGIN Imit.]
Used to represent the sound of a (mechanical) cash register, esp. with reference to making money.
> *Time* A surprisingly hearty *ka-ching* kicked off the holiday shopping season.

kadai *noun* var. of KARAHI.

kadaitcha /kəˈdʌɪtʃə/ *noun*. *Austral*. Also **kurd-**. L19.
[ORIGIN Perh. from Arrernte *gwerdaje*.]
1 A malignant supernatural being. L19.
2 A special feathered shoe worn by an Aborigine on a mission of vengeance. Also ***kadaitcha shoe***. L19.
3 A mission of vengeance; the ritual accompanying such a mission. L19.
4 A man empowered to carry out vengeance. Also ***kadaitcha man***. E20.

Kaddish /ˈkadɪʃ/ *noun*. E17.
[ORIGIN Aramaic *qaddīš* holy.]
An ancient Jewish doxology regularly recited in the synagogue, including brief prayers for the welfare of Israel and concluding with a prayer for universal peace.

kade *noun* var. of KED *noun*¹.

Kadet *noun* var. of CADET *noun*².

Kadhakali *noun* var. of KATHAKALI.

kadi *noun* var. of CADI.

kadin /ˈkɑːdɪn/ *noun*. M19.
[ORIGIN Turkish *kadın* formed as KHATUN.]
hist. A woman of the Sultan of Turkey's harem.

kadish /ˈkɑːdɪʃ/ *noun*. E19.
[ORIGIN Syrian Arabic *kadīš* from Old Turkish *igdiş* a crossbreed, from *igid-* feed, rear; cf. Turkish *idiş* gelding.]
A part-bred Arabian horse; a nag; a gelding.

kadkhoda /kadˈkoːda, kadˈkəʊdə/ *noun*. M20.
[ORIGIN Persian *kadḵudā*, from *kad* house + *ḵudā* master. Cf. KEHAYA.]
The headman of an Iranian village.

kae /keɪ/ *noun*. *Scot. & N. English*. ME.
[ORIGIN Corresp. to Middle Dutch *ca*, *ka(e)* (Dutch *ka*), Old High German *chaha*, *chā* (Middle High German *kā*), Danish *kaa*, Norwegian *kaae*.]

A jackdaw.

kae /keɪ, kɑː/ *verb trans.* Long *obsolete* exc. *dial.* **M16.**
[ORIGIN Uncertain: perh. var. of CLAW *verb* or CA' *verb*.]
Only in ***kae me***, ***kae thee*** and ***kae me and I'll kae thee***: used as a suggestion or proposal of mutual help, service, flattery, etc.

kaemmererite *noun* var. of KÄMMERERITE.

kaempferol /ˈkampfərɒl, ˈkɛ-/ *noun.* **L19.**
[ORIGIN from mod. Latin *Kaempferia* genus name of the plant from which it was first obtained, from Engelbert *Kaempfer* (1651–1716), German traveller: see -OL.]
CHEMISTRY. A yellow flavonoid, $C_{15}H_{10}O_6$, which occurs in various plants.

kaersutite /kɛːˈsuːtʌɪt/ *noun.* **L19.**
[ORIGIN from *Kaersut* locality in Greenland where it was first found + -ITE[1].]
MINERALOGY. A dark variety of hornblende containing titanium, occurring in many volcanic rocks.

kafenion /kafəˈniːən/ *noun.* **M20.**
[ORIGIN Greek *kafeneio(n)*.]
A Greek coffee house.

Kaffeeklatsch /ˈkafeklatʃ/ *noun.* Also ***kaffee-klatch*** /ˈkafɪklatʃ/. **L19.**
[ORIGIN German, from *Kaffee* coffee + *Klatsch* gossip. Cf. KLATCH.]
Gossip over coffee cups; a coffee party.

kafferboom *noun* var. of KAFFIRBOOM.

Kaffir /ˈkafə/ *noun & adjective.* Chiefly *S. Afr.* Also (*arch.*) **Caffre**; **Kafir.** See also KAFIR. **M16.**
[ORIGIN Arabic *kāfir* unbeliever, from active pple of *kafara* be unbelieving.]
▸ **A** *noun.* **1** A non-Muslim. *derog.* Now *rare* or *obsolete.* **M16.**
2 a A member of a Bantu-speaking people, esp. the Xhosa, in South Africa. Now *rare* or *obsolete.* **L16.** ▸**b** A black African. Now *offensive*, and legally actionable in South Africa. **M19.** ▸**c** ***White Kaffir***, a white person who has adopted a black African way of life. *derog. offensive.* **E20.**
3 Bantu; *spec.* Xhosa. **E19.**
4 In *pl.* South African mining shares. *Stock Exchange slang.* **L19.**
▸ **B** *attrib.* or as *adjective.* Black African. Now *offensive* exc. in some collocations below. **L18.**
Kaffir beer an alcoholic drink brewed from malted Kaffir corn. **Kaffirboetie** /ˈkafəbʊtiː/ (*derog. & offensive*) a white South African who shows concern for the welfare of black South Africans. **Kaffir bread** any of several southern African cycads with edible pith. **Kaffir corn** a variety of sorghum, *Sorghum bicolor* var. *caffrorum*, grown in southern Africa, esp. for making beer; = MABELE. **Kaffir crane** = *CROWNED crane*. **Kaffir finch** a S. African bishop bird or widow bird, *esp.* the red bishop, *Euplectes orix*, and the sakabula, *E. progne*. **Kaffir lily** (**a**) an ornamental plant of the iris family, *Schizostylis coccinea*, bearing spikes of flowers resembling gladioli; (**b**) = CLIVIA. **Kaffir lime** a SE Asian citrus tree, *Citrus hystrix*, with green fruit and aromatic leaves that are used in Thai and Indonesian cooking. **Kaffir melon** an indigenous southern African melon, *Citrullus caffer*. **Kaffir orange** any of several small trees of the genus *Strychnos* (family Loganiaceae), esp. *S. pungens*; the globose fruit of such a tree, with an edible pulp but poisonous seeds. **Kaffir piano** *offensive* a southern African marimba or xylophone. **Kaffir plum** (the red edible fruit of) an ornamental southern African tree, *Harpephyllum caffrum* (family Anacardiaceae). **Kaffir pot** = POTJIE. **Kaffir tea** (**a**) any of various South African plants used to make medicinal teas, esp. *Helichrysum nudifolium*, of the composite family; (**b**) an infusion of the leaves of such a plant; *spec.* = *ROOIBOS tea*.

kaffirboom /ˈkafəbʊəm/ *noun. S. Afr.* Also **kaffer-**. **E19.**
[ORIGIN from KAFFIR + Afrikaans *boom* tree.]
Any of several southern African kinds of coral tree, esp. *Erythrina caffra* and *E. lysistemon*, the red seeds of which are used as beads.

kaffiyeh *noun* var. of KEFFIYEH.

Kaffrarian /kəˈfrɛːrɪən/ *adjective.* Also (*arch.*) **C-**. **E19.**
[ORIGIN from *Kaffraria* (see below) formed as KAFFIR (prob. orig. named by Arab seafarers): see -AN.]
Of, pertaining to, or characteristic of Kaffraria, a region along the SE coast of South Africa.

Kafir /ˈkafə/ *noun.* **M19.**
[ORIGIN formed as KAFFIR.]
A member of a people inhabiting the Hindu Kush mountains of NE Afghanistan.
– COMB.: **Kafir harp** a simple harp with four or five strings.

Kafkaesque /kafkəˈɛsk/ *adjective.* **M20.**
[ORIGIN from *Kafka* (see below) + -ESQUE.]
Of or pertaining to the Austrian writer Franz Kafka (1883–1924) or his writings; similar to or suggestive of the nightmarish atmosphere or situations portrayed in his stories.

kaftan /ˈkaftan, kafˈtɑːn/ *noun.* Also **c-**. **L16.**
[ORIGIN Turkish, from Persian *kaftān*, partly through French *cafetan*.]
1 An Eastern man's long tunic with a waist girdle. **L16.**
2 A long loose dress; a loose-fitting shirt. **M20.**

kago /ˈkɑːgo, ˈkɑːgəʊ/ *noun.* Pl. **-os.** **E18.**
[ORIGIN Japanese.]
A kind of Japanese litter, orig. consisting of basketwork slung on a pole and carried on the shoulders of bearers, later made of wood.

kagoule *noun* var. of CAGOULE.

kagu /ˈkɑːguː/ *noun.* **M19.**
[ORIGIN Melanesian.]
A very rare nocturnal crested gruiform bird, *Rhynochetus jubatus* of New Caledonia, drab grey with display patterns beneath the wings and a red bill.

kagura /ˈkɑːgʊrə/ *noun.* **L19.**
[ORIGIN Japanese.]
A form of traditional sacred music and dance performed at Shinto festivals.

Kahal /ˈkaːhal/ *noun.* **E20.**
[ORIGIN Hebrew *qāhāl* assembly, community.]
(The governing body of) any of the former localized Jewish communities in Europe.

kahawai /ˈkɑːwʌɪ/ *noun.* Chiefly *NZ.* **M19.**
[ORIGIN Maori.]
= ***Australian salmon*** s.v. AUSTRALIAN *adjective*.

kahikatea /kaˌhɪkəˈtiːə, kʌɪkəˈtiːə/ *noun.* **E19.**
[ORIGIN Maori.]
A New Zealand coniferous tree, *Dacrycarpus dacrydioides* (family Podocarpaceae). Also called ***white pine***.

kahili /kəˈhiːli, kɑː-/ *noun.* **M19.**
[ORIGIN Hawaiian *kāhili*.]
A feather standard, mounted on a tall pole, symbolic of royalty in Hawaii and used on ceremonial occasions.

Kahn /kɑːn/ *noun.* **E20.**
[ORIGIN Reuben Leon *Kahn* (1887–1979), Lithuanian-born US bacteriologist.]
MEDICINE. ***Kahn test***, ***Kahn reaction***, a diagnostic test for syphilis devised by Kahn in which serum or spinal fluid is mixed with antigen from beef heart and examined for flocculation.

kahuna /kəˈhuːnə/ *noun.* **L19.**
[ORIGIN Hawaiian.]
In Hawaii: a priest, a wise man; a minister; a sorcerer.

kai /kʌɪ/ *noun. NZ colloq.* **M19.**
[ORIGIN Maori.]
Food.
kai moana /ˈməʊanə/ food from the sea, esp. fish, shellfish, and seaweed.
■ **kaikai** /ˈkʌɪkʌɪ/ *noun* food; feasting; a feast: **M19.**

kaid /kɑːˈiːd/ *noun.* Also (*arch.*) **c-**. **E19.**
[ORIGIN from Arabic *qā'id* leader: see ALCAIDE.]
= ALCAIDE.

kaikomako /kʌɪkəʊˈmɑːkəʊ/ *noun.* Pl. same, **-os.** **M19.**
[ORIGIN Maori.]
A New Zealand tree, *Pennantia corymbosa* (family Icacinaceae), which bears panicles of fragrant white flowers and black berries.

kail *noun* var. of KALE.

kailyard *noun* var. of KALEYARD.

kaim *noun* var. of KAME.

kaimakam /kʌɪməˈkɑːm/ *noun.* Also †**caimacam**, **qaimaqam.** **E17.**
[ORIGIN Turkish *kaymakam*, from Arabic *qā'im maqām* one standing in the place of another.]
In the Ottoman Empire: a lieutenant, a deputy, esp. in the army or the government; *spec.* an official deputizing for the grand vizier. In modern Turkey: the governor of a kaza.

kain /kʌɪn/ *noun*[1]. Pl. **-s**, same. **L18.**
[ORIGIN Malay.]
In Malaysia and Indonesia: (a piece of) cloth, esp. for use as clothing; a sarong. Freq. with postpositive adjective.

> J. KIRKUP Round their waists they wore . . kain songket which is a silver or gold-threaded sarong.

kain *noun*[2] var. of CAIN *noun*[1].

kainga /kɑːˈɪŋgə, ˈkɑːɪŋə/ *noun. NZ.* **E19.**
[ORIGIN Maori.]
A Maori place of residence, settlement, or village.

kainic /ˈkʌɪnɪk/ *adjective.* **M20.**
[ORIGIN from Japanese *kainin*, from *kainin-sō*, name of the source alga: see -IC.]
kainic acid, a neurotoxic organic acid extracted from the red alga *Digenea simplex* and used as an anthelmintic.

kainite /ˈkʌɪnʌɪt, ˈkeɪ-/ *noun.* Also **-it** /-ɪt/. **M19.**
[ORIGIN German *Kainit*, from Greek *kainos* new, recent (as being of recent formation): see -ITE[1].]
A white monoclinic mineral which is a double salt consisting of hydrated magnesium sulphate and potassium chloride, and is used as a fertilizer.

kainogenesis *noun* var. of CAENOGENESIS.

kairomone /ˈkʌɪrəməʊn/ *noun.* **L20.**
[ORIGIN from Greek *kairos* opportunity, advantage, after PHEROMONE.]
BIOLOGY. A chemical secreted and released by an organism which acts as a signal to the advantage of an organism of a different species.

kairos /ˈkʌɪrɒs/ *noun.* **M20.**
[ORIGIN Greek = right or proper time.]
Fullness of time; the propitious moment, esp. for decision or action.

kaiseki /kʌɪˈsɛːkiː/ *noun.* **E20.**
[ORIGIN Japanese, from *kai* (from *kaichu* kimono pocket) + *seki* stone.]
A style of traditional Japanese cuisine in which a series of very small, intricate dishes are prepared; a meal served in this style.

Kaiser /ˈkʌɪzə/ *noun.*
[ORIGIN Old English *cāsere* = Old Frisian *keisar*, Old Saxon *kēsur*, *-ar*, Old Norse *keisari*, Gothic *kaisar*, from Germanic from Greek *kaisar* from Latin CAESAR; in Middle English partly from Old Norse; in mod. use from German *Kaiser* (cf. Dutch *keizer*, †*keiser*, †*keser*).]
(The title of) an emperor, *spec.* †(**a**) a Roman Emperor, (**b**) *hist.* a Holy Roman Emperor, (**c**) an Austrian or German Emperor.
– PHRASES & COMB.: **Kaiser Bill moustache**, **Kaiser moustache** *colloq.* a moustache with the ends turned up, as worn by Wilhelm II, Kaiser of Germany (1888–1918). **kaiser roll** *N. Amer.* a type of bread roll. **Kaiser's war** *the* First World War. **king or Kaiser** *arch.* any powerful earthly ruler.
■ **Kaiserism** *noun* (*hist.*) political absolutism, esp. with ref. to the German Empire **E20.** **Kaiserist** *noun* (*hist.*) an adherent of Kaiserism **E20.** **Kaisership** *noun* the position or reign of a Kaiser **M19.**

k'ai shu /ˈkʌɪ ʃuː/ *noun phr.* **L19.**
[ORIGIN Chinese *kǎishū*, from *kǎi* model + *shū* write.]
The usual script used for the Chinese language, suitable for everyday purposes.

kaitaka /kʌɪˈtɑːkə/ *noun. NZ.* **L19.**
[ORIGIN Maori.]
A flaxen Maori cloak.

kaizen /kʌɪˈzɛn/ *noun.* **L20.**
[ORIGIN Japanese, lit. 'improvement', from *kai* alter + *zen* good.]
Continuous improvement of working practices, personal efficiency, etc., as a business philosophy.

kajang /ˈkɑːdʒaŋ/ *noun & adjective.* Also (earlier) **cajang**, †**cadjan.** **L17.**
[ORIGIN Malay & Javanese.]
▸ **A** *noun.* Matting or roofing made from the dried leaves of palms or pandanus; a mat, piece of roofing, awning, etc., made from this. **L17.**
▸ **B** *attrib.* or as *adjective.* Made from the dried leaves of palms or pandanus; made from kajang(s). **E18.**

K

Kajar *noun* var. of QAJAR.

kajaten *noun* see KIAAT.

kajawah /kəˈdʒɑːwə, ˈkadʒəwə/ *noun.* **M17.**
[ORIGIN Urdu *kajāwah*, *kaja-*, Persian *kajāwa*.]
In some Eastern countries: a kind of litter for women consisting of a large pannier or wooden frame, a pair of which are carried by a camel.

kaka /ˈkɑːkɑː/ *noun.* **L18.**
[ORIGIN Maori.]
A New Zealand parrot, *Nestor meridionalis*, which has a long beak and is olive-brown, varied with red or yellow.
– COMB.: **kaka-beak**, **kaka-bill** a climbing leguminous New Zealand plant, *Clianthus puniceus*, with vivid red flowers; also called ***glory pea***.

kakaki /kəˈkɑːki/ *noun.* **M20.**
[ORIGIN Hausa.]
A kind of W. African trumpet.

kakapo /ˈkɑːkəpəʊ/ *noun.* Pl. same, **-os.** **M19.**
[ORIGIN Maori.]
A large yellow and brownish-green nocturnal flightless parrot, *Strigops habroptilus*, of New Zealand. Also called ***ground parrot***, ***owl parrot***.

kakar /ˈkɑːkə/ *noun.* Also **-ur.** **L19.**
[ORIGIN Prob. imit.]
= MUNTJAC.

kakariki /kɑːkəˈriːki/ *noun. NZ.* **M19.**
[ORIGIN Maori.]
Either of two New Zealand parakeets, the red-fronted parakeet, *Cyanoramphus novaezelandiae*, and the yellow-fronted parakeet, *C. auriceps*.

kakemono /kɑːkɪˈməʊnəʊ/ *noun.* Pl. **-os.** **L19.**
[ORIGIN Japanese, from *kake* hanging + *mono* thing.]
A Japanese unframed wall picture, usu. painted or inscribed on silk or paper.

kaki /ˈkɑːki/ *noun.* **E18.**
[ORIGIN Japanese.]
The Japanese persimmon, *Diospyros kaki*, native to China and Japan and the kind most often cultivated.

Kakiemon /kəˈkiːeɪmɒn/ *adjective.* **L19.**
[ORIGIN See below.]
Designating, characteristic of, or in the style of a kind of porcelain first made by the Japanese potter Sakaida Kakiemon (1596–1666) at Arita, characterized by sparse asymmetrical designs painted over a glazed white ground.

kakistocracy /kakɪˈstɒkrəsi/ *noun.* **E19.**
[ORIGIN from Greek *kakistos* worst + -CRACY, after ARISTOCRACY.]
The government of a state by the worst citizens.

kakke /ˈkake/ *noun.* **L19.**
[ORIGIN Japanese.]
Beriberi.

kakkerlak /ˈkakəlak/ *noun*. Now *rare* or *obsolete*. **L17.**
[**ORIGIN** Dutch from German *kakerlak* from Spanish *cucaracha* **COCKROACH**.]
1 In SE Asia, esp. Java: an albino. **L17.**
2 A cockroach. **E19.**

kakotopia /kakəˈtəʊpɪə/ *noun*. **E20.**
[**ORIGIN** from Greek *kakos* bad, evil (cf. **CACO-**) + U)**TOPIA**.]
= **DYSTOPIA**.

kakur *noun* var. of **KAKAR**.

kakuro /ˈkakərəʊ, kəˈkjʊərəʊ/ *noun*. **E21.**
[**ORIGIN** Blend of Japanese *kasan* addition and *kurosu*, repr. a pronunc. of **CROSS** *noun*.]
A number puzzle in which players have to insert numbers into a crossword-like grid, with numbered clues and some blank squares.

kala-azar /kɑːlə-əˈzɑː/ *noun*. **L19.**
[**ORIGIN** Assamese, from *kālā* black + *āzār* disease.]
MEDICINE. A disease of tropical and subtropical regions caused by a protozoan of the genus *Leishmania* and transmitted by sandflies of the genus *Phlebotomus*, usu. involving emaciation, enlargement of the spleen and liver, anaemia, and fever; visceral leishmaniasis.

Kalamata /kaləˈmɑːtə/ *noun*. **M20.**
[**ORIGIN** A city in southern Greece.]
Used *attrib.* to designate the large, elongated fruit of an olive cultivar traditionally grown around Kalamata, having a purplish-black colour when cured.

kalamkari /ˈkʌləmkɑːri/ *noun*. **L20.**
[**ORIGIN** Hindi *kalamkārī*, lit. 'painting'.]
A type of cotton cloth printed by hand, orig. made in southern India.

kalanchoe /kalənˈkəʊɪ/ *noun*. **M19.**
[**ORIGIN** mod. Latin (see below) from French, ult. from Chinese *gāláncài*.]
Any of various chiefly African succulent shrubs and herbs of the genus *Kalanchoe* (family Crassulaceae), often grown as house or greenhouse plants, bearing usu. red, pink, or white flowers in terminal panicles and sometimes producing miniature plants from the edge of the leaves.

Kalashnikov /kəˈlaʃnɪkɒf, -ˈlɑːʃ-/ *noun & adjective*. **L20.**
[**ORIGIN** M. T. *Kalashnikov* (b. 1919), its Russian developer.]
(Designating) a type of rifle or sub-machine gun made in Russia.

kalashy, **kalasi**, **kalassi** *nouns* vars. of **KHALASSI**.

kale /keɪl/ *noun*. Also **kail**. **ME.**
[**ORIGIN** North. form of **COLE** *noun*[1].]
1 Any of various edible cruciferous plants of the genus *Brassica*; *spec.* a hardy cabbage-like vegetable, consisting of cultivars of *B. oleracea* and *B. napus*, with leaves which do not form a compact head (also called ***borecole***). **ME.**
curled kale, **curly kale**, **Scotch kale** a variety of kale in which the leaves are curled and crimped like parsley. **seakale**: see **SEA** *noun*.
2 Broth in which Scotch kale or cabbage forms a principal ingredient; *Scot.* soup made with various kinds of vegetables. **LME.**
3 Money. *N. Amer. slang*. **E20.**
– **COMB.**: **kale-bell** (*Scot.*) the dinner bell; **kale-runt**, **kale-stock** the stem of a kale plant (cf. **CASTOCK**); **kale-time** *Scot.* dinner time; **kale-worm** *Scot. & N. English* a caterpillar, *esp.* that of the cabbage white butterfly.

kaleej *noun* var. of **KALIJ**.

kaleidoscope /kəˈlʌɪdəskəʊp/ *noun & verb*. **E19.**
[**ORIGIN** from Greek *kalos* beautiful + *eidos* form + **-SCOPE**.]
▸ **A** *noun*. **1** An optical toy consisting of a tube containing an arrangement of mirrors and pieces of coloured glass or paper which produce a constantly changing pattern of coloured reflections as the observer looks into the tube and rotates it. **E19.**
2 A constantly changing group of bright colours or coloured objects; a thing which constantly shifts and changes. **E19.**

K. WATERHOUSE The word *challenging* drops into the kaleidoscope of phrases he's tumbling around. J. WAIN He was no longer the centre of a flashing kaleidoscope of the clever, the beautiful, the worldly.

▸ **B** *verb trans. & intrans.* See or appear as in a kaleidoscope; move into or in a kaleidoscopic pattern. **L19.**

E. PIZZEY A painting .. over the dining-room mantelpiece whirled round her head, and kaleidoscoped into oblivion.

■ **kaleidoˈscopic** *adjective* **M19.** **kaleidoˈscopically** *adverb* **M19.**

kalendar *noun* var. of **CALENDAR** *noun*.

kalends *noun pl.* var. of **CALENDS**.

kaleyard /ˈkeɪljɑːd/ *noun & adjective*. *Scot.* Also **kail-**. **M16.**
[**ORIGIN** from **KALE** + **YARD** *noun*[1].]
▸ **A** *noun*. A cabbage garden, a kitchen garden, *esp.* one attached to a small cottage. **M16.**
▸ **B** *attrib.* or as *adjective*. (Usu. **K-**.) Designating or pertaining to a group of late 19th-cent. fiction-writers, including J. M. Barrie (1860–1937), who portrayed local town life in Scotland and made much use of the vernacular. **L19.**
■ **kaleyarder** *noun* a writer of the Kaleyard School **L19.**

kalgan /ˈkɑːlgɑːn/ *noun & adjective*. **M20.**
[**ORIGIN** *Kalgan* (see below).]
(Designating) a fur obtained from a lamb from the area of Kalgan (now called Zhangjiakou), a city in Hebei province, China.

kali /ˈkeɪlʌɪ, ˈkali/ *noun*. **L16.**
[**ORIGIN** Colloq. Arabic *qalī* calcined ashes of Salsola etc.: cf. **ALKALI**.]
1 Any of several plants of the genus *Salsola*, of the goosefoot family; *esp.* the prickly saltwort, *S. kali*. **L16.**
†**2** Soda ash; = **ALKALI** 1; vegetable alkali, potash. **L18–E19.**

kalian /kaˈljɑːn/ *noun*. **M19.**
[**ORIGIN** Persian *ḳalyān* from Arabic *ġalayān*: cf. **CALEAN**.]
An Iranian type of hookah.

kalicine /ˈkalɪsiːn/ *noun*. **L19.**
[**ORIGIN** Irreg. from mod. Latin *kalium* potassium + *-c-* + **-INE**[5].]
MINERALOGY. Native potassium bicarbonate, $KHCO_3$, a monoclinic mineral occurring as white crystals.
■ Also **kaˈlicinite** *noun* **E20.**

kalij /kɑːˈlɪdʒ/ *noun*. Also **kaleej** /kəˈliːdʒ/. **M19.**
[**ORIGIN** Pahari.]
More fully ***kalij pheasant***. A pheasant, *Lophura leucomelana*, of SE Asia and the Himalayan region.

kalimba /kəˈlɪmbə/ *noun*. **M20.**
[**ORIGIN** Bantu.]
A musical instrument played with the thumbs, consisting of metal strips along a small hollow piece of wood.

kalkoentjie /kalˈkʊɪŋki, -tʃi/ *noun*. *S. Afr.* Also **-tje**. **M19.**
[**ORIGIN** Afrikaans, from *kalkoen* turkey + *-tjie* dim. suffix.]
1 A pipit of the open veld, *Macronyx capensis*. **M19.**
2 Any of several plants of the iris family with scarlet flowers like a turkey's wattles, esp. *Gladiolus alatus*. **E20.**

kallidin /ˈkalɪdɪn/ *noun*. **M20.**
[**ORIGIN** from **KALLIKREIN** + **PEPT**)**ID**(**E** + **-IN**[1].]
BIOCHEMISTRY. A naturally occurring decapeptide, orig. confused with bradykinin, which causes contraction of smooth muscle and vasodilation.

kallikrein /ˈkalɪkriːɪn, -kriːn/ *noun*. **M20.**
[**ORIGIN** from Greek *kallikreas* **PANCREAS** + **-IN**[1].]
BIOCHEMISTRY. Any of various enzymes which release a kinin from a plasma protein precursor, so promoting vasodilation; orig. and *esp.* that found in the human pancreas and body fluids.

kallitype /ˈkalɪtʌɪp/ *noun*. *obsolete* exc. *hist.* **L19.**
[**ORIGIN** from Greek *kalli-* combining form (see **-I-**) of *kallos* beauty + **-TYPE**.]
A type of photographic process using a ferric salt developed with silver nitrate.

kalmia /ˈkalmɪə/ *noun*. **M18.**
[**ORIGIN** mod. Latin (see below), from Pehr *Kalm* (1716–79), Swedish botanist + **-IA**[1].]
Any of several N. American shrubs of the genus *Kalmia*, of the heath family, with evergreen leaves and clusters of pink or white flowers; *esp.* mountain laurel, *K. latifolia*, and sheep laurel, *K. angustifolia*.

Kalmyk /ˈkalmɪk/ *noun & adjective*. Also **Kalmuck** /ˈkalmʌk/. **E17.**
[**ORIGIN** Russian *kalmyk*.]
▸ **A** *noun*. Pl. **-s**, same.
1 a A member of a Mongolian people living on the NW shores of the Caspian Sea. **E17.** ▸**b** The language of this people, a western form of Mongolian. **E19.**
2 (**k-**.) A kind of shaggy cloth, resembling bearskin. **M19.**
▸ **B** *attrib.* or as *adjective*. Of or pertaining to the Kalmyks or their language. **L18.**
■ **Kalˈmykian** *adjective* (*rare*) **E18.**

kalon /ˈkalən/ *noun*. *literary*. Now *rare*. **M18.**
[**ORIGIN** Greek.]
The ideal good; the *summum bonum*.

HENRY FIELDING Good fame is a species of the Kalon and it is by no means fitting to neglect it.

kalong /ˈkɑːlɒŋ/ *noun*. **E19.**
[**ORIGIN** Javanese.]
Any of several fruit bats of SE Asia and Indonesia; *esp.* the large common flying fox, *Pteropus vampyrus*.

kalpa /ˈkalpə/ *noun*. **L18.**
[**ORIGIN** Sanskrit.]
In Indian cosmology: an aeon, a great age of the world, a cycle of *yugas*; *spec.* in **HINDUISM**, a period of 4,320 million years.

kalpack, **kalpak** *nouns* vars. of **CALPAC**.

kalsilite /ˈkalsɪlʌɪt/ *noun*. **M20.**
[**ORIGIN** from *K, Al, Si* chem. symbols for potassium, aluminium, silicon + **-LITE**.]
MINERALOGY. A rare hexagonal silicate of potassium and aluminium, similar to nepheline, found in some lavas.

kalsomine /ˈkalsəmʌɪn/ *noun & verb*. **M19.**
[**ORIGIN** Unknown.]
▸ **A** *noun*. A kind of white or coloured wash for walls; = **CALCIMINE**. **M19.**
▸ **B** *verb trans. & intrans.* Whitewash with kalsomine. **M19.**

kama *noun* var. of **KAAMA**.

kamachili /kɑːməˈtʃiːli/ *noun*. **M19.**
[**ORIGIN** Tagalog *kamatsilé* from Mexican Spanish.]
A tropical American leguminous tree, *Pithecellobium dulce*, with edible pods and bark that yields a yellow dye.

kamacite /ˈkaməsʌɪt/ *noun*. **L19.**
[**ORIGIN** from Greek *kamak-*, *kamax* vine-pole + **-ITE**[1].]
MINERALOGY. An alloy of iron and nickel occurring in meteorites as bar-shaped masses.

kamagraphy /kəˈmagrəfi/ *noun*. **M20.**
[**ORIGIN** French *kamagraphie*: see **-GRAPHY**.]
A process for making copies of original paintings, using a special press and treated canvas, which reproduces the colour and texture of the brushstrokes.
■ **kamagraph** /ˈkaməgrɑːf/ *noun* [back-form.] (a printing press for producing) a reproduction painting copied by kamagraphy **M20.**

kamahi /ˈkɑːməhi/ *noun*. *NZ*. **M19.**
[**ORIGIN** Maori.]
A tall forest tree, *Weinmannia racemosa* (family Cunoniaceae), with racemes of small cream-coloured flowers and dark wood.

Kamakura /ˈkɑːməkʊərə/ *adjective*. **E20.**
[**ORIGIN** See below.]
Designating or pertaining to the era of Japanese history (1192–1333) during which the seat of military government was at Kamakura (a city on S. Honshu) esp. as a period or artistic production.

kamala /ˈkamələ/ *noun*. **E19.**
[**ORIGIN** Sanskrit, prob. of Dravidian origin.]
1 A tree of the spurge family, *Mallotus philippensis*, of India and SE Asia. Also ***kamala tree***. **E19.**
2 A fine reddish-orange powder made from the fruit capsules of this, used locally as an orange dye and an anthelmintic. **M19.**

Kamares /kəˈmɑːriːz/ *adjective & noun*. **L19.**
[**ORIGIN** from Greek *Kamarais* a Minoan cave-sanctuary on Mount Ida in Crete, where the pottery was found.]
(Designating or pertaining to) a type of Minoan pottery from the middle Bronze Age, characterized by the use of red, white, and yellow ornaments on a black ground, depicting abstract or stylized plant designs.

kamassi /kəˈmasi/ *noun*. **L18.**
[**ORIGIN** Afrikaans *kammassie*, prob. from Nama.]
(The hard yellow wood of) a southern African evergreen tree, *Gonioma kamassi* (family Apocynaceae).

Kama Sutra /kɑːmə ˈsuːtrə/ *noun & adjectival phr.* **L19.**
[**ORIGIN** Sanskrit, from *kāma* love, desire + *sūtra* **SUTRA**.]
▸ **A** *noun phr.* (The title of) an ancient Sanskrit treatise on the art of love and sexual technique; a sex manual. **L19.**
▸ **B** *adjectival phr.* Sexually explicit; sensual. **M20.**

Kamba /ˈkambə/ *noun & adjective*. **L19.**
[**ORIGIN** Bantu. See also **WAKAMBA**.]
▸ **A** *noun*. Pl. same, **-s**.
1 A member of a people of central Kenya, related ethnically to the Kikuyu. **L19.**
2 The Bantu language of this people. **L19.**
▸ **B** *attrib.* or as *adjective*. Of or pertaining to the Kamba or their language. **E20.**

Kamchadal /ˈkamtʃədal/ *noun & adjective*. **M18.**
[**ORIGIN** Russian.]
▸ **A** *noun*. Pl. **-s**, same.
1 A member of a non-Russian people inhabiting the Kamchatka peninsula on the Pacific coast of Siberia. **M18.**
2 The language of this people, now virtually extinct. **M20.**
▸ **B** *attrib.* or as *adjective*. Of or pertaining to the Kamchadals or their language. **E20.**

Kamchatkan /kamˈtʃatk(ə)n/ *noun & adjective*. **L18.**
[**ORIGIN** from *Kamchatka* (see below) + **-AN**.]
▸ **A** *noun*. A native or inhabitant of the Kamchatka peninsula on the Pacific coast of Siberia; a Kamchadal. **L18.**
▸ **B** *adjective*. Of or pertaining to Kamchatka or its inhabitants. **M19.**

kame /keɪm/ *noun*. Also **kaim**. **LME.**
[**ORIGIN** Var. of **COMB** *noun*[1].]
1 = **COMB** *noun*[1]. *Scot. & N. English*. **LME.**
2 A steep and sharp hill ridge; *spec.* in *GEOLOGY*, a ridge or mound of sand and gravel deposited on or near a glacier. **L18.**

kameeldoorn /kəˈmɪəldʊən/ *noun*. *S. Afr.* Also **-doring** /-dʊərɪŋ/. **E19.**
[**ORIGIN** Afrikaans *kameeldoring*, from Dutch *kameel* camel + *doorn* thorn.]
= ***CAMEL*-thorn** (b).

kameez /kəˈmiːz/ *noun*. Also **-ze**, (earlier) **camise** /-s, -z/. Pl. **-es**, same. **E19.**
[**ORIGIN** Arabic *qamīṣ*, perh. from late Latin *camisia*: see **CHEMISE**.]
A loose long-sleeved shirt or tunic worn, esp. by Muslims, in the Indian subcontinent, and by some Muslims elsewhere.
SHALWAR ***kameez***.

kamerad /ˈkaməraːd, *foreign* kaməˈraːt/ *interjection*. **E20.**
[ORIGIN German, lit. 'comrade', from French *camerade, camarade*: see COMRADE.]
Used by a German-speaking soldier notifying to an enemy a wish to surrender.

kami /ˈkaːmi/ *noun*. Pl. same. **E17.**
[ORIGIN Japanese.]
A Shinto god or deity. Also, the Japanese Emperor, a Japanese lord.

kamik /ˈkamɪk/ *noun*. **L19.**
[ORIGIN Inupiaq.]
A long sealskin boot worn by Eskimos.

kamikaze /kamɪˈkaːzi/ *noun & adjective*. **L19.**
[ORIGIN Japanese = divine wind, formed as KAMI + *kaze* wind.]
▸ **A** *noun*. **1** In Japanese tradition, the gale that destroyed the fleet of the invading Mongols in 1281. **L19.**
2 In the Second World War, (a crewman of) a Japanese aircraft, usu. loaded with explosives, making a deliberate suicidal crash on an enemy target; a suicide pilot or plane. **M20.**
3 SURFING. A deliberately taken wipeout. **M20.**
▸ **B** *adjective*. Of, pertaining to, or characteristic of a kamikaze; reckless, dangerous, potentially self-destructive. **M20.**

Spectator The suicidal self confidence of kamikaze pilots ramming an aircraft-carrier. *Evening Standard* The kamikaze liberals who prefer glorious defeat. *Daily Mail* A kamikaze roller-skater who weaves his way through the traffic.

Kamilaroi /kəˈmɪlərɔɪ/ *noun & adjective*. Pl. of noun same. **M19.**
[ORIGIN The name in Kamilaroi.]
A member of, of or pertaining to, a group of Australian Aboriginal peoples of northern New South Wales and southern Queensland; (of) the language of these peoples.

kämmererite /ˈkɛmərərʌɪt, ˈkam-/ *noun*. Also **kaem-**. **M19.**
[ORIGIN from A. A. *Kämmerer* (1789–1858), Prussian surveyor of mines + -ITE[1].]
MINERALOGY. A reddish or lavender-coloured variety of chlorite, containing chromium.

kampong /kamˈpɒŋ/ *noun*. Also (earlier) **c-**; **kampung** /-ˈpʌŋ/. **L18.**
[ORIGIN Malay: see COMPOUND *noun*[2].]
In Malaysia: a village, an enclosure.

Kampuchean /kampʊˈtʃiːən/ *adjective & noun*. **L20.**
[ORIGIN from *Kampuchea* Khmer name of Cambodia (used officially between 1975 and 1989) + -AN.]
(A native or inhabitant) of Cambodia. Cf. CAMBODIAN.

kampung *noun* var. of KAMPONG.

Kan *noun* var. of GAN.

Kan. *abbreviation*.
Kansas.

kana /ˈkaːnə/ *noun*. Pl. same. **E18.**
[ORIGIN Japanese, from *ka* temporary, non-regular + *na* name, writing.]
(A character or syllabary in) Japanese syllabic writing. Cf. HIRAGANA, KATAKANA.

kanaka /kəˈnakə, -ˈnaːkə/ *noun*. **M19.**
[ORIGIN Hawaiian = person, human being.]
A South Sea Islander, *esp.* (*hist.*) one shipped to Queensland, Australia, for forced labour on the sugar plantations.

kanamycin /kanəˈmʌɪsɪn/ *noun*. **M20.**
[ORIGIN from mod. Latin *kanamyceticus* (see below) + -IN[1]: cf. -MYCIN.]
Any of several broad-spectrum antibiotics related to neomycin which are produced by the bacterium *Streptomyces kanamyceticus*.

Kanarese /kanəˈriːz/ *noun & adjective*. Also **C-**. **M19.**
[ORIGIN from *Kanara* (see below) + -ESE.]
▸ **A** *noun*. Pl. same.
1 = KANNADA *noun*. **M19.**
2 A member of a Kannada-speaking people of Kanara in western India. **L19.**
▸ **B** *adjective*. Of or pertaining to Kanara or its people; *spec.* = KANNADA *adjective*. **M19.**

kanari /kəˈnaːri/ *noun*. **L18.**
[ORIGIN Malay *kenari*.]
Any of several SE Asian trees of the genus *Canarium* (family Burseraceae), producing edible nuts from which oil is extracted; *esp.* the Java almond, *C. luzonicum*.

kanat *noun* var. of QANAT.

kanban /ˈkanban/ *noun*. **L20.**
[ORIGIN Japanese, from *kan* see + *ban* board.]
1 A card used for ordering parts etc. in a Japanese just-in-time manufacturing system. **L20.**
2 In full ***kanban system***. A Japanese just-in-time manufacturing system in which parts etc. are ordered on cards. **L20.**

kanchil /ˈkaːntʃɪl, ˈkan-/ *noun*. **E19.**
[ORIGIN Malay *kancil*.]
The smallest chevrotain, *Tragulus javanicus*, native to forests in Borneo, Java, and Indo-china.

Kandyan /ˈkandɪən/ *adjective & noun*. **M19.**
[ORIGIN from *Kandy* (see below) + -AN.]
▸ **A** *adjective*. Of, pertaining to, or characteristic of the town or former kingdom of Kandy in Ceylon (Sri Lanka), or its inhabitants. **M19.**
▸ **B** *noun*. A native or inhabitant of Kandy. **M19.**

Kanesian /kəˈniːʒ(ə)n/ *noun & adjective*. **E20.**
[ORIGIN from *Kanesh* an ancient city of Asia Minor + -IAN.]
(Of) the principal dialect of Hittite. Also called ***Nesite***.

kang /kaŋ/ *noun*. **L18.**
[ORIGIN Chinese *kàng*.]
In China: a kind of stove for warming rooms; also, a brick or wooden structure for sleeping on, warmed from below by a fire.

kanga /ˈkaŋgə/ *noun*[1]. *Austral. colloq.* **E20.**
[ORIGIN Abbreviation.]
A kangaroo.

kanga *noun*[2] var. of KHANGA.

kangany /kanˈgaːni/ *noun*. Also **-ni**. **E19.**
[ORIGIN Tamil *kankāni*, from *kaṇ* eye + *kāṇ-* see.]
hist. An overseer or headman of a gang of local labourers in Ceylon (Sri Lanka), southern India, or Malaysia.

kangaroo /kaŋgəˈruː/ *noun*. Pl. **-s**, (in sense 1) same. **L18.**
[ORIGIN Guugu Yimidhirr (an Australian Aboriginal language of NE Queensland) *gangurru*.]
1 Any of various herbivorous marsupial mammals of the family Macropodidae, of Australia, New Guinea, and adjacent islands, which have small forelimbs, powerful hind limbs and long feet enabling a leaping bipedal gait, and a long tail for balance; *esp.* any of the larger kinds of the genus *Macropus*. Cf. WALLABY. **L18.**
grey kangaroo, ***rat-kangaroo***, ***red kangaroo***, ***tree kangaroo***, etc.
2 An Australian, *esp.* one representing Australia in sport; *spec.* a member of the Australian international rugby league team. *colloq.* **L19.**
3 In Britain, a parliamentary closure by which some amendments are selected for discussion and others excluded. Also ***kangaroo closure***. **E20.**
– COMB.: **kangaroo apple** *Austral.* (the edible fruit of) any of several Australian plants of the genus *Solanum*, of the nightshade family, esp. *S. laciniatum*, *S. vescum* (the gunyang), and *S. aviculare* (the poroporo of New Zealand); **kangaroo beetle** a bright, metallic, jumping leaf beetle of the genus *Sagra*, with enlarged hind legs; **kangaroo care** a method of caring for a premature baby in which the infant is held in skin-to-skin contact with a parent as much as possible. ***kangaroo closure***: see sense 3 above; **kangaroo court** (orig. *US*) an improperly constituted court with no legal standing held by strikers, mutineers, etc.; **kangaroo dog** a large dog trained to hunt kangaroos; **kangaroo fly** *Austral.* a small irritating fly; **kangaroo grass** a tall fodder grass, *Themeda australis*, found in Australasia, southern Asia, and Africa; **kangaroo justice** the procedure or product of a decision of a kangaroo court; **kangaroo mouse** (***a***) a marsupial mouse; (***b***) any small N. American desert rodent of the genus *Microdipodops*; **kangaroo paw** any of several Australian plants of the genus *Anigozanthos* (family Haemodoraceae), with showy woolly red or green flowers; **kangaroo rat** (***a***) a rat-kangaroo; (***b***) any of various small burrowing rodents of the genus *Dipodomys*, of the southern US and Mexico, with elongated hind feet; **kangaroo thorn** a spiny Australian leguminous shrub, *Acacia armata*, used for hedges; **kangaroo vine** an Australian evergreen vine, *Cissus antarctica*, with dark green heart-shaped leaves, grown as a house plant.

kangaroo /kaŋgəˈruː/ *verb intrans.* **E19.**
[ORIGIN from the noun.]
1 Hunt kangaroos. Chiefly as ***kangarooing*** *verbal noun & ppl adjective*. **E19.**
2 Jump or move like a kangaroo; make a great jump (*lit. & fig.*). **M19.**
▪ **kangarooer** *noun* a person who hunts kangaroos **M19.**

kangha /ˈkʌŋhə/ *noun*. **L20.**
[ORIGIN Punjabi *kanghā*.]
A comb worn in the hair as one of the five distinguishing signs of the Sikh Khalsa, symbolizing cleanliness.

K'ang-Hsi /kaŋˈʃiː/ *adjective*. **E20.**
[ORIGIN Royal name of Hsüan-Yeh (see below).]
Designating or pertaining to Chinese pottery and porcelain of the reign of Hsüan-Yeh, emperor of China (1661–1722), notable for very fine blue and white wares and the development of *famille verte* and *famille noire*.

Kango /ˈkaŋgəʊ/ *noun*. Pl. **-os**. **E20.**
[ORIGIN Uncertain: perh. suggested by *kangaroo*.]
(Proprietary name for) a kind of mechanical hammer. Also ***Kango hammer***.

kangri /ˈkaːŋgri/ *noun*. **E20.**
[ORIGIN Hindi *kāgṛī*: cf. Kashmiri *kāġürü*.]
A small wicker-covered clay-lined pot filled with glowing charcoal, carried next to the skin, esp. by Kashmiris, to keep warm.

Kanjar /ˈkandʒə/ *noun*. **L19.**
[ORIGIN Unknown.]
A member of any of various small Gypsy communities in the Indian subcontinent.

kanji /ˈkandʒi, ˈkaːn-/ *noun*. Pl. same. **E20.**
[ORIGIN Japanese, from *kan* Chinese + *ji* letter, character.]
(Any of) the set of borrowed and adapted Chinese ideographs used in the Japanese writing system. Cf. KANA.

kankar *noun* var. of KUNKUR.

kankerbos /ˈkaŋkəbɒs/ *noun*. *S. Afr.* Also **-bossie** /-bɒsi/. **E20.**
[ORIGIN Afrikaans.]
= ***cancer bush*** s.v. CANCER *noun*.

kankie /ˈkaŋki/ *noun*. **M18.**
[ORIGIN Akan.]
In W. Africa: a kind of bread made from maize flour.

Kannada /ˈkanədə/ *noun & adjective*. **M19.**
[ORIGIN Kannada *Kannaḍa*.]
▸ **A** *noun*. The Dravidian language of Kanara and Karnataka in western India, closely allied to Telugu. **M19.**
▸ **B** *attrib.* or as *adjective*. Of or pertaining to Kannada. **M19.**

kanoon /kəˈnuːn/ *noun*. **E19.**
[ORIGIN Persian *qānūn* from Arabic, ult. from Greek *kanōn*.]
A plucked musical instrument of the dulcimer or psaltery type, in the classic form with seventy-two strings, now with fifty to sixty.

kan-pei *interjection* var. of GANBEI.

kanpu *noun* var. of GANBU.

kans /kaːns/ *noun*. **L19.**
[ORIGIN Hindi *kāṃs* from Sanskrit *kāśa*.]
In the Indian subcontinent: a coarse grass, *Saccharum spontaneum*, used for thatching.

Kans. *abbreviation*.
Kansas.

Kansa /ˈkanzə/ *noun & adjective*. Also **Kansas** /ˈkanzəs/. **E18.**
[ORIGIN Illinois from Kansa *kkᑴze*.]
▸ **A** *noun*. Pl. **Kansa**, **Kansas** /ˈkanzəz, -zəs/. A member of a Siouan people formerly of Kansas and now of Oklahoma; the language of this people. Also called ***Kaw***. **E18.**
▸ **B** *attrib.* or as *adjective*. Of or pertaining to the Kansa or their language. **E19.**

Kansan /ˈkanz(ə)n/ *noun & adjective*. **M19.**
[ORIGIN from *Kansas* (see below) + -AN. Cf. KANSA.]
▸ **A** *noun*. **1** A native or inhabitant of the state of Kansas in the Middle West of the US. **M19.**
2 GEOLOGY. One of the Pleistocene glaciations in N. America. **M20.**
▸ **B** *adjective*. Of or pertaining to Kansas; *spec.* (GEOLOGY) designating or pertaining to the Kansan. **L19.**
▪ †**Kansian** *noun* a Kansan **M–L19.**

Kansas *noun & adjective* see KANSA.

kantar /kanˈtaː/ *noun*. Also **c-**. **M16.**
[ORIGIN Arabic *qinṭār*, pl. *qanāṭīr*, from (prob. through Syriac *qantĕr*) Latin *centenarius* CENTENARY. Cf. QUINTAL, Old French *quantar, canter*, medieval Latin *cantar(i)um*, Italian *cantaro*.]
An Arab unit of weight having wide local variations, but in Egypt equal to about 45 kg.

kantele /ˈkantɪli/ *noun*. **E20.**
[ORIGIN Finnish.]
A form of zither used in Finland and the adjoining part of Russia.

Kantian /ˈkantɪən/ *adjective & noun*. **L18.**
[ORIGIN from *Kant* (see below) + -IAN.]
▸ **A** *adjective*. Of or pertaining to the German philosopher Immanuel Kant (1724–1804) or his philosophical principles or views, esp. the view that the phenomenal world derives its structure from the nature of the mind that perceives it. **L18.**
▸ **B** *noun*. An adherent or student of the philosophical principles or views of Kant. **L18.**
▪ **Kantianism** *noun* (adherence to) Kantian principles or views **L18.** **Kantism** *noun* (now *rare*) Kantianism **E19.**

kantikoy /ˈkantɪkɔɪ/ *noun*. Also **c-** & other vars. **L17.**
[ORIGIN Delaware *kə̀ntke:w* lit. 'he dances'.]
Among Algonquian Indians: a ceremonial dance; a party with dancing.

KANU /ˈkaːnuː/ *abbreviation*.
Kenya African National Union.

kanuka /ˈkaːnʊkə/ *noun*. *NZ*. **E20.**
[ORIGIN Maori.]
A small white-flowered evergreen tree, *Leptospermum ericoides*, of the myrtle family. Also called ***white tea tree***.

Kanuri /kəˈnuːri/ *noun*. Pl. same. **L19.**
[ORIGIN Kanuri.]
A member of a group of peoples living in the region of Lake Chad, in Niger and NE Nigeria; the language of these peoples.

kanzu /ˈkanzuː/ *noun*. **E20.**
[ORIGIN Kiswahili.]
A long white cotton or linen robe worn by E. African men.

kaoliang /keɪəʊljaŋ/ *noun*. **E20.**
[ORIGIN Chinese *gāoliang*, from *gāo* (Wade–Giles *kao*) high + *liáng* fine grain.]
A variety of sorghum, *Sorghum bicolor* var. *nervosum*, grown for grain in China and Manchuria.

K

kaolin /ˈkeɪəlɪn/ *noun*. **E18.**
[**ORIGIN** French from Chinese *gāolǐng* lit. 'high hill', a place in Jiangxi province where it is found.]
A fine white clay resulting from the decomposition of feldspar, used to make porcelain and china, as a filler in paper and textiles, and in medicinal adsorbents and poultices. Also (**MINERALOGY**), any of a group of clay minerals which typically occur in such clay, *esp.* kaolinite.
■ **kaoˈlinic** *adjective* **L19.**

kaolinise *verb* var. of **KAOLINIZE**.

kaolinite /ˈkeɪəlɪnʌɪt/ *noun*. **M19.**
[**ORIGIN** from **KAOLIN** + **-ITE**[1].]
MINERALOGY. A white or grey clay mineral which is the chief constituent of kaolin.
■ **kaolinitic** /keɪəlɪˈnɪtɪk/ *adjective* of the nature of or containing kaolinite or other clay minerals of the kaolin group **L19.**

kaolinize /ˈkeɪəlɪnʌɪz/ *verb trans.* Also **-ise**. **L19.**
[**ORIGIN** formed as **KAOLIN** + **-IZE**.]
GEOLOGY. Convert into kaolin. Chiefly as ***kaolinized*** *ppl adjective*.
■ **kaoliniˈzation** *noun* **L19.**

kaon /ˈkeɪɒn/ *noun*. **M20.**
[**ORIGIN** from *ka* (repr. pronunc. of the letter **K, κ**) + **-ON**.]
PARTICLE PHYSICS. Any of a group of mesons which have masses several times those of the pions and non-zero hypercharge, and on decaying usu. produce two or three pions, or a muon and a neutrino. Also called ***K-meson***, ***K-particle***.
■ **kaˈonic** *adjective* of or pertaining to a kaon; (of an atom) having a kaon orbiting the nucleus: **M20.**

kapa *noun* see **TAPA** *noun*[1].

kapai /ˈkɑːpʌɪ/ *adjective & adverb*. *NZ*. **M19.**
[**ORIGIN** Maori *ka pai*.]
Good; well, fine. Also as *interjection*, expr. pleasure or approval.

K

kaparring /kəˈparɪŋ/ *noun*. *S. Afr.* **M19.**
[**ORIGIN** Afrikaans from Javanese *gamparan*.]
A traditional form of wooden sandal worn by Cape Malays.

kapellmeister /kəˈpɛlmʌɪstə/ *noun*. **M19.**
[**ORIGIN** German, from *Kapelle* court orchestra from medieval Latin *capella* **CHAPEL** + *Meister* master.]
Chiefly *hist.* The leader or conductor of a court orchestra, an opera, a choir, etc.

Kapenaar *noun* var. of **KAAPENAAR**.

kapok /ˈkeɪpɒk/ *noun*. **M18.**
[**ORIGIN** Malay *kapuk*.]
A large tropical tree, *Ceiba pentandra* (family Bombacaceae) (also ***kapok tree***); the silky fibre surrounding the seeds of this tree, used to stuff mattresses, cushions, etc.
– **NOTE:** Formerly pronounced /ˈkɑːpək/.

Kaposi /kəˈpəʊsi/ *noun*. **L19.**
[**ORIGIN** M. K. *Kaposi* (1837–1902), Hungarian dermatologist.]
Used in *possess.* (now chiefly in ***Kaposi's sarcoma***) & *attrib.* to designate a disease involving multiple malignant tumours usu. of the lymph nodes or the skin, often associated with defective immunity.

kappa /ˈkapə/ *noun*. **LME.**
[**ORIGIN** Greek.]
1 The tenth letter (Κ, κ) of the Greek alphabet. **LME.**
2 **BIOLOGY.** An infective and independently reproducing particle (now usu. regarded as a commensal bacterium) which occurs within cells of some strains of the ciliate *Paramecium aurelia*, and produces a substance toxic to *Paramecium* cells lacking such particles. Also, such particles collectively. **M20.**

kappie /ˈkapi/ *noun*. *S. Afr.* **M19.**
[**ORIGIN** Afrikaans from Dutch *kapje* dim. of *kap* hood.]
A sun bonnet with a large brim to protect the face.

kapu /ˈkapu/ *adjective & noun*. **M20.**
[**ORIGIN** Hawaiian.]
= **TABOO** *adjective & noun*.

kapur /ˈkapə/ *noun*. **M20.**
[**ORIGIN** Malay.]
Any of various large dipterocarp timber trees of the genus *Dryobalanops*, esp. *D. aromatica*, native to Malaya, Sumatra, and Borneo; the wood of such a tree.

kaput /kəˈpʊt/ *adjective*. *slang*. **L19.**
[**ORIGIN** German *kaputt* from French (*être*) *capot* (be) without tricks in piquet etc.: cf. **CAPOT** *noun*[1] & *verb*.]
Finished, worn out; dead, destroyed; rendered useless or unable to function; broken.

kara /ˈkɑːrə/ *noun*. **L20.**
[**ORIGIN** Punjabi *karā*.]
A steel bangle worn on the right wrist as one of the five distinguishing signs of the Sikh Khalsa, symbolizing loyalty, commitment, and unity with God.

Karabagh /ˈkarəbɑː/ *noun & adjective*. **E20.**
[**ORIGIN** A region now forming part of Nagorno-Karabakh in Azerbaijan, SW Asia.]
(Designating) a thick knotted carpet or rug of the type originally made in Karabakh, usu. with a floral pattern but occas. with an animal one.

†**karabe** *noun*. **M16–L18.**
[**ORIGIN** Ult. from Arabic *kahrabā'* from Persian *kahrubā* amber (lit. 'attracting straw').]
= **AMBER** *noun* 2.

karabiner /karəˈbiːnə/ *noun*. **M20.**
[**ORIGIN** Abbreviation of German *Karabiner-haken* spring hook. Cf. **KRAB**.]
A metal oval or D-shaped coupling link with a closure protected against accidental opening, used in mountaineering.

karaburan /karabʊˈran, karəˈbjʊər(ə)n/ *noun*. **E20.**
[**ORIGIN** Turkish, from *kara* black + *buran* whirlwind.]
A hot dusty wind which blows in central Asia.

karahi /kʌˈrʌɪ/ *noun*. Also **kadai** /kʌˈdʌɪ/, **karai**. **L19.**
[**ORIGIN** Hindi *karāhī*]
A small bowl-shaped frying pan with two handles, used in Indian cookery (esp. for preparing balti dishes).

Karaite /ˈkɛːrəʌɪt/ *noun & adjective*. Also (earlier) †**C-**. **E18.**
[**ORIGIN** from Hebrew *Qārā'īm* scripturalists, from *qārā'* read: see **-ITE**[1].]
▸**A** *noun*. A member of a Jewish sect founded in the 8th cent. and located chiefly in the Crimea and neighbouring areas, and in Israel, which rejects rabbinical tradition in favour of literal interpretation of the Scriptures. **E18.**
▸**B** *adjective*. Of or pertaining to this sect. **E20.**
■ **Karaism** *noun* the religious system of the Karaites **L19.**

karaka /kəˈrakə, ˈkarəkə/ *noun*. **M19.**
[**ORIGIN** Maori.]
A New Zealand tree, *Corynocarpus laevigata* (family Corynocarpaceae), with orange berries and poisonous seeds which are edible after roasting.

Kara-Kalpak /ˈkarəkalˌpak/ *noun & adjective*. Also **Karakalpak**. **E18.**
[**ORIGIN** Kyrgyz, from *kara* black + *kalpak* cap.]
▸**A** *noun*. Pl. **-s**, same.
1 A member of a Turkic people inhabiting a region south of the Aral Sea in Uzbekistan. **E18.**
2 The Kazakh dialect of this people. **L19.**
▸**B** *attrib.* or as *adjective*. Of or pertaining to the Kara-Kalpaks or their dialect. **M19.**

karakia /karəˈkiːə/ *noun & verb*. *NZ*. Pl. same, **-s**. **M19.**
[**ORIGIN** Maori.]
▸**A** *noun*. A Maori incantation. **M19.**
▸**B** *verb trans.* Utter a karakia for or over; pray for. **M19.**

karakul /ˈkarəkʊl/ *noun & adjective*. Also **caracul**. **M19.**
[**ORIGIN** Russian *karakul'*, from the name of an oasis in Uzbekistan and of two lakes in Tajikistan, app. ult. from Turkic.]
▸**A** *noun*. **1** (An animal of) a breed of sheep with a coarse wiry fleece. **M19.**
2 (Cloth or fur resembling) the glossy curled fleece of a young lamb of this breed. Also called ***Persian lamb***. **L19.**
▸**B** *attrib.* or as *adjective*. Of or pertaining to the karakul or karakul. **L19.**

Kara-Kyrgyz /ˈkarəkɪəˌgɪz, -ˌkəːgɪz/ *noun & adjective*. Pl. same. **L19.**
[**ORIGIN** Kyrgyz, from *kara* black + as **KYRGYZ**.]
= **KYRGYZ**.

karamat *noun & adjective* var. of **KRAMAT**.

Karamojong /karəˈməʊdʒɒŋ/ *noun & adjective*. Also **Kari-** /karɪ-/, (earlier) **-jo** /-dʒəʊ/. **E20.**
[**ORIGIN** Nilotic.]
▸**A** *noun*. Pl. same, **-s**. A member of a Nilotic people of Karamoja in NE Uganda; the language of this people. **E20.**
▸**B** *attrib.* or as *adjective*. Of or pertaining to the Karamojong or their language. **E20.**

karamu /ˈkarəmuː/ *noun*. **M19.**
[**ORIGIN** Maori.]
Any of various Australasian trees and shrubs of the genus *Coprosma*, of the madder family, some of which produce edible fruits.

karana /ˈkʌrənə/ *noun*. **M20.**
[**ORIGIN** Sanskrit *karaṇa* action, posture.]
Any of the 108 basic postures in Indian dance.

karanga /ˈkarəŋə/ *noun*. *NZ*. **E20.**
[**ORIGIN** Maori.]
A (Maori) ritual chant of welcome.

Karankawa /kəˈraŋkəwə/ *noun & adjective*. Also **Carancahua** /-hwə/. **E19.**
[**ORIGIN** Amer. Spanish *Carancahuases* (pl.) prob. from Karankawa.]
▸**A** *noun*. Pl. same, **-s**. A member of an American Indian people of the Gulf coast of Texas; the language of this people. **E19.**
▸**B** *attrib.* or as *adjective*. Of or pertaining to the Karankawa or their language. **E19.**
■ **Karankawan** *adjective & noun* **L19.**

karanteen /kar(ə)nˈtiːn/ *noun*. *S. Afr.* **E20.**
[**ORIGIN** Unknown.]
Either of two small marine fishes of the family Sparidae, *Crenidens crenidens* (more fully ***white karanteen***), and the bamboo fish, *Sarpa salpa* (more fully ***striped karanteen***).

karaoke /karəˈəʊki, karɪ-/ *noun*. **L20.**
[**ORIGIN** Japanese, from *kara* empty + *oke* abbreviation of *ōkesutora* orchestra.]
A form of entertainment (originating in Japan) in which one or more people sing popular songs as soloists against pre-recorded backing music; (in full ***karaoke music***) such pre-recorded backing music.
– **COMB.:** **karaoke bar**, **karaoke club**: providing karaoke facilities for customers (esp. in Japan); **karaoke machine**: for reproducing the music and at the same time giving a display of the words; ***karaoke music***: see above.

karat *noun* see **CARAT**.

karate /kəˈrɑːti/ *noun*. **M20.**
[**ORIGIN** Japanese, lit. 'empty hand', i.e. weaponless, from *kara* empty + *te* hand.]
A Japanese system of unarmed combat using the hands and feet as weapons.
– **COMB.:** **karate-chop** *noun & verb* (strike with) a sharp slanting blow of the hand.
■ ***karateka*** /kəˈrɑːtɪkɑː/ *noun* an exponent of or expert in karate **M20.**

karaya /kəˈrʌɪə/ *noun*. **L19.**
[**ORIGIN** Hindi *karāyal* resin.]
In full ***karaya gum***, ***gum karaya***. A gum exuded by the Indian tree *Sterculia urens* (family Sterculiaceae), with uses similar to tragacanth.

karee *noun* var. of **KARREE**.

karela /kəˈreɪlə/ *noun*. **M19.**
[**ORIGIN** Hindi *karelā* from Sanskrit *kāravella*.]
In the Indian subcontinent: (the fruit of) the balsam pear, *Momordica charantia*.

Karelian /kəˈriːlɪən/ *noun & adjective*. Also **C-**. **M19.**
[**ORIGIN** from *Karelia* (see below) + **-AN**.]
▸**A** *noun*. **1** A native or inhabitant of Karelia, a region in eastern Finland and the adjoining part of Russia. **M19.**
2 The Finno-Ugric language of this people. **L19.**
▸**B** *adjective*. Of or pertaining to Karelia, its people, or their language. **M19.**

Karen /kəˈrɛn/ *noun & adjective*. In sense A.1 also (earlier) †**Carian(er)**. **M18.**
[**ORIGIN** Burmese *ka-reng* wild unclean man.]
▸**A** *noun*. **1** A member of a non-indigenous people scattered throughout Myanmar (Burma), esp. in the east. **M18.**
2 The language of this people. **M19.**
▸**B** *attrib.* or as *adjective*. Of or pertaining to the Karens or their language. **M19.**

karez /ˈkɑːrɛz/ *noun*. Also ***-ze***. **L19.**
[**ORIGIN** Pashto from Persian.]
= **QANAT**.

karezza /kəˈrɛtsə/ *noun*. Also **c-**. **L19.**
[**ORIGIN** Italian *carezza* caress.]
Sexual intercourse in which ejaculation is avoided.

Karimojong *noun & adjective* var. of **KARAMOJONG**.

Karitane /karɪˈtɑːni/ *adjective*. *NZ*. **E20.**
[**ORIGIN** A township in the South Island of New Zealand.]
Designating, pertaining to, or involving the system of antenatal and postnatal care for mothers and babies initiated by the Royal New Zealand Society for the Health of Women and Children. Cf. **PLUNKET** *adjective*[2].

karkun *noun* var. of **CARCOON**.

karma /ˈkɑːmə, ˈkəːmə/ *noun*. **E19.**
[**ORIGIN** Sanskrit *karman* action, effect, fate.]
In **BUDDHISM & HINDUISM**, the sum of a person's actions, esp. intentional actions, regarded as determining that person's future states of existence; in **JAINISM**, subtle physical matter which binds the soul as a result of bad actions. Now also *gen.*, fate or destiny following as effect from cause.

> *Yoga & Health* The good Karmas from your past have helped you. J. **DIDION** Whatever happens it's in her karma.

– **COMB.:** ***karma marga*** /-ˈmɑːgə/ [*mārga* path] a strict adherence to Hindu precepts in order to attain a better life in one's next incarnation; ***karma yoga*** /-ˈjəʊgə/ the attainment of perfection through disinterested action; ***karma yogi*** /-ˈjəʊgi/ an exponent of ***karma yoga***.
■ **karmic** *adjective* of or pertaining to karma **L19.**

karmadharaya /kɑːməˈdɑːrəjə, kəː-/ *noun*. **M19.**
[**ORIGIN** Sanskrit, formed as **KARMA** + *dhāraya* holding, bearing.]
LINGUISTICS. A compound in which the first element describes the second, as ***highway***, ***steamboat***, etc.

Karman /ˈkɑːmən/ *noun*. **E20.**
[**ORIGIN** Theodore von *Kármán* (1881–1963), Hungarian-born physicist and aeronautical engineer.]
PHYSICS. Used *attrib.* to designate a vortex street in which the vortices of one line are situated opposite points midway between those of the other line.

Karmathian /kɑːˈmeɪθɪən/ *noun & adjective*. Also **C-**. E19.
[ORIGIN from Ḥamdān *Karmaṭ* its founder + -IAN.]
▸ **A** *noun*. A member of a Muslim sect founded in the 9th cent. E19.
▸ **B** *adjective*. Of or pertaining to this sect. E20.

Karnata /kəˈnɑːtə/ *adjective & noun*. Also (now *rare*) **C-**. L18.
[ORIGIN Alternative name for *Karnataka*: see KARNATAKA.]
▸ **A** *noun*. = KANNADA *noun*. Now *rare*. L18.
▸ **B** *adjective*. = KARNATAKA. E19.

Karnataka /kəˈnɑːtəkə/ *adjective*. E19.
[ORIGIN See below. Cf. CARNATIC, KARNATA.]
Of or pertaining to the state of Karnataka (formerly Mysore) in SW India, its language (Kannada), or its music.

Karnaugh /ˈkɑːnɔː/ *noun*. M20.
[ORIGIN Maurice *Karnaugh* (b. 1924), US physicist.]
MATH. & LOGIC. ***Karnaugh map***, ***Karnaugh diagram***, a diagram that consists of a rectangular array of squares each representing a different combination of the variables of a Boolean function.

karo /ˈkɑːrəʊ/ *noun*. Pl. same, **-os**. M19.
[ORIGIN Maori.]
An evergreen shrub or small tree native to New Zealand, *Pittosporum crassifolium* (family Pittosporaceae), with leathery leaves and clusters of small crimson flowers.

Karok /kəˈrɒk/ *noun & adjective*. M19.
[ORIGIN from Karok *karuk* upstream.]
▸ **A** *noun*. Pl. **-s**, same. A member of a N. American Indian people of the Klamath river valley in NW California; the language of this people. M19.
▸ **B** *attrib.* or as *adjective*. Of or pertaining to the Karoks or their language. L19.

Karoo /kəˈruː/ *noun & adjective*. Also **-rr-**, **k-**. L18.
[ORIGIN Nama.]
▸ **A** *noun*. Any of certain elevated semi-desert plateaux in southern Africa; terrain of this kind. L18.
▸ **B** *attrib.* or as *adjective*. GEOLOGY. Designating or pertaining to a series of Triassic rocks in southern Africa, chiefly fossiliferous sandstone mixed with volcanic matter. L19.

karoshi /kəˈrəʊʃi/ *noun*. L20.
[ORIGIN Japanese, from *ka* excess + *rō* labour + *shi* death.]
In Japan, death caused by overwork.

kaross /kəˈrɒs/ *noun*. *S. Afr.* Also †**kross**. M18.
[ORIGIN Afrikaans *karos*, perh. from Nama.]
A cloak or sleeveless jacket like a blanket made of hairy animal skins, worn by the indigenous peoples of southern Africa. Also, a rug of sewn skins.

karree /kəˈriː/ *noun*. Also **karee**. E19.
[ORIGIN Afrikaans from Nama *karib*.]
Either of two willow-like southern African trees of the genus *Rhus*, *R. lancea* and *R. viminalis* (family Anacardiaceae). Also ***karree-boom*** /-bʊəm/ [Afrikaans *boom* = tree].

Karren /ˈkar(ə)n/ *noun pl.* L19.
[ORIGIN German.]
PHYSICAL GEOGRAPHY. The furrows or fissures of a Karrenfeld; terrain characterized by these. Cf. LAPIÉS.

Karrenfeld /ˈkar(ə)nfɛlt, -fɛld/ *noun*. Pl. **-felder** /-fɛldə/, **-felds** /-fɛldz/. L19.
[ORIGIN German, from KARREN + *Feld* field.]
PHYSICAL GEOGRAPHY. An area or landscape, usu. of limestone bare of soil, which has been eroded by solution so as to have an extremely dissected surface with conspicuous furrows and fissures, often separated by knifelike ridges. Cf. LAPIÉS.

karri /ˈkari/ *noun*. M19.
[ORIGIN Nyungar.]
A tall eucalyptus, *Eucalyptus diversicolor*, of western Australia; the hard red timber of this tree.

Karroo *noun* var. of KAROO.

karrozzin /kəˈrɒtsɪn/ *noun*. Also **car(r)ozzi**. E20.
[ORIGIN Maltese from Italian *carrozza*.]
A horse-drawn cab used in Malta.

Karshuni *noun* var. of GARSHUNI.

karst /kɑːst/ *noun*. L19.
[ORIGIN German *der Karst* (perh. rel. to Slovene *Krâs*) a limestone plateau region in Slovenia, SE Europe.]
PHYSICAL GEOGRAPHY. A kind of topography characteristic of areas of relatively soluble rock (usu. limestone) and mainly underground drainage, marked by numerous abrupt ridges, gorges, fissures, swallow holes, and caverns; a region dominated by such topography.
tower karst: see TOWER *noun*[1].
– ATTRIB. & COMB.: In the sense 'characteristic of or of the nature of karst', as ***karst land***, ***karst scenery***, ***karst topography***, etc. Special combs., as **karst tower** a steep-sided often flat-topped conical hill characteristic of tropical and subtropical karst.
■ **karstic** *adjective* of the nature of karst; pertaining to or characteristic of karst: E20. **karstifiˈcation** *noun* development of karst or karstic features; alteration into karst: M20. **karstify** *verb trans.* subject to karstification (chiefly as ***karstified***, ***karstifying*** *ppl adjectives*) M20. **karsting** *noun* = KARSTIFICATION E20.

kart /kɑːt/ *noun*. M20.
[ORIGIN Abbreviation.]
= GO-KART.
■ **karting** *noun* = GO-KARTING M20.

kartel *noun* var. of KATEL.

karuna /ˈkʌrʊnə/ *noun*. M19.
[ORIGIN Sanskrit *karuṇā*.]
BUDDHISM. Loving compassion.

karyo- /ˈkarɪəʊ/ *combining form*.
[ORIGIN from Greek *karuon* nut: see -O-.]
BIOLOGY. Of or pertaining to the nucleus of an animal or plant cell.
■ **karyˈogamy** *noun* fusion of cell nuclei L19. **karyogram** *noun* an idiogram; a karyotype: M20. **karyokiˈnesis** *noun* division of a cell nucleus during mitosis L19. **karyokiˈnetic** *adjective* of or pertaining to karyokinesis L19. **karyˈolysis** *noun* dissolution of a cell nucleus L19. **karyoˈlytic** *adjective* of or pertaining to karyolysis L19. **karyomere** *noun* a vesicle containing a single chromosome, formed in some cells at division E20. **karyomiˈtosis** *noun* karyokinesis L19. **karyomiˈtotic** *adjective* karyokinetic L19. **karyoplasm** *noun* nucleoplasm L19. **karyoˈplasmic** *adjective* of or pertaining to karyoplasm E20. **karyoˈrrhexis** *noun* [Greek *rhēxis* bursting] fragmentation of a cell nucleus L19. **karyosome** *noun* a densely staining chromatin body within a cell nucleus, *esp.* one distinct from a nucleolus: L19.

karyology /karɪˈɒlədʒi/ *noun*. L19.
[ORIGIN from KARYO- + -LOGY.]
BIOLOGY. **1** The characteristic features of the nuclei *of* a particular cell type, species, strain, etc. L19.
2 The branch of biology that deals with cell nuclei and (esp.) chromosomes. M20.
■ **karyoˈlogic** *adjective* (chiefly *US*) M20. **karyoˈlogical** *adjective* E20. **karyoˈlogically** *adverb*. E20.

karyotin /ˈkarɪətɪn/ *noun*. E20.
[ORIGIN from KARYO- + *-tin*, after *chromatin*.]
BIOLOGY. = CHROMATIN.

karyotype /ˈkarɪətʌɪp/ *noun & verb*. E20.
[ORIGIN from KARYO- + -TYPE.]
BIOLOGY. ▸**A** *noun*. **1** The chromosomal constitution of a cell (and hence of an individual, species, etc.) represented by the number, size, shape, etc., of the chromosomes (usu. as at metaphase). E20.
2 A systematized (esp. photographic) representation of the chromosomes of a cell or cells. M20.
▸ **B** *verb trans.* Determine or investigate the karyotype of (a cell, species, etc.). M20.
■ **karyoˈtypic**, **karyoˈtypical** *adjectives* of or pertaining to a karyotype M20. **karyoˈtypically** *adverb* M20.

karzy *noun* var. of KHAZI.

kasbah /ˈkazbɑː/ *noun*. Also **c-**. M18.
[ORIGIN French *casbah* from Maghribi pronunc. of Arabic *qaṣaba* fortress.]
(The Arab quarter surrounding) a N. African castle or fortress citadel.

kasha /ˈkaʃə/ *noun*[1]. Also (earlier) †**c-**. E19.
[ORIGIN Russian.]
1 A porridge made from cooked buckwheat or other grains. E19.
2 A beige colour resembling that of buckwheat groats. M20.

Kasha /ˈkaʃə/ *noun*[2]. E20.
[ORIGIN Unknown.]
(Proprietary name for) a soft napped fabric made from wool and hair. Also, a cotton lining material.

Kashan /kəˈʃɑːn/ *noun & adjective*. E20.
[ORIGIN A province and town in central Iran.]
(Designating) a finely woven rug, usu. of wool or silk, made in Kashan.

Kashgai /ˈkaʃgʌɪ/ *noun & adjective*. Also **Qashgai** & other vars. L19.
[ORIGIN Turkic.]
▸ **A** *noun*. Pl. **-s**, same. A member of a Turkic people living around Shiraz in Iran. L19.
▸ **B** *adjective*. Of or pertaining to the Kashgais. E20.

Kashgar /ˈkaʃgɑː/ *adjective*. L19.
[ORIGIN See below.]
Of or pertaining to Kashgar, a city and district of Sinkiang-Uighur (formerly East Turkestan) in China; *spec.* (***a***) designating the Turkic language of Kashgar; (***b***) designating a type of Turkish carpet associated with Kashgar.

Kashmir /ˈkaʃmɪə, kaʃˈmɪə/ *noun & adjective*. L19.
[ORIGIN See KASHMIRI. Cf. CASHMERE.]
▸ **A** *noun*. **1** = CASHMERE 1. *rare*. L19.
2 = KASHMIRI *noun* 2. *rare*. L19.
▸ **B** *attrib.* or as *adjective*. **1** = KASHMIRI *adjective*. L19.
Kashmir goat a goat of a Himalayan breed yielding fine soft wool (used to make cashmere).
2 Designating a Caucasian rug or carpet with a flat napless surface and loose ends of yarn on the back. Also called ***Soumak***. E20.
■ **Kashmirian** *adjective & noun* (now *rare* or *obsolete*) (***a***) *adjective* = KASHMIRI *adjective*; (***b***) *noun* = KASHMIRI *noun* 2: L18.

Kashmiri /kaʃˈmɪəri/ *adjective & noun*. L19.
[ORIGIN from KASHMIR + -I[2].]
▸ **A** *adjective*. Of or pertaining to Kashmir, a disputed territory in the western Himalayas, formerly a separate state but now divided between India and Pakistan. L19.
▸ **B** *noun*. **1** The Dard language of Kashmir. L19.
2 A native or inhabitant of Kashmir. M20.

Kashrut /kaʃˈruːt/ *noun*. Also **-ruth** /-ˈruːθ/. E20.
[ORIGIN Hebrew = legitimacy (in religion), formed as KOSHER *adjective*.]
The body of Jewish religious laws relating to the suitability of food, ritual objects, etc.; the observance of these laws.

Kashube /kəˈʃuːb/ *noun*. Also **Kaszube**. L19.
[ORIGIN from *Kashubia* (Polish *Kaszuby*): see below.]
1 A member of the Slavonic people inhabiting Kashubia, a region of Poland west and north-west of Gdańsk. L19.
2 The dialect of this people, Kashubian. M20.

Kashubian /kəˈʃuːbɪən/ *noun & adjective*. Also (earlier) **Cassub-** /kəˈsuːb-/; **Kaszub-**. M19.
[ORIGIN formed as KASHUBE + -AN.]
▸ **A** *noun*. **1** The Lechitic dialect of Kashubia. M19.
2 = KASHUBE *noun* 1. M20.
▸ **B** *adjective*. Of or pertaining to Kashubia, its people, or their dialect. E20.

Kassite /ˈkasʌɪt/ *noun & adjective*. L19.
[ORIGIN from Assyrian *kaššu* + -ITE[1].]
▸ **A** *noun*. **1** A member of an Elamite people from the Zagros mountains in Iran, who ruled Babylon from the 18th to the 12th cent. BC. L19.
2 The language of this people. M20.
▸ **B** *adjective*. Of or pertaining to the Kassites or their language. L19.

kasturi /kaˈstuːri/ *noun*. Also **-ra** /-rə/. M19.
[ORIGIN Sanskrit *kastūrī*.]
A Himalayan musk deer.

Kaszube *noun*, **Kaszubian** *noun & adjective* vars. of KASHUBE, KASHUBIAN.

kat *noun* var. of KHAT.

kat- *prefix* see CATA-.

kata /ˈkɑːtɑː/ *noun*. M20.
[ORIGIN Japanese.]
A system of basic exercises or postures and movements used to teach and improve the execution of techniques in judo and other martial arts.

kata- *prefix* see CATA-.

katabasis /kəˈtabəsɪs/ *noun*. *literary*. Pl. **-ases** /-əsiːz/. M19.
[ORIGIN Greek, from *kata* down + *basis* going. Cf. ANABASIS.]
A military retreat, *esp.* that of the Greeks under Xenophon, related in his *Anabasis*.

katabatic /katəˈbatɪk/ *adjective*. In sense 1 **c-**. L19.
[ORIGIN Greek *katabatikos*, from *katabainein* go down: see -IC. Cf. ANABATIC.]
†**1** MEDICINE. Gradually declining in severity. *rare*. Only in L19.
2 METEOROLOGY. Of a wind: caused by local downward motion of (esp. cool dense) air. Opp. ANABATIC. L19.

katabolic *adjective*, **katabolism** *noun* vars. of CATABOLIC, CATABOLISM.

katabothron *noun* etc., see KATAVOTHRON.

katakana /katəˈkɑːnə/ *noun*. Also **-gana**. E18.
[ORIGIN Japanese, from *kata* side + *kana* KANA.]
An angular form of kana, used in modern Japanese mainly for writing words of foreign origin and for emphasis. Cf. HIRAGANA.

katana /kəˈtɑːnə/ *noun*. Also (earlier) †***cattan***. E17.
[ORIGIN Japanese, prob. from *kata* one side + *na* blade.]
A long single-edged sword used by Japanese samurai.

Katangese /kataŋˈgiːz/ *noun & adjective*. M20.
[ORIGIN from *Katanga* (see below) + -ESE.]
▸ **A** *noun*. Pl. same. A native or inhabitant of Katanga (Shaba), a province in the SE of the Democratic Republic of Congo (Zaire). M20.
▸ **B** *adjective*. Of or pertaining to Katanga or the Katangese. M20.

katathermometer /katəθəˈmɒmɪtə/ *noun*. E20.
[ORIGIN from *kata-* var. of CATA- + THERMOMETER.]
A thermometer with an enlarged bulb used to determine the cooling power of ambient air or the rate of airflow by measuring the time taken for the indicated temperature to fall by a specified amount.

†**katatonia** *noun* var. of CATATONIA.

katavothron /katəˈvɒθrən/ *noun*. *arch.* Also **c-**, **-both-** /-ˈbɒθ-/, **-thra** /-θrə/. Pl. **-thra** /-θrə/, **-thrai** /-θrʌɪ/, **-throns**. E19.
[ORIGIN mod. Greek *katabothra*, pl. *-thrai*, *-thres*, from Greek *kata* down + *bothros* hole (*-v-* repr. mod. Greek pronunc., *-on* from misunderstanding sing. as neut pl.).]
A subterranean channel or deep hole formed by the action of water; a swallow hole.

K

Kate Greenaway /keɪt ˈɡriːnəweɪ/ *adjectival phr.* L19.
[ORIGIN Kate (Catherine) *Greenaway* (1846–1901), English artist and illustrator of children's books.]
Designating (a garment in) a style of children's clothing modelled on Kate Greenaway's drawings.

katel /ˈkɑːt(ə)l/ *noun. S. Afr.* Also (*arch.*) **cartle**; **kartel**. M19.
[ORIGIN Afrikaans, app. from Portuguese *catel*, *catle* little bed from Malay *katil* from Tamil *kaṭṭil* bedstead. Cf. KATIL.]
A lightweight portable bed or hammock, used in an ox wagon.

kat' exochen /kat ˈɛksəʊtʃɛn/ *adverbial phr.* Now *rare*. L16.
[ORIGIN Greek *kat' exokhēn*.]
Pre-eminently.
– NOTE: Usu. found in untransliterated Greek characters.

Kathak /ˈkʌtək/ *noun & adjective*. Also (esp. in sense A.2) **k-**. M20.
[ORIGIN Sanskrit *kathaka* professional storyteller, from *kathā* story.]
▸ **A** *noun*. Pl. **-s**, (in sense 1) same.
1 A member of a northern Indian caste of storytellers and musicians. M20.
2 A type of northern Indian classical dance alternating passages of mime with passages of dance; an example of this. M20.
▸ **B** *attrib.* or as *adjective*. Of or pertaining to the Kathak or Kathak. M20.

Kathakali /kɑːtəˈkɑːli, kʌtəˈkʌli/ *noun*. Also (*rare*) **Kadh-**. E20.
[ORIGIN Malayalam *kathakaḷi*, from Sanskrit *kathā* story + Malayalam *kaḷi* play.]
A southern Indian dance drama based on Hindu literature, characterized by stylized costume and make-up, and frequent use of mime.

katharevousa /ˌkaθərəˈvuːsə, kaθəˈrɛvʊsə/ *noun*. E20.
[ORIGIN mod. Greek *kathareuousa* fem. of *kathareuōn* pres. pple of Greek *kathareuein* be pure, from *katharos* pure.]
The purist form of modern Greek (at one time, but since 1976 no longer, the language officially used by the state).

Katharine *noun* see CATHERINE.

katharometer /kaθəˈrɒmɪtə/ *noun*. E20.
[ORIGIN from Greek *katharos* pure + -OMETER.]
An instrument for detecting a gas or measuring its concentration in a mixture by measuring changes in thermal conductivity.

katharsis *noun*, **kathartic** *adjective & noun* see CATHARSIS, CATHARTIC.

kathenotheism /kəˈθɛnəʊˌθiːɪz(ə)m/ *noun*. M19.
[ORIGIN from Greek *kath ena* one by one + *theos* god + -ISM.]
Vedic polytheism, in which each god in turn for a period of time is considered single and supreme.

Katherine *noun* see CATHERINE.

katheter *noun*, **kathetometer** *noun* vars. of CATHETER, CATHETOMETER.

kathi /ˈkɑːði/ *noun*. M20.
[ORIGIN Malay *kadi* from Arabic *qāḍī* CADI.]
A judge in Islamic law, who also functions as a registrar of Muslim marriages, divorces, etc.

Kathleen Mavourneen /ˌkaθliːn məˈvɔːniːn/ *noun & adjective. Austral. & NZ slang.* E20.
[ORIGIN Title of a song one line of which is 'it may be for years, and it may be forever.']
▸ **A** *noun*. An open-ended jail sentence. Also, a habitual criminal. E20.
▸ **B** *adjective*. Open-ended, of indeterminate duration. E20.

†**kathode** *noun*, †**kathodic** *adjective*, †**kathodo-** *combining form* vars. of CATHODE, CATHODIC, CATHODO-.

kati /ˈkati/ *noun*. Also **katti**. E18.
[ORIGIN Malay.]
In Malaysia: = CATTY *noun*.

katil /ˈkɑːt(ə)l/ *noun. S. Afr.* M20.
[ORIGIN Malay: see KATEL.]
A bier used by Cape Malays in funeral ceremonies.

katipo /ˈkatɪpəʊ/ *noun*. Pl. same, **-os**. M19.
[ORIGIN Maori.]
A venomous black New Zealand spider, *Latrodectus katipo*, with a red spot on its back.

katjiepiering /ˈkatʃɪˈpɪərɪŋ, ˈkʌkɪ-/ *noun*. L18.
[ORIGIN Afrikaans from Malay *kacapiring*.]
Any of various southern African gardenias, esp. *Gardenia thunbergia* and *G. jasminoides*.

katonkel /kəˈtɒŋk(ə)l/ *noun. S. Afr.* M19.
[ORIGIN Afrikaans from Malay *ketangkai*.]
Either of two marine game fishes of the family Scombridae, the seir, *Scomberomorus commerson*, and the bonito, *Sarda sarda*.

Kat stitch /ˈkat stɪtʃ/ *noun phr.* E20.
[ORIGIN from *Kat* pet form of female forename *Katherine*, *C-*, after Catherine of Aragon, said to have invented the stitch: see STITCH *noun*[1].]
LACE-MAKING. A stitch which forms a star-shaped ground net.

katsuo /ˈkatswo/ *noun*. Pl. same. E18.
[ORIGIN Japanese, perh. from *kata* hard + *uo* fish.]
A bonito, *Katsuwonus pelamis*, important as a food fish in Japan, fresh or dried.
▪ ***katsuobushi*** /katswoˈbuʃi/ *noun*, pl. same, a dried quarter of this fish L19.

katsura /katˈsʊərə/ *noun*. E20.
[ORIGIN Japanese.]
1 A type of Japanese wig worn mainly by women. E20.
2 In full ***katsuramono*** /katˌsʊərəˈməʊnəʊ/ [*mono* piece, play]. A type of romantic Noh play with a woman as the central character. E20.

Kattern /ˈkatəːn/ *noun & verb intrans.* Also **C-**. M18.
[ORIGIN Alt. of St *Catherine* of Alexandria, the patron saint of spinners, martyred in AD 307.]
hist. (Celebrate) the feast day of St Catherine, 25 November.

katti *noun* var. of KATI.

katun /ˈkɑːtuːn/ *noun*. E20.
[ORIGIN Maya.]
A period of twenty years, each of 360 days, in the calendar of the Mayan Indians.

katydid /ˈkeɪtɪdɪd/ *noun*. Also **c-**. L18.
[ORIGIN Imit.]
Any of various large N. American bush crickets, the males of which make a characteristic sound.

Katyusha /kəˈtjuːʃə/ *noun*. M20.
[ORIGIN Russian.]
A type of Russian rocket mortar.
– COMB.: **Katyusha rocket** launched from a Katyusha.

katzenjammer /ˈkats(ə)ndʒamə/ *noun. US colloq.* M19.
[ORIGIN German, from *Katzen* (combining form of *Katze* cat) + *Jammer* distress, wailing.]
1 A hangover; a severe headache. M19.
2 *transf. & fig.* Confusion, disorder; clamour, uproar. L19.

kauch /kɑːx/ *noun. Scot.* Also **kiaugh** /kjɑːx/ & other vars. L18.
[ORIGIN Unknown.]
Trouble, worry.

kau-kau /ˈkaʊkaʊ/ *noun*. Pl. same. M20.
[ORIGIN from Melanesian pidgin, perh. ult. from Chinese.]
In New Guinea: the sweet potato.

kaumatua /kaʊˈmɑːtʊə/ *noun. NZ.* M19.
[ORIGIN Maori.]
A Maori elder.

kauri /ˈkaʊri/ *noun*. E19.
[ORIGIN Maori.]
A tall coniferous New Zealand tree, *Agathis australis*; the hard timber of this tree.
– COMB.: **kauri gum** the fossil resin of the kauri, used as a varnish.

kausia /ˈkɔːsɪə, ˈkaʊsɪə/ *noun*. M19.
[ORIGIN Greek.]
GREEK ANTIQUITIES. A low broad-brimmed felt hat worn in ancient Macedonia.

kava /ˈkɑːvə/ *noun*. L18.
[ORIGIN Tongan.]
A shrub, *Piper methysticum* (family Piperaceae), of the West Pacific islands; a narcotic fermented drink made esp. in Fiji from its macerated roots. Cf. YANGGONA.

kavadi /ˈkɑːvədi/ *noun*. M20.
[ORIGIN Tamil *kāvaṭi*.]
A decorated arch carried on the shoulders as an act of penance in Malaysian Hindu religious practice.

kavass /kəˈvɑːs, kəˈvas/ *noun*. Also (*arch.*) **c-**, **-w-**. E19.
[ORIGIN Turkish *kavas* guard from Arabic *qawwās* bowman, from *qaws* bow.]
In Turkey: orig., an armed officer, servant, or courier; now usu., a uniformed guard or messenger at an embassy, consulate, etc.

kavir /kəˈvɪə/ *noun*. Also **kev-**. L19.
[ORIGIN Persian.]
A salt desert or (occas.) saline swamp in Iran; terrain characterized by such a feature.
the Kavir the great central salt desert of Iran.

Kavirondo /kɑːvɪˈrɒndəʊ/ *noun & adjective*. L19.
[ORIGIN An area of Kenya, of unknown origin.]
▸ **A** *noun*. Pl. same, **-os**.
1 A member of any of the Nilotic and Bantu-speaking peoples inhabiting the Kavirondo area of Kenya. L19.
2 The Nilotic or Bantu language of any of these peoples. L19.
▸ **B** *attrib.* or as *adjective*. Of or pertaining to the Kavirondo, its people, or (any of) their languages. L19.
Kavirondo crane = CROWNED *crane*.

Kaw /kɔː/ *noun & adjective. US.* Pl. of noun **-s**, same. E19.
[ORIGIN from traders' N. Amer. French abbreviation of KANSA.]
= KANSA.

kawakawa /ˈkɑːwəkɑːwə/ *noun*[1]. M19.
[ORIGIN Maori.]
1 A shrub or small tree, *Macropiper excelsum*, of the pepper family, native to New Zealand and neighbouring islands. Also called ***pepper tree***. M19.
2 A variety of nephrite. *NZ.* L19.

kawakawa /kɑːvəˈkɑːvə/ *noun*[2]. L19.
[ORIGIN Hawaiian.]
The little tuna, *Euthynnus affinis*, of the Pacific Ocean.

Kawasaki /kɑːwəˈsɑːki/ *noun*. L20.
[ORIGIN Tomisaku *Kawasaki*, Japanese paediatrician, who first described the condition in 1967.]
Used *attrib.* in *Kawasaki disease*, *Kawasaki syndrome*, to designate a disease in young children, of unknown cause, which is characterized by a rash, fever, conjunctival infection, dryness and redness of the lips, and glandular swelling, and which can give rise to heart damage.

kawass *noun* var. of KAVASS.

Kawi /ˈkawi/ *noun*. E19.
[ORIGIN Sanskrit *kavi* poet.]
The classic or poetic language of Java and Bali, in which the ancient indigenous language is mixed with many words of Sanskrit origin.

kay /keɪ/ *interjection*. M20.
[ORIGIN Abbreviation.]
= OK *interjection*.

kaya /ˈkʌɪə/ *noun*. L19.
[ORIGIN Japanese.]
A Japanese coniferous tree, *Torreya nucifera*, related to the yew, with large edible seeds the oil of which is used in cooking. Also, the wood of this tree.

kayak /ˈkʌɪak/ *noun*[1]. M18.
[ORIGIN Inupiaq *qayaq*.]
▸ **A** *noun*. **1** An Eskimo canoe, made of a framework of light wood covered with sealskins, and having a small watertight opening in the top to admit a single man. M18.
2 A small covered canoe modelled on this, used for touring or sport. M20.
▸ **B** *verb intrans.* Travel by kayak, paddle a kayak. L19.
▪ **kayaker** *noun* a person who kayaks M19. **kayakist** *noun* a kayaker M20.

kayak /ˈkʌɪak/ *noun*[2]. *Canad.* Also **kiack**. M19.
[ORIGIN Perh. from (the same root as) KAYAK *noun*[1].]
= ALEWIFE 2.

Kayan /ˈkʌɪən/ *noun & adjective*. M19.
[ORIGIN Kayan.]
▸ **A** *noun*. Pl. **-s**, same.
1 A member of a people of Sarawak and Borneo. M19.
2 The Indonesian language of this people. L19.
▸ **B** *attrib.* or as *adjective*. Of or pertaining to the Kayans or their language. M19.

kayles /keɪlz/ *noun pl.* Now *dial. & hist.* Also **kyles** /kʌɪlz/. Sing. form used only in comb. ME.
[ORIGIN Middle Dutch & mod. Dutch *kegel*, †*keyl-* (in *keylbane* skittle-alley) = Old High German *kegil* (German *Kegel*) tapering stick, cone, skittle.]
A variety of ninepins or skittles; the set of wooden or bone pins used in this.

kaylied /ˈkeɪlʌɪd, ˈkeɪlɪd/ *adjective. dial. & slang.* M20.
[ORIGIN Unknown.]
Extremely drunk.

kayo /ˈkeɪəʊ/ *adjective & noun*[1]. *slang.* E20.
[ORIGIN Reversal of pronunc. of OK under the influence of KAYO *verb & noun*[2].]
▸ **A** *adjective*. = OK *adjective*. E20.
▸ **B** *noun*. Pl. **-o(e)s**. = OK *noun*. M20.

kayo /ˈkeɪəʊ/ *verb & noun*[2]. *colloq.* E20.
[ORIGIN Repr. pronunc. of KO.]
Chiefly BOXING. ▸ **A** *verb trans.* Knock out; stun or fell, esp. with a blow. E20.
▸ **B** *noun*. Pl. **-o(e)s**. A knockout; a knockout blow. M20.

Kayser–Fleischer ring /ˈkʌɪzəflʌɪʃə rɪŋ/ *noun phr.* M20.
[ORIGIN from Bernhard *Kayser* (1869–1954) & Bruno *Fleischer* (1874–1965), German ophthalmologists.]
MEDICINE. A pigmented ring around the cornea, usu. brownish, caused by copper deposition and diagnostic of Wilson's disease.

kaza /ˈkɑːzə/ *noun*. Also **c-**. L19.
[ORIGIN Turkish, from Arabic *kaza* from Arabic *qaḍā*: see CADI.]
In Turkey: formerly, a judicial district; now, an administrative district governed by a kaimakam.

kazachoc /kazəˈtʃɒk/ *noun*. Also **kozatchok**. E20.
[ORIGIN Russian, dim. of *kazak* COSSACK.]
A Slavonic, chiefly Ukrainian, dance with a fast and usu. quickening tempo, and employing the step *prisiadka*.

Kazak /kəˈzɑːk/ *adjective & noun*. E20.
[ORIGIN from *Kazakh*, a town in Azerbaijan.]
(Designating) a type of thick durable Caucasian wool rug, characterized by large geometric designs in striking colours.

Kazakh /kəˈzɑːk/ *noun & adjective*. M19.
[ORIGIN Russian, formed as COSSACK.]
▸ **A** *noun*. Pl. **-s**, **-i** /-i/.
1 A member of a Turkic people of central Asia, esp. of Kazakhstan. M19.
2 The language of this people. E20.
▸ **B** *attrib.* or as *adjective*. Of or pertaining to the Kazakhs or their language. L19.

kazi /ˈkɑːziː/ *noun*. E17.
[ORIGIN Arabic *qāḍī* CADI (repr. a pronunc.).]
A cadi in some parts of central and SE India and the Indian subcontinent.

kazillion *noun* var. of GAZILLION.

kazoo /kəˈzuː/ *noun*. Also **g-** /g-/. L19.
[ORIGIN App. imit. of the sound produced.]
A toy or (now) jazz musical instrument consisting of a tube with a membrane at each end or over a hole in the side, which produces a buzzing noise when blown into.
■ **kazooer** *noun* M20. **kazooist** *noun* L20.

KB *abbreviation*.
King's Bench.

KBE *abbreviation*.
Knight Commander (of the Order) of the British Empire.

KC *abbreviation*[1].
1 King's College.
2 King's Counsel.

kc *abbreviation*[2].
Kilocycle(s); kilocycles per second.

KCB *abbreviation*.
Knight Commander (of the Order) of the Bath.

KCIE *abbreviation*.
Knight Commander (of the Order) of the Indian Empire.

KCMG *abbreviation*.
Knight Commander (of the Order) of St Michael and St George.

kc/s *abbreviation*.
Kilocycles per second.

KCSI *abbreviation*.
Knight Commander (of the Order) of the Star of India.

KCVO *abbreviation*.
Knight Commander of the Royal Victorian Order.

KD *abbreviation*.
Knocked down.

KE *abbreviation*.
Kinetic energy.

kea /ˈkiːə/ *noun*. M19.
[ORIGIN Maori.]
A large brownish-green parrot of the Southern Alps of New Zealand, *Nestor notabilis*, which has an omnivorous diet including carrion and is known to attack sheep.

Keating's /ˈkiːtɪŋz/ *noun*. L19.
[ORIGIN from Thomas *Keating*, 19th-cent. Brit. chemist + -'s[1].]
In full ***Keating's powder***. (Proprietary name for) a type of insect powder.

Keatsian /ˈkiːtsɪən/ *adjective & noun*. M19.
[ORIGIN from *Keats* (see below) + -IAN.]
▸ **A** *adjective*. Of, pertaining to, or characteristic of the English poet John Keats (1795–1821) or his work. M19.
▸ **B** *noun*. An admirer or student of Keats or his work. L19.
■ **Keatsiˈana** *noun pl.* [-ANA] publications or other items concerning or associated with Keats E19.

kebab /kɪˈbab, kə-, -ˈbɑːb/ *noun & verb*. Also ***kabob**, (earlier, now *rare*) **cabob**, /kəˈbɒb/. L17.
[ORIGIN Arabic *kabāb* (perh. ult. from Persian), partly through Urdu, Persian, & Turkish.]
▸ **A** *noun*. **1** A dish consisting of pieces of meat, fish, or vegetables grilled or roasted on a skewer or spit. L17.
DONER KEBAB. SHISH KEBAB.
2 *PHYSICAL CHEMISTRY*. Each of the platelike crystallites in a shish kebab polymer structure. L20.
▸ **B** *verb trans. colloq.*
1 Stab or transfix with a spear or skewer. L20.
2 Subject to sharp criticism or critical analysis. L20.

kebaya /kəˈbɑːjə/ *noun*. Also (earlier) †***cabaia*** & other vars. L16.
[ORIGIN from Arabic *qabāya* repr. colloq. pronunc. of *qbā'a* fem. of *qbā'* tunic, gown, shirt: in early use through Portuguese *cabaya* or Persian, in mod. use through Malay *kebaya*.]
1 A light loose tunic of a type worn in SE Asia by women or (formerly) by men. L16.
SARONG *kebaya*.
2 A short tight-fitting long-sleeved jacket, together with a sarong the traditional dress of Malay and Indonesian women. M20.

kebbie /ˈkɛbi/ *noun*. *Scot. & N. English*. E19.
[ORIGIN Unknown.]
A staff or stick with a hooked head.

kebbuck /ˈkɛbək/ *noun*. *Scot.* LME.
[ORIGIN Perh. from Gaelic *càbag*.]
A whole cheese.

keck /kɛk/ *noun*. *obsolete* exc. *dial.* E17.
[ORIGIN from KEX, taken as a pl.]
(The dry hollow stem of) a large umbelliferous plant; = KEX.

keck /kɛk/ *verb intrans*. Now *dial.* E17.
[ORIGIN Imit.]
1 Retch; feel an inclination to vomit; (foll. by *at*) reject (food, medicine, etc.) with loathing, express strong dislike or disgust. E17.
2 Of a bird: make an abrupt call, cluck, cackle. M18.

keckle /ˈkɛk(ə)l/ *verb trans*. E17.
[ORIGIN Unknown.]
NAUTICAL. Protect (a hemp cable or hawser) with old rope in order to prevent chafing in the hawsehole.

kecks /kɛks/ *noun pl. slang & dial.* L19.
[ORIGIN Alt. of *kicks* (see KICK *noun*[1] 11a).]
Trousers, knickers, or underpants.

kecksie /ˈkɛksi/ *noun*. Chiefly *dial.* Also **-y**. L16.
[ORIGIN from *kexes* pl. of KEX, taken as = *kexies*.]
= KECK *noun*, KEX.

SHAKES. *Hen. V* Hateful docks, rough thistles, kecksies, burs.

ked /kɛd/ *noun*[1]. Also **kade** /keɪd/. L16.
[ORIGIN Unknown.]
Any of various bloodsucking hippoboscid flies parasitic on birds and mammals; *esp.* (more fully ***sheep ked***) a wingless flat-bodied fly, *Melophagus ovinus*, which infests sheep.

Ked /kɛd/ *noun*[2]. E20.
[ORIGIN Perh. alt. of *ped-* in *pedal* etc.]
(Proprietary name, in pl., for) a soft-soled canvas shoe.

keddah *noun* var. of KHEDA.

kedge /kɛdʒ/ *noun*. E18.
[ORIGIN from the verb.]
In full ***kedge anchor***. A small anchor with an iron stock for warping or hauling off after grounding.

kedge /kɛdʒ/ *verb*. L15.
[ORIGIN Perh. specialized use of CADGE *verb* 1.]
NAUTICAL. **1** *verb intrans. & trans*. Warp or tow (a ship) by hauling in a hawser attached to a small anchor dropped at some distance. L15.
2 *verb intrans*. Of a ship: move by means of kedging. M19.
■ †**kedger** *noun* = KEDGE *noun* L15–E18.

kedgeree /ˈkɛdʒəriː/ *noun*. M17.
[ORIGIN Hindi *khicṛī* from Sanskrit *khiccā* dish of boiled rice and sesame.]
1 An Indian dish of rice boiled with split pulses, onions, eggs, and seasonings. M17.
2 In European cookery, a dish made of boiled rice, eggs, fish, and seasonings. E19.
3 *transf. & fig.* A mixture, a jumble. E20.
– COMB.: **kedgeree-pot** a large earthenware container for holding water and for cooking.

kedlock /ˈkɛdlək/ *noun*. *obsolete* exc. *dial.* ME.
[ORIGIN App. repr. Old English *cedele* dog's mercury, of unknown origin.]
1 Any of several yellow-flowered cruciferous weeds, esp. charlock, *Sinapis arvensis*. ME.
2 = KEX. L17.

keech /kiːtʃ/ *noun*[1]. *obsolete* exc. *dial.* L16.
[ORIGIN Unknown.]
1 A lump of congealed fat; the fat of a slaughtered animal rolled up into a lump. L16.
2 A cake, *spec.* a large pastry made with chopped apples and raisins. L17.

keech /kiːx/ *noun*[2]. *Scot. colloq.* E19.
[ORIGIN Var. of CACK *noun*.]
Excrement.

keek /kiːk/ *verb & noun*. Now only *Scot. & N. English*. Also (earlier) †**kike**. LME.
[ORIGIN Perh. rel. to Middle Dutch *kīken*, *kieken* (Dutch *kijken*), Low German *kīken* look, peep. Cf. also PEEK *verb*[1] & *noun*[1].]
▸ **A** *verb intrans*. Peep, esp. surreptitiously as through a narrow opening, or round a corner. Formerly also, glance, gaze. LME.

A. GRAY He keeked between the stems of sorrel.. at the midden.

▸ **B** *noun*. A peep, a surreptitious glance. E17.
– COMB.: **keeking glass** a looking glass; **keek-keek** *interjection* a call used in hide-and-seek.
■ **keeker** *noun* (*a*) a person who peeps; *spec.* (*b*) an overseer or inspector in a coal pit; (*c*) in *pl.*, the eyes: E19.

keel /kiːl/ *noun*[1]. ME.
[ORIGIN Old Norse *kjǫlr* from Germanic.]
1 *NAUTICAL*. The lengthwise timber or metal structure along the base of a ship or boat, on which the framework of the whole is built up, and which in boats and small vessels forms a prominent central ridge on the undersurface which provides lateral stability. ME.
bar-keel, ***bilge keel***, ***drop-keel***, ***plate-keel***, etc. ***false keel***: see FALSE *adjective*. **on an even keel** (*a*) with the keel horizontal or level; (*b*) *fig.* balanced, stable. SLIDING ***keel***. ***vertical keel***: see VERTICAL *adjective*.
2 A ship, a vessel. *poet.* M16. ▸**b** A yacht built with a permanent keel instead of a centreboard. L19.
3 A central ridge along the back or convex surface of an animal or plant organ or structure. L16. ▸**b** *ORNITHOLOGY*. A prominent ridge along the sternum or breastbone of most birds (carinates), to which the flight muscles are attached; the carina. M18. ▸**c** *BOTANY*. The two lower petals of a papilionaceous flower, fused together round the stamens and styles to form a boat-shaped structure. L18. ▸**d** A prominent sternum in a dog. M20.
4 That part of anything which corresponds in position, form, etc., to a ship's keel; the bottom or undersurface; a keel-like lower part; *spec.* a longitudinal structure running the length of the underside of an aircraft's fuselage or a seaplane's float. E18.
5 a [Norwegian *kjøl*.] *The* spinal ridge of mountains stretching down the centre of Norway. M19. ▸**b** *ARCHITECTURE*. A ridge or edge on a rounded moulding. L19.
6 (Usu. **K-**.) *The* constellation Carina. E20.
– COMB.: **keel-bill** the smooth-billed ani, *Crotophaga ani*, of the W. Indies; **keel-block** any of the short pieces of timber etc. supporting the keel of a vessel in a shipyard or dry dock; **keel-plate** any of the plates forming the keel of a metal ship.
■ **keelage** *noun* (*rare*) a toll or due payable by a ship on entering or anchoring in a harbour LME. **keelless** /-l-l-/ *adjective* L19. **keel-like** /-l-l-/ *adjective* resembling (that of) a keel E19.

keel /kiːl/ *noun*[2]. ME.
[ORIGIN Middle Low German *kēl*, Middle Dutch *kiel* ship, boat (mod. *keel*) = Old English *ċēol*, Old Saxon, Old High German *kiol* (Dutch *kiel*, German *Kiel*), Old Norse *kjóll*, from Germanic.]
Chiefly *hist.* **1** A flat-bottomed boat, esp. of a kind used on the rivers Tyne and Wear in NE England for carrying coal and loading colliers; a lighter. ME. ▸**b** The quantity of coal carried in a keel, approx. 19.2 tonnes. M18.
2 = CHIULE. E17.
– COMB.: **keel-bully** *dial.* a member of the crew of a keel; a Tyneside lighterman; **keelman** *noun*[1] a person who works on a keel or barge.

keel /kiːl/ *noun*[3]. Chiefly *Scot.* L15.
[ORIGIN Unknown.]
A variety of red ochreous iron ore used for marking sheep, stone, timber, yarn, etc.; ruddle. Also, a mark made with this.
– COMB.: **keelman** *noun*[2] a dealer in ruddle.
■ **keely** *adjective* (*rare*) containing much keel; of the nature of keel: E18.

keel /kiːl/ *verb*[1]. *obsolete* exc. *dial.*
[ORIGIN Old English *cēlan* = Old Frisian *kēla* (Dutch *koelen*), Old High German *kuolen* (German *kühlen*), Old Norse *kœla*, from Germanic, from base of COOL *adjective*.]
1 *verb trans*. Cool (now only *lit.*, formerly also *fig.*). OE. ▸**b** *spec.* Cool (a hot or boiling liquid) by stirring, skimming, or pouring in something cold, in order to prevent it from boiling over. LME.
2 *verb intrans*. Become or grow cool (*lit.* & *fig.*). ME.

keel /kiːl/ *verb*[2] *trans*. Chiefly *Scot.* E16.
[ORIGIN from KEEL *noun*[3].]
Mark with ruddle.

keel /kiːl/ *verb*[3]. E19.
[ORIGIN from KEEL *noun*[1].]
1 *verb trans*. Turn up the keel of, capsize (a boat etc.); overturn, upset (a person, animal, or thing). Freq. foll. by *over*. E19.
2 *verb intrans*. Turn or be turned over; capsize; fall over or be felled as if by shock. Usu. foll. by *over*. M19.

L. MACNEICE The ship keeled over and sank. A. JUDD He keeled off the table on to his back.

3 *verb intrans*. Of a ship: roll on its keel. M19.

keelboat /ˈkiːlbəʊt/ *noun*. L17.
[ORIGIN from KEEL *noun*[1], *noun*[2] + BOAT *noun*.]
†**1** A small keel. L17–M18.
2 A large flatboat used on American rivers. *US*. L18.
3 A yacht built with a permanent keel instead of a centreboard. L19.
– COMB.: **keelboatman** *US* a person who works on a keelboat.

keeled /kiːld/ *adjective*. L18.
[ORIGIN from KEEL *noun*[1] + -ED[2].]
Having a keel; *spec.* (*a*) (of a boat) built with a keel; (*b*) *BIOLOGY* (of an organ or structure) having a central ridge, carinate.
keeled scraper [translating French *grattoir caréné*] *ARCHAEOLOGY* a prehistoric flint tool having a central ridge on its upper surface.

keeler /ˈkiːlə/ *noun*[1]. *rare*. ME.
[ORIGIN from KEEL *noun*[2] + -ER[1].]
A person who works on a keel or barge.

keeler /ˈkiːlə/ *noun*[2]. *obsolete* exc. *dial.* LME.
[ORIGIN from KEEL *verb*[1] + -ER[1].]
A vessel for cooling liquids; a shallow tub used for household purposes.

keelhaul /ˈkiːlhɔːl/ *verb & noun*. M17.
[ORIGIN Dutch *kielhalen*, from *kiel* (see KEEL *noun*[2]) + *halen* HALE *verb*[1].]
▸ **A** *verb trans*. Haul (a person) through the water under the keel of a ship, as a punishment (*obsolete* exc. *hist.*). Now also *fig.*, rebuke or reprimand severely. M17.
▸ **B** *noun*. An act of keelhauling. M19.

K

keelie /ˈkiːli/ *noun*. Chiefly *Scot. & N. English*. LME.
[ORIGIN Perh. formed as GILLIE *noun*^{1}. Sense 2 perh. a different word.]
1 A disreputable person living in a town or city, now esp. Glasgow. LME.
2 A sparrowhawk or kestrel. E19.
– NOTE: In isolated use before 19.

keeling /ˈkiːlɪŋ/ *noun*. L19.
[ORIGIN from KEEL *noun*^{1} + -ING^1.]
The material or make of a ship's keel.

keelivine /ˈkiːlɪvʌɪn/ *noun*. *Scot. & N. English*. Also **keely-**. M17.
[ORIGIN Unknown.]
A pencil, orig. *spec.* a blacklead pencil. Also ***keelivine pen***.

keelson /ˈkiːls(ə)n, ˈkɛl-/ *noun*. Also **kelson** /ˈkɛl-/, (orig.) †**kelswayn** & other vars. ME.
[ORIGIN Rel. to and perh. from Low German *kielswin*, from *kiel* KEEL *noun*^{1} + (prob.) *swin* SWINE, used, like *cat, dog, horse*, for a timber.]
1 NAUTICAL. A lengthwise timber or metal structure running internally along the bottom of a ship, parallel with and bolted to the keel, fastening the floor timbers or plating and the keel together. ME. ▸**b** A structure in the hull of a flying boat or the float of a seaplane, analogous to the keelson of a ship's hull. E20.
2 = KEEL *noun*^{1} 1. *rare*. M19.

keelyvine *noun* var. of KEELIVINE.

Keemun /ˈkiːmuːn/ *noun*. L19.
[ORIGIN A district in China.]
A black tea grown in Keemun, China.

keen /kiːn/ *noun*. M19.
[ORIGIN Irish CAOINE, formed as KEEN *verb*^{2}.]
An Irish funeral song accompanied by wailing in lamentation for the dead.

D. M. DAVIN I am contributing my funeral keen, my personal lament.

keen /kiːn/ *adjective & adverb*.
[ORIGIN Old English *cēne* = Middle Low German *kône* (Dutch *koen*), Old High German *kuoni* (German *kühn*) bold, brave, Old Norse *kœnn* skilful, expert, from Germanic.]
▸ **A** *adjective*. †**1** Wise, learned, clever. Cf. sense 7b below. OE–LME.
†**2 a** Brave, valiant, daring. OE–E17. ▸**b** Mighty, powerful, strong. *poet. & rhet.* OE–E16. ▸**c** (Esp. of a wild animal) fierce, savage; harsh, cruel. OE–E17. ▸**d** Proud, insolent; heinous. ME–L16.
3 Of a blade etc.: having a very sharp edge or point; able to cut or pierce with ease. Of an edge or point: extremely sharp. ME. ▸**b** Of a price: competitive. M20.

M. SHADBOLT When the axe was . . keen, he began to chop wood. M. CONEY It was a good knife with a keen blade.

4 a Of cold (or formerly, heat): piercing, intense. Of wind, air, etc.: very sharp, biting. ME. ▸**b** Of sound: piercing, shrill. Of light: vivid, clear. Of scent: strong. ME. ▸**c** Of something touched: causing pain, smarting, stinging. Of a taste: acrid, pungent. Now *rare*. LME. ▸**d** Excellent. *colloq.* (orig. *US*). E20.

a O. MANNING Up above . . into the bare rock fields where the cold was keen. *Lancaster Guardian* Early frosts . . assist the colouring of the leaves—a keen frost will hasten their fall. **b** A. SILLITOE He liked soap that was keen to the smell.

5 a Of a circumstance, a thought, an emotion, etc.: causing acute pain or deep distress. ME. ▸**b** Of language: severe, incisive, cutting. ME.

a T. GRAY Keen Remorse with blood defil'd. DICKENS Mr. Tremlow . . had betrayed the keenest mental terrors. **b** GIBBON They pointed their keenest satire against a despicable race.

6 Of a person: eager, interested, impassioned, fervent. Of desire, emotion, etc.: intense. Also foll. by *about, for, to do*. Freq. in ***keen on*** (colloq.), very interested in; much attracted by, in love with. ME.

R. DAHL The farmers didn't stop for lunch; they were too keen to finish the job. F. HOWERD I wasn't too keen on the way he said 'perhaps'. B. PYM She was a bit keen on me at one time. D. PRATER His wife was . . a keen cyclist. M. DRABBLE They were young and keen and full of ideas.

7 a Of the eyes or eyesight: sharp, penetrating. Of the ears or hearing, or the nose or smell, etc.: acute, highly sensitive. Also, of a person or animal: sharp *of* sight, smell, hearing, etc. ME. ▸**b** Of a person: intellectually acute. Of the mind or a mental process: endowed or conducted with great acumen. ME. ▸**c** Of the face or appearance: suggestive of perceptiveness or acumen. L18.

a J. MARQUAND My observation had never been so keen. R. CROMPTON William's keen eye had been searching out each detail. I. ASIMOV If our noses were a little keener . . we could probably tell which world we were on with one sniff. **b** LD MACAULAY Nature had given him a keen understanding.

– PHRASES: (*as*) ***keen as mustard***: see MUSTARD *noun* 1. ***keen on***: see sense 6 above.
▸ †**B** *adverb*. Keenly. LME–M17.
■ **keenly** *adverb* OE. **keenness** /-n-n-/ *noun* LME.

keen /kiːn/ *verb*^{1} *trans. rare*. L16.
[ORIGIN from KEEN *adjective & adverb*.]
Make keen; sharpen.

R. DAHL Keens the dog up before a race. G. SEYMOUR The very solitude of the wood . . keened and sharpened his senses.

keen /kiːn/ *verb*^{2}. M19.
[ORIGIN from Irish *caoinim* I wail.]
1 *verb intrans.* Utter or sing a keen; wail or lament bitterly for a dead person. M19.

F. FORSYTH The body of Johnny was taken by his own people who keened over him. A. ALVAREZ It was his turn to keen and cry.

2 *verb trans.* Lament (a death, a loss, etc.) by keening. M19.
3 *verb trans.* Utter (a cry etc.) in a shrill wailing tone. L19.

keener /ˈkiːnə/ *noun*^{1}. E19.
[ORIGIN from KEEN *verb*^{2} + -ER^1.]
A person who keens; *spec.* a professional mourner at Irish wakes and funerals.

keener /ˈkiːnə/ *noun*^{2}. *N. Amer.* M19.
[ORIGIN from KEEN *adjective* + -ER^1.]
A shrewd person; a person who drives a hard bargain. Also, an eager person.

Keene's cement /kiːnz sɪˈmɛnt/ *noun phr.* M19.
[ORIGIN Richard Wynn *Keene*, who patented the plaster in 1838.]
A kind of plaster of Paris containing alum or another salt, which sets to a very hard white finish.

keep /kiːp/ *noun*. ME.
[ORIGIN from the verb.]
†**1** Care, heed, notice. Chiefly in ***take keep***, (foll. by *of, to do*, or *obj. clause*). ME–L19.

A. BARCLAY What God hath done for you ye take no keepe.

2 Care in tending, watching, or preserving; charge. Orig. in †***take keep***. *arch.* ME.

KEATS If from shepherd's keep a lamb strayed far.

3 An article which serves for containing or retaining something; *esp.* (**a**) (now *dial.*) a clasp or similar fastening; (**b**) *rare* a reservoir for fish; a weir or dam for retaining water. LME. ▸**b** MINING. Each of a set of movable iron supports on which the cage rests when at the top of the shaft of a coalmine. M19.
4 *hist.* The innermost and strongest structure or central tower of a medieval castle, serving as a last defence; a stronghold, a donjon. M16.
5 The action of keeping or maintaining a person or thing; the fact of being kept. M18. ▸**b** The food required to keep a person or animal; provender, pasture; maintenance, support. Now chiefly in ***earn one's keep***. E19.

M. R. MITFORD Our old spaniel . . and the blue grey-hound . . were sent out to keep for the summer. **b** J. R. LOWELL You're so darned lazy, I don't think you're hardly worth your keep.

– PHRASES: **earn one's keep** *fig.* do enough to justify what one receives; provide a sufficient return. **for keeps** *colloq.* (orig. *US*) (*a*) to keep for good; completely, altogether; in deadly earnest; (*b*) CRICKET defensively, in order to remain at the wicket. **in good keep** well kept, in good condition. **in low keep** in poor condition.

keep /kiːp/ *verb*. Pa. t. & pple **kept** /kɛpt/. LOE.
[ORIGIN Unknown.]
▸ †**I** *verb trans.* (with *genit.* in Old English, afterwards with *direct obj.*). Early senses: see also KEP.
1 Seize, lay hold of; snatch, take. LOE–L15.
2 Try to catch or get. LOE–ME.
3 Take in, receive, contain, hold. LOE–ME.
4 Take in with the eyes, ears, or mind; take note of, see, observe; watch. LOE–L17.
5 Watch for, await; lie in wait for; intercept. LOE–L15.
6 Meet; encounter; greet, welcome. Only in ME.
▸ **II** *verb trans.* (in early use also *verb intrans.*).
†**7** *verb intrans. & trans.* Have regard (for), care (for), (foll. by *of* (orig. *genit.*), *to do*, simple *obj.*); take care, attend *to*. LOE–L16.
8 *verb trans.* Pay due regard to; observe, abide by, (a law, custom, promise, agreement, set time, etc.). LOE.

G. ORWELL If you kept small rules, you could break the big ones. E. O'BRIEN He kept the dinner appointment.

9 *verb trans.* Observe with due formality and in the prescribed manner (a religious rite, ceremony, etc.); celebrate, solemnize. ME. ▸**b** Observe by attendance, residence, performance of duty, or in some prescribed or regular way. In later use chiefly in ***keep chapels***, ***keep halls*** (at college or school), ***keep terms***, ***keep residence***, etc., and in ***keep early hours***, ***keep late hours***, ***keep regular hours***, etc. LME.

V. WOOLF He seldom spoke of the dead, but kept anniversaries with singular pomp. C. V. WEDGWOOD Being Sunday the Commissioners kept it as a fast. **b** THACKERAY He kept his chapels, and did the college exercises. J. I. M. STEWART They kept long hours in the Bodleian Library.

10 *verb trans.* Guard, defend, protect, (*from*). *arch.* exc. in ***keep goal***, ***keep wicket*** below. ME.

G. M. BROWN They've left a boy To keep the door of the fold, I hope.

†**11** *verb refl. & intrans.* Take care, beware, *that*. ME–E16.
12 *verb trans.* **a** Take care of, look after, tend, have charge of (a thing, *arch. & dial.* a person or animal). ME. ▸**b** Maintain or preserve (a place etc.) in proper order. LME.

a JOSEPH STRUTT David, who kept his father's sheep.

13 *verb trans.* Provide with food, clothing, and other requisites of life; maintain, support. Also foll. by *in* a thing regularly provided. ME. ▸**b** Maintain in return for sexual favours. Earlier as KEEPING *noun* 4b. M16.

R. DAVIES My father had died, and the shop could keep her. K. GRENVILLE With a trade behind him, he could marry Sal and keep her.

14 *verb trans.* Preserve in being or operation; continue to have, practise, etc. ME. ▸**b** Carry on, continue to cause, (a disturbance, etc.). Now usu. ***keep up***. LME.

SHAKES. *1 Hen. IV* Two stars keep not their motion in one sphere. P. LARKIN All afternoon . . For miles inland, A slow and stopping curve southwards we kept.

keep company, ***keep guard***, ***keep a lookout***, ***keep order***, ***keep pace***, ***keep silence***, ***keep the peace***, ***keep time***, ***keep tune***, etc.

15 *verb trans.* With compl.: maintain, or cause to continue in a specified condition, state, place, position, action, or course. ME.

J. RHYS A little muff to keep your hands warm. E. O'BRIEN Think of anything, so long as the mind keeps itself occupied. *Femina* Be alert. Keep your eyes and ears open. A. BROOKNER People upon whom Blanche could rely to keep the party going.

16 *verb trans.* Cause or induce to remain in a place; detain; *spec.* (now usu. more fully ***keep in jail***, ***keep prisoner***, etc.) hold in custody, prevent from escaping. ME.

V. WOOLF I'm sorry I'm late . . I got kept.

17 *verb trans.* Hold back, restrain, (*from*). ME.

Black & White I shall not be able to keep myself from strangling her. ROBERT ANDERSON There's something between fathers and sons that keeps them from being friends.

18 *verb trans.* Put aside for future use; reserve, store. ME.

R. H. MOTTRAM Two Canadian majors . . came to claim the table . . and found it kept for them. E. WAUGH If you don't mind . . we will keep our business until after luncheon.

19 *verb trans.* Retain in one's possession or control; continue to have, hold, or possess. ME. ▸**b** *verb trans.* Have habitually in stock or on sale. L16.

E. M. FORSTER England will never keep her trade overseas unless she is prepared to make sacrifices. D. BARNES He . . laid a paper-cutter between the pages to keep his place. B. BETTELHEIM A parent . . should keep his cool in times of trouble.

20 *verb trans.* Stay in, refrain from leaving, (a place); *esp.* be confined to (one's bed, room) by sickness. ME. ▸**b** Stay in one's position in or on, against opposition or in spite of circumstances or conditions. LME.

M. KEANE Jane still kept her bed but grew a little stronger every day. W. GOLDING The parson keeps his cabin. We shall see little of him. **b** W. FAULKNER The streets where no horse could have kept its feet.

21 *verb trans.* Withhold possession or use of (a thing) or the knowledge of (a fact) *from* a person. LME.

T. WASHINGTON Where they would not receive his salvation, the same for ever shalbe kept from them. DAY LEWIS If my father . . had worries, they were kept from me.

22 *verb trans.* Continue to follow (a way, path, course, etc.), so as not to lose it or get out of it. LME.

Field How the driver kept the track is a marvel.

23 *verb trans.* Carry on, conduct, as presiding officer or a chief actor (an assembly, court, fair, market, etc.). LME.

HENRY FIELDING His wife . . began to keep an assembly, or . . to be 'at home' once a week.

24 *verb trans.* Carry on and manage, conduct as one's own, (a business, shop, etc.). E16.

G. GREENE Mr. Verloc . . keeps a tiny independent cinema in the East End.

25 *verb trans.* Maintain continuously (a record, diary, accounts, etc.) by making the requisite entries. M16.

J. CONRAD In those books he intended to keep . . a record of his rising fortunes.

26 *verb trans.* Maintain in one's service, or for one's use or enjoyment; own and manage (animals). M16.

G. GREENE The doctor kept his own cows. O. MANNING Your father kept a good cellar. R. DAVIES At the top of the class structure were . . families who kept 'maids'.

▸ **III** *verb intrans.* (Chiefly with ellipsis of refl. pronoun.)
27 Reside, dwell, live, lodge. Now *colloq.* (esp. CAMBRIDGE UNIV. & *US*). LME.

E. M. W. TILLYARD He kept in the historic set of rooms . . once occupied by the poet Gray.

28 Remain for a time in a particular place or spot. LME. ▸**b** Of a school: be in session. *US*. M19.

GEO. ELIOT He suggested that she should keep in her own room.

29 Remain in good condition, last without spoiling; *fig.* admit of being reserved for another occasion. LME.

F. MARRYAT He brought home more venison than would keep in the hot weather. CONAN DOYLE Your story, however, can keep.

30 Continue, go on, in a specified course or action. **M16.** ▸**b** Go on *doing*. **L18.**

W. FAULKNER Just keep right on up the road past the schoolhouse. **b** B. ENGLAND They were both tired . . but they kept going. *Sunday (Kolkata)* The bills . . keep piling up.

31 With compl.: remain or continue in a specified condition, state, place, position, action, or course. **M16.**

E. BOWEN I kept out of debt for more than a year. I. MURDOCH I usually keep clear of Soho. A. BULLOCK Bevin kept in constant and close touch with Arthur Deakin.

32 *CRICKET.* = ***keep wicket*** below. **M19.**

– PHRASES: (A selection of cross-refs. only is included: see esp. other nouns.) **how are you keeping?** *colloq.* in what state is your health? ***keep an eye on***: see EYE *noun*. ***keep a secret***: see SECRET *noun*. **keep goal** act as goalkeeper in football etc. ***keep house***: see HOUSE *noun*[1]. ***keep in touch***: see TOUCH *noun*. ***keep one's balance***: see BALANCE *noun*. ***keep one's distance***: see DISTANCE *noun*. ***keep the wolf from the door***: see WOLF *noun*. ***keep time***: see TIME *noun*. ***keep track of***: see TRACK *noun*. **keep wicket** act as wicketkeeper in cricket.

– WITH ADVERBS IN SPECIALIZED SENSES: **keep abreast** (cause to) proceed at an equal pace (*lit. & fig.*) (foll. by *with*, *of*). **keep away** (***a***) (cause to) remain absent or at a distance; (***b***) *NAUTICAL* (cause to) sail off the wind or to leeward. **keep back** (***a***) restrain, detain; hold back forcibly; (***b***) withhold; retain or reserve designedly; conceal; (***c***) hold oneself or remain at the back. **keep down** (***a***) cause to remain at a low level (***keep one's head down***: see HEAD *noun*); *fig.* hold in subjection; (***b***) retain (food etc.) in one's stomach without vomiting; (***c***) (cause to) remain low in amount, number, or degree; (***d***) lie low, stay hidden. **keep in** (***a***) confine in a place, esp. in school after hours; not utter or give vent to; *fig.* refrain from giving voice to; (***b***) keep (a fire) burning; (***c***) (now *colloq.*) remain on good terms *with*; (***d***) ***keep one's hand in***: see HAND *noun*. **keep off** (***a***) hinder from coming near, ward off; avert; (***b***) stay at a distance; **keep on** (***a***) continue to hold, wear, occupy, employ, etc.; (***b***) continue or persist in a course of action; *esp.* go on *doing*; (***c***) ***keep on at***, nag or pester (a person) continually (*to do*). **keep out** cause to remain outside; prevent from getting in. **keep over** reserve, hold over. **keep together** (cause to) remain associated or united (***keep body and soul together***: see BODY *noun*). **keep under** hold in subjection or under control. **keep up** (***a***) keep shut up or confined; (***b***) support, prevent from sinking or falling; (***c***) maintain in a worthy or effective condition; support; keep in repair; keep burning; (***d***) maintain, retain, preserve (a quality, state of things, accomplishment, etc.); keep from deteriorating or disappearing; (***keep up appearances***: see APPEARANCE); (***e***) continue, go on with (an action, a course of action); ***keep it up***, prolong a party; (***f***) prevent from going to bed; (***g***) ***keep up to***, prevent from or insist on not falling below (a level, standard, principle, etc.); keep informed of; (***h***) continue alongside, keep abreast; proceed at an equal pace *with* (*lit. & fig.*); ***keep up with the Joneses***, strive not to be outdone by one's neighbours; (***i***) continue to maintain a friendship or acquaintance; keep in touch (*with*).

– WITH PREPOSITIONS IN SPECIALIZED SENSES: **keep at** work persistently at; continue to occupy oneself with; also ***keep at it***. **keep from** (***a***) remain absent or away from; (***b***) restrain oneself from. **keep off** avoid, stay away from; ***keep off the grass***: see GRASS *noun*. **keep to** (***a***) adhere to, abide by (a promise, agreement, etc.); (***b***) confine or restrict oneself to; ***keep to oneself***, (*colloq.*) ***keep oneself to oneself***, avoid the society of others. **keep with** remain with, associate with; keep up with.

– COMB.: **keep-fit** *adjective & noun* (***a***) *adjective* designating or pertaining to exercises etc. designed to keep people fit and healthy; (***b***) *noun* keep-fit exercises; keep-fit class; **keep-left** *adjective* designating a sign etc. directing traffic to the left of the road; **keepnet** *ANGLING* a net for keeping fish alive until they are returned to the water; **keep-out** *adjective* designating a sign prohibiting entry.

keepable /ˈkiːpəb(ə)l/ *adjective*. **LME.**
[ORIGIN from KEEP *verb* + -ABLE.]
†**1** Of a law: able to be observed. Only in **LME.**
2 Durable, long-lasting. Now only, (of a foodstuff etc.) able to last without deterioration. **L16.**
■ **keepaˈbility** *noun* **L19.**

keeper /ˈkiːpə/ *noun*. **ME.**
[ORIGIN from KEEP *verb* + -ER[1].]
▸ **I** from KEEP *verb* I, II.
1 A person who has charge or oversight of a person or thing; *esp.* (***a***) an attendant in a prison, *arch.* lunatic asylum, etc.; (***b***) the custodian of a museum, art gallery, etc. **ME.** ▸†**b** A nurse; a person who has charge of the sick. **LME–M17.** ▸**c** An officer who has the charge of a forest, woods, or grounds; now *esp.* = ***gamekeeper*** s.v. GAME *noun*. **LME.** ▸**d** *SPORT.* A wicketkeeper; a goalkeeper. **M18.**

SIR W. SCOTT The herds without a keeper strayed. U. SINCLAIR A keeper came to him with the word that his time was up. R. V. JONES One of the keepers in the botany department of the Natural History Museum.

bookkeeper, ***door-keeper***, ***gamekeeper***, ***goalkeeper***, ***housekeeper***, ***time-keeper***, ***wicketkeeper***, etc.

2 A person or thing which keeps or retains something. **ME.**

SHAKES. *Rich. II* He is a flatterer, A parasite, a keeper-back of death.

3 A person who observes or keeps a command, law, promise, etc. **LME.**
4 A person who owns or carries on some establishment or business. **LME.**
hotel-keeper, ***shopkeeper***, etc.

5 A mechanical device for keeping something in place; a clasp, catch, etc. Freq., a loop securing the end of a buckled strap. **M16.** ▸**b** A bar of soft iron placed across the poles of a horseshoe magnet to prevent loss of power. **M19.** ▸**c** A ring that keeps another (esp. a wedding ring) on the finger; a guard ring. **M19.** ▸**d** A simple ring worn in the ears to keep a pierced hole open. **M20.**
†**6** A man who keeps a mistress. **L17–M19.**
▸ **II** from KEEP *verb* III.
7 A person who continues or remains *at* a place. *rare*. **E17.**
8 A fruit, or other product, that keeps (well or badly). **M19.**

– PHRASES: ***finders keepers***: see FINDER *noun*. **Keeper of the Great Seal** an officer in England and Scotland (in England now the Lord Chancellor) who has the custody of the Great Seal. **Keeper of the Privy Seal** (***a***) *hist.* in England, the Lord Privy Seal; (***b***) a similar officer in Scotland and the Duchy of Cornwall. **Lord Keeper (of the Great Seal)** = ***Keeper of the Great Seal*** above.
■ **keepering** *noun* the work of a gamekeeper **M19.** **keepership** *noun* the office or position of a keeper **M16.**

keeper /ˈkiːpə/ *verb trans.* **E20.**
[ORIGIN from the noun or back-form. from KEEPERING *noun*.]
Look after as a gamekeeper.

keeping /ˈkiːpɪŋ/ *noun*. **ME.**
[ORIGIN from KEEP *verb* + -ING[1].]
▸ **I** The action of KEEP *verb* I, II.
1 Observance of a rule, command, ordinance, institution, practice, promise, etc. **ME.**
2 The action of looking after, guarding, or defending someone or something; custody, charge, guardianship. **ME.** ▸**b** Guard, defence. Esp. in ***at one's keeping***, ***on one's keeping***, ***upon one's keeping***, on one's guard. *obsolete* exc. *dial.* **ME.** ▸**c** Wicketkeeping; goalkeeping. **M19.**

HOBBES The Book of the Law was in their keeping.

goalkeeping, ***time-keeping***, ***wicketkeeping***, etc. ***safe keeping***: see SAFE *adjective*.

3 Maintenance of a thing or person in good condition; the condition in which a thing is kept. **ME.**
4 a Maintenance, sustenance with food; food, fodder. **ME.** ▸**b** The maintaining of a mistress or lover; the fact or condition of being so maintained. **LME.**
5 The maintaining of a state or condition. **ME.**
peacekeeping etc.
†**6** Confinement, imprisonment; prison. **ME–E16.**
7 The action of retaining as one's own; the owning and managing of animals, a business, etc.; in *pl.*, things kept or retained. **ME.**
bee-keeping etc.
8 Reservation for future use; preservation. **LME.**
9 *PAINTING.* The maintenance of proper perspective in a picture; the maintenance of harmony of composition. **E18.** ▸**b** *gen.* Agreement, harmony. Esp. in ***in keeping (with)***, ***out of keeping (with)***. **L18.**

b A. BRIGGS His methods were in keeping with the reformation of manners.

▸ **II** The action of KEEP *verb* III.
10 Staying or remaining in a place or in a certain condition; *spec.* remaining sound. Formerly also, persistence in an activity. **LME.**

– COMB.: **keeping room** (esp. *CAMBRIDGE UNIV.* & *US*) a living room, a parlour.

keeping /ˈkiːpɪŋ/ *ppl adjective*. **LME.**
[ORIGIN from KEEP *verb* + -ING[2].]
That keeps; *esp.* (of a fruit) that keeps well.

keepsake /ˈkiːpseɪk/ *noun & adjective*. **L18.**
[ORIGIN from KEEP *verb* + SAKE *noun*[1]: cf. *namesake*.]
▸ **A** *noun*. A thing kept or given to be kept for the sake of, or in remembrance of, the giver; *spec.* (*hist.*) a literary annual consisting of collections of verse, prose, and illustrations, of a type common in the early part of the 19th cent. **L18.**
▸ **B** *adjective*. Constituting or resembling a keepsake; *spec.* (*arch.*) having the inane prettiness of faces in keepsakes or the affected literary style of such books. **M19.**

keertan *noun* var. of KIRTAN.

keeshond /ˈkeɪshɒnd/ *noun*. Pl. **-honden** /-hɒnd(ə)n/, **-honds**. **E20.**
[ORIGIN Dutch, from *Kees* pet form of male forename Cornelius + *hond* dog.]
A breed of dog of Dutch origin, which is a variety of the spitz, with long thick grey hair; a dog of this breed.

keester *noun* var. of KEISTER.

keeve /kiːv/ *noun*. Also **kive** /kʌɪv/.
[ORIGIN Old English *cȳf*, perh. from Germanic but no corresp. forms in the cognate langs.]
A tub, a vat; *spec.* a vat for holding liquid in brewing and bleaching; *MINING* a vessel in which tin or copper ore is washed.

kef *noun* see KIEF.

keffiyeh /kəˈfiː(j)ə/ *noun*. Also **kaff-**, **kuf-** & other vars. **E19.**
[ORIGIN Arabic *kūfiyya* (colloq.) *keffiyya*.]
A kerchief worn as a headdress by Bedouin Arabs.

kefir /kəˈfɪə, ˈkɛfə/ *noun*. Also **kephir**. **L19.**
[ORIGIN Caucasian name.]
An effervescent liquor resembling kumis, prepared from fermented milk and employed as a medicine or food for invalids.
– COMB.: **kefir grains** a composite substance used in the Caucasus to ferment milk.

keftedes /kɛfˈtɛðiːz/ *noun pl.* Also **-dhes**. **E20.**
[ORIGIN Greek *kephtes*, pl. *kephtedes* from Turkish *köfte* from Persian KOFTA.]
In Greek cookery: small meatballs made with herbs and onions.

Keftian /ˈkɛftɪən/ *noun & adjective*. **E20.**
[ORIGIN formed as KEFTIU + -AN.]
ANCIENT HISTORY. ▸ **A** *noun*. = KEFTIU. **E20.**
▸ **B** *adjective*. Of or pertaining to the Keftiu. **E20.**

Keftiu /ˈkɛftjuː/ *noun*. Pl. same. **E20.**
[ORIGIN Place name in Egyptian records, perh. identical with Caphtor: see CAPHTOR.]
ANCIENT HISTORY. A member of an E. Mediterranean people named in Egyptian records, sometimes identified as the Cretans. Usu. in *pl.*

keg /kɛg/ *noun*. **E17.**
[ORIGIN Later form of CAG *noun*.]
1 A small barrel or cask, usu. of less than 10 gallons (approx. 45.5 litres) or (*US*) 30 gallons. **E17.**
2 *spec.* A barrel of beer; beer. *Austral. & NZ slang*. **L19.**
3 In full ***keg beer***, ***keg bitter***, etc. Beer etc. to which carbon dioxide has been added, served from a sealed metal container. **M20.**

Kegel /ˈkeɪg(ə)l/ *noun*. **L20.**
[ORIGIN Dr Arnold *Kegel* (1894–1976), US physician.]
Used ***attrib.*** to designate an exercise performed to strengthen a woman's pelvic floor muscles.

kegger /ˈkɛgə/ *noun*. *US slang*. **M20.**
[ORIGIN from KEG *noun* + -ER[1].]
1 A party at which beer is served, esp. from the keg. **M20.**
2 A keg of beer. **L20.**

kegler /ˈkɛglə, ˈkeɪglə/ *noun*. *N. Amer.* **M20.**
[ORIGIN German, from *Kegel* skittle.]
A person who plays tenpin bowling, skittles, ninepins, etc.

kehaya /kɛhəˈjɑː/ *noun*. *obsolete* exc. *hist.* **L16.**
[ORIGIN Ottoman Turkish *kehya*, *kyāhya* corrupt forms of Persian *kadḵhudā*: see KADKHODA.]
A Turkish steward, viceroy, deputy, agent, etc.; a local governor; a village chief.

kehilla /kəˈhɪlə, kɛhiˈlɑː/ *noun*. Pl. ***-llot(h)*** /-ˈlaʊt/. **L19.**
[ORIGIN (Yiddish *kĕhilĕ* from) Hebrew *qĕhillāh* community.]
The Jewish community in a town or village.

kehua /ˈkɛːhʊɑː/ *noun*. *NZ*. **M19.**
[ORIGIN Maori.]
A ghost, a spirit.

keif *noun* see KIEF.

keiretsu /keɪˈrɛtsuː/ *noun*. **M20.**
[ORIGIN Japanese, lit. 'system, order of descent'.]
In Japan: a linked conglomeration of businesses; a hierarchy of suppliers, subcontractors, etc. owned or part-owned by a parent company which they serve.

keister /ˈkiːstə, ˈkʌɪstə/ *noun*. *N. Amer. slang*. Also **kee-**, **key-** /ˈkiː-/. **L19.**
[ORIGIN Unknown.]
1 a A suitcase, a satchel; a handbag; a tool case; a sample case. **L19.** ▸**b** A strongbox in a safe; a safe. **E20.**
2 The buttocks. **M20.**

R. PERLE I've had it up to my keister with all these leaks.

keitloa /ˈkeɪtləʊə/ *noun*. *rare*. **M19.**
[ORIGIN Setswana *kgetlwa*, *kh-*.]
The black rhinoceros, *Diceros bicornis*.

Kekchi /ˈkɛktʃi/ *noun & adjective*. **E19.**
[ORIGIN Maya.]
▸ **A** *noun*. Pl. same, **-s**. A member of an ancient people of the Mayan empire or their modern descendants who now live in Guatemala; the language of these people. **E19.**
▸ **B** *attrib.* or as *adjective*. Of or pertaining to the Kekchi or their language. **M20.**

Kekulé /ˈkɛkʊleɪ/ *noun*. **E20.**
[ORIGIN Friedrich August *Kekulé* (1829–96), German chemist.]
CHEMISTRY. Used ***attrib.*** to designate formulae or structures which represent benzene and related molecules as having a closed ring of six carbon atoms linked by alternate double and single bonds.

kel /kɛl/ *noun*. *slang*. **E20.**
[ORIGIN Abbreviation.]
= KELLY 2. Earlier as ***Darby kel*** s.v. DARBY 4.

kelch /kɛltʃ/ *noun*. *slang*. *derog.* Also **kelt** /kɛlt/, **keltz** /kɛlts/. **E20.**
[ORIGIN Unknown.]
A white person.

K

keld /kɛld/ *noun. N. English.* ME.
[ORIGIN Old Norse *kelda*.]
A well, a spring; a deep, still, smooth part of a river.
– NOTE: Frequent in place names in Cumbria and Yorkshire in N. England.

kelebe /ˈkɛləbi/ *noun.* M19.
[ORIGIN Greek *kelebē*.]
GREEK ANTIQUITIES. A wide-mouthed vessel with a broad flat rim and two handles connecting this to the body but not extending above the rim.

kelek /ˈkɛlɪk/ *noun.* L17.
[ORIGIN Turkish.]
A raft or float used on rivers in Turkey, Kurdistan, etc., formed of inflated sheepskins, bundles of reeds, etc.

kelewang *noun* var. of KLEYWANG.

kelim *noun* var. of KILIM.

kell /kɛl/ *noun. obsolete* exc. *dial.* ME.
[ORIGIN Var. of CAUL *noun*[1].]
1 A woman's hairnet, cap, or headdress. ME.
2 A long cloak or garment; a shroud. LME.
3 Gossamer threads forming a kind of film on grass. E16.
4 An enveloping membrane; a caul. M16.

Keller /ˈkɛlə(r)/ *noun.* E20.
[ORIGIN German = cellar.]
A beer cellar in Austria or Germany.

Kelly /ˈkɛli/ *noun.* Also **k-**. L19.
[ORIGIN Prob. from the common Irish surname (from Irish *Ó Ceallaigh*). See also KEL.]
1 In full ***Kelly pool***. A type of pool using fifteen balls. *N. Amer.* L19.
2 = BELLY *noun* 2, 4. Earliest as ***Darby Kelly*** s.v. DARBY 4. *rhyming slang.* E20.
3 A man's hat; *spec.* a derby hat. *slang* (chiefly *US*). E20.
4 OIL INDUSTRY (**k-**). The joint of a drill string which passes through a hole in the rotary table and has a square cross-section so that it is turned by the table. E20.
5 ***Kelly's eye***, number one in the game of bingo. *colloq.* E20.
6 In full ***Kelly green***. A light green colour. Orig. *US.* M20.
– PHRASES: ***swing Kelly***: see SWING *verb*.

K

keloid /ˈkiːlɔɪd/ *noun & adjective.* Also **ch-**. M19.
[ORIGIN French *chéloïde*, *kél-*, from Greek *khēlē* claw of a crab: see -OID.]
MEDICINE. ▸**A** *noun.* (An area of) thickened raised scar tissue that tends to increase in extent. Formerly also, the condition of having this. M19.
▸**B** *adjective.* Designating or consisting of such a scar or tissue. L19.

kelong /ˈkeɪlɒŋ/ *noun.* L19.
[ORIGIN Malay.]
A large fish trap built with stakes, common along the coasts of the Malay peninsula and in other parts of Malaysia and Indonesia. Also, a building erected over such a trap.

kelp /kɛlp/ *noun.* LME.
[ORIGIN Unknown.]
1 Any of various large brown seaweeds, chiefly members of the orders Fucales and Laminariales, which are burnt for the substances found in the ashes; such seaweed collectively; spec. *Macrocystis pyrifera* of the Pacific coast of America, the largest of the seaweeds. LME.
2 The calcined ashes of seaweed used for the salts of sodium, potassium, and iodine which they contain, esp. (formerly) in the manufacture of soap and glass. M17.
– COMB.: **kelp crab** a spider crab, *Pugettia producta*, found on the Pacific coast of N. America; **kelpfish** (*a*) a scaled blenny, *Gibbousia montereyensis*, of tidal pools and kelp beds on the Pacific coast of the US; (*b*) any of several coastal fishes of Australia and New Zealand, esp. of the percoid family Chironemidae.
■ **kelping** *noun* the collection or manufacture of kelp E19.

kelper /ˈkɛlpə/ *noun & adjective.* In senses A.2, B. also **K-**. E19.
[ORIGIN from KELP + -ER[1].]
▸**A** *noun.* **1** A manufacturer of kelp. E19.
2 A native or inhabitant of the Falkland Islands in the S. Atlantic, the shores of which abound in kelp. M20.
▸**B** *adjective.* Of or pertaining to the Falkland Islands or their inhabitants. M20.

kelpie /ˈkɛlpi/ *noun*[1]. *Scot.* Also **kelpy**. L17.
[ORIGIN Perh. from Gaelic *cailpeach*, *colpach* bullock, colt.]
A water spirit or demon assuming various shapes, usu. that of a horse, reputed to haunt lakes and rivers and to take delight in the drowning of travellers etc. Also ***water-kelpie***.

kelpie /ˈkɛlpi/ *noun*[2]. *Austral. & NZ.* L19.
[ORIGIN App. from the name of a particular bitch, *King's Kelpie* (*c* 1870).]
A smooth-coated, prick-eared, Australian breed of sheep-dog derived from imported Scottish collies; a dog of this breed.

kelpy *noun* var. of KELPIE *noun*[1].

kelson, †**kelswayn** *nouns* see KEELSON.

kelt /kɛlt/ *noun*[1]. ME.
[ORIGIN Unknown.]
A salmon, sea trout, or other fish (in bad condition) after spawning, before returning to the sea.

kelt /kɛlt/ *noun*[2] *& adjective. Scot. & N. English. obsolete* exc. *hist.* E16.
[ORIGIN Gaelic, Irish *cealt* clothes: cf. KELTER *noun*[1].]
(Made of) a kind of heavy woollen cloth formerly used for outer garments by country people in Scotland and N. England.

Kelt *noun*[3] var. of CELT *noun*[1].

kelt *noun*[4] var. of KELCH.

kelter /ˈkɛltə/ *noun*[1] *& adjective. Scot. & N. English.* Now *rare.* E16.
[ORIGIN Irish *celtair* (mod. *cealtair*) cloak: cf. KELT *noun*[2].]
(Made of) coarse cloth used for outer garments.

kelter /ˈkɛltə/ *noun*[2]. *dial.* M19.
[ORIGIN Unknown.]
Rubbish; nonsense.

kelter *noun*[3] var. of KILTER *noun*[1].

Keltic *adjective* var. of CELTIC.

keltz *noun* var. of KELCH.

Kelvin /ˈkɛlvɪn/ *noun.* Also **k-**. L19.
[ORIGIN Sir William Thomson, Ld *Kelvin* (1824–1907), Brit. physicist and inventor.]
1 (**K-**.) Used *attrib.* and in *possess.* to designate instruments and concepts devised by Kelvin. L19.
degree Kelvin = sense 1 above. **Kelvin balance** an instrument for measuring the current passing through a set of horizontal coils by balancing the electromagnetic force produced by the current with a sliding weight. **Kelvin bridge**, **Kelvin double bridge** a modification of the Wheatstone bridge used for measuring low resistances. **Kelvin scale** a scale of absolute temperature defined thermodynamically, orig. with the freezing and boiling points of water 100 degrees apart, but later modified to make the triple point of water exactly 273.16 degrees. **Kelvin's law**: that the most economical cross-sectional area of an electrical conductor used as a transmission line is that for which the cost of the energy dissipated in any period is equal to the charges during the same period on the capital cost of the line. **Kelvin temperature** a temperature on the Kelvin scale.
†**2** (**k-**.) A kilowatt-hour. L19–E20.
3 (**k-**.) The SI unit of thermodynamic temperature, one degree of the Kelvin scale (equal in magnitude to the degree Celsius). (Symbol K.) E20.

Kemalism /ˈkɛm(ə)lɪz(ə)m/ *noun.* E20.
[ORIGIN from *Kemal* (see below) + -ISM.]
The political, social, and economic policies advocated by the Turkish soldier and statesman Kemal Atatürk (*c* 1880–1938), which aimed to create a modern republican secular Turkish state out of a part of the Ottoman Empire.
■ **Kemalist** *noun & adjective* (*a*) *noun* an advocate or adherent of Kemalism; (*b*) *adjective* of or pertaining to Kemalism or Kemalists: M20.

kemb /kɛm/ *verb trans. obsolete* exc. *dial.* Pa. t. & pple **kembed**, **kempt** /kɛm(p)t/.
[ORIGIN Old English *cemban*, from Germanic base of COMB *noun*[1]. Repl. by COMB *verb*, but survives in KEMPT *adjective*, UNKEMPT.]
1 = COMB *verb* 1a. OE.
†**2** = COMB *verb* 1b. ME–E18.

kemp /kɛmp/ *noun*[1]. *obsolete* exc. *dial.*
[ORIGIN Old English *cempa* = Old Frisian *kempa*, *kampa*, Old Saxon *kempio*, Old High German *kempfo*, from West Germanic.]
1 A big, strong, and brave warrior or fighter; a champion; a pugnacious person. OE.
2 A stalk of the ribwort plantain, *Plantago lanceolata*, used in a children's game in which the stalks with their flower heads are struck against each other. *Scot.* L16.

kemp /kɛmp/ *noun*[2]. LME.
[ORIGIN Old Norse *kampr* beard, moustache, whisker.]
Orig., a coarse or stout hair, as those of the eyebrows. Now, (a) hair of this kind occurring among wool.

kemp /kɛmp/ *verb & noun*[3]. *Scot. & N. English.* LME.
[ORIGIN Middle Dutch *kempen*, *kimpen*, Low German *kämpen*, Old High German *chemfan*, Old Norse *keppa*, from Germanic.]
▸**A** *verb intrans.* Fight or contend *with*; *spec.* compete or strive (*with*) in doing a piece of work, esp. in reaping. LME.
▸**B** *noun.* A contest, esp. between reapers. L18.
■ **kemper** *noun* (*a*) *Scot.* a person who competes or strives for victory, esp. in reaping; (*b*) *arch.* = KEMP *noun*[1] 1: M17.

kempas /ˈkɛmpəs/ *noun.* M19.
[ORIGIN Malay.]
A leguminous timber tree, *Koompassia malaccensis*, native to Malaya, Sumatra, and Borneo; the wood of this tree.

Kempeitai /ˈkɛmpeɪtʌɪ/ *noun.* M20.
[ORIGIN Japanese *kenpeitai*.]
The Japanese military secret service in the period 1931–45.

kempt /kɛm(p)t/ *adjective.* OE.
[ORIGIN pa. pple of KEMB *verb*.]
(Of hair or wool) combed, neatly brushed or trimmed; *transf.* neat, tidy. Cf. UNKEMPT.

S. SPENDER Gardens as well kempt as a short hair-cut. W. SANSOM The kempt yellow gravel of drives. *Sunday Express* Perfectly kempt in a blue cardigan and striped shirt.

kempt *verb pa. t. & pple*: see KEMB *verb*.

kempy /ˈkɛmpi/ *noun. Scot. & N. English.* E16.
[ORIGIN from KEMP *noun*[1] + -Y[6].]
= KEMP *noun*[1] 1.

kempy /ˈkɛmpi/ *adjective.* E19.
[ORIGIN from KEMP *noun*[2] + -Y[1].]
(Of wool) having many kemps; resembling kemps.

ken /kɛn/ *noun*[1]. M16.
[ORIGIN from the verb.]
†**1** The distance that bounds the range of ordinary vision, esp. at sea; a marine measure of about 32 kilometres or 20 miles. M16–E17.
2 Range of knowledge or mental perception. M16. ▸**b** Look, gaze. Now *rare.* M17.

P. ARROWSMITH Sex . . was something beyond his ken, which he never consciously thought about.

3 Range of sight or vision. Now *rare.* L16.

KEATS Then felt I like some watcher of the skies When a new planet swims into his ken.

†**4** Sight or view *of* something; possibility or capacity of seeing. L16–M18.

SHAKES. *Lucr.* To drown in ken of shore.

ken /kɛn/ *noun*[2]. *slang.* M16.
[ORIGIN Unknown.]
A house, *esp.* one where thieves, beggars, etc., meet or lodge.

ken /kɛn/ *noun*[3]. Pl. same. E18.
[ORIGIN Japanese.]
A Japanese unit of length equal to six *shaku*, approximately 2 metres or yards.

ken /kɛn/ *noun*[4]. Pl. same. L19.
[ORIGIN Japanese.]
A territorial division of Japan; a prefecture.

ken /kɛn/ *noun*[5]. L19.
[ORIGIN Japanese, lit. 'fist'.]
A Japanese game of forfeits played with the hands and with gestures.

ken /kɛn/ *verb.* Infl. **-nn-**. Pa. t. & pple **kenned**, **kent** /kɛnt/.
[ORIGIN Old English *cennan* = Old Frisian *kenna*, *kanna*, Old Saxon *kennian*, Old High German (Dutch, German) *kennen*, Old Norse *kenna*, Gothic *kannjan*, from Germanic, from Indo-European base also of CAN *verb*[1], KNOW *verb*.]
▸**I** Causative.
†**1** *verb trans.* Make known, declare; impart the knowledge of (something). OE–E17.
†**2** *verb trans.* Direct, teach, or instruct (a person); teach or show how *to do*. ME–M16.
†**3** *verb trans.* Direct, guide, or show the way *to* a place or person. ME–L16.
▸**II** Non-causative.
4 *verb trans.* See; catch sight of; look at, scan. *arch.* ME.
5 *verb trans.* Recognize, identify; be able to distinguish (one person or thing *from* another). Now *Scot. & N. English.* ME.
†**6** *verb trans.* Get to know, ascertain, find out. ME–E17.
7 *verb trans.* Know; be acquainted with; understand; be aware *that*. Now chiefly *Scot.* ME.

G. MACDONALD I dinna ken what ye mean, Alec. T. H. WHITE He kens the difference yet of right and wrong. *Scottish Field* Perhaps the authorities . . didnae ken his faither, for they made his son Professor of . . Astronomy!

8 *verb intrans.* Have knowledge (*of*, *about*); know how (*to do*). Now *Scot.* ME.
9 *verb trans.* †**a** Acknowledge, admit to be genuine, valid, etc. ME–L17. ▸**b** SCOTS LAW (now *hist.*). Recognize as legal heir or successor *to* an estate; *spec.* recognize (a widow) as entitled to a terce of a late husband's estate. LME.
– COMB.: **ken-mark** a mark by which something can be recognized, *esp.* a brand.

kenaf /kəˈnaf/ *noun.* L19.
[ORIGIN Persian, var. of *kanab* HEMP.]
= AMBARI.

kench /kɛn(t)ʃ/ *noun. US.* M19.
[ORIGIN Unknown.]
A box or bin used for salting sealskins or fish.

Kendal /ˈkɛnd(ə)l/ *noun.* LME.
[ORIGIN A town in Cumbria, NW England.]
1 Used *attrib.* to designate things, esp. textiles, originating in or associated with Kendal in England. LME.

Daily Telegraph They . . included in their packs 'iron rations' of chocolate, raisins and Kendal mint cake.

Kendal cotton: see COTTON *noun*[2]. **Kendal green** *hist.* (*a*) = sense 2 below; (*b*) the green colour of Kendal cloth.
†**2** A kind of rough green woollen cloth. LME–L17.

kendo /ˈkɛndəʊ/ *noun.* E20.
[ORIGIN Japanese, from *ken* sword + *dō* way.]
A Japanese sport of fencing with two-handed staves of split bamboo.

keneme *noun* var. of CENEME.

Kenilworth ivy /ˈkɛn(ə)lwəːθ ˈʌɪvi/ *noun phr.* L19.
[ORIGIN *Kenilworth* Castle, Warwickshire, England.]
= ***ivy-leaved toadflax*** s.v. IVY *noun*.

Kenite /ˈkiːnʌɪt/ *noun & adjective*. M16.
[ORIGIN from Hebrew *qēnī* adjective assoc. with *qayin* a weapon made of metal, Arabic *qayn*, Aramaic *qaynāyā* smith, metalworker: see -ITE[1].]
▸ **A** *noun*. A member of an ancient nomadic people from S. Palestine, freq. mentioned in the Bible. M16.
▸ **B** *adjective*. Of or pertaining to the Kenites. E20.

kennedya /kɛˈniːdɪə/ *noun*. M19.
[ORIGIN mod. Latin (see below), from Lewis *Kennedy* (d. 1818), English nurseryman.]
Any of various climbing leguminous plants of the genus *Kennedia*, with showy esp. crimson flowers, native to Australia.

kennel /ˈkɛn(ə)l/ *noun*[1] & *verb*. ME.
[ORIGIN from Anglo-Norman noun = Old French *chenil* (cf. Anglo-Latin *canillum, kenillum*), from Latin *canis* dog.]
▸ **A** *noun*. **1** A small structure for a dog to shelter or live in; a house or range of buildings in which a pack of hounds are kept. Also (usu. in *pl.*, freq. treated as *sing.*), an establishment where dogs are bred or boarded. ME. ▸**b** The hole or lair of a fox or other animal. Now *rare*. M18. ▸**c** A small and mean dwelling or hut, a hovel. M19.

W. HOLTBY The . . retriever bitch who drowsed with her head hanging out of the wooden kennel. R. RENDELL I've never left her since she was a puppy . . . I couldn't put her in kennels. She'd fret.

2 A pack of hounds or of other animals. LME. ▸**b** *fig.* A pack, crew, or gang of people. *arch.* L16.
– COMB.: **Kennel Club** an organization which establishes dog breeds, records pedigrees, issues the rules for dog shows and trials, etc.; a branch of this organization; **kennelmaid**, **kennelman** a woman, man, who works in a kennels.
▸ **B** *verb*. Infl. **-ll-**, *-l-.
1 *verb intrans.* Shelter or live in a kennel; retire into a kennel or lair. M16. ▸**b** Foll. by *up*: return to one's kennel; *colloq.* keep quiet, shut up. E20.
2 *verb trans.* Put into or keep in a kennel or kennels; *colloq.* shut *up*, lodge, hide. L16.
■ **kennelling** *noun* (*a*) the action of the verb; (*b*) provision of kennels: E18.

kennel /ˈkɛn(ə)l/ *noun*[2]. L16.
[ORIGIN Later form of CANNEL *noun*[1]. Cf. CANAL *noun*, CHANNEL *noun*[1].]
A surface drain in a street; a gutter.

Kennelly layer /ˈkɛn(ə)lɪ ˌleɪə/ *noun phr.* E20.
[ORIGIN Arthur Edwin *Kennelly* (1861–1939), US electrical engineer.]
= ***E-layer*** s.v. E, E. Also ***Kennelly–Heaviside layer*** [see HEAVISIDE LAYER].

kennetic /kɛˈnɛtɪk/ *adjective*. M20.
[ORIGIN from KEN *verb* after KINETIC *adjective*.]
Of or pertaining to the nature or acquisition of knowledge. Chiefly in ***kennetic inquiry***.

kennetjie /ˈkɛnəki, -tʃi/ *noun*. *S. Afr.* M20.
[ORIGIN Afrikaans.]
Tipcat; a tipcat.

kenning /ˈkɛnɪŋ/ *noun*[1]. Now *Scot. & N. English*. ME.
[ORIGIN from KEN *verb* + -ING[1].]
†**1** Teaching, instruction. ME–M16.
†**2** Sign, token; appearance. Only in ME.
†**3** = KEN *noun*[1] 4. LME–L17.
4 a Mental cognition; knowledge, understanding; awareness, recognition. LME. ▸**b** A small but perceptible amount, a little. L18.
†**5 a** = KEN *noun*[1] 1. L15–L17. ▸**b** = KEN *noun*[1] 3. M16–E17.

kenning /ˈkɛnɪŋ/ *noun*[2]. L19.
[ORIGIN Old Norse, from *kenna* know, perceive, from Germanic base of KEN *verb*.]
A poetic phrase used instead of the simple name of a thing in Old Norse, Old English, and other Germanic poetry, as *oar-steed* for 'ship', *storm of swords* for 'battle'.

keno /ˈkiːnəʊ/ *noun & interjection*. E19.
[ORIGIN Unknown.]
▸ **A** *noun*. A game of chance resembling bingo or lotto, based on the drawing of numbers and covering of corresponding numbers on cards. E19.
▸ **B** *interjection*. Expr. encouragement or approval. *US slang*. M19.

kenogenesis *noun* var. of CAENOGENESIS.

kenosis /kɪˈnəʊsɪs/ *noun*. L19.
[ORIGIN Greek *kenōsis* an emptying, with ref. to *Philippians* 2:7 *heauton ekenōse* lit. 'emptied himself'.]
CHRISTIAN THEOLOGY. Christ's full or partial renunciation of his divine nature or powers in his incarnation.
■ **kenotic** /kɪˈnɒtɪk/ *adjective* of or pertaining to kenosis; involving or accepting the doctrine of kenosis: L19. **kenoticism** /kɪˈnɒtɪsɪz(ə)m/ *noun* the doctrine of or belief in the kenosis of Christ L19. **kenoticist** /kɪˈnɒtɪsɪst/ *noun* a person who believes in the doctrine of kenosis L19.

Kensington /ˈkɛnzɪŋt(ə)n/ *noun*. L19.
[ORIGIN A borough of London, now part of the Royal Borough of Kensington and Chelsea.]
1 ***Kensington outline stitch***, ***Kensington stitch***, = ***split stitch*** s.v. SPLIT *adjective*. L19.
2 Speech supposedly characteristic of Kensington, London. M20.

B. MASON The 'both' came out purest Kensington as 'beeouth'.

■ **Kensingtonian** /kɛnzɪŋˈtəʊnɪən/ *noun & adjective* (a native or inhabitant) of Kensington L19.

Kensitite /ˈkɛnzɪtʌɪt/ *noun & adjective*. L19.
[ORIGIN from *Kensit* (see below) + -ITE[1].]
ECCLESIASTICAL HISTORY. ▸**A** *noun*. A follower of John Kensit (1853–1902), a Low Church extremist who objected to alleged Romanizing aspects of the Anglican Church. L19.
▸ **B** *attrib.* or as *adjective*. Of or pertaining to Kensitites or Kensitism. E20.
■ **Kensitism** *noun* M20.

kenspeck /ˈkɛnspɛk/ *adjective*. *dial.* L16.
[ORIGIN Of Scandinavian origin: cf. Old Norse *kennispeki* faculty of recognition, Middle Swedish *kännespaker*, Swedish *känspak*, Norwegian *kjennespak* quick at recognizing, from Old Norse *kenna* KEN *verb* + *spak-*, *spek-* wise, wisdom.]
= KENSPECKLE.

kenspeckle /ˈkɛnspɛk(ə)l/ *adjective*. *Scot. & N. English*. M16.
[ORIGIN formed as KENSPECK + -LE[1].]
Easily recognizable, conspicuous.

kent /kɛnt/ *noun*[1] & *verb*[1]. *Scot. & N. English*. E17.
[ORIGIN Perh. var. of QUANT *noun, verb*.]
▸ **A** *noun*. A shepherd's staff; a long pole, *esp.* one used in vaulting ditches etc. or for punting. E17.
▸ **B** *verb intrans. & trans.* Punt (a boat etc.). E19.

Kent /kɛnt/ *noun*[2]. E19.
[ORIGIN See KENTISH.]
In full ***Kent sheep***. (An animal of) a breed of hardy sheep having a long coarse fleece.

kent *verb*[2] *pa. t. & pple*: see KEN *verb*.

kentallenite /kɛnˈtalnʌɪt/ *noun*. E20.
[ORIGIN from *Kentallen*, a village in SW Scotland + -ITE[1].]
GEOLOGY. A dark coarse-grained mafic rock consisting of olivine and augite with orthoclase, plagioclase, and biotite.

kente /ˈkɛntə/ *noun*. Also **K-**. M20.
[ORIGIN Twi = cloth.]
More fully ***kente cloth***. In Ghana: a brightly coloured banded material; a long garment made from this material, loosely draped on or worn around the shoulders and waist.

kentia /ˈkɛntɪə/ *noun*. L19.
[ORIGIN mod. Latin (see below), from William *Kent* (d. 1828), botanical collector + -IA[1].]
Any of various pinnate-leaved palms of the former genus *Kentia*, native to Australia and some Pacific islands; esp. *Howeia forsterana* and *H. belmoreana*, freq. grown as house plants.

Kenticism /ˈkɛntɪsɪz(ə)m/ *noun*. M18.
[ORIGIN from *Kent* (see KENTISH) after *Anglicism* etc.]
A word, idiom, or expression peculiar to the Kentish dialect, *spec.* of the Old and Middle English periods.

†**kenting** *noun*. M17–L18.
[ORIGIN App. from *Kent* (see KENTISH) + -ING[1].]
A kind of fine linen cloth orig. made in Kent.

Kentish /ˈkɛntɪʃ/ *adjective & noun*. OE.
[ORIGIN from *Cent* Kent (see below) from Latin *Cantium* from Celtic noun meaning either 'border' or 'white': see -ISH[1].]
▸ **A** *adjective*. Of, pertaining to, or characteristic of Kent, a county in SE England, and one of the supposed seven kingdoms of the Angles and Saxons. OE.
Kentish crow *local* a hooded crow. **Kentish fire** rhythmic hand clapping, either as applause or as a demonstration of impatience or dissent. **Kentish glory** a large, orange-brown and white patterned moth, *Endromis versicolora*. **Kentish nightingale** a blackcap. **Kentish plover** a small plover, *Charadrius alexandrinus*, resembling a pale ringed plover and of worldwide distribution. **Kentish rag** a hard compact limestone found in Kent, used for paving and building. **Kentish tern** a Sandwich tern.
▸ **B** *noun*. **1** *pl.* The natives or inhabitants of Kent. *rare*. OE.
2 The dialect of Kent *spec.* of the Old and Middle English periods. M19.

†**kentle** *noun* var. of QUINTAL.

kentledge /ˈkɛntlɪdʒ/ *noun*. E17.
[ORIGIN Old French *quintelage* ballast, with assim. to *kentle* obsolete var. of QUINTAL: see -AGE.]
NAUTICAL. Pig iron or other heavy material used as permanent ballast.

Kentuck /ˈkɛntʌk/ *adjective & noun*. *US*. E19.
[ORIGIN Abbreviation of KENTUCKY.]
= KENTUCKIAN.

Kentuckian /kɛnˈtʌkɪən/ *noun & adjective*. *US*. L18.
[ORIGIN from KENTUCKY + -IAN.]
▸ **A** *noun*. A native or inhabitant of Kentucky, a south-eastern state of the US. L18.
▸ **B** *adjective*. Of or pertaining to Kentucky. E19.

Kentucky /kɛnˈtʌki/ *noun*. L18.
[ORIGIN See below.]
Used *attrib.* to designate things from or associated with the state of Kentucky in the south-eastern US.
Kentucky bluegrass the grass *Poa pratensis*, grown for fodder in the central US. **Kentucky coffee tree** a N. American leguminous tree, *Gymnocladus dioicus*, the seeds of which can be used as a substitute for coffee. **Kentucky Derby** a horse race for three-year-olds run annually at Louisville in Kentucky. **Kentucky rifle** a long-barrelled muzzle-loading flintlock rifle. **Kentucky warbler** an olive-green and yellow warbler, *Geothlypsis formosa*, of the eastern US.

kentum *adjective* var. of CENTUM *adjective*.

Kenya /ˈkɛnjə/ *noun*. M20.
[ORIGIN See below.]
Used *attrib.* to designate people or things from or associated with Kenya, a country in E. Africa.
Kenya Asian = ***Kenyan Asian*** s.v. KENYAN *adjective*. **Kenya coffee** a mild coffee grown in Kenya.

Kenyah /ˈkɛnjə/ *noun & adjective*. M19.
[ORIGIN Kenyah.]
▸ **A** *noun*. Pl. **-s**, same. A member of one of the aboriginal peoples inhabiting parts of Borneo and Sarawak; the Indonesian language of this people. M19.
▸ **B** *attrib.* or as *adjective*. Of or pertaining to the Kenyahs or their language. E20.

Kenyan /ˈkɛnjən/ *noun & adjective*. M20.
[ORIGIN from KENYA + -AN.]
▸ **A** *noun*. A native or inhabitant of Kenya. M20.
▸ **B** *adjective*. Of, pertaining to, or characteristic of Kenya or its people. M20.
Kenyan Asian an Asian, esp. one from India or Pakistan, resident or formerly resident in Kenya.
■ **Kenyaniˈzation** *noun* in Kenya, the replacement of settlers and Asians by Kenyan Africans in government posts, the civil service, etc. M20. **Kenyanize** *verb trans.* make Kenyan in character, organization, etc. L20.

kep /kɛp/ *verb & noun*. *Scot. & N. English*. LME.
[ORIGIN Differentiated form of KEEP *verb* (cf. senses 5, 6 & pa. t. *kept*).]
▸ **A** *verb trans.* Infl. **-pp-**.
1 Meet, intercept; stop the course of; receive the force of (a blow). LME.
2 Catch so as to prevent from falling; catch (falling liquid) as in a vessel. L15.
▸ **B** *noun*. **1** = CATCH *noun*[1] 2. E18.
2 A chance, an opportunity. L18.
3 = CATCH *noun*[1] 4. E20.

kephal-, **kephalo-** *combining forms* see CEPHALO-.

kephir *noun* var. of KEFIR.

kepi /ˈkɛpi, ˈkeɪpi/ *noun*. M19.
[ORIGIN French *képi* from Swiss German *Käppi* dim. of *Kappe* cap.]
A French military cap with a flat circular top which slopes towards the front and a horizontal peak.

Kepler /ˈkɛplə/ *noun*. E18.
[ORIGIN Johann *Kepler* (1571–1630), German astronomer.]
ASTRONOMY. Used in *possess.* and *attrib.* to designate things discovered or investigated by Kepler.
Kepler problem = ***Kepler's problem*** below. **Kepler's equation** the equation $\theta = \phi - e \sin \phi$ relating the mean anomaly θ of a planet to the eccentric anomaly ϕ and the eccentricity e of the orbit. **Kepler's law** each of three propositions: (*a*) that the planets move in ellipses having the sun at one focus; (*b*) that the radius vector of a planet sweeps out equal areas in equal times; (*c*) that the square of a planet's orbital period is directly proportional to the cube of its mean distance from the sun. **Kepler's problem** the problem of solving Kepler's equation for the eccentric anomaly of a planet in a known orbit given the mean anomaly, i.e. of finding the position of the planet at any given time.

Keplerian /kɛˈplɪərɪən/ *adjective*. M19.
[ORIGIN from KEPLER + -IAN.]
Of or pertaining to Kepler or his discoveries and investigations; *spec.* (*a*) designating or pertaining to the free motion of a body in the gravitational field of another more massive body (described by a trajectory that is an ellipse or other conic section); (*b*) designating a refracting telescope with a positive objective and eyepiece, giving an inverted image.

kept /kɛpt/ *ppl adjective*. L17.
[ORIGIN from KEEP *verb*. Earlier in UNKEPT.]
That has been or is being kept; *spec.* (esp. of a woman) maintained or supported in return for sexual favours.

kept *verb pa. t. & pple* of KEEP *verb*.

ker- /kə/ *prefix*. *colloq.* (orig. *US*). M19.
[ORIGIN Imit.]
Forming nouns and interjections imit. of the sound or the effect of the fall of some heavy body, as ***kerchunk***, ***kerflop***, ***kerplunk***, ***kerslam***, ***kersplash***, ***kerthump***, ***kerwhop***, etc.

kerasin /ˈkɛrəsɪn/ *noun*. L19.
[ORIGIN Irreg. from Greek *keras* horn + -IN[1].]
BIOCHEMISTRY. A cerebroside normally found in the brain and accumulated in the liver, spleen, and elsewhere in individuals with Gaucher's disease.

K

keratectasia /kɛrətɛkˈteɪzɪə/ *noun*. **L19.**
[ORIGIN from KERATO- + ECTASIA.]
OPHTHALMOLOGY. Protrusion of part of the cornea.

keratectomy /kɛrəˈtɛktəmi/ *noun*. **L19.**
[ORIGIN from KERATO- + -ECTOMY.]
MEDICINE. Surgical excision of part of the cornea; an instance of this.

keratin /ˈkɛrətɪn/ *noun*. **M19.**
[ORIGIN from Greek *kerat-*, *keras* horn + -IN[1].]
BIOCHEMISTRY. Any of a group of fibrous proteins which have a structure cross-linked by disulphide bonds and form the chief structural constituent of skin, nails, hair, feathers, horn, etc.

keratinisation *noun*, **keratinise** *verb* vars. of KERATINIZATION, KERATINIZE.

keratinization /ˌkɛrətɪnʌɪˈzeɪʃ(ə)n, kəˌrat-/ *noun*. Also **-isation**. **L19.**
[ORIGIN formed as KERATINIZE + -ATION.]
The process of becoming keratinous; *esp.* the hardening of the cells of the skin, hair, etc., by deposition of keratin.

keratinize /ˈkɛrətɪnʌɪz, kəˈrat-/ *verb*. Also **-ise**. **L19.**
[ORIGIN from Greek *keratinos* horny + -IZE.]
1 *verb intrans.* Become keratinous. **L19.**
2 *verb trans.* Make keratinous, subject to keratinization. Freq. as ***keratinized*** *ppl adjective*. **E20.**

keratino- /ˈkɛrətɪnəʊ/ *combining form* of KERATIN: see -O-.
■ **keraˈtinocyte** *noun* an epidermal cell which produces keratin **M20.** **keratiˈnolysis** *noun* chemical breakdown of keratin **E20.** **keratinoˈlytic** *adjective* bringing about keratinolysis **M20.** **keratinoˈphilic** *adjective* (*BOTANY*) (chiefly of a fungus) growing on keratinous material, as hair, feathers, etc. **M20.**

keratinous /kəˈratɪnəs/ *adjective*. **L19.**
[ORIGIN from KERATIN + -OUS.]
Of the nature of or like horn; consisting of or containing keratin.

K

keratitis /kɛrəˈtʌɪtɪs/ *noun*. **M19.**
[ORIGIN from KERATO- + -ITIS.]
MEDICINE. Inflammation of the cornea.

kerato- /ˈkɛrətəʊ/ *combining form*. Before a vowel **kerat-**.
[ORIGIN Greek, from *kerat-*, *keras* horn: see -O-. Cf. CERATO-.]
Chiefly *MEDICINE.* **1** Of or relating to keratinous or horny tissues.
2 Of or pertaining to the cornea of the eye.
■ **keratoacanˈthoma** *noun*, pl. **-mas**, **-mata** /-mətə/, [Greek *akantha* thorn] a nodular growth of the skin which usu. heals spontaneously **M20.** **keratoconjuncˈtival** *adjective* of or pertaining to the cornea and the conjunctiva **M20.** **keratoconjunctiˈvitis** *noun* (a condition involving) inflammation of the cornea and conjunctiva **L19.** **keratoˈconus** *noun* [Latin *conus* cone] *OPHTHALMOLOGY* a condition of the eye in which the cornea develops a rounded apex **M20.** **keratoˈderma** *noun* a local or general thickening of the horny layer of the epidermis **M20.** **keratoˈdermia** *noun* keratoderma **E20.** **keraˈtogenous** *adjective* producing horn or keratin **L19.** **keratoˈhyalin(e)** *noun* (*BIOCHEMISTRY*) an amorphous protein found in association with keratin **L19.** **keraˈtoma** *noun*, pl. **-mas**, **-mata** /-mətə/, = KERATOSIS **L19.** **keratomalacia** /-məˈleɪʃ(ɪ)ə/ *noun* softening of the cornea associated esp. with vitamin A deficiency **L19.** **keraˈtometer** *noun* (*OPHTHALMOLOGY*) an instrument for measuring the curvature of the cornea by observing images reflected in it (also called ***ophthalmometer***) **L19.** **keratoˈmetric** *adjective* pertaining to or obtained with a keratometer **L19.** **keraˈtometry** *noun* measurement of the curvature of the cornea **L19.** **keratomiˈleusis** *noun* [Greek *smileusis* carving] surgical reshaping of the cornea to correct a refractive error **M20.** **keratoplasty** *noun* (an instance of) surgery performed on the cornea, *esp.* corneal transplantation **M19.** **keraˈtosis** *noun*, pl. **-toses** /-ˈtəʊsiːz/, a horny growth, esp. on the skin; a condition marked by such growths: **L19.** **keraˈtotic** *adjective* of or pertaining to keratosis **M20.**

keratolysis /kɛrəˈtɒlɪsɪs/ *noun*. **L19.**
[ORIGIN from KERATO- + -LYSIS.]
MEDICINE. Loosening or (partial) destruction of keratinous tissue, esp. that of the skin, through disease or chemical action. Also, destruction of corneal tissue.
■ **keratoˈlytic** *adjective & noun* (*MEDICINE*) (an agent) able to soften or destroy keratinous material **L19.**

keratophyre /ˈkɛrətəfʌɪə/ *noun*. **L19.**
[ORIGIN from KERATO- + *-phyre* as in *granophyre*.]
GEOLOGY. Any of various fine-grained sodium-rich igneous rocks, typically albitic trachytes.

keratotomy /kɛrəˈtɒtəmi/ *noun*. **L19.**
[ORIGIN from KERATO- + -TOMY.]
Surgical incision into the cornea. Chiefly as ***radial keratotomy*** (see RADIAL *adjective*).

kerb /kəːb/ *noun & verb*. Also †**kirb**. **M17.**
[ORIGIN Var. of CURB *noun*.]
▸ **A** *noun* **1** **a** = CURB *noun* 6. **M17.** ▸**b** = CURB *noun* 9. **E18.**
2 = CURB *noun* 1. **L17.**
3 A stone edging of stone to a pavement or raised path; = CURB *noun* 8. **E19.**

J. GALLOWAY We were standing at the kerb to get over the street.

4 = CURB *noun* 5. **M19.**
– COMB.: **kerb-crawl** *verb intrans.* engage in kerb-crawling; **kerb-crawler** a (usu. male) person who engages in kerb-crawling; **kerb-crawling** the practice of driving slowly by the edge of a road, harassing or soliciting esp. female passers-by; **kerb drill** precautionary procedure, esp. looking to right and left, made before crossing a road and often taught to children; **kerb market** (a place for) the sale of securities after hours or of shares not dealt with on a stock exchange; **kerb service** = *curb service* s.v. CURB *noun*; **kerbside** the side of a road or pavement nearer the kerb; a kerb; **kerbstone** any of the stones forming a kerb; a kerb; ***kerbstone market*** = ***kerb market*** above; **kerb weight** the weight of a car without occupants or baggage.
▸ **B** *verb trans.* Provide with a kerb. **M19.**
■ **kerbing** *noun* (**a**) the action of the verb; (**b**) the stones collectively forming a kerb: **M19.**

†**kerch** *noun*[1]. **LME–L18.**
[ORIGIN formed as CURCH.]
= KERCHIEF 1.

Kerch /kəːtʃ/ *noun*[2]. Also **Kertch**. **M20.**
[ORIGIN See below.]
Used *attrib.* to designate a type of ancient red-figured Greek pottery found in Kerch, a town in the Crimea, S. Ukraine.

kercher /ˈkəːtʃə/ *noun*. *obsolete* exc. *dial.* **LME.**
[ORIGIN Syncopated from Old French *couvrechier*, *cuevre-*, erron. forms of *couvrechief* etc.: see KERCHIEF.]
= KERCHIEF.

kerchief /ˈkəːtʃɪf/ *noun*. **ME.**
[ORIGIN Anglo-Norman *courchef* = Old French *cuevre-chief*, (also mod.) *couvre-chef*, from *couvrir* COVER *verb*[2] + *chief* head (see CHIEF *noun*): cf. COVERCHIEF.]
1 A cloth or scarf used to cover the head, esp. by a woman; a covering for the neck or shoulders, a neckerchief, a cravat. **ME.**
2 A cloth used for any of various other purposes; *spec.* a handkerchief. **LME.**
■ **kerchiefed** *adjective* covered with or wearing a kerchief **E17.**

ker-ching *noun & interjection* var. of KA-CHING.

kêrel /ˈkɛːr(ə)l/ *noun*. *S. Afr. colloq.* Also **kerel**. **L19.**
[ORIGIN Afrikaans from Dutch = CARL *noun*: cf. CHURL.]
A fellow, a chap, a young man; a boyfriend.

kereru /ˈkɛrəruː/ *noun*. **L19.**
[ORIGIN Maori.]
The New Zealand pigeon, *Hemiphaga novaeseelandiae*. Also called ***kuku***.

Keres /ˈkɛrɛs/ *noun & adjective*. Pl. of noun same. **E19.**
[ORIGIN Amer. Spanish *Queres* from Amer. Indian.]
Of or pertaining to, a member of, a Pueblo Indian people inhabiting parts of New Mexico; (of) the language of this people, forming the Keresan group.

Keresan /ˈkɛrəs(ə)n/ *adjective & noun*. **L19.**
[ORIGIN from KERES + -AN.]
▸ **A** *adjective*. Of or pertaining to the Keres of New Mexico; *spec.* designating or pertaining to a linguistic group constituted by Keres. **L19.**
▸ **B** *noun*. The linguistic group constituted by Keres. **M20.**

kerf /kəːf/ *noun*.
[ORIGIN Old English *cyrf* from West Germanic, from base of CARVE: cf. Old Norse *kurfr* chip, *kyrfa* cut. See also CARF.]
1 The act of cutting or carving; a cut, a stroke. Now *rare*. **OE.**
2 The result of cutting; an incision, notch, slit, etc., made by cutting, esp. by a saw. **LME.**
3 The cut end or surface on a felled or pruned tree. **LME.**
4 A piece or quantity cut off; a cutting. **L17.**
■ **kerfed** *adjective* having incisions or slits **L19.**

kerfuffle /kəˈfʌf(ə)l/ *noun*. *colloq.*, orig. *Scot.* Also **ca-**, **cu(r)-**. **E19.**
[ORIGIN Perh. from CURFUFFLE *verb*, but cf. Irish *cíor thuathail* confusion, disorder.]
Fuss, commotion, disorder, agitation.

J. M. FLEMING The kerfuffle over the stolen jewels last week. M. GEE In the kerfuffle, he didn't hear the front door.

Kerguelen /ˈkəːɡɪlɪn/ *noun*. **M19.**
[ORIGIN A group of islands in the southern Indian Ocean, from Yves Joseph de *Kerguelen*-Tremarec, 18th-cent. French navigator.]
Kerguelen cabbage, †***Kerguelen land cabbage***, †***Kerguelen's land cabbage***, a cabbage-like cruciferous plant, *Pringlea antiscorbutica*, confined to Kerguelen and neighbouring islands.

keri *noun* var. of QERE.

Kerman *adjective & noun* var. of KIRMAN.

Kermanji /kəˈmɑːndʒi/ *noun*. **L19.**
[ORIGIN Kurdish *kurmānjī*.]
= KURDISH *noun*.

Kermanshah *noun & adjective* var. of KIRMANSHAH.

kermes /ˈkəːmɪz/ *noun*. **L16.**
[ORIGIN French *kermès* from Arabic *qirmiz* (= sense 2 below). Cf. CRIMSON, ARMOZEEN.]
1 More fully ***kermes oak***. A small evergreen oak, *Quercus coccifera*, of the Mediterranean region. **L16.**
2 (The dried bodies of) adult females of the scale insect *Kermes ilicis*, which form hard berry-like galls on the kermes oak, used to make dye and (formerly) medicines; the scarlet dye made from these. Cf. ALKERMES. **E17.**
3 *CHEMISTRY & PHARMACOLOGY.* A vermilion compound, precipitated antimony trisulphide. Also more fully ***kermes mineral***. Now *rare* or *obsolete*. **M18.**

kermesse /kəˈmɛs/ *noun*. **L19.**
[ORIGIN French, formed as KERMIS.]
1 = KERMIS. **L19.**
2 *CYCLING.* A circuit race. **M20.**

kermis /ˈkəːmɪs/ *noun*. Also **kirmess**. **L16.**
[ORIGIN Dutch *kermis*, †*-misse*, from *kerk* CHURCH *noun* + *misse* MASS *noun*[1]: orig. = mass on annual anniversary of dedication of a church, when a fair was held. Cf. KERMESSE.]
In the Low Countries, parts of Germany, etc.: an annual fair or carnival. Also (*US*), a similar fair or bazaar, usu. for charitable purposes.

kern /kəːn/ *noun*[1]. Also **kerne**. Pl. **-s**, same. **LME.**
[ORIGIN Irish *ceithearn* from Old Irish *ceithern* band of foot soldiers. Cf. earlier CATERAN.]
1 *hist.* A light-armed Irish foot soldier. Formerly also a band of kerns. **LME.**
2 A rustic, a peasant. *arch.* **L15.**

kern /kəːn/ *noun*[2]. **L16.**
[ORIGIN Rel. to KERN *verb*[1] & KERNEL *noun*[1]: perh. already in Old English: cf. Norwegian *kyrne* grain & CURN; in sense 3 extracted from German *Kernzähler* nucleus counter.]
†**1** The kernel (of a nut). *rare*. Only in **L16.**
2 A grain (of wheat, sand, etc.). *rare*. **M18.**
3 *METEOROLOGY.* A suspended dust particle, *esp.* one which acts as a nucleus for condensation. **M20.**
– COMB.: **kern counter** [German *Kernzähler*] a device in which a sample of air is supersaturated to make kerns visible (by causing condensation) for counting.

kern /kəːn/ *noun*[3]. **L17.**
[ORIGIN Perh. from French *carne* corner, Norman-Picard var. of Old French *charne* from Latin *cardin-*, *cardo* hinge.]
TYPOGRAPHY. A part of a metal type projecting beyond the body or shank, as parts of some italic letters; a part of a printed character that overlaps its neighbours.

kern /kəːn/ *verb*[1]. *obsolete* exc. *dial.* **ME.**
[ORIGIN from Germanic base of CORN *noun*[1]: prob. already in Old English.]
1 *verb intrans.* Of corn: form the hard grains in the ear, seed. **ME.**
†**2** *verb trans.* Cause to granulate; make (salt) into grains. **L16–E18.** ▸**b** Sprinkle or preserve with salt. **E17–L19.**
3 *verb intrans.* Of salt etc.: crystallize in grains, become granular. **M17.**

kern /kəːn/ *verb*[2] *trans.* **L17.**
[ORIGIN from KERN *noun*[3].]
TYPOGRAPHY. Cast (metal type) with a kern or kerns; make (esp. selected characters) overlap neighbouring characters. Now also, modify the spacing between (characters) as specified by the manufacturer.

kerne *noun* var. of KERN *noun*[1].

kernel /ˈkəːn(ə)l/ *noun*[1] & *verb*[1].
[ORIGIN Old English *cyrnel* dim. of *corn* seed: see CORN *noun*[1], -EL[1].]
▸ **A** *noun*. **1** A seed, *esp.* one in a fruit; a pip, a stone. *obsolete* exc. *dial.* **OE.**
2 The softer (usu. edible) part contained within the hard shell of a nut or of a fruit stone. **OE.**

fig.: J. VIORST Anxiety contains a kernel of hope.

3 A rounded swelling in any part of the body; *esp.* an enlarged lymph node **OE.**
4 The seed and hard husk of a grain, esp. wheat. **ME.** ▸†**b** A granule, as of sand or salt. **LME–E19.**
5 A gland or glandular body; a tonsil; a lymphatic gland or ganglion. Now *rare* or *obsolete*. **LME.**
6 The nucleus, core, or centre of something. Also (*fig.*), the essential part; the gist of a narrative, the basis of a system, etc. **M16.** ▸**b** *LINGUISTICS.* The stem or common basis of a set of inflectional forms, as *lach-* in the German verb *lachen*. **L19.** ▸**c** *PHYSICS.* = CORE *noun*[1] 12. **E20.** ▸**d** *MATH.* A (given) function of two or more variables from which an integrand is obtained by multiplying by one or more other functions each of just one of the variables. **E20.** ▸**e** *MATH.* The set of all the elements of a group that are mapped by a given homomorphism into the identity element. **M20.** ▸**f** *LINGUISTICS.* In full ***kernel sentence***. In early transformational grammar, a basic or core sentence that results from the application of only a few (obligatory) transformations, and to which other sentences may be related by further transformations; a set of such sentences. **M20.** ▸**g** *COMPUTING.* The most basic level or core of an operating system of a computer, responsible for resource allocation, file management, and security. **L20.**

J. GALSWORTHY The kernel of life was in . . saving for his children. *Ski Survey* The front of an avalanche . . does not have the same speed as the kernel following behind.

▸ **B** *verb*. Infl. **-ll-**, ***-l-**.
†**1** *verb intrans.* Form kernels or seed; (of land) produce grain or corn. **LME–E18.**
2 *verb trans.* Enclose as a kernel in its shell. **M17.**
■ **kernelled** *adjective*[1] †(**a**) full of kernels or glands; (**b**) having a kernel: **LME.** **kernelless** /-l-l-/ *adjective* (*rare*) without a kernel **L19.**

kernelly *adjective* †(*a*) consisting of or full of glands, glandular; (*b*) resembling a kernel: LME.

kernel /ˈkəːn(ə)l/ *noun*[2] & *verb*[2]. *obsolete* exc. *hist.* Also †**carnel**. ME.
[ORIGIN Old French *carnel*, *quernel* (mod. *créneau*): see CRENEL *noun*, *verb*.]
▸ †**A** *noun*. An indentation or embrasure in the battlement of a wall; = CRENEL *noun*. Also (usu. in *pl.*), battlements. ME–L17.
▸ **B** *verb trans.* Infl. **-ll-**, *****-l-**. Provide with embrasures or battlements; crenellate. ME.
■ **kernelled** *adjective*[2] (*rare*) having battlements or embrasures, crenellated E18.

kernicterus /kəːˈnɪkt(ə)rəs/ *noun*. Also (earlier) †**-ikt-**. E20.
[ORIGIN German *Kernikterus*, from *Kern* nucleus + *Ikterus* jaundice.]
MEDICINE. The staining and permanent damaging of brain cells with bilirubin, often causing deafness and athetosis, which may occur in haemolytic disease of the newborn.
■ **kernicteric** *adjective* pertaining to or afflicted with kernicterus M20.

Kernig's sign /ˈkəːnɪgz sʌɪn/ *noun phr.* E20.
[ORIGIN V. M. *Kernig* (1840–1917), Russian physician.]
MEDICINE. Resistance to straightening of the leg at the knee in a patient lying supine with the hips fully flexed, an indication of meningitis.

†**kernikterus** *noun* see KERNICTERUS.

kernite /ˈkəːnʌɪt/ *noun*. E20.
[ORIGIN from *Kern* County, California + -ITE[1].]
MINERALOGY. A hydrated monoclinic form of sodium borate which occurs as large transparent crystals and is a major source of borax.

kernos /ˈkəːnɒs/ *noun*. Pl. **-noi** /-nɔɪ/. E20.
[ORIGIN Greek.]
ARCHAEOLOGY. An ancient Mediterranean and Middle Eastern baked clay vessel having small cups around the rim or fixed in a circle to a central stem.

kero /ˈkɛrəʊ/ *noun*. *Austral.* & *NZ colloq.* M20.
[ORIGIN Abbreviation.]
Kerosene.

kerogen /ˈkɛrədʒ(ə)n/ *noun*. E20.
[ORIGIN from Greek *kēros* wax + -GEN.]
GEOLOGY. A complex fossilized organic material found in oil shale and other sedimentary rock, which is insoluble in common organic solvents and yields petroleum products on distillation.

kerosene /ˈkɛrəsiːn/ *noun* & *verb*. Also **-ine**. M19.
[ORIGIN Irreg. from Greek *kēros* wax + -ENE, -INE[5].]
▸ **A** *noun*. A petroleum distillate containing liquid hydrocarbons which boils in the range 150° to 300°C, and is used as a fuel for tractors and jet engines, and in domestic heaters; paraffin oil. M19.
▸ **B** *verb trans.* Saturate with kerosene. L19.

Kerr /kəː/ *noun*. E20.
[ORIGIN John *Kerr* (1824–1907), Scot. physicist.]
PHYSICS. Used *attrib.* to designate things studied or devised by Kerr.
Kerr cell a transparent cell containing a liquid across which a voltage may be applied to produce a strong Kerr (electro-optical) effect, used to vary the plane of polarization of light and hence (when placed between crossed Polaroids) the intensity of a beam. **Kerr effect** (*a*) the rotation of the plane of polarization of light when reflected from a magnetized surface (more fully ***Kerr magneto-optical effect***); (*b*) the production of birefringence in a substance by an electric field (more fully ***Kerr electro-optical effect***).

kerria /ˈkɛrɪə/ *noun*. E19.
[ORIGIN mod. Latin (see below), from William *Ker* or *Kerr* (d. 1814), English botanical collector: see -IA[1].]
1 A deciduous yellow-flowered shrub, *Kerria japonica*, of the rose family, native to China and Japan and freq. cultivated esp. in its double-flowered version. E19.
2 ***white kerria***, a closely related shrub, *Rhodotypos scandens*, which bears white flowers. E20.

Kerry /ˈkɛri/ *noun*[1]. L18.
[ORIGIN See sense 1 below.]
1 Used *attrib.* to designate things originating in or associated with Kerry, a county in SW Ireland. L18.
Kerry Blue (**terrier**) (a dog of) a breed of medium-sized terrier with a long silky grey-blue coat. **Kerry cow** (an animal of) a breed of small black dairy cattle.
2 A Kerry cow; a Kerry Blue terrier. E19.

Kerry /ˈkɛri/ *noun*[2]. E20.
[ORIGIN A town and neighbouring range of hills in the Welsh county of Powys.]
More fully ***Kerry Hill*** (***sheep***). (An animal of) a breed of sheep having a thick fleece and black markings near the muzzle and feet.

kersey /ˈkəːzi/ *noun* & *adjective*. Now *rare*. LME.
[ORIGIN Prob. from *Kersey* in Suffolk: cf. Anglo-Latin *pannus cersegus*, *carsea*, Anglo-Norman *drap de kersy*.]
▸ **A** *noun*. Pl. **-seys**, **-sies**.
1 A kind of coarse cloth woven from short-stapled wool. LME.
2 A make or variety of kersey (usu. in *pl.*). Formerly also, a piece of kersey of a definite size. LME.
3 In *pl.* Trousers made of kersey. M19.
▸ **B** *attrib.* or as *adjective*. **1** Made of kersey. L16.
T. KENEALLY He had good kersey breeches on.
†**2** *fig.* Plain, homely. *rare* (Shakes.). Only in L16.

kerseymere /ˈkəːzɪmɪə/ *noun* & *adjective*. L18.
[ORIGIN Alt. of CASSIMERE, by assoc. with KERSEY.]
▸ **A** *noun*. **1** A medium-weight twilled woollen cloth. L18.
2 In *pl.* & (occas.) *sing.* Trousers made of kerseymere. M19.
▸ **B** *attrib.* or as *adjective*. Made of kerseymere. E19.

Kertch *noun* var. of KERCH *noun*[2].

keruing /ˈkɛrʊɪŋ/ *noun*. E20.
[ORIGIN Malay *keruing*.]
The light or dark brown hardwood timber of several trees of the genus *Dipterocarpus* (family Dipterocarpaceae), found in western Malaysia, Sabah, and Indonesia.

kerygma /kɪˈrɪgmə/ *noun*. Pl. **-mata** /-mətə/. L19.
[ORIGIN Greek *kērugma*, from *kērussein* proclaim.]
CHRISTIAN CHURCH. *The* preaching of the Gospels; the element of proclamation as contrasted with didache (teaching) in the communication of the Christian gospel.
■ **kerygˈmatic** *adjective* belonging to or of the nature of preaching E20. **kerygˈmatically** *adverb* M20.

kesh /keɪʃ/ *noun*. L20.
[ORIGIN Punjabi *keś*.]
The uncut hair and beard worn as one of the five distinguishing signs of the Sikh Khalsa, symbolizing dedication.

kest /kɛst/ *verb trans.* & *intrans.* *dial.* Pa. t. & pple **kest**, **kested**. L16.
[ORIGIN Var. of CAST *verb*.]
= CAST *verb*; *esp.* (*a*) cast aside, throw away; (*b*) outdo.

kestrel /ˈkɛstr(ə)l/ *noun*. LME.
[ORIGIN Perh. from French *casserelle* dial. var. of *crécerelle*, †*cresserelle* (dial. *cristel*), from synon. *crécelle* lit. 'rattle', of imit. origin.]
Any of several falcons distinguished by the habit of hunting by sustained hovering; esp. *Falco tinnunculus*, widely distributed in the Old World, and (more fully ***American kestrel***) the American sparrowhawk, *F. sparverius*.
NANKEEN ***kestrel***.

Keswick /ˈkɛzɪk/ *noun*. E19.
[ORIGIN A town in Cumbria, NW England, where John Sander, who first introduced it, lived.]
In full ***Keswick codling***, ***Keswick codlin***. A variety of cooking apple which has a greenish skin tinged with red.

ket /kɛt/ *noun*[1]. *obsolete* exc. *dial.* ME.
[ORIGIN Old Norse *kjǫt* flesh (Icelandic *ket*, *kjöt*, Swedish *kött*, Danish *kød*, *kjød*).]
Raw flesh, carrion; *fig.* trash, rubbish.

ket /kɛt/ *noun*[2]. M20.
[ORIGIN from BRAC)KET *noun*: cf. BRA *noun*[2].]
QUANTUM MECHANICS. A vector in Hilbert space symbolized by |⟩, *esp.* one representing the state of a quantized system. Freq. ***ket vector***. Cf. BRA *noun*[2].

ket- *combining form* see KETO-.

keta /ˈkiːtə/ *noun*. Pl. same. E19.
[ORIGIN Russian.]
= CHUM *noun*[4].

ketal /ˈkiːtal/ *noun*. E20.
[ORIGIN from KETO- + -AL[2].]
CHEMISTRY. A compound of the general formula $R^1R^2C(OR^3)OR^4$, where the Rs are alkyl groups. Cf. ACETAL.

ketamine /ˈkɛtəmiːn, ˈkiːt-/ *noun*. M20.
[ORIGIN from KETO- + AMINE.]
A synthetic crystalline compound, $C_{13}H_{16}NOCl$, used as an anaesthetic and analgesic drug and also illicitly as a hallucinogen.

ketazine /ˈkiːtəziːn/ *noun*. L19.
[ORIGIN from KETO- + AZINE.]
CHEMISTRY. A compound of the general formula $R^1R^2C{=}NN{=}CR^3R^4$ (where the Rs are alkyl groups), made esp. by reaction of hydrazine with two ketone molecules.

ketch /kɛtʃ/ *noun*. M17.
[ORIGIN Later form of CATCH *noun*[2].]
NAUTICAL. A two-masted, fore-and-aft rigged sailing vessel (formerly used esp. for coastal trading) in which the mizzenmast is shorter than the mainmast and stepped forward of the rudder post.
bomb-ketch: see BOMB *noun* 3.

ketch *verb* see CATCH *verb*.

ketchup /ˈkɛtʃəp, -ʌp/ *noun*. Also *****catsup** /ˈkatsə-/, (now *rare*) **catchup** /ˈkatʃ-/. L17.
[ORIGIN Perh. from Chinese (Cantonese) *k'ē chap* tomato juice.]
A spicy sauce, now usu. of a thick consistency, made from tomatoes, or from mushrooms, walnuts, etc., and used as a relish with meat, fish, etc. Freq. with specification, as ***mushroom ketchup***, ***tomato ketchup***, etc.

ketene /ˈkiːtiːn/ *noun*. Also (earlier) **-en** /-(ə)n/. E20.
[ORIGIN from KETONE + -ENE.]
CHEMISTRY. A pungent colourless gas, $CH_2{=}C{=}O$, having wide applications in synthesis owing to its high reactivity; any substituted derivative of this, with the structure $:C{=}C{=}O$.

kethib /kəˈθiːb, -t-/ *noun*. Also **-bh**, ***K-***. M17.
[ORIGIN Hebrew *kĕṯīḇ* written.]
A traditional reading in the Hebrew text of the Old Testament and Hebrew Scriptures which is unintelligible or unsuitable for public reading and for which a *qere* is substituted.

Kethubim /kɛθuːˈviːm, kɛt-/ *noun pl.* L17.
[ORIGIN Hebrew *kĕṯuḇīm* writings.]
= HAGIOGRAPHA.

ketimine /ˈkiːtɪmiːn/ *noun*. E20.
[ORIGIN from KETO- + IMINE.]
CHEMISTRY. A compound of the general formula $RR'C{=}NH$ (where the Rs are alkyl groups), formed e.g. by the action of ammonia on a ketone.

keto- /ˈkiːtəʊ/ *combining form*. Before a vowel also **ket-**. In sense 2 also as attrib. adjective **keto**.
[ORIGIN from KETONE: see -O-.]
1 Chiefly CHEMISTRY & MEDICINE. Of a ketone or ketones.
2 CHEMISTRY. Designating or containing a ketone group, esp. as opp. to an enolic group.
■ **keto acid** *noun* a compound whose molecule contains both a ketone group and a carboxylic acid group E20. **ketoaciˈdosis** *noun* acidosis due to enhanced production of ketone bodies M20. **keto-compound** *noun* a compound containing a ketone group L19. **keto-ˈenol**, **keto-eˈnolic** *adjectives* designating tautomerism between keto and enol forms of a compound E20. **ketoˈgenesis** *noun* metabolic production of ketone bodies E20. **ketoˈgenic** *adjective* producing ketone bodies; *spec.* (of a diet) rich in fats and low in carbohydrates, sometimes used therapeutically in epilepsy to produce ketosis; ***ketogenic steroid***, ***17-ketogenic steroid***, a steroid which yields a (17-)ketosteroid on oxidation: E20. **α-ketoˈglutarate** *noun* a salt or ester of α-ketoglutaric acid E20. **α-ketogluˈtaric** *adjective*: ***α-ketoglutaric acid***, a dibasic keto acid, $HOOC{\cdot}CO{\cdot}CH_2{\cdot}CH_2{\cdot}COOH$, formed by oxidation and decarboxylation of isocitric acid in the Krebs cycle E20. **ketoˈhexose** *noun* a ketone with six carbon atoms L19. **ketoˈpentose** *noun* a ketone with five carbon atoms E20. **ketoˈsteroid** *noun* a steroid whose molecule contains a ketone group, *esp.* (in full ***17-ketosteroid***) one with this group at the carbon atom designated 17 M20. **keˈtoxime** *noun* an oxime of a ketone, a compound of the general formula $RR'C{=}NOH$ (where the Rs are alkyl groups) L19.

ketol /ˈkiːtɒl/ *noun*. L19.
[ORIGIN from KETO- + -OL.]
CHEMISTRY. A compound having a hydroxyl group attached to a carbon atom adjacent to or near a carbonyl group.
■ **keˈtolic** *adjective* M20.

ketolysis /kɪˈtɒlɪsɪs/ *noun*. M20.
[ORIGIN from KETO- + -LYSIS.]
BIOCHEMISTRY. The metabolic decomposition of ketone bodies.
■ **ketolytic** /kiːtə(ʊ)ˈlɪtɪk/ *adjective* of, pertaining to, or causing ketolysis E20.

ketonaemia /kiːtə(ʊ)ˈniːmɪə/ *noun*. Also *****-nemia**. E20.
[ORIGIN from KETONE + -AEMIA.]
MEDICINE. The presence of an abnormally high concentration of ketone bodies in the blood.

ketone /ˈkiːtəʊn/ *noun*. M19.
[ORIGIN German *Keton* alt. of *Aketon* ACETONE.]
CHEMISTRY. Any of a class of compounds typified by acetone, which have the general structure $RR'C{=}O$ (where the Rs are alkyl groups), and are formed esp. by the partial oxidation of secondary alcohols.
– COMB.: **ketone body** BIOCHEMISTRY each of the three related compounds acetone, acetoacetic acid, and β-hydroxybutyric acid, which are produced in fatty-acid and amino-acid metabolism; **ketone group** the carbonyl group $:C{=}O$ when attached to two carbon atoms in a molecule.
■ **ketonic** /kɪˈtɒnɪk/ *adjective* of or pertaining to ketones; of the nature of a ketone: L19. **ketoniˈzation** *noun* the process of changing from an enol form into a keto form M20. **ketonize** *verb intrans.* undergo ketonization M20.

ketonemia *noun* see KETONAEMIA.

ketonuria /kiːtə(ʊ)ˈnjʊərɪə/ *noun*. E20.
[ORIGIN from KETONE + -URIA.]
MEDICINE. The excretion of abnormally large amounts of ketone bodies in the urine.

ketosis /kɪˈtəʊsɪs/ *noun*. E20.
[ORIGIN from KETO- + -OSIS.]
MEDICINE. The increased metabolic production of ketone bodies, usu. associated with a predominance of fat metabolism as in starvation and in diabetes mellitus.
■ **ketotic** /kɪˈtɒtɪk/ *adjective* affected or associated with ketosis M20.

kettle /ˈkɛt(ə)l/ *noun*.
[ORIGIN Old English *ċetel*, (West Saxon) *ċietel* = Old Norse *ketill*, Old Saxon (Dutch) *ketel*, Old High German *kezzil* (German *Kessel*), from Germanic from Latin *catillus* dim. of *catinus* deep vessel for serving or cooking food, repl. in Middle English by forms from Old Norse.]
▸ **I 1** A vessel, usu. of metal, for boiling water or other liquids; *spec.* (*a*) a covered vessel with a spout and handle, used to boil water for domestic purposes (also ***tea kettle***);

K

(*b*) (in full ***fish kettle***) a long usu. oval pan for cooking fish in liquid. Also, a kettle and its contents; the contents of a kettle; as much as a kettle will hold, a kettleful. OE.

L. CODY She put the kettle on for tea.

electric kettle, ***jug kettle***, ***maslin kettle***, ***whistling kettle***, etc. **kettle of fish** (*a*) *Scot. dial.* = sense 2 above; (*b*) a state of affairs: in ***a pretty kettle of fish***, ***a fine kettle of fish***, ***a nice kettle of fish***, etc., a mess, an awkward state of affairs; ***a different kettle of fish***, ***another kettle of fish***, a different state of affairs or matter altogether.

2 A picnic or excursion at which fish is cooked out of doors. *Scot. dial.* L17.
3 A bowl-shaped or saucer-shaped vessel in which operations are carried out on low-melting metals, glass, plastics, etc., in the liquid state. E19.
4 A deep circular hollow scoured out in a rocky riverbed, under a glacier, etc.; a pothole. Also (PHYSICAL GEOGRAPHY) = ***kettle hole*** below. M19.
5 A watch. *slang* (chiefly *criminals'*). M19.
▸ †**II 6** = KETTLEDRUM. *rare* (Shakes.). Only in E17.
– COMB.: **kettle-bottom** (*a*) a hill with broad flat top and sloping sides; (*b*) NAUTICAL a ship with a flat floor; **kettle-holder** a piece of cloth etc. used to protect the hand from the heat of a kettle handle; **kettle hole** PHYSICAL GEOGRAPHY a deep, often circular depression in the ground formed by the melting of an ice block trapped in glacial deposits; **kettle lake** PHYSICAL GEOGRAPHY a lake in a kettle hole; **kettle moraine** PHYSICAL GEOGRAPHY a moraine in which there are numerous kettle holes.
■ **kettleful** *noun* as much as a kettle will hold M19. **kettler** *noun* †(*a*) a person who mends kettles; (*b*) a colour-mixer's assistant who boils dyestuffs: E17.

kettledrum /ˈkɛt(ə)ldrʌm/ *noun & verb*. M16.
[ORIGIN from KETTLE *noun* + DRUM *noun*[1].]
▸ **A** *noun*. **1** MUSIC. A percussion instrument, a hollow brass or copper hemisphere over the edge of which parchment or (now) plastic is stretched and tuned to a definite note. Formerly also, a player on this instrument, a kettledrummer. M16.
2 An afternoon tea party, smaller than a drum (DRUM *noun*[1] 4). *colloq.* (now *hist.*). M19.
▸ **B** *verb intrans.* Infl. **-mm-**. Beat a kettledrum; make a noise like a kettledrum. M19.
■ **kettledrummer** *noun* a person who plays the kettledrum M17.

kettle-pins, **kettles** *nouns* var. of KITTLE-PINS, KITTLES.

kettle-stitch /ˈkɛt(ə)lstɪtʃ/ *noun*. E19.
[ORIGIN German *Kettelstich*, from *Kettel* small chain + *Stich* stitch.]
In bookbinding: a knot made at the head and tail of a book in sewing it, by which the thread holding one sheet is fastened to the thread in the next.

ketubah /kətuːˈbɑː/ *noun*. M19.
[ORIGIN Hebrew *kĕtubbāh* written statement.]
A formal Jewish marriage contract which includes financial provisions for the wife in the event of the husband's death or of divorce.

ketyl /ˈkiːtʌɪl, -tɪl/ *noun*. E20.
[ORIGIN from KETO- + -YL.]
CHEMISTRY. A salt of a metal with a free-radical anion of the formula RR′CO⁻ (where the Rs are alkyl groups), formed by dissolving a metal in a ketone.

Keuper /ˈkɔɪpə/ *noun & adjective*. M19.
[ORIGIN German, orig. a miners' term.]
GEOLOGY. (Designating or pertaining to) a European series of sedimentary rocks of Upper Triassic age, represented in England chiefly by marls and sandstones.

keurboom /ˈkɪəbʊəm/ *noun*. M18.
[ORIGIN Afrikaans, from *keur* choice + *boom* tree.]
Any of several small southern African leguminous trees of the genus *Virgilia*, esp. *V. capensis*, with pinnate leaves and drooping clusters of usu. mauve scented flowers.

keV *abbreviation*.
Kilo-electronvolt.

kevel /ˈkɛv(ə)l/ *noun*[1]. *obsolete* exc. *Scot. & N. English*. Also **kewl** /kjuːl/. ME.
[ORIGIN Old Norse *kefli* round stick, small roller, gag, rel. to *kafli* piece.]
1 A bit for a horse's mouth. Also, a gag. ME.
2 A rounded piece of wood; a staff, a cudgel. E19.

kevel /ˈkɛv(ə)l/ *noun*[2]. ME.
[ORIGIN Old Northern French *keville* = Old French & mod. French *cheville* pin, peg.]
1 A pin or hasp for fastening something. *obsolete* exc. *hist.* ME.
2 NAUTICAL. A large cleat fitted to the gunwale of a ship and used in belaying ropes. ME.

kevel /ˈkɛv(ə)l/ *noun*[3]. *Scot. & N. English*. ME.
[ORIGIN Unknown.]
A kind of hammer for rough-hewing or breaking stone. Also ***kevel-hammer***, ***kevel-mell***.

Kevenhuller /ˈkɛv(ə)nhʊlə/ *noun*. *obsolete* exc. *hist.* Also **Khev-**. M18.
[ORIGIN A. von *Khevenhüller* (1683–1744), Austrian field marshal.]
1 In full ***Kevenhuller cock***. A high peaked cock given to hats worn by men in the mid 18th cent. M18.
2 In full ***Kevenhuller hat***. A hat worn cocked in this fashion. M18.

kevir *noun* var. of KAVIR.

Kevlar /ˈkɛvlɑː/ *noun*. L20.
[ORIGIN Unknown.]
(Proprietary name for) a synthetic fibre of high-tensile strength used esp. as a reinforcing material for rubber in tyres etc.

kewl *noun* var. of KEVEL *noun*[1].

kewpie /ˈkjuːpi/ *noun*. Orig. *US*. Also **K-**, **cupie**. E20.
[ORIGIN from CUP(ID + -IE.]
In full ***kewpie doll***. (Proprietary name for) a chubby doll with a curl or topknot on its head; *transf.* a person resembling such a doll.

kex /kɛks/ *noun*. Now *dial.* ME.
[ORIGIN Perh. of Celtic origin: cf. Welsh *cegid*, Cornish *kegaz*, Breton *kegid*. See also KECK *noun*, KECKSIE.]
1 The dry, usu. hollow stalk of a large umbellifer (as cow parsley, hogweed, wild angelica, etc.) or similar plant. ME. ▸†**b** Such stalks collectively or as a material. M16–E18.
2 An umbelliferous plant with a hollow stalk. LME.
†**3** The hard case of a chrysalis. Only in 17.
†**4** A weak spiritless person. E17–E18.
■ **kexy** *adjective* like a kex; dry and brittle; withered, sapless: E17.

key /kiː/ *noun*[1] & *adjective*.
[ORIGIN Old English *cǣġ*, *cæġe* = Old Frisian *kei*, *kay*, of unknown origin.]
▸ **A** *noun* **I 1** An instrument fitting into a lock for locking or unlocking it, usu. made of metal and with more or less elaborate incisions etc. to fit the wards of the lock; a similar instrument for operating a switch in the form of a lock. OE.

A. S. NEILL I tried the lock with one of my own keys, and managed to open the trunk. W. WHARTON She has a key and lets herself in. J. GORES A. . Mustang with the driver's window open and the key in the ignition.

2 A key as representing the power of custody, control, admission, etc.; a key as a symbol of office. OE.
3 THEOLOGY. [With allus. to *Matthew* 16:19] *sing.* & (usu.) in *pl.* The ecclesiastical authority regarded by Roman Catholics as conferred by Christ on St Peter and transmitted to the Popes as his successors; the disciplinary or spiritual power of priests as successors of the Apostles. OE.

LD MACAULAY Lewis . . was . . accused by the Pope of encroaching on the spiritual power of the keys.

4 a A thing that opens up the way to something; *esp.* a sure means to or *to* a desired objective. OE. ▸**b** A place which from the strategic advantages of its position gives control over a territory, sea, etc. LME.

a R. FORD A supply of cigars, these keys to Spanish hearts. C. GEBLER Self-understanding is the key to any sort of self-improvement. **b** T. MO Those heights are the keys to the city.

5 A solution or explanation of what is unknown, mysterious, or obscure; *spec.* (*a*) an alphabetical or other system for the interpretation of a cipher, an allegorical statement, etc.; (*b*) a text explaining the abbreviations or symbols used in a book, the figures in a photograph or picture, etc.; (*c*) (a part of) a book containing solutions of mathematical or other problems, translations of exercises in a foreign language, etc. OE. ▸**b** CHESS. A move in the solution of a problem which determines the style of the whole solution. E19. ▸**c** A scheme for identifying a plant, animal, etc., by selecting one alternative in each of successive pairs or sets of contrasted characters. M19. ▸**d** The device used to key or distinguish an advertisement. Orig. *US*. E20.

F. BURNEY I felt his meaning, though I had no key to it.

6 MUSIC. A system of notes definitely related to each other, based on a particular note and predominating in a piece of music; the sum of melodic and harmonic relations existing between the tones of such a system, tonality. Formerly also = KEYNOTE *noun* 1. LME.

J. PLAYFORD To shew in what Key the Song was set, and how each Musical Key had relation . . to another. A. HOPKINS Certain keys have emotional connotations in composers' minds.

major key, ***minor key***, ***natural key***, etc.

7 *transf.* & *fig.* **a** (High or low) tone (of the voice); pitch. L16. ▸**b** Intensity (of feeling or action); (prevailing) tone or style (of thought or expression). Freq. in ***in key***, ***out of key*** below. L16. ▸**c** Tone or relative intensity of colour. M19.

a W. BLACK Loudly discoursing—in a high shrill and plaintive key—of his troubles. **b** M. B. KEATINGE In a high key of spirits in consequence of the reception he was favoured with. W. STUBBS The writs to the barons are shorter but in the same key. **c** J. RUSKIN Harmonies of amber-colour and purple are full of exquisite beauty in their chosen key.

▸ **II** A mechanical device resembling the key of a lock.
8 a A thing that holds together or joins the parts of a structure; *esp.* the keystone of an arch. ME. ▸†**b** *fig.* A leading person or thing; *esp.* a cardinal point or principle. M16–L17. ▸**c** The part of a first coat of plaster which passes between the laths and secures the rest; the roughness of a surface which enables plaster etc. to adhere to it. E19.

9 A pin, bolt, or wedge inserted between other pieces, esp. to fasten various parts together; = COTTER *noun*[1]. LME.
10 a Each of the levers or buttons pressed down or otherwise moved by the fingers to produce the notes in playing any of various musical instruments, as an organ, piano, flute, concertina, etc. L15. ▸**b** Each of a set of levers or buttons pressed by the fingers to operate a typewriter, word processor, computer terminal, etc. Also, a lever etc. operating a mechanical device for making or breaking an electric circuit, used in telegraphy etc. M19.

a J. BALDWIN He touched a black key on the piano and it made a dull sound.

b carriage return key, ***shift key***, etc.

11 An instrument for grasping and turning a screw, peg, or nut, esp. (*a*) for winding a clock, watch, or clockwork machine, (*b*) for turning the wrest pins of a piano, (*c*) for turning a valve or stopcock. E17. ▸**b** An instrument for extracting teeth, esp. molars. *obsolete* exc. *hist.* M19.
▸ **III 12** In *pl.* More fully ***House of Keys***. A body of twenty-four members which forms the elective branch of the legislature of the Isle of Man. LME.
▸ **IV 13** The dry winged fruit of an ash, elm, sycamore, etc., usu. growing in bunches; = SAMARA. E16.
– PHRASES ETC.: **golden key** a bribe to obtain admission. **Greek key** each of the bends of which a Greek fret consists, suggestive of a key. ***high-key***: see HIGH *adjective*. ***House of Keys***: see sense 12 above. **in key** in harmony, consonant (*with*). **key of the sea** the pelican's foot shell. ***latchings key***: see LATCHING 2. ***low-key***: see LOW *adjective*. ***master key***: see MASTER *noun*[1] & *adjective*. **out of key** out of harmony, not consonant (*with*). **silver key** = ***golden key*** above. ***SKELETON key***. **St Peter's keys** the cross keys borne in the papal arms. ***under lock and key***: see LOCK *noun*[2].
▸ **B** *attrib.* or as *adjective*. Of paramount or crucial importance. Cf. earlier KEYNOTE, KEYSTONE. L19.

Physics Bulletin Two ideas were key in the discovery of the kinoform. S. MIDDLETON He'd assembled a jig-saw only to find that key pieces were missing. S. KITZINGER The sexual tie is a key one in defining who a woman is.

– COMB. & SPECIAL COLLOCATIONS: **key-block** a block used in the printing of chiaroscuro and colour pictures to give the outline, and to provide a guide for the accurate registration of the tint or colour blocks; **key-bugle**: fitted with keys to increase the number of its sounds; **key-clog** a piece of wood tied to a key, to prevent its being lost; **key-cold** *adjective* (now *rare*) extremely cold (*lit.* & *fig.*), *esp.* cold in death; **key-colour** the leading colour in a picture; **key-drawing** (in lithography and colour printing) an outline drawing which is transferred on to the key plate and used as a guide to printing the colours; **key grip** CINEMATOGRAPHY & TELEVISION the person in a film crew who is in charge of the camera equipment; **keyholder** a person who keeps the key or keys of a workshop, factory, etc.; **key industry** an industry essential to the carrying on of others; **key light** the main source of light in a photograph or film; **keylogger** a computer program that records every keystroke made by a computer user, esp. in order to gain fraudulent access to passwords and other confidential information; **key man** a person who plays a leading or important role in a group, an industry, etc.; **key map**: in bare outline, to simplify the use of a full map; **key money** a payment required from an incoming tenant for the provision of a key to the premises; **key move** CHESS = sense A.5b above; **keypad** a miniature keyboard or set of buttons for operating a portable electronic device, a telephone, etc.; **keypal** *slang* a person with whom one becomes friendly by exchanging emails; **key plate** (*a*) a plate of metal surrounding a keyhole; (*b*) (in colour-printing from a metal surface) the outline plate answering to a keystone in lithography; **key ring** a ring on which keys can be hung; **key signature** MUSIC a group of sharps or flats after the clef at the beginning of each staff, indicating the key in which the piece is to be performed; **Key Stage** (in the UK) any of the four fixed stages into which the national curriculum is divided, each having its own prescribed course of study; **keyway** MECHANICS a groove cut in a shaft or in the boss of a wheel to receive a key; **keyword** (*a*) a word serving as a key to a code, cipher, etc.; (*b*) a word or thing of great importance or significance; *spec.* (in an information-retrieval system) any informative word in the title or text of a document etc. chosen as indicating its main content; ***keyword-in-context*** *adjective*, designating an index or concordance in which keywords are listed alphabetically, preceded and followed by a fixed amount of context; **key worker** an employee who provides a vital service, esp. in the police, health, or education sectors.
– NOTE: Until *c* 1700 pronounced to rhyme with *day*, *way*, etc. The modern pronunc. is app. of northern origin.

key /kiː/ *noun*[2]. L17.
[ORIGIN Var. of CAY, infl. in spelling and pronunc. by *key* var. of QUAY *noun*.]
A low island, sandbank, or reef, such as one of those common in the W. Indies or off the coast of Florida.
– COMB.: **Key lime** [named after the Florida *Keys*] a small yellowish lime with a sharp flavour.

†**key** *noun*[3] see QUAY *noun*.

key /kiː/ *verb*. LME.
[ORIGIN from KEY *noun*[1].]
▸ **I** *verb trans.* **1** Lock with a key; lock up; fasten securely. *rare*. LME.
2 Fasten by means of a pin, wedge, bolt, etc. L16. ▸**b** Cause (plaster, glued surfaces, pigments, etc.) to adhere; roughen (a surface) to help the adhesion of plaster etc. L19.
3 Regulate the pitch of (the strings of a musical instrument, a stringed instrument); *fig.* give a certain tone or intensity to (a feeling or thoughts). Foll. by *up*: stimulate,

K

raise to a high pitch; cause to be nervous, excited, or tense. Foll. by *down*: lower in pitch or intensity. **M17.** ▸**b** Fix the strings of a musical instrument on the pegs or keys. **L19.**
4 Insert the keystone in (an arch). Also foll. by *in*. Now *rare* or *obsolete*. **M18.**
5 Distinguish (an advertisement) by some device, as the form of the address given, which will identify the publication generating particular responses. Orig. *US*. **E20.**
6 *ELECTRONICS*. Switch from one state to another (usu. on or off), by means of a key or relay, as in telegraphic transmission; provide with a means for doing this. **E20.**
7 Set out (kinds of plant, animal, etc.) in a key for the purposes of identification (freq. foll. by *out*). Also, identify by means of a key. **E20.**
8 Cause to fit *in with* something else or *into* a group, pattern, etc. **M20.**
9 Transfer or operate on (data), set (copy), or produce (text), by manipulating the keys of a keyboard. Also foll. by *in* etc. **M20.**
▸ **II** *verb intrans.* **10** Fit *into* a group or *in with* something else. **M20.**

E. BOWEN Lean young skyscrapers.. key in with Rome's general virtuosity.

11 Be identified as or *as* a given species if one follows a key. Usu. foll. by *out*. **M20.**
■ **keyer** *noun* a person who or thing which keys something, *spec.* (*ELECTRONICS*) a device for switching a signal supply on and off **M20.**

keyaki /kɪˈɑːki/ *noun*. **E20.**
[ORIGIN Japanese.]
(The pale lustrous wood of) a Japanese tree, *Zelkova serrata*, of the elm family.

keyboard /ˈkiːbɔːd/ *noun & verb*. **E19.**
[ORIGIN from KEY *noun*[1] + BOARD *noun*.]
▸ **A** *noun*. **1** *MUSIC*. A row of keys for producing the notes in an organ, piano, or similar instrument. **E19.** ▸**b** In *pl*. Keyboard instruments. *colloq.* **L20.**
shifting keyboard: see SHIFTING *adjective* 1.
2 The set of keys on a typewriter, computer, etc. **M19.**
– COMB.: **keyboard instrument** a musical instrument having a keyboard or keyboards.
▸ **B** *verb trans. & intrans.* Enter (data) by means of a keyboard. **M20.**
■ **keyboarder** *noun* a person who operates a (computer) keyboard, a person who enters data on a keyboard **M20.** **keyboardist** *noun* a player on a keyboard instrument **L20.**

keyed /kiːd/ *adjective*. **M16.**
[ORIGIN from KEY *noun*[1], *verb*: see -ED[2], -ED[1].]
1 Having a key or keys. **M16.**
2 Secured, fastened, or strengthened by means of a key; (of an arch) constructed with a keystone. **E19.**
3 ***keyed-up***, nervous, excited, tense. **L19.**

keyhole /ˈkiːhəʊl/ *noun & verb*. **L16.**
[ORIGIN from KEY *noun*[1] + HOLE *noun*[1].]
▸ **A** *noun*. **1** A hole by which a key is inserted in a lock. **L16.**

L. CODY Do come in.. unless you want to stay outside with your ear to the keyhole.

2 In carpentry or engineering: a hole made to receive a peg or key. **E18.**
– COMB.: **keyhole limpet** a limpet of the family Fissurellidae, having a shell with an aperture at the apex; **keyhole saw** a saw with a long narrow blade for cutting small holes such as keyholes; **keyhole surgery**: performed through a very small hole with the aid of a fibrescope and special instruments.
▸ **B** *verb intrans.* Of a bullet: strike the target in such a way as to make a keyhole-shaped hole. **L19.**

keyless /ˈkiːlɪs/ *adjective*. **E19.**
[ORIGIN from KEY *noun*[1] + -LESS.]
Having no key or keys.

Keynesian /ˈkeɪnzɪən/ *adjective & noun*. **M20.**
[ORIGIN from *Keynes* (see below) + -IAN.]
▸ **A** *adjective*. Of or pertaining to the English economist John Maynard Keynes (1883–1946) or his economic theories, esp. regarding state control of the economy through money and taxes. **M20.**
▸ **B** *noun*. An adherent of Keynes's economic theories. **M20.**
■ **Keynesianism** *noun* **M20.**

keynote /ˈkiːnəʊt/ *noun & verb*. **M18.**
[ORIGIN from KEY *noun*[1] + NOTE *noun*[2].]
▸ **A** *noun*. **1** *MUSIC*. The first note of the scale of any key, which forms the basis of, and gives its name to, the key; the tonic. **M18.**
2 *fig.* The prevailing tone or idea of a speech, piece of writing, course of action, etc. **L18.**

M. SEYMOUR-SMITH The key-note of her character was obstinacy.

– COMB.: **keynote address**, **keynote speech** (orig. *US*) a speech, usu. an opening address, designed to state the main concerns of a conference or (at a political rally) arouse enthusiasm or promote unity.
▸ **B** *verb trans.* Express the prevailing tone or idea of (something); deliver the keynote speech of (a conference etc.). *colloq.* (orig. *US*). **M20.**
■ **keynoter** *noun* (orig. *US colloq.*) a person who delivers a keynote speech **E20.**

keypunch /ˈkiːpʌn(t)ʃ/ *noun & verb*. **M20.**
[ORIGIN from KEY *noun*[1] + PUNCH *noun*[1].]
▸ **A** *noun*. A keyboard device for transferring data by means of punched holes or notches in cards or paper tape. **M20.**
▸ **B** *verb trans. & intrans.* Produce holes or notches in (a card or paper tape) by means of a keypunch; put (text) into the form of punched cards or paper tape by means of a keypunch. **M20.**
■ **keypunchable** *adjective* able to be represented on punched cards or paper tape **L20.** **keypuncher** *noun* (*a*) = KEYPUNCH *noun*; (*b*) a person who operates a keypunch: **M20.**

keyster *noun* var. of KEISTER.

keystone /ˈkiːstəʊn/ *noun & verb*. **M17.**
[ORIGIN from KEY *noun*[1] + STONE *noun*.]
▸ **A** *noun*. **1** The wedge-shaped block or central voussoir at the summit of an arch built of stone. **M17.**
2 *fig.* The central principle of a system, course of action, etc., on which all the rest depends. **E19.**

Times The Third Reich.. would have as its keystone the conception of the people and the national idea.

3 *PRINTING*. In colour lithography, a stone which bears the key-drawing, not normally used in the printing. **M19.**
4 (Usu. **K-**.) [from *Keystone Kop* below.] A police officer. Usu. in *pl*. *N. Amer. slang*. **M20.**
– COMB.: **keystone effect** *CINEMATOGRAPHY & TELEVISION* a form of distortion by which a rectangular object produces a trapezial image, resulting from the line of projection (of light or electrons) not being normal to the screen; **Keystone Kop** a comically bumbling policeman featured in films produced by the Keystone Film Company (formed 1919); usu. in *pl.*; **Keystone State** *US* the state of Pennsylvania, the seventh of the original thirteen states.
▸ **B** *verb trans.* *CINEMATOGRAPHY & TELEVISION*. Distort by a keystone effect. Chiefly as ***keystoning*** *verbal noun*. **M20.**

keystroke /ˈkiːstrəʊk/ *noun & verb*. **E20.**
[ORIGIN from KEY *noun*[1] + STROKE *noun*[1].]
▸ **A** *noun*. A depression of a key on a keyboard, esp. as a measure of work. **E20.**
▸ **B** *verb trans.* = KEY *verb* 9. **M20.**
■ **keystroker** *noun* a person who operates the keys of a keyboard, esp. of a keypunch **L20.**

KG *abbreviation*[1].
Knight (of the Order) of the Garter.

kg *abbreviation*[2].
Kilogram(s).

KGB *abbreviation*. *hist.*
Russian *Komitet Gosudarstvennoĭ Bezopasnosti* Committee of State Security, the state security police of the former USSR 1954–91.

kgotla /kəˈgɒtlə/ *noun*. Also (earlier) ***kotla*** /ˈkɒtlə/, ***khotla***. **M19.**
[ORIGIN Setswana.]
An assembly of tribal elders among certain Bantu-speaking peoples; a place where such assemblies are held. Cf. KUTA.

Kgs *abbreviation*.
Kings (in the Bible).

khabar /ˈkʌbə/ *noun*. Also ***khubber***. **M19.**
[ORIGIN Urdu & Persian *ḵabar* from Arabic]
In the Indian subcontinent: information, news, rumour.

khad *noun* var. of KHUD.

khadar /ˈkɑːdə/ *noun*. Also **-ir**. **M19.**
[ORIGIN Hindi *khādar*.]
In the Indian subcontinent: a flood plain; land susceptible to flooding.

khadi /ˈkadi/ *noun & adjective*. Also **khaddar** /ˈkadə/. **E20.**
[ORIGIN Punjabi *khaddar*, Hindi *khādar*, *khādī*.]
(Made of) homespun handwoven cotton (or silk) cloth of the Indian subcontinent.

khadir *noun* var. of KHADAR.

khair /ˈkʌɪə/ *noun*. **M19.**
[ORIGIN Hindi *khair*, Sanskrit *khadira*.]
An Indian leguminous tree, *Acacia catechu*, from which catechu is obtained.

khaki /ˈkɑːki/ *adjective & noun*. **M19.**
[ORIGIN Urdu *ḵākī* dust-coloured, from *ḵāk* dust from Persian.]
▸ **A** *adjective*. Dust-coloured; dull brownish yellow. Also, made of khaki. **M19.**

B. GELDOF Now in Africa he donned his casual lightweight khaki tropical gear. T. O. ECHEWA Green khaki shorts with frayed hems.

▸ **B** *noun*. **1** Dust-colour; dull brownish yellow. **M19.**
2 A dull yellowish-brown fabric, orig. of stout twilled cotton, later also of wool, etc., used esp. for army uniforms. **M19.**

Sunday Express Some are in civilian clothes, the rest in army khaki.

3 A soldier dressed in khaki; *spec.* (*S. Afr. slang*) a British soldier in the Boer War of 1899–1902. **L19.**
4 In *pl.* Khaki trousers; khaki clothes. **M20.**
– COMB.: **khaki bos** /bɒs/, **khaki bush** *S. Afr.* any of several weeds of the composite family supposedly introduced by British troops in the Boer War; esp. *Tagetes minuta*, native to S. America; **khaki election** a general election won by appeal to war spirit or to the military vote; *spec.* (*hist.*) that won in 1900, during the Boer War, by the Conservatives under Lord Salisbury; **khaki weed** a S. American plant of the amaranth family, *Alternanthera repens*, naturalized in southern Africa and Australia.
■ **khakied** *adjective* dressed in khaki **E20.**

khalassi /kəˈlasi/ *noun*. Also **-ashi**, **-asi**, **ka-**; †**clashee**, †**clashy**. **L18.**
[ORIGIN Urdu *ḵalāṣī*, *kalāšī*.]
A native of the Indian subcontinent of inferior rank, *esp.* one employed as a seaman.

Khaldian /ˈkaldɪən/ *noun & adjective*. **L19.**
[ORIGIN from *Khaldis*, *Khaldi* the supreme god in Urartu + -AN, -IAN.]
▸ **A** *noun*. **1** = URARTIAN *noun* 1. **L19.**
2 = URARTIAN *noun* 2. **E20.**
▸ **B** *adjective*. = URARTIAN *adjective*. **E20.**

khalif *noun* var. of CALIPH.

khalifa /kəˈliːfə/ *noun*. In sense 2 also **ch-**. **E18.**
[ORIGIN Arabic *ḵalīfa*: see CALIPH.]
1 Chiefly *hist.* = CALIPH. **E18.**
2 A Malay ceremony in which a dancer pierces his person with swords, orig. as a demonstration of Islamic faith. *S. Afr.* **M19.**

khalifate *noun* var. of CALIPHATE.

Khalkha /ˈkɑːlkə/ *noun & adjective*. Also **-ka**. **L19.**
[ORIGIN Unknown.]
▸ **A** *noun*. **1** A member of a section of the Mongolian people, constituting the bulk of the population of Outer Mongolia. **L19.**
2 The language of these people, a demotic form of Mongolian adopted as the official language of the Mongolian People's Republic. **E20.**
▸ **B** *attrib.* or as *adjective*. Of or pertaining to the Khalkhas or their language. **L19.**

khalsa /ˈkɑːlsə/ *noun*. Also **-ah**. **L18.**
[ORIGIN Urdu from Persian *ḵāl(i)ṣa* crown land, revenue department, from fem. of Arabic *ḵāliṣ* pure, free (from), belonging (to).]
1 The governmental revenue department in a state in the Indian subcontinent. **L18.**
2 (**K-**.) The fraternity of warriors into which Sikh males are initiated at puberty. **L18.**

khama *noun* var. of KAAMA.

khamsin /ˈkamsɪn/ *noun*. Also **ham-** /ˈham-/. **L17.**
[ORIGIN Arabic *ḵamāsīn*, from *ḵamsīn*, *-sūn* fifty (see below).]
An oppressive hot southerly wind, which blows in Egypt at intervals for about fifty days in March, April, and May, and fills the air with sand from the desert.

khan /kɑːn, kan/ *noun*[1]. **LME.**
[ORIGIN Old French *chan* or medieval Latin *ca(a)nus* from Turkic (hence Mongolian, Arabic, Persian) *ḵān* lord, prince, identified with *ḵa'an* var. of *ḵāḵān* supreme ruler: cf. CHAGAN, CHAM *noun*.]
Orig., any of the various successors of Genghis Khan, supreme rulers over Turkish, Tartar, and Mongol peoples and emperors of China in the Middle Ages; later, an Ottoman sultan. Also, a principal noble of the Mughal empire; a ruler, official, or man of rank in Afghanistan, Persia, or other Muslim countries of central Asia. Formerly also used as a polite form of address affixed to a Muslim name (and now a common surname among Muslims of the Indian subcontinent).
■ **khanate** *noun* (*hist.*) a district governed by a khan; the position of khan: **L18.**

khan /kɑːn, kan/ *noun*[2]. Also **han** /hɑːn/, †**cane**. **LME.**
[ORIGIN Persian *ḵān*.]
A caravanserai.

khana /ˈkɑːnə/ *noun*. **E19.**
[ORIGIN Hindi *khānā*, from Sanskrit *khād-* eat.]
In the Indian subcontinent: food; a meal.

khanda *noun* var. of KHANJAR.

khanga /ˈkaŋgə/ *noun*. Also **kanga**. **M20.**
[ORIGIN Kiswahili.]
In E. Africa: a fabric printed in various colours and designs with borders, used esp. for women's clothing.

khanjar /ˈkandʒə/ *noun*. Also **han-** /ˈhan-/, **khanda** /ˈkandə/. **E17.**
[ORIGIN (Persian, Turkish, Urdu) *ḵanjar* from Arabic]
A dagger worn in certain Muslim countries, esp. in southern Arabia.

khanjee /ˈkɑːndʒiː/ *noun*. Also **han-** /ˈhɑːn-/. **M19.**
[ORIGIN Turkish *hānji*, formed as KHAN *noun*[2] + *-ji* agent-suffix.]
The keeper of a caravanserai.

khansama /ˈkɑːnsəmɑː, kɑːnˈsɑːmə/ *noun*. Also ***-man*** /-mən/. **E17.**
[ORIGIN Urdu *ḵānsāmā*, Urdu & Persian *ḵānsāmān*, from *ḵān* master, KHAN *noun*[1] + *sāmān* household goods.]
In the Indian subcontinent: a male servant combining the functions of house steward and butler.

K

Khanty /ˈkanti/ *noun & adjective*. Also **-ti**. Pl. of noun same. M20.
[ORIGIN Russian from Khanty *Xanti*.]
A member of, or pertaining to, a people living in the Ob River basin in western Siberia; (of) the Ob-Ugrian language of this people. Earlier called ***Ostyak***.

khanum /ˈkɑːnəm/ *noun*. M17.
[ORIGIN Persian *ḵānum* from Turkish *hanım*, from *hān* KHAN *noun*[1] + *-ım* 1st person sing. possess. suffix.]
In certain parts of the Middle East and the Indian subcontinent: a lady of high rank, *hist.* the wife of a khan. Now also used as a polite form of address affixed to a Muslim woman's name.

khapra /ˈkaprə/ *noun*. L19.
[ORIGIN Hindi *khaprā*, from Sanskrit *kharpara* thief.]
In full ***khapra beetle***. A small brownish-black dermestid beetle, *Trogoderma granarium*, native to India and found widely elsewhere as a pest of stored grain.

kharif /kaˈriːf/ *noun*. E19.
[ORIGIN Persian & Urdu from Arabic *ḵarīf* autumn, autumnal rain.]
In the Indian subcontinent: the autumn crop, sown at the beginning of the summer rains.

Kharoshti /kəˈrɒʃti/ *noun*. L19.
[ORIGIN Sanskrit *kharoṣṭī* from Semitic: cf. Hebrew *ḥāraṣ* cut, engrave.]
One of the two oldest alphabets in the Indian subcontinent, derived from Aramaic and used for about seven centuries from *c* 300 BC in NW India and central Asia. Cf. BRAHMI.

Kharri *noun*, **Kharrian** *adjective & noun* vars. of HURRI, HURRIAN.

Khasi /ˈkɑːsi/ *noun & adjective*. Also **Khasia** /ˈkɑːsɪə/, **Khasiya** /ˈkɑːsɪjə/. L18.
[ORIGIN from the *Khasi* Hills (see below).]
▸ **A** *noun*. **1** A member of a Mongolian people inhabiting the Khasi and Jaintia Hills in NE India. L18.
2 The Mon-Khmer language of this people. M19.
▸ **B** *attrib.* or as *adjective*. Of or pertaining to the Khasis or their language. E19.

Khaskura /ˈkaskʊrə/ *noun*. E20.
[ORIGIN Newari *Khas-kurā*, from Sanskrit *Khasa*, name of a people + Newari *kurā* speech.]
The Nepali language.

khassadar /ˈkasədɑː/ *noun*. E20.
[ORIGIN Afghan Persian *ḵāṣṣa-dār*, from *ḵāṣṣa* possessions of the authorities + *-dār* holding, holder: cf. Persian *ḵāṣṣa-bardār* (from *bardār* raiser).]
An irregular tribal police officer on the North-West Frontier of India.

khat /kɑːt/ *noun*. Also **kat**, **qat**. M19.
[ORIGIN Arabic *qāt*.]
A shrub, *Catha edulis*, of the spindle tree family, cultivated in Arabia for its leaves, which are chewed or infused as a stimulant; the narcotic drug obtained from these leaves.

khatib /kaˈtiːb/ *noun*. E17.
[ORIGIN Arabic *ḵaṭīb*.]
A Muslim preacher, with responsibility for delivering the *khutbah*.

Khatri /ˈkʌtriː, ˈkatri/ *noun*. M17.
[ORIGIN Hindi *khat(t)rī* from Sanskrit *kṣatriya* KSHATRIYA.]
= KSHATRIYA.

Khatti *noun* var. of HATTI.

khatun /ˈkɑːtuːn/ *noun*. M19.
[ORIGIN Turkic *katūn*, Persian *ḵātūn* perh. from Sogdian *xwat'yn* queen.]
In certain parts of the Middle East: a lady of high rank; *hist.* a queen. Also used as an honorific title affixed to a Muslim woman's name.

khaya /ˈkʌɪjə, ˈkeɪjə/ *noun*. E20.
[ORIGIN mod. Latin (see below), from Wolof *xay*.]
Any of various tropical African trees of the genus *Khaya* (family Meliaceae); the timber of such a tree (also called ***African mahogany***).

khayal /kəˈjɑːl/ *noun*. Also ***khyal*** /kɪˈɑːl/. L19.
[ORIGIN Hindi *khayāl*.]
A traditional type of song from the northern part of the Indian subcontinent, usu. containing two main themes.

Khazar /kəˈzɑː/ *noun & adjective*. Also **Ch-**. M19.
[ORIGIN Unknown.]
▸ **A** *noun*. A member of a Turkish people who occupied a large part of southern Russia from the 8th to the 11th cent. and who converted to Judaism. M19.
▸ **B** *attrib.* or as *adjective*. Of or pertaining to the Khazars. L19.

khazi /ˈkɑːzi/ *noun*. *slang*. Also **karzy**. M20.
[ORIGIN Alt. of Italian *casa* house.]
A lavatory.

kheda /ˈkeɪdə, ˈkɛdə/ *noun*. Also **keddah**, **kheddah**. L18.
[ORIGIN Assamese & Bengali *khedā*.]
In the north of the Indian subcontinent: an enclosure for the capture of wild elephants.

Khedive /kɪˈdiːv/ *noun*. M19.
[ORIGIN French *khédive* from Ottoman Turkish *kedıv* from Persian *ḵadīw* prince, var. of *ḵudaiw* petty god, from *ḵudā* god.]
hist. (The title of) the viceroy of Egypt under Turkish rule, 1867–1914.
■ **Khedival**, **Khedivial** *adjectives* of or pertaining to the Khedive L19. **Khedivate**, **Khediviate** *nouns* the office or authority of the Khedive L19.

kheer /ˈkɪə/ *noun*. *Indian*. M19.
[ORIGIN Hindi *khīr* from Sanskrit *kṣīrī*.]
An Indian dessert consisting of rice and sugar boiled in milk or coconut milk, often flavoured with cardamom and ground nuts.

khet /keɪt/ *noun*. M19.
[ORIGIN Hindi from Sanskrit *kṣetra*.]
In the Indian subcontinent: a tract of cultivated land; a plantation.

Khevenhuller *noun* var. of KEVENHULLER.

khidmutgar /ˈkɪdmʌtgɑː/ *noun*. Also **khit-** /ˈkɪt-/. M18.
[ORIGIN Urdu from Persian *ḵidmatgār*, from Arabic *ḵidma(t)* service + Persian *-gār* agent-suffix.]
In the Indian subcontinent: a male servant who waits at table.

Khilafat /kɪˈlɑːfət/ *noun & adjective*. E20.
[ORIGIN Persian, Turkish from Arabic *ḵilāfa(t)* caliphate.]
▸ **A** *noun*. The spiritual and temporal headship of Islam. E20.
▸ **B** *attrib.* or as *adjective*. *hist.* Designating or pertaining to a Muslim movement set up in India in 1919 orig. to champion the claims of the Sultan of Turkey to the Khilafat. E20.

khilat /ˈkɪlʌt, kəˈlɑːt/ *noun*. L17.
[ORIGIN Urdu, Persian *ḵil'at*, from Arabic *ḵil'a(t)*.]
hist. In India etc.: a set of clothes presented by a person of rank as a mark of distinction; *transf.* any handsome present made by an acknowledged superior.

Khirbet Kerak /ˈkɑːbət ˈkɛrak/ *adjective*. M20.
[ORIGIN A Syrian town by Lake Tiberias.]
ARCHAEOLOGY. Designating a red and black, highly burnished type of early Bronze Age pottery first found at Khirbet Kerak in the 1940s.

khitmutgar *noun* var. of KHIDMUTGAR.

Khlyst /klɪst, xlɪst/ *noun*. Also **Khlist**. Pl. **-sti**, **-sty**, /-sti/. M19.
[ORIGIN Russian (pl. *khlysty*) lit. 'whip'.]
A member of a sect of ascetic Russian Christians, formed in the 17th cent., who believed that Christ could be reincarnated in human beings through their suffering.

Khmer /kmɛː/ *noun & adjective*. L19.
[ORIGIN Khmer.]
▸ **A** *noun*. Pl. **-s**, same.
1 A native or inhabitant of the ancient kingdom of Khmer in SE Asia, which reached the peak of its power in the 11th cent., or the modern country corresponding to it, Cambodia. L19.
2 The largely monosyllabic language spoken in Cambodia, belonging to the Mon-Khmer group of the Austro-Asiatic family. E20.
▸ **B** *attrib.* or as *adjective*. Of or pertaining to the Khmers or their language. M20.
– PHRASES: **Khmer Rouge** /ruːʒ/, pl. **-s -s** (pronounced same), [French = red] (a member of) a Communist movement active in Cambodia in the late 1960s and the 1970s, holding power there 1975–9.

Khoikhoi /ˈkɔɪkɔɪ/ *noun & adjective*. Also **Khoi-Khoin** /-kɔɪn/. L18.
[ORIGIN Nama, lit. 'men of men'.]
▸ **A** *noun*. Pl. same. A member of a group of indigenous peoples of South Africa and Namibia, including the Nama and the ancestors of the Griquas. L18.
▸ **B** *adjective*. Of or pertaining to the Khoikhoi or their languages. L19.
– NOTE: Now preferred to ***Hottentot***, which is regarded as offensive.

Khoisan /ˈkɔɪsɑːn/ *noun & adjective*. M20.
[ORIGIN from KHOI(KHOI + SAN *noun*[2] & *adjective*.]
▸ **A** *noun*. A southern African language family including Nama (Khoikhoi) and San. M20.
▸ **B** *adjective*. Designating or pertaining to (peoples who speak languages of) this family. M20.

khoja /ˈkəʊdʒə/ *noun*. E17.
[ORIGIN (Turkish *hoca* from) Persian *ḵ*[w]*āja*.]
1 A teacher in a Muslim school; a Muslim scribe or clerk. E17.
2 (**K-**.) A member of an Ismaili Muslim sect found mainly in western India. L19.

kho-kho /ˈkəʊkəʊ/ *noun*. L19.
[ORIGIN Marathi *khō-khō*.]
An Indian game of tag with two teams of twelve people.

Khond *noun & adjective* var. of KOND.

khor /kɔː/ *noun*. L19.
[ORIGIN Repr. a pronunc. of Arabic *ḵawr* low land between two stretches of higher ground, (colloq.) wadi.]
In Sudan and neighbouring regions: a dry watercourse or ravine.

Khorassan /kɒrəˈsɑːn/ *noun & adjective*. Also **Khurasan** /kʊrəˈsɑːn/. E20.
[ORIGIN A province in NE Iran.]
(Designating) a Persian carpet or rug with vivid colouring and a fine silky texture, of a type made in NE Iran.

Khotan /kəʊˈtɑːn/ *adjective*. L19.
[ORIGIN See KHOTANESE.]
Designating a type of carpet or rug made in Khotan, usu. with Chinese geometrical patterns or stylized natural designs.

Khotanese /kəʊtəˈniːz/ *noun & adjective*. L19.
[ORIGIN from *Khotan* (see below) + -ESE.]
▸ **A** *noun*. Pl. same.
1 A native or inhabitant of the city or district of Khotan in Chinese Turkestan. L19.
2 The Iranian language of Khotan. M20.
▸ **B** *adjective*. Of or pertaining to the Khotanese or their language. M20.

khotla *noun* var. of KGOTLA.

khoum /kuːm/ *noun*. L20.
[ORIGIN Arabic *ḵums* one-fifth.]
A monetary unit of Mauritania, equal to one-fifth of an ouguiya.

Khrushchevism /ˈkrʊstʃəfɪz(ə)m/ *noun*. M20.
[ORIGIN from *Khrushchev* (see below) + -ISM.]
The practice or principles of the Russian statesman Nikita Sergeevich Khrushchev (1894–1971), notable for his denunciation of Stalin and his advocacy of peaceful coexistence with the Western powers.
■ **Khrushchevian** /ˈkrʊstʃəfɪən, krʊsˈtʃɒfɪən/ *adjective* of, pertaining to, or characteristic of Khrushchev or his policies M20.

khubber *noun* var. of KHABAR.

khud /kʌd/ *noun*. Also **khad**. M19.
[ORIGIN Hindi *kaḍ*.]
In the Indian subcontinent: a deep ravine or chasm; a precipitous cleft or descent in a hillside.

khula /kuːˈlɑː/ *noun*. M20.
[ORIGIN Arabic *ḵul* retreat, renunciation.]
In Islamic law: a form of divorce initiated by the wife, effected by the return of her husband's wedding gift. Cf. TALAQ.

Khurasan *noun & adjective* var. of KHORASSAN.

Khurri *noun*, **Khurrian** *adjective & noun*, vars. of HURRI, HURRIAN.

khus-khus *noun* var. of CUSCUS *noun*[3].

khutbah /ˈkʊtbə/ *noun*. E19.
[ORIGIN Arabic *ḵuṭba*.]
A form of sermon, consisting of homily and supplication, delivered in mosques before the midday Friday prayer, at the time of the two main Muslim festivals, and on other exceptional occasions.

khyal *noun* var. of KHAYAL.

Khyber /ˈkʌɪbə/ *noun*. *rhyming slang*. M20.
[ORIGIN *Khyber Pass*, the chief pass in the Hindu Kush mountains between Afghanistan and NW Pakistan.]
More fully ***Khyber Pass***. = ARSE *noun* 1.

kHz *abbreviation*.
Kilohertz.

ki /kiː/ *noun*. M19.
[ORIGIN Hawaiian = Polynesian TI *noun*[1].]
A shrub of the agave family, *Cordyline fruticosa*, found in China and the Pacific islands, the fermented root of which yields an alcoholic drink. Cf. TI *noun*[1].

kiaat /kɪˈɑːt/ *noun*. *S. Afr.* Also (earlier) **kajaten** /kʌɪˈɑːt(ə)n/, & other vars. E19.
[ORIGIN Afrikaans from Malay *kajaten* wood, teak.]
More fully ***kiaat hout*** /həʊt/ [Afrikaans = wood]. A leguminous tree, *Pterocarpus angolensis*, of southern Africa; the wood of this tree, resembling teak.

kiack *noun* var. of KAYAK *noun*[2].

kiang /kɪˈaŋ/ *noun*. Also **kyang**. M19.
[ORIGIN Tibetan *kyang*, *rkyang*.]
A wild ass, *Equus hemionus*, of a subspecies native to the Tibetan plateau. Also called ***dziggetai***. Cf. KULAN, ONAGER.

kia ora /kɪə ˈɔːrə/ *interjection*. *NZ*. L19.
[ORIGIN Maori.]
(A greeting) expr. good will, or wishing good health.

kiap /ˈkiːʌp, ˈkiːap/ *noun*. E20.
[ORIGIN Pidgin English, from *captain* or German *Kapitän*.]
In Papua New Guinea: a white patrol or police officer.

K

kiasu /ˈkiːəsuː/ *noun & adjective. SE Asian.* L20.
[ORIGIN Chinese, lit. 'scared to lose'.]
▸ **A** *noun.* A grasping, selfish attitude. L20.
▸ **B** *adjective.* Very anxious not to miss an opportunity; grasping. L20.

kiaugh *noun* var. of KAUCH.

kiawe /kiːˈaveɪ/ *noun.* E20.
[ORIGIN Hawaiian.]
A S. American mesquite, *Prosopis juliflora*, naturalized in Hawaii. Also ***kiawe-tree***.

kibbeh /ˈkɪbeɪ, ˈkɪbiː/ *noun.* E19.
[ORIGIN Arabic *kubba(h)* ball, lump.]
In Middle Eastern cookery: a dish consisting of a ground mixture of meat, bulgar or rice, and spices, served raw or shaped into dumplings and then fried or grilled.

kibble /ˈkɪb(ə)l/ *noun*[1]. LME.
[ORIGIN Middle High German, German *Kübel* from medieval Latin *cupellus*, *-ppa* corn measure, drinking vessel, from *cuppa* CUP *noun*.]
MINING. A large wooden or (later) iron or steel bucket, for conveying ore or rubbish to the surface.

kibble /ˈkɪb(ə)l/ *noun*[2]. L16.
[ORIGIN Uncertain: perh. from the surname *Kibble*.]
In full ***kibble-hound***. A breed of hound related to the beagle; a dog of this breed.

kibble /ˈkɪb(ə)l/ *noun*[3]. L19.
[ORIGIN Perh. alt. of COBBLE *noun*, but partly from KIBBLE *verb*.]
1 In *pl.* = COBBLE *noun* 2. L19.
2 *sing.* & in *pl.* Coarsely ground grain, pulses, etc.; (chiefly *N. Amer.*) dry pet food containing coarsely ground grain. E20.

kibble /ˈkɪb(ə)l/ *verb trans.* L18.
[ORIGIN Unknown.]
Grind (esp. grain) coarsely; crush into small pieces.
■ **kibbler** *noun* (a person who operates or tends) a machine which kibbles or grinds grain, pulses, etc., coarsely L19.

kibbutz /kɪˈbʊts/ *noun.* Pl. **-im** /-ɪm/, (occas.) **-es**. M20.
[ORIGIN mod. Hebrew *qibbūṣ* gathering.]
A collective (esp. farming) settlement in Israel, owned communally by its members, and organized on cooperative principles.
■ **kibbutznik** *noun* a member of a kibbutz M20.

kibe /kʌɪb/ *noun & verb.* LME.
[ORIGIN Unknown.]
▸ **A** *noun.* **1** A chapped or ulcerated blister or chilblain, *esp.* one on the heel. Now *arch. & dial.* LME.

SHAKES. *Haml.* The toe of the peasant comes so near the heel of the courtier, he galls his kibe.

on the kibes of following on the heels of.
2 *transf.* A sore on the foot of a horse, sheep, etc. Now *rare* or *obsolete*. M17.
▸ **B** *verb trans.* Affect with blisters or chilblains. Chiefly as ***kibed*** *ppl adjective.* Now *dial.* L15.
■ **kiby** *adjective* (now *dial.*) affected with blisters or chilblains E16.

kibitka /kɪˈbɪtkə/ *noun.* L18.
[ORIGIN Russian, from Turkic *kebit*, *kibit* (ult. from Sogdian *kpyd*) + Russian suffix *-ka*.]
1 A circular tent made of lattice work and covered with thick felt, formerly used by Tatars; *transf.* a Tatar household or family. L18.
2 A Russian wagon or sledge with a rounded cover or hood. L18.

kibitz /ˈkɪbɪts/ *verb intrans. slang* (chiefly *N. Amer.*). E20.
[ORIGIN Yiddish from German *kiebitzen*, from *Kiebitz* lapwing, pewit, interfering onlooker at cards.]
1 Look on at cards, or some other activity, esp. offering unwanted advice. E20.

Life Dulles kibitzes briefly at the card game. T. CLANCY A task on which over a hundred staff members had already kibitzed.

2 Chat, engage in banter; mess *around*. M20.

National Observer (US) Crowded places . . full of people who argue and kibitz.

■ **kibitzer** *noun* a person who kibitzes; a busybody, a meddler: E20.

kiblah /ˈkɪblə/ *noun.* Also **q-**, **-a**. M17.
[ORIGIN Arabic *qibla* that which is opposite.]
1 (The direction of) the place to which Muslims must turn for prayer, now the Kaaba at Mecca. M17.
2 = MIHRAB 2. L18.

kiboko /kɪˈbəʊkəʊ/ *noun.* Pl. **-os**. E20.
[ORIGIN Kiswahili = hippopotamus.]
A strong heavy whip made of hippopotamus hide.

kibosh /ˈkʌɪbɒʃ/ *noun & verb. slang.* Also **ky-**. M19.
[ORIGIN Unknown.]
▸ **A** *noun.* **1** ***put the kibosh on***, put an end to; dispose of finally. M19.

C. SANDBURG Put the kibosh on 'em so they'll never come back.

2 Nonsense. L19.
▸ **B** *verb trans.* Put an end to; finish off. M19.

Kichaga /kɪˈtʃagə/ *noun & adjective.* L19.
[ORIGIN Bantu, from *ki-* prefix + *Chaga* CHAGGA.]
(Of) the Bantu language of the Wachagga.

kick /kɪk/ *noun*[1]. M16.
[ORIGIN from KICK *verb*[1].]
▸ **I** **1** An act of kicking; a blow or thrust with the foot; *spec.* an act of striking a ball with the foot. M16.

M. GEE A touch on . . his calf, a very slight kick, it felt like a foot. *Evening Telegraph (Grimsby)* Knowles took the kick . . with the ball careering on to the bar.

corner kick, ***drop kick***, ***penalty kick***, ***place kick***, etc.
2 *fig.* A grave or humiliating setback; a severe criticism or punishment. Esp. in ***a kick in the pants***, ***a kick in the teeth***. E17. ▸**b** An objection; an expression or display of opposition. M19.

LYTTON His . . policy was wittily described . . as a 'quick alternation of kicks and kindness'.

3 A fashion, a fad; the latest style; an (esp. temporary) interest in or enthusiasm for a specified subject, manner of behaving, etc. *slang.* L17.

M. DUFFY They're still all on the health food kick.

4 A recoil of a gun when discharged. E19.

M. MITCHELL The back kick of the pistol made her reel.

5 A jerk, a jolt; jerking motion. Also, a sudden surge of electricity. M19.
6 A sudden strong stimulant effect, esp. caused by alcohol or a drug. Also, a thrill, an excitement, a pleasure; a cause of excitement etc. M19.

J. KEROUAC It's just kicks . . . We're having a good time. H. WOUK I get a kick out of giving the press the slip. B. BOVA They drank something chalky white, thick; it had an alcoholic kick to it.

7 A person who kicks (well or badly), a (*good* or *bad*) kicker, esp. in rugby and American football. M19.
8 Ability or disposition to kick or rebel. L19.

K. WEATHERLY This blow was a better one, and it took some kick out of the roo.

9 *ATHLETICS.* A sudden burst of speed, esp. towards the end of a middle-distance race. M20.

G. A. SHEEHAN The runner with the kick will beat his opponent.

▸ **II** **10** A sixpence. *arch. slang.* L17.
11 In *pl.* ▸**a** Breeches, trousers, pants, knickers. Cf. KICKSEYS. *slang & dial.* L17. ▸**b** Shoes. *slang* (orig. *US*). L19.
12 A pocket. *slang.* M19.

F. DONALDSON At any moment I might be in the chips with 40,000 dollars in my kick.

– PHRASES: **for kicks** purely for (esp. reckless) pleasure or excitement. ***free kick***: see FREE *adjective*. ***high kick***: see HIGH *adjective*. **more kicks than halfpence** more harshness than kindness. ***top kick***: see TOP *adjective*.
– COMB.: **kick-boxer** a person who participates in kick-boxing; **kick-boxing** a form of boxing incorporating elements of karate, esp. kicking with bare feet; **kick drum** a bass drum played using a pedal; **kick plate** a metal plate at the base of a door or panel to protect it from damage or wear; **kick-pleat** a pleat in a narrow skirt to allow more freedom of movement; **kicksorter** *colloq.* an instrument that registers the number of electrical pulses received in each of a set of amplitude ranges; a pulse-height analyser; **kickstand** a metal prop, attached to the frame, for holding up a bicycle or motorcycle, when not in use; **kick-start** *noun & verb* (*a*) *noun* a device allowing the starting of a motorcycle etc. by a downward thrust on a pedal; a method or an act of starting a motorcycle etc. in this way; (*b*) *verb trans. & intrans.* start (an engine) in this way; *fig.* start or restart (a process etc.) by providing some initial impetus; **kick-starter** a device allowing the kick-starting of an engine etc.; **kick-tail** *noun & adjective* (designating) a sharp upward slope at the rear of a skateboard or a skateboard having this; **kick-turn** a standing turn in skiing; **kick-wheel** a potter's wheel worked by a foot pedal.

kick /kɪk/ *noun*[2]. M19.
[ORIGIN Uncertain: perh. a use of KICK *noun*[1] but cf. NICK *noun*[1] 10.]
An indentation in the bottom of a glass bottle which diminishes the internal capacity and increases stability. Cf. KICK-UP 5.

kick /kɪk/ *verb*[1]. LME.
[ORIGIN Unknown.]
1 *verb intrans.* Strike out with the foot. Also, raise the leg vigorously, esp. in dancing. LME.

P. MATTHIESSEN In the vicinity of females, the male 'kicks'—a loose twitch of the leg. R. INGALLS She . . kicked and thrashed while they dragged her along the sidewalk.

2 *verb intrans. fig.* Express anger, defiance, or dislike; rebel; object strongly. Usu. foll. by *against*, *at*. LME.

M. MCLUHAN I find my lecture schedule . . heavier . . but nothing to kick about. E. CRANKSHAW In childhood this great disciplinarian had kicked against all discipline.

3 *verb trans.* Strike (something or someone) with the foot. L16. ▸**b** Reproach or be annoyed with (oneself). L19.

A. MASON A foot kicked him hard in the ribs. M. MCCONNELL To get a space shuttle off the ground, you can't just . . kick the tires. **b** L. OLIVIER I . . was beginning to kick myself for my lack of perception.

4 *verb trans.* Impel, drive, or move (as) by kicking. Usu. with adverb (phr.). L16. ▸**b** Dismiss, discharge, reject (esp. a suitor). *US slang.* E19.

W. WHARTON She kicked her only daughter out of the house at sixteen. A. L. ROWSE Vansittart . . was kicked out of the way for Cadogan, more amenable to Chamberlain.

5 *verb intrans. & trans.* (with *it*). Die. Formerly foll. by *up*. Cf. ***kick the bucket*** s.v. BUCKET *noun*[2]. *slang.* M17.

F. DHONDY The confusion only started when he kicked it. Died, I mean.

6 *verb trans. transf.* Strike (something) with a violent impact (chiefly in ***kick the beam*** s.v. BEAM *noun*). Of a gun: strike in the recoil. M17.

Guns Review That little gun tends to kick the user very hard.

7 *verb intrans. transf.* ▸**a** Of a gun: recoil when fired. M19. ▸**b** *CRICKET.* (Of a ball) rebound almost vertically from the pitch; (of a pitch or a bowler) cause a ball to do this. Also foll. by *up*. M19. ▸**c** *TELEGRAPHY.* Of a relay: break contact momentarily. E20.
8 *verb trans. FOOTBALL.* Score (a goal) by a kick. M19.
9 *verb trans. & intrans.* Give up or overcome (a habit, esp. drug-taking). *colloq.* M20.

N. MAILER It's easier to give up the love of your life than to kick cigarettes.

– PHRASES: ***alive and kicking***: see ALIVE *adjective*. **kick against the pricks** *fig.* rebel, be recalcitrant, esp. to one's own hurt. **kick a person's ass** (*slang*, chiefly *N. Amer.*) dominate, defeat, or punish a person. **kick ass** (*slang*, chiefly *N. Amer.*) act forcefully or in a domineering manner. ***kick down the ladder***: see LADDER *noun* 2. ***kick one's heels***: see HEEL *noun*[1]. **kick over the traces** (of a horse) get a leg over the traces and become out of control; *fig.* (of a person) throw off usual restraints. ***kick the beam***: see BEAM *noun*. ***kick the bucket***: see BUCKET *noun*[2]. ***kick the habit***: see HABIT *noun*. ***kick the hindsight(s) off***, ***kick the hindsight(s) out of***: see HINDSIGHT 2. ***kick the shit out of***: see SHIT *noun*. ***kick the tar out of***: see TAR *noun*[1] 1.
– WITH ADVERBS IN SPECIALIZED SENSES: **kick about**, **kick around** (*a*) *colloq.* walk or wander about, esp. aimlessly; (*b*) ***be kicking about***, ***be kicking around***, (of a thing) lie around, esp. untidily; be available, unused, or unwanted; (*c*) (chiefly *N. Amer.*) kick (a thing) in all directions; *fig.* treat (a person) harshly, unfairly, or contemptuously; (*d*) discuss or examine in an informal or unstructured way, try out (a subject, idea, etc.). **kick back** (*a*) = BACKFIRE *verb* 2; (*b*) *colloq.* give a refund or rebate (to). **kick down** operate a kick-down device (see below). **kick in** (*a*) break down (a door etc.) by kicking against the outer side; *spec.* (*US slang*) break into (a building etc.); (*b*) *slang* (orig. *US*) contribute (money, one's share, etc.); (*c*) become activated; come into effect. **kick off** (*a*) throw off (a shoe etc.) by kicking; (*b*) *verb intrans.* (*FOOTBALL*) begin or resume a match; *fig.* start, begin (*with*); (*c*) *slang* die. **kick on** *Austral. & NZ slang* continue to play well; gain or maintain momentum. **kick out** (*a*) expel, eject, esp. with a kick; (*b*) *SURFING* perform a kick-out (see below). **kick up** raise (dust etc.) (as) by kicking; *fig.* make (a disturbance or nuisance) (***kick up a row***: see ROW *noun*[3]; ***kick up a shindy***: see SHINDY 2; ***kick up a stour***: see STOUR *noun*); (see also sense 7b above). **kick upstairs** *colloq.* remove (a person) from the scene of action by promotion to an ostensibly higher post.
– COMB.: **kick-about** an informal form of football; an informal game of football; **kick-and-rush** *adjective* designating football played with more vigour than skill; **kick-ass** *adjective* (*slang*, chiefly *N. Amer.*) rough, aggressive, powerful; **kick-ball** (a) football; **kick-down** *noun & adjective* (designating) a device operated by the foot, *spec.* (on a motor vehicle with automatic transmission) for changing to a lower gear by fully depressing the accelerator pedal; **kick-in** *FOOTBALL* a practice at goal-shooting before the start of a match; **kick-off** (*a*) *FOOTBALL* the start or resumption of a match; (*b*) *fig.* the start, the beginning; an inaugural or opening event; **kick-out** *SURFING* a manoeuvre executed by thrusting down on the rear of one's surfboard and pivoting it on its tail so as to ride up and over the top of a wave; **kick-the-can**, **kick-the-tin** a children's game in which a tin can is kicked.
■ **kickable** *adjective* M17. **kiˈckee** *noun* [-EE[1]] a person who is kicked E19. **kickish** *adjective* (*obsolete* exc. *dial.*) given to kicking; irritable: L16. **kickster** *noun* a person whose behaviour is governed principally or solely by the desire for pleasure or excitement M20. **kicky** *adjective* (*a*) *Scot.* inclined or apt to kick or provide kicks; *spec.* clever, lively; provoking, annoying; (*b*) *CRICKET* causing the ball to kick; (*c*) *N. Amer. colloq.* exciting: L18.

kick /kɪk/ *verb*[2] *trans. slang.* L18.
[ORIGIN Perh. a use of KICK *verb*[1].]
Ask (a person) *for* something; obtain by asking.

Kickapoo /ˈkɪkəpuː/ *noun & adjective.* L17.
[ORIGIN Kickapoo *kiikaapoa*.]
▸ **A** *noun.* Pl. **-s**, same.
1 A member of an Algonquian people now of Kansas, Oklahoma, and Mexico. L17.
2 The language of this people. M20.
▸ **B** *attrib.* or as *adjective.* Of or pertaining to the Kickapoos or their language. E19.

kickback /ˈkɪkbak/ *noun. colloq.* M20.
[ORIGIN from KICK *verb*[1] + BACK *adverb*.]
1 A refund, a rebate; the return of (esp. stolen) money, goods, etc.; a payment (usu. illegal) made to a person who has facilitated a transaction, appointment, etc. M20.

D. FRANCIS Order extensively from him and in return receive a sizable commission. A kickback.

2 A strong reaction or repercussion; an undesirable result. M20.

Listener One of the kick-backs . . is . . the over-administering of education.

3 *RAILWAYS.* A section of track sloping sharply upwards so as to reverse the direction of a wagon etc. by the force of gravity. M20.

K

4 Surplus preservative released from timber during the preservation process. M20.

kicker /ˈkɪkə/ *noun*. M16.
[ORIGIN from KICK *verb*[1] + -ER[1].]
1 A person who or thing which kicks; *spec.* a horse given to kicking. M16. ▸**b** *fig.* A person who protests, objects, or rebels. Chiefly *US*. L19.
2 MINING. Earth left in place in first cutting a vein, to support its sides. M18.
3 CRICKET. A ball that rebounds more sharply than usual from the pitch. L19.
4 POKER. A high third card retained in the hand with a pair at the draw. L19.
5 (A boat driven by) an outboard motor. *N. Amer. colloq.* E20.
6 PRINTING. A device which, as newspapers come off the press, pushes one out of line at regular intervals so as to create separate batches of a specified number. M20.

†**kickie-wickie** *noun*. *rare* (Shakes.). Only in E17.
[ORIGIN Fanciful.]
A wife.

kicking /ˈkɪkɪŋ/ *verbal noun* & *ppl adjective*. M16.
[ORIGIN from KICK *verb*[1] + -ING[1].]
▸ **A** *verbal noun*. The action of KICK *verb*[1]; an instance of this, *spec.* an assault in which the victim is kicked repeatedly. M16.

J. KING Though I got a kicking it gives me a bit of respect from the other lads.

▸ **B** *ppl adjective*. Lively and exciting. *slang*.

C. J. STONE It was a full-on, kicking party till sunrise.

– COMB.: **kicking plate** a metal plate fixed to the lower part of a door etc. to prevent damage or wear; **kicking strap** (*a*) a strap adjusted to prevent a horse from kicking in harness; (*b*) NAUTICAL a rope lanyard fixed to the boom to prevent it from rising.

kickseys /ˈkɪksɪz/ *noun pl. arch. slang*. Also **kicksies**. E19.
[ORIGIN from KICK *noun*[1].]
Breeches; trousers. Cf. KICK *noun*[1] 11a.

K

kickshaw /ˈkɪkʃɔː/ *noun* & *adjective*. *arch.* Orig. †**quelque chose**. L16.
[ORIGIN French *quelque chose* something.]
▸ **A** *noun*. **1** A fancy dish in cookery, usu. French, as opp. to a familiar, substantial English dish. Usu. *derog.* L16.
2 Something dainty or elegant, but impractical; a toy, a trifle. E17.
3 A frivolous person. *obsolete* exc. *dial.* M17.
▸ **B** *attrib.* or as *adjective*. Frivolous, trifling. M17.
▪ **kickshawed** *adjective* consisting of or treated with kickshaws E17.

kicksies *noun pl.* var. of KICKSEYS.

kick-up /kɪˈkʌp, ˈkɪkʌp/ *noun*. L18.
[ORIGIN from KICK *verb*[1] + UP *adverb*[1].]
1 A violent disturbance or row. L18.
2 A dance, a party. *colloq.* (orig. *US*). L18.
3 An act of kicking a leg or the legs in the air. M19.
4 MINING. A device for overturning and emptying trams, wagons, etc. L19.
5 = KICK *noun*[2]. E20.

kid /kɪd/ *noun*[1]. ME.
[ORIGIN Old Norse *kið* rel. to Old High German *chizzī*, *kizzīn* (German *Kitze*), from Germanic.]
1 A young goat. ME. ▸**b** A young antelope or similar animal; formerly *spec.*, a roe deer in its first year. ME.

M. MILNER A mother goat appearing with her three kids.

2 The flesh of a young goat as food. LME.
3 The skin of a kid, lamb, etc., esp. made into a soft pliable leather used chiefly to make gloves and shoes; in *pl.*, gloves or shoes made of this. L15.

H. E. BATES A final look at her hands, their coarseness hidden . . by the clean white kid.

VICI *kid*.

4 a A child, esp. a young child. *colloq.* L16. ▸**b** N. AMER. HISTORY. An indentured servant, esp. on a plantation. Cf. KIDNAP. E18. ▸**c** An expert young criminal, esp. a fighter, a thief, etc. *slang*. Now *rare*. E19. ▸**d** A young person. Also used as a familiar form of address. *colloq.* (orig. *US*). L19.

L. DUNCAN What would the kids at school think? P. ROTH He was a good father to the kids. **d** J. D. MACDONALD We can't talk here, kid. J. BRODSKY We were young, we were kids.

d our kid *colloq.* one's (only) younger brother or sister.
5 *sing.* & in *pl.* With *the*: two stars in the constellation Auriga, represented as kids held in the hand of the charioteer. Also ***kid-star***. *rare*. E17.
– COMB.: **kid brother** *colloq.* (orig. *US*) a person's younger brother; **kidflick** *slang* a film for children; **kid glove** a glove made of kidskin (***handle with kid gloves***, handle or treat gently, delicately, discreetly, or gingerly); **kid-glove** *adjective* characterized by wearing kid gloves or (*fig.*) by dainty, delicate, discreet, or gingerly treatment; **kid-gloved** *adjective* (*a*) wearing kid gloves; (*b*) = ***kid-glove*** above; **kid sister** *colloq.* (orig. *US*) a person's younger sister; **kidskin** the skin of a kid, lamb, etc., made into leather; ***kid-star***: see sense 5 above; **kids' stuff**, **kid's stuff** *colloq.* (orig. *US*) something suitable for children; a very simple or trivial task etc.; **kidvid** *slang* television or video programmes for children.
▪ **kiddish** *adjective* (*rare*) †(*a*) of, pertaining to, or resembling a kid; (*b*) *slang* childish: M16. **kiddo** *noun* (*colloq.*), pl. **-os**, a young person or child (freq. as a familiar form of address) L19. **kidlet** *noun* a young child L19. **kidling** *noun* (*a*) a small young goat; (*b*) a small child or baby: L16.

kid /kɪd/ *noun*[2]. *obsolete* exc. *dial.* ME.
[ORIGIN Unknown.]
A faggot or bundle of twigs, brushwood, gorse, etc., used for burning, or as a prop for loose soil etc.

kid /kɪd/ *noun*[3]. M18.
[ORIGIN Perh. var. of KIT *noun*[1].]
1 A small wooden tub for domestic use; *esp.* a sailor's mess tub. M18.
2 A box or wooden pen on the deck of a fishing vessel to receive fish as they are caught. *US*. L19.

kid /kɪd/ *noun*[4]. *colloq.* L19.
[ORIGIN from KID *verb*[3].]
Deception, falsehood, pretence. Also (*Austral.* & *NZ slang*), nonsense.
no kid = ***no kidding*** s.v. KID *verb*[3] 2.

kid /kɪd/ *adjective*. Long *arch. rare*. Also **kyd**. ME.
[ORIGIN pa. pple of KITHE.]
Made known, mentioned; famous, renowned; notorious.

kid /kɪd/ *verb*[1] *intrans*. Infl. **-dd-**. LME.
[ORIGIN from KID *noun*[1].]
Give birth to a kid.

kid /kɪd/ *verb*[2] *trans*. *obsolete* exc. *dial.* Infl. **-dd-**. E16.
[ORIGIN from KID *noun*[2].]
Bind up (brushwood etc.) in bundles or faggots. Also, prop up or secure (loose soil etc.) using bundles of twigs etc.

kid /kɪd/ *verb*[3]. *colloq.* Infl. **-dd-**. E19.
[ORIGIN Perh. from KID *noun*[1] in sense 'make a kid or goat of' or 'make a child of'.]
1 *verb trans.* Deceive or hoax (a person); joke with or tease (a person). Also foll. by *along*, *on*. E19.

H. MAYHEW He kids them on by promising three times more than the things are worth. F. DONALDSON I don't seem able to kid myself that is real literature. J. UPDIKE My nose looks like a strawberry; Toby kids me about it.

2 *verb intrans.* Deceive, pretend, joke with, tease. Also foll. by *around*. E19.

J. DIDION You have to kid around with them, be more fun. W. WHARTON I thought she was kidding, but she's serious.

no kidding that is the truth.
▪ **kiddingly** *adverb* in a kidding manner, teasingly M20.

†**kid** *verb*[4] *pa. pple*: see KITHE.

kidang *noun* var. of KIJANG.

kidder /ˈkɪdə/ *noun*[1]. *colloq.* L19.
[ORIGIN from KID *verb*[3] + -ER[1].]
A person who kids another or others; a hoaxer, a joker, a teaser, a deceiver.

kidder *noun*[2] var. of KIDDIER.

Kidderminster /ˈkɪdəmɪnstə/ *noun*. L17.
[ORIGIN A town in Worcestershire, England.]
1 Used *attrib.* to designate things originating or produced in Kidderminster, *spec.* a kind of pileless reversible carpet in which the pattern is formed by the intersection of two cloths of different colours. L17.
2 Kidderminster carpeting, a Kidderminster carpet. M18.

kiddie /ˈkɪdi/ *noun*. *colloq.* Also **-y**. L16.
[ORIGIN from KID *noun*[1] + -IE.]
1 A young goat. L16.
2 A young criminal or other person who assumes a flash manner and style of dress. *arch.* L18.
3 A child; a young person. M19.
– COMB.: **kiddie brother** = ***kid brother*** s.v. KID *noun*[1]; **kiddie car** (orig. *US*) (*a*) a small toy car for a child to ride; (*b*) a pram; **kiddie-porn** child pornography; **kiddie sister** = ***kid sister*** s.v. KID *noun*[1]; **kiddiewink**, **kiddiewinkie** (chiefly *joc.*) a small child.

kiddier /ˈkɪdɪə/ *noun*. *obsolete* exc. *dial.* Also **kidder** /ˈkɪdə/. M16.
[ORIGIN Unknown.]
A person who buys provisions from the producers and sells them at a market; = BADGER *noun*[1].

kiddle /ˈkɪd(ə)l/ *noun*. Now *rare*. ME.
[ORIGIN Anglo-Norman *kidel* (whence Anglo-Latin *kidellus*), Old French *quidel*, *guidel* (mod. French *guideau*).]
A dam, weir, or barrier in a river, having an opening fitted with nets etc. for catching fish. Also, a barrier constructed of stakes and nets on a sea beach for the same purpose.

kiddush /ˈkɪdʊʃ/ *noun*. Also **K-**. M18.
[ORIGIN Hebrew *qiddūš* sanctification.]
A ceremony of prayer and blessing over wine, performed by the head of a Jewish household at the meal ushering in the Sabbath (on a Friday night) or a holy day or at the lunch preceding it.

kiddushin /kɪˈduːʃiːn/ *noun*. Also **K-**. L19.
[ORIGIN Aramaic *qiddūšīn*.]
JUDAISM. The section of the Mishnah dealing with betrothal and marriage. Also, the Jewish ceremony of betrothal; the gift given by a Jewish groom to effect a betrothal.

kiddy *noun* var. of KIDDIE.

kidnap /ˈkɪdnap/ *verb* & *noun*. L17.
[ORIGIN Back-form. from KIDNAPPER.]
▸ **A** *verb trans.* Infl. **-pp-**, ***-p-**. Carry off by illegal force or fraud, abduct, (a person, esp. a child) formerly, to provide servants or labourers for the American plantations, now esp. to obtain ransom. L17.
▸ **B** *noun*. An act of kidnapping someone. M20.

R. CROMPTON It's a kidnap . . We'll get a ransom on it. *Eastern Daily Press (Norwich)* The kidnap victim . . was taken from his home.

kidnapper /ˈkɪdnapə/ *noun*. Also ***-naper**. M17.
[ORIGIN from KID *noun*[1] + NAPPER *noun*[2].]
A person who kidnaps someone.

kidney /ˈkɪdni/ *noun*. ME.
[ORIGIN Uncertain: perh. from elem. rel. to COD *noun*[1] + EY *noun*.]
1 Either of a pair of glandular organs of rounded shape with a shallow indentation on one side, situated in humans in the back of the abdominal cavity, which maintain the composition of the blood, removing waste nitrogenous and other matter and excreting it as urine. Also, a similar gland in vertebrates and some invertebrates, those of cattle, sheep, and pigs being used as food. ME.
2 *fig.* Orig., a temperament, a constitution, a disposition. Now also, a kind, sort, or class (of person). ME.

W. HOLTBY Here he lacked men of his own kidney.

3 Something resembling a kidney, esp. in shape; *spec.* †(*a*) *rare* an ovary; (*b*) an oval variety of potato; also ***kidney potato***. L16.
– COMB. & PHRASES: **artificial kidney** = ***kidney machine*** below; **kidney bean** (*a*) any of several bean plants with kidney-shaped seeds, *esp.* a dwarf French bean, *Phaseolus vulgaris*; (*b*) the seed of such a plant, esp. when of a dark red variety; **kidney dish** a kidney-shaped dish, esp. used as a receptacle in surgery; **kidney fern** a New Zealand fern, *Cardiomanes reniforme*, with kidney-shaped leaves; **kidney graft** the operation of transplanting a kidney from one person to another; **kidney machine** a machine for effecting dialysis of the blood; also called ***artificial kidney***, ***haemodialyser***; **kidney ore** haematite occurring as kidney-shaped masses; **kidney-piece** a cam on a watch wheel with a kidney-shaped outline; ***kidney potato***: see sense 3 above; **kidney punch** BOXING an illegal punch to the kidney area; **kidney-shaped** *adjective* shaped like a kidney, with one side concave and the other convex; **kidney stone** (*a*) a kidney-shaped stone, a cobble; (*b*) a renal calculus; **kidney table**: having a kidney-shaped top; **kidney vetch** a leguminous plant, *Anthyllis vulneraria*, of chalk grassland and sea cliffs, with heads of usu. bright yellow flowers; also called ***lady's fingers***; **kidney worm** either of two parasitic nematodes, *Stephanurus dentatus*, which infests pigs, and *Dioctophyma renale*, which infests humans, dogs, and other mammals; ***pulpy kidney*** (***disease***): see PULPY 1.

kidology /kɪˈdɒlədʒi/ *noun*. *colloq.* M20.
[ORIGIN Irreg. from KID *verb*[3] + -OLOGY.]
The art or practice of kidding people; deliberate deception, mockery, or teasing.

J. GALLOWAY It wasn't doing the boy any favours . . just kidology to make out it was.

kidult /ˈkɪdʌlt/ *adjective* & *noun*. *slang* (freq. *derog.*). M20.
[ORIGIN Blend of KID *noun*[1] and ADULT.]
▸ **A** *adjective*. Designating or pertaining to television programmes, films, etc., intended to appeal to both children and adults. M20.
▸ **B** *noun*. An adult with childish tastes in television viewing etc. M20.

kief /kiːf/ *noun*. In sense 1 also **kef** /kɛf/, **keif** /keɪf/; in sense 2 also **kif**. E19.
[ORIGIN Arabic *kayf* (repr. colloq. pronunc.).]
1 A state of drowsiness or dreamy intoxication produced by the use of cannabis etc. Also, the enjoyment of idleness. E19.
do kief, **make kief** pass the time in idleness.
2 In Morocco and Algeria: cannabis or some other substance smoked to produce dreamy intoxication. L19.

Kieffer /ˈkiːfə/ *noun*. L19.
[ORIGIN Peter *Kieffer* (1812–90), US horticulturist, who developed it.]
In full ***Kieffer pear***. A disease-resistant variety of pear, a hybrid between the common pear, *Pyrus communis*, and the Chinese pear, *P. pyrifolia*.

kiekie /ˈkiːkiː/ *noun*. M19.
[ORIGIN Maori.]
A New Zealand climbing plant, *Freycinetia banksii* (family Pandanaceae), with edible bracts and leaves used for weaving baskets etc.

kielbasa /kiːlˈbasə, kjɛl-/ *noun*. M20.
[ORIGIN Polish *kiełbasa* sausage.]
A type of highly seasoned Polish sausage.

kiepersol /ˈkɪpəs(ə)l, -sɒl/ *noun*. Also **kippersol**. L19.
[ORIGIN Afrikaans from KITTISOL sunshade, umbrella, with ref. to the shape of its crown.]
Any of several small southern African trees of the genus *Cussonia*, of the ivy family, with leaves in tufts at the ends of the branches and with a root which is chewed for its sap.

kier /kɪə/ *noun*. **L16**.
[**ORIGIN** Old Norse *ker* vessel, tub = Old High German *kar*, Gothic *kas*.]
A vat; *spec.* †(*a*) a brewing vat; (*b*) a large vat in which cloth is boiled, bleached, etc.
■ **kierful** *noun* **L19**. **kiering** *noun* boiling in a kier or vat **E20**.

kierie /ˈkɪri/ *noun*. *S. Afr.* Also (earlier) †**kirri**. **M18**.
[**ORIGIN** Nama.]
A short club or knobbed stick used as a weapon by indigenous peoples of South Africa. Cf. **KNOBKERRIE**.

Kierkegaardian /kɪəkəˈɡɑːdɪən, -ˈɡɔːd-/ *adjective & noun*. **M20**.
[**ORIGIN** from *Kierkegaard* (see below) + **-IAN**.]
▸ **A** *adjective*. Of or pertaining to the Danish philosopher Søren Kierkegaard (1813–55) or his philosophy, esp. as criticizing traditional Christianity and idealism from an existentialist position. **M20**.
▸ **B** *noun*. An adherent or student of Kierkegaard's philosophy. **M20**.

kieselguhr /ˈkiːz(ə)lɡʊə/ *noun*. **L19**.
[**ORIGIN** German, from *Kiesel* gravel (see **CHESIL**) + **GUHR**.]
A soft diatomaceous earth used as an absorbent in explosives, a filtering medium, etc.

kieserite /ˈkiːzərʌɪt/ *noun*. **M19**.
[**ORIGIN** from D. G. *Kieser* (1779–1862), German physician + **-ITE**[1].]
MINERALOGY. Hydrated magnesium sulphate, occurring naturally as a white fine-grained monoclinic mineral, esp. in salt mines.

Kievan /ˈkiːɛf(ə)n, -v-/ *adjective*. **M20**.
[**ORIGIN** from *Kiev* (see below) + **-AN**.]
Of or pertaining to the Ukrainian city of Kiev, esp. in the historical period (*c* 900–*c* 1150) when it dominated European Russia.
■ Also **Kievian** *adjective* **E20**.

kiewiet /ˈkiːvɪt/ *noun*. *S. Afr.* Also **-wit**. **L18**.
[**ORIGIN** Afrikaans: imit.]
The crowned lapwing, *Vanellus coronatus*, of southern and eastern Africa.
■ Also **kiewietjie** /ˈkiːviki/ *noun* [Afrikaans *-tjie* dim. suffix] **L19**.

kif *noun* see **KIEF**.

†**kiff** *noun*. **L16–E18**.
[**ORIGIN** Alt.]
= **KITH** *noun* 3.

kijang /kɪˈdʒaŋ/ *noun*. Also **kidang** /kɪˈdaŋ/. **L18**.
[**ORIGIN** Malay *kijang*, Javanese *kidang*.]
A barking deer or muntjac.

kikar /ˈkɪkə/ *noun*. **L19**.
[**ORIGIN** Hindi *kīkar*.]
In the Indian subcontinent: = **BABUL**.

kike /kʌɪk/ *noun*[1]. *slang* (*derog. & offensive*). **E20**.
[**ORIGIN** Unknown.]
A Jew.

kike *verb & noun*[2] see **KEEK**.

kikoi /kɪˈkɔɪ/ *noun*. **M20**.
[**ORIGIN** Kiswahili.]
In E. Africa: a distinctive striped cloth with an end fringe, worn round the waist.

Kikongo /kɪˈkɒŋɡəʊ/ *noun & adjective*. **L19**.
[**ORIGIN** Kikongo, from *ki-* prefix + **KONGO**.]
(Of) the Bantu language of the Kongo people, used in the Congo and adjacent areas.

Kikuchi /kɪˈkuːtʃi/ *noun*. **M20**.
[**ORIGIN** Seishi *Kikuchi* (1902–74), Japanese physicist.]
PHYSICS. ***Kikuchi lines***, ***Kikuchi pattern***, lines in an electron diffraction pattern which are attributed to the elastic scattering of previously inelastically scattered electrons and may be used to determine the orientation of crystals.

Kikuyu /kɪˈkuːjuː/ *noun & adjective*. Pl. of noun same, **-s**. **M19**.
[**ORIGIN** Bantu.]
1 Of or pertaining to, a member of, a people constituting the largest ethnolinguistic group in Kenya. **M19**.
Kikuyu grass a creeping perennial grass, *Pennisetum clandestinum*, native to the highlands of Kenya and cultivated elsewhere as a lawn and fodder grass.
2 (Of) the Bantu language of this people. **E20**.

kilderkin /ˈkɪldəkɪn/ *noun*. **LME**.
[**ORIGIN** from Middle Dutch *kinderkin* var. of *kin(n)eken*, *-kijn*, dim. of *kintal*, *quintal* **QUINTAL**: see **-KIN**.]
1 A cask for liquids, fish, butter, etc., containing half a barrel, or 16 or 18 gallons. **LME**.
2 This filled with some commodity; the quantity contained in this, esp. as a measure of capacity. **LME**.

kilhig /ˈkɪlhɪɡ/ *noun*. *US*. **E20**.
[**ORIGIN** Unknown.]
A short stout pole used as a lever or brace to direct the fall of a tree.

kilian /ˈkɪlɪən/ *noun*. Also **-ll-**, **K-**. **M20**.
[**ORIGIN** Unknown.]
A fast ice dance executed by a pair of skaters side by side.

kilim /kɪˈliːm/ *adjective & noun*. Also **ke-**. **L19**.
[**ORIGIN** Turkish *Kılım* from Persian *gelīm*.]
(Designating) a pileless woven carpet, rug, etc., made in Turkey, Kurdistan, and neighbouring areas.

Kilkenny /kɪlˈkɛni/ *noun*. **E19**.
[**ORIGIN** A county and city in Leinster in the Republic of Ireland.]
Used *attrib.* to designate things found in or associated with Kilkenny.
Kilkenny cat either of a pair of cats fabled to have fought until only their tails remained; *fig.* either of a pair of combatants who fight until they annihilate each other. **Kilkenny marble** a grey limestone which becomes dark blue or black when polished.

kill /kɪl/ *noun*[1]. **ME**.
[**ORIGIN** from **KILL** *verb*[2].]
▸ **I** †**1** A stroke, a blow. *rare*. Only in **ME**.
▸ **II** **2** An act of killing an animal hunted as prey or game; an animal killed as prey or game. **M19**.

R. DAHL Always being right up with the hounds . . for fear that she might miss a kill. R. K. NARAYAN It'd do them good to watch their mother hunt and share a fresh kill.

in at the kill present at or benefiting from the killing of an animal or (*fig.*) the successful conclusion of an enterprise.
3 *TENNIS* etc. An act of striking a ball so that it cannot be returned. Cf. **KILL** *verb*[2] 11. **E20**.
4 *MILITARY*. An act of destroying or disabling an enemy aircraft, submarine, etc.; an aircraft etc. destroyed in this way. *colloq.* **M20**.

Royal Air Force News A tally of 27 enemy aircraft 'kills', eight probably destroyed and six damaged.

5 An act of bringing something to an end; a victory; a knockout in boxing etc. *colloq.* **M20**.
quick kill: see **QUICK** *adjective & adverb*.
– **COMB.**: **kill ratio** *US* the proportion of casualties on each side in a military action; **kill zone** = ***killing zone*** s.v. **KILLING** *noun*.

kill /kɪl/ *noun*[2]. *US local*. **M17**.
[**ORIGIN** Dutch *kil*, Middle Dutch *kille* riverbed, channel.]
A stream, a creek, a tributary river.

kill /kɪl/ *noun*[3]. **E19**.
[**ORIGIN** Irish, Gaelic *cill* from Old Irish *cell* (from Latin *cella* **CELL** *noun*[1]) cell, church, burial place (esp. as 1st elem. of place names).]
hist. The cell of a Celtic monk or hermit; an ancient Irish or Scottish church or monastic settlement.

kill *noun*[4] & *verb*[1] see **KILN**.

kill /kɪl/ *verb*[2]. **ME**.
[**ORIGIN** Prob. from Germanic word rel. to **QUELL** *verb*[1] & already in Old English.]
▸ **I** †**1** *verb trans. & intrans.* Strike, hit, beat. Only in **ME**.
2 *verb trans.* Put to death; cause the death of, deprive of life. **ME**. ▸**b** Procure (meat) by killing animals. Now *rare*. **M16**.

J. C. MORISON Bentley did kill his adversary dead. LE ROI JONES He's dead because I killed him. V. CANNING Nearly killed myself on the tower ladder.

3 *verb trans.* Expel, suppress, destroy, (a feeling, desire, thought, reaction, etc.); subdue, neutralize, nullify (an effect, a quality, etc.). **ME**.

O. W. HOLMES Quantities of black tea to kill any extra glass of red claret he may have swallowed. D. W. JERROLD [He] detected his wife painfully endeavouring to kill a laugh. W. BLACK You have killed her faith as well as ruined her life. E. F. BENSON There was something in Edgar that, for her, killed romance. J. C. COX The high blank walls . . kill the grace of the lancet windows.

4 *verb trans.* Deprive (an organism, a substance, a process, etc.) of vitality, activity, effect, etc. Now also, destroy, break, or ruin (a thing). **L15**.

A. YOUNG Potatoes have quite killed the land.

5 *verb trans.* **a** Cause severe pain or suffering to; overexert (esp. oneself, *doing*). **E16**. ▸**b** Overwhelm (a person) by a strong impression, as of admiration, anger, delight, grief, etc.; impress, thrill; convulse with laughter, *refl.* laugh heartily. **M17**.

a A. BROOKNER The girls in the workroom complain. I could kill Christian Dior. B. EMECHETA Twenty five kobo would not kill him, but he worked very hard for his money too. *New Yorker* Her new shoes are killing her. **b** Q He's a genius . . like Chaplin. I've never seen anybody kill an audience like them. *Melody Maker* During the Elton John tour in the States . . man, we killed them night after night.

6 *verb trans.* Prevent the passing of (a bill) in Parliament. **E17**.
7 *verb trans.* Spend (time) engaged in some activity, esp. while waiting for a specific event. **E18**.

L. STEPHEN Tapestry, in which ladies employed their needles by way of killing time. B. EMECHETA He had killed his waiting time by going daily to the farm with his father.

8 *verb trans.* Consume; eat or drink; *spec.* consume the entire contents of (a bottle of liquor). *colloq.* **M19**.

B. SCHULBERG We . . topped off the evening by killing the second bottle of Scotch.

9 *verb trans.* Cancel or delete (text etc.) from a book, journal, etc., before publication, or from a computer file. In *JOURNALISM*, suppress or deny (a story etc.). *colloq.* **M19**.

B. T. BRADFORD I'll have the story killed and the journalist fired immediately.

10 *verb trans.* Extinguish, turn off (a light, an engine etc.), put out (a cigarette etc.). *colloq.* **M19**.

C. HOPE The coach turned into a large parking lot and the driver killed the engine. *Arena* If we kill the light now . . we might be able to go right back to sleep.

11 *verb trans.* In *TENNIS* etc., strike (a ball) so that it cannot be returned. In *FOOTBALL*, *HOCKEY*, etc., stop (a ball) dead. **L19**.
12 *verb trans.* *METALLURGY*. Treat (molten steel) so as to prevent the evolution of oxygen on solidification, *spec.* by adding a reducing agent. Freq. as ***killed*** *ppl adjective*. **L19**.
▸ **II** **13** *verb intrans.* Cause a death or deaths. **M16**.

AV *Exod.* 20:13 Thou shalt not kill. F. HARRIS If looks could kill, he'd have had short shrift.

14 *verb intrans.* Of an animal: yield meat *well* etc. when slaughtered. **M19**.
– **PHRASES**: ***dressed to kill***: see **DRESS** *verb* 6a. **kill or cure** (of a remedy etc.) drastic, extreme. ***kill the goose that lays the golden eggs***, ***kill the goose that laid the golden eggs***: see **GOOSE** *noun*. ***kill two birds with one stone***: see **BIRD** *noun*. **kill with kindness** harm or spoil (a person) by mistaken or excessive kindness or overindulgence. ***shoot to kill***: see **SHOOT** *verb*.
– **WITH ADVERBS IN SPECIALIZED SENSES**: **kill off** (*a*) remove or get rid of by killing, destroy completely; (*b*) (of an author) represent (a fictional character) as killed or dead, write the death of into a plot. **kill out** (*a*) cull by killing; (*b*) (of an animal) yield a specified amount of meat when slaughtered (foll. by *at* the amount).
– **COMB.**: **killbuck** (*obsolete* exc. *dial.*) a fierce-looking man; **kill-cow** *noun & adjective* (*obsolete* exc. *dial.*) (*a*) *noun* a bully, a braggart; a terrible, great, or important person; a serious, terrible, or tragic event; †(*b*) *adjective* bragging, bullying; terrifying; **kill-crazy** *adjective* (*colloq.*) insanely desiring to kill, murderous; **kill-devil** (*obsolete* exc. *hist.*) (*a*) rum; (*b*) *ANGLING* an artificial bait made to spin in the water like a wounded fish; **killjoy** a person who or thing which dampens or destroys enjoyment or pleasure; **kill-lamb** *US* sheep laurel or lambkill, *Kalmia angustifolia*; **kill-time** an activity intended to consume spare time; a tactic used in sport etc. to allow time to elapse with no change of score.
■ **killable** *adjective* (*a*) able to be killed, easy to kill; (*b*) fit to be killed for food etc.: **E19**.

K

killadar /ˈkɪlədɑː/ *noun*. **L18**.
[**ORIGIN** Urdu & Persian *ḳil'adār* from Arabic *qal'a* fort, castle + Persian *-dār* holding, holder.]
hist. In India, the commandant or governor of a fort or castle.

Killamook *noun & adjective* see **TILLAMOOK**.

Killarney /kɪˈlɑːni/ *noun*. **M19**.
[**ORIGIN** A town in Co. Kerry, Ireland.]
Used *attrib.* to designate things found in or associated with Killarney.
Killarney fern a bristle fern, *Trichomanes speciosum*, formerly abundant in the neighbourhood of Killarney.

killas /ˈkɪləs/ *noun*. **L17**.
[**ORIGIN** Prob. from Cornish.]
A clay slate of Devonian age, found in Cornwall lying over granite.

killcrop /ˈkɪlkrɒp/ *noun*. *rare*. **M17**.
[**ORIGIN** Low German *kilkrop*, German *Kielkropf*, 2nd elem. corresp. to **CROP** *noun*.]
An insatiable child, supposed in folklore to be a fairy changeling.

killdeer /ˈkɪldɪə/ *noun*. Pl. same, **-s**. Also **-dee** /-diː/. **M18**.
[**ORIGIN** Imit. of the bird's call.]
A large brown and white plover, *Charadrius vociferus*, of N. America.

killer /ˈkɪlə/ *noun & adjective*. **LME**.
[**ORIGIN** from **KILL** *verb*[2] + **-ER**[1].]
▸ **A** *noun* **I** **1** A person who or thing which kills. **LME**.

I. MURDOCH She wanted to be the victim not the killer. *British Medical Journal* Might this be relevant to Alzheimer's disease, now America's number four killer?

impulse killer, ***revenge killer***, etc. ***ladykiller***, ***painkiller***, etc. ***humane killer***: see **HUMANE** *adjective*. ***SERIAL killer***.
2 *ANGLING*. An effective bait. **L17**.
3 = ***killer whale*** below. **E18**.
false killer a whale, *Pseudorca crassidens*, which resembles a killer whale with a smaller dorsal fin and without the white markings.
4 An impressive, admirable, or formidable person or thing; a hilarious joke; a decisive blow. *colloq.* **E20**.

ALAN BENNETT You're a killer Dad, you really are. *New Yorker* So I gave him a dirty look at one point—a real killer.

▸ **II** **5** A cow, sheep, etc., reared for slaughter. Usu. in *pl.* *colloq.* (chiefly *Austral.* & *NZ*). **L19**.
▸ **B** *attrib.* or as *adjective*. **1** That kills, deadly. **L19**.

I. ILLICH Death has paled into a metaphorical figure, and killer diseases have taken his place.

2 Impressive, admirable, formidable. *slang*. **L20**.

Arena Woody Allen can still knock out killer one liners. *City Limits* Sometimes James Brown's albums stank, but there was always one killer track.

– **COMB. & SPECIAL COLLOCATIONS**: **killer app** (*colloq.*, orig. & chiefly *COMPUTING*) a feature, function, or application of a new technology or product which is presented as virtually indispensable or much superior to rival products; **killer bee** *colloq.*, chiefly *US* an Africanized honeybee; **killer cell** PHYSIOLOGY a white blood cell (a type of lymphocyte) which destroys infected or cancerous cells and parasites (see also NATURAL *killer cell*); **killer-diller** *noun & adjective* (*slang*) (*a*) *noun* = sense A.4 above; (*b*) *adjective* = sense B.2 above; **killer instinct** (*a*) an innate tendency to kill, a homicidal tendency; (*b*) *fig.* a keenly competitive or ruthless streak; **killer submarine**: designed to hunt and destroy enemy submarines under water; **killer whale** a predatory toothed whale, *Orcinus orca*, with black and white markings and a high narrow dorsal fin.

– NOTE: Recorded earlier in ME as a surname.

killian *noun* var. of KILIAN *noun*.

killick /ˈkɪlɪk/ *noun*. Also **-ock** /-ək/. M17.
[ORIGIN Unknown.]
NAUTICAL. **1** A heavy stone held in a wooden anchor-shaped frame, used on a small vessel as a substitute for an anchor. Also, a small anchor. M17.
2 A leading seaman's badge, bearing the symbol of an anchor; a leading seaman. *colloq.* E20.

killifish /ˈkɪlɪfɪʃ/ *noun*. Pl. **-es** /-ɪz/, (usu.) same. E19.
[ORIGIN App. from KILL *noun*[2] + FISH *noun*[1].]
Any of several small, often brightly coloured toothcarps of the families Cyprinodontidae and Poeciliidae; *esp.* any of the genus *Fundulus*, found esp. in sheltered rivers and estuaries of eastern N. America. Also called ***topminnow***.

killiki(n)nick *noun* var. of KINNIKINNICK.

killing /ˈkɪlɪŋ/ *noun*. LME.
[ORIGIN from KILL *verb*[2] + -ING[1].]
1 The action of KILL *verb*[2]; an instance of this. LME.

> *Christian Aid News* Fr. Josimo . . had been witness to the expulsions, torture . . and killings of peasants for many years. *attrib.*: *Soldier* Flanders is the killing ground in which the fate of the countries of Europe has been decided.

2 A large profit; a quick and profitable success in business etc. *slang*. L19.

> J. O'FAOLAIN The old man . . had made a killing in real estate.

K

– COMB.: **killing bottle**: containing poisonous vapour for killing captured insects etc.; **killing circle** the area within which the shot from a gun is sufficiently compact to kill game; **killing field(s)** a place where a heavy loss of life has occurred, esp. as the result of massacre or genocide during a time of warfare or violent civil unrest: often with ref. to Cambodia in the 1970s, through the film *The Killing Fields* (1984); **killing time** (*a*) the time at which an animal is (ready to be) killed; (*b*) SCOTTISH HISTORY any of the periods during which many Covenanters were put to death; **killing zone** (*a*) the area of a military engagement with a high concentration of fatalities; (*b*) the area of the human body where entry of a projectile would kill, esp. as indicated on a target for shooting practice.

killing /ˈkɪlɪŋ/ *adjective & adverb*. LME.
[ORIGIN from KILL *verb*[2] + -ING[2].]
▸ **A** *adjective*. **1** That kills; deadly, destructive. LME.

> *Daily Colonist* The wind . . will be followed . . by calm, cold weather with killing frosts. B. EMECHETA Anything is possible to the man with a killing weapon.

2 *hyperbol.* **a** Overwhelming; *spec.* (*a*) crushing, oppressive; (*b*) very beautiful or attractive; (*c*) arduous, exhausting. E17. ▸**b** Excruciatingly funny, hilarious. *colloq.* M19.

> **a** H. ROBBINS He couldn't keep working at a pace like that forever. It was killing. P. L. FERMOR Their floppy hats were worn at killing angles.

▸ **B** *adverb*. = KILLINGLY. L17.

> R. L. STEVENSON The ocean breeze blew killing chill.

■ **killingly** *adverb* in a killing manner L16. **killingness** *noun* M19.

killock *noun* var. of KILLICK.

killogie /kɪˈləʊgi/ *noun*. *Scot.* Now *rare*. Also **-logy**. E16.
[ORIGIN from *kill* var. of KILN *noun* + LOGIE.]
The covered space in front of the fireplace of a kiln, providing a draught for the fire and sheltering the person attending it.

Kilmarnock /kɪlˈmɑːnək/ *noun*. M17.
[ORIGIN A town in SW Scotland.]
▸ **I 1** Used *attrib.* to designate things originating or found in Kilmarnock. M17.
Kilmarnock bonnet, **Kilmarnock cap** a cap resembling a tam-o'-shanter. **Kilmarnock willow** a pendulous cultivar of the goat willow, *Salix caprea*.
▸ **II 2** A Kilmarnock cap or bonnet. E19.

kiln /kɪln/ *noun & verb*. Also (now *Scot.*) **kill** /kɪl/. OE.
[ORIGIN Latin *culina* kitchen, stove.]
▸ **A** *noun*. An industrial furnace, oven, etc., for burning, baking, or drying, *spec.* (*a*) for calcining lime, (*b*) for baking bricks, (*c*) for firing pottery, (*d*) for drying grain, hops, etc. OE.
progressive kiln: see PROGRESSIVE *adjective*. **set the kiln on fire** cause a serious commotion or turmoil.
– COMB.: **kiln-dry** *verb trans.* dry in a kiln.
▸ **B** *verb trans.* Burn, bake, or dry in a kiln. E16.
■ **kilnful** *noun* the amount a kiln can hold LME.

Kilner jar /ˈkɪlnə dʒɑː/ *noun phr.* M20.
[ORIGIN Manufacturer's name.]
(Proprietary name for) a type of preserving jar.

kilo /ˈkiːləʊ/ *noun*. Pl. **-os**. L19.
[ORIGIN French, abbreviation of *kilogramme*, *kilomètre*.]
1 = KILOGRAM. L19.
2 = KILOMETRE. L19.

kilo- /ˈkɪləʊ, ˈkiːləʊ/ *combining form*.
[ORIGIN French, from Greek *khilioi* thousand: see -O-.]
Used in names of units of measurement to denote a factor of one thousand, as ***kilojoule***, ***kilolitre***, ***kilopascal***, etc., or (in COMPUTING) a factor of 1,024 (2^{10}), as ***kilobyte*** etc. Abbreviation ***k***.
■ **kilobase** *noun* (BIOCHEMISTRY) a unit of size of nucleic acid chains, equal to one thousand base pairs (also ***kilobase-pair***) L20. **kilobit** *noun* (COMPUTING) a unit of memory size equal to 1,024 bits M20. **kilobuck** *noun* (*slang*) a thousand dollars M20. **kilocalorie** *noun* = CALORIE (a) L19. **kilocycle** *noun* (*a*) a thousand cycles (of some periodic phenomenon); (*b*) = KILOHERTZ: E20. **kilohertz** *noun* a thousand hertz or cycles per second E20. **kilovolt** *noun* a thousand volts L19. **kilovoltage** *noun* voltage expressed in kilovolts M20. **kilowatt** *noun* a thousand watts (***kilowatt-hour***, a unit of energy equal to that produced in one hour by a power of one kilowatt (= 3.6 million joule)) L19. **kilowattage** *noun* power expressed in kilowatts M20.

kilobyte /ˈkɪləbʌɪt/ *noun*. L20.
[ORIGIN from KILO- + BYTE.]
COMPUTING. A unit of memory size equal to 1,024 (2^{10}) bytes.

kilogram /ˈkɪləgram/ *noun*. Also **-gramme**. L18.
[ORIGIN French *kilogramme*, formed as KILO- + GRAM *noun*[2].]
A fundamental unit of mass or (*loosely*) weight in the metric system (equal to approx. 2.205 lb), orig. defined as the mass of a cubic decimetre of pure water, now as an SI unit defined as equal to the mass of a unique standard cylinder of platinum-iridium alloy kept at Sèvres near Paris. Also, (in full ***standard kilogram***) this or a similar object acting as a standard mass. (Symbol kg.)
– COMB.: **kilogram calorie** = CALORIE (a); **kilogram-force**, pl. **kilograms-force**, a unit of force or weight equal to the weight of a mass of one kilogram under standard gravity; **kilogram-metre** a unit of energy equal to that required to raise a mass of one kilogram to the height of one metre under standard gravity.

kilometre /ˈkɪləmiːtə, kɪˈlɒmɪtə/ *noun*. Also ***-meter**. L18.
[ORIGIN French *kilomètre*, formed as KILO- + METRE *noun*[2].]
A unit of length or distance equal to one thousand metres, equivalent to approx. 3280.84 feet or approx. five-eighths of a mile.
■ **kiˈlometrage** *noun* the number of kilometres covered or travelled L20. **kiloˈmetric** *adjective* pertaining to a kilometre or kilometres; marking a distance of a kilometre: M19.

kiloton /ˈkɪlətʌn/ *noun*. M20.
[ORIGIN from KILO- + TON *noun*[1].]
One thousand tons; usu. *spec.*, a unit of explosive power, equal to that of one thousand tons of TNT.

Kilroy /ˈkɪlrɔɪ/ *noun*. M20.
[ORIGIN Perh. from James J. *Kilroy*, a US shipyard worker who wrote 'Kilroy was here' on sections of warships he had inspected at Quincy, Mass.]
(The name of) a mythical person, popularized by American servicemen in the Second World War, who left such inscriptions as 'Kilroy was here' on walls all over the world.

kilt /kɪlt/ *noun*. M18.
[ORIGIN from the verb.]
A kind of skirt reaching to the knee, usu. made of pleated tartan cloth, as traditionally worn by men from the Scottish Highlands. Now also, any similar garment worn elsewhere or by women and children.
■ **kilted** *adjective* wearing a kilt E19.

kilt /kɪlt/ *verb*. ME.
[ORIGIN Of Scandinavian origin: cf. Swedish dial. *kilta* to swathe, Danish *kilte (op)* tuck (up), Old Norse *kilting* a skirt, *kjalta* the lap.]
1 *verb trans.* Tuck up (skirts) round the body. Also foll. by *up*. ME.

> D. H. LAWRENCE She, with her skirts kilted up, flew round at her work, absorbed.

2 *verb trans.* Tie or hoist up (a thing); hang (a person). Now *rare* or *obsolete*. L17.
3 *verb intrans.* Go quickly, hasten, as if with the skirts kilted up. *Scot.* E19.
4 *verb trans.* Gather in vertical pleats. L19.
■ **kilting** *noun* (*a*) the action of the verb; (*b*) clothing or material tucked up or gathered in pleats: E16.

kilta /ˈkɪltə/ *noun*. L19.
[ORIGIN Unknown.]
In the Indian subcontinent, esp. in the Himalayan region: a kind of long conical wicker basket carried on the back.

kilter /ˈkɪltə/ *noun*[1]. Also **kelter** /ˈkɛltə/. E17.
[ORIGIN Unknown.]
Good condition or order; good state of health or spirits. Chiefly in ***out of kilter***, ***in kilter***, ***in good kilter***.

> *Outrage* Daylight saving throws everyone's body clock out of kilter.

kilter /ˈkɪltə/ *noun*[2]. L19.
[ORIGIN Prob. var. of KELTER *noun*[2].]
An unorthodox poker hand containing no card higher than nine, nor any ace, pair, flush, or straight.

kiltie /ˈkɪlti/ *noun & adjective*. *colloq.* M19.
[ORIGIN from KILT *noun* + -IE.]
▸ **A** *noun*. A person, esp. a Highland soldier, wearing a kilt. M19.
▸ **B** *adjective*. Kilted. E20.

kimberlite /ˈkɪmbəlʌɪt/ *noun*. L19.
[ORIGIN from *Kimberley*, diamond-mining centre in South Africa + -ITE[1].]
GEOLOGY. A rare intrusive blue-green igneous rock, a porphyritic mica-peridotite, which occurs in South Africa and Siberia and is a source of diamonds. Also called ***blue ground***.

kimchi /ˈkɪmtʃi/ *noun*. L19.
[ORIGIN Korean.]
A raw strongly flavoured cabbage pickle, the Korean national dish.

Kimeridge *noun* var. of KIMMERIDGE.

kim-kam /ˈkɪmkam/ *adjective & adverb*. Now chiefly *dial.* L16.
[ORIGIN App. redupl. of CAM *adjective & adverb* with vowel variation: cf. FLIMFLAM, JIMJAM.]
Crooked(ly), awkward(ly), perverse(ly).

kimmer *noun* var. of CUMMER.

Kimmeridge /ˈkɪmərɪdʒ/ *noun*. Also (earlier) **Kimer-**. M18.
[ORIGIN A village on the Dorset coast of SW England.]
GEOLOGY. Used *attrib.* to designate sedimentary deposits of Jurassic age which are especially well developed near Kimmeridge.
Kimmeridge clay (a bed of) a fossiliferous clay containing bituminous shale which forms deposits extending across much of southern England and parts of Europe. **Kimmeridge coal** bituminous shale from the Kimmeridge clay which can be burnt as fuel.
■ **Kimmeˈridgian** *adjective & noun* (designating or pertaining to) a division of the Upper Jurassic including the Kimmeridge clay M19.

kimnel /ˈkɪmn(ə)l/ *noun*. Long *obsolete* exc. *dial.* ME.
[ORIGIN App. rel. to COOMB *noun*[1].]
A tub used for brewing, kneading, salting meat, and other household purposes.

ki-mon /ˈkiːmɒn/ *noun*. L19.
[ORIGIN Japanese, from *ki* demon, devil + *mon* gate.]
In Japanese tradition (taken from Chinese geomancy): the north-east, the traditional source of evil.

kimono /kɪˈməʊnəʊ/ *noun & adjective*. M17.
[ORIGIN Japanese, from *ki* wearing + *mono* thing.]
▸ **A** *noun*. Pl. **-os**. A long Japanese robe with wide sleeves, tied with a sash. Now also, in Western countries, a garment (esp. a dressing gown) modelled on this. M17.
▸ **B** *attrib.* or as *adjective*. Resembling or characteristic of a kimono. E20.
■ **kimonoed** *adjective* wearing a kimono L19.

Kim's game /ˈkɪmz geɪm/ *noun phr.* E20.
[ORIGIN from *Kim* (the eponymous hero of) a book by Rudyard Kipling (1865–1936), in which a similar game is played.]
A memory-testing game in which players try to remember as many as possible of a set of objects briefly shown to them.

kin /kɪn/ *noun & adjective*.
[ORIGIN Old English *cyn(n* = Old Frisian *kin*, *ken*, *kon*, Old Saxon, Old High German *kunni* (Dutch *kunne*), Old Norse *kyn*, Gothic *kuni*, from Germanic, from Indo-European base also of Greek *genos*, Latin *genus* race, GENUS.]
▸ **A** *noun*. **I** Family, race, blood relations.
1 A group of people descended from a common ancestor; *spec.* a family, a clan. Formerly also, the progeny *of* a specified ancestor. Long *rare*. OE.
2 a *collect.* One's family, one's relatives; relatives; *transf.* people or things of a similar kind. OE. ▸**b** A member of one's family, a relative. *arch.* OE.

> **a** E. INGERSOLL The martens . . , skunks, otters and their kin of the family Mustelidae. G. STEIN These relatives of hers . . were the only kin she had. A. TOFFLER We expect ties with our immediate family, and to a lesser extent with other kin. A. BURGESS George . . gave a great dinner for his kin at the Midland Hotel. *Sunday Times* The middle-classes and their kin.

3 Ancestral stock; family. Esp. in ***of good kin***, ***of noble kin***. Long *obsolete* exc. *dial.* OE.
4 The quality, condition, or fact of being related by birth or descent; kinship, consanguinity. Now *rare* or *obsolete*. LME.
▸ **II** Class, group, division.
†**5** A natural class, group, or division of people, animals, plants, etc., with shared attributes or ancestry; *spec.* a race, a species. OE–E16. ▸†**b** A kind of (person or thing). OE–L16.
– PHRASES: ***kissing kin***: see KISSING *ppl adjective*. ***kith and kin***: see KITH *noun* 3. **near of kin** closely related. **next of kin** the living person or persons standing in the nearest degree of relationship to another, and entitled to share in his or her personal estate in case of intestacy. **of kin** (*a*) (long *rare*) by birth or descent; (*b*) related by blood or in character, akin. ***store the kin***: see STORE *verb*.
– COMB.: **kin group** a group of people related by blood or marriage; **kin selection** BIOLOGY a form of natural selection in which an apparently disadvantageous characteristic (esp. altruistic behaviour) increases in the population due to increased survival

of individuals genetically related to those possessing the characteristic.
▸ **B** *pred. adjective*. Related; akin (*to*). **L16.**

> SHAKES. *Tr. & Cr.* One touch of nature makes the whole world kin.

kin /kɪn/ *aux. verb*. Chiefly *US* (*black English & dial.*). **L19.**
[**ORIGIN** Repr. a pronunc. of **CAN** *verb*[1].]
Can; be able to.

-kin /kɪn/ *suffix*.
[**ORIGIN** from or after Middle Dutch *-kijn*, *-ken*, German *-chen*, as in Middle Dutch *husekijn*, *huusken*, German *Häuschen* little house.]
Forming dim. nouns, as ***catkin***, ***lambkin***, ***manikin***.

kina /ˈkiːnə/ *noun*[1]. *NZ*. **M20.**
[**ORIGIN** Maori.]
An edible sea urchin, *Evechinus chloroticus*.

kina /ˈkiːnə/ *noun*[2]. Pl. **-s**, same. **L20.**
[**ORIGIN** Tok Pisin = mother-of-pearl shell, used in exchange, from Tolai, any broad flat seashell.]
The basic monetary unit of Papua New Guinea, equal to 100 toea.

kinaesthesia /kɪnɪsˈθiːzɪə, kʌɪn-/ *noun*. Also ***kines-**. **L19.**
[**ORIGIN** from Greek *kinein* move + *aisthēsis* sensation: see **-IA**[1].]
The faculty of being aware of the position and movement of parts of the body, by means of sensory nerves (proprioceptors) within the muscles, joints, etc.; the sensation producing such awareness.
▪ **kinaesthesiˈometer** *noun* an instrument for measuring kinaesthetic sensitivity **L19.** **kinaesthesis** *noun* = **KINAESTHESIA L19.** **kinaesthetic** /-ˈθɛtɪk/ *adjective* of or pertaining to kinaesthesia; involving or utilizing kinaesthesia: **L19.** **kinaesthetically** *adverb* by means of kinaesthesia **M20.**

kinaki /kɪˈnaki/ *noun*. *NZ*. **E19.**
[**ORIGIN** Maori.]
A Maori relish; a tasty or savoury addition to a Maori meal.

kinase /ˈkʌɪneɪz/ *noun*. **E20.**
[**ORIGIN** from Greek *kinein* move + **-ASE**.]
BIOCHEMISTRY. **1** A substance which converts an inactive precursor into an active enzyme. Now *rare* or *obsolete*. **E20.**
2 Any of various enzymes that catalyse the transfer of a phosphate group from ATP to another molecule. **M20.**

kinchin /ˈkɪntʃɪn/ *noun*. *slang*. Now *rare* or *obsolete*. **M16.**
[**ORIGIN** German *Kindchen* dim. of *Kind* child: cf. **-KIN**.]
A young child. Orig. & usu. in *comb.* (see below).
– **COMB.**: †**kinchin-cove** a young boy; **kinchin-lay** the practice of stealing money from children sent on errands; †**kinchin-mort** [see **MOT** *noun*[1]] a young girl.

kincob /ˈkɪŋkɒb/ *noun & adjective*. **E18.**
[**ORIGIN** Urdu & Persian *kamkāb* gold or silver brocade, alt. of *kamkā* damask silk, from older Chinese *kjəmχwa* ornate (applied to brocade), from *kjəm* gold + *χwa* flower, decoration.]
(Made of) a rich Indian fabric, embroidered with gold or silver.

kind /kʌɪnd/ *noun*. Also †**kynd**.
[**ORIGIN** Old English *cynd(e)*, earlier *ġecynd(e)*, from Germanic, from bases of **Y-**, **KIN** *noun*.]
▸ **I** Nature.
1 (The regular course of) nature; the established order of things. Long *arch*. **OE.**

> W. MORRIS O ye who sought to find Unending life against the law of Kind.

2 Innate character, native constitution; natural disposition. Long *rare*. **OE.**

> H. T. BUCKLE For as to the men themselves, they merely acted after their kind.

†**3** Natural state, form, or condition; a natural property or quality. **OE–LME.**
4 A manner, a way, a fashion; *spec.* the manner natural or proper to a person or thing. *arch*. **OE.**

> T. HALE Being in no kind desirous that his Majesty should be under any Obligation.

5 Character regarded as determining the class to which a thing belongs; generic or specific nature. **E17.**

> D. LESSING There was a difference in degree but not in kind.

▸ **II** A class, a sort, a type.
6 A group of animals or plants having a common origin; a race. Now *literary*. **OE.**

> THOMAS SMITH Without this society of man and woman the kind of man could not long endure. DEFOE They would sooner starve than eat any Thing that lived on human kind.

7 A class of individuals or objects distinguished by common essential characteristics; a genus, a species; a sort, a variety. (After *these* or *those* pl. sometimes same.) **OE.** ▸**b** *collect.* A sex. Long *rare*. **M16.** ▸**c** A literary genre. **M17.**

> GOLDSMITH Of the bear, there are three different kinds. J. BUCHAN The shutters . . were the kind that lock with a key. S. BELLOW A bronchial infection of a rare kind. D. JOHNSON The bartender was my kind of person. **b** R. HUNTFORD Emily took the revenge of her kind by mothering her man. **c** G. HOUGH The impetus to the theory of kinds was initially given by Aristotle.

▸ **III** Descent, birth, sex.
†**8 a** One's native place or position; a natural entitlement; a birthright, a heritage. **OE–M17.** ▸**b** Birth, descent. **OE–M17.**
†**9 a** Gender; sex. **OE–L16.** ▸**b** The sexual organs. *rare*. **OE–ME.** ▸**c** Semen. **LME–M16.**
†**10 a** Offspring, progeny; descendants. **OE–L16.** ▸**b** (A generation of) a family; a clan, tribe, etc. **ME–L17.**
11 Ancestral race or stock; family. *arch*. **ME.**

> SHAKES. *Per.* She's such a one that, were I well assur'd Came of gentle kind and noble stock, I'd wish no better choice.

– **PHRASES**: **a kind of** a person or thing resembling or roughly equivalent to (another). ***all kind of***, ***all kinds of***: see **ALL** *adjective*. †**by kind** by nature, naturally. ***Communion in both kinds***, ***Communion in one kind***: see **COMMUNION** 5. **in kind** (*a*) in goods or labour as opp. to money; (*b*) in a similar form, likewise. **kind of** somewhat, to some extent (cf. **KINDA**). ***kissing kind***: see **KISSING** *ppl adjective*. **law of kind** *arch.* the natural order of things, nature. **nothing of the kind** not at all like the thing in question; (expr. denial) in no way, not at all. **of a kind** (*a*) *derog.* scarcely worthy of a specified term or description; (*b*) (of two or more persons or things) similar in some important respect. **of its kind** within the limitations of the class to which it belongs. **one's own kind** (the) people with whom one has a great deal in common. ***SOMETHING* of the kind**. ***these kind of***: see **THESE** *adjective* 1. ***the worst kind***: see **WORST** *adjective, adverb, & noun*. ***those kind of***: see **THOSE** *adjective* 2.
– **COMB.**: **kind payment** payment in kind, payment in goods or labour as opp. to money.
▪ **kinda**, **-er** /ˈkʌɪndə/ *adverb* (*non-standard*) [repr. a pronunc.: see **A** *preposition*[2]] somewhat, to some extent, = ***kind of*** above **M19.**

kind /kʌɪnd/ *adjective & adverb*.
[**ORIGIN** Old English *ġe)cynd(e)* from Germanic, from base of **KIND** *noun*.]
▸ **A** *adjective*. **I** Natural, native.
†**1** Implanted by or conforming to nature; proper, appropriate. **OE–L17.**
2 †**a** Of an heir, inheritance, etc.: lawful, rightful. **OE–E18.** ▸**b** Native, indigenous. Long *obsolete* exc. *Scot.* **ME.** ▸†**c** Of a person: related to oneself; one's own. **ME–E16.** ▸†**d** Having a specified character or position by nature or birth. **LME–L16.**
▸ **II** Good by nature.
3 †**a** Well-born, of gentle birth; well-bred. **ME–L19.** ▸**b** Of a good kind; having the natural qualities well developed. *obsolete* exc. *dial.* **ME.**
4 Having or displaying a gentle, sympathetic, or benevolent disposition; showing consideration for others. Formerly also, courteous. (Foll. by *to*.) **ME.**

> J. RULE The kindest thing Evelyn could do was to ignore her nervousness. A. BURGESS Mother Andrea had a sweet face and was kind and gentle. *fig.*: R. CHURCH The winter . . of damp and sulphurous fogs, had not been kind to her.

5 Of a person, action, etc.: affectionate, loving, fond; intimate. Now *rare* exc. *dial.* **ME.**

> POPE Do lovers dream, or is my Delia kind.

†**6** Acceptable, agreeable, pleasant. **ME–L18.**
7 Grateful, thankful. *obsolete* exc. *dial.* **LME.**
8 Soft, tender; easy to work. *dial. & techn.* **M18.**
▸ **B** *adverb*. Kindly. *colloq.* **E17.**

kindergarten /ˈkɪndəɡɑːt(ə)n/ *noun*. **M19.**
[**ORIGIN** German, lit. 'children's garden'.]
1 Orig., a school teaching young children according to a method devised by Friedrich Fröbel (see **FROEBEL**) for developing their intelligence by means of interesting objects, exercises with toys, games, singing, etc. Now, any nursery school. **M19.**
2 *hist.* The group of young men with imperialist ideals recruited by Lord Milner, High Commissioner of South Africa, to help with reconstruction work after the second Boer War of 1899–1902. **E20.**
▪ **kindergartener** *noun* a teacher or pupil at a kindergarten **L19.**

Kinder, Kirche, Küche /ˈkɪndər ˈkɪrçə ˈkyçə/ *noun phr. pl.* Freq. *iron.* **L19.**
[**ORIGIN** German, lit. 'children, church, kitchen'.]
The domestic and religious concerns traditionally regarded as appropriate for a woman.

kinderspiel /ˈkɪndəʃpiːl/ *noun*. **E20.**
[**ORIGIN** German, lit. 'children's play'.]
A dramatic piece performed by children.

kind-hearted /kʌɪndˈhɑːtɪd/ *adjective*. **M16.**
[**ORIGIN** from **KIND** *adjective* + **HEARTED**.]
Having a kind disposition.
▪ **kind-heartedly** *adverb* **E20.** **kind-heartedness** *noun* **L16.**

kindle /ˈkɪnd(ə)l/ *noun*. **ME.**
[**ORIGIN** App. from **KIND** *noun* + **-LE**[1].]
1 A litter of kittens. Formerly also, the young of any animal; a young one. Long *rare*. **ME.**
2 ***in kindle***, (of a hare, rabbit, etc.) pregnant, with young. Chiefly *dial.* **L19.**

kindle /ˈkɪnd(ə)l/ *verb*[1]. **ME.**
[**ORIGIN** from Old Norse *kynda* + **-LE**[3], suggested by Old Norse *kindill* candle, torch.]
▸ **I** *verb trans.* **1** Set fire to (combustible material); ignite; light (a flame, a fire). **ME.**

> D. M. THOMAS She . . kindled a fire in the stove.

2 Inflame, arouse, inspire, (an emotion, feeling, etc.); give rise to (trouble etc.). **ME.**

> D. DELILLO I'm happy to say I've kindled an interest. A. BROOKNER She . . never did anything to kindle the emotions of other drivers.

3 Excite, stir up (a person, the imagination, etc.). Also foll. by *to*, *to do*. **ME.**
4 Make bright or glowing as with fire. **E16.**
▸ **II** *verb intrans.* **5** Begin to burn; catch fire. **ME.**

> *New York Times* To-day, a light kindles in the long night of horror in El Salvador.

6 (Of an emotion, feeling, etc.) rise, be aroused, be excited; (of a person) become impassioned or excited, respond with animation. **ME.**

> J. REED They greeted him with an immense crusading acclaim, kindling to the daring of it. G. GREENE His imagination kindled with a more daring project.

7 Become bright or glowing like fire. **L18.**
▪ **kindler** *noun* **LME.**

kindle /ˈkɪnd(ə)l/ *verb*[2] *trans. & intrans.* Now chiefly *dial.* **ME.**
[**ORIGIN** App. from **KIND** *noun* + **-LE**[3], or from **KINDLE** *noun*.]
Of a hare, rabbit, etc.: give birth to (young).

kindless /ˈkʌɪndlɪs/ *adjective*. Now *rare*. **ME.**
[**ORIGIN** from **KIND** *noun* + **-LESS**; in sense 2 as if from **KIND** *adjective*.]
†**1** Without natural power, feeling, etc.; unnatural. **ME–E17.**
2 Devoid of kindness. **M19.**

kindlily /ˈkʌɪndlɪli/ *adverb*. **E19.**
[**ORIGIN** from **KINDLY** *adjective* + **-LY**[2].]
In a kindly manner.

kindliness /ˈkʌɪndlɪnɪs/ *noun*. **LME.**
[**ORIGIN** formed as **KINDLILY** + **-NESS**.]
1 The quality or habit of being kindly. **LME.**
†**2** Mildness of climate etc. that is favourable to vegetation. **M17–L18.**

kindling /ˈkɪndlɪŋ/ *noun*[1]. **ME.**
[**ORIGIN** from **KINDLE** *verb*[1] + **-ING**[1].]
1 The action of **KINDLE** *verb*[1]; an instance of this. **ME.**
2 Material for lighting a fire. **E16.**
– **COMB.**: **kindling wood** dry wood suitable for lighting fires.

kindling /ˈkɪndlɪŋ/ *noun*[2]. Now chiefly *dial.* **ME.**
[**ORIGIN** from **KINDLE** *verb*[2] + **-ING**[1].]
1 The action of **KINDLE** *verb*[2]; an instance of this. **ME.**
2 (A member of) a brood or litter; progeny, offspring. **ME.**

kindly /ˈkʌɪndli/ *adjective*. **OE.**
[**ORIGIN** from **KIND** *noun* + **-LY**[1].]
▸ **I** Pertaining to nature or birth.
1 a Existing or occurring according to (the laws of) nature; natural (*to*); proper, suitable. Long *obsolete* exc. *Scot.* **OE.** ▸†**b** Implanted by nature; innate. **OE–E17.**
2 Having a hereditary right to a position, tenancy, etc.; rightful, lawful; (of a child) legitimate. Now *rare*. **OE.** ▸**b** Native, indigenous. *obsolete* exc. *Scot.* **E17.**
†**3** Belonging to one by birth; hereditary. **ME–M17.**
▸ **II** Good by nature.
4 Of good natural qualities; excellent of its kind; healthy, thriving. Now *arch. & dial.* **LME.**
5 Acceptable, agreeable, pleasant; *spec.* (of climate, conditions, etc.) benign, favourable to growth. **LME.**

> A. WEST They . . sat about in deck chairs in kindly weather.

6 Having or displaying a friendly benevolent disposition; kind, good-natured. **E16.**

> DAY LEWIS Aunt Alice I remember as a kindly, comfortable, clucking woman. A. N. WILSON Tibba in the most matter-of-fact and yet kindly way had . . taken control.

kindly /ˈkʌɪndli/ *adverb*. **OE.**
[**ORIGIN** from **KIND** *adjective* + **-LY**[2].]
1 †**a** In accordance with nature; characteristically. Later also, thoroughly, exactly. **OE–L16.** ▸**b** In a manner appropriate to the nature of a thing; properly, fittingly; readily, spontaneously; successfully. Now *rare* exc. *dial.* **LME.**
2 In a kind manner; sympathetically, considerately, benevolently; affectionately. **ME.**
3 In a way that pleases or is agreeable to the recipient. Now chiefly in polite requests and (*iron.*) in demands. **L16.**

> J. K. TOOLE Will you kindly go away? A. MACLEAN If not, kindly refrain from sending pointless signals.

– **PHRASES**: **take kindly** accept as a kindness, be pleased by. **take kindly to** find acceptable, pleasant, or endearing. **thank kindly** thank heartily and appreciatively.

kindness /ˈkʌɪn(d)nɪs/ *noun*. **ME.**
[**ORIGIN** from **KIND** *adjective* + **-NESS**.]
1 The quality or habit of being kind; kind nature or disposition; kind behaviour or treatment. **ME.**

> COLERIDGE I have never forgotten the kindness . . which I received from yourself and Mr. C.

kill with kindness: see **KILL** *verb*[2]. ***milk of human kindness***: see **MILK** *noun*.

K

2 A kind deed, a considerate act. Formerly also, a benefaction. ME.

DICKENS Do a kindness to the sweet dear that is withering away.

3 A feeling of fondness or affection; good will, favour. Now *arch.* LME.

G. HEYER Her ladyship has a kindness for Drusilla.

†**4** A natural inclination or aptitude. *rare.* LME–L17.
†**5** Kinship; close relationship. LME–L17.
†**6** Hereditary right, *spec.* to a tenancy. *Scot.* E16–M17.

kindred /ˈkɪndrɪd/ *noun & adjective.* ME.
[ORIGIN from KIN *noun & adjective* + -RED, with phonet. devel. of *d* between *n* and *r* as in *thunder*.]
▶ **A** *noun* **1 a** Relationship between people, esp. by blood or descent; kinship. ME. ▸**b** *fig.* Affinity of character; resemblance. L16.
2 A group of people related by blood; a family, a clan, a tribe. Now *rare.* ME. ▸†**b** The family or descendants *of* a specified ancestor. ME–M17. ▸†**c** A generation. ME–M16. ▸†**d** Descent, pedigree. LME–L16.
†**3** Ancestral stock; family. ME–E16.
4 a *collect.* One's family or relatives. ME. ▸†**b** A kinsman, a kinswoman. LME–E18.
▶ **B** *attrib.* or as *adjective.* **1** Allied in nature or properties; possessing similar qualities; cognate. ME.
kindred spirit a person whose character and outlook have much in common with one's own; in *pl.*, people whose character and outlook have much in common.
2 a Related by birth or marriage. M16. ▸**b** Of, pertaining to, or done by relatives. L16.
■ **kindredness** *noun* kindredship M19. **kindredship** *noun* the quality or state of being akin; kinship: M18.

kindy /ˈkɪndi/ *noun. Austral. & NZ colloq.* M20.
[ORIGIN Abbreviation.]
A kindergarten.

kine /kʌɪn/ *noun*[1]. M20.
[ORIGIN Back-form. from KINESICS.]
An isolable element of body movement or gesture made in non-vocal communication.

kine *noun*[2] see COW *noun*[1].

kine *adjective*, **kinema** *noun* see CINE *adjective*, CINEMA.

kinematic /kɪnɪˈmatɪk, kʌɪn-/ *adjective.* M19.
[ORIGIN from Greek *kinēmat-*, *kinēma* movement (from *kinein* move) + -IC.]
Of or pertaining to kinematics; relating to pure motion, considered without reference to force or mass; *spec.* (MECHANICS) designating a set of mechanical elements the relative position and motion of any one of which is uniquely determined by the relative position and motion of the other(s).
kinematic viscosity: see VISCOSITY 2.
■ **kinematical** *adjective* = KINEMATIC M19. **kinematically** *adverb* as regards or by means of kinematics L19.

kinematics /kɪnɪˈmatɪks, kʌɪn-/ *noun pl.* M19.
[ORIGIN formed as KINEMATIC + -ICS.]
1 The branch of mechanics that deals with pure motion, considered without reference to the objects in motion, or to the forces acting on them. Treated as *sing.* Cf. KINETICS 1. M19.
2 The kinematic features or properties of something. Treated as *sing.* or *pl.* M20.

kinematograph *noun & verb*, **kinematographic** *adjective*, **kinematography** *noun* see CINEMATOGRAPH etc.

kineme /ˈkʌɪniːm/ *noun.* M20.
[ORIGIN from Greek *kinē(sis* movement + -EME.]
A meaningful unit of body movement or gesture made in non-vocal communication.

kinep *noun* var. of GUINEP.

kinescope /ˈkɪnɪskəʊp/ *noun & verb.* Chiefly *US.* M20.
[ORIGIN from Greek *kinē(sis* movement + -SCOPE: orig. a proprietary name.]
TELEVISION. ▶**A** *noun.* **1** A kind of television picture tube. M20.
2 A film recording of a television broadcast; a telerecording. M20.
▶ **B** *verb trans.* Make a telerecording of. M20.

kinesic /kɪˈniːsɪk, kʌɪ-/ *adjective.* M20.
[ORIGIN from Greek *kinēs(is* movement + -IC.]
Of or pertaining to communication effected non-vocally through movements or gestures.
■ **kinesically** *adverb* M20.

kinesics /kɪˈniːsɪks, kʌɪ-/ *noun pl.* (usu. treated as *sing.*). M20.
[ORIGIN formed as KINESIC + -ICS.]
The branch of knowledge that deals with the way body movements and gestures convey meaning non-vocally; such movements and gestures.

kinesiology /kɪˌniːsɪˈɒlədʒi, kʌɪ-/ *noun.* L19.
[ORIGIN from Greek *kinēsis* movement + -OLOGY.]
1 The branch of science that deals with the mechanics of (human) bodily movement. L19.
2 In full ***applied kinesiology***. A technique of alternative therapy which uses tests of muscle strength as part of a holistic approach to identify and treat underlying health problems. M20.
■ **kinesioˈlogic**, **kinesioˈlogical** *adjectives* M20. **kinesiologist** *noun* M20.

kinesis /kɪˈniːsɪs, kʌɪ-/ *noun.* Pl. **kineses** /-siːz/. E17.
[ORIGIN Greek *kinēsis* movement.]
1 *gen.* Motion; a kind of movement. *rare.* E17.
2 BIOLOGY. An undirected movement of an organism that occurs in response to a particular kind of stimulus. E20.
3 ZOOLOGY. Mobility of the bones of the skull, as in some birds and reptiles. M20.

kinesthesia *noun* see KINAESTHESIA.

kinetheodolite /ˌkɪnɪθɪˈɒdəlʌɪt, ˌkʌɪ-/ *noun.* M20.
[ORIGIN from Greek *kinē(sis* movement + THEODOLITE.]
A telescope used to follow the path of a projectile, aircraft, etc., and mounted so that its elevation and azimuth angles are indicated.

kinetic /kɪˈnɛtɪk, kʌɪ-/ *adjective.* M19.
[ORIGIN Greek *kinētikos*, from *kinein* move: see -IC.]
1 Of, pertaining to, or relating to motion; due to or resulting from motion. M19. ▸**b** BIOLOGY. Of, pertaining to, or of the nature of a kinesis. E20. ▸**c** *fig.* Active, dynamic, full of energy. M20.

c H. G. WELLS They were at least kinetic, they wanted to make things happen.

2 CHEMISTRY. Of, pertaining to, or governed by the kinetics of a reaction. L19.
3 CYTOLOGY. Pertaining to or involved in mitotic division; undergoing division. Cf. KINESIS 1. L19.
4 PHONETICS. Of a consonant, vowel, etc.: changing in quality during utterance as opp. to being held constant. M20.
5 (Of art, a work of art) depending on movement for its effect; of, pertaining to, or producing works of this kind. M20.
– SPECIAL COLLOCATIONS: **kinetic energy** energy which a body possesses by virtue of being in motion (cf. ***potential energy*** s.v. POTENTIAL *adjective*). **kinetic heating** heat generated by the compression and acceleration of air by a fast-moving body. **kinetic theory** a theory which explains physical properties of matter in terms of the motions of constituent particles; *spec.* either of those theories relating respectively to heat and the gaseous state.
■ **kinetically** *adverb* in a kinetic manner, as regards kinetics E20.

kineticist /kɪˈnɛtɪsɪst, kʌɪ-/ *noun.* M20.
[ORIGIN from KINETICS + -IST.]
1 Chiefly CHEMISTRY. An expert in or student of kinetics. M20.
2 A kinetic artist. L20.
■ **kineticism** *noun* kinetic art M20.

kinetics /kɪˈnɛtɪks, kʌɪ-/ *noun pl.* Exc. in sense 2b, usu. treated as *sing.* M19.
[ORIGIN from KINETIC + -ICS.]
1 The branch of dynamics that deals with the relations between the motions of bodies and the forces acting on them. Cf. DYNAMICS 1, STATICS 1. M19.
2 CHEMISTRY. The branch of physical chemistry that deals with the mechanisms and rates of chemical processes. Also (***gas kinetics***), the science of the properties of gases as systems of moving particles. L19. ▸**b** Usu. treated as *pl.* Those aspects of a process that relate to its rate; the details of the way a reaction occurs, esp. as regards its rate. E20.

kinetin /ˈkʌɪnɪtɪn/ *noun.* M20.
[ORIGIN from KINETO- + -IN[1].]
BIOCHEMISTRY. A synthetic compound, 6-furfurylaminopurine, $C_{10}H_9N_5O$, having the properties of a plant growth hormone or kinin.

kineto- /kɪˈniːtəʊ, kʌɪ-/ *combining form.*
[ORIGIN Greek, from *kinētos* movable: see -O-.]
Moving, associated with movement.
■ **kinetochore** *noun* [Greek *khōros* place] CYTOLOGY = CENTROMERE M20. **kinetoˈdesma** *noun*, pl. **-mas**, **-mata** /-mətə/, BIOLOGY (in ciliates and flagellates) a thin fibre consisting of a number of fibrils each terminating in a kinetosome M20. **kinetoˈgenesis** *noun* the (theoretical) origination of animal structures in animal movements L19. **kinetograph** *noun* (*hist.*) an early form of film camera, the resulting images being viewed through a kinetoscope L19. **kinetoˈnucleus** *noun* (BIOLOGY) = KINETOPLAST E20. **kinetoplast** *noun* (BIOLOGY) a mass of mitochondrial DNA lying close to a kinetosome in some protozoa, esp. trypanosomes E20. **kinetoscope** *noun* †(**a**) *rare* a sort of moving panorama; (**b**) *hist.* an early motion-picture device in which the images were viewed through a peephole: M19. **kinetosome** *noun* (BIOLOGY) a cytoplasmic structure which forms the base of a cilium or flagellum E20.

kinety /ˈkʌɪnəti/ *noun.* M20.
[ORIGIN French *cinétie*, from Greek *kinētikos* KINETIC: see -Y[3].]
BIOLOGY. In ciliates and flagellates, a kinetodesma together with its associated kinetosomes.

kinfolk /ˈkɪnfəʊk/ *noun.* Chiefly *N. Amer.* Also **-folks.** L19.
[ORIGIN from KIN *noun & adjective* + FOLK.]
= KINSFOLK.

king /kɪŋ/ *noun.* Also (esp. in titles) **K-.**
[ORIGIN Old English *cyning*, later *cyng*, *cing* = Old Frisian *kining*, *kon-*, *ken-*, Old Saxon, Old High German *kuning* (Dutch *koning*, German *König*), from Germanic, prob. from bases of KIN *noun*, -ING[3].]
1 A male sovereign (esp. hereditary) ruler of an independent state, a male monarch. Also, the head of a region, a tribe, etc., having the status of such a ruler. OE. ▸**b** Any of the kings of Israel and Judah. In *pl.* (treated as *sing.*) (**K-**), each of two (formerly four) books of the Old Testament and Hebrew Scriptures dealing with the history of the kings (also ***Book of Kings***). LME.

W. S. GILBERT Britain set the world ablaze In good King George's glorious days. W. S. CHURCHILL We have a King and Queen . . at the summit of . . the British nation.

2 (Usu. **K-.**) God or Christ regarded as omnipotent. Freq. in ***King of heaven***, ***King of bliss***, ***King of glory***, etc. OE.

H. F. LYTE Praise, my soul, the King of heaven.

3 A woman who rules or bears herself like a king, a queen. *rare.* ME.
4 A person pre-eminent in a given sphere or class; *esp.* (preceded by specifying word) a great merchant, manufacturer, etc., of the thing indicated, a magnate. ME.

Sunday Times Carlos Lehder Rivas, the reputed Columbian cocaine king.

gold king, ***railway king***, etc.
5 An animal, plant, fruit, or other thing regarded as supreme or outstandingly excellent in its class. Also (orig. *US*), a thing of outstanding economic importance. LME.

Times Cheap coal could still be the energy king.

6 †**a** [translating Latin *rex*.] A queen bee. LME–E18. ▸**b** A fully developed male termite. L19.
7 In games. ▸**a** CHESS. The piece which each player must protect against the moves made by the other, so as to prevent it from being finally checkmated. LME. ▸**b** CARDS. One card in each suit, bearing the representation of a king, ranking immediately above the queen and usu. below the ace (but orig. the highest card in the pack). M16. ▸**c** BILLIARDS. An ivory peg formerly placed at one end of the table. *obsolete* exc. *hist.* L17. ▸**d** DRAUGHTS. A piece with an extra capacity of moving, made by crowning an ordinary piece that has reached the opponent's baseline. E19.
8 Any of certain people holding symbolic or pretended supreme authority; *esp.* the chief player in any of certain children's games (see below). M16.
9 *ellipt.* **a** A toast in which the king's health is drunk. M18. ▸**b** (Usu. **K-.**) The British national anthem in the reign of a male monarch, 'God Save the King'. M20.
10 *techn.* **a** In *pl.* One of the classes into which fullers' teasels are sorted. L18. ▸**b** A kind of salmon fly for angling. L18.
– PHRASES & COMB.: ***Book of Kings***: see sense 1b above. ***divine right of kings***: see DIVINE *adjective* 2. **King Alfred daffodil** a commonly grown yellow trumpet daffodil. **king and country**: the objects of allegiance for a patriot whose head of state is a king. **King at Arms** = ***King of Arms*** below. **kingbolt** a main or large bolt in a mechanical structure; *esp.* (**a**) an iron rod in a roof, used instead of a king post; (**b**) a vertical bolt passing through the axle of a horse-drawn carriage or railway coach and forming a pivot on which the axle swings in taking curves. **King Caesar** an old children's game in which two sets of players run between opposite bases and another player tries to catch them. **king carp** a variety of the common carp, *Cyprinus carpio*, covered with uniform scales. **King Charles** = ***King Charles's spaniel*** below. **King Charles's head** [the obsession of Mr Dick in Dickens's *David Copperfield*] an obsession, an *idée fixe*. **King Charles's spaniel** a small black-and-tan breed of spaniel; a dog of this breed. **king cobra** a large, venomous, hooded Indian snake, *Ophiophagus hannah*; also called ***hamadryad***. **King Country** *NZ* an extensive region in the North Island of New Zealand, inhabited by certain Maori tribes under a king following the New Zealand Wars of the 1860s. **king crab** (**a**) = ***HORSESHOE crab***; (**b**) any of various very large crabs of the family Lithodidae, which resemble the spider crabs and are found in cold waters of the N. Pacific. **kingcup** (**a**) the marsh marigold, *Caltha palustris*; (**b**) *dial.* any of several buttercups found in meadows. **king devil** *US* a European hawkweed, *Hieracium praealtum*, a troublesome weed in parts of N. America. **King Edward** (**VII potato**) an oval variety of potato with a white skin mottled with red. ***king-EIDER***. **king fern** *NZ* a large fern, *Marattia salicina*, with fronds up to 4.5 metres long. **king-hit** *noun & verb* (*Austral. & NZ slang*) (**a**) *noun* a knockout blow, a hard punch; a hard fighter, a bully, a leader; (**b**) *verb trans.* punch hard, knock out. **king-hunter** any of various African and Australian kingfishers which do not feed on fish. **King James Bible**, **King James Version** the Authorized Version of the Bible (1611). **King Log** [with ref. to the fable of Jupiter and the frogs] a ruler going to an extreme of laissez-faire (cf. ***King Stork*** below). **king lory** = ***king parrot*** below. **king mackerel** a game fish of the American Atlantic coast, *Scomberomorus cavalla*; also called ***Spanish mackerel***, ***kingfish***. **kingmaker** a person who controls the appointment of kings or (*transf.*) other people of authority through his or her political influence; *spec.* an epithet of Richard Neville, Earl of Warwick, in the reigns of Henry VI and Edward IV. **king-nut** *US* a kind of hickory, *Carya laciniosa*, with a large nut. **King of Arms** (the title of) each of three chief heralds of the College of Arms, viz. Garter, Norroy and Ulster, Clarenceux (see also LYON ***King of Arms***). **king of beasts** the lion. **king of birds** the eagle. **King of Kings** (**a**) a king who has lesser kings under him (esp. as a title adopted by Eastern rulers); (**b**) God. **king of terrors** death personified. **King of the Castle** a children's game involving dislodging a player from a mound. **king of the herrings** any of various fishes popularly supposed to lead shoals of herring, *esp.* the oarfish, *Regalecus glesne*. ***King of the Romans***: see ROMAN *noun*[1]. ***king of the vultures***: see VULTURE *noun*. ***king or Kaiser***: see KAISER. **king parrot** any of various small Australasian

K

parrots of the genus *Alisterus*. **king penguin** a large penguin, *Aptenodytes patagonica*, of the Falklands and other Antarctic islands. **king post** CARPENTRY an upright post in the centre of a roof truss, extending from the ridge to the tie beam. **king prawn** any of several large prawns of the genus *Penaeus*, obtained esp. in Australian waters. **king rail** a large rail, *Rallus elegans*, of freshwater marshes in eastern N. America. ***king* ROOIBEKKIE**. **king salmon** the Chinook salmon, *Oncorhynchus tshawytscha*. ***King's Attorney***: see ATTORNEY *noun* 2. **king's bad bargain** NAUTICAL a lazy or incompetent sailor. **King's Bench** (*a*) see BENCH *noun* 3b; (*b*) (in full ***King's Bench prison***) a former prison for debtors and criminals jailed by the supreme courts at Westminster etc. **king's bishop**, **king's knight**, **king's rook** CHESS the bishop etc. on the king's side of the board at the start of a game. **king's blue** cobalt blue. ***King's bounty***: see BOUNTY 4. ***King's Champion***: see CHAMPION *noun*[1]. ***King's Counsel***: see COUNSEL *noun* 7b. **king's cushion** *Scot.* a seat made by the crossed hands of two people. ***king's evil***: see EVIL *noun*[1] 5b. **King's Friends** *hist.* a political party (*c* 1760–80) which sought to increase the power of the Crown in order to maintain political stability. **king's gambit** CHESS: in which a sacrifice of the king's bishop's pawn is offered. ***King's Guide***: see GUIDE *noun* 1c. **king's hard bargain** NAUTICAL = *king's bad bargain* above. ***King's highway***: see HIGHWAY 1. **king's-hood** *Scot.* the reticulum or second stomach of a ruminant. **kingside** *noun & adjective* (CHESS) (*a*) *noun* = *king's side* below; (*b*) *adjective* made or done on the king's side of the board; (of a piece) situated on that side. **king-size** *adjective & noun* (*a*) *adjective* (esp. of a cigarette) of a size larger than normal; (*b*) *noun* a king-size cigarette. **king-sized** *adjective* = *king-size adjective* above. ***king's knight***: see *king's bishop* above. ***King's Messenger***: see MESSENGER *noun*. **kingsnake** any of various large N. American colubrid snakes of the genus *Lampropeltis*, which prey on other snakes. **king's pawn** CHESS the pawn immediately in front of the king at the start of a game; ***king's pawn opening***: in which White begins by advancing the king's pawn two squares. **king's peg** a mixture of brandy and champagne. ***King's Proctor***: see PROCTOR *noun* 3. ***King's quarantain***: see QUARANTAIN 1. **king's ransom** a very large sum of money. ***King's Remembrancer***: see REMEMBRANCER 1a. ***king's rook***: see *king's bishop* above. **King's Scholar** a scholar in a school founded by royal charter (esp. Eton College). ***King's Scout***: see SCOUT *noun*[3]. **king's ship** *hist.* (*a*) a ship of the fleet provided and maintained out of royal revenue, a ship of the Royal Navy; (*b*) a warship equipped at public expense. **king's side** CHESS the half of the board on which both kings stand at the start of a game. **king's silver** *hist.* money paid in the Court of Common Pleas for licence to levy a fine. **king's spear** any of several tall plants of the lily family, esp. *Asphodeline lutea*, with dense racemes of yellow flowers. **King Stork** [see *King Log* above] a ruler going to an extreme of active oppression. ***king's truce***: see TRUCE *noun*. **king's yellow** orpiment or yellow arsenic used as a pigment. **king vulture** a neotropical vulture, *Sarcorhamphus papa*, having a brightly coloured head. **King William's cravat** a cravat of the kind worn by King William III (1689–1702). **King Willow** the game of cricket personified (cf. WILLOW *noun* 5). **kingwood** any of several tropical woods used in marquetry, esp. those of *Dalbergia cearensis* (family Leguminosae) and *Astronium fraxinifolium* (family Anacardiaceae). ***Lyon King of Arms***. ***Pearly King***: see PEARLY *adjective*. ***silver king***: see SILVER *noun & adjective*. ***take the King's* SHILLING**. ***the king over the water***: see WATER *noun*. ***the King's colour***: see COLOUR *noun* 7. ***the King's English***: see ENGLISH *adjective & noun*. ***the kings of Cologne***: see ***the three kings*** below. ***the King's peace***: see PEACE *noun*. ***the King's Serjeant***: see SERGEANT. ***the King's speech***: see SPEECH *noun*. ***the sport of kings***: see SPORT *noun*. **the three kings** three wise men or Magi (*Matthew* 2:1–12); also ***the kings of Cologne***, ***the three kings of Cologne*** [because their bodies were believed to be preserved at that city]. ***turn King's evidence***: see EVIDENCE *noun*.

■ **kinghood** *noun* kingship; the rank, authority, or office of king; kingly spirit or character: ME. **kingless** *adjective* ME. **kinglessness** *noun* M19. **kinglike** *adjective & adverb* (*a*) *adjective* resembling, characteristic of, or befitting a king; kingly, regal; (*b*) *adverb* like a king, in a manner befitting a king: LME. **kingling** *noun* (freq. *derog.*) a petty king L16.

king /kɪŋ/ *verb*. LME.
[ORIGIN from the noun.]
1 *verb intrans. & trans.* (with *it*). Act the part of a king; rule, govern. LME.

> *Times* Matchan kinged over his 165-acres domain.

2 *verb trans.* Make (a person) into a king. L16.
3 *verb trans.* Rule over (a country) as king. *rare*. L16.

> SHAKES. *Hen. V* She is so idly king'd, Her sceptre so fantastically borne.

kingbird /ˈkɪŋbəːd/ *noun*. Also **king bird**. M18.
[ORIGIN from KING *noun* + BIRD *noun*.]
†1 A darling. *N. Amer. rare*. M–L18.
2 Any of several N. American tyrant flycatchers of the genus *Tyrannus*. L18.
3 A bird of paradise, *Cicinnurus regius*. Now usu. ***king bird of paradise***. L18.
4 A royal bird; an eagle. *poet.* M19.

kingcraft /ˈkɪŋkrɑːft/ *noun*. M17.
[ORIGIN from KING *noun* + CRAFT *noun*.]
The art of ruling as a king, esp. in the use of clever or crafty tactics in dealing with subjects.

kingdom /ˈkɪŋdəm/ *noun & verb*.
[ORIGIN Old English *cyningdōm* = Old Saxon *kuningdōm*, Old Norse *konungdómr*, from Germanic bases of KING *noun*, -DOM.]
▸ **A** *noun*. †1 Kingly function, authority, or power; sovereignty, kingship. OE–L17.

> SHAKES. *Rich. III* Else my kingdom stands on brittle glass.

2 An organized community having a king as its head; a monarchical state or government. ME.

> BURKE The opinion that all the kingdoms of Europe were at a remote period elective.

Middle Kingdom: see MIDDLE *adjective*. ***New Kingdom***: see NEW *adjective*. ***Old Kingdom***: see OLD *adjective*. ***United Kingdom***: see UNITED *adjective*.

3 The territory or country subject to a king; the area over which a monarch's rule extends; a realm. ME. ▸**b** *The* Scottish local government area (formerly county) of Fife, which was one of the seven Pictish kingdoms. E18.
4 *transf. & fig.* **a** More fully ***the kingdom of God***, ***the kingdom of heaven***. The spiritual sovereignty of God or Christ, or the sphere over which this extends, in heaven or on earth. ME. ▸**b** The spiritual rule or realm of evil or infernal powers. ME. ▸**c** A realm or sphere in which a condition or quality is supreme. LME. ▸**d** Any sphere in which one has dominion like that of a king. Esp. in ***come into one's kingdom*** [cf. *Luke* 23:42], acquire power, attractiveness, etc. L16. ▸**e** Anything compared to a country ruled by a king; a domain. L16.

> **a** *Christadelphian* We . . pray that we may be able to help one another . . towards the Kingdom. **c** V. S. PRITCHETT The kingdoms of fantasy and mirth are long-lasting and not of this world. **d** S. T. FELSTEAD Towards the end of the 'eighties, the music-hall had come into its kingdom.

a kingdom come [from *thy kingdom come* in the Lord's Prayer] (*a*) *colloq.* the next world, eternity; ***till kingdom come***, for an indefinitely long period; (*b*) the millennial kingdom of Christ.

5 A province of nature; *esp.* each of the three traditional divisions (animal, vegetable, and mineral) into which natural objects have been classified; BIOLOGY the highest category in most systems of taxonomic classification. L17.
▸ **B** *verb trans.* †1 With *it*: pose as a kingdom. *rare*. Only in E17.
2 Take possession of, as a kingdom. L19.
■ **kingdomed** *adjective* (*a*) provided with or constituted as a kingdom; (*b*) (as 2nd elem. of comb.) divided into (so many) kingdoms: E17.

kingfish /ˈkɪŋfɪʃ/ *noun*. Pl. **-es** /-ɪz/, (usu.) same. M18.
[ORIGIN from KING *noun* + FISH *noun*[1].]
1 Any of various fishes notable for their size, appearance, or value as food; *esp.* (*a*) the opah, *Lampris guttatus*; (*b*) = ***YELLOWTAIL kingfish***; (*c*) = ***king mackerel*** s.v. KING *noun*; (*d*) a barb (*Menticirrhus*); (*e*) the barracouta, *Thyrsites atun*; (*f*) a trevally of the genus *Caranx*. M18.
2 A leader, a boss. Freq. as a nickname. *US slang*. M20.

kingfisher /ˈkɪŋfɪʃə/ *noun & adjective*. Also (earlier) †**king's-fisher**. ME.
[ORIGIN from KING *noun* + FISHER.]
▸ **A** *noun*. **1** A small European bird, *Alcedo atthis*, with a long beak and brilliant blue and orange plumage, feeding on fish and aquatic animals which it captures by diving; any bird of the family Alcedinidae, most members of which feed in this manner. ME.
malachite kingfisher, ***pied kingfisher***, etc.
2 = ***kingfisher blue*** below. E20.
– COMB.: **kingfisher blue** (of) a brilliant blue colour.
▸ **B** *adjective*. Of kingfisher blue. M20.

Kingite /ˈkɪŋʌɪt/ *noun & adjective*. M19.
[ORIGIN from KING *noun* + -ITE[1].]
NZ HISTORY. ▸**A** *noun*. A follower of the Maori king, after whom the King Country was named. M19.
▸ **B** *attrib.* or as *adjective*. Of or pertaining to the Kingites. L19.

kingklip /ˈkɪŋklɪp/ *noun*. *S. Afr.* E19.
[ORIGIN Afrikaans from Dutch *koningklipvisch*, from *koning* king + *klipvisch* KLIPFISH.]
More fully ***kingklipfish***. Any of various edible serranid marine fishes, esp. *Epinephelus andersoni*.

King Kong /kɪŋ ˈkɒŋ/ *noun*. M20.
[ORIGIN An apelike monster in the film of that name.]
(A nickname for) a person of outstanding size or strength.

kinglet /ˈkɪŋlɪt/ *noun*. E17.
[ORIGIN from KING *noun* + -LET.]
1 A petty king; a king ruling over a small territory. Usu. *derog.* E17.
2 Any of several tiny birds of the genus *Regulus*; esp. *R. satrapa* and *R. calendula* (family Sylviidae), of N. America, and (formerly) the goldcrest, *R. regulus*. M19.

kingly /ˈkɪŋli/ *adjective & adverb*. LME.
[ORIGIN from KING *noun* + -LY[1].]
▸ **A** *adjective*. **1** Of the rank or nature of a king or kings. LME.

> E. PEYTON The Divine Catastrophe of the Kingly Family of the House of Stuarts.

2 Of or belonging to a king; held, exercised, or issued by a king. LME. ▸**b** Of government: monarchical. M17.

> B. EMECHETA His kingly eyes shone and his was the voice of authority. *New Yorker* President Reagan . . held sway over the American political scene with an almost kingly authority.

3 Having the character or quality of a king; kinglike, majestic. LME.

> DRYDEN A generous, laudable, and kingly pride.

▸ **B** *adverb*. In a kingly manner; royally, regally. LME.

> J. CLEVELAND This Way he could not but dye Kingly, at least, like a Gentleman.

■ **kingliness** *noun* L15.

kingpin /ˈkɪŋpɪn/ *noun*. E19.
[ORIGIN from KING *noun* + PIN *noun*.]
†1 The tallest (central) pin in the game of kayles. Only in E19.
2 = ***kingbolt*** s.v. KING *noun*. Freq. (*fig.*), a thing holding together a complex system or arrangement; the most important person in a party, organization, etc. M19.

> *Daily Telegraph* The owner of three shops was the kingpin behind a wholesale shoplifting plot.

†**king's-fisher** *noun* see KINGFISHER.

kingship /ˈkɪŋʃɪp/ *noun*. ME.
[ORIGIN from KING *noun* + -SHIP.]
1 The office of king; the fact of being king; reign as a king. ME.
2 The rule of a king; monarchical government. M17.
3 With possess. adjective as ***his kingship*** etc.: his etc. majesty. M17.
4 The territory of a king, a kingdom. M19.

kingsman /ˈkɪŋzmən/ *noun*. Pl. **-men**. Also **king's man**, pl. **king's men** /mɛn/; **K-**. E17.
[ORIGIN from KING *noun* + -'S[1] + MAN *noun*.]
▸ **I** *hist.* **1** ***the King's Men***, a company of actors under the patronage of James I. E17.
2 A partisan of the king; a royalist. M17.
3 A person who supported the British cause at the time of the American Revolution. *US*. L18.
4 A customs officer. E19.
▸ **II** **5** A member of King's College, Cambridge. E19.

kingston /ˈkɪŋst(ə)n/ *noun*. *obsolete* exc. *local*. M17.
[ORIGIN Unknown.]
The monkfish, *Squatina squatina*.

Kingston valve /ˈkɪŋst(ə)n valv/ *noun phr.* M19.
[ORIGIN John *Kingston*, 19th-cent. Brit. dockyard foreman, its inventor.]
NAUTICAL. A kind of conical valve for closing an orifice in a ship's side below the waterline, opening outwards with a screwing action.

kingy /ˈkɪŋi/ *noun*. M20.
[ORIGIN from KING *noun* + -Y[6].]
A children's chasing game played with a ball, the winner being declared 'king'.

†**kinic** *adjective* var. of QUINIC.

kinin /ˈkʌɪnɪn/ *noun*. M20.
[ORIGIN from Greek *kinein* set in motion + -IN[1]. In sense 1 after BRADYKININ.]
BIOCHEMISTRY. **1** Any of a group of low molecular-weight peptides formed in body tissue in response to injury, which have local effects including pain and vasodilation. M20.
2 Any of a class of compounds that (with auxins) control plant growth and development. Also called **cytokinin**. M20.
■ **kiˈninogen** *noun* a biologically inactive precursor of a kinin (sense 1) M20.

kinjal /kɪnˈdʒɑːl/ *noun*. M19.
[ORIGIN Caucasian Turkic (= Russian *kinzhal*) formed as KHANJAR.]
In the Caucasus, Kurdistan, etc.: a dagger.

kink /kɪŋk/ *noun*[1]. *Scot. & N. English*. Also (earlier) **ch-** /tʃ-/. ME.
[ORIGIN from KINK *verb*[1].]
A fit of laughter or coughing that catches the breath. Formerly also, whooping cough.

kink /kɪŋk/ *noun*[2]. L17.
[ORIGIN Middle & mod. Low German *kinke* (Dutch *kink*) from base meaning 'bend': cf. Icelandic (Old Norse) *kikna* bend at the knees.]
1 A short twist in a rope, thread, wire, etc., where it is bent back on itself, *esp.* one stiff enough to cause obstruction (orig. NAUTICAL); a tight wave in human or animal hair. Also (*transf.*), a crick in the neck. L17. ▸**b** A sudden bend in a line, course, etc., that is otherwise straight or smoothly curved. L19.

> *Hairdo Ideas* A special planning technique that takes the kink out of curls.

2 *fig.* **a** A mental twist or quirk. Now chiefly, a bizarre sexual practice or preference. E19. ▸**b** A clever idea for or method of doing something. Chiefly *US*. E19.

> **a** T. JEFFERSON Adair . . had his kink. He believed . . the Indians of America to be descended from the Jews. R. DAVIES You know that homosexuality is an O.K. kink nowadays.

3 A person who has bizarre sexual tastes or is given to bizarre sexual practices; *loosely* an eccentric. Orig. *US*. M20.

> *Independent* He was a bit of a kink. He liked to be caned.

■ **kinkless** *adjective* without a kink; *spec.* (ELECTRONICS) (of a tetrode) designed so as to have a smooth characteristic curve: M20.

kink /kɪŋk/ *verb*[1] *intrans. Scot. & N. English.* Also (earlier) **ch-** /tʃ-/.
[ORIGIN Old English *cincian*, app. a nasalized var. of Germanic base repr. by Middle High German *kīchen* to gasp: cf. KINKCOUGH.]
Gasp convulsively for breath in a fit of coughing (esp. whooping cough) or laughing.

kink /kɪŋk/ *verb*[2]. L17.
[ORIGIN Prob. from Dutch *kinken*, formed as KINK *noun*[2].]
1 *verb intrans.* Form a kink; (of a rope etc.) twist or curl stiffly, esp. at one point, so as to catch or get entangled; (of something straight) take a sudden backward bend. L17.

W. GOLDING The river kinks violently in a right angle then gets back on course again.

2 *verb trans.* Cause to kink, twist stiffly; make kinky. Usu. in *pass.* E19.

Punch The sinister kinked logic governing the behaviour of the characters. A. S. BYATT A middle-aged man with . . long, kinked, greasy fringes of hair.

kinkajou /ˈkɪŋkədʒuː/ *noun.* L18.
[ORIGIN French *quincajou*, alt. of French CARCAJOU Ojibwa *kwi:nkwaʔa:ke:* wolverine. Cf. QUICKHATCH.]
A fruit-eating arboreal Central and S. American mammal, *Potos flavus*, related to the raccoon, with a prehensile tail.

kinkcough /ˈkɪŋk-kɒf/ *noun. Scot. & N. English.* Also **ch-** /tʃ-/. LME.
[ORIGIN from KINK *verb*[1] + COUGH *noun*.]
Whooping cough.

kinkey *adjective & noun* var. of KINKY.

kinkhost /ˈkɪŋkhɒst/ *noun. obsolete* exc. *Scot.* ME.
[ORIGIN from KINK *verb*[1] + HOAST *noun*, perh. through Middle Low German *kinkhōste*.]
= KINKCOUGH.

K

kinkle /ˈkɪŋk(ə)l/ *noun.* M19.
[ORIGIN from KINK *noun*[2] + -LE[1].]
A slight kink or twist.
■ **kinkled** *adjective* having kinkles or kinks; (of hair) frizzed: L19.

kinky /ˈkɪŋki/ *adjective & noun.* Also **-ey**. M19.
[ORIGIN from KINK *noun*[2] + -Y[1].]
▸ **A** *adjective.* **1** Having kinks or twists; (of hair) tightly curled. M19.

M. ANGELOU My real hair . . would take the place of the kinky mass . . Momma wouldn't let me straighten.

2 *fig.* **a** Strange, eccentric. *colloq.* L19. ▸**b** Of property: dishonestly come by. *criminals' slang.* E20. ▸**c** Having or marked by bizarre sexual tastes or practices; (of clothing etc.) suggestive of bizarre sexual tastes. *colloq.* M20.

a E. M. FORSTER This jaundiced young philosopher, with his kinky view of life, was too much for him. **c** *Listener* One of the girls—a buxom specimen in kinky patent leathers. F. WARNER Kinky sex makes them feel inadequate. *Chicago Sun* The impression that these lascivious men are all *child porn, kinky weirdos.*

▸ **B** *noun.* **1** A person with kinky hair. *colloq.* Usu. *derog.* E20.
2 An object dishonestly obtained. *criminals' slang.* E20.
3 A person with bizarre sexual tastes. *colloq.* M20.
■ **kinkily** *adverb* M20. **kinkiness** *noun* E20.

kinless /ˈkɪnlɪs/ *adjective.* M17.
[ORIGIN from KIN *noun* + -LESS.]
Having no relatives or kindred.

kinnikinnick /ˌkɪnɪkɪˈnɪk/ *noun.* Also **killi-** /ˌkɪlɪ-/, **-kinik**, & other vars. L18.
[ORIGIN Delaware (Unami) *kələk:əni:k:an* admixture.]
1 A mixture used by N. American Indians as a substitute for tobacco or for mixing with it, usu. consisting of dried sumac leaves and the inner bark of dogwood or willow. L18.
2 Any of the various plants used for this, *esp.* bearberry, *Arctostaphylos uva-ursi.* E19.

kino /ˈkiːnəʊ/ *noun.* Pl. **-os**. L18.
[ORIGIN App. from a W. African lang.]
The astringent gum of certain tropical trees and other plants, used locally in medicine, tanning, etc.; orig. (in full ***African kino***, GAMBIA KINO) that of a W. African leguminous tree, *Pterocarpus erinaceus*, now esp. (in full ***East Indian kino***, ***Malabar kino***) that of a related tree of India and Sri Lanka, *P. marsupium*. Also, any of the trees or plants which yield this gum.
Bengal kino (the gum of) the dhak tree, *Butea monosperma.* **Jamaican kino** (the gum of) the sea grape, *Coccoloba uvifera.*

kino- /ˈkʌɪnəʊ/ *combining form* of Greek *kinein* set in motion: see -O-.
■ **kino'cilium** *noun*, pl. **-lia** /-lɪə/, BIOLOGY a cilium which is capable of moving; *spec.* one borne singly on each hair cell of the maculae of the inner ear amid many stereocilia: M20. **kinoplasm** *noun* (BIOLOGY) a supposed kind of fibrillar cytoplasm formerly held to give rise to the active parts of a cell (e.g. the membrane and mitotic apparatus) L19.

†**kinone** *noun* var. of QUINONE.

†**kinovic** *adjective* var. of QUINOVIC.

-kins /kɪnz/ *suffix.*
[ORIGIN Extension of -KIN.]
Forming dim. nouns expr. endearment, as ***babykins***, ***boykins***. Formerly also in certain oaths, as ***bodikins***.

kinsfolk /ˈkɪnzfəʊk/ *noun pl.* Also (now *rare*) **-folks**. LME.
[ORIGIN from KIN *noun* + -'S[1] + FOLK.]
The people to whom one is related by blood (or by marriage); (one's) relatives. Cf. KINFOLK, KINSPEOPLE.

kinship /ˈkɪnʃɪp/ *noun.* M19.
[ORIGIN from KIN *noun* + -SHIP.]
1 a Blood relationship. M19. ▸**b** ANTHROPOLOGY. The recognized ties of relationship (by descent, marriage, etc.) forming the basis of social organization in a culture. M19.

a A. J. P. TAYLOR Their father . . claimed kinship with the Thompsons.

2 Similarity of characteristics or origins; (an) affinity. L19.

P. V. WHITE No evidence of intellectual kinship in any of her small circle of acquaintance. M. FITZHERBERT He felt a kinship with the despised Christians.

– COMB.: **kinship group** ANTHROPOLOGY a unit of social organization based on kinship.

kinsman /ˈkɪnzmən/ *noun.* Pl. **-men**. LOE.
[ORIGIN from KIN *noun* + -'S[1] + MAN *noun*.]
A man of one's own kin; an adult male relative; in *pl.* also, kinsfolk.
■ **kinsmanly** *adjective* appropriate to or characteristic of a kinsman M19. **kinsmanship** *noun* M19.

kinspeople /ˈkɪnzpiːp(ə)l/ *noun pl. US.* L18.
[ORIGIN from KIN *noun* + -'S[1] + PEOPLE *noun*.]
= KINSFOLK.

kinswoman /ˈkɪnzwʊmən/ *noun.* Pl. **-women** /-wɪmɪn/. ME.
[ORIGIN from KIN *noun* + -'S[1] + WOMAN *noun*.]
A woman of one's own kin; an adult female relative.

†**kintal** *noun* var. of QUINTAL.

kinzigite /ˈkɪntsɪgʌɪt/ *noun.* L19.
[ORIGIN from *Kinzig*, a valley in Germany + -ITE[1].]
GEOLOGY. A metamorphic schistose rock containing garnet, biotite, and varying amounts of quartz, plagioclase, sillimanite, and cordierite.

Kioko /kɪˈəʊkəʊ/ *noun & adjective.* Pl. of noun same, **-os**. L19.
[ORIGIN Bantu.]
Of or pertaining to, a member of, an African people inhabiting the Democratic Republic of Congo (Zaire) and Angola; (of) the Bantu language of this people.

kiore /kɪˈɔːreɪ/ *noun.* M19.
[ORIGIN Maori.]
= ***POLYNESIAN rat***. Also ***kiore rat***.

kiosk /ˈkiːɒsk/ *noun.* E17.
[ORIGIN French *kiosque* from Turkish *köşk* from Persian *kušk* pavilion.]
1 An open pavilion or summer house of light construction in Turkey, Iran, etc. E17.
2 A similar structure used as a shelter or bandstand in gardens and parks elsewhere. M19.
3 A light, often movable, booth from which newspapers, refreshments, cigarettes, tickets, etc., are sold. Also (*Austral. & NZ*), a building in which refreshments are served in a park etc. M19.
4 More fully ***telephone kiosk***. A booth or box in which a public telephone is installed. E20.

Kiowa /ˈkʌɪəwə/ *noun & adjective.* E19.
[ORIGIN Amer. Spanish *Caygua* from Kiowa *kɔ́ygú* (pl.).]
▸ **A** *noun.* Pl. **-s**, same.
1 A member of a N. American Indian people of the southern plains of the US. E19.
2 The language of this people. M19.
▸ **B** *attrib.* or as *adjective.* Of or pertaining to the Kiowa or their language. E19.
Kiowa Apache a member of, of or pertaining to, an Athabaskan people associated with the Kiowa; (of) the language of this people.

kip /kɪp/ *noun*[1]. LME.
[ORIGIN Uncertain: perh. rel. to Middle Dutch *kip*, *kijp* pack or bundle (of hides).]
The hide of young or small sheep or cattle as used for leather; a set or bundle of such hides, containing a specific number (usu. 30 or 50).

kip /kɪp/ *noun*[2]. L16.
[ORIGIN Uncertain: cf. Low German *Kippe* point, peak, tip.]
1 The sharp point of a hill; a jutting outcrop of rock; something pointed or beaked; *spec.* the hooked tip of the lower jaw of a breeding male salmon (cf. KIPPER *noun*[1] 1, KYPE). *Scot.* L16.
2 GYMNASTICS. A basic movement in which the body is rapidly straightened from an inverted pike position by pushing the hips forward and the legs back. *US.* E20.

kip /kɪp/ *noun*[3]. *slang.* M18.
[ORIGIN Uncertain: cf. Danish *kippe* hovel, tavern, *horekippe* brothel.]
1 A brothel. M18.
2 A cheap lodging house, a dosshouse; a lodging, a bed. L19.
3 A sleep, a nap; the action of sleeping. L19.
– COMB.: **kip house** a cheap lodging house, a dosshouse; **kip-shop** a dosshouse; a brothel.

kip /kɪp/ *noun*[4]. *Austral. & NZ.* L19.
[ORIGIN Uncertain: cf. KIPPEEN.]
A small piece of wood from which coins are spun in the game of two-up.

kip /kɪp/ *noun*[5]. Orig. *US.* E20.
[ORIGIN Prob. from KI(LO- + P(OUND *noun*[1].]
ENGINEERING. A unit of force equal to a weight of 1,000 lb (approx. 453.6 kg), used in expressing loads.

kip /kɪp/ *noun*[6]. Pl. same, **-s**. M20.
[ORIGIN Thai.]
The basic monetary unit of Laos, equal to 100 ats.

kip /kɪp/ *verb*[1] *intrans. slang.* Infl. **-pp-**. L19.
[ORIGIN from KIP *noun*[3].]
Go to bed, sleep; lie or settle *down* to sleep.

K. AMIS I . . kipped for a spell in the library. Nobody ever disturbed you there. M. FORSTER He could never live in one place for long, preferring to kip down where he found himself.

kip /kɪp/ *verb*[2] *intrans. US.* Infl. **-pp-**. E20.
[ORIGIN from KIP *noun*[2].]
GYMNASTICS. Perform a kip.

kipa(h) *noun* var. of KIPPA.

Kipchak /kɪpˈtʃɑːk/ *noun & adjective.* Pl. of noun same, **-s**. E19.
[ORIGIN Russian from Turkish *Kıpçak*.]
Of or pertaining to, a member of, a Turkic people (now extinct) of central Asia and the region north of the Caucasus (also called ***Cumans***, ***Polovtsy***) or *loosely* any of various nomadic Turkic-speaking peoples of these areas; (of) the language of the original Kipchak (also called ***Cuman***); (designating or pertaining to) the north-western group of Turkic languages and dialects.

Kiplingese /kɪplɪŋˈiːz/ *noun.* L19.
[ORIGIN from *Kipling* (see below) + -ESE.]
The literary style and characteristics of the writer Rudyard Kipling (1865–1936).
■ **Kiplingesque** *adjective* resembling Kipling in style L19. **Kiplingesquely** *adverb* M20. **'Kiplingism** *noun* views or style of expression characteristic of Kipling L19. **'Kiplingite** *noun & adjective* (**a**) *noun* an admirer or student of Kipling or his work; (**b**) *adjective* characteristic of Kipling: L19. **'Kiplingize** *verb trans.* make like Kipling E20.

kippa /kɪˈpɑː/ *noun.* Also ***kipa(h)***, ***kippah***. M20.
[ORIGIN mod. Hebrew *kippāh*.]
A skullcap, usu. of crocheted thread, worn by Orthodox male Jews.

kippage /ˈkɪpɪdʒ/ *noun. Scot.* M16.
[ORIGIN Aphet. from French *équipage* EQUIPAGE *noun*.]
1 The crew of a ship. Cf. EQUIPAGE *noun* 1. *obsolete* exc. *hist.* M16.
2 Disorder, confusion; a state of excitement or irritation. E19.

kippah *noun* var. of KIPPA.

kippeen /kɪˈpiːn/ *noun. Irish.* Also **kippin** /ˈkɪpɪn/. M19.
[ORIGIN Irish *cipín*: cf. Gaelic *cipean* stump, peg, stick or dibble for planting.]
A stick or dibble used for planting; a short thin stick.

kipper /ˈkɪpə/ *noun*[1] *& adjective*[1].
[ORIGIN Old English *cypera*, used once with *leax* salmon (LAX *noun*[1]) = Old Saxon *kupiro*, perh. connected with COPPER *noun*[1] *& adjective*, from the colour of the male salmon.]
▸ **A** *noun.* **1** A male salmon or sea trout during the breeding season. Cf. KIP *noun*[2] 1, SHEDDER *noun.* OE.
2 A kippered fish, now esp. a herring. ME.
3 a A person, *esp.* a young or small person, a child. *slang.* E20. ▸**b** An English person, *spec.* an immigrant in Australia or New Zealand. *Austral. & NZ slang.* M20.
4 A torpedo. Cf. FISH *noun*[1] 1b. *nautical slang.* M20.
– COMB.: **kipper tie** a brightly coloured and very wide necktie.
▸ †**B** *adjective.* Designating or characteristic of a male salmon or sea trout at the breeding season; unhealthy, thin. LME–E19.

kipper /ˈkɪpə/ *noun*[2]. *Austral.* L18.
[ORIGIN Dharuk *gibarra*.]
A young Aboriginal male who has been initiated and is admitted to the rights of manhood.

kipper /ˈkɪpə/ *adjective*[2]. *N. English.* L17.
[ORIGIN Perh. symbolic. See also CHIPPER *adjective*.]
Nimble; lively; cheerful; eager.

kipper /ˈkɪpə/ *verb trans.* L18.
[ORIGIN from KIPPER *noun*[1].]
Cure (herring etc.) by splitting open, salting, and drying in the open air or in smoke.

fig.: P. LIVELY His white moustache was kippered a delicate tan on the right hand side.

■ **kipperer** *noun* E20.

kipper-nut /ˈkɪpənʌt/ *noun.* L16.
[ORIGIN from unkn. 1st elem. + NUT *noun*.]
The pignut, *Conopodium majus.*

kippersol *noun* var. of KIEPERSOL.

kippin *noun* var. of KIPPEEN.

Kipp's apparatus /ˈkɪps apəˈreɪtəs/ *noun phr.* L19.
[ORIGIN P. J. *Kipp* (1808–64), German chemist.]
CHEMISTRY. An apparatus for the controlled generation of a gas (esp. hydrogen sulphide) by the action of a liquid on a solid at room temperature, consisting of three glass bulbs in which the pressure of evolved gas is balanced against a head of liquid.

kipsie /ˈkɪpsi/ *noun. Austral. slang.* Also **-sy.** E20.
[ORIGIN from KIP *noun*[3] + -SY.]
A house, a home; a shelter, a lean-to.

Kipsigis /ˈkɪpsɪgɪs/ *noun & adjective.* M20.
[ORIGIN Kipsigis.]
▸ **A** *noun.* Pl. same.
1 A member of a people inhabiting western Kenya. M20.
2 The Nilotic language of this people. M20.
▸ **B** *attrib.* or as *adjective.* Of or pertaining to the Kipsigis or their language. M20.

kipsy *noun* var. of KIPSIE.

Kir /kɪə, kəː/ *noun.* M20.
[ORIGIN Canon Félix *Kir* (1876–1968), mayor of Dijon in France, who is said to have invented the recipe.]
(Proprietary name for) a drink made from dry white wine and cassis.
Kir royale [French = royal Kir] a cocktail made from cassis and champagne or sparkling white wine.

†**kirb** *noun & verb* var. of KERB.

Kirby /ˈkəːbi/ *noun.* E19.
[ORIGIN Charles *Kirby*, 17th-cent. English fish hook maker.]
Used *attrib.* and (formerly) in *possess.* to designate a design of fish hook originated by Kirby.

kirby grip /ˈkəːbɪgrɪp/ *noun.* Also (proprietary) **Kirbigrip.** E20.
[ORIGIN from *Kirby*, Beard & Co. Ltd, original manufacturers + GRIP *noun*[1].]
A type of sprung hairgrip.

Kirchhoff's law /ˈkɪətʃɒfs lɔː, *foreign* ˈkɪrxhɔfs/ *noun phr.* M19.
[ORIGIN G. R. *Kirchhoff* (1824–87), German physicist.]
1 ELECTRICITY. Either of two laws concerning electric networks in which steady currents are flowing: (**a**) (***Kirchhoff's first law***) that the algebraic sum of the currents in all the conductors that meet in a point is zero; (**b**) (***Kirchhoff's second law***) that the algebraic sum of the products of current and resistance in each part of any closed path in a network is equal to the algebraic sum of the electromotive forces in the path. M19.
2 PHYSICS. The law that the absorptivity of a body for radiant energy of any particular wavelength is equal to its emissivity at the same temperature for the same wavelength. E20.

Kirghiz, Kirgiz *nouns & adjectives* vars. of KYRGYZ.

kiri /ˈkɪəri/ *noun.* E18.
[ORIGIN Japanese.]
A Chinese tree, *Paulownia tomentosa* (also ***kiri tree***); the wood of this tree, esp. as used for cabinetwork in Japan.

kirin /ˈkɪərɪn/ *noun.* Also ***K-***. E18.
[ORIGIN Japanese, formed as KYLIN.]
A mythical beast of composite form resembling a unicorn, freq. portrayed in Japanese pottery and art.

Kiriwinian /kɪrɪˈvɪnɪən/ *noun & adjective.* E20.
[ORIGIN from *Kiriwina* (see below) + -IAN.]
▸ **A** *noun.* A native or inhabitant of Kiriwina, the largest of the Trobriand Islands. E20.
▸ **B** *adjective.* Of or pertaining to Kiriwina. E20.

kirk /kəːk/ *noun & verb. Scot. & N. English.* In sense A.2 also **K-.** ME.
[ORIGIN Old Norse *kirkja* from Old English *ċir(i)ċe* CHURCH *noun*.]
▸ **A** *noun.* **1** = CHURCH *noun.* ME.

> M. LEITCH The sound of hymn-singing . . coming from a kirk somewhere in his own country.

2 *The* Church of Scotland as opp. to the Church of England or the Episcopal Church in Scotland. M16.
– PHRASES: ***Free Kirk***: see FREE *adjective, noun, & adverb.* **Kirk of Scotland** *hist. & colloq.* the Church of Scotland. ***Wee Free Kirk***: see WEE *adjective.*
– COMB.: **kirk-assembly** the assembly of the Church of Scotland; **kirkman** a clergyman; a member of the Church of Scotland; **kirk-master** (now *N. English*) a churchwarden; ***kirk session***: see SESSION *noun*; **kirk-town** *Scot.* (**a**) the village, hamlet, or (area of) town in which a parish church is situated; (**b**) = GLEBE 2b; **kirkyard** *Scot.* a churchyard.
▸ **B** *verb trans.* = CHURCH *verb* 1. Now *Scot.* LME.
■ **kirkless** *adjective* (*Scot.*) = CHURCHLESS E19. **kirkward(s)** *adverb* = CHURCHWARDS LME.

kirkin head /ˈkəːkɪnhɛd/ *noun.* E18.
[ORIGIN App. from arbitrary alt. of KIRK + HEAD *noun*.]
ARCHITECTURE. = JERKIN HEAD.

Kirlian /ˈkəːlɪən/ *noun.* L20.
[ORIGIN S. D. and V. K. *Kirlian*, 20th-cent. Russian electricians.]
Used *attrib.* to designate (pictures obtained by) a process of recording corona discharges from the surfaces of objects directly on to photographic material.

Kirman /kɪəˈmaːn, kə-/ *adjective & noun.* Also **Ker-.** L19.
[ORIGIN A province and town in SE Iran.]
(Designating) a carpet or rug made in Kirman, usu. having soft delicate colouring and naturalistic designs.

Kirmanshah /kəˈmaːnʃaː, kəːmanˈʃaː/ *noun & adjective.* Also **Ker-.** E20.
[ORIGIN A city in western Iran.]
(Designating) a carpet or rug made in Kirman, usu. one with a white field and flowered medallion and borders.
– NOTE: Erroneously named, by confusion with KIRMAN.

kirmess *noun* var. of KERMIS.

kirn /kəːn/ *noun*[1] *& verb. Scot. & N. English.* ME.
[ORIGIN Var. of CHURN, infl. by Old Norse *kirna*.]
▸ **A** *noun.* A churn. ME.
▸ **B** *verb trans. & intrans.* = CHURN *verb. Scot.* M16.

kirn /kəːn/ *noun*[2]. *Scot. & N. English.* Now *rare.* L16.
[ORIGIN Unknown.]
1 A feast held on the completion of a harvest, a harvest home. L16.
2 The last handful of corn cut on the harvest field. L18.
get the kirn, win the kirn gain the distinction of cutting down the last armful of corn; succeed in finishing the harvest.
– COMB.: **kirn-baby, kirn-dolly** a crude doll made from the last handful of corn, a corn dolly.

kirpan /kəːˈpaːn/ *noun.* E20.
[ORIGIN Punjabi & Hindi *kirpān* from Sanskrit *kṛpāṇa* sword.]
The dagger or short sword worn (sometimes in miniature form) as one of the five distinguishing signs of the Sikh Khalsa, symbolizing determination to defend the truth.

kirri *noun* see KIERIE.

kirsch /kɪəʃ/ *noun.* M19.
[ORIGIN German, abbreviation of *Kirsch(en)wasser*: see KIRSCHWASSER.]
An alcoholic spirit distilled, chiefly in Germany and Switzerland, from the fermented juice of cherries.

kirschenwasser *noun* var. of KIRSCHWASSER.

Kirschner value /ˈkɪəʃnə ˌvaljuː/ *noun phr.* E20.
[ORIGIN Aage *Kirschner* (1870–1952), Danish chemist.]
A number expressing the proportion of certain fatty acids (esp. butyric acid) in a fat.

kirschwasser /ˈkɪəʃvasə/ *noun.* Also (now *rare*) **kirschen-** /ˈkɪəʃ(ə)n-/. E19.
[ORIGIN German, from *Kirsche* cherry + *Wasser* water.]
= KIRSCH.

kirsh *noun* var. of QURSH.

Kir-Shehr /kəːʃɪə/ *noun & adjective.* Also **Kirshehir.** E20.
[ORIGIN A town in central Turkey.]
(Designating) a brightly coloured prayer rug made in Kir-Shehr.

kirtan /ˈkɪətən/ *noun.* Also **keer-.** L19.
[ORIGIN Sanskrit *kīrtana*.]
In the Indian subcontinent: a devotional song or hymn.

kirtle /ˈkəːt(ə)l/ *noun & verb.* Now *arch.* or *hist.*
[ORIGIN Old English *cyrtel* = Old Norse *kyrtill* tunic, from Germanic, ult. prob. from Latin *curtus* short: see CURT, -LE[1].]
▸ **A** *noun.* **1** A man's tunic or coat, usu. reaching to the knees or lower. OE.
2 A woman's gown or outer petticoat. OE.
▸ **B** *verb trans.* Cover or clothe (as) with a kirtle. L19.
■ **kirtled** *adjective* wearing a kirtle M17.

kisaeng /ˈkiːsaŋ, -ɛŋ/ *noun.* L19.
[ORIGIN Korean.]
A trained female entertainer, the Korean equivalent of a geisha.

kisan /kɪˈsaːn/ *noun.* M20.
[ORIGIN Hindi *kisān* from Sanskrit *kṛṣāṇa* person who ploughs.]
In the Indian subcontinent: a peasant, an agricultural worker.

kish /kɪʃ/ *noun*[1]. L18.
[ORIGIN Irish *cis, ceis* basket, hamper.]
In Ireland: a large wickerwork basket or cart body with removable wickerwork sides, used chiefly for carrying turf.

kish /kɪʃ/ *noun*[2]. E19.
[ORIGIN Uncertain: cf. French *chiasse* (dial. *quiasse*) scum on metal.]
METALLURGY. A floating scale of impure graphite, formed on molten iron during smelting.

kishke /ˈkɪʃkə/ *noun.* Also **-ka, -keh.** M20.
[ORIGIN Yiddish from Polish *kiszka* or Ukrainian *kishka*: cf. Russian *kishka*.]
1 Beef intestine casing stuffed with a savoury filling. M20.
2 *sing.* & in *pl.* The guts. *slang.* M20.

Kisii /ˈkɪsiː/ *noun & adjective.* Pl. of noun same. E20.
[ORIGIN Bantu.]
Designating or pertaining to, a member of, a people living in Kisii, a district on the east side of Lake Victoria, Kenya; (of) the Bantu language of this people.

kiskadee /kɪskəˈdiː/ *noun.* Also **keskidee** /kɛskɪˈdiː/. L19.
[ORIGIN Imit. of the bird's call.]
Any of various tyrant flycatchers of Central and S. America; *esp.* (more fully ***great kiskadee***) the large *Pitangus sulphuratus*, which has a black and white striped head and yellow underparts.

Kislev /ˈkɪslɛf/ *noun.* Also †**Casleu, Kislew.** LME.
[ORIGIN Hebrew *Kislēw*.]
In the Jewish calendar, the third month of the civil and ninth of the religious year, usu. coinciding with parts of November and December.

kismet /ˈkɪzmɛt, -mɪt, -s-/ *noun.* E19.
[ORIGIN Turkish *kısmet* from Arabic *qisma(t)* division, portion, lot, fate.]
Destiny, fate.

> N. HORNBY What chance did I stand against kismet?

kiss /kɪs/ *noun.*
[ORIGIN Old English *coss* from Germanic base of KISS *verb*, refashioned after KISS *verb*.]
1 A touch or caress given with slightly pursed lips as an expression of affection, sexual desire, greeting, etc., or reverence; an act of kissing. OE.

> C. S. LEWIS I never could endure the embrace or kiss of my own sex. J. C. OATES He . . pressed upon her anxious lips a warm, passionate, husbandly kiss.

2 *fig.* A light touch or impact. L16. ▸**b** BILLIARDS & SNOOKER etc. A light touching of one ball by another. M19.

> DAY LEWIS The . . feeling which the cold kiss of the dew spreads through one's whole body.

3 A representation of a kiss in the form of an x, esp. at the close of a letter. M18.

> C. FREMLIN A row of 'x's', hurried kisses, all he had time to scribble.

4 A small cake or piece of confectionery; a sweet, a chocolate. E19.
5 A drop of sealing wax accidentally let fall beside the seal of a letter. *colloq.* Now *rare.* E19.
– PHRASES: ***blow a kiss***: see BLOW *verb*[1]. ***butterfly kiss. deep kiss***: see DEEP *adjective.* ***French kiss***: see FRENCH *adjective.* **kiss of peace** ECCLESIASTICAL a ceremonial kiss, esp. in the Eucharist, as a sign of unity. **the kiss of death** a seemingly kind or well-intentioned action, look, association, etc., which brings disastrous consequences. **the kiss of life** the mouth-to-mouth method of artificial respiration.
– COMB.: **kiss-curl** a small flat curl worn on the forehead, in front of the ear, or at the nape of the neck; **kiss impression** PRINTING: by which ink is deposited on to paper by letterpress printing using the lightest possible contact; **kissproof** *adjective* (esp. of lipstick) not greatly affected or harmed by kissing.
■ **kissless** *adjective* E18.

kiss /kɪs/ *verb.* Pa. t. & pple **kissed**, (*arch.*) **kist.**
[ORIGIN Old English *cyssan* = Old Frisian *kessa*, Old Saxon *cussian* (Dutch *kussen*), Old High German *kussen* (German *küssen*), Old Norse *kyssa*, from Germanic.]
1 *verb trans.* Press or touch (esp. a person's lips or face) with slightly pursed lips to express affection, sexual desire, greeting, etc., or reverence. OE. ▸**b** *transf.* Of a bird: touch lightly with the bill in a supposed caress. LME.

> D. H. LAWRENCE She leaned forward and kissed him, with a slow, luxurious kiss, lingering on the mouth. L. CODY She did not like being kissed. G. VIDAL He kissed her averted cheek and left the room.

2 *verb intrans.* Of two people: exchange a kiss or kisses. ME.

> H. FAST When had they last kissed or embraced?

3 *fig.* **a** *verb intrans.* Usu. of two things: touch lightly. ME. ▸**b** *verb trans.* Touch or brush against lightly. LME.

> **b** R. GRAVES My arrow kissed his shoulder and glanced off.

4 BILLIARDS & SNOOKER etc. ▸**a** *verb trans.* Cause a ball to touch (another ball) lightly; (of a ball) touch (another ball) lightly. L16. ▸**b** *verb intrans.* Of two balls: knock together lightly. L19.
5 *verb trans.* Bring into a certain state or position by kissing; take *away*, remove *from*, by kissing. E17.
6 *verb trans.* Express by kissing. Also with cognate obj., give (a kiss). M19.

> TENNYSON We will kiss sweet kisses, and speak sweet words. W. MAXWELL Bedtime came and I kissed my mother good night.

– PHRASES, & WITH ADVERBS IN SPECIALIZED SENSES: **(as) easy as kiss my hand, (as) easy as kiss your finger**, & vars., very easy. **kiss and be friends, kiss and make up** become reconciled. **kiss and tell** recount one's sexual exploits. **kiss a person's arse, kiss a person's behind, kiss a person's bum** *coarse slang* behave obsequiously towards (a person). **kiss better** *colloq.* comfort (a sick or injured person, esp. a child) by kissing him or her, esp. on the sore or injured part of the body, kiss as a gesture of removing pain. **kiss goodbye (to)** say goodbye (to) with a kiss; (foll. by *to*) resign oneself to the loss of. **kiss hands** kiss the hand(s) of the monarch etc. as a ceremonial duty, esp. on taking up an official appointment. **kiss my arse** *coarse slang* go away!, go to hell! **kiss off** *slang* (chiefly *N. Amer.*) (**a**) dismiss, get rid of, kill; (**b**) go away, die. **kiss the book**: i.e. the Bible, New Testament, or Gospels, in taking an oath (cf. BOOK *noun* 4a). **kiss the cup** take a sip of liquor; drink. **kiss the dirt, kiss the dust** be overthrown or killed; submit. **kiss the ground** prostrate oneself in homage; *fig.* be overthrown. ***kiss the Pope's toe***: see TOE *noun.* **kiss the rod** accept chastisement or correction submissively.
– COMB.: **kiss-in-the-ring** a children's game in which all the players stand in a ring with hands joined except for one who runs round and touches one of the opposite sex, who then pursues and tries to kiss him or her; **kiss-me-quick** (**a**) *hist.* a

K

small bonnet standing far back on the head; (**b**) ***kiss-me-quick hat***, a hat bearing the words 'kiss-me-quick' (or some other, usu. joc., phrase) on the front; **kiss-off** *slang* (chiefly *N. Amer.*) a dismissal; a thing marking the end of a relationship etc.
■ **kissa'bility** *noun* the quality of being kissable, suitable for being kissed L19. **kissable** *adjective* able to be kissed, suitable for kissing, such as to invite kissing E19. **kissably** *adverb* in a manner which invites kissing L19. **kissage** *noun* (*literary* or *joc.*) kissing L19. **kissy** *adjective* (*colloq.*) characterized by or given to kissing; ***play kissy-face*** (*US*), engage in light amorous kissing: E20.

Kissagram *noun* see KISSOGRAM.

kissar /ˈkɪsə/ *noun*. M19.
[ORIGIN Repr. colloq. pronunc. of Arabic *qīṭār*, *qītār* KITAR.]
A kind of lyre used in Ethiopia and other parts of N. Africa.

kissel /ˈkɪs(ə)l, kiˈsjɛl/ *noun*. E20.
[ORIGIN Russian *kisel'*, from same base as *kislyĭ* sour.]
A dessert dish made from fruit juice or purée boiled with sugar and water and thickened with potato or cornflour.

kisser /ˈkɪsə/ *noun*. M16.
[ORIGIN from KISS *verb* + -ER¹.]
1 A person who kisses; the giver of a kiss. M16.
J. KRANTZ Lester . . was one terrific kisser.
2 The mouth; the face. Orig. *boxing slang*. M19.
JANE OWEN Karen took a swing at her, she ducked and Neil caught it right in the kisser.

Kissi /ˈkɪsi/ *noun & adjective*. L19.
[ORIGIN Kissi.]
▸ **A** *noun*. Pl. same, **-s**. A member of an agricultural people inhabiting the regions of Guinea, Sierra Leone, and Liberia near the headwaters of the Niger; the Niger-Congo language of this people. L19.
▸ **B** *attrib.* or as *adjective*. Of or pertaining to the Kissi or their language. M20.

K

kissing /ˈkɪsɪŋ/ *verbal noun*. ME.
[ORIGIN from KISS *verb* + -ING¹.]
The action of KISS *verb*.
when the kissing has to stop when the honeymoon period finishes; when one is forced to recognize harsh realities.
– COMB.: **kissing ball**, **kissing bough**, **kissing bunch**, **kissing bush** a Christmas wreath or ball of evergreens hung from the ceiling, under which a person may be kissed; **kissing comfit** a perfumed comfit for sweetening the breath; **kissing gate** a small gate swinging in a U- or V-shaped enclosure, so as to allow only one person to pass at a time; †**kissing strings** *hist.* a woman's bonnet strings or cap strings tied under the chin with the ends hanging loose; **kissing time** the time to kiss (freq. a joc. reply to children who ask the time).

kissing /ˈkɪsɪŋ/ *ppl adjective*. L16.
[ORIGIN from KISS *verb* + -ING².]
That kisses (a person or thing).
kissing bug *US* a bloodsucking reduviid bug, spec. *Melanolestes picipes*, which can inflict a painful bite on humans. **kissing cousin** a relative or friend with whom one is on close enough terms to greet with a kiss. **kissing gourami** [from the fish's habit of touching objects with its lips pursed as if for a kiss] a small SE Asian gourami, *Helostoma temminckii*, often kept in aquaria. **kissing kin**, **kissing kind** = *kissing cousin* above.
■ **kissingly** *adverb* M19.

kissogram /ˈkɪsəgram/ *noun*. Also (proprietary) **Kissagram**. L20.
[ORIGIN from KISS *noun* or *verb* + -O- + -GRAM.]
A novelty greetings message sent through a commercial agency, delivered (usu. by a provocatively dressed young woman) with a kiss.
attrib.: *News on Sunday* Emma . . once worked as a kissogram girl.

kist /kɪst/ *noun*¹ & *verb*. *Scot.* & *N. English*. ME.
[ORIGIN Old Norse *kista*: see CHEST *noun*.]
▸ **A** *noun*. **1** A chest, a trunk, a coffer. ME.
kist o' whistles (now *rare*) an organ.
2 A coffin; *esp.* a stone coffin, a sarcophagus. ME. ▸**b** ARCHAEOLOGY. = CIST *noun*¹. M19.
3 A chest or place in which money is kept, a treasury; a store of money. *rare*. E17.
4 A basket. *rare*. E18.
▸ **B** *verb trans.* Put into a chest, esp. a coffin. M17.
■ **kistful** *noun* (*rare*) as much as a kist will hold M17.

kist /kɪst/ *noun*². M18.
[ORIGIN Urdu *ḳist* from Persian *ḳisṭ* from Arabic = portion, instalment.]
In the Indian subcontinent: an instalment (of a yearly land revenue or other payment).
– COMB.: ***kistbandi*** [Urdu, Persian *bandī* settlement] an agreement to pay a debt in specified instalments.

kistvaen /ˈkɪstvʌɪn/ *noun*. Also **c-**. E18.
[ORIGIN Welsh *cistfaen*, from *cist* chest (CIST *noun*¹) + *faen* (*maen*) stone.]
ARCHAEOLOGY. A stone burial chamber.

Kiswa /ˈkɪswə/ *noun*. L16.
[ORIGIN Arabic = attire, apparel, curtaining.]
The black cloth covering the walls of the Kaaba, made annually in Egypt and brought to Mecca with the pilgrimage caravan, now usu. made of black brocade with the Islamic creed outlined in the weave and a gold-embroidered band bearing Koranic texts.

Kiswahili /kiːswəˈhiːli, kɪswɑː-/ *noun & adjective*. M19.
[ORIGIN Bantu, from *ki-* prefix + SWAHILI.]
(Of) a major language of the Bantu family, spoken widely and used as a lingua franca in E. Africa and the Democratic Republic of Congo (Zaire); Swahili.

kit /kɪt/ *noun*¹. ME.
[ORIGIN Middle Dutch *kitte* (Dutch *kit* tankard), of unknown origin.]
1 a A cylindrical wooden tub, barrel, or pail, with or without a lid and usu. having a handle or handles. ME. ▸**b** A basket or box, esp. for holding fish. Also, the contents of a kit, as a measure of weight. M19.
2 a A collection of articles forming part of the equipment of a soldier; the bag or knapsack containing these with or without its contents. Now also (*gen.*), a set of clothing needed for any specific purpose, esp. for sport; a costume, an outfit, a uniform. L18. ▸**b** A collection of personal effects or necessaries, esp. as packed up for travelling. E19. ▸**c** Orig., the outfit of tools required by a workman, esp. a shoemaker. Now also, a set of articles or equipment needed for any specific purpose. M19. ▸**d** More fully ***drum kit***. An outfit of drums, cymbals, and other percussion devices and accessories used by a drummer in a pop, rock, or jazz group etc. E20. ▸**e** A quantity of printed matter on a specified topic for students etc. M20.
a H. BAILEY Roland's returned kit, including his bullet-holed tunic and blood-stained vest. B. BEHAN Geordie came round with the kits—blue jackets, shorts, shoes, shirts. *attrib.*: E. BLUNDEN The first kit inspection proved that we were short of . . rifles, leather equipment, gas masks. **c** *fig.*: B. EMECHETA Our little secrets make us women; they are part of our survival kit.
a football kit etc. **c** ***bicycle-repair kit***, ***first-aid kit***, ***tool kit***, etc.
3 A number of things or persons viewed as a whole; a set, a lot, a collection. Esp. in ***the whole kit***. *N. Amer. slang*. L18.
4 A set of parts or constituents from which a thing may be assembled or made. M19.
attrib.: *Sunday Times* Jumpers available in either kit form or ready made.
model aircraft kit, ***wine-making kit***, etc.
– PHRASES: **get one's kit off** *colloq.* take off all of one's clothes. HATTED ***kit***. **the whole kit and boodle** *slang* the whole set or lot, everything, everyone (also ***the whole kit and*** CABOODLE).
– COMB.: **kitbag** a stout usu. cylindrical bag in which to carry a soldier's, traveller's, or sports player's kit; **kit car** a car sold in parts for assembly by the owner; **kit furniture**: sold in parts for assembly by the owner; **kitset** *NZ* the components and aids for assembling an article or model.
■ **kitless** *adjective* M19.

kit /kɪt/ *noun*². Now *rare*. E16.
[ORIGIN Uncertain: perh. from first syll. of Latin *cithara*, Greek *kithara* CITHER.]
hist. A small fiddle, esp. as used by a dancing master.

kit /kɪt/ *noun*³. M16.
[ORIGIN Abbreviation of KITTEN *noun*.]
A young cat, a kitten; the young of certain other animals as the fox, badger, beaver, and ferret.

kit /kɪt/ *noun*⁴. *NZ*. M19.
[ORIGIN Maori *kete*.]
A basket plaited from flax.
■ **kitful** *noun* as much or as many as a kit will hold L19.

kit /kɪt/ *noun*⁵. L19.
[ORIGIN App. from German dial. *Kitte*, *Kütte* covey, flight of doves etc.]
A school or small flying group of pigeons.

kit /kɪt/ *verb*¹ *trans.* Infl. **-tt-**. E18.
[ORIGIN from KIT *noun*¹.]
1 Put or pack (esp. fish) in a kit or kits. E18.
2 Equip (a person or thing) with a uniform, an outfit, equipment, etc.; provide with a kit. Freq. foll. by *out*, *up*. E20.
Sunday Express Ramblers kitted out with boots and rucksacks. A. MARS-JONES We'll see about getting you kitted up with the documents . . that you'll be needing.

kit /kɪt/ *verb*² *intrans.* & *trans.* *rare*. Infl. **-tt-**. M18.
[ORIGIN from KIT *noun*³.]
Of a cat, ferret, beaver, etc.: bear (young), kitten.

Kitab /kɪˈtɑːb/ *noun*. L19.
[ORIGIN Arabic *kitāb* piece of writing, record, book.]
The Koran. Also, among Muslims, the sacred book of any of certain other revealed religions, as Judaism or Christianity.

kitar /kɪˈtɑː/ *noun*. *rare*. M17.
[ORIGIN Arabic *qītār* from Greek *kithara* CITHARA: cf. KISSAR.]
An Arabian form of guitar or lute.

Kit-cat /ˈkɪtkat/ *noun & adjective*. Also **-Cat**, (sense 3) **k-**. E18.
[ORIGIN from *Kit* (= Christopher) *Cat* or *Catling*, keeper of the pie-house in London where the club orig. met. Sense 3 from a series of portraits of the club's founders.]
1 (Designating) a club of Whig politicians and men of letters founded in the reign of James II. E18.
2 A member of this club. E18.
3 (Designating or pertaining to) a portrait of less than half length but including the hands (usu. 36 × 28 in.). M18.

kitchen /ˈkɪtʃɪn, -tʃ(ə)n/ *noun, adjective, & verb*.
[ORIGIN Old English *cyċene* (Middle Low German *kökene*, Middle Dutch *cokene*, Dutch *keuken*), Old High German *chuhhina* (Middle High German *Küchen*, German *Küche*), from West Germanic from late Latin *coquina*, from *coquere* cook.]
▸ **A** *noun* **I 1** The room or part of a house in which food is prepared and cooked; a place fitted with apparatus for cooking. OE.
D. PRATER A tiny kitchen where he could prepare his porridge.
2 Cookery; a culinary establishment; the cuisine of a particular country etc. L17.
G. BERKELEY On breaking up of the Duke's kitchen, one of his under-cooks may be got.
3 A part of a casino at Monte Carlo where gamblers place smaller bets than in the *salles privées*. M20.
4 The percussion section of an orchestra or band. *slang*. M20.
5 A set of matching units for use in storing and preparing food, often with cooker, refrigerator, etc., esp. as sold together. M20.
Which? A fitted kitchen built from manufactured units.
▸ **II 6** Food, as meat, cheese, butter, etc., eaten with bread or other plain fare as a relish; drink taken with food. Chiefly *Scot.* & *N. Irish*. LME.
– PHRASES: **hell's kitchen** an area or place regarded as very disreputable or unpleasant; *spec.* a district of New York City once regarded as the haunt of criminals. ***Pullman kitchen***: see PULLMAN 5. **thieves' kitchen** a place inhabited or used by thieves or other criminals.
▸ **B** *attrib.* or as *adjective*. Of or pertaining to a kitchen; used or found in a kitchen. LME.
– COMB. & SPECIAL COLLOCATIONS: **kitchen cabinet** (orig. *US*) (**a**) a group of unofficial advisers (orig. of the president of the US) popularly believed to have greater influence than elected or appropriate officials; a private or unofficial group of advisers thought to be unduly influential; (**b**) a cabinet for domestic and culinary utensils etc. in a kitchen; **kitchen-diner** a room serving both as a kitchen and as a dining room; **kitchen Dutch** (now *rare*) [translating Dutch *kombuis-Hollands*] the dialect of Afrikaans spoken by people of mixed ethnicity in the Western Province of South Africa; *derog.* Afrikaans; **kitchen evening** *Austral.* & *NZ* an evening event at which guests bring gifts of kitchenware to a bride-to-be (cf. *kitchen tea* below); **kitchen-fee** (now *Scot.*) dripping; tallow; **kitchen garden** a garden or a part of a garden in which vegetables and sometimes fruit or herbs are grown esp. for domestic use; **kitchen-gardener** a person who tends a kitchen garden; **kitchen-gardening** the tending of a kitchen garden; **Kitchen Kaffir** (now regarded as *offensive*) former name for FANAKALO; **kitchen-knave** *arch.* a boy employed in a kitchen, a cook's boy; **kitchen-Latin** inferior Latin, dog Latin; **kitchen maid** a female servant employed in a kitchen, usu. under a cook; **kitchen midden** [translating Danish *kjøkkenmødding*, *køkken-* from *køkken* kitchen] ARCHAEOLOGY a prehistoric refuse heap associated with a site of human habitation, consisting chiefly of shells and animal bones, but also sometimes containing stone implements and other relics; **kitchen paper** absorbent paper used for drying and cleaning purposes in a kitchen etc., often sold as a roll; **kitchen-parlour** a room serving both as kitchen and parlour; †**kitchen-physic** *joc.* nourishment for an invalid (as a form of treatment); **kitchen-plot** = *kitchen garden*; **kitchen police** in the US army, enlisted men detailed to help the cook, wash dishes, etc.; the work of such men; **kitchen shower** *N. Amer.* = *kitchen tea* below; **kitchen sink** a sink in a kitchen, in which dirty dishes, vegetables, etc., are washed (freq. used as a symbol of women's enslavement to the kitchen or of the drab and mundane); ***everything but the kitchen sink***, everything possible or imaginable; **kitchen-sink** *adjective* designating or pertaining to art, esp. drama, dealing with domestic reality, esp. in its drab or sordid aspects; **kitchen stove** a stove in a kitchen; ***everything but the kitchen stove*** = ***everything but the kitchen sink*** above; **kitchen-stuff** refuse or waste from a kitchen, *esp.* dripping; **kitchen tea** *Austral., NZ, & S. Afr.* a party to which guests bring gifts of kitchenware for a bride-to-be (cf. ***kitchen evening*** above); **kitchenware** utensils for use in a kitchen; **kitchen wench** *arch.* a girl employed in a kitchen, a kitchen maid.
▸ **C** *verb trans.* †**1** Entertain in the kitchen, supply with food. *rare* (Shakes.). Only in L16.
2 Serve as relish for; make palatable, season. Also, use sparingly as relish with food; make (food) go far. *Scot.* E18.
■ **kitchenable** *adjective* suitable for cooking and eating E20. **kitcheny** *adjective* of, pertaining to, or suggestive of a kitchen L19.

kitchener /ˈkɪtʃɪnə/ *noun*¹. LME.
[ORIGIN from KITCHEN *noun* + -ER¹.]
1 A person employed in a kitchen; *esp.* in a monastery, the person in charge of the kitchen. LME.
2 A cooking range fitted with various appliances such as ovens, plate-warmers, water heaters, etc. L19.

Kitchener /ˈkɪtʃɪnə/ *noun*² & *adjective*. E20.
[ORIGIN from *Kitchener* (see below).]
▸ **A** *noun*. **1** A man thought to resemble the British soldier Horatio Herbert Kitchener (1850–1916), first Earl Kitchener of Khartoum, esp. in having an imposing and taciturn personality. E20.
2 *hist.* A soldier recruited while Kitchener was Secretary of State for War (1914–16). E20.
▸ **B** *attrib.* or as *adjective*. Of, pertaining to, or characteristic of Kitchener or soldiers recruited when he was Secretary of State for War. E20.

E. BLUNDEN The first Kitchener battalion . . to hold the sector. A. CADE A drooping Kitchener moustache.

Kitchener bun *Austral.* a cream-filled bun coated with cinnamon and sugar.

kitchenette /kɪtʃɪˈnɛt/ *noun*. Orig. *US*. **E20**.
[ORIGIN from KITCHEN *noun* + -ETTE.]
A small kitchen; an alcove or a part of a room fitted as a kitchen.

Kitchen rudder /ˈkɪtʃɪn ˈrʌdə, ˈkɪtʃ(ə)n/ *noun phr.* **E20**.
[ORIGIN J. G. A. *Kitchen*, Englishman who patented the device in 1914.]
A steering device for small craft consisting of a pair of curved deflectors either side of the propeller whose position is altered to change the course or speed of the vessel.

kite /kʌɪt/ *noun*.
[ORIGIN Old English *cȳta*, from base also of Middle High German *Küze* (German *Kauz*) screech owl & other words echoing various cries.]
1 Any of various medium-sized birds of prey of the genus *Milvus* and related genera (family Accipitridae), with long wings, forked tail, and soaring flight; *esp.* (more fully ***red kite***) a reddish-brown European kite, *Milvus milvus*. **OE**.
black kite, ***brahminy kite***, ***swallow-tailed kite***, ***whistling kite***, etc.
2 A person who preys on or exploits others, a sharper, a shark; a worthless or contemptible person, a wretch. *arch.* **M16**.

SHAKES. *Lear* Detested kite! thou liest.

3 A toy consisting of a light frame covered with a light thin material, usu. in the form of an isosceles triangle with a circular arc as base or a quadrilateral symmetrical about the longer diagonal and having a tail for balance, flown in the wind at the end of a long string. Also, a modification of a toy kite designed to support a person in the air or to form part of an unpowered aircraft. **M17**. ▸**b** An aeroplane. *slang* (orig. MILITARY). **E20**.

L. DURRELL Children flying their coloured kites in the quick fresh evening wind.

fly a kite: see FLY *verb*. ***go fly a kite***: see FLY *verb*. ***high as a kite***: see HIGH *adjective*.
4 a A bill of exchange used for raising money on credit; an accommodation bill. *slang*. **E19**. ▸**b** A letter, a communication, *esp.* an illicit one; *spec.* a letter or verbal message smuggled into, out of, or within a prison. *slang*. **M19**. ▸**c** A cheque, *esp.* a fraudulent one. *slang*. **E20**.
5 NAUTICAL. **a** In *pl.* The highest sails of a ship, set only in a light wind. Also ***flying kites***. **M19**. ▸**b** On a minesweeper: a device attached to a sweep wire submerging it to the requisite depth when it is towed over a minefield. **E20**.
6 GEOMETRY. A quadrilateral figure symmetrical about one diagonal. **L19**.
– COMB.: **kite balloon** a balloon anchored to the ground with a long string or wire, used for scientific or other purposes; **kite bar** a bar or stripe of an undesirable colour in the plumage of a fancy pigeon; **kiteboarding** = *kitesurfing* below. **kitefish** = ***moonfish*** (d) s.v. MOON *noun*[1]; **kite-flyer** a person who flies a kite (*lit. & fig.*); **kite-flying** (**a**) the flying of a kite on a string; (**b**) the raising of money by writing or passing fraudulent or unbacked cheques; (**c**) the trying out of a proposal etc.; the making of an announcement or taking of a step in order to ascertain public opinion; **kite-man** a person who obtains money against bills of exchange or cheques that will not be honoured; **Kitemark** a kite-shaped mark granted for use on goods approved by the British Standards Institution; **kite-mark** *verb trans.* use the Kitemark on; **kite-photograph** a photograph taken by means of a camera attached to a kite or kite balloon; **kite's-foot tobacco** a bright-coloured variety of tobacco; **kitesurfing** the sport or pastime of riding on a modified surfboard while holding on to a specially designed kite.

kite /kʌɪt/ *verb*. **M19**.
[ORIGIN from the noun.]
1 a *verb intrans.* Fly, soar, or move through the air like a kite; *fig.* move quickly, rush, rise quickly, (foll. by *around*, *off*, *up*, etc.). **M19**. ▸**b** *verb trans.* Cause to fly high like a toy kite. **M19**.

a T. PYNCHON Birds in the sunlight kiting behind him.

2 a *verb trans. & intrans.* Write or use (a cheque, bill, or receipt) fraudulently or without cover; raise (money) by dishonest means. *slang*. **M19**. ▸**b** *verb trans. & intrans.* Send (a communication); *spec.* smuggle (a letter) into, out of, or within a prison. *slang*. **E20**.

a A. MILLER Dozens of small businessmen with seven-year sentences for kiting not very large checks. *New Yorker* Even if loans were kited . . what did that imply?

kitenge /kɪˈtɛŋgi/ *noun*. Also **vi-** /vɪ-/. **M20**.
[ORIGIN Kiswahili *kitengele*.]
In E. Africa: a fabric, usu. of cotton and printed in various colours and designs with distinctive borders, used esp. for women's clothing.

kit fox /ˈkɪtfɒks/ *noun*. **E19**.
[ORIGIN Prob. from KIT *noun*[3] with ref. to its small size: see FOX *noun*.]
The swift fox, *Vulpes velox*; *esp.* the form of this inhabiting the south-western US and northern Mexico (sometimes regarded as a distinct species, *V. macrotis*).

kith /kɪθ/ *noun*.
[ORIGIN Old English *cȳþþ*, earlier *cȳþþu* = Old High German *chundida* from Germanic, from base also of KITHE: cf. COUTH. See also KIFF.]
†**1 a** Knowledge; information. **OE–LME**. ▸**b** Knowledge of how to behave; rules of etiquette. **LME–E19**.
†**2** One's native land or region, home; *gen.* a country, a region. **OE–E16**.
3 *collect.* One's friends, acquaintances, neighbours, or fellows; later also, kin. *arch.* exc. in ***kith and kin***, (orig.) country and kinsfolk, friends and relatives, (now also) one's relatives, one's family. **OE**.

E. O'BRIEN She . . had neither kith nor kin of her own. G. PRIESTLAND There are the Falkland islanders—our own kith and kin.

■ **kithless** *adjective* **M18**.

kithara *noun* var. of CITHARA.

kithe /kʌɪð/ *verb*. Now *Scot.* & *N. English*. Also **kythe**. Pa. pple **kithed**, **kythed**; †**kid**, †**kyd**. See also KID *adjective*.
[ORIGIN Old English *cȳþan* = Old Frisian *kētha*, Old Saxon *kuþian*, Old High German *kunden*, Old Norse *kynna*, Gothic *kunþjan*, from Germanic, from base also of KITH: cf. COUTH.]
1 *verb trans.* †**a** Proclaim, declare, tell. **OE–M16**. ▸**b** Show, reveal, make manifest; prove, demonstrate. **ME**.
†**2** *verb trans.* Exhibit or display (a feeling, quality, etc.); exercise, practise, perform. **OE–E18**.
†**3** *verb trans.* Acknowledge, confess; recognize. **OE–E17**.
4 *verb intrans.* Show oneself or itself, become manifest, appear. **ME**.
■ **kithing** *noun* (*rare*) (**a**) the action of the verb; (**b**) an act of showing or telling, a proclamation, a manifestation: **ME**.

kitling /ˈkɪtlɪŋ/ *noun*. Now *dial.* **ME**.
[ORIGIN Perh. from Old Norse *ket(t)lingr* (Norwegian *kjetling*) kitten.]
†**1** The young of any animal; a cub, a whelp. **ME–E17**.
2 A young cat, a kitten. **LME**.
3 A child, a young person, an offspring; a person thought to resemble a kitten, *spec.* a soft effeminate man. **L15**.

kitsch /kɪtʃ/ *noun & adjective*. Also **K-**. **E20**.
[ORIGIN German.]
▸ **A** *noun*. Art or artefacts perceived as being of poor quality, esp. when garish or sentimental; these enjoyed in a perverse or self-conscious way; the qualities associated with such art or artefacts. **E20**.

JILLY COOPER Flying ducks were only acceptable if they were outside and moving. Now they've become *kitsch*. *Listener* A galloping fancy for Victoriana, a sophisticated and uncritical taste for Kitsch and the cute.

▸ **B** *adjective*. Of the nature of or pertaining to kitsch; garish, sentimental, tasteless. **M20**.

Listener Director Jeremy Mortimer does offer irony . . with some brilliantly kitsch use of Country music. J. CAREY They rented a kitsch house in Pacific Palisades, Los Angeles, with luminous dogs as lamps.

■ **kitschily** *adverb* in a kitsch manner **L20**. **kitschiness** *noun* the quality or condition of being kitsch **L20**. **kitschy** *adjective* possessing the characteristics of kitsch **M20**.

kittel /ˈkɪt(ə)l/ *noun*. **L19**.
[ORIGIN Yiddish (German = overall, smock), from Middle High German *ki(e)tel* cotton or hempen outer garment.]
A white cotton or linen robe worn by orthodox Jews on certain holy days; such a robe used as a shroud.

kitten /ˈkɪt(ə)n/ *noun & verb*. **LME**.
[ORIGIN from Anglo-Norman var. of Old French *chitoun*, *chet-* (mod. *chaton*) dim. of *chat* CAT *noun*[1]: the ending assim. to -EN[1].]
▸ **A** *noun*. **1** A young cat. **LME**.

M. ANGELOU Frankel turned around like a kitten trying to catch its tail.

2 The young of certain other animals, as the fox, ferret, beaver, and rabbit. **L15**.
3 More fully ***kitten moth***. Any of certain moths of the genus *Furcula* (family Notodontidae), with furry bodies. **E19**.
alder kitten, ***poplar kitten***, ***sallow kitten***.
4 A girl or young woman, *esp.* a coy or flirtatious one. **L19**.
– PHRASES & COMB.: **have kittens** (*fig.*) *colloq.* be or become very angry, anxious, or upset. **kitten heel** a type of low stiletto heel.
▸ **B** *verb intrans.* Of a cat, ferret, beaver, etc.: give birth to a kitten or kittens. **LME**.
■ **kittenhood** *noun* the state, condition, or period of being a kitten **M19**. **kittenlike** *adjective* resembling a kitten, kittenish **M19**.

kittenish /ˈkɪt(ə)nɪʃ/ *adjective*. **M18**.
[ORIGIN from KITTEN + -ISH[1].]
Like a kitten or that of a kitten; playful, lively; coy, flirtatious.

DICKENS She was all girlishness, and playfulness, and wildness, and kittenish buoyancy.

■ **kittenishly** *adverb* **L19**. **kittenishness** *noun* **E20**.

†**kittisol** *noun*. **L16–L19**.
[ORIGIN Portuguese & Spanish *quitasol*, from *quitar* take away + *sol* sun. Cf. PARASOL.]
A sunshade, a parasol, an umbrella; *spec.* a Chinese umbrella made of bamboo and oiled paper.

Kittitian /kɪˈtɪʃ(ə)n/ *noun & adjective*. **M20**.
[ORIGIN from St *Kitts* (see below) + *-itian* as in *Haitian*.]
▸ **A** *noun*. A native or inhabitant of the island of St Kitts in the W. Indies. **M20**.
▸ **B** *adjective*. Of or pertaining to St Kitts or its inhabitants. **L20**.

kittiwake /ˈkɪtɪweɪk/ *noun*. Orig. *Scot.* **E17**.
[ORIGIN Imit. of the bird's cry.]
A small maritime gull of the genus *Rissa*, spec. *R. tridactyla*, of the N. Atlantic and Arctic Oceans.

kittle /ˈkɪt(ə)l/ *adjective*. Orig. *Scot. & N. English*. **M16**.
[ORIGIN from KITTLE *verb*[1].]
Ticklish (*lit. & fig.*); difficult to deal with or manage; risky, precarious; capricious, rash, erratic in behaviour.
kittle cattle (people who or animals which are) capricious, rash, or erratic in behaviour; (things which are) difficult to use or deal with.

kittle /ˈkɪt(ə)l/ *verb*[1] *trans.* Now *dial.* (chiefly *Scot.*).
[ORIGIN Old English (in *kitelung* noun) corresp. to Old Saxon *kitilon* (Dutch *kittelen*), Old High German *kizzilōn* (German *kitzeln*), Old Norse *kitla*, from Germanic: superseded in Middle English by forms from Old Norse.]
1 Tickle, touch as if tickling (a person or thing). **OE**.
2 Stimulate, excite, rouse, please. **ME**.
3 Puzzle with a question etc., perplex. **E19**.
■ **kittly** *adjective* (*Scot.*) ticklish; causing a tickling sensation; difficult, puzzling: **E19**.

kittle /ˈkɪt(ə)l/ *verb*[2]. Now *Scot.* & *N. English*. **M16**.
[ORIGIN Perh. back-form. from KITLING, but cf. Norwegian *kjetla* in same sense.]
1 *verb intrans.* = KITTEN *verb*. **M16**.
2 *verb intrans. & trans.* (in *pass.*). Be engendered or produced; come into being. **E19**.

kittle-pins /ˈkɪt(ə)lpɪnz/ *noun*. *obsolete* exc. *dial.* Also **kettle-** /ˈkɛt(ə)l-/. **M17**.
[ORIGIN 1st elem. rel. to KITTLES.]
The game skittles.

kittles /ˈkɪt(ə)lz/ *noun*. Now *rare* or *obsolete*. Also **kettles** /ˈkɛt(ə)lz/. **L16**.
[ORIGIN Unknown: cf. KITTLE-PINS.]
The game skittles.

K

kittul /ˈkɪtuːl/ *noun*. **L17**.
[ORIGIN Sinhalese *kitul*.]
The jaggery palm, *Caryota urens*; a fibre obtained from the leaf stalks of this, used for making ropes, brushes, etc.

kitty /ˈkɪti/ *noun*[1]. **E18**.
[ORIGIN Abbreviation of KITTEN *noun* + -Y[6].]
(A pet name for) a kitten or a cat.

J. C. OATES Followed along after the cat, calling *Here kitty*.

kitty /ˈkɪti/ *noun*[2]. **E19**.
[ORIGIN Unknown.]
1 A prison, a jail. *N. English*. **E19**.
2 A pool of money in some card games etc. made up of contributions from each player and used as winnings or for refreshments etc. Also, a sum of money made up of contributions by people involved in a common activity, a reserve fund. **L19**.

B. BAINBRIDGE Every Friday the two men put money into a kitty towards its . . purchase. *Scotsman* Even in times of vastly reduced income . . the wives . . were blamed if the kitty ran dry.

scoop the kitty: see SCOOP *verb* 5a.
3 BOWLS. The jack. **L19**.

kiva /ˈkiːvə/ *noun*. **L19**.
[ORIGIN Hopi *kíva*.]
A chamber, built wholly or partly underground, used by male Pueblo Indians for religious rites etc. Cf. ESTUFA.

kive *noun* var. of KEEVE.

kiver /ˈkɪvə, ˈkiː-/ *noun*. *obsolete* exc. *dial.* **ME**.
[ORIGIN App. from *kive* var. of KEEVE.]
A shallow wooden vessel or tub.

Kiwanis /kɪˈwɑːnɪs/ *noun*. **E20**.
[ORIGIN Unknown.]
In full ***Kiwanis Club***. A N. American society of business and professional men formed for the maintenance of commercial ethics and as a social and charitable organization.
■ **Kiwanian** *noun* a member of a Kiwanis Club **E20**.

kiwi /ˈkiːwiː/ *noun*. In sense 2 **K-**. **M19**.
[ORIGIN Maori.]
1 Any of several dark brown or grey tailless, flightless, nocturnal ratite birds of the genus *Apteryx*, of New Zealand forest and scrub, having a long bill and hairlike feathers, a national emblem of New Zealand. **M19**.
2 A New Zealander, esp. a soldier or member of a national sports team. *colloq.* **E20**.

Telegraph (Brisbane) 10-wicket haul leads Kiwis to Test victory. *attrib.*: M. S. POWER He . . managed to affect the nasal Kiwi twang almost to perfection.

3 A non-flying member of an air force. *arch. slang*. **E20**.
4 In full ***kiwi fruit***. The sweet brown-skinned oval fruit of either of two eastern Asian plants of the genus *Actinidia*,

A. deliciosa, with green flesh, and *A. chinensis*, with yellow flesh. Also called ***Chinese gooseberry***. M20.

ki-yi /kʌɪˈjʌɪ/ *verb & noun. US colloq.* M19.
[ORIGIN Imit.]
▸ **A** *verb intrans.* Pres. pple **ki-yi-ing**; pa. t. **ki-yi-ed**. (Of a dog) howl, yelp; howl or yelp like a dog. M19.
▸ **B** *noun.* **1** The howl or yelp of a dog; a whoop or shout resembling this. L19.
2 A dog. L19.

Kizil /kɪˈzɪl/ *noun & adjective.* Pl. of noun **-s**, same. L19.
[ORIGIN Turkish *kızıl* red.]
Of or pertaining to, a member of, a Turkic people of southern Siberia.

Kizilbash /ˈkɪzɪlbɑːʃ/ *noun.* M17.
[ORIGIN Turkish *kızılbaş*, formed as KIZIL + *baş* head.]
1 A Persianized Turk in Iran or Afghanistan. M17.
2 A member of any of several cultural or religious minorities in Asian Turkey. E20.

kJ *abbreviation.*
Kilojoule(s).

Kjeldahl /ˈkɛldɑːl/ *noun.* L19.
[ORIGIN Johann *Kjeldahl* (1849–1900), Danish chemist.]
BIOCHEMISTRY. Used *attrib.* and in *possess.* to designate a method of estimation of nitrogen in organic substances by treatment with concentrated sulphuric acid and conversion of the resulting ammonium sulphate to ammonia, which is then titrated.
Kjeldahl flask a glass flask with a round bottom and a long wide neck, used in the Kjeldahl method.

KKK *abbreviation.*
Ku Klux Klan.

kl *abbreviation.*
Kilolitre(s).

Klaas's cuckoo /ˈklɑːsɪz ˈkʊkuː/ *noun phr.* Also **Klaas' cuckoo**. M19.
[ORIGIN *Klaas*, a servant of the French explorer François Le Vaillant (1753–1824).]
A bronze and green cuckoo, *Chrysococcyx klaas*, of sub-Saharan Africa. Cf. MIETJIE.

klaberjass /ˈklabəjas/ *noun.* Also **clobiosh** /ˈklɒbɪjɒʃ/ & other vars. L19.
[ORIGIN German from Dutch *klaverjas*.]
CARDS. A two-handed card game distantly related to bezique, in which points are scored for winning value cards in tricks and for declaring combinations.

Klamath /ˈklaməθ/ *noun & adjective.* Pl. of noun **-s**, same. E19.
[ORIGIN Chinook *łámał* Klamath.]
Of or pertaining to, a member of, a Penutian people of the Oregon–California border; (of) the language of this people.
Klamath weed *US* common St John's wort, *Hypericum perforatum*, naturalized as a weed in the US.

Klan /klan/ *noun & adjective.* M19.
[ORIGIN Abbreviation.]
▸ **A** *noun.* The Ku Klux Klan. M19.
– COMB.: **Klansman** a member of the Ku Klux Klan.
▸ **B** *attrib.* or as *adjective.* Of or pertaining to the Ku Klux Klan. E20.

Klang /klaŋ/ *noun.* L19.
[ORIGIN German = sound.]
MUSIC. A tone composed of fundamental and overtones.
– COMB.: ***Klangfarbe*** /-farbə, -fɑːbə/ [German *Farbe* colour] musical quality of a note, timbre; ***Klangfarbenmelodie*** /-farbənmeloˌdiː, -fɑːbənˌmɛlədi/ melody of timbres.

klapmatch *noun* var. of CLAPMATCH.

klapper /ˈklapə/ *noun. S. Afr.* M19.
[ORIGIN Perh. from Afrikaans from Malay *kelapa* coconut, or from Afrikaans *klapper* rattle.]
= ***Kaffir orange*** s.v. KAFFIR.

klatch /klatʃ/ *noun.* Also ***Klatsch***. M20.
[ORIGIN German *Klatsch* gossip.]
A social gathering, a party, *spec.* a coffee party. Cf. KAFFEEKLATSCH.

klaxon /ˈklaks(ə)n/ *noun & verb.* Orig. *US.* E20.
[ORIGIN Name of the original manufacturers.]
▸ **A** *noun.* (Proprietary name for) an electric horn or warning hooter, orig. one on a motor vehicle. E20.

J. LE CARRÉ He heard the klaxons, . . moaning out . . like the howl of starving animals.

▸ **B** *verb intrans.* Sound a klaxon. E20.

Kleagle /ˈkliːɡ(ə)l/ *noun.* Also **k-**. E20.
[ORIGIN from KL(AN + EAGLE *noun.*]
An officer of the Ku Klux Klan.

klebsiella /klɛbzɪˈɛlə/ *noun.* E20.
[ORIGIN mod. Latin (see below), from *Klebs* (see KLEBS–LÖFFLER) + -I- + -ELLA.]
MEDICINE & BACTERIOLOGY. Any of various Gram-negative coliform bacteria of the genus *Klebsiella*, which includes several associated with respiratory, urinary, and wound infections.

Klebs–Löffler /klɛbzˈləːflə/ *noun.* L19.
[ORIGIN T. A. E. *Klebs* (1834–1913) and F. A. J. *Löffler* (1852–1915), German bacteriologists.]
MEDICINE & BACTERIOLOGY. Used *attrib.* to designate the coryneform bacillus *Corynebacterium diphtheriae*, which causes diphtheria in humans and similar diseases in other animals.

Kleenex /ˈkliːnɛks/ *noun.* Orig. *US.* Also **k-**. Pl. same, **-es** /-ɪz/. E20.
[ORIGIN Invented name.]
(Proprietary name for) an absorbent disposable paper tissue, used esp. as a handkerchief.

L. CODY She mopped the puddle in her saucer with a piece of Kleenex. P. LIVELY She got out a Kleenex and blew her nose.

kleft *noun* var. of KLEPHT.

Klein bottle /ˈklʌɪn bɒt(ə)l/ *noun phr.* M20.
[ORIGIN Felix *Klein* (1849–1925), German mathematician.]
MATH. A closed surface both sides of which, at any point, are parts of the same continuous surface, freq. represented in three dimensions as a bottle with the neck passed through the side and joined to a hole in the base.

Kleinian /ˈklʌɪnɪən/ *adjective & noun.* M20.
[ORIGIN from *Klein* (see below) + -IAN.]
▸ **A** *adjective.* Of or pertaining to the psychoanalyst Melanie Klein (1882–1960) or her theories, esp. concerning child psychoanalysis, or her school of psychoanalysis which stressed people's need for social relationships. M20.
▸ **B** *noun.* An advocate of the theories of Melanie Klein; an adherent of the Kleinian school of psychoanalysis. M20.

klendusity /klɛnˈdjuːsɪti/ *noun.* M20.
[ORIGIN from Greek *kleis* bar, bolt + *endusis* entry + -ITY.]
BOTANY. Ability of a plant to escape infection through the possession of some inhibiting property.
■ **klendusic** *adjective* exhibiting klendusity M20.

klep /klɛp/ *noun. slang.* L19.
[ORIGIN Abbreviation.]
= KLEPTOMANIAC.

klepht /klɛft/ *noun.* Also **kleft**. E19.
[ORIGIN mod. Greek *klephtēs* from Greek *kleptēs* thief.]
A Greek brigand or bandit. Also, a Greek fighter for independence, *spec.* against the Turks in the 15th cent. or during the war of independence (1821–8).
■ **klephtic** *adjective* M19.

klepto /ˈklɛptəʊ/ *noun. slang.* Pl. **-os**. M20.
[ORIGIN Abbreviation.]
= KLEPTOMANIAC.

kleptocracy /klɛpˈtɒkrəsi/ *noun.* E19.
[ORIGIN from Greek *klepto-* (see KLEPTOMANIA) + -CRACY.]
(Government by) a ruling body of thieves; a nation ruled by thieves.
■ **ˈkleptocrat** *noun* a member of a kleptocracy, a thieving ruler M20.

kleptolagnia /klɛptə(ʊ)ˈlaɡnɪə/ *noun.* E20.
[ORIGIN formed as KLEPTOMANIA + Greek *lagneia* lust, after ALGOLAGNIA.]
PSYCHIATRY. The practice of achieving sexual arousal through stealing; the compulsive urge to steal for this purpose.

kleptomania /klɛptə(ʊ)ˈmeɪnɪə/ *noun.* M19.
[ORIGIN from Greek *klepto-* combining form of *kleptēs* thief, rel. to *kleptein* steal + -MANIA.]
The compulsive urge to steal, usu. without regard for need or profit.
■ **kleptomaniac** *noun & adjective* (**a**) *noun* a person affected with kleptomania; (**b**) *adjective* affected with kleptomania, characteristic of a kleptomaniac: M19.

kleptoparasite /klɛptə(ʊ)ˈparəsʌɪt/ *noun.* Also **c-**. L20.
[ORIGIN formed as KLEPTOMANIA + PARASITE *noun.*]
ZOOLOGY. A bird, insect, or other animal which habitually robs others (of a different species) of food.
■ **kleptoparaˈsitic** *adjective* M20. **kleptoparasitism** *noun* the behaviour of a kleptoparasite M20. **kleptoparasitize** *verb trans.* habitually rob (another animal) of food L20.

kleruch *noun* var. of CLERUCH.

kletterschuh /ˈklɛtəʃuː/ *noun.* Pl. **-schuhe** /-ʃuːə/. E20.
[ORIGIN German, lit. 'climbing shoe'.]
A light boot worn esp. for rock-climbing. Usu. in *pl.*

kleywang /ˈkleɪwaŋ/ *noun.* Also **kelewang** /ˈkɛlɪwaŋ/. L18.
[ORIGIN Malay *kelewang*.]
A single-edged Indonesian sword.

klezmer /ˈklɛzmə/ *noun.* Pl. same, **klezmorim** /ˈklɛzmərɪm/. M20.
[ORIGIN Yiddish, contr. of Hebrew *kĕlēy zemer* musical instruments.]
A member of a group of musicians playing traditional eastern European Jewish music; (in full ***klezmer music***) this type of music.

klick /klɪk/ *noun. slang* (orig. *US* MILITARY). Also **klik**. M20.
[ORIGIN Unknown.]
A kilometre.

T. CLANCY Have the 4th pull back about thirty klicks.

– NOTE: Orig. used in the Vietnam War.

klieg /kliːɡ/ *noun.* E20.
[ORIGIN A. T. & J. H. *Kliegl* (1872–1927 & 1869–1959), US inventors.]
CINEMATOGRAPHY & TELEVISION. In full ***klieg light***. A kind of arc lamp invented for use in film studios; a powerful electric light used in filming.
– COMB.: **klieg eye(s)** an eye condition caused by exposure to very bright light, characterized by watering and conjunctivitis.

klik *noun* var. of KLICK.

Klinefelter /ˈklʌɪnfɛltə/ *noun.* M20.
[ORIGIN H. F. *Klinefelter* (b. 1912), US physician.]
MEDICINE. Used *attrib.* and in *possess.* to designate a syndrome affecting males in which the cells have an extra X chromosome (in addition to the normal XY), characterized by a tall thin physique, small infertile testes, eunuchoidism, and gynaecomastia.

Kling /klɪŋ/ *noun.* Now *rare*. E17.
[ORIGIN Malay *Keling* Tamil trader or settler (derog.) from Sanskrit *Kaliṅga* an old name for a strip of coast along the Bay of Bengal.]
An Indian settler in Malaysia. Also †***Kling man***.

Klingon /ˈklɪŋɒn/ *noun.* M20.
[ORIGIN Invented name.]
1 A member of a warlike humanoid alien species in the US television series *Star Trek* and its derivatives and sequels. M20.
2 The language of the Klingons. L20.
– NOTE: The Klingon language, created by Dr Marc Okrand for a film in 1984, is used and studied by enthusiasts of *Star Trek*.

klino- /ˈklʌɪnəʊ/ *combining form* of Greek *klinein* to lean, slope: see -O-. Cf. CLINO-.
■ **klinokiˈnesis** *noun* (BIOLOGY) variation in the rate of turning M20. **klinokiˈnetic** *adjective* (BIOLOGY) of or pertaining to klinokinesis M20. **klinostat** *noun* a revolving device on or in which germinating seeds or growing plants can be placed so as to counteract the directional influence of gravity, light, etc., on their growth L19.

klip /klɪp/ *noun. S. Afr. colloq.* E19.
[ORIGIN Afrikaans from Dutch = rock, stone.]
1 ***blink klip*** [BLINK *adjective*]. Powdered micaceous iron ore, formerly used as a cosmetic. E19.
2 A stone, a pebble. M19.
3 A diamond. Also ***blink klip***. L19.

klipbok /ˈklɪpbɒk/ *noun.* Also **-buck** /-bʌk/. L19.
[ORIGIN Afrikaans, from Dutch *klip* rock + *bok* buck.]
= KLIPSPRINGER.

klipdas /ˈklɪpdas/ *noun. S. Afr.* M19.
[ORIGIN Afrikaans, formed as Dutch *klip* rock + DAS *noun.*]
= DASSIE 1.

klipfish /ˈklɪpfɪʃ/ *noun.* Pl. **-es** /-ɪz/, (usu.) same. L18.
[ORIGIN Partial translation of Dutch *klipvisch* (mod. *-vis*) or Danish *klipfisk* rockfish.]
1 Any of various brightly coloured viviparous marine fishes of the family Clinidae, which live in shallow water or rock pools. Cf. KINGKLIP. *S. Afr.* L18.
2 A codfish split open, boned, salted, and dried. M19.

klipkous /ˈklɪpkəʊs/ *noun. S. Afr.* M18.
[ORIGIN Afrikaans, from Dutch *klip* rock + *kous* stocking.]
= ABALONE.

klippe /ˈklɪpə/ *noun.* E20.
[ORIGIN German = partly submerged or buried rock.]
GEOLOGY. A part of a nappe which has become detached from its parent mass by sliding or by erosion of intervening parts.

klipspringer /ˈklɪpsprɪŋə/ *noun.* L18.
[ORIGIN Afrikaans, from Dutch *klip* rock + *springer* SPRINGER.]
A small antelope, *Oreotragus oreotragus*, inhabiting rocky terrain in sub-Saharan Africa.

klister /ˈklɪstə/ *noun.* M20.
[ORIGIN Norwegian = paste.]
SKIING. A soft wax for applying to the running surface of skis to facilitate movement, used esp. when the temperature is above freezing.

klompie /ˈklɒmpi/ *noun. S. Afr.* Also **-pje**. M19.
[ORIGIN Afrikaans from Dutch *klompje* dim. of *klomp*: see CLUMP *noun.*]
1 A group, a cluster, esp. of animals or of shrubs or trees. *colloq.* M19.
2 A type of hard yellow brick, orig. imported from the Netherlands. Also ***klompie brick***. E20.

Klondike /ˈklɒndʌɪk/ *noun & verb.* Also **-dyke**. L19.
[ORIGIN A region and river in the Yukon, NW Canada, the scene of a gold rush in the years following 1896; a name also given to a herring fishery off the west coast of Scotland.]
▸ **A** *noun.* **1** A source of valuable material or of wealth. L19.
2 CARDS. A variety of patience. *N. Amer.* E20.
▸ **B** *verb trans.* Also **k-**. Export (fish, esp. mackerel or herring) while fresh, freq. to a foreign factory ship. Chiefly *Scot.* E20.
■ **Klondiker** *noun* (**a**) a prospector in the Klondike; (**b**) (chiefly *Scot.*) an exporter of or dealer in fresh fish, esp. mackerel or herring; a ship used for exporting fresh fish: L19.

K

klong /klɒŋ/ *noun*. L19.
[ORIGIN Thai.]
In Thailand: a canal.

klonkie /ˈklɒŋki/ *noun*. *S. Afr.* M20.
[ORIGIN Afrikaans, blend of *klein* small & *jong* boy + dim. suffix *-kie*.]
A black or Coloured boy.

klooch *noun* var. of KLOOTCH.

kloof /kluːf/ *noun*. *S. Afr.* M18.
[ORIGIN Dutch = cleft: see CLOVE *noun*[4].]
A deep valley, a ravine, a gorge.

klootch /kluːtʃ/ *noun*. *N. Amer. dial.* Now regarded as *offensive*. Also **klooch**. M19.
[ORIGIN Chinook Jargon *klootchman* from Nootka *ło·csma* woman, wife.]
In full ***klootchman***. A N. American Indian woman.

klop *noun & verb* see CLOP.

klops /klɒps/ *noun*. Pl. same, **-se** /-sə/. M20.
[ORIGIN German.]
A type of meatball or meat loaf.

kludge /klʌdʒ/ *noun & verb*. *slang* (orig. *US*). M20.
[ORIGIN Prob. symbolic: cf. BODGE, FUDGE *verb*.]
▸ **A** *noun*. An ill-matched assortment of parts put together to fulfil a specific purpose; *spec.* in COMPUTING, an improvised machine, system, or program, a hastily or awkwardly contrived solution to a fault or bug, a badly structured system in need of redesign. M20.
▸ **B** *verb trans*. Improvise or put together (a device, program, etc.) from an ill-matched assortment of parts. L20.

†**klumene** *noun*. M19–E20.
[ORIGIN from mod. Latin *kalium* potassium (because orig. derived from potassium carbide) + -ENE.]
CHEMISTRY. = ACETYLENE.

klunk /klʌŋk/ *noun*. *US slang*. Also **c-**. M20.
[ORIGIN Unknown.]
= KLUTZ.

klutz /klʌts/ *noun & verb*. *N. Amer. slang*. M20.
[ORIGIN Yiddish from German *Klotz* wooden block. Cf. CLOT *noun*.]
▸ **A** *noun*. A clumsy awkward person, *esp.* one considered socially inept; a fool. M20.

J. CHANCELLOR Many Nixon haters believed that the crook had been replaced by the klutz.

▸ **B** *verb intrans*. Foll. by *about*, *around*: behave awkwardly or foolishly, move clumsily. L20.
■ **klutziness** *noun* awkwardness of manner, foolishness L20. **klutzy** *adjective* awkward in manner, foolish M20.

Kluxer /ˈklʌksə/ *noun*. *US slang*. L19.
[ORIGIN from Ku *Klux* Klan + -ER[1].]
A member of the Ku Klux Klan.

klydonograph /klʌɪˈdəʊnəɡrɑːf/ *noun*. E20.
[ORIGIN from Greek *kludōn* wave, billow + -O- + -GRAPH.]
ELECTRICITY. An instrument used to determine photographically the voltage and polarity of a surge, by means of a point electrode resting on film behind which is a plate electrode.

klystron /ˈklʌɪstrɒn/ *noun*. M20.
[ORIGIN from Greek *klus-* stem of *kluzein* wash or break over + -TRON.]
ELECTRONICS. An electron tube for amplifying or generating microwave signals using the energy of a beam of electrons whose velocities have been modulated by a high-frequency voltage so that they collect into bunches.
klystron oscillator, ***klystron tube***. ***reflex klystron***: see REFLEX *noun & adjective*.

km *abbreviation*.
Kilometre(s).

km/h *abbreviation*.
Kilometres per hour.

kn. *abbreviation*.
NAUTICAL. Knot(s).

knab *noun* see NOB *noun*[2].

knab /nab/ *verb*[1]. *obsolete* exc. *dial.* Also **nab**. Infl. **-bb-**. M17.
[ORIGIN Imit.: cf. KNAP *verb*[2], KNUB *verb*.]
1 *verb trans*. Bite lightly, nibble, nip. M17.
2 *verb intrans*. Bite, nibble, (*on*, *upon*). M17.

knab *verb*[2] see NOB *verb*[1].

†**knabby** *adjective & noun* see NOBBY *adjective & noun*.

knack /nak/ *noun*[1]. Now *Scot.* LME.
[ORIGIN Imit.: cf. Dutch *knak*, German *Knack(e)*.]
A sharp sound or blow; *fig.* a jibe, a taunt.

knack /nak/ *noun*[2]. LME.
[ORIGIN Ult. imit., but perh. immed. from Dutch, Low German *knak*. Cf. KNACK *noun*[1].]
▸ **I 1** A trick, *esp.* a clever or (formerly) a deceitful one. LME.

E. O'BRIEN She mastered the knack of walking backward.

2 An intuitive or acquired talent or skill for doing something cleverly and successfully; the ability to deal with or do something in the best way. L16.

R. CROMPTON It's jus' a knack. It jus' wants practice. *Observer* I only hope I've got my mother's knack of dealing with awkward questions. R. ELLMANN His knack for drawing was shown in some illustrations he made. P. BARKER He's got the knack of talking to your Dad.

3 A habit of acting or speaking in a particular way, a tendency to do a certain thing. L17.

R. HARLING He always had a knack of falling out with anyone in time. L. VAN DER POST This dreaming process had a knack of following through into my waking imagination.

▸ **II 4** An ingenious contrivance; a trinket, a trifle, a knick-knack. *arch.* M16.
■ **knacky** *adjective* artful, clever, adroit, ingenious E18.

knack /nak/ *verb*. *obsolete* exc. *dial.* LME.
[ORIGIN Imit.: for senses 3 & 4 cf. Dutch *knakken*, Middle High German *knacken*, *gnacken*, etc.]
1 †**a** *verb trans*. Sing in a lively or ornate way, trill, (a song). Only in LME. ▸**b** *verb intrans*. Speak in a lively way, chatter; talk mincingly. E16.
2 *verb trans*. Mock or taunt (a person). Chiefly *Scot.* LME.
3 *verb trans*. Strike (things) together so as to produce a sharp abrupt noise; gnash (the teeth); snap (the fingers). L15. ▸**b** Break or crack (something) with a sharp sound. M16.
4 *verb intrans*. Make a sharp abrupt noise, as when stones are struck together. E17.

knacker /ˈnakə/ *noun*[1]. LME.
[ORIGIN from KNACK *verb* + -ER[1].]
†**1** A person who sings in a lively way. Only in LME.
2 A thing that makes a sharp cracking noise; *spec.* a castanet. Usu. in *pl.* *obsolete* exc. *dial.* E17.
3 A testicle. Usu. in *pl.* *slang*. M19.

knacker /ˈnakə/ *noun*[2]. L16.
[ORIGIN Uncertain: in sense 1 perh. orig. maker of the smaller articles of harness (from KNACK *noun*[2] + -ER[2]).]
1 A harness-maker; a saddler. *dial.* L16.
2 An old worn-out horse. *dial.* L18.
3 A buyer of old or worn-out horses for slaughter. E19. ▸**b** A buyer of old houses, ships, etc., for their materials. L19.

fig.: J. CAREY The knacker's yard of language. This is where clichés come to die.

■ **knackery** *noun* a knacker's yard or business M19.

knacker /ˈnakə/ *verb trans*. *slang*. L19.
[ORIGIN from KNACKER *noun*[1] 3 or KNACKER *noun*[2] 3.]
Kill; castrate. Now usu., exhaust, wear out; damage severely, ruin.

B. BEAUMONT Roger Uttley had knackered his back bending . . to pick up a piece of apple pie.

■ **knackered** *adjective* dead; castrated; (now usu.) exhausted, worn out: L19.

knackwurst /ˈnakwəːst, *foreign* ˈknakvʊrst/ *noun*. Also **knock-** /ˈnɒk-/. M20.
[ORIGIN German, from *knacken* make a cracking noise + *Wurst* sausage.]
A type of short fat highly seasoned German sausage.

knag /naɡ/ *noun*. LME.
[ORIGIN German (orig. Low German) *Knagge* knot, peg.]
1 A short projection from the trunk or branch of a tree, as a dead branch; a peg, a hook. LME.
2 A knot in wood; the base of a branch. M16.
3 A pointed rock or crag. Now *dial.* M16.
†**4** Any of the knobs or points of a stag's horn; a tine. L16–M17.
■ †**knagged** *adjective* knobbed, toothed, jagged LME–E18. **knaggy** *adjective* knotty, rough, rugged, jagged M16.

knaidel /ˈkneɪd(ə)l/ *noun*. Also **knei-**. Pl. **-dlach** /-dlax/. M20.
[ORIGIN Yiddish *kneydel* from Middle High German, German KNÖDEL.]
A type of dumpling eaten esp. in Jewish households during Passover. Usu. in *pl.*

knallgas /ˈknalɡas/ *noun*. L19.
[ORIGIN German, from *Knall* bang, detonation + *Gas* gas.]
CHEMISTRY. An explosive mixture of gases, esp. one of two volumes of hydrogen with one of oxygen.

knap /nap/ *noun*[1]. Chiefly *dial.*
[ORIGIN Old English *cnæp(p)*, perh. cogn. with Old Norse *knappr* knob etc.: cf. KNOP.]
The crest or summit of a hill or of rising ground; a small hill or hillock; a stretch of rising ground.

knap /nap/ *noun*[2]. Now *dial.* LME.
[ORIGIN Imit.: cf. KNAP *verb*[1]. See also NAP *noun*[4].]
An abrupt stroke or blow, a sharp knock.

knap *noun*[3] see KNAPE.

†**knap** *noun*[4] var. of NAP *noun*[2].

knap /nap/ *verb*[1]. Now *dial.* exc. ARCHAEOLOGY. Infl. **-pp-**. LME.
[ORIGIN Imit.: cf. Dutch & German (orig. Low German) *knappen* crack, crackle, KNAP *noun*[2].]
1 *verb trans. & intrans.* Strike (a thing or person) with a hard short sound; knock, rap. LME.
2 *verb trans*. Break (esp. a stone, *spec.* a flint) with a sharp blow from a hammer etc.; snap, crack, (something). M16.
3 *verb trans. & intrans.* Speak or say, esp. affectedly; utter, chatter. *Scot. & N. English*. L16.
4 *verb trans*. Break, strike, or knock *off* smartly. E17.

knap /nap/ *verb*[2] *intrans. & trans.* Now *dial.* Infl. **-pp-**. L16.
[ORIGIN Uncertain: cf. KNAB *verb*[1], Dutch & German (orig. Low German) *knappen* bite.]
Bite, nip, snap (at), nibble.

†**knap** *verb*[3] var. of NAP *verb*[2].

knape /neɪp/ *noun*. Long *obsolete* exc. *dial.* In sense 3 also **knap** /nap/.
[ORIGIN Old English *cnapa* = Old Saxon *cnapo*, Old High German *knappo* (German *Knappe* page, squire). Obscurely rel. to KNAVE.]
†**1** = KNAVE 1. OE–E17.
†**2** = KNAVE 2. OE–M16.
3 = KNAVE 3. LME.

knapped /napt/ *adjective*. M19.
[ORIGIN from KNAP *verb*[1] + -ED[1].]
Of flint, a flint: broken by a sharp blow.

B. W. ALDISS A fine church . . refaced with knapped flint in the eighteen-eighties.

knapper /ˈnapə/ *noun*. Chiefly *dial.* L18.
[ORIGIN from KNAP *verb*[1] + -ER[1].]
A person who or thing which shapes or breaks stones, esp. flints.

knapsack /ˈnapsak/ *noun*. E17.
[ORIGIN Middle Low German, from Dutch *knapzak* (German *Knappsack*), prob. from German *knappen* bite (cf. KNAP *verb*[2]) + *zak* SACK *noun*[1].]
A bag of canvas or other weatherproof material with shoulder straps, carried on the back esp. by soldiers and hikers.

A. RANSOME The knapsacks on their backs, . . were heavy and uncomfortable.

– COMB.: **knapsack pump**, **knapsack sprayer** a sprayer consisting of a hand-held nozzle supplied from a pressurized reservoir that is carried on the back like a knapsack.
■ **knapsacked** *adjective* equipped with a knapsack or knapsacks E20. **knapsacking** *noun* travelling with a knapsack L19.

knapweed /ˈnapwiːd/ *noun*. Orig. †**knopweed**. LME.
[ORIGIN from KNOP *noun* + WEED *noun*[1]. For the change of vowel cf. *strop*, *strap*.]
Any of several plants of the genus *Centaurea*, of the composite family, related to the thistles, with heads of usu. purple flowers and hard globular involucres; *esp.* (more fully ***lesser knapweed***) hardhead, *C. nigra*, and (more fully ***greater knapweed***) *C. scabiosa*, of chalk grassland.

knar /nɑː/ *noun*. Also **knaur** /nɔː/, **gn-**. See also KNUR. ME.
[ORIGIN Middle Low German, Middle Dutch, Middle High German *knorre* (Dutch *knorr*, German *Knorren*) knobbly protuberance.]
1 A rugged rock or stone. Now *dial.* ME.
2 A knot in wood; *spec.* a bark-covered protuberance on the trunk or root of a tree. LME.
3 A burly thickset person. Long *obsolete* exc. *Scot.* LME.
■ **knarred** *adjective* knotted, gnarled M19. **knarry** *adjective* (long *arch. rare*) having knars or knots, knotty LME.

knarl /nɑːl/ *noun*. *rare*. L16.
[ORIGIN App. deriv. of KNAR: cf. GNARL *noun*, KNURL *noun*.]
†**1** A tangle, a knot. Only in L16.
2 A hunchbacked person, a dwarf. *dial.* E19.

knaur *noun* var. of KNAR.

knave /neɪv/ *noun*.
[ORIGIN Old English *cnafa* = Old High German *knabo* (German *Knabe* boy) from West Germanic. Obscurely rel. to KNAPE.]
†**1** A male child, a boy. Latterly only more fully ***knave-bairn***, ***knave-child***. OE–E19.
2 A boy employed as a servant; a male servant; a person of low status, a menial. *arch.* OE.
3 An unprincipled or disreputable person, esp. a man. ME. ▸**b** A fellow, a chap. *joc.* M16.

F. DONALDSON He is far more fool than knave.

4 CARDS. The lowest court card of each suit, bearing the representation of a male youth; a jack. M16.
– COMB.: ***knave-bairn***, ***knave-child***: see sense 1 above; ***knave noddy***: see NODDY *noun*[2].
■ **knaveship** *noun* †(**a**) *Scot.* a quantity of corn or meal given as a fee to a miller's servant; (**b**) *arch.* (with possess. adjective, as ***his knaveship*** etc.) a mock title given to a disreputable person: L15. **knavish** *adjective* characteristic of a knave LME. **knavishly** *adverb* L15. **knavishness** *noun* E16.

knavery /ˈneɪv(ə)ri/ *noun*. E16.
[ORIGIN from KNAVE + -ERY.]
1 Unprincipled or deceitful behaviour, trickery; an unprincipled deed or practice. *arch.* E16.
†**2** A trick, a jest; roguishness, playfulness. L16–M17. ▸**b** Frippery, finery. *rare* (Shakes.). Only in L16.

K

knawel /ˈnɔːɪl/ *noun*. L16.
[ORIGIN German *Knauel*, *Kneuel*.]
A low-growing plant of the genus *Scleranthus*, of the pink family, with clusters of small petalless flowers; *esp.* (more fully ***annual knawel***), *S. annuus*, a weed frequent in sandy soil.

knead /niːd/ *verb*.
[ORIGIN Old English *cnedan* = Old Saxon *knedan* (Dutch *kneden*), Old High German *knetan* (German *kneten*), from West Germanic.]
1 *verb trans.* Work into a homogeneous plastic mass by successively drawing out, folding over, and pressing together; *esp.* work (moistened flour or clay) into dough or paste; make (bread, pottery, etc.) by this process. OE.
S. ORBACH The Italian mama kneading the pasta.
2 *verb trans.* Blend or weld together; manipulate, mould, form. LME.
H. ROGERS Inconsistencies . . incapable . . of being kneaded into any harmonious system. B. TAYLOR Knead and shape her to your thought.
3 *verb trans.* & *intrans.* **a** Massage or squeeze with the hands, as if working dough etc. E17. ▸**b** Esp. of a cat: paw (a thing or person) repetitively with alternate front paws. M20.
a M. AMIS With quivering finger-tips I kneaded my forehead and scalp. **b** V. CANNING The cat woke me up by kneading determinedly on my chest.
■ **kneadable** *adjective* E19. **kneader** *noun* ME.

knee /niː/ *noun*.
[ORIGIN Old English *cnēo(w)* = Old Frisian *kniu*, *knē*, *knī*, Old Saxon *knio* (Dutch *knie*), Old High German *kneo*, *kniu* (German *Knie*), Old Norse *kné*, Gothic *kniu*, from Germanic from Indo-European, from base also of Latin *genu*, Greek *gonu*.]
▸**I** A joint.
1 The joint between a person's thigh and lower leg; the region around this joint. Also, the upper surface of the thighs of a sitting person, the lap. OE. ▸**b** A damaged condition of the knee. (Earliest in ***housemaid's knee*** s.v. HOUSEMAID.) M19.
M. DRABBLE He organised himself into a sitting position, his arms around his knees. A. BROOKNER Those rules that girls are supposed to learn at their mother's knee. M. IGNATIEFF In the garden, holding Lionel on her knee. J. FORD Humbly on my knees I kiss your gracious hand. H. BROOKE My knees trembled . . ; a swimming came before my eyes.
2 A joint in an animal limb corresponding or analogous to the human knee; *spec.* (**a**) the carpal articulation of the foreleg of a quadruped; (**b**) the tarsal articulation or heel of a bird. LME.
3 The part of a garment covering the knee. LME.
▸**II** Something resembling the knee.
4 A piece of timber with a natural or artificial angular bend, *spec.* one used as a support in carpentry and shipbuilding; a piece of metal of similar shape and use. LME.
5 A part of a hill, tree, etc., regarded as corresponding to a human knee. Also (*rare*), a natural prominence, as a rock or crag. L16.
6 BOTANY. **a** The node of a grass. Now *dial.* L17. ▸**b** A conical protuberance on the roots of the bald cypress and tupelo, rising above the water in which the tree grows. L19.
7 An abrupt obtuse or approximately right-angled bend in a graph between parts where the slope varies smoothly. L19.
– PHRASES: **across one's knee** (of a person, esp. a child) face-down on or on to the knee to be spanked. **bend the knee**, **bow the knee** kneel, esp. in submission. **bring a person to his or her knees** bring a person to a difficult position or to submission. ***housemaid's knee***: see HOUSEMAID *noun*. **knee by knee** side by side and close together. **knee to knee** (**a**) = *knee by knee* above; (**b**) facing each other with the knees touching. ***on bended knee(s)***: see BEND *verb*. ***on the knees of the gods***: see GOD *noun*. ***the bee's knees***: see BEE *noun*[1]. ***water on the knee***: see WATER *noun*.
– COMB.: **knee-action** (**a**) the action or coordination of movement of the knee joint of a horse; (**b**) exaggerated raising of the knee by an athlete; (**c**) a form of independent front-wheel suspension in a motor vehicle; **knee-bend** *noun* & *verb* (**a**) *noun* an act of bending the (human) knee; *spec.* a physical exercise in which the body is raised and lowered without use of the hands; (**b**) *verb intrans.* perform a knee bend or knee bends; **kneeboard** *noun* & *verb* (**a**) *noun* a short surfboard ridden in a kneeling position; (**b**) *verb intrans.* ride a kneeboard; **knee bone** the patella, the kneecap; **knee-boot**: reaching to the knee; **knee-boss** *hist.* a piece of armour used to protect the knee, consisting of a cap of leather etc.; **knee brace** a strut fixed diagonally as reinforcement between two parts of a structure that meet at right angles; **knee-braced** *adjective* supported by a knee brace; **knee-breeched** *adjective* wearing knee breeches; **knee breeches**: reaching down to or just below the knee; **knee-deep** *adjective* (**a**) immersed *in* to the knee, *fig.* deeply involved *in*; (**b**) (covered with water etc.) so deep as to reach to the knee; **knee-halter** *verb trans.* (chiefly *S. Afr.*) restrain (an animal, esp. a horse) by fastening a cord or halter from its head to its knees; **knee-high** *adjective* immersed in or reaching as high as the knees (***knee-high to a grasshopper***); **kneehole** a space for the knees between the drawers of a desk etc.; a desk having a kneehole; **knee-holly**, **knee-holm** butcher's broom, *Ruscus aculeatus*; **knee-jerk** *noun* & *adjective* (**a**) *noun* a sudden involuntary kick caused by a blow on the tendon just below the knee and used as a test of reflexes; (**b**) *adjective* predictable, automatic, stereotyped; **knee joint** (**a**) the joint between the femur and the tibia in the leg; (**b**) MECHANICS a joint formed of two pieces hinged together endwise, a toggle joint; **knee-length** *adjective* reaching to the knee; **knee-pan** = KNEECAP *noun* 2; **knee-piece** (**a**) a bent piece of timber used as a support in carpentry and shipbuilding; (**b**) *hist.* a flexible piece of armour used to protect the knee; **knee-plate** (**a**) *hist.* a broad steel plate worn as a protection for the thigh; (**b**) an angled metal plate used as a support in shipbuilding; **knee-rafter** a rafter the lower end of which is bent downwards; a diagonal brace between a rafter and a tie beam; **knee-roof** = *curb roof* s.v. CURB *noun*; **knee-slapper** *N. Amer.* an uproariously funny joke; **knee-strings**: worn round the knee at the bottom of knee breeches; **knees-up** *colloq.* [from 'Knees up, Mother Brown', a popular song by H. Weston, B. Lee, and I. Taylor] a lively party or gathering, a celebration; **knee timber** timber having a natural angular bend, suitable for use as a support in shipbuilding or carpentry; **knee-trembler** *slang* an act of sexual intercourse between people in a standing position.
■ **kneelike** *adjective* resembling a knee (in shape or function) L19.

knee /niː/ *verb*. Pa. t. & pple **kneed**. LOE.
[ORIGIN from the noun.]
1 †**a** *verb intrans.* Kneel or bow, esp. in reverence or submission (*to*). LOE–E17. ▸**b** *verb trans.* Show reverence or submission to by kneeling or bending the knee. *arch.* L16.
2 *verb trans.* Make (one's way) on one's knees. *rare.* E17.
3 *verb trans.* CARPENTRY etc. Fasten (timbers) with a knee or knees. E18.
4 **a** *verb trans.* Give a kneelike or angular bend to. *Scot.* E19. ▸**b** *verb intrans.* Bend at an angle. *Scot.* E19.
5 *verb trans.* Disable (an animal) by making a cut in the knee. *US.* M19.
6 *verb trans.* Strike or touch with the knee; *spec.* strike (a person), esp. in the groin, deliberately with the knee. L19.
R. B. PARKER I kneed him in the groin.
– NOTE: Not recorded between ME and L16 (when re-formed).

kneecap /ˈniːkap/ *noun* & *verb*. M17.
[ORIGIN from KNEE *noun* + CAP *noun*[1].]
▸**A** *noun*. **1** A cap or protective covering for the knee; *spec.* a flexible piece of armour covering the knee. M17.
2 The convex bone in front of the knee joint, the patella. M19.
▸**B** *verb trans.* Infl. **-pp-**. Shoot (a person) in the knee or leg as a punishment, esp. for betraying or defying a terrorist group. L20.

kneed /niːd/ *adjective*. L16.
[ORIGIN from KNEE *noun*, *verb*: see -ED[2], -ED[1].]
1 **a** Having an angle like a knee; having or fixed with a knee or knees for support. L16. ▸**b** BOTANY. Bent at the nodes; geniculate. L16.
2 Having knees (of a specified kind). M17.
3 Of trousers: bulging at the knees. L19.

kneel /niːl/ *verb intrans.* Pa. t. & pple **kneeled**, **knelt** /nɛlt/.
[ORIGIN Old English *cnēowlian*, corresp. to Middle & mod. Low German *knēlen*, Dutch *knielen*: cf. KNEE *noun*, *verb*.]
1 Fall, support oneself, or (less commonly) rise on one's knees or a knee, esp. in reverence or submission (*to* a person, God, etc.). Also with indirect pass., ***be knelt to***. OE.
TENNYSON Good people, you do ill to kneel to me. M. SCAMMELL He would kneel before the icon and recite his prayers. D. H. LAWRENCE Women were kneeling on the stones, filling red jars.
2 Foll. by *down*: go down on the knees. Foll. by *up*: rise or support oneself on the knees with the body and thighs upright. ME.
W. WHARTON He kneels down and begins gathering up his tools.
– NOTE: The form *knelt* (after *felt*, *dealt*) dates only from 19.
■ **kneeler** *noun* (**a**) a person who kneels, esp. in reverence; (**b**) a cushion, hassock, or low bench used for kneeling on, esp. in prayer: LME. **kneeling** *noun* (**a**) the action of the verb; an instance of this; (**b**) a place or space for kneeling in a place of worship: ME.

kneesie /ˈniːzi/ *noun*. *colloq.* Also **-sy**. M20.
[ORIGIN Joc. dim. of pl. of KNEE *noun*: see -IE.]
sing. & in *pl.* Amorous play with the knees. Cf. FOOTSIE *noun*[1].

kneidel *noun* var. of KNAIDEL.

Kneipe /ˈknaɪpə/ *noun*. Pl. ***-pen*** /-pən/, ***-pes***. M19.
[ORIGIN German.]
In Germany: a lively social gathering of young people, esp. students, in a bar or restaurant; a public house, a bar.

Kneipp /nʌɪp/ *noun*. L19.
[ORIGIN Sebastian *Kneipp* (1821–97), Bavarian priest.]
Used *attrib.* to designate (a system of) hydropathic treatments advocated by Kneipp, *spec.* walking barefoot through dewy grass.

†**kneiss** *noun* see GNEISS.

knell /nɛl/ *noun*.
[ORIGIN Old English *cnyll* rel. to KNELL *verb*. See also KNOLL *noun*[2].]
1 The sound made by a bell when struck or rung, esp. when rung slowly and solemnly (as) for a death or at a funeral. OE.
SIR W. SCOTT The heavy knell, the choir's faint swell, Came slowly down the wind.
2 *fig.* A sound, an announcement, or an event regarded as portending death or the end of something. E17.
SOUTHEY As if with the Inchcape Bell, The fiends below were ringing his knell. J. GALSWORTHY When . . Dartie had that financial crisis . . the knell of all prosperity seemed to have sounded.
DEATH ***knell***.

knell /nɛl/ *verb*. *arch.*
[ORIGIN Old English *cnyllan*: present form (from late Middle English) perh. by assoc. with BELL *noun*[1]. See also KNOLL *verb*.]
1 *verb trans.* Strike with a resounding blow, knock. Long *obsolete* exc. *Scot.* OE.
†**2** *verb trans.* Ring (a bell), esp. slowly and solemnly (as) for a death or at a funeral; toll (a bell). OE–M17.
3 *verb intrans.* (Of a bell) ring, esp. for a death or at a funeral, toll; *transf.* & *fig.* sound ominously or dolefully, reverberate. LME.
4 *verb trans.* **a** Summon or call (as) by a knell. LME. ▸**b** Proclaim (as) by a knell. M19.

knelt *verb pa. t.* & *pple*: see KNEEL.

Knesset /ˈknɛsɛt/ *noun*. M20.
[ORIGIN Hebrew, lit. 'gathering'.]
The parliament of the state of Israel.

knevel *noun* & *verb* var. of NEVEL.

knew *verb pa. t.* of KNOW *verb*.

knez /knɛz/ *noun*. Pl. ***knezes*** /ˈknɛzɪz/, same. L16.
[ORIGIN Slavonic (Serbian and Croatian *knêz*, Russian *knyaz'*, Bulgarian *knez*, etc.) from Old Church Slavonic *kŭnęzĭ*, from Germanic noun meaning 'king'.]
Formerly in Slavonic countries: a prince, a ruler; a lord, a nobleman.

knick /nɪk/ *noun*[1] & *verb*. *Scot.* L16.
[ORIGIN Imit.: cf. (with the noun) Middle Dutch *cnic* (Dutch *knik*), Middle Low German, German *Knick*, (with the verb) Middle Dutch *cnicken* (Dutch *knikken*), Middle Low German, German *knicken*.]
▸**A** *noun*. A cracking or clicking sound made (as) with the fingers. Long *obsolete* exc. *Scot.* L16.
▸**B** *verb trans.* & *intrans.* Make a cracking or clicking sound with (the fingers etc.). M18.

knick /nɪk/ *noun*[2]. Also **nick**. M20.
[ORIGIN German = bend, kink, break.]
PHYSICAL GEOGRAPHY. **1** = KNICKPOINT. M20.
2 The angle formed by a pediment and the adjacent mountain slope. M20.

knicker *noun*[1] see KNICKERS.

knicker *noun*[2] var. of NICKER *noun*[3].

knickerbocker /ˈnɪkəbɒkə/ *noun*. M19.
[ORIGIN Diedrich *Knickerbocker*, pretended author of W. Irving's *History of New York* (1809).]
1 (**K-**.) A descendant of the original Dutch settlers of the New Netherlands (later divided into New York and New Jersey); a New Yorker. M19.
2 In *pl.* ▸**a** Short loose-fitting trousers gathered in at the knee or calf. M19. ▸**b** = KNICKERS 2. L19.
– COMB.: **Knickerbocker Glory** a quantity of ice cream served with fruit, jelly, cream, etc., in a tall glass; **knickerbocker yarn** yarn flecked with different colours.
■ **knickerbockered** *adjective* wearing knickerbockers M19.

knickers /ˈnɪkəz/ *noun pl.* In attrib. use & in comb. usu. in sing. **knicker** (otherwise *rare*). L19.
[ORIGIN Abbreviation of *knickerbockers*: see KNICKERBOCKER.]
1 Knickerbockers. Also, a boy's short trousers. *colloq.* (now *N. Amer.*). L19.
J. UPDIKE A trio of them were gathered in knickers and Scots caps on a felt putting green.
2 A pair of women's or girls' pants worn as underwear, covering the body from the waist or hips to the tops of the thighs (orig. to the knees). Also ***pair of knickers***. L19. ▸**b** As *interjection*. Expr. surprise, contempt, disbelief, etc. *colloq.* L20.
V. GLENDINNING She dressed exotically in a crimson silk shawl over frilled knickers. *Melody Maker* Laugh? That's an easy one. The knickers are still wet.
French knickers: see FRENCH *adjective*. **get one's knickers in a twist** *colloq.* become agitated or upset.
– COMB.: **knicker yarn** = *KNICKERBOCKER* ***yarn***.
■ **knickered** *adjective* wearing knickerbockers or knickers L19.

knick-knack /ˈnɪknak/ *noun*. Also **nick-nack**. L16.
[ORIGIN Redupl. of KNACK *noun*[2] with vowel variation.]
†**1** A petty trick, an artifice, a subterfuge. L16–L17.
2 A repeated knocking or cracking sound; an instrument producing such a sound. Now *rare*. M17.
3 A small dainty article of furniture, dress, etc.; any trifling frivolous object more for ornament than use; a trinket. L17.
I. COLEGATE Tables crowded with knick-knacks and framed photographs. *Sunday Express* Holding her latest knick-knack—a . . full-size replica of the America's Cup.
■ **knick-ˈknackatory** *noun* (now *rare*) [after *conservatory* etc.] a repository of knick-knacks E18. **knick-ˈknackery** *noun* a knick-knack or trifling ornament; knick-knacks collectively: L18. **knick-knacket** *noun* (*Scot.*) a little knick-knack L18. **knick-knackish** *adjective* of the nature of a knick-knack, trifling E19.

knick-knacky *adjective* (*a*) given to acquiring knick-knacks; (*b*) of the nature of a knick-knack, affected, trifling: L18.

knickpoint /ˈnɪkpɔɪnt/ *noun*. Also **n-**. E20.
[ORIGIN Partial translation of German *Knickpunkt*, from *Knick* KNICK *noun*² + *Punkt* point.]
PHYSICAL GEOGRAPHY. A break of slope in a river profile, esp. where a new curve of erosion arising from rejuvenation intersects an earlier curve.

knicks /nɪks/ *noun pl. colloq.* L19.
[ORIGIN Abbreviation.]
= KNICKERS.

knife /nʌɪf/ *noun*. Pl. **knives** /nʌɪvz/.
[ORIGIN Late Old English *cnīf* from Old Norse *knífr* = Old Frisian, Middle Low German *knīf*, Middle Dutch *cnijf* (Dutch *knijf*), from Germanic word of unknown origin.]
1 A cutting instrument composed of a blade (usu. of metal with usu. one long edge sharpened) and a handle into which this is fixed either rigidly or with a joint. LOE. ▸**b** Such an instrument used as a weapon. ME. ▸**c** Such an instrument used in surgery. Chiefly in ***the knife***, surgery, a surgical operation. L19.

ARNOLD BENNETT He ate a little of the lean . . ; then he . . laid down his knife and fork. *fig.*: *Observer* I was skinned by the icy knives of the wind. **b** SHAKES. *Tr. & Cr.* Thou lay'st in every gash that love hath given me The knife that made it. **c** *Listener* No one knows what can happen once the patient is under the knife.

bread knife, ***butter knife***, ***carving knife***, ***fish knife***, ***flick knife***, ***palette knife***, ***paperknife***, ***penknife***, ***sheath knife***, ***steak knife***, etc.

2 A sharpened cutting blade forming part of a machine. M19.

– PHRASES: **before one can say knife** *colloq.* very quickly or suddenly. **get one's knife into** persecute, be persistently malicious or vindictive towards. ***long knife***: see LONG *adjective*¹. †**pair of knives** a set of two knives, esp. as carried in a sheath. **that one could cut with a knife** *colloq.* (of an accent) marked, heavily dialectal; (of an atmosphere) oppressive, tense. ***the run of one's knife***: see RUN *noun*. **twist the knife** *fig.* increase existing suffering, worsen an injury already inflicted.

– COMB.: **knife-bar**: holding the knives in a cutting machine; **knife-blade** (*a*) the blade of a knife; (*b*) *MOUNTAINEERING* a long thin piton; **knife-board** (*a*) a board on which knives are cleaned; (*b*) *colloq.* (*hist.*) the double bench on the roof of an early type of bus; **knife-boy**: employed to clean table knives; **knife-edge** (*a*) the edge of a knife; (*b*) a steel wedge on which a pendulum etc. swings; (*c*) a sharp mountain ridge, an arête; (*d*) *fig.* a position of extreme danger or uncertainty; **knife-edged** *adjective* having a thin sharp edge like a knife; **knifefish** any of various narrow-bodied fishes; *spec.* any of various neotropical freshwater fishes of the families Gymnotidae and Rhamphichthyidae, allied to the electric eel, with a long bladelike anal fin; **knife-grinder** (*a*) a person who grinds knives and cutting tools in the process of manufacture; (*b*) a travelling sharpener of knives and cutting tools; (*c*) an instrument for grinding cutting tools; **knife-guard** a small hinged metal arm on the back of a carving fork to protect the hand against the slipping of the knife; **knife-machine**: for cleaning knives; **knifeman** a person who uses a knife as a tool or weapon; **knife pleat** a narrow flat pleat on a skirt etc.; **knife-pleated** *adjective* having knife pleats; **knifepoint** the pointed end of a knife, esp. as directed at a person as a threat (***at knifepoint***, under threat of injury or an ultimatum etc.); **knife rest** (*a*) a metal or glass rest or support for a carving knife at table; (*b*) *military slang* a barrier made of barbed wire and timber; **knife switch** *ELECTRICITY*: operated by the movement of a conducting blade or set of blades hinged at one end; **knife-thrower** a person who throws knives at targets as an entertainment, esp. in a circus; **knife-throwing** the throwing of knives at targets, esp. as a circus act; **knife-work** the use of knives as weapons or instruments.

■ **knifeful** *noun* as much as a knife will hold or carry M19. **knifeless** *adjective* (*rare*) LME. **knifelike** *adjective* resembling a knife, having a sharp blade M19.

knife /nʌɪf/ *verb*. M19.
[ORIGIN from the noun Cf. KNIVE *verb*.]
1 *verb trans.* Cut or stab with a knife; *techn.* trim with a knife. M19.

CONAN DOYLE I would have thought no more of knifing him than of smoking this cigar. S. KITZINGER Rape . . is violence, just as much as being knifed.

2 *verb trans.* (Attempt to) bring about the defeat of (a person) in an underhand way. *slang*. L19.
3 *verb intrans.* Move as with the action of a knife cutting or passing through. E20.

Coarse Angler The line knifed up . . through the brown water of the loch.

■ **knifer** *noun* (*a*) a person who carries or uses a knife as a weapon; (*b*) a person who trims the soles and heels of shoes and boots: L19.

knifey /ˈnʌɪfi/ *noun*. *colloq.* (chiefly *Scot.*). Also **-fie**. L19.
[ORIGIN from KNIFE *noun* + -Y⁶.]
= MUMBLE-THE-PEG.

knifey /ˈnʌɪfi/ *adjective*. M19.
[ORIGIN from KNIFE *noun* + -Y¹.]
Resembling the edge of a knife in narrowness or sharpness.

knifie *noun* var. of KNIFEY *noun*.

knight /nʌɪt/ *noun & verb*.
[ORIGIN Old English *cniht* = Old Frisian *knecht*, *kniucht*, Old Saxon *knecht*, Old High German *kneht* (Dutch *knecht*, German *Knecht*), from West Germanic word of unknown origin.]
▸ **A** *noun*. †**1** A boy, a youth. Only in OE.
†**2** A boy or youth employed as an attendant or servant; a male servant or attendant of any age. OE–ME.
3 a *hist.* In the Middle Ages: a male military servant of a person of high rank; a feudal tenant holding land from a superior in exchange for military service; *spec.* a man, usu. a noble, raised to honourable military rank esp. by a monarch after service as a page and squire, and ranking below a baron; such a man serving or attending a woman of rank, esp. as her champion in a war or tournament. OE. ▸**b** *fig.* A man devoted to the service of a woman, cause, etc. ME. ▸**c** *hist.* In full ***knight of the shire***. A gentleman representing a shire or county in parliament, orig. either of two of the rank of knight. LME. ▸**d** A man awarded a title (now non-hereditary) by a sovereign in recognition of personal merit or services rendered, ranking below a baronet, and entitled to be styled *Sir*. M16.

a C. S. LEWIS The blood went back to a Norman knight whose bones lie at Battle Abbey. T. H. WHITE 'I shall have to have a lady-love . . ' added the future knight . . 'so that I can . . do deeds in her honour.' **b** SHAKES. *Rom. & Jul.* O, find him! give this ring to my true knight. TENNYSON In all your quarrels will I be your knight.

a ***Knight of the Bath***, ***Knight of the Garter***, ***Knight of the Thistle***, etc.

4 Orig. (in ancient history or mythology), a person holding a position or rank similar to that of the medieval knight. Later *spec.* (*a*) *ROMAN HISTORY*. [translating Latin *eques* horseman] a member of the class orig. forming the Roman army's cavalry, later of great wealth and political importance; (*b*) *GREEK HISTORY*. [translating Greek *hippeus* horseman] a citizen of the second class at Athens in the constitution of Solon. ME. ▸†**b** [translating Latin *miles*.] An ordinary soldier. ME–M16.
5 *CHESS*. Each of the four pieces (two per player) moving to the next but one square of the opposite colour, and usu. having the upper part shaped like a horse's head. ME.
†**6** *NAUTICAL*. Either of two strong posts or bitts on a deck, having sheaves through which the jeers or halyards were passed. LME–M17.

– COMB. & PHRASES: ***knight bachelor***: see BACHELOR 1; ***knight banneret***: see BANNERET *noun*¹; ***knight commander***: see COMMANDER 2c; **knight-head** *NAUTICAL* either of two large timbers rising obliquely from the keel behind the stem of a vessel and supporting the bowsprit; ***Knight HOSPITALLER***; **knight in shining armour** a chivalrous rescuer or helper, esp. of a woman; ***knight marshal***: see MARSHAL *noun*¹; **Knight of Columbus** *N. Amer.* a member of a society of Roman Catholic men founded at New Haven, Connecticut, in 1882; ***Knight of the Holy Sepulchre***: see SEPULCHRE *noun* 1; **knight of the post** *arch.* [with allus. to a whipping post] a man making his living by giving false evidence; a notorious perjurer; **knight of the road** (*a*) a highwayman; (*b*) a commercial traveller; (*c*) a tramp; (*d*) a lorry driver; a taxi driver; **knight of the shire** (*a*) see sense 3c above; (*b*) *joc.* a Conservative member for a country constituency who has been knighted for political services; ***knight of the spigot***: see SPIGOT *noun* 1; **knight service** (*a*) *hist.* the tenure of land on condition of military service; (*b*) (good) service such as was rendered by a knight; ***Knight Templar***: see TEMPLAR *noun* 1, 1b; ***Teutonic Knights***, ***Teutonic Order*** (***of Knights***): see TEUTONIC *adjective* 2; ***white knight***: see WHITE *adjective*.

▸ **B** *verb trans.* Confer a knighthood on. ME.

H. BAILEY Her husband, Sir George Catlin, was knighted in 1970.

■ **knightage** *noun* (*a*) knights collectively; (*b*) a list and account of knights: M19. **knightess** *noun* (*rare*) (*a*) a woman who fights like a knight; (*b*) a female member of a knightly order: M16. **knightlike** *adjective & adverb* (*a*) *adjective* resembling or befitting a knight; (*b*) *adverb* = KNIGHTLY *adverb*: LME. **knightling** *noun* (*rare*) a petty or insignificant knight M17. **knightship** *noun* (now *rare*) †(*a*) military service; †(*b*) knightly character; valour; (*c*) the rank or position of a knight: ME.

knight errant /nʌɪt ˈɛr(ə)nt/ *noun phr.* Also **knight-errant**. Pl. **knights errant**, **knight-errants**. LME.
[ORIGIN from KNIGHT *noun* + ERRANT *adjective*.]
1 A medieval knight wandering in search of chivalrous adventures. LME.

G. BERKELEY From what giants and monsters would these knight-errants undertake to free the world?

2 *transf.* A man of a chivalrous, adventurous, or quixotic nature. M18.

H. H. ASQUITH The Victorians . . were not a race of knights errant. *fig.*: *Your Business* Design—the knight errant of British business.

■ **knight-errantry** *noun* (*a*) the practice or conduct of a knight errant; (*b*) *rare* the body of knights errant: M17. **knight-errantship** *noun* (*rare*) the condition of a knight errant; (with possess. adjective, as ***your knight-errantship*** etc.) a mock title of respect given to a knight errant: M17.

knighthood /ˈnʌɪthʊd/ *noun*. OE.
[ORIGIN from KNIGHT *noun* + -HOOD.]
†**1** Boyhood, youth. Only in OE.
2 The rank or dignity of a knight; an award of this. ME. ▸**b** A man with this rank; a knight. *rare*. L16.

R. H. SHERARD The middle class contempt for the title of knighthood. E. LINKLATER He had been offered a knighthood for his official War History of the submarines.

3 The profession or vocation of a medieval knight. ME. ▸†**b** [translating Latin *militia*.] Military service; warfare. ME–M16.

R. A. VAUGHAN The old virtues of knighthood—its truth and honour, its chastity and courage.

4 The character and qualities befitting a medieval knight. ME.
5 Knights collectively. LME.

knightly /ˈnʌɪtli/ *adjective*. OE.
[ORIGIN from KNIGHT *noun* + -LY¹.]
†**1** Boyish. Only in OE.
2 Having the rank or qualities of a medieval knight. Now *rare*. LME.
3 Of a thing, action, etc.: of, pertaining to, or befitting a medieval knight. LME.

DRYDEN Preferr'd above the rest, By him with knightly deeds.

4 Consisting of knights. M19.

J. A. MICHENER That was the report circulated through the knightly circles of Europe.

■ **knightlihood** *noun* (*rare*) LME. **knightliness** *noun* L16.

knightly /ˈnʌɪtli/ *adverb*. LME.
[ORIGIN from KNIGHT *noun* + -LY².]
After the fashion of or in a manner befitting a medieval knight.

SHAKES. *Rich. II* Say . . why thou comest thus knightly clad in arms.

kniphofia /nɪˈfəʊfɪə, nʌɪ-; nɪpˈhəʊfɪə/ *noun*. M19.
[ORIGIN mod. Latin (see below), from Johann Hieronymus *Kniphof* (1704–63), German botanist + -IA¹.]
Any of various tall ornamental plants of the genus *Kniphofia*, of the lily family, native to southern and eastern Africa and bearing long spikes or dense racemes of red, yellow, or orange flowers. Also called ***red-hot poker***, ***torch lily***. Cf. TRITOMA.

K

knish /knɪʃ/ *noun*. M20.
[ORIGIN Yiddish from Russian (also *knysh*) kind of bun or dumpling.]
A baked or fried dumpling made of flaky dough filled with chopped liver, potato, or cheese.

knit /nɪt/ *noun*. L16.
[ORIGIN from the verb.]
1 a The style or stitch in which a thing is knitted; a knitted fabric; knitted work; knitwear. L16. ▸**b** A knitted garment. Freq. in *pl.* M20.

a *New York Post* Whip up . . day dress in low-cost knit. *Daily Telegraph* Coco Chanel . . seized upon the freedom of knit as early as 1913. **b** *Shetland Times* Warm chunky knits, very welcome in present weather conditions.

2 A contraction or wrinkle of the brow. L19.

knit /nɪt/ *verb*. Infl. **-tt-**. Pa. t. & pple **knitted**, (esp. in senses 3–6) **knit**.
[ORIGIN Old English *cnyttan* = Middle Low German, Middle Dutch *knutten* (German dial. *knütten*), from West Germanic verb, from base of KNOT *noun*¹.]
▸ **I 1** *verb trans.* Tie in or with a knot; fasten, bind, attach, or join (as) by knotting. Now *arch. & dial.* OE. ▸†**b** Fasten or bundle up; *fig.* reprove, silence. Also foll. by *up*. ME–L16. ▸†**c** Geld (a ram) by tying the scrotum. E17–M18.
2 *verb trans. & intrans.* Orig., form (a net) by knotting string in an open mesh pattern. Later, make (a garment, blanket, etc.) by interlocking and entwining a successive series of loops of yarn, esp. wool, using long needles or a machine, *spec.* by bringing the yarn from the back through the next loop in a plain or garter stitch; make (a stitch or a row of stitches) in this way. ME.

DYLAN THOMAS Knit one slip one knit two together Pass the slipstitch over. P. MORTIMER You couldn't have knitted a tea-cosy out of that wool. M. WEST Lotte would be waiting . . knitting placidly at the fireside. J. UPDIKE Her russet knit sweater has ridden up from the waist of her slacks. E. O'BRIEN She knit his socks in cable stitch.

3 a *verb trans.* Combine or unite closely; bind, join, or connect firmly. Freq. foll. by *together*. Now chiefly *fig.* ME. ▸**b** *verb intrans.* Join; grow together; unite; *spec.* (of the parts of a broken bone) become joined, heal. L15. ▸**c** *verb intrans.* Of bees: cluster together in a mass. Now *dial.* L16.

a POPE There, where the juncture knits the channel bone. J. CONRAD The unspoken loyalty that knits together a ship's company. **b** K. KESEY I can't get back in togs till the fracture knits and I get the cast off. *Sunday Times* A very clingy, tightly-knit atmosphere where everybody knows each other's business.

4 *verb trans.* Interlace, intertwine; weave or plait together. Now *rare* or *obsolete*. LME.
5 a *verb trans.* Draw (the brows) closely together to form folds or wrinkles. LME. ▸**b** *verb intrans.* Of the brows: draw closely together. M16.

a SHAKES. *2 Hen. VI* He knits his brow and shows an angry eye. **b** J. HARVEY Whenever Hawkins said something that displeased Riley, his bushy eyebrows knit and met in one.

6 *verb trans. & intrans.* Make or become compact or firm by close contraction or combination of parts. LME. ▸**b** *verb intrans. spec.* Of fruit etc.: form, set. Of a tree or flower: form fruit. LME. ▸†**c** Of a female animal: conceive. E17–L18.

G. SANTAYANA His languid figure grew somewhat better knit.

7 *verb trans.* Constitute or establish (a covenant, agreement, etc.). LME.
8 *verb trans.* Foll. by *up*: ▸**a** Tie or fasten up; make, repair, or finish off (a garment etc.) by knitting. LME. ▸**b** Conclude, finish, end. M16.

a SHAKES. *Macb.* Sleep that knits up the ravell'd sleeve of care. R. C. TRENCH We see how entirely his own life is knit up with his child's. **b** J. A. FROUDE The tragedy was being knitted up in the deaths of the last actors in it.

▸**II 9** *verb intrans.* Of beer, wine, etc.: effervesce, form froth. Now *rare* or *obsolete*. M18.
– COMB.: **knitbone** the plant comfrey, *Symphytum officinale*, reputed to mend broken bones; a herbal tea made from this; **knitwork** knitted work; knitting.
■ **knitter** *noun* (*a*) a person or thing which ties or unites something; (*b*) a person who knits garments etc.: ME.

knitch /nɪtʃ/ *noun*. Long *dial.* Also **nitch**.
[ORIGIN Old English *ġe)cnyċċe* cogn. with Low German *knuck(e*, German *Knocke* bundle of heckled flax.]
†**1** A bond. Only in OE.
2 A bundle of wood, hay, corn, etc.; a sheaf; a faggot. ME.
■ **knitchel** *noun* a small bundle E16.

knitch *verb* see NITCH *verb*.

knitting /ˈnɪtɪŋ/ *noun*. LME.
[ORIGIN from KNIT *verb* + -ING[1].]
1 The action of KNIT *verb*. LME. ▸†**b** A tie, a fastening, a knot. LME–L16.
2 The product of knitting; knitted work; *esp.* a garment etc. in the process of being made by knitting. L19.

A. CHRISTIE Taking her knitting out of its embroidered . . bag.

– PHRASES: *double knitting*: see DOUBLE *adjective & adverb*.
– COMB.: **knitting case** (*a*) = *knitting sheath* below; (*b*) a case for keeping knitting needles in; **knitting machine**: used for mechanically knitting garments etc.; **knitting needle**, **knitting pin** a thin pointed rod of steel, wood, plastic, etc., usu. with a knob at one end, used esp. in pairs in knitting; **knitting sheath** a cylindrical sheath for holding a knitting needle steady; **knitting wire** *Scot.* = *knitting needle* above.

knittle /ˈnɪt(ə)l/ *noun*. LME.
[ORIGIN from KNIT *verb*: see -LE[1].]
A string or cord for tying or fastening. Long only *spec.* (*a*) NAUTICAL a small line made of yarn; (*b*) *dial.* a drawstring.

knitwear /ˈnɪtwɛː/ *noun*. E20.
[ORIGIN from *knit* pa. pple of KNIT *verb* + WEAR *noun*.]
Knitted garments collectively.

knive /nʌɪv/ *verb trans. & intrans.* M19.
[ORIGIN from KNIFE *noun* after *strife*, *strive*, etc.]
= KNIFE *verb*.

knives *noun* pl. of KNIFE *noun*.

knob /nɒb/ *noun & verb*. LME.
[ORIGIN Middle Low German *knobbe* knot, knob, bud: cf. Flemish *knobbe(n* lump of bread etc., Dutch *knobbel* bump, knot, & KNOP, KNUB *noun*, NOB *noun*[1].]
▸**A** *noun*. **1** A rounded lump or protuberance, esp. at the end or on the surface of a thing; *spec.* a handle of a door or drawer shaped like this, a similar attachment for pulling, turning, etc. LME. ▸**b** ARCHITECTURE. A carved boss, esp. at the end of a raised moulding or at the intersection of ribs. M18. ▸**c** The penis. *coarse slang*. L20.

M. ANGELOU I had my hand on the knob when the door burst open. T. O. ECHEWA Peering into the car's interior . . at the knobs and buttons on its instrument panel. P. ROTH Remember the knobs on the top of the maple bedposts?

with knobs on *slang* that and more (used in retort to an insult, to express emphatic agreement, etc.).
2 A prominent isolated rounded mound or hill; any hill. Cf. KNOT *noun*[1] 12. Chiefly *US*. M17.
3 A small usu. round piece *of* butter, sugar, coal, etc. L17.
4 = NOB *noun*[1] 1. *slang*. E18.
– COMB.: **knob-cone (pine)** a Californian pine, *Pinus attenuata*; **knob-nosed** *adjective* having a knob-shaped nose; **knobstick** (*a*) = KNOBKERRIE; (*b*) *arch.* = BLACKLEG *noun* 3; **knobwood** a small southern African tree, *Zanthoxylum capense*, of the rue family, which bears spine-tipped protuberances on its trunk.
▸**B** *verb*. Infl. **-bb-**.
1 *verb intrans.* Form a knob or knobs; bulge (*out*). M16.
2 *verb trans.* Hit, strike. Cf. NOB *verb*[1]. *slang*. E19.
3 *verb trans.* Provide with a knob or knobs. L19.
■ **knobbed** *adjective* provided with or having a knob or knobs; formed into or ending in a knob: LME. **knoblike** *adjective* resembling (that of) a knob E19.

knobber /ˈnɒbə/ *noun*. L17.
[ORIGIN from KNOB *noun* + -ER[1].]
= KNOBBLER.

knobble /ˈnɒb(ə)l/ *noun*. LME.
[ORIGIN from KNOB *noun* + -LE[1]. Cf. Dutch, Low German *knobbel* knob, knot. Cf. KNUBBLE *noun*, NUBBLE *noun*.]
A small knob.
■ **knobbled** *adjective* L19.

knobble *verb* var. of KNUBBLE *verb*.

knobbler /ˈnɒblə/ *noun*. L17.
[ORIGIN from KNOBBLE *noun* + -ER[1].]
A male deer in its second year; a brocket.

knobbly /ˈnɒbli/ *adjective*. Also **n-**. M17.
[ORIGIN from KNOBBLE *noun* + -Y[1]. Cf. KNUBBLY, NUBBLY.]
Full of or covered with knobbles; of the nature of a knobble.

Listener A knobbly-knees competition at Butlin's.

knobby /ˈnɒbi/ *adjective & noun*. LME.
[ORIGIN from KNOB *noun* + -Y[1].]
▸**A** *adjective*. **1** Full of or covered with knobs. LME.
2 Of the nature of a knob, knob-shaped. M18.
▸**B** *noun*. An opal. *Austral.* E20.
■ **knobbiness** *noun* E17.

knobkerrie /ˈnɒbkɛri/ *noun*. Also **-kerry**, **-kierie** /-kɪəri/. M19.
[ORIGIN from KNOB *noun* + KIERIE, after Afrikaans *knopkierie*.]
A short thick stick with a knobbed head, used as a weapon or missile esp. by indigenous peoples of South Africa.

knock /nɒk/ *noun*[1]. ME.
[ORIGIN from the verb.]
1 An act of knocking; a blow, a thump; the sound of this; *spec.* a rap or a succession of raps at a door to call attention or gain admittance. ME. ▸**b** A misfortune, a setback, a financial or emotional blow; an adverse criticism. M17. ▸**c** *spec.* A knocking noise in an engine, esp. (in an internal-combustion engine) caused by the detonation of fuel within the cylinder; faulty combustion of this kind; pinking. L19.

M. WEST The knock at the door startled Merdelius. R. INGALLS She . . gave the prearranged knock on the door. *Press & Journal (Aberdeen)* He took a bad ankle knock . . and it is very swollen. **b** T. WILLIAMS Hard knocks my vanity's been given. *Times* The firm . . have had their fair share of knocks.

knock-for-knock agreement an agreement between motor insurance companies by which each pays its own policyholders irrespective of liability. *postman's knock*: see POSTMAN *noun*[1] 1. **b** *school of hard knocks*: see SCHOOL *noun*[1]. **take a knock** suffer a setback; be criticized adversely. **take the knock** bear or accept responsibility.
2 A clock. *Scot.* LME.
3 CRICKET. An innings; a spell at batting in a match or at practice; the score achieved by a player during this. *colloq.* L19.

Club Cricketer He . . averaged 36.75 in four innings . . thanks largely to a knock of 72. *Cricketer International* He scored two first-class hundreds . . and played an especially memorable knock against Nottinghamshire.

4 An act of copulation. *slang*. M20.
– COMB.: **knockmeter** an instrument for measuring the intensity of knock in the cylinder of an internal-combustion engine; **knock rating** (the determination of) the insusceptibility of a fuel to knock.

knock /nɒk/ *noun*[2]. ME.
[ORIGIN In sense 1 from Gaelic, Irish *cnoc* knoll, hillock. With sense 2 cf. Danish dial. *knock* hillock.]
1 A hill; a hillock, a knoll. *Scot.* Now only *poet.* or in place names. ME.
2 A sandbank. *dial.* L16.

knock /nɒk/ *verb*.
[ORIGIN Old English *cnocian* = Middle High German *knochen*, Old Norse *knoka*, of imit. origin.]
1 *verb intrans.* Strike a hard surface with an audible sharp blow; *spec.* strike esp. a door to call attention or gain admittance (foll. by *at*, *on*). Formerly also, deliver a blow or blows. OE. ▸**b** *verb trans.* (with *it* or cognate obj.) give (a knock); convey by knocking. E17.

SHAKES. *Tam. Shr.* What's he that knocks as he would beat down the gate? M. BALDWIN If you knocked at every house You wouldn't find a man who could recognise a louse. D. ADAMS He knocked on the inner door. *fig.*: P. ROTH How tempted I would have been to yield, if opportunity had only knocked. **b** J. H. NEWMAN A visitant Is knocking his dire summons at my door.

2 *verb trans.* Give a hard blow or blows to; hit, strike, beat, hammer; make (a hole etc.) by beating or hammering. OE. ▸**b** Copulate with (a woman); father (a child) on a woman (foll. by *out of*). *slang*. L16. ▸**c** Rob (esp. a safe or till). *slang*. M18. ▸**d** Make a strong (esp. favourable) impression on. *slang*. L19. ▸**e** Speak ill or slightingly of, criticize, disparage, find fault with. *colloq.* L19.

CONAN DOYLE He knocked a hole . . in the lath and plaster ceiling. K. HULME She leans back . . and knocks the edge of the portrait. B. ZEPHANIAH I used to knock a drum and make a sound. M. MOORCOCK She knocked the lever at the back of the chimney. **d** W. SOYINKA I want to launch it on this tour. Man, it will knock them. **e** V. SETH Don't knock what you haven't tried. *Daily Mirror* Until we . . actually win something . . we will never stop people knocking us.

3 *verb trans.* Drive or bring (a thing) violently against or *against* something else. ME.

SHAKES. *Hen. V* I'll knock his leek about his pate.

4 *verb intrans.* **a** Come into violent collision with something; *colloq.* move energetically, clumsily, noisily, or randomly *about*, *along*, *around*, etc. M16. ▸**b** Of a mechanism etc.: make a rattling or thumping noise, esp. as a result of parts being loose and striking each other. Also *spec.*, (of an internal-combustion engine), suffer from knock caused by faulty combustion, (of fuel) give rise to knock in an engine. M19.

a G. ALLEN Knocking up and down all over the country. **b** P. G. WODEHOUSE The engine was not humming so smoothly. It had begun to knock.

5 *verb trans.* Drive or force *away*, *into*, *off*, *out*, etc., by means of a blow or blows or by striking. E17.

DEFOE I knocked pieces into the wall of the rock. J. T. STORY Suddenly somebody bounced into me, nearly knocking me flying. P. CAMPBELL I knocked an ashtray off the windowsill. B. PYM People surged forward, nearly knocking them over. R. INGALLS She's knocked the wind out of you. J. MORTIMER She had knocked her kitchen and living room together. *Grimsby Evening Telegraph* Watson . . knocked the ball past two defenders on the line.

– PHRASES: *knock all of a heap*: see HEAP *noun*. *knock cold*: see COLD *adjective*. *knock for six*: see SIX *noun* 4. *knock hell out of*: see HELL *noun*. *knock into a cocked hat*: see *cocked hat* s.v. COCK *verb*[1]. **knock into the middle of next week** *colloq.* send (a person) flying, esp. with a blow. *knock off one's perch*: see PERCH *noun*[2]. *knock one's block off*: see BLOCK *noun* 6b. **knock one's head against** *fig.* come into collision with (unpleasant facts or conditions) (*knock one's head against a brick wall*: see WALL *noun*[1]). **knock on the head** (*a*) stun or kill by a blow on the head; (*b*) *colloq.* put an end to (a scheme etc.). **knock on wood**, **knock wood** *fig.* (*N. Amer.*) touch wood. *knock* PRISCIAN'S *head*. *knock rotten*: see ROTTEN *adverb*. *knock the socks off*: see SOCK *noun*[1]. *knock the* STUFFING *out of*. *knock the tar out of*: see TAR *noun*[1] 1. **knock sideways** *colloq.* disconcert; astonish. *knock silly*: see SILLY *adjective* 6. **knock spots off** *colloq.* defeat easily. **knock the bottom out of** *fig.* make invalid or useless, prove to be worthless. *knock the hindsight(s) off*, *knock the hindsight(s) out of*: see HINDSIGHT 2. *knock the shit out of*: see SHIT *noun*. *knock wood*: see *knock on wood* above. *you could have knocked me down with a feather*: see FEATHER *noun*.
– WITH ADVERBS IN SPECIALIZED SENSES: **knock about**, **knock around** (*a*) strike repeatedly; treat roughly; (*b*) *colloq.* wander or roam aimlessly; lead a wandering adventurous life; (*c*) lie around, be available or in the vicinity; (*d*) be a habitual companion of, be associated *with* socially; (*e*) strike (a ball or balls) casually or half-heartedly; (see also sense 4 above). **knock back** (*a*) *colloq.* eat or esp. drink (esp. alcohol) quickly or in large quantities; (*b*) *Austral.* & *NZ colloq.* refuse, rebuff; (*c*) reverse the progress of, check; *fig.* (*colloq.*) disconcert; (*d*) work (risen bread dough) by vigorous kneading and throwing down, to expel air before baking. **knock down** (*a*) hit and knock to the ground; *spec.* (in *pass.*) be hit and knocked to the ground by a vehicle; demolish; (*b*) dispose of (an article) to or *to* a bidder at an auction by a knock with a hammer; (*c*) *colloq.* lower the price of; lower (a price); (*d*) *arch. colloq.* call upon *for* an action etc.; (*e*) take (machinery, furniture, etc.) to pieces for transportation; (*f*) *Austral.* & *NZ slang* spend (a pay cheque etc.) freely; (*g*) *US slang* steal (esp. passengers' fares); (*h*) *US* cause (a ship) to list heavily beyond recovery (usu. in *pass.*); (*i*) *N. Amer.* earn, get paid. **knock off** (*a*) finish or stop work; (*b*) finish or stop (work etc.); (*knock it off!* leave off! stop it!); (*c*) *colloq.* dispatch or dispose of (business); complete or do hastily; *spec.* produce (a literary work, painting, etc.) in a hurried and perfunctory fashion; (*d*) deduct from or *from* an amount or sum; (*e*) CRICKET score (runs) to ensure victory; (*f*) *slang* steal, rob; (*g*) *slang* kill; (*h*) *slang* arrest (a person); (*i*) *slang* copulate with, seduce, (a woman); (see also sense 5 above). **knock on** RUGBY drive or knock (a ball) with the hand or arm in the direction of the opponent's goal line (in contravention of the rules); **knock out** (*a*) stun with a blow, knock unconscious; (*b*) *spec.* knock down (a boxing opponent) for a count of 10, so disqualifying him or her; (*c*) defeat, esp. in a competition involving various stages; (*d*) *colloq.* make roughly or hastily; (*e*) *US*, *Austral.*, & *NZ slang* earn; (*f*) get rid of; destroy; (*g*) *colloq.* exhaust (oneself) through effort; (*h*) *slang* please greatly, astonish (freq. in *pass.*); (*i*) empty (a tobacco pipe) by tapping; (see also sense 5 above). **knock over** *slang* rob, burgle. **knock together** put together or assemble hastily or roughly. **knock under** give in, submit. **knock up** (*a*) drive upwards with a blow; BOOKBINDING & PRINTING even the edges of (a pile of loose sheets) by striking them against a hard surface; (*b*) make, put together, or arrange hastily; (*c*) gain, earn, accumulate; *spec.* (CRICKET) score (runs) rapidly; (*d*) waken, rouse, by knocking at the door; (*e*) exhaust or make ill (usu. in *pass.*); (*f*) become exhausted or ill; (*g*) *slang* (orig. *US*) make (a woman) pregnant; (*h*) play tennis, squash, etc., for practice, esp. before a match.
– COMB.: **knock-back** (chiefly *Austral.* & *NZ colloq.*) a refusal, a rebuff; **knock-kneed** *adjective* having knock knees; **knock knees** an abnormal condition in which the legs curve inwards at the knee so as to touch when the feet are apart; **knock-me-down** *adjective* (*fig.*) overbearing; violent; **knock-off** (*a*) *slang* a robbery; a stolen object, *collect.* stolen objects; (*b*) *slang* a copy or reproduction of a design etc., *esp.* one made illegally; (*c*) *colloq.* the time when one's work finishes for the day; **knock-stone** a stone or cast-iron plate on which ore is broken; **knock-up** *noun & adjective* (designating) a practice game in tennis, squash, etc., esp. before a match.

knockabout /ˈnɒkəbaʊt/ *adjective & noun*. Also **knock-about**. M19.
[ORIGIN from *knock about* s.v. KNOCK *verb*.]
▸**A** *adjective*. **1** Designating a general labourer or handyman on a station or farm. *Austral.* & *NZ*. M19.
2 Wandering vagrant; *spec.* (*Austral.* & *US*) designating a tramp or layabout. L19.
3 Of a garment, clothing, etc.: suitable for rough use. L19.
4 Esp. of comedy: rough, boisterous; slapstick. L19.

V. CRONIN This free-and-easy, almost knockabout atmosphere pleased Catherine. *Listener* Mother-in-law jokes, double entendres and slices of knockabout farce.

5 Designating a sloop-rigged sailing yacht or a sailing yacht without a bowsprit; *gen.* designating any small yacht or dinghy. Chiefly *N. Amer.* **L19.**
▸ **B** *noun.* **1** A general labourer or handyman on a station or farm. *Austral. & NZ.* **L19.**
2 A tramp, a layabout. *Austral. & US.* **L19.**

T. K. WOLFE Alcoholics, psychopaths, knockabouts .. were arrested in the Bronx.

3 A knockabout comic performer or performance. **L19.**

knock-down /ˈnɒkdaʊn/ *adjective & noun.* Also **knockdown. L17.**
[ORIGIN from *knock down* s.v. KNOCK *verb*.]
▸ **A** *adjective.* **1** Such as to knock someone or something down or to the ground; *fig.* irresistible, overwhelming. **L17.**

T. HOOPER An aerosol fly killer—one containing a pyrethrum knock-down ingredient.

2 Of furniture etc.: easily dismantled and reassembled; sold in separate parts requiring to be assembled. **L18.**
3 Of a price: reserve (at an auction); low. Of an article: sold at the reserve price, sold cheaply. **L19.**

Guardian BEA will be able to offer seats on scheduled flights .. at knock-down prices. D. EDGAR The Roneo. I got it, knock-down, from the Catholic Association.

▸ **B** *noun.* **1** A thing, *spec.* a blow, that knocks a person down; an act of knocking someone or something down; an instance of being knocked down. Formerly also (*fig.*), strong liquor. **L17.** ▸**b** The heeling of a ship by the force of the wind. **L19.**

S. B. FLEXNER Amateur Athletic Club rules .. redefined a *round* by making it not dependent on a knock-down. *fig.*: *Times* Prices slipped ... Oil shares took the brunt of the knock-down.

2 An introduction (to a person). *US, Austral., & NZ slang.* **M19.**
– COMB.: **knock-down-and-drag-out**, **knock-down-drag-out** *adjectives & nouns* (designating) a free-for-all fight.

knocker /ˈnɒkə/ *noun.* **LME.**
[ORIGIN from KNOCK *verb* + -ER[1].]
1 A person who or thing which knocks; *esp.* a person who knocks at a door in order to call attention or gain admittance. **LME.**
2 A hinged metal or wooden usu. ornamental instrument fastened to and used for knocking at a door. Also ***door knocker***. **L16.**
3 A person of striking appearance. Cf. STUNNER 2. *slang.* Now *rare.* **E17.**
4 A knock-down blow. *rare.* Long *dial.* **L17.**
5 A spirit or goblin supposedly living in a mine and indicating the presence of ore by knocking. *dial.* **M18.**
6 A person who continually finds fault. *colloq.* **L19.**
7 Either of two pads inset near the heel of a pair of hand shears. *Austral. & NZ slang.* **L19.**
8 A person who sells or buys from door to door; the action of selling or buying from door to door. Cf. RAPPER *noun*[1] 6. **M20.**
9 In *pl.* A woman's breasts. *coarse slang.* **M20.**

N. MAILER Look at the knockers on her, Murray says.

– PHRASES: ***oil the knocker***: see OIL *verb.* **on the knocker** (*a*) (engaged in buying or selling) from door to door; (*b*) on credit; (*c*) *Austral. & NZ colloq.* promptly. **up to the knocker** *slang* in good condition; to perfection.
– COMB.: **knocker-up** *hist.* a person employed to rouse early workers by knocking at their doors or windows.

knocking /ˈnɒkɪŋ/ *noun.* **ME.**
[ORIGIN from KNOCK *verb* + -ING[1].]
1 The action of KNOCK *verb*; an instance of this. **ME.**
2 MINING, in *pl.* Pieces of ore broken off by hammering or chiselling. **M18.**
– COMB.: **knocking copy** advertising or publicity intended to discredit a competitor's product; **knocking shop** *slang* a brothel.

knock-on /*as noun* nɒkˈɒn, *as adjective* ˈnɒkɒn/ *noun & adjective.* **M19.**
[ORIGIN from KNOCK *verb* + ON *adverb*.]
▸ **A** *noun.* RUGBY. An act of knocking on. **M19.**
▸ **B** *adjective.* **1** PHYSICS. Ejected or produced as a result of the collision of an atomic or subatomic particle with an atom. **M20.**
2 Of a mechanical part of a vehicle etc.: that may be attached or fastened by knocking or striking. **M20.**
– COMB.: **knock-on effect** a secondary, indirect, or cumulative effect.

knockout /ˈnɒkaʊt/ *adjective & noun.* Also **knock-out. E19.**
[ORIGIN from *knock out* s.v. KNOCK *verb*.]
1 (Designating or pertaining to) an auction at which a group of bidders cooperate to keep the bidding low and then sell the purchases amongst themselves. *slang.* **E19.**
2 (Designating) a blow etc. capable of knocking a person, esp. a boxer, unconscious. **L19.**

C. ODETS Joe's eyes glitter; his face is hard and flushed. He has won by a knockout. *Health & Strength* The gallant Frenchman .. pounded into a knockout defeat in four rounds.

knockout drops *colloq.* a liquid drug added to a drink to make the drinker unconscious. **technical knockout**: see TECHNICAL *adjective.*
3 (Designating) a competition or the system used in it in which the defeated competitors in each round are eliminated. **L19.**
4 (A person or thing) of outstanding or superb quality. *colloq.* **L19.**

B. BAINBRIDGE 'Did you enjoy the Hermitage?' .. 'It was a bloody knockout'. E. LEONARD I hear she's a knockout Twenty years old, gorgeous.

5 MECHANICS. (Designating or pertaining to) a piece designed to be knocked out to form a hole, or a device for knocking out or ejecting an object from a mould etc. **L19.**

knockwurst *noun* var. of KNACKWURST.

Knödel /ˈknøːd(ə)l/ *noun.* Also ***Knoe-***. Pl. same, ***-eln*** /-əln/. **E19.**
[ORIGIN German.]
In southern Germany and Austria: a type of dumpling.

Knoevenagel /ˈknɔːvənɑːg(ə)l/ *noun.* **E20.**
[ORIGIN Emil *Knoevenagel* (1865–1921), German chemist.]
CHEMISTRY. ***Knoevenagel reaction***, ***Knoevenagel's reaction***, ***Knoevenagel condensation***, the reaction of an aldehyde or ketone with malonic acid or a related compound to yield an acid with the group ·CHCHCOOH, which occurs in the presence of ammonia or an amine as catalyst.

Knole /nəʊl/ *adjective.* **M20.**
[ORIGIN *Knole* Park (see below).]
Designating a sofa with adjustable sides allowing conversion into a bed, designed after an original (*c* 1605–20) at Knole Park, Kent.

knoll /nəʊl/ *noun*[1].
[ORIGIN Old English *cnoll* corresp. to Middle Dutch *knolle* clod, ball (Dutch *knol* turnip, tuber), Middle High German *knolle* clod (German *Knolle* clod, lump, tuber), Old Norse *knollr* mountain summit (Norwegian *knoll* clod, tuber). See also KNOWE.]
1 The summit or rounded top of a mountain or hill. *obsolete* exc. *dial.* **OE.**
2 A small hill; a hillock, a mound. **OE.**
†**3** A turnip. *dial.* **L17–L19.**
4 A lump, a large piece. *Scot.* **E19.**
■ **knolly** *adjective* containing many knolls or hillocks **E19.**

knoll /nəʊl/ *noun*[2]. Now *arch. & dial.* **LME.**
[ORIGIN Prob. imit. alt. of KNELL *noun*. Cf. KNOLL *verb*.]
†**1** A large church bell. Only in **LME.**
2 The action or an act of tolling a bell; the toll of a large bell. **L15.**

knoll /nəʊl/ *verb.* **ME.**
[ORIGIN Prob. imit. alt. of KNELL *verb*. Cf. KNOLL *noun*[2].]
1 *verb intrans.* Of a bell or clock: sound, toll, chime. Now chiefly *dial.* **ME.** ▸**b** *verb trans.* Indicate by ringing, toll out. *rare.* **M19.**
2 *verb trans.* Ring or toll (a bell). Now *arch. & dial.* **LME.** ▸†**b** Ring a knell for. *rare* (Shakes.). Only in **L16.**
3 *verb trans.* Summon by the sound of a bell. **E17.**
■ **knoller** *noun* a person who rings or tolls a bell **E17.**

Knoop /nuːp, knuːp/ *noun.* **M20.**
[ORIGIN Frederick *Knoop* (1878–1943), US instrument-maker.]
Used *attrib.* to designate an indentation test devised by Knoop and the pyramidal diamond indenter used in it.

knop /nɒp/ *noun.* **ME.**
[ORIGIN Middle Low German, Middle Dutch *knoppe* (Dutch *knop*) = Old Frisian *knop*, Old High German *knoph* (German *Knopf* knob, knot, button). Cf. KNAP *noun*[1].]
1 A small rounded (esp. ornamental) protuberance; a knob, a boss, a stud, a tassel, etc. **ME.** ▸†**b** A swelling on the skin; a wart, a pimple, a callus. **M16–E19.** ▸**c** An ornamental loop or tuft formed in a strand of yarn. **E20.**
2 The kneecap; the elbow joint. *obsolete* exc. *dial.* **LME.**
3 A flower bud. *arch.* **LME.**
■ **knopped** *adjective* (*a*) having knops, knobby; (*b*) formed into a knop or knob: **LME.**

knopper /ˈnɒpə/ *noun.* Pl. **-ern** /-ən/, **-ers. L19.**
[ORIGIN German = gall nut.]
More fully ***knopper gall***. A kind of oak gall having the form of a sterile, malformed acorn, caused by the gall wasp *Andricus quercuscalicis*.

†**knopweed** *noun* see KNAPWEED.

knorhaan *noun* var. of KORHAAN.

knorr /nɔː/ *noun.* **L19.**
[ORIGIN Old Norse *knǫrr* (merchant) ship.]
hist. A large wide cargo ship with a single sail, used in medieval northern Europe.

knosp /nɒsp/ *noun. rare.* **E19.**
[ORIGIN German *Knospe* bud, boss, knob.]
An ornamental knob, boss, or stud, *esp.* one in the form of a bud.

Knossian /ˈknɒsɪən, ˈknəʊ-/ *adjective.* **L19.**
[ORIGIN from Greek *Knōssos* Knossos (see below) + -IAN.]
Of or pertaining to Knossos, the principal city of Minoan Crete and site of the ruins of a vast labyrinthine palace of the 18th to the 14th cents. BC.

knot /nɒt/ *noun*[1].
[ORIGIN Old English *cnotta* = Dutch *knot*, Middle Low German *knotte*, Middle High German *knotze* knob, knot, from West Germanic.]
▸ **I 1** An intertwining of a rope, string, or other flexible thing, esp. to form a secure fastening or an obstruction when drawn tight; a set method of tying such a fastening; a representation of such an intertwining, esp. a monogram, as a heraldic badge. Also, a tangle in hair, knitting, etc. **OE.** ▸**b** A ribbon etc. tied as an ornament to be worn on or attached to a garment. **LME.** ▸†**c** ASTRONOMY. The star α Piscium, which is situated between the two parts of the constellation Pisces. **M16–E18.**

R. BOLTON One knot in a thread will stay the Needle's Passage as well as five hundred. R. CROMPTON Can you tie knots what can't come untied? J. L. WATEN Gleaming black hair, gathered in a heavy knot at the back. J. HELLER The knot of his tie is inches down. F. DONALDSON His .. head adorned by a white handkerchief, tied in a knot at each corner. J. CRACE I tied it in a firm knot. K. GIBBONS She would .. comb out the knots for me. Where did you get this pretty hair?

granny knot, ***love-knot***, ***Matthew Walker knot***, ***reef knot***, ***slip knot***, etc.
2 A definite quantity or measure of thread, yarn, etc. *obsolete* exc. *hist.* **LME.**
3 A design or figure formed of crossing lines. Now *rare* or *obsolete.* **LME.**
4 A flower bed laid out in an intricate design; *gen.* any laid-out garden plot. Now chiefly *Scot. & dial.* exc. in ***knot garden*** below. **L15.**
5 NAUTICAL. Any of a number of divisions marked by knots at fixed intervals on a log line and used as a measure of speed (orig. from the rate the knots run out while a sand-glass is running). Hence, a unit of measurement equal to one nautical mile per hour (1.15 mph, 1.85 kph) used esp. to express the speed of ships, aircraft, currents, and winds. **M17.** ▸**b** A nautical mile. *colloq.* **M18.**

J. A. MICHENER His engine could deliver only six knots forward while the river was flowing four knots in the opposite direction. J. D. MACDONALD Tropical storm Ella .. still holding course and speed, with winds approaching fifty knots. **b** F. MARRYAT We were going twelve knots an hour, and running away from them.

6 *hist.* More fully ***porter's knot***. A double shoulder pad and forehead loop formerly used by London market porters for carrying loads. **E18.**
7 PHYSICAL GEOGRAPHY. An elevated point or region where several mountain chains meet. **M19.**
8 MATH. A closed unicursal curve in three dimensions; *spec.* one which, on being distorted in any way so as to bring it into a plane without passing one part through another, will always have nodes. **L19.**
▸ **II** *fig.* from sense 1.
9 A difficulty, a complex or confusing problem. **OE.** ▸**b** *spec.* The main point in a problem; the complication in the plot of a story etc. **LME.**

J. C. POWYS What a knot of paradox and contradiction life is. **b** GLADSTONE The very knot of the difficulty not yet overcome.

10 Something forming or maintaining a union; a tie, a bond, a link; *spec.* a marriage. **ME.**
†**11** An obligation; a binding condition; a restriction. **LME–E19.**
▸ **III** *transf.* **12** A hill of moderate height; *esp.* a rocky hill or summit. Chiefly in place names. Cf. KNOB *noun* 2. **ME.**
13 A carved knob or embossed ornament; a boss; an ornamental stud or fastening. **ME.**
14 A hard, esp. rounded, swelling or growth in human or animal tissue; a hard contracted lump, as in a muscle; a mass formed by concretion or coagulation within a substance; *fig.* a contorted mass or lump as felt in the stomach or throat. **ME.**

J. CLARE Insects of mysterious birth .. Doubtless brought by moisture forth, Hid in knots of spittle white. B. MOORE Her legs were thick and knots of varicose veins stood out under her stockings. W. WHARTON I think they're anxious. I know I am. My stomach's twisted, curled in knots.

15 A thickened part or protuberance in the stem, branch, or root of a plant; a node; a hard mass formed in a tree trunk at the intersection with a branch; the resulting round cross-grained mark in a board or plank. Also (now only *dial.*), a bud. **LME.**

V. WOOLF He dug the point of it .. into a knot in the table. A. HIGGINS Wooden walls with knots in the planks, some of which had dropped out.

16 A small group or cluster (*of* persons or things). **LME.**

E. WHARTON The great hall was empty but for the knot of dogs by the fire. D. DELILLO See that knot of people? He's right in the middle. R. THOMAS A few yards away .. the press had already formed a restless knot.

– PHRASES: **at a rate of knots** *colloq.* very fast. ***encased knot***: see ENCASE *verb.* ***French knot***: see FRENCH *adjective.* ***Gordian knot***: see GORDIAN *adjective* 1. ***Grecian knot***: see GRECIAN *adjective.* ***porter's knot***: see sense 6 above. †**seek a knot in a bulrush**, †**seek a knot in a rush** seek or make difficulties where there are none. ***Sehna knot.*** **tie in knots** baffle or confuse completely. ***tie the knot***: see TIE *verb*[1]. ***Windsor knot***: see WINDSOR *adjective* 1.

K

– COMB.: **knotberry** *local* the cloudberry, *Rubus chamaemorus*; **knot garden** an intricately designed formal garden; **knot-head** *noun & adjective* (*N. Amer.*) (designating) a stupid person or animal; **knothole** (*a*) a hole in a board or plank where a knot has fallen out; (*b*) a hollow formed in a tree trunk by the decay of a branch; (*c*) a hole formed by the excavation of clay; **knot-stitch** a stitch by which ornamental knots are made; **knotweed** (*a*) = KNOTGRASS 1; (*b*) any of various other plants belonging to or formerly included in the genus *Polygonum*, esp. = *Japanese knotweed* s.v. JAPANESE *adjective*; **knotwork** ornamental work consisting of or (*spec.* in architecture) representing cords etc. intertwined and knotted together.

■ **knotless** *adjective* LME.

knot /nɒt/ *noun*[2]. LME.
[ORIGIN Uncertain: perh. imit. of the bird's call. Cf. GNAT *noun*[2].]
A short-billed, Arctic-breeding sandpiper, *Calidris canutus*. Also (in full ***great knot***), a larger sandpiper, *C. tenuirostris*, which breeds in Siberia.

knot /nɒt/ *verb*. Infl. **-tt-**. LME.
[ORIGIN from KNOT *noun*[1].]
1 a *verb intrans.* Form lumps, knobs, or knots; become knotty. Formerly of plants: form nodes; bud; begin to develop fruit. Long *obsolete* exc. *Scot.* LME. ▸**b** *verb trans.* Form lumps, knobs, or knots on or in; make knotty; *esp.* furrow or knit (the brows). E16.

> **b** O. WISTER Perplexity knotted the Virginian's brows.

2 *verb trans.* Tie in a knot; form a knot or knots in; secure with a knot. M16. ▸**b** *verb intrans.* Form a knot or knots; be or become twisted into a knot. Chiefly *fig.* E17.

> G. ORWELL She . . put her clothes on, knotted the scarlet sash about her waist. J. KOSINSKI Her long hair . . had knotted itself into innumerable thick braids impossible to unravel. E. WILSON It is a good idea to knot the gold thread . . to prevent it from constantly slipping out. J. KRANTZ Even his tie was perfectly knotted. **b** J. POYER His stomach knotted tighter until nausea caught at . . his throat.

3 *verb trans. & intrans.* Unite or gather closely together *spec.* in a knot or group; assemble, congregate. Now *rare*. E17.

> G. GREENE A small group of middle-aged, bowler-hatted businessmen knotted at the far corner.

4 *verb intrans.* Make knots for fringing. E18. ▸**b** *verb trans.* Make (a fringe) with knots. M18.

knotgrass /ˈnɒtɡrɑːs/ *noun*. E16.
[ORIGIN from KNOT *noun*[1] + GRASS *noun*.]
1 Any of several weeds of the genus *Polygonum* (family Polygonaceae), esp. *Polygonum aviculare*, with wiry jointed creeping stems and small pinkish or whitish flowers in the axils of the leaves. E16.
2 Any of various other plants with jointed stems; *spec.* (*a*) fiorin grass, *Agrostis stolonifera*; (*b*) *US* joint-grass, *Paspalum distichum*; (*c*) a variety of false oat with swollen basal internodes, *Arrhenatherum elatius* subsp. *bulbosum*. L16.
whorled knotgrass a small creeping plant of damp sandy places, *Illecebrum verticillatum*, of the pink family.
3 Either of two small noctuid moths, *Acronicta rumicis*, and (in full ***light knotgrass***) *A. menyanthidis*. Also ***knotgrass moth***. E19.

knotted /ˈnɒtɪd/ *adjective*. ME.
[ORIGIN from KNOT *noun*[1], *verb*: see -ED[2], -ED[1].]
1 Having a knot or knots tied in it; fastened with a knot. ME. ▸**b** *fig.* Complex, intricate; twisted as in a knot. M17.

> A. SILLITOE He wore a knotted tie over a white collar. N. FREELING Every kind of . . junk held together with knotted bits of string.

2 Characterized by knobs or protuberances; gnarled; (of the brows) furrowed, knitted. LME. ▸**b** Formed into a compact close mass esp. of blossom. Long *dial.* exc. in ***knotted*** MARJORAM. E17. ▸**c** Decorated with knots or bosses. M19.

> TOLKIEN A huge man with . . great bare arms and legs with knotted muscles. *New Yorker* My father's hands . . are brown and knotted.

3 Of a garden: laid out in an intricate design. L16.
– PHRASES: **get knotted!** *colloq.* go away! stop annoying me! nonsense!
■ **knottedness** *noun* the fact or manner of being formed into a knot E20.

knotter /ˈnɒtə/ *noun*. E18.
[ORIGIN from KNOT *noun*[1], *verb* + -ER[1].]
1 A person who or machine which ties knots. E18.
2 With prefixed numeral: a boat or ship capable of a speed of a specified number of knots. E20.

knotting /ˈnɒtɪŋ/ *noun*. LME.
[ORIGIN from KNOT *verb*, *noun*[1] + -ING[1].]
1 The action of tying a knot or tying something in a knot or knots. LME. ▸**b** The tying of knots in yarn to form a decorative network or pattern; work made in this way. L17.
2 The formation of knots or lumps; the production of buds etc. LME.
3 A preparation applied to knots in boards etc. prior to painting to prevent resin from oozing through; the application of this. E19.

4 The process of removing knots or lumps from cloth, pulp, etc. L19.

knotty /ˈnɒti/ *adjective*. ME.
[ORIGIN from KNOT *noun*[1] + -Y[1].]
1 Having knots, full of knots; tied or entangled in knots. ME.

> SHAKES. *Haml.* Make . . Thy knotty and combined locks to part, And each particular hair to stand on end.

2 *fig.* Difficult, complex, hard to explain, puzzling. ME.

> M. PUZO The relief of a conscientious administrator who has solved a knotty personnel problem.

3 Having many knots or lumps, covered with knots or lumps; gnarled; (of a board etc.) containing knots. LME.

> F. RAPHAEL Pamela had her warm hands on Fagin's knotty joints. A. LURIE On the wall over the knotty pine sideboard.

4 *fig.* Hard and rough in character. Now *rare*. M16.
– COMB.: †**knotty-pated** *adjective* (*rare*, Shakes.) stupid.
■ **knottily** *adverb* L17. **knottiness** *noun* LME.

knout /naʊt, nuːt/ *noun & verb*. *hist.* M17.
[ORIGIN French from Russian *knut* from Old Norse *knútr* rel. to KNOT *noun*[1].]
▸ **A** *noun.* A scourge or whip used in imperial Russia, often causing death. M17.
▸ **B** *verb trans.* Flog with a knout. M18.

know /nəʊ/ *noun*[1]. L16.
[ORIGIN from KNOW *verb*.]
The fact of knowing; knowledge. Now chiefly in ***in the know***, having secret or inside information.

know *noun*[2] var. of KNOWE.

know /nəʊ/ *verb*. Pa. t. **knew** /njuː/; pa. pple **known** /nəʊn/.
[ORIGIN Old English *cnāwan*, earlier *gecnāwan*, corresp. to Old High German *-cnāen*, *-cnāhen*, Old Norse pres. indic. *kná*, pl. *knegum*. An orig. reduplicating verb from Indo-European base repr. also by CAN *verb*[1], KEN *verb*, and Latin (*g*)*noscere*, *cognoscere*, Greek *gignōskein*.]
▸ **I** Recognize, admit.
1 *verb trans.* Recognize, perceive; identify; *spec.* perceive (a thing or person) as identical with something or someone already perceived or considered. OE. ▸**b** Distinguish; be able to distinguish (one thing) *from* another. M20.

> SCOTT FITZGERALD I knew I had guessed right about those missing hours. J. MORTIMER The Fanners were known as good landlords. *Sunday Times* The art of dressing is to know what you look good in. **b** E. F. BENSON Lady Heron, who did not know a picture from a statue.

†**2** *verb trans.* Acknowledge; admit the claims or authority of. Also, own, confess. ME–M16.
3 *verb trans.* In biblical use: take notice of, regard; care for; approve. LME.
▸ **II** Be acquainted with, have experience of.
4 *verb trans.* **a** Be acquainted with (a thing, a place, a person); be familiar with by experience, or through information. Also, become familiar with. ME. ▸**b** *refl.* Understand oneself. ME. ▸**c** Have experience of (an occurrence, an emotion, a circumstance, etc.); have experienced or undergone. Also, be subject to, undergo. ME.

> MILTON I know each lane, and every alley green . . of this wilde Wood. J. RHYS I am longing to know all your plans and where you are. **b** *Notes & Queries* The folly of that impossible precept 'Know thyself'. **c** THACKERAY I never knew a man die of love. R. BROOKE We, who have known shame. J. BUCHAN The purple gloom which is all the night that Laverlaw knows in early July.

5 *verb trans.* Be personally acquainted with (a person); be familiar or friendly with. ME. ▸†**b** *verb trans.* In *pass.* Be personally acquainted or familiar *with*. ME–M16. ▸†**c** *verb intrans.* Of two people: be (mutually) acquainted. Only in E17.

> E. BOWEN Can't say I ever knew him. **c** SHAKES. *Cymb.* Sir, we have known together in Orleans.

6 *verb trans.* Have sexual intercourse with. Now *arch.* or *joc.* ME.
▸ **III** Come to apprehend, learn.
7 *verb trans.* Be aware or apprised of (something), esp. through observation, inquiry, or information. Formerly also, become cognizant of, learn. ME. ▸**b** *verb intrans.* Be aware of a fact. ME.

> GOLDSMITH An enemy whom he knew more powerful than himself. N. SHUTE I don't know that she could manage by herself. W. M. HAILEY All languages which are known not to be attached to any of the above Units. E. WELTY You'll know when it starts, all right, because of the bang! G. JOSIPOVICI You showed no surprise . . it was as if you had known I would be coming.

8 *verb trans.* Be conversant with (a body of facts, principles, a method of action, etc.), esp. through instruction, study, or practice; have learned; be able to recall; be versed or skilled in. Formerly also, learn. ME. ▸**b** Have a good command of (a language, subject, etc.). M19.

> W. TREVOR There was more information that he had known but forgotten until now. C. ISHERWOOD We both knew Newbolt's Vitae Lampada by heart, we'd learnt it at school.

9 *verb intrans.* Have understanding or knowledge. ME.

> R. KIPLING The boy has devised . . it so that no hint is given except to those who know!

10 *verb trans.* Comprehend as fact or truth; understand with clearness and certainty. Freq. opp. ***believe***. ME.
†**11** *verb trans.* Make (a thing) known or familiar. Also, tell or disclose a thing to (a person). Only in ME.
– PHRASES: **all one knows (how)** everything in one's power, all one can. **and knows it** *colloq.* and is clearly aware of what has been stated. **before one knows where one is** very soon, very quickly, with baffling speed. **be not to know** (*a*) have no way of learning; (*b*) be not to be told. *dear knows*: see DEAR *interjection*. **don't I know it** *colloq.* I am well aware of it, don't tell me. **don't you know?** *colloq.* (expr. emphasis) wouldn't you say?, isn't it? **do you know something?**, **you know something?** *colloq.* shall I tell you something?, listen to this. *every schoolboy knows*: see SCHOOLBOY *noun*. **for all I know**, **for all you know**, etc., as far as I am, you are, etc., aware or concerned. *for reasons best known to oneself*: see REASON *noun*[1]. *get to know*: see GET *verb*. *give to know*: see GIVE *verb*. **God knows** (*a*) certainly, indeed, it is true; (*b*) I have no idea, no one knows. *if you know what I mean*: see MEAN *verb*[1]. *if you must know*: see MUST *verb*[1]. **I knew it** I was sure this would happen. **I know what** *colloq.* I have an idea, suggestion, etc. **I want to know!** *US colloq.* well, well! **I wouldn't know (about that)** I cannot be expected to know (about that), don't ask me (about that). *know a hawk from a handsaw*, *know a hawk from a heronshaw*: see HAWK *noun*[1]. *know all the answers*: see ANSWER *noun*. **know as** be familiar with under the name of; in *pass.*, be commonly called. **know a thing or two** be experienced or shrewd. *know better*, *know better than that*, *know better than to do*: see BETTER *adverb*. *know by name*: see NAME *noun*. *know enough to come in out of the rain*: see RAIN *noun*[1]. *know from nothing*: see *not know from nothing* below. **know how** understand the way, have the expertise or ability (*to do* something). *know how many beans make five*: see BEAN *noun*. *know inside out*: see INSIDE *noun*. *know like a book*: see BOOK *noun*. *know like the back of one's hand*: see BACK *noun*[1]. **know little and care less**, **know nothing and care less** be completely unconcerned *about*; be studiously ignorant. *know one's distance*: see DISTANCE *noun*. *know one's onions*: see ONION *noun*. *know one's own mind*: see MIND *noun*[1]. *know one's place*: see PLACE *noun*[1]. **know one's stuff** *colloq.* be fully acquainted with or well up in something. *know one's way about*, *know one's way around*: see WAY *noun*. *know something backward(s)*: see BACKWARD *adverb*. **know the reason why** demand (and get) an explanation. *know the ropes*: see ROPE *noun*[1]. **know the score** be aware of what is going on. *know the time of day*: see TIME *noun*. **know too much** be in possession of too much important information to be allowed to live or continue as normal. *know to speak to*: see SPEAK *verb*. *know what one is talking about*: see TALK *verb*. **know what one likes** have fixed or definite tastes in art, poetry, etc., without necessarily having the knowledge or informed opinion to support them. **know what's what** be experienced or shrewd; be aware of what is going on. *know whereof one speaks*: see WHEREOF *rel. adverb & conjunction*. **know where one is (with)**, **know where one stands (with)** know how one is regarded (by someone); know the opinions (of someone) on an issue. **know who's who** be aware of the identity, status, etc., of each person. *let a person know*: see LET *verb*[1] 12. **not if I know it** only against my will. *not know from a bar of soap*: see SOAP *noun*[1]. *not know from Adam*: see ADAM *noun*. *not know from Eve*: see EVE *noun*[1]. **not know from nothing**, **know from nothing** *N. Amer. colloq.* be totally ignorant. *not know one's arse from one's elbow*: see ARSE *noun* 1. *not know shit from* SHINOLA. *not know what hit one*: see HIT *verb*. *not know what to do with oneself*: see DO *verb*. *not know which way to turn*, *not know where to turn*: see TURN *verb*. **not want to know** not be interested. *one never knows*: see *you never know* below. **that's all you know (about it)** you are more ignorant than you think. **what do you know (about that)?**, **wouldn't you know?**, **wouldn't you just know?** expr. mild surprise; well I never!, fancy that! **wouldn't you like to know?**, **wouldn't he like to know?**, etc., I have no intention of telling you, him, etc., in spite of your, his, etc., curiosity. **you know** (*a*) indicating that the person being addressed ought to be aware of something unstated; (*b*) used as a conversation filler: you see. *you know something?*: see *do you know something?* above. **you know what?** I am going to tell you something. *you know what I mean*: see MEAN *verb*[1]. *you must know*: see MUST *verb*[1]. **you never know**, **one never knows** something unexpected or surprising may occur, nothing is certain.
– WITH PREPOSITIONS IN SPECIALIZED SENSES: **know about** have information about. †**know for** (*rare*, Shakes.) be aware of. **know of** †(*a*) be or become assured of; learn of or about; (*b*) be aware of; (*c*) ***not that I know of***, not so far as I am aware.
– COMB.: **know-little** *rare* a simpleton; *you-know-what*, *you-know-who*: see YOU *pronoun*.
■ **knower** *noun* a person who knows ME.

knowable /ˈnəʊəb(ə)l/ *adjective & noun*. LME.
[ORIGIN from KNOW *verb* + -ABLE.]
▸ **A** *adjective.* That may be known; able to be comprehended, ascertained, or recognized. Formerly also, that may know. LME.
▸ **B** *absol.* as *noun.* That which is knowable; a knowable thing. M17.
■ **knowaˈbility** *noun* M19. **knowableness** *noun* M17.

know-all /ˈnəʊɔːl/ *noun & adjective*. Also **know-it-all** /ˈnəʊɪtɔːl/. L19.
[ORIGIN from KNOW *verb* + ALL *noun*.]
▸ **A** *noun.* A person who seems to know everything; a (would-be) smart and clever person. L19.

> S. MIDDLETON They were smug Conservative voters, know-alls.

▸ **B** *adjective.* Full of knowledge; smugly or arrogantly knowledgeable. Also, deaf to advice or instruction. L19.

> P. G. WODEHOUSE These know-it-all directors make me tired.

K

knowbot /ˈnəʊbɒt/ *noun*. L20.
[ORIGIN Blend of KNOW *verb* and ROBOT.]
COMPUTING. A program designed to search through large numbers of databases in response to requests for information by users of a network.
– NOTE: Proprietary name in the US.

knowe /naʊ/ *noun*. Also **know**. E16.
[ORIGIN Alt. of KNOLL *noun*[1].]
A hillock, a knoll, a piece of rising ground.

know-how /ˈnəʊhaʊ/ *noun*. M19.
[ORIGIN from *know how* s.v. KNOW *verb*.]
Technical expertise; practical ability or invention.

B. BAINBRIDGE They have manpower, resources, know-how. A. GUINNESS My own lack of know-how and swift rash judgements hampered the allied cause.

knowing /ˈnəʊɪŋ/ *noun*. ME.
[ORIGIN from KNOW *verb* + -ING[1].]
†1 Acknowledgement; recognition. Only in ME.
†2 Personal acquaintance. Only in ME.
3 The action of getting to understand, the fact of understanding; knowledge. ME.
4 The state or fact of being aware or informed of something; cognizance. ME. ▸†b Something known, an experience. *rare* (Shakes.). Only in E17.
there is no knowing no one can tell, one cannot know.

knowing /ˈnəʊɪŋ/ *adjective*. LME.
[ORIGIN from KNOW *verb* + -ING[2].]
1 a That knows, having knowledge; understanding, intelligent, well-informed; conscious; mentally perceptive. LME. ▸b Skilled or versed *in* something. M17.

M. ARNOLD A matter which does not fall within the scope of our ordinary knowing faculties. B. JOWETT He is the most knowing of all living men.

2 Of a person, an action, a look, etc.: having or showing discernment or cunning; shrewd, cunning. E16.

N. COWARD I've always been sophisticated, far too knowing. D. WELCH I saw the nurses exchange superior and knowing smiles.

3 Informed, aware. (Foll. by †*of*, *to*.) *arch*. M17.
4 Showing awareness of current fashions, style, etc. *colloq*. *obsolete* exc. as passing into sense 2. L18.
■ **knowingly** *adverb* (*a*) in a knowing manner; (*b*) consciously, intentionally: LME. **knowingness** *noun* E18.

know-it-all *noun & adjective* see KNOW-ALL.

knowledgable *adjective* var. of KNOWLEDGEABLE.

knowledge /ˈnɒlɪdʒ/ *noun*. ME.
[ORIGIN Prob. from KNOWLEDGE *verb*.]
▸ †I Rel. to KNOWLEDGE *verb* and early uses of KNOW *verb*.
1 Acknowledgement; confession. ME–M16.
2 Recognition. ME–E17.
3 Legal cognizance; judicial investigation or inquiry. Chiefly *Scot*. LME–M18.
4 *gen*. Cognizance, notice. Only in ***take knowledge of***, take cognizance of, notice. Only in E17.
▸ II Rel. to later uses of KNOW *verb*.
5 The fact of knowing a thing, state, person, etc.; acquaintance; familiarity gained by experience. ME.

M. BRETT These stories can be difficult to understand without some knowledge of the background.

†6 Personal acquaintance, friendship. Also, those with whom one is acquainted. LME–E17.
7 Sexual intercourse. Foll. by *of*, †*with*. *obsolete* exc. in ***carnal knowledge*** s.v. CARNAL *adjective* 2. LME.
8 Acquaintance with a fact or facts; a state of being aware or informed; awareness, consciousness. LME.

L. GORDON The small rain of spring seems to carry some knowledge of human sorrow. B. MOORE These things were done without my knowledge.

9 Chiefly PHILOSOPHY. Intellectual perception of fact or truth; clear and certain understanding or awareness, esp. as opp. to opinion. Formerly also, intelligence, intellect. (Foll. by *of*.) LME. ▸†b MEDICINE. Diagnosis. M16–M17.

D. HARTLEY The Infinite Power, Knowledge, and Goodness of God.

10 Understanding of a branch of learning, a language, etc.; (a) theoretical or practical understanding *of* an art, science, industry, etc. LME.

V. SACKVILLE-WEST All craftsmen share a knowledge. J. KRANTZ Billy's knowledge of housekeeping was limited.

11 *gen*. The fact or condition of being instructed, or of having information acquired by study or research. Also, a person's range of information; learning, erudition. LME.

Time Knowledge can be shared; experience cannot.

†12 Notice, intimation; information. LME–E18.
13 †a A sign or mark by which something is recognized, or distinguished; a token. L15–M16. ▸b A perception, intuition, or other cognition. Usu. in *pl*. Now *rare* or *obsolete*. M16. ▸c A branch of learning; a science, an art. Usu. in *pl*. Now *rare*. L16.
14 The sum of what is known. M16.
– PHRASES: ***carnal knowledge*** (***of***): see CARNAL *adjective* 2. **come to a person's knowledge** become known to a person. ***common knowledge***: see COMMON *adjective*. **grow out of knowledge**, **grow out of one's knowledge** (now *rare*) cease to be known, become unfamiliar. ***hearsay knowledge***: see HEARSAY *noun*. ***immediate knowledge***: see IMMEDIATE *adjective* 3. ***knowledge by acquaintance***, ***knowledge of acquaintance***: see ACQUAINTANCE 3. ***knowledge by description***: see DESCRIPTION 1b. ***mediate knowledge***: see MEDIATE *adjective* 2b. ***take knowledge of***: see sense 4 above. **to one's knowledge** (*a*) so far as one is aware; (*b*) as one knows for certain. ***to the best of one's knowledge***: see BEST *adjective* etc. ***tree of knowledge*** (***of good and evil***): see TREE *noun*.
– COMB.: **knowledge base** COMPUTING the underlying set of facts, assumptions, and inference rules which a computer system has available to solve a problem; a store of information (as in a database) available to draw on; **knowledge-based** *adjective* (of an academic discipline) founded on an accumulation of facts, non-empirical; (of a computer system) incorporating a set of facts, assumptions, or inference rules derived from human knowledge; **knowledge box** *joc*. the head; **knowledge economy**: in which growth is dependent on the quantity, quality, and accessibility of the information available, rather than the means of production; **knowledge factory** *derog*. a university, college, etc., which places emphasis on vocational training or which over-emphasizes factual knowledge; **knowledge industry** (*derog*. or *joc*.) the development and use of knowledge, *spec*. in universities, polytechnics, etc.; **knowledge management** the handling of information and resources in such a way as to promote efficiency, competence, and innovation within a commercial organization. **knowledge worker** a person whose job involves handling or using information.
– NOTE: Orig. corresp. to the earliest senses of KNOWLEDGE *verb*, then used as noun of action corresp. to KNOW *verb*, in which role it has partially replaced KNOWING *noun*.
■ **knowledged** *adjective* (*rare*) provided with knowledge M16. **knowledgeless** *adjective* (*rare*) M19.

†**knowledge** *verb*.
[ORIGIN Old English *cnāwelǣċing* (for *-ung*) verbal noun, from (*ge*)*cnāwan* KNOW *verb* + *-lǣċan*, from *-lac*: see -LOCK. Simple verb recorded early in Middle English.]
1 *verb trans*. a = ACKNOWLEDGE 1. OE–M17. ▸b = ACKNOWLEDGE 3. ME–L16. ▸c = ACKNOWLEDGE 4. LME–L18. ▸d Recognize; MEDICINE diagnose (an illness). M16–E17.
2 *verb trans*. & *intrans*. Have sexual intercourse with or *with*. Only in ME.
3 *verb intrans*. Make confession. LME–E16.
■ †**knowledging** *noun* (*a*) the action of the verb; (*b*) = KNOWLEDGE *noun*: OE–L16.

knowledgeable /ˈnɒlɪdʒəb(ə)l/ *adjective*. Also **-dgable**. E17.
[ORIGIN In sense 1 from KNOWLEDGE *verb*, in sense 2 from KNOWLEDGE *noun*: see -ABLE.]
†1 Able to be perceived or recognized; recognizable; noticeable. Only in E17.
2 Possessing or showing knowledge; well-informed; intelligent. Also, aware *of*. E19.

D. ROWE Despite the wise and knowledgeable advice from kindly child-rearing experts, many parents . . still beat . . children.

■ **knowledgeaˈbility** *noun* M20. **knowledgeableness** *noun* L19. **knowledgeably** *adverb* M19.

knowledgement /ˈnɒlɪdʒm(ə)nt/ *noun*. *arch*. Also **-dgm-**. E17.
[ORIGIN from KNOWLEDGE *verb* + -MENT.]
†1 Formal acknowledgement; legal cognizance. E–M17.
2 Knowledge, cognizance. M17.

known /nəʊn/ *adjective & noun*. ME.
[ORIGIN pa. pple of KNOW *verb*.]
▸ A *adjective*. 1 Learned, apprehended mentally; familiar, *esp*. familiar to all, generally known or recognized. Also, identified as such. ME.

A. CHRISTIE Billy Kellett? . . He's known to the police. F. HOWERD I was leaving surroundings where I had become known and was accepted. I. DRUMMOND His face was not recognised in the rogues' gallery, nor did his description tally with any known criminal. *Sunday Express* There are 700 known species of holly in the world.

†2 Possessed of knowledge; acquainted with something; learned *in*. LME–M17.
▸ B *absol*. as *noun*. †1 An acquaintance. Only in ME.
2 A well-known person. Also, a known criminal. M19.
3 ***the known***, that which is known, all known things. M19.

known *verb pa. pple* of KNOW *verb*.

know-nothing /ˈnəʊnʌθɪŋ/ *noun & adjective*. In senses A.2, B.2 also **Know-Nothing**. E19.
[ORIGIN from KNOW *verb* + NOTHING *noun*.]
▸ A *noun* 1 a A person who knows nothing, an ignorant person. E19. ▸b A person who holds that nothing can be known; an agnostic. E19.
2 US HISTORY. A member of a political party in the US, prominent from 1853 to 1856, which supported exclusion of immigrants from government, and whose members preserved its original secrecy by denying its existence. M19.
▸ B *attrib*. or as *adjective* 1 a That knows nothing; grossly ignorant. E19. ▸b That holds that nothing can be known; agnostic. E19.
2 US HISTORY. Of or pertaining to the American Know-Nothings. M19.
■ **know-nothingism** *noun* (*a*) wilful ignorance; agnosticism; (*b*) the political doctrine of the American Know-Nothings: M19. **know-nothingness** *noun* the state or quality of knowing nothing; complete ignorance: L19.

Knoxian /ˈnɒksɪən/ *noun & adjective*. E18.
[ORIGIN from *Knox* (see below) + -IAN.]
▸ A *noun*. An adherent of John Knox (*c* 1505–72), the Scottish reformer mainly responsible for establishing the Presbyterian Church, or his beliefs. E18.
▸ B *adjective*. Of or pertaining to John Knox or his beliefs. E20.

Knt *abbreviation*.
Knight.

knub /nʌb/ *noun*. Now chiefly *dial*. See also NUB *noun*[1]. L16.
[ORIGIN Middle Low German *knubbe* var. of *knobbe* KNOB *noun*.]
1 A small lump, a protuberance, a knob; *esp*. a small swelling on the body, a boil. L16.
2 The innermost wrapping of a silkworm cocoon. E19.

knub /nʌb/ *verb trans*. *dial*. Now *rare* or *obsolete*. Also (earlier) †**n-**. Infl. **-bb-**. E17.
[ORIGIN Imit.: cf. KNAB *verb*[1]. See also KNUBBLE *verb*.]
1 = KNUBBLE *verb*. E17.
†2 Bite gently, nibble. Only in M17.

knubble /ˈnʌb(ə)l/ *noun*. *dial*. Now *rare* or *obsolete*. L17.
[ORIGIN from KNUB *noun* + -LE[1]. Cf. KNOBBLE *noun*, NUBBLE *noun*.]
A small knob. Formerly also, a knuckle.

knubble /ˈnʌb(ə)l/ *verb trans*. *dial*. Now *rare* or *obsolete*. Also (earlier) †**n-**; **knob-**. L17.
[ORIGIN from KNUB *verb* + -LE[3]. See also NOBBLE.]
Strike with the knuckles or fist, beat.

knubbly /ˈnʌbli/ *adjective*. *dial*. M19.
[ORIGIN from KNUBBLE *noun* + -Y[1]. Cf. KNOBBLY, NUBBLY.]
Full of or covered with knubs or small protuberances.

knuck /nʌk/ *noun*. E19.
[ORIGIN Abbreviation of KNUCKLE *noun*, KNUCKLER.]
1 A thief, a pickpocket. Cf. KNUCKLE *noun* 2b. *slang*. Now *rare* or *obsolete*. E19.
2 In *pl*. (treated as *sing*.). A game of marbles in which the winner can shoot a marble at the loser's knuckles. *US*. M19.
3 A knuckleduster. L19.

knuckle /ˈnʌk(ə)l/ *noun*. ME.
[ORIGIN Middle Low German *knökel*, corresp. to Old Frisian *knok(e)le*, Middle Dutch *knokel*, *knökel* (Dutch *kneukel*), Middle High German *knuchel*, *knüchel* (German *Knöchel*), dim. of base of Middle Low German *knoke* (Dutch *knok*), Middle High German *knoche* (German *Knochen*) bone, perh. ult. rel. to KNEE *noun*.]
1 The end of a bone at a joint, the more or less rounded protuberance formed when a joint is bent, as in the knee, elbow, and vertebral joints. Formerly also, a fist. Now only *Scot*. & *dial*. exc. as below. ME.
2 *spec*. The hard protuberance formed on the back of the hand by a finger joint when the fingers are bent or the hand is shut, *esp*. that at the root of a finger. LME. ▸†b A pickpocket. Cf. KNUCK 1. L18–M19.

S. BECKETT I stuck in my forefinger up to the knuckle. D. FRANCIS He gripped his binoculars so hard that his knuckles showed white. J. RATHBONE Her hands showed signs of much age, being knotted at the knuckles.

3 Something shaped, angled, or protruding like a knuckle bone. LME.

S. R. CROCKETT I . . sat on a solid knuckle of rock that shot up from the ribs of the mountain.

4 The projection of the carpal or tarsal joint of a quadruped; a joint of meat consisting of this with the parts above and below it. E17.
5 A knuckleduster. M19.

A. S. NEILL Savage assaults with . . brass knuckles.

– PHRASES: **go the knuckle** *Austral*. *slang* fight, punch. **near the knuckle** *colloq*. verging on the indecent. ***rap on the knuckles***, ***rap over the knuckles***: see RAP *verb*[1] 1.
– COMB.: **knuckleball** BASEBALL a slow pitch which moves erratically, made by gripping the ball with the fingertips; **knuckleballer** BASEBALL a player who pitches a knuckleball; **knuckle-bow** a guard on a sword hilt to cover the knuckles; **knuckle-deep** *adverb* (now *rare*) up to the knuckles; *fig*. very deeply; **knuckle-dragger** *colloq*. a stupid or loutish man; **knuckle-dragging** *adjective* (*colloq*.) (of a man) stupid or loutish; **knuckledust** *verb trans*. strike with a knuckleduster; **knuckleduster** a metal guard worn over the knuckles in fist fighting to protect them and increase the force of a blow; **knuckle-end** the lower or small end of a leg of mutton or pork; **knucklehead** a slow-witted or stupid person; **knuckle joint** (*a*) a joint at a knuckle (on the hand of a person, or the limb of an animal); (*b*) MECHANICS a joint connecting two parts of a mechanism, in which a projection in one fits into a recess in the other; **knuckle sandwich** *slang* a punch in the mouth; **knuckle timber** SHIPBUILDING a timber having or forming an acute angle; **knuckle-walker** a primate, e.g. the gorilla and chimpanzee, having a quadrupedal gait in which the knuckles (rather than the tips of the fingers or flat of the palm) make contact with the ground; **knuckle-walking** the practice of walking with the gait of a knuckle-walker.
■ **knuckled** *adjective* having knuckles LME. **knuckler** *noun* (*a*) *slang* a pickpocket; (*b*) BASEBALL a knuckleball: M19. **knucklesome**

K

adjective (rare) knuckly **E20**. **knuckly** *adjective* having large or prominent knuckles **M19**.

knuckle /ˈnʌk(ə)l/ *verb*. **M18**.
[ORIGIN from the noun.]
▶ **I** *verb intrans.* **1** Place one's knuckles on the ground in playing at marbles. Usu. foll. by *down*. **M18**.
2 Acknowledge oneself beaten; give way, give in, submit. Usu. foll. by *down* or *under* (*to*). **M18**.
R. ELLMANN They had knuckled under to Queensbury's threats.
3 Foll. by *down*: apply oneself earnestly (*to*). **M19**.
4 Protrude or project like a knuckle. *rare*. **M19**.
5 FARRIERY. Of the knee or fetlock: project *over* or *forwards* through weakness of the ligaments. **L19**.
▶ **II** *verb trans.* **6** Strike, press, or rub with the knuckles. **L18**.
P. GALLICO He reached over and knuckled Clary gently under . . the chin. A. CARTER She finished . . crying, knuckling her eyesockets like a child. Z. TOMIN I knuckled a signal . . on a small black door.
7 Propel (a marble etc.) from between the knuckle of the thumb and the bent forefinger. **E19**.

knuckle bone /ˈnʌk(ə)lbəʊn/ *noun*. **LME**.
[ORIGIN from KNUCKLE *noun* + BONE *noun*.]
1 A bone forming a knuckle; *spec.* the rounded end at the joint of a finger bone. **LME**.
2 a A limb bone of an animal with a ball-like knob at the joint-end; the rounded end of such a bone. Also, a knuckle of meat. **LME**. ▶**b** A metacarpal or metatarsal bone of a sheep; in *pl.*, (such bones used in) a game of jacks. **M18**.

Knudsen /ˈknʊds(ə)n/ *noun*. **M20**.
[ORIGIN M. H. C. *Knudsen* (1871–1949), Danish physicist.]
PHYSICS. Used **attrib.** and in **possess.** to designate apparatus, phenomena, and concepts connected with (***a***) low density fluid flow; (***b***) OCEANOGRAPHY a method of determining the salinity of seawater by titration with silver nitrate.
Knudsen flow the flow, from an orifice or through a tube, of a rarefied gas with a high Knudsen number, so that resistance to flow arises mainly from collisions of molecules with the walls of the orifice or tube rather than with each other. **Knudsen gas**: having a Knudsen number much greater than one. **Knudsen gauge**, **Knudsen manometer** an instrument for measuring the absolute pressure of a rarefied gas. **Knudsen number** the ratio of the mean free path of molecules in a gas to a length derived from the dimensions of the vessel or orifice through which it flows.

knur /nəː/ *noun*. Also **-rr**. **LME**.
[ORIGIN Var. of KNAR.]
1 A hard excrescence or swelling in the flesh. *obsolete* exc. *Scot. dial.* **LME**.
2 A knot or hardened excrescence on the trunk of a tree, a knar; a hard concretion in stone; any swollen formation. **M16**.
3 = KNURL 2. *N. English*. **L17**.
4 A wooden ball used in a game (***knur and spell***) resembling trapball; a similar ball used in other games. *N. English*. **M19**.

knurl /nəːl/ *noun & verb*. Also **n-**. **E17**.
[ORIGIN App. a deriv. of KNUR. Cf. GNARL *noun*, KNARL.]
▶ **A** *noun*. **1** A small projection or excrescence; a knot, knob, etc.; a small bead or ridge, *esp.* any of a series worked on a metal surface. **E17**.
2 A thickset stumpy person. *Scot. & dial.* **L17**.
▶ **B** *verb trans.* Make knurls on the edge of (a coin, a screw head, etc.); mill, crenate. **L19**.
■ **knurled** *adjective* having knurls; crenated, milled: **E17**. **knurling** *noun* (***a***) the action of the verb; (***b***) knurled work: **E17**. **knurly** *adjective* (***a***) having knurls or knots; (***b***) *Scot. & dial.* stumpy, thickset: **E17**.

knurr *noun* var. of KNUR.

knut /kəˈnʌt, nʌt/ *noun*. *arch. slang*. **E20**.
[ORIGIN Alt. of NUT *noun*.]
A fashionable or showy young man, = NUT *noun* 6.

KO *abbreviation*.
1 Kick-off.
2 Knocked out; knockout.

ko /kəʊ/ *noun*[1]. *NZ*. Pl. same, **kos**. **M19**.
[ORIGIN Maori.]
A Maori digging stick.

Ko /kəʊ/ *noun*[2]. **L19**.
[ORIGIN Chinese *gē* (Wade-Giles *ko*) elder brother.]
CERAMICS. In full ***Ko ware***, ***Ko yao*** /jaʊ/ [*yáo* pottery]. A crackled Song ware closely related to Kuan ware. Also, any of various other crackled porcelains.

ko /kəʊ/ *noun*[3]. Pl. **kos**. **M20**.
[ORIGIN Chinese *gē* (Wade-Giles *ko*) spear, lance.]
CHINESE ANTIQUITIES. A dagger, a halberd.

koa /ˈkəʊə/ *noun*. **E19**.
[ORIGIN Hawaiian.]
A Hawaiian forest tree, *Acacia koa*; the dark wood of this, used in cabinetmaking. Also ***koa tree***, ***koa-wood***.

koala /kəʊˈɑːlə/ *noun*. **L18**.
[ORIGIN Dharuk *gula*.]
An Australian arboreal marsupial, *Phascolarctos cinereus*, which resembles a small bear, has thick ash-grey fur, and feeds on eucalyptus leaves. Also ***koala bear***.
– NOTE: The form *koala bear* is widely used but zoologically incorrect.

koan /ˈkəʊɑːn/ *noun*. **M20**.
[ORIGIN Japanese *kōan*, from Chinese *gōngàn* official business.]
ZEN BUDDHISM. A riddle without a solution, used to demonstrate the inadequacy of logical reasoning and provoke sudden enlightenment.

kob /kɒb/ *noun*[1]. **L18**.
[ORIGIN Wolof *kooba*.]
In full ***kob antelope***. A grazing antelope, *Kobus kob*, native to African savannah.
UGANDA ***kob***.

kob /kɒb/ *noun*[2]. *S. Afr.* **E20**.
[ORIGIN Abbreviation.]
= MEAGRE *noun*[1]. Also called ***kabeljou***, ***salmon bass***.

koban /ˈkəʊban/ *noun*. **E17**.
[ORIGIN Japanese *ko-ban*, from *ko* little + *ban* part, share, division: cf. OBAN.]
An oblong gold or silver coin with rounded corners, formerly used in Japan; the sum of money represented by this, one-tenth of an oban.

kobellite /ˈkəʊb(ə)lʌɪt/ *noun*. **M19**.
[ORIGIN from Franz von *Kobell* (1803–82), German mineralogist + -ITE[1].]
MINERALOGY. A monoclinic sulphide of lead, bismuth, and antimony, usu. occurring as lead-grey radiated masses.

kobo /ˈkəʊbəʊ/ *noun*. Pl. same. **L20**.
[ORIGIN Alt. of COPPER *noun*[1].]
A monetary unit of Nigeria, equal to one-hundredth of a naira.

kobold /ˈkəʊbəld/ *noun*. **M19**.
[ORIGIN German: cf. COBALT.]
In German folklore, a familiar spirit, supposed to haunt houses and help the occupants, a brownie; also, an underground spirit, a goblin, a gnome.

Koch /kɒx, kɒk/ *noun*. **L19**.
[ORIGIN Robert *Koch* (1843–1910), German bacteriologist.]
MEDICINE. Used in **possess.** and **attrib.** to designate things discovered or introduced by Koch.
Koch postulates = ***Koch's postulates*** below. **Koch's bacillus** (chiefly *hist.*) the tubercle bacillus, first isolated by Koch. **Koch's postulates** a set of four criteria which should be satisfied before a given disease is attributed with certainty to any particular microorganism. **Koch-Weeks bacillus** [J. E. *Weeks* (1853–1949), US ophthalmologist] the bacterium *Haemophilus aegyptius*, which is a common cause of infectious conjunctivitis.

kochia /ˈkəʊkɪə, ˈkɒtʃɪə/ *noun*. **L19**.
[ORIGIN mod. Latin (see below), from Wilhelm D. J. *Koch* (1771–1849), German botanist: see -IA[1].]
Any of various plants formerly included in the genus *Kochia*, of the goosefoot family; esp. *Bassia* (formerly *Kochia*) *scoparia*, a shrubby Eurasian plant grown for its decorative foliage which turns deep fiery red in the autumn.

KO'd /keɪˈəʊd/ *abbreviation*.
Knocked out.

Kodak /ˈkəʊdak/ *noun & verb*. **L19**.
[ORIGIN Arbitrary name invented by the manufacturer.]
▶ **A** *noun*. **1** (Proprietary name for) a camera of a range produced by Kodak Ltd. Also, any small camera. **L19**.
2 *transf.* A photograph taken with a Kodak. **L19**.
▶ **B** *verb trans. & intrans.* Photograph with a Kodak; *fig.* describe or capture quickly or vividly. Now *rare*. **L19**.
■ **Kodaker** *noun* (now *rare*) **L19**.

Kodiak /ˈkəʊdɪak/ *noun*. **L19**.
[ORIGIN An island off Alaska.]
In full ***Kodiak bear***. A brown bear (*Ursus arctos*) of a subspecies endemic to some islands off Alaska, notable for the large size of individuals.

koechlinite /ˈkəːklɪnʌɪt/ *noun*. **E20**.
[ORIGIN from Rudolf *Koechlin* (1862–1939), Austrian museum curator + -ITE[1].]
MINERALOGY. An orthorhombic molybdate of bismuth usu. occurring as greenish-yellow plates or soft white to yellow masses.

koeksister /ˈkʊksɪstə/ *noun*. *S. Afr.* **E20**.
[ORIGIN Afrikaans *koe(k)sister*, perh. from *koek* cake + *sissen* sizzle.]
A plaited doughnut dipped in syrup, a traditional South African confection.

koel /ˈkəʊəl/ *noun*. **E19**.
[ORIGIN Hindi *koël*, *koil* from Sanskrit KOKILA.]
Any of certain cuckoos of the genera *Eudynamys* and *Urodynamys*; *spec.* (***a***) *E. scolopacea* of southern and SE Asia; (***b***) *E. cyanocephala* of Australia.

koelreuteria /kəːlrɔɪˈtɪərɪə/ *noun*. **L18**.
[ORIGIN mod. Latin (see below), from Joseph G. *Koelreuter* (1733–1806), German naturalist: see -IA[1].]
A deciduous tree of the eastern Asian genus *Koelreuteria* (family Sapindaceae); esp. the widely cultivated *K. paniculata*, which has large panicles of yellow flowers and pinnate leaves which turn bright yellow in autumn.

koenenite /ˈkəːnənʌɪt/ *noun*. **E20**.
[ORIGIN from Adolf von *Koenen* (1837–1915), German geologist + -ITE[1].]
MINERALOGY. A trigonal hydroxide and chloride of magnesium, aluminium, and sodium, which forms pale yellow scales when pure, but is normally red owing to enclosed haematite.

koettigite /ˈkəːtɪgʌɪt/ *noun*. **M19**.
[ORIGIN from Otto *Köttig*, 19th-cent. German chemist + -ITE[1].]
MINERALOGY. A monoclinic hydrated arsenate of zinc, containing also cobalt and nickel, usu. forming red or pink prisms.

kofta /ˈkɒftə, ˈkəʊftə/ *noun*. **L19**.
[ORIGIN Urdu & Persian *koftah* pounded meat.]
In Middle Eastern and Indian cookery: a savoury ball made with minced meat, paneer, or vegetables.

koftgari /ˈkəʊftgəriː/ *noun*. **L19**.
[ORIGIN Urdu & Persian *kuft-garī* beaten work.]
A kind of damascene work of the Indian subcontinent, in which a pattern traced on steel is inlaid with gold.

koha /ˈkəʊha/ *noun*. *NZ*. **L20**.
[ORIGIN Maori.]
A gift, a donation.

kohanga reo /ˌkɔːhaŋə ˈreɪəʊ/ *noun*. *NZ*. **L20**.
[ORIGIN Maori, lit. 'language nest'. Cf. TE REO.]
A preschool educational institution in which the language of instruction is Maori.

kohekohe /kəʊɪˈkəʊɪ/ *noun*. **M19**.
[ORIGIN Maori.]
A tall forest tree, *Dysoxylum spectabile* (family Meliaceae), native to New Zealand, bearing panicles of fragrant white flowers.

kohen /ˈkɒhɛn, kɔɪn/ *noun*. Pl. **kohanim** /ˈkɒhɛnɪm, ˈkɔɪnɪm/. Also **c-**, pl. **-s**. **L19**.
[ORIGIN Hebrew, lit. 'priest'.]
JUDAISM. A member of the priestly caste, having certain rights and duties in the synagogue.

koh-i-noor /ˈkəʊɪnʊə/ *noun*. Also (earlier) †**Cohi Noor**. **E19**.
[ORIGIN from Persian *kūh* mountain + *i* of + Arabic *nūr* light.]
1 A famous Indian diamond, part of the British Crown jewels since 1849; *transf.* any magnificent large diamond. **E19**.
2 *fig.* Something that is the most precious or most superb *of* its kind. **L19**.

kohl /kəʊl/ *noun & verb*. **L18**.
[ORIGIN Arabic *kuḥl*: see ALCOHOL.]
▶ **A** *noun*. A powder, usu. consisting of antimony sulphide or lead sulphide, used as eye make-up and as eye ointment, esp. in Eastern countries. **L18**.
A. S. BYATT She had her father's big black eyes, outlined in Kohl.
▶ **B** *verb trans.* Darken with kohl. **M20**.

kohlrabi /kəʊlˈrɑːbi/ *noun*. **E19**.
[ORIGIN German *Kohlrabi* from (with assim. to *Kohl* COLE *noun*[1]) Italian *cauli* or *cavoli rape*, pl. of *cavolo rapa* (whence French *chou-rave*), repr. medieval Latin *caulorapa*: see COLE *noun*[1], RAPE *noun*[3].]
A variety of cabbage, *Brassica oleracea* var. *gongylodes*, with an edible turnip-shaped base to its stem.

Kohlrausch's law /ˈkəʊlraʊʃɪz lɔː/ *noun phr.* **L19**.
[ORIGIN Friedrich Wilhelm *Kohlrausch* (1840–1910), German physicist.]
PHYSICAL CHEMISTRY. A law stating that the equivalent electrical conductivity of an electrolyte (strictly, at infinite dilution) is the sum of independent contributions from the cation and the anion present in the electrolyte.

Kohs block /ˈkəʊz blɒk/ *noun phr.* **M20**.
[ORIGIN from Samuel *Kohs* (1890–1984) US psychologist + BLOCK *noun*.]
PSYCHOLOGY. Any of several coloured cubes making up a set, from which a subject is required to form specified patterns.

kohua /ˈkɔːhʊə/ *noun*. *NZ*. **M19**.
[ORIGIN Maori.]
A Maori earth oven or hangi. Also, a three-legged iron pot or kettle.

koi /kɔɪ/ *noun*. Pl. same. **E18**.
[ORIGIN Japanese.]
A carp (in Japan). Now *esp.* a carp of a large ornamental variety bred in Japan. Also ***koi carp***.

koi-cha /ˈkɔɪtʃə/ *noun*. **E18**.
[ORIGIN Japanese, from *koi* thick, strong, dark + *cha* tea.]
In Japan: powdered tea mixed to a thick brew and drunk ceremonially.

koi hai /kɔɪˈhʌɪ/ *noun*. *colloq.* (now chiefly *hist.*). Also ***qui hi*** /kwʌɪˈhʌɪ/. **E19**.
[ORIGIN from Urdu, Hindi *koī hai* is anyone there? (used to call a servant).]
A British resident in the Indian subcontinent, esp. in Bengal.

koilonychia /kɔɪləˈnɪkɪə/ *noun*. **E20**.
[ORIGIN from Greek *koilos* hollow + *onukhos*, *onux* nail + -IA[1].]
MEDICINE. A condition of the fingernails in which the outer surfaces are concave instead of convex; spoon-nail.

K

koine /ˈkɔɪniː/ *noun*. L19.
[ORIGIN Greek *koinē* fem. sing. of *koinos* common, ordinary.]
1 The common literary language of the Greeks from the close of classical Attic to the Byzantine era. L19.
2 LINGUISTICS. A language or dialect common to a wide area in which different languages or dialects are, or were, used locally; a lingua franca. L19.
D. WHITELOCK The general use of the West Saxon literary *koine*.
3 A set of cultural or other attributes common to various groups. E20.
— NOTE: In Greek characters in L19; transliterated from E20.

koinonia /kɔɪˈnəʊnɪə/ *noun*. E20.
[ORIGIN Greek *koinōnia* communion, fellowship.]
THEOLOGY. Christian fellowship or communion, with God or, more commonly, with fellow Christians.

koji /ˈkəʊdʒi/ *noun*. L19.
[ORIGIN Japanese *kōji*.]
An enzyme preparation derived from various moulds used to cause fermentation in the production of saké, soy sauce, etc.

kojic /ˈkəʊdʒɪk/ *adjective*. E20.
[ORIGIN from KOJI + -IC.]
CHEMISTRY. ***kojic acid***, a crystalline pyrone derivative produced from dextrose by some fungi of the genus *Aspergillus*, with mild antibacterial properties.

kokako /ˈkɔːkəkəʊ/ *noun*. Pl. same, **-os**. L19.
[ORIGIN Maori.]
A New Zealand wattlebird, *Callaeas cinerea*.

kokam *noun* var. of KOKUM.

kokanee /ˈkəʊkani/ *noun*. L19.
[ORIGIN Shuswap *kəknæxʷ*.]
A sockeye salmon of a non-migratory dwarf subspecies found in lakes in western N. America. Also ***kokanee salmon***. Also called ***silver trout***.

koker /ˈkəʊkə/ *noun*. M19.
[ORIGIN Dutch.]
In Guyana: a sluice gate, a lock gate; the water between such gates.

kokerboom /ˈkʊəkəbʊəm/ *noun*. *S. Afr.* L18.
[ORIGIN Afrikaans, from Dutch *koker* quiver + *boom* tree.]
A small aloe tree, *Aloe dichotoma*, the branches of which were formerly used by the Nama to make quivers for arrows.

kokeshi /ˈkəʊkəʃiː/ *noun*. Pl. same. M20.
[ORIGIN Japanese, from *ko* small + *ke* tiny + *shi* child.]
A kind of wooden Japanese doll.

kokila /ˈkəʊkɪlə/ *noun*. L18.
[ORIGIN Sanskrit. Cf. KOEL.]
In the Indian subcontinent: the Indian koel, *Eudynamys scolopacea*.

kokko /ˈkəʊkəʊ/ *noun*. Also **koko**. M19.
[ORIGIN Burmese.]
1 A large deciduous leguminous tree, *Albizia lebbeck*, which bears heads of yellowish-white flowers and is native to tropical Asia, though naturalized in Africa and the Caribbean. Also called ***East Indian walnut***, ***lebbek***, ***siris***. M19.
2 The dark brown wood of this tree. M20.

koklass /ˈkəʊkləs, ˈkɒklas/ *noun*. Also **-as**. Pl. same. M19.
[ORIGIN from var. of Nepali *phakrās*.]
More fully ***koklass pheasant***. A pheasant, *Pucrasia macrolopha*, which has a long crest and is native to the Himalayan region and China.

koko *noun* var. of KOKKO.

kokopu /ˈkɔːkəpuː/ *noun*. *NZ*. L19.
[ORIGIN Maori.]
A small freshwater fish of the genus *Galaxias*.

kokowai /ˈkɔːkɔːwʌɪ/ *noun*. *NZ*. M19.
[ORIGIN Maori.]
Red ochre or burnt red clay used by Maori to decorate wood.

kok-saghyz /kɒksəˈgɪz/ *noun*. M20.
[ORIGIN Russian *kok-sagyz*, from Turkic *kök* root + *sagiz* gum, resin.]
A dandelion, *Taraxacum kok-saghyz*, native to Turkestan, the roots of which yield a latex.

koku /ˈkəʊkuː/ *noun*. Pl. same. E18.
[ORIGIN Japanese.]
A Japanese unit of capacity equal to ten *to*, used for liquids and solids, esp. rice, and containing approximately 40 gallons (180 litres) or 5 bushels.

kokum /ˈkəʊkəm/ *noun*. Also **-am**. M19.
[ORIGIN Hindi *kokam*.]
In full ***kokum butter***, ***kokum oil***. An edible semi-solid oil derived from the tropical Asian plant *Garcinia indica* (family Guttiferae).

Kol /kəʊl/ *noun & adjective*. L18.
[ORIGIN Unknown.]
▶ **A** *noun*. Pl. **-s**, same. A member of any of various Munda-speaking peoples of the north-east of the Indian subcontinent. L18.
▶ **B** *attrib*. or as *adjective*. Of or pertaining to the Kols. M19.

kola *noun* var. of COLA *noun*[1].

kolach /ˈkɒlatʃ/ *noun*. Pl. **-che** /-tʃiː/, **-ches** /-tʃɪz/. E20.
[ORIGIN Czech *koláč*, from *kolo* wheel, circle.]
A small tart or pie popular in the Czech Republic and Slovakia, topped or filled with fruit.

Kolam /ˈkəʊlɑːm/ *noun & adjective*. M19.
[ORIGIN Ethnic name.]
▶ **A** *noun*. Pl. **-s**, same. A member of a Dravidian people of central India. M19.
▶ **B** *attrib*. or as *adjective*. Of or pertaining to this people. L19.
■ **Kolami** *noun & adjective* (of) the language of this people M19.

Kolarian /kəʊˈlɛːrɪən/ *noun & adjective*. M19.
[ORIGIN from *kolar*, an ancient name for India + -IAN.]
= MUNDA.

Kolbe /ˈkɒlbə/ *noun*. L19.
[ORIGIN A. W. H. *Kolbe* (1818–84), German chemist.]
CHEMISTRY. Used *attrib*. and in *possess*. to designate two reactions used in synthesis: (***a***) the electrolysis of a salt of a carboxylic acid, R·COOH, to yield an alkane R_2; (***b***) the reaction of sodium phenoxide with carbon dioxide to yield sodium salicylate.

kolbeckite /ˈkɒlbɛkʌɪt/ *noun*. E20.
[ORIGIN from Friedrich *Kolbeck* (1860–1943), German mineralogist + -ITE[1].]
MINERALOGY. A rare blue monoclinic hydrated phosphate of scandium, usu. containing calcium, aluminium, and other elements.

Koli /ˈkəʊli/ *noun & adjective*. Also †**Koolee**. E19.
[ORIGIN Ethnic name.]
▶ **A** *noun*. Pl. **-s**, same. A member of an aboriginal people of Gujarat in western India. Earlier as COOLIE *noun* 1. E19.
▶ **B** *attrib*. or as *adjective*. Of or pertaining to the Kolis. M19.

kolinsky /kəˈlɪnski/ *noun*. M19.
[ORIGIN from *Kola* a port in NW Russia + pseudo-Russ. ending *-insky*.]
(The fur of) a weasel, *Mustela sibirica*, native to northern and eastern Eurasia, Japan, and Taiwan.

kolkhoz /ˈkɒlkɒz, kʌlkˈhɔːz/ *noun*. Pl. same, **-zes** /-zɪz/, **-zy** /-zi/. E20.
[ORIGIN Russian, from *kol(lektivnoe khoz(yaĭstvo* collective farm.]
In countries of the former USSR: a collective farm.

kollergang /ˈkɒləgaŋ/ *noun*. L19.
[ORIGIN German = crushing action.]
A crushing machine used in milling paper pulp.

kolm /kɒlm/ *noun*. M20.
[ORIGIN Swedish.]
PETROGRAPHY. A form of cannel coal with a relatively high content of metals, found in Swedish shales.

Kol Nidre /kɒl ˈniːdreɪ/ *noun*. L19.
[ORIGIN Aramaic *kol niḏrē* all the vows (the opening words of the prayer).]
An Aramaic prayer annulling vows made before God, sung by Jews at the opening of the Day of Atonement service on the eve of Yom Kippur. Also, the service or the melody at or to which this prayer is sung.

kolo /ˈkəʊləʊ/ *noun*. Pl. **-os**. L18.
[ORIGIN Croatian = wheel.]
A Slavonic dance performed in a circle.

Koma /ˈkəʊmə/ *noun & adjective*. Pl. of noun same. E20.
[ORIGIN Local name.]
Of or pertaining to, a member of, a people living near the border of Sudan and Ethiopia along the Blue Nile and its tributaries; (of) their language.
■ **Koman** *noun & adjective* (designating) a group of languages of Sudan and Ethiopia that includes Koma M20.

komatiite /kəˈmatɪʌɪt/ *noun*. M20.
[ORIGIN from *Komati* river in southern Africa + -ITE[1].]
GEOLOGY. Any of a class of ultramafic extrusive igneous rocks typically displaying a distinctive texture of criss-crossing sheaves of elongated crystals of olivine.
■ **komatiitic** /kəmatɪˈɪtɪk/ *adjective* L20.

komatik /ˈkɒmətɪk/ *noun*. E19.
[ORIGIN Inupiaq (Inuit) *qamutik*.]
A dog sledge used by the people of Labrador.

†**kombaars** *noun* see KOMBERS.

kombé /ˈkɒmbeɪ/ *noun*. M19.
[ORIGIN Nyanja.]
The juice obtained from the seeds of a central African climbing plant, *Strophanthus kombe* (family Apocynaceae), which is a source of the drug strophanthin.

kombers /ˈkɒmbəːs/ *noun*. *S. Afr.* Also †**-baars**. E19.
[ORIGIN Afrikaans from Dutch *kombaars* ship's blanket.]
A blanket, a rug.

kombu /ˈkɒmbuː/ *noun*. L19.
[ORIGIN Japanese *konbu*, lit. 'tangle'.]
A brown seaweed of the genus *Laminaria*, used in Japanese cooking, esp. as a base for stock.

komfoor /kɒmˈfɔː/ *noun*. *S. Afr.* M19.
[ORIGIN Dutch from Picard form of Old French *chaufoire* kettle for hot water.]
A small brazier or stove; a chafing dish.

Komi /ˈkəʊmi/ *noun & adjective*. Pl. of noun same. L19.
[ORIGIN Komi.]
Of or pertaining to, a member of, a people of northern central Russia, esp. of the Komi Republic; (of) the Finno-Ugric language of the Komi. Also called ***Zyrian***.

komitadji, **komitaji** *nouns* vars. of COMITADJI.

Kommandatura /kəmɑːndəˈtʊərə/ *noun*. M20.
[ORIGIN Alt. of German *Kommandantur* commandant's headquarters, command post, after Russian *komendatura*.]
The centre of operation of a military government.

Kommers /kəˈmɛrs/ *noun*. Pl. **-e** /-ə/. M19.
[ORIGIN German from Latin *commercium*: see COMMERCE *noun*.]
A social gathering of German students.

Komodo /kəˈməʊdəʊ/ *noun*. E20.
[ORIGIN An Indonesian island.]
Komodo dragon, ***Komodo monitor***, a large monitor lizard, *Varanus komodoensis*, native to Komodo and neighbouring islands.

Komondor /ˈkɒməndɔː/ *noun*. L20.
[ORIGIN Hungarian.]
A sheepdog of a Hungarian breed with a dense white coat.

Komsomol /ˈkɒmsəmɒl/ *noun*. M20.
[ORIGIN Russian *komsomol*, short for *Kommunisticheskiĭ Soyuz Molodëzhi* Communist Union of Youth.]
hist. (A member of) the Communist youth organization of the USSR.

kona /ˈkəʊnə/ *noun*. M19.
[ORIGIN Hawaiian, lit. 'leeward', the wind being of opposite direction to the prevailing north-easterlies.]
A stormy southerly or south-west wind in the Hawaiian Islands.

konak /kəʊˈnɑːk/ *noun*. M19.
[ORIGIN Turkish = halting place, inn.]
A large house, palace, or official residence, in Turkey or the former Ottoman Empire.

konaki /kəʊˈnaki, ˈkəʊnaki/ *noun*. *NZ*. E20.
[ORIGIN Maori *kōneke* sledge.]
A horse-drawn wooden sledge.

Kond /kɒnd/ *noun & adjective*. Also **Kh-**. M19.
[ORIGIN Dravidian *Konḍa*.]
▶ **A** *noun*. **1** A member of a Dravidian people inhabiting Orissa in eastern India. M19.
2 The language of this people. L19.
▶ **B** *attrib*. or as *adjective*. Of or pertaining to the Konds or their language. M19.

Konditorei /ˌkɒnditoˈraɪ/ *noun*. Pl. same, **-en** /-ən/. M20.
[ORIGIN German, from *Konditor* confectioner.]
Confectionery; a shop selling confectionery or rich pastries.

Kondratieff /kɒnˈdrɑːtjɛf/ *noun*. Also **-iev**. M20.
[ORIGIN N. D. *Kondratieff* (1892–c 1935), Russian economist.]
ECONOMICS. ***Kondratieff cycle***, ***Kondratieff wave***, each of a series of supposed cycles or waves of economic expansion and contraction lasting from forty to sixty years.

konfyt /kɒnˈfeɪt/ *noun*. *S. Afr.* M19.
[ORIGIN Afrikaans = Dutch *konfijt*, prob. from French CONFITURE.]
Fruit preserved in sugar; preserve, jam.

Kongo /ˈkɒŋgəʊ/ *noun & adjective*. Pl. of noun same, **-os**. M19.
[ORIGIN Kikongo.]
Of or pertaining to, a member of, a people of the region of the Congo (Zaire) River in west central Africa; (of) the Bantu language of this people, Kikongo.

kongoni /kɒŋˈgəʊni/ *noun*. E20.
[ORIGIN Kiswahili.]
Esp. in E. Africa: the hartebeest, *Alcelaphus buselaphus*.

kongsi /ˈkɒŋsi/ *noun*. M19.
[ORIGIN Chinese *gōngsī* (Wade–Giles *kungszu*) company, corporation.]
In the Malay archipelago: an association, a partnership, *esp*. an association of Chinese people from the same area.

koniaku /kɒnˈjakuː/ *noun*. Also (earlier) **konjak** /ˈkɒnjak/. L19.
[ORIGIN Japanese *konnyaku*, *konyaku*.]
A South Asian plant, *Amorphophallus konjac*, of the arum family (Araceae); (flour obtained from) the starchy root of this, used in Japanese cooking.

konimeter /kəˈnɪmɪtə/ *noun*. E20.
[ORIGIN from Greek *konis* dust + -METER.]
A kind of impinger which directs a measured volume of air on to a slide to which any dust particles will adhere.

konini /ˈkɔːniːni/ *noun*. *NZ*. M19.
[ORIGIN Maori.]
A New Zealand fuchsia, *Fuchsia excorticata*; *collect*. the berries of this shrub.

konjak *noun* see KONIAKU.

Konkani /ˈkəʊŋkəni/ *noun & adjective*. L19.
[ORIGIN Marathi & Hindi *kõkṇī*, from Sanskrit *koṅkaṇa* Konkan (see below).]
▶ **A** *noun*. Pl. **-s**, same.

K

1 A native or inhabitant of the Konkan, a coastal region of western India; a member of the Konkani-speaking community of Goa and the Konkan. L19.
2 An Indo-Aryan language that is the main language of Goa. E20.
▸ **B** *attrib.* or as *adjective.* Of or pertaining to the Konkanis or their language. L19.

kono /ˈkəʊnəʊ/ *noun*[1]. L19.
[ORIGIN Korean *konu*.]
A Korean board game between two players, each having an equal number of pieces and trying to block or capture those of the opponent.

Kono /ˈkəʊnəʊ/ *noun*[2] & *adjective*. E20.
[ORIGIN Mande.]
▸ **A** *noun.* Pl. **-os**, same.
1 A member of a Mande people of Sierra Leone. E20.
2 The language of the Konos, having affinities with Vai. E20.
▸ **B** *attrib.* or as *adjective.* Of or pertaining to the Konos or their language. E20.

koodoo *noun* var. of KUDU.

kook /kuːk/ *noun* & *adjective*. *slang*. M20.
[ORIGIN Prob. abbreviation of CUCKOO *noun* 3 or *adjective* 2.]
▸ **A** *noun.* 1 A crazy or eccentric person. M20.
Black World These marchers were . . a bunch of kooks.
2 SURFING. A bad or inexperienced surfer. M20.
▸ **B** *attrib.* or as *adjective.* Crazy, eccentric. M20.

kooka /ˈkʊkə/ *noun*. *Austral. slang*. E20.
[ORIGIN Abbreviation.]
= KOOKABURRA.

kookaburra /ˈkʊkəbʌrə/ *noun*. M19.
[ORIGIN Wiradhuri *guguburra*.]
Any of certain arboreal kingfishers of the genus *Dacelo*, of Australia and New Guinea; *spec.* the large brown *D. novaeguineae*, distinguished by its peculiar laughing cry (also called ***laughing jackass***).

K

kooky /ˈkʊki/ *adjective*. *slang*. Also **-ie**. M20.
[ORIGIN from KOOK + -Y[1].]
Crazy, eccentric.
E. L. WALLANT I feel like dropping . . this kooky life and marrying a . . tired businessman.
■ **kookily** *adverb* M20. **kookiness** *noun* M20.

†**Koolee** *noun* & *adjective* var. of KOLI.

Koori /ˈkʊri/ *noun*. *Austral.* Also **-ie**. M19.
[ORIGIN Awabakal *gurri* person.]
An Aborigine.

Kootenai *noun* & *adjective* var. of KUTENAI.

kootie *noun* var. of COOTIE *noun*.

kop /kɒp/ *noun*. M19.
[ORIGIN Afrikaans from Dutch *kop* head: cf. COP *noun*[1].]
1 A prominent hill or peak. Freq. in place names. *S. Afr.* M19.
2 SOCCER (**K-**.) A high bank of terracing for standing spectators, usu. supporting the home side, orig. and esp. that formerly at the ground of Liverpool Football Club; the spectators massed on such terracing. Also more fully ***Spion Kop*** /ˈspʌɪən/ [*Spioen Kop*, site of a battle in South Africa during the Boer War]. E20.
■ **Koppite**, **Kopite**, *noun* (SOCCER) a spectator who frequents a Kop M20.

kopa Maori /kɒpə ˈmaʊri/ *noun phr.* *NZ.* Also **copper Maori**. E19.
[ORIGIN from Maori *kāpura* fire, *kopa* oven + MAORI.]
A Maori earth oven or hangi.

kopdoek /ˈkɒpdʊk/ *noun*. *S. Afr.* E20.
[ORIGIN Afrikaans, formed as KOP + DOEK.]
A headcloth or headscarf.

kopek /ˈkəʊpɛk, ˈkɒp-/ *noun*. Also **-eck**, **copek**. E17.
[ORIGIN Russian *kopeĭka* dim. of *kop'ë* lance (from figure of a tsar (orig. Ivan IV) bearing a lance instead of sword).]
A monetary unit of Russia and some other countries of the former USSR, equal to one-hundredth of a rouble; a coin of this value.

kopi /ˈkəʊpi/ *noun*. *Austral.* L19.
[ORIGIN Baagandji (an Australian Aboriginal language of the border region of New South Wales and South Australia) *gabi*.]
Gypsum- or selenite-bearing rock or mud; powdered gypsum.

kopiyka /kɒˈpiːkə/ *noun*. L20.
[ORIGIN Ukrainian, from Russian *kopeĭka* KOPEK.]
A monetary unit of Ukraine, equal to one-hundredth of a hryvna.

kopje *noun* var. of KOPPIE.

Koplik's spot /ˈkɒplɪks ˌspɒt/ *noun phr.* Also **Koplik spot**. L19.
[ORIGIN from Henry *Koplik* (1858–1927), US paediatrician.]
MEDICINE. A small greyish-yellow spot, usu. with a red halo, numbers of which occur on the buccal mucosa in the early stages of measles.

koppa /ˈkɒpə/ *noun*. LME.
[ORIGIN Greek.]
A letter (ϙ) between pi and rho of the original Greek alphabet, later displaced by kappa, but retained as a numeral.

koppel /ˈkʌp(ə)l, ˈkɒp-/ *noun*. L19.
[ORIGIN Yiddish.]
A skullcap worn by male Jews, a yarmulke.

koppie /ˈkɒpi/ *noun*. *S. Afr.* Also **kopje**. M19.
[ORIGIN Afrikaans from Dutch *kopje* dim. of *kop* head. Cf. KOP.]
A small hill, *esp.* any of the flat-topped or pointed hillocks characteristic of the veld.

kora /ˈkɔːrə/ *noun*. L18.
[ORIGIN from a W. African lang.]
A stringed W. African instrument resembling a harp.

koradji /ˈkɒrədʒi, kəˈradʒi/ *noun*. *Austral.* Also (earlier) **coradgee** & other vars. L18.
[ORIGIN Dharuk *garraaji*.]
An Aborigine skilled in traditional medicine.

Koran /kɔːˈrɑːn, kə-/ *noun*. Also **Qur'an** /kəˈrɑːn/. E17.
[ORIGIN Arabic *qur'ān* recitation, reading, from *qara'a* read, recite: cf. Syriac *keryānā* scripture reading (in Christian liturgy). See also earlier ALCORAN.]
The sacred book of Islam, believed by Muslims to be the word of God as revealed in Arabic to Muhammad, and arranged after the latter's death; a copy of this.
■ **Koranic** /-ˈrɑːnɪk, -ˈranɪk/ *adjective* E19.

Korana /kəˈrɑːnə/ *noun* & *adjective*. Also **Kora** /ˈkɔːrə/, **Koranna**. E19.
[ORIGIN Unknown.]
▸ **A** *noun.* Pl. same, **-s**.
1 A member of a group of Nama peoples in southern Africa. E19.
2 The language of these peoples. L19.
▸ **B** *attrib.* or as *adjective.* Of or pertaining to the Korana or their language. M19.

Koranko /kəˈraŋkəʊ/ *noun* & *adjective*. Pl. of noun same, **-os**. E19.
[ORIGIN Mande.]
1 Of or pertaining to, a member of, a Mande people of Guinea and Sierra Leone. E19.
2 (Of) the language of this people. L19.

Koranna *noun* & *adjective* var. of KORANA.

kordax /ˈkɔːdaks/ *noun*. Also **c-**. M16.
[ORIGIN Greek.]
A dissolute dance of ancient Greek comedy.

kore /ˈkɔːreɪ/ *noun*. E20.
[ORIGIN Greek *korē* = maiden.]
A Greek statue of a draped maiden.

Korean /kəˈriːən/ *noun* & *adjective*. Also (earlier) †**C-**. E17.
[ORIGIN from *Korea* (see below) + -AN.]
▸ **A** *noun.* 1 A native or inhabitant of Korea in eastern Asia, now divided into the Republic of Korea (or South Korea) and the Democratic People's Republic of Korea (North Korea). E17.
2 The agglutinative language of Korea, of uncertain affinity. E19.
3 *ellipt.* A Korean chrysanthemum. M20.
▸ **B** *adjective.* Of or pertaining to Korea or its language. E17.
Korean chrysanthemum a late-flowering hybrid chrysanthemum developed from *Dendranthema zawadskii* and other Far Eastern species. **Korean pine** a slow-growing pine with dark green leaves, *Pinus koraiensis*, native to Korea and Japan.
■ **Koreanize** *verb trans.* give a Korean character to M20.

Koreish /kəˈrʌɪʃ/ *noun pl.* & *adjective*. Also (earlier) †**Coreis(h)**; **Quraysh**, **Qureysh**, & other vars. M17.
[ORIGIN Arabic *qurayš* Koreish, *qurašī* Koreishite.]
▸ **A** *noun pl.* The tribe which inhabited Mecca in the time of Muhammad and to which he belonged. M17.
▸ **B** *attrib.* or as *adjective.* Of or pertaining to the Koreish. L19.
■ **Koreishite** *noun* a member of the Koreish E18.

korero /ˈkɔːrərəʊ/ *noun*. *NZ.* Pl. same, **-os**. E19.
[ORIGIN Maori.]
Talk, conversation, discussion; a conference.

korfball /ˈkɔːfbɔːl/ *noun*. E20.
[ORIGIN Dutch *korfbal*, from *korf* basket + *bal* ball.]
A game of Dutch origin, resembling basketball but in which players are not permitted to run with the ball, played between teams of mixed sexes (usu. six male and six female on each).

korhaan /kɔːˈhɑːn, kəˈrɑːn/ *noun*. *S. Afr.* Also **kn-** /kn-/. M18.
[ORIGIN Afrikaans, from *kor-*, *knor-* imit. base (cf. Dutch *korren* coo, *knorren* grumble, snarl) + *haan* cock. Cf. Dutch *korhaan* woodcock.]
A bustard.

kori /ˈkɔːri/ *noun*[1]. E19.
[ORIGIN Setswana *kgori*.]
In full ***kori bustard***. A bustard, *Choriotis kori*, of sub-Saharan Africa.

kori /ˈkɔːri/ *noun*[2]. M19.
[ORIGIN Sindhi *korī* = Hindi *kolī* from Sanskrit *kolika* from Tamil *kōṭikar*.]
A member of a low Hindu caste of weavers of northern India.

korimako /kɒrɪˈmɑːkəʊ/ *noun*. *NZ.* Pl. same, **-os**. M19.
[ORIGIN Maori.]
A New Zealand honeyeater, *Anthornis melanura*. Also called ***bellbird***, ***makomako***.

korin /ˈkɔːrɪn/ *noun*. M19.
[ORIGIN App. from a W. African lang.]
The red-fronted gazelle, *Gazella rufifrons*, native to Africa from Senegal to Sudan. Also ***korin gazelle***.

Kōrin /ˈkɔːrɪn/ *noun*. L19.
[ORIGIN See below.]
Kōrin school, ***Kōrin style***, a school of decorative traditional Japanese painting typified by the work of the Japanese artist Kōrin Ogata (1658–1716).

koringkriek /ˈkɔːrɪŋkrɪk/ *noun*. *S. Afr.* E20.
[ORIGIN Afrikaans, from Dutch *koorn* corn + *kriek(en)* chirp.]
A long-horned grasshopper.

korkir *noun* var. of CORKIR.

Korku /ˈkɔːkuː/ *noun* & *adjective*. M19.
[ORIGIN Munda.]
▸ **A** *noun.* Pl. **-s**, same. A member of a Munda people of the central provinces of India; the language of this people. M19.
▸ **B** *attrib.* or as *adjective.* Of or pertaining to the Korkus or their language. M19.

korma /ˈkɔːmə/ *noun*. L19.
[ORIGIN Urdu *kormā*, *kormah* from Turkish *kavurma*.]
A mildly spiced Indian dish of meat or fish marinaded in yogurt or curds.
chicken korma etc.

kornelite /ˈkɔːnəlʌɪt/ *noun*. L19.
[ORIGIN from *Kornel* Hlavacsek, late 19th-cent. Czech engineer + -ITE[1].]
MINERALOGY. A violet to pale pink monoclinic hydrated ferric sulphate, usu. occurring as needles or fibrous aggregates.

kornerupine /ˈkɔːnərʊpiːn/ *noun*. L19.
[ORIGIN from A. N. *Kornerup* (1857–81), Danish geologist + -INE[5].]
MINERALOGY. A green orthorhombic silicate of aluminium and magnesium, usu. occurring in prismatic aggregates.

koro /ˈkɔːrəʊ/ *noun*. Pl. same. E19.
[ORIGIN Japanese *kōro* incense-pot, censer.]
An elaborate Japanese vase, usu. of bronze, jade, or porcelain, in which incense is burned.

koromiko /kɒrəˈmiːkəʊ/ *noun*. Pl. same, **-os**. M19.
[ORIGIN Maori.]
Any of various New Zealand shrubs of the genus *Hebe*, of the figwort family, esp. *H. salicifolia*.

korowai /ˈkɒrəwʌɪ/ *noun*. *NZ.* E19.
[ORIGIN Maori.]
A Maori cloak or cape of flax, ornamented with black twisted thrums. Also ***korowai mat***.

korrigan /ˈkɒrɪg(ə)n/ *noun*. M19.
[ORIGIN Breton (Vannes dial.), fem. of *korrig* gnome, dim. of *korr* dwarf.]
In Breton folklore, a fairy or witch noted esp. for stealing children.

korrigum /ˈkɒrɪg(ə)m/ *noun*. E19.
[ORIGIN from Saharan: cf. Kanuri *kargun*.]
A topi (antelope) of the W. African subspecies.

Korsakoff /ˈkɔːsəkɒf/ *noun*. E20.
[ORIGIN S. S. *Korsakoff* (1854–1900), Russian psychiatrist.]
MEDICINE. Used in *possess.* to designate a psychotic syndrome, often the result of chronic alcoholism, characterized by disorientation, memory loss for recent events, and consequent confabulation.

koru /ˈkɔːruː/ *noun*. *NZ.* M20.
[ORIGIN Maori.]
A stylized fern-leaf motif in Maori carving and tattooing.

koruna /ˈkɒrʊnə/ *noun*. E20.
[ORIGIN Czech = crown.]
The basic monetary unit of the Czech Republic and Slovakia, equal to 100 halers or haliers.

Korwa /ˈkɔːwə/ *noun* & *adjective*. M19.
[ORIGIN Munda.]
▸ **A** *noun.* Pl. same, **-s**.
1 A member of a Munda people of the Chota Nagpur area of India. M19.
2 The language of the Korwa. L19.
▸ **B** *attrib.* or as *adjective.* Of or pertaining to the Korwa or their language. M19.

Koryak /ˈkɔːjak/ *noun* & *adjective*. E18.
[ORIGIN Russian *Koryaki* (pl.).]
▸ **A** *noun.* Pl. **-s**, same.
1 A member of a people inhabiting the northern part of the Kamchatka peninsula on the Pacific coast of Siberia. E18.
2 The Palaeo-Siberian language of this people. L19.
▸ **B** *attrib.* or as *adjective.* Of or pertaining to the Koryaks or their language. L18.

kos /kɒs/ *noun*. Also **koss**, **coss**, †**course**. Pl. same. E17.
[ORIGIN Hindi from Sanskrit *krośa* lit. 'cry, shout'.]
In the Indian subcontinent: a measure of length varying in different parts, usu. between 3 and 4 km (2 to 2½ miles).

kosh *noun & verb* var. of COSH *noun*[1] *& verb*.

Koshare /kə(ʊ)ˈʃɑːriː/ *noun*. Pl **-s**, same. L19.
[ORIGIN Keresan *k'ɨ̄:ṣari*.]
A member of a Pueblo Indian clown society representing ancestral spirits in rain and fertility ceremonies.

kosher /ˈkəʊʃə/ *adjective, noun, & verb*. M19.
[ORIGIN Hebrew *kāšēr* fit, proper.]
▸ **A** *adjective*. **1** Of food: prepared according to the Jewish law. M19.

R. HAYMAN Meat cannot be *kosher* unless the animals' throats have been cut by the authorized butcher.

2 That sells or prepares such food; where such food is cooked or eaten. L19.

Guardian The last kosher butcher left for Israel.

3 Correct, genuine, legitimate. *colloq*. L19.

T. PYNCHON They got the contracts. All drawn up in most kosher fashion. L. CODY Everything seemed fairly kosher until this morning.

▸ **B** *noun*. **1** *ellipt*. Kosher food; a kosher shop. L19.
2 The Jewish law regarding food. Chiefly in ***keep kosher***. M20.
▸ **C** *verb trans*. Prepare (food) according to the Jewish law. L19.

Kosovar /ˈkɒsəvɑː/ *noun & adjective*. M20.
[ORIGIN Albanian.]
▸ **A** *noun*. A native or inhabitant of the region of Kosovo, bordering Serbia, Montenegro, Albania, and Macedonia, esp. one whose native language is Albanian. M20.
▸ **B** *adjective*. Of or relating to Kosovo or the Kosovars. L20.
■ **Kosovan** *noun & adjective* L20.

kosso *noun* var. of KOUSSO.

kotal /ˈkəʊtal/ *noun*. E19.
[ORIGIN Persian & Pashto from Mongolian.]
In Afghanistan and adjacent regions: a pass over a mountain; a col; the ridge or summit of a pass.

kotatsu /kəʊˈtatsuː/ *noun*. L19.
[ORIGIN Japanese.]
A wooden frame placed over a central hearth or charcoal brazier in Japanese houses and covered with a thick quilt to give an enclosed area for warming the hands and feet. Also, the hearth or brazier and the cover together.

kotla *noun* see KGOTLA.

koto /ˈkəʊtəʊ/ *noun*. Pl. **-os**. L18.
[ORIGIN Japanese.]
A long Japanese zither, now usu. having thirteen silk strings, usu. played on the floor.

kotow *noun & verb* var. of KOWTOW.

kotuku /ˈkɔːtʊkʊ, ˈkəʊtəkuː/ *noun*. *NZ*. M19.
[ORIGIN Maori.]
The white heron or great egret, *Egretta alba*.

kotwal /kəʊtˈwɑːl/ *noun*. Also **c-**. L16.
[ORIGIN Hindi *koṭvāl* from Sanskrit *koṭṭapāla*.]
In the Indian subcontinent: a chief officer of police for a city or town; a town magistrate.

kotwali /kəʊtˈwɑːli/ *noun*. M19.
[ORIGIN Hindi *koṭvālī*, formed as KOTWAL.]
In the Indian subcontinent: a police station.

kou /kəʊ/ *noun*. E19.
[ORIGIN Hawaiian.]
A Hawaiian tree, *Cordia subcordata*, of the borage family; the dark brown wood of this tree.

koulan *noun* see KULAN.

koulibiac *noun* var. of COULIBIAC.

koumiss /ˈkuːmɪs/ *noun*. Also **kumis(s)**. L16.
[ORIGIN French *koumis*, German *Kumiss*, Polish *kumys*, Russian *kumys* from Tartar *kumiz*.]
A fermented liquor prepared from mare's or other milk, used as a drink and medicine esp. by central Asian nomadic tribes; a spirituous liquor distilled from this.

kouprey /ˈkuːpreɪ/ *noun*. M20.
[ORIGIN Khmer.]
A rare large grey wild ox, *Bos sauveli*, native to the forests of Indo-China.

koura /ˈkəʊərə/ *noun*. *NZ*. M19.
[ORIGIN Maori.]
A freshwater crayfish, *Paranephrops planifrons*.

kourbash *noun & verb* var. of KURBASH.

kouros /ˈkuːrɒs/ *noun*. Pl. **-roi** /-rɔɪ/. E20.
[ORIGIN Greek (Ionic form of *koros* boy).]
GREEK ANTIQUITIES. A sculptured representation of a youth.

kouskous *noun* var. of COUSCOUS *noun*[1].

kousso /ˈkʊsəʊ/ *noun*. Also ***kosso*** /ˈkɒsəʊ/. M19.
[ORIGIN Amharic.]
The dried flowers of an Ethiopian tree, *Hagenia abyssinica* (family Rosaceae), used as a remedy for tapeworm.

kovsh /kɒvʃ/ *noun*. Pl. **-shi** /-ʃi/. L19.
[ORIGIN Russian.]
In Russia: a ladle or container for drink.

kowhai /ˈkəʊwʌɪ, ˈkɔːfʌɪ/ *noun*. M19.
[ORIGIN Maori.]
Any of a number of leguminous shrubs or small trees of the genus *Sophora*; esp. *S. tetraptera*, native to New Zealand and Chile, which bears racemes of golden-yellow flowers (also called ***locust tree***).

kowtow /kaʊˈtaʊ/ *noun & verb*. Also **kotow** /kəʊˈtaʊ/. E19.
[ORIGIN Chinese *kētóu* (Wade–Giles *k'ot'ou*), from *kē* knock, strike + *tóu* head.]
▸ **A** *noun*. The action or practice, formerly customary in China, of touching the ground with the forehead as a sign of extreme respect, submission, or worship; *fig*. an act of obsequious respect. E19.
▸ **B** *verb intrans*. Perform the kowtow; *fig*. act in an obsequious manner. M19.

S. CONRAN She couldn't stand the way that Robert kowtowed to her father.

■ **kowtower** *noun* M20.

koyan /kəʊˈjɑːn/ *noun*. L18.
[ORIGIN Malay.]
A unit of weight of the Malay peninsula equal to 40 *piculs* and equivalent to approximately 5,330 lb (2.42 tonnes).

kozatchok *noun* var. of KAZACHOC.

KP *abbreviation*.
1 Kitchen police(man). *US*.
2 Knight (of the Order) of St Patrick.

kph *abbreviation*. Also **k.p.h.**
Kilometres per hour.

Kr *symbol*.
CHEMISTRY. Krypton.

kra /krɑː/ *noun*. E19.
[ORIGIN Malay *kera*.]
The long-tailed or crab-eating macaque, *Macaca fascicularis*, of SE Asia.

kraak porselein /krɑːk ˈpɔːsɪleɪn/ *noun phr*. Also **kraak porcelain** /ˈpɔːs(ə)lɪn/. M20.
[ORIGIN Dutch, from *kraak* carrack (the type of Portuguese ship from which the porcelain was first captured in 1603) + *porselein* PORCELAIN.]
Blue and white Chinese porcelain of the Wan-li period (1573–1619) or later in the 17th cent.; a European imitation of this.

kraal /krɑːl/ *noun & verb*. M18.
[ORIGIN Afrikaans from Portuguese *curral*. Cf. CORRAL *noun* and CRAWL *noun*[1].]
▸ **A** *noun*. **1** In southern Africa: a village of huts enclosed by a fence or stockade, and often having a central space for cattle etc.; the community of such a village. M18.
2 In southern Africa: an enclosure for cattle or sheep, a stockade, a pen, a fold. L18.
3 In Sri Lanka: an enclosure into which wild elephants are driven; the process of capturing elephants by driving them into an enclosure. L19.
4 = CRAWL *noun*[1] 2. M20.
▸ **B** *verb trans*. Enclose in a kraal or stockade. E19.

krab /krab/ *noun*. *colloq*. M20.
[ORIGIN Abbreviation & contr.]
= KARABINER.

kraft /krɑːft/ *noun*. E20.
[ORIGIN Swedish = strength, in *kraftpapper* kraft paper.]
More fully ***kraft paper***. A strong smooth brown paper made from unbleached soda pulp.

Krag /krag/ *noun*. *colloq*. L19.
[ORIGIN O. H. *Krag*: see KRAG-JØRGENSEN.]
= KRAG-JØRGENSEN.

kragdadig /kraxˈdɑːdɪx/ *adjective*. *S. Afr*. Also (in attrib. use) ***-dige***. M20.
[ORIGIN Afrikaans = Dutch *krachtdadig*.]
Forceful, vigorous in wielding power, unyielding.
■ ***kragdadigheid*** /-heɪt/ *noun* [*-heid* -HOOD] forcefulness, vigour in wielding power M20.

Krag-Jørgensen /kragˈjəːg(ə)ns(ə)n/ *noun*. E20.
[ORIGIN from O. H. *Krag* (1837–1912) and E. *Jørgensen*, Norwegian firearm designers. Cf. earlier KRAG.]
A type of rifle (and carbine) introduced in Denmark and Norway in the late 19th cent. and adopted in the US.

krai /krʌɪ/ *noun*. Also **kray**. M20.
[ORIGIN Russian *kraĭ*.]
In countries of the former USSR: a second-order administrative division, a region, a territory.

krait /krʌɪt/ *noun*. L19.
[ORIGIN Hindi *karait*.]
Any of several brightly coloured venomous elapid snakes of the genus *Bungarus*, of the Indian subcontinent and SE Asia. See also ***SEA krait***

kraken /ˈkrɑːk(ə)n/ *noun*. M18.
[ORIGIN Norwegian.]
A mythical sea monster of enormous size, said to appear off the coast of Norway.

krakowiak /krəˈkəʊvɪak/ *noun*. L19.
[ORIGIN Polish, from *Kraków* (Cracow) in Poland.]
= CRACOVIENNE.

Krama *noun* var. of KROMO.

kramat /kraˈmɑːt, ˈkrɑːmət/ *noun & adjective*. Also **karamat** /kəˈrɑːmət/. L18.
[ORIGIN Malay *keramat* (adjective) sacred, holy, (noun) holy place, holy person, from Arabic *karāma* miracle worked by a saint other than a prophet.]
▸ **A** *noun*. A Muslim holy place or place of pilgrimage. L18.
▸ **B** *adjective*. Sacred to Muslims. M20.

krameria /krəˈmɪərɪə/ *noun*. M19.
[ORIGIN mod. Latin genus name, from J. G. H. *Kramer* (d. 1742), Austrian botanist + -IA[1].]
= RHATANY.

kran /krɑːn/ *noun*. L19.
[ORIGIN Persian *krān*.]
hist. An Iranian (Persian) coin and monetary unit.

krans /krɑːns/ *noun*. *S. Afr*. Also **krantz** /krants/. L18.
[ORIGIN Afrikaans from Dutch = coronet, chaplet from Old High German, Middle High German, German *Kranz* coronet, circle, encircling ring of mountains, from a base meaning 'ring'.]
A wall of rock encircling a mountain or summit; a precipitous or overhanging cliff above a river, valley, etc.

Krapfen /ˈkrapf(ə)n/ *noun*. Pl. same. M19.
[ORIGIN German.]
In Germany and German-speaking countries: a fritter or doughnut.

K ration /ˈkeɪ raʃ(ə)n/ *noun phr*. M20.
[ORIGIN from initial letter of surname of Ancel Keys (1904–2004), US physiologist + RATION *noun*.]
An issue of compressed or dehydrated food etc. for use in the absence of regular supplies, esp. as given to soldiers in the Second World War.

kratogen /ˈkratədʒ(ə)n, ˈkreɪt-/ *noun*. E20.
[ORIGIN from Greek *kratos* strength + -GEN.]
GEOLOGY. = CRATON.
■ **kratoˈgenic** *adjective* E20.

kraurosis /krɔːˈrəʊsɪs/ *noun*. Pl. **-roses** /-ˈrəʊsiːz/. L19.
[ORIGIN from Greek *krauros* brittle, dry + -OSIS.]
MEDICINE. Atrophy, *spec*. of the skin of the vulva.
■ **kraurotic** /-ˈrɒtɪk/ *adjective* affected with kraurosis L19.

kraut /kraʊt/ *noun*. M19.
[ORIGIN German = vegetable, cabbage. Cf. earlier SAUERKRAUT.]
1 Sauerkraut. M19.
2 (Usu. **K-**.) A German, *esp*. a German soldier. *slang*. *derog*. *offensive*. E20.

Krautrock /ˈkraʊtrɒk/ *noun*. L20.
[ORIGIN from KRAUT + ROCK *noun*[3].]
An experimental style of rock music associated with German groups of the 1970s, characterized by improvisation and strong, hypnotic rhythms.

Krav Maga /krɑːv ˈmɑːgə/ *noun*. L20.
[ORIGIN Hebrew, lit. 'contact combat'.]
A form of self-defence and physical training developed by the Israeli army.

kraw-kraw *noun* var. of CRAW-CRAW.

kray *noun* var. of KRAI.

Krebs cycle /ˈkrɛbz sʌɪk(ə)l/ *noun phr*. Also **Krebs' cycle**. M20.
[ORIGIN Sir Hans Adolf *Krebs* (1900–81), German-born Brit. biochemist.]
BIOCHEMISTRY. A cyclic sequence of enzyme-catalysed metabolic reactions which occur in mitochondria as part of aerobic cell respiration, in which oxaloacetic acid is acetylated, oxidized, and ultimately regenerated by a series of reactions in which ADP is converted to the energy-rich ATP. Also called ***tricarboxylic acid cycle***.

kreef /kriːf, krɪəf/ *noun*. *S. Afr*. Pl. same. M19.
[ORIGIN Afrikaans from Dutch *kreeft* lobster.]
A southern African crayfish or spiny lobster, *Jasus lalandii*.

kremlin /ˈkrɛmlɪn/ *noun*. M17.
[ORIGIN French from Russian *kreml'* citadel.]
A citadel or fortified enclosure within a Russian town or city, *esp*. (**K-**) that of Moscow; (**K-**) *the* government of the former USSR.
■ **Kremliˈnology** *noun* the study and analysis of Soviet policies M20. **Kremliˈnologist** *noun* a student or analyst of Soviet policies M20.

Kremnitz white *noun phr*. var. of CREMNITZ WHITE.

Krems white /krɛmz ˈwʌɪt/ *noun phr*. M19.
[ORIGIN from *Krems* a town of N. Austria + WHITE *noun*.]
A white lead pigment used as a paint base; Cremnitz white.

kreng /krɛŋ/ *noun*. Also **crang** /kraŋ/. E19.
[ORIGIN Dutch *kreng*, Middle Dutch *crenge* carrion, of unknown origin.]
WHALING. The carcass of a whale from which the blubber has been removed.

krennerite /ˈkrɛnərʌɪt/ *noun*. L19.
[ORIGIN from J. S. *Krenner* (1839–1920), Hungarian mineralogist + -ITE[1].]
MINERALOGY. A rare orthorhombic telluride of gold, usu. containing silver, and found in yellow or white prismatic crystals with a metallic lustre.

kreophagous *adjective* var. of CREOPHAGOUS.

kreplach /ˈkrɛplɑːx/ *noun pl.* L19.
[ORIGIN Yiddish *kreplech* pl. of *krepel* from dial. German *Kräppel* fritter, cogn. with KRAPFEN.]
Triangular noodles filled with chopped meat or cheese and served with soup.

kretek /ˈkrɛtɛk/ *noun*. M20.
[ORIGIN Indonesian *keretek*.]
An Indonesian (esp. Javanese) cigarette containing cloves.

kreutzer /ˈkrɔɪtsə/ *noun*. M16.
[ORIGIN German *Kreuzer*, from *Kreuz* CROSS *noun* after medieval Latin *denarius crucigerus* lit. 'cross-bearing penny': see -ER[1]. Cf. CRAZIA.]
A small silver or copper coin, originally stamped with a cross and formerly current in parts of Germany and in Austria.

kriegie /ˈkriːgi/ *noun*. *slang*. M20.
[ORIGIN Abbreviation of German *Kriegsgefangener* prisoner of war: see -IE.]
A prisoner of war, *esp.* an Allied prisoner of war in Germany during the Second World War.

kriegspiel /ˈkriːgspiːl/ *noun*. L19.
[ORIGIN German, from *Krieg* war + *Spiel* game.]
1 A war game in which blocks representing troops etc. are moved about on maps. L19.
2 A form of chess with an umpire and two players, in which each player plays at a separate board and has only limited information about the other's moves. L19.

krieker /ˈkriːkə/ *noun*. US. M19.
[ORIGIN German *Kriecher* creeper.]
The pectoral sandpiper, *Calidris melanotos*.

K

Krilium /ˈkrɪlɪəm/ *noun*. M20.
[ORIGIN from *kril-* alt. of *a)cryl(onitrile* + -IUM.]
(Proprietary name for) any of various mixtures of polyacrylate salts and other carboxylated polymers used to improve the texture of soil and its resistance to erosion.

krill /krɪl/ *noun*. Also **kril**. Pl. same. E20.
[ORIGIN Norwegian *kril* small fish fry.]
A small shrimplike planktonic crustacean of the order Euphausiacea, important as food for fish, and for some whales and seals. Chiefly as *collect. pl.*

krimmer /ˈkrɪmə/ *noun*. Also **c-**. M19.
[ORIGIN German, from *Krim* (Russian *Krym*) Crimea (see CRIMEAN): see -ER[1].]
The grey or black furry fleece of young lambs from the Crimean area; a cloth resembling this. Cf. ASTRAKHAN, KARAKUL.

Krio /ˈkriːəʊ/ *noun & adjective*. M20.
[ORIGIN Prob. alt. of CREOLE.]
(Of or pertaining to) an English-based creole language of Sierra Leone.

kris /kriːs/ *noun*. Pl. **kris(s)es**. Also **crease**, **creese**. L16.
[ORIGIN Malay *keris*, partly through Dutch *kris*, German *Kris*, Spanish, Portuguese *cris*, French *criss*, etc.]
A Malay or Indonesian dagger with a straight or wavy blade.

Krishnaism /ˈkrɪʃnəɪz(ə)m/ *noun*. L19.
[ORIGIN from Sanskrit *Kṛṣṇa* Krishna (see below) + -ISM.]
The worship of or belief in the Hindu god Krishna (an incarnation of Vishnu).

Kriss Kringle /krɪs ˈkrɪŋg(ə)l/ *noun*. US. Now *rare*. M19.
[ORIGIN Prob. alt. of German *Christkindl* Christmas present, (colloq.) Christ-child. Cf. CHRISTINGLE.]
Santa Claus.

kriti /ˈkrɪti/ *noun*. E20.
[ORIGIN Sanskrit *kṛti* a composition.]
In the music of the southern part of the Indian subcontinent, a song, often devotional in character, which is deliberately composed and not an improvisation on a set theme.

Kromayer lamp /ˈkrəʊmʌɪə lamp/ *noun phr.* E20.
[ORIGIN Ernst *Kromayer* (1862–1933), German dermatologist.]
MEDICINE. A water-cooled mercury vapour lamp used for local ultraviolet irradiation.

kromesky /krə(ʊ)ˈmɛski, ˈkrɒmɛski/ *noun*. M19.
[ORIGIN Polish *kromeczka* small slice.]
A croquette made of minced meat or fish rolled in bacon etc. and fried.

Kromo /ˈkrəʊməʊ/ *noun*. Also **Krama** /ˈkrɑːmə/. E19.
[ORIGIN Javanese *krama*, Indonesian *kromo*.]
In Indonesia: the polite form of Javanese, used by those of lower status when addressing social superiors. Cf. NGOKO.

krona /ˈkrəʊnə/ *noun*. Pl. **-nor** /-nə/. L19.
[ORIGIN Swedish = CROWN *noun*. Cf. KRÓNA, KRONE, KROON.]
The basic monetary unit of Sweden, equal to 100 öre.

króna /ˈkrəʊnə/ *noun*. Pl. **-nur** /-nə/. L19.
[ORIGIN Icelandic = CROWN *noun*. Cf. KRONA, KRONE, KROON.]
The basic monetary unit of Iceland, equal to 100 aurar.

krone /ˈkrəʊnə/ *noun*. Pl. in branch I **-ner** /-nə/, in branch II **-nen** /-nən/. L19.
[ORIGIN Danish & German = CROWN *noun*. Cf. KRONA, KRÓNA, KROON.]
▸**I 1** The basic monetary unit of Denmark and Norway, equal to 100 øre. L19.
▸**II** *hist.* **2** A gold coin of the German Empire worth ten marks. L19.
3 A silver coin of the Austrian Empire worth 100 hellers. L19.

kronen, **kroner** *nouns pl.* see KRONE.

kronor *noun* pl. of KRONA.

krónur *noun* pl. of KRÓNA.

kroon /kruːn/ *noun*. E20.
[ORIGIN Estonian = CROWN *noun*. Cf. KRONA, KRÓNA, KRONE.]
The basic monetary unit of Estonia.

†**kross** *noun* var. of KAROSS.

Kru /kruː/ *noun & adjective*. Also **Kroo**. Pl. of noun same. M19.
[ORIGIN W. African.]
Of or pertaining to, a member of, a people of the coast of Liberia; (of) the language of this people, or the group of languages including it.

krug /krʊg/ *noun*. M19.
[ORIGIN German.]
In Germany and German-speaking countries: a beer mug, a tankard.

Krugerism /ˈkruːgərɪz(ə)m/ *noun*. L19.
[ORIGIN from *Kruger* (see below) + -ISM.]
hist. The policy of Stephanus Johannes Paulus *Kruger* (1825–1904), who led the Afrikaners to victory in the First Boer War and served as President of the Transvaal from 1883 to 1899.
■ **Krugerite** *noun & adjective* (**a**) *noun* an adherent of Kruger or his policy; (**b**) *adjective* of or pertaining to Krugerism or Krugerites: L19.

krugerrand /ˈkruːgərand, -rɑːn, kruːgəˈrɑːnt/ *noun*. M20.
[ORIGIN formed as KRUGERISM + RAND *noun*[2].]
A South African gold coin bearing the image of President Kruger, valued as an investment.

Krukenberg tumour /ˈkrʊkənbəːg ˈtjuːmə/ *noun phr.* E20.
[ORIGIN Friedrich Ernst *Krukenberg* (1871–1946), German scientist.]
MEDICINE. A secondary ovarian carcinoma usu. associated with a primary growth in the stomach.

krummholz /ˈkrʌmhɒlts/ *noun*. E20.
[ORIGIN German = elfin-tree, lit. 'crooked wood'.]
= ***elfin-wood*** s.v. ELFIN *adjective*.

krummhorn /ˈkrʌmhɔːn, ˈkrʊm-/ *noun*. Also **crumhorn**. L17.
[ORIGIN German, from *krumm* crooked, curved + *Horn* HORN *noun*.]
MUSIC. **1** A medieval and Renaissance wind instrument with a double reed and a curved end. L17.
2 An organ reed stop, usu. of 8-ft pitch, suggestive of a krummhorn or clarinet in tone; = CREMONA *noun*[1], CROMORNE. L19.

Krupp /krʌp/ *noun*. L19.
[ORIGIN Alfred *Krupp* (1812–87), German metallurgist, founder of a steel and armament works at Essen in Germany.]
A gun made at a Krupp factory in Germany.

kryo- *combining form* see CRYO-.

krypton /ˈkrɪptɒn/ *noun*. L19.
[ORIGIN Greek *krupton* neut. of *kruptos* hidden, concealed.]
A colourless odourless gaseous chemical element, atomic no. 36, which is one of the noble gases, occurring as a trace constituent of the earth's atmosphere and used in lasers and other optical devices (symbol Kr).

krytron /ˈkrʌɪtrɒn/ *noun*. L20.
[ORIGIN from obscure 1st elem. + -TRON.]
ELECTRONICS. A high-speed solid-state switching device which is triggered by a pulse of coherent light.

KS *abbreviation*.
1 Kansas.
2 King's Scholar.

Kshatriya /ˈkʃatrɪə/ *noun*. L18.
[ORIGIN Sanskrit *kṣatriya*, from *kṣatra* rule.]
A member of the second of the four main Hindu castes. Cf. KHATRI.

K. St J. *abbreviation*.
Knight (of the Order) of St John.

KT *abbreviation*[1].
1 Knight (of the Order) of the Thistle.
2 Knight Templar.

Kt *abbreviation*[2].
Knight.

kt *abbreviation*[3].
NAUTICAL. Knot(s).

K/T *abbreviation*.
GEOLOGY. Cretaceous/Tertiary.

Ku *symbol*.
CHEMISTRY. Kurchatovium.

Kuan /kwɑːn/ *noun*. E19.
[ORIGIN Chinese *guān* (Wade–Giles *kuān*) an official.]
1 ***Kuan Hua*** /hwɑː/ [*huà* speech], = MANDARIN *noun*[1] 2. E19.
2 ***Kuan Yin*** /jɪn/, a goddess of Chinese Buddhism, to whom intercession for aid or protection is made; a representation of this goddess. M19.
3 In full ***Kuan ware***, ***Kuan yao*** /jaʊ/ [*yáo* pottery]. A type of thickly glazed celadon made in predominantly greyish colours at Hangchow during the Song dynasty; pottery resembling this produced elsewhere in China. L19.

Kuba /kuːˈbɑː/ *noun & adjective*. E20.
[ORIGIN A town in NE Azerbaijan.]
= KABISTAN.

Ku-band /ˈkɛɪjuːband/ *noun*. L20.
[ORIGIN from *Ku* (arbitrary serial designation) + BAND *noun*[2].]
TELECOMMUNICATIONS. A microwave frequency band used for satellite communication and broadcasting, using frequencies of about 12 gigahertz for terrestrial reception and 14 gigahertz for transmission.

kubong /ˈkuːbɒŋ/ *noun*. E19.
[ORIGIN Malay.]
A flying lemur.

kuccha *noun* var. of KACCHA.

Kuchaean /kʊˈtʃiːən/ *noun & adjective*. Also **Kuchean**. M20.
[ORIGIN French *koutchéen*, from *Kucha* a town in Xinjiang (Sinkiang), China: see -AN, -EAN.]
(Of) the western dialect of Tocharian, Tocharian B.

Kuchen /ˈkuːxən/ *noun*. Pl. same. M19.
[ORIGIN German = cake.]
In Germany or among German- or Yiddish-speaking people: a cake; *esp.* a cake taken with coffee.

kudos /ˈkjuːdɒs/ *noun*. L18.
[ORIGIN Greek = praise, renown.]
Glory, fame, renown.

J. COLVILLE British troops are getting hardly any kudos. R. FRAME The kudos of Cambridge and a double first didn't cancel out Surbiton.

— NOTE: Sometimes incorrectly taken to be a pl. form, with a sing. form *kudo*.

kudu /ˈkuːduː, ˈkʊdʊ/ *noun*. Also **koodoo**. Pl. **-s**, same. L18.
[ORIGIN Afrikaans *koedoe* from Xhosa *i-qudu*.]
Either of two large white-striped greyish-brown African antelopes with spiral horns, *Tragelaphus strepsiceros* (more fully ***greater kudu***), of sub-Saharan savannah and *T. imberbis* (more fully ***lesser kudu***), of E. Africa and Arabia.

kudzu /ˈkʊdzuː/ *noun*. L19.
[ORIGIN Japanese *kuzu*.]
In full ***kudzu vine***. A climbing leguminous plant, *Pueraria lobata*, of China and Japan, cultivated elsewhere for fodder, as an ornamental, and to prevent soil erosion.

kuei /ˈkuːeɪ/ *noun*. M20.
[ORIGIN Chinese *guī* (Wade–Giles *kuei*).]
A bronze Chinese food vessel, usu. with two handles and often surmounted by animal heads.

Kufic /ˈkjuːfɪk/ *adjective*. Also **C-**. E18.
[ORIGIN from *Kufa* (see below, Arabic *al-Kūfa*) + -IC.]
Of or pertaining to the ancient city of Kufa south of Baghdad; *spec.* designating an early form of Arabic script freq. found in inscriptions and attributed to the scholars of Kufa.

kufiyeh *noun* var. of KEFFIYEH.

kuge /ˈkuːgə/ *noun*. Also **-é**. Pl. same. L16.
[ORIGIN Japanese.]
In feudal Japan: the nobility attached to the imperial court at Kyoto; a court noble.

kugel /ˈkuːg(ə)l/ *noun*. M19.
[ORIGIN Yiddish = ball, from Middle High German *kugel(e)* ball, globe.]
In Jewish cookery: a kind of pudding; *esp.* a savoury pudding, usu. of potatoes or other vegetables, served as a separate course or as a side dish.

Kugelhupf *noun* var. of GUGELHUPF.

kuia /ˈkuːɪə/ *noun*. NZ. Pl. same. L19.
[ORIGIN Maori.]
An elderly Maori woman. Freq. as a form of address.

Kuiper belt /ˈkʌɪpə bɛlt/ *noun phr.* L20.
[ORIGIN Gerard P. *Kuiper* (1905–73), Dutch-born US astronomer.]
ASTRONOMY. A region of the solar system beyond the orbit of Neptune, believed to contain many comets, asteroids, and other small bodies made largely of ice.

Kuki /ˈkuːki/ *noun*[1] *& adjective*. L18.
[ORIGIN Prob. from a Sino-Tibetan lang.]
▸**A** *noun*. Pl. **-s**, same. A member of any of several peoples inhabiting the hills of Manipur and Mizoram, on the border of India and Myanmar (Burma); the language of these peoples. L18.

▸ **B** *attrib.* or as *adjective*. Of or pertaining to the Kukis or their language. **E19.**

kuki /ˈkuːki/ *noun*[2]. **M19.**
[**ORIGIN** Maori from **COOK** *noun*.]
NZ HISTORY. A slave of a Maori chieftain.

Ku Klux /ˈkuːklʌks, ˈkjuː-/ *noun*. **M19.**
[**ORIGIN** Abbreviation.]
1 A member of the Ku Klux Klan. **M19.**
2 The Ku Klux Klan. **L19.**
■ **Ku Kluxism** *noun* **L19.**

Ku Klux Klan /kuːklʌksˈklan, kjuː-/ *noun*. **M19.**
[**ORIGIN** Perh. from Greek *kuklos* circle + alt. of **CLAN** *noun*.]
1 An American secret society of white people, founded in the Southern states after the Civil War of 1861–5 to defend the southern way of life, which developed into an organization to intimidate black people through terrorism and murder. **M19.**
2 A group held to resemble the Ku Klux Klan. **M20.**
– **COMB.:** **Ku Klux Klansman** a member of the Ku Klux Klan.
– **NOTE:** Although the original Ku Klux Klan was outlawed by the American Congress in 1871, a similar organization still exists.
■ **Ku Klux Klanner** *noun* a member of the Ku Klux Klan **E20.**

kukri /ˈkʊkri/ *noun*. **E19.**
[**ORIGIN** Nepali *khukuri*.]
A curved knife broadening towards the point and usu. with the sharp edge on the concave side, used by Gurkhas.

kuku /ˈkuːkuː/ *noun*. *NZ*. **M19.**
[**ORIGIN** Maori. Cf. **KUKUPA**.]
= **KERERU**.

kukui /kʊˈkuːi/ *noun*. **E19.**
[**ORIGIN** Hawaiian.]
An evergreen tree, *Aleurites moluccana*, of the spurge family, native to the Moluccas and S. Pacific islands, with large seeds which yield an oil used for lighting and other purposes. Also called ***candleberry***, ***candlenut***.

kukumakranka /ˌkʊkʊməˈkraŋkə/ *noun*. **L18.**
[**ORIGIN** Nama.]
Any of various small bulbous plants of the southern African genus *Gethyllis*, of the daffodil family, bearing fragrant white flowers; the fragrant underground fruit of this, used to scent rooms or to flavour brandy for medicinal use.

kukupa /ˈkuːkuːpə/ *noun*. *NZ*. **M19.**
[**ORIGIN** Maori. Cf. **KUKU**.]
= **KERERU**.

kula /ˈkuːlə/ *noun*. **E20.**
[**ORIGIN** Melanesian.]
In some Pacific communities, esp. in the Trobriand Islands: an inter-island system of ceremonial exchange of items as a prelude to or concomitant of regular trading.

Kulah /ˈkuːlə/ *noun*[1] & *adjective*. **L19.**
[**ORIGIN** A town in western Turkey.]
(Designating) a type of Turkish rug of a large size with a long loose pile.

kulah /ˈkuːlə/ *noun*[2]. **E20.**
[**ORIGIN** Persian *kulāh* cap.]
A conical cap of felt or lambskin worn by Muslims in the Middle East.

kulak /ˈkuːlak/ *noun*. **L19.**
[**ORIGIN** Russian, lit. 'fist, tight-fisted person' from Turkic *kol* hand.]
Orig., a well-to-do Russian farmer or trader. Later, a peasant proprietor working for his own profit in the Soviet Union.

kulan /ˈkuːlən/ *noun*. Also (earlier) **koulan**. **L18.**
[**ORIGIN** Turkic.]
A wild ass, *Equus hemionus*, of a subspecies native to the central Asian steppes. Cf. **KIANG**, **ONAGER**.

kulchur /ˈkʌltʃə/ *noun*. *joc.* or *derog.* **M20.**
[**ORIGIN** Repr. pronunc.]
= **CULTURE** *noun* II.

Kulin /kʊˈliːn/ *noun* & *adjective*. **M19.**
[**ORIGIN** Sanskrit *kulīna* well-born, from *kula* family.]
In the NE of the Indian subcontinent: (designating) a brahmin of the highest class.
■ **Kulinism** *noun* (chiefly *hist.*) polygamy as practised by Kulins **L19.**

Kullah /kəˈlɑː/ *noun*. **E19.**
[**ORIGIN** Pegu *Goḷa* Indian Buddhist immigrant from Sanskrit *Gauḍa* ancient name of part of the NE of the Indian subcontinent.]
In Myanmar (Burma): a foreigner, now *esp.* a European.

Kultur /kʊlˈtuːr/ *noun*. **E20.**
[**ORIGIN** German, from Latin *cultura* or French *culture* **CULTURE** *noun*.]
German civilization and culture, esp. (*derog.*) seen as racialist, authoritarian, and militaristic.
– **COMB.:** ***Kulturgeschichte*** /-gəʃɪçtə/ [*Geschichte* history] the history of the cultural development of a country etc.; history of civilization; ***Kulturkampf*** /-kampf/ [*Kampf* struggle] the conflict in 19th-cent. Germany between the civil and ecclesiastical authorities for the control of schools and Church appointments; ***Kulturkreis*** /-kraɪs/, pl. ***-se*** /-zə/, [*Kreis* sphere] a cultural group; a cultural complex; ***Kulturstaat*** /-ʃtaːt/, pl. ***-en*** /-ən/, [*Staat* State] a civilized country; ***Kulturträger*** /-trɛːgər/, pl. same, [*Träger* carrier] an agent of cultural transmission.

kulturny /kʊljˈturnɪj, kʊlˈtəːni/ *adjective*. **M20.**
[**ORIGIN** Russian *kul'turnyĭ*, from *kul'tura* from Latin *cultura* or French *culture* **CULTURE** *noun*.]
In countries of the former USSR: cultured, civilized; good mannered, well behaved. Cf. **NEKULTURNY**.

Kuman *noun* & *adjective* var. of **CUMAN**.

kumara /ˈkuːmərə/ *noun*. *NZ*. Also **-era**. **L18.**
[**ORIGIN** Maori.]
The sweet potato, *Ipomoea batatas*.

Kumbh Mela /kʊm ˈmeɪlɑː/ *noun phr.* **M19.**
[**ORIGIN** Sanskrit, from *kumbh* pitcher (the name given to the sign Aquarius of the zodiac) + *mela* assembly.]
A Hindu festival and assembly which is held once every twelve years (in January or February, whilst the sun is in Aquarius) at four locations in India and at which pilgrims bathe in the waters of the Ganges and Jumna Rivers.

kumbuk /ˈkʌmbʌk, ˈkʊmbʊk/ *noun*. **M19.**
[**ORIGIN** Sinhalese.]
An evergreen tree of southern India and Sri Lanka, *Terminalia arjuna* (family Combretaceae); the wood of this tree.

kumera *noun* var. of **KUMARA**.

kumis, **kumiss** *nouns* vars. of **KOUMISS**.

kumite /ˈkuːmɪteɪ/ *noun*. **L20.**
[**ORIGIN** Japanese, lit. 'sparring'.]
In martial arts: freestyle fighting.

kumkum /ˈkʊmkʊm/ *noun*. **M20.**
[**ORIGIN** Sanskrit *kuṅkuma* saffron.]
A red powder used ceremonially, esp. by Hindu women to make a small distinctive mark on the forehead; the mark so made.

kümmel /ˈkʊm(ə)l/ *noun*. **M19.**
[**ORIGIN** German, repr. Middle High German, Old High German *kumil* var. of *kumīn* **CUMIN**.]
A sweet liqueur flavoured with caraway and cumin seeds.

kumpit /ˈkʊmpɪt/ *noun*. **M20.**
[**ORIGIN** Prob. from Maranao *kompit*.]
A trading vessel of the Philippines.

kumquat /ˈkʌmkwɒt/ *noun*. Also **c-**. **L17.**
[**ORIGIN** Chinese (Cantonese) *kam kwat* lit. 'gold orange'.]
1 A small citrus fruit, like a miniature orange, from any of several Far Eastern trees of the genus *Fortunella*, esp. *F. japonica* and *F. margarita*; the tree producing this, cultivated in China and Japan. **L17.**
2 More fully ***native kumquat***. A citrus tree of NE Australia, *Eremocitrus glauca*; the plum-sized acid fruit of this. *Austral.* **L19.**

kumri /ˈkʊmri/ *noun*. **L19.**
[**ORIGIN** Kannada *kumari*.]
A system of shifting cultivation practised in Karnataka, in SW India. Also called ***podu***.

Kumyk /ˈkuːmɪk/ *noun* & *adjective*. **L18.**
[**ORIGIN** See below.]
▸ **A** *noun*. Pl. same, **-s**.
1 A member of a Turkic people of the Kumyk plateau in the Caucasus. **L18.**
2 The language of this people. **L20.**
▸ **B** *attrib.* or as *adjective*. Of or pertaining to the Kumyk or their language. **M20.**

Kuna /ˈkuːnə/ *noun*[1] & *adjective*. Also **C-**. **M19.**
[**ORIGIN** Kuna.]
▸ **A** *noun*. Pl. **-s**, same.
1 A member of an American Indian people of the isthmus of Panama. **M19.**
2 The Chibchan language of this people. **E20.**
▸ **B** *attrib.* or as *adjective*. Of or pertaining to the Kuna or their language. **M19.**

kuna /ˈkuːnə/ *noun*[2]. Pl. **kune**, **kunas**. **L20.**
[**ORIGIN** Croatian, lit. 'marten' (marten furs being formerly used as a medium of exchange).]
The basic monetary unit of Croatia, equal to 100 lipa.

kunai /ˈkuːnʌɪ/ *noun*. *Austral.* **M20.**
[**ORIGIN** Name in New Guinea.]
Lalang grass, *Imperata cylindrica*.

kunbi /ˈkuːnbi/ *noun*. **L16.**
[**ORIGIN** Marathi *kuṇbī*, *kuḷambī*, Hindi *kurmī*, from Sanskrit *kuṭumbin*.]
A member of a Hindu agricultural caste.

kundalini /ˈkʊndəlɪniː/ *noun*. **L19.**
[**ORIGIN** Sanskrit *kuṇḍalinī* lit. 'snake'.]
YOGA. **1** The latent (female) energy which lies coiled at the base of the spine. **L19.**
2 In full ***kundalini yoga***. A type of meditation which aims to direct and release this energy. **M20.**

kune *noun* pl. of **KUNA** *noun*[2].

kung fu /kʊŋˈfuː, kʌŋ-/ *noun*. **L19.**
[**ORIGIN** Chinese *gongfu* (Wade–Giles *kung fu*), from *gong* (*kung*) merit + *fu* master.]
The Chinese form of karate.

kungu /ˈkʌŋguː/ *noun*. **M19.**
[**ORIGIN** Nyanja *nkungu*.]
In full ***kungu fly***. Any of various dipteran flies whose larvae live in E. African lakes, above which the flies can form large swarms.
– **COMB.:** **kungu cake** a kind of cake made from the bodies of large numbers of these gnats compressed together.

kunkur /ˈkʌŋkə/ *noun*. Also **-ker**, **kankar**. **L18.**
[**ORIGIN** Hindi *kaṅkar* from Sanskrit *karkara*.]
In the Indian subcontinent: a coarse, often nodular, limestone used to make lime and in road-building.

Kunstforscher /ˈkʊnstfɔrʃər/ *noun*. Pl. same. **L19.**
[**ORIGIN** German, from *Kunst* art + *Forscher* researcher.]
An art historian.

Kunstgeschichte /ˈkʊnstgəˌʃɪçtə/ *noun*. **L19.**
[**ORIGIN** German, from *Kunst* art + *Geschichte* history.]
The history of art, art history.

Kunsthistoriker /ˈkʊnsthɪsˌtoːrikər/ *noun*. Pl. same. **M20.**
[**ORIGIN** German, from *Kunst* art + *Historiker* historian.]
An art historian.

Künstlerroman /ˈkynstlərоˌmaːn/ *noun*. Pl. ***-e*** /-ə/. **M20.**
[**ORIGIN** German, from *Künstler* artist + *Roman* novel.]
A *Bildungsroman* about an artist.

Kunstprosa /ˈkʊnstproːza/ *noun*. **M20.**
[**ORIGIN** German, from *Kunst* art + *Prosa* prose.]
Literary prose, ornate and stylized prose.

kunzite /ˈkʌntsʌɪt, ˈkʌnzʌɪt/ *noun*. **E20.**
[**ORIGIN** from George F. *Kunz* (1856–1932), US gemmologist + **-ITE**[1].]
MINERALOGY. A lilac-coloured gem variety of spodumene which fluoresces or changes colour when irradiated.

Kuomintang /kwəʊmɪnˈtaŋ, gwəʊ-/ *noun*. Also **Guomindang** /gwəʊmɪnˈdaŋ/. **E20.**
[**ORIGIN** Chinese *guómíndǎng* (Wade–Giles *kuo min tang*) national people's party, from *guó* nation + *mín* people + *dǎng* party.]
A Chinese nationalist radical party founded in 1912, holding power from 1928 until succeeded by the Communist Party in 1949, and subsequently forming the central administration of Taiwan.

K

Kuo-yu /ˈkwəʊjuː/ *noun*. **M20.**
[**ORIGIN** Chinese = national language, from *guó* (Wade–Giles *kuo*) nation + *yu* language.]
A form of Mandarin, the predecessor of modern standard Chinese, adopted for official use.

kupfernickel /ˈkʊpfənɪk(ə)l/ *noun*. **L18.**
[**ORIGIN** German, from *Kupfer* **COPPER** *noun*[1] + *Nickel*: see **NICKEL** *noun*.]
MINERALOGY. = **NICCOLITE**.

Kupferschiefer /ˈkʊpfəʃiːfə/ *noun*. **M19.**
[**ORIGIN** German, from *Kupfer* **COPPER** *noun*[1] + *Schiefer* shale, slate.]
GEOLOGY. (A stratum of) a bituminous brown or black copper-bearing shale of the Permian series.

Kupffer cell /ˈkʊpfə sɛl/ *noun phr.* Also **Kupffer's cell** /ˈkʊpfəz/. **E20.**
[**ORIGIN** Karl Wilhelm von *Kupffer* (1829–1902), Bavarian anatomist.]
ANATOMY. Each of the phagocytic cells which line the sinusoids of the liver and are involved in the breakdown of red blood cells. Usu. in *pl.*

†**kuphar** *noun* var. of **GUFA**.

Kur /kuːr/ *noun*. Pl. ***-ren*** /-rən/. **L19.**
[**ORIGIN** German = a cure.]
A cure, a medicinal drinking of the waters at a spa in Germany or a German-speaking country; a spa.

kura /ˈkʊrə/ *noun*. **L19.**
[**ORIGIN** Japanese.]
In Japan: a fireproof storehouse.

kurakkan /ˈkʊrəkɑːn/ *noun*. **L17.**
[**ORIGIN** Sinhalese.]
In Sri Lanka: the finger millet or ragi, *Eleusine coracana*, used to make flour which forms a staple food of poorer villagers.

kurbash /ˈkʊəbaʃ/ *noun* & *verb*. Also **kour-**. **E19.**
[**ORIGIN** Arabic *kurbāj*, *kirbāj* from Turkish *kırbaç* whip.]
▸ **A** *noun*. A whip of (esp. hippopotamus) hide formerly used as an instrument of punishment in Turkey and Egypt. **E19.**
▸ **B** *verb trans.* Flog with a kurbash. **M19.**

kurchatovium /kəːtʃəˈtəʊvɪəm/ *noun*. **M20.**
[**ORIGIN** from I. V. *Kurchatov* (1903–60), Russian nuclear physicist + **-IUM**.]
(A name proposed for) a very unstable radioactive transuranic chemical element, atomic no. 104, produced artificially (symbol Ku). Cf. **RUTHERFORDIUM**.

Kurd /kəːd/ *noun*. **E17.**
[**ORIGIN** Kurdish.]
A member of a mainly pastoral Islamic people living in Kurdistan, a region in contiguous areas of Turkey, Iraq, Iran, and Syria.

kurdaitcha *noun* var. of **KADAITCHA**.

Kurdish /ˈkəːdɪʃ/ *noun & adjective*. E19.
[ORIGIN from KURD + -ISH[1].]
▸ **A** *noun*. The Iranian language of the Kurds. E19.
▸ **B** *adjective*. Of or pertaining to the Kurds or their language. M19.

Kurdistan /kəːdɪˈstɑːn/ *noun*. M20.
[ORIGIN See KURD.]
More fully ***Kurdistan rug***. A rug with a geometric design, handwoven in Kurdistan.

Kuren *noun* pl. of KUR.

kurgan /kʊəˈgɑːn/ *noun*. L19.
[ORIGIN Russian, of Turkic origin: cf. Turkish *kurgan* castle, fortress.]
A prehistoric sepulchral tumulus or barrow such as is found in Siberia and central Asia.

Kurhaus /ˈkuːrhaʊs/ *noun*. Pl. ***-häuser*** /-hɔyzər/. M19.
[ORIGIN German, formed as KUR + *Haus* HOUSE *noun*[1].]
In Germany and German-speaking countries: a building at a health resort where medicinal water is dispensed; a pump room.

kuri /ˈkʊri/ *noun*. NZ. M19.
[ORIGIN Maori = dog.]
= ***MAORI dog***. Also, a mongrel; *slang* an unpleasant or disliked person.

Kuril /kʊˈriːl/ *noun & adjective*. Also **-ile**. M18.
[ORIGIN Russian.]
▸ **A** *noun*. An Ainu. Now *rare*. M18.
▸ **B** *attrib*. or as *adjective*. Of or pertaining to the Ainu. Chiefly *spec*. designating or pertaining to a chain of small islands stretching northwards from Japan to the Kamchatka peninsula. E19.
■ **Kuˈrilian** *noun & adjective* M19.

Kurnai *noun & adjective* var. of GANAY.

Kurort /ˈkuːrɔrt/ *noun*. Pl. ***-e*** /-ə/. M19.
[ORIGIN German, formed as KUR + *Ort* place.]
In Germany and German-speaking countries: a health resort, a spa, a watering place.

Kuroshio /kʊrə(ʊ)ˈʃiːəʊ/ *noun*. Also **-siwo** /-ˈsiːwəʊ/ & other vars. L19.
[ORIGIN Japanese, from *kuro* black + *shio* tide.]
Usu. with *the*: (the name of) a warm ocean current flowing north-eastwards past Japan. Also called ***Japan current***, ***Japanese current***.

kurper /ˈkəːpə/ *noun*. *S. Afr.* M19.
[ORIGIN Afrikaans from Dutch *karper* carp.]
Any of various carplike freshwater fishes, esp. of the genera *Sandelia* and *Tilapia*.

kurrajong /ˈkʌrədʒɒŋ/ *noun*. *Austral*. Also **c-**. E19.
[ORIGIN Dharuk *garrajung*.]
Any of various Australian trees with tough bark which yields a fibre, *esp*. (more fully ***black kurrajong***), *Brachychiton populneus*.

Kurrichane thrush /kʌrɪˈtʃaneɪ θrʌʃ/ *noun phr*. E20.
[ORIGIN *Kurrichane*, a place in Transvaal, South Africa.]
A thrush, *Turdus libonyanus*, of central and southern Africa.

Kursaal /ˈkuːrzaːl, ˈkʊəsɑːl/ *noun*. Pl. ***-säle*** /-zɛːlə/, ***-saals*** /-sɑːlz/. M19.
[ORIGIN German, formed as KUR + *Saal* hall, room.]
Esp. in Germany and German-speaking countries: a public building at a health resort, provided for the use and entertainment of visitors.

kurta /ˈkəːtə/ *noun*. E20.
[ORIGIN Urdu & Persian *kurtah*.]
A loose shirt or tunic worn esp. by Hindu men and women.

kurtosis /kəːˈtəʊsɪs/ *noun*. E20.
[ORIGIN Greek *kurtōsis* a bulging, convexity, from *kurtos* bulging, convex: see -OSIS.]
STATISTICS. The degree of sharpness of the peak of a frequency-distribution curve, *spec*. as measured by the quantity μ_4/μ_2^2 or its excess over 3 (μ_4 and μ_2 being the fourth and the second moments about the mean of the distribution).

kuru /ˈkʊruː/ *noun*. M20.
[ORIGIN Name in New Guinea.]
MEDICINE. A fatal viral brain disease found among certain peoples of New Guinea.

Kurukh /ˈkʊrʊk/ *noun & adjective*. L19.
[ORIGIN Kurukh.]
▸ **A** *noun*. Pl. same, **-s**.
1 A member of an aboriginal people of the northern Indian subcontinent, now esp. of the state of Bihar. Also called ***Oraon***. L19.
2 The Dravidian language of this people. E20.
▸ **B** *attrib*. or as *adjective*. Of or pertaining to the Kurukh or their language. E20.

kuruma /kʊˈruːmə/ *noun*. E18.
[ORIGIN Japanese.]
Orig., a type of Japanese covered carriage drawn by two oxen. Later, a Japanese rickshaw.
■ **kurumaya** /kʊruːˈmɑːjə/ *noun* a person who pulls a kuruma L19.

Kurume /kʊˈruːmeɪ/ *noun*. E20.
[ORIGIN A town on the Japanese island of Kyushu, where the azalea was first developed.]
In full ***Kurume azalea***. Any of a group of small evergreen azalea hybrids, chiefly derived from the Japanese *Rhododendron kiusianum* and *R. kaempferi*.

kurus /kəˈruːʃ/ *noun*. Also †**grouch**. Pl. same. L19.
[ORIGIN Turkish *kuruş* from German GROSCHEN.]
A monetary unit of Turkey, equal to one-hundredth of a Turkish lira.

kurvey /kəːˈveɪ/ *verb intrans*. *S. Afr.* L19.
[ORIGIN from Dutch *karwei* hard work, big job from Middle Dutch *corweie* from French CORVÉE.]
Carry goods in an ox wagon.

kurveyor /kəːˈveɪə/ *noun*. *S. Afr.* L19.
[ORIGIN Dutch *karweier*, formed as KURVEY: see -ER[1], -OR.]
A travelling trader, a carrier.

Kushan /ˈkʊʃɑːn, kʊˈʃɑːn/ *noun & adjective*. Also **Kushana** /kʊˈʃɑːnə/. L19.
[ORIGIN Prakrit *kuṣāna* adjective from Iranian.]
▸ **A** *noun*. Pl. **-s**, same. A member of an Iranian dynasty who invaded the Indian subcontinent and established a powerful empire in the north-west between the 1st and 3rd cents. AD. L19.
▸ **B** *attrib*. or as *adjective*. Of or pertaining to this people, esp. their dynasty. L19.

Kushite *noun & adjective* var. of CUSHITE.

Kushitic *noun & adjective* var. of CUSHITIC.

kusimanse /kuːsɪˈmansi/ *noun*. Also **c-**. M19.
[ORIGIN App. from a W. African lang.]
A small dark-brown burrowing long-nosed mongoose, *Crossarchus obscurus*, of W. African forests.

kusti /ˈkʊstiː/ *noun*. M19.
[ORIGIN Persian *kustī* girdle, cincture, Gujarati *kusti*, *kasti*.]
A cord worn round the waist by Parsees, consisting of seventy-two threads to represent the chapters of one of the portions of the Zend-Avesta.

kuta /ˈkuːtə/ *noun*. M20.
[ORIGIN Setswana.]
= KGOTLA.

Kutani /kʊˈtɑːni/ *noun*. L19.
[ORIGIN The village of *Kutani-mura* in the former province of Kaga, Japan.]
In full ***Kutani ware***. A kind of gold and dark red Japanese porcelain.

kutcha /ˈkʌtʃə/ *adjective & noun*. Also **c-**, **kacha**. E19.
[ORIGIN Hindi *kaccā* raw, crude, uncooked.]
▸ **A** *adjective*. In the Indian subcontinent: slight, makeshift, unfinished; built of dried mud. E19.
▸ **B** *noun*. Dried mud used as a building material in the Indian subcontinent. M19.

kuteera *noun* var. of KUTIRA.

Kutenai /ˈkuːtəneɪ, -ni/ *noun & adjective*. Also **-ay** & other vars. E19.
[ORIGIN Blackfoot *Kotonáai-*.]
▸ **A** *noun*. Pl. **-s**, same. A member of a N. American Indian people of the Rocky Mountains; the language of this people. E19.
▸ **B** *attrib*. or as *adjective*. Of or pertaining to the Kutenais or their language. L19.

kutira /kəˈtɪərə/ *noun*. Also **kuteera**. M19.
[ORIGIN Hindi *katīrā*.]
In full ***kutira gum***. A gum obtained from an Indian shrub, *Cochlospermum religiosum* (family Bixaceae), used as a substitute for tragacanth. Also, a gum from several trees of the genus *Sterculia* (family Sterculiaceae).

kutnahorite /kʊtnəˈhɔːrʌɪt/ *noun*. Also **kutno-**. E20.
[ORIGIN German *Kutnohorit*, from *Kutná Hora* a town in Bohemia: see -ITE[1].]
MINERALOGY. A rare hexagonal carbonate of calcium and manganese, also containing magnesium and iron, usu. occurring as pink rhombohedra.

kuttar /kʌˈtɑː/ *noun*. L17.
[ORIGIN Sanskrit *kaṭṭāra*.]
In the Indian subcontinent: a short dagger with a handle of two parallel bars, joined by a crosspiece forming the part grasped by the hand.

Kuvasz /ˈkuːvaʃ, -s/ *noun*. Pl. **-ok** /-ɒk/, **-es** /-ɪz/. M20.
[ORIGIN Hungarian from Turkish *kavas* guard: see KAVASS.]
A breed of large white long-coated dog, orig. from Hungary, used as a guard dog; a dog of this breed.

Kuwaiti /kʊˈweɪti/ *noun & adjective*. E20.
[ORIGIN Arabic *kuwaytī*, from *al-Kuwayt* Kuwait (see below): see -I[2].]
▸ **A** *noun*. **1** A native or inhabitant of Kuwait, an Arab sheikhdom on the north-west coast of the Persian Gulf. E20.
2 The dialect of Arabic spoken in Kuwait. M20.
▸ **B** *adjective*. Of or pertaining to Kuwait or the Kuwaitis. M20.

kuzushi /kʊˈzʊʃi/ *noun*. M20.
[ORIGIN Japanese, from *kuzusu* destroy, pull down.]
JUDO. The fact or state of being unbalanced by one's opponent; a loss of the initiative.

kV *abbreviation*.
Kilovolt(s).

kVa *abbreviation*.
Kilovolt-ampere(s).

kvass /kvɑːs/ *noun*. Also **kvas**, **quass**. M16.
[ORIGIN Russian *kvas*.]
In Russia and some countries to the west: a fermented drink, low in alcohol, made from rye flour or bread with malt; rye beer.

kvell /kvɛl/ *verb intrans*. *US slang*. M20.
[ORIGIN Yiddish *kveln* from German *quellen* gush, well up.]
Boast; feel proud or happy; gloat.

> T. CLANCY Everyone he'd just pointed to *kvelled* a little at being singled out for the cameras.

kvetch /kvɛtʃ/ *noun & verb*. *N. Amer. slang*. M20.
[ORIGIN As noun from Yiddish *kvetsh*, as verb from Yiddish *kvetshn*, from German *Quetsche* crusher, presser, *quetschen*, crush, press.]
▸ **A** *noun*. An objectionable person; *spec*. someone who complains a great deal, a fault-finder. M20.
▸ **B** *verb intrans*. Complain, whine. Chiefly as ***kvetching*** *verbal noun*. M20.

> N. COHN My friends . . would not stop kvetching until I gave it a shot.

■ **kvetcher** *noun* M20.

kvutza /ˈkvʊtsɑː, kvʊtˈsɑː/ *noun*. E20.
[ORIGIN mod. Hebrew *qĕbhūṣāh* from Hebrew = group.]
In Israel: a communal and cooperative settlement, which, with others, may form a kibbutz.

kW *abbreviation*.
Kilowatt(s).

Kwa /kwɑː/ *noun & adjective*. Also (now *rare*) **Qua**. M19.
[ORIGIN Kwa.]
▸ **A** *noun*. Pl. same. The group of related languages, spoken from Ivory Coast to Nigeria, which includes Akan, Ewe, Igbo, and Yoruba. Also (*rare*), a member of a Kwa-speaking people. M19.
▸ **B** *attrib*. or as *adjective*. Of or pertaining to this group of languages. E20.

KWAC /kwak/ *abbreviation*.
Keyword and context.

kwacha /ˈkwɑːtʃə/ *noun*. Pl. same, **-s**. M20.
[ORIGIN Bantu = dawn.]
1 The dawn: used as a Zambian nationalist slogan. M20.
2 The basic monetary unit of Zambia and Malawi, equal to 100 ngwee in Zambia, 100 tambala in Malawi. M20.

kwai-lo /ˈkwʌɪləʊ/ *noun*. *derog*. M20.
[ORIGIN Chinese (Cantonese) (*faan*) *kwai ló* lit. '(foreign) devil fellow': cf. FOREIGN *devil*.]
In China, a foreigner, *esp*. a European.

kwaito /ˈkwʌɪtəʊ/ *noun*. *S. Afr.* L20.
[ORIGIN Either from the *Amakwaito*, a group of 1950s township gangsters, or from Afrikaans *kwaai* angry, vicious, (slang) excellent.]
A style of South African popular music similar to hip hop.

Kwakiutl /ˈkwɑːkjʊt(ə)l/ *noun & adjective*. M19.
[ORIGIN Kwakiutl *Kʷágut*.]
▸ **A** *noun*. Pl. same, **-s**.
1 A member of a N. American Indian people of the north-western coast. M19.
2 The language of this people. L19.
▸ **B** *attrib*. or as *adjective*. Of or pertaining to the Kwakiutl or their language. L19.

kwanga /ˈkwaŋgə/ *noun*. E20.
[ORIGIN Bantu.]
In the Congo (Zaire): a kind of bread made of manioc.

kwanza /ˈkwanzə/ *noun*. Pl. same, **-s**. L20.
[ORIGIN Perh. from Kiswahili = first.]
The basic monetary unit of Angola, equal to 100 lweis.

Kwanzaa /ˈkwanzɑː/ *noun*. *N. Amer.* L20.
[ORIGIN from Kiswahili *matunda ya kwanza*, lit. 'first fruits (of the harvest)', from *kwanza* first.]
A secular festival observed by many African Americans from 26 December to 1 January as a celebration of their cultural heritage and traditional values.
– NOTE: The festival was instigated in 1966 by Maulana 'Ron' Karenga, a black power activist.

kwashiorkor /kwɒʃɪˈɔːkɔː, kwa-/ *noun*. M20.
[ORIGIN Local name in Ghana.]
A form of malnutrition caused by severe protein and energy deficiency, chiefly affecting young (esp. newly weaned) children in tropical Africa, and producing apathy, oedema, loss of pigmentation, diarrhoea, and other symptoms.

kwedini /kwiːˈdɪni/ *noun*. *S. Afr.* E20.
[ORIGIN Xhosa, voc. of *ikwedini* boy.]
A young African (esp. Xhosa) boy.

kweek /kwiːk/ *noun*. *S. Afr.* E20.
[ORIGIN Afrikaans from Dutch = couch grass: cf. QUICK *noun*[2], QUITCH.]
In full ***kweek grass***. A grass propagating by underground runners, *esp.* dog's tooth grass, *Cynodon dactylon*.

kwela /ˈkweɪlə/ *noun*. M20.
[ORIGIN Afrikaans, perh. from Zulu *khwela* climb, mount.]
A popular dance, and its accompanying music, resembling jazz, of central and southern Africa.

kWh *abbreviation*.
Kilowatt-hour(s).

KWIC /kwɪk/ *abbreviation*.
Keyword in context.

KWOC /kwɒk/ *abbreviation*.
Keyword out of context.

KY *abbreviation*. Also **Ky.**
Kentucky.

kya /ˈkʌɪə/ *noun*. E20.
[ORIGIN Zulu *-khaya* place of abode.]
In South Africa, Zimbabwe, etc.: an African's hut; the living accommodation of an African servant.

kyack /ˈkʌɪak/ *noun*. *US*. E20.
[ORIGIN Unknown.]
A kind of packsack consisting of two containers hung on either side of a packsaddle.

kyang *noun* var. of KIANG.

kyanise *verb* var. of KYANIZE.

kyanite /ˈkʌɪənʌɪt/ *noun*. Also **c-** /s-/. L18.
[ORIGIN from Greek *kuan(e)os* dark blue + -ITE[1].]
MINERALOGY. A triclinic aluminium silicate mineral usu. occurring as blue, greenish or colourless tabular crystals and used in heat-resistant ceramics.

kyanize /ˈkʌɪənʌɪz/ *verb trans*. Also **-ise**. M19.
[ORIGIN from J. H. *Kyan* (1774–1850), Irish inventor + -IZE.]
Impregnate (wood) with a solution of corrosive sublimate as a preservative. Chiefly as ***kyanized*** *ppl adjective*, ***kyanizing*** *verbal noun*.

kyat /kiːˈɑːt/ *noun*. Pl. same, **-s**. M20.
[ORIGIN Burmese.]
The basic monetary unit of Myanmar (Burma) since 1952, equal to 100 pyas.

kybosh *noun & verb* var. of KIBOSH.

kyd *adjective* var. of KID *adjective*.

†**kyd** *verb pa. pple*: see KITHE.

kye /kʌɪ/ *noun*. *nautical slang*. E20.
[ORIGIN Unknown.]
1 A mean person. E20.
2 Cocoa, drinking chocolate. E20.

kyle /kʌɪl/ *noun*[1]. Long *obsolete* exc. *dial.* LME.
[ORIGIN Old Norse *kýli*.]
A sore, an ulcer, a boil.

kyle /kʌɪl/ *noun*[2]. *Scot.* M16.
[ORIGIN Gaelic *caol*, genit. *caoil* narrow strait or sound, from *caol* narrow.]
A narrow channel between two islands, or between an island and the mainland; a sound, a strait.

kyles *noun pl.* var. of KAYLES.

kylie /ˈkʌɪli/ *noun*. *Austral.* M19.
[ORIGIN Nyungar *garli*.]
Esp. in western Australia: a boomerang.

kylikes *noun* pl. of KYLIX.

kylin /ˈkiːlɪn/ *noun*. M19.
[ORIGIN Chinese *qílín*, from *qí* male + *lín* female.]
A mythical animal of composite form figured on Chinese and Japanese pottery, a Chinese unicorn. Cf. KIRIN.

kylix /ˈkʌɪlɪks, ˈkɪl-/ *noun*. Pl. **-ikes** /-ɪkiːz/. Also **c-**, pl. **-ices** /-ɪsiːz/. M19.
[ORIGIN Greek *kulix*.]
GREEK ANTIQUITIES. A shallow cup with a tall stem, a tazza.

kyloe /ˈkʌɪləʊ/ *noun*. *Scot.* E19.
[ORIGIN Gaelic *gaidhealach* Gaelic, Highland.]
(An animal of) the breed of Highland cattle.

kymogram /ˈkʌɪmə(ʊ)gram/ *noun*. E20.
[ORIGIN formed as KYMOGRAPH: see -GRAM.]
A recording made with a kymograph; *esp.* in PHONETICS, a recording of pressure variations produced during articulation.

kymograph /ˈkʌɪmə(ʊ)grɑːf/ *noun*. M19.
[ORIGIN from Greek *kumo-* combining form of *kuma* wave (see -O-) + -GRAPH.]
1 An instrument for recording variations in pressure e.g. of blood in the blood vessels, of air during respiration or speech, etc., by the trace of a stylus on a rotating cylinder; a recording manometer. M19.
2 MEDICINE. An apparatus for recording the movement of the heart or other internal organs on an X-ray plate or film. Also called ***roentgenkymograph***. M20.
■ **kymoˈgraphic** *adjective* pertaining to or made with a kymograph L19. **kymoˈgraphically** *adverb* by means of a kymograph M20. **kymography** /kʌɪˈmɒgrəfi/ *noun* the technique or process of using a kymograph M20.

†**kynd** *noun* var. of KIND *noun*.

†**kynded** *adjective*. *rare* (Spenser). Only in L16.
[ORIGIN from KIND *noun* + -ED[2].]
Begotten, sprung.

kynurenic /kʌɪnjʊˈrɛnɪk, kɪ-/ *adjective*. L19.
[ORIGIN from Greek *kun-*, *kuon* dog + *-uren-* irreg. from *ouron* urine: see -IC.]
BIOCHEMISTRY. ***kynurenic acid***, an organic acid that results from metabolism of tryptophan and is excreted in the urine of humans and various animals; 4-hydroxyquinoline-2-carboxylic acid, $C_{10}H_7NO_3$.
■ **kynurenine** /kʌɪˈnjʊərəniːn, kɪ-/ *noun* an amino acid, $H_2N{\cdot}C_6H_4{\cdot}COCH_2CH(NH_2)COOH$, which is a precursor of kynurenic acid in tryptophan metabolism M20.

kyogen /ˈkjəʊgɛn/ *noun*. Pl. same. L19.
[ORIGIN Japanese *kyōgen*, lit. 'crazy words'.]
A comic interlude presented between performances of Noh plays.

kyoodle /kʌɪˈ(j)uːd(ə)l/ *verb intrans*. *US dial. & colloq.* E20.
[ORIGIN Imit.]
Make a loud noise; bark, yap.

kype /kʌɪp/ *noun*. M20.
[ORIGIN Var. of KIP *noun*[2], perh. infl. by PIKE *noun*[1].]
A hook formed on the lower jaw of adult male salmon and trout during the breeding season; a kip.
■ **kyped** *adjective* possessing a kype M20.

kyphoscoliosis /ˌkʌɪfəskəʊlɪˈəʊsɪs/ *noun*. Pl. **-oses** /-ˈəʊsiːz/. L19.
[ORIGIN formed as KYPHOSIS + SCOLIOSIS.]
MEDICINE. A combination of kyphosis and scoliosis; backward and lateral curvature of the spine.
■ **kyphoscoliotic** /-ˈɒtɪk/ *adjective* E20.

kyphosis /kʌɪˈfəʊsɪs/ *noun*. Pl. **-phoses** /-ˈfəʊsiːz/. Also (earlier) †**c-**. M19.
[ORIGIN Greek *kuphōsis* humpbacked condition, from *kuphos* bent, hunchbacked: see -OSIS.]
MEDICINE. Outward curvature of the spine, an excessive amount of which causes a hunched back. Cf. LORDOSIS, SCOLIOSIS.
■ **kyphotic** /kʌɪˈfɒtɪk/ *adjective* pertaining to or affected with kyphosis L19.

Kyrgyz /kɪəˈgiːz, ˈkəːgɪz/ *noun & adjective*. Also **Kirg(h)iz**. See also KARA-KYRGYZ. E17.
[ORIGIN Russian *Kirgiz* from Turkish *Kırgız*.]
▸ **A** *noun*. Pl. same, **-es** /-ɪz/.
1 A member of a widespread people of west central Asia, now chiefly inhabiting Kyrgyzstan. E17.
2 The Turkic language of this people. L19.
▸ **B** *attrib.* or as *adjective*. Of or pertaining to the Kyrgyz or their language. M19.
Kyrgyz pheasant = MONGOLIAN *pheasant*.

Kyrie /ˈkɪrɪeɪ/ *noun*. E16.
[ORIGIN Abbreviation of KYRIE ELEISON.]
1 = KYRIE ELEISON 1. E16.
†**2** = KYRIE ELEISON 2. Only in 16.

Kyrie eleison /ˌkɪrɪeɪ ɪˈleɪɪzɒn, -sɒn, -s(ə)n/ *noun*. ME.
[ORIGIN medieval Latin from Greek *Kuriē eleēson* Lord, have mercy.]
1 The words ('Lord, have mercy') of a short repeated invocation or response used in the Roman Catholic, Greek Orthodox, and Anglican Churches, esp. at the beginning of the Eucharist. Also, a musical setting of these words, esp. as the first movement of a mass. ME.
†**2** A complaint; a scolding. E16–M17.

kyrielle /kɪrɪˈɛl/ *noun*. M17.
[ORIGIN French *kyrielle*, Old French *kyriele* from medieval Latin *kirieles* (pl.) from *Kyrie eleison*: see KYRIE ELEISON.]
†**1** A long rigmarole. Only in M17.
2 A kind of French verse divided into short equal couplets ending with the same word, which serves for a refrain. L19.

kyte /kʌɪt/ *noun*. *Scot. & N. English*. M16.
[ORIGIN Unknown.]
The belly, the stomach, the paunch.

kythe *verb* var. of KITHE.

kyu /kjuː/ *noun*. M20.
[ORIGIN Japanese *kyū* class.]
Each of the (numbered) grades of the less advanced level of proficiency in judo, karate, and other martial (or orig. martial) arts, (also ***kyu grade***); a person who has reached (a specified grade of) this level. Cf. DAN *noun*[4].

kyudo /ˈkjuːdəʊ/ *noun*. M20.
[ORIGIN Japanese, lit. 'way of the bow', from *kyū* bow + *dō* way, method.]
The Japanese martial art of longbow archery, incorporating set rhythmic movements and practised in a meditative state.

K

Ll

L, l /ɛl/.
The twelfth letter of the modern English alphabet and the eleventh of the ancient Roman one, corresp. to Greek *lambda* and ult. Semitic *lamed*. The sound normally represented by the letter is a lateral consonant, voiced alveolar before a vowel or /j/, voiced velar in final position, before most consonants or syllabically, partially or wholly devoiced following stressed /p, k/. In certain combinations the l has become silent having modified the preceding vowel, as *-alf* /ɑːf/, *-alm* /ɑːm/, *-olk* /əʊk/. See also **ELL** *noun*[2]. Pl. **L's**, **Ls**.
▸ **I 1** The letter and its sound.
2 The shape of the letter; an object shaped like the letter L; *esp.* (**a**) an extension of a building at right angles to the main block; (**b**) a pipe-joint connecting two pipes at right angles, an elbow joint. Cf. **ELL** *noun*[2].
L-head, **L-headed** *adjectives* designating (a reciprocating internal-combustion engine having) L-shaped combustion chambers, in which the valves are situated in a side arm. **L-shaped** *adjective* having a shape or a cross-section like the capital letter L.
▸ **II** Symbolical uses.
3 Used to denote serial order; applied e.g. to the twelfth (also freq. the eleventh, either I or J being omitted) group or section, sheet of a book, etc.
4 The roman numeral for fifty. ▸**b** *LXX*, the roman numeral for seventy; *spec.* the Septuagint.
5 a *CHEMISTRY.* Orig. *l*, now only as a small capital ʟ: as *prefix* denoting (a compound having) a configuration about an asymmetric atom analogous to that of a standard reference molecule (now ʟ-glyceraldehyde for organic compounds). Also, as ʟ(+), ʟ(−), further denoting respectively laevo- or dextrorotation of polarized light by the compound. [Extended use of l- = laevorotatory.] ▸**b** *PHYSICS.* (Cap. L.) Used to designate the series of X-ray emission lines of an excited atom of longer wavelength than the K-series (cf. K, K 3c), arising from electron transitions to the atomic orbit of second lowest energy, with principal quantum number 2; hence ***L-shell***, this orbit; ***L-electrons***, electrons in this shell; ***L-capture***, the capture by an atomic nucleus of one of the L-electrons. ▸**c** *PHYSICS.* Denoting the quantum number of the orbital angular momentum of one electron (*l*) or an assemblage of electrons (*L*). ▸**d** *BACTERIOLOGY.* (Cap. L.) The designation (now chiefly as ***L-form***) of an atypical form of certain bacteria which lacks a cell wall, exhibits a very variable shape, and somewhat resembles a mycoplasma. ▸**e** ***L-band***, a frequency band of electromagnetic waves used for radar, extending from 390 to 1550 megahertz.
▸ **III 6** Abbrevs.: **L** = Lake; Lance (in ranks of the British army); large; Latin; learner(-driver), ***L-plate***, a learner plate; left; Liberal (in politics); [Latin] *libra* pound of money (repr. by the conventional sign £, as £100; see also **L.S.D.**); Licentiate (in academic degrees); (*TAXONOMY*) Linnaeus; Lire. **l** = left; length; line (in references); litre(s). ***l-*** (*CHEMISTRY*) = laevorotatory (cf. sense 5a above).

LA *abbreviation.*
1 Library Association.
2 Local authority.
3 Los Angeles.
4 Louisiana.

La *symbol.*
CHEMISTRY. Lanthanum.

la *noun* see **LAH**.

La /la/ *adjective* (*def. article*). Also **la**. **M19.**
[**ORIGIN** French or Italian, fem. def. article, from Latin *illa* fem., *ille* that.]
Used preceding the name of a prima donna, or (freq. *joc.* or *iron.*) the name of any woman. Cf. **THE** *adjective* 6.

> P. G. WODEHOUSE La Brinkmeyer badly needed a toad in her bed.

La **SERENISSIMA**.

la /lɑː, lɔː/ *interjection.* **L16.**
[**ORIGIN** Natural exclam. Cf. **LO** *interjection*[1], **WELLAWAY**.]
1 Introducing or accompanying a conventional phrase, or calling attention to an emphatic statement. In later use, a mere expression of surprise. *arch.* **L16.**

> W. CONGREVE O la now! I swear and declare, it shan't be so. V. W. MASON La! how you startled me!

†**2** Redupl. **la la**. Expr. derision. **L16–E17.**

La. *abbreviation.*
Louisiana.

L-A *abbreviation.*
Latin America.

laager /ˈlɑːɡə/ *noun.* **M19.**
[**ORIGIN** Afrikaans = German *Lager*, Dutch *leger*: see **LEAGUER** *noun*[1].]
A camp, an encampment; *S. AFR. HISTORY* a Boer camp marked out and protected by a circle of wagons; *transf.* & *fig.* a defensive position, *esp.* one protected by armoured vehicles; an entrenched policy, viewpoint, etc., under attack from opponents.

> *Armed Forces* Syrian commandos staged a night attack on an Israeli vehicle laager. *attrib.*: *Economist* Sanctions might create a laager mentality.

laager /ˈlɑːɡə/ *verb.* **L19.**
[**ORIGIN** from the noun.]
1 *verb trans.* Form (wagons) into a laager; encamp (people) in a laager. Also foll. by *up*. **L19.**

> C. FULLER Van Rensburg's wagons were not laagered, but scattered about. *fig.*: *Cape Times* Are we . . going to keep ourselves laagered when other countries in Africa get together?

2 *verb intrans.* Form a laager; make a camp in a laager. Also foll. by *up*. **L19.**

> *Tablet* We stopped firing at about seven o'clock, and laagered up for the night.

laagte /ˈlɑːxtə/ *noun. S. Afr.* Also **leegte**. **M19.**
[**ORIGIN** Afrikaans from Dutch = a valley, from *laag* **LOW** *adjective*.]
A valley or shallow dip in the veld.

laari *noun* see **LARI**.

lab /lab/ *noun*[1]. Long *obsolete* exc. *dial.* **LME.**
[**ORIGIN** Prob. imit. Cf. Dutch *labben* blab, tell tales, **BLAB** *noun*[1], *verb*[1].]
A sneak, a telltale.

lab /lab/ *noun*[2]. **L19.**
[**ORIGIN** Abbreviation.]
A laboratory.

> *attrib.*: *Listener* An honest lab assistant loses his job for refusing to work on a poison gas project.

lab coat a white protective coat worn by workers in a laboratory.

Lab /lab/ *noun*[3] *& adjective.* **L19.**
[**ORIGIN** Abbreviation.]
(Of or pertaining to) the Labour Party.

Lab /lab/ *noun*[4]. *colloq.* Chiefly *N. Amer.* Also **l-**. **M20.**
[**ORIGIN** Abbreviation.]
A Labrador (dog).

Labadist /ˈlabədɪst/ *noun.* **L17.**
[**ORIGIN** French *Labadiste*, from *Labadie* (see below) + **-IST**.]
ECCLESIASTICAL HISTORY. A follower of the French mystic Jean de Labadie (1610–74), who seceded from the Roman Church and founded a sect holding quietist views.

labakh *noun* var. of **LEBBEK**.

laban /ˈlaban/ *noun.* Also ***leban*** /ˈlɛban/, ***leben*** /ˈlɛbən/. **L17.**
[**ORIGIN** Arabic = milk.]
A drink consisting of coagulated sour milk.

Labanotation /ˈlɑːbənəʊˌteɪʃ(ə)n/ *noun.* **M20.**
[**ORIGIN** from *Laban* (see below) + **NOTATION**.]
A system of dance notation devised by the Hungarian-born dancer and choreographer Rudolf von Laban (1879–1958).

labaria /ləˈbɑːrɪə/ *noun.* Also (earlier) **labarri** /ləˈbɑːri/. **E19.**
[**ORIGIN** Amer. Spanish, perh. from Carib.]
In Guyana: any of several poisonous coral snakes or pit vipers, *esp.* the fer de lance, *Bothrops atrox*, and the bushmaster, *Lachesis muta*.

Labarraque /labəˈrak/ *noun.* Now *rare* or *obsolete*. **E19.**
[**ORIGIN** Antoine Germain *Labarraque* (1777–1850), French pharmacist.]
Labarraque's liquid, ***Labarraque's solution***, Javelle water.

labarri *noun* see **LABARIA**.

labarum /ˈlabərəm/ *noun.* **E17.**
[**ORIGIN** Late Latin, whence Byzantine Greek *labaron*.]
The imperial standard of Constantine the Great (306–337), with Christian symbols added to Roman military symbols; *gen.* a symbolic banner.

†**labdacism** *noun* var. of **LAMBDACISM**.

labdanum /ˈlabdənəm/ *noun.* **E16.**
[**ORIGIN** medieval Latin form of **LADANUM**.]
= **LADANUM**.

labefaction /labɪˈfakʃ(ə)n/ *noun.* **E17.**
[**ORIGIN** from Latin *labefact-* pa. ppl stem of *labefacere* weaken, from *labi* fall + *facere* make: see **-FACTION**.]
A shaking, weakening; overthrow, downfall.

label /ˈleɪb(ə)l/ *noun.* **ME.**
[**ORIGIN** Old French = ribbon, fillet (also *lambel*, mod. *lambeau* rag), prob. from Germanic form rel. to **LAP** *noun*[1], with dim. suffix.]
▸ **I** A strip or band.
1 *HERALDRY.* A temporary mark of cadency now distinguishing the eldest son of a family during the lifetime of his father or grandfather, consisting of a band across the upper part of the shield having (usu. three or five) dependent points. Formerly also, each of the dependent points. **ME.**
2 A narrow strip of cloth etc.; a fillet, a ribbon; the infula of a mitre. **ME.**
†**3** A small strip of paper or parchment attached to a document as a supplementary note; a codicil. **LME–M17.**
†**4** *ASTRONOMY & SURVEYING.* In an astrolabe or a circumferentor: a narrow brass rule used chiefly in taking altitudes. **LME–L17.**
†**5** *gen.* A slip or strip of anything. **LME–L17.**
6 A narrow strip of material attached to a document to carry the seal. **L15.**
7 *ARCHITECTURE.* A moulding over a door, window, or other opening; a dripstone. **E19.**
▸ **II 8** A slip of paper, cardboard, metal, etc., (intended to be) attached to an object and carrying information, instructions, etc., concerning it; *spec.* a piece of fabric sewn inside a garment bearing the brand name, size, etc. (Now the usual sense.) **L17.** ▸**b** An adhesive postage stamp or bill stamp. **M19.** ▸**c** A circular piece of paper on the centre of a gramophone record giving details of the record. **E20.**

> A. K. GREEN Poison . . bought at a drug-store usually has a label on the bottle. R. HUGHES A number of labels . . which he was pasting onto the various . . packages. **b** DAVID POTTER Stamps to collect the postage due on underpaid letters are . . described as Postage Due Labels.

9 *fig.* A short classifying phrase or name applied to a person, work of art, idea, etc. **L19.** ▸**b** In a dictionary entry, a word or phrase indicating the area, content, category, etc., of the word being defined. **E20.**

> P. BROOK We rush to give them a label. *Atlantic Monthly* The Democratic governors . . are all progressive pragmatists. That's the label I give myself.

10 A brand name; a brand-named product, the manufacturer of a brand-named product; *spec.* (a section of) a recording company producing records under a distinctive name. **E20.**

> *Making Music* We . . decided to put out a single, and started a label.

11 *BIOLOGY & CHEMISTRY.* A substance (as a distinctive isotope, or a dye) used to label another substance (see **LABEL** *verb* 2). **M20.**
12 *COMPUTING.* **a** An arbitrary name for a statement in a program which facilitates reference to it elsewhere in the program. **M20.** ▸**b** A set of data recorded on a reel of magnetic tape describing its contents and serving for identification by a computer. **M20.**
– **COMB.**: **labelmate** a fellow musician or group recording for the same record label; **label-stop** *ARCHITECTURE* a boss or corbel supporting the end of a label or dripstone.

label /ˈleɪb(ə)l/ *verb trans.* Infl. **-ll-**, ***-l-**. **E17.**
[**ORIGIN** from the noun.]
1 Affix a label to, mark with a label. **E17.** ▸**b** *fig.* Describe or designate as with a label; categorize. **M19.**

> K. WILLIAMS A cleaning fluid . . which he'd mistakenly labelled 'Cough Syrup'. C. S. FORESTER He was labelled at once as the midshipman who was seasick in Spithead. **b** *New Republic* The amendment has been labeled a punitive measure.

2 *BIOLOGY & CHEMISTRY.* Make (a substance, a molecule, or a constituent atom) experimentally recognizable but essentially unaltered in behaviour, so that its path may be followed or its distribution ascertained, esp. by replacing a constituent atom by one of a different isotope, identifiable by its radioactivity or its different mass, or by attaching a (usu. fluorescent) dye to the molecule. Cf. **LABEL** *noun* 11. **M20.**
▪ **labeller** *noun* **L19.**

labella *noun* pl. of **LABELLUM**.

labelled /ˈleɪb(ə)ld/ *adjective.* Also ***labeled**. **L16.**
[**ORIGIN** from **LABEL** *noun*, *verb*: see **-ED**[2], **-ED**[1].]
1 *HERALDRY.* Of a mitre: having labels or infulae (of a particular tincture). **L16.**
2 *ARCHITECTURE.* Having a label or dripstone. **M19.**
3 Marked with a ticket bearing the name, description of contents, etc., of the article. **L19.**

4 BIOLOGY & CHEMISTRY. Of an atom: of a different isotope (of the element normally present). Of a molecule or substance: made recognizable by labelling (see LABEL *verb* 2). M20.

labellum /lə'bɛləm/ *noun*. Pl. **-lla** /-lə/. E19.
[ORIGIN Latin, dim. of *labrum* lip.]
1 ENTOMOLOGY. Either of a pair of lobes terminating the proboscis of certain insects. E19.
2 BOTANY. The lowest segment of the inner whorl of perianth segments of an orchid, usu. larger and different in shape from the remainder. M19.

labia *noun* pl. of LABIUM.

labial /'leɪbɪəl/ *adjective & noun*. L16.
[ORIGIN medieval Latin *labialis*, from Latin *labia* lips: see -AL[1].]
▸ **A** *adjective*. **1** Of or pertaining to the lips; *spec.* (PHONETICS) designating those sounds which require complete or partial closure of the lips for their formation, as the consonants /p/, /b/, /m/, /f/, /v/, /w/, and vowels for which the lips are rounded. L16.
labial pipe MUSIC a flue pipe in an organ.
2 ANATOMY etc. Pertaining to, of the nature of, associated with, or situated on a lip or labium. M17.
▸ **B** *noun*. **1** PHONETICS. A labial sound. M17.
2 A labial part or organ, as any of the scales which border the mouth of a fish or reptile. L19.
■ **labialism** *noun* (PHONETICS) the tendency to labialize sounds; labial pronunciation: L19. **labi'ality** *noun* (PHONETICS) the quality of being labial L19. **labially** *adverb* (*a*) PHONETICS with a labial sound or utterance; (*b*) towards the lips: E20.

labialize /'leɪbɪəlʌɪz/ *verb trans.* Also **-ise**. M19.
[ORIGIN from LABIAL + -IZE.]
PHONETICS. Make (a sound or sounds) labial in character; round (a vowel).
■ **labiali'zation** *noun* the action of labializing, the condition of being labialized; rounding of a vowel: M19.

labiate /'leɪbɪət/ *adjective & noun*. E18.
[ORIGIN mod. Latin *labiatus*, from LABIUM: see -ATE[2].]
▸ **A** *adjective*. **1** BOTANY. ▸**a** Of a corolla or calyx: = ***two-lipped*** s.v. TWO *adjective*. E18. ▸**b** Belonging to the family Labiatae, consisting of herbaceous plants and undershrubs usu. with two-lipped flowers and square stalks (e.g. the mints, ground ivy, the dead-nettles). M19.
2 ANATOMY & ZOOLOGY. Resembling a lip or labium in shape, function, etc. L19.
▸ **B** *noun*. BOTANY. A plant of the family Labiatae. M19.
■ **labiated** *adjective* (now *rare* or *obsolete*) = LABIATE *adjective* 1a, 2 E18.

labile /'leɪbɪl, -ʌɪl/ *adjective*. LME.
[ORIGIN Late Latin *labilis*, from *labi* fall: see -ILE.]
1 Liable to lapse. Of a person: apt to err or sin; THEOLOGY liable to fall from innocence. LME.

> G. CHEYNE All creatures being . . free, must necessarily, . . be labile, fallible and peccable. *Forum* These funds are no more labile than any other form of trust.

2 Liable to undergo displacement in position or change in nature, form, chemical composition, etc.; unstable; *esp.* in CHEMISTRY (of an attached ligand or group) readily displaced by another, (of a bond) readily broken. E17. ▸**b** PSYCHOLOGY. Emotionally or behaviourally unstable. M20.
■ **la'bility** *noun* (chiefly SCIENCE) the quality or state of being labile M16.

labilize /'leɪbɪlʌɪz/ *verb trans.* Also **-ise**. E20.
[ORIGIN from LABILE + -IZE.]
CHEMISTRY. Make labile (esp. a chemical bond or group).
■ **labili'zation** *noun* M20. **labilizer** *noun* a labilizing agent M20.

labio- /'leɪbɪəʊ/ *combining form*.
[ORIGIN from Latin *labium* lip + -O-.]
1 PHONETICS. Forming nouns and adjectives with the sense '(a sound) formed with the lips and (some other organ)', as ***labio-nasal*** etc.
2 ANATOMY. Forming chiefly adjectives with the sense 'of or pertaining to the lips and (some other part)', as ***labio-alveolar***, ***labioglossolaryngeal***, ***labioglossopharyngeal***, ***labio-lingual***, ***labio-mental*** [Latin *mentum* chin], etc.
■ **labio'dental** *adjective & noun* (a sound) formed with the lips and teeth M17. **labiomancy** *noun* lip-reading L17. **labio'palatal** *adjective & noun* (a sound) formed with the lips and the hard palate L19. **labio'velar** *adjective & noun* (a sound) formed with the lips and the soft palate L19.

labium /'leɪbɪəm/ *noun*. Pl. **-ia** /-ɪə/. L16.
[ORIGIN Latin = lip: cf. LABRUM.]
1 ANATOMY. A liplike structure; *spec.* (chiefly in pl.) the two pairs of folds of skin on either side of the vulva. L16.
labia majora /mə'dʒɔːrə/ the larger, outer pair of labia of the vulva. **labia minora** /mɪ'nɔːrə/ the smaller, inner pair of labia of the vulva.
2 ENTOMOLOGY. The fused mouthpart which forms the floor of the mouth or underlip. E19.
3 BOTANY. The lip, esp. the lower or anterior lip, of a labiate corolla. Cf. GALEA. E19.

lablab /'lablab/ *noun*. E19.
[ORIGIN Arabic *lablāb*.]
A leguminous plant, *Lablab purpureus*, grown as a pulse and animal fodder in India, Egypt, and other tropical countries. Also called ***bonavist***, ***Egyptian bean***, ***hyacinth bean***.

labor *noun & adjective* see LABOUR *noun & adjective*.

laboratorial /lab(ə)rə'tɔːrɪəl/ *adjective*. M19.
[ORIGIN from LABORATORY + -AL[1].]
Of or pertaining to a laboratory.

laboratory /lə'bɒrət(ə)ri, 'lab(ə)rət(ə)ri/ *noun*. E17.
[ORIGIN medieval Latin *laboratorium*, from Latin *laborat-* pa. ppl stem of *laborare*: see LABOUR *verb*, -ORY[1].]
1 A room or building set aside and equipped for scientific experiments or research (orig. and esp. in chemistry), for teaching science, or for the development or production of chemical or medicinal products. See also ***language laboratory*** s.v. LANGUAGE *noun*[1]. E17.
2 A department of an arsenal where ammunition, explosives, etc., are produced or examined. E18.
3 METALLURGY. The hearth of a reverberatory furnace. M19.
– COMB.: **laboratory animal** any animal (e.g. rat, monkey, mouse) commonly used for experiments in a laboratory; **laboratory frame (of reference)** NUCLEAR PHYSICS: in which measurements of particle velocity etc. are made with respect to a laboratory regarded as stationary; **laboratory school** US: at which student teachers are trained and classroom techniques demonstrated.

labored *adjective*, **laborer** *noun*, **laboring** *adjective* see LABOURED *adjective* etc.

laborious /lə'bɔːrɪəs/ *adjective*. LME.
[ORIGIN Old French & mod. French *laborieux* from Latin *laboriosus*, from *labor*: see LABOUR *noun*, -IOUS.]
1 Industrious, assiduous, hard-working. Now *rare* or *obsolete*. LME. ▸†**b** = LABOURING *ppl adjective* 1. M16–L18.
2 Characterized by or involving labour or exertion. LME.

> C. DARWIN The laborious breathing necessary in high regions. S. E. FERRIER A most laborious and long-winded letter.

3 Entailing labour in construction or execution. Of literary style etc.: not fluent. M16.

> J. CRACE Equipped with . . neat, laborious handwriting, and a skill with ledgers.

4 Giving birth with difficulty. Of labour: difficult. M17.
■ **labori'osity** *noun* (*rare*) M17. **laboriously** *adverb* L15. **laboriousness** *noun* M17.

Laborism *noun*, **Laborist** *noun & adjective*, etc., see LABOURISM etc.

laborous /'leɪb(ə)rəs/ *adjective*. LME.
[ORIGIN formed as LABORIOUS: see -OUS.]
†**1** = LABORIOUS 1, 2, 3. LME–L18.
2 = LABOURING *ppl adjective*. *Scot.* M16.

laborsome *adjective* see LABOURSOME.

labour /'leɪbə/ *noun & adjective*. Also ***labor**. ME.
[ORIGIN Old French *labo(u)r* (mod. *labeur* ploughing) from Latin *labor* toil, trouble, suffering.]
▸ **A** *noun* **I** **1** Exertion of the faculties of the body or mind, esp. when painful or compulsory; physical or mental toil. ME. ▸†**b** Physical exercise. L16–M17.

> AV *Ps.* 104:23 Man goeth forth unto his worke: and to his labour. D. FRANCIS Physics . . they took to be unacceptably hard mental labour.

2 An instance of bodily or mental exertion; a task (to be) performed. ME.

> W. S. CHURCHILL Work with the United Nations in the more fruitful labours of peace.

3 The outcome, product, or result of work. Freq. in *pl. arch.* ME.

> SWIFT My labours, which cost me so much thought and watching.

†**4** Trouble or pains taken; *esp.* the exertion of influence to further a matter or obtain a favour. LME–M17.
5 Childbirth; the period from the onset of regular uterine contractions until the expulsion of the placenta. L16.

> V. CRONIN After a difficult labour, Catherine gave birth to a healthy child.

6 (Physical) work considered as required for the execution of a task or as supplying the wants of the community; the contribution of the worker to production. L18. ▸**b** ***the Labour***, = ***Labour Exchange*** (b) below. *colloq.* M20.

> G. M. TREVELYAN Farms worked by a single family without hired labour. **b** L. HENDERSON I'm going for a job the Labour picked out for me.

7 Workers (esp. manual workers) considered as a social class or a political force. Freq. *attrib.* M19.

> *Encycl. Brit.* Organised labour seldom gained . . public sympathy.

8 (**L-**.) *ellipt.* The Labour Party. E20.

> ALDOUS HUXLEY Tell Brett . . to vote Labour, our only hope. J. BUCHAN The Left Wing of Labour blessed it cordially.

▸ **II** **9** A group of moles. L15.
– PHRASES: ***direct labour***: see DIRECT *adjective*. ***division of labour***: see DIVISION 2. FORCED ***labour***. ***free labour***: see FREE *adjective*. ***hard labour***: see HARD *adjective*. **Herculean labour** = ***Labour of Hercules*** below. **in labour** (of a woman) giving birth. **labour in vain** fruitless efforts. **Labour of Hercules** a task requiring enormous strength or persistence. **labour of love** a task undertaken for the love of a person or for the work itself. **lost labour** = ***labour in vain*** above. ***organized labour***: see ORGANIZED 3a.
– COMB.: **labour brigade** a unit or group of workers, *esp.* one organized by the state or a local authority; **labour camp** a penal settlement where the prisoners must work as labourers; **labour day** (*a*) in China and the former USSR, a unit of labour calculated according to the expected productivity of a worker; (*b*) (***Labour Day***) a day celebrated in honour of workers, often as a public holiday (in many places on 1 May, in N. America on the first Monday of September); **Labour Exchange** (*a*) *hist.* an establishment for the exchange of the products of labour without the use of money; (*b*) (also ***labour exchange***) (*hist. & colloq.*) an employment exchange; **labour force** (*a*) the body of workers employed at a particular place or time; (*b*) the number of people in the population in employment or seeking work; **labour hero**, **labour heroine** a title awarded to a male, female, worker who achieves a high output; **labour-intensive** *adjective* (of a process or industry) having labour as the largest factor or cost; **labour market** the supply of labour considered with reference to the demand for it; **labour movement** the effort by organized labour to improve conditions for workers; the organizations and individuals involved in this; **labour-only** *adjective* (of a subcontractor, subcontracting) supplying only the labour for a particular piece of work; ***labour pains***: see PAIN *noun*[1] 3b; **Labour Party** the political party formed in Britain in 1906 by a federation of trade unions and socialist groups to represent labour in Parliament; any of various similar parties in other countries (***Independent Labour Party***: see INDEPENDENT *adjective*); **labour relations** the relations between management and labour; **labour-saving** *adjective* designed to reduce or eliminate work; **labour spy** US a person employed or enlisted by a company to report on the activities of workers; **labour theory of value** the theory that the value of a commodity should be determined by the amount of labour used in its production; **labour ward** a room in a hospital set aside for childbirth; **Labour Weekend** NZ the long weekend preceding and including Labour Day.
▸ **B** *adjective*. Of or pertaining to a Labour Party, *esp.* the British Labour Party. E20.

> J. BUCHAN A young Labour member from the Midlands.

labour /'leɪbə/ *verb*. Also ***labor**. LME.
[ORIGIN Old French & mod. French *labourer* (now chiefly = plough) from Latin *laborare*, from *labor* LABOUR *noun*.]
▸ **I** *verb trans.* **1** Till, cultivate (the ground); work (a mine). Now *arch. & dial.* LME.
2 Work on; produce or execute with labour. *arch.* LME.

> DRYDEN They . . labour Honey to sustain their Lives.

3 Elaborate, work out in (excessive) detail. Now usu., treat or insist on (a point, a question, etc.) at (inordinate) length. LME.

> A. POWELL Perhaps it is tedious to labour the point.

4 Work for or with a view to (a result); work hard for (a cause etc.). *arch.* LME. ▸†**b** Bring into a specified condition or position by strenuous exertion. L15–L17.

> BURKE How much I wished for, and how earnestly I laboured, that re-union. **b** H. MONTAGU To labour the eye to see darknesse.

†**5** Endeavour to influence or persuade (a person); advocate (a matter) strenuously. LME–M17.
†**6** **a** Make tired, weary; burden, distress. LME–E18. ▸**b** Work (an animal); use (the body, its parts, occas. the mind) in some work. L15–L19.
†**7** Work by beating, rubbing, pounding, etc. L15–M17.
8 Belabour, beat, thrash. *obsolete* exc. *dial.* L16.
▸ **II** *verb intrans.* **9** Exert oneself physically or mentally; toil, esp. hard or against difficulties; do (esp. manual) work to earn one's living. LME.

> M. WEBB I'd laboured . . a long while, and labour brings a thing near the heart's core. Z. MEDVEDEV His . . parents laboured in a steel mill.

10 Exert oneself, strive (*for*, *to do*). LME. ▸†**b** Exert one's influence in urging a suit or to obtain something desired. Foll. by *to* (a person). L15–L16.

> W. MARCH Rhoda . . laboured so diligently to improve her penmanship.

11 Move or travel, esp. with difficulty or against obstacles. LME. ▸**b** Of a ship: roll or pitch heavily at sea. E17. ▸**c** Of an engine: work noisily and with difficulty, esp. when under load. M20.

> J. STEINBECK A stilted heron laboured up into the air. **b** BYRON The ship labour'd so, they scarce could hope To weather out much longer.

12 Be burdened or troubled, as by disease, shortage of food, etc.; suffer from some disadvantage or defect. Foll. by *under* (also †*of*, *with*, *on*, *in*). LME.

> C. KINGSLEY You are labouring under an entire misapprehension.

†**13** Of a woman: be in labour, give birth. LME–L18.
■ †**labourable** *adjective* (chiefly of land) able to be worked L15–M18.

labourage /'leɪb(ə)rɪdʒ/ *noun*. Also ***laborage**. ME.
[ORIGIN Old French & mod. French, from *labourer* LABOUR *verb*: see -AGE. In sense 3 from LABOUR *noun*.]
†**1** Labouring, labour, work. ME–M17.
†**2** Ploughing; ploughed or cultivated land. L15–E16.
3 Payment for labour. E19.

L

laboured /ˈleɪbəd/ *adjective*. Also ***labored**. LME.
[ORIGIN from LABOUR *verb* + -ED[1].]
†**1** Learned. Only in LME.
†**2 a** Worn with use. Only in M16. ▸**b** Used for work; hard worked. L16–E18.
†**3** Cultivated, tilled, ploughed; (of a mine) worked. L16–M19.
4 Produced or accomplished with labour; performed with great effort. Now freq. *derog.*, tediously elaborated, lacking spontaneity, heavy. L16.

JOHN FOSTER Other writing of a laboured and tedious kind. M. KINGSLEY The laboured beat of the engines.

■ **labouredly** *adverb* L19. **labouredness** *noun* M20.

labourer /ˈleɪb(ə)rə/ *noun*. Also ***laborer**. ME.
[ORIGIN from LABOUR *verb* + -ER[1].]
1 A person who performs (esp. unskilled) physical labour as a service or for a livelihood; *spec.* one who assists a skilled worker. ME.

A. BRIEN The labourers who slave in the mills and warehouses.

bricklayer's labourer, dock labourer, farm labourer, mason's labourer, etc. ***casual labourer***: see CASUAL *adjective*. **labourer-in-trust** *hist.* an officer ranking next below a clerk of works supervising repairs to royal palaces and other state buildings.
2 *gen.* A person who does work of any kind, a worker. LME.
3 ENTOMOLOGY. A worker insect. *rare*. E17.

labouring /ˈleɪb(ə)rɪŋ/ *ppl adjective*. Also ***laboring**. LME.
[ORIGIN from LABOUR *verb* + -ING[2].]
1 That labours; *esp.* (of a person) performing or engaged in unskilled labour. LME. ▸†**b** Of an animal: used for work. E16–E19.
2 Working hard; striving or struggling against pressure or some obstacle. Of a ship: rolling or pitching heavily. LME. ▸†**b** Of the moon: eclipsed. E–M17.
3 Of a woman: in labour. M16.
– SPECIAL COLLOCATIONS: **labouring class(es)** = ***working class(es)*** s.v. WORKING *adjective*. **labouring oar**: the hardest to pull; ***ply the labouring oar, pull the labouring oar, tug the labouring oar***, do much of the work.
■ **labouringly** *adverb* laboriously M19.

Labourism /ˈleɪbərɪz(ə)m/ *noun*. Also ***-bor-**, **l-**. E20.
[ORIGIN from LABOUR *noun* + -ISM.]
(The holding or advocacy of) the principles of a Labour Party or the labour movement.

Labourist /ˈleɪbərɪst/ *noun & adjective*. Also **l-**, ***-bor-**. E20.
[ORIGIN from LABOUR *noun* + -IST.]
▸ **A** *noun*. A supporter of the interests of Labour in politics; an advocate of Labourism. E20.
▸ **B** *adjective*. Of or pertaining to the interests of labour or *spec.* the British Labour Party. E20.

Labourite /ˈleɪbərʌɪt/ *noun & adjective*. Also **l-**, ***-bor-**. L19.
[ORIGIN from LABOUR *noun* + -ITE[1].]
= LABOURIST; (esp. of a Member of Parliament) of the Labour Party.

labourless /ˈleɪbəlɪs/ *adjective*. Also ***labor-**. E17.
[ORIGIN from LABOUR *noun* + -LESS.]
Without labour; requiring or doing no labour.

laboursome /ˈleɪbəs(ə)m/ *adjective*. Also ***labor-**. M16.
[ORIGIN from LABOUR *noun* + -SOME[1].]
†**1** Industrious, hard-working. M16–E17.
2 Requiring, entailing, or accompanied by labour. Now *dial. rare*. L16.
3 Of a ship: apt to pitch and roll violently in a heavy sea. L17.
■ **laboursomely** *adverb* M16. **laboursomeness** *noun* M16.

labra *noun* pl. of LABRUM.

labradoodle /ˈlabrəˌduːd(ə)l/ *noun*. M20.
[ORIGIN from LABRADOR + POODLE *noun*.]
A dog that is a cross-breed of a Labrador retriever and a poodle.

Labrador /ˈlabrədɔː/ *noun*. M19.
[ORIGIN A large peninsula in eastern Canada.]
1 Used *attrib.* to designate things found in or associated with Labrador. M19.
Labrador current a surface current running along the northern shore of Baffin Island and continuing southward until it meets the Gulf Stream off the coast of Newfoundland. **Labrador dog** = ***Labrador retriever*** below. **Labrador duck** a sea duck of the Labrador coast, *Camptorhynchus labradorius*, extinct since *c* 1875; also called ***pied duck***. **Labrador feldspar** = LABRADORITE. **Labrador hornblende** = ENSTATITE. **Labrador retriever** a medium-sized, black or yellow, short-coated retriever of a breed developed in Newfoundland and Labrador. **Labrador spar**, **Labrador stone** = LABRADORITE. **Labrador tea** a low-growing shrub, *Ledum palustre*, of the heath family, which has leathery evergreen leaves used locally in Canada as a tea substitute.
2 *ellipt.* A Labrador retriever. E20.

labradorescence /ˌlabrədɔːˈrɛs(ə)ns/ *noun*. E20.
[ORIGIN from LABRADORITE + -ESCENCE.]
MINERALOGY. The brilliant play of colours exhibited by some specimens of feldspars, esp. labradorite.

Labradorian /labrəˈdɔːrɪən/ *noun & adjective*. M19.
[ORIGIN from LABRADOR + -IAN.]
▸ **A** *noun*. A native or inhabitant of Labrador in Eastern Canada. M19.
▸ **B** *adjective*. Of or pertaining to Labrador. L19.

labradorite /labrəˈdɔːrʌɪt/ *noun*. E19.
[ORIGIN from LABRADOR + -ITE[1].]
MINERALOGY. A triclinic silicate of the plagioclase feldspar series which may show a bluish or multicoloured iridescence due to microscopic internal planes of reflection.

labral /ˈleɪbr(ə)l/ *adjective*. L19.
[ORIGIN from LABRUM + -AL[1].]
ZOOLOGY. Of or pertaining to a labrum or liplike part.

labret /ˈleɪbrɪt/ *noun*. M19.
[ORIGIN from LABRUM + -ET[1].]
A piece of stone, bone, shell, etc., inserted in the lip as an ornament.
■ **labreˈtifery** *noun* the practice of wearing labrets L19.

labroid /ˈleɪbrɔɪd/ *adjective & noun*. M19.
[ORIGIN from mod. Latin *Labrus* genus name + -OID.]
ZOOLOGY. ▸**A** *adjective*. Pertaining or belonging to the wrasse family Labridae of perciform fishes of temperate and tropical seas worldwide, or to a closely related family. M19.
▸ **B** *noun*. A labroid fish. M19.

labrum /ˈleɪbrəm/ *noun*. Pl. **labra** /ˈleɪbrə/. E18.
[ORIGIN Latin = lip, cogn. with *labium* rel. to Greek *laptein* LAP *verb*[1].]
ZOOLOGY. A lip, a liplike part; *esp.* a part forming the upper border or covering of the mouth in insects, crustaceans, etc.

labrys /ˈlabrɪs/ *noun*. E20.
[ORIGIN Greek *labrus*.]
CLASSICAL ANTIQUITIES. The sacred double-headed axe of ancient Crete; a representation of this.

laburnum /ləˈbəːnəm/ *noun*. M16.
[ORIGIN Latin.]
Any of several small leguminous trees of the genus *Laburnum*, esp. *L. anagyroides* and *L. alpinum* and their hybrids, bearing long pendulous racemes of bright yellow flowers followed by pods of poisonous seeds. Also, the dark wood of these trees.

labyrinth /ˈlab(ə)rɪnθ/ *noun*. LME.
[ORIGIN French *labyrinthe* or Latin *labyrinthus* from Greek *laburinthos* of unknown origin.]
1 A structure consisting of a complex network of tunnels, paths, etc., through which it is difficult to find one's way, a maze; *spec.* (***the Labyrinth***) in GREEK MYTHOLOGY, the maze constructed by Daedalus to contain the Minotaur. LME. ▸**b** A maze formed by paths bordered by high hedges, usu. as a feature in a garden. E17.
2 *transf.* & *fig.* A complex or confusing situation; an intricate system; a complicated arrangement esp. of streets or buildings. M16.

H. ARENDT There are . . few guides . . through the labyrinth of inarticulate facts. R. MACAULAY The real Trebizond . . was in the labyrinth of narrow streets.

3 ANATOMY & ZOOLOGY. A complex cavity hollowed out of each temporal bone, containing the organs of hearing and balance; the inner ear. Also, any of various other organs of intricate structure, as the accessory respiratory organs of certain fishes. L17.
bony labyrinth. membranous labyrinth: see MEMBRANOUS *adjective* 1.
4 ENGINEERING & ELECTRICITY. Any of various devices containing or consisting of winding passages; *esp.* a series of chambers designed to absorb unwanted vibrations in a loudspeaker. M19.
– COMB.: **labyrinth fish** a fish of the perciform suborder Anabantidae, most members of which (including the gouramis and Siamese fighting fish) have a labyrinth-like accessory breathing organ above the gill chambers.
■ **labyˈrinthal** *adjective* (*rare*) M17. †**labyrinthial** *adjective* M16–E18. **labyˈrinthian** *adjective* L16. **labyˈrinthic** *adjective* M17. **labyrinthical** *adjective* (*rare*) E17.

labyrinth /ˈlab(ə)rɪnθ/ *verb trans*. E19.
[ORIGIN from the noun.]
Enclose in or as in a labyrinth; arrange in the form of a labyrinth.

labyrinthiform /labəˈrɪnθɪfɔːm/ *adjective*. M19.
[ORIGIN from LABYRINTH *noun* + -I- + -FORM *noun*.]
Having the form of a labyrinth; of a sinuous or intricate structure; ICHTHYOLOGY having a labyrinth or accessory breathing organ above the gill chamber.

labyrinthine /labəˈrɪnθʌɪn, -ɪn/ *adjective*. M17.
[ORIGIN formed as LABYRINTHIFORM + -INE[1].]
1 Pertaining to or of the nature of a labyrinth; intricate, complicated, involved. M17.
2 Pertaining to the labyrinth or inner ear. L19.

labyrinthitis /ˌlab(ə)rɪnˈθʌɪtɪs/ *noun*. E20.
[ORIGIN formed as LABYRINTHIFORM + -ITIS.]
MEDICINE. Inflammation of the labyrinth or inner ear.

labyrinthodont /labəˈrɪnθədɒnt/ *noun & adjective*. M19.
[ORIGIN from mod. Latin *Labyrinthodontia* (see below), from Greek *laburinthos* LABYRINTH *noun* + -ODONT.]
PALAEONTOLOGY. ▸**A** *noun*. Any of various large fossil amphibians of the Palaeozoic and Triassic order Labyrinthodontia, characterized by teeth of labyrinthine structure having the enamel deeply folded. M19.
▸ **B** *adjective*. Of or having labyrinthine teeth; *spec.* of or pertaining to the order Labyrinthodontia. M19.

LAC *abbreviation*.
Leading Aircraftman.

lac /lak/ *noun*[1]. Also †**lack**, (earlier) †**lacca**. See also LAKE *noun*[3]. LME.
[ORIGIN (medieval Latin *lac*, *lac(c)a* from) Portuguese *lac(c)a* from Hindi *lākh*, Persian *lāk*. Cf. SHELLAC.]
1 The dark-red resinous encrustation secreted as a protective covering by the females of certain homopteran insects (esp. *Laccifer lacca*) parasitic on SE Asian trees, used (esp. in the Indian subcontinent) to make shellac and dye. LME.
seed-lac: ground in water to remove the dye. **stick-lac** untreated lac encrusted on twigs.
†**2** The varnish made from lac. Also, any of various resinous wood varnishes. Cf. LACQUER *noun* 2, 3. L16–E18.
3 Ware coated with lac or lacquer. M17.
†**4** The colour of lac; crimson. Also, a pigment prepared from lac. Cf. LAKE *noun*[3] 1. L17–M18.
– COMB.: **lac-dye** a brilliant scarlet dye prepared from lac; **lac insect** any lac-producing insect, esp. *Laccifer lacca*.

lac /lak/ *noun*[2]. M20.
[ORIGIN Abbreviation of LACTOSE.]
BIOLOGY. Used (usu. *attrib.* and printed in italics) orig. to denote the ability (of normal individuals) or inability (of mutants) of the bacterium *Escherichia coli* to metabolize lactose, and now also to designate (the parts of) the genetic system involved in this ability. Also, a *lac*[+] bacterium; the *lac* operon.
– COMB.: **lac operon** a group of adjacent genes in *E. coli* which, in the presence of lactose, cause the synthesis of the enzymes required for lactose metabolism.

lac *noun*[3] var. of LAKH.

†**lacca** *noun* see LAC *noun*[1].

laccase /ˈlakeɪz/ *noun*. L19.
[ORIGIN from medieval Latin *lacca* LAC *noun*[1] + -ASE.]
BIOCHEMISTRY. A copper-containing enzyme which oxidizes hydroquinones to quinones, involved in the setting of lac.

laccolite /ˈlakəlʌɪt/ *noun*. L19.
[ORIGIN from Greek *lakkos* reservoir + -LITE.]
GEOLOGY. = LACCOLITH.
■ **laccoˈlitic** *adjective* L19.

laccolith /ˈlakəlɪθ/ *noun*. L19.
[ORIGIN formed as LACCOLITE + -LITH.]
GEOLOGY. A concordant mass of igneous rock thrust up through sedimentary beds, and giving a domed form to the overlying strata.
■ **laccoˈlithic** *adjective* of, pertaining to, or characteristic of a laccolith L19.

lace /leɪs/ *noun & adjective*. ME.
[ORIGIN Old French *laz*, *las* (mod. *lacs* noose) from Proto-Romance from Latin *laqueus* noose.]
▸ **A** *noun*. †**1** A net, a noose, a snare. Chiefly *fig.* ME–E17.
2 A cord, a line, a string, a thread, a tie. *obsolete* exc. as in sense 3 below. ME.
3 *spec.* ▸**a** A cord or leather strip used to draw together opposite edges (chiefly of garments or footwear) by being passed in and out through eyelet holes (or around hooks, studs, etc.) and pulled tight. ME. ▸†**b** A cord from which a sword, hat, etc., hangs about the body. LME–L16.

a AV *Exod.* 28:28 Bind the brestplate . . unto the rings . . with a lace of blewe. C. GEBLER I slipped my feet into my shoes and began to tie my laces.

a bootlace, shoelace, etc.
†**4** In building: a tie beam; a brace. ME–E17.
5 Ornamental trimming for dresses, coats, etc. Now only in ***gold lace, silver lace***, a braid formerly made of gold or silver wire, now of silk or thread with a thin wrapping of gold or silver. ME.
6 A delicate ornamental openwork fabric made by twisting, looping, or knotting threads by hand or machine. M16.

B. MASON My eyes on the . . petticoat lace below her skirt. *fig.*: L. MACNEICE The brown lace sinking In the empty glass of stout.

blonde lace, bobbin lace, Irish lace, Medici lace, mignonette lace, Nottingham lace, Valenciennes lace, etc. ***iron lace***: see IRON *noun & adjective*.
7 A small quantity of spirits etc. mixed with some other drink, esp. coffee. E18.
▸ **B** *attrib.* or as *adjective*. Made of lace. L19.
– COMB. & SPECIAL COLLOCATIONS: **lacebark (tree)** any of several trees and shrubs with lacelike inner bark; *esp.* (***a***) a W. Indian evergreen shrub, *Lagetta lagetto* (family Thymelaeaceae); (***b***) *NZ* = HOUHERE; **lace-border** a geometrid moth, *Scopula ornata*, with a broad lacelike border to the wings; **lacebug** any insect of the family Tingidae of small plant-feeding bugs with lacelike wings; **lacecap** *noun & adjective* (a hydrangea) having corymbs made up of small fertile flowers or a mixture of these with larger sterile ones, giving the effect of lace; **lace curtain** a window curtain made of lace which lets in light but makes seeing into the room difficult; **lace-curtain** *adjective* having social pretensions, genteel; **lace-fern** any of several finely cut ferns; *esp.* a small N. American fern, *Cheilanthes gracillima*, having the underside of the frond covered with matted wool; **lace glass** Venetian glass

with lacelike designs; **lace-leaf (plant)** = *lattice leaf (plant)* s.v. LATTICE *noun*; **lace lizard**, **lace monitor** any Australian lizard of the genus *Varanus*, esp. the large arboreal *V. varius*; **lace pillow** a pillow or cushion placed on the lap of a person making lace by hand; †**lace-shade** a lace veil; **lacewing (fly)**, **lace-winged fly** any of various predatory neuropteran insects with delicate lacelike wings, esp. a member of the families Chrysopidae (*green lacewing*) or Hemerobiidae (*brown lacewing*); **lacewood** the wood of the American plane, *Platanus occidentalis*, or a similar wood, suitable for ornamental use.
■ **lacelike** *adjective* resembling lace L18. **lacery** *noun* (*rare*) lacelike work L19.

lace /leɪs/ *verb*. ME.
[ORIGIN Old French *lacier* (mod. *lacer*) from Proto-Romance base of LACE *noun*.]
1 a *verb trans.* Fasten or tighten with, or as with, a lace or string, now usu. with a lace or laces passed alternately through two rows of eyelet holes or around two rows of hooks, studs, etc. (Foll. by *up*, also *down, on, together*.) ME. ▸**b** *verb intrans.* Of a garment etc.: be fastened by means of laces. L18.

a W. WHARTON I can even lean over to lace my boots.

†**2** *verb trans.* Catch as in a noose or snare; entangle, ensnare. LME–L15.
3 *verb trans.* Fasten (a person) *into* a garment etc. by means of a lace or laces; compress the waist of (a person) by drawing corset laces tight. LME. ▸**b** *verb intrans.* Tighten or pull *in* corset laces; compress one's waist by so doing. L19.

T. HARDY He couldn't have moved from bed, So tightly laced in sheet and quilt . . He lay. E. FEINSTEIN Women were supposed to lace themselves tightly in silk.

4 a *verb trans.* Thread *with* a lace, string, etc. LME. ▸**b** *verb trans.* Pass (a cord etc.) in and out *through* holes, a fabric, etc. In BOOKBINDING, attach (the boards) to a sewn volume by passing the cords used through perforations in them (foll. by *in*). M17. ▸**c** *verb trans.* Intertwine. L19. ▸**d** *verb intrans.* Pass *across* a gap or *about* an object in a manner resembling or suggestive of lacing. L19. ▸**e** *verb trans.* Pass (film or tape) between the guides and other parts of a projector, tape recorder, etc., so that it runs from one spool to the other. Usu. foll. by *up*. M20.

a *fig.*: H. GEORGE We . . lace the air with telegraph wires. **c** T. O'BRIEN Sarah laced her fingers through mine. **d** H. G. WELLS A flimsy seeming scaffolding that laced about the . . Council House.

5 *verb trans.* Ornament or trim with laces or with lace. L16.

SWIFT Have I not . . laced your backs with gold.

6 *verb trans.* **a** Diversify with streaks of colour. Now freq. *fig.* L16. ▸**b** Flavour or fortify (a drink) with a dash of spirits, honey, etc.; add an extra ingredient to (a foodstuff), either to enhance or to adulterate it. (Foll. by *with*.) L17.

a H. CARPENTER A reputation for lacing his instruction . . with tags of Latin verse. **b** R. L. STEVENSON A jug of milk, which she had . . laced with whiskey. *Daily Telegraph* She laced his steak and kidney pie with . . weedkiller.

7 *verb trans. & intrans.* with *into*. Beat, thrash; abuse physically or verbally. *colloq.* L16.

E. WALLACE He laced me with a whip. *Time* Reviewers laced into the play.

†**8** *verb trans.* COOKERY. Make a number of incisions in (the breast of a bird). M17–L18.
– COMB.: **lace-up** *adjective & noun* (*a*) *adjective* (of footwear etc.) fastening with a lace or laces; (*b*) *noun* a lace-up shoe or boot (usu. in *pl.*).

laced /leɪst/ *adjective*. LME.
[ORIGIN from LACE *verb* + -ED¹.]
†**1** Wearing a necklace. Only in LME.
2 Of shoes etc.: made to be fastened or tightened with a lace or laces. E16.
†**3** Of a plant: entwined with a climbing plant. M16–M17.
4 Ornamented or trimmed with lace or laces. L16.
5 Of a drink: mixed with a small quantity of spirits etc. L17.
6 Marked with streaks of colour. Of a bird: having the edges of the feathers coloured differently from the general surface. M19.
– SPECIAL COLLOCATIONS: †**laced mutton** *slang* a prostitute. **laced valley** BUILDING a valley between the slopes of two adjoining roofs in which the end tile of each row abuts against a tile one and a half times the normal width laid diagonally on the valley board.

Lacedaemonian /ˌlasɪdɪˈməʊnɪən/ *noun & adjective*. Also **-demonian**. LME.
[ORIGIN from Latin *Lacedaemonius*, Greek *Lakedaimonios* + -AN.]
GREEK HISTORY. ▸**A** *noun*. A native or inhabitant of Lacedaemon, an area comprising the ancient Greek city of Sparta and its surroundings. LME.
▸**B** *adjective*. Of or pertaining to Lacedaemon or its inhabitants. Of speech etc.: laconic. M16.

lacerate /ˈlasərət/ *adjective*. M16.
[ORIGIN Latin *laceratus* pa. pple, formed as LACERATE *verb*: see -ATE².]
1 Mangled, torn, lacerated. M16.
2 BOTANY & ZOOLOGY. Having the edge or point irregularly cut as if torn; jagged. L18.

lacerate /ˈlasəreɪt/ *verb trans.* LME.
[ORIGIN Latin *lacerat-* pa. ppl stem of *lacerare*, from *lacer* mangled, torn: see -ATE³.]
Rip, mangle (esp. flesh or tissues); tear to pieces, tear up; *fig.* afflict, distress, harrow.

B. ENGLAND Jagged edges that lacerated their arms . . leaving slivers of . . cane . . in the flesh. V. NABOKOV He was lacerated with pity.

■ **lacerable** *adjective* able to be lacerated M17. **laceˈration** *noun* the action or process of lacerating flesh etc.; an instance of this; an open wound in which the skin (and underlying tissue) has been torn rather than cut: L16. **lacerative** *adjective* (*rare*) tending to lacerate M17.

Lacerta /ləˈsəːtə/ *noun*. L18.
[ORIGIN Latin *lacerta* lizard.]
(The name of) an inconspicuous constellation of the northern hemisphere, on the edge of the Milky Way between Cygnus and Andromeda; the Lizard.

lacertian /ləˈsəːtɪən, -ʃ(ə)n/ *adjective & noun*. E19.
[ORIGIN formed as LACERTA + -IAN.]
= LACERTILIAN.

lacertid /ləˈsəːtɪd/ *noun & adjective*. L19.
[ORIGIN formed as LACERTA + -ID³.]
ZOOLOGY. ▸**A** *noun*. A lizard of the Old World family Lacertidae, to which most European lizards belong. L19.
▸**B** *adjective*. Of, pertaining to, or designating this family. M20.

lacertilian /lasəˈtɪlɪən/ *adjective & noun*. M19.
[ORIGIN from mod. Latin *Lacertilia* (see below), from Latin *lacerta* lizard + -IL + -IAN.]
▸**A** *adjective*. Of, pertaining to, or characteristic of the reptilian suborder Lacertilia, which comprises the lizards; lizard-like, saurian. M19.
▸**B** *noun*. A reptile of the suborder Lacertilia; a lizard. M19.

lacertine /ləˈsəːtʌɪn/ *adjective*. M19.
[ORIGIN from Latin *lacerta* lizard + -INE¹.]
1 = LACERTILIAN. M19.
2 Of ornament: consisting of intertwined lizard-like figures. M19.

lacet /ləˈsɛt, leɪ-/ *noun*¹. L19.
[ORIGIN from LACE *noun* + -ET¹.]
A braid used to form designs on laces.

lacet /lasɛ/ *noun*². Pl. pronounced same. L19.
[ORIGIN French = lace, hairpin bend: see -ET¹.]
A hairpin bend in a road.

lachenalia /laʃəˈneɪlɪə/ *noun*. L18.
[ORIGIN mod. Latin (see below), from Werner de *la Chenal* (1736–1800), Swiss botanist + -IA¹.]
A small bulbous southern African plant of the genus *Lachenalia*, of the lily family, bearing thick, often spotted leaves, and spikes or racemes of tubular or bell-shaped flowers. Also called ***Cape cowslip***.

laches /ˈlaːtʃɪz/ *noun*. LME.
[ORIGIN Anglo-Norman *laches(se)* = Old French *laschesse* (mod. *lâchesse* cowardice), from *lasche* (mod. *lâche*): see LASH *adjective*, -ESS².]
†**1** Slackness, remissness, negligence. Also, an act or habit of neglect. LME–L15.
2 LAW. Delay in asserting a right, claiming a privilege, or making application for redress such as to bar its being granted. Also (now *rare*), negligence in the performance of a legal duty. L16. ▸**b** *gen.* Culpable negligence. M19.

Lachmann's law /ˈlaxmənz lɔː/ *noun phr.* E20.
[ORIGIN Karl *Lachmann* (1793–1851), German philologist.]
The rule that in Latin, a short root vowel in the present-tense stem of a verb is lengthened in the past participle if the present-tense stem ends in a voiced plosive.

lachryma Christi /ˌlakrɪmə ˈkrɪstʌɪ, -ti/ *noun phr.* L17.
[ORIGIN mod. Latin, lit. 'Christ's tear(s)', in Italian *lagrima* (or *-me*) *di Cristo*.]
A white, red, or pink Italian wine originally from grapes grown near Mount Vesuvius, now also produced elsewhere in Italy.

lachrymal /ˈlakrɪm(ə)l/ *adjective & noun*. Also (now the usual form in ANATOMY & MEDICINE etc.) **lacri-**, **lacry-**. LME.
[ORIGIN medieval Latin *lachrymalis*, *lacrimalis*, from Latin *lacrima* (earlier *lacruma*) tear, rel. to Greek *dakru* tear: see -AL¹.]
▸**A** *adjective*. **1** ANATOMY & PHYSIOLOGY. Connected with the secretion of tears; pertaining to or associated with an organ etc. involved in this process. LME.
lacrimal bone ANATOMY a small bone forming part of the orbit. *lacrimal* CARUNCLE.
2 Of or pertaining to tears; occas., characterized by, or indicative of, weeping. Of a vase: (conjectured to be) intended to contain tears. E19.
▸**B** *noun* **1 a** A lacrimal organ. Now only in *pl.* Now *rare*. LME. ▸**b** ANATOMY. A lacrimal bone. L19.
2 In *pl.* Fits of weeping. M18.
3 = LACHRYMATORY *noun* 1. M18.

lachrymary /ˈlakrɪməri/ *adjective & noun*. Also **lacri-**, **lacry-**. E18.
[ORIGIN from Latin *lacrima* (see LACHRYMAL) + -ARY¹.]
= LACHRYMATORY.

lachrymate /ˈlakrɪmeɪt/ *verb intrans.* Also **lacri-**, **lacry-**. E17.
[ORIGIN Latin *lacrimat-* pa. ppl stem of *lacrimare* weep, from *lacrima*: see LACHRYMAL, -ATE³.]
Now chiefly MEDICINE & PHYSIOLOGY. Weep; produce tears.

lachrymation /lakrɪˈmeɪʃ(ə)n/ *noun*. Also **lacri-**, **lacry-**. L16.
[ORIGIN Latin *lacrimatio(n-)*, formed as LACHRYMATE: see -ATION.]
The action or an act of weeping; a flow of tears.

lachrymator /ˈlakrɪmeɪtə/ *noun*. Also **lacri-**, **lacry-**. E20.
[ORIGIN formed as LACHRYMATE: see -OR.]
A substance (usu. as a gas, vapour, or dust) which causes irritation and copious watering on contact with the eyes.

lachrymatory /ˈlakrɪmət(ə)ri/ *noun & adjective*. Also **lacri-**, **lacry-**. M17.
[ORIGIN from Latin *lacrima* (see LACHRYMAL), after CHRISMATORY: see -ORY¹.]
▸**A** *noun*. **1** A phial of a kind found in ancient Roman tombs and conjectured to be intended to hold tears. M17.
2 A pocket handkerchief. *joc.* E19.
▸**B** *adjective*. Of or pertaining to tears; tending to cause tears. Of a vase: (conjectured to be) intended to contain tears. M19.

lachrymist /ˈlakrɪmɪst/ *noun*. Also **lacri-**, **lacry-**. E17.
[ORIGIN formed as LACHRYMATORY + -IST.]
A person who (frequently) weeps.

lachrymogenic /ˌlakrɪməˈdʒɛnɪk/ *adjective*. Also **lacri-**, **lacry-**. E20.
[ORIGIN formed as LACHRYMATORY + -O- + -GENIC.]
Giving rise to tears or weeping; lachrymatory.

lachrymose /ˈlakrɪməʊs/ *adjective*. Also **lacri-**, **lacry-**. M17.
[ORIGIN Latin *lacrimosus*, from *lacrima*: see LACHRYMAL, -OSE¹.]
†**1** Resembling tears; liable to exude in drops. Only in M17.
2 Tearful, inclined to weep. Of the eyes: full of tears. E18. ▸**b** Calculated to provoke tears; sad, mournful. E19.

b S. SONTAG The notorious lachrymose novel about the lovelorn egotist who shoots himself.

■ **lachrymosely** *adverb* M19. **lachryˈmosity** *noun* the quality or condition of being lachrymose L19.

lachrymous /ˈlakrɪməs/ *adjective*. *rare*. Also **lacri-**, **lacry-**. L15.
[ORIGIN Latin *lacrima* (see LACHRYMAL) + -OUS.]
†**1** Of an ulcer: weeping. Only in L15.
2 = LACHRYMOSE 2. M19.

Lachsschinken /ˈlaxsʃɪŋkən/ *noun*. E20.
[ORIGIN German, from *Lachs* salmon + *Schinken* ham.]
Cured and smoked loin of pork.

L

lacing /ˈleɪsɪŋ/ *noun*. LME.
[ORIGIN from LACE *verb* + -ING¹.]
1 The action of LACE *verb*. LME.
2 Something that laces or fastens; a fastening, a tie; a shoestring. LME. ▸**b** Rope used to attach a sail to a gaff or boom, a bonnet to a sail, etc. M19.
3 Ornamental openwork trimming or braiding. L16. ▸**b** The coloured border on the petal of a flower. Also, a similar marking on the feathers of a bird. M19.
4 A small quantity of spirits added to another drink. M19.
– COMB.: **lacing course** BUILDING a special course built into an arch or wall in order to bond different parts together and give added strength.

lacinia /ləˈsɪnɪə/ *noun*. Pl. **-niae** /-nɪiː/. L17.
[ORIGIN Latin = fringe, hem, rag, strip of cloth.]
1 BOTANY. A slash in a leaf, petal, etc.; a slender lobe between such slashes. L17.
2 ENTOMOLOGY. The inner distal lobe of the maxilla. Cf. GALEA. E19.

laciniate /ləˈsɪnɪət/ *adjective*. M18.
[ORIGIN formed as LACINIA + -ATE².]
BOTANY & ZOOLOGY. Cut into deep and narrow irregular segments; jagged, slashed.
■ **laciniated** *adjective* = LACINIATE M17. **laciniˈation** *noun* laciniate condition; a deep or irregular segment: M19.

lacis /ˈlasi/ *noun*. E16.
[ORIGIN French = net, network.]
1 A kind of lace made by darning patterns on net. E16.
2 ANATOMY. A network of cells surrounding the juxtaglomerular apparatus in a renal corpuscle. Chiefly in ***lacis cell***. M20.

lack /lak/ *noun*¹. ME.
[ORIGIN Corresp. to (& perh. partly from) Old Frisian *lek* blame, Middle Dutch, Middle Low German *lak* deficiency, fault, blame (Dutch *lak* calumny). Prob. already in Old English (cf. Anglo-Latin *lacca*, *laccum*).]
†**1** A defect; a moral failing, an offence, a crime. ME–L16.
2 A shortage or absence *of* (usu. something desirable or necessary); an instance of this. ME.

A. BELL It was a lack of security . . which was so worrying. *Punch* The tranquillity, . . convenience and joyfulness, notable lacks at Heathrow.

a painful lack: see PAINFUL 1. **for lack of**, **from lack of**, **through lack of** for want of. **no lack (of)** enough, plenty (of).

3 A fault that brings disgrace; disgrace, shame. (Often coupled with *shame*.) *Scot. arch.* LME. ▸†**b** Blame, censure for a fault. LME–M16.
4 The state of being in want; indigence, poverty. Also, the condition of lacking food; famine, starvation. M16.
†**5** The absence of a person or thing. M16–E17.
6 A thing wanted; something of which a need is felt. *rare.* M16.

†**lack** *noun*². M17–E19.
[ORIGIN Aphet. from ALACK.]
good lack!: expr. dissatisfaction, regret, surprise, etc.

†**lack** *noun*³ var. of LAC *noun*¹.

†**lack** *adjective.* LME.
[ORIGIN Perh. from Old Norse *lakr* defective. Cf. LACK *noun*¹.]
1 Deficient in quality; inferior, poor. *Scot.* LME–M19.
2 Deficient in quantity; short, wanting. L15–M17.

lack /lak/ *verb.* ME.
[ORIGIN Rel. to LACK *noun*¹. Cf. Middle Dutch *laken* be wanting, blame, Old Danish *lakke* deprecate.]
▸ **I 1** *verb intrans.* Be wanting or missing; be deficient in quantity or degree. ME.

> AV *Gen.* 18:28 Peraduenture there shall lacke fiue of the fiftie righteous. *BMX Action* Another part that usually lacks on . . bikes is the stem . . that won't hold bars.

2 *verb trans.* **a** Be without; have too little of; be deficient in. ME. ▸†**b** With *cannot*: do or go without. M–L16. ▸†**c** Perceive the absence of; miss. *rare* (Shakes.). Only in E17.

> I. McEwan He lacked the concentration for sustained thought. M. Piercy If they will let me have the two hundred I still lack.

3 *verb intrans.* Want *for* something; be in need (†*of*). E16.

> AV *Prov.* 28:27 He that giveth vnto the poore, shall not lacke.

▸ †**II 4** *verb trans.* Find fault with, abuse, blame, reproach. In weaker sense: deprecate, disparage. *Scot. & N. English.* ME–M19.
to lack to blame, blameworthy.
– COMB.: **lackland** *adjective & noun* (designating) a person owning no land or ruling no territory (orig. with cap. initial, as a designation of John, King of England 1199–1216); **lack-Latin** *adjective & noun* (*arch.*) (a person) knowing little or no Latin (chiefly in ***Sir John Lack-Latin***, a name for an ignorant priest); **lackwit** a stupid person.

L

lackadaisical /lakəˈdeɪzɪk(ə)l/ *adjective.* M18.
[ORIGIN from LACKADAISY: see -ICAL.]
Feebly sentimental, affectedly languishing; dreamily idle, listless, unconcerned, unenthusiastic.

> M. Beadle Homeward bound in a lackadaisical Indian-summer mood.

▪ **lackadaisiˈcality** *noun* the quality of being lackadaisical; an instance of this: E19. **lackadaisically** *adverb* E19. **lackadaisicalness** *noun* E19.

lackadaisy /ˈlakədeɪzi/ *interjection & adjective.* M18.
[ORIGIN Extended form of LACKADAY. Cf. UP-A-DAISY.]
▸ **A** *interjection.* = LACKADAY. M18.
▸ **B** *adjective.* = LACKADAISICAL. L18.

lackaday /ˈlakədeɪ/ *interjection. arch.* L17.
[ORIGIN Aphet. from *alack-a-day*: see ALACK.]
Expr. surprise, regret, or grief.

> D. M. Mulock Ah! lackaday! it's a troublesome world!

lacker *noun, verb* vars. of LACQUER *noun, verb.*

lackey /ˈlaki/ *noun & verb.* Also **lacquey.** E16.
[ORIGIN French *laquais*, †*alaquais* rel. to Catalan *alacay* (whence also Spanish (*a*)*lacayo*, Portuguese *lacayo*) = Spanish, Portuguese ALCAIDE.]
▸ **A** *noun.* **1** A (liveried) servant; a footman, a valet; a menial. E16.

> A. N. Wilson Herzen . . had a lackey to carry his books.

2 A hanger-on, a camp follower. *arch.* M16.
3 An obsequious person; a toady. Now *spec.* a servile political follower. L16.

> C. H. Spurgeon It is right to be obliging, but . . not every man's lackey. *American Mercury* American bankers . . have already stepped into the role of lackeys of British Imperialism.

4 Any of several lasiocampid moths, esp. *Malacosoma neustria*, having caterpillars with coloured stripes resembling a footman's livery. Also more fully ***lackey moth***. M19.
▸ **B** *verb.* **1** *verb intrans.* Behave or function as a lackey. M16.

> T. Dekker The Minutes (that lackey at the heeles of Time).

2 *verb trans.* Serve, esp. in a menial capacity; run errands for, dance attendance on. L16.

> *Quarterly Review* He had lacqueyed and flattered Walpole.

▪ **lackeyism** *noun* the service or attendance of lackeys, the behaviour of a lackey M19. **lackeyship** *noun* the condition or position of a lackey; lackeys collectively: M19.

lacking /ˈlakɪŋ/ *adjective.* L15.
[ORIGIN from LACK *verb* + -ING².]
1 Of a thing: not available, missing; in short supply. L15.

> J. Tyndall Flour was lacking to make the sacramental bread.

2 Deficient (*in* a specified quality), inadequate; *colloq.* deficient in intelligence. Formerly also, disabled. M17.

> R. Ingalls He's thought it wholly lacking in psychological interest.

3 In need; poor, destitute. E19.

lacklustre /ˈlaklʌstə/ *adjective.* Also ***-luster.** L16.
[ORIGIN from LACK *verb* + LUSTRE *noun*¹.]
Lacking in lustre or brightness, dull; lacking in vitality, force, or conviction, uninspired.

> Shakes. *A.Y.L.* He drew a dial from his poke, And, looking on it with lack-lustre eye, Says [etc.]. Dickens A faint lack-lustre shade of grey. T. Berger Her expression tended towards the lackluster, though her blue eyes were . . bright enough.

Laconian /ləˈkəʊnɪən/ *noun & adjective.* L16.
[ORIGIN from Latin *Laconia* (from Greek *Lakōn* Laconia: see below) + -AN.]
▸ **A** *noun.* **1** A native or inhabitant of Laconia, a territory of ancient Greece and now a department of modern Greece, the capital of which is Sparta. L16.
2 The dialect of ancient Greek spoken in Laconia. M19.
▸ **B** *adjective.* Of or pertaining to Laconia, its inhabitants, or its dialect; Lacedaemonian, Spartan. E17.

laconic /ləˈkɒnɪk/ *adjective & noun.* In sense A.1 **L-.** M16.
[ORIGIN Latin *Laconicus* from Greek *Lakōnikos*, from *Lakōn*: see LACONIAN, -IC.]
▸ **A** *adjective.* **1** Of or pertaining to Laconia (see LACONIAN) or its inhabitants; Lacedaemonian, Spartan. Now *rare.* M16.
2 Using few words, concise, terse, (the Spartans being known for their terse speech). L16.

> B. Adams She . . treated dramatic revelation with laconic disinterest. M. Atwood For Roz, this was the best part—her laconic mother, screaming her head off, and in public too.

▸ **B** *noun.* †**1** A laconic speaker. Only in 17.
2 Laconic or concise speech; in *pl.*, brief or concise sentences. *rare.* E18.
▪ **laconically** *adverb* E17. **laconicism** /ləˈkɒnɪsɪz(ə)m/ *noun* (**a**) brevity in speech or writing; (**b**) a short pithy sentence: M17.

laconicum /ləˈkɒnɪkəm/ *noun.* Pl. **-ca** /-kə/. E17.
[ORIGIN Latin, neut. of *Laconicus* (because a type of room first used by Spartans): see LACONIC.]
ROMAN ANTIQUITIES. The sweating room in a Roman bath.

Laconise *verb* var. of LACONIZE.

laconism /ˈlakənɪz(ə)m/ *noun.* In sense 2 **L-.** L16.
[ORIGIN Greek *lakōnismos*, from *lakōnizein* LACONIZE: see -ISM.]
1 = LACONICISM. L16.
2 *GREEK HISTORY.* Partiality for the Spartans or the Spartan interest. *rare.* M17.

Laconize /ˈlakənʌɪz/ *verb.* Also **-ise.** E17.
[ORIGIN Greek *lakōnizein*, from *Lakōn*: see LACONIAN, -IZE.]
GREEK HISTORY. **1** *verb intrans.* Favour the Spartans; imitate the customs or mode of speech of the Spartans; side with the Spartans in politics. E17.
2 *verb trans.* Bring under Spartan dominion or the Spartan form of government. L19.

lacquer /ˈlakə/ *noun.* Also **lacker.** L16.
[ORIGIN French †*lacre* sealing wax, from Portuguese *la*(*c*)*ca* formed as LAC *noun*¹.]
†**1** = LAC *noun*¹ 1. L16–E18.
2 A varnish consisting of shellac dissolved in alcohol with some (gold) colouring matter, used chiefly as a coating for brass. L17.
3 Any of various resinous wood varnishes capable of taking a hard polish, esp. (more fully ***Japan lacquer***, ***Japanese lacquer***) that obtained from the lacquer tree, *Rhus verniciflua* (see below). L17. ▸**b** Decorative ware made of wood coated with this, often inlaid with ivory, mother-of-pearl, etc. L19.
4 A coating material consisting of polymer dissolved in solvent which dries without chemical change. M19.
5 A kind of fixative for a hairstyle, usu. applied as an aerosol spray. M20.
6 In full ***lacquer disc***. A metal or glass disc coated with lacquer on which a groove is cut by a recording stylus, and from which the master disc is made. M20.
– COMB.: ***lacquer disc***: see sense 6 above; **lacquer tree** a tree of the cashew family, *Rhus verniciflua*, cultivated in Japan for lacquer and wax; **lacquerware** = sense 3b above; **lacquerwork** (the making of) lacquerware.

lacquer /ˈlakə/ *verb trans.* Also **lacker.** L17.
[ORIGIN from the noun.]
Cover or coat with lacquer; varnish; (of a material) serve as a varnish for. Also foll. by *over*.
▪ **lacquerer** *noun* a person who lacquers wood etc. M19. **lacquering** *noun* the action or process of coating wood etc. with lacquer; lacquer laid on wood etc.: L17.

lacquey *noun & verb* var. of LACKEY.

lacrimae rerum /ˌlakrɪmʌɪ ˈreɪrəm, ˈrɪərəm/ *noun.* E20.
[ORIGIN Latin, lit. 'tears for the way things are' (Virgil *Aeneid* I).]
The sadness of life; tears for the sorrows of life.

lacrimal *adjective & noun*, **lacrimary** *adjective & noun*, etc., see LACHRYMAL etc.

lacrosse /ləˈkrɒs/ *noun.* M19.
[ORIGIN from French (*le jeu de*) *la crosse* (the game of) the hooked stick.]
A ball game (orig. played by N. American Indians) in which the ball is thrown, carried, and caught with a long-handled stick with a shallow net at the end, called the crosse.
– COMB.: **lacrosse-stick** = CROSSE.

lacrymal *adjective & noun*, **lacrymary** *adjective & noun*, etc., vars. of LACHRYMAL etc.

lactalbumin /lakˈtalbjʊmɪn/ *noun.* L19.
[ORIGIN from LACTO- + ALBUMIN.]
BIOCHEMISTRY. Orig., the fraction of milk proteins obtained after the removal of casein and soluble in a salt solution. Now usu. ***α-lactalbumin***, a protein or mixture of closely similar proteins occurring in this fraction.

lactam /ˈlaktam/ *noun.* L19.
[ORIGIN from LACT(ONE + AM(IDE.]
CHEMISTRY. A cyclic amide analogous to a lactone, characterized by the group ·NH·CO· as part of a ring.
– COMB.: **lactam ring** a ring of the kind characteristic of lactams.

lactamase /ˈlaktəmeɪz/ *noun.* M20.
[ORIGIN from LACTAM + -ASE.]
BIOCHEMISTRY. ***β-lactamase***, any of various bacterial enzymes which cause the breaking of the C–N bond in the lactam ring of penicillins and cephalosporins (so rendering them ineffective as antibiotics).

lactamide /ˈlaktəmʌɪd/ *noun.* M19.
[ORIGIN from LACTO- + AMIDE.]
CHEMISTRY. The amide of lactic acid.

lactarium /lakˈtɛːrɪəm/ *noun.* E19.
[ORIGIN mod. Latin, use as noun of neut. of Latin *lactarius*: see LACTARY.]
An establishment for the sale of milk; a dairy.

lactary /ˈlakt(ə)ri/ *adjective. rare.* M17.
[ORIGIN Latin *lactarius* from *lac*, *lact-* milk: see -ARY¹.]
Of or pertaining to milk.

lactase /ˈlakteɪz/ *noun.* L19.
[ORIGIN from LACTOSE + -ASE.]
BIOCHEMISTRY. An enzyme which catalyses the hydrolysis of lactose to glucose and galactose.

lactate /ˈlakteɪt/ *noun.* L18.
[ORIGIN from LACTIC + -ATE¹.]
CHEMISTRY. A salt or ester of lactic acid.

lactate /lakˈteɪt/ *verb intrans.* L19.
[ORIGIN Back-form. from LACTATION: see -ATE³.]
Secrete or discharge milk. Earliest & chiefly as ***lactating ppl adjective.***

> E. Gellhorn Another function of oxytocin . . : the ejection of milk from the lactating mammillary gland. A. Storr Some primitive societies forbid sexual intercourse with a lactating woman.

▪ **lactated** *adjective* combined with a milk-product L19.

lactation /lakˈteɪʃ(ə)n/ *noun.* M17.
[ORIGIN Late Latin *lactatio*(*n-*), from *lactat-* pa. ppl stem of *lactare* suckle, from *lact-*, *lac* milk: see -ATION.]
1 The action or process of suckling young; the period of milk secretion normally following childbirth. M17.
2 The process of secreting milk from the mammary glands. M19.
▪ **lactational** *adjective* E20.

lacteal /ˈlaktɪəl/ *adjective & noun.* M17.
[ORIGIN from Latin *lacteus* (from *lact-*, *lac* milk) + -AL¹.]
▸ **A** *adjective.* **1** Of or pertaining to milk; consisting of or resembling milk. M17.
2 *ANATOMY.* Of a vessel etc.: carrying a milky fluid, esp. chyle. M17.
▸ **B** *noun. ANATOMY.* Any of the small blind-ended lymph vessels of the small intestines, which convey chyle containing absorbed fats into the lymphatic system. Usu. in *pl.* L17.

lacteous /ˈlaktɪəs/ *adjective.* M17.
[ORIGIN formed as LACTEAL + -OUS.]
1 Of the nature of milk. M17.
2 Resembling milk; of the colour of milk. M17.

lactescent /lakˈtɛs(ə)nt/ *adjective.* M17.
[ORIGIN Latin *lactescent-* pres. ppl stem of *lactescere*, from *lactere* be milky, from *lact-*, *lac* milk: see -ESCENT.]
1 Becoming milky; having a milky appearance. M17.
2 *BOTANY.* Yielding a milky juice. L17.
3 Producing or secreting milk. L18.
▪ **lactescence** *noun* a milky appearance, milkiness L17.

lactic /ˈlaktɪk/ *adjective.* L18.
[ORIGIN from Latin *lact-*, *lac* milk + -IC.]
1 Chiefly *CHEMISTRY & BIOCHEMISTRY.* Of, pertaining to, or derived from milk. L18.
lactic acid a colourless hygroscopic organic acid, $CH_3·CH(OH)·COOH$, present in sour milk and formed metabolically esp. as the end product of glycolysis; 2-hydroxypropanoic acid. **lactic fermentation**: (esp. of milk) due to bacterial conversion of lactose to lactic acid.
2 Of bacteria: producing lactic acid. Of dairy products, wine, etc.: containing an unusually high proportion of lactic acid. E20.

lactiferous /lak'tɪf(ə)rəs/ *adjective*. **L17**.
[**ORIGIN** formed as **LACTIC** + **-I-** + **-FEROUS**.]
1 *ANATOMY & ZOOLOGY* etc. Producing, secreting, or transporting milk. **L17**.
2 *BOTANY*. Conveying or yielding a milky juice. **L17**.

lactifuge /'laktɪfjuːdʒ/ *noun*. **M19**.
[**ORIGIN** formed as **LACTIC** + **-FUGE**.]
MEDICINE. A drug which retards the secretion of milk.

lactim /'laktɪm/ *noun*. **L19**.
[**ORIGIN** from **LACT(ONE** + **IM(IDE**.]
CHEMISTRY. Any of the class of cyclic imines which are tautomeric isomers of the lactams and are characterized by the group ·N=C(OH)· as part of a ring.

lacto- /'laktəʊ/ *combining form*.
[**ORIGIN** from Latin *lact-*, *lac* milk: see **-O-**.]
1 Of, pertaining to, or derived from milk.
2 Chiefly *CHEMISTRY*. Relating to or derived from lactic acid or lactose.
■ **lactoba'cillus** *noun*, pl. **-lli**, any of various rod-shaped Gram-positive bacteria of the genus *Lactobacillus* which convert carbohydrates to lactic acid in the gut and in fermenting natural (esp. dairy) products **E20**. **lacto'bionate** *noun* a salt of lactobionic acid **E20**. **lactobi'onic** *adjective* [**BI-** + **-ONIC**]: ***lactobionic acid***, a syrupy organic acid produced by oxidation of lactose **L19**. **lactocele** *noun* (*MEDICINE*) = **GALACTOCELE** **M19**. **lactochrome** *noun* (*BIOCHEMISTRY*) a yellow-orange pigment orig. extracted from milk and now identified with riboflavin **L19**. **lacto'ferrin** *noun* (*BIOCHEMISTRY*) a bactericidal iron-binding protein found esp. in milk **M20**. **lacto'flavin** *noun* (*BIOCHEMISTRY*) = **RIBOFLAVIN** **M20**. **lac'tometer** *noun* an instrument for measuring the relative density of milk **E19**. **lacto'nitrile** *noun* a yellow liquid, CH_3·CH(OH)·CN, the nitrile of lactic acid, used in the manufacture of acrylonitrile **L19**. **lacto-ovo-vege'tarian** *adjective & noun* (*a*) *adjective* (of a diet) consisting only of dairy products, eggs, and vegetables; (*b*) *noun* a person who subsists on such a diet: **M20**. **lactope'roxidase** *noun* a peroxidase occurring in milk and saliva **M20**. **lacto'phenol** *noun* a solution of phenol and lactic acid in glycerol and distilled water, used for mounting biological specimens **L19**. **lacto'protein** *noun* a protein which occurs normally in milk **M19**. **lactoscope** *noun* an instrument for measuring the quality of milk from its translucence **M19**.

lactogenic /laktə(ʊ)'dʒɛnɪk/ *adjective*. **M20**.
[**ORIGIN** from **LACTO-** + **-GENIC**.]
PHYSIOLOGY. Pertaining to or initiating the secretion of milk.
■ **'lactogen** *noun* a lactogenic hormone; *spec.* = **PROLACTIN**: **M20**. **lactogenesis** *noun* the initiation of milk secretion **M20**.

lactoglobulin /laktə(ʊ)'glɒbjʊlɪn/ *noun*. **L19**.
[**ORIGIN** from **LACTO-** + **GLOBULIN**.]
BIOCHEMISTRY. Orig., the fraction of milk proteins obtained after the removal of casein and precipitated in a salt solution. Now usu. **β-*lactoglobulin***, a protein or mixture of closely similar proteins occurring in the lactalbumin fraction of milk.

lactol /'laktɒl/ *noun*. **E20**.
[**ORIGIN** from **LACTO-** + **-OL**.]
CHEMISTRY. Any of the class of cyclic hemiacetals formed by the internal reaction of a hydroxyl and a carbonyl group (esp. in a sugar) and characterized by a ring containing a ·C(OH)·OC· group.

lactone /'laktəʊn/ *noun*. **M19**.
[**ORIGIN** from **LACTO-** + **-ONE**.]
CHEMISTRY. †**1** A volatile liquid obtained on heating lactic acid. Only in **M19**.
2 Any of the class of cyclic esters formed (as) by the elimination of a molecule of water from a carboxylic acid, and characterized by the group ·O·CO· as part of a ring. **L19**.

lactonic /lak'tɒnɪk/ *adjective*. **L19**.
[**ORIGIN** formed as **LACTONE** + **-IC**.]
CHEMISTRY. **1** ***lactonic acid***: ▸†**a** = ***GALACTURONIC acid***. Only in **L19**. ▸**b** = ***LACTOBIONIC acid***. **M20**.
2 Containing the characteristic ring structure of a lactone. **L19**.

lactonize /'laktənʌɪz/ *verb trans. & intrans.* Also **-ise**. **E20**.
[**ORIGIN** from **LACTONE** + **-IZE**.]
CHEMISTRY. Change into a lactone.
■ **lactoni'zation** *noun* **E20**.

lactose /'laktəʊz, -s/ *noun*. **M19**.
[**ORIGIN** from **LACTO-** + **-OSE**².]
A disaccharide sugar, $C_{12}H_{22}O_{11}$, composed of a glucose and a galactose unit, which is present in milk and is used in food processing and pharmaceutical manufacture. Also called ***milk sugar***.

lactosuria /laktə(ʊ)'sjʊərɪə/ *noun*. **M19**.
[**ORIGIN** from **LACTOSE** + **-URIA**.]
MEDICINE. The presence of lactose in the urine.

lacto-vegetarian /ˌlaktəʊvɛdʒɪ'tɛːrɪən/ *adjective & noun*. **E20**.
[**ORIGIN** from **LACTO-** 1 + **VEGETARIAN**.]
▸ **A** *adjective*. Consisting of or subsisting on vegetables and milk products (and formerly, eggs) only. **E20**.
▸ **B** *noun*. A person who subsists on a lacto-vegetarian diet. **E20**.
■ **lacto-vegetarianism** *noun* **M20**.

lactulose /'laktjʊləʊz, -s/ *noun*. **M20**.
[**ORIGIN** from **LACTO-** + *-ul-* + **-OSE**², perh. after *cellulose*.]
BIOCHEMISTRY & PHARMACOLOGY. A synthetic disaccharide sugar, $C_{12}H_{22}O_{11}$, composed of a fructose and a glucose unit, used as a laxative.

lactyl /'laktʌɪl, -tɪl/ *noun*. **M19**.
[**ORIGIN** from **LACTIC** + **-YL**.]
CHEMISTRY. The radical $CH_3CH(OH)CO$· derived from lactic acid. Usu. in *comb.*

lacuna /lə'kjuːnə/ *noun*. Pl. **-nae** /-niː/, **-nas**. **M17**.
[**ORIGIN** Latin, from *lacus* **LAKE** *noun*².]
1 A hiatus, a blank, a missing portion, esp. in a manuscript or text. **M17**.

> D. WILSON The context which fills up the numerous lacunae of the time-worn inscription. M. MEYER These two weeks provide another infuriating lacuna in our knowledge of Ibsen's life.

2 *techn.* A gap, a depression; a space or cavity, *esp.* within or between the tissues of an organism; *spec.* in *ANATOMY*, any of the small cavities in bone which contain the osteocytes. **E18**.
■ **lacunal** *adjective* pertaining to or of the nature of a lacuna (in tissue etc.) **M19**. **lacunate** *adjective* (*a*) = **LACUNAL**; (*b*) having many lacunae: **M20**.

lacunar /lə'kjuːnə/ *noun*. Pl. **lacunars**, **lacunaria** /lakjʊ'nɑːrɪə, -'nɛːrɪə/. **L17**.
[**ORIGIN** Latin, formed as **LACUNA**: see **-AR**¹.]
ARCHITECTURE. A vault or ceiling consisting of recessed panels; any of the panels in such a vault or ceiling.

lacunar /lə'kjuːnə/ *adjective*. **L19**.
[**ORIGIN** from **LACUNA** + **-AR**¹.]
= **LACUNAL**.
■ Also **lacunary** *adjective* **M19**.

lacune /lə'kjuːn/ *noun*. Now *rare*. **E18**.
[**ORIGIN** Alt.]
= **LACUNA**.

lacunose /lə'kjuːnəʊs/ *adjective*. **E19**.
[**ORIGIN** Latin *lacunosus*, from **LACUNA**: see **-OSE**¹.]
1 *BOTANY & ZOOLOGY*. Having many lacunae or depressions; furrowed, pitted. **E19**.
2 Of a manuscript: full of gaps or hiatuses. *rare*. **L19**.

lacustrian /lə'kʌstrɪən/ *adjective*. *rare*. **M19**.
[**ORIGIN** formed as **LACUSTRINE**: see **-IAN**.]
Of, pertaining to, or of the nature of a lake-dweller; lake-dwelling.

lacustrine /lə'kʌstrʌɪn, -rɪn/ *adjective*. **E19**.
[**ORIGIN** from Latin *lacus* **LAKE** *noun*² after *palustris* marshy.]
1 Of or pertaining to a lake or lakes. **E19**.
2 Of plants and animals: growing in or inhabiting lakes. **M19**. ▸**b** Of or pertaining to lake dwellings or lake-dwellers. **M19**.
3 *GEOLOGY*. Originating by deposition at the bottom of a lake. **M19**.

LACW *abbreviation*.
Leading Aircraftwoman.

lacy /'leɪsi/ *adjective*. **E19**.
[**ORIGIN** from **LACE** *noun* + **-Y**¹.]
Made of or resembling lace.
■ **lacily** *adverb* **M20**. **laciness** *noun* **E20**.

lad /lad/ *noun*. **ME**.
[**ORIGIN** Unknown.]
1 A boy, a youth, a young man; a young son. In extended use: any man (sometimes *iron.*), a fellow; *esp.* (*colloq.*) a workmate, drinking companion, etc., (usu. in *pl.*). Also used as a familiar form of address (also ***my lad***). **ME**.

> J. O'HARA A mere strip of a lad, hardly more than a boy. *Beano* Time for your bath, lad!

lad of wax: see **WAX** *noun*¹. **the lads** the members of a team or a group of men of any age sharing a common interest on equal terms; *spec.* the rank-and-file members of a trade union.
2 a A man of humble birth and position; a menial, a labourer. Long *obsolete* exc. *dial.* **ME**. ▸**b** A stable worker of any age and (in mod. use) either sex, esp. in a racing stable. **M19**.
3 A high-spirited or roguish man or boy, a daredevil. Esp. in ***a bit of a lad***, ***quite a lad***. **M16**.

> R. DAHL He's . . a genius . . . He's a bit of a lad too . . . Terrific womaniser.

4 A male sweetheart. *Scot.* **E18**.
– **COMB.**: **lad-bairn** *Scot.* a male child; **lad's love** the aromatic plant southernwood, *Artemisia abrotanum*.
■ **laddie** *noun* (a form of address or endearment to) a lad **M16**. **laddish** *adjective* of or pertaining to a lad or lads; like a lad: **M19**. **laddo** *noun* (*colloq.*, orig. *Irish*), pl. **-os**, (a form of address or mode of reference to) a lad **L19**. **ladhood** *noun* the state of being a lad **L19**.

Ladakhi /lə'dɑːki/ *noun & adjective*. **M19**.
[**ORIGIN** Ladakhi.]
▸ **A** *noun*. **1** A native or inhabitant of Ladakh, a district of eastern Kashmir. **M19**.
2 The language of Ladakh, a dialect of Tibetan. **L19**.
▸ **B** *attrib.* or as *adjective*. Of or pertaining to Ladakh, the Ladakhis, or their language. **L19**.

ladang /lə'dɑːŋ/ *noun*. **L18**.
[**ORIGIN** Malay.]
In the Malay archipelago: a piece of land under dry cultivation, often a jungle clearing.

ladanum /'ladənəm/ *noun*. **M16**.
[**ORIGIN** Latin *ladanum*, *ledanum* from Greek *ladanon*, *lēdanon*, from *lēdon* mastic: cf. **LABDANUM**.]
A gum resin which exudes from plants of the genus *Cistus*, esp. *C. ladanifer* and *C. incanus* subsp. *creticus*, much used in perfumery and for fumigation.

ladder /'ladə/ *noun*. Also (*dial.*) **lether** /'lɛðə/.
[**ORIGIN** Old English *hlǣd(d)er* = Old Frisian *hlēdere*, Middle Dutch *lēdere* (Dutch *leer*), Old High German *leitara* (German *Leiter*), from West Germanic.]
1 A (fixed or portable) device usu. made of wood, metal, or rope, consisting of a series of bars ('rungs') or steps between two supports, and used as a means of climbing up or down. **OE**. ▸**b** *spec.* The steps to a gallows. *obsolete* exc. *hist.* **M16**.

> R. K. NARAYAN He put up the ladder and climbed to the loft.

extension ladder, ***rope ladder***, ***scaling ladder***, ***stepladder***, etc. **see a hole through a ladder**, **see through a ladder** see something obvious. ***snakes and ladders***: see **SNAKE** *noun* 1b. **b climb the ladder**, **mount the ladder**, **go up the ladder** be hanged. **groom of the ladder** the hangman.
2 A hierarchical structure perceived as resembling a ladder. **ME**.

> R. DAHL He bounced up the ladder . . to the top job . . , Archbishop of Canterbury!

kick down the ladder reject or disown the friends or associations that have helped one to rise in the world. ***social ladder***: see **SOCIAL** *adjective*.
3 *gen.* Anything resembling a ladder in appearance or function. **ME**.
fish ladder: see **FISH** *noun*¹.
4 In knitted garments or stockings or tights: a vertical strip of unravelled fabric. **M19**.

> J. C. OATES Her silk stockings broke . . in . . runs and ladders.

5 *NAUTICAL*. A series of range-finding shots up to or back to the target. **E20**.
6 A league table or ranking order of contestants. **M20**.

> *Star (Sheffield)* She . . reached number nine in the junior ladder at the . . Squash Club.

7 An opportunity or advantageous move in an undertaking (with ref. to the board game of snakes and ladders). **M20**.
– **COMB.**: **ladder-back (chair)**: in which the back is formed of horizontal pieces of wood; **ladder-back woodpecker**, **ladder-backed woodpecker** a woodpecker of Mexico and adjoining regions with black and white barred markings, *Picoides scalaris*; **ladder competition** (*a*) = ***ladder tournament*** below; (*b*) *CHESS* a competition in which players receive and accumulate points according to the merits of their proposed solutions to a series of problems, until a predetermined number of points is achieved; **ladder fern** any of various chiefly tropical ferns of the genus *Nephrolepis*, which spread by creeping rhizomes, producing new crowns; **ladder point**: (in a competition or tournament) which contributes towards improvement in a competitor's ranking; **ladder polymer**: in which pairs of straight-chain molecules are joined by recurring cross-links; **ladder-proof** *adjective* (of a fabric) not liable to ladder; **ladder shell** a wentletrap, esp. *Epitonium groenlandicum*; **ladder stitch** a crossbar stitch in embroidery; **ladder-stop** at the top and toe of a stocking, a band of openwork designed to prevent a ladder; **ladder tournament** a tournament in which players are placed in ranking order and move up by successfully challenging the player ranked next above; **ladder truck** a vehicle for carrying fire ladders and hooks; **ladder way** a way by which one descends or ascends by means of a ladder in the deck of a ship or the shaft of a mine.

ladder /'ladə/ *verb*. **LME**.
[**ORIGIN** from the noun.]
1 *verb trans.* Scale with a ladder or ladders; provide with a ladder or ladders. **LME**.
2 a *verb intrans.* Of a garment, esp. of stockings or tights: develop a ladder. **E20**. ▸**b** *verb trans.* Cause a ladder in (a garment). Cf. earlier **LADDERED** 3. **M20**.
3 *verb intrans.* *NAUTICAL*. Fire shots in a ladder. Freq. as ***laddering*** *verbal noun*. **E20**.

laddered /'ladəd/ *adjective*. **E17**.
[**ORIGIN** from **LADDER** *noun*, *verb*: see **-ED**², **-ED**¹.]
†**1** Of a rope: made into a ladder. Only in **E17**.
2 Scaled with a ladder or ladders; provided with a ladder or ladders. **L19**.
3 Of a garment, esp. of stockings or tights: that has developed a ladder, that has been laddered. **E20**.

lade /leɪd/ *noun*¹. Chiefly *dial.* **L17**.
[**ORIGIN** Uncertain: perh. from **LADE** *verb*.]
A board or rail fixed to the side of a cart or wagon to give greater width.

lade /leɪd/ *noun*². **E18**.
[**ORIGIN** Sense 1 extracted from English place names in *-lade* (*Cricklade*, *Lechlade*, etc.), repr. Old English *gelād* channel, **LODE**. Sense 2 app. a var. of **LEAD** *noun*², perh. conf. with a Scot. & north. form of **LODE**.]
1 A channel, a watercourse, the mouth of a river. **E18**.
2 A channel for leading water to a mill wheel; a mill race. Chiefly *Scot.* **E18**.

L

lade /leɪd/ *verb*. Pa. pple & ppl adjective **laden** /ˈleɪd(ə)n/ (the usual form in branch I), **laded** (the only form in branch II).
[ORIGIN Old English *hladan* = Old Frisian *hlada*, Old Saxon, Old High German *hladan* (Dutch, German *laden*), Old Norse *hlaða*, Gothic *-hlaþan*, from West Germanic base also of LAST *noun*[2].]
▸ **I** Load.
1 *verb trans.* Put the cargo on board (a ship). Also, put a load in or on (a vehicle, a beast of burden, a person, etc.) (now only as ***laden ppl adjective***). OE. ▸**b** Load (a person) *with* gifts etc., (a tree, branch) *with* fruit; fill abundantly. Now only as ***laden ppl adjective.*** L15. ▸**c** Burden, weigh down *with*. Now only as ***laden ppl adjective***, burdened (*with* sin, sorrow, etc.). *arch.* M16.
2 *verb trans.* Put or place on or in something as a burden, freight, or cargo. Now only, ship (goods) as cargo. OE. ▸**b** *verb intrans.* Of a ship: take on cargo. LME.
†**3** *verb trans.* Load or charge (a gun). Also, load (cartridges) in a gun. M–L17.
▸ **II** Draw water.
4 *verb trans.* Take up (water or other fluids) from a river, a vessel, etc., with a ladle, scoop, etc.; bale. OE. ▸**b** *verb trans.* Empty by baling. *obsolete* exc. *dial.* M16. ▸**c** *verb intrans.* Scoop up liquid, bale. E17.
†**5** *verb trans.* Of a ship: let in (water). LME–M16.
■ **lader** *noun* (now *rare* or *obsolete*) M16.

†**lade-bord** *noun & adjective* see LARBOARD.

laden *pa. pple & ppl adjective* see LADE *verb*.

laden /ˈleɪd(ə)n/ *verb trans.* E16.
[ORIGIN from LADE *verb* + -EN[5]. Perh. partly Scot. var. of LOADEN *verb*[1].]
Load, burden.

ladette /laˈdɛt/ *noun. colloq.* L20.
[ORIGIN from LAD + -ETTE.]
A young woman who enjoys social drinking, sport, or other activities customarily considered to be male-oriented, and typically displays attitudes or behaviour regarded as irresponsible or brash.

la-di-da /lɑːdɪˈdɑː/ *noun, adjective, & adverb. colloq.* Usu. *derog.* Also **lah-de-da**. L19.
[ORIGIN Imit. of the style of pronunciation referred to. Cf. LARDY-DARDY.]
▸ **A** *noun.* (A person given to) pretentious speech, manners, or behaviour. L19.
▸ **B** *adjective.* Characteristic or imitative of the upper classes; (affectedly) genteel or refined. L19.
▸ **C** *adverb.* In an affected or excessively refined manner; genteelly. M20.

la-di-da /ˈlɑːdɪdɑː/ *verb intrans. colloq.* Also **lah-de-da**. E20.
[ORIGIN from the noun.]
Use affected manners or speech.

la-di-da /ˈlɑːdɪdɑː/ *interjection. colloq.* E20.
[ORIGIN from the noun.]
Expr. derision, esp. of a person's pretentious speech or manner. Also (*US*), expr. scorn or lack of concern.

ladify *verb* var. of LADYFY.

Ladik /laˈdiːk/ *noun & adjective.* E20.
[ORIGIN A village in Turkey.]
(Designating) a type of prayer rug made in the district around Ladik.

Ladin /ləˈdiːn/ *noun & adjective.* M19.
[ORIGIN Latin *Latinus* LATIN *adjective & noun*.]
(Designating or pertaining to) the Rhaeto-Romance dialect spoken in northern Italy.

lading /ˈleɪdɪŋ/ *noun.* LME.
[ORIGIN from LADE *verb* + -ING[1].]
1 The action of LADE *verb*. LME.
bill of lading: see BILL *noun*[3].
2 Freight, cargo. E16.

ladino /ləˈdiːnəʊ/ *noun*[1]. E20.
[ORIGIN Italian.]
In full ***ladino clover***. A large fast-growing variety of white clover (*Trifolium repens*), native to northern Italy and cultivated elsewhere, esp. in the US, as a fodder crop.

ladino /laˈdiːnəʊ/ *adjective & noun*[2]. In senses A.3, B.3 usu. **L-**. M19.
[ORIGIN Spanish from Latin *Latinus* LATIN *adjective & noun*.]
▸ **A** *adjective.* **1** Wild, vicious, cunning. M19.
2 Of or pertaining to a ladino or ladinos. M20.
3 Of or pertaining to Ladino. M20.
▸ **B** *noun.* Pl. **-os**.
1 A vicious or unmanageable horse, steer, etc.; a stray animal. L19.
2 In Central America: a mestizo or white person. L19.
3 A language based on Old Spanish and written in modified Hebrew characters, used by some Sephardic Jews, esp. in Mediterranean countries. L19.

ladle /ˈleɪd(ə)l/ *noun.*
[ORIGIN Old English *hlædel*, from *hladan* LADE *verb*: see -EL[1].]
1 A large spoon with a long handle and cup-shaped bowl, used chiefly for serving or pouring liquids; the contents of such a spoon, a ladleful. OE. ▸**b** A vessel for transporting molten metal or glass in a foundry etc. LME. ▸**c** A long-handled instrument for charging a cannon etc. with loose powder. *obsolete* exc. *hist.* L15. ▸**d** In (Scottish) Presbyterian churches: a small wooden box at the end of a long wooden handle used for taking up the collection and Communion tokens. E19.
2 A float-board of a water wheel. Also ***ladle board***. LME.
3 A tax on grain etc. brought to a burgh market for sale; the amount payable in cash or kind (also ***ladle dues***). Also, the vessel used as the measure in assessing this. *Scot. obsolete* exc. *hist.* L16.
■ **ladleful** *noun* as much as a ladle will hold LME.

ladle /ˈleɪd(ə)l/ *verb trans.* E16.
[ORIGIN from the noun.]
1 Equip (a watermill) with ladle boards. Long *obsolete* exc. *hist.* E16.
2 Lift out or up with a ladle; transfer to another receptacle using a ladle. Foll. by *out*: distribute, esp. lavishly. M16.

> H. ROTH His mother.. began ladling out the steaming yellow pea-soup into the bowls. R. BROOKE But it's absurd to ladle out indiscriminate praise, as most people do.

■ **ladler** *noun* (*a*) (*Scot., obsolete* exc. *hist.*) a collector of ladle dues; (*b*) a person who ladles something: M17.

la dolce vita *noun phr.* see DOLCE VITA.

ladrone /ləˈdrəʊn, *in sense 1* ˈladrən/ *noun.* In sense 1 also **laidron** /ˈleɪdrən, ˈladrən/. M16.
[ORIGIN Spanish *ladrón* formed as LATRON.]
1 A dishonest or idle person. *Scot.* M16.
2 A highwayman in Spain or Spanish America. M19.

lady /ˈleɪdi/ *noun & adjective.*
[ORIGIN Old English *hlǣfdīge*, from *hlāf* LOAF *noun*[1] + Germanic base meaning 'knead'. Cf. DEY *noun*[1], DOUGH *noun*.]
▸ **A** *noun.* **I** As a designation for a woman (or girl).
1 A mistress in relation to servants; the female head of a household. OE.

> SWIFT When you are sent on a Message, deliver it in your own Words.. not in the Words of your.. Lady.

2 A woman to whom obedience or feudal homage is due: the feminine designation corresponding to *lord*. Now chiefly *poet.* OE. ▸**b** A woman who is the object of chivalrous devotion, one loved and courted by a man. Cf. sense 6 below. LME.

> MILTON Here ye shall have greater grace, To serve the Lady of this place. **b** TENNYSON Never a line from my lady yet.

3 *spec.* The Virgin Mary; an image or representation of the Virgin. Now only ***Our Lady***. OE.
4 A woman of superior position in society, or to whom such a position is conventionally or by courtesy attributed. Now, the feminine equivalent of ***gentleman***, freq. as a more courteous synonym for 'woman'. In extended use: any woman (freq. *iron.* or *derog.*). ME. ▸**b** Used as a form of address to a woman (now *colloq.*). In *pl.*, used as the normal form of address to a number of women. ME.

> C. STEAD She had been nurtured in the idea that she was to be a great lady. S. PLATH Irwin had a queer, old-world habit of calling women ladies.

5 a As an honorific title, used preceding the names of goddesses, allegorical figures, personifications, etc. Now *arch.* exc. in ***Lady Luck***, = FORTUNE *noun* 1. ME. ▸**b** Used preceding titles of honour or designations of dignified office, as an added mark of respect. *arch.* exc. in ***Lady Mayoress***, the wife or consort of a Lord Mayor. LME. ▸**c** Used preceding a name to form part of the customary designation of a woman (or girl) of rank, (*a*) as a less formal substitute for Marchioness (of), Countess (of), Viscountess, Baroness; (*b*) preceding the forename of the daughter of a duke, marquess, or earl; (*c*) preceding the husband's forename of the wife or widow of the holder of a courtesy title in which *Lord* precedes a forename; (*d*) preceding the surname of the wife or widow of a baronet or knight. LME. ▸**d** Used preceding a designation of relationship, by way of respectful address or reference. *arch.* or *joc.* E16.

> **b** SIR W. SCOTT They call me Lady Abbess, or Mother. **c** H. JACOBSON You say her name is Lady Ilchester?

6 A wife, a consort. Also, a female companion or lover. Cf. sense 2b above. ME.

> C. WATERTON The unfortunate governor and his lady lost their lives. D. DELILLO His current lady.

7 A courteous, refined, or genteel woman. M19.
▸ **II** *transf.* **8** †**a** A queen at chess. LME–L15. ▸**b** A queen in a pack of playing cards. *colloq.*, orig. *US*. E20.
9 Any of various butterflies. E17.
10 A calcareous structure in the stomach of a lobster, forming part of the masticatory apparatus and fancifully supposed to resemble the outline of a seated woman. M17.
11 A roofing slate of a small size. Cf. COUNTESS 2, DUCHESS 4. E19.
▸ **B** *attrib.* or as *adjective*. **1** Female, esp. (*a*) with names of occupations etc., esp. those traditionally associated with men, (*b*) (freq. *joc.*) of an animal. E17.

> DICKENS Our observant lady readers. G. R. SIMS The dog.. had five beautiful puppies.. it being a lady-dog.

2 Genteel; (esp. in titles of servants) having or claiming the status of gentlewoman. E19.

> R. M. CRAWSHAY Two lady-helps and.. a strong person.. to do the roughest work.

– PHRASES ETC.: ***find the lady***: see FIND *verb*. ***fine lady***: see FINE *adjective*. ***FIRST lady***. ***hunt the lady***: see HUNT *verb*. ***iron lady***: see IRON *noun & adjective*. **Ladies' Aid (Society)** †(*a*) during the American Civil War, a women's organization devoted to sending garments, bandages, etc., to the soldiers; (*b*) *N. Amer.* an organization of women who support the work of a church by fund-raising, arranging social activities, etc. **ladies and gentlemen**: used as a (formal) form of address to a mixed audience or company. **ladies' cabin**, **ladies' car**, **ladies' carriage** on public transport, a compartment etc. reserved for females. **ladies' chain** a figure in a quadrille etc. **ladies' cloakroom** a cloakroom or lavatory for females. **ladies' fingers** = ***lady's finger*** below. **Ladies' Gallery** a gallery in the House of Commons reserved for women. **ladies' man** a man who is fond of female company. **ladies' night** a function at a men's club etc. to which women are invited. **ladies' room** = ***ladies' cloakroom*** above. **ladies who lunch** [title of a song by S. Sondheim (b. 1930)] affluent women with enough free time to meet for lunch in restaurants; *spec.* women who organize and take part in fashionable lunches to raise funds for charitable projects. **Lady altar** an altar in a Lady chapel. **Lady Baltimore (cake)** *US*. [the wife of Lord Baltimore, founder of Maryland] a layered white butter cake filled with raisins, nuts, etc. **Lady Bountiful** [orig. a character in Farquhar's play *The Beaux' Stratagem*] a patronizingly generous wealthy woman. **ladyboy** (in Thailand) a transvestite or transsexual. **lady-chair** a seat formed by the hands of two people standing facing each other, each person grasping one of his or her own wrists and one of the opposite person's. **Lady chapel** a chapel dedicated to the Virgin Mary, in a church or cathedral, often situated east of the high altar. **Lady Chatterley** /ˈtʃatəli/ [with allus. to the character in D. H. Lawrence's novel *Lady Chatterley's Lover*] a sexually promiscuous woman, *esp.* one attracted to a man considered socially inferior. **lady-clock**, **lady-cow** (*obsolete* exc. *dial.*) a ladybird. **Lady Day** a day kept in celebration of some event in the life of the Virgin Mary, now *spec.* 25 March, the feast of the Annunciation and one of the quarter days in England, Wales, and Ireland. **lady fern** a delicate fern, *Athyrium filix-femina*, of damp shady places; any fern of the genus *Athyrium*. **ladyfish** any of various marine fishes; *esp.* (*a*) the tenpounder, *Elops saurus*; (*b*) the bonefish, *Albula vulpes*. **lady-fly** (*obsolete* exc. *dial.*) a ladybird. **lady-in-waiting** a lady attending a queen or princess. **ladykiller** a practised and habitual seducer, a dangerously attractive man. **lady-love** a female sweetheart or lover. ***Lady Luck***: see sense 5a above. **Lady Macbeth** /məkˈbɛθ/ [with allus. to the character in Shakes. *Macb.*] a remorseless or melodramatic woman, *esp.* one leading or assisting a weak man. ***Lady Mayoress***: see sense 5b above. **Lady Muck** *colloq.* (*derog.*) a socially pretentious woman. **lady of easy virtue** a prostitute or sexually promiscuous woman. ***lady of leisure***: see LEISURE *noun*. **lady of pleasure** a prostitute, a courtesan. **lady of the bedchamber** = ***lady-in-waiting*** above. **lady of the manor** the mistress of a manor house. **lady of the night** (*a*) (with hyphens) BOTANY a W. Indian shrub, *Brunfelsia americana* (family Solanaceae), bearing white flowers which are particularly fragrant at night; (*b*) a prostitute. **lady orchid**, **lady orchis** a rare British orchid, *Orchis purpurea*, of woodland on chalk, with dark purple helmet and whitish labellum. ***lady's bedstraw***: see BEDSTRAW 2. **lady's companion** a small case or bag arranged to hold implements for needlework etc. **lady's cushion** the mossy saxifrage, *Saxifraga hypnoides*. **lady's delight** *US* the wild pansy, *Viola tricolor*. **lady's ear-drops** *dial.* & *US* any of several garden fuchsias. **lady's finger** (*a*) *sing.* & in *pl.* the kidney vetch, *Anthyllis vulneraria*; (*b*) a sponge finger; (*c*) *sing.* & (usu.) in *pl.* okra. **lady's horse**, **lady's hunter**: (*a*) trained to carry a woman riding side-saddle; (*b*) suitably mannered for a lady. **lady's laces** ribbon grass, *Phalaris arundinadea* var. *picta*; also called ***painted grass***. **lady's maid** a lady's personal maidservant. **lady's man** = ***ladies' man*** above. **lady's mantle** any of various plants of the genus *Alchemilla*, of the rose family, with roundish palmately lobed leaves and cymes of tiny green flowers; *esp.* any plant belonging to the *A. vulgaris* aggregate species. **lady-smock** = ***lady's smock*** below. **lady's slipper (orchid)** any of several European and N. American orchids of the genus *Cypripedium*, with a large inflated labellum likened to a shoe; *esp.* (in Europe) *C. calceolus*. **lady's smock** (*a*) the cuckooflower, *Cardamine pratensis*; (*b*) *dial.* hedge bindweed, *Calystegia sepium*. **lady's thistle** the milk thistle, *Silybum marianum*. †**lady's traces** = ***lady's tresses*** below. **lady's tresses** any of several small orchids of the genus *Spiranthes*, with a spirally twisted row or rows of greenish-white flowers; *esp.* (in full ***autumn lady's tresses***) *S. spiralis*; ***creeping lady's tresses*** = GOODYERA. **Lady Superior** the head of a convent or nunnery in certain orders. **lady's waist** *Austral.* & *NZ colloq.* a small gracefully shaped glass; a drink served in such a glass. ***lady ware***: see WARE *noun*[2] 4b. **lady wife** *colloq.* (used to refer to) a person's wife. ***leading lady***: see LEADING *adjective*. ***lord and lady***, ***lords and ladies***: see LORD *noun*. **my lady**: a form of address used chiefly by servants etc. to a holder of the title 'lady'. ***naked ladies***: see NAKED *adjective*. ***old lady***: see OLD *adjective*. ***Our Lady***: see sense A.3 above. ***Our Lady's*** PSALTER. ***PAINTED lady***. ***pink lady***: see PINK *adjective*[2]. ***scarlet lady***: see SCARLET *adjective*. **the ladies** the female sex, *spec.* the female members of any group or party. **the Ladies**, **the Ladies'** (treated as *sing.*) a public lavatory for females, a ladies' cloakroom. **the lady of the house** the mistress of a household; a housewife. **the lady of the lamp**, **the lady with the lamp** (popular name for) Florence Nightingale (1820–1910), founder of the modern nursing profession; any female nurse. ***The Visitation of our Lady***: see VISITATION 4. ***walking lady***: see WALKING *ppl adjective*. ***White Lady***: see WHITE *adjective*. ***young lady***: see YOUNG *adjective*.
■ **ladydom** *noun* the realm of ladies M19. **ladyhood** *noun* the state or condition of being a lady; the qualities of a lady; ladydom: E19. **ladyish** *adjective* resembling a lady; affectedly refined or delicate M19. **ladykin** *noun* a little lady (occas. as a term of endearment) (cf. earlier LAKIN *noun*[2]) M19. **ladyless** *adjective* L15.

lady /ˈleɪdi/ *verb trans.* E17.
[ORIGIN from the noun.]
†**1** Raise to the rank of a lady; address as 'lady'; make lady-like or feminine. E–M17.
2 With *it*: play the lady or mistress. *rare.* E17.

ladybird /ˈleɪdɪbəːd/ *noun.* L16.
[ORIGIN from LADY *noun* + BIRD *noun.*]
1 A (female) sweetheart; a darling. Now *rare.* L16.
2 †**a** A kind of butterfly. Only in L16. ▸**b** Any of numerous usu. predatory brightly coloured beetles of the family Coccinellidae, of which the most familiar kinds are brownish red with black spots. L17.
3 The pintail (duck), *Anas acuta. dial.* L19.

ladybug /ˈleɪdɪbʌg/ *noun. dial. & N. Amer.* L17.
[ORIGIN from LADY *noun* + BUG *noun*[2].]
= LADYBIRD 2b.

ladyfy /ˈleɪdɪfʌɪ/ *verb trans.* Also **ladify**. E17.
[ORIGIN from LADY *noun* + -FY.]
Make a lady of; give the title of 'Lady' to.
■ **ladyfied** *adjective* (*colloq.*) having the airs of a fine lady L19.

ladylike /ˈleɪdɪlʌɪk/ *adjective.* M16.
[ORIGIN from LADY *noun* + -LIKE.]
1 Suitable for or appropriate to a lady; *derog.* effeminately delicate or graceful. M16.

K. ATKINSON Mrs Carter's ladylike tones cracked into indecorous Yorkshire when she tried to shout.

2 Having the appearance or manners of a lady; *derog.* (esp. of a man) effeminately delicate or fastidious. E17.
■ **ladylikeness** *noun* M19.

ladyship /ˈleɪdɪʃɪp/ *noun.* ME.
[ORIGIN from LADY *noun* + -SHIP.]
1 The condition of being a lady; rank as a lady. ME.
2 With possess. adjective (as ***her ladyship*** etc.): a title of respect given to a lady; *iron.* a mode of reference or address to a woman thought to be giving herself airs. LME.

laen /leɪn/ *noun.*
[ORIGIN Old English *lǣn*: see LOAN *noun*[1].]
LAW (now *hist.*). In Anglo-Saxon England, an estate held as a benefice.
– COMB.: **laen-land** land held as a laen.

Laestrigon *noun*, **Laestrigonian** *noun & adjective* vars. of LESTRIGON, LESTRIGONIAN.

Laetare /liːˈtɛːri, lʌɪˈtɑːri/ *noun.* L19.
[ORIGIN Latin *laetare* imper. sing. of *laetari* rejoice.]
In full ***Laetare Sunday***. The fourth Sunday of Lent.

laetic /ˈliːtɪk/ *adjective.* M19.
[ORIGIN Late Latin *laeticus*, from *laetus* joyful, ult. from Germanic base of LET *verb*[1]: see -IC.]
hist. Of, pertaining to, or designating a class of non-Roman cultivators under the later Roman Empire, who occupied lands for which they paid tribute.

Laetrile /ˈleɪtrʌɪl, -rɪl/ *noun.* Also **l-**. M20.
[ORIGIN from LAE(VOROTATORY + NI)TRILE.]
(Proprietary name for) a substance that has been used to treat cancer with controversial results and is identical with or related to amygdalin.

laevo- /ˈliːvəʊ/ *combining form.* Also ***levo-**.
[ORIGIN from Latin *laevus* left + -O-.]
Turning or turned to the left; *CHEMISTRY* laevorotatory. Opp. DEXTRO-.
■ **laevotarˈtaric** *adjective*: ***laevotartaric acid***, the laevorotatory form of tartaric acid M19. **laevoˈtartrate** *noun* a laevorotatory tartrate M19.

laevorotatory /liːvəʊˈrəʊtət(ə)ri/ *adjective.* Also ***levo-**. L19.
[ORIGIN from LAEVO- + ROTATORY.]
CHEMISTRY. Having or relating to the property (possessed by some compounds) of rotating the plane of polarized light to the left, i.e. anticlockwise when viewed in the opposite direction to that of propagation. Opp. DEXTROROTATORY.
■ **laevoroˈtation** *noun* (the property of) rotating the plane of polarized light in this direction L19.

laevulinic /liːvjʊˈlɪnɪk/ *adjective.* Also ***lev-**. L19.
[ORIGIN formed as LAEVULOSAN + -IN[1] + -IC.]
CHEMISTRY. ***laevulinic acid***, a crystalline keto acid, $CH_3CO(CH_2)_2COOH$, orig. obtained by heating laevulose.

laevulosan /ˈliːvjʊləsan/ *noun.* Also ***lev-**. M19.
[ORIGIN from LAEVULOSE + -AN.]
CHEMISTRY. †**1** An anhydride of laevulose. M–L19.
2 A polysaccharide composed chiefly of laevulose residues. E20.

laevulose /ˈliːvjʊləʊz, -s/ *noun.* Also ***lev-**. L19.
[ORIGIN formed as LAEVO- + -ULE + -OSE[2].]
CHEMISTRY. The laevorotatory (and predominant naturally occurring) form of fructose. Cf. DEXTROSE.

lafayette /lɑːfeɪˈɛt/ *noun. US.* M19.
[ORIGIN Marquis de *Lafayette* or *La Fayette* (1757–1834), French soldier and statesman who fought in the American War of Independence.]
A sciaenid fish of N. American Atlantic coasts and rivers, *Leiostomus xanthurus*, now more commonly called ***spot***.

Laffer curve /ˈlafə kəːv/ *noun phr.* L20.
[ORIGIN Arthur *Laffer* (b. 1942), US economist.]
ECONOMICS. A supposed relationship between economic activity and the rate of taxation, which suggests that there is an optimum tax rate which maximizes tax revenue.

LAFTA *abbreviation.*
Latin American Free Trade Association.

lag /lag/ *noun*[1]. In sense 2 also †**lage**. ME.
[ORIGIN Unknown. Cf. LAG *verb*[3].]
1 A narrow marshy meadow, usu. beside a stream. Long *obsolete* exc. *dial.* ME.
2 Water, urine. *arch. slang.* M16.
†**3** ***lag of duds***, a 'wash' of clothes. *slang.* M16–E18.

lag /lag/ *noun*[2]. E16.
[ORIGIN Rel. to LAG *adjective.* Cf. LAG *verb*[2].]
1 The last or hindmost person (in a race, game, sequence of any kind). *slang.* Now *rare.* E16.
†**2** In *pl.* What remains in a vessel after the liquor is drawn off; dregs, lees. E16–E18.
†**3** The lowest class. (Cf. ***lag-end*** s.v. LAG *adjective*) *rare* (Shakes.). Only in E17.
4 The condition of lagging. M19. ▸**b** A period of time separating any phenomenon or event from an earlier one to which it is related (causally or in some other way) (freq. ***time lag***); (the amount of) a retardation in a current or other movement. See also ***jet lag*** s.v. JET *noun*[2]. M19.

b *Economist* A . . lag must occur between the dates when . . losses are incurred and compensation is paid. *Nature* A . . lag between the addition of bicarbonate and the . . attainment of the maximum rate. M. GORDON A season . . behind, but that small lag was death.

b angle of lag the fraction of a complete cycle, multiplied by 360° or 2π radians, by which a sinusoidal electric current lags behind the associated sinusoidal voltage. **lag of the tide** the interval by which the tidewave falls behind the mean time in the first and third quarters of the moon (cf. PRIMING *noun*[2]). ***leads and lags***: see LEAD *noun*[2].
– COMB.: **lag fault** *GEOLOGY* a type of overthrust formed when the uppermost of a series of rocks moves more slowly than the lower ones; **lag phase** *BIOLOGY* the period elapsing between the inoculation of a culture medium etc. with bacteria and the commencement of their exponential growth; **lag time** the period of time elapsing between one event and a later, related, event, esp. between a cause and its effect; (the extent of) a lag.

lag /lag/ *noun*[3]. *dial.* E17.
[ORIGIN Unknown.]
1 A flock of geese. *rare.* E17.
2 A goose. Freq. as *interjection*, used in driving farmyard geese. E19.
– NOTE: The primary sense is prob. 2, which may be attested earlier in GREYLAG.

lag /lag/ *noun*[4]. L17.
[ORIGIN Prob. of Scandinavian origin: cf. Icelandic *laggar*, Swedish *lagg* stave, Old Norse *lǫgg* rim of a barrel, from Germanic base of LAY *verb*[1].]
1 A stave of a barrel. Now *dial.* L17.
2 Each of the staves or laths forming the covering of a band drum or a steam boiler or cylinder, or the upper casing of a carding machine; (a piece of) any insulating cover for a boiler etc. Also, each of the wooden crossbars in a loom used to control the weaving of fabric designs. M19.
– COMB.: **lag bolt**, **lag-screw** a woodscrew with a flat or bolt head used to secure a lag to a cylinder or drum.

lag /lag/ *noun*[5]. *slang.* E19.
[ORIGIN Unknown. Cf. LAG *verb*[4].]
1 A term of imprisonment or (formerly) transportation. E19.
2 A convict. Formerly also, a person sentenced to transportation. E19. ▸**b** A hardened or habitual prisoner, a recidivist. Freq. ***old lag***. E20.

lag /lag/ *adjective. obsolete* exc. *dial.* LME.
[ORIGIN Perh. a children's & dial. alt. of LAST *adjective.* Cf. LAG *noun*[2], *verb*[2].]
Last, hindmost; belated, lingering behind, lagging, tardy. Also as *interjection*, claiming the last turn in a children's game. (Earliest in ***lag-man*** below.)
– COMB.: **lag-end** the hinder or latter part, the fag end. †**lag-man** the last person, the one who brings up the rear.

lag /lag/ *verb*[1] *trans.* Long *obsolete* exc. *dial.* Infl. **-gg-**. LME.
[ORIGIN Unknown.]
Make wet and muddy; bedraggle.

lag /lag/ *verb*[2]. Infl. **-gg-**. M16.
[ORIGIN Rel. to LAG *adjective.* Cf. LAG *noun*[2].]
1 *verb intrans.* Progress too slowly; fail to keep pace with others; hang back, fall behind, remain in the rear. Freq. foll. by *behind* (adverb or preposition), *after.* M16.

K. LINES Very soon they lagged on the steep upward track. K. M. E. MURRAY Britain had lagged behind the Germans in philological study.

2 *verb trans.* Hinder, retard, tire. *obsolete* exc. *dial.* L16.
3 *verb trans.* Fall behind; be or occur after. M20.

Daily Telegraph Unemployment lags changes in output.

– COMB.: **lag-last** a person who lags or lingers to the very last.
■ **laggingly** *adverb* in a slow or lingering manner E19.

lag /lag/ *verb*[3]. *slang.* Infl. **-gg-**. Also †**lage**. M16.
[ORIGIN Unknown. Cf. LAG *noun*[1].]
†**1** *verb trans.* Wash, wash *off.* Only in M16.
2 *verb trans.* Adulterate (spirits) with water. E19.
3 *verb intrans.* Urinate. E19.

lag /lag/ *verb*[4]. *arch. slang.* Infl. **-gg-**. L16.
[ORIGIN Unknown. Cf. LAG *noun*[5].]
1 *verb trans. & intrans.* Carry off, steal. L16.
2 *verb trans.* Sentence to prison or (formerly) transportation. E19.
3 *verb trans.* Catch, apprehend, arrest. M19.

lag /lag/ *verb*[5] *trans.* Infl. **-gg-**. L19.
[ORIGIN from LAG *noun*[4]. Cf. earlier LAGGER *noun*[3], LAGGING *noun*[2].]
Cover (a boiler, pipe, etc.) with insulating material.

Science News Liquid oxygen tanks . . have to be lagged to reduce the loss of oxygen by boiling.

lagan /ˈlag(ə)n/ *noun.* Also **lig-** /ˈlɪg-/. M16.
[ORIGIN Old French (whence medieval Latin *laganum*) perh. from Old Norse *lagn-*, as in *lagn*, genit. *lagnar* dragnet, from Germanic base of LAY *verb*[1].]
LAW. Goods or wreckage lying on the bed of the sea. Cf. FLOTSAM, JETSAM.
■ **lagander** *noun* (long *obsolete* exc. *hist.*) an official who took charge of lagan or wreckage E16.

lagar /laˈgar, laˈgɑː/ *noun.* Pl. ***-res*** /-res, -rɪz/. M19.
[ORIGIN Spanish from Latin *lacus* vat for freshly pressed wine. Cf. LAKE *noun*[2] 4.]
In Spain and Portugal: a large (usu. stone) trough in which grapes are trodden.

lagarto /ləˈgɑːtəʊ/ *noun.* Long *rare.* Pl. **-os**. M16.
[ORIGIN Spanish: see ALLIGATOR.]
An alligator.

Lag b'Omer /lɑːg ˈbəʊmə/ *noun.* L19.
[ORIGIN Hebrew *lāg* pronunc. of the letters LG (*lamed*, *gimel*) symbolizing 33 + *bā* in the + *ʿōmer* OMER.]
A Jewish festival held on the 33rd day of the Omer, traditionally regarded as celebrating the end of a plague in the 2nd cent. AD.

†**lage** *noun, verb* see LAG *noun*[1], *verb*[3].

lagen /ˈlag(ə)n/ *noun. obsolete* exc. *hist.* L16.
[ORIGIN Latin *lagona*, *lagena* flagon from Greek *lagunos*.]
A liquid measure equal to several pints.

lagena /ləˈdʒiːnə/ *noun.* Pl. **-nae** /-niː/. L19.
[ORIGIN Latin: see LAGEN.]
ZOOLOGY. An extension of the saccule of the ear in some vertebrates, corresponding to the cochlear duct in mammals.
■ **lagenar** *adjective* M20.

lageniform /ləˈdʒiːnɪfɔːm/ *adjective.* E19.
[ORIGIN formed as LAGENA + -I- + -FORM.]
BOTANY & ZOOLOGY. Shaped like a bottle or flask.

lager /ˈlɑːgə/ *noun.* M19.
[ORIGIN German *Lager-Bier* beer brewed for keeping, from *Lager* storehouse.]
A kind of effervescent beer, orig. German or Czech, which is light in colour and body; a drink of this. Also (esp. in early use) ***lager beer***.
– COMB.: **lager lout** *colloq.* a young man who behaves badly as a result of excessive drinking.

lager /ˈlɑːgə/ *verb trans.* M20.
[ORIGIN German *lagern* to store.]
Store (beer) to mature.

lagerstätte /ˈlɑːgəʃtɛtə/ *noun.* Pl. **-atten** /-ɛtən/. L20.
[ORIGIN German *Lagerstätte* mineral deposit, from *Lager* store, stock + *Stätte* place, site.]
PALAEONTOLOGY. A fossil deposit of exceptional richness or interest.

lagetto /ləˈgɛtəʊ/ *noun. W. Indian.* Pl. **-os**. L17.
[ORIGIN Amer. Spanish *lageto*.]
The lacebark tree, *Lagetta lagetto*.

laggard /ˈlagəd/ *adjective, noun, & verb.* E18.
[ORIGIN from LAG *verb*[2] + -ARD.]
▸ **A** *adjective.* Lagging behind, hanging back, loitering, slow. E18.

T. WILLIAMS While love made her brilliant, . . it made me laggard and dull.

▸ **B** *noun.* A person who lags behind; a lingerer, a loiterer. E19.
▸ **C** *verb intrans.* Hang back, loiter. M19.
■ **laggardly** *adjective* having the character or spirit of a laggard; hesitant, slow: M20. **laggardly** *adverb* (*rare*) in a slow or hesitant manner M19. **laggardness** *noun* M19.

lagger /ˈlagə/ *noun*[1]. E16.
[ORIGIN from LAG *verb*[2] + -ER[1].]
A person who lags or hangs back; a lingerer, a loiterer.

lagger /ˈlagə/ *noun*[2]. *slang.* Now *rare.* E19.
[ORIGIN from LAG *verb*[4] or *noun*[5] + -ER[1].]
A convict or ex-convict.

L

lagger /ˈlagə/ *noun*[3]. **E19.**
[ORIGIN from (the same root as) LAG *verb*[5] + -ER[1].]
A person who installs and maintains insulation for pipes, boilers, etc.

laggin /ˈlagɪn/ *noun*. *Scot. & N. English*. **E16.**
[ORIGIN from Old Norse *lǫgg*: see LAG *noun*[4].]
1 The projecting part of the staves at the bottom part of a cask or other hooped vessel. **E16.**
2 The inner angle of a wooden dish, between the sides and the bottom. **L18.**

lagging /ˈlagɪŋ/ *noun*[1]. *slang*. Now *rare*. **E19.**
[ORIGIN from LAG *verb*[4] + -ING[1].]
A sentence or term of imprisonment or penal servitude, *spec.* a term of three years.

lagging /ˈlagɪŋ/ *noun*[2]. **M19.**
[ORIGIN from (from the same root as) LAG *verb*[5] + -ING[1].]
1 *sing.* & (now *rare*) in *pl.* Insulation material for boilers, pipes, etc. **M19.**
2 The action of covering a boiler, pipe, etc., with insulation. **L19.**

lagniappe /laˈnjap/ *noun*. *US*. **M19.**
[ORIGIN Louisiana French from Spanish *la ñapa*.]
Something given as a bonus or gratuity; extra reward.

> S. J. PERELMAN Since the ship was calling there anyway, the trip would be pure lagniappe. *Time* A tasty lagniappe: a special dividend of $2.50 per share on top of the regular . . dividend.

for lagniappe as a bonus; into the bargain; for good measure.

lagomorph /ˈlagəmɔːf/ *noun*. **L19.**
[ORIGIN from Greek *lagōs* hare + -MORPH.]
ZOOLOGY. Any of the herbivorous mammals constituting the order Lagomorpha, which includes the hares, rabbits, and pikas.

lagoon /ləˈguːn/ *noun & verb*. Also (earlier) †**laguna**, †**lagune**. **E17.**
[ORIGIN Italian, Spanish *laguna* (partly through French *lagune*), from Latin LACUNA: see -OON.]
▸ **A** *noun*. **1** An area of salt or brackish water separated from the sea by low sandbanks or a similar barrier; *spec.* any of those in the neighbourhood of Venice, Italy. **E17.**
2 The stretch of water within an atoll or inside a barrier reef. **M18.**
3 A freshwater (esp. stagnant) lake or pond. *US, Austral., & NZ*. **M18.**
4 A shallow pool constructed for the treatment and concentration of sewage and slurry. **E20.**
▸ **B** *verb trans.* Treat and concentrate (sewage and slurry) in lagoons. **E20.**
■ **lagoonal** *adjective* of or characteristic of a lagoon or lagoons **E20.**

lagophthalmos /lagɔfˈθalməs/ *noun*. Also (earlier) **-mus**. **E17.**
[ORIGIN (mod. Latin *lagophthalmus*) from Greek *lagōphthalmos* adjective, from *lagōs* hare (from the supposed inability of hares to close their eyes) + *ophthalmos* eye.]
Inability to close the eyes (as a symptom of disease).
■ **lagophthalmia** *noun* = LAGOPHTHALMOS **L17.** **lagophthalmic** *adjective* pertaining to or affected with lagophthalmos **L19.**

Lagrange /ləˈgrɒ̃ʒ, lɑː-/ *noun*. **M19.**
[ORIGIN Joseph Louis *Lagrange* (1736–1813), Italian-born mathematician who worked in Prussia and France.]
MATH. Used *attrib.* and in *possess.* to designate various concepts introduced by Lagrange or arising out of his work.
Lagrange equation, **Lagrange's equation** each of a set of equations of motion in classical dynamics relating the total kinetic energy of a system to a set of generalized coordinates, forces acting, and time.

Lagrangian /ləˈgrɒ̃ʒɪən, lɑː-/ *adjective & noun*. Also **-ean**. **M19.**
[ORIGIN from LAGRANGE + -IAN.]
MATH. & ASTRONOMY. ▸ **A** *adjective*. Of or pertaining to the work of J. L. Lagrange (see LAGRANGE); of the kind introduced by Lagrange or associated with his work. **M19.**
Lagrangian function the difference between the kinetic energy and the potential energy of a system expressed as a function of generalized coordinates, their time derivatives, and time. **Lagrangian point** each of five points in the orbital plane of two bodies (e.g. a planet and a moon) at which a third body of negligible mass will remain stationary relative to the others.
▸ **B** *noun*. A Lagrangian function. **M20.**

Lagting /ˈlɑːgtɪŋ/ *noun*. **M19.**
[ORIGIN Norwegian.]
A functional division of the Norwegian Parliament, operating primarily for law-making purposes.

†**laguna**, †**lagune** *nouns* vars. of LAGOON.

lah /lɑː/ *noun*. Also (earlier) **la**. **ME.**
[ORIGIN from Latin *la(bii)*: see UT.]
MUSIC. The sixth note of a scale in a movable-doh system; the note A in the fixed-doh system.

lahar /ˈlɑːhɑː/ *noun*. **E20.**
[ORIGIN Javanese.]
GEOLOGY. A mud-flow of volcanic ash mixed with water.

lah-de-da *noun, adjective, & adverb, verb* vars. of LA-DI-DA *noun* etc., *verb*.

Lahnda /ˈlɑːndə/ *noun & adjective*. **E20.**
[ORIGIN Punjabi *lahandā*, *lahandī* western, of the west.]
(Designating or pertaining to) an Indo-Aryan language of the western Punjab and adjacent areas of Pakistan.

Lahu /lɑːˈhuː/ *noun & adjective*. Pl. of noun same, **-s**. **E20.**
[ORIGIN Lahu.]
A member of, of or pertaining to, an aboriginal people of the Lolo group in SW China, esp. Yunnan; (of) the Tibeto-Burman language of this people.

lai /leɪ/ *noun*[1]. **L18.**
[ORIGIN Old French: see LAY *noun*[2].]
Any of a number of short narrative poems concerned with love and magic written in England, in either English or French, between the 12th and the 15th cents. Also, a medieval French lyric associated with the *trouvères* of northern France. Also ***Breton lai***.

Lai /lʌɪ/ *noun*[2] *& adjective*. **L19.**
[ORIGIN Lai.]
▸ **A** *noun*. Pl. **-s**, same.
1 A member of a people living in the Chin hills of Myanmar (Burma). **L19.**
2 The language of this people. **E20.**
▸ **B** *attrib.* or as *adjective*. Of or pertaining to the Lais or their language. **L19.**

laic /ˈleɪɪk/ *adjective & noun*. **M16.**
[ORIGIN Late Latin *laicus* from Greek *laikos*, from *laos* people: see -IC. Cf. LAY *adjective*.]
▸ **A** *adjective*. Of or pertaining to a layman or the laity; non-clerical, secular, temporal. **M16.**
▸ **B** *noun*. A member of the laity; a person who is not an ecclesiastic. **L16.**
■ **laical** *adjective* **L15.** **laically** *adverb* **L19.**

laich /leɪx/ *noun, adjective, & adverb*. *Scot.* Also **laigh**. **LME.**
[ORIGIN Scot. form of LOW *adjective*.]
▸ **A** *noun*. A piece of low-lying ground; a hollow. **LME.**
▸ **B** *adjective*. On or near the ground, not elevated; inferior in rank or quality; not loud. **LME.**
▸ **C** *adverb*. In a low position; to a low point; in a low tone. **LME.**

laicise *verb* var. of LAICIZE.

laicism /ˈleɪɪsɪz(ə)m/ *noun*. **L18.**
[ORIGIN from LAIC + -ISM.]
The principle of control by members of the laity; secularism.

laicity /leɪˈɪsɪti/ *noun*. **E20.**
[ORIGIN from LAIC + -ITY.]
The principles of the laity; the rule or influence of the laity; the fact of being lay.

laicize /ˈleɪɪsʌɪz/ *verb trans.* Also **-ise**. **L19.**
[ORIGIN from LAIC + -IZE.]
Withdraw clerical character or status from; secularize; *spec.* place (a school etc.) under lay control; make (an office) tenable by members of the laity.

> *Pall Mall Gazette* To laicize the names of the Paris streets, and banish . . the word 'Sainte'. M. WEST When his priestly vocation no longer satisfied him he had asked to be laicised.

■ **laiciˈzation** *noun* **L19.** **laicizer** *noun* **L19.**

laid /leɪd/ *ppl adjective*. **M16.**
[ORIGIN pa. pple of LAY *verb*[1].]
1 That has been laid. Also with adverbs, as *by, down, off, on, out, up*. **M16.**

> H. DE WINDT In the midst of beautifully laid-out gardens, is the . . Palace of the Raja. *Architectural Review* Central heating, lighting, cooking, . . laid-on water and drainage. *Daily Telegraph* Laid-off workers at Coventry are receiving . . £5 unemployment benefit. *Country Life* Reaping a small field of badly laid corn. E. PIZZEY Sitting down to a properly laid table. *Armed Forces* The imperative need to observe laid-down procedures to the letter.

get laid *slang* have sexual intercourse. **laid paper**: having a ribbed appearance made by parallel wires in the mould or on the dandy roller. **laid work** embroidery consisting of strands of silk etc. laid on the material and held in place by tiny stitches.
2 Of rope: having strands twisted in a specified manner or style, as ***cable-laid***, ***hawser-laid***, etc. **M17.**
3 Of a scheme: deliberately contrived. *obsolete* exc. in ***best-laid***. **L17.**
4 ***laid-back***, inclined backwards; *fig.* (orig. *US*), relaxed, casual, nonchalant, detached; (of music) mellow, subdued. **E20.**

laid *verb pa. t. & pple* of LAY *verb*[1].

Laïdes *noun pl.* of LAÏS.

laidly /ˈleɪdli/ *adjective*. Now *arch. & Scot.* Also †**laily**. **ME.**
[ORIGIN North. var. of LOATHLY *adjective*.]
Offensive, hideous, repulsive.

laidron *noun* see LADRONE.

laigh *noun, adjective, & adverb* var. of LAICH.

laik /leɪk/ *verb intrans.* *obsolete* exc. *dial.* Also **lake**.
[ORIGIN Old English *lācan* corresp. to Old Norse *leika*, Gothic *laikan* play, repl. in Middle English by forms from Old Norse.]
†**1** Exert oneself, move quickly, leap, spring; fight. **OE–LME.**
2 Play, sport; take time off work. Also foll. by *about, away*. **ME.**

laika /ˈlʌɪkə/ *noun*. Pl. **laiki** /ˈlʌɪki/. **E20.**
[ORIGIN Russian *laĭka*, from *laĭ* bark.]
A dog belonging to a group of Asiatic breeds of the spitz type, characterized by a pointed muzzle, pricked ears, and a stocky body with a tail curling over the back.

†**laily** *adjective* var. of LAIDLY *adjective*.

lain /leɪn/ *noun*. *obsolete* exc. *dial.* **L16.**
[ORIGIN Perh. from pa. pple of LIE *verb*[1].]
A layer, a stratum.

lain *verb pa. pple* of LIE *verb*[1].

lair /lɛː/ *noun*[1].
[ORIGIN Old English *leger* = Old Frisian *leger* situation, Old Saxon *legar* bed (Dutch *leger* bed, camp, LEAGUER *noun*[1]), Old High German *leger* bed, camp (German *Lager*, infl. by *Lage* situation), Gothic *ligis*, from Germanic base of LIE *verb*[1].]
†**1** The action or fact of lying or lying down. **OE–M18.**
2 A grave, a tomb. Now only *Scot.*, a plot in a graveyard. **OE.**
3 A place where one sleeps; a bed, a couch. **OE.**

> CARLYLE Wretchedness . . shivers hunger-stricken into its lair of straw.

4 A resting place for domestic animals; *spec.* an enclosure or large shed for cattle on the way to market. **LME.**
5 A place of rest or concealment for a wild animal; *transf.* a (secret) retreat or base. **LME.**

> J. HILTON The tribesmen Kept you in some lair in the mountains.

beard the lion in his lair: see BEARD *verb* 1.
6 *AGRICULTURE*. Nature or kind of soil, with reference to its effect on the quality of crops, or of the animals pastured upon it. **LME.**

lair /lɛː/ *noun*[2]. *obsolete* exc. *dial.* **ME.**
[ORIGIN Old Norse *leir*.]
Clay, mire, mud.

lair /lɛː/ *noun*[3]. *Austral. & NZ slang*. Also **lare**. **E20.**
[ORIGIN Back-form. from LAIRY *adjective*[2].]
A flashily dressed man; a show-off.

lair /lɛː/ *verb*[1]. **ME.**
[ORIGIN from LAIR *noun*[1].]
†**1** *verb trans.* Prostrate, lay on the ground. Only in **ME.**
2 **a** *verb intrans.* Lie, repose (*on* a bed, *in* a lair). **L16.** ▸**b** *verb trans.* Place in a lair; serve as a lair for. **L17.**

lair /lɛː/ *verb*[2]. *obsolete* exc. *dial.* **M16.**
[ORIGIN from LAIR *noun*[2].]
1 *verb trans.* Cause or allow to sink in mire or a morass. **M16.**
2 *verb intrans.* Stick or sink in mire or bog. **L16.**

lair /lɛː/ *verb*[3]. *Austral. & NZ slang*. Also **lare**. **E20.**
[ORIGIN from LAIR *noun*[3] or *lairy* var. of LEERY *adjective*[2].]
1 *verb intrans.* Act in a flashy or knowing manner. **E20.**
2 *verb trans.* Dress flashily, dress *up*. Freq. as pa. pple in ***laired up***, ***all laired up***. **M20.**

lairage /ˈlɛːrɪdʒ/ *noun*. **L19.**
[ORIGIN from LAIR *noun*[1] or *verb*[1] + -AGE.]
The placing of cattle in a lair or lairs; space, or a place, where cattle may be rested or kept on the way to market.

laird /lɛːd/ *noun*. *Scot.* **LME.**
[ORIGIN Scot. var. of LORD *noun*.]
A landowner, esp. of a large estate; *hist.* a holder of land directly from the king.
■ **lairdie** *noun* a petty laird **M18.** **lairdly** *adjective* having the rank or quality of a laird **L19.** **lairˈdocracy** *noun* [after *aristocracy*] lairds as forming a ruling class **M19.** **lairdship** *noun* (**a**) the estate of a laird; (**b**) the condition or dignity of being a laird; (**c**) lairds collectively: **M17.**

lairy /ˈlɛːri/ *adjective*[1]. *obsolete* exc. *dial.* **ME.**
[ORIGIN from LAIR *noun*[2] + -Y[1].]
Boggy, miry, swampy. Formerly also, earthly, filthy.

lairy *adjective*[2] var. of LEERY *adjective*[2].

Laïs /ˈlʌɪɪs/ *noun*. Now *rare*. Pl. **Laïdes** /ˈlʌɪɪdiːz/. **L16.**
[ORIGIN Either of two celebrated Greek courtesans of the 5th and 4th cents. BC.]
(A name for) a beautiful and accomplished temptress.

laisse /lɛs/ *noun*. Pl. pronounced same. **L19.**
[ORIGIN French.]
In Old French verse: a distinct section of a poem.

laisser-aller, **laisser-faire**, **laisser-passer** *nouns* vars. of LAISSEZ-ALLER etc.

laissez-aller /lɛseɪˈaleɪ, *foreign* lɛseale/ *noun*. Also **laisser-**. **E19.**
[ORIGIN French, lit. 'allow to go'.]
Absence of restraint; unconstrained ease and freedom.

> THACKERAY With some justice, though with a good deal too much laissez-aller of tongue. *attrib.*: DICKENS A magnificent high-handed laissez-aller neglect.

laissez-faire /lɛseɪˈfɛː, *foreign* lɛsefɛːr/ *noun*. Also **laisser-**. **E19.**
[ORIGIN French, lit. 'allow to do'.]
Government abstention from interference in the actions of individuals, esp. in commerce; *gen.* non-interference or indifference.

Atlantic Monthly Frequently characterized as an exacting conductor.. Evans has since become alarmingly laissez-faire. *attrib.*: G. M. TREVELYAN The slum-landlords.. according to the prevalent laissez-faire philosophy, were engaged from motives of self-interest.

■ **laissez-faireism** /lɛseɪˈfɛːrɪz(ə)m/ *noun* belief in or practice of laissez-faire **M19**. **laissez-faireist**, **-fairist** /lɛseɪˈfɛːrɪst/ *noun* a believer in laissez-faire, a practitioner of laissez-faire **M20**.

laissez-passer /lɛseɪˈpɑːseɪ, *foreign* lɛsepɑse (*pl. same*)/ *noun*. Also **laisser-**. **E20**.
[ORIGIN French, lit. 'allow to pass'.]
A permit to travel or to enter a particular place, a pass.

Times He has been granted.. a laissez-passer to the Greek military zone. Y. MENUHIN Music has been my laissez-passer to foreign lands.

lait *noun* var. of LATE *noun*[1].

lait /leɪt/ *verb*. *obsolete* exc. *dial.* **ME**.
[ORIGIN Old Norse *leita*.]
1 *verb trans.* Look or search for; seek, try to find. **ME**.
2 *verb intrans.* Look, search. Also, hesitate in speech. **ME**.

laitance /ˈleɪt(ə)ns/ *noun*. **E20**.
[ORIGIN French, from *lait* milk: see -ANCE.]
A milky scum appearing on the surface of freshly laid cement.

laithe *noun* var. of LATHE *noun*[2].

laity /ˈleɪɪti/ *noun*. **LME**.
[ORIGIN from LAY *adjective* + -ITY.]
▸ **I** Treated as *sing.* & (usu.) *collect. pl.*
1 The body of people not in ecclesiastical orders as opp. to the clergy; lay people collectively. **LME**.

D. CUPITT Christianity makes a sharper distinction than other faiths between the clergy and the laity.

2 Those people not following some particular profession or occupation, or not knowledgeable in some particular subject. **M19**.

G. B. SHAW All professions are conspiracies against the laity.

▸ **II 3** The condition or state of being a lay person. **E17**.

lakatoi /ˈlakətɔɪ/ *noun*. Pl. same, **-s**. **L19**.
[ORIGIN Papuan.]
A vessel made by the Motu of New Guinea by lashing together three or more large dugout canoes and adding a deck and superstructure.

lake /leɪk/ *noun*[1]. *obsolete* exc. *dial.*
[ORIGIN Old English *lacu* from Germanic.]
A small stream of running water. Also, a channel for water.

lake /leɪk/ *noun*[2]. **LOE**.
[ORIGIN Old French *lac* from Latin *lacus* lake, pool, tank, pit, trough; perh. later assim. to LAKE *noun*[1].]
1 A pond, a pool. Now *US*. **LOE**.
2 A large body of water entirely surrounded by land; an ornamental stretch of water in a park etc. **ME**. ▸**b** *transf.* A stored surplus of a liquid commodity. Freq. with specifying word, esp. *wine*. Cf. MOUNTAIN 2b. **L20**.

JULIETTE HUXLEY One very severe winter the lake froze right over its eastern end. *fig.*: D. DELILLO A great dark lake of male rage.

go and jump in the lake, ***go jump in the lake***: see JUMP *verb*. ***Great Lakes***: see GREAT *adjective*. ***jump in the lake***: see JUMP *verb*. **the Lakes** = ***Lake District*** below.
†**3 a** A pit; occas., a grave. **ME–E16**. ▸**b** An underground dungeon; a prison. Only in **LME**.
†**4** [After Latin *lacus*.] A wine vat. **LME–M17**.
– COMB.: **lake-basin** (***a***) a depression which contains, or has contained, a lake; (***b***) the area drained by all the streams entering a lake; **Lake Country** = ***Lake District*** below; **lake-crater** a crater which contains or has contained a lake; **Lake District** *spec.* the region round the lakes in Cumbria in NW England; **lake-dweller** a prehistoric inhabitant of a lake dwelling; **lake dwelling** a prehistoric hut built upon piles driven into the bed or shore of a lake; **lakefront** the land along the edge of a lake; ***lake* HERRING**; **Lake poetry**: written by the Lake Poets; **Lake Poets** the poets Coleridge, Southey, and Wordsworth, who lived in the Lake District; **lake salmon** = ***lake trout*** (b) below; **Lake School** the Lake Poets; **lake settlement** a prehistoric settlement with lake dwellings; **lakeside** *noun & attrib. adjective* (located at) the side of a lake; **lake trout** (***a***) a large, pale, partly migrating form of the trout, *Salmo trutta*, occurring in N. European lakes; (***b***) the salmonid *Salvelinus namaycush*, occurring in N. American lakes; **lake village** a prehistoric village made up of lake dwellings; **lakeweed** water pepper, *Persicaria hydropiper*.
■ **lakeless** *adjective* having no lakes **L19**. **lakelet** *noun* a small lake **L18**.

lake /leɪk/ *noun*[3]. **E17**.
[ORIGIN Var. of LAC *noun*[1].]
1 A purplish-red pigment originally obtained from lac, later from cochineal treated with a metallic compound. Also, the colour of this. **E17**.
2 Any pigment obtained by the combination of an organic colouring matter with a metallic oxide, hydroxide, or salt; *spec.* the insoluble product of a soluble dye and a mordant. **L17**.
crimson lake, ***green lake***, ***Indian lake***, ***madder lake***, ***purple lake***, etc.

lake /leɪk/ *verb*[1] *trans.* Now *rare* or *obsolete*. **L19**.
[ORIGIN from LAKE *noun*[3].]
Make (blood or blood cells) lake-coloured, *spec.* by causing haemolysis.

lake *verb*[2] var. of LAIK.

Lakeland /ˈleɪklənd/ *noun & adjective*. Also **l-**. **E19**.
[ORIGIN from LAKE *noun*[2] + LAND *noun*[1].]
1 (Of or pertaining to) an area of lakes, *spec.* the English Lake District. **E19**.

J. MUNRO A woman.. whose Lakeland accent was difficult for him to understand.

2 In full ***Lakeland terrier***. A rough-coated, red or black and tan terrier with a stocky body and a broad muzzle, belonging to a breed developed in Lakeland. **E20**.

T. HORNER A good Lakeland will hang on to his quarry with tremendous grip.

■ **Lakelander** *noun* a native or inhabitant of Lakeland **L19**.

laker /ˈleɪkə/ *noun*. In senses 1, 2 also **L-**. **L18**.
[ORIGIN from LAKE *noun*[2] + -ER[1].]
†**1** A visitor to the English Lake District. **L18–E19**.
2 A Lake Poet. *arch. colloq.* **E19**.
3 A fish living in or taken from a lake; *spec.* = ***lake trout*** (b) s.v. LAKE *noun*[2]. *N. Amer.* **E19**.
4 A person accustomed to sailing on a lake. **M19**.
5 A boat constructed for sailing on the Great Lakes of N. America. **L19**.

lakh /lak/ *noun*. Also **lac**. **E17**.
[ORIGIN Hindi *lākh* from Sanskrit *lakṣa* mark, token, 100,000.]
In the Indian subcontinent: one hundred thousand; occas., an indefinite large number.

J. MASTERS Wouldn't it be wonderful if someone gave us a lakh of rupees. *Times of India* The cyclone has left.. a trail of destruction.. leaving lakhs of people in desolation.

lakin /ˈleɪkɪn/ *noun*[1]. *obsolete* exc. *dial.* **LME**.
[ORIGIN Perh. from Old Norse *leika* toy: cf. LAIK.]
A plaything, a toy. Formerly also, a baby.

†**lakin** *noun*[2]. *colloq.* **L15–E17**.
[ORIGIN Contr. of LADY *noun* + -KIN. Cf. LADYKIN.]
by lakin, ***by our lakin***, by Our Lady.

lakish /ˈleɪkɪʃ/ *adjective*. **L16**.
[ORIGIN from LAKE *noun*[2] + -ISH[1].]
1 †**a** Having many lakes or pools. Only in **L16**. ▸†**b** Inhabiting a lake. **M–L17**. ▸**c** Like a lake. **L19**.
2 Of or pertaining to the Lake Poets; resembling the productions of the Lake Poets. **E19**.

Lakist /ˈleɪkɪst/ *noun*. *arch. colloq.* **E19**.
[ORIGIN from LAKE *noun*[2] + -IST.]
A member or adherent of the Lake School of poetry; a Lake Poet.

Lakota /ləˈkəʊtə/ *noun & adjective*. Pl. of noun **-s**, same. **M19**.
[ORIGIN Lakota *lakhóta*.]
A member of, of or pertaining to, a Sioux people of western South Dakota; (of) the dialect of this people. Also called ***Teton***.

lakoum *noun* var. of LOKUM.

laksa /ˈlɑːksa/ *noun*. **L20**.
[ORIGIN Malay.]
A Malaysian dish of Chinese origin, consisting of rice noodles served in a curry sauce or hot soup.

laksamana /laksəˈmɑːnə/ *noun*. **E17**.
[ORIGIN Malay from Sanskrit *lakṣmana* lit. 'having fortunate tokens' (the name of a mythical hero, Rama's half-brother).]
(The title formerly given to) a high dignitary or admiral in the Malay kingdoms.

lakum *noun* var. of LOKUM.

laky /ˈleɪki/ *adjective*. **M19**.
[ORIGIN from LAKE *noun*[3] + -Y[1].]
Of the colour of lake, purplish-red.

la-la /lɑːˈlɑː, ˈlɑːlɑː/ *adjective*. Now *rare* or *obsolete*. **L18**.
[ORIGIN from *la la* redupl. of LA *interjection*.]
So-so, not very good, poor.

la-la /lɑːˈlɑː, ˈlɑːlɑː/ *verb*. **E20**.
[ORIGIN formed as LA-LA *adjective*.]
1 *verb intrans.* Sing or say the syllable *la* repeatedly, esp. in place of the words or notes of a tune. **E20**.
2 *verb trans.* Sing (a song) in this way. **E20**.

lalang /ˈlɑːlaŋ/ *noun*. Also **-ll-**. **L18**.
[ORIGIN Malay.]
A large coarse grass, *Imperata cylindrica*, which overruns pastures and forest clearings in Old World tropics.

lalapaloosa, **lalapalooza** *nouns* vars. of LALLAPALOOSA.

laldy /ˈlaldi/ *noun*. *Scot.* **L19**.
[ORIGIN Uncertain: perh. rel. to Old English *læl* whip, weal.]
A beating, a thrashing; punishment. Now chiefly *fig.*, esp. in ***give it laldy***, do something with vigour or enthusiasm.

-lalia /ˈleɪlɪə/ *suffix*.
[ORIGIN Repr. Greek *lalia* speech, chatter.]
Used in forming words denoting various disorders or unusual faculties of speech, as in ***dyslalia***, ***echolalia***, ***glossolalia***, ***idiolalia***, etc.

Lalique /laˈliːk/ *noun & adjective*. **E20**.
[ORIGIN See below.]
(Designating) jewellery or decorative glassware made by or in the style of the French designer René Lalique (1860–1945).

lall /lal/ *verb intrans. rare.* **L19**.
[ORIGIN Imit., after Latin *lallare*: see LALLATION.]
Speak childishly or unintelligibly, utter meaningless sounds. See also LALLING.

Lallan /ˈlalən/ *adjective & noun*. *Scot.* As noun now usu. **Lallans** /ˈlalənz/. **E18**.
[ORIGIN Repr. a pronunc. of LOWLAND.]
▸ **A** *adjective*. Of or pertaining to the Scottish Lowlands. **E18**.
▸ **B** *noun*. The Lowland Scots dialect; now *esp.* a revived and modified form of the spoken dialect as a literary language. **L18**.

lallang *noun* var. of LALANG.

Lallans *noun* see LALLAN.

lallapaloosa /laləpəˈluːsə, -zə/ *noun*. *US slang.* Also **lala-**, **lolla-** /lɒlə-/, **-za** /-zə/, **-zer** /-zə/, & other vars. **L19**.
[ORIGIN Fanciful.]
Something outstandingly good of its kind; an excellent or attractive person or thing.

S. J. PERELMAN All agreed that Luba Pneumatic was a lollapaloosa, the Eighth Wonder of the World. *New Yorker* Palms, marble statues, and indoor fountains galore—a lalapalooza.

lallation /laˈleɪʃ(ə)n/ *noun*. **M17**.
[ORIGIN Latin *lallatio(n-)*, from *lallat-* pa. ppl stem of *lallare* sing lullaby: see -ATION.]
1 Infantile or imperfect speech, *esp.* the repetition of meaningless sounds by babies; idioglossia. **M17**.
2 Pronunciation of what should be the phoneme /r/ as if /l/. Also called ***lambdacism***. **M19**.

lalling /ˈlalɪŋ/ *noun*. *rare.* **L19**.
[ORIGIN from (the same root as) LALL *verb* + -ING[1].]
= LALLATION.

lallygag *noun & verb* var. of LOLLYGAG.

lam /lam/ *noun*. *N. Amer. slang.* **L19**.
[ORIGIN from the verb.]
Escape, flight. Chiefly as below.
on the lam on the run. **take it on a lam**, **take it on the lam** run away, escape.

lam /lam/ *verb*. Infl. **-mm-**. **L16**.
[ORIGIN Perh. of Scandinavian origin: cf. Norwegian, Danish *lamme* lame, paralyse.]
1 *verb trans.* Beat soundly, thrash, strike. Now *colloq.* **L16**.

D. L. SAYERS If you're thinkin' of.. lammin' a millionaire on the head, don't do it.

2 *verb intrans.* Strike, attack with blows etc., (foll. by *into* a person); hit *out*. *colloq.* **L19**.

CONAN DOYLE Lam out with your whip as hard as you can lick. R. H. MORRIESON Once Pop really lammed into her, gave her one helluva hiding.

3 *verb intrans.* Run off, escape. *slang* (chiefly *US*). **L19**.
■ **lamming** *noun* (***a***) the action of the verb; (***b***) a beating, a thrashing: **E17**. **lamster** *noun* (*slang*, chiefly *US*) a fugitive, a person on the run **E20**.

Lam. *abbreviation*.
Lamentations (in the Bible).

lama /ˈlɑːmə/ *noun*. **M17**.
[ORIGIN Tibetan *bla-ma* (the *b* is silent).]
A Buddhist religious teacher of Tibet or Mongolia.
DALAI LAMA. ***grand lama***: see GRAND *adjective*[1]. ***PANCHEN Lama***. TASHI LAMA.
■ **lamaic** *adjective* pertaining to or characteristic of lamas **E19**. **lamaism** *noun* the system of doctrine and observances inculcated and maintained by lamas; (**L-**) Tibetan Buddhism: **E19**. **lamaist** *noun & adjective* (***a***) *noun* a person who professes lamaism; (***b***) *adjective* of or pertaining to lamaists or lamaism: **E19**. **lamanism** *noun* = LAMAISM **M18**. **lamasery** *noun* a monastery of lamas **M19**.

lamantin /ləˈmantɪn/ *noun*. **M17**.
[ORIGIN French.]
The manatee.

Lamarckian /ləˈmɑːkɪən/ *adjective & noun*. **E19**.
[ORIGIN from *Lamarck* (see below) + -IAN.]
▸ **A** *adjective*. Of or pertaining to the French naturalist Jean Baptiste Lamarck (1744–1829) or his theory of organic evolution, which he ascribed to heritable modifications produced in the individual by habit, instinctive propensity, and the direct action of the environment. **E19**.
▸ **B** *noun*. A person who holds Lamarckian views. **M19**.
■ **Lamarckianism** *noun* = LAMARCKISM **L19**. **Lamarckism** *noun* the theory of the origin of species proposed by Lamarck **L19**.

lamb /lam/ *noun*.
[ORIGIN Old English *lamb* = Old Frisian, Old Saxon, Old High German *lamb* (Dutch *lam*, German *Lamm*), Old Norse, Gothic *lamb* (in Gothic 'sheep'), from Germanic.]
1 A young sheep. **OE**.

MILTON Ewes and their bleating Lambs. *Proverb*: One might as well be hanged for a sheep as a lamb.

L

2 *fig.* **a** A young member of a flock, esp. of the Church. *arch.* OE. ▸**b** A person who is as meek, gentle, innocent, or weak as a lamb. Also used as a term of endearment. OE. ▸**c** A simpleton; a person who is cheated; *esp.* a person who loses money in speculation. LME.

a J. WESLEY One who was as hot as any of the lambs at the tabernacle; but she is now a calm, reasonable woman. **b** G. PUTTENHAM It is comely for a man to be a lambe in the house, and a Lyon in the field. P. BOWLES But my dear lamb, whatever are you going to *do* all day? **c** W. GLADDEN The 'lambs' are shorn in this . . stock market alone at eight hundred million dollars a year.

3 Lambskin. LME.
4 The flesh of a lamb used as food. LME.

J. MASTERS The smell of roasting lamb was all over the place.

– PHRASES: *as meek as a lamb*: see MEEK *adjective* 1b. *beaver lamb*: see BEAVER *noun*[1]. **Holy Lamb** Jesus Christ; *HERALDRY* = AGNUS DEI 2. *Immaculate Lamb*: see IMMACULATE *adjective*. **like a lamb** gently, compliantly. *MUTTON dressed as lamb*. *paschal lamb*: see PASCHAL *adjective*. *Persian lamb*: see PERSIAN *adjective*. *SHORN lamb*. **the Lamb (of God)** Jesus Christ. *twin lamb disease*: see TWIN *adjective & noun*.

– COMB.: **lamb-creep** a hole in a hedge or hurdle just large enough for lambs to get in and out of the fold; **lamb fries** *US* lamb's testicles as food; **lambkill** *N. Amer.* the sheep laurel, *Kalmia angustifolia*; **lamb-pie** (*a*) a pie containing lamb; (*b*) (*obsolete* exc. *dial.*) a beating, a thrashing; *eat lamb-pie*, be beaten; **lamb's ears** a labiate garden plant, *Stachys byzantina*, with purple flowers and whitish woolly leaves; **lamb's fry** (*a*) lamb's offal, esp. testicles; (*b*) *Austral. & NZ* lamb's liver as food; **lamb's lettuce** the common corn salad vegetable, *Valerianella locusta*; **lamb's quarter(s)** the weed fat hen, *Chenopodium album*; **lamb's tails** hazel catkins; **lamb's tongue** the hoary plantain, *Plantago media*, a common plant of chalk grassland; *lamb succory*: see SUCCORY 2; *lamb-suckle*: see SUCKLE *noun*[1] 1.

■ **lambie** *noun* a little lamb (used as a term of endearment, esp. for a child) M17. **lambkin** *noun* (*a*) a young or small lamb; (*b*) (a term of endearment for) a young vulnerable person: ME. **lamblike** *adjective* resembling a lamb; gentle, meek: L16. **lambling** *noun* a small or young lamb L16.

lamb /lam/ *verb*. L16.
[ORIGIN from the noun.]
1 *verb intrans.* Give birth to a lamb. L16.
lambing season, *lambing time*, etc.
2 *verb trans.* In *pass.* Of a lamb: be born. M17.
3 *verb trans.* Of a shepherd: tend (ewes) at lambing time. Also foll. by *down*. M19.
4 *verb trans.* Foll. by *down*: induce or encourage (a person) to spend money recklessly; spend (money), esp. recklessly. *Austral. & NZ*. M19.

lamba /ˈlambə/ *noun*[1]. E18.
[ORIGIN Malagasy *làmba*.]
A large piece of cloth worn as a cloak by Madagascans.

Lamba /ˈlambə/ *noun*[2] *& adjective*. Also **Ilamba** /ɪˈlambə/. E20.
[ORIGIN Bantu.]
▸ **A** *noun*. Pl. same, **-s**. A member of a people of northern Zambia and the Democratic Republic of Congo (Zaire); the Bantu language of this people. E20.
▸ **B** *attrib.* or as *adjective*. Of or pertaining to the Lamba or their language. E20.

lambardar /lambəˈdɑː, lʌm-/ *noun*. Also ***lum-*** /lʌm-/. M19.
[ORIGIN Urdu *lambardār*, from *lambar* rank (from English NUMBER *noun*) + Persian *-dār* holding, holder.]
An official headman and tax gatherer of a village in the Indian subcontinent.

lambaste /lamˈbeɪst/ *verb trans.* Also **-bast**. M17.
[ORIGIN from LAM *verb* + BASTE *verb*[3].]
1 Beat, thrash. M17.
2 *fig.* Scold, castigate; criticize severely. L19.

A. TOFFLER Intellectuals . . have lambasted television, in particular, for standardizing speech, habits, and tastes. B. NEIL Lambasting me with some choice Italian words.

lambda /ˈlamdə/ *noun*. E17.
[ORIGIN Greek.]
▸ **I 1** The eleventh letter (Λ, λ) of the Greek alphabet. E17.
▸ **II 2** *CHEMISTRY*. A millionth of a litre. Usu. written λ. M20.
3 *NUCLEAR PHYSICS*. More fully ***lambda particle***. A neutral hyperon (or its antiparticle) which has a mass 2183 times that of the electron, a spin of ½, and zero isospin, and on decaying usually produces a nucleon and a pion; orig. also, any of several similar charged hyperons. Freq. written Λ. M20.
4 *MICROBIOLOGY*. A bacteriophage originally isolated from *Escherichia coli*, used in genetic research. Freq. written λ. M20.
– COMB.: **lambda point** *PHYSICS* (*a*) the temperature (approximately 2.18 K) below which liquid helium in equilibrium with its vapour is superfluid, and at which there is a sharp maximum in its specific heat; (*b*) any temperature at which the specific heat of a substance exhibits similar behaviour (freq. written as ***λ point***).

lambdacism /ˈlamdəsɪz(ə)m/ *noun*. Also †**labd-**. M17.
[ORIGIN Late Latin *la(m)bdacismus* from Greek *la(m)bdakismos*, from *la(m)bda* (see LAMBDA) + *-ismos* -ISM with hiatus-filling *k*.]
1 Too frequent repetition of the phoneme /l/ or letter *l* in speaking or writing. M17.
2 Pronunciation of what should be the phoneme /r/ (*r*) as if /l/ (*l*). Also called ***lallation***. M19.

lambdoid /ˈlamdɔɪd/ *adjective*. L16.
[ORIGIN from LAMBDA + -OID.]
1 *ANATOMY*. = LAMBDOIDAL. L16.
2 *MICROBIOLOGY*. Relating to or mutated from bacteriophage lambda. M20.

lambdoidal /lamˈdɔɪd(ə)l/ *adjective*. M17.
[ORIGIN formed as LAMBDOID + -AL[1].]
Resembling the Greek letter lambda (Λ) in form; *spec.* in *ANATOMY*, designating or pertaining to the suture connecting the two parietal bones with the occipital.

lambeau /lɑ̃bo/ *noun*. Pl. ***-eaux*** /-o/. M16.
[ORIGIN French: see LABEL *noun*.]
A strip or fillet hanging from a headdress or garment. In *HERALDRY*, each of the dependent points of a label; (occas.) a label.

Lambeg /ˈlambɛg/ *noun*. M20.
[ORIGIN A village near Belfast, N. Ireland.]
In full ***Lambeg drum***. A large drum of a type traditionally beaten by Orangemen on ceremonial occasions.
■ **Lambegger** *noun* a person who beats such a drum M20.

lambent /ˈlambənt/ *adjective*. M17.
[ORIGIN Latin *lambent-* pres. ppl stem of *lambere* lick: see -ENT.]
1 Of a flame or light: playing lightly upon a surface without burning it; shining with a soft clear light and without fierce heat. M17. ▸**b** Of eyes, the sky, etc.: softly radiant. E18. ▸**c** *fig.* Of wit, style, etc.: lightly brilliant. L19.

THACKERAY The lambent lights of the starry host of heaven. B. T. BRADFORD A log spurted and flared . . , the lambent flames illuminating the shadowed face. **b** E. FIGES The garden was . . lambent with green and gold. M. M. R. KHAN Her mellow soulful lambent gaze masks a determined vengeful hating. **c** J. MORLEY A humour now and then a little sardonic, but more often genial and lambent.

2 Licking, that licks. Now *rare*. E18.
■ **lambency** *noun* the state or quality of being lambent; an instance or occurrence of this: E19. **lambently** *adverb* E19.

†**lamber** *noun*[1] *& adjective*. Chiefly *N. English*. LME–E19.
[ORIGIN French *l'ambre* the amber.]
(Made of, or of the colour of) amber.

lamber /ˈlamə/ *noun*[2]. E19.
[ORIGIN from LAMB *verb* + -ER[1].]
A person who looks after ewes when lambing.

Lambert /ˈlambət/ *noun*. In sense 3 **l-**. L19.
[ORIGIN Johann Heinrich *Lambert* (1728–77), German mathematician.]
1 *CARTOGRAPHY*. Used *attrib.* & in *possess.* to designate certain map projections devised by Lambert, *spec.* a conical conformal projection having two standard parallels along which the scale is true. L19.
2 *PHYSICS*. ***Lambert's law***: (*a*) that the intensity of the light emitted by an element of area of a perfectly diffusing surface is proportional to the cosine of the angle between the direction of emission and the normal to the surface; (*b*) that layers of equal thickness absorb an equal fraction of the light traversing them. L19.
3 (**l-**.) A unit of luminance equal to one lumen per square centimetre (equivalent to approximately 3180 candelas per square metre). E20.

Lambeth /ˈlambəθ/ *noun & adjective*. M19.
[ORIGIN A South London borough.]
▸ **I 1** Designating events etc. associated with the palace of the Archbishop of Canterbury in Lambeth, the Archbishop of Canterbury himself, or the Church of England generally. M19.
Lambeth Conference an assembly of the Anglican bishops, usu. held decennially at Lambeth Palace. **Lambeth degree** a degree *honoris causa* conferred by the Archbishop of Canterbury. ***Lambeth Quadrilateral***: see QUADRILATERAL 3.
▸ **II 2** (Designating) a kind of glazed and painted earthenware manufactured in Lambeth from the 17th to the 19th cent. L19.
3 ***Lambeth Walk*** [a street in Lambeth], a social dance with a walking step, popular in the late 1930s (following its creation for the revue *Me and my Girl*). M20.

Lambic /lɑ̃bik/ *noun*. L19.
[ORIGIN French: cf. *alambic* a still.]
A strong draught beer brewed in Belgium.

†**lambitive** *adjective & noun*. M17–E18.
[ORIGIN from Latin *lambit-* pa. ppl stem of *lambere* lick + -IVE.]
(A medicine) taken by licking up with the tongue.

lamboys /ˈlambɔɪz/ *noun*. M16.
[ORIGIN Perh. from LAMBEAU.]
In Tudor armour: a series of metal plates resembling a skirt or skirts.

lambrequin /ˈlambrɪkɪn/ *noun*. E18.
[ORIGIN French, from Dutch dim. of *lamper* veil: see -KIN.]
1 A piece of material worn over a helmet as a covering, in *HERALDRY* esp. represented with one end (which is cut or jagged) pendent or floating. E18.
2 A cornice with a valance of pendent labels or pointed pieces, placed over a door or window; a short curtain or piece of drapery (with the lower edge either scalloped or straight) suspended for ornament from a mantelshelf. *US*. L19.
3 *CERAMICS*. Ornamentation consisting of solid colour with a lower edge of jagged or scalloped outline. L19.

Lamb shift /ˈlam ʃɪft/ *noun phr.* M20.
[ORIGIN Willis E. *Lamb* (b. 1913), US physicist.]
PHYSICS. A displacement of energy levels in hydrogen and hydrogen-like atoms such that those differentiated only by different values of orbital angular momentum are not coincident, as predicted by Dirac's theory, but separated by a very small amount.

lambskin /ˈlamskɪn/ *noun & adjective*. LME.
[ORIGIN from LAMB *noun* + SKIN *noun*.]
▸ **A** *noun* **1 a** The skin or hide of a lamb with the wool on; this dressed and used for clothing etc. LME. ▸**b** Leather prepared from the skin of a lamb. M18.
†**2** A heavy blow. L16–E17.
– COMB.: †**lambskinman** *slang* a magistrate, a judge.
▸ **B** *attrib.* or as *adjective*. Made of lambskin. LME.

lambswool /ˈlamzwʊl/ *noun & adjective*. Also **lamb's-wool**. M16.
[ORIGIN from LAMB *noun* + -'S[1] + WOOL *noun*.]
▸ **A** *noun*. **1** Soft fine wool from a lamb used for knitted garments or hosiery; clothing material made of this. M16.
2 A drink consisting of hot ale mixed with the pulp of roasted apples, sweetened and spiced. L16.
▸ **B** *adjective*. Made of lambswool. M19.

lamburger /ˈlambəːgə/ *noun*. M20.
[ORIGIN from LAMB *noun* + BURGER.]
A hamburger made from minced lamb.

lamdan /ˈlʌmdən/ *noun*. E20.
[ORIGIN Hebrew *lamdān* lit. 'person who has learned', from *lāmaḏ* learn.]
A person learned in Jewish law; a Talmudic scholar.

lame /leɪm/ *noun*[1]. ME.
[ORIGIN from the adjective.]
†**1** Lameness; infirmity. ME–E16.
2 An outsider; a person unskilled in the behaviour patterns of a particular group. *US slang*. M20.

J. WAMBAUGH They're a couple of lames trying to groove with the Kids.

lame /leɪm/ *noun*[2]. *obsolete* exc. *hist.* L16.
[ORIGIN Old French & mod. French from Latin *lam(m)ina*, *lamna*. Cf. LAMIN, LAMINA.]
A thin plate, esp. of metal; a thin piece of any substance, a lamina; *spec.* any of the small overlapping steel plates used in old armour.

F. WILKINSON Gauntlets were produced with extra lames, or plates, to give additional flexibility . . to the hand.

lame /leɪm/ *adjective*.
[ORIGIN Old English *lama* = Old Frisian *lam*, *lom*, Old Saxon *lamo* (Dutch *lam*), Old High German *lam* (German *lahm*), Old Norse *lami*, from Germanic adjective meaning 'weak in the limbs', rel. to Old High German *luomi* dull, slack, gentle.]
1 Disabled; weak, infirm. Foll. by *on*, *of* the affected part. *arch.* OE. ▸**b** Imperfect, defective, unsatisfactory, (foll. by *of*, *in* the defective part). Now chiefly of an excuse, narrative, etc.: weak, unconvincing. LME. ▸**c** Of a person: unskilled in the fashionable behaviour of a particular group; socially inept. *colloq.* M20.

E. GRIMSTONE A Germaine . . who was lame of halfe his body, and simple. **b** SHAKES. *Oth.* Being not deficient, blind, or lame of sense. *TV Guide (Canada)* It suffers from weak jokes, lame characters and—understandably—canned laughter. **c** *Time* Anyone who does not know that is obviously lame . . . or perhaps just over 25.

2 *spec.* Disabled through injury to, or defect in, a limb. Now only, disabled in the foot or leg, so as to walk awkwardly and with difficulty. Also foll. by *in*, †*of*, †*on*, †*with* the affected part. OE. ▸**b** Of a limb (now only of the leg or foot): functioning imperfectly or painfully. ME. ▸**c** Of footsteps: halting. Also *fig.* (of metrical feet or verses): metrically defective. LME.

D. CAUTE Rodney says Thumper is lame in his right foreleg. *absol.*: AV *Job* 29:15 I was eyes to the blind, and feet was I to the lame. **b** S. JOHNSON Her present qualifications for the niceties of needlework being dim eyes and lame fingers.

– SPECIAL COLLOCATIONS & COMB.: **lamebrain** *colloq.* a dull-witted or stupid person. **lamebrained** *adjective* dull-witted, stupid. *lame duck*: see DUCK *noun*[1].
■ **lamely** *adverb* L16. **lameness** *noun* M16. **lamer** *noun* (*colloq.*, chiefly *US*) a stupid, inept, or contemptible person M20.

lame /leɪm/ *verb trans.* ME.
[ORIGIN from LAME *adjective*: earliest as pa. pple after Old Norse *lamiðr*.]
Make lame; cripple, disable.

lamé /ˈlɑːmeɪ/ *noun & adjective*. E20.
[ORIGIN French, formed as LAME *noun*[2].]
(Made of) a brocaded fabric consisting of silk or other yarns interwoven with metallic threads.

lamel /ˈlam(ə)l/ *noun*. Now *rare* or *obsolete*. L17.
[ORIGIN Anglicized from LAMELLA.]
= LAMELLA.

lamella /lə'mɛlə/ *noun*. Pl. **-llae** /-liː/, **-llas**. L17.
[ORIGIN Latin, dim. of *lam(m)ina*: see LAME *noun*[2].]
A thin plate, scale, layer, or film; any of the individual layers in a lamellar structure, as in some bones, shells, metals, rocks, etc.; *spec.* (*a*) any of the radiating gills of an agaric; (*b*) ZOOLOGY any of the sheets of tissue in the gill of an animal; (*c*) BOTANY any of the photosynthetic membranes in a chloroplast; (*d*) ORNITHOLOGY any of the fine plates in the bill of a lamellirostral bird.
middle lamella: see MIDDLE *adjective*.
■ **lamellate** /'lam(ə)lət/ *adjective* (*a*) lamellated; (*b*) ENTOMOLOGY (of an antenna) lamellicorn: E19. **lamellated** /'lam(ə)leɪtɪd/ *adjective* arranged in or having layers or thin sheets E18.

lamellar /lə'mɛlə/ *adjective*. L18.
[ORIGIN from LAMELLA + -AR[1].]
1 Consisting of, characterized by, or arranged in lamellae or thin plates or layers. L18.
2 PHYSICS. = LAMINAR 2. M20.

lamellibranch /lə'mɛlɪbraŋk/ *noun & adjective*. M19.
[ORIGIN from mod. Latin *Lamellibranchia* (see below), from Latin LAMELLA + -I- + Greek *bragkhia* gills.]
ZOOLOGY. ▸**A** *noun*. A bivalve mollusc (class Bivalvia, formerly Lamellibranchia); *spec.* any of those with lamellated gills, which comprise the subclass Lamellibranchia. M19.
▸**B** *adjective*. Pertaining to or of the nature of a lamellibranch. M19.
■ Also **lamelli'branchiate** *adjective & noun* M19.

lamellicorn /lə'mɛlɪkɔːn/ *adjective & noun*. M19.
[ORIGIN from mod. Latin *Lamellicornia* former taxonomic name, from Latin LAMELLA + -I- + *cornu* horn.]
ENTOMOLOGY. ▸**A** *adjective*. Of, pertaining to, or designating the beetle superfamily Scarabaeoidea whose members typically have antennae with lamelliform segments and include the dung beetles, chafers, and stag beetles. M19.
▸**B** *noun*. A lamellicorn beetle. M19.

lamelliform /lə'mɛlɪfɔːm/ *adjective*. E19.
[ORIGIN from LAMELLA + -I- + -FORM.]
Having the form or structure of a lamella or thin plate.

lamellipodium /ləmɛlɪ'pəʊdɪəm/ *noun*. Pl. **-dia** /-dɪə/. L20.
[ORIGIN from LAMELLA + -I-, after *pseudopodium*.]
CYTOLOGY. A flattened extension of a cell, used in amoeboid locomotion or in adhesion to the substrate.

lamellirostral /ləmɛlɪ'rɒstr(ə)l/ *adjective*. M19.
[ORIGIN from LAMELLA + -I- + Latin *rostrum* beak + -AL[1].]
ORNITHOLOGY. Of a bird, as a duck, flamingo, etc.: having a beak edged with fine plates for filtering food particles from water.

lamellose /lə'mɛləʊs/ *adjective*. M18.
[ORIGIN from LAMELLA + -OSE[1].]
= LAMELLAR *adjective* 1.

lament /lə'mɛnt/ *noun*. M16.
[ORIGIN Latin *lamenta* (pl.) wailing, weeping, groans, laments, or from the verb.]
1 An (esp. passionate) expression of sorrow or anguish. Also *poet.* lamentation. M16.

> MILTON A voice of weeping heard, and loud lament. H. SPURLING The book is full of laments for the damage done by 'telephones and newspapers and bicycles'.

2 A poem or song of grief, an elegy; *esp.* a dirge performed at a death or funeral. L17.

> D. STEWART Solemn and melancholy airs or Laments as they call them.

lament /lə'mɛnt/ *verb*. LME.
[ORIGIN French *lamenter* or Latin *lamentari*, from *lamenta*: see LAMENT *noun*.]
1 *verb trans.* Express or (now) feel profound sorrow for or concerning; mourn the loss of; bewail. LME. ▸**b** *refl.* Feel sorry for oneself; bemoan one's fate. *arch.* M18.

> F. RAPHAEL He lamented—and sought to alleviate, . . the fate of his servants. P. FERGUSON 'Cissie had hardly a civil word to say to me,' lamented Jessie. B. GILROY The house was full of people . . lamenting her passing. **b** A. B. JAMESON He began to lament himself because of the robbery.

2 *verb intrans.* Express (or feel) profound grief; mourn passionately. Foll. by *for*, *over*, (rarely) *after*. LME.

> R. KNOLLES Greatly lamented for by all the Christians in Syria. M. SPARK She was crying and lamenting so much that any form of rational inquiry was useless.

†**3** *verb trans.* Cause grief to, distress. L16–E18.
■ **lamenter** *noun* L16. **lamentingly** *adverb* in a passionately mournful manner, so as to express profound grief E17.

lamentable /'laməntəb(ə)l/ *adjective*. LME.
[ORIGIN Old French & mod. French, or Latin *lamentabilis*, from *lamentari*: see LAMENT *verb*, -ABLE.]
1 Full of or expressing sorrow or grief; mournful, doleful. Now *arch. rare*. LME.

> N. HAWTHORNE The lamentable friends, trailing their long black garments.

2 That is to be lamented; pitiable, regrettable. LME. ▸**b** Contemptible, deplorable; wretchedly bad. M17.

> LD MACAULAY Another Macdonald, destined to a lamentable and horrible end. **b** *Oban Times* A lamentable clutter of buildings . . and brutal modern extensions to pleasant old houses.

■ **lamentableness** *noun* L16. **lamentably** *adverb* L15.

lamentation /lamən'teɪʃ(ə)n/ *noun*. LME.
[ORIGIN Old French & mod. French, or Latin *lamentatio(n-)*, from *lamentat-* pa. ppl stem of *lamentari*: see LAMENT *verb*, -ATION.]
1 The action of lamenting; bewailing, mourning; (in weakened sense) regret. LME.

> SHELLEY There shall be lamentation heard in Heaven As o'er an angel fallen. J. MCCOSH Another subject of general lamentation is the evil produced by party spirit.

2 An instance of this; a lament. LME.

> W. IRVING The lamentations of women who had lost some relative in the foray.

Lamentations (of Jeremiah) (the name of) a book of the Old Testament and Hebrew Scriptures, traditionally ascribed to the prophet Jeremiah, which laments the destruction of Jerusalem by the Chaldeans.

lamented /lə'mɛntɪd/ *adjective*. E17.
[ORIGIN from LAMENT *verb* + -ED[1]. Earlier in UNLAMENTED.]
Mourned for; lamented; regretted.
the late lamented (a mode of reference to) a person recently dead.

lamento /la'mento/ *noun*. Pl. **-ti** /-ti/. M20.
[ORIGIN Italian.]
MUSIC. An elegiac or mourning song; in Italian opera, a tragic aria.

lamentoso /lamen'toːzo/ *adverb & adjective*. L19.
[ORIGIN Italian.]
MUSIC. (A direction:) in a mournful style.

lametta /la'mɛta/ *noun*. M19.
[ORIGIN Italian, dim. of *lama* = LAME *noun*[2].]
Brass, silver, or gold foil or wire; *spec.* thin strips of metallic foil used as Christmas decorations.

lamia /'leɪmɪə/ *noun*. Pl. **-ias**, **-iae** /-iiː/. LME.
[ORIGIN Latin from Greek = mythical monster, carnivorous fish.]
A mythical monster supposed to have the body of a woman, and to prey on human beings and suck the blood of children. Also, a witch, a she-demon.

lamin /'lamɪn/ *noun*. L15.
[ORIGIN formed as LAMINA. Cf. also LAME *noun*[2].]
A lamina; a thin plate or layer of metal etc.; a plate of metal used as an astrological instrument or as a charm.

lamina /'lamɪnə/ *noun*. Pl. **-nae** /-niː/. M17.
[ORIGIN Latin *la(m)mina*. Cf. LAME *noun*[2], LAMIN.]
1 A thin plate or layer of a metal or other material; ANATOMY & BIOLOGY a thin layer of bone, membrane, or other tissue. M17. ▸**b** BOTANY. The flat, expanded portion of a leaf, petal, or thallus. Opp. ***unguis***. M18.
2 GEOLOGY. The thinnest separable layer of a sedimentary rock deposit. M19.
3 MATH. A plane sheet of negligible thickness. M19.

laminable /'lamɪnəb(ə)l/ *adjective*. L18.
[ORIGIN from LAMINATE *verb* + -ABLE.]
Able to be formed into thin plates or layers.
■ **laminability** *noun* M19.

laminagraph /'lamɪnəgrɑːf/ *noun*. Also **lamino-**. M20.
[ORIGIN from LAMINA + -GRAPH.]
MEDICINE. = TOMOGRAPH.
■ **lamina'graphic** *adjective* M20. **laminagram** *noun* = TOMOGRAM M20. **lami'nagraphy** *noun* M20.

laminal /'lamɪn(ə)l/ *adjective*. E19.
[ORIGIN from LAMINA + -AL[1].]
1 = LAMINAR 1. *rare*. E19.
2 PHONETICS. Produced by the blade of the tongue. M20.

laminar /'lamɪnə/ *adjective*. E19.
[ORIGIN from LAMINA + -AR[1].]
1 Consisting of or arranged in laminae. E19.
2 PHYSICS. Of the flow of a fluid: smooth and regular, not turbulent, the direction of motion at any point remaining constant as if the fluid were moving in a series of layers of different velocity sliding over one another without mixing. L19. ▸**b** Of a body: having a shape that tends to produce laminar flow in the adjacent fluid. M20.

laminaran /'lamɪnəran/ *noun*. M20.
[ORIGIN formed as LAMINARIA + -AN.]
BIOCHEMISTRY. A polysaccharide which occurs in laminaria and other brown algae.

laminaria /lamɪ'nɛːrɪə/ *noun*. M19.
[ORIGIN mod. Latin (see below), from Latin *lam(m)ina* LAMINA + *-aria* -ARY[1].]
Any brown seaweed of the genus *Laminaria*, with long thin flat fronds; *collect.* seaweed of this genus. Also called ***oarweed***, ***kelp***.
■ **laminarian** *adjective* of or pertaining to laminaria; *spec.* designating the littoral zone, extending from low-water mark to a depth of about 27.5 m. or 90 ft, in which laminaria grows: M19.

laminarin /'lamɪnərɪn/ *noun*. M20.
[ORIGIN formed as LAMINARIA + -IN[1].]
BIOCHEMISTRY. = LAMINARAN.

laminarize /'lamɪnərʌɪz/ *verb trans.* Also **-ise**. M20.
[ORIGIN from LAMINAR + -IZE.]
AERONAUTICS. Design so as to maximize the surface area over which the flow in the boundary layer is laminar.
■ **laminari'zation** *noun* M20.

laminary /'lamɪn(ə)ri/ *adjective*. M19.
[ORIGIN from LAMINA + -ARY[1].]
= LAMINAR *adjective* 1.

laminate /'lamɪnət/ *adjective & noun*. M17.
[ORIGIN from LAMINA + -ATE[2].]
▸**A** *adjective*. Having the form of or consisting of a lamina; provided with a lamina or laminae. M17.
▸**B** *noun*. A manufactured laminated structure or material; *esp.* a (rigid or flexible) material made by bonding a number of different layers together, as laminated plastic. M20.

> *Scientific American* Metal laminates . . are constructed . . of . . layers. K. WATERHOUSE He . . makes for the buffet car, already, in his head, tapping coins on laminate.

laminate /'lamɪneɪt/ *verb*. M17.
[ORIGIN from LAMINA + -ATE[3].]
1 *verb trans.* Beat or roll (metal) into thin plates. M17.
2 *verb trans. & intrans.* Separate or split into layers. M17.
3 *verb trans.* Cover or coat with laminae or a laminate. L17.
4 *verb trans.* Make by bonding layers of material together; unite into a laminate. M19.
■ **laminator** *noun* a machine, person, or organization that makes (plastic) laminates M20.

laminated /'lamɪneɪtɪd/ *adjective*. M17.
[ORIGIN from LAMINATE *verb* + -ED[1].]
Consisting of, arranged in, or provided with laminae or a laminate; formed or manufactured in a succession of layers; *spec.* (of a worktop etc.) coated with a protective laminate.

> F. RAPHAEL An orange coffee-machine hissed on the laminated work-surface. *Which?* Laminated glass consists of two sheets of . . glass with tough plastic interleaved between them.

laminated plastic material made by bonding together layers of cloth, paper, etc., that have been impregnated or coated with a synthetic resin.

lamination /lamɪ'neɪʃ(ə)n/ *noun*. L17.
[ORIGIN formed as LAMINATED: see -ATION.]
1 The action or process of laminating something; the manufacture of laminates. L17.
2 The condition of being laminated or layered; laminated structure. M18.
3 A layer of a laminated material or object. M19.

laminboard /'lamɪnbɔːd/ *noun*. E20.
[ORIGIN from LAMIN(ATED + BOARD *noun*.]
(A) composite board consisting of numerous thin strips of wood glued face to face between two facing sheets of wood or laminated plastic.

laminectomy /lamɪ'nɛktəmi/ *noun*. L19.
[ORIGIN from LAMINA + -ECTOMY.]
Surgical removal of one or more of the posterior arches of the vertebrae (each arch being formed by the junction of two laminae), esp. as a method of access to the spinal canal; an instance of this.

lamington /'lamɪŋt(ə)n/ *noun*. *Austral. & NZ*. E20.
[ORIGIN App. from Lord *Lamington*, Governor of Queensland, Australia, 1895–1901.]
A square of sponge cake dipped in chocolate or jam and grated coconut.

laminitis /lamɪ'nʌɪtɪs/ *noun*. M19.
[ORIGIN from LAMINA + -ITIS.]
VETERINARY MEDICINE. Inflammation of the laminae of the hoof of a horse or other hoofed animal.

lamino- /'lamɪnəʊ/ *combining form*. M20.
[ORIGIN from LAMIN(AL + -O-.]
PHONETICS. Forming adjectives and corresp. nouns denoting sounds produced with the blade of the tongue and some other point of articulation, as ***lamino-dental***, ***lamino-palatal***.

laminose /'lamɪnəʊs/ *adjective*. E19.
[ORIGIN from LAMINA + -OSE[1].]
Consisting of or having the form of laminae.

laminous /'lamɪnəs/ *adjective*. L17.
[ORIGIN from LAMINA + -OUS.]
= LAMINOSE.

lamish /'leɪmɪʃ/ *adjective*. L16.
[ORIGIN from LAME *adjective* + -ISH[1].]
Somewhat lame.

lamium /'leɪmɪəm/ *noun*. L17.
[ORIGIN mod. Latin (see below) from Latin from Greek *lamia* gaping mouth (with ref. to the shape of the flowers).]
Any plant of the labiate genus *Lamium*, which includes several kinds of dead-nettle.

Lammas /'laməs/ *noun*.
[ORIGIN Old English *hlāfmæsse*, from *hlāf* LOAF *noun*[1] + *mæsse* MASS *noun*[1]; later interpreted as from LAMB *noun* + MASS *noun*[1].]
1 August, *spec.* as (*a*) celebrated in the early English Church as a harvest festival, at which loaves of bread

made from the first ripe corn were consecrated, (*b*) observed in Scotland as one of the quarter days; also ***Lammas Day***. Also (*arch.*), the part of the year in which Lammas occurs.
latter Lammas: see LATTER *adjective*.
– COMB.: ***Lammas day***: see above; **Lammas growth** FORESTRY a shoot produced by a tree in summer, after a pause in growth; **Lammas-land** *hist.* private land available for common use after Lammas until the following spring; **Lammas shoot** = ***Lammas growth*** above; **Lammas wheat** winter wheat.

lammergeier /ˈlaməɡʌɪə/ *noun*. Also **-geyer**. E19.
[ORIGIN German *Lämmergeier*, from *Lämmer* pl. of *Lamm* lamb + *Geier* vulture.]
A long-winged, long-tailed vulture, *Gypaetus barbatus*, inhabiting lofty mountains in southern Europe, Asia, and Africa. Also called ***bearded vulture***.

lammervanger /ˈlaməvaŋə, -faŋə/ *noun*. *S. Afr.* M19.
[ORIGIN Afrikaans, from *lam* lamb + *vanger* catcher.]
An eagle, esp. one believed to prey on lambs. Also, = LAMMERGEIER.

lammie /ˈlami/ *noun*. Also **lammy**. L19.
[ORIGIN Perh. from LAMB *noun* + -IE, with allus. to the wool used in making the garment.]
A thick quilted woollen overgarment worn by sailors in cold weather. Also more fully ***lammie coat***, ***lammie suit***.

Lamout *noun & adjective* var. of LAMUT.

lamp /lamp/ *noun*. ME.
[ORIGIN Old French & mod. French *lampe* from late Latin *lampada* from accus. of Latin *lampas* from Greek *lampas*, *lampad-* torch, rel. to *lampein* to shine.]
1 Orig., a vessel in which oil is burnt at a wick to provide illumination. Now *gen.*, (a device, often consisting of a holder and shade, designed to hold or enclose) a source of artificial illumination, as a candle, a gas jet, or (usu.) an electric bulb. Also, a device producing infrared, ultraviolet, or other radiation, esp. for therapeutic purposes. ME. ▸**b** A torch. LME.
Argand lamp, ***astral lamp***, ***bicycle lamp***, ***desk lamp***, ***flash lamp***, ***headlamp***, ***indicator lamp***, ***mercury lamp***, ***standard lamp***, ***table lamp***, etc. ***the lady of the lamp***, ***the lady with the lamp***: see LADY *noun* & *adjective*. ***Slave of the Lamp***: see SLAVE *noun*[1] 1. ***smell of the lamp***: see SMELL *verb* 8a.

2 A celestial object producing or reflecting light, *esp.* the sun or the moon. *poet.* LME. ▸**b** In *pl.* The eyes. Formerly *poet.*, now *slang*. L16.
3 A source or centre of spiritual or intellectual light. E16.
– COMB.: **lampblack** *noun & verb* (*a*) *noun* a pigment consisting of finely divided, almost pure carbon, obtained by collecting the soot produced by burning oil or gas; (*b*) *verb trans.* paint, smear, or coat with lampblack; **lampbrush** *attrib. adjective* (CYTOLOGY) (of a chromosome) having numerous paired lateral loops of DNA, which give the whole chromosome the appearance of a bottle-brush; ***lamp chimney***: see CHIMNEY *noun* 6; **lamp-holder** a device for supporting or securing a lamp, esp. an electric one; **lamp-house** the part of a photographic enlarger or projector which houses the light source; **lamplit** *adjective* lit by a lamp or lamps; **lamp oil** (*a*) oil for burning in a lamp; (*b*) nocturnal study or work; **lamp post** a tall post supporting a street lamp (***between you and me and the lamp post***: see BETWEEN *preposition*); **lamp shell** a brachiopod; **lamp-socket** = ***lamp-holder*** above; **lamp standard** a post or other strong support for a lamp; a lamp post.
■ **lampful** *adjective* (*poet.*) (of the sky) starry L16. **lampist** *noun* a person skilled or employed in making or maintaining lamps M19. **lampless** *adjective* E17. **lamplet** *noun* a small lamp E17.

lamp /lamp/ *verb*[1]. L16.
[ORIGIN from the noun.]
1 *verb trans.* Provide with a lamp or lamps. L16.
2 *verb intrans.* Shine. E17.
3 *verb trans.* Light as with a lamp. E19.
4 *verb trans.* See, look at, recognize, watch. *slang*. Orig. *US*. L19.

lamp /lamp/ *verb*[2] *intrans.* *Scot.* E17.
[ORIGIN Unknown.]
Move quickly with long steps.

lamp /lamp/ *verb*[3] *trans.* Chiefly *N. English*. E19.
[ORIGIN Of uncertain origin; perh. rel. to LAM *verb*.]
Hit or beat (a person).

> C. BROOKMYRE Tell me, I'll lamp him one.

lampadedromy /lampəˈdɛdrəmi/ *noun*. M19.
[ORIGIN Greek *lampadēdromia*, from *lampad-*, *lampas* torch + *-dromia* running.]
GREEK HISTORY. A torch race.

lampadephoria /ˌlampadəˈfɔːrɪə/ *noun*. Also **-do-**. M19.
[ORIGIN Greek *lampadēphoria*, *-do-*, from *lampad-*, *lampas* torch + *phor-* stem of *pherein* bear, carry: see -IA[1].]
GREEK HISTORY. = LAMPADEDROMY.

lampadite /ˈlampədʌɪt/ *noun*. M19.
[ORIGIN from W. A. *Lampadius* (1772–1842), German chemist + -ITE[1].]
MINERALOGY. A cupriferous variety of wad.

lampadomancy /ˈlampədəmansi/ *noun*. M17.
[ORIGIN from Greek *lampad-*, *lampas* torch + -O- + -MANCY.]
Divination by the observation of lamps or candles.

lampas /ˈlampəs/ *noun*[1]. LME.
[ORIGIN In sense 1 prob. from Dutch †*lampers* (now *lamfer*); in sense 2 from French *lampas*, *-asse*, which may be a different word.]
†**1** A kind of crape. LME–M16.
2 An expensive patterned silk, originally imitating Indian painted and resist-dyed textiles, later imported from China, Iran (Persia), and France. M19.

lampas /ˈlampəs/ *noun*[2]. Also **-ss**; **-ers** /-əz/. E16.
[ORIGIN Old French & mod. French, prob. from dial. *lāpā* throat, *lāpē* gums, from nasalized var. of Germanic base of LAP *verb*[1].]
VETERINARY MEDICINE. A disease of horses, in which there is swelling of the fleshy lining of the roof of the mouth behind the front teeth.

lamper /ˈlampə/ *noun*. L19.
[ORIGIN from LAMP *noun* + -ER[1].]
1 A person who trims and maintains household lamps. *rare*. L19.
2 A person who hunts at night, using a bright lamp to dazzle a hunted animal. Cf. LAMPING *noun*. L20.

lamper-eel /ˈlampəriːl/ *noun*. E16.
[ORIGIN Prob. from var. of LAMPREY + EEL *noun*.]
A lamprey. Also (*US*), an eelpout. Cf. ***LAMPREY-eel***.

lampern /ˈlampən/ *noun*. ME.
[ORIGIN Old French *lampreion* etc., dim. of *lampreie* LAMPREY.]
A lamprey, *Lampetra fluviatilis*, of rivers and coastal waters of NW Europe. Also called ***river lamprey***.

lampers *noun* var. of LAMPAS *noun*[2].

lamping /ˈlampɪŋ/ *noun*. L20.
[ORIGIN from LAMP *noun*, *verb*[1] + -ING[1].]
A method or the practice of nocturnal hunting, using a bright light to dazzle the hunted animal so as to bewilder it and make it easy to catch or kill.

lamping /ˈlampɪŋ/ *adjective*. L16.
[ORIGIN from LAMP *verb*[1] + -ING[2].]
Flashing, resplendent.

lampion /ˈlampɪən/ *noun*. M19.
[ORIGIN French from Italian *lampione* augm. of *lampa* (from French *lampe*) LAMP *noun*.]
An oil lamp, often of coloured glass, used in illuminations.

lamplight /ˈlamplʌɪt/ *noun*. LME.
[ORIGIN from LAMP *noun* + LIGHT *noun*.]
Light from a lamp or lamps.

lamplighter /ˈlamplʌɪtə/ *noun*. M18.
[ORIGIN from LAMP *noun* + LIGHTER *noun*[2].]
1 *hist.* A person employed to light (gas) street lamps. M18.
2 A device used for lighting a lamp. M19.
3 = CRAPPIE. *N. Amer.* L19.

lampoon /lamˈpuːn/ *noun & verb*. M17.
[ORIGIN French *lampon*, perh. from *lampons* let us drink (used as a refrain), 1st person pl. imper. of *lamper* gulp down, guzzle, nasalized form of *laper* LAP *verb*[1]: see -OON.]
▸**A** *noun*. A virulent or scurrilous satire against a person, a satirical attack. M17.
▸**B** *verb trans.* Abuse or satirize virulently or scurrilously, esp. in writing. M17.
■ **lampooner** *noun* L17. **lampoonery** *noun* the practice of writing lampoons; the quality of a lampoon, scurrility: E18. **lampoonist** *noun* L19.

lamprey /ˈlampri/ *noun*. ME.
[ORIGIN Old French *lampreie* (mod. *lamproie*) from medieval Latin *lampreda*, whence also Old English *lamprede*, Old High German *lampreta*, perh. alt. of *lampetra* prob. from Latin *lambere* lick + *petra* stone (with allus. to the lamprey attaching itself to stones). Cf. LIMPET.]
Any of various predatory cyclostome fishes of the family Petromyzontidae, which inhabit rivers and coastal waters, and have an eel-like body without scales or paired fins and a jawless mouth like a sucker with horny teeth and rough tongue.
river lamprey, ***sea lamprey***.
– COMB.: **lamprey-eel** the sea lamprey, *Petromyzon marinus* (cf. LAMPER-EEL).

lampro- /ˈlamprəʊ/ *combining form* of Greek *lampros*, bright, shining: see -O-.
■ **lamproˈphyllite** *noun* [Greek *phullon* leaf] MINERALOGY a monoclinic silicate of sodium, strontium, and titanium, usu. occurring as golden-brown prisms L19.

lamprophyre /ˈlamprəfʌɪə/ *noun*. L19.
[ORIGIN from LAMPRO- + Greek *porphureos* purple: cf. PORPHYRY.]
GEOLOGY. Any of a class of porphyritic igneous rocks consisting of a fine-grained feldspathic groundmass with phenocrysts esp. of biotite.
■ **lamproˈphyric** *adjective* L19.

lampshade /ˈlampʃeɪd/ *noun & adjective*. M19.
[ORIGIN from LAMP *noun* + SHADE *noun*.]
▸**A** *noun*. A shade placed over a lamp to diffuse or direct the light. M19.
▸**B** *attrib.* or as *adjective*. Resembling or suggestive of a lampshade. M19.

> *Daily Chronicle* The young ladies of gay Bohemia in . . lampshade hats.

lampyrid /ˈlampɪrɪd/ *noun & adjective*. L19.
[ORIGIN mod. Latin *Lampyridae* (see below), from Latin *lampyris* glow-worm from Greek *lampuris*, from *lampein* shine: see -ID[3].]
▸**A** *noun*. Any insect of the coleopteran family Lampyridae, which includes the glow-worms and fireflies. L19.
▸**B** *adjective*. Of, pertaining to, or designating this family. E20.

Lamut /laˈmuːt/ *noun & adjective*. Also **-out**. E18.
[ORIGIN Unknown.]
▸**A** *noun*. **1** A member of a branch of the Tungus people living on the shores of the Sea of Okhotsk. E18.
2 The language of this people, belonging to the Manchu-Tungus family. L18.
▸**B** *attrib.* or as *adjective*. Of or pertaining to the Lamuts or their language. L18.

LAN /lan/ *abbreviation*.
COMPUTING. Local area network.

lanai /ləˈnʌɪ/ *noun*. Also (earlier) †**ranai**. E19.
[ORIGIN Hawaiian.]
A porch or veranda, orig. in Hawaii; a roofed structure with open sides near a house.

lanarkite /ˈlanəkʌɪt/ *noun*. M19.
[ORIGIN from *Lanarkshire*, former Scot. county + -ITE[1].]
MINERALOGY. A monoclinic oxide and sulphate of lead occurring as greenish-white, grey, or yellowish crystals.

lanate /ˈleɪneɪt/ *adjective*. M18.
[ORIGIN Latin *lanatus*, from *lana* wool: see -ATE[2].]
BOTANY & ENTOMOLOGY. Having a woolly covering or surface.

Lancashire /ˈlaŋkəʃə/ *noun*. L16.
[ORIGIN A county in NW England.]
1 Used *attrib.* to designate things made in or associated with Lancashire. L16. ▸**b** In full ***Lancashire cheese***. A white semi-hard cheese. L19.
Lancashire hotpot a dish of meat, onion and potato, resembling Irish stew.
2 a A breed of shorthorn cattle from Lancashire; an animal of this breed. M19. ▸**b** A variety of canary developed in Lancashire, with pale yellow plumage. L19.

Lancaster /ˈlaŋkəstə, -kastə/ *noun & adjective*. M19.
[ORIGIN See below.]
hist. (Designating) a cannon or rifle with a slightly oval bore designed by the English gunsmith Charles Lancaster (1820–78).

Lancaster cloth /ˈlaŋkəstə klɒθ, ˈlaŋkastə/ *noun phr.* M20.
[ORIGIN from *Lancaster* (see LANCASTRIAN) + CLOTH.]
A light washable cloth waterproofed with a linseed oil compound.

Lancasterian /laŋkaˈstɪərɪən/ *adjective*. E19.
[ORIGIN from *Lancaster* (see below) + -IAN.]
hist. Of or pertaining to the English educationalist Joseph Lancaster (1778–1838), or the monitorial form of instruction which he established in schools.

Lancastrian /laŋˈkastrɪən/ *noun & adjective*. M16.
[ORIGIN from *Lancaster* a city in NW England, formerly the county town of Lancashire + -IAN.]
1 *hist.* (An adherent or supporter) of the family descended from John of Gaunt (1340–99), Duke of Lancaster, fourth son of Edward III, esp. in the Wars of the Roses. Cf. YORKIST. M16.
2 (A native or inhabitant) of Lancaster or Lancashire in NW England. L18.

lance /lɑːns/ *noun*. Also (earlier, now only in sense 5) **launce**. ME.
[ORIGIN Old French & mod. French from Latin *lancea*, of alien (prob. Celtic) origin.]
1 a *hist.* A spear with a long wooden shaft and an iron or steel head, held by a charging horseman. ME. ▸**b** A similar weapon used for spearing fish, harpooning whales, etc. E18.

> **a** GIBBON The lance was the . . peculiar weapon of the knight. *fig.*: F. H. BURNETT He liked the big . . trees, with the late afternoon sunlight striking golden lances through them.

break a lance: see BREAK *verb*.
2 a A mounted soldier armed with a lance; a lancer. LME. ▸**b** *hist.* A man-at-arms with his attendant archers, foot soldiers, etc. E19. ▸**c** = ***lance corporal*** below. *colloq.* L19.
a FREELANCE.
†**3** A branch of a tree, a shoot. LME–M17.
4 MEDICINE. A lancet. Now *rare*. L15.
5 More fully ***sand lance***. = ***sand eel*** s.v. SAND *noun*. E17.
6 A small thin case containing a firework. M17.
7 a A thin metal pipe through which oxygen etc. is passed in order to burn away metal, concrete, etc., using heat generated by burning the metal to be cut or the pipe itself. Also ***thermic lance***. E20. ▸**b** METALLURGY. In full ***oxygen lance***. A metal pipe through which oxygen may be injected into molten metal or directed on to its surface. M20.
8 A rigid tube at the end of a hose for pumping or spraying liquid. M20.
– COMB.: **lance bombardier** the rank in the Royal Artillery corresponding to lance corporal in the infantry; **lance corporal** (*a*) *hist.* an acting corporal receiving the pay of a private; (*b*) the lowest rank of non-commissioned army officer; **lancejack** *military slang* a lance corporal, a lance bombardier; **lance-oval** *adjective* narrowly oval; **lance sergeant** a corporal acting as a sergeant; **lance snake** = FER DE LANCE; **lancewood** (the tough elastic wood of) any of various trees, *esp.* (*a*) *Oxandra lanceolata* (family Annonaceae) of the W. Indies; (*b*) *Pseudopanax crassifolius* (family Araliaceae) of New Zealand.
■ **lanced** *adjective* having a lance; shaped like a lance: L18.

lance /lɑːns/ *verb*. **ME**.
[**ORIGIN** Old French & mod. French *lancer*, †*-ier*, formed as **LANCE** *noun*: cf. **LAUNCH** *verb*.]
1 *verb trans.* Fling, hurl, launch, throw (a dart, fire, a look, etc.); shoot out (the tongue); put forth (blossoms). Also foll. by *forth, out, up*. Now *poet.* **ME**.

M. P. SHIEL The torpedo-boat lances one of her . . needles of steel.

2 *verb intrans.* **a** Bound, move quickly, rush. *obsolete* exc. *dial.* **ME**. ▸†**b** (Of leaves or fire) spring, shoot up; (of pain) shoot. **LME–M18**. ▸**c** Launch, push *out*. *rare*. **E16**.
3 *verb trans.* Pierce (as) with a lance; cut, gash; slit, slit open. Now *rare* or *obsolete*. **LME**.
4 *verb trans.* Make an incision in (the gums, an abscess, etc.) with a lancet or other sharp instrument. **L15**.

B. MALAMUD The surgeon had lanced the sores on his feet. *fig.*: R. BOYLE The Orator . . is more sollicitous to tickle their Ears, than . . to launce their Consciences.

5 *verb trans.* Cut (a hole) or inject (oxygen) by means of an oxygen lance. **M20**.

lancegay /ˈlɑːnsgeɪ/ *noun*. *obsolete* exc. *hist.* Also †**launce-**. **LME**.
[**ORIGIN** Old French *lancegaye*, perh. alt. of *l'archegaye* javelin, lance, by assoc. with *lance* **LANCE** *noun*: cf. **ASSEGAI**.]
A kind of lance.

lance-knight /ˈlɑːnsnʌɪt/ *noun*. Also †**-knecht**. **E16**.
[**ORIGIN** German *Lanzknecht* alt. of *Landsknecht* (see **LANSQUENET**) after *Lanz* **LANCE** *noun*.]
hist. A mercenary foot soldier, *esp.* one armed with a lance or pike.

lancelet /ˈlɑːnslɪt/ *noun*. **M16**.
[**ORIGIN** from **LANCE** *noun* + **-LET**.]
†**1** *SURGERY*. A lancet. **M16–M17**.
2 Any of a number of small elongated fishlike chordates of the family Branchiostomidae, that burrow in underwater sand etc. **M19**.

lanceolate /ˈlɑːnsɪələt/ *adjective*. **M18**.
[**ORIGIN** Late Latin *lanceolatus*, from Latin *lanceola* dim. of *lancea* **LANCE** *noun*: see **-ATE**[2].]
Shaped like a spearhead; narrow and tapering to each end; *BOTANY & ZOOLOGY* tapering from near the base.
■ Also **lanceolated** *adjective* **M18**.

lancepesade /lɑːnspɪˈzɑːd/ *noun*. Also †**lance-prisade**; **lanceprisado** /lɑːnsprɪˈzɑːdəʊ/, pl. **-do(e)s**. **M16**.
[**ORIGIN** French †*lancepessade* (now *anspessade*) from Italian *lancia spezzata* soldier on a forlorn hope, devoted adherent, lit. 'broken lance', from *lancia* **LANCE** *noun* + *spezzata* fem. pa. pple of *spezzare* break; vars. in *-pris-* are due to assoc. with Spanish, Italian *presa* seizure, capture.]
hist. **1** A member of a class of experienced soldiers separate from ordinary companies. **M16**.
2 A non-commissioned officer of the lowest grade; a lance corporal. **E17**.

lancer /ˈlɑːnsə/ *noun*. **L16**.
[**ORIGIN** French *lancier*, from *lance* **LANCE** *noun*: see **-ER**[2]. Cf. late Latin *lancearius*.]
1 A (cavalry) soldier armed with a lance (*hist.*); a soldier belonging to any of several regiments still officially called Lancers. **L16**.
2 In *pl.* (treated as *sing.*). A kind of quadrille for 8 or 16 pairs; a piece of music for this. **M19**.

lances *nouns* pls. of **LANCE** *noun*, **LANX**.

lancet /ˈlɑːnsɪt/ *noun*. **LME**.
[**ORIGIN** Old French & mod. French *lancette*, dim. of *lance* **LANCE** *noun*: see **-ET**[1].]
†**1** A (small) lance. **LME–M18**.
2 A surgical knife, usu. broad, two-edged, and with a sharp point, used for bleeding, opening abscesses, etc. **LME**.
3 *ARCHITECTURE*. **a** More fully ***lancet light***, ***lancet window***. A high narrow window with a lancet arch. **L18**. ▸**b** More fully ***lancet arch***. An arch with a head resembling the blade of a lancet. **E19**.
– **COMB.**: ***lancet arch***: see sense 3b above; **lancetfish** (*a*) a surgeon fish; (*b*) any of various long slender spiny-finned predatory marine fishes of the family Alepisauridae; ***lancet light***, ***lancet window***: see sense 3a above.
■ **lanceted** *adjective* (of a window) having a lancet arch; (of a church) having lancet windows: **M19**.

lanciform /ˈlɑːnsɪfɔːm/ *adjective*. **M19**.
[**ORIGIN** from **LANCE** *noun* + **-I-** + **-FORM**.]
Shaped like a lance.

lancinate /ˈlɑːnsɪneɪt/ *verb trans.* *rare*. **E17**.
[**ORIGIN** Latin *lancinat-* pa. ppl stem of *lancinare* tear, rel. to *lacer*: see **LACERATE** *verb*, **-ATE**[3].]
Pierce, tear.

lancinating /ˈlɑːnsɪneɪtɪŋ/ *adjective*. **M18**.
[**ORIGIN** from **LANCINATE** + **-ING**[2].]
Chiefly of pain: acute, piercing.

Lancs. *abbreviation*.
Lancashire.

land /land/ *noun*[1].
[**ORIGIN** Old English *land* (= Old Frisian, Old Saxon (Dutch), Old Norse, Gothic *land*), Old High German *lant* (German *Land*), from Germanic.]
1 The solid part of the earth's surface, as distinguished from the sea or water, or from the air. **OE**.
2 a Ground or soil, esp. with ref. to its use or properties. **OE**. ▸**b** ***the land***, the (cultivable) earth regarded as a repository of natural resources and the chief source of human sustenance or livelihood. **LME**. ▸**c** An area of ground under cultivation; a field. Freq. in *pl.* *S. Afr.* **M18**.

b G. B. SHAW You must nationalize the land and put a stop to this shameless exploitation.

a arable land, ***badland(s)***, ***flatland***, ***ploughland***, ***stubble land***, etc.
3 A part of the earth's surface marked off by natural or political boundaries; a territory, a country, a nation, a state. Also (*fig.*), a realm, a domain. **OE**.
4 Ground or territory held as public or private property, landed property, (in *LAW* usu. together with any buildings etc. above the ground and any minerals, mines, etc., beneath it). In *pl.*, territorial possessions. **OE**.

G. BERKELEY A convenient house with a hundred acres of land adjoining to it. LD MACAULAY Their lands had been divided by Cromwell among his followers.

†**5** The country, as opp. to the town. **OE–L18**.
6 a A strip of arable land or pasture divided from other similar strips by furrows (formerly freq. taken as a local unit of measure). **LME**. ▸**b** Chiefly *ENGINEERING*. An area or space left between adjacent grooves, holes, etc., in a surface, as (*a*) the top of a tooth on various metal-cutting tools immediately behind the cutting edge; (*b*) the space between the grooves of a rifle bore; (*c*) the space between the furrows of a millstone; (*d*) the space between the grooves of a gramophone record. **M19**.
7 A tenement building, usu. divided into flats for different households. *Scot.* **LME**.
8 A stretch of country of undefined extent. Usu. with specifying word, as ***highland***, ***lowland***, ***mountain land***, etc. **E17**.

W. WHARTON As I've gone north, the traffic has picked up and the land has flattened out.

9 *euphem.* = **LORD** *noun* 5: in exclamatory phrs. *US*. **M19**.
the land knows, ***good land***, ***land's sake***, ***for the land's sake***.
– **PHRASES**: **be on the land** *Austral.* be engaged in rural (usu. agricultural) occupations. **by land** by way of the land, on or over the land (as a mode of travel or conveyance), on foot or using a vehicle etc. ***common land***: see **COMMON** *adjective*. ***fast land***: see **FAST** *adjective*. ***firm land***: see **FIRM** *adjective*. ***happy land***: see **HAPPY** *adjective*. ***height of land***: see **HEIGHT** *noun*. ***Holy Land***: see **HOLY** *adjective*. **how the land lies** *fig.* what the situation is. **in the land of the living** alive. **land ahoy!**, **land ho!** *interjections* (*NAUTICAL*): announcing the sighting of land from the sea. ***land of cakes***: see **CAKE** *noun*. ***Land of Little Sticks***: see ***Land of the Little Sticks*** below. ***land of the broad acres***: see **BROAD** *adjective* 2. ***land of the Covenant***: see **COVENANT** *noun*. **Land of the Free** *US* the United States of America. **Land of the Little Sticks**, **Land of Little Sticks** *Canad.* [Chinook *stik* wood, tree, forest] the subarctic tundra region of northern Canada, characterized by its stunted vegetation. **Land of the Long White Cloud** *NZ* New Zealand. **land of the midnight sun** (that part of) any of the most northerly European countries in which it never gets fully dark during the summer months. **land of the rising sun** Japan. ***lands and tenements***: see **TENEMENT** 2. **land to** *NAUTICAL* just within sight of land, when at sea. ***law of the land***: see **LAW** *noun*[1]. ***lie of the land***: see **LIE** *noun*[2]. ***live off the land***: see **LIVE** *verb*. ***Never Never Land***: see **NEVER**. ***no man's land***: see **NO** *adjective*. ***promised land***: see **PROMISE** *verb*. ***red land***: see **RED** *adjective*. ***the fat of the land***: see **FAT** *noun*[2]. ***the Flowery Land***: see **FLOWERY** *adjective* 1. ***the land***: see sense 2b above. ***the land of Nod***: see **NOD** *noun*. ***ure of land***: see **URE** *noun*[2]. ***white land***: see **WHITE** *adjective*. ***wide brown land***: see **WIDE** *adjective*. ***within land***: see **WITHIN** *adverb, preposition, adjective, & noun*. ***yard of land***: see **YARD** *noun*[2] 4.
– **ATTRIB. & COMB.**: In the senses 'belonging, attached to, or characteristic of the land', 'situated or taking place on land (as opp. to on the sea or water or in the air)', 'living on land (as opp. to on or in water)', as ***land battle***, ***land-bird***, ***land-engine***, ***land-journey***, ***land-monster***, ***land-plant***, ***land-prospect***, ***land-snail***, ***land-soldier***, etc. Special combs., as **land agency** (*a*) the occupation of a land agent; (*b*) an agency for the sale etc. of estates; **land agent** (*a*) a steward or manager of landed property; (*b*) an agent for the sale of land; **land army** (*a*) an army that fights on land; (*b*) (also with cap. initials) a corps of women established in Britain in 1917 for work on the land esp. in wartime; **land-bred** *adjective* (*a*) brought up on land (as opp. to on sea); (*b*) native, indigenous; ***land breeze***: see **BREEZE** *noun*[2] 2; **land bridge** (*a*) a connection (usu. prehistoric) between two land masses; (*b*) an overland route linking countries more directly than other routes; †**land-carrack** (*a*) a coasting vessel; (*b*) a prostitute; **land-carriage** (the cost of) carriage or transport by land; **land-community** joint or common ownership of land; **land connection** = ***land bridge*** (a) above; **land crab** any crab of the tropical and subtropical family Gecarcinidae, many members of which spend much time on land; *esp.* (in full ***blue land crab***) a New World crab, *Cardisoma guanhumi*; **land cress** a winter cress, *Barbarea verna*, native to SW Europe and grown as a salad plant (cf. **WATERCRESS**); **land district** *US* any of the districts into which a state or territory is divided for matters connected with land; **land drain** a drain made of porous or perforated piping, placed in a gravel-filled trench, and used for subsoil drainage; **land-end** (now *dial.*) a piece of ground at the end of a land in a ploughed field; **land-fast** *adjective* firmly attached to the shore; **land fever** *N. Amer.* eager desire for, or excitement about, securing land; **landfill** (*a*) the disposal of refuse by burying it under layers of earth; (*b*) refuse disposed of under layers of earth, an area filled in by this process; †**land-fish** *fig.* an unnatural creature; **land-floe** a sheet of sea ice extending from the land; **land-flood**: caused by the overflowing of a river or other inland water; **land-folk** the people of a land or country; **land force** an armed force serving on land, as opp. to a naval or air force; in *pl.*, the soldiers composing such a force; **landform** (*a*) a physical feature of the earth's surface; (*b*) (***land-form***) a species (of organism) found on land; **land-fyrd** (*obsolete* exc. *hist.*) a land force; **land gavel** *hist.* land tax; rent for land, ground rent; **land girl** a member of the Land Army; **land-grabber** an illegal seizer of land, *esp.* (*IRISH HISTORY*) a person who took a farm after the eviction of the previous tenant; **land grant** a grant of public land; ***land-grant college*** (*US*), a college set up with federal aid; **landholder** a proprietor, holder, or occupier of land; **land-hunger** keen desire for the acquisition of land; **land-hungry** *adjective* eager to acquire land; **land-ice** ice attached to the shore, as distinguished from floe ice; **land-jobber** a person who buys and sells land on speculation; **land law** (*a*) (long *obsolete* exc. *hist.*) the law of a country, the law of the land; (*b*) the law, or a law, governing real property; **Land League** *IRISH HISTORY* an association of Irish tenant farmers etc. set up in 1879 (and suppressed in 1881), which sought to have rents reduced and ultimately to bring about radical land reform; **Land-leaguer** *IRISH HISTORY* a member of or sympathizer with the Land League; **Land-leaguism** *IRISH HISTORY* the principles or practice of the Land League; **land-leech** a large terrestrial leech of the tropical genus *Haemodipsa*; **land legs** the ability to walk comfortably on land after being at sea, in a train, etc.; **landline** (*a*) *noun* an overland means of telecommunication, esp. a conventional telecommunications connection by cable; (*b*) *verb trans.* transmit over a landline; **landlocked** *adjective* (*a*) (almost) enclosed or surrounded by land; (*b*) hemmed in or limited by surrounding land; **land-looker** *US* = **CRUISER** 2a; **land mass** a large continuous area of land, esp. of continental size; **land-measure** †(*a*) measurement of land; (*b*) a unit of measure or system of such units used in stating the area of land; **land measurement** the art or process of measuring the area of fields, farms, etc.; **land-measurer** a person whose occupation is land measurement; **land-measuring** = ***land measurement*** above; **landmine** (*a*) an explosive mine used on land; (*b*) a bomb dropped by parachute from an aircraft; **land mullet** a large burrowing lizard, *Egernia major*, of the skink family, with shiny fish-like scales, native to the coastal regions of eastern Australia; **land office** *US* an office recording dealings in public land; ***land-office business*** (*colloq.*), enormous trade; **landowner** an owner or proprietor of land; **landowning** *noun & adjective* owning land, being the proprietor of land; **land-pike** *US* (*a*) = ***hellbender*** s.v. **HELL** *noun*; (*b*) a thin, inferior type of pig; **landplane** an aircraft which can only operate from or alight on land (opp. ***seaplane***); **land-poor** *adjective* (*US*) poor through the burden of taxation resulting from owning much land; **landrail** the corncrake; **land-rat** (*a*) a rat that lives on land; †(*b*) a contemptible person, a thief; **Land Registry** (a building or office housing) a government department with which titles to or charges upon land must be registered; **land-right** (*obsolete* exc. *hist.*) = ***land law*** (a) above; **Landrover** (proprietary name for) a sturdy four-wheel-drive motor vehicle designed esp. for work in rough or agricultural country; ***land scrip***: see **SCRIP** *noun*[2] 2b; **land-service** service as a soldier on land; **land-shark** *slang* (*a*) a person who makes a living by exploiting seamen when they are ashore; (*b*) = ***land-grabber*** above; **land ship** (*a*) a vehicle on land (esp. a tank) regarded as resembling in function a ship on the sea; (*b*) a ship erected and kept on land for training purposes; **land-sick** *adjective* (*a*) sick through the sight of land; sick of being on land; (*b*) ill from being on land again after a long sea voyage; (*c*) *NAUTICAL* (of a ship) impeded in its movements by being close to land; **land speed** (*a*) speed (of an aircraft) relative to the ground; (*b*) speed on the ground (e.g. in a motor vehicle); **land spring** a spring which comes into action and overflows only intermittently, usu. after heavy rains; **land-steward** a person who manages a landed estate for the owner; **land-stream** a current in the sea due to river waters; **land-surveying** the process, art, or profession of measuring, and making plans of, landed property; **land-surveyor** a person whose profession is land-surveying; **land-swell** the roll of the water near the shore; **land-take** the action of taking land, or an area of land taken, for colonization or development; **land tax** *hist.* a tax levied on landed property; **land-thief** a person who robs land or robs on land; **landtie** a rod, beam, or piece of masonry securing or supporting a wall etc. by connecting it with the ground; **land-value** the economic value of land in all respects, esp. as a basis for rating or taxation; **land-war** (*a*) a war waged on land, as opp. to a naval or air war; (*b*) a dispute or struggle concerning land; **land-wash** (*a*) the wash of the tide near the shore; (*b*) (orig. *N. Amer.*) the part of a beach covered by water at high tide; **land-water** (*a*) water flowing through or over land, as opp. to seawater; (*b*) = ***land-flood*** above; (*c*) water free from ice along a frozen shore; **land wheel** the wheel of a plough that runs on the unploughed land; **land-wind** a wind blowing seaward from the land; **land wire** = ***landline*** above; **land yacht** a vehicle with wheels and a sail or sails for recreational use on a beach etc.

Land /lant, land/ *noun*[2]. Pl. ***Länder*** /ˈlɛndər/, ***Lands*** /landz/. **E20**.
[**ORIGIN** German.]
A semi-autonomous unit of local government in Germany and Austria.

land /land/ *verb*. **ME**.
[**ORIGIN** from **LAND** *noun*[1].]
1 *verb trans. & intrans.* Bring or come to land; put or go ashore; disembark. **ME**. ▸**b** *verb trans.* In *pass.* Be given the status of a landed immigrant. *Canad.* **E20**.

MRS H. WARD His hansom landed him at the door of a great mansion. C. ISHERWOOD The Soviet fleet will make an immediate dash for Swinemünde and begin to land troops. E. SAINTSBURY Charles Edward Stuart . . landed on the west coast of Scotland in 1745.

2 *verb trans.* *ANGLING*. Bring (a fish) to land, esp. with a hook or net. **E17**. ▸**b** *fig.* Catch (a person); gain or win (money, a

L

prize, etc.); obtain (a job etc.), esp. against strong competition. M19.

K. KESEY George told the doctor he'd have to land his fish or cut it loose. **b** C. P. SNOW Neither he nor Kate could understand how she had finally landed him. S. HASTINGS Back in England he managed to land a job in the City. *Today's Golfer* Putts . . good enough to land the claret jug, the title and the £75,000 first prize.

3 *verb trans. & intrans.* Bring to or arrive at a specified place, point or position; put in or end (*up*) in a specified (esp. unfortunate) position or situation. M17. ▸**b** *verb trans. & intrans.* Set down or alight (from a vehicle). Now *rare* or *obsolete*. L17. ▸**c** *verb trans.* Establish (a person) in a safe or favourable situation. *slang.* M19. ▸**d** *verb trans. & intrans.* (Cause to) fall to the ground or strike a surface from above. M19. ▸**e** *verb intrans. & trans.* Alight on, or bring under control to, earth or some other surface after a flight. L19.

I. MURDOCH Liza's . . lack of common sense constantly landed her in scrapes. N. ANNAN His business failed, he landed in a debtors' gaol. S. MIDDLETON It was past eleven o'clock when he landed upstairs. **d** J. B. MORTON He went through the parlour floor and landed in the scullery below. **e** K. W. GATLAND Instead of landing the entire space-ship, a secondary rocket will descend to the surface. F. HERBERT A hawk landed on the sand near his outstretched hand. V. S. NAIPAUL To land at La Guaira airport . . was to come down to a different country.

land on one's feet = *fall on one's feet* s.v. FALL *verb*.

4 a *verb trans.* Bring (a horse etc.) first past the winning post. *colloq.* M19. ▸**b** *verb intrans.* Win a race. *colloq.* M19.

a *Times* Sheikh Muhammad . . landed two winners.

5 a *verb trans.* Encumber or burden (a person) *with*. M19. ▸**b** *verb trans. & intrans.* (foll. by *out*). Strike (a blow). L19.

a *Punch* Spinks and I were landed with this . . job just as we were about to leave. **b** HARPER LEE It was easy to grab his front hair and land one on his mouth.

– WITH ADVERBS IN SPECIALIZED SENSES: **land on** (of an aircraft) touch down on the deck of an aircraft carrier. **land up** (*a*) *verb phr. intrans.* come eventually to a specified state; (*b*) *verb phr. trans.* fill or block up (a watercourse, pond, etc.) with earth; silt up.

L

landammann /ˈlandəmən/ *noun*. Also **-man**, **L-**. L17.
[ORIGIN Swiss German, from *Land* LAND *noun*[2] + *Amman(n)* = German *Amtmann*, from *Amt* office + *Mann* man.]
The chief magistrate in certain Swiss cantons. Formerly also, the chief officer in certain smaller administrative districts of Switzerland.

landau /ˈlandɔː, -aʊ/ *noun*. M18.
[ORIGIN from *Landau* in Germany, where first made.]
Chiefly *hist.* A four-wheeled horse-drawn carriage, with folding front and rear hoods enabling it to travel open, half-open, or closed. Also ***landau carriage***.

landaulet /landɔːˈlɛt, -də-/ *noun*. In sense 2 also **-lette**. L18.
[ORIGIN from LANDAU + -LET.]
Chiefly *hist.* **1** A small landau. L18.
2 A type of car with a leather hood above the rear seats. E20.

landbank /ˈlan(d)baŋk/ *verb intrans.* L20.
[ORIGIN from LAND BANK.]
Accumulate land for future development or investment potential. Chiefly as ***landbanking*** *verbal noun*.

land bank /ˈlandbaŋk/ *noun*. L17.
[ORIGIN from LAND *noun*[1] + BANK *noun*[3].]
1 A bank which issues currency using land as security. L17.
2 In full ***federal land bank***. Any of a number of banks providing mortgages on farmland, financed by issuing public bonds. *US*. E20.
3 COMMERCE. The total amount of land accumulated and held by a private corporation or government body, esp. for future development; a corporation etc. accumulating land for development. M20.

land-boc /ˈlandbəʊk/ *noun*. Long *obsolete* exc. *hist.* OE.
[ORIGIN from LAND *noun*[1] + *bōc* BOOK *noun*.]
A charter or deed by which land was granted.

landdrost /ˈland(d)rɒst/ *noun*. M18.
[ORIGIN Afrikaans, from Dutch *land* LAND *noun*[1] + *drost* bailiff.]
hist. A district magistrate in South Africa.

lande /lɑ̃d/ *noun*. Pl. pronounced same. L18.
[ORIGIN French: cf. LAUND.]
A tract of wild land, a moor, esp. in SW France.

landed /ˈlandɪd/ *adjective*. OE.
[ORIGIN from LAND *noun*[1], *verb*: see -ED[1], -ED[2].]
1 Possessing (an estate in) land. OE.

G. ORWELL The Anglican Church . . was simply a preserve of the landed gentry.

2 Consisting of land or in the possession of land; (of revenue) derived from land. E18.
3 That has landed or has been landed. M19.
4 Of an engineering tool etc.: having a land between grooves etc. M20.
– SPECIAL COLLOCATIONS: **landed immigrant** *Canad.*: admitted to Canada for permanent residence. **landed interest** interest in land as a possession; the owners and holders of land. **landed plunger**: forming an accurate seal when mated with a corresponding mould.

lander /ˈlandə/ *noun*[1]. M19.
[ORIGIN from LAND *verb* + -ER[1].]
1 a A person who lands or goes ashore. M19. ▸**b** A spacecraft designed to be landed on the surface of a planet or the moon. M20.
2 MINING. The person who receives the kibble at the mouth of a shaft. M19.

lander *noun*[2] see LAUNDER *noun*.

Länder *noun pl.* see LAND *noun*[2].

landfall /ˈlan(d)fɔːl/ *noun*. E17.
[ORIGIN from LAND *noun*[1] + FALL *noun*[2].]
1 The arrival at or sighting of land from the sea. Now also, (an) arrival at land after a flight over the sea. E17. ▸**b** A place on land sighted or reached after a journey over the sea. L19. ▸**c** A place where an undersea pipeline reaches land. L20.

C. RYAN Wreathed by flak bursts, the huge armada made landfall over the Dutch coast. **b** T. BRASSEY The Bahamas will be for ever memorable as the landfall of Columbus. **c** *Selling Today* Aberdeen, the nearest landfall and port to the Forties field.

make a good landfall, **make a bad landfall** meet with land in accordance with or contrary to one's navigational intentions.
2 An unexpected inheritance of land. M18.

landgravate *noun* var. of LANDGRAVIATE.

landgrave /ˈlan(d)greɪv/ *noun*. Also (esp. in titles) **L-**. LME.
[ORIGIN Middle Low German (= Middle High German *lantgrâve*, German *Landgraf*), from *land* LAND *noun*[2] + *grave* GRAVE *noun*[2].]
hist. A count with jurisdiction over a German territory.
■ **landgraveship** *noun* = LANDGRAVIATE M17. **landgravine** /ˈlan(d)grəviːn/ *noun* the wife of a landgrave; a female ruler of a landgraviate: L17.

landgraviate /landˈgreɪvɪət/ *noun*. Also **landgravate** /ˈlan(d)grəveɪt/ E17.
[ORIGIN medieval Latin *landgraviatus*, from LANDGRAVE: see -I-, -ATE[1].]
hist. The office, jurisdiction, or territory of a landgrave.

landing /ˈlandɪŋ/ *noun*. LME.
[ORIGIN from LAND *verb* + -ING[1].]
1 The action of LAND *verb*; an instance of this. LME.
automatic landing: see AUTOMATIC *adjective* 2. ***happy landings***: see HAPPY *adjective*.
2 A place for disembarking, loading, or unloading; a landing place. LME.
3 A platform or resting place at the top of a staircase or between two flights of stairs; a passage or antechamber at the top of a flight of stairs. L18. ▸**b** Stone used in or suitable for making staircase landings. M19.
– COMB.: **landing beam** AERONAUTICS a radio beam to guide aircraft when landing; **landing card** a card issued to a passenger on an international flight or voyage, to be surrendered on arrival; **landing craft** (*a*) MILITARY a naval vessel designed for putting troops, tanks, etc., ashore; (*b*) ASTRONAUTICS the section of a spacecraft used for the final descent to the surface of a planet or the moon; **landing flap** AERONAUTICS a flap that can be lowered to increase the lift and the drag to make possible lower speeds for take-off and landing; **landing gear** (*a*) see GEAR *noun* 5c; (*b*) the retractable support at the front of a semi-trailer that supports it when not attached to the tractor; **landing light** (*a*) a light on a runway to guide an aircraft in a night landing (usu. in *pl.*); (*b*) a light attached to an aircraft to illuminate the ground for a night landing; **landing net**: for landing a fish that has been hooked; **landing pad** (*a*) a small area of an airfield or heliport, where helicopters land and take off; (*b*) a cushioned or strengthened foot which supports a hovercraft, spacecraft, etc., on the ground; **landing run** (*a*) the distance an aircraft travels in contact with the ground during landing; (*b*) that part of a flight during which a pilot prepares to land; **landing stage** a (floating) platform, for the landing of passengers and goods; **landing strip** an airstrip; **landing ticket** = *landing card* above; **landing wire** AERONAUTICS a wire on a biplane or light monoplane designed to take the weight of a wing when the aircraft is on the ground.

landing place /ˈlandɪŋpleɪs/ *noun*. E16.
[ORIGIN from LANDING + PLACE *noun*[1].]
1 a A place for the landing of passengers and goods. E16. ▸**b** A place where a bird, insect, aircraft, etc., can or does land. L18.
2 = LANDING *noun* 3. Now *rare* or *obsolete*. E17.

land-junker /ˈlandjʊŋkə/ *noun*. Now *rare* or *obsolete*. M19.
[ORIGIN German: see LAND *noun*[1], JUNKER *noun*[1].]
A country squire.

landlady /ˈlan(d)leɪdi/ *noun*. M16.
[ORIGIN from LAND *noun*[1] + LADY *noun*, after *landlord*.]
1 A woman who lets land or (part of) a building to a tenant. M16.
2 A woman who keeps a public house, lodgings, or a boarding house. M17.

†**land-leaper** *noun*. LME–E18.
[ORIGIN from LAND *noun*[1] + LEAPER, after Middle Dutch *landlooper*: see LAND-LOPER.]
= LAND-LOPER.

ländler /ˈlɛndlə/ *noun*. L19.
[ORIGIN German.]
An Austrian peasant dance, similar to a slow waltz; a piece of music for this dance.

landless /ˈlandlɪs/ *adjective*. LOE.
[ORIGIN from LAND *noun*[1] + -LESS.]
1 Not possessing land, having no landed property. LOE.
2 Having no land on its surface or within its bounds. *rare.* E17.
■ **landlessness** *noun* M19.

land-loper /ˈlandləʊpə/ *noun*. *arch.* Latterly chiefly *Scot.* Also **-louper** /-laʊpə/. L16.
[ORIGIN Middle Dutch *landlooper* (Dutch *landloper* tramp), from *land* LAND *noun*[1] + *loopen* run: see LEAP *verb*. Cf. LAND-LEAPER, LOAFER.]
1 A vagrant. Formerly also, a renegade. L16.
†**2** = LANDLUBBER. L16–E18.
■ **landloping** *adjective* wandering, vagrant L16.

landlord /ˈlan(d)lɔːd/ *noun*. OE.
[ORIGIN from LAND *noun*[1] + LORD *noun*.]
1 A lord or owner of land, a person who lets land to a tenant. Later also, a person who lets (part of) a building. OE.

S. HASTINGS He was a good landlord, the tenants' cottages were always kept in repair.

2 A person (esp. a man) who keeps a public house, lodgings, or a boarding house. L17.

Which? We visited . . 2,232 pubs and asked the landlords about the drinks they served.

3 A private host or entertainer. Chiefly *Scot.* E18.
■ **landlordism** *noun* (chiefly *hist.*) the (esp. Irish) system whereby land is owned by landlords to whom tenants pay a fixed rent; the advocacy or practice of this system: M19. **landlordly** *adjective* pertaining to or characteristic of a landlord or landlords M19. **landlordry** *noun* (long *rare*) landlords collectively L16. **landlordship** *noun* the position of or a post as a landlord E19.

land-louper *noun* var. of LAND-LOPER.

landlubber /ˈlandlʌbə/ *noun*. L17.
[ORIGIN from LAND *noun*[1] + LUBBER.]
A person with little or no experience of the sea or sailing; a person who lives on land.
■ **landlubberly** *adjective* characteristic of a landlubber M19.

landman /ˈlandmən/ *noun*. Pl. **-men**. OE.
[ORIGIN from LAND *noun*[1] + MAN *noun*: cf. LANDSMAN *noun*[1].]
†**1** A native of a particular country. *rare.* OE–M17.
2 A countryman, a peasant. Now *rare* or *obsolete*. ME.
3 = LANDSMAN *noun*[1] 2. Now *rare* or *obsolete*. L15.
†**4** A man possessing landed property. M16–E18.
5 = ***leaseman*** s.v. LEASE *noun*[3]. *US.* E20.

landmark /ˈlandmɑːk/ *noun*, *verb*, & *adjective*. OE.
[ORIGIN from LAND *noun*[1] + MARK *noun*[1].]
▸ **A** *noun*. **1** (An object marking) the boundary of a country, an estate, etc. OE.

BURKE When . . he returned to . . his estates, . . he found none of the ancient landmarks removed.

2 A conspicuous object in a landscape, serving as a (navigational) guide; any prominent object in a neighbourhood or district. L16.

W. STYRON I gave up pointing out the landmarks of the capital, abandoning the tour-guide approach. I. MURDOCH She could not remember the way and kept looking for landmarks.

3 An object, event, etc., which marks a period, (a stage in) a development, or a turning point. M19.

P. LARKIN This has never been done before . . . I therefore salute a landmark in publishing history. *Woman & Home* Another landmark came in February when Sarah achieved her wings as a qualified pilot.

▸ **B** *verb trans.* Be or act as a landmark to; provide with a landmark. E20.
▸ **C** *attrib.* or as *adjective*. That is or serves as a landmark; signifying an important change, development, etc. M20.

W. FAULKNER There was no territory . . that he did not know—bayou, ridge, landmark trees. R. C. A. WHITE Landmark cases embodying sweeping reforms of the law.

land-marshal /ˈlandmɑːʃ(ə)l/ *noun*. Also **L-**. L17.
[ORIGIN from LAND *noun*[1] + MARSHAL *noun*[1], repr. in sense 1 Swedish *landtmarskalk*, in sense 2 German *Landmarschall*.]
hist. **1** In Sweden: the speaker or president of the assembly of the first estate. L17.
2 In Austria, Prussia, etc.: the marshal of a province. E18.

landmen *noun* pl. of LANDMAN.

landnam /ˈlandnəm/ *noun*. M20.
[ORIGIN Danish = occupation of land.]
ARCHAEOLOGY. The clearance of forested land for (usu. short-term) agricultural purposes; evidence of this provided by sudden changes in pollen spectra.

landnám /ˈlandnɑːm/ *noun*. M19.
[ORIGIN Old Norse *land-nám*, from *land* land, territory + *nám* from *nema* to take.]
hist. Land-take, esp. with ref. to the Norse colonization of Iceland.

landocracy /lanˈdɒkrəsi/ *noun*. *joc.* M19.
[ORIGIN from LAND *noun*[1]: see -CRACY.]
A class of people with political power based on possession of land.

landrace /ˈlandreɪs/ *noun*. **M20.**
[**ORIGIN** Danish = national breed.]
A breed of large white pig, originally developed in Denmark; an animal of this breed.

Landry /ˈlɑːndri, *foreign* lɑ̃dri/ *noun*. **L19.**
[**ORIGIN** J. B. *Landry* (1826–65), French physician.]
MEDICINE. ***Landry's paralysis***, ***Landry's disease***, orig., any acute ascending paralysis, now *spec*. = **GUILLAIN–BARRÉ SYNDROME**.

Landsborough grass /ˈlandzbərə grɑːs/ *noun phr.* Now *rare* or *obsolete*. **L19.**
[**ORIGIN** from William *Landsborough* (1826–86), Austral. explorer.]
= ***Flinders grass*** s.v. **FLINDERS** *noun*[2] 2.

landscape /ˈlan(d)skeɪp/ *noun, adjective, & adverb*. Also †**landskip**, †**lantskip**. **L16.**
[**ORIGIN** Middle Dutch *lantscap*, Dutch *landschap* landscape, province; *-skip* after Dutch pronunc.: see **LAND** *noun*[1]. Cf. **-SHIP**.]
▸ **A** *noun*. **1** A picture of natural (esp. inland) scenery (cf. **SEASCAPE**). Formerly also, the scenery forming the background of a portrait etc. **L16.** ▸†**b** A sketch, an outline; a bird's-eye view, a map. **M17–E18.** ▸†**c** *fig.* An epitome *of* some quality. **M17–E19.**
2 Natural scenery; the pictorial representation of scenery, esp. as an artistic genre. **E17.**
3 a (A view presented by) an expanse of terrain or district which is visible from a particular place or direction; an expanse of (country) scenery. **M17.** ▸**b** *GEOGRAPHY*. A tract or region of land with its characteristic topographical features, esp. as shaped or modified by (usu. natural) processes and agents. **L19.**

> **a** B. **MOORE** The landscape, hilly, empty . . gradually began to change. **b** N. **CALDER** The sculpture of landscapes by water, ice and wind. *fig.*: *Scientific American* Trade unions have become a prominent feature of the industrial landscape.

– **COMB.**: **landscape architect** a practitioner of landscape architecture; **landscape architecture** (the art of) planning and designing the open-air environment, esp. with ref. to the harmonious fitting of buildings, roads, etc., into the landscape; **landscape gardener** a practitioner of landscape gardening; **landscape gardening** (the art of) laying out ornamental grounds or grounds imitating natural scenery; **landscape-marble** a variety of marble with markings resembling shrubbery or trees; **landscape painter** an artist who paints landscapes.

▸ **B** *adjective & adverb*. Of a page, book, etc., or the manner in which it is set or printed: having or in a rectangular shape with the width greater than the height. Opp. **PORTRAIT** *adjective & adverb*. **E20.**

landscape /ˈlan(d)skeɪp/ *verb*. **M17.**
[**ORIGIN** from **LANDSCAPE** *noun, adjective, & adverb*.]
1 *verb trans.* Represent as a landscape; depict. Now *rare* or *obsolete*. **M17.**
2 *verb trans.* & *intrans.* Lay out (a garden etc.) as a landscape; conceal or enhance the appearance of (a building, road, etc.) by means of landscape architecture. **E20.**
■ **landscaper** *noun* a person skilled in landscape architecture or landscape gardening **M20.** **landscapist** *noun* (*a*) a painter of landscapes; (*b*) a landscaper: **E19.**

Landseer /ˈlan(d)sɪə/ *noun*. **L19.**
[**ORIGIN** Sir Edwin *Landseer* (1802–73), English painter.]
A black and white Newfoundland dog of a type once painted by Landseer. Also more fully ***Landseer Newfoundland***.

landside /ˈlan(d)sʌɪd/ *noun, adjective, & adverb*. **M16.**
[**ORIGIN** from **LAND** *noun*[1] + **SIDE** *noun*.]
▸ **A** *noun*. †**1** The shore. Only in **M16.**
2 The flat side of a plough which is turned towards the unploughed land. **M18.**
3 The landward side of something. **M19.**
4 The side or sections of an airport to which the public has admittance. **M20.**
▸ **B** *adjective*. Designating or pertaining to the landside of an airport. **L20.**
▸ **C** *adverb*. To or towards the landside of an airport. **L20.**

†**landskip** *noun* var. of **LANDSCAPE** *noun*.

landsknecht *noun* see **LANSQUENET**.

landsleit *noun* pl. of **LANDSMAN** *noun*[2].

landslide /ˈlan(d)slʌɪd/ *noun*. **M19.**
[**ORIGIN** from **LAND** *noun*[1] + **SLIDE** *noun*.]
1 A landslip, an avalanche. **M19.**
2 An overwhelming majority of votes for one party or candidate in an election. **L19.**

landslip /ˈlan(d)slɪp/ *noun*. **L17.**
[**ORIGIN** from **LAND** *noun*[1] + **SLIP** *noun*[3].]
The sliding down of a mass of land on a mountain, cliff, etc.; land which has so fallen.

Landsmål /ˈlantsmɔːl/ *noun*. Now *rare*. Also ***-maal***. **L19.**
[**ORIGIN** Norwegian, from *land* country + *mål* language.]
= **NYNORSK**. Cf. **BOKMÅL**, **RIKSMÅL**.

landsman /ˈlan(d)zmən/ *noun*[1]. Pl. **-men**. **OE.**
[**ORIGIN** from **LAND** *noun*[1] + **-'S**[1] + **MAN** *noun*.]
1 †**a** A native of a particular country. **OE–LME.** ▸**b** A fellow countryman. **L16.**
2 A person living or working on land as opp. to a seaman; (*obsolete* exc. *hist.*) a sailor on his first sea voyage. **M17.**

landsman /ˈlɒntsmɒn/ *noun*[2]. Pl. ***landsleit*** /ˈlɒntslʌɪt/. **M20.**
[**ORIGIN** Yiddish, from Middle High German *lantsman*, *lantman* a native: cf. **LANDMAN**.]
Among Jews: a fellow Jew; a compatriot.

landsmen *noun* pl. of **LANDSMAN** *noun*[1].

Landsturm /ˈlantʃtʊrm/ *noun*. Pl. ***-stürme*** /-ʃtyrmə/. **E19.**
[**ORIGIN** German, lit. 'land-storm'.]
hist. In Germany and German-speaking countries: a general levy in time of war; an auxiliary militia force.

landswoman /ˈlan(d)swʊmən/ *noun*. Pl. **-women** /-wɪmɪn/. **M19.**
[**ORIGIN** from **LAND** *noun*[1] + **-'S**[1] + **WOMAN** *noun*, after **LANDSMAN** *noun*[1].]
A woman living on the land or skilled in working on it.

landward /ˈlandwəd/ *noun, adverb, & adjective*. **LME.**
[**ORIGIN** from **LAND** *noun*[1] + **-WARD**.]
▸ **A** *noun*. The direction or position of the land. Only in ***to landward***, ***to the landward***, †(*a*) *Scot.* in the country, as opp. to the town; (*b*) (*obsolete* exc. *dial.*) towards the land, on the land side (*of*); & in ***landward-bred*** below. **LME.**
– **COMB.**: **landward-bred** *adjective* (*Scot.*) country-bred.
▸ **B** *adjective*. **1** Belonging to or inhabiting the country; rural, rustic. *Scot.* **M16.**
2 Facing the land, as opp. to the sea. **M19.**
▸ **C** *adverb*. Towards the land. **E17.**
■ **landwards** *noun & adverb* †(*a*) *noun* = **LANDWARD** *noun* (only in ***to landwards***, ***to the landwards***); (*b*) *adverb* = **LANDWARD** *adverb*: **L16.**

Landwehr /ˈlantveːr/ *noun*. **E19.**
[**ORIGIN** German, lit. 'land-defence'.]
MILITARY. In Germany and some other countries: that part of the organized land forces of which continuous service is required only in time of war; the army reserve.

lane /leɪn/ *noun*[1]. See also **LOAN** *noun*[2].
[**ORIGIN** Old English *lane* = Old Frisian *lana*, *laen*, Middle Dutch *lāne* (Dutch *laan*). Ult. origin unknown.]
1 A narrow path or road between hedges, banks, etc.; a narrow road or street between houses or walls. **OE.**

> R. K. **NARAYAN** He . . stole along by-ways and lanes. M. **LOWRY** There was a lane branching to the left . . , no more than a cart-track at first. *Proverb*: It's a long lane that has no turning.

2 (A thing resembling) a narrow or comparatively narrow way, channel, or passage, *esp.* a passage between two lines of people or through a crowd. **LME.** ▸**b** A channel or path designated for use or regularly used by shipping or aircraft, esp. on busy routes. **M19.** ▸**c** *SPORT*. A path or channel allocated to an individual (esp. a sprinter or swimmer) in a race, usu. marked out and separated from parallel paths etc. by lines or ropes. **E20.** ▸**d** A division along a road, marked out by painted lines and used to segregate traffic according to speed, intended direction, type of vehicle, etc. **E20.** ▸**e** In tenpin bowling etc.: a long narrow strip of floor down which a ball is bowled. **M20.**

> **b** P. **NORMAN** We traverse sea lanes crowded, like a busy street, with . . liners and cargo ships and . . tankers. *Aircraft Illustrated* For flights in British airspace, air traffic control lanes . . are established. **c** *Marathon & Distance Runner* The gun went, the six athletes in their own lanes were released into the . . bend. *Swimming Times* In the 6-lane . . pool provided for competition. **d** R. **DAHL** A policeman on a motor-cycle loomed up alongside us on the inside lane. ***attrib.***: *Evening Post (Bristol)* Better lane discipline by all traffic would make roundabouts safer for all.

3 A long narrow enclosure from which kangaroos, cattle, etc., are driven into a pen or pound. *Austral.* **M19.**
4 *ASTRONOMY*. A narrow band or strip in the sky, in the image of a galaxy, etc., that differs markedly from its immediate surroundings, e.g. in containing no observable stars. **L19.**

> *Nature* A small, irregular, diffuse nebulosity . . with a prominent dark lane.

– **PHRASES**: ***fast lane***: see **FAST** *adjective*. **in lane** in the appropriate or correct lane. ***lover's lane***: see **LOVER** *noun*. ***memory lane***: see **MEMORY** *noun*. ***red lane***: see **RED** *adjective*. **the lane** *slang* the throat.
■ **laned** *adjective* divided into (a specified number of) lanes **L19.**

lane *adjective, adverb, & noun*[2] see **LONE** *adjective* etc.

Lane's Prince Albert /leɪnz prɪns ˈalbət/ *noun phr.* **L19.**
[**ORIGIN** from John *Lane*, 19th-cent. English horticulturist, who introduced it, and *Prince Albert* (see **ALBERT**).]
A large green variety of cooking apple.

langar /ˈlʌŋgər/ *noun*. *Indian*. **M20.**
[**ORIGIN** Hindi.]
Among Sikhs: a communal free kitchen or meal.

långbanite /ˈlɔːŋbənʌɪt/ *noun*. **L19.**
[**ORIGIN** from *Långban*, a locality in Sweden + **-ITE**[1].]
MINERALOGY. A trigonal silicate and oxide of antimony, ferric iron, and manganese, black with a metallic lustre.

langbeinite /ˈlaŋbʌɪnʌɪt/ *noun*. **L19.**
[**ORIGIN** from A. *Langbein*, 19th-cent. German chemist + **-ITE**[1].]
MINERALOGY. A sulphate of potassium and magnesium crystallizing in the cubic system, which occurs in marine salt deposits and is made synthetically, and is used in the production of fertilizers.

langeleik /ˈlaŋəlʌɪk/ *noun*. Pl. ***-en*** /-ən/. Also ***langleik*** /ˈlaŋlʌɪk/. **E20.**
[**ORIGIN** Norwegian.]
An early Norwegian stringed instrument, resembling the zither.

langer /ˈlaŋə/ *noun*. *Irish slang*. **L20.**
[**ORIGIN** Of uncertain origin.]
The penis. Also, a stupid or contemptible person.

Langerhans /ˈlaŋəhanz/ *noun*. **L19.**
[**ORIGIN** Paul *Langerhans* (1847–88), German anatomist.]
ANATOMY. **1** ***islet of Langerhans***, ***island of Langerhans***, any of a number of groups of cells in the pancreas which secrete insulin and some other hormones. **L19.**
2 ***Langerhans cell***, ***cell of Langerhans***, a kind of dendritic or stellate cell found in the epidermis and characterized by the presence of cytoplasmic granules. **L19.**

†**langfad** *noun* see **LYMPHAD**.

Langhans /ˈlaŋhanz/ *noun*. **L19.**
[**ORIGIN** Theodor *Langhans* (1839–1915), German pathologist.]
ANATOMY & MEDICINE. Used ***attrib.***, in ***possess.***, and with *of* to designate (*a*) (a cell of) an inner layer of large cuboidal cells covering chorionic villi beneath the syncytial layer; (*b*) a distinctive kind of polynuclear giant cell observed esp. in tuberculosis and related granulomatous conditions.

Langi *noun & adjective* var. of **LANGO**.

langite /ˈlaŋgʌɪt/ *noun*. **M19.**
[**ORIGIN** from V. von *Lang* (1838–1921), Austrian physicist + **-ITE**[1].]
MINERALOGY. A blue or bluish-green orthorhombic basic sulphate of copper, resembling brochantite.

lang-kale /ˈlaŋkeɪl/ *noun*. *Scot.* **E18.**
[**ORIGIN** from *lang* var. of **LONG** *adjective*[1] + **KALE**.]
= ***Scotch kale*** s.v. **KALE** 1.

langlauf /ˈlaŋlaʊf/ *noun*. Also **L-**. **E20.**
[**ORIGIN** German, lit. 'long run'.]
Cross-country skiing; a cross-country skiing race.
■ **langlaufer** *noun* a competitor in (a) langlauf. **E20.**

L

langleik *noun* var. of **LANGELEIK**.

langley /ˈlaŋli/ *noun*. **M20.**
[**ORIGIN** Samuel P. *Langley* (1834–1906), US astronomer.]
METEOROLOGY. A unit of solar energy flux per unit area, equal to one (small) calorie per square centimetre (approx. 41,900 joule per square metre).

Langmuir /ˈlaŋmjʊə/ *noun*. **M20.**
[**ORIGIN** Irving *Langmuir* (1881–1957), US physicist.]
Used ***attrib.*** to designate concepts introduced by Langmuir or arising out of his work.
Langmuir adsorption isotherm, **Langmuir isotherm** *PHYSICS* a curve showing the relationship between the extent of adsorption of a gas on a surface and the gas pressure. **Langmuir–Blodgett film** [Katherine B. *Blodgett* (1898–1979), US physicist and chemist] *CHEMISTRY* a monomolecular layer of an organic material which can be used to build extremely small electronic devices. **Langmuir cell** *OCEANOGRAPHY* each of the cells within which water circulates in Langmuir circulation. **Langmuir circulation** *OCEANOGRAPHY* the large-scale organized motion, due to convection currents, which takes place near the surface of large bodies of water.

Lango /ˈlaŋəʊ/ *noun & adjective*. Also **-ngi** /-ŋi/. **E20.**
[**ORIGIN** Nilotic.]
▸ **A** *noun*. Pl. same.
1 A member of a village-dwelling people of the Nile region of Uganda. **E20.**
2 The Nilotic language of this people. **E20.**
▸ **B** ***attrib.*** or as *adjective*. Of or pertaining to the Lango or their language. **E20.**

Langobard /ˈlaŋgəbɑːd/ *noun & adjective*. *hist.* **L18.**
[**ORIGIN** Late Latin *Langobardus*: see **LOMBARD** *noun*[1]. Cf. earlier **LONGOBARD**.]
▸ **A** *noun*. = **LOMBARD** *noun*[1] 1. **L18.**
▸ **B** ***attrib.*** or as *adjective*. Of or pertaining to the (Germanic) Lombards. **M20.**
■ **Lango'bardian** *adjective* **E20.** **Lango'bardic** *adjective & noun* (*a*) *adjective* of or pertaining to the Langobards or their language; (*b*) *noun* the West Germanic language of the Langobards: **E18.**

langooty *noun* see **LANGOTI**.

langosta /laŋˈgɒstə/ *noun*. Chiefly *US*. **L19.**
[**ORIGIN** Spanish from popular Latin alt. of Latin *locusta* **LOCUST** *noun*.]
1 = **LOCUST** *noun* 1. Now *rare* or *obsolete*. **L19.**
2 = **LANGOUSTE**. **E20.**

langostino /lango'stino, laŋgəˈstiːnəʊ/ *noun*. Pl. ***-os*** /-ɔs, -əʊz/. **E20.**
[**ORIGIN** Spanish, formed as **LANGOSTA** + *-ino* **-INE**[1].]
= **LANGOUSTINE**.

langoti /lʌŋˈgəʊti/ *noun*. Also (now *rare*) ***-gooty*** /-ˈguːti/. **E19.**
[**ORIGIN** Hindi *lāgoṭī*.]
In the Indian subcontinent: a kind of loincloth.

langouste /ˈlɒŋguːst, *foreign* lɑ̃gust (*pl. same*)/ *noun.* **M19.**
[**ORIGIN** French from Old Provençal *lagosta* from popular Latin alt. of Latin *locusta* **LOCUST** *noun*.]
A lobster; *esp.* the spiny lobster, *Palinurus vulgaris.*

langoustine /ˈlɒŋgustiːn, *foreign* lɑ̃gustin (*pl. same*)/ *noun.* **M20.**
[**ORIGIN** French, formed as **LANGOUSTE**: see **-INE**[1].]
The Norway lobster, esp. as food.

langrage /ˈlaŋgrɪdʒ/ *noun.* **M18.**
[**ORIGIN** Origin of 1st elem. unkn.: see **-AGE**.]
Case-shot loaded with pieces of iron of irregular shape, formerly used to damage the rigging and sails of enemy ships.
■ Earlier †**langrel** *noun* **L16–M19.**

langsat /ˈlaŋsat/ *noun.* **L18.**
[**ORIGIN** Malay.]
(The edible fruit of) a SE Asian tree, *Lansium domesticum* (family Meliaceae).

langsuir /ˈlaŋsjʊə/ *noun.* Also **-suyar.** **L19.**
[**ORIGIN** Malay.]
In Malaysian folklore: a female vampire with a whinnying cry, that preys on newborn children.

lang syne /laŋ ˈsʌɪn/ *adverbial & noun phr. Scot.* **E16.**
[**ORIGIN** from *lang* Scot. form of **LONG** *adverb* + **SYNE** *adverb*.]
(The days of) long ago. Now *rare* exc. in **AULD** *lang syne.*

language /ˈlaŋgwɪdʒ/ *noun*[1]. **ME.**
[**ORIGIN** Old French & mod. French *langage* (Anglo-Norman also *language*, after *langue* tongue, speech) from Proto-Gallo-Romance, from Latin *lingua* tongue, language: see **-AGE**.]
1 a A system of human communication using words, written and spoken, and particular ways of combining them; any such system employed by a community, a nation, etc. **ME.** ▸**b** *transf.* A mode of communication by inarticulate sounds used by lower animals, birds, etc. **ME.** ▸**c** *transf.* A non-verbal method of human communication, as gesture or facial expression, hand-signing, etc.; a means of artistic expression, as dance, music, or painting. **E17.** ▸**d** A way of interpreting or ordering experience shared by a group, a community, etc.; a common code or pattern of behaviour. **E20.** ▸**e** *LINGUISTICS.* = **LANGUE** 3. **E20.** ▸**f** *COMPUTING.* Any of various systems of precisely defined symbols and rules for writing programs or representing instructions and data. **M20.**

a J. MARQUAND I answered him in Chinese, a language which I knew..Joyce did not understand. **c** R. G. COLLINGWOOD A dispute between Italian peasants is conducted..in a highly elaborated language of manual gesture. *Observer* He sends Edith flowers, rather too many..and speaking not quite the right language. **f** *Which Micro?* Most home computers speak the same language..called BASIC.

c *body language, eye language, sign language*, etc.
2 The form of words used in communicating something; manner or style of expression. **ME.** ▸**b** The professional or specialized vocabulary of a discipline, a group of people, etc. **E16.** ▸**c** The style of a literary composition or of a non-verbal work of art. Also, the wording of a document, statute, etc. **E18.** ▸**d** More fully *bad language.* Coarse or vulgar expressions. **M19.**

M. FOOT More than ever before or after, Churchill's language fitted the time. **b** R. K. NARAYAN I'm picking up the railway language quite successfully. **c** W. COWPER A tale should be judicious, clear, succinct, The language plain. *Listener* The structural and harmonic tension of Mahler's later musical language. **d** T. KENEALLY 'I want t'do a fuckin' good job.' 'No language in here!'

3 a Power or faculty of speech; ability to speak a foreign language. Now *rare.* **LME.** ▸**b** Human communication using a system of words and particular ways of combining them. **L16.**

a W. COWPER Oh that those lips had language! **b** J. UGLOW At the most crucial moments, language may fail. We have to move into silence.

†**4 a** The act of speaking or talking; the use of speech. **LME–E16.** ▸**b** That which is said, talk, report, *esp.* censorious or opprobrious words. **LME–M17.**
5 a A community of people having the same form of speech, a nation. *arch.* **LME.** ▸**b** A national division or branch of a religious and military Order. Long *rare* exc. *hist.* **E18.**
– **PHRASES**: *artificial language*: see **ARTIFICIAL** *adjective* 1. *bad language*: see sense 2d above. *command of language*: see **COMMAND** *noun.* *dead language*: see **DEAD** *adjective* 9. *first language*: see **FIRST** *adjective.* **language of flowers** a method of expressing sentiments through a set of symbolic meanings attached to different flowers. *MATERNAL language. MIXED language. MODERN languages. natural language*: see **NATURAL** *adjective. plain language*: see **PLAIN** *adjective*[1] *& adverb. private language*: see **PRIVATE** *adjective. second language*: see **SECOND** *adjective.* **speak someone's language**, **speak the same language** have a mutual understanding, get on well, have a similar outlook. **strong language**: indicating violent emotion. **talk someone's language**, **talk the same language** = *speak someone's language* above.
– **COMB.**: **language area** (*a*) an area of the cerebral cortex regarded as especially concerned with the use of language; (*b*) a region where a particular language is spoken; **language arts** those subjects (as reading, writing, spelling, etc.) taught in schools to develop oral and written communication skills; **language-game** *PHILOSOPHY* a complete but limited system of communication, which may form part of the existing use of language; **language lab**, **language laboratory** a classroom equipped with tape recorders etc., where foreign languages are learned by means of repeated oral practice; **language loyalty**, **language maintenance** *LINGUISTICS* the preservation of a native language or dialect by an individual or group in a community where another language is dominant; **language-particular** *adjective* = *language-specific* below; **language planning** the preparation of a normative orthography, grammar, and dictionary for a non-homogeneous speech community; official promotion or encouragement of a particular language, vocabulary, etc.; **language shift** *LINGUISTICS* a move from one (usu. native) language or dialect to another (usu. culturally dominant) by an individual or speech community; **language-specific** *adjective* (*LINGUISTICS*) distinctive to a particular language; **language universal** *LINGUISTICS* a linguistic feature shared by all languages.
■ **languageless** *adjective* **E17.**

language *noun*[2] var. of **LANGUID** *noun.*

language /ˈlaŋgwɪdʒ/ *verb trans.* **E17.**
[**ORIGIN** from **LANGUAGE** *noun*[1].]
†**1** Express in words. **E–M17.**
2 *transf.* Express by sign or gesture. **E19.**

languaged /ˈlaŋgwɪdʒd/ *adjective.* **ME.**
[**ORIGIN** from **LANGUAGE** *noun*[1], *verb*: see **-ED**[2], **-ED**[1].]
1 Skilled *in* a language or languages. Also *well languaged.* **ME.**
2 Having a language or languages. Freq. with specifying word: characterized by or expressed in a specified kind of language or languages. **L15.**
†**3** Expressed in language, worded. **M17–L17.**

langue /lɑ̃g/ *noun.* Pl. pronounced same. **ME.**
[**ORIGIN** French from Latin *lingua* tongue, language.]
†**1** A language. *rare.* **ME–M17.**
2 = **LANGUAGE** *noun*[1] 5b. Long *rare* exc. *hist.* **L18.**
3 *LINGUISTICS.* A language viewed as an abstract system used by a speech community, in contrast to the actual linguistic behaviour of individuals. Opp. **PAROLE** *noun* 4. **E20.**

langued /laŋgd/ *adjective.* **LME.**
[**ORIGIN** from French *langué* (from *langue* tongue + *-é* pa. ppl suffix) + **-ED**[1].]
HERALDRY. Of a charge: having a tongue of a specified tincture.

langue de boeuf /lɑːŋ də ˈbəːf/ *noun phr. obsolete* exc. *hist.* **LME.**
[**ORIGIN** French, lit. 'oxtongue'.]
†**1** A rough-leaved plant; *esp.* (**a**) bugloss; (**b**) oxtongue. **LME–M18.**
2 A type of medieval pike or halberd, with a head shaped like an oxtongue. **LME.**

langue de chat /lɑːŋ də ˈʃɑː, *foreign* lɑ̃g də ʃa/ *noun phr.* Pl. **langues de chat** (pronounced same). **L19.**
[**ORIGIN** French, lit. 'cat's tongue'.]
A long thin piece of chocolate; a long finger-shaped biscuit.

langue d'oc /lɑ̃g dɔːk/ *noun phr.* **E18.**
[**ORIGIN** Old French & mod. French, formed as **LANGUE** + *de* of + *oc* yes (from Latin *hoc*).]
The language of medieval France south of the Loire, generally characterized by the use of *oc* to mean 'yes', and the basis of modern Provençal. Cf. **LANGUE D'OÏL.**

Languedocian /laŋgəˈdəʊʃ(ə)n/ *adjective & noun.* **M18.**
[**ORIGIN** from *Languedoc* (see below) + **-IAN**.]
▸ **A** *adjective.* Of or pertaining to Languedoc, a former province in the south of France. **M18.**
▸ **B** *noun.* **1** A native or inhabitant of Languedoc. **M18.**
2 The language of Languedoc, a dialect of Provençal. **E19.**

langue d'oïl /lɑ̃g dɔi/ *noun phr.* Also ***langue d'oui*** /lɑ̃g dwi/. **E18.**
[**ORIGIN** Old French & mod. French, formed as **LANGUE** + *de* of + *oïl* (now *oui*) yes (from Latin *hoc ille*).]
The language of medieval France north of the Loire, generally characterized by the use of *oïl* to mean 'yes', and the basis of standard modern French. Cf. **LANGUE D'OC.**

langues de chat *noun phr.* pl. of **LANGUE DE CHAT.**

languet /ˈlaŋgwɪt/ *noun.* **LME.**
[**ORIGIN** Old French *languete* (mod. *languette*), dim. of *langue* tongue: see **-ETTE**.]
†**1** The tongue of a balance. Only in **LME.**
†**2** A tongue-shaped ornament. **LME–M16.**
†**3** A thong used to tie a shoe. **LME–L18.**
†**4** An instrument for spreading or rolling salve etc. **L16–E19.**
5 A tongue-shaped part of an implement; *spec.* (**a**) a narrow blade projecting at the edge of a spade; (**b**) a small piece of metal on a sword hilt which overhangs the scabbard. **E17.**
†**6** A narrow projecting piece of land; a tongue. Only in **17.**
7 *ZOOLOGY.* A small tonguelike process, rows of which occur along the dorsal edge of the branchial sac of a tunicate. **M19.**
8 A flat plate placed in an organ flue pipe on the top of the foot, opposite the mouth. Cf. **LANGUID** *noun* 2. **M19.**

languid /ˈlaŋgwɪd/ *noun.* Also **language** /ˈlaŋgwɪdʒ/. **L17.**
[**ORIGIN** Alt. of **LANGUET**.]
†**1** = **LANGUET** 3. Only in **L17.**
2 = **LANGUET** 8. **M19.**

languid /ˈlaŋgwɪd/ *adjective.* **L16.**
[**ORIGIN** French *languide* or Latin *languidus*, from *languere*: see **LANGUISH** *verb*, **-ID**[1].]
1 Of a person, an animal, etc.: faint, weak, fatigued; idle, inert. **L16.**

R. THOMAS Suddenly he felt weak, languid and almost comfortable in his exhaustion.

2 Of energy, motion, etc.: weak, slow-moving. **M17.**

LD MACAULAY Two rivers met, the one gentle, languid.

3 a Of style, language, an idea: wanting force or vividness, uninteresting. **L17.** ▸**b** Of a person, actions, etc.: spiritless, apathetic, sedentary. **E18.**

b R. P. JHABVALA Her manner..was mostly languid and indifferent.

4 Of trade or some other activity: sluggish, inactive. **M19.**
■ **languidly** *adverb* **M17.** **languidness** *noun* **M17.**

languish /ˈlaŋgwɪʃ/ *verb & noun.* **ME.**
[**ORIGIN** Old French & mod. French *languiss-* lengthened stem of *languir* from Proto-Romance var. of Latin *languere* languish, rel. to *laxus* **LAX** *adjective*: see **-ISH**[2].]
▸ **A** *verb.* **1** *verb intrans.* Of a living thing: weaken; be or become faint, feeble, or ill; suffer. **ME.** ▸**b** Exist under conditions which debilitate or depress. Usu. foll. by *in*, *under.* **L15.**

E. JONES The patient..is languishing in a semi-conscious state. **b** *Independent* The grandmother languishes in an old people's home.

2 *verb intrans.* Droop in spirits; pine with love, grief, etc. Also foll. by *for*, *to do.* **ME.** ▸**b** Assume a sentimentally tender or languid look or expression. **E18.**

DE QUINCEY The poor nuns..were languishing for some amusement. V. SACKVILLE-WEST She trembled for joy in his presence, languished in his absence.

3 *verb intrans.* Of an appetite, activity, interest, etc.: slacken, lose vigour or intensity. Formerly also, (of light, colour, sound, etc.) become dim or indistinct. **LME.**

P. L. FERMOR Talk would languish and a pensive gloom descend.

4 *verb trans.* Pass (a period of time) in languishing. Usu. foll. by *out.* Now *rare.* **E17.**
▸ **B** *noun.* **1** The action or state of languishing. **LME.**
2 A tender look or gesture. *rare.* **E18.**
■ **languisher** *noun* **L16.**

languishing /ˈlaŋgwɪʃɪŋ/ *noun.* Now *rare.* **LME.**
[**ORIGIN** from **LANGUISH** + **-ING**[1].]
The action of **LANGUISH** *verb*; languor. Also, an attack of languor or faintness, esp. proceeding from disease.

languishing /ˈlaŋgwɪʃɪŋ/ *adjective.* Now *rare.* **ME.**
[**ORIGIN** formed as **LANGUISHING** *noun* + **-ING**[2].]
1 Declining; suffering; becoming faint, feeble, or ill. **ME.** ▸**b** Of an illness or death: lingering. **E17.**
2 a Pining with love or grief. **LME.** ▸**b** Of behaviour, a look: sentimental. **L17.**
3 Weary; bored; slow. Also, uninteresting. **M17.**
■ **languishingly** *adverb* **L16.**

languishment /ˈlaŋgwɪʃm(ə)nt/ *noun.* Now *rare.* **M16.**
[**ORIGIN** formed as **LANGUISHING** *noun* + **-MENT**.]
1 Sorrow, esp. when caused by love or longing; grief, depression; mental pain or distress; a feeling of such sorrow etc. **M16.** ▸**b** Longing, tenderness; an expression of this. **L17.**

B. W. PROCTER That inward languishment of mind, which dreams Of some remote and high accomplishment. M. O. W. OLIPHANT Love-agonies and languishments beyond the reach of words.

2 Sickness, weakness, or suffering; a bout or fit of this. **L16.** ▸**b** Weariness, lassitude; decline, decay; inertness. **E17.**

languor /ˈlaŋgə/ *noun & verb.* **ME.**
[**ORIGIN** Old French (mod. *langueur*) from Latin, from *languere*: see **LANGUISH**.]
▸ **A** *noun.* †**1** Disease, illness. **ME–E17.**
†**2** Distressed condition; suffering, sorrow, longing. **ME–L16.**
3 a Faintness, fatigue; inertia, lassitude. **LME.** ▸**b** Tenderness of mood, feeling, etc.; lassitude of spirit caused by sorrow, lovesickness, etc. **M18.**

a A. WILSON Vin had replaced his usual languor by an attempt to sit in an erect, military fashion. **b** S. ROGERS A softer..light pervades the whole And steals a pensive languor o'er the soul.

4 a A heaviness or stillness of the air, sky, etc. **M18.** ▸**b** Lack of activity or interest, esp. in art, scholarship, trade, etc. **M18.**

a R. L. STEVENSON The boom of distant surges disturbed the languor of the afternoon.

▸ **B** *verb intrans.* Languish. **ME.**
■ **languorous** *adjective* **L15.** **languorously** *adverb* **L19.**

L

langur /ˈlaŋɡə, lanˈɡʊə/ *noun*. **E19**.
[**ORIGIN** Hindi *laṅgūr*, from Sanskrit *lāṅgūla* having a tail.]
Any of several long-tailed herbivorous cercopithecoid monkeys of India and eastern Asia, of the *Presbytis* and related genera.
douc langur, ***entellus langur***, ***Hanuman langur***, etc.

laniariform /lanɪˈɛːrɪfɔːm/ *adjective*. **M19**.
[**ORIGIN** from LANIARY + -I- + -FORM.]
Shaped like a laniary tooth.

laniary /ˈlanɪəri/ *adjective & noun*. **E19**.
[**ORIGIN** Latin *laniarius* pertaining to a butcher, from *lanius* butcher, from *laniare* tear, rend: see -ARY[1].]
▸ **A** *adjective*. Of a tooth: adapted for tearing, canine. **E19**.
▸ **B** *noun*. A canine tooth. **M19**.

laniate /ˈlanɪeɪt/ *verb trans. rare*. **E18**.
[**ORIGIN** Latin *laniat-* pa. ppl stem of *laniare*: see LANIARY, -ATE[3].]
Tear to pieces.

laniferous /ləˈnɪf(ə)rəs/ *adjective*. **M17**.
[**ORIGIN** from Latin *lanifer*, from *lana* wool: see -FEROUS.]
Wool-bearing; woolly.

lanigerous /ləˈnɪdʒ(ə)rəs/ *adjective*. **E17**.
[**ORIGIN** from Latin *laniger*, from *lana* wool: see -GEROUS.]
Wool-bearing; woolly.

La Niña /lɑː ˈniːnjə, la ˈniːnjə/ *noun phr*. **L20**.
[**ORIGIN** Spanish, lit. 'the girl child', after EL NIÑO.]
A cooling of the water in the equatorial Pacific, which occurs at irregular intervals, and is associated with widespread changes in weather patterns complementary to those of El Niño, but less extensive and damaging in their effects.

lanista /ləˈnɪstə/ *noun*. Pl. **-stae** /-stiː/. **M19**.
[**ORIGIN** Latin.]
ROMAN HISTORY. A trainer of gladiators.

lank /laŋk/ *adjective, noun, & verb*.
[**ORIGIN** Old English *hlanc* from Germanic base repr. also by Middle & mod. High German *lenken* bend, turn, Old English *(h)lanca* hip, loin, Old High German *lancha*. Cf. FLINCH *verb*[1], LINK *noun*[2].]
▸ **A** *adjective*. **1** Not filled out or plump; shrunken, spare; tall and lean. **OE**.
T. C. WOLFE He was a tall lank boy, and his half-fare age might be called to question.
2 Of grass: long and flaccid. **M17**.
3 Chiefly of hair: without curl or wave, straight, flat; dull, lifeless. **L17**.
K. VONNEGUT The banners hung lank in the windless day. D. LODGE The girls' hair was lank and greasy from neglect.
▸ **B** *noun*. †**1** Leanness, scarcity, thinness. **M17–E18**.
2 A lanky or lean person. **L19**.
▸ **C** *verb trans. & intrans*. Make or become lank. **E16**.
■ **lankly** *adverb* **E17**. **lankness** *noun* **E17**.

lanky /ˈlaŋki/ *adjective & noun*. **L17**.
[**ORIGIN** from LANK *adjective* + -Y[1].]
▸ **A** *adjective*. Awkwardly or ungracefully lean and long. Formerly also, (of hair) somewhat lank. **L17**.
▸ **B** *noun*. (A nickname for or form of address to) a lanky person. **M19**.
■ **lankily** *adverb* **E20**. **lankiness** *noun* **L19**.

lanner /ˈlanə/ *noun*. **LME**.
[**ORIGIN** Old French & mod. French *lanier*, perh. use as noun of *lanier* cowardly, from derog. use of *lanier* weaver from Latin *lanarius* wool-merchant, from *lana* wool: see -ER[2].]
A falcon, *Falco biarmicus*, found in Africa and countries bordering on the Mediterranean; in *FALCONRY*, the female of this. Also ***lanner falcon***.

lanneret /ˈlanərɪt/ *noun*. **LME**.
[**ORIGIN** Old French & mod. French *laneret* dim. of LANNER: see -ET[1].]
FALCONRY. The male of the lanner.

lanolin /ˈlan(ə)lɪn/ *noun*. **L19**.
[**ORIGIN** from Latin *lana* wool + *ol(eum* oil + -IN[1].]
The fatty matter which permeates sheep's wool, extracted as a yellowish viscous mixture of esters and used as a basis for ointments. Also called ***wool fat***, ***wool oil***, ***wool wax***.

lanose /ˈleɪnəʊs/ *adjective*. **M19**.
[**ORIGIN** Latin *lanosus*, from *lana* wool: see -OSE[1].]
Chiefly *BOTANY & ZOOLOGY*. Of the nature of or resembling wool; woolly.
■ **la'nosity** *noun* **L19**.

lanosterol /ləˈnɒstərɒl/ *noun*. **E20**.
[**ORIGIN** from Latin *lana* wool + -O- + -STEROL.]
BIOCHEMISTRY. An unsaturated sterol, $C_{30}H_{50}O$, which is an intermediate in the bodily synthesis of cholesterol and in the form of esters is a major component of lanolin.

lansfordite /ˈlansfədʌɪt/ *noun*. **L19**.
[**ORIGIN** from *Lansford*, a town in Pennsylvania, USA + -ITE[1].]
MINERALOGY. A hydrate of magnesium carbonate which crystallizes in the monoclinic system and usu. occurs in colourless stalactitic forms.

lansquenet /ˈlɑːnskənɛt, ˈlans-/ *noun*. Also (in sense 1 now the usual form) **landsknecht** /ˈlan(d)sknɛkt/. **E17**.
[**ORIGIN** (French from) German *Landsknecht*, from genit. of *Land* LAND *noun*[2] + *Knecht* soldier. Cf. LANCE-KNIGHT.]
1 *hist*. A member of a class of mercenary soldiers in the German and other Continental armies in the 16th and 17th cents. **E17**.
2 A gambling card game of German origin. **L17**.

lant /lant/ *noun*. Now *rare*.
[**ORIGIN** Old English *hland*, *hlond*.]
Urine, *esp*. stale urine used for various industrial purposes.

lantana /lanˈtɑːnə/ *noun*. **L18**.
[**ORIGIN** mod. Latin (see below), from the specific name of the wayfaring tree, *Viburnum lantana*, to which it bears a superficial resemblance.]
Any of various shrubs and perennial herbs of the genus *Lantana*, of the verbena family, chiefly native to subtropical America, bearing axillary heads of red, yellow, white, or varicoloured flowers; esp. *L. camara*, grown in gardens and a weed in some tropical countries.

lanterloo /ˈlantəluː/ *noun*. **M17**.
[**ORIGIN** French *lantur(e)lu*, orig. the meaningless refrain of a popular 16th cent. song.]
1 = LOO *noun*[1]. *obsolete* exc. *dial. & hist*. **M17**.
2 Used as a meaningless refrain. *rare*. **M20**.

lantern /ˈlantən/ *noun & verb*. Also (*arch*.) **lanthorn** /ˈlantɔːn/. **ME**.
[**ORIGIN** Old French & mod. French *lanterne* from Latin *lanterna* from Greek *lamptēr* torch, lamp (from *lampein* shine: cf. LAMP *noun*), after *lucerna* lamp.]
▸ **A** *noun*. **1** (A lamp consisting of) a transparent case, usu. of glass, horn, paper, etc., containing and protecting a light. **ME**.
J. HILTON Light was from paper lanterns, motionless in the still air. R. K. NARAYAN There was a dark patch between the light from the shop and the dim lantern.
2 *fig*. A thing which or (formerly) person who metaphorically gives light. **ME**.
G. BANCROFT The lantern of science has guided us on the track of time.
3 *ARCHITECTURE*. A square, curved, or polygonal structure on the top of a dome or a room, with the sides glazed or open, so as to admit light; a similar structure used for ventilation or some other purpose. **LME**.
4 The chamber at the top of a lighthouse, in which the light is placed. Formerly also, a lighthouse. **L15**.
5 *MECHANICS*. A form of lantern-shaped cogwheel, a trundle. **M17**.
6 The megrim, *Lepidorhombus whiffiagonis*. Cf. ***lanternfish*** below. *local*. **L17**.
7 **a** The hollow projection on the head of a lantern fly. **M18**. ▸**b** More fully ***Aristotle's lantern***. The framework supporting the masticatory apparatus of certain echinoids. **M19**.
– **PHRASES**: ***Chinese lantern***: see CHINESE *adjective*. ***dark lantern***: see DARK *adjective*. ***magic lantern***: see MAGIC *adjective*. **parish lantern** the moon.
– **COMB.**: **lantern bug** = ***lantern fly*** below; **lantern clock** a 17th-cent. wall clock worked by weights and surmounted by a bell in a frame; **lanternfish** (*a*) *local* = sense 6 above; (*b*) = MYCTOPHID *noun*; **lantern fly** any of numerous chiefly tropical hemipteran insects of the family Fulgoridae, in many of which the head bears a hollow projecting structure once thought to be luminous; **lantern-jawed** *adjective* having lantern jaws; **lantern jaws** long thin jaws, giving a hollow appearance to the cheeks; **lantern-light** (*a*) the light from a lantern; (*b*) *ARCHITECTURE* a glazed frame in the side of a lantern; (*c*) a skylight; **lantern-man** (*a*) a person who carries a lantern; †(*b*) *spec*. a nightman; **lantern shell** (the translucent shell of) a bivalve mollusc of the genus *Thracia*; **lantern slide** a slide for projection by a magic lantern etc.; **lantern wheel** = sense 5 above.
▸ **B** *verb trans*. **1** **a** Enclose as in a lantern. **L18**. ▸**b** Provide or light with a lantern or lanterns. **L18**.
2 Put to death by hanging on a lamp post. *rare*. **E19**.
■ **lanternist** *noun* a person who uses a magic lantern **L19**.

lanthanide /ˈlanθənʌɪd/ *noun*. **E20**.
[**ORIGIN** from LANTHANUM + -IDE.]
Any of the series of chemical elements having an atomic number between 57 (lanthanum) and 71 (lutetium) inclusive, which form part of the group of transition metals, have similar chemical properties, and occur together in monazite, gadolinite, and certain other minerals. Cf. ***rare earth*** s.v. RARE *adjective*[1].

lanthanum /ˈlanθənəm/ *noun*. **M19**.
[**ORIGIN** from Greek *lanthanein* lie hidden + -IUM.]
A metallic chemical element, atomic no. 57, which is the first element of the lanthanide series (symbol La).
■ **lanthana** *noun* lanthanum oxide, La_2O_3, a white solid **L19**. **lanthanite** *noun* (*MINERALOGY*) an orthorhombic hydrated carbonate of lanthanum and cerium, usu. occurring as colourless or pale pinkish or yellowish tabular crystals **M19**. **lanthanoid**, **lanthanon** *nouns* = LANTHANIDE **M20**.

lanthorn *noun & verb* see LANTERN *noun & verb*.

†**lantskip** *noun* var. of LANDSCAPE *noun*.

lanuginous /ləˈnjuːdʒɪnəs/ *adjective*. **L16**.
[**ORIGIN** from Latin *lanuginosus*, from *lanugo* down, from *lana* wool: see -OUS.]
Chiefly *BOTANY & ZOOLOGY*. Covered with down or fine soft hair; of the nature of down; downy.
■ Also **lanuginose** *adjective* **L17**.

lanugo /ləˈnjuːɡəʊ/ *noun*. **LME**.
[**ORIGIN** Latin: see LANUGINOUS.]
†**1** The fibrous pith of a reed stem. *rare*. Only in **LME**.
2 Fine soft hair or down, *spec*. that covering the human fetus; a covering resembling this. **L17**.

lanx /laŋks/ *noun*. Pl. **lances** /ˈlansiːz/. **LME**.
[**ORIGIN** Latin.]
ANTIQUITIES. A large dish or bowl.

lanyard /ˈlanjəd/ *noun*. Also (earlier) †**lanyer**. **LME**.
[**ORIGIN** Old French & mod. French *lanière*, earlier *lasniere*, from *lasne*, perh. blend of *laz* LACE *noun* and *nasle* from Germanic (whence also German *Nestel* string, lace): final syll. assoc. with YARD *noun*[2].]
1 *NAUTICAL*. A short length of rope or line attached to something to secure it; *spec*. one used to secure the shrouds and stays of a sailing ship. **LME**.
†**2** A lace, a strap, a thong, a lash. **L15–E19**.
3 A cord attached to a breech mechanism for firing a gun. Also, a cord used to start an engine etc. **E19**.
W. BOYD He jerked the lanyard on the motor and with a clatter the engine started up again.
4 A cord passed around the neck, wrist, shoulder, etc., on which a knife, whistle, etc., may be secured. **M19**.
Washington Post Young staff members with whistles dangling from the lanyards around their necks.

Lao /laʊ/ *noun & adjective*. **M18**.
[**ORIGIN** Lao. Cf. LAOTIAN.]
▸ **A** *noun*. Pl. same, **-s**.
1 A member of a Tai people of Laos and NE Thailand. **M18**.
2 The Shan language of this people. **M20**.
▸ **B** *attrib*. or as *adjective*. Of or pertaining to the Lao or their language. **E19**.

Laocoön /leɪˈɒkəʊɒn/ *noun*. **E17**.
[**ORIGIN** Greek *Laokoōn*, a legendary Trojan priest (Virgil *Aeneid* II).]
A statue of the death struggle of Laocoön and his two sons, who were crushed to death by two sea serpents. Also (*transf*.), a person resembling such a statue in action or appearance; a (death-)struggle.
DICKENS Scrooge . . making a perfect Laocoön of himself with his stockings. ***attrib***.: G. GREENE The desperate contortions of a director caught in the Laocoön coils of an impossible script.

Laodicean /ˌleɪə(ʊ)dɪˈsiːən/ *noun & adjective*. **E17**.
[**ORIGIN** from Latin *Laodicea* (from Greek *Laodikeia*) (see below) + -AN. See -EAN.]
▸ **A** *noun*. A native or inhabitant of the city of Laodicea in Asia Minor. Also (after *Revelation* 3:16), a person who is lukewarm or indifferent, esp. in religion or politics. **E17**.
▸ **B** *adjective*. Of or pertaining to Laodicea. Also, lukewarm or indifferent, esp. in religion or politics. **M17**.
■ **Laodiceanism** *noun* lukewarmness, indifference, esp. in religion or politics **L18**.

laogai /laʊˈɡʌɪ/ *noun*. **L20**.
[**ORIGIN** Chinese, lit. 'reform through labour'.]
A system of labour camps in China, many of whose inmates are political dissidents.

Laotian /ˈlaʊʃ(ə)n, lɑːˈəʊʃ(ə)n/ *adjective & noun*. **M19**.
[**ORIGIN** from *Laos* (see below), prob. after *Mars*, *Martian*: see -IAN. Cf. LAO.]
▸ **A** *adjective*. Of or pertaining to Laos, a country in SE Asia. **M19**.
▸ **B** *noun*. **1** A native or inhabitant of Laos, *spec*. a Lao. **M19**.
2 = LAO *noun* 2. **M19**.

lap /lap/ *noun*[1].
[**ORIGIN** Old English *læppa*, corresp. to Old Frisian *lappa*, Old Saxon *lappo*, Old High German *lappa*, with *pp* for *pf* from Low German (German *Lappen*): cf. Old Norse *leppr* clout, rag, lock of hair.]
1 A part of a garment etc. which hangs down or projects and can be folded over; a flap, a lappet. **OE**.
JAS. HOGG Wiped his eyes . . with the lap of his plaid. B. HINES One lap of MacDowall's shirt curved out from beneath his sweater . . like half an apron.
2 **a** A lobe of the ear, liver, lungs, etc. *obsolete* exc. in ***ear-lap*** s.v. EAR *noun*[1]. **OE**. ▸†**b** A fold of flesh or skin. **LME–E17**.
3 †**a** The fold of a robe (e.g. a toga) over the breast, which served as a pocket or pouch. Also, the bosom. **ME–M17**. ▸**b** The front portion of a skirt when held up to contain or catch something. **ME**. ▸**c** A form of loincloth worn by Indians in Guyana. **M18**.
4 **a** The front portion of the body from the waist to the knees of a person seated, considered with its covering garments as the place *in* or *on* which a child is nursed or an object held. **ME**. ▸**b** *transf*. A hollow among hills. **M17**.
a R. P. JHABVALA He was sitting upright in bed and on his lap lay a large wooden board. A. BROOKNER She lifted the cat off her lap and brushed down her skirt.
– **PHRASES**: **drop in a person's lap**, **drop into a person's lap** shift or impose (a task, responsibility, etc.) to or on (to) someone. **drop into the lap of** become the responsibility of. **fall into**

one's lap come into one's possession, come within one's grasp. **in the lap of luxury** in opulent or luxurious circumstances, surroundings, etc. ***in the lap of the gods***: see GOD *noun*. **throw in a person's lap**, **throw into a person's lap** = *drop in a person's lap* above.

– COMB.: **lap belt** a safety belt across the lap; **lap-board** a board to lay on the lap, as a substitute for a table; **lap dance** an erotic dance or striptease performed close to, or sitting on the lap of, a paying customer; **lap dancer** a performer of lap dances; **lap desk** a portable writing case or surface, *esp.* one for use on the lap; **lapdog** a pet dog of a kind small enough to sit on the lap; **lap-held** *adjective & noun* = **laptop** below; **lap-iron** a piece of iron used as a lapstone; **lap portable** a laptop computer; **lap robe** a rug or cloth to cover the lap of a seated person, esp. in a vehicle; **lap steel (guitar)** a pedal steel guitar; **lapstone** a shoemaker's stone held in the lap to beat leather on; **lap strap** a safety strap across the lap; **lap-table** = *lap-board* above; **laptop** *adjective & noun* [after DESKTOP] (designating) a computer small and light enough to be used on one's lap.

■ **lapful** *noun* as much or as many as will fill a person's lap E17.

lap /lap/ *noun*[2]. LME.

[ORIGIN from LAP *verb*[1].]

1 The action or an act of lapping; an amount lapped up; a lick, a smack, a taste. LME.

2 Something that is lapped up; *spec.* (**a**) liquid food for dogs; (**b**) *slang & dial.* a weak drink or thin liquid food (cf. ***cat-lap*** s.v. CAT *noun*[1]); (**c**) *slang* drink, liquor in general. M16.

3 A lapping sound, as that of wavelets on a beach. L19.

lap /lap/ *noun*[3]. L17.

[ORIGIN from LAP *verb*[2]. Cf. LAP *noun*[4].]

1 A bundle, esp. of hay or straw. *obsolete* exc. *dial.* L17.

2 a The amount by which one thing overlaps or covers another; the overlapping part. E19. ▸**b** In a steam engine, the distance a slide valve moves beyond what is needed to stop the passage of steam. M19. ▸**c** METALLURGY. A defect consisting of a superficial seam formed when a projecting part is accidentally folded over and pressed against the surface of the metal in rolling etc. E20.

> **a** Z. M. PIKE Those logs were joined together by a lap of about two feet at each end.

3 a A layer or sheet, usu. wound on a roller, into which cotton, wool, or flax is formed during its manufacture. E19. ▸**b** In warp knitting, a loop of yarn on a needle. L19.

4 The act of encircling, or the length of rope, silk, thread, etc., required to encircle, a drum or reel. M19.

5 One circuit of a racetrack etc. M19.

> *Chicago Tribune* Barney started to burn up the track and opened a big gap, leading the first lap. D. DELILLO I . . swim laps in the college pool.

– PHRASES: **half lap** a means of joining rails, shafts, etc., by halving the thickness of the ends to be joined and fitting them together; a joint so formed. **lap of honour** a ceremonial circuit of a racetrack, football pitch, etc., by a winner or winners, or by any contestant(s) to receive applause. **last lap** the final section of a journey etc.

– COMB.: **lap dissolve** CINEMATOGRAPHY & TELEVISION a fade-out of a scene that overlaps with a fade-in of a new scene, so that one appears to dissolve into the other; **lap joint** = *half lap* above; **lap-join** *verb trans.* join by means of a lap joint; **lapstrake** *noun & adjective* (**a**) *noun* a clinker-built boat; (**b**) *adjective* clinker-built; **lap weld**: in which the parts to be joined overlap one another; **lap-weld** *verb trans.* join with a lap weld; **lap winding** a kind of armature winding in which the two ends of each coil are connected to adjacent commutator segments, so that each coil overlaps the next.

lap /lap/ *noun*[4]. E19.

[ORIGIN Perh. same word as LAP *noun*[3].]

1 A rotating disc for cutting or polishing gems or metal. E19.

2 A polishing tool of a special shape, coated or impregnated with an abrasive substance. L19.

lap /lap/ *verb*[1]. Infl. **-pp-**.

[ORIGIN Old English *lapian*, corresp. to Middle Low German, Middle Dutch *lapen*, Old High German *laffan*, from Germanic, rel. to Latin *lambere*, Greek *laptein* lick, lap; partly from Old French & mod. French *laper*.]

1 *verb intrans.* Take up liquid with the tongue. OE.

2 *verb trans.* Of an animal or (*rare*) a person: take up or *up* (liquid etc.) with the tongue; drink up, *up* or *down* greedily. ME. ▸**b** *fig.* Receive or consume avidly. Foll. by *up*. L19.

> R. JARRELL A puppy laps water from a can. **b** *Listener* The Indian Embassy in Bonn will lap up information about Eastern Germany.

3 *verb intrans. & trans.* Of water: move or wash against (the shore etc.) with a rippling or splashing sound like that made in lapping liquid. Also foll. by *in*, *up*. E19.

> B. UNSWORTH He watched the gleaming water lap against its containing wall.

lap /lap/ *verb*[2]. Infl. **-pp-**. ME.

[ORIGIN from LAP *noun*[1].]

1 a *verb trans.* Coil, fold, wrap (material, a garment, a limb, etc.). (Foll. by *about*, *in*, *round*.) ME. ▸**b** *verb intrans.* Wrap *about*, *round*. Now chiefly *dial.* M16.

> **a** SWIFT He would lap a Piece of it about a Sore Toe. A. S. BYATT The anaconda was lapped about herself in one corner of her box.

2 *verb trans.* Enfold in a wrap or wraps, swathe; bind up, tie round. (Foll. by *in*, *over*, *round*, *up*.) ME.

> C. READE A good dozen of spices lapped in flax paper. *transf.*: J. BUCHAN The moorlands lap it round as the sea laps a reef.

3 *verb trans. fig.* ▸†**a** Include; implicate; wrap *up* in a disguise. ME–M17. ▸**b** Of conditions or influences: enfold, surround, esp. with soothing or seductive effect. ME.

> **b** L. MORRIS I who was . . Only a careless boy lapt round with ease.

4 *verb trans.* Fold, fold *up*, *together*; roll *up*. Foll. by *into*. *obsolete* exc. *dial.* LME.

5 *verb trans.* Enfold caressingly; nurse, fondle; surround with soothing care, protection, etc. Now usu. in *pass.* LME.

> E. M. GOULBURN Moses has been lapped in royal luxury from his infancy.

6 *verb trans.* Cause to overlap; lay (something) *on*, *over* another thing so as partly to cover it. E17.

7 *verb intrans.* Project; *fig.* extend beyond a limit. Foll. by *over* (adverb). M17.

†**8** *verb intrans.* Lie on something, so as to cover partially or project over it. Foll. by *on to*, *over* (preposition), *upon*. L17–M19.

9 a *verb trans.* Lead (a competitor in a race) by one or more laps; overtake to become one or more laps ahead. M19. ▸**b** *verb trans. & intrans.* Of a competitor, a vehicle, etc., in a race: travel over (a distance) as a lap; traverse. E20.

> **a** *New Yorker* I could have gone faster . . but it didn't seem nice to lap too many people. *fig.*: *Times* We are constantly being lapped in the wages race. **b** *Daily Express* There are many machines entered which could lap all day at sixty-five miles an hour. P. EVANS Just lapping the track gently.

lap /lap/ *verb*[3] *trans.* Infl. **-pp-**. L19.

[ORIGIN from LAP *noun*[4].]

Polish with a lap.

lapageria /lapəˈdʒɪərɪə/ *noun*. M19.

[ORIGIN mod. Latin (see below), from Joséphine Tascher de *la Pagerie* (1763–1814), empress of France: see -IA[1].]

A climbing Chilean shrub, *Lapageria rosea* (family Smilacaceae), bearing large bell-shaped pendulous red or white flowers.

laparo- /ˈlapərəʊ/ *combining form*.

[ORIGIN from Greek *lapara* soft part of the body (between ribs and hip), flank, from *laparos* slack, loose: see -O-.]

MEDICINE. Of or pertaining to the abdomen, abdominal.

■ **laparoscope** *noun* an instrument used for examining the abdomen; *spec.* a tube for insertion into the peritoneal cavity, with a source of light at the inserted end and a means of forming an image of the illuminated region at the other end: M19. **laparoˈscopic** *adjective* pertaining to or obtained by laparoscopy M20. **lapaˈroscopist** *noun* a person who uses a laparoscope M20. **lapaˈroscopy** *noun* †(**a**) examination of the loins or abdomen; (**b**) examination of the inside of the peritoneal cavity by means of a laparoscope inserted through a small incision; an operation in which a laparoscope is used: M19. **lapaˈrotomize** *verb trans.* perform a laparotomy on E20. **lapaˈrotomy** *noun* (an instance of) a surgical operation in which a substantial opening is made into the peritoneal cavity, esp. for exploratory purposes M19.

lapel /ləˈpɛl/ *noun*. M17.

[ORIGIN from LAP *noun*[1] + -EL[2].]

That part of the front of a coat etc. which is folded over towards either shoulder.

■ **lapelled** *adjective* (**a**) provided with a (specified kind of) lapel; (**b**) folded over so as to form a lapel: M18.

†**laperkin** *noun* see LATTERKIN.

lapicide /ˈlapɪsʌɪd/ *noun*. M17.

[ORIGIN Latin *lapicida* for *lapidicida*, from *lapid-*, *lapis* stone: see -CIDE.]

A person who cuts stones, or inscriptions on stone.

■ Also †**lapicidary** *noun*: only in L16.

lapidary /ˈlapɪd(ə)ri/ *noun & adjective*. LME.

[ORIGIN Latin *lapidarius* adjective, in late Latin as noun = stonecutter, from *lapid-*, *lapis* stone: see -ARY[1]. For sense A.2 cf. medieval Latin *lapidarium* book of gems.]

▸ **A** *noun* **1 a** A cutter, polisher, or engraver of gems or precious stones. LME. ▸†**b** An expert in the nature and kinds of gems; a connoisseur of lapidary work. LME–L18.

2 A treatise on (precious) stones. *obsolete* exc. *hist.* LME.

– COMB.: **lapidary-mill**, **lapidary's-mill**, **lapidary's-wheel**, **lapidary-wheel** the grinding and polishing apparatus of a lapidary.

▸ **B** *adjective* **1 a** Engraved on stone. E18. ▸**b** Of style etc.: characteristic of or suitable for inscriptions; dignified, concise. E18.

> **b** *Academy* A stanza [which] has a lapidary dignity as of something carved in stone.

2 Concerned with stones. Now *rare*. M19.

> J. BARNES I . . wrote a lapidary volume issued in a handwritten edition of one.

■ **lapiˈdarian** *adjective* (**a**) skilled in the knowledge of stones; (**b**) inscribed in stone; characteristic of such an inscription: L17. **lapidarist** *noun* = LAPIDARY *noun* 1 E17.

lapidate /ˈlapɪdeɪt/ *verb trans. literary*. E17.

[ORIGIN Latin *lapidat-* pa. ppl stem of *lapidare*, from *lapid-*, *lapis* stone: see -ATE[3].]

Throw stones at; stone to death.

■ **lapiˈdation** *noun* stoning to death; pelting with stones: E17.

lapideous /ləˈpɪdɪəs/ *adjective*. Now *rare*. M17.

[ORIGIN from Latin *lapideus* (from *lapid-*, *lapis* stone) + -OUS.]

Of the nature of stone, stony.

lapidescent /lapɪˈdɛs(ə)nt/ *adjective*. Now *rare* or *obsolete*. M17.

[ORIGIN Latin *lapidescent-* pa. ppl stem of *lapidescere* become stony, formed as LAPIDEOUS: see -ESCENT.]

That is in the process of becoming stone; (of spring water etc.) tending to turn into stone, petrifying.

■ †**lapidescence** *noun* M17–L18.

lapidicolous /lapɪˈdɪk(ə)ləs/ *adjective*. L19.

[ORIGIN from Latin *lapid-*, *lapis* stone + -I- + -COLOUS.]

ECOLOGY. Esp. of a beetle: living under stones or similar objects.

■ **laˈpidicole** *noun* a lapidicolous animal M20.

lapidific /lapɪˈdɪfɪk/ *adjective*. Now *rare* or *obsolete*. M17.

[ORIGIN French *lapidifique* or medieval Latin *lapidificare*: see LAPIDIFY, -IC.]

Adapted to or concerned with the making of stones.

lapidification /ləˌpɪdɪfɪˈkeɪʃ(ə)n/ *noun*. LME.

[ORIGIN from medieval Latin *lapidificat-* pa. ppl stem of *lapidificare*: see LAPIDIFY, -FICATION.]

The process of hardening or of turning into stone.

lapidify /ləˈpɪdɪfʌɪ/ *verb*. M17.

[ORIGIN French *lapidifier* or medieval Latin *lapidificare*, from Latin *lapid-*, *lapis* stone: see -FY.]

†**1** *verb intrans.* Become stone. Only in M17.

2 *verb trans.* Make or turn into stone. L18.

lapidist /ˈlapɪdɪst/ *noun*. Long *rare*. M17.

[ORIGIN from Latin *lapid-*, *lapis* stone + -IST.]

= LAPIDARY *noun* 1.

lapiés /ˈlapjɛz, ˈlapɪeɪz/ *noun pl.* Also **lapies**. E20.

[ORIGIN French dial. *lapiaz*, *lapiés* (sing. *lapié*) ult. from Latin *lapis* stone.]

PHYSICAL GEOGRAPHY. = KARREN. Also (treated as *sing.*) = KARRENFELD.

lapillus /ləˈpɪləs/ *noun*. Pl. **-lli** /-lʌɪ/. M18.

[ORIGIN Latin, dim. of *lapis* stone; in pl. also from Italian *lapilli*, pl. of *lapillo*.]

Orig., a small stone or pebble. Now (GEOLOGY), a fragment of rock or lava ejected from a volcano, *spec.* one between 2 and 64 mm in size. Usu. in *pl.*

lapis /ˈlapɪs/ *noun*. LME.

[ORIGIN Latin.]

1 Stone; *spec.* the philosopher's stone. *rare* exc. in phrs. LME.

2 = LAPIS LAZULI. E19.

– PHRASES: ***lapis Armenus*** /ɑːˈmiːnəs/ [= Armenian] *hist.* = AZURITE 2. ***lapis calaminaris*** /kaləmɪˈnɑːrɪs/ [medieval Latin, from *calamina* CALAMINE] *hist.* = CALAMINE. ***lapis ollaris*** /ɒˈlɑːrɪs/ [= preserved in jars] *hist.* = POTSTONE.

lapis lazuli /ˈlapɪs ˈlazjʊlʌɪ, -li/ *noun phr.* LME.

[ORIGIN from Latin *lapis* stone + medieval Latin *lazuli* genit. of *lazulum*, varying with *lazur*, *lazurius*, from Persian *lāžward* lapis lazuli: cf. AZURE *noun & adjective*.]

A blue semi-precious stone composed chiefly of a sulphur-containing silicate of sodium and aluminium; *hist.* a pigment consisting of crushed grains of this, the original ultramarine; the colour ultramarine. Cf. LAPIS 2.

Lapita /ləˈpiːtə/ *adjective*. M20.

[ORIGIN A site in New Caledonia.]

ARCHAEOLOGY. Designating a type of decorated pottery found throughout Polynesia and dating from the first millennium BC.

Lapith /ˈlapɪθ/ *noun*. Pl. **-ths**, **-thae** /-θiː/. E17.

[ORIGIN Latin *Lapithae* (pl.) from Greek *Lapithai*.]

GREEK MYTHOLOGY. A member of a people of Thessaly known for their wars with the centaurs.

Laplace /lɑːˈplɑːs/ *noun*. E19.

[ORIGIN Pierre Simon, Marquis de *Laplace* (1749–1827), French astronomer and mathematician.]

MATH. Used *attrib.* and in *possess.* to designate concepts and mathematical expressions devised by Laplace or arising out of his work.

Laplace equation = ***Laplace's equation*** below. **Laplace operator** = LAPLACIAN *noun*. **Laplace's equation** the equation $\nabla^2 V = 0$, *esp.* its representation in Cartesian coordinates, $\partial^2 V/\partial x^2 + \partial^2 V/\partial y^2 + \partial^2 V/\partial z^2 = 0$, where V is a function of x, y, and z. **Laplace's operator** = LAPLACIAN *noun*. **Laplace transform** a function $\bar{f}(x)$ related to a given function $g(t)$ by the equation $\bar{f}(x) = \int_0^\infty \exp(-xt)\, g(t)\, dt$. **Laplace transformation** the transformation by which a Laplace transform is obtained from a given function.

Laplacian /lɑːˈplɑːsɪən/ *adjective & noun*. Also **-cean**, **l-**. M19.

[ORIGIN from LAPLACE + -IAN.]

▸ **A** *adjective*. Of or pertaining to Laplace; originating with Laplace. M19.

▸ **B** *noun*. The differential operator ∇^2 ('del squared') that occurs in Laplace's equation. M20.

Lapland /ˈlaplənd, -land/ *noun*. L16.

[ORIGIN Swedish *Lappland*, formed as LAPP + *land* LAND *noun*[1].]

Used ***attrib.*** to designate things found in or associated with Lapland, the region which forms the most north-

erly portion of the Scandinavian peninsula, divided between Finland, Norway, Sweden, and Russia.
Lapland bunting a bunting, *Calcarius lapponicus*, of northern circumpolar regions. **Lapland longspur** *N. Amer.* = *Lapland bunting*.
■ **Laplander** *noun* a native or inhabitant of Lapland, a Lapp **E17**. **Laplandish** *adjective & noun* (**a**) *adjective* of or pertaining to Lapland, the Lapps, or Lappish; (**b**) *noun* Lappish: **L17**.

lap-lap /ˈlaplap/ *noun*[2]. **M20.**
[**ORIGIN** Local name.]
A loincloth of a kind worn by Australian Aborigines and in New Guinea.

lap-lap /ˈlaplap/ *verb intrans. & noun*[1]. Infl. **-pp-**. **M19.**
[**ORIGIN** Imit. redupl. of **LAP** *verb*[1], *noun*[2].]
(Make) a repeated lapping sound.

Laporte rule /laˈpɔːt ruːl/ *noun phr.* **M20.**
[**ORIGIN** O. *Laporte* (1902–71), German-born US physicist.]
PHYSICS. The rule that electron transitions in atoms occur only between states whose *l* quantum numbers differ by ±1 or (alternatively) between states of opposite parity (a rule which holds for electric dipole transitions).

Lapp /lap/ *noun & adjective.* **L16.**
[**ORIGIN** Swedish, perh. orig. a term of contempt (cf. Middle High German *lappe* simpleton), in medieval Latin *Lappo(n-)*.]
▸ **A** *noun.* **1** A member of the indigenous population of the extreme north of Scandinavia. **L16.**
2 The language of the Lapps, Lappish. **L19.**
▸ **B** *adjective.* Of or pertaining to the Lapps or Lappish. **E19.**
– **NOTE:** Although *Lapp* is still widely used, the people themselves prefer to be called *Sami*.

lappa /ˈlapə/ *noun. W. Afr.* **M20.**
[**ORIGIN** Hausa, from Arabic *laffa* wrap up, cover.]
A woman's shawl, wrap, or skirt.

lapper /ˈlapə/ *noun*[1]. **E17.**
[**ORIGIN** from **LAP** *verb*[1] + **-ER**[1].]
A person who or animal which laps, or takes up liquid with the tongue.

lapper /ˈlapə/ *noun*[2]. **M18.**
[**ORIGIN** from **LAP** *verb*[2] + **-ER**[1].]
A person who laps or folds up linen.

lapper /ˈlapə/ *noun*[3]. **L19.**
[**ORIGIN** from **LAP** *verb*[3] + **-ER**[1]]
A person who uses a lap or lapidary's wheel.

lappet /ˈlapɪt/ *noun.* **LME.**
[**ORIGIN** from **LAP** *noun*[1] + **-ET**[1].]
1 A lobe of the ear, liver, lung, etc. **LME.** ▸**b** A fold or pendent piece of flesh, skin, membrane, etc., esp. on some animals. **E17.**
2 A loose or overlapping part of a garment; a flap, a fold; a lapel. **L16.**

SWIFT Lifting up the lappet of his coat.

3 An attached or hanging part of an item of headgear; *spec.* (now *rare*) a streamer attached to a woman's headdress. Also, in clerical dress, = **BAND** *noun*[2] 2b. **E17.**

E. A. PARKES A sealskin cap with ear lappets.

4 *gen.* A loose hanging part of anything. **L17.**

S. T. WARNER A lappet of hair dangles . . over her left eye.

5 In full ***lappet moth***. Any of several mostly brown velvety lasiocampid moths whose caterpillars have lappets on their sides; *spec.* a common Eurasian moth, *Gastropacha quercifolia*. **E19.**
6 *WEAVING.* **a** A figure woven on cloth by means of needles placed in a sliding frame; cloth bearing such figures. **M19.** ▸**b** A mechanism for producing such figures. **L19.**
7 *ART.* A repeated motif used as a decorative border on Chinese ceramics etc. **E20.**
– **COMB.:** ***lappet moth***: see sense 5 above; **lappet-weaving** a method of weaving in which figures are produced on the surface of cloth by means of needles placed in a sliding frame.
■ **lappeted** *adjective* (of a person) wearing lappets; (of a headdress) provided with lappets: **L18.**

lappie /ˈlapi/ *noun. S. Afr.* **L19.**
[**ORIGIN** Afrikaans, from *lap* rag + dim. suffix *-ie*.]
A rag, a cloth.

lapping /ˈlapɪŋ/ *noun*[1]. **LME.**
[**ORIGIN** from **LAP** *verb*[1] + **-ING**[1].]
The action of **LAP** *verb*[1].

lapping /ˈlapɪŋ/ *noun*[2]. **LME.**
[**ORIGIN** from **LAP** *verb*[2] + **-ING**[1].]
1 The action of wrapping. Also, a wrapping; trappings, wraps. *obsolete* exc. *dial.* **LME.** ▸†**b** Folding in the arms; embracing, caressing. **LME–E17.**
2 The action of overlapping or of causing an overlap; a part that overlaps. **E17.**
3 *COMMERCE.* A method of embezzlement by which (esp. repeated) credits are recorded in accounts as deferred. **M20.**

lapping /ˈlapɪŋ/ *noun*[3]. **L19.**
[**ORIGIN** from **LAP** *verb*[3] + **-ING**[1].]
The action or process of polishing or grinding on a lap.

Lappish /ˈlapɪʃ/ *adjective & noun.* **M19.**
[**ORIGIN** from **LAPP** + **-ISH**[1].]
▸ **A** *adjective.* Of or pertaining to the Lapps; *spec.* designating or pertaining to the Finno-Ugric language of the Lapps. **M19.**
▸ **B** *noun.* The Lappish language. **L19.**

Lapponian /laˈpəʊnɪən/ *noun & adjective. arch.* **E17.**
[**ORIGIN** from medieval Latin *Lappo(n-)* (see **LAPP**) + **-IAN**.]
= **LAPP**.

Lapponic /laˈpɒnɪk/ *adjective.* **E19.**
[**ORIGIN** formed as **LAPPONIAN** + **-IC**.]
= **LAPPISH** *adjective*.

Lapponoid /ˈlapənɔɪd/ *adjective.* **M20.**
[**ORIGIN** formed as **LAPPONIAN** + **-OID**.]
ANTHROPOLOGY. Of physical, esp. cranial, features: characteristic of or associated with early Lapp peoples.

Lapsang /ˈlapsaŋ/ *noun.* **M20.**
[**ORIGIN** Abbreviation.]
= **LAPSANG SOUCHONG**.

lapsang souchong /ˈlapsaŋ ˈsuːʃɒŋ/ *noun.* **L19.**
[**ORIGIN** from invented 1st elem. + **SOUCHONG**.]
A variety of souchong tea with a smoky flavour. Also ***lapsang souchong tea***.

lapsarian /lapˈsɛːrɪən/ *noun & adjective.* **E20.**
[**ORIGIN** from Latin *lapsus* fall, **LAPSE** *noun* + **-ARIAN**, or back-form. from *infralapsarian*, *postlapsarian*, *sublapsarian*, etc.]
THEOLOGY. ▸**A** *noun.* A believer in the doctrine of the Fall of Man from innocence. **E20.**
▸ **B** *adjective.* Of or pertaining to the Fall of Man. **E20.**

lapse /laps/ *noun.* **LME.**
[**ORIGIN** Latin *lapsus*, from *laps-* pa. ppl stem of *labi* glide, slip, fall, rel. to *labare* slip, *labor* **LABOUR** *noun*.]
1 *LAW.* The termination of a right or privilege (orig. to ecclesiastical patronage) through disuse or failure to follow appropriate procedures. **LME.**
2 The gliding or passing away *of* time, one's life, etc.; an interval *of* time elapsed. **LME.** ▸**b** A gliding or flow of water. Also, a gentle downward motion. *arch.* **M17.**

M. O. W. OLIPHANT A lapse of a hundred years is not much in the story of . . Florence. F. NORRIS The fountain made itself heard, . . marking off the lapse of seconds, the progress of hours.

3 A slip of the memory, the tongue, the pen, etc.; a mistake, a slight error. **L15.**

V. BROME Freud now made a long . . attempt to justify his lapse of memory. J. VIORST Expecting to be betrayed, we seize on every flaw and lapse.

4 A weak or careless deviation or falling from what is right; a moral slip. **L15.** ▸**b** *THEOLOGY.* A falling away *from* the faith or *into* heresy. **M17.**

E. MANNIN His occasional alcoholic lapses shouldn't be held against him. LD MACAULAY The hero sank again into a voluptuary; and the lapse was deep and hopeless.

†**the Lapse** (**of Man**) *THEOLOGY* = ***the Fall*** (***of Man***) s.v. **FALL** *noun*[2].
5 A decline to a lower state or degree. Formerly also, a fall in temperature. **M16.**
6 A falling into ruin. *rare.* **E17.**
– **COMB.:** **lapse rate** *METEOROLOGY* the rate of fall of atmospheric temperature with altitude.

lapse /laps/ *verb.* **LME.**
[**ORIGIN** Partly from Latin *lapsare*, from *laps-* (see **LAPSE** *noun*); partly from the noun.]
▸ **I** *verb intrans.* **1 a** Of time: pass *away*. **LME.** ▸**b** *gen.* Glide or pass effortlessly; descend gradually. **L18.** ▸**c** Of water: flow gently. Also, (of a person or a vessel) float, glide gently over water. **M19.**

c DICKENS Rippling waves that lapsed in silver hush Upon the beach.

2 †**a** Fall into error, heresy, or sin. **E–M17.** ▸**b** Fall (*away* or *back*) into an inferior or previous state; fail to maintain a position or state, esp. through absence of effort or influence. Foll. by *from*, *into*. **M17.**

b V. S. NAIPAUL The system became hard to maintain and he had allowed it to lapse. R. K. NARAYAN He blurted out a couple of questions . . and lapsed into silence. J. M. COETZEE It was only . . work that could keep him from lapsing into gloominess. *Daily Telegraph* Puttnam is a working-class lad made good and he still lapses into Cockney idiom.

3 a *LAW.* Of a right, privilege, etc.: become void, revert *to* someone, through non-fulfilment of conditions, absence of heirs, etc. **E18.** ▸**b** *COMMERCE.* Of a contract, agreement, policy, etc.: become void or ineffective, usu. through the withdrawal of one party or the failure to pay a premium. **M19.**

b A. JOHN I failed to produce the goods . . and our contract lapsed. *Times* Sketchley's $33-a-share offer . . has lapsed.

▸ **II** *verb trans.* †**4** Pounce on as an offender, apprehend. *rare* (Shakes.). Only in **E17.**
†**5** Cause to slip or fall; let slip, let pass. **M17–E18.**
6 Allow (a right etc.) to lapse; cause or allow (a contract, agreement, policy, etc.) to become void or ineffective, esp. through non-payment; forfeit, lose (esp. a member or one's membership) usu. through breach of rules. **M17.**

Daily Mail They were told that they would be lapsed from their union for being in arrears. *Observer* The trouble and expense of lapsing one policy and starting another.

■ **lapsable** *adjective* (long *rare*) **L17.** **lapser** *noun* **L17.**

lapsus /ˈlapsəs/ *noun.* Pl. same. **E17.**
[**ORIGIN** Latin: see **LAPSE** *noun*.]
A lapse, a slip, an error. Chiefly in phrs. below.
lapsus calami /ˈkaləmʌɪ/ a slip of the pen. ***lapsus linguae*** /ˈlɪŋgwʌɪ/ a slip of the tongue.

Laputan /ləˈpjuːt(ə)n/ *adjective.* **M19.**
[**ORIGIN** from *Laputa* (see below) + **-AN**. Cf. **LAPUTIAN**.]
Of or pertaining to Laputa, the flying island in Swift's *Gulliver's Travels*, whose inhabitants were addicted to visionary projects; visionary, fanciful, absurd.

Laputian /ləˈpjuːʃ(ə)n/ *noun. rare.* (Swift). **E18.**
[**ORIGIN** formed as **LAPUTAN** + **-IAN**.]
An inhabitant of Laputa (see **LAPUTAN**).

lapwing /ˈlapwɪŋ/ *noun.*
[**ORIGIN** Old English *hlēapewince*, formed as **LEAP** *verb* + base (meaning 'move sideways or from side to side') of **WINK** *verb*[1], assim. to **LAP** *verb*[2], **WING** *noun*: named from its manner of flight.]
Any of several mostly black and white plovers of the genus *Vanellus*, which have a crested head, wattles, and wing spurs and occur in most temperate and tropical regions except N. America; *spec.* the peewit or green plover, *V. vanellus*, of Europe and Asia.
wattled lapwing: see **WATTLED** 2.

laquais de place /lakɛ də plas/ *noun phr.* Now *rare*. Pl. same. **L18.**
[**ORIGIN** French, lit. 'place servant': see **LACKEY**, **PLACE** *noun*[1].]
A manservant temporarily hired during a visit to a foreign city.

laquear /ˈlakwɪɑː/ *noun.* Pl. ***-ria*** /-rɪə/. **E18.**
[**ORIGIN** Latin *laqueare* panelled ceiling.]
ARCHITECTURE. A ceiling consisting of panelled recessed compartments, with bands between the panels.

lar /lɑː/ *noun.* In sense 1 also **L-**. Pl. **lars**, **lares** /ˈlɑːriːz/. **L16.**
[**ORIGIN** Latin, pl. *lares*.]
1 *ROMAN HISTORY.* A household or ancestral god. Freq. in *pl.*, the protective gods of a house; household gods; also, the home. Cf. **PENATES**. **L16.**
lares and penates the home.
2 More fully ***lar gibbon***. The common or white-handed gibbon, *Hylobates lar*, of Thailand and Malaysia. **E19.**

lararium /ləˈrɛːrɪəm/ *noun.* Pl. ***-ria*** /-rɪə/. **E17.**
[**ORIGIN** Latin, from *lares*: see **LAR**.]
ROMAN HISTORY. The part of a Roman house where the images of lares or household gods were kept; a private shrine or chapel.

La Raza /laˈrasa/ *noun phr.* **M20.**
[**ORIGIN** Mexican Spanish from Spanish = the race.]
Mexican-Americans collectively, as a group with a strong sense of racial and cultural identity.

larboard /ˈlɑːbɔːd, -bəd/ *noun & adjective. arch.* Also (earlier) †**lade-bord** & other vars. **LME.**
[**ORIGIN** Perh. from **LADE** *verb* (referring to the side on which cargo was received) + alt. of **BOARD** *noun*, after **STARBOARD**.]
NAUTICAL. ▸**A** *noun.* = **PORT** *noun*[5]. **LME.**
▸ **B** *attrib.* or as *adjective*. Belonging to or situated on the port side of a vessel. **L15.**

larbolins /ˈlɑːbəlɪnz/ *noun pl.* **M18.**
[**ORIGIN** Contr. of **LARBOARD** + **-LING**[1] + **-S**[1]. Cf. **STARBOLINS**.]
NAUTICAL. The crew members of the port watch.

larceny /ˈlɑːs(ə)ni/ *noun.* **L15.**
[**ORIGIN** Anglo-Norman, from Old French *larcin* from Latin *latrocinium*, from *latro(n-)* brigand, robber, (earlier) mercenary soldier, from Greek *latron* pay, *latreus* mercenary, *latreuein* serve.]
gen. Theft; an act or instance of theft; *LAW* theft of personal property (replaced as a statutory crime in English law by ***theft***).
grand larceny, **petty larceny** *LAW* (now *hist.*): of personal property to a value greater, less, than a legally specified amount.
■ **larcener** *noun* a larcenist **M17.** **larcenist** *noun* a person who commits larceny **E19.** **larcenous** *adjective* pertaining to or characterized by larceny, thievish **M18.**

larch /lɑːtʃ/ *noun*[1]. **M16.**
[**ORIGIN** Middle High German *larche* var. of *lerche* (German *Lärche*) from Old High German from Latin *laric-*, *larix*, prob. of alien origin.]
1 Any of various deciduous coniferous trees of the genus *Larix*; spec. *L. decidua*, native to the Alps and cultivated for its tough durable timber. Also ***larch tree***. **M16.**
2 The wood of these trees. **M19.**
– **COMB.:** **larch blister**, **larch canker** a disease caused by the fungus *Trichoscyphella willkommii*, which causes cankers on the bark of larch trees; **larch gum**: similar to gum arabic and extracted from a N. American larch, *Larix occidentalis*; ***larch leaf cast***: see **LEAF** *noun*[1]; **larch needle-cast** a disease caused by the fungus *Mycosphaerella laricina*, which attacks and kills the foliage of larch trees; **larch sawfly** a sawfly, *Pristiphora erichsonii*, whose larvae feed on the leaves of larch trees; ***larch tree***: see sense 1 above.

larch *noun*[2] see **LURCH** *noun*[3].

larchen /ˈlɑːtʃ(ə)n/ *adjective. poet.* **E19.**
[**ORIGIN** from **LARCH** *noun*[1] + **-EN**[4].]
Consisting of larches, that is a larch.

L

lard /lɑːd/ *noun*. ME.
[ORIGIN Old French & mod. French = bacon from Latin *lar(i)dum* rel. to Greek *larinos* fat.]
†**1** The fat of a pig; (fat) bacon or pork. ME–E18.
2 The internal fat of the abdomen of a pig, esp. when rendered and clarified for use in cooking and pharmacy. Also, any fatty preparation based on or resembling this. ME. ▸**b** The internal fat of another animal. L15.
– PHRASES: ***bladder of lard***: see BLADDER *noun* 3.
– COMB.: **lardass** *N. Amer. slang* a person with large buttocks, a fat person; **lard-bladder** *colloq.* a fat person; **lard oil** a clear oil expressed from lard.

lard /lɑːd/ *verb trans*. ME.
[ORIGIN Old French & mod. French *larder*, formed as LARD *noun*. Cf. INTERLARD.]
1 *COOKERY*. Insert strips of bacon or pork in the substance of (meat, poultry, etc.) before cooking. ME.
larding needle, **larding pin**: for piercing meat so that bacon or pork can be inserted.
2 Smear or cover with lard or fat; grease. *rare*. LME.
E. BOWEN Hair that though sternly larded would never stay down.
3 Stick all over *with*; cover, line, or strew *with*. Now *arch. rare*. M16.
LYTTON Larding himself with sharp knives and bodkins.
4 Intersperse or garnish (speech or writing) with particular words, expressions, ideas, etc.; interlard. M16.
J. WAIN Larding his essays with phony quotations. *Nature* The organizers have larded their ban with varying expressions of regret.
†**5** Enrich with or as with fat; fatten. L16–L17.
6 Adulterate with lard. L19.

lardaceous /lɑːˈdeɪʃəs/ *adjective*. E19.
[ORIGIN from LARD *noun* + -ACEOUS.]
MEDICINE. Resembling lard; = AMYLOID *adjective* 2.

larder /ˈlɑːdə/ *noun*. ME.
[ORIGIN Anglo-Norman *larder*, Old French *lardier*, medieval Latin *lardarium*, formed as LARD *noun* + -ER².]
†**1** A supply of meat; meat in storage. ME–L15.
2 A room or cupboard for the storage of food (orig. esp. meat). LME.
3 A store of food hoarded by an animal; *spec.* the collection of prey impaled by a shrike. E20.
– COMB.: **larder beetle** a small brown dermestid beetle, *Dermestes lardarius*, whose larvae can be very destructive to stored meat and hides; also called ***bacon beetle***.

larderellite /lɑːdəˈrɛlʌɪt/ *noun*. M19.
[ORIGIN from Francesco de *Larderel* (1789–1858), Italian industrialist + -ITE¹.]
MINERALOGY. A monoclinic hydrated ammonium borate, occurring in fumarolic deposits as a white powder.

larderer /ˈlɑːd(ə)rə/ *noun*. Now *rare*. L15.
[ORIGIN Anglo-Norman (Anglo-Latin *larderarius*), formed as LARDER + -ER². Cf. LARDINER.]
A person who has charge of a larder.

lardiner /ˈlɑːdɪnə/ *noun*. *obsolete* exc. *hist*. ME.
[ORIGIN Anglo-Norman, alt. of LARDERER, or from Anglo-Latin *lardinarius*, *-erius*.]
1 = LARDER 1. *Scot. & N. English*. ME.
2 An official who has charge of a larder. ME.

lardon /ˈlɑːdən/ *noun*. Also **lardoon** /lɑːˈduːn/. LME.
[ORIGIN Old French & mod. French, formed as LARD *noun*: see -OON.]
COOKERY. A strip of bacon or pork used to lard meat.

lardy /ˈlɑːdi/ *adjective*. M17.
[ORIGIN from LARD *noun* + -Y¹.]
1 Obese; unattractively fat. *colloq*. M17.
S. STEWART Dave . . had dragged his lardy body into a vertical position.
2 Full of or containing lard; like lard. L19.
– COMB.: **lardy cake** a kind of cake made with bread dough, lard, currants, etc.

lardy-dardy /lɑːdɪˈdɑːdi/ *adjective*. *colloq*. M19.
[ORIGIN Imit. of a style of pronunciation: cf. LA-DI-DA *adjective*.]
= LA-DI-DA *adjective*.

lare *noun*, *verb* vars. of LAIR *noun*³, *verb*³.

laree *noun* var. of LARI.

lares *noun pl.* see LAR.

larf /lɑːf/ *verb intrans. & trans. & noun*. *non-standard*. M19.
[ORIGIN Repr. a pronunc.]
Esp. representing cockney speech: (a) laugh.

Largactil /lɑːˈgaktɪl/ *noun*. M20.
[ORIGIN Unknown.]
(Proprietary name for) the drug chlorpromazine.

largamente /lɑːgəˈmɛnti/ *adverb & adjective*. M19.
[ORIGIN Italian = broadly.]
MUSIC. A direction: in a slow dignified style.

large /lɑːdʒ/ *adjective*, *adverb*, *& noun*. ME.
[ORIGIN Old French & mod. French (now = broad, wide) from Latin *larga* fem. of *largus* abundant, bountiful.]
▸**A** *adjective* **I 1** Liberal in giving; generous; munificent; open-handed. Also, liberal in expenditure, prodigal, lavish. (Foll. by *of*, *in*.) Cf. sense 5b below. Long *obsolete* exc. *dial*. ME.
SHAKES. *2 Hen. VI* The poor King Reignier, whose large style Agrees not with the leanness of his purse. DRYDEN Large of his treasures.
▸**II** Ample, wide, great.
†**2** Ample in quantity; copious, abundant. ME–M17.
R. HAKLUYT The Kings of France and England gave large money towards the maintenance of the army.
3 Ample in spatial extent; spacious, roomy, capacious. *obsolete* exc. as in sense 8 below. ME.
COVERDALE *1 Kings* 4:29 God gaue Salomon maruelous greate wyszdome and vnderstondinge, and a large hert. *fig.*: J. S. BLACKIE The brain by knowledge grows, the heart Is larger made by loving.
†**4** Extensive in transverse dimension; broad, wide. ME–E18.
MILTON Southward through Eden went a River large.
5 a Of an abstract thing: wide in range or capacity; comprehensive, wide-ranging. ME. ▸**b** Of a person: generous or unstinting in an action, possessing or displaying an attribute to the full. Foll. by *in*, †*of*. Cf. sense 1 above. LME.
a J. WESLEY How good Thou art, How large thy Grace! LD MACAULAY A good reason for giving large powers to a trustworthy magistrate. W. S. CHURCHILL Neither side in the Crimean War was inspired by large strategic views. **b** F. M. PEARD He was large in his offers of friendship towards a young nephew of Mr. Pritchard's.
6 a Of a discourse, narrative, etc.: lengthy. Now *rare* or *obsolete*. ME. ▸†**b** Of a person: prolix. E17–L18.
a J. L. MOTLEY He fell into large and particular discourse with the deputies.
†**7** Of a measure of space or time: (more than) full, good. Of the time of day: fully come. LME–M18.
8 Of considerable or relatively great size or extent; big, great; extensive; of a kind or variety of greater size than the ordinary. LME. ▸**b** Of a movement, pace, etc.: covering a good extent of ground at a step. LME. ▸**c** Of a meal: heavy, abundant. M18. ▸**d** *MEDICINE*. (Of a sound heard in auscultation) full, sonorous (now *rare*); (of the pulse) full. M19. ▸**e** That is engaged in a particular occupation on a large scale. L19.
D. H. LAWRENCE The stones of the large house were burdened with ivy. G. GREENE The pyjamas she was wearing were too large for her. I. MURDOCH She . . spent a large part of her week-ends in showing them London. U. BENTLEY The houses of most of the boys were small and the families large. **b** J. KOSINSKI It was difficult to adjust my small steps to the large, measured stride of the soldier. **c** B. PYM We ate a large tea and ate much. **e** J. G. PATON Large farmers and small farmers.
a large order: see ORDER *noun*. ***in a large measure***, ***in large measure***: see MEASURE *noun*. ***large as life***, ***larger than life***: see LIFE *noun*. **law of large numbers** a law stating that the result of a series of statistical trials approaches the true probability of the observed outcome more closely as the number of trials increases.
9 Of speech or manner: pompous, imposing, grandiose. E17.
SHAKES. *Lear* And your large speeches may your deeds approve.
▸**III** Not restricted, free.
†**10** Indulgent, lax; not strict or rigorous. LME–M18.
J. STRYPE When King Henry was large towards the Protestants, Cranmer was so also.
†**11** Having or observing few or no restrictions or limitations. LME–L18.
MILTON Leaving my dolorous Prison I enjoy Large liberty to round this Globe of Earth.
†**12** Of speech etc.: free, unrestrained; licentious, improper. LME–L16.
SHAKES. *Much Ado* The man doth fear God, howsoever it seems not in him by some large jests he will make.
13 *NAUTICAL*. Of the wind: crossing the line of a sailing ship's course in a favourable direction, esp. on the beam or quarter. L16.
J. NARBOROUGH As . . the Wind grew large, we might alter our Course when we would.
– COMB. & SPECIAL COLLOCATIONS: ***large CALORIE***; **large-eyed** *adjective* having a large eye or large eyes; characterized by wide open eyes; **large-handed** *adjective* (*a*) having large hands; †(*b*) grasping, rapacious; (*c*) open-handed, generous; **large-hearted** *adjective* magnanimous, generous, having wide sympathies; ***large intestine***: see INTESTINE *noun*; **large-minded** *adjective* having a liberal or generous mind; marked by breadth of ideas; not narrow-minded; **largemouth bass**, **large-mouthed bass** a N. American freshwater bass, *Micropterus salmoides* (family Centrarchidae), introduced elsewhere as a game fish; **large print** printing in large bold characters designed to be more easily read by partially sighted people; **large-scale** *adjective* drawn to a large scale, on a large scale, extensive, widespread, relating to large numbers; ***large TORTOISESHELL***; **large type** = ***large print*** above.
▸**B** *adverb*. †**1** Amply; fully, by a great deal; abundantly. Chiefly *Scot. & N. English*. ME–E18.
†**2** Liberally, generously. ME–M17.
3 Freely, unrestrainedly, boldly. Now *US*. LME.
4 Of speech and writing: at length, fully. *obsolete* exc. in ***writ large*** (after Milton). LME.
MILTON *New Presbyter* is but *Old Priest* writ Large.
5 Orig., transversely, across. Now *spec*. (*NAUTICAL*) with the wind large, with the wind on the quarter or abaft the beam. LME.
†**6** With big steps; with ample gait. M17–E18.
– PHRASES: ***by and large***: see BY *adverb*. **go large**, **lead large** (in a naval or military manoeuvre) break off from a set course and go straight ahead. ***writ large***: see WRITE *verb*.
▸**C** *noun*. **1** (Large) size, (large, full) extent. Long *obsolete* exc. in phrs. below. LME.
2 Liberty. Long *obsolete* exc. in ***at large*** below. LME.
†**3** Liberality, bounty. LME–M16.
4 *MUSIC*. The longest note recognized in the early notation, equivalent to two or three long notes, according to the rhythm employed; the character denoting this, ◡ or ⌒. L15.
– PHRASES: **at large** (*a*) at liberty, free; †(*b*) not fixed, unsettled; (*c*) at length, in full; †(*d*) in full size (as opp. to a model or abridged form); (*e*) as a whole, in general, altogether; (*f*) in a general way, without particularizing (***AMBASSADOR-at-large***); †(*g*) over a wide area, abroad; (*h*) without a specific aim. †**at one's large** at liberty. **in large** on a large scale. **in the large** (*a*) = ***in large*** above; (*b*) in general, as a whole.
■ **largish** *adjective* somewhat large L18.

large /lɑːdʒ/ *verb*. ME.
[ORIGIN from the adjective. Cf. Old French *largir* and (for sense 2) French *larguer*.]
†**1** *verb trans*. Enlarge, increase, widen. ME–M17.
2 *verb intrans*. *NAUTICAL*. Of the wind: become large (see LARGE *adjective* 13). E17.

largely /ˈlɑːdʒli/ *adverb*. ME.
[ORIGIN from LARGE *adjective* + -LY².]
1 Liberally, generously, bountifully. *arch*. ME.
2 To a great extent; extensively, greatly, considerably, abundantly, much. Now usu., principally, on the whole. ME.
E. M. FORSTER For so young a man he had read largely. E. BOWEN Constructed largely of glass and blistered white paint, Waikiki faced the sea boldly. E. WAUGH In my experience the more responsible posts in the army are largely filled by certifiable lunatics.
†**3** At (great) length, in full, fully. LME–M19.
4 With a wide or general application; in a broad sense. *arch*. LME.
†**5** Freely, without restraint. LME–M16.
6 In large characters, letters, or outlines. Now *rare*. E17.
7 With lofty demeanour; loftily, pompously. M19.

largen /ˈlɑːdʒ(ə)n/ *verb trans. & intrans. poet*. M19.
[ORIGIN from LARGE *adjective* + -EN⁵.]
Make or grow large or larger.

largeness /ˈlɑːdʒnɪs/ *noun*. ME.
[ORIGIN from LARGE *adjective* + -NESS.]
†**1** Liberality, open-handedness, generosity; prodigality. ME–E17.
2 (Great) size, volume, or bulk; bigness, extensiveness. ME.
†**3** Breadth, width. LME–M18.
4 The quality of not being circumscribed or limited in scope, range, or capacity; wide-ranging quality. Opp. ***narrowness***. LME.
†**5** Lengthiness, prolixity. M16–M17.
†**6** Freedom, scope, opportunity. *rare*. Only in M17.
7 Lofty bearing, pomposity. L19.

largesse /lɑːˈʒɛs, -ˈdʒɛs/ *noun*. Also **-ess**. ME.
[ORIGIN Old French & mod. French from Proto-Romance, from Latin *largus*: see LARGE *adjective*, -ESS².]
1 Liberality, generosity, munificence. Long *obsolete* exc. *hist*. ME.
2 Liberal bestowal of gifts; money or other gifts freely bestowed, esp. by a person in a high position on some special occasion. ME. ▸**b** An act of such giving; a free gift of money etc. M16.
H. WOUK His relish for power and his satisfaction in bestowing largesse. CLIVE JAMES The . . artists who received the largesse of the Whitlam regime seem . . to represent a return to insularity. *fig.*: L. MACNEICE The watch-fires glow and spread their red largesse of flames. **b** T. ARNOLD His triumphs were followed by various largesses of provisions and money to the populace.
†**3** Freedom, liberty. LME–L16.
– NOTE: Formerly more fully naturalized: in 19 usu. spelled *-ess* and with stress on 1st syll.

larghetto /lɑːˈgɛtəʊ/ *adverb*, *adjective*, *& noun*. E18.
[ORIGIN Italian, dim. of LARGO.]
MUSIC. ▸**A** *adverb & adjective*. A direction: in fairly slow time. E18.
▸**B** *noun*. Pl. **-os**. A movement or passage played in this way. L19.

largition /lɑːˈdʒɪʃ(ə)n/ *noun*. Now *rare*. M16.
[ORIGIN Old French *largicion* or its source Latin *largitio(n-)*, from *largit-* pa. ppl stem of *largiri* be bountiful, from *largus*: see LARGE *adjective*, -ITION.]

L

The bestowal of gifts or largesse; bountiful giving; an instance of this.

largo /ˈlɑːgəʊ/ *adverb, adjective, & noun.* L17.
[ORIGIN Italian = broad.]
MUSIC. ▸**A** *adverb & adjective.* A direction: in slow time and with a broad dignified treatment. L17.
▸**B** *noun.* Pl. **-os**. A movement or passage played in this way. M18.

lari /ˈlɑːriː/ *noun.* Also **laree**, (in sense 1) †**larin**, (in sense 2) **laari**. Pl. **-s**, same. L16.
[ORIGIN Persian *lārī*, from *Lār* a town on the north of the Persian Gulf.]
1 A kind of Persian and Arabic coin consisting of a strip of metal bent over in the form of a hook. *obsolete* exc. *hist.* L16.
2 A monetary unit of the Maldives, equal to one-hundredth of a rufiyaa. L20.
3 The basic monetary unit of Georgia, equal to 100 tetri. L20.

Lariam /ˈlarɪəm/ *noun.* L20.
[ORIGIN Prob. from partial rearrangement of MALARIA.]
(Proprietary name for) the antimalarial drug mefloquine.

lariat /ˈlarɪət/ *noun.* M19.
[ORIGIN from Spanish *la reata*, from *la* the + *reata*, from *reatar* tie again, from *re-* RE- + *atar* from Latin *aptare* adjust, from *aptus*: see APT. Cf. RIATA.]
A lasso; a rope for tethering animals, esp. used by cowboys.

larin *noun* see LARI.

larix /ˈlarɪks/ *noun.* M16.
[ORIGIN Latin: see LARCH *noun*[1].]
†**1** A Middle Eastern plant, *Camphorosma monspeliaca*, of the goosefoot family, used medicinally. M16–M17.
2 A tree of the genus *Larix*; a larch. L16.

lark /lɑːk/ *noun*[1]. Also (chiefly *Scot. & N. English*) **laverock** /ˈlav(ə)rək/.
[ORIGIN Old English *lāferce*, older *lǣwerce*, *lāuricæ*, corresp. to Middle Low German, Middle Dutch *lēwer(i)ke* (Dutch *leeuwerik*), Old High German *lērihha* (German *Lerche*), Old Norse *lævirki* (perh. from English): ult. origin unknown.]
Any of various small brown singing birds of the family Alaudidae, with an elongated hind claw; *spec.* the skylark, *Alauda arvensis*. Also (with specifying word), any of various birds resembling but not related to the true larks.

B. W. PROCTER Be constant.. As larks are to the morn or bats to eve.

crested lark, *horned lark*, *meadow lark*, *shorelark*, *skylark*, *titlark*, *woodlark*, etc. **get up with the lark**, **rise with the lark** get up out of bed very early.
– COMB.: **lark bunting** a bunting, *Calamospiza melanocorys*, of the N. American plains; **lark-heel** (*a*) = *lark's heel* below; (*b*) a projecting heel; **lark's heel** (*a*) larkspur; (*b*) nasturtium; **lark sparrow** a N. American ground-nesting sparrow, *Chondestes grammacus*.
▪ **larker** *noun*[1] (*obsolete* exc. *hist.*) a person whose occupation is catching larks M17.

lark /lɑːk/ *noun*[2]. *colloq.* E19.
[ORIGIN from LARK *verb*.]
1 A period of lively amusement; an amusing incident, a (practical) joke. E19.

P. G. WODEHOUSE I hadn't meant to go at first, but I turned up for a lark. J. KRANTZ She had.. thought it might be something of a lark to edit a film in her house.

2 An affair, a type of activity, a line of business. M20.

A. SILLITOE This long-distance running lark is the best of all, because it makes me think so good. J. FOWLES If you think you take me in with all this lying in bed lark you're mistaken.

▪ **larkish** *adjective* of the nature of a lark; playful, silly: E19. **larksome** *adjective* given to larking; playful: L19.

lark /lɑːk/ *verb. colloq.* E19.
[ORIGIN Uncertain: perh. alt. of LAIK, but cf. SKYLARK *verb*.]
1 *verb intrans.* Play tricks, frolic (freq. foll. by *about*). Formerly *esp.* ride in a frolicsome manner, ride across country. E19.

THACKERAY Jumping the widest brooks, and larking over the newest gates in the country. W. S. MAUGHAM Stick to your work and don't go larking about with the girls.

2 *verb trans.* Make fun of, tease (a person); ride (a horse) across country. Now *rare* or *obsolete*. M19.
▪ **larker** *noun*[2] a person given to larking about E19.

larkspur /ˈlɑːkspəː/ *noun.* L16.
[ORIGIN from LARK *noun*[1] + SPUR *noun*[1].]
Any of numerous annual plants native to the Mediterranean that constitute the genus *Consolida*, of the buttercup family; esp. *C. ajacis*, grown for its blue, pink, or white flowers. Also (now only with specifying word), any plant of the related genus *Delphinium*.

larky /ˈlɑːki/ *adjective. colloq.* E19.
[ORIGIN from LARK *noun*[2] + -Y[1].]
Inclined or ready for a lark; given to larking about; frolicsome, playful.
▪ **larkiness** *noun* L19.

larm /lɑːm/ *noun.* Long *rare* or *obsolete*. M16.
[ORIGIN Aphet.]
= ALARM *noun*.

Larmor /ˈlɑːmə/ *noun.* E20.
[ORIGIN Sir Joseph *Larmor* (1857–1942), Irish-born physicist.]
PHYSICS. Used *attrib.* and in *possess.* to designate concepts arising from Larmor's work.
Larmor frequency: of Larmor precession. **Larmor precession** precession (about the direction of magnetic flux) of the rotational axis of a particle rotating in a magnetic field. **Larmor radius**: of the helical path of a free charged particle spiralling about magnetic field lines.

larmoyant /lɑːˈmɔɪənt/ *adjective. rare.* E19.
[ORIGIN French, pres. pple of *larmoyer* be tearful: see -ANT[1].]
Given to tears, lachrymose.

larn *verb* see LEARN *verb*.

larnax /ˈlɑːnaks/ *noun.* Pl. **larnakes** /ˈlɑːnəkiːz/. L19.
[ORIGIN Greek.]
GREEK ANTIQUITIES. A chest, ossuary, urn, or coffin, usu. of terracotta and freq. ornamented with designs.

Larnian /ˈlɑːnɪən/ *adjective & noun.* M20.
[ORIGIN from *Larne* a town in Co. Antrim, N. Ireland + -IAN.]
ARCHAEOLOGY. (Designating or pertaining to) a late Mesolithic and early Neolithic culture of Northern Ireland.

larnite /ˈlɑːnʌɪt/ *noun.* E20.
[ORIGIN formed as LARNIAN + -ITE[1].]
MINERALOGY. A rare monoclinic mineral consisting of a metastable phase of dicalcium silicate.

larrigan /ˈlarɪg(ə)n/ *noun. N. Amer.* L19.
[ORIGIN Unknown.]
A long boot made of undressed leather.

larrikin /ˈlarɪkɪn/ *noun & adjective.* Chiefly *Austral.* M19.
[ORIGIN Unknown.]
▸**A** *noun.* A (usu. juvenile) street rowdy, a hooligan. M19.
▸**B** *attrib.* or as *adjective.* Of the nature of or characteristic of a larrikin. L19.
▪ **larrikinism** *noun* rowdy behaviour, hooliganism L19.

larrup /ˈlarəp/ *verb trans. dial. & colloq.* E19.
[ORIGIN Uncertain: perh. rel. to LATHER *verb*, LEATHER *verb*.]
Beat, flog, thrash.
▪ **larruping** *noun* (*a*) the action of the verb; (*b*) a thrashing, a beating: L19.

larry /ˈlari/ *noun*[1]. *dial.* L19.
[ORIGIN Unknown.]
(A state of) confusion, excitement.

Larry /ˈlari/ *noun*[2]. *colloq.* E20.
[ORIGIN Unknown: form that of pet form of male forename *Lawrence*.]
as happy as Larry, extremely happy.

larum /ˈlɛːrəm, ˈlar(ə)m/ *noun & verb.* LME.
[ORIGIN Aphet. from ALARUM *noun*.]
▸**A** *noun.* **1** A call to arms, a battle cry; a warning sound. Also, a tumultuous noise; a hubbub, an uproar. Now chiefly *poet.* LME. ▸†**b** A state of frightened surprise; = ALARM *noun* 1. Only in L16.
2 The alarm of a clock or watch. *obsolete* exc. *dial.* L16.
▸**B** *verb trans.* Sound as an alarm; give the alarm to. *obsolete* exc. *poet. & dial.* L16.

larva /ˈlɑːvə/ *noun.* Pl. **-vae** /-viː/. M17.
[ORIGIN Latin = ghost, mask.]
1 A disembodied spirit; a ghost, a spectre. *obsolete* exc. *hist.* M17.
2 An insect in a state of development (displaying little or no similarity to the adult) lasting from the time of its leaving the egg until its transformation into a pupa; a grub, a caterpillar. Also, an immature form in other animals that undergo some sort of metamorphosis, e.g. amphibians, coelenterates, copepods, tapeworms, etc. M18.

larval /ˈlɑːv(ə)l/ *adjective.* M17.
[ORIGIN Latin *larvalis*, formed as LARVA + -AL[1].]
†**1** Of the nature of or pertaining to a ghost or spirit. Only in M17.
2 Of, pertaining to, or characteristic of a larva; of the nature of or in the condition of a larva. M19.

larvated /ˈlɑːveɪtɪd/ *adjective.* Now *rare* or *obsolete*. E17.
[ORIGIN from mod. Latin *larvatus*, from Latin LARVA: see -ATE[2], -ED[1].]
Masked, concealed.

†**larve** *noun.* E17.
[ORIGIN French formed as LARVA.]
1 = LARVA 1. E17–M19.
2 A mask. M–L17.
3 = LARVA 2. M18–M19.

larvi- /ˈlɑːvi/ *combining form* of Latin LARVA: see -I-.
▪ **larviˈcidal** *adjective* of the nature of a larvicide; that kills larvae: E20. **larvicide** *noun* a preparation adapted to kill larvae; a predator that kills larvae: E20. **larviform** *adjective* having the form of a larva M19. **larˈviparous** *adjective* producing young in the condition of larvae E19. **larvipoˈsition** *noun* the deposition of a larva (rather than an egg) by a female insect E20. **larˈvivorous** *adjective* feeding on larvae L19.

larvikite /ˈlɑːvɪkʌɪt/ *noun.* Also (earlier) †**laur-**. L19.
[ORIGIN from *Larvik* (formerly *Laurvik*), a seaport in Norway + -ITE[1].]
GEOLOGY. An augite-containing syenite, often used as a decorative stone, that has a coarse texture dominated by rhombs of soda or soda-lime feldspar.

lary *adjective* var. of LEERY *adjective*[2].

laryngal /ləˈrɪŋg(ə)l/ *adjective & noun.* M19.
[ORIGIN from mod. Latin *laryng-*, LARYNX + -AL[1].]
(A sound) produced in the larynx. Cf. LARYNGEAL.

laryngeal /ləˈrɪndʒɪəl/ *adjective & noun.* L18.
[ORIGIN from mod. Latin *laryngeus* (formed as LARYNGAL) + -AL[1].]
▸**A** *adjective.* **1** ANATOMY & MEDICINE. Of or pertaining to the larynx; affecting or seated in the larynx; (of an instrument) used to treat or examine the larynx. L18.
2 Of a speech sound: made in the larynx with only the front part of the vocal cords vibrating, giving a very low frequency and producing what is known as 'creaky voice'. E20. ▸**b** PHILOLOGY. of or pertaining to laryngeals (see sense B.2 below). M20.
▸**B** *noun.* **1** A laryngeal nerve or artery. L19.
2 A laryngeal sound; *spec.* (PHILOLOGY) a reconstructed phonetic element with a laryngeal quality thought to have existed in Proto-Indo-European and to have left traces in extant Indo-European languages. M20.
▪ **laryngealist** *noun* (PHILOLOGY) an adherent of the theory that there were laryngeals in Proto-Indo-European M20. **laryngealiˈzation** *noun* the action or fact of being laryngealized M20. **laryngealized** *adjective* (of a sound) produced in or affected by the larynx M20.

laryngectomy /larɪnˈdʒɛktəmi/ *noun.* L19.
[ORIGIN from LARYNGO- + -ECTOMY.]
Surgical removal of the larynx; an instance of this.
▪ **laryngectomee** *noun* a person who has undergone laryngectomy M20.

larynges *noun pl.* see LARYNX.

laryngismus /larɪnˈdʒɪzməs/ *noun.* E19.
[ORIGIN mod. Latin, formed as LARYNGITIS: see -ISM.]
MEDICINE. Spasmodic closure of the vocal cords, often with noisy indrawing of breath.

laryngitis /larɪnˈdʒʌɪtɪs/ *noun.* E19.
[ORIGIN from mod. Latin *laryng-*, LARYNX + -ITIS.]
Inflammation of the lining membrane of the larynx.
▪ **laryngitic** /-ˈdʒɪtɪk/ *adjective* L19.

laryngo- /ləˈrɪŋgəʊ/ *combining form* of mod. Latin *laryng-*, LARYNX: see -O-. Before a vowel **laryng-**.
▪ **laryngoˈfissure** *noun* surgical incision of the larynx through the midline of the thyroid cartilage L19. **laryngoˈpharynx** *noun* (the larynx together with) the lower part of the pharynx L19. **laryngophone** *noun* a throat microphone E20. **laryngospasm** *noun* spasmodic closure of the larynx M19. **laryngoˈtracheal** *adjective* pertaining to both the larynx and the trachea L19. **laryngotracheobronˈchitis** *noun* inflammation of the larynx, trachea, and bronchi; *spec.* an acute febrile disease (a form of croup) that causes such inflammation and occurs chiefly in young children M20.

laryngology /larɪŋˈgɒlədʒi/ *noun.* M19.
[ORIGIN from LARYNGO- + -LOGY.]
The branch of medicine that deals with the larynx and its diseases.
▪ **laryngoˈlogical** *adjective* L19. **laryngologist** *noun* L19.

laryngoscope /ləˈrɪŋgəskəʊp/ *noun.* M19.
[ORIGIN formed as LARYNGOLOGY + -SCOPE.]
An instrument which enables an observer to inspect a patient's larynx.
▪ **laryngoscopic** /-ˈskɒpɪk/ *adjective* of or pertaining to the laryngoscope or its use M19. **laryngoˈscopically** *adverb* L19. **laryngoscopist** /larɪŋˈgɒskəpɪst/ *noun* a person who uses, or is skilled in using, the laryngoscope M19. **laryngoscopy** /larɪŋˈgɒskəpi/ *noun* inspection of the larynx; the use of a laryngoscope: M19.

laryngotomy /larɪŋˈgɒtəmi/ *noun.* M17.
[ORIGIN Greek *laruggotomia*, from *larugg-*, *larugx* LARYNX: see -TOMY.]
Surgical incision into the larynx from without, esp. (through the cricoid cartilage) in order to provide an aperture for respiration; an instance of this.

larynx /ˈlarɪŋks/ *noun.* Pl. **larynges** /ləˈrɪndʒiːz/, **larynxes**. L16.
[ORIGIN mod. Latin from Greek *larugx*, *larugg-*.]
ANATOMY & ZOOLOGY. A hollow cartilaginous and muscular organ forming the upper part of the trachea or windpipe, and holding the vocal cords in humans and most mammals.

lasagne /ləˈzanjə, -ˈsan-, -ˈsɑːn-/ *noun.* Also **-gna**. M19.
[ORIGIN Italian, pl. of *lasagna*, ult. from Latin *lasanum* chamber pot, perh. also cooking pot.]
Pasta in the form of long wide strips; an Italian dish consisting of this and a sauce.
lasagne verdi /ˈvəːdi/ [green] lasagne coloured and flavoured with spinach.

lascar /ˈlaskə/ *noun. arch.* E17.
[ORIGIN Persian & Urdu *laškarī* soldier, from *laškar* army, camp, (cf. LASHKAR) through Portuguese *lascari*, *lascarin*, pl. *-res* (repl. *-is*, *-ins*). Cf. LASCARINE.]

1 (Usu. **L-**.) A sailor from India or SE Asia. **E17**.

> LONGFELLOW The . . surf, O'er the coral reefs of Madagascar, Washes the feet of the swarthy Lascar.

2 In the Indian subcontinent: a menial soldier; *spec.* (more fully ***gun-lascar***) one employed to do menial work in the artillery. **L18**.

> WELLINGTON We can get neither recruits, servants, lascars, coolies, or bullock drivers.

†**lascarine** *noun*. Also **L-**. **L16–E19**.
[ORIGIN Portuguese *lascarin*: see LASCAR.]
A soldier from India or Ceylon (Sri Lanka). Also, a non-European police officer in India or Ceylon.

†**lasce** *noun* see LASS.

lascivious /lə'sɪvɪəs/ *adjective*. **LME**.
[ORIGIN from late Latin *lasciviosus*, from Latin *lascivia* licentiousness, from *lascivus* sportive, lustful, wanton: see -OUS.]
1 Inclined to lust, lustful, lecherous, wanton. **LME**.

> MILTON Hee on Eve Began to cast lascivious Eyes. DENNIS POTTER He did not want any lascivious comments or dirty-minded ogling.

2 Conducive to or encouraging lust or lechery. Formerly also, voluptuous, luxurious. **L16**.

> J. T. STORY She made . . a lewd movement with her hips as a kind of lascivious promise.

■ **lasciviously** *adverb* **M16**. **lasciviousness** *noun* **M16**.

lascivity /lə'sɪvɪti/ *noun*. Long *rare*. **L15**.
[ORIGIN French *lascivité* from Latin *lascivitat-*, from *lascivus*: see LASCIVIOUS, -ITY.]
Lasciviousness, lust.

lase /leɪz/ *verb intrans*. **M20**.
[ORIGIN Back-form. from LASER *noun*², as though this were an agent noun in -ER¹.]
Of a substance or device: emit coherent light as (in) a laser; operate as the working substance of a laser.

laser /'leɪsə/ *noun*¹. *obsolete* exc. *hist.* & in ***laserwort*** below. **ME**.
[ORIGIN Latin, from *laserpicium* the plant yielding the resin, also called *silphium* (= Greek *silphion*).]
A gum resin obtained from the plant silphium, credited in classical times with great medicinal properties.
– COMB.: **laserwort** any of various umbelliferous plants of the genus *Laserpitium*, esp. *L. latifolium*.

laser /'leɪzə/ *noun*². **M20**.
[ORIGIN Acronym, from *light amplification by the stimulated emission of radiation*, after MASER.]
A device that can emit a very intense, narrow, parallel beam of highly monochromatic and coherent light (or other electromagnetic radiation) by using light to stimulate the emission of more light of the same wavelength and phase by excited atoms or molecules. Cf. MASER.

> *attrib.*: *Daily Telegraph* A laser beam . . can weld a detached retina back into place.

– COMB.: **laser angioplasty** MEDICINE: involving the use of a laser to burn away blocking tissue; **laserdisc**: on which signals or data are recorded to be reproduced by directing a laser beam on to the surface and detecting the reflected or transmitted light; **laser printer** a printer in which a laser is used to form a pattern of dots on a photosensitive drum corresponding to the pattern of print required on a page; **LaserVision** (proprietary name for) a video system in which the signals are on a laserdisc.

lash /laʃ/ *noun*¹. **ME**.
[ORIGIN from LASH *verb*¹. Cf. LASH *noun*².]
1 A stroke with a thong, whip, etc. Formerly also, a sudden or violent blow, a sweeping stroke. **ME**.
2 The flexible part of a whip. **LME**. ▸**b** *The* punishment of flogging. **M16**. ▸**c** A whip, a scourge. Chiefly *poet.* & *rhet.* **M17**.
3 An eyelash. Usu. in *pl.* **L18**.

> DICKENS Long dark lashes . . concealed his downcast eyes.

– PHRASES: **have a lash (at)** *Austral.* & *NZ* make an attempt (at), have a go (at).
– COMB.: **lash rope** *N. Amer.* a rope for lashing a pack or load on a horse or vehicle.
■ **lashed** *adjective*¹ having eyelashes, usu. of a specified kind **L18**. **lashless** *adjective* having no eyelashes **E19**.

lash /laʃ/ *noun*². **LME**.
[ORIGIN Perh. LASH *noun*¹ substituted for other words of similar sound; or perh. var. of LATCH *noun*¹.]
1 A string, a cord, a thong. Long *rare*. **LME**.
2 WEAVING. = LEASH *noun* 7a. **M18**.

LASH /laʃ/ *noun*³. Also **Lash**, **lash**. **M20**.
[ORIGIN Acronym, from *lighter aboard ship*.]
Used *attrib.* to designate a ship, or system of shipping, in which loaded barges are placed directly on board the ship.

lash /laʃ/ *adjective*. Long *obsolete* exc. *dial.* **LME**.
[ORIGIN Old French *lasche* (mod. *lâche*) from Proto-Romance var. of Latin *laxus* lax. See also LUSH *adjective*.]
1 Culpably negligent or remiss, lax. **LME**.
2 Soft, watery, tender. **LME**.
3 Slack, relaxed, without energy. **E16**.

lash /laʃ/ *verb*¹. **ME**.
[ORIGIN Perh. imit.]
▸ **I** Move swiftly or suddenly (now freq. coloured by branch II).
1 *verb intrans.* Make a sudden movement; dash, dart, spring; (of rain etc.) pour, rush. Usu. foll. by adverb or adverbial phr. **ME**.

> J. RUSKIN A lizard . . one expects . . to lash round the shaft and vanish. J. LE CARRÉ A strong sea wind lashed at his city suit. *impers.*: *Woman's Own* It could have lashed down with rain the whole time.

2 †**a** *verb trans.* Assail, attack. Only in **ME**. ▸**b** *verb intrans.* Let fly, rush (*at*); strike or hit *out* violently; (of a horse) kick *out*. **LME**.

> **b** I. MURDOCH We lashed out, hoping that our blows were falling . . upon the unrighteous. I. MCEWAN The other lashed back and . . scratched the first man's eye.

3 *verb trans.* Dash, throw, apply liberally. **ME**.

> *Hair Flair* The lotions we lash on our hair, the potions we put on our face.

4 *verb trans.* Lavish, squander. Usu. foll. by *out*. **E16**. ▸†**b** Pour *out* or *forth* impetuously (words etc.). **E16–M17**.
5 *verb intrans.* Of a person: rush into excess; break out into violent language; be lavish. Foll. by *out*. **M16**.

> J. WAIN You're abroad now. Why don't you lash out a bit?

▸ **II** *spec.* with ref. to LASH *noun*¹.
6 *verb trans.* Beat or strike with a lash etc.; flog, scourge. Also *transf.*, beat on or against. **LME**. ▸**b** *fig.* Castigate in words, rebuke, satirize. **L16**.

> P. THEROUX The rain lashed Jerry's face. **b** *Time* Bob Bergland . . lashes Earl Butz's laissez-faire policies.

7 *verb trans.* Urge or drive by, or as by, lashes. **L16**.
lash oneself into a fury work oneself into a rage.
■ **lashed** *adjective*² (**a**) beaten with or as with a whip; (**b**) *colloq.* drunk, intoxicated: **E17**. **lashingly** *adverb* in a lashing manner; by means of lashing: **L16**.

lash /laʃ/ *verb*² *trans.* **LME**.
[ORIGIN Perh. of Low German origin: cf. Middle Dutch *lasche* rag, patch, gusset, Dutch *laschen* patch, sew together, scarf (timber).]
†1 Lace (a garment). **LME–E17**.
2 Chiefly NAUTICAL. Fasten with cord, rope, twine, etc., (*to* something). Also foll. by *down, on, together*. Formerly also, truss (clothes). **E17**.

> *Independent* Ferries often put to sea in calm waters without lashing vehicles down. J. M. COETZEE His mattock was a sharp stone lashed to a stick.

– COMB.: **lashed-up** *adjective* improvised; **lash-up** (**a**) a makeshift or hastily contrived improvisation; (**b**) a failure, a fiasco.

lasher /'laʃə/ *noun*. **E17**.
[ORIGIN from LASH *verb*¹, *verb*² + -ER¹.]
1 A person who or (less commonly) a creature or thing which uses a lash. **E17**.
father-lasher: see FATHER *noun*.
2 NAUTICAL. A rope used for fastening, a lashing. **M17**.
3 On the River Thames in southern England: the body of water that rushes over an opening in a barrier or weir; (the opening in) a weir. **L17**. ▸**b** The pool into which this water falls. **M19**.

> J. K. JEROME The pool under Sandford lasher . . is a very good place to drown yourself in.

lashing /'laʃɪŋ/ *noun*¹. **LME**.
[ORIGIN from LASH *verb*¹ + -ING¹.]
1 The action of **LASH** *verb*¹; beating, flogging; an instance of this. Foll. by *out*: lavishing, squandering. **LME**.
2 In *pl.* Large quantities, plenty, abundance, (*of*). Orig. *Irish*. **E19**.

> J. P. DONLEAVY Porridge with lashings of milk and sugar.

lashing /'laʃɪŋ/ *noun*². **M17**.
[ORIGIN from LASH *verb*² + -ING¹.]
Chiefly NAUTICAL. The action of LASH *verb*²; the action of fastening something with a rope. Also, a rope used for fastening.
soul and body lashing: see SOUL *noun*.

lashkar /'laʃkɑː/ *noun*. In sense 1 usu. †**leskar**. **E17**.
[ORIGIN Persian & Urdu *laškar* army, camp: cf. LASCAR.]
†1 A camp of Indian soldiers. **E–M17**.
2 A body of armed Pathan men. **L19**.

LASIK /'leɪzɪk/ *noun*. **L20**.
[ORIGIN Acronym, from *laser-assisted in situ keratomileusis*.]
Corrective eye surgery in which a flap of the corneal surface is raised and a thin layer of underlying tissue is removed using a laser.

lasiocampid /ˌleɪsɪə(ʊ)'kampɪd/ *noun & adjective*. **L19**.
[ORIGIN mod. Latin *Lasiocampidae* (see below), from *Lasiocampa* genus name, from Greek *lasios* hairy, shaggy + *kampē* caterpillar: see -ID³.]
▸ **A** *noun*. Any moth of the large family Lasiocampidae, which includes eggars, lackeys, and lappet moths, and the larvae of which are called tent caterpillars. **L19**.
▸ **B** *adjective*. Of, pertaining to, or designating this family. **E20**.

lask /lɑːsk/ *noun*¹. **M16**.
[ORIGIN Anglo-Norman var. of Old French *lasche*, from *lascher*: see LASK *verb*.]
Looseness of the bowels, diarrhoea; an attack of this; = LAX *noun*² 2. Now only in veterinary use.

lask /lɑːsk/ *noun*². **M19**.
[ORIGIN Perh. from Middle Dutch *lasche* (mod. *lasch*) piece cut out, flap.]
A slice of fish used to bait a fish hook.

lask /lɑːsk/ *verb*. **ME**.
[ORIGIN Anglo-Norman var. of Old French *lascher* (mod. *lâcher*) loosen, from Proto-Romance alt. of Latin *laxare*, from *laxus* LAX *adjective*.]
†1 *verb trans.* Lower in quality, quantity, or strength, relax; thin (the blood); shorten (life); alleviate (pain). Only in **ME**.
†2 *verb intrans.* Suffer from diarrhoea. **M16–M17**.
3 *verb intrans.* NAUTICAL. Sail large with a quartering wind. *arch.* **E17**.

lasket /'lɑːskɪt/ *noun*. **E18**.
[ORIGIN Perh. alt. of French *lacet* (see LATCHET *noun*¹) in same sense, after GASKET.]
NAUTICAL. Any of the loops or rings of cord by which a bonnet is attached to the foot of a sail.

†**laso** *noun & verb* var. of LASSO.

laspring /'laspriŋ/ *noun*. **M18**.
[ORIGIN Perh. from LAX *noun*¹ + PINK *noun*², interpreted as contr. of *last spring*.]
A young salmon. Also ***gravel laspring***.

lasque /lɑːsk/ *noun*. **L17**.
[ORIGIN Perh. from Persian *lašk* piece.]
A flat, ill-formed, or veiny diamond. Also ***lasque diamond***.

lass /las/ *noun*. Chiefly *Scot.*, *N. English*, & *poet.* Also (earlier) †**lasce**. **ME**.
[ORIGIN Ult. from Old Norse *laskura* (fem.) unmarried, from base repr. by Old Swedish *løsk kona* unmarried woman.]
1 A girl, a young woman. **ME**. ▸**b** *spec.* A maidservant. **L18**. ▸**c** (Used as a playful form of address to) a female animal, e.g. a mare or bitch. **M19**.

> B. CASTLE I talked to the lass who represents the young Socialists on the N.E.C.

2 A girlfriend, a sweetheart. **L16**.

> W. COWPER There might ye see . . the shepherd and his lass.

3 A female member of the Salvation Army. Also ***hallelujah lass***. *colloq.* **L19**.
– COMB.: †**lass-lorn** *adjective* forsaken by one's lass or sweetheart.

Lassa /'lasə/ *noun*. **L20**.
[ORIGIN A village in NE Nigeria (where first reported in 1969).]
1 ***Lassa fever***, an acute febrile virus disease that occurs in tropical Africa with a high mortality rate. **L20**.
2 ***Lassa virus***, the virus causing this disease. **L20**.

'lasses /'lasɪz/ *noun*. *US colloq.* **L18**.
[ORIGIN Abbreviation.]
= MOLASSES.

lassi /'lʌsi, 'lasi/ *noun*. **L19**.
[ORIGIN Hindi *lassī*.]
In the Indian subcontinent: a drink made from a buttermilk or yogurt base with water.

lassie /'lasi/ *noun*. Also **lassy**. **E18**.
[ORIGIN from LASS + -IE.]
1 (A term of endearment for) a girl, a young woman. Chiefly *Scot.* **E18**.
2 = LASS 3. *colloq.* **E20**.

lassitude /'lasɪtjuːd/ *noun*. **LME**.
[ORIGIN French from Latin *lassitudo*, from *lassus* weary: see -TUDE.]
Weariness of body or mind; languor; lack of energy resulting from fatigue; disinclination to exert or interest oneself; an instance of this.

> B. GELDOF We were . . doing something new in reaction to the lassitude of the more established bands.

lasso /lə'suː, 'lasəʊ/ *noun & verb*. Also †**laso**, †**lazo**. **M18**.
[ORIGIN Spanish *lazo* (repr. Amer. Spanish pronunc.) = Old French *laz*: see LACE *noun & adjective*.]
▸ **A** *noun*. Pl. **-o(e)s**.
1 A long rope, esp. of untanned hide, with a noose at one end now used chiefly in the western US for catching cattle and wild horses. **M18**.
2 *hist.* A girth placed round a cavalry horse with a lasso or long rope attached, for use in drawing guns etc. Also ***lasso harness***. **M19**.
– COMB.: **lasso-cell** ZOOLOGY a nematocyst or stinging cell of a coelenterate; a similar cell of a ctenophore, which with others exudes a long sticky thread; ***lasso harness***: see sense 2 above.
▸ **B** *verb trans.* **1** Catch (as) with a lasso. **E19**.
2 MILITARY. Draw (guns etc.) with lasso harness. **M19**.
■ **lassoer** *noun* **L19**.

lassock /'lasək/ *noun*. *Scot.* **E19**.
[ORIGIN from LASS + -OCK.]
A little girl.

lassy *noun* var. of LASSIE.

lassy me /ˈlasi miː/ *interjection. slang.* M19.
[ORIGIN Perh. contr. of *Lord save me*.]
Expr. surprise.

last /lɑːst/ *noun*[1].
[ORIGIN Old English *lāst* (masc., sense 1), *lǣst* (fem., sense 2), *lǣste* (sense 3) = Middle Low German *lēst(e*, Dutch *leest*, Old High German *leist* (German *Leisten*) a last, Old Norse *leistr* foot, sock, Gothic *laists* footprint, track, from Germanic base meaning 'follow': cf. LAST *verb*[1].]
†1 A footstep, a track, a trace. Latterly only in ***not a last***, nothing, not at all. OE–L15.
†2 A boot. Only in OE.
3 A shoemaker's model of the foot, for shaping and repairing boots and shoes. OE.
stick to one's last refrain from meddling in matters one does not understand.

last /lɑːst/ *noun*[2].
[ORIGIN Old English *hlæst* = Old Frisian *hlest*, Middle & mod. Low German, Middle Dutch & mod. Dutch *last*, Old High German *hlast* (German *Last*), from West Germanic base repr. also by Old Norse *hlass* load, from Germanic base of LADE *verb*.]
†1 A load, a burden, a weight carried. OE–LME.
2 A commercial denomination of weight, capacity, or quantity, varying for different kinds of goods and in different localities, e.g. 12 sacks of wool, 12 barrels of cod, 10 quarters of malt or grain. ME. ▸†**b** *transf.* A huge indefinite number. LME–E18.
†3 A unit in the measurement of a ship's burden equal to 2 tons (occas. 1 ton). M17–L18.

last /lɑːst/ *noun*[3]. *obsolete* exc. *hist.* LOE.
[ORIGIN Anglo-Latin *lastum*, *lestum* (Domesday Book *lest*), used for LATHE *noun*[1].]
= LATHE *noun*[1]. Also, an administrative assembly in Kent (more fully ***last-court***).

last /lɑːst/ *noun*[4]. ME.
[ORIGIN from LAST *verb*[1].]
1 Continuance, duration. Now *rare*. ME.
2 Power of holding on or out; staying power. E17.

last /lɑːst/ *verb*[1].
[ORIGIN Old English *lǣstan*, corresp. to Old Frisian *lāsta*, *lēsta* fulfil, Old Saxon *lēstian* execute, Old High German, German *leisten* afford, yield, Gothic *laistjan* follow, from Germanic, from base also of LAST *noun*[1].]
†1 *verb trans.* Orig., follow (a leader); pursue (a course, a practice). Later, carry out (a command, a promise); pay (tribute); maintain (peace). OE–L15.
2 *verb intrans.* Of a state of things, a process, a period of time: continue, endure, go on. OE. ▸†**b** With compl. preposition phr.: continue in a specified condition, course of action, etc. ME–M17.

L. HELLMAN We must have had a lot of wine because our lunch lasted long after everybody left. H. BAILEY A short sharp war, which would last perhaps six months. **b** MILTON Whence in perpetual fight they needs must last Endless, and no solution will be found.

3 **a** *verb intrans.* Hold out; continue fresh, unbroken, unimpaired, effective, etc. Of a person (also foll. by *out*): manage to continue in a post, a course of action, etc.; remain alive. ME. ▸**b** *verb trans. & intrans.* Of provisions, resources, etc.: remain sufficient for the needs of (a person etc.) throughout a period. ME. ▸**c** *verb trans.* Continue in vigour as long as or longer than (now usu. foll. by *out*); hold out under or against. ME.

G. GREENE His prose, unlike his poetry, has not lasted well. M. N. COX Is this relief temporary or will it last? W. BOYD If I radically trim my budget I can last for another three weeks. **b** T. F. POWYS Mr Mayhae garnered and stowed away enough humility to last any man a lifetime. P. BOWLES He finished his cigarette slowly, making it last. J. RHYS I've enough cash to last for two or three months.

c ***last the pace***: see PACE *noun*[1].
†4 *verb intrans.* Extend in space; reach, stretch. ME–L16.

last /lɑːst/ *verb*[2] *trans.* E17.
[ORIGIN from LAST *noun*[1].]
Put (a boot or shoe) on a last.

last /lɑːst/ *adverb, adjective, & noun*[5].
[ORIGIN Old English *latost*, (Northumbrian) *lætest*, corresp. to Old Frisian *letast*, *lest*, Old Saxon *latst*, *last*, *letist* (Dutch *laatst*, *lest*, Old High German *lazzōst*, *lezzist* (German *letzt*), Old Norse *latastr*), from Germanic superl. of base of LATE *adjective, adverb*: see -EST[1]. *Latest* is a new formation on *late*.]
▸ **A** *adverb*. **1** After all others in a series; at the end. OE.

E. O'NEILL Paul comes out last carrying an accordion.

2 On the occasion next before the present; most recently. ME.

SHELLEY When did you see him last? W. S. CHURCHILL Nearly ten days have passed since I last addressed you.

3 As the final thing to be mentioned or considered; in the last place, lastly. ME.

SHAKES. *2 Hen. IV* First my fear, then my curtsy, last my speech.

4 In the end, finally. M17.

DRYDEN Pleas'd with his Idol, he . . Adores; and last, the Thing ador'd, desires.

▸ **B** *adjective*. **1** Following all the others in time, order, series, succession, or enumeration; subsequent to all others in occurrence, existence, etc.; *emphatic* last in order of likelihood, suitability, preference, etc. (With a cardinal numeral now placed before the numeral, exc. when in sense 'last-mentioned', formerly usu. after the numeral.) ME. ▸**b** Extreme or remotest in space or position. Formerly also, rearmost. Now *rare*. LME.

H. B. STOWE It's the last night we may be together. E. O'NEILL The cockney seems about to challenge this last statement. E. BOWEN The Major was making his last round through the orchards before shutting up the house. DAY LEWIS She was the last of a clan which had been founded some centuries before. A. WILSON The subject of his wife's illness was the last thing that Bernard wished to discuss. R. K. NARAYAN I . . read the Oxford edition from the first page to the last. *Fast Forward* Uncle Buck is the last person you'd choose to look after the kids.

2 *spec.* Belonging to the final stages, esp. of a person's life or the world's existence; relating to death or the end of the world. ME.

J. H. NEWMAN Hosius . . with his last breath, abjured the heresy. V. BRITTAIN The last moments of men who had died in hospital.

3 Occurring or presenting itself next before the present or existing time; most recent, latest. (With a common noun after *the* or (emphasizing recentness) *this* or *these* or without article or demonstrative; with the name of a month, of a day of the week, etc., placed before or (more formally) after the noun.) ME.

MARVELL Having writ to you last post. R. GRAVES It was half-past three On Easter Tuesday last. M. BRADBURY Howard had fetched it last time. M. AMIS These last few days I've had no time for reading.

4 Remaining or arrived at after others have disappeared or have been removed, exhausted, or spent; the only remaining. LME.

M. DICKENS She . . would count the change to the last halfpenny. J. KRANTZ Vito waited until the last man had left.

5 Reaching its ultimate limit; attaining a degree beyond which one cannot go; utmost, extreme. Now chiefly in ***of the last importance***. LME.

LD MACAULAY Their Church was suffering the last excess of injury and insult. J. P. MAHAFFY Rowing . . was of the last importance in their naval warfare.

6 After which there is nothing to be done or said; final, conclusive, definitive. Now only in ***last word*** below. M17.

S. JOHNSON Whatever shall be the last decision of the law.

▸ **C** *absol.* as *noun*. **1** After prepositions, esp. *at*: the last point of time, the end (see phrs. below). ME.
2 The last person or thing of a category, series, etc.; the one coming at the end of a series arranged in order of rank or estimation, the lowest. (Foll. by *of*.) LME.

POPE Oh may some spark of your celestial fire The last, the meanest of your sons inspire. J. K. JEROME To give the lad time between each lesson to forget what he learned at the last.

3 *spec.* The last day or last moments of life; the end of life, death. Chiefly with possess. LME.

C. J. LEVER As he drew nigh his last his sufferings gave little intervals of rest.

4 *The* concluding, last remaining, or most recent part *of* a thing; *spec.* (now *N. Amer.*) *the* last day *of* a month. M16.

E. O'NEILL Turin comes in . . and overhears the last of her prayer. DYLAN THOMAS She's down to the last of the elderflower wine.

5 With a demonstrative, relative, etc., adjective: the last-mentioned person or thing. M16.

W. DAMPIER With a Fireship and 3 Tenders, which last had not a constant crew.

6 With possess. adjective: one's last performance of a certain act (implied by the verb). Esp. in ***breathe one's last*** (sc. *one's last breath*). L16.

ADDISON The swans . . now sung their last, and dy'd.

7 With a possess.: a person's most recent letter. Now chiefly in commercial use. L16.

W. CONGREVE By your last from Dublin I may guess this will find you at Kilkenny.

8 *The* last mention or sight of a person or thing. Esp. in ***hear the last of***, ***see the last of***. *colloq.* M19.

– SPECIAL COLLOCATIONS, PHRASES, & COMB. (of adverb, adjective, & noun): **at last** in the end, finally; after a long time, at length. **at long last** eventually but only after much delay. **at the last** *arch.* = *at last* above. **at the long last** (now *rare* or *obsolete*) = *at long last* above. ***every last***: see EVERY *adjective* 1. ***first and last***: see FIRST *adverb*. ***first or last***: see FIRST *adverb*. **four last things** (THEOLOGY) *the* four things (death, judgement, heaven, and hell) studied in eschatology. ***from first to last***: see FIRST *noun*. ***have the last laugh***: see LAUGH *noun*. **if it's the last thing I do** (in emphasizing one's intention or desire to do a thing) even if I die after doing that. †**in the last** *rare* finally, in the end. ***in the last analysis***: see ANALYSIS 1. **last across (the road)** a children's game in which the object is to be the last to cross a road (or railway) in the path of an approaching vehicle (or train). ***last assize(s)***: see ASSIZE *noun* 3. **last but not least** last in order of mention or occurrence but not of importance. **last but one** (the one) immediately preceding the final or most recent. **last but two** (the) next but one before the final or most recent. **last day** (**a**) (now *dial.*) yesterday; (**b**) (*Last Day*) *the* Day of Judgement. **last days** (**a**) *the* concluding period in the life or history *of* a person etc.; (**b**) *the* period including and immediately preceding the Last Judgement. ***last ditch***: see DITCH *noun*. **last-ditch** *adjective* (of opposition, resistance, etc.) maintained to the end; (of an effort etc.) made at the last minute in an attempt to avert disaster. **last end** *arch. & dial.* the very end; *esp.* the end of life, death. **last evening** yesterday evening. ***last gasp***: see GASP *noun*. †**last hand** the finishing touches. **last home** the grave. ***last honours***: see HONOUR *noun*. **last hurrah** (orig. *US*) the final act in a politician's career; *transf.* any final performance or effort. **last in, first out** (**a**) (of a system of employment) in which those most recently recruited are the first to be made redundant; (**b**) (of a system of accounting) in which the goods most recently acquired by a company are valued as though they are the first to be sold; (**c**) COMPUTING (designating or pertaining to) a procedure in which the item removed from a buffer, queue, etc., is always the one most recently added. ***Last Judgement***: see JUDGEMENT 2. ***last lap***: see LAP *noun*[3]. **last man** CRICKET the batsman who goes in to bat last. **last minute** the time immediately before a critical event. **last-minute** *adjective* performed, occurring, bought, etc. at the latest possible time. **last moment** = *last minute* above. **last-moment** *adjective* = *last-minute adjective* above. †**last morning** yesterday morning. **last name** a surname. **last night** yesterday night. ***last office(s)***: see OFFICE *noun* 5. ***last of the Mohicans***: see MOHICAN *noun*. †**last past** (**a**) (with dates) = sense B.3 above; (**b**) (of a period of time) extending to the present, (the) past (year etc.). ***last post***: see POST *noun*[6]. ***last quarter***: see QUARTER *noun* 7b. ***last resort***: see RESORT *noun*. **last rites**, **last sacraments** (ROMAN CATHOLIC CHURCH) *the* sacraments (the Eucharist and extreme unction) administered to the dying. ***last sleep***: see SLEEP *noun*. ***last straw***: see STRAW *noun*. **Last Supper**: eaten by Jesus and his disciples on the eve of the Crucifixion. **last thing (at night)** as one's final act before going to bed. **last things** = *four last things* above. **last trump** the trumpet call that some believe will wake the dead on the Day of Judgement. ***last will and testament***: see WILL *noun*[1]. **last word** (**a**) *the* final pronouncement on a subject, after which there is nothing more to be said; ***have the last word***, speak in such a way as to close an argument; (**b**) (*fig.*) *the* finest, most advanced, etc., example of its kind; *the* latest fashion. **last words** a person's last recorded remark before dying; ***famous last words***, (an ironical comment on or rejoinder to) an overconfident or boastful assertion that may well be proved wrong by events. ***on one's last legs***: see LEG *noun*. ***pay one's last respects***: see RESPECT *noun*. **second last** = *last but one* above. ***Seven Last Words***: see WORD *noun*. ***the last rose***: see ROSE *noun*. **third last** = *last but two* above. **to the last** up to the end; *esp.* up to the last moment of life.

lastage /ˈlɑːstɪdʒ/ *noun. obsolete* exc. *hist.* LME.
[ORIGIN Anglo-Norman, Old French & mod. French *lestage* (medieval Latin *lestagium*), from *lest* LAST *noun*[2].]
1 A toll payable by traders attending fairs and markets. LME.
†2 The ballast of a ship. LME–M18.
3 A payment for liberty to load a ship; a port duty levied at so much per last of cargo. LME.

laster /ˈlɑːstə/ *noun*[1]. E18.
[ORIGIN from LAST *verb*[1] + -ER[1].]
A person who or thing which lasts; *spec.* (**a**) a fruit that keeps well; (**b**) a person who has staying power.

laster /ˈlɑːstə/ *noun*[2]. L19.
[ORIGIN from LAST *noun*[1] or *verb*[2] + -ER[1].]
A worker who shapes a boot or shoe by fixing the parts smoothly on a last.

Lastex /ˈlastɛks/ *noun*. Also **l-**. M20.
[ORIGIN from E)LAST(IC + -*ex* (arbitrary ending).]
(Proprietary name for) an elastic yarn formed from a combination of rubber or man-made elastomeric fibres with silk, cotton, or rayon, used in the manufacture of corsetry etc.

lasting /ˈlɑːstɪŋ/ *noun*[1]. ME.
[ORIGIN from LAST *verb*[1] + -ING[1].]
The action of LAST *verb*[1]; continuance, duration, permanence.
– COMB.: **lasting power** staying power.

lasting /ˈlɑːstɪŋ/ *adjective & noun*[2]. ME.
[ORIGIN from LAST *verb*[1] + -ING[2].]
▸ **A** *adjective*. **1** Of long continuance, persistent; permanent, enduring. In early use freq. everlasting. ME.

M. FITZHERBERT Deep & lasting friendships. M. SCAMMELL His decision was to make a lasting impression on Solzhenitsyn.

2 Of a material substance: durable. Formerly, of provisions, fruit, etc.: keeping well. ME.

G. BERKELEY Our black cloth is neither so lasting, nor of so good a dye as the Dutch.

3 Of a racehorse: possessed of staying power. *slang.* E19.
▸ **B** *absol.* as *noun*. A durable kind of cloth; = EVERLASTING *noun* 3. M18.
■ **lastingly** *adverb* ME. **lastingness** *noun* ME.

lastly /ˈlɑːstli/ *adverb*. LME.
[ORIGIN from LAST *adjective* + -LY[2].]
1 At the end; finally. Now only, as the last in a series of items, operations, points in a discourse, etc.; in conclusion. LME.

T. HARDY A coat was laid on . . ; then another coat for increased blackness; and lastly a third.

†2 Very lately, recently. L16–M17.
†3 Decisively, once and for all. E–M17.

L

MILTON I for his sake will leave Thy bosom . . and for him lastly die.

lasya /ˈlɑːsjə/ *noun*. M20.
[ORIGIN Sanskrit *lāsya*.]
A graceful Indian style of female dancing.

lat /lɑːt/ *noun*[1]. E19.
[ORIGIN Hindi *lāṭh*, *lāṭ*.]
1 A staff, a pole. *rare*. E19.
2 An obelisk or a columnar monument in the Indian subcontinent; *spec.* any of the ancient Buddhist columns of Eastern India. L19.

lat /lɑːt/ *noun*[2]. Pl. **lati** /ˈlɑti/, **lats**. E20.
[ORIGIN from 1st syll. of *Latvija* Latvia.]
A unit of gold currency established by the state of Latvia in August 1922 and discontinued in 1941.

lat /lat/ *noun*[3]. *slang*. E20.
[ORIGIN Abbreviation.]
= LATRINE. Usu. in *pl.*

lat /lat/ *noun*[4]. *slang*. M20.
[ORIGIN Abbreviation.]
= LATISSIMUS. Usu. in *pl.*

lat *noun*[5] see LATH *noun*.

lat. *abbreviation*.
Latitude.

Latakia /latəˈkiːə/ *noun*. E19.
[ORIGIN See below.]
In full ***Latakia tobacco***. A fine kind of tobacco produced near and shipped from Latakia, a port in Syria.

latania /ləˈteɪnɪə, ləˈtanɪə/ *noun*. L18.
[ORIGIN In sense 1 from Spanish Amer. In sense 2 from mod. Latin (see below) from French LATANIER, the name used in Mauritius.]
1 = LATANIER 1. *US*. L18.
2 Any of several fan palms of the genus *Latania*, native to Mauritius and neighbouring islands. M19.

latanier /ləˈtanɪə/ *noun*. E19.
[ORIGIN French: cf. LATANIA.]
1 Any of several fan palms found in the southern US and Central America; *esp.* the cabbage palmetto, *Sabal palmetto*. *US*. E19.
2 (The Mauritian name for) any of several fan palms; *esp.* = LATANIA 2. E20.

L

latch /latʃ/ *noun*[1]. ME.
[ORIGIN In sense 1 prob. from LATCH *verb*[1]. In sense 2 prob. from Old French *lache* var. of *laz* LACE *noun*: cf. LATCHET *noun*[1].]
1 A fastening for a door or gate, consisting of a small bar which falls or slides into a catch, and is lifted by a lever, string, etc., from outside. Now also (more fully ***night-latch***), a small spring lock for an outer door, which catches when the door is closed and is worked from the outside by a key. ME.

B. BEHAN Someone pushed the door but the latch was on, and he had to knock.

off the latch unlatched, ajar. **on the latch** fastened by a latch only, not locked.

2 **a** A loop or noose for securing a thing; a snare. Also, a leather thong. *obsolete* exc. *dial.* LME. ▸**b** ELECTRONICS. A logic circuit which retains whatever output state results from a momentary input signal until reset by another signal (also ***latch circuit***). Also called ***toggle circuit***, ***toggle***. M20.

– COMB.: **latch bolt** a spring-loaded bolt; ***latch circuit***: see sense 2b above; **latchkey** a key to open the spring lock of an outer door; ***latchkey child***, a child given such a key as a means of entering home after school while his or her parents are still out at work; **latch-string** a string fastened to a latch and passed through a hole in the door, so that the latch may be raised from outside; *esp.* (*US*) such a string left hanging out as a sign of welcome.

†**latch** *noun*[2] see LURCH *noun*[3].

latch /latʃ/ *verb*[1].
[ORIGIN Old English *læċċan* from Germanic, from base rel. to those of Greek *lazesthai*, Latin *laqueus* noose.]
†1 *verb trans.* Take hold of, grasp, seize, esp. with the hand or claws; clasp, embrace; *fig.* grasp with the mind, comprehend. OE–E17. ▸†**b** Put or strike swiftly *off*, *out*, *up*; dart *out* (the tongue). ME–M16.
†2 *verb trans.* Take with force; capture, seize (a person, goods). OE–M16.
3 *verb trans.* Be the recipient of, get, receive. Now only (*dial.*), become infected with, catch (a disease). ME.

SHAKES. *Macb.* I have words That would be howl'd out in the desert air, Where hearing should not latch them.

4 *verb trans.* Intercept the fall of, catch (something falling); catch or receive *in* (a receptacle). *obsolete* exc. *dial.* M16.
5 *verb intrans.* Alight, settle. *dial.* E19.
6 *verb intrans.* Foll. by *on* (adverb): (***a***) attach oneself *to* a person as a constant companion; give one's adherence *to* an idea etc.; (***b***) get wise (*to* a fact etc.), understand. *colloq.* (orig. *US*). M20.

New Yorker Mr. Kelly has latched on to a sound . . idea.

– COMB.: **latch-pan** (chiefly *dial.*) a pan placed under a joint to catch the drippings.

latch /latʃ/ *verb*[2]. LME.
[ORIGIN from LATCH *noun*[1].]
1 *verb trans.* Fasten or secure with a latch. LME.

P. THEROUX The shutters of the hut were down and latched.

2 *verb intrans.* Of a door etc.: shut so that the latch catches. M20.

T. S. ELIOT Please *shut the door after you*, so it latches.

latchet /ˈlatʃɪt/ *noun*[1]. LME.
[ORIGIN Old French *lachet* var. of *lacet*, from *laz* LACE *noun*: see -ET[1].]
1 A narrow strip of something; a loop. Now only (*Scot.*), a loop of string used to keep a bricklayer's line horizontal; a tingle. LME.
2 *spec.* A narrow thong or lace for fastening a shoe or sandal. Now *arch.* (esp. in allusion to *Mark* 1:7) & *dial.* LME.

AV *Mark* 1:7 There commeth one mightier than I after me, the latchet of whose shooes I am not worthy to stoupe downe, and vnloose.

†3 NAUTICAL. = LASKET. L15–E17.

latchet /ˈlatʃɪt/ *noun*[2]. Also **-ett**. L19.
[ORIGIN Unknown.]
The European red gurnard, *Aspitrigla cuculus*. Also (*Austral.*), a flying gurnard, *Pterygotrigla polyommata*.

latching /ˈlatʃɪŋ/ *noun*. LME.
[ORIGIN from LATCH *verb*[1] + -ING[1].]
†1 The action of LATCH *verb*[1]. Only in LME.
2 NAUTICAL. = LASKET. Also ***latchings key***. Usu. in *pl.* L18.

late /leɪt/ *noun*[1]. Long *obsolete* exc. *Scot.* Also **lait**. ME.
[ORIGIN Partly from Old Norse *lát* letting (as in *blóð-lát* blood-letting), (in pl.) manners, sounds, partly from Old Norse *læte* (only in nom. & accus.) manner, sound, both from Germanic base of LET *verb*[1].]
†1 Appearance, aspect; outward manner or bearing. ME–L15.
2 In *pl.* Manners, behaviour; *esp.* unruly behaviour or actions, goings-on. ME.
†3 Voice, sound. Only in ME.

late /leɪt/ *adjective* & *noun*[2]. Compar. **later**, LATTER; superl. **latest**, LAST *adjective*.
[ORIGIN Old English *læt* = Old Frisian *let*, Old Saxon *lat*, Old High German *laz* (German *lass*), Old Norse *latr*, Gothic *lats*, from Germanic, from Indo-European base repr. also by Latin *lassus* weary: rel. to LET *verb*[2].]
▸**A** *adjective* **I 1** Slow, tardy; tedious. Now *dial.* OE.
2 Occurring, coming, or being after the proper, right, or customary time; delayed or deferred in time. Freq. *impers.* in ***it is late***, ***it was too late***, etc. (Foll. by *for*, *to do*.) OE. ▸**b** Of a plant, fruit, etc.: flowering or ripening at an advanced season of the year. LME. ▸**c** Of a fruit etc.: backward in ripening. Of a season: prolonged or deferred beyond its proper time. M17. ▸**d** Of a woman: whose menstrual period has failed to occur at the expected time. *colloq.* M20.

E. WAUGH Trust me . . . It is not too late to escape. J. STALLWORTHY Light woke me early, but the trams were late. A. MACLEAN I was quite ten minutes late for my appointment. **b** *Stock & Land* (*Melbourne*) There are still some late sunflowers to be harvested. **c** D. H. LAWRENCE If the season is late . . then mid-September sees the corn still standing in stook.

too late a week: see WEEK *noun*.

3 (Occurring) far on in the course of the day, esp. well on into the evening or night (freq. *impers.* in ***it is late*** etc.). Also (*colloq.*), of a person: keeping late hours, going to bed late. OE.

G. GREENE Once the iron roof crumpled as a late vulture settled for the night. J. OSBORNE It is late afternoon, the end of a hot day. M. AYRTON This . . documentary, intended for late showing when children . . are presumed to be in bed. W. WHARTON It's getting late, time for the old man to go home.

4 Belonging to an advanced stage in a period, the development of a person or thing, the history of a science, language, etc. LME. ▸**b** *attrib.* Of a period, season, etc.: that is at an advanced stage. Also, of a writer, composer, etc.: that is writing, composing, etc., at an advanced stage in his or her artistic development. L18.

D. ROCK Late but beautiful Flemish stained glass. H. H. FURNESS *The Tragedie of Coriolanus* is classed among the late plays [of Shakespeare]. **b** J. M. MURRY The late autumn of 1818. V. S. NAIPAUL He was in his late thirties. *Listener* This prevents him from over-praising early Waugh at the expense of late. D. ROWE Devastating childhood experiences which laid the foundations for anxiety and panic attacks in later life.

b the late Bronze Age, ***late Victorian times***, etc.

5 **a** Of a person: recently deceased. LME. ▸**b** That was recently (the holder of an office etc.) but is not now. LME.

a A. BROOKNER Her late husband was a Wing Commander in the Royal Air Force. **b** A. J. TOYNBEE Brasilia . . is only about 600 miles from the late capital, Rio de Janeiro.

6 Recent in date; that has recently happened or occurred; recently made, performed, completed; of recent times; belonging to a recent period. Now chiefly in ***of late years***. LME.

T. HARDY Stables fitted with every late appliance.

▸**II** Special uses of superl. ***latest***.

7 = LAST *adjective*. Now *arch.* & *poet.* LME.

SOUTHEY I had her latest look of earthly love, I felt her hands last pressure.

8 Most recent; newest, most up to date. L16.

A. TOFFLER Doctors . . complain that they cannot keep up with the latest developments. M. MOORCOCK Accordions . . would play the tunes of the moment, as well as the latest songs from France.

– SPECIAL COLLOCATIONS & COMB.: **late blight** a disease of potatoes caused by the fungus *Phytophthora infestans*; = ***potato blight*** s.v. POTATO *noun*. **latecomer** a person who arrives late; a recent arrival, a newcomer. **late cut** CRICKET a cut, but with the actual stroke delayed until after the usual moment. **late dinner** (esp. in Victorian society) the main evening meal, held later than the children's dinner. **late fee** an increased fee paid in order to secure the dispatch of a letter posted after the advertised time of collection. **late hours**: after most people have gone to bed; esp. in ***keep late hours***. ***late Latin***: see LATIN *noun*. **late licence** a licence allowing a public house, nightclub, etc., to serve alcohol beyond the usual hours. **late mark**: indicating that a pupil is late for school. **late-model** *adjective* (*N. Amer.*, of a car) recently made. **late night** a night when one goes to bed after the usual time. **late-tackling** (FOOTBALL etc.) tackling an opponent illegally, when he or she is no longer in possession of the ball. **late unpleasantness** *the* war that took place recently; *spec.* (*US*) *the* American Civil War. **late wood** a denser section of the annual ring of a tree, formed late in the growing season.

▸**B** *noun*. The fact of being late or recent. Chiefly & now only in ***of late***, lately, recently. ME.

■ **lateness** *noun* OE.

late /leɪt/ *adverb*. Compar. **later**; superl. **latest**, LAST *adverb*.
[ORIGIN Old English *late* = Old High German *laz*, *lazzo*, from *lat-* stem of Old English *læt* LATE *adjective*.]
†1 Slowly. OE–LME.
2 At or to an advanced stage in a period, esp. of the day, the year, or a lifetime. Also, after the proper or expected time. OE. ▸**b** In compar.: at a later stage within a period; subsequently. Also ***later on***. M16. ▸**c** In *compar.* as *interjection*. [Ellipt. for (*I'll*) *see you later*.] Farewell for the present. *US slang*. M20.

J. BUCHAN The snow lay late that year. C. P. SNOW I got back from Germany late in September. B. PYM A middle-aged man who had been ordained late in life. L. CODY The show started ten minutes late. *Proverb*: Better late than never. **b** M. WEST Merdelius promised to call later in the week. R. ELLMANN Neither now nor later would he hesitate to take risks.

3 At or to a late hour of the day; *esp.* (until) far on in the evening or night. ME.

V. WOOLF His mother had taken him for a burglar when he came home late. N. MITFORD The day after a dance, Nancy was allowed to sleep late.

4 **a** Recently, of late, not long ago. Now *poet.* ME. ▸**b** Not long since (but not now); recently (but no longer). Cf. LATE *adjective* 5b. LME.

a BYRON To Ianthe, Those climes where I have late been straying. **b** *Daily Telegraph* His father is robustly played by John Paul, late of 'Doomwatch'.

– PHRASES: ***early and late***: see EARLY *adverb*. ***late in the day***: see DAY *noun*. ***soon or late***: see SOON *adverb*. ***sooner or later***: see SOON *adverb*.

lated /ˈleɪtɪd/ *adjective*. *poet.* L16.
[ORIGIN from LATE *adjective* + -ED[1].]
= BELATED.

lateen /ləˈtiːn/ *adjective* & *noun*. Also **latine**, **latteen**. M16.
[ORIGIN French *latine* (in *voile latine* Latin sail, so named as used in the Mediterranean) fem. of *latin* LATIN *adjective*.]
▸**A** *adjective*. Designating a triangular sail suspended by a long yard at an angle of about 45 degrees to the mast, or a vessel, yard, etc., possessing or used with such a sail. M16.
lateen mizzen, ***lateen rig***, etc.
▸**B** *noun*. A lateener. M19.
■ **lateener** *noun* a vessel with a lateen rig L19.

lateish *adjective* & *adverb* var. of LATISH.

lately /ˈleɪtli/ *adverb*. OE.
[ORIGIN from LATE *adjective* + -LY[2].]
†1 Slowly, tardily, sluggishly; reluctantly, sparingly. OE–LME.
2 Within recent times; recently, of late. L15.

N. COWARD What have you been doing lately? During these last years? J. KRANTZ Lately he had taken to waking in the night.

†3 After the usual or proper time; at a late hour, late. E16–E17.

latemost /ˈleɪtməʊst/ *adjective*. Now *arch.* *rare*. OE.
[ORIGIN from LATE *adjective* + -MOST.]
Last.

laten /ˈleɪt(ə)n/ *verb intrans.* & *trans.* L19.
[ORIGIN from LATE *adjective* + -EN[5].]
Become or make late.

latency /ˈleɪt(ə)nsi/ *noun*. M17.
[ORIGIN from LATENT *adjective*: see -ENCY.]
1 Latent condition, nature, or existence; *spec.* in BIOLOGY, that of a disposition or faculty which remains concealed until the necessary conditions for its development are supplied. M17. ▸**b** In psychoanalytic theory: a condition when sexual feelings are held to be sublimated or

repressed, lasting from the age of five to puberty. Freq. in *latency period*. E20.
2 a Delay between a stimulus and a response, esp. in muscle; a latent period. L19. ▸**b** *COMPUTING*. More fully ***latency time***. The delay before a transfer of data begins following an instruction for its transfer, esp. to or from a rotating storage device. M20.

La Tène /la ˈtɛn/ *adjective*. L19.
[ORIGIN A district at the east end of the Lake of Neuchâtel, Switzerland, where remains of this culture were first discovered.]
Designating or pertaining to a culture (lasting from the 5th to the 1st cent. BC) of the second Iron Age of central and western Europe, and the style of art associated with it.

lateness /ˈleɪtnɪs/ *noun*. OE.
[ORIGIN from LATE *adjective* + -NESS.]
The quality or condition of being late, esp. of being advanced in a period or behind the proper time.

latensification /leɪˌtɛnsɪfɪˈkeɪʃ(ə)n/ *noun*. M20.
[ORIGIN from LATENT *adjective* + INTENSIFICATION.]
PHOTOGRAPHY. Intensification of an existing latent image on a photographic film or plate by treatment with a chemical, prolonged exposure to light, or other means.

latent /ˈleɪt(ə)nt/ *adjective & noun*. LME.
[ORIGIN Latin *latent-* pres. ppl stem of *latere* lie hidden: see -ENT.]
▸ **A** *adjective*. **1** Hidden, concealed; present or existing, but not manifest, exhibited, or developed. (Now esp. of a quality, formerly also of a material thing.) Opp. ***patent***. LME. ▸**b** That is really but not overtly what is implied by the noun; disguised. M17.

> M. L. KING Often white liberals are unaware of their latent prejudices. A. FRASER Troubles . . had certainly brought out in him virtues which might otherwise have remained latent. **b** Z. TOMIN I suppose that at best I am a very latent bisexual.

2 *MEDICINE*. Of a disease: in which the usual symptoms are not (yet) manifest. L17.
3 Of a fingerprint: of a kind not normally visible to the naked eye. E20.
– SPECIAL COLLOCATIONS: **latent ambiguity** *LAW* a doubt as to the meaning of a document, not patent from the document itself, but raised by the evidence of some extrinsic and collateral matter. **latent energy** = *potential energy* s.v. POTENTIAL *adjective*. **latent heat**: required to convert a solid into a liquid, or a liquid into a vapour, without change of temperature. **latent image** *PHOTOGRAPHY* the invisible image formed in a photographic emulsion by exposure and rendered visible by development. **latent learning** *PSYCHOLOGY*: that has taken place without any incentive (such as rewards or punishments) and is not manifested until there is a goal to be achieved. **latent partner**: whose name does not appear as a member of a firm or company. **latent period**: between a stimulus and a response, esp. (*a*) *MEDICINE* between infection (or exposure to radiation) and the manifestation of symptoms; (*b*) *PHYSIOLOGY* between a stimulus (as the arrival of a nerve impulse) and the response. **latent root** *MATH*. an eigenvalue of a matrix. **latent virus**: causing no apparent disease in one organism but capable of doing so when transmitted to another.
▸ **B** *noun*. A latent fingerprint. E20.
▪ **latently** *adverb* M16. **latentness** *noun* M17.

later *adjective, adverb* see LATE *adjective, adverb*.

-later /lətə/ *suffix*.
[ORIGIN Greek *-latrēs* worshipper.]
Used (usu. preceded by **-o-**) to form agent nouns with the sense '(excessive) worshipper' corresp. to abstract nouns in ***-latry***, as ***idolater***, ***Mariolater***, ***bardolater***.

laterad /ˈlatərad/ *adverb*. Now *rare*. E19.
[ORIGIN from Latin *later-*, *latus* side + -AD[3].]
ANATOMY. Towards the side.

lateral /ˈlat(ə)r(ə)l/ *adjective, noun, & verb*. LME.
[ORIGIN Latin *lateralis*, from *later-*, *latus* side: see -AL[1].]
▸ **A** *adjective*. **1** Of or pertaining to the side or sides; situated at or issuing from the side or sides; towards the side, directed sideways. LME.
†**2** Existing or moving side by side. Of winds: coming from the same half (eastern or western) of the horizon. E–M17.
3 a *ANATOMY & ZOOLOGY*. Situated on one side or other of an organ or organism, esp. in the region furthest from the median plane. (Foll. by *to*.) Opp. ***medial***. E18. ▸**b** *MEDICINE*. Of a disease or condition: affecting the side or sides of the body; confined to one side of the body. E18. ▸**c** *CRYSTALLOGRAPHY*. Designating or pertaining to those axes of a crystal (form) which are inclined to the main or vertical axis. E19. ▸**d** *PHYSICS*. Acting or placed at right angles to the line of motion or of strain. E19.
4 Designating or pertaining to a branch of a family descended from a brother or sister of a person in direct line. L18.
5 *PHONETICS*. Of (articulation of) a consonant (e.g. English *l*): formed by or involving partial closure of the air passage by the tongue, which is so placed as to allow the breath to flow on one or both sides of the point of contact. M19.
– SPECIAL COLLOCATIONS & COMB.: **lateral-cut** *adjective* (of a gramophone record) with undulations made by a cutting stylus that moved from side to side (opp. ***hill and dale*** s.v. HILL *noun*). **lateral line (system)** a system of organs in fish and aquatic amphibians situated on the head and along the sides of the body and sensitive to vibrations and pressure changes. ***lateral malleolus***: see MALLEOLUS 2. **lateral moraine**: situated at the side of a glacier. **lateral plate** *BIOLOGY* the unsegmented ventral part of the mesoderm in the early vertebrate embryo. **lateral thinking** a way of thinking which seeks the solution to intractable problems through unorthodox methods, or elements which would normally be ignored by logical thinking. **lateral ventricle** *ANATOMY* each of two fluid-filled chambers in the centre of each cerebral hemisphere of the brain.
▸ **B** *noun*. †**1** Each of two or more lateral winds. Only in M17.
2 A lateral or side part, branch, tooth, projection, etc. M18.
3 *PHONETICS*. A lateral consonant. M20.
4 *AMER. FOOTBALL*. A sideways pass. M20.
▸ **C** *verb intrans*. Infl. **-ll-**, ***-l-**. *AMER. FOOTBALL*. Make a sideways pass. M20.

lateralise *verb* var. of LATERALIZE.

laterality /latəˈralɪti/ *noun*. M17.
[ORIGIN from LATERAL *adjective* + -ITY.]
1 The quality of having (distinct) sides, (right- or left-) sidedness; *spec*. the dominance of the right-hand or left-hand member of a pair of bodily organs as regards a particular activity or function (such as the hands in writing, or the cerebral hemispheres in controlling speech). M17.
2 *PHONETICS*. Lateral articulation. M20.

lateralize /ˈlat(ə)rəlʌɪz/ *verb trans*. Also **-ise**. M19.
[ORIGIN from LATERAL *adjective* + -IZE.]
1 Move to the side; place in a lateral position. Chiefly as ***lateralized*** *ppl adjective*. M19.
2 In *pass*. Be largely under the control of one (usu. specified) side of the brain. M20.
3 *PHONETICS*. Make (a consonant) lateral. Chiefly as ***lateralized*** *ppl adjective*. M20.
▪ **laterali'zation** *noun* laterality, esp. of cerebral activity; diagnostic localization of a lesion or pathological process to one or other side of the brain; the property of being lateralized: E20.

laterally /ˈlat(ə)rəli/ *adverb*. LME.
[ORIGIN from LATERAL *adjective* + -LY[2].]
At, to, or from the side; in a lateral or sideways direction.

lateralwards /ˈlat(ə)r(ə)lwədz/ *adverb*. E20.
[ORIGIN from LATERAL *adjective* + -WARDS.]
ANATOMY. Laterally; to or from the median plane of the body.
▪ Also **lateralward** *adverb* M20.

Lateran /ˈlat(ə)rən/ *adjective*. ME.
[ORIGIN Latin *Laterana*, *-um*, from the ancient Roman family of the Plautii *Laterani*.]
Of or pertaining to a district of Rome, originally the site of a palace belonging to the Plautii Laterani, afterwards the palace of the popes of the same name, and a cathedral church dedicated to St John; *spec*. designating or pertaining to each of the five general councils of the Western Church held in the Lateran Palace between 1123 and 1512.

latera recta *noun phr*. pl. of LATUS RECTUM.

laterisation *noun* var. of LATERIZATION.

laterite /ˈlatərʌɪt/ *noun*. E19.
[ORIGIN from Latin *later* brick + -ITE[1].]
A clayey (usu. red) soil or soil horizon characterized by a high proportion of sesquioxides, esp. of aluminium and iron, and a low proportion of bases and silica, formed by chemical weathering in tropical and subtropical regions; *esp*. one which hardens or has hardened on exposure to air; *loosely* any of various other reddish or iron-rich surface materials in the tropics and subtropics.
▪ **lateritic** /latəˈrɪtɪk/ *adjective* resembling, of the nature of, or approaching the composition of laterite M19.

lateritious /latəˈrɪʃəs/ *adjective*. Now *rare*. M17.
[ORIGIN from Latin *lateritius*, *-icius*, from *later* brick: see -ITIOUS[1].]
Chiefly *MEDICINE*, of urinary deposits: of the colour of brick, brick-red.

lateritization /ˌlat(ə)rɪtʌɪˈzeɪʃ(ə)n/ *noun*. Also **-isation**. E20.
[ORIGIN from LATERITE + -IZATION.]
The formation of laterite and lateritic soils; the weathering or soil-forming process that results in this.
▪ **'lateritize** *verb trans*. convert into laterite (usu. in *pass*.) E20.

laterization /latərʌɪˈzeɪʃ(ə)n/ *noun*. Also **-isation**. E20.
[ORIGIN formed as LATERITIZATION.]
= LATERITIZATION.
▪ **'laterize** *verb trans*. = LATERITIZE E20.

latero- /ˈlatərəʊ/ *combining form*.
[ORIGIN from Latin *later-*, *latus* side + -O-.]
Forming words with the senses 'pertaining to the side (and another part), pertaining to the side of (a specified structure)', as ***latero-anterior***, ***latero-cervical***, ***latero-posterior***, *adjectives*, 'on or towards the side', as ***lateroflexion***, ***lateroversion***.
▪ **latero'flexion** *noun* (*ANATOMY*) abnormal bending or curvature to one side M19. **latero'version** *noun* (*ANATOMY*) abnormal displacement (of an organ, esp. the uterus) to one side M19.

laters /ˈleɪtəz/ *interjection*. *colloq*. (chiefly *N. Amer*.). L20.
[ORIGIN from *later* (compar. of LATE *adjective*, *adverb*) + -S[3].]
Goodbye for now; see you later.

lates /ˈleɪtiːz/ *noun*. Pl. same. M20.
[ORIGIN mod. Latin from Greek *latos* Nile perch.]
A fish of the genus *Lates*, comprising large percoid food fishes; *esp*. = ***NILE perch***.

latest /ˈleɪtɪst/ *noun*. L19.
[ORIGIN Absol. use of superl. of LATE *adjective*.]
1 The most advanced possible hour, the most distant possible date. Only in ***at latest***, ***at the latest***. L19.
2 *The* most recent news, fashion, etc. With possess.: a person's most recent achievement, (esp. reprehensible) action, etc. *colloq*. L19.
latest word: see WORD *noun*.

latest *adjective, adverb* see LATE *adjective, adverb*.

late wake /ˈleɪtweɪk/ *noun*. E18.
[ORIGIN Alt. of LYKE WAKE after LATE *adjective*.]
= LYKE WAKE.

†**lateward** *adverb & adjective*. LME.
[ORIGIN from LATE *adjective* + -WARD.]
▸ **A** *adverb*. **1** Of late, recently. LME–M17.
2 Late, after the proper time or season. L16–M17.
▸ **B** *adjective*. Late, slow; *esp*. (of fruit, a crop, etc.) late in maturing, (of a season) backward. LME–M18.

latex /ˈleɪtɛks/ *noun & adjective*. Pl. **latexes**, **latices** /ˈleɪtɪsiːz/. M17.
[ORIGIN Latin = liquid, fluid.]
▸ **A** *noun*. †**1** *MEDICINE*. Any of various body fluids; *esp*. the watery part of the blood and other secretions. M17–M18.
2 *BOTANY*. A milky liquid found in many plants, e.g. of the poppy, spurge, and dogbane families, which exudes when the plant is cut and coagulates on exposure to the air; *spec*. that of *Hevea brasiliensis* or other plants used to produce rubber. M19.
3 A dispersion in water of particles of a polymer that is formed during polymerization and is used to make paints, coatings, etc. M20.
▸ **B** *attrib*. or as *adjective*. Consisting of or containing latex; pertaining to latex. L19.
latex paint: having a latex as its binding medium.

lath /lɑːθ/ *noun*. Pl. **-ths** /-θs, -ðz/. Also (earlier, now *dial*.) **lat** /lat/.
[ORIGIN Old English *lætt* (corresp. to Middle Dutch *latte*, Dutch *lat*, German dial. *Latz*), *lat*; repl. in Middle English in general use by forms with *-þþ-* (prob. already in Old English, corresp. to Old High German *latta* (German *Latte*)).]
1 A thin narrow strip of wood; *spec*. one used to form a groundwork upon which to fasten the slates or tiles of a roof or the plaster of a wall or ceiling, or in the construction of latticework or trelliswork and Venetian blinds. OE. ▸**b** Wood or metal in thin narrow strips, used in building (chiefly as a groundwork for a coating of plaster) to form a wall or partition. Freq. in ***lath and plaster***. L15. ▸**c** (A thin narrow piece of wood used for) an imitation weapon. *arch*. L16.

> **c** SHAKES. *Tit. A*. Have your lath glued within your sheath Till you know better how to handle it.

2 The part of an arbalest or crossbow which bends the bow. *obsolete* exc. *hist*. M16.
3 *transf*. A slender or fragile thing or person. M17. ▸**b** *MINERALOGY*. A thin narrow elongated mineral crystal. E20.

> F. BURNEY 'Thin as Dr. Lind' says the King. Lind was . . a mere lath.

– COMB.: **lath-nail** a nail for fixing laths on battens.

L

lath /lɑːθ/ *verb trans*. LME.
[ORIGIN from the noun.]
Cover (a wall or ceiling) with laths for plastering. Also foll. by *over*.

lathe /leɪð/ *noun*[1]. *obsolete* exc. *hist*.
[ORIGIN Old English *læþ*, corresp. to Old Norse *lāð* landed possession, land, rel. to Germanic base in Gothic *unlēds* unlanded, poor, Old English *unlæd(e* wretched.]
Each of the administrative districts (latterly five in number) into which Kent was formerly divided, each comprising several hundreds.

lathe /leɪð/ *noun*[2]. *obsolete* exc. *N. English*. Also **laithe**. ME.
[ORIGIN Old Norse *hlaða* rel. to *hlaða* LADE *verb*.]
A barn.

lathe /leɪð/ *noun*[3]. ME.
[ORIGIN Prob. from Old Danish *lad* stand, supporting framework, as in *drejelad* turning lathe, *savelad* saw-bench, perh. a special use of *lad* pile, heap from Old Norse *hlað* rel. to *hlaða* LADE *verb*.]
1 A machine for turning wood, metal, ivory, etc., in which the article to be turned is held in a horizontal position by means of adjustable centres and rotated against the tools with which it is cut to the required shape. Also ***turning lathe***. ME.
capstan lathe, ***pole lathe***, etc.
2 ***potter's lathe***, a machine for throwing and turning pottery, the article being placed on a revolving horizontal disc. E18.
– COMB.: **lathe-bed** the lower framework of a lathe, having a slot from end to end in which one or both of the heads may be moved backwards or forwards; **lathe-head** the headstock of a lathe.

lathe /leɪð/ *noun*[4]. LME.
[ORIGIN Rel. to Swedish *lad*, formed as LATHE *noun*[3], German *Lade*: see also LAY *noun*[5].]
WEAVING. The movable swing frame or batten of a loom.

lathe /leɪð/ *verb trans. obsolete* exc. *dial.*
[ORIGIN Old English *laþian* = Old Frisian *lathia*, *ladia*, Old Saxon *laþian*, Old High German *ladōn* (German *laden*) Old Norse *laða*, Gothic *laþōn*: cogn. with Gothic *laþaleikō* willingly.]
Invite, call. Chiefly as ***lathing*** *verbal noun*.

lathee *noun* var. of LATHI.

lathen /ˈlɑːθ(ə)n/ *adjective*. *rare*. M19.
[ORIGIN from LATH *noun* + -EN[4].]
Made of lath.

lather /ˈlɑːðə, ˈlaðə/ *noun*[1].
[ORIGIN Old English *lēaþor* = Old Norse *lauðr*, from Germanic, from Indo-European base also of Greek *loutron* bath. Later from LATHER *verb*.]
†**1** Washing soda; froth from this. Only in OE.
2 A froth or foam made by the agitation of a mixture of soap and water. L16. ▸**b** *transf.* Violent perspiration, *esp.* the frothy sweat of a horse. M17. ▸**c** *fig.* A state of agitation, anxiety, irritation, etc., such as induces sweat. M19.

E. PIZZEY His hands were gently rubbing the shampoo into a rich lather. **b** M. WEBB There came one riding all in a lather to tell of the great victory. **c** N. SAHGAL Why get into a lather about what you can't undo?

3 The action of lathering or applying lather to something. E17.
– COMB.: **lather-boy** *hist.* a boy employed in a barber's shop to lather the chins of customers.

lather /ˈlɑːθə/ *noun*[2]. ME.
[ORIGIN from LATH *noun*, *verb* + -ER[1].]
A person who makes or fixes laths.

lather /ˈlɑːðə, ˈlaðə/ *verb*.
[ORIGIN Old English *lēþran*, *līeþran* = Old Norse *leyðra*, from Germanic, from base of LATHER *noun*[1]. From 16 assim. in form to LATHER *noun*[1].]
1 *verb trans.* Cover (as) with a lather; apply lather to; wash in or with a lather; in *pass.* = sense 2 below. OE.

M. MITCHELL Uncle Peter . . drove to the hospital, making trip after trip until the old horse was lathered. A. MILLER Roy would snarl . . his jaws lathering.

2 *verb intrans.* Now chiefly of a horse: become covered with foam or frothy sweat. ME.
3 *verb intrans.* Produce and form a lather or froth. E17.
4 *verb trans.* Beat, thrash; *fig.* defeat soundly. *colloq.* L18.
■ **latherer** *noun* a person who applies lather; *esp.* (*hist.*) = ***lather-boy*** s.v. LATHER *noun*[1]: L19.

lathery /ˈlɑːð(ə)ri, ˈlað-/ *adjective*. E19.
[ORIGIN from LATHER *noun*[1] + -Y[1].]
Covered with or resembling lather; *fig.* unsubstantial. Of a horse: covered with frothy sweat.

lathi /ˈlɑːtiː/ *noun*. Also ***lathee***. M19.
[ORIGIN Hindi *lāṭhī*.]
In the Indian subcontinent: a long heavy iron-bound stick, usu. of bamboo, used as a weapon.

lathing /ˈlɑːθɪŋ/ *noun*. ME.
[ORIGIN from LATH *verb* + -ING[1].]
1 The action of LATH *verb*. ME.
2 Lath; work in lath. E16.

lathy /ˈlɑːθi/ *adjective*. L17.
[ORIGIN from LATH *noun* + -Y[1].]
1 Esp. of a person: resembling a lath; long and very thin. L17.
2 Made of lath (and plaster). E19.

lathyrism /ˈlaθɪrɪz(ə)m/ *noun*. L19.
[ORIGIN from LATHYRUS + -ISM.]
MEDICINE. A tropical disease marked by tremors, muscular weakness, and paraplegia, commonly attributed to continued consumption of the seeds of the grass pea, *Lathyrus sativus*.

lathyrus /ˈlaθɪrəs/ *noun*. M18.
[ORIGIN mod. Latin (see below) from Greek *lathuros* a kind of vetch.]
Any of various leguminous plants constituting the genus *Lathyrus*, resembling vetches but with hairy styles and usu. winged stems.

lati *noun pl.* see LAT *noun*[2].

Latian /ˈleɪʃ(ə)n/ *adjective & noun*. L16.
[ORIGIN from Latin *Latium* (see LATIN *adjective & noun*) + -AN.]
▸ **A** *adjective*. Of or pertaining to Latium; *literary* Latin. L16.
▸ **B** *noun*. A native or inhabitant of Latium. L17.

latices *noun pl.* see LATEX.

laticiferous /latɪˈsɪf(ə)rəs/ *adjective*. M19.
[ORIGIN from Latin *latici-* combining form of LATEX + -FEROUS.]
BOTANY. Conducting or containing latex; (of tissue) containing laticiferous tubes or vessels.

laticlave /ˈlatɪkleɪv/ *noun*. M17.
[ORIGIN Late Latin *laticlavium*, *-vus*, from *latus* broad + *clavus* purple stripe. (In classical Latin *latus clavus*.)]
ROMAN ANTIQUITIES. A badge consisting of two broad purple stripes on the edge of the tunic, worn by senators and other people of high rank.

†**latifund** *noun* see LATIFUNDIUM.

latifundia *noun* pl. of LATIFUNDIUM.

latifundist /latɪˈfʌndɪst/ *noun*. Also in Spanish form **latifundista** /ˌlatɪfʌnˈdɪstə/. M20.
[ORIGIN Spanish *latifundista*, from *latifundio*: see LATIFUNDIUM, -IST.]
The owner of a latifundium in Spain or Latin America.

latifundium /lɑːtɪˈfʌndɪəm, lat-, leɪt-/ *noun*. Pl. **-dia** /-dɪə/. Orig. anglicized as †**-fund**. M17.
[ORIGIN Latin, from *latus* broad + *fundus* landed estate; partly from Spanish *latifundio* from Latin.]
A large landed estate or ranch, freq. worked by slaves or people of semi-servile status; *esp.* one in Spain or Latin America or (*hist.*) in ancient Rome. Usu. in *pl.*

latigo /ˈlatɪɡəʊ/ *noun*. *US*. Pl. **-o(e)s**. L19.
[ORIGIN Spanish.]
A strap for tightening a cinch.

latimer /ˈlatɪmə/ *noun*. Long *obsolete* exc. *hist.* ME.
[ORIGIN Anglo-Norman (whence Anglo-Latin *latimerus*, *-rius*, earlier *latimarius*) = Old French *latimier* alt. of *latinier* (Anglo-Latin *latinarius*), from *Latin* Latin: see -ER[2]. Cf. LATINER.]
An interpreter.

latimeria /latɪˈmɪərɪə/ *noun*. M20.
[ORIGIN mod. Latin, from Marjorie E. D. Courtenay-*Latimer* (1907–2004), South African museum curator + -IA[1].]
ZOOLOGY. Any coelacanth of the extant deep-sea genus *Latimeria*.

Latin /ˈlatɪn/ *adjective & noun*. OE.
[ORIGIN Latin *Latinus*, from *Latium*: see below, -INE[1]. Cf. LIDDEN.]
▸ **A** *adjective*. **1** Pertaining to, characteristic of, composed in, or using Latin (see sense B.1 below). OE.

SHAKES. *L.L.L.* Remuneration! O, that's the Latin word for three farthings.

2 Of or pertaining to ancient Latium, the area of central Italy which included Rome, or its inhabitants. ME.
3 *spec.* Designating or pertaining to the branch of the Christian church which once used Latin in all its rites; Roman Catholic. M16.
4 *hist.* Of or pertaining to the peoples of western Europe, viewed in their relations with the Ottoman Empire and with the Saracens and Turks. *arch.* L18.
5 Pertaining to or characteristic of the European and American peoples speaking languages developed from Latin; *spec.* Latin American. M19. ▸**b** Of, pertaining to, or characteristic of Latin American music or dance. M19.

R. W. EMERSON The Teutonic tribes have a national singleness of heart, which contrasts with the Latin races. V. GLENDINNING He was extrovert, physical, unstable, and very Latin. **b** DEREK ROBINSON He stood . . snapping his fingers to a Latin beat.

– SPECIAL COLLOCATIONS & COMB.: **Latin America** the countries in Central and S. America in which Spanish or Portuguese is the dominant language. **Latin American** *adjective & noun* (**a**) *adjective* belonging to or derived from Latin America; *spec.* designating a class of ballroom dancing consisting of dances of Latin American origin or inspiration, such as the rumba, samba, cha-cha-cha, etc.; (**b**) *noun* a native or inhabitant of a Latin American country. **Latin cross** a plain cross with the lowest member longer than the other three. **Latin language** = sense B.1 below. **Latin letter** a letter of the Roman alphabet. **Latin Quarter** [French *Quartier Latin*] the district of Paris on the left or south bank of the Seine, where Latin was spoken in the Middle Ages, and where students and artists live and the principal university buildings are situated. **Latin rights** [Latin *ius Latii*] *ROMAN HISTORY* a set of privileges, falling short of full citizenship, enjoyed by inhabitants of Latium and from 89 BC on extended to people outside Italy. **Latin rite** a religious ceremonial using Latin, esp. in the Roman Catholic Church. **Latin square** an arrangement of letters etc. each occurring n times, in a square array of n^2 compartments so that no letter appears twice in the same row or column; such an arrangement used as the basis of experimental procedures in which it is desired to control or allow for two sources of variability while investigating a third.
▸ **B** *noun*. **1** The Italic language (orig. the dialect of Latium) spoken in ancient Rome and its empire, which was used internationally in the Middle Ages as a medium of communication among educated people. With specifying word: a particular form, phase, etc., of Latin. OE. ▸†**b** A translation into Latin, as a school exercise. Usu. in *pl.* L15–L17.

B. MOORE Mass . . said in Latin because Latin was the language of the Church.

ecclesiastical Latin, ***popular Latin***, etc.

2 A native or inhabitant of Latium; *ROMAN HISTORY* a person who enjoyed the Latin rights. Formerly also, a speaker of Latin, a Latin author, (usu. in *pl.*). LME.
3 A member or adherent of the Latin Church, *esp.* one living in Asia. Now *rare*. LME.
4 *hist.* A person belonging to any of the Western nations of Europe during the Crusades. *arch.* L18.
5 A native or inhabitant of any of the various countries in Europe (France, Italy, Spain, etc.) and America whose language is developed from Latin; *spec.* a Latin American. L19.
– PHRASES: **classical Latin**: before about AD 200, *esp.* between about 100 BC and AD 14. ***dog Latin***: see DOG noun. **late Latin**: from about 150 to 600. ***law Latin***: see LAW *noun*[1]. ***Low Latin***: see LOW *adjective & noun*[4]. **medieval Latin**: from about 600 to 1500. **modern Latin**: since 1500, used esp. in scientific classification. **Old Latin**: before about 100 BC. ***pig Latin***: see PIG *noun*[1]. ***silver Latin***: see SILVER *noun & adjective*. **thieves' Latin** the secret language or slang of thieves. ***Vulgar Latin***: see VULGAR *adjective*.
– COMB.: **Latin school** *US* a school offering Latin (and sometimes Greek) as part of the syllabus.
■ **Latiˈnesque** *adjective* resembling Latin, having a Latin character L19. **Latinish** *adjective* (*rare*) resembling Latin E17. **Latinless** *adjective* without knowledge of Latin M16. **Latinly** *adverb* (now *rare*) (**a**) in (good or pure) Latin; (**b**) in the style of the Latin peoples: LME.

Latin /ˈlatɪn/ *verb trans.* Long *arch.* M16.
[ORIGIN from LATIN *adjective & noun*.]
Translate into Latin.

Latinate /ˈlatɪneɪt/ *adjective*. E20.
[ORIGIN from LATIN *adjective & noun* + -ATE[2].]
Of, pertaining to, or derived from Latin; having the character of Latin; (occas.) resembling a native of a Latin country.

latine *adjective* var. of LATEEN.

Latiner /ˈlatɪnə/ *noun*. *colloq.* M17.
[ORIGIN from LATIN *noun*, *verb* + -ER[1]. Cf. LATIMER.]
A person proficient in Latin; a person who speaks Latin; *Scot.* a pupil studying Latin.

Latinic /ləˈtɪnɪk/ *adjective*. M19.
[ORIGIN from LATIN *adjective & noun* + -IC.]
Derived from or resembling Latin; Latinate. Also, of or pertaining to the ancient Latians or the modern Latin nations.
■ Also **Latinical** *adjective* L19.

Latinise *verb* var. of LATINIZE.

Latinism /ˈlatɪnɪz(ə)m/ *noun*. L16.
[ORIGIN medieval Latin *latinismus*, formed as LATIN *adjective & noun*: see -ISM.]
1 An idiom or form of expression characteristic of Latin, esp. one used by a writer in another language; conformity in style to Latin models. L16.
2 The influence or authority of the Latin Church. E20.

Latinist /ˈlatɪnɪst/ *noun*. M16.
[ORIGIN medieval Latin *latinista*, formed as LATIN *adjective & noun*: see -IST. Cf. French *latiniste*.]
1 An expert in or student of Latin. Formerly also, a writer of Latin. M16.
2 A theologian of the Latin Church. M16.
■ **Latiˈnistic** *adjective* pertaining to or characterized by Latinism; characteristic of a Latinist: E19.

Latinity /ləˈtɪnɪti/ *noun*. LME.
[ORIGIN Latin *Latinitas*, *-tat-*, formed as LATIN *adjective & noun*: see -ITY. Cf. Old French & mod. French *latinité*.]
1 Latin speech; the way in which a person speaks or writes Latin; the use of Latin. LME.
2 *ROMAN HISTORY*. The status of enjoying Latin rights. L19.
3 Latin character. E20.

Latinize /ˈlatɪnʌɪz/ *verb*. Also **-ise**. L16.
[ORIGIN Late Latin *latinizare*, formed as LATIN *adjective & noun*: see -IZE. Cf. French *latiniser*.]
1 *verb trans.* Give a Latin form to (a word etc. of another language); fill (a language) with words or idioms of Latin origin. L16. ▸**b** *verb intrans.* Use words or idioms from Latin. M17.
2 *verb trans.* Convert (a person, a people) to the ideas, customs, etc., of the Latins, or to the rites etc. of the Latin Church. E17.
3 *verb trans.* Transcribe in Roman letters. M19.
■ **Latiniˈzation** *noun* M19. **Latinizer** *noun* E17.

Latino /ləˈtiːnəʊ/ *noun & adjective*. *N. Amer.* Fem. **-na** /-nə/. M20.
[ORIGIN Amer. Spanish, prob. special use of Spanish *latino* LATIN *adjective & noun*.]
▸ **A** *noun*. Pl. **-os**, fem. **-as**. A Latin American inhabitant of the United States. M20.
▸ **B** *adjective*. Of or pertaining to the Latin American inhabitants of the United States. L20.

Latino- /ˈlatɪnəʊ/ *combining form*.
[ORIGIN from Late Latin *Latinus* LATIN *adjective* + -O-.]
Forming compounds with the sense 'partly Latin and partly —', as ***Latino-Faliscan***, ***Latino-Jazz***, ***Latino-Sabellian***.

Latino sine flexione /ˈlatɪnəʊ ˌsɪnɪ flɛksɪˈəʊnɪ/ *noun phr.* E20.
[ORIGIN Latin (*Latino* abl. of *Latinus* LATIN *adjective*) = in Latin without inflection.]
An artificial language intended for international use, in which nouns are taken from the ablative case of Latin nouns.

latish /ˈleɪtɪʃ/ *adjective & adverb*. Also **lateish**. E17.
[ORIGIN from LATE *adjective*, *adverb* + -ISH[1].]
▸ **A** *adjective*. Somewhat late. E17.
▸ **B** *adverb*. At a somewhat late hour. E19.

latissimus /lɑːˈtɪsɪməs/ *noun*. Pl. **-mi** /-mʌɪ, -miː/. E17.
[ORIGIN mod. Latin, ellipt. for *musculus latissimus dorsi* lit. 'the broadest muscle of the back'.]
ANATOMY. More fully ***latissimus dorsi*** /ˈdɔːsʌɪ, -siː/. Either of a pair of large, roughly triangular muscles covering the lower part of the back, from the sacral, lumbar, and lower thoracic vertebrae to the armpits.

latitant /ˈlatɪt(ə)nt/ *adjective & noun*. Now *rare*. M17.
[ORIGIN Latin *latitant-* pres. ppl stem of *latitare* frequentative of *latere* be hidden: see -ANT[1].]
▸ **A** *adjective*. That lies concealed; lurking; latent. Formerly *spec.*, hibernating. M17.
▸ **B** *noun*. A person who is in hiding, esp. from a legal process. L19.
■ **latitancy** *noun* M17.

latitat /ˈlatɪtat/ *noun*. *obsolete* exc. *hist.* M16.
[ORIGIN Latin, 3rd person sing. of pres. indic. of *latitare*: see LATITANT.]
LAW. A writ summoning a defendant assumed to be in hiding to answer in the Court of King's or Queen's Bench.

latitation /latɪˈteɪʃ(ə)n/ *noun*. Now *rare*. E17.
[ORIGIN Latin *latitatio(n-)*, from *latitat-* pa. ppl stem of *latitare*: see LATITANT, -ATION.]
The fact of lying concealed; hiding, lurking.

latitude /ˈlatɪtjuːd/ *noun*. LME.
[ORIGIN Latin *latitudo*, *-din-*, from *latus* broad: see -TUDE. Cf. Old French & mod. French *latitude*.]
▸ **I** Breadth, width.
1 Transverse dimension; extent as measured from side to side; breadth of a surface, as opp. to length. Also, spaciousness. Now only *joc.* LME. ▸†**b** A tract or area as defined by its breadth; a wide compass or extent. LME–L18.

R. L'ESTRANGE 'Tis Field of a Huge Latitude that the Devil has to Dance . . in.

2 †**a** The range within which something may vary. LME–L18. ▸**b** Extent, range, scope. Also, great or full extent. Now *rare*. E17. ▸**c** *PHOTOGRAPHY*. The range of exposures for which an emulsion, printing paper, etc., will give acceptable contrast. L19.

a R. KIRWAN Few stones admit of a greater latitude of composition. **b** H. L. MANSEL The . . passage of Locke . . when understood in its proper latitude.

3 Freedom from narrow restrictions; liberality of construction or interpretation; tolerated variety of action or opinion. E17. ▸†**b** Laxity of conduct or principle. L17–E18.

L. TRILLING A considerable latitude in our selection of . . books.

▸ **II** *techn.* (opp. LONGITUDE).
4 *GEOGRAPHY*. **a** The angular distance on its meridian of any place on the earth's surface from the equator (quantitatively identical with the elevation of the pole above the horizon, and with the declination of the zenith). LME. ▸**b** Angular distance on a meridian. Only in ***degree of latitude***, ***minute of latitude***, etc. E17. ▸**c** A locality as defined by parallels of latitude; a region, a clime. Usu. in *pl.* M17.

a *transf.*: D. FRANCIS The silencer reached the latitude of my heart. **c** A. HARDY In all latitudes from the polar seas to the tropics.

5 *ASTRONOMY*. **a** Angular distance from the ecliptic, corresp. to terrestrial latitude (also ***celestial latitude***) or from a similar line of reference. Cf. DECLINATION 4a. LME. ▸**b** The angular distance of a point on the surface of a celestial object from the equator. L19.

latitudinal /latɪˈtjuːdɪn(ə)l/ *adjective*. LME.
[ORIGIN formed as LATITUDE + -AL[1].]
1 Relating to breadth or width. Formerly of (esp. abdominal) muscles: transverse. *rare*. LME.
2 Pertaining to or depending on geographical latitude; corresponding to lines of latitude. L18.
■ **latitudinally** *adverb* in respect of breadth or latitude M19.

latitudinarian /ˌlatɪtjuːdɪˈnɛːrɪən/ *noun & adjective*. M17.
[ORIGIN formed as LATITUDE + -ARIAN, after *trinitarian* etc.]
▸ **A** *noun*. A person who practises or favours latitude in opinion or action, esp. in religion; *spec.* (*ECCLESIASTICAL HISTORY*) any of a group of 17th-cent. divines who, while attached to episcopal government and liturgical forms of worship, regarded them basically as not of fundamental importance. Also, a person who, though not a sceptic, has no preference among creeds and forms of Church government or worship. M17.
▸ **B** *adjective*. Allowing, favouring, or characterized by latitude in opinion or action, esp. in religion; characteristic of a latitudinarian. L17.
■ **latitudinarianism** *noun* latitudinarian doctrine, opinions, or practice, esp. in religion L17.

latitudinary /latɪˈtjuːdɪn(ə)ri/ *adjective*. *rare*. L17.
[ORIGIN formed as LATITUDINARIAN + -ARY[1].]
= LATITUDINARIAN *adjective*.

latitudinous /latɪˈtjuːdɪnəs/ *adjective*. M19.
[ORIGIN formed as LATITUDE + -OUS.]
1 Characterized by latitude of interpretation. M19.
2 = LATITUDINAL *adjective* 2. E20.

lative /ˈleɪtɪv/ *adjective & noun*. M20.
[ORIGIN from Latin *lat-* pa. ppl stem of *ferre* bring + -IVE.]
GRAMMAR. ▸**A** *adjective*. Designating, being in, or pertaining to the case used in some languages, e.g. of the Finno-Ugric group, to express motion up to or as far as. Cf. ALLATIVE. M20.
▸ **B** *noun*. *The* lative case; a word, form, etc., in the lative case. M20.

latke /ˈlʌtkə/ *noun*. E20.
[ORIGIN Yiddish, from Russian *latka* earthenware cooking vessel, (dial.) dish cooked in such a vessel.]
In Jewish cookery: a pancake, *esp.* one made with grated potato.

latomy /ˈlatəmi/ *noun*. *rare*. Also in Greek form **latomia** /ləˈtəʊmɪə/. M17.
[ORIGIN Greek *latomia*, from *laas*, *las* stone + *-tomia* -TOMY.]
GREEK HISTORY. A stone quarry; *spec.* (*collect. sing.* & in *pl.*) the quarries at Syracuse, used as a prison.

laton *noun* var. of LATTEN.

Latonian /ləˈtəʊnɪən/ *adjective & noun*. L16.
[ORIGIN from Latin *Latonius*, from *Latona* (see below) from Greek (Aeolic) *Latōn*, (Attic) *Lētō*: see -AN.]
▸ **A** *adjective*. Of or pertaining to Latona, in classical mythology the mother of Apollo and Diana. L16.
▸ **B** *noun*. ***the Latonian***, Apollo. *poet.* E19.

latosol /ˈlatəsɒl/ *noun*. M20.
[ORIGIN from LATERITE + -O- + -SOL.]
A lateritic soil.

latoun *noun* see LATTEN.

latrant /ˈleɪtr(ə)nt/ *adjective*. *literary*. E18.
[ORIGIN Latin *latrant-* pres. ppl stem of *latrare* to bark: see -ANT[1].]
Barking like a dog.

latration /ləˈtreɪʃ(ə)n/ *noun*. *literary*. E17.
[ORIGIN medieval Latin *latratio(n-)*, from Latin *latrat-* pa. ppl stem of *latrare*: see LATRANT, -ATION.]
The barking of a dog; a bark.

latreutic /ləˈtruːtɪk/ *adjective*. *rare*. M19.
[ORIGIN Greek *latreutikos* pertaining to divine worship, from *latreuein*: see LATRIA.]
Of the nature of latria.
■ Also **latreutical** *adjective* E17.

latria /ləˈtrʌɪə/ *noun*. E16.
[ORIGIN Late Latin from Greek *latreia*, from *latreuein* wait on, serve with prayer.]
ROMAN CATHOLIC CHURCH. The highest form of worship, due to God alone; the veneration properly given to God. Cf. DULIA, HYPERDULIA.

latrine /ləˈtriːn/ *noun*. ME.
[ORIGIN French from Latin *latrina* contr. of *lavatrina*, from *lavare* wash.]
A lavatory, *esp.* a communal one in a camp, barracks, hospital, etc.
– COMB.: **latrine rumour** *military slang* a baseless rumour believed to originate in gossip in the latrines.
– NOTE: In isolated use before 17, rare before 19.
■ **latrinogram** *noun* (*military slang*) = LATRINE ***rumour*** M20.

†**latrociny** *noun*. LME.
[ORIGIN Latin *latrocinium*, from *latro*: see LATRON. Cf. LARCENY.]
1 Highway robbery, freebooting, plundering. LME–M17.
2 A band of robbers. L15–M18.

latron /ˈleɪtrən/ *noun*. Long *arch.* L16.
[ORIGIN Latin *latro(n-)*: see LARCENY. Cf. LADRONE.]
A robber, a brigand.

-latry /lətri/ *suffix*.
[ORIGIN Greek *-latreia* worship: cf. LATRIA.]
Used (usu. preceded by -O-) in sense '(excessive) worship' in words of Greek origin or formed from Greek elements, as ***idolatry***, ***demonolatry***, ***Mariolatry***; also in jocular formations, as ***bardolatry***.

LATS /*freq.* lats/ *abbreviation*.
MEDICINE. Long-acting thyroid stimulator.

latte /ˈlateɪ/ *noun*. L20.
[ORIGIN Italian, lit. 'milk'.]
A drink of caffè latte.

latteen *adjective & noun* var. of LATEEN.

latten /ˈlat(ə)n/ *noun & adjective*. Also **laton**, (*arch.*) **latoun**. ME.
[ORIGIN Old French *laton*, *leiton* (mod. *laiton*), of unknown origin.]
▸ **A** *noun*. **1** A yellow alloy resembling or identical with brass, hammered into thin sheets and used esp. to make monumental brasses and church ornaments. Now *arch.* or *hist.* ME.
black latten: rolled and unpolished. **roll latten**: polished on both sides. **shaven latten** a very thin form of latten.
2 Any metal made in thin sheets; *esp.* tin plate (more fully ***white latten***). Now *dial.* E17.
▸ **B** *attrib.* or as *adjective*. Made or consisting of latten. L15.
■ **lattener** *noun* a worker in or maker of latten ME.

latter /ˈlatə/ *adjective, adverb, & noun*.
[ORIGIN Old English *lætra* (fem. & neut. *-re*) adjective, *lator* adverb, compar. of LATE *adjective*, *adverb*. *Later* is a new formation on *late*.]
▸ **A** *adjective*. †**1** Slower. OE–ME.
2 Further on in time or order; nearer the end; *arch.* belonging to a later or more advanced period (now chiefly with ref. to a period of the year or its produce). ME.

AV *Joel* 2:23 We forbeare to descend to latter Fathers. A. C. SWINBURNE Pale as grass, or latter flowers.

Latter Prophets: see PROPHET.
3 Belonging to the final stages, esp. of a person's life or of the world's existence; = LAST *adjective* 2. Now chiefly in ***latter days***. *arch.* E16. ▸**b** Recent. Chiefly in ***these latter days***, the recent past. E17.

T. JEFFERSON All the latter years of aged men are overshadowed with its gloom.

4 The second mentioned of two (opp. ***former***); (more loosely) the last mentioned of several. Also, mentioned at or near the end of a preceding clause or sentence. M16.

A. A. MILNE On Wednesday and on Saturday, But mostly on the latter day. *Guardian* The Berlin Wall stands unbreached, passes are needed to get into Bethlehem and Father Christmas has been arrested . . . It's the latter item that fascinates me.

– SPECIAL COLLOCATIONS & COMB.: **latter-day** *adjective* belonging to more recent times, modern; ***Latter-day Saint***, a member of the Mormon Church (officially called the Church of Jesus Christ of the Latter-day Saints). **latter end** (*a*) the concluding part of a period etc.; the end of life, (one's) death; (*b*) *joc.* the buttocks. **latter Lammas** *joc.* a day that will never come. †**latter-will** *Scot.* a person's last will and testament. See also LATTERMATH.
▸ †**B** *adverb*. **1** More slowly. OE–LME.
2 Later. ME–L16.
▸ **C** *noun*. *The* second mentioned of two (or, more loosely, *the* last mentioned of several) persons or things. Also, *the* person or thing mentioned at or near the end of the preceding clause or sentence. E17.

F. R. WILSON A nave and chancel, with a small vestry on the north side of the latter. T. CAPOTE Two . . lawyers . . replaced Schultz, the latter having resigned from the case. *Oxford Mail* Three accompanied pieces by Bruckner, Brahms and Schubert of which the latter was the most winning.

latterkin /ˈlatəkɪn/ *noun*. Orig. †**laperkin**. L17.
[ORIGIN Unknown.]
A glazier's tool, for widening the grooves in the leads of lattice windows.

latterly /ˈlatəli/ *adverb*. M18.
[ORIGIN from LATTER *adjective* + -LY[2].]
In the later stages of a period, esp. a person's life; of late, recently.

HOR. WALPOLE He died . . at Hammersmith, though latterly he resided chiefly at Bath. H. GUNTRIP Fairbairn has latterly turned his attention to the problems of psychotherapy.

lattermath /ˈlatəmaːθ, -maθ/ *noun*. Chiefly *dial.* M16.
[ORIGIN from LATTER *adjective* + MATH *noun*[1].]
The second mowing, the aftermath; the second crop of grass etc.

lattermost /ˈlatəməʊst/ *adjective*. E19.
[ORIGIN from LATTER *adjective* + -MOST.]
Last.

lattice /ˈlatɪs/ *noun & verb*. ME.
[ORIGIN French *lattis*, from *latte* LATH *noun*.]
▸ **A** *noun*. **1** A structure of laths or strips of metal etc. crossed and fastened together, with open spaces left between, used as a screen, e.g. in window openings; a window, gate, screen, etc., so constructed. ME. ▸**b** A lattice (usu. painted red) as a mark of a public house or inn; a public house, an inn. Also ***red lattice***. *arch.* L16. ▸**c** Lattices collectively; = ***latticework*** below. L16.

C. ISHERWOOD The iron lattices were drawn down over the bank windows.

2 *transf.* Something with an open interlaced structure like that of a lattice. M17. ▸**b** *HERALDRY*. = TRELLIS *noun* 1b. *rare*. E19. ▸**c** In textile manufacture: a latticework apron or conveyer used to carry material into or out of a machine. L19. ▸**d** *ELECTRICITY*. A network having four impedances and two pairs of terminals, each terminal of one pair being connected by an impedance to each of the other pair. Also more fully ***lattice network***. M20.
3 a Any regular arrangement of points or pointlike entities that fills a space, area, or line; *spec.* a crystal lattice, a space lattice. L19. ▸**b** An array of fuel and moderator in the core of a nuclear reactor. M20.
a BRAVAIS LATTICE. ***crystal lattice***: see CRYSTAL *noun & adjective*. ***primitive lattice***: see PRIMITIVE *adjective & noun*. ***space lattice***: see SPACE *noun*.
4 *MATH*. A partially ordered set in which every pair of elements has an infimum and a supremum. M20.
– COMB.: **lattice beam** = *lattice girder* below; **lattice conduction** *PHYSICS* transfer of energy between the vibrating atomic nuclei in a crystal lattice; **lattice conductivity** *PHYSICS* that part of the thermal conductivity of a crystalline substance arising from lattice conduction; **lattice constant** *CRYSTALLOGRAPHY* the length of a side, or the size of an angle, of the unit cell of a lattice; *spec.* the length of each of the sides of the unit cell of a cubic lattice; **lattice energy** *PHYSICS* the energy required to separate the ions of a crystal to an infinite distance from one another; **lattice filter** *ELECTRICITY* a filter consisting of components connected so as to form a lattice network; **lattice frame**, **lattice girder** a girder consisting of two horizontal bars connected by diagonal bars, usu. crossed so as to resemble latticework; **lattice leaf (plant)** a monocotyledonous aquatic plant of Madagascar, *Aponogeton madagascariensis* (family Aponogetonaceae), in which the submerged leaves are reduced to a network of veins; ***lattice***

L

network: see sense 2d above; **lattice plane** *PHYSICS* a plane containing lattice points; a layer of atoms or molecules in a crystal; **lattice point** (*a*) *MATH.* a point on a graph or in space having integral coordinates; (*b*) any of the points of which a lattice, esp. a crystal lattice, is composed; **lattice site** a (specified) location in the molecular lattice structure of a metal, crystal, etc.; **lattice vibration** *PHYSICS* (*a*) an oscillation of an atom or molecule about its equilibrium position in a crystal lattice; (*b*) a lattice wave; **lattice wave** *PHYSICS* a displacement of atoms or molecules from their equilibrium position in a crystal which travels as a wave through the crystal; **lattice window**: a window with a lattice or composed of small diamond-shaped panes set in leadwork; **latticework** interlacing laths or strips of metal etc. forming a lattice.

▶ **B** *verb trans.* **1** Provide (as) with a lattice or latticework. Also foll. by *up, over.* **LME.**

> L. BLUE Lattice the top with thin strips of tinned red pimento . . and anchovy fillets.

2 Form into a lattice, arrange as a lattice. **M20.**
■ **latticewise** *adverb* in the form of a lattice or latticework **M16.**

latticed /ˈlatɪst/ *adjective.* **M16.**
[**ORIGIN** from **LATTICE** *noun, verb*: see **-ED**[2], **-ED**[1].]
1 Provided with a lattice or latticework. **M16.**
2 Shaped or arranged like a lattice; *esp.* (*BOTANY & ZOOLOGY*) having a conformation or marking resembling latticework. **L16.** ▸**b** *HERALDRY.* Bearing a charge representing or resembling latticework, trellised. *rare.* **E18.**

latticinio /latiˈtʃiːnjo, latɪˈtʃiːnjəʊ/ *noun.* Also **-no** /-no, -nəʊ/. **M19.**
[**ORIGIN** Italian, lit. 'dairy produce', from medieval Latin *lacticinium*.]
An opaque white glass used in threads to decorate clear Venetian glass.

latus /ˈleɪtəs/ *noun.* Now *rare* or *obsolete.* **L16.**
[**ORIGIN** Late Latin from Greek *latos*.]
(The classical name of) the Nile perch, *Lates niloticus.* Cf. **LATES.**

latus rectum /leɪtəs ˈrɛktəm/ *noun phr.* Pl. **latera recta** /lat(ə)rə ˈrɛktə/. **E18.**
[**ORIGIN** Latin = right side.]
GEOMETRY. (The length of) a straight line passing through the focus of a conic at right angles to the transverse or major axis.

Latvian /ˈlatvɪən/ *adjective & noun.* **E20.**
[**ORIGIN** from *Latvia* (see below), Latvian & Lithuanian *Latvija* + **-AN.**]
▶ **A** *adjective.* Of or pertaining to Latvia, a Baltic state between Estonia and Lithuania, its people, or their language. **E20.**
▶ **B** *noun.* **1** A native or inhabitant of Latvia. **E20.**
2 The Baltic language of Latvia. **E20.**

lau /laʊ/ *noun.* **E20.**
[**ORIGIN** Dinka & Nuer.]
A water monster reputed to live in the swamps of the Nile valley.

lauan /ˈlaʊən, laˈwɑːn/ *noun.* **L19.**
[**ORIGIN** Tagalog *lawá'an, láwan*.]
The lightweight hardwood timber produced by various Philippine trees of the genus *Shorea* (family Dipterocarpaceae) or closely related genera.

laubmannite /ˈlaʊbmənʌɪt/ *noun.* **M20.**
[**ORIGIN** from Heinrich *Laubmann* (1865–1951), German mineralogist + **-ITE**[1].]
MINERALOGY. An orthorhombic basic phosphate of ferrous and ferric iron forming yellow- to grey-green crystals.

laud /lɔːd/ *noun*[1]. **ME.**
[**ORIGIN** Old French *laude*, pl. *laudes* from Latin *laudes* pl. of *laus* praise.]
1 *ECCLESIASTICAL.* In *pl.* (treated as *sing. & pl.*). The first of the daytime canonical hours of prayer, orig. appointed for daybreak; the office, with which may be said the original night office of matins, appointed for this hour. **ME.**
2 Praise, high commendation. Now *rare* exc. in hymns. **LME.** ▸**b** A cause or subject for praise. *rare.* **M16.**

> J. M. NEALE All glory, laud, and honour To thee, Redeemer, King.

3 A hymn, an ascription of praise. **M16.**

laud /laˈud/ *noun*[2]. Pl. ***laudes*** /laˈudes/. **L19.**
[**ORIGIN** Spanish *laúd* from Arabic *al-ʿūd*: see **LUTE** *noun*[1].]
A Spanish lute.

laud /lɔːd/ *verb trans.* **LME.**
[**ORIGIN** Latin *laudare*, from *laud-*, *laus* praise.]
Praise highly, sing or speak the praises of (orig. as an act of worship); celebrate.

> P. GAY He lauded Jung's writings, peppering his enthusiasms with shrewdly placed criticisms.

laudable /ˈlɔːdəb(ə)l/ *adjective.* Also ***-ible.** **LME.**
[**ORIGIN** Latin *laudabilis*, formed as **LAUD** *verb*: see **-ABLE, -IBLE.**]
1 Praiseworthy, commendable. In early use also, of the nature of praise, laudatory. **LME.**

> *Dun's Review* Every new regulation—no matter how laudable its goal—has a price.

†**2** Satisfactory; healthy, sound, wholesome; *MEDICINE* (of pus) creamy and inoffensive. **E16–L19.**
■ **laudaˈbility** *noun* (*rare*) **LME.** **laudableness** *noun* **L17.** **laudably** *adverb* **LME.**

laudanine /ˈlɔːdəniːn/ *noun.* **L19.**
[**ORIGIN** from **LAUDANUM** + **-INE**[5].]
CHEMISTRY. An alkaloid derived from opium with analgesic properties.
■ **laudanosine** /lɔːˈdanəsiːn/ *noun* an alkaloid, laudanine methyl ether, which occurs in opium and is a strong tetanic poison **L19.**

laudanum /ˈlɔːd(ə)nəm, ˈlɒ-/ *noun.* **M16.**
[**ORIGIN** mod. Latin, used by Paracelsus as the name of a costly medicament in which opium was early suspected to be the active ingredient, perh. var. of Latin **LADANUM**, or suggested by Latin *laudare* **LAUD** *verb*.]
1 Orig., any of various preparations in which opium was the main ingredient. Later, an alcoholic solution of morphine, formerly commonly used as a painkiller. **M16.**
†**2** = **LADANUM. M16–E18.**

laudation /lɔːˈdeɪʃ(ə)n/ *noun.* **LME.**
[**ORIGIN** Old French *laudacion* or Latin *laudatio(n-)*, from *laudat-* pa. ppl stem of *laudare* **LAUD** *verb*: see **-ATION.**]
The giving of praise; an instance of this, a eulogy.

laudative /ˈlɔːdətɪv/ *adjective & noun. rare.* **LME.**
[**ORIGIN** Latin *laudativus*, from *laudat-*: see **LAUDATION, -IVE.**]
▶ **A** *adjective.* Expressive of praise; laudatory. (Foll. by *of*.) **LME.**
▶ †**B** *noun.* A laudative expression or discourse; a eulogy. Only in **17.**

laudator /lɔːˈdeɪtə/ *noun.* Now *rare.* **E19.**
[**ORIGIN** Latin, from *laudat-*: see **LAUDATION, -OR.**]
= **LAUDER.**

laudator temporis acti /lɔːˌdeɪtə ˌtɛmp(ə)rɪs ˈaktʌɪ/ *noun phr.* Pl. ***laudatores temporis acti*** /lɔːdəˌtɔːriːz/. **M18.**
[**ORIGIN** Latin *laudator temporis acti (se puero)* a praiser of past times, (when he himself was a boy) (Horace *Ars Poetica*).]
A person who holds up the past as a golden age.

laudatory /ˈlɔːdət(ə)ri/ *adjective.* **M16.**
[**ORIGIN** Late Latin *laudatorius*, formed as **LAUDATOR**: see **-ORY**[2].]
Expressive of praise; eulogistic. (Foll. by *of*.)
■ **laudatorily** *adverb* **M19.**

lauder /ˈlɔːdə/ *noun.* **E17.**
[**ORIGIN** from **LAUD** *verb* + **-ER**[1].]
A person who praises: a eulogist.

laudes *noun* pl. of **LAUD** *noun*[2].

Laudian /ˈlɔːdɪən/ *adjective & noun.* **L17.**
[**ORIGIN** from *Laud* (see below) + **-IAN.**]
Chiefly *hist.* ▶**A** *adjective.* Of, pertaining to, or characteristic of William Laud, Archbishop of Canterbury 1633–45, noted for his advocacy of pre-Reformation liturgical practices and his opposition to Calvinism; favouring the tenets or practices of Laud; instituted by Laud. **L17.**
▶ **B** *noun.* A follower of Laud. **E18.**
■ **Laudianism** *noun* the principles and practice of Laud and his followers **L19.**

laudible *adjective* see **LAUDABLE.**

Laudism /ˈlɔːdɪz(ə)m/ *noun.* **M19.**
[**ORIGIN** from William *Laud* (see **LAUDIAN**) + **-ISM.**]
= **LAUDIANISM.**
■ **Laudist** *noun* = **LAUDIAN** *noun* **M18.**

Laue /ˈlaʊə/ *noun.* **E20.**
[**ORIGIN** Max von *Laue* (1879–1960), German physicist.]
CRYSTALLOGRAPHY. Used *attrib.* with ref. to a method of X-ray diffraction in which a narrow beam of X-rays is directed at a thin crystal and the resulting diffraction pattern recorded on a photographic film.
Laue method, ***Laue pattern***, etc.

Laufen /ˈlaʊf(ə)n/ *adjective.* **E20.**
[**ORIGIN** A town in Germany near Salzburg.]
Designating a minor glacial retreat following the last major (Würm) glaciation in the Alps.

laugh /lɑːf/ *noun.* **L17.**
[**ORIGIN** from the verb.]
1 The action of laughing; inclination to laugh. *rare.* **L17.**

> S. J. DUNCAN Mr. Pratte had very blue eyes with a great deal of laugh in them.

2 A burst of laughter; a bout of laughing. Also, a person's characteristic manner of laughing. **E18.**

> J. AUSTEN Elinor could have forgiven everything but her laugh.

barrel of laughs: see **BARREL** *noun.* **for laughs**, **for a laugh** merely for one's amusement or as a joke. **get the laugh on**, **get the laugh over** = ***have the laugh on*** below. **good for a laugh** that can be trusted to raise a laugh. **have the last laugh** be vindicated after being initially held up to ridicule. **have the laugh on**, **have the laugh over** be in a position to enjoy the discomfiture of (an opponent). **have the laugh on one's side** be in a position to enjoy the discomfiture of an opponent. ***holy laugh***: see **HOLY** *adjective.* ***play for laughs***: see **PLAY** *verb.* ***raise a laugh***: see **RAISE** *verb.* **the laugh is on me** the tables are turned and now I am the person exposed to ridicule.

3 a A laughing stock. *rare.* **E19.** ▸**b** An amusing thing, circumstance, or person; (freq. *iron.*) a joke. *colloq.* **L19.**

– **COMB.:** **laugh-line** (*a*) *THEATRICAL* a comic line received with laughter; (*b*) = ***laughter-line*** s.v. **LAUGHTER** *noun*[1]; **laugh track** a recording of audience laughter added to a soundtrack.

laugh /lɑːf/ *verb.*
[**ORIGIN** Old English *hlæhhan*, (West Saxon) *hliehhan* = Old Frisian *hlakkia*, Old High German *hlahhan, hlahhēn* (Dutch, German *lachen*), Old Norse *hlæja*, Gothic *hlahjan*, from Germanic, ult. from Indo-European imit. base (cf. Greek *klōssein* to cluck).]
1 *verb intrans.* Make the spasmodic inarticulate sounds, the movements of the facial muscles, shaking of the sides, etc., which are the instinctive expressions of lively amusement, scorn, exultation, etc., or reactions to certain physical sensations, such as that produced by tickling. Also, have one of the emotions expressed by laughing. **OE.** ▸**b** Of water, scenery, corn, etc.: be lively with movement or the play of light and colour as if expressing joyous feeling. *poet. & rhet.* **LME.**

> M. WEST Jean Marie laughed—a gusty chuckle of genuine amusement. **b** S. BARING-GOULD This mountain plateau laughs with verdure.

†**2** *verb trans.* Laugh or mock at, deride. **OE–M17.**
3 *verb trans.* Utter (a laugh) as an expression of amusement etc. Also, utter or say laughingly. **LME.**

> C. E. RIDDELL 'What a flatterer ladies must have found you', laughed Miss Pousnett.

4 *verb trans.* With obj. & compl. or adverbial phr.: bring into a given state or position by laughing; *esp.* persuade (a person) *out of* a belief, a solemn mood, etc., by laughter or mockery. **LME.**

> J. TRAPP Whose whole life is to eat, and drink . . and laugh themselves fat. A. W. HARE Is there anybody . . who has not . . been laught out of what he ought to have done.

– **PHRASES:** **be laughing** *colloq.* be in a position to exult, be fortunate or successful. ***enough to make a cat laugh***: see **CAT** *noun*[1]. †**laugh and lay down**, †**laugh and lie down** an obsolete card game. **laugh in a person's face** show open contempt for a person. ***laugh in one's sleeve***: see **SLEEVE** *noun.* ***laugh like a drain***: see **DRAIN** *noun.* **laugh one's head off** laugh heartily or uncontrollably (*at*). **laugh on the other side of one's face**, **laugh on the other side of one's mouth**, **laugh on the wrong side of one's face**, **laugh on the wrong side of one's mouth** be discomfited after premature exultation. **laugh out of court** dismiss as absurd. **laugh to scorn** *arch.* ridicule, deride. ***laugh up one's sleeve***: see **SLEEVE** *noun.*
– **WITH ADVERBS & PREPOSITIONS IN SPECIALIZED SENSES:** **laugh at** — (*a*) laugh in response to, see the funny side of; (*b*) deride, make fun of. **laugh away** †(*a*) let go with a laugh; (*b*) = ***laugh off*** below; (*c*) while away (time) with laughter. **laugh down** subdue or silence with laughter. **laugh off** dismiss (a misfortune, an embarrassment, etc.) with a laugh. †**laugh out** brazen out with laughter. **laugh over** — (preposition) laugh as one thinks about. †**laugh over** (adverb) discuss with laughter or merriment.

laughable /ˈlɑːfəb(ə)l/ *adjective.* **L16.**
[**ORIGIN** from **LAUGH** *verb* + **-ABLE.**]
Calculated to excite laughter; ludicrous, absurd.

> B. VINE Her I could never betray. The idea is laughable, a stupid joke. J. BANVILLE I felt . . like a village idiot, sad and laughable and yet in a way pathetically endearing.

■ **laughableness** *noun* **M19.** **laughably** *adverb* **E19.**

laugher /ˈlɑːfə/ *noun.* **LME.**
[**ORIGIN** from **LAUGH** *verb* + **-ER**[1].]
1 A person who laughs, a person who likes to laugh. Also, a scoffer. **LME.**
2 A variety of the domestic pigeon, so called from its peculiar note. **M18.**
3 A highly amusing or absurd remark, situation, etc.; a (baseball) match so easily won as to be laughable. *US slang.* **M20.**

laughful /ˈlɑːfʊl, -f(ə)l/ *adjective.* **E19.**
[**ORIGIN** from **LAUGH** *noun* + **-FUL.**]
Full of laughter or merriment.

laugh-in /ˈlɑːfɪn/ *noun.* **M20.**
[**ORIGIN** from **LAUGH** *verb* + **-IN**[2].]
A demonstration, event, or situation marked by or devised for communal laughter or merriment.

laughing /ˈlɑːfɪŋ/ *noun.* **ME.**
[**ORIGIN** from **LAUGH** *verb* + **-ING**[1].]
The action of **LAUGH** *verb*; laughter.
– **COMB.:** **laughing death** = **KURU**; ***laughing game***: see **GAME** *noun* 2b; **laughing gas** nitrous oxide used as an anaesthetic (so called from the exhilarating effect it produces when inhaled); **laughing matter** a fit subject for laughter (***no laughing matter***, a serious matter); **laughing muscle** the muscle that produces the facial contortions of laughter; **laughing stock** an object of derisive laughter or general ridicule.

laughing /ˈlɑːfɪŋ/ *adjective.* **ME.**
[**ORIGIN** from **LAUGH** *verb* + **-ING**[2].]
That laughs. Freq. in names of animals, so called from their cry or appearance.
laughing crow = ***laughing thrush*** below. **laughing dove** an African dove, *Stigmatopelia senegalensis.* **laughing goose** the white-fronted goose, *Anser albifrons.* **laughing gull** a N. American gull, *Larus atricilla*; also (*dial.*), the herring gull, the black-headed gull. ***laughing hyena***: see **HYENA** 1a. ***laughing jackass***: see **JACKASS** 2. **laughing owl** a rare owl of New Zealand, *Sceloglaux albifacies.* **laughing thrush** any of various Asian babblers, chiefly of the genus *Garrulax.*

L

■ **laughingly** *adverb* (*a*) in a laughing manner, with laughter; (*b*) *iron.* with laughable inappropriateness: M16.

laughsome /ˈlɑːfs(ə)m/ *adjective*. E17.
[ORIGIN from LAUGH *noun* + -SOME[1].]
Given to laughing; (of a thing) comic, laughable.

laughter /ˈlɑːftə/ *noun*[1].
[ORIGIN Old English *hleahtor* = Old High German *hlahtar* (whence German *Gelächter*), Old Norse *hlátr*, from Germanic, from base of LAUGH *verb*.]
1 The action of laughing, the sound of laughing. Also, a person's manner of laughing. OE. ▸**b** An instance of this; a laugh. Now *rare*. OE.
R. P. JHABVALA He made another joke whereupon they dissolved in relieved laughter. **b** GOLDSMITH They broke out into a laughter for four or five several times successively.
HOMERIC *laughter*. *rock with laughter*: see ROCK *verb*[1].
2 A subject for laughter. *poet.* L16.
SHAKES. *1 Hen. IV* Argument for a week, laughter for a month, and a good jest for ever.
– COMB.: **laughter-line** any of the small wrinkles at the corners of the eyes or mouth supposedly formed by years of intermittent laughter.
■ **laughterless** *adjective* E19.

laughter /ˈlɑːftə/ *noun*[2]. Long *obsolete* exc. *dial.* LME.
[ORIGIN Old Norse *láttr* from Germanic, from base of LAY *verb*[1].]
The whole number of eggs laid by a fowl before she is ready to sit; a clutch of eggs.

laughworthy /ˈlɑːfwəːði/ *adjective*. *rare*. E17.
[ORIGIN from LAUGH *noun* + -WORTHY.]
Deserving to be laughed at; ridiculous.

laughy /ˈlɑːfi/ *adjective*. *rare*. M19.
[ORIGIN from LAUGH *noun* or *verb* + -Y[1].]
Inclined to or full of laughter. Also, comic, laughable.

lauhala /laʊˈhɑːlə/ *noun*. E19.
[ORIGIN Hawaiian, from *lau* leaf + *hala* screw pine.]
A Polynesian screw pine, *Pandanus tectorius*; (the material plaited from) its dried leaves.

laulau /ˈlaʊlaʊ/ *noun*. M20.
[ORIGIN Hawaiian, redupl. of *lau* leaf.]
A portion of a Hawaiian dish of meat or fish wrapped in leaves and steamed or baked. Also, the wrapping of leaves for this dish.

laumontite /ˈlɔːm(ə)ntʌɪt/ *noun*. E19.
[ORIGIN from Gillet de *Laumont* (1747–1834), French mineralogist + -ITE[1].]
MINERALOGY. A monoclinic hydrous silicate of aluminium and calcium, occurring as white crystals which lose water and crumble when exposed to the air.

†**launce** *noun*[1]. *rare*. Only in L16.
[ORIGIN Latin *lanc-*, *lanx*, Italian *lance*.]
A scale, a balance.
SPENSER Need teacheth her . . That fortune all in equall launce doth sway.

launce *noun*[2] see LANCE *noun*.

†**launcegay** *noun* var. of LANCEGAY.

launch /lɔːn(t)ʃ/ *noun*[1]. LME.
[ORIGIN from the verb.]
1 A sudden leap or rapid motion. Now chiefly *dial.*, a long stride. LME.
†**2** The action or an act of lancing; a prick. M–L16.
3 A ramp or slipway from which a boat is launched. E18.
4 The action or an act of launching a vessel into the sea, esp. for the first time and with appropriate ceremonies; *fig.* the action or an act of launching a person into a business, career, etc. M18. ▸**b** The starting off of a bird in flight. M19. ▸**c** The launching of an aircraft or spacecraft. M20. ▸**d** (An instance of) the launching of a new product on the market. M20.
J. CLELAND Making this launch into the wide world, by repairing to London. **d** *Marketing Week* Two new . . magazine launches are announced this month.
– COMB.: **launch pad** = *LAUNCHING pad*; *launch window*: see WINDOW *noun* 3c.
– NOTE: Formerly pronounced /lɑːn(t)ʃ/.

launch /lɔːn(t)ʃ/ *noun*[2]. L17.
[ORIGIN Spanish *lancha* pinnace, perh. of Malay origin: cf. Portuguese *lanchara* from Malay *lancharan*, from *lanchar* quick, nimble.]
1 *hist.* A longboat of a man-of-war, more flat-bottomed than that of a merchant ship. L17.
2 More fully ***motor launch***, ***steam launch***, etc. A small motor boat carried on a cruising yacht; a similar boat, usu. partly open, used as a pleasure boat. M19.
– COMB.: **launchman** a man who operates a launch.
– NOTE: Formerly pronounced /lɑːn(t)ʃ/.

launch /lɔːn(t)ʃ/ *verb*. ME.
[ORIGIN Anglo-Norman *launcher*, Old Northern French *lancher*, var. of Old French *lancier* LANCE *verb*.]
▸ **I** *verb trans.* †**1** Pierce, wound; cut, slit; make (a wound) by piercing; cut with a lancet, lance. ME–L17.
DRYDEN Nine Bulls were launch'd by his victorious arm.
2 Discharge with force, hurl (a missile etc.); *fig.* utter (criticism, threats, etc.) with vehemence. ME. ▸**b** Dart forward (a weapon, limb, etc.). Now only, dart *out* (something long and flexible). LME. ▸**c** *refl.* Hurl oneself forward or down, rush, precipitate oneself. L17.
W. IRVING Much as they thirsted for his blood, they forbore to launch a shaft. W. E. H. LECKY He launched from the pulpit the most scathing invectives. **c** T. PAINE A spider can launch itself from the top, as playful amusement.
3 Cause (a vessel) to move from land into the water; *esp.* set afloat (a newly built vessel) for the first time, often with ceremonies. LME. ▸**b** Start (now esp. a rocket, spacecraft, etc.) on its course; release (a balloon or its contents) into the air at the beginning of a flight. E17.
DAY LEWIS He launched his coble into a rough sea.
4 *fig.* Start (a person) *in*, *into*, or *on* a business, career, etc. Also foll. by *out*. E17. ▸**b** Set on foot, initiate (a course of action, scheme, etc.); mount (a campaign, an offensive); bring before the public (a new publication, radio or television programme, etc.); formally introduce (a product etc.) on to the market. L19.
C. ISHERWOOD He was going to put up the money to launch Sally upon a stage career. **b** J. AGATE Barry Neame was giving a luncheon-party to launch Maurice Healy's new book. H. L. MENCKEN I marvel that no one tries to launch a royalist movement in the United States. H. KISSINGER A new assault was launched in the direction of Tehepone. *Kuwait Times* Gavaskar and Krishna Srikkanth launched the Indian innings.
5 NAUTICAL. Move (heavy goods) by pushing. Formerly, hoist (a yard). E17.
▸ **II** *verb intrans.* **6** Make a sudden or rapid motion; rush, plunge. Now only (*dial.*), take long strides, bound. ME. ▸†**b** *transf.* Shoot, sprout. Also, project. LME–L17.
7 Of people in a vessel: put out to sea. Freq. foll. by *out*, (*arch.*) *forth*. M16.
C. THIRLWALL Before any Greek navigator ventured . . to launch out beyond Sicily.
8 Enter boldly, eagerly, or without restraint into or *into* a new (freq. ambitious) enterprise, financial outlay, etc.; plunge into or *into* a long recital, a tirade, etc. Freq. foll. by *forth*, *out*. M16.
A. JESSOPP The small man . . is . . slow to launch out into expense. *Observer* Why must a dancer launch out as a choreographer as well? K. WILLIAMS He launched into a long account of his Australian tour.
9 a Of a ship: be launched, pass into the water. Now *rare*. M17. ▸**b** Of a new programme, product, etc.: be launched. L20.
b *Daily Telegraph* The first weekly issue of the Sunday Mirror magazine launches this weekend.
10 Propel a boat with a pole; *spec.* (in wildfowling) punt across mud. E19.
– NOTE: Formerly pronounced /lɑːn(t)ʃ/.

launcher /ˈlɔːn(t)ʃə/ *noun*. E19.
[ORIGIN from LAUNCH *verb* + -ER[1].]
1 A person who launches. E19.
2 A person who launches something or someone. L19.
3 A device or structure that launches something or is used for launching; *spec.* (*a*) a structure that holds a rocket or missile during launching; (*b*) a rocket from which a satellite is released into orbit. E20.

launching /ˈlɔːn(t)ʃɪŋ/ *verbal noun*. LME.
[ORIGIN from LAUNCH *verb* + -ING[1].]
The action of LAUNCH *verb*; an instance of this.
– COMB.: **launching pad** the area on which a rocket stands for launching; *fig.* a starting point for a (freq. ambitious) enterprise, career, etc.; **launching ways** the beds of timber blocks, sloping gradually towards the water, on which the bilge keels of a ship rest after completion of construction.

laund /lɔːnd/ *noun*. Now *arch.* & *dial.* ME.
[ORIGIN Old French *launde* (mod. *lande*) wooded district, heath. See also LAWN *noun*[2].]
An open space among woodland, a glade; untilled ground, pasture.

launder /ˈlɔːndə/ *noun*. Also (now chiefly in sense 2c) **lander** /ˈlɑːndə/. ME.
[ORIGIN Contr. of LAVENDER *noun*[1].]
†**1** A person who washes linen. ME–E17.
2 a A trough for water, either cut in the earth or formed of wood etc.; *esp.* in MINING, one for washing ore. M17. ▸**b** A gutter for rainwater. M17. ▸**c** METALLURGY. A channel for conveying molten metal from a furnace or container to a ladle or mould. E20.

launder /ˈlɔːndə/ *verb*. L16.
[ORIGIN from the noun.]
1 *verb trans.* Wash (clothes, linen, etc.); wash, perhaps starch, and usu. also iron (clothes, linen, etc.). L16.
2 *verb intrans.* Of a fabric or garment etc.: admit of being laundered; bear laundering without damage to the texture, colour, etc. E20.
Daily Mail This hard wearing fabric, which launders perfectly.
3 *verb trans. fig.* Treat or process (something) to make it appear acceptable. M20. ▸**b** Transfer (funds or goods) to conceal a dubious or illegal origin, later recovering them from apparently legitimate sources. Also, reduce the tax payable on (profits) by selling assets or transferring funds to a loss-making subsidiary, for later selling back. L20.
Toronto Sun There is nothing we can do to launder the rhetoric of Soviet leaders. **b** *Police Review* 'Dirty money' which is 'laundered' through Swiss or Caribbean bank accounts, reappearing as apparently legitimate capital.
■ **launderer** *noun* LME.

launderette /lɔːndəˈrɛt, lɔːnˈdrɛt/ *noun*. Also **laundrette** /lɔːnˈdrɛt/. M20.
[ORIGIN from LAUNDER *verb* + -ETTE.]
An establishment with automatic washing machines for the use of customers.

laundermat /ˈlɔːndəmat/ *noun*. Chiefly *N. Amer.* M20.
[ORIGIN from LAUNDER *verb* + -MAT. Cf. LAUNDROMAT.]
A launderette.

Launder-Ometer /lɔːnˈdrɒmɪtə, lɔːndəˈrɒmɪtə/ *noun*. Orig. *US*. Also **launderometer**. E20.
[ORIGIN from LAUNDER *verb* + -OMETER.]
(Proprietary name for) a machine for carrying out standardized laundering tests on fabrics, detergents, etc.

laundress /ˈlɔːndrɪs/ *noun*. M16.
[ORIGIN from LAUNDER *noun* or LAUNDERER + -ESS[1].]
1 A woman employed to launder clothes etc. M16.
2 *hist.* A female caretaker of chambers in the Inns of Court. L16.

laundrette *noun* var. of LAUNDERETTE.

Laundromat /ˈlɔːndrəmat/ *noun*. Orig. *US*. Also **l-**. M20.
[ORIGIN Alt. formed as LAUNDERMAT.]
An automatic washing machine. Also, (US proprietary name for) a launderette.

laundry /ˈlɔːndri/ *noun* & *verb*. E16.
[ORIGIN Contr. of LAVENDRY.]
▸ **A** *noun*. **1** The action or process of laundering clothes, linen, etc.; the laundering work presented by a particular quantity of clothes etc. E16. ▸**b** *fig.* The action of laundering funds etc. L20.
J. RULE I'm doing the landlady's laundry and cleaning this week.
2 An establishment where clothing etc. is laundered. L16. ▸**b** *fig.* An establishment where funds etc. are laundered. L20.
b *New York Times* Bahamian companies provided a convenient 'laundry' for illegitimate mob money looking . . to reach legitimate usage.
Chinese laundry: see CHINESE *adjective*.
3 Articles of clothing etc. that need to be, or have been, laundered. E20.
T. K. WOLFE There was laundry hanging all along the shower curtain rod.
– COMB.: **laundry list** *fig.* (*colloq.*) a long or exhaustive list of people or things; **laundryman**, **laundrywoman** (*a*) a launderer of clothes, linen, etc.; (*b*) a person who collects and delivers laundry.
▸ **B** *verb trans.* = LAUNDER *verb* 1. L19.

laura /ˈlɔːrə/ *noun*. Also ***lavra*** /ˈlavrə/. E18.
[ORIGIN Greek = lane, passage, alley.]
CHRISTIAN CHURCH. A group of huts or cells inhabited by reclusive monks in Egypt and the Middle East. In the Orthodox Church, a monastery consisting of separate cells; a large monastery.

Laura Ashley /lɔːrə ˈaʃli/ *adjective*. L20.
[ORIGIN Brit. fashion and textile designer (1925–85).]
Of a garment, fabric, etc.: characteristic of the style of Laura Ashley; *spec.* having a small floral pattern. Also (*fig.*), frilly, feminine, sentimental.
■ **Laura Ashleyish** *adjective* L20.

Laurasia /lɔːˈreɪʒə/ *noun*. M20.
[ORIGIN mod. Latin, from *Laur(entia* the ancient land mass corresp. to N. America (formed as LAURENTIAN *adjective*[1]) + *Eur)asia* (see EURASIAN *adjective* & *noun*).]
GEOLOGY. A supercontinent thought to have existed in the northern hemisphere and to have broken up in Mesozoic or late Palaeozoic times to form N. America, Europe, and most of Asia. Also, these land masses collectively as they exist today.
■ **Laurasian** *adjective* M20.

laurate /ˈlɔːreɪt/ *noun*. L19.
[ORIGIN from LAURIC + -ATE[1].]
CHEMISTRY. A salt or ester of lauric acid.

†**laureat** *adjective* & *noun* var. of LAUREATE *adjective* & *noun*.

laureate /ˈlɒrɪət, ˈlɔː-/ *adjective* & *noun*. Also †**-at**. LME.
[ORIGIN Latin *laureatus*, from *laurea* laurel tree, laurel crown, use as noun of fem. of *laureus* adjective, from *laurus* LAUREL *noun*, or from medieval Latin *laureat-* pa. ppl stem of *laureare* crown with laurels: see -ATE[2].]
▸ **A** *adjective* **1 a** Of a crown or wreath: consisting of

laurel, imitating a crown or wreath composed of laurel. LME. ▸b Crowned with laurel, wearing a laurel crown or wreath as a symbol of distinction or eminence. E17.
2 Distinguished for excellence as a poet. Now chiefly in *POET laureate*. LME. ▸b *gen.* Worthy of special distinction or honour, pre-eminent in a certain sphere. E16.
3 Of a thing: worthy of a laurel wreath; deserving to be honoured for eloquence etc. In later use also, of or pertaining to poets. LME.
▸ **B** *noun*. †**1** Glory, honour, distinction. Only in L15.
2 a (Also **L-**.) = *POET laureate*. E16. ▸b *transf.* A person who is pre-eminent or worthy of special distinction in a certain sphere. E19. ▸c A eulogist, a court panegyrist. M19. ▸d A person awarded an honour for achieving distinction, a graduate. L19.

b HARTLEY COLERIDGE Herrick was the laureate of flowers and perfumes.

d *Nobel laureate*: see NOBEL 2.
■ **laureateship** *noun* the position or office of (poet) laureate L18.

laureate /ˈlɒrɪeɪt, ˈlɔː-/ *verb trans.* LME.
[ORIGIN In sense 1 from medieval Latin *laureare* (see LAUREATE *adjective & noun*); in sense 2 from the adjective: see -ATE[3].]
1 Crown with laurel as a mark of honour; crown as victor, poet, etc.; confer honourable distinction upon. LME.
2 *spec.* ▸a Confer a university degree on; in *pass.*, graduate. M17. ▸b Appoint to the office of poet laureate. E18.

laureation /lɒrɪˈeɪʃ(ə)n, lɔː-/ *noun*. E17.
[ORIGIN medieval Latin *laureatio(n-)*, from *laureat-* pa. ppl stem of *laureare*: see LAUREATE *adjective & noun*, -ATION.]
The action of crowning someone with laurel or making someone laureate; the creation of a poet laureate. In Scottish universities, graduation or admission to a degree, now *spec.* an honorary degree.

laurel /ˈlɒr(ə)l/ *noun & adjective*. Also (earlier) †**laurer**. ME.
[ORIGIN Old French *lorier* (mod. *laurier*) from Provençal *laurier*, from *laur* (= Old French *lor*, Catalan *llor*, etc.) from Latin *laurus*, prob. of Mediterranean origin. The later form is due to dissimilation of *r . . r* to *r . . l*: cf. Spanish *laurel*.]
▸ **A** *noun*. **1** A tree or shrub of the genus *Laurus* (family Lauraceae); *spec.* (more fully ***bay laurel***) the bay tree, *L. nobilis*. ME.
2 *collect. sing.* & in *pl.* The foliage of this tree (real or imaginary) as an emblem of victory or of distinction in poetry etc. Esp. ***reap one's laurels***, ***win one's laurels***. LME. ▸b A branch or wreath of this tree (real or imaginary). LME. ▸†c The dignity of poet laureate. E18–E19. ▸d = ***laurel-green*** below. E20.
look to one's laurels beware of losing one's pre-eminence. **repose on one's laurels**, **rest on one's laurels**, **retire on one's laurels** cease to strive for further glory.
3 a Any of various trees and shrubs having leaves resembling those of the bay tree; *esp.* (more fully ***common laurel***, ***cherry laurel***) *Prunus laurocerasus*, an evergreen shrub of the rose family much grown in shrubberies. E17. ▸b Any of various trees and shrubs of the family Lauraceae, related to the bay tree. M17.
a ***Japanese laurel***, ***mountain laurel***, ***spurge laurel***, etc. **b** ***camphor laurel***.
4 NUMISMATICS. Any of various English gold pieces (esp. those of 20 shillings) on which the monarch's head was figured with a wreath of laurel. E17.
– COMB.: **laurel-bottle** a bottle containing crushed laurel leaves, used by entomologists for killing insects; **laurel-cherry** = ***cherry laurel***, sense 3 above; **laurel-green** *noun & adjective* (of) the medium green colour of bay tree leaves; **laurel magnolia** *US* either of two magnolias, the evergreen *Magnolia grandiflora* and the sweet bay, *M. virginiana*; **laurel oak** *US* either of two oaks, *Quercus laurifolia* and *Q. imbricaria*; **laurel-water** the water obtained by distillation from the leaves of the cherry laurel and containing a small proportion of prussic acid.
▸ †**B** *adjective*. Crowned or wreathed with laurel; *fig.* renowned. L16–E17.

laurel /ˈlɒr(ə)l/ *verb trans.* Infl. **-ll-**, ***-l-**. M17.
[ORIGIN from the noun.]
Wreathe with laurel, adorn with or as with laurel; *fig.* honour, acclaim.

laurelled /ˈlɒr(ə)ld/ *adjective*. Also ***-eled**. M17.
[ORIGIN from LAUREL *noun*, *verb*: see -ED[2], -ED[1].]
Adorned, crowned, or wreathed with laurel; *fig.* honoured, illustrious. Also, covered with a growth of laurel, made of laurel.

Laurence /ˈlɒr(ə)ns/ *noun*. Also **Lawrence**. L18.
[ORIGIN Male forename.]
1 Laziness personified, a lazy person. Also ***Lazy Laurence*** *obsolete* exc. *dial.* L18.
2 The shimmer reflected from the earth's surface on hot days; a mirage. *US colloq.* E20.

Laurentian /lɒˈrɛnʃ(ə)n/ *adjective*[1]. M19.
[ORIGIN from Latin *Laurentius* Laurence, Lawrence, from the St Lawrence River + -AN.]
GEOLOGY. Designating or pertaining to a geological region in eastern Canada of Precambrian age (the ***Laurentian Shield***) or the period in which it was formed; *esp.* designating a group of granites found north-west of the St Lawrence River.

Laurentian /lɒˈrɛnʃ(ə)n/ *adjective*[2]. M19.
[ORIGIN from Lorenzo (*Laurentius*) de' Medici (1449–92), Florentine nobleman + -AN.]
Designating or pertaining to the library in Florence founded by Lorenzo de' Medici, or manuscripts preserved there.

Laurentian *adjective*[3] & *noun* var. of LAWRENTIAN.

†**laurer** *noun & adjective* see LAUREL *noun & adjective*.

lauric /ˈlɔːrɪk/ *adjective*. L19.
[ORIGIN from mod. Latin genus name *Laurus* laurel + -IC.]
CHEMISTRY. ***lauric acid***, a saturated fatty acid, $CH_3(CH_2)_{10}COOH$, which occurs as a glyceride in laurel oil, coconut oil, and other vegetable fats. Also called ***dodecanoic acid***.
■ **lauroyl** /ˈlɔːrəʊʌɪl, -əʊɪl/ *noun* the radical $CH_3(CH_2)_{10}CO·$ M20.

laurustine /ˈlɔːrəstʌɪn/ *noun*. L17.
[ORIGIN Anglicized from LAURUSTINUS.]
= LAURUSTINUS.

laurustinus /lɒrəˈstʌɪnəs, lɔː-/ *noun*. E17.
[ORIGIN mod. Latin *laurus tinus*, i.e. Latin *laurus* laurel + *tinus* laurustinus.]
A Mediterranean evergreen winter-flowering shrub, *Viburnum tinus*, of the honeysuckle family.

lauryl /ˈlɒrɪl, -rʌɪl, ˈlɔː-/ *noun*. E20.
[ORIGIN from LAURIC + -YL.]
CHEMISTRY. A radical $CH_3(CH_2)_{10}CH_2·$, derived from lauric acid; dodecyl. Usu. in *comb.*
– COMB.: **lauryl alcohol** a crystalline low-melting alcohol, $CH_3(CH_2)_{10}CH_2OH$, which is obtained by reduction of coconut oil and whose sulphate esters are used in detergents.

Lausitz /ˈlaʊsɪts/ *adjective*. E20.
[ORIGIN German name of Lusatia: see LUSATIAN *noun & adjective*.]
ARCHAEOLOGY. Designating or pertaining to an urnfield culture which flourished in central Europe during the later Bronze Age.

lautenclavicymbel /ˈlaʊt(ə)nklavɪˌsɪmb(ə)l/ *noun*. Also **-al**. L19.
[ORIGIN German *Lautenklavizimbel*, from *Laute* lute + *Klavizimbel* harpsichord, formed as CLAVICYMBAL.]
hist. A type of harpsichord with gut rather than metal strings. Also called ***lute harpsichord***.

lauter /ˈlaʊtə/ *adjective & verb*. E20.
[ORIGIN from German *läutern* purify, refine, strain.]
BREWING. ▸ **A** *adjective*. Involved in, used in, or resulting from the refining process. E20.
– COMB.: **lautermash** refined liquid, wort.
▸ **B** *verb trans.* Refine, filter. Chiefly as ***lautering*** *verbal noun*. M20.

LAUTRO /ˈlaʊtrəʊ/ *abbreviation*.
Life Assurance and Unit Trust Regulatory Organization.

Lauwine /laʊˈviːnə, ˈlɔːwɪn/ *noun*. Now *rare*. Also ***Lawine*** /ˈlɑːviːnə/. E19.
[ORIGIN (Orig. Swiss) German *Lawine*, †*Lauwin(e*, etc., of unknown origin.]
An avalanche.
– NOTE: Formerly more fully naturalized.

LAV *abbreviation*.
MEDICINE. Lymphadenopathy-associated virus.

lav /lav/ *noun*. *colloq.* E20.
[ORIGIN Abbreviation.]
= LAVATORY *noun* 3. Cf. LAVVY.

lava /ˈlɑːvə/ *noun*. M18.
[ORIGIN Italian (orig. Neapolitan dial.) = lava stream from Vesuvius, (formerly) stream caused by sudden rain, from Latin *lavare* to wash.]
1 The fluid or semi-fluid magma or molten rock which flows from a volcano or other fissure in the earth. M18.

Scientific American The magma is erupted at the surface as lava.

2 A stream or flow of molten rock issuing from a volcanic crater or fissure. M18.

Sunday Express Composed of solidified lavas from ancient volcanoes, this . . mountain is the highest point in the land.

3 a The hard igneous rock resulting from the cooling of volcanic lava. M18. ▸b A kind of lava; a bed of solidified lava. L18.
– COMB.: ***lava bomb***: see BOMB *noun* 4; **lava flow** a mass of flowing or solidified lava; **lava lamp** a transparent electric lamp containing a viscous liquid in which a brightly coloured waxy substance is suspended, rising and falling in irregular and constantly changing shapes; **lava tube**, **lava tunnel** a natural tunnel within a solidified lava flow, formerly occupied by flowing molten lava; **lava ware** a type of stoneware with the semi-vitreous appearance of lava.
■ **laval** *adjective* L19.

lavabo /ləˈveɪbəʊ, *in sense* 2 ˈlavəbəʊ/ *noun*. Pl. **-o(e)s**. M18.
[ORIGIN Latin = I will wash.]
1 ECCLESIASTICAL. **a** In the Eucharist: the ritual washing of a celebrant's hands at the offertory. M18. ▸b The small towel used to wipe the celebrant's hands. M18. ▸c The basin used for the washing. M18.
2 a A washing trough used in some medieval monasteries. L19. ▸b A wash-hand basin. E20. ▸c = LAVATORY *noun* 4. M20.

lavage /ˈlavɪdʒ, laˈvɑːʒ/ *noun & verb*. L18.
[ORIGIN French, from *laver* to wash: see -AGE.]
▸ **A** *noun*. **1** An act of washing, a wash. L18.
2 MEDICINE. The washing out of a body cavity or a wound with water or a medicated solution. L19.
▸ **B** *verb trans.* MEDICINE. Cleanse or irrigate (an organ). M20.

lava-lava /ˈlɑːvəlɑːvə/ *noun*. L19.
[ORIGIN Samoan.]
In Samoa and some other Pacific islands: a wrap-around skirtlike garment worn by either sex.

lavaliere /ləˈvaljɛː/ *noun*. Also **-(l)lière**, **-lier** /-lɪə/, **L-**. L19.
[ORIGIN Louise de *la Vallière* (1644–1710), French courtesan.]
1 Used *attrib.* to designate any of various items of women's clothing in styles associated with the reign of Louis XIV of France. L19.
2 A pendent necklace. E20.
3 A loosely tied cravat. M20.
4 A small microphone worn hanging around the neck. Also ***lavaliere microphone***. M20.

†**lavament** *noun*. LME–E19.
[ORIGIN medieval Latin *lavamentum*, from Latin *lavare* to wash: see -MENT. Cf. LAVEMENT.]
An act of washing; a wash, a lotion.

lavandera /lavanˈdera/ *noun*. M19.
[ORIGIN Spanish.]
In Spain and Spanish-speaking countries: a washerwoman.

lavaret /lavarɛ (*pl. same*), ˈlav(ə)rət/ *noun*. M19.
[ORIGIN French.]
A form of the freshwater houting, *Coregonus lavaretus*, occurring in central European lakes.

lavash /ləˈvaʃ, ləˈvɑːʃ/ *noun*. Pl. same. M17.
[ORIGIN Partly from Armenian *lawa*, partly from Ottoman Turkish, Persian *lava*.]
A type of unleavened or slightly leavened Middle Eastern flatbread.

lavatera /lavəˈtɛːrə, ləˈvɑːt(ə)rə/ *noun*. M18.
[ORIGIN mod. Latin (see below), from the brothers *Lavater*, 17th- and 18th-cent. Swiss physicians and naturalists.]
Any of various herbs or shrubs constituting the genus *Lavatera*, of the mallow family, bearing pink, white, or purple flowers; *esp.* the tree mallow, *L. arborea*.

lavation /ləˈveɪʃ(ə)n/ *noun*. LME.
[ORIGIN Latin *lavatio(n-)* washing, from *lavat-* pa. ppl stem of *lavare* wash: see -ATION.]
The action of washing, an instance of this; water for washing.

lavatorial /lavəˈtɔːrɪəl/ *adjective*. M19.
[ORIGIN from LAVATORY *noun* + -AL[1].]
1 Of or pertaining to washing. M19.
2 Of or pertaining to lavatories; *spec.* (**a**) designating or pertaining to a style of architecture or decoration alleged to resemble that used for public lavatories; (**b**) (of conversation, humour, etc.) making undue reference to lavatories and their use. M20.

ALAN ROSS Endless lavatorial town hall corridors. *Reader's Report* Many poets, when talking about their art, drop . . into . . obstetrical and even lavatorial imagery.

lavatory /ˈlavət(ə)ri/ *noun*. LME.
[ORIGIN Late Latin *lavatorium*, from Latin *lavat-*: see LAVATION, -ORY[1].]
1 A vessel for washing; a laver, a bath. Also (ECCLESIASTICAL), a piscina. LME. ▸†b *fig.* A means of spiritual cleansing or purification. LME–M17.
†**2** A lotion, a wash. LME–L17.
3 ECCLESIASTICAL. The ritual washing of a celebrant's hands at the offertory (cf. LAVABO 1a) or (formerly) after the cleansing of the vessels following the Eucharist. E16.
4 Orig., a room with washing facilities. Now, a room, building, or compartment fitted for people to urinate and defecate in, usu. with facilities for washing the hands and face; also, any place or facility provided for urination and defecation. M17. ▸b An appliance for urinating and defecating into, usu. flushed by water. M20.

J. P. DONLEAVY And a toilet bowl wedged between two walls, the lavatory. M. SPARK Freddy went to the lavatory, not from need, but in case there should be a long journey ahead. **b** *attrib.*: K. WILLIAMS You're sitting on this freshly painted lavatory seat and the cistern overflows.

†**5** A laundry. M17–L19.
– COMB.: **lavatory humour** unsavoury or crude humour making undue reference to lavatories, lavatorial humour; **lavatory paper** = ***toilet paper*** s.v. TOILET *noun*; **lavatory style** a lavatorial style of architecture.

lavatory /ˈlavət(ə)ri, ləˈveɪt(ə)ri/ *adjective*. M19.
[ORIGIN from the noun.]
Of or pertaining to washing.

lave /leɪv/ *noun*. *obsolete* exc. *Scot.*
[ORIGIN Old English *lāf* = Old Frisian *lāva*, Old Low German *lēva*, Old High German *leiba*, Old Norse *leif*, Gothic *laiba* from Germanic base also of LEAVE *verb*[1].]
What is left; the remainder, the rest.

lave /leɪv/ *adjective. obsolete* exc. in comb. below. LME.
[ORIGIN Cf. Old Norse *lafa* to droop.]
Of ears: drooping, hanging.
– COMB.: **lave-eared** *adjective* having lave-ears; **lave-ears** drooping or hanging ears (esp. of a horse), lop-ears.

lave /leɪv/ *verb.* Now chiefly *poet.*
[ORIGIN Old English *lafian* = Middle Dutch & mod. Dutch *laven*, Old High German *labōn*, German *laben* refresh, from Latin *lavare* wash. Coalesced in Middle English with forms from Old French & mod. French *laver* from Latin *lavare*.]
1 *verb trans.* Wash, orig. *spec.* by pouring water on; bathe. OE. ▸**b** *verb intrans.* Bathe. E18.

J. UPDIKE Several Tuareg women . . were laving Sheba's feet.

2 *verb trans.* Pour (out), sprinkle, ladle. Foll. by *into, on, upon.* OE.
3 *verb trans.* Draw (water) out or up with a bucket, scoop, etc.; bale. (Foll. by *out, up.*) *obsolete* exc. *dial.* ME.
4 *verb trans.* Of a river or body of water: wash against, flow along or past. E17.

W. DE LA MARE When calm waters lave a rock-bound coast.

laveer /lə'vɪə/ *verb intrans. obsolete* exc. *literary.* L16.
[ORIGIN Dutch *laveeren*, earlier †*loveren* from French †*loveer* (now. *louvoyer*), from *lof* windward, LUFF *noun*[1]: see -EER.]
NAUTICAL. Beat to windward, tack.

lavement /'leɪvm(ə)nt/ *noun.* M17.
[ORIGIN Old French & mod. French, from *laver* to wash: see LAVE *verb*, -MENT. Cf. LAVAMENT.]
1 The action of washing or cleansing. *rare.* M17.
2 *MEDICINE.* A cleansing solution, *esp.* an enema. Now *rare.* L18.

†**lavender** *noun*[1]. ME–M16.
[ORIGIN Old French *lavandier* (masc.), *-iere* (fem.) from Proto-Romance var. of Latin *lavanda* things to be washed, use as noun of neut. pl. of gerundive of *lavare* to wash: see -ER[2].]
= LAUNDER *noun* 1.

lavender /'lav(ə)ndə/ *noun*[2] & *adjective.* ME.
[ORIGIN Anglo-Norman *lavendre*, ult. dissimilated form of medieval Latin *lavendula* etc., of unknown origin.]
▸**A** *noun.* **1** Any of various small labiate shrubs constituting the genus *Lavandula*, with spikes of purple flowers and narrow oblong or lanceolate leaves, native to the Mediterranean region; *spec.* any of those grown in gardens or cultivated for perfume, esp. *Lavandula angustifolia*, *L. latifolia*, and their hybrid. ME.
2 The flowers and stalks of cultivated lavender, dried and placed among linen, clothes, etc., to scent them and preserve them from moths. L16.
3 *ellipt.* Lavender-blue. M19.
4 *fig.* Effeminacy, homosexuality, homosexual tendencies. E20.

New Republic Rick is so hard-boiled that any touch of lavender is wiped away.

5 *CINEMATOGRAPHY.* Positive stock, or a positive print, used for producing duplicate negatives; a print made from such a negative. M20.
– PHRASES: ***French lavender***: see FRENCH *adjective.* **lay up in lavender** preserve carefully for future use. **oil of lavender** the oil obtained by distillation of the blossoms of cultivated lavender, used in medicine and perfumery. ***sea lavender***. ***spike lavender***: see SPIKE *noun*[2].
– COMB.: **lavender bag** a bag containing dried lavender; **lavender-blue** (of) the colour of lavender flowers, a pale blue with a trace of red; **lavender cotton** a greyish aromatic shrub of the composite family, *Santolina chamaecyparissus*, grown for ornament; **lavender oil** = ***oil of lavender*** above; †**lavender rays** ultraviolet radiation; **lavender soap** soap perfumed with lavender; **lavender water** perfume made from distilled lavender, alcohol, and ambergris.
▸**B** *adjective.* **1** Of the colour or fragrance of lavender flowers. M19.
2 *fig.* Refined, genteel, sentimental. E20. ▸**b** Of or pertaining to homosexuality; (of a man) homosexual, effeminate. *colloq.* M20.
■ **lavendery** *adjective* perfumed with lavender, fragrant L19.

lavender /'lav(ə)ndə/ *verb trans.* E19.
[ORIGIN from the noun.]
Perfume with lavender; put lavender among (linen etc.). Also, launder.

†**lavendry** *noun.* ME–M16.
[ORIGIN Old French *lavanderie* (cf. Latin *lavandaria* things to be washed): see -RY.]
= LAUNDRY *noun* 1, 2. Also, a washerwoman, a laundress.

lave net /'leɪv nɛt/ *noun phr.* L19.
[ORIGIN Origin of 1st elem. unkn.]
A kind of fishing net used chiefly in shallow water.

laver /'leɪvə, 'lɑːvə/ *noun*[1]. LOE.
[ORIGIN Latin.]
†**1** A water plant mentioned by Pliny. Also called ***sion***. LOE–E17.
2 Formerly, any of various marine algae. Now, one that is edible, *esp.* (more fully ***purple laver***) *Porphyra umbilicalis*. E17.
– COMB.: **laver bread** a Welsh food made from the fronds of *Porphyra umbilicalis*, which are boiled, dipped in oatmeal, and fried.

laver /'leɪvə/ *noun*[2]. ME.
[ORIGIN Old French *laveor, laveoir* (mod. *lavoir*) formed as LAVATORY *noun*.]
1 A basin or bowl for washing; (occas.) any vessel for water. Formerly also, a piscina or a washing trough in a monastic cloister. Now only *poet.* & *rhet.* ME. ▸**b** In biblical translations and allusions: a large bronze vessel used by Jewish priests for washing. M16. ▸**c** The basin of a fountain. *arch.* E17.
2 The baptismal font. Also *fig.*, the spiritual purification of baptism; any spiritually cleansing agency. LME.
†**3** A process or instance of washing. Only in L17.
– COMB.: **laver-pot** *HERALDRY* a jug with a handle and a lid.

laver /'leɪvə/ *noun*[3]. E19.
[ORIGIN Perh. var. of LEVERS.]
HERALDRY. A charge representing a ploughshare. Also ***laver cutter***.

Laverack /'lav(ə)rak/ *noun.* L19.
[ORIGIN Edward *Laverack* (d. 1877), English dog-breeder.]
In full ***Laverack setter***. (A dog of) a breed of English setter having long white fur flecked with other colours.

laverock *noun* see LARK *noun*[1].

Laves phase /'lɑːvəs feɪz/ *noun phr.* M20.
[ORIGIN from Fritz-Henning *Laves* (1906–78), German crystallographer + PHASE *noun*.]
METALLURGY. Any of a group of intermetallic compounds of composition approximately AB_2 in which the relative sizes of the A and B atoms allow a stable packing arrangement with unusually high coordination numbers.

lavish /'lavɪʃ/ *adjective.* LME.
[ORIGIN Old French *lavasse* deluge of rain (cf. Old French *lavis* torrent of words), from *laver* wash, pour: see -ISH[1].]
1 a Spending, producing, or giving without moderation; unstinting; extravagant, prodigal. (Foll. by *of, in, with.*) LME. ▸**b** Spent, given, or produced in unstinted profusion; abundant. L16. ▸**c** Sumptuous, rich, luxurious. L19.

a E. A. FREEMAN The people . . were . . most lavish in gifts to holy places. M. WEST Herman was lavish with compliments. **b** J. A. MICHENER The two Cobb boys . . passed among the guests, treating each with lavish deference. **c** *Which?* They've poured money into the pubs . . with large sums spent . . on lavish decor. S. NAIPAUL Their food was not only plentiful but lavish.

2 a Of speech etc.: unrestrained, effusive. L15. ▸†**b** Of conduct or disposition: unrestrained, wild, licentious. L16–M17. ▸**c** Of grass or wheat: rank, overgrown. *dial.* E18.
■ **lavishly** *adverb* LME. **lavishness** *noun* L15.

lavish /'lavɪʃ/ *verb.* M16.
[ORIGIN from the noun.]
†**1** *verb intrans.* Be extravagant, plunge *into* (excess); be excessive with words, exaggerate. M16–L17. ▸**b** Of rain: pour *along* in torrents. Only in M19.
2 *verb trans.* Give or spend profusely or excessively. (Foll. by *in, on, upon.*) M16.

W. S. CHURCHILL He was astonished at the vast sums which were being lavished upon the masonry. R. GRAVES If I lavished extravagant praise on her, she deserved it all.

■ **lavishingly** *adverb* (now *rare*) in a lavish manner L16. **lavishment** *noun* (now *rare*) the action of lavishing M17.

lavolta /lə'vɒltə/ *noun.* L16.
[ORIGIN from Italian *la* the + *volta* turn.]
hist. A lively dance for couples in 3/4 time, in which each partner lifts the other clear of the ground in turn.

lavra *noun* var. of LAURA.

lavvy /'lavi/ *noun.* M20.
[ORIGIN Abbreviation.]
= LAVATORY *noun* 3. Cf. LAV.

law /lɔː/ *noun*[1].
[ORIGIN Old English *lagu* (pl. *laga*) from Old Norse pl. of *lag* something laid down or fixed, ult. from Germanic base of LAY *verb*[1], LIE *verb*[1].]
▸**I** A rule of conduct imposed by secular authority.
1 (Usu. with *the*.) The body of rules, whether formally enacted or customary, which a particular state or community recognizes as governing the actions of its subjects or members and which it may enforce by imposing penalties. Orig. also, a code or system of rules of this kind. OE. ▸†**b** What the law awards; what is due according to the law. LME–L16. ▸**c** Personified as an agent uttering or enforcing the rules of which it consists. Also *colloq.* (orig. *US*), a police officer, the police; a sheriff. E16.

SHAKES. *Merch. V.* The Venetian law Cannot impugn you as you do proceed. L. R. BANKS Even my dad, that's so strict, breaks the law sometimes. **c** DICKENS If the law supposes that, . . the law is a ass—a idiot. *Times* I enquired of the Law where I might cash a cheque. *Orlando (Florida) Sentinel* The students now know they could get . . in trouble with the law.

2 Any of the body of individual rules in force in a state or community. In early use only in *pl.*, with a collect. sense approaching sense 1. OE.

SHAKES. *Hen. VIII* His faults lie open to the laws; let them, Not you, correct him. R. CAMPBELL A stupid law prevents them entering town in their native garb. J. RATHBONE Laws are not for governments, they are for the governed.

3 a Laws regarded as obeyed or enforced; controlling influence of laws; a state of respect for or observance of the laws. Freq. in ***law and order***. ME. ▸**b** Laws regarded collectively as a social system; rules or injunctions that must be obeyed; something which has the binding force or effect of laws. ME. ▸**c** Laws regarded as a class of objects or as a subject of study; that department of knowledge of which laws are the subject matter; (*sing.* & in *pl.*) jurisprudence. Also (with specifying word), any of the branches into which this collective body may be divided as it affects particular spheres of activity. LME.

a V. SETH A nation . . In its own birth resisted law. *Proverb*: Necessity has (*or* knows) no law. **b** TENNYSON You knew my word was law, and yet you dared To slight it. G. ORWELL His actions are not regulated by law or by any clearly formulated code of behaviour. **c** J. H. NEWMAN Men learned in the law. W. CATHER He was going . . to read law in the office of a Swedish lawyer.

4 a (Usu. with *the*.) The profession which is concerned with the exposition of the law, with pleading in the courts, and with the transaction of business requiring skilled knowledge of law; the profession of a lawyer. ME. ▸**b** Legal knowledge; legal acquirements. M17.

a OED Three of his brothers are in the law. **b** R. CHURCH Coke thoroughly disliked Bacon. He thought lightly of his law.

5 The action of the courts, as a means of providing redress of grievances or enforcing claims; judicial remedy; recourse to the courts, litigation. ME.
6 The statute and common law. Opp. EQUITY 3. L16.
7 (Predicatively.) A correct decision or opinion on a legal matter; (with *good, bad*, etc.) a legal judgement considered from the point of view of correctness. M18.

W. BLACKSTONE If it be found that the former decision is manifestly absurd or unjust, it is declared, not that such a sentence was bad law, but that it was not law.

▸**II** Chiefly *CHRISTIAN CHURCH*. Divine commandments.
8 The body of commandments considered to express the will of God with regard to the conduct of intelligent creatures, whether revealed in Scripture, innate in the mind, or demonstrable by reason. Also, a particular commandment. Freq. in ***God's law***, ***law of nature*** (cf. sense 15 below), ***law of reason***, etc. OE.

AV *Ps.* 1:2 His delight is in the Law of the Lord.

9 The system of moral and ceremonial precepts contained in the Pentateuch; the ceremonial portion of the system considered separately. Also (in expressed or implied opposition to ***the Gospel***), the Mosaic dispensation; the system of divine commands and penalties imposed for disobedience contained in the Scriptures. More explicitly ***the law of Moses***, ***the Mosaic law***, etc. OE. ▸**b** (L-.) *The* five books of the Pentateuch taken together, in the Jewish religion constituting the first and most important of the three canonical divisions of the Hebrew Scriptures (the others being the Prophets and the Hagiographa or Writings). LME.

J. CUMMING By what he suffered, I escape the law's curse. C. RAPHAEL The sense of purpose which Moses unfolded found form in the 'Law', the Kings and the Prophets.

†**10** A religious system; a faith or creed. ME–L17.
▸**III** A rule or procedure not derived from an external commanding authority.
†**11** Custom, customary rule or usage; habit, practice. Also, a particular (esp. criminal) practice. ME–L16.
†**12** What is or is considered right or proper; justice or correctness of conduct. Only in ME.
13 A rule of action or procedure; any of the rules defining correct procedure in an art or department of action, social context, or in a game etc. Also, the code or body of rules recognized in a specified department of action etc. ME.

T. JACKSON Unto Satan . . he did vouchsafe the benefit of the law of Armes or duel. L. ADDISON Contrary to all . . Laws of Hospitality. E. R. CONDER A moral law states what ought to be.

14 An allowance in time or distance made to an animal that is to be hunted, or to one of the competitors in a race, in order to ensure equal conditions; a start; *gen.* indulgence, mercy. *arch.* E17.

G. WHITE When the devoted deer was separated from his companions, they gave him . . law . . for twenty minutes. GEO. ELIOT I will never grant One inch of law to feeble blasphemies.

▸**IV** A regularity in the material world.
15 A principle deduced from observation, applicable to a defined group or class of phenomena, and generally expressible by the statement that a particular phenomenon always occurs if certain conditions are present; *esp.* (with specifying word(s)) such a principle formulated in a particular case or associated with a particular discoverer.

L

Also (with ref. to the physical world) ***law of nature*** (cf. sense 8 above). **M17.** ▸**b** A (freq. jocular) precept or rule of action, or statement of cause and effect in everyday life. **M20.**

> J. TYNDALL As regards the motion of the surface of a glacier, two laws are to be borne in mind. B. STEWART A perfect gas obeys Gay Lussac's law. **b** *New York Times* The first law for officeholders is . . 'Get re-elected.' H. MCCLOY I call this Julian's Law: a great man's intimates are never as great as he is.

Bode's law, Grassmann's law, Grimm's law, Kepler's laws, Ohm's law, Stefan–Boltzmann law, Trouton's law, etc. **b** ***Murphy's law, Parkinson's law, Sod's law,*** etc.

16 *MATH.* The rule or principle on which a series, or the construction of a curve, etc., depends. **E19.**
17 The state of being describable by natural laws; order and regularity in the natural world. **M19.**

> J. B. MOZLEY In the argument against miracles the first objection is that they are against law.

– PHRASES ETC.: **at law** according to the laws (***sue at law***: see SUE 12). ***bad law***: see BAD *adjective*. **be a law unto oneself** be guided by one's own sense of what is right; habitually disregard custom or the usual norms. ***blue laws***: see BLUE *adjective*. **both laws** *hist.* the civil and the canon laws. ***brother-in-law***: see BROTHER *noun*. ***canon law***: see CANON *noun*[1]. ***case law***: see CASE *noun*[1]. ***civil law***: see CIVIL *adjective*. ***court of law***: see COURT *noun*[1] 11. ***criminal law***: see CRIMINAL *adjective* 2. ***DAUGHTER-in-law***. ***father-in-law***: see FATHER *noun*. ***first law of THERMODYNAMICS***. **give law (to)** *arch.* exercise undisputed control (over); impose one's will (on). **go to law** take legal action, make use of the courts of law. **have the law on**, †**have the law of** take legal action against. ***international law***: see INTERNATIONAL *adjective*. ***inverse square law***: see INVERSE *adjective*. ***law of averages***: see AVERAGE *noun*[2] 5. ***law of excluded middle, law of excluded third***: see EXCLUDE *verb* 5. ***law of GRAVITATION***. ***law of honour***: see HONOUR *noun*. ***law of nations***: see NATION *noun*[1]. **law of nature** = ***natural law*** below. ***law of parsimony***: see PARSIMONY 2b. ***law of sewers***: see SEWER *noun*[1]. **law of the jungle** the supposed code of survival in jungle life; a system in which brute force and self-interest are paramount. **law of the land** (*a*) *arch.* the custom of the country concerned; (*b*) the laws in force in the country concerned. **law of the Medes and Persians** [*Daniel* 6:12] a law, or system of laws, that cannot be altered. **lay down the law** be dogmatic or authoritarian. ***limb of the law***: see LIMB *noun*[1]. ***lynch law***: see LYNCH *noun*[1]. ***man of law***: see MAN *noun*. ***martial law***: see MARTIAL *adjective*. ***moral law***: see MORAL *adjective*. ***mother-in-law***: see MOTHER *noun*[1]. **natural law** (*a*) = sense 8 above; (*b*) an observable law relating to natural phenomena. †**new law** the Gospel. †**old law** the Mosaic dispensation; the Old Testament. ***Oral Law***: see ORAL *adjective*. ***periodic law***: see PERIODIC *adjective*[1] 2. ***personal law***: see PERSONAL *adjective*. ***presumption of law***: see PRESUMPTION 2. ***public law***: see PUBLIC *adjective & noun*. ***Rejoicing of the Law, Rejoicing over the Law***: see REJOICING 1b. ***Roman law***: see ROMAN *adjective*. ***rule of law***: see RULE *noun*. ***Salic law***: see SALIC *adjective*[1]. ***second law of THERMODYNAMICS***. ***SERGEANT of law***. ***sister-in-law***: see SISTER *noun*. ***son-in-law***: see SON *noun*[1]. ***square law***: see SQUARE *adjective*. ***strong arm of the law***: see STRONG *adjective*. **take the law into one's own hands** seek to redress a grievance by one's own methods, esp. by force. **take the law of** *arch.* = ***have the law on*** above. ***third law of THERMODYNAMICS***. ***wage one's law, wage the law***: see WAGE *verb* 3a. ***wager of law***: see WAGER *noun* 5a.

– COMB.: **law-abiding** *adjective* obedient to the law; **law-abidingness** obedience to the law; ***law agent***: see AGENT *noun* 2; **law book**: (*a*) containing a code of laws; (*b*) on the subject of law; **law-borrow(s)**, **law-burrow(s)** *SCOTS LAW* (*a*) legal security required from a person that he or she will not injure the person, family, or property of another; (*b*) a person standing surety for another; **lawbreaker** a person who breaks the law; **lawbreaking** *noun & adjective* (of, engaged in) breaking the law; ***law-burrow(s)***: see ***law-borrow(s)*** above; **law centre** a publicly funded centre providing legal advice; **law-church** *arch.* (*derog.*) the Established Church; **Law Commission** a body of legal advisers responsible for systematically reviewing the law of England and Wales or of Scotland and advising on reform; **Law Commissioner** a member of one of the Law Commissions; **law court** a court of law; **law-day** (*a*) *hist.* the day of the meeting of a sheriff's court, court leet, or other court; (the session of) such a court; (*b*) *hist.* the day appointed for the discharge of a bond; (*c*) *US* a day on which educational publicity is given to legal matters in some states; **law French** the non-standard variety of Norman French used in English law books from the medieval period to the 18th cent.; **lawgiver** a person who makes or codifies laws; **lawgiving** the making or codifying of laws, legislation; **law-hand** a style of handwriting formerly used for legal documents; **law-keeper** †(*a*) a guardian of the law; (*b*) a law-abiding person; **law Latin** the non-standard Latin of early English statutes; **Law Lord** (*a*) any of the members of the House of Lords qualified to take part in its judicial business; (*b*) *colloq.* (in Scotland) any of the judges of the Court of Session or High Court of Justiciary who have by courtesy the style of 'Lord'; **lawmaker** = ***lawgiver*** above; **law merchant** [medieval Latin *lex mercatoria*] *hist.* the body of rules regulating trade and commerce between different countries; **law office** *N. Amer.* a lawyer's office; **law officer** a public functionary employed in the administration of the law, or to advise the Government in legal matters; *spec.* (more fully ***Law Officer of the Crown***), in England and Wales either the Attorney General or the Solicitor General, in Scotland either the Lord Advocate or the Solicitor General for Scotland; **Law Society** a professional body representing solicitors (in the UK and some Commonwealth jurisdictions); **law station** *slang* a police station; **law stationer** a trader who stocks stationery etc. required by lawyers, formerly often also taking in documents for fair copying or engrossing; **lawsuit** an action in law; a prosecution of a claim by litigation; **law term** (*a*) a word or expression used in law; (*b*) each of the periods appointed for the sitting of the courts of law.

■ **law-worthy** *adjective* (*hist.*) having a standing in the courts of law; within the purview of the law: **E19.**

law /lɔː/ *noun*[2]. *Scot. & N. English.* **ME.**
[ORIGIN Var. of LOW *noun*[1].]
A hill, *esp.* one more or less round or conical. Chiefly in names, as ***North Berwick Law, Cushat Law.***

†**law** *noun*[3]. *Scot.* **LME–M16.**
[ORIGIN Prob. from Old Norse *lag* (see LAW *noun*[1]).]
Share of expense; a charge, a bill.
– NOTE: Survives in LAWING.

law /lɔː/ *verb.* **OE.**
[ORIGIN from LAW *noun*[1].]
1 *verb trans.* †**a** Ordain (laws); establish as a law; make lawful. **OE–M17.** ▸**b** Command or impose as law; control (as) by law. *rare.* **L18.**
2 a *verb intrans.* & †*trans.* (with *it*). Go to law, litigate. **L15.** ▸**b** *verb trans.* Take legal action against. **M17.**

> **a** J. FLETCHER Ye must law and claw before ye get it. GEO. ELIOT People who inherited estates that were lawed about.

3 *verb trans.* Expeditate (a dog) and so render incapable of doing mischief. *obsolete* exc. *hist.* **M16.**

law /lɔː/ *interjection.* Now *colloq.* Also **laws** /lɔːz/. **L16.**
[ORIGIN Rel. to LO *interjection*[1], LA *interjection*, or alt. of LOR'. Cf. LAWK.]
Expr. chiefly astonishment or admiration, or (often) surprise at being asked a question; orig. chiefly asseverative.
■ Also **lawsy** *interjection* (chiefly *US*) **L19.**

lawdy *interjection* var. of LORDY.

lawful /ˈlɔːfʊl, -f(ə)l/ *adjective.* **ME.**
[ORIGIN from LAW *noun*[1] + -FUL.]
1 Observant of law or duty; law-abiding, faithful, loyal. Now *rare.* **ME.**
2 Appointed, sanctioned, or recognized by law; legally qualified or entitled. **ME.** ▸**b** Of a marriage: legally valid. Of offspring: legitimate. **LME.** ▸†**c** In exclamations as an intensive. *dial.* **L18–M19.**

> THOMAS MORTON She is my wife . . . My lawful, wedded wife.

3 According or not contrary to law or rules, permitted by law. **LME.** ▸†**b** Permissible; allowable, justifiable. **L16–E18.**

> D. PARKER Guns aren't lawful; Nooses give; Gas smells awful; You might as well live. *Guardian* The sellers were in lawful possession of the goods.

†**4** Pertaining to or concerned with law. **LME–M17.**
5 Describable or governed by laws of nature. **M20.**
■ **lawfully** *adverb* **ME.** **lawfulness** *noun* **ME.**

Lawine *noun* var. of LAUWINE.

lawing /ˈlɔːɪŋ/ *noun. Scot. arch.* **M16.**
[ORIGIN from LAW *noun*[3] + -ING[1].]
A reckoning or bill at a public house.

lawk /lɔːk/ *interjection. arch.* Also **lawks** /lɔːks/. **M18.**
[ORIGIN Alt. of LORD *noun*, perh. also rel. to LACK *noun*[2]. Cf. LAW *interjection.*]
Expr. surprise, consternation, etc.
– COMB.: **lawkadaisy** = LACKADAISY; **lawkamercy**, **-mussy** Lord have mercy!

lawless /ˈlɔːlɪs/ *adjective.* **ME.**
[ORIGIN from LAW *noun*[1] + -LESS.]
1 a Without law; having no laws, or enforcement of laws; ignorant of law. **ME.** ▸**b** Exempt from law, not within the province of law. Formerly also, in the position of an outlaw. **ME.**

> W. IRVING Commercial feuds in the lawless depths of the wilderness.

2 Regardless of or disobedient to law; uncontrolled by law, unbridled, licentious. **ME.**

> LD MACAULAY He should be protected against lawless violence. R. K. NARAYAN Ramani was eccentric and lawless in his tastes. G. GORER One of the most lawless populations in the world has turned into one of the most law-abiding.

■ **lawlessly** *adverb* **L16.** **lawlessness** *noun* **L16.**

lawlike /ˈlɔːlʌɪk/ *adjective.* **M16.**
[ORIGIN from LAW *noun*[1] + -LIKE.]
1 Like law, having a resemblance to law, or to legal phraseology or proceedings. Now *rare.* **M16.**
2 Resembling a law of nature. Also, such as to be a law of nature if established as true. **M20.**

lawman /ˈlɔːmən/ *noun.* Pl. **-men.** **OE.**
[ORIGIN from LAW *noun*[1] + MAN *noun*, partly after Old Norse *lagamaðr, lǫgmaðr.*]
1 *LAW* (now *hist.*). An officer in Anglo-Saxon England, *spec.* (*a*) a person whose official duty it was to declare the law; (*b*) In the five Danish boroughs, any of a number of magistrates or aldermen. **OE.**
2 *hist.* The president of the supreme court in Orkney or Shetland. **M16.**
3 A man of law, a lawyer. Now *rare.* **M16.**
4 A law-enforcement officer; a sheriff, a policeman. *colloq.* **M20.**

lawn /lɔːn/ *noun*[1] *& adjective.* **LME.**
[ORIGIN Prob. from *Laon*, a city in France, important for linen manufacture.]
▸ **A** *noun.* **1** A kind of fine linen or cotton; in *pl.*, pieces or sorts of this. **LME.** ▸**b** *spec.* This fabric used for the sleeves worn by a bishop. Hence, the dignity or office of a bishop. **M17.**
†**2** A garment or other article made of lawn. **L15–E19.**
3 = ***lawn sieve*** below. **M19.**
▸ **B** *attrib.* or as *adjective.* Made of lawn. **L15.**
– SPECIAL COLLOCATIONS & COMB.: **lawn sieve** a fine sieve of silk or other fabric, used esp. for clay. **lawn-sleeved** *adjective* wearing lawn sleeves; of or pertaining to a bishop or bishops. **lawn sleeves** sleeves of lawn as forming part of episcopal dress; the office or dignity of a bishop; a bishop or bishops.
■ **lawned** *adjective* arrayed in lawn, wearing lawn sleeves **L18.**

lawn /lɔːn/ *noun*[2] *& verb.* **M16.**
[ORIGIN Alt. of LAUND *noun.*]
▸ **A** *noun.* **1** An open space between woods; a glade. = LAUND *noun*. Now *arch. & dial.* exc. with ref. to the New Forest. **M16.**

> J. THOMSON The thistly lawn, the thick-entangled broom.

2 (A stretch of) untilled ground; (an extent of) grass-covered land. *obsolete* exc. as passing into sense 3. **E17.**

> MILTON The Shepherds on the Lawn . . Sate simply chatting in a rustick row.

3 An area of grass-covered ground which is kept mown and smooth, in a garden, park, etc.; such ground. Also, an area planted with low-lying herbs etc., esp. camomile. **M18.**

> R. W. EMERSON The beautiful lawns and gardens of the colleges. B. RUBENS The neat square of lawn that fronted the house.

4 *BIOLOGY.* A layer of bacteria or other cells uniformly distributed over the surface of a culture medium. **M20.**
– COMB.: **lawn chair** *N. Amer.* a folding chair for use out of doors; **lawn edger** a powered appliance for trimming the grass at the edge of a lawn; **lawn meet** the meeting of a hunt in the grounds of a private house; **lawnmower** a machine with a rotating blade or blades for cutting the grass on a lawn; **lawn party** a party held on a lawn, a garden party; **lawn sand** a top-dressing of sand and other components, used as a fertilizer and weedkiller for lawns; ***lawn tennis***: see TENNIS *noun* 2.
▸ **B** *verb trans.* Turn (ground) into lawn; lay with lawn. **M18.**

lawny /ˈlɔːni/ *adjective*[1]. **L16.**
[ORIGIN from LAWN *noun*[1] + -Y[1].]
1 Made of lawn. **L16.** ▸**b** Dressed in lawn; of or pertaining to a bishop or bishops. **M17.**
2 Resembling lawn. **E17.**

lawny /ˈlɔːni/ *adjective*[2]. **E17.**
[ORIGIN from LAWN *noun*[2] + -Y[1].]
Resembling a lawn; covered with smooth green turf. Formerly also, containing lawns or glades.

Lawrence *noun* var. of LAURENCE.

Lawrencian *adjective & noun* var. of LAWRENTIAN.

lawrencium /lɒˈrɛnsɪəm/ *noun.* **M20.**
[ORIGIN from Ernest O. *Lawrence* (1901–58), US physicist + -IUM.]
A radioactive transuranic metallic element, atomic no. 103, produced artificially. (Symbol Lr, formerly Lw.)

Lawrentian /lɒˈrɛnʃɪən, -ʃ(ə)n/ *adjective & noun.* Also **Laurentian**, **Lawrencian.** **E20.**
[ORIGIN from *Lawrence* (see below), Latin *Laurentius* + -IAN.]
▸ **A** *adjective.* **1** Of or pertaining to the British military leader and author Thomas Edward Lawrence ('Lawrence of Arabia') (1888–1935), his actions, or his works. **E20.**
2 Of or pertaining to the English author David Herbert Lawrence (1885–1930), or his work or style of writing. **M20.**
▸ **B** *noun.* An admirer or student of T. E. or D. H. Lawrence or the work of either. **M20.**
■ **Lawrenti'ana** *noun pl.* [-ANA] publications or other items concerning or associated with D. H. Lawrence **M20.**

lawrightman /ˈlɔːrʌɪtmən/ *noun. obsolete* exc. *hist.* Pl. **-men.** **LME.**
[ORIGIN from LAW *noun*[1] + RIGHT *noun*[1] + MAN *noun*, translating Old Norse *lǫgréttu-maðr.*]
In Orkney and Shetland: a local official responsible mainly for the supervision of weights and measures (in Shetland) or for keeping the peace (in Orkney).

laws *interjection* var. of LAW *interjection*.

Lawson cypress *noun phr.* var. of LAWSON'S CYPRESS.

lawsoniana /ˌlɔːsəʊnɪˈɑːnə/ *noun.* **M20.**
[ORIGIN mod. Latin specific epithet, formed as LAWSON'S CYPRESS.]
= LAWSON'S CYPRESS.

Lawson's cypress /ˈlɔːs(ə)nz ˈsʌɪprəs/ *noun phr.* Also **Lawson cypress.** **M19.**
[ORIGIN Peter (d. 1820) and his son Charles (1794–1873) *Lawson*, Scot. nurserymen, who first cultivated the plant.]
A cypress, *Chamaecyparis lawsoniana*, native to the western US, that is widely planted as an ornamental shrub or tree.

lawting /ˈlɔːtɪŋ/ *noun. obsolete* exc. *hist.* **L15.**
[ORIGIN Old Norse *lǫgþing*, from *lǫg* LAW *noun*[1] + *þing* THING *noun*[2].]
The former Supreme Court of Judicature in Orkney and Shetland.

lawyer /ˈlɔːjə, ˈlɔɪə/ *noun & verb.* LME.
[ORIGIN from LAW *noun*[1] + -YER.]
▸ **A** *noun.* **1** A person with knowledge of the law; a member of the profession of the law; *esp.* a solicitor or barrister. LME.
†**2** A lawgiver. M16–M17.
3 a Either of two birds, the black-necked stilt, *Himantopus mexicanus*, and the avocet, *Recurvirostra americana*. *US.* E19. ▸**b** Either of two fishes: the burbot, *Lota lota*, and the bowfin, *Amia calva*. *US.* M19.
4 A thorny creeping plant, a bramble, a briar (*dial.*); *Austral. & NZ* = ***bush lawyer*** s.v. BUSH *noun*[1]. M19.
– PHRASES ETC.: ***bush lawyer***: see BUSH *noun*[1]. COMMON LAWYER. ***criminal lawyer***: see CRIMINAL *adjective* 2. **lawyer's wig** = SHAGGY *ink cap*. PENANG LAWYER. *PHILADELPHIA* ***lawyer***. *SEA-****lawyer***.
– COMB.: **lawyer cane**, **lawyer vine** *Austral. & NZ* a thorny climbing plant, esp. *Calamus australis*.
▸ **B** *verb intrans.* Follow the profession of lawyer; act as a lawyer. Chiefly as ***lawyering*** *verbal noun.* L17.
▪ **lawyer-like** *adjective & adverb* (*a*) *adjective* resembling a lawyer or the practice of a lawyer; (*b*) *adverb* in the manner of a lawyer: L16. **lawyerly** *adjective* lawyer-like; of or pertaining to lawyers: M17.

lax /laks/ *noun*[1]. Now *rare.*
[ORIGIN Old English *læx*, (West Saxon) *leax* = Low German *las*, Old High German *lahs* (German *Lachs*), Old Norse (Swedish, Danish) *lax*, from Germanic. Cf. LOX *noun*[2].]
A salmon; *esp.* a Swedish or Norwegian salmon.

lax /laks/ *noun*[2]. *obsolete* exc. *dial.* LME.
[ORIGIN Perh. from LAX *verb.*]
†**1** (Treatment of illness by) a laxative medicine, an aperient. LME–M16.
2 Looseness of the bowels, diarrhoea. LME.
†**3** Relief, release. *rare.* Only in L18.

lax /laks/ *noun*[3]. *colloq.* M20.
[ORIGIN Contr.]
= LACROSSE.

lax /laks/ *adjective & adverb.* LME.
[ORIGIN Latin *laxus* loose, cogn. with SLACK *adjective.*]
▸ **A** *adjective.* **1** Of the bowels: loose. Formerly also, (of a person) having loose bowels. LME.
2 a Loose in texture; loosely cohering or compacted; porous. LME. ▸**b** *BOTANY.* Esp. of an inflorescence: having the parts distant from each other or in an open or loose arrangement. L18.

> **a** T. H. GREEN Those organs which possess a lax structure . . as the lungs.

3 Loose-fitting, worn loosely; careless of one's dress or appearance. *rare.* LME.
4 Not strict or severe; vague, not precise or exact. L15.

> J. R. GREEN Richard [Cromwell] was known to be lax and godless in his conduct. M. EDWARDES Discipline was lax, and bad practices were widely in evidence.

5 Slack; not tense or rigid; (of bodily constitution or mental powers) lacking in tone or tension. Now *rare.* M17. ▸**b** Of the limbs etc.: relaxed, without muscular tension. M19. ▸**c** *PHONETICS.* Of a speech sound: pronounced with the vocal muscles relaxed. Cf. TENSE *adjective* 1b. E20.

> **b** R. WEST A two-day-old calf, lax on the ground, like a great skein of fawn-coloured silk.

▸ †**B** *adverb.* So as to have ample room. *rare* (Milton). Only in M17.
▪ **laxly** *adverb* LME. **laxness** *noun* LME.

lax /laks/ *verb trans.* LME.
[ORIGIN Latin *laxare*, from *laxus* LAX *adjective.*]
1 Make lax; loosen, relax. *obsolete* exc. *Scot.* LME.
2 *PHONETICS.* Articulate (a speech sound) with the vocal muscles relaxed. M20.

laxation /lakˈseɪʃ(ə)n/ *noun.* LME.
[ORIGIN Late Latin *laxatio(n-)*, from Latin *laxat-* pa. ppl stem of *laxare*: see LAX *verb*, -ATION.]
The action or an act of loosening or relaxing something; the state of being loosened or relaxed; *MEDICINE* defecation. Also, administration of a laxative.

laxative /ˈlaksətɪv/ *adjective & noun.* LME.
[ORIGIN Old French & mod. French *laxatif, -ive* or late Latin *laxativus*, from Latin *laxat-*: see LAXATION, -ATIVE.]
▸ **A** *adjective.* **1** Of medicine etc.: tending to cause evacuation of the bowels. LME.
2 Of the bowels etc.: loose. Of a disease: characterized by looseness of the bowels. Now *rare.* LME. ▸**b** *transf.* Unable to contain one's speech or emotions. Now *rare* or *obsolete.* E17.
▸ **B** *noun.* **1** A laxative medicine. LME.
†**2** (A) looseness of the bowels. *rare.* LME–E16.
▪ **laxativeness** *noun* E17.

laxist /ˈlaksɪst/ *noun & adjective.* M19.
[ORIGIN from LAX *adjective* + -IST.]
▸ **A** *noun.* A person who favours lax views or interpretation; a person who is not a rigorist. M19.
▸ **B** *attrib.* or as *adjective.* Of or pertaining to laxists. L19.

laxity /ˈlaksɪti/ *noun.* E16.
[ORIGIN French *laxité* or Latin *laxitas*, from *laxus* LAX *adjective*: see -ITY.]
1 Looseness, esp. of the bowels; slackness, absence of tension. E16.
2 Looseness of texture or cohesion. E17.
3 Lack of strictness or severity; vagueness; lack of precision; an instance of this. E17.

> R. L. STEVENSON How are you, the apostle of laxity, to turn . . about into the Rabbi of precision. R. MACAULAY Laxity among the rich encourages immorality among the poor.

Laxton /ˈlakst(ə)n/ *noun.* Also **Laxton's** /ˈlakst(ə)nz/. E20.
[ORIGIN *Laxton* Brothers (see below).]
Any of several varieties of fruit bred and introduced by Laxton Brothers, a firm of English nurserymen.
Laxton's Superb a popular, late-ripening variety of red-skinned eating apple.

laxy /ˈlaksi/ *adjective.* Long *rare.* E18.
[ORIGIN from LAX *adjective* + -Y[1].]
= LAX *adjective* 2.

lay /leɪ/ *noun*[1]. Long *obsolete* exc. *dial.*
[ORIGIN Old English *lagu* from Germanic, perh. also infl. by Old French *lai* pool from late Latin *lacus.*]
A lake, a pool.

lay /leɪ/ *noun*[2]. ME.
[ORIGIN Old French & mod. French *lai* corresp. to Provençal *lais*: ult. origin unknown.]
1 A short lyric or narrative poem intended to be sung; a narrative poem; a song. ME. ▸**b** The song of birds. *poet.* LME.

> E. HUXLEY: W. S. Gilbert's lay of the two Englishmen wrecked on a desert island. N. FRYE One can never spontaneously burst into song, however doleful a lay.

†**2** A tune. Only in 16.

†**lay** *noun*[3]. LME–L18.
[ORIGIN Perh. aphet. from ALLAY *noun*[1].]
Alloy. Freq. in ***lay metal***, a kind of pewter.

lay /leɪ/ *noun*[4]. M16.
[ORIGIN from LAY *verb*[1].]
1 The action of imposing a tax; an assessment, a rate, a tax. Now *dial.* M16.
†**2** A wager, a bet, a stake. L16–M18.

> DEFOE By venturing my life upon an even lay with him.

3 The resting place of an animal. Also, a bed of oysters or mussels. L16.

> F. FRANCIS The boatman will probably know . . the lay of the trout.

†**4** A layer, a stratum; a course of masonry etc. L16–M18.
5 Rate or terms of purchase or remuneration. *US local.* E18.
6 A line or plan of business, occupation, etc.; a (particular) job. *slang.* E18.

> G. B. SHAW So blackmail is the game . . . There's nothing to be got out of me on that lay.

7 a The position or direction in which something, esp. country, lies; lie of the land etc. E19. ▸**b** The direction or amount of twist in the strands of a rope etc. E19. ▸**c** *PRINTING.* The arrangement of type in a compositor's case. Also, the position of the print on a sheet of paper. L19.

> **a** N. MARSH Did she tell you anything that supports our theory or sets us off on another lay?

8 A share in a venture; *esp.* an individual's proportion of the proceeds of a whaling voyage. M19.
9 The laying of eggs. Chiefly in ***in lay***, (of a hen) in a condition to lay eggs; ***point of lay*** s.v. POINT *noun*[1]. L19.
10 A woman (occas. a man) who is readily available for sexual intercourse; an act of sexual intercourse. Cf. LAY *verb*[1] 3b. *slang* (orig. *US*). M20.

> J. O'HARA Then you turn around and pay him back by giving his girl a lay. S. BELLOW She wanted to give her heart once and for all, . . and quit being an easy lay.

– COMB.: **lay-edge** *PRINTING* the edge of a sheet of paper which is used to determine the correct position of the sheet in a press; **lay gauge** an attachment on a printing press that keeps the paper in the correct position.

lay /leɪ/ *noun*[5]. *dial.* L18.
[ORIGIN Alt. of LATHE *noun*[4].]
WEAVING. The batten of a loom; = LATHE *noun*[4].

lay *noun*[6] var. of LEY *noun*[1].

lay /leɪ/ *adjective.* ME.
[ORIGIN Old French *lai* (now repl. by *laïque*) formed as LAIC.]
1 Of a person: non-clerical; not in ecclesiastical orders. ME.

> *New York Times* Particular attention must now be given to women, both lay and religious.

2 †**a** Uninstructed, unlearned. *rare.* ME–M16. ▸**b** Non-professional, not expert, not professionally trained or qualified, esp. in law or medicine. E19.

> **b** *Times* Any interest on the part of lay people in medical matters is regarded as . . interference.

3 Pertaining to or characteristic of a lay person or the laity; done by a lay person or the laity. E17.

> W. COWPER With reverend tutor clad in habit lay.

– SPECIAL COLLOCATIONS: **lay analysis** psychoanalysis undertaken by an analyst who has not been medically trained. **lay analyst** a person who practises psychoanalysis without medical training. **lay bishop** †(*a*) *derog.* a person who sets up as a teacher of morality; (*b*) a lay rector. **lay brother**, **lay sister** a man, woman, who has taken the habit and vows of a religious order, but is employed mostly in manual labour and is excused other duties. **lay clerk** (*a*) an adult singer in a cathedral or collegiate church; (*b*) a parish clerk. **lay communion** (*a*) membership of a Church as a lay person; (*b*) the communicating of the laity in the Eucharist. **lay deacon** a person in deacon's orders who also follows a secular employment. **lay elder** a non-clerical elder of a Church. **lay preacher** a preacher (esp. in the Methodist Church) who is not ordained. ***lay reader***: see READER 1b. **lay rector** a layman receiving rectorial tithes. ***lay sister***: see ***lay brother*** above. ***lay*** *VICAR.*

lay /leɪ/ *verb*[1]. Pa. t. & pple **laid** /leɪd/.
[ORIGIN Old English *leċġan* = Old Frisian *ledza*, *leia*, Old Saxon *leggian* (Dutch *leggen*), Old High German *lecken*, *legen* (German *legen*), Old Norse *legja*, Gothic *lagjan*, from Germanic base also of LIE *verb*[1].]
▸ **I** Prostrate.
1 *verb trans.* Bring or cast down from an erect position; strike down; make prostrate. Formerly also, abase, humble. Now only with compl. denoting prostration or extension on a surface. OE. ▸**b** Of wind or rain: beat down (crops). L16.

> BROWNING We check the fire by laying flat Each building in its path. TENNYSON Like flaws in summer laying lusty corn.

2 *verb trans.* Cause (the sea, a wind, a cloud of dust, etc.) to subside; allay (anxiety), appease (anger, appetite, etc.). Now chiefly *arch. & dial.* exc. in ***lay the dust***. ME. ▸**b** Cause (a ghost) to cease appearing. L16.

> SHAKES. *Two Gent.* See how I lay the dust with my tears. A. F. DOUGLAS-HOME The mistrust of the Archbishop was never laid. **b** B. HARTE For now that the ghosts of my heart are laid. *transf.*: *Times* We must lay the myth that the RPO was . . more eligible for penalisation than . . other orchestras.

3 *verb trans.* **a** Deliver (†oneself, a mother) of a child; bring to bed *of* a child. *obsolete* exc. *dial.* LME. ▸**b** Have sexual intercourse with (esp. a woman). Cf. LAY *noun*[4] 10. *slang* (orig. *US*). M20.
4 *verb trans.* *HORTICULTURE* = LAYER *verb* 1a. Now *rare* or *obsolete.* M16. ▸**b** Trim (a hedge) back, cutting the branches half through, bending them down, and interweaving them. Chiefly *dial.* M18.
5 *verb trans.* Orig., bring down, reduce, (a swelling). Now, smooth down, cause to lie evenly. L16.
6 *verb trans.* *NAUTICAL.* Sail out so far as to bring (land etc.) below the horizon. Opp. ***raise***. L16.
▸ **II** Deposit.
7 *verb trans.* Place in a position of rest *on* the ground or any other supporting surface; deposit in some specified place. OE. ▸**b** In the British Parliament: place (documents) on the table in order to give information to the House of Commons. E20.

> G. GREENE I laid the newspaper flat on the table. DAY LEWIS At a level crossing I laid pins on the line. **b** *Hansard* His Majesty's Government have been willing to lay the complete records.

8 *verb trans.* **a** Deposit *in* the grave; bury. Freq. in ***lay one's bones*** below. OE. ▸**b** Place (a person etc.) in a recumbent posture in a specified place. ME.

> **a** YEATS In Drumcliff churchyard Yeats is laid. TOLKIEN They had laid their fallen comrades in a mound. **b** M. ARNOLD The bent grass where I am laid.

9 *verb trans. & intrans.* Of a hen bird etc.: eject (an egg) from its body. See also ***lay an egg*** below. OE.

> ADDISON When she has laid her Eggs in such a manner that she can cover them. B. MACDONALD Black chickens which were supposed to lay as well as the White Leghorn.

†**10** *verb trans.* With adverbial phr. as compl.: deposit as a pledge or in pawn; mortgage (lands). ME–L17. ▸**b** Give up (a person) as a hostage; give up (a hostage). ME–M16.
11 *verb trans.* Put down as a wager; stake (a sum, one's head, life, etc.). Also, stake something on (a wager, a bet). ME. ▸**b** *verb intrans.* Wager, bet; announce one's readiness to bet. LME. ▸**c** *verb trans.* Bet on (a horse etc.). L19.

> ARNOLD BENNETT I lay anything he had opened the safe before and read the will before. J. COLVILLE The invasion may be pending (though I'll lay 10–1 against).

†**12** *verb trans.* Relinquish, sacrifice, (one's life). ME–M16.
†**13** *verb trans.* Lose the faculty of (speech). *N. English.* ME–M17.
▸ **III** Place, set, apply.
14 *verb trans.* Place close *to*; put *to* for a purpose, apply. OE. ▸†**b** Attach, add, annex *to*. OE–E19. ▸†**c** Put *in* or commit *to* prison. ME–M16. ▸**d** Put (hounds) *on* a scent. L18.

> SHAKES. *Macb.* By each at once her choppy finger laying Upon her skinny lips. E. M. FORSTER She laid her face against the tree.

15 *verb trans.* Place (one's hand or hands) on or apply (one's hand or hands) to a person or thing, esp. for purposes of appropriation or in violence. OE. ▸**b** *gen.* Place (one's arms, legs, etc.) in a specified position. LME.

L

Book of Common Prayer Or have laid violent hands upon themselves. DICKENS Laying hands on the article as if it were a Bottle. **b** D. H. LAWRENCE Louis . . laid his head a little on one side.

16 *verb trans.* Place (affection, hope, confidence, value) *on* or *in* a person or thing. *arch.* ME.

CONAN DOYLE Neither now or at any time have I laid great store upon my life.

17 *verb trans.* Arrange (a snare, a trap, an ambush) ready for operation, set. ME. ▸**b** *verb intrans.* Set an ambush or a trap *for*; lie in wait *for*. L15. ▸†**c** *verb trans.* Set watch or guard in (a place); search (a place) *for*. M16–M17.

b M. KINGSLEY The men go and lay for a rubber-hunter.

18 *verb trans.* Bring into a specified state, esp. of subjection, passivity, or exposure to view or danger. ME. ▸**b** NAUTICAL. Foll. by *aboard*: run into or alongside (a ship), usu. for boarding. Also, bring (a ship) into a specified position, as *alongside* another vessel etc. L16.

J. COLLIER It lays him at the mercy of chance and humour. C. M. YONGE He was laid under orders to follow the commands of the Spanish king.

19 *verb trans.* †**a** Post or station (a body of soldiers etc.); station (post horses) along a route. Also, beset (a place) with soldiers. LME–M19. ▸**b** Locate (a scene) in a particular place. Formerly also, assign to a specified locality. L16.

b W. COWPER I never framed a wish or formed a plan . . But there I laid the scene.

20 *verb trans.* MILITARY. Set (a gun, esp. a large one) in the correct position to hit a mark, aim. L15.

K. DOUGLAS I crammed shells into the six-pounder as fast as Evan could lay and fire it.

21 *verb refl.* & *intrans.* Orig., set oneself *against*. Later, apply oneself *to*. M16.

CARLYLE When Friedrich laid himself to engineering, I observe, he did it well.

▸ **IV** Impose as a burden.

22 *verb trans.* Impose (a penalty, command, obligation, tax, etc.) as a burden. Also (*N. Amer. slang*), inflict (an experience, emotion, etc.). Freq. foll. by *on*. OE. ▸†**b** Assess, rate, tax, (a person). ME–E18.

H. L. MENCKEN Not many of them returned in taxes the extra expense they laid on the community.

23 *verb trans.* Cause (blame, †aspersions, †ridicule) to fall *on*. ME.

W. IRVING The good wives . . never failed . . to lay the blame on Dame van Winkle.

24 *verb trans.* Bring (a stick etc.) down *on*; inflict (blows) *on*. ME.

J. A. FROUDE What if my son wishes to lay a stick on my back?

25 *verb intrans.* Deal blows; make an attack. Chiefly foll. by prepositions: see below. ME.

GOLDSMITH Rascal! replied the Tyrant, give me the Stick; and . . he laid on the unresisting Slave.

†**26** *verb trans.* Strike, beat (a person) *on* the face, *over* the head, etc. ME–E18.

J. ARBUTHNOT The cook laid them over the pate with a ladle.

▸ **V** Dispose or arrange in proper relative position over a surface.

27 *verb trans.* Place (a foundation, a floor, bricks, a submarine cable, etc.) in the horizontal position; place (a carpet) in position on the floor. OE. ▸**b** Set out (a table), spread (a tablecloth), place (plates, cutlery, etc.) in order in preparation for a meal; set out a table ready *for* (a meal) in this way. Also, place fuel ready for lighting (a fire). Formerly also, prepare (a bed) for sleeping in. ME. ▸**c** PRINTING. Fill (a case) with new sorts. L17.

W. BRONK Looking at stones the Incas laid. *fig.*: M. EDGEWORTH She laid the cornerstone of all her future misfortunes at that very instant. **b** G. GREENE No table was laid for dinner. P. H. JOHNSON You can come and lay the table. We'll eat in the kitchen.

28 *verb trans.* Orig., establish (a law), settle, lay down (a principle). Later, fix the outlines of, arrange, devise, (a plan, a plot, a scheme). OE. ▸**b** *verb intrans.* Orig., make arrangements or plans *for*. Later (now *dial.* & *US*), plan or intend *to do*. LME. ▸†**c** *verb trans.* Contrive, arrange. E17–E18.

C. THIRLWALL His schemes also were more artfully laid.

29 *verb trans.* †**a** Direct (one's steps). Only in OE. ▸†**b** Apply or devote (one's power, affection, possessions) *to*. Also foll. by *into*. ME–E17. ▸**c** NAUTICAL. Set (a course *for*). M17.

c C. FRANCIS The wind freshened and shifted . . , so that *Gulliver G* was able to lay her course.

†**30** *verb trans.* Set down *in* writing; put into or express *in* (a particular form of language). ME–L18.

31 *verb trans.* Cover or coat (a material, an object, etc.), *with* something, esp. for ornamentation. LME.

J. A. FROUDE My bath-room is . . a part of the veranda laid with zinc.

32 *verb trans.* Twist yarn to form (a strand), or strands to form (a rope). LME.

33 *verb trans.* Sharpen (a cutting instrument) with a steel. *dial.* L15.

34 *verb trans.* ART. Put (colour etc.) on a surface in layers; put or arrange (colours, †a picture) on canvas. L15.

▸ **VI** Present, put forward.

35 *verb trans.* Bring forward as a charge, accusation, or imputation; impute, attribute (a fault etc.) *to*. *arch.* ME.

SOUTHEY That . . you should lay to me Unkind neglect. G. W. DASENT He had . . to lay his sleeplessness on something, . . so he laid it on the lobster salad.

36 *verb trans.* Put forward, allege, (a claim, †reason, †example, etc.). LME. ▸**b** Orig., assign (a date). Later (LAW), state or describe *as*; fix (damages) *at* a certain amount. Now *rare*. LME. ▸**c** Present (an information, indictment, etc.) in legal form. L18.

W. S. MAUGHAM She was careful to make it plain . . that she laid no claims on him.

▸ **VII 37** *verb intrans.* = LIE *verb*[1] I, II. Now chiefly *dial.* & *non-standard*. ME. ▸**b** NAUTICAL. Of a ship: lie in a specified position. M16.

Word Study I was just laying there minding my own business. R. ADAMS So even if you *was* to have to lay down for a bit. *Rescue News* The flints were . . just laying on the beach.

– PHRASES: ***kill the goose that lays the golden eggs***: see GOOSE *noun*. **lay about one** hit out on all sides (*lit.* & *fig.*). **lay a charge** make an accusation. ***lay a finger on***: see FINGER *noun*. **lay a ground** ART spread a coating over a surface, as a basis for colours. **lay an egg** *colloq.* (*a*) (of an aircraft) drop a bomb; (*b*) (orig. *US*) (of a performer or performance) fail badly. **lay an eye on** *US* = *lay eyes on* below. ***lay by the heels***: see HEEL *noun*[1]. ***lay claim to***: see CLAIM *noun* 1. **lay dead** *colloq.* (chiefly *US*) remain inactive, lie low, do nothing in particular. **lay emphasis on**, **lay stress on**, **lay weight on** emphasize, treat as being particularly important. **lay eyes on** set eyes on, look at; catch sight of. **lay hands on** (*a*) seize, appropriate; (*b*) do violence to (esp. oneself); (*c*) confirm or ordain by placing one's hands on the head of (a candidate). **lay hold of**, **lay hold on** seize, grasp, *fig.* benefit from (an opponent's weak point etc.). †**lay home to** assault, attack, (*lit.* & *fig.*). ***lay in a person's dish***: see DISH *noun* 1. ***lay in pledge***, ***lay in to pledge***: see PLEDGE *noun*. **lay it on a person** *N. Amer. slang* give information to a person. ***lay low***: see LOW *adjective* & *noun*[4]. ***lay one's account with*** etc.: see ACCOUNT *noun*. **lay one's bones** be buried *in* a specified place. ***lay oneself wide open***: see WIDE *adverb*. ***lay one's finger on***: see FINGER *noun*. ***lay one's hands on***: see HAND *noun*. ***lay on one's oars***: see OAR *noun*. ***lay on the line***: see LINE *noun*[2]. ***lay on the table***: see TABLE *noun*. ***lay open to***: see OPEN *adjective*. ***lay pipe***, ***lay pipes***: see PIPE *noun*[1]. **lay siege to** besiege; attack (*lit.* & *fig.*). ***lay something at a person's door***: see DOOR *noun*. ***lay stress on***: see *lay emphasis on* above. ***lay the saddle upon the right horse***: see SADDLE *noun*. ***lay to heart***: see HEART *noun*. **lay to rest** put to rest, bury, (*lit.* & *fig.*). ***lay to sleep***: see SLEEP *noun*. ***lay to someone's charge***: see CHARGE *noun*. ***lay to wed***: see WED *noun* 2. ***lay violent hands on***: see VIOLENT *adjective*. ***lay wait***: see WAIT *noun* 4. ***lay waste***: see WASTE *adjective*. ***lay weight on***: see *lay emphasis on* above.

– WITH ADVERBS IN SPECIALIZED SENSES: **lay abroad** *arch.* spread out; spread (a net). **lay aside** (*a*) put (a garment, weapon, etc.) away from one; put on one side; (***lay aside the tomahawk***: see TOMAHAWK *noun*); (*b*) cease to use or think of or practise; †(*c*) put out of the way, get rid of; (*d*) set (money etc.) apart *for* future use; (*e*) in *pass.*, be incapacitated for work by illness. **lay away** (*a*) = *lay aside* (a), (b) above; (*b*) *rare* bury; (*c*) place (hides) flat in a large vat or pit to steep in strong tan liquor, as the final stage in the tanning process. **lay back** (*a*) cause to slope back from the vertical; (*b*) *colloq.* (chiefly *US*) lie or lean back, recline, relax. **lay by** (*a*) = *lay aside* (a), (b) above; †(*b*) = *lay aside* (c) above; (*c*) put away in store; store up; save (money); (*d*) put away for future disposal or safety; (*e*) in *pass.* be incapacitated by illness; (*f*) *US* work (a crop or field) for the last time, before leaving it to grow without further husbandry. **lay down** (*a*) put down on the ground or other surface, after holding or carrying; put off, discard (a garment, armour); ***lay down arms***, ***lay down one's arms***: see ARM *noun*[2]; (*b*) resign, relinquish (office, power, dignity, hopes, etc.); cease to bear (a name); discontinue (a custom, a fashion); (*c*) place in a recumbent or prostrate position, cause to lie down; (*d*) put down (money) as a wager or a payment; †(*e*) cast down, overthrow; (*f*) NAUTICAL (of the wind or sea) make (a ship etc.) lie on its side; (*g*) (begin to) construct (a road, a railway, etc.); ***lay down a keel***, begin to construct a ship; (*h*) establish, formulate definitely (a principle, a rule); prescribe (a course of action, limits, etc.); ***lay down the law***: see LAW *noun*[1]; (*i*) set down (a plan) on paper etc.; delineate; †(*j*) put down in writing; treat of; (*k*) NEEDLEWORK (*arch.*) run and fell (a seam); trim, embroider; (*l*) convert (arable land) into pasture; put (land) *under* grass, clover, etc. (also foll. by *in*, *to*, *with*); (*m*) store (wine) in a cellar; (*n*) *US* give up; cease to act; fail; withdraw; (*o*) *Jazz slang* set up or establish (a certain beat); (*p*) make a recording of (esp. popular music). **lay fast** †(*a*) put in fetters, imprison (also ***lay fast by the feet***); (*b*) make unable to proceed or escape. †**lay forth** (*a*) stretch out in a prostrate position; display openly; (*b*) put or bring forward in argument etc.; reveal, make clear. **lay in** (*a*) place in store; provide oneself with a stock of; †(*b*) put in (a claim); (*c*) enclose or reserve (a meadow) for hay; (*d*) HORTICULTURE place in position (the new wood of a trained tree); (*e*) paint (a picture etc.) in the first unfinished stage; (*f*) NAUTICAL unship (oars); (*g*) BASKETBALL bounce (the ball) off the backboard into the basket. **lay off** †(*a*) take off, take away; †(*b*) NAUTICAL steer (a ship) away from the shore; (of a ship) remain stationary outside a harbour; (*c*) mark or separate off (land etc.), esp. for a specific purpose; (*d*) (orig. *dial.* & *US*) discontinue; discharge (an employee) permanently or temporarily, esp. owing to shortage of work; (*e*) in decorating, work over a painted etc. surface with brushstrokes going in the same direction; (*f*) desist from (doing something); abstain from or stop using (something); stop bothering (a person); freq. *absol.* in *imper.*: cut it out! stop it!; (*g*) NAUTICAL & AERONAUTICS indicate on a chart etc., work out (a course); (*h*) (of a bookmaker) insure against a substantial loss resulting from (a large bet) by placing a similar bet with another bookmaker; (*i*) (FOOTBALL & HOCKEY etc.) pass (the ball) to a teammate who can make progress with it. **lay on** (*a*) impose (a command, a penalty, a tax); (*b*) deal blows with vigour; make a vigorous attack; (*c*) inflict (blows); ply (a lash etc.) vigorously; (*d*) (also ***lay it on***) increase the charge for goods etc.; formerly also, be lavish in expense; (*e*) apply a coat of (paint, varnish, etc.) to a surface; ***lay on thick***, ***lay it on thick***, ***lay on with a trowel***, ***lay it on with a trowel***, do (something) to excess, flatter, eulogize, etc., lavishly; (*f*) PRINTING place (the sheets of paper) on the type to be printed; (*g*) put (hounds) on a scent; (*h*) NEEDLEWORK place (thread) on a material before couching it down with a separate thread; (*i*) provide pipes, cables, etc., for the supply of (water, gas, electricity, telephonic communication, etc.); make available (refreshments, entertainment, a means of transport, etc.); (*j*) *N. Amer. slang* give (something) to a person; (*k*) (FOOTBALL & HOCKEY etc.) make (a pass) with accuracy so that a teammate can readily make the next move; (*l*) *verb phr. trans.* & *intrans.* (ANGLING) lower (a weight or shot) to rest with the hook and bait on the bed of the river, stream, etc. **lay out** (*a*) extend at length; take out and expose to view, the air, etc.; lay so as to project outwards; (*b*) stretch out and prepare (a body) for burial or cremation; *slang* kill (a person); *colloq.* put (a person) temporarily out of action; knock unconscious; ***lay out cold***: see COLD *adjective*; (*c*) spend (money); †(*d*) employ or exercise (powers, effort); (*e*) ***lay oneself out***, take pains; (*f*) ***lay out for*** (now *rare* or *obsolete*), look out for; take measures to win or get; (*g*) scheme, plan *to* effect some purpose; (*h*) (now *rare* exc. *US*) display, expose; set forth, expound, demonstrate; (*i*) apportion (land) for a purpose; dispose, arrange, (grounds, streets, a garden, etc.) according to a plan; (*j*) plan or map out; (*k*) NAUTICAL occupy a position on a yard towards the yardarms for the purpose of manipulating the sails. **lay over** (*a*) overlay; (*b*) *US colloq.* miss, allow to pass by; postpone; place a temporary embargo on; (*c*) *US colloq.* excel, outdo; (*d*) *N. Amer. colloq.* lie over; break one's journey and stop, esp. overnight. **lay to** (*a*) place in juxtaposition; †(*b*) put or bring into action; bring to bear; (*c*) NAUTICAL come to a stationary position with the head towards the wind; = ***lie to*** s.v. LIE *verb*[1]. **lay together** (*a*) place in juxtaposition; add together; ***lay their heads together***: see HEAD *noun*; †(*b*) concoct, compose (a story). **lay up** †(*a*) vomit up; (*b*) AGRICULTURE throw up (land) in ridges as a preparation for sowing; reserve (land) for hay; (*c*) put away for safety; store up (goods, provisions); put by; save; ***lay up in lavender***: see LAVENDER *noun*[2]; (*d*) confine to a house or bed through illness etc.; freq. in *pass.*, be (taken) ill; (*e*) take (a ship, a vehicle, etc.) out of service; (*f*) = sense 32 above; (*g*) NAUTICAL lay a course; (*h*) assemble or stack (plies or layers) in the arrangement required for the manufacture of plywood or other laminated material (usu. prior to bonding into a single structure).

– WITH PREPOSITIONS IN SPECIALIZED SENSES: **lay at** (now chiefly *dial.*) aim blows or an attack at; attack, assail, (*lit.* & *fig.*). **lay before** place in front of (a person); bring to the notice of, submit to the consideration of. †**lay from** put away from (oneself); take *one's fingers* off (something). **lay into** *colloq.* belabour. †**lay off** = ***lay from*** above. **lay on** attack vigorously, beat soundly. †**lay to** assault, attack, press hard (*lit.* & *fig.*).

– COMB.: **layback** (*a*) the receding position of the nose of certain breeds of dog, esp. the bulldog; (*b*) MOUNTAINEERING a method of climbing a crack in a rock etc. by leaning back with the feet against the (rock) face; (*c*) in various sports, the movement or position of leaning backwards or lying on one's back; **laybacking** MOUNTAINEERING the activity of climbing a crack by means of a layback; **laybarge** a barge designed for laying underwater pipelines; **lay-bed** (*a*) (now *dial.*) a grave; †(*b*) a layer, a stratum; **lay-down** *noun* (*a*) *slang* a certainty, a sure thing; (*b*) *slang* a remand in custody; (*c*) *dial.* & *non-standard* a lie-down, a rest; **lay-down** *adjective* (*a*) designating a collar which is folded over and does not stand up; (*b*) designating a hand or contract at cards (esp. bridge) which is such that success is possible against any defence, so that no harm would be done by exposing the player's cards on the table; **layflat** *adjective* & *noun* (designating) a tube, tubing, etc., that can lie or be laid flat; **lay-in** BASKETBALL a shot made at the top of a jump, usu. by bouncing the ball off the backboard into the basket; **lay-off** (*a*) a rest, a respite; a period during which a worker is temporarily dismissed or given leave; (*b*) a part of the year during which activity in a particular business or game is partly or completely suspended; (*c*) the (esp. temporary) dismissal of a number of workers from a factory etc., usually for economic reasons; **layover** †(*a*) an additional cloth laid over a tablecloth; (*b*) *N. Amer.* a stop or stay in a place, esp. overnight; a halt, a rest, a delay; **lay-up** (*a*) a period during which a person or thing is (temporarily) out of employment or use; (*b*) the operation of laying up in the manufacture of laminated material; the assembly of layers ready for bonding so produced; (*c*) BASKETBALL (also ***lay-up shot***) an attempt to score from free play; a shot made directly into the basket without bouncing the ball off the backboard.

– NOTE: The use in branch VII, avoided in standard English, is probably encouraged by confusion with LAY *verb*[2], the pa. t. of LIE *verb*[1].

lay *verb*[2] *pa. t.* of LIE *verb*[1].

layabout /ˈleɪəbaʊt/ *noun*. M20.

[ORIGIN from LAY *verb*[1] + ABOUT *adverb*.]

A habitual loafer or idler.

N. BAWDEN He wasn't lazy, not a layabout. *attrib.*: *Punch* Any old-fashioned plot about layabout art-lecturers getting mixed up with funny spies.

layaway /ˈleɪəweɪ/ *noun*. L19.

[ORIGIN from *lay away* s.v. LAY *verb*[1].]

1 TANNING. = LAYER *noun* 5. Freq. *attrib.* L19.

2 = LAY-BY 2b. *N. Amer.* M20. ▸**b** An article reserved for a customer who has paid a deposit. *N. Amer.* L20.

L

b unclaimed layaway a reserved and partly paid-for article offered for sale at a reduced price on the customer's failing to complete the purchase.

lay-by /ˈleɪbʌɪ/ *noun*. Pl. **lay-bys**. **E19**.
[**ORIGIN** from *lay by* s.v. **LAY** *verb*¹.]
1 a A part of a river, canal, etc., in which barges are put aside out of use. **E19**. ▸**b** A railway siding. **M19**. ▸**c** A length of roadway at the side of a carriageway on which vehicles can park without obstructing other traffic. **M20**.
2 a Something laid by or saved; savings. **L19**. ▸**b** A system of paying a deposit to secure an article for later purchase. Chiefly *Austral. & NZ*. **M20**.

lay-day /ˈleɪdeɪ/ *noun*. **L18**.
[**ORIGIN** from **LAY** *verb*¹ + **DAY** *noun*: cf. German *Liegetage* (pl.) lay-days, (days of) demurrage.]
COMMERCE. **1** Any of a certain number of days allowed for the loading and unloading of cargo. **L18**.
2 A day on which a boat is delayed in port, e.g. by bad weather. **M20**.

layer /ˈleɪə/ *noun*. **ME**.
[**ORIGIN** from **LAY** *verb*¹ + **-ER**¹.]
1 a A person who lays stones; a mason. Long *obsolete* exc. *hist*. **ME**. ▸**b** *gen*. A person who or thing which lays something or someone. **M16**. ▸**c** A hen that lays eggs. Freq. with specifying word. **E18**. ▸**d** = ***gun-layer*** s.v. **GUN** *noun*. **L19**.

> **b** N. FAIRFAX Layers of plots and traps. R. LEIGHTON The Lord Himself is the layer of this corner stone. **c** *Poultry World* A . . deep drinking trough essential for the adult layer.

2 A region of matter that is thin in relation to its lateral extent, *esp*. one adjacent to or covering a surface; a thickness of clothing worn over or under another; a stratum, a course, a bed. **E17**. ▸**b** A formation of aircraft, esp. bombers, flying at the same height. **M20**.

> P. DAVIES Old stars blast off an outer layer into space.

MALPIGHIAN ***layer***. **NEPHELOID** ***layer***. **PILIFEROUS** ***layer***. **PLEXIFORM** ***layer***. **PRISMATIC** ***layer***. **REVERSING** ***layer***. ***scattering layer***: see **SCATTERING** *ppl adjective* 2. **VISCERAL** ***layer***. ***vitelline layer***: see **VITELLINE** 2.

3 HORTICULTURE. A shoot fastened down and partly covered with earth to take root while still attached to the parent plant. **E17**. ▸**b** A crop of, or field containing, sown grass or clover; = **LEY** *noun*¹. Chiefly *dial*. **L18**. ▸**c** *collect*. Plants of a specific kind forming part of a hedge. Chiefly *dial*. **L18**.
4 An oyster bed. **M17**.
5 A large vat or pit in which hides are placed flat to steep in strong tan liquor as the final stage in the tanning process. **L18**.
6 CARTOGRAPHY. An area depicted in a particular tint chosen to represent all land between two specified heights. **E20**.
– **COMB.**: **layer cake** a cake consisting of layers of sponge held together by a sweet filling, and usu. iced; **layer cloud** *METEOROLOGY* a sheetlike cloud having little vertical depth but considerable horizontal extent; **layer colour** *CARTOGRAPHY* a colour used in the layer system of showing relief; **layer-cut** *noun & verb* (*a*) *noun* a haircut with the hair in overlapping layers; (*b*) *verb trans*. cut (hair) in overlapping layers; **layer dressing** the wearing of layers of clothes of varying lengths such that each layer shows beneath the one outside it; **layer-out** a person who prepares a body for burial or cremation; **layer pit** = sense 5 above; **layer-pudding** a steamed pudding consisting of layers of suet crust pastry with a sweet filling; **layer shading** *CARTOGRAPHY* the use of layer tints to show relief; **layer system** *CARTOGRAPHY* the representation of land between different heights or contours by different colours or tints that are graded so as to show relief at a glance; **layer tint** *CARTOGRAPHY* a layer colour, or a tint of such a colour; **layer vat** = sense 5 above.

layer /ˈleɪə/ *verb*. **E18**.
[**ORIGIN** from the noun.]
1 HORTICULTURE. **a** *verb trans*. Propagate (a plant) as a layer. **E18**. ▸**b** *verb intrans*. Bend down a layer to the ground and cover it partly with earth to take root and propagate the plant. **L18**. ▸**c** = **LAY** *verb*¹ 4b. **L19**.
2 *verb intrans*. Of crops: be laid flat as by wind or rain through weakness of growth. **L19**.
3 *verb trans*. Place or insert as a layer; arrange in layers. **E20**. ▸**b** Cut (hair) in overlapping layers. **M20**.

layered /ˈleɪəd/ *adjective*. **M19**.
[**ORIGIN** from **LAYER** *noun*, *verb*: see **-ED**², **-ED**¹.]
Divided into layers; having layers (of a specified character or number); covered with layers; *CARTOGRAPHY* having relief shown by the layer system; (of dress) worn in layers; (of hair) cut in overlapping layers.

layering /ˈleɪərɪŋ/ *noun*. **E18**.
[**ORIGIN** from **LAYER** *verb* + **-ING**¹.]
The action of **LAYER** *verb*; *spec*. (*a*) *HORTICULTURE* the method or activity of propagating a plant as a layer; (*b*) *CARTOGRAPHY* = ***layer shading*** s.v. **LAYER** *noun*; the use on a distribution map of shading etc. to represent distribution in layers; (*c*) = ***layer dressing*** s.v. **LAYER** *noun*

layette /leɪˈjɛt/ *noun*. **M19**.
[**ORIGIN** French, dim. of Old French *laie* drawer, box from Middle Dutch *laege*: see **-ETTE**.]
A set of clothing, toilet articles, and bedclothes for a newborn child.

lay-fee /ˈleɪfiː/ *noun*. *obsolete* exc. *hist*. **ME**.
[**ORIGIN** Anglo-Norman *lai fe*: see **LAY** *adjective*, **FEE** *noun*².]
1 A fee or estate in land held in consideration of secular services, as distinguished from an ecclesiastical fee. **ME**.
†**2** The laity, lay people collectively. **LME–M17**.

lay figure /leɪ ˈfɪɡə/ *noun phr*. **L18**.
[**ORIGIN** from **LAY**(**MAN** *noun*² + **FIGURE** *noun*.]
1 A jointed figure of a human body used by artists as a model for arranging drapery on etc. **L18**.

> W. S. MAUGHAM The look of a lay figure in a studio.

2 A person lacking in individuality, a nonentity; an unrealistic character in a novel etc. serving only to advance the plot. **M19**.

> G. GREENE She isn't a lay figure, the audience see enough of her . . to feel the shock of her murder.

laygear /ˈleɪɡɪə/ *noun*. **M20**.
[**ORIGIN** from **LAY**(**SHAFT** + **GEAR** *noun*.]
ENGINEERING. The set of gearwheels on a layshaft. Also ***laygear cluster***.

laying /ˈleɪɪŋ/ *noun*. **ME**.
[**ORIGIN** from **LAY** *verb*¹ + **-ING**¹.]
1 The action of **LAY** *verb*¹. **ME**.
2 A thing that is laid; a layer, a bed, a stratum. **LME**. ▸**b** An oyster bed. **M19**.
– **COMB.**: **laying house** (*a*) a building in which rope is made; (*b*) a building in which laying hens are kept; **laying mash**, **laying meal** a special food for laying hens.

laying /ˈleɪɪŋ/ *adjective*. **L16**.
[**ORIGIN** from **LAY** *verb*¹ + **-ING**².]
Esp. of a hen: that lays.

laylight /ˈleɪlʌɪt/ *noun*. **M20**.
[**ORIGIN** from **LAY** *verb*¹ + **LIGHT** *noun*.]
A window or light made of glazed panels and set into a ceiling to provide natural or artificial light.

laylock *noun & adjective* see **LILAC**.

layman /ˈleɪmən/ *noun*¹. Pl. **-men**. **LME**.
[**ORIGIN** from **LAY** *adjective* + **MAN** *noun*.]
1 A person who is not a cleric; a member of the laity. **LME**.

> T. S. ELIOT None of my people, . . Whether layman or clerk, shall you touch.

2 A person without professional or special knowledge in a particular subject, esp. law or medicine. **L15**.

> G. STEINER There is no use trying to explain to the layman the reality-concepts of modern mathematics or physics. A. STORR Another feature of psychotherapy which the layman finds hard to understand.

†**layman** *noun*². Pl. **-men**. **L17–L18**.
[**ORIGIN** Dutch *leeman*, from *led* (now *lid*) limb, joint (cf. **LITH** *noun*¹) + *man* **MAN** *noun*.]
= **LAY FIGURE**.

laymen *noun*¹, *noun*² pls. of **LAYMAN** *noun*¹, *noun*².

layout /ˈleɪaʊt/ *noun*. **M19**.
[**ORIGIN** from ***lay out*** s.v. **LAY** *verb*¹.]
1 The planning or disposition of land, streets, etc.; land laid out; the plan or disposition of a house, factory, garden, etc.; the way in which plans, printed matter, etc., are arranged or set out. **M19**. ▸**b** A drawing showing the design of a proposed piece of printing, sometimes with specifications for production; the preparation of such drawings; the design details of a cartoon film. **E20**.
2 Something arranged or set out in a particular way; the tools or apparatus pertaining to some occupation etc.; *US slang* the equipment used for smoking opium. **M19**. ▸**b** A scheme, a plan, an arrangement; a course of action. Orig. & chiefly *US*. **M19**. ▸**c** A number of people associated in some way; a party or gang (of people); a family. Freq. *derog*. *US colloq. & dial*. **M19**.
3 a In faro, the representation in enamel etc. of a suit of cards on a green cloth, on which stakes are laid. **M19**. ▸**b** The arrangement formed by the cards laid out on the table in any of various card games, esp. patience; a tableau. **M19**.

Laysan /leɪˈzɑːn, -ˈzan/ *noun*. **L19**.
[**ORIGIN** An island in the Hawaiian archipelago.]
Used *attrib*. to designate birds native to Laysan.
Laysan albatross an albatross, *Diomedea immutabilis*, of the N. Pacific. **Laysan duck** = ***Laysan teal*** below. **Laysan finch** a Hawaiian honeycreeper, *Telespyza cantans*, a large finchlike bird noted for its song. **Laysan rail** an extinct rail, *Porzanula palmeri*. **Laysan teal** a mallard of the subspecies *Anas platyrhynchos laysanensis*.

layshaft /ˈleɪʃɑːft/ *noun*. **L19**.
[**ORIGIN** Prob. from **LAY** *verb*¹ + **SHAFT** *noun*.]
A short secondary or intermediate shaft driven by gearing from the main shaft of an engine; *spec*. one inside a gearbox that transmits the drive from the input shaft to the output shaft.

laystall /ˈleɪstɔːl/ *noun*. *arch*. **E16**.
[**ORIGIN** from **LAY** *verb*¹ + **STALL** *noun*¹.]
†**1** A burial place. **E–M16**.
2 A (public) refuse heap. **M16**.

laywoman /ˈleɪwʊmən/ *noun*. Pl. **-women** /-wɪmɪn/. **E16**.
[**ORIGIN** from **LAY** *adjective* + **WOMAN** *noun*.]
A female member of the laity; a woman without professional or special knowledge in a particular subject, esp. law or medicine.

Laz /lɑːz/ *noun & adjective*. Also **Laze** /ˈlɑːzə/. **M19**.
[**ORIGIN** Laz.]
▸ **A** *noun*. Pl. **Laz**, **Lazes** /ˈlɑːzɪz, -zəz/.
1 A member of a group of Caucasian peoples of NE Turkey. **M19**.
2 The S. Caucasian language of this people. **M20**.
▸ **B** *attrib*. or as *adjective*. Of or pertaining to the Laz or their language. **M20**.
■ **Lazic** *adjective* **M20**.

lazar /ˈlazə/ *noun & adjective*. *arch*. **ME**.
[**ORIGIN** medieval Latin *lazarus*, an application of the name *Lazarus* (*Luke* 16:20), partly through Old French *lasdre* (mod. *ladre*).]
▸ **A** *noun*. **1** A poor and diseased person, *esp*. a leper. **ME**.
†**2** Discoloured and decaying matter in cheese. **L16–E18**.
– **COMB.**: **lazar-house** = **LAZARETTO** 1.
▸ **B** *adjective*. Of a person: poor and diseased; leprous. **LME**.
■ **lazarlike** *adjective* resembling a poor and diseased person, leprous **E17**.

lazaret /lazəˈrɛt/ *noun*. Also **-ette**. **E17**.
[**ORIGIN** French formed as **LAZARETTO**.]
1 = **LAZARETTO** 1. **E17**.
2 = **LAZARETTO** 2. **E18**.
3 = **LAZARETTO** 3. **L19**.

lazaretto /lazəˈrɛtəʊ/ *noun*. Pl. **-os**. **M16**.
[**ORIGIN** Italian, dim. of **LAZZARO**.]
1 An isolation hospital for people with infectious diseases, esp. those with leprosy. **M16**.
2 A building or ship for quarantine. **E17**.
3 NAUTICAL. The after part of a ship's hold, used for stores. **E18**.

Lazarist /ˈlazərɪst/ *noun*. **M18**.
[**ORIGIN** French *Lazariste*, from *Lazare* Lazarus: see **LAZAR**, **-IST**.]
CHRISTIAN CHURCH. A member of the Congregation of the Priests of the Mission founded by St Vincent de Paul in 1624, and established a few years later in the College of St Lazare at Paris.

Lazarite /ˈlazərʌɪt/ *noun*. Now *rare* or *obsolete*. **M16**.
[**ORIGIN** from *Lazarus* (see **LAZAR**) + **-ITE**¹.]
CHRISTIAN CHURCH. †**1** A member of a religious order taking its name from Lazarus. Only in **M16**.
2 = **LAZARIST**. **E18**.

Lazarus /ˈlaz(ə)rəs/ *noun*. *rare*. **L15**.
[**ORIGIN** Personal name used allusively: see **LAZAR**.]
A person with leprosy; a beggar.

laze /leɪz/ *noun*¹. *colloq*. **M19**.
[**ORIGIN** from **LAZE** *verb*.]
The action of lazing; an instance of this; a spell of lazing.

Laze *noun*² *& adjective* var. of **LAZ**.

laze /leɪz/ *verb*. **L16**.
[**ORIGIN** Back-form. from **LAZY** *adjective*.]
1 *verb intrans*. Lie, move, or act in a sleepy listless fashion; enjoy oneself lazily. **L16**.

> D. WIGODER He . . shouted that I had lazed around for long enough. *Holiday Which?* You . . may spot a turtle or a mantra ray, lazing on the sea bed.

2 *verb trans*. Orig., indulge (oneself) in indolence. Later, pass (time) *away* lazily. **E17**.

†**lazo** *noun & verb* var. of **LASSO**.

lazule /ˈlazjuːl/ *noun*. Now *rare* or *obsolete*. **L16**.
[**ORIGIN** medieval Latin *lazulum*: see **LAPIS LAZULI**.]
More fully ***lazule-stone***. = **LAPIS LAZULI**.

lazuli /ˈlazjʊlʌɪ, -li/ *noun*. **M17**.
[**ORIGIN** from **LAPIS**) **LAZULI**.]
= **LAPIS LAZULI**.
– **COMB.**: **lazuli bunting**, **lazuli finch** a small cardinal grosbeak of western N. America, *Passerina amoena*, the male of which has a brilliant blue head and back.

lazulite /ˈlazjʊlʌɪt/ *noun*. **E19**.
[**ORIGIN** formed as **LAZULI** + **-ITE**¹.]
MINERALOGY. A hydrous phosphate of aluminium and magnesium, occurring as blue monoclinic crystals. Also (*poet*.), lapis lazuli.
■ **lazuˈlitic** *adjective* **M19**.

lazurite /ˈlazjʊrʌɪt/ *noun*. **L19**.
[**ORIGIN** from medieval Latin *lazur* from Arabic *lāzaward* (see **AZURE** *noun & adjective*): see **-ITE**¹.]
MINERALOGY. A rare silicate of sodium and aluminium occurring as blue crystals of the cubic system and as the chief constituent of lapis lazuli.

lazy /ˈleɪzi/ *adjective*. **M16**.
[**ORIGIN** Perh. of Low Dutch origin: cf. Low German *lasich* languid, idle.]
1 a Of a person etc.: disinclined to work, not disposed to action or effort; idle; inactive, slothful. **M16**. ▸**b** *transf*. Of a

thing, place, or condition: characterized by or inducing laziness. E17.

R. LAWLER And you, yer lazy sod, lollin' there. Git on out into me kitchen. M. ROBERTS Bring the wine over, Helen. I'm too lazy to move. **b** LONGFELLOW The great dog.. Hangs his head in the lazy heat.

2 Orig. (of a literary style etc.), languid, having little energy. Later (now esp. of a river), sluggish, slow-moving. M16.

H. BELLOC In the courtyard.. a lazy fountain leaped and babbled. B. PEARSON Two lagoons fed by a creek that was lazy when it wasn't in flood.

†**3** Bad, worthless. *dial.* L17–L18.

– SPECIAL COLLOCATIONS & COMB.: **lazy arm** a type of boom from which a microphone may be slung. **lazy-back** †(*a*) a sluggard; (*b*) the place at the surface of a mine where coals are loaded and stacked for sale; (*c*) (chiefly *hist.*) a high bar on the back of a carriage seat; a movable backrest on a gig etc.; (*d*) ***lazy-back chair***, a chair with a reclining back. **lazy-bed** a bed about two metres or six feet wide, on which potatoes etc. for cultivation are laid, and covered with earth taken from a trench up to a metre or three feet wide on each side. **lazy-board** *US* a short board on the left side of a wagon, used by teamsters to ride on. **lazy daisy (stitch)** a petal-shaped embroidery stitch. **lazy dog** *US military slang* a type of fragmentation bomb designed to explode in mid-air and scatter steel pellets at high speed over the target area. **lazy eight** an aerobatic manoeuvre in which an aircraft executes an S-shaped path which, when viewed laterally, resembles a figure 8 lying on its side. **lazy eye** an amblyopic eye in which underuse has contributed to its poor vision, *esp.* the unused eye in squint. **lazy jack** (*a*) a device resembling a lazy tongs; (*b*) NAUTICAL any of various small ropes extending vertically from the topping lifts to the boom for holding a fore-and-aft sail when taking it in. *Lazy* LAURENCE. **Lazy Susan** (orig. *US*) a revolving stand on a table to hold condiments etc.; a muffin stand. **lazy tongs** a device for grasping objects at a distance, comprising a system of several pairs of levers crossing and pivoted at their centres like scissors, so connected that the movement of the first pair is communicated to the last, which is fitted with ends like those of a pair of tongs.

▪ **lazyhood** *noun* laziness M19. **lazily** *adverb* L16. **laziness** *noun* L16. **lazyish** *adjective* somewhat lazy L19.

lazy /ˈleɪzi/ *verb.* E17.
[ORIGIN from LAZY *adjective.*]
1 *verb intrans.* = LAZE *verb* 1. E17.
2 *verb trans.* = LAZE *verb* 2. L19.

lazybones /ˈleɪzɪbəʊnz/ *noun. colloq.* Pl. same. L16.
[ORIGIN from LAZY *adjective* + BONE *noun* + -S¹.]
A lazy person.

lazzaro /ˈlazərəʊ/ *noun.* Pl. **-ri** /-ri/. M17.
[ORIGIN Italian, formed as LAZAR.]
= LAZZARONE.

lazzarone /lazəˈrəʊni/ *noun.* Pl. **-ni** /-ni/. L18.
[ORIGIN Italian, augm. of LAZZARO.]
In Naples and other Italian cities: a person who subsists on the proceeds of odd jobs, an idler, a beggar.

lb *abbreviation.*
Latin *Libra* a pound or pounds (weight).

l.b. *abbreviation.*
CRICKET. Leg bye(s).

LBC *abbreviation.*
London Broadcasting Company.

L/Bdr *abbreviation.*
Lance Bombardier.

LBO *abbreviation.*
COMMERCE. Leveraged buyout.

l.b.w. *abbreviation.*
CRICKET. Leg before wicket.

LC *abbreviation. US.*
Landing craft.

l.c. *abbreviation.*
1 Letter of credit.
2 Latin *Loco citato* in the passage previously cited.
3 TYPOGRAPHY. Lower case.

LCC *abbreviation.*
hist. London County Council.

LCD *abbreviation.*
1 MATH. Least or lowest common denominator.
2 Liquid crystal display (freq. *attrib.*, esp. with redundant *display*).

LCJ *abbreviation.*
Lord Chief Justice.

LCM *abbreviation.*
1 Landing craft, mechanized. *US.*
2 MATH. Least or lowest common multiple.

L/Cpl *abbreviation.*
Lance Corporal.

LCT *abbreviation. US.*
Landing craft, tank.

LD *abbreviation*¹.
Lethal dose (usu. followed by a numeral indicating that the dose kills that percentage of a sample, as ***LD50***).

Ld *abbreviation*².
Lord.

Ldg *abbreviation.*
Leading (Seaman etc.).

LDL *abbreviation.*
BIOCHEMISTRY. Low-density lipoprotein.

LDS *abbreviation.*
Licentiate in Dental Surgery.

LE *abbreviation.*
MEDICINE. Lupus erythematosus.

-le /(ə)l/ *suffix*¹ (not productive).
[ORIGIN Repr. Old English *-el, -ela, -(e)le* in nouns and *-ol, -ul, -el* in adjectives, from Germanic, with many Indo-European cognates. See also -EL¹.]
Forming nouns from nouns with (orig.) dim. sense, as ***bramble***, or denoting an appliance, as ***thimble***, ***handle***; forming nouns from verbs, denoting an agent, as ***beadle***, or an instrument, as ***bridle***, ***girdle***, and adjectives from verbs with the sense 'apt or liable (to do)', as ***brittle***, ***fickle***, ***nimble***. In some nouns, as ***riddle***, repr. a back-form. from *-els*, taken as pl.

-le /(ə)l/ *suffix*² (not productive).
Forming nouns with (orig.) dim. sense, and repr. Old French *-el* from Latin *-ellum* dim. suffix, as ***castle***, ***mantle***, Old French *-el* from Latin *-ale* neut. sing. of *-alis* adjectival suffix, as ***cattle***, Old French *-aille* from Latin *-alia* neut. pl. of *-alis* adjectival suffix, as ***battle***, and Old French *-eille* from Latin *-icula* dim. suffix, as ***bottle***. Cf. -EL².

-le /(ə)l/ *suffix*³ (not productive).
[ORIGIN Repr. Old English *-lian* from Germanic.]
Forming verbs with frequentative or dim. sense, as ***babble***, ***crumple***, ***dazzle***, ***giggle***, ***nestle***, ***twinkle***, ***wrestle***.

LEA *abbreviation.*
Local Education Authority.

lea /liː/ *noun*¹. Now chiefly *poet.* exc. in place names. Also †**ley**. See also LEY *noun*².
[ORIGIN Old English *lēah*, *lēa* corresp. to Old High German *lōh* grove (Middle High German = low brushwood, scrubland), from Germanic from Indo-European base repr. also by Latin *lucus* grove, Lithuanian *laũkas* field, Sanskrit *lokás* open space.]
A tract of open ground, *esp.* grassland.

lea /liː/ *noun*². LME.
[ORIGIN Perh. deriv. of French *lier* bind, tie, from Latin *ligare*, but cf. LEASE *noun*².]
A measure of yarn of varying quantity.

lea *noun*³ see LEY *noun*¹.

lea /liː, leɪ/ *adjective.* Now *dial.* Also **ley**, **lay** /leɪ/. OE.
[ORIGIN Perh. from base of LAY *verb*¹, LIE *verb*¹.]
Of land: fallow, unploughed.

leach /liːtʃ/ *noun*¹. *arch.* LME.
[ORIGIN Old French *lesche* (mod. *lèche*).]
†**1** A slice (of meat etc.); a strip. LME–E16.
2 A dish consisting of sliced meat, eggs, fruits, and spices in jelly etc. LME.

leach /liːtʃ/ *noun*². M17.
[ORIGIN App. from LEACH *verb*¹.]
1 The saturated brine which drains from the salt in salt extraction, or is left behind when salt is extracted. Earliest in †***leach-brine***. M17.
2 A perforated vessel or trough used for making lye from wood ashes by pouring water over them. *obsolete* exc. *dial.* L17.
3 TANNING. A pit in which a tanning liquid is mixed. L18.

Leach /liːtʃ/ *noun*³. M19.
[ORIGIN William *Leach* (1790–1836), English naturalist.]
Leach's petrel, ***Leach's storm petrel***, a storm petrel of the N. Atlantic and N. Pacific, *Oceanodroma leucorhoa*, which flies in a distinctive darting manner close to the sea.

leach /liːtʃ/ *verb*¹.
[ORIGIN Old English *leċċan* from West Germanic, from base also of LAKE *noun*¹.]
†**1** *verb trans.* Water, wet. *rare.* OE–L16.
†**2** *verb intrans.* Soften, melt. *rare.* Only in E17.
3 a *verb trans.* Cause (a liquid) to percolate through some material. *rare.* L18. ▸**b** *verb trans.* Subject (soil, ores, etc.) to the action of percolating water etc. which removes soluble constituents; *fig.* slowly deprive *of.* M19.
4 *verb trans.* Take (a substance) *away*, *out*, by percolation. M19.
5 *verb intrans.* Be subject to the action of percolating water; (of a liquid or solute) pass through or *out* by percolation. L19.
▪ **leachaˈbility** *noun* ability to be leached out M20. **leachable** *adjective* able to be leached out M20. **leachate** *noun* (a quantity of) liquid that has percolated through a solid and leached out some of the constituents M20. **leacher** *noun* (*a*) = LEACH *noun*² 3; (*b*) a person who leaches something: L19. **leachy** *adjective* (of a soil) unable to hold water; very porous: L19.

leach /liːtʃ/ *verb*² *trans. arch.* LME.
[ORIGIN from LEACH *noun*¹.]
Cut (meat etc.) in slices; slice.

lead /lɛd/ *noun*¹ & *adjective.*
[ORIGIN Old English *lēad* = Old Frisian *lād*, Middle Low German *lōd* (Dutch *lood*) lead, Middle High German *lōt* (German *Lot*) plummet, solder, from West Germanic.]
▸ **A** *noun.* **1** A soft, heavy, malleable, bluish-grey metal that is a chemical element, atomic no. 82, occurring in galena and other minerals (symbol Pb). OE.

SHAKES. *Macb.* A heavy summons lies like lead upon me. COLERIDGE The ship went down like lead.

milled lead, ***pig-lead***, ***pot-lead***, ***sheet lead***, etc.

2 a A large pot, cauldron, or kettle, a large open vessel used in brewing and various other operations, (orig., one made of lead). Now *dial.* OE. ▸**b** A lead milk pan. *dial.* M18.
3 The metal made into an object, e.g. a seal, the plummet of a plumb line, a pipe, a lead coffin. Now *esp.* (more fully ***cold lead***) bullets. ME.
4 NAUTICAL. A lump of lead suspended on a line to discover the depth of water; a sounding lead. ME.
5 a In *pl.* The sheets or strips of lead used to cover a roof; a lead roof. ME. ▸**b** A strip of lead between panes in lattice or stained-glass windows, a calm. Usu. in *pl.* E18.
6 Graphite, used as a material for pencils; a thin stick of graphite within a pencil, or for filling a propelling pencil. Cf. ***blacklead*** s.v. BLACK *adjective.* E19.
7 TYPOGRAPHY. A thin strip, usu. of type metal, less than type-high, of varying thickness and length, used to separate lines of type. E19.
– PHRASES ETC.: ***arm the lead***: see ARM *verb*¹. **as heavy as lead** very heavy. ***blacklead***: see BLACK *adjective*. **cast the lead** lower a sounding lead from a ship. ***cold lead***: see sense 3 above. **lead in one's pencil** *slang* (esp. male sexual) vigour. ***mock lead***: see MOCK *adjective*. ***potter's lead***: see POTTER *noun*¹. ***red lead***: see RED *adjective*. ***sugar of lead***: see SUGAR *noun* & *adjective*. **swing the lead** *slang* idle, shirk; malinger. **take the lead out of one's pants** *slang* hurry up, act promptly. TETRAETHYL ***lead***. ***white lead***: see WHITE *adjective*.
▸ **B** *attrib.* or as *adjective.* Made (wholly or partly) of lead, consisting of lead. LME.
– SPECIAL COLLOCATIONS & COMB.: **lead-acid** *adjective* designating a secondary cell or battery in which the anode and cathode are plates or grids of lead (or lead alloy) coated with lead dioxide and spongy lead respectively, both immersed in dilute sulphuric acid. **lead-ash**, **lead-ashes** litharge. **lead-back** *US* the dunlin. **lead balloon** a failure, an unsuccessful venture. **lead bronze**: containing lead, used in bearings. **lead bullion** a mixture of lead and other heavy metals formed during the extraction of lead. **lead-burn** *verb trans.* weld (pieces of lead). **lead-burning** the welding of lead. **lead cell** a lead-acid cell. **lead chamber** a large vessel made of welded sheet lead, used in the manufacture of sulphuric acid from sulphur dioxide, air, and steam using oxides of nitrogen as catalysts. **lead comb**: made of lead, used to darken the hair. **lead crystal** = ***lead glass*** below. **lead flat** a flat roof made of sheet lead laid across joists and boarding. **lead glance** galena. **lead glass** glass containing a substantial proportion of lead oxide, making it more refractive. **lead glaze** POTTERY: containing lead oxide. **lead light** a window in which small panes are fixed in lead calms, a leaded light. **lead line** (*a*) a sounding lead, a plumb line; (*b*) a line loaded with lead weights, running along the bottom of a net; (*c*) MEDICINE a bluish-grey line along the gums at their junction with the teeth, indicating lead poisoning; (*d*) a narrow strip of lead between two pieces of stained glass; a calm. **lead-line** *verb trans.* put lead lines in (stained-glass work). **leadman** (*a*) a dealer in lead; (*b*) a lead-miner. **lead-mill** (*a*) a factory for producing milled or sheet lead; (*b*) a lead plate used for grinding gemstones. **lead-nail**: used to fasten a sheet of lead on a roof (usu. in *pl.*). **lead ochre** = MASSICOT. **lead paper** a test paper treated with a preparation of lead. **lead-papered** *adjective* covered with or containing lead paper. **lead pencil**: of graphite, often enclosed in cedar or other wood. **lead-pipe cinch** *US colloq.* a complete certainty. **lead-plant** *US* a leguminous shrub, *Amorpha canescens*, formerly believed to indicate the presence of lead ore. **lead-plaster** = DIACHYLON. **lead poisoning** acute or chronic poisoning by the absorption of lead into the body. **lead ratio** the ratio of the quantity of lead in a rock sample to that of its radioactive parents uranium and thorium, from which the age of the sample may be determined. ***lead shot***: see SHOT *noun*¹. **lead-spar** = CERUSSITE. **lead-swing** *verb intrans.* (*slang*) = ***swing the lead*** above. **lead-swinger** *slang* a shirker, a malingerer. ***lead*** TETRAETHYL. **lead-tin** *noun* & *adjective* (an alloy) containing lead and tin. **lead-tree** (*a*) a tropical leguminous tree, *Leucaena latisiliqua*; (*b*) a dendritic crystalline deposit of metallic lead or zinc in lead acetate solution. **lead-vitriol** = ANGLESITE. **lead-wash**, **lead-water** MEDICINE a dilute solution of lead acetate. **lead wool** lead in a fibrous state, used for caulking pipe joints. **leadwort** (*a*) any of various mainly tropical perennial herbs and shrubs of the genus *Plumbago*, with tubular calyx and five-lobed corolla, esp. *P. europaea* of southern Europe; (*b*) any member of the family Plumbaginaceae, which includes this genus and also the thrifts and sea lavenders.

lead /liːd/ *noun*². ME.
[ORIGIN from LEAD *verb*¹.]
1 a The action of LEAD *verb*¹; leading, direction, guidance. *obsolete* exc. *dial.* ME. ▸**b** Direction given by going in front; example, precedent. Esp. in ***follow the lead of***. M19. ▸**c** A guiding indication; a clue to the solution of something. M19. ▸**d** JOURNALISM. A summary or outline of a newspaper story; a guide to a story that needs further development or exploration; the first (often the most important) item in a newspaper etc. Cf. ***lead story*** below. E20.
2 a A man-made watercourse, *esp.* one leading to a mill (also called ***mill-leat***). M16. ▸**b** A (garden) path; an alley.

L16. ▸**c** A channel in an ice field. E19. ▸**d** A thong, strap, or cord for leading or controlling a dog etc. L19.

3 The front or leading place; the place in front *of* (something); freq. in ***take the lead***, ***take a lead***. Also, the position or function of leading, leadership. L16. ▸**b** The front section of a flock of sheep or herd of cattle. *Austral. & NZ.* E20.

Daily Mirror Scholes' goal in the 54th minute put United in the lead. *Nature* Europe has taken the lead in research into urban wind power.

4 a *CURLING.* The first player; the stone first played. Also, the course along which the stones are propelled. L17. ▸**b** *BOWLS.* The advantage of throwing the jack and bowling first. M18. ▸**c** *BOXING.* The first punch delivered (of two or more). E20.

5 a *BELL-RINGING.* The position of the first of a set of changing bells. L17. ▸**b** *MUSIC.* The giving out of a phrase or passage by one of the voices or instruments in a piece, to be followed in harmony by the others. L19. ▸**c** *MUSIC.* The most prominent part in a piece played by an orchestra, esp. a jazz band; the player or instrument that plays this; the leader of a section of an orchestra. Also, the start of a passage played by a particular instrument. Freq. *attrib.* M20.

6 *CARDS.* The action, privilege, or obligation of playing the first card in a round or trick. Also, the card (to be) played first in a round or trick; the suit to which the first card belongs. M18.

7 *MINING.* **a** = LODE 5. E19. ▸**b** An alluvial deposit of gold along the bed of an ancient river. M19.

8 (A person who plays) the leading or principal part in a play or film. E19.

Vanity Fair Silvers kept playing the same role, the affable best pal of the male lead. *attrib.*: *Screen International* Best film, best direction, best lead actress.

9 The distance which ballast, coal, soil, etc. has to be conveyed to its destination. M19.

10 *NAUTICAL.* The direction in which a rope runs fair to the deck. Cf. ***fairlead*** s.v. FAIR *adjective & adverb.* M19.

11 *ELECTRICITY.* A conductor (usu. a wire) conveying electric current from a source to an appliance. L19.

12 *ELECTRICITY.* The angle through which the brushes are shifted around a commutator from the neutral point. L19.

13 *HOROLOGY.* The action of a tooth of a toothed wheel in impelling another tooth or a pallet. L19.

14 A piece of railway track connecting a switch to a frog. E20.

15 *MECHANICS.* The axial distance travelled by a screw in one turn. E20.

– PHRASES: **give a lead (to)** (*HUNTING* etc.) go first in jumping a fence etc. to give encouragement (to the rest); *fig.* provide (with) a clue. **have a lead on**, **gain a lead on** have, acquire, a position in front of or an advantage over. ***juvenile lead***: see JUVENILE *adjective.* **leads and lags** the hastening or delaying of payment to take advantage of expected changes in the exchange rate. **return the lead** *CARDS* lead the suit already led by one's partner.

– ATTRIB. & COMB.: In the sense 'leading,' as ***lead guitarist***, ***lead singer***, etc. Special combs., as **lead-bars** the bars to which the traces of front coach horses are attached; **lead counsel** *US* the senior of two or more lawyers acting for the same party; **lead-horse**, **lead-mule** a horse or mule that is guided or controlled by a lead; **lead-reins** the reins of the front coach horses; **lead-rope** a rope used as a lead for a horse etc.; **lead-screw**: that moves the carriage of a lathe; **lead sheet** *US slang* a sheet of music with the melodic line and lyric only; *transf.* an overcoat; **lead story**: given greatest prominence in a newspaper etc.; **lead time**: between the initiation and completion of a process of production or development.

lead /liːd/ *verb*[1]. Pa. t. & pple **led** /lɛd/.

[ORIGIN Old English *lǣdan* = Old Frisian *lēda*, Old Saxon *lēdjan* (Dutch *leiden*), Old High German, German *leiten*, Old Norse *leiða*, from Germanic, from base also of LOAD *noun*.]

▸ **I** Conduct.

1 *verb trans.* Cause to go along with oneself; *spec.* †(**a**) bring or take (a person or animal) to a place (also foll. by *away*, *down*, etc.); (**b**) convey, usu. in a cart or other vehicle; now only *N. English*, cart (coal, corn, stones, turf, etc.). †(**c**) (of a natural agent, e.g. the wind) carry. OE. ▸**b** Bring forward, adduce (testimony). Formerly also, initiate (an action) at law. Now only *SCOTS LAW.* ME.

JOSEPH HALL Causing the Clouds to lead in store of rain. W. B. STONEHOUSE One shilling a load is the price . . for leading a cart-load of warp. **b** *Times* It would be strange if evidence competent to prove the offender's guilt . . could not be led in a hearing.

2 *verb trans.* Of a person or (*transf.*) a circumstance, motive, etc.: accompany and show the way to (a person); *esp.* direct or guide by going on in advance. Freq. with *away*, *in*, *out*, etc. OE.

C. RAYNER Mrs Miller led Freddy . . up the first flight of stairs. K. LAING Sackey's long strides led him far ahead.

3 *verb trans.* Of a commander: march at the head of and direct the movement of (troops). Also foll. by *on*. OE.

H. BAILEY Victor . . had been blinded at Arras, leading his platoon into battle.

4 *verb trans.* Direct the course of (a person) by holding the hand or some part of the body or clothing; conduct (an animal) by means of a cord, halter, bridle, etc. Also foll. by *away*, *in*, *off*, etc. OE. ▸**b** *verb trans. fig.* Guide by persuasion as contrasted with commands or threats. L16. ▸**c** *verb intrans.* Submit to being led. E17.

J. HERRIOT Five dogs were being led round the perimeter. B. BREYTENBACH The workers who can still see lead their blind comrades by the hand. **b** G. PUTTENHAM Princes may be lead but not driuen. **c** *Time* These people lead real easy.

5 With inanimate thing as obj.: ▸**a** *verb trans.* Guide the course or direction of (something flexible); draw or pass (a rope etc.) *over* a pulley, *through* a hole, etc. Formerly also, trace (a line, a boundary). OE. ▸**b** *verb trans.* Conduct (water etc.) through a channel or pipe. Also foll. by *away*, *forth*, *off*, *out*. ME. ▸†**c** *verb trans.* Steer (a boat); drive (a carriage). LME–M16. ▸**d** *verb intrans. NAUTICAL.* Of a rope: admit of being led. M19.

6 *verb trans.* Guide with reference to action or opinion; bring by persuasion or counsel *to* or *into* a condition, bring by argument etc. *to* a conclusion; induce *to do*. ME. ▸**b** *LAW.* Put a question to (a witness) in such a way as to suggest the answer required. Cf. ***leading question*** s.v. LEADING *adjective.* M19.

Law Reports There was nothing in the prospectus to lead him to such a conclusion. M. BARING It was Master C. who had led him into mischief. W. ABISH Her appearance, her surname . . led him to assume that she was of German extraction.

7 a *verb trans. & intrans.* Of a thoroughfare etc.: serve as a passage or approach for (a person) *to* or *into* a place. ME. ▸**b** *verb intrans.* Foll. by *to*: tend towards as a consequence; end in. LME. ▸**c** *verb intrans.* Form a channel *into*; form a connecting link *to* (something). M19.

a J. STEINBECK The rutted sandy road that led through the brushy country. *fig.*: R. K. NARAYAN Staying in Malgudi would not lead him anywhere. **b** ANTHONY SMITH Damage to a part of the cortex invariably led to speech disorder. *Christian Aid News* These policies have led to increased bank lending.

†**8** *verb trans.* Conduct (affairs); manage, govern. ME–L16.

†**9** *verb trans.* Deal with, treat. As pa. pple: circumstanced, situated, in a specified condition. ME–L15.

▸ **II** Carry on.

†**10** *verb trans.* Engage in, perform (a dance, a song); utter sounds of (joy or mournfulness). OE–L15.

11 *verb trans.* Go through and experience, pass, (a period of time, now usu. a life or a particular kind of life). OE. ▸†**b** Pass through (pain, suffering); bear, endure. ME–L15.

T. FULLER He led his old age in London. L. HELLMAN Julia was leading a strange life.

▸ **III** Precede, be foremost. (Cf. sense 2.)

12 *verb trans.* Have the first place in. LME. ▸**b** *verb intrans. & trans.* Have the lead (over) in a race, match, game, etc.; be ahead (of). L18. ▸**c** *verb trans.* Outnumber. L20.

P. BAILEY May our country ever lead The world, for she is worthiest. *Harper's Magazine* Of the causes . . pneumonia led the list. **b** *Oxford Mail* An Abingdon side who led 6–3 at half-time. *Daily Telegraph* Northants, with seven wickets standing, lead Kent by 90 runs. **c** *Times* Advancing issues led declines by a ratio of only three to two.

13 *verb trans.* Take the principal part in (proceedings of any kind); be at the head of (a party, a movement); have the official initiative in the proceedings of (a deliberative body). Also, set (a fashion). M17. ▸**b** Perform one's part in (singing, a musical performance) so as to give the cue to others; give the cue to (other singers or performers) by performing one's part. M19.

T. FULLER They should rather lead a fashion of thrift, than follow one of riot. D. DELILLO She led a more or less daily protest against . . her mother's habits. M. FOOT He lacked the . . sympathy to understand the Labour movement which he aspired to lead. **b** G. MANVILLE FENN He . . led the chorus.

14 *verb intrans.* **a** *BELL-RINGING.* Be the first of the changing bells. L17. ▸**b** *MUSIC.* In a fugue etc.: introduce a subject which is taken up by the other parts successively. L19.

15 *CARDS.* **a** *verb intrans.* Play the first card in a round or trick. Also foll. by *off*. L17. ▸**b** *verb trans.* Play (a specified card) as first player; play a card of (a specified suit). Also foll. by *out*. M18.

b *Bridge Magazine* Now he leads a low spade which South wins.

16 a *verb trans.* Of a barrister: act as leading counsel in (a case); act as leader to (another barrister). E19. ▸**b** *verb intrans.* Appear as leading counsel (*for* the prosecution, defence, the plaintiff, the defendant). M19.

b A. TROLLOPE Of course I must lead in defending her.

17 *verb intrans. BOXING.* Direct a punch at one's opponent, esp. as the first of a series of punches. Freq. with *with*. L19.

18 *verb trans. SHOOTING.* Aim ahead of (a moving target) so that the target and the missile reach the same point simultaneously. L19.

19 *verb intrans.* Give prominence to an event, story, etc. Foll. by *on*, *with*. E20.

Times For Princess Margaret's wedding *The Times* . . did not even lead with the story.

– PHRASES: **lead a person a chase** give a pursuer trouble by one's speed or circuitous course. ***lead a person a dance***: see DANCE *noun.* **lead a person a difficult life**, **lead a person an uncomfortable life**, etc., subject a person to a life of constant difficulty, discomfort, etc. ***lead apes (in hell)***: see APE *noun.* **lead by the nose** cause to obey submissively. **lead captive** take away or escort as a prisoner. **lead in prayer** guide (a congregation) in public prayers. ***lead large***: see LARGE *adverb.* ***lead the dance***: see DANCE *noun.* **lead the prayers (of a congregation)** = ***lead in prayer*** above. ***lead the ring***: see RING *noun*[1]. **lead the van** be in the forefront. **lead the way** go in advance of others, take the lead in an expedition or course of action. **lead up the garden (path)** lead on, entice; mislead, deceive. **lead with one's chin** (of a boxer) leave one's chin unprotected; *fig.* behave or speak incautiously.

– WITH ADVERBS & PREPOSITIONS IN SPECIALIZED SENSES: **lead away** induce to follow unthinkingly (usu. in *pass.*). **lead off** *verb phr. trans. & intrans.* (**a**) take the first steps in (a dance, a ball); (**b**) begin (a performance), open (a conversation, a discussion) (freq. foll. by *with*). **lead on** (**a**) *verb phr. trans.* induce gradually to advance; entice or beguile into going to greater lengths; (**b**) *verb phr. intrans.* direct conversation *to* a subject. **lead out** take the first steps in (a dance); conduct (a partner) into the dance. **lead through** (**a**) *verb phr. trans.* (*CARDS*) force to be played before an opponent; (**b**) *verb phr. intrans.* (of two climbers) act alternately as leader over successive stretches of rock. **lead up** (**a**) *verb phr. trans.* (now *rare* or *obsolete*) = ***lead out*** above; (**b**) *verb phr. intrans.* form a gradual introduction *to*; direct one's talk gradually *to* a topic or point; (**c**) *verb phr. intrans.* (foll. by *to*) lead a card and so allow the safe play of (a card held by another player).

lead /lɛd/ *verb*[2]. LME.

[ORIGIN from LEAD *noun*[1].]

1 *verb trans.* Cover with lead. Also foll. by *over*. LME.

2 *verb trans.* Arm, load, or weight with lead. L15.

3 *verb trans.* **a** Fix (glass in a window) with lead calms. Also foll. by *in*, *up*. M16. ▸**b** Set or fasten *in* firmly with molten lead. L18.

†**4** *verb trans.* Line (pottery) with lead or lead glaze; glaze. Also foll. by *over*. M16–L17.

5 *verb trans. PRINTING.* Separate (lines of type) by inserting leads; *loosely* in photocomposition or computer-assisted setting, space out (lines). M19.

6 *verb intrans. NAUTICAL.* Use a sounding lead; take soundings. M19.

7 *verb trans.* In *pass.* Of a gun barrel: become foul with a coating of lead. L19.

8 *verb trans.* Smooth the inside of (a gun barrel) with a lap of lead. L19.

leadable /ˈliːdəb(ə)l/ *adjective. rare.* M19.

[ORIGIN from LEAD *verb*[1] + -ABLE.]

Able to be led, amenable to being led.

■ **leadableness** *noun* L19.

leadbeater /ˈlɛdbiːtə, -bɛtə/ *noun. Austral.* L19.

[ORIGIN from LEADBEATER'S COCKATOO.]

= LEADBEATER'S COCKATOO.

Leadbeater's cockatoo /ˈlɛdbɛtəz kɒkəˈtuː, -biːt-/ *noun phr.* M19.

[ORIGIN Benjamin *Leadbeater*, 19th-cent. English naturalist.]

The pink cockatoo, *Cacatua leadbeateri*.

Leadbeater's possum /ˈlɛdbɛtəz ˈpɒsəm, -biːt-/ *noun phr.* Also (earlier, now *rare*) **Leadbeater's opossum**. E20.

[ORIGIN from John *Leadbeater* (c 1832–88), Austral. taxidermist.]

A small Australian possum, *Gymnobelideus leadbeateri*, which has grey and white fur with dark markings and is only found in eastern Victoria.

leaded /ˈlɛdɪd/ *adjective.* ME.

[ORIGIN from LEAD *noun*[1], *verb*[2]: see -ED[2], -ED[1].]

1 Covered, lined, loaded, or weighted with lead. ME.

2 Of a pane of glass: fitted into lead calms. M19.

3 *TYPOGRAPHY.* Having the lines of type separated by leads; *loosely* having extra space between lines. M19.

4 Affected by lead poisoning. L19.

5 Containing added lead; *spec.* (of petrol) containing tetraethyl lead. M20.

leaden /ˈlɛd(ə)n/ *adjective.* OE.

[ORIGIN from LEAD *noun*[1] + -EN[4].]

1 Consisting or made of lead. OE.

E. YOUNG Night . . stretches forth Her leaden sceptre o'er a slumb'ring world.

2 Of a cold dull grey colour. LME.

S. J. PERELMAN It was the season of the southwest monsoon, marked by leaden, overcast skies.

leaden flycatcher a small grey-green Australasian flycatcher, *Myiagra rubecula*.

3 *transf. & fig.* **a** Of base quality or composition; of little value. L16. ▸**b** Weighing like lead; oppressively burdensome or numbing. Of the limbs: hard to drag along, moving slowly and heavily. L16. ▸**c** Lacking animation; inert, spiritless, depressing. L16.

a C. MARLOWE Base leaden Earles, that glory in your birth. **b** POPE Leaden slumbers press his drooping eyes. O. MANNING The heat now had a leaden weight so even the flies were stilled. **c** *Opera Now* Some of the chorus singing . . is ill-defined and leaden.

■ **leadenly** *adverb* L19. **leadenness** /-n-n-/ *noun* E17.

L

leaden /ˈlɛd(ə)n/ *verb. rare.* **M16.**
[ORIGIN from LEAD *noun*[1] + -EN[5] or from LEADEN *adjective*.]
†**1** *verb trans.* Fasten with molten lead. Only in **M16.**
2 *verb intrans.* Press down like lead. Only as ***leadening*** *ppl adjective.* **M19.**
3 *verb trans.* Make leaden or dull. **L19.**

Leadenhall Street /ˈlɛd(ə)nhɔːl striːt/ *noun phr.* **E19.**
[ORIGIN A street in the City of London, which from 1648 to 1861 contained the headquarters of the East India Company.]
hist. The East India Company.

leader /ˈliːdə/ *noun.* **ME.**
[ORIGIN from LEAD *verb*[1] + -ER[1].]
▸ **I** A person or an animal.
1 A person who conducts others, precedes others as a guide, leads a person by the hand or an animal by a cord, etc. **ME.** ▸†**b** The driver of a vehicle. Latterly *dial.*, a carter. **ME–L19.**

DRYDEN Ample Plains, Where oft the Flocks without a Leader stray.

follow-my-leader: see FOLLOW *verb*.
2 A person who leads an armed body. **ME.**
3 A person who guides others in action or opinion; a person who takes the lead in a business, enterprise, or movement. Freq. *spec.*, the official head or chief spokesman of a nation, a political party, a deliberative body, etc. Formerly also, a chieftain, a ruler. **LME.** ▸**b** A barrister whose status (in England, that of a King's or Queen's Counsel) entitles him to lead a case. Also, the senior counsel of a circuit. **M19.** ▸**c** The foremost member of a profession; more widely, a person of eminent position and influence. **M19.** ▸**d** *spec.* (Usu. **L-**.) [translating German *Führer*, Italian *Duce*, Spanish *Caudillo*.] The head of an authoritarian state. **E20.**

Daily Telegraph Mr. Brezhnev, the Soviet Communist party leader. M. ANGELOU Martin King had been a hero and a leader to me.

Leader of the House (*a*) (in the House of Commons) an MP chosen from the party in office to plan the Government's legislative programme and arrange the business of the House; (*b*) (in the House of Lords) the peer who acts as spokesman for the Government. **Leader of the Opposition** the MP chosen to lead the main opposition party in the House of Commons.
4 *MUSIC.* A person who leads a choir or band of dancers, musicians, or singers; *spec.* the first violin in an orchestra. Also (*US*), a conductor. **M16.**
5 a The first person in a file; any of the front people in a moving body. In *SURVEYING*, the person at the forward end of the chain. **E17.** ▸**b** Any of the front horses, cattle, or dogs in a team; the front horse in a tandem. **L17.** ▸**c** The player, team, etc., that has the lead in a race, match, etc. **L20.**
6 a *CARDS.* The first player in a round. Also, a person who leads from a particular suit. **L17.** ▸**b** *CURLING.* The first player. **L18.**
7 In full ***class-leader***. The presiding member of a Methodist class. **M18.**
▸ **II** A thing.
8 A thing which leads; *colloq.* a remark or question intended to lead conversation, a feeler. **ME.** ▸**b** *COMMERCE.* An article that attracts buyers; *esp.* = ***loss-leader*** s.v. LOSS *noun*. **M19.** ▸**c** A share that is leading the movement of prices on a stock exchange. **M20.**
9 *BOTANY.* The growing tip of the main stem or of a principal branch of a tree or shrub. Also, a bine. **L16.**
10 *MINING.* A small and insignificant vein, which leads to or indicates the proximity of a larger and better one. **M17.**
11 A tendon. **E18.**
12 a *ENGINEERING.* The one of a set of wheels connected directly to the source of power. **E19.** ▸**b** In *pl.* = ***leading wheels*** s.v. LEADING *adjective*. **L19.** ▸**c** *NAUTICAL.* = ***leading-block*** s.v. LEADING *noun*[1]. **L19.**
13 *TYPOGRAPHY.* Each of a series of dots or dashes to guide the eye in lists etc. Usu. in *pl.* **E19.**
14 a A main agricultural drain. **M19.** ▸**b** A tributary. **M19.**
15 *JOURNALISM.* = ***leading article*** (a) s.v. LEADING *adjective*. **M19.**

Wales The Welsh weeklies have often masterly leaders on politics and literature.

16 A quick-match enclosed in a paper tube for the purpose of conveying fire rapidly to an explosive. **M19.**
17 *ANGLING.* A length of material connecting the end of a fishing line to a hook or fly. **M19.** ▸**b** A net so placed as to intercept fish and lead them into a pound, weir, trap net, etc. **L19.**
18 A pipe to conduct water. *Scot. & US.* **M19.**
19 A short length of blank or uncoated film or recording tape attached at the beginning or end of a reel for purposes of threading or identification. **E20.**
20 *METEOROLOGY.* In full ***leader stroke***. A preliminary stroke of lightning that ionizes the path taken by the much brighter return stroke that follows. **M20.**
– COMB.: **leader board** a scoreboard, esp. at a golf course, on which the names etc. of the leading competitors are displayed; ***leader stroke***: see sense 20 above; **leader tape** (a length of) uncoated tape intended for use as a leader on a reel of magnetic tape.
■ **leadered** *adjective* made the subject of a leading article **L19.** **leaderene** *noun* (*joc.*) [with female ending after forenames like *Marlene*] a female leader, esp. of an autocratic character (orig. as a nickname given to Margaret Thatcher (b. 1925) when leader of the Conservative Opposition in Britain, 1975–9) **L20.** **leaderess** *noun* (now *rare*) a female leader **L16.** **leadeˈrette** *noun* a short editorial paragraph printed after the principal leader(s) in a newspaper **L19.** **leaderless** *adjective* **L19.** **leaderly** *adjective* (*rare*) having the qualities of a leader **E20.** **leadership** *noun* (*a*) the office or position of leader, esp. of a political party; (*b*) the action of leading or influencing; ability to lead or influence; (*c*) the leaders of a group collectively: **E19.**

leadhillite /ˈlɛdhɪlʌɪt, lɛdˈhɪlʌɪt/ *noun.* **M19.**
[ORIGIN from *Leadhills*, Scotland + -ITE[1].]
MINERALOGY. A monoclinic basic sulphate and carbonate of lead occurring as whitish pearly crystals.

lead-in /ˈliːdɪn/ *noun.* **E20.**
[ORIGIN from LEAD *verb*[1] + IN *adverb*.]
1 In full ***lead-in wire***: ▸**a** A wire that leads in from outside, *esp.* one connecting an outdoor aerial with an indoor receiver or transmitter. **E20.** ▸**b** A wire in an electric lamp that carries the current between the cap and the filament or electrode. **E20.**
2 An introduction, an opening. **E20.**

leading /ˈliːdɪŋ/ *noun*[1]. **ME.**
[ORIGIN from LEAD *verb*[1] + -ING[1].]
1 The action of LEAD *verb*[1]. **ME.**
2 A small or lateral vein in a lead mine. Cf. LEADER 10. **M17.**
3 A directing influence or guidance; *spec.* (esp. in the Society of Friends) a spiritual indication of the proper course of action in any case. **E19.**
– COMB.: **leading block** *NAUTICAL* a single block used to bring the hauling part of a rope or the fall of a tackle into a more convenient direction; **leading rein**: to lead a horse or other animal; **leading staff**: to lead a bull by means of a ring through its nose; **leading string** (*a*) in *pl.*, strings for guiding and supporting children when learning to walk (***be in leading strings*** (*fig.*), be in a state of helpless dependence); (*b*) a cord for leading an animal.

leading /ˈlɛdɪŋ/ *noun*[2]. **LME.**
[ORIGIN from LEAD *verb*[2] + -ING[1].]
1 The action of covering, framing, or mending something with lead. **LME.**
2 Leadwork; *spec.* the calms of a window collectively. **E19.**
3 *TYPOGRAPHY.* The placing of leads between lines of type; the amount of blank space between lines of print. **M19.**
4 Lead deposit on a surface; *esp.* fouling in a gun from lead bullets. **L19.**

leading /ˈliːdɪŋ/ *adjective.* **L16.**
[ORIGIN from LEAD *verb*[1] + -ING[2].]
1 That goes first or is in front. **L16.**
2 That guides, directs, or leads (*to* something). **E17.**
3 That takes the lead; chief, principal, prominent. **E17.**

E. KUZWAYO He . . was honoured . . to speak to a leading member of the Soweto community. *Financial Times* Barclays Bank, Britain's leading issuer of Visa credit cards.

– SPECIAL COLLOCATIONS & COMB.: **leading aircraftman**: holding the rank next above aircraftman. **leading article** (*a*) an article in a newspaper appearing as the expression of editorial opinion; (*b*) a principal article of trade. ***leading case***: see CASE *noun*[1]. **leading counsel** a King's or Queen's Counsel; the senior of two or more barristers appearing for the same party. **leading dog** *Austral. & NZ*: trained to run ahead of a flock of sheep to control its speed. **leading edge** (*a*) the forward edge of a moving body, esp. an aircraft wing or propeller blade; (*b*) *ELECTRONICS* the part of a pulse in which the amplitude increases; (*c*) *fig.* the forefront or vanguard, esp. of technological development (freq. *attrib.*). **leading-in wire** = LEAD-IN 1. **leading lady** the actress or film star who plays the principal female part in a play or film. **leading light** (*a*) *NAUTICAL* a leading mark illuminated at night; (*b*) *fig.* a person of importance and influence in a specified sphere. **leading man** the actor or film star who plays the principal male part in a play or film. **leading mark** *NAUTICAL* any of a set of conspicuous objects on land which a pilot has to keep visually in line in order to bring a vessel safely in and out of harbour. **leading note** *MUSIC* the seventh note of the diatonic scale (leading upwards to the tonic). **leading question** (*a*) (esp. *LAW*) a question put in such a way as to suggest the answer required; (*b*) (in weakened use) an awkward or pointed question; an important point. **leading rating**, (*hist.*) **leading seaman** a seaman in the Royal Navy holding the rank next below petty officer. **leading shoot** *BOTANY* = LEADER 9. **leading tone** *MUSIC* (*US*) = ***leading note*** above. **leading wheels** the front pair of wheels in a locomotive, placed before the driving wheels. **leading wind** *NAUTICAL* a fair wind, *esp.* one blowing abaft the beam.
■ **leadingly** *adverb* (*rare*) **M19.**

†**leadish** *adjective.* **LME–L18.**
[ORIGIN from LEAD *noun*[1] + -ISH[1].]
Somewhat like lead.

leadless /ˈlɛdlɪs/ *adjective.* **E19.**
[ORIGIN from LEAD *noun*[1] + -LESS.]
Containing or using no lead, devoid of lead.

lead-off /ˈliːdɒf/ *noun.* **L19.**
[ORIGIN from ***lead off*** s.v. LEAD *verb*[1].]
A commencement; a thing which leads off, the first of a series.

lead-out /ˈliːdaʊt/ *noun & adjective.* **E20.**
[ORIGIN from LEAD *verb*[1] + OUT *adverb*.]
▸ **A** *noun.* An act of leading something or someone out. **E20.**
▸ **B** *attrib.* or as *adjective. ELECTRONICS.* Designating or pertaining to a conductor by which current may enter or leave an electronic device. **M20.**

leadsman /ˈlɛdzmən/ *noun.* Pl. **-men**. **L18.**
[ORIGIN from LEAD *noun*[1] + -'S[1] + MAN *noun*.]
The sailor who casts the lead in taking soundings.

lead-up /ˈliːdʌp/ *noun.* **M20.**
[ORIGIN from ***lead up*** s.v. LEAD *verb*[1].]
A thing which leads up to something else.

leadwork /ˈlɛdwəːk/ *noun*[1]. **M17.**
[ORIGIN from LEAD *noun*[1] + WORK *noun*.]
1 Plumber's or glazier's work. **M17.**
2 In *pl.* (freq. treated as *sing.*). An establishment for smelting lead ore. **E18.**

leadwork /ˈliːdwəːk/ *noun*[2]. **E20.**
[ORIGIN from unkn. 1st elem. + WORK *noun*.]
sing. & in *pl.* Fancy stitches used as an ornamental filling in lace-making.

leady /ˈlɛdi/ *adjective.* **LME.**
[ORIGIN from LEAD *noun*[1] + -Y[1].]
Resembling lead, esp. in colour.

leaf /liːf/ *noun*[1]. Pl. **leaves** /liːvz/.
[ORIGIN Old English *lēaf*, corresp. to Old Frisian *lāf*, Old Saxon *lōf* (Dutch *loof*), Old High German *loup* (German *Laub*), Old Norse *lauf*, Gothic *laufs*, from Germanic.]
▸ **I** The organ of a plant etc.
1 Any of the relatively broad flat usu. green outgrowths of a vascular plant, produced laterally from a stem or branch or springing from the base of the stem, which function as the principal organ in photosynthesis (in their fullest form consisting of an expanded part, attached to the stem by a stalk); *popularly* the expanded part only. **OE.**

A. A. MILNE I was shaking like an aspen leaf. V. S. NAIPAUL The stacked-up, wet beech leaves slowly turning to compost.

five-leaf: see FIVE *adjective*. *FOLIAGE* ***leaf***. ***juvenile leaf***: see JUVENILE *adjective*. ***rough leaf***: see ROUGH *adjective*. ***seed leaf***: see SEED *noun*. ***true leaf***: see TRUE *adjective* etc. ***walking leaf***: see WALKING *ppl adjective*.
2 The leaves of a tree or plant collectively; foliage. **OE.** ▸†**b** [Cf. French *vin de deux feuilles*.] In the description of wine: a season, a year. **L16–E18.**

F. BROOKE The year began in March with the coming of the leaf. *fig.*: SHAKES. *Macb.* I have lived long enough. My way of life Is fall'n into the sear, the yellow leaf.

fall of the leaf: see FALL *noun*[2]. **in leaf**, **in full leaf** having (all) its leaves expanded. ***yellow leaf***: see YELLOW *adjective*.
3 *popularly.* A petal, esp. of a rose. **LME.**
4 A representation of a leaf; (esp. *ARCHITECTURE*) an ornament in the form of a leaf. **LME.**
5 *spec.* ▸**a** The dried leaves of the tobacco plant, or of other plants used for smoking. **E17.** ▸**b** The green leaves of the tea plant. **L19.**
a in the leaf (of tobacco) uncut and with the stems left on. ***wrapper leaf***: see WRAPPER *noun* 1b.
▸ **II** An object resembling a leaf.
6 Each of the subdivisions of a folded sheet of paper, parchment, etc., after trimming; *esp.* any of a number of such subdivisions (each containing one page on each side of the fold) which compose a book or manuscript, a folio; a single sheet of paper, esp. stationery. Also, the matter printed or written on a leaf. **OE.**

M. LEITCH He put the folded slip between the leaves of the book.

loose-leaf: see LOOSE *adjective*. **take a leaf out of a person's book** base one's conduct on what a person does. **turn over a new leaf** adopt a different (now always a better) line of conduct.
7 A layer of fat inside an animal; *esp.* that surrounding the kidneys of a pig. **LME.**
8 A very thin sheet of metal (esp. gold or silver) or other material produced by beating out or splitting; a lamina of horn, marble, wood, etc. Also, a thin piece of soap or other detergent (larger than a flake). **LME.** ▸**b** Each of the metal strips of a leaf spring. **E20.** ▸**c** Each of the solid layers of a cavity wall. **M20.**
gold leaf: see GOLD *noun*[1] & *adjective*. ***silver leaf***: see SILVER *noun & adjective*.
9 A hinged part or any of a series of parts connected at one side or end by a hinge. Now usu. *spec.*, (*a*) each of two or more parts of a door, gate, or shutter turning on hinges; (*b*) a hinged flap at the side of a table, able to be raised when required for use; any movable addition to the top of a table; (*c*) the part of a drawbridge or bascule bridge which is raised on a hinge; (*d*) a hinged sight on the barrel of a rifle. **LME.**

V. SACKVILLE-WEST The table had been extended by the addition of several leaves. *Daily Telegraph* It takes two footmen to open a front door, one for each leaf.

10 Each of the teeth of a pinion. **E18.**
11 The brim of a hat. Chiefly *Irish*. **M18.**
12 *WEAVING.* A set of heddles stretched between the same two shafts. **M19.**

L

eight-leaf twill (& with other numerals): woven on eight etc. leaves of heddles.
13 *ZOOLOGY.* An organ or part resembling a leaf, as the external ear of a mammal or the nasal appendage of a leaf-nosed bat. **M19.**
14 *MATH. & COMPUTING* = ***leaf node*** below. **M20.**
– **COMB.:** **leaf arrowhead** *ARCHAEOLOGY* an arrowhead shaped like a leaf, usu. of the Neolithic period and made of flint; **leaf-bed** a layer of leaves sometimes found in subsoil; **leaf beet** any of several varieties of beet (chard, seakale beet, spinach beet) of which the midribs or leaves are cooked as a vegetable; **leaf beetle** any beetle of the very varied family Chrysomelidae, comprising usu. robust compact beetles with smooth elytra in bright or metallic colours; **leafbird** any bird of the southern Asian family Irenidae; *esp.* a bright green bird of the genus *Chloropsis*; **leaf blight** any of several plant diseases causing the death of foliage; **leaf blister** (***a***) a disease of certain fruit trees caused by a parasitic mite; (***b***) a disease of pear trees caused by the fungus *Taphrina bullata*, in which the leaves develop brown blisters; **leaf blotch** any of several plant diseases indicated by discoloured patches on foliage; *esp.* (*US*) = ***black spot*** (a) s.v. **BLACK** *adjective*; **leaf-brown** *adjective & noun* (having) the colour of dead leaves; **leaf bud** a bud from which leaves are produced; **leaf butterfly** a butterfly which resembles a leaf, e.g. one of the genus *Kallima*; **leaf cast** any of several fungal diseases causing conifers to shed their needles, e.g. ***larch leaf cast***, due to *Meria laricis*, and ***pine leaf cast***, due to *Lophodermium pinastri*; **leaf curl** any of several plant diseases characterized by curling leaves, *esp.* (more fully ***peach leaf curl***) a disease of peach, almond, and nectarine trees caused by the fungus *Taphrina deformans*; **leafcutter** (***a***) (in full ***leafcutter bee***) any of various solitary bees of the family Megachilidae which cut fragments from leaves to line their nests; (***b***) (in full ***leafcutter ant***) any of various chiefly tropical American ants of the genus *Atta* which use pieces cut from leaves to cultivate fungus for food; **leaf-cutting** a leaf used as a cutting in the propagation of certain plants, e.g. begonias; **leaf-cutting ant**, **leaf-cutting bee** = *leafcutter* (b), (a) above; **leaf fall** the shedding of leaves by a plant; **leaf fat** the fat occurring in layers round a pig's kidneys; **leaf-flea** a plant louse; **leaf folder** = ***leaf roller*** below; **leaf-frog** any American tree frog of the genus *Phyllomedusa* or related genera; **leaf-gap** *BOTANY* an area of parenchyma in the stem immediately above the point at which a leaf trace diverges from it; **leaf gelatin**: manufactured in sheet form for cooking purposes; **leaf-gold** = ***gold leaf*** s.v. **GOLD** *noun*[1] & *adjective*; **leaf green** *adjective & noun* (having) the colour of green leaves; **leafhopper** any leaping homopteran insect of the superfamily Cicadelloidea, whose members suck the sap of plants and often spread disease; **leaf insect** any of various insects of the family Phyllidae (order Phasmida) which closely resemble leaves in shape and colour; **leaf lard**: made from the leaf fat of a pig; **leaf-louse** a plant louse, an aphid; **leaf miner** any insect (esp. a fly of the family Agromyzidae) whose larvae eat their way between the cuticles of leaves; **leaf monkey** any of various monkeys of S. or SE Asia of the subfamily Colobinae (family Cercopithecidae); a colobine; **leaf mould** (***a***) topsoil or compost consisting largely of decayed leaves; (***b***) a disease of tomatoes caused by the fungus *Cladosporium fulvum*; **leaf node** *MATH. & COMPUTING* a node or vertex in a tree connected to only one other node or vertex; **leaf-nosed** *adjective* (esp. of a bat) having a leaflike appendage on the snout; *spec.* designating a bat of the Old World family Hipposideridae, or the New World family Phyllostomatidae; **leaf-opposed** *adjective* (of a flower etc.) arising opposite a leaf; **leaf peeper** *US colloq.* a person who visits particular areas, especially in New England, to view the autumn foliage; **leaf-point** *ARCHAEOLOGY* a projectile point shaped like a leaf, made of flint or some similar rock, found in various Palaeolithic and later cultures; **leaf protein** protein present in leaves, esp. when extracted for use as a possible dietary supplement; **leaf roll** a virus disease of potatoes marked by upward curling of the leaves; **leaf roller** any insect (esp. a tortricid moth) whose larvae roll up the leaves of plants which they infest; **leaf scald** (***a***) = ***leaf scorch*** below; (***b***) a disease of sugar cane caused by the bacterial pathogen *Xanthomonas albilineans*; **leaf-scale** a scale on a plant stem which develops into a leaf; **leaf scar** a cicatrix left on the bark by the separation of the leaf stalk of a fallen leaf; **leaf scorch** (***a***) a plant disease caused by a deficiency of potassium, which makes leaves shrivel and turn brown at the edges; (***b***) any of several fungal diseases producing similar effects; **leaf-shaped** *adjective* having the shape of a leaf; ***leaf-shaped arrowhead*** = ***leaf-arrowhead*** above; **leaf sheath** a flattened expansion of the petiole in some plants, which embraces the stem; **leaf shutter** *PHOTOGRAPHY*: composed of a ring of thin plates which swivel to admit light through a central aperture (cf. ***iris diaphragm*** s.v. **IRIS** *noun* 4b); **leaf soil** = ***leaf mould*** (a) above; **leaf-spine**: formed from a modified leaf; **leaf spot** any of numerous fungal and bacterial plant diseases which cause leaves to develop discoloured spots; **leaf spring**: consisting of a number of strips of metal curved slightly upwards and clamped together one above the other; **leaf stalk** a petiole; **leaf-tendril**: formed from a modified leaf or part of a leaf; **leaf-tobacco** raw tobacco with the stalks still on it; **leaf trace** *BOTANY* a vascular bundle extending from the stele to the base of a leaf; **leaf warbler** any small green or yellow Old World woodland warbler of the genus *Phylloscopus*.
■ **leaflike** *adjective* resembling (that of) a leaf **E19.**

leaf /liːf/ *noun*[2]. *military slang.* **M19.**
[**ORIGIN** Var. of **LEAVE** *noun*[1].]
Leave of absence; furlough.

leaf /liːf/ *verb.* **E17.**
[**ORIGIN** from **LEAF** *noun*[1].]
1 *verb intrans.* Bear leaves or foliage, come into leaf. Also (*N. Amer.*) foll. by *out*. **E17.**
2 a *verb trans.* Turn the leaves of (a book or papers), esp. in a casual manner. Also foll. by *over*. Now *US*. **M17.** ▸**b** *verb intrans.* Turn the leaves of a book or papers, esp. in a casual manner. Usu. foll. by *through*. **E20.**

> **b** D. **LESSING** One tattered old magazine, the sort of thing you leaf through at the dentist.

3 *verb trans.* Cover or shade with foliage. *rare.* **M19.**
4 *verb trans.* Give a number in sequence to (a leaf of a book). **L19.**

leafage /ˈliːfɪdʒ/ *noun.* **L16.**
[**ORIGIN** from **LEAF** *noun*[1] + -**AGE**.]
1 Leaves collectively; foliage. **L16.**
2 The representation of leaves or foliage, esp. as ornamentation. **E18.**

leafed /liːft/ *adjective.* **M16.**
[**ORIGIN** from **LEAF** *noun*[1] + -**ED**[2]: cf. **LEAVED** *adjective*.]
1 Having leaves or foliage; bearing (a specified kind of) foliage. Chiefly after a descriptive or numeral adjective **M16.**
†**2** Of a door, book, etc.: having (a specified number of) leaves. **L16–E17.**
3 Of a hat: (broad-)brimmed. **M19.**

leafery /ˈliːf(ə)ri/ *noun.* **M19.**
[**ORIGIN** from **LEAF** *noun*[1] + -**ERY**.]
Leafage, foliage.

leafit /ˈliːfɪt/ *noun.* Now *rare.* **L18.**
[**ORIGIN** from **LEAF** *noun*[1] + *-it*, perh. = -**ET**[1].]
= **LEAFLET** *noun* 1.

leafless /ˈliːflɪs/ *adjective.* Also (earlier) †**leaveless**. **L15.**
[**ORIGIN** from **LEAF** *noun*[1] + -**LESS**.]
Without a leaf; lacking leaves or foliage.
leafless tree *slang* the gallows.
■ **leaflessness** *noun* **E19.**

leaflet /ˈliːflɪt/ *noun & verb.* **L18.**
[**ORIGIN** from **LEAF** *noun*[1] + -**LET**.]
▸ **A** *noun* **1** †**a** *BOTANY.* A sepal. **L18–M19.** ▸**b** *BOTANY.* Each of the divisions of a compound leaf. **E19.** ▸**c** *popularly.* A young leaf. Also (*rare*), a petal. **M19.**

> **b** A. T. **THOMSON** The leaves are . . pinnate, with a terminal leaflet a little larger than the rest.

2 *ANATOMY & ZOOLOGY.* An organ or part resembling a thin leaf or sheet; *spec.* the thin flap of a valve in the heart or a blood vessel. **E19.**
3 A small sheet of paper or a sheet folded into two or more leaves but not stitched, containing printed matter (often advertisements), usu. distributed free of charge. **M19.**

> *Which?* BAR publish a leaflet on their arbitration scheme.

– **COMB.:** **leaflet raid** a raid in which leaflets are dropped from an aircraft.
▸ **B** *verb intrans. & trans.* Distribute printed leaflets to (a community, neighbourhood, etc.). **M20.**
■ **leafle'teer** *noun* (freq. *derog.*) a writer or distributor of leaflets **L19.**

leafy /ˈliːfi/ *adjective.* In sense 1 also (earlier, now *poet.*) **leavy** /ˈliːvi/. **LME.**
[**ORIGIN** from **LEAF** *noun*[1] + -**Y**[1]: cf. **LEAVY**.]
1 Covered with leaves, having many leaves; (of a place) rich in foliage from the abundance of trees or bushes. Also, made or consisting of leaves. **LME.** ▸**b** Of a part of a plant: leaflike, foliaceous. **L17.** ▸**c** Producing broad-bladed leaves, as distinct from other kinds of foliage. **L19.**

> **COLERIDGE** In the leafy month of June. A. **MILLER** Brooklyn Heights was like a quiet, leafy village. *Power Farming* The leafy top growth of the plant.

leafy spurge a European spurge, *Euphorbia esula*, with numerous long linear leaves.
2 Of a substance: consisting of thin sheets; laminate. **M18.**
■ **leafiness** *noun* **E17.**

league /liːɡ/ *noun*[1]. *arch.* **LME.**
[**ORIGIN** Either from late Latin *leuca*, *leuga*, late Greek *leugē* (of Gaulish origin), or from Provençal *lega* = Old French & mod. French *lieue*.]
A variable measure of distance, usu. estimated at about five kilometres or three miles.

league /liːɡ/ *noun*[2]. **LME.**
[**ORIGIN** Partly from French *ligue* from Italian *liga*, Latinized form of *lega*, from *legare* bind from Latin *ligare*; partly immed. from Italian *lega*.]
1 A military, political, or commercial compact made between parties for their mutual protection and assistance in matters of common interest; a body of states or people associated in such a compact. **LME.** ▸**b** An association of individuals, clubs, or societies for some common political, sporting, or other purpose; *spec.* a group of sports clubs or a class of contestants who compete with one another for a championship. **M19.** ▸**c** *transf. & fig.* A group showing a certain level of competence or ability. **M20.**

> **ROBERT WATSON** Exciting the princes of the league of Munster to take the field against the Spaniards. **c** M. **AMIS** She was fairly formidable, a bit out of my league really. J. J. **HENNESSY** They were . . moving into a new league, where they could command . . what music they wanted. *Bulletin (Sydney)* If East-West wants to play in the big league it must shape up to heavy competition.

b ***Delian League***, ***Gaelic League***, ***Hanseatic League***, ***Ivy League***, etc. ***baseball league***, ***cricket league***, ***football league***, ***rugby league***, etc.
2 *gen.* A covenant, a compact, an alliance. Now *rare.* **E16.**
3 *BASKET-MAKING.* A single continuous cane used as a combined bottom stick and upright. **E20.**
– **PHRASES:** *big league*: see **BIG** *adjective.* **Holy League** any of several leagues in European history, as that formed by Pope Julius II against the French in 1511. **in league with** having a compact with, allied or conspiring with. ***Land League***: see **LAND** *noun*[1]. **League of Nations** an association of states, dominions, and colonies established by the treaty of peace of 1919 to promote international cooperation, peace, and security, now replaced by the United Nations. ***Little League***: see **LITTLE** *adjective.* ***major league***: see **MAJOR** *adjective.* ***minor league***: see **MINOR** *adjective & noun.* ***Muslim League***: see **MUSLIM** *adjective.* ***Primrose League***: see **PRIMROSE** *noun.* ***Solemn League and Covenant***: see **COVENANT** *noun* 6. **the League** *hist.* (***a***) a league formed in 1576 under the direction of the Guises, to prevent the accession of Henry IV to the French throne; (***b***) the League of Nations.
– **COMB.:** **league football** football played in leagues, *spec.* (*Austral.*) rugby league or Australian Rules football; **league table** a list of the members of a competitive league in ranking order; any list of ranking order; *transf.* a systematic comparison of performance in any field of competitive activity.
■ **leaguite** *noun* = **LEAGUER** *noun*[2] **M19.**

league /liːɡ/ *verb trans. & intrans.* **L16.**
[**ORIGIN** from **LEAGUE** *noun*[2]. Cf. French *liguer*.]
Form (into) or join a league (*with*); confederate.

> W. **DRUMMOND** To league a people is to make them know their strength & power. **SHELLEY** Where kings first leagued against the rights of men. H. **ADAMS** Count 'Loweis' . . leagued with the Counts of Flanders, . . and Toulouse, against Philip Augustus.

leaguer /ˈliːɡə/ *noun*[1]. **L16.**
[**ORIGIN** Dutch *leger* camp, corresp. to Old English *leger* **LAIR** *noun*[1]. Cf. **LAAGER** *noun*.]
1 A military camp, *esp.* one engaged in a siege; a besieging force. **L16.**

> R. **CAPELL** Here was the German leaguer, whither . . the Germans withdrew behind wire.

2 A military siege. **L16.**

> J. L. **MOTLEY** The Harlem siege, and . . the more prosperous leaguer of Alkmaar.

– **PHRASES:** **in leaguer** in camp, engaged in a siege. **lie leaguer** (now *rare*) be resident as an ambassador, agent, etc.
– **COMB.:** **leaguer-lady**, **leaguer-lass** *euphem.* a woman attached to a military camp, providing various (esp. sexual) services.

leaguer /ˈliːɡə/ *noun*[2]. **L16.**
[**ORIGIN** from **LEAGUE** *noun*[2] + -**ER**[1].]
A member of a league.

> *Cape Times* There are few American major leaguers earning less than $30 000 a year.

leaguer /ˈliːɡə/ *noun*[3]. *obsolete* exc. *S. Afr.* **L17.**
[**ORIGIN** Perh. from Dutch *ligger* tun, from *liggen* **LIE** *verb*[1]. Cf. German *Leger* freshwater cask(s) on board ship.]
A measure of liquid, as water, wine, oil, etc.; a cask of corresponding size.

> *Naval Chronicle* The largest casks are called leaguers. *Cape Times* Two lorries . . carrying a 5-leaguer tank of wine (some 800 gallons).

leaguer /ˈliːɡə/ *verb.* **L16.**
[**ORIGIN** from **LEAGUER** *noun*[1].]
1 *verb intrans. & refl.* Lodge, lie; *spec.* encamp, set one's leaguer. Now *rare.* **L16.**

> B. **MONTGOMERY** We were leaguering as an Army beyond that once-dreaded position.

2 *verb trans.* Besiege, beleaguer. Chiefly as ***leaguered***, ***leaguering*** *ppl adjectives.* **E18.**

> **COLERIDGE** That the voice of truth . . though leagured round By envy . . Be heard. W. **SARGENT** His . . defence of Detroit against Pontiac and his leaguering hordes.

leak /liːk/ *noun.* **L15.**
[**ORIGIN** Prob. of Low German or Dutch origin, with **LEAK** *verb*, *adjective*, ult. from Germanic var. of base of **LACK** *noun*[1]: the noun is repr. by Middle Dutch *lek*, German dial. *Lech* a crack, Old Norse *leki*.]
1 a A hole, crack, etc. (orig. in a ship) through which a liquid, gas, powder, etc., enters or escapes. **L15.** ▸**b** *transf. & fig.* A breach or defect which allows the gradual loss of valuable materials or qualities. **L16.** ▸**c** *PHYSICS.* A path or component of relatively high resistance through which a small (freq. controlled) flow of current, gas, etc., may occur. **L19.** ▸**d** An improper or deliberate disclosure of (secret or confidential) information. **E20.**

> **a** Sir W. **SCOTT** Rent was the sail, and strain'd the mast, And many a leak was gaping fast. J. **WILCOX** The workmen will be here to fix a leak in the roof. *Chemical Engineering* The instrument is to test for leaks in sealed gas-filled objects. **b** P. G. **HAMERTON** An able finance minister . . has found means of closing a great leak in the treasury. **d** D. O. **SELZNICK** There have been leaks about previous discussions. *Encounter* What we have . . is security punctuated by leaks.

2 a The action or an act of leaking; an escape of fluid, gas, radiation, flux, etc., through a hole or crack, or by permeation of an intended barrier; leakage of electric charge or current. **E19.** ▸**b** An act of urinating. Cf. **LEAK** *verb* 2b. *slang.* **M20.**

L

a *Academy* In hydrogen the leak was slowest... The rate of leak in the halogens is.. very rapid. *Times* Burst pipes.. caused a minor radiation leak at one of the country's.. nuclear power stations.

b take a leak urinate.

– COMB.: **leakproof** resistant to leaks, watertight.

†**leak** *adjective*. OE–L18.

[ORIGIN Old English (*h*)*lec*, later formed as LEAK *noun*: the adjective is repr. by Middle Dutch *lek*, German dial. *lech*, Old Norse *lekr*.]

= LEAKY.

leak /liːk/ *verb*. LME.

[ORIGIN formed as LEAK *noun*; the verb is repr. by Middle Dutch *lēken*, Old High German *lëchen*, Middle High German, German dial. *lechen* crack, become leaky, Old Norse *leka*.]

1 *verb intrans.* Pass (*out, away, forth*) by a leak or leakage. LME.

J. WOODWARD A Crack, through which a small quantity of the Liquor leak'd forth. E. POLLARD A particle can 'leak' through any but an infinitely thick wall.

2 *verb intrans. & trans.* Allow (fluid etc.) to pass in or out through a leak. E16. ▸**b** *verb intrans.* Urinate. *slang*. L16.

JOHN ROSS The starboard boiler began to leak. M. PIERCY The attic roof leaks.. into a pail.

†**3** *verb trans.* In *pass.* Have sprung a leak; be emptied (*out*) by leakage. E17–M18.

4 *verb trans.* BREWING. Cause (liquor) to run *over, on, off*, gradually. *obsolete* exc. *dial.* L17.

5 a *verb intrans.* Of a secret etc.: transpire, become known. Also foll. by *out*. L18. ▸**b** *verb intrans. & trans.* Disclose or allow the disclosure of (secret or confidential information). M19.

a *Time* They claimed the Campbell allegation had somehow leaked to the Atlanta newspaper. W. TREVOR We could get into terrible trouble.. if any of this leaked out. **b** J. COLVILLE An alarming communiqué to the effect that the French had leaked about the project. *Herald (Melbourne)* Daniel Ellsberg.. was charged with leaking the secret Pentagon papers.

■ **leaker** *noun* M20.

leakage /ˈliːkɪdʒ/ *noun*. L15.

[ORIGIN from LEAK *verb* + -AGE.]

1 The action of leaking; admission or escape of fluid etc. through a leak; loss of fluid etc. by leaking. L15.

G. ANSON Jars.. are liable to no leekage, unless they are broken. *Science* The leakage of helium through Pyrex glass at elevated temperatures has been noted.

2 Allowance made for waste of fluid etc. by leaking. L16.

S. SMILES The lightermen claimed as their right the perquisites of 'wastage' and 'leakage'.

3 a *transf. & fig.* Diminution resulting from gradual waste or escape; unexplained continuous disappearance of something. M17. ▸**b** PHYSICS. The passage of radiation, magnetic flux, etc., across a boundary, or through an intended barrier; a gradual escape of electric charge or current. M19. ▸**c** The improper or deliberate disclosure of (secret or confidential) information. L19.

a C. WILSON The problem with neurotics.. is a kind of *leakage* of energy. **b** *Consumers Digest* One of the best companies hasn't yet built Appliance Leakage Current Interrupters. *Which?* We test for microwave leakage.

4 Fluid etc. which leaks. M17.

W. IRVING The drippings of the kitchen and the leakage of the tap-room.

leakance /ˈliːk(ə)ns/ *noun*. L19.

[ORIGIN from LEAK *verb* + -ANCE, as contr. of *leakage conductance*.]

ELECTRICITY. Conductance attributable to leakage or imperfect insulation.

leaky /ˈliːki/ *adjective*. E17.

[ORIGIN from LEAK *noun* + -Y¹.]

1 a Having a leak or leaks; allowing fluid etc. to pass through a hole or fissure. E17. ▸**b** *fig.* (Of a person) unable to keep a secret; (of memory) not retentive. L17. ▸**c** Passing urine frequently or in large quantities; incontinent. E18. ▸**d** Of a person: inclined to weep, lachrymose. E20.

a *US News & World Report* Hoang Nhu Tran and his Family fled Vietnam on a leaky boat. **b** W. SOMERVILLE But be thou, my Muse! No leaky Blab. M. WARNOCK Other people have memories 'like a sieve',.. notoriously leaky.

2 ELECTRICITY. Retaining electric charge only with gradual loss; connected to or having a high resistance that acts as a leak. E20.

3 GENETICS. Designating a mutant gene that has some residual activity of the wild type; designating a protein with reduced activity compared with that produced by the wild type. Cf. HYPOMORPHIC. M20.

– COMB.: **leaky-grid detection** ELECTRICITY: in which the signal is applied to the grid of a valve through a series capacitor and a resistor connected as a grid leak or in parallel with the capacitor.

■ **leakiness** *noun* E17.

L

leal /liːl/ *adjective & adverb*. Now *Scot. & N. English* or *literary*. ME.

[ORIGIN Anglo-Norman *leal*, Old French *leel*: see LOYAL.]

▸ **A** *adjective*. **1** Loyal, faithful, honest. ME.

R. GRAVES Now you vow to be leal and true.

2 True, genuine; real, actual; exact, accurate. ME.

J. LOUTHIAN The said Witnesses to bear leal and soothfast Witnessing.

3 Lawful; just, fair. LME.

– COMB.: **leal-hearted** *adjective* loyal, faithful, honest.

▸ **B** *adverb*. **1** Loyally, faithfully. ME.

2 Truly, exactly, accurately; perfectly, thoroughly. LME.

■ **leally** *adverb* loyally, faithfully, truly ME. **lealty** *noun* (*arch.*) faithfulness, loyalty M19.

lea-land /ˈliːland/ *noun*. Now *dial.* Also **lay-** /ˈleɪ-/. ME.

[ORIGIN from LEA *adjective* + LAND *noun*¹.]

Fallow land; land laid down to grass.

leam /liːm/ *noun & verb*. Now *Scot. & N. English*.

[ORIGIN Old English *lēoma* = Old Saxon *liom*, Old Norse *ljómi*, from Germanic noun whence also Gothic *lauhmuni* lighting, from Germanic from Indo-European base also of Latin *lux*, *lumen* light.]

▸ **A** *noun*. Light, flame; a flash, ray, or gleam of light; brightness, gleam. OE.

▸ **B** *verb intrans.* Shine, gleam; light *up*. ME.

†**leamer** *noun* var. of LIMER *noun*¹.

lean /liːn/ *noun*¹. LME.

[ORIGIN from the verb.]

1 A thing to lean or rest on; a support. Long *obsolete* exc. *Scot.* LME.

2 The action or condition of leaning; inclination. L18.

lean /liːn/ *noun*². LME.

[ORIGIN from the adjective.]

The lean part of meat; lean meat.

Nursery rhyme: Jack Sprat could eat no fat, his wife could eat no lean.

lean /liːn/ *adjective*.

[ORIGIN Old English *hlǣne* from Germanic, perh. rel. to Lithuanian *klýnas* scrap, fragment, Latvian *kleins* feeble.]

1 Thin, not plump or fat; not fleshed out. OE. ▸**b** Of a ship: built on clean tapering lines. M18.

R. GRAVES The lean captain of a trading-vessel envies the big-paunched wine-shop proprietor.

2 *fig.* Meagre, poor in quality; (of diet) not nourishing; (of employment) unremunerative. ME.

E. BLUNDEN The day's meals.. were still substantial despite the lean supplies. *Times* He went through a lean patch.. but has since come back strongly.

3 *techn.* Of various materials, as soil, mortar, fuel, etc.: low in essential or valuable elements or qualities. ME.

4 Scantily provided. Formerly also, short *of*. ME.

5 Of meat: containing little or no fat. LME.

M. PYKE Meat is made of.. the fat, and the lean or protein part.

6 TYPOGRAPHY. Of (a stroke in) a letter: thin, slender. Now *rare*. L17.

7 Of industry, a company, etc.: economical, efficient. L20.

Observer Industry was now leaner and fitter and in a much better position to compete.

– SPECIAL COLLOCATIONS & COMB.: **lean-burn** *adjective* designating (the technology associated with) an internal-combustion engine designed to run on a lean mixture and so reduce pollution. **lean mixture** vaporized fuel containing a high proportion of air. **lean times**, **lean years**, etc., times, years, etc., of scarcity.

■ **leanish** *adjective* M17. **leanly** *adverb* L16. **leanness** /-n-n-/ *noun* OE.

lean /liːn/ *verb*. Pa. t. & pple **leaned** /liːnd/, **leant** /lɛnt/.

[ORIGIN Old English *hleonian*, *hlinian*, corresp. to Old Frisian *lena*, Old Saxon *hlinon* (Dutch *leunen*), Old High German (*h*)*linēn* (German *lehnen*), from Germanic base rel. to that of Greek *klimax* ladder, CLIMAX, Latin *clivus* declivity, Sanskrit *çri* lean, with *-n-* formative as in Greek *klinein* to lean, slope, Latin *inclinare* INCLINE *verb*.]

1 *verb* †*intrans. & refl.* Recline, lie (*down*), rest. *obsolete* exc. *Scot.* OE.

2 *verb intrans.* **a** Bend or incline in a particular direction. (Foll. by *back, over, towards*, etc.) OE. ▸**b** Move or be situated obliquely; swerve (*aside*). LME.

a H. JACOBSON I leaned towards them so as not to miss a single word. **b** R. L. STEVENSON The gigs had leaned to their right.

3 *verb intrans.* **a** Incline against an object for support; support oneself or be supported *on*, (*up*) *against* something. ME. ▸**b** Press *upon*; lay emphasis *upon*. M18.

a G. GREENE She leant against the door and tried to steady herself.

4 *verb intrans. fig.* Rely or depend *on*. ME.

P. CASEMENT Trainees.. often lean too heavily upon the advice or comments of a supervisor.

5 *verb trans.* **a** Cause to lean or rest, prop (*against, on*, etc.). ME. ▸**b** Cause to bend or incline. LME.

a P. THEROUX Haddy rolled the barrel.. into the junkpile and leaned a log against it. **b** E. B. BROWNING I would lean my spirit o'er you.

6 *verb intrans.* Incline or tend *towards* or *to* some quality or condition. Also, have a tendency favourable *to*. LME.

POPE There's not a blessing Individuals find, But some way leans and hearkens to the Kind.

7 *verb intrans.* **a** Incline or tend in thought, affection, or conduct; be disposed *to, towards*. M16. ▸†**b** Defer *to* an opinion. M16–E17.

a G. KEILLOR I lean toward this theory. **b** SHAKES. *Cymb.* You lean'd unto his sentence with what patience Your wisdom may inform you.

– PHRASES & COMB.: **lean against** (chiefly LAW) be unfavourable to, not countenance. **lean on** *colloq.* put pressure on (a person) in order to force him or her to do something. **lean-over** an inclination down or forward; something over which one can lean. ***lean over backward(s)***: see BACKWARD *adverb* 1. **lean to one side** *fig.* (POLITICS) (of a political party, diplomatic policy, etc.) be biased towards a particular, esp. socialist, country, party, etc. **lean upon** MILITARY be close up to something serving as a protection.

■ **leaner** *noun* M16.

leangle /ˈliːaŋg(ə)l/ *noun*. *Austral.* Also **leeangle**, **liangle**, & other vars. M19.

[ORIGIN Wemba-wemba and Wuywurung *lia* tooth.]

A wooden club bent at the striking end.

leaning /ˈliːnɪŋ/ *noun*. OE.

[ORIGIN from LEAN *verb* + -ING¹.]

1 The action of LEAN *verb*. OE.

2 *fig.* An inclination, a bias; a tendency. L16.

W. TREVOR He had no political leanings himself, neither Republican nor imperialist.

– COMB.: **leaning note** MUSIC = APPOGGIATURA; **leaning stock** a support (*lit. & fig.*); *spec.* the ledge on which an organ pipe rests.

leant *verb pa. t. & pple*: see LEAN *verb*.

lean-to /ˈliːntuː/ *noun & adjective*. LME.

[ORIGIN from LEAN *verb* + TO *adverb*.]

▸ **A** *noun*. Pl. **-tos**.

1 A building whose roof leans against another building or against a wall; a penthouse. LME.

R. MACAULAY A small.. man crept out of a lean-to which was propped against a ruined wall.

2 *transf.* A temporary shelter, supported or free-standing, of brushwood, canvas, etc.; a rudimentary tent or hut. Chiefly *Canad.* L19.

▸ **B** *attrib.* or as *adjective*. Pertaining to or of the nature of a lean-to. Also, placed so as to lean against something. M17.

lean-to building, lean-to porch, lean-to room, lean-to shed, etc.

leap /liːp/ *noun*¹. Also (*Scot. & Irish*) **lep** /lɛp/.

[ORIGIN Old English *hlȳp* from Germanic base of LEAP *verb*. Cf. Old Frisian *hlēp*, Dutch *loop*, Old High German *hlouf* (German *Lauf*), Old Norse *hlaup*. Partly directly from the verb.]

1 a An act or the action of leaping; a bound, a jump, a spring. OE. ▸**b** *transf. & fig.* An abrupt change or movement (*from, to, up* etc.); a sudden transition. Later *spec.*, a sudden increase or advance (*to, up*, etc.). OE.

a P. G. WODEHOUSE She sprang onto the pavement with a gay leap. **b** N. ARMSTRONG That's one small step for man, one giant leap for mankind. D. PRATER He began to prepare for his leap into the unknown. *Financial Times* The crucial factor was.. the leap in the oil price.. with rises in other.. prices.

2 A thing to be leaped over or from. Also, a place or distance leaped. Freq. in place names, as ***Smuggler's Leap, Lover's Leap***. ME.

3 An act or the action of springing on a female in copulation; an act of copulation. Now *rare*. E17.

4 MUSIC. A passing from one note to another by an interval greater than one degree of the scale; an interval greater than one degree of the scale. Cf. STEP *noun*¹ 4b. L17.

5 MINING. A fault or dislocation of strata. M18.

6 The sudden fall of a river to a lower level. M18.

H. I. JENKINSON The water makes five or six leaps in its descent.

– PHRASES: **by leaps (and bounds)** by sudden transitions; with startlingly rapid progress or increase. **leap forward** a marked or notable advance (***Great Leap (Forward)***: see GREAT *adjective*). ***leap in the dark***: see DARK *noun*¹.

– COMB.: **leap day** an intercalary day in the calendar, *esp.* that of a leap year (29 February); **leap second** a second which on particular occasions is inserted into (or omitted from) the atomic scale of reckoning time in order to bring it into correspondence with solar time; **leap year** a year having one intercalary day (now 29 February) more than the common year of 365 days (perh. so called because fixed festivals after February in a leap year fall two days of the week, instead of the usual one day, later than in the preceding year).

leap /liːp/ *noun*². *obsolete* exc. *dial.*

[ORIGIN Old English *lēap* = Old Norse *lauper*.]

A basket; *spec.* a basket in which to catch or keep fish.

leap /liːp/ *verb*. Pa. t. & pple **leaped** /liːpt/, **leapt** /lɛpt/. Also (*Scot. & Irish*) **lep** /lɛp/, pa. t. & pple **lept**, pres. pple **lepping**.

[ORIGIN Old English *hlēapan* = Old Frisian (*h*)*lāpa*, Old Saxon *-hlōpan* (Dutch *loopen*), Old High German *loufan* (German *laufen* run), Old Norse *hlaupa* (whence LOUP *verb*), Gothic *-hlaupan*, from Germanic. Cf. WALLOP *verb*.]

1 *verb intrans.* **a** Rise with both (or all) feet suddenly from a standing place, alighting in some other position; jump, spring. Freq. foll. by *aside, down, in*, etc. OE. ▸**b** Spring to one's seat *upon* a horse, *into* the saddle. (Foll. by *up*.) OE. ▸**c** Of a fish: spring from the water. LME.

a M. SCAMMELL They would leap naked into the Volga to swim. *Proverb*: Look before you leap. **c** J. MCPHEE A salmon.. leaps into the air.. ten pounds of fish jumping.. high into the air.

2 *verb intrans.* Spring sportively up and down; jump, esp. with joy, mirth, etc.; dance, skip. OE.

M. PIERCY I leap and twirl and prance.

3 *verb intrans.* Run; rush, throw oneself. Also foll. by *forth, out*, etc. Long *rare*. LOE.
4 *verb intrans.* Spring suddenly *to* or *upon* one's feet; rise with a bound *from* a sitting or recumbent position. Freq. foll. by *up*. ME.

G. VIDAL Burden leapt to his feet.

5 *verb intrans.* **a** *transf. & fig.* Of a thing: spring, move with a leap or bound; *esp.* fly, by explosive or other force. ME. ▸**b** Of the heart, (*rare*) the pulse: beat vigorously, bound, throb. E16. ▸**c** MINING. Of a vein of ore: be dislocated. M18. ▸**d** Of frost: melt or thaw suddenly. *colloq.* M19.

a P. ABRAHAMS The high ceiling collapsed.. sending massive tongues of fire leaping at the sky. **b** H. ROTH David's heart leaped in secret joy.

6 *fig.* **a** *verb intrans.* Pass abruptly from one condition or position to another. Also foll. by *back, down, up*. ME. ▸**b** *verb intrans.* Pass *over* without pausing. L16. ▸**c** *verb intrans. & trans.* MUSIC. Pass from one note to another (by an interval greater than one degree of the scale). L19.

a H. KELLER The fire leaped into life. *Private Eye* Sir Michael .. leapt into the Press denouncing the sentences. **b** A. HAMILTON I can perceive several Things worth noticing, they have neglected or leapt over.

7 *verb trans.* Spring over; pass from one side to the other by leaping (*lit. & fig.*); *spec.* (of a bridge) span, extend across. LME.

New Yorker A railroad bridge and two highway bridges leap the Atchafalaya.

8 *verb trans. & intrans.* Spring on (a female) in copulation; copulate with (a female). Now *rare*. LME.

J. BARTH Confronted with that battery of eager bosoms and delicious behinds,.. the urge to.. leap those fine girls was terrific.

9 *verb trans.* Cause (an animal) to take a leap. L17.

W. H. RUSSELL [He] had leaped his horse across a deep nullah.

– PHRASES: **be ready to leap out of one's skin** be delighted, eager, or surprised. **leap at** make a spring at in order to seize; *fig.* exhibit eagerness for. **leap out of one's skin** be extremely delighted, eager, or surprised. **leap to the eye** be immediately apparent.
■ **leapable** *adjective* E20.

leaper /ˈliːpə/ *noun.* OE.
[ORIGIN from LEAP *verb* + -ER[1].]
†**1** A runner; a dancer. OE–L16.
2 A person who or animal which leaps or jumps; an animal which uses leaping as a mode of progression. ME.

leapfrog /ˈliːpfrɒɡ/ *noun & adjective.* L16.
[ORIGIN from LEAP *verb* + FROG *noun*[1].]
▸ **A** *noun.* **1** A game in which one player places his or her hands on the bent back or shoulders of another and vaults over him or her with legs apart, typically then becoming the one, or the last of a line, to be leaped over while the (first) bent-over player becomes the leaper. Also, a vault of this kind. L16.
2 *fig.* The taking of turns in moving to the front, the action or process of leapfrogging; *spec.* (**a**) MILITARY a method of maintaining constant communication with a moving command by keeping one instrument in operation while another moves past it to a position in front; (**b**) competition for higher wages by leapfrogging. E20.
▸ **B** *attrib.* or as *adjective.* Of the nature or style of leapfrog, a leapfrog, or leapfrogging. E17.

Time Sequential or 'leap-frog' bypasses around two blocked sections of the arteries.

leapfrog /ˈliːpfrɒɡ/ *verb.* Infl. **-gg-**. L19.
[ORIGIN from the noun.]
1 *verb intrans.* **a** Leap or vault as at leapfrog. L19. ▸**b** MILITARY. Of detachments or units, esp. in an attack: go in advance of each other by turns. E20. ▸**c** Demand higher wages every time a group of comparable wage-earners has succeeded in pulling level or getting ahead. Chiefly as ***leapfrogging*** *verbal noun & ppl adjective.* M20.

R. KIPLING He.. tried to leapfrog into the saddle. *fig.*: A. POWELL Through column-writing and minor editorships, he had.. leapfrogged into a.. promising position in Fleet Street. **c** *New York Times* Direct controls may check 'leapfrogging' by unions.. to .. maintain.. wages relative to those of other workers.

2 *verb trans.* Leap or vault over as at leapfrog; move in front of by leapfrogging. L19.

A. J. BARKER The two rear companies were picked up.. and leapfrogged to the head of the main column.

leaping /ˈliːpɪŋ/ *verbal noun.* OE.
[ORIGIN from LEAP *verb* + -ING[1].]
The action of LEAP *verb*; an instance of this.
– COMB.: **leaping head**, **leaping horn** the lower pommel on a side-saddle, against which the left knee presses in leaping; †**leaping house** a brothel; **leaping time** *rare* the time of activity, youth.

leaping /ˈliːpɪŋ/ *ppl adjective.* OE.
[ORIGIN from LEAP *verb* + -ING[2].]
That leaps. Formerly also, that runs or dances.
Cape leaping hare, **leaping hare** = SPRINGHAAS. **leaping ague** chorea.

leapt *verb pa. t. & pple*: see LEAP *verb*.

lear /lɪə/ *noun*[1]. Now *Scot. & N. English*. LME.
[ORIGIN from *lear* var. of LERE *verb*. Cf. LORE *noun*[1].]
Instruction, learning. Formerly also, a piece of instruction, a lesson; a doctrine, a religion.
– COMB.: **lear-father** a master in learning; a person who has influenced others.

†**lear** *noun*[2]. LME.
[ORIGIN Old French *loiure, lieure*, (also mod.) *liure* from Latin *ligatura* LIGATURE *noun*.]
1 Tape; binding for the edges of fabric. LME–M18.
2 A thickening for sauces, soups, etc.; a thickened sauce. LME–M19.

lear /lɪə/ *noun*[3]. L15.
[ORIGIN Perh. extended use of LAIR *noun*[1] 6.]
Colour (of sheep or cattle) due to the nature of the soil.

lear *noun*[4] var. of LEER *noun*[4].

lear *verb* var. of LERE.

learn /ləːn/ *verb.* Pa. t. & pple **learned** /ləːnd/, **learnt** /ləːnt/. Also (now *dial. & joc.*) **larn** /lɑːn/.
[ORIGIN Old English *leornian* = Old Frisian *lernia, lirnia*, Old Saxon *līnon*, Old High German *lernēn, lirnēn* (German *lernen*) from West Germanic, from base also of LORE *noun*[1].]
▸ **I** Acquire knowledge.
1 *verb trans. & intrans.* Acquire knowledge of (a subject) or skill in (an art etc.) as a result of study, experience, or instruction; acquire or develop an ability *to do*. OE.

G. STEIN Lena could first.. learn how to do things. B. MONTGOMERY We learnt by bitter experience. S. DELANEY Oh Jo, you're only a kid. Why don't you learn from my mistakes? R. P. JHABVALA She had learned a lot and was very wise and provident now. D. WIGODER From my clumsy fall I learned to be more cautious.

2 *verb trans. & intrans.* Become acquainted with or informed of (a fact); hear (*of*), ascertain. ME.

T. HARDY He.. held up his watch to learn the time. *Times* One learnt by chance that they were in lowly jobs. G. GREENE When Rembrandt wants to marry.. we learn for the first time of an impediment.

▸ **II** Impart knowledge. Now *non-standard*.
3 *verb trans.* Give instruction to, teach. ME. ▸**b** Give instruction in, teach (a thing) *to* a person. *rare*. LME.

H. MAYHEW My mother learned me to needlework and knit.

†**4** *verb trans.* Inform (a person) of something. Foll. by obj. clause or double obj. LME–L17.

SHAKES. *Tr. & Cr.* Learn me the proclamation.

– PHRASES ETC.: **I am yet to learn**, **I have yet to learn** I am unaware (usu. with implication of disbelief). **I'll learn you** *non-standard*: a warning of impending punishment. **learn by heart**, **learn by rote** commit to memory (a formulaic information, a passage of prose or verse). **learning machine** a computer etc. designed to improve its ability to solve problems or perform tasks by making use of information from previous attempts. ***learn one's lesson***: see LESSON *noun* 6. **learn the hard way** learn by painful experience. ***learn the ropes***: see ROPE *noun*[1]. **learn-to-—** *attrib. adjective* designating a course of lessons or step-by-step instructions in a subject or skill. ***live and learn***: see LIVE *verb*.
– WITH ADVERBS IN SPECIALIZED SENSES: **learn off** commit to memory, learn by heart. **learn out** (now *dial.*) find out, discover. **learn up** make oneself familiar with by study etc.
■ **learnaˈbility** *noun* the quality or fact of being learnable M20. **learnable** *adjective* able to be learned, easily learned E17.

learned /ˈləːnɪd, *in branch II* ləːnd/ *adjective.* Compar. (*arch.*) **learneder**; superl. (*arch.*) **learnedest**. ME.
[ORIGIN from LEARN + -ED[1].]
▸ **I** from LEARN II.
1 Of a person: that has been taught; educated; now *spec.* having profound knowledge gained by study, deeply read, erudite. Foll. by *in*. ME. ▸**b** *spec.* Knowledgeable in law. Now a courtesy title for lawyers in courts of law, the House of Commons, etc., esp. in ***my learned friend*** etc. L15.

R. DAHL Dr. Hugh Alderson Fawcett was a keen and learned archaeologist.

2 Pursued or studied chiefly by people of learning; (of a word) introduced into the language by people of learning; showing or characterized by learning; scholarly. L16.

G. W. KITCHIN Words of very different origin.. the one popular, the other learned. E. WILSON Those.. learned families .. managed not merely to set up the classics but to edit and elucidate them too.

learned journal, ***learned paper***, ***learned society***, etc.
▸ **II** from LEARN I.
3 That has been learned. (*rare* before M20). LME.

Physiology & Behaviour Replication was made of a study suggesting transfer of a learned response from 1 rat to another.

learned helplessness PSYCHIATRY a condition (thought to be one of the underlying causes of depression) in which a person suffers from a chronic sense of powerlessness arising from a traumatic event or persistent failure to succeed.
■ **learnedly** *adverb* M16. **learnedness** *noun* (earlier in UNLEARNEDNESS) M17.

learner /ˈləːnə/ *noun.* OE.
[ORIGIN from LEARN + -ER[1].]
1 A person who is learning a subject or skill, a person under instruction; a disciple. In early use also, a scholar, a learned person. OE.
2 *spec.* A person who is learning a foreign language. L19.
3 A person who is learning to drive a motor vehicle and has not yet passed a driving test. M20.
– COMB.: **learner driver** = sense 3 above; **learner plate** a sign showing a red L, attached to a motor vehicle in order to designate the driver a learner (freq. in *pl.*); **learner's dictionary** a simple dictionary designed for the use of foreign students.

learnfare /ˈləːnfɛː/ *noun. N. Amer.* L20.
[ORIGIN from LEARN + WEL)FARE, after WORKFARE.]
A welfare system in which attendance at school, college, or a training programme is necessary in order to receive benefits.

learning /ˈləːnɪŋ/ *noun.* OE.
[ORIGIN from LEARN + -ING[1].]
1 The action of LEARN *verb*. OE. ▸**b** Education; schooling. *obsolete* exc. *dial.* LME.
2 Knowledge acquired by systematic study; the possession of such knowledge. ME.

Proverb: A little learning is a dangerous thing.

3 A thing learned or taught; a lesson, an instruction; information; a doctrine; a maxim; a branch of learning; an acquired skill. LME.
– PHRASES: ***latent learning***: see LATENT *adjective*. ***new learning***: see NEW *adjective*. ***open learning***: see OPEN *adjective*. ***revival of learning***: see REVIVAL 1a.
– COMB.: **learning curve** a graph showing progress in learning; the rate at which something is learned or experience is acquired; **learning difficulties**, **learning disability** difficulty in acquiring knowledge and skills to the normal level, esp. because of mental disability or cognitive disorder; **learning-disabled** *adjective* having a learning disability; **learning resource** a material for (esp. self-)education, e.g. a microfilm or audiovisual aid, made accessible in a library, school, etc. (freq. in *pl.*); **learning set** PSYCHOLOGY an ability to solve problems of a particular type which is acquired through experience in solving such problems.
– NOTE: *Learning difficulties* became prominent in L20. It covers general conditions such as Down's syndrome as well as more specific ones such as dyslexia. Considered more positive than terms such as *mentally handicapped*, it is now the standard accepted term in Britain in official contexts. *Learning disability* is the equivalent in North America; in Britain it tends to refer specifically to conditions in which the IQ is impaired.

learnt *verb pa. t. & pple*: see LEARN.

leary *adjective* var. of LEERY *adjective*[2].

lease /liːz/ *noun*[1]. *obsolete* exc. *dial.* Also **leaze**.
[ORIGIN Old English *lǣs* from Germanic, perh. from base of LET *verb*[1]. Occas. conf. with pl. of LEA *noun*[1].]
(A) pasture; (a) meadowland; (a) common.

lease /liːs/ *noun*[2]. LME.
[ORIGIN App. var. of LEASH *noun*, perh. partly from French *lisse, lice* (in sense 2a).]
WEAVING. **1** A certain quantity of thread. Long *obsolete* exc. *Scot.* LME.
2 **a** = LEASH *noun* 7a. E19. ▸**b** The crossing of the warp threads in a loom; the place at which the warp threads cross. Freq. in ***keep the lease***, separate the threads alternately. M19.

lease /liːs/ *noun*[3]. LME.
[ORIGIN Anglo-Norman *les* = Old French *lais, leis*, from spec. use of *lesser, laissier* (mod. *laisser*) let, leave from Latin *laxare*, from *laxus* loose, LAX *adjective*.]
1 A contract between parties by which one conveys property, esp. lands (later also rights, services, etc.) to the other for a prescribed term, or at will, usu. in consideration of a periodic payment; the instrument by which such a conveyance is made. LME.

Law Times The lease.. had been lent.. to the plaintiff.. for perusal. E. KUZWAYO The 99-year leases.. are now seen as an insecure piece of legislation. F. WYNDHAM My mother.. was .. trying to secure the lease of a small house in Knightsbridge. *fig.*: SHAKES. *Macb.* Our high-plac'd Macbeth Shall live the lease of nature.

2 A piece of land held on lease. *N. Amer., Austral., & NZ.* L19.

M. MACHLIN There had also been several good shows of natural gas on neighbouring leases.

– PHRASES: ***missive of lease***: see MISSIVE *noun* 2. **new lease of life**, (*N. Amer.*) **new lease on life** a substantially improved prospect of living, or of use after repair. ***wet lease***: see WET *adjective*.
– COMB.: **leaseman** an agent in the oil industry who negotiates leases of land for drilling and related matters.

†**lease** *adjective & noun*[4].
[ORIGIN Old English *lēas*, from Germanic base also of -LESS, LOOSE *adjective*.]
▸ **A** *adjective.* Untrue, false; lying. OE–LME.
▸ **B** *noun.* An untruth, a falsehood. OE–L16.

L

lease /liːz/ *verb*[1] *trans. & intrans. obsolete* exc. *dial.*
[ORIGIN Old English *lesan* = Old Frisian *lesa* read, Old Saxon, Old High German *lesan* (Dutch *lezen*, German *lesen* gather, read), Old Norse *lesa*, Gothic *galisan* gather, from Germanic.]
1 Glean. OE.
2 Pick, esp. in separating good seeds etc. from bad. LME.
■ **leaser** *noun*[1] ME.

lease /liːz/ *verb*[2] *intrans. obsolete* exc. *Scot. & N. English*. OE.
[ORIGIN from LEASE *adjective*.]
Tell lies.
■ **leaser** *noun*[2] OE. **leasing** *noun* lying, falsehood; a lie: OE.

lease /liːs/ *verb*[3]. L15.
[ORIGIN Anglo-Norman *lesser*: see LEASE *noun*[3].]
1 *verb trans.* & (*rare*) *intrans.* Take a lease of (a property etc.); hold (a property etc.) by a lease. L15.

J. P. HENNESSY The land . . did not belong to Mr. Trollope but was only leased from Lord Northwick.

2 *verb trans.* Grant the possession or use of by a lease; let *out* on a lease. L16.

A. MILLER Our landlord was . . planning to lease out our . . apartment to two families. *New York Times* T. Talbot Bond Co . . . sells and leases office equipment.

■ **leasee** *noun* (*rare*) = LESSEE L16. **leaser** *noun* (*rare*) = LESSEE L19. **leasor** *noun* (*rare*) = LESSOR L15.

lease /liːz/ *verb*[4] *trans.* L19.
[ORIGIN from *leas* pl. of LEA *noun*[2].]
Divide (yarn or thread) into leas.

leaseback /ˈliːsbak/ *noun & adjective*. M20.
[ORIGIN from LEASE *verb*[3] + BACK *adverb*.]
A seller's action in taking out a lease on a property from the buyer, as part of the terms of the sale. Freq. in ***sale and leaseback***.

leasehold /ˈliːshəʊld/ *noun & adjective*. E18.
[ORIGIN from LEASE *noun*[3] after *freehold*.]
▸ **A** *noun*. A tenure by lease; real estate so held. E18.
▸ **B** *attrib.* or as *adjective*. Held by lease. E18.

What Mortgage If you are buying a leasehold property—a flat, for instance.

■ **leaseholder** *noun* a person who possesses leasehold property M19.

lease-lend /liːsˈlɛnd/ *adjective, noun, & verb*. M20.
[ORIGIN from LEASE *verb*[3] + LEND *verb*.]
▸ **A** *adjective & noun*. (Designating or pertaining to) an arrangement between parties for exchanging reciprocal aid, orig. *spec.* one of 1941 whereby armaments, supplies, and services were exchanged among the Allies during the Second World War. M20.
▸ **B** *verb trans.* Pa. t. & pple **-lent** /-lɛnt/. Supply by means of a lease-lend arrangement. M20.

leash /liːʃ/ *noun & verb*. ME.
[ORIGIN Old French *lesse*, (also mod.) *laisse*, from spec. (let (a dog) run on a slack lead) use of *lesser*, *laissier*: see LEASE *noun*[2].]
▸ **A** *noun*. **1** A thong or lead by which a dog, orig. *spec.* a hound or hunting dog, is held. ME. ▸**b** A harness for restraining a young child while walking etc. Chiefly *N. Amer.* M20.

SIR W. SCOTT She led three greyhounds in a leash. D. CARNEGIE What do you mean by letting that dog run loose . . without a . . leash?

strain at the leash pull hard at a restraining leash; *fig.* be eager or impatient to begin (chiefly as ***straining at the leash***).
2 A set of three hounds, hawks, hares, etc. ME.

Hounds Although the tally was a leash the last brave hare beat us. *transf.*: TENNYSON Then were I wealthier than a leash of Kings.

3 *fig.* A restraint; control. Esp. in ***in leash***, ***out of leash***. ME.
†**4** A snare, a noose. *rare*. LME–E19.
5 FALCONRY. A thong or string passed through the varvels of the jesses to secure a hawk. LME.
6 A lash with a thong, whip, etc. *Scot.* Long *rare*. E16.
7 WEAVING. **a** Any of the cords with an eye in the middle to receive the warp thread, which run between the parallel laths of the heddle of a loom. M18. ▸**b** = LEASE *noun*[2] 2b. L19.
– COMB.: **leash law** †(**a**) a regulation in hunting or coursing; (**b**) (chiefly *N. Amer.*) a regulation by which a dog etc. must be kept on a leash in public.
▸ **B** *verb trans.* **1** Orig., beat with a leash. Now (*dial.*), whip. E16.
2 Attach or tie by a leash. L16.
3 Link (*together*), esp. in threes. M19.

leasow /ˈliːsəʊ, ˈlɛzə/ *noun & verb*. Now *dial.*
[ORIGIN Old English *lǣswe* oblique form of *lǣs* LEASE *noun*[1].]
▸ **A** *noun*. = LEASE *noun*[1]. OE.
▸ **B** *verb trans. & intrans.* Pasture, graze. Long *rare*. OE.

least /liːst/ *adjective, noun, & adverb*.
[ORIGIN Old English *lǣst* contr. of *lǣsest* from Germanic, from bases of LESS *adjective*, -EST[1].]
▸ **A** *adjective*. **1** Smallest; less than any other in size or degree; *colloq.* fewest. OE.

L. STERNE A fix'd star of the least magnitude. J. M. MURRY A part, and not the least part, of Keats' share of that burden.

2 Lowest in position or importance; meanest. *arch.* OE.

P. SIDNEY I am poore and least of all.

3 *the least*, any, however slight: usu. in neg. and hypothetical contexts. LME.

T. MEDWIN The least noise often scares away . . game of the forest. *Times* Impolite men are not the least bit fanciable.

4 In the names of animals and plants: smallest among several bearing the same name. Cf. LESSER *adjective* 2a. M17.
▸ **B** *absol.* as *noun*. **1** That which is least; the least quantity or amount. ME. ▸**b** *the least* (adverbial), = sense C.1 below. M17.

SHAKES. *Mids. N. D.* Love, therefore, and tongue-tied simplicity In least speak most to my capacity. OED The very least I can do is to apologize for the mistake.

†**2** A most minute quantity or part. M17–E19.

T. STANLEY There being in Nature no least which cannot be divided.

▸ **C** *adverb*. **1** In the lowest degree; less than any other, or than at any other time. ME.

SHAKES. *Lear* Thy youngest daughter does not love thee least. MILTON Mammon, the least erected Spirit that fell From Heav'n. G. BERKELEY Alciphron has made discoveries where I least expected it.

2 = ***at least*** below. *colloq.* L19.

M. TWAIN Yes, least I reckon so.

– PHRASES & SPECIAL COLLOCATIONS: **at least**, **at the least** (**a**) not less than, at the minimum; (**b**) at any rate, at all events; if nothing else. ***circle of least confusion***: see CIRCLE *noun* 1. **in the least** at all; in the slightest degree. ***last but not least***: see LAST *adjective*. **law of least action** PHYSICS = ***principle of least action*** below. **least chipmunk** a small brown striped chipmunk, *Tamias minimus*, widespread in N. America. ***least common denominator***: see DENOMINATOR 1. ***least common multiple***: see MULTIPLE *noun* 1. **least flycatcher** a small migratory American flycatcher, *Empidonax minimus*, with grey and yellow plumage. **least of all** especially not. **least said, soonest mended** talking will not improve matters. ***method of least squares***: see SQUARE *noun*. ***not least***: see NOT *adverb*. **principle of least action** PHYSICS the principle that an actual trajectory of a physical system is always such that, in comparison with any slightly different motion between the same end points, the integral over the trajectory of the momentum with respect to distance has a minimum (or a maximum) value. **principle of least constraint** ENGINEERING the principle that the motions of a set of interconnected masses vary as little as possible from those they would exhibit if separate. ***principle of least squares***: see SQUARE *noun*. **to say the least** (**of it**) to put it mildly.

leastways /ˈliːstweɪz/ *noun & adverb*. Also (earlier) **-way**. LME.
[ORIGIN from LEAST *adjective* + WAY *noun* + -S[1]: see -WAYS. Cf. LEASTWISE.]
▸ †**A** *noun*. ***at least way***(***s***), ***at the least way***(***s***), ***in least way***(***s***), ***in the least way***(***s***), at least. LME–E17.
▸ **B** *adverb*. Or rather, at least. *dial. & colloq.* E19.

I. RANKIN Nobody much in tonight though, not yet leastways.

leastwise /ˈliːstwʌɪz/ *noun & adverb*. LME.
[ORIGIN from LEAST *adjective* + -WISE. Cf. LEASTWAYS.]
▸ †**A** *noun*. ***at leastwise***, at least. LME–L17.
▸ **B** *adverb*. = LEASTWAYS *adverb*. Now *rare*. E19.

leat /liːt/ *noun*. Chiefly *dial. & techn.* L16.
[ORIGIN Repr. in Old English *wæter*) *gelǣt* water channel, from base of *lǣtan* LET *verb*[1].]
A channel made to carry water for a mill etc.

leath /liːθ/ *noun & verb*. Long *obsolete* exc. *dial.* ME.
[ORIGIN Unknown.]
▸ **A** *noun*. **1** Cessation, rest. ME.
2 MINING. A soft part in a vein. M18.
▸ **B** *verb*. **1** *verb trans.* Soften, relax. ME.
†**2** *verb intrans.* Cease, abate. Only in ME.

leather /ˈlɛðə/ *noun & adjective*.
[ORIGIN Old English *leþer* (in compounds) = Old Frisian *lether*, Old Saxon *leþar* (Dutch *leer*), Old High German *ledar* (German *Leder*), Old Norse *leðr*, from Germanic from Indo-European base also of Old Irish *lethar* (mod. *leathar*), Welsh *lledr*, Breton *ler*.]
▸ **A** *noun*. **1** Animal skin treated by tanning or a similar process. OE. ▸**b** A kind of leather. Usu. in *pl.* M19.
buff leather, ***japanned leather***, ***morocco leather***, ***patent leather***, ***Russia leather***, ***Spanish leather***, ***Turkey leather***, ***upper leather*** etc.
2 Skin (now *slang*); *spec.* the skin on the ear flap of a dog. Formerly also, a bag or pouch of skin. ME.
3 A thing made wholly or largely of leather; a piece of leather, as one for polishing. LME. ▸**b** *spec.* = ***stirrup leather*** s.v. STIRRUP *noun*. M16. ▸**c** The ball in cricket or football. *slang*. M19. ▸**d** A wallet, a purse. *slang*. L19.
chamois leather, ***wash leather***, etc.
4 **a** In *pl.* Articles of clothing made of leather, as shoes, leggings, breeches, etc.; *spec.* leather clothes for wearing on a motorcycle. M19. ▸**b** Leather clothing, esp. as intended to express extreme masculinity, aggression, or sadomasochistic tendencies, or to arouse sexual (esp. homosexual) desire. M20.

a R. RENDELL The boy . . , dressed in leathers now and carrying a crash helmet.

5 A brown colour like that of leather. L19.
– PHRASES: ***hell for leather***: see HELL *noun*. ***leather and prunella***: see PRUNELLA *noun*[2]. **lose leather** *slang* suffer abrasion of the skin. ***pull leather***: see PULL *verb*. ***tough as leather***: see TOUGH *adjective*.
▸ **B** *attrib.* or as *adjective*. **1** Made of leather; resembling leather. OE.
2 Of, pertaining to, or wearing leather clothing. M20.

P. THEROUX She saw . . another gang of leather boys howling at a cornered Asian. W. BAYER You go to bars. Ever go to a leather bar?

– SPECIAL COLLOCATIONS & COMB.: **leatherback** (**turtle**) a large marine turtle, *Dermochelys coriacea*, with a thick leathery carapace; also called ***trunk-turtle***. **leather beetle** a dermestid beetle, *Dermestes maculatus*; also called **hide beetle**. **leather breeches** (**beans**) *US dial.* dried beans or bean pods; dried beans cooked in their pods. **leather carp** an abnormal scaleless variety of the carp. **leathercloth** cloth coated on one side with a waterproof varnish; a synthetic product simulating leather. **leather-coat** a russet apple. **leather-flower** a N. American climbing plant, *Clematis viorna*, with thick leathery purplish sepals. **leather-hard** *adjective* (of unfired pottery) dried and hardened enough to be trimmed or decorated with slip, but not enough to be fired. **leather-head** (**a**) *slang* a stupid person; (**b**) *Austral.* any of various friarbirds. **leather-headed** *adjective* (*slang*) stupid, slow-witted. **leather-headedness** *slang* stupidity. **leather-hunting** *Cricket slang* fielding, esp. when the batsman is hitting out freely. **leatherleaf** a N. American low evergreen shrub, *Chamaedaphne calyculata*, of the heath family, with leathery leaves. **leather medal** (orig. *US*) a derisory award. **leatherneck** *slang* (**a**) NAUTICAL a soldier; (**b**) *US* a marine; (**c**) *Austral.* = ROUSEABOUT *noun* 2. **Leather-Stocking** a N. American frontiersman. **leather-turtle** = ***leatherback*** above. **leatherwood** a N. American shrub, *Dirca palustris* (family Thymelaeaceae), with a very tough bark; also called ***moosewood***.
■ **leatheˈrette** *noun* imitation leather made from cloth, paper, etc. L19. **leather-like** *adverb & adjective* (**a**) *adverb* (*rare*) in the manner of leather; (**b**) *adjective* resembling leather, esp. in appearance: L16. **leatheroid** *noun* a fabric, resembling leather, made from chemically treated cotton paper L19.

leather /ˈlɛðə/ *verb*. ME.
[ORIGIN from LEATHER *noun & adjective*.]
1 *verb trans.* Cover or fit with leather. ME.
2 *verb trans.* Beat, flog, *spec.* with a leather belt. E17. ▸**b** *verb intrans.* Foll. by *away*, *on*: work unremittingly (*at*). M19.

TENNYSON I'd like to leather 'im black and blue.

■ **leathered** *adjective* (**a**) covered or fitted with leather(s); (**b**) made into, or like, leather: ME. **leathering** *noun* (**a**) the action of the verb; (**b**) *colloq.* a beating, a flogging; (**c**) a covering or strip of leather: E16.

leatherjacket /ˈlɛðədʒakɪt/ *noun*. L18.
[ORIGIN from LEATHER *noun & adjective* + JACKET *noun*.]
1 Any of various thick-skinned marine fishes, as the carangid *Oligoplites saurus*, and various filefishes and triggerfishes (family Balistidae). L18.
2 *Austral.* A kind of pancake. M19.
3 Any of various Australian trees with a tough bark, esp. *Ceratopetalum apetalum* (family Cunoniaceae). L19.
4 A burrowing crane fly larva, *esp.* one of the genus *Tipula*. L19.
5 A person, esp. a member of a gang, wearing a leather jacket. M20.

leathern /ˈlɛð(ə)n/ *adjective*. *arch.* OE.
[ORIGIN from LEATHER *noun* + -EN[4].]
Made of leather; leathery.
leathern convenience (latterly *joc.*) a large horse-drawn carriage.

leathery /ˈlɛð(ə)ri/ *adjective*. M16.
[ORIGIN from LEATHER *noun* + -Y[1].]
Resembling leather in appearance or texture.
leathery turtle = ***leatherback*** (***turtle***) s.v. LEATHER *noun & adjective*.
■ **leatheriness** *noun* E20.

leathwake /ˈliːθweɪk/ *adjective*. Long *obsolete* exc. *N. English*.
[ORIGIN Old English *liþewāc*, *leoþuwāc*, formed as LITH *noun*[1] + *wāc* soft, pliant (see WEAK *adjective*).]
Having supple joints; *gen.* pliant, soft.

leave /liːv/ *noun*[1].
[ORIGIN Old English *lēaf* from West Germanic base also of Middle High German *loube*, German †*Laube*, from Germanic base also of LIEF.]
1 Permission (*to do*). OE. ▸**b** More fully ***leave of absence***. Permission to be absent from one's normal duties, employment, etc.; (authorized) absence from work etc.; a period of such absence. L18.

W. H. IRELAND Upon which subject I shall beg leave to dwell a little. H. JAMES The young girl gave him gracious leave to accompany her. W. S. CHURCHILL Free to say what they like in print without prior leave of the Government. **b** R. K. NARAYAN I'll have to apply to my office for leave. A. WEST The . . platform was crowded with soldiers and airmen going home on leave from the camps. J. BERMAN Dick announces his plan to take a leave from the clinic.

b ***compassionate leave***, ***maternity leave***, ***paternity leave***, ***sabbatical leave***, ***shore leave***, ***sick leave***, etc.
2 Farewell, departure. Formerly also, permission to depart. Chiefly in ***take leave*** (***of***), ***take one's leave*** (***of***) below. ME.

MILTON And Satan bowing low . . Took leave. *fig.*: B. FRANKLIN I now took leave of printing, as I thought, for ever.

– PHRASES: **by your leave** (freq. *iron.*) with your permission. ***French leave***: see FRENCH *adjective*. **get one's leave** (*obsolete* exc. *Scot.*) be

discharged or dismissed from one's job etc. **give a person his or her leave** (*obsolete* exc. *Scot.*) discharge or dismiss a person from a job. *leave of absence*: see sense 1b above. **take leave of one's senses** have a mental aberration, go mad. **take leave to** venture to, presume to. **take leave (of)**, **take one's leave (of)** †(*a*) obtain permission to depart (from a person); (*b*) say goodbye (to). TICKET OF LEAVE. **without so much as a by your leave** without even apologizing or asking permission; brusquely. **with your leave** = *by your leave* above.
– COMB.: **leave-breaker** a sailor who exceeds his leave of absence; **leave-taker** a person saying goodbye; **leave-taking** the action or an act of saying goodbye.

leave /liːv/ *noun*[2]. L19.
[ORIGIN from the verb.]
The position in which the balls are left for the next stroke in billiards, croquet, etc.

leave /liːv/ *verb*[1]. Pa. t. & pple **left** /lɛft/.
[ORIGIN Old English *lǣfan* = Old Frisian *lēva*, Old Saxon *-leian*, Old High German *leiban* (cf. Old High German *bilīban*, German *bleiben* remain), Old Norse *leifa*, Gothic *-laibjan*, from Germanic verb meaning 'remain', from base also of LAVE *noun*.]
1 *verb trans.* **a** (Arrange to) transfer possession of at one's death *to* an heir or successor; bequeath (*to*). Also in *indirect pass.* OE. ▸**b** Have remaining on one's death; be survived by. OE.

ADDISON I was left a thousand pounds by an uncle. J. BUCHAN My father died a year ago and left me the business. L. WHISTLER He made a new will, leaving everything to me. **b** R. BROOKE Then they died. They left three children. E. BROCK When he died he left two meerschaum pipes / and a golden sovereign on a chain.

†**2** *verb intrans.* Remain (*behind*, *over*); continue in one place. OE–M16.
3 a *verb trans.* Allow to remain; let remain in the same place or in a specified condition by refraining from consuming or otherwise acting on. In *pass.*, remain. OE. ▸**b** *verb trans.* Of a mathematical operation: yield as a remainder. LME. ▸†**c** *verb intrans.* Not to consume the whole of one's portion of food etc. Also foll. by *over*. Only in E17.

E. LINKLATER She pours her brother's whisky into what's left of her lager. H. MOORE The parts he disliked he would alter and the parts he didn't dislike he'd leave. **b** O. HENRY One from four leaves three.

4 *verb trans.* **a** Put down, deposit; place and keep; hand in and have kept; deposit and (deliberately or inadvertently) omit to remove; deposit or entrust (a thing or matter) to be attended to, delivered, collected, etc., in one's absence. ME. ▸**b** Cause to be in a specified condition. LME. ▸**c** Deposit or cause to remain as a trace or record. M18.

a J. G. COZZENS He realized that he must have left his hat somewhere—in the taxi? L. HELLMAN Willy had phoned and left the name of a man who made fine riding boots. M. ANGELOU Some of the workers would leave their sacks at the store. **b** E. WAUGH I know I look awful . . . The adjutant left me in no doubt on that subject. R. DAHL Two hours of writing fiction leaves this particular writer absolutely drained. E. FEINSTEIN His death left her an orphan. **c** I. MURDOCH My steps as I crossed the pavement left moist sticky traces.

5 *verb trans.* **a** Omit to do, abstain from dealing with, esp. so that another agent may be able to; commit, refer (something) *to* a person. ME. ▸**b** Allow (a person or thing) *to do* something or something *to be done* or dealt with without interference or assistance or in one's absence; *colloq.* (chiefly *US*) let (a person or thing) do something. E16. ▸**c** Postpone (a decision, action, etc.). M16.

a J. C. POWYS We'd better leave theology to people who're too old for anything else. *Observer* It is left to the New Parliament to make a European electoral law. **b** A. CHRISTIE I left her to have a wash and brush up. J. O'FAOLAIN Ah, leave her go.

6 *verb trans.* Go away, depart, move away, from (a place, person, or thing); deviate from (a line of road, etc.); pass (an object) so that it is in a specified relative position or direction. ME.

J. GALSWORTHY It was enough to make a man get up and leave the table. G. GREENE Men who leave a bar unobtrusively when other people enter.

7 *verb trans.* Stop doing or resign from (a job etc.); terminate one's relation to or connection with (a place, person, institution, etc.); abandon. ME. ▸†**b** Part with, lose (one's breath, life). ME–M17.

C. SIMMONS After nine years of marriage, Winifred left Buckram. *Sunday Express* Around this time South Africa was leaving the Commonwealth.

8 *verb trans.* Cease, desist from (a habit, activity, etc.); drop (a subject). ME. ▸†**b** *verb intrans.* Stop; cease (*to*); break off a narrative. ME–E17.

G. GREENE She said she had read my books and left the subject there.

9 *verb intrans.* Depart, set off, go away; abandon one's place of residence etc.; stop doing or resign from one's job etc. M16.

J. LE CARRÉ She watched him leave, perhaps to make sure he really went. I. MURDOCH Adelaide was clever at school, but left at fifteen and became a clerk.

– PHRASES & COMB.: **be well left** be well provided for by inheritance. **get left** *colloq.* be deserted or worsted. **leave a card on** make a formal call on (a person). *leave alone*: see ALONE 1. *leave a person cold*: see COLD *adjective*. *leave a person cool*: see COOL *adjective*. **leave a person to his or her own devices** let a person tackle a problem etc. without help or interference. **leave a person to it** *colloq.* let a person get on with a job etc. without help or interference. **leave away from** not bequeath to. **leave be** *colloq.* refrain from disturbing; not interfere with. *leave flat*: see FLAT *adjective* 6. **leave for dead** (*a*) abandon as being beyond rescue; (*b*) *Austral. & NZ slang* outdistance, excel by far. **leave go (of)**, **leave hold (of)** *colloq.* let go (of), cease holding. *leave in the lurch*: see LURCH *noun*[1] 2. **leave it at that** abstain from further comment or action. **leave it out** *slang* stop it. **leave it to a person**, **leave it with a person** let a person deal with a matter etc.; put a person in charge of a matter etc. *leave much to be desired*: see *leave something to be desired* below. *leave no stone unturned*: see STONE *noun*. **leave nothing to chance** arrange every detail carefully. *leave oneself wide open*: see WIDE *adverb*. *leave one's visiting card*: see VISITING *verbal noun*. *leave out of account*: see ACCOUNT *noun*. **leave something to be desired**, **leave much to be desired**, etc., fail to meet a standard; be (very etc.) unsatisfactory. *leave standing*: see STANDING *adjective*. **leave the room** *euphem.* go to the lavatory. *leave to stew*, *leave to stew in one's own juice*: see STEW *verb*. *leave to the* MERCY *of*. **leave up to** let (a choice, action, etc.) be the prerogative or responsibility of. *leave well alone*: see WELL *adjective*. **leave word (with)** entrust with a message. *left holding the baby*: see HOLD *verb*. **left-luggage (office)** a place at a railway station etc. where luggage may be deposited for later retrieval.
– WITH ADVERBS & PREPOSITIONS IN SPECIALIZED SENSES: **leave aside** omit, ignore, not consider. **leave behind** (*a*) not take with one at one's departure, go away without; (*b*) cause to remain as a trace or record; (*c*) outstrip. **leave for** (*a*) set off to travel to (a place etc.); (*b*) abandon, depart from, in favour of a new (person or pursuit). **leave from** = *leave away from* above. **leave off** (*a*) cease from *doing*; not wear; discontinue (an action, habit, etc.); make an end, stop; (of a narrative) come to an end; (*b*) set (a person) down (from a vehicle), drop (a person) off. **leave out** (*a*) leave in a visible or accessible place; leave outdoors; (*b*) omit; ignore. **leave out of** exclude from. **leave over** (*a*) allow to remain; (*b*) postpone for subsequent consideration or action.
■ **leavable** *adjective* L19. **leaver** *noun* a person who has just left or is about to leave a position etc., *spec.* a boy or girl who has just left or is about to leave school: M16.

leave /liːv/ *verb*[2] *intrans.* ME.
[ORIGIN from LEAF *noun*[1] with voicing before the verbal inflection.]
= LEAF *verb* 1.

†**leave** *verb*[3] *trans. rare* (Spenser). Only in L16.
[ORIGIN Old French & mod. French *lever*: see LEVY *noun*[1].]
Raise (an army).

leaved /liːvd/ *adjective*. ME.
[ORIGIN from LEAF *noun*[1], LEAVE *verb*[2]: see -ED[2], -ED[1].]
1 Bearing leaves, in leaf; having leaves (of a specified number or kind). ME.

C. BRONTË The great dining-room, whose two-leaved door stood open. E. DIEHL After the flat book form had become . . usual, papyrus . . was made up into leaved books.

†**2** Reduced to a leaf or thin plate; laminated. M16–M17.
3 Resembling a leaf of a plant. M19.

†**leaveless** *adjective* see LEAFLESS.

leaven /ˈlɛv(ə)n/ *noun*. Also **levain**. ME.
[ORIGIN Old French *levain* from Proto-Gallo-Romance use of Latin *levamen* lit. 'means of raising', only in sense 'alleviation, relief', from *levare* lighten, relieve, raise, from *levis* light.]
1 A substance or agent which produces fermentation; *spec.* (*a*) yeast added to dough to make it rise; (*b*) dough reserved from an earlier batch to start a later one fermenting. ME.
2 *fig.* **a** An agency which exercises a transforming influence from within (chiefly with allusion to the Gospels, e.g. *Matthew* 13:33, 16:6). LME. ▸**b** A tempering or modifying element; an admixture (of some quality etc.). L16.

a M. L. KING You are to be that vitally active leaven in the lump of the nation. **b** A. C. SWINBURNE Pleasure with pain for leaven. *Manchester Examiner* We should remember their temptations and mix a large leaven of charity with our judgements.

– PHRASES: **of the same leaven** of the same sort or character. *old leaven*: see OLD *adjective*.
■ **leavenless** *adjective* L19.

leaven /ˈlɛv(ə)n/ *verb trans.* LME.
[ORIGIN from the noun.]
1 Ferment (dough etc.) with leaven. LME.

AV 1 *Cor.* 5:6 Know ye not that a little leauen leaueneth the whole lumpe?

2 *fig.* Permeate with a transforming influence; imbue or mingle *with* some tempering or modifying element. Formerly also (*rare*), debase or corrupt by admixture. M16.

J. GROSS Those useful wealthy eccentrics who did so much to leaven the conformism of Victorian culture.

Leavers *noun* var. of LEVERS.

leaves *noun* pl. of LEAF *noun*[1].

leaving /ˈliːvɪŋ/ *noun*. ME.
[ORIGIN from LEAVE *verb*[1] + -ING[1].]
1 In *pl.* & †*sing.* What is left or remains; things left over, esp. as worthless. ME.

Graphic Their leavings—what they did not touch—made a luxurious supper for all my waiters.

2 The action of LEAVE *verb*[1]. LME.
leaving certificate, *leaving examination*, *leaving party*, etc.
– COMB.: **leaving shop** *slang* an unlicensed pawnshop.

Leavisian /liːˈvɪsɪən/ *noun & adjective*. M20.
[ORIGIN from *Leavis* (see below) + -IAN.]
▸ **A** *noun.* An admirer, supporter, or student of the English literary critic Frank Raymond Leavis (1895–1978). M20.
▸ **B** *adjective.* (Characteristic) of F. R. Leavis or his writings. M20.

Leavisite /ˈliːvɪsʌɪt/ *adjective & noun*. Freq. *derog.* M20.
[ORIGIN formed as LEAVISIAN + -ITE[1].]
▸ **A** *noun.* = LEAVISIAN *noun*. M20.
▸ **B** *adjective.* (Characteristic of the work) of F. R. Leavis (see LEAVISIAN) or his disciples. M20.

leavy *adjective* see LEAFY.

leban *noun* var. of LABAN.

Lebanese /lɛbəˈniːz/ *noun & adjective*. E20.
[ORIGIN from *Lebanon* (see below) + -ESE.]
▸ **A** *noun.* Pl. same. A native or inhabitant of Lebanon, a coastal country in the eastern Mediterranean. E20.
▸ **B** *adjective.* Of or pertaining to Lebanon or its inhabitants. E20.

lebbek /ˈlɛbɛk/ *noun*. Also **labakh** /ˈlabak/ & other vars. M18.
[ORIGIN Arabic *labak*.]
= KOKKO 1.

leben *noun* var. of LABAN.

Lebensform /ˈleːbənsfɔrm; ˈleɪb(ə)nsfɔːm, -z-/ *noun*. Pl. **-en** /-ən/. M20.
[ORIGIN German, lit. 'form of life'.]
A sphere of human social activity involving values; a style or aspect of life.

Lebenslust /ˈleːbənslʊst; ˈleɪb(ə)nslʊst, -nz-, -lʌst/. *noun*. L19.
[ORIGIN German.]
Zest for life, *joie de vivre*.

Lebensraum /ˈleːbənsraʊm; ˈleɪ-, -z-/ *noun*. E20.
[ORIGIN German.]
Space for living, room to exist and function freely; *spec.* (*hist.*) territory which many German nationalists in the mid 20th cent. claimed was needed for the survival and healthy development of the nation.

Lebensspur /ˈleːbənsʃpuːr; ˈleɪb(ə)nspʊə, -z-/. *noun*. Pl. **-ren** /-rən/. M20.
[ORIGIN German, from *Leben* life + *Spur* trace, track.]
GEOLOGY. A small track, burrow, cast, etc., left in sediment by a living organism; *esp.* one preserved in fossil form in sedimentary rock, a trace fossil. Usu. in *pl.*

Lebenswelt /ˈleːbənsvɛlt, ˈleɪ-/ *noun*. Pl. **-en** /-ən/. M20.
[ORIGIN German.]
= ***lifeworld*** s.v. LIFE *noun*.

Leber /ˈleɪbə/ *noun*. L19.
[ORIGIN Theodor *Leber* (1840–1917), German ophthalmologist.]
MEDICINE. ***Leber's atrophy***, ***Leber's disease***, hereditary optic atrophy, a rare condition, in which partial blindness in both eyes sets in rapidly, typically affecting young men.

leberwurst /ˈleɪbəwəːst/ *noun*. M19.
[ORIGIN German.]
(A) liver sausage.

lebes /ˈlɛbiːz/ *noun*. Pl. same. M19.
[ORIGIN Greek *lebēs*.]
GREEK ANTIQUITIES. A deep round-bottomed bowl for holding wine.

Lebkuchen /ˈlebkuːxən/ *noun*. Pl. same. M19.
[ORIGIN German, from Middle High German *kuoche* KUCHEN.]
A type of biscuit with a texture resembling that of cake, usu. glazed and containing spices and honey; a biscuit of this type.

Leboyer /ləˈbwajeɪ, *foreign* ləbwaje/ *noun*. L20.
[ORIGIN Frédérick *Leboyer* (b. 1918), French obstetrician.]
Used *attrib.* with ref. to a manner of childbirth involving gentle delivery and handling with minimum intervention and minimum stimulation of the baby.

lecanomancy /ˈlɛk(ə)nə(ʊ)ˌmansi/ *noun*. L16.
[ORIGIN from Greek *lekanomanteia*, from *lekanē* dish, pan, pot: see -MANCY.]
Divination by inspecting water in a basin.

leccer /ˈlɛkə/ *noun*. *slang* (now *joc.*). Also **lecker**. L19.
[ORIGIN Alt.: see -ER[6].]
A lecture. Freq. in *pl.*

lech /lɛk/ *noun*[1]. Now *rare*. M18.
[ORIGIN Welsh *llech* (flat) stone. Cf. CROMLECH.]
A Celtic monumental stone.

lech /lɛtʃ/ *noun*[2]. Now *colloq.* Also **letch**. L18.
[ORIGIN Uncertain: now interpreted as back-form. from LECHER *noun*. Cf. LECH *verb*.]
1 A strong desire or longing, *esp.* a sexual one; a lustful look. L18.
2 A lecherous person. M20.

L

Lech /lɛk/ *noun*[3] *& adjective*. Also **Lekh**. M19.
[ORIGIN German from Old Polish.]
▸ **A** *noun*. Pl. same, **-s**. A member of an early Slavonic people once inhabiting the region around the upper Oder and Vistula, whose descendants are the Poles. M19.
▸ **B** *attrib.* or as *adjective*. Of or pertaining to the Lechs. L19.
▪ **Lechish** *noun & adjective* [German *lechisch*] = LECHITIC L19. **Le'chitic** *noun & adjective* [German *lechitisch*] (*a*) *noun* a group of W. Slavonic languages held by some to have once formed a single sub-dialect within the Slavonic group; (*b*) *adjective* = LECH *adjective*: M20.

lech /lɛtʃ/ *verb intrans. colloq.* Also **letch**. E20.
[ORIGIN Back-form. from LECHER *noun*.]
Behave lecherously; feel (esp. sexual) desire (foll. by *after*); look lustfully (*at*).

> *Marie Claire* You can't be leching at a girl while waiting for your date.

lechaim *interjection* var. of LECHAYIM.

Le Chatelier /lə ʃaˈtɛljeɪ/ *noun*. E20.
[ORIGIN Henry *Le Chatelier* (1850–1936), French chemist.]
1 CHEMISTRY. ***Le Chatelier's principle***, ***Le Chatelier principle***: if a constraint (such as a change in pressure, temperature, or concentration of a reactant) be applied to a system in equilibrium, the equilibrium will shift so as to tend to counteract the effect of the constraint. E20.
2 Used *attrib.* with ref. to a test for the soundness (freedom from expansion) of cement. E20.

lechatelierite /ləʃəˈtɛlɪərʌɪt, ləʃatɛˈlɪərʌɪt/ *noun*. E20.
[ORIGIN from LE CHATELIER + -ITE[1].]
Naturally occurring vitreous silica, formed when siliceous material is intensely heated (as by lightning).

lechayim /ləˈxajim/ *interjection*. Also ***lechaim*** /ləˈxʌɪm/ & other vars. M20.
[ORIGIN Hebrew *lĕ-ḥayyīm*.]
A drinking toast: to life!

leche *noun* var. of LECHWE.

lecheguilla *noun* var. of LECHUGUILLA.

lechenaultia *noun* var. of LESCHENAULTIA.

lecher /ˈlɛtʃə/ *noun*[1] *& verb*. Also †**letcher**. ME.
[ORIGIN Old French *lichiere* (nom.), *lecheor*, *-ur* (accus.), from *lechier* live in debauchery or gluttony (mod. *lécher* lick), from Frankish from West Germanic base of LICK *verb*.]
▸ **A** *noun*. A man of promiscuous sexual desires or behaviour. ME.
▸ **B** *verb intrans.* Behave like a lecher; copulate. LME–M18.

Lecher /ˈlɛtʃə, *foreign* ˈlɛçər/ *noun*[2]. L19.
[ORIGIN Ernst *Lecher* (1856–1926), Austrian physicist.]
PHYSICS. Used *attrib.* and (formerly) in *possess.* to designate a device for measuring a high-frequency electric oscillation, consisting of two parallel wires joined by a sliding contact, positions of maximum response or absorption being separated by a distance equal to half the wavelength of the oscillation.

lecherous /ˈlɛtʃ(ə)rəs/ *adjective*. Also †**letcherous**. ME.
[ORIGIN Old French *lecheros*, from *lecheor*: see LECHER *noun*[1], -OUS.]
1 Given to lechery, lustful and promiscuous; (of behaviour, thought, etc.) characteristic of a lecher. ME.
†**2** Of a person: fond of luxurious living, gluttonous. Of food: rich, mouth-watering. L15–M16.
▪ **lecherously** *adverb* ME. **lecherousness** *noun* M16.

lechery /ˈlɛtʃ(ə)ri/ *noun*. Also †**leachery**, †**letcherie**, **-ery**. ME.
[ORIGIN Old French *lecherie*, from *lecheor*: see LECHER *noun*[1], -Y[3].]
Lustful and promiscuous sexual indulgence. Formerly also, an instance of this.

lechuguilla /lɛtʃəˈɡɪl(j)ə/ *noun*. Also **lecheg-**. M19.
[ORIGIN Mexican Spanish from Spanish = wild lettuce, dim. of *lechuga* LETTUCE.]
Any of several fibrous agaves of Mexico and the southern US, esp. *Agave lecheguilla*, used as a source of ixtle.

lechwe /ˈlɛːtʃwi/ *noun*. Also **leche** /ˈlɛtʃi/ & other vars. M19.
[ORIGIN Prob. from Bantu.]
A grazing antelope, *Kobus leche*, of flood plains in central southern Africa.
NILE ***lechwe***.

-lecithal /ˈlɛsɪθ(ə)l/ *suffix*.
[ORIGIN from Greek *lekithos* yolk of an egg: see -AL[1].]
EMBRYOLOGY. Forming adjectives with the sense 'having a yolk (of a specified type)', as ***alecithal***, ***homolecithal***, ***telolecithal***, etc.

lecithin /ˈlɛsɪθɪn/ *noun*. M19.
[ORIGIN from Greek *lekithos* yolk + -IN[1].]
BIOCHEMISTRY. Any of a group of natural phospholipids which are esters of a phosphatidic acid with choline; such phospholipids collectively; a mixture containing these, used commercially as a food emulsifier etc.
▪ **lecithinase** /-z/ *noun* = PHOSPHOLIPASE E20.

lecithotrophic /ˌlɛsɪθəˈtrəʊfɪk, ˌlɛkɪ-, -ˈtrɒfɪk-/ *adjective*. M20.
[ORIGIN formed as LECITHIN + -O- + -TROPHIC.]
ZOOLOGY. Of the larvae of certain marine invertebrates: feeding on the yolk of the egg from which they have emerged.

lecker *noun* var. of LECCER.

Leclanché /ləˈklɑ̃ːʃeɪ/ *noun*. L19.
[ORIGIN Georges *Leclanché* (1839–82), French chemist.]
PHYSICS. ***Leclanché battery***, ***Leclanché cell***, a primary electrochemical cell with a zinc cathode in contact with zinc chloride, ammonium chloride as the electrolyte, and a carbon anode in contact with a mixture of manganese dioxide and carbon powder.

lect /lɛkt/ *noun*. L20.
[ORIGIN from -LECT.]
LINGUISTICS. A variety within a language; a form of speech defined by a homogeneous set of rules.

-lect /lɛkt/ *suffix*. M20.
[ORIGIN from DIA)LECT.]
Forming nouns denoting a variety within a language, a form of speech defined by a homogeneous set of rules, as ***acrolect***, ***basilect***, ***idiolect***, ***sociolect***, etc.

lectern /ˈlɛkt(ə)n, -əːn/ *noun*. ME.
[ORIGIN Old French *letrun* from medieval Latin *lectrum*, from Latin *legere* read.]
A stand or desk, usu. with a sloping top or front that can hold an open book, notes, etc., from which a person can read: *esp.* (*a*) one in a church for use by a lector, cantor, or preacher; (*b*) one for a lecturer's notes.

lectin /ˈlɛktɪn/ *noun*. M20.
[ORIGIN from Latin *lect-* pa. ppl stem of *legere* choose, select + -IN[1].]
BIOCHEMISTRY. Any of various proteins, usu. of plant origin, which bind specifically to certain sugars or saccharide residues and so cause agglutination of particular cell types.

lectio difficilior /ˌlɛktɪəʊ dɪfɪˈkɪlɪɔː/ *noun phr.* Pl. **lectiones difficiliores** /lɛktɪˌəʊneɪz dɪfɪkɪlɪˈɔːreɪz/. M20.
[ORIGIN Word-order var.]
= DIFFICILIOR LECTIO.

lection /ˈlɛkʃ(ə)n/ *noun*. ME.
[ORIGIN Latin *lectio(n-)*, from *lect-* pa. ppl stem of *legere* read: see -ION. Cf. Old French *lection*.]
†**1** = ELECTION. ME–M16.
2 †**a** A particular way of reading or interpreting a passage. M16–E18. ▸**b** TEXTUAL CRITICISM. A reading found in a particular copy or edition of a text. M17.
3 An extract from a sacred book, appointed to be read at religious services; a lesson. E17.

lectionary /ˈlɛkʃ(ə)n(ə)ri/ *noun*. L18.
[ORIGIN medieval Latin *lectionarius*, *-arium*, from Latin *lect-*: see LECTION, -ARY[1].]
A book of extracts from sacred books appointed to be read at religious services. Also, a list of extracts to be so read.

lectiones difficiliores *noun phr.* pl. of LECTIO DIFFICILIOR.

lectisternium /lɛktɪˈstəːnɪəm/ *noun*. Also (earlier) anglicized as †**lectistern**. L16.
[ORIGIN Latin, from *lectus* couch, bed + -I- + *sternere* spread.]
ROMAN HISTORY. A sacrificial banquet at which food was set before images of gods, placed on couches.

lector /ˈlɛktɔː/ *noun*. LME.
[ORIGIN Latin, from *lect-*: see LECTION, -OR.]
1 ECCLESIASTICAL. A person commissioned as, or ordained to the office of, a liturgical reader. LME.
2 A person who reads; *spec.* a reader or lecturer in a college or university, now esp. one in a European country, as Germany or France, or in a foreign country teaching his or her native language. LME.
▪ **lectorate** *noun* (ECCLESIASTICAL) the position or office of lector L19. **lectorship** *noun* the office of lector, a post as a lector E17.

lectotype /ˈlɛktətʌɪp/ *noun*. E20.
[ORIGIN from Greek *lektos* chosen + -TYPE.]
TAXONOMY. A specimen from the material originally used to describe a species and later selected as the type in the absence of a holotype.

lectric /ˈlɛktrɪk/ *noun & adjective*. *colloq.* Also **'lectric**. M20.
[ORIGIN Aphet.]
= ELECTRIC.

lectrice /lɛkˈtriːs, ˈlɛktriːs/ *noun*. L19.
[ORIGIN French from Latin *lectrix* fem. of Latin LECTOR.]
1 A woman engaged as an attendant or companion to read aloud. L19.
2 A female lecturer. M20.

lecture /ˈlɛktʃə/ *noun*. LME.
[ORIGIN Old French, or medieval Latin *lectura*, from *lect-*: see LECTION, -URE.]
1 The action or an act of reading. Also, a text to be read. *arch.* LME.

> J. CONRAD He had evolved from the lecture of the letters a definite conviction.

†**2** = LECTION 2. LME–L17.
3 a An address or discourse on a particular subject; *esp.* (*a*) a formal discourse delivered to students etc. by a teacher at a college or university; (*b*) an expository or catechetical sermon delivered outside the regular order of liturgical services. Also, the delivering of formal discourses as a method of instruction. M16. ▸**b** (An endowment for) a regular series of lectures; a lectureship. Now *rare*. E17.

> **a** R. ELLMANN Attending Ruskin's lectures on Florentine art. **b** J. BANDINEL The Lecture founded by the late rev. and pious John Bampton M.A.

4 A lengthy reprimand, a reproving speech. Formerly also, a (moral) lesson or example. M16.

> E. YOUNG Heaven means to make one half of the species a moral lecture to the other. J. RULE His mother's . . little lectures about trying to be kinder to his sister.

wormwood lecture: see WORMWOOD *adjective*.
– COMB.: **lecture circuit** a regular itinerary for lecturers on tour; **lecture-recital** a lecture illustrated by music; ***lecture theatre***: see THEATRE *noun* 5a.
▪ **lectu'rette** *noun* a short lecture M19.

lecture /ˈlɛktʃə/ *verb*. L16.
[ORIGIN from the noun.]
1 *verb intrans.* & †*trans.* with *it*. Give a lecture or lectures; hold a post as a lecturer. L16.
2 *verb trans.* Give a lecture or lectures to (an audience); instruct or entertain by lecture. Formerly also, stir *up* by lectures or sermons. L17.
3 *verb trans.* Rebuke or reprimand at length. E18.
▪ **lectu'ree** *noun* (*rare*) a person who attends or receives a lecture or lectures E20.

lecturer /ˈlɛktʃ(ə)rə/ *noun*. L16.
[ORIGIN from LECTURE *verb* + -ER[1].]
1 ANGLICAN CHURCH. An ordained stipendiary minister, usu. appointed locally to preach regular lectures (chiefly *hist.*). Formerly also = LECTOR *noun* 1. L16.
2 A person who lectures, esp. in a college or university. Now also, (the grade of) a person with an academic teaching post below the rank of professor. E17.
visiting lecturer: see VISITING *ppl adjective*.
▪ **lecturership** *noun* (*rare*) a lectureship L19.

lectureship /ˈlɛktʃəʃɪp/ *noun*. M17.
[ORIGIN from LECTURE *noun* + -SHIP.]
The position or office of lecturer; a post as a lecturer.

lecturess /ˈlɛktʃ(ə)rɛs/ *noun*. Now *rare*. E19.
[ORIGIN from LECTURER: see -ESS[1].]
A female lecturer, a lectrice.

lecythus /ˈlɛsɪθəs/ *noun*. Pl. ***-thi*** /-θʌɪ/. M19.
[ORIGIN Late Latin formed as LEKYTHOS.]
GREEK ANTIQUITIES. = LEKYTHOS.

LED /ɛliːˈdiː/ *noun*. Also **led**. M20.
[ORIGIN Acronym, from *light-emitting diode*.]
A light-emitting diode, a semiconductor diode that emits light when a voltage is suitably applied.

led /lɛd/ *adjective*. L16.
[ORIGIN pa. pple of LEAD *verb*[1].]
1 That has been or is led. L16.
2 That follows slavishly or sycophantically. *arch.* L17.

led *verb pa. t. & pple* of LEAD *verb*[1].

†**ledden** *noun* var. of LIDDEN.

ledeburite /ˈleɪdəbjʊrʌɪt/ *noun*. E20.
[ORIGIN from Adolf *Ledebur* (1837–1906), German metallurgist + -ITE[1].]
METALLURGY. The eutectic of the iron/iron carbide system, composed of austenite and cementite and occurring in cast iron.

†**leden** *noun* var. of LIDDEN.

lederhosen /ˈleɪdəhəʊz(ə)n/ *noun pl.* M20.
[ORIGIN German, from *Leder* leather + *Hosen* pl. of *Hose* trouser.]
Leather shorts, esp. as traditionally worn in Alpine regions of Bavaria etc.

ledge /lɛdʒ/ *noun & verb*[1]. ME.
[ORIGIN Uncertain: perh. from an early form of LAY *verb*[1].]
▸ **A** *noun*. **1** A bar or strip of wood or other material fixed across a door, gate, chair, etc. Now *dial.* ME. ▸**b** NAUTICAL. Any of several pieces of timber fixed transversely across a wooden ship between beams supporting the deck. L17.
2 A raised edge around a board, tray, etc. Now *rare* or *obsolete*. M16.
3 A narrow horizontal surface projecting from a wall etc. or formed by the top of a vertical structure. M16. ▸**b** A shelflike projection from the side of a rock, a mountain, etc. M18. ▸**c** METEOROLOGY. A layer in the ionosphere in which the ionization increases less rapidly with height than in the regions immediately above and below it. M20.

> J. T. MICKLETHWAITE The ledge of the pulpit. I. MCEWAN Geraniums on window ledges.

4 GEOLOGY. A ridge esp. of rocks, beneath the sea near the shore. Formerly also, a range of mountains or hills. M16.

5 a ARCHITECTURE. A string course; a moulding. E17. ▸**b** MINING. A stratum of metal-bearing rock. Also, a vein of quartz etc. M19.
– COMB.: **ledge-door** = *LEDGED door*; **ledge-handle** ARCHAEOLOGY a handle resembling a ledge, found on pottery.
▸ **B** *verb intrans.* Form a ledge. *rare.* L16.
■ **ledgeless** *adjective* E19. **ledging** *noun* a ledge; *collect.* ledges: E19. **ledgy** *adjective* having many ledges, consisting of ledges (of rock) L18.

ledge /lɛdʒ/ *verb*[2] *trans.* Long *obsolete* exc. *dial.* Also †**lege**. ME.
[ORIGIN Aphet.]
Allege.

ledged /lɛdʒd/ *adjective.* M16.
[ORIGIN from LEDGE *noun* + -ED[2].]
Having or provided with a ledge or ledges.
ledged door an unframed door consisting of vertical boards fixed to horizontal ledges.

ledgement /ˈlɛdʒm(ə)nt/ *noun.* Also **-dgm-**. LME.
[ORIGIN App. from LEDGE *noun* + -MENT.]
ARCHITECTURE. **1** A string course. LME.
2 The representation of a structure in two dimensions as though the surfaces of the structure were laid flat in a manner revealing their relative dimensions and positions. M19.

ledger /ˈlɛdʒə/ *noun, adjective, & verb.* Also (now the usual form in ANGLING & MUSIC) **leger**, (now only in sense A.3) **lieger** /ˈliːɡə/. LME.
[ORIGIN Some early forms corresp. in sense to Dutch *legger, ligger* (from *leggen* LAY *verb*[1], *liggen* LIE *verb*[1]), on which the English forms were prob. modelled with phonet. accommodation to early forms of LAY *verb*[1], LIE *verb*[1] with /dʒ/: see -ER[1].]
▸ **A** *noun* **1** †**a** A large bible or breviary. LME–L17. ▸**b** A record book, a register. M16. ▸**c** The principal book of a set of account books used for recording financial transactions etc., containing debtor-and-creditor accounts. L16.
c *nominal ledger*: see NOMINAL *adjective*.
2 a A flat stone slab covering a grave. E16. ▸**b** A lower millstone. Now *dial.* E16.
3 a A resident ambassador; a (permanent) representative. *obsolete* exc. *hist.* M16. ▸†**b** A person permanently in a place; a resident. L16–M17.
4 a A horizontal timber in a scaffolding, lying parallel to the face of the building. L16. ▸**b** A wooden rod laid across a thatch to hold it in place. E20.
5 ANGLING. A bait fished on the bottom without a float. M17.
▸ **B** *attrib.* or as *adjective.* Remaining or resting in a place; resident, esp. as an ambassador etc.; permanent; standing, stationary. *obsolete* exc. as below. M16.
– SPECIAL COLLOCATIONS & COMB.: **ledger bait** = sense A.5 above. **ledger book** a record book, a register, an account book. **ledger line** MUSIC a line added above or below the staff for a note or group of notes higher or lower than the staff can accommodate. **ledger-millstone** (now *dial.*) = sense A.2b above. **ledger-pole** = sense A.4a above. **ledger space** MUSIC: between the stave and a ledger line or between ledger lines. **ledger-stone** = sense A.2a above. **ledger-tackle** ANGLING: using a (lead) weight to keep the bait on the bottom.
▸ **C** *verb.* ANGLING.
1 *verb intrans.* Use a ledger bait. L17.
2 *verb trans.* Fix (tackle or bait) for fishing on the bottom without a float. L20.

ledgment *noun* var. of LEDGEMENT.

ledum /ˈliːdəm/ *noun.* M19.
[ORIGIN mod. Latin (see below) from Greek *lēdon* mastic.]
Any of several dwarf shrubs of the genus *Ledum*, of the heath family, native to cold north temperate regions; *esp.* Labrador tea.

lee /liː/ *noun*[1] *& adjective.*
[ORIGIN Old English *hlēo, hlēow-* = Old Frisian *hlī*, Old Saxon *hleo, hlea*, Old Norse *hlé*, from Germanic (whence also Old Norse *hlý*). Naut. use mainly from Old Norse. See also LEW, LUKE *adjective*.]
▸ **A** *noun.* **1** *sing.* or (*rare*) in *pl.* Protection, shelter. OE.
J. WAIN In the lee of this behemoth, David was . . well hidden.
†**2** A sheltered position or condition. Also, calmness, peace, tranquillity. LME–M17.
3 Chiefly NAUTICAL. The sheltered side of an object. Also, the side of a ship, the land, an eminence, etc., that is turned or faces away from the wind. LME.
R. HUGHES Manoeuvring . . to the schooner's lee and clambering on board.
†**4** A river. *rare* (Spenser). Only in L16.
– PHRASES: **lee ho!**, **lee o!**: a helmsman's warning that the vessel is coming about. **on lee**, **on the lee**, **under lee**, **under the lee** NAUTICAL to leeward. **under the lee (of)** under the protection (of), under the shelter (of).
▸ **B** *attrib.* or as *adjective.* **1** Sheltered, esp. from the wind. *obsolete* exc. *dial.* LME.
2 Situated or occurring on the sheltered side of a vessel or other object. E16.
3 Moving in the direction of the prevailing wind. Freq. in ***lee tide***. E18.
– COMB. & SPECIAL COLLOCATIONS: **leeboard** a vertical wooden board, fixed to the side of a flat-bottomed sailing vessel and lowered into the water to diminish the drift to leeward; **lee gauge**: see ***have the lee gauge of*** s.v. GAUGE *noun* 2; ***lee helm***: see HELM *noun*[2]; **lee-room** room for a ship to deviate from or manoeuvre within its course; a safety margin; **lee shore** a shore that the wind blows on, that is to the lee of a passing vessel; **lee side** (**a**) = sense A.3 above; (**b**) GEOLOGY the downstream side of a mound of rock which has undergone erosion by a glacier; **lee wave** METEOROLOGY a standing wave generated on the sheltered side of an obstacle by an air current passing over or around it.
■ **leemost** *adjective* furthest to leeward E17.

†**lee** *noun*[2]. Pl. LEES. LME–E19.
[ORIGIN Old French *lie* = Provençal, Portuguese *lia*, Spanish *lía*, medieval Latin pl. *liae* from Gaulish (cf. Old Irish *lige*).]
= LEES.

leeangle *noun* var. of LEANGLE.

leech /liːtʃ/ *noun*[1]. *arch.*
[ORIGIN Old English *lǣce* = Old Frisian *letza, leischa*, Old Saxon *lāki*, Old High German *lāhhi*, Old Swedish *läkir*, Gothic *lēkeis*, from Germanic from Indo-European (cf. Irish *liaigh*).]
A physician, a healer.
– COMB.: **leechcraft** the art of healing; medical science.
■ **leechdom** *noun* a medicine, a remedy OE.

leech /liːtʃ/ *noun*[2].
[ORIGIN Old English *lǣce*, (Kentish) *lȳce* = Middle Dutch *lake, lieke, leke*, assim. to LEECH *noun*[1].]
1 Any annelid worm of the class Hirudinea, comprising forms with a sucker at each end; *esp.* one that sucks blood, as *Hirudo medicinalis*, formerly used for drawing blood. OE.
horseleech, ***medicinal leech***, etc.
2 *fig.* A rapacious exploitative person. L18.
– PHRASES: **like a leech** persistently.
– COMB.: **leech-extract** an anticoagulant extract prepared from leeches, containing hirudin; †**leech-glass** MEDICINE a glass tube to hold a leech when applying it to a particular spot.
■ **leechlike** *adjective* resembling (that of) a leech L17.

leech /liːtʃ/ *noun*[3]. L15.
[ORIGIN Perh. rel. to Old Norse *lík* a naut. term of uncertain meaning (cf. Swedish *lik*, Danish *lig* bolt rope).]
NAUTICAL. Either vertical edge of a square sail; the aft edge of a fore-and-aft sail.
after leech, ***mast leech***, ***weather leech***, etc.
– COMB.: **leech line** a rope attached to the leech, used to truss a sail up to a yard; **leech rope** that part of a bolt rope which borders the leech.

leech /liːtʃ/ *verb*[1] *trans.* Now *arch. rare.* ME.
[ORIGIN from LEECH *noun*[1].]
Cure, heal.
■ **leecher** *noun* a physician LME. **leechery** *noun* the art or practice of healing E17.

leech /liːtʃ/ *verb*[2]. E19.
[ORIGIN from LEECH *noun*[2].]
1 *verb trans.* Apply leeches to medicinally. E19.
2 *verb trans. fig.* Drain of energy, money, etc. E20.
3 *verb intrans.* Attach oneself like a leech, be parasitic. Foll. by *on* (*to*). M20.
R. K. NARAYAN He left college, and . . was still leeching on his father.

Leech lattice /liːtʃ ˈlatɪs/ *noun phr.* L20.
[ORIGIN J. *Leech* (1925–92), Brit. mathematician.]
MATH. A set of points in 24-dimensional Euclidean space regularly arranged such that each point has exactly 196,560 nearest neighbours.

Leeds /liːdz/ *noun & adjective.* M19.
[ORIGIN A city in W. Yorkshire, England.]
(Designating) creamware of a type originally made at Leeds.

Lee-Enfield /liːˈɛnfiːld/ *noun & adjective.* E20.
[ORIGIN from J. P. *Lee* (1831–1904), US designer of the bolt action + *Enfield* (see ENFIELD).]
(Designating) a type of bolt-action rifle formerly used by the British army.

†**leeful** *adjective.* ME–E19.
[ORIGIN from LEAVE *noun*[1] + -FUL.]
Permissible, right, lawful; just.

leegte *noun* var. of LAAGTE.

leek /liːk/ *noun.*
[ORIGIN Old English *lēac*, corresp. to Middle Dutch *looc* (Dutch *look*), Old High German *louh* (German *Lauch*), Old Norse *laukr* from Germanic base also of Finnish *laukka*, Old Church Slavonic *lukŭ*.]
1 A plant, *Allium porrum*, of the lily family, allied to the onion but with flat overlapping leaves forming an elongated cylindrical bulb which is eaten as a vegetable. Also, this as the Welsh national emblem. OE. ▸†**b** Used as a type of something of little value. ME–L18.
eat the leek, **eat one's leek** submit to humiliation under compulsion. ***houseleek***: see HOUSE *noun*[1] *& adjective*.
2 With specifying words: any of various other plants of the genus *Allium* or (formerly) other genera. LME.
sand leek: see SAND *noun*. ***sectile leek***: see SECTILE 1. ***wild leek***: see WILD *adjective, noun, & adverb*.
3 ***green leek***, any of various green parrots, *esp.* the superb parrot, *Polytelis swainsoni*. M19.
– COMB.: **leek-green** *noun & adjective* (of) a very pale green.
■ **leeky** *adjective* (**a**) leek-green; (**b**) full of leeks: M16.

lee-lone /ˈliːləʊn/ *noun.* Chiefly *dial.* Also **-lane** /-leɪn/. L19.
[ORIGIN Emphasized form of LONE *noun*[2].]
One's individual self; *one's* own. Chiefly in ***by one's lee-lone***.

Lee–Metford /liːˈmɛtfəd/ *noun & adjective.* L19.
[ORIGIN from J. P. Lee (see LEE–ENFIELD) + W. E. *Metford*.]
(Designating) a type of rifle in use before the Lee–Enfield rifle.

leep /liːp/ *verb trans.* L19.
[ORIGIN Hindi *līp, līpna*, from Sanskrit *lip-* smear.]
In the Indian subcontinent: wash with cow dung and water.

†**leer** *noun*[1].
[ORIGIN Old English *hlēor* = Old Saxon *hleor* etc., Old Norse *hlýr* pl.]
1 The face, the countenance. Also, the look or appearance of the face and skin, the complexion. OE–E19.
SHAKES. *Tit. A.* Fie, treacherous hue . . Here's a young lad framed of another leer.
2 The cheek. OE–L16.

leer /lɪə/ *noun*[2]. Long *rare* exc. *dial.* LME.
[ORIGIN Unknown. Cf. LIRE *noun*[1].]
The flank, the loin; the hollow under the ribs.

leer /lɪə/ *noun*[3]. L16.
[ORIGIN from the verb.]
A sideways glance; a sly, malign, or lascivious smile or look.
P. TOYNBEE The old man looks . . appreciatively at the nurses; even manages a . . leer.

leer /lɪə, lɛː/ *noun*[4]. Also **lear**, **lehr**. M17.
[ORIGIN Unknown.]
A slow-cooling heated tunnel for annealing glass.
– COMB.: **leer man** a person who works at a leer.

leer /lɪə/ *adjective*[1].
[ORIGIN Old English (earlier in *lǣrnes* LEERNESS) = Old Saxon, Old High German *lāri* (Dutch *laar*, German *leer*), from West Germanic.]
1 Empty. Formerly also, clear *of*. Long *arch. rare.* OE.
2 Having no burden or load; (of a horse) without a rider. *obsolete* exc. *dial.* LME.
3 Having an empty stomach; hungry, faint through lack of food. *dial.* M19.
■ **leerness** *noun* (long *arch. rare*) emptiness OE.

†**leer** *adjective*[2]. E17–E19.
[ORIGIN App. from the verb.]
Looking sideways or askance; indirect; sly.

leer /lɪə/ *verb intrans.* M16.
[ORIGIN Perh. from LEER *noun*[1], with the idea of glancing over one's cheek.]
1 Look sideways or askance. Now only, look or gaze with a sly, malign, or lascivious expression. M16.
C. LAMB Slily leering down the table. S. KITZINGER A woman . . is leered at by men who look her body up and down.
2 Walk stealthily or with averted looks; slink *away*, *off*. Now *rare.* M16.
Landfall The youth leering off to his first booze-up.
■ **leeringly** *adverb* in a leering manner E18.

leervis /ˈlɪərfəs/ *noun. S. Afr.* Also **-fish** /-fɪʃ/. Pl. same. M19.
[ORIGIN Afrikaans, from *leer* leather + *vis* fish.]
A large carangid game fish, *Hypacanthus amia*, found off the Atlantic coast of southern Africa.

leery /ˈlɪəri/ *adjective*[1]. *obsolete* exc. *dial.* L17.
[ORIGIN from LEER *adjective*[1] + -Y[1].]
= LEER *adjective*[1].

leery /ˈlɪəri/ *adjective*[2]. *slang.* Also **l(e)ary**, **lairy** /ˈlɛːri/. E18.
[ORIGIN Perh. from LEER *adjective*[2] + -Y[1].]
1 Wide awake, knowing, sharp, streetwise. Also, shy, doubtful, suspicious, wary, (*of*, *about*). E18.
New Yorker If a hawk . . plows into a snowbank, he will be leery of snow.
2 Flashily dressed; showy, trashy. *Austral. & NZ.* L19.
■ **leerily** *adverb* M19. **leeriness** *noun* doubt, suspicion, mistrust L19.

lees /liːz/ *noun pl.* LME.
[ORIGIN Pl. of LEE *noun*[2].]
1 The sediment of wine or some other liquids. LME.
H. MAYHEW The scum and lees of all broths and soups.
2 *fig.* The basest part, dregs, refuse. L16.
H. MELVILLE My body is but the lees of my better being.
– PHRASES: **drain the lees**, **drain to the lees**, **drink the lees**, **drink to the lees** drain or drink to the last drop, drain or drink to the very end. **on the lees**, **upon the lees** *fig.* sedentary; freq. in ***settle on the lees***, ***settle upon the lees***, become sedentary.

leesome /ˈliːs(ə)m/ *adjective*[1]. *obsolete* exc. *Scot.* ME.
[ORIGIN from LIEF *adjective* + -SOME[1].]
Lovable; pleasing; pleasant.

†**leesome** *adjective*[2]. Chiefly *Scot.* LME–M18.
[ORIGIN from LEAVE *noun*[1] + -SOME[1].]
Lawful, permissible, right.

leet /liːt/ *noun*[1]. *obsolete* exc. *hist.* ME.
[ORIGIN Anglo-Norman *lete*, Anglo-Latin *leta*, of unknown origin.]
1 A court of record which the lords of certain manors were empowered by charter or prescription to hold once or twice a year. Also ***court leet***. ME.

L

2 The jurisdiction of a leet; the district over which this jurisdiction extended. LME.

leet /liːt/ *noun*[2]. Now chiefly *Scot.* LME.
[ORIGIN Prob. from Anglo-Norman, Old French *lit(t)e* var. of *liste* LIST *noun*[3].]
A list of people designated as eligible for some office. Freq. in ***short leet*** s.v. SHORT *adjective*.

leet /liːt/ *noun*[3]. Long *dial. rare.* E17.
[ORIGIN Repr. Old English *gelǣte* junction, from Germanic base of LET *verb*[1].]
A meeting of ways, a crossroads. Only in ***two-way leet***, ***three-way leet***, ***four-way leet***.

leetle /ˈliːt(ə)l/ *adjective. joc.* L17.
[ORIGIN Alt.]
Little.

leeward /ˈliːwəd, ˈljuːəd/ *noun, adjective, & adverb.* M16.
[ORIGIN from LEE *noun*[1] + -WARD.]
▸ **A** *noun*. = LEE *noun*[1] 3. Chiefly in ***to leeward***. M16.
▸ **B** *adjective*. †**1** Of a ship: that makes much leeway. E17–M18.
2 Situated on the side sheltered from the wind; having a direction away from the wind. (Foll. by *of*.) Opp. ***windward***. M17.
▸ **C** *adverb*. Towards the lee or sheltered side. L18.
■ **leewardly** *adjective* (of a ship) liable to drift to leeward when sailing close to the wind E17. **leewardmost** *adjective* furthest to leeward L17.

leeway /ˈliːweɪ/ *noun.* M17.
[ORIGIN from LEE *noun*[1] + WAY *noun*.]
1 Lateral drift of a ship to leeward of the desired course; the amount of deviation produced by such drift. M17.

F. CHICHESTER Because of the . . leeway caused by the gale, I had been driven back . . towards Europe.

make leeway drift to leeward. **make up leeway** correct or compensate for leeway; *fig.* struggle out of a bad position, recover lost time.
2 *fig.* Freedom of action within set limits; room allowed for this; a safety margin. L19.

J. J. HENNESSY For all the rigidity of the . . rules there was some leeway for personal expression. A. WEST She's . . late now and half an hour is her usual amount of leeway.

L

left /lɛft/ *adjective, adverb, & noun.*
[ORIGIN Old English *lyft-* in *lyftādl* (disease) paralysis, Kentish *left*, corresp. to East Frisian *luf*, Dutch dial. *loof* weak, worthless, Middle Dutch, Low German *luchter*, *lucht*, *luft*, Northern Frisian *leeft*, *leefter* left: ult. origin unknown.]
▸ **A** *adjective*. †**1** Weak. Only in OE.
2 Designating that side of the body which is usually the weaker of the two and which is in the position of west if one is facing north, its individual parts, and (occas.) their clothing; designating the corresponding side of any other body or object. ME.

MILTON Who stooping op'nd my left side, and took From thence a Rib. E. WAUGH Pins and needles in my left leg. G. GREENE Kay . . winked her left eye.

have two left feet be awkward or clumsy.
3 That has the relative position of the left side with respect to the right. (Sometimes with ref. to the direction in which an object is considered to face, sometimes with ref. to an object's appearance to a spectator.) In pred. use usu. foll. by *of*; in attrib. use now chiefly replaced by ***left-hand***, exc. in certain special collocations (see below). ME. ▸**b** MATH. Designating an entity whose definition involves two elements in a conventionally defined order, opposite to that designated as right. M20.

I. MURDOCH Is he on the left side of the road or the right side?

4 (Also **L-**.) Of or pertaining to the left in politics, philosophy, etc. See sense C.2 below. M19.

T. E. LAWRENCE We are the more liberal ('left' in the Parliamentary sense).

– SPECIAL COLLOCATIONS: **left arm** CRICKET a player who bowls with the left arm. **left back** in FOOTBALL & HOCKEY etc., (the position of) a back who plays primarily on the left of the pitch. ***left bank***: see BANK *noun*[1] 1. ***left bower***: see BOWER *noun*[5]. **left brain** the left-hand side of the human brain, believed to be associated with linear and analytical thought. **left-brained** *adjective* having the left as the dominant or more efficient part of the brain. **left centre** in FOOTBALL & HOCKEY etc., (the position of) a player who plays primarily to the left of the centre of the pitch. **left defender** in FOOTBALL & HOCKEY etc., a left half who plays deep. **left flank** = LEFT WING *noun phr.* 2. **left half(-back)** in FOOTBALL & HOCKEY etc., (the position of) a halfback who plays primarily on the left of the pitch. **left midfield** in FOOTBALL & HOCKEY etc., the midfield players who play primarily on the left of the pitch. **left turn** a turn that brings a person's front to face as his or her left side did before; a turn or turning to the left.
– COMB.: **left-brained** *adjective* having the left as the dominant or more efficient part of the brain (see ***left brain*** above); **left-eye** *adjective* having both eyes on the left-hand side of the head; *spec.* designating flatfish (flounders) of the family Bothidae; **left-eyed** *adjective* (**a**) having the left as the dominant or more efficient eye; (**b**) = ***left-eye*** above; **left-footed** *adjective* having the left as the dominant or more efficient foot; **left-footer** *slang* (*derog.*) a Roman Catholic.
▸ **B** *adverb*. On or towards the left side; in the direction of the left; (of rotary motion) anticlockwise. ME.

Birmingham Post It is just a case of looking left and right.

eyes left: see EYE *noun*. **left, right, and centre**, (also) **right and left**, **right, left, and centre** in all directions; on all sides; indiscriminately. ***stage left***: see STAGE *noun* 4.
– COMB.: **left-leaning** *adjective* sympathetic towards the left in politics.
▸ **C** *noun*. **1** The left-hand part, side, region, or direction. ME.

G. GREENE Rimmer moved a hand to the left, a hand to the right. F. SWINNERTON Peters . . who sat on her left, was as tongue-tied as Turnbull on her right.

true left: see TRUE *adjective, noun, & adverb*.
2 MILITARY. The left wing of an army. Also (in *pl.*), the soldiers whose place is on the left. E18.
3 Orig., those members of comparatively radical opinions in a Continental legislature, by custom seated on the left of the president. Now, (the views and aims of) any party or group favouring radical, reforming, or socialist views. Also, the more advanced or innovating section of a philosophical, religious, etc., group. M19.

T. BENN He moved . . to the Left . . arguing for world peace, human rights and civil liberties.

New Left: see NEW *adjective*. ***Old Left***: see OLD *adjective*.
4 A shoe etc. for the left foot; a glove etc. for the left hand. M19.
5 A shot fired at game with the left barrel of a double-barrelled shotgun; a creature hit by such a shot. Earliest in ***right-and-left*** s.v. RIGHT *noun*[1]. M19.
6 Chiefly BOXING. (A blow dealt with) the left hand. M19.

G. F. FIENNES Out shot a telescopic left, and I had the shiner of all time for weeks.

7 FOOTBALL & HOCKEY etc. (The position of) a player who plays primarily on the left side of the pitch. Chiefly in ***inside left***, ***outside left***. L19.
8 A left turn. L20.

G. F. SIMS Straight on is Fort Mason . . . We make a left on to Lombard.

hang a left: see HANG *verb*.
■ **leftish** *adjective* inclined to the political, philosophical, etc., views of the left M20. **leftishness** *noun* M20. **leftism** *noun* the political, philosophical, etc., views or principles of the left; profession of left-wing views: E20. **leftist** *noun & adjective* (**a**) *noun* an adherent of the left; a person who professes to be left-wing; (**b**) *adjective* of or pertaining to leftism or the left: E20. **leftmost** *adjective* situated furthest to the left M19. **leftness** *noun* the condition of being on the left M16.

left *verb pa. t. & pple* of LEAVE *verb*[1].

left field /lɛft ˈfiːld/ *noun & adjectival phr.* As adjective also **left-field**. M19.
[ORIGIN from LEFT *adjective* + FIELD *noun*.]
▸ **A** *noun phr.* **1** BASEBALL. (A fielder in) the part of the outfield to the left of the batter when facing the pitcher. M19.
2 *fig.* A position away from the centre of activity or interest, or (*US*) from the left in politics; a state of ignorance, confusion, or unreality. *colloq.* M20.

Time An increasing number of candidates are emerging from left field to give voters surprising options.

▸ **B** *adjective*. That is outside the mainstream of fashion, unconventional. *colloq.* L20.

Christian Science Monitor Occasional left-field productions like . . 'Dr. Strangelove'.

■ **left-fielder** *noun* (BASEBALL) a fielder in the left field M19.

left hand /lɛft ˈhand/ *noun & adjectival phr.* As adjective also **left-hand**. ME.
[ORIGIN from LEFT *adjective* + HAND *noun*.]
▸ **A** *noun phr.* **1** The hand of the left side. ME.

J. STEINBECK Kino carried a bundle in his left hand.

marry with the left hand marry morganatically.
2 (The region or direction on) the left side of a person or thing. ME.

C. JONES Place of every Suit in your Hand the worst of it to the Left-hand.

▸ **B** *adjectival phr.* **1** On or to the left side; done with the left hand. ME.

M. ATWOOD He drove with . . the left-hand window open.

Fleming's left-hand rule: see FLEMING *noun*[2]. **left-hand drive** a motor-vehicle steering system with the steering wheel and other controls fitted on the left side; a vehicle with such steering. **left-hand marriage** a morganatic marriage. **left-hand rope**: laid up and twisted anticlockwise. **left-hand rule** PHYSICS = ***Fleming's left-hand rule*** s.v. FLEMING *noun*[2]. **left-hand screw** a screw which rotates anticlockwise when inserted; any equivalent spiral.
2 Ambiguous, questionable; sinister. Now *rare*. L16.

left-handed /lɛftˈhandɪd, *esp. attrib.* ˈlɛfthandɪd/ *adjective & adverb.* LME.
[ORIGIN from LEFT HAND + -ED[2].]
▸ **A** *adjective*. **1** Having the left hand more serviceable than the right; using the left hand by preference. LME.

Pall Mall Gazette A left-handed bowler is nearly always a right-handed bat.

2 *fig.* †**a** Disabled. LME–M17. ▸**b** Clumsy, inept. LME.

b A. BLOMFIELD Spiritual men are generally left-handed in secular affairs.

3 Ambiguous, doubtful; questionable. E17.

J. STEVENS 'Tis not safe trusting a Left Handed Man with Money. A. DOUGLAS 'I'm not trying to date you.' 'Well, that's a left-handed compliment,' she complained.

4 Inauspicious, sinister, malign. Long *rare*. E17.
5 Of or pertaining to the left hand; *spec.* (**a**) designating or pertaining to a marriage in which the bridegroom gives the bride his left hand instead of his right (as was the custom at morganatic weddings in Germany), morganatic; (**b**) (of an implement) adapted or designed for use by a left-handed person; (**c**) (of an action) performed with the left hand. M17.
6 Characterized by a leftward direction or rotation; (of a screw) that is turned anticlockwise to drive it in; laevorotatory; (of a shell) sinistral. Cf. LAEVO-. E19.
▸ **B** *adverb*. Towards the left; with the left hand. M19.

Horse & Hound The fox ran . . left-handed over the Waltham Lane.

■ **left-handedly** *adverb* L19. **left-handedness** *noun* M17.

left-hander /lɛftˈhandə/ *noun.* M19.
[ORIGIN formed as LEFT-HANDED + -ER[1].]
1 A blow delivered with the left hand. M19.
2 A left-handed person. L19.
3 A left-handed compliment. M20.

Times 'Not bad' might appear a good enough specimen of the simplest type of left-hander.

4 A left-hand turn or bend. L20.

leftie *noun & adjective* var. of LEFTY *noun & adjective*.

leftover /ˈlɛftəʊvə/ *adjective & noun.* L19.
[ORIGIN from *left* pa. pple of LEAVE *verb*[1] + OVER *adverb*.]
▸ **A** *adjective*. Remaining over; not used up or disposed of. L19.
▸ **B** *noun*. **1** A thing remaining over; *esp.* a portion of some article of food left over from a meal. Usu. in *pl.* L19.
2 A survivor. E20.

leftward /ˈlɛftwəd/ *adverb & adjective.* L15.
[ORIGIN from LEFT *adjective* + -WARD.]
▸ **A** *adverb*. On or in the direction of the left side; towards the left. L15.

Listener I was rather Conservative as a young man. I've moved gently leftward.

▸ **B** *adjective*. Situated on the left; directed or tending towards the left; executed from right to left. E19.

Times In the borough elections the leftward movement . . has been repeated.

■ **leftwardness** *noun* (*rare*) M20. **leftwards** *adverb* = LEFTWARD *adverb* L19.

left wing /lɛft ˈwɪŋ/ *noun & adjectival phr.* As adjective also **left-wing**. M16.
[ORIGIN from LEFT *adjective* + WING *noun*.]
▸ **A** *noun phr.* **1** The division on the left side of an army or fleet in battle array. M16.
2 FOOTBALL & HOCKEY etc. (The position of) a player on the left side of the centre(s); the part of the field in which a left wing normally plays. L19.
3 The radical or socialist section of a group or political party; the more liberal or progressive section of a right-wing or conservative group or political party. L19.

JAMES WHITE A massive purge of the left wing of the fascist party.

▸ **B** *adjective*. Of or pertaining to the left wing, esp. in politics. L19.

P. ARROWSMITH She was too young, modern and Left Wing to hold conventional views about sex.

■ **left-ˈwinger** *noun* (**a**) a player on the left wing; (**b**) POLITICS an adherent of the left wing: L19. **left-ˈwingery** *noun* adherence to the left wing, the beliefs or practices of the left wing M20. **left-ˈwingism** *noun* = LEFT-WINGERY E20.

lefty /ˈlɛfti/ *adjective & noun. colloq.* Also **leftie**. L19.
[ORIGIN from LEFT *noun* + -Y[6].]
▸ **A** *adjective*. **1** Left-handed. L19.
2 Of or pertaining to the left in politics etc. M20.
▸ **B** *noun*. **1** A left-handed person, esp. a sportsperson. E20.
2 POLITICS. An adherent of the left. M20.

leg /lɛɡ/ *noun.* ME.
[ORIGIN Old Norse *leggr* (cf. Swedish *lägg*, Danish *læg* calf of the leg, Latin *lacertus* muscles) from Germanic. Superseded *shank*.]
▸ **I 1** Each of the limbs of support and locomotion in an animal body; *esp.* either of the two lower limbs of the human body. Also, the part of this from the hip to the ankle, or (*spec.* in ANATOMY) from the knee to the ankle. ME. ▸**b** (A part of) a leg of an animal or bird used as food. LME. ▸**c** ***leg up***, ***leg-up***, a lift by the leg to help a person climb up or get over an obstacle; a help in a difficulty, an aid to progress. Orig. & esp. in ***give a person a leg up***. *colloq.* M19.

C. STEAD His legs were shaking, and he stumbled at every step. A. HARDY A terrestrial animal . . larger than an elephant would have . . legs so thick . . it could not walk. I. MCEWAN Mary was . . scratching the calf and ankle of one leg. **b** D. LEAVITT I bought a leg of lamb to freeze.

2 A gesture of deferential respect made by drawing back one leg and bending the other; a bow, a scrape. Freq. in ***make a leg***. Now *arch.* or *joc.* L16.
3 = BLACKLEG *noun* 2. *arch. slang.* E19.
4 CRICKET. The side of the pitch on which the batsman stands, esp. the part which lies behind or roughly in line with him or her (also ***leg side***). Also, (the area occupied by) a fielder who plays on this side of the pitch. E19.

Times His attempt to sweep to leg at a straight enough ball.

5 A woman. *slang* (chiefly *US*). *derog.* M20.
▸**II** A thing resembling a leg or acting as a support.
6 An artificial leg. Also ***peg leg***, ***wooden leg***, etc. LME.
7 Chiefly HERALDRY. A representation or figure of a leg, esp. bent at the knee. LME.
8 A part of a garment which covers a leg. LME.

DICKENS Put my hunk of bread-and-butter down the leg of my trousers.

9 †**a** The stem of an earthenware or glass vessel. Only in L15. ▸**b** Each of the comparatively long and slender supports of a piece of furniture etc. E17. ▸**c** Each of the columns extending below the main deck of an oil rig, used to float and stabilize the vessel or to rest it on the seabed. M20.

b M. BRADBURY A number of tables with gunmetal legs and bright yellow tops.

10 Esp. SHIPBUILDING & MINING. A bar, pole, etc., used as a support or prop. L15.
11 NAUTICAL. Any of various short ropes which branch out into two or more parts. E17.
12 **a** Either of the sides of a triangle, viewed as standing on a base; either of the two parts on each side of the vertex of a curve. M17. ▸**b** Each of the branches of a forked, jointed, or curved object. L17. ▸**c** A strand of the network connecting the patterns in lace. Usu. in *pl.* M19. ▸**d** MINING. Either of the two nearly vertical lateral prolongations of the saddle of a quartz reef. L19. ▸**e** BROADCASTING. A supplementary network attached to a main network and providing coverage for a particular region; a group of stations in a network. *US.* M20.

b *Croquet* It cannot effect the stroke . . on account of the leg of a hoop intervening.

13 **a** NAUTICAL. A run made on a single tack. M19. ▸**b** *gen.* A part of, or stage in, a journey, race, competition, etc. E20. ▸**c** STOCK EXCHANGE. A stage or period of an account or market. L20.

a H. ALLEN Captain Bittern . . fetched a tremendous leg away across the Atlantic. **b** *Sunday Graphic* Mrs. Morrow-Tait . . arrives at Malta from Marseilles . . on the second leg of her round-the-world tour. **c** *Times* Equities ended the first leg of the two week account on a . . firm note.

– PHRASES: **abdominal leg** ENTOMOLOGY = PROLEG. ***a bone in one's leg***: see BONE *noun*. ***an arm and a leg***: see ARM *noun*[1]. ***cost an arm and a leg***: see COST *verb* 1. **change leg** (of a horse) change step. **dance a person off his or her legs**, **run a person off his or her legs**, **walk a person off his or her legs** cause a person to dance, run, walk, etc., to exhaustion. **false leg** ENTOMOLOGY = PROLEG. ***feel one's legs***: see FEEL *verb*. **get one's leg over** *slang* engage in sexual intercourse. ***hang a leg***: see HANG *verb*. ***Harry long legs***: see HARRY *noun*[2]. **have legs** *US colloq.* (of a book, film, play, etc.) have lasting popularity. **have no legs** *colloq.* have insufficient momentum to reach a desired point. **have the legs of** travel faster than. †**heave up the leg** = *lift the leg* below. ***keep one's legs***: see KEEP *verb*. **lay one's leg over** *slang* = ***get one's leg over*** above. **leg before wicket** CRICKET illegal obstruction of the ball by the batsman with a part of the body other than the hand, for which he or she can be given out. **legs eleven** *joc.* eleven orig. & esp. in the game of bingo. ***leg up***: see sense 1c above. **lift the leg**, **lift up the leg** *slang* (esp. of a dog) urinate. **long leg** CRICKET (the position of) a fielder on the leg side at a long distance from the wicket. ***middle leg***: see MIDDLE *adjective*. **no leg to stand on**, **not a leg to stand on** no support whatever. ***on one's hind legs***: see HIND *adjective*. **on one's last legs** at the end of one's life or resources. **on one's legs** (*a*) standing; (of a public speaker etc.) standing up and orating; (*b*) well enough to stand or walk; (*c*) *fig.* prosperous, established. **pull a person's leg** *colloq.* tease a person, deceive a person playfully or humorously. ***red leg***: see RED *adjective*. ***run a person off his or her legs***: see ***dance a person off his or her legs*** above. SEA ***legs***. **shake a leg** (*a*) make a start; hurry up; (*b*) begin dancing. **shake a loose leg** lead an irregular life. **short leg** CRICKET (the position of) a fielder on the leg side at a short distance from the wicket. **show a leg** get out of bed; make one's appearance. **square leg** CRICKET (the position of) a fielder on the leg side about square with the wicket (***short square leg***: see SHORT *adjective*). ***straight leg***: see STRAIGHT *adjective*[1] & *adverb*[1]. **stretch one's legs** †(*a*) increase one's stride, walk fast; (*b*) exercise the legs by walking. **take to one's legs** run (away). ***talk the hind legs off a*** DONKEY. ***walk a person off his or her legs***: see ***dance a person off his or her legs*** above. ***walking leg***: see WALKING *verbal noun*. ***walking on two legs***, ***walking with two legs***: see WALKING *noun*. ***white leg***: see WHITE *adjective*. ***with one's tail between one's legs***: see TAIL *noun*[1].

– COMB.: **leg bail** (*a*) [BAIL *noun*[1]] ***give leg bail*** (joc.), run away; (*b*) [BAIL *noun*[2]] CRICKET the bail nearest the batsman; **leg bone** the shin bone, the tibia; **leg break** CRICKET a ball which deviates from the leg side after bouncing; such a deviation; ***leg bye***: see BYE *noun* 3; **leg-cutter** CRICKET a fast leg break; **leg drive** (*a*) ROWING drive imparted by movement of the rower's legs; (*b*) CRICKET a drive to the leg side; ***leg glance***: see GLANCE *noun*[1] 2b; **leg guard** a protection for the leg; CRICKET a covering for the knee, shin, and ankle, worn as a protection against injury from the ball; †**leg-harness** armour for the leg; **leg iron** a shackle or fetter for the leg; **leg man**, **leg woman** an assistant who does legwork; **leg-of-mutton** *adjective* resembling a leg of mutton, esp. in shape; ***leg-of-mutton sail***, a triangular mainsail; ***leg-of-mutton sleeve***, a sleeve very full on the arm but close-fitting at the wrist; **leg-over** *slang* sexual intercourse; **leg-pad** CRICKET a leg guard; **leg-pull** a playful or humorous deception; **leg-puller** a person given to leg-pulling; **leg-pulling** the action or an act of deceiving a person playfully or humorously; **leg-rest** a support for the leg of a seated invalid; **leg-ring** an aluminium strip secured round a bird's leg to identify it; **legroom** space for the legs, *spec.* in a car; **leg-rope** *verb & noun* (*Austral. & NZ*) (*a*) *verb trans.* catch or secure (an animal) by the leg with a noosed rope; (*b*) *noun* a noosed rope used for catching and securing animals; **leg-show** *colloq.* a theatrical production in which dancing girls display their legs; ***leg side***: see sense A.4 above; **leg slip** CRICKET (a fielder in) a position to stop a ball glancing off the bat to the leg side behind the wicket; **leg spin** CRICKET a type of spin which causes the ball to turn from the leg side after bouncing; **leg-spinner** CRICKET a ball bowled with a leg spin; a leg spin bowler; **leg stump** CRICKET = ***leg bail*** (b) above; **leg theory** CRICKET a theory that favours bowling to leg with a concentration of fielders on the leg side; **leg trap** CRICKET a group of fielders stationed for catches near the wicket on the leg side; ***leg-up***: see sense 1c above; **leg warmer** either of a pair of tubular (usu. knitted) garments, orig. worn by dancers at rehearsal, covering the leg from ankle to thigh, but often worn gathered from the ankle to below the knee (usu. in *pl.*); ***leg woman***: see ***leg man*** above; **legwork** work which involves running errands, going from place to place gathering information, etc.; **leg-worm** = ***Guinea worm*** s.v. GUINEA 1.

■ **leglet** *noun* (*a*) a little leg; (*b*) an ornament or band worn round the leg: E19.

leg /lɛɡ/ *verb trans.* Infl. **-gg-**. E17.
[ORIGIN from the noun.]
▸**I** **1** Foll. by *it*: use the legs; walk fast, run. E17.

Golf Illustrated The . . coach broke down and . . David legged it up to the clubhouse to find . . alternative transport.

2 Chiefly *hist.* Propel (a boat) through a canal tunnel by thrusting the legs against the walls; navigate (a tunnel) in this way. Also foll. by *through*. M19.
▸**II** **3** **a** Hit with gunshot or otherwise injure on the leg. E19. ▸**b** Seize or hold by the leg. L19.

a *Shooting Times* I legged a hare and it went into that hedge.

legacy /ˈlɛɡəsi/ *noun.* LME.
[ORIGIN Old French *legacie* from medieval Latin *legatia* legateship, from *legatus* LEGATE *noun*: see -CY. In Branch II repr. also medieval Latin *legantia*, from *legare* bequeath: cf. LEGANTINE *adjective*.]
▸**I** Legateship, legation.
†**1** The function or office of a delegate or deputy, esp. a papal legate. LME–E18.
†**2** A body of people sent as a deputation to a monarch etc.; the act of sending such a body. LME–L16.
†**3** The message or business committed to a delegate or deputy. LME–M17.
▸**II** **4** A sum of money, or a specified article, given to another by will; a bequest. LME. ▸**b** *transf.* & *fig.* A tangible or intangible thing handed down by a predecessor; a long-lasting effect of an event or process. L16.

C. HOPE Perhaps a rich relative would die and leave him a legacy. **b** J. WAIN The legacy of Victorian industrialism—slums, ignorance, densely crowded streets. S. BRETT The scar on her thumb, legacy of an accident with a kitchen knife.

†**5** The action or an act of bequeathing; bequest. L15–E17.
– COMB.: **legacy-hunter**, **legacy-monger** a person who is attentive to old and rich people in the hope of obtaining a legacy.

†**legacy** *verb trans.* M16.
[ORIGIN from the noun.]
1 Give or leave as a legacy. M16–M17.
2 Bequeath a legacy to. L18–L19.

legal /ˈliːɡ(ə)l/ *adjective & noun.* LME.
[ORIGIN Old French & mod. French *légal* or Latin *legalis*, from *leg-*, *lex* law: see -AL[1]. Cf. LEAL *adjective*, LOYAL.]
▸**A** *adjective.* **1** CHRISTIAN CHURCH. ▸**a** Of or pertaining to the Mosaic law. LME. ▸**b** Of or pertaining to the law of works, i.e. salvation by works, as opp. to salvation by faith. Formerly also (of a person), upholding the law of works. M17.
2 **a** Of or pertaining to law; falling within the province of law. E16. ▸**b** Belonging to or characteristic of the profession of the law. E19.

a C. ACHEBE The paper I signed has no legal force. **b** OED Whether he is a lawyer or not, he seems to have a legal mind.

3 **a** Required or appointed by law; founded on or deriving authority from law. E17. ▸**b** Recognized by law as distinguished from equity. E19.

a K. WATERHOUSE He has not . . explicitly acknowledged her legal right to do it.

a ***legal separation*** etc.
4 Permitted, or not forbidden, by law; lawful. M17. ▸**b** Allowed by or in accordance with a particular set of rules; permissible. M20.

F. ASTAIRE Betting on the animals away from the race course is legal in England. **b** *Pool Magazine* If you got a red and three yellows on the first legal shot.

5 Pertaining to or designating stationery (often yellow) that measures 22 × 35.5 cm (8.5 × 14 inches). *N. Amer.* L19.
– SPECIAL COLLOCATIONS: **legal aid** official assistance allowed under certain conditions towards the expense of litigation. **legal beagle** *colloq.* a lawyer, *spec.* one who is keen and astute. **legal cap** *US* ruled writing paper used chiefly for drafting legal documents. **legal capacity** a person's authority under law to engage in a particular undertaking or maintain a particular status. **legal charity** *hist.* relief dispensed under the Poor Laws. **legal eagle** *colloq.* = ***legal beagle*** above. **legal fiction** an assumption that something is true even though it may be untrue, made esp. in judicial reasoning to develop the law. **legal holiday** *US* a public holiday established by law. **legal man** [law Latin *legalis homo*] a man who has full legal rights. **legal memory** the period of legal prescription, in England reckoned from the commencement of the reign of Richard I (1189). **legal person** a person who has full legal rights. **legal proceedings** (steps taken in) a legal action or lawsuit. ***legal separation***: see SEPARATION 5. **legal tender** coin or other money which a creditor is bound by law to accept when tendered in payment of a debt.
▸**B** *noun.* **1** A thing connected with law; a legal formality; a legal notice. E16.

Sunday Sun (Brisbane) Do your own legals. Arrange your own divorce, . . will, . . estates & probate.

2 The exact taxi fare without any tip. *slang.* E20.
■ **lega'lese** *noun* (*colloq.*) the abstruse and complicated language of legal documents E20. **legally** *adverb* in a legal manner; lawfully; from the point of view of law: M16. **legalness** *noun* (*rare*) legality M17.

legalise *verb* var. of LEGALIZE.

legalism /ˈliːɡ(ə)lɪz(ə)m/ *noun.* M19.
[ORIGIN from LEGAL *adjective* + -ISM.]
1 CHRISTIAN CHURCH. Adherence to the Mosaic law as opp. to the gospel; the doctrine of justification by works; teaching influenced by that doctrine. M19.
2 Attribution of great importance to law or formulated rule; strict adherence to the letter rather than the spirit of law. L19.

legalist /ˈliːɡ(ə)lɪst/ *noun.* M17.
[ORIGIN from LEGAL *adjective* + -IST.]
1 CHRISTIAN CHURCH. An adherent of legalism. M17.
2 A person versed in the law; a person who views things from a legal standpoint. E19.
■ **lega'listic** *adjective* of or pertaining to legalists or legalism; characterized by legalism: L19. **lega'listically** *adverb* M20.

legality /liːˈɡalɪti, lɪ-/ *noun.* LME.
[ORIGIN French *légalité* or medieval Latin *legalitas*, from Latin *legalis*: see LEGAL, -ITY.]
1 The quality or state of being legal or in conformity with the law. Also, observance of the law; strict adherence to law or rule, legalism. LME.

A. BRIEN She had never doubted the legality of the union between the lady and the gentleman.

2 An obligation imposed by law; a legal procedure. Usu. in *pl.* M19.

Redbook Buying a home . . is a transaction fraught with legalities.

■ **legali'tarian** *adjective* advocating or insisting on conformity with the law M20. **legali'tarianism** *noun* (*a*) advocacy of or insistence on conformity with the law; (*b*) legal egalitarianism: M20.

legalize /ˈliːɡ(ə)lʌɪz/ *verb trans.* Also **-ise**. E18.
[ORIGIN from LEGAL *adjective* + -IZE.]
Make legal or conformable to law; make authoritative under law; sanction.
■ **legali'zation** *noun* E19.

legantine /ˈlɛɡəntɪn/ *adjective.* Now *rare.* M16.
[ORIGIN Alt. of medieval Latin *legatinus* (formed as LEGATE *verb*) after Latin *legant-* pres. ppl stem of *legare* bequeath: see -INE[1]. Cf. medieval Latin *legantia* for *legatio* LEGACY *noun*.]
= LEGATINE.

legatary /ˈlɛɡət(ə)ri/ *noun & adjective.* Now *rare.* M16.
[ORIGIN Latin *legatarius*, from *legatum* bequest, formed as LEGATE *verb*: see -ARY[1].]
▸**A** *noun.* A person to whom a bequest is left; a legatee. M16.
▸**B** *adjective.* Of or pertaining to a bequest; of the nature of a bequest. L17.

legate /ˈlɛɡət/ *noun.* LOE.
[ORIGIN Old French & mod. French *légat* from Latin *legatus* use as noun of pa. pple of *legare*: see LEGATE *verb*, -ATE[1].]
1 Orig., an ecclesiastic deputed to represent the Pope and vested with his authority. Now *spec.* a cardinal sent as papal ambassador extraordinary on special missions to states acknowledging the supreme spiritual authority of the Pope. LOE. ▸**b** *hist.* A governor of a province of the Papal States. M17.
legate a latere /ɑː ˈlatəri/ [Latin = by a third party] a papal legate of the highest class and fullest powers.
2 *gen.* An ambassador, a delegate, a messenger. LME.
3 ROMAN HISTORY. (The deputy of) a general or governor of a province. L15.
■ **legateship** *noun* the office of legate, the dignity of a legate, a post as a legate M16.

legate /lɪˈɡeɪt/ *verb trans.* L15.
[ORIGIN Latin *legat-* pa. ppl stem of *legare* bequeath, (also) send as an envoy: see -ATE[3].]
Give by will, bequeath. Freq. in ***give and legate***.
■ **lega'tee** *noun* a person to whom a legacy has been bequeathed (***residuary legatee***: see RESIDUARY 1) L17.

L

legatine /ˈlɛɡətɪn/ *adjective*. E17.
[ORIGIN from LEGATE *noun* + -INE[1]. Cf. LEGANTINE.]
Of or pertaining to a legate; having the authority of a legate.

legation /lɪˈɡeɪʃ(ə)n/ *noun*. LME.
[ORIGIN Old French & mod. French *légation* or Latin *legatio(n-)*, formed as LEGATE *verb*: see -ATION.]
1 The object for which a legate is sent, a legate's mission or commission. LME.
2 The action of sending a (papal) legate; the fact of being sent as a legate. LME.
3 A body of deputies sent on a mission; a diplomatic minister (now esp. one ranking below ambassador) and his or her entourage. E17. ▸**b** The official residence or office of a diplomatic minister. M19.

LD MACAULAY The report which the English legations made of what they had seen . . in Russia.

4 The position or office of legate, a legateship. E17.

W. FORSYTH He wrote . . to request that he might have a legation given him.

5 *hist.* A province of the Papal States, governed by a legate. M19.
■ **legationary** *adjective* of or pertaining to a legation, qualified or ready to go on a legation M19.

legative /ˈlɛɡətɪv/ *adjective*. M16.
[ORIGIN Late Latin *legativus*, formed as LEGATE *verb*: see -IVE.]
Of or pertaining to a legate; empowering a person as a representative conferring the authority of a legate.

legato /lɪˈɡɑːtəʊ/ *adjective, adverb, & noun*. M18.
[ORIGIN Italian, pa. pple of *legare* bind from Latin *ligare*.]
MUSIC. ▸**A** *adjective & adverb*. Smooth(ly) and connected(ly), with no breaks between successive notes. Freq. as a direction. M18.
▸**B** *noun*. A legato style of performance; a piece or passage (to be) played legato. L19.

legator /lɪˈɡeɪtə/ *noun*. M17.
[ORIGIN Latin, formed as LEGATE *verb*: see -OR.]
A person who gives something by will, a testator.
■ **legaˈtorial** *adjective* of or pertaining to a legator or testator L19.

L

†**lege** *verb* var. of LEDGE *verb*[2].

legend /ˈlɛdʒ(ə)nd/ *noun & adjective*. ME.
[ORIGIN Old French & mod. French *légende* from medieval Latin *legenda* lit. 'things to be read', neut. pl. of gerundive of *legere* read, taken as fem. sing.: see -END.]
▸**A** *noun*. **1** The story of the life of a saint. Long *rare*. ME.
2 A collection of saints' lives or similar stories. Now chiefly in ***the Golden Legend***, ***the Legend***, a 13th-cent. collection of saints' lives written by Jacobus de Voragine, Archbishop of Genoa. ME.
†**3** A story, a history, an account. LME–L17.
†**4** A list, a record. LME–E17.
5 ECCLESIASTICAL. A lectionary. *obsolete* exc. *hist.* LME.

E. C. THOMAS The Legend containing Scriptures, Homilies, and Lives of the Saints.

6 a A writing, an inscription, a motto, *esp.* one on a coin or medal. L15. ▸**b** A written explanation accompanying an illustration, map, etc. E20.

a B. MALAMUD Fidelman went among the graves, reading legends on tombstones. **b** P. KAVANAGH The principal legend on the note stated that all stuff delivered must be 'according to sample'.

7 A traditional tale popularly regarded as historical; an inauthentic story popularly regarded as true. E17. ▸**b** Such stories collectively. M19. ▸**c** A person about whom such stories are told; a subject of legend; a very famous or notorious person. Freq. in ***a legend in one's (own) lifetime***, ***a legend in one's (own) time***. M20.

R. LANE-FOX Legends of Persian atrocity went far beyond the truth. D. L. SAYERS There is a legend that she personally ironed our old butler's back for lumbago. **b** JAN MORRIS Bishop Moberly . . whose wife only once, so legend says, called him by his Christian name. **c** W. RAEPER Hawker was . . a legend by this time in his work of seeking to rescue . . sailors.

8 NAUTICAL. An estimate or statement of legend displacement, speed, etc. See sense B.2 below. M20.

W. S. CHURCHILL Ask your people to give you a legend for a 16-inch-gun ship.

▸**B** *attrib.* or as *adjective*. **1** Of the nature of a legend; very well known, legendary. E17.

EuroBusiness Jacques Calvet, whose protectionist views towards the Japanese were legend.

2 NAUTICAL. Designating the estimated or planned displacement, speed, etc., of a ship before construction or testing. E20.
■ **legended** *adjective* (*rare*) (**a**) bearing a legend or inscription; (**b**) celebrated in legends: M19. **legendist** *noun* a writer of legends M17. **legendry** *noun* legends collectively M19.

legendary /ˈlɛdʒ(ə)nd(ə)ri/ *noun & adjective*. E16.
[ORIGIN medieval Latin *legendarius* adjective, *-ium* noun, from *legenda*: see LEGEND, -ARY[1].]
▸**A** *noun*. †**1** A collection of legends, esp. of lives of saints. Only in 16.
2 A writer of legends. E17.
▸**B** *adjective*. **1** Pertaining to or of the nature of a legend; based on a legend; celebrated or related in legend, very famous or notorious. L16.

D. ADAMS College porters are legendary for . . such feats of memory.

legendary age, **legendary period**: of which the accounts are mostly of the nature of legends.
2 Of a writer: relating legends. M17.
■ **legenˈdarily** *adverb* according to legend, notably, notoriously M20.

Legendre /ləˈʒɑ̃drə/ *noun*. L19.
[ORIGIN A. M. *Legendre* (1752–1833), French mathematician.]
MATH. Used *attrib.* and in *possess.* to designate various expressions investigated by Legendre, esp. the differential equation $(1 - x^2)\,d^2y/dx^2 - 2x\,dy/dx + n(n + 1)y = 0$, its solutions, and associated functions.
Legendre coefficient, ***Legendre function***, ***Legendre polynomial***, ***Legendre's coefficient***, ***Legendre's function***, ***Legendre's polynomial***, etc.
■ **Legendrian** *adjective* L19.

Leger /ˈlɛdʒə/ *noun*[1]. L19.
[ORIGIN Abbreviation.]
1 = ***St Leger*** s.v. SAINT *noun & adjective*. L19.
2 A stand or section of a racecourse, *esp.* one some distance from the winning post. *Austral.* L20.

leger *adjective, noun*[2], *& verb* see LEDGER.

legerdemain /lɛdʒədɪˈmeɪn/ *noun*. LME.
[ORIGIN French *léger de main*, from *léger* light + *de* of + *main* hand.]
1 Sleight of hand; juggling; conjuring. LME.

COLERIDGE The professors of legerdemain . . pull out ribbon after ribbon from their mouth.

2 *transf. & fig.* Trickery, deception. M16.

M. ANDERSON The trial itself was shot full of legerdemain, pre-arranged to lead the jury astray.

†**3** An instance of legerdemain. M16–M17.
■ **legerdemainist** *noun* a juggler, a conjuror, a trickster M19.

legerity /lɪˈdʒɛrɪti/ *noun*. Now *rare*. M16.
[ORIGIN French *légèreté*, from *léger* from Proto-Gallo-Romance from Latin *levis* light: see -ITY.]
Lightness (*lit. & fig.*); nimbleness.

M. BEERBOHM Alighting with the legerity of a cat, he . . was off, like a streak of . . lightning.

†**lege talionis** *adverbial phr.* L16–M18.
[ORIGIN Latin (*lege* abl. of *lex*): see LEX TALIONIS.]
According to the *lex talionis*.

leggat *noun* var. of LEGGET.

legged /lɛɡd, ˈlɛɡɪd/ *adjective*. LME.
[ORIGIN from LEG *noun* + -ED[2].]
Having legs, esp. of a specified kind, number, or (HERALDRY) tincture. Freq. as 2nd elem. of comb., as ***bow-legged***, ***long-legged***, ***two-legged***, etc.

legger /ˈlɛɡə/ *noun*[1]. M19.
[ORIGIN from LEG *verb* + -ER[1].]
Chiefly *hist.* A person who propels a barge through a canal tunnel by thrusting his or her legs against the walls.

legger /ˈlɛɡə/ *noun*[2]. E20.
[ORIGIN from LEG *noun* + -ER[1].]
In a slaughterhouse, a butcher who works on the legs of the carcasses.

legger /ˈlɛɡə/ *noun*[3]. *US colloq.* E20.
[ORIGIN Abbreviation.]
= BOOTLEGGER. Also as 2nd elem. of comb., an illegal seller (of the thing specified).

leggero *adjective & adverb* var. of LEGGIERO.

legget /ˈlɛɡət/ *noun*. Also **-at**. M16.
[ORIGIN Unknown.]
In thatching, a tool made from a flat board attached to a handle and studded with nails, used for dressing and driving reeds into place.

leggiero /lɛˈdʒɛːrəʊ, *foreign* lɛdˈdʒɛːro/ *adjective & adverb*. Also **leggero**. L19.
[ORIGIN Italian.]
MUSIC. Light(ly) and graceful(ly). Freq. as a direction.

legging /ˈlɛɡɪŋ/ *noun*. Also **-in** /-ɪn/. M18.
[ORIGIN from LEG *noun* + -ING[3].]
1 In *pl.* (an overgarment consisting of) protective coverings for the legs, usu. from ankle to knee; also, tight-fitting stretch trousers for women and girls; *sing.* (*rare*) either leg of a pair of leggings. M18.
2 CRICKET. A leg guard. Usu. in *pl.* Now *rare* or *obsolete*. M19.
■ **legginged** *adjective* having leggings M19.

leggo /lɛˈɡəʊ/ *verb intrans.* (*imper.*). *non-standard*. L19.
[ORIGIN Contr.]
Let go.

leggy /ˈlɛɡi/ *adjective*. L18.
[ORIGIN from LEG *noun* + -Y[1].]
1 Having (particularly) long legs; *slang* (of a woman) attractive, sexy. L18.

Z. TOMIN He squeezes his leggy body into what little space is left under the table. *Listener* A couple of leggy dollybirds.

2 Characterized by a display of legs. *slang*. M19.

Daily Telegraph Christmas . . concerts, leggy burlesques.

3 Of a plant: long-stemmed. M19.

legh *noun* var. of LEIGH.

leghaemoglobin /ˌlɛɡhiːməˈɡləʊbɪn/ *noun*. Also *****-hemo-**. M20.
[ORIGIN from LEG(UME + HAEMOGLOBIN.]
BIOCHEMISTRY. A red pigment in the root nodules of legumes which facilitates nitrogen fixation and has a structure similar to haemoglobin.

Leghorn /lɛˈɡɔːn, ˈlɛɡhɔːn/ *adjective & noun*. Esp. in sense 1 also **l-**. M18.
[ORIGIN Anglicized from Italian *Legorno*, now *Livorno* (repr. Latin *Liburnus*), a port in Tuscany, western Italy.]
1 (Designating) a fine straw plaiting of a kind originally imported from Livorno; (designating) a hat made from such plaiting. M18.
2 (A bird of) a breed of small hardy domestic fowl. M19.

legible /ˈlɛdʒɪb(ə)l/ *adjective*. LME.
[ORIGIN Late Latin *legibilis*, from *legere* read: see -IBLE.]
1 Of writing: clear enough to be read; easily deciphered. LME.
2 Of a literary composition: accessible to readers; easy to read, readable. *rare*. LME.
3 *transf. & fig.* Clear, discernible. E17.
■ **legiˈbility** *noun* the quality or condition of being legible L17. **legibleness** *noun* legibility E18. **legibly** *adverb* L16.

legion /ˈliːdʒ(ə)n/ *noun & adjective*. ME.
[ORIGIN Old French *legiun*, *-ion* (mod. *légion*) from Latin *legio(n-)*, from *legere* choose, levy: see -ION.]
▸**A** *noun* **1 a** *hist.* A body of infantry in the Roman army, ranging in number from 3,000 to 6,000 (at the time of Marius), and usu. combined with many cavalry. ME. ▸**b** Any of various (esp. Continental) military bodies of modern times. L16.
2 *gen.* An armed host, (a part of) an army. *literary*. ME.
3 A vast host or multitude, esp. of angels or spirits. ME.

AV *Matt.* 26:53 He shall presently giue me more then twelue legions of Angels. M. L. KING We are marching no longer by ones and twos but in legions of thousands.

4 Any of various national associations of ex-servicemen and (now) ex-servicewomen instituted after the First World War. E20.
American Legion, ***Royal British Legion***, ***Canadian Legion***, etc.
– PHRASES: **foreign legion** a body of foreign volunteers in the French army, in the 19th and early 20th cents., employed in the colonies or on distant expeditions and famed for their audacity and endurance. **Legion of Honour** a French order of distinction, founded by Napoleon in 1802, conferred as a reward for civil or military services. **legion of the lost** (**ones**) people who are destitute or abandoned.
– COMB.: **Legion disease**, **Legion fever** (esp. *Journalists' slang*) = ***legionnaires' disease*** s.v. LEGIONNAIRE.
▸**B** *adjective*. **1** Innumerable, widespread. Esp. (with allus. to *Mark* 5:9) in ***my name is legion***, ***their name is legion***, etc. L17.

Times The inaccuracies were so legion.

2 *attrib.* Of or pertaining to a national legion of ex-servicemen and ex-servicewomen. M20.
■ **legioned** *adjective* (*poet.*) arrayed in legions E19.

legionaire *noun* var. of LEGIONNAIRE.

legionary /ˈliːdʒ(ə)n(ə)ri/ *adjective & noun*. LME.
[ORIGIN Latin *legionarius*, from *legio(n-)*: see LEGION, -ARY[1].]
▸**A** *adjective*. **1** Of or pertaining to a legion. LME.
2 Constituting or consisting of a legion or legions. M17.
▸**B** *noun*. **1** A soldier of a legion; a member of a legion. L16.
2 A member of the Legion of Honour. E19.

legionella /liːdʒəˈnɛlə/ *noun*. Pl. **-llae** /-liː/. L20.
[ORIGIN mod. Latin, from LEGION + -ELLA.]
A bacterium of the genus *Legionella*, comprising rod-shaped aerobic Gram-negative forms; *esp.* one that causes legionnaires' disease.

legionnaire /liːdʒəˈnɛː/ *noun*. Also **legionaire**. E19.
[ORIGIN French *légionnaire*, from *légion* LEGION *noun*.]
A member of a legion; *esp.* (usu. **L-**) a member of a named legion, as the American Legion, the Royal British Legion, or the French Foreign Legion.
legionnaires' disease [from an outbreak at a convention of the American Legion in Philadelphia in 1976] a severe form of bacterial pneumonia (often accompanied by mental confusion) caused by *Legionella pneumophila* and associated esp. with infected water systems in buildings.

legislate /ˈlɛdʒɪsleɪt/ *verb*. E18.
[ORIGIN Back-form. from LEGISLATOR, LEGISLATION.]
†**1** *verb trans.* Make laws for. *rare*. Only in E18.
2 *verb intrans.* Make or enact laws; make provision by laws *for*. E19.

Which? The Government should legislate for standard quantities of wine.

3 *verb trans.* Create or destroy by legislation; drive or change by legislation *into*, *out of*. M19.

Lancashire Life It could be legislated out of existence.

legislation /lɛdʒɪsˈleɪʃ(ə)n/ *noun*. **M17**.
[**ORIGIN** from late Latin *legis latio(n-)*, i.e. *legis* genit. of *lex* law + *latio(n-)* proposing (a law), from *latus*: see **LEGISLATOR**, **-ATION**.]
1 The action of making or giving laws; the enactment of laws; an instance of this. **M17**.

Guardian The best legislation is not legislation which results in a lot of cases going to the High Courts.

2 The enactments of a legislator or legislature collectively; the whole body of enacted laws. **M19**.

M. BRETT The framework for the system . . is enshrined in legislation.

— PHRASES: ***subordinate legislation***: see **SUBORDINATE** *adjective* 2.
■ **legislational** *adjective* **E19**.

legislative /ˈlɛdʒɪslətɪv/ *adjective & noun*. **M17**.
[**ORIGIN** from **LEGISLATION**, **LEGISLATOR**: see **-ATIVE**. Cf. French *législatif*.]
▸ **A** *adjective*. **1** That legislates, that has the function of legislating, that has the power to legislate. **M17**.

A. TOFFLER Congresses, . . parliaments, city councils—legislative bodies in general.

2 Of or pertaining to legislation. **M17**.

H. D. THOREAU Those who go to soirees and legislative halls must have new coats.

3 Enacted or appointed by legislation. **L18**.

J. MCPHEE The Homestead Act and other legislative provisions.

▸ **B** *noun*. The power of legislating; the body in which this power is vested, the legislature. Now *rare*. **M17**.
■ **legislatively** *adverb* in a legislative manner; by legislation: **M17**.

legislator /ˈlɛdʒɪsleɪtə/ *noun*. **L15**.
[**ORIGIN** from Latin *legis lator*, i.e. *legis* genit. of *lex* law + *lator* proposer, mover, agent noun from *latus* pa. pple of *tollere* raise.]
A person who makes laws (for a people or nation); a member of a legislative body.
■ **legislatorial** /ˌlɛdʒɪsləˈtɔːrɪəl/ *adjective* (**a**) of or pertaining to a legislator or legislation; (**b**) having the power to legislate, acting as a legislator or legislature: **L18**. **legislaˈtorially** *adverb* **E19**. **legislatorship** *noun* the position of legislator **M17**. **legislatress** *noun* (now *rare*) a female legislator **E18**. **legisˈlatrix** *noun* (now *rare*) = **LEGISLATRESS** **L17**.

legislature /ˈlɛdʒɪslətʃə/ *noun*. **L17**.
[**ORIGIN** from **LEGISLATOR** + **-URE**, after **JUDICATURE**.]
1 The power that makes or enacts laws; a body of people empowered to make or enact the laws of a country or state. **L17**.

W. LIPPMANN The existing laws of property and contracts had not been formally enacted by a legislature.

†**2** The exercise of the power of legislation. **E–M18**.

legist /ˈliːdʒɪst/ *noun*. **LME**.
[**ORIGIN** Old French & mod. French *légiste* or medieval Latin *legista*, from Latin *leg-*, *lex* law: see **-IST**.]
1 A person knowledgeable in the law. **LME**.
2 *spec*. A member of a group of legal philosophers in the early Han dynasty in China. **M20**.
■ †**legister** *noun* [Old French *legistre* var. (infl. by *ministre* etc.) of *legiste* **LEGIST**] = **LEGIST** 1 **ME–M16**.

legit /lɪˈdʒɪt/ *noun & adjective*. *colloq*. **L19**.
[**ORIGIN** Abbreviation of **LEGITIMATE** *adjective & noun*.]
▸ **A** *noun*. **1** A legitimate actor. **L19**.
2 The legitimate theatre, legitimate drama. **L19**.
3 A legitimate child. **M20**.
4 ***on the legit***, within the law. **M20**.
▸ **B** *adjective*. **1** Of or pertaining to the legitimate theatre or legitimate drama. **E20**.
2 Lawful, legal. **M20**.

legitim *adjective & noun* var. of **LEGITIME**.

legitimacy /lɪˈdʒɪtɪməsi/ *noun*. **L17**.
[**ORIGIN** from **LEGITIMATE** *adjective*: see **-ACY**.]
1 The fact of being a legitimate child. **L17**. ▸†**b** Genuineness. Only in **L17**.
2 Legal right to govern or to sovereignty; *spec*. the fact or principle of strict hereditary succession to a throne. **E19**.
3 Conformity to law, rule, or principle; lawfulness; conformity to sound reasoning, logicality. **M19**.

legitimate /lɪˈdʒɪtɪmət/ *adjective & noun*. **LME**.
[**ORIGIN** medieval Latin *legitimatus* pa. pple of *legitimare* legitimize, from Latin *leg-*, *lex* law: see **-ATE**[2].]
▸ **A** *adjective*. **1** (Of a child) having the status of one born to parents lawfully married to each other, entitled in law to full filial rights; (of a parent) lawfully married to the other parent of a child; (of status, descent, etc.) of or through such parents or children. **LME**. ▸†**b** Genuine, not spurious. **M16–E19**.

R. ELLMANN Lady Wilde presented her husband with three legitimate offspring to match his three illegitimate ones. A. N. WILSON Sergey did the decent thing . . and married her, giving her children legitimate status.

2 a Conformable to, sanctioned or authorized by, law or principle; lawful; justifiable; proper. **M17**. ▸**b** Normal, regular; conformable to a recognized standard type; *HORSE-RACING* designating flat-racing as opp. to hurdle-racing or steeplechasing. **M17**. ▸**c** Designating or pertaining to art considered to have aesthetic merit or serious intent, esp. (**a**) conventional theatre or drama as opp. to musical comedy, farce, etc.; (**b**) classical music as opp. to jazz or popular music. **L18**. ▸**d** Sanctioned by the laws of reasoning; logically admissible or inferable. **L18**. ▸**e** Of a monarch, sovereignty, etc.: justified or validated by the strict principle of hereditary right. **E19**.

a H. KISSINGER The only legitimate war aim left for the United States was to get its prisoners back. W. VAN T. CLARK We must act in a reasoned and legitimate manner, not as a lawless mob. **b** *New Yorker* I grew up exposed to the wealthy . . and . . wealthy people became legitimate to me. **c** S. BRETT I am an actor in the legitimate theatre; these are mere variety artistes.

▸ **B** *noun*. **1** A legitimate child. **L16**.
2 A supporter or advocate of strict hereditary succession to a throne, a legitimist. Also, a legitimate monarch. **E19**.
3 a The legitimate theatre. **L19**. ▸**b** An actor in the legitimate theatre. Cf. earlier **LEGIT** *noun* 1. **M20**.
■ **legitimately** *adverb* **L16**. **legitimateness** *noun* legitimacy **E17**.

legitimate /lɪˈdʒɪtɪmeɪt/ *verb trans*. **L15**.
[**ORIGIN** medieval Latin *legitimat-* pa. ppl stem of *legitimare*: see **LEGITIMATE** *adjective & noun*, **-ATE**[3].]
1 Make lawful, legalize; authorize by legal enactment. **L15**.

Daily Colonist No nation in world history has ever legitimated the use of marijuana.

2 Give the status of a legitimate child to, as by subsequent marriage; establish the legitimacy of (a person) by an authoritative declaration or decree. **L16**.

Daily Telegraph The child of an adulterous union could be legitimated by the subsequent marriage of its parents.

3 Affirm or show to be legitimate; authorize or justify by word or example; serve as justification for. **E17**.

J. N. ISBISTER He constantly makes appeal to . . science to justify and legitimate his theoretical conclusions.

legitimation /lɪˌdʒɪtɪˈmeɪʃ(ə)n/ *noun*. **LME**.
[**ORIGIN** medieval Latin *legitimatio(n-)*, formed as **LEGITIMATE** *verb*: see **-ATION**. Cf. Old French & mod. French *légitimation*.]
1 An authoritative declaration or decree of legitimacy; a document of authorization. *rare*. **LME**.
†**2** Legitimacy, authenticity. **M16–L17**.
3 The action or process of legitimating someone. **M16**.

BOSWELL Legitimation by subsequent marriage.

4 The action or process of legitimating something. **M16**.
5 A legitimating authority; a justification. **M20**.

legitimatize /lɪˈdʒɪtɪmətʌɪz/ *verb trans*. Also **-ise**. **L18**.
[**ORIGIN** from **LEGITIMATE** *adjective* + **-IZE**.]
= **LEGITIMIZE**.

DICKENS He married her in good earnest, and legitimatized . . all the other children.

■ **legitimatiˈzation** *noun* **L20**.

legitime /ˈlɛdʒɪtɪm/ *adjective & noun*. Also **-im**. **LME**.
[**ORIGIN** Old French & mod. French *légitime* adjective & noun from Latin *legitimus*, from *leg-*, *lex* **LAW** *noun*[1].]
▸ †**A** *adjective*. **1** = **LEGITIMATE** *adjective* 1. **LME–E17**.
2 = **LEGITIMATE** *adjective* 1. **LME–L18**.
▸ **B** *noun*. †**1** *pl*. Those of legitimate birth. Only in **LME**.
2 *CIVIL & SCOTS LAW*. The portion of a deceased person's estate to which a child of his or hers is legally entitled, regardless of the terms of the will. **L17**.

legitimise *verb* var. of **LEGITIMIZE**.

legitimism /lɪˈdʒɪtɪmɪz(ə)m/ *noun*. **L19**.
[**ORIGIN** French *légitimisme*, formed as **LEGITIME**: see **-ISM**.]
Support of legitimate authority, esp. of a claim to a throne on the grounds of strict hereditary succession; adherence to legitimist claims or views.

legitimist /lɪˈdʒɪtɪmɪst/ *noun & adjective*. **M19**.
[**ORIGIN** French *légitimiste*, formed as **LEGITIME**: see **-IST**.]
▸ **A** *noun*. A supporter of legitimate authority, esp. of a claim to a throne on the grounds of strict hereditary succession; *spec*. in France, a supporter of the elder Bourbon line, driven from the throne in 1830. **M19**.
▸ **B** *attrib*. or as *adjective*. Of or pertaining to legitimists or legitimism. **M19**.

L. ADAMIC Washington . . was legitimist. It wanted no revolution in Yugoslavia.

legitimity /lɛdʒɪˈtɪmɪti/ *noun*. *rare*. **E19**.
[**ORIGIN** French *légitimité*, formed as **LEGITIME**: see **-ITY**.]
Legitimacy.

legitimize /lɪˈdʒɪtɪmʌɪz/ *verb trans*. Also **-ise**. **M19**.
[**ORIGIN** from Latin *legitimus* (see **LEGITIME**) + **-IZE**.]
Make (esp. a child) legitimate; serve as a justification for.
■ **legitimiˈzation** *noun* **M19**.

leglen /ˈlɛglən/ *noun*. *Scot*. **E18**.
[**ORIGIN** Perh. alt. of **LAGGIN**.]
A milk pail.

legless /ˈlɛglɪs/ *adjective*. **LME**.
[**ORIGIN** from **LEG** *noun* + **-LESS**.]
1 Having no legs. In early use also, lacking a leg. **LME**.
2 Drunk, *esp*. too drunk to stand. *slang*. **L20**.

V. SETH If I don't share the bottle, Helen will be legless by the time we play our scale.

■ **leglessness** *noun* **M19**.

Lego /ˈlɛgəʊ/ *noun*. **M20**.
[**ORIGIN** from Danish *leg godt* play well, from *lege* play.]
(Proprietary name for) a constructional toy consisting of interlocking plastic building blocks.

legong /lɛˈgɒŋ/ *noun*. **E20**.
[**ORIGIN** Indonesian.]
(A participant in) a stylized Balinese dance performed esp. by young girls.

legrandite /ləˈgrɑːndʌɪt/ *noun*. **M20**.
[**ORIGIN** from *Legrand*, a 20th-cent. Belgian mine manager + **-ITE**[1].]
MINERALOGY. A hydrated arsenate of zinc occurring as yellow transparent monoclinic crystals.

leguan /ˈlɛgjʊən/ *noun*. Also **leguaan**. **L18**.
[**ORIGIN** Prob. from French *l'iguane* the iguana. Cf. **LIKKEWAAN**.]
= **IGUANA** 2.

leguleian /lɛgjʊˈliːən/ *noun & adjective*. **M17**.
[**ORIGIN** from Latin *leguleius* pettifogger (from *leg-*, *lex* law) + **-AN**.]
▸ **A** *noun*. A lawyer. *derog*. **M17**.
▸ **B** *adjective*. Of or pertaining to petty questions of law or law language. *rare*. **L17**.
■ **leguleious** *adjective* (*rare*) = **LEGULEIAN** *adjective* **M17**.

legume /ˈlɛgjuːm/ *noun*. **M17**.
[**ORIGIN** French *légume* from Latin *legumen*, from *legere* gather: so called because the fruit may be gathered by hand.]
1 The fruit or edible portion of any leguminous plant (bean, pea, etc.) grown for food; any vegetable used as food. Usu. in *pl*. **M17**.
2 A leguminous plant. **L17**.
3 The pod or seed vessel of a leguminous plant. **L18**.

legumen /lɪˈgjuːmən/ *noun*. Pl. **-mens**, **-mina** /-mɪnə/. **LME**.
[**ORIGIN** Latin: see **LEGUME**.]
1 = **LEGUME** 1. **LME**.
2 = **LEGUME** 2. **L17**.
3 = **LEGUME** 3. **M18**.

legumin /lɪˈgjuːmɪn/ *noun*. **M19**.
[**ORIGIN** from **LEGUME** + **-IN**[1].]
BIOCHEMISTRY. A protein resembling casein, found in leguminous and other seeds.

legumina *noun pl*. see **LEGUMEN**.

leguminose /lɪˈgjuːmɪnəʊs/ *adjective*. **L17**.
[**ORIGIN** formed as **LEGUMINOUS**: see **-OSE**[1].]
= **LEGUMINOUS**.

leguminous /lɪˈgjuːmɪnəs/ *adjective*. **LME**.
[**ORIGIN** from Latin *leguminosus*, from *legumin-*, *legumen* **LEGUME**: see **-OUS**.]
1 Of or pertaining to pulse; (of a vegetable or crop) of the nature of pulse. **LME**.
2 *BOTANY*. Of or pertaining to the Leguminosae, a large family which includes peas, beans, mimosas, and other plants bearing legumes or pods, freq. with nitrogen-fixing nodules on the roots and pinnate or trifoliate leaves. **L17**. ▸**b** Like that of a leguminous plant. **L17**.
— NOTE: In isolated use before **M17**.

lehr *noun* var. of **LEER** *noun*[4].

Lehrjahr /ˈleːrjaːr/ *noun*. Pl. **-e** /-ə/. **M19**.
[**ORIGIN** German, from *lehr(en* teach + *Jahr* years.]
A year of apprenticeship or learning. Usu. in *pl*., one's apprenticeship.

lehua /leɪˈhuːə/ *noun*. **L19**.
[**ORIGIN** Hawaiian.]
An evergreen tree, *Metrosideros collina*, of the myrtle family, native to the Polynesian and Melanesian islands of the Pacific Ocean and bearing panicles of scarlet flowers. Cf. **OHIA**.

lei /leɪ/ *noun*[1]. **M19**.
[**ORIGIN** Hawaiian.]
A Polynesian garland made of flowers, feathers, shells, etc., often given as a symbol of affection.

lei /leɪ/ *noun*[2]. **E20**.
[**ORIGIN** Chinese *léi*.]
ARCHAEOLOGY. An urn-shaped Chinese bronze wine vessel of the Shang period to *c* 250 BC.

lei *noun*[3] pl. of **LEU**.

Leibnitz *noun*, **Leibnitzian** *adjective & noun* vars. of **LEIBNIZ**, **LEIBNIZIAN**.

Leibniz /ˈlʌɪbnɪts/ *noun*. Also **-tz**. **M19**.
[**ORIGIN** G. W. *Leibniz* (1646–1716), German philosopher and mathematician.]
1 *MATH*. ***Leibniz's theorem***, ***Leibniz theorem***, the theorem that the *n*th derivative of a product of two functions may be expressed as a sum of products of the derivatives of the individual functions, the coefficients being the same as those occurring in the binomial theorem. **M19**.

L

2 *PHILOSOPHY.* ***Leibniz's law***, the principle of the identity of indiscernibles. **M20.**

Leibnizian /lʌɪbˈnɪtsɪən/ *adjective & noun.* Also **-tz-**. **M18.**
[ORIGIN formed as LEIBNIZ + -IAN.]
▸ **A** *adjective.* Pertaining to or characteristic of Leibniz or his philosophy; regarding matter as a multitude of monads and assuming pre-established harmony between everything. **M18.**
▸ **B** *noun.* A follower or adherent of Leibniz. **M18.**

Leicester /ˈlɛstə/ *noun.* **L18.**
[ORIGIN A city in Leicestershire, central England.]
1 In full ***Leicester sheep***. (An animal of) a valuable long-woolled variety of sheep orig. bred in Leicestershire, England. In *Austral. & NZ* freq. more fully ***English Leicester***. See also ***Border Leicester*** s.v. BORDER *noun.* **L18.**
2 (An animal of) a long-horned variety of cattle, orig. bred in Leicestershire. **M19.**
3 In full ***Leicester cheese***. A firm-textured usu. orange-coloured full milk cheese of a type orig. made in Leicestershire. Also ***Red Leicester***. **L19.**

Leichhardt /ˈlʌɪkɑːt/ *noun.* **M19.**
[ORIGIN F. W. L. *Leichhardt* (1813–48), German explorer of Australia.]
In full ***Leichhardt pine***, ***Leichhardt tree***. A tree of the madder family, *Nauclea orientalis*, which is native to Australia and India and bears heads of yellow flowers.

Leics. *abbreviation.*
Leicestershire.

Leidenfrost /ˈlʌɪd(ə)nfrɒst/ *noun.* **M19.**
[ORIGIN J. G. *Leidenfrost* (1715–94), German physicist.]
PHYSICS. Used *attrib.* and in *possess.* with ref. to a phenomenon in which liquid, in contact with a surface whose temperature exceeds some critical value (the ***Leidenfrost point***), forms a vapour layer which insulates it from the surface.

leigh /liː/ *noun.* Also **legh**. **L18.**
[ORIGIN Unknown.]
= ***Irish deer*** s.v. IRISH *adjective.*

†**leighton** *noun.* **OE–L18.**
[ORIGIN formed as LEEK + TOWN *noun.*]
A garden.

leio- /ˈlʌɪəʊ/ *combining form* of Greek *leios* smooth, forming chiefly nouns and adjectives in *BIOLOGY & MEDICINE*: see **-O-**.
■ **leiomyˈoma** *noun*, pl. **-mas**, **-mata** /-mətə/, *MEDICINE* a myoma arising from smooth muscle **L19.** **leiomyosarˈcoma** *noun*, pl. **-mas**, **-mata** /-mətə/, *MEDICINE* a malignant sarcoma arising from smooth muscle, *esp.* a uterine fibroid **E20.** **leioˈphyllous** *adjective* (*BOTANY*) having smooth leaves **L19.** **leiotrichous** /lʌɪˈɒtrɪkəs/ *adjective* smooth-haired; having straight lank hair: **M19.** **leiotrichy** /lʌɪˈɒtrɪki/ *noun* the fact or condition of being leiotrichous **E20.**

leir *verb* see LERE *verb.*

Leishman /ˈliːʃmən/ *noun.* **E20.**
[ORIGIN W. B. *Leishman* (1865–1926), Brit. pathologist.]
MEDICINE. **1** ***Leishman body***, ***Leishman's body***, an ovoid structure consisting of a single non-flagellated leishmania found in the macrophages of people with leishmaniasis. Also ***Leishman–Donovan body***. **E20.**
2 ***Leishman stain***, ***Leishman's stain***, a mixture of eosin and methylene blue used to stain blood smears. **E20.**

leishmania /liːʃˈmeɪnɪə/ *noun.* Pl. **-ia**, **-iae** /-ɪiː/, **-ias**. **E20.**
[ORIGIN mod. Latin (see below), from LEISHMAN + -IA[1].]
ZOOLOGY & MEDICINE. **1** Any protozoon of the genus *Leishmania* (family Trypanosomidae), comprising pathogenic species occurring as non-flagellated Leishman bodies in human macrophages, and as flagellated individuals in the alimentary canal of sandflies, which act as vectors. **E20.**
2 Any flagellate of the family Trypanosomidae when existing in a leishmanial form. **E20.**
■ **leishmanial**, **leishmanian** *adjectives* caused by leishmaniae; typical of a leishmania as it occurs in humans and other mammals (i.e. as a Leishman body): **E20.** **leishmaniasis** /-məˈnʌɪəsɪs/, *noun*, pl. **-ases** /-əsiːz/, infection with or a disease caused by species of *Leishmania*, principally kala-azar and oriental sore **E20.** **leishmaniˈosis** *noun*, pl. **-oses** /-ˈəʊsiːz/, = LEISHMANIASIS **E20.** ˈ**leishmanoid** *noun* (in full ***dermal leishmanoid***) a condition occurring as a sequel to kala-azar and characterized by an eruption of whitish patches on the skin **E20.**

Leisler's bat /ˌlʌɪzləz ˈbat/ *noun phr.* **E20.**
[ORIGIN T. P. *Leisler*, 19th-cent. German zoologist.]
A small black vespertilionid bat, *Nyctalus leisleri*, of N. Africa and Eurasia. Also called ***lesser noctule***.

leister /ˈliːstə/ *noun & verb.* **M16.**
[ORIGIN Old Norse *ljóstr* (Norwegian dial. *lioster*, Swedish *ljuster*, Danish *lyster*), from *ljósta* to strike.]
▸ **A** *noun.* A pronged spear for striking and catching fish, chiefly salmon. **M16.**
▸ **B** *verb trans.* Spear with a leister. **M19.**

leisurable /ˈlɛʒ(ə)rəb(ə)l/ *adjective.* Now *rare.* **L16.**
[ORIGIN from LEISURE *noun & adjective* + -ABLE, after *comfortable*: cf. PLEASURABLE.]
1 Carried out without haste, deliberate; having leisure, leisurely. **L16.**
2 Of the nature of leisure, not requiring haste. **E17.**
■ **leisurably** *adverb* **M16.**

leisure /ˈlɛʒə/ *noun & adjective.* **ME.**
[ORIGIN Anglo-Norman *leisour*, Old French *leisir* (mod. *loisir*) from Proto-Romance use as noun of Latin *licere* be allowed.]
▸ **A** *noun* **1 a** (The state of having) time at one's own disposal; free or unoccupied time. **ME.** ▸**b** A period or spell of unoccupied time. Now *rare* or *obsolete.* **LME.**

> **a** J. RUSKIN The first volume . . took the best of the winter's leisure.

†**2** Freedom or opportunity (*to do*). **ME–M17.**
†**3** Leisureliness, deliberation. **ME–L17.**
4 Opportunity afforded by freedom from occupations (*to do*, *for*). **LME.**

> **a** P. G. WODEHOUSE The wolf at the door left little leisure for careful thought. W. STYRON He would also have the leisure to start a project which he had always cherished.

5 Time remaining, sufficient time. Now *rare* or *obsolete.* **M16.**

> SIR W. SCOTT He found himself unexpectedly in Eachin's close neighbourhood, with scarce leisure to avoid him.

– PHRASES: **at leisure** (***a***) with free or unoccupied time at one's disposal; (***b***) without haste, with deliberation. **at one's leisure** when one has unoccupied time at one's disposal; at one's ease or convenience. **attend a person's leisure**, **attend upon a person's leisure** *arch.* wait until a person is unoccupied. †**by leisure** in a leisurely manner; at one's leisure; by degrees. **gentleman of leisure** = ***man of leisure*** below. **lady of leisure** a woman of independent means or whose time is free from obligations to others. **man of leisure** a man of independent means or whose time is free from obligations to others. **stay a person's leisure**, **stay upon a person's leisure** *arch.* = ***attend a person's leisure*** above.
▸ **B** *attrib.* or as *adjective.* Of or pertaining to leisure, having leisure; free, unoccupied. **LME.**

> W. T. MILLS The ancient priesthood gathered to itself all the functions of the leisure and professional classes. F. RAPHAEL A vermilion track-suit . . and Puma leisure shoes.

– SPECIAL COLLOCATIONS & COMB.: **leisure centre**, **leisure complex** a building having sporting facilities, bars, etc. **leisurewear** informal clothes, *esp.* tracksuits, sportswear, etc.
■ **leisureful** *adjective* having much leisure, leisurely **LME.** **leisureless** *adjective* **M16.**

leisure /ˈlɛʒə/ *verb. rare.* **E20.**
[ORIGIN from the noun.]
1 *verb intrans.* Have or enjoy leisure. **E20.**
2 *verb trans.* Make leisurely. **E20.**

leisured /ˈlɛʒəd/ *adjective.* **E16.**
[ORIGIN from LEISURE *noun* + -ED[2].]
1 Characterized by or having leisure; leisurely. **E16.**

> Y. MENUHIN Tours were comparatively leisured; a few days were spent at each stopping place.

2 Having ample leisure. Esp. in ***the leisured class***(***es***). **L18.**

leisurely /ˈlɛʒəli/ *adjective.* **E17.**
[ORIGIN from LEISURE *noun* + -LY[1].]
1 Having leisure; able to proceed without haste. **E17.**

> F. DONALDSON One of those leisurely souls who believe in taking time over one's packing.

2 Of an action or agent: performed or operating at leisure or without haste; deliberate. **E17.**

> P. G. WODEHOUSE Her gaze was moving easily about the room, taking in each picture . . in a leisurely inspection.

■ **leisureliness** *noun* **E19.**

leisurely /ˈlɛʒəli/ *adverb.* **L15.**
[ORIGIN from LEISURE *noun* + -LY[2].]
At leisure, without haste; with deliberate motion or action.

> J. K. TOOLE The slowly rocking streetcars . . seemed to be leisurely moving toward no special destination.

leitmotif /ˈlʌɪtməʊtiːf/ *noun.* Also **-iv**. **L19.**
[ORIGIN German, from *leit-* leading + *Motiv* MOTIVE *noun.*]
1 *MUSIC.* A theme associated throughout a work with a particular person, situation, or sentiment. **L19.**
2 *gen.* A recurrent idea or image in a literary work etc. **L19.**

> H. ACTON She longed for a place of her own: this was the leitmotiv of her letters. J. BERMAN Staircase imagery functions as a leitmotif in Eliot's writings.

lek /lɛk/ *noun*[1] *& verb.* **L19.**
[ORIGIN Perh. from Swedish *leka* to play: cf. LAIK.]
ZOOLOGY. ▸**A** *noun.* A patch of ground which the males of certain species of bird use solely for communal breeding displays and to which the females come to mate; such a gathering or display. **L19.**
▸ **B** *verb intrans.* Infl. **-kk-**. Take part in a lek. **L19.**

lek /lɛk/ *noun*[2]. Pl. **lekë** /ˈlɛkə/, **-s**, same. **E20.**
[ORIGIN Albanian.]
The basic monetary unit of Albania, now equal to 100 qintars.

lekach /ˈlɛkax/ *noun.* **M20.**
[ORIGIN Yiddish.]
A Jewish cake traditionally made with honey.

lekane /lɛˈkɑːni/ *noun.* **E20.**
[ORIGIN Greek *lekanē* a bowl, a dish.]
GREEK ANTIQUITIES. A shallow bowl, usu. with handles and a cover.

lekanis /lɛˈkɑːnɪs/ *noun.* Pl. ***-ides*** /-ɪdiːz/. **E20.**
[ORIGIN Dim. of LEKANE.]
= LEKANE.

lekë *noun pl.* see LEK *noun*[2].

Lekh *noun & adjective* var. of LECH *noun*[3] *& adjective.*

lekker /ˈlɛkə/ *adjective. S. Afr. colloq.* **E20.**
[ORIGIN Afrikaans from Dutch (cf. German *lecker*) rel. to Dutch *likken* LICK *verb.*]
Pleasant, sweet, nice; good, excellent.

lekythos /ˈliːkɪθɒs, ˈlɛ-/ *noun.* Pl. ***-thoi*** /-θɔɪ/. **M19.**
[ORIGIN Greek *lēkuthos*. See also LECYTHUS.]
GREEK ANTIQUITIES. A vase or flask with a narrow neck.

LEM *abbreviation.*
Lunar excursion module.

leman /ˈlɛmən, ˈliː-/ *noun. arch.* Pl. **-s**. **ME.**
[ORIGIN from LIEF *adjective* + MAN *noun.*]
1 A lover, a sweetheart. Formerly (occas.), a husband or wife. **ME.**
2 An illicit lover, now *esp.* a mistress. **ME.**
■ **lemanless** *adjective* (*rare*) **M18.** **lemanry** *noun* (now *rare*) illicit love **L15.**

lemel *noun* var. of LIMAIL.

lemma /ˈlɛmə/ *noun*[1]. Pl. **lemmas**, **lemmata** /ˈlɛmətə/. **L16.**
[ORIGIN Latin from Greek *lēmma*, pl. *lēmmata*, something taken for granted or assumed, theme, argument, title, from base also of *lambanein* take.]
1 An axiom or demonstrated proposition used in an argument or proof. **L16.**
2 The argument or subject of a literary work, prefixed as a heading; the heading or theme of a scholium or annotation. Also, a motto attached to a picture etc. **E17.**
3 A word or phrase defined in a dictionary, glossed in a glossary, entered in a word list, etc.; the form of a word or phrase chosen to represent all inflectional and spelling variants in a dictionary entry etc. **M20.**

lemma /ˈlɛmə/ *noun*[2]. Pl. **lemmas**, **lemmata** /ˈlɛmətə/. **M18.**
[ORIGIN Greek, from *lepein* to peel.]
†**1** The husk or shell of a fruit. Only in **M18.**
2 *BOTANY.* The lower bract of the floret of a grass. Cf. PALEA 2. **E20.**

lemmata *nouns pl.* see LEMMA *noun*[1], *noun*[2].

lemmatical /ləˈmatɪk(ə)l/ *adjective. rare.* **M17.**
[ORIGIN from Latin *lemmat-*, LEMMA *noun*[1] + -IC + -AL[1].]
Of or pertaining to a lemma; of the nature of a lemma.
■ Also **lemmatic** *adjective* (*rare*) **M20.**

lemmatize /ˈlɛmətʌɪz/ *verb trans.* Also **-ise**. **M20.**
[ORIGIN formed as LEMMATICAL + -IZE.]
Sort into lemmas, sort so as to group together inflected or variant forms of the same word.
■ **lemmatiˈzation** *noun* **M20.**

lemme /ˈlɛmi/ *verb intrans.* (*imper.*). *colloq.* **L19.**
[ORIGIN Contr.: cf. GIMME.]
Let me.

> C. E. MONTAGUE Lemme alone. I'm an old man. C. WESTON Okay, man, lemme think.

lemming /ˈlɛmɪŋ/ *noun.* **E18.**
[ORIGIN Norwegian, Danish *lemming*, rel. to Swedish *lämmel*, Norwegian *lemen(de)*, Old Norse *lómundr*.]
1 Any of several small short-tailed Arctic rodents of the genus *Lemmus* and related genera of the family Muridae, noted for their fluctuating populations and, esp. in the Norway lemming (see below), periodic mass migrations. Formerly also ***lemming mouse***, ***lemming rat***. **E18.**
bog lemming: of the American genus *Synaptomys*. **collared lemming**: of the genus *Dicrostonyx*. **Norway lemming** a Scandinavian lemming, *Lemmus lemmus*. **steppe lemming** any central Asian vole of the genus *Lagurus*.
2 *fig.* A person bent on a headlong rush, esp. towards disaster; a person unthinkingly joining a mass migration; an unthinking person. **M20.**

> *Listener* Some lemmings . . learn sooner than others. The exodus to . . Yorkshire began several years ago. *attrib.*: D. F. HORROBIN This lemming unconcern may have dangerous consequences.

■ **lemming-like** *adjective* resembling (that of) a lemming; headlong, suicidal, unthinking: **M20.**

lemna /ˈlɛmnə/ *noun.* **L18.**
[ORIGIN mod. Latin *Lemna* (see below) from Greek *lemna*.]
Any of various aquatic plants of the genus *Lemna* (family Lemnaceae); = ***duckweed*** s.v. DUCK *noun*[1].

Lemnian /ˈlɛmnɪən/ *adjective.* **L16.**
[ORIGIN from Latin *Lemnius*, Greek *Lēmnios*, from *Lēmnos* (see below) + -AN.]
Of or pertaining to the Aegean island of Lemnos.
Lemnian earth a grey or yellowish-red clay formerly used in medicine.

†**lemnisc** *noun. rare.* Only in E18.
[ORIGIN formed as LEMNISCUS.]
1 A ribbon. E18.
2 = LEMNISCUS 1. E18.

lemniscate /lɛmˈnɪskət/ *noun & adjective.* L18.
[ORIGIN from mod. Latin *lemniscata* fem. of Latin *lemniscatus* adjective, adorned with ribbons, formed as LEMNISCUS: see -ATE².]
MATH. ▸**A** *noun.* A type of Cassinian oval with two symmetrical loops across a central node (as the figure 8), defined by the equation $r^2 = 2a^2 \cos 2\theta$. L18.
▸**B** *adjective.* Of or pertaining to lemniscates; of the nature of a lemniscate. L19.

lemniscus /lɛmˈnɪskəs/ *noun.* Pl. **-sci** /-skʌɪ, *in sense 1 also* -sʌɪ/. M19.
[ORIGIN Latin from Greek *lēmniskos* ribbon. Cf. earlier LEMNISC.]
1 The character ÷ used by ancient textual critics in their annotations. M19.
2 ZOOLOGY. Either of the two ribbon-like internal appendages associated with the proboscis of acanthocephalans. M19.
3 ANATOMY. A band or bundle of fibres in the central nervous system, *esp.* any of those connecting sensory nuclei to the thalamus. M19.

lemon /ˈlɛmən/ *noun¹, adjective, & verb.* LME.
[ORIGIN Old French & mod. French *limon* (now restricted to the lime), corresp. to Spanish *limón*, Portuguese *limão*, Italian *limone*, medieval Latin *limo, limon-*, from Arabic *līmūn, laymūn* collect. (sing. *-ūna*) fruits of the citron kind. Cf. LIME *noun³*.]
▸**A** *noun.* **1** The ovate pale yellow acid fruit of the tree *Citrus limon*, much used for making drinks and as a flavouring. LME.
2 The tree which bears this fruit, a widely cultivated member of the rue family. Also ***lemon tree***. E17.
3 Preceded by specifying word: any of several other plants bearing yellow fruit like lemons. M18.
4 The colour of a lemon; pale yellow. L18.
5 a Formerly, a person with a tart or snappy disposition. Now usu., a simpleton, a loser; a person easily deluded or taken advantage of. *slang.* M19. ▸**b** A thing which is bad, unsatisfactory, or disappointing; *esp.* a substandard or defective car. *slang* (orig. *US*). E20. ▸**c** The head. *slang.* E20. ▸**d** An informer, a person who turns state's evidence. *US slang.* M20.
6 A lemon-flavoured soft drink; lemonade or lemon juice. L19.
– PHRASES ETC.: **hand a person a lemon** pass off a substandard article as good; swindle a person, do a person down. ***oranges and lemons***: see ORANGE *noun*. ***salt of lemon***: see SALT *noun¹* 2c. ***sweet lemon***: see SWEET *adjective & adverb*. **the answer is a lemon** a reply is unsatisfactory or non-existent. ***water lemon***: see WATER *noun*.
▸**B** *adjective.* Of or resembling the colour, flavour, or fragrance of a lemon; pale yellow. M17.
– COMB. & SPECIAL COLLOCATIONS: ***lemon balm***: see BALM *noun¹* 6; **lemon cheese** a conserve made from lemons, butter, eggs, and sugar; **lemon-colour** (of) a pale yellow; **lemon-coloured** *adjective* pale yellow; **lemon curd** = ***lemon cheese*** above; **lemon drop** a boiled sweet flavoured with lemon; **lemon-game** *US slang* a type of confidence trick in which the victim is led to believe that he or she can win at pool against a player who is in fact expert; **lemon geranium** a pelargonium, *Pelargonium crispum*, grown for its lemon-scented leaves; **lemon grass** a lemon-scented grass, *Cymbopogon citratus*, native to southern India and Sri Lanka, which yields an oil used in perfumery and cookery; **lemon law** *N. Amer. colloq.* a law requiring the manufacturer or seller to repair or replace a defective car; **lemon meringue (pie)** an open pie consisting of a pastry case with a lemon filling and a topping of meringue; **lemon oil** an essential oil obtained from the rind of lemons, used in cooking and perfumery; **lemon plant** = ***lemon verbena*** below; **lemon-scented** *adjective* having a smell suggestive of lemons; ***lemon-scented verbena*** = ***lemon verbena*** below; **lemon squash** a drink made from lemons and other ingredients, often sold in concentrated form; **lemon-squeezer** (*a*) an instrument for extracting the juice from a lemon; (*b*) *NZ colloq.* a hat with a peaked crown and broad flat brim, worn ceremonially by New Zealand troops; **lemon thyme** a lemon-scented cultivated variety of thyme, *Thymus* × *citriodorus*, grown as a herb; **lemon verbena** a S. American shrub of the verbena family, *Aloysia triphylla*, grown for its lemon-scented leaves; **lemonwood** (*a*) *NZ* a small New Zealand evergreen tree, *Pittosporum eugenioides* (family Pittosporaceae), with leaves that are fragrant when crushed; (*b*) (the light-coloured wood of) any of several tropical American trees, esp. the Cuban *Calycophyllum candidissimum*, of the madder family; **lemon yellow** (of) a pale yellow.
▸**C** *verb trans.* Flavour with lemon. M18.
■ **lemonish** *adjective* somewhat resembling the colour, flavour, or fragrance of a lemon E18.

lemon /ˈlɛmən/ *noun².* M19.
[ORIGIN French *limande*, beside *lime* (cf. Italian *lima, limanda*), of unknown origin.]
In full ***lemon dab***, ***lemon sole***. A common flatfish of the eastern N. Atlantic, *Microstomus kitt*, of the flounder family, an important food fish. Also (by assoc. with LEMON *noun¹*), any of various mostly yellowish flatfishes.

lemonade /lɛməˈneɪd/ *noun.* M17.
[ORIGIN French *limonade*, from *limon* lemon: see -ADE.]
A drink made of lemon juice and water, sweetened with sugar; a synthetic carbonated drink flavoured with lemon.

lemony /ˈlɛməni/ *adjective.* M19.
[ORIGIN from LEMON *noun¹* + -Y¹.]
1 Of or resembling the flavour or fragrance of a lemon. M19.
2 Irritated, angry. *Austral. slang.* M20.

lempira /lɛmˈpɪərə/ *noun.* M20.
[ORIGIN *Lempira*, 16th-cent. chieftain who opposed the Spanish conquest of Honduras.]
The basic monetary unit of Honduras, equal to 100 centavos.

lemur /ˈliːmə/ *noun.* Pl. (in sense 1) **lemures** /ˈlɛmjʊriːz/, (in sense 2) **lemurs**. M16.
[ORIGIN (mod. Latin from) Latin *lemures* (pl.) shades of the dead.]
1 Chiefly ROMAN MYTHOLOGY. In *pl.*, the spirits of the dead, ghosts. Now occas. *sing.*, a ghost. M16.
2 ZOOLOGY. Any mammal of the prosimian family Lemuridae, comprising long-tailed, sharp-muzzled, arboreal animals found chiefly in Madagascar. Also, any related primate, as the indri and the loris. L18.
flying lemur, mongoose lemur, ring-tailed lemur, woolly lemur, etc.
■ **lemurid** /ˈliːmjʊrɪd, ˈlɛm-/ *noun* a member of the family Lemuridae L19. **lemuriform** /lɪˈmjʊərɪfɔːm/ *adjective & noun* (an animal) resembling a lemur L19. **lemurine** /ˈliːm-, ˈlɛm-/ *adjective & noun* = LEMUROID M19.

lemurian /lɪˈmjʊərɪən/ *adjective.* L19.
[ORIGIN from (the same root as) LEMUR + -IAN.]
1 (**L-**.) Of or pertaining to Lemuria, a hypothetical continent formerly supposed to have existed in the Jurassic period, stretching from Africa to SE Asia. Now *rare* or *obsolete*. L19.
2 Of or pertaining to lemurs; characteristic of lemurs. L19.

lemuroid /ˈliːmjʊrɔɪd, ˈlɛm-/ *adjective & noun.* L19.
[ORIGIN from LEMUR + -OID.]
▸**A** *adjective.* Designating or pertaining to the prosimian suborder Lemuroidea, of which the genus *Lemur* is the type. Also, resembling the lemurs. L19.
▸**B** *noun.* A lemuroid animal. L19.

Lenape /ˈlɛnəpi, ləˈnɑːpi/ *noun & adjective.* E18.
[ORIGIN Delaware *lənáːpeː*, from *lən-* ordinary + *-aːpeː* man.]
▸**A** *noun.* Pl. same, **-s**.
1 A member of the Delaware or any of various subgroups of the Delaware. E18.
2 The Algonquian language of any of these peoples. L19.
▸**B** *attrib.* or as *adjective.* Of or pertaining to the Lenape or their language(s). M19.

lenate /ˈliːneɪt, lɪˈneɪt/ *verb trans. & intrans.* E20.
[ORIGIN from Latin *lenis* soft + -ATE³.]
= LENITE.
■ **leˈnation** *noun* E20.

lend /lɛnd/ *noun. Scot., dial., & colloq.* L16.
[ORIGIN from the verb.]
A loan.

> RODDY DOYLE I thought you wanted a lend of one of me blouses or something.

lend /lɛnd/ *verb.* Pa. t. & pple **lent** /lɛnt/.
[ORIGIN Old English *lǣnan* = Old Frisian *lēna, lēnia*, Dutch *leenen*, Old High German *lēhanōn* (German *lehnen* enfeoff), from Germanic base also of LOAN *noun¹*: inf. with *-d* from late Middle English after verbs, as *bend, send*, having an analogous pa. t. & pple.]
1 *verb trans.* Grant the temporary use of (a thing) on the understanding that it or its equivalent shall be returned. Now also foll. by *out*. OE. ▸**b** *spec.* Grant the use of (money) at interest. OE. ▸**c** *verb intrans.* Make a loan or loans. OE.

> *Spectator* 20,000 books of reference (which are not, of course, to be lent out). A. MILLER Manny . . had a policy of never lending tools. R. ELLMANN Pater would get into trouble later for lending Flaubert's books to undergraduates. **b** C. HOPE The banks are falling over each other to lend him money.

2 *verb trans.* **a** Give, grant, or impart (something abstract or temporary). OE. ▸†**b** Hold out (a hand) to be taken. LME–E17. ▸**c** Give or deal (a blow). Now *dial.* LME. ▸**d** Grant the use or support of (a part of the body). L16.

> **a** R. CROMPTON He certainly lends an interest to life. M. FLANAGAN They found new ways of lending support to each other.

3 *verb refl.* Accommodate or adapt oneself *to*. Of a thing: admit of being applied *to* a purpose or subjected *to* a certain treatment. M19.

> E. BOWEN Lewis did not lend himself to the subterfuge. M. WARNOCK Brain activity . . lends itself to being described as a series of happenings or events.

– PHRASES: ***lend a hand***: see HAND *noun*. **lend an ear** listen, pay attention. ***lend colour to***: see COLOUR *noun*. **lending library** (a part of) a library from which books may be borrowed (with or without direct payment). **lend one's ears** = ***lend an ear*** above. ***lend wings to***: see WING *noun*. ***minimum lending rate***: see MINIMUM *adjective*. ***Public Lending Right***: see PUBLIC *adjective & noun*.
■ **lendable** *adjective* E17.

lender /ˈlɛndə/ *noun.* LOE.
[ORIGIN from LEND *verb* + -ER¹.]
A person who lends; *esp.* a person who or institution which makes a business of lending money at interest.
lender of last resort an institution that will lend money, usu. at a high rate of interest, to a borrower unable to obtain a loan elsewhere.

lending /ˈlɛndɪŋ/ *noun.* ME.
[ORIGIN from LEND *verb* + -ING¹.]
1 The action of LEND *verb*; *esp.* the lending of money at interest. ME.
2 †**a** In *pl.* Money advanced to soldiers when regular pay cannot be given. L16–M17. ▸**b** *gen.* A thing lent. E17.

lend-lease /lɛndˈliːs/ *adjective, noun, & verb.* M20.
[ORIGIN from LEND *verb* + LEASE *verb³*.]
= LEASE-LEND.

lene /ˈliːn/ *adjective & noun.* Now *rare* or *obsolete.* E18.
[ORIGIN formed as LENIS.]
▸**A** *adjective.* †**1** HEBREW GRAMMAR. Of a point within a Hebrew letter: denoting absence of aspiration. Only in E18.
2 PHONETICS. Of a consonant: voiceless and plosive; (occas. simply) plosive. M18.
▸**B** *noun.* PHONETICS. A (voiceless) plosive consonant. M18.

lenes *noun* pl. of LENIS *noun*.

†**leng** *noun* see LING *noun¹*.

†**leng** *verb* var. of LING *verb*.

†**lenger** *adjective & adverb.*
[ORIGIN Old English *lengra* from Germanic compar. of base of LONG *adjective¹*: see -ER³.]
▸**A** *adjective.* Longer. OE–M16.
▸**B** *adverb.* Longer. ME–L16.

lengha /ˈlɛŋgə/ *noun.* L20.
[ORIGIN Punjabi.]
An outfit worn by Indian women, comprising a long full skirt, choli, and dupatta.

length /lɛŋθ, lɛŋkθ/ *noun.*
[ORIGIN Old English *lengþu* = Dutch *lengte*, Old Norse *lengd*, from Germanic, from base also of LONG *adjective¹*: see -TH¹.]
1 Extent from beginning to end, esp. of a period of time, a speech, etc. OE. ▸**b** An instance of this; a period or duration of time, *esp.* a long period. LME.

> I. WATT Sentences . . of fairly usual length. C. HOPE The length of military service was indefinite. **b** R. K. NARAYAN She was welcome to stay any length of time.

2 The linear extent of any thing as measured from end to end; the greater of two or greatest of three dimensions of a body or figure. Also, the extent of a garment in a vertical direction when worn. LOE. ▸**b** An instance of this. E18.

> R. P. JHABVALA He looked down the length of the table. **b** J. AGEE The inward wall . . was hung solid with cassocks of all lengths. A. KOESTLER Relationship between the lengths of the sides of a right-angled triangle.

3 The distance or extent between the extremities of something specified. ME. ▸**b** The full extent of one's body. L16. ▸**c** SPORT. The distance between the nose and tail of a horse etc., or between the bow and stern of a boat, used in expressing the winning margin or lead in a race. M17. ▸**d** SWIMMING. The distance from end to end of a swimming pool; this distance as an amount swum. Cf. WIDTH 1b. E20.

> **b** TENNYSON All her fair length upon the ground she lay. **c** *Horse & Hound* Holborn Head passed the post three lengths clear.

4 a The quality or fact of being long; substantial duration or extent. Opp. ***shortness***. LME. ▸**b** Verbosity, lengthiness. Now *rare*. L16.

> **a** J. BAYLEY 'The Turn of the Screw' . . in spite of its length has . . the characteristics . . of a short story.

5 a Distance to a location or destination; distance travelled. Now *Scot.* LME. ▸**b** *fig.* A degree or extreme to which a course of action or an opinion can be taken. L17.

> **b** M. ANGELOU Disappointment drives our young men to some desperate lengths.

†**6** Reach, range. LME–E17.
7 a A (long) stretch or extent of land, hair, etc. L16. ▸**b** A piece of material etc. of a certain or distinct extent. M17. ▸**c** The penis. Also, an act of sexual intercourse. *slang.* M20.

> **b** A. T. ELLIS She had posted off a length of pale blue silk.

8 THEATRICAL. A portion of an actor's part, consisting of forty-two lines. M18.
9 BREWING. The quantity of liquid drawn off from a certain amount of malt. M18.
10 PROSODY. Quantity, esp. long quantity, of a sound or syllable. Opp. ***shortness***. M18.
11 a CRICKET. The distance from the batsman at which a (well-bowled) ball pitches; the consistent reaching of a (good) distance by the bowler. M18. ▸**b** TENNIS & BADMINTON etc. The quality of making shots to the back of the court; the consistent achievement of such play. E20.

> **a** P. WARNER Rhodes . . was accurate in his length.

12 BRIDGE. Four or more cards of the same suit held in one hand. E20.
13 MATH. The number of components in any connected sequence. M20.
– PHRASES: ***at arm's length***: see ARM *noun¹*. ***at full length***: see FULL *adjective*. **at length** (*a*) after a long time, at or in the end; (*b*) for a

L

long time, in detail, fully, (also ***at great length, at some length***, etc.). †**at the length** = *at length* above. †**draw out in length** prolong, protract. **draw out to a great length** prolong, protract. ***full length***: see FULL *adjective*. ***measure one's length, measure out one's length***: see MEASURE *verb*. ***not the length of a street***: see STREET *noun*. †**of length** long. **slip someone a length** (of a man) have sexual intercourse with someone. **the length and breadth** (throughout) the whole area, (in) all parts or directions. **the length of** *Scot.* as far as.

– COMB.: **lengthman** a person appointed to maintain a certain stretch of road, railway, or canal; **length-mark** (*a*) a phonetic symbol used to indicate the length of a sound, esp. to indicate that a vowel sound is long; (*b*) a macron indicating length; **lengthsman** = *lengthman* above.

■ **lengthful** *adjective* (*poet.*, now *rare*) long E17.

lengthen /ˈlɛŋθ(ə)n, -ŋkθ-/ *verb*. LME.
[ORIGIN from LENGTH + -EN[5].]
1 *verb trans.* Make longer, extend; prolong. Also foll. by *out*. LME. ▸**b** Make phonetically or prosodically long. M17.

J. WAIN A garrulous chairman lengthened out a . . meeting into nearly three hours.

lengthen one's grip: see GRIP *noun*[1]. ***lengthen one's stride***: see STRIDE *noun* 1a.
2 *verb intrans.* Become longer. LME.

C. MORGAN The young shoots were lengthening. DENNIS POTTER The awkward pause lengthened between them.

■ **lengthened** *adjective* made longer; long: L16. **lengthener** *noun* M16.

lengthways /ˈlɛŋθweɪz, -ŋkθ-/ *adverb*. L16.
[ORIGIN from LENGTH + -WAYS.]
In the direction of or parallel to the length of something; along the length.

lengthwise /ˈlɛŋθwʌɪz, -ŋkθ-/ *adverb & adjective*. L16.
[ORIGIN from LENGTH + -WISE.]
▸ **A** *adverb*. = LENGTHWAYS. L16.
▸ **B** *adjective*. Following the direction of the length. L19.

lengthy /ˈlɛŋθi, ˈlɛŋkθi/ *adjective*. L17.
[ORIGIN from LENGTH + -Y[1].]
1 (Of a composition, speech, etc.) of unusual length, excessively detailed, prolix; (of a period of time) long, extended, tedious. L17.

A. CARTER Ranulph Hazard, during all his lengthy marital and extramarital career, had produced no issue. A. GRAY I have replaced the lengthy chapter headings with snappier titles of my own.

2 Physically long. Now *rare*. M18.
– NOTE: Orig. an Americanism.
■ **lengthily** *adverb* L18. **lengthiness** *noun* E19.

L

Lengua /ˈlɛŋgwə/ *noun & adjective*. E19.
[ORIGIN Spanish, lit. 'tongue'.]
▸ **A** *noun*. Pl. same, **-s**.
1 A member of a S. American Indian people inhabiting the Paraguayan Gran Chaco area. E19.
2 The language of this people. E20.
▸ **B** *adjective*. Of or pertaining to the Lengua. E20.

lenient /ˈliːnɪənt/ *adjective*. M17.
[ORIGIN Latin *lenient-* pres. ppl stem of *lenire* soothe, from *lenis* soft, mild, smooth: see -ENT. Cf. French †*lénient*.]
1 Emollient, soothing, relaxing. *arch.* M17.
2 Merciful, mild, tolerant; not disposed to or characterized by severity. Also, (of punishment) mild. (Foll. by *to*, *towards*, *with*.) L18.

K. GRAHAME Supposing you were to say . . three years for the furious driving, which is lenient. *Daily Express* William's much-loved nanny . . was sacked for being too lenient with him.

■ **lenience** *noun* lenient action or behaviour, indulgence L18. **leniency** *noun* the quality of being lenient L18. **leniently** *adverb* M19.

lenify /ˈliːnɪfʌɪ/ *verb trans*. Now *rare*. M16.
[ORIGIN Late Latin *lenificare*, from Latin *lenis*: see LENIENT, -FY.]
1 Alleviate, mitigate, soothe (suffering, emotion, etc.). M16.
†**2** Soothe, soften (a part of the body); relieve (an ailment). L16–E18.

Leninism /ˈlɛnɪnɪz(ə)m/ *noun*. E20.
[ORIGIN from *Lenin*, the assumed name of Vladimir Il'ich Ulyanov (1870–1924), leader of the Bolsheviks and founder of the Soviet State, + -ISM.]
The political and economic doctrines of Marx as interpreted and applied by Lenin to the governing of the Soviet Union, to international proletarian revolution, and to the dictatorship of the working class. See also ***Marxism–Leninism*** s.v. MARXISM *noun*[1] (also called ***Marxist–Leninism***).
– COMB.: **Leninism–Stalinism** Lenin's doctrines as interpreted and applied by Stalin.

Leninist /ˈlɛnɪnɪst/ *adjective & noun*. E20.
[ORIGIN formed as LENINISM + -IST.]
▸ **A** *adjective*. Of, pertaining to, or characteristic of Lenin, his followers, or his doctrines. E20.
▸ **B** *noun*. A follower or adherent of Lenin or his doctrines. E20.
– COMB.: **Leninist–Marxist** *adjective* = ***Marxist–Leninist*** s.v. MARXIST *noun*[1] & *adjective*[1]; **Leninist–Stalinist** *adjective* of, pertaining to, or characteristic of Leninism–Stalinism.
■ Also **Leninite** *adjective & noun* E20.

lenis /ˈliːnɪs, ˈleɪnɪs, ˈlɛnɪs/ *adjective & noun*. E20.
[ORIGIN Latin: see LENIENT. Cf. LENE.]
PHONETICS. ▸**A** *adjective*. Of a consonant: weakly articulated; *spec.* designating the less or least strongly articulated of two or more homorganic consonants. See also earlier ***spiritus lenis*** s.v. SPIRITUS 1a. E20.
▸ **B** *noun*. Pl. **lenes** /-iːz/. A lenis consonant. M20.
– NOTE: Opp. *fortis*.

lenite /ˈliːnʌɪt, lɪˈnʌɪt/ *verb trans. & intrans*. E20.
[ORIGIN Back-form. from LENITION.]
Esp. in Celtic languages: make or become lenis in articulation.
■ **leˈnitable** *adjective* M20.

lenitic /lɪˈnɪtɪk/ *adjective*. E20.
[ORIGIN from Latin *lenitas* mildness, from *lenis* (see LENIENT): see -IC.]
ECOLOGY. Of freshwater organisms or habitats: inhabiting or situated in still water. Cf. LOTIC.

lenition /lɪˈnɪʃ(ə)n/ *noun*. LME.
[ORIGIN formed as LENIS + -ITION, in sense 2 after German *Lenierung*.]
†**1** A relief, a mitigation. *rare*. LME–M16.
2 In Celtic languages: the process or result of a consonant's becoming lenis or lost; weakening of articulation. E20.

lenitive /ˈlɛnɪtɪv/ *noun & adjective*. LME.
[ORIGIN medieval Latin *lenitivus*, from Latin *lenit-* pa. ppl stem of *lenire* soften, formed as LENIS: see -IVE. Cf. Old French & mod. French *lénitif*, *-ive*.]
▸ **A** *noun*. **1** A soothing medicine or medical appliance. LME.
2 Anything that mitigates or soothes; a palliative. E17.
▸ **B** *adjective*. **1** Of a medicine or medical appliance: soothing, gently laxative. Now *rare*. LME.
2 Of a person, a person's disposition, etc.: lenient, mild, gentle. Now *obsolete* exc. *Scot.* E17.
■ **lenitively** *adverb* E17.

lenity /ˈlɛnɪti/ *noun*. LME.
[ORIGIN Old French *lénité* or Latin *lenitas*, formed as LENIS: see -ITY.]
Lenience, gentleness, mercifulness; an instance of this.

leno /ˈliːnəʊ/ *noun & adjective*. Also †**lino**. Pl. of noun **-os**. L18.
[ORIGIN French *linon*, from *lin* flax: cf. LINE *noun*[1], LINEN.]
(Of) a kind of cotton gauze, used for veils, curtains, etc.; (designating) the type of weave used for this fabric.
– COMB.: **leno loom** a loom which produces leno weave.

lens /lɛnz/ *noun*. L17.
[ORIGIN Latin = lentil: so called on account of its shape.]
1 A piece of glass or other transparent substance with one or two surfaces curved or otherwise shaped to cause regular convergence or divergence of light passing through it; such a piece, or combination of pieces, as forming part of a camera etc. L17. ▸**b** *spec.* A piece of glass or plastic enclosed in a frame for wearing in front of the eyes. Also, a contact lens. L19.
contact lens: see CONTACT *noun* 4. ***simple lens***: see SIMPLE *adjective* 9. ***supplementary lens***: see SUPPLEMENTARY *adjective*. ***zoom lens***: see ZOOM *noun*.
2 a ANATOMY. The transparent elastic biconvex structure behind the iris of the eye by which light is focused on to the retina. Also ***crystalline lens***. E18. ▸**b** ZOOLOGY. Any of the facets of a compound eye. M19.
3 A biconvex body of any material, as rock, ice, water, etc. L19.
4 A structure or device analogous to a glass lens for focusing or otherwise modifying the direction of sound, electrons, radiation, etc. E20.
acoustic lens, ***gravitational lens***, etc.
– COMB.: **lens cap** a protective cap that fits over the end of a lens tube; **lens coating** a thin transparent coating applied to a lens to reduce reflection of light at its surface; **lens hood** a tube with outwardly sloping sides fitted to a camera lens to shield it from unwanted light; **lensman** = ***cameraman*** s.v. CAMERA; **lens paper**, **lens tissue** a kind of soft thin absorbent paper suitable for wiping lenses; **lens turret** a rotatable mounting fitted to the front of a camera and carrying several lenses; **lenswork** = ***camerawork*** s.v. CAMERA.
■ **lensless** *adjective* L19. **lenslet** *noun* a small lens, *esp.* one of many in a compound eye or lenticular film M20.

lens /lɛnz/ *verb*. E20.
[ORIGIN from the noun.]
1 *verb intrans.* GEOLOGY. Of a body of rock: become gradually thinner along a particular direction to the point of extinction. Usu. foll. by *out*. E20.
2 *verb trans.* = FILM *verb* 2. *US slang*. M20.
■ **lensing** *noun* (*a*) the action of the verb; (*b*) ASTRONOMY & PHYSICS an effect resembling that of a lens, *esp.* the bending of radiation by a strong gravitational field: E20.

lensed /lɛnzd/ *adjective*. M19.
[ORIGIN from LENS *noun*, *verb*: see -ED[2], -ED[1].]
1 Provided with a lens or lenses. M19.
2 ASTRONOMY. Of (an image of) a celestial object: having an appearance affected by a gravitational lens situated between the object and the observer. L20.

lensoid /ˈlɛnzɔɪd/ *adjective*. M20.
[ORIGIN from LENS *noun* + -OID.]
= LENTOID *adjective*.

Lent /lɛnt/ *noun*[1]. ME.
[ORIGIN Abbreviation of LENTEN.]
1 The season of spring. *obsolete* exc. in *comb.* below. ME.
2 ECCLESIASTICAL. The period of 40 weekdays from Ash Wednesday to Easter Eve, devoted to fasting and penitence in commemoration of Jesus's fasting in the wilderness. ME.
†**3 a** A period of fasting prescribed by any religious system. LME–L18. ▸**b** A period or indulgence of 40 days. L15–M16.
4 In *pl.* The boat races held in the spring term at Cambridge University. L19.
– COMB.: **Lent lily** the wild daffodil, *Narcissus pseudonarcissus*; **Lent term** the term in some universities etc. in which Lent falls, the spring term.

lent /lɛnt/ *noun*[2]. *obsolete* exc. *dial.* LME.
[ORIGIN pa. pple of LEND *verb*.]
The action of lending; a loan.

lent /lɛnt/ *adjective*. LME.
[ORIGIN (Old French from) Latin *lentus* slow, calm.]
†**1** Chiefly of a fever or a fire: slow. LME–L18.
2 MUSIC. In slow time. Now *rare*. E18.

lent *verb pa. t. & pple* of LEND *verb*.

-lent /lənt/ *suffix* (not productive).
[ORIGIN Latin *-lentus* -ful.]
In and forming adjectives with the sense 'full of, characterized by', as ***pestilent***, ***violent***. Cf. -ULENT.

lentamente /lɛntəˈmɛnti/ *adverb*. M18.
[ORIGIN Italian, from *lento* from Latin *lentus* slow.]
MUSIC. Slowly, in slow time.

lente /ˈlɛnti/ *adjective*. M20.
[ORIGIN Latin = slowly.]
MEDICINE. Of a substance, esp. insulin: that is metabolized or absorbed gradually when introduced into the body.

Lenten /ˈlɛnt(ə)n/ *noun & adjective*. Also **l-**.
[ORIGIN Old English *lencten* prob. from base also of Middle Low German, Middle Dutch, Dutch *lente*, German *Lenz*, etc., spring, from Germanic base of LONG *adjective*[1] (with ref. to the lengthening of the days in spring). As adjective now interpreted as from LENT *noun*[1] + -EN[4].]
▸ †**A** *noun*. **1** Spring; = LENT *noun*[1] 1. OE–ME.
2 = LENT *noun*[1] 2. OE–M17.
▸ **B** *attrib.* or as *adjective*. **1** Of or pertaining to Lent, observed or taking place in Lent. OE.

H. R. LANDON The annual Lenten concerto, which took place on 16 and 17 April.

2 Appropriate to Lent; (of food etc.) meagre, plain; (of appearance or facial expression) mournful, dismal. L16.

G. BRENAN Our cities are sad and sordid places, our food Lenten.

– SPECIAL COLLOCATIONS: **Lenten corn** corn sown about Lent. **Lenten face** a dismal look or countenance. **Lenten fare** food without meat. **Lenten-kail** *Scot.* broth made without meat. **Lenten pie** a pie containing no meat. **Lenten rose** a variety of *Helleborus orientalis*, blooming in late winter and early spring.

lentic /ˈlɛntɪk/ *adjective*. M20.
[ORIGIN from Latin *lentus* (see LENT *adjective*) + -IC.]
ECOLOGY. = LENITIC.

lenticel /ˈlɛntɪsɛl/ *noun*. M19.
[ORIGIN mod. Latin *lenticella* (French *lenticelle*) dim. of Latin *lent-*, *lens* lentil.]
BOTANY. A pore in the bark of woody stems and in some roots which allows the passage of gases.
■ **lentiˈcellate** *adjective* producing or bearing lenticels M19.

lenticle /ˈlɛntɪk(ə)l/ *noun*. L19.
[ORIGIN formed as LENTICULE.]
GEOLOGY. A lenticular piece or mass of rock, a small lentil.

lenticular /lɛnˈtɪkjʊlə/ *adjective & noun*. LME.
[ORIGIN Latin *lenticularis*, formed as LENTICULE: see -AR[1].]
▸ **A** *adjective*. **1** Shaped like a lentil or a (usu. biconvex) lens. LME.
2 Of or pertaining to a lens; using a lens or lenses. L19.
3 PHOTOGRAPHY. (Of a film, screen, etc.) embossed with minute, usu. cylindrical, lenses so that two or more images can be interspersed; designating a method of colour photography using such a film together with filters. M20.
– SPECIAL COLLOCATIONS: **lenticular cloud** METEOROLOGY a lens-shaped cloud with sharp, occas. iridescent, outlines usu. associated with lee waves. **lenticular galaxy** ASTRONOMY: having a flattened shape and dense centre like a spiral galaxy, but without spiral arms. **lenticular gland** BOTANY = LENTICEL. **lenticular nucleus** ANATOMY = ***LENTIFORM nucleus***.
▸ †**B** *noun*. A surgical knife with a lenticular shape. LME–E19.
■ **lenticuˈlarity** *noun* lenticular form or quality E20.

lenticulated /lɛnˈtɪkjʊleɪtɪd/ *adjective*. E20.
[ORIGIN from LENTICULE + -ATE[3] + -ED[1].]
Embossed with minute lenses; = LENTICULAR *adjective* 3.

lenticulation /lɛnˌtɪkjʊˈleɪʃ(ə)n/ *noun*. E20.
[ORIGIN from LENTICULE + -ATION.]
PHOTOGRAPHY. **1** The condition of being lenticulated. E20.
2 Each of the minute lenses of a lenticular film. M20.

lenticule /ˈlɛntɪkjuːl/ *noun*. L19.
[ORIGIN Latin *lenticula*: see LENTIL, -CULE.]
1 A lentil-shaped object. L19.
2 PHOTOGRAPHY. = LENTICULATION 2. M20.

lentiform /ˈlɛntɪfɔːm/ *adjective*. E18.
[ORIGIN from Latin *lent-*, *lens* lentil + -I- + -FORM.]
Shaped like a lentil or a (usu. biconvex) lens; lenticular.
■ **lentiform nucleus** ANATOMY the lower of the two grey nuclei of the corpus striatum.

lentigo /lɛnˈtʌɪɡəʊ/ *noun*. Pl. **lentigines** /lɛnˈtɪdʒɪniːz/. LME.
[ORIGIN Latin, formed as LENTIFORM.]
A freckle, a pimple; *spec*. a small brown hyperpigmented patch of skin usu. occurring on the face or hands, esp. of elderly people. Also, the condition of having such patches.
■ **lentiginous** /lɛnˈtɪdʒɪnəs/ *adjective* covered with freckles, affected with lentigo L16.

lentil /ˈlɛnt(ə)l/ *noun*. ME.
[ORIGIN Old French & mod. French *lentille* from Proto-Romance from Latin *lenticula* dim. of *lent-*, *lens* lentil.]
1 Any of the small rounded seeds of a leguminous plant, *Lens culinaris*, used in soups, stews, etc. (usu. in *pl.*); the plant itself, cultivated for food in Mediterranean countries. ME. ▸†**b** In *pl.* In full ***water lentils***, ***lentils of the water***. Duckweed (genus *Lemna*). E16–E17.
†**2** In *pl.* Freckles or spots on the skin. M16–L17.
3 GEOLOGY. A mass of rock shaped like a biconvex or plano-convex lens; *spec*. one regarded as a subdivision of a formation. L19.

lentiscus /lɛnˈtɪskəs/ *noun*. Pl. **-sci** /-skiː/, **-scuses**. LME.
[ORIGIN Latin: see LENTISK.]
= LENTISK.

lentisk /lɛnˈtɪsk/ *noun*. LME.
[ORIGIN Latin *lentiscus*, prob. of alien origin.]
The mastic tree, *Pistacia lentiscus*.

lentitude /ˈlɛntɪtjuːd/ *noun*. E17.
[ORIGIN Latin *lentitudo*, from *lentus* slow: see -TUDE.]
Slowness, lethargy.

lentivirus /ˈlɛntɪvʌɪrəs/ *noun*. L20.
[ORIGIN from Latin *lentus* slow + -I- + VIRUS.]
BIOLOGY & MEDICINE. Any of a group of retroviruses producing illnesses characterized by a delay in the onset of symptoms after infection.

lento /ˈlɛntəʊ/ *adverb & adjective*. E18.
[ORIGIN Italian.]
1 *adverb & adjective*. MUSIC. (A direction:) in slow time, slower than adagio. E18.
2 *adjective*. Pronounced more slowly than in normal speech. M20.

lentoid /ˈlɛntɔɪd/ *adjective & noun*. L19.
[ORIGIN from Latin *lent-*, *lens* lentil + -OID.]
▸ **A** *adjective*. Shaped like a lens or lentil, biconvex. L19.
▸ **B** *noun*. BIOLOGY. A lens-shaped or spherical structure composed of retinal cells adhering together. M20.

lentor /ˈlɛntə, -ɔː/ *noun*. E17.
[ORIGIN Latin = viscosity, from *lentus*: see LENT *adjective*, -OR. Sense 2 cf. Old French & mod. French *lenteur*.]
†**1** Clamminess, tenacity, or viscidity of the blood etc. E17–M19. ▸**b** A viscid component of the blood. Only in E18.
2 Slowness, lack of vitality. M18.

Lenz's law /ˈlɛntsɪz lɔː, ˈlɛnz-/ *noun phr*. M19.
[ORIGIN from H. F. E. *Lenz* (1804–65), German physicist.]
ELECTRICITY. The law that the direction of an induced current is always such as to oppose the change in the circuit or the magnetic field that produces it.

Leo /ˈliːəʊ/ *noun*. In sense 1 †**l-**. Pl. **-os**. OE.
[ORIGIN Latin: see LION.]
†**1** A lion. OE–ME.
2 (The name of) a conspicuous constellation on the ecliptic just north of the celestial equator, between Cancer and Virgo; ASTROLOGY (the name of) the fifth zodiacal sign, usu. associated with the period 23 July to 22 August (see note s.v. ZODIAC); the Lion. OE. ▸**b** ***Leo Minor***, (the name of) an inconspicuous constellation immediately north of Leo; the Little Lion. E18.

attrib.: E. KIRK Leo people are fine conversationalists.

3 A person born under the sign Leo. L19.

S. PLATH The astrologer at her elbow (a Leo).

Leonardesque /liːənɑːˈdɛsk/ *adjective*. M19.
[ORIGIN from *Leonardo* da Vinci (see below) + -ESQUE.]
Characteristic of or resembling the works of the Tuscan artist Leonardo da Vinci (1452–1519).

Leonberg /ˈliːənbəːɡ/ *adjective & noun*. E20.
[ORIGIN A town in SW Germany.]
(Designating) a breed of large dog, a cross between a St Bernard and a Newfoundland, often golden in colour; (designating) a dog of this breed.
■ **Leonberger** *noun* a Leonberg dog M20.

leone /liːˈəʊn/ *noun*. M20.
[ORIGIN from Sierra *Leone*, a country on the coast of W. Africa.]
The basic monetary unit of Sierra Leone, equal to 100 cents.

Leonese /liːəˈniːz/ *adjective & noun*. M19.
[ORIGIN from *León* (see below) + -ESE.]
▸ **A** *adjective*. Of or pertaining to the Spanish province and former kingdom of León or the town of León in this area. M19.
▸ **B** *noun*. Pl. same.
1 A native or inhabitant of León. M19.
2 The Spanish dialect of León, having affinities with Portuguese. M19.

Leonid /ˈliːənɪd/ *noun & adjective*. L19.
[ORIGIN from Latin *leo(n-)*, lion + -ID².]
ASTRONOMY. (Designating) any of a shower of meteors seeming to radiate from the constellation Leo in November.

leonine /ˈliːənʌɪn/ *adjective*¹. LME.
[ORIGIN Old French & mod. French *léonin*, *-ine* or Latin *leoninus*, *-ina*, from *leo(n-)* LION: see -INE¹.]
1 Resembling a lion, like that of a lion, lion-like. LME. ▸**b** MEDICINE. Designating the lion-like facial appearance characteristic of leontiasis. E19.

J. HELLER A splendid . . old man with a massive leonine head and an angry shock of wild white hair.

2 Of or pertaining to a lion. E16.

Leonine /ˈliːənʌɪn/ *adjective*² & *noun*. In senses A.2, B. also **l-**. LME.
[ORIGIN from male forename *Leo*, formed as LEONINE *adjective*¹.]
▸ **A** *adjective*. **1** Of or pertaining to any of the popes named Leo. LME.
Leonine City the part of Rome in which the Vatican stands, walled and fortified by Pope Leo IV.
2 Designating or pertaining to a kind of medieval Latin verse in hexameter or elegiac metre with internal rhyme. Now also, designating English verse with internal rhyme. M17.
▸ **B** *noun*. In *pl.* Leonine verse. M19.

leontiasis /liːɒnˈtʌɪəsɪs/ *noun*. *rare*. Pl. **-ases** /-əsiːz/. M18.
[ORIGIN mod. Latin from Greek, from *leont-*, *leōn* LION: see -IASIS.]
MEDICINE. Orig., a supposedly lion-like appearance of the face due to lepromatous leprosy. Now, a similar condition (more fully ***leontiasis ossea*** /ˈɒsɪə/ [Latin *osseus* bony]) arising from Paget's disease (of the facial bones).

leopard /ˈlɛpəd/ *noun & adjective*. Also (*arch.*) **libbard** /ˈlɪbəd/. ME.
[ORIGIN Old French (mod. *léopard*) from late Latin *leopardus* from late Greek *leopardos*, also *leontopardos*, from *leōn*, *leont-* LION + *pardos* PARD *noun*¹.]
▸ **A** *noun*. **1** A large carnivorous mammal of the cat family, *Panthera pardus*, of Africa and southern Asia, having a yellowish-fawn coat with dark brown or black spots grouped in rosettes. Cf. PANTHER. ME. ▸**b** Any of various other related animals. Usu. with specifying word. L18.

AV *Jer.* 13:23 Can the Ethiopian change his skinne? or the leopard his spots?

b black leopard a leopard of a black-coated variety found in SE Asia. ***clouded leopard***: see CLOUD *verb* 3. ***snow leopard***: see SNOW *noun*¹.
2 a HERALDRY. In medieval blazon: lion passant guardant, as in the arms of England. ME. ▸**b** A figure of a leopard in painting, heraldry (in post-medieval blazon), etc. ME.
3 The fur of the leopard. Also, the skin of the leopard; a coat made from this. L15.

Vogue A suède coat lined and trimmed with leopard. E. MCBAIN Two furs. A leopard and an otter.

– COMB.: **leopard cat** any of several small spotted cats, *esp.* the wild cat of SE Asia, Japan, and Taiwan, *Felis bengalensis*; **leopard frog** *US* a N. American frog, *Rana pipiens*, that is green with black pale-ringed blotches; also called ***meadow frog***; **leopard lily** (orig. *US*) any of several spotted lilies, esp. *Lilium pardalinum* (cf. PANTHER-*lily*); **leopard-man** a member of a leopard society (see below); **leopard moth** a large European goat moth, *Zeuzera pyrina*, that is white with black spots; **leopard's bane** any of various yellow-rayed plants of the genus *Doronicum*, of the composite family, much grown in gardens for their early flowers, esp. *D. pardalianches*; **leopard seal** an Antarctic seal, *Hydrurga leptonyx*, with a partly spotted coat; **leopard-skin** *adjective* (*a*) made of leopard skin or of material resembling leopard skin; (*b*) ***leopard-skin chief***, ***leopard-skin priest***, among the Nuer people of E. Africa, a mediator or arbitrator who settles disputes; **leopard snake** a colubrid snake of central Europe and western Asia, *Elaphe situla*, with blotched brown markings; **leopard society** in W. Africa, a secret society whose members dress as leopards and attack people in the manner of leopards; **leopard-tortoise** a large spotted African land tortoise, *Testudo pardalis*; **leopard-tree** (*a*) = ***letter-wood*** s.v. LETTER *noun*¹; (*b*) = ***leopard-wood*** (b) below; **leopard-wood** (*a*) (the wood of) a S. American tree of the fig family, *Brosimum guianense*; (*b*) *Austral.* (the wood of) either of two trees with spotted bark, *Flindersia maculosa* and *F. collina*, of the rue family.
▸ **B** *adjective*. Made of leopard skin or of material resembling leopard skin. L18.
■ **leopardess** *noun* a female leopard M16.

Leopardian /liːəˈpɑːdɪən/ *adjective*. L19.
[ORIGIN from *Leopardi* (see below) + -IAN.]
Of, pertaining to, or characteristic of the Italian poet and scholar Count Giacomo Leopardi (1798–1837) or his work.

leopon /ˈlɛp(ə)n/ *noun*. M20.
[ORIGIN Blend of LEOPARD and LION.]
ZOOLOGY. An animal born of a mating between a leopard and a lion.

leotard /ˈliːətɑːd/ *noun*. L19.
[ORIGIN Jules *Léotard* (1830–70), French trapeze artist.]
A close-fitting one-piece garment, usu. covering the torso and arms, worn by gymnasts, dancers, etc.; a similar fashion garment.
■ **leotarded** *adjective* L20.

lep *noun*, *verb* see LEAP *noun*¹, *verb*.

lepak /ˈlɛpak/ *verb intrans*. *SE Asia*. Infl. **-k-**. L20.
[ORIGIN from Malay *lepa* lazy.]
Spend one's time aimlessly loitering or loafing around.

Lepcha /ˈlɛptʃə/ *noun & adjective*. E19.
[ORIGIN Nepali *lāpche*.]
▸ **A** *noun*. Pl. **-s**, same.
1 A member of a people of Sikkim in India. Also called ***Rong***. E19.
2 The Tibeto-Burman language of this people. M19.
▸ **B** *attrib*. or as *adjective*. Of or pertaining to the Lepchas or their language. E19.

leper /ˈlɛpə/ *noun*¹. Now *rare* or *obsolete*. ME.
[ORIGIN Old French & mod. French *lèpre* from late Latin LEPRA.]
Leprosy.

leper /ˈlɛpə/ *adjective & noun*². LME.
[ORIGIN Prob. from attrib. use of LEPER *noun*¹.]
▸ †**A** *adjective*. Affected with leprosy, leprous. LME–L16.
▸ **B** *noun*. **1** A person with leprosy. Now usu. avoided in medical use. LME.
2 A person who is shunned, esp. on moral grounds; an outcast. E19.

E. WAUGH No one knows papa. He's a social leper. *Sunday Express* They are the lepers in every prison—child molesters, rapists.

– COMB.: **leper house** a refuge or hospital for people with leprosy.

lepid /ˈlɛpɪd/ *adjective*. Now *rare* or *obsolete*. E17.
[ORIGIN Latin *lepidus*.]
Witty, amusing; charming, elegant.

lepido- /ˈlɛpɪdəʊ/ *combining form* of Greek *lepid-*, *lepis* scale: see -O-.
■ **lepidocrocite** /-ˈkrəʊsʌɪt/ *noun* [Greek *krokis* fibre] MINERALOGY a red to reddish-brown orthorhombic hydroxide of ferric iron, usu. occurring as scaly or fibrous dipyramidal crystals E19. **lepidoˈdendron** *noun* [Greek *dendron* tree] a fossil plant of the genus *Lepidodendron*, common in coal measures, and characterized by the presence on the trunk of leaf scars M19. **lepidomelane** /-mɛˈleɪn/ *noun* [Greek *melanos* black] MINERALOGY a ferroan variety of biotite, usu. occurring in aggregations of small black scales M19. **lepidoˈsaurian** *adjective & noun* (*a*) *adjective* designating or pertaining to the large group of reptiles which have a scaly skin, including all living lizards and snakes; (*b*) *noun* a reptile of this group: L19. **lepidoˈsiren** *noun* the S. American lungfish, *Lepidosiren paradoxa* M19. **lepidotrichium** /-ˈtrɪkɪəm/ *noun*, pl. **-chia** /-kɪə/, [Greek *trikh-*, *thrix* hair] ICHTHYOLOGY any of the bony rays supporting the outer part of the fins in most teleost fishes E20.

lepidolite /ˈlɛpɪdəlʌɪt, lɪˈpɪdəlʌɪt/ *noun*. L18.
[ORIGIN from LEPIDO- + -LITE.]
MINERALOGY. A kind of mica containing lithium.

Lepidoptera /lɛpɪˈdɒpt(ə)rə/ *noun pl*. L18.
[ORIGIN mod. Latin, from LEPIDO- + Greek *pteron* wing: see -A³.]
(Members of) a large order of insects having four scale-covered wings, comprising butterflies and moths.
■ **lepidopter** *noun* an insect of this order E19. **lepidopteral** *adjective* lepidopteran E19. **lepidopteran** *adjective & noun* (*a*) *adjective* of or pertaining to the order Lepidoptera; (*b*) *noun* a lepidopteran insect: M19. **lepidopterist** *noun* a person who studies Lepidoptera E19. **lepidopterous** *adjective* lepidopteran L18. **lepidoptery** *noun* = LEPIDOPTEROLOGY M20.

lepidopterology /ˌlɛpɪdɒptəˈrɒlədʒi/ *noun*. L19.
[ORIGIN from LEPIDOPTERA + -OLOGY.]
The branch of entomology that deals with Lepidoptera.
■ **lepidopteroˈlogical** *adjective* L19. **lepidopterologist** *noun* L19.

lepidote /ˈlɛpɪdəʊt/ *adjective*. Now *rare*. M19.
[ORIGIN mod. Latin *lepidotus* from Greek *lepidōtos*, from *lepid-*, *lepis* scale.]
Chiefly BOTANY. Covered with scurfy scales.

leporine /ˈlɛpərʌɪn/ *adjective*. M17.
[ORIGIN Latin *leporinus*, from *lepor-*, *lepus* hare: see -INE¹.]
Of, pertaining to, or resembling a hare, harelike.

lepospondyl /lɛpəˈspɒndɪl/ *noun*. M20.
[ORIGIN from mod. Latin *Lepospondyli* (see below), from Greek *lepos* husk + *spondulos* vertebra.]
Any amphibian of the fossil suborder Lepospondyli, distinguished by vertebrae shaped like hourglasses.
■ **lepospondylous** *adjective* E20.

lepper /ˈlɛpə/ *noun*. *dial.* & *slang*. E20.
[ORIGIN Var. of LEAPER.]
A horse or dog that jumps, *esp.* one used for hunting or racing.

lepra /ˈlɛprə/ *noun*. **LME.**
[**ORIGIN** Late Latin, classical Latin *leprae* pl., from Greek *lepra* use as noun of fem. of *lepros* scaly, from *lepos*, *lepis* scale.]
MEDICINE. Orig., any disease characterized by scaling of the skin, *esp.* psoriasis. Now, leprosy.

leprechaun /ˈlɛprəkɔːn/ *noun*. **E17.**
[**ORIGIN** Irish *leipreachán* alt. of Middle Irish *luchrupán* alt. of Old Irish *luchorpán*, from *lu* small + *corp* body.]
In Irish folklore, a small, usu. mischievous being of human form, often associated with shoemaking or buried treasure.

leprolin /ˈlɛprəlɪn/ *noun*. **E20.**
[**ORIGIN** from **LEPROSY** + *-lin*, after **TUBERCULIN**.]
MEDICINE. = **LEPROMIN**.

leprologist /lɪˈprɒlədʒɪst/ *noun*. **E20.**
[**ORIGIN** from **LEPRA** + **-OLOGIST**.]
A medical expert in leprous diseases.

leproma /lɛˈprəʊmə/ *noun*. Pl. **-mas**, **-mata** /-mətə/. **L19.**
[**ORIGIN** from **LEPRA** + **-OMA**.]
MEDICINE. Any of the swellings of the skin, nerves, or mucous membranes characteristic of one of the principal forms of leprosy.
■ **lepromatous** *adjective* of the nature of a leproma; characterized by or exhibiting lepromas: **L19.**

lepromin /ˈlɛprəmɪn/ *noun*. **M20.**
[**ORIGIN** from **LEPROMA** + **-IN**[1].]
MEDICINE. A boiled saline extract of lepromatous tissue, used in testing resistance to leprosy.

lepropbil /ˈlɛprəfɪl/ *noun*. **M20.**
[**ORIGIN** from **LEPROSY** + **-PHIL**.]
A person who is attracted to people with leprosy.
■ **lepro'philia** *noun* attraction to people with leprosy **M20.**

leprophobia /lɛprəˈfəʊbɪə/ *noun*. **L19.**
[**ORIGIN** from **LEPROSY** + **-PHOBIA**.]
Irrational fear of leprosy; *spec.* an irrational belief that one has leprosy.

leprosarium /lɛprəˈsɛːrɪəm/ *noun*. Pl. **-ia** /-ɪə/. **M19.**
[**ORIGIN** from late Latin *leprosus* **LEPROUS** + **-ARIUM**.]
A hospital for people with leprosy.

leprose /ˈlɛprəʊs/ *adjective*. **M19.**
[**ORIGIN** formed as **LEPROSARIUM** or from **LEPRA**: see **-OSE**[1].]
BOTANY. Having a scaly or scurfy appearance; *esp.* (of lichen) in which the thallus adheres like a scurf.

leprosery /lɛˈprɒsəri/ *noun*. Also **-rie**. **L19.**
[**ORIGIN** French *léproserie*, from *lépreux* or late Latin *leprosus*: see **LEPROUS**, **-ERY**.]
A leper house; a leper colony.

leprosy /ˈlɛprəsi/ *noun*. **M16.**
[**ORIGIN** from **LEPROUS** + **-Y**[3], repl. **LEPRY**.]
1 = ***Hansen's disease*** s.v. **HANSEN** 2. In biblical translations and allusions, any disfiguring skin disease. **M16.**
2 *fig.* Moral corruption or contagion. **L16.**

leprous /ˈlɛprəs/ *adjective*. **ME.**
[**ORIGIN** Old French *lepro(u)s* (mod. *lépreux*) from late Latin *leprosus*, formed as **LEPRA**: see **-OUS**.]
1 Affected with leprosy. Also (*fig.*), foul, obscene; morally corrupt or corrupting. **ME.** ▸†**b** Causing or inducing leprosy. *rare*. **M16–E17.** ▸**c** Pertaining to, resembling, or accompanying leprosy. **M17.**

F. W. **FARRAR** Her literature . . a leprous fiction which poisoned every virtue.

2 Covered with whitish scales; *BOTANY* = **LEPROSE**; pale, unhealthy-looking. **E17.**

YEATS You that have no living light, but dropped from a last leprous crescent of the moon.

■ **leprously** *adverb* **E17.** **leprousness** *noun* **L15.**

†**lepry** *noun*. **ME–M17.**
[**ORIGIN** from **LEPER** *noun*[2] + **-Y**[3].]
= **LEPROSY**.

lepta *noun pl.* see **LEPTON** *noun*[1].

lepto- /ˈlɛptəʊ/ *combining form* of Greek *leptos* fine, small, thin, delicate: see **-O-**. Opp. **PACHY-**.
■ **leptomenin'gitis** *noun* inflammation of the leptomeninges **M19.** **leptomeninx** /-ˈmiːnɪŋks/ *noun*, pl. **-meninges** /-mɪˈnɪndʒiːz/, (*ANATOMY*) *sing.* & (usu.) in *pl.*, the arachnoid and pia mater considered together **L19.** **lepto'nema** *noun* [Greek *nēma* thread] *CYTOLOGY* = **LEPTOTENE** **E20.** **leptopro'sopic** *adjective* [Greek *prosōpon* face] having a long narrow face **L19.** **leptorrhine** /ˈlɛptərʌɪn/ *adjective* [Greek *rhin-*, *rhis* nose] *ANTHROPOLOGY* (of the nose) long and narrow; having such a nose: **L19.** **leptotene** *noun* [**-TENE**] *CYTOLOGY* the first stage of the prophase of the first meiotic division, in which the chromosomes are visible as fine slender threads **E20.**

leptocaul /ˈlɛptəkɔːl/ *noun* & *adjective*. **M20.**
[**ORIGIN** from **LEPTO-** + Greek *kaulos* stem, stalk.]
BOTANY. (A tree) having or characterized by a relatively thin primary stem and branches. Cf. **PACHYCAUL**.
■ **lepto'caulous** *adjective* = **LEPTOCAUL** *adjective* **M20.** **leptocauly** *noun* development of this type **M20.**

leptocephalus /lɛptə(ʊ)ˈsɛf(ə)ləs, -ˈkɛf-/ *noun*. Pl. **-li** /-lʌɪ, -liː/. **M18.**
[**ORIGIN** mod. Latin, from **LEPTO-** + Greek *kephalē* head.]
The transparent leaf-shaped larva of an eel or of certain other fishes.
– **NOTE**: Orig. erron. regarded as a fish of a distinct genus, *Leptocephalus*.

leptokurtic /lɛptə(ʊ)ˈkəːtɪk/ *adjective*. **E20.**
[**ORIGIN** from **LEPTO-** + Greek *kurtos* bulging + **-IC**.]
STATISTICS. Of a frequency distribution or its graphical representation: having greater kurtosis than the normal distribution.
■ **leptokur'tosis** *noun* the property of being leptokurtic **E20.**

leptome /ˈlɛptəʊm/ *noun*. Now *rare*. **L19.**
[**ORIGIN** German *Leptom*, from Greek *leptos* thin: see **-OME**.]
BOTANY. The conducting tissue of the phloem. Cf. **HADROME**.

leptomonad /lɛpˈtɒmənad/ *noun* & *adjective*. **E20.**
[**ORIGIN** from **LEPTOMONAS** + **-AD**[1].]
ZOOLOGY. (Designating) any trypanosome when existing in an elongated form (assumed only in the invertebrate host and in culture) with a flagellum emerging from the anterior end. Also = **LEPTOMONAS**.

leptomonas /lɛpˈtɒmənas/ *noun* & *adjective*. Pl. same. **E20.**
[**ORIGIN** mod. Latin (see below), from **LEPTO-** + Greek *monas* **MONAD**.]
ZOOLOGY. (Designating) any trypanosome of the genus *Leptomonas*, which includes species parasitic in insects etc. and existing in both leptomonad and leishmanial forms. Also = **LEPTOMONAD**.

lepton /ˈlɛptɒn/ *noun*[1]. Pl. **-ta** /-tə/, **-tons**. **E18.**
[**ORIGIN** Greek (sc. *nomisma* coin), neut. of *leptos* small.]
An ancient Greek coin of small value, a mite; in modern Greece until 2002, a monetary unit equal to one-hundredth of a drachma.

lepton /ˈlɛptɒn/ *noun*[2]. **M20.**
[**ORIGIN** from Greek *leptos* small + **-ON**.]
PARTICLE PHYSICS. Any of a class of subatomic particles (including electrons, muons, and neutrinos) which do not take part in the strong interaction. Cf. **HADRON**.
– **COMB.**: **lepton number** a quantum number assigned to subatomic particles that is ± 1 for leptons and 0 for other particles and is conserved in all known interactions.
■ **lep'tonic** *adjective* of, pertaining to, or involving leptons **M20.**

leptoquark /ˈlɛptəʊkwɑːk/ *noun*. **L20.**
[**ORIGIN** from **LEPTON** *noun*[2] + **QUARK** *noun*[2].]
PARTICLE PHYSICS. Any of several hypothetical subatomic particles with some properties of a lepton and some of a quark.

leptosomic /lɛptə(ʊ)ˈsəʊmɪk/ *adjective*. **M20.**
[**ORIGIN** from **LEPTO-** + Greek *sōma* body + **-IC**.]
Designating or possessing a type of physique characterized by leanness and tallness.
■ **'leptosome** *noun* (a person with) a leptosomic physique **M20.**

leptospira /lɛptə(ʊ)ˈspʌɪrə/ *noun*. Pl. **-rae** /-riː/. **E20.**
[**ORIGIN** mod. Latin (see below), from **LEPTO-** + Greek *speira* coil.]
BACTERIOLOGY. Any spirochaete bacterium of the genus *Leptospira*, which includes *L. icterohaemorrhagiae*, a parasite of rats and the cause of Weil's disease in humans.
■ **leptospiral** *adjective* pertaining to, characteristic of, or caused by leptospirae; ***leptospiral jaundice***, infectious or spirochaetal jaundice, Weil's disease: **E20.** **'leptospire** *noun* = **LEPTOSPIRA** **M20.** **leptospi'rosis** *noun*, pl. **-roses** /-ˈrəʊsiːz/, infection with, or a disease caused by, leptospirae **E20.**

Lepus /ˈlɛpəs/ *noun*. **M17.**
[**ORIGIN** Latin *lepus* hare, Lepus.]
(The name of) a constellation of the southern hemisphere immediately south of Orion; the Hare.

lere /lɪə/ *verb*. *obsolete* exc. *Scot.* Also **lear**, (*Scot.*) **leir**.
[**ORIGIN** Old English *læran* = Old Frisian *lēra*, Old Saxon *lērian* (Dutch *leeren*), Old High German *lēren* (German *lehren*), Old Norse *læra*, Gothic *laisjan*, from Germanic base also of **LORE** *noun*[1], **LEARN**.]
†**1** *verb trans.* Teach; = **LEARN** *verb* 3. **OE–M19.**
†**2** *verb trans.* Inform, tell; = **LEARN** *verb* 4. **ME–M17.**
†**3** *verb trans.* & *intrans.* Acquire knowledge of (something); = **LEARN** *verb* 1. **ME–E19.**
4 *verb intrans.* Acquire knowledge, become informed. **ME.**
■ **lered** *ppl adjective* (*obsolete* exc. *dial.*) = **LEARNED** **ME.**

lerky /ˈləːki/ *noun*. *local*. **E20.**
[**ORIGIN** Unknown.]
A children's noisy outdoor game in which players hide and then come out to try and kick a tin can etc.

lerp /ləːp/ *noun*. **M19.**
[**ORIGIN** Wemba-wemba *lerep*.]
A sweet secretion produced by insect larvae on the leaves of eucalypts and other plants; the scales produced by its solidification, eaten by Australian Aborigines.

lerret /ˈlɛrɪt/ *noun*. *dial.* **E19.**
[**ORIGIN** Unknown.]
A boat suitable for heavy seas, used around the Isle of Portland in Dorset, SW England.

T. **HARDY** The trip in the stern of the lerret had quite refreshed her.

lerve *noun* var. of **LURVE**.

les /lɛz/ *noun* & *adjective*. *slang*. Also **lez**, pl. of noun **-z(z)es**, **L-**. **E20.**
[**ORIGIN** Abbreviation: cf. **LESBO**, **LEZZY**.]
= **LESBIAN** *adjective* 2, *noun* 2.

Lesbian /ˈlɛzbɪən/ *adjective* & *noun*. In senses A.2, B.2 now usu. **l-**. **M16.**
[**ORIGIN** from Latin *Lesbius*, Greek *Lesbios*, from *Lesbos* (see below) + **-AN** (senses A.2 & B.2 from the alleged homosexuality of Sappho, poetess of Lesbos (*c* 600 **BC**): cf. **SAPPHIC**).]
▸ **A** *adjective*. **1** Of or pertaining to the island of Lesbos in the northern Aegean. **M16.**
Lesbian rule *hist.* a mason's rule made of lead, which could be bent to fit curved surfaces; *fig.* a principle allowing flexibility.
2 Of a woman: homosexual. Also, of, pertaining to, or characterized by female homosexuality. **L19.**

D. **LESSING** Thinking that two women, friends on a basis of criticism of men are Lesbian. *Atlantic Monthly* Two girls who discover in themselves the first stirrings of Lesbian attraction.

▸ **B** *noun*. **1** A native or inhabitant of Lesbos. **L16.**
2 A female homosexual. **L19.**

Pink Paper The discrimination faced by lesbians and gay men in the workplace.

■ **lesbianism** *noun* female homosexuality **L19.** **lesbic** *adjective* = **LESBIAN** *adjective* 2 **L19.**

lesbigay /ˈlɛzbɪˌgeɪ/ *adjective* & *noun*. *colloq.* **L20.**
[**ORIGIN** Orig. from **LESBI(AN)** + **GAY**; later from **LES(BIAN)**, **BI(SEXUAL)**, + **GAY**.]
▸ **A** *adjective*. Pertaining to or designating lesbians, bisexuals, and male homosexuals collectively. **L20.**
▸ **B** *noun*. A lesbian, bisexual, or male homosexual. **L20.**

lesbo /ˈlɛzbəʊ/ *noun*. *slang*. Also **L-**. Pl. **-os**. **M20.**
[**ORIGIN** Abbreviation: see **-O**. Cf. **LES**, **LEZZY**.]
= **LESBIAN** *noun* 2.

leschenaultia /lɛʃəˈnəʊtɪə/ *noun*. Also **lech-**. **E19.**
[**ORIGIN** mod. Latin (see below), from L. T. *Leschenault* de la Tour (1773–1826), French botanist and traveller: see **-IA**[1].]
Any of various herbaceous plants and evergreen shrubs of the Australian genus *Leschenaultia* (family Goodeniaceae), bearing red, blue, white, or yellow flowers.

Lesch–Nyhan syndrome /lɛʃˈnʌɪhən ˌsɪndrəʊm/ *noun phr.* **M20.**
[**ORIGIN** from Michael *Lesch* (b. 1939) and William L. *Nyhan* (b. 1926), US physicians.]
MEDICINE. A rare hereditary syndrome which affects young boys (usu. causing early death) and is marked by compulsive self-mutilation of the head and hands, together with mental disability and involuntary muscular movements.

lese /liːz/ *verb*. *obsolete* exc. *dial.* Pa. t. **lore** /lɔː/; pa. pple **lorn** /lɔːn/. **ME.**
[**ORIGIN** Repr. Old English *-lēosan* as in *forlēosan* **FORLESE**.]
1 *verb trans.* Lose. **ME.**

BACON Flowers Pressed or Beaten, do lese the Freshness and Sweetness of their Odour.

†**2** *verb intrans.* Lose, be a loser. **ME–E17.**
3 *verb trans.* Destroy; bring to ruin or perdition; spoil. **ME.**
†**4** *verb intrans.* Come to ruin; be ruined or lost. *rare*. **ME–L15.**
†**5** *verb trans.* Forsake, desert, abandon. Cf. earlier **LORN** *adjective* 2. *rare* (Spenser). Only in **L16.**

SPENSER Neither of them she found where she them lore.

lesed /liːzd/ *adjective*. *obsolete* exc. (*rare*) *SCOTS LAW*. **LME.**
[**ORIGIN** from Latin *laesus* pa. pple of *laedere* injure, hurt + **-ED**[1].]
Damaged, injured.

lese-majesty /liːzˈmadʒɪsti/ *noun*. Also ***lèse-majesté*** /lɛzmaʒɛste/. **LME.**
[**ORIGIN** French *lèse-majesté* from Latin *laesa majestas* hurt or violated majesty (i.e. of the sovereign people), from *laesa* fem. pa. pple of *laedere* injure, hurt, *majestas* **MAJESTY**.]
1 The insulting of a monarch or other ruler. Also, treason. **LME.**
2 *transf.* Presumptuous behaviour, disrespect. **M17.**

Lesghian /ˈlɛzgɪən/ *noun* & *adjective*. Also **Lezgian**. **M19.**
[**ORIGIN** from Russian *Lezgin*: see **-IAN**.]
▸ **A** *noun*. **1** A member of a people of the NE Caucasus. Formerly also, a member of a mountain people of Dagestan. **M19.**
2 The Ibero-Caucasian language of these people. **L19.**
▸ **B** *adjective*. Of or pertaining to the Lesghians or their language. **L19.**

lesion /ˈliːʒ(ə)n/ *noun* & *verb*. **LME.**
[**ORIGIN** Old French & mod. French *lésion* from Latin *laesio(n-)*, from *laes-* pa. ppl stem of *laedere* injure, hurt: see **-ION**.]
▸ **A** *noun*. **1** Injury, harm; a wound, a blemish. **LME.**
2 Orig., damage to property or rights. Now (chiefly *SCOTS LAW*), injury or loss used as grounds for annulling a contract. **M16.**
3 *MEDICINE* & *BIOLOGY*. A pathological change in the functioning or structure of an organ, body, organism, etc. **M18.**
▸ **B** *verb trans.* *MEDICINE* & *BIOLOGY*. Cause a lesion or lesions in (an animal, organ, etc.). **M20.**

†**leskar** *noun* see **LASHKAR**.

lespedeza /lɛspɛˈdiːzə/ *noun*. **L19.**
[**ORIGIN** mod. Latin (see below), from (by a misreading) V. M. de *Céspedes* (fl. 1785), Spanish governor of eastern Florida.]
Any of various leguminous herbs and shrubs of the genus *Lespedeza*, native to N. America and eastern Asia; *esp.* a plant of this kind used in the southern US as a

fodder crop and to control soil erosion. Also called ***bush clover, Japan clover***.

less /lɛs/ *adjective* (in mod. usage also classed as a ***determiner***), ***adverb, preposition, noun, & conjunction***. As conjunction also **'less**.

[ORIGIN Old English *lǣssa* = Old Frisian *lēssa* from Germanic (whence also Old English *lǣs* = Old Frisian *lēs* adverb), from Indo-European base also of Greek *loisthos* last. As conjunction partly abbreviation of UNLESS. Cf. LEAST.]

▸ **A** *adjective*. A compar. of ***little***.

1 a A smaller number of; fewer. Now *non-standard*. OE. ▸**b** Of number, amount, degree, etc.: not so great (as something mentioned or implied). Formerly also of physical size and material objects: smaller. (In attrib. use ***lesser*** is more usual.) Opp. (in mod. English) ***greater***. LOE. ▸**c** Of smaller quantity or amount; not so much. ME.

b JOSEPH HARRIS 19 is less than 20. BYRON And then the sighs he would suppress.. grew less and less. A. N. WILSON Their number was less than ten. **c** G. GREENE Things would have been different.. if Margaret had been less artist, more woman. E. BOWEN Mrs. Kearney could do with a little less weight and Miss Kevin.. with a little more. P. THEROUX Going without food he needed less sleep. W. BOYD With less reluctance than usual .. Temple allowed his father-in-law to grasp his hand.

2 Of lower status or rank; inferior. *obsolete* exc. in phrs. like ***no less a person than***. OE.

3 Designating the smaller, inferior, or (after Latin use) younger of two persons or things of the same name. *obsolete* exc. in ***James the Less*** and imitations of this. OE.

†**4** With words expressing or implying a neg.: more. *rare* (Shakes.). Only in E17.

▸ **B** *adverb*. To a smaller extent; in a lower degree; to an inferior extent, amount, etc. OE.

M. ARNOLD The less practised eye of sanguine youth. H. JAMES It didn't matter if one was a little more or a little less understood. G. VIDAL It looked smaller and less tidy than he had expected. J. MITCHELL It.. applied less in Shrieve's colony than in others.

▸ **C** *preposition*. With the subtraction of; minus. Orig. following the quantity to be subtracted. OE.

Times Cost of paint.. Less VAT input tax.. £500.

▸ **D** *noun*. A smaller amount, quantity, or number (*than* one that is mentioned or implied, *of* something). OE.

C. H. SPURGEON The less said about her the better. J. CONRAD In less than two minutes he was back in the brig. W. FAULKNER The face.. showed less of the ravages of passions.. than his own.

▸ **E** *conjunction*. Unless. Now *US dial. & colloq.* ME.

— PHRASES (of adjective, adverb, & noun): **do less than** do anything other than (freq. in neg. contexts). **do no less** do nothing else or other (*than*). **in less than no time** *colloq.* very soon, very quickly. ***know little and care less***, ***know nothing and care less***: see KNOW *verb*. †**less in** inferior in point of. **less is more**: expr. the view that a minimalist approach in matters of aesthetics is more effective. **less of** †(***a***) = *less in* above; (***b***) ***less of a*** —, a — to a smaller extent; (***c***) *colloq.* (as imper.) let us have less of, desist from (an action). **less than** (***a***) not at all, by no means; †(***b***) unless. ***more haste, less speed***: see HASTE *noun*. ***more or less***: see MORE *adjective* etc. **much less**: introducing a statement or suggestion regarded as still more unacceptable than one that has just been denied. ***NE'ER the less***. ***no less***: see NO *adverb*². †**nothing less** least of all things, anything rather (than the thing in question). **nothing less than** †(***a***) far from being, anything rather than; (***b***) the very same thing as; quite equal to. ***not the less***: see NOT *adverb*. **still less** = *much less* above. **the less** a thing which or person who is smaller or less (of two things compared).

less /lɛs/ *verb*. Long *rare*. ME.

[ORIGIN from LESS *adjective*.]

†**1** *verb intrans.* = LESSEN *verb* 1. ME–E17.

2 *verb trans.* = LESSEN *verb* 2. ME.

-less /lɪs/ *suffix*.

[ORIGIN Old English *-lēas* from *lēas* devoid (of), free (from), from Germanic base also of LOOSE *adjective*.]

1 Forming adjectives & adverbs from nouns with the sense 'free from, lacking (a), without (a)', as ***doubtless***, ***fearless***, ***hatless***, ***powerless***.

2 Forming adjectives from verbs with the senses 'unable to be —ed', as ***countless***, ***tireless***; 'that does not —', as ***fadeless***.

■ **-lessly** *suffix*: forming corresp. adverbs. **-lessness** *suffix*: forming corresp. nouns.

lessee /lɛˈsiː/ *noun*. L15.

[ORIGIN Anglo-Norman *lessee*, Old French *lessé*, pa. pples of *lesser* (mod. *laisser*): see LEASE *noun*³, -EE¹.]

A person to whom a lease is granted; a person holding property under a lease, a tenant.

■ **lesseeship** *noun* the condition or position of a lessee E19.

lessen /ˈlɛs(ə)n/ *verb*. LME.

[ORIGIN from LESS *adjective* + -EN⁵; superseded LESS *verb*.]

1 *verb intrans.* Become less in size, quantity, amount, scope, etc.; decrease. LME. ▸**b** Decrease in apparent size as a result of increasing distance. E17.

PERCY WHITE Amongst the lessening throng of dancers. D. JOHNSON Soon the rain lessened.

2 *verb trans.* Make less in size, quantity, amount, scope, etc.; diminish. LME.

J. C. POWYS The car.. lessened its pace the moment he stood still. A. HARDING Only time would lessen my feeling for my cousin.

3 *verb trans.* Represent as less; extenuate, palliate (a fault); disparage, belittle. *arch.* LME.

†**4** *verb trans.* Lower the dignity, position, or character of; humble; degrade, demean. LME–L18.

†**5** *verb trans.* In *pass.* Suffer loss or curtailment *of*; be reduced *in* (some quality). LME–L18.

lessen /ˈlɛs(ə)n/ *conjunction*. *US dial.* L19.

[ORIGIN Repr. a pronunc. of *less than*.]

Unless.

lesser /ˈlɛsə/ *adjective, noun, & adverb*. ME.

[ORIGIN from LESS *adjective* + -ER³: a double compar.]

▸ **A** *adjective*. **1** Not so great or much (as something mentioned or implied); inferior, of lower status or worth; smaller. Chiefly, & now only, *attrib.* ME.

A. DESAI The lesser functionaries of the camp to whom the commandant left the daily routine. F. WELDON Lesser men do that, who don't have the same sensitivities. DENNIS POTTER He did not call out, nor make any lesser sign of distress.

2 *spec.* ▸**a** Designating the smaller of two similar or related plants, animals, anatomical parts, or places. Opp. ***greater*** (see GREAT *adjective* 7e). Cf. LEAST *adjective* 4. E17. ▸**b** MUSIC. Designating a minor interval. Now *rare*. L17.

a ***Lesser Antilles***, ***lesser celandine***, ***lesser noctule***, ***lesser omentum***, ***lesser spotted woodpecker***, etc.

— SPECIAL COLLOCATIONS: **Lesser Asia** *arch.* Asia Minor. ***Lesser BAIRAM***. ***Lesser Bear***: see BEAR *noun*¹ 2. **lesser breed** people of inferior status. ***lesser diesis***: see DIESIS 1. ***Lesser Dog***: see DOG *noun* 5. ***lesser doxology***: see DOXOLOGY 2. ***Lesser Entrance***: see ENTRANCE *noun*. ***lesser evil***: see EVIL *noun*¹. ***lesser fry***: see FRY *noun*¹. **lesser light** [*Genesis* 1:16] a person of less eminence or importance. ***Lesser Wain***: see WAIN *noun*¹ 2.

▸ **B** *absol.* as *noun*. The lesser person or thing. L15.

lesser of two evils: see EVIL *noun*¹.

▸ **C** *adverb*. = LESS *adverb*. Long *obsolete* exc. in ***lesser-known adjective*** L16.

■ **lesserness** *noun* (*rare*) M16.

lesses /ˈlɛsɪz/ *noun pl.* *arch.* LME.

[ORIGIN Old French & mod. French *laisses* (mod. also *laissées*), from *laisser* to leave.]

HUNTING. The droppings of a beast of prey.

lessest /ˈlɛsɪst/ *adjective & noun*. *obsolete* exc. *dial.* M16.

[ORIGIN from LESS *adjective* + -EST¹.]

(The) least.

lessive /ˈlɛsɪv/ *noun*. *rare*. L18.

[ORIGIN Old French & mod. French from late Latin *lixiva* use as noun of pl. of *lixivus* var. of *lixivius*: see LIXIVIUM.]

A lye of wood ashes, soap suds, etc., used in washing.

lessness /ˈlɛsnɪs/ *noun*. *rare*. LME.

[ORIGIN from LESS *adjective* + -NESS.]

The quality or condition of being less; inferiority.

lesson /ˈlɛs(ə)n/ *noun*. ME.

[ORIGIN Old French & mod. French *leçon* formed as LECTION.]

†**1** Matter intended to be read or listened to; a public reading, a lecture; a course of lectures. ME–E18.

2 CHRISTIAN CHURCH. A passage of Scripture or other religious writing (appointed to be) read during a liturgical service (usually, a passage other than the Gospel at the Eucharist); *esp.* either of two such passages (see ***first lesson***, ***second lesson*** below) in Anglican matins and evensong. ME.

first lesson: from the Old Testament and forming the first of two in matins and evensong. ***proper lesson***: see PROPER *adjective* 2. **second lesson**: from the New Testament and forming the second of two in matins and evensong.

†**3** The action of reading to oneself; study (*of*). ME–L15.

4 A portion of a book or dictated matter to be studied by a pupil for repetition to the teacher; something that is learned or intended to be learned. ME.

R. K. NARAYAN I could hear my classmates shouting their lessons in unison. S. COOPER Knots had been another of her father's favourite lessons.

5 A continuous portion of teaching given to a pupil or class at one time; any of the portions into which a course of instruction is divided. ME.

E. BLISHEN Every lesson was an hour long. N. HINTON The bell rang for the first lesson.

give lessons give systematic instruction (*in* a subject) over a period. ***take lessons***: see TAKE *verb*.

6 An occurrence from which instruction may be gained; an instructive example; a rebuke or punishment calculated to prevent a repetition of an offence. LME.

G. STEIN It was a lesson to poor Mrs. Haydon not to do things any more for anybody.

learn one's lesson *fig.* be wiser as a result of an unpleasant, painful, etc., experience. **read a person a lesson** *fig.* reprimand or punish a person. **teach a person a lesson** *fig.* punish a person.

†**7** A musical exercise or composition. L16–E19.

— COMB.: **lesson-piece** a piece of material on which to practise needlework.

lesson /ˈlɛs(ə)n/ *verb trans.* *arch.* M16.

[ORIGIN from the noun.]

Give a lesson or lessons to, instruct, teach; admonish, rebuke. Also, bring *into* or *to* (a certain state) by giving a lesson or lessons.

lessor /lɛˈsɔː, ˈlɛsɔː/ *noun*. LME.

[ORIGIN Anglo-Norman *lesso(u)r*, from *lesser*: see LEASE *noun*³, -OR.]

A person who grants a lease.

lessy *noun & adjective* var. of LEZZY.

lest /lɛst/ *conjunction*.

[ORIGIN Old English *þȳ lǣs þe* whereby less that (*þȳ* THE *adverb*, *lǣs* less, *þe* rel. particle), late Old English *þe lǣste*, from which the first word was lost by aphesis in Middle English.]

1 A neg. particle of intention or purpose, introducing a subjunct. clause expr. something to be prevented or guarded against: in order that.. not. Also †***lest that***. OE.

R. KIPLING Lord God of Hosts, be with us yet, Lest we forget, lest we forget. M. SINCLAIR She drew in her breath lest he should hear it now.

2 After verbs of fearing or phrs. indicating apprehension or danger, introducing a subjunct. clause expr. the event that is feared: that. OE.

F. CLISSOLD I felt a strong inclination to sleep, and feared lest I should drop down.

leste /ˈlɛstə/ *noun*. M19.

[ORIGIN Portuguese = east wind.]

A hot dry east wind in Madeira and the Canary Islands.

lestobiosis /ˌlɛstəʊbʌɪˈəʊsɪs/ *noun*. E20.

[ORIGIN from Greek *lestēs* robber + -O- + Greek *biōsis* way of life, after *symbiosis* etc.]

ZOOLOGY. A form of symbiosis found among certain social insects in which a small species inhabits the nest of a larger one and feeds on the food stored there, or on the brood of the larger species.

■ **lestobiotic** /-ˈɒtɪk/ *adjective* exhibiting lestobiosis E20.

Lestrigon /ˈlɛstrɪɡ(ə)n/ *noun*. Also **Lae-** /ˈliː-, ˈlʌɪ-/. Pl. **Lestrigones** /lɛˈstrɪɡəniːz/, **Lestrigons**. L16.

[ORIGIN (Latin *Laestrygones* pl. from) Greek *Lestrugones*.]

= LESTRIGONIAN *noun*. Formerly also *transf.*, a cannibal, a monster.

Lestrigonian /lɛstrɪˈɡəʊnɪən/ *noun & adjective*. Also **Lae-** /liː-, lʌɪ-/. M16.

[ORIGIN formed as LESTRIGON + -IAN.]

▸ **A** *noun*. A member of a cannibal people of southern Italy in Homer's *Odyssey*. M16.

▸ **B** *adjective*. Of or pertaining to the Lestrigonians. E17.

let /lɛt/ *noun*¹. ME.

[ORIGIN from LET *verb*².]

1 Hindrance, obstruction; a thing that hinders, an impediment. *arch.* exc. in ***let or hindrance***, ***without let*** (***or hindrance***). ME.

2 TENNIS & FIVES etc. Obstruction of the ball in a way specified in the rules, on account of which it must be served again; an instance of this. In TENNIS also, (a ruling requiring) an additional serve when a line judge and umpire disagree on the outcome of the previous play. E19.

let /lɛt/ *noun*². L17.

[ORIGIN from LET *verb*¹.]

The action or an act of letting accommodation or a property for hire or rent.

— NOTE: Rare before 19.

let /lɛt/ *verb*¹. Infl. **-tt-**. Pa. t. & pple **let**.

[ORIGIN Old English *lǣtan* = Old Frisian *lēta*, Old Saxon *lātan* (Dutch *laten*), Old High German *lāzan* (German *lassen*), Old Norse *láta*, Gothic *lētan*, from Germanic (orig. redupl.) verb from base rel. to that of LATE *adjective*.]

▸ **I** Leave; allow to pass.

†**1** *verb trans.* Allow to remain, leave behind; refrain from taking away, using, consuming, occupying, etc. OE–M17.

†**2 a** *verb trans.* Leave undone; leave out, omit; omit or forbear *to do*. Cf. LET *verb*² 2. OE–M17. ▸**b** *verb intrans.* Desist, forbear. (Foll. by *of*, *from*.) Cf. LET *verb*² 2. ME–M16.

†**3** *verb trans.* Leave (a task, responsibility, bequest) *to* someone else. OE–E17.

4 *verb trans.* Allow the escape of (confined fluid); shed (tears, blood); emit (breath, a sound, etc.). Now *rare* exc. in ***let blood*** s.v. BLOOD *noun*. OE.

5 a *verb trans.* Grant the possession and use of (land, a building, a room, movable property) to or *to* another in consideration of rent or hire; award (a contract). Formerly also, lend (money) at interest. OE. ▸**b** *verb intrans.* Of property etc.: be let. L18.

a S. SPENDER The West End is full of shops to let. P. NORMAN So she gravitated upwards, letting the ground floor to tenants. *Daily Telegraph* The contract has been let for the M40.. road. **b** O. ONIONS That the old place should suddenly let over his head seemed.. the slightest of risks.

6 *verb trans.* Set free, liberate. Also with adjective compl. Long *obsolete* exc. in ***let loose*** below. OE.

†**7** *verb trans. & intrans.* (with *of*). Omit or cease to speak of. Only in ME.

†**8** *verb trans.* Leave, abandon, forsake; abandon *to* the flames. ME–L16.

L

†**9** *verb trans.* Lose (one's life, virtue, honour, etc.). ME–L16.
10 *verb trans.* Allow to pass or go. Foll. by *to, into*, etc. LME.

A. T. ELLIS She felt that she had let it into her mind something evil.

▸ **II** Uses with a following inf. (usu. without *to*).
11 a *verb trans.* Not prevent or forbid; permit, allow. Also *ellipt.* with inf. understood. OE. ▸†**b** *verb intrans.* Give permission. M16–E18.

a J. KEBLE If they be indulged and let to run wild. M. MORRIS They might march directly down upon Montrose's left flank—if Montrose would let them. J. STEINBECK He stood aside and let the doctor and his man enter. I. MURDOCH He never let himself doze in the mornings. *Daily Mirror* You're letting her spoil your sex life.

12 *verb trans.* Cause. Now only foll. by *know* exc. as passing into sense 11a above. OE.

Financial Times He has let it be known that he might be available to help.

13 *verb trans.* In *imper.* (with noun or pronoun as obj.) as aux. verb, with inf. serving as 1st or 3rd person imper. of the following verb, in exhortations, commands, and assumptions to be made. Also *ellipt.* with inf. understood. ME. ▸**b** *ellipt.* Let *us* etc. go. *arch.* L16.

E. NESBIT 'There are steps down,' said Jimmy . . . 'Don't let's,' said Kathleen. R. P. JHABVALA Let us be thankful for small mercies. **b** SIR W. SCOTT Let us home ere the storm begins to rage.

▸ **III** Behave, appear, think.
†**14 a** *verb trans.* With compl.: regard as. With obj. and inf., or clause: consider *to be, that* (a person or thing) *is*. OE–LME. ▸**b** *verb intrans.* Think. ME–L15.
†**15** *verb intrans.* Behave, conduct oneself; have (a particular) behaviour or appearance; make *as though*, pretend. LOE–L18.
†**16** *verb intrans.* Think (highly, lightly, much, etc.) *of*. Also foll. by *by, to*. LOE–E17.

– PHRASES: (A selection of cross-refs. only is included: see esp. other verbs.) ***let alone***: see ALONE 1. ***let a person blood***: see BLOOD *noun*. **let a person have it** *slang* direct a blow or shot at a person; assail with blows or words. **let at** (now *Scot.*) discharge missiles at, assail. **let be** (*a*) *verb phr. trans.* = ***let alone*** (a) s.v. ALONE 1 above; (*b*) *verb phr. intrans.* desist; (*c*) *verb phr. trans.* (chiefly *Scot.*) = ***let alone*** (b) s.v. ALONE 1 above. ***let drive***: see DRIVE *verb* 11. **let drop** (*a*) = ***let fall*** (b) below; (*b*) ***let it drop***, let the matter end there, not continue with the matter (freq. in *imper.*). **let 'em all come** *colloq.*: expr. cheerful defiance. **let fall** (*a*) lower, cause to fall; (*b*) = DROP *verb* 11; †(*c*) allow to lapse; proceed no further with; (*d*) GEOMETRY draw (a perpendicular) to a line from a point not on it (foll. by *on*); (*e*) shed (tears). ***let fly***: see FLY *verb*. **let go** (*a*) allow to escape or go free, set at liberty; release; (*b*) relax or relinquish (one's hold); (*c*) relax or relinquish one's hold (*of*); (*d*) dismiss from one's thoughts; cease to attend to or control; ***let it go at that***: see GO *verb*; (*e*) cease to restrain; chiefly *refl.*, give way to enthusiasm, an impulse, etc.; also, cease to take trouble about one's appearance, habits, etc.; (*f*) drop (an anchor); (*g*) dismiss (an employee). **let know** inform (a person). **let loose** set free, set at large, (esp. something fierce or uncontrollable); ***all hell let loose***: see HELL *noun*. ***let me see***: see SEE *verb*. ***let pass***: see PASS *verb*. ***let rip***: see RIP *verb*[1]. **let's** *colloq.* let us; ***let's pretend***, a game of pretence or make-believe; ***let's you and me, let's you and I, let's us*** (*US colloq.*), let us do. **let slip** (*a*) *verb phr. trans.* & *intrans.* loose (a hound) from the lease in order to begin the chase; (*b*) *verb phr. trans.* allow to escape through carelessness; fail to take (an opportunity); ***let slip through one's fingers***: see FINGER *noun*. ***let stew, let stew in one's own juice***: see STEW *verb*. ***let the world wag (as it will)***: see WAG *verb*. ***let walk***: see WALK *verb*[1]. ***let well alone***: see WELL *adjective*. ***let wit***: see WIT *verb*. ***not let the grass grow under one's feet***: see GRASS *noun*.

– WITH ADVERBS IN SPECIALIZED SENSES: **let down** (*a*) *verb phr. trans.* lower; cause or allow to descend by gradual motion or short stages; lower in status, intensity, or strength; ***let a person down gently, let a person down easily*** (*colloq.*), treat considerately so as to spare a person's self-respect; avoid humiliating a person abruptly; ***let one's hair down***: see HAIR *noun*; (*b*) *verb phr. trans.* disappoint; fail in supporting, aiding, or justifying (a person, team, etc.); freq. in ***let the side down*** s.v. SIDE *noun*; (*c*) *verb phr. intrans.* (*US*) diminish, deteriorate; relax; (*d*) *verb phr. trans.* (of a cow) give (milk); (*e*) *verb phr. intrans.* (of an aircraft or a pilot) descend prior to making a landing. (*f*) *verb phr. trans.* lengthen (a garment); lower (a hem) in order to lengthen a garment; (*g*) *verb phr. trans.* deflate (a tyre). **let in** (*a*) allow to enter; give admittance to (a person), esp. into a dwelling; open the door of a dwelling to; *refl.* enter the dwelling where one lives, usually by means of a key; (*b*) ***let in on***, allow to share (confidential information, privileges, etc.); (*c*) insert into the surface or substance of a thing; (*d*) *arch.* give rise to; (*e*) *colloq.* involve in loss or difficulty by fraud, financial failure, etc.; ***let in for***, involve in, commit to, (something unpleasant or unexpected); (*f*) in driving a motor vehicle, engage (the clutch) by releasing one's pressure on the clutch pedal. **let off** (*a*) discharge (a gun, a firework) with an explosion; *fig.* crack (a joke); ***let off steam***: see STEAM *noun*; (*b*) allow to go or escape; excuse from punishment, a duty, etc.; punish lightly *with* a specified punishment; (*c*) let or lease (property) in portions; (*d*) allow to alight from a bus etc. **let on** *colloq.* (*a*) reveal, divulge, disclose, or betray a fact by word or look (foll. by *to* a person, *that* or *why* something is the case); (*b*) pretend (*that, to do*). **let out** (*a*) *verb phr. trans.* give egress to; cause, allow, or enable to go out or escape by an opening, esp. through a doorway; set free, liberate; release from prison or confinement; *fig.* excuse or release from an obligation; ***let the cat out of the bag***: see CAT *noun*[1]; (*b*) ***let out of***, permit to be absent from (esp. one's sight); (*c*) *verb phr. trans.* give vent to (anger etc.); give expression to (a thought); (*d*) *verb phr. trans.* release (a reef) so as to increase the size of a sail; make (a garment) fuller or looser by allowing extra material at the seams; alter (the seams) in order to increase the fullness or size of a garment; (*e*) *verb phr. trans.* put out to hire or contract; distribute among several tenants or hirers; *arch.* lend (money) at interest; (*f*) *verb phr. trans.* divulge, disclose; freq. with clause as obj.; (*g*) *verb phr. intrans.* & *trans.* strike out with (the fist, the heels, etc.); give way to invective, use strong language; (*h*) *verb phr. trans.* & *intrans.* (*colloq.*) give (a horse) its head; drive (a motor vehicle) very fast; (*i*) *verb phr. trans.* in driving a motor vehicle, release (the clutch), (*j*) *verb phr. intrans.* (*N. Amer.*) (of a class, meeting, entertainment, etc.) finish, come to an end. **let through** allow to pass. **let up** *colloq.* (*a*) become less intense or severe; cease; ***let up on*** (*US*), cease to have to do with; (*b*) relax one's efforts.

– WITH PREPOSITIONS IN SPECIALIZED SENSES: **let into** (*a*) allow to enter; (*b*) insert into the surface or substance of; (*c*) introduce to the knowledge of, make acquainted with. **let off** excuse from (a punishment, duty, etc.).

– COMB.: **let's-pretend** *adjective* pretended, counterfeit; imaginary.
■ **letting** *noun* (*a*) the action of the verb; an instance of this; freq. with adverb or verb; (*b*) a property that is let or available for letting: LME.

let /lɛt/ *verb*[2]. *arch.* Infl. **-tt-**. Pa. t. & pple **let, letted**.
[ORIGIN Old English *lettan* = Old Frisian *letta*, Old Saxon *lettian* (Dutch *letten*), Old High German *lezzen*, Old Norse *letja*, Gothic *latjan*, from Germanic base of LATE *adjective*.]
1 *verb trans.* Hinder, prevent, obstruct. Now chiefly in ***let and hinder***. (Foll. by *from*, †*of*, †*to do*, †*that*.) OE.

Daily Telegraph A Church let and hindered from striking out boldly on new paths.

†**2** *verb intrans.* & *trans.* Check or withhold oneself, desist, forbear; omit *to do*. (Not always distinguishable from LET *verb*[1] 2.) Only in ME.
†**3** *verb intrans.* Be a hindrance. LME–M17.

-let /lɪt, lət/ *suffix*.
[ORIGIN Orig. from Old French *-elette*, from *-et(e)* -ET[1] added to words in *-el* -EL[2] 1 (also = Latin *-ale* -AL[1]).]
Forming nouns from nouns.
1 Denoting a smaller or lesser kind, as ***booklet, flatlet, starlet***.
2 Denoting an article worn on the part of the body signified by the base, as ***anklet, necklet***.
– NOTE: Words from Old French include *bracelet, chaplet, crosslet, frontlet, gauntlet, hamlet, mantelet*. Early English formations are *armlet, ringlet, townlet* (all M16). The suffix became common only in 18 (*cloudlet, leaflet, streamlet*), and prolific in 19.

letch /lɛtʃ/ *noun*[1]. Now *rare*. L18.
[ORIGIN Perh. from LATCH *verb*[1], infl. by LECH *noun*[2].]
A craving, a longing.

letch *noun*[2], *verb*, †**letcher** *noun* & *verb*, etc., vars. of LECH *noun*[2] etc.

let-down /ˈlɛtdaʊn/ *noun* & *adjective*. M18.
[ORIGIN from ***let down*** s.v. LET *verb*[1].]
▸ **A** *noun*. **1** A disappointment; a drawback, a disadvantage. M18.

A. LURIE They sent me to Fresh Air Camp. What a let-down. J. HELLER He felt a melancholy let-down at the thought she might not care.

2 The descent of an aircraft or spacecraft prior to landing. M20.
3 The flow of milk in a nursing mother or a cow as a reflex response to suckling or massage. M20.
▸ **B** *attrib. adjective*. Able to be let down or lowered. M20.

let-go /ˈlɛtgəʊ/ *noun*. Pl. **-o(e)s**. M17.
[ORIGIN from ***let go*** s.v. LET *verb*[1].]
An act of letting go.

lethal /ˈliːθ(ə)l/ *adjective* & *noun*. L16.
[ORIGIN Latin *lethalis*, from *lethum* var. of *letum* death, by assoc. with Greek *lēthē*: see LETHE, -AL[1].]
▸ **A** *adjective*. **1** THEOLOGY. Causing or resulting in spiritual death; entailing damnation. Formerly esp. of sin: mortal. L16.
2 Causing or capable of causing death, deadly; resulting in death. E17. ▸**b** GENETICS. Of an allele or chromosomal abnormality (such as a deletion): resulting in the death of an individual possessing it before the normal span or before sexual maturity; capable of causing such premature death when homozygous. E20.

A. G. GARDINER I struck a swift, lethal blow with my right hand.

3 Of or pertaining to death. E17.
4 *fig.* Harmful, damaging; destructive, devastating. Also, (of a shot in football etc.) very accurate. M19.

V. BROME An aching head—the result of one particularly lethal champagne party.

– SPECIAL COLLOCATIONS: **lethal chamber**: in which to kill people or animals by means of a toxic gas. **lethal dose** the amount of a toxic substance that causes death in people or animals. **lethal injection**: administered for the purposes of euthanasia or as a means of capital punishment.
▸ **B** *noun*. GENETICS. A lethal allele or chromosomal abnormality. E20.
■ **lethally** *adverb* M17.

lethality /lɪˈθalɪti/ *noun*. M17.
[ORIGIN from LETHAL + -ITY.]
The condition or quality of being lethal; ability to cause death.

lethargic /lɪˈθɑːdʒɪk/ *adjective* & *noun*. LME.
[ORIGIN Latin *lethargicus* from Greek *lēthargikos*, from *lēthargos*: see LETHARGY, -IC.]
▸ **A** *adjective*. **1** Affected with lethargy; of or pertaining to lethargy. LME.

O. MANNING The city was lethargic, the palace dormant. G. GORDON Edward, not an especially lethargic man, was worn out by the time he reached the office.

2 Causing lethargy. E18.
▸ †**B** *noun*. A lethargic person. LME–M18.
■ **lethargical** *adjective* = LETHARGIC *adjective* 1 E17. **lethargically** *adverb* M17. **lethargicalness** *noun* M17.

lethargize /ˈlɛθədʒʌɪz/ *verb trans.* Also **-ise**. E17.
[ORIGIN from LETHARGY + -IZE.]
Affect with lethargy.

lethargy /ˈlɛθədʒi/ *noun* & *verb*. LME.
[ORIGIN Old French *litargie* (mod. *léthargie*) from late Latin *lethargia* (medieval Latin *litargia*, after medieval Greek pronunc.) from Greek *lēthargia*, from *lēthargos* forgetful, from *lēth-* base of *lanthanesthai* forget.]
▸ **A** *noun*. **1** A condition of torpor, inertness, or apathy; lack of vitality. LME.
2 MEDICINE. A pathological state of sleepiness or deep unresponsiveness and inactivity. Now *rare*. LME.
▸ **B** *verb trans.* = LETHARGIZE. *rare*. E17.

Lethe /ˈliːθi, -iː/ *noun*. M16.
[ORIGIN Latin from Greek *lēthē* forgetfulness, oblivion, from *lēth-*: see LETHARGY.]
1 In Greek mythology, a river in Hades whose water produced, in those who drank it, forgetfulness of the past (freq. in allusive phrs.); oblivion, forgetfulness of the past. M16.
†**2** Death. *rare* (Shakes.). Only in L16.

Lethean /liːˈθiːən/ *adjective*. E17.
[ORIGIN from Latin *Lethaeus* from Greek *lēthaios*, from *lēthē*: see LETHE, -AN.]
Of or pertaining to the mythological River Lethe; pertaining to or causing oblivion.

lethed /liːθt/ *adjective*. *rare*. E17.
[ORIGIN Perh. from Latin *lethum* death + -ED[2].]
Dead (*lit.* & *fig.*).

†**Lethe'd** *adjective*. *rare* (Shakes.). Only in E17.
[ORIGIN from LETHE + -ED[2].]
Lethean.

lether *noun* see LADDER *noun*.

lethiferous /lɪˈθɪf(ə)rəs/ *adjective*. M17.
[ORIGIN from Latin *let(h)ifer*, from *let(h)um* death: see -FEROUS.]
= LETHAL *adjective* 2.

let-in /ˈlɛtɪn/ *adjective*. L19.
[ORIGIN from ***let in*** s.v. LET *verb*[1].]
TYPOGRAPHY. Designating a note at the side of a text and protruding into it, next to a row of indented lines.

let-off /ˈlɛtɒf/ *noun*. E19.
[ORIGIN from ***let off*** (a), (b) s.v. LET *verb*[1].]
1 A display of festivity, a festive occasion. *arch.* E19.
2 A release or exemption from punishment or duty. M19. ▸**b** CRICKET. A batsman's escape from dismissal when a fielder misses an opportunity to get him or her out. M19.
3 The action of pulling the trigger of a rifle. E20.

let-out /ˈlɛtaʊt/ *noun* & *adjective*. M19.
[ORIGIN from ***let out*** s.v. LET *verb*[1].]
▸ **A** *noun*. **1** An entertainment on a large or lavish scale. *Irish*. M19.
2 An opportunity of avoiding a difficulty, an embarrassing situation, etc.; an excuse. E20.
– COMB.: **let-out clause**: specifying a circumstance in which the terms of an agreement, contract, etc., shall not apply.
▸ **B** *adjective*. Of a fur garment: made by cutting a fur and reassembling the pieces to make a longer narrower whole. M20.

le tout Paris *noun phr.* var. of TOUT PARIS.

let-pass /lɛtˈpɑːs/ *noun*. M17.
[ORIGIN from ***let pass*** s.v. PASS *verb*.]
A permit allowing passage.

Lett /lɛt/ *noun*. L16.
[ORIGIN German *Lette* from Latvian *Latvi*.]
1 A member of a people living near the Baltic, chiefly in Latvia; a Latvian. L16.
2 Latvian, Lettish. M19.

lettable /ˈlɛtəb(ə)l/ *adjective*. E17.
[ORIGIN from LET *verb*[1] + -ABLE.]
Able to be let; suitable for letting.

letter /ˈlɛtə/ *noun*[1]. ME.
[ORIGIN Old French & mod. French *lettre* from Latin *littera* letter of the alphabet, (in pl.) epistle, document, literature, culture.]
▸ **I** An alphabetic character.
1 A character representing one or more of the elementary sounds of the speech of a language; any of the symbols that compose an alphabet. ME. ▸**b** Such characters collectively. Long *obsolete* exc. in ***before the letter*** below. LME. ▸**c** In *pl.* (*colloq.*), a degree, qualification, or honour denoted by its initial letters following the name

L

of the holder; such letters. In *sing.* (*US*), a school or college honour for achievement in sport, denoted similarly by an abbreviation or monogram representing the name of the school etc. L19.

> R. HOGGART SILENCE, in letters nine inches high and four inches across.

block letters, ***capital letters***, etc.

2 PRINTING. In *pl.* & *sing.*, types. Also, a font of type; a particular style of printed characters. Now *rare.* M16.

▶ **II** Something written.

†**3** An inscription, a document, a text; a written warrant or authority; in *pl.*, writings, written records. ME–L18.

4 *sing.* & (*arch.*) in *pl.* A written, typed, or printed communication addressed to a person, organization, etc., and usually sent by post or messenger. ME. ▸**b** *sing.* & (usu.) in *pl.* A formal or legal document of this kind. ME. ▸**c** An article, report, etc., describing the social, political, or cultural situation of the correspondent, esp. for a newspaper. L18.

> **c** K. MARTIN Dore was an excellent correspondent, who for many years had written paragraphs about Parliament, mainly for the London Letter.

air letter, ***chain letter***, ***day letter***, ***form letter***, ***love letter***, etc.

5 The precise terms or strict verbal interpretation of a statement or document; the signification that lies on the surface. Cf. SPIRIT *noun* 7c. ME.

> *New Yorker* Even according to the strictest letter of the law, kissing and embracing are permitted. H. CARPENTER Ritual laws governed daily conduct, and religion was of the letter rather than the spirit. *Shetland Times* The council . . obliged BP to stick by the letter of its lease.

6 In *pl.* Literature in general; acquaintance with literature; learning, erudition. Also, authorship. ME.

> W. S. CHURCHILL It was . . the Augustan Age of English letters.

7 In full ***French letter***. A condom. M19.

– PHRASES: ***ascending letter***: see ASCENDING 1. ***beautiful letters***. **before the letter** a proof before letters, = PROOF *noun* 13. ***begging letter***: see BEG *verb*. ***black letter***: see BLACK *adjective*. **commonwealth of letters**, **republic of letters** authors collectively; literature. ***dead letter***: see DEAD *adjective* etc. ***Dear John letter***: see DEAR *adjective*[1]. ***descending letter***: see DESCENDING *adjective* 1. ***dominical letter***: see DOMINICAL *adjective* 2. ***French letter***: see sense 7 above. ***initial letter***: see INITIAL *adjective*. **in letter and in spirit** in form and substance. ***Latin letter***: see LATIN *adjective*. **letter by letter** taking each letter in its turn. ***letter*** CERTIFICATORY. ***letter missive***: see MISSIVE *adjective* 1. **letter of advice** COMMERCE a letter notifying the drawing of a bill on or the consignment of goods to the recipient. ***letter of attorney***: see ATTORNEY *noun*. **letter of comfort** an assurance about a debt, short of a legal guarantee, given to a bank by a third party. ***letter of credence***: see CREDENCE 2. ***letter of credit***: see CREDIT *noun*. **letter of intent** a document containing a declaration of the intentions of the writer. **letter of introduction**: written by one person and given to another to introduce him or her to the addressee. ***letter of marque (and reprisal)***: see MARQUE *noun*[1]. ***letter of protection***: see PROTECTION 3. ***letter of recommendation***: see RECOMMENDATION 1. ***letter of slains***: see SLAIN *noun*. ***letters*** AVOCATORY. ***letter of*** TRANSMITTAL. ***letters dimissory***: see DIMISSORY 2. ***letters missive***: see MISSIVE *adjective* 1. ***letters of administration***: see ADMINISTRATION 4. ***Letters of Orders***: see ORDER *noun*. ***letters patent***: see PATENT *adjective* 1. ***letter testimonial***: see TESTIMONIAL *adjective* 1. **man of letters** a scholar, a writer. ***missive letter***: see MISSIVE *adjective* 1. ***nundinal letter***: see NUNDINAL. ***open letter***: see OPEN *adjective*. ***pastoral letter***: see PASTORAL *adjective*. **profession of letters** authorship. ***proof before letters***: see PROOF *noun* 13. ***red-letter day***: see RED *adjective*. ***republic of letters***: see ***commonwealth of letters*** above. ***revival of letters***: see REVIVAL 1a. ***Samian letter***: see SAMIAN *adjective*. ***scarlet letter***: see SCARLET *adjective*. ***Sunday letter***. ***the will of the summons letters***: see WILL *noun*[1]. **to the letter** with adherence to every detail; in accordance with a strict literal interpretation (*of*). ***white letter***: see WHITE *adjective*. ***woman of letters***: see WOMAN *noun*.

– COMB.: **letter-balance** a balance for weighing a letter; **letter bomb** an explosive device sent through the post as a terrorist's weapon; **letterbox** (*a*) a box in which letters are kept; (*b*) a public receptacle into which letters are dropped for collection and subsequent delivery by post; a receptacle into which letters are dropped when delivered; a slit in a door through which letters may be put; (*c*) a person or place through which spies pass information; (*d*) a format for presenting widescreen films on a standard television screen in which the image is displayed in approximately its original proportions across the middle of the screen, leaving blank areas above and below; **letter-card** a card with a gummed edge which can be folded and sealed to serve in place of a letter and its envelope; **letter carrier** a person who carries letters; *spec.* (*N. Amer.*) a postman, a postwoman; **letterform** the graphic form of a letter of an alphabet; **letter-founder** (now *rare*) a type founder; **letterhead** a printed heading on a sheet of letter paper containing the address etc. of an organization or individual; paper with such a heading; **letter heading** a printed heading on a letterhead; **letter-man** †(*a*) a Chelsea pensioner who was entitled to extra pay on the ground of a letter from the monarch; (*b*) *US* a person who has received a letter for sport; **letter-office** a post office; **letter paper** paper for writing letters, esp. business ones; **letter-perfect** *adjective* (*a*) THEATRICAL knowing one's part to the letter; (*b*) literally correct, verbally exact; *fig.* flawless, unexceptionable; **letter-plate** a plate for fixing to the outside of a door or wall and having a rectangular aperture through which letters may be put; **letterpress** (*a*) printed text as opp. to or accompanying illustrations; (*b*) matter printed from a raised surface, as opp. to lithography etc.; **letter-quality** *adjective* (esp. of a printer attached to a computer) producing print of a quality suitable for business letters; (of a letter etc.) printed to this standard; **letter-scale** a scale for weighing letters; **letter-space** *noun* & *verb* (TYPOGRAPHY) (*a*) *noun* a space inserted between the letters of a word; (*b*) *verb intrans.* insert extra space between the letters of a word; **letter-spaced** *adjective* (TYPOGRAPHY) having extra space between the letters of a word; **letter-weight** a paperweight; **letter-wood** the wood of the S. American tree *Brosimum aubletii*, of the mulberry family, which is red-brown, marked with irregular black spots; the tree itself; also called ***leopard-wood***; **letter-word** a runic symbol or ideogram signifying both the name for something and a specific single letter; a word wholly or partly consisting of a letter or letters which are abbreviations in themselves; **letter-writer** a person who writes letters.

letter /ˈlɛtə/ *noun*[2]. LME.

[ORIGIN from LET *verb*[1] + -ER[1].]

A person who lets something; (with suffixed adjective, verb, etc.) a person who lets loose, lets go, etc.

> JONSON A careless letter-go Of money. H. MAYHEW The letters of rooms are the most exacting in places crowded with the poor.

blood-letter etc.

letter /ˈlɛtə/ *verb*. LME.

[ORIGIN from LETTER *noun*[1].]

†**1** *verb trans.* Instruct in letters or learning. Only in LME.

2 *verb trans.* Exhibit, classify, or distinguish by means of letters. M17.

3 *verb intrans.* Write letters. Chiefly as LETTERING. M17.

4 *verb trans.* Write, paint, etc., letters on; write, paint, etc., (a word or words) on; inscribe. E18.

> J. GARDNER He drove an old blue Chevy truck with his name and phone number lettered on the door.

■ **letterer** *noun* a person who practises or is skilled in lettering; a calligrapher: E20.

lettered /ˈlɛtəd/ *adjective*. ME.

[ORIGIN from LETTER *noun*[1], *verb*: see -ED[2], -ED[1].]

1 Acquainted with or instructed in letters; learned, literate, educated. ME. ▸**b** Of or pertaining to learning or learned people; characterized by learning or literary culture. E18.

> **b** DISRAELI A man of lettered tastes.

2 Inscribed with letters; *spec.* (of a book) having the title etc. on the back or spine in gilt or coloured letters. M17.

Letterer-Siwe /lɛt(ə)rəˈsiːvə/ *noun*. M20.

[ORIGIN from Erich *Letterer* (1895–1982) & Sture *Siwe* (1897–1966), German physicians.]

MEDICINE. Used *attrib.* and in *possess.* to designate a usu. fatal histiocytosis of the reticuloendothelial system, occurring in early childhood.

letteret /ˈlɛt(ə)rɪt/ *noun*. E19.

[ORIGIN from LETTER *noun*[1] + -ET[1].]

A little or short letter.

lettergram /ˈlɛtəgram/ *noun*. E20.

[ORIGIN from LETTER *noun*[1] + TELE)GRAM.]

Chiefly *hist.* A telegram meant to be delivered with the ordinary mail.

lettering /ˈlɛt(ə)rɪŋ/ *noun*. M17.

[ORIGIN from LETTER *verb*, *noun*[1] + -ING[1].]

1 The action of writing letters; letter-writing. Now *rare*. M17.

2 Letters written, painted, etc., on something. Also, the action or art of forming letters; calligraphy. E19.

> F. RAPHAEL Tasteful lettering pointed out the multi-storey car park.

– COMB.: **lettering piece** a piece of leather on the spine of a book bearing the title.

letterless /ˈlɛtəlɪs/ *adjective*. L16.

[ORIGIN from LETTER *noun*[1] + -LESS.]

†**1** Not written down. Only in L16.

2 Unacquainted with letters or literature; illiterate. E17.

3 Having no letters or correspondence. M18.

4 Having no letters inscribed or appended. M19.

letterset /ˈlɛtəsɛt/ *noun*. M20.

[ORIGIN from *letter*(*press* s.v. LETTER *noun*[1] + OFF)SET *noun*.]

A method of printing in which ink is transferred from a raised surface to a blanket wrapped round a cylinder and from it to the paper etc.

Lettic /ˈlɛtɪk/ *adjective* & *noun*. *arch.* M19.

[ORIGIN from LETT + -IC.]

▶ **A** *adjective*. Of or pertaining to the Letts or Latvians; *spec.* = BALTIC *adjective* 2. M19.

▶ **B** *noun*. The Latvian language. M19.

lettiga /lɛˈtiːgə/ *noun*. E19.

[ORIGIN Italian from Latin *lectica* litter, from *lectus* bed.]

A kind of sedan chair in which two people are carried facing one another.

Lettish /ˈlɛtɪʃ/ *adjective* & *noun*. *arch.* M18.

[ORIGIN from LETT + -ISH[1].]

▶ **A** *adjective*. Of or pertaining to the Letts or Latvians or their language; Latvian. M18.

▶ **B** *noun*. Latvian. M19.

Letto- /ˈlɛtəʊ/ *combining form*. *arch.* M19.

[ORIGIN mod. Latin *Letto*, from LETT: see -O-.]

Used with adjectives & nouns referring to other languages or peoples, with the sense 'Lettish or Latvian and —', as ***Letto-Lithuanian***, ***Letto-Slavonic***, etc.

lettre /lɛtr/ *noun*. Pl. pronounced same. E18.

[ORIGIN French: see LETTER *noun*[1].]

The French for 'letter', occurring in various phrases used in English.

■ ***lettre bâtarde*** /batard/ [French = bastard] bastarda L19. ***lettre de cachet*** /də kaʃɛ/, pl. ***lettres de cachet***, [lit. 'of seal'] (*a*) *hist.* a warrant issued in the France of the *ancien régime* for the imprisonment of a person without trial at the pleasure of the monarch; (*b*) an official order for imprisonment, exile, etc.: E18. ***lettre de forme*** /də fɔrm/ [lit. 'of shape or form'] textura L19. ***lettre de somme*** /də sɔm/ [lit. 'of sum or total'] rotunda L19.

lettrine /lɛˈtriːn/ *noun*. M20.

[ORIGIN French, formed as LETTER *noun*[1]: see -INE[1].]

An initial letter, *esp.* a decorated one; an initial letter standing out from a painted background.

lettrism /ˈlɛtrɪz(ə)m/ *noun*. Also in French form ***lettrisme*** /lɛtrism/. M20.

[ORIGIN French, formed as LETTER *noun*[1]: see -ISM.]

A movement in French art and literature characterized by a repudiation of meaning and the use of letters (sometimes invented) as isolated units.

■ **lettrist**, ***lettriste*** /lɛtrist (*pl. same*)/ *noun* & *adjective* (*a*) *noun* an exponent or advocate of lettrism; (*b*) *adjective* pertaining to or characteristic of lettrism or lettrists: M20.

lettuce /ˈlɛtɪs/ *noun*. ME.

[ORIGIN Old French *letuës*, *laituës* pl. of *laituë* (mod. *laitue*) from Latin *lactuca*, from *lac(t-)* milk, with ref. to the milky juice of the plant.]

1 Any plant of the genus *Lactuca* of the composite family; *esp.* (also ***garden lettuce***) the cultivated species *L. sativa*, whose leaves are much used as a salad; such plants or their leaves collectively. Also, any of various plants resembling true lettuces. ME.

> H. SPURLING Bowls of the lettuce and radishes . . began to appear on Ivy's table.

cabbage lettuce, ***cos lettuce***, ***iceberg lettuce***, ***sea lettuce***, etc.

2 Money. *slang* (orig. *US*). E20.

– COMB.: **lettuce green** a medium shade of green.

■ **lettuce-like** *adjective* resembling (that of) a lettuce L19.

letty /ˈlɛti/ *noun*. *slang*. M19.

[ORIGIN Italian *letto* from Latin *lectus*.]

A bed; a lodging.

scarper the letty: see SCARPER 2.

let-up /ˈlɛtʌp/ *noun*. M19.

[ORIGIN from *let up* s.v. LET *verb*[1].]

A diminution in intensity or severity; a cessation, a break. (Foll. by *in*.)

> *Nature* There is little prospect of a letup in fuel shortages for the next few years.

Letzeburgesch /lɛtsəˈbɔrgɛʃ/ *noun* & *adjective*. Also **-isch** /-ɪʃ/. E20.

[ORIGIN from local name for Luxembourg + *-esch* -ISH[1].]

= LUXEMBURGISH.

leu /ˈleɪuː/ *noun*. Pl. **lei** /leɪ/. L19.

[ORIGIN Romanian = lion.]

The basic monetary unit of Romania, equal to 100 bani.

Leucadian /l(j)uːˈkeɪdɪən/ *noun* & *adjective*. E17.

[ORIGIN from *Leucadia* (see below) + -IAN.]

Chiefly *hist.* ▶**A** *noun*. A native or inhabitant of Leucadia (mod. Leukas or Levkas), an island in the Ionian Sea. E17.

▶ **B** *adjective*. Of or pertaining to Leucadia. M20.

leucine /ˈluːsiːn/ *noun*. Also (now *rare*) **-in** /-ɪn/. E19.

[ORIGIN from Greek *leukos* white + -INE[5], -IN[1].]

BIOCHEMISTRY. A hydrophobic amino acid, $(CH_3)_2CHCH_2$-$CH(NH_2)COOH$, which occurs in proteins and is essential in the human diet; 2-amino-4-methylpentanoic acid.

leucite /ˈluːsʌɪt/ *noun*. L18.

[ORIGIN formed as LEUCINE + -ITE[1].]

MINERALOGY. A potassium aluminosilicate, crystallizing in the tetrahedral system and usu. found as grey or white glassy trapezohedra in volcanic rocks.

■ **leucitic** /-ˈsɪtɪk/ *adjective* containing or of the nature of leucite M19.

leuco- /ˈluːkəʊ/ *combining form*. Before a vowel also **leuc-**. Also (esp. MEDICINE & *US*) **leuk(o)-**. In sense 2 also as attrib. adjective **leuco**.

[ORIGIN from Greek *leukos* white: see -O-.]

1 Forming nouns and adjectives with the sense 'white, pale'; *esp.* in MEDICINE, repr. LEUCOCYTE; in CHEMISTRY, forming names of colourless compounds chemically transformable to coloured ones.

2 Chiefly DYEING. Designating the reduced, water-soluble colourless form of a dye which is fixed on the fibre and subsequently oxidized to the dye proper by the air.

■ **leucoblast** *noun* (BIOLOGY) a spheroidal cell from which a leucocyte develops L19. **leuco'blastic** *adjective* (BIOLOGY) containing or involving leucoblasts E20. **leuco'cidin** *noun* a bacterial leucotoxin L19. **leuco'cratic** *adjective* (PETROGRAPHY) (of a rock) light-coloured; rich in felsic minerals: E20. **leucoderm** *noun* & *adjective* (a person who is) white-skinned, Caucasian E20. **leuco'derma**, **leuco'dermia** *nouns* (MEDICINE) an acquired local depigmentation of the skin of unknown cause; cf. VITILIGO: L19. **leuco'dermic** *adjective* (*a*) pertaining to or exhibiting leucoderma; (*b*) (naturally) white-skinned, Caucasian: L19. †**leucopathy** *noun* = ALBINISM M–L19. **leuco'penia** *noun* (MEDICINE) a reduction in the number of

L

white cells in the blood L19. **leucophore** *noun* (ZOOLOGY) a type of guanophore, an iridocyte E20. **leuco'plakia** *noun* [Greek *plak-*, *plax* flat surface] MEDICINE white patches appearing on the tongue or on other mucous membranes L19. **leucoplast**, **leuco'plastid** *nouns* (BIOLOGY) a colourless starch-accumulating organelle found in plant cells L19. **leucopoiesis** /-pɔɪˈiːsɪs/ *noun* (PHYSIOLOGY) the production of leucocytes in the bone marrow E20. **leucopoietic** /-ˈɛtɪk/ *adjective* (PHYSIOLOGY) of or pertaining to leucopoiesis E20. **leucopterin** /luːˈkɒptərɪn/ *noun* (CHEMISTRY) a white pterin pigment found esp. in certain butterflies E20. **leuco'tactic** *adjective* (PHYSIOLOGY) pertaining to or promoting leucotaxis M20. **leuco'taxin**, **-ine** *noun* (PHYSIOLOGY) a substance found in injured tissue and inflammatory exudates which causes an increase in the permeability of capillaries, and attracts leucocytes M20. **leuco'taxis** *noun* (PHYSIOLOGY) movement of leucocytes in a particular direction M20. **leuco'toxin** *noun* (MEDICINE) a substance which destroys leucocytes E20.

leucocyte /ˈluːkə(ʊ)sʌɪt/ *noun*. Also **leuko-**. L19.
[ORIGIN from LEUCO- + -CYTE.]
PHYSIOLOGY. Any of various colourless nucleated amoeboid cells of the blood, lymph, connective tissue, etc. Also called ***white blood cell***, ***white blood corpuscle***, ***white cell***, ***white corpuscle***.
■ **leucocytic** /-ˈsɪtɪk/ *adjective* of or pertaining to leucocytes; characterized by the presence of leucocytes: L19. **leucocy'tosis** *noun*, pl. **-toses** /-ˈtəʊsiːz/, an increase in the number of leucocytes in the blood M19.

leucoma /luːˈkəʊmə/ *noun*. Also **leuk-**. E18.
[ORIGIN mod. Latin from Greek *leukōma*, formed as LEUCO- + -OMA.]
MEDICINE. (The condition of having) a white opacity in the cornea of the eye, usu. as a result of inflammation. Also called ***albugo***.
■ **leucomatous** *adjective* affected with leucoma L19.

leucon /ˈluːkɒn/ *noun*. L19.
[ORIGIN mod. Latin genus name, formed as LEUCO-.]
ZOOLOGY. A grade of sponge structure of the leuconoid type; a leuconoid sponge. Cf. ASCON, SYCON.
■ **leuconoid** *adjective & noun* (*a*) *adjective* designating, of, or pertaining to a sponge of the most complex type, composed of a mass of flagellated chambers and water canals; (*b*) *noun* a sponge of this type: E20.

†**leucophlegmacy** *noun*. Also in Latin form **-matia**. M16–M18.
[ORIGIN medieval Latin *leucophlegmasia*, formed as LEUCO- + late Latin *phlegma*: see PHLEGM, -ACY.]
Dropsy.
■ †**leucophlegmatic** *adjective* dropsical M17–M19.

leucorrhoea /luːkəˈriːə/ *noun*. Also ***-rrhea**. L18.
[ORIGIN from LEUCO- + -RRHOEA.]
MEDICINE. A mucous or mucopurulent discharge from the vagina. Also called ***the whites***, ***white flux***.
■ **leucorrhoeal**, **leucorrhoeic** *adjectives* of, pertaining to, or affected with leucorrhoea E19.

leucoses *noun* pl. of LEUCOSIS.

leucosin /ˈluːkə(ʊ)sɪn/ *noun*. Also **leuk-**. L19.
[ORIGIN from Greek *leukos* white + -IN¹.]
BIOCHEMISTRY. **1** An albumin found in some cereal grains. L19.
2 A polysaccharide found in storage vesicles in cells of some golden algae. E20.

leucosis /luːˈkəʊsɪs/ *noun*. In sense 2 **leuk-**. Pl. **-oses** /-əʊsiːz/. E18.
[ORIGIN Greek *leukōsis*, from *leukoun* make white, from *leukos* white: see -OSIS.]
MEDICINE. **1** Whiteness; the process of becoming white. *rare*. E18.
2 Chiefly VETERINARY MEDICINE. Leukaemia; a leukaemic disease of animals, *esp.* any of a group of malignant viral diseases of poultry (***avian leucosis***, ***fowl leucosis***) or of cattle (***bovine leucosis***). E20.
■ **leucotic** /-ˈkɒtɪk/ *adjective* of, pertaining to, or affected with leucosis L19.

leucotomy /luːˈkɒtəmi/ *noun*. E18.
[ORIGIN from LEUCO- + -TOMY.]
†**1** Surgical cutting of the sclera of the eye. Only in E18.
2 Surgical cutting of tracts of white nerve fibres in the brain; orig. *spec.*, prefrontal lobotomy; an instance of this. E18.
■ **'leucotome** *noun* an instrument used to perform leucotomy M20. **leucotomize** *verb trans.* perform leucotomy on M20.

leucotriene *noun* var. of LEUKOTRIENE.

leucous /ˈluːkəs/ *adjective*. Now *rare* or *obsolete*. M19.
[ORIGIN from Greek *leukos* white + -OUS.]
Having a white skin; albino.

leud /l(j)uːd/ *noun*. Pl. **leudes** /ˈl(j)uːdiːz/, **leuds**. M18.
[ORIGIN Repr. medieval Latin *leudes* from Old Saxon *liudi* people, nation.]
hist. In the Frankish kingdoms: a person holding land by feudal tenure; a vassal.

leuk- *combining form* see LEUCO-.

leukaemia /luːˈkiːmɪə/ *noun*. Also ***-kemia**. M19.
[ORIGIN from LEUK- + -AEMIA.]
MEDICINE. Any of a group of malignant progressive diseases characterized by the gross overproduction of (freq. immature or abnormal) leucocytes, which accumulate and suppress other haemopoietic activity.

leukaemic /luːˈkiːmɪk/ *adjective & noun*. Also ***-kemic**. L19.
[ORIGIN from LEUKAEMIA + -IC.]
▸ **A** *adjective*. Affected with leukaemia; characteristic of or resembling leukaemia; *spec.* marked by an excess of leucocytes in the blood. L19.
▸ **B** *noun*. An individual with leukaemia. M20.

leukaemogenic /luːˌkiːməˈdʒɛnɪk/ *adjective*. Also ***-kemo-**. M20.
[ORIGIN from LEUKAEMIA + -O- + -GENIC.]
MEDICINE. Capable of producing leukaemia; pertaining to the production of leukaemia.
■ **leu'kaemogen** *noun* a leukaemogenic substance or agent M20. **leukaemogenesis** *noun* the production or development of leukaemia M20.

leukaemoid /luːˈkiːmɔɪd/ *adjective*. Also ***-kemoid**. E20.
[ORIGIN from LEUKAEMIA + -OID.]
MEDICINE. Of a symptom or condition: resembling (that found in) leukaemia but due to some other cause.

leukemia *noun*, **leukemic** *adjective & noun*, etc., see LEUKAEMIA etc.

leuko- *combining form* see LEUCO-.

leukocyte *noun* var. of LEUCOCYTE.

leukosin *noun* var. of LEUCOSIN.

leukosis *noun* see LEUCOSIS.

leukotriene /luːkəˈtrʌɪiːn/ *noun*. Also **leuco-**. L20.
[ORIGIN from LEUCO- + TRIENE.]
BIOCHEMISTRY. Any of a group of biologically active metabolites of arachidonic acid, orig. isolated from leucocytes, which contain three conjugated double bonds.

leukovirus /ˈluːkəʊvʌɪrəs/ *noun*. M20.
[ORIGIN from LEUKO- + VIRUS.]
Any of a group of pleomorphic retroviruses which cause leucosis or tumours in mammals and birds.

lev /lɛv/ *noun*. Also **leva** /ˈlɛvə/. Pl. **leva**, **levas**, **levs**. L19.
[ORIGIN Bulgarian, var. of *lăv* lion.]
The basic monetary unit of Bulgaria, equal to 100 stotinki.

Lev. *abbreviation*.
Leviticus (in the Bible).

levada /lɛˈvɑːdə/ *noun*. L19.
[ORIGIN Portuguese = mill-stream, sluice.]
In Madeira: a canal for irrigation.

levade /ləˈvɑːd/ *noun*. M20.
[ORIGIN French, from *lever* raise: see -ADE.]
A dressage movement (superseding the *pesade*) in which the horse raises its forequarters with the forelegs drawn up, and balances on its hind legs which are placed well forward under the body and deeply bent.

levain *noun* var. of LEAVEN *noun*.

Levallois /ləˈvalwɑː/ *noun & adjective*. E20.
[ORIGIN A suburb of northern Paris.]
ARCHAEOLOGY. (Designating or characterized by) a technique of working flint or other rocks, developed in the Lower and Middle Palaeolithic periods, in which a block is trimmed so that a flake of predetermined size and shape can be struck from it.
■ **Levall'oisean** *adjective* designating, pertaining to, or characterized by this technique; pertaining to or characteristic of such a culture: M20.

levallorphan /liːvəˈlɔːfan/ *noun*. M20.
[ORIGIN from *levo-* var. of LAEVO- + ALL(YL + M)ORPHINE + -AN.]
PHARMACOLOGY. A morphine analogue and opioid antagonist which is used to counteract the effects of some narcotics.

levan /ˈliːvan/ *noun*. E20.
[ORIGIN from LEVO- + -AN, after *dextran*.]
BIOCHEMISTRY. A fructan, *esp.* any of a class of fructans produced by bacteria and grasses.

levancy /ˈlɛv(ə)nsi/ *noun*. L17.
[ORIGIN from LEVANT *adjective*¹: see -ANCY.]
LAW (now *hist.*). The fact of being levant. Only in ***levancy and couchancy***.

Levant /lɪˈvant/ *noun*¹. In sense 3 also **l-**. L15.
[ORIGIN French, pres. pple of *lever* raise, used as noun for the point where the sun rises: see -ANT¹.]
1 The countries of the East; *spec.* the eastern part of the Mediterranean, with its islands and neighbouring countries. Now *arch.* or *hist.* L15.
2 = LEVANTER *noun*¹ 2. Now *rare* or *obsolete*. E17.
3 = ***Levant morocco*** s.v. LEVANT *adjective*². L19.

†**levant** *noun*². *slang*. E18–E19.
[ORIGIN Transf. use of LEVANT *noun*¹ sense 1. Cf. French *faire voile en Levant* be stolen or spirited away. Cf. LEVANT *verb*.]
An act of absconding after losing a bet, a bet made with the intention of absconding if it is lost. Only in ***come the levant***, ***run a levant***, ***throw a levant***.

levant /ˈlɛv(ə)nt/ *adjective*¹. LME.
[ORIGIN French, pres. pple of *lever* raise, *se lever* rise: see -ANT¹.]
LAW (now *hist.*). Of an animal: rising. Only in ***levant and couchant***, (*a*) (of cattle) turned out day and night on common land; (*b*) (of straying animals) having stayed for a day and a night (the necessary period before the landowner might distrain them).

Levant /lɪˈvant/ *adjective*². Also **l-**. E16.
[ORIGIN Attrib. use of LEVANT *noun*¹.]
1 Pertaining to or obtained from the Levant. Now chiefly *arch.* or *hist.* E16.
Levant morocco a high-grade large-grained morocco leather. **Levant wormseed** = SANTONICA.
2 East, eastern, easterly. Opp. PONENT *adjective* 1. *arch.* L16.

levant /lɪˈvant/ *verb intrans. slang*. E17.
[ORIGIN formed as LEVANT *noun*².]
Abscond, run away, esp. with (gambling) debts unpaid.

Levanter /lɪˈvantə/ *noun*¹. In sense 2 also **l-**. M17.
[ORIGIN from LEVANT *noun*¹ + -ER¹.]
1 = LEVANTINE *noun*. *rare*. M17.
2 A strong easterly wind in the Mediterranean. L18.

levanter /lɪˈvantə/ *noun*². *slang*. L18.
[ORIGIN from LEVANT *verb* + -ER¹.]
A person who absconds, esp. after losing a bet.

Levantine /lɪˈvantʌɪn, ˈlɛv(ə)n-, -tɪn/ *noun & adjective*. Now chiefly *arch.* or *hist.* E17.
[ORIGIN from LEVANT *noun*¹ + -INE¹.]
▸ **A** *noun*. A native or inhabitant of the Levant. E17.
▸ **B** *adjective*. Of or pertaining to the Levant or its inhabitants; (of a ship) trading to the Levant. In early use, pertaining to the east, eastern. E17.
■ **Levantinism** /lɪˈvantɪnɪz(ə)m/ *noun* the spirit or culture of the Levant M20. **levantinize** /lɪˈvantɪnʌɪz/ *verb trans.* make Levantine in form or character E20.

levari facias /lɪˌvɑːrʌɪ ˈfeɪʃɪas/ *noun phr.* E17.
[ORIGIN Latin = cause to be levied, from *levari* be levied (from *levare* raise) + *facias* cause, 2nd person sing. pres. subjunct. of *facere* do, make.]
LAW (now *hist.*). A writ ordering a sheriff to distrain the defendant's goods and income from lands against payment of the sum for which judgement has been given.

levas *noun pl.* see LEV.

levator /lɪˈveɪtə/ *noun*. E17.
[ORIGIN Latin = a person who lifts, from *levat-* pa. ppl stem of *levare* lift: see -OR.]
1 ANATOMY. A muscle which raises a limb or organ. Also ***levator muscle***. E17.
†**2** SURGERY. An elevator for lifting depressed broken bone. L17–L18.

leveche /lɛˈvɛtʃi/ *noun*. L19.
[ORIGIN Spanish.]
A hot, dry, more or less southerly wind of SE Spain, the local counterpart of the sirocco.

levee /ˈlɛvi, ˈlɛveɪ/ *noun*¹ *& verb*¹. L17.
[ORIGIN French *levé* var. of *lever* rising, use as noun of *lever* (inf.) rise. Cf. COUCHEE.]
▸ **A** *noun* **1 a** *hist.* A reception of visitors on rising from bed; a morning assembly held by a person of distinction. L17. ▸**b** *hist.* An afternoon assembly for men only held by (a representative of) the British monarch. M18. ▸**c** A reception or assembly at any time of day. Now *arch.* exc. *N. Amer.* M18.
†**2** The company assembled at a levee. Only in 18.
†**3** The action of rising, *spec.* from one's bed. E18–E19.
▸ †**B** *verb trans.* Attend the levees of; pursue at levees. Only in 18.

levee /ˈlɛvi, lɪˈviː/ *noun*² *& verb*². *US*. E18.
[ORIGIN French *levée* fem. of *levé* pa. pple of *lever* raise: see LEVY *noun*¹.]
▸ **A** *noun*. **1** An embankment to prevent the overflow of a river. E18. ▸**b** PHYSICAL GEOGRAPHY. A low broad ridge of sediment running alongside a river channel. Also, any similar natural embankment, as one formed by a mud flow, lava flow, or submarine current. L19.
2 A landing place, a pier, a quay. M19.
▸ **B** *verb trans.* Raise a levee or embankment along (a river) or in (a district). Also, shut or keep *off* by means of a levee. M19.

J. PALMER Islands in the river might be *leveed* and successfully cultivated.

■ **leveed** *adjective* (of a district) surrounded by or provided with levees; (of a river) having a (natural) levee or levees: M20.

levée en masse /ləvɛ ɑ̃ mas/ *noun phr.* Pl. ***levées en masse*** (pronounced same). E19.
[ORIGIN French.]
A mass mobilization (orig. in Revolutionary France) in response to the threat of invasion. Cf. ***levy in mass*** s.v. LEVY *noun*¹ 2.

Economist An immediate *levée en masse*, . . the calling up now of every able-bodied man.

level /ˈlɛv(ə)l/ *noun*. ME.
[ORIGIN Old French *livel* (later *nivel*, mod. *niveau*) from Proto-Romance var. of Latin *libella* dim. of *libra* balance, scales.]
▸ **I 1** An instrument which indicates a line parallel to the plane of the horizon, used to determine whether a surface is horizontal; *spec.* a surveying instrument for

giving a horizontal line of sight. ME. ▸**b** (Usu. **L-**.) *The* constellation Norma. L19.

spirit level, ***stride level***, etc.

2 A horizontal position; the condition of being horizontal. LME.

DEFOE The rising of the water brought me a little more upon a level.

3 a A (nearly) horizontal passage or gallery in a mine, *esp.* one used for drainage. M16. ▸**b** A level tract of land, a stretch of country without hills; *spec.* (in proper names) any of various large expanses of level country. E17. ▸**c** A (more or less) level or flat surface. M17. ▸**d** A floor or storey in a building; a stratum in the earth. M20.

c TENNYSON By zig-zag paths.. Came on the shining levels of the lake. **d** N. MOSLEY Our house is on four levels. *London Archaeologist* Post-medieval levels deserve greater attention.

4 Position as marked by a horizontal line; a (real or imaginary) horizontal line or plane in relation to which elevation is measured. M16. ▸**b** A position (on a real or imaginary scale) in respect of amount, intensity, extent, etc.; a relative height, amount, or value. L19. ▸**c** *PHYSICS.* More fully ***energy level***. (The energy value associated with) each of a set of discrete states of a quantized system; *spec.* a state or group of states of an atom characterized by the quantum numbers *n*, *L*, *S*, and *J* (cf. STATE *noun* 3b, TERM *noun* 13c). E20. ▸**d** *STATISTICS.* In full ***level of confidence***, ***level of significance***. A number chosen as the maximum (or minimum) value of the probability with which any statistical result must be false (or true) for that result to be accepted as having been demonstrated. E20. ▸**e** *BROADCASTING & RECORDING.* The volume of a sound or the strength of a signal as it shows up in different pieces of equipment. M20.

M. BRADBURY It rains.. and the level of the lake rises. **b** *Nature* That could result in dangerous levels.. of sulphates in city air. *Daily Telegraph* New.. starts are down to 40 per cent. of their level.. last year.

sea level etc.

5 A plane or standard in social, moral, or intellectual matters. E17. ▸**b** A layer or position in a hierarchy. M20. ▸**c** A facet or layer of significance, esp. in a literary or artistic work; any of various shades of meaning which may be perceived. M20. ▸**d** The aspect or aspects of a subject, situation, etc., being considered at any particular time. M20.

C. STEAD This stupid conversation, which she thought beneath Miss Aiden's level. P. BROOK He is there, on our level, attainable. **b** *Guardian* On instructions from director-level, the estimates.. had been prepared. B. EMECHETA Professorial class, .. those on salary level sixteen. **c** *Books* On the surface, it is .. pacy... On another level, it explores.. agonizing moral decisions. **d** C. F. HOCKETT Selection and preliminary ordering of data determine the *range* of analysis; the choice of criteria fixes the *level* of analysis. K. WATERHOUSE Conversation,.. seemingly on a personal level, flows easily.

▸†**II 6** That which a weapon is aimed at; a mark. Also (*fig.*), an aim, a purpose. E16–E17. ▸**b** The action of aiming; aim. Also, the line of fire, the range of the missile. M16–E18.

– PHRASES: ***advanced level***: see ADVANCED 2. ***black level***: see BLACK *adjective*. ***dumpy level***: see DUMPY *adjective*[2]. ***energy level***: see sense 4c above. **find one's level** reach one's right (social, intellectual, etc.) place in relation to one's associates. ***level of confidence***, ***level of significance***: see sense 4d above. **on a level** on a horizontal line or plane. **on a level with** on the same plane as; *fig.* the equal of. **on the level** (*a*) on the flat, horizontal; (*b*) (*colloq.*, orig. *US*) honest(ly), truthful(ly), straightforward(ly). ***ordinary level***: see ORDINARY *adjective*. **take a level** *SURVEYING* ascertain the elevation of a piece of land. ***trophic level***: see TROPHIC *adjective* 2. ***white level***: see WHITE *adjective*.

– COMB.: **level-free** *adjective* (of a mine) able to be worked or drained by means of levels; **level test**: of a recording or broadcast signal level to determine whether the settings or positions of equipment should be changed; **level tube** the glass tube of a spirit level.

level /ˈlɛv(ə)l/ *adjective & adverb*. LME.

[ORIGIN from the noun.]

▸ **A** *adjective*. **1** Horizontal; perpendicular to the plumb line. LME. ▸**b** Lying, moving, or directed in an (approximately) horizontal plane. M17.

2 Having an even surface; flat; not bumpy. M16. ▸**b** Of a quantity of a dry substance or ingredient: even with the brim of the measure; not rounded or heaped. M20.

J. CONRAD A great plain as level as the sea. C. MACKENZIE Turf recently disturbed was trodden level again. **b** E. CRAIG A heaped spoonful equals 2 level or liquid spoonfuls.

3 a Lying in the same horizontal plane as something else; on a level *with*. Also *fig.*, consistent *with*, equal *to*. M16. ▸**b** Of two or more things: situated in the same level or plane. E17.

a R. DAHL The flame is absolutely level with my eyes. **b** B. BYARS She sat down.. so that their heads were level.

4 †**a** In equipoise, balanced, steady. L16–E17. ▸**b** Of the head (as the seat of the mind): well balanced, not agitated or confused, sensible. Orig. *US*. M19.

b *Woman & Home* It's vital to keep a level head if you're to be of help.

5 Of even, equable, or uniform quality, tone, or style; of even tenor. M17.

J. RULE I've actually tried to meet your level gaze. *Running* Run at a level pace.

6 Of a contest: even, with no competitor having the advantage. E19.

– COMB., SPECIAL COLLOCATIONS, & PHRASES: **level crossing** a place at which a road and a railway, or two railways, cross each other at the same level; **level-dyeing** a process designed to prevent uneven absorption of the colouring matter in dyeing; **level-headed** *adjective* having a level head, mentally well balanced, cool, sensible; **level-headedness** the quality or state of being level-headed; **level pegging** equality in a contest, equality of scores or achievements, the fact of being neck and neck; ***level playing field***; **one's level best**, (*US colloq.*) **one's levelest** one's very best, the most one can possibly do.

▸ **B** *adverb*. With direct aim; on a level *with*; horizontally. E17.

■ **levelly** *adverb* E17. **levelness** *noun* M17.

level /ˈlɛv(ə)l/ *verb*[1]. Infl. **-ll-**, ***-l-**. LME.

[ORIGIN from the noun.]

▸ **I 1** *verb trans.* Make (a surface) level or even; remove or reduce irregularities in the surface of. LME. ▸**b** Foll. by *out*: extend on a level. M17. ▸**c** *LINGUISTICS.* Reduce or obliterate a phonetic or morphological difference between (related forms), esp. by analogy. L19.

W. GASS The land is flat because the winds have leveled it.

2 *verb trans.* Place (two or more things) on the same level or (horizontal) plane. M16.

W. PHILLIPS Gunpowder leveled peasant and prince.

3 a *verb trans.* Bring or reduce to the level or standard of something else (foll. by *to*); put on a level *with*. E17. ▸**b** *verb intrans.* Be on a level or par *with*. *rare*. E17. ▸**c** *verb trans. & intrans.* Bring or move *up* or *down* to the level of something (expressed or implied); standardize. M18.

a W. H. PRESCOTT Aristocracy was levelled.. to the condition of the peasant. **c** F. R. LEAVIS The modern world of mass-production and levelling-down,.. hostile.. to all distinction of spirit. *Independent* Conservatives.. in favour of 'levelling up', not down.

4 *verb trans.* Beat or knock down; lay low, raze to the ground. E17. ▸**b** *transf. & fig.* Reduce or remove (inequalities) to produce evenness or equality; smooth *away*, *out*. M17.

P. EGAN Davis caught his adversary, and.. levelled him. *Independent* The earthquake levelled 90 per cent of the houses. **b** B. C. BRODIE Circumstances of trial, which.. level all artificial distinctions. *Times* The question of their co-operating.. to level out the production of cars.

5 *verb trans. & intrans.* Foll. by *off*, *out*: bring (an aircraft) into horizontal flight; (of an aircraft) assume horizontal flight; *transf. & fig.* (cause to) cease ascending or descending, increasing or decreasing. M20.

Literary Digest A 'pancake landing' occurs when the ship is leveled off several feet above the ground. *Times* Yields have been tending to level off, or even fall.

▸ **II 6** *verb trans.* Aim (a missile weapon); bring (a weapon) to the proper level for firing or striking. L15. ▸†**b** Shoot (a missile) *out* (*of* a weapon). L16–M17. ▸**c** *transf. & fig.* Direct (one's gaze) *at*, (satire, criticism, an accusation, etc.) *at* or *against*. L16. ▸†**d** Aim or intend (a thing) *to do*. Usu. in *pass*. E18–E19.

E. L. RICE He comes quickly down the steps.. levelling his revolver at the crowd. **c** M. SINCLAIR A look through his glasses, leveled at each member of his household. M. FOOT The charge could never be.. levelled against Nye.

level one's aim take aim.

7 *verb intrans.* Aim, take aim, (*lit. & fig.*). *arch.* L15. ▸†**b** Guess *at*. Only in L16.

W. DAMPIER When they shoot.., they level, and fire. T. SHERIDAN The Author in this Satyr levels at Nero.

8 *verb intrans.* Be honest or truthful; tell the truth, speak frankly, behave honestly or deal straightforwardly (*with*). *slang* (orig. *US*). E20.

R. CRAWFORD I'll level with you, I've been paid to find your brother. S. BELLOW He wouldn't answer. Lawyers level only among themselves.

▸ **III 9** *verb trans. & intrans.* *SURVEYING.* Ascertain the differences of level in (a piece of land); determine the height of a point or points relative to a given horizontal plane. L16.

level /ˈlɛv(ə)l/ *verb*[2]. *obsolete* exc. *dial.* Infl. **-ll-**. E16.

[ORIGIN Perh. alt. of LEVY *verb* by assoc. with LEVEL *verb*[1].]

= LEVY *verb*.

leveler *noun*, **leveling** *noun*, *adjective* see LEVELLER etc.

leveller /ˈlɛv(ə)lə/ *noun*. Also ***leveler**. L16.

[ORIGIN from LEVEL *verb*[1] + -ER[1].]

1 a A person who takes soundings or levels. Also, an instrument for taking levels. L16. ▸**b** A person who or thing which levels ground. E18. ▸**c** *BOXING.* A knock-down blow. E19.

2 An advocate of the abolition of social distinctions. Orig. & *spec.* (**L-**) a radical dissenter in 17th-cent. England, professing egalitarian principles. M17.

3 A thing which brings all people to a common level. M17.

■ **levelism** *noun* the principle of abolishing distinctions in society; in early use *spec.* the principles advocated by the Levellers: M17.

levelling /ˈlɛv(ə)lɪŋ/ *verbal noun*. Also ***leveling**. L16.

[ORIGIN from LEVEL *verb*[1] + -ING[1].]

The action of LEVEL *verb*[1]; an instance of this.

– COMB.: **levelling instrument** an instrument used in surveying and consisting essentially of a telescope fitted with a spirit level; **levelling pole**, **levelling rod** an instrument consisting essentially of a graduated pole with a vane sliding upon it, used in levelling; **levelling screw** a screw used to adjust parts of a contrivance to an exact level; **levelling staff** = ***levelling pole*** above.

levelling /ˈlɛv(ə)lɪŋ/ *ppl adjective*. Also ***leveling**. M17.

[ORIGIN from LEVEL *verb*[1] + -ING[2].]

That levels something; *esp.* bringing all to the same social, moral, or intellectual level. Also, of or pertaining to levellers and their principles.

lever /ˈliːvə/ *noun*. ME.

[ORIGIN Anglo-Norman *lever*, Old French & mod. French *levier* alt. of Old French *leveor*, from *lever* raise.]

1 A bar resting on a pivot, used to raise or dislodge some heavy or firmly fixed object; a crowbar; *MECHANICS* a simple machine consisting of a rigid bar which pivots about a fulcrum and may be used to transmit force applied at a second point to move a resistant load at a third, esp. with mechanical advantage. ME. ▸†**b** *gen.* A bar, a pole, a rod. ME–E17.

2 A projecting arm or handle by which a mechanism is operated or adjusted. M19.

Toronto Sun A simple flip of a lever will enable the bike to be folded.

3 In full ***lever watch***. A watch with a lever escapement. M19.

4 *fig.* A means of exerting moral force; a means of effecting something. M19.

Christian Aid News The Government has sometimes used our aid as a lever to coax countries.

– COMB.: **lever escapement** *WATCHMAKING* an escapement in which the connection between the escape wheel and the balance is made by means of a separate lever; **lever frame** the frame in a railway signal box in which the operating levers are mounted and interlocked; **lever watch**: see sense 3 above; **leverwood** the American hop hornbeam, *Ostrya virginica*.

lever /ˈliːvə/ *verb*. M19.

[ORIGIN from the noun.]

1 *verb intrans.* Apply a lever; work with a lever. M19.

2 *verb trans.* Lift, push, or otherwise move with or as with a lever; move or raise (oneself, another) awkwardly or with difficulty. Also, bring into a specified condition by or as by applying a lever. L19.

C. MACKENZIE Joseph.. levered up the lid.. with a chisel. A. MACLEAN I levered Smithy into a sitting position.

leverage /ˈliːv(ə)rɪdʒ/ *noun & verb*. E18.

[ORIGIN from LEVER *noun* + -AGE.]

▸ **A** *noun*. **1** The action of levering; the way of applying a lever. Also, a system of levers. E18.

2 The power of a lever; the mechanical advantage gained by the use of a lever. M19. ▸**b** *fig.* Advantage for accomplishing a purpose; increased power of action. M19.

3 *COMMERCE.* **a** The proportion of a company's total capital to ordinary shares; the effect of this on share prices. M20. ▸**b** The earning potential created by the ratio of capital to shares; the use of borrowed capital to enhance this. M20.

▸ **B** *verb trans.* **1** = LEVER *verb* 2. M20.

2 Use borrowed capital for (investment), expecting profits made to be greater than the interest payable. Chiefly as ***leveraged*** *ppl adjective*. M20.

leveraged buyout the buyout of a company (by its management) using borrowed capital.

lever de rideau /ləve də rido/ *noun phr.* Pl. ***levers de rideau*** (pronounced same). M19.

[ORIGIN French.]

= ***curtain-raiser*** s.v. CURTAIN *noun*.

leveret /ˈlɛv(ə)rɪt/ *noun*. LME.

[ORIGIN Anglo-Norman, dim. of *levre*, Old French & mod. French *lièvre* from Latin *lepus*, *lepor-* hare: see -ET[1].]

1 A young hare; *spec.* one in its first year. LME.

†**2** *transf. & fig.* A pet; a mistress. E–M17.

levers /ˈliːvəz/ *noun*[1]. Long *obsolete* exc. *dial.*

[ORIGIN Old English *læfer*. Cf. LAVER *noun*[3].]

Any of various plants with long flat leaves; *esp.* the yellow flag, *Iris pseudacorus*.

Levers /ˈliːvəz/ *noun*[2]. Also **Leavers**. E19.

[ORIGIN John *Levers* (1786–1848).]

Used ***attrib.***, ***absol.***, and in ***possess.*** in names of lace-making machinery developed by Levers, and of lace thus produced.

levers de rideau *noun phr.* pl. of LEVER DE RIDEAU.

L

†**levet** *noun*. E17–E18.
[ORIGIN Perh. from Italian *levata*, from *levare* raise.]
A trumpet call etc. to rouse soldiers and others in the morning; a reveille.

levi *noun* see LEVI'S.

leviable /ˈlɛvɪəb(ə)l/ *adjective*. Also **levy-**. L15.
[ORIGIN from LEVY *verb* + -ABLE.]
1 Of a duty, tax, etc.: able to be levied. L15.
2 Of a person: able to be called on for payment of a contribution. Of a thing: able to be seized in execution. L19.

leviathan /lɪˈvʌɪəθ(ə)n/ *noun & adjective*. As noun freq. also **L-**. LME.
[ORIGIN Late Latin (Vulgate) from Hebrew *liwyātān*.]
▸ **A** *noun*. **1** An (imaginary or real) aquatic animal of enormous size; a sea monster. LME. ▸**b** *fig.* A man of vast and formidable power or enormous wealth. E17. ▸**c** Anything very large of its kind; *esp.* a huge ship. E19.
MILTON Leviathan, Hugest of living Creatures. **b** DE QUINCEY So potent a defendant as this leviathan of two counties.
2 [After *Isaiah* 27:1.] Satan. LME.
R. WEST As the Almighty pointed out to Job, nothing can be done about . . leviathan.
3 [After a book by Hobbes, 1651.] The commonwealth, the state. In later use, a totalitarian or bureaucratic regime. M17.
▸ **B** *adjective*. Huge, monstrous. E17.
■ **leviaˈthanic** *adjective* (*rare*) huge as a leviathan M19.

Levied /ˈliːvʌɪd/ *adjective*. Also **Levi'd**. M20.
[ORIGIN from LEVI'S + -ED².]
Clad in Levi's; wearing Levi's.

levier /ˈlɛvɪə/ *noun*. Also **levy-**. L15.
[ORIGIN from LEVY *verb* + -ER¹.]
A person who levies something.

levigate /ˈlɛvɪgeɪt/ *verb trans.* Pa. pple †**-ate** (earlier), **-ated**. M16.
[ORIGIN Latin *levigat-* pa. ppl stem of *levigare* make smooth, polish: see -ATE³.]
†**1** Lighten, alleviate. Only in M16.
†**2** Make smooth; polish. M16–M19.
3 Reduce to a fine smooth powder; make a smooth paste of (*with* some liquid). M16.
■ **levigator** *noun* a thick metal polishing disc, used to smooth a lithographic stone E20.

levigation /lɛvɪˈgeɪʃ(ə)n/ *noun*. L15.
[ORIGIN from Latin *levigatio(n-)*, formed as LEVIGATE: see -ATION.]
The grinding of a substance in a mortar or on a slab, esp. with a liquid; the action of levigating something.

levin /ˈlɛvɪn/ *noun*. *arch.* ME.
[ORIGIN Prob. Old Norse, perh. from 1st elem. of Old Swedish *liughnelder* (Swedish *ljungeld*, Danish *lygnild*) lightning flash, from Germanic base of LIGHT *noun*.]
Lightning; a flash of lightning. Also, any bright light or flame.

levir /ˈliːvə/ *noun*. M19.
[ORIGIN Latin = Old English *tācor*, Homeric Greek *daēr*, Sanskrit *devṛ* husband's brother, brother-in-law.]
ANTHROPOLOGY. A brother-in-law; a person acting as such under the custom of the levirate.

levirate /ˈliːvɪrət/ *noun*. E18.
[ORIGIN formed as LEVIR + -ATE¹.]
The custom among ancient Hebrews and some other peoples, which obliged a dead man's brother or next of kin under certain circumstances to marry his widow.
■ **leviˈratic** *adjective* pertaining to or in accordance with the levirate E20.

Levi's /ˈliːvʌɪz/ *noun pl.* Also **Levis**, **l-**, in attrib. use **levi**. E20.
[ORIGIN *Levi* Strauss: see below.]
(Proprietary name for) a type of blue denim jeans or overalls patented and produced by Levi Strauss (1829–1902) as working clothes in the 1860s and adopted as a fashion garment in the 20th cent.

levitate /ˈlɛvɪteɪt/ *verb*. L17.
[ORIGIN from Latin *levis* light, after GRAVITATE: see -ATE³.]
1 *verb intrans.* Rise by virtue of lightness. *rare* in *gen.* sense. L17. ▸**b** Chiefly SPIRITUALISM. Rise and float in the air through supernatural agency. L19.
b CARYL CHURCHILL Joy will cause the . . population to levitate two feet off the ground.
2 *verb trans.* Make lighter or of less weight. *rare*. L17.
3 *verb trans.* **a** Chiefly SPIRITUALISM. Cause to levitate. L19. ▸**b** Cause (something heavier than the surrounding fluid) to rise or remain suspended without visible means (e.g. using magnetic forces). M20.
a A. LANG The levitated boy . . flew over a garden. **b** *Observer* Levitated trains would hover five inches above a metal track, held aloft by advanced repelling magnets.
■ **levitant** *noun* = LEVITATOR L19. **levitative** *adjective* adapted for or capable of levitation L19. **levitator** *noun* a person who believes in levitation or professes ability to practise it L19.

levitation /lɛvɪˈteɪʃ(ə)n/ *noun*. M17.
[ORIGIN from LEVITATE + -ATION.]
1 The action or process of levitating or being levitated; an instance of this. M17.
H. G. WELLS The invisibility of all the machinery gave an extraordinary effect of independent levitation. *Listener* A standing offer of £1,000 to any medium who can produce physical phenomena such as . . levitation . . under test conditions. *Observer* 'Magnetic levitation' . . could turn out to be the most important advance in transport technology.
†**2** The action or process of becoming lighter. Also, the quality of being comparatively light; buoyancy. L17–M18.
■ **levitational** *adjective* E20.

Levite /ˈliːvʌɪt/ *noun*. ME.
[ORIGIN Christian Latin *levita*, *levites*, from Greek *levitēs*, from *Levi*, from Hebrew *lēwī* Levi: see -ITE¹.]
1 A member of the ancient Jewish tribe of Levi, esp. of that part of it which provided assistants to the priests in worship in the temple. ME.
†**2** A deacon. LME–E17.
†**3** A member of the clergy; a domestic chaplain. Usu. *derog.* M17–M19.

Levitic /lɪˈvɪtɪk/ *adjective*. M17.
[ORIGIN formed as LEVITICAL: see -IC.]
= LEVITICAL.

Levitical /lɪˈvɪtɪk(ə)l/ *adjective*. M16.
[ORIGIN from late Latin (Vulgate) *leviticus* from Greek *levitikos* from *levitēs*: see LEVITE, -ICAL.]
1 Of or pertaining to the Levites. M16.
2 Of or pertaining to the ancient Jewish system of ritual administered by the Levites. Also, of or pertaining to the biblical Book of Leviticus. M16.
Levitical degrees the degrees of consanguinity within which marriage is forbidden (*Leviticus* 18:6–18).
■ **Leviticalism** *noun* Levitical tenets and practice L19. **Levitically** *adverb* in a Levitical manner, according to Levitical law M17.

levity /ˈlɛvɪti/ *noun*. M16.
[ORIGIN Latin *levitas*, from *levis* light: see -ITY.]
1 A tendency to make light of serious matters; frivolity; inappropriate jocularity. Now also, an instance of this. M16. ▸**b** Lack of constancy or resolution; instability, fickleness. E17. ▸**c** Undignified behaviour, impropriety; an instance of this. E17.
R. W. EMERSON But politics . . cannot be treated with levity. J. K. JEROME He had not meant to be funny, . . levity was not his failing. **b** GIBBON Forgot, with the levity of Barbarians, the services which they had . . received. **c** SWIFT Those . . little levities so commonly incident to young ladies.
2 The quality or fact of having comparatively little weight; lightness. *arch.* L16. ▸**b** A property formerly believed to exist in varying degrees in all substances and which made them tend to rise, as substances possessing gravity tend to sink. Cf. GRAVITY 4a. *obsolete* exc. *hist.* E17.
M. SOMERVILLE Hydrogen . . rises in the air on account of its levity.

levo- *combining form* see LAEVO-.

levodopa /liːvə(ʊ)ˈdəʊpə/ *noun*. L20.
[ORIGIN from *levo-* var. of LAEVO- + DOPA.]
BIOCHEMISTRY & PHARMACOLOGY. = *L-dopa* s.v. DOPA.

levorotatory *adjective* see LAEVOROTATORY.

levulinic *adjective* see LAEVULINIC.

levulosan, **levulose** *nouns* see LAEVULOSAN, LAEVULOSE.

levy /ˈlɛvi/ *noun*¹. ME.
[ORIGIN Old French & mod. French *levée* use as noun of fem. pa. pple of *lever*, from Latin *levare* raise, from *levis* light.]
1 a The collection of an assessment, duty, or tax (formerly also, of a debt or fine). ME. ▸**b** A tax, *esp.* one raised for a particular purpose; a call for or contribution of so much per member of a society. M17.
DISRAELI The sole object of the Government was to settle the legal levy of the duties. **b** W. E. COLLINSON The compulsory levy made by the Trade Unions.
b *capital levy*: see CAPITAL *adjective* & *noun*².
2 The enrolling or conscription of men for war. E17. ▸**b** A body of men enrolled; in *pl.*, the men enrolled. E17.
b E. A. FREEMAN The Danes put the irregular . . levies to flight.
levy in mass conscription of all able-bodied men (cf. LEVÉE EN MASSE).
– COMB.: **levy-money** †(*a*) a gratuity paid to recruits on enlistment; (*b*) contributions called for from the members of a society.

levy /ˈlɛvi/ *noun*². *US local. arch.* E19.
[ORIGIN Contr. of *eleven* (*pence* or *-penny bit*).]
= BIT *noun*² 4b.

levy /ˈlɛvi/ *verb trans.* LME.
[ORIGIN from LEVY *noun*¹, or directly from Old French & mod. French *lever*.]
1 Raise (contributions, taxes) or impose (a rate, toll, fee, etc.) as a levy. Foll. by †*of*, *on*, *upon*. LME. ▸**b** Impose (service) *upon*; demand (a person's attendance). M19. ▸**c** Impose a levy on (a person). E20.
2 †**a** Raise (a sum of money) as a profit or rent; collect (a debt). Also, take the revenues of (land). LME–M18. ▸**b** Raise (a sum of money) by legal execution or process. Foll. by *on* (*the goods of*). E16. ▸**c** Extort (esp. blackmail). M19.
†**3** Set up (a fence, weir, etc.); erect (a house). LME–M18.
4 Begin to wage (war), commence (hostilities). Foll. by *against*, *on*, *upon*. LME.
5 LAW. ***a levy a fine***, enter into a collusive suit for the transfer of land. *obsolete* exc. *hist.* L15. ▸**b** Draw up (an objection, protest) in due form. M17.
6 Enlist (armed men), raise (an army). L15.
†**7** Raise (a siege); break up (a camp). M16–E17.

levyable *adjective*, **levyer** *noun* vars. of LEVIABLE, LEVIER.

lew /ljuː, luː/ *noun*, *adjective*, & *verb*. Now *dial.* Also **loo** /luː/.
[ORIGIN Old English *hlēow-* stem of *hlēo*: see LEE *noun*¹. See also LEW-WARM.]
▸ **A** *noun*. **1** Lee, shelter; something giving shelter. OE.
2 Warmth, heat. *obsolete* exc. *Scot.* L16.
▸ **B** *adjective*. †**1** Warm; sunny. Only in OE.
2 Lukewarm, tepid. ME.
3 Sheltered from the wind. L17.
▸ **C** *verb*. **1** *verb trans. & intrans.* Make or become warm or tepid. OE.
2 *verb trans.* Shelter. M17.

lewd /luːd, ljuːd/ *adjective*. OE.
[ORIGIN Unknown.]
†**1** Lay, not in holy orders, not clerical. OE–E19.
†**2** Unlearned, unlettered, untaught. Of speech or art: crude, artless. ME–E17.
3 Belonging to or characteristic of the common people; common, low, vulgar. Long *rare*. LME.
†**4** Foolish, unskilful, bungling; ill-bred, bad-mannered. LME–E18.
†**5** Bad, worthless, poor, sorry. LME–L17.
6 Vile, evil, wicked, good-for-nothing, worthless. *obsolete* exc. as passing into sense 7. LME.
7 Crude and offensive in a sexual way; indecent, obscene. LME.
P. FUSSELL Lewd seaside postcards. S. FALUDI Sometimes the men would yell lewd things.
■ **lewdly** *adverb* LME. **lewdness** *noun* LME. **lewdster** *noun* (*rare*) a lascivious person L16.

lewis /ˈluːɪs/ *noun*¹. LME.
[ORIGIN Prob. from Old French *lous*, pl. of *lou(p)* (lit. 'wolf') a kind of siege engine.]
An iron contrivance for gripping heavy blocks of stone for lifting, consisting of three pieces arranged to form a dovetail, the outside pieces being fixed in a dovetail mortise by the insertion of the middle piece.

Lewis /ˈluːɪs/ *noun*². E20.
[ORIGIN Col. Isaac Newton *Lewis* (1858–1931), US soldier.]
In full ***Lewis gun***, ***Lewis machine-gun***. A light magazine-fed, gas-operated, air-cooled machine gun.

Lewis /ˈluːɪs/ *noun*³. M20.
[ORIGIN Gilbert Newton *Lewis* (1875–1946), US chemist.]
CHEMISTRY. Used **attrib.** and in **possess.** to designate the theory proposed by Lewis that atoms can combine to form molecules by sharing electrons.
Lewis acid a compound or ionic species which can accept an electron pair from a donor compound. **Lewis base** a compound or ionic species which can donate an electron pair to an acceptor compound.

lewis *noun*⁴ see LOUIS *noun*¹.

lewis /ˈluːɪs/ *verb trans.* M19.
[ORIGIN from LEWIS *noun*¹.]
Fasten by means of, or after the manner of, a lewis.

lewisia /luːˈɪzɪə, -ˈɪsɪə/ *noun*. M19.
[ORIGIN mod. Latin (see below), from Capt. Meriwether *Lewis* (1774–1809), US explorer + -IA¹.]
Any plant of the genus *Lewisia*, of the purslane family, comprising small flowering perennials native to western N. America, with fleshy leaves in a basal rosette and thick starchy roots.

Lewisian /luːˈɪsɪən/ *adjective*. M19.
[ORIGIN from *Lewis* (see LEWISMAN) + -IAN.]
GEOLOGY. Of, pertaining to, or characteristic of Lewis in the Outer Hebrides; *spec.* designating the oldest rocks in Britain, a group of Precambrian gneisses in NW Scotland.

lewisite /ˈluːɪsʌɪt/ *noun*. E20.
[ORIGIN from Winford Lee *Lewis* (1878–1943), US chemist + -ITE¹.]
A powerful vesicant and respiratory irritant developed for use in chemical warfare; 2-chlorovinyldichloroarsine, $ClCH{=}CHAsCl_2$, a dark oily liquid or vapour.

Lewisman /ˈluːɪsmən/ *noun*. Pl. **-men**. E20.
[ORIGIN from *Lewis* (see below) + MAN *noun*.]
A native or inhabitant of Lewis, the northern section of the island of Lewis with Harris in the Outer Hebrides off the NW coast of Scotland.

lewth /luːθ/ *noun*. *obsolete* exc. *dial.* OE.
[ORIGIN from LEW *adjective* + -TH¹.]
Warmth; shelter.

lew-warm /'lju:wɔ:m, 'lu:-/ *adjective.* Now *dial.* LME.
[ORIGIN from LEW *adjective* + WARM *adjective.*]
Lukewarm.

lex domicilii /ˌlɛks dɒmɪ'sɪlɪʌɪ/ *noun phr.* E19.
[ORIGIN Latin = law of the domicile.]
LAW. The law of the country in which a person is domiciled, as determining the right to make a will, succeed to property, etc.

lexeme /'lɛksi:m/ *noun.* M20.
[ORIGIN from LEX(ICON + -EME.]
LINGUISTICS. A lexical unit in the vocabulary of a language; a morpheme representing such a unit.
■ **le'xemic** *adjective & noun* (*a*) *adjective* of or pertaining to lexemes; (*b*) *noun* in *pl.*, the branch of linguistics that deals with lexemes: M20.

lex fori /lɛks 'fɔ:rʌɪ/ *noun phr.* E19.
[ORIGIN Latin = law of the court.]
LAW. The law of the country in which an action is brought, as regulating procedure, evidence, execution of judgements, etc.

lexical /'lɛksɪk(ə)l/ *adjective.* M19.
[ORIGIN from Greek *lexikos* (see LEXICON) + -AL[1].]
1 Of or pertaining to the words or vocabulary of a language. Freq. opp. ***grammatical.*** M19.

G. A. MILLER In the Oxford English Dictionary there are nearly half a million lexical units.

lexical meaning the meaning of a base in a paradigm or abstracted from particular grammatical contexts, e.g. of *love* in or as represented by *loves, loved, loving*, etc.
2 Pertaining to or of the nature of a lexicon or dictionary. L19.
■ **lexically** *adverb* (*a*) in respect of vocabulary; (*b*) according to lexicons of a language; in the manner of a lexicon: M19.

lexicalize /'lɛksɪk(ə)lʌɪz/ *verb trans.* Also **-ise.** M20.
[ORIGIN from LEXICAL + -IZE.]
LINGUISTICS. Represent by a unit or distinction in the lexicon or vocabulary of a language. Usu. in *pass.*
■ **lexicali'zation** *noun* M20.

lexico- /'lɛksɪkəʊ/ *combining form.* M20.
[ORIGIN Greek *lexiko-*, from *lexikos*: see LEXICON, -O-.]
LINGUISTICS. Forming compounds with the sense 'partly lexical and partly —', as in ***lexico-grammatical, lexico-statistic*** *adjectives.*

lexicographer /lɛksɪ'kɒgrəfə/ *noun.* M17.
[ORIGIN from late Greek *lexikographos*, formed as LEXICO-: see -GRAPHER.]
A writer or compiler of a dictionary or dictionaries.

lexicography /lɛksɪ'kɒgrəfi/ *noun.* L17.
[ORIGIN formed as LEXICO- + -GRAPHY.]
The art or practice of writing dictionaries.
■ **lexico'graphic** *adjective* = LEXICOGRAPHICAL E19. **lexico'graphical** *adjective* of or pertaining to lexicography L18. **lexico'graphically** *adverb* L19. †**lexicographics** *noun pl.* lexicographical writings: only in E18.

lexicology /lɛksɪ'kɒlədʒi/ *noun.* E19.
[ORIGIN formed as LEXICO- + -LOGY.]
The branch of knowledge that deals with words, their form, meaning, and (sometimes) history; the branch of linguistics that deals with the structure and content of the lexicon.
■ **lexico'logical** *adjective* of or pertaining to lexicology M19. **lexico'logically** *adverb* M20. **lexicologist** *noun* L19.

lexicon /'lɛksɪk(ə)n/ *noun.* E17.
[ORIGIN mod. Latin from Greek *lexikon* (sc. *biblion* book) neut. sing. of *lexikos* pertaining to words, from *lexis* phrase, word, diction from *legein* speak.]
1 A dictionary, *esp.* one of Greek, Hebrew, Syriac, or Arabic. E17. ▸**b** The vocabulary of some department of knowledge or sphere of activity; the vocabulary or word-stock of a region, a particular speaker, etc. Also, a list of words or names. M17.

b M. SCAMMELL That uniquely broad . . earthy lexicon that instantly identifies . . Solzhenitsyn's mature literary style. *New York Times* The President . . has decided to begin testing— 'routine' testing—of immigrants . . . In Mr. Reagan's lexicon 'routine' means 'mandatory, compulsory'.

2 *LINGUISTICS.* The complete set of elementary meaningful units in a language; the words etc. which would be in a complete dictionary (but without definitions). M20.
3 (**L-**.) (Proprietary name for) a game played with cards marked with the letters of the alphabet, the object being to form as long a word as possible. M20.
■ **lexiconize** *verb* (*a*) *verb intrans.* compile a lexicon; (*b*) *verb trans.* reduce to the form of a lexicon: L19.

lexicostatistic /ˌlɛksɪkəʊstə'tɪstɪk/ *adjective.* M20.
[ORIGIN from LEXICO- + STATISTIC *adjective.*]
LINGUISTICS. Of or pertaining to the statistics of vocabulary.
■ **lexicostatistical** *adjective* M20. **lexicostatistically** *adverb* M20.

lexicostatistics /ˌlɛksɪkəʊstə'tɪstɪks/ *noun.* M20.
[ORIGIN from LEXICO- + STATISTICS.]
The branch of linguistics that deals with the statistics of vocabulary; *spec.* = GLOTTOCHRONOLOGY.

lexigram /'lɛksɪgram/ *noun.* L20.
[ORIGIN from Greek LEXIS + -GRAM.]
A symbol representing a word; *esp.* one used in learning a language.

lexigraphy /lɛk'sɪgrəfi/ *noun.* E19.
[ORIGIN from Greek LEXIS + -GRAPHY.]
A system of writing in which each character represents a word, as in Chinese. Also (*rare*), the art of defining words.
■ **lexi'graphic** *adjective* pertaining to or characterized by lexigraphy M19. **lexi'graphical** *adjective* (*a*) = LEXIGRAPHIC; †(*b*) giving a diagrammatic representation of items in a list: E19. **lexi'graphically** *adverb* M19.

Lexiphanes /lɛk'sɪf(ə)ni:z/ *noun. literary.* M18.
[ORIGIN Greek *Lexiphanēs* phrase-monger (title of one of Lucian's dialogues), from LEXIS + *phan-*, *phainein* to display.]
A person who uses bombastic phraseology.
■ **Lexiphanic** /-'fanɪk/ *adjective* indulging in or marked by bombastic phraseology M18. **Lexiphanicism** /-'fanɪsɪz(ə)m/ *noun* (an instance of) bombastic phraseology M18.

lexis /'lɛksɪs/ *noun.* M20.
[ORIGIN Greek: see LEXICON.]
1 The diction or wording, in contrast to other elements, of a piece of writing. M20.
2 *LINGUISTICS.* Items of lexical, as opp. esp. to grammatical, meaning; the total word-stock of a language. Also, the branch of knowledge that deals with words as lexical items. M20.

lex loci /lɛks 'ləʊsʌɪ/ *noun phr.* L18.
[ORIGIN Latin = law of the place.]
LAW. The law of the country in which some event material to a case took place. Freq. foll. by a defining word or phr. ***lex loci contractus*** /kɒn'traktjʊs/ [= of a contract] the law of the country in which a contract was made. ***lex loci delicti*** /də'lɪktʌɪ/ [= of an offense] the law of the country in which a tort was committed.

lexotactics /lɛksəʊ'taktɪks/ *noun.* M20.
[ORIGIN Irreg. from LEX(EME + -O- + TACTICS.]
The branch of linguistics that deals with the ordering of lexemes in a language. Cf. MORPHOTACTICS, PHONOTACTICS.

lex talionis /ˌlɛks talɪ'əʊnɪs/ *noun phr.* M17.
[ORIGIN Latin, from *lex* law + *talionis* genit. of *talio(n-)* (see TALION). Cf. earlier LEGE TALIONIS.]
The (supposed) law of retaliation; the retributive theory of punishment, based on the Mosaic principle 'an eye for an eye, a tooth for a tooth'.

ley /leɪ/ *noun*[1]. Also **lay**, (now *rare*) **lea** /li:/. LME.
[ORIGIN Absol. use of LEA *adjective.*]
Land that has remained untilled for some years, *spec.* (*AGRICULTURE*) land put down to grass or clover for a limited period of years; a piece of such land.
– COMB.: **ley farming** the alternate growing of crops and grass.

ley /li:, leɪ/ *noun*[2]. E20.
[ORIGIN Specialized use of var. of LEA *noun*[1].]
A hypothetical straight line connecting prehistoric sites etc., freq. regarded as the line of an ancient track and credited by some with paranormal properties. Now usu. more fully ***ley line.***

leycesteria /lɛ'stɪərɪə/ *noun.* M19.
[ORIGIN mod. Latin (see below), from William *Leyster* (fl. 1820), Chief Justice of Bengal + -IA[1].]
Any of several Himalayan shrubs of the genus *Leycesteria*, of the honeysuckle family, with flowers in the axils of conspicuous purple bracts; esp. *L. formosa*, sometimes planted as cover for game.

Leyden /'lʌɪd(ə)n, 'leɪd(ə)n/ *noun.* M18.
[ORIGIN A city in the Netherlands (now *Leiden*).]
Chiefly *hist.* ***Leyden jar***, †***Leyden bottle***, †***Leyden phial***, an early electrical capacitor consisting of a glass bottle partly coated inside and outside with tinfoil.

Leydig /'lʌɪdɪg/ *noun.* E20.
[ORIGIN Franz von *Leydig* (1821–1908), German anatomist.]
ANATOMY. ***Leydig cell***, ***Leydig's cell***, ***cell of Leydig***, an interstitial cell of the testis, believed to be the site of androgen production. Usu. in *pl.*

Leyland cypress /'leɪlənd 'sʌɪprəs/ *noun phr.* Also **Leyland's cypress** /-ləndz/. M20.
[ORIGIN Christopher John *Leyland* (1849–1926), Brit. horticulturist.]
A vigorous ornamental hybrid cypress, × *Cupressocyparis leylandii*, much grown as a screening plant.

leylandii /leɪ'landɪʌɪ/ *noun.* Pl. same. L20.
[ORIGIN mod. Latin taxonomic name.]
The Leyland cypress.

lez *noun & adjective* var. of LES.

Lezgian *noun & adjective* var. of LESGHIAN.

lezzy /'lɛzi/ *noun & adjective. slang.* Also **lezzie**, **lezzer** /'lɛzə/. M20.
[ORIGIN Abbreviation: see -Y[6]. Cf. LES, LESBO, LIZZIE 1b.]
= LESBIAN *adjective & noun.*

LF *abbreviation.*
Low frequency.

LGV *abbreviation.*
Large goods vehicle

LH *abbreviation.*
BIOCHEMISTRY. Luteinizing hormone.

l.h. *abbreviation.*
Left hand.

Lhasa /'lɑ:sə/ *noun.* E20.
[ORIGIN The capital of Tibet.]
In full ***Lhasa apso*** /'apsəʊ/, pl. **-os**. (An animal of) a breed of small long-coated dog, often gold or grey and white, originating at Lhasa. Formerly also ***Lhasa terrier.***

LHD *abbreviation.*
Left-hand drive.

lhiamba /lɪ'ambə/ *noun.* Also ***li-***. M19.
[ORIGIN Bantu (cf. Kikongo *diamba*).]
In southern central Africa: marijuana, cannabis.

LI *abbreviation.*
1 Light Infantry.
2 Long Island.

Li *symbol.*
CHEMISTRY. Lithium.

li /li:/ *noun*[1]. Pl. same. L16.
[ORIGIN Chinese *lǐ*.]
A Chinese unit of distance, equal to about 0.6 km (0.4 mile).

li /li:/ *noun*[2]. L17.
[ORIGIN Chinese *lǐ*.]
In neo-Confucianism, correct observance of the rules governing behaviour to others, regarded as needed to maintain a person's harmony with the moral principles of nature.

li /li:/ *noun*[3]. Pl. same. M20.
[ORIGIN Chinese *lǐ*.]
An ancient Chinese bronze or pottery cooking vessel, with (usu. three) hollow legs.

liability /lʌɪə'bɪlɪti/ *noun.* L18.
[ORIGIN from LIABLE *adjective* + -ITY.]
1 *LAW.* The condition of being liable or answerable by law or equity. L18.
limited liability: see LIMITED *adjective.* ***STRICT liability.***
2 The condition of being liable or subject *to* something, apt or likely *to do* or *to suffer*, something undesirable. E19.
3 A thing for which a person is liable; *esp.* in *pl.*, the debts or pecuniary obligations of a person or company. M19.
4 *transf. & fig.* A person who or thing which puts one at a disadvantage, a hindering responsibility, a handicap. Freq. opp. ***asset.*** M20.

M. ATWOOD I had been twelve, which was a liability when other people were fifteen. *Lancaster Guardian* British Rail want to close it because it is a maintenance liability.

liable /'lʌɪəb(ə)l/ *pred. adjective.* LME.
[ORIGIN Perh. from Anglo-Norman, from Old French & mod. French *lier* bind (see LIAISON), but late and not in Anglo-Norman or Anglo-Latin records.]
1 *LAW.* Bound or obliged by law or equity; answerable at law (*for*, †*to*); subject *to* a tax, penalty, etc.; bound in law *to do.* LME. ▸**b** Of land: subject to taxation. Now *rare* or *obsolete.* E17.

F. DONALDSON If I spend more than six months in this country I'm liable to pay income tax. *Woman & Home* All drug companies will become strictly liable for injuries caused by their products. *Which?* Goods brought in from a non-EC country are liable to import duty.

2 a Susceptible, exposed, or open *to* (something undesirable). Formerly also *gen.*, subject *to* (any influence or change). L16. ▸**b** Apt or likely *to do* (exc. *dial. & N. Amer.* chiefly something undesirable), *to be —ed.* L17.

a ADDISON He . . found that though they were Objects of his Sight, they were not liable to his Touch. A. STORR Although everyone, in varying degree, is liable to depression . . some persons are peculiarly susceptible. **b** *Farmer & Stockbreeder* Salesmanship . . is liable to be overrated. W. WHARTON Without his glasses, he's liable to smash into a tree.

†**3** Subject or subservient *to*; attached or belonging *to.* L16–E17.
†**4** Suitable, apt, (*to do*). Only in L16.

SHAKES. *John* Finding thee . . Apt, liable to be employ'd in danger.

†**5** Incident *to.* M17–M18.

E. HAYWOOD The faults of inadvertency are liable to us all.

■ **liableness** *noun* (now *rare*) M17.

liaise /lɪ'eɪz/ *verb intrans. colloq.* (orig. *military slang*). E20.
[ORIGIN Back-form. from LIAISON.]
Establish communication or cooperation, act as a link, (*with, between*).

liaison /lɪ'eɪz(ə)n, -zɒn, -zɒ̃/ *noun.* M17.
[ORIGIN French, from *lier* bind from Latin *ligare* + -ISON.]
1 *COOKERY.* A binding or thickening agent for sauces, consisting chiefly of the yolks of eggs. Formerly, the process of binding or thickening. M17.
2 An intimate relation or connection; *spec.* an illicit sexual relationship, esp. between a man and a married woman. E19.

L

R. THOMAS Her antidote . . had been party after party . . and dangerous, discreet liaisons.

3 Communication and cooperation, orig. *spec.* between military forces or units, esp. during a battle or campaign. **E19.**

B. B. SCHOFIELD The liaison between the two services was as good as it could be. A. W. MYERS Mind and body must be working in liaison.

4 *PHONETICS.* The pronunciation of a normally silent final consonant before a vowel (or mute *h*) beginning the following word, esp. in French. **L19.**

Daily Chronicle The nightly false 'liaison' made by a clever actress . . . 'Take Lady Agatha-r-out,' she says.

– COMB.: **liaison officer** an officer in the armed services concerned with the liaison of units etc.

liamba *noun* var. of LHIAMBA.

liana /lɪˈɑːnə/ *noun.* Also **liane** /lɪˈɑːn/. **L18.**
[ORIGIN French *liane*, †*liène*, orig. = clematis, perh. from dial. French *liener* bind sheaves, from French *lien* bond, tie; alt. after Latin or Spanish models.]
Any long woody climbing plant that twines round trees, esp. in a tropical rainforest; the stem of such a plant.

liang /ljaŋ/ *noun.* Pl. same. **E19.**
[ORIGIN Chinese *liǎng*.]
A Chinese weight equal to about 38 grams (1⅓ oz); this weight in silver as a monetary unit. Also called ***tael***.

liangle *noun* var. of LEANGLE.

liar /ˈlʌɪə/ *noun.*
[ORIGIN Old English *lēogere* (= Old High German *liugari*, Old Norse *ljúgari*), from *lēogan* LIE *verb*[2] + -ER[1]: see -AR[3].]
1 A person who lies or tells a falsehood; an untruthful person. **OE.**
paradox of the liar, **the liar (paradox)** *LOGIC* the paradox involved in a speaker's statement that he or she is lying or is a (habitual) liar.
2 In *pl.*, or in full ***liar dice***. A gambling game resembling poker dice, in which the thrower conceals the dice thrown and sometimes declares a false score. **M20.**

L

liard /ljɑː, ljɑːd/ *noun.* **M16.**
[ORIGIN French, of unknown origin.]
hist. A small coin formerly current in France, worth a quarter of a sou. Also, (the type of) a coin of small value.

lias /ˈlʌɪəs/ *noun.* In sense 1 orig. **lyas**; in sense 2 usu. **L-**. **LME.**
[ORIGIN Old French *liais* hard limestone, prob. from *lie* LEE *noun*[2].]
1 A kind of blue argillaceous limestone rock, esp. as it occurs in SW England. **LME.**
2 *GEOLOGY.* ***the Lias***, a series of fossiliferous strata forming the lowest division of the Jurassic system, and including blue argillaceous limestones. **E19.**
■ **liassic** /lʌɪˈasɪk/ *adjective* (*GEOLOGY*) of or pertaining to the Lias **M19.**

liatris /lʌɪˈatrɪs, ˈlʌɪətrɪs/ *noun.* **E19.**
[ORIGIN mod. Latin (see below), of unknown origin.]
Any of various N. American plants of the genus *Liatris*, of the composite family, cultivated for their long spikes of purple or white flower heads. Also called ***blazing star***.

Lib /lɪb/ *noun*[1] & *adjective. colloq.* Also **l-**. **L19.**
[ORIGIN Abbreviation.]
= LIBERAL *adjective* 5, *noun* 2. See also LIB-LAB.
Lib Dem *colloq.* a Liberal Democrat, Liberal Democratic.

lib /lɪb/ *noun*[2]. *colloq.* **M20.**
[ORIGIN Abbreviation.]
Liberation, esp. from social discrimination.
Gay Lib: see GAY *adjective*. ***Men's Lib***: see MAN *noun*. ***women's lib***: see WOMAN *noun*.

lib /lɪb/ *verb*[1] *trans. obsolete* exc. *dial.* Infl. **-bb-**. **LME.**
[ORIGIN Perh. from Germanic base repr. also by Middle Dutch *lubben* maim, geld, and already in Old English. See also GLIB *verb*[2].]
Castrate, geld.

†**lib** *verb*[2] *intrans. criminals' slang.* Infl. **-bb-**. **M16–M19.**
[ORIGIN Unknown.]
Sleep.

libament /ˈlɪbəm(ə)nt/ *noun. arch.* **L16.**
[ORIGIN Latin *libamentum*, from *libare*: see LIBATE, -MENT.]
A drink-offering, a libation.

libate /lʌɪˈbeɪt/ *verb trans. & intrans. literary.* **M19.**
[ORIGIN Latin *libat-* pa. ppl stem of *libare* pour out, rel. to Greek *leibein* pour drop by drop: see -ATE[3].]
Pour out (wine etc.) in honour of a god. Also, make a libation to (a god).

libation /lʌɪˈbeɪʃ(ə)n/ *noun.* **LME.**
[ORIGIN Latin *libatio(n-)*, formed as LIBATE: see -ATION.]
1 The action or an act of pouring out of wine or other liquid in honour of a god; liquid so poured out; a drink-offering. **LME.**

T. O. ECHEWA Everyone pours libations . . to the spirits of the ancestors.

2 *transf.* Liquid poured out to be drunk; a potation. *joc.* **M18.**

J. AGATE Further libations being indicated, my . . bottle of whiskey . . was now requisitioned.

■ **libationary** *adjective* = LIBATORY *adjective* **L19.** **libationer** *noun* a person who pours out libations to a god etc. **E20.**

libatory /ˈlʌɪbət(ə)ri/ *noun & adjective.* **E17.**
[ORIGIN As noun from ecclesiastical Latin *libatorium*, formed as LIBATE; as adjective from LIBATION after *vibratory*, *vibration*: see -ORY[1], -ORY[2].]
▸ †**A** *noun.* A vessel used in libation. Only in **E17.**
▸ **B** *adjective.* Pertaining to or consisting of libations. **M19.**

libbard *noun & adjective* see LEOPARD.

†**libbege** *noun. criminals' slang.* **M16–M19.**
[ORIGIN Uncertain: cf. LIB *verb*[2].]
A bed.

libber /ˈlɪbə/ *noun. colloq.* **L20.**
[ORIGIN from LIB *noun*[2] + -ER[1].]
An advocate of liberation, a liberationist; *esp.* = ***women's liberationist*** s.v. WOMAN *noun*.

libbet /ˈlɪbɪt/ *noun*[1]. *obsolete* exc. *dial.* **M16.**
[ORIGIN Perh. rel. to Old French *libe*, *libbe* block of stone: see -ET[1].]
A thick length of wood; a stick used to beat or throw at something.

libbet /ˈlɪbɪt/ *noun*[2]. *obsolete* exc. *dial.* Also **lippet** /ˈlɪpɪt/. **L16.**
[ORIGIN Uncertain: perh. var. of LAPPET.]
A torn piece, a shred, a fragment. Formerly, the lobe of the ear.

libeccio /lɪˈbɛtʃəʊ/ *noun.* **M17.**
[ORIGIN Italian, from Latin *Lib-*, *Libs* (also *Lips*) from Greek *Lib-*, *Lips*.]
(The Italian name for) the south-west wind.

libel /ˈlʌɪb(ə)l/ *noun.* **ME.**
[ORIGIN Old French (mod. *libelle*) from Latin *libellus* dim. of *liber* book: see -EL[2].]
1 A formal document, a written declaration or statement. *obsolete* exc. *hist.* (as occasional rendering of Latin *libellus*). **ME.**
2 a *CIVIL & ADMIRALTY LAW.* A writing or document containing a plaintiff's allegations and instituting a suit. **ME.** ▸**b** *SCOTS LAW.* A formal statement setting out the grounds on which either a civil or criminal prosecution is made; an indictment. **LME.** ▸**c** *ECCLESIASTICAL LAW.* The initial pleading, or the plaintiff's written declaration or charges, in a plenary case. **M16.**
b ***subsumption of the libel***: see SUBSUMPTION 1b.
3 A little book; a (short) treatise or piece of writing. Also (by confusion), = LABEL *noun* 8. Now only *Scot.* **LME.**
†**4** A leaflet, bill, or pamphlet posted up or publicly circulated; *spec.* one assailing or defaming the character of some person. **E16–L18.**
5 a A false and defamatory statement; *transf.* a thing or circumstance that tends to bring undeserved discredit *on* a person, a country, etc. by misrepresentation etc. **E17.** ▸**b** *LAW.* A false and defamatory statement in writing, film, or other permanent form; the act or offence of publishing such a statement. Cf. SLANDER *noun* 1. **M17.**

a R. RENDELL She bore not the least resemblance to the Marquise of Tai and it would have been a cruel libel to suggest it.

b ***criminal libel***: see CRIMINAL *adjective*. ***public libel***: see PUBLIC *adjective & noun*. ***seditious libel***: see SEDITIOUS 2.

libel /ˈlʌɪb(ə)l/ *verb.* Infl. **-ll-**, ***-l-**. **LME.**
[ORIGIN from the noun: cf. medieval Latin *libellare* in sense 2.]
†**1** *verb intrans.* Institute a suit against or *against* a person. **LME–L16.**
2 *verb trans.* **a** *ECCLESIASTICAL & SCOTS LAW.* Specify in a libel; institute a suit against (a person) by means of a libel. **L15.** ▸**b** *ADMIRALTY LAW.* Bring suit against (a vessel or cargo or its owner). **E19.**
†**3** *verb intrans.* Make libellous accusations or statements; spread defamation. Foll. by *against*, *on*. **L16–M17.**
4 *verb trans.* Defame by the circulation of libellous statements; accuse falsely and maliciously; *spec.* (*LAW*), publish a libel against. **E17.**

POPE But what so pure, which envious tongues will spare? Some wicked wits have libell'd all the fair.

libelee, **libeler** *nouns*, etc., see LIBELLEE etc.

libellant /ˈlʌɪb(ə)l(ə)nt/ *noun.* Also ***libelant**. **E18.**
[ORIGIN from LIBEL *verb* + -ANT[1], after *appellant* etc.]
LAW. A person who institutes a suit in an ecclesiastical or admiralty court.

libellee /lʌɪbəˈliː/ *noun.* Also ***libelee**. **M19.**
[ORIGIN from LIBEL *verb* + -EE[1].]
LAW. A person against whom a libel has been filed. Also, a person who is the object of a libel.

libeller /ˈlʌɪb(ə)lə/ *noun.* Also ***libeler**. **L16.**
[ORIGIN from LIBEL *verb* + -ER[1].]
A person who publishes a libel or libels.

libellist /ˈlʌɪb(ə)lɪst/ *noun.* Also ***libelist**. **L18.**
[ORIGIN from LIBEL *noun* + -IST.]
= LIBELLER.

libellous /ˈlʌɪb(ə)ləs/ *adjective.* Also ***libelous**. **E17.**
[ORIGIN from LIBEL *noun* + -OUS.]
Containing or constituting a libel, of the nature of a libel. Also, engaged in libels.
■ **libellously** *adverb* **M19.**

libellula /lɪˈbɛljʊlə/ *noun.* **M18.**
[ORIGIN mod. Latin (see below), dim. of *libella* dragonfly, perh. from Latin *libella* scales (see LEVEL *noun*).]
ENTOMOLOGY. Any of several dragonflies of the genus *Libellula* or the family Libellulidae.
■ **libellulid** *noun* a dragonfly of the family Libellulidae **M19.**

libelous *adjective* see LIBELLOUS.

liber /ˈlʌɪbə/ *noun.* Now *rare.* **M18.**
[ORIGIN Latin = inner bark, parchment, book.]
BOTANY. = PHLOEM.

liberal /ˈlɪb(ə)r(ə)l/ *adjective & noun.* **ME.**
[ORIGIN Old French & mod. French *libéral* from Latin *liberalis*, from *liber* free: see -AL[1].]
▸ **A** *adjective.* **1** Orig., suitable for a free man or (in later use) a gentleman or person of social standing. Now only of education, culture, etc., usu. with an admixture of sense 4: directed to a general broadening of the mind, not restricted to the requirements of technical or professional training. **ME.**

C. MIDDLETON Agriculture was held the most liberal employment in old Rome. BURKE They are permitted . . to emerge out of that low rank into a more liberal condition. LD MACAULAY Countries which neither mercantile avidity nor liberal curiosity had ever impelled any stranger to explore.

2 Free in giving; generous, open-handed. (Foll. by *of*.) **ME.** ▸**b** Given or offered unstintingly; (of a meal, a helping, etc.) ample, lavish. **LME.** ▸**c** Of a part of the body, outline, etc.: full, large. **E17.**

M. C. CLARKE With Cassio he is patronising, and liberal of his advice. R. K. NARAYAN He was very liberal in entertaining me. **b** J. WAIN It seemed big to us, with its liberal allowance of bedrooms.

3 †**a** Free from restraint in speech or action; unrestrained by prudence or decorum. **LME–E18.** ▸**b** Of passage etc.: freely permitted, not interfered with. Long *arch.* **M16.** ▸**c** Of interpretation: inclining to laxity or indulgence; not rigorous. Of a translation: free, not literal. **L18.**

a SHAKES. *Haml.* Daisies, and long purples That liberal shepherds give a grosser name.

4 Unprejudiced, open-minded; *esp.* free from bigotry or unreasonable prejudice in favour of traditional opinions or established institutions, open to the reception of new ideas. Of a member or branch of a Church or religion: regarding many traditional beliefs as dispensable, invalidated by modern thought, or liable to change. **L18.**

JAS. MILL Liberal enquiries into the literature . . of the Hindus. W. P. ROBERTS I maintain that Liberal Protestantism . . is not anti-dogmatic.

5 Favourable to or respectful of individual rights and freedoms; *spec.* (in politics) favouring free trade and gradual political and social reform that tends towards individual freedom or democracy. Also (usu. **L-**), belonging to the Liberal Party of Great Britain or any analogous party so named in another country. **E19.**

J. BARZUN The liberal doctrine that school children have rights to freedom and individuality. C. SAGAN Holland was the most liberal and least authoritarian nation in Europe during this time. A. STORR The conditions of his imprisonment were sufficiently liberal to allow him visits to his . . family.

– SPECIAL COLLOCATIONS & COMB.: ***liberal arts***: see ART *noun*[1]. **Liberal Christian** (*a*) *US* a Unitarian; also, a Universalist; (*b*) a Christian who rejects or considers unimportant many traditional beliefs. **Liberal Democrat** a member of a British political party (formerly the ***Social and Liberal Democrats***) formed from the Liberal Party and members of the Social Democratic Party. **Liberal Democratic** *adjective* of or pertaining to the Liberal Democrats. **Liberal Judaism** a progressive movement in Judaism that abandons many of the traditional observances of Judaic law. **Liberal-Labour** *adjective* of or pertaining to (people associated with or sympathetic to) both Liberal and Labour parties. **Liberal Party** any of various political parties professing to favour progressive legislation; *esp.* (*hist.*) a British political party which replaced the old Whig Party *c* 1860 and was one of the two dominant parties in Britain until *c* 1920 (in 1988 merged with the Social Democratic Party under the title the ***Social and Liberal Democrats***, now ***Liberal Democrats***). **liberal studies** a broadly based additional course in arts subjects taken by students studying for a qualification in science, technology, or the humanities. **Liberal Unionist** a member of the party formed by those Liberals who would not support W. E. Gladstone's measure for Irish Home Rule in 1886.
▸ **B** *noun.* †**1** The leader of a gang of criminals. *criminals' slang.* Only in **M17.**
2 Orig. (*derog.*), an extreme Whig. Later, a person of liberal principles or ideas; *esp.* (usu. **L-**) a member of the Liberal Party of Great Britain or of an analogous party of another country. **E19.** ▸**b** A person who holds liberal views in theology. **E19.**

ARNOLD BENNETT Every Briton is at heart a Tory—especially every British Liberal. *New Yorker* I don't think he's a liberal . . he wants to see the poor work for their money.

■ **liberally** *adverb* in a liberal manner; *esp.* lavishly, profusely: **LME.** **liberalness** *noun* **LME.**

liberalise *verb* var. of LIBERALIZE.

liberalism /ˈlɪb(ə)r(ə)lɪz(ə)m/ *noun*. E19.
[ORIGIN from LIBERAL + -ISM.]
(The holding of) liberal opinions in politics or theology; (**L-**) the political tenets characteristic of a Liberal.
■ **liberalist** *noun & adjective* (*a*) *noun* an advocate of liberalism; (*b*) *adjective* of or pertaining to liberalists or liberalism: E19. **libera'listic** *adjective* of or pertaining to liberalism, of the nature of or inclining towards liberalism M19.

liberality /lɪbəˈralɪti/ *noun*. ME.
[ORIGIN Old French & mod. French *libéralité* or Latin *liberalitas*, from *liberalis*: see LIBERAL, -ITY.]
1 The quality of being liberal or free in giving; generosity, munificence. ME. ▸**b** An instance of this; a liberal gift or bounty. Now *rare*. E16.
R. ELLMANN He dispensed money with liberality.
2 Breadth of mind; freedom from prejudice; liberal-mindedness. E19.
F. RAPHAEL The rampant liberality of Sixties London.

liberalize /ˈlɪb(ə)r(ə)lʌɪz/ *verb*. Also **-ise**. L18.
[ORIGIN from LIBERAL *adjective* + -IZE.]
1 *verb trans.* **a** Make liberal; imbue with liberal ideas or principles; make liberal-minded; free from narrowness; enlarge the intellectual range of. L18. ▸**b** (Freq. **L-**.) Make Liberal in politics. M19. ▸**c** Remove restrictions on (the import of goods, outflow of capital, etc.). M20.
2 *verb intrans.* Favour liberal opinions; be or become liberal in one's ideas or principles. E19.
■ **liberali'zation** *noun* M19. **liberalizer** *noun* M19.

liberate /lɪbəˈreɪti/ *noun*. *obsolete* exc. *hist*. LME.
[ORIGIN Use as noun of medieval Latin imper. pl. of *liberare* to free, liberate (see LIBERATE *verb*), the word with which the writs began.]
LAW. Any of various writs requiring something to be paid or someone or something to be delivered up or handed over.

liberate /ˈlɪbəreɪt/ *verb trans*. Pa. pple & ppl adjective **-ated**, (earlier) †**-ate**. L16.
[ORIGIN Latin *liberat-* pa. ppl stem of *liberare*, from *liber* free: see -ATE[3].]
1 Set free, set at liberty; free, release *from* (something); *CHEMISTRY* set free from combination. L16.
G. F. KENNAN To liberate from every kind of slavery . . the toiling masses of the world.
2 Free (a country etc.) from enemy occupation. Also *iron.*, subject to a new tyranny. M20.
R. WHELAN They found the town liberated and German prisoners rounded up.
3 Loot (property); misappropriate. *slang*. M20.
J. DIDION She knows where they could liberate a Signal Corps generator.
4 Free from social conventions, esp. ones based on sex. Freq. as ***liberated*** *ppl adjective*. Cf. EMANCIPATE *verb* 2. M20.
U. BENTLEY You're all supposed to be liberated women, why leave it up to the man? H. KUREISHI Men wanted young women - what a liberated age it was!

liberation /lɪbəˈreɪʃ(ə)n/ *noun*. LME.
[ORIGIN Old French & mod. French *libération* or Latin *liberatio(n-)*, formed as LIBERATE *verb*: see -ATION.]
The action or an act of liberating someone or something or of setting someone free from bondage or oppression; the condition of being liberated.
Gay Liberation: see GAY *adjective*. ***Men's Liberation***: see MAN *noun*. ***women's liberation***: see WOMAN *noun*.
– COMB.: **Liberation Society** a 19th-cent. society which campaigned for the disestablishment of the Church of England and the repeal of discriminatory legislation against Nonconformists; **liberation theologian** a person who teaches liberation theology; **liberation theology** a theory, originating among Latin American theologians, which interprets liberation from social, political, and economic oppression as an anticipation of eschatological salvation.
■ **liberationism** *noun* the principles or practice of liberationists L19. **liberationist** *noun* (*a*) a sympathizer with the aims of the Liberation Society; (*b*) an advocate of women's liberation: M19.

liberative /ˈlɪb(ə)rətɪv/ *adjective*. M19.
[ORIGIN formed as LIBERATE *verb* + -IVE.]
Liberating; favouring liberation.

liberator /ˈlɪbəreɪtə/ *noun*. M17.
[ORIGIN Latin, formed as LIBERATE *verb*: see -OR.]
A person who liberates a people or country; a deliverer.

liberatory /ˈlɪb(ə)rət(ə)ri/ *adjective*. L16.
[ORIGIN formed as LIBERATOR + -ORY[2].]
= LIBERATIVE.

liberatress /ˈlɪbəreɪtrɪs/ *noun*. L18.
[ORIGIN from LIBERATOR + -ESS[1].]
A female liberator.

liberi *noun* pl. of LIBERO.

Liberian /lʌɪˈbɪərɪən/ *adjective*[1]. L18.
[ORIGIN from *Liberius* (see below) + -AN.]
Of or pertaining to Liberius (Pope, 352–66) or the period of his pontificate.
Liberian calendar a calendar attributed to the pontificate of Liberius. **Liberian catalogue** a list of the Popes up to and including Liberius.

Liberian /lʌɪˈbɪərɪən/ *adjective*[2] *& noun*. M19.
[ORIGIN from *Liberia* (see below), from Latin *liber* free (as founded as a settlement for freed black slaves from the US) + -AN.]
▸**A** *adjective*. Of or pertaining to the W. African state of Liberia or its people. M19.
▸**B** *noun*. A native or inhabitant of Liberia. Also, a Liberian ship. M19.

libero /ˈliːbero/ *noun*. Pl. **-ri** /-ri/. M20.
[ORIGIN Italian, lit. 'free'.]
SOCCER. = SWEEPER 7.

libertarian /lɪbəˈtɛːrɪən/ *noun & adjective*. L18.
[ORIGIN from LIBERTY *noun*[2] + -ARIAN, after *unitarian* etc.]
▸**A** *noun*. **1** A person who holds the doctrine of the freedom of the will, as opp. to that of necessity. L18.
2 A person who approves of or advocates liberty. L19.
▸**B** *adjective*. **1** Believing in free will. L19.
2 Advocating liberty. E20.
■ **libertarianism** *noun* the principles or doctrines of libertarians M19.

liberticide /lɪˈbəːtɪsʌɪd/ *noun & adjective*. L18.
[ORIGIN French, from *liberté*: see LIBERTY *noun*[2], -CIDE.]
▸**A** *noun*. **1** A destroyer of liberty. L18.
2 The destruction of liberty. *rare*. E19.
▸**B** *adjective*. Destructive of liberty. L18.
■ **liberti'cidal** *adjective* = LIBERTICIDE *adjective* L18.

libertinage /ˈlɪbətɪnɪdʒ/ *noun*. E17.
[ORIGIN from LIBERTINE + -AGE.]
1 = LIBERTINISM 1. E17.
2 = LIBERTINISM 2. M17.

libertine /ˈlɪbətiːn, -tɪn, -tʌɪn/ *noun & adjective*. LME.
[ORIGIN Latin *libertinus*, from *libertus* freedman, from *liber* free; in sense 2 after French *libertin*: see -INE[1].]
▸**A** *noun*. **1** *ROMAN HISTORY*. A freedman; a person manumitted from slavery. Also, the son of a freedman. LME.
2 A member of any of various antinomian sects of the early 16th cent., which arose in France and elsewhere in Continental Europe (usu. in *pl.*); *gen.* a freethinker. M16.
JOSEPH PARKER The intellectual libertine who denies everything that cannot be certified by the senses.
3 *transf.* A person who follows his or her own inclinations; a person who is not restricted or confined by convention etc. L16.
CHARTERED ***libertine***.
4 A man (occas., a woman) who is not restrained by morality, esp. in sexual relations; a person who leads a dissolute life, a licentious person. L16.
R. CHRISTIANSEN Don Giovanni is no mere libertine, but a man . . driven to excess by his contempt for the . . mediocrity around him.
▸**B** *adjective*. **1** Acknowledging no law in religion or morals; freethinking. L16.
2 Free or unrestrained in disposition, habit, conduct or language. Now *rare* or *obsolete*. L16. ▸†**b** Of literary composition, translation: extremely free. M17–M18.
3 Manumitted from slavery. *rare*. E17.
4 Characterized by habitual disregard of morality, esp. with regard to sexual relations; licentious, dissolute; characteristic of or resembling a libertine. E17.
A. S. BYATT One tends to think that those who are brought up libertine will compensate by growing strict.

libertinism /ˈlɪbətɪnɪz(ə)m/ *noun*. E17.
[ORIGIN from LIBERTINE + -ISM.]
1 Disregard of moral restraint, esp. in sexual relations; licentious or dissolute practices or habits of life. E17.
2 Freethinking. M17.
3 Freedom of life or conduct; unrestrained liberty. *rare*. M17.

libertinous /lɪˈbəːtɪnəs/ *adjective*. *rare*. M17.
[ORIGIN formed as LIBERTINE + -OUS.]
= LIBERTINE *adjective*.

Liberty /ˈlɪbəti/ *noun*[1]. L19.
[ORIGIN Messrs *Liberty* & Co., a London drapery firm.]
(Proprietary name) used *attrib.* to designate materials, styles, etc., characteristic of textile fabrics or articles sold by Messrs Liberty.

liberty /ˈlɪbəti/ *noun*[2]. LME.
[ORIGIN Old French & mod. French *liberté* from Latin *libertat-*, *-tas*, from *liber* free: see -TY[1].]
1 Exemption or release from captivity, bondage, or slavery. LME. ▸**b** *THEOLOGY*. Freedom from the bondage of sin, or of the law. LME.
AV *Isa.* 61:1 To proclaime libertie to the captiues.
2 Exemption or freedom from arbitrary, despotic, or autocratic rule or control. LME.
R. H. TAWNEY The theocracy of Massachusetts, merciless alike to religious liberty and to economic licence. ISAIAH BERLIN The liberty of some must depend on the restraint of others. *personified*: H. HALLAM Liberty never wore a more unamiable countenance than among these burghers, who abused the strength she gave them.
3 The condition of being able to act in any desired way without restraint; power to do as one likes. LME. ▸**b** *PHILOSOPHY*. The condition of being free from the control of fate or necessity. Now chiefly opp. ***necessity***. M16.
A. DE MORGAN We have a glorious liberty in England of owning neither dictionary, grammar nor spelling-book.
4 Free opportunity, range, or scope *to do* (or †*of doing*) something; *gen.* leave, permission. LME. ▸**b** Unrestricted use of a thing; access to or permission to go anywhere within the limits of a place. Chiefly in ***have the liberty of***. (Cf. FREEDOM 8b.) Now *rare* or *obsolete*. E17. ▸**c** *NAUTICAL*. Leave of absence. Cf. ***liberty man*** below. M18.
H. MARTINEAU Bid him come in and wait for liberty to talk. **b** DEFOE They allowed him the liberty of the town.
5 *LAW*. **a** A privilege or exceptional right granted to a subject by the sovereign power. Cf. FRANCHISE *noun* 4b. LME. ▸**b** In *pl.* Privileges, immunities, or rights enjoyed by prescription or by grant. LME. ▸**c** *hist.* A district having such privileges etc.; *spec.* (*a*) the district over which a corporation's privilege extended; (*b*) a district within the limits of a county, but exempt from the jurisdiction of the sheriff, and having a separate commission of the peace; (*c*) a district containing several manors held by a single lord; (*d*) *sing.* & in *pl.*, a district controlled by a city though outside its boundary; (*e*) an area outside a prison where some prisoners were sometimes allowed to reside. LME.
b W. H. PRESCOTT The liberties of the commons were crushed at the fatal battle of Villalar.
6 Formerly, unrestrained action, conduct, or expression; freedom of behaviour or speech, beyond what is granted or recognized as proper; licence. Now only, an instance of this, an overstepping or setting aside of rules or conventions. M16.
J. KNOX John the Baptist, whom Herode . . had beheaded for the libertie of his tonge. B. JOWETT Thucydides has rarely . . allowed himself liberties not to be found somewhere in other writers.
– PHRASES: **at liberty** (*a*) not in captivity or confinement; esp. in ***set at liberty***, liberate, set free; (*b*) free *to do, move, think*, etc.; (*c*) (of a person or thing) unoccupied, disengaged. †**at one's liberty** (*a*) at one's own choice, as one pleases; (*b*) in one's power, at one's disposal. ***cap of liberty***: see CAP *noun*[1]. ***civil liberty***: see CIVIL *adjective*. ***liberty of CONSCIENCE***. ***liberty of the press***: see PRESS *noun*[1]. **natural liberty** the state in which everyone is free to act as he or she thinks fit, subject only to the laws of nature. **take a liberty**, **take liberties** be unduly or improperly familiar *with* a person (sometimes *euphem.*); use freedom in dealing *with* rules, facts, etc. **take the liberty** presume or venture *to do*, take the presumptuous step *of doing*. ***tree of liberty***: see TREE *noun*.
– COMB.: **liberty act** a circus act performed by liberty horses; **liberty boat** *NAUTICAL* a boat carrying liberty men; **liberty bodice** (proprietary name for) a girl's or woman's underbodice designed with reinforcing strips; **liberty bond** any of a series of interest-bearing war bonds issued by the US government in 1917–18; **liberty boy** a noisy zealot for liberty; *US* a supporter of a freedom movement; **liberty cabbage** *US* sauerkraut; **liberty cap** (*a*) = ***cap of liberty*** s.v. CAP *noun*[1]; (*b*) a common small European toadstool, *Psilocybe semilanceata*, which contains psilocybin; **liberty day** *NAUTICAL*: on which part of a ship's crew are allowed to go ashore; **Liberty Hall** a place where one may do as one likes; **liberty horse** a horse that performs in a circus without a rider; **Liberty loan** any of the four issues of liberty bonds; **liberty man** *NAUTICAL* a sailor having leave to go ashore; **liberty-pole** a tall mast or staff with a Phrygian cap or other symbol of liberty on the top; **Liberty ship** a type of merchant vessel built in the US by rapid mass-production methods during the Second World War; **liberty tree** = ***tree of liberty*** s.v. TREE *noun*.

liberty /ˈlɪbəti/ *verb trans*. Long *obsolete* exc. *dial*. LME.
[ORIGIN from the noun.]
†**1** Endow with liberties or privileges. Only in LME.
2 Give liberty to; allow to run loose. L15.

liberum arbitrium /ˌliːbərʊm ɑːˈbɪtrɪəm, ˌlʌɪbərəm/ *noun phr*. M17.
[ORIGIN Latin (Livy) = free judgement, free will.]
Full power to decide; freedom of action.

liberum veto /ˌliːbərʊm ˈviːtəʊ, ˌlʌɪbərəm/ *noun phr*. L18.
[ORIGIN from Latin *liberum* neut. of *liber* free + VETO *noun*.]
A veto possessed by each member of a legislative etc. body requiring unanimity.

libidinal /lɪˈbɪdɪn(ə)l/ *adjective*. E20.
[ORIGIN from Latin *libidin-*, LIBIDO lust + -AL[1].]
PSYCHOANALYSIS. Of or pertaining to libido.
■ **libidinally** *adverb* M20.

libidinous /lɪˈbɪdɪnəs/ *adjective*. LME.
[ORIGIN from Latin *libidinosus*, formed as LIBIDINAL: see -OUS.]
Given to, full of, or characterized by lust or lechery; lustful, lecherous.
■ **libidinously** *adverb* E17. **libidinousness** *noun* E17.

libido /lɪˈbiːdəʊ, lɪˈbʌɪdəʊ/ *noun*. E20.
[ORIGIN Latin = desire, lust.]
PSYCHOANALYSIS. Psychic drive or energy, *esp.* that associated with the sexual instinct.

†**libken** *noun*. *criminals' slang*. M16–E19.
[ORIGIN from LIB *verb*[2] + KEN *noun*[2].]
A place to sleep in.

L

Lib-Lab /lɪbˈlab/ *adjective & noun*. E20.
[ORIGIN from LIB *noun*[1] & *adjective* + LAB *noun*[3] & *adjective*.]
▸ **A** *adjective*. = ***Liberal-Labour*** s.v. LIBERAL *adjective*. E20.
▸ **B** *noun*. A Liberal-Labour politician. E20.
■ **Lib-Labbery** *noun* Liberal-Labour politics M20.

LIBOR /ˈlʌɪbɔː/ *abbreviation*.
London Interbank Offered Rate.

Libra /ˈliːbrə, ˈlɪb-, ˈlʌɪb/ *noun*. In sense 2 **l-**. OE.
[ORIGIN Latin *libra* pound, balance, Libra.]
1 (The name of) a constellation of the southern hemisphere, on the ecliptic between Scorpio and Virgo; ASTROLOGY (the name of) the seventh zodiacal sign, usu. associated with the period 23 September to 22 October (see note s.v. ZODIAC); the Scales, the Balance. OE. ▸**b** A person born under the sign Libra. M20.

attrib.: A. LEO This causes Libra persons to love harmony.

2 ROMAN HISTORY. A unit of weight, equivalent to a pound of 12 ounces (0.34 kg). LME.

libral /ˈlʌɪbr(ə)l/ *adjective*. *rare*. M17.
[ORIGIN Latin *libralis*, formed as LIBRA: see -AL[1].]
Weighing a (Roman) pound.

Libran /ˈliːbrən, ˈlɪb-, ˈlʌɪb-/ *noun*. E20.
[ORIGIN from LIBRA + -AN.]
ASTROLOGY. = LIBRA *noun* 1b.

librarian /lʌɪˈbrɛːrɪən/ *noun*. L17.
[ORIGIN from Latin *librarius* concerned with books, (as noun) bookseller, scribe, from *libr-*, *liber* book, + -AN.]
†**1** A scribe, a copyist. L17–E18.
2 A person in charge of a library; an assistant in a library; a person trained or qualified to work in a library. E18.
■ **librarianess** *noun* (*rare*) a female librarian M19. **librarianship** *noun* the profession or work of a librarian; a position as a librarian: E19.

librarious /lʌɪˈbrɛːrɪəs/ *adjective*. *rare*. M17.
[ORIGIN formed as LIBRARIAN + -OUS.]
Of or pertaining to books.

library /ˈlʌɪbrəri, -bri/ *noun*. LME.
[ORIGIN Old French & mod. French *librairie* (mod. = bookshop, book trade) from Proto-Romance alt. of Latin *libraria* bookshop, use as noun of *librarius*: see LIBRARIAN, -ARY[1], -Y[3].]
1 A large organized collection of books for reading or reference, for use by the public or by a specific group; an individual's collection of books. LME. ▸**b** A mass of learning or knowledge; a source or the sources providing knowledge or learning. LME. ▸**c** A collection of films, gramophone records, computer routines etc., esp. when organized or sorted for some specific purpose. E20. ▸**d** GENETICS. A collection of bacterial cultures each transfected with a piece of genetic material, esp. forming a complete set representing a chromosome or genome; a collection of genes so transfected. Also, the set of genes common to a group of organisms. L20.

R. GRAVES Collecting a library of the pagan Classics. K. CLARK His brother . . had a large library, but his books were chosen for their instructive texts. **b** J. HAWTHORNE Cards and men formed the library of the Duchess of Marlborough.

2 A building or room containing such a collection of books, films, records, music, etc.; an institution or organization holding such a collection. LME. ▸**b** A theatre-ticket agency. *slang*. E19.

A. RADCLIFFE The library occupied the west side of the chateau. R. QUIRK Our bookshelves and libraries are full of books on the use of words.

3 A series of books, gramophone records, etc., issued by a publisher in similar bindings etc. as a set. L17.
– PHRASES: **circulating library** a small library with books lent to a group of subscribers in turn. ***free library***: see FREE *adjective*. ***lending library***: see LEND *verb*. ***public library***: see PUBLIC *adjective*. ***reference library***: see REFERENCE *noun*. ***travelling library***: see TRAVELLING *ppl adjective*. ***twopenny library***: see TWOPENNY *adjective* 2.
– COMB.: **library binding** a special strong binding of books for lending libraries; **library edition** an edition of good size and print and strongly bound; *spec*. a uniform edition of a writer's works; **library-frame glasses**, **library glasses** spectacles with heavy frames suitable for use when reading; **library school** a college teaching librarianship; **library science** librarianship as a subject of study; **library spectacles** = ***library-frame glasses*** above; **library steps** a stepladder for use in a library.

librate /ˈlʌɪbreɪt/ *noun*. E17.
[ORIGIN medieval Latin *librata (terrae)* a pound's worth (of land), from *libra* pound: see -ATE[1].]
hist. A piece of land worth a pound a year.

librate /ˈlʌɪbreɪt/ *verb*. E17.
[ORIGIN Latin *librat-* pa. ppl stem of *librare*, from *libra* balance: see -ATE[3].]
†**1** *verb trans*. Weigh. E–M17.
2 *verb intrans*. Oscillate like the beam of a balance; move from side to side or up and down. L17. ▸**b** Oscillate or waver *between* one thing and another. E19.
3 *verb intrans*. Of a bird etc.: be poised, balance itself. L18.
■ **libratory** *adjective* oscillatory M17.

libration /lʌɪˈbreɪʃ(ə)n/ *noun*. E17.
[ORIGIN Latin *libratio(n-)*, formed as LIBRATE *verb*: see -ATION.]
1 The action of librating; (a) motion like that of the beam of a balance oscillating upon its pivot; the state of being balanced or in equilibrium. E17.
2 ASTRONOMY. A real or apparent oscillating motion; *spec*. an irregularity of the moon's motion which makes it possible to see more than about 59 per cent of its surface from the earth. M17.
†**3** The action of weighing. M17–L18.
■ **librational** *adjective* of or pertaining to (the moon's) libration L19.

libretto /lɪˈbrɛtəʊ/ *noun*. Pl. **-ttos**, **-tti** /-ti/. M18.
[ORIGIN Italian, dim. of *libro* book.]
The text of an opera or other long vocal composition.
■ **librettist** *noun* a writer of a libretto or librettos M19.

libriform /ˈlʌɪbrɪfɔːm/ *adjective*. L19.
[ORIGIN from Latin *libr-*, LIBER + -FORM.]
BOTANY. Of certain xylem fibres: resembling the phloem or inner bark.

Librium /ˈlɪbrɪəm/ *noun*. Also **l-**. M20.
[ORIGIN Unknown.]
PHARMACOLOGY. (Proprietary name for) the tranquillizer chlordiazepoxide.

Libyan /ˈlɪbɪən/ *noun & adjective*. L15.
[ORIGIN from Latin *Libya* + -AN.]
▸ **A** *noun*. A native or inhabitant of Libya, a country in N. Africa. L15.
▸ **B** *adjective*. Of or pertaining to Libya; *poet*. N. African. E16.
■ †**Libyc** *adjective* [Greek *Libukos*] = LIBYAN *adjective* M16–M17.

Libyo- /ˈlɪbɪəʊ/ *combining form*. L19.
[ORIGIN from LIBY(AN + -O-.]
Libyan and —, as ***Libyo-Phoenician***.

licca /ˈlɪkə/ *noun*. M18.
[ORIGIN Unknown.]
In full ***licca tree***. A West Indian tree, *Zanthoxylum spinosum*, of the rue family.

lice *noun pl*. see LOUSE *noun*.

licence /ˈlʌɪs(ə)ns/ *noun*. Also ***license**. LME.
[ORIGIN Old French & mod. French from Latin *licentia* liberty, freedom, licentiousness, (in medieval Latin) authority, permission, from *licent-* pres. ppl stem of *licere* be allowed: see -ENCE.]
1 Liberty, esp. *to do* something; leave, permission. Formerly also, exemption *from* something. LME. ▸†**b** *spec*. Leave or permission to depart. Chiefly in ***take one's licence***. L15–M16.

W. BLACKSTONE The king . . may . . prohibit any of his subjects from going into foreign parts without licence. K. WATERHOUSE He seized on it as licence to raise . . the point of information.

2 Formal, usu. printed or written, permission from an authority to do something (esp. marry, print or publish a book, preach, drive on a public road, or carry on some trade (esp. in alcoholic liquor)), or to own something (esp. a dog, gun, or television set); a document giving such permission; a permit. LME. ▸**b** In some universities and colleges, a certificate of competence in a faculty. M16.

G. ORWELL They had had a pub, but they had lost their licence for allowing gambling. *Shetland Times* They are also looking for people using black and white licences for colour television.

driving licence, ***marriage licence***, ***road fund licence***, ***television licence***, etc. ***late licence***: see LATE *adjective*.
3 Liberty of action conceded or acknowledged; freedom; an instance of this. LME. ▸**b** Excessive liberty or disregard for law or propriety; an instance of this. LME. ▸**c** Licentiousness. E18.

D. STOREY You . . put down your thoughts . . and allow your imagination a little licence. B. T. BRADFORD Old people believe . . age gives them the licence to say exactly what they think. **b** S. SASSOON The thriftless licence of war-time behaviour. A. BEVAN We must distinguish between freedom and licence. **c** G. M. TREVELYAN Churchmen and Dissenters co-operated against the licence of the age.

4 A writer's or artist's irregularity in grammar, metre, perspective, etc., or deviation from fact, esp. for effect; an example of this. Freq. in ***poetic licence***. M16.
– COMB.: **licence number**, **licence plate** *N. Amer*. a registration number or number plate of a motor vehicle.
■ **licenceless** *adjective* not possessing a licence E20.

licence *verb*, **licenced** *adjective* vars. of LICENSE *verb*, LICENSED.

license *noun* see LICENCE *noun*.

license /ˈlʌɪs(ə)ns/ *verb trans*. Also **licence**. LME.
[ORIGIN from the noun: spelling with *-s-* after *practice*, *practise* etc.]
1 Allow, give permission to, (a person) *to do*, †*that*; permit or allow (a thing) to be done. Now *rare*. LME.

A. W. KINGLAKE Lord Stratford was licensed to do no more than send a message to an Admiral.

2 Grant (a person) a licence or formal permission *for*, *to do*; grant formal permission for, authorize, (an action or practice). LME. ▸**b** Authorize the publication of (a book) or the performance of (a play). E17. ▸**c** Authorize the use of (a thing, esp. premises) for a specific purpose. L18.

M. PATTISON A patent of Henry II . . licenses the sale of Rhenish wine. V. S. NAIPAUL A little notice said that Beharry was licensed to sell spirituous liquors. *Which?* The Council ensures that all conveyances it licenses, have met its professional requirements. **c** M. E. BRADDON In which there is . . not even a cottage licensed for the sale of ale. J. LE CARRÉ An old . . hotel with a lift licensed for three persons at a time.

†**3** Give leave of departure to; dismiss *from*; send away *to*. LME–E19.
4 Allow complete freedom or liberty to. *obsolete* exc. as LICENSED *adjective* 1. E17.
■ **licensable** *adjective* E17. **licenˈsee** *noun* a person to whom a licence is granted, esp. to sell alcoholic liquor M19. **licenser** *noun* a person who licenses something; *esp*. an official who licenses the publication of books or the performance of plays according to censorship rules: M17. **licensor** *noun* (LAW) = LICENSER M19.

licensed /ˈlʌɪs(ə)nst/ *adjective*. Also **licenced**. L16.
[ORIGIN from LICENSE *verb* + -ED[1] or LICENCE *noun* + -ED[2].]
1 Allowed complete freedom or liberty; privileged. L16.
2 To whom or for which a licence has been granted; having a licence; *esp*. (of premises) licensed for the sale of alcoholic liquor. M17.
licensed victualler an innkeeper licensed to sell alcoholic liquor etc.

licensure /ˈlʌɪs(ə)nsjʊə/ *noun*. Chiefly *N. Amer*. M19.
[ORIGIN from LICENSE *verb* + -URE.]
The granting of a licence esp. to carry on a trade or profession.

licentiate /lʌɪˈsɛnʃɪət/ *noun*. L15.
[ORIGIN medieval Latin *licentiatus* use as noun of pa. pple of *licentiare*: see LICENTIATE *verb*, -ATE[1].]
1 The holder of a university or college licence; *spec*. & now only in some foreign universities, the holder of a particular degree between bachelor and master or doctor. Now usu., the holder of a certificate of competence from a particular body or college to practise a particular profession. L15.

B. BAINBRIDGE A Fellow of the Royal College of Surgeons and a Licentiate of the Apothecaries' Company.

2 Esp. in Presbyterian Churches, a person with a licence to preach but as yet no appointment. M19.
■ **licentiateship** *noun* the status or qualification of a licentiate L19.

licentiate /lʌɪˈsɛnʃɪeɪt/ *verb trans*. Pa. pple & ppl adjective **-ated**, (earlier) †**-ate**. LME.
[ORIGIN Orig. pa. pple, from medieval Latin *licentiatus* pa. pple of *licentiare*, from *licentia*: see LICENCE *noun*, -ATE[2], -ATE[3].]
1 Allow, permit, (something); allow (a person) *to do*, †*that*. Now *rare* or *obsolete*. LME.
†**2** Grant a licence to (a person), esp. to preach. Cf. LICENTIATION. Chiefly *Scot*. M17–M18.
■ ˌ**licentiˈation** *noun* (now *rare*) †(***a***) the action of allowing something; (***b***) the action of granting a licence to practise medicine: M17.

licentious /lʌɪˈsɛnʃəs/ *adverb & adjective*. LME.
[ORIGIN from Latin *licentiosus*, from *licentia*: see LICENCE *noun*, -OUS.]
▸ †**A** *adverb*. With licence or liberty; freely. Only in LME.
▸ **B** *adjective*. **1** Lawless, lax, immoral. Now usu. *spec*., immoral or promiscuous in sexual relations. M16.

L. KINSALE He is all that is worst in the aristocracy. Profligate, licentious and godless.

2 Disregarding commonly accepted rules or conventions; deviating freely from grammatical or literary correctness. *arch*. M16.
■ **licentiously** *adverb* M16. **licentiousness** *noun* M16.

lich /lɪtʃ/ *noun*. *arch*. exc. (in var. forms) in LYCHGATE, LYKE WAKE. Also **lych**, **lyke** /lʌɪk/.
[ORIGIN Old English *līc* = Old Frisian *līk*, Old Saxon *līc* (Dutch *lijk*), Old High German *līh* (German *Leiche*), Old Norse *lík*, Gothic *leik*, from Germanic.]
†**1** A living body. Also, the trunk, the torso. OE–LME.
2 A dead body, a corpse. Formerly also, a wake. OE.
– COMB.: **lich-house** a mortuary; **lich owl** a screech owl (its cry supposedly portending a death); **lich-path** a path along which a corpse has been carried to burial, in some districts supposedly establishing a right of way; †**lich-rest** a burial place, a tomb; **lich-stone** a stone to place the coffin on at the lychgate; †**lich-way** = ***lich-path*** above.

lichanos /ˈlɪkənɒs/ *noun*. L17.
[ORIGIN Greek *likhanos* lit. 'forefinger'.]
In ancient Greek music, the third note up in a lower tetrachord, immediately above the parhypate.

lichee *noun* var. of LYCHEE.

lichen /ˈlʌɪk(ə)n/ *noun*. Pl. **-s**, same. E17.
[ORIGIN Latin from Greek *leikhēn*.]
1 Any of a large group of composite organisms formed by association of algal cells with a fungus, and occurring as encrusting or branching friable growths on surfaces, to which they give a green, grey, or yellow colour; orig. also, a liverwort. Also *collect*., such organisms growing as a crust or clump. E17.
2 MEDICINE & VETERINARY MEDICINE. Any of various unrelated skin conditions usu. characterized by (small) tough excrescences over a more or less limited area. E17.
lichen planus /ˈpleɪnəs/ [Latin = flat] a skin disorder characterized by an eruption of wide, flat, shiny, purple pimples.

– COMB.: **lichen-starch** lichenin; **lichen substance** any of about 65 compounds, mostly acids, which occur uniquely in lichens.
■ **liche'nicolous** *adjective* inhabiting lichens M19. **lichenification** /lʌɪˌkɛnɪfɪˈkeɪʃ(ə)n, ˌlʌɪk(ə)nɪfɪ-/ *noun* (MEDICINE & VETERINARY MEDICINE) hardening and thickening of the skin caused by scratching or other continued irritation; an area of skin so affected: L19. **lichenin** *noun* a glucan resembling cellulose and occurring esp. in lichens M19. **lichenism** *noun* the symbiosis between alga and fungus which occurs in lichens L19. **lichenist** *noun* = LICHENOLOGIST M19. **liche'nivorous** *adjective* lichen-eating M19. **lichenless** *adjective* M19. **lichenoid** *adjective* resembling (a) lichen M19. **lichenose** *adjective* of the nature of a lichen M19. **licheny** *adjective* overgrown with lichens; lichened: E19.

lichen /ˈlʌɪk(ə)n/ *verb trans.* M19.
[ORIGIN from the noun.]
Cover with lichen. Chiefly as ***lichened*** *ppl adjective.*

lichenized /ˈlʌɪk(ə)nʌɪzd/ *adjective.* Also **-ised**. M19.
[ORIGIN from LICHEN *noun* + -IZE + -ED[1].]
1 Covered with lichens. *rare.* M19.
2 Of a fungus or alga: living or adapted to live as a component of a lichen. M20.

lichenology /lʌɪkəˈnɒlədʒi/ *noun.* M19.
[ORIGIN from LICHEN *noun* + -OLOGY.]
The branch of botany that deals with lichens.
■ **licheno'logical** *adjective* M19. **lichenologist** *noun* M19.

lichenometry /lʌɪkəˈnɒmɪtri/ *noun.* M20.
[ORIGIN from LICHEN *noun* + -O- + -METRY.]
GEOLOGY. The dating of moraines or other recently exposed surfaces by measurement of the area of lichen growing on them.
■ **licheno'metric**, **licheno'metrical** *adjectives* M20.

lichenous /ˈlʌɪk(ə)nəs/ *adjective.* E19.
[ORIGIN from LICHEN *noun* + -OUS.]
1 MEDICINE. Pertaining to or of the nature of the skin condition lichen. E19.
2 Of, pertaining to, consisting of, or resembling lichen; covered with lichen. M19.

lichgate *noun* var. of LYCHGATE.

-licious /ˈlɪʃəs/ *suffix. colloq.*
[ORIGIN from DE)LICIOUS.]
Forming adjectives designating someone or something delightful or extremely attractive, as *bootylicious.*

licit /ˈlɪsɪt/ *adjective.* L15.
[ORIGIN Latin *licitus* pa. pple of *licere* be allowed.]
Allowable, permitted; lawful.
■ **licitly** *adverb* L15. **licitness** *noun* L18.

licitation /lɪsɪˈteɪʃ(ə)n/ *noun.* E17.
[ORIGIN Latin *licitatio(n-)*, from *licitat-* pa. ppl stem of *licitari* bid at an auction: see -ATION.]
Now US LAW. The action of putting something up for sale to the highest bidder.
– NOTE: Only in Dicts. before 20.

lick /lɪk/ *noun.* L16.
[ORIGIN from the verb.]
1 An act of licking; as much as may be taken by licking; *transf.* a small quantity or amount (*of* something). L16. ▸**b** A place to which animals go to lick earth impregnated with salt; a block of salt for animals to lick, a lick-log. Also ***salt lick***. Chiefly *N. Amer.* M18.

b D. TUKE Licks . . can be placed in a manger for greedy feeders.

a lick *N. Amer. colloq.* a bit (usu. in neg. contexts). **a lick and a promise** *colloq.* a hasty performance of a task, esp. of washing oneself.

2 A smart blow; *transf.* an attack, an attempt. L16. ▸**b** In *pl.* A beating (*Scot. & N. English*); *colloq.* critical or censorious remarks, criticism. L18.

R. L. STEVENSON I wish I had had a lick at them with the gun first. O. MANNING The man . . gave his horse a lick and the creature trotted for nearly a hundred yards. **b** P. ABRAHAMS I saw one take licks like that in slavery time; he died. *Time* A Star is Born does not deserve the licks it has got.

3 (A) speed, (a) pace; a burst of speed, a spurt. *colloq.* E19.

D. ADAMS Smoke billowed down out of it at an incredible lick. *Aviation News* The pilot . . took off down the aerodrome at a fair lick.

4 In jazz, rock music, etc.: a short solo or phrase. Freq. in ***hot licks***. M20.

lick /lɪk/ *verb.*
[ORIGIN Old English *liccian* = Old Saxon *liccon, leccon* (Dutch *likken*), Old High German *leckōn* (German *lecken*), from West Germanic, from Indo-European base repr. also by Greek *leikhein*, Latin *lingere*.]
1 *verb trans.* Pass the tongue over (something), with the object of tasting, moistening, removing something, etc.; take *in, up, off*, etc., by licking; make *clean* etc. by licking. OE. ▸†**b** *verb trans.* & *intrans.* (with *of, on*). Lap with the tongue, drink, sip, (a liquid). ME–L18.

A. CHAMBERS Morgan licked dribbling coffee from the side of his plastic mug. B. BYARS Simon had licked the icing off one of the Christmas cupcakes. L. CODY She watched one of the men licking cigarette papers and sticking them together. R. K. NARAYAN The goat . . licked the plate dry. C. HOPE Her face was chalky white, the lips dry and she licked them in her sleep. *Living* Two bad habits . . are cleaning lenses in tap water and licking them clean. **b** W. COWPER Lie there, and feed the fishes, which shall lick Thy blood.

2 *verb intrans. & trans. transf. & fig.* Of an inanimate object (esp. a wave, flame, etc.): lap (*at*) like a tongue, play lightly over or *over*, etc. OE.

J. H. NEWMAN The tide of human beings . . licking the base of the hill. V. CRONIN Flames from the fire . . were already licking at the staircase. G. M. FRASER The flames were licking towards the catwalk leading to the north-west tower.

3 *verb trans.* **a** Beat, thrash; drive (something) *out of* (a person) by beating. *slang.* M16. ▸**b** Defeat, get the better of, surpass, (a person); solve (a problem), overcome (a difficulty). *slang* (chiefly *N. Amer.*). L18.

a C. DARWIN How these poor dogs must have been licked. **b** E. O'NEILL You've finally got the game of life licked. H. ROBBINS The guy had guts. 'Try not to worry,' he said. 'We'll find a way to lick the bastards yet.'

4 *verb trans.* Paint with cosmetics; give a smooth or smart finish to (a picture). Now *rare* or *obsolete.* L16.
5 *verb intrans. & trans.* (with *it*). Run, ride, or move at full speed. *slang* (chiefly *N. Amer.*) & *dial.* M19.

A. P. GASKELL He sped her along. Boy, she can lick.

– PHRASES: **lick a person's arse** (*coarse slang*), **lick a person's boots**, **lick a person's shoes** behave sycophantically towards a person, be servile. ***lick creation***: see CREATION 4. **lick into fits** defeat thoroughly. **lick into shape** make presentable or efficient. **lick one's chops** *fig.* (**a**) = ***lick one's lips*** below; (**b**) *Jazz slang* warm up before a session. **lick one's lips** *fig.* (**a**) look forward to something with relish; (**b**) show one's satisfaction. **lick one's wounds** *fig.* be in retirement after defeat. ***lick the trencher***: see TRENCHER *noun*[1]. †**lick whole** heal by licking.
– COMB.: †**lick-dish** = ***lickspittle*** *noun* below; **lick hole** *Austral.* a place where lick-logs are placed for stock to lick; **lick-log** a block of salt for stock, esp. cattle, to lick; ***stand up to one's lick-logs***, make a firm stand; **lick-penny** a thing that uses up money; **lickpot** (long *obsolete* exc. *W. Indian*) the first finger; **lickspittle** *noun & verb* (**a**) *noun* a sycophant, a parasite; (**b**) *verb trans.* behave sycophantically towards; †**lick-trencher** = ***lickspittle*** *noun* above.
■ **licking** *noun* (**a**) the action of the verb; (**b**) *colloq.* a beating: LME. **licking** *adjective* (**a**) that licks; (**b**) *slang* splendid: M17.

licken /ˈlɪk(ə)n/ *verb intrans.* Long *obsolete* exc. *dial.* M16.
[ORIGIN Alt. of LIPPEN *verb.*]
Foll. by *to*: trust to, depend on.

licker /ˈlɪkə/ *noun.* LME.
[ORIGIN from LICK *verb* + -ER[1].]
1 A person who or thing which licks or (*spec.*) beats or defeats another. LME.
2 ***licker-in***, the cylinder in a carding machine which receives the cotton, wool, etc., from the feed rollers and passes it on to the main cylinder. M19.

lickerish /ˈlɪkərɪʃ/ *adjective.* Also **liquorish**. L15.
[ORIGIN Alt. of LICKEROUS, with -ISH[1] for -OUS.]
1 Fond of delicious food; greedy; *fig.* eagerly desirous, longing. (Foll. by †*after, for, to do.*) L15. ▸**b** Lecherous, lustful. E17.
2 Pleasant to the palate; sweet; tempting. Formerly also, (of a cook) skilful. L16.
■ **lickerishly** *adverb* M17. **lickerishness** *noun* L16.

†**lickerous** *adjective.* ME.
[ORIGIN Anglo-Norman var. of Old French *lecheros* LECHEROUS: see -OUS.]
1 = LICKERISH 2. ME–L17.
2 = LICKERISH 1. LME–M17. ▸**b** = LICKERISH 1b. LME–E17.
■ †**lickerously** *adverb* ME–L16. †**lickerousness** *noun* LME–M17.

lickety /ˈlɪkəti/ *noun & prefix. colloq.* (chiefly *N. Amer.*). E19.
[ORIGIN Fanciful extension of LICK *noun, verb.*]
▸ †**A** *noun.* ***as fast as lickety***, at full speed, headlong. Only in E19.
▸ **B** *prefix.* Forming adverbs, chiefly with verb stems, with the sense 'at full speed, headlong', as ***lickety-cut***, (esp.) ***lickety-split***, etc. M19.

licorice *noun* var. of LIQUORICE.

lictor /ˈlɪktə/ *noun.* LME.
[ORIGIN Latin, perh. rel. to *ligare* bind.]
ROMAN HISTORY. An officer attending a consul or other magistrate, bearing the fasces, and executing sentence on offenders.

licuala /lɪkjʊˈɑːlə/ *noun.* L19.
[ORIGIN mod. Latin (see below), from Makasarese *lekowala*.]
Any of various small palm trees of the genus *Licuala* with fan-shaped leaves and prickly stalks, native to Malaysia, New Guinea, and northern Australia.

lid /lɪd/ *noun.*
[ORIGIN Old English *hlid* = Old Frisian *hlid*, Middle Low German *lit* (*lid-*) (Dutch *lid*), Old High German *(h)lit* (now in German *(Augen)lid* eyelid), Old Norse *hlið* gate, gateway, gap, from Germanic, from base meaning 'cover'.]
1 A hinged or detachable cover for an upward-facing opening or esp. the top of a container; *dial.* the top crust of a pie. OE. ▸**b** A door, shutter, or similar means for closing an aperture. Now *dial.* exc. in ***port-lid*** s.v. PORT *noun*[3] 2b. ME.

E. WELTY A candy box with the picture of a pretty girl on the dusty lid. V. S. NAIPAUL Below the sloping lid of the desk . . were my father's records. *New Yorker* A greedy man in a good kitchen before dinner, lifting all the lids.

2 Either of the upper and lower folds of skin that meet when the eye is closed; an eyelid. ME.

D. JACOBSON She will be wearing green eye-shadow . . on her lids. B. T. BRADFORD Her alert green eyes, wise and shrewd under the wrinkled lids, missed nothing.

3 *transf.* **a** Either of the two sides or covers of a book. Chiefly *dial. & US.* L16. ▸**b** BOTANY & ZOOLOGY. An operculum. L17. ▸**c** MINING. A roof stone covering a pipe or cylindrical vein of ore (also **lid-stone**). Also, a flat piece of wood reinforcing the roof of a shaft. Chiefly *dial.* M18. ▸**d** A hat, a cap; *spec.* a motor cyclist's crash helmet. *slang.* L19. ▸**e** An ounce of marijuana. *slang.* M20.
– PHRASES: **put the lid on**, **put the tin lid on** *colloq.* (**a**) be the culmination of; (**b**) put a stop to. **take the lid off** *colloq.* expose (a scandal etc.).
■ **lidless** *adjective* without a lid; *poet.* vigilant: LME.

lid /lɪd/ *verb trans.* Infl. **-dd-**. ME.
[ORIGIN from the noun.]
Cover with a lid.

lidar /ˈlʌɪdɑː/ *noun.* M20.
[ORIGIN from LIGHT *noun* + RADAR.]
A detection system which works on the principle of radar, but uses light from a laser.

lidded /ˈlɪdɪd/ *adjective.* OE.
[ORIGIN from LID *noun, verb*: see -ED[2], -ED[1].]
1 Having a lid; covered (as) with a lid. OE.
2 *spec.* Of the eyes: having lids, covered with lids. Chiefly as 2nd elem. of comb., as ***half-lidded***, ***heavy-lidded***, ***high-lidded***. E19.

lidden /ˈlɪd(ə)n/ *noun.* Long *obsolete* exc. *dial.* Also †**led(d)en**.
[ORIGIN Old English *lǣden* repr. a Celtic or early Proto-Romance pronunc. of Latin *Latinum* Latin, conf. with Old English *leden* (sense 2), from *leode* people.]
†**1** Latin. Only in OE.
2 †**a** The language of a people etc.; a tongue. OE–ME. ▸†**b** (A form of) speech or utterance; a way of speaking, a language; *poet.* birdsong. ME–E17. ▸**c** Noise, chatter. L17.

liddle /ˈlɪd(ə)l/ *adjective. nursery & dial.* L19.
[ORIGIN Repr. a pronunc.]
= LITTLE *adjective.*

Lide /lʌɪd/ *noun. obsolete* exc. *dial.*
[ORIGIN Old English *hlȳda*, cogn. with *hlūd* LOUD *adjective.*]
The month of March.

lidgate /ˈlɪdgeɪt, ˈlɪdʒɪt/ *noun. obsolete* exc. *dial.* OE.
[ORIGIN from LID *noun* + GATE *noun*[1].]
A gate, *esp.* one set up between pasture and ploughed land or across a road to prevent cattle from straying.

lidia /ˈliðja/ *noun.* L19.
[ORIGIN Spanish, lit. 'fight'.]
A bullfight, esp. the earlier stages in which the *cuadrilla* prepares the bull for the *faena*.
■ ***lidiador*** /liðjaˈðɔr/ *noun*, pl. ***-dores*** /-ˈðɔːres/, a bullfighter L19.

lido /ˈliːdəʊ, ˈlʌɪ-/ *noun.* Pl. **-os**. L17.
[ORIGIN Italian *Lido*, a bathing beach near Venice, from *lido* shore, beach from Latin *litus*.]
A bathing beach, orig. *spec.* that near Venice; a resort; a public open-air swimming pool.

lidocaine /ˈlɪdəkeɪn/ *noun.* M20.
[ORIGIN from ACETANI)LID(E + -O- + -CAINE.]
PHARMACOLOGY. = LIGNOCAINE.

lie /lʌɪ/ *noun*[1].
[ORIGIN Old English *lyġe* from Germanic, assim. to LIE *verb*[2].]
1 An act or instance of lying; an intentional false statement; an untruth. OE. ▸**b** Something that deceives; an imposture. M16.

J. CARY I had committed some fault and told a lie about it. **b** N. O. BROWN Sublimation . . is a lie and cannot survive confrontation with the truth.

2 A charge of falsehood. *obsolete* exc. in ***give the lie to*** below. L16.

SHAKES. *Rich. II* That lie shall lie so heavy on my sword.

3 An anecdote, a tale, a tall story. Orig. & chiefly *black English.* M20.
– PHRASES: **act a lie** deceive without verbal lying. **give the lie to** accuse (a person) directly of lying; serve to show the falsity of (a supposition etc.). ***nail a lie***: see NAIL *verb.* ***officious lie***. **tell a lie** utter a lie. ***white lie***: see WHITE *adjective.*
– COMB.: **lie detector** an instrument intended to indicate when a person is lying by detecting changes in his or her physiological characteristics.

lie /lʌɪ/ *noun*[2]. In sense 4 also **lye**. L17.
[ORIGIN from LIE *verb*[1].]
1 Manner of lying; direction or position in which something lies; direction and amount of slope or inclination; *fig.* the position or aspect (of affairs etc.). L17. ▸**b** The position of a golf ball to be struck (freq. with specifying word). Also, the angle of the head of a golf club when the ball is to be struck. L18.

S. BARING-GOULD The horizontal lie of the chalk beds. **b** *Times* Pitching cleverly short of the green from an awkward lie.

lie of the land *fig.* state of affairs, how matters are tending. **b** ***hanging lie***: see HANGING *adjective.*

2 A mass that lies; a stratum, a layer. E18.

3 a Room to lie or take cover. *rare.* **M19.** ▸**b** The place of cover of an animal or bird. **L19.**
4 A railway siding. Chiefly *Scot.* **M19.**
5 An act or period of lying. Chiefly with adverbs (see below). **M19.** ▸**b** A *long* etc. period of resting or lying, esp. in bed. Cf. ***lie-in*** below. Chiefly *Scot.* **E20.**
– **COMB.:** **lie-down** *colloq.* a rest (on a bed etc.); **lie-in** *colloq.* (***a***) = a period or act of lying in bed in the morning after one's usual time for getting up (cf. sense 5 above); (***b***) a form of protest in which the participants lie down on the ground and refuse to move; **lie-up** the fact of lying inactive in a place. See also combs. s.v. **LIE** *verb*[1]

Lie /liː/ *noun*[3]. **M20.**
[**ORIGIN** Sophus *Lie* (1842–99), Norwegian mathematician.]
MATH. **1** ***Lie algebra***, a vector space over a field in which a product operation is defined such that, for all x, y, z in the space, $x \times y$ is bilinear, $x \times x = 0$, and $(x \times y) \times z + (y \times z) \times x + (z \times x) \times y = 0$. **M20.**
2 ***Lie group***, a topological group in which it is possible to label the group elements by a finite number of coordinates in such a way that the coordinates of the product of two elements are analytic functions of the coordinates of those elements, and the coordinates of the inverse of an element are analytic functions of the coordinates of that element. **M20.**

lie /lʌɪ/ *verb*[1]. Pa. t. **lay** /leɪ/, pres. pple **lying** /ˈlʌɪɪŋ/, pa. pple **lain** /leɪn/. Also (now *dial.*) **lig** /lɪɡ/, infl. **-gg-**. See also **LIG**.
[**ORIGIN** Old English *liċġan* = Old Frisian *lidz(i)a*, Old Saxon *liggian* (Dutch *liggen*), Old High German *liggen*, Old Norse *liggja*, from Germanic, from Indo-European base repr. also by Greek *lektron*, *lekhos*, Latin *lectus* bed.]
▸ **I** *verb intrans.* **1** Of a person or animal: have the body in a more or less horizontal position along the ground, a surface, etc. Freq. with compl. expr. condition. **OE.** ▸**b** Orig., be dead. Later, (of a dead body) be extended on a bier etc.; be buried (in a specified place). **OE.** ▸†**c** Lie sick, stay in bed through illness etc. **ME–L16.** ▸**d** Be in bed for the purpose of sleeping or resting. **ME.** ▸**e** Have sexual intercourse *with. arch.* **ME.**

SCOTT FITZGERALD A stretcher on which lies a drunken woman. DAY LEWIS The long white forenoons of childhood, as I lay ill or convalescent. G. GREENE The boy lay asleep . . in his teak bunk. **b** J. BETJEMAN Beneath the Abbey bells . . . Here, where England's statesmen lie. **e** P. O'BRIAN Woman, wilt thou lie with me?

2 Be or remain in a specified state of subjection, misery, captivity, etc.; be kept *in* prison. **OE.**

LD MACAULAY The defendant . . was lying in prison as a debtor.

3 Take a recumbent or prostrate position (chiefly with adverbs: see below). Formerly also, lean or hang *over* (a wall). **ME.**

B. BAINBRIDGE He . . went upstairs to lie on the couch.

4 a Reside, stay; *esp.* sleep or pass the night (in a place), lodge temporarily. *arch.* **ME.** ▸**b** *spec.* Of troops etc.: be encamped *at, in, near*, a place; have or take up a position. **ME.** ▸†**c** Live under specified circumstances or engaged in some specified occupation. (Foll. by *at, about*.) **M16–E18.**

GOLDSMITH He was to lie that night at a neighbour's. **b** T. FAIRFAX At Wakefield . . lay three thousand of the enemy.

5 Be or remain in a state of inactivity or concealment. Freq. with compl. (adjective or pa. pple). **ME.** ▸**b** Of a game bird: not rise. **L18.**

DICKENS Do you mean to . . let me lie here till this hunt is over?

lie close, ***lie doggo***, ***lie low***, ***lie perdu***, etc.

6 †**a** Foll. by *at, on*: importune, urge. **M16–M18.** ▸†**b** Foll. by *on*: oppress, harass. **L16–L17.** ▸**c** Apply oneself vigorously and steadily *to* (also foll. by †*at*). **L16.**
▸ **II** *verb intrans.* †**7** Of land, landed possessions: appertain *to*. **OE–E17.**
8 Be situated (in space), have a (specified) position, (of an event, experience, etc.) be disposed in time. Freq. with adjective or adverbial compl. **LOE.** ▸**b** Of a road, a course of travel, etc.: extend, have a (specified) direction; lead *through, by, along, among*, etc. **LOE.** ▸**c** Of the wind: remain in a specified quarter. **E17.** ▸**d** Be spread out or extended to the view; (of a period of time, a sequence of events, etc.) extend back into the past or forward into the future. **M18.** ▸**e** Of a competitor in a race: occupy a specified ordinal position. **M20.**

G. GREENE I am not to this day absolutely sure of where . . Jones's home lay. A. MACLEAN A small village lay at the head of the lake. **b** CARLYLE Our course lay along the Valley of the Rhone. **d** J. PAYN What a future seemed to lie before him! **e** D. FRANCIS He took the first half mile without apparent effort, lying about sixth.

9 ***NAUTICAL.*** **a** Of a ship: float in a berth or at anchor. **LOE.** ▸**b** Steer in a (specified) direction. **L16.**

a J. CONRAD The English ship . . was lying in Hyères Roads.

10 Of a material thing: be placed usu. more or less horizontally on the ground or other surface; (of a building etc.) be overthrown or fallen. **ME.** ▸**b** Be deposited, remain permanently in a specified place. **LME.** ▸**c** Of snow: settle and remain unmelted on the ground etc. **L17.**

J. STEINBECK Boxes of lettuce lay on her porch. I. MURDOCH We tilted the cage until it lay entirely upon its side. **c** *Times* North London had its heaviest snowfall of the winter . . but the snow did not lie.

11 Remain unworked, unused, untouched, or undiscovered. Freq. foll. by compl. **ME.**

GLADSTONE Rarely within the living memory has so much skill lain barren.

lie fallow, ***lie idle***, ***lie waste***, etc.

12 Of an abstract thing: exist, be found, reside, be arranged or related, in some specified position or order. **ME.** ▸†**b** Belong or pertain *to* a person (to do); pertain *to* a thing. **ME–M17.** ▸**c** Rest or be imposed as a charge, obligation, etc., *on* a person; be incumbent *on*; weigh *on* (one's mind etc.). **ME.** ▸**d** Be set *at stake*; hang or depend *on* a doubtful issue etc. Long *rare.* **L16.** ▸†**e** Of thoughts, inclinations, activities, etc.: have a specified direction. **M17–E19.**

G. M. TREVELYAN His strongest appeal lay in the strength, beauty and accuracy of his pictures of nature. C. HILL There could no longer be any doubt where real power lay. **c** DEFOE These Things . . lay upon my Mind. CASTLEREAGH It lay upon them to offer terms to us. **d** SHAKES. *All's Well* He persists As if his life lay on't.

13 Chiefly ***LAW.*** Of an action, charge, claim, etc.: be admissible or sustainable. **ME.**

A. CRUMP In which case no action for damages would lie.

14 Of the wind etc.: be or become still, subside. Long *obsolete* exc. *dial.* **L17.**
▸ **III** *verb trans.* **15** Cause to lie, lay. Now *rare.* **OE.** ▸**b** ***NAUTICAL.*** Lay (a course). **L16.**
– **PHRASES:** ***here lies our way***, ***here lies your way***: see **WAY** *noun*. ***how the wind lies***: see **WIND** *noun*[1]. ***let sleeping dogs lie***: see **DOG** *noun*. **lie heavy on** be a weight on (one's stomach or conscience). ***lie in one's way***: see **WAY** *noun*. **lie in ruins**, **lie in the dust** be overthrown or fallen (*lit. & fig.*). ***lie in state***: see **STATE** *noun*. ***lie in the bed one has made***: see **BED** *noun*. ***lie in the dust***: see ***lie in ruins*** above. ***lie in wed***: see **WED** *noun* 2. ***lie like a log***: see **LOG** *noun*[1]. ***lie on the stomach***: see **STOMACH** *noun*. ***lie on the table***: see **TABLE** *noun*. ***lie to wed***: see **WED** *noun* 2. ***lie upon the wager***: see **WAGER** *noun* 3. ***there lies your way***: see **WAY** *noun*.
– **WITH ADVERBS IN SPECIALIZED SENSES:** **lie about** lie here and there; be left carelessly out of place or in disorder. **lie ahead** be going to happen, be in store. **lie along** (***a***) be prostrate at full length, lie outstretched on the ground (*arch.*); extend along a surface; (***b***) ***NAUTICAL*** (of a ship) lean to one side under the pressure of a wind abeam. **lie around** = ***lie about*** above. **lie back** lean backwards against some support; recline so as to rest; ***lie back and enjoy it*** (iron.), relax and accept the inevitable. **lie by** †(***a***) have a concubine; (***b***) ***NAUTICAL*** = ***lie to*** below; also, arrange the sails of a ship during a gale so that heavy seas do not break aboard; (***c***) remain unused, be laid up in store; (***d***) keep quiet or retired; remain inactive, rest. **lie down** (***a***) assume a lying position; have a brief rest in or on a bed etc.; *fig.* give up, be remiss or lazy; ***take lying down***, receive (a beating, defeat, etc.) in an abject manner, without resistance or protest (chiefly in neg. contexts); ***lie down and die***, give up completely; ***lie down under***, accept without protest; †(***b***) be brought to bed *of* a child. **lie in** (***a***) be brought to bed in childbirth (*of* a child); †(***b***) amount to, cost, (a certain sum); (***c***) *colloq.* lie in bed in the morning after one's usual time for getting up. **lie off** ***NAUTICAL*** (of a ship) stand some distance away from the shore or another ship. **lie over** (***a***) be held over or deferred to a future occasion; (***b***) *US* break one's journey; stop. **lie to** ***NAUTICAL*** (of a ship) come almost to a stop with its head near the wind by backing or shortening sail. **lie up** (***a***) go into or be in hiding; take to one's bed or remain in one's room through illness; (of a ship) go into dock or be out of commission; (***b***) ***NAUTICAL*** lay or shape one's course.
– **WITH PREPOSITIONS IN SPECIALIZED SENSES:** **lie in** (***a***) rest or centre in; depend on; be in the power of (*to do*); ***as far as in me lies*** etc., to the best of my etc. power; (***b***) consist in, have its ground or basis in; (***c***) be contained or comprised in (a specified room or compass). **lie under** be subject to (some disadvantage or obligation); ***lie under sentence of death***, be condemned to death. **lie with** be the office or province of a person *to do* something; (see also sense 1e above).
– **COMB.:** **lie-abed** *arch.* a person who lies in bed; a late riser; a sluggard; **lie-about** an idle person, a layabout; **lie-by** (***a***) a neutral; (***b***) (now *dial.*) a concubine, a mistress. (See also combs. of **LIE** *noun*[2].)
■ **lier** *noun* **M16.**

lie /lʌɪ/ *verb*[2]. Pa. t. & pple **lied** /lʌɪd/, pres. pple **lying** /ˈlʌɪɪŋ/.
[**ORIGIN** Old English *lēogan* = Old Frisian *liāga*, Old Saxon *liogan* (Dutch *liegen*), Old High German *liogan* (German *lügen*), Old Norse *ljúga*, Gothic *liugan*, from Germanic base also of **LIE** *noun*[1].]
1 *verb intrans.* Make an intentionally false statement, tell a lie or lies (*to* a person). **OE.**

G. GREENE The train was very full, he said, though Myatt knew he lied. I. MURDOCH It seems so terrible to lie to him . . about things which just aren't true.

lie in one's teeth: see **TOOTH** *noun*. ***lie in one's throat***: see **THROAT** *noun*. ***lie like a trooper***: see **TROOPER** 1.

2 *verb intrans.* Of a thing: present a false statement; convey a false impression; be deceptive. **ME.**

A. PRICE The ground never lies, you can't put a spade in it without leaving a mark.

3 *verb trans.* †**a** Utter (a falsehood); say or allege (something) falsely. **ME–E16.** ▸**b** Get (oneself, a person, etc.) *into* or *out of* by lying. **E18.**

b *Punch* Go on tamely to allow yourself to be lied into Party blindness.

†**4** *verb trans.* Accuse of lying. Only in **LME.**
5 *verb intrans.* Talk, gossip; tell tall stories, exchange anecdotes. Orig. & chiefly *black English.* **M20.**

lié /lje, ˈliːeɪ/ *pred. adjective.* **M19.**
[**ORIGIN** French, pa. pple of *lier* to bind.]
Connected (*with*), intimately acquainted (*with*).

Liebchen /ˈliːpçən, ˈliːbtʃ(ə)n/ *noun.* **L19.**
[**ORIGIN** German.]
A person who is very dear to another; a sweetheart, a pet, a darling. Freq. used as a term of endearment.

lieber Gott /ˈliːbər ɡɔt/ *noun phr.* **L19.**
[**ORIGIN** German.]
Dear God. Chiefly as *interjection.*

Lieberkühn /ˈliːbəkyːn/ *noun.* **M19.**
[**ORIGIN** J. N. *Lieberkühn* (1711–56), German anatomist.]
ANATOMY. ***crypt of Lieberkühn***, ***gland of Lieberkühn***, ***Lieberkühn's gland***, etc., any of the minute tubular glands found at the base of the villi in the small intestine. Usu. in *pl.*
■ **Lieberˈkühnian** *adjective* **M19.**

Liebestod /ˈliːbəstoːt/ *noun.* Also ***l-***. **L19.**
[**ORIGIN** German, lit. 'love's death'.]
An aria or a duet in an opera etc. proclaiming the suicide of lovers; such a suicide.

Liebfraumilch /ˈliːbfraʊmɪlk, *foreign* ˈliːpfraʊmɪlç/ *noun.* **M19.**
[**ORIGIN** German, from *lieb* dear + *Frau* lady, (i.e. the Virgin Mary, patroness of the convent where it was first made) + *Milch* **MILK** *noun*.]
A mild white Rhine wine.

Liebig /ˈliːbɪɡ/ *noun.* **M19.**
[**ORIGIN** Baron Justus von *Liebig* (1803–73), German chemist.]
1 More fully ***Liebig's extract* (*of beef*)**. A highly concentrated extract containing the soluble constituents of beef. Now *rare.* **M19.**
2 ***Liebig condenser***, ***Liebig's condenser***, a common distillation device consisting of two concentric tubes, a coolant (usu. water) being passed through the outer tube to condense vapour in the inner one. **M19.**

Liebling /ˈliːplɪŋ, ˈliːb-/ *noun.* **M19.**
[**ORIGIN** German.]
= **LIEBCHEN.**

lied /liːd, -t/ *noun.* Pl. **lieder** /ˈliːdə/. Also **L-**. **M19.**
[**ORIGIN** German.]
A song; *esp.* a song characteristic of the German Romantic period, usu. for solo voice with piano accompaniment.
– **COMB.:** **liederabend** /-ɑːbənt/ [German *Abend* evening] an evening recital of such songs.

Liederkranz /ˈliːdəkrants/ *noun. US.* **E20.**
[**ORIGIN** German, lit. 'choral society'.]
(Proprietary name for) a strong-flavoured soft cheese.

lief /liːf/ *adjective, noun, & adverb.* Now *arch. & dial.*
[**ORIGIN** Old English *lēof* = Old Frisian *liāf*, Old Saxon *liob*, *liof* (Dutch *lief*), Old High German *liub*, *liup* (German *lieb*), Old Norse *ljúfr*, Gothic *liufs*, from Germanic, rel. to **LEAVE** *noun*[1], **LOVE** *noun*.]
▸ **A** *adjective.* **1** Beloved, dear, agreeable, acceptable, precious. **OE.**

TENNYSON I charge thee, quickly go again As thou art lief and dear. E. POUND This most lief lady.

2 Not disagreeable; not unwilling. Freq. in ***lief or loath***. **OE.**

R. W. DIXON Now hence must I . . be I loth or lief.

†**3** Desirous, willing, glad. (Foll. by *of, to do*.) **ME–E16.**
▸ †**B** *noun.* A beloved, a dear person; a friend, a sweetheart; a wife. Also (as a form of respectful address), sir, lord. **OE–M17.**
▸ **C** *adverb.* Gladly, willingly. **ME.**

A. E. HOUSMAN Where shall one halt to deliver This luggage I'd lief set down? C. DAY He said . . he would as lief go around in a wheelbarrow.

■ **liefly** *adverb* †(***a***) beautifully; dearly, kindly; (***b***) *rare* willingly, gladly: **OE.**

liege /liːdʒ/ *adjective, noun, & verb.* **ME.**
[**ORIGIN** Old French & mod. French *lige* (Old French also *liege*) from medieval Latin *leticus*, *laeticus* from *letus*, *litus*, prob. from Germanic.]
▸ **A** *adjective* **1 a** *hist.* Of a superior: entitled to feudal allegiance and service (now *rare* exc. in ***liege lord*** below). Of a vassal: bound to give feudal service and allegiance (cf. **LIEGEMAN**). **ME.** ▸**b** Loyal, faithful. *rare.* **L15.**
liege lord a feudal superior, a sovereign.
2 *hist.* Of or pertaining to the bond between feudal superior and vassal. **LME.**
▸ **B** *noun.* **1** *hist.* The superior to whom a vassal owes feudal allegiance and service; a liege lord. **LME.**

BROWNING My liege, do not believe it! I am yours.

2 A vassal who owes feudal allegiance and service to a superior, a liegeman (*hist.*); *transf.* a loyal subject of a sovereign. Usu. in *pl.* **LME.**

L

SIR W. SCOTT Her Majesty, being detained by her gracious desire to receive the homage of her lieges. J. TEY The Chief Constable . . sent a request to the Home Office for troops to protect the lieges.

▸ **C** *verb trans.* †**1** Give (homage etc.) as a liegeman. Only in L17.

2 Foll. by *it*: rule over like a liege lord. *rare*. M19.

■ **liegedom** *noun* the condition of being a liege E19. **liegeless** *adjective* (*rare*) (**a**) not subject to a superior; free; (**b**) disregardful of obligations to a superior: E19.

liegeman /ˈliːdʒmən/ *noun*. Pl. **-men**. LME.
[ORIGIN from LIEGE *adjective* + MAN *noun*: cf. medieval Latin *homo ligeus*, Old French *home* (mod. *homme*) *lige*.]

1 *hist.* A vassal owing feudal allegiance and service to a liege lord. LME.

2 A person who serves another as though sworn to do so, a faithful follower or subject. E19.

Liégeois /lɪˈeɪʒwɑː/ *noun & adjective*. Pl. of noun same. L16.
[ORIGIN French, from *Liège* (see below).]
(A native or inhabitant) of Liège, a city and province in Belgium.

lieger *noun & adjective* see LEDGER *noun & adjective*.

lien /liːn, ˈliːən, ˈlʌɪən/ *noun*. M16.
[ORIGIN French from Old French *loien* from Latin *ligamen* bond, from *ligare* to tie.]
LAW. A right to keep possession of property belonging to another person until a debt due by that person is discharged.

fig.: T. LUNDBERG The assets are free of any lien or encumbrances. *Rolling Stone* A sport on which television already had a lien.

■ **lienor** *noun* (*US Law*) a person holding a lien L19.

lieno- /lʌɪˈiːnəʊ/ *combining form*.
[ORIGIN from Latin *lien* spleen: see -O-.]
= SPLENO-, as ***lieno-renal***.

lientery /ˈlʌɪənt(ə)ri/ *noun*. Now *rare* or *obsolete*. Also (earlier) in mod. Latin form **lienteria** /lʌɪənˈtɪərɪə/. LME.
[ORIGIN Old French & mod. French *lientérie* or medieval Latin *lienteria* from Greek *leienteria*, from *leios* smooth + *entera* bowels: see -Y³.]
MEDICINE. A form of diarrhoea in which the food passes through the bowels partially or wholly undigested; an instance or kind of this.

■ **lien'teric** *adjective* L17.

lierne /lɪˈəːn/ *noun*. LME.
[ORIGIN French, perh. transf. use of *lierne* clematis, dial. var. of *liane*: see LIANA.]
ARCHITECTURE. A short rib connecting the bosses and intersections of vaulting ribs.

Liesegang /ˈliːzəgaŋ/ *noun*. E20.
[ORIGIN R. E. *Liesegang* (1869–1947), German chemist.]
PHYSICAL CHEMISTRY. ***Liesegang ring***, ***Liesegang figure***, each of a set of concentric rings of precipitate produced by the diffusion together of two solutions that react to form a slightly soluble precipitate. Usu. in *pl.*

lieu /ljuː, luː/ *noun*. ME.
[ORIGIN Old French & mod. French from Latin LOCUS *noun*[1] place.]
in lieu, in the place, instead, (*of*).

Lieut. *abbreviation*.
Lieutenant.

lieutenancy /lɛfˈtɛnənsi, *l(j)uːˈtɛnənsi/ *noun*. LME.
[ORIGIN from LIEUTENANT: see -ANCY.]

1 The position, rank, office, or authority of a lieutenant. LME.

†**2** The district or province governed by a lieutenant. L16–E18.

3 The term of a lieutenant's office. M17.

†**4** Delegated authority or command. Only in M17.

5 The body of deputy lieutenants in a county. Also, in the City of London, the body of commissioners (now usu. appointed annually) performing some of the duties of a Lord Lieutenant. L17.

lieutenant /lɛfˈtɛnənt, *l(j)uːˈtɛnənt/ *noun*. LME.
[ORIGIN Old French & mod. French, formed as LIEU + TENANT *noun*. Cf. LOCUM TENENS.]

1 A person who takes the place of another; *esp.* an officer (civil or military) acting for a superior; a representative, a substitute; a trusty assistant, a henchman. LME. ▸†**b** [translating Latin *legatus*, *proconsul*, *suffectus*, etc.] A consul suffect, a legate, a proconsul. LME–M18.

E. LINKLATER With Rod were his two most trusted lieutenants.

2 **a** An officer in the army or (US etc.) air force, ranking next below a captain. M16. ▸**b** A naval officer ranking next below a lieutenant commander. L16. ▸**c** An officer in the Salvation Army ranking next below a captain. L19.

a R. KIPLING Lieutenant Corkram . . rode by. **b** F. MARRYAT The Admiralty . . had . . promoted him to the rank of lieutenant.

3 In the US etc., a police or prison officer ranking next below a captain. E20.

– PHRASES ETC.: ***captain-lieutenant***: see CAPTAIN *noun*. ***deputy lieutenant***. **first lieutenant** (**a**) a naval officer with executive responsibility for a ship etc.; (**b**) in the US etc. army or air force, an officer ranking next below a captain. ***flag lieutenant***: see FLAG *noun*[4]. ***flight lieutenant***: see FLIGHT *noun*[1]. **Lieutenant of the Tower** the acting commandant of the Tower of London. ***Lord Lieutenant***: see LORD *noun*. **second lieutenant** an army or (formerly) naval officer ranking next below a (first) lieutenant. SUB-LIEUTENANT.

– COMB.: **lieutenant colonel** an army officer ranking next below a colonel, having the actual command of a regiment; **lieutenant colonelcy** the office or rank of lieutenant colonel; **lieutenant commander** a naval officer ranking below a commander and above a lieutenant; **lieutenant governor** the acting or deputy governor of a state, province, etc., under a governor or governor general.

■ †**lieutenantry** *noun* lieutenancy M16–L18. **lieutenantship** *noun* (now *rare*) the rank or position of a lieutenant LME.

lieutenant general /lɛfˌtɛnənt ˈdʒɛn(ə)r(ə)l/ *noun phr.* L15.
[ORIGIN from LIEUTENANT + GENERAL *adjective* (later taken as noun), after French *lieutenant général*.]

†**1** *gen.* A person exercising a delegated rule or command over some extensive region or department; the vicegerent of a kingdom etc. L15–E18.

2 A person acting as deputy to a general; an army officer ranking below a general and above a major-general. L16.

life /lʌɪf/ *noun*. Pl. **lives** /lʌɪvz/.
[ORIGIN Old English *līf* corresp. to Old Frisian, Old Saxon *līf* life, person (Dutch *lijf* body), Old High German *līb* life (German *Leib* body), Old Norse *líf* life, body, from Germanic, from base the weak grade of which appears in LIVE *verb*.]

▸ **I** **1** The condition, quality, or fact of being a living organism; the condition that characterizes animals and plants (when alive) and distinguishes them from inanimate matter, being marked by a capacity for growth and development and by continued functional activity; the activities and phenomena by which this is manifested. OE. ▸**b** Continuance or prolongation of animate existence (as opp. to death). OE. ▸**c** Animate existence as dependent on sustenance or favourable physical conditions. Formerly also, a livelihood, a person's living. Long *rare* or *obsolete*. ME.

JONATHAN MILLER The start of life is traditionally identified with the first breath. P. DAVIES Today we understand how man, and even . . how life has arisen on Earth. **b** BYRON No bugle awakes him with life-and-death call. **c** AV *Deut.* 20:19 The tree of the field is mans life.

bird-life, ***pond-life***, etc.

2 *fig.* A condition of power, activity, or happiness; *esp.* (chiefly in biblical and religious use) the condition of a person freed from the state of sin equated with spiritual death; salvation; regenerate condition. OE.

CARLYLE If our Bodily Life is a burning, our Spiritual Life is a being-burnt, a Combustion.

3 A being's, esp. a person's, animate existence viewed as a possession of which one is deprived by death. OE.

P. S. BUCK Her Life would not easily pass from her body. *Financial Times* Political violence claims an average of almost nine lives a day.

4 The cause or source of living; the animating principle; a person who or thing which makes or keeps a thing alive. ME.

T. TRYON Water and Air are the true life and Power of every Being. *Melody Maker* Offstage . . Dudley doesn't strike you as being the life and soul of the party.

5 **a** A living being, a person. Long *rare* exc. as passing into sense 3. ME. ▸**b** Vitality as embodied in an individual person or thing. *arch.* L16. ▸**c** Living things and their activity; *spec.* human presence or activity. E18.

c DICKENS Very little life was to be seen on either bank. K. WATERHOUSE The office area, though brightly lit, is empty of life. D. ATTENBOROUGH It was only the dinosaurs that disappeared, not the whole of animal life.

6 Energy; liveliness; animation, vivacity, spirit; *CRICKET* that quality in the pitch which causes the ball to rise abruptly or unevenly after pitching. L16.

LYTTON There was no lustre in her eye, no life in her step. M. CONEY She was full of life, full of vitality and youth.

7 The or *the* living form or (esp. nude) model; living semblance; life-size. L16.

W. HOLLAR He was drawing a figure after the life. *New Yorker* Unlike Acord, . . she preferred to draw from life.

▸ **II** **8** The animate existence of an individual in respect of its duration; the period from birth to death, from birth to a particular time, or from a particular time to death. OE. ▸**b** The time for which an inanimate thing exists or continues to function or be saleable or valid; *spec.* in *PHYSICS* (more fully ***mean life***), the average duration of existence of a type of particle or state (equal to the period in which the population decreases by a factor *e*, approx. 2.718). Cf. ***half-life*** s.v. HALF-. E18. ▸**c** Imprisonment or (formerly) transportation for life; a life sentence. *slang*. M19.

E. BAKER Man's life can be separated into . . four stages of childhood, youth, middle years . . old age. **b** E. RUTHERFORD A radioactive life of less than a minute. **c** *Times* Its . . turbo-jet engines will be permitted an initial 'life' . . of 1,000 hours. J. C. OATES A backwoods woman come to visit her husband, sentenced to Powhatassie for life.

9 A chance to live after a narrowly escaped death. Chiefly with ref. to the nine lives traditionally attributed to the cat. Usu. in *pl.* Cf. sense 11 below. M16.

10 A person considered with regard to the probable future duration of his or her life, esp. for insurance purposes; any particular amount of expectation of life. L17.

11 In various games, esp. card games, any of a specified number of successive chances each player has before being put out. Also (*CRICKET & BASEBALL* etc.), the continuation of a batsman's innings or a batter's turn at bat after a chance has been missed of getting him or her out. E19.

J. SNOW Walters . . was given a life by another blunder by Rowan.

▸ **III** **12** The series of actions and occurrences constituting the history of an individual from birth to death; the course of (human) existence from birth to death. Also (*THEOLOGY*), either of the two states of human existence separated by death. OE. ▸**b** A particular manner or course of living. Freq. with specifying word. OE. ▸**c** The active part of human existence; the business and active pleasures of the world. Also, the position of participating in the affairs of the world, of being a recognized member of society. L18.

MILTON To know That which before us lies in daily life. **b** R. CAMPBELL Few people enjoyed *living* so much as Aunt Jessie . . though her life was . . truly tough. DAY LEWIS Living . . the same enclosed, garrison life . . as the Anglo-Indians in India. **c** C. MACKENZIE I've got a fancy . . to show you a bit of life.

13 A written account of a person's history; a biography. ME.

S. SASSOON He had written the lives of several Generals. B. BAINBRIDGE The book was a life of Mozart.

– PHRASES: **a bad life** a person assessed for life-insurance purposes as not likely to exceed his or her expectation of life. **a good life** a person assessed for life-insurance purposes as likely to exceed his or her expectation of life. **a matter of life and death** something on which it depends whether one shall live or die; *fig.* something of vital importance (cf. ***life-and-death*** *adjective* below). **anything for a quiet life** any concession to ensure that one is not disturbed. **as large as life**, **large as life** (**a**) life-size; (**b**) in person, esp. prominently. ***book of life***: see BOOK *noun*. ***the BREATH of life***. **bring to life** recover from unconsciousness or inactivity, impart animation to. **come to life** emerge from unconsciousness or inactivity; become animated. ***decrement of life***: see DECREMENT 2b. ***depart from life***, ***depart from this life***, ***depart this life***: see DEPART *verb*. ***dog's life***: see DOG *noun*. ***double life***: see DOUBLE *adjective & adverb*. ***downhill of life***: see DOWNHILL *noun* 1. ***ELIXIR of life***. **eternal life**, **everlasting life**: in heaven. **expectation of life** the average period that a person at a specified age, in a known state of health, etc., may be expected to live, esp. as derived from statistics of the population at large. ***fact of life***: see FACT *noun*. ***for dear life***: see DEAR *adjective*[1]. **for life** for the remaining period of the person's life. ***for ONCE in one's life***. **for one's life** for dear life, (as if) to escape death. **for the life of me** even if my life depended on it (I could not etc.). **frighten the life out of** terrify. ***future life***: see FUTURE *adjective & noun*. **get a life** *colloq.* start living a fuller or more interesting existence; stop being so boring, conventional, studious, etc. (freq. in *imper.*). **get the fright of one's life**, **have the fright of one's life** be frightened as never before. **have the time of one's life** enjoy oneself as never before. ***high life***: see HIGH *adjective*. **how's life?** *colloq.* how are things going? **in life** to be experienced anywhere. ***large as life***: see ***as large as life*** above. **larger than life** more than life-size; exaggerated. ***lead a person a difficult life***, ***lead a person an uncomfortable life***: see LEAD *verb*[1]. ***life and limb***: see LIMB *noun*[1]. ***light of one's life***: see LIGHT *noun*. ***line of life***: see LINE *noun*[2]. ***live one's own life***: see LIVE *verb*. ***long of life***: see LONG *adjective*[1]. ***lose one's life***: see LOSE *verb*. ***loss of life***: see LOSS *noun*. **make life easy (for)** not create problems (for). ***middle life***: see MIDDLE *adjective*. **my life** *arch.* my beloved, my dearest. ***natural life***: see NATURAL *adjective*. ***new lease of life***, ***new lease on life***: see LEASE *noun*[3]. **not on your life** *colloq.* most certainly not. **on life** *arch.* alive. ***other life***: see OTHER *adjective*. ***plague the life out of***: see PLAGUE *verb*. ***pride of life***: see PRIDE *noun*[1]. ***private life***: see PRIVATE *adjective*. **put some life into it** act, perform, more energetically. **save a person's life** prevent a person's dying or being killed; *hyperbol.* provide much-needed relief for a person, esp. oneself, from exhaustion, boredom, etc. ***secret life***: see SECRET *adjective & noun*. ***see life***: see SEE *verb*. ***sell one's life dear(ly)***: see SELL *verb*. ***slice of life***: see SLICE *noun*[1] 3. ***staff of life***: see STAFF *noun*[1]. ***state of life***: see STATE *noun*. ***still life***: see STILL *adjective*. **take life** kill a person or an animal. **take one's life in one's hands** *colloq.* risk one's life. **take one's own life** kill oneself, commit suicide. ***the change of life***: see CHANGE *noun* 1. ***the facts of life***: see FACT *noun*. ***the kiss of life***: see KISS *noun*. **the life** *US slang* prostitution (freq. in ***in the life***). ***the life of RILEY***. **the life of the mind** intellectual or aesthetic pursuits, the realm of the imagination. ***the story of my life***, ***the story of his life***, etc.: see STORY *noun*[1]. ***the struggle for life***: see STRUGGLE *noun*. **this life** [translating Vulgate *haec vita*, in *1 Corinthians* 15:19] life on earth; ***depart from this life***: see DEPART *verb*. **this is the life** *colloq.*: expr. contentment. ***time of life***, ***time of one's life***: see TIME *noun*. **to the life** with lifelike representation; with fidelity to the original. ***tree of life***: see TREE *noun*. **true to life** providing an accurate representation of behaviour etc. ***unitive life***: see UNITIVE *adjective* 1. ***university of life***: see UNIVERSITY 1. **upon my life!** *arch.*: expr. of assertion. ***walk in life***, ***walk of life***: see WALK *noun*[1]. ***water of life***: see WATER *noun*. ***way of life***: see WAY *noun*. ***within an inch of one's life***: see INCH *noun*[1]. ***you bet your life***: see BET *verb* 2. ***your money or your life***: see MONEY *noun*.

– COMB.: **life-affirming** emotionally or spiritually uplifting; **life-and-death** *adjective* involving life and death; vitally important (cf. ***a matter of life and death*** above); **life assurance** = ***life insurance*** below; **lifebelt** a belt of buoyant or inflatable material for supporting the body in water; **lifeblood** (**a**) the blood necessary to life; *fig.* the vitalizing influence, the vital factor; (**b**) *colloq.*

L

an involuntary twitching of the lip or eyelid; **lifeboat** (*a*) a boat of special construction launched from land for rescuing those in distress at sea; a ship's small boat for abandoning ship in an emergency; (*b*) *US slang* a pardon, a commutation of sentence; (*c*) a system of support organization arranged by the Bank of England for secondary banks in danger of collapse; **life-breath** the breath which supports life; *fig.* an inspiring influence, a sustaining principle; *lifebuoy*: see BUOY *noun* 1b; **life coach** a person employed to help people attain their goals in life; **life cord** (*arch. rare*) = *life-string* below; **life cycle** (*a*) BIOLOGY (an account of) the series of developmental stages through which an organism passes from its initial state (egg) to the same state in the next generation; (*b*) the course of human, cultural, etc., existence from beginning through development and productivity to decay and ending; **life-day** *arch.* a day etc. of a person's life; freq. in *pl.* (occas. *sing.*), a person's life or lifetime, (all) the days of (one's) life; **life-estate** property that a person holds for life but cannot dispose of further; **life-everlasting** an American everlasting, *Anaphalis margaritacea*, grown for ornament; **life expectancy**, **life expectation** = *expectation of life* above; **life-expired** (esp. of railway vehicles) worn out or outdated; **life force** vital energy, a driving force or influence; **life form** (*a*) BIOLOGY a habit or vegetative form exhibited by any particular plant or which characterizes a group of plants; (*b*) a living organism; any kind of living thing; **life-giver** a person who or thing which gives life; **life-giving** *noun & adjective* (*a*) *noun* the giving of life; (*b*) *adjective* that gives life; **life-gun** a gun used for sending life-saving apparatus to ships; **life history** BIOLOGY = *life cycle* above; *transf.* (an account of) the series of stages in the existence of an inanimate thing; the story of a person's life, esp. when told at tedious length; **life-hold** *adjective* designating property which is held for life; **life imprisonment** imprisonment for life; **life-in-death** (*a*) a phantom state, a condition of being or seeming to be neither alive nor dead; something having the form or appearance of the supernatural, an apparition, a spectre; (*b*) = *death-in-life* s.v. DEATH *noun*; **life insurance** insurance for payment on the death of the insured person; **life interest** a right to a life-estate; **life jacket** a jacket of buoyant or inflatable material for supporting the body in water; **life list** ORNITHOLOGY a list of the kinds of bird recorded by a person during his or her life; **life member** a person who has acquired lifelong membership of a society etc.; **life membership** the status or position of a life member; **life net** *US* a safety net held to catch people forced by fire etc. to escape from buildings by jumping; **life office** an office or company dealing in life insurance; **life-or-death** *adjective* = *life-and-death adjective* above; **life partner** a person with whom one is in a long-term heterosexual or homosexual relationship; **life peer** a peer whose title cannot be inherited; **life peerage**: held by a life peer; **life-plant** a plant of the stonecrop family, *Kalanchoe pinnata*, which will produce young plants from the leaves even after the leaves are removed from the plant; **life policy** a life-insurance policy; **life preserver** (*a*) (long *rare* or *obsolete*) a person who preserves life; (*b*) a lifebuoy, lifebelt, or other contrivance used in saving life at sea; (*c*) a short stick with a heavily loaded end; **life raft** a raft, usu. an inflatable one, for conveying people, esp. as a substitute for a boat in an emergency; **liferent** *noun & verb* (SCOTS LAW) (*a*) *noun* a rent or income which a person is entitled to receive for life, usually for support; a right to use and enjoy (property) during one's life; (*b*) *verb trans.* assign in liferent; use and enjoy property during one's life; **liferenter** SCOTS LAW a person who is entitled to or enjoys a liferent; **liferentrix** a female liferenter; **life ring** *N. Amer.* a lifebuoy; **life-save** *verb trans.* save from death or serious difficulty, esp. drowning; act towards as a lifesaver; **lifesaver** (*a*) a person who or thing which may save a person etc. from death or serious difficulty; *esp.* (*Austral. & NZ*) = LIFEGUARD 4; (*b*) *fig.* a quality, characteristic, or circumstance that helps a person to endure adversity; **life-saving** *adjective & noun* of or pertaining to, the action of, saving a person etc. from death or serious difficulty, esp. from drowning; **life science** any of the sciences (such as zoology, bacteriology, or physiology) which deal with living organisms; such sciences collectively; **life scientist** an expert in or student of a life science; **life sentence** a sentence of imprisonment for life; *transf.* an illness, obligation, etc.; **life-size** *adjective & noun* (*a*) *adjective* of the size of life; (of a picture or statue) equal in size to the original; (*b*) *noun* the size of someone or something; a life-size portrait or statue; **life-sized** *adjective* = *life-size adjective* above; **life skill** a skill that is necessary or desirable for full participation in everyday life; **lifespan** a lifetime; the period of duration or existence (of an animate or inanimate thing); **life-spring** *arch.* the spring or source of life; **life-string** *arch.* a nerve etc. supposed to be essential to life; in *pl.*, things essential to the support of life; **lifestyle** (*a*) a person's basic character as established early in childhood which governs his or her reactions and behaviour; (*b*) an individual's or group's way of life; a way or style of living; *lifestyle drug*: used to improve quality of life (e.g. by alleviating impotence or baldness) rather than treat a disease or life-threatening condition; **life-support** *adjective* (of equipment) allowing vital functions to continue in an adverse environment or during severe disablement, as in giving assisted ventilation to a paralysed patient; **life's-work** the work of a lifetime; a task pursued throughout a person's whole life; **life table** a table of statistics relating to expectation of life; **life tenancy**: terminating with the holder's death; **life tenant** the holder of a life tenancy; **life test**: made on a sample of components under specified conditions, over a set period or until failure occurs, to determine their reliability; **life-test** *verb trans.* perform a life test on; **life-tide** *arch. rare* (*a*) a lifetime; (*b*) the tide or stream of life; **life-tree** = *tree of life* s.v. TREE *noun*; **life vest** *US* = *life jacket* above; **lifeway** (orig. *N. Amer.*) a way or manner of life; **life-while** *arch.* a lifetime; **life-work** = *life's-work* above; **lifeworld** PHILOSOPHY. [translating German LEBENSWELT] all the immediate experiences, activities, and contacts that make up the world of an individual, or of a corporate, life; **life-writer** *rare* a biographer; **life-writing** (the writing of) biography.

■ **lifeward** *adverb* in the direction of life, towards life M19. **lifey** *adjective* (*a*) characteristic of or belonging to life; (*b*) lively, spirited: LME.

life /lʌɪf/ *verb trans. rare.* L19.
[ORIGIN from the noun.]
Give life to.

lifeful /ˈlʌɪf-fʊl, -f(ə)l/ *adjective & noun.* Now *rare.* ME.
[ORIGIN from LIFE *noun* + -FUL.]
▸**A** *adjective.* Full of life; having much vitality or animation; giving or bestowing life or vitality. ME.
▸**B** *noun.* An amount sufficient to fill a lifetime. M19.
■ **lifefully** *adverb* LME. **lifefulness** *noun* M19.

lifeguard /ˈlʌɪfɡɑːd/ *noun.* M17.
[ORIGIN from LIFE *noun* + GUARD *noun*, prob. after Dutch †*lijfgarde*, German *Leibgarde*, (1st elem. meaning body).]
1 A bodyguard of soldiers. M17.
The Life Guards in the British army, a regiment of the Household Cavalry, now merged with the Horse Guards and the Dragoon Guards in the Household Cavalry.
2 The guard or protection of a person's life; a protecting agent or influence. Now *rare* or *obsolete.* M17.
3 A device attached to the front of a railway engine for sweeping small obstructions from the track. M19.
4 An expert swimmer employed to rescue bathers from drowning. Orig. *US.* L19.
– COMB.: **lifeguardman** a member of a lifeguard; **Life Guardsman** a soldier belonging to the Life Guards.

lifeless /ˈlʌɪflɪs/ *adjective.*
[ORIGIN Old English, formed as LIFE *noun* + -LESS.]
1 That has ceased to live; no longer living; dead. OE. ▸**b** Unconscious. Chiefly *hyperbol.* M17.

> M. SHADBOLT The bird lay limp . . . It was already quite lifeless. **b** DISRAELI Mrs. Felix Lorraine sank lifeless into his arms.

2 Not endowed with or possessing life; inanimate. OE.

> SHAKES. *A.Y.L.* That which here stands up Is but a quintain, a mere lifeless block.

3 Lacking animation, vigour, or activity. ME.

> E. BOWEN The flags had dropped and hung lifeless down their poles. B. PYM Marcia's short, stiff, lifeless hair.

4 Devoid of life or living beings. M18.

> BROWNING Treeless, herbless, lifeless mountain.

■ **lifelessly** *adverb* M19. **lifelessness** *noun* E18.

lifelike /ˈlʌɪflʌɪk/ *adjective & adverb.* E17.
[ORIGIN from LIFE *noun* + -LIKE.]
▸**A** *adjective.* **1** Likely to live. *rare.* E17.
2 Like or resembling life; exactly like a living or real original, closely resembling the person or thing represented. E18.
▸**B** *adverb.* With animation or liveliness. *rare.* M19.
■ **lifelikeness** *noun* M19.

lifeline /ˈlʌɪflʌɪn/ *noun.* E18.
[ORIGIN from LIFE *noun* + LINE *noun*[2].]
1 A line or rope for use in life-saving, e.g. attached to a lifebuoy or used by firefighters. E18. ▸**b** A diver's signalling line. L19.

> *Ilkeston Advertiser* The lifelines—easier to use and more accurate than lifebelts—were provided. *fig.*: G. ORWELL The public schoolman . . clings to the Old School Tie as to a lifeline.

2 *fig.* In CLASSICAL MYTHOLOGY, the thread supposedly spun by the Fates, determining the length of a person's life (formerly also called ***line of life***). Also, an essential supply route, a line of communication, etc. M19.

> *Sun (Baltimore)* As they [the Japanese] went along, they . . got themselves into a position where they could threaten the American life line to Australia. B. UNSWORTH Battistella, his lifeline in this too, brought him the gossip of the coffee house.

3 PALMISTRY. A line on the palm of the hand supposed to indicate one's length of life. L19.

> M. MCCARTHY He felt a sharp pain in . . his palm, the part bounded by his lifeline.

lifelong /ˈlʌɪflɒŋ/ *adjective & adverb.* M18.
[ORIGIN from LIFE *noun* + LONG *adjective*[1].]
▸**A** *adjective.* **1** = LIVELONG *adjective. rare.* M18.
2 Lasting a lifetime. E19.
▸**B** *adverb.* For a lifetime. *rare.* M19.

lifemanship /ˈlʌɪfmənʃɪp/ *noun.* M20.
[ORIGIN from LIFE *noun* + -MANSHIP.]
Skill in getting the edge over, or acquiring an advantage over, another person or persons.

lifer /ˈlʌɪfə/ *noun. slang.* E19.
[ORIGIN from LIFE *noun* + -ER[1].]
1 A person serving a sentence of imprisonment or (formerly) transportation for life. E19.

> J. C. HOLMES A letter from a lifer describing sex practices in the penitentiary.

2 A sentence of imprisonment for life. M19.

> E. WALLACE My husband got a lifer two years ago.

3 A person who leads a life of a specified character. Freq. as 2nd elem. of comb. E20.

> *Listener* Members may be 'arty-crafty' and 'simple-lifers'.

4 A life peer. M20.

lifesome /ˈlʌɪfs(ə)m/ *adjective.* Now *rare.* L16.
[ORIGIN from LIFE *noun* + -SOME[1].]
†**1** Fraught with life. Only in L16.
2 Full of life or animation, lively. L17.
■ **lifesomely** *adverb* L17. **lifesomeness** *noun* M19.

lifetime /ˈlʌɪftʌɪm/ *noun.* ME.
[ORIGIN from LIFE *noun* + TIME *noun.*]
1 The duration of a person's life, the (remaining) time during which a person is alive; *colloq.* an exceedingly long time. ME.

> C. ODETS My father never said one word to my mother in her whole lifetime. *attrib.*: *Country Life* The gifts tax . . would be a tax on lifetime gifts.

the chance of a lifetime, **the opportunity of a lifetime**: such as occurs only once in a person's life.
2 The duration of a thing or a thing's usefulness etc.; = LIFE *noun* 8b. M19.

> P. DAVIES Such clusters only have a finite lifetime, at the end of which they collapse.

Liffe /ˈlɪfi, lʌɪf/ *abbreviation.*
London International Financial Futures Exchange.

LIFO /ˈliːfəʊ/ *abbreviation.*
COMPUTING. Last in, first out.

lift /lɪft/ *noun*[1]. *obsolete* exc. *Scot. & poet.*
[ORIGIN Old English *lyft*, corresp. to Old Saxon, Old High German *luft* (Dutch *lucht*, German *Luft*), Old Norse *lopt* (see LOFT *noun*), Gothic *luftus*, from Germanic.]
Orig., the air, the atmosphere. Later, the sky, the upper regions. Also in *pl.*, the (seven) heavens.

lift /lɪft/ *noun*[2]. ME.
[ORIGIN from LIFT *verb.*]
▸**I 1** The quantity or weight, esp. of paper, that can be lifted at one time. Also (*Scot.*), a large quantity. ME.

> A. TROLLOPE I have used up three lifts of notepaper already.

2 A particular joint or cut of meat, esp. of beef. *dial.* E16.
3 A hingeless gate that is removed or opened by lifting. *dial.* L17.
4 An area of rising ground. E19.

> J. R. GREEN A mere lift of higher ground with a few grey cottages dotted over it.

5 A fingerprint that has been lifted. *US.* M20.
▸**II 6** NAUTICAL. In *pl.* Ropes reaching from each masthead to their respective yardarms to steady and suspend the ends. ME.
7 Any of the layers of leather etc. in the heel of a boot or shoe. Also, a built-up heel or device worn in a boot or shoe to make the wearer appear taller. L17.
8 An apparatus for raising or lowering people or things from one floor or level to another; an ascending chamber or compartment; a hoist. Also, the well or vertical opening in which such an apparatus works. M19. ▸**b** An apparatus for carrying people up and down a mountain etc. M20.

> ALDOUS HUXLEY Lenina Crowne shot up seventeen stories, turned to the right as she stepped out of the lift.

express lift: see EXPRESS *adjective*. ***paternoster lift***: see PATERNOSTER *noun* 4. **b** ***chairlift***, ***ski lift***, etc.
9 A set of pumps in a mine; the section of a shaft occupied by one such set. M19.
▸**III 10** The action or an act of lifting; a raising, a rising; the distance through which a thing is lifted and moved; the distance or extent to which something rises. LME. ▸**b** A free ride as a passenger in another person's vehicle. E18. ▸**c** The removal of a corpse from a house for burial or cremation; the starting of a funeral procession. *Scot. & N. English.* L19.

> E. K. KANE We continue perched up, just as we were after our great lift of last December. J. R. LOWELL An almost imperceptible lift of the eyebrow. **b** E. WAUGH A man in a newspaper van offered me a lift as far as Elstree.

dead lift: see DEAD *adjective* etc.
11 An act of lifting or stealing. Formerly also, a shift, a trick. *obsolete* exc. *dial. & slang.* L16.
12 *fig.* A rise in social status, prosperity, etc.; promotion; a rise in price; an act of helping, or a circumstance that helps, someone or something to a higher or more advanced position. E17. ▸**b** An elevating influence or effect; a cheering or encouraging influence or effect, a sense of elation. L18.

> LEIGH HUNT I shall set myself more on a level with these gentry . . by a lift in my fortunes. *Manchester Examiner* The extension of the franchise . . has given an incalculable forward lift to the principles of the Alliance. *Times* A lift in the dividend at Wilson (Connelly) earned its shares a rise. **b** *Practical Gardening* Fresh flowers are wonderful for . . giving us a lift when we feel a bit low. P. THEROUX The sugary breakfast . . gave him a lift.

†**13** The action of cutting a pack of cards; each of the portions into which a pack is divided by cutting. L17–E18.
14 ENGINEERING. The action of lifting a load through a vertical distance, or one of several successive distances. Also (MINING), a set of inclined workings following the slope of the beds. E18.

15 The act or habit of carrying the head, neck, eyes, etc., aloft; elevated carriage. **M19.**

R. D. BLACKMORE The proud lift of her neck was gone.

16 *PROSODY.* A stressed element in a line of alliterative verse. **L19.**

17 a The upward pressure which the air exerts on an aircraft etc. counteracting the force of gravity; the force on an aerofoil at right angles to its direction of motion through a fluid; upwardly-moving air which provides sufficient upward force to support a glider or carry it higher (freq. in ***in lift***). **E20.** ▸**b** The (maximum) weight that an aircraft can raise. **E20.**

a *Nature* Most flying insects depend, for their lift and thrust, on conventional aerofoil action. **b** *Daily Telegraph* The Puma.. helicopter, which has a total lift of up to 5,500 lb.

18 *DANCING.* A movement in which a dancer lifts another in the air. **E20.**

K. AMBROSE With the invention of each new ballet, new lifts are devised.

19 Transport by air; a number of people or an amount of supplies so transported. **M20.**
airlift.

20 The establishment by a sheepdog of control over a flock of sheep. **M20.**

21 *AUDIO.* A relative amplification of signals within a particular part of the audible range, esp. the bass. **M20.**

22 *SPORT.* A movement by which a weightlifter lifts a weight or a wrestler lifts an opponent. **M20.**

▸ †**IV 23** A person who lifts or takes away and appropriates something; a thief. *slang.* **L16–M17.**

– COMB.: **lift-bridge** a bridge on a canal etc. that may be raised to allow the passage of a boat; **lift coefficient** *AERODYNAMICS* a ratio representing the lift developed by unit area of an aerofoil in relation to the air speed; **lift-fan** a fan in a hovercraft which provides the air cushion; **lift-gate** (*a*) = sense 2 above; (*b*) a gate opening on to a lift in a building etc.; (*c*) *US* in a motor vehicle, a hinged back panel that opens upwards, a hatchback; **lift-slab** *attrib. adjective* designating a labour-saving system of building whereby precast components are raised by jacks to the position desired; **lift truck** = *fork-lift truck* s.v. FORK *noun*; **lift valve** a valve which opens by the valve head moving (vertically) out of its (horizontal) seat; **lift-web** a strip of webbing joining the harness and the rigging lines of a parachute; **lift wire** *AERONAUTICS* a wire on a biplane or light monoplane that extends from the wing to the fuselage and is designed to transmit part of the lift to the latter during flight.

■ **liftless** *adjective* not provided with a lift **E20.**

lift /lɪft/ *verb.* ME.

[ORIGIN Old Norse *lypta* = Middle High German, German *lüften*, from Germanic base of LIFT *noun*[1].]

1 *verb trans.* Raise into the air from the ground, or to a higher position, hoist (also foll. by *up*, *aloft*, etc.); pick up and bring to a lower position (usu. foll. by *down*); pick up and bring *out* etc. **ME.** ▸†**b** Bear, support. *rare.* Only in **L16.** ▸**c** Take up and hold or carry, pick up; *GOLF* pick up (a ball) during play. See also sense 6 below. **L16.** ▸**d** Help (sick or weak cattle) to stand up. Earlier as LIFTING *noun* 2. **L19.** ▸**e** Perform cosmetic surgery on (esp. the face or breasts) to reduce sagging; perform a facelift on. **E20.** ▸**f** *SPORT.* Win, carry off, (a prize, trophy, etc.). **E20.** ▸**g** *PRINTING.* Raise (lines of type), esp. in moving types from a composing stick to a galley, or in preparation for the distribution of used type. **M20.**

E. O'NEILL Lifting Mary to the floor. R. G. COLLINGWOOD I felt as if a veil had been lifted and my destiny revealed. A. PATON He.. lifts her from the floor to the chair. G. ORWELL He lay flat on his belly and tried to lift his weight by his hands. *Observer* This has to be lifted up and down when inserting paper. N. LUARD The Belgian unlocked the trunk, stood by the porter while he lifted out two suitcases. **c** D. STOREY Pulling at his mother's skirt and asking to be lifted. **f** *Belfast Telegraph* The third Second Division side in five years to lift the FA cup.

2 *verb trans. fig.* Elevate to a higher plane of thought or feeling; stimulate morally or spiritually, uplift. Freq. foll. by *up*. **ME.** ▸**b** Raise in dignity, rank, or estimation; exalt. Also foll. by *up*. Now *rare*. **ME.** ▸**c** Cheer (*up*), encourage. Also (*arch.*), make arrogant, puff *up* (with pride). **LME.** ▸**d** Raise in price, value, or amount. **E20.**

STEELE It lifts an heavy empty Sentence, when there is added to it a lascivious Gesture of Body. J. CARLYLE With so rich a husband she would be able to lift them out of all their difficulties. P. H. KOCHER He.. is lifted up to live above himself. **b** H. L. MENCKEN Those of the academic moiety seldom lift themselves above the level of mere pedagogues. **c** AV *2 Chron.* 26:16 But when he was strong, his heart was lifted vp to his destruction. G. BOYCOTT You take brilliant catches standing back, you lift and inspire the team. **d** *Times* Better than expected trading news from Reed International lifted the price 16p to 254p.

3 *verb intrans.* Rise; *esp.* (of a ship etc.) rise when riding on the waves. Also, admit of being raised (*up*). **LME.** ▸**b** Be or become visible above or against a surrounding landscape. **L16.** ▸**c** Of a floor etc.: swell or warp upwards; bulge. **L18.** ▸**d** *NAUTICAL.* Of a sail: ruffle slightly when caught by the wind on the leech. **E19.** ▸**e** Of clouds, fog, etc.: disperse, rise. Also (*N. Amer.*), of rain etc.: cease temporarily. **M19.** ▸**f** *PRINTING.* Of a forme of type: stay in one piece when raised from the surface on which it has been assembled. **M19.** ▸**g** Of an aircraft etc.: rise off or *off* the ground. **L19.** ▸**h** Rise in tone or volume of sound. **E20.**

R. KIPLING The big liner rolled and lifted. *Daily Express* The window-seat top lifts up. *Times* Hopes of future Government contracts caused the shares to lift 3p to 63p. **b** H. BELLOC The chestnuts made a dark belt from which the tall graces of the birches lifted. **d** E. PEACOCK The thick fog had lifted. J. C. OATES One of those.. storms that can last for a week without lifting. **g** H. G. WELLS The aëropile.. lifted clean and rose. *Scientific American* On July 21, 1969, *Eagle* lifted off from the moon. **h** J. GALSWORTHY The sounds of conversation lifting round him.

4 *verb trans.* Take up or collect (rents or moneys) as due; levy (contributions, fines, etc.); draw (wages, profits, etc.). Now *dial.* **LME.**

†**5** *verb trans.* Carve (a roasted swan). **LME–E19.**

6 *verb trans.* Pick up (a portable object) with dishonest intentions; steal (esp. cattle); steal (something) from a shop etc. *slang.* **E16.** ▸**b** Plagiarize (a passage, title, etc.). *colloq.* **E20.**

R. KIPLING He has lifted the Colonel's mare that is the Colonel's pride. T. KENEALLY She got six months for lifting a.. figurine from a store. E. REVELEY He had had to resort to.. lifting a wallet like a common pick-pocket. **b** CLIVE JAMES The lines about Leonidas are lifted straight from the *Imitations* version of Rauben's 'Die Tauben'.

†**7** *verb intrans.* Foll. by *at*: pull at (something) in an attempt at raising (*lit. & fig.*); rise in opposition to. **M16–E18.**

J. LOCKE Like the Body strain'd by lifting at a Weight too heavy.

8 *verb trans.* Take up and remove, take away; drive (cattle) away or to market; strike (a tent etc.); *Scot.* remove (a corpse) for burial or cremation; *fig.* discontinue, remove, (restrictions, an embargo, etc.). **M16.** ▸**b** *verb trans. HUNTING.* Move (hounds) from a lost scent in order to find the scent again elsewhere. Also, disperse (scent). **L18.** ▸**c** *verb trans.* Get rid of, pay off (a mortgage). *US.* **M19.** ▸**d** *verb trans.* Give a lift to in a carriage, motor vehicle, etc. **L19.** ▸**e** *verb trans. & intrans. ARTILLERY.* Increase (the range of fire) from that being used at a given point in an attack. **E20.** ▸**f** *verb trans.* Of a sheepdog: establish control over a flock of sheep. **E20.** ▸**g** *verb trans.* Arrest, take into custody. **E20.** ▸**h** *verb trans.* Evacuate (soldiers) from a beach etc.; airlift. **M20.** ▸**i** *verb trans.* Take an impression of (fingerprints) for identification purposes. *US.* **M20.**

I. L. IDRIESS His gang lifted their cattle... and got safely across to the Paroo. *Nature* If the embargo is.. lifted, it will take.. weeks for the oil to reach United States ports. **b** J. MASEFIELD The hounds were lifted and on his line. **d** M. SHARP Up she drove, lifted by Mr. Simnel the chemist, Taunton-bound. **e** A. FARRAR-HOCKLEY Some aghast to see the supporting artillery fire already lifting ahead of them. **g** *Times* If you have a father who is lifted, he has sons.. who will take his place. **h** J. MASEFIELD The first men lifted were not always soldiers. *Daily Telegraph* Medical supplies.. were being lifted in by helicopter.

9 *verb intrans.* Cut a pack of cards to determine the dealer. Now *rare* or *obsolete*. **L16.**

10 *verb trans.* Bear or carry in an elevated position; hold high. **L17.**

MILTON There the Capitol thou seest Above the rest lifting his stately head.

11 *verb trans.* Take up out of the ground (*Scot.* in *gen.* sense); *HORTICULTURE* dig up (potatoes, bulbs, etc.). **M19.**

Times Nurseries.. cannot lift and pack all their orders in a month.

12 *verb trans.* Hit (a ball) into the air; (of a batsman) hit a ball bowled by (a bowler) into the air. **L19.**

Daily Telegraph W. G. lifted Spofforth round to the leg boundary.

– PHRASES: ***lift a finger***: see FINGER *noun*. **lift one's elbow** = ***crook one's elbow*** s.v. CROOK *verb* 1. ***lift one's eyes***: see ***lift up one's eyes*** below. **lift one's game** improve one's game, begin to play better. **lift one's hand** *spec.* raise one's hand in taking an oath, or in hostility *against* (a person); *slang* to do a stroke of work (usu. in neg. contexts). ***lift one's hands***: see ***lift up one's hands*** below. ***lift the leg***: see LEG *noun*. ***lift the roof***: see ROOF *noun*. **lift up one's eyes**, **lift one's eyes** give an upward direction to the eyes, look up (*lit. & fig.*). **lift up one's hands**, **lift one's hands**: esp. in prayer, thanksgiving, etc. **lift up one's head** (*a*) raise one's head; (*b*) *fig.* recover vigour after prostration. **lift up one's voice** (*a*) sing, speak; (*b*) cry out. †**lift up the head of** bring out from prison; restore to liberty, dignity, etc. **lift up the heart of** raise the thoughts or desires of; encourage. ***lift up the horn***: see HORN *noun*. ***lift up the leg***: see LEG *noun*.

– COMB.: **liftback** a type of hatchback car; **lift-on** *adjective* made to lift on; ***lift-on, lift-off***, (designating) a method of hoisting containers from one vessel or vehicle to another; **lift-out** *adjective* made to lift out; **lift-up** *adjective* made to lift up.

■ **liftable** *adjective* (earlier in UNLIFTABLE) **M19.**

lifter /ˈlɪftə/ *noun.* M16.

[ORIGIN from LIFT *verb* + -ER[1].]

1 A person who lifts something (*lit. & fig.*). **M16.** ▸**b** A person who takes something up dishonestly; a thief. **L16.**
b cattle lifter, ***shoplifter***, etc.

2 A thing, esp. part of a contrivance or appliance, which lifts or is used for lifting. **L16.** ▸**b** *MINING.* A beam to which the head of a stamp is fastened in a stamp mill. **L17.** ▸**c** *CRICKET.* A ball, usu. one from a fast bowler, that rises sharply after striking the pitch. **M20.**

lifting /ˈlɪftɪŋ/ *noun.* ME.

[ORIGIN from LIFT *verb* + -ING[1].]

1 The action of LIFT *verb*; an instance of this (*lit. & fig.*). **ME.**
shoplifting.

2 The raising of sick or weak cattle to enable them to stand. **E19.**

3 In competitive walking, the raising of the rear heel before the front foot touches the ground. **M19.**

4 *COMMERCE.* In *pl.* The amount of a product, esp. mineral oil, transported through or out of a particular place, or by a particular means. **L20.**

– COMB.: **lifting beam** a beam, fitted to a crane hook, to which a load may be attached in two or more places; **lifting plate** an iron plate fastened on to the face of a pattern and provided with a hole into which a lifting screw can be inserted; **lifting screw** *noun*[1] a hook with a threaded shank which can be screwed into an object to facilitate its lifting; (see also ***lifting screw*** s.v. LIFTING *ppl adjective*); **lifting tape** *US* a kind of tape used for taking fingerprints.

lifting /ˈlɪftɪŋ/ *ppl adjective.* ME.

[ORIGIN from LIFT *verb* + -ING[2].]

That lifts; *AERONAUTICS* providing lift.

lifting body a (wingless) spacecraft with a shape designed to produce lift, so that aerodynamic control of its flight is possible within the atmosphere. **lifting bridge** a bridge of which either a part or the whole may be raised at one end to allow boats to pass. **lifting screw** *noun*[2] a rotor operating in a horizontal plane so as to provide lift for an aircraft; (see also ***lifting screw*** S.V. LIFTING *noun*).

lift-off /ˈlɪftɒf/ *adjective & noun.* E20.

[ORIGIN from LIFT *verb* + OFF *adverb*.]

▸ **A** *adjective.* Removable by lifting. **E20.**

Country Life The lift off tray is divided into nine crenellated compartments.

lift-on, lift-off: see ***lift-on*** s.v. LIFT *verb*.

▸ **B** *noun.* **1** A parachutist's method of leaving an aircraft by opening the parachute while standing on a wing, so as to be carried away by the air current. **M20.**

2 The vertical take-off of a rocket, helicopter, etc.; the moment at which an aircraft begins to leave the ground; *fig.* initiation or commencement of activity; getting off the ground (of a project or scheme). **M20.**

J. A. MORRIS The launch vehicle exploded soon after lift-off. *Daily Telegraph* Shell has lift-off with its space promotion.

Lifu /ˈliːfuː/ *noun & adjective.* M19.

[ORIGIN *Lifu* Island (see below).]

(Of) a Melanesian language spoken on Lifu Island, the largest of the Loyalty Islands in the SW Pacific.

■ **Lifuan** *noun & adjective* (a native or inhabitant) of Lifu Island **L19.**

lig /lɪɡ/ *verb intrans.* Infl. -gg-. OE.

[ORIGIN Var. of LIE *verb*[1].]

1 See LIE *verb*[1]. **OE.**

2 Idle or lie about. Also, take advantage of free parties or other benefits offered by companies for publicity purposes. *slang.* **M20.**

ligament /ˈlɪɡəm(ə)nt/ *noun.* LME.

[ORIGIN Latin *ligamentum*, from *ligare* bind, tie: see -MENT.]

1 A binding, a band, a tie; *SURGERY* a bandage, a ligature. Long only *fig.* (*arch.*), a bond of union. **LME.**

2 *ANATOMY.* A short band of tough flexible fibrous tissue which binds together bones or cartilages; any membranous fold which supports an organ and keeps it in position. **LME.** ▸**b** *ZOOLOGY.* Any similar part in lower organisms; *spec.* the elastic substance which holds together the valves of a bivalve shell. **L18.**

cruciate ligament: see CRUCIATE *adjective*. ***nuchal ligament***: see NUCHAL *adjective*. ***THYRO-ARYTENOID ligaments***.

■ **liga'mental** *adjective* = LIGAMENTOUS **L16.** **liga'mentary** *adjective* = LIGAMENTOUS **M18.** **liga'mentous** *adjective* of, pertaining to, of the nature of, or characteristic of a ligament or ligaments; composed of fibrous connective tissue: **L17.**

ligan *noun* var. of LAGAN.

ligand /ˈlɪɡ(ə)nd/ *noun.* M20.

[ORIGIN from Latin *ligandus* gerundive of *ligare* bind: see -AND.]

CHEMISTRY. An ion, atom, etc. (capable of) forming a coordination complex with a central (usu. a metal) atom; a molecule that selectively binds to another.

– COMB.: **ligand field** the electrostatic field produced by the ligands in the vicinity of the central atom.

■ **ligancy** *noun* = ***COORDINATION number*** (a) **M20.** **liganded** *adjective* bound to a ligand or ligands **M20.**

ligase /ˈlɪɡeɪz/ *noun.* M20.

[ORIGIN from Latin *ligare* bind + -ASE.]

BIOCHEMISTRY. An enzyme which catalyses the linking together of two molecules, esp. with a simultaneous conversion of ATP to ADP. Cf. SYNTHASE.

ligate /lɪˈɡeɪt/ *verb trans.* L16.

[ORIGIN Latin *ligat-* pa. ppl stem of *ligare* tie, bind: see -ATE[3].]

Bind with a ligature or bandage; *esp.* in *SURGERY*, tie up (an artery etc.) to stop bleeding.

ligation /lɪˈɡeɪʃ(ə)n/ *noun.* LME.

[ORIGIN Late Latin *ligatio(n-)*, formed as LIGATE: see -ATION.]

1 The action or process of binding; the condition of being bound. Long *obsolete* exc. as in *gen.* sense. **LME.**

2 The action or an act of binding with a ligature; *esp.* in *SURGERY*, the operation of ligating a bleeding artery etc. **LME.**

L

tubal ligation: see TUBAL 2.
3 A thing used in binding; a bandage, a tie. *arch.* **L16.**

ligature /ˈlɪɡətʃə/ *noun & verb.* **LME.**
[**ORIGIN** Late Latin *ligatura*, formed as LIGATE: see -URE.]
▸ **A** *noun.* **1** A thing used in binding or tying; a band, a tie; *esp.* (**a**) SURGERY a thread or cord used to tie up a bleeding artery etc.; (**b**) an adjustable band securing the reed to the mouthpiece in instruments of the clarinet family. **LME.** ▸**b** *fig.* A bond of union. **E17.** ▸†**c** Binding quality; something having this quality. **L17–E18.**
2 = LIGAMENT 2. Now *rare*. **LME.**
3 The action or an act of binding or tying; the result or place of such an action. **M16.**
4 MUSIC. A note form representing two or more notes to be sung to one syllable; a tie, a slur. **L16.**
5 A character or type formed by two or more letters joined together; a monogram. Also, a stroke connecting two letters. **L17.**
▸ **B** *verb trans.* = LIGATE. **E18.**

ligeance /ˈliːdʒ(ə)ns/ *noun.* **LME.**
[**ORIGIN** Old French (also *legiance*) (in medieval Latin *ligantia*, *-entia*, *leg-*), from *lige* LIEGE: see -ANCE.]
1 The allegiance of a liegeman or subject. *arch.* **LME.**
2 The jurisdiction of a monarch over his or her subjects or lieges; the territories subject to a monarch. Now *rare* or *obsolete*. **LME.**

liger /ˈlʌɪɡə/ *noun.* **M20.**
[**ORIGIN** Blend of LION and TIGER *noun*.]
An animal born of a mating between a lion and a tigress. Cf. TIGON.

ligger /ˈlɪɡə/ *noun. dial.* **LME.**
[**ORIGIN** from LIG + -ER[1].]
1 A coverlet; a mattress. **LME.**
2 **a** A plank; a beam; *spec.* = LEDGER *noun* 4a. **LME.** ▸**b** A branch laid on the top of a plashed hedge. **E19.** ▸**c** = LEDGER *noun* 4b. **M20.**
3 ANGLING. A line with a float and bait which is left in the water, as used in pike-fishing. **E19.**
4 A person who takes advantage of free parties etc. offered by companies for publicity purposes. *slang.* **L20.**

light /lʌɪt/ *noun.*
[**ORIGIN** Old English *lēoht*, (Anglian) *līht* = Old Frisian *liacht*, Old Saxon, Old High German *lioht* (Dutch, German *Licht*), from West Germanic, ult. from Indo-European base repr. also by Greek *leukos* white, Latin *lux* light. See also LITE *noun*[2].]
1 The natural agent which emanates from the sun, an intensely heated object, etc., and stimulates sight (now recognized as electromagnetic radiation: see sense e below); the medium or condition of space in which this is present and in which vision is possible (opp. ***darkness***); *spec.* the illumination proceeding from the sun in daytime; daylight, daytime. **OE.** ▸**b** An individual appearance of brightness as an object of perception. **OE.** ▸**c** The quantity or quality of illumination in a place; a person's fair or usual share of this. **M16.** ▸**d** Vivacity, enthusiasm, or inspiration in a person's face, esp. in the eyes. **L16.** ▸**e** PHYSICS etc. Electromagnetic radiation having a wavelength between about 400 and 750 nm, which is visible to the human eye; invisible electromagnetic radiation outside this range, *esp.* ultraviolet radiation. **E18.** ▸**f** The sensation produced (as) by the impinging of visible radiation on the retina. **E19.**

A. RANSOME Coming out . . into the light after being . . in the darkness inside the hill. J. HERSEY After dark, they worked by the light of the city's fires. J. STEINBECK A match flared, and in its momentary light Kino saw . . the men were sleeping. FRANK THOMPSON Starting at early light from the old fort. H. E. BATES We skated . . on into the evening by the light of fires. J. FOWLES She had only a candle's light to see by. **b** DAY LEWIS The whole picture . . is bathed in a brooding, sub-aqueous light. J. BERGER The lamps cast bright distinct circles of light. **c** F. WYNDHAM In some lights his markings appeared to be charcoal on cream. **d** J. B. PRIESTLEY Then the light died out of her face. S. BRETT The old light of paranoia gleamed in Alex's eye. **e** P. DAVIES Light takes an enormous length of time to travel between galaxies.

2 The state of being visible or exposed. **OE.**

E. A. FREEMAN He breaks forth into full light in the course of the next year.

3 Power of vision, eyesight (now *poet.*); in *pl.* (now *slang*), the eyes. **OE.**

R. GRAVES The light of both his eyes was quenched . . with red-hot needles. R. B. PARKER How come somebody punched your lights out over her?

4 A source of illumination, as the sun or esp. a lighted candle, a (now usu. electric) lamp, a beacon, etc.; a lighthouse; in *pl.*, illuminations. Formerly also *collect.*, the candles etc. used to light a place. **OE.** ▸**b** *spec.* A traffic light. Usu. in *pl.* **E20.**

C. ISHERWOOD One by one, the lights go out and there is total blackness. M. SPARK He saw below . . the lights of a car. E. ARDIZZONE The light of the lighthouse was out. D. FRANCIS The lights shone bright in the early winter evening. *attrib.*: L. DUNCAN It lit up her face as though she had pressed a light switch. **b** R. MACAULAY As the lights changed I saw a bus dashing up. S. BRILL They crashed into a car that was stopped at a light.

courtesy light, ***klieg light***, ***obstruction light***, ***reversing light***, ***traffic-light***, etc.

5 **a** Spiritual or religious illumination; in the Christian Church, God as the source of this; *spec.* in the Society of Friends, the inward revelation of Christ in the soul. **OE.** ▸**b** Mental illumination; elucidation, enlightenment, knowledge. Freq. in ***cast light on***, ***shed light on***, ***throw light on***, help explain. **OE.** ▸**c** In *pl.* Pieces of information, facts which explain a subject; the opinions, information, and capacities forming a person's intellect or mental ability. Freq. in ***according to one's lights***. **E16.** ▸**d** In a puzzle, the answer to a clue; *spec.* (**a**) a line in an acrostic puzzle; (**b**) the item filling the spaces in a crossword puzzle as the answer to a clue. **M19.**

a J. WESLEY I found such a light . . as I never remember to have had before. **b** A. BRINK The . . search for new light on the deaths of Gordon and Jonathan. *Music* The . . book . . throwing light on many areas of the profession hitherto surrounded in mystery.

6 A window or opening in a wall for the admission of light; *spec.* (**a**) any of the perpendicular divisions of a mullioned window; (**b**) a subdivision of a window with tracery. **LME.** ▸**b** Any of the (usu. openable) panes of glass forming the roof or side of a greenhouse or the top of a frame. **M18.**

M. GIROUARD Its row of first-floor oriel windows with arched central lights. *Do-It-Yourself* Fit locks on all ground floor lights. **b** *Gardener* Once the seedlings have germinated, remove the frame lights.

7 An eminent person; a person notable for virtue, intellect, etc. **LME.**

J. O'HARA In the 'prelims' one sees the lesser known lights of the boxing fraternity.

8 (Any of) the bright parts of a picture etc. suggesting illumination; comparative lightness as represented pictorially; *transf.* & *fig.* quieter or less dramatic passages in music or literature, providing artistic contrast (freq. in ***light and shade***: cf. SHADE *noun* 4). **E17.** ▸**b** A lighter glint in the hair, a highlight. **M20.**

W. M. CRAIG A light is made brighter by being opposed to a dark. TENNYSON The lights and shadows fly!

9 The aspect in which a thing is regarded or judged. **L17.**

T. S. ELIOT I am glad that you have come to see it in that light. J. HELLER We can't afford a situation that might put us in a bad light. H. MACMILLAN He tried to see matters in an objective light.

10 A flame or spark serving to ignite a combustible substance; a device producing this, as a taper, match, etc. **L17.**

S. THEMERSON I struck a match and gave him a light for his cigarette.

11 LAW. The light falling on the windows of a house, the obstruction of which by a neighbour is illegal. **M18.**
12 MECHANICS. An aperture, a clear space. **L18.**

– PHRASES: ***ancient lights***: see ANCIENT *adjective* 4. **appear in the light of** seem to be. ***black light***: see BLACK *adjective*. **bring to light** reveal. ***cast light on***: see sense 5b above. ***cold light***: see COLD *adjective*. **come to light** (**a**) be revealed; (**b**) *Austral.* & *NZ colloq.* produce, come up, *with*. ***Dutch light***: see DUTCH *adjective*. **festival of lights** (**a**) = HANUKKAH; (**b**) = DIWALI. ***FIRST light***. ***green light***: see GREEN *adjective*. ***have one's name in lights***: see NAME *noun*. ***hide one's light under a bushel***: see BUSHEL *noun*. ***inner light***: see INNER *adjective*. **in the light of** having regard to; drawing information from. ***leading light***: see LEADING *adjective*. ***lesser light***: see LESSER *adjective*. ***light at the end of the tunnel***: see TUNNEL *noun*. **light of day** (**a**) daylight, sunlight; (**b**) general notice; public attention. **light of one's life** (chiefly *joc.*) a much-loved person. **lights out** (**a**) bedtime in a school etc.; (**b**) MILITARY the last bugle call of the day. ***NEON light***. ***New Light***: see NEW *adjective*. ***NORTH light***. ***Northern Lights***: see NORTHERN *adjective*. ***Old Light***: see OLD *adjective*. **out like a light** deeply asleep or unconscious. ***polar light***: see POLAR *adjective*. **put out a person's light**, **quench a person's light** kill a person. ***raking light***: see RAKE *verb*[2]. ***red light***: see RED *adjective*. ***rising of the lights***: see RISING *noun*. **see the light** (**a**) come into the world, be brought out or published; (**b**) reach a full understanding or realization, esp. of Christianity. ***shed light on***: see sense 5b above. ***SHINING light***. ***sound and light***: see SOUND *noun*[2]. ***Southern Lights***: see SOUTHERN *adjective*. **stand in a person's light** stand so as to cut out (some of) the light a person is seeing by; *fig.* prejudice a person's interests or chances. ***strike a light!***: see STRIKE *verb*. ***strobe light***: see STROBE *adjective*. ***sweetness and light***: see SWEETNESS 1. ***throw light on***: see sense 5b above. ***top light***: see TOP *adjective*. ***Vauxhall light***: see VAUXHALL *adjective* 1. ***visible light***: see VISIBLE *adjective*. ***Wood's light***: see WOOD *noun*[3] 2. ***yellow light***: see YELLOW *adjective*.

– COMB.: **light barrier** [after *sound barrier*] the speed of light as the limiting speed attainable by any object; **lightboat** = *lightship* below; **light box** a box with a side of translucent glass and containing an electric light, so as to provide an evenly lighted flat surface; **light bulb** a glass bulb containing gas and a metal filament, giving light when an electric current is passed through; **light buoy**: equipped with a warning light which flashes intermittently; **light cone** PHYSICS a surface in space-time, represented as a cone in three dimensions, comprising all the points from which a light signal would reach a given point (at the apex) simultaneously, and which therefore appear simultaneous to an observer at the apex; **light cord** a cord which operates an electric light when pulled; **light curve** ASTRONOMY a graph showing the variation in the light received over a period of time from a variable star or other celestial object; **light day** ASTRONOMY the distance travelled by light in a day; **light-demander** a tree needing full light; **light-demanding** *adjective* (of a tree) needing full light; **light due** a toll on ships for the maintenance of lighthouses and lightships; **lightfast** *adjective* resistant to discoloration by light; **lightfastness** the quality of being lightfast; **light fixture** a flex, socket, etc., for use with a light bulb; **light-grasp** ASTRONOMY light-gathering power (of a telescope); **light guide** a transparent cylinder or strip along which light can travel with little loss by means of total internal reflection; an optical fibre; **light gun** = ***light pen*** below; **light-man** (**a**) a person in charge of the light in a lighthouse or lightship; (**b**) a linkman; **light meter** an instrument for measuring the intensity of light, esp. to show the correct photographic exposure; ***light microscope***: see MICROSCOPE *noun* 1; **light minute** ASTRONOMY the distance travelled by light in one minute; **light-money** money paid in light dues; **Lightmonger** a member of a City of London Livery Company representing the lighting industry (usu. in *pl.*); **light organ** the structure in a luminescent animal that emits light; **light pen** a hand-held penlike photosensitive device that may be used to transmit information to a data-processing system by placing or moving the tip on a surface, esp. the screen of a terminal etc.; **lightproof** *adjective* capable of resisting the harmful effects of (esp. intense) light; **light quantum** PHYSICS = PHOTON 2; **light-scattering** scattering of light, *spec.* of monochromatic light by a solution as a method of investigating the molecular weight and conformation of dissolved polymers; **light second** ASTRONOMY the distance travelled by light in one second; **lightship** a moored or anchored ship with a warning beacon light; **light show** a display of changing coloured lights for entertainment; **light station** a group of buildings comprising a lighthouse and associated housing for personnel, supplies, and equipment; **light table** a table top or other flat surface incorporating a light box; **light-tight** *adjective* impervious to light; **light-time** ASTRONOMY the time taken by light to travel from a distant source to the observer; **light trap** (**a**) PHOTOGRAPHY a device for excluding light from a room without preventing access into it; (**b**) a trap for night-flying insects; **light-trapped** *adjective* provided with a light trap; **light value** PHOTOGRAPHY a number representing on an arbitrary scale the intensity of light from a particular direction; **light valve** an electrical device which regulates the amount of light passing through it, used esp. in cinematography; **light well** a shaft designed to admit light from above into inner rooms or a staircase of a building; **light year** (**a**) ASTRONOMY the distance light travels in a year, approximately 9.46×10^{12} km (5.88×10^{12} miles); (**b**) *sing.* & (usu.) in *pl.*, a long distance, a great amount.

light /lʌɪt/ *adjective*[1].
[**ORIGIN** Old English *lēocht*, *līht* = Old Frisian *li(u)cht*, Old Saxon *-liht* (Dutch *licht*), Old High German *līht(i)* (German *leicht*), Old Norse *léttr*, Gothic *leihts*, from Germanic, from Indo-European base repr. also by LUNG. See also LITE *adjective*[2].]
▸ **I** Not physically weighty.
1 Of little weight; of relatively low in weight; of little weight due to lack of quality; (esp. of traffic) not abundant, sparse. **OE.** ▸**b** Of low relative density; *spec.* (of bread, pastry, etc.) properly risen, not dense. **ME.** ▸**c** Deficient in weight; below the standard or legal weight. **L15.**

R. BRADBURY Their luggage . . was light enough to be entirely empty. R. BRAUTIGAN A girl in a light summer dress. B. GILROY She was so light, he could pick her up . . like a baby. *Los Angeles Times* Light traffic . . at the time of the accident was . . the reason more vehicles were not involved.

2 (Of a vehicle, vessel, or aeroplane) lightly built; adapted for light loads and fast movement; bearing a small or comparatively small load; unladen, without cargo; (of a locomotive) with no train attached. **ME.** ▸†**b** Delivered (*of* a child). *rare* exc. in compar. Chiefly *Scot.* **ME–E20.**

THACKERAY My Lord Mohun sent to London for a light chaise he had. *Aviation News* Among the cluster of American light types appeared a couple of sailplanes.

3 Chiefly MILITARY. Lightly armed or equipped. **LME.**
▸ **II** Expressing the action or appearance of something physically light.
4 Having little momentum or force; acting or moving gently or without heavy pressure or violence. **OE.**

J. RUSKIN A painter's light execution of a background. H. E. BATES Her feet were light, no one heard. I. MURDOCH The garden was being caressed . . by the light rain. B. PYM She's got a light hand with pastry.

5 (Of food or drink) small in amount, easy to digest, not rich; (of wine, beer, etc.) containing little alcohol. Also, containing relatively few calories (cf. LITE *adjective*[2]). **OE.**

LYTTON The . . family were assembled at the last and lightest meal of the day. P. V. PRICE These wines are light in terms of body character. *Super Marketing* The new Goodalls Dressings are . . 'lighter', containing only 190 calories.

6 (Of soil) friable, porous, workable; (of a cloud) fleecy, vaporous. **ME.**
7 **a** Of a building: having the appearance of lightness; graceful, delicate, elegant. **M18.** ▸**b** PRINTING. Of type: having letters made up of thin strokes, not bold. **L19.**
8 (Of a syllable) unstressed, of little sonorousness; (of rhythm) consisting largely of unstressed syllables. **L19.**
▸ **III** Of little importance; not serious.
9 Of little importance; slight, trivial. *spec.* (of a sin) venial. **OE.** ▸**b** Of small value; cheap; (of a price) low. Now only *spec.* (**a**) COMMERCE (of a currency, investment, profit, etc.) low in value or price; (**b**) BRIDGE low, short of points for a traditional bid. **ME.**

LD MACAULAY Against the lighter vices the ruling faction waged war. I. MURDOCH To provide staff of any description in response to a department's lightest wish. *Financial Times* There are still a few operators whose lightest word can move individual stocks.

10 Characterized by levity, frivolous, unthinking. Foll. by †*of*. ME. ▸**b** Of a woman or a woman's behaviour: immoral, promiscuous. LME.

R. L. STEVENSON I made some light rejoinder. D. STOREY She was like a girl, or a woman just grown, light, uncaring. L. BLUE We touched many deep things in a light way.

▸ **IV** Having the quick action resulting from lightness.
11 Moving readily; agile, nimble, quick. *arch.* OE.
12 *fig.* That moves or is moved easily; fickle, shifty; facile, ready (esp. of belief). Foll. by *of*, *to do*. Now *rare*. ME.
▸ **V** That does not weigh heavily on or oppress the senses or feelings.
13 Easy to bear or endure. OE.
14 Of work, a task, etc.: easy to perform or accomplish; requiring little exertion. Also, slight in amount and so undemanding. OE.

Chicago Tribune This position is based in . . Chicago and requires light travel. V. BRITTAIN The nursing was now very light; most of our patients were convalescent.

15 Of sleep, a trance, or a person asleep: easily disturbed. OE.

DICKENS I am a light sleeper; and it's better to be up than lying awake. E. WAUGH I had roused Julia from the light trance in which she sat.

16 Of literature, an artistic production, etc.: requiring little mental effort, not profound or serious; amusing, entertaining. ME.

L. URIS A small orchestra played some light dinner music. A. BROOKNER I am not going to confide . . . Light conversation is all that is called for.

▸ **VI 17** Free from the weight of care or sorrow; cheerful, merry. ME.

C. POTOK I felt light and happy and completely at ease.

18 Dizzy, giddy, delirious; = LIGHT-HEADED 1. Now chiefly *dial.* LME.

C. ACHEBE He felt somewhat light in the head.

– PHRASES: **light o' love** a fickle woman; a prostitute. **light on** *colloq.* deficient in, short of. **make light of** treat as unimportant. **make light work of** do quickly and easily. ***the light** FANTASTIC **toe***. ***trip the light** FANTASTIC*.

– SPECIAL COLLOCATIONS & COMB.: **light-armed** *adjective* with light weapons or armour. ***light-bob***: see BOB *noun*[5]. **light bread** *US* (*a*) white bread; (*b*) any yeast-raised bread. **lighter-than-air** *adjective* (of an aircraft) weighing less than the air it displaces. **light-fingered** *adjective* given to stealing. ***light flyweight***: see FLY *noun*[1]. **lightfoot** *adjective & noun* (*a*) *adjective* (*poet.*) light-footed; (*b*) *noun* (a name for) a hare or a deer. **light-footed** *adjective* nimble. **light-footedly** *adverb* nimbly. **light hand** *fig.* a capacity for or instance of tactful management. **light-handed** *adjective* having a light, delicate, or deft touch. **light-handedness** the quality of being light-handed. ***light heavyweight***: see HEAVYWEIGHT. **light-heeled** *adjective* nimble. **light horse** (a soldier of) the light-armed cavalry. **light horseman** a soldier of the light horse. **light infantry**: with light weapons. **light industry** the manufacture of small or light articles. **light-limbed** *adjective* nimble. ***light** MIDDLEWEIGHT*. **light-minded** *adjective* frivolous. **light-mindedness** the quality of being light-minded. **light oil** any of various fractions of relatively low relative density obtained by the distillation of coal tar, wood tar, petroleum, etc. **light-skirts** *arch.* a prostitute or promiscuous woman. **light touch** *fig.* a capacity for or instance of delicate or tactful treatment. **light water** (*a*) water containing the normal proportion (or less) of deuterium oxide (about 0.02 per cent); ***light water reactor***, a nuclear reactor in which the moderator is light water; (*b*) a foam formed by water and a fluorocarbon surfactant which floats on flammable liquids lighter than water and is used in firefighting. ***light** WELTERWEIGHT*.

light /lʌɪt/ *adjective*[2].
[ORIGIN Old English *lēoht*, *līht* = Old Frisian *liācht*, Old Saxon, Old High German *lioht* (Dutch, German *licht*), ult. formed as LIGHT *noun*.]
1 †**a** Bright, shining, luminous; *esp.* (of a fire) burning brightly, blazing. OE–M18. ▸**b** Of a place, the time of day, etc.: having a considerable or sufficient amount of light, not dark. Formerly also, brightly illuminated. OE.

a J. JORTIN He piled these ancient books together and set them all on a light fire. **b** R. HUGHES If only it had been light they could have been happy enough exploring.

2 Pale, approaching white in colour. LME.

G. VIDAL Not a dark sullen blue but a light and casual blue. J. BARNES The dining hall . . where the light pine of my youth had been darkened by time.

light knotgrass: see KNOTGRASS 3. **light red** *spec.* (of) a pale red or reddish-orange pigment produced from iron oxide; ***light red silver ore***: see SILVER *noun & adjective*. **Light Sussex** (a bird of) a white variety of domestic fowl.

light /lʌɪt/ *verb*[1]. Pa. t. & pple **lighted**, **lit** /lɪt/.
[ORIGIN Old English *līhtan* = Old Frisian *lichta*, Middle Dutch *lichten*, Old High German *lihten*, Old Norse *létta*, from Germanic base also of LIGHT *adjective*[1].]
▸ **I** Lighten.
1 *verb trans.* Make light or lighter, lessen the weight of. Formerly also *fig.*, mitigate, assuage. Long *obsolete* exc. *Scot.* OE.
2 *verb trans.* Relieve *of* a material load or burden; unload (a ship); (latterly *dial.*) deliver *of* a child. Formerly also *fig.*, relieve *of* pain, sorrow, etc.; comfort, cheer. Now *rare* or *obsolete*. OE. ▸†**b** *verb intrans.* Become (more) cheerful. Only in ME.
†**3** *verb trans.* Lessen the effect or influence of; *Scot.*, slight, undervalue. E17–E19.
4 *verb trans. & intrans.* NAUTICAL. Move or lift (a sail etc.) *along* or *over*. M19.
▸ **II** Descend. Cf. ALIGHT *verb*.
5 *verb intrans.* Descend *from* a horse or vehicle; dismount. Also foll. by *off*, *down*. *arch.* OE.

BYRON Stern Hassan . . from his horse Disdains to light.

†**6** *verb intrans. & refl.* Of a person: descend, esp. from heaven or to hell. ME–M16.
7 *verb intrans.* Fall and settle or land on a surface. ME.

SIR W. SCOTT A feather just lighted on the ground can scarce be less concerned. W. VAN T. CLARK One of the coins lit on its edge and started rolling.

8 *verb intrans.* Of a blow, bullet, etc.: land, strike, (foll. by *on*, *upon*). Formerly also *gen.*, come *to* a person; arrive *at* a place; lodge or be situated *in* some position. Now *rare*. ME. ▸**b** Come or fall *into* a person's possession or company. Now *rare* or *obsolete*. M16. ▸**c** Turn out (*well*, *happily*, etc.); happen, occur. Now *dial.* E17.
9 Foll. by *on*, *upon*: (***a***) (of a thing) fall or descend upon as a piece of good or bad luck; (***b***) (of a person) happen to come across, chance upon. ME.

E. A. FREEMAN I have . . only once lighted on the use of the word in the singular. P. SCOTT Luck had lighted on our shoulders.

†**10** *verb intrans.* [Perh. in antithesis to sense 5, or merely transf. from sense 8.] Mount *on* horseback; climb *into* the saddle. LME–L16.
▸ **III 11** *verb intrans.* Foll. by *out*: depart, get out. *colloq.* M19.
12 *verb intrans.* Foll. by *in*, *into*: attack. *colloq.* L19.

light /lʌɪt/ *verb*[2]. Pa. t. & pple **lighted**, **lit** /lɪt/.
[ORIGIN Old English *līhtan* = Old Saxon *liuhtian*, Gothic *liuhtjan*, from Germanic base also of LIGHT *noun*.]
1 *verb intrans.* †**a** Be luminous; shine; be alight or burning. OE–L18. ▸**b** Of day: grow light, break. Long *obsolete* exc. *W. Indian*. OE.

a GOLDSMITH The taper which was lighting in the room was burnt out.

2 *verb trans.* Set burning (a candle, lamp, etc.); kindle (a fire); ignite. Also foll. by *up*, (rare) *off*. ME. ▸**b** *verb intrans.* Begin to burn, be lighted. LME. ▸**c** *verb intrans.* Foll. by *up*: set burning or begin to smoke a cigarette, pipe, etc. *colloq.* M19.

D. H. LAWRENCE When dark fell, the vendors lighted their torch-lamps. J. STEINBECK George walked to the fire pile and lighted the dry leaves. R. GRAVES Four tallow candles had just been lighted. P. MORTIMER I lit the cigarette. J. BERGER Every winter afternoon a fire is still lit. **b** G. GREENE The gas-main . . had been hit, and the gas wouldn't light properly. *transf.*: A. CARY The eve had just begun to light.

light a shuck: see SHUCK *noun*[2] 1.
3 *verb trans.* Provide with light or lighting; illuminate, esp. brightly or suddenly (freq. foll. by *up*). ME. ▸**b** *verb trans. & intrans. transf.* (Cause to) gleam or brighten with animation. Usu. foll. by *up*. M18.

J. STEINBECK One of them carried a lantern which lighted the ground. M. GIROUARD A Gothic-arched window was naturally adapted to light a vaulted building. J. BARNES The sun lit up that corner of the room. I. MURDOCH The scene was lit by oil lamps. F. SPALDING He . . saw life . . as if lit up on a stage. **b** DISRAELI A smile . . lighted up her face. W. BESANT I see the faces of all light up with satisfaction.

4 *verb trans.* Provide (a person) with light to see the way etc. ME.

S. O'FAOLÁIN She took a candle and lit me upstairs to bed. B. CHUTE It's turned dark. I'll light you home.

5 *verb trans.* Enlighten spiritually or intellectually. *arch.* ME.
■ **lightable** *adjective* able to be lighted L19.

light /lʌɪt/ *adverb*[1].
[ORIGIN Old English *lēohte* = Old Saxon, Old High German *līhto*, corresp. to the adjectival forms of LIGHT *adjective*[1].]
In a light manner; lightly as opp. to heavily; *esp.* with a light or the minimum load; *spec.* (of a locomotive running) with no rolling stock attached.

CECIL ROBERTS To travel in America one must travel light. *Railway Magazine* His engine ran light from Orpington to Kent House.

†**light** *adverb*[2]. OE–E18.
[ORIGIN Old English *lēohte* (= Old High German *liohto*), formed as LIGHT *adjective*[2].]
Brightly, clearly.

lightage /ˈlʌɪtɪdʒ/ *noun*. E17.
[ORIGIN from LIGHT *noun* + -AGE.]
†**1** A toll paid by a ship coming to a port where there is a lighthouse. E17–L18.
2 Provision of (artificial) light. M19.

lighted *verb*[1], *verb*[2] see LIGHT *verb*[1], *verb*[2].

lighten /ˈlʌɪt(ə)n/ *verb*[1]. LME.
[ORIGIN from LIGHT *adjective*[1] + -EN[5]; in sense 5 an extension of LIGHT *verb*[1].]
▸ **I 1** *verb trans.* Relieve of or *of* a load or burden; unload (a ship). *arch.* LME.

R. G. COLLINGWOOD This . . leaves the audience's mind . . not loaded with pity and fear but lightened of them.

2 *verb trans. fig.* Remove a burden from, relieve (the heart or mind). Formerly also, cheer, comfort. Now *rare*. LME.

Christian Aid News One day our hearts will be lightened.

3 *verb trans.* Make lighter or less heavy; lessen the pressure of; alleviate, mitigate. Also foll. by *up*. L15. ▸**b** HORSEMANSHIP. Make lighter or more free in movement. E18.

A. MILLER Start off with a couple of your good stories to lighten things up. M. L. KING His ready good humor lightened many tense moments. L. DEIGHTON Lightened by the loss of the great twelve cylinder Merlin the port wing tilted upwards. Q. CRISP Something—anything—that will . . lighten the terrible financial burden. J. DIDION You might try lightening up the foot on the gas pedal.

4 *verb intrans.* Become lighter or less heavy; ease up or *up*; (foll. by *up*) (of a person) become more cheerful (freq. in *imper.*). E18.

O. E. RÖLVAAG His mood lightened and brightened as he figured things out. J. C. OATES The rain lightened; and then suddenly increased. *Irish Press* He does lighten up occasionally in the company of his . . underling. D. LEAVITT Just lighten up . . . Don't be so worried all the time.

▸ †**II 5** Descend, light *upon*. LME–E18.
■ **lightener** *noun*[1] †(***a***) *N. English* = LIGHTER *noun*[1]; (***b***) a person who or thing which lightens or alleviates something: M16.

lighten /ˈlʌɪt(ə)n/ *verb*[2]. ME.
[ORIGIN from LIGHT *adjective*[2] + -EN[5].]
1 *verb trans.* Give light to; make bright or luminous; light up. ME. ▸†**b** In biblical translations and allusions: remove blindness or dimness from (the eyes). ME–M16.

F. O'BRIEN No beam of sun lightened the dull blackness of the clouds.

2 *verb trans.* Shed spiritual light on; enlighten spiritually. *arch.* ME.
†**3** *verb trans.* Kindle, ignite. ME–M17.
4 *verb intrans.* Shine, burn brightly; be or grow luminous or light; become paler. LME.

HUGH MILLER The low-browed clouds that lightened and darkened . . as the flames rose and fell. A. WILSON A great rocky plateau . . lightening to a lemon yellow. E. LINKLATER Presently the sky began to lighten.

5 *verb intrans.* Flash lightning, emit flashes of lightning. Usu. *impers.* in ***it lightens***, ***it is lightening***, etc. LME. ▸**b** *verb trans.* Cause to flash *out* or *forth*. Now *rare*. L16.

M. SINCLAIR It thundered and lightened.

6 *verb trans. & intrans.* Light up with animation etc.; brighten. L18.

E. K. KANE The gloom of several countenances was perceptibly lightened.

■ **lightener** *noun*[2] LME.

lightening /ˈlʌɪt(ə)nɪŋ/ *noun*[1]. See also LIGHTNING *noun*. ME.
[ORIGIN from LIGHTEN *verb*[2] + -ING[1].]
1 See LIGHTNING *noun*. ME.
2 The action of LIGHTEN *verb*[2]; an instance of this. ME.
lightening before death a revival of the spirits supposedly occurring just before death.

lightening /ˈlʌɪt(ə)nɪŋ/ *noun*[2]. LME.
[ORIGIN from LIGHTEN *verb*[1] + -ING[1].]
The action of LIGHTEN *verb*[1]; an instance of this; MEDICINE a drop in the level of the womb during the last weeks of pregnancy as the head of the fetus engages in the pelvis.

lighter /ˈlʌɪtə/ *noun*[1] & *verb*. LME.
[ORIGIN from LIGHT *verb*[1] + -ER[1], or from Dutch *lichter*.]
▸ **A** *noun*. A boat, usu. a flat-bottomed barge, used for transferring or transporting goods from a ship to a wharf or another ship. LME.
– COMB.: **lighterman** a worker on a lighter.
▸ **B** *verb trans.* Transfer or transport (goods) in a lighter. E19.
■ **lighterage** *noun* (the charge made for) the transferral or transport of goods by a lighter L15.

lighter /ˈlʌɪtə/ *noun*[2]. M16.
[ORIGIN from LIGHT *verb*[2] + -ER[1].]
1 A person who lights candles etc. Also ***lighter-up***. M16.
2 A thing for lighting a candle, fire, etc.; a device for lighting a cigarette etc., a cigarette lighter. E19.

lightful /ˈlʌɪtfʊl, -f(ə)l/ *adjective*. LME.
[ORIGIN from LIGHT *noun* + -FUL.]
Full of light; bright.
■ **lightfulness** *noun* L16.

light-headed /lʌɪtˈhɛdɪd/ *adjective*. LME.
[ORIGIN from LIGHT *adjective*[1] + HEADED *adjective*.]
1 Frivolous; thoughtless; fickle. LME.
2 Dizzy, giddy; delirious. M16.
■ **light-headedly** *adverb* L19. **light-headedness** *noun* E18.

L

light-hearted /lʌɪtˈhɑːtɪd/ *adjective*. LME.
[ORIGIN from LIGHT *adjective*[1] + HEARTED.]
1 Having a light heart; cheerful. LME.
2 Not serious; (unduly) casual; thoughtless. M19.
▪ **light-heartedly** *adverb* M19. **light-heartedness** *noun* E19.

lighthouse /ˈlʌɪthaʊs/ *noun*. E17.
[ORIGIN from LIGHT *noun* + HOUSE *noun*[1].]
A tower or other structure with a powerful light (orig. a beacon) at the top, situated on the coast or offshore to warn or guide ships.

lighting /ˈlʌɪtɪŋ/ *noun*. OE.
[ORIGIN from LIGHT *verb*[2] + -ING[1].]
1 Illumination, the provision of light; *spec.* equipment in a room, street, etc. for producing light, lights collectively. OE.
2 Lightning. Long *dial.* ME.
3 Kindling, ignition. LME.
4 The arrangement or effect of light. M19.
– COMB.: **lighting bridge** THEATRICAL a narrow platform over a stage, on which lights are operated; **lighting cameraman** CINEMATOGRAPHY a person in charge of the lighting of sets being filmed; **lighting plot** THEATRICAL a diagrammatic list showing the lighting to be used in each scene; **lighting tower** THEATRICAL a tall structure on which lights are fixed; **lighting-up time** the time when lights are switched on; *esp.* the time when lights on vehicles are required by law to be switched on.

lightish /ˈlʌɪtɪʃ/ *adjective*. M17.
[ORIGIN from LIGHT *adjective*[2] + -ISH[1].]
Somewhat light.

lightless /ˈlʌɪtlɪs/ *adjective*. OE.
[ORIGIN from LIGHT *noun* + -LESS.]
1 Receiving no light; dark. OE.
2 Giving or producing no light. ME.
▪ **lightlessness** *noun* M19.

lightly /ˈlʌɪtli/ *adjective*. Chiefly *Scot.* Long *rare* or *obsolete*. OE.
[ORIGIN from LIGHT *adjective*[1] + -LY[1].]
Frivolous, contemptible; contemptuous, disparaging.

lightly /ˈlʌɪtli/ *verb trans.* Chiefly *Scot.* LME.
[ORIGIN from LIGHTLY *adjective*.]
Make light of, despise, disparage.

lightly /ˈlʌɪtli/ *adverb*. OE.
[ORIGIN from LIGHT *adjective*[1] + -LY[2].]
1 With little weight; with little pressure, force, or violence; gently; in no great quantity or thickness; sparsely; in no great degree. OE. ▸**b** Of sleeping: not deeply. OE.

SHAKES. *Rich. III* They love his Grace but lightly. M. SINCLAIR Leaning back in his armchair.. his hands joined lightly at the finger-tips. J. P. DONLEAVY I'll knock lightly so's not to be rude. DAY LEWIS The adult world pressed only lightly upon me. E. BOWEN Samples—only lightly wrapped.. in thin paper. J. LEASOR I then ordered black coffee.. and two lightly boiled eggs. J. M. COETZEE 'Cheer up!' said the man,.. punching him lightly on the shoulder. **b** J. CARLYLE I sleep lightly enough for such emergency.

2 Without careful consideration; without strong reason. OE.

J. BUCHAN Something in the.. voice.. forbade Vernon to dismiss lightly this extraordinary tale. T. CAPOTE I will request the judge to set the death penalty. This.. decision has not been arrived at lightly.

3 With a lack of concern; carelessly, indifferently; slightingly. ME.

D. H. LAWRENCE She took her responsibilities lightly. B. PYM 'Oh, I don't suppose I shall see anything of her..' I said lightly.

4 With agility, nimbly. Formerly also, quickly; promptly; immediately. ME.

J. HAYWARD He lightly vaulting off his saddle, drew out his sword. O. MANNING Simon moved lightly among the stalls.

5 Easily, readily. *arch.* ME.

SIR W. SCOTT That's lightly said, but no sae lightly credited.

6 Without depression; cheerfully, merrily, lightheartedly. LME.

E. PEACOCK The old man.. chatted lightly with Basil.

†**7** As may easily or is apt to happen; probably; commonly. LME–L17.
– PHRASES: **get off lightly** be acquitted or escape with little or no punishment. **take lightly** not be serious about.

lightmans /ˈlʌɪtm(ə)ns/ *noun*. *slang*. Now *rare* or *obsolete*. M16.
[ORIGIN from LIGHT *adjective*[2]: for 2nd elem. cf. DARKMANS, TOGEMANS.]
The day.

lightness /ˈlʌɪtnɪs/ *noun*[1]. LOE.
[ORIGIN from LIGHT *adjective*[2] + -NESS.]
†**1** Brightness, light. LOE–E19.

H. LATIMER They were vnapte to receyue the bryghte lyghtnes of the truthe.

2 The condition or state of being light or illuminated; the quality of being light or pale (in colour). ME.

LYTTON The first thing that struck Walter in this apartment was its remarkable lightness. A. BROOKNER There was lightness in the sky that promised a change of season.

lightness /ˈlʌɪtnɪs/ *noun*[2]. ME.
[ORIGIN from LIGHT *adjective*[1] + -NESS.]
1 The quality or fact of having little weight; the fact of having a light load; smallness in quantity or amount. ME. ▸**b** Of bread, pastry, etc.: the quality or fact of being properly risen. M19.
2 Levity, fickleness, frivolity, thoughtlessness. ME. ▸†**b** Wantonness. E16–M17.
3 Agility, nimbleness, quickness. ME.
†**4** Ease, facility, readiness, esp. of belief. ME–M18.
5 Freedom from depression or sorrow, cheerfulness, mirth, light-heartedness. ME.
6 Absence of force or pressure in action or movement. LME.
7 Grace, elegance, delicacy. E19.

lightning /ˈlʌɪtnɪŋ/ *noun & adjective*. ME.
[ORIGIN Specialized use of LIGHTENING *noun*[1], now differentiated in spelling.]
▸ **A** *noun*. **1** The sudden bright light produced by electric discharge between clouds or between a cloud and the ground; (now *rare*) a flash of lightning, a thunderbolt. ME.

Y. MENUHIN When we were safely in the studio.. lightning split the sky.. illuminating woods and mountains. MERLE COLLINS Two more quick stabs of lightning Thunder crashed again, insistently.

ball lightning, *forked lightning*, *sheet lightning*, *summer lightning* etc. **like lightning**, **like greased lightning** with the greatest conceivable speed. *ride the lightning*: see RIDE *verb*.
2 Gin. Also, any strong, esp. low-quality, alcoholic spirit. Chiefly *US slang*. L18.
Jersey lightning: see JERSEY *noun*[1]. *white lightning*: see WHITE *adjective*.
3 In *pl.* A top grade of white jute. E20.
▸ **B** *attrib.* or as *adjective*. Very quick. M17.

E. WELTY The trick was not to miss the lightning visits of Dr. Courtland. V. BROME They were given a lightning tour of New York.

– COMB. & SPECIAL COLLOCATIONS: **lightning arrester** a device to protect telegraphic apparatus etc. from lightning or other voltage surges; **lightning beetle** *US* = *lightning-bug* below; **lightning box**: used to produce stage lightning; **lightning bug** *N. Amer.* a firefly; **lightning chess**: in which moves must be made at very short intervals; **lightning conductor** a metallic rod or wire fixed to the top or other exposed point of a building, or the mast of a ship, to divert lightning into the earth or sea; **lightning-proof** *adjective* protected from lightning; **lightning rod** = *lightning conductor* above; **lightning stone** = FULGURITE; **lightning strike** a strike by workers at short notice, esp. without official union backing.

lightning /ˈlʌɪtnɪŋ/ *verb intrans.* E20.
[ORIGIN from the noun.]
= LIGHTEN *verb*[2] 5.

lights /lʌɪts/ *noun pl.* ME.
[ORIGIN Use as noun of LIGHT *adjective*[1]: see -S[1]. See also LITE *noun*[2]. Cf. LUNG.]
The lungs. Now only, the lungs of sheep, pigs, bullocks, etc., used as food, esp. for pets.
scare the lights out of, **scare the liver and lights out of** scare greatly.

lightsome /ˈlʌɪts(ə)m/ *adjective*[1]. ME.
[ORIGIN from LIGHT *adjective*[1] + -SOME[1].]
1 Having the effect or appearance of lightness; *esp.* light, graceful, elegant. ME.
2 Light-hearted, cheerful, merry. ME. ▸**b** Flighty, frivolous. M16.
3 Lively, nimble, quick. E17.
▪ **lightsomely** *adverb* M16. **lightsomeness** *noun*[1] ME.

lightsome /ˈlʌɪts(ə)m/ *adjective*[2]. LME.
[ORIGIN from LIGHT *noun* + -SOME[1].]
1 Radiant with light; luminous. LME.
2 Esp. of a room, building, etc.: permeated with light; well lit, bright. LME.
3 Clear, manifest. Now *rare*. M16.
†**4** Light-coloured. L16–L17.
▪ **lightsomeness** *noun*[2] LME.

lightweight /ˈlʌɪtweɪt/ *noun & adjective*. L18.
[ORIGIN from LIGHT *adjective*[1] + WEIGHT noun.]
▸ **A** *noun*. **1** A weight at which boxing etc. matches are made, intermediate between featherweight and welterweight, in the amateur boxing scale now being between 57 and 60 kg, though differing for professionals, wrestlers, and weightlifters, and according to time and place; a boxer etc. of this weight; *gen.* a person or thing of below average weight. Formerly also, a horse carrying a light weight in a handicap race. L18.
2 *fig.* An unimportant or superficial person or thing. L19.
3 A garment, usu. a suit, made from lightweight material. L20.
▸ **B** *adjective*. Light in weight; (of a coin) deficient in weight; (of a boxer etc.) that is a lightweight, of or pertaining to lightweights; *fig.* unimportant, superficial, trivial. E19.

Melody Maker Tastier than the lightweight singles of their past. *New Yorker* In the warmest weather our lightweight poplin suit maintains its.. crisp appearance.

– PHRASES: **junior lightweight** (of) a weight in professional boxing of between 57.1 and 59 kg; (designating) a boxer of this weight.

lightwood /ˈlʌɪtwʊd/ *noun*[1]. M19.
[ORIGIN from LIGHT *adjective*[1] + WOOD *noun*[1].]
Any of various trees so called from the lightness of their wood; *esp.* (in Australia) *Acacia implexa* and *A. melanoxylon*.

lightwood /ˈlʌɪtwʊd/ *noun*[2]. *N. Amer.* & *W. Indian*. L17.
[ORIGIN from LIGHT *noun* (or LIGHT *verb*[2]) + WOOD *noun*[1].]
1 Any wood used in lighting a fire; *esp.* (in the southern US) resinous pinewood. L17.
2 Any of various trees which burn with a brilliant flame; *esp.* candle-wood, *Amyris balsamifera*. L19.

lign-aloes /lʌɪnˈaləʊz/ *noun*. Also **lign-aloe**. LME.
[ORIGIN Late Latin *lignum aloes* wood of the aloe (*aloes* genit. of *aloe*). Cf. LINALOE.]
1 The bitter drug aloes; = ALOE 3. LME.
2 Aloes wood; = ALOE 1. E17.
3 = LINALOE. M19.

ligneous /ˈlɪgnɪəs/ *adjective*. E17.
[ORIGIN from Latin *ligneus*, from *lignum* wood: see -OUS, -EOUS.]
1 Of the nature of wood; woody. Chiefly of plants and their texture (opp. ***herbaceous***). E17.
2 Made or consisting of wood, wooden. Chiefly *joc.* E19.

ligni- /ˈlɪgni/ *combining form* of Latin *lignum* wood: see -I-. Cf. LIGNO-.
▪ **lig'nicolous** *adjective* (BOTANY & ZOOLOGY) (**a**) living or growing on wood (as some mosses, fungi, etc.); (**b**) living in wood (as certain bivalves, termites, etc.): M19. **ligniform** *adjective* of the form or appearance of wood L18. **lig'nivorous** *adjective* wood-eating E19.

lignify /ˈlɪgnɪfʌɪ/ *verb trans.* & *intrans.* E19.
[ORIGIN from Latin *lignum* wood + -I- + -FY.]
BOTANY. Make or become woody. Chiefly as ***lignified*** *ppl adjective*.
▪ **lignifi'cation** *noun* the process of becoming woody E19.

lignin /ˈlɪgnɪn/ *noun*. E19.
[ORIGIN formed as LIGNIFY + -IN[1].]
A cross-linked phenolic polymer which combines with cellulose to give woody plant tissue its rigidity.
– COMB.: **lignin sulphonate** a salt of a lignosulphonic acid, used industrially as a dispersant, binder, etc.

lignite /ˈlɪgnʌɪt/ *noun*. E19.
[ORIGIN formed as LIGNIFY + -ITE[1].]
GEOLOGY. A brown, fossil deposit of late Cretaceous or Tertiary age, having a visibly ligneous structure; brown coal.
▪ **lig'nitic** *adjective* pertaining to or of the nature of lignite M19. **ligni'tiferous** *adjective* (of a bed or stratum) producing lignite M19.

ligno- /ˈlɪgnəʊ/ *combining form* of Latin *lignum* wood, or of LIGNIN: see -O-. Cf. LIGNI-.
▪ **ligno'cellulose** *noun* the complex of lignin and cellulose formed in woody plant cell walls E20. **lignocellu'losic** *adjective* pertaining to or containing lignocellulose M20. **ligno'ceric** *adjective* (CHEMISTRY): ***lignoceric acid***, a long-chain fatty acid, $CH_3(CH_2)_{22}COOH$, which is a minor component of natural fats; *n*-tetracosanoic acid: L19. **ligno'sulphonate** *noun* = ***LIGNIN sulphonate*** E20. **lignosul'phonic** *adjective*: ***lignosulphonic acid***, any of various compounds in which sulphonic acid groups are attached to lignin molecules, formed in the sulphite process for producing wood pulp E20.

lignocaine /ˈlɪgnəkeɪn/ *noun*. M20.
[ORIGIN from LIGNO- (with ref. to earlier name XYLOCAINE) + -CAINE.]
PHARMACOLOGY. An aromatic amide used as a local anaesthetic for the gums and mucous membranes.

lignose /ˈlɪgnəʊs/ *adjective & noun*. Now *rare* or *obsolete*. L17.
[ORIGIN Latin *lignosus*, from *lignum* wood: see -OSE[1].]
▸ **A** *adjective*. = LIGNEOUS. L17.
▸ **B** *noun*. = LIGNOCELLULOSE. L19.

lignous /ˈlɪgnəs/ *adjective*. Now *rare* or *obsolete*. M17.
[ORIGIN formed as LIGNOSE + -OUS.]
= LIGNEOUS.

lignum /ˈlɪgnəm/ *noun*[1]. LME.
[ORIGIN Latin = wood.]
With specifying word: a tree; wood.
– COMB.: **lignum aloes** = LIGN-ALOES 2.

lignum /ˈlɪgnəm/ *noun*[2]. *Austral. colloq.* L19.
[ORIGIN Alt. of mod. Latin POLYGONUM *noun*[1].]
Any of various tough wiry plants of the genus *Muehlenbeckia*, allied to the genus *Polygonum* (the knotweeds) and formerly included in it.

lignum vitae /lɪgnəm ˈvʌɪtiː, ˈviːtʌɪ/ *noun*. L16.
[ORIGIN Latin = wood of life.]
1 = GUAIACUM 1. Also, any of several other trees with hard heavy wood. L16.
2 = GUAIACUM 2. L16.
3 = GUAIACUM 3. Long *rare* or *obsolete*. E17.

ligroin /ˈlɪgrəʊɪn/ *noun*. L19.
[ORIGIN Unknown.]
CHEMISTRY. A volatile petroleum fraction with a boiling point between about 60 and 150°C, used as a solvent.

ligula /ˈlɪgjʊlə/ *noun*. Pl. **-lae** /-lʌɪ, -liː/. M18.
[ORIGIN Latin = strap, spoon, var. of LINGULA: see -ULE.]
1 A narrow strap-shaped part in a plant; *esp.* = LIGULE 2(a). Now *rare* or *obsolete*. M18.

2 A strap-shaped part in an insect; *spec.* the distal part of the labium, usu. lobed. M18.
■ **ligular** *adjective* pertaining to or resembling a ligula L19.

ligularia /lɪgjʊˈlɛːrɪə/ *noun*. M19.
[ORIGIN mod. Latin (see below), from Latin LIGULA (with ref. to the shape of the ray florets) + *-aria* -ARY[1].]
Any of various ornamental herbaceous plants of the Eurasian genus *Ligularia*, of the composite family, grown for their showy yellow-rayed flowers.

ligulate /ˈlɪgjʊlət/ *adjective*. M18.
[ORIGIN from LIGULA + -ATE[2].]
Having the form of a ligule, strap-shaped; BOTANY (of a floret of a plant of the composite family) extended on one side to form a flat strap-shaped limb (opp. ***tubular***).
■ Also **ligulated** *adjective* M18.

ligule /ˈlɪgjuːl/ *noun*. E17.
[ORIGIN Latin LIGULA.]
†**1** A Roman measure approximately equivalent to a small spoonful. Only in E17.
2 A narrow strap-shaped part of a plant; *spec.* (***a***) a membranous scale occurring on the inner side of the leaf sheath at its junction with the blade in most grasses and sedges; also, a scale on the upper surface of a leaf in the selaginellas; (***b***) the blade formed by a ligulate floret. E19.

ligure /ˈlɪgjʊə/ *noun*. *obsolete* exc. *hist.* Also †**ligury** & other vars. ME.
[ORIGIN Late Latin (Vulgate) *ligurius*, from Septuagint Greek *ligurion* one of the stones in the high priest's breastplate.]
A kind of precious stone.

AV *Exod.* 28:19 And the third row a Lygure, an Agate, and an Amethist.

Ligurian /lɪˈgjʊərɪən/ *adjective & noun*. E17.
[ORIGIN from Latin *Liguria* (see below) + -AN.]
▸ **A** *noun*. A native or inhabitant of Liguria, now a region in NW Italy, formerly an ancient country extending from NE Spain to NW Italy and including Switzerland and SE Gaul. Also, the pre-Italic Indo-European language of the ancient Ligurians; the Gallo-Italian dialect of modern Liguria. E17.
▸ **B** *adjective*. Of or pertaining to Liguria, the Ligurians, or their language. M17.

†**ligury** *noun* var. of LIGURE.

ligustrum /lɪˈgʌstrəm/ *noun*. M17.
[ORIGIN Latin.]
= PRIVET 1.

Lihyanite /liːˈjɑːnʌɪt/ *noun & adjective*. M20.
[ORIGIN from Arabic *lihyān* the name of an ancient tribe + -ITE[1].]
(Of) an early form of Arabic known only from north Arabian inscriptions of the 2nd and 1st cents. BC, written in a southern Semitic alphabet.
■ Also **Lihyani** /liːˈjɑːniː/ *noun & adjective* E20.

likable *adjective* var. of LIKEABLE.

like /lʌɪk/ *noun*[1]. ME.
[ORIGIN from LIKE *verb*[1].]
†**1** *sing.* & in *pl.* (One's) good pleasure. ME–E17.
2 In *pl.* Feelings of affection or preference for particular things; things liked or preferred; predilections. Chiefly coupled with ***dislikes***. L18.

like /lʌɪk/ *noun*[2]. ME.
[ORIGIN from LIKE *adjective* etc.]
1 With qualifying possess.: a person or thing of the same kind, one's counterpart, one's equal, one's match. ME.

E. W. MACBRIDE 'Sports'.. which breed true when crossed with their like. *Guardian* The recent murder.. was the work of Mr Mohtashemi or his like.

2 A thing considered in respect of its likeness to something else; an instance of similarity. Chiefly in proverbial expressions, as ***like breeds like***, ***like will to like***. LME.
3 ***the like***, a similar thing or things. LME.
and the like and similar things, et cetera. **or the like** or another thing or other things of the same kind. **the likes of** *colloq.* such a person or such people as (***the likes of me***, persons as humble as I; ***the likes of you***, persons as distinguished as you).
4 *sing.* & (usu.) in *pl.* Likelihood, probability. *rare* exc. *dial.* E17.
5 GOLF. The same number of strokes as one's opponent; a stroke that makes one's score for a hole equal to that of one's opponent. Chiefly in ***the like***. Cf. ODD *noun* 3. L18.

like /lʌɪk/ *adjective, preposition, adverb, & conjunction*. ME.
[ORIGIN Old Norse *líkr* aphet. from *glíkr*: see ALIKE *adjective*. Cf. earlier LIKENESS.]
▸ **A** *adjective*. **1** Having the same characteristics or qualities as some other person or thing; of approximately identical shape, size, etc., with something else; similar. Now usu. *attrib.*; also (*arch.*) foll. by *to*, *with*, †*as*. ME. ▸**b** Like each other, mutually similar. LME.

M. TWAIN Claws like to a bat's but broader. *Lancet* Farmer's lung and like conditions. **b** TENNYSON No two dreams are like. H. M. ROSENBERG There is a mutual repulsion between like charges.

2 *pred.* **a** That may reasonably be expected *to do*, likely to *do*. Now chiefly *colloq.* ME. ▸**b** Apparently about *to do*. Now *colloq.* M16.

a A. E. HOUSMAN We're like to meet no more. **b** SIR W. SCOTT The eldest man seemed like to choke with laughter.

3 Apt, suitable. Chiefly *pred.* Long *obsolete* exc. *Scot.* LME.
4 In accordance with appearances, probable, likely. Now *dial.* LME.

SHAKES. *Rom. & Jul.* Is it not like that I, So early waking.. shall I not be distraught?

5 Of a portrait etc.: bearing a faithful resemblance to the original. Now only *pred.* M16.
– COMB.: **like-minded** *adjective* having similar tastes, opinions, etc.; **like-mindedness** the state of being like-minded.
▸ **B** *preposition*. (Retaining an adjectival character and able to be qualified by adverbs of degree and compared.)
1 Having the same characteristics or qualities as; of approximately identical shape, size, etc., as; similar to. Orig. with dat. obj. ME. ▸**b** Similar to that or those of. *non-standard*. LME.

J. PRIESTLEY There was nothing like it in the philosophy of Plato. G. GREENE I think.. I am very like Napoleon IV. I. MURDOCH It was rather like the inside of a wardrobe. **b** J. BUCHAN The bent and heather of the Cheviots were like my domestic hills.

2 In the manner of, in the same way as; to the same degree as. (With obj. of preposition the subj. of the verbal action understood.) ME. ▸**b** In the manner or to the extent that one would or could. (With obj. of preposition the obj. of the verbal action understood: cf. sense D. below.) *colloq.* L17.

F. BURNEY She sings like her, laughs like her. *Punch* What was the use of his talking like that? D. HAMMETT 'You can't say that.' 'Like hell I can't.' DAY LEWIS Like flaming swords they barred my way. **b** R. KIPLING At least she did not treat me like a child. A. MAUPIN Why was this.. dowager talking to her like an equal.

like a lamb, ***like a red rag to a bull***, ***like a shag on a rock***, ***like a shot***, ***like nothing on earth***, ***like smoke***, ***like stink***, ***like steam***, etc.

†**3** In accordance with. LME–L16.
4 With certain verbs of perception: having the perceived quality of (something) so as to suggest its presence or occurrence. L16.

SIR W. SCOTT That sounds like nonsense, my dear.

†**5** As well as, as also. *rare*. L16–M17.
6 Characteristic of; such as one might expect from. M17.

DICKENS It would be like his impudence.. to dare to think of such a thing.

7 Of the kind represented by; such as. L19.

J. B. PRIESTLEY It.. offers you fantastic little old streets like Mary-Le-Port Street and Narrow Wine Street.

▸ **C** *adverb*. **1** Foll. by *to*: in the manner of, in the same way as; to the same degree as. *arch.* LME.

SHAKES. *Sonn.* Then my state, Like to the lark.. arising.., sings hymns at heaven's gate.

2 Equally, alike. Now *poet.* & only qualifying adjectives & adverbs. LME.
3 Qualifying an adjective: in the manner of a person who or thing which is. Now only *colloq.* in certain phrs. E16.
like crazy, ***like mad***, etc.
4 Likely, probably. *rare* exc. in ***like enough***, ***very like***, ***like as not***, ***as like as not***. L16.
5 So to speak; as it were. Also used as a filler of little or no meaning. *colloq.* L18.

LYTTON If your honour were more amongst us, there might be more discipline like. ALAN BENNETT He hasn't passed his examinations like. *New Society* I'm just dreading the first day, like. *New Yorker* Some guy dumped a bucket of Gatorade on us, and then, like, everyone was screaming.

▸ **D** *conjunction*. **1** As if, as though. Now *non-standard*. E16.

W. FAULKNER It looked like I was going to get shut of it. M. MACHLIN They all treat me like I was some weirdo.

2 In the same way that; as. *colloq.* E16.

D. L. SAYERS Like I was saying to your lady. G. GREENE He had to humiliate him like he humiliated my mother. M. MCCARTHY In the library there was.. a white piano, like in a night club.

– PHRASES (of all parts of speech): (A selection of cross-refs. only is included: see esp. other nouns.) **anything like** in any way resembling (chiefly in neg. contexts). **as like as not**, **like as not** *colloq.* very likely. ***as like as two peas***: see PEA *noun*[1] 1. **be like that** (***a***) be of the nature, character, or habit indicated; (***b***) (with stress on *that*, accompanied by or implying the crossing of fingers) be on very friendly or intimate terms. ***feel like***: see FEEL *verb*. ***in like manner***: see MANNER *noun*[1]. †**in like wise** in the same manner, similarly, likewise. **like another** (of a thing) that is ordinary; that is only one of a number of similar things, possibilities, etc. ***like anything***: see ANYTHING *pronoun*. **like as** *arch.* in the same way as (now only with following clause); just as if. ***like as not***: see ***as like as not*** above. **like** BILLY-O. ***like crazy***: see CRAZY *adjective*. **like enough** quite likely, very likely. ***like hang***: see HANG *noun*. **like — like —** as — as — is, so is —. ***like mad***: see MAD *adjective*. **like so** *colloq.* in this way. ***like wild***: see WILD *adjective, noun, & adverb*. ***look like***: see LOOK *verb*. **more like** *colloq.* nearer (a specified number or quantity); (also ***more like it***) nearer what is required or expected. **nothing like** in no way resembling, *esp.* in no way as good or effective as. ***same like***: see SAME *adverb*. ***sleep like a log***, ***sleep like a top***: see SLEEP *verb*. **something like** (***a***) in some way resembling, approximately; (***b***) *ellipt.* (*colloq.*) (with stress on *like*) what such a thing should be, a fine example; (***c***) *ellipt.* (*colloq.*) in a tolerably adequate manner. ***tell it like it is***: see TELL *verb*. **what is — like?** what is the nature or character of —?

like /lʌɪk/ *verb*[1].
[ORIGIN Old English *līcian* = Old Frisian *līkia*, Old Saxon *līkon* (Dutch *lijken*), Old High German *līhhēn*, Old Norse *líka*, Gothic *leikan*, from Germanic, from base also of LICH *noun*.]
1 a *verb trans.* (orig. with dat. obj.). Be pleasing to, suit, (a person). Now *arch.* & *dial.* OE. ▸†**b** *verb intrans.* Be pleasing, be liked or approved. OE–E17.

SIR W. SCOTT At first.. it liked me ill. D. G. ROSSETTI I rode sullenly Upon a certain path that liked me not.

†**2** *verb refl.* & *intrans.* Take pleasure; delight *in* something. ME–M16.
3 *verb intrans.* Be pleased, be glad. *obsolete* exc. *Scot.* ME.
†**4** *verb intrans.* Be in good condition; get on, thrive, (*well*, *better*, etc.). Latterly chiefly as ***liking*** *ppl adjective*. ME–L19.
5 *verb trans.* **a** Find agreeable, congenial, or satisfactory; feel attracted to or favourably impressed by (a person); have a taste for, take pleasure in, (a thing, *doing*, *to be*, *to do*, etc.). Also ***like well*** (now *arch.* exc. with qualification, e.g. *very*, or as compar. *better* or superl. *best*). ME. ▸**b** Find it agreeable, feel inclined, (*to do*, *to be*). In conditional use (***should like*** etc.): expr. desire, derision, or scepticism. ME. ▸**c** Prefer, choose to have, (a thing, *to do*, †*that*; a person or thing *to do*, *to be*, adjectival compl. (with *to be* understood), (*to be*) *done*). M16. ▸**d** In interrog. with *how*: feel about, regard, (a person or thing, *doing*, (in conditional use) *to do*). L16. ▸**e** With conditional aux.: wish to have. E19.

a H. B. STOWE I may *like* him well enough; but you don't *love* your servants. D. H. LAWRENCE He sang in the choir because he liked singing. T. F. POWYS An English gentleman never likes to be beaten. A. RANSOME Nobody much likes steak-and-kidney pudding.. eaten all cold and greasy at six. J. STEINBECK When there is a parade he likes to carry the flag. E. BOWEN They had from the first liked Rodney better than Edward. **b** J. LOCKE He may either go or stay, as he best likes. SHELLEY If you would like to go, We'll visit him. DICKENS I should like to see you do it, sir. E. WAUGH I should like to go with them and drink beer. **c** S. COLVIN The sonatas of Haydn were the music he liked Severn best to play to him. A. CARNEGIE He would like me to explain how I had been able to steer clear of these.. troubles. **d** C. LAMB The Chorics (how do you like the word?) of Samson Agonistes. LYTTON How do you like sharing the mirth of the groundlings? J. TICKELL How would you like to be half-starved for a bit? **e** S. T. WARNER Wouldn't Mr. Fortune like a girl too?

6 *verb intrans.* Derive pleasure *of* a person or thing; approve *of*, become fond *of*. *obsolete* exc. *dial.* LME.
7 *verb intrans.* Entertain feelings of affection. *arch.* L16.
– PHRASES: **and like it** (after an imper.) and any complaint will be unheeded. **if you like** *colloq.* if you wish to express it or consider it in that way; indeed, perhaps. **I like that!** *iron.*: expr. surprise or disgust at another's impudence, conceit, etc. ***know what one likes***: see KNOW *verb*. **like it or not** *colloq.* whether it is acceptable or not. ***like to hear oneself speak***, ***like to hear oneself talk***: see HEAR *verb*. ***not like the look of***: see LOOK *noun*. ***wouldn't you like to know***, ***wouldn't he like to know***: see KNOW *verb*.

like /lʌɪk/ *verb*[2]. LME.
[ORIGIN from LIKE *adjective* etc.]
†**1** *verb trans.* Make in a certain likeness; represent as like to; compare to; make a likeness of. LME–E17.
2 *verb intrans.* Orig., seem, pretend. Later, look like or be near to doing something or to being treated in a specified manner. Foll. by *to do*. Now *non-standard*, chiefly in ***had liked to do***. LME.

SHAKES. *Much Ado* We had lik'd to have had our two noses snapp'd off.

-like /lʌɪk/ *suffix*.
[ORIGIN from LIKE *adjective* etc.]
Forming (***a***) adjectives from nouns & (chiefly *Scot.*) adjectives, with the sense 'similar to, characteristic of, befitting, (one who is), resembling (that of)', as ***doglike***, ***ladylike***, ***shell-like***; ***gluey-like***; (***b***) (now *colloq.*) adverbs from nouns & adjectives, with the senses 'in the manner of', 'like one who is', as ***coward-like***; ***strangelike***.
– NOTE: A hyphen is usual in less common words of more than one syllable and in all words ending in *-l*.

likeable /ˈlʌɪkəb(ə)l/ *adjective*. Also **likable**. M18.
[ORIGIN from LIKE *verb*[1] + -ABLE.]
Esp. of a person: easy to like; pleasant, agreeable.
■ **likeaˈbility** *noun* E19. **likeableness** *noun* M19.

likelihead /ˈlʌɪklɪhɛd/ *noun*. Long *arch.* LME.
[ORIGIN from LIKELY + -HEAD[1].]
1 = LIKELIHOOD 2. Chiefly in ***by likelihead***, in all likelihood. LME.
†**2** = LIKELIHOOD 1. Only in LME.

likelihood /ˈlʌɪklɪhʊd/ *noun*. LME.
[ORIGIN from LIKELY + -HOOD.]
†**1** Likeness, similarity; an instance of this, a resemblance. LME–L17.
2 The quality or fact of being likely; an instance of this, a (good) chance. (Foll. by *of*, †*to do*.) LME.

H. CARPENTER There is every likelihood that she knew his books. A. STORR Association with other criminals carried the likelihood of reinforcing.. crime as a way of life.

L

in all likelihood, †**in likelihood** in all probability, very probably. **the likelihood** the probable fact.
†**3** A thing that is likely, a probability; a ground of probable inference, an indication. Freq. in *pl.* **M16–M17.**
4 The quality of offering a prospect of success; promise. Now only as an echo of Shakes. **M16.**

SHAKES. *1 Hen. IV* A fellow of no mark nor likelihood.

5 *STATISTICS.* A function of the variable parameters of a family of probability distributions that depends on a fixed set of data and equals the probability of the data, if these are assumed to relate to a population whose distribution has the given parameters. **E20.**
– **COMB.:** **likelihood ratio** *STATISTICS* the ratio of two likelihoods based on alternative hypotheses about the parameters of a distribution, used in testing these hypotheses.

likeliness /ˈlʌɪklɪnɪs/ *noun.* Now *rare.* **LME.**
[**ORIGIN** from LIKELY + -NESS.]
†**1** = LIKELIHOOD 1. **LME–E18.**
2 = LIKELIHOOD 2. **LME.**
†**3** = LIKELIHOOD 4. **LME–M18.**

likely /ˈlʌɪkli/ *adjective & adverb.* **ME.**
[**ORIGIN** Old Norse (*g*)*likligr*, from *likr* LIKE *adjective* etc. + *-ligr* -LY¹.]
▸ **A** *adjective.* **1** Having an appearance of truth or fact; that looks as if it would happen, be realized, or prove to be what is alleged or suggested; probable; to be reasonably expected *to do*, *to be*, (with impers. *it*) *that.* **ME.**

E. M. FORSTER I hope that none of your friends are likely to come in. *Listener* In a television studio, where the acoustic is liklier to be drier. A. THWAITE It seems likely that St Paul's was the church Edmund was going to. H. BAILEY Officers .. were six times as likely to be killed as their men. G. GREENE His life provided models for behaviour in any likely circumstance. *Lancaster Guardian* Surveys carried out last winter have helped to predict likely road conditions.

a likely story: expr. disbelief of another's statement. **as likely as not** quite probably. **not likely** *colloq.* certainly not (more strongly ***not bloody likely***; see also ***not PYGMALION likely***).
†**2** Having a resemblance, similar; resembling an original. **LME–M17.**
3 Apparently suitable or qualified (*for* a thing); apparently able or fitted (*to do*, *to be*). **LME.**

C. BURNEY Lely gave me these papers as the likelyest man to get them perfected. G. LORD He made a wide arc .. until he came to a likely camp site.

4 Having the appearance or giving evidence of vigour or ability; giving promise of success or excellence. **LME.**

Birmingham Post The department has ten jobs on offer to likely boys and girls.

†**5** Seemly, becoming, appropriate. **LME–M18.**
6 Good-looking. Chiefly *US & dial.* **LME.**
▸ **B** *adverb.* †**1** In a like or similar manner, similarly; (with ref. to portraiture) with close resemblance. **LME–L16.**
2 Probably, in all probability. Now chiefly *N. Amer., Scot., & dial.*, & in ***most likely***, ***very likely***. **LME.**

B. JOWETT You may be very likely right in that. D. MARQUIS A middle-aged person has likely learned how to have a little fun.

†**3** In a fit manner, suitably, reasonably. **LME–L17.**

liken /ˈlʌɪk(ə)n/ *verb.* **ME.**
[**ORIGIN** from LIKE *adjective* etc. + -EN⁵.]
1 *verb trans.* Represent as similar, point out the similarity of. Foll. by *to.* **ME.** ▸**b** In *pass.* Be associated by repute with another, esp. as a lover or future spouse. Foll. by *with*, *to*. Long *obsolete* exc. *Scot.* **M16.**

ANTHONY SMITH Plato likened memory to a wax tablet.

†**2** *verb intrans. & trans.* Be or become similar *to*, be or become like. **ME–M19.**
3 *verb trans.* Make like. *rare.* **LME.**
■ **likening** *noun* (*a*) the action of the verb; †(*b*) a comparison, a simile: **ME.**

likeness /ˈlʌɪknɪs/ *noun.*
[**ORIGIN** Old English (*ġe*)*līcnes*, formed as ALIKE *adjective* + -NESS.]
†**1** A person's stature. Only in **OE.**
2 A visual representation of a person or thing; a copy, an image, a portrait. Also, a person who closely resembles another. **OE.**

DYLAN THOMAS On receiving your photograph I went immediately to have my own likeness taken.

3 A shape or form like or identified as something, a semblance or guise *of.* **ME.**

SHELLEY The likeness of a throned king came by. E. A. FREEMAN Spalato is putting on the likeness of a busy modern town.

4 The quality or fact of being like; (a) resemblance, (a) similarity. (Foll. by *between*, *to*, †*with*.) **ME.**

H. JAMES She seemed to see a far-away likeness to the vaguely-remembered image of her mother.

catch a likeness: see CATCH *verb*.
†**5** A comparison; a parable. Only in **ME.**

liker /ˈlʌɪkə/ *noun.* Now *rare.* **M16.**
[**ORIGIN** from LIKE *verb*¹ + -ER¹.]
A person who likes something or someone.

Likert scale /ˈlʌɪkət skeɪl/ *noun phr.* **M20.**
[**ORIGIN** Rensis *Likert* (1903–81), US psychologist.]
PSYCHOLOGY. A scale used to represent people's attitudes to a topic.

likesome /ˈlʌɪks(ə)m/ *adjective.* *obsolete* exc. *dial.* **M16.**
[**ORIGIN** from LIKE *verb*¹ + -SOME¹.]
Agreeable, pleasant.

†**likeways** *adverb.* **M16–E18.**
[**ORIGIN** from LIKE *adjective* + -WAYS.]
= LIKEWISE.

likewise /ˈlʌɪkwʌɪz/ *adverb.* **LME.**
[**ORIGIN** Abbreviation of ***in like wise*** s.v. LIKE *adjective* etc.]
1 In the like manner, similarly. Now only in ***do likewise***. **LME.**
2 Also, as well, moreover, too; in return, conversely. **E16.**

F. SWINNERTON On the floor above, young Bertram Thornycroft was likewise in high glee. *Sunday Express* That is what Denis gives .. me and, likewise, what I try to give to him.

liking /ˈlʌɪkɪŋ/ *noun.* **OE.**
[**ORIGIN** from LIKE *verb*¹ + -ING¹.]
†**1** The fact of being to one's taste or of being liked. **OE–L16.**
†**2** Pleasure, enjoyment; an instance of this; *spec.* sensuality, sexual desire. **ME–E18.**
3 The bent of the will; what one wishes or prefers, (a person's) pleasure. Now *rare* exc. in ***to one's liking*** below. **ME.**
on liking, **upon liking** (now *rare*) on approval or trial. **to one's liking** according to one's wish, to one's taste.
4 The condition of being fond of or not averse to a person or thing; favourable regard, a fondness, a taste, a fancy. (Foll. by *for*, *to* a person.) **ME.**

A. KOESTLER Sympathy for his own body, for which usually he had no liking, played over him. E. FERRARS He's too stiff and prickly for my liking. R. WHELAN Capa and Dinah took an immediate liking to him.

†**5** Bodily condition, esp. good or healthy condition. **ME–M18.**
†**6** An object liked, (one's) beloved. **LME–M17.**

likkewaan /ˈlɪkəvɑːn/ *noun.* **E20.**
[**ORIGIN** Afrikaans formed as LEGUAN.]
= IGUANA 2.

Likud /lɪˈkuːd, -ˈkʊd/ *noun.* **L20.**
[**ORIGIN** Hebrew *likkūd* union, (mod.) coalition.]
A coalition of right-wing Israeli political parties, formed in 1973.

likuta /lɪˈkuːtə/ *noun.* Pl. **makuta** /məˈkuːtə/. **M20.**
[**ORIGIN** Kikongo.]
A former monetary unit of Zaire (formerly of the Congo) equal to one-hundredth of a zaire.

lil /lɪl/ *noun.* *slang & dial.* Also **lill**. **E19.**
[**ORIGIN** Romany.]
1 A book. **E19.**
2 A currency note. **M19.**

lil /lɪl/ *adjective.* *colloq.* **L19.**
[**ORIGIN** Repr. an informal pronunc.]
Little.

lila /ˈliːlɑː/ *noun.* **E19.**
[**ORIGIN** Sanskrit *līlā* play, amusement.]
In Hindu mythology and theology, the spontaneous playful activity exercised by God in all his actions, esp. in the creation of the universe; a sacred dance drama re-enacting this.

lilac /ˈlʌɪlək/ *noun & adjective.* Also (now *dial.*) **laylock** /ˈleɪlɒk/. **E17.**
[**ORIGIN** Obsolete French (now *lilas*) ult. from Persian *līlak* (whence also Turkish *leylâk*) var. of *nīlak* bluish, from *nīl* blue + dim. suffix *-ak*.]
▸ **A** *noun.* **1** A shrub or small tree, *Syringa vulgaris*, of the olive family, cultivated for its fragrant blossoms, which are typically of a pale pinkish-violet colour; *collect.* flowering sprays of this plant. Also (usu. with specifying word), (flowering sprays of) any of various other shrubs or trees belonging to this genus or thought to resemble the lilac. **E17.**
Persian lilac the azedarac, *Melia azedarach*.
2 A pale pinkish-violet colour. **L18.**
3 The scent of lilac, esp. as used in cosmetics. **L19.**
▸ **B** *adjective.* Of the colour lilac. **E19.**

Country Life Full-skirted lilac dress.

lilac-breasted roller a roller, *Coracias caudata*, of eastern and southern Africa.
■ **lilacky** *adjective* resembling or suggestive of lilac, of a colour resembling lilac **M19.**

lilangeni /liːlaŋˈgeɪni/ *noun.* Pl. **emalangeni** /ˌɪmalaŋˈgeɪni/. **L20.**
[**ORIGIN** Bantu, from *li-* sing. prefix (*ema-* pl. prefix) + *-langeni* member of royal family.]
The basic monetary unit of Swaziland, equal to 100 cents.

liliaceous /lɪlɪˈeɪʃəs/ *adjective.* **M18.**
[**ORIGIN** from late Latin *liliaceus*, from *lilium* LILY: see -ACEOUS.]
Pertaining to or characteristic of lilies, lily-like; *spec.* (*BOTANY*) of or pertaining to the family Liliaceae, which includes the genus *Lilium*, the lilies.

lilied /ˈlɪlɪd/ *adjective.* **E17.**
[**ORIGIN** from LILY + -ED².]
1 Resembling a lily in fairness of complexion. **E17.**

BROWNING Of just-tinged marble, like Eve's lilied flesh.

2 Covered with lilies, having many lilies. **M17.** ▸**b** Embellished with fleurs-de-lis. **L18.**

GEO. ELIOT Its lilied pool and grassy acres specked with deer.

lilipi /ˈlɪlɪpi/ *noun.* **L18.**
[**ORIGIN** Unknown.]
Chiefly *NZ HISTORY.* Boiled flour as an article of food.

lilium /ˈlɪlɪəm/ *noun.* **E20.**
[**ORIGIN** Latin: see LILY.]
= LILY *noun* 1.

lill /lɪl/ *noun*¹. *Scot.* **E18.**
[**ORIGIN** Uncertain: cf. Dutch *lul*.]
Any of the holes of a woodwind instrument.

lill *noun*² var. of LIL *noun.*

lill /lɪl/ *verb trans. & intrans.* Long *obsolete* exc. *dial.* **M16.**
[**ORIGIN** Symbolic: cf. LOLL *verb*.]
Esp. of an animal: hang (the tongue) *out* or out.

Lille lace /liːl ˈleɪs/ *noun phr.* **M19.**
[**ORIGIN** from *Lille*, a city in northern France.]
A kind of pillow or bobbin lace.

Lillet /ˈliːleɪ/ *noun.* **M20.**
[**ORIGIN** French surname.]
A French white wine aperitif resembling vermouth; a glass of this.
– **NOTE:** Proprietary name in the US.

lilli-pilli *noun* var. of LILLY-PILLY.

Lilliput /ˈlɪlɪpʌt/ *attrib. adjective.* **M18.**
[**ORIGIN** *Lilliput*, an imaginary country in Swift's *Gulliver's Travels* (1726), inhabited by people six inches high.]
Diminutive, Lilliputian.

Lilliputian /lɪlɪˈpjuːʃ(ə)n/ *noun & adjective.* **E18.**
[**ORIGIN** from LILLIPUT + -IAN.]
▸ **A** *noun.* In Swift's *Gulliver's Travels*: an inhabitant of Lilliput; a person of diminutive size, character, or mind. **E18.**
▸ **B** *adjective.* Of or pertaining to Lilliput or its inhabitants; of diminutive size; petty. **E18.**
■ **lilliputianize** *verb trans.* dwarf **L19.**

lilly-pilly /ˈlɪlɪˌpɪli/ *noun.* Also **lilli-pilli**. **M19.**
[**ORIGIN** Unknown.]
An Australian evergreen tree, *Acmena smithii*, of the myrtle family, with edible purplish to white berries; the timber or the fruit of this tree.

Li-Lo /ˈlʌɪləʊ/ *noun.* Also **Lilo**. Pl. **-os**. **M20.**
[**ORIGIN** Alt. of *lie low*.]
(Proprietary name for) an inflatable plastic or rubber mattress.

lilt /lɪlt/ *noun.* **L17.**
[**ORIGIN** from the verb.]
1 A song, a tune, *esp.* one of a cheerful or merry character. Chiefly *Scot.* **L17.**
2 The rhythmical cadence or swing of a tune or of verse; a characteristic inflection or rhythm in the voice. **M19.**
3 A springing action; a light springing step. **M19.**

lilt /lɪlt/ *verb.* Orig. *Scot. & N. English.* **LME.**
[**ORIGIN** Rel. to Low German, Dutch *lul* pipe (Dutch *lullepijp* bagpipe).]
†**1** *verb trans.* Sound (an alarm); lift up (the voice). **LME–E16.**
2 *verb trans.* Sing cheerfully or merrily; strike *up* (a song); tune *up* (pipes). **E18.**
3 *verb intrans.* Sing or sound cheerfully or merrily; sing or speak with a lilt. Freq. as ***lilting ppl adjective***. **E18.**

SIR W. SCOTT Jenny, whose shrill voice I have heard .. lilting in the Tartarean regions of the kitchen.

4 *verb intrans.* Move with a lilt. Chiefly as ***lilting ppl adjective***. **L18.**

Longman's Magazine Swinging down the street with an easy lilting stride.

5 *verb intrans.* Of music or speech: have a lilt. Chiefly as ***lilting ppl adjective***. **E19.**

W. H. AUDEN Or west to the Welsh Marches; to the lilting speech and the magicians' faces.

lily /ˈlɪli/ *noun & adjective.* **OE.**
[**ORIGIN** Latin *lilium* from (the same root as) Greek *leirion*, perh. of non-Indo-European origin.]
▸ **A** *noun.* **1** Any plant of the genus *Lilium* (family Liliaceae), comprising tall bulbous plants bearing large showy trumpet-shaped flowers on a tall slender stem, and often grown for ornament; *esp.* (without qualification) = ***MADONNA lily***. Also, a flower or flowering stem of such a plant. **OE.** ▸**b** In biblical translations: any of one or

more conspicuous Palestinian flowers, variously identified as a lily, tulip, anemone, gladiolus, etc. LME. ▸c With specifying word: any of various plants of other genera of the family Liliaceae or of related families, esp. the Amaryllidaceae. Also, any of certain unrelated plants with similarly conspicuous flowers. M16.

b AV *Matt.* 6:28 Consider the lilies of the field . . . Euen Solomon in all his glory was not arayed like one of these.

martagon lily, tiger lily, Turk's-cap lily, etc. **c arum lily, belladonna lily, day lily, Guernsey lily, Kaffir lily, Lent lily, May lily, Peruvian lily, St Bruno's lily, water lily,** etc.

2 *fig.* **a** A person or thing of exceptional whiteness, fairness, or purity; *sing.* & in *pl.*, the white of a beautiful complexion. LME. ▸b A person one despises; *esp.* a man regarded as lacking masculinity. E20.

3 A representation of the flower; *spec.* the heraldic fleur-de-lis, esp. with ref. to the arms of the old French monarchy (also ***golden lilies***); *the* royal arms of France, *the* French (Bourbon) dynasty. LME. ▸†b The fleur-de-lis which was used to mark north on a compass. E–M17. ▸c In *pl.* = ***lily-feet*** below. Also ***golden lilies***. M19.

– PHRASES: **gild the lily** embellish excessively, add ornament where none is needed. **lily of the valley**, (*arch.*) **lily of the vale** [translating Vulgate *lilium convallium* (*S. of S.* 2:1) translating Hebrew, an unidentified plant] a May-flowering woodland plant, *Convallaria majalis*, of the lily family, with two large leaves and racemes of white bell-shaped fragrant flowers; the scent of this plant, esp. as used in cosmetics. **paint the lily** [Shakes. *John*] = ***gild the lily*** above.

▸ **B** *adjective.* **1** White or fair as a lily; lily-white. L15.

2 Pale, pallid, colourless, bloodless. L16.

– COMB. (of noun & adjective): **lily bell**, **lily cup** the flower of the lily of the valley; **lily feet** the bound feet of a Chinese woman; **lily flower** the flower of the white lily; **lily-footed** *adjective* having lily feet; **lily-iron** a harpoon with a detachable head used in killing swordfish; **lily liver** the supposedly white liver of cowards; **lily-livered** *adjective* cowardly; **lily pad** the broad flat leaf of a water lily as it lies on the water; **lily-pond**: in which water lilies grow; **lily pot** a flowerpot with a lily in it; a representation of this, esp. as a religious emblem of purity and innocence; an ornamental vase resembling the lily pot of religious art, *esp.* a tobacco jar; **lily-trotter** a jacana, *esp.* an African one; **lily-turf** = MONDO *noun*[1].

■ **lily-like** *adjective* resembling (that of) a lily M17.

lily-white /ˈlɪlɪwʌɪt/ *adjective & noun.* ME.

[ORIGIN from LILY + WHITE *adjective*.]

▸ **A** *adjective.* **1** As white as a lily. ME.

2 In favour of, committed to, or pertaining to a policy of racial segregation. E20.

3 Irreproachable, lacking faults or imperfections. M20.

▸ **B** *noun.* A chimney sweep. *slang.* Now *rare* or *obsolete*. L17.

Lima /ˈliːmə/ *noun.* M18.

[ORIGIN The capital of Peru.]

In full ***Lima bean***. A bean plant, *Phaseolus limensis* (or *P. lunatus*), native to tropical S. America; the large flat white edible seed of this plant; a butter bean.

limaceous /lʌɪˈmeɪʃəs/ *adjective.* M17.

[ORIGIN formed as LIMAX + -ACEOUS.]

Of or pertaining to the genus *Limax* of slugs. Formerly, resembling a snail.

limaces *noun* pl. of LIMAX.

limaciform /lʌɪˈmeɪsɪfɔːm/ *adjective.* E19.

[ORIGIN formed as LIMAX + -I- + -FORM.]

Having the form of a slug.

limacine /ˈlʌɪməsʌɪn, -sɪn/ *adjective.* L19.

[ORIGIN formed as LIMAX + -INE[1].]

Resembling a slug or a snail.

limaçon /ˈlɪməsɒn/ *noun.* Also **-con**. L16.

[ORIGIN French = snail shell, spiral staircase, etc., from Old French & mod. French *limace* formed as LIMAX: see -OON.]

†**1** A kind of spiral military manoeuvre. Only in L16.

2 MATH. Any of a series of closed curves represented by the formula $r = a \cos \theta + b$, which when $a = b$ gives a cardioid; the locus of a point on a line a fixed distance from the intersection of the line with a circle, as the line rotates about a fixed point on the circle. L19.

limail /ˈliːm(ə)l/ *noun.* Now only *techn.* Also **lemel**. LME.

[ORIGIN Old French & mod. French *limaille*, from *limer* to file from Latin *limare*.]

Metal filings.

liman /liːˈmɑːn/ *noun.* M19.

[ORIGIN Russian = estuary, from Turkish from mod. Greek *limeni* from Greek *limēn*.]

A shallow lagoon at the mouth of a river behind a bar or spit, characteristic of the Black Sea.

limation /lʌɪˈmeɪʃ(ə)n/ *noun.* Now *rare*. E17.

[ORIGIN Late Latin *limatio(n-)*, from Latin *limat-* pa. ppl stem of *limare* to file: see -ATION.]

Filing; *fig.* the process of refining or improving the appearance of something.

limax /ˈlʌɪmaks/ *noun.* Pl. **limaces** /lʌɪˈmeɪsiːz/. LME.

[ORIGIN Latin *limax*, *limac-* slug, snail.]

Orig., a slug. Now, a slug of the genus *Limax* or the family Limacidae containing it.

limb /lɪm/ *noun*[1].

[ORIGIN Old English *lim* corresp. to Old Norse *limr*, prob. rel. to LITH *noun*[1].]

1 An organ or part of the body. Long *obsolete* exc. *dial.* OE.

2 A projecting part of a human or animal body such as a leg, arm, or wing. OE. ▸b *spec.* A leg of an animal or person; (now *joc.*) a leg of an object. LME.

C. BLACKWOOD He had an artificial limb, for he had lost a leg in the war. M. SCAMMELL They climbed down from . . the lorries and stretched their stiff limbs. **b** J. F. COOPER His limbs were guarded with long leggings.

3 Orig., a member; a section, a branch; an element, a component part. Now only, a member of something regarded metaphorically as a body. OE.

A. W. KINGLAKE An army is but the limb of a nation.

4 A large branch of a tree. OE.

5 *spec.* A projecting section of a building; each of the branches of a cross; a member or clause of a sentence; a spur of a mountain range; the part of a compound core of a transformer, electromagnet, etc., on which a coil is wound. L16.

6 [from *devil's limb* etc. below] A mischievous person, esp. a child. *colloq.* E17.

A. WEST Off it, you young limb, and out of there.

7 Either half of an archery bow. E19.

– PHRASES: **devil's limb**, **fiend's limb** †(*a*) an agent or scion of the Devil; (**b**) (now *dial.*) a mischievous wicked person. **life and limb** all the bodily faculties (***with life and limb***, without grave injury). **limb of the Devil**, **limb of Satan**, **limb of hell** = ***devil's limb*** above. **limb of the law** *derog.* a legal functionary; a lawyer, a police officer. **out on a limb** in an isolated or stranded position; at a disadvantage. PHANTOM ***limb***. **tear limb from limb** dismember violently.

– COMB.: **limb-bud** a small protuberance in an embryo from which a limb develops.

■ **limblike** *adjective* resembling (that of) a limb L19.

limb /lɪm/ *noun*[2]. LME.

[ORIGIN Old French & mod. French *limbe* or Latin LIMBUS.]

†**1** = LIMBO *noun*[1] 1. *Scot.* LME–L18.

2 SCIENCE. An edge; *spec.* (***a***) the graduated edge of a scientific instrument, esp. a quadrant; (***b***) the edge of the disc of a celestial object, esp. of the sun and moon. LME. ▸b BOTANY. The lamina or expanded portion of a monopetalous corolla or of a petal or sepal. Also, the lamina or blade of a leaf. M18.

†**3** A border. *rare*. LME.

– COMB.: **limb-darkening** ASTRONOMY the apparent darkening of the face of the sun towards its edge.

limb /lɪm/ *verb trans.* M17.

[ORIGIN from LIMB *noun*[1].]

†**1** *refl.* Provide oneself with limbs. *rare* (Milton). Only in M17.

2 Dismember. L17.

3 Remove branches from (a tree). M19.

Limba /ˈlɪmbə/ *noun*[1] *& adjective.* E20.

[ORIGIN Limba.]

▸ **A** *noun.* Pl. **-s**, same.

1 A member of a W. African people inhabiting Sierra Leone and Guinea. E20.

2 The Niger-Congo language of the Limbas. E20.

▸ **B** *attrib.* or as *adjective.* Of or pertaining to the Limbas or their language. E20.

limba /ˈlɪmbə/ *noun*[2]. M20.

[ORIGIN Gabon name *limbo*.]

(The timber of) a tall W. African hardwood tree, *Terminalia superba*. Also called ***afara***.

limbal /ˈlɪmb(ə)l/ *adjective.* M20.

[ORIGIN from LIMBUS + -AL[1].]

Of or pertaining to the limbus of the cornea.

limbate /ˈlɪmbeɪt/ *adjective.* E19.

[ORIGIN Late Latin *limbatus*, from Latin LIMBUS: see -ATE[2].]

BIOLOGY. Having an edge of a different colour from the rest.

limbeck /ˈlɪmbɛk/ *noun & verb. arch.* LME.

[ORIGIN Aphet. from ALEMBIC.]

▸ **A** *noun.* = ALEMBIC *noun*. LME.

▸ †**B** *verb trans.* = ALEMBIC *verb*; *fig.* rack (the brain). L16–M17.

limbed /lɪmd/ *adjective.* ME.

[ORIGIN from LIMB *noun*[1] + -ED[2].]

Having limbs. Chiefly as 2nd elem. of comb., as ***straight-limbed***, ***well-limbed***, etc.

limber /ˈlɪmbə/ *noun*[1]. Orig. †**lymo(u)r**; also †**limmer**. LME.

[ORIGIN Perh. from Old French & mod. French *limon*, medieval Latin *limo(n-)* shaft.]

1 The shaft of a cart or carriage. *obsolete* exc. *dial.* LME.

2 MILITARY. *sing.* & (orig.) †in *pl.* The detachable forepart of a gun carriage, consisting of two wheels and an axle, a pole for the horses, and a frame which holds one or two ammunition boxes. L15.

– COMB.: **limber-box**, **limber-chest** MILITARY the ammunition box carried by a limber.

limber /ˈlɪmbə/ *noun*[2]. E17.

[ORIGIN Old French & mod. French *lumière* light, limber, from Proto-Romance, from pl. of Latin *luminare* light, lamp, from *lumin-*, *lumen* light.]

NAUTICAL. Each of the holes made in the floor timbers of a ship to allow bilge water to run through to the lowest point for pumping (also more fully ***limber hole***); in *pl.*, any passage serving the same purpose.

– COMB.: ***limber hole***: see above; **limber rope**: passing through the limber holes, and moved to and fro to clear them.

limber /ˈlɪmbə/ *adjective.* M16.

[ORIGIN Perh. from LIMBER *noun*[1] with allus. to the to-and-fro motion of shafts and limbers.]

1 Easily bent; flexible, pliant, supple. M16.

fig.: SHAKES. *Wint. T.* You put me off with limber vows.

2 Of a person, movement, etc.: bending or moving easily; lithe and nimble. L16.

DISRAELI A limber and graceful figure. G. SANTAYANA Selling his polo-ponies, some of which . . were no longer quite keen and limber enough.

3 Limp, flaccid; flabby. Now chiefly *dial.* L16.

R. PRICE A sheriff that can't even serve his wife, limber as beeswax soon's he hits the bed.

– COMB. & SPECIAL COLLOCATIONS: †**limberham** (***a***) a supple-jointed person; *fig.* an obsequious person; (***b***) a foolish man who keeps a mistress, like the hero of Dryden's play *Mr Limberham*; **limberneck** a kind of botulism affecting poultry; **limber pine** a small pine of the Rocky Mountains, *Pinus flexilis*, with flexible branches.

■ **limberly** *adverb* L19. **limberness** *noun* M16.

limber /ˈlɪmbə/ *verb*[1]. M18.

[ORIGIN from LIMBER *adjective*.]

1 *verb trans.* Make limber. Also foll. by *up*. M18.

2 *verb intrans.* Exercise to make oneself limber, esp. in preparation for athletic activity etc. Usu. foll. by *up*. E20.

Successful Slimming A gentle jog or on-the-spot limbering-up.

limber /ˈlɪmbə/ *verb*[2]. M19.

[ORIGIN from LIMBER *noun*[1].]

MILITARY. **1** *verb intrans.* Fasten together the two parts of a gun carriage, as a preparation for moving away. Usu. foll. by *up*. M19.

2 *verb trans.* Attach the limber to (a gun). Usu. foll. by *up*. M19.

limbi *noun* pl. of LIMBUS.

limbic /ˈlɪmbɪk/ *adjective.* L19.

[ORIGIN French *limbique*, formed as LIMB *noun*[2]: see -IC.]

ANATOMY. Designating or pertaining to a lobe of the cerebrum forming the edge of the medial part of the cortex; of or pertaining to the limbic system.

limbic system a part of the brain that includes the limbic lobe and is concerned with basic emotions and with autonomic and olfactory functions.

limbless /ˈlɪmlɪs/ *adjective.* L16.

[ORIGIN from LIMB *noun*[1] + -LESS.]

Having no limbs, or fewer than the normal number of limbs.

limb-meal /ˈlɪmmiːl/ *adverb. arch. & dial.* OE.

[ORIGIN from LIMB *noun*[1] + -MEAL.]

Limb from limb, limb by limb; piecemeal.

limbo /ˈlɪmbəʊ/ *noun*[1]. Pl. **-os**. LME.

[ORIGIN Latin, abl. sing. of LIMBUS, in phrs. like *in limbo*, *e* (= out of) *limbo*.]

1 CHRISTIAN CHURCH. A region supposed in some beliefs to exist on the border of Hell as the abode of the just who died before Christ's coming and of unbaptized infants. LME. ▸†b Hell, Hades. L16–M17.

2 Prison, confinement. Formerly also, pawn. *slang.* L16.

3 An unfavourable place or condition, likened to limbo; *esp.* a condition of neglect or oblivion to which people or things are consigned when regarded as superseded, useless, or absurd; an intermediate or indeterminate condition; a state of inaction or inattention pending some future event. M17.

E. HUXLEY Legally, the Irish occupy a curious limbo. U. LE GUIN A fever that . . left him in a limbo between reason and unreason. JAN MORRIS Hav remained in a kind of limbo until . . the League of Nations declared its mandate. *Independent* These prisoners are totally in limbo . . No one is responsible for their welfare.

– COMB.: †**limbo-lake** the abode of spirits or tormented souls.

limbo /ˈlɪmbəʊ/ *noun*[2]. Pl. **-os**. L19.

[ORIGIN Zulu *ulembu* web, limbo.]

S. AFR. HISTORY. A kind of coarse calico.

limbo /ˈlɪmbəʊ/ *noun*[3]. Pl. **-os**. M20.

[ORIGIN from LIMBER *adjective*, *verb*[1].]

A W. Indian dance in which the dancer bends backwards and passes under a horizontal bar progressively lowered to just above the ground.

limbric /ˈlɪmbrɪk/ *noun.* M20.

[ORIGIN Unknown: *-bric* perh. from CAMBRIC.]

A closely woven cotton cloth of light to medium weight.

Limbu /ˈlɪmbuː/ *noun & adjective.* E19.

[ORIGIN Limbu.]

▸ **A** *noun.* Pl. **-s**, same.

1 A member of a people of eastern Nepal. E19.

2 The Tibeto-Burman language of this people. E20.

L

▸ **B** *attrib.* or as *adjective*. Of or pertaining to the Limbus or their language. M19.

Limburger /ˈlɪmbəːɡə/ *noun*. M19.
[ORIGIN Dutch & German, from *Limburg*, a province of NE Belgium: see -ER[1].]
A soft white cheese with a characteristic strong smell, orig. made in Limburg. Also ***Limburger cheese***.

limburgite /ˈlɪmbəːɡʌɪt/ *noun*. L19.
[ORIGIN from *Limburg*, a hamlet in Baden-Württemberg, Germany + -ITE[1].]
GEOLOGY. A dark, very basic extrusive igneous rock consisting of phenocrysts of pyroxene and olivine in an alkali-rich glassy groundmass.

limbus /ˈlɪmbəs/ *noun*. Pl. **-bi** /-bʌɪ/. LME.
[ORIGIN Latin = edge, border, (in medieval Latin) region on the border of hell.]
1 = LIMBO *noun*[1] 1. Now *rare*. LME.
2 *techn.* A border, a margin; *spec.* (*ANATOMY*) the margin of the cornea; *BOTANY* = LIMB *noun*[2] 2b. L17.

lime /lʌɪm/ *noun*[1].
[ORIGIN Old English *līm* corresp. to Middle Dutch *līm* (Dutch *lijm*), Old High German *līm* (German *Leim*), Old Norse *lím*, from Germanic var. of base of LOAM *noun*, ult. rel. to Latin *limus* mud.]
1 Orig., any adhesive substance, e.g. glue, paste. Later *spec.* = BIRDLIME *noun* 1; *fig.* a thing that entraps or holds a person. Now *poet.* OE.
2 Mortar or cement used in building. Freq. coupled with *stone*. *obsolete* exc. *Scot.* OE.

> SHAKES. *Rich. II* King Richard lies Within the limits of yon lime and stone.

3 The alkaline earth, calcium oxide, a brittle white caustic solid which is obtained by heating limestone, combines with water with the evolution of much heat, and is used as a refractory and a constituent of mortar, a source of slaked lime, and in many industrial processes; also called ***quicklime***. Also, slaked lime; (in phrs.) calcium; *AGRICULTURE* any calcium-containing fertilizer. OE.

> L. MACNEICE No lime has been laid on the land for forty years.

4 A vat containing a solution of lime for removing the hair from skins; such a solution. L19.
– PHRASES: **carbonate of lime** *arch.* calcium carbonate (cf. LIMESTONE). **lime and hair** a kind of plasterer's cement to which hair is added to bind the mixture closely together. ***white lime***: see WHITE *adjective*.
– COMB.: **lime-ash** *dial.* a composition of ashes and lime used as a rough kind of flooring for kitchens etc.; **limeburner** a person whose occupation is calcining limestone to obtain lime; **lime-cast** a covering or layer of lime mortar; **limekiln** a kiln in which limestone is calcined to obtain lime; **limepit** (*a*) a pit where limestone is quarried or calcined; (*b*) a pit containing lime for steeping hides to remove hair or fur; **lime-pot** (*a*) a pot for holding lime, birdlime, or limewash; †(*b*) a pot in which limestone was calcined; **lime-rock** limestone; **lime-rubbish** broken mortar from old walls etc. used as a dressing for land; **lime-sink** a rounded depression in the earth found in limestone districts; **lime soap** a mixture of insoluble calcium salts of fatty acids formed as a precipitate when soap is used in hard water, manufactured for various industrial purposes; **lime-soda** *adjective* designating a process for softening water by treatment with lime and sodium carbonate; **lime sulphur** an insecticide and fungicide containing calcium polysulphides which is made by boiling lime and sulphur in water; **lime-twig** *noun* & *verb* (*a*) *noun* a twig smeared with birdlime for catching birds; †(*b*) *verb trans.* entangle, ensnare; **limewash** *noun* & *verb* (*a*) *noun* a mixture of lime and water used for coating walls etc.; (*b*) *verb trans.* whitewash with such a mixture; **lime water** a solution of calcium hydroxide, formerly used medicinally; **lime-work** †(*a*) stucco; (*b*) = ***lime-works*** below; **lime-works** a place where lime is made.

lime /lʌɪm/ *noun*[2]. E17.
[ORIGIN Alt. of *line* var. of LIND.]
(More fully ***lime tree***) any of various deciduous trees of the genus *Tilia* (family Tiliaceae), esp. *T.* × *vulgaris*, a common ornamental tree with heart-shaped leaves and many small fragrant yellowish flowers; also called ***linden***. Also, the wood of these trees.

lime /lʌɪm/ *noun*[3]. M17.
[ORIGIN French from Spanish *lima* from Arabic *līma*: cf. LEMON *noun*[1].]
1 A globular citrus fruit that is smaller and greener than the lemon and has a more acid taste; the small spiny tree, *Citrus aurantiifolia* (family Rutaceae), of tropical regions which bears this fruit. M17. ▸**b** Any of various other trees, esp. of the family Rutaceae. M18.
b sweet lime a tree, *Citrus limetta*, resembling the lemon but with an insipidly sweet fruit.
2 *ellipt.* Lime-green. E20.
3 *ellipt.* Lime juice. Earlier in LIMEY. M20.
gin and lime etc.
– COMB.: **lime-green** *noun* & *adjective* (of) a pale green colour like that of a lime; **lime juice** (a preparation of) the juice of the lime as a drink, formerly given to prevent scurvy on long sea voyages; **lime-juicer** (cf. LIMEY) †(*a*) *Austral.* & *NZ slang* a person who has recently emigrated to Australia from Britain; (*b*) *US* a British ship or sailor; **lime marmalade**: made from limes; **lime punch**: made with lime juice instead of more usual lemon juice.

lime /lʌɪm/ *noun*[4]. *colloq.* L19.
[ORIGIN Abbreviation.]
= LIMELIGHT. Freq. in *pl.*

lime /lʌɪm/ *verb*[1]. LOE.
[ORIGIN from LIME *noun*[1].]
▸**I 1** *verb trans.* Join together, unite. LOE.
2 *verb trans.* Smear with a sticky substance, *spec.* with birdlime to catch birds. ME.
3 *verb trans.* Catch with birdlime. Freq. *fig.*, entrap, ensnare. *arch.* ME.
†**4** *verb trans.* Foul, defile. LME–L16.
▸**II** †**5** *verb trans.* Coat with limewash. LME–E17.
†**6** *verb intrans.* Put lime into wine. *rare* (Shakes.). Only in L16.
7 *verb trans.* & *intrans.* Dress (land, crops, etc.) with lime to improve growth. E17.
8 *verb trans.* Steep (skins) in lime and water. L17.
9 *verb trans.* Give (wood) a bleached effect by treating it with lime. Chiefly as ***limed*** *ppl adjective*. M20.

lime /lʌɪm/ *verb*[2] *intrans.* *W. Indian.* L20.
[ORIGIN Unknown: rel. to LIMER *noun*[3].]
Spend one's time idly in the street.

limeade /lʌɪmˈeɪd/ *noun*. L19.
[ORIGIN from LIME *noun*[3] + -ADE.]
A drink made from lime juice sweetened with sugar.

Limehouse /ˈlʌɪmhaʊs/ *verb intrans.* *slang.* E20.
[ORIGIN A district of E. London, England, where Lloyd George made such speeches.]
Make fiery speeches, esp. political ones.

limeless /ˈlʌɪmlɪs/ *adjective*. E18.
[ORIGIN from LIME *noun*[1] + -LESS.]
Having or containing no lime (calcium oxide).

limelight /ˈlʌɪmlʌɪt/ *noun* & *verb*. E19.
[ORIGIN from LIME *noun*[1] + LIGHT *noun*.]
▸**A** *noun*. **1** The intense white light produced by heating lime in an oxy-hydrogen flame, formerly used in theatres to light up important players and scenes and so direct attention to them; a lamp producing such light (cf. DRUMMOND LIGHT). E19.
2 ***the limelight***, the full glare of publicity; people's full attention. L19.

> E. LEWIS We earned . . a nice little sum out of Tutankhamen when he was in the limelight. P. USTINOV A puppy will steal the limelight from even a well-loved dog.

▸**B** *verb trans.* Pa. t. & pple **-lighted**, **-lit**. Illuminate with limelight or other strong light; make a focus of publicity or attention. E20.

limen /ˈlʌɪmɛn, ˈliː-/ *noun*. M17.
[ORIGIN Latin = threshold; in sense 2 translating German *Schwelle*.]
†**1** A threshold. Only in M17.
2 *PSYCHOLOGY*. The minimum strength of a stimulus required to produce a sensation; the minimum amount by which one stimulus has to differ from another for the difference to be perceptible. L19.

Limenian /lɪˈmiːnɪən/ *noun*. E19.
[ORIGIN from Amer. Spanish *limeño*, *-ña*, from *Lima*: see below, -IAN.]
A native or inhabitant of Lima, the capital of Peru.
■ ***limeño*** /liˈmeɲo/ *noun*, pl. **-os** /-ɔs/, a male Limenian M20. ***limeña*** /liˈmeɲa/ *noun* a female Limenian L19.

limer /ˈliːmə/ *noun*[1]. *obsolete* exc. *hist.* Also †**leam-**. ME.
[ORIGIN Anglo-Norman = Old French *liemier* (mod. *limier*), formed as LYAM.]
A hound; a bloodhound; a mongrel.

limer /ˈlʌɪmə/ *noun*[2]. E17.
[ORIGIN from LIME *verb*[1] + -ER[1].]
A person who limes something; a person who sets snares with birdlime; a person who limewashes walls etc. Also, a brush used for limewashing.

limer /ˈlʌɪmə/ *noun*[3]. *W. Indian.* L20.
[ORIGIN Unknown: rel. to LIME *verb*[2].]
A person who spends time idly in the streets.

Limerick /ˈlɪm(ə)rɪk/ *adjective* & *noun*. E19.
[ORIGIN The chief town of County Limerick, Ireland.]
▸**A** *adjective*. **1** Designating gloves of fine leather formerly made at Limerick. E19.
2 Designating (the pattern of) a fish hook in which the wire is bent abruptly through a large angle behind the barb but thereafter is bent more shallowly to the point at which it continues as the straight shank. E19.
3 Designating a type of embroidered lace originally made at Limerick. M19.
▸**B** *noun*. **1** A Limerick fish hook. M19.
2 Limerick lace. L19.
3 (Usu. **l-**.) A humorous or comic five-line stanza with the rhyme scheme *aabba*, there being three feet in the *a* lines and two in the *b* lines. L19.

limes /ˈlʌɪmiːz/ *noun*. Pl. **limites** /ˈlʌɪmɪtiːz/. M16.
[ORIGIN Latin = LIMIT *noun*.]
Now *ARCHAEOLOGY*. A boundary; *spec.* the boundary of the Roman Empire, esp. in the north of Europe.

limestone /ˈlʌɪmstəʊn/ *noun* & *adjective*. LME.
[ORIGIN from LIME *noun*[1] + STONE *noun*.]
▸**A** *noun*. A sedimentary rock composed chiefly of calcium carbonate, which yields lime when calcined and is used as a building material and in the making of cement; a species or (formerly) a piece of this rock. LME.
▸**B** *attrib.* or as *adjective*. Made or consisting of limestone. L17.
LITHOGRAPHIC ***limestone***. *MILIOLITE* ***limestone***.
– COMB.: **limestone fern**, **limestone polypody** a fern of limestone rocks and screes, *Gymnocarpium robertianum*, with greyish glandular fronds.

Limey /ˈlʌɪmi/ *adjective* & *noun*. *colloq. derog.* Also **l-**. L19.
[ORIGIN from LIME *noun*[3] (with ref. to *lime juice*) + -Y[6].]
▸**A** *adjective*. In former British colonies and the US: English, British. L19.

> D. LODGE Can't understand a word because of the guy's Limey accent.

▸**B** *noun*. **1** An English or British ship or sailor; an Englishman, a Briton. *N. Amer.* E20.
2 In some former British colonies: an English immigrant. M20.

limicole /ˈlʌɪmɪkəʊl/ *noun*. M20.
[ORIGIN from Latin *limus* mud + -I- + -COLE.]
An oligochaete worm living in mud or water.

limicoline /lʌɪˈmɪkəlʌɪn, -lɪn/ *adjective*. L19.
[ORIGIN from mod. Latin *Limicolae* (see below), formed as LIMICOLE: see -INE[1].]
Of or pertaining to the suborder Charadrii of waders or shorebirds (formerly the order Limicolae).

liminal /ˈlɪmɪn(ə)l/ *adjective*. L19.
[ORIGIN from Latin *limin-* LIMEN + -AL[1].]
1 Of, pertaining to, or constituting a transitional or initial stage of a process. Also, marginal, incidental, insignificant. L19.
2 Of, pertaining to, or situated at a limen; occupying a position on, or on both sides of, a boundary or threshold. L19.
■ **limiˈnality** *noun* M20.

liminary /ˈlɪmɪn(ə)ri/ *adjective*. Now *rare*. E17.
[ORIGIN French *liminaire* from Latin *liminaris*, formed as LIMINAL: see -ARY[2].]
Preliminary, preparatory.

liminess /ˈlʌɪmɪnɪs/ *noun*. E20.
[ORIGIN from LIMY + -NESS.]
The quality or state of being limy.

limit /ˈlɪmɪt/ *noun*. LME.
[ORIGIN Latin *limit-*, *limes*.]
1 Orig., a boundary, a frontier; an object serving to define a boundary, a landmark. Now *spec.* a boundary or terminal point considered as confining or restricting. Usu. in *pl.* LME.

> L. CODY They reached the lower limits of Hampstead Heath. JAYNE PHILLIPS After dusk you could get outside the city limits.

2 Any of the fixed points between which the possible or permitted extent, amount, duration, etc., of something is confined; a bound which may not be passed or beyond which something ceases to be possible or allowable. LME.

> H. JAMES He had perhaps reached the limits of legitimate experimentation. R. MACAULAY There *is* a limit to the patience of bishops. H. MOORE There was no barrier, no limit to what a young provincial student could . . do.

†**3** A tract, a region; in *pl.*, the bounds, territories. L15–L18.
4 Limitation, restriction within limits. Chiefly in ***without limit***. L16.
5 Prescribed time; the prescribed period of repose after childbearing. *rare* (Shakes.). E17.
6 *ASTRONOMY*. The greatest heliocentric latitude of a planet. E18.
7 *MATH.* A finite quantity to which the sum of a converging series progressively approximates; a fixed value to which a function can be made to approach continually, so as to differ from it by less than any assignable quantity; either of the two values of a variable between which a definite integral is taken. M18.
8 A greatest or smallest permitted or allowed amount; *spec.* (*a*) *CARDS* an agreed maximum stake or bet; (*b*) the maximum concentration of alcohol in the blood that the law allows in the driver of a motor vehicle. M19.

> L. DUNCAN Punished to the full limit of the law. R. LARDNER Two is my limit and I've already exceeded it. *Daily Express* Divorcee Lorna was double the legal limit.

age limit, ***speed limit***, ***weight limit***, etc.
9 The worst imaginable or tolerable. *colloq.* E20.

> G. B. SHAW Really! your father does seem to be about the limit.

– PHRASES: ***frozen limit***: see FROZEN *ppl adjective* 2. **go the limit** behave in an extreme way; last the stated number of rounds or the full time, as in a boxing match; allow sexual intercourse. ***limit of*** *PROPORTIONALITY*. **off-limits** out of bounds; forbidden. **over the limit** having exceeded a prescribed limit. ***proportional limit***: see PROPORTIONAL *adjective* 1. ***Rayleigh limit***: see RAYLEIGH 1. ***Roche limit***, ***Roche's limit***: see ROCHE *noun*[2]. ***territorial limit***: see TERRITORIAL *adjective*. ***the sky is the limit***: see SKY *noun*. **within limits** to a moderate extent; with some degree of freedom. **without limit** unrestrictedly.
– COMB.: **limit bid** *BRIDGE* a call which shows that the strength of the caller's hand does not exceed a certain value; **limit dog**: shown in a class limited to dogs having certain required qualifications; **limit gauge** *ENGINEERING*: used for determining whether a dimension of a manufactured item falls within the specified tolerance; **limit man**: who receives the longest start allowed in a handicap;

limit point *MATH.* a point every neighbourhood of which contains a point belonging to a given set; **limit switch** *ENGINEERING* a switch preventing the travel of an object past some predetermined point and mechanically operated by the motion of the object itself.

limit /ˈlɪmɪt/ *verb.* LME.
[ORIGIN Old French & mod. French *limiter* or Latin *limitare*, formed as LIMIT *noun*.]
1 *verb trans.* Assign, make *over*, within limits (also foll. by *away*); appoint, fix definitely; specify. (Foll. by *to*, *upon*, *to do*.) Now *rare* or *obsolete*. LME. ▸†**b** Appoint (a person) *to* an office; assign (a duty) *to* a person. LME–M17. ▸†**c** Allot, apportion. Usu. foll. by *out*. M16–M17.

MARVELL Neither do I believe we can finish it.. within the time limited us.

2 *verb trans.* Confine within limits, set bounds to; restrict. (Foll. by *to*.) LME.

G. M. TREVELYAN The Ten Hours Bill limited the daily work of women and youths in textile factories. L. CODY Such space as there was was further limited by green filing-cabinets. J. MCDOUGALL I shall limit mystery here to giving a glimpse into a psychic scene.

3 *verb trans.* Serve as a limit or boundary to; mark off *from*. Now *rare* exc. as ***limiting ppl adjective***. L16.

A. HOLMES Domes and basins represent the limiting cases in which the beds dip in all directions.. from, or.. towards, the centre. *Science News* This chamber is the limiting factor in rocket design.

■ **limitable** *adjective* L16.

limitary /ˈlɪmɪt(ə)ri/ *adjective.* E17.
[ORIGIN Senses 1, 3 from LIMIT *noun* + -ARY[2]; sense 2 from Latin *limitaris*, formed as LIMIT *noun*.]
1 Subject to limits; limited, restricted. E17.
2 Of or pertaining to a limit or boundary; situated on a boundary. M17.
3 Serving as a limit or boundary; limiting, confining, containing. (Foll. by *of*.) E19.

limitate /ˈlɪmɪteɪt/ *pa. pple & ppl adjective.* L16.
[ORIGIN Latin *limitatus* pa. pple of *limitare* LIMIT *verb*: see -ATE[2].]
▸ †**I** *pa. pple* **1** Limited. Only in L16.
▸ **II** *ppl adjective.* **2** Of land: divided up by boundaries. *rare.* M19.
3 *BOTANY.* Bounded by a distinct line. L19.

limitation /lɪmɪˈteɪʃ(ə)n/ *noun.* LME.
[ORIGIN Latin *limitatio(n-)*, from *limitat-* pa. ppl stem of *limitare* LIMIT *verb*: see -ATION.]
1 The action or an act of limiting. LME. ▸†**b** *spec.* The action of determining the boundaries of a country or the contour of a figure. L16–E18.
†**2 a** An allotted space; the district or circuit of an itinerant officer or preaching friar; the region belonging to a particular nation; *fig.* one's allotted sphere. LME–M16. ▸**b** An allotted time. *rare* (Shakes.). Only in E17.
3 A point or respect in which a thing, esp. a person's ability, is limited; a limiting provision or circumstance. E16.

H. J. S. MAINE He was heir to the earldom of Tyrone according to the limitations of the patent. E. F. BENSON 'He does love discussion,' said Lucia. 'I know... Don't you?'.. 'I like it, with limitations.' P. ROSE Mr Taylor.. considering his limitations, was behaving remarkably well.

have one's limitations, **have its limitations** lack talent or ability in some respects.
4 = LIMIT *noun* 1, 2. Freq. in *pl.* E16.
5 The condition of being limited. L16.

C. LYELL The limitation of groups of distinct species to regions separated.. by certain natural barriers.

6 *LAW.* The legal specification of a period within which an action must be brought or a period for which an estate shall continue or a law operate; a period so specified. L16. **statute of limitations**: prescribing a period of limitation for the bringing of actions of certain kinds.

limitative /ˈlɪmɪtətɪv/ *adjective.* M16.
[ORIGIN medieval Latin *limitativus*, from *limitat-*: see LIMITATION, -IVE.]
Tending to limit; limiting, restrictive.

limited /ˈlɪmɪtɪd/ *adjective & noun.* M16.
[ORIGIN from LIMIT *verb* + -ED[1]. Earlier in UNLIMITED.]
▸ **A** *adjective.* †**1** Appointed, fixed. M16–M17.
2 Confined within definite limits; restricted in scope, extent, amount, etc.; (of an amount or number) small; (of an income) low; (of monarchy, government, etc.) exercised under limitations of power prescribed by a constitution. E17.

E. BOWEN Her time in London was limited. *New Yorker* The Bicentennial carpet is now being shown at a limited number of fine stores. M. HUNTER Because of the narrator's limited vocabulary, there is no scope for.. adventure in language. E. PIZZEY Like many young working-class girls.. the choices open to her were very limited. *Which?* A very limited amount of wine—say one white and one red.

– SPECIAL COLLOCATIONS: **limited company**: whose members' liability for its debts are legally limited to the extent of their investment. **limited edition** an edition of a book, or reproduction of an object, limited to some specific number of copies. **limited liability** *LAW* liability that is limited by law (***limited liability company*** = ***limited company*** above). **limited partner** a partner in a company etc. whose liability towards its debts is legally limited and who does not take an active part in its running. **limited partnership** a partnership in which the liability of some partners is legally limited to the extent of their investment. **limited train** *US* a train consisting of a small number of cars and making few stops; an express train. **limited war**: in which the weapons used, the nations or territory involved, or the objectives pursued are restricted.
▸ **B** *noun.* **1** A limited train. *US colloq.* L19.
2 A limited company. E20.
■ **limitedly** *adverb* E17. **limitedness** *noun* M17.

limiter /ˈlɪmɪtə/ *noun.* LME.
[ORIGIN from LIMIT *verb* + -ER[1].]
1 A friar licensed to beg within certain limits. Also ***friar limiter***. *obsolete* exc. *hist.* LME.
2 A person who or thing which limits something or someone. L15. ▸**b** *ELECTRONICS.* A device whose output is restricted to a certain range of values irrespective of the size of the input. E20.

limites *noun* pl. of LIMES.

limitless /ˈlɪmɪtlɪs/ *adjective.* L16.
[ORIGIN from LIMIT *noun* + -LESS.]
Having or admitting of no limits; unlimited; unbounded, unrestricted.

JANET MORGAN The garden seemed limitless to Agatha, most of whose childhood world it composed. J. M. COETZEE There are times when I feel my strength to be limitless.

■ **limitlessly** *adverb* M19. **limitlessness** *noun* M19.

limitrophe /ˈlɪmɪtrəʊf/ *noun & adjective.* L16.
[ORIGIN French from late Latin *limitrophus*, formed as LIMIT *noun* + Greek *-trophos* supporting, from *trephein* support, nourish.]
▸ **A** *noun.* A borderland. Long *rare.* L16.
▸ **B** *adjective.* Situated on a frontier; adjacent *to* another country. M18.

limma /ˈlɪmə/ *noun.* L17.
[ORIGIN Late Latin from Greek *leimma* remnant, lemma, from *leipein* leave.]
MUSIC. The semitone of the Pythagorean scale.

limmer /ˈlɪmə/ *noun*[1] *& adjective. Scot. & N. English.* LME.
[ORIGIN Perh. rel. to LIMB *noun*[1].]
▸ **A** *noun.* **1** A criminal or disreputable person. LME.
2 A prostitute or promiscuous woman. M16.
▸ **B** *adjective.* Disreputable, dishonest. E16.

†**limmer** *noun*[2] var. of LIMBER *noun*[1].

limmu /ˈlɪmuː/ *noun.* M19.
[ORIGIN Assyrian.]
The year of office to which an Assyrian eponym gave his name; the office of an Assyrian eponym.

limn /lɪm/ *verb.* Now *literary.* LME.
[ORIGIN Alt. of LUMINE.]
1 *verb trans. & †intrans.* Illuminate (a manuscript etc.). Now *rare.* LME.
†**2** *verb trans.* Adorn or embellish with gold or bright colour; depict in gold etc. M16–M17.
3 *verb trans. & †intrans.* Paint (a picture or portrait); portray (a subject); *fig.* depict, make visible. Formerly *spec.* paint in watercolour or distemper. L16.

H. ROBBINS Rocco's face was limned in the dim glow from the match. J. STRACHEY The image of the loosened rose-spray clearly limned in the rain pool.

4 *verb trans.* Portray or represent (esp. a person) in words. L16.

Publishers Weekly Virginia Woolf's sharp wit, which could limn Ottoline Morell perfectly.

limner /ˈlɪmnə/ *noun.* ME.
[ORIGIN Alt. of †*luminer*, from LUMINE + -ER[2].]
1 *hist.* An illuminator of manuscripts. ME.
2 A painter, *esp.* a portrait painter. Now *literary.* L16.

limnetic /lɪmˈnɛtɪk/ *adjective.* L19.
[ORIGIN from Greek *limnētēs* living in marshes, from *limnē*: see LIMNO-, -IC.]
Of, pertaining to, or living in the open part of a freshwater lake or pond, away from the margin or bottom; = PELAGIC 4.

limnic /ˈlɪmnɪk/ *adjective.* M20.
[ORIGIN German *limnisch*, from Greek *limnē*: see LIMNO-, -IC.]
GEOLOGY. Formed or laid down in an inland body of standing fresh water such as a lake or a swamp.

limning /ˈlɪmɪŋ, ˈlɪmnɪŋ/ *noun.* LME.
[ORIGIN from LIMN + -ING[1].]
1 a Painting. LME. ▸**b** A painting, a portrait. L17.
2 The action or art of illuminating manuscripts etc. L15.

limno- /ˈlɪmnəʊ/ *combining form.*
[ORIGIN from Greek *limnē* pool, marshy lake + -O-.]
Of, pertaining to, or occurring in fresh water, esp. fresh standing water.
■ **limnograph** *noun* an apparatus for automatically recording the variations of level in a lake L19. **limˈnometer** *noun* an apparatus for measuring the variations of level in a lake M19. **limnoplankton** *noun* plankton found in fresh water L19.

limnology /lɪmˈnɒlədʒi/ *noun.* L19.
[ORIGIN from LIMNO- + -LOGY.]
The physical, chemical, geological, and biological aspects of lakes and other bodies of fresh standing water or (more widely) all inland water; the branch of science that deals with these.
■ **limnoˈlogical** *adjective* L19. **limnoˈlogically** *adverb* from the point of view of limnology E20. **limnologist** *noun* E20.

limnoria /lɪmˈnɔːrɪə/ *noun.* M19.
[ORIGIN mod. Latin from Greek *Limnoreia* water nymph.]
A marine isopod crustacean of the genus *Limnoria*, which includes *L. lignorum*, the gribble.

limo /ˈlɪməʊ/ *noun. colloq.* Pl. **-os**. M20.
[ORIGIN Abbreviation.]
= LIMOUSINE.

Limoges /lɪˈməʊʒ/ *adjective.* M19.
[ORIGIN See below.]
Designating painted enamels, porcelain, etc., made in Limoges, a city in central France.

limon /limɔ̃/ *noun.* L19.
[ORIGIN French from Latin *limus* mud.]
GEOLOGY. A fine sandy soil, probably of similar origin to loess, which is widespread in northern France and Belgium.

limoncello /lɪmɒnˈtʃɛləʊ/ *noun.* L20.
[ORIGIN Italian, from *limone* lemon + dim. suffix *-cello*.]
A lemon-flavoured Italian liqueur.

limonene /ˈlɪməniːn/ *noun.* E20.
[ORIGIN German *Limonen*, from *Limone* lemon: see -ENE.]
A colourless liquid terpene, $C_{10}H_{16}$, occurring in lemon, orange, and other essential oils and used in flavouring, as a solvent and wetting agent, etc.

limonite /ˈlʌɪmənʌɪt/ *noun.* E19.
[ORIGIN German *Limonit*, prob. from Greek *leimōn* meadow, after the earlier German name *Wiesenerz* lit. 'meadow-ore': see -ITE[1].]
MINERALOGY. An amorphous secondary material now recognized as a mixture of hydrous ferric oxides and important as an iron ore.
■ **limoˈnitic** *adjective* containing or resembling limonite L19.

limonium /lɪˈməʊnɪəm/ *noun.* M16.
[ORIGIN mod. Latin = Latin *limonion* from Greek *leimōnion* neut. of *leimōnios*, from *leimōn* meadow: see -IUM.]
Orig., any wintergreen of the genus *Pyrola*, esp. *P. rotundifolia*. Now, any plant of the genus *Limonium* (family Plumbaginaceae); sea lavender.

limous /ˈlʌɪməs/ *adjective.* Now *rare.* LME.
[ORIGIN from Latin *limosus*, from *limus* mud: see -OUS.]
Muddy; slimy.

Limousin /ˈlɪmʊzã/ *noun & adjective.* M17.
[ORIGIN See below.]
▸ **A** *noun.* **1** A native or inhabitant of the former province of Limousin in central France or of the region round Limoges; the dialect of this region. M17.
2 (An animal of) a French breed of beef cattle. L20.
▸ **B** *adjective.* Of or pertaining to Limousin. E18.

limousine /ˈlɪməziːn, lɪməˈziːn/ *noun.* E20.
[ORIGIN French, from fem. of LIMOUSIN; orig. a caped cloak worn in Limousin.]
1 A large luxurious car, often with a separate compartment for the driver. Orig., a car with a roof that projected over an outside driving seat. E20.
2 A passenger vehicle for carrying people over a fixed route to and from an airport. *N. Amer.* M20.
– COMB.: **limousine liberal** *US* a wealthy liberal.

limp /lɪmp/ *noun*[1]. M18.
[ORIGIN Unknown.]
MINING. An instrument for separating refuse from ore in the operation of jigging.

limp /lɪmp/ *noun*[2]. E19.
[ORIGIN from LIMP *verb*.]
The action of limping; a limping gait; a propensity to limp.

Daily Telegraph The little girl has a limp in one leg and will undergo physiotherapy.

limp /lɪmp/ *adjective.* E18.
[ORIGIN Prob. of dial. origin; perh. ult. rel. to LIMP *verb*, the basic sense being 'hanging loose'.]
1 Lacking firmness or stiffness, flaccid; flexible, pliant; (of a fabric) unstiffened. E18.

E. WAUGH The Emperor's colours hung limp in the sultry air. K. KESEY His breath explodes out of him, and he falls back limp against the wall.

2 Designating or having a book cover that is not stiffened with board. M19.
3 Lacking will, firmness, strictness, nervous energy, etc. M19.

E. WAUGH He talked five hours and left me limp. P. KURTH The failure of the tribunal.. to confront its experts with these limp, layman's objections.

– SPECIAL COLLOCATIONS & COMB.: **limp wrist** *US slang* a homosexual or effeminate man; **limp-wrist**, **limp-wristed** *adjectives* (*slang*) effeminate; weak, feeble.
■ **limply** *adverb* M19. **limpness** *noun* M18.

L

limp /lɪmp/ *verb intrans.* LME.
[ORIGIN Prob. back-form. from LIMPHALT: cf. Middle High German *limpfen*.]
†1 Fall short *of*. Only in LME.
2 Walk lamely. L16.

J. CONRAD The man limped down the ladder. J. FRAME Tom eased himself from his bed and limped from the room. *fig.*: G. GREENE How slowly time limps by in childhood.

3 Of verse: be metrically defective. M17.
4 Of a damaged ship, aircraft, etc.: proceed slowly or with difficulty. E20.

J. BARTH A divided rig . . would leave . . hope of limping bravely to port.

■ **limper** *noun* M17. **limping** *adjective* that limps; LAW (of a relationship or status) legal or recognized in one country but not in another: L16. **limpingly** *adverb* L16. **limpingness** *noun* M18.

limpet /ˈlɪmpɪt/ *noun*.
[ORIGIN Old English *lempedu* (cf. Old High German *lampfrida*) from medieval Latin *lampreda*, *-rida* limpet: see LAMPREY.]
1 Any of various marine gastropod molluscs with a shallow conical shell and a broad muscular foot that sticks tightly to rocks; *esp.* (more fully ***common limpet***) *Patella vulgata*. OE. ▸**b** *fig.* A clinging person. E20.
2 In full ***limpet bomb***, ***limpet mine***, etc. A type of explosive device attached magnetically to a ship's hull. M20.

†**limphalt** *adjective*. OE–M16.
[ORIGIN from Germanic base from Indo-European base also of Sanskrit *lámbate* hangs down or loose, sinks + HALT *adjective*.]
Lame, limping.

limpid /ˈlɪmpɪd/ *adjective*. LME.
[ORIGIN Latin *limpidus*, prob. rel. to *lympha* LYMPH.]
1 (Esp. of liquids) free from turbidity or suspended matter; clear, transparent. LME.

WILKIE COLLINS The eyes are of that soft, limpid, turquoise blue. D. H. LAWRENCE The morning was of a lovely limpid gold colour. E. WAUGH Two corpses . . rotated slowly . . in the limpid morning sunlight.

2 *transf.* & *fig.* Free from obscurity, complication, or guile; pure. M17.

B. PYM The limpid notes of a recorder playing 'Brother James's Air'.

■ **limˈpidity** *noun* M17. **limpidly** *adverb* L19. **limpidness** *noun* M17.

L

limpish /ˈlɪmpɪʃ/ *adjective*. L19.
[ORIGIN from LIMP *adjective* + -ISH¹.]
Somewhat limp.

limpkin /ˈlɪm(p)kɪn/ *noun*. L19.
[ORIGIN from LIMP *verb* + -KIN, with ref. to the bird's limping gait.]
A wading bird, *Aramus guarauna*, of S. America and south-eastern N. America, similar to but larger than a rail and living chiefly in marshes.

limpsy /ˈlɪm(p)si/ *adjective*. *dial.* & *US*. E19.
[ORIGIN from LIMP *adjective* + -SY.]
Limp.

limulus /ˈlɪmjʊləs/ *noun*. Pl. **-li** /-lʌɪ, -liː/. M19.
[ORIGIN mod. Latin from Latin *limulus* somewhat oblique, from *limus* oblique.]
A horseshoe crab of the genus *Limulus*.
■ **limuloid** *adjective* & *noun* (a crustacean) resembling a horseshoe crab M19.

limy /ˈlʌɪmi/ *adjective*. M16.
[ORIGIN from LIME *noun*¹ + -Y¹.]
1 Besmeared with birdlime. M16.
2 Of the nature of lime (calcium oxide), resembling lime. M17.
3 Consisting of or containing lime. L17.

lin /lɪn/ *verb*. Long *obsolete* exc. *Scot.* & *N. English*. Infl. **-nn-**.
[ORIGIN Old English *linnan* = Old High German *bilinnan*, Old Norse *linna*, Gothic *aflinnan*, from Germanic, from base also of LITHE *adjective*.]
†1 *verb intrans.* Cease (*to do*), leave off; desist (*from*); (of the wind) drop. OE–E18. ▸**b** Fail, omit, *to do*. Only in E18.
2 *verb trans.* Cease from, leave off, discontinue. ME.

linable /ˈlʌɪnəb(ə)l/ *adjective*. Also **lineable**. L17.
[ORIGIN from LINE *noun*² or *verb*² + -ABLE.]
(Able to be) ranged in a straight line.

linac /ˈlɪnak/ *noun*. M20.
[ORIGIN from *lin*ear *ac*celerator.]
PHYSICS. A linear (i.e. straight) particle accelerator.

linage /ˈlʌɪnɪdʒ/ *noun*. Also **lineage**. L19.
[ORIGIN from LINE *noun*² + -AGE.]
1 Position (of figures) in line. L19.
2 The number of lines in printed or written matter. L19.
3 Payment according to the number of lines in printed or written matter. Also, the charge made (by a newspaper etc.) according to the number of lines occupied by an advertisement etc. L19.

linaloe /lɪˈnaləʊ/ *noun*. Also **linaloa** /lɪnəˈləʊə/. L19.
[ORIGIN Mexican Spanish *lináloe* from Spanish = LIGN-ALOES.]
The aromatic wood of several Mexican trees of the genus *Bursera* (family Burseraceae), esp. *B. aleoxylon*.

linalool /lɪˈnaləʊɒl/ *noun*. L19.
[ORIGIN from LINALOE + -OL.]
CHEMISTRY. A fragrant liquid alcohol, $C_{10}H_{18}O$, found in various natural oils (including those of linaloe, rose, and orange) and used in perfumery.
■ ˈ**linalyl** *noun* the radical $C_{10}H_{17}$· present in ethers and esters of linalool E20.

linamarin /lɪnəˈmarɪn/ *noun*. L19.
[ORIGIN from Latin *linum* flax + *amarus* bitter + -IN¹.]
CHEMISTRY. A bitter, toxic, cyanogenic glucoside which occurs in flax, cassava, and other plants.

linaria /lʌɪˈnɛːrɪə/ *noun*. L16.
[ORIGIN mod. Latin (see below), from Latin *linum* flax (with ref. to the leaf-shape) + *-aria* -ARY¹.]
Any of several plants of the genus *Linaria*, of the figwort family, with spurred flowers and linear leaves; *esp.* yellow toadflax, *L. vulgaris*.

linarite /lɪˈnɑːrʌɪt, ˈlɪnərʌɪt/ *noun*. M19.
[ORIGIN from *Linares*, a town in southern Spain + -ITE¹.]
MINERALOGY. A monoclinic sulphate of lead and copper, $PbCu(SO_4)(OH)_2$, occurring as brilliant blue prisms.

linch /lɪn(t)ʃ/ *noun*¹. Long *obsolete* exc. in comb.
[ORIGIN Old English *lynis* = West Frisian *lins*, Old Saxon *lunisa* (Dutch *luns*, *lens*), Middle High German *luns(e)*, German *Lünse* rel. to Old High German *lun(a)* (German dial. *lunn*, *lon*): cf. Old High German *luning* linchpin.]
A linchpin.
– COMB.: **linch-drawer** *dial.* a tool for drawing out linchpins; **linch-hoop** a ring on the spindle of a carriage axle, held in place by the linchpin; LINCHPIN.

linch /lɪn(t)ʃ/ *noun*². *dial.* Also **lynch**. L16.
[ORIGIN Repr. Old English *hlinc*: see LINK *noun*¹.]
A rising ground; a ridge; a ledge, esp. on the side of a chalk down; an unploughed strip serving as a boundary between fields.

linch /lɪn(t)ʃ/ *verb trans.* L19.
[ORIGIN from LINCH *noun*¹.]
Fasten (as) with a linchpin.

linchpin /ˈlɪn(t)ʃpɪn/ *noun*. Also **lynch-**. LME.
[ORIGIN from LINCH *noun*¹ + PIN *noun*.]
1 A pin passed through an axle end to keep a wheel in position. LME.
2 A person or thing vital to an enterprise, organization, etc. L20.

Lincoln /ˈlɪŋk(ə)n/ *noun*. ME.
[ORIGIN The county town of Lincolnshire, a county in eastern England.]
▸ **I** *attrib.* **1** Designating things originating in or associated with Lincoln. ME.
†**Lincoln farthing** a hearth tax payable at Lincoln. **Lincoln green** a bright green cloth of a kind originally made at Lincoln. **Lincoln imp** a grotesque carving in Lincoln cathedral; an ornament etc. representing this. **Lincoln Longwool** (an animal of) a breed of sheep characterized by its large size and long fleece. **Lincoln Red** (an animal of) a breed of red shorthorn cattle producing both milk and beef. **Lincoln wool** wool from a Lincoln Longwool.
▸ **II** *ellipt.* **2** (An animal of) a variety of sheep originally bred in Lincolnshire. Also, a Lincoln Longwool, a Lincoln Red. M19.

Lincolnesque /lɪŋk(ə)nˈɛsk/ *adjective*. E20.
[ORIGIN from *Lincoln* (see below) + -ESQUE.]
Resembling or having the qualities of Abraham Lincoln (1809–65), sixteenth president of the US.

Lincolnian /lɪŋˈkəʊnɪən/ *adjective*. M19.
[ORIGIN formed as LINCOLNESQUE + -IAN.]
= LINCOLNESQUE.
■ **Lincolniana** /lɪŋkəʊnɪˈɑːnə, lɪŋˌkəʊnɪ-/ *noun pl.* [-ANA] publications or other items concerning or associated with Abraham Lincoln E20.

Lincoln rocker /ˈlɪŋk(ə)n ˌrɒkə/ *noun phr. US*. M20.
[ORIGIN from Abraham *Lincoln* (see LINCOLNESQUE) + ROCKER.]
A type of rocking chair with a straight upholstered back and seat and open arms, popular in the mid 19th cent.

Lincolnshire /ˈlɪŋk(ə)nʃə/ *noun*. E20.
[ORIGIN A county in eastern England.]
Used *attrib.* to designate things originating in or associated with Lincolnshire.
Lincolnshire Curly-Coat, **Lincolnshire Curly-Coated** (an animal of) an extinct breed of pig having a light-coloured curly or woolly coat. **Lincolnshire Longwool** = LINCOLN *Longwool*. **Lincolnshire Red** = LINCOLN *Red*.

lincomycin /lɪŋkə(ʊ)ˈmʌɪsɪn/ *noun*. M20.
[ORIGIN from mod. Latin *lincolnensis* (see below) + -MYCIN.]
PHARMACOLOGY. An antibiotic produced by the bacterium *Streptomyces lincolnensis* and effective against Gram-positive bacteria, esp. staphylococci and streptococci.

Lincrusta /lɪŋˈkrʌstə/ *noun*. Also **l-**. L19.
[ORIGIN from Latin *linum* flax + *crusta* rind, bark, after *linoleum*.]
(Proprietary name for) a kind of wallpaper covered with embossed linoleum.

Lincs. *abbreviation*.
Lincolnshire.

lincture /ˈlɪŋktʃə/ *noun*. Long *rare*. E17.
[ORIGIN formed as LINCTUS + -URE, or from a medieval Latin formation in *-ura*.]
= LINCTUS.

linctus /ˈlɪŋktəs/ *noun*. L17.
[ORIGIN medieval Latin (classical Latin = licking, from *lingere* to lick), after late Latin *electuarium* ELECTUARY.]
A syrupy liquid medicine, now *esp.* a soothing cough mixture.

†**lind** *noun*. Also **line**. OE–L18.
[ORIGIN Old English *lind(e)* corresp. to Old Saxon *lind(i)a* (Dutch *linde*), Old High German *linta* (German *Linde*), Old Norse *lind*, prob. rel. to Greek *elatē* silver fir. See also LINN *noun*².]
A lime tree; *gen.* a tree of any kind.

Lindabrides /lɪnˈdabrɪdiːz/ *noun*. *arch.* M17.
[ORIGIN A lady in the 16th-cent. romance *Mirror of Knighthood*.]
A lady-love, a sweetheart, a mistress.

lindane /ˈlɪndeɪn/ *noun*. M20.
[ORIGIN from Teunis van der *Linden* (1884–1965), Dutch chemist + -ANE.]
A toxic colourless crystalline compound, the gamma isomer of benzene hexachloride, $C_6H_6Cl_6$, used chiefly as an insecticide powder or spray.
– NOTE: A proprietary name for this substance is GAMMEXANE.

Linde /ˈlɪndə/ *noun*. E20.
[ORIGIN Carl P. G. R. von *Linde* (1842–1934), German physicist.]
Used *attrib.* to designate a process for liquefying gases (esp. atmospheric oxygen and nitrogen) by means of repeated cycles of compression, cooling, and expansion.

linden /ˈlɪndən/ *noun*. L16.
[ORIGIN Partly from LINDEN *adjective*, partly (in comb. *linden tree*) from Dutch *lindeboom*, †*lindenboom*, German *Lindenbaum*, from *linde* (see LIND) + *boom*, *Baum* tree.]
A lime tree. Also ***linden tree***.

†**linden** *adjective*. OE–ME.
[ORIGIN from LIND + -EN⁴.]
Made of the wood of the lime tree.

lindorm *noun* var. of LINDWORM.

lindworm /ˈlɪndwəːm/ *noun*. Also **lindorm** /ˈlɪndɔːm/. E19.
[ORIGIN Danish & Swedish *lindorm* a kind of mythical serpent, from Swedish *lind* flexible + *orm* snake, serpent (cf. WORM *noun*). Cf. LINGWORM.]
A monstrous and evil serpent or dragon of Scandinavian mythology.

lindy /ˈlɪndi/ *noun*. Also **L-**. M20.
[ORIGIN Nickname of C. A. *Lindbergh* (1902–74), the American pilot who in 1927 was the first to make a solo non-stop transatlantic flight: see -Y⁶.]
In full ***Lindy Hop***. A dance originating as a form of the jitterbug among black people in Harlem, New York.

line /lʌɪn/ *noun*¹. Now chiefly *dial.*
[ORIGIN Old English *līn* = Old Saxon, Old High German *līn* (Dutch *lijn-*, German *Lein*), Old Norse *lín*, Gothic *lein*, from Germanic from or corresp. to Latin *linum* rel. to Greek *linon*.]
1 The fibre of the flax plant. Now only, flax fibre of a fine and long staple, which has been separated by the hackle from the tow; occas., a similar fibre of other plants. OE.
2 Flax spun or woven; linen thread or cloth. OE.
3 The flax plant. LME.
†4 The seed of flax; linseed. M–L16.

line /lʌɪn/ *noun*².
[ORIGIN Old English *line* = Middle Dutch *line* (Dutch *lijn*), Old High German *līna* (German *Leine* cord), Old Norse *lína*, prob. from Germanic from Latin *linea*; partly from Old French & mod. French *ligne* from Proto-Romance var. of Latin *linea*, *linia* orig. use as noun (sc. *fibra* FIBRE) of fem. of *lineus* pertaining to flax, from *linum* flax: see LINE *noun*¹.]
▸ **I 1** A (piece of) rope, cord, or wire, esp. as serving a specified purpose. OE. ▸**b** A fishing line. ME. ▸†**c** In *pl.* Strings or cords for snaring birds. ME–M18. ▸**d** A cord used for measuring, or for levelling or straightening. ME. ▸**e** A clothes line. M18. ▸**f** In *pl.* Reins. *dial.* & *US*. E19. ▸**g** A telegraph or telephone wire or cable; a connection by means of this; an individual telephone number or extension. Also, any wire or cable serving as a conductor of electric current. M19.

I. SHAW In the bow, with the neat coiled spirals of lines. **b** L. HELLMAN A line on a fishing reel that tangled and couldn't be untangled. **d** W. C. BRYANT Trees then he felled . . and carefully He smoothed their sides, and wrought them by a line. **e** R. ADAMS Letting her drop, limp as an old garment fallen from a line. **f** *Budget (Ohio)* When the horses took off . . . He jumped on the wagon and grabbed the lines. **g** J. MASTERS Macaulay was on the line. A. BRINK The call came through. A very bad line, her voice . . almost unrecognisable.

clew-line, ***clothes line***, ***dragline***, ***fishing line***, ***lifeline***, ***plumb line***, ***shroud line***, ***spurling line***, etc. **g** ***chatline***, ***helpline***, etc.
†2 Rule, canon, precept; standard of life or practice. *rare*. ME–E17.

AV *Ps.* 19:4 Their line is gone out through all the earth, and their words to the end of the world.

3 In *pl.* One's appointed lot in life (orig. with ref. to *Psalms* 16:6). E17.

J. G. WHITTIER My brother's lines have indeed fallen unto him in a pleasant place.

†**4** A cord in the body. *rare*. E17–L18.
5 A spider's thread. *poet*. M18.

W. COWPER Spun as fine As bloated spiders draw the flimsy line.

▸**II 6** A row of characters either written, printed, or displayed on a VDU; any of the rows of characters in a piece of text; in *pl.*, the contents or sense of what is written, printed, or displayed. OE. ▸**b** A unit of poetry written etc. as continuous text, usu. on one line; a verse; in *pl.*, verses, poetry. Also (in *pl.*), a specified amount of text to be written out as a school punishment. M16. ▸**c** PRINTING. A row of letterforms and spacing material produced by a composition system. M17. ▸**d** A few words in writing; *esp.* a short letter. M17. ▸**e** In *pl.* = MARRIAGE ***lines***. Also (*dial.*), a certificate of church membership etc. E19. ▸**f** In *pl.* The words of an actor's part. L19.

C. WOLFE We carved not a line, and we raised not a stone. T. HARDY Not a line of her writing have I, Not a thread of her hair. S. PLATH My hand made big, jerky letters . . and the lines sloped down the page. **b** C. S. LEWIS If my lines rhymed and scanned and got on with the story I asked no more. E. BLISHEN One could cane them; give them lines. **d** D. L. SAYERS To write a few lines to the Dowager Duchess. **e** R. KIPLING I want . . The name, an' lines to show, An' not to be an 'ore. **f** M. AMIS I felt the uneasiness of a good actor with bad lines.

7 A row of people or things; *N. Amer.* a queue. M16. ▸**b** In certain team games, as American football, ice hockey, etc.: a row of players. L19. ▸**c** A row of machines or workstations progressively assembling or performing a succession of operations on a product during manufacture or processing. E20. ▸**d** In a business etc. organization, the chain of command or responsibility; the employees concerned directly with production as opp. to the provision of advisory and ancillary services. E20.

W. IRVING A line of trading posts from the Mississippi and the Missouri across the Rocky mountains. J. REED There was a long line of people waiting to be let in.

breadline etc. **c** ***assembly line***, ***production line***.

8 MILITARY. A trench, a rampart; in *pl.* (also *collect. sing.*), a connected series of fieldworks, defences, etc. Also, a row of huts or tents in a camp. M17. ▸**b** *hist.* In the First World War, the trenches collectively; the front line. Freq. in ***up the line*** below. E20.

SLOAN WILSON A hundred men dropped behind the German lines to destroy a bridge. **b** S. SASSOON Up in the line one somehow lost touch with such humanities.

9 a NAUTICAL. A body of ships in formation one after the other. E18. ▸**b** MILITARY. A wide-fronted shallow formation of troops or armoured vehicles etc. in adjacent columns. E19.

a T. CAMPBELL While the sign of battle flew On the lofty British line. **b** LYTTON Suddenly the lines of the Moors gave way.

10 A regular succession of buses, ships, aircraft, etc., plying between certain places; a company conducting a business providing this. Orig. *US*. L18.

Scotsman The first vessel of the new direct line to Jamaica from England. A. GRAHAM-YOOLL The Houlder Brothers Shipping line . . had been prominent in the meat trade for almost one century.

▸**III 11** A long narrow stroke or mark drawn or engraved on a surface or shown on a VDU. ME. ▸**b** A mark limiting an area of play on a court or pitch for a game; *spec.* a mark that must be crossed in order to score; in racing, a mark on the track (actual or imaginary) at the winning post. M16. ▸**c** Each of (usu. five) horizontal parallel equidistant strokes forming a stave in musical notation. E17. ▸**d** Any of the lines employed in a picture; chiefly *collect.* or in *gen.* sense, character of draughtsmanship or method of rendering form in art. E17. ▸**e** The total effect of the disposition of the limbs, body, and head of a dancer, gymnast, skater, fencer, etc., in movement or repose. E20. ▸**f** Instrumental or vocal melody; a structured sequence of notes or tones. E20. ▸**g** Each of the narrow horizontal strips forming a television picture. E20.

W. M. CRAIG An expression of forms only by simple lines. B. MALAMUD A heavy line was drawn on which to sign his name. **f** R. H. MYERS His music has line . . and the enormous merit of condensation. *Melody Maker* I consider jazz to be a lot of horns and one of those top speed bass lines.

b ***goal line***, ***halfway line***, ***penalty line***, ***service line***, ***22 metre line***, etc.

12 a A thing resembling a drawn stroke or mark, esp. in a natural object, as a thin band of colour; a suture, a ridge. ME. ▸**b** A furrow or seam in the face or hands; PALMISTRY a mark on the palm of the hand supposed to indicate one's fate, temperament, or abilities. M16. ▸**c** A narrow peak or trough of intensity in a spectrum, appearing as a fine straight black or bright band transverse to the length of the spectrum (cf. ***Fraunhofer lines***, ***Fraunhofer's lines*** s.v. FRAUNHOFER 1). Also, a component of emitted radiation at a discrete wavelength or narrow range of wavelengths, represented by such a band. M19.

a J. TYNDALL Along the faces of the sections the lines of stratification were clearly shown. **b** I. ZANGWILL There were lines of premature age on the handsome face. A. FRASER Already the characteristic deep lines . . had formed from nostril to chin.

13 A circle of the terrestrial or celestial sphere. Now *rare*. LME.

MILTON Under the Ethiop Line By Nilus head. POPE Where spices smoke beneath the burning Line.

14 a MATH. A continuous extent of length without thickness, freq. repr. by a drawn line (sense 11); the track of a moving point. LME. ▸**b** A curve connecting all points having a common property. Usu. with specifying word. E19.

15 A straight line (sense 14) imagined as drawn between two points, or between some point and the observer; *spec.* the (usu. imaginary) continuous horizontal mark through the feet of most letters. LME.

16 A contour, an outline; lineament. LME. ▸**b** FASHION. The outline or dominant features of composition of a dress or suit. E20.

SHELLEY The dim long line before Of a grey and distant shore. **b** *Times* The curved line was seen in all the long coats. *Vogue* Overall, a clear narrowing of the silhouette, . . presaging an even sparer line for autumn.

b ***A-line***, ***empire-line***, etc.

17 A direction as indicated by marks on a surface, a row of people or things, etc. Freq. in ***come into line***, ***bring into line*** below. L15. ▸**b** MILITARY. An arrangement of companies side by side. L18. ▸**c** A particular policy or set of policies which a politician may maintain or expect others to follow; = ***party line*** s.v. PARTY *noun*. Orig. *US*. L19. ▸**d** A marked tendency, a policy or trend; *colloq.* a glib or superficially attractive mode of address or behaviour, plausible talk. E20. ▸**e** The point spread for a number of football games on which bets may be laid. *US colloq.* M20.

E. HOYLE When your Adversary has a Bishop and one Pawn on the Rook's Line. G. A. LAWRENCE Get the horses in line, to start them for the farmer's Cup. **b** TENNYSON And he call'd 'Left wheel into line!' **c** G. F. KENNAN He had to follow . . the line his government had laid down for him. H. MACMILLAN His intervention followed the line of an article which had already appeared in the Daily Express. **d** A. L. ROWSE He has a fine line in Churchillian invective. *Globe & Mail (Toronto)* Try that line on your spouse. 'Dear, we're not going to save money.'

†**18** Degree, rank, station. E16–L18.

G. A. BELLAMY She had received a more liberal education than is usually bestowed upon English women in the middle line of life.

19 A limit, a boundary. L16. ▸**b** BRIDGE. A line across a scorecard. Chiefly in ***above the line***, ***below the line*** below. E20. ▸**c** The boundary between a credit and a debit in an account. M20.

C. ISHERWOOD For her, the line between reality and hallucination is getting very thin.

Maginot Line, ***Mason–Dixon line***, ***Plimsoll line***, ***Wallace's line***, etc.

20 One twelfth of an inch. M17.

21 In *pl.* **a** The outlines, plan, or draft of a building etc.; *spec.* in SHIPBUILDING, the outlines of a vessel as shown in its horizontal, vertical, and oblique sections. L17. ▸**b** *fig.* Plan of action, procedure, etc. M18.

G. SEMPLE The principal Lines of my Design of a Bridge suitable to that Place. C. READE Her extravagant poop that caught the wind, and her lines like a cocked hat reversed. **b** L. STRACHEY He laid down the lines for a radical reform in the . . administration of the army.

▸**IV 22** A lineage, a stock, a race. ME. ▸**b** A breed or variety of animal or plant universally characterized by some feature whose strength is the criterion for continued selection by breeders. Cf. ***line-bred***, ***line breeding*** below. E19.

H. BELLOC His line survives to-day. J. CLAVELL Our Queen's the third of the Tudor line.

23 A continuous series of people in chronological succession, *esp.* several generations of a family. Freq. with specifying word. ME.

W. COWPER In the line Of his descending progeny. J. T. STORY The Gladstones originally came from a long line of East Anglian politicians.

direct line, ***female line***, ***male line***.

▸**V 24** A course of action, procedure, life, thought, or conduct. ME.

DISRAELI I should then have inherited some family line of conduct, both moral, and political. G. C. LEWIS The Protectionists . . have taken no line in the matter.

25 A track, a course, a direction; a route. LME. ▸**b** A single track of a railway (freq. in ***the up line***, ***the down line***). Also, a branch or route of a railway or the whole system of railways under one management. E19. ▸**c** A settlement road, a bush road. Chiefly *Canad.* & *NZ*. E19. ▸**d** The straight or direct course in the hunting field or round a racetrack (also ***racing line***). M19. ▸**e** A row of traps or of poison bait. M19. ▸**f** A pipe or tube (of great or indefinite length in relation to its thickness). M19. ▸**g** In GOLF, the direction of the hole from the position of a player's ball. In CRICKET, the direction of flight of the ball from the bowler's hand. L19.

W. COWPER Though . . the shaft . . err but little from the intended line. I. ZANGWILL They ran on parallel lines that never met. **b** J. MASTERS An engine whistling . . a mile up the line.

b ***belt line***, ***branch line***, ***main line***, ***shunt line***, etc.

†**26** In *pl.* Goings on, caprices or fits of temper. *rare* (Shakes.). L16–E17.

27 A department of activity; a kind or branch of business or occupation. M17.

DICKENS Mr Augustus Cooper was in the oil and colour line. B. PYM Memorial services were not much in Edwin's line.

28 COMMERCE. (An order for, the stock in hand of) a particular design or class of goods. M19. ▸**b** The amount which one underwriter (or one company) accepts as his or her share of the total value of the subject matter covered by insurance. L19. ▸**c** A dose of a powdered narcotic or hallucinatory drug, as cocaine, heroin, etc., laid out in a line for use. *slang*. L20.

S. UNWIN They are mostly content with quick-selling lines such as Annuals. H. FAST Fritz Alcheck . . carried a line of men's haberdashery. **c** *Observer* Everybody I know takes heroin . . . Every party . . has smack available, lines and lines of it.

— PHRASES: (A selection of cross-refs. only is included.) **above the line** (**a**) BRIDGE (of points) scored for game, honours, overtricks, rubber, or for the failure of opponents to fulfil their contract; (**b**) ECONOMICS (spent etc.) on items of current expenditure; ADVERTISING in the mass media; CINEMATOGRAPHY (incurred etc.) before filming begins. **all along the line**, **all down the line**, **all the way down the line** at every point. **below the line** (**a**) BRIDGE (of points) scored for tricks bid and won, and counting towards the game; (**b**) ECONOMICS (spent etc.) on items of capital expenditure; ADVERTISING on means of promotion other than the mass media; CINEMATOGRAPHY (incurred etc.) during and after filming. ***bottom line***: see BOTTOM *adjective*. **bring into line** cause to agree, conform, or cooperate. **by rule and line** with precision. **come into line** agree, conform, cooperate. ***contour line***: see CONTOUR *noun* 2. **do a line with** *Austral.* & *NZ colloq.* (try to) enter into an amorous relationship with. ***dotted line***. **draw the line at** refuse to go as far as or beyond. ***equinoctial line***: see EQUINOCTIAL *adjective* 1. ***first line***. ***Fraunhofer lines***, ***Fraunhofer's lines*** see FRAUNHOFER 1. ***front line***: see FRONT *noun* & *adjective*. **get a line on** acquire information about (a thing), come to know. **get one's lines crossed**, **get the lines crossed** have a misunderstanding, become confused. **give a person line enough** let a person continue unhindered for a time in order to secure or detect him or her later. **hard lines** (usu. *colloq.*) bad luck, hardship. ***heaving line***: see HEAVE *verb*. ***hold the line***: see HOLD *verb*. ***hook, line, and sinker***: see HOOK *noun*. ***hotline***: see HOT *adjective*. **in line** so as to form a straight line (*with*); ***in line with***, in accordance with. **in one's line** suited to one's capacity, taste, etc. ***lateral line***: see LATERAL *adjective* etc. **lay it on the line**, **put it on the line** (**a**) hand over money; (**b**) state (something) clearly, plainly, or categorically. **lay on the line**, **put on the line** place (one's career etc.) at risk. **line abreast** NAUTICAL a number of parallel ships ranged on a line crossing the keels at right angles. **line ahead** NAUTICAL a number of ships following one another in a line. **line astern** (in) an aircraft formation in which a number of planes follow one another in a line. **line by line**, **line for line** from beginning to end, seriatim. ***line of battle***: see BATTLE *noun*. **line of beauty** the curve (resembling a slender elongated S) held by Hogarth to be a necessary element in all beauty of form. **line of business** *spec.* in the 18th- and 19th-cent. theatre, the kind of part for which an actor or actress was specifically engaged. ***line of country***: see COUNTRY *noun*. **line of credit** a loan by one country to another, to be utilized by the second for buying goods from the first; credit extended by a bank to a commercial concern to a certain amount; the amount so extended. ***line of defence***: see DEFENCE *noun* 3. **line of fire** the expected path of gunfire, a missile, etc. ***line of flotation***: see FLOTATION 1. **line of force** PHYSICS a curve whose direction at each point is that of the electric etc. force there. **line of fortune** = ***line of life*** (b) below. ***line of least*** RESISTANCE. **line of life** (**a**) CLASSICAL MYTHOLOGY the thread spun and cut by the Fates, determining the length of a person's life (cf. LIFELINE 2); (**b**) = LIFELINE 3. ***line of march***: see MARCH *noun*³. ***line of metal***: see METAL *noun* 7. ***line of sight***: see SIGHT *noun*. ***line of vision***: see VISION *noun*. ***long line***: see LONG *adjective*¹. ***loxodromic line***: see LOXODROMIC *adjective*. ***meridian line***: see MERIDIAN *adjective* 3. **not one's line** not one's vocation or calling, not among one's pursuits or interests. **on the line** (**a**) at risk; (**b**) (of a picture) exhibited with its centre about level with the spectator's eye. ***open line***: see OPEN *adjective*. **out of line** not in alignment with, discordant; ***step out of line***, ***get out of line***, etc., behave in an unconventional, discordant, or inappropriate manner. **out of one's line** unsuited to one's capacity, taste, etc. ***outside line***: see OUTSIDE *adjective*. **pay on the line** pay promptly. ***pure line***: see PURE *adjective*. ***put it on the line***: see ***lay it on the line*** above. ***put on the line***: see ***lay on the line*** above. **read between the lines** discover a meaning or purpose in a piece of writing etc. not obvious or explicitly expressed. ***red line***: see RED *adjective*. **ride the line** *US* make the circuit of the boundary of a cattle drift in order to drive in stray cattle. ***right line***: see RIGHT *adjective*. ***second line***: see SECOND *adjective*. **ship of the line** a line-of-battle ship. **shoot a line** *colloq.* put on an act, talk pretentiously, boast. ***soft line***: see SOFT *adjective*. **somewhere along the line** at some point (in time). **stand in line** *N. Amer.* form a queue. ***the end of the line***: see END *noun*. **the line** (**a**) the equinoctial line; *spec.* (**L-**) the Equator; (**b**) *US* the Mason–Dixon line; (**c**) in the British army, the regular and numbered regiments as distinguished from the Guards and the auxiliary forces; in the US army, the regular fighting force of all arms; (**d**) *Canad.* the US–Canadian border. ***thin blue line***: see THIN *adjective*. ***toe the line***: see TOE *verb* 2. **up the line** MILITARY to the battlefront. ***visual line***: see VISUAL *adjective*. ***wet one's line***: see WET *verb*. ***white line***: see WHITE *adjective*. ***yellow line***: see YELLOW *adjective*. ***YRAST line***. ***Z line***: see Z, z 6.

L

– **COMB.:** **line angle** DENTISTRY the angle at the junction of two surfaces of a tooth or cavity; **line-at-a-time printer** = *line printer* below; **linebacker** AMER. FOOTBALL a player just behind the defensive line (***middle linebacker***: see MIDDLE *adjective*); **linebacking** AMER. FOOTBALL playing as a linebacker; **line blanking** TELEVISION the suppression of signals that would contribute to the picture during flyback of the scanning spot between the transmission of successive lines; **line block** a block bearing a design in relief from which an illustration made up of lines without variations in tone may be printed; an illustration printed in this way; **line-boat** a boat used for line-fishing; **line-book** (*a*) PRINTING (*obsolete* exc. *hist.*) a book in which compositors kept account of the lines of set type credited and debited to them; (*b*) RAF *slang* a record of boasts; **line-bred** *adjective* produced by line breeding; **line breeding** selective breeding of animals for some desired feature by mating within a related line; **line-camp** *N. Amer.* a camp, esp. a cabin, for ranch hands in an outlying part of a large ranch; **line-casting** *adjective* (of a composing machine) that casts type a line at a time; **line dance** a type of country and western dance in which dancers line up in a row without partners and follow a choreographed pattern of steps to music; **line-dance** *verb intrans.* perform a line dance; **line dancer** a person who dances a line dance; **line drawing** a drawing done with a pen or pencil, a drawing in which images are produced from variations of lines; **line-drawn** *adjective* made by line drawing; **line drive** BASEBALL a ball driven straight and low above the ground; **line drop** ELECTRICAL ENGINEERING the voltage drop between two points on a transmission line; **line editor** COMPUTING a program that enables the editing of one line at a time on a VDU display; **line-ending** (*a*) = *line-filling* below; (*b*) the end of a line of poetry; **line-engraved** *adjective* made by line engraving; **line engraver** a practitioner of line engraving; **line engraving** the art of engraving, by lines incised on the plate, as distinguished from etching and mezzotint; an engraving executed in this manner; **linefeed** (*a*) the action of advancing paper in a printing machine or text on a screen by the space of one line; (*b*) the distance from the bottom of one line of type to the bottom of the next; **line-fence** *N. Amer.* a boundary fence between two farms or ranches; **line-filling** a flourish or ornament in the blank space at the end of a line of manuscript; **line finder** TELEPHONY a selector which searches for the calling subscriber's line when he or she lifts the receiver so that the line can be connected to a group of selectors available to any caller; **line-finishing** = *line-filling* above; **line-firing** MILITARY firing by a body of men in line; **line fisherman** a person who practises line-fishing; **line-fishing** fishing with a line as opp. to a net; fishing with a long line with many baited hooks attached at intervals; **line frequency** TELEVISION the number of scanning lines produced per second; **line gale** *US* = *line-storm* below; **line gauge** PRINTING a ruler showing the size of a type or types; **line graph**: in which the values of the variables are represented by a (continuous) line (cf. ***bar chart*** s.v. BAR *noun*[1]); **line haul** *US slang* a scheduled truck route or movement of freight; **line integral** MATH. the integral, taken along a line, of any differential that has a continuously varying value along that line; **line-integration** the operation of finding a line integral; **line judge** a linesman in a tennis match; **line loss** ELECTRICAL ENGINEERING loss of electrical energy along a transmission line; **line manager** a manager to whom an employee is directly responsible; **line officer** an officer holding command in a line regiment; **line pin** any of the specially pins used to fasten a bricklayer's line; **line pipe** pipe specially manufactured for use in pipelines; **line printer** a machine that prints output from a computer a line at a time; **line regiment** a regular and numbered regiment in the British army, a regiment of the line; **line-ride** *verb intrans.* (*US*) perform the action of line-riding; **line-rider** *US* a person engaged in line-riding; **line-riding** *US* the action of riding the line (see ***ride the line*** above); **line scan** (a device or technique using or involving) the motion of a scanning beam or spot along a line, or over an object or scene line by line; **line-sequential** *adjective* designating a system of colour television in which each line of the picture is in one of the three primary colours, the colour changing for each successive line; **line shaft**, **line shafting** a shaft, shafting, of relatively great length from which a number of separate machines are driven by countershafts or endless belts; **lineside** *adjective* adjacent to a railway line; **line-soldier** a soldier of a line regiment, a linesman; **line space** the space between the rows of characters in text; a space equivalent to a line of text; ***line-space lever***, ***line-space mechanism***, etc., a device that turns the platen of a typewriter to a new line of writing; **line-spacing** *noun & adjective* (*a*) *noun* the space between successive lines of text; (*b*) *adjective* designating or pertaining to the device that moves the platen to a new line; **line spectrum** a spectrum consisting of separate isolated lines; an emission (of light, sound, or other radiation) composed of a number of discrete frequencies or energies; **line squall** a squall, consisting of a violent straight blast of cold air with snow or rain, occurring along a cold front; **line standard** (*a*) a standard of length in the form of a bar marked with two lines, the distance between which (under specified conditions) is the standard length; (*b*) the number of lines constituting a complete television picture; **line-storm** *US* an equinoctial storm; **line-synchronizing** *adjective* designating a pulse transmitted in a television signal which causes the scanning process in the receiver to remain in synchrony with that at the transmitter; **line-width** PHYSICS the width of a spectral line as measured by the difference in wavelength, wave number, or frequency between its two limits; **line-wire** TELEGRAPHY the wire which connects the stations of a telegraph line; **line-work** (*a*) drawing or designing executed with the pen or pencil (as opp. to wash etc.); (*b*) copy or reproduction consisting of solid elements as distinct from halftone; (*c*) work as a lineman.

†**line** *noun*[3] var. of LIND.

line /lʌɪn/ *verb*[1] *trans.* LME.
[ORIGIN from LINE *noun*[1], with ref. to the use of linen as a lining material. Cf. medieval Latin *lineare*, *liniare*.]
1 Cover the inside surface of (a garment, box, etc.) with a layer of usu. different material; cover (a garment, box, etc.) on the inside; cover with an (adhesive) inside layer. LME. ▸**b** COOKERY. Cover the inside of (a dish, tin, etc.) *with* pastry etc. prior to baking. E19.

S. BELLOW His coat, once lined with fox, turned dry and bald. *fig.*: W. COWPER And poplar that with silver lines his leaf. **b** *Evening Post (Nottingham)* Line a flan dish with short crust pastry and bake blind.

2 Fill the cavity of (one's purse, stomach, etc.), esp. plentifully; cram, stuff. E16.

J. G. WHITTIER No bridegroom's hand be mine to hold That is not lined with yellow gold.

line one's pocket, **line one's purse** make money esp. by corrupt means.

†**3** Strengthen by placing something alongside; reinforce, fortify. L16–M18.

SHAKES. *Hen. V* To line and new repair our towns of war.

4 Cover the outside of; overlay, drape, pad; NAUTICAL add a layer of wood to. Now *rare* or *obsolete*. L16.

C. MARSHALL If the bed gets over cool, line it, or cover round with straw.

5 Serve or be used as a lining for. E18.

M. BRADBURY Howard's study is lined with bookshelves.

6 a BOOKBINDING. Glue on the back of (a book) a paper covering continuous with the lining of the back of the cover. L19. ▸**b** CABINET MAKING. Foll. by *up*: put a moulding round (the top of a piece of furniture). L19.

line /lʌɪn/ *verb*[2]. LME.
[ORIGIN from LINE *noun*[2].]
1 *verb trans.* Tie with a line, string, or cord. *rare*. LME.
2 *verb trans.* Measure or test with a line, cut to a line. LME.
3 *verb trans.* Trace *out* the outlines of (something to be constructed) (*lit.* & *fig.*); trace (as) with a line or lines; delineate, sketch; put *in* with a hard pencil the permanent lines of (a freehand drawing). LME.

SHAKES. *A.Y.L.* All the pictures fairest lin'd Are but black to Rosalinde. A. YARRANTON Here is a way plainly lined out to cheat the Rats and Mice.

4 *verb trans.* Mark in, off, out, with a line or lines; impress lines on; cover with lines. M16.

DICKENS This entry was afterwards lined through. *Expositor* The pale wronged face, lined with melancholy resignation.

5 *verb trans.* **a** Post troops etc. along (a hedge, road, etc.); (of troops) form an open or close line along (a pass etc.); (of persons or things) stand at fairly short intervals along (a street, wall, etc.). L16. ▸**b** Foll. by *out*: transplant (seedling trees) from beds into lines in a nursery for further growth. M20.

a GIBBON The ramparts were lined with trembling spectators. G. ORWELL The trees lined the road in close, dusty ranks.

6 a *verb trans.* Draw (persons or things) *up* or up in line (*with*); *US* assign (a person) *to* certain work; aim (a weapon) in a direct line *on* an object. Foll. by *up*: arrange, produce, or make ready, esp. *for* a particular person or purpose. L18. ▸**b** *verb intrans.* Form a line with others; fall into line; spread *out* in line. Foll. by *up*: be arranged in a line or lines; measure up (*to*). L18. ▸**c** *verb trans.* & *intrans.* BASEBALL. Hit (a ball) straight and low above the ground; play (a shot) as a line drive. Freq. foll. by *out*. L19.

a A. ALVAREZ The same bottles of hair lotion . . were lined above the basin in his father's dressing-room. K. AMIS You've got some scheme lined up for visiting places of . . historical interest. P. BARKER The women were lined up facing each other. **b** A. TROLLOPE She struggled to line up to the spirit of her promises and she succeeded. R. C. HUTCHINSON We all lined up outside the office to get our pay. **c** *Globe & Mail (Toronto)* Frank White lined a drive to centre field.

7 *verb trans.* Follow the line of flight of (bees). *US*. E19.
8 *verb trans.* & *intrans.* **a** Catch (fish) with a hook and line. *US. rare*. M19. ▸**b** Guide or control (a boat or canoe) from the bank or shore of a stretch of inland water by means of a rope or ropes. *N. Amer.* E20.
9 *verb trans.* Read out (a metrical psalm, a hymn) line by line for a congregation to sing. Also foll. by *out*. M19.
– **COMB.:** **line-up** a line of people for inspection; an arrangement of people in a team, nations in an alliance, etc.; the personnel or configuration of a band etc.

line /lʌɪn/ *verb*[3] *trans.* LME.
[ORIGIN Old French & mod. French *ligner*, *aligner* LINE *verb*[2], but sense-development obscure.]
Of a dog, wolf, etc.: copulate with, cover, (a bitch).

linea /ˈlɪnɪə/ *noun*. Pl. ***-eae*** /-ɪiː/. E17.
[ORIGIN Latin = LINE *noun*[2].]
ANATOMY. With mod. Latin specifying word: any of various (apparent) lines or linear structures in or on the body.
linea alba /ˈalbə/ [white] a tendinous line running from the breastbone to the pubis, where the flat abdominal muscles are attached.

lineable *adjective* var. of LINABLE.

lineae *noun* pl. of LINEA.

lineage /ˈlɪnɪɪdʒ/ *noun*[1]. ME.
[ORIGIN Old French & mod. French *lignage*, †*linage*, from Proto-Romance, from Latin LINEA: see -AGE.]
1 Lineal descent from an ancestor; ancestry, pedigree. ME.

TOLKIEN Aragorn is descended in direct lineage . . from Isildur Elendil's son himself. *transf.*: R. P. GRAVES His high lineage was that of the great classical scholars who had preceded him.

2 †**a** The people through whom one's lineal descent is traced; one's ancestors collectively. ME–M16. ▸**b** The descendants of a specified ancestor collectively. ME. ▸**c** A family or people viewed with reference to its descent; a tribe, a clan; *spec.* in ANTHROPOLOGY, a line of descent from a single ancestor, a social group tracing its descent from a single ancestor. LME.

b H. COX The dignity of the peerage . . was confined to the lineage of the person ennobled. **c** R. FIRTH The Tikopia lineages are patrilineal.

3 BIOLOGY. A sequence of species each of which is considered to have evolved from its predecessor. M20.

lineage *noun*[2] var. of LINAGE.

lineal /ˈlɪnɪəl/ *adjective* & *noun*. LME.
[ORIGIN Old French & mod. French *linéal* from late Latin *linealis*, from Latin LINEA: see -AL[1].]
▸ **A** *adjective*. **1** Of or pertaining to a line or lines; consisting of lines; (of writing) arranged in regular lines. LME. ▸**b** Of a measure: relating to a single dimension of space; linear. L17.

W. ROBERTS This way of writing may be as swift, lineal, and legible, as the operations of daylight. T. HOLCROFT They were not . . ignorant of lineal perspective. **b** R. RAYMOND The claim is 1,000 feet lineal measurement in length.

2 a Of descent, ancestry, etc.: that is in the direct line (opp. ***collateral***). LME. ▸**b** Pertaining to or transmitted by the direct line of descent. L15. ▸**c** Of a person: lineally descended (*from*, *to*, †*of*). *rare*. L16.

a J. LOCKE The Prime and Ancient Right of Lineal Succession to any thing. T. HARDY You are the lineal representative of the ancient and knightly family of the d'Urbervilles. S. BECKETT Seven male relations, lineal and collateral.

▸ **B** *noun*. †**1** Genealogy, pedigree. Only in LME.
2 A person who is related in the direct line. Usu. in *pl. rare*. M18.
■ **line'ality** *noun* the quality of being lineal; *esp.* uniformity of direction of a way of writing: E19.

lineally /ˈlɪnɪəli/ *adverb*. LME.
[ORIGIN from LINEAL + -LY[2].]
1 In the direct line of descent; by lineal descent. LME.
2 In a (direct) line. Now *rare*. LME.
3 Orig., by means of lines; graphically. Later, with regard to the lines or outline of a thing; line for line. E17.

lineament /ˈlɪnɪəm(ə)nt/ *noun*. LME.
[ORIGIN Latin *lineamentum*, from *lineare* make straight, (in medieval Latin) delineate, from LINEA: see -MENT.]
1 †**a** A part of the body, considered with respect to its contour or outline, a distinctive physical feature. LME–M18. ▸**b** *fig.* In *pl.* Distinctive features or characteristics. Now chiefly as passing into sense 2. M17.

a SWIFT What lineaments divine we trace Through all his figure, mien, and face! **b** LD MACAULAY Some lineaments of the character of the man were early discerned in the child.

2 A part of the face viewed with respect to its outline; a facial feature. Usu. in *pl.* E16.

F. O'CONNOR He made out the lineaments of the face—a mouth, . . a straight nose.

†**3** A line; a delineation, a diagram, an outline, a sketch. L16–E19. ▸**b** A minute portion, a trace; in *pl.*, elements, rudiments. L17–E19.

D. HUME The broken lineaments of the piece . . are carefully studied. **b** J. PINKERTON The paste . . encloses some lineaments of black mica.

■ †**lineamental** *adjective* of the nature of a sketch or imperfect outline; pertaining to lineaments: E17–L18.

linear /ˈlɪnɪə/ *adjective*. M17.
[ORIGIN Latin *linearis*, formed as LINEA + -AR[1].]
1 Of or pertaining to a line or lines. M17.

Pall Mall Gazette That linear hardness which never appears in nature.

2 Resembling a line; very narrow in proportion to its length, and of uniform breadth; BOTANY (of a leaf) long and narrow. M17.
3 Arranged or measured along a (straight) line; extended in a line or in length; *spec.* in MATH. & PHYSICS, involving measurement in one dimension only; able to be represented by a straight line on a graph (in Cartesian coordinates); involving or exhibiting directly proportional change in two related quantities. E18. ▸**b** Progressing in a single direction by regular steps or stages, sequential. M20.

J. MCPHEE It is a linear community: cabins spaced along the river. **b** P. MATTHIESSEN The Australian aborigines distinguish between linear time and a 'Great Time' of dreams . . in which all is present in this moment.

4 Consisting of lines; involving the use of lines; in lines; (of depiction) using clear outlines, expressed in lines rather than masses. M19. ▸**b** MUSIC. = HORIZONTAL *adjective* 4. M20.

Crafts Certain linear kinds of image . . are . . not suitable for tapestry.

– SPECIAL COLLOCATIONS: **Linear A** the earlier and undeciphered form of two forms of Bronze Age writing found in Crete and parts of Greece and recording a form of Mycenaean Greek (opp. ***Linear B*** below). **linear accelerator** a particle accelerator in which the particles travel in straight lines rather than in closed loops. **linear algebra** *MATH.* a finite-dimensional vector space, with multiplication defined and distributive over addition, in which (λ **a**) **b** = λ (**ab**) = **a** (λ **b**) for any scalar λ of the associated field and any vectors **a** and **b**; the branch of algebra that deals with the properties of these entities. **Linear B** the later of two forms of Bronze Age writing found in Crete and parts of Greece and recording a form of Mycenaean Greek (opp. ***Linear A*** above). **linear equation** an equation of the first degree (i.e. not having terms raised to higher than the first power). **linear motor**: producing linear rather than rotary motion by means of a magnetic field. **linear search** *COMPUTING* a search carried out in the order in which items are stored in a file.

linearise *verb* var. of LINEARIZE.

linearity /lɪnɪˈarɪti/ *noun*. M18.
[ORIGIN from LINEAR + -ITY.]
1 The quality or condition of being linear; a linear arrangement or formation. M18.
2 *MATH. & PHYSICS.* The property of being representable by a line; proportionality of two related quantities (such as input and output). E20.

linearize /ˈlɪnɪərʌɪz/ *verb trans.* Also **-ise**. L19.
[ORIGIN from LINEAR + -IZE.]
Represent in a linear form; transform *into* a linear figure; make linear.
■ **lineari'zation** *noun* L19. **linearizer** *noun* a person who or thing which linearizes something; *esp.* a device which linearizes the response of a measuring instrument or other mechanism L20.

linearly /ˈlɪnɪəli/ *adverb*. M19.
[ORIGIN from LINEAR + -LY[2].]
1 In a way that involves only terms of one dimension; in a linear or proportional manner. M19.
2 In a linear direction; by linear measurement; by means of lines. L19.

lineate /ˈlɪnɪət/ *ppl adjective*. M17.
[ORIGIN Latin *lineatus* pa. pple, formed as LINEATE *verb*: see -ATE[2].]
Marked with lines.

lineate /ˈlɪnɪeɪt/ *verb trans.* Long *rare*. M16.
[ORIGIN Latin *lineat-* pa. ppl stem of *lineare* reduce to a line, (in medieval Latin) delineate, from LINEA: see -ATE[3].]
1 Mark with lines. M16.
†**2** Delineate; represent by drawing or by description. E–M17.

lineation /lɪnɪˈeɪʃ(ə)n/ *noun*. LME.
[ORIGIN Latin *lineatio(n-)*, formed as LINEATE *verb*: see -ATION.]
1 The action or process of drawing lines or marking something with lines; an instance of this; a contour, an outline. Also, a marking or line on a surface, esp. of the skin. LME. ▸**b** Linear markings; an arrangement or group of lines. M16.
2 A division into lines. M19.
3 *GEOLOGY.* A linear feature observed in rock etc. M20.

lined /lʌɪnd/ *adjective*[1]. LME.
[ORIGIN from LINE *verb*[1] + -ED[1].]
1 That has been lined or given a lining. LME.
fur-lined, ***silk-lined***, etc.
2 *HERALDRY.* Of the lining of a mantle etc.: of a different tincture from the garment itself. L17.

lined /lʌɪnd/ *adjective*[2]. E17.
[ORIGIN from LINE *noun*[2], *verb*[2]: see -ED[2], -ED[1].]
1 Marked with lines, having lines traced or impressed on the surface. Also (as 2nd elem. of comb.), composed of a certain kind or number of lines. E17.

J. STEINBECK Her face was hard and lined and leathery with fatigue. M. ATWOOD The pad of lined paper I was writing on.

five-lined, ***right-lined***, ***straight-lined***, etc.
2 *HERALDRY.* Of an animal: having a line or leash attached to its collar. E18.

line-in /ˈlʌɪnɪn/ *noun*. L20.
[ORIGIN from LINE *noun*[2] + IN *adverb*.]
An input socket in an electrical device.

lineless /ˈlʌɪnlɪs/ *adjective*. L16.
[ORIGIN from LINE *noun*[2] + -LESS.]
†**1** On whom no bounds can be set. *rare*. Only in L16.
2 Having no lines. L18.

lineman /ˈlʌɪnmən/ *noun*. Pl. **-men**. M19.
[ORIGIN from LINE *noun*[2] + MAN *noun*.]
1 A person employed for the maintenance of a railway, telegraph, or telephone line. M19.
2 A person who carries the line in surveying. *rare*. M19.
3 A line fisherman. L19.
4 *AMER. FOOTBALL.* A forward. L19.

linen /ˈlɪnɪn/ *adjective & noun*.
[ORIGIN Old English *līnen*, *lǣnnen* = Old Frisian (Dutch) *linnen*, Old Saxon, Old High German *līnīn* (German *leinen*), from West Germanic, formed as LINE *noun*[1]: see -EN[4].]
▸ **A** *adjective*. Made of flax or cloth woven from flax. OE.

W. WOOD Our Returns are chiefly in Linnen and Linnen Yarn. J. STEINBECK Alice patted the cuts with a linen handkerchief dipped in warm water.

▸ **B** *noun*. **1** *collect.* Garments or other articles made or originally usually made of linen, as sheets, cloths, shirts, undergarments, etc. ME.

KEATS And still she slept an azure-lidded sleep, In blanched linen, smooth, and lavender'd. *Birmingham Post* His linen is as carefully selected as his wine list.

wash one's dirty linen in public be indiscreet about one's domestic quarrels, private disagreements, etc.
2 Cloth woven from flax. LME. ▸**b** A particular kind of such cloth. Usu. in *pl.* M18.

E. SAINTSBURY Chemical properties necessary for the bleaching of linen and other materials made from flax.

3 Something made of linen; a linen garment. Now usu. in *pl.* M16. ▸**b** Orig., a piece or pieces of linen, *esp.* strips of linen for use as bandages. Later (in *pl.*), grave-clothes. *obsolete* exc. *Scot.* L16.

L. HELLMAN Dresses . . a tan linen, and . . a white net for Babbie. *Woman's Own* She personally saw to her husband and son's linens.

4 *ellipt.* = ***linen-draper*** (b) below. *slang*. M20.
– COMB. & SPECIAL COLLOCATIONS: **linen-armourer** (*a*) (*obsolete* exc. *hist.*) a maker of gambesons and similar adjuncts to armour; †(*b*) *joc.* a tailor; **linen basket**: for soiled clothes; **linen-cupboard** a cupboard for bedlinen and table linen; the contents of such a cupboard; **linen-draper** (*a*) a trader who deals in linens, calicos, etc.; (**b**) *rhyming slang* a newspaper; **linen duster** a duster (see DUSTER 3) made of linen; **linenfold** (a) carved or moulded ornament representing a fold or scroll of linen; **linen-hall** a market hall for the sale of linens; **linen-panel**: one decorated with linenfold; **linen-press** a frame or receptacle for pressing or holding linen; **linen shower** *N. Amer.* a party at which a bride-to-be is given presents of household linen etc.; **linen tea** a tea arranged in order to provide house linen for a crèche, day nursery, etc.
■ **linenless** *adjective* M19.

lineolate /ˈlɪnɪəleɪt/ *adjective*. M19.
[ORIGIN from Latin *lineola* dim. of *linea* LINE *noun*[2] + -ATE[2].]
BOTANY & ZOOLOGY. Marked with minute lines.
■ Also **lineolated** *adjective* E19.

line-out /ˈlʌɪnaʊt/ *noun*. L19.
[ORIGIN from LINE *verb*[2], *noun*[2] + OUT *adverb*.]
1 *RUGBY UNION.* A formation of parallel lines of opposing forwards at right angles to the touchline for the throwing in of the ball; a play in which the ball is thrown in to such a formation. L19.
2 An output socket in an electrical device. L20.

liner /ˈlʌɪnə/ *noun*[1]. E17.
[ORIGIN from LINE *verb*[1] + -ER[1].]
1 A person who lines or fits a lining to something. E17.
2 A lining in an appliance, device, or container, *esp.* a removable one. M19. ▸**b** A paper or board for covering another similar material by adhesion etc. as part of the finished product. E20.
3 A lining of a garment, *esp.* one made of a man-made fibre. M20. ▸**b** A disposable lining for a baby's nappy. Also ***nappy liner***. M20.
4 In full ***liner note***. The text printed on the sleeve of a gramophone record, a sleeve note. M20.
– COMB.: **linerboard** a paperboard used as a facing on fibreboard; ***liner note***: see sense 4 above.

liner /ˈlʌɪnə/ *noun*[2]. LME.
[ORIGIN from LINE *noun*[2], *verb*[2] + -ER[1].]
▸ **I 1** An official appointed to mark out boundaries of properties in a burgh. *Scot.* LME.
2 A person employed to paint lines on the wheels etc. of a vehicle, esp. a carriage. E19.
3 A writer of miscellaneous news items paid for at so much per line. Now chiefly in PENNY-A-LINER. M19.
4 = LINESMAN 1. L19.
▸ **II 5** A threshed sheaf of corn. Long *obsolete* exc. *dial.* E17.
6 a A line-of-battle ship. E19. ▸**b** A ship belonging to a line of passenger ships. M19. ▸**c** An aircraft belonging to a regular line, used esp. for passenger transport. Also, a spaceship. E20. ▸**d** Any of a fleet of lorries; a container lorry. Also, a container train (chiefly in ***Freightliner*** s.v. FREIGHT *noun*, ***liner train*** below). M20.

b R. P. JHABVALA Both loved the fun to be had on an ocean liner. *Sunday Express* The supposedly unsinkable liner rammed an iceberg on . . her maiden voyage. **c** *New Scientist* The Boeing liner will have rather more than twice the capacity of the Concorde.

7 *BASEBALL.* A ball which, when struck, flies through the air in a nearly straight line not far from the ground. M19.
8 a A fine paintbrush used for outlining etc. L19. ▸**b** A cosmetic used for tinting a part of the face; a brush or pencil for applying this; *spec.* = ***eyeliner*** s.v. EYE *noun*. E20.

b *Slimming* Her eyes aren't circled any more by hard black liner.

9 A picture exhibited on the line, with its centre about level with the spectator's eye. *colloq.* L19.
10 A boat engaged in sea-fishing with lines as opp. to nets. E20.
11 An advertisement occupying a specified number of lines of print; *colloq.* a spoken passage of a specified number of lines in a play etc. Usu. as 2nd elem. of comb., preceded by a numeral (cf. ***one-liner*** s.v. ONE *adjective*). E20.
one-liner, ***two-liner***, etc.
12 A ferret held on a leash or line while rabbiting. E20.
– COMB.: **liner train** a fast through-running freight train made up of detachable containers on permanently coupled wagons.

linesman /ˈlʌɪnzmən/ *noun*. Pl. **-men**. M19.
[ORIGIN from LINE *noun*[2] + -'S[1] + MAN *noun*.]
1 A soldier belonging to a regiment of the line. M19.
2 = LINEMAN 1. L19.
3 a An umpire's or referee's assistant who decides whether or not a ball falls within the area of play on a court or pitch. L19. ▸**b** = LINEMAN 4. M20.
4 A person who attends to the upkeep of roadside verges. L19.

liney *adjective* var. of LINY.

ling /lɪŋ/ *noun*[1]. Also (earlier) †**leng**. ME.
[ORIGIN Prob. of Dutch or Low German origin; cf. Dutch *leng*, earlier *lenghe*, *linghe* rel. to LONG *adjective*[1] (cf. Old Norse *langa*, Swedish *långa*, Danish *lange*).]
1 Any of several long slender predacious gadoid fishes of the genus *Molva*, esp. *M. molva*, an important food fish found chiefly in the E. Atlantic. ME.
blue ling: see BLUE *adjective*.
2 Any of various other usu. slender fishes; *spec.* (***a***) *US* the burbot; (***b***) *Austral.* the beardie; (***c***) *Austral. & NZ* the pinkish-white cusk-eel *Genypterus blacodes*. M19.
– COMB.: **lingcod** *N. Amer.* a large food and sporting fish, *Ophiodon elongatus*, of the greenling family, found in the N. Pacific; also called ***cultus-cod***.

ling /lɪŋ/ *noun*[2]. ME.
[ORIGIN Old Norse *lyng*, of unknown origin.]
Any of various plants of the heath family, esp. *Calluna vulgaris*, heather. Formerly also, ground having much heather, heathland.
– COMB.: **ling bird** the meadow pipit, *Anthus pratensis*.

ling /lɪŋ/ *noun*[3]. M19.
[ORIGIN Chinese *ling*.]
A water chestnut, *Trapa bicornis*, native to China, the seeds of which are much eaten as food.

†**ling** *verb*. Also (earlier) **leng**.
[ORIGIN Old English *lengan* = Middle Low German *lengen*, Old High German *lengen* (German *längen*), Old Norse *lengja*, from Germanic, from base also of LONG *adjective*[1].]
1 *verb trans.* Lengthen, prolong; delay. OE–ME.
2 *verb intrans.* Linger, remain; continue in some condition. ME–L16.

-ling /lɪŋ/ *suffix*[1].
[ORIGIN Old English from Germanic, formed as -LE[1] + -ING[3]. In sense 2 from Old Norse.]
1 (Not productive.) Forming nouns from nouns with the sense 'a person or thing belonging to or concerned with', as ***hireling***, ***sapling***, etc.; nouns from adjectives with the sense 'a person or thing having the quality of being', as ***darling***, ***youngling***, ***sibling***, etc., (and similarly from an adverb, ***underling***); and nouns from verbs with the sense 'a person or thing undergoing', as ***shaveling***, ***starveling***.
2 Forming nouns from nouns with the sense 'a diminutive person or thing', as ***gosling***, ***duckling***; now freq. *derog.*, as ***godling***, ***lordling***, ***princeling***.

-ling /lɪŋ/ *suffix*[2] (not productive). Also **-lings** /-lɪŋz/.
[ORIGIN Old English *-ling* from Germanic base = extend.]
Forming adverbs of direction or extent from nouns, as ***grovelling***, and adjectives of condition or position from adverbs, as ***darkling***.

Lingala /lɪŋˈɡɑːlə/ *noun & adjective*. Also **Ngala** /(ə)ŋˈɡɑːlə/. E20.
[ORIGIN Bantu.]
(Of or pertaining to) a Bantu language of the Democratic Republic of Congo (Zaire), widely used as a lingua franca in the north and east of that country.

lingam /ˈlɪŋɡam/ *noun*. Also **linga** /ˈlɪŋɡə/. E18.
[ORIGIN Sanskrit *liṅga* sign, (sexual) characteristic. Var. infl. by Tamil *ilinkam*.]
A Hindu sacred object constituting a symbol of the god Siva, *spec.* (the representation of) a phallus.

lingberry *noun* var. of LINGONBERRY.

ling chih /ˈlɪŋ dʒə/ *noun phr.* E20.
[ORIGIN Chinese *língzhī* (Wade–Giles *ling chih*), from *líng* divine + *zhī* fungus.]
A motif on Chinese ceramic ware, esp. a representation of the fungus *Polyporus lucidus*, symbolizing longevity or immortality.

linge /lɪndʒ/ *verb trans. obsolete* exc. *dial.* E17.
[ORIGIN Unknown.]
Beat, thrash.

lingel /ˈlɪŋɡ(ə)l/ *noun*[1]. Now *dial.* Also **lingle**. LME.
[ORIGIN Old French *lignoel*, *ligneul* from popular Latin from Latin *linea* LINE *noun*[2].]
A shoemaker's waxed thread.

L

lingel /ˈlɪŋɡ(ə)l/ *noun*[2]. Now *dial.* Also **lingle**. LME.
[ORIGIN App. repr. Anglo-Norman from Latin *lingula* strap etc. dim. of *lingua* tongue: see -EL[2].]
†**1** *collect. sing.* The leather straps etc. of a horse's harness. Only in LME.
2 A thong, a latchet. M16.
†**3** A flat blade or spoon, a spatula. L16–E17.

lingenberry *noun* var. of LINGONBERRY.

linger /ˈlɪŋɡə/ *verb*. ME.
[ORIGIN Frequentative of LING *verb*: see -ER[5].]
†**1** *verb intrans.* Dwell, abide, stay (in a place). Only in ME.
2 *verb trans.* **a** Foll. by *forth*, *on*, *out*: draw out, prolong, protract by loitering or dallying. Also, idle or fritter *away* (time etc.). L15. ▸**b** Pass (life) sadly or wearily. *arch. rare.* E18.
a T. BROWN The first linger away their lives in perpetual drudgery. SIR W. SCOTT Half measures do but linger out the feud. **b** POPE Far from gay cities, and the ways of men, I linger life.
3 *verb intrans.* Stay behind, postpone one's departure; stay on in or not leave a place at the expected or right time, esp. because of reluctance to go. M16. ▸**b** Proceed at a slow pace; loiter, dawdle. E19. ▸**c** *fig.* Spend a long time *over* or *on* a subject or *round* a place. M19.
D. H. LAWRENCE Kate lingered to hear the end of this hymn. W. S. CHURCHILL Leslie . . lingered in the city with the Scottish cavalry till the day was lost. E. J. HOWARD Emma stayed to clear the table, and Dan lingered with her. **b** DICKENS He was never lingering or loitering, but always walking swiftly. **c** A. P. STANLEY I linger round a subject. D. H. LAWRENCE They measured the rooms, and lingered over every consideration.
4 *verb intrans.* Of a person: drag *on* one's existence in a state of illness, wretchedness, etc.; languish. M16.
RIDER HAGGARD He lingered for nearly two years.
5 *verb intrans.* Be slow to do or begin something; hesitate, delay. M16.
E. A. FREEMAN Malcolm lingered in his preparations.
6 *verb trans.* †**a** Cause to linger; prolong, draw out (the time etc.); delay, defer. M16–M17. ▸†**b** Keep waiting, put (a person) *off*. M16–E17.
a SHAKES. *Oth.* He goes into Mauritania . . unless his abode be linger'd here by some accident. R. SANDERSON Secure ones may linger their repentance till it be too late.
7 *verb intrans.* Have a longing or craving, hanker (*after*). M17.
N. BACON The Cardinal finding the King's mind to linger after another Bedfellow.
8 *verb intrans.* Esp. of illness: be slow to pass away, be protracted; hang *on*. M18. ▸**b** Be slow in coming or accruing. M19. ▸**c** Of an action or condition: be protracted (tiresomely or painfully), drag on. M19.
E. EDWARDS When the Plague had departed from most parts of London, it often lingered in the Tower. B. JOWETT But he has still a doubt lingering in his mind. M. L. KING The bitterly cold winter of 1962 lingered throughout the opening months of 1963. A. C. CLARKE These beliefs still survived, and would linger on for generations. **b** TENNYSON Knowledge comes, but wisdom lingers. **c** C. THIRLWALL As the siege of Ithome lingered, the Spartans called on their allies for aid.
■ **lingerer** *noun* M16.

lingerie /ˈlãʒ(ə)ri, *foreign* lɛ̃ʒri/ *noun*. M19.
[ORIGIN French, from *linge* linen: see -ERY.]
Orig., linen articles collectively; all the articles of linen, lace, etc., in a woman's wardrobe or trousseau. Now, women's underwear and nightclothes.

lingering /ˈlɪŋɡ(ə)rɪŋ/ *adjective*. M16.
[ORIGIN from LINGER *verb* + -ING[2].]
1 *gen.* That lingers. M16.
2 Esp. of illness: slow, painfully protracted. Formerly also, of a poison: characterized by slow action. L16.
■ **lingeringly** *adverb* L16.

lingle *noun*[1], *noun*[2] vars. of LINGEL *noun*[1], *noun*[2].

lingo /ˈlɪŋɡəʊ/ *noun*[1]. *colloq.* (orig. *joc.* & *derog.*). Pl. **-o(e)s**. M17.
[ORIGIN Prob. from Portuguese *lingoa* var. of *lingua* from Latin LINGUA.]
A foreign speech or language; the vocabulary of a special subject or class of people.
W. SAFIRE It was not until the 1960's that 'freak out' blossomed into drug lingo. E. FIGES 'German is a hideous lingo,' muttered Claude.

lingo /ˈlɪŋɡəʊ/ *noun*[2]. Pl. **-os**. M18.
[ORIGIN Perh. var. of LINGOT.]
WEAVING. A weight in a Jacquard loom.

lingo *noun*[3] var. of LINGOA.

lingoa /lɪŋˈɡəʊə/ *noun*. Also ***lingo*** /ˈlɪŋɡəʊ/. E19.
[ORIGIN Moluccan Malay *linggua*.]
A large SE Asian leguminous tree, *Pterocarpus indicus*; the wood of this tree (also called ***Burmese rosewood***, ***amboyna wood***).

lingoa geral *noun phr.* var. of LINGUA GERAL.

lingonberry /ˈlɪŋɡ(ə)nbɛri/ *noun*. Also **lingberry** /ˈlɪŋbɛri/, **lingenberry**. M20.
[ORIGIN from Swedish *lingon* cowberry + BERRY *noun*[1].]
The cowberry, *Vaccinium vitis-idaea*, esp. in Scandinavia, where the berries are much used in cookery. Also, an Arctic variety of this occurring in Russia and N. America.

lingot /ˈlɪŋɡət/ *noun*. *arch.* L15.
[ORIGIN French, from *l'* the + INGOT.]
1 = INGOT 2. L15.
†**2** = INGOT 1. M16–L17.

-lings *suffix* var. of -LING[2].

lingua /ˈlɪŋɡwə/ *noun*. L17.
[ORIGIN Latin = tongue, language.]
1 A language. L17.
2 = LINGO *noun*[2]. *rare.* L18.
3 ANATOMY & ZOOLOGY. The tongue; an organ resembling the tongue in form or function; *spec.* in ENTOMOLOGY, the central portion of the hypopharynx. E19.

†**lingua-** *combining form* see LINGUO-.

linguacious /lɪŋˈɡweɪʃəs/ *adjective*. *rare.* M17.
[ORIGIN Latin *linguaci-*, *linguax* loquacious, formed as LINGUA + -ACIOUS.]
1 Talkative, loquacious. M17.
†**2** Linguistic. Only in E19.

lingua franca /lɪŋɡwə ˈfraŋkə/ *noun phr.* Pl. **lingua francas**, **lingue franche** /lɪŋɡwɪ ˈfraŋki/. L17.
[ORIGIN Italian = Frankish tongue.]
A mixture of Italian with French, Greek, Arabic, Turkish, and Spanish, used in the Levant (now *hist.*). Also, any language serving as a medium between different nations etc. whose own languages are not the same; a system of communication providing mutual understanding.
K. A. PORTER Ric and Rac could not understand the words, but they knew . . the lingua franca of gallantry.

lingua geral /lɪŋɡwə dʒəˈrɑːl/ *noun phr.* Also **lingoa geral**. M19.
[ORIGIN Portuguese *lingua geral* general language.]
A trade language based on Tupi and used as a lingua franca in Brazil.

lingual /ˈlɪŋɡw(ə)l/ *adjective* & *noun*. LME.
[ORIGIN medieval Latin *lingualis*, formed as LINGUA + -AL[1].]
▸ **A** *adjective*. †**1** Tongue-shaped. Only in LME.
2 Chiefly ANATOMY & ZOOLOGY. Of, pertaining to, or involving the tongue or a tonguelike part; situated on or towards the tongue. M17.
lingual nerve a sensory nerve (a branch of the fifth cranial nerve) supplying the tongue. **lingual ribbon** the odontophore of a mollusc.
3 PHONETICS. Of a sound: formed by the tongue. M17.
4 Pertaining to the tongue as the organ of speech; pertaining to language or languages. L18.
▸ **B** *noun*. **1** PHONETICS. A lingual sound. M17.
2 ANATOMY. The lingual nerve. L19.
■ **lingualize** *verb trans.* make lingual L19. **lingually** *adverb* (ANATOMY) towards the tongue L19.

Linguaphone /ˈlɪŋɡwəfəʊn/ *noun*. Also **l-**. E20.
[ORIGIN from LINGUA + *-phone*, after GRAMOPHONE.]
(Proprietary name for) a language-teaching system based on the use of sound recordings in conjunction with textbooks.

linguatulid /lɪŋˈɡwatjʊlɪd/ *noun* & *adjective*. E20.
[ORIGIN mod. Latin *Linguatulida* former name of the group, from *Linguatula* (see below), from Latin *linguatus* lit. 'having a tongue', formed as LINGUA: see -ATE[2], -ID[3].]
▸ **A** *noun*. = PENTASTOMID *noun*; *spec.* one of the genus *Linguatula*, which parasitizes carnivorous mammals, esp. canids. E20.
▸ **B** *adjective*. = PENTASTOMID *adjective*. E20.

lingue franche *noun phr. pl.* see LINGUA FRANCA.

Linguet /ˈlɪŋɡwət/ *noun*. Also **l-**. M20.
[ORIGIN from Latin *lingua* tongue + -ET[1].]
PHARMACOLOGY. A tablet that is retained in the mouth, usu. under the tongue, while its ingredients are absorbed through the oral tissues.
– NOTE: Proprietary name in the US.

linguiform /ˈlɪŋɡwɪfɔːm/ *adjective*. M18.
[ORIGIN from LINGUA + -I- + -FORM.]
ANATOMY, BOTANY, & ZOOLOGY. Shaped like a tongue.

linguine /lɪŋˈɡwiːni/ *noun pl.* M20.
[ORIGIN Italian, pl. of *linguina* dim. of *lingua* tongue from Latin.]
Pasta in the form of tongue-shaped ribbons; an Italian dish consisting largely of this and usu. a sauce.

linguist /ˈlɪŋɡwɪst/ *noun*. L16.
[ORIGIN from Latin LINGUA + -IST.]
1 A person skilled in foreign languages. Freq. with specifying word. L16.
P. GROSSKURTH Abraham, . . well known as a gifted linguist. R. DEACON Blackwell was . . a linguist with a command of twenty languages.
†**2** A person who speaks freely and eloquently; a skilful speaker. L16–L17.
ANTHONY WOOD Richard Martin . . was a plausible Linguist, and eminent for Speeches spoken in Parliaments.
3 An expert in or student of language or linguistics. E17.
D. HARTLEY A Light in which Grammarians and Linguists alone consider Words. N. CHOMSKY A linguist studying English might propose several possible rules of question-formation.
mathematical linguist: see MATHEMATICAL *adjective*. ***structural linguist***.
4 = INTERPRETER 2. Now *rare* or *obsolete*. E17.
P. THOMAS This Evening came . . a Chinese Interpreter or Linguist.

linguister /ˈlɪŋɡwɪstə/ *noun*. Now *US*. M17.
[ORIGIN from LINGUIST + -ER[1].]
1 = LINGUIST 4. M17.
2 = LINGUIST 3. *rare.* L19.

linguistic /lɪŋˈɡwɪstɪk/ *adjective* & *noun*. M19.
[ORIGIN formed as LINGUIST + -IC. Cf. French *linguistique*, German *Linguistik*.]
▸ **A** *adjective*. Of or pertaining to the knowledge or study of languages; of or pertaining to language or languages. M19.
J. B. CARROLL The study of verbal behavior . . has . . been called . . *linguistic psychology*. V. S. NAIPAUL The knowledge I brought . . was linguistic. I knew that 'avon' originally meant only 'river'.
linguistic analysis (**a**) the analysis of language structures in terms of a particular theory of language; (**b**) PHILOSOPHY analysis of language as the medium of thought. **linguistic analyst** a person who practises linguistic analysis. **linguistic anthropology** anthropological research based on the study of the language of a selected group. **linguistic atlas** a set of tables or maps recording regional or dialectal variations of pronunciation, vocabulary, or inflectional forms. **linguistic geography** the branch of knowledge that deals with the geographical distribution of languages, dialects, etc.
▸ **B** *noun*. = LINGUISTICS. *rare.* M19.
■ **linguistical** *adjective* linguistic E19. **linguistically** *adverb* M19. **linguistician** /-ˈtɪʃ(ə)n/ *noun* an expert in or student of linguistics L19.

linguistics /lɪŋˈɡwɪstɪks/ *noun*. M19.
[ORIGIN from LINGUISTIC: see -ICS.]
The branch of knowledge that deals with language.
applied linguistics, ***area linguistics***, ***historical linguistics***, ***mathematical linguistics***, ***structural linguistics***, ***systemic linguistics***, ***text linguistics***, ***theoretical linguistics***, etc. ***ethnolinguistics***, ***psycholinguistics***, ***sociolinguistics***, etc.

linguistry /ˈlɪŋɡwɪstri/ *noun*. *rare.* L18.
[ORIGIN formed as LINGUIST + -RY.]
Linguistics.

lingula /ˈlɪŋɡjʊlə/ *noun*. Pl. **-lae** /-liː/. M17.
[ORIGIN Latin, partly from *lingere* lick, partly dim. of LINGUA: see -ULE. Cf. LIGULA.]
1 A device or (now usu.) anatomical structure resembling a small tongue; *spec.* in ANATOMY, a projection from the anterior cerebellum. M17.
2 Any (extant or fossil) inarticulate brachiopod of the genus *Lingula*. Now chiefly as mod. Latin genus name. M19.
■ **lingular** *adjective* (ANATOMY) of or pertaining to a lingula M19.

lingulate /ˈlɪŋɡjʊleɪt/ *adjective*. M19.
[ORIGIN Latin *lingulatus*, formed as LINGULA + -ATE[2].]
Tongue-shaped.

linguo- /ˈlɪŋɡwəʊ/ *combining form* of Latin LINGUA tongue: see -O-. Also †**lingua-**.
■ **linguo'dental** *adjective* & *noun* = INTERDENTAL *adjective* 2, *noun* M17.

lingworm /ˈlɪŋwəːm/ *noun*. Also **lyngorm** /ˈlɪŋɔːm/. L19.
[ORIGIN Old Norse *lyngormr*, from *lyng* heather + *ormr* serpent, snake (cf. WORM *noun*). Cf. LINDWORM.]
A fabulous serpent of Scandinavian mythology.

lingy /ˈlɪŋi/ *adjective*. M17.
[ORIGIN from LING *noun*[2] + -Y[1].]
Having much ling or heather; covered with ling.

linhay /ˈlɪni/ *noun*. *dial.* L17.
[ORIGIN Unknown.]
A shed or other farm building open in front, usually with a lean-to roof.

liniment /ˈlɪnɪm(ə)nt/ *noun*. LME.
[ORIGIN Late Latin *linimentum*, from Latin *linire* smear, anoint: see -MENT.]
†**1** Something used for smearing or anointing. LME–L17.
2 *spec.* An embrocation, usu. made with oil. LME.

linin /ˈlʌɪnɪn/ *noun*. M19.
[ORIGIN Greek *linon* thread + -IN[1].]
CYTOLOGY (now chiefly *hist.*). A lightly staining substance which forms a network of fine threads around the chromatin in an interphase nucleus.

lining /ˈlʌɪnɪŋ/ *noun*[1]. LME.
[ORIGIN from LINE *verb*[1] + -ING[1].]
1 The material with which a garment is lined; the inner or undersurface of material used to line a garment, esp. for protection or warmth. LME. ▸**b** In *pl.* Knickers, underpants; underclothes. Chiefly *dial.* E17.
J. RATHBONE A black velvet coat with . . scarlet silk lining.

L

2 *fig.* Contents; what is inside. **LME.**

SHAKES. *Rich. II* The lining of his coffers shall make coats To deck our soldiers for these Irish wars. J. BURROUGHS I was sure to return at meal-time with a lining of berries in the top of my straw hat.

3 Any material occurring or placed next beneath an outer one; an inside layer or surface. **E18.**

P. PARISH The stomach can get 'upset' if its lining is irritated (e.g. by aspirin or alcohol).

silver lining: see SILVER *noun & adjective*.

4 The action of providing something with a lining. Also foll. by *up*. **M19.**

lining /ˈlʌɪnɪŋ/ *noun*[2]. **L16.**
[ORIGIN from LINE *verb*[2] + -ING[1].]
1 Chiefly *MILITARY*. Arranging in line, alignment. **L16.**
2 The official marking of the boundaries of burghal properties in a Scottish royal burgh. Also (more fully ***decree of lining***), permission to erect or alter a building according to specified conditions. **L16.**
3 The use of a measuring line or of a stretched cord for alignment. **E19.**
4 The action of tracing (*out*) lines. **E19.**
5 The giving out of a hymn (by the precentor) line by line. Also foll. by *out*. **M19.**
6 Fishing with a line as opp. to a net. **M19.**

linish /ˈlɪnɪʃ/ *verb trans.* **L20.**
[ORIGIN from LIN(EN *noun* + FIN)ISH *verb*.]
Polish or remove excess material from (an object) by contact with a moving continuous belt coated with abrasive material. Chiefly as ***linishing*** *verbal noun*.
■ **linisher** *noun* a machine for linishing things **M20.**

link /lɪŋk/ *noun*[1].
[ORIGIN Old English *hlinc* (whence also LINCH *noun*[2]), perh. deriv. of base of LEAN *verb*.]
1 Rising ground; a ridge, a bank. *obsolete* exc. *dial.* **OE.**
2 In *pl.* Level or gently undulating sandy ground near a seashore, with turf, coarse grass, etc. (*Scot.*); (treated as *sing.* or *pl.*, more fully ***golf links***) a golf course, *esp.* one on such ground. **LME.**
– COMB.: **linksland** ground suitable or used for a golf links.
■ **linky** *adjective* (*rare*) resembling a link or links **M19.**

link /lɪŋk/ *noun*[2]. **LME.**
[ORIGIN Old Norse *hlekkr* (Icelandic *hlekkur*, Old Swedish *lænker*), from Germanic, rel. to Middle Low German *lenkhake* pot-hook, Middle High German *gelenke* (collect.) flexible parts of the body, (also mod.) *gelenk* joint, link.]
1 Any of a series of rings or loops forming a chain. Formerly also (in *pl.*), chains, fetters. **LME.** ▸**b** A chain. Long *obsolete* exc. *dial.* **L16.** ▸**c** Any of the hundred divisions of a surveyor's chain; a length equal to this (7.92 inches, approx. 20.1 cm). **M17.** ▸**d** = ***cufflink*** s.v. CUFF *noun*[1]. **E19.**

L. T. C. ROLT Short links between each of the main links of the suspension chains. *fig.*: R. V. JONES I had . . forged out every link in the chain of evidence. **d** S. BELLOW His shirt cuffs were soiled; he turned them underside up and transferred the links.

2 Something looped, or forming part of a chainlike arrangement; a loop. **LME.** ▸**b** Any of the divisions of a chain of sausages or black puddings. Usu. in *pl.* Now chiefly *dial.* **LME.** ▸**c** A joint of the body. Long *obsolete* exc. *Scot.* **E16.** ▸**d** In *pl.* The windings of a stream; the land along such windings. *Scot.* **L18.**

SHAKES. *2 Hen. IV* Now, Sir, a new link to the bucket must needs be had. **b** B. BAINBRIDGE Links of sausages coiled on a newspaper.

3 A connecting part; *esp.* a thing or a person serving to establish or maintain a connection; a member of a series; a means of connection or communication. **LME.** ▸**b** A means of travel or transport between two places. **M19.** ▸**c** A system or unit of contact by radio or telephone between two points. **E20.** ▸**d** [translating Russian *zveno*.] A small labour unit on a collective farm in the countries of the former USSR. **M20.** ▸**e** *FOOTBALL & HOCKEY*. A linkman. **M20.** ▸**f** *COMPUTING*. = POINTER 3d. **M20.**

N. FRYE The connecting link between . . the poem . . and what unites it to other forms of poetic experience. A. BEVAN The last link with medieval society was broken. **b** P. THEROUX There is no road or rail link through the Darien Gap between Panama and Columbia.

– PHRASES: **let out the links** act with more power, put more into something. *MISSING* ***link***. ***weak link***, ***weakest link***: see WEAK *adjective*.
– COMB.: **link buttons** a pair of buttons linked by a thread etc.; **link road** a road serving to link two or more major roads or centres; **link rod** (*a*) a rod which joins the levers on the steered stub axles of a motor vehicle; (*b*) each of the rods which connect pistons to wrist pins on the master rod in a radial internal-combustion engine; **linkspan** a bridge hinged at one end and used in loading and unloading a ship etc.; **link-verb** *GRAMMAR* a copular verb; **link-word** *GRAMMAR* any part of speech performing a linking function; **linkwork** (*a*) work composed of or arranged in links; (*b*) a kind of gearing whereby motion is transmitted by links as opp. to wheels or bands.

link /lɪŋk/ *noun*[3]. **E16.**
[ORIGIN Perh. from medieval Latin *linchinus* alt. of *lichinus* wick, match from Greek *lukhnos* light.]
1 *hist.* A torch made esp. of tow and pitch for lighting the way along dark streets. **E16.** ▸**b** A link boy. **M19.**
†**2** The material of such a torch used as blacking. **L16–E18.**
– COMB.: **link boy**: employed to carry a link; LINKMAN *noun*[1].

Link /lɪŋk/ *noun*[4]. **M20.**
[ORIGIN Edward *Link*, its Amer. inventor.]
In full ***Link trainer***. A flight simulator on which pilots are trained.

link /lɪŋk/ *adjective*. **L19.**
[ORIGIN Yiddish from German = left.]
Among Jews: not pious, not orthodox (in religion).

link /lɪŋk/ *verb*[1]. **LME.**
[ORIGIN from LINK *noun*[2].]
1 *verb trans.* Connect or join (two things or one thing to another) with or as with a link. (Foll. by *together, to, with*.) **LME.** ▸**b** Clasp, intertwine, (hands or arms). **M19.** ▸**c** Connect causally, associate in speech, thought, etc., *with* or *to*. **M20.**

D. ATTENBOROUGH A . . blood-vessel and a nerve cord run . . through all the segments, linking and coordinating them. R. DAVIES The automobile was linking the villages with towns, and the towns with cities. **b** P. H. JOHNSON His hands linked like an old man's behind his back. S. MIDDLETON They linked arms, filling the pavement. **c** E. L. DOCTOROW Her name was linked with dozens of men around town.

2 *verb intrans.* Be joined or connected (as) with a link, esp. in friendship, marriage, etc. Also foll. by *together*. **M16.** ▸**b** Go arm in arm, or hand in hand. **E19.**

SHAKES. *3 Hen. VI* For I were loath To link with him that were not lawful chosen. BURKE No one generation could link with the other.

– WITH ADVERBS IN SPECIALIZED SENSES: **link up** connect, combine, (*with*).
– COMB.: **link-up** an act or result of linking up.
■ **linker** *noun* **M19.**

link /lɪŋk/ *verb*[2] *intrans. Scot. & N. English.* **E18.**
[ORIGIN Uncertain: perh. rel. to LINK *verb*[1]. Cf. Norwegian *linka* toss or bend the body.]
Move nimbly, pass quickly along.
link off pass away, disappear quickly.

linkage /ˈlɪŋkɪdʒ/ *noun*. **L19.**
[ORIGIN from LINK *noun*[2], *verb*[1] + -AGE.]
1 The state of being linked; a system of links. Also, a link; a connection; the process of linking or connecting. **L19.** ▸**b** The linking together of different political issues as a negotiating tactic. **M20.**

Time She had made the proper linkages to British Victorianism and German romantic philosophy. **b** *Time* The real stumbling block is 'linkage'—the relationship between an Egyptian-Israeli treaty and a wider Middle East settlement.

2 *GENETICS*. (An) association between characters in inheritance such that they tend to be inherited together, owing to the location of their respective alleles on the same chromosome; formerly called ***coupling***, ***gametic coupling***. Also, the amount or degree of this association (between 50 per cent and 100 per cent). Cf. REPULSION 3c. **E20.**
– COMB.: ***linkage map***: see MAP *noun*[1] 1b.

linked /ˈlɪŋkt/ *adjective*. **LME.**
[ORIGIN from LINK *noun*[2], *verb*[1]: see -ED[2], -ED[1].]
1 Connected (as) by links; joined, associated. Formerly also, made or fashioned with links. **LME.**
linked list *COMPUTING* an ordered set of data elements, each of which contains a pointer to its successor.
2 *MILITARY*. Of two infantry battalions or regiments: joined together to form a regimental district. **L19.**
3 Of industries: allied to and dependent on one another. **M20.**
■ **linkedness** *noun* (*rare*) interconnection **E20.**

linking /ˈlɪŋkɪŋ/ *adjective*. **L19.**
[ORIGIN from LINK *verb*[1] + -ING[2].]
1 That links or joins together; *GRAMMAR* copulative. **L19.**
linking r a word-final *r* sound, represented in spelling, that is pronounced before a vowel but in standard British English no longer before a consonant or pause, as in *bar opens* /bɑːr ˈəʊpənz/ as opp. to *bar closes* /bɑː ˈkləʊzɪz/ (cf. ***intrusive r*** s.v. INTRUSIVE *adjective* 2).
2 *BROADCASTING & CINEMATOGRAPHY*. Of music, camera shots, commentary, etc.: providing continuity between programmes, scenes, etc. **M20.**

linkman /ˈlɪŋkmən/ *noun*[1]. Pl. **-men**. **E18.**
[ORIGIN from LINK *noun*[3] + MAN *noun*.]
hist. A man employed to carry a link to light the way.

linkman /ˈlɪŋkmən/ *noun*[2]. Pl. **-men**. **E20.**
[ORIGIN from LINK *noun*[2] + MAN *noun*.]
1 A person serving as a link between groups of people etc. **E20.**
2 *BROADCASTING*. A person providing continuity in a radio or television programme consisting of several items. **M20.**
3 *FOOTBALL & HOCKEY*. A player between the forwards and half-backs or strikers and backs. **M20.**

lin-lan-lone /ˈlɪnlanləʊn, lɪnlanˈləʊn/ *noun*. **L19.**
[ORIGIN Imit.]
Repr. the sound of a chime of three bells.

linn /lɪn/ *noun*[1]. Chiefly *Scot.*
[ORIGIN Old English *hlynn*, but largely from Gaelic *linne*, Irish *linn* (earlier *lind*) = Welsh *llyn* lake, pool, Old Cornish *-lin*, Breton *lin*.]
1 A torrent running over rocks; a cascade, a waterfall. **OE.**
2 A pool, *esp.* one into which a cataract falls. **M16.**
3 A precipice, a ravine with precipitous sides. **L18.**

linn /lɪn/ *noun*[2]. Now *dial. & US*. **L15.**
[ORIGIN Alt. of LIND.]
The linden or lime; the wood of this tree.

Linn. *abbreviation*.
TAXONOMY. Linnaeus.

linnaea /lɪˈniːə/ *noun*. **M19.**
[ORIGIN mod. Latin (see below), from *Linnaeus*: see LINNAEAN.]
A slender trailing plant, *Linnaea borealis*, of the honeysuckle family, which bears two pink pendulous flowers and is found in coniferous woods in northern latitudes. Also called ***twinflower***.

Linnaean /lɪˈniːən/ *adjective & noun*. Also **Linnean**. **M18.**
[ORIGIN from *Linnaeus*, Latinized form of *Linné* (see below) + -AN.]
▸ **A** *adjective*. Of or pertaining to the Swedish naturalist Linnaeus (Carl von Linné, 1707–78), the founder of modern systematic botany and zoology, or his binomial system of nomenclature for the classification of plants and animals; instituted by Linnaeus; adhering to the system of Linnaeus. **M18.**
▸ **B** *noun*. A follower of Linnaeus; a person who adopts the Linnaean system. **L18.**
– NOTE: Spelled *Linnean* in *Linnean Society*.

Linnean *adjective & noun* var. of LINNAEAN.

linnet /ˈlɪnɪt/ *noun*. **E16.**
[ORIGIN Old French (Walloon, Picard) *linette*, earlier *linot* (mod. *linot*, *linotte*), from *lin* flax from Latin *linum*. Cf. LINTWHITE.]
A small common migratory Eurasian songbird, *Acanthis cannabina*, of the passerine family Fringillidae, with brown or grey plumage, formerly kept as a pet. Also (usu. with specifying word), any of several similar songbirds.
green linnet: see GREEN *adjective*. **mountain linnet** = TWITE. ***pine linnet***: see PINE *noun*[2]. ***rose linnet***: see ROSE *adjective*.

linnet-hole /ˈlɪnɪthəʊl/ *noun*. **M17.**
[ORIGIN from alt. of French LUNETTE + HOLE *noun*[1].]
GLASS-MAKING. = LUNETTE 9.

lino /ˈlʌɪnəʊ/ *noun*[1]. Pl. **-os**. **E20.**
[ORIGIN Abbreviation.]
= LINOLEUM.

lino /ˈlʌɪnəʊ/ *noun*[2]. **E20.**
[ORIGIN Abbreviation.]
= LINOTYPE.

†**lino** *noun*[3] var. of LENO.

linocut /ˈlʌɪnəʊkʌt/ *noun*. **E20.**
[ORIGIN from LINO(LEUM + CUT *noun*[2].]
(A print made from) a design cut in relief on a piece of linoleum.
■ **linocutter** *noun* a person who makes a linocut; a tool for making linocuts: **E20.** **linocutting** *noun* the making of linocuts **E20.**

linography /lʌɪˈnɒɡrəfi/ *noun*. **L19.**
[ORIGIN from Latin *linum* flax + -OGRAPHY.]
A process of photographing on linen or calico to produce a representation to be coloured.
■ **linograph** *noun* a picture produced by linography **L20.**

linoleic /lɪnə(ʊ)ˈliːɪk, -ˈleɪɪk/ *adjective*. **M19.**
[ORIGIN from Latin *linum* flax + OLEIC.]
CHEMISTRY. ***linoleic acid***, a polyunsaturated fatty acid, $C_{17}H_{31}COOH$, which occurs as a glyceride in linseed oil and other drying oils, and is essential in the human diet. Cf. LINOLENIC.
■ **liˈnoleate** *noun* a salt or ester of linoleic acid **M19.** **liˈnolein** *noun* a glyceride of linoleic acid occurring in linseed oil **E20.**

linolenic /lɪnə(ʊ)ˈlɛnɪk, -ˈliːnɪk/ *adjective*. **L19.**
[ORIGIN from German *Linolen(saüre)*, from *Linolsaüre* LINOLEIC ***acid*** with inserted *-en* -ENE: see -IC.]
CHEMISTRY. ***linolenic acid***, a polyunsaturated fatty acid, $C_{17}H_{29}COOH$ (with one more double bond than the related linoleic acid), which occurs as a glyceride in linseed oil and other drying oils, and is essential in the human diet.
■ **liˈnolenate** *noun* a salt or ester of linolenic acid **E20.**

linoleum /lɪˈnəʊlɪəm/ *noun*. **L19.**
[ORIGIN from Latin *linum* flax + *oleum* oil.]
Canvas backing thickly coated with a preparation of linseed oil and powdered cork etc., used esp. as a floor-covering; a piece or example of this.
■ **linoleumed** *adjective* **L19.**

Linotype /ˈlʌɪnə(ʊ)tʌɪp/ *noun*. Also **l-**. **L19.**
[ORIGIN Alt. of *line o' type*.]
PRINTING. (Proprietary name for) a composing machine producing lines of words as single strips of metal, used esp. for newspapers.
■ **linotypist** *noun* a person who uses a Linotype machine **L20.**

L

linoxyn /lɪˈnɒksɪn/ *noun*. L19.
[ORIGIN from Latin *linum* flax + OXY- + -IN[1].]
CHEMISTRY. Any of various gelatinous or resinous substances obtained by oxidation of linseed oil by air.

linsang /ˈlɪnsaŋ/ *noun*. E19.
[ORIGIN Javanese & Malay.]
Either of two SE Asian forest animals related to civets, *Prionodon pardicolor* (more fully ***spotted linsang***) and *P. linsang* (more fully ***banded linsang***). Also (more fully ***African linsang***, ***Guinea linsang***), the related W. African mammal *Poiana richardsonii*.

linseed /ˈlɪnsiːd/ *noun*. OE.
[ORIGIN from LINE *noun*[1] + SEED *noun*.]
The seed of flax. Formerly also (*rare*), the flax plant.
– COMB.: **linseed cake** linseed pressed into cakes and used as cattle food; **linseed meal** ground linseed; **linseed oil** a desiccant oil extracted from linseed and used in paint and varnish; **linseed poultice** a poultice made of linseed or linseed meal.

linsey /ˈlɪnzi/ *noun & adjective*. LME.
[ORIGIN Prob. from *Lindsey* in Suffolk, southern England, said to be the original place of manufacture.]
Orig., (made of) a coarse linen fabric. Later, (made of) linsey-woolsey.

linsey-woolsey /lɪnzɪˈwʊlzi/ *noun & adjective*. L15.
[ORIGIN from LINSEY + WOOL *noun* + *-sey* jingling termination. Cf. WINCEY.]
▸ **A** *noun*. **1** Orig., a textile material of wool and linen. Now, a dress material of coarse inferior wool woven on a cotton warp. L15. ▸**b** A garment of this material. L19.
2 *fig.* A strange medley in talk or action; confusion, nonsense. L16.
▸ **B** *attrib.* or as *adjective*. Made of linsey-woolsey; *fig.* appearing to constitute a strange medley, confused, nonsensical. M16.

Linson /ˈlɪns(ə)n/ *noun*. M20.
[ORIGIN from *Linwood*, Scotland, where first made + R. & W. Watson, the first manufacturers.]
(Proprietary name for) a tough fibrous paper fabric used esp. in bookbinding as a cheaper substitute for cloth.

linstock /ˈlɪnstɒk/ *noun*. *obsolete* exc. *hist.* L16.
[ORIGIN Dutch *lontstok*, from *lont* match + *stok* stick, assim. to LINT.]
A staff with a head to hold a lighted match, and used to fire a cannon.

L

lint /lɪnt/ *noun*. LME.
[ORIGIN Perh. from Old French *linette* linseed, from *lin* flax: see -ETTE, -ET[1].]
1 The flax plant. Now only *Scot.* LME.
2 Flax prepared for spinning. Also, the refuse of this, used as a combustible. Chiefly *Scot.* LME.
3 A soft material used esp. for dressing wounds, orig. made by ravelling or scraping linen cloth. Formerly also in *pl.*, pieces of this material. LME. ▸**b** Orig., a particle of fluff. Later, fluff. E17.
4 Netting for fishing nets. Now *dial.* & *US*. E17.
5 The material which forms the bulk of the fibres in the cotton boll (cf. LINTER), which is separated from the cotton-seeds by ginning and which after processing is the ordinary cotton of commerce. L19.
– COMB.: **lint-head** *US dial.* a worker in a cotton mill; *derog.* a person of whom one disapproves; **lint-scraper** *hist.* a person employed to scrape lint (for hospital use); *slang*, *derog.* a young surgeon.
■ **linty** *adjective* †(*a*) resembling lint (*lit.* & *fig.*); (*b*) full of lint or fluff: E17.

lintel /ˈlɪnt(ə)l/ *noun*. ME.
[ORIGIN Old French (mod. *linteau*) from Proto-Romance, infl. by late Latin *liminare*, from Latin *limin-*, *limen* threshold.]
ARCHITECTURE. A horizontal support of timber, stone, metal, or concrete across the top of a door, window, or other opening.
■ **lintelled** *adjective* provided with a lintel E19.

linter /ˈlɪntə/ *noun*. *US*. E20.
[ORIGIN from LINT + -ER[1].]
1 A machine for removing the short fibres from cotton-seeds after ginning. E20.
2 In *pl.* The short fibres removed from the cotton-seeds after ginning. E20.

lintern /ˈlɪntən/ *noun*. Long *obsolete* exc. *dial.* Also (earlier) **linton**. M16.
[ORIGIN Alt.]
= LINTEL.

lintie /ˈlɪnti/ *noun*. *Scot.* L18.
[ORIGIN from LINT(WHITE + -IE, -Y[6].]
= LINNET.
rose lintie: see ROSE *adjective*.

linton *noun* see LINTERN.

lintwhite /ˈlɪntwʌɪt/ *noun*. Chiefly *Scot.*
[ORIGIN Old English from LINE *noun*[1] + *-twige* as in Old High German *zwigôn* pluck.]
= LINNET.

linum /ˈlʌɪnəm/ *noun*. M19.
[ORIGIN mod. Latin (see below), use as genus name of Latin *linum* flax.]
Any of various plants constituting the genus *Linum* (family Linaceae), which includes the cultivated flax, *L. usitatissimum*; *esp.* one grown for ornament.

linuron /ˈlɪnjʊrɒn/ *noun*. M20.
[ORIGIN from *lin-* of unknown origin + UR(EA + *-on* (arbitrary ending).]
An agricultural herbicide consisting of a cyclic derivative of urea.

Linux /ˈlɪnʌks, ˈlʌɪnʌks/ *noun*. L20.
[ORIGIN from the name of *Linus* Benedict Torvalds (b. 1969), Finnish software engineer, who wrote the first version of the system, + -X, as in UNIX.]
COMPUTING. A computer operating system modelled on Unix, whose source code is publicly available at no charge.
– NOTE: Proprietary name in the US.

liny /ˈlʌɪni/ *adjective*. Also **liney**. E19.
[ORIGIN from LINE *noun*[2] + -Y[1].]
1 Of the nature of or resembling a line or streak, thin, meagre. E19.
2 Full of lines, marked with lines. E19.

Linzertorte /ˈlɪntsərtɔrtə, ˈlɪntsətɔːtə/ *noun*. Pl. ***-ten*** /-t(ə)n/. E20.
[ORIGIN German, from *Linzer* adjective of the Austrian city *Linz* + *Torte* tart, pastry, cake (cf. TORTE).]
A kind of pastry with a jam filling, decorated on top with strips of pastry in a lattice pattern.

lion /ˈlʌɪən/ *noun & adjective*. ME.
[ORIGIN Anglo-Norman *liun* (French *lion*) from Latin *leo*, *leon* from Greek *leōn*, replacing earlier LEO.]
▸ **A** *noun*. **1** A large powerful carnivorous feline, *Panthera leo*, found in sub-Saharan Africa and parts of India (formerly more widely) and having a tawny or yellowish brown coat, a tufted tail, and (in the male) a shaggy mane; the male of this (cf. LIONESS); this animal as the type of strength, majesty, and courage, the 'king of beasts'. See also ***ant lion*** s.v. ANT *noun*, SEA LION. ME.

E. HALL We must . . fight together like lions. J. HOWELL Like the month of March, which entreth like a Lion.

2 *fig.* **a** A person who is strong, courageous, or fiercely brave. ME. ▸**b** A fiercely cruel, tyrannical, or rapacious creature or person. ME. ▸**c** (**L-**.) A member of a Lions Club (see below). E20.
3 An image or picture of a lion, esp. as a heraldic emblem, or as a sign for inns etc. ME. ▸**b** (**L-**.) The lion as the national emblem of Great Britain; *fig.* the British nation. Also ***British Lion***. L17. ▸**c** (**L-**.) A member of a British Isles rugby union team touring abroad. Also ***British and Irish Lion***. M20.

R. WEST Let's stop off at the Red Lion . . they do a posh tea.

4 A gold coin current in Scotland down to the reign of James VI. Also = HARD-HEAD 5. *obsolete* exc. *hist.* LME.
5 (Usu. **L-**.) (The name of) *the* constellation and zodiacal sign Leo; ***Little Lion***, (the name of) *the* constellation Leo Minor. LME.
6 **a** In *pl.* Things of note, celebrity, or curiosity (in a town etc.); sights worth seeing. Esp. in ***see the lions***, ***show the lions***. L16. ▸**b** A person of note or celebrity who is much sought after. E17. ▸†**c** A visitor to Oxford University. *slang*. L18–E19.

a B. H. MALKIN The churches were the best lions we met with. **b** A. S. DALE At fifty Shaw was a literary lion with a colourful public image. B. MASON Whenever Glad could bag a visiting lion . . . she would command The Friends to entertain.

– PHRASES: **a lion in the way**, **a lion in the path** [*Proverbs* 26:13] a danger or obstacle, esp. an imaginary one. ***beard the lion in his den***, ***beard the lion in his lair***: see BEARD *verb* 1. ***British and Irish Lion***: see senses 3c above. *foreign* ***British Lion***: see sense 3b above. ***Little Lion***: see sense 5 above. **mountain lion** = PUMA. ***Nemean lion***. **the lion's mouth** (a type of) a place of great peril. **the lion's provider** the jackal. **the lion's share** the largest or principal portion. ***twist the lion's tail***: see TWIST *verb*.
– COMB.: **lion ant** = *ant-lion* s.v. ANT *noun*; **lion dance** a traditional Chinese dance in which the dancers are masked and costumed to resemble lions; **lion dog** (*a*) (a dog belonging to) any of several breeds resembling miniature lions in colour or type of fur; (*b*) = ***ridgeback*** s.v. RIDGE *noun*[1]; **lionhead** a variety of goldfish having an enlarged head; **lionheart** a courageous person, freq. [translating French *Cœur de Lion*] as a sobriquet of Richard I, King of England 1189–99; **lionhearted** *adjective* having the heart or courage of a lion; courageous; magnanimously brave; **lion-hunter** a person who hunts lions; a person who is given to lionizing celebrities; **lion-huntress** a female lion-hunter; **Lions Club** any of numerous associated clubs devoted to social and international service, the first of which was founded in Chicago in 1917; **lion's ear** any of various plants of the African genus *Leonotis*, of the mint family, esp. *L. leonurus*, cultivated for its showy orange flowers borne in axillary clusters; **lion's foot** a plant of the Eurasian genus *Leontopodium*, of the composite family, *esp.* edelweiss, *L. alpinum*; **lion's heart** = ***obedient plant*** s.v. OBEDIENT 1; **lion's leaf** any plant of the Eurasian genus *Leontice*, of the berberis family, esp. *L. leontopetalum*; **lion's tail** the plant *Leonotis leonurus* (see ***lion's ear*** above); **lion's turnip** = ***lion's leaf*** above; **lion-tailed macaque** a SW Indian macaque, *Macaca silenus*; **lion tamarin** a tamarin of the genus *Leontopithecus*, esp. (more fully ***golden lion tamarin***) *Leontopithecus rosalia* of SE Brazil, with long silky golden fur; **lion-tawny** *noun & adjective* (of) the tawny colour characteristic of lions.
▸ **B** *attrib.* or as *adjective*. Like a lion, characteristic of a lion; strong, brave, or fierce as a lion. M16.

MILTON The bold Ascalonite Fled from his Lion ramp. TENNYSON Strong mother of a Lion-line.

■ **lionhood** *noun* the state or condition of being a lion M19. **lionish** *adjective* resembling, characteristic of, or of the nature of a lion; brave or fierce as a lion: M16. **lionism** *noun* the practice of lionizing; the condition of being treated as a celebrity: M19. **lion-like** *adjective & adverb* (*a*) *adjective* resembling a lion; characteristic or suggestive of a lion; (*b*) *adverb* in the manner of a lion: M16. **lionship** *noun* M18.

lioncel /ˈlʌɪənsɛl/ *noun*. Now *rare*. E17.
[ORIGIN Old French (mod. *lionceau*), dim. of *lion* LION: see -EL[2].]
Chiefly HERALDRY. A young or small lion; *spec.* each of two or more lions appearing together in arms.

lionel /ˈlʌɪən(ə)l/ *noun*. Now *rare* or *obsolete*. M17.
[ORIGIN Old French, dim. of *lion* LION: see -EL[2].]
HERALDRY. = LIONCEL.

lioness /ˈlʌɪənɪs/ *noun*. ME.
[ORIGIN Old French *lion(n)esse*, *leonesse* (mod. *lionne*), from *lion* LION: see -ESS[1].]
1 A female lion. ME.
2 †**a** A lady visitor to Oxford University. Cf. LION *noun* 6c. *slang*. E–M19. ▸**b** A female celebrity; a woman who is lionized. Cf. LION *noun* 6b. L19.

lionet /ˈlʌɪənɪt/ *noun*. Now *rare*. L16.
[ORIGIN Old French, dim. of *lion* LION: see -ET[1].]
A young lion.

lionize /ˈlʌɪənʌɪz/ *verb*. Also **-ise**. E19.
[ORIGIN from LION + -IZE.]
1 *verb trans.* Treat (a person) as a celebrity; make a lion of. E19.

D. SOBEL Galileo found himself lionised as another Columbus for his conquests.

2 *verb trans. & intrans.* See the chief sights of (a place); visit or go over (a place of interest). Now *rare*. E19. ▸**b** *verb trans.* Show the chief sights of a place to (a person); show the chief sights of (a place). Now *rare*. E19.
■ **lioniˈzation** *noun* M19. **lionizer** *noun* E19.

lionly /ˈlʌɪənli/ *adjective*. *rare*. M17.
[ORIGIN from LION + -LY[1].]
Lion-like.

lip /lɪp/ *noun*.
[ORIGIN Old English *lippa* = Old Frisian *lippa*, Middle Low German, Middle Dutch *lippe* (whence German *Lippe*), from Germanic, from base also of synon. Old Saxon *lepor*, Old High German *leffur*, *lefs* (German dial. *Lefze*), from Indo-European base also of Latin *labia*, *labra* lips.]
▸ **I** **1** Either of the two fleshy parts which in humans and animals form the upper and lower edges of the mouth opening. OE. ▸**b** The condition or strength of a wind instrumentalist's lips; embouchure. L19.

SHAKES. *Mids. N. D.* When she drinks, against her lips I bob. MILTON From his Lip Not Words alone pleas'd her. R. L. STEVENSON A cry rose to his lips. DAY LEWIS The set of the lips suggests a certain inward firmness. A. GERAS She . . remembered his lips on the back of her neck. R. B. PARKER I . . licked a little salt off my upper lip. **b** E. LEONARD He could have this job if he promised not to play his horn anymore. Well, he had lost his lip anyway.

†**2** Language. Chiefly in ***of one lip*** (a Hebraism). LME–L17.
3 **a** Impertinent talk; impudence, cheek. *colloq.* E19. ▸**b** A lawyer, *esp.* a criminal lawyer. *US slang*. E20.

a B. ASHLEY You wanna watch your lip, son. G. NAYLOR You were standing there, handing him all that lip.

▸ **II** A thing resembling the lips of the mouth.
4 The margin of a cup or other vessel, or of a bell; the edge of an opening or cavity, e.g. of the crater of a volcano; a (projecting) edge or rim. LME.

M. R. MITFORD A small brown pitcher with the lip broken. J. HILTON The moon . . swung over the lip of some shadowy eminence. J. S. HUXLEY A splendid waterfall with . . primroses growing near its lip. T. MORRISON The women . . shrieked at the lip of the open grave.

5 Each of the edges of a wound. LME.
6 = LABIUM 1, 2, LABRUM. LME.
7 Each of the edges of the aperture of a spiral shell. L17.
8 Either of the upper and lower edges of the aperture of an organ pipe. E18.
9 BOTANY. Either of the two divisions of a two-lipped corolla or calyx (see ***two-lipped*** s.v. TWO *adjective*). Also = LABELLUM 2. L18.
– PHRASES: **bite one's lip** †(*a*) show vexation; (*b*) repress an emotion, stifle laughter etc. ***curl one's lip***, ***curl the lip***: see CURL *verb*. ***hang on a person's lips***: see HANG *verb*. ***lick one's lips***: see LICK *verb*. †**make a lip**, †**make up a lip** make a face *at*; pout or poke fun *at*. ***pass a person's lips***: see PASS *verb*. ***seal a person's lips***: see SEAL *verb*[1]. ***stiff upper lip***: see STIFF *adjective*. **to the lips** (immersed etc.) very deeply.
– COMB.: **lip brush** a small brush used to apply lipstick; **lip-deep** *adjective* (*a*) deeply immersed (chiefly *fig.*); (*b*) of the nature of lip service; insincere, superficial; **lip gloss** a glossy cosmetic applied to the lips; **lip-labour** (*a*) empty or futile talk; †(*b*) kissing; **lipline** the outline of a person's lips; **lipliner** a cosmetic applied to the outline of the lips, mainly to prevent the unwanted spreading of lipstick or lip gloss; **lip microphone**: for use close to a speaker's lips; **lip-read** *verb trans. & intrans.* understand (a speaker, speech) solely by observing the movement of the lips; **lip-reader** a person who lip-reads; **lipsalve** (*a*) a preparation (now usu. in stick form) to prevent or relieve sore lips; (*b*) *fig.* flat-

tering speech; **lip service** service that is proffered but not performed; insincere expressions of support, respect, etc. (chiefly in ***pay lip service to***); **lip-strap**: passing from one cheek of a horse's bit through a ring in the curb chain to the other cheek; **lip-sync**, **-synch** *noun & verb* (*a*) *noun* (in film etc. acting) movement of a performer's lips in synchronization with a pre-recorded soundtrack; (*b*) *verb trans. & intrans.* perform (esp. a song) on film using this technique; **lip-work** = ***lip-labour*** above; **lip-worship** worship that consists only in words.
■ **lipless** *adjective* LME. **liplike** *adjective* resembling (that of) a lip M19.

lip /lɪp/ *verb*. Infl. **-pp-**. E17.
[ORIGIN from the noun.]
▸ **I 1** *verb trans.* Touch with the lips, apply the lips to; *poet.* kiss; touch lightly, (of water) lap. E17.

SHAKES. *Ant. & Cl.* A hand that kings Have lipp'd, and trembled kissing. *Chambers's Journal* Some little bay lipped by the Arctic current.

2 *verb trans.* Say, utter; *esp.* pronounce with the lips only, murmur softly. Also, (*colloq.*) sing. L18.

KEATS Salt tears were coming when I heard my name Most fondly lipp'd. B. HINES Billy opened his book, .. and began to lip the words.

3 *verb trans.* Insult, abuse, be impudent to (someone). *dial. & colloq.* L19.
4 *verb trans.* Take to the lips; taste, sip, nibble. M20.

B. BREYTENBACH Slowly we lipped and sipped our kümmel.

▸ **II** †**5** *verb trans.* Edge or overlay the lip of (a vessel). Only in E17.
6 *verb intrans.* Rise to, cover, or flow over the lip or brim of a vessel; (of a vessel) have liquid flowing over its brim or edge. Chiefly *Scot.* E18.

R. L. STEVENSON The gunwale was lipping astern. J. MASEFIELD The water .. left a trail, Lipped over on the yard's bricked paving.

7 *verb trans.* Notch on the lip or edge. E19.
8 *verb trans.* Fill in the interstices of (a wall). *Scot.* E19.
9 *verb trans.* Serve as a lip or margin to. Cf. LIPPED *adjective*. M19.
10 *verb intrans.* Chiefly MEDICINE. Of bone: grow out (abnormally) or project at an extremity or edge. L19.
11 *verb trans.* GOLF. Drive the ball just to the lip or edge of (a hole); (of a ball) reach the edge of (a hole) but fail to drop in. L19.

lip- *combining form* see LIPO-.

lipa /ˈliːpə/ *noun*. Pl. same, **-s**. L20.
[ORIGIN Croatian, lit. 'lime tree'.]
A monetary unit of Croatia, equal to one-hundredth of a kuna.

lipaemia /lɪˈpiːmɪə/ *noun*. Also ***-pem-**. L19.
[ORIGIN from LIPO- + -AEMIA.]
MEDICINE. The presence in the blood of an abnormally high concentration of emulsified fat.
■ **lipaemic** *adjective* characterized by lipaemia L19.

lipase /ˈlɪpeɪz, ˈlʌɪp-/ *noun*. L19.
[ORIGIN from LIPO- + -ASE.]
BIOCHEMISTRY. An enzyme which catalyses the hydrolysis of fats and oils to fatty acids and alcohols.

lipectomy /lʌɪˈpɛktəmi, lɪ-/ *noun*. L20.
[ORIGIN from LIP(O- + -ECTOMY.]
Any surgical procedure to remove unwanted body fat, usu. by suction.

lipemia *noun* see LIPAEMIA.

lipid /ˈlɪpɪd/ *noun*. Also (earlier, now *rare*) **-ide** /-ʌɪd/. E20.
[ORIGIN French *lipide*, formed as LIPO- + -IDE.]
BIOCHEMISTRY. Any of the large group of fats and fatlike compounds (including oils, waxes, steroids, etc.) which occur in living organisms and are soluble in certain organic solvents but only sparingly soluble in water; (an ester or other derivative of) a fatty acid.
■ **lipiˈdosis** *noun*, pl. **-doses** /-ˈdəʊsiːz/, MEDICINE a disorder characterized by an excessive accumulation of lipids in tissue M20.

Lipizzaner *noun* var. of LIPPIZANER.

lipo- /ˈlɪpəʊ, ˈlʌɪpəʊ/ *combining form*. Before a vowel **lip-**.
[ORIGIN from Greek *lipos* fat: see -O-.]
Chiefly BIOCHEMISTRY & MEDICINE. Forming nouns and adjectives with the sense 'fat, lipid'.
■ **lipochrome** *noun* any naturally occurring pigment which is soluble in fats or fat solvents L19. **lipoˈdystrophy** *noun* any of various disorders of fat metabolism or of the distribution of fat in the body E20. **lipoˈfuscin** *noun* any of various brownish pigments, esp. those deposited in certain body tissues during old age E20. **lipoˈgenesis** *noun* the metabolic formation of fat L19. **liˈpolysis** *noun* the hydrolytic breakdown of fat E20. **lipoˈlytic** *adjective* having the property of decomposing or hydrolysing fats L19. **lipoˈlytically** *adverb* as regards lipolysis E20. **lipophile**, **lipoˈphilic** *adjectives* having an affinity for lipids; readily dissolving, or soluble in, lipids: M20. **lipoˈphobic** *adjective* tending to repel lipids; not readily soluble in lipids: M20. **lipopoly ˈsaccharide** *noun* a complex molecule containing both lipid and polysaccharide parts M20. **lipoprotein** *noun* any of a group of proteins, present esp. in blood plasma and lymph, that have a molecule including a lipid component E20. **liposarˈcoma** *noun*, pl. **-mas**, **-mata** /-mətə/, a sarcoma of fatty tissue L19.

lipogram /ˈlɪpəgram/ *noun*. E18.
[ORIGIN Back-form. from Greek *lipogrammatos*: see LIPOGRAMMATIC, -GRAM.]
A composition from which the writer systematically omits a certain letter or certain letters.

lipogrammatic /ˌlɪpə(ʊ)grəˈmatɪk/ *adjective*. M18.
[ORIGIN from Greek *lipogrammatos* lacking a letter, from *lip-* weak stem of *leipein* leave, be lacking + *grammat-*, *gramma* letter: see -IC.]
Of or pertaining to a lipogram; of the nature of a lipogram.
■ **lipoˈgrammatist** *noun* a writer of lipograms E18.

lipography /lɪˈpɒgrəfi/ *noun*. L19.
[ORIGIN from Greek *lip-* (see LIPOGRAMMATIC) + -OGRAPHY.]
The omission of a letter or syllable in writing, *esp.* the scribal error of writing once what should be written twice.

lipoic /lɪˈpəʊɪk/ *adjective*. M20.
[ORIGIN from LIPO- + -IC.]
BIOCHEMISTRY. ***lipoic acid***, a sulphur-containing cyclic carboxylic acid, $C_8H_{14}O_2S_2$, which is a cofactor in the metabolic decarboxylation of pyruvate.
■ **lipoate** /ˈlɪpəʊeɪt/ *noun* a salt or ester of lipoic acid M20.

lipoid /ˈlɪpɔɪd/ *adjective & noun*. L19.
[ORIGIN from LIPO- + -OID.]
BIOCHEMISTRY & MEDICINE. ▸**A** *adjective*. Resembling or of the nature of fat. L19.
▸ **B** *noun*. A fatlike substance; a lipid. E20.
■ **liˈpoidal** *adjective* resembling or containing fat E20. **lipoiˈdosis** *noun*, pl. **-doses** /-ˈdəʊsiːz/, = LIPIDOSIS M20.

lipoma /lɪˈpəʊmə/ *noun*. Pl. **-mas**, **-mata** /-mətə/. M19.
[ORIGIN from LIPO- + -OMA.]
MEDICINE. A benign tumour of fatty tissue.
■ **lipomaˈtosis** *noun* abnormal deposition of fat in other tissue; growth of lipomas: L19.

liposculpture /ˈlɪpə(ʊ)ˌskʌlptʃə, ˈlʌɪ-/ *noun*. L20.
[ORIGIN from LIPO- + SCULPTURE *noun*.]
The use of liposuction, esp. to accentuate specific bodily features.

liposome /ˈlɪpəsəʊm/ *noun*. E20.
[ORIGIN from LIPO- + -SOME³.]
BIOLOGY. **1** A fatty globule suspended in the cytoplasm of a cell. Now *rare*. E20.
2 A minute artificial spherical sac consisting of one or more layers of phospholipid enclosing an aqueous core, used experimentally to represent biological membranes. M20.

liposuction /ˈlɪpə(ʊ)ˌsʌkʃ(ə)n, ˈlʌɪ-/ *noun*. L20.
[ORIGIN from LIPO- + SUCTION.]
A technique of cosmetic surgery in which particles of excess fat are removed through incisions using a vacuum pump.

lipothymy /lɪˈpɒθɪmi/ *noun*. Now *rare* or *obsolete*. Also in Latin form **lipothymia** /lɪpəˈθʌɪmɪə/. E17.
[ORIGIN from mod. Latin *lipothymia* from Greek *lipothumia*, from *lip-* (see LIPOGRAMMATIC) + -o- + *thumos* animation, spirit: see -Y³.]
Fainting, swooning; an instance of this.
■ **lipoˈthymic** *adjective* L17.

lipotropic /lɪpə(ʊ)ˈtrəʊpɪk, -ˈtrɒpɪk/ *adjective*. M20.
[ORIGIN from LIPO- + -TROPIC.]
PHYSIOLOGY. Tending to prevent or remove an accumulation of excess fat in the liver.
■ **lipotropism** *noun* lipotropic property or phenomena M20.

lipped /lɪpt/ *adjective*. LME.
[ORIGIN from LIP *noun* + -ED².]
Having or provided with a lip or lips; having lips of a specified kind; BOTANY labiate.

lippen /ˈlɪp(ə)n/ *verb*. Chiefly *Scot.* ME.
[ORIGIN Unknown. See also LICKEN.]
1 *verb intrans.* Confide, rely, trust. Foll. by *to*, *till*, (occas.) *in*, *into*, *of*, *on*. ME.
2 *verb trans.* Entrust. Foll. by *to*, *till*. LME.
3 *verb trans.* Expect with confidence. LME.

lipper /ˈlɪpə/ *verb & noun*. *dial.* & NAUTICAL. E16.
[ORIGIN Perh. frequentative LAP *verb*¹: see -ER⁵.]
▸ **A** *verb intrans.* Of water: ripple. E16.
▸ **B** *noun*. A rippling or slight ruffling of the surface of the sea. E16.

Lippes loop /ˈlɪpɪz luːp/ *noun phr.* M20.
[ORIGIN Jack *Lippes* (b. 1924), US obstetrician.]
An intrauterine contraceptive device in the shape of a double S.

lippet *noun* var. of LIBBET *noun*².

lippie *noun* var. of LIPPY *noun*.

lipping /ˈlɪpɪŋ/ *noun*. M19.
[ORIGIN from LIP *verb* + -ING¹.]
1 The action of LIP *verb*. M19. ▸**b** MEDICINE. Abnormal outgrowth of bone at a joint. L19.
2 An edging strip fixed to a board, door, etc.; the action of fixing such a strip. M20.

lippitude /ˈlɪpɪtjuːd/ *noun*. Now *rare*. LME.
[ORIGIN Latin *lippitudo*, from *lippus* bleary-eyed: see -TUDE.]
Soreness or bleariness of the eyes; an instance of this.

Lippizaner /lɪpɪtˈsɑːnə, lɪpɪˈzeɪnə/ *noun*. Also **Lipizzaner**. E20.
[ORIGIN German, from *Lippiza* (see below).]
(An animal of) a fine white breed of horse developed at the former Austrian Imperial stud at Lippiza near Trieste, and used esp. in dressage at the Spanish Riding School, Vienna.

lippy /ˈlɪpi/ *noun*. *colloq.* Also **lippie**.
[ORIGIN from LIP(STICK + -Y⁶.]
Lipstick.

lippy /ˈlɪpi/ *adjective*. L19.
[ORIGIN from LIP *noun* + -Y¹.]
1 Impertinent, insolent; talkative, verbose. *colloq. & dial.* L19.
2 Of a dog: having (unusually) hanging lips. L19.

lipstick /ˈlɪpstɪk/ *noun & verb*. L19.
[ORIGIN from LIP *noun* + STICK *noun*¹.]
▸ **A** *noun*. A stick of cosmetic for colouring the lips, usu. a shade of pink or red. L19.
▸ **B** *verb trans. & intrans.* Apply lipstick to (the lips). E20.
■ **lipsticky** *adjective* covered or sticky with lipstick M20.

Liptauer /ˈlɪptaʊə/ *noun*. E20.
[ORIGIN German, from *Liptó* a place in Slovakia.]
A soft cheese originally made in Hungary, usu. coloured and flavoured with paprika and other seasonings. Also ***Liptauer cheese***.

†**liquable** *adjective*. L15–M18.
[ORIGIN Latin *liquabilis*, from *liquare*: see LIQUATE, -ABLE.]
Able to be liquefied or melted.

†**liquamen** *noun*. LME.
[ORIGIN Latin, from *liquare*: see LIQUATE.]
1 A substance reduced to a liquid state. LME–E19.
2 A fluid for administering medicine. *rare*. Only in L19.

liquate /lɪˈkweɪt/ *verb*. M17.
[ORIGIN Latin *liquat-* pa. ppl stem of *liquare* make liquid, rel. to Latin LIQUOR *noun*: see -ATE³.]
1 *verb trans. & intrans.* Make or become liquid, melt. M17–E18.
†**2** *verb trans.* METALLURGY. Separate or purify (metals) by melting. M19.

liquation /lɪˈkweɪʃ(ə)n/ *noun*. L15.
[ORIGIN Late Latin *liquatio(n-)*, formed as LIQUATE: see -ATION.]
1 METALLURGY. The action or process of separating or purifying metals by melting. L15.
†**2** The process of making or becoming liquid; the condition of being melted; the capacity to be melted. E17–E18.

liquefaction /lɪkwɪˈfakʃ(ə)n/ *noun*. LME.
[ORIGIN Late Latin *liquefactio(n-)*, from Latin *liquefact-* pa. ppl stem of *liquefacere* LIQUEFY: see -FACTION.]
1 The action or process of liquefying; the state of being liquefied; reduction to a liquid state. LME.
†**2** *fig.* A 'melting' of the soul by religious ardour. E16–E18.

liquefactive /lɪkwɪˈfaktɪv/ *adjective*. LME.
[ORIGIN medieval Latin *liquefactivus*, from *liquefact-*: see LIQUEFACTION, -IVE.]
Having the effect of liquefying.

liquefy /ˈlɪkwɪfʌɪ/ *verb*. Also **liquify**. LME.
[ORIGIN Old French & mod. French *liquéfier* from Latin *liquefacere* make liquid, melt (pass. *liquefieri*), from *liquere* rel. to Latin LIQUOR *noun*: see -FY.]
1 *verb trans.* Make liquid; melt; convert (a gas) to a liquid state. Formerly also, dissolve. LME.
2 *verb intrans.* Become liquid. Formerly also, become dissolved. L16. ▸**b** Become intoxicated. *joc.* E19.
3 *verb trans.* Pronounce (a consonant) as a liquid. Now *rare* or *obsolete*. E18.
■ **liquefiable** *adjective* M16. **liquefied** *adjective* (*a*) that has (been) liquefied; (*b*) *joc.* drunk, intoxicated: L16. **liquefier** *noun* E19.

liquesce /lɪˈkwɛs/ *verb intrans. rare*. M19.
[ORIGIN Latin *liquescere*: see LIQUESCENT.]
Become liquid; *fig.* merge *into*.

liquescent /lɪˈkwɛs(ə)nt/ *adjective*. E18.
[ORIGIN Latin *liquescent-* pres. ppl stem of *liquescere* become liquid, from *liquere* rel. to Latin LIQUOR *noun*: see -ESCENT.]
That is in the process of becoming liquid (*lit.* & *fig.*); liable to become liquid.

B. MALAMUD A thin-faced boy with brown liquescent eyes out of Murillo.

■ **liquescence** *noun* L19. **liquescency** *noun* (*rare*) M17.

liqueur /lɪˈkjʊə/ *noun*. M18.
[ORIGIN French = LIQUOR *noun*.]
1 Any of various strong sweet alcoholic spirits flavoured with aromatic substances, usu. drunk after a meal. Also, a glass of such a drink. M18.

Z. MDA Even with the fuel of the cherry liqueur, the dances had become languid.

2 *ellipt.* A liqueur glass; a liqueur chocolate. E20.
– COMB.: **liqueur brandy**, **liqueur whisky**: of supposed special quality, intended to be drunk straight in small quantities like a liqueur; **liqueur chocolate** a chocolate with a liqueur filling; **liqueur glass** a very small drinking glass used for liqueurs; ***liqueur whisky***: see ***liqueur brandy*** above.

L

liquid /ˈlɪkwɪd/ *adjective & noun*. LME.
[ORIGIN Latin *liquidus*, from *liquere*, rel. to LIQUOR *noun*: see -ID[1].]
▸ **A** *adjective*. **1** Of a material substance: in that state (familiar as the normal condition of water, milk, etc.) in which it flows and takes a shape determined by its container while occupying the same volume (rather than dispersing like a gaseous substance); (of a gas) in such a state by reason of low temperature or high pressure. Also, composed of a substance in this condition. LME. ▸**b** Watery; (occas.) filled with tears. *poet.* L16.

SPENSER Which feedes each living plant with liquid sap. SHAKES. *Mids. N. D.* Decking with liquid pearl the bladed grass. G. GORDON He . . squirted liquid soap into the sink. **b** POPE Meanwhile our vessels plough the liquid plain.

2 Not fixed or stable, fluid. Of movement: facile, unconstrained. LME.

E. O. M. DEUTSCH The liquid nature, so to speak, of its technical terms. *New Yorker* A tall Bedouin . . walking with long, liquid strides.

3 a Of an account or debt: undisputed. Now only *SCOTS LAW*, = LIQUIDATE *adjective*. E16. ▸†**b** Of a proof, exposition, etc.: clear, evident, manifest. E17–E18.
4 Of light, fire, air, the eyes, etc.: clear, transparent, bright (like pure water). L16.

DRYDEN They That wing the liquid Air, or swim the Sea. T. GRAY The insect youth . . , Eager to . . float amid the liquid noon. R. P. JHABVALA The Rawul's eyes were not the usual kind of liquid brown.

5 Of sound: flowing, pure and clear in tone; free from harshness or discord; *PHONETICS* of the nature of a liquid (see sense B.1 below). E17.

J. BURROUGHS The liquid and gurgling tones of the bobolink. H. SWEET 'Liquid' voiced consonants . . unaccompanied by buzz. R. THOMAS Laura tried to get her stiff tongue around the soft, liquid sounds.

6 (Of assets etc.) able to be easily converted into cash; (already) in the form of cash. Also, having ready cash or liquid assets. Cf. FROZEN *adjective* 2c. L19.

N. FREELING Were they realizing assets, gathering up all the liquid money they could find?

L

▸ **B** *noun*. **1** *PHONETICS*. A voiced frictionless continuant consonant, *spec.* an oral rather than a nasal one (denoted by the letters *l*, *m*, *n*, and *r*, *spec.* the letters *l* and *r*). M16.
2 A liquid substance; liquid matter. In *pl.* freq., liquid food. E18.
noble liquid: see NOBLE *adjective*.
– SPECIAL COLLOCATIONS & COMB.: **liquid compass** a form of magnetic compass in which the card and needle are mainly supported by floating in a liquid. **liquid crystal** *PHYSICAL CHEMISTRY* a turbid liquid that exhibits double refraction (indicative of some degree of ordering in its internal structure) and exists as a distinct state of certain pure substances between the melting point and some higher temperature, at which it becomes an ordinary liquid; ***liquid crystal display***, a visual display, esp. of segmented numbers or letters, in which liquid crystals are made visible by temporarily modifying their capacity to reflect light. **liquid drop** a small drop of liquid, *spec.* (*PHYSICS*) as a model for the theoretical description of an atomic nucleus. **liquid fire** a very fiery (in taste) or highly combustible liquid; *esp.* one that can be sent as a burning jet in warfare. **liquid lunch** *colloq.* a midday meal at which alcoholic drink rather than food is consumed. **liquid manure** a water extract of manure used as a fertilizer. **liquid measure** a unit for expressing the volume of liquids. **liquid paper** (also **Liquid Paper**, US proprietary name) correction fluid. **liquid paraffin** *PHARMACOLOGY* an almost tasteless and odourless oily liquid that consists of hydrocarbons obtained from petroleum and is used as a laxative and in dressings. **liquid petroleum** *US* = ***liquid paraffin*** above. **liquid rheostat**: that uses an electrolyte solution as the resistive element. **liquid starter** a liquid rheostat used as a starter of an electric motor. ***liquid storax***: see STORAX 1.
■ **liquidly** *adverb* †(*a*) clearly, plainly; (*b*) in a liquid manner; after the manner of a liquid: E17. **liquidness** *noun* M16. **liquidy** *adjective* (*rare*) of a liquid nature; somewhat liquid: LME.

liquidambar /lɪkwɪdˈambə/ *noun*. L16.
[ORIGIN mod. Latin, app. irreg. from Latin *liquidus* LIQUID *adjective* + medieval Latin *ambar* AMBER.]
1 A resinous gum which exudes from the bark of trees of the genus *Liquidambar* (see below); liquid storax. Cf. AMBER *noun* 4. L16.
2 Any of various trees of the genus *Liquidambar* of the witch-hazel family, esp. *L. orientalis* of Asia Minor, and *L. styraciflua*, the sweet gum of N. America. M18.

liquidate /ˈlɪkwɪdeɪt/ *adjective*. Now only *Scot*. M16.
[ORIGIN medieval Latin *liquidatus* pa. pple, formed as LIQUIDATE *verb*: see -ATE[2].]
LAW. Of a debt or other sum: ascertained and fixed in amount by written agreement or the decree of a court. Cf. LIQUID *adjective* 3a.

liquidate /ˈlɪkwɪdeɪt/ *verb*. Pa. pple **-ated**, (earlier) †**-ate**. M16.
[ORIGIN medieval Latin *liquidat-* pa. ppl stem of *liquidare*, from Latin *liquidus*: see LIQUID, -ATE[3]. The financial senses are due to Italian *liquidare*, French *liquider*, sense 6 after Russian *likvidirovat'*.]
†**1** *verb trans.* Determine and apportion by agreement or by litigation; reduce to order, set out clearly (accounts). Cf. LIQUIDATE *adjective*. M16–L18.
†**2** *verb trans.* **a** Clear away, resolve (objections). *rare.* E17–M19. ▸**b** Make clear or plain; render unambiguous; settle. M17–L18.
3 *verb trans.* Liquefy, melt; *fig.* dissipate, waste. *rare.* M17.
4 *verb trans.* Clear off, pay, (a debt). E18.
5 a *verb trans.* Ascertain and set out clearly the liabilities of (a company or firm) and arrange the apportioning of the assets; wind up. Also, convert to liquid assets. L19. ▸**b** *verb intrans.* Go into liquidation. L19.
6 *verb trans.* Put an end to or get rid of, esp. by violent means; wipe out; kill. E20.

B. BETTELHEIM Even before an extermination policy went into effect, the Gestapo had been liquidating unfit persons. L. DEIGHTON Do German communities still exist in Russia? I thought Stalin liquidated them . . in the forties.

■ **liquidator** *noun* (*a*) a person appointed to conduct the winding up of a company; (*b*) a person who implements a policy of liquidation: M19.

liquidation /lɪkwɪˈdeɪʃ(ə)n/ *noun*. M16.
[ORIGIN French, from *liquider* liquidate, or directly from LIQUIDATE *verb*: see -ATION. Cf. medieval Latin *liquidatio(n-)* making clear, explaining.]
†**1** *LAW*. The action or process of ascertaining and apportioning the amounts of a debt etc. M16–M18.
2 The clearing off or settling of a debt. L18.
3 The action or process of winding up the affairs of a company etc.; the state or condition of being wound up; esp. in ***go into liquidation***. Also, the selling of certain assets in order to achieve greater liquidity. M19.
4 The action or fact of partaking of an alcoholic drink. *rare*. L19.
5 The action or process of abolishing or eliminating something or someone; the doing away with or killing of unwanted people. E20.
6 *CHESS*. A rapid exchange of pieces leading to simplification of the position. M20.

liquidise *verb* var. of LIQUIDIZE.

liquidity /lɪˈkwɪdɪti/ *noun*. E17.
[ORIGIN French *liquidité* or medieval Latin *liquiditas*, or directly from LIQUID *adjective*: see -ITY.]
1 The quality or condition of being liquid. E17.
2 Clearness or purity of tone. E19.
3 The interchangeability of assets and money; availability of liquid assets. E20.
– COMB.: **liquidity preference** the holding of assets in money or near money in preference to securities or interest-bearing investments; **liquidity ratio** the proportion of total assets which is held in liquid or cash form.

liquidize /ˈlɪkwɪdʌɪz/ *verb*. Also **-ise**. M19.
[ORIGIN from LIQUID *adjective* + -IZE.]
1 *verb trans. & intrans.* Make or become liquid. M19.
2 *verb trans.* Purée, emulsify, or blend (food), *esp.* in a liquidizer. M20.
■ **liquidizer** *noun* a machine used in the preparation of food, to make purées, emulsify, etc. M20.

liquidus /ˈlɪkwɪdəs/ *noun*. E20.
[ORIGIN Latin = LIQUID *adjective*.]
A line or surface in a phase diagram, or a temperature (corresponding to a point on the line or surface), above which a mixture is entirely liquid and below which it consists of liquid and solid in equilibrium. Also ***liquidus curve***, ***liquidus surface***, ***liquidus temperature***.

liquify *verb* var. of LIQUEFY.

liquor /ˈlɪkə/ *noun*. ME.
[ORIGIN Old French *licur*, *licour* (mod. LIQUEUR) from Latin *liquor* rel. to *liquare* liquefy, filter, *liqui* flow, *liquere* be fluid.]
1 A liquid; matter in a liquid state; a fluid. *obsolete* exc. as below. ME.

SHAKES. *Temp.* Yond . . black cloud, . . looks like a foul bombard that would shed his liquor.

2 Liquid for drinking; beverage, drink. Now usu. (a kind of) alcoholic drink, esp. produced by distillation. ME. ▸**b** A drink of an intoxicating beverage. *slang* (chiefly *US*). M19.

M. PUZO There was also plenty of liquor; champagne . . . , scotch, rye, brandy.

3 The water in which meat has been boiled; broth, sauce; the fat in which bacon, fish, etc., has been fried; the liquid contained in oysters. LME.

J. GRIGSON Simmer 4 oysters . . in their own liquor.

†**4** Grease or oil for lubricating purposes. Cf. LIQUOR *verb* 1. *dial.* M–L16.
5 A liquid of a particular kind used or produced in a chemical or industrial process etc. Also, the liquid part of a secretion; *MEDICINE* = ***liquor amnii*** below. M16. ▸**b** *BREWING*. Water. M18. ▸**c** *PHARMACOLOGY*. An aqueous solution of a particular substance. L18. ▸**d** The liquid produced by infusion of a tea. L19.

Nature Lignins are produced . . in waste liquors from pulping processes.

– PHRASES: **in liquor** intoxicated. ***liquor amnii*** /lɪkwɔːr ˈamnɪʌɪ, lʌɪkwɔːr, lʌɪkər/ [Latin] *MEDICINE* amniotic fluid. ***malt liquor***: see MALT *noun*[1] & *adjective*. ***mother liquor***: see MOTHER *noun*[1]. ***VINOUS liquor***.
■ **liquorless** *adjective* M19. **liquorous** *adjective* †(*a*) liquid; (*b*) full of (alcoholic) liquor; redolent of liquor: L17.

liquor /ˈlɪkə/ *verb*. E16.
[ORIGIN from the noun.]
1 *verb trans.* Cover or smear with a liquor; *esp.* lubricate or dress with grease or oil. Now *rare*. E16.
†**liquor a person's hide** thrash or beat a person.
2 *verb trans.* Supply with liquor to drink; ply with liquor. Also ***liquor up***. Now *slang*. M16.
3 *verb trans.* Steep in, soak, or treat with a liquor; steep (malt) in water. M18.
4 *verb intrans.* Drink alcoholic liquor. Also ***liquor up***. *slang*. M19.
5 *verb intrans.* Of tea: produce an infusion (of a specified quality). Chiefly as ***liquoring*** *ppl adjective*. L19.

liquorice /ˈlɪk(ə)rɪs, -rɪʃ/ *noun*. Also **licorice**. ME.
[ORIGIN Anglo-Norman *lycorys*, Old French *licoresse*, *-ece*, from (with assim. to *licor* LIQUOR *noun*) late Latin *liquiritia* from Greek *glukurrhiza*, from *glukus* sweet + *rhiza* root.]
1 The rhizome (also ***liquorice-root***) of the plant *Glycyrrhiza glabra* (see below); a preparation made from the evaporated juice of this, used medicinally and as a sweet, usu. in the form of a black chewy substance. ME.
2 The leguminous plant *Glycyrrhiza glabra*, native to the Mediterranean region and central and SW Asia. ME.
3 With specifying word: a preparation which resembles or is used as a substitute for the true liquorice; (the root of) a plant providing this. LME.
Indian liquorice: see INDIAN *adjective*. **wild liquorice** a Eurasian milk-vetch of calcareous hedge banks and scrub, *Astragalus glycyphyllus*, with axillary racemes of cream-coloured flowers.
– COMB.: ***liquorice-root***: see sense 1 above; **liquorice-stick** a stick of liquorice, as a sweet; **liquorice vetch** = ***wild liquorice*** above.

liquorish /ˈlɪkərɪʃ/ *adjective*[1]. L19.
[ORIGIN from LIQUOR *noun* + -ISH[1].]
Fond of or indicating fondness for liquor.
■ **liquorishly** *adverb* M19. **liquorishness** *noun* L18.

liquorish *adjective*[2] var. of LICKERISH.

liquorist /ˈlɪkərɪst/ *noun*. M19.
[ORIGIN French *liquoriste*, formed as LIQUEUR: see -IST.]
A person who makes liqueurs.

lira /ˈlɪərə, *foreign* ˈliːra/ *noun*. Pl. **lire** /ˈlɪəri, ˈlɪəreɪ, *foreign* liːre/, (occas.) **liras**. E17.
[ORIGIN Italian from Provençal *liura* = French LIVRE, Italian *libbra*, from Latin *libra* pound.]
1 The basic monetary unit of Italy, San Marino, and the Vatican City State until the introduction of the euro in 2002, equal to 100 centesimi. Also, the basic monetary unit of Malta, equal to 100 cents. E17.
2 The basic monetary unit of Turkey, equal to 100 kurus. L19.

lirate /ˈlʌɪərət/ *adjective*. L19.
[ORIGIN from Latin *lira* ridge + -ATE[2].]
ZOOLOGY. Of a shell: having ridges.
■ **liˈration** *noun* lirate marking E20.

lire /ˈlʌɪə/ *noun*[1]. Long *obsolete* exc. *Scot. & N. English*.
[ORIGIN Old English *lira* rel. to Old Norse *lær*, Swedish *lår* thigh, Old Norse *leggr* leg. Cf. LEER *noun*[2].]
Flesh, muscle, brawn.
■ **liry** *adjective* L15.

lire *noun*[2] *pl.* see LIRA.

lirella /lɪˈrɛlə/ *noun*. M19.
[ORIGIN mod. Latin (= French *lirelle*), dim. of Latin *lira* furrow: see -ELLA.]
BOTANY. The narrow apothecium, with a furrow along the middle, found in some lichens.
■ **lirelliform** *adjective* shaped like a lirella M19.

†**liriconfancy** *noun*. M16–M18.
[ORIGIN Alt. of Latin *lilium convallium*, infl. by FANCY *noun & adjective*.]
The lily of the valley, *Convallaria majalis*.

liriodendron /lʌɪrɪəˈdɛndrɒn/ *noun*. E19.
[ORIGIN mod. Latin (see below), from Greek *leirion* lily + *dendron* tree.]
Either of two trees of the genus *Liriodendron*, of the magnolia family; *esp.* the tulip tree, *L. tulipifera*, of the eastern US.

liripipe /ˈlɪrɪpʌɪp/ *noun*. Also (the usual form in sense 1) **-poop** /-puːp/. M16.
[ORIGIN medieval Latin *liripipium*, *lero-* variously explained as 'tippet of a hood', 'cord', 'shoelace', of unknown origin. Forms in *-poop* unexpl. See also LURRY *noun*.]
1 A thing to be learned and acted or spoken; one's lesson, one's role. Long *arch. rare*. M16.
2 A silly person. Long *arch. rare*. E17.
3 A long tail of a hood, esp. in old academic or clerical dress or attached to a medieval chaperon; a very long tippet. E17.

lirk /ləːk/ *noun & verb*. *Scot. & N. English*. LME.
[ORIGIN Unknown.]
▸ **A** *noun*. A fold in the skin; a wrinkle. LME.
▸ **B** *verb intrans. & trans.* Wrinkle. L17.

lis /liːs/ *noun*[1]. Pl. same, (*rare*) **lisses**. E17.
[ORIGIN French = lily.]
HERALDRY. = FLEUR-DE-LIS 2.

lis /lɪs/ *noun*[2]. **M18.**
[ORIGIN Latin = quarrel, dispute.]
LAW. A lawsuit; a process or action at law.
lis pendens /ˈpɛndɛnz/ a suit (elsewhere) pending; a formal notice that legal action is pending.

lis /lɪs/ *noun*[3]. Also **liss**. Pl. **lisses**. **M19.**
[ORIGIN Irish *lios*, Old Irish *lis*, *less* = Welsh *llys*.]
ARCHAEOLOGY. In Ireland, a circular enclosure having an earthen wall, often used as a fort.

Lisbon /ˈlɪzb(ə)n/ *noun*. **M17.**
[ORIGIN The capital of Portugal, Portuguese *Lisboa*.]
1 *gen. attrib.* Designating things found or made in, associated with, or obtained from Lisbon. **M17.**
2 *hist.* More fully ***Lisbon wine***. A Portuguese white wine imported from Lisbon. **E18.**
†**3** More fully ***Lisbon sugar***. A kind of soft sugar. **M18–E19.**
4 A kind of lemon with a relatively sour taste. **L19.**

lisente *noun* pl. of SENTE.

-lish /lɪʃ/ *suffix*. **L20.**
[ORIGIN from ENG)LISH.]
Forming nouns designating a blend of a particular language with English, as used by native speakers of the first language, as ***Hinglish***, ***Japlish***, etc.

li shu /ˈliː ʃuː/ *noun phr.* **L19.**
[ORIGIN Chinese *lì shū* clerical writing.]
In Chinese calligraphy, a form of script developed during the Han dynasty and widely adopted for official and educational purposes.

lisk /lɪsk/ *noun*. Long *obsolete* exc. *dial.* **ME.**
[ORIGIN Prob. of Scandinavian origin: cf. Middle Swedish *liuske*, Danish *lyske*.]
The loin or flank. Also, the groin.

lisle /lʌɪl, liːl/ *noun*. Also (formerly usu.) **L-**. **M16.**
[ORIGIN *Lisle*, former name of a town in NE France (now *Lille*).]
1 *attrib.* Made in, associated with, or obtained from Lille, France. Chiefly & now only *spec.* designating or made of a fine smooth cotton thread, used for stockings etc. **M16.**
2 (Cloth made from) lisle thread. **M16.**

lisp /lɪsp/ *noun*[1]. **E17.**
[ORIGIN from the verb.]
1 The action or an act of lisping; a lisping pronunciation. **E17.**
2 *transf.* A sound resembling a lisp, as the rippling of water, the rustle of leaves. **M19.**
■ **lispy** *adjective* characterized by a lisp, inclined to lisp **M19.**

Lisp /lɪsp/ *noun*[2]. Also **LISP**. **M20.**
[ORIGIN from *list processor*: see s.v. LIST *noun*[3].]
COMPUTING. A high-level programming language devised for list processing.

lisp /lɪsp/ *verb*.
[ORIGIN Old English (*ā*)*wlyspian*, from *wlisp*, *wlips* (adjective) lisping: cf. Middle Low German *wilspen*, *wlispen* (Dutch *lispen*), Old High German *lisp* stammering, *lispen* lisp (German *lispeln*). Of imit. origin.]
1 *verb intrans.* Substitute sounds approaching /θ/ and /ð/ for the sibilants /s/ and /z/ in speaking; (esp. of a child) speak with imperfect pronunciation. **OE.**

> *fig.*: W. DE LA MARE Each leaf to its sisters lisps softly.

2 *verb trans.* Utter with a lisp or lispingly. Also foll. by *out*. **E17.**
■ **lisper** *noun* **LME.**

lisping /ˈlɪspɪŋ/ *ppl adjective*. **M16.**
[ORIGIN from LISP *verb* + -ING[2].]
That lisps; (of a sound or utterance) characterized by a lisp or lisping.
■ **lispingly** *adverb* **M17.**

lispound /ˈlɪspaʊnd/ *noun*. **E16.**
[ORIGIN Low German, Dutch *lispund*, for *livsch pund* lit. 'Livonian pound'.]
hist. A unit of weight used in the Baltic trade, and in Orkney and Shetland, varying at different periods and in different localities from 12 to 30 pounds (approx. 5½ to 13½ kg).

†**liss** *noun*[1].
[ORIGIN Old English *līþs*, *liss*, from *līþe* LITHE *adjective*.]
1 Remission, release; mitigation, abatement; cessation, end. **OE–L19.**
2 Tranquillity, peace, rest; joy, delight. **OE–LME.**

liss *noun*[2] var. of LIS *noun*[3].

liss /lɪs/ *verb*. *obsolete* exc. *Scot.* & *N. Irish*.
[ORIGIN Old English *lissian*, formed as LISS *noun*[1].]
†**1** *verb trans.* Subdue; mitigate, relieve (pain etc.). **OE–M16.**
†**2** *verb trans.* Relieve (*of* pain etc.); comfort. **LME–L15.**
3 *verb intrans.* Abate, cease; be relieved *of*. **LME.**

Lissajous /ˈlɪsaʒuː/ *noun*. **L19.**
[ORIGIN Jules Antoine *Lissajous* (1822–80), French physicist.]
Used *attrib.* and in *possess.* to designate the plane figures (mostly crossed loops and simple curves) traced by a point executing two independent simple harmonic motions at right angles to one another and with frequencies in a simple numerical ratio.

lisse /liːs/ (*pl. same*) *noun & adjective*. **M19.**
[ORIGIN French = smooth (in *crêpe lisse*).]
(Of) a kind of silk or cotton gauze.

lissoir /ˈliːswɑː; *foreign* liswaːr/ (*pl. same*) *noun*. **E20.**
[ORIGIN French, from *lisser* to smooth + *-oir*, -ORY[1].]
ARCHAEOLOGY. A smoothing, polishing tool.

lissom /ˈlɪs(ə)m/ *adjective*. Also **lissome**. **L18.**
[ORIGIN Contr. formed as LITHESOME.]
Supple, limber; lithe and agile.
■ **lissomly** *adverb* **E20.** **lissomness** *noun* **M19.**

list /lɪst/ *noun*[1] & *adjective*.
[ORIGIN Old English *līste* = Middle Dutch *lijste* (Dutch *lijst*), Old High German *līsta* (German *Leiste*), from Germanic. In tilting repr. Old French *lisse* (mod. *lice*).]
▸ **A** *noun*. **I** Border, edging, strip.
1 a *gen.* A border, a hem, a bordering strip. Long *rare*. **OE.** ▸†**b** A lobe of an ear. **M16–M17.**
2 A strip of cloth or other fabric; *spec.* the selvedge or edge of a cloth, usually of different material from the body of the cloth. **ME.** ▸**b** Such selvedges collectively; material used for the selvedge of cloth. **M16.**
3 †**a** A band or strip of any material; a line or band conspicuously marked on a surface. **LME–L18.** ▸**b** A section of hair of a head or on a beard. **M19.**
4 A stripe of colour. **L15.**
5 *ARCHITECTURE.* A small square moulding or ring encircling the foot of a column, between the torus below and the shaft above (cf. LISTEL). Formerly also, a spiral line of a volute. **M17.**
▸ **II** Boundary.
†**6** A limit, a boundary. Freq. in *pl.* **LME–M17.**
7 a In *pl.* (†sometimes treated as *sing.*). The palisades or other barriers enclosing a space set apart for tilting; a space so enclosed for tilting matches or tournaments. **LME.** ▸**b** *transf.* & *fig.* A place or scene of combat or contest. **L16.**
b enter the lists make or accept a challenge, esp. to controversy (foll. by *against*).
†**8 a** *sing.* & in *pl.* An encircling palisade; a railed or staked enclosure. **L16–M18.** ▸**b** In *pl.*, the starting place of a race (= Latin *carceres*). Also *sing.*, a racecourse or exercising ground for horses. **L16–M18.**
▸ **B** *attrib.* or as *adjective*. Made of list or material used for selvedges. **M17.**

list /lɪst/ *noun*[2]. **ME.**
[ORIGIN from LIST *verb*[1].]
†**1** Pleasure, joy, delight. **ME–L16.**
2 Appetite, craving; desire, longing; inclination. Foll. by *to* a thing, *to do*. *arch.* **ME.**
3 (One's) desire or wish; (one's) good pleasure. *arch.* **ME.**

list /lɪst/ *noun*[3]. **L16.**
[ORIGIN French *liste* = Spanish, Italian *lista*, presumably formed as LIST *noun*[1] (from a strip of paper).]
A catalogue or roll consisting of a row or series of names, figures, words, etc.; *spec.* (***a***) in early use, a catalogue of the names of people engaged in the same duties or connected with the same object; (***b***) a catalogue of the soldiers of an army or of a particular arm; (***c***) a catalogue of the titles of the books (to be) published by a particular publisher; (***d***) an official register of buildings of architectural or historical importance that are statutorily protected from demolition or major alteration; (***e***) in the National Health Service, a general practitioner's register of patients; (***f***) *COMPUTING* a formalized representation of the concept of a list, used for the storage of data or in list processing.
housing list, ***reading list***, ***transfer list***, ***waiting list***, ***wine list***, etc. ***active list***: see ACTIVE *adjective* 5. ***backlist***: see BACK-. ***blacklist***: see BLACK *adjective*. ***civil list***: see CIVIL *adjective*. ***free list***: see FREE *adjective*. ***linked list***: see LINKED *adjective* 1. ***LLOYD'S List***. ***Reserved List***: see RESERVED 3. ***RETIRED list***. ***secret list***: see SECRET *adjective* & *noun*. ***shortlist***: see SHORT *adjective*. ***sick list***: see SICK *adjective*. ***white list***: see WHITE *adjective*.
– COMB.: **list broker** a trader in mailing lists; **list broking** trading in mailing lists; **list price** the price shown for an article in a printed list issued by the maker, or by the general body of makers of the particular class of goods; **list processing** *COMPUTING* the manipulation and use of chained lists and of data in them; **list processor** *COMPUTING* a processing system, language, etc., for use in list processing; **list system** a system of voting, common in Continental western Europe, in which voters cast their vote for a list of candidates rather than for an individual candidate; **list vote**, **list voting** a vote cast, voting, under a list system.

list /lɪst/ *noun*[4]. **M17.**
[ORIGIN Unknown.]
1 *NAUTICAL.* A careening or inclination of a ship to one side (owing to a leak, shifting cargo, etc.). **M17.**

> S. J. PERELMAN The ship had developed a dangerous list to port.

2 *transf.* A leaning over (of a building etc.). **L18.**

> E. HEMINGWAY The lovely *campanile* . . that has damn near as much list on it as the leaning tower of Pisa.

list /lɪst/ *verb*[1] *trans.* *arch.* 3 sing. pres. **list**, **listeth**, (*pers.*) **lists**; pa. **list**, **listed**.
[ORIGIN Old English *lystan* = Old Saxon *lustian* (Dutch *lusten*), Old High German *lusten* (German *lüsten*), Old Norse *lysta*, from Germanic, from base of LUST *noun*.]
1 *impers.* (In Old English with *accus.* or *dat.*) Be pleasing to. **OE.**

> W. RALEIGH When it listeth him to call them to an account. P. FLETCHER When me list to sadder tunes apply me.

2 *pers.* Desire, like, wish, (*to do*). **ME.**

> S. RICHARDSON Let them think what they list. SIR W. SCOTT We will, if your ladyship lists, leave him. H. ALLEN We shall make as many detours as we list.

list /lɪst/ *verb*[2]. *arch.*
[ORIGIN Old English *hlystan*, ult. from Germanic base repr. also by LISTEN *verb*.]
1 *verb intrans.* Listen (*to*, *unto*). **OE.**
2 *verb trans.* Listen to, hear. **ME.**

list /lɪst/ *verb*[3] *trans.* **ME.**
[ORIGIN from LIST *noun*[1]. Cf. Old French *lister* put a list on (cloth), Dutch *lijsten*.]
†**1** Put a list or edge round (an object); put as a list *upon*; fix list on the edge of (a door). **ME–L19.**
†**2** Enclose; shut *in* with rails etc. **L15–M16.**
3 *CARPENTRY.* Cut away the sappy edge of (a board); shape (a block or stave) by chopping. **M17.**
4 *AGRICULTURE.* Prepare (land) for a crop by making ridges and furrows with a lister or beds and alleys with a hoe. *US.* **L18.**

list /lɪst/ *verb*[4]. In senses 3, 4 now also **'list**. **E17.**
[ORIGIN from LIST *noun*[3]. In senses 3, 4 now aphet. from ENLIST.]
1 *verb trans.* Set down together or enter in a list; make a list of; catalogue, register; *spec.* (***a***) approve (a stock or other security) for dealing on a stock exchange (usu. in *pass.*); (***b***) *N. Amer.* place (a property) in the hands of a real-estate agent for sale or rent; add to the list of properties advertised by a real-estate agent; (***c***) enter (a name and address) in a telephone directory; (***d***) protect (a building etc.) by inclusion in a statutory preservation register; (***e***) *COMPUTING* display or print out (a program, the contents of a file, etc.). **E17.** ▸**b** *verb intrans.* Be specified in a list (*at*, *for* a price). **M20.**

> SCOTT FITZGERALD I tried . . to list the quotations on an interminable amount of stock. *Listener* The Stock Exchange now lists the Shares of the Houston Natural Gas Corporation. F. SPALDING Kenneth Clark, writing on the 'New Romanticism in British Painting' . . listed Sutherland, Piper and Moore as the leading figures.

2 *verb trans.* Include as if in a list or catalogue; categorize *among*, *in*, *under*, *with*, etc.; report, mention. **E17.**

> SWIFT It is under this class I have presumed to list my present treatise. *Anderson (S. Carolina) Independent* McGee listed the time of death as approximately 10 a.m. Tuesday.

blacklist: see BLACK *adjective*.
3 *verb trans.* Enter on the list of a military body; appoint formally to a post in a military body. In later use *spec.* enlist (oneself, another) for military service. *arch.* **M17.**

> STEELE A Drum passing by, . . I listed myself for a Soldier. R. KIPLING There's a Legion that never was 'listed. *transf.*: J. BENTHAM Men whose affections are already listed against the law in question.

4 *verb intrans.* Have one's name entered on the list of a military body; enlist for military service. *arch.* **M17.**

> W. BLACKSTONE If any officer and soldier . . shall desert, or list in any other regiment. *transf.*: T. HOOD When first the scholar lists in learning's train.

list /lɪst/ *verb*[5] *intrans.* **E17.**
[ORIGIN from LIST *noun*[4].]
(Of a ship) careen, heel, or incline to one side; *transf.* (of a building etc.) lean over.

> A. SCHLEE The deck listed with the weight of passengers. J. C. OATES Sauntering about with the baby on her hip, listing to one side.

listable /ˈlɪstəb(ə)l/ *adjective*. Orig. *US.* **M17.**
[ORIGIN from LIST *verb*[4] + -ABLE.]
Able to be listed or put on a list.

listed /ˈlɪstɪd/ *adjective*[1]. **ME.**
[ORIGIN from LIST *verb*[3], *noun*[1]: see -ED[1], -ED[2].]
▸ **I 1** Bordered, edged; striped; (of colours) arranged in bands or stripes. **ME.**
2 Provided with a list or selvedge. **M16.**
3 Covered or edged with list. **E19.**
4 *BASKET-MAKING.* Having an extra (decorative) skein on a handle. **E20.**
▸ **II 5** Enclosed, fenced in; *spec.* (of ground) enclosed in or converted into lists for tilting; (of a combat) fought in the lists. **LME.**
6 Engaged in the lists. *poet.* **M18.**

listed /ˈlɪstɪd/ *adjective*[2]. **M17.**
[ORIGIN from LIST *verb*[4] + -ED[1].]
1 Enlisted for military service. *arch.* **M17.**
2 Included in a list, directory, or catalogue; *spec.* (of a building) protected from demolition or major alteration by being included in an official list of buildings of architectural or historical importance; (of a company) having

L

its shares quoted on the main market of the London Stock Exchange. E20.

Western Mail (Cardiff) The thatched cottage . . is 18th century in part and it is a grade two listed building. M. BRETT The Stock Exchange . . requires that listed companies produce figures showing profits.

listel /ˈlɪst(ə)l/ *noun*. L16.
[ORIGIN Italian *listello* (whence also French *listel*) dim. of *lista* LIST *noun*[1].]
ARCHITECTURE. A small list or fillet.

listen /ˈlɪs(ə)n/ *noun*. LME.
[ORIGIN from the verb.]
†1 Hearing, sense of hearing. Only in LME.
2 The action or an act of listening; a spell of listening or attentive hearing. Also ***listen-in***. L18.

G. MANVILLE FENN She was often on the watch, and always on the listen. P. BAIR 'Did you have a nice talk?' 'I had a long listen'.

listen /ˈlɪs(ə)n/ *verb*.
[ORIGIN Old English *hlysnan* corresp. to Middle High German *lüsenen*, from West Germanic, from Germanic base repr. also by LIST *verb*[2].]
1 *verb trans.* Hear attentively; pay attention to (a person speaking or some utterance). Now *arch. & poet.* OE.

TENNYSON Listening the lordly music.

2 *verb intrans.* **a** Give attention with the ear to some sound or utterance or person speaking; make an effort to hear something. ME. ▸**b** Give attention with the ear *to, unto*; (in extended use) pay heed *to*, yield *to* a temptation or request. ME.

a D. H. LAWRENCE She stood and listened, and it seemed to her she heard sounds from the back of the cottage. *Radio Times* We sat listening . . with a portable set. H. ROTH Listen, I have an idea. **b** R. GRAVES Listen to those doors banging. D. LESSING I've listened to you two talk all my life. J. SIMMS My teacher is a fine critic and I listen carefully to him.

a listen good: see GOOD *adjective*. **b *listen to reason***: see REASON *noun*[1].
3 *verb intrans.* Sound (in a certain way), convey a certain impression *to* a listener. *US*. E20.
– WITH ADVERBS & PREPOSITIONS IN SPECIALIZED SENSES: **listen for** be eager or make an effort to catch the sound of; endeavour to hear or to hear of. **listen in** use a radio receiving set to listen to a broadcast programme etc., listen secretly to or tap a telephonic communication, listen to the conversation etc. of others, (foll. by *to, on*). **listen out** listen eagerly or carefully, listen for a sound on a radio receiver etc.; ***listen out for*** = ***listen for*** above.

L

listenable /ˈlɪs(ə)nəb(ə)l/ *adjective*. E19.
[ORIGIN from LISTEN *verb* + -ABLE.]
1 Willing to listen. Now *rare*. E19.
2 Easy or pleasant to listen to. E20.
■ **listenaˈbility** *noun* M20.

listener /ˈlɪs(ə)nə/ *noun*. E17.
[ORIGIN from LISTEN *verb* + -ER[1].]
1 A person who listens; an attentive hearer. Also ***listener-in***. E17.

LD MACAULAY The streets were stopped up . . by groups of talkers and listeners. *Daily Chronicle* By the magic of wireless it was, perhaps, the listeners-in who heard it first. R. JARRELL He was a remarkably polite listener, and nodded all the time you spoke. R. THOMAS You just sit there and listen. You're a pretty good listener, aren't you?

2 The ear. *arch. slang*. E19.
3 FORTIFICATION. = LISTENING ***gallery***. E19.
■ **listenership** *noun* the estimated number of listeners to a broadcast radio programme M20.

listening /ˈlɪs(ə)nɪŋ/ *noun*. ME.
[ORIGIN from LISTEN *verb* + -ING[1].]
1 The action of LISTEN *verb*; an instance of this. Also ***listening-in***. ME.

TENNYSON Lonely listenings to my mutter'd dream. *Saturday Evening Post* These telephones were connected with a listening-in device concealed behind a picture on the wall.

2 With qualifying adjective: broadcast, recorded, or other matter for listening to, esp. with reference to its quality or kind. M20.

Church Times Other incidents in his life also made interesting listening.

– COMB.: **listening gallery** FORTIFICATION an advanced trench or gallery used to listen to the movements of an enemy; **listening post** MILITARY an advanced position used to discover movements or the disposition of an enemy; *transf.* a station for intercepting electronic communications, a position from which to listen.

lister /ˈlɪstə/ *noun*[1]. L17.
[ORIGIN from LIST *verb*[4] + -ER[1].]
1 A person who enlists others for military service. *arch.* L17.
2 A person who makes out a list. L17.

lister /ˈlɪstə/ *noun*[2]. *US*. L19.
[ORIGIN from LIST *verb*[3] + -ER[1].]
A double-mould board plough which throws up ridges and at the same time plants and covers seed in the furrows.

listeria /lɪˈstɪərɪə/ *noun*. Pl. **-s**, same. M20.
[ORIGIN mod. Latin (see below), from Joseph *Lister* (1827–1912), English surgeon: see -IA[1].]
BACTERIOLOGY. A bacterium of the genus *Listeria*, esp. *L. monocytogenes*, a widespread pathogen of people and animals.
■ **listerial**, **listeric** /lɪˈstɛrɪk/ *adjectives* caused by or derived from listerias M20. **listeriˈosis** *noun* infection with, or a disease caused by, listerias (contracted esp. by the ingestion of contaminated food or silage) M20.

listful /ˈlɪstfʊl, -f(ə)l/ *adjective*. *arch.* L16.
[ORIGIN from LIST *verb*[2] + -FUL.]
Inclined to listen, attentive.

listing /ˈlɪstɪŋ/ *noun*[1]. LME.
[ORIGIN from LIST *noun*[1] + -ING[1].]
1 A selvedge, a border; material used for the selvedge of cloth. LME.
2 BASKET-MAKING. Extra (decorative) skeining on a handle. E20.

listing /ˈlɪstɪŋ/ *noun*[2]. M17.
[ORIGIN from LIST *verb*[4] + -ING[1].]
1 The action of enlisting someone; enrolment. *arch.* M17.
2 The action of listing someone or something; the drawing up of a list. M17.
3 An entry in a catalogue, telephone directory, timetable, or other list or register (freq. in *pl.*); a list; COMPUTING a printed or displayed copy of a program or of the contents of a file. E20.

Times The consortium says that it intends to retain a Stock Exchange listing. E. LEONARD He remembered from the TV listings that both movies first came out in 1957. *New Yorker* A real-estate agent . . who . . had a listing just a couple of houses down from Jennifer's.

listless /ˈlɪs(t)lɪs/ *adjective*. LME.
[ORIGIN from LIST *noun*[2] + -LESS.]
Characterized by unwillingness to move, act, or make any exertion; marked by languid indifference. Formerly also, without relish or inclination for some specified object or pursuit (foll. by *of*).

S. RAVEN James' growing indifference was reflected in the boys' bored and listless play. N. BAWDEN She was so listless, all her old sparkle gone. A. HUTSCHNECKER Humiliation and a sense of futility caused apathetic, listless, states of mind.

■ **listlessly** *adverb* L17. **listlessness** *noun* M17.

LISTSERV /ˈlɪstsəːv/ *noun*. Also **listserv**. L20.
[ORIGIN from LIST *noun*[3] + SERV(ER.]
COMPUTING. (Proprietary name for) an electronic mailing list of people who wish to receive specified information from the Internet.

Lisu /ˈliːsuː/ *noun & adjective*. L19.
[ORIGIN Yi (Lisu).]
▸**A** *noun*. Pl. same, **-s**. A member of a Tibeto-Burman people of the mountainous SW region of China; the Yi dialect of this people. L19.
▸**B** *adjective*. Designating or pertaining to the Lisu or their dialect. E20.

Lisztian /ˈlɪstɪən/ *adjective & noun*. L19.
[ORIGIN from *Liszt* (see below) + -IAN.]
▸**A** *adjective*. Of, pertaining to, or characteristic of the Hungarian pianist and composer Ferenc (Franz) Liszt (1811–86) or his music. L19.
▸**B** *noun*. An interpreter, student, or admirer of Liszt or his music. M20.

lit /lɪt/ *noun*. *obsolete* exc. *dial.* ME.
[ORIGIN Old Norse *litr*: cf. LITMUS.]
1 A colour, a dye; a stain. ME.
2 Dye stuff; a batch of dyeing. ME.

lit /lɪt/ *adjective*. E19.
[ORIGIN pa. pple of LIGHT *verb*[2].]
1 That has been lit; lighted, illumined. Also foll. by *up*. E19.
2 Drunk, intoxicated. Freq. foll. by *up*. *slang*. E20.

lit /lɪt/ *verb*[1]. *obsolete* exc. *dial.* Infl. **-tt-**. Pa. pple & ppl adjective. **lit**, **litted**. ME.
[ORIGIN Old Norse *lita*, formed as LIT *noun*.]
1 *verb trans.* Colour, dye; stain. ME.
2 *verb intrans.* Blush deeply. E19.

lit *verb*[2], *verb*[3] *pa. t. & pple*: see LIGHT *verb*[1], *verb*[2].

lit. /lɪt/ *noun & adjective*. *colloq.* Also **Lit.**, & without point. M19.
[ORIGIN Abbreviation.]
▸**A** *noun*. Literature (earliest in ENG. LIT.). Formerly also, a student or devotee of literature; a literary magazine. M19.
▸**B** *adjective*. Literary. L19.
lit. crit. literary criticism. **lit. sup.** a literary supplement.

litaneutical /lɪtəˈnjuːtɪk(ə)l/ *adjective*. M19.
[ORIGIN from Greek *litaneutikos*, from *litaneuein* pray: see LITANY, -AL[1].]
Of the nature of a litany.

litany /ˈlɪt(ə)ni/ *noun*. ME.
[ORIGIN Old French *letanie* (mod. *litanie*) from ecclesiastical Latin *litania* from Greek *litaneia* prayer, entreaty, from *litaneuein* pray, from *litanos* suppliant, from *litē* supplication: see -Y[3].]
1 CHRISTIAN CHURCH. A series of supplications, deprecations, or intercessions in which the clergy lead and other people respond, the same formula of response usu. being repeated for several successive clauses (used either as part of a service or by itself, in the latter case often in procession). ME.
the Litany that form of 'general supplication' appointed for use in the *Book of Common Prayer*.
2 *transf.* A form of supplication (e.g. in non-Christian worship) resembling a litany; a continuous repetition or long enumeration, a repeated formula, a long series. LME.

W. GOLDING Our crew . . invoked Allah and a whole litany of what I supposed were saints. H. BAILEY 'A generation gone,' went the litany of the time. *Sunday Times* The reform of any socialist system is likely to involve a litany of words and phrases such as skills, market economy, mobility of labour.

– COMB.: **litany-desk**, **litany-stool** a low movable prayer desk at which a minister kneels while reciting the litany.

litas /ˈliːtas/ *noun*. Pl. same. E20.
[ORIGIN Lithuanian.]
The basic monetary unit of Lithuania, equal to 100 centas.

litchi *noun* var. of LYCHEE.

lite /liːt, lɪt/ *noun*[1], *adjective*[1], & *adverb*. Long *arch. & dial.*
[ORIGIN Old English *lȳt* (noun, adjective, & adverb) = Old Saxon *lūt* (noun). Partly from Old Norse *litt* (adverb) contr. of *lítit* neut. of *lítill* LITTLE *adjective*.]
▸**A** *noun*. **1** Little, not much; *a* little. OE.
2 Few. OE.
▸**B** *adjective*. **1** Few; *a* few. OE.
2 Little in amount; not much of. ME.
3 Little in magnitude; small. ME.
▸**C** *adverb*. Little; in a small degree, to a small extent. OE.

lite /lʌɪt/ *noun*[2] & *adjective*[2]. Now *colloq.* L16.
[ORIGIN Var. of *light*. Now usu. a deliberate respelling.]
▸**A** *noun*. **1** In *pl.* = LIGHTS. Chiefly *dial.* L16.
2 A light. L20.
3 (Proprietary name for) a light beer with relatively few calories. L20.
▸**B** *adjective*. Light; *spec.* (proprietary) designating a light beer with relatively few calories. L16.

-lite /lʌɪt/ *suffix*.
[ORIGIN French *-lite*, German *-lit(h)*, repr. Greek *lithos* stone. Cf. -LITH.]
Forming names of minerals, rocks, mineral structures, etc., esp. as an alternative to -ITE[1] for stems ending in a vowel (***geikielite***, ***phonolite***).

liter *noun* see LITRE.

literacy /ˈlɪt(ə)rəsi/ *noun*. L19.
[ORIGIN from LITERATE: see -ACY. After earlier ILLITERACY.]
The quality or state of being literate; knowledge of letters; condition in respect to education, *esp.* ability to read and write.
– COMB.: COMPUTER ***literacy***; **literacy hour** a period in school set aside for developing reading skills, introduced as a daily requirement in English primary schools in 1998.

literae humaniores /ˌlɪtərʌɪ hjuːˌmanɪˈɔːriːz/ *noun phr.* Also **litterae humaniores**. M18.
[ORIGIN Latin = more humane letters.]
The humanities, secular learning as opp. to divinity; *esp.* at Oxford University, the school or subject of Greek and Roman classical literature, philosophy, and ancient history.

literal /ˈlɪt(ə)r(ə)l/ *adjective & noun*. LME.
[ORIGIN Old French & mod. French *littéral* or late Latin *lit(t)eralis*, from *lit(t)era* LETTER *noun*[1]: see -AL[1].]
▸**A** *adjective*. **I 1** Designating or pertaining to a sense or interpretation of a text, orig. esp. the Bible, obtained by taking words in their primary or customary meaning, and applying the ordinary rules of grammar, without mysticism, allegory, or metaphor; designating or pertaining to the etymological or a primary sense of a word. LME.

S. BECKETT True there was never much talk of the heart, literal or figurative. N. PODHORETZ The literal meaning of *Torah lishma* may be 'learning for its own sake', but the true, the theological meaning of the idea is 'studying the revealed word of God for the sake of heaven.' F. SPALDING His literal illustration of *The Song of Songs* aroused a Catholic controversy.

2 (Of a translation, version, transcript, etc.) representing the very words of the original, verbally exact; (of a representation in art or literature) exactly copied, true to life, realistic. L16.

DRYDEN The common way . . is not a literal Translation, but a kind of Paraphrase. F. HOYLE These extremely literal animal forms are accompanied by symbolic human figures.

3 That is so in its literal sense, without metaphor, exaggeration, or inaccuracy; literally so called; *colloq.* so called with some exaggeration etc. M17.

E. A. FREEMAN The literal extirpation of a nation is an impossibility. G. A. BIRMINGHAM Do you suppose that the Prime Minister, when he thinks he'll have to go to war with Germany, tells the literal truth?

4 Free from figures of speech, exaggeration, inaccuracy, distortion, or allusion. M18.

A. N. WILSON It is not safe to take Tolstoy's diaries as a literal record of events.

5 Of a person, a person's mind: apt to take literally what is spoken or written figuratively or with humorous exaggeration or irony; unimaginative, matter-of-fact. L18.

H. ALLEN You assured ships with honest, literal, and unimaginative persons.

▸ **II 6** Of or pertaining to letters of the alphabet; of the nature of a letter or letters, alphabetical. LME. ▸**b** Of a misprint or (occas.) scribal error: involving a letter or letters. E17. ▸**c** *MATH.* Performed by means of letters; denoted or expressed by a letter or letters; algebraic but not numerical. Now *rare*. L17.

†**7** Of or pertaining to literature or letters; literary. LME–E17.

– COMB.: **literal-minded** *adjective* having a literal mind, characteristic of a person with a literal mind, unimaginative; **literal-mindedness** the quality or state of being literal-minded.

▸ **B** *noun*. **1** *PRINTING*. A misprint, a typographical error. E17.

†**2** A literal interpretation or meaning. Only in M17.

3 *COMPUTING*. An operand which directly specifies a value, or defines itself rather than serving as an address or label; a character that is treated as data rather than as a symbolic name. M20.

literalise *verb* var. of LITERALIZE.

literalism /ˈlɪt(ə)r(ə)lɪz(ə)m/ *noun*. M17.
[ORIGIN from LITERAL *adjective* + -ISM.]
1 The disposition to literal interpretation. M17.
2 The disposition to literal representation in art or literature. M19.
3 Literal translation as a principle; a peculiarity of expression due to this. L19.

literalist /ˈlɪt(ə)r(ə)lɪst/ *noun*. M17.
[ORIGIN formed as LITERALISM + -IST.]
A person who insists on or is given to literal interpretation. Also, in art or literature, a person who depicts or describes things realistically, an exact copyist.
■ **literaˈlistic** *adjective* pertaining to or characteristic of a literalist or literalism L19.

literality /lɪtəˈralɪti/ *noun*. M17.
[ORIGIN formed as LITERALISM + -ITY.]
The quality or fact of being literal; literalness; an instance of this.

literalize /ˈlɪt(ə)r(ə)lʌɪz/ *verb trans*. Also **-ise**. E19.
[ORIGIN formed as LITERALISM + -IZE.]
Make literal; represent or accept as literal.
■ **literaliˈzation** *noun* M19. **literalizer** *noun* L19.

literally /ˈlɪt(ə)rəli/ *adverb*. L15.
[ORIGIN formed as LITERALISM + -LY².]
In a literal manner, in the literal sense; so as to represent the very words of the original; so as to depict or describe the thing realistically; (emphasizing the use of a word or phrase) without metaphor, exaggeration, distortion, or allusion, *colloq.* with some exaggeration etc., emphatically.

STEELE Others repeat only what they hear from others as literally as their parts or zeal will permit. T. HARDY A tone expressing that these words signified . . about one hundred times the amount of meaning they conveyed literally. G. GREENE He had only two pounds in his pocket—not literally in his pocket because . . they had been taken away from him. K. AMIS Literally hundreds of men were always pestering her to marry them. R. M. PIRSIG He literally had to move heaven and earth to arrive at this systematic understanding.

literalness /ˈlɪt(ə)r(ə)lnɪs/ *noun*. M17.
[ORIGIN formed as LITERALISM + -NESS.]
The quality or fact of being literal.

literarily /ˈlɪt(ə)rərɪli/ *adverb*. E19.
[ORIGIN from LITERARY + -LY².]
In a literary manner or respect.

literariness /ˈlɪt(ə)rərɪnɪs/ *noun*. L19.
[ORIGIN formed as LITERARILY + -NESS.]
The quality or fact of being literary.

literarism /ˈlɪt(ə)rərɪz(ə)m/ *noun*. M20.
[ORIGIN from LITERARY + -ISM.]
= LITERARYISM.

literary /ˈlɪt(ə)rəri/ *adjective & noun*. M17.
[ORIGIN Latin *lit(t)erarius*, from *lit(t)era* LETTER *noun*¹: see -ARY¹.]
▸ **A** *adjective*. †**1** Pertaining to the letters of the alphabet. M17–L18.
2 Of, pertaining to, or of the nature of literature; of or pertaining to books and written compositions; (of a word or idiom) used chiefly in books or by writers, not colloquial; *esp.* pertaining to or having the characteristics of that kind of written composition valued on account of its qualities of form or emotional effect. Formerly also, of or pertaining to the humanities or polite learning. M18.

LD MACAULAY The parliamentary conflict on the great question of a standing army was preceded by a literary conflict. G. GREENE The long pompous literary oath full of words too difficult for Taylor to pronounce. B. EMECHETA She had already cultivated the taste for wide reading and . . was always in the mood for literary talk. D. HALBERSTAM He was not much interested in literary style and he did not care about good writing.

3 Acquainted with or versed in literature; *spec.* engaged in literature as a profession, occupied in writing books. Of a society etc.: consisting of people engaged or interested in literature. L18.

4 Of painting, sculpture, etc.: that depicts or represents a story. E20.

– SPECIAL COLLOCATIONS & COMB.: **literary adviser** a person who gives advice or information on literary matters. **literary agency**: that acts for authors in dealing with publishers etc. **literary agent**: who acts for an author in dealing with publishers etc. **literary critic** a person who engages in literary criticism. **literary-critical** *adjective* pertaining to or of the nature of literary criticism. **literary criticism** the art or practice of estimating the qualities and character of literary works. **literary editor** (*a*) the editor of the literary section of a newspaper; (*b*) the editor of a book of collected writings. **literary-editorship** the post or function of a literary editor. ***literary executor***. **literary history** the history of the treatment of, and references to, a specified subject in literature. **literary property** (*a*) property which consists in written or printed compositions; (*b*) the exclusive right of publication as recognized and limited by law.

▸ **B** *noun*. A literary club or society; a literary person. *US*. E20.
■ **literaryism** *noun* addiction to literary forms; an instance of this, a form of expression belonging to literary language: L19.

litera scripta /lɪtərə ˈskrɪptə/ *noun phr*. M19.
[ORIGIN Latin.]
The written word.

literate /ˈlɪt(ə)rət/ *adjective & noun*. LME.
[ORIGIN Latin *lit(t)eratus*, from *lit(t)era* LETTER *noun*¹: see -ATE².]
▸ **A** *adjective*. **1** Acquainted with letters or literature; able to read and write; educated; (usu. as 2nd elem. of comb.) competent or knowledgeable in a specified area. LME. *COMPUTER-literate*.
2 Of or pertaining to literature or letters, literary. *arch*. M17.
▸ **B** *noun*. **1** A liberally educated or learned person. M16.
2 *spec.* In the Anglican Church, a person admitted to holy orders without having obtained a university degree. E19.
3 A person who can read and write (opp. an ***illiterate***); (usu. as 2nd elem. of comb.) a person who is competent or knowledgeable in a specified area. L19.
■ **literately** *adverb* M20.

literati /lɪtəˈrɑːtiː/ *noun pl*. E17.
[ORIGIN Latin *lit(t)erati* pl. of *lit(t)eratus* LITERATE *adjective*. Cf. LITERATO, LITERATUS.]
Men or women of letters; the learned class as a whole.

attrib.: HELEN FIELDING Am invited to a glittering literati launch of *Kafka's Motorbike* next week at the Ivy.

literatim /lɪtəˈreɪtɪm, -ˈrɑːtɪm/ *adverb*. M17.
[ORIGIN medieval Latin *lit(t)eratim*, from *lit(t)era* LETTER *noun*¹, after GRADATIM. Cf. VERBATIM.]
Letter for letter; literally.

literation /lɪtəˈreɪʃ(ə)n/ *noun*. E20.
[ORIGIN from Latin *lit(t)era* LETTER *noun*¹ + -ATION.]
The representation of sounds or words by a letter or letters, spelling.

literatist /ˈlɪt(ə)rətɪst/ *noun*. Now *rare*. M17.
[ORIGIN from LITERATE *adjective* + -IST.]
A person engaged in literary pursuits; a writer, an author.

literato /lɪtəˈrɑːtəʊ/ *noun sing*. Corresp. pl. LITERATI. E18.
[ORIGIN Italian *litterato* (now usu. *letterati*) formed as LITERATE.]
A member of the literati; a man of letters, a learned man. Cf. LITERATUS.

literator /ˈlɪt(ə)reɪtə/ *noun*. M17.
[ORIGIN Latin *lit(t)erator* teacher of letters, grammarian, sciolist, from *lit(t)era* LETTER *noun*¹: see -ATOR.]
†**1** A pretender to learning, a sciolist. Only in M17.
†**2** A bibliographer. Also, a literary or textual critic. M18–M19.
3 = LITTÉRATEUR. L18.

literature /ˈlɪt(ə)rətʃə/ *noun*. LME.
[ORIGIN (French *littérature* from) Latin *lit(t)eratura*, from *lit(t)era* LETTER *noun*¹: see -URE.]
1 Acquaintance with books; polite or humane learning; literary culture. Now *arch. rare*. LME.

S. JOHNSON His literature was unquestionably great. He read all the languages which are considered either as learned or polite.

2 Literary work or production; the realm of letters. L18.

LYTTON Ah, you make literature your calling, sir?

3 a Literary productions as a whole; the body of writings produced in a particular country or period. Now also *spec.* that kind of written composition valued on account of its qualities of form or emotional effect. E19. ▸**b** The body of books and writings that treat of a particular subject. M19. ▸**c** Printed matter of any kind. *colloq.* L19.

a S. SPENDER Trying to distinguish the kind of writing which is literature from that which is worthless. J. PLAMENATZ The quality of a literature does not always improve . . as population increases and literacy spreads. **b** J. BARZUN It is possible to master the literature of a subject. *Holiday Which?* It's . . not as spectacular as the tourist literature suggests. **c** V. BRITTAIN A suitcase full of informative literature.

a ***American literature***, ***English literature***, ***Russian literature***, etc. ***Wisdom literature***: see WISDOM.

literatus /lɪtəˈrɑːtəs/ *noun sing*. *rare*. Corresp. pl. LITERATI. E18.
[ORIGIN formed as LITERATE.]
A member of the literati; a man of letters, a learned man. Cf. LITERATO.

literose /ˈlɪtərəʊs/ *adjective*. *rare*. L19.
[ORIGIN Late Latin *lit(t)erosus*, from *lit(t)era* LETTER *noun*¹: see -OSE¹.]
Studiedly or affectedly literary.
■ **liteˈrosity** *noun* L19.

lith /lɪθ/ *noun*¹. Now *arch. & dial.*
[ORIGIN Old English *liþ* = Old Saxon *liþ*, Old Frisian *lith* (Dutch *lid*), Old High German *lid* (German *Glied*), Old Norse *liðr*, Gothic *liþus*, from Germanic; prob. rel. to LIMB *noun*¹.]
1 A limb. OE.
2 A joint; *spec.* the last joint or the tip of a finger. OE.
3 A segment of an orange etc. Also, each of the rings at the base of a cow's horn. Chiefly *Scot.* L18.

lith /lɪθ/ *noun*² *& adjective*. M20.
[ORIGIN Abbreviation of LITHOGRAPHY, LITHOGRAPHIC.]
(Designating or pertaining to) a photographic film thinly coated with emulsion, for producing images of extremely high contrast and density and used extensively in lithographic printing.

-lith /lɪθ/ *suffix*.
[ORIGIN from Greek *lithos* stone. Cf. -LITE.]
PALAEONTOLOGY, ARCHAEOLOGY, & MEDICINE. Forming nouns with the sense 'stone, stony structure', as ***batholith***, ***coccolith***, ***gastrolith***, ***monolith***, ***otolith***. Cf. -LITHIC.

lithaemia /lɪˈθiːmɪə/ *noun*. Now *rare*. Also ***-themia**. L19.
[ORIGIN from LITHIC *adjective*¹ + -AEMIA.]
= HYPERURICAEMIA.
■ **lithaemic** *adjective* of, pertaining to, or affected with lithaemia L19.

L

litham /liːˈθɑːm/ *noun*. M19.
[ORIGIN Arabic *liṯām* veil for the mouth.]
A cloth wound round the lower part of the face covering the mouth and sometimes part of the nose, worn by Bedouins.

litharge /ˈlɪθɑːdʒ/ *noun*. ME.
[ORIGIN Old French *litarge* (mod. *lith-*) from Latin *lithargyrus* from Greek *litharguros*, from *lithos* stone + *arguros* silver.]
CHEMISTRY. **1** Lead monoxide, PbO, a toxic red or yellow solid prepared by oxidation of lead in air and used as a pigment and in making glass and ceramics. Also †***litharge of lead***. Cf. MASSICOT. ME. ▸†**b** Any of various impure ores or mixtures containing lead monoxide. LME–L18.
†**2** White lead; red lead. M16–E19.

lithe /lʌɪð/ *noun*¹. Long *obsolete* exc. *Scot.* ME.
[ORIGIN from LITHE *adjective*.]
1 A calm, a lull. ME.
2 Shelter. M18.

lithe /lʌɪð/ *noun*². *obsolete* exc. *dial.* L17.
[ORIGIN from LITHE *verb*¹.]
Oatmeal and water used to thicken broth.

lithe /lʌɪð/ *adjective & verb*¹.
[ORIGIN Old English *līþe* = Old Saxon *līþi*, Old High German *lindi* (German *lind*) soft, gentle, from West Germanic, from Germanic from Indo-European base also of Old Norse *linr* soft, yielding, Old English *linnan* LIN *verb*.]
▸ **A** *adjective*. **1** Of a person, action, etc.: gentle, meek, mild. Long *Scot. rare*. OE.
2 Of a thing: mild, soft; agreeable, mellow. *obsolete* exc. *dial.* OE. ▸†**b** Of weather: calm, serene. Of water: smooth, still. ME–L16. ▸**c** Comfortable, sheltered. *Scot.* LME.
3 Easily bent, flexible; (of a person) supple, agile, (gracefully) slim and muscled. ME.

D. H. LAWRENCE He had that fine, lithe physique, suggestive of much animal vigour. V. SETH John . . talking to a lithe nymphet.

4 Of broth etc.: smooth, thick. Chiefly *dial.* M17.
▸ **B** *verb trans*. †**1** Make gentle or mild; assuage, relieve, soothe; make supple; subdue. OE–M17.
2 Make thick; thicken (broth etc.). Long *Scot. rare*. L17.
■ **lithely** *adverb* OE. **litheness** *noun* ME.

lithe /lʌɪð/ *verb*². Now *arch. & dial.* ME.
[ORIGIN Old Norse *hlýða*, from *hljóð* listening, sound, rel. to Gothic *hliuma* sense of hearing, Old English *hlēoþor* sense of hearing, music, Old High German *hlūdar*, from Germanic var. of base of LIST *verb*², LISTEN *verb*.]
1 *verb intrans*. Hearken, listen. ME.
2 *verb trans*. Hear (something). LME.

lithemia *noun* see LITHAEMIA.

lither /ˈlɪðə/ *adjective & adverb*. Now *arch. & dial.*
[ORIGIN Old English *lȳþre* from Germanic base also of 1st elem. of Middle High German, German *liederlich*: cf. Middle Low German *lüder* lewd man.]

▸ **A** *adjective*. †**1** Wicked, bad. OE–M16.
†**2** Ill-looking, worthless, poor, sorry. Of a part of the body: withered, paralysed. OE–E17.
3 Lazy, sluggish, spiritless. LME.
4 Pliant, supple; (of the air) yielding, allowing (swift) movement. Also, agile, nimble. M16.
▸ †**B** *adverb*. Badly, wickedly; ill, poorly. OE–ME.
■ †**litherly** *adjective* (*a*) idle, lazy; (*b*) spiteful, mischievous: L16–E19. †**litherly** *adverb* OE–E17. †**litherness** *noun* ME–E18.

lithesome /ˈlʌɪðs(ə)m/ *adjective*. M18.
[ORIGIN from LITHE *adjective* + -SOME[1]. See also LISSOM.]
Supple, agile, lissom.

lithia /ˈlɪθɪə/ *noun*[1]. E19.
[ORIGIN Alt. of LITHION after *soda*, *potassa*, etc.]
CHEMISTRY. Lithium oxide, Li_2O, a white hygroscopic alkaline solid.
– COMB.: **lithia-emerald** = HIDDENITE; **lithia-mica** = LEPIDOLITE; **lithia-tourmaline** any variety of tourmaline which contains lithium; **lithia water** mineral water containing dissolved salts of lithium.

lithia /ˈlɪθɪə/ *noun*[2]. *rare*. E19.
[ORIGIN mod. Latin, from Greek *lithos* stone: see -IA[1].]
MEDICINE. Lithiasis; *esp*. the formation of concretions in the sebaceous glands of the eyelid.

lithian /ˈlɪθɪən/ *adjective*. M20.
[ORIGIN from LITHIUM + -IAN.]
MINERALOGY. Having a constituent element partly replaced by lithium.

lithiasis /lɪˈθʌɪəsɪs/ *noun*. Pl. **-ases** /-əsiːz/. M17.
[ORIGIN medieval Latin from Greek, from *lithos* stone: see -IASIS.]
MEDICINE. The formation of stony concretions or calculi in the body, esp. in the gall bladder or the urinary system.

lithiated /ˈlɪθɪeɪtɪd/ *adjective*. L18.
[ORIGIN In sense 1 from LITHIC *adjective*[1], in sense 2 from LITHIA *noun*[1]: see -ATE[3], -ED[1].]
†**1** CHEMISTRY. Combined with uric acid. L18–L19.
2 Chiefly of mineral water: impregnated with lithium salts. E20.

L

lithic /ˈlɪθɪk/ *adjective*[1]. L18.
[ORIGIN Greek *lithikos*, from *lithos* stone: see -IC.]
1 CHEMISTRY & MEDICINE. Orig., = URIC. Now (*arch*.), of or pertaining to stones in the bladder. L18.
2 *gen*. Of, pertaining to, or resembling stone; consisting of stone; ARCHAEOLOGY of or pertaining to stone artefacts. M19.
■ **lithate** *noun* = URATE *noun* E19.

lithic /ˈlɪθɪk/ *adjective*[2]. L19.
[ORIGIN from LITHIUM + -IC.]
Chiefly CHEMISTRY. Of, pertaining to, or containing lithium.

-lithic /ˈlɪθɪk/ *suffix*.
[ORIGIN formed as -LITH + -IC: cf. Greek *lithikos* of stone.]
Forming adjectives with the sense 'of or pertaining to stone', as ***granolithic***, ***megalithic***; *spec*. in ARCHAEOLOGY, designating or pertaining to a particular cultural period that is a division of the Stone Age, as ***Mesolithic***, ***Neolithic***, ***Palaeolithic***.

lithification /ˌlɪθɪfɪˈkeɪʃ(ə)n/ *noun*. L19.
[ORIGIN from LITHIFY + -FICATION.]
GEOLOGY. The process of compaction of a sediment into stone.
■ Also **lithiˈfaction** *noun* L19.

lithify /ˈlɪθɪfʌɪ/ *verb trans*. L19.
[ORIGIN from Greek *lithos* stone + -I- + -FY.]
Form into stone. Chiefly as ***lithified*** *ppl adjective*.

†**lithion** *noun*. E–M19.
[ORIGIN Use as noun of neut. of Greek *lithios* stony, from *lithos* stone.]
CHEMISTRY. = LITHIA *noun*[1].

lithiophilite /lɪθɪˈɒfɪlʌɪt/ *noun*. L19.
[ORIGIN from LITHIUM + -O- + Greek *philos* friend + -ITE[1].]
MINERALOGY. A pink or brown orthorhombic phosphate of lithium and magnesium, often containing iron and forming a series with triphylite.

lithium /ˈlɪθɪəm/ *noun*. E19.
[ORIGIN from LITHIA *noun*[1]: see -IUM.]
A soft light highly reactive chemical element, atomic no. 3, which is a member of the alkali metal group and is found esp. in the minerals spodumene and lepidolite (symbol Li).

litho /ˈlʌɪθəʊ, ˈlɪθ-/ *noun*, *adjective*, & *verb*. *colloq*. L19.
[ORIGIN Abbreviation.]
▸ **A** *noun*. Pl. **-os**. = LITHOGRAPH *noun*, LITHOGRAPHY. L19.
▸ **B** *adjective*. = LITHOGRAPHIC. E20.
▸ **C** *verb trans*. = LITHOGRAPH *verb*. M20.

litho- /ˈlɪθəʊ/ *combining form*. Before a vowel **lith-**.
[ORIGIN Greek *lithos* stone: see -O-.]
Of or pertaining to stone or rock, or a calculus.
■ **lithochroˈmatic** *adjective* of, pertaining to, or produced by lithochromatics L19. **lithochroˈmatics** *noun* the art of taking impressions from stone painted with oil colours M19. **lithochrome** *adjective* lithochromatic M19. **lithochromy** *noun* painting on stone M19. **lithoclast** *noun* †(*a*) a stone-breaker; (*b*) SURGERY (now *rare*) an instrument for breaking up stone in the bladder: E19. **lithofacies** *noun* (GEOLOGY) a facies distinguished by its lithology M20. **lithoˈgenesis** *noun* (GEOLOGY) the formation of (esp. sedimentary) rock E20. **liˈthogenous** *adjective* (*a*) ZOOLOGY (of an animal) that secretes coral; (*b*) GEOLOGY (of a sediment) resulting from the breakdown of rock: M19. **lithoglyph** *noun* an engraving on stone; the art of engraving on stone: M19. **liˈtholatrous** *adjective* stone-worshipping L19. **liˈtholatry** *noun* stone-worship L19. **lithoneˈphrotomy** *noun* (MEDICINE) = NEPHROLITHOTOMY L19. **lithoˈphagic** *adjective* = LITHOPHAGOUS M20. **liˈthophagous** *adjective* (ZOOLOGY) stone-eating; *esp*. (of a mollusc) that bores through stone; (of a bird etc.) that swallows stones to aid digestion: E19. **lithophane** *noun* [Greek *-phanēs* appearing] a kind of ornamentation of porcelain visible when held to the light, produced by pressing designs into it when soft; an object so decorated: E20. **lithophanic** /-ˈfanɪk/ *adjective* pertaining to lithophanes or lithophany E19. ***lithophanie*** /litɔfani (*pl. same*)/ *noun* [French] (*a*) = LITHOPHANE; (*b*) = LITHOPHANY: M19. **liˈthophany** *noun* the art or process of making lithophanes M19. **lithophile** *adjective* (GEOLOGY & CHEMISTRY) designating an element which commonly occurs combined as a silicate, and is supposed to have become concentrated in the earth's outer layers E20. **liˈthophilous** *adjective* (BOTANY & ZOOLOGY) that thrives in stony places or on rocks M19. **lithopone** *noun* [Greek *ponos* (a thing produced by) work] a mixture of zinc sulphide and barium sulphate used as a white pigment in paints, leathers, etc. (now largely superseded by titanium dioxide) L19. **lithosere** *noun* (ECOLOGY) a plant succession originating on bare rock E20. **lithosol** *noun* (SOIL SCIENCE) an azonal soil consisting largely of imperfectly weathered rock fragments M20. **lithoˈstatic** *adjective* (GEOLOGY) designating pressure exerted by overlying rock M20. **lithotint** *noun* (chiefly *hist*.) the art or process of printing tinted pictures by lithography; a picture so printed: M19.

lithocyst /ˈlɪθəsɪst/ *noun*. M19.
[ORIGIN from LITHO- + CYST.]
1 ZOOLOGY. = STATOCYST. Now *rare* or *obsolete*. M19.
2 BOTANY. A cell containing a cystolith. L19.

lithodipyra /ˌlɪθə(ʊ)dɪˈpʌɪ(ə)rə/ *noun*. L18.
[ORIGIN from LITHO- + DI-[2] + Greek *pur* fire, with the sense 'stone twice fired'.]
= COADE STONE.

lithodomous /lɪˈθɒdəməs/ *adjective*. M19.
[ORIGIN from mod. Latin *Lithodomus* (see below), from Greek *lithodomos* mason, formed as LITHO- + *domos* building: see -OUS.]
ZOOLOGY. Living in rock; *spec*. designating or pertaining to stone-boring mussels of the genus *Lithodomus*.

lithograph /ˈlɪθə(ʊ)grɑːf, ˈlʌɪ-/ *noun*. E19.
[ORIGIN Back-form. from LITHOGRAPHY.]
1 A lithographic print. E19.
2 An inscription on stone. *rare*. M19.

lithograph /ˈlɪθə(ʊ)grɑːf, ˈlʌɪ-/ *verb trans*. E19.
[ORIGIN formed as LITHOGRAPH *noun*.]
1 Print, produce, or portray by lithography. E19.
2 Write or engrave on stone. *rare*. L19.

lithographer /lɪˈθɒgrəfə/ *noun*. L17.
[ORIGIN from LITHO- + -GRAPHER.]
†**1** A person who writes about stones. Only in L17.
2 A person who practises lithography. E19.

lithographic /lɪθə(ʊ)ˈgrafɪk/ *adjective*. E19.
[ORIGIN from LITHOGRAPHY + -IC.]
Of, pertaining to, or produced by lithography; engraved on stone.
lithographic limestone a compact fine-grained yellowish limestone used in lithography. **lithographic offset** = OFFSET *noun* 7. **lithographic paper**: suitable for lithographic printing. **lithographic stone** = ***lithographic limestone*** above. **lithographic varnish** a preparation of linseed oil used in inks for lithographic printing.
■ **lithographical** *adjective* (*rare*) = LITHOGRAPHIC E19. **lithographically** *adverb* by means of lithography E19.

lithography /lɪˈθɒgrəfi/ *noun*. E18.
[ORIGIN In sense 1 from mod. Latin *lithographia*; in sense 2 from German *Lithographie*, formed as LITHO- + -GRAPHY.]
†**1** A description of stones or rocks. Only in E18.
2 The art or process of making a print using greasy ink on porous stone or (now usu.) a metal or plastic plate or roller which has been treated to accept the ink only where it is required for printing. E19.
3 ELECTRONICS. In the manufacture of integrated circuits and semiconductor devices, a process used to define areas for subsequent etching or deposition, in which a surface layer of energy-sensitive material is selectively exposed to X-rays or electrons and then etched to form a resist layer that has the required pattern. L20.

lithoid /ˈlɪθɔɪd/ *adjective*. M19.
[ORIGIN Greek *lithoeidēs*, formed as LITHO-: see -OID.]
Of the nature or structure of stone.
■ Also **liˈthoidal** *adjective* M19.

Lithol /ˈlɪθɒl/ *noun*. E20.
[ORIGIN Unknown.]
CHEMISTRY. (Proprietary name for) any of various azo dyes. ***Lithol red***, ***Lithol yellow***, etc.

lithology /lɪˈθɒlədʒi/ *noun*. E18.
[ORIGIN from LITHO- + -LOGY.]
1 GEOLOGY. The general physical characteristics of a rock, esp. as discernible without a microscope; the branch of geology that deals with these characteristics. Cf. PETROLOGY. E18.
2 The branch of medicine that deals with calculi. *rare*. E19.
■ **lithoˈlogic** *adjective* E19. **lithoˈlogical** *adjective* L18. **lithoˈlogically** *adverb* with regard to lithology M19. **lithologist** *noun* M18.

lithomancy /ˈlɪθə(ʊ)mansi/ *noun*. M17.
[ORIGIN from LITHO- + -MANCY.]
Divination by signs derived from a stone or stones, esp. a lodestone.

lithomarge /ˈlɪθə(ʊ)mɑːdʒ/ *noun*. M18.
[ORIGIN mod. Latin *lithomarga*, formed as LITHO- + Latin *marga* marl.]
GEOLOGY. Orig., any of various soft claylike minerals, including kaolin. Now usu., a smooth hardened reddish deposit containing kaolinite and formed by the degradation of basalts.

lithontriptic /lɪθɒnˈtrɪptɪk/ *adjective* & *noun*. Now *rare* or *obsolete*. Also †**-thriptic**. M17.
[ORIGIN French *lithontriptique* or mod. Latin *lithontripticus* (later *-thrypticus*), from Greek LITHO- + *thruptein* break up, infl. by Greek *tripsis* rubbing, grinding: cf. LITHOTRIPSY.]
MEDICINE. (A medicine) having the property of breaking down calculi; lithotritic.

lithophone /ˈlɪθəfəʊn/ *noun*. L19.
[ORIGIN from LITHO- + -PHONE.]
†**1** MEDICINE. An instrument for rendering audible the contact of a sound or probe with a vesical calculus. *rare*. Only in L19.
2 MUSIC. Any of various percussion instruments made of marble or other stone. M20.

†**lithophyta** *noun* pl. of LITHOPHYTON.

lithophyte /ˈlɪθə(ʊ)fʌɪt/ *noun*. L18.
[ORIGIN from LITHO- + -PHYTE.]
1 ZOOLOGY. A polyp with a calcareous skeleton; a stony coral. L18.
2 BOTANY. A plant which grows on bare stone or rock. L19.
■ **lithophytic** /-ˈfɪtɪk/, **lithophytous** /-ˈfʌɪtəs/ *adjectives* E19.

†**lithophyton** *noun*. Pl. **-ta**. M17–M18.
[ORIGIN mod. Latin, formed as LITHO- + Greek *phuton* plant.]
A coral.

lithoprint /ˈlɪθə(ʊ)prɪnt, ˈlʌɪ-/ *verb trans*. M20.
[ORIGIN from LITHO(GRAPHY + PRINT *verb*.]
Chiefly *hist*. Print (esp. a typescript copy) by photolithography.

lithops /ˈlɪθɒps/ *noun*. M20.
[ORIGIN mod. Latin (see below), from LITHO- + Greek *ops* face.]
Any of various small succulent plants of the genus *Lithops* (family Aizoaceae), native to deserts in southern Africa and resembling small pairs of stones.

lithospermum /lɪθə(ʊ)ˈspəːməm/ *noun*. Also (earlier) †**-mon**. M16.
[ORIGIN (mod. Latin from) Greek *lithospermon*, formed as LITHO- + *sperma* seed.]
Any of various plants of the borage family included or formerly included in the genus *Lithospermum*, bearing white, yellow, or blue flowers and polished stony nutlets; *esp*. one grown for ornament.

lithosphere /ˈlɪθə(ʊ)sfɪə/ *noun*. M19.
[ORIGIN from LITHO- + -SPHERE.]
Formerly, the rocky part of the earth; the earth's crust. Now *spec*. the rigid outer portion of the earth including the crust and the outermost mantle, above the asthenosphere.
■ **lithoˈspheric** *adjective* L20.

lithostratigraphy /ˌlɪθə(ʊ)strəˈtɪgrəfi/ *noun*. M20.
[ORIGIN from LITHO- + STRATIGRAPHY.]
GEOLOGY. The branch of stratigraphy that deals with the relationship between lithology and stratigraphic position of strata.
■ **lithostratiˈgraphic**, **lithostratiˈgraphical** *adjectives* M20.

lithotomy /lɪˈθɒtəmi/ *noun*. M17.
[ORIGIN Late Latin *lithotomia* from Greek *lithotomia*, formed as LITHO- + -TOMY.]
†**1** A quarry. Only in M17.
2 Surgical incision into the bladder, kidney, etc., for the purpose of removing a stone; an instance of this. E18.
– COMB.: **lithotomy position** a supine position of the body, with the legs raised in stirrups, flexed and apart, used orig. for lithotomy and subsequently also in childbirth.
■ **lithoˈtomic** *adjective* E19. **lithoˈtomical** *adjective* L19. **lithotomist** *noun* M17.

lithotripsy /ˈlɪθə(ʊ)trɪpsi/ *noun*. M19.
[ORIGIN from LITHO- + Greek *tripsis* rubbing, grinding + -Y[3]: cf. LITHONTRIPTIC.]
MEDICINE. The operation of breaking or wearing down stones in the bladder, kidney, etc., by mechanical or ultrasonic means.
■ **lithotripter** *noun* a machine which generates and focuses ultrasonic waves to shatter stones in the bladder or kidney L20. **lithoˈtriptic** *adjective* M19. **lithotriptor** *noun* (*rare*) = LITHOTRITE E19.

lithotrity /lɪˈθɒtrɪti/ *noun*. **E19.**
[ORIGIN from LITHO- + Latin *tritor* rubber (from *terere* rub) + -Y[3]: cf. LITHOTRIPSY.]
MEDICINE. The operation of crushing a stone in the bladder into minute particles which can be expelled through the urethra; mechanical lithotripsy.
■ **ˈlithotrite** *noun* an instrument for lithotrity **M19.** **lithoˈtritic** *adjective* **M19.** **lithotritor** *noun* (now *rare* or *obsolete*) = LITHOTRITE **E19.**

lithotype /ˈlɪθə(ʊ)tʌɪp, *in senses 1, 2 also* ˈlʌɪ-/ *noun*. **L19.**
[ORIGIN from LITHO- + -TYPE.]
1 *PRINTING*. A stereotype made with shellac, sand, tar, and linseed oil, and pressed while hot on a plaster mould taken from type. **L19.**
2 A lithographed fingerprint. **L19.**
3 *GEOLOGY*. An individual lithological character or category; *esp.* any of several lithologically distinct types of coal. **M20.**

lithsman /ˈlɪθsmən/ *noun*. Pl. **-men**. **LOE.**
[ORIGIN Old Norse *liðsmaðr* (accus. *-mann*), from *liðs* genit. of *lið* host + *maðr* MAN *noun*.]
hist. A sailor in the navy under the Danish kings of England.

Lithuanian /lɪθjʊˈeɪnɪən, lɪθʊ-/ *noun & adjective*. **L16.**
[ORIGIN from *Lithuania* (see below) + -AN.]
▸ **A** *noun*. A native or inhabitant of Lithuania, the most southern of the three Baltic states; the language of Lithuania, belonging to the Baltic language group. **L16.**
▸ **B** *adjective*. Of or pertaining to Lithuania, its people, or its language. **L18.**
■ **Lithuanic** *adjective & noun* Lithuanian **M19.**

lithy /ˈlɪði/ *adjective*. Long *obsolete* exc. *dial.*
[ORIGIN Old English *liþig* = Old Norse *liðugr* yielding, nimble, Middle Dutch *ledech*, German *ledig* unoccupied, vacant: ult. origin unknown.]
1 Flexible; supple; lithe; soft. **OE.**
†**2** Weak, feeble. **LME–M16.**

litigable /ˈlɪtɪgəb(ə)l/ *adjective*. **M18.**
[ORIGIN from LITIGATE + -ABLE.]
That may become the subject of litigation.

litigant /ˈlɪtɪg(ə)nt/ *adjective & noun*. **M17.**
[ORIGIN French, from Latin *litigant-* pres. ppl stem of *litigare*: see LITIGATE, -ANT[1].]
▸ **A** *adjective*. Engaged in a lawsuit or dispute. Chiefly qualifying *party*. Freq. *postpositive*. **M17.**
▸ **B** *noun*. A person engaged in a lawsuit or dispute. **M17.**

litigate /ˈlɪtɪgeɪt/ *verb*. **E17.**
[ORIGIN Latin *litigat-* pa. ppl stem of *litigare*, from *lit-*, *lis* strife, lawsuit: see -ATE[3].]
1 *verb intrans.* Be a party to or counsel in a lawsuit; carry on a lawsuit; go to law. Formerly also *gen.*, dispute. **E17.**
2 *verb trans.* Make the subject of a lawsuit, contest at law; *gen.* contest (a point etc.). **M18.**

litigation /lɪtɪˈgeɪʃ(ə)n/ *noun*. **M16.**
[ORIGIN Late Latin *litigatio(n-)*, formed as LITIGATE: see -ATION.]
1 *gen.* Disputation. Now *rare*. **M16.**
2 The action or process of carrying on a lawsuit; legal proceedings. Also, an instance or (formerly) type of legal proceedings. **M17.** ▸**b** The practice of going to law. **L18.**

litigator /ˈlɪtɪgeɪtə/ *noun*. **L19.**
[ORIGIN from LITIGATE + -OR.]
A person who litigates; *spec.* (*US*) a trial lawyer.

S. BRILL The Solicitor General (the federal government's top litigator). *Guardian* A series of steps which allow solicitors to qualify as advocates and non-solicitors to become litigators.

litigiosity /lɪˌtɪdʒɪˈɒsɪti/ *noun*. **M19.**
[ORIGIN from Latin *litigiosus* (see LITIGIOUS) + -ITY.]
CIVIL & SCOTS LAW. The quality or fact of being litigious.

litigious /lɪˈtɪdʒəs/ *adjective*. **LME.**
[ORIGIN Old French & mod. French *litigieux* or Latin *litigiosus*, from *litigium* litigation, rel. to *litigare*: see LITIGATE, -OUS.]
1 Fond of or given to litigation or carrying on lawsuits; *gen.* (now *rare*) fond of disputes, argumentative. **LME.**
2 Disputable, questionable, contentious. Long only *spec.* disputable at law; that is or is liable to become the subject of a lawsuit; (*CIVIL & SCOTS LAW*) (of property) respecting which an action or diligence is pending, and which therefore may not be alienated. **LME.**
3 Of or pertaining to lawsuits or litigation. **L16.**
■ **litigiously** *adverb* **L16.** **litigiousness** *noun* **M17.**

litiscontestation /ˌlʌɪtɪskɒntɛˈsteɪʃ(ə)n/ *noun*. **LME.**
[ORIGIN from Latin *litis* (genit. of *lis* lawsuit) + *contestatio(n-)* (see CONTESTATION).]
CIVIL & SCOTS LAW. The formal entry of a suit in a court of law. Also, the establishment and joinder of contentious issues.

litmus /ˈlɪtməs/ *noun*. **ME.**
[ORIGIN Old Norse *lit-mosi* (formed as LIT *noun* + *mosi* moss), Middle Dutch *lijkmoes*.]
A soluble blue powder obtained from various lichens which turns red in acidic conditions and blue in alkaline over a range of pH 4.5–8.3.
– COMB.: **litmus blue** a blue pigment prepared from litmus; **litmus paper** unsized paper stained blue with litmus, to serve as a test for acids, reddened by an acid, to serve as a test for alkalis; **litmus test** a test for acids or alkalis using litmus paper; *fig.* a simple test to establish true character.

litoptern /lɪˈtɒptəːn/ *noun*. **E20.**
[ORIGIN from mod. Latin *Litopterna* (see below), from Greek *litos* smooth + *pternē* heel bone.]
PALAEONTOLOGY. Any extinct S. American ungulate mammal of the order Litopterna.

litotes /lʌɪˈtəʊtiːz/ *noun*. **L16.**
[ORIGIN Late Latin from Greek *litotēs*, from *litos* single, simple, meagre.]
RHETORIC. Ironical understatement, *spec.* in which an affirmative is expressed by the negative of the contrary, as *no small amount*, *no mean feat*, etc. Also called ***meiosis***.

lit-par-lit /liparli, liːpɑːˈliː/ *adjective & adverb*. **L19.**
[ORIGIN French, lit. 'bed by bed'.]
GEOLOGY. ▸**A** *adjective*. Designating or resulting from the intrusion of innumerable narrow, more or less parallel, sheets or tongues of magma into the bedding of rocks. **L19.**
▸ **B** *adverb*. In the manner of *lit-par-lit* intrusion. **E20.**

litre /ˈliːtə/ *noun*. Also ***liter**. **L18.**
[ORIGIN French, alt. of LITRON.]
A unit of capacity and volume in the metric system, now defined as one cubic decimetre (formerly as the volume of one kilogram of water under standard conditions) and equivalent to 1,000 cubic centimetres or approx. 1.75 pints.
■ **litreage** *noun* quantity or consumption in litres **L20.**

†**litron** *noun*. **E18–E19.**
[ORIGIN French from medieval Latin *litra* from Greek *litra* a Silician monetary unit.]
A unit of volume equal to a sixteenth of an old French bushel.

litster /ˈlɪtstə/ *noun*. Now *rare* or *obsolete*. **LME.**
[ORIGIN from LIT *verb*[1] + -STER.]
A dyer.

Litt.D. *abbreviation*.
Latin *Litterarum doctor* Doctor of Letters.

litten /ˈlɪt(ə)n/ *noun*. *obsolete* exc. *dial.* **OE.**
[ORIGIN from LICH + TOWN *noun*, contr. in late Middle English.]
A graveyard, a churchyard. Also ***church-litten***.

litten /ˈlɪt(ə)n/ *ppl adjective*. *pseudo-arch.* **E19.**
[ORIGIN from LIGHT *verb*[2] + -EN[6].]
Lighted, lit. Usu. as 2nd elem. of comb., as ***red-litten***, ***star-litten***, etc.

litter /ˈlɪtə/ *noun*. **ME.**
[ORIGIN Anglo-Norman *litere*, Old French & mod. French *litière* from medieval Latin *lectaria*, from Latin *lectus* (whence French *lit*) bed.]
†**1** A bed. **ME–L15.**
2 A form of conveyance containing a couch shut in by curtains and carried on two or more persons' shoulders or by beasts of burden (now chiefly *hist.*); *spec.* a stretcher or portable bed for transporting the sick or wounded. **ME.**

R. MACAULAY He was carried out on a golden litter. A. MASON A covered litter, borne by four slaves, its occupant quite invisible. F. NORRIS A litter was improvised, and throwing their coats over the body, the party carried it back. *attrib.*: *Sun (Baltimore)* First to be unloaded . . were the litter cases—seriously wounded and dying.

3 Straw, rushes, etc., used as bedding (now only for animals). Also, straw and dung together; *spec.* (in full ***cat litter***) grains of an absorbent material for lining a box for a cat to urinate and defecate in. **LME.** ▸**b** Straw etc. used for the protection of plants or (formerly) for thatch or as a component of plaster. **LME.** ▸**c** Decomposing but still recognizable vegetable debris from plants etc. forming a distinct layer above the soil, esp. in a forest. **E20.**
deep litter: see DEEP *adjective*.
4 A group of young (mammalian) animals comprising all those born at one birth. Formerly also, an act of giving birth to young. **LME.**

P. NORMAN Then Melody had her second litter of puppies.

5 Odds and ends or discarded material lying about; a state of untidiness; an accumulation *of* (disordered things). Now *esp.* refuse or rubbish discarded in an open or public place. **M18.**

CONAN DOYLE The rack . . was covered with a formidable litter of rods, reels and baskets. V. WOOLF Cigarette ends, little bits of paper, orange peel, all the litter of the day.

– COMB.: **litter basket**, **litter bin**: for the disposal of waste paper and other litter; **litterbug** a person who carelessly leaves litter in a public place; **litterfall** *ECOLOGY* the fall of leaves and other vegetable matter from plants to form litter; **litter lout** = ***litterbug*** above.
■ **littery** *adjective* of or pertaining to litter; marked by the presence of litter; untidy: **E19.**

litter /ˈlɪtə/ *verb*. **LME.**
[ORIGIN from the noun.]
1 *verb trans.* Provide (a horse etc.) with litter or straw as bedding. Also foll. by *down*. **LME.** ▸**b** *verb intrans.* Lie down on litter as bedding. *rare*. **M17.**
2 *verb trans. & intrans.* Of an animal or (occas., *derog.*) a person: give birth to (young). **L15.**
†**3** *verb trans.* Mix (plaster) (as) with litter; plaster. *rare*. **M16–M19.**
4 *verb trans.* Carry in a litter. *rare*. **E18.**
5 *verb trans.* Spread litter or straw on (the floor) or in (a stable). Also foll. by *down*. **E18.**
6 *verb trans.* **a** Strew *with* objects scattered untidily; leave as litter, scatter untidily *about* or *on*. Usu. in ***pass.*** **E18.** ▸**b** Of things: lie about untidily on. **M19.**

a F. A. KEMBLE Firewood and shavings lay littered about the floors. W. GERHARDIE The table was littered with bottles of the very best wine. V. S. PRITCHETT A piece of waste ground littered with tins and rubbish. C. FRANCIS The entire south Cornish coast is littered with wrecks. *fig.*: J. P. HOWES I would not like anyone to imagine we litter the texts of our dictionaries with typesetting codes. **b** E. TAYLOR The room looked extremely neat, except for all the papers littering the table. I. BANKS Ruined arches, fallen lintels, collapsed walls littered the slopes of sand.

■ **litterer** *noun* a person who throws or drops litter **E20.**

litterae humaniores *noun phr.* var. of LITERAE HUMANIORES.

littérateur /lɪtərɑːˈtəː, *foreign* literatœːr (*pl. same*)/ *noun*. **E19.**
[ORIGIN French from Latin *litterator*: see LITERATOR.]
A writer of literary or critical works, a literary person.

littering /ˈlɪt(ə)rɪŋ/ *noun*. **LME.**
[ORIGIN from LITTER *noun* or *verb* + -ING[1].]
1 The straw of an animal's bed; a layer of this. **LME.**
2 The action of LITTER *verb*. **M16.** ▸**b** The action of throwing or dropping litter. **M20.**
3 *collect.* Odds and ends scattered about. **L19.**

little /ˈlɪt(ə)l/ *adjective, noun, & adverb*.
[ORIGIN Old English *lȳtel*, *lytel* = Old Saxon *luttil* (Dutch *luttel*), Old High German *luzzil* (Middle High German, German dial. *lützel*), from West Germanic adjective, from base repr. also by Old English *lyt* adverb 'little'.]
▸ **A** *adjective*. Compar. LESS *adjective*, LESSER, **littler**; superl. LEAST, **littlest**.
▸ **I** Small; not great.
1 Of a material object, area of space, etc.: small in size, not large or big. Of a person: short in stature. **OE.** ▸**b** *attrib.* Designating the smaller or smallest of things of the class specified; forming names of animals (esp. birds), towns, rivers, streets, districts, etc., that are less large or important, later established, or suggestive of another or others of that name. Opp. GREAT *adjective* 7b. **OE.** ▸**c** *iron.* Big, considerable. Usu. preceded by *some*. **L16.**

L. STERNE Green taffeta, lined with a little bit of white quilted satin. J. CONRAD Depend on me to pick up the least little bit of a hint. HARPER LEE A big cake and two little ones on Miss Maudie's kitchen table. A. N. WILSON They had been talking . . of getting a little cottage. W. TREVOR I think we might have a little drink. D. DELILLO It's a little bitty thing but it shoots real bullets. **c** SHAKES. *Rich. III* Since I am crept in favour with myself, I will maintain it with some little cost. *Times* Movement out from . . London . . by teachers who have been there for some little time.

b ***little auk***, ***little gull***, ***little owl***, etc. ***Little Clarendon Street***, ***Little Malvern***, ***Little Ouse***, etc. ***Little Africa***, ***Little England***, ***Little Italy***, ***Little Switzerland***, ***Little Venice***, etc.
2 *spec.* Young; (esp. of a sibling) younger. **OE.**

I. MURDOCH She recalled a little girl, but . . the years seemed to have brought about a young woman. *Rolling Stone* Her sister . . remembers her once beating up a bully to protect their little brother. K. GIBBONS When I was little I would think of ways of killing my daddy.

3 Of a collective unity: having few members, inhabitants, etc.; small in number. **OE.**

KEATS What little town by river or sea shore . . Is emptied of this folk, this pious morn? J. MORLEY In the realm of . . letters, Voltaire is one of the little band of great monarchs.

4 Of distance or (a period of) time: short. Also qualifying a specific length of duration or distance with emphatic force. *arch.* exc. in ***a little while***. **OE.**
5 Of a thing: not of great importance or interest; trifling, trivial. Of a person: inferior in rank or condition (now *rare*). **ME.** ▸**b** Paltry, mean, contemptible. **L15.**

LD MACAULAY Every little discontent appears to him to portend a revolution. D. ROWE When you're depressed . . . Even the littlest thing hurts. **b** C. CLARKE They do this with the little cunning of little minds.

6 Of an abstract thing: small in quantity, duration, degree, intensity, etc. **ME.** ▸†**b** Having the quality or performing the action indicated to a slight extent only. Foll. by *of*. **LME–E16.** ▸**c** Of an agent or noun indicating occupation: that is such on a small scale. **LME.**

GOLDSMITH Upon that I proceed, . . though with very little hopes to reclaim him. DICKENS Tiny Tim . . had a plaintive little voice. E. C. STEDMAN A little poem, 'The Flower'. J. CONRAD Seating himself with a little spring on the . . parapet. SCOTT FITZGERALD She gave a little sigh . . so small that he did not notice it. M. MCCARTHY She did not seem to realize the little social nuances. **c** A. YOUNG A much larger capital than any little farmer can possess.

7 Used as an extension of various of the above senses to convey emotional overtones, as affection, amusement,

L

condescension, disparagement, etc., not implied by *small*. ME.

G. B. SHAW It was that awful little curate. G. B. SHAW Oh dear! My poor little brain is giving way. J. PORTER To sink or swim all on my little own! D. FRANCIS I have destroyed better things than your father's little racing stables. R. RENDELL They can't wait to get their hot little hands on rich capitalists' property. *New Yorker* Come and meet Mr. Haelkamp. He's the little painter we're beginning to collect.

▸ **II** Opp. ***much***. (In mod. usage also classed as a *determiner*.)
8 Not much; only a slight amount or degree of; scarcely any. OE. ▸**b** That is scarce or absent. Now *rare*. OE.

J. M. MURRY His poetic gift has little or no admixture of non-poetic elements. G. GREENE His own books took up so little room. W. GOLDING There had seemed little light all day. A. MCCOWEN My father . . was a man of . . very little education. Q. CRISP He seemed to have little difficulty in finding engagements for me. A. SCHLEE I . . had little idea how to conduct myself. **b** WORDSWORTH God help me for my little wit!

9 Preceded by *a*: a small quantity of; some though not much. Also (*rare*, Shakes.) without *a*. ME.

POPE A little learning is a dang'rous thing. LD MACAULAY By a little patience . . such a toleration might have been obtained. D. H. LAWRENCE Not even a little wind flickered the willows of the islets. R. K. NARAYAN Won't you come and have a little coffee with us? I. MURDOCH Mitzi had saved a little money. G. GORDON I was glad to have a little time . . to collect myself.

†**10** Few, not many. ME–M17.

– SPECIAL COLLOCATIONS, PHRASES, & COMB.: ***a little bird***: see BIRD *noun*. ***a little wee***: see WEE *adjective*. ***great cry and little wool***: see CRY *noun*. ***have little scruple***: see SCRUPLE *noun*. ***Land of Little Sticks***, ***Land of the Little Sticks***: see LAND *noun*[1]. **laugh like little Audrey** laugh heartily (esp. at a serious situation). ***Little Bear***: see BEAR *noun*[1] 2. **little black dress** a simple black dress suitable for most relatively formal social engagements. **little-boy**, **little-boyish** *adjectives* pertaining to, suited to, or resembling (that of) a small boy. **little-boy-lost** *adjective* resembling (that of) a small boy who has lost his way. **little boys' room** *euphem.* a men's lavatory. ***little CASSINO***. **little chief hare** *N. Amer.* [translating Chipewyan *bucka-thrae-ggayaze*] a N. American pika, *Ochotona princeps*. **little death** a weakening or loss of consciousness, *spec.* in sleep or during an orgasm. ***Little Dipper***: see DIPPER 5a. ***Little Dog***: see DOG *noun* 5. **little-ease** *hist.* a prison cell too small to stand or lie full length in. **little end** MECHANICS the smaller end of a connecting rod, attached to the piston. **Little Englander** (chiefly *hist.*) a person opposed to an imperial role or policy for Britain. **Little Englandism** (chiefly *hist.*) opposition to an imperial role or policy for Britain. ***Little Entrance***: see ENTRANCE *noun*. **little finger** either of the outermost and smallest fingers. **Little Gem** a small compact variety of lettuce of the cos type. **little-girl**, **little-girlish** *adjectives* pertaining to, suited to, or resembling (that of) a little girl. **little-girl-lost** *adjective* resembling (that of) a small girl who has lost her way. **little girls' room** *euphem.* a women's lavatory. **little go** (*a*) *hist.* a private and illegal lottery; (*b*) *arch. slang* the first examination for the degree of BA at the Universities of Oxford and Cambridge. **little grebe** a small dumpy grebe, *Tachybaptus ruficollis*, with a trilling call, occurring widely in the Old World; also called ***dabchick***. **little green man** an imaginary person of peculiar appearance, esp. from outer space. ***little Hitler***: see HITLER *noun* 2. **Little Horse** *the* constellation Equuleus. **little house** (now *Austral., NZ, & dial.*) a privy, a lavatory. **little ice age** METEOROLOGY any period of comparatively cold climate occurring outside the major glacial periods; *spec.* (freq. with cap. initials) such a period which reached its peak during the 17th cent. **little Joe** in the game of craps, a throw of four. **Little League** *N. Amer.* a baseball league for children between the ages of 8 and 12. ***Little Lion***: see LION *noun* 5. **little magazine** a literary magazine, usu. with experimental writing and in small format. **little man** (*a*) (esp. *joc.*) (as a form of address) a boy; (*b*) a person working or producing on a small scale; (*c*) the ordinary 'man in the street'; (*d*) (now *dial.*) the little finger. **Little Mary** *colloq.* the stomach. ***little master***: see MASTER *noun*[1] 19. **Little Masters** a group of 16th-cent. German engravers, followers of Dürer, named from the size of their prints. ***little mastery***: see MASTERY 5. **little neck (clam)** *US*. [from *Little Neck*, Long Island, NY State] a small variety of quahog. ***little old***: see OLD *adjective*. **little ones** young children or animals. ***little Parliament***: see PARLIAMENT *noun*. **little people** (*a*) fairies; (*b*) children; (*c*) the poor; ordinary people. ***little ray of sunshine***: see RAY *noun*[1]. ***Little Red Book***: see RED *adjective*. **Little Russian** *noun & adjective* (*hist.*) (*a*) *noun* a Ukrainian; the Ukrainian language; (*b*) *adjective* Ukrainian. ***little scarlet***: see SCARLET *noun* 5. **little science** scientific or technological investigation not requiring large resources. **little season** the fashionable season in London in the winter. **little skate** a small rounded skate, *Raja erinacea*, which has a densely thorny black back and is common in the NW Atlantic. ***little slam***: see SLAM *noun*[2]. ***little stranger***: see STRANGER *noun* 5c. **little theatre**: esp. for experimental productions. ***little tin god***: see TIN *noun & adjective*. **little toe** either of the outermost and smallest toes. ***little Turk***: see TURK *noun*[1]. **little-worth** *adjective* (now *arch. & Scot.*) of little worth. ***much cry and little wool***: see CRY *noun*. ***no little***: see NO *adjective*. ***one's little all***: see ALL *noun* 8. ***poor little rich boy***, ***poor little rich girl***: see POOR *adjective*. ***set little store by***: see STORE *noun*. ***that little lot***: see LOT *noun*. ***the little corporal***: see CORPORAL *noun*[2] 1. **the little woman** (*colloq.*, freq. *derog.*) one's wife. ***the patter of little feet***: see PATTER *noun*[2]. ***this little lot***: see LOT *noun*. ***turn round one's little finger***, ***twist round one's little finger***, ***wind round one's little finger***, ***wrap round one's little finger***: see FINGER *noun*. ***ye gods and little fishes***: see GOD *noun*. ***your little game***: see GAME *noun*.

▸ **B** *absol.* as *noun*. **I** *absol.* **1 a** Those that are little. Chiefly with *the*. OE. ▸**b** That which is little; the little qualities, aspects, etc. Chiefly with *the*. L18.

2 Not much, only a small amount (*of the, my, this*, etc.). Qualified by a demonstr. or possess.: (the) small amount, (so) small a quantity. OE.

OED He showed little of the amiability which was ascribed to him. I. MURDOCH She knew little about jewels. B. MALAMUD A shrug that may mean much or little. C. RAYNER We ate so little. A. THWAITE She knew the value of education though she had little herself. K. WATERHOUSE There seems little else to be said.

▸ **II 3** *A* small quantity, piece, or portion (*of the, my, this*, etc.); *arch.* a small thing; a trifle (usu. in *pl.*). OE.

T. GODWIN He drank a little of the wine. DISRAELI Let me recommend you a little of this pike! A. TATE Not a little of it comes from the comfortable habit of citing a passage in the Preface to *Lyrical Ballads*. N. COWARD Would you like some brandy? . . Just a little. I. MURDOCH Out of so much, can we not salvage a little.

4 *A* short time or distance. Chiefly in ***after a little***, ***for a little***, ***in a little***. OE.

– PHRASES: **a little** (*a*) to a little or slight extent; in a small degree; (*b*) for or at a short time or distance. **a little — somewhat —**, rather —. **by little and little** *arch.* = *little by little* below. **in little** (*a*) on a small scale; †(*b*) *spec.* (PAINTING) in miniature. ***know little and care less***: see KNOW *verb*. **little by little** by degrees, gradually. **little or nothing** hardly anything. ***make little of***: see MAKE *verb*. **not a little** a great deal. ***say little for***: see SAY *verb*[1]. ***see little of***: see SEE *verb*.

▸ **C** *adverb*. **1** To only a small extent or degree; not much. Also, infrequently, rarely. OE.

W. S. MAUGHAM She cared little what he spoke of. J. BUCHAN He is old and can go about very little. S. BEDFORD They entertained their neighbours as little as possible. G. GREENE It is awful how little we change. E. BLISHEN We thought little of the concert hall, a university lecture room. *Cornwall Review* St. Just-in-Penwith . . seems to have been little influenced by the outside world. V. S. NAIPAUL I walked . . down little-used lateral lanes on the hillsides.

2 Not at all; hardly. Only with verbs of knowing, thinking, or caring, etc. Freq. preceding the verb modified, with periphrastic *do*. ME.

M. EDGEWORTH He little imagined of how much consequence it might be. T. HARDY You only knew me as a governess; you little think what my beginnings were. G. GREENE Little did they know that the story . . had already reached the ears of the drinkers. *New Yorker* 'Little did they imagine,' she said.

†**3** A little time (before); for only a little time. ME–E17.

little /ˈlɪt(ə)l/ *verb trans. & intrans. obsolete* exc. *poet.* OE.
[ORIGIN from LITTLE *adjective*.]
Make or become little; diminish.

littleness /ˈlɪt(ə)lnɪs/ *noun*. OE.
[ORIGIN from LITTLE *adjective* + -NESS.]
1 Smallness of quantity, stature, degree, extent, etc. OE.
2 Absence of greatness or importance; triviality; meanness, pettiness; an instance of this. LME.

littler *adjective* see LITTLE *adjective*.

Littler's blue /lɪtləz ˈbluː/ *noun phr.* M20.
[ORIGIN William *Littler* (1724–84), English potter.]
A rich blue colour applied to porcelain or stoneware.

Little's disease /ˈlɪt(ə)lz dɪˌziːz/ *noun phr.* L19.
[ORIGIN William John *Little* (1810–94), English physician.]
MEDICINE. A form of congenital cerebral palsy causing bilateral spastic weakness of the limbs.

littlest *adjective* see LITTLE *adjective*.

littlie *noun* var. of LITTLY.

littling /ˈlɪtlɪŋ/ *noun*. *dial.* OE.
[ORIGIN from LITTLE *adjective* + -LING[1].]
A young child or animal.

littlish /ˈlɪtlɪʃ/ *adjective*. Chiefly *dial.* M19.
[ORIGIN from LITTLE *adjective* + -ISH[1].]
Rather little.

littly /ˈlɪtli/ *noun*. Also **littlie**. L19.
[ORIGIN from LITTLE *adjective* + -Y[6], -IE.]
A small child or person; *esp.* (in *pl.*), small children, the young children of a family etc.

littoral /ˈlɪt(ə)r(ə)l/ *adjective & noun*. M17.
[ORIGIN Latin *littoralis* var. of *litoralis*, from *litor-*, *litus* shore: see -AL[1].]
▸ **A** *adjective*. **1** Of or pertaining to the shore of the sea, a lake, etc.; existing or occurring on or adjacent to the shore. M17.
2 ECOLOGY & GEOLOGY. Designating, of, or pertaining to the zone of the shore extending from the high-water mark to the low-water mark (= INTERTIDAL), or (occas.) to the edge of the continental shelf; (of an organism) living in this zone; (of a sediment) deposited in this zone. Also, designating or pertaining to the region of a lake near the shore in which rooted vegetation occurs; = INFRALITTORAL (b). M17.
▸ **B** *noun*. A littoral area; the coast. E19.

littorinid /lɪˈtɒrɪnɪd/ *noun & adjective*. M20.
[ORIGIN mod. Latin *Littorinidae* (see below), from *Littorina* genus name: see -ID[3].]
▸ **A** *noun*. A marine snail of the family Littorinidae, which includes the periwinkles. M20.
▸ **B** *adjective*. Of, pertaining to, or designating this family. M20.

litui *noun* pl. of LITUUS.

liturgic /lɪˈtəːdʒɪk/ *adjective & noun*. M17.
[ORIGIN medieval Latin *liturgicus* from Greek *leitourgikos*, from *leitourgia*: see LITURGY, -IC.]
▸ **A** *adjective*. = LITURGICAL. M17.
▸ **B** *noun*. †**1** A liturgical book. Only in L17.
2 In *pl.* (treated as *sing.*). The branch of knowledge that deals with liturgies, their form, origin, etc. Also called ***liturgiology***. M19.

liturgical /lɪˈtəːdʒɪk(ə)l/ *adjective*. M17.
[ORIGIN formed as LITURGIC: see -ICAL.]
Of or pertaining to (forms of) public worship or *spec.* the Liturgy or Eucharist. Also, of or pertaining to liturgics.
liturgical colours: used in ecclesiastical vestments, hangings for an altar, etc., varying according to the season, festival, or kind of service. **Liturgical Movement** a movement advocating the restoration of the active participation by the people in the official worship of the Church.
■ **liturgically** *adverb* from a liturgical point of view; in a liturgy, in liturgical worship: M19.

liturgiology /lɪˌtəːdʒɪˈɒlədʒi/ *noun*. M19.
[ORIGIN from LITURGY + -OLOGY.]
Liturgics.
■ **liturgioˈlogical** *adjective* L19. **liturgiologist** *noun* M19.

liturgise *verb* var. of LITURGIZE.

liturgism /ˈlɪtədʒɪz(ə)m/ *noun*. E20.
[ORIGIN from LITURGY + -ISM.]
Excessive concern with liturgy or liturgical detail.

liturgist /ˈlɪtədʒɪst/ *noun*. M17.
[ORIGIN from LITURGY + -IST.]
1 A person who uses or advocates the use of a liturgy. M17.
2 An authority on liturgies; a compiler of liturgies. M17.
3 A person who celebrates divine worship. M19.
■ **liturˈgistical** *adjective* L19.

liturgize /ˈlɪtədʒʌɪz/ *verb intrans. rare*. Also **-ise**. E19.
[ORIGIN from LITURGY + -IZE.]
Perform a liturgical act.

liturgy /ˈlɪtədʒi/ *noun*. M16.
[ORIGIN French *liturgie* or late Latin *liturgia* from Greek *leitourgia* public service, worship of the gods, from *leitourgos* public servant, minister, from var. of *lēitos* public, from *lēos* Ionic form of *lāos* people + *-ergos* performing.]
1 (**L-**.) The service of the Eucharist of the Orthodox Church; a specified type or form of Eucharistic service. M16.
Liturgy of the Presanctified: see PRESANCTIFY.
2 A form of public worship, esp. in the Christian Church; a set of formularies for the conduct of this. L16. ▸**b** ***the Liturgy***, the *Book of Common Prayer*. E17.

transf.: D. ACHESON The Council of Foreign Ministers . . had developed a liturgy and tradition of its own.

3 GREEK HISTORY. A public office or duty performed gratuitously by a rich Athenian. M19.

lituus /ˈlɪtjʊəs/ *noun*. Pl. **litui** /ˈlɪtjʊʌɪ/. E17.
[ORIGIN Latin.]
1 ROMAN ANTIQUITIES. The crooked staff or wand carried by an augur. Also, a curved trumpet, a clarion. E17.
2 MATH. A plane spiral having (in polar coordinates) the formula $r^2\theta = a$, with a tail that approaches the polar axis asymptotically. M18.

Litvak /ˈlɪtvɒk/ *noun*. L19.
[ORIGIN Yiddish from Polish *Litwak* Lithuanian.]
A Jew from Lithuania or its neighbouring regions.

Litzendraht /ˈlɪtsəndraːt/ *noun*. E20.
[ORIGIN German, from *Litze* braid, cord, lace, strand + *Draht* wire.]
= LITZ WIRE.

Litz wire /lɪts ˈwʌɪə/ *noun phr.* E20.
[ORIGIN Partial translation of LITZENDRAHT.]
ELECTRICITY. Wire composed of many fine strands twisted together and individually insulated, so as to reduce the increase in resistance at high frequencies.

livable *adjective* var. of LIVEABLE.

live /lʌɪv/ *adjective*. M16.
[ORIGIN Aphet. from ALIVE, repl. earlier LIVES *adjective*.]
1 a That is alive; living, as opp. to dead. Chiefly *attrib.* M16. ▸**b** Actual, genuine; not pretended or pictured or toy. Chiefly in ***a real live***. Usu. *joc.* L19. ▸**c** Corresponding to actual facts. E20. ▸**d** Of a performance etc.: heard or watched at the time of its occurrence, as opp. to recorded on film, tape, etc.; given in front of a public audience as opp. to in a recording studio etc. Also, (of a recording, a film, etc.) made of a live performance. M20.

a P. THEROUX We had got used to Father looking like a live scarecrow. **d** A. ROAD Recording . . can never be quite as nail-biting as live transmission. *Guardian* No doubt the video is not quite the same as watching the race live.

2 Of a coal, embers, etc.: flaming, glowing. E17.

Z. TOMIN There must be a live lump of coal somewhere, burning itself out.

3 *transf. & fig.* Full of life or active power; busy, lively; alert, energetic. Also, (of a question, an issue, etc.) of current interest, not obsolete or exhausted. M17.

L

M. ARNOLD All the live murmur of a Summer's day. *Sun (Baltimore)* Another live issue—the question of setting up a . . buffer zone in Korea.

4 (Of a mineral or rock) still forming part of the earth's mass, unwrought; (of air) in its native state, pure. **M17.**
5 Containing unexpended energy; (of a shell) unexploded; (of a match) unkindled. **L18.** ▸**b** *ELECTRICITY.* (Of a rail, wire, etc.) connected to a source of electrical power, carrying a voltage; (of a microphone etc.) switched on, receptive to sound. **L19.**
6 Of a machine part or piece of apparatus, esp. an axle: that moves or imparts movement. **E19.**
7 *ACOUSTICS.* Of a room or enclosure: having a relatively long reverberation time. Cf. DEAD *adjective* 15. **M20.**
— SPECIAL COLLOCATIONS & COMB.: **live action** *CINEMATOGRAPHY* action involving real people or animals, as opp. to animation, titles, etc. **live bait** *ANGLING* a living worm, small fish, etc., used as bait. **livebearer** any of numerous small, chiefly freshwater, American fishes of the family Poeciliidae, members of which (including the guppies, swordtail, mollies, and platies) have internal fertilization and give birth to live young. **live-bearing** *adjective* bearing live young, not laying eggs; viviparous. **live-birth**: in which the child is born alive. **live-born** *adjective* born alive. **live fence** (orig. *US*) a hedge. **live load** a temporary or varying load on a structure, *esp.* the weight of people or goods in a building or vehicle (cf. *dead load* s.v. DEAD *adjective*). **live oak**: of the evergreen species *Quercus virginiana*, of the southern US. **live steam**: from a boiler at full pressure. **livestock** animals kept or dealt in for use or profit. **live weight** the weight of an animal before it has been slaughtered and prepared as a carcass. **live wire** *fig.* an energetic or forceful person.
■ **liveness** *noun* **L19.**

live /lɪv/ *verb.*
[ORIGIN Old English *libban* & *lifian*, corresp. to Old Frisian *libba*, *lifa*, Old Saxon *libbian*, *lebon*, Old High German *lebēn* (German *leben*), Old Norse *lifa* live, remain, Gothic *liban*, from Germanic base rel. to that of LIFE *noun*, LEAVE *verb*[1].]
1 *verb intrans.* **a** Be alive; have animal or vegetable life. **OE.** ▸**b** *fig.* Of a thing: exist, be found. *poet.* **L16.**

H. BAILEY She had only two more years to live.

2 *verb intrans.* Supply oneself with food; feed, subsist. Foll. by *by*, *on*, *upon*. **OE.**

AV *Matt.* 4:4 Man shall not live by bread alone. I. MURDOCH Carel was a vegetarian and lived on grated carrot and eggs and cheese.

3 *verb intrans.* Procure oneself the means of subsistence; depend on for a livelihood. Foll. by *by*, *off*, *on*, *upon*. **OE.**

A. JESSOPP Those luxuries which the big man consumes . . the small man lives by. C. ISHERWOOD He left him all his money, not very much, but enough to live on, comfortably. ANTHONY SMITH Primitive *Homo*, living off the countryside.

4 *verb intrans.* Spend or lead one's life; conduct oneself in a specified way, esp. with ref. to moral behaviour, personal aims or principles, or personal conditions. **OE.** ▸**b** *verb trans.* with cognate obj. Lead (one's life) in a specified way. **OE.**

O. BLACKALL Rules . . to observe and live by. P. CAMPBELL The family lived in considerable comfort. I. MURDOCH Adelaide lived in a perpetual state of anxiety. J. C. OATES No intention whatsoever of living as their families had lived. **b** J. MORLEY Montaigne—content to live his life, leaving many questions open.

5 *verb intrans.* Continue in life; be alive for a longer or shorter period; have one's life prolonged. Also foll. by *on*. **OE.** ▸**b** Escape spiritual death. Now *rare.* **LME.** ▸**c** *fig.* Of a thing: survive, continue. *poet.* & *rhet.* **M18.**

Academy Lord Carnarvon did not live to put the final touches to his translation. **c** P. KAVANAGH His pleasure did not live long.

6 *verb intrans.* Endure, last through; *spec.* (of a vessel) escape destruction, remain afloat. **ME.**
7 *verb intrans.* Make one's home; dwell, reside; *transf.* (of an object) have its place. Also, spend much non-working time *in* a room etc. **ME.**

D. H. LAWRENCE They'd lived next door to us when I was a little lad. J. CANNAN I couldn't find any brandy. Do you know where it lives? H. BAILEY The poor live in caravans, the bourgeoisie in solid brick houses.

8 *verb trans.* Express in one's life; carry out in one's life the principles etc. of. **M16.**

J. JORTIN To say who is the Lord . . is to deny God . . and live a lie. *Grimsby Evening Telegraph* How can a man like this hope to negotiate with Iceland . . whose people virtually live fish?

9 *verb intrans.* Continue in the memory; escape obliteration or oblivion. **L16.**

R. W. DIXON So would he . . give me those kind looks which live in me. C. H. SISSON To live in the memory of men is one of the most persistent . . wishes of mankind.

10 *verb intrans.* Enjoy life intensely or abundantly. **E17.**

N. HINTON He couldn't wait to get out of school and really start living.

— PHRASES: **he'll live**, **I'll live**, etc., (freq. *joc.*) no need for worry or concern. *how the other half lives*: see HALF *noun*. *I'll live*: see *he'll live* above. **live and learn** continually discover new facts as life goes on. **live and let live** be tolerant of others and be so tolerated. *live by one's wits*: see WIT *noun*. **live dangerously** take risks habitually. *live extempore*: see EXTEMPORE *adverb*. *live for the MOMENT*. *live high off the hog*, *live high on the hog*: see HOG *noun*. *live in each other's pockets*: see POCKET *noun*. **live in oneself** rely on oneself for company etc., live in isolation. *live in sin*: see SIN *noun*[1]. *live in the MOMENT*. **live it up** live gaily and extravagantly. *live like a lord*: see LORD *noun*. **live off the country**, **live off the land** subsist on the produce of the land. **live on air** (appear to) eat nothing. **live one's own life** follow one's own plans or principles; live independently. *live on one's hump*: see HUMP *noun*. *live on one's nerves*: see NERVE *noun*. **live out of a suitcase** live temporarily with one's belongings still packed. *live over the brush*: see BRUSH *noun*[2] 3. *live over the shop*: see SHOP *noun*. *live rough*: see ROUGH *adverb*. *live tally*: see TALLY *noun*. **live to oneself** = *live in oneself* above. *live to tell the tale*: see TALE *noun*. **live within oneself** = *live in oneself* above. **live with oneself** retain one's self-respect. **long live** — *interjection* expr. loyalty. **where one lives** *US slang* at or to the right or vital point. *well to live*: see WELL *adjective*. *will to live*: see WILL *noun*[1].
— WITH ADVERBS & PREPOSITIONS IN SPECIALIZED SENSES: **live down** overcome (a prejudice, scandal, etc.) by a blameless course of life. **live in**, **live out** reside in, away from, one's place of employment. **live through** survive, remain alive at the end of. **live to** survive and reach (a certain age etc.). **live together** cohabit, esp. as man and wife. **live up to** (*a*) act in full accordance with (principles, rules, etc.); (*b*) push expenditure to the full limits of (one's fortune). **live well** (*a*) have plenty; be in comfortable circumstances; (*b*) live a virtuous life. **live with** (*a*) reside with, *esp.* cohabit with as man and wife; (*b*) tolerate, accept.
— COMB.: **lived-in** *adjective* occupied, inhabited; comfortable, homely; **live-for-ever** = LIVELONG *noun*; **live-in** *adjective* & *noun* (*a*) *adjective* resident, esp. in one's place of employment or as a person's lover, common-law spouse, etc.; (of an item of clothing) able to be worn continually; very comfortable or practical; (*b*) *noun* a live-in employee, lover, etc.; **live-out** *adjective* residing away from one's place of employment.

liveable /ˈlɪvəb(ə)l/ *adjective.* Also **livable**. **E17.**
[ORIGIN from LIVE *verb* + -ABLE.]
†**1** Likely to live. *rare.* Only in **E17.**
†**2** Conducive to comfortable living. Only in **M17.**
3 Of a house, a room, a locality, etc.: that may be lived in; suitable for living in. **E19.**
4 Of life: that can be lived; bearable, supportable. **M19.**
5 Of a person: easy to live with or *with*; companionable, sociable. **M19.**
■ **livea'bility** *noun* (*a*) suitability for habitation; (*b*) survival expectancy, esp. of poultry: **E20.** **liveableness** *noun* **M19.**

lived /lʌɪvd/ *adjective.* **LME.**
[ORIGIN from *live* infl. form of LIFE *noun* + -ED[2].]
Having a certain kind or length of life, as ***low-lived***, etc.
— NOTE: Earliest in LONG-LIVED; see also SHORT-LIVED.

†**livelihead** *noun.* **LME.**
[ORIGIN from LIVELY *adjective* + -HEAD[1].]
1 Liveliness; vivacity. **LME–E18.** ▸**b** Living form. Also, condition of being alive. **M–L16.**
2 Means of living; inheritance; livelihood. **L15–L16.**

livelihood /ˈlʌɪvlɪhʊd/ *noun*[1].
[ORIGIN Old English *līflād*, from *līf* LIFE *noun* + *lād* course, way (see LOAD *noun*, LODE), assim. in 16 to LIVELY *adjective* and -HOOD.]
†**1** Lifetime; kind or manner of life; conduct. **OE–L16.**
2 A means of living, a source of maintenance. **ME.** ▸†**b** Sustenance, food, nourishment. **ME–L17.**

B. HEAD Men made a livelihood transporting goods across country by wagon. *Forbes* There are a lot of people who depend on me for their livelihood.

†**3** Income, revenue, a stipend; in *pl.*, emoluments. **LME–E17.**
†**4** Property yielding an income, landed or inherited property; an estate, an inheritance. **LME–E17.**

†**livelihood** *noun*[2]. **M16–M17.**
[ORIGIN from LIVELY *adjective* + -HOOD.]
Liveliness.

livelong /ˈlɪvlɒŋ/ *noun.* **L16.**
[ORIGIN from LIVE *verb* + LONG *adverb*: cf. *live-for-ever* s.v. LIVE *verb*.]
Any of several plants which retain their form or greenness for a long time; *esp.* (*a*) orpine, *Sedum telephium*; †(*b*) pearly everlasting, *Anaphalis margaritacea*.

livelong /ˈlɪvlɒŋ/ *adjective. poet.* & *rhet.* **LME.**
[ORIGIN Orig. from LIEF *adjective* + LONG *adjective*[1] (cf. German *die liebe lange Nacht*). In 16 interpreted as from LIVE *adjective* or *verb* + LONG *adjective*[1], and alt. in form.]
Of a period of time: very long or apparently very long; whole, entire.

STEELE Here I sit moping all the live-long Night.

lively /ˈlʌɪvli/ *adjective.* **OE.**
[ORIGIN from LIFE *noun* + -LY[1].]
▸ **I** †**1** Having life; living, live, animate. **OE–M17.** ▸**b** Of or pertaining to a living person; (of instruction etc.) delivered orally. **M16–E18.**
†**2** Of or pertaining to life; necessary to life, vital. **OE–M17.**
3 Full of action or interest; lifelike, animated; vivid, stimulating. **ME.**

J. GILMOUR A valley lively with flocks, herds, tents. M. WEST The discussion was so lively that it was a quarter to one before Mendelius was able to escape. *Holiday Which?* They are . . aimed at young people looking for a lively holiday in the sun.

4 Full of life; vigorous, energetic, active, brisk. **ME.**

B. TARKINGTON His mother took a lively interest in everything.

look lively move (more) quickly or energetically (freq. in *imper.*).
5 Of colour, light, etc.: vivid, bright, fresh. **LME.**
6 Vivacious, jolly, sociable. **L16.**

D. WIGODER She was lively, laughed gaily, talked easily.

7 Exciting, dangerous, difficult. *joc.* **L18.**

Law Times The Press is making things lively for Her Majesty's judges.

▸ **II** **8** *NAUTICAL.* Of a boat etc.: rising lightly to the waves. **L17.**
■ **livelily** *adverb* **M16.** **liveliness** *noun* **LME.**

lively /ˈlʌɪvli/ *adverb.* **OE.**
[ORIGIN formed as LIFE *noun* + -LY[2].]
†**1** So as to impart life. Only in **OE.**
†**2** As a living person or thing. **LME–L16.**
3 With animation, actively, briskly, nimbly, vigorously. Now chiefly in ***step lively***, = ***look lively*** s.v. LIVELY *adjective* 4. **LME.** ▸†**b** With feeling. **L16–M18.**
4 In a lifelike manner; vividly. Now *rare.* **LME.** ▸†**b** Clearly, plainly. **M16–L17.**

liven /ˈlʌɪv(ə)n/ *verb trans.* & *intrans. colloq.* **E18.**
[ORIGIN from LIFE *noun* + -EN[5]. Cf. ENLIVEN.]
Make or become (more) lively; brighten, cheer. Also foll. by *up*.

A. BROOKNER Things livened up a little when the cousins . . arrived.

■ **livener** *noun* a thing that enlivens; *spec.* an alcoholic drink: **L19.**

liver /ˈlɪvə/ *noun*[1] & *adjective.*
[ORIGIN Old English *lifer* = Old Frisian *livere*, Middle Dutch *lever* (Dutch *lever*), Old High German *lībara* (German *Leber*), Old Norse *lifr*, from Germanic.]
▸ **A** *noun.* **1** A large lobed glandular organ in the abdomen of vertebrate animals which secretes bile, detoxifies the blood, and is important in the metabolism and storage of major nutrients. Also, the flesh of the liver of some animals, used as food. **OE.** ▸**b** Any of various analogous glandular organs or tissues in invertebrates. **M19.**

J. RULE Silver set down a plate of eggs, chicken livers, and toast.

2 *fig.* & *allus.* **a** The seat of love or other passionate emotion, as anger, bitterness, etc. *arch.* **LME.** ▸**b** The seat of cowardice. **L16.**

a DRYDEN When Love's unerring Dart Transfixt his Liver, and inflam'd his Heart.

3 *CHEMISTRY.* = HEPAR. *arch.* **L17.**
4 A diseased or disordered condition of the liver. Freq. with specifying word, as ***hobnail liver***. **E19.**
5 *ellipt.* = ***liver colour*** below. **M19.**
— PHRASES: *LILY liver*. **liver of sulphur** a liver-coloured mixture containing potassium sulphide and used as a lotion to treat skin diseases. *scare the liver and LIGHTS out of*. *white liver*: see WHITE *adjective*.
▸ **B** *adjective.* Liver-coloured. **M19.**
— COMB. & SPECIAL COLLOCATIONS: **liver chestnut** a dark kind of chestnut horse; **liver colour** the colour of liver, dark reddish-brown; **liver-coloured** *adjective* of liver colour; *liver fluke*: see FLUKE *noun*[1] 2; **liver-hearted** *adjective* cowardly; **liverleaf** *N. Amer.* = HEPATICA 2; **liver pad** a pad or plaster for the area of the liver; **liver rot** disease of the liver; (*esp.* in *VETERINARY MEDICINE*) a type of anaemia caused by the liver fluke; distomiasis; fascioliasis; **liver salts**: intended to be taken in water etc. to relieve dyspepsia or biliousness; **liver sausage** (a) soft sausage filled with cooked liver etc.; **liver spot** any of several skin conditions causing brown spots or patches of melanin, *esp.* chloasma or (now usu.) lentigo; any of the brown spots on the skin characteristic of these conditions; **liver-spotted** *adjective* having liver-coloured spots or liver spots; †**liver-vein** (*a*) the basilic vein; (*b*) *allus.* the conduct of someone in love; **liver-wing** the right wing of a fowl etc. which, when dressed for cooking, has the liver tucked under it; *joc.* the right arm; **liverwurst** /-wəːst/ [German *Wurst* sausage: cf. LEBERWURST] = *liver sausage* above.
■ **livered** *adjective* †(*a*) coagulated, clotted; (*b*) (as 2nd elem. of comb.) having a liver of a specified kind, as ***lily-livered***, ***white-livered***, etc.: **ME.** **liverless** *adjective* **L16.**

liver /ˈlɪvə/ *noun*[2]. **LME.**
[ORIGIN from LIVE *verb* + -ER[1].]
1 A person who lives or is alive (now *rare*). Also (chiefly *US*), a resident, a dweller. **LME.** ▸**b** = LIVIER 1a. *Canad.* **M18.**
2 With qualifying adjective: a person who lives in a specified way, for a long time, etc. **LME.**

HUGH WALPOLE To be an artist was . . synonymous with being a loose liver and an atheist. D. HEWETT The Brewsters were long livers. The old man looked good for another thirty years.

— PHRASES: *free-liver*: see FREE *adjective*. **good liver** (*a*) a virtuous person; (*b*) a person given to good living.

liver /ˈlɪvə/ *verb trans.* & *intrans. obsolete* exc. *dial.* **ME.**
[ORIGIN Partly from Old French *livrer* (see LIVERY *noun*), partly aphet. from DELIVER *verb*.]
= DELIVER *verb.*

liverance /ˈlɪv(ə)r(ə)ns/ *noun. obsolete* exc. *dial.* **ME.**
[ORIGIN Partly from Old French *livrance* delivery, sort of homage, from *livrer* (see LIVERY *noun*). Partly aphet. from DELIVERANCE.]
Delivery, distribution; deliverance, release.

liverish /ˈlɪv(ə)rɪʃ/ *adjective.* **M18.**
[ORIGIN from LIVER *noun*[1] + -ISH[1].]
1 Resembling liver. **M18.**

S. MILLER It [a photograph album] was old, a liverish red worn almost to pink at its edges.

2 Suffering from a disorder of the liver. Also, peevish, bad-tempered. L19.

E. S. CONNELL Liverish prostitutes hawking greasy nostrums.

■ **liverishness** *noun* E20.

Liverpool /ˈlɪvəpuːl/ *noun & adjective.* M19.
[ORIGIN A city in NW England, on the River Mersey.]
(Designating) delftware and porcelain manufactured in Liverpool in the 18th cent.

Liverpudlian /lɪvəˈpʌdlɪən/ *noun & adjective.* M19.
[ORIGIN formed as LIVERPOOL (with joc. substitution of *puddle* for *pool*) + -IAN.]
(A native or inhabitant) of the city of Liverpool in NW England.

liverwort /ˈlɪvəwəːt/ *noun.* LOE.
[ORIGIN from LIVER *noun*[1] + WORT *noun*[1], translating medieval Latin *hepatica*.]
1 Orig., the thalloid bryophyte *Marchantia polymorpha*, lobed like the liver. Now, any bryophyte of the class Hepaticae, with a capsule splitting open into four valves and either thalloid or mosslike (foliose) in form. LOE.
2 = HEPATICA 2. Now *US*. L16.

livery /ˈlɪv(ə)ri/ *noun & verb.* ME.
[ORIGIN Anglo-Norman *liveré*, Old French & mod. French *livrée*, use as noun of fem. pa. pple of *livrer* dispense, deliver, from Latin *liberare* LIBERATE *verb*, (in medieval Latin) deliver up, hand over: see -Y[5].]
▸ **A** *noun* **1** **a** *hist.* The dispensing of food, provisions, or clothing to retainers or servants; *gen.* provision, allowance. ME. ▸**b** *hist.* The food or provisions so dispensed; an allowance or ration of food that is served out. ME. ▸**c** Allowance of provender for horses. Now *rare* exc. in ***at livery***, ***livery stable***, below. LME.
2 Orig., clothing, *esp.* distinctive clothing or a distinctive item of clothing worn by the retainers or servants of a particular employer, for recognition. More widely, a distinctive badge or outfit worn by a member of a City Company, a servant, an official, etc. ME. ▸**b** *transf. & fig.* A distinctive guise, marking, or outward appearance. ME. ▸**c** An emblem, device, or distinctive colour scheme on a vehicle, product, etc., indicating its owner or manufacturer. M20.

A. SETON Two boys in white livery marched through the gate. A. CARTER The valet sat up on the box in a natty black and gold livery. **b** G. BERKELEY Clothing themselves in the livery of other men's opinions. **c** K. WARREN The 14 vehicles were in a new livery, basically light grey and green.

3 *collect.* **a** Retainers or servants in livery. Now *rare* or *obsolete*. LME. ▸**b** A livery company; the members of a livery company. E16.

b *Times* A dinner given by the Distillers' Company for the ladies and livery yesterday.

4 *LAW* (now *hist.*). The legal delivery of property into a person's possession; a writ allowing this. LME.
†**5** **a** *gen.* The action of handing over or conveying something into a person's hands; delivery of goods, money, a writ, etc. LME–M18. ▸**b** Delivery or dealing of blows. Only in LME.
6 **a** = ***livery stable*** below. *US*. M19. ▸**b** A horse kept at livery; a horse (and carriage) hired from a livery stable. Also, stabling at a livery stable. L19.
– PHRASES: **at livery** (of a horse) stabled, fed, and groomed for the owner at a fixed charge. **in livery** wearing a particular livery. **livery of seisin** *LAW* (now *hist.*) an early means of granting freehold land or property by any of a number of symbolic gestures, as giving the grantee a piece of turf from the land, standing on the land and inviting the grantee to enter, etc. **out of livery** dressed in livery; wearing plain clothes. **take up one's livery** become a liveryman.
– COMB.: **livery company** any of the London City companies which formerly had a distinctive costume; **livery cupboard** *hist.* (*a*) a cupboard in which allowances of food were served out; (*b*) an ornamental buffet or sideboard; **livery servant** a servant who wears livery; **livery stable** a stable where horses are kept at livery or let out for hire.
▸ **B** *verb trans.* Array in a livery. *rare*. L16.
■ **liveried** *adjective* dressed in or provided with a livery M17.

livery /ˈlɪvəri/ *adjective.* M18.
[ORIGIN from LIVER *noun*[1] + -Y[1].]
1 Of the consistency or colour of liver; (of soil) heavy, tenacious. M18.
2 = LIVERISH 2. *colloq.* M20.

liveryman /ˈlɪv(ə)rɪmən/ *noun.* Pl. **-men**. L17.
[ORIGIN from LIVERY *noun* + MAN *noun*.]
1 A liveried retainer or servant. Now *rare* or *obsolete*. L17.
2 A member of a livery company. L17.
3 A keeper of or attendant in a livery stable. M19.

lives *noun* pl. of LIFE *noun*.

†**lives** *adjective.* OE–E17.
[ORIGIN Old English *lifes* genit. sing. of *līf* LIFE *noun*: see -'S[1]. Cf. LIVE *adjective*.]
Alive; live, living.

liveware /ˈlʌɪvwɛː/ *noun.* M20.
[ORIGIN from LIVE *adjective* + WARE *noun*[2].]
Working personnel, as distinct from the inanimate or abstract things they work with; *spec.* computer personnel or users.

liveyer(e) *nouns* see LIVIER.

livid /ˈlɪvɪd/ *adjective.* LME.
[ORIGIN French *livide* or Latin *lividus*, from *livere* be bluish: see -ID[1].]
1 Of a bluish-leaden colour; discoloured as by a bruise; black and blue. LME.

J. UPDIKE Her left leg showed a livid ripple of varicose vein.

2 Of a colour: having a bluish or greyish tinge. E19.
3 Furiously angry, as if pale with rage. *colloq.* E20.

R. CHANDLER Orrin would be absolutely livid Mother would be furious too.

■ **liˈvidity** *noun* LME. **lividness** *noun* M17.

livier /ˈlɪvjə, *in sense 3 also* ˈlʌɪ-/ *noun. dial.* In sense 1a also (now usu.) **livyer**, **liveyer(e)**. M19.
[ORIGIN Prob. alt. of LIVER *noun*[2]: see -IER.]
1 **a** A resident or a permanent settler in Newfoundland or Labrador. Cf. earlier LIVER *noun*[2] 1b. *Canad.* M19. ▸**b** *gen.* An inhabitant, a dweller. L19.
2 A living person. L19.
3 A person who holds a tenement on a lease for a life or lives. L19.

living /ˈlɪvɪŋ/ *noun*[1]. ME.
[ORIGIN from LIVE *verb* + -ING[1].]
1 **a** The action of LIVE *verb*; the fact of being alive or of dwelling in a specified place. ME. ▸**b** The action of leading one's life in a particular (moral, physical, etc.) manner. ME. ▸†**c** One's lifetime. LME–L16.

a G. JOSIPOVICI The ordinary complements to daily living, the plates, the cups, the bowls.

2 **a** A livelihood; a means of maintenance or support. Formerly also, an income, an endowment. ME. ▸†**b** Food; in *pl.*, victuals. LME–M19. ▸**c** The action, process, or method of gaining one's livelihood. M16.

a N. GORDIMER This cocky miss who played the guitar . . as if the world owed her a living. E. LEONARD Maureen wouldn't a cared what you did for a living.

a earn a living, ***get a living***, ***make a living***, etc.

3 †**a** Property, *esp.* landed estate. Also (in *pl.*), estates, possessions. LME–E19. ▸**b** A holding of land, a tenement. *obsolete* exc. *dial.* L16.
4 *ECCLESIASTICAL.* A position as a vicar or rector with income or property or both. LME.

R. MACAULAY On his last return to Anglicanism, he had accepted a country living.

– PHRASES: ***cost of living***: see COST *noun*[2]. **good living** a high standard of life, esp. with regard to food and drink. ***gracious living***: see GRACIOUS *adjective*. **plain living and high thinking** frugal and philosophic life. ***standard of living***: see STANDARD *noun*.
– COMB.: **living area** = ***living space*** (c) below; **living floor** *ARCHAEOLOGY* a well-defined single horizon containing contemporary (esp. prehistoric) material suggesting domestic occupation; **living-in**, **living-out** residing in, out of, an employer's premises; **living room** (*a*) a room for general day use; (*b*) = LEBENSRAUM; **living space** (*a*) = LEBENSRAUM; (*b*) space for accommodation; (*c*) an area in a room or house for general day use; **living standard** the level of consumption in terms of food, clothing, services, etc., estimated for a person, group, or nation; **living wage** a wage on which it is possible to live without undue hardship.
■ **livingless** *adjective* (*rare*) without a living L19.

living /ˈlɪvɪŋ/ *adjective & noun*[2]. OE.
[ORIGIN from LIVE *verb* + -ING[2].]
▸ **A** *adjective*. **1** *pred. & postpositive*. Not dead; alive, when alive. OE.

R. B. PEAKE You are the only man living that can serve my brother.

2 That lives or has life; that is real. Also, contemporary, now existent. OE. ▸**b** *transf.* (Of water) flowing, running; (of a coal, embers, etc.) live; (of a rock or stone) = LIVE *adjective* 4. LME. ▸**c** Of a language: still in vernacular use. L17.

DICKENS By the living Lord it flashed upon me . . that she had done it. T. K. WOLFE There was no way to explain this to a living soul. *Independent* He is living proof that the party can change its way.

3 With specifying word: that passes life in a specified manner. LME.
4 Of or pertaining to a living person or what is living. L17.

J. CRACE She is . . interested in living folklore.

5 = LIVELY *adjective* 4–7. E18.
– SPECIAL COLLOCATIONS: **living chess**: in which living people act as the chess pieces. ***living daylights***: see DAYLIGHT. **living dead** *the* undead; *the* class of people leading an empty or miserable existence. **living-dead** *adjective* experiencing living death. **living death** an empty or miserable existence. **living fossil** a plant or animal that has survived relatively unchanged since the extinction of the others of its group, known only as fossils. ***living image***: see IMAGE *noun*. **living memory** the memories of some people still living. **living newspaper** a theatrical documentary consisting of a series of short social or political scenes. **living picture** (*a*) = *TABLEAU vivant*; (*b*) a motion picture. **living skeleton** a very emaciated person. **living theatre** theatre consisting of live stage performances, as opp. to cinema. **living will** a written declaration by a person setting out the circumstances in which artificial means of maintaining his or her life should be withdrawn.
▸ **B** *noun collect. pl.* *The* class of living people. OE.

D. A. DYE Hey, Taylor. You back among the living?

in the land of the living: see LAND *noun*[1].
■ **livingly** *adverb* LME. **livingness** *noun* L17.

Livingstone daisy /ˌlɪvɪŋstən ˈdeɪzi/ *noun phr.* M20.
[ORIGIN from unidentified proper name + DAISY.]
A dwarf mesembryanthemum, *Dorotheanthus bellidiformis*, native to southern Africa, bearing daisy-like flowers in many colours.

Livonian /lɪˈvəʊnɪən/ *noun & adjective.* L16.
[ORIGIN from medieval Latin *Livonia* (see below) + -IAN.]
▸ **A** *noun.* **1** A native or inhabitant of Livonia, a former Baltic province of Russia, now divided between Estonia and Latvia. L16.
2 The Baltic language of the Livonians. E19.
▸ **B** *adjective.* Of or pertaining to Livonia, the Livonians, or their language. M18.

livor /ˈlʌɪvɔː/ *noun. arch.* LME.
[ORIGIN Latin.]
1 Discoloration of the skin, as from bruising or in a corpse. LME.
†**2** Ill will, malignity, spite. Only in 17.

Livornese /lɪvɔːˈniːz/ *noun & adjective.* E19.
[ORIGIN from *Livorno* (see LEGHORN) + -ESE.]
▸ **A** *noun.* Pl. same. A native or inhabitant of the city of Livorno (Leghorn) in west central Italy. E19.
▸ **B** *adjective.* Of or pertaining to Livorno. E19.

livraison /livrɛzɔ̃/ *noun.* Pl. pronounced same. E19.
[ORIGIN French from Latin *liberatio(n-)* LIBERATION.]
A part, number, or fascicle of a work published by instalments.

livre /ˈliːvrə/ *noun.* M16.
[ORIGIN French from Latin *libra* pound: cf. LIRA.]
An old French monetary unit, worth one pound of silver.

livre de chevet /liːvrə də ʃəvɛ/ *noun phr.* Pl. ***livres de chevet*** (pronounced same). E20.
[ORIGIN French, lit. 'book of the bedhead'.]
A bedside book; a favourite book.

livre de circonstance /liːvrə də sirkɔ̃stɑ̃ːs/ *noun phr.* Pl. ***livres de circonstance*** (pronounced same). M20.
[ORIGIN French.]
A book composed or adapted for the occasion.

livres de chevet, ***livres de circonstance*** *noun phrs.* pls. of LIVRE DE CHEVET, LIVRE DE CIRCONSTANCE.

livret /ˈliːvrɪt/ *noun. rare.* LME.
[ORIGIN French, from *livre* book: see -ET[1].]
A small book.

livyer *noun* see LIVIER.

liwa /ˈliːwɑː/ *noun.* E20.
[ORIGIN Arabic *liwā'* banner, flag, province.]
hist. A province or large administrative district in any of several Arabic-speaking countries, esp. Iraq.

lixivia *noun* pl. of LIXIVIUM.

lixivial /lɪkˈsɪvɪəl/ *adjective & noun.* M17.
[ORIGIN from LIXIVI(UM + -AL[1].]
▸ **A** *adjective.* Of, pertaining to, or of the nature of (a) lye. Also, alkaline. Now *rare*. M17.
▸ †**B** *noun.* A lye; an alkali. Only in L17.

†**lixiviate** *adjective & noun.* M17–E19.
[ORIGIN formed as LIXIVIAL: see -ATE[2].]
= LIXIVIAL.

lixiviate /lɪkˈsɪvɪeɪt/ *verb trans.* M17.
[ORIGIN mod. Latin *lixiviat-* pa. ppl stem of *lixiviare*, formed as LIXIVIUM: see -ATE[3].]
1 Impregnate with lye. Now *rare* or *obsolete*. M17.
2 Separate (a substance) into soluble and insoluble constituents by percolation of liquid, usu. water; leach. M18.
■ **lixiviˈation** *noun* M18.

lixivium /lɪkˈsɪvɪəm/ *noun. arch.* Pl. **-ia** /-ɪə/. M17.
[ORIGIN Late Latin, use as noun of Latin *lixivius* made into lye, from *lix* ashes, lye.]
A solution obtained by leaching; lye; *spec.* water containing alkaline salts leached from wood ashes.
■ **lixivious** *adjective* (now *rare* or *obsolete*) of, pertaining to, or of the nature of (a) lye M17.

lizard /ˈlɪzəd/ *noun.* LME.
[ORIGIN Old French *lesard*, *-arde* (mod. *lézard*, *-arde*) repr. Latin *lacertus*, *lacerta*, app. identical with *lacertus* muscle: see -ARD.]
1 Any of numerous mostly small reptiles which have an elongated body, a long tail, four legs, and a scaly or granulated skin and belong to the order Lacertilia; *ZOOLOGY* any reptile of the order Lacertilia, which also includes limbless forms (e.g. slow worms). Also (now *loosely*), any related or similar animal, as a crocodilian or dinosaur; *arch.* a newt. LME. ▸**b** With specifying word: any

L

of various species of the genus *Lacerta* or other lacertilian genera. L17. ▸**c** Lizard skin. L19.
flying lizard, ***monitor lizard***, ***sleeping lizard***, ***viviparous lizard***, etc.
2 Chiefly HERALDRY. A figure or charge representing a lizard. LME.
3 (Usu. **L-**.) (The name of) *the* constellation Lacerta. L18.
4 NAUTICAL. A piece of rope having a thimble or block spliced into one or both ends. L18.
5 A fancy variety of canary. Also ***lizard canary***. M19.
6 A musterer of sheep; a person who maintains boundary fences. *Austral. & NZ slang*. L19.
– PHRASES: ***lounge lizard***: see LOUNGE *noun*[1].
– COMB.: ***lizard canary***: see sense 5 above; **lizard cuckoo** any of several W. Indian lizard-eating cuckoos of the genus *Saurothera*; **lizardfish** any of various fishes of the family Synodontidae, found in warm seas and having large pelvic fins on which they rest; **lizard-green** *noun & adjective* (of) a colour resembling that of the green lizard; **lizard orchid** a rare British orchid, *Himantoglossum hircinum*, having greenish flowers with a very long narrow central lobe to the labellum; **lizard-skin** *adjective* made of the skin of a lizard; **lizard's tail** a US swamp plant, *Saururus cernuus* (family Saururaceae), with long tapering spikes of apetalous flowers.
■ **lizard-like** *adverb & adjective* (*a*) *adverb* (*rare*) in the manner of a lizard; (*b*) *adjective* resembling (that of) a lizard: L16. **lizardly** *adjective* (*rare*) resembling a lizard L19.

Lizzie /ˈlɪzi/ *noun*. Also **l-**. E20.
[ORIGIN Pet form of the female forename *Elizabeth*. In sense 1b infl. by LEZZY; in sense 3 alt. of *Lisbon*.]
1 a An effeminate young man. Also ***Lizzie boy***. *slang*. E20. ▸**b** A lesbian. *slang*. M20.
2 More fully ***tin Lizzie***. A car, *esp.* an early model of a Ford. *colloq.* E20.
3 Lisbon wine. *arch. slang*. M20.
4 ***busy Lizzie***, a balsam, *Impatiens walleriana*, native to E. Africa, with usu. red, pink, or white flowers and much grown as a house plant. M20.

LJ *abbreviation*.
Lord Justice.

L JJ *abbreviation*.
Lords Justices.

LL *abbreviation*.
1 Latin *legum* of laws (in academic degrees).
2 Lord Lieutenant.

ll. *abbreviation*.
Lines (in references).

'll *verb* see WILL *verb*[1].

llama /ˈlɑːmə/ *noun*. E17.
[ORIGIN Spanish from Quechua.]
1 A S. American cud-chewing mammal, *Llama glama*, which belongs to the same family as camels but is smaller and humpless, and is found only domesticated as a beast of burden and a source of soft woolly fur and meat. E17.
2 The wool of the llama; a material made from this. M19.

llanero /lɑːˈnɛːrəʊ, lj-/ *noun*. Pl. **-os**. E19.
[ORIGIN S. Amer. Spanish, from LLANO.]
An inhabitant of a llano.

llano /ˈlɑːnəʊ, ˈljɑː-/ *noun*. Pl. **-os**. E17.
[ORIGIN Spanish from Latin *planum* PLANE *noun*[3].]
A level treeless plain in the south-western US and the northern parts of S. America.

LLB *abbreviation*.
Latin *Legum baccalaureus* Bachelor of Laws.

LLD *abbreviation*.
Latin *Legum doctor* Doctor of Laws.

LLM *abbreviation*.
Latin *Legum magister* Master of Laws.

Lloyd-Georgian /lɔɪdˈdʒɔːdʒɪən/ *adjective & noun*. *hist.* E20.
[ORIGIN from *Lloyd George* (see below) + -IAN.]
▸**A** *adjective*. Of, pertaining to, or associated with the British Liberal statesman and Prime Minister Lloyd George (1863–1945). E20.
▸**B** *noun*. A follower or adherent of Lloyd George or his policies. E20.

lloydia /ˈlɔɪdɪə/ *noun*. M19.
[ORIGIN mod. Latin (see below), from Edward Lhwyd or *Lloyd* (1660–1709), Welsh antiquary + -IA[1].]
Any of various small bulbous alpine plants constituting the genus *Lloydia* of the lily family, and bearing white or yellow flowers; *esp.* the Snowdon lily, *L. serotina*.

Lloyd Morgan's canon /lɔɪd ˈmɔːg(ə)nz ˌkanən/ *noun phr.* Also **Lloyd Morgan canon**. M20.
[ORIGIN from C. *Lloyd Morgan* (1852–1936), Brit. psychologist + CANON *noun*[1].]
The principle that the behaviour of an animal should not be interpreted in terms of a higher psychological process if it can be explained in terms of a lower one.

Lloyd's /lɔɪdz/ *noun*. E19.
[ORIGIN from Edward *Lloyd*, who supplied shipping information to clients meeting in his coffee house in London from 1688.]
An incorporated association of underwriters in London who undertake insurance (orig. marine insurance only) with individual liability.
Lloyd's List a daily publication devoted to shipping news. **Lloyd's Register (of Shipping)** an annual classified list of ships over a certain tonnage; the independent society which publishes this.

LM *abbreviation*[1].
1 PROSODY. Long metre.
2 Lunar module.

lm *abbreviation*[2].
Lumen(s).

LME *abbreviation*.
London Metal Exchange.

LMS *abbreviation*.
1 London Mathematical Society.
2 *hist.* London, Midland, and Scottish (Railway).
3 London Missionary Society

LMT *abbreviation*.
Local mean time.

ln *abbreviation*.
Modern Latin *Logarithmus naturalis* natural logarithm.

LNB *abbreviation*.
TELECOMMUNICATIONS. Low-noise blocker, a circuit on a satellite dish which selects the required signal from the transmission.

LNE *abbreviation*. Also **LNER**.
hist. London and North-Eastern (Railway).

LNG *abbreviation*.
Liquefied natural gas.

Lo /ləʊ/ *noun*. *US*. Now *rare*. Pl. **Los**. L19.
[ORIGIN from the line '*Lo*, the poor Indian' in Pope's *Essay on Man*, a use of LO *interjection*[1].]
An American Indian. Also ***Mr Lo***, ***Mrs Lo***.

lo /ləʊ/ *interjection*[1].
[ORIGIN Old English *lā* natural exclam. (cf. LA *interjection*); from Middle English partly from imper. of LOOK *verb*.]
Orig., oh! Later, used to direct attention to a surprising fact or sight; see! look! Now *arch.* exc. in ***lo and behold*** (chiefly *joc.*).

lo /ləʊ/ *interjection*[2]. *colloq.* Also **'lo**. E20.
[ORIGIN Abbreviation.]
Hello.

loa /ˈləʊə/ *noun*[1]. M19.
[ORIGIN mod. Latin (see below), app. from a Bantu lang. of Angola.]
A filarial worm of the genus *Loa*, found in tropical Africa and infecting the eyes and subcutaneous tissues in humans; an eye worm.

loa /ˈləʊə/ *noun*[2]. Pl. same, **-s**. M20.
[ORIGIN Haitian creole *lwa*, from Yoruba *oluwa* lord, owner.]
A god in the voodoo cult of Haiti.

loach /ləʊtʃ/ *noun*. LME.
[ORIGIN Old French & mod. French *loche*, of unknown origin.]
Any of numerous small slender freshwater cyprinoid fishes of the family Cobitidae, found in Europe and Asia.
spined loach, ***stone loach***: see STONE *noun*, *adjective*, & *adverb*.

load /ləʊd/ *noun*. Also †**lode**. See also LODE.
[ORIGIN Old English *lād* = Old High German *leita* course, leading, procession (German *Leite*), Old Norse *leið* way, course, from Germanic, from base also of LEAD *verb*[1].]
▸ **I 1** See LODE. OE.
▸ **II** †**2** Carriage, carrying. Also, an act of placing a burden for carrying on or in something. OE–E16. ▸**b** [from the verb.] COMPUTING. The action or an act of loading a program. Usu. *attrib.* M20.
3 a A thing laid on or taken up by a person or animal, or put in a vehicle or vessel, to be carried; a burden; (usu. with preceding noun) an amount which is usu. or actually carried, or which can be carried, by a specified vehicle etc. ME. ▸**b** The quantity of a particular substance which it is customary to load at one time; a unit of measure or weight based on this. LME. ▸**c** The (amount of) material carried along by a stream; the material carried by various other natural agents of transportation, as glaciers, winds, and ocean currents. L19. ▸**d** A quantity of items washed or to be washed in a washing machine or dishwasher at one time. M20.

a R. K. NARAYAN She wasn't asking him to carry the load on his head. K. GIBBONS He.. picks up the next load of strangers. ALAN BENNETT I've got to pick up a load of.. windcheaters.

cartload, ***horse-load***, ***lorryload***, etc.
4 *fig.* A burden of affliction, sin, responsibility, etc.; a thing which weighs down, oppresses, or impedes a person. LME.

D. W. JERROLD With this thought, a load was lifted from the old man's heart.

5 a A material object or a force which acts or is conceived as a weight, clog, etc. L16. ▸**b** The charge of a firearm. L17. ▸**c** The resistance which machinery offers when driven by a dynamo or motor. L19. ▸**d** BUILDING & ENGINEERING. The force exerted on a structure or part of one. L19. ▸**e** The electric power that a generating system is delivering or required to deliver at any moment. L19. ▸**f** ELECTRONICS. An impedance or circuit that receives the output of a transistor or other device, or in which the output is developed. E20.

b Z. GREY He had used up all the loads in Wright's gun.

6 One's fill of alcoholic drink. Freq. in ***get a load on*** below. *colloq.* L16.
7 A great quantity or number (*of*); plenty, a lot. Freq. in *pl.* *colloq.* E17.

K. ISHIGURO There's always loads on in London. *Independent* What a load of old cobblers. *New York Times* A rambling summer camp where you had loads of fun.

8 = DOSE *noun* 4. *slang*. M20.
9 An amount of work, teaching, etc., to be done by a person. Freq. with preceding noun M20.

J. C. HEROLD His teaching load amounted to three and a half hours daily.

caseload etc.
10 The quantity of semen ejaculated at orgasm. *slang*. L20.
– PHRASES: **a load off a person's mind** a source of anxiety removed; ***take a load off a person's mind***, bring a person relief from anxiety. ***dead load***: see DEAD *adjective* etc. **get a load of** *slang* look at, perceive, make oneself aware of, scrutinize; listen carefully to; freq. in *imper.* **get a load on**, **have a load on** *slang* become or be drunk. †**lay on load** deal heavy blows; *fig.* speak with emphasis or exaggeration; emphasize (the fact) *that*; exaggerate; be extravagant. ***like a load of bricks***: see BRICK *noun*. ***live load***: see LIVE *adjective*. **take a load off (one's feet)** sit or lie down. **under load** MECHANICS & ELECTRICITY subjected to a load. ***useful load***: see USEFUL *adjective* 1.
– COMB.: **load displacement**, **load draught** the displacement or draught of a vessel when laden; **load factor** (*a*) the ratio of the average or actual amount of work, power, etc., to the maximum possible; (*b*) the ratio of the weight of an aircraft to the maximum weight the wings can support; also, the reciprocal of this; (*c*) the ratio of the number of seats occupied in an aircraft to the number available; the weight of freight carried as a proportion of the maximum that can be carried; **load line** (*a*) a Plimsoll line; (*b*) ELECTRONICS a straight line that crosses the characteristic curves of a transistor or valve and has a gradient and position determined by the load, so that it represents the possible operating conditions of the device; **loadmaster** the member of an aircraft's crew who is responsible for the cargo; **load-shedding** a temporary curtailment of the supply of electricity to an area to avoid excessive load on the generating plant; **loadspace** space in a motor vehicle for carrying a load; **load-waterline** the line of flotation of a ship when fully laden; the Plimsoll line.

load /ləʊd/ *verb*. Pa. pple **-ed**, (*arch. & dial.*) **-en**. L15.
[ORIGIN from the noun.]
1 a *verb trans.* Place on a person or animal, or on or in a vehicle, as a load for transport; put on board as cargo. Formerly, carry (hay etc.). L15. ▸**b** *verb intrans.* Take on a load or cargo; (of a vehicle) fill with passengers. Also foll. by *up*. E18.

a *Beano* Load your goodies on my cart, Mr. Baker. A. BROOKNER The chauffeur loads the suitcases into the car. **b** *Australian Financial Review* More than 10 huge bulk carriers have waited .. to load at Port Hedland.

2 *verb trans.* Put a load on or in; provide with a burden or cargo; charge *with* a load. Also foll. by *up*. E16.

JAYNE PHILLIPS We are kept busy loading and unloading the supply ships. *Sunday Express* After loading up the Land Rover... Titus, our driver/guide, sped south.

3 *verb trans. fig.* **a** Weigh down, burden, oppress *with* affliction, sin, responsibility, etc.; impede, encumber. E16. ▸**b** Overwhelm *with* abuse, reproaches, etc. Formerly also, throw blame upon; charge *with* something opprobrious. M17.

a J. GALSWORTHY We load our houses with decoration. G. GREENE Every day.. had loaded her with something to decide.

4 *verb trans.* **a** Add weight to; be a weight or burden on; bear down or oppress *with* a material weight; weight with lead; increase the resistance to the working of (a machine). L16. ▸**b** Adulterate by adding something to increase weight or density; make (light or thin wine) appear full-bodied by adulteration. M19. ▸**c** Give a bias to (dice, a roulette wheel). (Earlier as LOADED 1b.) E20. ▸**d** ELECTRICITY. Provide with additional inductance in order either to reduce the distortion and attenuation of signals (in the case of a telephone line etc.), or to reduce the resonant frequency (in the case of an aerial); provide with a load consisting of any kind of impedance. E20.

a J. WAIN Two middle-aged women.. began to load the rack with parcels.

5 *verb trans.* Supply in excess or overwhelming abundance *with*. Also foll. by *up with*. Usu. in *pass.* L16.

SIR W. SCOTT Old Torquil.. loaded him with praises.

6 *verb trans.* **a** Heap or pile *on*. *rare*. L16. ▸**b** PAINTING. Lay (colour) on thickly in opaque masses. M19.
7 a *verb trans. & intrans.* Put a charge of ammunition into (a firearm); in *pass.*, have one's firearm loaded. E17. ▸**b** *verb*

L

trans. Insert a photographic film or plate in (a camera); insert (a film etc.) *into* a camera. L19. ▸**c** *verb trans.* Fill (a pipe) with tobacco; place items for washing in (a washing machine or dishwasher). E20. ▸**d** *verb trans.* COMPUTING. Transfer (a program or data) into memory, or into the central processor from a more remote part of memory. M20. ▸**e** *verb trans.* Take up a quantity of paint on (a paintbrush). L20.

a R. NICHOLS Soon we shall load and fire and load. **b** *SLR Camera* Take a roll of film . . and load it into your camera.

8 *verb refl. & intrans.* Increase (an insurance premium) by adding a charge to provide for expenses, an increased risk, etc.; charge (a particular life) with a loaded premium. Chiefly as LOADING 3. M19.
9 *verb refl. & intrans.* STOCK EXCHANGE. Buy in large quantities. L19.
10 PSYCHOLOGY. **a** *verb trans.* Weight the relative contribution of (a factor). M20. ▸**b** *verb intrans.* Be correlated. (Foll. by *on*.) L20.
– PHRASES: **load the bases** BASEBALL place base-runners on all three bases. **loading dose** MEDICINE a dose sufficiently large that increasing it produces no increase in its effects.
– COMB.: **load-and-go** COMPUTING an operating technique in which the loading and execution of a program, and any intervening processes, form one continuous operation.

loadability /ləʊdəˈbɪlɪti/ *noun.* M20.
[ORIGIN from LOAD *verb* + -ABILITY.]
The degree of ease with which goods may be loaded or transported.

loadberry /ˈləʊdb(ə)ri/ *noun. dial.* M18.
[ORIGIN Rel. to Norwegian dial. *ladberg*, Old Norse *hlaðberg*.]
In Shetland: a flat rock forming a natural landing place; *spec.* a small enclosed landing place for the unloading of boats.

loaded /ˈləʊdɪd/ *adjective.* M17.
[ORIGIN from LOAD *verb* + -ED¹.]
1 That has been loaded; bearing or carrying a load; laden; charged. M17. ▸**b** Weighted, esp. with lead; (of dice) weighted or biased so that some faces come uppermost more often than others. L18. ▸**c** *fig.* Charged with some hidden implication or underlying suggestion; biased, prejudiced. M20.

b J. M. ROBERTSON One is flogged to death with loaded whips. **c** *Listener* An ill-prepared or a loaded question.

loaded down weighed down with a load. **loaded with** having a load of, *colloq.* having much or many.
2 **a** Drunk. Chiefly *pred. slang.* M19. ▸**b** Drugged; under the influence of drugs. Chiefly *pred. US slang.* E20.
3 Well prepared (*for* a thing). Chiefly in ***loaded for bear*** s.v. BEAR *noun*¹ 1. *US.* L19.
4 Wealthy. *slang.* M20.
5 Esp. of a car: well fitted out; having optional extras. *N. Amer. colloq.* M20.

loaden /ˈləʊd(ə)n/ *verb*¹ *trans. obsolete* exc. *dial.* M16.
[ORIGIN from LOAD *noun* + -EN⁵. Cf. LADEN *verb.*]
Load.

loaden *verb*² *pa. pple*: see LOAD *verb.*

loader /ˈləʊdə/ *noun*¹. ME.
[ORIGIN from LOAD *verb* + -ER¹.]
1 **a** A person who loads something; a person whose task it is to load guns; (*obsolete* exc. *dial.*) a carrier. ME. ▸**b** A machine or device for loading things; COMPUTING a program which controls the loading of other programs. L19.

a *Scottish Sunday Express* Passengers were delayed yesterday when loaders walked out at . . Heathrow Airport.

2 With preceding noun or adjective: a gun, machine, vessel, etc., that is loaded in the specified way. M19.

Independent The vessel . . is a stern loader.

front-loader etc.

loading /ˈləʊdɪŋ/ *noun.* LME.
[ORIGIN from LOAD *verb* + -ING¹.]
1 The action of LOAD *verb.* LME. ▸**b** MEDICINE. The administration of a large amount, esp. a loading dose, of a substance. M20.

b *Journal of Neurochemistry* No 5-hydroxytryptophan was detected in the brain after tryptophan loading.

2 The load or cargo of a vehicle, vessel, etc. Now *rare.* L15.
3 **a** An amount added to an insurance premium to load it. M19. ▸**b** *Austral. & NZ.* An amount added to a basic wage or salary in recognition of some special factor. M20.
4 A substance used to load another; *spec.* in PAPER-MAKING, one added to modify the quality of the paper. L19.
5 BUILDING & ENGINEERING. The loads collectively that act on a structure or part of one. E20.

J. S. FOSTER Types of floor structure which impose an even distribution of loading on the wall.

6 The weight of an aircraft divided by its wing area (in full ***wing loading***) or by the power of its engines (in full ***power loading***). E20.
7 The maximum current or power that an electrical appliance is meant to take. M20.
8 PSYCHOLOGY. The extent to which a factor or variable contributes to or is correlated with some resultant quality or overall situation, usu. represented by a number arrived at by statistical analysis of test results. M20.
9 The concentration or amount of one substance in another. M20.

Nature An increase in the stratospheric dust loading.

10 The number of passengers carried by a vehicle or vessel. M20.

Railway World Apart from poor loadings on 6 September, patronage has been good.

– COMB.: **loading bay** a bay or recess in a building where vehicles are loaded and unloaded; **loading coil** an inductance coil used in the loading of telephone lines or aerials; **loading gauge** (*a*) the maximum height and width allowed for railway vehicles to ensure adequate clearance through bridges and tunnels; (*b*) a device suspended over railway lines for checking the dimensions of rolling stock; **loading rod** a ramrod; **loading shovel** a vehicle with a power-operated shovel for digging out material and carrying it short distances.

†**loadsome** *adjective. rare.* L16–M19.
[ORIGIN from LOAD *noun* + -SOME¹.]
Burdensome.

loadstar *noun* var. of LODESTAR.

loadstone *noun* var. of LODESTONE.

loadum /ˈləʊdəm/ *noun. obsolete* exc. *hist.* L16.
[ORIGIN Perh. contr. of *load him*.]
A card game, an ancestor of hearts, the aim of which was to avoid taking tricks or penalty cards in tricks.

loaf /ləʊf/ *noun*¹. Pl. **loaves** /ləʊvz/.
[ORIGIN Old English *hlāf* = Old High German *leip* (German *Laib*, †*Leib*), Old Norse *hleifr* loaf, Gothic *hlaifs* bread, from Germanic.]
1 Bread. *obsolete* exc. *dial.* OE.
2 A portion of bread baked in one mass; any of the portions, of uniform size and shape, into which a batch of bread is divided. OE.
cottage loaf, ***fruit loaf***, ***granary loaf***, ***wholemeal loaf***, etc.
3 A moulded conical mass of sugar; a sugarloaf. LME.
†**4** *gen.* A mass or lump of anything. LME–L17.
5 A head on a cabbage. E19.
6 (A mass of) minced or chopped meat moulded into the shape of a loaf and cooked, usu. to be eaten cold in slices. Usu. with preceding noun. L19.
beef loaf, ***ham loaf***, ***meat loaf***, etc.
7 A person's head; the mind, common sense. Esp. in ***use one's loaf***. *slang.* E20.
– PHRASES: **brown loaf**: of brown bread. ***French loaf***: see FRENCH *adjective.* ***holy loaf***: see HOLY *adjective.* **loaf of bread**, **loaf o' bread** *rhyming slang* dead. **loaves and fishes** [after *John* 6:26] personal profit as a motive for religious profession or public service. **mushroom loaf**, **oyster loaf** the crust of a loaf or roll of bread filled with a stuffing of mushrooms or oysters. **white loaf**: of white bread.
– COMB.: **loaf-bread** (now *dial.*) bread made in the form of loaves; ordinary bread as opp. to cake or wafers; **loaf-cake** a plain cake made in the form of a loaf; **loaf-eater** *hist.* a household servant in pre-Conquest England; **loaf sugar** refined sugar made into a loaf-shaped mass.

loaf /ləʊf/ *noun*². M19.
[ORIGIN from LOAF *verb*².]
An act or spell of loafing.

loaf /ləʊf/ *verb*¹ *intrans.* L16.
[ORIGIN from LOAF *noun*¹.]
Of a cabbage: form a head.

loaf /ləʊf/ *verb*². M19.
[ORIGIN Prob. back-form. from LOAFER.]
1 *verb intrans.* Spend time idly, loiter; saunter. Freq. foll. by *about*, *around*. M19.

G. B. SHAW He shuts the door; yawns; and loafs across to the sofa. M. J. BRUCCOLI He dressed in his slacks and a sweater and loafed while waiting. D. ADAMS He was a poet and preferred loafing about under trees with a bottle of laudanum.

2 *verb trans.* Fritter (time) *away*. M19.

loafer /ˈləʊfə/ *noun.* M19.
[ORIGIN Perh. from German *Landläufer* tramp, from *Land* LAND *noun*¹ + *laufen* (dial. *lofen*) to run. Cf. LAND-LOPER.]
1 A person who loafs. M19.
2 = LOBO. Also ***loafer wolf***. *N. Amer.* L19.
3 (L-.) **a** (Proprietary name for) a shoe like a moccasin for casual wear. Usu. in *pl.* M20. ▸**b** (Proprietary name for) a type of jacket for informal wear. M20.
■ **loaferdom** *noun* the state of being a loafer L19. **loaferism** *noun* (now *rare*) the practice of loafing M19.

loam /ləʊm/ *noun & adjective.*
[ORIGIN Old English *lām* = Middle Dutch & mod. Dutch *leem*, Middle Low German *lēm* (whence German *Lehm*) rel. to Old High German *leimo* (German dial. *leimen*), from West Germanic, from var. of base of LIME *noun*¹, rel. to Latin *limus* mud.]
▸ **A** *noun.* †**1** Clay, clayey earth, mud. OE–M17.
2 Clay moistened with water so as to form a paste that can be moulded into shape; *spec.* a mixture of moistened clay, sand, chopped straw, etc., used in making bricks, plastering walls, grafting, etc. ME.
3 Earth, soil. *arch.* ME.
4 (A) very fertile soil composed chiefly of clay, sand, and humus; GEOLOGY (a) friable mixture of sand, silt, clay, and usu. humus. M17.

C. LYELL Cliffs, composed . . of alternating strata of blue clay, gravel, loam, and fine sand. F. NORRIS The Quien Sabe ranch—some four thousand acres of rich clay and heavy loams.

red loam: see RED *adjective.*
▸ **B** *attrib.* or as *adjective.* Made or consisting of loam. E16.
■ **loamless** *adjective* (esp. of potting compost) containing no loam L19.

loam /ləʊm/ *verb.* E17.
[ORIGIN from the noun.]
†**1** *verb trans.* Cover or plaster with loam. E17–E18.
2 *verb intrans. & trans.* Search (a region) for gold by washing the loam from the foot of a hill until the increasing number of gold grains leads to the lode. *Austral. & NZ.* E20.

Loamshire /ˈləʊmʃə/ *noun.* M19.
[ORIGIN from LOAM *noun* + SHIRE *noun*.]
(The name of) an imaginary rural English county in some fiction; in *pl.*, a regiment from this county.

loamy /ˈləʊmi/ *adjective.* ME.
[ORIGIN from LOAM *noun* + -Y¹.]
†**1** Formed of earth. *rare.* Only in ME.
2 Of or pertaining to loam; consisting of or resembling loam. L16.
■ **loaminess** *noun* E18.

loan /ləʊn/ *noun*¹. ME.
[ORIGIN Old Norse *lán* corresp. to Old English *lǣn* LAEN, Middle Dutch *lēne* (Dutch *leen*), Old High German *lēhan* (German *Lehn*, *Lehen*), from Germanic base also of LEND *verb*.]
†**1** A gift or grant from a superior. ME–L15.
2 A thing that is lent; *esp.* a sum of money lent to an individual, organization, etc., often at interest. ME. ▸**b** A word, custom, etc., adopted by one people from another. M18.

J. WILCOX She was in the middle of discussing a loan with a client at the bank. J. N. ISBISTER He remained very poor, dependent . . upon loans made to him by his wealthier friends.

3 **a** The action or an act of lending; the state of being lent. Freq. in ***on loan***, acquired or given as a loan. ME. ▸†**b** The action of hiring or letting. E17–L18.

a J. ADAMS I am much obliged to you . . for the loan of this precious collection of memorials.

4 **a** A contribution of money, formerly often a forced one, from a private individual or public body towards the expenses of the state, the amount of which is acknowledged by the Government as a debt; a sum of money so contributed. LME. ▸**b** An arrangement by which a Government receives advances of money on specified conditions, esp. the payment of stipulated interest. M18.
– PHRASES: ***savings and loan***: see SAVING *noun* 3. ***soft loan***: see SOFT *adjective.* ***subordinated loan***: see SUBORDINATE *verb* 2.
– COMB.: †**loan-bank** an establishment from which poor people could borrow money at low interest; **loan-blend** a compound word consisting of both native and foreign elements; **loan capital** the part of the capital of a company etc. that has to be repaid, usu. at a stipulated rate of interest, irrespective of profits; **loan collection** a collection of works of art, curiosities, etc., lent by their owners for exhibition; **loan-farm** *S. Afr.* a piece of land loaned to a farmer by the Government; **loanholder** a person who holds debentures or other acknowledgements of a loan; a mortgagee; **loan-money** †(*a*) money payable as a contribution to a government loan; (*b*) money advanced as a loan; **loan-monger** *derog.* a person who negotiates loans; **loan-office** (chiefly *US*) (*a*) an office for lending money to private borrowers; (*b*) an office for receiving subscriptions to a government loan; **loan-place** *S. Afr.* = ***loan-farm*** above; **loan shark** *colloq.* a person who lends money at exorbitant rates of interest; **loan-sharking** *colloq.* the lending of money at exorbitant rates of interest; **loan-shift** a change in the meaning of a word resulting from the influence of a foreign language; a word so affected; **loan translation** an expression adopted by one language from another in more or less literally translated form, a calque; **loanword** a word adopted or borrowed, usu. with little modification, from another language.

loan /ləʊn/ *noun*². *Scot. & N. English.* Also †**lone**. LME.
[ORIGIN Var. of LANE *noun*¹. Earlier in LOANING.]
1 A lane, a narrow path; *spec.* (*a*) a green lane through unenclosed fields, esp. one leading to common open ground (now chiefly in surviving names); (*b*) a street, a roadway. LME.
2 An open uncultivated piece of ground near a farmhouse or village on which cows are milked etc. E18.

loan /ləʊn/ *verb trans.* ME.
[ORIGIN from LOAN *noun*¹.]
Grant the loan of; lend (esp. money).

J. RULE She liked loaning her car to Walt. J. WILCOX You said you'd loan me a few bucks.

■ **loanable** *adjective* able to be loaned; available for loans: M19. **loanee** *noun* a person to whom a loan has been granted, a borrower M19. **loaner** *noun* (*a*) a lender; (*b*) (in full ***loaner car***) a car lent by a garage to a customer whose own car is kept for repair or service: L19.

L

loaning /ˈləʊnɪŋ/ *noun*. *Scot. & N. English*. Also **lonnin(g)** /ˈlɒn-/. ME.
[ORIGIN from LOAN *noun*² + -ING¹.]
= LOAN *noun*² 1.

†**loath** *noun*. OE.
[ORIGIN from LOATH *adjective* (orig. from the neut.). In sense 2 from LOATHE *verb*.]
1 A hateful or harmful thing; evil, harm; an annoyance, a trouble. OE–LME.
2 Dislike, hatred, ill will; disgust, loathing. ME–E18.

loath /ləʊθ/ *adjective*. Also **loth**.
[ORIGIN Old English *lāþ* = Old Frisian *leed*, Old Saxon *lēþ* (Dutch *leed*), Old High German *leid* (cf. German *Leid* sorrow, pain, *leider* (compar. of adjective) unfortunately), Old Norse *leiðr*, from Germanic.]
†1 Hostile, angry, spiteful. OE–LME.
†2 Repulsive, loathsome, unpleasant. (Foll. by dat., *to* a person.) OE–L16.
3 Disinclined, reluctant, unwilling. Chiefly *pred*. (Foll. by *to do*, *that*.) ME. ▸†b Displeased. *rare*. ME–L17.

GEO. ELIOT Lammeter isn't likely to be loth for his daughter to marry into my family. A. JOHN I was loath to leave this delightful inn. E. BOWEN Antonia, loth to have them out of her sight, . . came down to follow the two.

nothing loath not at all unwilling.
†4 Ugly. ME–M16.
– COMB.: **loath-to-depart** *arch*. a song expressing regret for departure; any tune played as a farewell.

loathe /ləʊð/ *verb*.
[ORIGIN Old English *lāþian* = Old Saxon *lēþon*, Old Norse *leiða*, from Germanic, from base of LOATH *adjective*.]
†1 **a** *verb intrans*. Be hateful, displeasing, or offensive. (Foll. by indirect obj., *to* a person). OE–L16. ▸**b** *verb trans*. Excite loathing or disgust in (a person); make (a person) loath *to do* or averse *from*. M16–M17.
2 *verb trans*. Formerly, grow weary of; feel aversion or dislike for. Now, have an intense aversion for; regard with utter abhorrence and disgust; detest. ME.

DAY LEWIS I still loathe artichokes. B. MASON From being generally disliked, Ginger Finucane was now loathed. JULIAN GLOAG If I didn't loathe taking pills . . I'd cheerfully swallow a few too many.

†3 *verb intrans*. Be or become disgusted, feel disgust. ME–E17.
■ **loather** *noun* E17. **loathing** *noun* the action of the verb; (an) intense dislike, disgust: ME. **loathingly** *adverb* in the manner of a person who feels a loathing E17.

loathful /ˈləʊðfʊl, -f(ə)l/ *adjective*. LME.
[ORIGIN from LOATH *noun* + -FUL.]
1 Loathsome. Now *rare*. LME.
2 Retiring, bashful. Long *obsolete* exc. *Scot*. M16.

loathly /ˈləʊðli/ *adjective*. OE.
[ORIGIN from LOATH *adjective* + -LY¹. See also LAIDLY.]
Loathsome, repulsive, hideous, horrible.
– NOTE: Rare after 16 until revived as a literary word in 19.
■ **loathliness** *noun* (now *rare*) LME.

loathly /ˈləʊðli/ *adverb*. Now *rare*. OE.
[ORIGIN from LOATH *adjective* + -LY².]
†1 In a manner to cause loathing; foully, hideously. OE–E17. ▸**b** With abhorrence or detestation. ME–E17.
2 Reluctantly, unwillingly. LME.

loathness /ˈləʊθnɪs/ *adjective*. Long *rare*. ME.
[ORIGIN from LOATH *adjective* + -NESS.]
The quality or condition of being loath; reluctance, disinclination.

loathsome /ˈləʊðs(ə)m/ *adjective*. ME.
[ORIGIN from LOATH *noun* + -SOME¹.]
Arousing disgust or loathing; offensive to the senses; hateful, distasteful, repulsive.
■ **loathsomely** *adverb* LME. **loathsomeness** *noun* (*a*) the quality of being loathsome; (*b*) a loathsome thing; †(*c*) a feeling of loathing, disgust: ME.

loathy /ˈləʊði/ *adjective*. *arch*. LME.
[ORIGIN from LOATH *noun* + -Y¹.]
†1 = LOATH *adjective* 3. Only in LME.
2 = LOATHSOME. L15.

loaves *noun* pl. of LOAF *noun*¹.

lob /lɒb/ *noun*¹ & *adjective*. ME.
[ORIGIN Prob. from various Low Dutch words: cf. East Frisian *lob(be* hanging lump of flesh, Dutch †*lobbe*, *lubbe* hanging lip, *lobbes* bumpkin.]
▸ **A** *noun*. **1** A pollack, a saithe. Long *obsolete* exc. *Scot*. ME.
2 A country bumpkin; a clown, a lout. Now *dial*. LME.
3 A pendulous object. *rare*. L17.
4 A lump, a large piece; a nugget of gold. Chiefly *dial*. E19.
– COMB.: **lob-tail** *verb intrans*. (of a whale) raise its tail in the air and beat the water with it (chiefly as ***lob-tailing*** *verbal noun*).
▸ **B** *attrib*. or as *adjective*. Rustic; loutish; clumsy. Now *dial*. E16.

lob /lɒb/ *noun*². Also **lobb**. L17.
[ORIGIN Unknown.]
A step in a mine; any of a series of veins of ore descending stepwise. Usu. in *pl*.

lob /lɒb/ *noun*³. *criminals' slang*. Also **lobb**. E18.
[ORIGIN Unknown.]
A box; a till.

lob /lɒb/ *noun*⁴. M19.
[ORIGIN from LOB *verb*.]
1 CRICKET. A slow underhand ball. M19.
2 In many ball games: a ball struck in a high arc, a stroke sending the ball in a high arc. L19.

lob /lɒb/ *verb*. Infl. **-bb-**. L16.
[ORIGIN from LOB *noun*¹. Cf. LOP *verb*².]
†1 *verb intrans*. Behave like a lout. Only in L16.
2 *verb trans*. Cause or allow to hang heavily. Now *rare*. L16.
3 *verb intrans*. Move heavily or clumsily; (of a cab-driver) travel slowly in search of a fare. E19.

B. HINES The hawk lobbed off her perch, and . . reached the shelf behind the door.

4 **a** *verb trans. & intrans*. Throw, esp. heavily or clumsily; toss or bowl with a slow movement; *spec*. in many ball games, strike (the ball) in a high arc. M19. ▸**b** *verb trans*. Deceive or defeat (an opponent) with a lobbed ball. E20.

a *Football News* Worrall quickly lobbed the ball in front of the empty goal. S. MIDDLETON He moodily lobbed three stones at the rock tower.

5 *verb intrans*. Arrive; drop *in*. *Austral. slang*. E20.

Lobachevskian /lɒbəˈtʃɛvskɪən, -ˈtʃɛf-/ *adjective*. L19.
[ORIGIN from Nikolai *Lobachevsky* (1793–1856), Russian mathematician: see -IAN.]
MATH. Designating, of, or pertaining to a non-Euclidean hyperbolic geometry in which space is everywhere negatively curved. Cf. RIEMANNIAN.

lobar /ˈləʊbə/ *adjective*. M19.
[ORIGIN from LOBE + -AR¹.]
Of or pertaining to a lobe; designating an acute form of pneumonia most commonly caused by pneumococcal infection and affecting one lobe of a lung.

lobate /ˈləʊbeɪt/ *adjective*. M18.
[ORIGIN from LOBE + -ATE².]
Chiefly BOTANY, ZOOLOGY, & GEOLOGY. Having or characterized by lobes, lobed.
■ Also **lobated** *adjective* E18.

lobation /lə(ʊ)ˈbeɪʃ(ə)n/ *noun*. M19.
[ORIGIN from LOBATE + -ATION.]
The formation of lobes; the condition of being lobate.

lobato- /lə(ʊ)ˈbeɪtəʊ/ *combining form*. M19.
[ORIGIN from LOBATE + -O-.]
Lobate and —, as ***lobato-digitate***, ***lobato-foliaceous*** adjectives, etc.

lobb *noun* var. of LOB *noun*², *noun*³.

lobbier *noun* var. of LOBBYER.

lobby /ˈlɒbi/ *noun*. M16.
[ORIGIN medieval Latin *lobia*: see LODGE *noun*.]
†1 A monastic cloister. Only in M16.
2 A passage or corridor connected with one or more apartments in a building; an anteroom, an entrance hall; the foyer of a hotel. L16.

G. MARKSTEIN In the lobby of the officers' club the wives were having a whist drive. J. THURBER I chanced to be in the lobby of the theatre between acts.

3 **a** In the Houses of Parliament, a hall adjacent to one or other debating chamber where members of the House concerned can meet non-members; (more fully ***central lobby***) a hall between these two lobbies to which the public has access; in the Houses of Parliament and some other legislatures, either of two corridors either side of a debating chamber into which members go, and thereby vote, during a division (more fully ***division lobby***). Also, the body of lobby correspondents. M17. ▸**b** A body of people seeking to influence legislators or public opinion on behalf of a particular interest or cause; influence of this kind; an event at which people go to a house of legislature to lobby its members. E19.

b *Economist* American . . interests have maintained their effective lobby against the project. *Listener* The vested privileges and subsidies of the powerful alcohol lobby.

4 AGRICULTURE. A small enclosure for cattle adjoining a farmyard. L18.
– COMB.: **lobby chest** *hist*. a low chest of drawers; **lobby correspondent** a political journalist who has access to MPs in the lobby of the House of Commons; any of a group of journalists who receive unattributable briefings from the Government.

lobby /ˈlɒbi/ *verb*. Orig. *US*. M19.
[ORIGIN from the noun.]
1 *verb trans*. Seek to influence (members of a house of legislature) in the exercise of legislative functions, orig. by frequenting the lobby; seek to win over to a cause. Also, procure the passing of (a bill etc.) *through* a legislature by such means. M19.

Which? Abroad, all Access/Visa can do is lobby their international organisations . . for a ban. A. BRIEN Write to the papers, organize petitions, lobby relatives, complain to the Governor.

2 *verb intrans*. Frequent the lobby of a house of legislature for the purpose of influencing members' votes; seek to gain support (*for* a cause). M19.

S. BRILL From the day . . Hoffa went off to jail, Fitzsimmons had lobbied for his release. V. BROME Between meetings, considerable lobbying went on behind the scenes.

lobbyer /ˈlɒbɪə/ *noun*. *US*. Also **lobbier**. M19.
[ORIGIN from LOBBY *verb* + -ER¹.]
= LOBBYIST.

lobby-gow /lɒbɪˈgaʊ/ *noun*. *US slang*. E20.
[ORIGIN Unknown.]
An errand boy, a messenger; a hanger-on, an underling, esp. in an opium den or in the Chinese quarter of a town.

lobbyist /ˈlɒbɪɪst/ *noun*. Orig. *US*. M19.
[ORIGIN from LOBBY *noun* + -IST.]
A person who lobbies, a supporter of a lobby.
■ **lobbyism** *noun* the system of lobbying L19.

lobcock /ˈlɒbkɒk/ *noun*. Now *dial*. M16.
[ORIGIN from LOB *noun*¹ + COCK *noun*¹.]
A country bumpkin; a lout, a boor; a heavy dull creature; a blundering fool.

lobe /ləʊb/ *noun*. LME.
[ORIGIN Late Latin *lobus* from Greek *lobos* lobe of the ear or liver, capsule, pod.]
1 A roundish projecting part, usually one of two or more similar portions into which an object is divided by a fissure; *esp*. one of the divisions of the liver, lungs, brain, or other organ. LME.

J. BRONOWSKI The main organisation of the brain is in the frontal lobes and the prefrontal lobes.

Roche lobe: see ROCHE *noun*².
2 BOTANY. A (chiefly rounded) projection or division of a leaf, petal, or other organ of a plant; *esp*. one extending less than halfway to the centre. Formerly also, a pod, a capsule. L17.
3 = ***ear lobe*** s.v. EAR *noun*¹. E18.
4 The larger or most important and projecting part of a cam wheel. M19.
5 GEOLOGY. A great marginal projection from the body of a continental ice sheet. L19.
6 A portion of the radiation pattern of an aerial which represents a group of directions of stronger radiation and is bounded on each side by directions in which there is minimum radiation. E20.
7 CALLIGRAPHY. A curved projecting part of a letter. M20.
– COMB.: **lobefin** a crossopterygian fish; **lobe-finned** *adjective* designating a crossopterygian fish.
■ **lobed** *adjective* having a lobe or lobes L18. **lobeless** *adjective* (*rare*) M19. **lobelike** *adjective* resembling (that of) a lobe M19.

lobectomy /ləʊˈbɛktəmi/ *noun*. E20.
[ORIGIN from LOBE + -ECTOMY.]
Surgical removal of a lobe, esp. of a lung or the brain; an instance of this.

lobelia /ləˈbiːlɪə/ *noun*. M18.
[ORIGIN from Matthias de *Lobel* (1538–1616), botanist to James I + -IA¹.]
1 Any of various chiefly tropical and subtropical herbaceous (rarely shrubby) plants of the genus *Lobelia* (family Campanulaceae), of which many species are cultivated in gardens; *esp*. the common blue-flowered bedding plant *L. erinus* and the red-flowered *L. fulgens*. M18.
2 (The dried stem and leaves of) Indian tobacco, *Lobelia inflata*, used medicinally. M19.
■ **lobeliˈaceous** *adjective* of or pertaining to the former family Lobeliaceae (now included in the Campanulaceae) M19. **ˈlobeline** *noun* (CHEMISTRY) an alkaloid, $C_{22}H_{27}NO_2$, obtained from Indian tobacco which has physiological effects similar to those of nicotine M19.

Lobel's catchfly /ləʊˈbɛlz ˈkatʃflʌɪ/ *noun phr*. M17.
[ORIGIN from M. de *Lobel*: see LOBELIA.]
= ***sweet-william catchfly*** s.v. SWEET *adjective*.

†**lobfish** *noun*. Pl. **-es**, (usu.) same. M16–E19.
[ORIGIN from LOB *noun*¹ + FISH *noun*¹.]
A kind of stockfish.

lobing /ˈləʊbɪŋ/ *noun*. L19.
[ORIGIN from LOBE + -ING¹.]
The formation or occurrence of lobes.

loblolly /ˈlɒblɒli/ *noun*. L16.
[ORIGIN Unknown.]
1 Thick gruel, esp. as a rustic or nautical dish or a simple medicinal remedy. Formerly also, the medicines of a ship's doctor. Now *dial*. L16. ▸**b** A mudhole. *US colloq*. M19.
2 A country bumpkin, a boor. Now *dial*. E17.
3 In full ***loblolly pine***. A long-leaved pine, *Pinus taeda*, of the southern US. M18.
– COMB.: **loblolly bay** a small ornamental evergreen tree, *Gordonia lasianthus*, of the tea family, native to the southern US; **loblolly boy** an attendant who assists a ship's surgeon and his mates in their duties; *dial*. an errand boy, a man of all work; ***loblolly pine***: see sense 3 above; **loblolly tree** *W. Indian* any of several tropical American trees of the genus *Cupania* (family Sapindaceae), so called from the softness of their wood.

lobo /ˈləʊbəʊ/ *noun*. *N. Amer*. Pl. **-os**. M19.
[ORIGIN Spanish from Latin *lupus* wolf.]
A large grey wolf of the south-western US. Also called ***loafer wolf***, ***loafer***.

L

lobola /lə'bəʊlə/ *noun*. Also **-lo** /-ləʊ/. **M19**.
[ORIGIN Bantu: cf. Xhosa *lobola* give a bride price.]
The bride price, usu. in cattle, traditionally given by many grooms in southern Africa to the parent or guardian of the bride; the custom of paying such a bride price.

lobopod /'ləʊbəpɒd/ *adjective & noun*. **M20**.
[ORIGIN from LOBOPODIUM.]
ZOOLOGY. ▸**A** *adjective*. Of a worm etc.: possessing a lobopodium. **M20**.
▸**B** *noun*. = LOBOPODIUM 2. **M20**.

lobopodium /ləʊbə'pəʊdɪəm/ *noun*. Pl. **-ia** /-ɪə/. **E20**.
[ORIGIN from mod. Latin *lobosus* having many or large lobes + PODIUM.]
ZOOLOGY. **1** A blunt or lobelike pseudopodium. **E20**.
2 A primitive blunt limb or limblike organ on some worms or wormlike animals. **M20**.
■ **lobopodial** *adjective* of the nature of or possessing a lobopodium **M20**.

lobotomy /lə'bɒtəmi/ *noun*. **M20**.
[ORIGIN from LOBE + -O- + -TOMY.]
Surgical incision into a lobe, esp. the frontal lobe of the brain, in the treatment of mental illness; an instance of this.
■ **lobotomi'zation** *noun* the action of lobotomizing someone; the state of being lobotomized: **L20**. **lobotomize** *verb trans*. perform a lobotomy on **M20**. **lobotomized** *adjective* (**a**) that has been lobotomized; (**b**) *slang* sluggish, stupefied: **M20**.

lobscouse /'lɒbskaʊs/ *noun*. *dial*. & *NAUTICAL*. **E18**.
[ORIGIN Corresp. to Dutch *lapskous*, Danish, Norwegian, German *lapskaus*: ult. origin unknown. Cf. LOBLOLLY. See also SCOUSE.]
A sailor's dish consisting of meat stewed with vegetables and ship's biscuit etc.
■ **lobscouser** *noun* a sailor **L19**.

Lob's pound /lɒbz 'paʊnd/ *noun phr*. *obsolete* exc. *dial*. **L16**.
[ORIGIN from LOB *noun*[1] + -'S[1] + POUND *noun*[2].]
Prison, the lock-up; *fig*. an entanglement, a difficulty.

lobster /'lɒbstə/ *noun*[1] & *verb*.
[ORIGIN Old English *loppestre*, *lopystre*, *lopustre* from Latin *locusta* crustacean, LOCUST, with *-stre* after agent nouns in -STER.]
▸**A** *noun*. **1** Any of several large marine decapod crustaceans of the genus *Homarus*, with stalked eyes, a long tail, and large pincers as the first pair of limbs; (usu. with specifying word) any similar crustacean of the same family, Nephropidae. **OE**. ▸**b** The flesh of a lobster as food. **L18**. ▸**c** A crayfish, *esp*. one with claws eaten as food. *Austral*. & *NZ*. **E19**.
2 A British soldier or marine; orig. *spec*. a member of a regiment of Roundhead cuirassiers (from their wearing jointed plate armour suggestive of a lobster's tail, later use after the red coat of a soldier's uniform). Also ***boiled lobster***. *derog*. **M17**.
3 (In full ***lobster moth***) a brown moth, *Stauropus fagi*, of the prominent family (Notodontidae); (in full ***lobster caterpillar***) the caterpillar of this, distinguished by some unusually long legs and a posterior end reflexed over the back. **E19**.
4 A slow-witted, awkward, or gullible person; a fool, a dupe; a bore. *US slang*. **L19**.
– PHRASES: ***boiled lobster***: see sense 2 above. ***NORWAY lobster***. **raw lobster** *slang*. [with allus. to the blue uniform, as opp. to the former red coats of 'boiled lobsters'] a police officer. ***SPINY lobster***. **unboiled lobster** *slang* = ***raw lobster*** above.
– COMB.: **lobster bisque** (the colour of) a thick cream soup made of lobster; **lobster boat** a boat used in lobster-fishing, with a well in which to keep the lobsters alive; ***lobster caterpillar***: see sense 3 above; ***lobster moth***: see sense 3 above; **lobster Newburg** lobster cooked in a thick cream sauce containing sherry or brandy; **lobster pot** a basket or similar structure serving as a trap to catch lobsters; **lobster shift** *US slang* = ***lobster trick*** below; **lobster-tail** a piece of armour jointed in the manner of a lobster's tail; **lobster thermidor** cooked lobster mixed with a cream sauce, returned to its shell, sprinkled with cheese, and browned; **lobster trick** *US slang* an overnight shift, esp. on a newspaper.
▸**B** *verb intrans*. Fish for lobsters. Chiefly as ***lobstering*** *verbal noun*. **L19**.
■ **lobsterish** *adjective* resembling a lobster; red-faced: **E20**. **lobsterling** *noun* a young lobster **E20**.

lobster /'lɒbstə/ *noun*[2]. **L19**.
[ORIGIN from LOB *verb* + -STER.]
A person who (habitually) lobs a ball.

lobstick *noun* var. of LOPSTICK.

lobular /'lɒbjʊlə/ *adjective*. **E19**.
[ORIGIN from LOBULE + -AR[1].]
Pertaining to, having the form of, or affecting a lobule or lobules.

lobulated /'lɒbjʊleɪtɪd/ *adjective*. **L18**.
[ORIGIN from LOBULE + -ATE[2] + -ED[1].]
Having lobules, consisting of lobules.
■ **lobulate** /-lət/ *adjective* = LOBULATED **M19**. **lobu'lation** *noun* the formation of lobules; a lobulated condition: **L19**.

lobulato- /lɒbjʊ'leɪtəʊ/ *combining form*. **M19**.
[ORIGIN from LOBULATE + -O-.]
Lobulated and —, as ***lobulato-crenate***.

lobule /'lɒbjuːl/ *noun*. **L17**.
[ORIGIN from LOBE + -ULE, after *globule* etc.]
Chiefly *ANATOMY*. A small lobe; a lobular subdivision of a lobe.

lobulus /'lɒbjʊləs/ *noun*. Pl. **-li** /-lʌɪ, -liː/. **M18**.
[ORIGIN mod. Latin dim. of Latin *lobus* LOBE, or Latinization of LOBULE.]
= LOBULE.

lobworm /'lɒbwəːm/ *noun*. **M17**.
[ORIGIN from LOB *noun*[1] + WORM *noun*.]
1 A large earthworm used for bait by anglers. **M17**.
2 A lugworm. **M19**.

locable /'ləʊkəb(ə)l/ *adjective*. *rare*. **M16**.
[ORIGIN medieval Latin *locabilis*, from Latin *locare* to place, from *locus* place: see -ABLE.]
Able to be localized or placed.

†**local** *noun*[1] var. of LOCALE.

local /'ləʊk(ə)l/ *adjective & noun*[2]. **LME**.
[ORIGIN Old French & mod. French from late Latin *localis*, from Latin LOCUS *noun*[1]: see -AL[1].]
▸**A** *adjective*. **1** Of or affecting a particular part of the body; of or pertaining to a particular place in a system, series, etc., or a particular part of an object. **LME**.
2 Belonging to or existing in a particular locality or neighbourhood, esp. a town, county, etc., as opp. to the country as a whole. **L15**. ▸**b** Limited or peculiar to a particular place or places. **E17**.

> D. WIGODER My local G.P. . . was waiting at the door of my house. L. CODY Anna dutifully followed her round the local shops. *USA Today* The history of the Cold War and local crises around the world. M. MILNER We took the plane to Athens, then the local bus to Delphi.

3 **a** Pertaining to or concerned with spatial position or extension. Now chiefly in ***local situation***. **L15**. ▸†**b** Having the attribute of spatial position. **M16–E18**. ▸**c** *GRAMMAR*. Esp. of a case: relating to place or situation. **M19**.

> J. PRIESTLEY The Cartesians . . maintain . . that spirits have no extension, nor local presence.

4 Of or pertaining to places (in the geographical sense) or an individual place as such. **E17**.

> RICHARD MORRIS The etymology of local names.

5 *MATH*. Of or pertaining to a locus. Now *rare*. **E18**.
– SPECIAL COLLOCATIONS: ***local ANAESTHESIA***. ***local anaesthetic***: see ANAESTHETIC *noun*. **local area network** a network joining computers in the same building or nearby buildings, by which they can communicate with each other with enhanced quality and speed owing to their proximity. **local authority** an administrative body in British local government. **local call** a telephone call within a prescribed area around a caller's local exchange. **local cluster** *ASTRONOMY* a cluster of stars, within the Galaxy, to which the sun belongs. **local colour** (**a**) *ART* the actual colour of a thing in ordinary daylight and uninfluenced by the proximity of other colours; (**b**) the detailed representation of the characteristic features of a place or period in order to convey a sense of actuality; such features themselves in real life, picturesque qualities. **local content** the part of a manufactured product that is made, supplied, or assembled locally. ***local derby***: see DERBY 2b. **local exchange** the telephone exchange to which a subscriber has a direct line. **local government** the administration of the affairs of a town, county, etc., by the elected representatives of those who live in it, as opp. to administration by the Government. **local group** *ASTRONOMY* the cluster of about twenty galaxies to which our own galaxy belongs. †**local motion** movement from place to place, motion of translation. **local option** (a) choice at local or district level whether to accept or reject state or national legislation, *spec*. any allowing or prohibiting the sale of alcoholic liquor. **local oscillator** an oscillator in a radio receiver etc. that generates oscillations for heterodyning with an incoming signal. **local paper** a newspaper distributed only in a certain area and usu. featuring local, as distinct from national, news. **local preacher** a lay member of the Methodist Church who is authorized to lead worship in the district in which he or she resides. **local pub** *colloq*. a public house convenient to a person's home, a public house serving a locality or community. **local radio** radio broadcasting that serves a local area only. **local talent** the talented people or (*colloq*.) the attractive women or men of a particular locality. **local time** (**a**) *ASTRONOMY* time as reckoned from the transit of the mean sun over the meridian of the place concerned; (**b**) time as reckoned throughout a particular country time zone, esp. with ref. to an event reported from it. **local veto**: on the sale of alcoholic liquor in a district under the exercise of a local option.
▸**B** *absol*. as *noun*. **1** A locally applied medicament. Only in **LME**.
2 **a** A person who is attached by occupation, function, etc., to some particular place or district; *esp*. = ***local preacher*** above. **E19**. ▸**b** An inhabitant of a particular locality regarded with ref. to that locality. **M19**.

> **b** H. JACOBSON She . . left him to bore the locals with his explanations of what everything in their village really meant.

3 An item of local interest in a newspaper; *collect*. matter of local interest. **M19**.
4 A postage stamp current only in a certain district. **L19**.
5 A train which serves the stations of a particular district or which stops at all or most of the stations on a line. **L19**.
6 A local branch of a trade union. *N. Amer*. **L19**.

> S. BRILL He did legal work for the Teamsters, serving the Detroit local.

7 = ***local pub*** above. *colloq*. **M20**.

> L. P. HARTLEY The first thing he usually does . . is to pay a visit to the local.

8 = ***local anaesthetic*** s.v. ANAESTHETIC *noun*. **M20**.
9 A person who trades in a financial market on his or her own account. **M20**.

local /'ləʊk(ə)l/ *verb trans*. Infl. **-ll-**, **-l-**. **L16**.
[ORIGIN from LOCAL *adjective*.]
SCOTS LAW. Apportion an increase in (a minister's salary) among different landholders; lay the charge of (such a salary) *on* a landholder or land.

lo-cal /ləʊ'kal/ *adjective*. *colloq*. **M20**.
[ORIGIN from alt. of LOW *adjective* + abbreviation of CALORIE.]
= ***low-calorie*** s.v. LOW *adjective*.

locale /ləʊ'kɑːl/ *noun*. Also †**local**. **L18**.
[ORIGIN French *local* noun (see LOCAL *adjective & noun*[2]) respelt to indicate stress. Cf. MORALE.]
A place, a locality, esp. with ref. to some event or circumstances connected with it; a venue.

localisable *adjective*, **localise** *verb*, **localised** *adjective* vars. of LOCALIZABLE etc.

localism /'ləʊk(ə)lɪz(ə)m/ *noun*. **E19**.
[ORIGIN from LOCAL *adjective* + -ISM.]
1 Something characteristic of a particular locality; a local idiom, custom, etc. **E19**.

> *Scientific American* Some of the varieties of speech are mere localisms.

2 Attachment to a locality, esp. to the place in which one lives; limitation of ideas, sympathies, and interests arising out of such attachment; preference for what is local; an instance of this state of mind. **M19**.

> C. LASCH The will to build a better society . . , along with traditions of localism, self-help, and community action.

localist /'ləʊk(ə)lɪst/ *noun & adjective*. **L17**.
[ORIGIN from LOCAL *adjective* + -IST.]
▸**A** *noun*. A person who tends to treat or regard things as local, to subject them to local conditions, etc.; a student of what is local. **L17**.
▸**B** *adjective*. Of or pertaining to localism or localists; parochial, provincial. **M20**.
■ **loca'listic** *adjective* **L19**.

localitis /ləʊkə'lʌɪtɪs/ *noun*. *colloq*. **M20**.
[ORIGIN from LOCAL *adjective* + -ITIS.]
Undue concern for or attention to a particular place or region to the detriment of others.

locality /ləʊ'kalɪti/ *noun*. **E17**.
[ORIGIN French *localité* or late Latin *localitas*, from *localis* LOCAL *adjective*: see -ITY.]
1 The fact or quality of having a position in space. **E17**.
2 †**a** An assessment, tax, or levy, *esp*. one for the expenses of war. *Scot*. **M–L17**. ▸**b** The localling of a minister's stipend; a decree enacting this; a stipend that is localled. *Scot*. **M17**.
†**3** The fact of belonging to a particular spot; in *pl*., local characteristics, feelings, or prejudices. **L18–E19**.
4 In *pl*. The features or surroundings of a particular place. **E19**.
5 *PHRENOLOGY*. The faculty of recognizing and remembering places. **E19**.
bump of locality: see BUMP *noun*[1].
6 The situation or position of an object; *esp*. the geographical place or situation of a plant, mineral, etc. **E19**.
7 An area or district considered as the site occupied by certain people or things or as the scene of certain activities; a neighbourhood. **M19**.

> W. TREVOR The girl's father . . was a man of some note in the locality. *Which?* Planning permission is intended to make sure a . . development fits in with the locality.

8 *PSYCHOLOGY*. The action of mentally locating a tactile stimulus. **L19**.

localizable /'ləʊk(ə)lʌɪzəb(ə)l/ *adjective*. Also **-isable**. **M19**.
[ORIGIN from LOCALIZE + -ABLE.]
Able to be localized.
■ **localiza'bility** *noun* **M20**.

localize /'ləʊk(ə)lʌɪz/ *verb*. Also **-ise**. **L16**.
[ORIGIN from LOCAL *adjective* + -IZE.]
1 *verb intrans*. **a** Adapt oneself to a place, comply temporarily with the requirements of a particular place. *rare*. **L16**. ▸**b** Be confined to or concentrated in one place, *spec*. (foll. by *in*, of a disease or a causative agent of disease) be confined to (a specified area of the body); *Austral*. settle down to live in one place. **M20**.

> **b** R. W. RAVEN The viruses of West Nile . . localized preferentially in the tumours of some patients.

2 *verb trans*. Make local in character; imbue with the characteristics of a particular place. Now *rare*. **L18**.
3 *verb trans*. Fix in a particular place or district or in a particular part of a whole; *esp*. restrict or confine *to* a particular place, make local in range or currency. **L18**.

L

▸**b** Concentrate (attention) *on* a particular spot. **E19.** ▸**c** Identify with a particular locality. **L19.**

Annual Register The policy of non-intervention . . had succeeded in its main object of localising the conflict.

4 *verb trans.* Attribute (in thought or statement) to a particular place; find or invent a locality for, ascertain the locality of. Also foll. by *to*. **E19.**

Brain A patient . . was unable to localize an object seen.

– **NOTE:** In isolated use before **L18.**
■ **locali'zation** *noun* the action or an act of localizing; the state of being localized: **E19. localizer** *noun* a person who or thing which localizes something; *spec.* in AERONAUTICS, a device for transmitting a narrow vertical radio beam along a runway by means of which an incoming aircraft can be brought into line with it and any lateral deviation automatically corrected: **L19.**

localized /ˈləʊk(ə)lʌɪzd/ *adjective*. Also **-ised**. **E19.**
[ORIGIN from LOCALIZE + -ED¹.]
Confined to or concentrated in a particular place or part; that has been localized.

B. SPOCK A haematoma, a localized haemorrhage under the scalp that sticks out as a distinct bump. *Financial Times* Midland Bank is carrying out a localized experiment with these 'smart' cards at Loughborough.

locally /ˈləʊk(ə)li/ *adverb*. **LME.**
[ORIGIN from LOCAL *adjective* + -LY².]
1 In respect to place or to position in space. **LME.**

Scientific American The extraneous points that minimize the length of the network locally are . . called Steiner points.

2 With regard to a particular place or part; in certain districts; *esp.* in the locality specified or alluded to. **M19.**

New York Times Craftsmen were hired locally or flown in from Colorado.

localness /ˈləʊk(ə)lnɪs/ *noun*. **M18.**
[ORIGIN from LOCAL *adjective* + -NESS.]
The quality of being local.

locanda /loˈkanda/ *noun*. Pl. **-de** /-de/. **M18.**
[ORIGIN Italian from medieval Latin (*camera*, *domus*) *locanda* (room, house) to be let.]
In Italy: a lodging house, an inn.

locant /ˈlɒk(ə)nt/ *noun*. **M20.**
[ORIGIN Latin *locant-* pres. ppl stem of *locare* LOCATE: see -ANT¹.]
CHEMISTRY. A number or letter in the name or cipher of a compound that indicates the position in its molecular structure of a constituent atom or group.

locate /lə(ʊ)ˈkeɪt/ *verb*. **E16.**
[ORIGIN Latin *locat-* pa. ppl stem of *locare* to place, let for hire, from LOCUS *noun*¹ place: see -ATE³.]
†**1** *verb trans.* LAW. Let out on hire. *rare*. **E16–L19.**
2 *verb trans.* Appoint the site of; assign (in thought or statement) to a particular place or position; station, position; US HISTORY survey and demarcate (a tract of land etc.), take possession of (a land claim, mine, etc.). **L16.**
3 *verb intrans.* Establish oneself or itself in a place; take up residence or business in a place; settle. Chiefly *N. Amer.* **M17.**

Fortune Many of America's biggest blue-chip corporations have located here.

4 *verb trans.* Fix or establish in a place (chiefly *N. Amer.*); in *pass.*, be situated, (of a quality etc.) be present *in*. **E19.** ▸**b** *verb trans.* Appoint (a minister) to a permanent pastoral charge of the Methodist Church. *US*. **E19.** ▸**c** *verb intrans.* Of a Methodist minister: take up a permanent pastoral charge; retire. *US*. **M19.**

F. MARRYAT We packed up and located ourselves about two miles from the common. E. CALDWELL A large . . duck pond located on the north side of the park. *Oban Times* Their plans to locate the system at Invergarry.

5 *verb trans.* Allocate, apportion. **E19.**
6 *verb trans.* Discover the exact place or locality of. **L19.**

J. BERMAN More than 3000 letters have been located, perhaps half the number he actually wrote.

■ **locatable** *adjective* **M19.**

location /lə(ʊ)ˈkeɪʃ(ə)n/ *noun*. **L16.**
[ORIGIN Latin *locatio(n-)*, formed as LOCATE: see -ATION.]
1 The action or process of locating something. **L16.**

W. H. PRESCOTT The Castilian officers, to whom the location of the camp had been intrusted.

2 The fact or condition of occupying a particular place; local position, situation; position in a series. **L16.**

M. SCAMMELL It was strictly forbidden to reveal the location of the camp.

3 A site, a place; *US* a tract of land surveyed and demarcated, *esp.* a mining claim; *S. Afr.* (during the time of apartheid) an area where black South Africans were obliged to live, usu. on the outskirts of a town or city; a township. **L18.** ▸**b** A place of settlement or residence. Chiefly *US*. **L18.** ▸**c** A farm, a sheep station; a homestead. *Austral. & NZ*. **E19.** ▸**d** CINEMATOGRAPHY. An actual place or natural setting where filming takes place, as opp. to one simulated in a studio. Freq. in ***on location***. **E20.** ▸**e** COMPUTING. (A unit of memory occupying) a position in memory. **M20.**

S. BELLOW Alone on the Rue Bonaparte, such an enviable location.

■ **locational** *adjective* **E20.**

locative /ˈlɒkətɪv/ *adjective & noun*. **E19.**
[ORIGIN formed as LOCATE + -IVE, after *nominative*, *accusative*, etc.]
▸ **A** *adjective*. **1** GRAMMAR. Designating, being in, or pertaining to a case in inflected languages expressing place or location. **E19.**
2 Of or pertaining to location; serving to locate something. *rare*. **E19.**
▸ **B** *noun*. GRAMMAR. *The* locative case; a word, form, etc., in the locative case. **E19.**

locator /lə(ʊ)ˈkeɪtə/ *noun*. Now *rare* or *obsolete*. **E17.**
[ORIGIN from LOCATE + -OR.]
1 LAW. A person who lets something for hire. **E17.**
2 *US & AUSTRAL.* HISTORY. A person who takes up a grant of land, opens a mine, etc. **L18.**
3 A thing which locates or is used for locating something. **E20.**

loc. cit. /lɒk ˈsɪt/ *adverbial phr.* **M19.**
[ORIGIN Abbreviation of Latin *loco citato* or *locus citatus* (in) the place cited.]
In the book etc. that has previously been quoted, in the passage already cited.

locellus /lə(ʊ)ˈsɛləs/ *noun*. Pl. **-lli** /-lʌɪ, -liː/. **M19.**
[ORIGIN Latin, dim. of LOCULUS compartment.]
BOTANY. A secondary cell; *esp.* a secondary compartment in the loculus of an anther or ovary.
■ **locellate** *adjective* divided into locelli **L19.**

loch /lɒk, lɒx/ *noun*¹. **LME.**
[ORIGIN Gaelic. Cf. LOUGH.]
In Scotland: a lake; (more fully ***sea loch***) an arm of the sea, esp. when narrow or partially landlocked.
– **COMB.:** **lochside** *noun & adjective* (situated or occurring at) the edge of a loch.

loch *noun*² var. of LOCHE.

Lochaber-axe /lɒˈkɑːbəraks, -ˈka-, -x-/ *noun*. **E17.**
[ORIGIN A district of the Highland region, NW Scotland.]
hist. A large halberd with a hook at the end.

lochage /ˈlɒkeɪdʒ/ *noun*. **E19.**
[ORIGIN Greek *lokhagos*, from *lokhos* lochus + *agein* to lead.]
GREEK HISTORY. The commander of a lochus.

lochan /ˈlɒk(ə)n, -x-/ *noun*. **L17.**
[ORIGIN Gaelic, dim. of LOCH *noun*¹.]
In Scotland: a small loch or lake.

loche /lɒʃ/ *noun*. Chiefly *Canad.* Also **loch**, **losh**. **E19.**
[ORIGIN French = LOACH.]
= BURBOT.

Loch Fyne /lɒk ˈfʌɪn, lɒx/ *adjectival phr.* **E20.**
[ORIGIN A sea loch in W. Scotland.]
Designating a type of fishing boat with a standing lug mainsail.

lochi *noun* pl. of LOCHUS.

lochia /ˈlɒkɪə, ˈləʊ-/ *noun pl.* (treated as *sing.* or †*pl.*). Orig. in French form †**lochies**. **L17.**
[ORIGIN mod. Latin from Greek *lokhia* use as noun of neut. pl. of *lokhios* pertaining to childbirth, from *lokhos* childbirth.]
Matter discharged from the uterus and vagina following childbirth.
■ **lochial** *adjective* **M18.**

Lochinvar /lɒkɪnˈvɑː, -x-/ *noun*. **L19.**
[ORIGIN The hero of a ballad in Sir Walter Scott's *Marmion*.]
A young male eloper.

Lochlann /ˈlɒklan, -x-/ *noun*. **M19.**
[ORIGIN Irish = Scandinavia, *Lochlannach* Scandinavian.]
hist. A Viking, a Norseman.

Loch Ness monster /lɒk nɛs ˈmɒnstə, lɒx/ *noun phr.* **M20.**
[ORIGIN See below.]
A monster alleged to exist in the waters of Loch Ness, in the Highland region of northern Scotland.

lochus /ˈlɒkəs/ *noun*. Pl. **-chi** /-kʌɪ/. **M19.**
[ORIGIN mod. Latin from Greek *lokhos*.]
GREEK HISTORY. A division of the army in Sparta and some other states.

lochy /ˈlɒki, -x-/ *adjective*. *rare*. **E19.**
[ORIGIN from LOCH *noun*¹ + -Y¹.]
Full of lochs.

loci *noun*¹ var. of LOCIE.

loci *noun*² pl. of LOCUS *noun*¹.

loci classici, ***loci desperati*** *noun phrs.* pls. of LOCUS CLASSICUS, LOCUS DESPERATUS.

locie /ˈləʊki/ *noun*. *N. Amer. & NZ colloq.* Also **loci**, **lokey**. **M20.**
[ORIGIN Abbreviation of LOCOMOTIVE *noun*: see -IE. Cf. LOCO *noun*².]
A railway engine, a locomotive.

loci poenitentiae, ***loci standi*** *noun phrs.* pls. of LOCUS POENITENTIAE, LOCUS STANDI.

lock /lɒk/ *noun*¹.
[ORIGIN Old English *locc* = Old Frisian, Old Saxon *lok*, Middle Dutch *locke* (Dutch *lok*), Old High German *loc* (German *Locke*), Old Norse *lokkr*, from Germanic. Perh. identical with LOCK *noun*².]
1 Any of the portions into which a head of hair, a beard, etc., naturally divides itself; a curl, a tress; in *pl.* (*literary*), the hair of the head. **OE.** ▸†**b** A lovelock; a tress of artificial hair. Only in **17.**

D. CARNEGIE He wore his hair so long that his auburn locks almost touched his shoulders. J. CARY Long black locks streamed down her forehead. E. LONGFORD Though this . . hair was turning from grey to white, Mrs. Arbuthnot snipped off two locks.

2 A tuft or flock of wool, cotton, etc. **ME.**
3 A quantity, usu. a small one, of any material, esp. hay or straw; a handful, an armful, a bundle. Now *dial.* **LME.**

T. HARDY I'll curl up to sleep in a lock of straw.

lock /lɒk/ *noun*².
[ORIGIN Old English *loc* = Old Frisian *lok* lock, Old Saxon *lok* hole, Old High German *loh* (German *Loch*) hole, Old Norse *lok* lid, end, conclusion (Gothic has *usluk* opening), from Germanic. Partly from LOCK *verb*¹.]
▸ **I** A fastener.
1 Orig., any fastener such as a bar, bolt, or latch. Later, a device for fastening a door, lid, etc., consisting of a bolt or system of bolts in a mechanism which can be operated only by means of a key of a particular shape; any fastener designed to be secure against people without the particular means or knowledge required to operate it. **OE.**

D. L. SAYERS He had new locks put on the doors.

oarlock, ***rowlock***, etc. ***combination lock***, ***mortise lock***, ***padlock***, ***Yale lock***, etc.
†**2** A hobble or shackle on the foot of a horse or other animal to prevent it from straying. **E16–L17.**
3 The mechanism in a firearm by means of which the charge is detonated. Also ***gunlock***. Earliest as 2nd elem. of comb. **M16.**
firelock, ***flintlock***, ***matchlock***, ***Miquelet lock***, etc.
4 = ROWLOCK. **M19.**
5 A device to keep a wheel from revolving, or from turning to right or left. **L19.**
▸ **II** A barrier, an enclosure.
†**6** A barrier on a river that can be opened or closed as required. **ME–M18.**
†**7** The passage or waterway between the piers of a bridge. **M16–E19.**
8 On a canal or river: a portion of the channel shut off at each end by folding gates provided with sluices to let the water in or out, and so raise or lower boats from one water level to another. **L16.**
9 = ***airlock*** (a) s.v. AIR *noun*¹. **L19.**
vapour lock: see VAPOUR *noun*.
▸ **III** Senses derived from LOCK *verb*¹.
10 An interlocked or jammed state, esp. of traffic. Formerly, an unintelligible or ambiguous discourse. **M16.**
11 a A wrestling hold that prevents an opponent from moving the part held; *fig.* a stratagem, a dodge, *esp.* a means of ensuring a person's compliance or cooperation; a difficulty, a dilemma. **E17.** ▸**b** RUGBY. (The position of) either of two players in the second row of a scrum, behind the hooker. Also ***lock forward***, LOCKMAN 3. **E20.**

a M. PUZO Gilly here has a lock on the federal judge who will try the case. **b** *Glasgow Herald* Catswell, six times at lock for Glasgow, will be making his first appearance as a district flanker.

12 A receiver of stolen goods; a house where stolen goods are received. *criminals' slang*. **L17.**
13 The turning of the front wheels of a vehicle from the line of direction of the rear wheels, as when changing direction (also ***steering lock***); the limit of such turning in each direction (more fully ***full lock***). **M19.**

L. MACNEICE The quick lock of a taxi. *Autocar* The 35ft. 3in. mean turning circle with 4.25 turns lock-to-lock is not excessive.

▸ **IV 14** (Also **L-**.) A hospital for the treatment of venereal disease. Also ***Lock-hospital***. Now *arch.* or *hist.* **L16.**
– **COMB. & PHRASES:** **lock and block (system)** a system of railway signalling by which a train does not enter a section of line until the preceding train has left it, the signal being locked at 'danger' and only released when the preceding train leaves the section; **lock-and-key** *adjective* involving structural complementarity or mutual specificity like that of a lock and its key; **lockbox** *N. Amer.* a delivery letterbox provided with a lock; **lockdown** *N. Amer.* the confining of prisoners to their cells, esp. in order to regain control during a riot; ***lock forward***: see sense 11b above; †**lock-hole** a keyhole; **lock-keeper** a person who looks after a lock on a canal or river; **lock-knit** *noun & adjective* (fabric) knitted with an interlocking stitch; **locknut** (*a*) a nut screwed down on another to prevent its breaking loose; (*b*) a nut designed to prevent accidental loosening once it has been tightened; **lock-saw** a long tapering saw for cutting the seat for a lock in a door; **lockstep** *noun & adjective* (*a*) *noun* marching with each person as close as possible to the person in front; *fig.* rigidity of procedure or operation (*in lockstep*, in exact synchronism, exactly parallel); (*b*) *adjective*

L

not amenable to alteration; **lock stitch** a stitch made by a sewing machine in which two threads are locked firmly together; **lock, stock, and barrel, stock, lock, and barrel** (*a*) absolutely everything; (*b*) *adverbial* in its entirety; **lock-washer** a washer which when compressed by the tightening of a nut exerts an outward force on the nut to prevent its becoming loose; **under lock and key** securely locked up.
■ **lockful** *noun* as much or as many as will fill a lock (on a canal etc.) E19. **lockless** *adjective* L16.

lock /lɒk/ *verb*[1]. ME.
[ORIGIN from LOCK *noun*[2].]
▶ **I 1 a** *verb trans.* Fasten (a door, drawer, etc.) with a lock and key; secure (a room, building, etc.) by locking the doors (usu. foll. by *up*). ME. ▸**b** *verb intrans.* Of a door etc.: have the means of being locked. L16.

a LD MACAULAY The reformers locked up the church and departed with the keys. G. GREENE Then he closed, locked, bolted and chained the door.

2 *verb trans.* Confine *in* a room, building, etc., with a lock; (foll. by *up*, *away*, (US) *down*) put under lock and key, make secure or inaccessible (as) in a locked receptacle. ME.

Peace News Prison officers . . refused to lock up a frail 75 year old man. G. NAYLOR He locked the circulars up in his desk. *Time* He was locked in the same Montluc prison. J. UGLOW Mrs. Pullet's medicines all have to be priced, valued and above all locked away.

3 *verb trans.* **a** Esp. of hills, ice, etc.: enclose, surround. Usu. in *pass.* LME. ▸**b** Of sleep, enchantment, etc.: overpower completely. Usu. foll. by *up*. E18.

a W. H. DIXON The vessel was locked in ice.

4 a *verb trans.* Fix or join firmly by fitting of parts into each other. Also foll. by *together*. LME. ▸**b** *verb trans.* Engage in a close embrace or close combat. Now only in *pass.* E17. ▸**c** *verb intrans.* Interlock, intertwine. L17.

a T. HEGGEN He sat down in the chair . . locked his hands behind his head. **b** R. GRAVES They stood there, . . locked in each other's arms. *fig.*: *Times* Mrs. Thatcher is locked in disagreement with other member states over future EEC spending.

a lock horns (of cattle) entangle the horns mutually in fighting; *fig.* (*N. Amer.*) engage in combat (*with*).

5 *verb trans.* Shut off (as) with a lock *from* a person; preclude or prevent *from* something (as) by locking. Also foll. by *up*. Now *rare*. E17.

6 *verb intrans.* Of a vehicle: allow the front wheels to turn to right or left. Of wheels: be capable of turning to right or left. M17.

R. BROUGHTON The road is narrow and the coach will not lock.

7 a *verb trans.* Fasten, make fast, fix; *techn.* fasten or engage (one part of a machine) *to* another. L17. ▸**b** *verb trans.* Immobilize (esp. a wheel). L17. ▸**c** *verb intrans.* Of a mechanism or joint: become locked, jam. M19.

b *Daily Telegraph* Letting in the clutch gently so as not to lock the driving wheels. **c** *Which?* Brakes satisfactory but front wheels lock early.

8 *verb trans. & intrans.* ELECTRONICS. (Cause to) keep *to* a particular frequency of operation. M20.

▶ **II 9** *verb intrans.* Provide locks for the passage of vessels. M18.

10 *verb intrans.* (Of a canal) pass by a lock *into*; (of a vessel) pass *down*, *in*, etc., through a lock; take a boat into a lock; (of a person) go *out* through an airlock. M18.

11 *verb trans.* **a** Pass (a vessel) *down*, *in*, etc., by means of a lock. M18. ▸**b** Provide (a canal etc.) with locks; shut *off* (part of a river) by means of a lock. M18.

– WITH ADVERBS IN SPECIALIZED SENSES: **lock in** trap or fix firmly or irrevocably. **lock on** (cause to) locate and then track automatically as a target or reference object (foll. by *to*). **lock out** (*a*) prevent the entry of (a person) by locking a door; (*b*) (of an employer) submit (employees) to a lockout; (*c*) ELECTRONICS temporarily prevent the operation or use of. **lock up** (*a*) MILITARY take a position in line or in file as close as possible to the next person; (*b*) invest (capital) in something that is not easily convertible into money; (*c*) PRINTING fix the type or pages in (a forme) ready for press; (*d*) make certain of (an outcome, prize, etc.); (see also senses 1a, 2, etc., above).
■ **lockable** *adjective* L19.

†**lock** *verb*[2] *trans.* L15–M19.
[ORIGIN Dutch *lokken* = German *locken*.]
Allure, entice.

-lock /lɒk/ *suffix* (not productive).
[ORIGIN Old English *-lac*.]
Forming nouns, mostly long obs., now only in ***wedlock***, with the sense 'actions or proceedings, practice'.

lockage /ˈlɒkɪdʒ/ *noun*. L17.
[ORIGIN from LOCK *noun*[2], *verb*[1] + -AGE.]
†**1** The means of locking or fitting pieces of timber together. Only in L17.
2 The amount of rise or fall effected by a (canal etc.) lock or series of locks. L18.
3 Payment levied for going through a lock. L18.
4 The construction and working of locks; locks collectively. E19.
5 The passage of a vessel through a lock. E20.

Lockean /ˈlɒkɪən/ *adjective & noun*. Also **Lockian**. E19.
[ORIGIN from *Locke* (see below) + -AN, -IAN.]
▶ **A** *adjective*. Of, pertaining to, or characteristic of the English empiricist philosopher and political theorist John Locke (1632–1704) or his ideas. E19.
▶ **B** *noun*. A follower or adherent of Locke. L19.
■ **Lockeanism** *noun* the philosophical doctrines of Locke or his followers M19.

locked /lɒkt/ *adjective*[1]. LME.
[ORIGIN from LOCK *noun*[1] + -ED[2].]
Having locks of hair.

locked /lɒkt/ *adjective*[2]. LME.
[ORIGIN from LOCK *verb*[1], *noun*[2]: see -ED[1], -ED[2].]
1 That has been locked; that has locked; *esp.* (also foll. by *up*) closed with a lock and key. LME.

British Medical Journal Limited movement in knee which becomes locked if moved much. A. JUDD The people . . had retreated behind locked doors and put out their lights.

2 Provide with a (pad)lock. L15.
3 Of a canal: provided with locks. E19.
– SPECIAL COLLOCATIONS & COMB.: **locked-coil** *adjective* designating a rope or cable which has the outer strands of such a shape as to lock together and form a smooth cylindrical surface. **locked groove** on a gramophone record, a circular groove into which the normal spiral groove runs. **locked jaw** (*a*) a jaw shut fast by spasmodic contraction of the muscles; (*b*) = LOCKJAW.

locker /ˈlɒkə/ *noun*. ME.
[ORIGIN from LOCK *noun*[2], *verb*[1] + -ER[1]; sense 2 prob. of Low Dutch origin (cf. Flemish *loker*).]
▶ **I 1** A thing that locks, closes, or fastens something. Now *rare* or *obsolete* exc. *techn.* ME.
▶ **II 2** A box, chest, or compartment with a lock, *esp.* any of a number for public use in a pavilion, gymnasium, sports centre, etc.; NAUTICAL a chest or compartment for clothes, stores, ammunition, etc. Also, a small cupboard attached to a bench, under a window seat, etc. LME.

E. PIZZEY They made their beds and tidied their lockers.

†**3** ECCLESIASTICAL. An aumbry in a church. Only in 16.
4 A compartment in a dovecote. E17.
▶ **III 5** A person who locks something; *spec.* an official in charge of a bonded warehouse, under the warehouse-keeper. Also with adverbs. E18.
– PHRASES: **a shot in one's locker**, **a shot in the locker** money in one's possession; a chance left; a thing in reserve but ready for use. ***DAVY JONES's locker***.
– COMB.: **locker room** a room containing a number of lockers in a pavilion, gymnasium, sports centre, etc.

locker /ˈlɒkə/ *verb intrans.* Chiefly *Scot. & N. English*. Now *rare* or *obsolete*. LME.
[ORIGIN Perh. from LOCK *noun*[1] + -ER[5].]
Curl. Chiefly as ***lockered***, ***lockering*** *ppl adjectives*.

locket /ˈlɒkɪt/ *noun*. LME.
[ORIGIN Old French *locquet* (mod. *loquet* latch) dim. of (chiefly Anglo-Norman) *loc* latch, lock, from Germanic base also of LOCK *noun*[2]: see -ET[1].]
†**1** An iron crossbar in a window. LME–L16.
2 A metal plate or band, esp. on a scabbard. LME.
†**3** A group of small jewels set in a pattern. M17–E18.
4 A small ornamental case containing a miniature portrait, a lock of hair, etc., and usu. hung round the neck. Formerly also, a small lock on a necklace etc. L17.
■ **locketed** *adjective* ornamented with a locket; set in a locket: L19.

lockfast /ˈlɒkfɑːst/ *adjective*. LME.
[ORIGIN Sense 1 from LOCK *noun*[2] + FAST *adjective*; sense 2 from LOCK *verb*[1] + FAST *adverb*.]
1 Fastened or secured by a lock. Chiefly *Scot.* LME.
2 Adapted for locking something securely. L19.

Lockian *adjective & noun* var. of LOCKEAN.

lock-in /ˈlɒkɪn/ *noun*. E20.
[ORIGIN from ***lock in*** s.v. LOCK *verb*[1].]
The act or fact of locking in a person or thing; the state of being locked in.

locking /ˈlɒkɪŋ/ *noun*. E17.
[ORIGIN from LOCK *verb*[1] + -ING[1].]
1 The action of LOCK *verb*[1]; an instance of this. Also with adverbs. E17.

P. O'DONNELL I'll see to the locking-up. *Motor Boat & Yachting* The steel hull will take all the knocks and bumps of continual locking. B. MOORE Heavy doors clanged shut and he heard a locking sound.

attrib.: ***locking plate***, ***locking ring***, etc.
2 A mechanism for locking something. M17.

Lockist /ˈlɒkɪst/ *noun*. Now *rare*. E18.
[ORIGIN from *Locke* (see LOCKEAN) + -IST.]
= LOCKEAN *noun*.

lockjaw /ˈlɒkdʒɔː/ *noun*. E19.
[ORIGIN Alt. of ***locked jaw*** s.v. LOCKED *adjective*[2].]
Trismus tetanus.
■ **lockjawed** *adjective* unable to speak, speechless E19.

lockman /ˈlɒkmən/ *noun*. Pl. **-men**. LME.
[ORIGIN from LOCK *noun*[2] + MAN *noun*.]
1 SCOTTISH HISTORY. A public executioner. LME.
2 In the Isle of Man, a coroner's summoner. M17.

3 RUGBY. = LOCK *noun*[2] 11b. E20.

lock-on /ˈlɒkɒn/ *noun*. M20.
[ORIGIN from ***lock on*** s.v. LOCK *verb*[1].]
1 (The commencement of) automatic tracking. M20.
2 The establishment of a rigid physical connection. M20.

lockout /ˈlɒkaʊt/ *noun*. M19.
[ORIGIN from ***lock out*** s.v. LOCK *verb*[1].]
1 The exclusion of employees by their employer from their place of work until certain terms are agreed to. M19.
2 ELECTRONICS. The automatic temporary prevention of the operation or use of a relay or other device. Usu. ***attrib.*** E20.

lockram /ˈlɒkrəm/ *noun*[1] *& adjective*[1]. *obsolete* exc. *hist.* L15.
[ORIGIN French *locrenan* from *Locronan* (lit. 'cell of St Ronan'), a village in Brittany where the fabric was formerly made. For the change of final *n* to *m* cf. *buckram*.]
▶ **A** *noun*. (An article made of) linen fabric for clothing and household use. L15.
▶ **B** *attrib.* or as ***adjective***. Made of lockram. M16.

lockram /ˈlɒkrəm/ *adjective*[2] *& noun*[2]. *dial.* E19.
[ORIGIN Perh. fig. use of LOCKRAM *noun*[1] *& adjective*[1].]
▶ **A** *adjective*. Nonsensical. E19.
▶ **B** *noun*. Nonsense. M19.

locksman /ˈlɒksmən/ *noun*[1]. Pl. **-men**. E18.
[ORIGIN from LOCK *noun*[2] + -'S[1] + MAN *noun*.]
†**1** A turnkey, a jailer; a public executioner. *Scot.* E18–E19.
2 A lock-keeper. M19.

locksman /ˈlɒksmən/ *noun*[2]. Pl. **-men**. M20.
[ORIGIN from LOCK *noun*[1] + -S[1] + MAN *noun*.]
In Jamaica, a Rastafarian who wears his hair long and plaited.

locksmith /ˈlɒksmɪθ/ *noun*. ME.
[ORIGIN from LOCK *noun*[2] + SMITH *noun*.]
A person who makes or mends locks.
■ **locksmithery** *noun* the locksmith's art E19. **locksmithing** *noun* M19.

lockspit /ˈlɒkspɪt/ *verb & noun*. M17.
[ORIGIN from LOCK *noun*[2], *verb*[1] + SPIT *noun*[3].]
▶ **A** *verb trans. & intrans.* Infl. **-tt-**. Mark out (ground) by a lockspit. M17.
▶ **B** *noun*. A cut or trench in the ground indicating the line further work should follow (in mining, fortifications, etc.). E18.

lock-up /ˈlɒkʌp/ *adjective & noun*. M18.
[ORIGIN from ***lock up*** s.v. LOCK *verb*[1].]
▶ **A** *adjective*. Esp. of a building or room: able to be locked up. M18.

Morecambe Guardian The accommodation provides lock-up shop plus freezer room.

▶ **B** *noun*. **1** The action or an act of locking something up, esp. a building for the night; the time at which a building is locked up. M19. ▸**b** The action of locking up capital; the unrealizable state of capital that is locked up; an amount of capital locked up. M19.
2 A place that can be locked up; *spec.* a building or room for the detention (usu. temporary) of offenders. M19. ▸**b** A lock-up garage. E20.

locky /ˈlɒki/ *adjective*. E17.
[ORIGIN from LOCK *noun*[1] + -Y[1].]
Of or pertaining to locks of hair; having many locks of hair.

loco /ˈləʊkəʊ/ *noun*[1]. Pl. **-os**. M19.
[ORIGIN Abbreviation of LOCOFOCO.]
US HISTORY. A Locofoco Democrat.

loco /ˈləʊkəʊ/ *noun*[2]. *colloq.* Pl. **-os**. M19.
[ORIGIN Abbreviation of LOCOMOTIVE *noun*. Cf. LOCIE.]
A railway engine, a locomotive.
– COMB.: **locoman** an engine driver; a man who works on the railways.

loco /ˈləʊkəʊ/ *noun*[3] *& adjective*. L19.
[ORIGIN Spanish = insane.]
▶ **A** *noun*. Pl. **-o(e)s**.
1 Any of several leguminous plants (chiefly species of *Astragalus*) found in the western and south-western US which cause loco disease (see below). L19.
2 = ***loco disease*** (a) below. L19.
– COMB.: **loco disease** (*a*) a disease in cattle, horses, etc., affecting the brain, caused by eating locoweed; (*b*) *Austral.* a similar disease affecting stock eating Darling pea, *Swainsona galegifolia*; **locoweed** (*a*) = sense 1 above; (*b*) *US slang* marijuana.
▶ **B** *adjective*. Crazy, insane, off one's head. *slang* (orig. *US*). L19.

loco-descriptive /ˌləʊkəʊdɪˈskrɪptɪv/ *adjective*. E19.
[ORIGIN from Latin LOCUS *noun*[1] place + -O- + DESCRIPTIVE.]
Descriptive of local scenery.

locoed /ˈləʊkəʊd/ *adjective*. *US*. L19.
[ORIGIN from LOCO *noun*[3] *& adjective* + -ED[2].]
Affected with or poisoned by loco; (of a person) = LOCO *adjective*.

locofoco /ˌləʊkəʊˈfəʊkəʊ/ *noun & adjective*. *US*. Pl. of noun **-os**. M19.
[ORIGIN Invented word, perh. from LOCO *noun*[2] + alt. of Italian *fuoco*, Spanish *fuego* fire.]
†**1** (Designating) a self-igniting cigar or match. M–L19.

2 (Usu. **L-**.) (Designating, pertaining to, or characteristic of) a member of the Democratic Party, esp. (*hist.*) the radical wing of it in and after 1835. **M19.**
■ **locofocoism** *noun* (*hist.*) the principles of the Locofoco party **M19.**

locomobile /ləʊkəˈməʊbɪl/ *noun*. Now *rare*. **L19.**
[**ORIGIN** from Latin *loco* (see **LOCOMOTIVE**) + *mobilis* **MOBILE** *adjective*.]
A steam-powered road vehicle.

locomote /ˈləʊkəməʊt/ *verb intrans. slang* exc. **SCIENCE. M19.**
[**ORIGIN** Back-form. from **LOCOMOTION**.]
Move about from place to place.

locomotion /ləʊkəˈməʊʃ(ə)n/ *noun*. **M17.**
[**ORIGIN** from Latin *loco* (see **LOCOMOTIVE**) + *motio(n-)* **MOTION** *noun*.]
1 The action or power, on the part of an organism or vehicle, of moving from place to place. **M17.**

> V. GORNICK Her legs were attached to her torso for the strict purpose of useful locomotion.

2 Movement from place to place, esp. by artificial means; travel. **L18.**

> D. JACOBSON For you riding is a sport, .. not a serious means of locomotion.

locomotive /ləʊkəˈməʊtɪv/ *adjective & noun*. **E17.**
[**ORIGIN** mod. Latin *locomotivus*, from Latin *loco* abl. of **LOCUS** *noun*[1] place + late Latin *motivus* **MOTIVE** *adjective*, after medieval Latin *in loco moveri* move by change of position in space.]
▸ **A** *adjective*. **1** Of, pertaining to, or effecting progressive motion by an organism or vehicle. **E17.** ▸**b** Of or pertaining to travel. *joc.* **L18.**
2 Having the power of progressive motion. **M17.** ▸**b** Of a person: constantly travelling from place to place. *joc.* **M18.**
locomotive engine an engine designed to travel under its own power, *esp.* one for drawing railway vehicles; a railway engine.
▸ **B** *noun*. **1** A locomotive engine, a railway engine; a mechanically propelled vehicle not designed to carry a load (other than its own fuel etc.) and with a weight greater than a legally specified minimum. **E19.**
2 In *pl.* The legs. *slang.* **M19.**
3 A cheer. *US slang.* **E20.**
■ **locomotively** *adverb* with regard to locomotion **M19.** **locomotiveness** *noun* the quality or fact of being locomotive; power of or fondness for locomotion: **E19.**

locomotor /ˈləʊkəməʊtə/ *noun & adjective*. **E19.**
[**ORIGIN** from Latin *loco* (see **LOCOMOTIVE**) + **MOTOR** *noun*. As adjective from French *locomoteur*.]
▸ **A** *noun*. A person who or thing which can move from place to place. **E19.**
▸ **B** *adjective*. Chiefly **BIOLOGY**. Of or pertaining to locomotion. **L19.**
locomotor **ATAXIA**.

locomotory /ləʊkəˈməʊt(ə)ri/ *adjective*. **M19.**
[**ORIGIN** formed as **LOCOMOTOR** + **MOTORY**.]
Pertaining to or having the power of locomotion.

locoum *noun* var. of **LOKUM**.

Locrian /ˈləʊkrɪən/ *adjective & noun*. **M16.**
[**ORIGIN** from Latin *Locris* (see below) + **-AN**.]
▸ **A** *noun*. A native or inhabitant of Locris, a division of ancient Greece. **M16.**
▸ **B** *adjective*. Of or pertaining to Locris or the Locrians. **M17.**
Locrian mode **MUSIC** an (unidentified) ancient Greek mode; (occas.) one of the church modes.

loculament /ˈlɒkjʊləm(ə)nt/ *noun*. Now *rare*. **M17.**
[**ORIGIN** Latin *loculamentum*, formed as **LOCULUS**.]
A little cell; *spec.* (**BOTANY**) any of the cells or compartments of a capsule or pericarp.

locular /ˈlɒkjʊlə/ *adjective*. **M19.**
[**ORIGIN** from **LOCUL(US** + **-AR**[1].]
= **LOCULATED**. Cf. earlier **BILOCULAR**.

loculated /ˈlɒkjʊleɪtɪd/ *adjective*. **E19.**
[**ORIGIN** from **LOCUL(US** + **-ATE**[2] + **-ED**[1].]
Having or divided into loculi.

locule /ˈlɒkjuːl/ *noun*. **L19.**
[**ORIGIN** French formed as **LOCULUS**.]
Chiefly **BIOLOGY**. = **LOCULUS**.

loculicidal /ˌlɒkjʊlɪˈsʌɪd(ə)l/ *adjective*. **E19.**
[**ORIGIN** from Latin **LOCULUS** + **-I-** + *caedere*, *-cid-* to cut (cf. **-CIDE**) + **-AL**[1].]
BOTANY. (Of the dehiscence of a fruit) occurring through the back or dorsal suture of the loculus; (of a carpel of fruit) that undergoes such dehiscence. Cf. **SEPTICIDAL**.
■ **loculicidally** *adverb* **M19.**

loculus /ˈlɒkjʊləs/ *noun*. Pl. **-li** /-lʌɪ, -liː/. **LME.**
[**ORIGIN** Latin, dim. of **LOCUS** *noun*[1] place: see **-CULE**.]
†**1** A purse. Only in **LME**.
2 A small chamber or cell in an ancient tomb. **L17.**
3 **BIOLOGY**. Any of a number of small cavities or cells separated from one another by septa; *esp.* (**BOTANY**) a cavity of an ovary or anther. **M19.**

locum /ˈləʊkəm/ *noun*[1]. **E20.**
[**ORIGIN** Abbreviation of **LOCUM TENENS**, **LOCUM-TENENCY**.]
1 A person who undertakes the professional duties of someone else in his or her absence, *esp.* a physician or member of the clergy who stands in for another; a person who holds office temporarily. **E20.**
2 The situation of a locum; a post as a locum. **E20.**

locum *noun*[2] var. of **LOKUM**.

locum-tenency /ləʊkəmˈtɛnənsi/ *noun*. **M19.**
[**ORIGIN** from **LOCUM TENENS**: see **-CY**.]
= **LOCUM** *noun*[1] 2.

locum tenens /ləʊkəm ˈtiːnɛnz, ˈtɛn-/ *noun phr*. Pl. **locum tenentes** /tɪˈnɛntiːz/. **M17.**
[**ORIGIN** medieval Latin, from Latin *locum* accus. of **LOCUS** *noun*[1] place + *tenens* pres. pple of *tenere* hold.]
1 = **LOCUM** *noun*[1] 1. **M17.**
2 = **LOCUM** *noun*[1] 2. **L19.**

locuplete /ˈlɒkjʊpliːt/ *adjective*. *rare*. **L16.**
[**ORIGIN** Latin *locuplet-*, *locuples*, from **LOCUS** *noun*[1] place + *plere* fill.]
Amply stocked, rich.

locus /ˈləʊkəs, ˈlɒkəs/ *noun*[1]. Pl. **loci** /ˈləʊsʌɪ, ˈlɒkiː/. **E18.**
[**ORIGIN** Latin = place.]
1 A place, a site; a position, a point, esp. in a text. Chiefly *techn.* **E18.** ▸**b** **GENETICS**. A position on a chromosome at which a particular gene is located; a gene. **E20.**

> M. H. ABRAMS The realm of Ideas is the ultimate locus not only of reality but of value. *Times Lit. Suppl.* Sind had been the locus of one of man's earliest urban societies.

2 **MATH**. The curve or other figure composed of all the points which satisfy a particular equation or are generated by a point, line, or surface moving in accordance with defined conditions. **E18.**
3 A subject, a topic. **M18.**
4 = **LOCUS STANDI**. **E20.**
– **PHRASES**: ***genius loci***: see **GENIUS** 5. ***locus in quo*** /ɪn ˈkwəʊ/ [Latin = in which] the locality of an event, esp. (**LAW**) the land on which a trespass has been committed. **locus of control** **PSYCHOLOGY** the perceived site of the controlling influence in a person's life and environment.

locus /ˈləʊkəs/ *noun*[2] *& verb*. *slang*. **L17.**
[**ORIGIN** Perh. from Spanish *loco*: see **LOCO** *noun*[3] *& adjective*.]
▸ **A** *noun*. A stupefying drink or ingredient. **L17.**
▸ **B** *verb trans*. Infl. **-s(s)-**. Stupefy with drink; get *away* under the influence of drink. Cf. **HOCUS** *verb* 2. **M19.**

locus ceruleus /ləʊkəs sɪˈruːlɪəs, ˌlɒkəs/ *noun phr*. Also **locus caeruleus**, **locus coeruleus**. **L19.**
[**ORIGIN** Latin *locus caeruleus* blue place.]
ANATOMY. An area on the floor of the fourth ventricle of the brain.

locus classicus /ˌləʊkəs ˈklasɪkəs, ˌlɒkəs/ *noun phr*. Pl. ***loci classici*** /ˌləʊsʌɪ ˈklasɪsʌɪ, ˌlɒkiː ˈklasɪkiː/. **M19.**
[**ORIGIN** Latin = classical place.]
A passage regarded as the principal authority on a subject or the origin of a quotation or saying; the best known occurrence of an idea or theme.

locus desperatus /ˌləʊkəs dɛspəˈreɪtəs, ˌlɒkəs dɛspəˈrɑːtəs/ *noun phr*. Pl. ***loci desperati*** /ˌləʊsʌɪ dɛspəˈreɪtʌɪ, ˌlɒkiː dɛspəˈrɑːtiː/. **E20.**
[**ORIGIN** Latin = hopeless place.]
A corrupt manuscript reading that defies interpretation.

locus poenitentiae /ˌləʊkəs piːnɪˈtɛnʃɪiː, ˌlɒkəs piːnɪˈtɛnʃɪʌɪ/ *noun phr*. Pl. ***loci poenitentiae*** /ˌləʊsʌɪ piːnɪˈtɛnʃɪiː, ˌlɒkiː piːnɪˈtɛnʃɪʌɪ/. **M18.**
[**ORIGIN** Latin = place of penitence.]
A place of repentance; **LAW** an opportunity for a person to withdraw from a commitment or contract, esp. an illegal one, so long as some particular step has not been taken.

locus standi /ləʊkəs ˈstandʌɪ, lɒkəs ˈstandiː/ *noun phr*. Pl. ***loci standi*** /ləʊsʌɪ ˈstandʌɪ, lɒkiː ˈstandiː/. **E19.**
[**ORIGIN** Latin = place of standing.]
A recognized or identifiable status, esp. in law; the right to be heard in a court of law.

locust /ˈləʊkəst/ *noun & verb*. **ME.**
[**ORIGIN** Old French & mod. French *locuste* from Latin *locusta* locust, crustacean (cf. **LOBSTER** *noun*[1] *& verb*).]
▸ **A** *noun*. **1** Any grasshopper of the family Acrididae (the short-horned grasshoppers); *esp.* any of several species of Africa and the warm parts of Asia and the Americas that form large migratory swarms highly destructive to vegetation. **ME.** ▸**b** *fig.* A person of devouring or destructive propensities. **M16.** ▸**c** A grasshopper of the family Tettigoniidae (long-horned grasshoppers). Chiefly *Austral.* **M19.** ▸**d** A cicada, esp. *Cicada septendecim*, the seventeen-year locust. *US & Austral.* **M19.**
2 The pod of the cassia, *Cassia fistula*; the pod of the carob tree, thought to resemble a locust. **E17.**
3 In full ***locust tree***. Any of various leguminous trees; *esp.* (***a***) = **CAROB** 2; (***b***) a tree of the W. Indies and Guyana, *Hymenaea courbaril*; (***c***) *N. Amer.* = **ACACIA** 2 (also ***black locust***); (***d***) *NZ* a kowhai, *Sophora tetraptera*. **E17.** ▸**b** A club of the wood of the N. American locust tree, formerly carried by US police. *US.* **M19.**
honey locust tree: see **HONEY** *noun*.
– **COMB.**: **locust bean** the fruit of the carob tree; **locust-berry** the fruit of a W. Indian tree, *Byrsonima coriacea* (family Malpighiaceae); the tree itself; **locust-bird** *S. Afr.* any of various birds (esp. certain pratincoles) that eat locusts, *spec.* (more fully ***great locust-bird***) the European white stork, *Ciconia ciconia*; **locust-eater** *S. Afr.* = ***locust-bird*** above; ***locust tree***: see sense 3 above; **locust years** years of poverty and hardship.
▸ **B** *verb intrans*. Swarm (and devour) as locusts do. *rare*. **L19.**

locusta /ləˈkʌstə/ *noun*. Now *rare* or *obsolete*. Pl. **-stae** /-stiː/. **LME.**
[**ORIGIN** Latin: see **LOCUST**.]
†**1** A locust. Only in **LME**.
2 **BOTANY**. The spikelet of a grass. **E18.**

locution /ləˈkjuːʃ(ə)n/ *noun*. **LME.**
[**ORIGIN** Old French & mod. French, or Latin *locutio(n-)*, from *locut-* pa. ppl stem of *loqui* talk, speak: see **-ION**.]
1 A form of expression; a phrase, an expression. **LME.**

> J. UPDIKE Critical prose, like the prose of business letters, has its set locutions and inevitable rhythms.

†**2** The action of speaking, utterance. **L15–M18.**
3 Speech as the expression of thought; style of discourse, expression. Now *rare*. **E16.**
■ **locutionary** *adjective* (**PHILOSOPHY & LINGUISTICS**) designating, pertaining to, or of the nature of an act of speaking or writing considered with reference only to its sense and reference (cf. **ILLOCUTIONARY**, **PERLOCUTIONARY**) **M20.**

locutor /ləˈkjuːtə/ *noun*. *rare*. **M19.**
[**ORIGIN** Latin, from *loqui*: see **LOCUTION**, **-OR**.]
A speaker.

locutory /ˈlɒkjʊt(ə)ri/ *noun*. **L15.**
[**ORIGIN** medieval Latin *locutorium*, from Latin *locut-*: see **LOCUTION**, **-ORY**[1].]
An apartment in a monastery set apart for conversation.
■ Also **locutorium** /lɒkjʊˈtɔːrɪəm/ *noun*, pl. **-ia** /-ɪə/, **L18.**

lod /lɒd/ *noun*. **M20.**
[**ORIGIN** from *logarithmic odds*.]
STATISTICS. The logarithm of the odds in favour of or against an event; the logarithm of the ratio of two odds. Usu. in *pl.* or more fully ***lod score***.

Loddon lily /ˈlɒd(ə)n ˈlɪli/ *noun phr*. **L19.**
[**ORIGIN** The *Loddon*, a tributary of the River Thames near Reading in southern England, on the banks of which the plant was once common.]
The summer snowflake, *Leucojum aestivum*.

lode /ləʊd/ *noun*. Also (now *rare*) **load**.
[**ORIGIN** Old English *lād*: see **LOAD** *noun*.]
▸ **I** **1** Orig., a course, a way, a journey. Later (*dial.*), a road, a lane. **OE.**
†**2** Guidance. Only in **ME**.
3 A watercourse, a (natural or man-made) channel; an open drain in fenny districts. Now *local*. **LME.**
4 A lodestone; *fig.* an object of attraction. **E16.**
5 **MINING**. A vein of metal ore. **E17.**
masterly lode, ***scovan lode***, etc.
▸ **II** See **LOAD** *noun*.

†**lodeman** *noun*. Pl. **-men**. **OE–M16.**
[**ORIGIN** from **LODE** + **MAN** *noun*.]
= **LODESMAN**.

lodemanage /ˈləʊdmanɪdʒ/ *noun*. **ME.**
[**ORIGIN** Anglo-Norman *lodmanage*, from **LODEMAN**: see **-AGE**.]
Pilotage; skill in navigation. Also, the cost of pilotage.

†**lodemen** *noun* pl. of **LODEMAN**.

loden /ˈləʊd(ə)n/ *noun & adjective*. Also **L-**. **E20.**
[**ORIGIN** German.]
▸ **A** *noun*. **1** A heavy waterproof woollen cloth. **E20.**
2 A coat or cloak made of this. **M20.**
3 A dark green colour in which the cloth is often made. **M20.**
▸ **B** *adjective*. Made of this cloth. **E20.**

lodesman /ˈləʊdzmən/ *noun*. Pl. **-men**. **ME.**
[**ORIGIN** Alt. of **LODEMAN** after *doomsman* etc.]
†**1** A leader, a guide. **ME–L16.**
2 *hist.* A pilot; a steersman. **ME.**

lodestar /ˈləʊdstɑː/ *noun*. Also **load-**. **ME.**
[**ORIGIN** from **LODE** + **STAR** *noun*[1]: cf. Old Norse *leiðastjarna*, Middle High German *leit(e)sterne*.]
1 A star that serves as a guide for navigation etc.; *esp.* the Pole Star. **ME.**
2 *fig.* A person or thing on which one's attention or hopes are fixed; a guiding principle. Also, an object of pursuit. **LME.**

> D. PARKER One who murmurs that his wife Is the lodestar of his life.

lodestone /ˈləʊdstəʊn/ *noun*. Also **load-**. **E16.**
[**ORIGIN** from **LODE** + **STONE** *noun*.]
1 Magnetite that is naturally magnetized; a piece of this used as a magnet. **E16.**
variation of the lodestone: see **VARIATION** 8.
2 *fig.* A thing that is a focus of attention or attraction. **L16.**

lodge /lɒdʒ/ *noun*. **ME.**
[**ORIGIN** Old French *loge* arbour, summer house, hut (in mod. French hut, cottage, theatre box, etc.) from medieval Latin *laubia*, *lobia* from Germanic (whence German *Laube* arbour), perh. from base of **LEAF** *noun*[1]. Cf. **LOBBY** *noun*.]
▸ **I** **1** A small house or dwelling, *esp.* a temporary one; a hut; a tent; an arbour. Now *dial.* **ME.** ▸†**b** A prison, a cell. **ME–E18.** ▸**c** A shed, an outhouse. *dial.* **E18.**
2 A workshop, *esp.* a mason's workshop. Long *obsolete* exc. *hist.* **ME.**

H. BRAUN Quarries having their own lodges capable of supplying ready-made such simple features as doorways.

3 A house in a forest, on a moor, etc., used for temporary accommodation by people hunting or shooting game. LME.

R. MACAULAY The Maxwells' shooting lodge stood in a fold of the moors.

4 A small house, at the entrance of a park or in the grounds of a mansion, occupied by a gatekeeper, gardener, etc.; a room or kiosk occupied by a porter at the entrance of a college, factory, etc. LME.
5 The den or lair of an animal, now *esp.* that of a beaver or otter. M16.
6 *gen.* A lodging, an abode; *esp.* a temporary one. Formerly also, a place where something can lodge. L16.
7 A meeting place for members of a branch of the Freemasons or some other societies; (the members of) a branch of Freemasons etc., a local branch of a trade union. Also, a meeting of a lodge of Freemasons etc. L17.

Daily Mail Men at 25 miners' union lodges . . have already defied a recommendation from their area delegates.

Grand Lodge the governing body of the Freemasons (and of some other societies), presided over by the grand master. ***Orange Lodge***: see ORANGE *adjective*[2].

8 The residence of the head of a college, esp. at Cambridge University. M18.
9 a A sump or pump room in a mine shaft. M18. **▸b** A mill dam. *dial.* M19.
10 A large house; a hotel. Chiefly as 2nd elem. of proper names. E19.
motor lodge: see MOTOR *noun & adjective*.
11 The tent of a N. American Indian; a wigwam, a tepee. Also, the number of Indians accommodated in one tent as a unit of enumeration, reckoned from four to six. E19.
▸ II Rendering related mod. Romance words.
†12 = LOGGIA. M17–E19.
13 = LOGE *noun* 2. *rare.* M18.
14 [Cf. Portuguese *loja*.] A storage room for wine. L19.

L

lodge /lɒdʒ/ *verb.* ME.
[ORIGIN Old French *logier* (mod. *loger*), formed as LODGE *noun*.]
▸ I *verb trans.* **†1** Place in tents or other temporary shelter; station (an army); *refl.* pitch one's tent, take up a military position. ME–L16.
2 Provide with sleeping quarters; receive into one's house for the night; provide with accommodation, establish as a resident (*in*). Formerly also, entertain (a guest). LME. **▸b** *refl.* Establish oneself, take up one's quarters. Formerly also, pass the night. LME. **▸c** Of a room, house, etc.: serve as a lodging or habitation for. Of a thing: contain; in *pass.*, be contained *in*. LME. **▸†d** *fig.* Harbour or entertain (a feeling or thought) in one's mind or heart. L16–E18. **▸e** Have as a lodger. M18.

LYTTON You lodge your horses more magnificently than yourself. M. COX The old Christopher Inn, where the . . boys were lodged. **c** T. CLARK The backwindow / lodges six housesparrows in the bricks Under the sill.

3 Discover the lair of (a buck or stag). L16.
4 Of rain or wind: flatten or bend (a standing crop). L16.

Scientific American Lodged plants often end up lying in the mud.

5 a Get (a thing) into an intended place; *esp.* succeed in causing (a weapon or blow) to reach a target. E17. **▸b** Throw (a thing) so as to be caught in flight; cause to become embedded, caught, or fixed in something; (of a current etc.) deposit in passing. E17. **▸c** Deposit in a specified place of custody or security. M17. **▸d** Vest or represent as residing in a specified person or thing; place (power etc.) *with* or *in the hands of* a person or body. L17. **▸e** Deposit in court or with an official a formal statement of (a complaint, objection, etc.); bring forward, allege, (an objection etc.). E18. **▸†f** Set or fasten in a socket etc. E18–E19.

b W. ABISH They inspected . . the bullets still lodged in the ceiling. E. RHODE This incident . . lodged itself in my mind. **c** B. STEWART Four authorized copies were made and lodged at the office of the Exchequer. **d** E. ARBER Selden lodges the Civil Power of England in the King and the Parliament. **e** W. GERHARDIE He would lodge a vigorous protest through the usual channels.

▸ II *verb intrans.* **†6** Encamp. LME–E17.
7 Remain or live in a place, esp. temporarily; *spec.* pass the night; (of a thing) have its seat, reside. Now *rare.* LME. **▸b** *spec.* Reside or live in another person's house, paying a sum of money periodically in return; be a lodger, live in lodgings. M18.

b R. MACAULAY Any cheap room where I could lodge for a few days.

8 Of a buck or stag: go to its lair. L15.
9 Become embedded, caught, or fixed in something. E17.

L. DURRELL The machine flew into the apricot-tree where it lodged precariously.

10 Of a standing crop: be bent or flattened by wind or rain. M17.

New Yorker The wheats . . tended to lodge.

■ **lodgeable** *adjective* able to be lodged in, suitable for lodging in L16. **lodged** *adjective* that has lodged; HERALDRY (of a beast of the chase, as a buck, hart, etc.) represented as lying on the ground with the head up: ME.

lodgement /ˈlɒdʒm(ə)nt/ *noun.* Also **-dgm-**. L16.
[ORIGIN Old French & mod. French *logement*, from *log(i)er*: see LODGE *verb*, -MENT.]
1 A place in which persons or things are lodged, located, or deposited, *esp.* a lodging house, lodgings; a place of shelter or protection; MILITARY quarters for soldiers. Now *rare.* L16.
2 MILITARY. A temporary defensive work made on a captured part of an enemy's fortifications to make good a position and provide protection. L17.
3 a MILITARY. The action of establishing oneself or making good a position in enemy territory; an area of enemy territory that is captured and held. E18. **▸b** A stable position gained, a foothold; the state or fact of being lodged. E18.

a C. RYAN Throughout the 82nd's vast lodgment . . a series of wild . . enemy attacks threatened disaster. **b** L. J. JENNINGS An intention which seems . . never to have held more than a temporary lodgment in his mind. W. DE LA MARE The claw of the tender bird Finds lodgement here.

4 The action of lodging something, esp. a sum of money, securities, etc.; a deposit of money. E18.

T. WOGAN Some unfortunate customer entering the bank with a large lodgment would . . find the place deserted.

5 The fact or process of becoming lodged; a place where something becomes lodged; a mass of matter that has become lodged. M18.

J. S. FOSTER They do not protrude into the cavity and provide lodgement for mortar droppings.

6 Accommodation in or provision of lodgings; lodging. *rare.* E19.

lodgepole /ˈlɒdʒpəʊl/ *noun & verb.* E19.
[ORIGIN from LODGE *noun* + POLE *noun*[1].]
▸ A *noun.* A pole used to support a wigwam or tepee. *N. Amer.* E19.
– COMB.: **lodgepole pine** a pine native to mountainous regions of north-west N. America, *Pinus contorta* var. *latifolia*.
▸ B *verb trans.* Beat with a lodgepole. M19.

lodger /ˈlɒdʒə/ *noun.* ME.
[ORIGIN from LODGE *verb* + -ER[1].]
†1 A person who lives in a tent. Only in ME.
2 A person who remains or lives in a place, esp. temporarily; a person who passes the night in a place. *arch.* E16.
†3 A person who lodges another, a host. M16–M17.
4 A person who lodges in another person's house, now esp. in part of a house that remains under the general control of the landlord. L16.

P. H. JOHNSON The top two floors of the house were kept furnished for lodgers.

5 A thing that lodges or becomes lodged. M19.
– COMB.: **lodger-franchise** *hist.* a right to vote conferred in 1867 on people in boroughs (and later in counties) occupying lodgings of an annual rental value of at least £10.
■ **lodgerdom** *noun* lodgers collectively; a district where many people live as lodgers: E20.

lodging /ˈlɒdʒɪŋ/ *noun.* ME.
[ORIGIN from LODGE *verb* + -ING[1].]
▸ I 1 a A place or building in which a person lodges or resides; a dwelling; *Scot.* a self-contained house. Formerly also, a bedroom; a (military) encampment. ME. **▸†b** A prison, a hospital; a prison cell. LME–L17. **▸†c** The lair of a buck or stag. L16–E17.
†2 Dwelling, abode, esp. of a temporary nature. Chiefly in ***make lodging***, ***take one's lodging***, ***take up one's lodging***. LME–E17.
3 Accommodation in hired rooms or a lodging house (freq. in ***board and lodging***); temporary or overnight accommodation. Formerly, permanent residential accommodation. LME. **▸†b** Material to lie or sleep on. L17–E18.
board and lodging: see BOARD *noun*.
4 In *pl.* **†a** Military quarters; a defensive position. LME–L17. **▸b** A room or set of rooms in another person's house or (formerly) an inn or hotel where a person lodges. M17. **▸c** An official residence; *esp.* that of the head of certain Oxford colleges. M17.
c Judges' lodgings a house which was the residence of the assize judge when he came for the assizes.
▸ II 5 The action of LODGE *verb.* E16.
– COMB.: **lodging house** a house in which lodgings are let (***model lodging house***: see MODEL *adjective* 1); **lodging room** (now *local*) a bedroom; **lodging turn** an occasion or period for which a railway employee has to lodge at the destination before returning to the place of departure.

lodgment *noun* var. of LODGEMENT.

lodh /ləʊd/ *noun.* L18.
[ORIGIN Hindi from Sanskrit *lodhra*.]
The bark of a shrub, *Symplocos racemosa* (family Symplocaceae), of southern and SE Asia used in dyeing (also ***lodh-bark***); the shrub itself.

lodicule /ˈlɒdɪkjuːl/ *noun.* M19.
[ORIGIN Latin *lodicula* dim. of *lodic-*, *lodix* coverlet: see -CULE.]
BOTANY. A green or white scale forming the lowest part of a grass flower.

loellingite *noun* var. of LÖLLINGITE.

loerie /ˈlʊəri/ *noun. S. Afr.* Also **lourie**. L18.
[ORIGIN Afrikaans from Dutch *lori* formed as LORY.]
Any of several southern African turacos or coucals.
VLEI ***loerie***.

loess /ˈləʊɪs, ləːs/ *noun.* M19.
[ORIGIN German *Löss* from Swiss German *lösch* loose, from *lösen* loosen.]
GEOLOGY. A fine yellowish-grey loam composed of material transported by the wind during and after the glacial period which forms extensive deposits from north central Europe to eastern China, in the American Midwest, and elsewhere.
■ **loessial**, **loessic** *adjectives* composed of loess E20.

lo-fi /ˈləʊfʌɪ/ *noun & adjective. colloq.* M20.
[ORIGIN from alt. of LOW *adjective* + *-fi*, after HI-FI: cf. ***low fidelity*** s.v. LOW *adjective*.]
AUDIO. (Designating, pertaining to, or characterized by) sound reproduction inferior to that produced by hi-fi.

loft /lɒft/ *noun.* LOE.
[ORIGIN Old Norse *lopt* air, sky, upper room, from Germanic. Cf. ALOFT, LIFT *noun*[1].]
▸ I †1 The air, the sky, the upper region. LOE–L16.

SPENSER And ever-drizling raine upon the loft.

2 An upper room, an attic, esp. for storage etc. rather than living accommodation; *US* any upstairs room. Formerly also, an apartment or room. ME. **▸b** A room over a stable esp. for the storage of hay and straw; a hayloft. M16.

Which? The Mansfield's house has . . 25mm of insulation in the loft.

hayloft, ***rood loft***, etc.
†3 a A floor or storey in a house. LME–M17. **▸b** A layer, a stratum. M16–L17.
4 Orig., a room or gallery at the top of a rood screen, a rood loft. Later (now chiefly *Scot.* in *gen.* sense), a gallery in a church or public room; *spec.* an organ loft. LME.

THACKERAY The two schools had their pews in the loft on each side of the organ.

5 A ceiling. Formerly also, a floor of a room. *obsolete* exc. *Canad. dial.* L16.
6 An upper storey; an upper level in a house. *N. Amer.* E18.
7 Chiefly SHIPBUILDING & NAUTICAL. A large room or gallery where something can be spread out for working on. Chiefly with specifying word. E18. **▸b** A place where sails are made; a sail loft. M20.
mould loft, ***rigging loft***, ***sail loft***, etc.
8 A pigeon house, a dovecote, (also ***pigeon-loft***). Also *collect.*, the pigeons kept in a loft. M18.
▸ II 9 Backward slope in the head of a golf club. L19.
10 The action of lofting a ball in golf etc.; a lofting hit or stroke. L19.
– COMB.: **loft conversion** the alteration of a loft, attic, etc., from storage space into a room suitable for living accommodation.

loft /lɒft/ *verb trans.* LME.
[ORIGIN from the noun.]
†1 Insert a layer of planks etc. in (a building) so as to separate the storeys; fit with a ceiling or floor. Also, provide with a loft or upper storey. LME–M17.
2 Store (goods or produce) in a loft. *rare.* E16.
3 Gently hit, throw, kick, or otherwise send (a ball etc.) high up; hit high up so as to clear (an obstacle); hit a delivery of a ball from (a bowler, pitcher, etc.) high up. Also, raise (something) to a higher position. M19.

Kerryman Cronin lofted in a high ball from over 60 metres.

4 Keep (pigeons) in a loft or flock. L19.

lofted /ˈlɒftɪd/ *adjective.* M16.
[ORIGIN from LOFT *noun*, *verb*: see -ED[2], -ED[1].]
1 Orig., fitted with an inner ceiling, floored. Later (*Scot. & N. English*), having one or more storeys above the ground floor. M16.
2 a Of a golf club: made with a backward slope in the head. L19. **▸b** Of a stroke etc.: that lofts a ball. Also (of a ball), that has been lofted. L19.

lofter /ˈlɒftə/ *noun*[1]. Now *rare.* L19.
[ORIGIN from LOFT *verb* + -ER[1].]
A golf club, *spec.* a number 8 iron, for lofting the ball.

lofter /ˈlɒftə/ *noun*[2]. L20.
[ORIGIN from LOFT *noun* + -ER[1].]
A decoy placed in a tree etc. to attract pigeons.

lofting /ˈlɒftɪŋ/ *noun.* E16.
[ORIGIN from LOFT *noun*, *verb* + -ING[1].]
1 A roofing, ceiling, or flooring, esp. in a mine. Now chiefly *dial.* E16.
2 The action of LOFT *verb.* M19.
3 SHIPBUILDING & AERONAUTICS. The activity of a loftsman, a loftsman's work. M20.

– **COMB.**: **lofting iron** (now *rare*) = LOFTER *noun*[1]; **lofting pole** a pole used to position a decoy for pigeons in a tree etc. (cf. LOFTER *noun*[2]).

loftsman /ˈlɒf(t)smən/ *noun*. Pl. **-men**. E20.
[ORIGIN from LOFT *noun* + -'S[1] + MAN *noun*.]
SHIPBUILDING & AERONAUTICS. A person who reproduces a draughtsman's specifications for a ship or aircraft in full size on the floor of a mould loft.

lofty /ˈlɒfti/ *adjective & noun*. ME.
[ORIGIN from LOFT *noun* + -Y[1], infl. by ALOFT.]
▸ **A** *adjective* **1 a** Exalted in dignity, character, or quality; of high rank; (of an expectation, aim, or wish) directed to a high object. ME. ▸**b** Consciously haughty, proud, aloof, dignified. L15. ▸**c** Of written or spoken language (and occas. of a writer or speaker): elevated in style or sentiment; sublime. M16. ▸**d** Majestic in sound, producing a majestic sound. L16.

a E. JENKINS Heir to one of the loftiest of the English peerages. E. JONES Those who have set themselves lofty goals and had great expectations. **b** F. BURNEY He appeared very lofty, and highly affronted. W. W. JACOBS Mr. John Blows stood listening to the foreman with an air of lofty disdain. **c** POPE The shades where . . lofty Denham sung. B. JOWETT I am willing to speak in your lofty strain.

2 Of a mountain, tree, building, etc.: extending to a great height in the air; of imposing altitude, towering. L16. ▸**b** Of flight: soaring to a great height. Of the brow: imposingly high. M18.

K. AMIS It was a lofty room with an immense window. M. L. KING The South's beautiful churches with their lofty spires pointing heavenward. **b** J. WESLEY Ye birds of lofty Wing, On high his Praises bear. W. S. LANDOR The kingly brow, arched lofty for command.

†**3** Of the wind, the sea: violent, high. E17–M18.
4 Massive, superior. Formerly also (of sheep), in good condition. *dial.* M17. ▸**b** Of wool and woollen fabrics: bulky and springy, resilient. L19.
▸ **B** *absol.* as *noun*. **1** *collect. pl.* The class of lofty people. *rare*. L16.

AV *Isa.* 5:15 The eyes of the loftie shall be humbled.

2 (**L-**.) (A nickname for) a very tall or (*iron.*) short person. M20.

Sunday Telegraph Scottie, Windmill and Lofty had all got themselves nicked.

■ **loftily** *adverb* M16. **loftiness** *noun* (**a**) the state of being lofty; (**b**) *rare* (with possess. adjective, as *your loftiness* etc.) a mock title of respect given to a tall person: M16.

log /lɒg/ *noun*[1]. ME.
[ORIGIN Unknown.]
▸ **I 1** A bulky mass of wood; *esp.* an unhewn portion of a felled tree, or a length cut off for use as firewood. ME. ▸**b** *SURFING*. A large or heavy surfboard. M20.

D. L. SAYERS He walked up to the fire and kicked the logs moodily. P. GALLICO He . . pulled her down between two logs of fallen trees.

2 a A heavy piece of wood, fastened to the leg of a person or an animal to impede movement. L16. ▸**b** *MILITARY HISTORY*. A form of punishment whereby a heavy weight was chained to an offender's leg to be dragged or carried around as the person moved. M19.

a DICKENS Here I am tied like a log to you.

3 A piece of quarried slate before it is split into layers. E18.

Times Collyweston slate is . . produced by the action of frost on the stone logs.

4 In *pl.* A jail, a lock-up. *Austral. slang*. L19.

R. BOLDREWOOD Ten minutes in the logs.

▸ **II 5** An apparatus for ascertaining the speed of a ship, consisting of a float attached to a line wound on a reel. Also, any other apparatus for the same purpose. L16.

F. CHICHESTER An old-fashioned log, which worked by timing the run-out of a given length of line.

6 a A book containing a detailed daily record of a ship's voyage; a logbook. E19. ▸**b** A systematic record of things done, found, experienced, etc., as (**a**) a record of discoveries or variations at successive depths in drilling a well; a graph or chart displaying this information; (**b**) a record with details of journeys kept by a lorry driver; (**c**) a record of what is broadcast by a radio or television station; (**d**) *COMPUTING* a sequential file of the transactions on a database. E20. ▸**c** A list or summary of claims for a wage increase etc. Freq. more fully *log of claims*. *Austral.* E20.

a *Yachting World* In theory, a navigator keeps everything in his log. **b** K. G. FENELON A daily log . . showing the nature of the work performed. *National Observer (US)* Newspapers run their own TV logs.

– **PHRASES**: (*as*) *easy as falling off a log*: see FALLING *verbal noun*. **fall like a log** fall in a helpless or stunned state. **heave the log**, **stream the log**, **throw the log** use a log to ascertain a ship's speed. **in the log** (of wood) unhewn. *King Log*: see KING *noun*. **lie like a log** lie motionless, lie in a helpless or stunned state. *log of claims*: see sense 6c above. *patent log*: see PATENT *adjective*. *rough log*: see ROUGH *adjective*. *round log*: see ROUND *adjective*. **sail by the log** calculate a ship's position by the log. *sleep like a log*: see SLEEP *verb*. *stream the log*, *throw the log*: see *heave the log* above.
– **COMB.**: **log-basket** a basket for holding logs by a fire; **log-board** a hinged pair of boards on which the particulars of a ship's log are noted for transcription into the logbook; **log cabin** (orig. *US*) (**a**) a cabin or small house built of logs; (**b**) a pattern in patchwork, quilting, etc., in which pieces of material are arranged to give the effect of pieces of wood formed into adjoining squares; **log canoe**: hollowed out of a single tree; **log-cock** *N. Amer.* = *PILEATED woodpecker*; **log flume** (**a**) a channel built to convey water for transporting logs or timber; (**b**) = FLUME *noun* 2b; **loghead** a stupid person; **logheaded** *adjective* stupid, dull, obtuse; **log house** (**a**) a house etc. built of logs; *US HISTORY* a prison; (**b**) = *log cabin* (b) above; **log line** a line of 100 fathoms or more forming part of a log for ascertaining the speed of a ship; the kind of line used for this purpose; **log-man** †(**a**) *gen.* a person who carries logs; (**b**) *US local* a person employed to cut and carry logs to a mill; **logrunner** any of various mainly Australasian ground-dwelling songbirds of the family Orthonychidae; *spec.* (also called *chowchilla*) either of two birds of the genus *Orthonyx*, which have stiffened tail feathers; **log sheet** a logbook in which the driver of a commercial motor vehicle enters particulars of working and rest hours; **log-work** (**a**) the arrangement of logs in the walls of a house or other building; (**b**) the keeping of a log or logbook.

log /lɒg/ *noun*[2] *& adjective*. M17.
[ORIGIN Abbreviation.]
▸ **A** *noun*. = LOGARITHM (freq. used preceding a number or algebraic quantity the logarithm of which is to be indicated). M17.
$\textbf{log}_e$ natural logarithm (of).
▸ **B** *adjective*. = LOGARITHMIC. L18.
– **COMB. & SPECIAL COLLOCATIONS**: **log-log** *adjective* (of a graph or graph paper) having or using a logarithmic scale along both axes; **log-normal** *adjective* (*STATISTICS*) such that the logarithm of the variate is distributed according to a normal distribution; **log-normally** *adverb* according to a log-normal distribution; **log table** a table of logarithms (usu. in *pl.*).

log /lɒg/ *verb*[1]. Infl. **-gg-**. E17.
[ORIGIN from LOG *noun*[1].]
†**1** *verb intrans.* Be like a log, be sluggish. Only in E17.
2 *verb trans.* Orig., bring (a tree) to the state of a log; deprive of branches. Later, cut (timber) into logs; (chiefly *N. Amer.*) clear (a region) of logs or trees (also foll. by *off*, *over*, *up*). L17. ▸**b** *verb intrans.* Fell timber and cut the wood into logs. Cf. earlier LOGGING *noun* 1. Orig. *US*. M19. ▸**c** *verb trans.* Foll. by *up*: pile (logs, debris, etc.) together for final clearance by burning after an initial bush burn has taken place. *NZ colloq.* L19.

H. D. THOREAU Only a little spruce and hemlock beside had been logged here. **b** C. L. SKINNER They always went upstream to log, and let the current bring down the timber.

3 *verb intrans.* Orig. (of water), lie heavily in a ship. Later, lie motionless like a log. M18.
4 *verb trans. MILITARY HISTORY*. Inflict on (an offender) the punishment of the log (LOG *noun*[1] 2b). E19.
5 *verb trans.* **a** Orig. *NAUTICAL*. Enter (esp. the distance made by a ship) as information in a log or logbook; *gen.* enter (information) in a regular record. Also foll. by *down*, *up*. E19. ▸**b** Esp. of a ship: achieve or cover (a certain distance); travel at (a certain speed). Also, attain as a cumulative total of time, distance, etc., which is entered in a regular record. L19. ▸**c** *NAUTICAL*. Fine. (From the entering of details of offenders and offences committed in a logbook.) L19.

a N. H. BISHOP Logging with pleasure my day's run at sixty-seven miles. D. CAUTE Female cousins . . neatly logged in Elizabeth's address book as Aunt This and Aunt That. **b** *Listener* The *Graf Zeppelin* was the first aircraft to log over a million miles. H. ALLEN She logs about ten knots in this breeze.

6 *verb trans.* Lay *out* (a road) with a layer of logs. L19.
7 *verb intrans. MINING*. Make a log support for a windlass. Foll. by *up*. *Austral.* L19.
8 *verb intrans. & trans.* **a** Foll. by *in*, *on*: go through the procedure, as entering a password or identification number at a terminal, which gives access to a computer system; gain access for (a person) by logging in. (Foll. by *to*.) M20. ▸**b** Foll. by *off*, *out*: go through the procedure, as entering a command at a terminal, which ends access to a computer system; end access for (a person) by logging off. M20.
– **COMB.**: **login**, **logon** (**a**) the action or an act of logging in to a computer system; (**b**) a password or code used when logging in; **logoff**, **logout** the action or an act of logging off from a computer system.

log /lɒg/ *verb*[2] *trans. & intrans.* Chiefly *dial.* Infl. **-gg-**. E19.
[ORIGIN Unknown. Earlier as LOGAN.]
Rock, move to and fro; oscillate. Chiefly as *logging ppl adjective*.
logging rock, **logging stone** = LOGAN.

-log *suffix* see -LOGUE.

logan /ˈlɒg(ə)n/ *adjective & noun*. M18.
[ORIGIN Var. of *logging* ppl adjective of LOG *verb*[2].]
(Designating, in *logan stone*) a poised heavy stone which rocks at a touch.

loganberry /ˈləʊg(ə)nb(ə)ri/ *noun*. L19.
[ORIGIN from J. H. *Logan* (1841–1928), US horticulturist + BERRY *noun*[1].]
A soft fruit resembling a blackberry but longer and reddish; the plant bearing this fruit, *Rubus loganobaccus*, apparently resulting from a cross between the Pacific dewberry, *Rubus ursinus*, and an American variety of raspberry. Cf. TAYBERRY, TUMMELBERRY, VEITCHBERRY.

logaoedic /lɒgəˈiːdɪk/ *adjective & noun*. M19.
[ORIGIN Late Latin *logaoedicus* from Greek *logaoidikos*, from *logos* saying, speech (see LOGOS) + *aoidē* song: see -IC.]
PROSODY. ▸**A** *adjective*. Designating any of various metres in which dactyls are combined with trochees. M19.
▸ **B** *noun*. A logaoedic verse. Usu. in *pl.* M19.

logarithm /ˈlɒgərɪð(ə)m, -rɪθ-/ *noun*. E17.
[ORIGIN mod. Latin *logarithmus*, from Greek *logos* relation, ratio (see LOGOS) + *arithmos* number.]
MATH. The power to which a fixed number or base must be raised in order to produce any given number; any of a series of such exponents tabulated as a means of simplifying computation by making it possible to replace multiplication and division of numbers by addition and subtraction of their corresponding exponents; *spec.* (more fully *common logarithm*) a logarithm to the base 10.
Napierian logarithm, **natural logarithm** a logarithm to the base *e* (2.71828 . . .).
■ **logaˈrithmal** *adjective* (*rare*) = LOGARITHMIC M17. †**logarithmetical** *adjective* = LOGARITHMIC E17–M19.

logarithmic /lɒgəˈrɪðmɪk/ *adjective*. L17.
[ORIGIN from LOGARITHM + -IC.]
MATH. Of or pertaining to logarithms; involving or employing logarithms; expressed by or as a logarithm; exponential.
logarithmic amplifier: that produces an output in logarithmic proportion to the input. **logarithmic cosine** the logarithm of a cosine. **logarithmic curve**: which forms a straight line when plotted against a logarithmic scale; an exponential curve. *logarithmic decrement*: see DECREMENT 3c. **logarithmic scale**: along which distances are proportional to the logarithms of the marked indices. **logarithmic sine** the logarithm of a sine. **logarithmic spiral** = *EQUIANGULAR spiral*. **logarithmic tangent** the logarithm of a tangent.
■ **logarithmical** *adjective* M17. **logarithmically** *adverb* by the use of logarithms; in logarithmic proportions: M18.

L

logatom /ˈlɒgətəm/ *noun*. M20.
[ORIGIN Arbitrary.]
TELEPHONY. A meaningless syllable formed usu. from initial and final consonants and a vowel, for use in testing telephone systems.

logbook /ˈlɒgbʊk/ *noun*. L17.
[ORIGIN from LOG *noun*[1] + BOOK *noun*.]
1 *NAUTICAL*. A book containing a detailed daily record of a ship's voyage (including the rate of progress as indicated by the log); *AERONAUTICS* a book in which particulars of aircraft flights, flying hours, etc., are recorded; *gen.* any book containing a detailed record. L17.
2 In the UK, a document (now officially called the *vehicle registration document*) recording the registration details of a motor vehicle. M20.

loge /lɔːʒ (*pl. same*), ləʊʒ/ *noun*. M18.
[ORIGIN French: see LODGE *noun*.]
1 a A booth, a stall. M18. ▸**b** A concierge's lodge. M20.
2 A box in a theatre, opera house, etc. M18.

-loger /lədʒə/ *suffix*.
[ORIGIN from (the same root as) -LOGY: see -ER[1].]
Forming nouns with the sense 'a person skilled in a specified branch of knowledge', as *astrologer*, *campanologer*, etc.; = -LOGIST.

loggat /ˈlɒgət/ *noun*. *obsolete* exc. *hist.* Also **logget**. M16.
[ORIGIN App. from LOG *noun*[1].]
1 A game in which thick sticks were thrown as close as possible to a mark (usu. in *pl.*); a missile used in this game. M16.
†**2** A pole, a heavy stake. E–M17.

logger /ˈlɒgə/ *noun*[1]. M18.
[ORIGIN from LOG *verb*[1] + -ER[1].]
1 A person who fells timber or cuts timber into logs; a lumberjack. *N. Amer.* M18.
2 More fully *data-logger*. An instrument for making a (continuous or intermittent) recording of the successive values of a number of different physical quantities. M20.

logger /ˈlɒgə/ *noun*[2]. *dial.* L18.
[ORIGIN Symbolic, from LOG *noun*[1]. Prob. earlier as 1st elem. of LOGGERHEAD.]
1 A block of wood for hobbling a horse. L18.
2 Lumpy matter. L19.

logger /ˈlɒgə/ *adjective*. *obsolete* exc. *dial.* L17.
[ORIGIN App. back-form. from LOGGERHEAD.]
Thick, heavy, stupid.

loggerhead /ˈlɒgəhɛd/ *noun*. L16.
[ORIGIN Prob. from LOGGER *noun*[2] + HEAD *noun*.]
1 A stupid person. *arch.* L16.
2 A head out of proportion to the body; a large or thick head. *colloq.* L16.

3 a In full ***loggerhead turtle***. A large-headed sea turtle, *Caretta caretta*, of warm seas worldwide. **M17.** ▸**b** In full ***loggerhead kingbird***. A W. Indian kingbird, *Tyrannus caudifasciatus*. **M17.** ▸**c** Any of various large-headed fishes, such as the bullhead. *dial.* **L17.** ▸**d** In full ***loggerhead shrike***. A shrike, *Lanius ludovicianus*, of the southern US and Mexico. **E19.** ▸**e** Any of various large moths. *dial.* **M19.**
4 An iron instrument with a long handle and a ball at the end heated for melting pitch etc. **L17.**
5 In *pl.* (treated as *sing.*). Knapweed. *dial.* **E19.**
6 A rounded wooden upright near the stern of a whaling boat to which a turn of the line may be caught. **M19.**
– PHRASES: **at loggerheads** disagreeing or disputing (*with*).
▪ **loggerheaded** *adjective* (**a**) stupid; (**b**) (esp. of an animal) having a large head: **L16.**

logget *noun* var. of LOGGAT.

loggia /ˈləʊdʒə, ˈlɒ-, -dʒɪə/ *noun*. **M18.**
[ORIGIN Italian = LODGE *noun*.]
1 A gallery or arcade having one or both of its sides open to the air. **M18.**
2 An open-sided extension to a house, a veranda. **E20.**

logging /ˈlɒɡɪŋ/ *noun*. **E18.**
[ORIGIN from LOG *verb*[1] + -ING[1].]
1 The action of felling timber or hewing timber into logs. Also, a quantity of timber felled. **E18.**
2 = LOGROLLING 1. **E19.**
3 The process of taking and recording information about something. **M20.**

loggy /ˈlɒɡi/ *adjective*. **E17.**
[ORIGIN from LOG *noun*[1] + -Y[1].]
†**1** Of a crop: of strong growth, rank. **E–M17.**
2 Heavy; sluggish in movement. **M19.**
3 Having many logs. **M19.**
▪ **logginess** *noun* a state of heaviness or sluggishness **E20.**

loghtan /ˈlɒxt(ə)n/ *noun*. **E18.**
[ORIGIN Uncertain: perh. from Old Manx *laughten* brown.]
In full ***Manx loghtan***. A four-horned breed of sheep with red-brown wool, native to the Isle of Man; a sheep of this breed.

logia *noun* pl. of LOGION.

logic /ˈlɒdʒɪk/ *noun*. **LME.**
[ORIGIN Old French & mod. French *logique* from late Latin *logica* from Greek *logikē* (*tekhnē* art) of reason, from *logos* reasoning, discourse: see LOGOS, -IC.]
1 *sing.* & (now *arch. rare*) in *pl.* (treated as *sing.* or *pl.*). The branch of philosophy that deals with forms of reasoning and thinking, esp. inference and scientific method. Also, the systematic use of symbolic techniques and mathematical methods to determine the forms of valid deductive argument. **LME.** ▸**b** In Hegelian philosophy, the fundamental science of thought and its categories (including metaphysics or ontology). **M19.**

J. S. MILL Logic is not the science of Belief, but .. of Proof, or Evidence.

2 a A system or scheme of logic. Also, an instance of the application of science or the art of reasoning to some particular branch of knowledge or investigation. **LME.** ▸**b** The inferential procedures or structure *of* some field of inquiry. **M19.**

a R. ADAMSON The metaphysical logic of Hegel, the empirical logic of Mill, the formal logic of Kant. **b** R. G. COLLINGWOOD As mathematics is the logic of physics, so law is the logic of politics.

a ***mathematical logic***: see MATHEMATICAL *adjective*. ***modal logic***: see MODAL *adjective* 1. ***symbolic logic***: see SYMBOLIC *adjective*.

3 a Logical argumentation; a chain of reasoning; the correct or incorrect use of reasoning. Also, ability in reasoning. **LME.** ▸**b** A means of convincing someone or proving something; the inexorable force or compulsion *of* a thing. Also, the necessary consequence *of* an argument, a decision, etc. **L17.**

a LD MACAULAY We should be sorry to stake our faith in a higher Power on Mr. Robert Montgomery's logic. E. V. NEALE Sir William Hamilton argues with overpowering learning and logic. **b** J. EADIE The logic of their facts was irresistible.

a ***chop logic***: see CHOP *verb*[2]

4 COMPUTING & ELECTRONICS. The system or principles underlying the representation of logical operations and two-valued variables by physical signals, esp. as in a computer; the (esp. conceptual) forms and interconnections of logic elements in a computer etc.; logical operations collectively, as performed by computers etc. **M20.**
– COMB.: **logic circuit** a circuit for performing logical operations, consisting of one or more logic elements; **logic element** a device (usu. electronic) for performing a logical operation, in which the past or present values of one or more inputs determine the values of one or more outputs according to a simple scheme usu. involving only two possible values for the signals; ***logic gate***: see GATE *noun*[1] 11b; **logic-tight** *adjective* impervious to logic or reason.

-logic /ˈlɒdʒɪk/ *suffix*.
[ORIGIN from or after Greek *-logikos*, from adjectives & nouns in *-logos*, *-logia* -LOGY: see -IC.]
Forming adjectives corresp. esp. to nouns in ***-logy***, with the sense 'pertaining to or derived from a particular branch of knowledge or experience'; = -LOGICAL.

logical /ˈlɒdʒɪk(ə)l/ *adjective & noun*. **LME.**
[ORIGIN medieval Latin *logicalis*, from late Latin *logica* LOGIC: see -ICAL.]
▸ **A** *adjective*. **1** Of or pertaining to logic or formal argument. **LME.** ▸**b** COMPUTING & ELECTRONICS. Of or pertaining to the logic of computers and similar equipment or the conceptual arrangement of software or data; designed to carry out processes which can be expressed in terms of symbolic logic. **M20.**
2 Not contravening the principles of logic; correctly reasoned. **L16.**
3 Of a person: capable of reasoning correctly. **M17.**

Edinburgh Review The strong and logical-minded Manning.

4 Characterized by reason; rational, reasonable. *rare*. **M17.**
5 That follows as a reasonable inference or natural consequence; deducible or defensible on the ground of consistency; reasonably believed or done. **M19.**

M. M. ATWATER Harold was the logical suspect—plenty of motive, the opportunity, it all checked. G. BROWN It would scarcely seem logical to have a Deputy Leader not in the Government.

– SPECIAL COLLOCATIONS: **logical addition** the formation of a logical sum. ***logical atom***: see ATOM *noun* 7. ***logical atomism***: see ATOMISM 2. **logical empiricism** = ***logical positivism*** below. **logical empiricist** = ***logical positivist*** below. **logical form** the form, as distinct from the content, of a proposition, argument, etc., which can be expressed in logical terms. **logical grammar** the rules of word use in a proposition on which its logical, as distinct from its purely grammatical, sense or meaning is held to depend. **logical implication** implication which is based on the formal and not the material relationship between propositions. **logical multiplication** the formation of a logical product. **logical necessity** the compulsion to believe that of which the opposite is inconceivable. **logical operation** an operation of the kind used in logic (such as conjunction or negation); any analogous (non-arithmetical) operation on numbers, esp. binary numbers, in which each digit of the result depends on only one digit in each operand. ***logical paradox***: see PARADOX *noun* 2c. **logical positivism** a form of positivism regarding all valid philosophical problems as solvable by logical analysis. **logical positivist** an adherent or student of logical positivism. **logical product** the conjunction of two or more propositions; the intersection of two or more sets; (written $p \vee q$, $p \cap q$, $p.q$, pq, p and q). **logical structure** the formal framework of logical rules to which a theory, language, proposition, etc., must conform in order to have truth value. **logical subject** the subject which is implied in a sentence or proposition, or which exists in the deep structure of a sentence. **logical sum** the disjunction of two or more propositions; the union of two or more sets; (written $p \wedge q$, $p \cup q$, p or q, $p + q$). **logical syntax** the system of sentence construction in a proposition on which its logical, as distinct from its purely grammatical sense or meaning, is held to depend. **logical truth** that which is true in logical or formal terms regardless of material meaning. **logical word** a word of the type which gives logical context or form to a proposition but which, by itself, is non-representational and without meaning.
▸ **B** *noun*. In *pl.* The subjects studied in a course of instruction in logic. *obsolete* exc. *hist.* **M16.**
▪ **logiˈcality** *noun* the quality of being logical **M19.** **logicalize** *verb trans.* make logical **M19.** **logically** *adverb* in a logical manner, according to the principles of logic or the laws of sound reasoning; ***logically perfect language***, a language in which the grammatical structure of sentences would be identical with their logical structure: **L16.** **logicalness** *noun* (*rare*) logicality **E18.**

-logical /ˈlɒdʒɪk(ə)l/ *suffix*.
[ORIGIN formed as -LOGIC: see -ICAL.]
Forming adjectives corresp. esp. to nouns in ***-logy***, with the sense 'pertaining to or derived from a particular branch of knowledge or experience', as ***pathological***, ***theological***, etc.
– NOTE: An adjective in *-logical* may exist alongside an adjective in *-logic* formed from the same base, but in such a case the adjective in *-logical* is likely to be more commonly used and to have a wider application (cf. -IC, -ICAL).

logician /ləˈdʒɪʃ(ə)n/ *noun*. **LME.**
[ORIGIN Old French & mod. French *logicien*, formed as LOGIC + -ICIAN.]
1 A writer on logic; a student of logic. **LME.**
mathematical logician etc.
2 A person skilled in reasoning. **L16.**

logicise *verb* var. of LOGICIZE.

logicism /ˈlɒdʒɪsɪz(ə)m/ *noun*. **M20.**
[ORIGIN from LOGIC + -ISM.]
The theory that a set of axioms for mathematics can be deduced from a primitive set of purely logical axioms.

logicist /ˈlɒdʒɪsɪst/ *noun & adjective*. **E20.**
[ORIGIN from LOGIC + -IST.]
▸ **A** *noun*. A (mathematical) logician; an adherent or student of logicism. **E20.**
▸ **B** *attrib.* or as *adjective*. Of or pertaining to logicists or logicism. **M20.**

logicize /ˈlɒdʒɪsʌɪz/ *verb*. Also **-ise**. **M19.**
[ORIGIN from LOGIC + -IZE, after *criticize*.]
1 *verb intrans.* Use logical argument, employ logic. **M19.**
2 *verb trans.* Turn into logic. **M19.**

logico- /ˈlɒdʒɪkəʊ/ *combining form*.
[ORIGIN from LOGIC, LOGIC(AL *adjective*: see -O-.]
Forming adjectives with the sense 'logical and —', as ***logico-mathematical***, ***logico-philosophical***, etc., and occas. nouns with the sense 'of logic, employing logic', as ***logico-analyst***.

logie /ˈləʊɡi/ *noun*. **M19.**
[ORIGIN App. from David *Logie*, the inventor.]
THEATRICAL. An ornament made of zinc, intended to give the effect of jewellery.

logion /ˈlɒɡɪɒn/ *noun*. Pl. **logia** /ˈlɒɡɪə/. **L19.**
[ORIGIN Greek = oracle, from *logos* word (see LOGOS).]
A traditional maxim of a religious teacher or sage; *esp.* in *pl.* (also **L-**), a supposed collection of the sayings of Jesus circulating in the early Church.
▪ **Logian** *adjective* (of a document etc.) containing the Logia of Jesus **E20.**

†**logist** *noun*. **L16–M18.**
[ORIGIN Latin *logista* or Greek *logistēs*, from *logizesthai*: see LOGISTIC *adjective*[1] & *noun*, -IST.]
An expert reckoner or accountant; *spec.* a member of a board of Athenian officials whose function was to examine the accounts of those who had completed a term of office in the magistracy.

-logist /lədʒɪst/ *suffix*.
[ORIGIN from (the same root as) -LOGY: see -IST.]
Forming nouns with the sense 'an expert in or student of the specified branch of knowledge, a person skilled in *—logy*', as ***etymologist***, ***geologist***, ***heresiologist***, ***ideologist***, ***zoologist***, etc.

logistic /ləˈdʒɪstɪk/ *adjective*[1] & *noun*. **E17.**
[ORIGIN Late Latin *logisticus* from Greek *logistikos*, from *logizesthai* reckon, formed as LOGOS: see -ISTIC. Cf. earlier LOGISTICAL *adjective*[1].]
▸ **A** *adjective*. †**1** Of or pertaining to reasoning; logical. **E–M17.**
2 Of or pertaining to reckoning or calculation. *rare*. **E18.**
3 a MATH. Logarithmic, exponential. Now *rare* or *obsolete* exc. in ***logistic curve*** below. **E18.** ▸**b** Of or pertaining to mathematical or symbolic logic. **E20.**
a logistic curve a sigmoidal curve used in population studies, which increases approximately exponentially for small values of the variable and approaches a constant value asymptotically for large values.
▸ **B** *noun*. †**1** = CALCULATOR 1. Only in **M17.**
2 = LOGISTICS *noun*[1]. Now *rare* or *obsolete*. **M17.** ▸**b** Mathematical or symbolic logic. **E20.**
3 MATH. A logistic curve. **E18.**
▪ **logistician** /-ˈstɪʃ(ə)n/ *noun* an expert in or student of mathematical or symbolic logic **M20.**

logistic /ləˈdʒɪstɪk/ *adjective*[2]. **M20.**
[ORIGIN from (the same root as) LOGISTICS *noun*[2].]
Of or pertaining to logistics; = LOGISTICAL *adjective*[2].

logistical /ləˈdʒɪstɪk(ə)l/ *adjective*[1]. **L16.**
[ORIGIN formed as LOGISTIC *adjective*[1]: see -ICAL.]
1 Of or pertaining to calculation. Long *rare*. **L16.**
2 Pertaining to or based on reasoning or disputation. Now *rare*. **M17.**
3 MATH. = LOGISTIC *adjective*[1] 3a. Long *rare* or *obsolete*. **M17.**
4 Of or pertaining to logicism. **M20.**

logistical /ləˈdʒɪstɪk(ə)l/ *adjective*[2]. **M20.**
[ORIGIN from (the same root as) LOGISTIC *adjective*[2]: see -ICAL.]
Of or pertaining to logistics; = LOGISTIC *adjective*[2].

logistically /ləˈdʒɪstɪk(ə)li/ *adverb*[1]. **E20.**
[ORIGIN from LOGISTIC *adjective*[2] or LOGISTICAL *adjective*[2]: see -ICALLY.]
From the point of view of logistics, with regard to logistics.

logistically /ləˈdʒɪstɪk(ə)li/ *adverb*[2]. *rare*. **M20.**
[ORIGIN from LOGISTIC *adjective*[1] or LOGISTICAL *adjective*[1]: see -ICALLY.]
With regard to mathematical or symbolic logic; in the manner of mathematical or symbolic logic.

logistics /ləˈdʒɪstɪks/ *noun*[1]. Now *rare* or *obsolete*. **E18.**
[ORIGIN from LOGISTIC *noun*: see -ICS.]
The art of arithmetical calculation; the elementary processes of calculation.

logistics /ləˈdʒɪstɪks/ *noun*[2] *pl.* **L19.**
[ORIGIN from French *logistique*, from *loger* quarter, LODGE *verb*: see -ICS.]
1 The organization of moving, lodging, and supplying troops and equipment. **L19.** ▸**b** The commercial activity of transporting goods to customers. **L20.**
2 The detailed organization and implementation of a plan or operation. **M20.**

LADY BIRD JOHNSON The vast logistics of deciding who was going to stay where. *Guardian* The logistics of interviewing the six women were tough.

logit /ˈlɒɡɪt/ *noun*. **M20.**
[ORIGIN Contr. of *logarithmic unit*.]
STATISTICS. The natural logarithm of the quotient of a probability and its complement.

– COMB.: **logit analysis** a form of regression analysis which makes use of logits.

logjam /ˈlɒɡdʒam/ *noun*. L19.
[ORIGIN from LOG *noun*[1] + JAM *noun*[4].]
1 A crowded mass of logs in a river; a place where logs become jammed. L19.
2 *fig.* An obstruction, a blockage; a delay; a deadlock. L19.

Listener Nothing is likely to break the Arab-Israeli log-jam until the Arabs achieve . . unity.

logo /ˈlɒɡəʊ, ˈləʊɡəʊ/ *noun*. Pl. **-os**. M20.
[ORIGIN Abbreviation of LOGOGRAM, LOGOTYPE.]
A symbol or device designed to represent an object, concept, or attitude; *esp.* an emblematic design adopted by an organization to identify its products.

S. KNIGHT In Italy the logo of the Brotherhood is the figure of a Black Friar. *Marketing Week* LWT's logo, previously orange, turquoise and white, now a crisp red, white and blue.

■ **logoed** *adjective* decorated with or identified by a logo L20.

logocentric /lɒɡə(ʊ)ˈsɛntrɪk/ *adjective*. M20.
[ORIGIN from Greek *logos* word, reason (see LOGOS) + -CENTRIC.]
1 Centred on reason. M20.
2 Centred on language; regarding the word as a fundamental expression of reality. L20.
■ **logocentrism** *noun* concentration on language; the belief that the word is a fundamental expression of reality: L20.

logodaedalist /lɒɡəˈdiːd(ə)lɪst/ *noun*. *rare*. E18.
[ORIGIN from mod. Latin *logodaedalus* from Greek *logodaidalos*, from *logos* word (see LOGOS) + *daidalos* skilful: see -IST.]
A person skilled in the use of words.
■ **logodaedaly** *noun* skill in using words E18.

logodiarrhoea /ˌlɒɡədʌɪəˈrɪə/ *noun*. *rare*. E18.
[ORIGIN from Greek *logos* word (see LOGOS) + DIARRHOEA. Cf. LOGORRHOEA.]
= ***verbal diarrhoea*** s.v. VERBAL *adjective*.
■ Earlier †**logodiarrhe** *noun* [cf. French *logodiarrhée*]: only in E17.

logogram /ˈlɒɡəɡram/ *noun*. E19.
[ORIGIN from Greek *logos* word (see LOGOS) + -GRAM.]
▸ **I 1** = LOGOGRIPH. *rare*. E19.
▸ **II 2** A sign, symbol, or character representing a word, as in shorthand or some ancient writing systems. Also, such a sign etc. used to represent part of a word. M19.
3 *gen.* A symbol or device designed to represent in simple graphic form an object, concept, or attitude; an organization's emblem or badge, a logotype. M20.

logograph /ˈlɒɡəɡrɑːf/ *noun*. L18.
[ORIGIN from Greek *logos* word (see LOGOS) + -GRAPH.]
†**1** = LOGOGRIPH. Only in L18.
2 = LOGOGRAPHER 2. *rare*. M19.
3 = LOGOGRAM 2. L19.
4 = LOGOTYPE 1. L19.
5 An instrument for giving a graphic representation of speech sounds. L19.

logographer /ləˈɡɒɡrəfə/ *noun*. M17.
[ORIGIN from late Latin *logographus* accountant from Greek *logographos* prose-writer, from *logos* word: see LOGOS, -GRAPHER.]
†**1** A lawyer's clerk; an accountant. M17–M18.
2 An early writer of (esp. Greek) traditional history in prose. M19.
3 A professional speech-writer in ancient Greece. M19.

logography /ləˈɡɒɡrəfi/ *noun*. L18.
[ORIGIN from Greek *logos* word (see LOGOS) + -GRAPHY.]
1 PRINTING. A method of composition involving the arrangement and composition of groups of letters or complete words as opp. to single letters. L18.
2 A method of longhand reporting employing several reporters each taking down a few words in succession. M19.
■ **logoˈgraphic** *adjective* (**a**) of or pertaining to logography; (**b**) consisting of characters or signs, each of which singly represents a group of characters, which may constitute a complete word: L18. **logoˈgraphical** *adjective* (*rare*) logographic E19. **logoˈgraphically** *adverb* L18.

logogriph /ˈlɒɡəɡrɪf/ *noun*. L16.
[ORIGIN French *logogriphe*, from Greek *logos* word (see LOGOS) + *griphos* fishing basket, riddle.]
A kind of enigma in which a certain word and other words that can be formed out of all or any of its letters are to be guessed from synonyms of them introduced into a set of verses. Also, an anagram, a puzzle involving anagrams.
■ **logoˈgriphic** *adjective* (*rare*) of or pertaining to logogriphs, of the nature of a logogriph E19.

logolatry /ləˈɡɒlətri/ *noun*. E19.
[ORIGIN from Greek *logos* word (see LOGOS) + -LATRY.]
Excessive admiration for words; unreasonable regard for words or for verbal truth.

logology /ləˈɡɒlədʒi/ *noun*. E18.
[ORIGIN from Greek *logos* word (see LOGOS) + -LOGY.]
†**1** The doctrine of the Logos. *rare*. E–M18.
2 The branch of knowledge that deals with words. E19.

logomachy /ləˈɡɒməki/ *noun*. M16.
[ORIGIN Greek *logomakhia*, from *logos* word (see LOGOS) + -MACHY.]
Contention about words; controversy turning on merely verbal points; an instance of this.

■ **logomachist** *noun* a person given to logomachy, a person who disputes about verbal subtleties E19.

logomaniac /lɒɡə(ʊ)ˈmeɪnɪak/ *noun*. L19.
[ORIGIN from Greek *logos* (see LOGOS) word + -MANIAC.]
A person who is obsessively interested in words.

logopaedics /lɒɡəˈpiːdɪks/ *noun*. Also ***-ped-**. E20.
[ORIGIN from Greek *logos* word (see LOGOS), after ORTHOPAEDICS.]
The branch of medicine that deals with speech disabilities and their treatment; speech therapy.

logophile /ˈlɒɡəfɪl, -fʌɪl/ *noun*. M20.
[ORIGIN from Greek *logos* word (see LOGOS) + -PHILE.]
A lover of words.

logophobia /lɒɡəˈfəʊbɪə/ *noun*. E20.
[ORIGIN from Greek *logos* word (see LOGOS) + -PHOBIA.]
Irrational fear or distrust of words.

logorrhoea /lɒɡəˈrɪə/ *noun*. Also ***-rrhea**. E20.
[ORIGIN from Greek *logos* word (see LOGOS) + -RRHOEA, prob. after DIARRHOEA.]
Abnormally rapid and voluble speech, as a symptom of mental illness; *gen.* an excessive flow of words, prolixity; = ***verbal diarrhoea*** s.v. VERBAL *adjective*.
■ **logorrhoeic** *adjective* of, pertaining to, or affected with logorrhoea M20.

Logos /ˈlɒɡɒs/ *noun*. L16.
[ORIGIN Greek = account, relation, ratio, reason(ing), argument, discourse, saying, speech, word, rel. to *legein* choose, collect, gather, say, used in a mystic sense by Hellenistic and Neoplatonist philosophers and by St John.]
1 CHRISTIAN THEOLOGY. The Word of God, the second person of the Trinity. L16.
2 A pervading cosmic idea or spirit of creativity or rationality. M17.

logothete /ˈlɒɡəθiːt/ *noun*. L18.
[ORIGIN medieval Latin *logotheta* or its source Greek *logothetēs* auditor, from *logos* account (see LOGOS).]
hist. Any of various functionaries under the Byzantine emperors; *esp.* (also in the Norman kingdom of Sicily) a high official with the function of a chancellor.

logotype /ˈlɒɡə(ʊ)tʌɪp/ *noun*. E19.
[ORIGIN from Greek *logos* word (see LOGOS) + TYPE *noun*.]
1 PRINTING. A type containing a word, or two or more letters, cast in one piece. E19.
2 An emblem or device used as the badge of an organization in display material. M20.
3 PRINTING. A single piece of type that prints such an emblem. M20.

logroll /ˈlɒɡrəʊl/ *verb*. Chiefly *US*. M19.
[ORIGIN Back-form. from LOGROLLING.]
1 *verb trans.* Procure the passing of (a bill) by logrolling. M19.
2 *verb intrans.* Practise logrolling. M19.

logroller /ˈlɒɡrəʊlə/ *noun*. Chiefly *N. Amer.* M19.
[ORIGIN from LOG *noun*[1] + ROLLER *noun*[1].]
1 A person who practises logrolling. M19.
2 A device for transporting logs in a sawmill. L19.

logrolling /ˈlɒɡrəʊlɪŋ/ *noun*. Chiefly *US*. E19.
[ORIGIN from LOG *noun*[1] + ROLLING *noun*, from the expression *You roll my log and I'll roll yours*.]
1 The practice of exchanging favours, esp. (**a**) in politics, of exchanging votes to mutual benefit, (**b**) of providing reciprocally favourable reviews, notices, etc., in literary publications. *colloq.* E19.
2 a The action of rolling logs to a required spot; the action of causing a floating log to rotate by treading, esp. as a competitive sport. M19. ▸**b** A meeting for cooperation in rolling logs for transportation etc. M19.

-logue /lɒɡ/ *suffix*. Also ***-log**.
[ORIGIN from or after French from Greek *-logos*, *-logon* speaking or treating of, from *logos*: see LOGOS.]
1 Forming nouns with the senses 'talk, kind of discourse', as ***dialogue***, ***monologue***, etc., and (occas.) 'compilation', as ***catalogue*** etc.
2 = -LOGIST, as ***ideologue***, ***Sinologue***, etc.

logwood /ˈlɒɡwʊd/ *noun*. L16.
[ORIGIN from LOG *noun*[1] + WOOD *noun*[1].]
1 (The heartwood of) a Central American and W. Indian leguminous tree, *Haematoxylum campechianum*. L16.
2 An extract of this wood, used for colouring and dyeing. L19.

logy /ˈləʊɡi/ *adjective*. *N. Amer.* M19.
[ORIGIN Uncertain: cf. Dutch *log* heavy, dull.]
Dull and heavy in motion or thought.

-logy /lədʒi/ *suffix*. E19.
[ORIGIN French *-logie* or medieval Latin *-logia* from Greek, from *logos*: see LOGOS, -Y[3].]
Forming nouns with the senses 'discourse' as ***tetralogy***, ***trilogy***, etc.; 'a characteristic of speech or language', as ***battology***, ***cacology***, ***dittology***, ***eulogy***, ***tautology***, etc.; 'a subject of study or interest, a branch of knowledge' (usu. with -O-: see -OLOGY), as ***archaeology***, ***geology***, ***sociology***, ***theology***, ***zoology***, etc.

Lohan /ˈləʊhɑːn/ *noun*. M19.
[ORIGIN Chinese *luóhàn* (Wade–Giles *Lo-han*).]
= ARHAT.

†**lohoch** *noun*. Pl. **-(e)s**. Also **looch**. M16–M19.
[ORIGIN medieval Latin *lohoc* from Arabic *laʿūq* electuary, from *laʿiqa* lick.]
MEDICINE. A linctus.

LOI *abbreviation*.
Lunar orbit insertion.

loiasis /ləʊˈʌɪəsɪs/ *noun*. E20.
[ORIGIN from LOA *noun*[1] + -IASIS.]
Infection with, or a disease caused by, loas.

loi-cadre /lwakadr/ *noun*. Pl. ***lois-cadres*** (pronounced same). M20.
[ORIGIN French.]
FRENCH POLITICS. A general outline law, the principles of which can be applied by the government in succeeding parallel situations.

loid /lɔɪd/ *noun & verb*. *criminals' slang*. Also **'loid**. M20.
[ORIGIN Abbreviation of CELLULOID *noun*.]
▸ **A** *noun*. A celluloid strip used by thieves to force open a spring lock. M20.
▸ **B** *verb trans.* Break open (a lock) by this method. M20.

loin /lɔɪn/ *noun*. ME.
[ORIGIN Old French *loigne* eastern var. of *longe* (mod. = loin of veal) from Proto-Romance, from Latin *lumbus* loin.]
sing. & (usu.) in *pl.* The part or parts of a human being or quadruped situated on both sides of the vertebral column, between the ribs and the pelvis (*biblical & arch.* as the part of the body that should be covered by clothing or as the seat of physical strength and of reproductive power). Also, a joint of meat which includes the vertebrae of the loins.

DAY LEWIS His satisfaction at inheriting blood which had not passed through any huckster's loin. M. AMIS His loins were rich in sons.

gird one's loins, ***gird up one's loins***: see GIRD *verb*[1].
– COMB.: **loincloth** a cloth worn round the loins, esp. as the sole garment.
■ **loined** *adjective* having loins (of a specified kind) M19.

loir /lɔɪə, *foreign* lwaːr (*pl. same*)/ *noun*. Now *rare* or *obsolete*. L18.
[ORIGIN Old French & mod. French from popular Latin var. of Latin *glir-*, *glis* dormouse.]
The fat or edible dormouse, *Glis glis*.

Loire /lwɑː/ *noun*. M20.
[ORIGIN The longest river in France.]
In full ***Loire wine***. A wine from grapes grown in the Loire valley.

lois-cadres *noun pl.* of LOI-CADRE.

loiter /ˈlɔɪtə/ *verb*. LME.
[ORIGIN Perh. from Middle Dutch *loteren* wag about, Dutch *leuteren* shake, totter, dawdle, from base repr. also by Middle Dutch *lutsen* wag about. Cf. German *lottern*.]
1 *verb intrans.* Waste time in idleness. Now *spec.* linger indolently on the way when on an errand, journey, etc.; linger idly about a place; dawdle. LME. ▸**b** Travel or proceed indolently and with frequent pauses. Foll. by adverb or adverbial phr. E18.

J. LE CARRÉ People . . loiter outside the house with nothing to do. **b** O. WISTER I loitered here and there, . . watching the cowboys.

2 *verb trans.* Allow (time etc.) to pass idly; waste carelessly or on trifles. Now only foll. by *away*, (occas.) *out*. M16.

OED We loitered away the rest of the day.

loiter with intent (to commit a felony).
■ **loiterer** *noun* M16. **loiteringly** *adverb* in a loitering manner M16.

Lokal /loˈkal/ *noun*. E20.
[ORIGIN German.]
In Germany or Austria: a local bar or nightclub.

lokanta /loˈkanta, lə(ʊ)ˈkantə/ *noun*. M20.
[ORIGIN Turkish from Italian *locanda*.]
In Turkey: a restaurant.

lokey *noun* var. of LOCIE.

lokoum *noun* var. of LOKUM.

Lok Sabha /ləʊk səˈbɑː/ *noun*. M20.
[ORIGIN from Sanskrit *lok* people + *sabhā* SABHA.]
The lower house of the Indian parliament. Cf. RAJYA SABHA.

lokshen /ˈlɒkʃ(ə)n/ *noun pl.* L19.
[ORIGIN Yiddish, pl. of *loksh* noodle.]
Noodles (in Jewish cookery).

lokum /lɒˈkuːm/ *noun*. Also ***-koum***, ***-c-***, ***la-*** /lə-/. E20.
[ORIGIN Abbreviation of Turkish *RAHAT lokum*.]
Turkish delight.

loligo /ləˈlʌɪɡəʊ/ *noun*. Pl. **-os**. E17.
[ORIGIN mod. Latin from Latin *lolligo*.]
A squid, *esp.* one of the genus *Loligo*. Now chiefly as mod. Latin genus name.

Lolita /ləˈliːtə/ *noun*. M20.
[ORIGIN The main character in a novel (1958) of the same name by Vladimir Nabokov (1899–1977).]
A sexually precocious schoolgirl.

loll /lɒl/ *noun*. **L16**.
[**ORIGIN** from the verb.]
1 A person who lolls. Formerly also, a thing that lolls, e.g. a tongue. **L16**.
2 The action or posture of lolling. **E18**.
3 A pet; a spoilt child. *dial.* **E18**.

loll /lɒl/ *verb*. **LME**.
[**ORIGIN** Symbolic: cf. **LILL** *verb*.]
1 *verb intrans.* Hang down loosely, droop, dangle, (also foll. by *down*). Now usu., lean idly, recline or rest in a relaxed attitude against something. **LME**.

V. SACKVILLE-WEST The housekeeper never lolled. She sat . . upright. P. H. JOHNSON The tired waiters lolled against the wall. G. SWIFT The boys are lolling about, reading comics. D. M. THOMAS Kolya . . was asleep, his head lolling on her shoulder.

2 *verb trans.* Let droop or dangle. Later *spec.* allow to rest idly or in a relaxed attitude. Formerly also foll. by *up*: hang. Now *rare*. **LME**.
3 a *verb trans.* Stick out (the tongue) in a pendulous manner. Also foll. by *out*. **E17**. ▸**b** *verb intrans.* Of the tongue: stick out pendulously, hang out. Usu. foll. by *out*. **L17**.

a D. WELCH The boy . . lolled out his tongue. **b** DENNIS POTTER Her tongue lolling out between her teeth.

■ **loller** *noun* **LME**. **lolling** *adjective* (**a**) that lolls; (**b**) HERALDRY (of a falcon or hawk) with wings raised and hanging down: **M16**. **lollingly** *adverb* **M19**.

lollapaloosa, **lollapalooza**, **lollapaloozer** *nouns* vars. of **LALLAPALOOSA**.

Lollard /ˈlɒləd/ *noun*. **LME**.
[**ORIGIN** Middle Dutch *lollaerd* lit. 'mumbler, mutterer', from *lollen* mumble: see **-ARD**.]
1 *hist.* Any of the heretics, from the 14th cent. to the Reformation, who were either followers of John Wyclif or held opinions similar to his, esp. on the necessity for the Church to aid people to live a life of evangelical poverty and imitate Jesus. **LME**.
2 A person who lolls; an idler. *rare*. **M17**.

E. B. BROWNING Learn to be a *Lollard* like me, and establish yourself on a sofa.

■ **Lollardism** *noun* the tenets and practice of the Lollards **E19**. **Lollardry** *noun* = **LOLLARDISM** **LME**. **Lollardy** *noun* = **LOLLARDISM** **LME**. **Lollardy** *adjective* (*rare*) characteristic of the Lollards **E16**.

löllingite /ˈlɔːlɪŋʌɪt/ *noun*. Also **loe-**. **M19**.
[**ORIGIN** from *Lölling*, Austria + **-ITE**[1].]
MINERALOGY. An arsenide of iron occurring as brilliant white bipyramidal crystals of the orthorhombic system.

lollipop /ˈlɒlɪpɒp/ *noun*. **L18**.
[**ORIGIN** Perh. from **LOLLY** *noun*[3] (though recorded earlier) + **POP** *noun*[1].]
1 Orig. (*dial.*), a sweet confection of a particular kind; in *pl.*, sweets in general. Now *spec.* a large sweet (esp. a boiled sweet), water ice, or similar confection, on a stick. **L18**.
2 *fig.* A showy or non-serious composition or performance. **M19**.

Gramophone The choice of music is admirable (no lush lollipops).

3 A circular sign used by a lollipop man etc. (see below). *colloq.* **M20**.
– COMB.: **lollipop lady**, **lollipop man**, **lollipop woman** *colloq.* an official using a circular sign on a stick to stop traffic so that children may cross a road, esp. near a school.

lollop /ˈlɒləp/ *verb & noun*. *colloq.* **M18**.
[**ORIGIN** Prob. from **LOLL** *verb*, by assoc. with **TROLLOP**.]
▸ **A** *verb intrans.* Lounge, sprawl; move or proceed in a lounging or ungainly way; bob or heave up and down; bound clumsily. **M18**.

B. PYM His old sealyham, who lolloped along like a little rocking-horse. M. BRADBURY The sea lolloped against the side of the ship. B. BAINBRIDGE I'm supposed to be her companion. Why else should I be lolloping about the Soviet Union?

▸ **B** *noun*. **1** The action or an act of lolloping. **M19**.
2 A trifling lazy person. **L19**.
■ **lollopy** *adjective* disposed to lollop, characterized by lolloping **M19**.

lollo rosso /ˌlɒləʊ ˈrɒsəʊ/ *noun*. **L20**.
[**ORIGIN** Italian, from *lòllo* (perh. from the name of the film actress Gina *Lollobrigida* (b. 1927)) + *rosso* red.]
A variety of lettuce having leaves with a ruffled red edge.

lolly /ˈlɒli/ *noun*[1]. *Canad. rare*. **L18**.
[**ORIGIN** Abbreviation of **LOBLOLLY**.]
Soft ice formed in turbulent water along a shore etc.; = **FRAZIL**. Also *lolly ice*.

lolly /ˈlɒli/ *noun*[2]. **M19**.
[**ORIGIN** Abbreviation of **LOLLIPOP**.]
1 A sweet. Exc. *Austral. & NZ* now *spec.* a lollipop or ice lolly. **M19**.
ice lolly, **iced lolly** a water ice or ice cream on a small stick.
2 An easy catch in cricket. *colloq.* **E20**.
3 Money. *colloq.* **M20**.

N. COWARD I hope to get some lolly from the serialization rights.

lolly /ˈlɒli/ *noun*[3]. *dial.* **L19**.
[**ORIGIN** Uncertain: perh. from use in pronunc. of *l* or from **LOLL** *verb*.]
The tongue.
– NOTE: Prob. much earlier and perh. the 1st elem. of **LOLLIPOP**.

lollygag /ˈlɒlɪgag/ *noun & verb*. *N. Amer. slang*. Also **lally-** /ˈlalɪ-/. **M19**.
[**ORIGIN** Unknown.]
▸ **A** *noun*. Foolishness, nonsense. **M19**.

E. L. WHEELER I kin get lots o' jobs if I'd take my pay in friendship an' all sech lollygag.

▸ **B** *verb intrans.* Infl. **-gg-**. Fool around; spend time aimlessly, idle; dawdle. Also, kiss and cuddle amorously, canoodle. **M19**.

Lolo /ˈləʊləʊ/ *noun & adjective*. **M18**.
[**ORIGIN** Lolo.]
▸ **A** *noun*. Pl. **-os**, same. A member of an aboriginal people of SW China; the Tibeto-Burman language of this people. Also called *Yi*. **M18**.
▸ **B** *attrib.* or as *adjective*. Of or pertaining to the Lolo or their language. **E20**.

loma /ˈləʊmə/ *noun*[1]. *US*. **M19**.
[**ORIGIN** Spanish from *lomo* back, loin, ridge.]
In the south-western US, a broad-topped hill or ridge.

Loma /ˈləʊmə/ *noun*[2] *& adjective*. **M20**.
[**ORIGIN** Loma.]
▸ **A** *noun*. Pl. **-s**, same. A member of a people inhabiting the border regions of Liberia, Sierra Leone, and Guinea; the Mande language of this people. **M20**.
▸ **B** *attrib.* or as *adjective*. Of or pertaining to the Loma or their language. **M20**.

Lombard /ˈlɒmbəd, -bɑːd/ *noun*[1] *& adjective*. **ME**.
[**ORIGIN** Middle Dutch, Middle Low German *lombaerd* or French *lombard* from Italian *lombardo* (medieval Latin *lombardus*) repr. late Latin *Langobardus*, *Longo-*, Latin *langobardi* (Tacitus) from Germanic, from base of **LONG** *adjective*[1] + ethnic name *Bardi*. Cf. **LANGOBARD**, **LONGOBARD**. See also **LUMBER** *noun*[2].]
▸ **A** *noun*. **1** *hist.* A member of a Germanic people from the lower Elbe who invaded Italy in the 6th cent. and founded a kingdom named Lombardy after them. **ME**.
2 A native or inhabitant of the region of Lombardy in north central Italy. Formerly *spec.* one engaged in banking, money-changing, or pawnbroking; hence any banker, money-changer, or pawnbroker. **LME**.
3 The Italian dialect of modern Lombardy. **L16**.
†**4** A bank, a money-changer's or moneylender's office; a pawnshop. Cf. **LUMBER** *noun*[2]. **E17–L18**.
▸ **B** *adjective*. Of or pertaining to the Lombards or Lombardy; Lombardic. **ME**.
– SPECIAL COLLOCATIONS & COMB.: **Lombard band** ARCHITECTURE a shallow pilaster dividing a wall into bays. **Lombard Street** [a street in London, orig. occupied by Lombard bankers and still containing many of the principal London banks] the money market, financiers as a body; ***Lombard Street to a China orange***, great wealth against one ordinary object, virtual certainty.
■ **Lomˈbardian** *adjective* = **LOMBARDIC** *adjective* **M19**. **Lombardism** *noun* a Lombardic idiom **E19**. **Lomˈbardo-** *combining form* [after Italian *Lombardo-Veneto*] Lombardic and —: **L19**.

lombard /ˈlɒmbəd/ *noun*[2]. **M19**.
[**ORIGIN** Spanish †*lombarda*.]
hist. A light cannon used in Spain in the 16th cent.

Lombardic /lɒmˈbɑːdɪk/ *adjective*. **L17**.
[**ORIGIN** from **LOMBARD** *noun*[1] + **-IC**.]
Of or pertaining to Lombardy or the Lombards; *spec.* designating or pertaining to the style of architecture which prevailed in northern Italy from the 7th to the 13th cent., a style of handwriting common in Italian manuscripts during the same period, and the school of painters, represented esp. by Leonardo da Vinci, Mantegna, and Luini, which flourished at Milan and other Lombard cities during the 15th and 16th cents.

Lombardy poplar /ˈlɒmbədi ˈpɒplə/ *noun phr.* **M18**.
[**ORIGIN** A region of north central Italy: see **LOMBARD** *noun*[1].]
A fastigiate variety of the black poplar, *Populus nigra* var. *italica*, widely planted in Europe and N. America, and orig. introduced to lowland Britain from Italy.

Lombrosian /lɒmˈbrəʊzɪən/ *noun & adjective*. **E20**.
[**ORIGIN** from *Lombroso* (see below) + **-IAN**.]
▸ **A** *noun*. An adherent or student of the Italian physician and criminologist Cesare Lombroso (1836–1909) and his theories of the physiology, psychology, and treatment of criminals. **E20**.
▸ **B** *adjective*. Of or pertaining to Lombroso or his theories. **M20**.

loment /ˈləʊmɛnt/ *noun*. **LME**.
[**ORIGIN** Latin *lomentum* bean-meal (orig. a cosmetic made of bean-meal), from *lavare* to wash.]
†**1** Bean-meal. Only in **LME**.
2 BOTANY. = **LOMENTUM**. **E19**.

lomentum /lə(ʊ)ˈmɛntəm/ *noun*. Pl. ***-ta*** /-tə/. **M19**.
[**ORIGIN** Latin: see **LOMENT**.]
BOTANY. The pod of some leguminous plants, breaking up when mature into sections each containing one seed.

lomi-lomi /ləʊmɪˈləʊmi/ *noun*. **M19**.
[**ORIGIN** Hawaiian, lit. 'masseur, masseuse', redupl. of *lomi* massage, from *lomi* rub with the hand.]
A type of massage practised among the Hawaiians.

London /ˈlʌndən/ *noun*. **ME**.
[**ORIGIN** The capital of England, and now of the UK.]
Used *attrib.* to designate things from or associated with London.
London bridge: a children's singing game (more fully ***London bridge is falling down***). **London broil** *N. Amer.* a grilled steak served cut diagonally in thin slices. **London clay** GEOLOGY a clay formation of the lower Eocene in SE England, esp. around London. **London fog** a dense fog once peculiar to London and large industrial towns. **London gin** a dry gin. **London ivy** *arch.* (**a**) the smoke of London, as clinging to and blackening buildings; (**b**) a thick London fog. ***London particular***: see **PARTICULAR** *noun*. ***London plane***: see **PLANE** *noun*[2] 1. **London pride** (**a**) (now *dial.*) sweet william, *Dianthus barbatus*; (**b**) a commonly cultivated saxifrage, *Saxifraga* × *urbium*, with panicles of white red-spotted flowers and rosettes of leathery leaves. **London purple** an insecticide containing arsenic trioxide and aniline. **London rocket** [so named from its springing up on the ruins after the Great Fire of London (1666)] a cruciferous plant, *Sisymbrium irio*, with yellow flowers. **London shrinking** a finishing process applied to fabric to prevent shrinkage. **London-shrunk** *adjective* finished by London shrinking.
■ **Londoner** *noun* a native or inhabitant of London **LME**. **Londonian** /lʌnˈdəʊnɪən/ *noun & adjective* (**a**) *noun* (*rare*) a Londoner; (**b**) *adjective* pertaining to or characteristic of London: **E19**. **Londonish** *adjective* pertaining to or characteristic of London, exhibiting features or aspects of London **M19**. **Londonism** *noun* a word, idiom, or pronunciation peculiar to London speech **E19**. **Londoniˈzation** *noun* the action or process of Londonizing something or someone **L19**. **Londonize** *verb trans.* make like London or its inhabitants, give a Londonish character to **L18**. **Londony** *adjective* suggestive of London or its characteristics **L19**.

†**lone** *noun*[1] var. of **LOAN** *noun*[2].

lone /ləʊn/ *adjective, adverb, & noun*[2]. Also (*Scot.*) **lane** /leɪn/. **LME**.
[**ORIGIN** Aphet. from **ALONE**.]
▸ **A** *adjective & adverb*. **I** *attrib.* **1** (Of a person, personal situation, etc.) companionless, solitary (chiefly *literary*). Also, standing apart from others, isolated. **LME**. ▸**b** Having a feeling of loneliness; lonesome. **M19**.

E. M. FORSTER Two lone females in an unknown town. M. ESSLIN A lone outsider, cut off and isolated. P. FERGUSON A lone sock curled amidst the dust. *Daily Express* Charles spent a lone holiday.

2 Now esp. of a woman: unmarried, single or widowed. **M16**.

Which? Lone parents . . are likely to lose out.

3 Only, sole. *rare*. **E17**.
4 Of a place: lonely; unfrequented, uninhabited. *poet.* **E17**.

POPE In some lone isle, or distant Northern land.

▸ **II** *pred. adjective & adverb*. **5** Alone, by oneself or itself. Now *dial.* **E17**.
– SPECIAL COLLOCATIONS & COMB.: **lone hand** in card games, esp. euchre, a hand played, or a player playing, against all the other players, or against the opposite side without help; ***play a lone hand*** (*fig.*), act on one's own without help. **lone pair** PHYSICAL CHEMISTRY a pair of electrons in the outer shell of an atom which are not involved in bonding. **lone ranger** [from the hero of a western] a person acting alone, esp. to uphold the right. **Lone Scout** a Scout who does not have a regular access to a Scout troop. **lone star** the single star on the state flag of Texas; ***Lone Star State***, the state of Texas. **lone wolf** a person who mixes little with others, a person who prefers to act alone. **lone-wolf** *verb intrans.* live, work, or act alone.
▸ **B** *noun*. (Also **lones**.) *One's* self, *one's* own. Chiefly in ***by one's lone***, ***on one's lone***. Chiefly *Scot. & N. English*. **LME**.

W. M. RAINE Why for do they let a sick man . . travel all by his lone.

■ **loneful** *adjective* (long *obsolete* exc. *dial.*) lonely, forlorn **M16**. **loneness** *noun* (now *rare*) solitariness; loneliness; lonesomeness: **L16**.

lonelihood /ˈləʊnlɪhʊd/ *noun*. *poet.* **M19**.
[**ORIGIN** from **LONELY** + **-HOOD**.]
Loneliness.

lonelily /ˈləʊnlɪli/ *adverb*. **M19**.
[**ORIGIN** from **LONELY** + **-LY**[2].]
In a lonely fashion.

loneliness /ˈləʊnlɪnɪs/ *noun*. **L16**.
[**ORIGIN** from **LONELY** + **-NESS**.]
1 The condition of being alone or solitary; isolation. **L16**.
2 The condition of being unfrequented; desolateness. **M18**.
3 Sadness at being alone; the sense of solitude; dejection arising from lack of friends or company. **E19**.

lonely /ˈləʊnli/ *adjective*. **L16**.
[**ORIGIN** from **LONE** *adjective* + **-LY**[1].]
1 Of a person, personal situation, etc.: companionless, unaccompanied, solitary. **L16**.

R. K. NARAYAN The Temptress Devil, who waylaid lonely wayfarers. C. C. TRENCH Frederick had spent a lonely childhood, with no relatives . . , no friends.

2 Of a place: unfrequented; desolate. **L16**.

J. A. MICHENER One of the loneliest and gloomiest sections of Texas.

3 Of a thing: isolated, standing apart. Chiefly *poet.* M17.

M. ARNOLD That lonely tree against the western sky.

plough a lonely furrow: see PLOUGH *verb*.

4 a Imparting a feeling of loneliness; dreary. M17. ▸**b** Dejected because of lack of friends or company; sad at the thought that one is alone; having a feeling of solitariness. E19.

a CONAN DOYLE My house is lonely. I . . and my bees have the estate all to ourselves. **b** A. MCCOWEN My Grandma Walkden died . . , and my grandfather was very lonely.

— COMB.: **lonely heart** a person suffering from loneliness; ***Miss Lonelyhearts***, (a pseudonym used by) a journalist giving advice in a newspaper or magazine to people who are lonely or in difficulties.

loner /ˈləʊnə/ *noun*. M20.
[ORIGIN from LONE *adjective* + -ER¹.]
A person who avoids company and prefers to be alone; an animal of solitary habits.

lones *noun* var. of LONE *noun*².

lonesome /ˈləʊns(ə)m/ *adjective & noun*. M17.
[ORIGIN from LONE *adjective* + -SOME¹.]
▸ **A** *adjective*. **1** Of a person etc.: solitary, lonely; now *esp.* having a feeling of solitude or loneliness, feeling lonely or forlorn. Also foll. by *for*. M17.

M. WEBB It seemed lonesome that night without Gideon. A. BEATTIE I got lonesome for you tonight.

2 Of a place etc.: unfrequented, desolate; now *esp.* causing feelings of loneliness, making one feel forlorn. M17.
▸ **B** *noun*. *One's* self, *one's* own. Chiefly in ***by one's lonesome, on one's lonesome***. *colloq.* L19.
■ **lonesomely** *adverb* L18. **lonesomeness** *noun* E18.

long /lɒŋ/ *adjective*¹ & *noun*.
[ORIGIN Old English *lang*, *long* = Old Frisian, Old Saxon *lang*, *long*, Old High German *lang* (Dutch, German *lang*), Old Norse *langr*, Gothic *laggs*, from Germanic.]
▸ **A** *adjective*. **I** With ref. to spatial measurement.
1 Great in measurement from end to end; not soon traversed. OE. ▸**b** Tall. Now *colloq.*, esp. *Scot.* OE. ▸**c** Designating a measure of length greater than the standard measure of that name. E17. ▸**d** Of action, vision, etc.: acting at or extending to a great distance. E17.

T. HARDY She could not have come a very long distance. I. MURDOCH Annette walked quickly, taking long strides. E. CALDWELL She has long brown hair hanging down her back. W. BOYD The long stretch of Government Road.

2 Having (a relative or specified) extension from end to end. Freq. with adverb or adverbial phr. expressing the amount of length. OE.

THOMAS HUGHES Pike, three inches long.

3 Having the length much greater than the breadth; elongated. OE.
▸ **II** With ref. to serial extent or duration.
4 Of a series, enumeration or succession, a speech, a sentence, a word, a literary work, etc.: having a great extent from beginning to end; not soon finished. OE. ▸**b** Of a number or thing numerically estimated: large; expressed by many digits; consisting of many individuals; CARDS (of a suit) of which a large number of cards (4 or more) are held or have been played, (of a card) of such a suit. M18.

G. VIDAL The treaty was very long. **b** *Black World* I'd quit pushing tomorrow, baby, but the money is so long.

5 (Of a period of time, or a process, state, or action) having a great extent in duration; that has continued or will continue in action, operation, or obligation for a long period, lasting. OE.

SCOTT FITZGERALD There was such a long pause. D. DUNN In the afternoon twilight of a long lunch in London. I. MURDOCH From long experience Barney could tell the . . boats apart. A. THWAITE I am not doomed to a long exile here.

6 PHONETICS & PROSODY. (Of a vowel (in mod. use also of a consonant or syllable)) having the greater of two recognized contrastive durations; (of a vowel or syllable) stressed; (of a vowel letter) representing in context a vowel with such duration (in English the sound of its alphabetical name, as *i* in *pile*, *u* in *cute*). OE.
7 Having (a relative or specified) extension serially or temporally. ME.

J. WILCOX I'm not going to do any paper longer than five pages.

8 Continuing too long; lengthy, prolix, tedious. ME.

POPE He is apt to be too long in his descriptions.

9 Of a point in time: distant, remote. Now only in ***long date*** below, and in legal phr. ***a long day***. LME. ▸**b** Of a bill of exchange, promissory note, etc.: maturing at a distant date, having a long time to run. M19.

10 Designating a period of time, a number, a weight, or a quantity greater than the usual period etc. of that name. Also, felt as excessive or unusual in duration. L16.

G. GREENE The law has . . , impressed it on me through three long days. A. ALVAREZ A long fortnight, sixteen days.

11 COMMERCE. Designating or pertaining to the buying of stocks, commodities, etc., in large quantities in expectation of a coming scarcity and rise in price. M19.

— PHRASES: ***a long row to hoe***: see ROW *noun*¹. ***as broad as it is long***: see BROAD *adjective* 1. ***at a long stay***: see STAY *noun*¹ 1. ***at long last***: see LAST *adverb, adjective, & noun*⁵. ***at long range***: see RANGE *noun*¹. ***by a long way***: see WAY *noun*. ***come a long way***: see WAY *noun*. ***cut a long story short***: see SHORT *adjective*. ***for a long season***: see SEASON *noun*. ***go a long way***: see WAY *noun*. **go long (on)** COMMERCE buy in large quantities in expectation of a coming scarcity and rise in price. ***have a face as long as a fiddle***: see FIDDLE *noun*. ***Land of the Long White Cloud***: see LAND *noun*¹. **long in the tooth** (orig. of a horse) displaying the roots of the teeth owing to the recession of the gums with increasing age; *gen.* old. **long of life** (now *rare*) of long life. **long on** *colloq.* well supplied with, having plenty of. ***the Long Forties***: see FORTY *noun* 1. ***the long green***: see GREEN *noun*. **the long robe** *fig.* (*arch.*) the legal profession (chiefly in ***of the long robe***); cf. ***the short robe*** s.v. SHORT *adjective, noun, & adverb*. ***think it long, think long***: see THINK *verb*².

— SPECIAL COLLOCATIONS & COMB.: **long acre** †(*a*) a long narrow field of an acre; (*b*) *NZ* a grass verge between a roadway and a fence. **long-acuminate** *adjective* (BOTANY) having a long tapering point. **long-and-short** *adjective* (*a*) ***long-and-short stitch***, in embroidery, a flat stitch used for shading; (*b*) ***long-and-short work*** (Archit.), alternation of tall quoins horizontal with slabs. **long arm** (*a*) an arm fully extended to reach something; ***make a long arm*** (colloq.), reach out the arm a long way; (*b*) a far-reaching power (freq. in ***the long arm of coincidence, the long arm of the law***); (*c*) (with hyphen or as one word) a long-barrelled gun, as a musket, rifle, etc.; (*d*) (with hyphen or as one word) a pole fitted with a hook, shears, etc., for use at a height beyond the ordinary reach of the arm. **long ball** (in sport) a ball hit, kicked, or thrown a long way. **long barrow** ARCHAEOLOGY an elongated Neolithic grave mound. **long-beard** (*a*) *rare* [pseudo-etymological rendering] a Lombard; (*b*) Spanish moss, *Tillandsia usneoides*. **longbill** a bird with a long bill, *esp.* a woodcock. **long bill** a bill containing a great number of items; a bill in which the charges are excessive. **long blow** *Austral. & NZ* a stroke of the shears in sheep-shearing which cuts away the fleece from rump to neck. **longboard** a type of long surfboard. **longboat** the largest boat belonging to a sailing vessel. **long bone** any of the main limb bones, *esp.* (in *pl.*) the femur, tibia, humerus, and radius. **longbow** a large bow drawn by hand and discharging a long feathered arrow, the chief weapon of English armies from the 14th cent. until the introduction of firearms (***draw the longbow, pull the longbow***, make exaggerated statements, tell invented stories). ***long-breathed***. **long card** in whist or bridge, a card of a suit held only by one player (usu. in *pl.*); (see also sense 4b above). **long-case (clock)** a weight-and-pendulum clock in a tall wooden case; also called ***grandfather clock***. **long chain** CHEMISTRY a relatively large number of atoms (usu. of carbon) linked together in a line (freq. *attrib.* with hyphen). **long chair** = CHAISE LONGUE. ***long chalk(s)***: see CHALK *noun*. **long chance**: involving considerable uncertainty or risk. **long cist** ARCHAEOLOGY a type of megalithic tomb having a long and narrow chamber to which there is direct entry. ***long clam***: see CLAM *noun*² 1(c). **long clay** *colloq.* a churchwarden pipe. **long cloth** cloth woven in unusually long pieces, *esp.* cotton or calico cloth of this kind made in the Indian subcontinent. **long clothes** the garments of a baby in arms. **long-coat** a coat reaching to the ankles; in *pl.* also (*arch.*) = ***long clothes*** above. **long corner** HOCKEY a penalty hit taken from a spot on the back line within 5 yards of the corner flag (opp. ***short corner***). **long cross** (*a*) PRINTING in a hand press, a bar dividing a chase the longest way; (*b*) NUMISMATICS a cross of which the limbs extend to the outer circle on a coin. **long date** a distant date for the maturing of a bill etc. **long-dated** *adjective* †(*a*) that has existed from a distant date; (*b*) extending to a distant date in the future; *esp.* not due for early payment or redemption, designating fixed-interest securities having redemption dates more than 15 years away. **long-day** *adjective* (*a*) having a long working day; (*b*) (of a plant) needing a long daily period of light to induce flowering. **longdog** *dial.* a greyhound. ***long dozen***: see DOZEN *noun* 1. ***long division***: see DIVISION 5. **long drawer** a drawer extending the full width of a chest, wardrobe, etc. **long dress** a floor- or ankle-length dress, usu. worn as evening dress. **long drink** a drink served in a tall glass; a large measure of liquid to drink. **long dung** = ***long manure*** below. **long ear** (*a*) *arch.* an ass (*lit. & fig.*); (*b*) [translating local name] a member of the people who once inhabited Easter Island and were distinguished by artificially lengthened ears. **long-eared** (*a*) having long ears; ***long-eared owl***, an owl, *Asio otus*, widespread in the northern hemisphere, having two earlike tufts on top of the head; (*b*) asinine, stupid. **long-ells** *hist.* a kind of coarse woollen cloth. ***Longer Catechism***: see CATECHISM 2. **long face** *colloq.* a dismal or exaggeratedly solemn facial expression. **long-faced** *adjective* (*colloq.*) having a dismal or exaggeratedly solemn facial expression. **long family**: having many children. **long field** CRICKET (*a*) long off or long on; (*b*) part of the field behind the bowler. **long figure** a heavy cost. **long finger** the middle finger; in *pl.* also the three middle fingers. ***long firm***: see FIRM *noun* 3. **long-footed** *adjective* having long feet; ***long-footed*** POTOROO. **long-fours** long candles, four of which weighed a pound. **long game** GOLF driving and other play to reach the green. **long glass** a full-length looking glass. **long grass** *spec.* grass or grasslike growth, typical of certain areas in Africa, tall enough to conceal large animals. **longhair** a person or animal (esp. a cat) with longer hair than usual (RUSSIAN ***longhair***); a person of a type regarded as characteristically having long hair; *spec.* (*a*) (freq. *derog.*) a clever person, an aesthete, an intellectual; a devotee of classical (as opp. to popular) music; (*b*) a hippy, a beatnik. **longhaired** *adjective* (*a*) having longer hair than usual; of a kind or breed characterized by relatively long hair; (*b*) (freq. *derog.*) that is a 'longhair', with aesthetic or intellectual pretensions. **longhand** ordinary handwriting, as distinguished from shorthand or typing or printing. **long handle** (CRICKET) the action or practice of hitting freely. **long-haul** *adjective* designating or pertaining to travel, transport of goods, or any effort made, over a long distance. **longhead** (*a*) a person who has a skull of more than average length; *spec.* in ANTHROPOLOGY a dolichocephalic person; (*b*) *colloq.* a shrewd person. **long-headed** *adjective* (*a*) of great discernment or foresight; shrewd; (*b*) having a long head; dolichocephalic. **long-headedness** the quality or state of being long-headed. **long hop** a ball bowled or thrown so that it makes a long flight after pitching or bouncing. **long-horned** *adjective* having long horns; ***long-horned beetle***, = LONGHORN 2; ***long-horned grasshopper***, = ***bush cricket*** s.v. CRICKET *noun*¹. **long hour**: indicated by any of the higher number of strokes on a clock etc. **longhouse** †(*a*) a privy, a lavatory; (*b*) a house of unusual length, *spec.* a long communal dwelling among certain peoples, as some N. American Indians and Indonesians. ***long*** HUNDREDWEIGHT. **long ink** PRINTING: of a consistency such that it can be drawn out. **long john** (*a*) *sing.* & (usu.) in *pl.* (*colloq.*) underpants with full-length legs; (*b*) (also with caps.) a long coffee table (also ***long john table***); (*c*) (***longjohn***) a tropical S. American tree of the knotgrass family, *Triplaris surinamensis*, so called from its long inflorescence. **long jump** an activity or athletic contest of jumping as far as possible along the ground in one leap from a running start. **long-jump** *verb intrans.* make or take part in a long jump. **long jumper** a person who long-jumps. **Long Knife** (*a*) a knife with a long blade, esp. used as a weapon; ***night of the long knives***: see NIGHT *noun*; (*b*) *N. AMER. HISTORY* (a name given by N. American Indians to) white settlers, esp. of Virginia, or white soldiers, in Canada, *spec.* a citizen of the US, (freq. in *pl.*). **longleaf pine** a pine of the southern US, *Pinus palustris*, with long leaves and cones. ***long leg***: see LEG *noun*. **long-legged** *adjective* (*a*) having long legs; *fig.* speedy; (*b*) NAUTICAL (of a ship) drawing a great deal of water. **long-legs** (*a*) = ***longshanks*** (b) below; (*b*) = DADDY-***long-legs***. **long lens**: with a great focal length. **long-life** *adjective* remaining usable or serviceable for an unusually long time. **long line** (*a*) a line of manuscript or type that runs across the page without columnar division; (*b*) in Old English verse, two half-lines considered as a unit; (*c*) (usu. ***longline***) a deep-sea fishing line. **longliner** (chiefly *N. Amer.*) a person who fishes with a longline; a fishing vessel which uses longlines. **long-lining** fishing with longlines. **longlist** (*a*) *noun* a list of selected names, esp. of candidates for a post, from which a shortlist is made; (*b*) *verb trans.* put on a longlist. **long-lugged** *adjective* (*Scot.*) having long ears; *fig.* eager to listen to secrets or scandal. **long-lunged** *adjective* = LONG-WINDED 2. **long manure** manure containing unclipped straw undecayed. **Long March** (*hist.*) *the* year-long retreat of the Chinese Communists across SW China during the period of Nationalist government. **long mark** a macron (placed over a vowel letter to indicate long quantity). **long measure** linear measure, the measure of length (metres, miles, etc.). **long memory**: that retains the recollection of events for a long period. **long metre** (*a*) a hymn stanza of four lines each containing eight syllables; (*b*) a quatrain of iambic tetrameters with alternate lines rhyming. **long mirror** = ***long glass*** above. **long-moss** = ***long-beard*** (b) above. **long-nebbed** *adjective* (*Scot.*) having a long nose; *fig.* curious, prying. **longneck** (*a*) an earthenware retort or still with a long neck; (*b*) a bird with a long neck, *esp.* a heron or a pintail duck; (*c*) ***longneck clam***: see CLAM *noun*² 1(c). **long-necked** *adjective* having a long neck; ***long-necked clam*** = ***longneck*** (c) above. **long nine** *hist.* a kind of long cheap cigar. **long nose** (*a*) *slang* the thumb to the nose, as a gesture of mockery (chiefly in ***make a long nose***); (*b*) (***long-nose***) any of various fishes having an elongated snout. **long-nosed** *adjective* having a long nose; ***long-nosed*** POTOROO. **long odds** very unequal stakes or chances in betting. ***long off***: see OFF *noun*. ***long on***: see ON *noun*. ***Long Parliament***: see PARLIAMENT *noun*. ***long pepper***: see PEPPER *noun*. **long-persistence** *adjective* designating a screen of a cathode-ray tube on which a spot remains luminous for some time after the beam has moved away. **long pig** [from Polynesian name] human flesh as food. **long-pod** a variety of broad bean which produces a very long pod. **long price** a heavy cost; high odds in betting. ***long primer***: see PRIMER *noun*¹ 3. **long pull** (*a*) PRINTING a pull on the bar of a wooden hand press almost to its fullest extent; (*b*) a practice in public houses of giving over-measure to attract custom. **long purples** *dial.* any of several plants with long spikes or racemes of purple flowers; *esp.* (*a*) early purple orchid, *Orchis mascula*; (*b*) purple loosestrife, *Lythrum salicaria*. **long purse** *colloq.* (a purse containing) plenty of money. **long rains** in tropical countries, the rainy season. **long-range** *adjective* having a long range, of or pertaining to a long period of future time. **long room** an assembly room in a private house or public building. **long rope** a skipping game using a rope of considerable length. ***long rough dab***: see ROUGH *adjective*. **long run** (*a*) a long period of continuous presentation (of a play, a broadcast programme, etc.); (*b*) ***in the long run***, in the end, over a long period of time, as the ultimate outcome (after all vicissitudes). **long-run** *adjective* taken or considered in the long run. **long s** a lower-case form of the letter s, written or printed ſ, not in general use after the early 19th cent. ***long sea***: see SEA *noun*. **long service** prolonged service in one post, esp. (MILITARY) enlistment for a long or the maximum period. **longshanks** (*a*) a tall or long-legged person, orig. *spec.* (**L-**) Edward I of England (1239–1307); (*b*) the black-winged stilt, *Himantopus himantopus*. **longship** *hist.* a ship accommodating a large number of rowers; a ship of war, a galley. **long-short** a long short story. **long short story** a short story of more than average length, a novella. **long shot** (*a*) a shot fired at a distance; a distant range; (*b*) something incredible or very unlikely; a far-fetched explanation; a wild guess; a bet laid against considerable odds; (*c*) a cinema or television shot which includes figures or scenery at a distance. **long sight** (*a*) capacity for seeing distant objects; (*b*) the defect of sight by which only comparatively distant objects are seen distinctly; hypermetropia. **long-sighted** *adjective* (*a*) having long sight; unable to distinguish nearby objects clearly; hypermetropic; (*b*) *fig.* having great foresight; far-seeing. **long-sightedly** *adverb* in a long-sighted manner. **long-sightedness** the condition of being long-sighted. **long sixes** long candles, six of which weighed a pound. **long sleeve** a sleeve extending below the elbow, esp. fully to the wrist. **long-sleeved** *adjective* having long sleeves. **long-sleever** *Austral. & NZ slang* a tall glass, a long drink. **long-spined** *adjective* having long spines; ***long-spined sea scorpion***: see SEA *noun*. **long-splice** a splice without significant thickening of the rope at the join. **longspur** any of several N. American buntings of the genus *Calcarius*; LAPLAND ***longspur***.

L

long-staple *adjective & noun* (designating) cotton having a long fibre. **longstop** CRICKET (the position of) a fielder who stands behind the wicketkeeper to stop the balls that pass him or her; *fig.* a last resort in an emergency etc. **long straw** unclipped straw (esp. as opp. to reed) for use in thatching. **long stroke** a piston or pump rod stroke which is longer than the average. **long sufferance** *arch.* patient endurance of a provocation or trial. **long suit** *fig.* [from sense 4b above] one's strong point. **long sweetening** *US* molasses or other liquid sweetening. **long-tackle** NAUTICAL a light two-block tackle for hoisting sails etc. **longtail boat** a long narrow boat of a kind used in Thailand, having the propeller mounted on a long shaft at the rear. **long-term** *adjective & adverb* (**a**) *adjective* lasting for or pertaining to a relatively long period of time; maturing or becoming effective only after a long period; (**b**) *adverb* over or at the end of a long period of time. **long-termer** a prisoner serving a long sentence. **long-termism** the making of decisions with a view to long-term aims or consequences. **long time** (adverbial) (**a**) ***a long time***, for a long time; also without *a* (*arch.* exc. *Jamaican* & in ***long time no see*** (*colloq.*) [joc. imitation of broken English], used as a greeting after prolonged separation); (**b**) ***this long time***, for a long time down to the present. **long-time** *adjective* that has been such for a long time; extending for a long time into the future, requiring a long time. **long-timer** = ***long-termer*** above. **long togs** NAUTICAL clothes worn on shore. **Long Tom** (**a**) *hist.* a gun of large size and long range; (**b**) a trough for washing gold-bearing deposits; (**c**) *Austral.* any marine fish of the family Belonidae, with elongated jaws; (**d**) *slang* a particularly high-powered telephoto camera lens. ***long ton***: see TON *noun*[1] 4. **long tongue** *fig.* a capacity to talk a lot. **long-tongued** *adjective* having much to say, loquacious, chattering, babbling. **long trousers**: reaching to the ankle. **long twelves** PRINTING (chiefly *hist.*) a duodecimo imposition scheme with the forme arranged in two rows of six long narrow type pages (as opp. to the standard three rows of four shorter and broader pages). **long vacation**, (*colloq.*) **long vac** the summer vacation of courts of law and universities, and similar institutions; a regular long holiday. **long verse** (**a**) = ***long line*** (b) above; (**b**) hexametric verse. **long view(s)** consideration of remote effects; ***take the long view***, have regard for more than current needs or concerns; plan for the future. **long waist** a low or deep waist of a dress or body. **long-waisted** *adjective* having a long waist. **longwall** *noun, adjective, & adverb* (MINING) (**a**) *noun & adjective* (pertaining to or involving) a single long face worked (usu. mechanically) along its whole length; (**b**) *adverb* by the longwall method. **long wave** a wave of relatively long wavelength; *spec.* in BROADCASTING, a radio wave with a wavelength between about one and ten kilometres. **long weekend** a weekend holiday of more than the usual length; *fig.* the period between the First and Second World Wars. ***long whist***: see WHIST *noun*[2]. **long-wings** the swift. **long-wool** (**a**) long-stapled wool, suitable for combing or carding; (**b**) (usu. ***longwool***) a sheep of a breed with long wool (***Lincoln Longwool***). **long-woolled** *adjective* (of a sheep) having long wool. **long word** *colloq.* a word that indicates a long time. **long years** *rhet.* many years. (See also combs. of LONG *adverb*.)

▸ **B** *noun*. **I** *absol.* **1** Much time; a long interval or period. (Passing into adverb, having a comparative & superlative, & modifiable by adverbs of degree.) OE.

> *Engineering* It will take . . ten times that long to get a train ready. E. O'NEILL Life at its longest is brief enough. B. PYM It seems to take so long to get everything.

2 *The* long explanation or recital. Chiefly in ***the long and the short of it***, the sum total or substance, the upshot. E16.

▸ **II** As count noun.

3 A long note in music; a long flash or dash in Morse code etc.; a long syllable or vowel; a mark indicating that a vowel or (formerly) a note is long. LME.

4 ARCHITECTURE. Each of a series of long blocks placed alternately with short ones in a vertical line. M19.

5 A long vacation. M19.

6 In *pl.* **a** Long clothes. M19. ▸**b** Long trousers. *colloq.* E20.

7 In *pl.* Long whist. *obsolete* exc. *hist.* M19.

8 COMMERCE. **a** A person who has bought stocks, commodities, etc., in expectation of a coming scarcity and rise in price. L19. ▸**b** In *pl.* Long-dated stocks. M20.

– PHRASES: **at longest**, **at the longest** on the longest estimate. **before long** before a long time has elapsed, soon, (also ***before much longer*** etc.). ERELONG. **for long** for a long time, esp. projecting into the future (also ***for a little longer*** etc.). **longs and shorts** (**a**) quantitative (esp. Latin or Greek) verses or versification; (**b**) ARCHITECTURE (the style of masonry with) alternate short and long blocks in a vertical line. **that long** *colloq.* that length of time, (in neg. contexts) much time. ***the long and the short of it***: see sense B.2 above.

▪ **longish** *adjective* somewhat long E17.

long /lɒŋ/ *adjective*[2]. Now *arch. & dial.* ME.
[ORIGIN Aphet. from ALONG *adjective*[1]. Cf. LONG *verb*[2].]
long of (†***long on***), attributable to, owing to, on account of, because of.

long /lɒŋ/ *verb*[1].
[ORIGIN Old English *langian* = Old Saxon *langon*, Middle Dutch *langen* seem long, desire, extend, offer (Dutch *langen* offer, present), Old High German *langēn* (impers.) (German *langen* reach, extend, suffice), Old Norse *langa* (impers. & pers.) desire, long, from Germanic, from base of LONG *adjective*[1].]

▸ †**I** **1** *verb intrans. & trans.* Lengthen. OE–L15.

▸ **II** †**2** *verb intrans. impers.* ***me longs***, ***me longeth***, etc., I have etc. a yearning desire. Foll. by *after, to, to do*. OE–LME.

3 *verb intrans.* Have a yearning desire; wish earnestly. Foll. by *for* (*after*), *to*, *do*. ME. ▸†**b** Foll. by adverb or adverbial phr. with a verb of motion implied: long to go. ME–M16.

> E. L. DOCTOROW She longed to have her ambitions aroused. M. AMIS He longed for him to be taken into care.

long /lɒŋ/ *verb*[2] *intrans.* Now *arch. rare.* Also **'long**. ME.
[ORIGIN formed as LONG *adjective*[2]; later taken as abbreviation of BELONG *verb*.]

1 Be appropriate; pertain, refer or relate, *to*, *unto*; belong *to*, *unto* as a member, part, inhabitant, dependent, etc. ME. ▸†**b** Be of concern *to* (a person); be fitting *to*. LME–M16.

†**2** Foll. by *to*, *unto*: be the property or rightful possession of; = BELONG *verb* 3. ME–L19.

long /lɒŋ/ *adverb*.
[ORIGIN Old English *lange*, *longe* = Old Frisian *lang(e)*, *long(e)*, Old Saxon, Old High German *lango* (Dutch *lang*, German *lange*), from Germanic base of LONG *adjective*[1].]

1 For or during a long time; in *compar.* & *superl.* or preceded by adverbs of comparison (*as, how, so, thus, too*, etc.), for or during the specified or implied length of time. OE.

> J. BUCHAN 'Have you known her long?' I asked . . . 'Since she was a child.' J. MITCHELL A series of . . kindly housekeepers (none of whom stayed very long). D. PRATER He . . would long remember their talk. N. GORDIMER I don't know how much longer I'll . . keep on that job.

2 *pred.* after *be* (passing into adjective & noun). (Occupied or delayed for) a long time. Foll. by *doing*, *in* (†*of*, †*a*) *doing*, (colloq.) *absol.* ME.

> SIR W. SCOTT They were not long of discovering the *tête-du-pont*. G. B. SHAW I shan't be long (He goes out).

3 At, from, or to a distant point of time (usu. foll. by *after*, *before*, (arch.) *ere*, *since* (adverbs, conjunctions, or prepositions)); in *compar.* (chiefly preceded by adverbs of degree, as *any, no, much, a little*, etc.), after the specified or implied point of time. ME.

> SCOTT FITZGERALD I'll have a new score on Broadway long before you've finished. G. ORWELL He had long grown used to sleeping . . on his face. G. VIDAL The roof of the temple had long since fallen in. S. COOPER By the time he . . found what he was looking for, his shirt was long dry.

4 Subjoined to noun phrs. expressing duration: throughout the length of (the period specified or implied). ME.

> B. JOWETT He was . . working all his life long. E. O'NEILL Unable to bear the thick silence a minute longer.

5 At or to a great or a specified distance in space; far. Now chiefly SPORT, of a ball etc. ME.

> W. MORRIS The fisher sits . . with a rod that reaches long.

– PHRASES: ***all day long***, ***all the day long***: see DAY *noun*. ***all night long***, ***all the night long***: see NIGHT *noun*. **as long as**, **so long as**, (*colloq.*) **long as** during the whole time that; provided that, if only. ***long live***: see LIVE *verb*. **no longer** not now as formerly. **not be long for this world** have only a short time to live. **so long** *colloq.* goodbye, *au revoir*. ***so long as***: see ***as long as*** above.

– COMB. (not always clearly distinguishable from combs. of LONG *adjective*[1]): **long-acting** *adjective* (PHARMACOLOGY) having effects that last a long time; **long-ago** *adjective & noun* (belonging to) the distant past; **long-continued** *adjective* continued or that has continued for a long period or space; **long-drawn** *adjective* (**a**) prolonged to a great or inordinate length (also ***long-drawn-out***); (**b**) (chiefly *poet.*) having great longitudinal extension; **long-fed** *adjective* (of cattle) fed a special diet to complete fattening for a long period before slaughter; **long-keeping** *adjective* able to be kept for a long time; **long-lasting** *adjective* that lasts for a long time; **long-living** *adjective* that lives for a long time; **long-play** *adjective* = ***long-playing*** below; **long-player** a long-playing record; **long-playing** *adjective* that plays for a long time; *spec.* designating or pertaining to a microgroove gramophone record designed to be played at 33⅓ revolutions per minute and lasting for about 10 to 30 minutes on each side; abbreviation ***LP***; **long-running** *adjective* continuing for a relatively long period of time; *spec.* (of a play) having a large number of consecutive performances.

long. *abbreviation*.
Longitude.

-long /lɒŋ/ *suffix*. Also †**-longs**.
[ORIGIN from LONG *adjective*[1].]
Forming adverbs and adjectives with the senses '-wise', 'foremost', (= -LING[2]), as ***headlong***, ***sidelong***, and 'lasting or throughout the specified time', as ***daylong***, ***lifelong***. (Earliest in ENDLONG.)

longaeval, **longaevous** *adjectives* vars. of LONGEVAL, LONGEVOUS.

longan /ˈlɒŋɡ(ə)n/ *noun*. M18.
[ORIGIN Chinese *lóngyǎn* lit. 'dragon's eye', from *lóng* dragon + *yǎn* eye.]
The edible fruit of an evergreen tree, *Dimocarpus longan* (family Sapindaceae), cultivated in China and SE Asia; the tree itself.

longanimity /lɒŋɡəˈnɪmɪti/ *noun*. Now *rare*. LME.
[ORIGIN Late Latin *longanimitas*, *-tat-*, from *longanimus*, from *longus* LONG *adjective*[1] + *animus* mind, after Greek *makrothumia*: see -ITY.]
Long-suffering; forbearance or patience under provocation etc.
▪ **longanimous** /lɒŋˈɡanɪməs/ *adjective* (*rare*) long-suffering; enduring, patient: E17.

long-distance /lɒŋˈdɪst(ə)ns/ *adjective, noun, adverb, & verb*. L19.
[ORIGIN from LONG *adjective*[1] + DISTANCE *noun*.]

▸ **A** *adjective*. To or from a long distance; (of a weather forecast) long-range; (of a telephone call, public transport, etc.) between distant places. L19.

▸ **B** *noun*. A long-distance telephone (call); a race distance of the longest category, now usu. 10,000 metres or 6 miles and longer. E20.

▸ **C** *adverb*. By long-distance telephone. M20.

▸ **D** *verb trans.* Make a long-distance telephone call to (a person); report long-distance. M20.

longe *noun, verb* vars. of LUNGE *noun*[1], *verb*[2].

longer /ˈlɒŋə/ *noun*[1]. *rare*. LME.
[ORIGIN from LONG *verb*[1] + -ER[1].]
A person who longs for someone or something.

longer /ˈlɒŋə/ *noun*[2]. *Canad.* L18.
[ORIGIN from LONG *adjective*[1] + -ER[1].]
A long pole or piece of timber used for fencing, a fishing stage, etc.

longeron /ˈlɒndʒərɒn/ *noun*. E20.
[ORIGIN French.]
AERONAUTICS. A frame member running lengthways along a fuselage.

longeval /lɒnˈdʒiːv(ə)l/ *adjective*. Also **-aeval**. L16.
[ORIGIN from Latin *longaevus* (see LONGEVITY) + -AL[1].]
Long-lived, long-lasting.

longevity /lɒnˈdʒɛvɪti/ *noun*. E17.
[ORIGIN Late Latin *longaevitas*, *-tat-*, from Latin *longaevus*, from *longus* LONG *adjective*[1] + *aevum* age: see -ITY.]
Long life; long duration of existence.

longevous /lɒnˈdʒiːvəs/ *adjective*. Now *rare*. Also **-aevous**. L17.
[ORIGIN from Latin *longaevus* (see LONGEVITY) + -OUS.]
Long-lived; living or having lived to a great age.

longhorn /ˈlɒŋhɔːn/ *noun*. M19.
[ORIGIN from LONG *adjective*[1] + HORN *noun*.]

1 (An animal of) a breed of beef cattle, often reddish, with long curved horns. M19.
Texas longhorn.

2 In full ***longhorn beetle***. Any of numerous usu. elongate beetles of the family Cerambycidae, having very long, slender, backwardly flexed antennae, and found worldwide esp. in woodland. M19.

3 = ***long-eared owl*** s.v. LONG *adjective*[1]. M19.

4 In full ***longhorn grasshopper***. = ***bush cricket*** s.v. CRICKET *noun*[1]. L19.

longi- /ˈlɒndʒi/ *combining form* of Latin *longus* LONG *adjective*[1]: see -I-.
▪ **longiˈpennate** *adjective* long-winged M19.

longicorn /ˈlɒndʒɪkɔːn/ *adjective & noun*. M19.
[ORIGIN from mod. Latin *Longicornia* former taxonomic name, from Latin *longus* LONG *adjective*[1] + -I- + Latin *cornu* horn.]
(Designating or pertaining to) a longhorn beetle; = CERAMBYCID.

longie /ˈlʌŋi/ *noun*. *Scot.* E19.
[ORIGIN Norn *longvi* from Old Norse *langvi* rel. to LOOM *noun*[3] (cf. Norwegian *lomvi*).]
The common guillemot, *Uria aalge*.

longiloquence /lɒnˈdʒɪləkw(ə)ns/ *noun*. *rare*. M19.
[ORIGIN from LONGI-, after BREVILOQUENCE.]
Speaking at great length.

longimanous /lɒnˈdʒɪmənəs/ *adjective*. *rare*. M17.
[ORIGIN from late Latin *longimanus*, from *longus* LONG *adjective*[1] + *manus* hand: see -OUS.]
Having long hands. Formerly also *fig.*, far-reaching.

†**longimetry** *noun*. L17–L18.
[ORIGIN from LONGI-, after ALTIMETRY.]
The art or process of measuring distances.

longing /ˈlɒŋɪŋ/ *noun*. OE.
[ORIGIN from LONG *verb*[1] + -ING[1].]
The action of LONG *verb*[1]; (a) yearning desire. (Foll. by *for*, *after*, *to do*.)
OCEANIC ***longing***. ***save one's longing***: see SAVE *verb*.

longing /ˈlɒŋɪŋ/ *adjective*. E16.
[ORIGIN from LONG *verb*[1] + -ING[2].]
That longs for someone or something; characterized by yearning desire.
▪ **longingly** *adverb* in a longing manner, with yearning desire LME. **longingness** *noun* (*rare*) M16.

longinquity /lɒnˈdʒɪŋkwɪti/ *noun*. Now *rare*. M16.
[ORIGIN Latin *longinquitas*, *-tat-*, from *longinquus* distant, from *longus* LONG *adjective*[1]: see -ITY.]

1 Long distance; remoteness. M16.

2 Remoteness of time, long continuance. E17.

longitude /ˈlɒndʒɪtjuːd, ˈlɒŋɡɪ-/ *noun*. LME.
[ORIGIN Latin *longitudo*, *-din-*, from *longus* LONG *adjective*[1]: see -TUDE. Cf. Old French & mod. French *longitude*.]

▸ **I** **1** **a** Length, longitudinal extent. Formerly also, tallness, height. Now chiefly *joc.* LME. ▸**b** Length of time; long continuance. Now *rare*. E17.

▸ **II** *techn.* (opp. LATITUDE).

2 GEOGRAPHY. The angular distance of any place on the earth's surface, east or west of a standard meridian (e.g. that of Greenwich), measured in degrees up to 180 degrees east or west, or in units of time (1 hour = 15 degrees); distance east or west measured as the angle between two meridians. Also (*esp.* in ASTRONOMY), angular

distance measured from a similar line of reference, e.g. on the surface of a celestial object. LME.
galactic longitude, ***heliographic longitude***, etc.
3 *ASTRONOMY.* Angular distance measured eastward on the ecliptic from the vernal equinoctial point to a circle at right angles to the ecliptic through a given point. LME.
geocentric longitude, ***heliocentric longitude***, etc.

longitudinal /lɒndʒɪ'tjuːdɪn(ə)l, lɒŋɡɪ-/ *adjective & noun.* LME.
[ORIGIN from LONGITUDE + -AL[1].]
► **A** *adjective.* **1** Extending or proceeding in the direction of the length of a body; running lengthwise. LME. ›**b** *PHYSICS.* Of a vibration, wave, etc.: involving displacement parallel to the direction of propagation. M19.

> C. DARWIN Several of the species are beautifully coloured with longitudinal stripes. R. F. CHAPMAN Running through the neck are longitudinal muscles.

2 Of or pertaining to length as a dimension; (of extent) in length. M18.

> W. COBBETT The number of longitudinal inches of the foot measure.

3 Of or pertaining to longitude; measured from east to west. L19.

> *Scholarly Publishing* The accurate relocation of the longitudinal position of France.

4 Involving information about an individual or group at different times throughout a long period. M20.

> B. J. UNDERWOOD We are interested in the longitudinal aspects, i.e., how they developed.

► **B** *noun.* †**1** *ANATOMY.* Either of two muscles of the epigastrium. Only in M16.
2 A longitudinal member; *spec.* (***a***) in iron and steel ships, a plate parallel or nearly so to the vertical keel; (***b***) a longeron, *esp.* one in an airship. M19.
■ **longitudinally** *adverb* in a longitudinal direction; in the direction of the length of an object; lengthways: E18.

long-lived /lɒŋ'lɪvd/ *adjective.* LME.
[ORIGIN Orig. from LONG *adjective*[1] + *live* infl. form of LIFE *noun* + -ED[1], later also taken as from LONG *adverb* + *lived* pa. pple of LIVE *verb*.]
Having a long life or existence; living or lasting a long time, durable.
■ **longlivedness** *noun* longevity L19.

longly /'lɒŋli/ *adverb.* Now *rare.* ME.
[ORIGIN from LONG *adjective*[1] + -LY[2].]
†**1** For a long while. ME–E17.
2 At considerable length, using many words. ME.
3 To a considerable length (in space). M17.

longness /'lɒŋnɪs/ *noun.* Now *rare.* OE.
[ORIGIN from LONG *adjective*[1] + -NESS.]
Length; long continuance.

Longobard /'lɒŋɡəbɑːd/ *noun & adjective. hist.* LME.
[ORIGIN Late Latin *Longobardus*: see LOMBARD *noun*[1] & *adjective*. Cf. LANGOBARD.]
► **A** *noun.* Pl. **-bards**, **-bardi** /-bɑːdiː/. = LOMBARD *noun*[1] 1. LME.
► **B** *adjective.* Of or pertaining to the (Germanic) Lombards. M19.
■ **Longo'bardian** *adjective & noun* M19. **Longo'bardic** *adjective* M19.

longo intervallo /ˌlɒŋɡəʊ ɪntə'valəʊ/ *adverbial phr.* L17.
[ORIGIN Latin = at a distance.]
At some remove; in spite of the gulf between.

†**-longs** *suffix* var. of -LONG.

longshore /'lɒŋʃɔː/ *adjective.* E19.
[ORIGIN Aphet. from *alongshore*: see ALONG *adjective*[2], *preposition*, & *adverb*.]
1 Existing on, frequenting, or directed along a shore; found or employed along a shore. E19.
2 *PHYSICAL GEOGRAPHY.* Moving, taking place, or laid down more or less parallel to a shore. M19.
– COMB.: **longshoreman** a person who frequents or is employed along a shore; a landsman engaged in loading and unloading cargoes, or in fishing for oysters etc., along a shore.
■ **longshoring** *noun* the type of work done at a port; the occupation of a longshoreman: E20.

longsome /'lɒŋs(ə)m/ *adjective.* Now *arch. & dial.* OE.
[ORIGIN from LONG *adjective*[1] + -SOME[1]. Cf. Old Saxon, Old High German *langsam* (Dutch *langzaam*, German *langsam*).]
Long, lengthy; long-lasting; *esp.* tediously long.
■ **longsomely** *adverb* LME. **longsomeness** *noun* OE.

long standing /lɒŋ 'standɪŋ, *as attrib. adjective* 'lɒŋstandɪŋ/ *noun phr. & adjective.* As adjective usu. **long-standing**. M16.
[ORIGIN from LONG *adjective*[1] + STANDING *noun*. As adjective partly attrib. use of noun, partly from LONG *adverb* + STANDING *adjective*.]
► **A** *noun phr.* Continuance for a long time in a settled and recognized position, rank, etc.; (now *rare*) an instance of this. Chiefly in ***of long standing***. M16.
► **B** *adjective.* Of long standing; that has existed for a long time, not recent. E19.

long-suffering /lɒŋ'sʌf(ə)rɪŋ, *as attrib. adjective* 'lɒŋ sʌf(ə)rɪŋ/ *noun & adjective.* E16.
[ORIGIN from LONG *adjective*[1] + SUFFERING *noun*. As adjective largely from LONG *adverb* + SUFFERING *adjective*.]
► **A** *noun.* Patient endurance of provocation or trial. E16.
► **B** *adjective.* Enduring provocation or trial with patience. M16.
■ **long-sufferingly** *adverb* L19.

long-tail /'lɒŋteɪl/ *noun.* L16.
[ORIGIN from LONG *adjective*[1] + TAIL *noun*[1].]
1 A long-tailed animal; formerly, a dog or horse with the tail uncut; a long-tailed bird, *spec.* (***a***) the long-tailed duck, *Clangula hyemalis*; (***b***) the white-tailed tropicbird, *Phaethon lepturus*; (***c***) *dial.* a pheasant. L16.
2 A native of the county of Kent in SE England (in allusion to the jocular imputation that the people of Kent had tails). Long *obsolete* exc. *dial.* E17.
– COMB.: **long-tail pair** *ELECTRONICS* orig., a pair of matched valves connected to a common large resistor; now usu., a pair of matched bipolar transistors with their emitters so connected.

long-tailed /'lɒŋteɪld/ *adjective.* L15.
[ORIGIN formed as LONG-TAIL + -ED[2].]
1 Having a long tail. L15.
2 Of a word: having a long termination. Formerly also (of a speech etc.), long-winded. *joc.* M16.
– SPECIAL COLLOCATIONS: **long-tailed duck** a marine duck, *Clangula hyemalis*, of Arctic regions, the male of which has elongated tail feathers. ***long-tailed jaeger***: see JAEGER *noun*[2]. ***long-tailed mag***: see MAG *noun*[1] 2. **long-tailed pair** *ELECTRONICS* = LONG-TAIL *pair*. ***long-tailed SKUA***. ***long-tailed tailorbird***: see TAILOR *noun*. **long-tailed tit** any of several small tits of the family Aegithalidae, esp. *Aegithalos caudatus*.

longueur /lɔ̃(ŋ)'ɡəː, *foreign* lɔ̃ɡœːr (*pl. same*)/ *noun.* L18.
[ORIGIN French = length.]
A lengthy or tedious passage of writing, music, etc.; a tedious stretch of time.

longwards /'lɒŋwədz/ *adverb.* L20.
[ORIGIN from LONG *adjective*[1] + -WARDS.]
PHYSICS. Towards longer wavelengths; on the long-wavelength side *of*.
■ Also **longward** *adverb* L20.

longways /'lɒŋweɪz/ *preposition & adverb.* M16.
[ORIGIN from LONG *adjective*[1] + -WAYS.]
► †**A** *preposition.* In the direction of the length of, along. M16–M17.
► **B** *adverb.* In the direction of the length of a thing; longwise, lengthways; longitudinally. L16.

long-winded /lɒŋ'wɪndɪd/ *adjective.* L16.
[ORIGIN from LONG *adjective*[1] + WIND *noun*[1] + -ED[2].]
1 Capable of continuing in action for a long time without being out of breath; long-breathed. L16.
2 (Of a person) given to tedious lengthiness in speech or writing, or to dilatoriness in action; (of speech etc.) tediously long. L16.
■ **long-windedly** *adverb* M19. **long-windedness** *noun* M19.

longwise /'lɒŋwʌɪz/ *adverb.* M16.
[ORIGIN from LONG *adjective*[1] + -WISE.]
Lengthwise, longitudinally, longways.

†**longwort** *noun* var. of LUNGWORT.

lonicera /lɒ'nɪs(ə)rə/ *noun.* L18.
[ORIGIN mod. Latin (see below), from Adam *Lonicer* (1528–86), German botanist.]
Any of various climbing shrubs of the genus *Lonicera* (family Caprifoliaceae), which includes the common honeysuckle, *L. periclymenum*; *esp.* a dense evergreen shrub, *L. nitidum*, much used as hedging.

Lonk /lɒŋk/ *noun.* M19.
[ORIGIN Dial. var. of 1st syll. of *Lancashire*.]
(An animal of) a variety of large mountain sheep which originated in Lancashire or Yorkshire in northern England; the wool of such sheep.

lonnin(g) *noun* var. of LOANING.

Lonsdale belt /lɒnzdeɪl 'bɛlt/ *noun phr.* E20.
[ORIGIN The title of Hugh Cecil Lowther (1857–1944), fifth earl of *Lonsdale*, who presented the first one.]
Any of various belts conferred on professional boxing champions of the UK.

lontar /'lɒntɑː/ *noun.* E19.
[ORIGIN Malay.]
= PALMYRA. Also, a manuscript written on leaves of this palm.

loo /luː/ *noun*[1]. L17.
[ORIGIN Abbreviation of LANTERLOO.]
1 A round card game in which a player who fails to take a trick or breaks any of the laws of the game is required to pay a certain sum to a pool; the fact of having to pay a sum to the pool at loo; the sum deposited in the pool. L17.
2 A party playing at loo; a social gathering for playing loo. Now *rare.* M18.
– COMB.: **loo table** a round table for playing loo on or resembling one for this purpose.

loo /luː/ *noun*[2]. *obsolete* exc. *hist.* L17.
[ORIGIN formed as LOUP *noun*[2].]
More fully ***loo mask***. A half-mask covering the upper part of the face, worn by women in the 17th cent.

loo /luː/ *noun*[3]. L19.
[ORIGIN Hindi *lūh*, *lū*, also *lūk(h)*, from Sanskrit *lūkṣa*, Prakrit *lūha*, *lukkha* dry.]
In Bihar and the Punjab: a hot dust-laden wind.

loo /luː/ *noun*[4]. *colloq.* M20.
[ORIGIN Unknown.]
A water closet, a lavatory.

loo *noun*[5], *adjective* var. of LEW *noun*, *adjective*.

loo /luː/ *verb*[1] *trans.* Long *obsolete* exc. *dial.* Pa. t. & pple **looed**, **loo'd**. M17.
[ORIGIN Aphet. from HALLOO *verb*.]
Incite by shouting 'halloo!'; urge *on* by shouts.

loo /luː/ *verb*[2] *trans.* Pa. t. & pple **looed**, (usu.) **loo'd**. L17.
[ORIGIN from LOO *noun*[1].]
1 Subject to a forfeit at the game of loo. L17.
2 *fig.* Defeat, thwart. Now *dial.* E18.

loo *verb*[3] var. of LEW *verb*.

loo /luː/ *interjection.* E17.
[ORIGIN Aphet. from HALLOO *interjection*.]
Inciting a dog to the chase; = HALLOO *interjection*.

looby /'luːbi/ *noun.* Now chiefly *dial.* LME.
[ORIGIN Uncertain: perh. rel. to LOB *noun*[1].]
An awkward, stupid, clownish person; a lout.
■ †**loobily** *adjective* loutish, awkward, clumsy: M17–L18.

†**looch** *noun* var. of LOHOCH.

looey /'luːi/ *noun. N. Amer. slang.* Also **looie**. E20.
[ORIGIN Abbreviation of LIEUTENANT (in N. Amer. pronunc.): see -Y[6], -IE.]
A lieutenant.

loof /luːf/ *noun*[1]. *Scot. & N. English.* LME.
[ORIGIN Old Norse *lófi* = Gothic *lofa*.]
The palm of the hand.

loof /luːf/ *noun*[2]. Now *rare.* M19.
[ORIGIN Arabic *lūf*: see LOOFAH.]
= LOOFAH.

loofah /'luːfə/ *noun.* Also **luffa** /'lʌfə/. L19.
[ORIGIN Arabic *lūfa* the plant, *lūf* the species.]
A coarse sponge made from the bleached vascular system of the fruit of a tropical gourd, *Luffa aegyptiaca*, used to cleanse and scrub the skin. Also, the gourd itself.

loogan /'luːɡ(ə)n/ *noun. arch. US slang.* E20.
[ORIGIN Unknown.]
A stupid or despicable person.

looie *noun* var. of LOOEY.

look /lʊk/ *noun.* ME.
[ORIGIN from the verb.]
1 The action or an act of looking; a glance of the eyes; a particular direction of the eyes in order to look at someone or something (foll. by *at*, for the purpose of examining or considering); *transf.* an examination, a consideration, (foll. by *at*). ME.

> A. LOOS Mons. Broussard . . took a good look at us. V. WOOLF The hat she stuck on without giving a look in the glass. K. TENNANT Then she saw me . . and if looks could have killed! D. EDEN 'What are you doing with that torch?' 'Just having a look round.' B. MONTGOMERY The whole question of mobilisation requires a new look. W. WHARTON She gives me a couple of long looks.

2 *sing.* & in *pl.* Personal appearance or aspect; an expression in the eyes or on the face; (now usu. in *pl.*) an impression given by a person's general appearance; in *pl.* sometimes *spec.* good looks. LME.

> J. GALSWORTHY The moustache, which imparted a somewhat military look to his face. RADCLYFFE HALL She had looks, too; he thought her a lovely creature. C. POTOK The look of surprise was gone from his face. R. L. FOX A venerable old man with a look of Homer. W. MAXWELL I studied the look in his hazel eyes.

3 The appearance of an inanimate or abstract thing, esp. as expressive of its quality or nature; a way in which a thing appears. M16. ›**b** An appearance, style, or effect (usu. of a specified kind) of dress, toilette, or decoration. M20.

> E. WAUGH By the look of them, they were . . cheap cigars. K. AMIS The table had . . a cheap, hasty look. **b** C. ACHEBE The crew . . aspire to the military look. *Hairdo Ideas* If you are considering a longer look, here's how to grow your hair.

– PHRASES: ***dirty look***: see DIRTY *adjective*. **for the look of the thing** *colloq.* for the sake of appearances. ***good looks***: see GOOD *adjective*. **have a look of** resemble vaguely, remind the spectator of the appearance of (a person or thing). ***new look***: see NEW *adjective*. **not like the look of** find (a situation etc.) disconcerting or alarming. ***throw a look***: see THROW *verb*. ***wet look***: see WET *adjective*.

look /lʊk/ *verb.*
[ORIGIN Old English *lōcian* = Old Saxon *lōkon*, Middle Dutch *loeken*, from West Germanic, rel. to Old High German *luogēn* (German dial. *lugen*) see, look, spy.]
► **I** Direct one's sight.

L

1 **a** *verb intrans.* Give a certain direction to one's sight; use one's ability to see; direct one's eyes to some person or object (foll. by *at*, (arch.) *on, upon*); occas. (now *colloq.*), give a look of surprise, stare; make a visual search or examination. Also, of the eye: be directed to some person or object. OE. ▸**b** *verb intrans.* Direct or apply one's mind; turn or fix one's attention or regard. (Foll. by *at*, (arch.) *on, upon.*) OE. ▸**c** *verb intrans.* In *imper.* Demanding attention or expostulating. Also ***look you***, (arch.) ***look ye*** (repr. popular speech ***look'ee***), (more brusque) ***look here***. See also LOOKIT, LOOKY. OE. ▸**d** *verb trans.* Direct (a look etc.) with the eyes; express by a look or glance, or by one's countenance; show or threaten by one's looks. L16.

> **a** G. BERKELEY When we look only with one eye. OED Yes, you may look! W. S. MAUGHAM Though the police looked with care, they had discovered no fingerprints. E. O'NEILL They'd run over you as soon as look at you. J. C. POWYS Resplendently dressed ladies looked significantly at each other. C. ISHERWOOD Looking grimly into the mirror. B. RUBENS He looked straight ahead of him. M. SARTON Go into the study and look at TV. E. WELTY Roy looked from one man to the other. V. S. NAIPAUL I liked to look; I noticed everything. **b** SHAKES. *Haml.* He that made us with such large discourse, Looking before and after. M. PATTISON The . . manner of looking at things varies. **c** R. CROMPTON 'Look here!' began one outlaw in righteous indignation. I. MURDOCH Look, there isn't anything to say, is there? **d** J. THOMSON They . . sigh'd, and look'd unutterable Things. A. E. HOUSMAN Look your last at me, For I come home no more. A. CHRISTIE Poirot looked a question. The lady explained.

2 *verb trans.* Take care, make sure, see, *that* or *how* something is done (*arch.*); use one's sight to ascertain or observe (now *spec.* at a glance) *who, what, how, whether*, etc. Formerly also, consider, ascertain, *who, when, whether*, etc.; try *if* something can be done etc. OE.

> SHELLEY When I call, Look ye obey the masters. J. H. NEWMAN He glanced from one article to another, looking who were the University-preachers.

†**3** *verb trans.* Take care of, keep, guard, watch over, preserve in safety; observe (a day). OE–LME.

4 *verb trans.* (Chiefly synonymous with *verb intrans.* with preposition.) Look at or towards; view, inspect, examine visually or (formerly) mentally; (now *rare*) bring by one's looks into a certain place or condition; search for, seek out. Now *dial.* exc. in ***look a person in the eye***, ***look a person in the face***, & in certain phrs. (see below). ME. ▸†**b** Consult or refer to (an author, a book, or a place in a text); search for (a word etc.) in a book of reference. ME–E19.

> SHAKES. *Cymb.* Thou hast look'd thyself into my grace. ALLAN RAMSAY He frown'd and look'd his watch. G. NORTH I was looking the sheep when the station rang.

5 *verb trans.* Expect to *do*, †*that*, †*a thing*; intend, seek, try, *to do*. Formerly also, wait for the time *when*, be curious to see *how, whether*, etc. E16.

> S. DANIEL His fortune gives him more than he could looke. A. E. HOUSMAN Two lovers looking to be wed.

▸ **II** Have a certain appearance.

6 *verb intrans.* (In some uses as copular verb.) Have the appearance of being; seem to the sight or the mind. Foll. by noun or adjective compl., inf., adverb (now chiefly *well, ill*, or indefinite in *how*). ME.

> *Manchester Examiner* Miss Anderson looked the part to perfection. J. CONRAD She doesn't look just a girl. I. MURDOCH He remained . . , looking the picture of health. J. BETJEMAN A gun-emplacement . . Looks older than the hill fort. P. CAMPBELL Calais to Troyes looked about 250 miles. E. REVELEY They even looked alike, both tall willowy . . types. P. FERGUSON It wasn't often that Lily looked beaten. A. BROOKNER How do you think she's looking?

good-looking, ***ill-looking***, etc.

▸ **III** Have an outlook, face a particular way.

7 *verb intrans.* Have or afford a particular outlook; face or turn (in a particular direction); face, front, or be turned *towards, into, on to*, etc. Cf. ***look out*** (c) below. M16.

> P. V. PRICE A vineyard that looks south . . will give wines that smile.

8 *verb intrans.* Show a tendency; tend, point, (in a particular direction). Formerly also (*rare*), tend or promise *to do*. E17.

> P. GREG All the facts look the other way.

– PHRASES ETC.: **here's looking at you**, (*arch.*) **here's looking towards you** *colloq.*: used as a toast. ***look a gift-horse in the mouth***: see GIFT *noun*. ***look alive***: see ALIVE 4. ***look a person in the eye***: see EYE *noun*. ***look a person in the face***: see FACE *noun*. **look as if**, (*colloq.*) **look as though** have an appearance suggesting the belief that; freq. *impers.* in ***it looks as if***, ***it looked as if***, etc. ***look babies***: see BABY *noun* 3. ***look big***: see BIG *adverb*. ***look daggers***: see DAGGER *noun*[1]. **look down one's nose at** be scornful or dismissive of, feel oneself to be superior to. ***look for trouble***: see TROUBLE *noun*. ***look good***: see GOOD *adjective*. **look like** (*a*) have the appearance of being; seem to be; (*b*) give promise of (esp. *doing*), threaten, show a likelihood of; usu. *impers.* in ***it looks like***, ***it looked like***, etc. ***look lively***: see LIVELY *adjective* 4. ***look one's age***: see AGE *noun* 1. **look oneself** appear to be in one's usual health. ***look on the bright side***: see BRIGHT *adjective* 1b. **look sharp** †(*a*) keep strict watch; (*b*) bestir oneself briskly, lose no time. ***look sick***: see SICK *adjective*. ***look small***: see SMALL *adjective*. **look the other way** ignore what one should notice. ***look the part***: see PART *noun*. †**look what** whatever. **look what you've done!** *colloq.*: rebuking a person immediately after an action. **look who's here!** *colloq.*: expr. surprise or pleasure at an arrival. ***look who's talking***: see TALK *verb*. **not know which way to look** be embarrassed. ***way of looking at it***, ***way of looking at things***: see WAY *noun*.

– WITH ADVERBS IN SPECIALIZED SENSES: **look about** be on the watch, be on the lookout; make a search *for*; let one's eyes rove. **look around** look about, look round (*for*). **look back** (*a*) turn and look at something in the direction from which one is going or from which one's face is turned; (*b*) direct the mind to something that is past, think on the past, (foll. by *into, on, upon, to*); (*c*) *colloq.* show signs of reversal, decline, or interrupted progress, be regretful or half-hearted about an enterprise one has begun, (usu. in neg. contexts). **look down** (*a*) foll. by *on, upon*: hold in contempt, scorn, consider oneself superior to; (*b*) COMMERCE tend downwards in price; (*c*) *arch.* quell or overcome by one's looks. **look forward to** await (an expected event), esp. with pleasure. **look in** (*a*) enter a room etc. for the purpose of seeing something; make a short call or visit (foll. by *on, upon* a person); (*b*) *colloq.* watch a television programme. **look on** direct one's looks towards an object in contemplation or observation; *esp.* be a mere spectator (and not a participator in the action). **look out** (*a*) look from within a building etc. to the outside; put one's head out of an aperture, e.g. a window, to look; (*b*) be on the watch, keep one's eyes open, (*for*); exercise vigilance, be prepared *for*; have care *for*; (*c*) have or afford an outlook (*on, over*, etc.); †(*d*) make a brief excursion; (*e*) find by looking, select by inspection. **look over** *verb phr. trans.* cast one's eyes over (a person or thing); scrutinize; inspect one by one or part by part. **look round** look about in every direction; look in another direction; go round looking at the features of a place; examine the possibilities etc. with a view to deciding on a course of action; search about *for*. **look sideways** look (*at*) or regard furtively or improperly; *spec.* glance amorously or suspiciously. **look through** (*a*) *verb phr. trans.* give (a person) a searching look or glance; examine or survey exhaustively or successively; †(*b*) become visible or obvious. **look up** (*a*) raise the eyes, turn the face upward; ***look up to*** (*fig.*), have a feeling of respect or veneration for; †(*b*) cheer up, take courage, be cheerful; (*c*) improve, esp. in price or prosperity; (*d*) search for; now *esp.* search for (something) in a dictionary or work of reference, among papers, etc., consult (a book etc.) in order to gain information; (*e*) *colloq.* call on, go to visit (a person), esp. for the first time or after loss of contact; (*f*) *arch.* direct vigilance to; (*g*) ***look up and down***, scrutinize the appearance of (a person) from head to foot. †**look upon** = ***look on*** above.

– WITH PREPOSITIONS IN SPECIALIZED SENSES: **look about** — turn one's eyes to or make searches in various parts of (a room etc.); go about observing in (a country, town, etc.); ***look about one***, turn one's eyes or attention to surrounding objects, consider or take account of one's position and circumstances. **look after** — (*a*) follow with the eye; look in the direction of (a person or thing departing); *fig.* think regretfully of (something past); †(*b*) anticipate with desire or fear; look forward to; (*c*) seek for, demand (qualities); (*d*) concern oneself with; attend to, take care of; (*e*) *rare* keep watch over. **look against** — look and be dazzled by. **look around** — = ***look round*** below. **look at** — (*a*) take or accept (a thing), become involved in, find (a person) attractive, show sexual interest in, (usu. in neg. contexts); (*b*) ***to look at***, in respect of appearance; ***not much to look at***; (*c*) ***to look at*** — (colloq.), judging from the appearance of —; (see also senses 1a, b above). **look for** — (*a*) expect, hope for, anticipate, be on the watch for; (*b*) seek, search for; ***look for a needle in a haystack***, ***look for a needle in a bottle of hay***: see NEEDLE *noun*; (*c*) *Scot.* look at, observe. **look into** — (*a*) direct one's sight to the interior of, examine the inside of, consult (a book etc.) in a cursory manner; (*b*) examine (a matter) minutely; investigate (a question); (*c*) enter (a house etc.) for a few moments in passing. **look on** — †(*a*) pay regard to; hold in esteem, respect; (*b*) regard or consider *as*; (*c*) regard with a specified expression or feeling; (see also senses 1a, b above). **look over** — (*a*) peruse or inspect cursorily; †(*b*) ignore, leave out of consideration; (*c*) *arch.* overlook, pardon, (a fault); (*d*) *Scot.* look after, take care of. **look round** — (*a*) inspect, scrutinize, search; go round looking at the features of (a place); (*b*) put one's head round (a door etc.) to look. **look through** — (*a*) direct one's sight through (an aperture, a transparent body, or something having interstices); pretend not to see (freq. ***look right through***, ***look straight through***); penetrate the dishonesty or pretence of; †(*b*) be visible through; (*c*) direct one's view over the whole of or to every one of; peruse cursorily from end to end; glance through (a book etc.). **look to** — (*a*) direct one's attention to; select for consideration; (in biblical translations) regard with favour; (*b*) attend to, take care of; concern oneself with guarding, preserving, or improving; ***look to it***, be careful, beware, take care or see *that*; ***look to one's hits***: see HIT *noun*; ***look to one's laurels***: see LAUREL *noun* 2; (*c*) keep watch over; (*d*) direct one's expectations to; rely on (a person etc.) *for* something; look forward to, expect, count on, aim at. **look unto** — *arch.* = ***look to*** above. **look upon** — = ***look on*** above; (see also senses 1a, b above).

– COMB. (partly from the noun): **look-ahead** *noun & adjective* (designating) an action of judging what can happen or is likely to happen in the (immediate) future; **look-and-say** *noun & adjective* (designating) a method of teaching reading by identifying each word as a whole (as opp. to treating a word as a series of separate letters); **look-around**, **look-round** an inspection, a scrutiny, a search; **look-on** *adjective* designating a fishing net pulled up as a test of the condition of others; ***look-round***: see ***look-around*** above; **look-through** PAPER-MAKING the appearance of paper when held up to light; **lookup** the action of systematic electronic information retrieval; a facility for this.

lookalike /ˈlʊkəlʌɪk/ *noun & adjective*. M20.

[ORIGIN from LOOK *verb* + ALIKE *adjective*.]

▸ **A** *noun*. A person or thing closely resembling another in appearance, a double; a product closely similar to or meant to be identified with another. (Freq. following the name of the person or thing resembled.) M20.

> L. GREENBAUM Except for the wife's stomach, the two women were look-alikes. M. PIERCY Burt Reynolds look-alikes in pick-up trucks. *Practical Computing* This Japanese PC look-alike has nothing new to offer.

▸ **B** *adjective*. Closely similar, esp. in appearance; identical. L20.

look-down /ˈlʊkdaʊn/ *noun*. M19.

[ORIGIN from LOOK *verb* or *noun* + DOWN *adverb*.]

1 A view or prospect downwards. *rare*. M19.

2 A silvery carangid fish, *Selene vomer*, of the tropical Atlantic, which has a distinctive high blunt forehead. Also called ***horse-head***. *US*. L19.

looked /lʊkt/ *adjective*. *obsolete* exc. *Scot.* L16.

[ORIGIN from LOOK *noun* + -ED[2].]

Having a look or appearance of a specified kind (usu. preceded by defining adjective or adverb). Now only in ***well-looked***.

looker /ˈlʊkə/ *noun & verb*. ME.

[ORIGIN from LOOK *verb* + -ER[1].]

▸ **A** *noun*. **1** A person who looks after or has charge of something; a shepherd, a farm bailiff, a steward; (as 2nd elem. of comb.) an official inspector of the specified thing. Now *dial.* ME.

2 A person who looks or directs the eyes. Also foll. by adverb or preposition. LME.

3 A person (occas. a thing) having an appearance or looks of a specified kind. L15. ▸**b** A good-looking person, esp. a woman; a strikingly attractive thing. *colloq.* L19.

> **b** J. COE Not much of a looker but she had the most fabulous contacts.

good-looker: see GOOD *adjective*.

– COMB.: **looker-in** (*a*) a person who looks in on another, a casual visitor; (*b*) a viewer of television; **looker-on** a person who looks on, a mere spectator, (cf. ***onlooker***); **looker-out** in the book trade, a person who looks out wanted volumes from stock; **looker-upper** *colloq.* a person who looks something up.

▸ **B** *verb trans. & intrans.* Tend and guard (farm animals). *dial.* L19.

look-in /ˈlʊkɪn/ *noun*. M19.

[ORIGIN from LOOK *verb* or *noun* + IN *adverb*.]

1 A hasty glance; a peep. *rare*. M19.

2 An informal call, a short visit. M19.

3 An opportunity to take part in something, esp. with a chance of success; a share of attention. *colloq.* L19.

looking /ˈlʊkɪŋ/ *noun*. ME.

[ORIGIN from LOOK *verb* + -ING[1].]

1 The action of LOOK *verb*; an instance of this. Also foll. by adverb or preposition. ME.

†**2** A person's look, expression, or appearance. ME–E17.

– COMB.: **looking-forward** an act of looking forward, an anticipation of future events; **looking-over** an inspection.

looking glass /ˈlʊkɪŋɡlɑːs/ *noun*. E16.

[ORIGIN from LOOKING + GLASS *noun*.]

▸ **I 1** A glass to look in, in order to see one's own face or figure; a mirror made of silvered glass. E16.

2 Plate glass; glass silvered for use as a mirror. Now *rare*. L17.

▸ **II 3** A chamber pot. *arch. slang*. E17.

– COMB. & PHRASES: **looking-glass carp** = ***mirror carp*** s.v. MIRROR *noun*; **looking-glass land**, **looking-glass world** an imaginary world or land in which everything is as it would be if seen reversed, through a looking glass; ***Venus's looking glass***: see VENUS.

lookism /ˈlʊkɪzəm/ *noun*. L20.

[ORIGIN from LOOK *noun* + -ISM.]

Prejudice or discrimination on the grounds of a person's appearance.

■ **lookist** *noun & adjective* L20.

lookit /ˈlʊkɪt/ *verb* (*imper.*). *N. Amer. colloq.* E20.

[ORIGIN Extension of LOOK *verb*. Cf. LOOKY.]

1 *verb intrans.* Demanding attention or expostulating. Cf. LOOK *verb* 1C. E20.

2 *verb trans.* Look at (something or someone). E20.

lookout /ˈlʊkaʊt/ *noun*. L17.

[ORIGIN from LOOK *verb* or *noun* + OUT *adverb*.]

1 **a** A person or party employed or stationed to look out; a reconnoitring boat or vessel. L17. ▸**b** A station or building from which a person or party can look out. Orig. NAUTICAL. E18.

> **a** A. NICOL 'Someone!' the look-out called.

2 The action or an act of looking out. Chiefly in ***keep a lookout*** (***for***), ***keep a good lookout*** (***for***), etc., ***on the lookout*** (***for***), ***upon the lookout*** (***for***). Orig. NAUTICAL. M18.

> S. BECKETT Parts would . . get lost if he did not keep a sharp look-out. R. INGALLS Advise residents . . to be on the look-out for this highly dangerous animal.

3 A more or less distant view; a prospect; a prospective condition, an outlook. L18.

> DICKENS 'He's going at the knees.' 'That's a bad look-out.' C. MACKENZIE I remember the look-out . . to an ocean of blue sky.

4 With possess.: a person's own concern, which others are not bound to consider. Chiefly after *be*. L18.

T. S. ELIOT If they haven't any contingency fund . . , that's their look-out.

look-over /ˈlʊkəʊvə/ *noun*. **E20**.
[**ORIGIN** from **LOOK** *verb* or *noun* + **OVER** *adverb*.]
An examination, a survey.

look-see /ˈlʊksiː/ *noun*. *slang*. **L19**.
[**ORIGIN** from **LOOK** *verb* or *noun* + **SEE** *verb*, from or imit. of pidgin English.]
A survey; a tour of inspection, a reconnaissance; an investigation.

look-up /ˈlʊkʌp/ *noun*. **M19**.
[**ORIGIN** from **LOOK** *verb* + **UP** *adverbs*.]
1 A call, a visit. *rare*. **M19**.
2 The action of looking something up in a dictionary, file, etc.; a facility for this; retrieval of information about items in an ordered collection. Freq. ***attrib***. **M20**.

looky /ˈlʊki/ *verb intrans*. (*imper*.). *N. Amer. colloq*. **L19**.
[**ORIGIN** Extension of **LOOK** *verb*, perh. repr. *look ye* (see **LOOK** *verb* 1c). Cf. **LOOKIT**.]
Demanding attention or expostulating. Chiefly in ***looky here***.

loom /luːm/ *noun*[1].
[**ORIGIN** Old English *gelōma*, formed as **Y-** + base also in *andlōman* (pl.) apparatus, furniture. Aphet. in Middle English.]
1 *gen*. An implement, a tool. *obsolete* exc. *Scot*. & *N. English*. **OE**. ▸†**b** The penis. **LME–M16**. ▸†**c** = **HEIRLOOM**. **LME–E19**.
2 An open vessel, as a bucket, tub, vat, etc. *obsolete* exc. *Scot*. **ME**.
3 A machine in which yarn or thread is woven into fabric by the crossing of vertical and horizontal threads (called respectively the warp and weft). **LME**.

fig.: T. NASHE Spiders . . wont to set vp their loomes in euery windowe.

circular loom, ***hand loom***, ***Jacquard loom***, ***power loom***, etc.
4 The art, business, or process of weaving. Chiefly *literary*. **L17**.

TENNYSON Display'd a splendid silk of foreign loom.

5 *ELECTRICITY*. **a** Flexible tubing fitted over an ordinary insulated wire to provide additional protection. **E20**. ▸**b** A group of parallel insulated wires bound together into a bundle. **M20**.

loom /luːm/ *noun*[2]. **L17**.
[**ORIGIN** Scandinavian: cf. Norwegian *lom*, *lumm*, Icelandic *hlummur* (Old Norse *hlumr*).]
The part of an oar between the rowlock and the grip for hands; *loosely* the handle of an oar.

loom /luːm/ *noun*[3]. Orig. *Shetland*. **L17**.
[**ORIGIN** Old Norse *lómr*.]
Any of several diving birds of northern seas, *esp*. a guillemot or a diver (cf. **LOON** *noun*[2]). Also, the flesh of these birds used as food.

loom /luːm/ *noun*[4]. **M19**.
[**ORIGIN** from **LOOM** *verb*[2].]
Chiefly *NAUTICAL*. An indistinct and exaggerated appearance or outline of an object or of land on the horizon, caused by refraction of light through mist etc. Also, a glow in the sky caused by reflection of light from a lighthouse etc.; a mirage over water or ice.

loom /luːm/ *verb*[1] *trans*. *rare*. **M16**.
[**ORIGIN** from **LOOM** *noun*[1].]
1 Weave (a fabric). **M16**.
2 ***loom the web***, mount the warp on a loom. **E19**.

loom /luːm/ *verb*[2] *intrans*. **M16**.
[**ORIGIN** Prob. of Low Dutch origin: cf. East Frisian *lōmen* (whence Swedish dial. *loma*) move slowly, rel. to Middle High German *lüemen* be weary, from *lüeme* slack, soft.]
1 Appear indistinctly, come into view in an enlarged and indefinite form, freq. threateningly, (*lit*. & *fig*.). Also foll. by *up*. Freq. with adjective compl., as ***loom large***. **M16**.

S. BARSTOW The bandstand . . looms up out of the dark. CLIVE JAMES Big ships loom at the ends of city streets. D. MURPHY The grey school buildings loomed out of the rain. R. SCRUTON Taxation has always loomed large among political issues.

†**2** Of a ship, the sea: move slowly up and down. *rare*. Only in **17**.

loomer /ˈluːmə/ *noun*. **L19**.
[**ORIGIN** from **LOOM** *verb*[1] + **-ER**[1].]
In weaving, an operative who mounts the warp on a loom.

loomery /ˈluːməri/ *noun*. **M19**.
[**ORIGIN** from **LOOM** *noun*[3] + **-ERY**.]
A place where looms or guillemots breed; a colony of looms.

looming /ˈluːmɪŋ/ *noun*. **E17**.
[**ORIGIN** from **LOOM** *verb*[2] + **-ING**[1].]
The action or an act of looming or coming indistinctly into view; a mirage over water or ice (cf. **LOOM** *noun*[4]).

loon /luːn/ *noun*[1]. Chiefly *Scot*. & *N. English*. **LME**.
[**ORIGIN** Unknown.]
1 A worthless, dishonest, or idle person. **LME**. ▸**b** A prostitute or promiscuous woman. **M16**.
2 A man of low birth or condition: contrasted with ***lord***. *arch*. **M16**.
3 *gen*. A fellow, a man; a boy, a youth. **M16**.
4 A boor, a lout. **E17**.

loon /luːn/ *noun*[2]. **M17**.
[**ORIGIN** Prob. from (the same root as) **LOOM** *noun*[3], alt. perh. by assim. to **LOON** *noun*[1]. In sense 2 perh. infl. by **LOONY** *noun*[2].]
1 Any bird of the diver family, *esp*. (more fully ***common loon***) the great northern diver, *Gavia immer*. Cf. **LOOM** *noun*[3]. Chiefly *N. Amer*. **M17**. ▸**b** The great crested grebe; the little grebe. **L17**.
(***as***) ***crazy as a loon*** (with allus. to the bird's actions in escaping from danger and its wild cry).
2 A crazy person; a simpleton. **L19**.

loon /luːn/ *noun*[3]. *colloq*. **L20**.
[**ORIGIN** from the verb.]
In *pl*. & more fully ***loon pants***, ***loon trousers***. Close-fitting casual trousers widely flared from the knees to the ankles.

loon /luːn/ *verb intrans*. *slang*. **M20**.
[**ORIGIN** Unknown.]
Esp. of a young person: spend one's leisure time in a pleasurable way, e.g. by dancing to popular music; lie or wander *about*.

looney *adjective & noun* var. of **LOONY** *adjective & noun*[2].

loonie /ˈluːni/ *noun*[1]. *Canad. colloq*. Also **-ny**. **L20**.
[**ORIGIN** from **LOON** *noun*[2] + **-IE**, **-Y**[6].]
The Canadian one-dollar coin introduced in 1987; the Canadian dollar.

loonie *adjective & noun*[2] var. of **LOONY** *adjective & noun*[2].

loony *noun*[1] var. of **LOONIE** *noun*[1].

loony /ˈluːni/ *adjective & noun*[2]. *colloq*. Also **looney**, **loonie**, (now *rare*) **luny**. **M19**.
[**ORIGIN** Abbreviation of **LUNATIC**: see **-Y**[6].]
▸ **A** *adjective*. Lunatic, crazed, daft, dazed, demented, foolish, silly; holding unacceptably radical political views. **M19**.

Truck & Driver A fractured leg didn't stop the madman . . pulling his loony stunts. L. MCMURTRY Nobody would be loony enough to hire you to cook. *Times* The loony left has been disastrous for the Labour Party.

▸ **B** *noun*. A person who is mentally ill; an eccentric or foolish person. **L19**.
– **COMB.**: ***loony bin***: see **BIN** *noun* 7; **loony-doctor** *slang* a doctor who treats mental illnesses, a psychiatrist; **loony tunes** [*Looney Tunes*, a US animated cartoon series beginning in the 1930s, featuring Bugs Bunny and other characters] *noun & adjective* (chiefly *US*) crazy or deranged (people).

loop /luːp/ *noun*[1]. **ME**.
[**ORIGIN** Unknown.]
1 = **LOOPHOLE**. **ME**.
†**2** An opening in the parapet of a fortification; an embrasure. **L15–L17**.

loop /luːp/ *noun*[2]. **LME**.
[**ORIGIN** Uncertain: cf. Irish *lúb*, Gaelic *lùb* a loop, a bend, etc.]
▸ **I 1** A portion of a string, rope, thread, etc., doubled or crossing itself so as to form an aperture, commonly fastened at the point of crossing or juncture (used e.g. as an ornament for dress or as part of a fastener taking a hook or button). **LME**.

E. LINKLATER Round his neck was the running loop of a rope. P. BOWLES He swung the box on one finger by the little loop . . in the string. R. INGALLS The dragon had his tail curled into loops. *Vogue* Shirt . . with loop for buttoning collar up.

2 A thing, course, or figure having more or less the shape of a loop, as a curved line that crosses itself traced or written on paper, a part of the apparent path of a planet, a deep bend of a river; a ring or curved piece of metal etc., as one employed for the insertion of a bolt, ramrod, or rope, as a handle for lifting. **LME**.

M. HUGHES The river meandered in a wide lazy loop. *Tennis* His fear of losing made him hit the ball in higher and higher loops. *New Yorker* Her handwriting was neat and sloping, loops on the letters that demanded them.

in the loop kept fully informed; included in a process. **out of the loop** not kept fully informed; excluded from a process.
▸ **II** *spec*. **3** (A looped part of) a stitch in knitting, crochet, etc. **L18**.
4 *ANATOMY & ZOOLOGY*. A looped vessel, fibre, or other structure. **M19**.
Henle's loop, ***loop of Henle***: see **HENLE**.
5 *MATH*. A closed curve (on a graph etc.). **M19**.
6 **a** A complete circuit or path for an electrical signal or current. **M19**. ▸**b** A railway or telegraph line diverging from, and afterwards returning to, the main line or circuit. **L19**.
7 *SKATING*. A curve crossing itself, or any of several elaborations upon this, made on a single edge. Also (in full ***loop jump***), a jump in which the skater makes a full turn in the air, taking off from and landing on the same edge. **M19**.
8 *PHYSICS*. The portion of a standing wave between two nodes. **L19**.
9 A configuration in fingerprints with lines shaped like simple loops. **L19**.
10 A vertically curved path described by an aeroplane, (orig.) a fairground machine, etc., with a climb and a dive between which the body of the plane etc. is upside down; a manoeuvre in which such a path is taken. **E20**.
loop the loop: see **LOOP** *verb*[1] 6. ***outside loop***: see **OUTSIDE** *adjective*.
11 A slack length of film etc. left between two mechanisms to allow for a difference between the supply and take-up motions; an endless strip of film or magnetic tape allowing continuous repetition. **E20**.
12 = ***loop aerial*** below. **E20**.
13 A sequence of control operations or activities in which each depends on the result of the previous one; *esp*. (more fully ***closed loop***) one in which there is feedback. **M20**.
open loop: see **OPEN** *adjective*.
14 *COMPUTING*. A sequence of instructions which is executed repeatedly (usu. with an operand that changes in each cycle) until some previously specified criterion is satisfied. **M20**.
15 A type of intrauterine contraceptive coil. **M20**.
LIPPES LOOP.
– **COMB.**: **loop aerial**, **loop antenna** an aerial consisting of one or more loops of wire; **loop diuretic** *MEDICINE* a powerful diuretic which inhibits resorption of water and sodium from the loop of Henle in the kidney; **loop film** an endless loop of cinematographic film; ***loop jump***: see sense 7 above; **loop-knit** *adjective* knitted with loop yarn; **loop-knot** †(***a***) a reef knot; (***b***) a single knot tied in a doubled cord etc., so as to leave a loop beyond the knot; **loop-lace** (***a***) a kind of ornament consisting of a series of loops; (***b***) a kind of lace consisting of patterns worked on a ground of fine net; **loop line** = sense 6b above; **loop pile** carpet pile with uncut loops; **loop stitch** *noun & verb* (***a***) *noun* a kind of fancy stitch consisting of loops; (***b***) *verb trans*. connect or attach by means of loop stitches; **loop system** a method of connecting electrical supply points (as lamp roses) by taking the wires to each point from terminals at its switch and at the previous supply point, instead of making a separate joint elsewhere in the circuit; **loop-work** work consisting of loops or looped stitches; **loop-worm** = **LOOPER** *noun*[1] 1; **loop yarn** yarn with one thread fastened in loops around another (usu. finer) thread.

loop /luːp/ *noun*[3]. Now *rare* or *obsolete*. Also **loup**. **L17**.
[**ORIGIN** formed as **LOUPE**.]
FOUNDING. A soft mass of wrought iron taken from the finery for hammering into a bloom.

L

loop /luːp/ *verb*[1]. **LME**.
[**ORIGIN** from **LOOP** *noun*[2].]
1 *verb trans*. Draw through a loop; encircle or enclose *in* or *with* a loop. **LME**.
2 *verb intrans*. Form a loop; *spec*. (of a caterpillar etc.) move by successive curving and straightening actions. Cf. earlier **LOOPER** *noun*[1] 1. **E19**.
3 *verb trans*. Put or form loops on; provide (a garment etc.) with loops. **M19**.
4 *verb trans*. Form into a loop or loops. **M19**.
5 *verb trans*. Fasten (*back*, *up*) by forming into a loop, or by means of an attached loop; join (*together*) or connect by means of a loop or loops; (foll. by *in*) connect (a wire, appliance, etc.) into an electric circuit by the loop system. **L19**.
6 *verb trans*. ***loop the loop***, (of an aeroplane or (orig.) a fairground machine) perform the feat of circling in a vertical loop (see **LOOP** *noun*[2] 10). **E20**.
7 *verb intrans*. *COMPUTING*. Execute a loop. **M20**.
– **COMB.**: **loop-in** a connection between two lengths of wire made at a terminal in the loop system; ***loop-in system*** = ***loop system*** s.v. **LOOP** *noun*[2]; **loop-the-loop** an act of looping the loop.
– **NOTE**: Rare before **M19**.

loop /lʊəp/ *verb*[2] *intrans*. *S. Afr*. **E19**.
[**ORIGIN** Afrikaans from Dutch *lopen* to walk.]
Walk. Freq. in *imper*., commanding an animal to start moving or (now usu.) a person or animal to leave.

looped /luːpt/ *adjective*[1]. **E16**.
[**ORIGIN** from **LOOP** *noun*[2], *verb*[2]: see **-ED**[2], **-ED**[1].]
1 Coiled or wreathed in loops. Formerly also, intertwined. **E16**.
†**2** Having or fastened with a loop. **L16–E17**.
3 Of lace: worked on a ground of fine net. **L17**.
4 Held in a loop, held *up* by a loop. **M19**.
5 Intoxicated, drunk. *slang* (chiefly *N. Amer*.). **M20**.

looped /luːpt/ *adjective*[2]. *rare*. **E17**.
[**ORIGIN** from **LOOP** *noun*[1] + **-ED**[2].]
Having loopholes.

looper /ˈluːpə/ *noun*[1]. **M18**.
[**ORIGIN** from (the same root as) **LOOP** *verb*[1] + **-ER**[1].]
1 The caterpillar of a geometrid moth, which moves by successive curving and straightening actions. **M18**.
2 A contrivance for making loops in a sewing machine etc.; an implement for looping strips together in making rag carpets. **M19**.
3 A person who loops the loop, or who has done so. **E20**.

looper /ˈlʊəpə/ *noun*[2]. *S. Afr*. (now *hist*.). **E19**.
[**ORIGIN** Afrikaans from Dutch, lit. 'runner'.]
Any of the lugs or pellets of buck shot, usu. made by cutting a ball in four. Usu. in *pl*.

loopful /ˈluːpfʊl, -f(ə)l/ *noun*. L19.
[ORIGIN from LOOP *noun*² + -FUL.]
Chiefly MICROBIOLOGY. The quantity of fluid, esp. of a bacterial suspension, which is contained in a loop of (platinum) wire.

loophole /ˈluːphəʊl/ *noun & verb*. L16.
[ORIGIN from LOOP *noun*¹ + HOLE *noun*¹.]
▸ **A** *noun*. **1** A narrow vertical slit in a wall etc. for shooting or looking through or for the admission of light and air. Formerly also, a porthole. L16.
2 *fig*. An outlet, a means of escape; *esp*. an ambiguity or omission in a statute, contract, etc. which affords opportunity for evading its intention. M17.

B. GELDOF We would have to find some legal loophole . . to get supplies . . here quickly.

▸ **B** *verb trans*. Cut loopholes in the walls of; provide with loopholes. M17.

loopy /ˈluːpi/ *adjective*. L18.
[ORIGIN from LOOP *noun*² + -Y¹.]
1 Crafty, deceitful. *Scot*. L18.
2 Full of loops; characterized by loops. M19.
3 Mad or eccentric; crazy. *colloq*. E20.

loose /luːs/ *noun*. E16.
[ORIGIN from LOOSE *verb, adjective*.]
▸ **I 1** ARCHERY. The action or an act of discharging an arrow. E16.
†**2** The conclusion or close of a matter. L16–M17.
3 A state or condition of looseness, laxity, or unrestraint; free indulgence; unrestrained action or feeling; abandonment. Now only in ***give a loose to***, (occas.) ***give loose to***, allow (a person) unrestrained freedom; give full vent or expression to (feelings etc.). L16.
†**4** An act of letting go or parting with something. E–M17.
†**5** The action or an act of getting free, liberation, release. M17–M18.
†**6** An impetuous course or rush. E–M19.
▸ **II 7** *The* state of being loose. Chiefly in ***on the loose***, (*a*) *arch*. living by prostitution; (*b*) enjoying oneself freely, free from ties or commitments; (*c*) escaped from confinement or imprisonment. L18.
8 RUGBY. *The* part of the play in which the ball travels freely from player to player. Chiefly in ***in the loose***. L19.

L

loose /luːs/ *adjective & adverb*. ME.
[ORIGIN Old Norse *lauss* = Old Frisian *lās*, Old Saxon, Old High German *lōs* (Dutch, German *los*), Gothic *laus*, from Germanic, from base also of LEASE *adjective*, -LESS.]
▸ **A** *adjective* **1 a** Free or released from bonds, fetters, or physical restraint; not confined or tethered; (of a horse etc.) running free. ME. ▸†**b** Loosely clothed; naked. LME–E18. ▸**c** Not bound together; not forming a bundle or package; not tied up or secured; having an end or ends hanging free; (of money, cash, etc.) in coins as opp. to notes, in relatively small denominations. L15. ▸**d** Free for disposal or acquisition; unattached, unappropriated, unoccupied. Now *esp*. (of a football or hockey ball) not in any player's possession. L15. ▸**e** Freed from an engagement, obligation, etc. Long *obsolete* exc. *dial*. M16. ▸**f** Of ideas, speech, etc.: unconnected, rambling, stray, random. Now *rare*. L17. ▸**g** Of an inanimate thing: not fastened or attached to that to which it belongs as a part or appendage, or with which it has previously been connected; detached. E18. ▸**h** Not joined to anything else. E19. ▸**i** GRAMMAR. Of a modifying clause or phrase: dispensable without loss of semantic or grammatical completeness. M20.

a A. PRICE There was a mass murderer loose. J. MCPHEE Cook's loose ones [dogs], running amok, could be counted on to . . drive the tied ones berserk. **c** G. GREENE He drew a loose match from his pocket. I. MCEWAN She tucked some loose strands of hair behind her ear.

g ***come loose***, ***get loose***, etc.
2 a Not rigidly or securely attached or fixed in place; ready to move in or come apart from the body to which it is joined or on which it rests. ME. ▸†**b** Of the eyes: not fixed, roving. E17–M19. ▸**c** Of a cough: producing phlegm or sputum with little difficulty. M19.

a R. DAHL He was up on the roof . . replacing some loose tiles. B. MOORE Loose chippings of stone rattled against the . . undercarriage.

3 Not tightly drawn or stretched; slack, relaxed, not tense; limber; *slang* uninhibited. ME. ▸**b** Of clothes: not clinging close to the figure or body; loosely fitting. LME. ▸**c** Of a person's build: ungainly, looking unsuited for brisk movement. M19.

MILTON What time the labour'd Oxe In his loose traces from the furrow came. P. ROTH Standing there as loose and as easy, as happy as I will ever be. *Running* The runners . . will need to keep loose and warm. J. WILCOX The loose flesh on the old woman's throat quivered. **b** R. CHANDLER The violet scarf was loose enough to show that he wore no tie. A. BROOKNER A loose sweater and a long jersey skirt. **c** DICKENS He was a strong, loose, round-shouldered, shuffling shaggy fellow.

4 a Lacking in retentiveness or power of restraint; (of the tongue) likely to speak indiscreetly; lax in principle, conduct, or speech, *esp*. promiscuous, dissolute, immoral. ME. ▸**b** Of the bowels, a person: tending to diarrhoea. E16.

a DRYDEN The scandal I have given by my loose writings. CARLYLE A rash young fool; carries a loose tongue. *International Herald Tribune* Senators, so loose when it comes to their own behavior, suddenly become twitching watchdogs for virtue.

5 Not close or compact in arrangement or structure; not dense or serried; straggling. LME. ▸**b** BOTANY. = LAX *adjective* 2b. L18. ▸**c** Designating or pertaining to exercise or play (esp. in football or hockey) in which those engaged are not close together or in which there is free movement. E19.

SHELLEY The loose array Of horsemen o'er the wide fields. J. A. MICHENER Instead of the compact bales . . . large, loose stacks . . now went to St. Louis. G. LORD The last census, . . had contained fifteen households scattered in a wide, loose circle. Z. TOMIN A cohesive body, not just a loose collection of signatories.

6 Not rigid, strict, correct, or careful; marked by inaccuracy or carelessness; inexact, indeterminate, vague; (of a translation) not close; (qualifying an agent noun) doing the specified act loosely. M16. ▸†**b** Not providing security, unsettled. Only in 17.

W. D. WHITNEY We are loose thinkers and loose talkers. R. G. COLLINGWOOD The problems of philosophy were, even in the loosest sense of that word, eternal. *Times* McGlew was getting methodically behind . . every ball and hitting anything loose. A. BURGESS Staid conservatism is as much an enemy of the language as loose slanginess.

7 Designating a stable etc. in which animals are kept untethered or in which they can move about freely. E19.

– PHRASES: (A small selection of cross-refs. only is included: see esp. other verbs.) ***all hell let loose***: see HELL *noun*. ***a screw loose***: see SCREW *noun*¹. ***cast loose***: see CAST *verb*. **cut loose** (*a*) free oneself, escape, (*from*); (*b*) begin to act freely. ***fast and loose***: see FAST *adjective*. ***have a tile loose***: see TILE *noun*. ***let loose***: see LET *verb*¹.

– SPECIAL COLLOCATIONS & COMB.: **loose back** a method of binding the spine of a book to make it open more easily. **loose-bodied** *adjective* (of a dress) loose-fitting. **loose box** a stall for a horse in which the animal can move about. **loose cannon** *fig*. a person or thing causing unintentional or misdirected damage. **loose change** a quantity of coins for casual use, kept or left in one's pocket etc. **loose coupling** ELECTRICITY: in which the interdependence between circuits is weak. **loose cover** a detachable cover for a chair, couch, or car seat. **loose end** *fig*. (*a*) a disconnected or uncompleted part, a final outstanding matter, (usu. in *pl*.); (*b*) ***at a loose end***, (*N. Amer*.) ***at loose ends***, without a definite occupation, with nothing to do. **loose-ended** *adjective* ended or finished off in a slack, untidy, or inconclusive way. **loose-endedness** the quality or state of being loose-ended. **loose-fill** loose insulating material, as vermiculite, for filling spaces between rafters etc. **loose fish** (*a*) WHALING a whale not attached to a harpoon and line and free for any person to take; (*b*) *slang* a person of irregular habits, a dissipated person. **loose-footed** *adjective* (NAUTICAL) (of a sail) not tightly held in at the foot, (of a boat) having such a sail. **loose forward** RUGBY a forward who plays at the back of the scrum. **loose head** RUGBY the forward in the front row of a scrummage closest to the scrum half as he (or she) puts the ball into the scrummage. **loose-housed** *adjective* kept in loose housing. **loose housing** (a method of housing cattle unconfined in) partly covered barns with access to a feeding area. **loose ice** ice through which a ship etc. can pass. **loose-knit** *adjective* connected in a tenuous or ill-defined way; not closely linked. **loose-leaf** *adjective* (of a notebook, ledger, etc.) made with each leaf separate for ready insertion or removal. **loose-limbed** *adjective* having supple limbs. **loose-lipped** *adjective* (*a*) = *loose-mouthed* below; (*b*) having full lips. **loose-mouthed** *adjective* loose-tongued; uninhibited in speech. **loose order** an arrangement of soldiers etc. with wide intervals between them. **loose rein** a rider's relaxed control of a horse, a control that is not rigorous, (chiefly in ***on a loose rein***). **loose scrum**, **loose scrummage** RUGBY a scrum formed by the players round the ball during play, and not ordered by the referee. †**loose shot** marksmen not attached to a company. **loose-skinned** *adjective* having skin wrinkled or hanging in folds. **loose smut** any of several diseases of cereals, esp. barley and wheat, caused by smut fungi of the genus *Ustilago*. **loose-tongued** *adjective* likely to speak indiscreetly, blabbing.

▸ **B** *adverb*. Loosely; with a loose hold. L15.
sit loose (to) be independent (of), be indifferent (to).
■ **loosely** *adverb* LME. **looseness** *noun* LME.

loose /luːs/ *verb*. ME.
[ORIGIN from the adjective.]
1 *verb trans*. Let loose or set free (*from*); release (*lit. & fig*.) from bonds, fetters, or physical restraint; free (the lips, tongue, etc.) from constraint. ME. ▸**b** *verb intrans*. In biblical allusions: set people free, release people. Chiefly in ***to bind and to loose***. LME.

AV *Isa*. 51:14 The captiue exile hasteneth that he may be loosed. W. DE LA MARE Loosed from remorse and hope and love's distress. *New Yorker* The industry's reluctance to loose information on the non-expert world.

2 a *verb trans*. Undo, untie, unfasten (fetters, a knot); break (a seal). ME. ▸**b** *verb trans*. Unlock or unpack (a chest etc.); unpack (goods) from a container. Chiefly *Scot*. LME. ▸**c** *verb trans*. Detach, cast loose, let go, (chiefly NAUTICAL, from moorings etc.). Formerly also, remove (an article of clothing) from the body. LME. ▸**d** *verb trans. & intrans*. Detach the team from (a plough etc.). *Scot*. L15. ▸†**e** *verb trans*. Unjoin or unclasp (hands). M–L16.

a SHELLEY Throw back their heads and loose their streaming hair. J. BUCHAN I broke one of the bootlaces . . and loosed the other.

3 *verb trans*. Weaken the adhesion or attachment of; make unstable or insecure in position. Now *arch. & Scot*. ME.

AV *Ecclus* 22:16 As timber girt and bound together in a building, cannot be loosed with shaking.

†**4** *verb trans*. Break up, dissolve, do away with. Chiefly *fig*. ME–E19.
†**5** *verb trans*. Break (faith); violate (a peace). LME–M16.
6 NAUTICAL. †**a** *verb trans*. Weigh (an anchor). LME–M16. ▸**b** *verb intrans*. Weigh anchor. E16.
7 a *verb trans*. Shoot or let fly (an arrow); let off (a gun); *transf. & fig*. give vent to, emit, cause or allow to proceed from one. LME. ▸**b** *verb intrans*. Shoot, let fly. Now usu. foll. by *off*. LME.

a C. CAUSLEY Occasionally he looses a scared glance. K. CROSSLEY-HOLLAND He . . loosed an arrow at a luckless bird. **b** *Daily News* Artillerymen dashed forward . . and loosed on the foe.

8 *verb trans*. Make loose or slack; relax. *arch*. exc. in ***loose hold*** (colloq.), let go. LME. ▸†**b** Relax or loosen (the bowels). LME–M17.
9 *verb trans*. Redeem, release or obtain by payment; pay for. *Scot*. LME.
10 *verb trans*. SCOTS LAW. Withdraw (an arrestment). E16.
†**11** *verb trans*. Solve, explain. L16–M17.
12 *verb intrans*. Finish working; (of a school, factory, etc.) close, disperse, break up. *dial*. L17.
■ **looser** *noun* E16.

loosen /ˈluːs(ə)n/ *verb*. ME.
[ORIGIN from LOOSE *adjective* + -EN⁵.]
▸ **I** *verb trans*. **1** Set free (*lit. & fig*.), release from bonds or physical restraint. Now chiefly (*fig*.), make (a person's tongue) talk more freely. ME.

F. TUOHY Tongues loosened . . by . . the urgency of getting their say.

2 Undo, untie, unfasten (bonds, a knot, etc.). Now *esp*. make looser or less tight, relax, slacken, *fig*. relax in point of severity or strictness. LME.

J. G. COZZENS Ernest relaxed more . . , consciously loosening each muscle. H. WILLIAMSON He dismounted to loosen the curb-chain, which had been hooked too tight under the animal's jaw. D. ATHILL Pain and exhaustion had loosened her grip on life.

loosen the purse strings: see PURSE STRING.
3 Weaken the adhesion or attachment of; unfix, detach. LME. ▸†**b** *fig*. Detach in affection, make a breach between. Only in E17.

LD MACAULAY A wall which time . . had so loosened that it shook in every storm. M. M. KAYE A breeze blowing through the branches loosened the petals and sent them floating down.

4 a Relieve the costiveness of, cause a free evacuation of (the bowels). L16. ▸**b** Make (a cough) produce phlegm or sputum with less difficulty. M19.
5 Make less coherent; separate the particles of. L17.

DRYDEN Iron Teeth of Rakes . . to move The crusted Earth and loosen it.

▸ **II** *verb intrans*. **6** Become loose or looser; relax. L17.

A. P. HERBERT The taut rope, loosening, scattered a shower of brilliant rain. M. PIERCY He had begun to warm towards me, to loosen. A. LURIE Garrett's tongue seemed to be loosening.

7 Foll. by *up*: **a** Give money willingly, talk freely. *N. Amer. colloq*. E20. ▸**b** Exercise the muscles before concentrated physical effort, limber up. M20.

a R. D. PAINE Someone will have to loosen up to pay for the damage. **b** M. RUSSELL I'll be twenty minutes loosening up . . . I'm after the exercise.

■ **loosener** *noun* (*a*) a thing which or person who loosens something; (*b*) CRICKET a (not very good) ball delivered before the bowler is fully loosened or warmed up: M17.

loosestrife /ˈluːsstrʌɪf/ *noun*. M16.
[ORIGIN from LOOSE *verb* + STRIFE *noun*, mistranslation of Latin *lysimachia*, *-ion*, as if from Greek *lusimakhos* 'loosing (i.e. ending) strife', instead of from *Lusimakhos* Lysimachus, its discoverer.]
Either of two tall upright summer-flowering plants growing by ponds and rivers, (*a*) (in full ***yellow loosestrife***) *Lysimachia vulgaris*, of the primrose family, bearing racemes of golden-yellow flowers; (*b*) (in full ***purple loosestrife***) *Lythrum salicaria* (family Lythraceae), with a long showy spike of purplish-red flowers. Also (usu. with specifying word), any of various other plants of the genus *Lysimachia* or the family Lythraceae.

loosey-goosey /luːsɪˈguːsi/ *adjective*. *N. Amer. colloq*. M20.
[ORIGIN Fanciful formation from LOOSE *adjective* + GOOSY *adjective*.]
Relaxed and comfortable.

J. D. PISTONE I couldn't be so loosey-goosey anymore, come and go as I pleased, pretend ignorance.

loosish /ˈluːsɪʃ/ *adjective*. E19.
[ORIGIN from LOOSE *adjective* + -ISH¹.]
Somewhat loose.

loot /luːt/ *noun*[1]. M19.
[ORIGIN Hindi *lūṭ*, *lūṭnā*, from Sanskrit *luṇṭ(h)-* rob.]
1 Goods (esp. articles of considerable value) taken from an enemy, a captured city, etc.; booty, plunder, spoil; illicit gains made by a public servant. Also, the action or process of looting. M19.
2 Money. *slang*. M20.

loot /luːt/ *noun*[2]. *US military slang*. L19.
[ORIGIN Abbreviation of LIEUTENANT (in N. Amer. pronunc.).]
A lieutenant.

loot *noun*[3] see LUTE *noun*[3].

loot /luːt/ *verb*. E19.
[ORIGIN from LOOT *noun*[1].]
1 *verb trans. & intrans.* Plunder, sack (a city, a building, etc.); rob (a house, shop, etc.) left unprotected after violent events. E19.
2 *verb trans.* Carry off as loot or booty; steal (goods). E19.
■ **lootable** *adjective* (*rare*) that may be looted or taken as loot, desirable as loot L19. **looter** *noun* M19.

lootie /ˈluːti/ *noun*. M18.
[ORIGIN Hindi *lūṭī*, formed as LOOT *noun*[1].]
hist. In the Indian subcontinent: a member of a body of native irregulars whose chief object in warfare was plunder; a member of a band of marauders or robbers. Usu. in *pl.*

lop /lɒp/ *noun*[1]. Now *dial.* LME.
[ORIGIN Prob. from Old Norse from base also of *hlaupa* LEAP *verb*.]
A flea.

lop /lɒp/ *noun*[2]. LME.
[ORIGIN Uncertain: perh. ult. rel. to Lithuanian *lùpti* to strip, to peel; later partly from LOP *verb*[1]. Cf. earlier LOPPED *adjective*, Anglo-Latin *loppa* (pl.).]
1 *collect.* The smaller branches and twigs of a tree; faggot-wood. Also, a branch that has been lopped off. LME.
lop and top, **lop and crop** the trimmings of a tree.
†**2** The action or process of lopping a tree or boughs. Only in L16.
– COMB.: **lop-wood** branches and twigs lopped from a tree.

lop /lɒp/ *noun*[3]. E19.
[ORIGIN Imit.: cf. LOP *verb*[3].]
NAUTICAL. A state of the sea in which the waves are short and lumpy.

lop /lɒp/ *noun*[4]. M19.
[ORIGIN Abbreviation of ***lop-eared*** s.v. LOP *verb*[2].]
A variety of rabbit with long drooping ears.

lop /lɒp/ *verb*[1]. Infl. **-pp-**. E16.
[ORIGIN from or rel. to LOP *noun*[2]. Cf. earlier LOPPED *adjective*, Anglo-Latin *loppare*.]
1 *verb trans.* Cut off the branches, twigs, etc., from (a tree); cut away the superfluous growth of, trim; occas., cut the top off (a tree). E16. ▸**b** *transf. & fig.* Cut off the head or a limb of (a person). (Foll. by †*away*, †*off*.) *arch.* E17.

S. JOHNSON A few strokes of an axe will lop a cedar.

2 *verb trans.* Cut off (the branches, twigs, etc.) from a tree. Freq. foll. by *away*, *off*. L16. ▸**b** *transf. & fig.* Cut off (a limb, the head) from the body; cut off from a whole, remove (items) as superfluous. (Foll. by *away*, *off*.) L16.

G. GREENE Somebody had lopped the branches for firewood. D. WIGODER To.. lop branches from overgrown trees. **b** *Times* Brownhills, which has been lopped off Miss Jennie Lee's constituency. A. HALEY The flash of a long knife lopped off his head cleanly at the shoulders.

3 *verb intrans.* Lop branches and twigs from a tree; cut off a limb, the head, or a part of any whole; make strokes *at* with the purpose of cutting something off. L16.

R. HAWKINS One plowing,.. another sowing, and lopping.

lop /lɒp/ *verb*[2]. Infl. **-pp-**. L16.
[ORIGIN Prob. symbolic: cf. LOB *verb*.]
1 *verb intrans.* Hang loosely or limply; droop; flop *about*; stick *out* ungracefully or in a lopsided way. L16. ▸**b** *verb trans.* Of an animal: let (the ears) hang or droop. E19.
2 *verb intrans.* Slouch, dawdle, hang *about*. L16.
3 *verb intrans.* Move with short bounds. L19.
– WITH ADVERBS IN SPECIALIZED SENSES: **lop down** *US colloq.* sit down, lie down.
– COMB.: **lop-ear** (*a*) a drooping ear; (*b*) = LOP *noun*[4]; **lop-eared** *adjective* (esp. of an animal) having drooping ears; **lop-ears** drooping ears; **lop-grass** *dial.* = ***soft brome*** s.v. SOFT *adjective*; **lop-rabbit** = LOP *noun*[4].

lop /lɒp/ *verb*[3] *intrans.* Infl. **-pp-**. L19.
[ORIGIN Imit.: cf. LOP *noun*[3].]
Of water: break in short lumpy waves.

lope /ləʊp/ *noun*. LME.
[ORIGIN Var. of LOUP *noun*[1].]
1 A leap. *obsolete* exc. *Scot.* LME.

R. NORTH I cannot do the Author Justice.. without taking a large Lope, over the next Reign.

2 A long bounding stride, a loping gait. E19.

E. L. DOCTOROW He.. ran along the top of the train in a kind of simian lope.

lope /ləʊp/ *verb intrans.* ME.
[ORIGIN Var. of LOUP *verb*.]
1 Leap, jump, spring, (*about*). *obsolete* exc. *dial.* ME.
2 Run (away). Now only *slang & dial.* LME.
3 Run with a long bounding stride. (Foll. by *along*, *away*.) E19.

V. WOOLF As I lay in the grass a hare loped past me. H. WILLIAMSON He went for long runs, loping along.

loper /ˈləʊpə/ *noun*. L15.
[ORIGIN from LOPE *verb* + -ER[1].]
†**1** A leaper, a dancer. Only in L15.
2 ROPE-MAKING. A swivel on which yarns are hooked at one end while being twisted into cordage. L18.
3 CABINETMAKING. A sliding rail to be pulled out to support the leaf of a bureau etc. M19.

loperamide /ləʊˈpɛrəmʌɪd/ *noun*. L20.
[ORIGIN Prob. from CH)LO(RO-[2] + PI)PER(IDINE + AMIDE.]
PHARMACOLOGY. An opiate drug which inhibits peristalsis and is used to treat diarrhoea.

lopez-root /ˈləʊpɛzˌruːt/ *noun*. L18.
[ORIGIN = mod. Latin *radix lopeziana*, orig. applied to the root of a related E. African plant discovered by Juan *Lopez* Pinheiro.]
The root of a SE Asian plant, *Toddalia asiatica*, of the rue family, used as a remedy for diarrhoea.

lophiodon /ləˈfʌɪədɒn/ *noun*. M19.
[ORIGIN mod. Latin (see below), from Greek *lophion* dim. of *lophos* crest + -ODON.]
PALAEONTOLOGY. A fossil ungulate mammal of the Eocene genus *Lophiodon* (cf. LOPHIODONT).

lophiodont /ˈləʊfɪədɒnt, ˈlɒf-/ *adjective & noun*. M19.
[ORIGIN formed as LOPHIODON.]
PALAEONTOLOGY. ▸**A** *adjective*. Pertaining to or resembling a lophiodon; of or characteristic of the family Lophiodontidae of Eocene ungulates, probably related to tapirs. M19.
▸**B** *noun*. An animal of the family Lophiodontidae. L19.

lophioid /ˈləʊfɪɔɪd, ˈlɒf-/ *adjective & noun*. M19.
[ORIGIN from mod. Latin *Lophius* genus name, app. from Greek *lophia* or *lophos* mane, dorsal fin: see -OID.]
ZOOLOGY. ▸**A** *adjective*. Of or pertaining to the family Lophiidae, which includes certain anglerfishes. M19.
▸**B** *noun*. A lophioid fish. M19.

lopho- /ˈləʊfəʊ, ˈlɒfəʊ/ *combining form* of Greek *lophos* crest, as ***lophobranchiate***, ***lophophore***, etc.: see -O-.

lophobranch /ˈləʊfə(ʊ)braŋk, ˈlɒf-/ *adjective & noun*. M19.
[ORIGIN formed as LOPHOBRANCHIATE.]
ZOOLOGY. = LOPHOBRANCHIATE.

lophobranchiate /ləʊfə(ʊ)ˈbraŋkɪət, lɒf-/ *adjective & noun*. M19.
[ORIGIN from LOPHO- + Greek *bragkhia* gills: see -ATE[2].]
ZOOLOGY. ▸**A** *adjective*. Belonging to or having the characteristics of the order Lophobranchii of bony fishes (e.g. sea horses and pipefishes) in which the gills are arranged in small lobes or tufts. M19.
▸**B** *noun*. A lophobranchiate fish. M19.

lophodont /ˈləʊfə(ʊ)dɒnt, ˈlɒf-/ *adjective & noun*. L19.
[ORIGIN from LOPHO- + -ODONT.]
ZOOLOGY. ▸**A** *adjective*. (Of a molar tooth) having (esp. transverse) ridges between the cusps; (of a dentition) characterized by such molar teeth. L19.
▸**B** *noun*. A herbivore with a lophodont dentition. L19.

lophophorate /ləˈfɒfəreɪt, ləʊfə(ʊ)ˈfɔːreɪt/ *noun & adjective*. M20.
[ORIGIN from LOPHOPHORE: see -ATE[2].]
ZOOLOGY. ▸**A** *noun*. Any of a group of sessile or sedentary coelomate invertebrates possessing a lophophore, including brachiopods, bryozoans, and phoronids. M20.
▸**B** *adjective*. Designating, pertaining to, or characteristic of a lophophorate. M20.

lophophore /ˈləʊfə(ʊ)fɔː, ˈlɒf-/ *noun*. M19.
[ORIGIN from LOPHO- + -PHORE.]
1 ZOOLOGY. A feeding organ in lophophorates, pterobranchs, etc., consisting of a circular, crescentic, or spiral ridge surrounding the mouth and bearing ciliated tentacles, usu. hydraulically linked to the coelom. M19.
2 A bird of the genus *Lophophorus*; = MONAL. *rare*. L19.
■ **lophoˈphoral** *adjective* of or pertaining to a lophophore L19.

lophotrichous /ləˈfɒtrɪkəs/ *adjective*. E20.
[ORIGIN from LOPHO- + -TRICH + -OUS.]
MICROBIOLOGY. Designating or characteristic of a bacterium in which several flagella occur as a crest or bundle at one end of the cell.

lopolith /ˈlɒpəlɪθ/ *noun*. E20.
[ORIGIN from Greek *lopas* basin + -O- + -LITH.]
GEOLOGY. A large intrusive mass similar to a laccolith but having the base centrally sunken.
■ **lopoˈlithic** *adjective* M20.

loppage /ˈlɒpɪdʒ/ *noun*. *rare*. L17.
[ORIGIN from LOP *verb*[1] + -AGE.]
The loppings from trees collectively; lop.

lopped /lɒpt/ *adjective*. ME.
[ORIGIN from LOP *noun*[2] or *verb*[1]: see -ED[2], -ED[1].]
1 That has been lopped; BOTANY & ZOOLOGY (now *rare* or *obsolete*) truncate. ME.

G. GREENE The lopped arm came into view.. the stump like a bludgeon of wood. I. MURDOCH A lopped tree trunk.. served as a seat.

2 HERALDRY. Of a branch etc.: couped to show the cross-section. *rare*. E19.

lopper /ˈlɒpə/ *noun*. M16.
[ORIGIN from LOP *verb*[1] + -ER[1].]
A person who lops the branches, twigs, etc., off trees; a person who lops something off.

lopper /ˈlɒpə/ *adjective*. *obsolete* exc. *Scot.* ME.
[ORIGIN Prob. from LOPPER *verb*.]
= LOPPERED.

lopper /ˈlɒpə/ *verb*. Now only *Scot. & N. English*. ME.
[ORIGIN Perh. from Old Norse *hlaup* coagulation (of milk or blood): see -ER[5].]
1 *verb intrans.* Esp. of milk: curdle, clot. ME. ▸**b** *verb trans.* Turn to curds; curdle; cause to clot. L19.
2 *verb intrans.* Dabble, besmear, cover with clotted matter. E19.
■ **loppered** *adjective* (esp. of milk or blood) clotted, coagulated, curdled ME.

lopping /ˈlɒpɪŋ/ *noun*. E16.
[ORIGIN from LOP *verb*[1] + -ING[1].]
1 The action of LOP *verb*[1]. E16.
2 In *pl.* Branches and shoots lopped from a tree; material for lopping. L16.

loppy /ˈlɒpi/ *noun*. *Austral. slang*. L19.
[ORIGIN Perh. from LOP *verb*[2] (see -Y[1]) or LOPPY *adjective*[1].]
A handyman on a rural station, a roustabout.

loppy /ˈlɒpi/ *adjective*[1]. *obsolete* exc. *dial.* L15.
[ORIGIN from LOP *noun*[1] + -Y[1].]
Full of or infested with fleas.

loppy /ˈlɒpi/ *adjective*[2]. M19.
[ORIGIN from LOP *verb*[2] + -Y[1].]
That hangs loosely; limp.

loppy /ˈlɒpi/ *adjective*[3]. L19.
[ORIGIN from LOP *verb*[3] + -Y[1].]
Of the sea: lumpy, choppy.

L

lopseed /ˈlɒpsiːd/ *noun*. *N. Amer.* E19.
[ORIGIN from LOP *verb*[2] + SEED *noun*.]
A plant of NE Asia and eastern N. America, *Phryma leptostachya*, of the verbena family, with spikes of small white or purplish flowers which droop against the stem when in seed.

lopsided /lɒpˈsʌɪdɪd/ *adjective*. E18.
[ORIGIN from LOP *verb*[2] + SIDE *noun* + -ED[2].]
That (appears to) lean on or towards one side; having one side lower or smaller than the other; (of a ship) disproportionately heavy on one side; unevenly balanced.

G. W. TARGET The boy trailed in, lopsided with the weight of the bag. E. BLISHEN This charming church, of which I'd made lopsided drawings in childhood. *fig.*: G. GREENE The novelist's philosophy will always be a little lopsided.

■ **lopsidedly** *adverb* L19. **lopsidedness** *noun* M19.

lopstick /ˈlɒpstɪk/ *noun*. *Canad.* Also **lob-** /ˈlɒb-/. E19.
[ORIGIN from LOP *noun*[2] or *verb*[1] + STICK *noun*[1].]
A tree which has had its branches lopped, usu. with the name of the lopper cut in its trunk.

loq. /lɒk/ *verb intrans.* (*3 sing. pres.*). M19.
[ORIGIN Abbreviation.]
= LOQUITUR.

loquacious /lɒˈkweɪʃəs/ *adjective*. M17.
[ORIGIN from Latin *loquaci-*, *loquax*, from *loqui* speak: see -ACIOUS.]
1 Given to much talking; talkative. M17.

R. K. NARAYAN Twenty words where one would do... He was becoming loquacious. B. GILROY His grief made him loquacious. He talked on about everything.

2 Of birds, water, etc.: chattering, babbling. Chiefly *poet.* L17.

POPE The chough, the sea-mew, the loquacious crow.

■ **loquaciously** *adverb* M19. **loquaciousness** *noun* E18.

loquacity /lɒˈkwasɪti/ *noun*. ME.
[ORIGIN French *loquacité* or Latin *loquacitas*, formed as LOQUACIOUS: see -ACITY.]
The condition or quality of being loquacious; talkativeness; an instance of this.

loquat /ˈləʊkwɒt/ *noun*. E19.
[ORIGIN Chinese (Cantonese) *luh kwat* lit. 'rush orange'.]
The fruit of a tree of the rose family, *Eriobotrya japonica*, native to China and Japan and cultivated in many warm countries; (in full ***loquat tree***) the tree itself. Also called ***Japanese medlar***.

loquency /ˈləʊkw(ə)nsi/ *noun. rare.* E17.
[ORIGIN Late Latin *loquentia*, formed as LOQUENT: see -ENCY.]
Talking, speech.
■ Also **loquence** *noun* L17.

loquent /ˈləʊkwənt/ *adjective. rare.* L16.
[ORIGIN Latin *loquent-* pres. ppl stem of *loqui* speak: see -ENT.]
That speaks.
■ **loquently** *adverb* L19.

loquitur /ˈlɒkwɪtə/ *verb intrans.* (*3 sing. pres.*). M19.
[ORIGIN Latin.]
Speaks (with the speaker's name added, as a stage direction or to inform a reader). Abbreviation LOQ.

lor' /lɔː/ *interjection. colloq.* Also **lor**. M19.
[ORIGIN Alt. of LORD *noun*. Cf. LORS.]
Expr. surprise, dismay, etc. Cf. LORD *noun* 5, LORDY.

TAFFRAIL Lor'! . . I do look a sight, and no mistake!

lora *noun* pl. of LORUM.

loral /ˈlɔːr(ə)l/ *adjective & noun.* L19.
[ORIGIN from LORE *noun*[2] + -AL[1].]
ZOOLOGY. = LOREAL.

Loran /ˈlɔːran, ˈlɒ-/ *noun.* M20.
[ORIGIN from *long-range navigation*.]
A radar navigation system by which a position is calculated from the time delay between signals from two pairs of synchronized radio transmitters. Cf. SHORAN.

lorate /ˈlɔːreɪt/ *adjective.* M19.
[ORIGIN from Latin LORUM + -ATE[2].]
BOTANY. Strap-shaped.

lorazepam /lɔːˈreɪzɪpam, -ˈrazə-/ *noun.* M20.
[ORIGIN from CH)LOR(O-[2] + *azepam*, after *diazepam* etc.]
PHARMACOLOGY. A drug of the benzodiazepine group, given as a tranquillizer and hypnotic.

lorcha /ˈlɔːtʃə/ *noun.* Also **lorch** /lɔːtʃ/. M17.
[ORIGIN Portuguese, of unknown origin.]
A fast sailing vessel with a hull of European shape but a Chinese rig.

lord /lɔːd/ *noun.*
[ORIGIN Old English *hlāford* from contr. of *hlāfweard* from Germanic, from base of LOAF *noun*[1] + WARD *noun*. See also LUD.]
► **I** A master, a ruler.
†**1** A master in relation to servants; the male head of a household. OE–E17.

AV *Matt.* 24:46 Blessed is that seruant, whome his Lord when he cometh, shall finde so doing.

2 A man (or boy) who has dominion over others as his subjects, or to whom service and obedience are due; a master, a ruler, a chief, a prince, a monarch. Now chiefly *rhet.* OE. ►**b** *fig.* A pre-eminent person or thing. ME. ►**c** An owner, a possessor, a proprietor (of land, houses, etc.). Cf. LANDLORD. Now only *poet. & rhet.* ME. ►**d** A magnate in some particular trade. E19.

MILTON Man over men He made not Lord. LD MACAULAY A race which reverenced no lord, no king but himself. **b** J. G. STRUTT The attribute of strength by which the lord of the woods is more peculiarly distinguished. **c** R. KIPLING He was . . lord of a crazy fishing-boat.

d *tobacco lord* etc.

3 *spec.* A feudal superior; the proprietor of a fee, manor, etc. OE.

T. KEIGHTLEY The rights of the Lord of a town extended to the levying of tolls.

4 A husband. Now only *poet. & joc.* OE.

C. PATMORE Love-mild Honoria . . With added loves of lord and child.

5 ***Lord*** (***God***) (usu. with *the*, exc. as *voc.*), God. Freq. as interjection and in exclamatory phrs. expr. surprise (originating from the use in invocations), dismay, etc. Cf. LAND *noun*[1] 9, LOR', LORDY, LORS, LUD. OE.

SHAKES. *Rich. II* The breath of worldly men cannot depose The deputy elected by the Lord. C. SIMEON This is the Lord's work and fit for a Sabbath-day. E. LEONARD They said, 'Oh, my Lord,' if he happened to mention he'd served time.

6 Jesus Christ. Freq. in ***Our Lord***, ***the Lord***. ME.

TENNYSON How loyal in the following of thy Lord!

7 ASTROLOGY. The planet that has a dominant influence over an event, period, region, etc. LME.
► **II** As a designation of rank or official dignity.
8 Orig., any man (or boy) of exalted position in a kingdom or commonwealth, *spec.* (*hist.*) a feudal tenant who derived a title, by military or other honourable service, directly from the king (cf. BARON 1). Now, a nobleman, a peer of the realm, or a person (as an archbishop or bishop) entitled by courtesy, office, etc., to the title ***Lord***, or some higher title. ME.
9 Used preceding a name to form part of the designation of a man (or boy) of rank, (***a***) as a less formal substitute for Marquess (of), Earl (of), Viscount, Baron, (never followed by *of*, e.g. ***the Earl of Derby*** but ***Lord Derby***); (***b***) preceding the forename, with or without the surname, of the younger son of a duke or marquess. LME.

C. C. F. GREVILLE I dined with Lord and Lady Frederick Fitz Clarence and Lord Westmoreland. H. WILSON Commoners, including Lord North, whose barony was a courtesy title.

10 Forming part of the title of office of any of various high officials in the law, government, armed services, etc., holding authority deputed from the monarch. Also, given as part of a title to individual members of a board appointed to perform the duties of some high office of state that has been put in commission. LME.
11 A mock title of dignity given to the person appointed to preside on certain festive occasions. Chiefly in ***Lord of Misrule*** s.v. MISRULE *noun*. M16.
12 A hunchback. *arch. slang.* L17.

– PHRASES & COMB.: ***by the Lord Harry***: see HARRY *noun*[2]. ***drunk as a lord***: see DRUNK *adjective*. ***First Lord of the Treasury***: see TREASURY 4. ***First Sea Lord***: see SEA. **House of Lords** (***a***) the upper legislative chamber of the UK, composed of peers and bishops; (***b***) a committee of specially qualified members of this assembly appointed as the ultimate appeal court; (***c***) the building where these bodies meet; (***d***) *slang* a lavatory. ***liege lord***: see LIEGE *adjective* 1. **live like a lord** live sumptuously, have a high standard of living. ***Lord Advocate***: see ADVOCATE *noun* 1. **lord and lady**, pl. **lords and ladies**, (orig. & chiefly *Canad.*) a harlequin duck (usu. in *pl.*). **lord and master** (***a***) (now chiefly *rhet.*) = sense 2 above; (***b***) *poet. & joc.* = sense 4 above. **Lord Bishop**: the formal title of a bishop, esp. a diocesan bishop of the Church of England. ***Lord bless me***, ***Lord bless my soul***, ***Lord bless you***: see BLESS *verb*[1]. ***Lord Chamberlain*** (***of the Household***): see CHAMBERLAIN 1. ***Lord Chancellor***: see CHANCELLOR. ***Lord Chief Justice***: see JUSTICE *noun*. ***Lord Clerk Register***: see REGISTER *noun*[1]. ***Lord Commissioner***: see COMMISSIONER 1. **Lord Derby** a large green- and yellow-skinned variety of cooking apple; the tree that produces it. ***Lord God***: see sense 5 above. ***Lord God of hosts***: see HOST *noun*[1]. ***Lord Great Chamberlain*** (***of England***): see CHAMBERLAIN 1. **Lord have mercy** (**on us**) *interjection* expr. astonishment. ***Lord High Admiral***: see ADMIRAL 2. ***Lord High Chancellor***: see CHANCELLOR. ***Lord High Commissioner***: see COMMISSIONER 1. ***Lord High Steward of England***, ***Lord High Steward of Scotland***: see STEWARD *noun* 8. ***Lord High Treasurer***: see TREASURER 1. **lord-in-waiting** a nobleman holding a certain office in attendance on the monarch. ***Lord Justice***, ***Lord Justice Clerk***, ***Lord Justice General***, ***Lord Justice of Appeal***: see JUSTICE *noun*. ***Lord Keeper*** (***of the Great Seal***): see KEEPER *noun*. **lord-lieutenancy** the position or office of a Lord Lieutenant. **Lord Lieutenant** (***a***) an official holding deputed authority from the monarch; *spec.* the chief executive authority and head of the magistracy in each county (formerly also having extensive powers with regard to the militia etc.); (***b***) *hist.* the viceroy of Ireland. ***Lord love you***, ***Lord love me***, ***Lord love a duck***: see LOVE *verb* 1. ***Lord* LYON**. ***Lord Marcher***: see MARCHER *noun*[1]. **Lord Mayor** (the title of) the head of the municipal corporation of London, Dublin, or York, later also of any of several other large cities; ***Lord Mayor's Day***, the day on which a Lord Mayor of London comes into office; ***Lord Mayor's Show***, a procession of decorated vehicles etc. in London on Lord Mayor's Day. **Lord Muck** *slang* a pompous self-opinionated man, a socially pretentious man. **Lord of Appeal** (**in Ordinary**) a member of the House of Lords committee appointed as the ultimate judicial appeal court. ***Lord of hosts***: see HOST *noun*[1]. ***Lord of Misrule***: see MISRULE *noun*. ***lord of regality***: see REGALITY 2a. ***Lord of Sabaoth***: see SABAOTH 1. ***Lord of the ascendant***: see ASCENDANT *noun* 1. **lord of the bedchamber** a nobleman holding a certain office in personal attendance on the monarch. **Lord of the Flies** (***a***) Beelzebub; (***b***) with allusive ref. to the title of the book (1954) by William Golding (1911–93), in which a group of schoolboys marooned on an uninhabited tropical island revert to savagery and primitive ritual. **lord of the manor** the lord or master of a manor house. ***lord of the soil***: see SOIL *noun*[1]. ***Lord Ordinary***: see ORDINARY *noun*. ***lord paramount***: see PARAMOUNT *adjective* 1. ***Lord President of the Council***: see PRESIDENT *noun*. ***Lord Privy Seal***: see PRIVY *adjective*. ***lord proprietary***: see PROPRIETARY *noun* 3. ***lord proprietor***: see PROPRIETOR 2. ***Lord Protector*** (***of the Commonwealth***): see PROTECTOR 2b. ***Lord Provost***: see PROVOST *noun*. ***Lord Rector***: see RECTOR 3b. **lords and ladies** (***a***) the cuckoo pint or wild arum, *Arum maculatum*; (***b***) see ***lord and lady*** above. **Lords Appellant**(**s**) *hist.* a group of nobles who brought charges of treason against certain supporters of Richard II. ***Lord's day***: see ***the Lord's day*** below. ***lords of creation***: see ***lords of the creation*** below. ***Lords of the Articles***: see ARTICLE *noun* 2. **lords of the creation**, **lords of creation** (***a***) humankind; (***b***) *joc.* men as opp. to women. ***Lords triers***: see TRIER 5. ***Lord Treasurer***: see TREASURER 1. ***Lord Warden***: see WARDEN *noun*[1] 11. ***Lord Woolton pie***: see WOOLTON PIE. ***mesne lord***: see MESNE *adjective*. **my lord** (***a***) *arch.* the ordinary title used in speaking to or of a nobleman; (***b***) *voc.* preceding a title or rank or office; (***c***) in *pl.* (not preceding a title), the form of address to a number of noblemen or bishops or to two or more judges of the Supreme Court sitting together in a court of law; (***d***) in *pl.* (not preceding a title), in official correspondence, the ministers composing a department of state collectively; (***e***) (not preceding a title) the polite or respectful form of address to a nobleman under the rank of duke, a bishop, or a judge of the Supreme Court. ***Our Lord***: see OUR *adjective* 1b. ***swear like a lord***: see SWEAR *verb*. **the Lords** the temporal and spiritual peers of Parliament, constituting the upper legislative body of the UK; the House of Lords. **the Lord's day**, **Lord's day** Sunday. ***the Lord's house***: see HOUSE *noun*[1]. **the Lord's Prayer** the prayer taught by Jesus to his disciples (*Matthew* 6:9–13, *Luke* 11:2–4). **the Lords spiritual** the bishops and archbishops sitting in the House of Lords. **the Lord's Supper** the Eucharist. ***the Lord's table***: see TABLE *noun* 13. **the Lords temporal** the peers of the realm sitting in the House of Lords. **treat like a lord** entertain sumptuously, treat with profound deference. ***year of Our Lord***: see YEAR *noun*[1].
■ **lord-dom** *noun* †(***a***) the position of being a lord, lordship; (***b***) *rare* the state of things characterized by the existence of lords: OE. **lordful** *adjective* (*rare*) having the bearing of a lord, lordly LME. **lordless** *adjective* OE. **lordlet** *noun* (*joc.*) a young, small, or minor lord L19. **lordlike** *adjective & adverb* (***a***) *adjective* resembling, befitting, or characteristic of a lord; lordly; †(***b***) *adverb* in the manner of a lord; domineeringly; sumptuously: LME. **lor'dolatry** *noun* (*joc.*) excessive admiration for a lord or lords M19.

lord /lɔːd/ *verb.* ME.
[ORIGIN from the noun.]
†**1** *verb intrans.* Exercise lordship, have dominion. ME–L15.
2 *verb trans.* Be or act as lord of; control, manage, rule. Now *rare.* LME.
3 *verb intrans.* & (chiefly) *trans.* with *it*. Behave in a lordly manner, assume airs of grandeur; domineer. Freq. foll. by *over*. M16.

P. USTINOV A mad monk lording it over an alleged parliament. A. BURGESS Laurence . . from the second class . . was able to observe Magnus lording it in first.

4 *verb trans.* Confer the title of ***Lord*** on; ennoble; address or speak of as 'lord'. E17.

lording /ˈlɔːdɪŋ/ *noun.* OE.
[ORIGIN from LORD *noun* + -ING[3].]
1 = LORD *noun* 2. Usu. in *pl.*, esp. as a form of address. *arch.* OE.
2 A little lord, a petty or minor lord. Chiefly *derog.* L16.

lordling /ˈlɔːdlɪŋ/ *noun.* ME.
[ORIGIN from LORD *noun* + -LING[1].]
= LORDING 2 (freq. *derog.*). Also occas. (*arch.*) = LORDING 1.

lordly /ˈlɔːdli/ *adjective & noun.* OE.
[ORIGIN from LORD *noun* + -LY[1].]
► **A** *adjective.* **1** Of or pertaining to a lord or lords; consisting of lords; administered by lords. Now *rare.* OE.

JOHN HALL Lordly or absolute Monarchy is the best and most natural Government. E. MIALL Pensioning off supernumerary members of lordly houses.

2 Of a person: having the character, attributes, appearance, or demeanour of a lord. Of an action: befitting a lord; honourable, noble. LME. ►**b** Haughty, imperious, lofty, disdainful. LME.

C. H. SPURGEON He is more lordly than all emperors and kings. F. RAPHAEL Byron's name is associated with lordly excess and romantic adventure. **b** L. STEPHEN A lordly indifference to making money by his writings.

3 Of a thing: fit for a lord; grand, magnificent, noble. L15.

H. G. DAKYNS Cyrus was flying at lordlier game than certain irrepressible hill tribes. C. MACKENZIE The lordly spread, of which a magnificent lobster was the *pièce de résistance*.

► **B** *absol.* as *noun*. A lordly person or thing. Now usu., *the lordly* people as a class. L15.
■ **lordlily** *adverb* E17. **lordliness** *noun* †(***a***) lordly state or condition; (***b***) lordly disposition; grandeur; arrogance: LME.

lordly /ˈlɔːdli/ *adverb. arch.* LME.
[ORIGIN from LORD *noun* + -LY[2].]
After the manner of a lord; in a lordly manner.

R. SAVAGE Lordly neglectful of a worth unknown. W. MORRIS In a land where few were poor, if none Were lordly rich.

lordosis /lɔːˈdəʊsɪs/ *noun.* Pl. **-doses** /-ˈdəʊsiːz/. E18.
[ORIGIN mod. Latin from Greek *lordōsis*, from *lordos* bent backwards: see -OSIS.]
1 MEDICINE. Backward curvature of the spine, an excessive amount of which causes concavity of the back. Cf. KYPHOSIS, SCOLIOSIS. E18.
2 ZOOLOGY. A posture assumed by some female mammals during mating, in which the back is arched downwards; the assumption of such a posture. M20.
■ **lordotic** /-ˈdɒtɪk/ *adjective* M19.

lordship /ˈlɔːdʃɪp/ *noun & verb.* OE.
[ORIGIN from LORD *noun* + -SHIP.]
► **A** *noun.* **1** The dignity and functions of a lord; dominion, rule, ownership *of*, *over*. OE.

G. BANCROFT Parliament had asserted an absolute lordship over the colonies. H. WILSON The first lordship of the Treasury.

2 The land or territory belonging to or under the jurisdiction of a lord; a domain, an estate, a manor. LME. ►†**b** A government, a province, a district. LME–L16.

LD MACAULAY The new envoy . . bore a title taken from the lordship of Zulestein.

3 With possess. adjective (as ***your lordship*** etc.): a title of respect given to a nobleman below the rank of a duke, to a judge, and to a bishop; *joc.* a mock complimentary or respectful designation for an ordinary person. LME.

W. CRUISE We must call that case to the consideration of your Lordships. RACHEL ANDERSON The stone dogs on his Lordship's terrace.

4 A percentage on the sale of a book; a royalty (on a mine or a book). *Scot.* M18.
► **B** *verb.* Infl. **-pp-**.
†**1** *verb intrans. & trans.* Exercise lordship (over); be a lord or ruler (of). ME–L15.
2 *verb trans.* Address as 'your lordship'. M18.

lordy /ˈlɔːdi/ *interjection.* Orig. *US.* Also **lawdy**. M19.
[ORIGIN from LORD *noun* + -Y[6].]
Expr. surprise, dismay, etc. Cf. LORD *noun* 5, LOR'.

N. MAILER Well, Lordy-me. N. FREELING A kidnapping . . . And lordy, it's the child of a magistrate.

lore /lɔː/ *noun*[1].
[ORIGIN Old English *lār* = Old Frisian *lāre*, Old Saxon, Old High German *lēra* (Dutch *leer*, German *Lehre*), from West Germanic base also of LEARN.]
1 The act of teaching; the condition of being taught; instruction, education; a piece of instruction; a lesson. Now *arch. & dial.* OE.
COLERIDGE We have learnt A different lore. J. M. NEALE In the Cross we found our pulpit, In the Seven great Words, our lore.
2 That which is taught; doctrine, teaching, *esp.* religious doctrine. Now *poet. & arch.* OE. ▸†**b** A doctrine, a precept; a creed, a religion. OE–L16.
SIR W. SCOTT Can piety the discord heal.. Can Christian lore, can patriot zeal?
3 Advice, counsel; an instruction, a command. Now *rare* or *obsolete*. ME.
MILTON Understanding rul'd not, and the Will Heard not her lore.
4 Orig., that which is learned; learning, scholarship, erudition; (now only *arch. & Scot.*: cf. LEAR *noun*[1]). Later, the body of traditional facts, anecdotes, or beliefs relating to some particular subject or held by a specific group. ME. ▸†**b** A branch of knowledge, a science. ME–M16.
R. C. A. WHITE Typical jury lore suggests that women are less likely to convict than men. ROSEMARY MANNING Edith was very knowledgeable in country lore.
■ **lored** *adjective* (*rare*) learned; stored with knowledge: M19. **loreless** *adjective* (*rare*) without learning or knowledge ME.

lore /lɔː/ *noun*[2]. E17.
[ORIGIN Latin LORUM.]
†**1** A strap, a thong, a rein. *rare*. E–M17.
2 ZOOLOGY. A long flat appendage or surface; *spec.* (**a**) a mouthpart in certain insects, as homopterans and hymenopterans; (**b**) the region between the eye and the side of the beak in a bird, or between the eye and the nostril in a snake; = LORUM. E19.

lore *verb pa. pple* of LESE.

loreal /ˈlɔːrɪəl/ *adjective & noun*. M19.
[ORIGIN from LORE *noun*[2] + -AL[1].]
ZOOLOGY. ▸**A** *adjective*. Of, pertaining to, or in the region of the lore; loral. M19.
▸**B** *noun*. A loreal plate, shield, etc. M19.

Lorelei /ˈlɔːrəlʌɪ, ˈlɒ-/ *noun*. E20.
[ORIGIN In German legend, a siren with long blond hair who sat on the *Lorelei* rock on the Rhine, and whose song lured boatmen to destruction.]
A dangerously fascinating woman, a temptress, a siren.

Lorentz /ləˈrɛnts/ *noun*. E20.
[ORIGIN H. A. *Lorentz* (1853–1928), Dutch physicist.]
PHYSICS. Used **attrib.** to designate various concepts and phenomena described by Lorentz or arising from his work.
Lorentz-covariant *adjective* covariant under a Lorentz transformation. **Lorentz contraction**, **Lorentz–FitzGerald contraction** = *FITZGERALD contraction*. **Lorentz force**: exerted on a charged particle by a magnetic field through which it is moving. **Lorentz-invariant** *adjective* invariant under a Lorentz transformation. **Lorentz transformation** the set of equations which in the special theory of relativity relate the space and time coordinates of one frame of reference to those of another moving rectilinearly with respect to it. **Lorentz triplet** a group of three spectral lines produced by the Zeeman effect.
■ **Lorentzian** *adjective & noun* (**a**) *adjective* of or pertaining to Lorentz or his theories, or the concepts arising out of his work; *spec.* designating (the graph of) a function having the same form as the expression, in classical radiation theory, for the intensity of a spectral emission line in terms of frequency; (**b**) *noun* a Lorentzian curve or function: M20.

Lorenz /ləˈrɛnts/ *noun*[1]. E20.
[ORIGIN L. V. *Lorenz* (1829–91), Danish physicist.]
PHYSICS. ***Lorenz constant***, ***Lorenz's constant***, ***Lorenz number***, the ratio $k/\sigma T$ (where k = thermal conductivity, σ = electrical conductivity, T = temperature), which has approximately the same value for many metallic elements over a wide range of temperatures.

Lorenz /ləˈrɛnts/ *noun*[2]. M20.
[ORIGIN M. O. *Lorenz* (1876–c 1970), US statistician.]
Lorenz curve, a curve in which cumulative percentage of the total of some variable (esp. national income) is plotted against cumulative percentage of a corresponding population ranked in increasing order of the size of share, so illustrating any inequality of distribution.

lorgnette /lɔːnˈjɛt, *foreign* lɔrɲɛt (*pl. same*)/ *noun*. E19.
[ORIGIN French, from *lorgner* to squint, ogle: see -ETTE.]
sing. & in *pl.* A pair of eyeglasses to be held in the hand, usu. by a long handle. Also, a pair of opera glasses.

lorgnon /ˈlɔːnjən, lɔrɲɔ̃ (*pl. same*)/ *noun*. M19.
[ORIGIN French, from *lorgner*: see LORGNETTE, -OON.]
sing. & in *pl.* A single or double eyeglass; a lorgnette. Also, a pair of opera glasses.

lorica /ləˈrʌɪkə/ *noun*. Pl. **-cae** /-siː, -kiː/, **-cas**. E18.
[ORIGIN Latin = breastplate formed as LORUM.]
1 ROMAN ANTIQUITIES. A cuirass or corselet of leather. E18.
†**2** The coping or protecting head of a wall. Only in E18.
3 A kind of cement or paste for coating a vessel before subjecting it to heat. Now *rare* or *obsolete*. M18.
4 ZOOLOGY. The stiff protective case or shell of some protozoans and rotifers. M19.

loricate /ˈlɒrɪkeɪt/ *adjective & noun*. E19.
[ORIGIN Latin *loricatus* pa. pple, formed as LORICATE *verb*: see -ATE[2].]
ZOOLOGY. ▸**A** *adjective*. Covered with protective plates or scales; having a lorica. E19.
▸**B** *noun*. A loricate animal. Formerly *spec.* (**a**) a crocodilian; (**b**) an armadillo, a pangolin. *rare*. M19.

loricate /ˈlɒrɪkeɪt/ *verb trans*. E17.
[ORIGIN Latin *loricat-* pa. ppl stem of *loricare*, formed as LORICA: see -ATE[3].]
Enclose in or cover with a protective coating.
■ **loriˈcation** *noun* (**a**) the action or an act of loricating something; (**b**) a defensive covering or casing: E18.

loricated /ˈlɒrɪkeɪtɪd/ *adjective*. E17.
[ORIGIN formed as LORICATE *verb* + -ED[1].]
Enclosed in or covered with a protective coating; ZOOLOGY = LORICATE *adjective*.

lorikeet /ˈlɒrɪkiːt/ *noun*. L18.
[ORIGIN from LORY + *-keet*, after *parakeet*.]
Any of various small brightly coloured lories of Australia and the Indo-Pacific islands, chiefly of the genera *Charmosyna*, *Glossopsitta*, and *Trichoglossus*.

lorilet /ˈlɒrɪlət, lɒrɪˈlɛt/ *noun*. *Austral*. M20.
[ORIGIN from LORY + -LET.]
Any of several very small, mainly green, short-tailed parrots of the genera *Opopsitta* and *Psittaculirostris*, native to rainforests in NE Australia and New Guinea. Also called ***fig parrot***.

lorimer *noun* var. of LORINER.

loriner /ˈlɒrɪnə/ *noun*. Also **-mer** /-mə/. ME.
[ORIGIN Old French *lorenier*, *-mier*, from *lorain* strap of a harness, from Proto-Romance, from Latin *lorum* strap, thong: see -ER[2].]
A maker of bits and metal mountings for horses' bridles and of stirrup irons; a spurrier; *gen.* a maker of small ironware, a worker in wrought iron. Now only in the title of one of the London livery companies.

†**loring** *noun*. *rare* (Spenser). Only in L16.
[ORIGIN from LORE *noun*[1] + -ING[1].]
Teaching, instruction.

loriot /ˈlɒrɪət/ *noun*. Long *rare*. L16.
[ORIGIN French, from *l'* the + *oriot* var. of *oriol* ORIOLE.]
The golden oriole, *Oriolus oriolus*.

loris /ˈlɔːrɪs/ *noun*. L18.
[ORIGIN French, perh. from Dutch †*loeris* clown, booby.]
Any of several small slow-moving nocturnal primates of the subfamily Lorisinae, with small ears, very short tails, and opposable thumbs, *esp.* (more fully ***slender loris***) *Loris tardigradus* of Sri Lanka and southern India, and (more fully ***slow loris***) *Nycticebus coucang* of SE Asia.
■ **lorisid** *noun & adjective* (**a**) *noun* a member of the family Lorisidae, which includes lorises, pottos, and bushbabies; (**b**) *adjective* of or pertaining to the family Lorisidae: M20. **lorisoid** *noun & adjective* (an animal) resembling a loris or related to the lorises M20.

lormery /ˈlɔːməri/ *noun*. *obsolete* exc. *hist*. LME.
[ORIGIN Old French *lormerie*, from *loremier*: see LORINER, -ERY.]
The small ironware produced by lorimers; a place for the making or selling of such ware.

lorn /lɔːn/ *adjective*. Now *arch. & joc*. ME.
[ORIGIN pa. pple of LESE.]
1 Lost, perished, ruined; doomed to destruction. *obsolete* exc. *dial*. ME.
SIR W. SCOTT If thou readest, thou art lorn! Better hadst thou ne'er been born!
2 Abandoned, left alone; bereft *of*; lonely, desolate; forlorn. L15.
W. OWEN Uncle.. has made overtures to me to add my lorn voice to the choir. D. PARKER Mrs. Ewing never vaunted her lorn condition, never shut herself within the shaded chambers of bereavement.
■ **lornness** /-n-n-/ *noun* forlornness M19.

lorn *verb pa. pple* of LESE.

Lorraine /lɒˈreɪn/ *noun*. M19.
[ORIGIN A region and former province in NE France.]
Chiefly HERALDRY. ***Lorraine cross***, ***cross Lorraine***, ***cross of Lorraine***, a cross with two horizontal limbs.

Lorrainer /lɒˈreɪnə/ *noun*. L17.
[ORIGIN formed as LORRAINE + -ER[2].]
A native or inhabitant of Lorraine in NE France.

lorry /ˈlɒri, ˈlʌri/ *noun*. M19.
[ORIGIN Perh. from the personal name *Laurie*.]
1 **a** A long flat low wagon without sides. Also, a truck or wagon used on a railway or tramway. M19. ▸**b** A large strong motor vehicle for transporting goods, troops, etc., *esp.* an open one with a flat platform. E20.
b ***army lorry***, ***articulated lorry***, ***goods lorry***, etc. **fall off a lorry**, **fall off the back of a lorry** (of goods etc.) be acquired in dubious circumstances from an unspecified source.
2 MINING. A running bridge over a pit. L19.
– COMB.: **lorry-bus** a lorry used as a vehicle for public transport; **lorry-hop** *verb* hitchhike by lorry; **lorry park** an open space or lot reserved for the parking of lorries.

lorry /ˈlɒri/ *verb trans*. E20.
[ORIGIN from LORRY *noun*.]
Transport or convey by means of a lorry or lorries.

lors /lɔːz/ *interjection*. *colloq*. M19.
[ORIGIN Alt. of LORD *noun*. Cf. LOR'.]
Expr. surprise, dismay, etc.

lorum /ˈlɔːrəm/ *noun*. Pl. **lora** /ˈlɔːrə/. L19.
[ORIGIN Latin = strap, thong.]
ZOOLOGY. = LORE *noun*[2] 2.

lory /ˈlɔːri/ *noun*. L17.
[ORIGIN Malay *lori*, *luri*, dial. var. of *nuri*: cf. Dutch *lori*, French *lori*.]
Any of various parrot-like birds with brilliant plumage of the family Loriidae, found in SE Asia and Australasia and feeding mainly on nectar with brush-tipped tongues. Cf. LOERIE.

LOS *abbreviation*.
Loss of signal.

losable /ˈluːzəb(ə)l/ *adjective*. Also **loseable**. LME.
[ORIGIN from LOSE *verb* + -ABLE.]
Able to be lost.

Los Angeleno /lɒs andʒəˈliːnəʊ/ *noun*. Also **-ino**. Pl. **-os**. M20.
[ORIGIN from *Los Angeles* after ANGELENO.]
= ANGELENO.

†**lose** *noun*[1]. ME–E19.
[ORIGIN Old French *los*, *loz*, *loos* from Latin *laudes* pl. of *laus* praise.]
Praise; renown, fame; reputation.

lose /luːz/ *noun*[2]. *slang*. L19.
[ORIGIN from LOSE *verb*.]
An instance of losing a race.
– COMB.: **lose bet**, **lose game**: in which the loser of the game wins the stakes.

lose /luːz/ *verb*. Pa. t. & pple **lost** /lɒst/.
[ORIGIN Old English *losian*, from *los* LOSS, later sense-development infl. by cognate LESE, pronunc. prob. infl. by LOOSE *adjective* etc.]
†**1** *verb intrans*. Perish; be lost or missing. OE–LME.
2 *verb trans*. †**a** Destroy, bring to perdition; be the ruin of. OE–E17. ▸**b** In *pass*. Be brought to destruction or ruin; perish, die or be dead; (of the soul) be damned; (of a ship etc.) disappear, perish at sea. ME. ▸**c** Ruin (a person) in another's estimation. Now *rare* or *obsolete*. E17.
a SHAKES. *Haml.* What to ourselves in passion we propose, The passion ending, doth the purpose lose. **b** *Law Times* The vessel.. sank in a short time, all hands being lost. **c** C. SEDLEY 'Twas I that lost you in each Roman mind.
3 *verb trans*. Become unable to find; cease to know the whereabouts of. OE. ▸†**b** Fail to retain in the mind or memory; forget. M16–E18. ▸**c** Cease to follow (the right track). Freq. in ***lose one's way*** below. M16. ▸**d** Fail to keep in sight; *poet*. cease to hear (a song etc.). L16. ▸**e** Draw away from, be no longer near or among; leave (another competitor) hopelessly behind in a race. L17.
TENNYSON Since her horse was lost I left her mine. J. MORLEY Humanity had lost its title-deeds and he had recovered them. **c** D. H. LAWRENCE He.. stumbled blindly.., having lost the path in the complete darkness. **d** T. HERBERT Wee.. got sight of the Carracke, and lost her for euer, in two houres after. TENNYSON Losing her carol I stood pensively. **e** POPE Here where the mountains less'ning as they rise Lose the low vales.
4 *verb trans*. Suffer the privation of (a possession, an attribute, a faculty, etc.); cease to possess or have through negligence or misadventure; be or become separated from by death or estrangement; be deprived of; *spec.* (**a**) suffer the loss of (blood) from one's blood vessels; (**b**) (of an army commander etc.) suffer the loss of (troops) by death, capture, etc.; (**c**) (of a doctor) fail to preserve the life of (a patient); (**d**) (of a woman) suffer the loss of (a child) in childbirth, miscarry (a child). ME. ▸**b** Of a thing: be deprived of or part with (a portion of itself, a quality, an appendage). Also foll. by *off*. ME. ▸**c** Fail to maintain (a position, a state of mind or body, etc.). L15. ▸†**d** Be deprived of the power or opportunity *to do*. Only in 17. ▸**e** Cease to suffer from, get rid of (a cold etc.); undergo a reduction of, shed (weight). Also, vomit up (a recently eaten meal). M17. ▸**f** In *pass*. Of an art: cease to be known or practised. Of a quality etc.: cease to be present. M17.
E. WAUGH My papa has just put all his money into a cinema film and lost it all. E. BOWEN They lost their colours and had five or six hundred slain. L. URIS For five consecutive years she lost children through early miscarriages. L. HELLMAN They had lost a brother in a yellow fever epidemic. **b** H. CAINE Her household duties had lost their interest. **c** MILTON They astonisht all resistance lost, All courage. **e** WILKIE COLLINS O! let me teach my heart to lose its fears. OED I have not yet lost my rheumatism.
5 *verb intrans*. Suffer loss or detriment; cease to possess something wholly or partly; incur disadvantage (foll. by *in*, †*of*); be worse off, esp. financially, as the result of a transaction (foll. by *by*, *on*). ME.
TENNYSON 'Tis better to have loved and lost Than never to have loved at all. OED Both armies lost heavily. J. CLEARY I've lost on every race so far.

L

6 *verb trans.* Spend (time, opportunities, etc.) to no purpose; waste. ME.

F. MARRYAT There is no time to be lost. G. BOOTHBY A.. fellow who never lost a chance of making himself objectionable. A. AYCKBOURN Of all the working days lost.. half are due to strikes and illness.

7 *verb trans.* Fail to obtain (something one might have had); miss (a train etc.); fail to catch (a quarry). ME. ▸**b** Fail to apprehend by sight or hearing; not catch (words etc.). L16. ▸†**c** Fail to attend. E18–M19.

JAS. HARRIS The swift-footed Salius lost the prize to young Euryalus. OED I did not lose a word of his speech. S. LEACOCK No, not the fish they caught; this was the big one that they lost. **b** SWIFT I lost church today.

8 *verb trans.* **a** Cause the loss of. ME. ▸**b** Cause (a person) to miss the course of an argument etc.; bewilder. Chiefly *colloq.* M17. ▸**c** Dispose of or discard as unnecessary or superfluous; kill. *colloq.* M20.

a E. A. FREEMAN The crimes of John lost him all the northern part of his French possessions. **b** P. CAREY I'm sorry.. but you've lost me. What was what deal?

9 *verb trans.* **a** Be deprived of (something) in a contest or game; forfeit (a stake); be defeated in (a game, a battle, a lawsuit); fail to carry (a motion). Also in CRICKET, have (a wicket) taken by an opponent. (Foll. by *to.*) ME. ▸**b** *verb intrans.* Be defeated; forfeit money, a stake, etc., by defeat in a game. M16.

a DICKENS The motion was lost by a majority of two. R. CAMPBELL I lost only one fight out of eight. G. BOYCOTT Bob Willis had lost his battle against a knee injury. **b** SHAKES. *Lear* Who loses and who wins; who's in, who's out. SWIFT She lost at one Sitting to the Tune of a hundred Guineas.

10 *verb refl.* (& in *pass.*). **a** Lose one's way, go astray, (*lit.* & *fig.*). M16. ▸**b** Lose identity, become merged (*in* something else), (*lit.* & *fig.*). E17. ▸**c** Become deeply absorbed or engrossed (*in* thought etc.); be bewildered, be overwhelmed (*in*). Formerly also, be or become distracted (from emotion or excitement). E17. ▸**d** Become hidden from view, become obscured, (*in* clouds etc.). L17.

a MILTON In wandring mazes lost. J. C. POWYS His mind went faster still.. losing itself in infinite perspectives. **b** J. AUSTEN All surprise was shortly lost in other feelings. C. LAMB I love to lose myself in other men's minds. **c** W. IRVING As I.. lose myself in melancholy musings. B. JOWETT He seemed to be lost in the contemplation of something great. **d** DRYDEN When the setting Stars are lost in Day. W. COWPER Rills that.. lose themselves at length In matted grass.

11 Of a clock etc.: **a** *verb intrans.* Run (increasingly) slow; indicate a time earlier than the correct time. M19. ▸**b** *verb trans.* Run slow by (a specified amount of time). M19.

– PHRASES: ***heads I win, tails you lose***: see HEAD *noun*. ***lose an eye***: see EYE *noun*. ***lose caste***: see CASTE 3. ***lose count***: see COUNT *noun*[1] 1. ***lose countenance***: see COUNTENANCE *noun*. ***lose face***: see FACE *noun*. ***lose flesh***: see FLESH *noun*. ***lose ground***: see GROUND *noun*. ***lose heart***: see HEART *noun*. **lose height** (of an aeroplane etc.) descend to a lower level in flight. ***lose interest***: see INTEREST *noun*. **lose it** *colloq.* lose control of one's temper or emotions; cease to be rational or effective. ***lose leather***: see LEATHER *noun*. **lose–lose** *adjective* (*colloq.*) denoting a situation which is disadvantageous or damaging to all those involved; **lose nothing in the telling** = ***not lose in the telling*** below. ***lose no time***: see TIME *noun*. ***lose one's balance***: see BALANCE *noun*. ***lose one's block***: see BLOCK *noun* 6b. ***lose one's grip***: see GRIP *noun*[1]. ***lose one's hair***: see HAIR *noun*. ***lose one's head***: see HEAD *noun*. ***lose one's heart***: see HEART *noun*. **lose one's life** be killed. ***lose one's market***: see MARKET *noun*. ***lose one's mind***: see MIND *noun*[1]. ***lose one's nerve***: see NERVE *noun*. ***lose one's rag***: see RAG *noun*[1]. ***lose one's seat***: see SEAT *noun*. ***lose one's shirt***: see SHIRT *noun*. ***lose one's stirrups***: see STIRRUP *noun*. ***lose one's temper***: see TEMPER *noun*. ***lose one's touch***: see TOUCH *noun*. ***lose one's voice***: see VOICE *noun*. **lose one's way** go astray (*lit.* & *fig.*). ***lose one's wool***: see WOOL *noun*. ***lose patience***: see PATIENCE *noun*. ***lose sight of***: see SIGHT *noun*. ***lose sleep over***: see SLEEP *noun*. ***lose the number of one's mess***: see MESS *noun*. ***lose the plot***: see PLOT *noun*. ***lose the scent***: see SCENT *noun*. **lose the way** = ***lose one's way*** above. ***lose touch* (*with*)**: see TOUCH *noun*. ***lose track of***: see TRACK *noun*. **lose way** (of a ship or boat) begin to move less quickly. ***lose weight***: see WEIGHT *noun*. **nothing to lose** *colloq.* no possibility of further loss. **not lose in the telling** (of a story) be, if anything, exaggerated. ***win the saddle or lose the horse***: see SADDLE *noun*. **you can't lose** etc., you etc. must inevitably profit.

– WITH ADVERBS IN SPECIALIZED SENSES: **lose out** *colloq.* be unsuccessful, suffer a loss, not get a fair chance or advantage, (foll. by *on*).

loseable *adjective* var. of LOSABLE.

losel /ˈləʊz(ə)l/ *noun & adjective*. Now *arch. & dial.* LME.
[ORIGIN App. from *los-* stem of LESE + -EL[1].]
▸ **A** *noun*. A worthless person; a profligate, a ne'er-do-well. LME.
▸ **B** *adjective*. Good-for-nothing, worthless. E17.
■ **loselry** *noun* worthless or profligate behaviour LME.

loser /ˈluːzə/ *noun*. ME.
[ORIGIN from LOSE *verb* + -ER[1].]
†**1** A destroyer. ME–E17.
2 A person who loses or suffers loss; *esp.* a person, horse, etc., that loses a race etc., an unsuccessful competitor. M16. ▸**b** A consistently unsuccessful person, a failure. M20.

SHAKES. *Haml.* You will draw both friend and foe, Winner and loser? LD MACAULAY He.. declared that he had been a loser by his mission. **b** E. FEINSTEIN Seryosha was a sick man, as well as a hopelessly weak one, a born loser.

bad loser, **poor loser** a person who is dejected or angered by losing a game etc. **good loser** a person who is not dejected or angered by losing a game etc.
3 BILLIARDS. A losing hazard. L19.
4 A convicted criminal, a person who has served a sentence in prison, esp. for a specified number of times. *US slang.* E20.

E. S. GARDNER He's a two-time loser.

5 BRIDGE. A card that will not take a trick. E20.

losh /lɒʃ/ *noun*[1]. Now *rare*. L16.
[ORIGIN Russian *los'*.]
An elk. Long *obsolete* exc. in ***losh hide***, ***losh leather***, the untanned hide of the elk, and later of the buffalo and ox, prepared with oil; a soft buff-coloured leather.

losh *noun*[2] var. of LOCHE.

†**losh** *verb intrans.* E17–M19.
[ORIGIN Perh. imit.]
Fall with a splash; go stumbling.

losh /lɒʃ/ *interjection*. *Scot.* L18.
[ORIGIN Alt. of LORD *noun*. Cf. LOR', LORS.]
Expr. surprise, dismay, etc.

losing /ˈluːzɪŋ/ *noun*. OE.
[ORIGIN from LOSE *verb* + -ING[1].]
The action of LOSE *verb*; an instance of this. In early use *spec.* perdition, destruction; the action of being lost or destroyed.
a losing streak: see STREAK *noun*.

losing /ˈluːzɪŋ/ *ppl adjective*. E16.
[ORIGIN from LOSE *verb* + -ING[2].]
That loses, that results in loss.
losing battle a battle in which defeat seems inevitable (*lit.* & *fig.*). **losing game** (*a*) a game in which defeat seems inevitable; (*b*) a game in which the loser of the game wins the stakes, a test of skill in forcing one's opponent to win. ***losing hazard***: see HAZARD *noun*.
■ **losingest** *adjective* (*N. Amer. colloq.*) losing more often than others of its kind, least successful L20.

loss /lɒs/ *noun*.
[ORIGIN Old English *los* corresp. to Old Norse *los* breaking up of the ranks of an army, from Germanic from base also of LESE, LEASE *adjective*, LOOSE *adjective*; later back-form. from *lost* pa. pple of LOSE *verb*.]
1 Perdition, ruin, destruction; the state or fact of being destroyed or ruined. *obsolete* exc. as passing into later senses. OE.

MILTON Thou hast.. quitted all to save A world from utter loss.

2 a Orig., the state of being a loser, defeat. Later, the losing of, or defeat in, a battle, game, or contest. ME. ▸**b** The fact of losing someone or something, deprivation of or failure to keep a possession, attribute, faculty, etc. Also, the fact of being deprived of a person by death, estrangement, etc.; the death of a person regretted; *spec.* miscarriage of a child. LME. ▸**c** Failure to take advantage or make good use of time, opportunities, etc. LME. ▸**d** Failure to gain or obtain something sought. E17.

a C. HOPE The Brahm family regarded the loss of the Great War as a tragedy. **b** LD MACAULAY The Papists of Ireland attributed to him the loss of their lands. M. N. COX King Lear's is the archetypal cry of devastating loss 'Thou'lt come no more.' J. MCDOUGALL The loss of control that is entailed in letting their thoughts wander freely. *Which?* Insurance which covers loss of luggage. **c** SIR W. SCOTT Instant reimbursement for loss of time. J. TYNDALL This error caused us the loss of an hour. **d** D. DYKE A word that signifieth.. losse of victory. OED I do not wish to risk the loss of my train.

3 MILITARY. The losing (by an army commander etc.) of troops by death, capture, etc.; *sing.* & in *pl.*, the number of troops so lost. ME.

D. A. THOMAS The losses were horrific.. about 8,000 men.

†**4** A cause or occasion of ruin or deprivation. *rare*. LME–M16.
5 A particular instance of losing; a person, thing, or amount lost; *spec.* an instance of losing blood. LME.

EVELYN Thus ended this incomparable Lady: our never to be sufficiently lamented losse. *Holiday Which?* Nowadays people who try to sell their timeshare commonly make a sizeable loss.

6 Diminution of one's possessions or advantages; detriment or disadvantage involved in being deprived of something, or resulting from a change of conditions; an instance of this. (Opp. *gain*.) LME.

AV *Phil.* 3:7 What things were gaine to me, those I counted losse for Christ. *Bella* A terrible sense of loss and grief filled Hilary.

†**7** REAL TENNIS. A lost chase. L16–E17.
†**8** Lack, default, want. E–M17.
– PHRASES: **a great loss** a person or thing whose loss is a severe blow (freq. in neg. contexts). **at a loss** (*a*) (of a hound) having lost the track or scent of a quarry, at fault; (*b*) (of a person) puzzled, not knowing what to do, (freq. foll. by *for, to do*); ***be at a loss for words***, not know what to say; (*c*) (of something sold) for less than the purchase price. ***consequential losses***: see CONSEQUENTIAL *adjective* 1. ***cut one's losses***: see CUT *verb*. ***dead loss***: see DEAD *adjective* etc. ***loss of face***: see FACE *noun*. **loss of life** (*a*) the fact of being put to death, esp. as a punishment; (*b*) *gen.* the destruction of human lives. ***profit and loss***: see PROFIT *noun*.
– COMB.: **loss adjuster** an insurance agent who assesses the amount of compensation arising from a loss; **loss-leader** an article put on sale at a non-profit-making price in order to attract potential buyers of other articles; **loss-maker** a business etc. consistently working at a loss; **loss-making** *verbal noun* the making of a loss (in business, etc.); **loss-making** *ppl adjective* that makes a loss; **loss-proof** *adjective* guaranteed against loss, inflation, fluctuation in market value, etc.

losset /ˈlɒsɪt/ *noun*. Chiefly *dial.* M17.
[ORIGIN Irish *losaid* (Old Irish *losat*) kneading trough.]
A wooden tray.

lossless /ˈlɒslɪs/ *adjective*. L16.
[ORIGIN from LOSS *noun* + -LESS.]
†**1** Without loss. L16–M17.
2 ELECTRICITY. Characterized by or causing no dissipation of electrical or electromagnetic energy. M20.

lossy /ˈlɒsi/ *adjective*. M20.
[ORIGIN from LOSS *noun* + -Y[1].]
ELECTRICITY. Characterized by or causing dissipation of electrical or electromagnetic energy.

lost /lɒst/ *adjective & noun*. LME.
[ORIGIN pa. pple of LOSE *verb*.]
▸ **A** *adjective*. **1** Of time, effort, opportunities, etc.: not used advantageously; spent in vain; wasted. LME.
2 Having gone astray, having lost the way; *fig.* bewildered, puzzled. Also, of which a person has been deprived; not retained in possession; no longer to be found. LME.
3 That has perished or been destroyed; ruined, esp. morally or spiritually; (of a soul) damned. M16.
4 Of a battle, game, etc.: in which a defeat has been sustained. E18.
– PHRASES: **be lost on** fail to influence or draw the attention of, not be noticed or appreciated by. **be lost without** be unable to cope without, have great difficulty if deprived of. **get lost** *slang* cease to be annoying, go away (usu. in *imper.*). ***legion of the lost ones***: see LEGION *noun*. ***lost in the shuffle***: see SHUFFLE *noun* 3b. ***lost in thought***: see THOUGHT *noun*[1]. **lost to** (*a*) that has passed from the possession of, that has been taken from; (*b*) no longer affected by a sense of duty, shame, etc., with regard to. ***no love lost between***: see LOVE *noun*.
– SPECIAL COLLOCATIONS: ***lost cause***: see CAUSE *noun*. **lost generation** the generation reaching maturity *c* 1915–25, a high proportion of whose men were killed in the First World War; any culturally or emotionally unstable generation. ***lost labour***: see LABOUR *noun*. **lost motion** imperfect transmission of motion between two parts of a machine which communicate one with the other, owing to faulty construction or looseness of the parts. **lost property** lost articles found but not claimed; ***lost property department***, ***lost property office***, an office, department, dealing with (the disposal of) lost property. **lost river** *US* a river which disappears into the ground and re-emerges elsewhere. **lost rock**, **lost stone** *US* an erratic boulder. ***Lost Tribes***: see TRIBE *noun*. **lost wax** = CIRE PERDUE. **lost weekend** a weekend spent in dissolute living.
▸ **B** *absol.* as *noun*. **1** An advertisement of a lost article. *rare*. M18.
2 *The* lost persons or things as a class. M19.
LEGION ***of the lost***.
■ **lostly** *adverb* (*rare*) M17. **lostness** *noun* E18.

lost *verb pa. t. & pple* of LOSE *verb*.

los von Rom /loːs fɔn ˈroːm/ *noun phr.* L19.
[ORIGIN German = free from Rome.]
A policy seeking to reduce the political influence of the Roman Catholic Church in Austria and Germany at the end of the 19th cent.; the movement concerned with this.

lot /lɒt/ *noun*.
[ORIGIN Old English *hlot* corresp. to Old Frisian *hlot*, Middle Low German, Middle Dutch & mod. Dutch *lot*, Old Norse *hlutr*, *hluti*, also Old English *hlȳt*, from Germanic. Rel. to German *Loos*, *Los*.]
1 Any of a set of objects used in a method of random selection to secure a decision in deciding disputes, dividing goods, choosing people for an office or duty, etc., by an appeal to chance or the divine agency supposed to be concerned in the results of chance. Now chiefly in ***cast lots***, ***draw lots***, etc. (usu. *between*, *for*, *who*, etc.). OE.

G. CHAPMAN Each markt his lot, and cast it in, to Agamemnons caske. TOLKIEN They now drew lots for the watches.

2 The action or an act of casting, drawing, etc., lots, to obtain a decision. Chiefly in ***by lot***. OE. ▸**b** The choice resulting from a casting, throwing, etc., of lots. ME. ▸†**c** *sing.* & in *pl.* A game of chance. Also, a divinatory appeal to chance. L16–L18.

R. HARRIS Let's put it to the Lot. **b** W. H. PRESCOTT The lot fell on Egmont to devise some suitable livery.

3 A portion, a share; *spec.* what is assigned by lot as a person's share or portion in an inheritance or a distribution of property; a division or share of property made by lot. OE. ▸†**b** A person's turn *to do* something (orig., as determined by lot). ME–M17.

F. W. ROBERTSON When the revenues of a cathedral.. fell to the lot of a monastery.

4 What is given to a person by fate or divine providence; *esp.* a person's destiny, fortune, or condition in life. **OE.**

> L. STRACHEY A child of the eighteenth century whose lot was cast in a new, . . unsympathetic age. S. BRETT It is the actor's lot to have his performances dissected by ill-informed critics.

5 *hist.* **a** An amount to be paid, a tax, a due. Chiefly in ***scot and lot***, ***lot and scot*** s.v. SCOT *noun*[2]. **OE.** ▸**b** A payment of lead ore as a royalty to the owner of a mine. **L15.**
†**6** A part, portion, or division of something; a number of things or persons forming part of a larger whole. (Cf. sense 10 below.) Only in **ME.**
7 Orig., a prize in a lottery. Later in the card game lottery, a card obtaining a prize for the holder. **M16.**
8 A number of persons or things of the same kind, or associated in some way; a quantity, a collection, a set. Now chiefly *colloq.* **L16.**

> W. BENHAM Their crew seem to have been a lazy lot. E. WAUGH They are a very decent generous lot of people.

9 A plot or portion of land assigned to a particular owner; a piece of land divided off or set apart for a particular purpose (freq. with specifying word). Also, each of the plots or portions into which a tract of land is divided when offered for sale. Chiefly *N. Amer.* **M17.** ▸**b** Land round a film studio where outside filming may be done. Chiefly *N. Amer.* **E20.** ▸**c** A car park; a plot of land used for parking vehicles for sale or hire. Chiefly *N. Amer.* **M20.**

> H. GEORGE A house and the lot on which it stands are alike property. SLOAN WILSON The possibility of subdividing her land into one-acre lots. **b** *Tucson Magazine* She is under contract with Universal and cannot do a series off the lot.

building lot, ***parking lot***, etc.
10 An article, or set of articles, offered separately at a sale; *esp.* each of the items at a sale by auction. **E18.** ▸**b** A person of a specified (usu. bad) kind. **M19.**

> J. B. MORTON An auction of a job lot of vegetables. B. BAINBRIDGE The catalogue comprised 228 lots.

11 A considerable number, quantity, or amount; *a* good or great deal; *sing.* & in *pl.*, a great quantity. (Foll. by *of*.) *colloq.* **E19.**

> A. H. CLOUGH You see lots of villas, six or seven at least, in ruins. *Listener* Mr Donoghue . . doesn't mean us, he means you lot. *Economist* Luddites who would halt technology and therefore a lot of economic growth.

– PHRASES: ***a lot on one's plate***: see PLATE *noun* 25. **across lots** *N. Amer. dial.* & *colloq.* over fields etc. as a short cut. **bad lot** a disreputable or vicious person. **cast in one's lot with**, **throw in one's lot with** associate oneself with, decide to share the fortunes of. **call to the lot of** become the duty, business, obligation, etc., of. **fall to the lot of** become the responsibility of (a person) *to do*. ***have a lot of time for***: see TIME *noun*. **have no part nor lot in**, **have neither part nor lot in** (with ref. to *Acts* 8:21) have no share in. ***lot and scot***: see SCOT *noun*[2]. ***odd lot***: see ODD *adjective*. ***round lot***: see ROUND *adjective*. ***say a lot for***: see SAY *verb*[1]. ***scot and lot***: see SCOT *noun*[2]. ***set a lot by***: see SET *verb*[1]. **that lot**, **this lot**, (chiefly *joc.* & *derog.*) **that little lot**, **this little lot** *colloq.* that, this, particular group or set. **that's the lot** *colloq.* there is no more to come, that is all there is. **that's your lot** *colloq.* there is no more to come to you, that is all you are going to get. **the lot**, **the whole lot** *colloq.* the whole of a certain number or quantity. ***this lot***, ***this little lot***: see ***that lot*** above. ***throw in one's lot with***: see ***cast in one's lot with*** above. **us lot**, **you lot**, etc. *colloq.* we, you, etc., as a group. ***Virgilian lots***: see VIRGILIAN *adjective* 1.
– COMB.: **lot attendant** (chiefly *N. Amer.*) a car park attendant; **lot-jumper** *US* a person who appropriates another's plot or allotment of land; ***lot-lead***: see sense 3b above; **lot-man** †(*a*) a pressed seaman; †(*b*) *rare* a pirate; (*c*) *Scot.* a person who threshes grain etc.; **lot-mead**, **lot-meadow** a common meadow, the shares in which are apportioned by lot.

lot /lɒt/ *verb*. Infl. **-tt-**.
[ORIGIN Old English *hlēotan* = Old Saxon *hliotan*, Old High German *liozan*, Old Norse *hlýta* cast lots, obtain by lot, from Germanic base also of LOT *noun*. Latterly directly from LOT *noun* (cf. French *lotir* cast lots etc.).]
▸ **I** *verb intrans.* **1** Cast lots *who, whether, for*. *rare.* **OE.**
†**2** Pay a lot or assessment. Only in ***scot and lot***, ***lot and scot*** s.v. SCOT *verb*. *Scot.* **LME–E18.**
3 Foll. by *on*: count on; rely on; look for, expect. Now *US.* **M17.**
▸ **II** *verb trans.* †**4** Obtain by lot, acquire a share in. Only in **OE.**
5 Divide (land) into lots, esp. for assignment to a private owner; portion *out* and allot (land *to* a person etc.). **LME.**
6 Assign *to* as a share or portion; assign as a person's lot or destiny. Also foll. by *out*. **LME.** ▸†**b** Appoint or allot to *do* or *be*. **L16–M17.**
†**7** Impose a tax or due on. Only in **M16.**
8 Divide or group into lots for sale. Also foll. by *out*. **E18.**
9 Cast lots for; divide, apportion, or distribute by lot. Now *rare.* **E18.**
10 Choose (pressed men) by lot for service. *obsolete* exc. *hist.* **M18.**
11 Portion *off* by lot. **M19.**

lota /ˈləʊtə, -tɑː/ *noun*. Also **lotah**. **E19.**
[ORIGIN Hindi *loṭā*.]
In the Indian subcontinent: a spheroidal water pot, usually made of polished brass.

lotaustralin /ləʊˈtaʊstrəlɪn/ *noun*. **M20.**
[ORIGIN from mod. Latin *Lot(us) austral(is* (see below) + -IN[1].]
CHEMISTRY. A toxic cyanogenic glucoside which occurs in various plants, esp. *Lotus australis* and *Trifolium repens* (white clover).

lote /ləʊt/ *noun*. *arch.* **E16.**
[ORIGIN Anglicization.]
= LOTUS (esp. sense 2).
– COMB.: **lote-tree** (*a*) the nettle tree, *Celtis australis*; (*b*) the jujube tree, *Ziziphus lotus*.

loth /ləʊt/ *noun*. **L17.**
[ORIGIN German = lead.]
A former unit of weight in the Netherlands, Germany, Austria, and Switzerland, equal to half the local ounce.

loth *adjective* var. of LOATH *adjective*.

Lotharingian /ləʊθəˈrɪndʒɪən/ *noun* & *adjective*. **E17.**
[ORIGIN from *Lotharingia* (see below) + -AN.]
▸ **A** *noun*. A native or inhabitant of the ancient duchy of Lotharingia in northern Europe, situated between the Rhine and the Scheldt from Frisia to the Alps. **E17.**
▸ **B** *adjective*. Of or pertaining to Lotharingia or its inhabitants, or modern Lorraine, a region in NE France. **L19.**

Lothario /ləˈθɛːrɪəʊ, -ˈθɑː-/ *noun*. Pl. **-os**. **M18.**
[ORIGIN A character in Rowe's *Fair Penitent* (1703).]
A selfish and irresponsible seducer; a libertine.

> D. L. SAYERS Men like Crutchley, with quantities of large white teeth, are practically always gay Lotharios.

loti /ˈləʊti, ˈluːti/ *noun*. Pl. **maloti** /məˈləʊti, -ˈluːti/. **L20.**
[ORIGIN Sesotho.]
The basic monetary unit of Lesotho, equal to 100 lisente.

lotic /ˈləʊtɪk/ *adjective*. **E20.**
[ORIGIN from Latin *lotus* washing, from *lot-* (see LOTION) + -IC.]
ECOLOGY. Of freshwater organisms or habitats: inhabiting or situated in rapidly moving water. Cf. LENITIC *adjective*.

lotiform /ˈləʊtɪfɔːm/ *adjective*. **L19.**
[ORIGIN from LOT(US + -I- + -FORM.]
ARCHITECTURE. Of a pillar, column, etc.: shaped like a lotus.

lotion /ˈləʊʃ(ə)n/ *noun*. **LME.**
[ORIGIN Old French & mod. French, or Latin *lotio(n-)* washing, from *lot-*, *laut-* pa. ppl stem of *lavare* wash: see -ION.]
1 A liquid medicinal or cosmetic preparation applied externally. **LME.**
†**2** **a** = LAVATORY *noun* 3. Only in **16.** ▸**b** *gen.* The action of washing the body, ablution, esp. with a medicinal or cosmetic preparation. **M16–L18.**
†**3** The passing of metals, medicines, etc., through water for cleansing or purification. **E17–L18.**
4 Alcoholic drink. *arch. slang.* **L19.**

Lotka–Volterra /ˌlɒtkəvɒlˈtɛrə/ *noun*. **M20.**
[ORIGIN A. J. *Lotka* (1880–1949), US statistician, and V. *Volterra* (1860–1940), Italian mathematician.]
Used *attrib.* with ref. to a mathematical model which uses coupled differential equations to predict the variation in time of two populations, *spec.* of a predator species and a prey species.

lotment /ˈlɒtm(ə)nt/ *noun*. *obsolete* exc. *dial.* **M17.**
[ORIGIN from LOT *verb* + -MENT.]
An allotment of land.

loto *noun* see LOTTO *noun*[1].

lotong /ləʊˈtɒŋ/ *noun*. **E19.**
[ORIGIN Malay.]
A leaf monkey of the genus *Presbytis*, esp. *P. obscura*.

Lotophagi /ləʊˈtɒfədʒʌɪ/ *noun pl.* **E17.**
[ORIGIN Latin from Greek *Lōtophagoi*, from *lōtos* LOTUS + *phagein* eat.]
The lotus-eaters of Greek legend.
■ **lotophagous** *adjective* (*rare*) lotus-eating, resembling the lotus-eaters **M19.**

lotos *noun* see LOTUS.

lotos-eater *noun* var. of LOTUS-EATER.

lottery /ˈlɒt(ə)ri/ *noun*. **M16.**
[ORIGIN Prob. from Dutch *loterij*, from *lot* LOT *noun* + *-erij* -ERY. Cf. French *loterie*, Italian *lotteria*.]
1 A means of raising money by selling numbered tickets and giving prizes to the holders of numbers drawn at random. **M16.**
2 *transf.* & *fig.* An enterprise or process whose success is governed by chance. **L16.**

> *She* You can appeal, but the procedure is something of a lottery.

†**3** Decision by casting or drawing of lots. Also, chance, issue of events as determined by chance. **L16–L17.**
†**4** A thing which comes to a person by lot or fortune. Only in **E17.**
5 A card game in which prizes are obtained by the holders of certain cards. **M19.**
– COMB.: **lottery wheel** a revolving mechanism used to shuffle the tickets in a lottery before the winning tickets are drawn.

lotto /ˈlɒtəʊ/ *noun*[1]. Also (earlier, now *rare*) **loto** /ˈləʊtəʊ/. **L18.**
[ORIGIN (French *loto* from) Italian *lotto*.]
1 A game of chance resembling bingo, in which numbers drawn as in a lottery are to be matched with numbers on a card, the winner being the first to have a card with a row of numbers all of which have been drawn. **L18.**
2 A lottery (in Italy). **E19.**

Lotto /ˈlɒtəʊ/ *noun*[2]. **M20.**
[ORIGIN Lorenzo *Lotto* (*c* 1480–1556), Italian painter.]
In full ***Lotto rug***. A kind of rug characterized by a pattern based on a design of octagons, as depicted in paintings by Lorenzo Lotto.

lotus /ˈləʊtəs/ *noun*. Also (esp. in sense 2) **lotos**. **L15.**
[ORIGIN Latin from Greek *lōtos*.]
1 Some kind of clover or trefoil (referred to by Homer as food for horses). *obsolete* exc. *hist.* & *poet.* **L15.**
2 A plant yielding a fruit represented by Homer as producing in those who ate it a state of dreamy forgetfulness and loss of all desire to return home, identified by later Greek writers with a N. African shrub (probably the jujube tree, *Ziziphus lotus*). **M16.**
3 A tree mentioned by classical writers, having a hard black wood (probably the nettle tree, *Celtis australis*). **M16.**
4 Any of several exotic water lilies; *esp.* (***a***) *Nymphaea lotus*, sacred in ancient Egypt, which has white flowers and pink outer petals; (***b***) *Nelumbo nucifera*, sacred in parts of southern Asia (and treated symbolically in Hindu and Buddhist thought), which has white or pink flowers; (***c***) (more fully ***American lotus***) the N. American water lily *Nelumbo lutea*, which has fragrant yellow flowers. **L16.** ▸**b** In full ***lotus position***. In Yoga, a cross-legged bodily position with the feet resting on the thighs, said to resemble the lotus blossom. Also called ***padmasana***. **M20.**
5 Any of various leguminous plants of the genus *Lotus*; *spec.* bird's-foot trefoil, *L. corniculatus*. **M18.**
– COMB.: **lotusbird** *Austral.* the jacana; **lotus capital**, **lotus-column** *EGYPTOLOGY*: shaped like a lotus, ornamented with lotuses; **lotus-land** the fabled land of the lotus-eaters; a land of ease and delight; ***lotus position***: see sense 4b above.

lotus-eater /ˈləʊtəsˌiːtə/ *noun*. Also **lotos-**. **M19.**
[ORIGIN from LOTUS + EATER.]
1 A member of a people represented by Homer as living on the fruit of the lotus and existing in a state of dreamy forgetfulness and idleness. **M19.**
2 A person given up to indolent enjoyment. **M19.**
■ **lotus-eat** *verb intrans.* give oneself up to indolent enjoyment (chiefly as ***lotus-eating*** *verbal noun* & *ppl adjective*) **M19.**

L

louche /luʃ, luːʃ/ *adjective*. **E19.**
[ORIGIN French = cross-eyed, squinting.]
Not straightforward. Now usu., dubious, shifty, disreputable.

> E. WAUGH I knew of a louche little bar quite near here. *Time* She plays loose—and even louche—types.

Loucheux /luːˈʃəː, -ˈʃuː/ *noun* & *adjective*. **E19.**
[ORIGIN Canad. French, formed as LOUCHE.]
▸ **A** *noun*. Pl. same. An Athabaskan people inhabiting the Yukon and Mackenzie River areas in Alaska and NW Canada; the language of this people. **E19.**
▸ **B** *attrib.* or as *adjective*. Of or pertaining to the Loucheux or their language. **E19.**

loud /laʊd/ *adjective*.
[ORIGIN Old English *hlūd* = Old Frisian *(h)lūd*, Old Saxon *hlūd* (Dutch *luid*), Old High German *hlūt* (German *laut*), from West Germanic from Indo-European, from base meaning 'hear', whence also Greek *kluein* hear, *klutos* famous, Latin *cluere* be famed.]
1 (Of a sound or voice) strongly audible, noisily or oppressively audible, making a powerful impression on the sense of hearing; that makes, or is able or liable to make, strongly audible sounds. **OE.** ▸**b** Of a place etc.: full of noise, re-echoing. **L16.**

> G. LYTTELTON Down the Steep it falls, In loud Cascades. A. RADCLIFFE The storm was now loud. T. CAMPBELL The loud waves lash'd the shore. C. POTOK A straight, loud voice that rang through the terrible silence. A. DAVIS An explosion a hundred times louder than the loudest . . thunderclap. B. ASHLEY Vibrations from a loud electric bell. **b** *Guardian* In a wood which had previously been loud with bird-song, an eerie silence prevailed.

2 **a** Clamorous, noisy; noisily aggressive; emphatic or vehement in expression. **M16.** ▸†**b** Chiefly of a lie: manifest, palpable, flagrant. **M16–L17.** ▸†**c** Of motives: pressing, urgent. Only in **E17.**

> **a** TENNYSON Men loud against all forms of power. S. BRILL Hoffa became louder and more bad-tempered.

3 Of smell or flavour: powerful, offensive. Now chiefly *US.* **M17.**

> MILTON The strong breath and loud stench of avarice.

4 Esp. of colour, pattern, dress, etc.: vulgarly obtrusive, flashy. **L18.**

> D. LODGE He is wearing his loudest check sports jacket.

– SPECIAL COLLOCATIONS & COMB.: **loud-hail** *verb trans.* & *intrans.* speak, call, or address through a loudhailer. **loudhailer** a megaphone or other electronic device for amplifying the voice, so that it can be heard at a distance. **loudmouth** *adjective*, *noun*, & *verb* (**a**) *adjective* loud-mouthed, noisy; (**b**) *noun* a person given to loud and self-assertive talk; (**c**) *verb intrans.* talk loudly and self-assertively, bluster. **loud-mouthed** *adjective* noisily self-assertive, vociferous. **loud pedal** = **sustaining pedal** (a) s.v. SUSTAINING. **loudspeaker** an instrument for converting variations in applied electrical impulses into corresponding sound waves (usu. music or voice) that are able to be heard at a distance from the instrument.

■ **loudish** *adjective* somewhat loud E19. **loudly** *adverb* L15.

loud /laʊd/ *adverb*.
[ORIGIN Old English *hlude*, from the adjective.]
1 Loudly, with a loud noise or voice; aloud. OE.

G. GREENE Better not talk so loud He may be listening. P. BOWLES They could hear the storm blowing louder than before.

loud and clear (esp. in radio or telecommunication) (heard or received) loudly and clearly; *gen.* without misunderstanding or uncertainty. †**loud and still** under all circumstances. **out loud** aloud, so as to be widely heard.
†**2** With *lie*: openly, blatantly. LME–E17.
3 Of smell: strongly, offensively. Chiefly *US*. L19.
– COMB.: **loud-spoken** *adjective* given to loud speaking.

louden /ˈlaʊd(ə)n/ *verb*. M18.
[ORIGIN from LOUD *adjective* + -EN[5].]
1 *verb trans.* Make loud or louder. M18.
2 *verb intrans.* Become loud, grow louder. E19.

M. PEAKE Steerpike . . could hear the loudening of the rain.

loudness /ˈlaʊdnɪs/ *noun*. LOE.
[ORIGIN from LOUD *adjective* + -NESS.]
The quality or condition of being loud; an instance of this. Also, the (great or small) extent to which a sound is heard as loud.
– COMB.: **loudness control** a device on an audio amplifier which corrects for the change in quality of reproduced sound at low volumes by boosting the bass (and often also the treble) relative to the middle frequencies.

Lou Gehrig's disease /luː ˈɡɛːrɪɡz dɪˌziːz/ *noun phr.* M20.
[ORIGIN Henry *Louis Gehrig* (1903–41), US baseball player, who died from the disease.]
MEDICINE. A progressive degeneration of the motor neurons of the central nervous system, leading to muscle wasting and paralysis; amyotrophic lateral sclerosis.

L

lough /lɒk, lɒx/ *noun*. OE.
[ORIGIN Irish *loch* = Gaelic LOCH *noun*[1].]
1 A lake, a pool. In early use also, a strait, a gulf. Now *rare* or *obsolete*. OE.
2 In Ireland: a lake, an arm of the sea. LME.

louis /ˈluːi/ *noun*[1]. Pl. same /-z/. Also (*arch.*) anglicized as **lewis** /luːɪs/, pl. same, **lewises**. M17.
[ORIGIN French from LOUIS *noun*[2] & *adjective*.]
hist. In full ***louis d'or*** /dɔː/ [= gold]. A French gold coin issued in the reign of Louis XIII (1640) and subsequently until the time of Louis XVI (1793). Later also, a 20-franc piece or Napoleon.

Louis /luːi/ *noun*[2] & *adjective*. Usu. in fuller phrs. as below. M19.
[ORIGIN French (see below).]
(Designating or pertaining to) any of the styles in architecture, furniture, decorative art, etc., characteristic of the reigns of several kings of France named Louis; *spec.* and in full: ***Louis Treize*** /treɪz/, Louis XIII, 1610–43; ***Louis Quatorze*** /kaˈtɔːz/, Louis XIV, 1643–1715; ***Louis Quinze*** /kãz/, Louis XV, 1715–74; ***Louis Seize*** /seɪz/, Louis XVI, 1774–93.

Louisianan /lʊˌiːzɪˈanən, -ˈɑː-/ *adjective & noun*. Also **-anian** /-ˈanɪən/. L18.
[ORIGIN from *Louisiana* (see below), from *Louis* XIV (see LOUIS *noun*[2] & *adjective*) + -IAN.]
▸ **A** *noun*. A native or inhabitant of Louisiana, a state of the southern US at the mouth of the Mississippi. L18.
▸ **B** *adjective*. Of or pertaining to the state of Louisiana. M19.

Louis Philippe /ˌluːɪfɪˈliːp/ *noun & adjective*. E20.
[ORIGIN See below.]
(Designating or pertaining to) the style of architecture, furniture, and interior decoration characteristic of the reign of Louis Philippe, King of France 1830–48.

lounder /ˈlʌndə/ *noun & verb*. *Scot.* E18.
[ORIGIN Perh. symbolic.]
▸ **A** *noun*. A heavy swingeing blow. E18.
▸ **B** *verb trans.* Beat, cudgel, thrash. Also, hurl with violence *on*. L18.
■ **loundering** *adjective* (of a blow etc.) swingeing, severe E18.

lounge /laʊn(d)ʒ/ *noun*[1]. L18.
[ORIGIN from LOUNGE *verb*[1].]
1 An act or spell of lounging; a leisurely walk, a saunter, stroll. Also, a lounging gait or manner of reclining. L18.

LYTTON Our life is a lounge from the cradle to the grave. W. BLACK When we went out for a lounge after luncheon.

2 **a** A place for lounging; a gathering of loungers. Now *rare*. L18. ▸**b** A sitting room of a house; a public sitting room in a hotel; a waiting room with seats at an airport. L19.

b J. BETJEMAN It's ever so close in the lounge dear. J. MUNRO They were in the departure lounge, waiting for their flight call. M. BRADBURY The English department faculty lounge, wherein the faculty were . . assembled. J. RULE There was no one she knew in the employees' lounge.

3 A kind of sofa or easy chair on which a person can lie at full length. M19.
– COMB.: **lounge bar** a separate bar in a public house which is more comfortably furnished than the public bar; **loungecore** [after ***HARD core***] *joc.* easy-listening music; **lounge lizard** (*slang*, orig. *US*) a man who spends his time idling in fashionable society, esp. in search of a wealthy patroness; **lounge suit** a man's formal suit for ordinary day wear; **loungewear** casual, comfortable clothing worn at home.

lounge *noun*[2] see LUNGE *noun*[2].

lounge /laʊn(d)ʒ/ *verb*[1]. Orig. *Scot.* E16.
[ORIGIN Perh. symbolic.]
1 *verb intrans.* Move indolently; slouch. Freq. with adverb E16.

LYTTON Vargrave lounged into the billiard-room.

2 *verb intrans.* Pass time indolently or without definite occupation; idle. L17.

G. K. CHESTERTON Like all ingrainedly idle men, he was very fond of lounging.

3 *verb intrans.* Recline casually or comfortably, loll. M18.

J. CARY He lounged across the bed, propped on one elbow. H. G. WELLS The vicar ceased to lounge and sat up.

4 *verb trans.* Pass (time etc.) *away* (rarely *out*) in idleness. L18.
■ **lounger** *noun* (**a**) a person who lounges, an idler; (**b**) an article of furniture or dress designed for use in relaxation: E16.

lounge *verb*[2] see LUNGE *verb*[1].

loungey /ˈlaʊndʒɪ/ *noun*. *colloq.* Also **loungy**. E20.
[ORIGIN from LOUNGE *noun*[1], *verb*[1] + -Y[1].]
1 Of a place: conducive to lounging; comfortable. E20.
2 Pertaining to easy-listening music. L20.

loup /laʊp/ *noun*[1]. *Scot.* See also LOPE *noun*. LME.
[ORIGIN Old Norse *hlaup*: see LEAP *noun*[1].]
= LEAP *noun*[1].

loup /lu/ *noun*[2]. Pl. pronounced same. M18.
[ORIGIN French, lit. 'wolf', from Latin *lupus*.]
1 In full ***loup de mer*** /də mɛːr/ [= sea wolf]. The sea bass, *Dicentrarchus labrax*, found off the coasts of western Europe and in the Mediterranean. M18.
2 A woman's light mask or half-mask for the face. Cf. earlier LOO *noun*[2]. M19.

loup *noun*[3] var. of LOOP *noun*[3].

loup /laʊp/ *verb intrans. & trans. Scot. & N. English.* See also LOPE *verb*. ME.
[ORIGIN Old Norse *hlaupa*: see LEAP *verb*.]
= LEAP *verb*.

loupe /luːp/ *noun*. LME.
[ORIGIN Old French & mod. French. See also LOOP *noun*[3].]
†**1** A precious stone of imperfect brilliance; *esp.* a sapphire. LME–M16.
2 A kind of small magnifier used by watchmakers or jewellers. L19.

loup-garou /ˈluːɡəruː/ *noun*. L16.
[ORIGIN French, from *loup* wolf (see LOUP *noun*[2]) + *garou* (from Old High German antecedent of Middle High German *werwolf* WEREWOLF).]
= WEREWOLF.

louping ill /ˈlaʊpɪŋˌɪl/ *noun*. LME.
[ORIGIN from LOUP *verb* + -ING[1] + ILL *noun*.]
VETERINARY MEDICINE. A viral disease of animals, esp. sheep, which causes a staggering gait often with spasmodic jumps.

lour /ˈlaʊə/ *noun*[1]. Also **lower**. ME.
[ORIGIN from the verb.]
1 A gloomy or sullen look; a frown, scowl. ME.
2 Gloominess of the sky, weather, etc.; threatening appearance; an instance of this. L16.

lour /ˈlaʊə/ *noun*[2]. *slang.* Now *rare* or *obsolete*. Also **lower**. M16.
[ORIGIN Unknown.]
Money.

lour /ˈlaʊə/ *verb intrans.* Also **lower**. ME.
[ORIGIN Unknown.]
1 Frown, scowl; look angry or sullen. Formerly also, be depressed or mournful. ME. ▸**b** Of the clouds, sky, etc.: look dark and threatening. Foll. by **on**, **over**, **upon**. L16.

J. GRANT His brows knit and his eyes loured. S. NAIPAUL Carmen lowered at the mob. **b** SHAKES. *Rich. III* The clouds that lour'd upon our house.

2 Crouch, lurk, skulk. Chiefly *Scot.* Now *rare*. LME.

lourd /lʊəd/ *adjective & noun*. Now *rare*. LME.
[ORIGIN Old French & mod. French = heavy, (formerly) foolish.]
▸ **A** *adjective*. Orig., sluggish, dull, coarse, stupid. Later, heavy; gloomy. LME.
▸ †**B** *noun*. A coarse fellow, a lout. Only in L16.

loure /lʊə/ *noun*. E18.
[ORIGIN French, also = kind of bagpipe.]
hist. A kind of rustic dance thought to have had a bagpipe accompaniment. Also, a slow baroque dance in 3/4 or 6/4 time.

lourie *noun* var. of LOERIE.

louring /ˈlaʊərɪŋ/ *adjective*. Also **lowering**. LME.
[ORIGIN from LOUR *verb* + -ING[2].]
1 Frowning, scowling; angry-looking, gloomy, sullen. LME.

D. H. LAWRENCE His boisterous humour gave way to lowering silences.

2 Of the clouds, sky, weather, circumstances, etc.: gloomy, dark, threatening. LME.

G. SANTAYANA Rather autumnal with lowering clouds and rain. *Daily Telegraph* The louring threat of nuclear warfare.

†**3** Lurking, skulking. LME–L16.
■ **louringly** *adverb* L16.

louro /ˈlʊərəʊ/ *noun*. Pl. **-os**. E19.
[ORIGIN Portuguese, lit. 'laurel', from Latin *laurus* LAUREL *noun*.]
Any of several tropical S. American hardwood timber trees belonging to the genera *Ocotea*, *Nectandra*, and related genera of the laurel family, *esp.* (in full ***red louro***) *Ocotea rubra*; the dense wood of these trees. Also (the wood of) any of several similar Brazilian trees of the genus *Cordia*, of the borage family.

loury /ˈlaʊəri/ *adjective*. Also **lowery**. M17.
[ORIGIN from LOUR *noun*[1] + -Y[1].]
Of the sky etc.: dull, gloomy, threatening.

louse /laʊs/ *noun*. Pl. **lice** /lʌɪs/; in sense 2 usu. **louses**.
[ORIGIN Old English *lūs*, pl. *lȳs* = Middle Low German, Middle Dutch, Old High German *lūs*, (Dutch *luis*, German *Laus*), Old Norse *lús*.]
1 Any small wingless insect of the order Siphunculata (or Anoplura) (more fully ***sucking louse***), parasitic on mammals, or the order Mallophaga (more fully ***biting louse***), parasitic mainly on birds; spec. *Pediculus humanus*, which infests the hair and skin of humans and has two forms living respectively on the head (more fully ***head louse***) and body (more fully ***body louse***). Also, any of various other small creatures held to resemble these. OE. ▸**b** As the type of something worthless or contemptible. L16.

M. KINGSLEY Sleep impossible—mosquitoes! lice!! **b** SWIFT 'Tis not that I value the money three skips of a louse. CHESTERFIELD I . . don't care a louse if I never see it again.

booklouse, ***crab louse***, ***water-louse***, ***woodlouse***, etc.
2 A contemptible or unpleasant person. M17.

R. KIPLING Why hast thou allowed this louse Lutuf to live so long? R. SILVERBERG Is he worth risking your life for? I thought you said he was a louse.

– COMB.: **louse-borne** *adjective* (of a disease) transmitted by lice; **louse-trap** *dial.* & *slang* a comb; **lousewort** any plant of the genus *Pedicularis*, of the figwort family; esp. *P. sylvatica* and (N. Amer.) *P. canadensis*, which bear pink or red flowers.

louse /laʊz, -s/ *verb*. LME.
[ORIGIN from the noun.]
1 *verb trans. & intrans.* Clear (a person, oneself, a garment) of lice, remove lice (from). LME.
†**2** *verb intrans.* Be infested with lice. *rare* (Shakes.). Only in E17.
3 *verb trans.* Foll. by *up*: infest with lice; spoil, mess up. *slang.* M20.
■ **louser** *noun* (**a**) a person who louses; (**b**) *slang* (also ***louser-up***) a person who spoils things; a contemptible person: L16.

louses *noun pl.* see LOUSE *noun*.

lousy /ˈlaʊzi/ *adjective*. ME.
[ORIGIN from LOUSE *noun* + -Y[1].]
1 Full of lice, infested with lice. ME. ▸†**b** Characterized by the presence of lice. E16–M19.
2 Vile, contemptible; disgusting; inferior, very bad; ill; in low health or spirits. LME.

THACKERAY I've been trying to write today & only squeezed out one lousy page. S. BECKETT The patients did sometimes feel as lousy as they sometimes looked. M. GEE I'm a lousy pianist. A. LURIE Polly would be able to take taxis when the weather was lousy.

3 Teeming *with*; abundantly supplied *with*. *slang.* M19.

V. M. YEATES Were not shipping magnates lousy with shekels? *Field & Stream* The lilies were lousy with pickerel.

■ **lousily** *adverb* E17. **lousiness** *noun* M16.

lout /laʊt/ *noun*. M16.
[ORIGIN Perh. from LOUT *verb*[1].]
A rough, crude, or ill-mannered person (esp. a man).

A. F. DOUGLAS-HOME The lout who tries to throw his weight about at the expense of weaker brethren. J. IRVING The sort of louts who hung around the station all day.

lager lout, ***litter lout***, etc.

lout /laʊt/ *verb*[1] *intrans.* Now *arch. & dial.*
[ORIGIN Old English *lūtan* = Old Norse *lúta* (Swedish *luta*, Danish *lude*), from Germanic.]
Bend or bow in deference (*to*); stoop; *fig.* submit (*to*).

lout /laʊt/ *verb*[2]. M16.
[ORIGIN from LOUT *noun* (but sense 2 may be a separate word).]
†**1** *verb trans.* Treat with contempt, mock. M16–M17.
2 *verb intrans.* Act loutishly; lounge (*about*, *off*, etc.). E19.

loutish /ˈlaʊtɪʃ/ *adjective*. M16.
[ORIGIN from LOUT *noun* + -ISH[1].]
Characteristic of a lout; ill-mannered, crude or rough in behaviour.
■ **loutishly** *adverb* L16. **loutishness** *noun* M16.

loutrophoros /luːtrəˈfɔːrɒs/ *noun*. Pl. **-roi** /-rɔɪ/. L19.
[ORIGIN Greek, from *loutron* water for a bath + *-phoros* -bearing.]
CLASSICAL ANTIQUITIES. A tall two-handled vessel used for carrying water to the nuptial bath.

louvre /ˈluvə/ *noun*. Also **-ver**. ME.
[ORIGIN Old French *lover*, *lovier* skylight, prob. from Germanic form rel. to base of LODGE *noun*.]
1 A structure like a turret on the roof of a medieval building, with side openings for ventilation etc. ME.
2 A hole in a roof for the passage of smoke; a chimney. *obsolete* exc. *dial.* LME.
3 *sing.* & (earlier) in *pl.* An arrangement of overlapping slats placed across an opening and usu. designed to admit air and some light but exclude rain. Also (*sing.*), an individual slat of such an arrangement. M16.
– COMB.: **louvre board** each of the slats making up a louvre (usu. in *pl.*).
■ **louvred** *adjective* (**a**) arranged like louvres; (**b**) provided with a louvre or louvres: M19.

lovable /ˈlʌvəb(ə)l/ *adjective*. Also **loveable**. LME.
[ORIGIN from LOVE *verb* + -ABLE.]
Inspiring or deserving love or affection; amiable; attractive, pleasing.
■ **lova'bility** *noun* M19. **lovableness** *noun* E19. **lovably** *adverb* E19.

lovage /ˈlʌvɪdʒ/ *noun*. LME.
[ORIGIN Alt., by assoc. with LOVE *noun* and ACHE *noun*[2] (= parsley), of Old French *levesche*, *luvesche* (mod. *livèche*) from late Latin *levisticum* (sc. *apium* parsley), for earlier *ligusticum* neut. of *ligusticus* Ligurian.]
An umbelliferous plant, *Levisticum officinale*, native to southern Europe, used as a culinary and medicinal herb. Also (more fully ***Scots lovage***, ***Scotch lovage***), a white-flowered umbellifer, *Ligusticum scoticum*, which grows on European rocky coasts.

lovat /ˈlʌvət/ *noun & adjective*. E20.
[ORIGIN *Lovat*, a place in the Highlands of Scotland.]
(Designating or made of) tweed of a muted green colour; (of) a muted green colour (also ***lovat-green***).

love /lʌv/ *noun*.
[ORIGIN Old English *lufu* = Old Frisian *luve*, Old High German *luba*, Gothic (*brōþru*) *lubō* (brotherly) love, from Germanic, from weak grade of base repr. also by Old Saxon *lubig* loving, Old High German *gilob* precious, Old English, Old Saxon, Old Norse *lof*, Old High German *lob* praise, from Indo-European base also of Latin *lubet* it is pleasing, *lubido* desire, Old Church Slavonic *ljubŭ* dear, *ljubiti* love, Sanskrit *lubhyati* desires. Rel. also to LIEF, LEAVE *noun*[1].]
1 That state of feeling with regard to a person which manifests itself in concern for the person's welfare, pleasure in his or her presence, and often also desire for his or her approval; deep affection, strong emotional attachment. (Foll. by *of*, *for*, *to*, *towards*.) OE. ▸**b** An instance of affection (now *rare*). Formerly also, an act of kindness. OE. ▸**c** Affectionate greetings (freq. as a closing formula in letters). M17.

SHAKES. *L.L.L.* My love to thee is sound, sans crack or flaw. JULIETTE HUXLEY I secretly adored my father and longed to be able to show him my love. B. GILROY The grandchildren's clothes washed and ironed with love. **c** SCOTT FITZGERALD I'd been writing letters . . and signing them: 'Love, Nick.'

brotherly love, ***mother love***, ***platonic love***, ***romantic love***, etc.

2 In Christian use: the benevolence and affection of God; the affectionate devotion due to God; regard and consideration prompted by a sense of a common relationship to God. OE.

AV *1 John* 4:16 God is loue, and hee that dwelleth in loue, dwelleth in God.

3 Strong predilection, liking, or fondness for, or devotion to something. Foll. by *of*, *for*, (arch.) *to*. OE.

C. A. LINDBERGH The army Air Corps is built up of men who fly for the love of flying. E. FEINSTEIN Marina's interest in gypsies was part of her love of everything exotic.

4 That feeling of attachment which is based on sexual qualities; sexual passion combined with liking and concern for the other. OE. ▸**b** An instance of being in love; in *pl.*, amatory relations, love affairs. L16.

MILTON Haile wedded Love, mysterious Law, true sourse Of human ofspring. S. JOHNSON It is commonly a weak man who marries for love. K. WATERHOUSE Love was a taboo subject in our country. **b** SWIFT The Colonel was cross'd in his first Love.

5 a (**L-**.) The personification of sexual affection, usu. masculine and more or less identified with Eros, Amor, or Cupid of classic mythology. ME. ▸**b** A cupid; a god of love; a figure or representation of a god of love. L16.

b W. M. PRAED Wher'er her step in beauty moves, Around her fly a thousand loves.

6 A beloved person; *esp.* one's sweetheart. Freq. (with or without *possess.*) as a form of intimate or (*colloq.*) friendly address. ME. ▸†**b** An illicit or clandestine lover. LME–E17. ▸**c** *gen.* An object of love; a person who or thing which is loved. M18. ▸**d** A charming or delightful person or thing. *colloq.* E19.

C. MARLOWE Liue with me and be my Loue. SHAKES. *Merch. V.* Whether Bassanio had not once a love. ALAN BENNETT Wash your hands, love, we're all ready. **c** D. WIGODER He introduced me to one of my greatest loves—classical music. J. RULE You were the great love of her life. **d** J. AUSTEN The garden is quite a love. P. CAREY Be a love and get back into your own bed.

7 Amorous sexual activity, sexual intercourse. Now chiefly in ***make love***, ***lovemaking*** below. LME.
†**8** A game of chance: = MORA *noun*[2]. L16–E18.
†**9** A material worn in mourning; a border of this. E17–E19.
10 In various games, esp. tennis, squash, etc.: no score, nil, nothing. M18.

– PHRASES ETC.: **apple of love** *arch.* = ***love apple*** below. ***boy's-love***: see BOY *noun*. **fall in love** develop a great (esp. sexual) love (mutually or *with* another). *FIRST* ***love***. **for love** without stakes, for nothing; for pleasure rather than profit. †**for all love(s)**, †**of all love(s)**: expr. strong adjuration or entreaty. **for the love of** for the sake of; on account of; ***for the love of Mike***: see MIKE *noun*[2] 3. ***free love***: see FREE *adjective*. **give one's love to** (**a**) send one's affectionate greeting to; (**b**) fall or be in love with. **in love** (**with**) enamoured (of), imbued with love (for); *transf.* very fond (of), much addicted (to). ***labour of love***: see LABOUR *noun*. ***light o' love***: see LIGHT *adjective*[1]. **love at first sight** the action or state of falling in love with a person who or *transf.* a thing which one has not previously seen. **love in a cottage** *arch.* marriage with insufficient means. **love's young dream** the relationship of young lovers; the object of someone's love; a man regarded as a perfect lover. **make love** (**a**) *arch.* pay amorous attention (*to*); (**b**) have sexual intercourse (foll. by *to*, *with*). **no love lost between** (two people etc.) †(**a**) mutual affection; (**b**) mutual dislike. **not for love or money** not at any price, by no means. ***of all love(s)***: see ***for all love(s)*** above. **out of love** (**with**) by no means or no longer in love (with); disgusted (with). ***tug of love***: see TUG *noun*[1] 3. ***tunnel of love***: see TUNNEL *noun* 4.

– COMB.: **love affair** †(**a**) in *pl.*, the experiences connected with being in love; (**b**) a romantic or sexual relationship between two people in love; *fig.* an intense enthusiasm or liking for something; **love apple** *arch.* a tomato; **love beads** (a necklace of) coloured beads worn as a symbol of universal love; **love-begotten** *adjective* (*arch.*) (of a child) illegitimate; **lovebird** (**a**) any of various small parrots said to display remarkable affection for their mates; *esp.* any member of the chiefly African genus *Agapornis*; *Austral.* a budgerigar; (**b**) *joc. & colloq.* in *pl.*, an affectionate couple, lovers; **lovebite** (a bruise on the skin due to) a sucking kiss; **love bush** *W. Indian* dodder; **love child** an illegitimate child; **love-curl** a lovelock, esp. on the forehead; **love-dart** ZOOLOGY a calcareous dart secreted by a snail's reproductive organs which is projected into the body of the snail's partner prior to copulation; †**loveday** a day appointed for a meeting to settle a dispute amicably; an agreement made on such a day; †**love-draught** a philtre; **love feast** among early Christians, a meal affirming brotherly love (cf. AGAPE *noun*); a religious service (esp. of Methodists) imitating this; **love game** a game in tennis etc. in which the loser fails to score a point; **love handles** *colloq.* deposits of excess fat at a person's waistline; **love–hate** *attrib. adjective* designating a relationship etc. marked by ambivalent feelings of love and hate existing towards the same object; **love hotel** (esp. in Japan) a hotel whose rooms can be hired for short periods of time, used for assignations between lovers; **love-in-a-mist** (**a**) a blue-flowered garden plant, *Nigella damascena*, with many delicate green bracts; (**b**) a W. Indian passion flower, *Passiflora foetida*; **love-in-idleness** heartsease, *Viola tricolor*; **love interest** a theme or episode in a story, film, etc., of which the main element is the affection of lovers; **love-juice** (**a**) a love potion, an aphrodisiac; (**b**) a sexual secretion; **love-knot** a knot or bow tied as a token of love; **love-lay** *poet.* a love song; **love letter** a letter written to express love; **love-lies-bleeding** an amaranth, *Amaranthus caudatus*, with drooping purple-red flowering spikes, cultivated as a garden plant; **love life** the aspect of a person's life involving relationships with lovers; **love-light** radiance (of the eyes) expressing love; **lovelock** a curl or lock of hair worn on the temple or forehead, or (formerly) in some other special way; **lovemaking** (**a**) *arch.* courtship; (**b**) amorous sexual activity, *esp.* sexual intercourse; **love match** a marriage or engagement of which the motive is love, not worldly advantage or convenience; **love-mate** a sweetheart, a lover; **love nest** a secluded retreat for (esp. illicit or clandestine) lovers; **love object** the person on whom love is centred; **love-pass**, **love-passage** *arch.* an incident involving love; **love-pat** a pat expressing or motivated by love; **love-play** wooing, caressing; *spec.* foreplay; **love potion** a philtre supposed to excite love; **love scene** an intimate scene between lovers, esp. in a story or play; **love seat** an armchair or small sofa designed for two occupants; **love song** a song of (romantic) love; **love-spoon** a wooden spoon, sometimes with a double bowl, carved for presentation to an intended wife; **love story** a story in which the main theme is the affection of lovers; **love-tap** a tap or gentle blow expressing or motivated by love; **love token** a thing given as a sign or token of love; **love-tree** the Judas tree, *Cercis siliquastrum*; **love vine** *US* (**a**) dodder; (**b**) = CORALLITA.
■ **lovelike** *adjective* (*rare*) (**a**) of a nature appropriate to love; †(**b**) lovely: E17.

love /lʌv/ *verb*. OE.
[ORIGIN from the noun.]
1 *verb trans.* Feel love for (a person, a thing personified); be very fond of, hold dear. OE. ▸**b** *spec.* Feel sexual love for; be in love with. OE. ▸**c** *verb intrans.* Feel love; *esp.* be in love. ME.

J. A. FROUDE A man who loved England well, but who loved Rome better. J. GARDAM He had loved the king and had ridden . . from the fells to Westminster for a coronation. J. NAGENDA Your old mother who loves you with all her heart. **b** SHAKES. *Oth.* I never knew woman love man so. **c** SHAKES. *Jul. Caes.* Love, and be friends. TENNYSON 'Tis better to have loved and lost, Than never to have loved at all.

I must love you and leave you *colloq.*: a formula of departure. **Lord love you**, **Lord love me**, **Lord love a duck**, etc. *interjections* expr. surprise, emphasis, etc. **loved one** a person beloved; *esp.* in *pl.*, one's family or relations. ***love paramour***: see PARAMOUR *adverb* 2. ***love to pieces***: see PIECE *noun*.

2 *verb trans.* **a** Be strongly attached to (a thing), be unwilling to part with or allow to perish (life, honour, etc.). OE. ▸**b** Take great pleasure in, be devoted or addicted to; *colloq.* like very much. Foll. by simple obj. *to do*, *doing* a person or thing *to do*. ME. ▸**c** Take pleasure in the existence of; admire greatly. ME.

a MARVELL As you loue your own affaires . . be pleased . . to let me know your minds. **b** H. GLASSE Some love a pig brought whole to table. P. V. WHITE He loved her to need him. MERLE COLLINS The Christmas plays she also loved. M. MILNER I have always loved drawing goats. *San Francisco Chronicle* He loves to bat, especially if he can put the ball out of the park. **c** BURKE I love firm government.

3 *verb trans.* Of a plant or (less usually) an animal: have a tendency to thrive in (a certain kind of situation). LME.

B. TAYLOR The violet loves a sunny bank.

4 *verb trans.* Embrace or caress affectionately. Freq. foll. by *up*. *colloq.* L19.

K. S. PRICHARD Why don't you give her a hug . . love her up a bit? B. HOLIDAY That dog . . began lapping me and loving me like crazy.

– COMB.: **loved-up** *slang* (**a**) under the influence of the drug Ecstasy, esp. with the result of feeling euphoric and affectionate; (**b**) in love, or behaving very amorously; **love-in** a gathering for the purpose of establishing and enjoying love relationships; **love-up** *slang* an act of caressing, hugging, or kissing.

loveable *adjective* var. of LOVABLE.

loveful /ˈlʌvfʊl, -f(ə)l/ *adjective*. Now *rare*. ME.
[ORIGIN from LOVE *noun* + -FUL.]
1 Full of love. ME.
†**2** Lovable. LME–L16.

Lovelace /ˈlʌvleɪs/ *noun*. M19.
[ORIGIN Robert *Lovelace*, a character in S. Richardson's novel *Clarissa Harlowe* (1747–8).]
A seducer.

loveless /ˈlʌvlɪs/ *adjective*. ME.
[ORIGIN from LOVE *noun* + -LESS.]
1 Without love; unloving; unloved. ME.
2 Unlovely. *rare*. E17.
■ **lovelessly** *adverb* E17. **lovelessness** *noun* M19.

loveling /ˈlʌvlɪŋ/ *noun*. *rare*. E17.
[ORIGIN from LOVE *noun or verb* + -LING[1].]
A lovely creature; an object of love; a darling.

lovelorn /ˈlʌvlɔːn/ *adjective*. M17.
[ORIGIN from LOVE *noun* + LORN *adjective*.]
Forsaken by one's love; pining from unrequited love.

lovely /ˈlʌvli/ *adjective & noun*. OE.
[ORIGIN from LOVE *noun* + -LY[1].]
▸ **A** *adjective* †**1 a** Loving, kind, affectionate. Also, amicable. OE–M17. ▸**b** Amorous. LME–L16.
2 Worthy of love; suited to attract love; spiritually or morally beautiful. OE.

SOUTHEY The life and death of that man were equally lovely. J. RUSKIN If his mind be . . sweetly toned, what he loves will be lovely.

3 Lovable or attractive on account of beauty; beautiful; *colloq.* delightful, pleasing, excellent, exquisitely beautiful. Also as *interjection*, expr. pleasure, commendation, etc. ME.

SHAKES. *Tam. Shr.* Till the tears that she hath shed . . Like envious floods o'er-run her lovely face. E. WAUGH You do know a lovely lot of stories. DYLAN THOMAS Thank you so much . . ; it was lovely of you. J. F. LEHMANN It was a hauntingly lovely September morning. A. CROSS 'I'll bring some wine . . .' 'Lovely.' J. SIMMS There was a lovely smell of rock cakes. E. PIZZEY It's lovely to see you looking so well.

lovely and — *colloq.* delightfully —, very —.

▸ **B** *noun*. A lovely person or thing. Now usu., a glamorously beautiful woman or girl. LME.

T. PYNCHON One of the girls, . . brown-haired lovely in a black knit leotard.

■ **lovelify** *verb trans.* (*rare*) make lovely L19. **lovelihead** *noun* (*arch. rare*) loveliness M17. **lovelily** *adverb* ME. **loveliness** *noun* the quality of being lovely, exquisite beauty: ME.

lovely /ˈlʌvli/ *adverb*. Now only *poet. & non-standard*. OE.
[ORIGIN from LOVE *noun* + -LY[2].]
†**1** Lovingly, affectionately. OE–L16.
2 Lovably, beautifully; in a lovely manner, delightfully, excellently, commendably. LME.

A. E. HOUSMAN How clear, how lovely bright. C. FREMLIN *Your mummy has taught you to eat up lovely.*

L

lover /ˈlʌvə/ *noun*. ME.
[ORIGIN from LOVE *verb* + -ER[1].]
1 A person who feels fondness or kindly regard towards another. Now *rare* exc. in Christian use (cf. LOVE *noun* 2). ME.

C. WESLEY Jesu, Lover of my Soul. H. BROOKE A stranger, but a very warm lover of yours.

2 A person (esp. a man) who is in love with someone; either of two people involved in a sexual relationship (outside of or without marriage), *spec.* an illicit or clandestine one. Freq. in *pl.*, a couple in love, sexual partners. Also (*colloq.*) as a form of intimate or friendly address. ME. ▸**b** A pimp. *US slang*. E20.

AV *Jer.* 3:1 Thou hast played the harlot with many louers. D. HEYES 'You got it, lover,' the waitress said. P. THEROUX There were lovers on this heath, plainly copulating. R. INGALLS She never has had lovers? She's always been alone?

3 A person who has an affection, predilection, fancy, or liking for a specified thing, activity, idea, etc. ME.

D. HUME Lovers of Liberty, but greater Lovers of Monarchy. L. GRIFFITHS We're all horse lovers but we're not daft as well. E. SAINTSBURY Lewis Carroll . . a great lover of children.

– COMB.: **lover boy** *slang* a (male) lover, an attractive man, a woman-chaser; freq. as a form of address; **lover's knot** = *love-knot* s.v. LOVE *noun*; **lovers' lane** a road or other secluded place to which lovers resort; **lovers' quarrel**, **lovers' tiff** a dispute between lovers (which therefore will not last long); **lovers' rock** a gentle, melodic style of reggae music usu. having lyrics about love.

■ **lovered** *adjective* (*rare*) having a lover (of a specified kind) L16. **lovering** *noun* (*colloq.*) amorous activity, fondling; courting: L19. **loverless** *adjective* E19. **loverlike** *adjective & adverb* like or as befits a lover M16.

loverly /ˈlʌvəli/ *adjective*[1]. E16.
[ORIGIN from LOVER + -LY[1].]
Like or befitting a lover.

loverly /ˈlʌvəli/ *adjective*[2]. *joc. & colloq.* E20.
[ORIGIN Repr. a cockney pronunc.]
Lovely.

loverly /ˈlʌvəli/ *adverb*. *rare*. L15.
[ORIGIN from LOVER + -LY[2].]
In the manner of a lover.

lovesick /ˈlʌvsɪk/ *adjective*. LME.
[ORIGIN from LOVE *noun* + SICK *adjective*.]
Languishing with romantic love.

J. M. MURRY Endymion's lovesick wanderings in search of the moon-goddess. L. GILLEN Idiotic of her to behave like a lovesick schoolgirl.

■ **lovesickness** *noun* E18.

lovesome /ˈlʌvs(ə)m/ *adjective*. Now *literary*. OE.
[ORIGIN from LOVE *noun* + -SOME[1].]
1 Worthy of or inspiring love; lovable. OE.
2 Lovable on account of beauty; lovely, beautiful. ME.

T. E. BROWN A garden is a lovesome thing, God wot!

3 Loving, friendly. ME.
4 Amorous. M16.
■ **lovesomeness** *noun* OE.

loveworthy /ˈlʌvwəːði/ *adjective*. ME.
[ORIGIN from LOVE *noun* + -WORTHY.]
Worthy to be loved, deserving love.
■ **loveworthiness** *noun* M19.

lovey /ˈlʌvi/ *noun*. *colloq.* M18.
[ORIGIN from LOVE *noun* + -Y[6].]
Used as a term of endearment: love, sweetheart. Cf. DOVEY.

lovey-dovey /ˈlʌvɪˌdʌvi, ˌlʌvɪˈdʌvi/ *noun & adjective*. *colloq.* E19.
[ORIGIN from LOVEY + DOVEY.]
▸ **A** *noun*. Used as a term of endearment: love, sweetheart. E19.
▸ **B** *adjective*. Fondly affectionate, *esp.* unduly so; sentimental. L19.

T. CALLENDER Everything went back lovey-dovey again between the two of them. D. FRANCIS She was never a lovey-dovey sort of mother.

■ **lovey-doveyness** *noun* E20.

loving /ˈlʌvɪŋ/ *noun*. LME.
[ORIGIN from LOVE *verb* + -ING[1].]
The action of LOVE *verb*; active love, affection.

loving /ˈlʌvɪŋ/ *adjective*. OE.
[ORIGIN from LOVE *verb* + -ING[2].]
That loves; feeling or showing love; affectionate. Freq. as 2nd elem. of comb.

ALDOUS HUXLEY Every loving word was treasured as a word . . from the depths of the heart. G. JEKYLL The rock-loving Campanulas. *Times* 20 fun-loving people to share Christmas.

loving cup a large, often silver, two-handled drinking cup passed round at banquets, the guests successively drinking from it. **loving kindness** kindness arising from a deep personal love, as (in Christian use) the active love of God for his creatures; affectionate tenderness and consideration. ***tender loving care***: see TENDER *adjective*.
■ **lovingly** *adverb* LME. **lovingness** *noun* L16.

low /ləʊ/ *noun*[1]. Now chiefly *dial.* See also LAW *noun*[2].
[ORIGIN Old English *hlāw*, *hlǣw*, corresp. to Old Saxon *hlēo*, *hlēw-*, Old High German *hleo*, Gothic *hlaiw*, from Germanic, ult. from Indo-European base meaning 'slope' (whence also LEAN *verb*).]
1 = LAW *noun*[2]. OE.
2 A grave mound; a tumulus. OE.

low /ləʊ/ *noun*[2]. Chiefly *Scot. & N. English*. Also **lowe**. ME.
[ORIGIN Old Norse *logi* = Old Frisian *loga*, from Germanic (rel. to German *Lohe* (also in *lichterloh* in a blaze)) from Indo-European base also of LIGHT *noun*.]
1 (A) flame. ME.
in a low, **on a low** on fire. **put the low to** set fire to. **take a low** catch fire.
2 A light. E19.

low /ləʊ/ *noun*[3]. M16.
[ORIGIN from LOW *verb*[1].]
The action or an act of lowing; a bovine animal's deep subdued resonant sound.

low /ləʊ/ *adjective & noun*[4]. ME.
[ORIGIN Old Norse *lágr* = Old Frisian *lēge*, *lēch*, Middle Dutch *lage*, *laech*, *lege*, *leech* (Dutch *laag*), Middle High German *læge* (German dial. *läg*) flat, from Germanic base rel. to base of LIE *verb*[1].]
▸ **A** *adjective*. **I 1** Of small or less than average upward extent; little; short. Now *rare* of a person exc. *Scot.* ME. ▸**b** Chiefly of clothing: cut so as to extend below the normal level, low-cut. M19.

D. H. LAWRENCE The kitchen, a long, low room. DAY LEWIS Five steps, flanked by low stone balustrades. **b** SCOTT FITZGERALD She wore a low gown which displayed the bright eczema of her chest and back.

2 Situated not far above the ground or a specified level or (formerly) under the earth's surface; not elevated in position. Also, designating a country or a district near the sea or not far above sea level (now only in fixed collocations, as ***the Low Countries***, ***Low German***, etc.: cf. LOWER *adjective* 2). ME. ▸**b** Dead (and buried). *arch.* ME. ▸**c** Of a curtsy, bow, etc.: in which the body is brought (relatively) close to the ground. M16. ▸**d** Of the sun, moon, a star, etc.: near the horizon. L17.

G. BERKELEY Trees . . in low and shady places do not yield so good tar.

3 Esp. of a river, a lake, etc.: below the usual vertical measurement; shallow. LME.
4 *PHONETICS*. Of a sound: produced with (part of) the tongue in a lowered position. M19.
▸ **II** *transf. & fig.* **5** Of or in a humble rank or position (now *derog.* of a person, passing into sense 5c); humble in disposition, meek (now *rare*). ME. ▸**b** Base, mean. ME. ▸**c** Coarse, vulgar; disreputable. L16.

C. THIRLWALL A young man of low birth . . had been . . acknowledged as king. E. WAUGH You are a distinguished man, . . not like these low soldiers. **b** JAS. ROBERTSON Flattery or fawning or other low arts. **c** B. WEBB There is nothing that is low or bad broadcasted. L. BLUE I also like low things such as liver and lights.

6 Of inferior quality, character, or style; unrefined, commonplace. ME. ▸**b** Chiefly *BIOLOGY*. Advanced to a lesser degree; having a simple or primitive organization. Usu. in compar.: see LOWER *adjective* 2c. M19.

C. KINGSLEY To discriminate between high art and low art they must have seen both.

7 a (Of a quality, condition, etc.) small or reduced in quantity, degree, or intensity; *spec.* (**a**) (of sound) not loud (see also sense 9 below); (**b**) (of heat) not of a high temperature; (of temperature) less likely to promote melting and the emission of radiation. LME. ▸**b** Of price, rate, quantity, value, etc.: not high, below what is regarded as normal or average; numerically small. E17. ▸**c** Of latitude: at a short distance from the equator. M18.

a W. FAULKNER White faces . . sharp in the low light. M. FRAYN The air temperature was low, but the woods . . were filled with . . sunlight. G. VIDAL Her voice became so low that he could barely hear her. M. GORDON I have a rather low tolerance for horrors. **b** *Manchester Examiner* Chinese workmen . . work for low wages. D. MURPHY The rent was so low . . because of the previous tenant's suicide.

8 Lacking physical strength or vigour; weak (through illness or poor nourishment). Now *esp.* dejected, dispirited, depressed. LME. ▸**b** Of diet etc.: providing little nourishment, poor. E18.

T. DREISER He was exceedingly low and not expected to live. P. BARKER She came out of hospital so low that for the first time . . she thought about suicide. **b** L. STRACHEY The low diet and constant bleedings . . were an error.

9 Of a voice, musical sound, etc.: not high or acute in pitch, not shrill; producing or produced by relatively slow vibrations. LME.
10 Of a stock of a commodity etc.: small or reduced in quantity; nearly exhausted. E18.

TOLKIEN The food would not last for ever: it was . . beginning to get low.

11 = LOW CHURCH *adjectival phr.* *colloq.* M19.
12 Of a date: relatively recent. Usu. in *compar. & superl.* E20.
▸ **III** After a verb, as the result of an action or process.
13 So as to be in a low position or on or to a low level. Chiefly in ***lay low***, ***lie low*** below. Passing into *adverb*. ME.
– PHRASES: ***burn low***: see BURN *verb*. ***high and low***: see HIGH *adjective, adverb, & noun*. **lay low** (**a**) lay flat; bring to the ground; *fig.* humble; (**b**) bury. **lie low** (**a**) crouch; be prostrate, be dead; *fig.* be humbled; (**b**) *colloq.* keep quiet or out of the way; make no intervention; bide one's time. **low on** *colloq.* short of. **low to paper** *PRINTING* (of type) of less than normal height. ***run low***: see RUN *verb*. ***the low toby***: see TOBY *noun*[2].
– SPECIAL COLLOCATIONS & COMB.: **low-alloy** *adjective* (*METALLURGY*) containing a small proportion of alloying elements. **low-born** *adjective* of humble birth. **lowboy** *N. Amer.* (**a**) a table with drawers and fairly short legs; (**b**) a low-slung trailer for transporting very tall or heavy loads. **low-bred** *adjective* having or characterized by vulgar manners. **low-browed** *adjective* (**a**) (of a person) having a low forehead; (**b**) (of rocks) overhanging; (of a doorway etc.) low, dark. **low-bush** *adjective* (*N. Amer.*) designating or pertaining to a plant that grows low to the ground; ***low-bush blackberry***, the N. American dewberry, *Rubus flagellaris*. **low-carbohydrate**, (*colloq.*) **low-carb** *adjective* (of food or drink) low in carbohydrates. **low-calorie** *adjective* (of food or drink) low in calories. **low-class** *adjective* (**a**) of low quality; (**b**) of low social class. **low comedian** an actor of low comedy. **low comedy**: in which the subject and treatment border on farce. **low-cut** *adjective* cut with a neckline that exposes the neck and upper part of the breast. **low-definition** *adjective* designating or providing a relatively unclear or indistinct image. **low-down** *noun & adjective* (**a**) *noun* (*colloq.*) the relevant information or fundamental facts *on*; (**b**) *adjective* abject, mean, despicable. ***Low Dutch***: see DUTCH *adjective, noun*[1]. **low-end** *adjective* (*COMMERCE*) of, pertaining to, or associated with the cheaper end of the market for a particular product. **low enema**: delivered into the rectum. ***lowest common denominator***: see DENOMINATOR 1. ***lowest common multiple***: see MULTIPLE *noun* 1. ***lowest terms***: see TERM *noun*. **low fidelity** *AUDIO* (the reproduction of) low-fidelity sound. **low-fidelity** *adjective* (*AUDIO*) designating, pertaining to, or characterized by sound reproduction inferior to high fidelity (cf. LO-FI). **low frequency** *spec.* a frequency of vibration or oscillations having a relatively small number of cycles per second; in *TELECOMMUNICATIONS* etc., a radio frequency in the range 30–300 kilohertz, *loosely* an audio (as opp. to a radio) frequency. **low gear** a gear of a motor vehicle providing a low ratio between the speed of the driven wheels and that of the driving mechanism and so a low speed to the vehicle itself. ***Low German***: see GERMAN *noun*[1] *& adjective*[1]. **low grade** *PHILOLOGY* a reduced form in an ablaut series, usu. pronounced /ə/. **low-grade** *adjective* of low quality. **low-hanging fruit** *colloq.* something easily achieved or overcome. **low-headed** *adjective* (of a tree) having a low crown of foliage. **low heels** low-heeled shoes. ***low keep***: see KEEP *noun*. **low-key** *adjective* (**a**) *PHOTOGRAPHY* consisting of dark tones; (**b**) *fig.* muted, restrained, not intense or prominent. **low-keyed** *adjective* = ***low-key*** (b) above. **Low Latin** [translating French *bas-latin*] late and medieval Latin. **low-level** *adjective* (**a**) situated near or below ground level; *fig.* low-ranking, unobtrusive; (**b**) designating mild radioactivity or mildly radioactive waste; (**c**) *COMPUTING* (of a programming language) containing only relatively simple instructions, close to machine language in form. **low-lived** *adjective* of, pertaining to, or living a low or disreputable life. **low-loader** a lorry with a low floor and (usu.) no sides for heavy loads. **low-loss** *adjective* (*ELECTRICITY*) characterized by or causing little dissipation of electric or electromagnetic energy. **low-lying** *adjective* at low altitude (above sea level etc.). ***low mass***: see MASS *noun*[1]. **low-maintenance** *adjective* (*colloq.*) (of a person) independent and not demanding a lot of attention. **low-melting** *adjective* melting at a relatively low temperature, esp. at little more than room temperature. **low men** dice loaded to turn up low numbers. **low-minded** *adjective* vulgar or ignoble in mind or character. **low-mindedness** the quality or state of being low-minded. **low-molecular** *adjective* (*CHEMISTRY*) having a low molecular weight. **low-necked** *adjective* (of a garment) having a low-cut neck. **low opinion** a very unfavourable opinion. **low-pass** *adjective* (*AUDIO* etc.) designating a filter that attenuates only those components with a frequency greater than some cut-off frequency. **low-pitched** *adjective* (**a**) (of a sound) low in pitch; (**b**) (of a roof) not very steep. **low point** the minimum or worst state reached. **low post** *BASKETBALL* an offensive position on the court close to the basket. **low-powered** *adjective* having little power or energy. **low pressure** (**a**) a low degree of activity or exertion; (**b**) an atmospheric condition with pressure below average. **low profile** a low-keyed and unobtrusive policy or attitude, a condition of behaving in a restrained or inconspicuous way. **low-profile** *adjective* (**a**) designating a motor-vehicle tyre which is wide in proportion to its height; (**b**) designating, having, or maintaining a low profile. ***low relief***: see RELIEF *noun*[2] 1. **low-rent** *adjective* (**a**) (of a property) costing relatively little to rent; (**b**) *transf.* (*N. Amer.*) inexpensive; having little prestige; shoddy. **low-residue** *adjective* (of a meal or diet) designed to produce relatively little faeces and urine. **low-rise** *adjective & noun* (a building) of one storey or few storeys. **low season** the period of fewest visitors at a resort etc. **low side window** *ARCHITECTURE* a small window lower than the other windows, found in some medieval churches. **low-slung** *adjective* (**a**) lower in height or closer to the ground than usual; (**b**) (of clothes, esp. trousers) cut to fit low on the hips rather than the waist; **low-spirited** *adjective* dejected, depressed. **low-spiritedness** the quality or condition of being low-spirited. **low spirits** dejection, depression. **Low Sunday** the Sunday after Easter. **low tech** *noun & adjective* (**a**) *noun* = ***low technology*** below; (**b**) *adjective* involved in, employing, or requiring only low technology. **low technology** less advanced or relatively unsophisticated technological development or equipment. **low tension** low voltage. **low tide** the time or level of the tide at its ebb. **low water** the tide at its lowest. **low-water mark** (**a**) the level reached at low water or in a drought or dry season; (**b**) a minimum recorded level or value. **Low Week** the week beginning with Low Sunday. **low-wines** the first spirit that comes off in the distillation process. **low-yield** *adjective* producing little, giving a low return; *spec.* (of a nuclear weapon) having a relatively low explosive force.
▸ **B** *noun*. **I** *absol.* **1** That which is low; those who are low or of humble birth. ME.
†**2** After *at*, *in*, *on* prepositions. The ground, the earth. Only in ME.

▸ **II 3** A piece of low-lying land; *spec.* in East Anglia, a hollow or valley between dunes; a pool left by the tide in such a hollow. **ME.**

> *Rolling Stone* The peaks, lows and riffs of these . . Nevada California border ranges.

4 The lowest trump card dealt or drawn. Chiefly in ***high-low-jack (and the game)***, = ALL FOURS 2. **E19.**
5 An area of low barometric pressure. Also, an area of low gravitational field strength. **L19.**
6 A low point or minimum in price, temperature, etc.; *spec.* a depression, a state of dejection. **E20.**

> F. L. ALLEN The Boston *literati* . . sank . . to new lows for all time. *New York Times* The United States dollar plunged yesterday to another post-war low. C. THUBRON Easy does it, Daniel, you're having one of your lows.

7 = ***low gear*** above. **M20.**

> A. HALL I dragged the manual into low to kill the rest of the speed.

low /ləʊ/ *verb*¹.
[ORIGIN Old English *hlōwan* = Old Saxon *hlōian* (Dutch *loeien*) (whence *hlōwinga* roaring), Old High German *hluoen*, from Germanic redupl. strong verb, from Indo-European repr. base also of Latin *clamare* shout.]
1 *verb intrans.* Of a bovine animal: (orig.) bellow; (now) utter a deep subdued resonant sound, moo. **OE.**

> W. VAN T. CLARK We could hear the cows lowing . . , a mellow sound at that distance. A. BRINK A single calf in a pen, lowing wretchedly at regular intervals.

2 *verb intrans. transf.* Make a loud noise, bellow. Now *rare*. **OE.**
3 *verb trans.* Orig., utter with a bellow. Now, utter with a deep murmur. **M16.**

low /ləʊ/ *verb*² *trans. obsolete* exc. *dial.* **ME.**
[ORIGIN from LOW *adjective*.]
1 Make or bring low. Chiefly *fig.*, abase, humble. **ME.**
2 Diminish, lessen, esp. in value. **ME.**
3 Hold or put in a lower position. **LME.**

low /ləʊ/ *verb*³ *intrans.* Chiefly *Scot.* & *N. English.* **ME.**
[ORIGIN Old Norse *loga*, from *logi* LOW *noun*².]
Flame, blaze, (*up*); glow; *fig.* burn with passion.

low /laʊ/ *verb*⁴ *trans. colloq.* Also (now usu.) **'low**. **LME.**
[ORIGIN Partly from Old French & mod. French *louer* from Latin *laudare* praise, approve; partly aphet. from ALLOW.]
= ALLOW I.

> G. V. GALWEY Wind's backed four points . . . We've got to 'low for it.

low /ləʊ/ *adverb.* **ME.**
[ORIGIN from LOW *adjective*.]
1 In a low position; on or not much above the ground or some other level. **ME.** ▸**b** *fig.* Humbly; in a low condition or rank; at a low rate. **LME.**

> J. MITCHELL They flew quite low over the bush. J. M. COETZEE He . . gathered the next tuft of lucerne, and cut it clean and low.

high and low: see HIGH *adjective, adverb, & noun.*
2 To a low point or position. Also, in a low direction. **ME.**

> J. STEINBECK The sun dropped low toward the horizon. G. GREENE They stoop low slipping between the tables.

3 In a low tone; not loudly, softly; with not much intensity. Also of singing etc.: at a low pitch, on low notes. **ME.**
blow high, blow low: see BLOW *verb*¹.
4 (To a point) far down in time; late. **M17.**
– COMB.: **low-flung** *adjective* (*arch. US colloq.*) of low character or standing.

lowan /ˈləʊən/ *noun. Austral.* **M19.**
[ORIGIN Wemba-wemba *lawan*.]
The mallee fowl.

lowance /ˈlaʊəns/ *noun.* Now *dial.* **M16.**
[ORIGIN Aphet. from ALLOWANCE.]
A limited portion of food or drink or its equivalent in money given in addition to wages.

lowball /ˈləʊbɔːl/ *noun & verb.* Chiefly *US.* **M19.**
[ORIGIN from LOW *adjective* + BALL *noun*¹.]
▸ **A** *noun.* **1** BASEBALL. A ball pitched so as to pass over the plate below the level of the batter. **M19.**
2 COMMERCE. (The action of offering) a deceptively or unrealistically low price or estimate. **M20.**
▸ **B** *verb trans.* COMMERCE. Reduce to a deceptive or unrealistically low price or level. **M20.**
■ **lowballer** *noun* **L20.**

lowbell /ˈləʊbɛl/ *noun & verb.* **L16.**
[ORIGIN Perh. from LOW *adjective* + BELL *noun*¹.]
▸ †**A** *noun.* **1** A small bell; *esp.* a cowbell, a sheep bell. **L16–M17.**
2 A bell used at night in fowling, to stupefy the birds with terror. **L16–E19.**
▸ **B** *verb trans.* †**1** Capture (birds) by the use of a lowbell; scare or bewilder as with a lowbell. **L16–M17.**
2 Deride by the jangling of tins, kettles, etc. *dial.* **M19.**
■ **lowbeller** *noun* **L16.**

lowbrow /ˈləʊbraʊ/ *noun & adjective. colloq.* (orig. *US*). **E20.**
[ORIGIN from LOW *adjective* + BROW *noun*¹, after HIGHBROW.]
▸ **A** *noun.* A person who is not, or does not claim or aim to be, highly intellectual or cultured. **E20.**
▸ **B** *adjective.* Not highly, or not pretentiously, intellectual or cultured. **E20.**

> H. CARPENTER Chapbooks, which played much the same part in society as lowbrow television drama does now.

■ **lowbrowism** *noun* lack of interest in intellectual or cultural matters **M20.**

Low Church /ləʊ ˈtʃəːtʃ/ *noun & adjectival phr.* **E18.**
[ORIGIN from LOW *adjective* + CHURCH *noun*, after LOW CHURCHMAN.]
▸ **A** *noun phr.* (The principles of) a section of the Church of England or (now also) any of various Nonconformist Churches laying little emphasis on ritual, priestly authority, and sacraments. **E18.**
▸ **B** *adjectival phr.* Of, pertaining to, or characteristic of (the principles of) this section or such a Church. **E18.**
■ **Low-'Churchism** *noun* Low-Church principles, doctrine, or practice **M19.**

Low Churchman /ləʊ ˈtʃəːtʃmən/ *noun phr.* Pl. **Low Churchmen**. **E18.**
[ORIGIN from LOW *adjective* + CHURCHMAN.]
An advocate of Low Church principles.

low-country /ˈləʊkʌntri/ *noun & adjective.* Also (in sense A.2 only) without hyphen. **L15.**
[ORIGIN from LOW *adjective* + COUNTRY.]
▸ **A** *noun.* **1** A region or district whose level is lower than that of the surrounding country. **L15.**
2 ***the Low Countries***, the Netherlands, Belgium, and Luxembourg. **M16.**
3 = LOWVELD. *S. Afr.* **L19.**
▸ **B** *attrib.* or as *adjective.* **1** (With cap. initials.) Of, pertaining to, or from the Low Countries. **E17.**
2 Of or pertaining to the low-country or (*S. Afr.*) the lowveld. **M19.**

lowe *noun* var. of LOW *noun*².

lower *noun*¹, *noun*² vars. of LOUR *noun*¹, *noun*².

lower /ˈləʊə/ *adjective, noun*³, *& adverb.* **ME.**
[ORIGIN from LOW *adjective* + -ER³.]
▸ **A** *adjective.* **1** Compar. of LOW *adjective.* **ME.**
2 *spec.* Designating a thing or person less high in position, degree, or status than, or situated below, another of the same. **L16.** ▸**b** Designating (part of) a region, river, etc., situated on less high land, or to the south, or towards the sea. Usu. opp. ***upper***. **E17.** ▸**c** BIOLOGY. Of an organism or group: less advanced, primitive in organization. Opp. ***higher***. **L18.** ▸**d** GEOLOGY & ARCHAEOLOGY. (Freq. **L-**.) Designating an older, and hence usu. deeper, part of a stratigraphic division, archaeological deposit, etc., or the period in which it was formed or deposited. Opp. ***upper***. **M19.**
lower intestine, ***lower lip***, etc. **b** ***Lower California***, ***Lower Egypt***, ***the lower Danube***, etc. **d** ***Lower Carboniferous***, ***Lower Triassic***, etc.
– SPECIAL COLLOCATIONS, PHRASES, & COMB.: ***lower case***: see CASE *noun*². **Lower Chamber** = ***Lower House*** below. ***Lower Chinook***: see CHINOOK 1. **lower-class** *adjective* of or pertaining to the lower or working class; *derog.* common, vulgar. **lower class(es)** (the members of) the working class. **lower court** a court subject to overruling by another on appeal etc. **lower deck** (*a*) the deck of a ship situated immediately above the orlop deck; (*b*) the petty officers and men of a ship collectively. **lower fourth**, **lower fifth** a lower division of a fourth, fifth, form in a secondary school. **Lower House** one of the houses of a legislature consisting of two houses, usu. the larger and more representative one, often dealing with legislation before the Upper House; *esp.* the House of Commons. ***lower jaw***: see JAW *noun*¹ 1. **lower orders** = ***lower classes*** above. ***lower pastern***: see PASTERN 2c. **lower regions** = ***lower world*** below. **lower school** in a secondary school, (the pupils in) the forms below the fifth. **lower second** the lower division of a second-class honours degree. **lower sixth** a lower division of a sixth form in a secondary school. **lower world** (*a*) earth as opp. to heaven; (*b*) hell; the realm of the dead. ***lower yield point***: see YIELD *verb*. ***the lower criticism***: see CRITICISM 2.
▸ **B** *noun.* **1** An inferior person or thing. **ME.**
2 A lower plate of artificial teeth. **L19.**
▸ **C** *adverb.* Compar. of LOW *adverb.* **M16.**
■ **lowermost** *adjective & adverb* lowest **M16.**

lower /ˈləʊə/ *verb*¹. **E16.**
[ORIGIN from LOWER *adjective*.]
1 a *verb trans.* Make lower, reduce the level of. **E16.** ▸**b** *verb trans.* Cause or allow to descend, let down gradually (a drawbridge, a person or thing suspended from above, etc.); haul down (a sail, a flag) (also (NAUTICAL) foll. by *away*). **M17.** ▸**c** *verb intrans.* NAUTICAL. Haul down a sail. Also foll. by *away*. **M18.** ▸**d** *verb trans.* Cause (one's eyes) to look downwards, cause (one's head, eyelids, etc.) to droop, esp. as an expression of humility, modesty, evasion, etc. **M19.** ▸**e** *verb trans.* Drink (beer etc.); empty (a bottle or glass of beer etc.) by drinking. *colloq.* **L19.**

> **a** D. LARDNER The water escapes . . until the level of C has been lowered to that of B. **b** B. PYM Adam Prince lowered himself carefully on to the ground. K. WILLIAMS He lowered the blinds in his car. M. ATWOOD He . . lowered the outboard motor into the water. **d** R. P. JHABVALA He had lowered his eyes as if afraid of embarrassing me. **e** L. GREX He could lower a whole bottle of three-star brandy.

2 *verb intrans.* Descend, sink. Formerly also, cower, crouch. Freq. foll. by *down*. **M16.** ▸**b** Slope downwards. **E19.**
3 *verb trans.* & *intrans.* Diminish, reduce, esp. in price. **L17.**

> B. SPOCK It looks as though teething lowers resistance. *Lancaster Guardian* The committee decided to lower the entrance fee.

4 *verb trans.* Make lower in quality or degree; lessen the intensity of. Formerly also, reduce the strength of, dilute (a liquid, the air, etc.). **M18.** ▸**b** MUSIC. Depress in pitch, flatten. **L19.** ▸**c** PHONETICS. Modify (a sound) by articulation with a lower tongue position. **L19.**

> I. MURDOCH Bruno had lowered his voice to a confidential whisper. *Which?* The 'flash-freeze' button . . lowers the temperatures in the freezer.

5 *verb trans.* Bring down in rank or estimation, degrade, dishonour, (esp. oneself). **L18.**

> LYTTON In marriage a man lowers a woman to his own rank. R. K. NARAYAN We have a status . . to keep. We can't lower ourselves unduly.

6 *verb trans.* Bring down to a lower position on a graduated scale. **M19.**

> B. STEWART It is possible to lower the freezing-point by various means.

– PHRASES: ***lower one's sights***: see SIGHT *noun.* **lower the boom** *N. Amer. slang* inflict a physical defeat *on* (a person), treat severely.
■ **lowerable** *adjective* **L19.** **lowerer** *noun* **L19.**

lower *verb*², **lowering** *adjective*, **lowery** *adjective* vars. of LOUR *verb*, LOURING, LOURY.

Lowestoft /ˈləʊstɒft/ *noun & adjective.* **L18.**
[ORIGIN A town in Suffolk, England.]
(Made from) a soft-paste porcelain made orig. in Lowestoft from 1757. Also ***Lowestoft porcelain***.
Oriental Lowestoft: see ORIENTAL *adjective.*

lowish /ˈləʊɪʃ/ *adjective.* **L17.**
[ORIGIN from LOW *adjective* + -ISH¹.]
Somewhat low.

lowland /ˈləʊlənd/ *noun & adjective.* **L15.**
[ORIGIN from LOW *adjective* + LAND *noun*¹. See also LALLAN.]
▸ **A** *noun.* In sense 2 **L-**.
1 Low-lying or level land; the low-lying part of a country or district. Usu. in *pl.* **L15.**
2 *spec.* **a** In *pl.* & †*sing.* *The* less mountainous southern and eastern region of Scotland. **L15.** ▸**b** In *pl.* *The* Low Countries. **L17.**
3 In *pl.* (treated as *sing.*). The dialect of the Scottish Lowlands, Lallans. *Scot.* **M19.**
▸ **B** *adjective.* Of, pertaining to, or inhabiting lowland; *spec.* (**L-**) of, pertaining to, or characteristic of (the people of) the Scottish Lowlands. **E16.**
■ **lowlander** *noun* a native or inhabitant of the low-lying part of a country or district; *spec.* (**L-**) a native or inhabitant of the Scottish Lowlands: **L17.**

lowlife /ˈləʊlʌɪf/ *adjective & noun.* **L18.**
[ORIGIN from LOW *adjective* + LIFE *noun*.]
▸ **A** *adjective.* Disreputable, vulgar. Now also, of or pertaining to the (criminal) underworld or an underclass. **L18.**
▸ **B** *noun.* Pl. **-lifes**, (occas.) **-lives** /-lʌɪvz/. A coarse vulgar person; a member of the (criminal) underworld or an underclass; such people collectively. **E20.**

lowlight /ˈləʊlʌɪt/ *noun & adjective.* **E20.**
[ORIGIN from LOW *adjective* + LIGHT *noun*, after *highlight*.]
▸ **A** *noun.* **1** A dark (esp. artificial) streak in lighter hair. **E20.**
2 A moment or feature of low interest or activity; a low point; a poor performance etc. **L20.**
▸ **B** *attrib.* or as *adjective.* PHOTOGRAPHY. Designating devices for use in conditions of little light, and operations performed in such conditions. **L20.**

lowlives *noun pl.* see LOW LIFE.

lowly /ˈləʊli/ *adjective.* Now chiefly *arch.* & *rhet.* **LME.**
[ORIGIN from LOW *adjective* + -LY¹.]
1 Humble in feeling or behaviour; humble in condition or quality; modest. **LME.** ▸**b** Low, mean, base. *rare.* **M18.**

> R. OWEN Her parents would not . . consider allowing their daughter to marry a man . . of lowly origin. D. ROWE The lowly status of children . . in poverty.

2 Low in position (usu. with allus. to sense 1). **L16.**

> E. K. KANE The sun, albeit from a lowly altitude, shone out.

3 Of a plant or animal: primitive, simple. **L19.**
■ **lowlihead** *noun* (*arch.*) humility, lowliness **LME.** **lowlily** *adverb* **ME.** **lowliness** *noun* **LME.**

lowly /ˈləʊli/ *adverb.* Now chiefly *arch.* or *rhet.* **ME.**
[ORIGIN from LOW *adjective* + -LY².]
1 In a lowly manner; humbly, modestly, meekly. **ME.**
2 In a low position or posture (in later use with allus. to sense 1). **ME.** ▸**b** In a low voice. Now *poet.* **LME.** ▸†**c** In an inferior manner, meanly. *rare* (Shakes.). Only in **E17.** ▸**d** With a low opinion. *rare.* **M18.**

lowmost /ˈləʊməʊst/ *adjective & adverb.* Now *dial.* **M16.**
[ORIGIN from LOW *adjective*, *adverb* + -MOST.]
Lowest.

L

lown /laʊn/ *adjective, adverb, & noun. Scot. & N. English.* LME.
[ORIGIN Old Norse (dial.) *logn*, earlier *lygn*.]
▸ **A** *adjective.* **1** Of the weather, water, a place: calm, quiet, still. Of a person, action, etc.: calm, gentle, silent, still. LME.
2 Sheltered; cosy, snug. E18.
▸ **B** *adverb.* Quietly, softly. M16.
▸ **C** *noun.* Quiet, calm, stillness. Also, shelter. L18.
■ **lownly** *adverb* calmly, quietly; in shelter: L18.

lown /laʊn/ *verb intrans. Scot. & N. English.* LME.
[ORIGIN from LOWN *adjective.*]
1 Become calm, calm. LME.
2 Shelter. LME.

lowness /ˈləʊnɪs/ *noun.* ME.
[ORIGIN from LOW *adjective* + -NESS.]
1 The quality or condition of being low. ME.
2 (Also **L-**.) With possess. adjective (as ***his lowness*** etc.): a mock title of rank. L18.

Lowry /ˈlaʊri/ *adjective.* M20.
[ORIGIN See below.]
Reminiscent or characteristic of the work of the British painter Lawrence Stephen Lowry (1887–1976); *esp.* matchstick, involving matchstick figures.
■ **Lowry'esque** *adjective* M20.

lowveld /ˈləʊvɛlt, -f-/ *noun.* L19.
[ORIGIN Partial translation of Afrikaans *Laeveld* low country.]
(A region of) veld situated at a low altitude; *spec.* the low-lying region of north-eastern South Africa and Swaziland.

lowy /ˈləʊi/ *noun. obsolete* exc. *hist.* L16.
[ORIGIN Old French *louée*, *lieuée* from medieval Latin *leucata*, *leugata*, from late Latin *leuca*, *leuga*: see LEAGUE *noun*[1], -Y[5].]
A district or area extending for about a league outside a town but still under its control.

lox /lɒks; ɛləʊˈɛks/ *noun*[1]. Also **LOX**. E20.
[ORIGIN Orig. from *l*iquid *ox*ygen explosive; later interpreted as repr. *l*iquid *ox*ygen.]
1 An explosive device which uses liquid oxygen as an oxidant. E20.
2 Liquid oxygen, esp. when used as a rocket propellant. M20.

L

lox /lɒks/ *noun*[2]. Chiefly *N. Amer.* M20.
[ORIGIN Yiddish *laks* from German *Lachs* salmon.]
Smoked salmon.

Loxa /ˈlɒksə/ *noun.* L18.
[ORIGIN A province (now Loja) of Ecuador.]
More fully ***Loxa bark***. Cinchona bark.

loxia /ˈlɒksɪə/ *noun.* E18.
[ORIGIN mod. Latin, from Greek *loxos* oblique: see -IA[1].]
A crossbill. Now chiefly as mod. Latin genus name.

loxodon /ˈlɒksədɒn/ *noun.* Now *rare.* M19.
[ORIGIN mod. Latin *Loxodonta* genus name, from Greek *loxos* oblique + -ODON (with ref. to the oblique ridges on the worn molars).]
ZOOLOGY. An African elephant.
■ Also **loxodont** *noun* L19.

loxodromic /lɒksəˈdrɒmɪk/ *noun & adjective.* L17.
[ORIGIN French *loxodromique*, from Greek *loxos* oblique + *dromos* course: see -IC.]
NAUTICAL & MATH. ▸ **A** *noun.* **1** A loxodromic line or table. L17.
2 In *pl.* The art or practice of sailing to a constant compass bearing. E18.
▸ **B** *adjective.* Of or pertaining to motion or alignment at a constant angle to the meridians, esp. sailing by the rhumb (on a constant compass bearing). E18.
loxodromic curve, **loxodromic line**, **loxodromic spiral** a rhumb line, a path which cuts the meridians at a constant angle (not a right angle).
■ **loxodrome** /ˈlɒksədrəʊm/ *noun* a loxodromic line, a rhumb line L19. **loxodromism** *noun* the tracing of or movement in a loxodromic line or curve M19. **loxodromy** /lɒkˈsɒdrəmi/ *noun* loxodromism; loxodromics; a loxodrome: M17.

loy /lɔɪ/ *noun.* M18.
[ORIGIN Irish *lái*.]
A long narrow asymmetric spade used in Ireland. Also, a similar tool for digging with a broad chisel point.

loyal /ˈlɔɪəl/ *adjective & noun.* M16.
[ORIGIN French from Old French *loial* later var. of *leial*, *leel* from Latin *legalis* LEGAL. Cf. LEAL.]
▸ **A** *adjective.* **1** Faithful or steadfast in allegiance, *spec.* to the legitimate monarch or government of one's country. Also, enthusiastically reverential to (the family of) the monarch. M16. ▸**b** *gen.* True or faithful to the obligations of duty, love, friendship, etc. L16.

W. S. CHURCHILL Charles set up his standard . . and called his loyal subjects to his aid. N. CHOMSKY A peasant-based guerilla force loyal to Sihanouk that will restore him to power. **b** M. ANGELOU One white New York club owner who had been a loyal friend to me. P. GROSSKURTH However loyal . . to Freud, he had a strong mind of his own.

2 Of a thing, action, etc.: characterized by or exhibiting loyalty. L16.
loyal toast a toast proposed and drunk to the monarch of one's country.
†**3** Legal; *spec.* (of a child) legitimate. Only in 17.
▸ **B** *noun.* Orig., a person bound by allegiance, a liege subject. Now *gen.*, a loyal subject. M16.
■ **loyalize** *verb trans.* make or keep loyal E17. **loyally** *adverb* E16. **loyalness** *noun* L16.

loyalist /ˈlɔɪəlɪst/ *noun & adjective.* L17.
[ORIGIN from LOYAL *adjective* + -IST.]
▸ **A** *noun.* A loyal person; a person who actively maintains allegiance to a monarch, government, cause, etc. Now chiefly (usu. **L-**), a supporter of political union with, or an opponent of political separation from, a particular state; *spec.* (***a***) *hist.* any of the colonists of the American revolutionary period who supported the British cause, many of whom afterwards migrated to Canada; (chiefly *Canad.*) a descendant of such a person; (***b***) an Irish or Northern Irish advocate or supporter of union between Great Britain and Northern Ireland or (before partition) the whole of Ireland. L17.

THACKERAY This resolute old loyalist . . was with the King whilst his house was . . being battered down. *Tribune* If re-elected she would . . be a strong Kinnock loyalist.

▸ **B** *attrib.* or as *adjective.* (Freq. **L-**.) Of or pertaining to a loyalist or Loyalists, characterized by loyalism. L19.

News on Sunday The bonfire was the first of dozens . . lit in Loyalist areas as part of the pre-July 12 celebrations.

■ **loyalism** /ˈlɔɪəlɪz(ə)m/ *noun* the principles, practices, or actions of a loyalist or (usu. **L-**) Loyalists M19.

loyalty /ˈlɔɪəlti/ *noun.* LME.
[ORIGIN Old French *loialté* (mod. *loyauté*), from *loial* LOYAL: see -TY[1].]
1 The fact or condition of being loyal; faithfulness to duty or in love, friendship, etc.; faithful allegiance to the legitimate monarch or government of one's country. LME.

J. W. KRUTCH Brand loyalty, or the refusal to be seduced from your devotion to a particular mark of goods. S. HASTINGS His love of France was fierce, his loyalty to the General absolute. P. LOMAS In times of crisis . . group loyalty is vital.

2 A feeling or example of this. Freq. in *pl.* E17.

M. ARNOLD Home of lost causes . . and impossible loyalties. JULIETTE HUXLEY For me it was a battle of loyalties between my family and Julian's exacting demands.

– COMB.: **loyalty card** an identity card issued by a retailer to its customers as part of a consumer incentive scheme, whereby credits are accumulated for future discounts every time a transaction is recorded.

†**loyn(e)** *noun* var. of LUNE *noun*[1].

Loyolite /ˈlɔɪəlʌɪt/ *noun.* M17.
[ORIGIN mod. Latin *Loyolita*, from St Ignatius *Loyola* (1491–1556), one of the founders of the Society of Jesus: see -ITE[1].]
A Jesuit.

lozen /ˈlɒz(ə)n/ *noun & adjective.* Chiefly *Scot.* LME.
[ORIGIN Prob. from Old French *loseingne* var. of *losenge* LOZENGE.]
▸ **A** *noun.* †**1** A thin cake made from pastry. Only in LME.
†**2** A lozenge-shaped figure. L15–L18.
3 A pane of glass, orig. a lozenge-shaped one. L16.
▸ **B** *attrib.* or as *adjective.* = LOZENGE *adjective.* E16.
■ **lozened** *adjective* = LOZENGED M16.

lozenge /ˈlɒzɪndʒ/ *noun & adjective.* ME.
[ORIGIN Old French *losenge* (mod. *losange*), prob. deriv. of word repr. by Provençal *lausa*, Spanish *losa*, Portuguese *lousa* slab, tombstone, and late Latin *lausiae* (*lapides*) stone slabs, slates, ult. of Gaulish or Iberian origin.]
▸ **A** *noun.* **1** A rhombus or diamond-shaped figure. In HERALDRY, a charge consisting of such a figure, less elongated than a fusil, and placed with its longer axis vertical; also, a lozenge-shaped shield upon which the arms of a spinster or widow are emblazoned. ME. ▸**b** Any of the lozenge-shaped facets of a cut precious stone. M18.
†**2** COOKERY. A lozenge-shaped cake; a lozenge-shaped ornament as a garnish. ME–L15.
3 A small (orig. lozenge-shaped) sweet or medicinal tablet made of flavoured sugar, for dissolving in the mouth. M16.
4 Any of the lozenge-shaped panes of glass in a casement. Cf. LOZEN 3. M17.
▸ **B** *attrib.* or as *adjective.* Lozenge-shaped; of, composed of, or ornamented with lozenges. Cf. LOZEN *adjective.* M17.
■ **lozenged** *adjective* ornamented with lozenge-shaped figures of alternate colours; divided into lozenge-shaped spaces: LME. **lozenger** *noun* †(***a***) = LOZENGE 1; (***b***) *US & N. English* = LOZENGE 3: E16. **lozengewise** *adverb* (esp. HERALDRY) so as to form a lozenge or in a lozenge pattern LME.

lozengy /ˈlɒzɪndʒi/ *adjective.* M16.
[ORIGIN Old French *losengié*, formed as LOZENGE: see -Y[5].]
1 HERALDRY. Of a field: covered with lozenges of alternate tinctures; divided into lozenges. Formerly also, (of a bearing) shaped like a lozenge. M16.
2 Resembling or shaped like a lozenge; composed of or divided into lozenges. E17.

Lozi /ˈləʊzi/ *noun & adjective.* In sense A.1 also (sing.) **Mulozi** /mʊ-/, (pl.) **Malozi** /mə-/. M20.
[ORIGIN Bantu.]
▸ **A** *noun.* Pl. **-zi**, **Lozis**.
1 A member of a people inhabiting Zambia. Earlier called ***Barotse***. M20.
2 The Bantu language of this people, Silozi. M20.
▸ **B** *attrib.* or as *adjective.* Of or pertaining to the Malozi or their language. M20.

LP *abbreviation.*
1 Long-playing (gramophone record).
2 METEOROLOGY. Low pressure.

LPG *abbreviation.*
Liquefied petroleum gas.

Lr *symbol.*
CHEMISTRY. Lawrencium.

LS *abbreviation.*
1 Letter (not autograph) signed; cf. ***ALS***.
2 Linnean Society.

l.s. *abbreviation.*
Latin *Locus sigilli* the place of the seal (on a document).

LSD /ɛlɛsˈdiː/ *noun.* M20.
[ORIGIN Abbreviation.]
Lysergic acid diethylamide (see LYSERGIC *adjective*), a synthetic derivative of lysergic acid which is a powerful hallucinogenic drug able to produce profound changes in perception and mood.

l.s.d. *abbreviation.*
hist. Pounds, shillings, and pence (in former British currency); money, riches.

LSE *abbreviation.*
London School of Economics.

LSI *abbreviation.*
Large-scale integration (of electronic microcircuits).

LT *abbreviation*[1].
Low tension.

Lt *abbreviation*[2].
1 Lieutenant.
2 Light.

LTA *abbreviation.*
Lawn Tennis Association.

Ltd *abbreviation.*
Limited (of a company).

LTM *abbreviation.*
Long-term memory.

LTP *abbreviation.*
PHYSIOLOGY. Long-term potentiation, a phenomenon whereby the transmission of nerve impulses along hippocampal pathways in the brain is facilitated for many hours by brief, high-frequency electrical stimulation of these pathways.

LTR *abbreviation.*
Long-term relationship.

Lu *symbol.*
CHEMISTRY. Lutetium.

lü /ljuː/ *noun.* Pl. same. M17.
[ORIGIN Chinese *lǜ*.]
In Chinese music: each of a series of standard bamboo pitch pipes used in ancient music; a fundamental pitch, each of the twelve semitone pitch notes within the octave (represented by these pipes).

luau /ˈluːaʊ/ *noun.* M19.
[ORIGIN Hawaiian *lū'au*.]
A Hawaiian party or feast usu. accompanied by some form of entertainment.

Luba /ˈluːbə/ *noun & adjective.* L19.
[ORIGIN Bantu.]
▸ **A** *noun.* Pl. same, **-s**. A member of a people of the Democratic Republic of Congo (Zaire); the Bantu language of this people. L19.
▸ **B** *attrib.* or as *adjective.* Of or pertaining to the Luba or their language. E20.

Lubavitcher /ˈluːbəˌvɪtʃə, luːˈbɒ-/ *noun.* M20.
[ORIGIN from *Lubavich*, a town in western Russia + -ER[1].]
A member of a Hasidic community founded in the 18th cent. which stresses piety and missionary work.

lubbard /ˈlʌbəd/ *noun. obsolete* exc. *Scot. & N. English.* M16.
[ORIGIN Alt. of LUBBER: see -ARD.]
= LUBBER.

lubber /ˈlʌbə/ *noun, adjective, & verb.* LME.
[ORIGIN Perh. from Old French *lobeor* swindler, parasite, from *lober* deceive, sponge on, mock (perh. from Frankish *lobon* praise) with assim. in sense to LOB *noun*[1].]
▸ **A** *noun.* **1** A big, clumsy, esp. idle person; a lout. Formerly also, a drudge. *arch. & dial.* LME.
2 NAUTICAL. A clumsy sailor; a person not used or suited to sea life. Cf. LANDLUBBER. L16.
– COMB.: **lubber fiend** a beneficent goblin supposed to perform chores etc. round the house or farm at night; **lubber-grasshopper** either of two large clumsy grasshoppers of the southern US, *Brachystola magna* and *Romalea microptera*; **Lubberland** an imaginary land of idleness and plenty; **lubber line**, **lubber mark**, **lubber point** NAUTICAL a vertical line marked on a compass, indicating a ship's forward direction; **lubber's hole** NAUTICAL a hole in the platform of a ship's top, used to avoid climbing the futtock shrouds.
▸ **B** *attrib.* or as *adjective.* Clumsy, stupid; loutish. M16.
▸ **C** *verb intrans.* Behave as a lubber; loaf about; NAUTICAL navigate a boat like a lubber. M16.

■ **lubberlike** *adjective* of, pertaining to, or characteristic of a lubber L16.

lubberly /ˈlʌbəli/ *adjective & adverb.* L16.
[ORIGIN from LUBBER *noun* + -LY[1].]
▸ **A** *adjective.* **1** Of the nature or characteristic of a lubber; loutish, clumsy, lazy, stupid. L16.
2 NAUTICAL. Resembling, pertaining to, or characteristic of a lubber; unseamanlike. L18.
▸ **B** *adverb.* In a lubberly manner; unskilfully, clumsily. L16.
■ **lubberliness** *noun* L16.

lube /luːb, ljuːb/ *noun & verb.* Chiefly *N. Amer. & Austral. colloq.* M20.
[ORIGIN Abbreviation.]
▸ **A** *noun.* **1** = LUBRICANT *noun.* M20.
2 = LUBRICATION. M20.
▸ **B** *verb trans.* = LUBRICATE. M20.

Lubecker /ˈluːbɛkə, ˈljuː-/ *noun.* E17.
[ORIGIN from *Lübeck* (see LUBISH) + -ER[1].]
hist. A merchant vessel from Lübeck in northern Germany.

Lubish /ˈluːbɪʃ, ˈljuː-/ *adjective. obsolete* exc. *hist.* M16.
[ORIGIN German *lübisch*, from *Lübeck* (see below) + *-isch* -ISH[1].]
Of or pertaining to Lübeck, a town in northern Germany; *spec.* designating a money of account formerly in extensive mercantile use in northern Germany.

lubra /ˈluːbrə, ˈljuː-/ *noun. Austral. offensive.* M19.
[ORIGIN Prob. from an Australian Aboriginal language of Tasmania.]
An Aboriginal woman.

lubric /ˈluːbrɪk, ˈljuː-/ *adjective.* Now *rare.* L15.
[ORIGIN Old French & mod. French *lubrique* or Latin *lubricus* slippery: see -IC.]
1 Smooth and slippery. Formerly also *fig.*, unsteady, unsettled. L15.
2 Lascivious; wanton. L15.
■ Also **lubrical** *adjective* E17.

lubricant /ˈluːbrɪk(ə)nt, ˈljuː-/ *noun & adjective.* E19.
[ORIGIN Latin *lubricant-* pres. ppl stem of *lubricare*: see LUBRICATE, -ANT[1].]
▸ **A** *noun.* A substance, usu. an oil, used to lubricate machinery etc.; a substance used to make motion or action smooth or to remove friction. E19.
▸ **B** *adjective.* Lubricating. E19.

lubricate /ˈluːbrɪkeɪt, ˈljuː-/ *verb.* E17.
[ORIGIN Latin *lubricat-* pa. ppl stem of *lubricare*, from *lubricus* slippery: see -ATE[3].]
1 *verb trans.* Make slippery or smooth; make smooth the motion or action of (something) by applying a fluid or unguent; *spec.* apply oil etc. to (a machine part etc.) so as to minimize friction and allow smooth running. E17. ▸**b** *gen.* Oil, grease. L18.

R. TATE All molluscous animals secrete a mucous fluid to lubricate the skin. *Practical Woodworking* Wax is used to lubricate the moving parts.

2 *verb intrans.* Act as a lubricant. E18.

Practical Hairstyling & Beauty Conditioner . . coats each hair with a small amount of oil which protects and lubricates.

3 *verb trans.* Affect, esp. make convivial or tipsy, with liquor; accompany (a meal etc.) with drink. Usu. in *pass.* Cf. OILED 3. E20.

Independent Dinners prepared by juvenile amateur cooks and lubricated by cheap supermarket plonk.

■ **lubriˈcation** *noun* the action of lubricating; the condition of being lubricated: E19. **lubriˈcational** *adjective* of, pertaining to, or for lubrication E20. **lubricative** *adjective* having the property of lubricating L19.

lubricator /ˈluːbrɪkeɪtə, ˈljuː-/ *noun.* M18.
[ORIGIN from LUBRICATE + -OR.]
1 A lubricating substance; a lubricant; *spec.* (PHOTOGRAPHY, now *rare*) an agent for glazing prints before burnishing. M18.
2 A device for lubricating a machine or instrument. M19.
3 A person who lubricates. L19.

lubricious /luːˈbrɪʃəs, ljuː-/ *adjective.* L16.
[ORIGIN from Latin *lubricus* slippery + -IOUS. Cf. (earlier) LUBRICOUS.]
1 Lecherous; wanton; licentious. L16.

Observer Displaying . . well-turned ankles to the lubricious gaze of the multitude. J. HELLER They fell immediately into an orgy of lubricious kissing.

2 Slippery, smooth; slimy, oily. M17. ▸**b** *fig.* Shifty; unstable, fickle, elusive. Formerly also, (*rare*), voluble, glib. M17.

R. FERGUSON How Lubricious a Friend and Changeable a Partizan he will be.

lubricity /luːˈbrɪsɪti, ljuː-/ *noun.* L15.
[ORIGIN Old French & mod. French *lubricité* or late Latin *lubricitas*, formed as LUBRICIOUS: see -ITY.]
1 Lechery, wantonness, licentiousness. Also, an instance of this. L15.
†**2** Looseness of the bowels. M16–M18.
3 Slipperiness, smoothness; oiliness. E17.
4 *fig.* Shiftiness; unsteadiness, instability; elusiveness. E17. ▸†**b** Volubility, glibness. E–M17.

lubricous /ˈluːbrɪkəs, ˈljuː-/ *adjective.* M16.
[ORIGIN formed as LUBRICIOUS + -OUS.]
= LUBRICIOUS.

lubrify /ˈluːbrɪfʌɪ, ˈljuː-/ *verb trans.* Now *rare.* LME.
[ORIGIN medieval Latin *lubrificare*, from Latin *lubricus* slippery: see -FY.]
Make slippery or smooth; lubricate.

lubritorium /luːbrɪˈtɔːrɪəm, ljuː-/ *noun.* Chiefly *US.* M20.
[ORIGIN from LUBRICATE etc. after *auditorium*, *sanatorium*, etc.: see -ORIUM.]
A greasing bay in a service station; a service station.

Lucan /ˈluːk(ə)n, ˈljuː-/ *adjective.* L19.
[ORIGIN from ecclesiastical Latin *Lucas*, Greek *Loukas* Luke + -AN.]
CHRISTIAN CHURCH. Of, pertaining to, or characteristic of the evangelist St Luke or the Gospel attributed to him.

Lucanian /luːˈkeɪnɪən, ljuː-/ *adjective & noun.* E17.
[ORIGIN from *Lucania* (see below) + -AN.]
Chiefly ROMAN HISTORY. ▸**A** *adjective.* Of, pertaining to, or belonging to Lucania, a region in southern Italy (now also called Basilicata). E17.
Lucanian cow, **Lucanian ox** *hist.* an elephant.
▸ **B** *noun.* A member of a Samnite tribe formerly inhabiting Lucania. E18.

lucanid /luːˈkeɪnɪd, ljuː-/ *adjective & noun.* E20.
[ORIGIN mod. Latin *Lucanidae* (see below), from *Lucanus* genus name, from Latin *Lucania*: see LUCANIAN, -ID[3].]
(Of, pertaining to, or designating) a stag beetle of the family Lucanidae.

lucarne /ˈluːkɑːn, ˈljuː-, *foreign* lykarn (*pl. same*)/ *noun.* M16.
[ORIGIN Old French & mod. French (also †*lucane*) from Provençal *lucana*, of unknown origin. See also LUTHERN.]
A skylight; a dormer window.

Lucas /ˈluːkəs, ˈluːkɑː, *foreign* lyka/ *noun.* M20.
[ORIGIN F. Édouard A. *Lucas* (1842–91), French mathematician.]
MATH. ***Lucas sequence***, ***Lucas series***, the sequence of integers 1, 3, 4, 7, . . . , formed in the same way as the Fibonacci numbers; a generalization of this series and the Fibonacci series, in which the *n*th term $u_n = pu_{n-1} - qu_{n-2}$ (where *p* and *q* are constants); ***Lucas number***, a number of the Lucas series.

Lucca /ˈluːkə, ˈlʌ-/ *adjective.* E18.
[ORIGIN A city in Tuscany, west central Italy (formerly also a province).]
1 Designating a variety of olive oil of a superior quality. E18.
2 Designating a type of processed lambskin used chiefly to make headgear. M20.

Luccan /ˈluːk(ə)n, ˈlʌ-/ *adjective & noun.* E20.
[ORIGIN from LUCCA + -AN. Cf. earlier LUCCHESE.]
▸ **A** *adjective.* Of or pertaining to the city or former province of Lucca, in west central Italy. E20.
▸ **B** *noun.* A native or inhabitant of Lucca. E20.

Lucchese /luːˈkiːz, -ˈkeɪsi, lʌ-/ *noun & adjective.* M17.
[ORIGIN Italian, from LUCCA + *-ese* -ESE.]
▸ **A** *noun.* Pl. same, **Lucchesi** /luːˈkeɪsi, lʌ-/. A native or inhabitant of the city or (formerly) province of Lucca in west central Italy. M17.
▸ **B** *adjective.* Of or pertaining to Lucca or the Lucchese. L19.

luce /luːs, ljuːs/ *noun.* Pl. same. LME.
[ORIGIN Old French *lus*, *luis* formed as LUCY.]
1 A pike, *esp.* a full-grown one; (occas.) this as a heraldic charge; = LUCY. LME.
2 ***luce of the sea***, ***sea-luce***, the European hake. L16.

lucence /ˈluːs(ə)ns, ˈljuː-/ *noun.* L15.
[ORIGIN from LUCENT: see -ENCE.]
= LUCENCY.

J. STEINBECK The pearly lucence of platinum or old pewter.

lucency /ˈluːs(ə)nsi, ˈljuː-/ *noun.* M17.
[ORIGIN from LUCENT: see -ENCY.]
Luminosity, brilliance.

W. BOYD The skyscrapers . . were hazy and indistinct against the soft lucency of the mid-afternoon sky.

lucent /ˈluːs(ə)nt, ˈljuː-/ *adjective.* LME.
[ORIGIN Latin *lucent-* pres. ppl stem of *lucere* shine: see -ENT.]
1 Shining, bright, luminous. LME.

L. ADAMIC The alpine sun had burnished their faces and naked forearms to a deep, lucent brown. *Holiday Which?* It's on a beautiful site and built from lucent pink stone.

2 Translucent, clear. E19.
■ **lucently** *adverb* E19.

lucern /luːˈsəːn, ljuː-/ *noun*[1]. Long *rare* or *obsolete.* M16.
[ORIGIN Prob. from early mod. German *lüchsern* adjective, from *Luchs* lynx.]
The lynx; the fur of this (formerly freq. in *pl.*), formerly held in high esteem.

lucern *noun*[2] var. of LUCERNE *noun*[2].

lucernal /luːˈsəːn(ə)l, ljuː-/ *adjective.* Now *rare* or *obsolete.* L18.
[ORIGIN formed as LUCERNE *noun*[1] + -AL[1].]
Designating a microscope in which the object is illuminated by a lamp or other artificial light.

lucerne /luːˈsəːn, ljuː-/ *noun*[1]. Long *obsolete* exc. *hist.* LME.
[ORIGIN Latin *lucerna*, from *luc-*, *lux* light.]
A lamp, a lantern.

lucerne /luːˈsəːn, ljuː-/ *noun*[2]. Also **-ern.** M17.
[ORIGIN French *luzerne* from mod. Provençal *luzerno* transf. use of *luzerno* glow-worm, with ref. to the shiny seeds.]
A leguminous plant, *Medicago sativa*, cultivated for fodder, which bears blue to violet flowers and trifoliate leaves. Also called ***alfalfa***.
TOWNSVILLE ***lucerne***.

lucet /ˈluːsɪt, ˈljuː-/ *noun.* M17.
[ORIGIN Unknown.]
A lyre-shaped tool formerly used in making cords and laces.

Lucianic /luːʃɪˈanɪk/ *adjective*[1]. E19.
[ORIGIN from Latin *Lucianus* from Greek *Loukianos* Lucian (see below) + -IC.]
Of, pertaining to, or characteristic of Lucian (fl. AD 160), a Greek writer of satyrical dialogues, or his witty scoffing style.
■ †**Lucianical** *adjective* = LUCIANIC *adjective*[1] M16–M17. **Lucianically** *adverb* L16.

Lucianic /luːʃɪˈanɪk/ *adjective*[2]. L19.
[ORIGIN formed as LUCIANIST *noun*[2] + -IC.]
ECCLESIASTICAL HISTORY. Of or pertaining to St Lucian of Antioch; *spec.* designating or pertaining to the text of the Greek Bible revised by him.

Lucianist /ˈluːʃ(ə)nɪst/ *noun*[1]. L16.
[ORIGIN formed as LUCIANIC *adjective*[1] + -IST.]
A student, follower, or imitator of the Greek satirist Lucian.

Lucianist /ˈluːʃ(ə)nɪst/ *noun*[2]. E18.
[ORIGIN from Latin *Lucianus* (see below) + -IST.]
ECCLESIASTICAL HISTORY. **1** A follower or adherent of Lucianus, a Marcionite of the 2nd cent. AD. Now *rare.* E18.
2 A follower or adherent of St Lucian of Antioch, a subordinationist theologian and teacher martyred in 312. E18.

lucible /ˈluːsɪb(ə)l, ˈljuː-/ *adjective. rare.* E17.
[ORIGIN Latin *lucibilis*, from *lucere* shine: see LUCID, -IBLE.]
Bright, lucent.

L

lucid /ˈluːsɪd, ˈljuː-/ *adjective.* L16.
[ORIGIN French *lucide* or Italian *lucido* from Latin *lucidus*, from *lucere* shine, be evident, from *luc-*, *lux* light: see -ID[1].]
1 Bright, luminous, resplendent (now *poet.*); ENTOMOLOGY & BOTANY smooth and shining; ASTRONOMY (of a star) visible to the naked eye. L16.
2 Translucent, clear. E17.

C. AIKEN In the cold blue lucid dusk before the sunrise, One yellow star sings.

3 [translating medieval Latin (pl.) *lucida intervalla*.] Designating or pertaining to an interval of sanity between periods of insanity or dementia, or (formerly) a temporary remission in a disease. Also *transf.*, designating an interval of calm or normality. E17.
4 Marked by clearness of reasoning or expression; easily understood. L18.

L. MACNEICE Housman . . is usually a lucid poet but the poem below is one of his few obscure ones. N. FREELING The notebooks are tangled but . . perfectly lucid.

5 Of a person: rational; sane. M19.

J. HIGGINS 'How's Malone?' . . 'Is he lucid?' 'Some of the time.'

6 PSYCHOLOGY. Of a dream: experienced with the dreamer feeling awake, aware of dreaming, and able to control events consciously. M20.
■ **lucidly** *adverb* E18. **lucidness** *noun* M17.

lucida /ˈluːsɪdə, ˈljuː-/ *noun.* E18.
[ORIGIN Latin (sc. *stella* star) fem. of *lucidus*: see LUCID.]
ASTRONOMY. The brightest star of a constellation.

lucidity /luːˈsɪdɪti, ljuː-/ *noun.* M17.
[ORIGIN Latin *luciditas*, from *lucidus*: see LUCID, -ITY.]
The quality or condition of being lucid; brightness, luminosity (now *poet.*); rationality; clarity of thought or expression.

lucifee /ˈluːsɪfiː/ *noun. Canad., & US local.* Also **-vee** /-viː/. L18.
[ORIGIN Alt. of French *loup cervier* from Latin *lupus cervarius*, from *lupus* wolf + *cervarius* that hunts stags (from *cervus* stag).]
The Canadian lynx, *Lynx canadensis.*

Lucifer /ˈluːsɪfə, ˈljuː-/ *noun.* In sense 3 **l-.** OE.
[ORIGIN Latin *lucifer* adjective light-bringing, from *luc-*, *lux* light, after Greek *phōsphoros* (see PHOSPHORUS): see -FER.]
1 The morning star; the planet Venus when in the sky before sunrise. Now *poet.* OE.
2 The rebel angel whose fall from heaven Jerome and other early Christian writers considered was alluded to in *Isaiah* 14:12 (where the word is an epithet of the king of Babylon); Satan, the Devil. Formerly also *allus.*, a person seeking to dethrone God. Now chiefly in ***as proud as Lucifer***. OE.
3 A friction match. Also more fully ***Lucifer match***. *arch.* M19.

luciferase /luːsɪfəreɪz, ljuː-/ *noun*. L19.
[ORIGIN formed as LUCIFER + -ASE.]
BIOLOGY. An enzyme which catalyses a reaction by which a luciferin produces light.

Luciferian /luːsɪˈfɪərɪən, ljuː-/ *noun & adjective*[1]. M16.
[ORIGIN from Latin *Lucifer* (see below) + -IAN.]
ECCLESIASTICAL HISTORY. ▸**A** *noun*. An adherent of the sect founded by Lucifer, bishop of Cagliari in the 4th cent. AD, who opposed the supposed leniency of the Church towards repentant Arians. M16.
▸**B** *adjective*. Of or pertaining to this sect. E17.

Luciferian /luːsɪˈfɪərɪən, ljuː-/ *adjective*[2]. Now *rare* or *obsolete*. L16.
[ORIGIN from LUCIFER + -IAN.]
Of or pertaining to Lucifer; Satanic, devilish; *esp.* excessively proud.

luciferin /luːˈsɪf(ə)rɪn, ljuː-/ *noun*. L19.
[ORIGIN formed as LUCIFER + -IN[1].]
BIOLOGY. A substance in an organism such as the glow-worm which can produce light when oxidized in the presence of a specific enzyme.

luciferous /luːˈsɪf(ə)rəs, ljuː-/ *adjective*. M17.
[ORIGIN formed as LUCIFER + -OUS.]
Bringing, conveying, or emitting light. Now chiefly *fig.*, affording illumination or insight; illuminating.

lucific /luːˈsɪfɪk, ljuː-/ *adjective*. E18.
[ORIGIN Late Latin *lucificus*, from Latin *luc-*, *lux* light: see -FIC.]
Producing light.

luciform /ˈluːsɪfɔːm, ˈljuː-/ *adjective*. Now *rare*. L17.
[ORIGIN medieval Latin *luciformis* (repr. Greek *augoeidēs*), from Latin *luc-*, *lux* light: see -FORM.]
Having the quality of light, luminous, (*spec.* as a quality of the body which is the vehicle of the soul in Neoplatonic philosophy).

lucifugous /luːˈsɪfjʊɡəs, ljuː-/ *adjective*. M17.
[ORIGIN from Latin *lucifugus*, from *luc-*, *lux* light + *fugere* to fly: see -OUS.]
ZOOLOGY & BOTANY. Shunning the light.

Lucina /luːˈsʌɪnə, -ˈsiːnə, ljuː-/ *noun*. LME.
[ORIGIN Latin, use as noun of fem. of *lucinus* adjective from *luc-*, *lux* light: see -INE[1].]
The Roman goddess who presided over childbirth; *transf.* (*literary*, now *rare*) a midwife.

Lucite /ˈluːsʌɪt, ˈljuː-/ *noun*. M20.
[ORIGIN from Latin *luc-*, *lux* light + -ITE[1].]
(Proprietary name for) a solid transparent plastic that is a methyl methacrylate resin. Also called ***Plexiglas***, ***Perspex***.

lucivee *noun* var. of LUCIFEE.

luck /lʌk/ *noun*. L15.
[ORIGIN Low German *luk* aphet. from *geluk*, in Middle Dutch *ghelucke* (Dutch *geluk*) = Middle High German *gelücke* (German *Glück* good fortune, happiness), from *ge-* Y- + base of unknown origin. Prob. orig. a gambling term.]
1 The action or effect of casual or uncontrollable events; the sum of fortuitous events affecting (favourably or unfavourably) a person's interests or circumstances; a person's apparent tendency to have good or ill fortune; the imagined tendency of chance to bring a succession of (favourable or unfavourable) events. L15. ▸†**b** A piece of *good*, *bad*, etc., fortune. M16–E17. ▸**c** Chance regarded as a cause or bestower of good or ill fortune. (Sometimes personified: cf. ***Lady Luck*** s.v. LADY *noun* 5a.) M16. ▸**d** An action or event regarded as bringing or presaging *good* or *bad* fortune. E20.

SHAKES. *Com. Err.* I have but lean luck in the match. J. DAVIDSON I don't allow it's luck and all a toss. E. O'NEILL I've tried to keep things going in spite of bad luck. **c** I. FLEMING As luck would have it, there were no vacancies and I had to turn him down. *Evening Telegraph (Grimsby)* Valentinos Joy . . had luck on his side. **d** OED You should never put boots on the table: it's bad luck.

2 Good fortune; success, prosperity, or advantage coming by chance rather than as the consequence of merit or effort. L15. ▸**b** An object, esp. an heirloom, on which the prosperity of a family etc. supposedly depends. L18. ▸**c** A piece of good fortune. Also, a lucky find. *Scot.* M19.

V. WOOLF What luck to find you alone. M. FITZHERBERT For an amateur journalist it was a great piece of luck. Z. TOMIN She had had all the luck. She had never had to get her hands dirty.

– PHRASES: **bad luck!**, **bad luck to you!**, **bad luck to it!**, etc. *colloq.*: expr. ill will, disappointment, etc. ***beginner's luck***: see BEGINNER 2. **devil's own luck** uncannily good luck. **down on one's luck** in a period of ill fortune. **for luck** to bring good luck. **good luck!**, **good luck to you!**, **good luck to it!**, etc. *colloq.*: expr. goodwill, encouragement, etc. **hard luck** worse fortune than one deserves. ***ill luck***: see ILL *adjective & adverb*. **in luck** fortunate, enjoying good luck. **just my luck**, **just his luck**, **just our luck**, etc., typical of my, his, our, etc., bad luck. **luck of the draw**: expr. resignation at the chance outcome of events etc. ***nigger luck***: see NIGGER *adjective & noun*. **no such luck** *colloq.* unfortunately not. **one's luck is in** luck is on one's side. **out of luck** having bad luck, in misfortune. **press one's luck**, **push one's luck** *colloq.* take undue risks. **ride one's luck** *colloq.* let favourable events take their course, not take undue risks. SALTASH LUCK. ***the best of British luck***: see BRITISH *adjective* 2. **the luck of the Irish** very good luck. ***tough luck***: see TOUGH *adjective*. **try one's luck** make a venture or attempt. **worse luck** *colloq.* unfortunately.
– COMB.: **luck-money**, **luck-penny** (*a*) a piece of money given or kept for luck; (*b*) *hist.* a certain sum required by local custom to be returned by the seller to the buyer, esp. in the sale of livestock.

luck /lʌk/ *verb intrans*. LME.
[ORIGIN Perh. from Dutch *lukken*, formed as LUCK *noun*.]
1 Chance, happen; turn out *well*, *ill*, etc. Also *impers.* in (*it*) *lucks* etc. *obsolete* exc. *dial.* LME. ▸**b** Be lucky; prosper, succeed. *obsolete* exc. *dial.* L16.
2 a Foll. by *upon*, *up on*: chance to find or meet with. *colloq.* L17. ▸**b** Foll. by *into*, *on to*: acquire by good fortune. *colloq.* M20.
3 Foll. by *out*: achieve success or advantage by good luck, esp. in a difficult or adverse situation. Also, experience (extreme) bad luck; be killed. *N. Amer. colloq.* M20.

luckie *noun* var. of LUCKY *noun*[1].

luckily /ˈlʌkɪli/ *adverb*. L15.
[ORIGIN from LUCKY *adjective* + -LY[2].]
In a lucky manner; with good luck, fortunately. Formerly also, successfully, prosperously. Now chiefly modifying a sentence or clause.

E. BOWEN Luckily for Francis, he had been left on shore. A. S. BYATT Luckily you never realise what you've let yourself in for until afterwards.

luckiness /ˈlʌkɪnɪs/ *noun*. M16.
[ORIGIN from LUCKY *adjective* + -NESS.]
The quality or condition of being lucky.

luckless /ˈlʌklɪs/ *adjective*. M16.
[ORIGIN from LUCK *noun* + -LESS.]
1 Having no luck or good fortune; unlucky, ill-starred, unfortunate. M16.
†**2** Presaging evil, ominous. L16–M17.
▪ **lucklessly** *adverb* M19. **lucklessness** *noun* M19.

lucky /ˈlʌki/ *noun*[1]. *Scot.* (now *dial.*). Also **-ie**. E18.
[ORIGIN from the adjective.]
(A name for) an elderly woman, *spec.* a grandmother; *joc.* a woman of any age; *spec.* the landlady of an alehouse. Used as a form of address and as a title preceding the proper name.

lucky /ˈlʌki/ *noun*[2]. *slang*. E19.
[ORIGIN Unknown.]
An act of escaping. Only in ***cut one's lucky***, ***make one's lucky***, get away, escape.

lucky /ˈlʌki/ *adjective*. LME.
[ORIGIN from LUCK *noun* + -Y[1].]
1 Having good luck, attended by good luck; *spec.* successful through luck as distinct from skill, design, or merit. Formerly also *gen.*, successful, prosperous. LME. ▸**b** Of a literary composition: unstudied in expression. E18.

G. B. SHAW He will be lucky to have any pay at all. L. DUNCAN You're a lucky boy to have the opportunity of growing up in her home. W. ABISH Lovely children, lovely husband, lovely house . . . You're a lucky woman. A. N. WILSON She was lucky . . if she saw anyone, apart from the congregation at church. J. NAGENDA She was like a gambler, . . and her lucky streak held throughout. P. CUTTING We regarded ourselves as among the lucky few who had escaped a kidnap attempt.

2 Of an event, circumstance, etc.: of the nature of good luck; occurring by chance and producing a happy or good result. Also (*rare*), occurring by chance, fortuitous. M16.

P. THEROUX It had been a lucky find at the Northampton dump. M. MOORCOCK A lucky V2 rocket destroyed the school.

3 Of an object: supposedly presaging or bringing good luck. M16.

QUEEN VICTORIA The new house seems to be lucky indeed. A. L. ROWSE He was born under a lucky star. W. BOYD 'I wasn't expecting you for two months.' 'Well, it's your lucky day, then.'

4 Of an amount: full, good. *dial.* M17.
– PHRASES: **lucky him**, **lucky you**, etc.: expr. envy at another's good fortune. ***strike lucky***: see STRIKE *verb*. ***thank one's lucky stars***: see STAR *noun*[1] *& adjective*.
– SPECIAL COLLOCATIONS & COMB.: **lucky bag** (*a*) a bag of sweets etc. with (wholly or partly) unspecified contents; (*b*) a bag containing different articles to be chosen as from a lucky dip. **Lucky Country** Australia. **lucky dip** a tub containing different articles concealed in wrapping or bran etc., and chosen at random by participants; *fig.* a miscellany or medley from which one obtains something by chance.

†**lucration** *noun*. M17–E19.
[ORIGIN Late Latin *lucratio(n-)*, from Latin *lucrat-*: see LUCRATIVE, -ATION.]
The action or an act of gaining.

lucrative /ˈluːkrətɪv, ˈljuː-/ *adjective*. LME.
[ORIGIN Latin *lucrativus*, from *lucrat-* pa. ppl stem of *lucrari* to gain, from *lucrum* gain: see -ATIVE.]
1 Yielding financial gain or profit; profitable. LME.

J. S. HUXLEY Aldous . . was busy writing film scripts, which he found more lucrative than essays and novels.

†**2** Of a person, action, etc.: intent on or directed towards profit; avaricious, covetous. M16–L18.
▪ **lucratively** *adverb* M19. **lucrativeness** *noun* E18.

lucre /ˈluːkə, ˈljuː-/ *noun*. Now *derog.* LME.
[ORIGIN French, or Latin *lucrum* gain.]
Financial gain or profit. Also, money. Formerly also, acquisition *of* or greed for profit or gain.

A. BLOND The only incentive to perform is the lure of lucre.

filthy lucre: see FILTHY *adjective*.

Lucretian /luːˈkriːʃ(ə)n, ˈljuː-/ *adjective*. E18.
[ORIGIN from *Lucretius* (see below) + -AN.]
Of, pertaining to, or characteristic of the Roman didactic poet Lucretius (Titus Lucretius Carus, *c* 94–*c* 55 BC) or his Epicurean philosophy.

†**lucriferous** *adjective*. M17–E18.
[ORIGIN from Latin *lucrum* LUCRE + -I- + -FEROUS.]
Lucrative.

†**lucrous** *adjective*. E16–L18.
[ORIGIN from Latin *lucrosus*, from *lucrum* LUCRE: see -OUS.]
Of or pertaining to lucre. Also, avaricious.

†**luctiferous** *adjective*. *rare*. M17–E19.
[ORIGIN from Latin *luctifer*, from *luctus* sorrow + *-ifer* bearing: see -FEROUS.]
Bringing sorrow; mournful.

lucubrate /ˈluːkjʊbreɪt, ˈljuː-/ *verb intrans*. *arch.* E17.
[ORIGIN Latin *lucubrat-* pa. ppl stem of *lucubrare*, from *luc-*, *lux* light: see -ATE[3].]
Work or study, esp. by artificial light at night. Also, express one's thoughts in writing, esp. laboriously and elaborately.
▪ **lucubrator** *noun* L18. **lucubratory** *adjective* of or pertaining to lucubration; elaborately meditative: M17.

lucubration /luːkjʊˈbreɪʃ(ə)n, ljuː-/ *noun*. *arch.* L16.
[ORIGIN Latin *lucubratio(n-)*, formed as LUCUBRATE: see -ATION.]
1 The action or an act of lucubrating. L16.
2 The product of (esp. nocturnal) study or work; *spec.* a literary work, esp. of a pedantic or overelaborate nature. Usu. in *pl.* E17.

luculent /ˈluːkjʊl(ə)nt, ˈljuː-/ *adjective*. LME.
[ORIGIN Latin *luculentus*, from *luc-*, *lux* light: see -ENT.]
1 Full of light; bright, clear, shining. Now *rare*. LME.
2 Of evidence, an argument: clear, convincing. Of an explanation: lucid. Formerly also, (of oratory, an orator, etc.) brilliant, admirable. M16.
▪ **luculently** *adverb* E17.

luculia /lʊˈkuːlɪə/ *noun*. E19.
[ORIGIN mod. Latin (see below), from local name of *Luculia gratissima*.]
Any of several evergreen shrubs of the genus *Luculia*, of the madder family, native to the Himalayas and Yunnan (SW China), with leathery leaves and corymbs of fragrant pink or white flowers.

Lucullan /luːˈkʌlən, lʊ-/ *adjective*. M19.
[ORIGIN Latin *Lucullanus*, from *Lucullus* (see below): see -AN.]
Of, pertaining to, or characteristic of Licinius Lucullus, a wealthy Roman general of the 1st cent. BC famous for his lavish banquets; profusely luxurious.
▪ Also **Lucullean** *adjective* [from Latin *Lucullеus*: see -EAN] E17. **Lucullian** *adjective* [from Latin *Lucullianus*: see -IAN] L19.

lucuma /ˈluːkjʊmə, ˈljuː-/ *noun*. L16.
[ORIGIN Spanish *lúcuma* from Quechua *loqma*.]
Any of various tropical American trees of the former genus *Lucuma*, now *Pouteria* (family Sapotaceae), which bear sweet fruit.

lucumo /ˈluːkjʊməʊ, ˈljuː-/ *noun*. Pl. **-os**. M19.
[ORIGIN Latin from an Etruscan title.]
ROMAN HISTORY. Any of a group of Etruscan nobles, combining the character, status, and duties of priest and prince.

lucumony /ˈluːkjʊməni, ˈljuː-/ *noun*. M18.
[ORIGIN French *lucumonie*, formed as LUCUMO: see -Y[3].]
ROMAN HISTORY. Each of the twelve states of the Etruscan federation.

lucus a non lucendo /ˌluːkʌs ɑː nɒn luːˈkɛndəʊ, ˌl(j)uːkʌs eɪ nɒn l(j)uːˈsɛndəʊ/ *noun phr.* E18.
[ORIGIN Latin, lit. 'a grove from its not shining', i.e. *lucus* (a grove) is derived from *lucere* (shine) because there is no light there.]
A paradoxical or otherwise absurd derivation; something of which the qualities are the opposite of what its name suggests. Also abbreviated to ***lucus a non***.

lucy /ˈluːsi/ *noun*. E17.
[ORIGIN Late Latin *lucius*.]
HERALDRY. A pike (fish).

lud /lʌd/ *noun*. E18.
[ORIGIN Repr. a pronunc.]
1 = LORD *noun* 5. Chiefly as *interjection*. *arch.* E18.
2 ***m'lud***, ***my lud*** = ***my lord*** (e) s.v. LORD *noun*, used as a form of address to a judge in a court of law. M19.

Luddism /ˈlʌdɪz(ə)m/ *noun*. E19.
[ORIGIN formed as LUDDITE + -ISM.]
1 *hist.* The practices of the Luddites. E19.
2 *transf.* (Also **l-**.) Intense dislike of or opposition to increased industrialization or the introduction of new technology, esp. in a place of work. M20.

L

Luddite /ˈlʌdʌɪt/ *noun & adjective*. **E19**.
[ORIGIN Perh. from Ned *Lud* an insane person who destroyed two stocking frames *c* 1779: see -ITE[1].]
▸ **A** *noun*. **1** *hist.* A member of the bands of English artisans who (1811–16) rioted against mechanization and destroyed machinery. **E19**.
2 *transf.* (Also l-.) A person opposed to increased industrialization or the introduction of new technology, esp. into a place of work. **L20**.
▸ **B** *adjective*. **1** *hist.* Of or pertaining to the Luddites or their beliefs. **E19**.
2 *transf.* (Also l-.) Characterized by opposition to increased industrialization or the introduction of new technology. **M20**.
■ **Ludditism** *noun* = LUDDISM **M19**.

luderick /ˈluːd(ə)rɪk, ˈlʌdrɪk/ *noun*. **L19**.
[ORIGIN Ganay *ludarag*.]
An edible herbivorous percoid fish, *Girella tricuspidata* (family Kyphosidae), of Australasian coastal waters and estuaries. Cf. PARORE.

Ludian /ˈluːdɪən, ˈljuː-/ *noun & adjective*. **M20**.
[ORIGIN formed as LUDIC *noun & adjective*[1] + -IAN.]
= LUDIC *noun & adjective*[1].

ludibrious /luːˈdɪbrɪəs, ljuː-/ *adjective*. Now *rare*. **L16**.
[ORIGIN from Latin *ludibriosus*, from *ludibrium* sport, jest, from *ludere* play: see -OUS.]
†**1** Apt to be a subject of jest or mockery. **L16–L17**.
2 Scornful, mocking. **M17**.

†**ludibry** *noun*. **E17–E18**.
[ORIGIN Latin *ludibrium*: see LUDIBRIOUS, -Y[4].]
Derision, contempt; an object of derision.

Ludic /ˈluːdɪk, ˈljuː-/ *noun & adjective*[1]. **E20**.
[ORIGIN from Olonetsian *lüüdi* (perh. from Russian *lyudi* people) + -IC.]
(Of) a language of the Finnish group of the Finno-Ugric language family, used by a small number of speakers in the Olonets region of NW Russia.

ludic /ˈluːdɪk, ˈljuː-/ *adjective*[2]. **M20**.
[ORIGIN French *ludique*, from Latin *ludere* to play, from *ludus* sport: see -IC.]
(Of play) spontaneous and without purpose; (of behaviour) undirected and spontaneously playful.

ludicro- /ˈluːdɪkrəʊ, ˈljuː-/ *combining form*. **M18**.
[ORIGIN formed as LUDICROUS: see -O-.]
Ludicrous and —.

ludicrous /ˈluːdɪkrəs, ˈljuː-/ *adjective*. **E17**.
[ORIGIN from Latin *ludicr-*, *ludicer*, perh. from *ludicrum* source of fun, witticism, sporting or theatrical show, from *ludere*: see LUDIC *adjective*[2], -OUS.]
†**1** Sportive; intended in jest, jocular; derisive. **E17–L18**.
†**2** Given to jesting; frivolous. Also, witty, humorous. **L17–E19**.
3 Ridiculous, laughably absurd. **L18**.

S. J. PERELMAN The effect of the trousers, at least three sizes too large for him, was .. ludicrous. B. PYM One of those ludicrous things that happen sometimes, reducing everything to the level of farce.

■ **ludiˈcrosity** *noun* ludicrousness **M19**. **ludicrously** *adverb* **L17**. **ludicrousness** *noun* the state or quality of being ludicrous **M17**.

ludification /ˌluːdɪfɪˈkeɪʃ(ə)n/ *noun*. Now *rare*. **LME**.
[ORIGIN Latin *ludificatio(n-)*, from *ludificat-* pa. ppl stem of *ludificare* delude, from *ludus* sport: see -FICATION.]
A deception; a mocking jest.

ludo /ˈluːdəʊ, ˈljuː-/ *noun*. **L19**.
[ORIGIN Latin = I play.]
A simple board game played with dice and counters in which the aim is to be the first to reach a destination.

Ludolph's number /ˈluːdɒlfs ˌnʌmbə/ *noun phr*. **L19**.
[ORIGIN *Ludolph* van Ceulen (1540–1610), German-born teacher.]
The number π, which Ludolph evaluated to 35 decimal places.
■ **Luˈdolphian** *adjective* of or pertaining to Ludolph; chiefly in ***Ludolphian number***, = LUDOLPH'S NUMBER: **L19**.

Ludwig's angina /ˌlʊdvɪgz anˈdʒʌɪnə/ *noun phr*. **M20**.
[ORIGIN W. F. von *Ludwig* (1790–1865), German surgeon.]
Severe inflammation of the tissues of the floor of the mouth (usu. caused by streptococci).

lues /ˈluːiːz, ˈljuː-/ *noun*. **M17**.
[ORIGIN Latin = plague.]
Syphilis (also more fully ***lues venerea*** /vəˈnɪərɪə/). Formerly also, a plague, a pestilence.
lues Boswelliana /-ˌbɒzwɛlɪˈeɪnə, -ˈɑːnə/ *joc.* [mod. Latin, formed as BOSWELL + *-iana* (fem.) -IAN] a biographer's tendency to magnify his or her subject, regarded as a disease.
■ **luetic** /-ˈɛtɪk/ *adjective* **L19**.

luff /lʌf/ *noun*[1]. **ME**.
[ORIGIN Old French *lof*, prob. from Low German or Dutch.]
NAUTICAL. †**1** A device for altering the course of a ship, as a spar operating on a sail etc. **ME–L15**.
†**2** The part or side of a ship facing the wind. **LME–E17**.
3 The edge of a fore-and-aft sail next to the mast or stay. **E16**.
4 The broadest part of a ship's bow, where the sides begin to curve in towards the stem. **E17**.
5 In full ***luff-tackle***. A purchase composed of a double and a single block. **M17**.
– PHRASES: **spring a luff**, **spring one's luff** bring the ship's head closer to the wind.

luff /lʌf/ *noun*[2]. *colloq.* **E19**.
[ORIGIN Repr. a pronunc. of the 1st syll.]
= LIEUTENANT.

luff /lʌf/ *verb*. **LME**.
[ORIGIN from LUFF *noun*[1], perh. through Dutch *loeven*.]
1 *verb intrans.* Bring the head of a ship nearer to the wind; steer or sail nearer the wind. Also foll. by *in*, *off*, *up*, etc. **LME**.
2 *verb trans.* Bring the head of (a ship) nearer to the wind; turn (the helm) to achieve this. **E17**.
3 *verb trans.* *SAILING*. Obstruct (another craft passing windward) by sailing closer to the wind. **L19**.
4 *verb trans.* Alter the inclination of (the jib of a crane or derrick); raise by moving (the jib) *in*; lower by moving (the jib) *out*. **E20**.
luffing crane a crane whose jib can be luffed in operation.

luffa *noun* var. of LOOFAH.

luftmensch /ˈlʊftmɛnʃ/ *noun*. Also ***-mensh***. Pl. ***-en*** /-(ə)n/. **E20**.
[ORIGIN Yiddish *luftmensh*, from *luft* (German *Luft*) air + *mensh* (German *Mensch*) person.]
An impractical visionary.

Luftwaffe /ˈlʊftvafə/ *noun*. **M20**.
[ORIGIN German, from *Luft* air + *Waffe* weapon.]
hist. The German air force up to the end of the Second World War.

lug /lʌg/ *noun*[1]. Now *dial.* **ME**.
[ORIGIN Unknown.]
1 A long stick or pole; a branch of a tree. **ME**.
2 A unit of length, more or less equal to a pole or perch, varying between 15 and 21 feet, but usu. 16½ feet (approx. 5.03 m). Also, a unit of area more or less equal to a square pole or perch. **M16**.

lug /lʌg/ *noun*[2]. **L15**.
[ORIGIN Prob. of Scandinavian origin: cf. Swedish *lugg* forelock, nap of cloth.]
1 Either of two flaps of a hat, for covering the ears. *Scot. & N. English*. **L15**.
2 An ear. Formerly also, the lobe of an ear. *Scot., N. English, & colloq.* **E16**.
3 A projection resembling an ear on an object by which it may be carried, fixed in place, etc. **E17**. ▸**b** Pressure used to extort money. Esp. in ***put the lug on***. *US slang*. **E20**.

E. LINKLATER The stack was stitched up so as to leave two lugs to carry it by. K. CLARK With pots .., such as casseroles, lugs .. facilitate easy gripping and lifting.

4 The side wall of a recessed fireplace; a (chimney) corner. *Scot. & N. English*. **L18**.
5 A tobacco leaf of low quality. **M19**.
6 In *pl.* Airs, affected manners. Chiefly in ***put on lugs***. *US slang*. **L19**.
7 A lout; a sponger. Chiefly *N. Amer. slang*. **M20**.

R. CHANDLER The girl snapped at me: 'Is this lug your partner?'

– COMB.: **lug-chair** an easy chair with side pieces for the head; **lughole** *dial. & colloq.* the orifice of the ear (cf. ***earhole*** s.v. EAR *noun*[1]); **lug-mark** *noun & verb trans.* = EARMARK; **lug sole** *N. Amer.* a shoe sole with deep indentations designed for a good grip.

†**lug** *noun*[3]. Only in **M16**.
[ORIGIN Cf. LUG *verb*, Low German *lug*, Dutch *log* slow, heavy, LOG *noun*[1].]
A heavy clumsy thing.
– NOTE: Perh. surviving in FUSTILUGS.

lug /lʌg/ *noun*[4]. **E17**.
[ORIGIN Unknown.]
= LUGWORM.

lug /lʌg/ *noun*[5]. **E17**.
[ORIGIN from the verb.]
1 The action or an act of lugging; a rough or hard pull. **E17**.

J. K. JEROME You give your ropes a lug that pulls all his pegs out.

2 A thing which is or needs to be lugged; *spec.* a box or crate used for shipping fruit. *US*. **E19**.

lug /lʌg/ *noun*[6]. **M19**.
[ORIGIN Abbreviation.]
= LUGSAIL.

lug /lʌg/ *verb*. Infl. **-gg-**. **LME**.
[ORIGIN Prob. of Scandinavian origin: cf. Swedish *lugga* pull a person's hair & LUG *noun*[2].]
1 *verb trans. gen.* Pull, give a pull to; pull *by* the ear, hair, etc.; *fig.* tease, worry, bait. *obsolete* exc. *dial.* **LME**.

POPE Mr. Lintott lugg'd the reins. Stopt Short, [etc.].

2 *verb trans.* Pull along with violent effort; drag, tug (something heavy). Also, carry with difficulty (something heavy) *around* or *about* with one. **LME**. ▸**b** *fig.* Introduce (a subject etc.) in a forced manner or irrelevantly. Usu. foll. by *in*. **E18**.

ALDOUS HUXLEY Spandrell had to .. push and lug the heavy body on to its side. G. GREENE He bent and heaved and .. lugged it ashore. A. MCCOWEN He lugged furniture about in a shop in Tonbridge. G. SWIFT I used to trail behind Dad, lugging his bag of clubs. **b** *Scotsman* Counsel for the other side had lugged in everything he could to prejudice the case.

3 *verb intrans.* Pull (hard), tug, (*at*, *on*). **LME**. ▸**b** Move heavily and slowly; drag. Now *rare*. **LME**.

BROWNING A whip awaits shirkers .. Who slacken their pace, sick of lugging At what don't advance for their tugging.

4 *verb intrans.* Foll. by *out*: draw one's sword; pull out money or a purse. *arch.* **L17**.
■ **luggable** *adjective* able to be lugged; *spec.* (of a computer) barely portable: **L20**.

Luganda /luːˈgandə, ljuː-/ *noun & adjective*. **L19**.
[ORIGIN Bantu, from *lu-* prefix + *ganda*. Cf. MUGANDA, BAGANDA.]
(Of) the Bantu language of the Baganda people, widely used in Uganda.

Lugbara /lʊgˈbɑːrə/ *noun & adjective*. Also **Lugwari** /lʌgˈwɑːri/. **E20**.
[ORIGIN Lugbara.]
▸ **A** *noun*. Pl. same, **-s**.
1 A member of a people inhabiting the border area of Uganda and the Democratic Republic of Congo (Zaire). **E20**.
2 The Sudanic language of this people. **M20**.
▸ **B** *attrib.* or as *adjective*. Of or pertaining to the Lugbara or their language. **E20**.

luge /luːʒ/ *verb & noun*. **L19**.
[ORIGIN Swiss French.]
▸ **A** *verb intrans.* Toboggan; ride or race on a luge. **L19**.
▸ **B** *noun*. A light toboggan for one or two people usu. ridden in a supine position; the sport in which these are raced. **E20**.

Luger /ˈluːgə/ *noun & adjective*. **E20**.
[ORIGIN George *Luger* (1849–1923), German engineer and firearms expert.]
(Proprietary name designating) a German type of automatic pistol.

luggage /ˈlʌgɪdʒ/ *noun*. **L16**.
[ORIGIN from LUG *verb* + -AGE, after *baggage*.]
1 Orig., what has to be lugged about; inconveniently heavy baggage. Now (*sing.* & (*rare*) in *pl.*), the baggage of a traveller or passenger; also, the baggage of an army. **L16**.

E. M. FORSTER Frieda and Helen and all their luggages had gone. JO GRIMOND The bus had to .. take the luggage—usually including a large trunk—to the station.

2 Bags, suitcases, etc., designed to hold the belongings of a traveller or passenger. **E20**.
– COMB.: **luggage locker** a locker at a railway station, air terminal, etc., for use by passengers. **luggage van** a railway carriage for travellers' belongings.
■ **luggaged** *adjective* loaded with luggage **M19**. **luggageless** *adjective* **M19**.

†**luggard** *noun*. *rare*. **E16–M19**.
[ORIGIN from LUG *verb* + -ARD.]
A sluggard.

lugged /lʌgd/ *adjective*. *obsolete* exc. *dial.* **L15**.
[ORIGIN from LUG *noun*[2] + -ED[2].]
Having lugs or ears.

luggee /lʌˈgiː/ *noun*. *rare*. **M19**.
[ORIGIN from LUG *verb* + -EE[1].]
A person who is lugged or pulled.

lugger /ˈlʌgə/ *noun*[1]. **E17**.
[ORIGIN from LUG *verb* + -ER[1].]
A person who lugs something.

lugger /ˈlʌgə/ *noun*[2]. **M18**.
[ORIGIN from (the same root as) LUG *noun*[6] + -ER[1].]
A small ship carrying two or three masts with a lugsail on each.

lugger /ˈlʌgə/ *verb trans.* *obsolete* exc. *dial.* **M17**.
[ORIGIN from LUG *verb* + -ER[5].]
Drag or carry about; *fig.* burden, tease.

luggie /ˈlʌgi/ *noun*. *Scot.* **E18**.
[ORIGIN from LUG *noun*[2] + -IE.]
A small wooden vessel with a lug or handle.

Lugol /ˈluːgɒl/ *noun*. **L19**.
[ORIGIN Jean *Lugol* (1786–1851), French physician.]
Lugol's iodine, ***Lugol's solution***, a solution of iodine and potassium iodide in water, used to administer iodine internally and as a biological stain.

lugsail /ˈlʌgseɪl/ *noun*. **L17**.
[ORIGIN Prob. from LUG *noun*[2] + SAIL *noun*[1].]
NAUTICAL. A four-cornered sail bent on a yard slung at a third or quarter of its length from one end.

lugubrious /lʊˈguːbrɪəs/ *adjective*. **E17**.
[ORIGIN from Latin *lugubris*, from *lugere* mourn: see -IOUS.]
Characterized by, expressing, or causing mourning; mournful; doleful, dismal.

L

T. Heggen Pulver was .. depressed by the news, and he lay in Robert's bunk .. and made lugubrious conversation. C. Blackwood The usual pained expression on her long lugubrious face. S. Chitty Aunt Leah was the cheerful one while Aunt Rosina .. was lugubrious and suffered from indigestion.

■ †**lugubre** *adjective* [French] = LUGUBRIOUS E18–M19. **lugubri'osity** *noun* (*rare*) M19. **lugubriously** *adverb* M19. **lugubriousness** *noun* L19. †**lugubrous** *adjective* = LUGUBRIOUS M17–E18.

Lugwari *noun & adjective* var. of LUGBARA.

lugworm /'lʌgwəːm/ *noun*. E19.
[ORIGIN from LUG *noun*⁴ + WORM *noun*.]
A polychaete worm of the genus *Arenicola*, which burrows in sandy beaches and is much used as fishing bait.

Luing /lɪŋ/ *noun & adjective*. L20.
[ORIGIN An island in the Hebrides, Scotland.]
▸ **A** *noun*. Pl. same. (An animal of) a breed of cattle derived from a crossing of the beef shorthorn and the Highland. L20.
▸ **B** *adjective*. Designating this breed of cattle. L20.

Luiseño /luːɪ'seɪnjəʊ/ *noun & adjective*. Also (earlier) **San Luiseño** /sɑːn/. M19.
[ORIGIN Spanish, from *San Luis Rey*, a mission in S. California.]
▸ **A** *noun*. Pl. same, **-os**. A member of a Shoshonean people of SW California; the language of this people. M19.
▸ **B** *attrib.* or as *adjective*. Of or pertaining to the Luiseño or their language. L19.

luke /luːk, ljuːk/ *adjective*. Now *dial.* ME.
[ORIGIN Perh. formed as LEE *noun*¹ & *adjective*, LEW. Cf. Old Norse *hlyr* warm, mild, rel. to Old High German *lão* (German *lau*).]
= LUKEWARM *adjective*.

lukewarm /'luːkwɔːm, luːk'wɔːm, lj-/ *adjective & noun*. LME.
[ORIGIN from LUKE + WARM *adjective*.]
▸ **A** *adjective*. **1** Moderately warm, tepid. LME.

J. Steinbeck He scooped lukewarm mush into two bowls. D. Leavitt Celia is treading the lukewarm blue water of Nathan's parents' swimming pool.

2 Of a person, action, attribute, etc.: having little warmth or depth of feeling; lacking enthusiasm; indifferent. LME.

M. Meyer The play .. attracted little notice, and such reviews as did appear were lukewarm.

▸ **B** *noun*. A lukewarm or unenthusiastic person. L17.
■ **lukewarmly** *adverb* E17. **lukewarmness** *noun* M16. **lukewarmth** *noun* the quality or state of being lukewarm L16.

lukiko /luː'kiːkəʊ/ *noun*. L19.
[ORIGIN Luganda = audience-hall, council.]
The council or parliament of the Baganda people of Uganda.

lulav /'luːlɑːv, 'lʊləv/ *noun*. Also **-b**. Pl. **-s**, **-im** /-ɪm/. L19.
[ORIGIN Hebrew *lûlāḇ* branch.]
A palm branch traditionally carried at the Jewish festival of Succoth.

lull /lʌl/ *noun*¹. M17.
[ORIGIN from LULL *verb*.]
1 †**a** Soothing drink. Only in M17. ▸**b** A thing which lulls; *spec.* a lulling sound. E18.
2 A brief period of intermission or quiescence in a storm (*lit. & fig.*) or in any activity. E19.

P. L. Fermor Even in a momentary lull, the rain was fierce. A. Brookner We were not busy in the shop: it was the lull before .. Christmas. J. Nagenda All this was very much the lull before the storm.

3 A lulled or stupefied condition. M19.

lull /lʌl/ *noun*². M19.
[ORIGIN Dutch *lul* tube.]
WHALING. A tube to convey blubber into the hold of a whaling ship.

lull /lʌl/ *verb*. ME.
[ORIGIN Imit. of sounds used to sing a child to sleep: cf. LULLABY etc. & Swedish *lulla*, Danish *lulle* hum a lullaby, Dutch *lullen*, also Middle Dutch *lollen* mutter, Latin *lallare* sing to sleep.]
1 *verb trans.* Soothe with sounds or caresses; induce to sleep or to pleasing quiescence. ME. ▸**b** Quiet (suspicion) by deception; delude into a sense of security (usu. in *pass.*). E17.

V. Nabokov I would lull and rock .. Lolita in my marble arms. T. Roethke I'm lulled into half-sleep By the lapping of water. **b** *Truck & Driver* Mantova .. had been lulled into a false sense of security.

†**2** *verb intrans.* Be lapped in soothing slumbers. LME–L16.
3 *verb trans.* Bring to a state of comparative quiescence (winds, sea, etc.). L17.
4 *verb intrans.* (Of the sea or wind) become lulled, or gradually diminished in force or power; become quiescent or inactive. E19.
■ **lullingly** *adverb* in a lulling manner, with lulling effect M19.

lulla /'lʌlə/ *interjection*. *arch.* Also **lullay** /'lʌleɪ/. ME.
[ORIGIN Imit.: see LULL *verb*.]
= LULLABY *interjection*. Now only in traditional songs.

lullaby /'lʌləbʌɪ/ *interjection, noun, & verb*. M16.
[ORIGIN formed as LULLA + *-by* as in BYE-BYE *noun, interjection*. Cf. *hushaby, rock-a-bye*.]
▸ **A** *interjection*. **1** Used to please or pacify a child or to send a child to sleep. (Sometimes preceded by *lulla*.) M16.
†**2** Goodbye, goodnight. L16–E17.
▸ **B** *noun*. A song or soothing refrain to pacify or put a child to sleep. L16.
▸ **C** *verb trans. & intrans.* Soothe (a child) with a lullaby; sing (a child) to sleep. L16.

lullay *interjection* var. of LULLA.

Lullian /'lʌlɪən/ *adjective*. M17.
[ORIGIN from *Lullius* (see below) + -AN.]
Of or pertaining to the Christian mystic Lullius (Ramón or Raymond Lull, 1234–1315), his writings, or his beliefs.
■ †**Lullianist** *noun* = LULLIST: only in E17.

Lullist /'lʌlɪst/ *noun*. M16.
[ORIGIN from *Lull* (see LULLIAN) + -IST.]
A follower of the Christian mystic Lullius (see LULLIAN).
■ **Lullism** *noun* the beliefs of Lullius or his followers E20.

lulu /'luːluː/ *noun*. *slang*. Freq. *iron.* L19.
[ORIGIN Uncertain: perh. from *Lulu* pet form of female forename *Louise*.]
A remarkable or wonderful person or thing.

luluai /'luːluːʌɪ/ *noun*. E20.
[ORIGIN Tolai.]
hist. In New Guinea: a man appointed by the (colonial) government to be responsible for the maintenance of order in a village; a village headman.

Lulworth skipper /'lʌlwəθ 'skɪpə/ *noun phr.* M19.
[ORIGIN from *Lulworth* Cove, Dorset + SKIPPER *noun*¹.]
A hesperiid butterfly, *Thymelicus acteon*, found along the Dorset and Devon coast of SW England and in central and southern Europe and NW Africa.

lum /lʌm/ *noun*. *Scot. & N. English*. E16.
[ORIGIN Perh. from Old French *lum* light (from Latin *lumen*): cf. French *lumière* in sense 'aperture, passage'.]
†**1** An opening in a roof; a skylight. Only in E16.
2 A chimney; a chimney top. E17.
– COMB.: **lum hat** a top hat.

luma /'luːma/ *noun*. Pl. same, **-s**. L20.
[ORIGIN Armenian.]
A monetary unit of Armenia, equal to one-hundredth of a dram.

lumachelle /luːmə'kɛl, ljuː-/ *noun*. Also †**-lla**, †**-lli**. L18.
[ORIGIN (French from) Italian *lumachella* little snail, from *lumaca* snail: see -EL².]
A dark-coloured compact limestone containing fossil shells which make it iridescent.

lumbago /lʌm'beɪgəʊ/ *noun & verb*. L17.
[ORIGIN Latin *lumbago*, *lumbagin-*, from *lumbus* loin.]
▸ **A** *noun*. Rheumatic pain in the lower muscles of the back. L17.
▸ **B** *verb trans.* Affect with lumbago. L18.
■ **lumbaginous** /-dʒɪnəs/ *adjective* of, pertaining to, or affected with lumbago M17.

†**lumbal** *adjective & noun*. L17–E19.
[ORIGIN mod. Latin *lumbalis*, from Latin *lumbus* loin: see -AL¹.]
= LUMBAR.

lumbar /'lʌmbə/ *noun & adjective*. LME.
[ORIGIN medieval Latin *lumbaris*, from Latin *lumbus* loin: see -AR¹.]
▸ **A** *noun*. †**1** A bandage used for a rupture. Only in LME.
2 An artery, vein, nerve, or vertebra situated in the lumbar region. M19.
▸ **B** *adjective*. Situated in or designating the region of the loins, esp. the small of the back; of, pertaining to, or performed on or within the spinal cord in this region. M17.
lumbar puncture the insertion of a cannula into the lumbar part of the spinal cord to withdraw cerebrospinal fluid or introduce a drug.

lumbardar *noun* var. of LAMBARDAR.

lumber /'lʌmbə/ *noun*¹. M16.
[ORIGIN Perh. from LUMBER *verb*¹, but at one time assoc. with LUMBER *noun*².]
1 Disused articles of furniture etc. taking up room inconveniently, or removed to be out of the way; useless odds and ends; useless or cumbrous material. M16.

Pope Loads of learned lumber in his head. R. Gittings An immense amount of accumulated lumber to pack and dispose.

2 Timber sawn into rough planks or otherwise partly prepared. Chiefly *N. Amer.* M17.
3 Superfluous fat, esp. in horses. E19.
– COMB.: **lumber baron** *N. Amer.* a leading or wealthy timber merchant; **lumber-camp** (chiefly *N. Amer.*) a camp in which lumberjacks live; **lumberjack** (chiefly *N. Amer.*) a person who fells forest trees, cuts them into logs, or transports them to a sawmill; **lumberjacket** a warm hip-length jacket fastening up to the neck, of a type worn by lumberjacks; **lumberman** (chiefly *N. Amer.*) a lumberjack; **lumber-port** (*a*) a porthole in the bow or stern of a ship for loading or unloading timber; (*b*) a seaport from which timber is shipped; **lumber-raft** a raft made of logs, boards, etc.; **lumber room** a room in which disused articles of furniture etc. are kept, a room for useless odds and ends; **lumber town** *N. Amer.* a town chiefly engaged in the timber trade; **lumber trade** (chiefly *N. Amer.*) the trade in rough timber; **lumber-wagon** *N. Amer.* a springless wagon of a type used for hauling timber; **lumber yard** *N. Amer.* a timber yard.

lumber /'lʌmbə/ *noun*². *slang*. E17.
[ORIGIN Alt. of LOMBARD *noun*¹.]
†**1** A pawnbroking establishment. E17–M18.
2 *in lumber*, in pawn, in pledge; *transf.* in prison, in trouble, in difficulties. L17.
3 A house or room, *spec.* where stolen property is hidden; a house used by criminals. M18.

lumber /'lʌmbə/ *verb*¹ *intrans.* LME.
[ORIGIN Perh. symbolic. Isolated Middle English use may be rel. to LAME *adjective*. Cf. LUMPER *verb*.]
1 Move in a clumsy or blundering manner; now *esp.* move heavily on account of unwieldiness of bulk and mass. Now chiefly with adverb or adverbial phr. LME.

R. K. Narayan I .. paused to observe .. a country cart lumbering along. G. Vidal When he walks he sort of lumbers. C. Thubron Water buffalo lumbered down sodden tracks.

2 Rumble, make a rumbling noise. *obsolete* exc. *US*. L15.

lumber /'lʌmbə/ *verb*². M17.
[ORIGIN from LUMBER *noun*¹.]
1 *verb trans.* Orig., cover, fill *up*, or obstruct with lumber; burden uselessly, encumber. Now usu., leave (someone) *with* something unwanted or unpleasant; get (someone) into trouble or difficulties; freq. in *pass.* M17.

E. Wallace If they lumbered you with the crime, it was because you was a mug. *Daily Mail* If you're lured into parting with your lolly, you could be lumbered.

2 *verb trans.* Heap or place together as lumber, without order or method; deposit as lumber. L17.
3 a *verb intrans.* Perform the labour or carry on the business of cutting and preparing forest timber. (Earlier as LUMBERING *noun*.) Chiefly *N. Amer.* E19. ▸**b** *verb trans.* Go over (ground) cutting down timber. M19.

lumber /'lʌmbə/ *verb*³ *trans.* *slang*. E19.
[ORIGIN from LUMBER *noun*².]
Deposit (property) in pawn; imprison, arrest.

lumberer /'lʌmb(ə)rə/ *noun*¹. L16.
[ORIGIN from LUMBER *verb*¹ + -ER¹.]
A person who moves clumsily or blunderingly; a person who moves heavily on account of unwieldiness of bulk and mass.

lumberer /'lʌmb(ə)rə/ *noun*². Chiefly *N. Amer.* E19.
[ORIGIN from LUMBER *verb*² + -ER¹.]
A person engaged in the lumber or timber trade.

lumberer /'lʌmb(ə)rə/ *noun*³. *slang*. E19.
[ORIGIN from LUMBER *verb*³ + -ER¹.]
A pawnbroker.

lumbering /'lʌmb(ə)rɪŋ/ *noun*. Chiefly *N. Amer.* M18.
[ORIGIN from LUMBER *verb*² + -ING¹.]
The lumber or timber trade; dealing or working in timber.

lumbering /'lʌmb(ə)rɪŋ/ *adjective*. L16.
[ORIGIN from LUMBER *verb*¹ + -ING².]
Ponderous in movement, inconveniently bulky.
■ **lumberingly** *adverb* M19.

lumberly /'lʌmbəli/ *adjective*. E19.
[ORIGIN from LUMBER *verb*² + -LY¹.]
Clumsy, cumbrous.

†**lumber-pie** *noun*. M17–M19.
[ORIGIN from var. of LOMBARD *adjective* (cf. LUMBER *noun*²) + PIE *noun*².]
A savoury pie made of meat or fish and eggs.

lumbersome /'lʌmbəs(ə)m/ *adjective*. E19.
[ORIGIN from LUMBER *verb*¹ + -SOME¹.]
Cumbrous, unwieldy.

lumbo- /'lʌmbəʊ/ *combining form*. L19.
[ORIGIN from Latin *lumbus* loin + -O-.]
Pertaining to or situated in the lumbar and — regions, or the lumbar region and —, as ***lumbo-aortic***, ***lumbosacral*** *adjectives*

lumbrical /lʌm'brʌɪk(ə)l/ *adjective & noun*. L17.
[ORIGIN mod. Latin *lumbricalis*, from Latin LUMBRICUS: see -AL¹.]
▸ **A** *adjective*. **1** ANATOMY. Designating certain fusiform muscles in the hand and the foot which assist in flexing and extending the digits. L17.
2 Pertaining to or resembling a worm. L17.
▸ **B** *noun*. = LUMBRICALIS. L19.

lumbricalis /lʌmbrɪ'keɪlɪs/ *noun*. Pl. **-les** /-liːz/. E18.
[ORIGIN mod. Latin: see LUMBRICAL.]
ANATOMY. A lumbrical muscle.

lumbriciform /lʌm'brʌɪsɪfɔːm, -'brɪs-/ *adjective*. E19.
[ORIGIN from Latin LUMBRICUS + -I- + -FORM.]
Vermiform.

L

lumbricine /ˈlʌmbrɪsʌɪn/ *adjective*. L19.
[ORIGIN mod. Latin *lumbricina*, from Latin LUMBRICUS: see -INE[1].]
ZOOLOGY. Of, pertaining to, or characteristic of the family Lumbricidae or the suborder Lumbricina of earthworms.

lumbricoid /ˈlʌmbrɪkɔɪd/ *adjective & noun*. M19.
[ORIGIN from LUMBRICUS + -OID.]
ZOOLOGY. (An organism) resembling a lumbricus.

lumbriculus /lʌmˈbrɪkjʊləs/ *noun*. Pl. **-li** /-lʌɪ, -liː/. E20.
[ORIGIN mod. Latin, dim. of Latin LUMBRICUS: see -CULE.]
ZOOLOGY. An aquatic oligochaete worm of the genus *Lumbriculus*, resembling an earthworm.

lumbricus /lʌmˈbrʌɪkəs, ˈlʌmbrɪkəs/ *noun*. Pl. **-ci** /-sʌɪ, -siː/. LME.
[ORIGIN Latin = worm.]
ZOOLOGY. An earthworm, *esp.* one of the genus *Lumbricus*. Also (now *rare*), an intestinal roundworm.

lumen /ˈluːmɛn, ˈljuː-/ *noun*. Pl. (in sense 1) **-mina** /-mɪnə/, (in sense 2) **-mens**. L19.
[ORIGIN Latin *lumen*, *lumin-* (a) light, an opening.]
1 a ANATOMY & BIOLOGY. A tubular passage or cavity in an organism or cell; the central space in an intestine, blood vessel, etc. L19. ▸**b** A tubular passage in a catheter or other surgical instrument. L19.
2 PHYSICS. The SI unit of luminous flux, equal to the flux emitted by a uniform point source of intensity one candela (formerly, one candle) into a solid angle of one steradian. (Symbol lm.) L19.

lumen siccum /luːmɛn ˈsɪkəm, ˈljuː-/ *noun phr.* E17.
[ORIGIN Latin, lit. 'dry light'.]
The objective light of rational knowledge or thought.

lumeter /ˈluːmiːtə, ˈljuː-/ *noun*. E20.
[ORIGIN from Latin LUMEN + -METER.]
= LUXMETER.

lumi- /ˈluːmi, ˈljuː-/ *combining form* of Latin *lumin-*, LUMEN light: see -I-.
■ **lumichrome** *noun* (CHEMISTRY) a compound, $C_{12}H_{10}N_4O_2$, formed by ultraviolet irradiation of riboflavin in acidic solution and showing a blue fluorescence M20. **lumiˈflavin** *noun* (CHEMISTRY) a compound, $C_{13}H_{12}N_4O_2$, formed by ultraviolet irradiation of riboflavin in alkaline solution and showing a yellow-green fluorescence M20. **lumirhoˈdopsin** *noun* (BIOCHEMISTRY) an orange intermediate that is formed when rhodopsin is bleached by light and changes spontaneously to metarhodopsin M20. **luˈmisterol** *noun* (BIOCHEMISTRY) a steroid alcohol, $C_{28}H_{44}O$, which is a stereoisomer of ergosterol and occurs as an intermediate when this is converted to vitamin D_2 by ultraviolet irradiation and warming M20.

lumina *noun pl.* see LUMEN.

luminaire /ˈluːmɪnɛː, ˈljuː-/ *noun*. E20.
[ORIGIN French: see LUMINARY *noun*.]
(A lighting unit consisting of) an electric light and its fittings.

Luminal /ˈluːmɪn(ə)l, ˈljuː-/ *noun*. E20.
[ORIGIN Prob. from Latin LUMEN (as a rendering of PHEN-) + -AL[2].]
PHARMACOLOGY. (Proprietary name for) the drug phenobarbitone.

luminal /ˈluːmɪn(ə)l, ˈljuː-/ *adjective*. L19.
[ORIGIN formed as LUMEN + -AL[1].]
Of or pertaining to a lumen.

luminance /ˈluːmɪn(ə)ns, ˈljuː-/ *noun*. L19.
[ORIGIN from (the same root as) LUMINANT: see -ANCE.]
1 Luminousness. L19.
2 PHYSICS. The amount of luminous flux emitted by unit area of a source into unit solid angle (the objective analogue of subjective brightness). M20.
3 The component of a television signal which carries information on the brightness of the image. M20.

luminant /ˈluːmɪn(ə)nt, ˈljuː-/ *noun & adjective*. Now *rare*. L19.
[ORIGIN Latin *luminant-* pres. ppl stem of *luminare*, from *lumin-*, LUMEN: see -ANT[1].]
▸ **A** *noun*. An illuminant. L19.
▸ **B** *adjective*. Illuminating, luminous. L19.

luminarist /ˈluːmɪn(ə)rɪst, ˈljuː-/ *noun*. Now *rare*. L19.
[ORIGIN French *luminariste*, from Latin *lumin-*, LUMEN: see -IST.]
ART. An adherent or practitioner of luminism.
■ **luminarism** *noun* the art or practice of luminarists, = LUMINISM 1 E20.

luminary /ˈluːmɪn(ə)ri, ˈljuː-/ *noun*. LME.
[ORIGIN Old French *luminarie* (mod. *-aire*) or late Latin *luminarium*, from Latin *lumin-*, LUMEN: see -ARY[1].]
1 a A lamp, an artificial light. LME. ▸**b** A natural light-giving body; *esp.* a celestial object, the sun or the moon. L15.
2 A source of intellectual, moral, or spiritual light; a prominent or influential person. LME.

> P. GROSSKURTH The leading luminaries sat around the . . table, the lesser figures . . behind them. *News on Sunday* A leading criminal lawyer said to be a luminary in the libel field.

luminate /ˈluːmɪneɪt, ˈljuː-/ *verb trans. arch.* Pa. pple & ppl adjective **-ated**, (earlier) †**-ate**. M16.
[ORIGIN Latin *luminat-* pa. ppl stem of *luminare*: see LUMINANT, -ATE[3].]
Light up, illuminate.
■ **lumiˈnation** *noun* (*rare*) a shedding or emission of light M17.

lumine /ˈluːmɪn, ˈljuː-/ *verb trans.* Now *rare*. LME.
[ORIGIN Old French *luminer* from Latin *luminare*: see LUMINANT. See also LIMN *verb*.]
Light up, illumine. In early use, illuminate (a manuscript etc.).
■ †**luminer** *noun* (see also LIMNER) ME–L15.

luminesce /luːmɪˈnɛs, ljuː-/ *verb intrans.* L19.
[ORIGIN Back-form. from LUMINESCENT.]
Be or become luminescent.

luminescence /luːmɪˈnɛs(ə)ns, ljuː-/ *noun*. L19.
[ORIGIN from (the same root as) LUMINESCENT: see -ENCE.]
1 The property of some substances of emitting light without being heated, as in fluorescence and phosphorescence. L19.
2 Light, or a glow, emitted by a luminescent object or surface. E20.

luminescent /luːmɪˈnɛs(ə)nt, ljuː-/ *adjective*. L19.
[ORIGIN from Latin *lumin-*, LUMEN + -ESCENT.]
Exhibiting or pertaining to luminescence.

luminiferous /luːmɪˈnɪf(ə)rəs, ljuː-/ *adjective*. E19.
[ORIGIN formed as LUMINESCENT: see -FEROUS.]
Producing or transmitting light. Chiefly *hist.* in ***luminiferous ether***.

luminise *verb* var. of LUMINIZE.

luminism /ˈluːmɪnɪz(ə)m, ˈljuː-/ *noun*. E20.
[ORIGIN from Latin *lumin-*, LUMEN + -ISM.]
ART. **1** A movement in painting concentrating on representing the effects of light. E20.
2 Use of light to produce an object of art. M20.
■ **luminist** *noun & adjective* (**a**) *noun* an adherent or practitioner of luminism; (**b**) *adjective* of or pertaining to luminists or luminism: E20.

luminize /ˈluːmɪnʌɪz, ˈljuː-/ *verb trans.* Also **-ise**. M20.
[ORIGIN formed as LUMINISM + -IZE.]
Make luminous; apply a luminous substance to.
■ **luminizer** *noun* M20.

luminol /ˈluːmɪnɒl, ˈljuː-/ *noun*. M20.
[ORIGIN from Latin *lumin-*, LUMEN + -OL.]
CHEMISTRY. A bicyclic hydrazide, $C_8H_7N_3O_2$, which gives a blue luminescence when oxidized in alkaline solution and is used in the determination of oxidizing agents and metal ions.

luminophore /ˈluːmɪnəfɔː, ˈljuː-/ *noun*. Also **-phor**. E20.
[ORIGIN formed as LUMINOL + -O- + -PHORE.]
1 A luminescent substance. E20.
2 A group of atoms in a molecule which is responsible for its luminescence. E20.

luminosity /luːmɪˈnɒsɪti, ljuː-/ *noun*. M17.
[ORIGIN from LUMINOUS: see -OSITY.]
1 The quality or condition of being luminous. M17. ▸**b** The effectiveness of light of any particular wavelength in producing the sensation of brightness. L19. ▸**c** ASTRONOMY. The intrinsic brightness of a celestial object (as distinct from its apparent brightness, diminished by distance); the rate of emission of electromagnetic radiation within any part of the spectrum. E20. ▸**d** PHYSICS. A parameter of a colliding beam accelerator equal to the ratio of the rate of interactions to the cross-section for the interaction. M20.
2 A luminous thing; a luminous point or area. M19.
– COMB.: **luminosity curve**: showing how emitted energy or perceived brightness varies with wavelength; **luminosity function** ASTRONOMY: giving the number or proportion of celestial objects with an absolute magnitude equal to or greater than any value.

luminous /ˈluːmɪnəs, ˈljuː-/ *adjective*. LME.
[ORIGIN Old French & mod. French *lumineux* or Latin *luminosus*, from *lumin-*, LUMEN: see -OUS.]
1 Full of light; emitting or casting light; shining, bright; luminescent. LME. ▸**b** Of a room etc.: well lit. Now *rare*. E17.

> A. C. CLARKE In the lightless abyss, many creatures carry constellations of luminous organs. M. SHADBOLT Tim's pale shirt, vaguely luminous in the gloom. J. CHEEVER Her skin had a luminous and pearly whiteness.

2 Shedding intellectual, moral, or spiritual light; (of a writer, literary style, etc.) clear and illuminating. LME.

> *Women's Review* Luminous prose, acute intellect and the insight of a spiritual healer.

■ **luminously** *adverb* E19. **luminousness** *noun* M17.

lumme /ˈlʌmi/ *interjection. colloq.* L19.
[ORIGIN Alt. of (*Lord*) *love me*.]
Expr. surprise or emphasis.

lummox /ˈlʌməks/ *noun. dial. & N. Amer. colloq.* E19.
[ORIGIN Unknown.]
A large, heavy, or clumsy person; an ungainly or stupid lout.

> K. REICHS I watched a lummox push his girlfriend against a wall.

lummy /ˈlʌmi/ *adjective. arch. slang.* M19.
[ORIGIN Unknown.]
First-rate.

lump /lʌmp/ *noun*[1]. ME.
[ORIGIN Unknown. Cf. Danish *lump(e)* lump, Norwegian, Swedish dial. *lump* block, stump, log; but what may be the original sense, 'shapeless piece', is seen also in Dutch *lomp*, †*lompe* rag, Dutch *lomp*, Low German *lump* coarse, rude (whence German *Lumpen* rag).]
1 A compact, shapeless, or unshapely piece or mass. ME. ▸**b** *ellipt.* A lump of sugar. L19.

> J. T. STORY The police . . had seen Maria feeding lumps of sugar to the racehorse. P. ABRAHAMS A woman gave each person a lump of thick porridge.

2 a A mass of clay taken up by a potter or sculptor for one operation, a mass of dough intended for one baking. ME. ▸**b** A mass of malleable iron. E16.
3 A heavy dull person, a lazy person; an ungainly person; a big sturdy person. ME.

> L. CODY She makes me feel like a big lump.

†**4** An aggregate of units; a heap, a clump, a cluster. LME–L18.
5 A protuberance, a swelling, an excrescence, *esp.* one caused by disease or injury in an animal body. LME. ▸**b** A feeling of tightness or pressure in the throat due to emotion. Chiefly in ***a lump in one's throat***, ***bring a lump to a person's throat***. *colloq.* M19.

> E. NESBIT There was a lump on his young brow as big as a turkey's egg. D. DELILLO Steffie was routinely examining her chest for lumps.

6 A great quantity, a lot. *slang & dial.* E16.

> R. D. BLACKMORE Colonel Harding owed him a lump of money.

†**7** The whole mass or quantity of something; the great majority. L16–E18.
8 A nipple on the barrel of a musket; an iron block under the barrel of certain types of breech-loading gun descending into a recess in the action. M19.
9 NAUTICAL. A wave of a choppy sea. M19.
10 *The* workhouse. *arch. slang.* L19.
11 A parcel of food given to a tramp or vagrant. *US slang.* E20.
12 In *pl.* Hard knocks, attacks. *slang.* M20.

> J. H. GRAY My father would . . take his verbal lumps, saying nothing.

13 *The* class of people in building or other trades who contract to do work for a lump sum, or who work as self-employed individuals for payment without deduction of tax. M20.
– PHRASES: **by the lump**, **in the lump** as a whole, in a general manner; without breaking down into units, in the mass; wholesale; for a lump sum. **lump of clay** the human body regarded as purely material, without a soul. ***lumps of delight***: see DELIGHT *noun* 4.
– COMB.: **lump-account** an account in which items are treated together without particulars or details; **lump coal** coal in lumps as mined; **lump sugar** loaf sugar broken into lumps or cut into cubes; **lump sum** (**a**) a sum covering or including a number of items; (**b**) a sum of money paid to cover the complete cost of something; **lump work** work contracted for as a single job for a lump sum.

lump /lʌmp/ *noun*[2]. M16.
[ORIGIN Middle Low German *lumpen*, Middle Dutch *lumpe*, perh. identical with LUMP *noun*[1].]
= LUMPFISH.

lump /lʌmp/ *verb*[1] *trans. obsolete* exc. *dial.* M16.
[ORIGIN Perh. rel. to Dutch *lompen*.]
Beat, thresh.

lump /lʌmp/ *verb*[2]. L16.
[ORIGIN Symbolic: cf. *dump*, *grump*, *mump*, etc.]
1 *verb intrans.* Look sulky or disagreeable. (In early use esp. in collocation with *lour*.) Long *obsolete* exc. *dial.* L16.
2 *verb trans.* Be displeased at (something that must be endured), put up with ungraciously, tolerate reluctantly. (Freq. in antithesis with ***like***.) *colloq.* E19.

> W. S. MAUGHAM If they don't like it they can lump it. J. S. HUXLEY There was no alternative accommodation . . ; we just had to lump it.

lump /lʌmp/ *verb*[3]. E17.
[ORIGIN from LUMP *noun*[1].]
1 *verb trans.* Put together in one mass, sum, or group, without discrimination or regard for particulars or details; treat as alike or like. Foll. by *together*, *with*, *in with*, *under*, etc. E17. ▸**b** *verb trans. & intrans.* TAXONOMY. Classify (plants or animals) disregarding minor variations as a basis for more taxa; conflate (taxa) in this way. L19.

> J. W. KRUTCH Under this designation is lumped without discrimination any aspiration toward distinction. G. PRIESTLAND Pop (in which I lump, indiscriminately, . . all kinds of electronic bumping and grinding). J. BARZUN Jung's lumping of dreams, legends and hearsay with recorded fact. J. UPDIKE In the present volume, the footnotes are cumbersomely lumped at the back. J. WAIN In that district all of us who were not Welsh were inevitably lumped together as foreigners.

2 *verb intrans.* Collect *together* into a lump; be formed or raised into lumps; coagulate. E17.
3 *verb trans.* †**a** Pay in a lump sum. *rare.* Only in M18. ▸**b** Lay the whole of (a particular sum of money) *on* a single object. M19.

L

4 *verb trans.* Melt down into a lump; form or raise into lumps; cover with lumps. **L18.**
5 *verb intrans.* Move heavily *along*; drop or sit heavily *down*. **M19.**
6 a *verb intrans.* Act as a lumper, load or unload cargoes. Chiefly as ***lumping*** *verbal noun.* (Cf. earlier **LUMPER** *noun* 1.) **M19.** ▸**b** *verb trans.* Load or unload (a ship, a cargo); *colloq.* carry or shift (something heavy) *about* etc. with effort or difficulty or roughly. **L19.**

A. BRIEN Can't keep lumping your favourite books backwards and forwards.

lumpectomy /lʌmˈpɛktəmi/ *noun.* **L20.**
[**ORIGIN** from **LUMP** *noun*[1] + **-ECTOMY.**]
Surgical removal of a lump from a woman's breast in a case of suspected or diagnosed cancer, the remainder of the breast being left intact; an instance of this.

lumped /lʌmpt/ *adjective.* **LME.**
[**ORIGIN** from **LUMP** *noun*[1], *verb*[3]: see **-ED**[2], **-ED**[1].]
1 Made, shaped, or raised into a lump. **LME.**
2 *ELECTRICITY.* (Containing impedances or circuit elements) localized at a particular point or points, rather than distributed uniformly throughout part of a circuit. **E20.**

lumpen /ˈlʌmpən/ *adjective & noun. derog.* **M20.**
[**ORIGIN** Back-form. from **LUMPENPROLETARIAT.**]
▸ **A** *adjective.* Ignorantly contented, boorish, stupid; uninterested in revolutionary advancement. Also joined to the noun qualified. **M20.**

A. BROOKNER Her lumpen immobility, her absorption in the cat. *Spectator* A lumpen-intelligentsia of déclassé students.

▸ **B** *noun collect. pl. The* class of those who are lumpen. **L20.**

lumpenproletariat /ˌlʌmpənprəʊlɪˈtɛːrɪət/ *noun. derog.* **E20.**
[**ORIGIN** German, from *Lumpen* rag (cf. **LUMP** *noun*[1]) + **PROLETARIAT.** Orig. used by Karl Marx.]
The poorest and least cohesive section of the proletariat, making no contribution to the workers' cause; the ignorantly contented lower orders of society uninterested in revolutionary advancement.
▪ **lumpenproletarian** *adjective & noun* of or pertaining to, a member of, the lumpenproletariat **M20.**

lumper /ˈlʌmpə/ *noun.* **L18.**
[**ORIGIN** from **LUMP** *verb*[3] or *noun*[1] + **-ER**[1].]
1 A labourer employed in loading and unloading cargoes, a docker; a person employed in unloading fish. **L18.**
2 A small contractor, a person who contracts for lump work. *slang.* **M19.**
3 A person (esp. a taxonomist) who attaches importance to similarities rather than differences in classification or analysis and so favours inclusive categories. Cf. **SPLITTER** *noun* 1b. **M19.**

lumper /ˈlʌmpə/ *verb intrans. obsolete* exc. *dial.* **E16.**
[**ORIGIN** Perh. symbolic. Cf. **LUMBER** *verb*[1].]
Move clumsily; stumble or blunder along.

lumpers /ˈlʌmpəz/ *noun pl. slang.* **M20.**
[**ORIGIN** from ***lump sum*** s.v. **LUMP** *noun*[1]: see **-ER**[6].]
A lump sum paid as compensation for loss of employment.

lumpfish /ˈlʌmpfɪʃ/ *noun.* Pl. **-es**, (usu.) same. **E17.**
[**ORIGIN** from **LUMP** *noun*[2] + **FISH** *noun*[1].]
A spiny-finned heavy-bodied fish, *Cyclopterus lumpus*, of the N. Atlantic, with modified pelvic fins forming a disc-shaped sucker with which it clings to objects with great force.

lumping /ˈlʌmpɪŋ/ *adjective.* **LME.**
[**ORIGIN** from **LUMP** *verb*[3] + **-ING**[2].]
1 †**a** Weighing heavy. Only in **LME.** ▸**b** Great, big. *colloq.* **E18.**

b R. CAMPBELL A most melancholy fellow with a great lumping text-book in his fist.

b a lumping pennyworth (now *dial.*) plenty for one's money.
2 *gen.* That lumps (something). **M18.**

lumpish /ˈlʌmpɪʃ/ *adjective.* **LME.**
[**ORIGIN** from **LUMP** *noun*[1] (& partly **LUMP** *verb*[3]) + **-ISH**[1].]
1 Stupidly dull or lethargic in action, thought, or feeling. Formerly also, low-spirited, dejected, melancholy. **LME.**

POPE The lumpish husband snoar'd away the night. F. DONALDSON The earlier letters . . were . . of that lumpish kind everyone writes to school-children.

2 Of cumbersome weight or bulk; not easily moved; *esp.* heavy and clumsy in appearance, shape, or movement. **M16.**

SIR W. SCOTT Swelling lumpish hills.

3 Full of lumps, in lumps, lumpy. **E18.**

A. N. WILSON Tugging away the soft bread . . in lumpish handfuls.

4 Of sound: dull and heavy. **M18.**

HENRY FIELDING He fell prostrated on the floor with a lumpish noise.

▪ **lumpishly** *adverb* **LME.** **lumpishness** *noun* **L16.**

lumpless /ˈlʌmplɪs/ *adjective.* **E20.**
[**ORIGIN** from **LUMP** *noun*[1] + **-LESS.**]
Having no lumps.

lumpsucker /ˈlʌmpsʌkə/ *noun.* **M18.**
[**ORIGIN** from **LUMP** *noun*[2] + **SUCKER** *noun.*]
= **LUMPFISH.**

lumpy /ˈlʌmpi/ *adjective.* **E18.**
[**ORIGIN** from **LUMP** *noun*[1] + **-Y**[1].]
1 Full of lumps; (of water) cut up by the wind into small waves. **E18.**

Listener A lumpy swell and a Force Eight wind. P. BAILEY If there's one thing I can't abide, it's lumpy porridge.

2 Having an outline or shape characterized by lumps or roundish protuberances; having a heavy and clumsy appearance. **E18.**

N. GORDIMER The legs had the ex-dancer's hard lumpy calves.

3 Intoxicated, drunk. *arch. slang.* **E19.**
– **SPECIAL COLLOCATIONS:** **lumpy jaw** actinomycosis affecting the jaw, common in cattle.
▪ **lumpily** *adverb* **L19.** **lumpiness** *noun* **E19.**

luna /ˈluːnə/ *noun.* **LME.**
[**ORIGIN** Latin = moon.]
1 (**L-**.) The moon (personified). **LME.**
2 †**a** *ALCHEMY.* The metal silver. **LME–M17.** ▸**b** *HERALDRY.* The tincture argent in the fanciful blazon of the arms of sovereign princes. **E18.** ▸**c** ***luna cornea*** /ˈkɔːnɪə/ [= horn], fused silver chloride. **E18.**
3 In full ***luna moth***. A large grey-green N. American saturniid moth, *Actias luna*, with crescent-shaped spots and long curved tails on the wings. **L19.**

lunabase /ˈluːnəbeɪs/ *noun.* **M20.**
[**ORIGIN** from Latin **LUNA** moon + **BASE** *noun*[1] (with ref. to **BASIC** *adjective* 2b).]
ASTRONOMY. The maria or lowlands of the moon (the dark-coloured regions as seen from the earth); the basaltic rock of which these are composed. Cf. **LUNARITE.**

lunacy /ˈluːnəsi/ *noun.* **M16.**
[**ORIGIN** from **LUNATIC**: see **-ACY.**]
1 Insanity, orig. of an intermittent kind supposed to be brought about by the changes of the moon. Formerly in *LAW*, such mental unsoundness as interferes with civil rights or transactions. **M16.**
commission of lunacy *hist.* a commission, issuing from a court, authorizing an inquiry as to the soundness of a person's mind. **Master in Lunacy** *hist.* a legal officer with the duty of investigating the mental condition of people alleged to be insane.
2 Mad folly, great foolishness. **L16.**

Luna Park /luːnə ˈpɑːk/ *noun phr.* **E20.**
[**ORIGIN** An amusement centre on Coney Island, Brooklyn, New York.]
An amusement centre, an entertainment park.

lunar /ˈluːnə/ *adjective & noun.* **LME.**
[**ORIGIN** Latin *lunaris*, formed as **LUNA**: see **-AR**[1].]
▸ **A** *adjective.* **1** Crescent-shaped; marked with crescent-shaped spots. **LME.**
2 Of or pertaining to the moon; situated in or on the moon; of or pertaining to travel to the moon. Formerly also, (supposedly) influenced by or dependent on the moon. **E17.** ▸**b** Monthly, menstrual. *rare.* **L17.** ▸**c** Having the character of the moon as opp. to that of the sun; not warmly bright; pale, pallid. **M18.**
3 [So called because the class includes *q*, the initial letter of Arabic *qamar* moon.] Of an Arabic consonant: before which the *l* of the article is not assimilated. Opp. **SOLAR** *adjective*[1] 4. **L18.**
4 Of or containing silver. **E19.**
– **SPECIAL COLLOCATIONS & COMB.:** **lunar caustic** fused silver nitrate. **lunar cycle** the Metonic cycle. **lunar day** the interval of time between two successive crossings of the meridian by the moon. **lunar distance** the angular distance of the moon from the sun, a planet, or a fixed star, used in calculating longitude at sea. **lunar-diurnal** *adjective* pertaining to the lunar day. ***lunar eclipse***: see **ECLIPSE** *noun* 1. **lunar excursion module**, **lunar module** a module designed to take an astronaut from an orbiting spacecraft to the moon's surface and back. **lunar month** (**a**) = ***SYNODIC month***; (**b**) a period of 28 days (four weeks). **lunar node** either of the two points at which the orbit of the moon cuts the ecliptic. **lunar observation** an observation of lunar distances in finding longitude at sea. **lunar orbit** (**a**) the orbit of the moon around the earth; (**b**) an orbit around the moon. ***lunar regular***: see **REGULAR** *noun* 4. **lunarscape** a picture or view of the moon's surface; the lunar landscape. **lunar year** a period of twelve lunar months (about 354⅓ days).
▸ **B** *noun.* †**1** A moonlike body, a satellite. Only in **M17.**
2 a A lunar distance; a lunar observation. **M19.** ▸**b** A look. *colloq.* **M19.**
3 The lunate bone. **M19.**
▪ **lunarnaut** *noun* [after **ASTRONAUT** etc.] a person who travels or has travelled to the moon **M20.**

lunaria /luːˈnɛːrɪə/ *noun.* Also (earlier, now *rare* or *obsolete*) **lunary** /ˈluːnəri/. **LME.**
[**ORIGIN** medieval Latin *lunaria*, from Latin **LUNA** moon + *-aria* **-ARY**[1].]
Any of several plants having a feature associated with the moon; *esp.* (**a**) the garden plant honesty, *Lunaria annua* (with ref. to the round shiny seed vessels); (**b**) *arch.* the fern moonwort, *Botrychium lunaria* (with ref. to the crescent-shaped segments of the barren fronds).

lunarian /luːˈnɛːrɪən/ *noun.* Now *rare.* **E18.**
[**ORIGIN** formed as **LUNAR** + **-IAN.**]
1 A (supposed) dweller in or on the moon. **E18.**
2 An observer or describer of the moon; a user of lunar observations in finding longitude. **E19.**

lunarite /ˈluːnərʌɪt/ *noun.* **M20.**
[**ORIGIN** formed as **LUNAR** + **-ITE**[1].]
ASTRONOMY. The uplands of the moon (the light-coloured regions as seen from the earth); the siliceous rock of which these are composed. Cf. **LUNABASE.**

lunarium /luːˈnɛːrɪəm/ *noun.* **L18.**
[**ORIGIN** mod. Latin, formed as **LUNAR** + **-IUM.**]
An instrument representing the phases and motions of the moon.

lunary *noun* see **LUNARIA.**

lunary /ˈluːnəri/ *adjective.* Now *rare.* **M16.**
[**ORIGIN** formed as **LUNAR**: see **-ARY**[2].]
1 = **LUNAR** *adjective* 2. **M16.**
2 = **LUNAR** *adjective* 1. **E17.**

lunate /ˈluːneɪt/ *adjective & noun.* **L18.**
[**ORIGIN** Latin *lunatus*, from Latin **LUNA** moon: see **-ATE**[2].]
▸ **A** *adjective.* Chiefly *ZOOLOGY & BOTANY.* Crescent-shaped; *spec.* (*ANATOMY*) designating one of the bones of the wrist. **L18.**
▸ **B** *noun.* A small prehistoric crescent-shaped stone (usu. flint) artefact or implement. **M20.**
▪ **lunated** *adjective* (now *rare*) = **LUNATE** *adjective* **L17.**

lunatic /ˈluːnətɪk/ *adjective & noun.* **ME.**
[**ORIGIN** Old French & mod. French *lunatique* from late Latin *lunaticus*, from Latin **LUNA** moon: see **-ATIC.**]
▸ **A** *adjective.* **1** Insane; orig., affected by an intermittent kind of insanity supposed to be brought about by the changes of the moon. Formerly in *LAW*, affected by such mental unsoundness as interferes with civil rights or transactions. **ME.** ▸**b** Madly foolish, wildly eccentric, frantic, idiotic; (of an action, appearance, etc.) indicating lunacy or mad folly. **E16.**
†**2 a** Influenced by the moon. **LME–L16.** ▸**b** Of a horse: affected with moon-blindness; moon-blind. **L16–M18.**
▸ **B** *noun.* **1** An insane person; a person of unsound mind; a madman. **LME.**
2 A madly foolish or idiotic person. **E17.**
– **COMB. & SPECIAL COLLOCATIONS:** **lunatic asylum** (chiefly *hist.*) a mental home or hospital; ***lunatic fringe***: see **FRINGE** *noun.*

lunatical /luːˈnatɪk(ə)l/ *adjective. rare.* **L16.**
[**ORIGIN** from **LUNATIC** + **-AL**[1].]
= **LUNATIC** *adjective.*
▪ **lunatically** *adverb* **L19.**

lunation /luːˈneɪʃ(ə)n/ *noun.* **LME.**
[**ORIGIN** medieval Latin *lunatio(n-)*, from **LUNA** moon: see **-ATION.**]
1 The time from one new moon to the next, constituting a lunar or synodic month. **LME.**
2 The time of full moon. **M16.**

lunch /lʌn(t)ʃ/ *noun & verb.* **L16.**
[**ORIGIN** In sense 1 perh. from Spanish *lonja* slice. In sense 2 abbreviation of **LUNCHEON.**]
▸ **A** *noun.* †**1** A (thick) piece; a hunk. **L16–L19.**
2 A meal taken around midday or early in the afternoon, *spec.* one lighter or less formal than the evening meal; a light refreshment taken between breakfast and a midday dinner or main meal; in some places, a light meal at any time of the day. **E19.**
Dutch lunch: see **DUTCH** *adjective.* ***LIQUID lunch.*** **out to lunch** *N. Amer. slang* insane; stupid, unaware; disorganized, incompetent; socially unacceptable. ***ploughman's lunch***: see **PLOUGHMAN** 2. ***SUNDAY lunch. working lunch***: see **WORKING.**
– **COMB.:** **lunch box** (**a**) a container for a packed meal; (**b**) *US slang* a fool, a simpleton, an inept person; (**c**) *slang* the male genitals, esp. when conspicuous in tight clothing; **lunch hour** a break of an hour or so for lunch, the hour at which lunch is (usu.) taken; **lunchmeat** *US* meat sold in slices for sandwiches; **lunch pail** *N. Amer.* a lunch box; **lunchroom** a restaurant with quick service of lunches; **lunchtime** the time at which lunch is (usu.) taken.
▸ **B** *verb.* **1** *verb intrans.* Take lunch. **E19.**
ladies who lunch: see **LADY** *noun & adjective.*
2 *verb trans.* Provide lunch for. **L19.**
▪ **luncher** *noun* **M19.** **lunchless** *adjective* **E20.**

luncheon /ˈlʌn(t)ʃ(ə)n/ *noun & verb.* **L16.**
[**ORIGIN** In sense A.1 prob. an extension of **LUNCH** *noun* 1 after *punch, puncheon, trunch, truncheon*. Other uses of unknown origin.]
▸ **A** *noun.* †**1** = **LUNCH** *noun* 1. **L16–L19.**
2 Orig., a light refreshment or lunch taken between two of the ordinary mealtimes, esp. between breakfast and a midday dinner or main meal. Now usu., a lunch taken around midday or early in the afternoon (now *formal*). Also (*US*), a late supper or other light meal. **M17.**
– **COMB.:** **luncheon car** on a railway train, a restaurant car where lunches are provided; **luncheon meat** a type of precooked meat containing preservatives, in loaf form for slicing etc.; **luncheon voucher** a money voucher given to an employee which is exchangeable for meals at certain restaurants or food from certain shops.
▸ **B** *verb intrans.* Take luncheon, lunch. **M19.**
▪ **luncheo'nette** *noun* a small restaurant or snack bar serving light lunches **E20.** **luncheonless** *adjective* **L19.**

Lunda /ˈlʌndə/ *noun & adjective*. Pl. of noun same, **-s**. L19.
[ORIGIN Bantu.]
Of or pertaining to, a member of, a people of Angola and Zambia; (of) the Bantu language of this people.

lundum /ˈlʊndəm/ *noun*. M20.
[ORIGIN Portuguese.]
A simple Portuguese song and dance originating from Africa, probably one of the sources from which fado developed.

Lundyfoot /ˈlʌndɪfʊt/ *noun*. E19.
[ORIGIN from *Lundy Foot*, a tobacconist in Dublin, Ireland, c 1776.]
A kind of snuff.

lune /luːn/ *noun*[1]. Also †**loyn(e)**. LME.
[ORIGIN Old French *loigne* var. of *longe* shortening of *allonge* lengthening, drawing out, from *allonger*, from *long* LONG *adjective*[1].]
A length of cord etc.; *spec*. a leash for a hawk.

lune /luːn/ *noun*[2]. *arch*. E17.
[ORIGIN Latin LUNA moon, in medieval Latin sense, whence also French *lune*, Middle High German *lūne* (German *Laune* whim, caprice).]
A fit of frenzy or lunacy; a mad freak or tantrum. Usu. in *pl*.

lune /luːn/ *noun*[3]. E18.
[ORIGIN French from Latin LUNA moon.]
1 GEOMETRY. A figure formed on a plane by arcs of two circles intersecting at two points; a figure formed on a sphere by two semicircles intersecting at diametrically opposite points. Also called ***lunule***, ***lunula***. E18.
2 Anything in the shape of a crescent or half moon. Now *rare*. E18.

lunel /luːˈnɛl/ *noun*. L18.
[ORIGIN from *Lunel* (see below).]
A sweet muscat wine produced around Lunel in the department of Hérault, southern France. Also ***lunel-wine***.

lunette /luːˈnɛt, ljuː-/ *noun*. L16.
[ORIGIN French, dim. of *lune* moon from Latin LUNA: see -ETTE.]
1 FARRIERY. A semicircular horseshoe for the front of the hoof only. Also ***lunette-shoe***. L16.
2 ARCHITECTURE. **a** An arched aperture in a concave ceiling for the admission of light. E17. ▸**b** A crescent-shaped or semicircular space in a ceiling, dome, etc., decorated with paintings or sculptures; a piece of decoration filling such a space. E18.
3 A blinker for a horse. M17.
4 In *pl*. Spectacles. Now *rare*. L17.
5 FORTIFICATION. A work larger than a redan, consisting of two faces forming a salient angle and two flanks. E18.
6 The figure or shape of a crescent moon. L18.
7 A watch glass of flattened shape. Also ***lunette glass***, ***lunette watch glass***. M19.
8 In the guillotine, the circular hole which receives the neck of the victim. M19.
9 Any of the flues connecting a glass furnace and its arch. (Earlier in LINNET-HOLE.) M19.
10 A crescent-shaped ornament. M19.
11 A ring or forked plate to or by which a field gun carriage or other vehicle for towing is attached. L19.
12 ROMAN CATHOLIC CHURCH. A circular case, fitting into an aperture in a monstrance, for holding the consecrated host. L19.
13 PHYSICAL GEOGRAPHY. A broad shallow mound of wind-blown material along the leeward side of a lake or dry lake basin, esp. in arid parts of Australia, and typically crescent-shaped with the concave edge along the lake shore. M20.

lung /lʌŋ/ *noun*.
[ORIGIN Old English *lungen* = Old Frisian *lungen*, Middle Low German *lunge*, Middle Dutch *longe* (Dutch *long*), Old High German *lungun* (German *Lunge*), corresp. to Old Norse *lunga*, from Germanic from Indo-European base repr. also by LIGHT *adjective*[1]. Named from their lightness: cf. LIGHTS.]
1 The respiratory organ which brings air into contact with the blood in many vertebrates, occurring usu. in pairs in the thorax and communicating through bronchi with the windpipe; a respiratory organ in some invertebrates. See also ***iron lung*** s.v. IRON *noun & adjective*. OE. ▸**b** *fig*. A place where fresh air can be breathed; in *pl*., the parks and open spaces in or close to a city. Foll. by *for*, *of*. E19.

> P. BARKER She was aware of the movement of her lungs, sucking in and expelling air. **b** L. MUMFORD The urban park . . the 'lungs' of the city. *South Wales Echo* The planners . . want the land to the west of Caerphilly to remain as a lung for the town.

†**2** *sing*. & in *pl*. A person who blows a fire; a chemist's assistant. E–M17.
– PHRASES: ***black lung***: see BLACK *adjective*. **lungs of oak**, **lungs of the oak** a tree lichen, *Lobaria pulmonaria*, formerly reputed to be of value in treating disorders of the lung. ***miner's lung***: see MINER.
– COMB.: **lung book** = ***book-lung*** s.v. BOOK *noun*; **lung-fever** pneumonia; **lung fluke** a parasitic trematode flatworm of the genus *Paragonimus*; **lung power** strength of voice; **lungworm** any of various nematode worms parasitic in the lungs of mammals, esp. of some farm and domestic animals. See also LUNGFISH.

■ **lungful** *noun* as much as will fill the lungs; *spec*. a quantity of inhaled cigarette smoke: M19. **lungless** *adjective* E17.

lunge /lʌn(d)ʒ/ *noun*[1]. Also **longe** /lʌn(d)ʒ, lɒn(d)ʒ/. E17.
[ORIGIN Old French & mod. French *longe* var. of Old French *loigne*: see LUNE *noun*[1].]
†**1** *gen*. A thong, a cord. Only in E17.
2 A long rope or rein used in training or exercising horses, by which a horse is held while being made to circle the trainer at a walk, trot, or canter. E18.
3 = ***lungeing-ring*** s.v. LUNGE *verb*[2]. M19.

lunge /lʌn(d)ʒ/ *noun*[2]. Also (now *rare* or *obsolete*) **lounge** /laʊn(d)ʒ/. M18.
[ORIGIN Aphet. from (the same root as) ALLONGE.]
1 A thrust with a sword (*spec*. in FENCING) or other weapon. M18.
2 A sudden forward movement; a plunge, a rush. M19.
3 An act of thrusting one foot forward with the knee bent while keeping the other foot fixed, as an exercise or gymnastic movement. L19.

lunge /lʌn(d)ʒ/ *noun*[3]. *N. Amer*. M19.
[ORIGIN Abbreviation of *muskellunge* var. of MASKINONGE.]
Either of two large N. American freshwater fishes, *Esox masquinongy*, a pike found in the Great Lakes, and (now *rare*) the N. American lake trout, *Salvelinus namaycush*.

lunge /lʌn(d)ʒ/ *verb*[1]. Also (now *rare* or *obsolete*) **lounge** /laʊn(d)ʒ/. M18.
[ORIGIN from LUNGE *noun*[2].]
1 *verb trans*. Deliver (a kick, a thrust) with a lunge. M18.
2 *verb intrans*. Make a lunge; FENCING make a thrust with a foil or rapier; BOXING deliver a blow from the shoulder. (Foll. by *at*.) E19.

> M. S. POWER Poppy Burn lunged to her feet and fled. J. FULLER A stallion tethered by each foot strained and lunged. *New York Times* He lunged at me, and I stabbed him.

3 *verb trans*. Drive or thrust (as) with a lunge. M19.

> F. T. BUCKLAND The scorpion instantly lunged his sting into him. R. B. PARKER I . . lunged the door inward.

lunge /lʌn(d)ʒ/ *verb*[2] *trans*. Also **longe** /lʌn(d)ʒ, lɒn(d)ʒ/. Pres. pple & verbal noun **-eing**. E19.
[ORIGIN from LUNGE *noun*[1].]
Train or exercise (a horse, occas. a rider) with a lunge or in a lungeing ring.
lungeing ring *adjective* a circular exercising ground in which a lunge is used.

lunged /lʌŋd/ *adjective*. L17.
[ORIGIN from LUNG + -ED[2].]
Having lungs, or something resembling lungs. Of a person usu. with prefixed adjective, as ***small-lunged***, ***weak-lunged***.

lungeous /ˈlʌn(d)ʒəs/ *adjective*. *dial*. L17.
[ORIGIN from LUNGE *noun*[2] or *verb*[1] + -OUS.]
†**1** Of a fall: heavy. Only in L17.
2 Of a person: rough-mannered, violent (in play). L18.

lunger /ˈlʌn(d)ʒə/ *noun*[1]. M19.
[ORIGIN from LUNGE *verb*[1] + -ER[1].]
A person who lunges.

lunger /ˈlʌŋə/ *noun*[2]. *arch*. *colloq*. L19.
[ORIGIN from LUNG + -ER[1].]
A person diseased or wounded in the lungs.

lungfish /ˈlʌŋfɪʃ/ *noun*. Pl. **-es** /-ɪz/, (usu.) same. L19.
[ORIGIN from LUNG *noun* + FISH *noun*[1].]
A fish able to breathe air using primitive lungs, a dipnoan; *esp*. any of the extant genera *Lepidosiren* of S. America, *Protopterus* of Africa, and *Neoceratodus* of Australia, having long thick bodies and filamentous fins, and living in shallow fresh water or swamps.
QUEENSLAND ***lungfish***.

lung-gom-pa /ˈlʊŋgompa/ *noun*. M20.
[ORIGIN Tibetan.]
A Tibetan monk able to walk many miles at great speed without stopping.

lungi /ˈlʊŋgiː/ *noun*. E17.
[ORIGIN Urdu *lungī*: cf. LANGOTI.]
In the Indian subcontinent: a cloth worn wound round the lower body with the end passed between the legs and tucked into the waist; cotton material of which such cloths are made. Also, a length of cotton cloth worn as a skirt in Myanmar (Burma), where it is part of the national dress of both sexes.

lungwort /ˈlʌŋwəːt/ *noun*. Also †**long-**. OE.
[ORIGIN from LUNG + WORT *noun*[1], from the reputed power of such plants to cure lung disorders.]
†**1** Any of a group of hawkweeds (*Hieracium murorum* and related forms) with leaves mostly in a basal rosette. In later use more fully ***French lungwort***, ***golden lungwort***. OE–L18.
†**2** White hellebore, *Veratrum album*; black hellebore, *Helleborus niger*. ME–E17.
3 Any of several spring-flowering plants of the genus *Pulmonaria*, of the borage family, with flowers of pink, blue, or white (often changing with age); *esp*. the common garden flower *P. officinalis*, with white spots on the leaves supposed to resemble the spots in a diseased lung. M16. ▸**b** With specifying word: any of various chiefly N. American plants of the allied genus *Mertensia*. L18.
b sea lungwort = ***oyster plant*** (a) s.v. OYSTER *noun*.
†**4** Great mullein, *Verbascum thapsus*. M16–E18.
†**5** = ANGELICA *noun*[1] 1. M16–M18.
6 A lichen, *Lobaria pulmonaria*, which grows on trees; = ***lungs of oak***, ***lungs of the oak*** s.v. LUNG. L16.

lungy /ˈlʌŋi/ *adjective*. *colloq*. L19.
[ORIGIN from LUNG + -Y[1].]
1 Affected with a disease of the lungs. L19.
2 Coming from the lungs. E20.

lunisolar /luːnɪˈsəʊlə/ *adjective*. L17.
[ORIGIN from Latin LUNA moon + -I- + SOLAR *adjective*[1].]
ASTRONOMY. Of or pertaining to the mutual relations of the sun and moon; resulting from the combined action of the sun and moon.
lunisolar period a cycle of 532 years, containing a whole number of both lunar cycles and solar cycles. ***lunisolar precession***: see PRECESSION 2a. **lunisolar year**: with divisions regulated by phases of the moon and an average length made to agree with the solar year.

lunitidal /luːnɪˈtʌɪd(ə)l/ *adjective*. M19.
[ORIGIN from Latin LUNA moon + -I- + TIDAL.]
Designating the interval between the time when the moon crosses a given meridian and the time of the following high tide at that meridian.

lunk /lʌŋk/ *noun*. *colloq*. (orig. *US*). M19.
[ORIGIN Abbreviation.]
= LUNKHEAD.

lunker /ˈlʌŋkə/ *noun*. *N. Amer*. *colloq*. E20.
[ORIGIN Unknown.]
An animal, esp. a fish, which is an exceptionally large example of its species.

lunkhead /ˈlʌŋkhɛd/ *noun*. *colloq*. (orig. *US*). M19.
[ORIGIN Prob. from alt. of LUMP *noun*[1] + HEAD *noun*.]
A slow-witted unintelligent person, a blockhead.
■ **lunkheaded** *adjective* L19.

lunt /lʌnt/ *noun & verb*. *Scot*. E16.
[ORIGIN Dutch *lont* match.]
▸ **A** *noun*. **1** A slow-burning match; a torch. E16.
2 Smoke (with flame), *esp*. the smoke from a pipe. Also, hot vapour. L18.
▸ **B** *verb*. **1** *verb intrans*. Smoke, emit smoke; blaze, glow; (of smoke) rise in wreaths, curl. L18.
2 *verb trans*. Kindle, light *up*; smoke (a pipe). E19.

lunula /ˈluːnjʊlə/ *noun*. Pl. **-lae** /-liː/. L16.
[ORIGIN Latin, dim. of LUNA moon: see -ULE.]
1 GEOMETRY. = LUNE *noun*[3] 1. L16.
2 ARCHAEOLOGY. A gold crescent-shaped neck ornament of the early Bronze Age. E18.
3 ANATOMY, ZOOLOGY, & BOTANY = LUNULE 3. E19. ▸**b** ANATOMY. A crescent-shaped region of thin tissue on each side of the nodule on each cusp of a valve in the heart or aorta. M19.
4 CONCHOLOGY. = LUNULE 4. M19.

lunular /ˈluːnjʊlə/ *noun & adjective*. L16.
[ORIGIN from LUNULA + -AR[1].]
GEOMETRY. ▸†**A** *noun*. A crescent-shaped figure. L16–L18.
▸ **B** *adjective*. Of or pertaining to a lunule; of the form of a lunule, crescent-shaped. E18.

lunulate /ˈluːnjʊleɪt/ *adjective*. M18.
[ORIGIN mod. Latin *lunulatus*, formed as LUNULA: see -ATE[2].]
ZOOLOGY & BOTANY. **1** Crescent-shaped. M18.
2 Having crescent-shaped markings. M19.

lunulated /ˈluːnjʊleɪtɪd/ *adjective*. E18.
[ORIGIN formed as LUNULATE + -ED[1].]
†**1** = LUNULATE 1. Only in 18.
2 = LUNULATE 2. L18.

lunule /ˈluːnjuːl/ *noun*. L16.
[ORIGIN formed as LUNULA: see -ULE.]
†**1** A mark shaped like a half moon. Only in L16.
2 GEOMETRY. = LUNE *noun*[3] 1. M18.
3 ANATOMY, ZOOLOGY, & BOTANY. A crescent-shaped mark, spot, etc.; *spec*. the pale area at the base of a fingernail. Cf. LUNULA 3. E19.
4 CONCHOLOGY. The crescent-shaped depression in front of the umbo of a shell; = LUNULA 4. E19.

lunulet /ˈluːnjʊlɪt/ *noun*. E19.
[ORIGIN from (the same root as) LUNULE + -ET[1].]
ZOOLOGY & BOTANY. A small crescent-shaped mark.

luny *adjective & noun* see LOONY *adjective & noun*[2].

Luo /ˈluːəʊ/ *noun & adjective*. E20.
[ORIGIN Luo.]
▸ **A** *noun*. Pl. same, **-s**.
1 A member of an E. African people of Kenya and the upper Nile valley. E20.
2 The Nilotic language of this people. M20.
▸ **B** *attrib*. or as *adjective*. Of or pertaining to the Luo or their language. M20.

lupanar /luːˈpeɪnə/ *noun*. *literary*. M19.
[ORIGIN Latin, from *lupa* prostitute, she-wolf, fem. of *lupus* wolf.]
A brothel.

L

lupara /lu'pa:ra, lu:'pɑ:rə/ *noun*. M20.
[ORIGIN Italian (slang), from *lupa* she-wolf.]
A sawn-off shotgun as used by the Mafia.

Lupercal /'lu:pəkal/ *noun*. Pl. **Lupercalia** /lu:pə'keɪlɪə/, **Lupercals**. L16.
[ORIGIN Latin, noun form of *lupercale* neut. of *lupercalis* pertaining to Lupercus (see below).]
†**1** An orgy. Only in L16.
2 ROMAN HISTORY. *sing.* & in *pl.* A festival held annually in February in honour of Lupercus, the Roman equivalent of the Greek god Pan. E17.
■ **Lupercalian** /lu:pə'keɪlɪən/ *adjective* of or pertaining to the Lupercalia L19.

lupin /'lu:pɪn/ *noun*. Also **lupine**. LME.
[ORIGIN Latin *lupinus*, *lupinum*.]
1 Any of various leguminous plants of the genus *Lupinus*, with palmate leaves and showy flowers in long terminal racemes; a flowering stem of such a plant. In early use, *esp.* the Mediterranean *Lupinus albus*, cultivated for its seed and for fodder; now usu., any of the ornamental kinds, with flowers in many colours, mainly derivatives and hybrids of the N. American *L. polyphyllus* and *L. arboreus*. LME.
Nootka lupin: see NOOTKA *adjective* 1. RUSSELL LUPIN. ***tree lupin***: see TREE *noun*.
2 In *pl.* The seeds of this plant. LME.

lupine *noun* var. of LUPIN.

lupine /'lu:pʌɪn/ *adjective*. M17.
[ORIGIN Latin *lupinus*, from *lupus* wolf: see -INE[1].]
Having the nature or qualities of a wolf.

lupinosis /lu:pɪ'nəʊsɪs/ *noun*. Pl. **-oses** /-əʊsi:z/. L19.
[ORIGIN from LUPIN + -OSIS.]
Poisoning of animals, esp. sheep, after ingestion of lupins, usu. caused by toxins produced by a fungus of the genus *Phomopsis* growing on the plants.

lupoid /'lu:pɔɪd/ *adjective*. M19.
[ORIGIN from LUPUS + -OID.]
MEDICINE. = LUPOUS 2.

lupous /'lu:pəs/ *adjective*[1]. M19.
[ORIGIN from (the same root as) LUPUS + -OUS.]
1 = LUPINE *adjective*. *rare*. M19.
2 MEDICINE. Pertaining to or resembling lupus. L19.

L

lupulin /'lu:pjʊlɪn/ *noun*. E19.
[ORIGIN from mod. Latin use as specific epithet (see below) of Latin *lupulus* a plant mentioned by Pliny (perh. wild hops): see -IN[1].]
A fine yellowish powder found under the scales of the calyx of the hop, *Humulus lupulus*; the bitter principle contained in this.
■ **lupu'linic** *adjective* M19.

lupulone /'lu:pjʊləʊn/ *noun*. Also **-on** /-ɒn/. E20.
[ORIGIN formed as LUPULIN + -ONE.]
CHEMISTRY. A crystalline cyclic ketone, $C_{26}H_{38}O_4$, that is one of the bitter-tasting constituents of hops and has strong antibiotic activity. Cf. HUMULONE.

lupus /'lu:pəs/ *noun*. In sense 3 **L-**. L16.
[ORIGIN Latin = wolf.]
†**1** A wolf. Only in L16.
2 Any of various ulcerous or erosive diseases of the skin; now *esp.* lupus vulgaris and lupus erythematosus (see below). Also called ***noli me tangere***. L16.
lupus erythematosus /ˌɛrɪθi:mə'təʊsəs/ [mod. Latin, from Greek *eruthēma*: see ERYTHEMA] an inflammatory disease of the skin giving rise to scaly red patches, esp. on the face, and sometimes (***systemic lupus erythematosus***) also involving internal organs. **lupus vulgaris** /vʌl'gɑ:rɪs/ [Latin = common] a chronic tuberculous disease of the skin giving rise to brownish nodules.
3 (The name of) a constellation of the southern hemisphere, lying partly in the Milky Way between Scorpius and Centaurus; the Wolf. L17.
4 The pike (fish). E18.

lur /lʊə/ *noun*[1]. Pl. **lurer** /'lʊərə/, **lurs**. L19.
[ORIGIN Danish, Norwegian, & Swedish. Cf. LURE *noun*[2].]
A Bronze Age musical instrument of the horn family found in Scandinavia.

Lur /lʊə/ *noun*[2]. M19.
[ORIGIN Prob. from Iranian.]
A member of an aboriginal people inhabiting Luristan in western Iran.

lurch /lə:tʃ/ *noun*[1]. M16.
[ORIGIN App. from French †*lourche* (also *l'ourche*) a game resembling backgammon, also in *demeurer lourche* be discomfited (originally in the game), prob. from Middle High German *lurz* (mod. dial. *lurtsch*) left (hand), wrong. Cf. earlier LURCH *verb*[1].]
†**1** A cheat, a swindle. M16–E17.
2 A state of discomfiture. Long *obsolete* exc. in ***leave in the lurch***, leave (a person) in adverse circumstances without assistance or in a position of unexpected difficulty. M16.

R. BROWNING He has left his sweetheart here in the lurch.

3 In various games, a concluding state of the score in which one player is greatly ahead of the other; a game or set of games in which the loser scores nothing; at cribbage, a game in which the winner scores 61 before the loser has scored 31 or 121 before the loser has scored 91; in whist, a treble. Now *rare* or *obsolete*. L16.
†**4** A game resembling backgammon. Only in 17.

lurch /lə:tʃ/ *noun*[2]. Now *rare* or *obsolete*. M16.
[ORIGIN from LURCH *verb*[2].]
†**1** An opportunity for eating more than others. Only in M16.
2 A state of concealment. Only in ***lie at lurch***, ***lie on the lurch***, lie concealed, lie in wait (*lit.* & *fig.*). L16.

lurch /lə:tʃ/ *noun*[3]. Orig. NAUTICAL. Also (earlier) †**larch**, †**latch**. L17.
[ORIGIN Unknown.]
1 A ship's sudden leaning over to one side; *gen.* a sudden unsteady movement or lean to one side, a stagger; a staggering gait. L17.

M. SCAMMELL Every lurch .. sent a spasm of agonizing pain coursing through his body. K. WATERHOUSE A lurch of panic as he realises he may be about to hear her voice.

2 A propensity, a penchant, a leaning. *US*. L18.
– NOTE: Rare, and only in *la-* forms, before 19.

lurch /lə:tʃ/ *verb*[1] *trans*. ME.
[ORIGIN Rel. to LURCH *noun*[1].]
1 Beat in a game of skill, sometimes by a specified number or proportion of points. (Cf. LURCH *noun*[1] 3.) ME. ▸**b** *fig.* Defeat. Now *rare* or *obsolete*. E18.
2 Leave in the lurch, disappoint, deceive. Now *rare* or *obsolete*. M17.
– NOTE: In isolated use before 17.

lurch /lə:tʃ/ *verb*[2]. LME.
[ORIGIN Perh. var. of LURK *verb*, infl. in meaning by LURCH *noun*[1].]
†**1** *verb intrans.* Remain in or about a place furtively or secretly, esp. with evil intent. Also, avoid company, sulk. LME–L18. ▸**b** Of a dog, esp. a greyhound: run from the line, not pursue a quarry energetically. Chiefly as ***lurching*** *verbal noun*. Only in 19.
2 *verb trans.* Orig., start before and prevent (a person) from obtaining a fair share of food, profit, etc. Later, defraud, cheat, rob. *arch.* M16.
†**3** *verb trans.* Secure (something) beforehand; engross, monopolize (a commodity). Also, get hold of by stealth, pilfer, steal. M16–M17. ▸†**b** *verb intrans.* Get hold of something by stealth; pilfer, steal. L16–M17.
4 *verb trans.* Pursue (rabbits etc.) with a lurcher. E18.

lurch /lə:tʃ/ *verb*[3] *intrans*. Orig. NAUTICAL. M19.
[ORIGIN from LURCH *noun*[3].]
Make a lurch; lean suddenly over to one side; progress lurchingly; move suddenly, unsteadily, and without purpose; stagger.

D. H. LAWRENCE The car lurched and bumped in the great gaps. A. MACLEAN Halliday was .. lurching unsteadily in my direction, bottle in one hand and glass in the other. P. L. FERMOR In the fickle fashion of the very drunk, they lurched away into the night. J. FULLER The boat lurched dangerously in the rocky inlet.

■ **lurchingly** *adverb* in a lurching manner M19.

lurcher /'lə:tʃə/ *noun*. E16.
[ORIGIN from LURCH *verb*[2] + -ER[1].]
1 A petty thief, a swindler. *arch.* E16.
†**2** A person who starts before and prevents another from obtaining a fair share, esp. of food; a glutton. M16–E17.
3 A crossbred dog, esp. the offspring of a greyhound and a collie or retriever, used esp. by poachers for pursuing hares and rabbits. M17.
4 A person who loiters or lies hidden in a suspicious manner; a spy. E18.
5 = BUM *noun*[1] 3. *slang*. *obsolete* exc. *hist.* L18.

lurdan /'lə:d(ə)n/ *noun* & *adjective*. *arch.* ME.
[ORIGIN Old French *lourdin*, from *lourd* heavy, *lort* foolish from Latin *luridus* LURID.]
▸ **A** *noun*. A dull, incapable, or idle person; a vagrant, an idler. ME.
▸ **B** *adjective*. Worthless, ill-bred, lazy. LME.

lure /lʊə, ljʊə/ *noun*[1]. ME.
[ORIGIN Old French *luere* (mod. *leurre*), from Germanic, prob. rel. to Middle High German *luoder*, German *Luder* bait.]
1 A falconer's apparatus for recalling a hawk, consisting of a bunch of feathers attached to a long cord or thong, within which the hawk finds its food while being trained. ME.

B. HINES Billy .. began to swing the lure. The hawk turned and stooped at it.

2 A thing which allures, entices, or tempts; the enticing quality *of* a pursuit etc. LME.

C. MCCULLOUGH The sound of his piper drawing him into battle was the sweetest lure in the world. D. LEAVITT There was the lure of the unknown, the unknowable.

3 **a** A trap, a snare. Chiefly *fig.* LME. ▸**b** A means of enticing fish or animals to be caught; a decoy. L17.

a DISRAELI The colonel fell into the lure only through his carelessness. **b** *National Observer* (US) I have fished with a good many lures.

4 HERALDRY. **a** A charge representing a hawk's lure, consisting of two birds' wings with the points directed downwards, and joined above by a ring attached to a cord. L16. ▸**b** *in lure*, (of wings) with the points downwards and joined at the top. E17.
5 The cry of a falconer recalling a hawk; *fig.* an alluring cry. M17.

lure /lʊə/ *noun*[2]. M19.
[ORIGIN Danish & Norwegian *lur*, Old Norse *lúr*. Cf. LUR *noun*[1].]
A long curved trumpet, used for calling cattle. Also called ***velour***.

lure /lʊə, ljʊə/ *verb*. LME.
[ORIGIN from LURE *noun*[1].]
1 *verb trans.* Recall (a hawk) by casting the lure; call (a hawk) to the lure. LME.
2 *verb trans.* Allure, entice, tempt. Also foll. by *out of*, *away from*, etc. LME.

S. BELLOW It was a mistake to be drawn or lured out of his taciturnity. C. SANDBURG Painted women under the gas lamp luring the farm boys.

†**3** *verb trans.* Train (a hawk) to come to the lure. Now *rare*. L15–L16.
4 *verb intrans.* Call to a hawk while casting the lure. Now *rare*. M16. ▸†**b** Call loudly (*at*). Only in 17.
†**5** *verb intrans.* Set a trap (*for*); entrap. L16–E18.
■ **luringly** *adverb* in a luring or enticing manner L19.

lurement /'lʊəm(ə)nt, 'ljʊə-/ *noun*. *rare*. L16.
[ORIGIN from LURE *verb* + -MENT.]
(An) allurement.

lurer *noun pl.* see LUR *noun*[1].

Lurex /'ljʊərɛks/ *noun*. Also **l-**. M20.
[ORIGIN Unknown.]
(Proprietary name for) a type of yarn which incorporates a metallic thread; fabric made from this yarn.

Lurgi /'lʊəgi, 'lə:gi/ *noun*. M20.
[ORIGIN from the *Lurgi* Gesellschaft für Wärmetechnik m.b.H., of Frankfurt, Germany.]
Used ***attrib.*** to designate a method of gasification suitable for low-grade coal such as lignite by reaction with steam and oxygen at high pressure.
Lurgi gas, ***Lurgi plant***, ***Lurgi process***.

lurgy /'lə:gi/ *noun*. *joc.* M20.
[ORIGIN Unknown.]
A (non-existent) highly infectious disease frequently referred to in the radio comedy series the Goon Show (see GOON *noun* 5); an unspecified minor illness. Chiefly in ***the dreaded lurgy***.

H. MACINNES I had caught the dreaded swamp lurgy.

lurid /'lʊərɪd, 'ljʊə-/ *adjective*. M17.
[ORIGIN Latin *luridus*, from base also of *luror* wan or yellow colour: see -ID[1].]
1 Pale and dismal in colour; wan and sallow; of a ghastly hue. M17.

J. A. SYMONDS A leaden glare .. makes the snow and ice more lurid.

2 Shining with a red glow or glare amid darkness. Also, vivid or glowing in colour. E18. ▸**b** *hyperbol.* Having an unnatural glare. M18.

T. WILLIAMS The kitchen now suggests that sort of lurid nocturnal brilliance. I. MCEWAN The first course was in place, each melon slice with its lurid cherry. **b** DISRAELI The lurid glare of the anaconda's eye.

3 BOTANY & ZOOLOGY. Yellowish- or dingy brown. Now *rare*. M18.
4 *fig.* Ominous; sensational, horrifying; showy, gaudy. M19.

M. ANGELOU The lurid tales we read. E. SAINTSBURY Macdonald paints a picture of poverty .. equalled only by Dickens in its lurid detail.

■ **luridly** *adverb* L18. **luridness** *noun* M18.

lurk /lə:k/ *noun*. Now chiefly *slang*. E19.
[ORIGIN from LURK *verb*.]
1 The action of prowling about. Chiefly in ***on the lurk***. *rare*. E19.
2 **a** A method of fraud. M19. ▸**b** A scheme, a dodge; a plan of action, a racket; a method of profitable business. Chiefly *Austral.* & *NZ*. L19. ▸**c** A job. *Austral.* & *NZ*. E20.
3 An idle person, a loafer. *dial.* M19.
4 A hiding place; a place frequented by a particular person or class of people. E20.

lurk /lə:k/ *verb intrans*. ME.
[ORIGIN Perh. from LOUR *verb* + frequentative suffix *-k* as in *talk*. Cf. Low German *lurken* shuffle along, Norwegian *lurka* sneak away.]
1 Be hidden; lie in ambush; conceal oneself, esp. furtively, *in*, *under*, *about*, etc. Formerly also, live in concealment or retirement. ME. ▸†**b** Shirk work; idle. M16–L18.

A. UTTLEY Something was behind the oak tree, hidden, lurking. A. SILLITOE Scorpions lurk under loose stones.

2 Move about secretively and furtively; steal *along*, *away*, *out*. Now *rare*. ME.

THACKERAY The main thoroughfare .. up which John lurks to bed.

3 Escape notice, exist unobserved, be latent. LME.

R. BURNS Where the bluebell and gowan lurk lowly unseen. G. CLARE Behind the imposing façade of former imperial splendour lurked defeat, poverty and fear.

†**4** Peer furtively or slyly. LME–E16.
5 Defeat in a game of chance. Chiefly as ***lurked*** *ppl adjective. slang.* E20.

C. MORGAN Four straight aces. Good enough? You're lurked, Sandford.

6 COMPUTING. Subscribe to an online forum (e.g. a bulletin board or mailing list) and read the postings of other members without oneself contributing any messages. L20.
■ **lurking** *adjective* that lurks; concealed, latent, semi-conscious: LME. **lurkingly** *adverb* M16. **lurky** *adjective* (*rare*) tending to lurk L19.

lurker /ˈləːkə/ *noun*[1]. ME.
[ORIGIN from LURK *verb* + -ER[1].]
1 A person who lurks. ME.
2 A begging impostor; a petty thief. *slang.* M19.

lurker /ˈləːkə/ *noun*[2]. E19.
[ORIGIN Unknown.]
One of a group of three boats used in pilchard-fishing, from which the fishing operation is directed.

lurry /ˈlʌri/ *noun. obsolete* exc. *dial.* L16.
[ORIGIN Alt. of LIRIPIPE.]
1 Something said by rote; a lesson, a set speech, patter. L16.
2 A confused assemblage or mass. E17.
3 A confusion of voices; a babel, a hubbub, an outcry. M17.

lurve /ləːv/ *noun. colloq.* Also **lerve**. M20.
[ORIGIN Alt. of LOVE *noun*, repr. pronunc. of *love* in popular romantic songs.]
Love; romantic infatuation; sexual attraction.

attrib.: V. WALTERS Girl's got the lurve fever.

Lusatian /luːˈseɪʃ(ə)n/ *noun & adjective.* M16.
[ORIGIN from medieval Latin *Lusatia* (see below) + -AN.]
▸ **A** *noun.* **1** A native or inhabitant of Lusatia, an area of eastern Germany between the Elbe and the Oder; *esp.* a Sorb. M16.
2 The West Slavonic language of Lusatia, Sorbian. L19.
▸ **B** *adjective.* Of or pertaining to Lusatia or its inhabitants or language, Sorbian. M19.

luscious /ˈlʌʃəs/ *adjective & noun.* LME.
[ORIGIN Perh. alt. of shortened form of DELICIOUS. Cf. also LUSH *adjective.*]
1 Richly sweet in taste or smell; *colloq.* delicious. LME.

A. G. GARDINER Pears that.. melted rich and luscious in the mouth. JULIETTE HUXLEY Fellows comfortably digested their luscious meal.

2 Excessively sweet, cloying, sickly; (esp. of language or literary style) overrich in sound, imagery, or voluptuous suggestion. M16.

T. BIRCH A luscious Style stuffed with gawdy Metaphors and Fancy. HAZLITT A stream of luscious panegyrics. M. DONOVAN Without the addition of water.. the resulting wine would be luscious and heavy.

3 Orig., appealing to a lascivious taste, salacious, voluptuous. Later, voluptuously attractive, sexually desirable. E17.

POPE Cantharides.. Whose use old Bards describe in luscious rhymes. E. PIZZEY A mole.. highlighted her luscious mouth.

■ **lusciously** *adverb* M16. **lusciousness** *noun* L16.

†**lush** *noun*[1]. *rare.* LME–L19.
[ORIGIN from LUSH *verb*[1].]
A stroke, a blow.

lush /lʌʃ/ *noun*[2]. *slang.* L18.
[ORIGIN Uncertain: perh. joc. from LUSH *adjective.*]
1 Liquor, alcoholic drink. L18.

N. MAILER Stoned with lush, with pot.

2 A drinking bout. M19.
3 A drunkard; *N. Amer.* an alcoholic. L19.

R. JAFFE For him to make her mother stay dry he first had to admit she was a lush.

– COMB.: **lushbum** a drunkard; **lush drum** a disreputable bar or pub; **lush-head** a drunkard, an alcoholic.

lush /lʌʃ/ *adjective.* LME.
[ORIGIN Perh. alt. of LASH *adjective* by assoc. with LUSCIOUS.]
1 Lax, flaccid; soft, tender. *obsolete* exc. *dial.* LME.

T. BLUNDEVILLE The flesh of.. all his bodie is lush and feeble.

2 Of vegetation, esp. grass: succulent and luxuriant. E17. ▸**b** Characterized by luxuriance of vegetation. E19. ▸**c** Luxurious; (of a woman) voluptuously attractive. M19.

SHELLEY In the warm hedge grew lush eglantine. E. HEMINGWAY The grass was lush underfoot. **b** LYTTON Hedges.. all lush with convolvulus and honeysuckle. **c** T. HARDY The aesthetic, sensuous, pagan pleasure in natural life and lush womanhood. D. LESSING The former hotel dining room, lush to the point of lubricity.

3 Of a colour: deep and rich. M18.
4 Very pleasing or good. *slang.* L20.

www.fictionpress.com Where did you get your skirt from? It's lush.

■ **lushly** *adverb* LME. **lushness** *noun* E20.

lush /lʌʃ/ *verb*[1]. *obsolete* exc. *dial.* ME.
[ORIGIN Perh. var. of LASH *verb*[1].]
1 *verb intrans.* Rush, dash; come *down* with a rush. ME.
2 Strike. ME.

lush /lʌʃ/ *verb*[2]. *slang.* E19.
[ORIGIN from LUSH *noun*[2].]
1 *verb trans.* Ply with alcoholic liquor. E19.
2 a *verb intrans. & trans.* (with *it*). Drink alcoholic liquor. E19. ▸**b** *verb trans.* Drink (alcoholic liquor). M19.
3 Foll. by *up*: **a** *verb intrans.* Get drunk. E20. ▸**b** *verb trans.* Ply with drink, make (a person) drunk. E20. ▸**c** *verb trans.* Provide with a luxurious standard of living. E20.
■ **lusher** *noun* an excessively self-indulgent person, *esp.* one who drinks to excess L19.

Lushai /ˈluːʃʌɪ/ *noun & adjective.* M19.
[ORIGIN Lushai.]
▸ **A** *noun.* Pl. same, **-s**.
1 A member of a group of Mizo people (of Mizoram in NE India). M19.
2 The Tibeto-Burman language of this group, the lingua franca of the Mizo. L19.
▸ **B** *adjective.* Of or pertaining to the Lushai or their language. M19.

lushburg /ˈlʌʃbəːg/ *noun.* Long *obsolete* exc. *hist.* ME.
[ORIGIN Alt. of *Luxembourg*: see LUXEMBOURGER.]
A base coin made in imitation of the sterling or silver penny and imported from Luxembourg in the reign of Edward III.

Lushington /ˈlʌʃɪŋt(ə)n/ *noun. arch. slang.* E19.
[ORIGIN The 'City of *Lushington*', a convivial society which met at the Harp Tavern, Russell Street, London, prob. with punning allus. to LUSH *noun*[2].]
Drunkenness. Also, a drunkard.

lushy /ˈlʌʃi/ *adjective*[1] *& noun. slang.* E19.
[ORIGIN from LUSH *noun*[2] + -Y[1], -Y[6].]
▸ **A** *adjective.* Intoxicated, drunk. E19.
▸ **B** *noun.* A drunkard, an alcoholic. M20.

lushy /ˈlʌʃi/ *adjective*[2]. *rare.* E19.
[ORIGIN from LUSH *adjective* + -Y[1].]
1 = LUSH *adjective* 3. E19.
2 = LUSCIOUS *adjective.* L19.

Lusian /ˈluːsɪən/ *adjective & noun. poet.* L18.
[ORIGIN Latin *Lusi-* in *Lusitania* (see LUSITANIAN) etc. + -AN.]
= LUSITANIAN.

Lusitanian /luːsɪˈteɪnɪən/ *adjective & noun.* L16.
[ORIGIN from Latin *Lusitania* (see below) + -AN.]
▸ **A** *adjective.* **1** Of or pertaining to Lusitania, an ancient province of Hispania, mainly corresponding to modern Portugal; (chiefly *poet.*) of or pertaining to Portugal. L16.
2 BOTANY & ZOOLOGY. Of, pertaining to, or designating a part of the flora and fauna of the British Isles found particularly also in SW Europe, esp. Portugal. E20.
▸ **B** *noun.* A native or inhabitant of Lusitania or (chiefly *poet.*) Portugal. E17.

lusk /lʌsk/ *adjective. obsolete* exc. *dial.* L18.
[ORIGIN from LUSK *verb & noun.*]
Lazy, sluggish.

†**lusk** *verb & noun.* ME.
[ORIGIN Unknown.]
▸ **A** *verb intrans.* Lie hidden; lie idly or at ease; skulk. ME–M17.
▸ **B** *noun.* An idle or lazy person, a sluggard. LME–L17.

†**luskish** *adjective.* E16–E19.
[ORIGIN from LUSK *noun* + -ISH[1].]
Slothful, lazy, sluggish.
■ †**luskishly** *adverb* M16–M17. †**luskishness** *noun* M16–M17.

lusky /ˈlʌski/ *adjective.* Long *obsolete* exc. *dial.* E17.
[ORIGIN from LUSK *noun* + -Y[1].]
Lazy, sluggish.

Luso- /ˈluːsəʊ/ *combining form.*
[ORIGIN from *Lusitania*: see LUSITANIAN, -O-.]
Forming adjectives and nouns with the senses 'of Lusitania or Portugal', 'Lusitanian or Portuguese and —', as ***Luso-Brazilian***, ***Luso-Hispanic***, etc.

lusophone /ˈluːsəfəʊn/ *adjective.* L20.
[ORIGIN from LUSO- + -PHONE.]
Portuguese-speaking.

lusory /ˈluːs(ə)ri/ *adjective.* Now *rare.* M17.
[ORIGIN Latin *lusorius* belonging to a player, from *lusor* player, from *lus-* pa. ppl stem of *ludere* play: see -ORY[2].]
Used as a pastime; playful, sportive; (of a composition) written in a playful style.

lust /lʌst/ *noun.*
[ORIGIN Old English *lust* corresp. to Old Frisian, Old High German, German *lust*, Old Norse *losti*, Gothic *lustus*, from Germanic base repr. also by LIST *verb*[1].]
†**1** Pleasure, delight (also foll. by *in, to, unto*). Also (*poet.*) a source of pleasure or delight. OE–E17. ▸**b** In *pl.* Pleasures. OE–LME. ▸**c** Liking towards a person. Foll. by *to.* LME–M16.
†**2** Desire, appetite, inclination; an instance of this. Foll. by *of, to, to do. obsolete* exc. as passing into sense 6. OE.

W. SCLATER I have neither lust nor leasure to enter the question.

3 A sensuous appetite or desire considered as sinful or leading to sin. Usu. in *pl.* OE.

R. NIEBUHR Man's lusts are fed by his imagination.

4 Strong (esp. uncontrollable) sexual appetite or desire. OE.

C. S. FORESTER He was hot with desire, dizzy with lust. S. KITZINGER So intensely sexual, that, driven by lust, they ravaged men's bodies and souls. R. CHRISTIANSEN Hogg had taken the noble principle of free love as an excuse to indulge mere lust.

†**5** Vigour, life. ME–L17.
6 A passionate desire *for, to do*; a passionate enjoyment *of.* L17.

H. J. LASKI The lust of power sets man against his neighbour to the profit of the rich. A. J. TOYNBEE The lust for taking human life had become obsessive—indeed, maniacal. J. WAIN They punched, elbowed, kicked and tore each other with a real lust to hurt.

lust /lʌst/ *verb.* ME.
[ORIGIN from the noun.]
†**1** *verb trans.* Please, delight. ME–M16.
†**2** *verb intrans.* Desire, choose, wish, (*to do*). LME–E17.
3 *verb intrans.* Have a strong or excessive (*spec.* sexual) desire, feel lust. Foll. by *after, for.* E16.

M. S. POWER I've seen them lusting for blood once they start hunting. P. D. JAMES He had a wife he lusted after but didn't love.

luster /ˈlʌstə/ *noun*[1]. Now *rare.* L16.
[ORIGIN from LUST *verb* + -ER[1].]
A person who lusts.

luster *noun*[2], *noun*[3], *verb* see LUSTRE *noun*[1], *noun*[2], *verb.*

lustered *adjective* see LUSTRED.

lustering *noun* see LUSTRING *noun*[2].

lustful /ˈlʌstfʊl, -f(ə)l/ *adjective.* OE.
[ORIGIN from LUST *noun* + -FUL.]
1 Having a strong or excessive desire; eagerly or inordinately desirous *of, to do. arch.* OE.
†**2** Delightful, pleasurable. Only in ME.
3 Vigorous, lively. *arch.* M16.
4 Full of or characterized by lust; pertaining to or manifesting lust. L16.

DENNIS POTTER Arthur was indeed a lustful psychotic,.. perpetually hard in the loins.

■ **lustfully** *adverb* OE. **lustfulness** *noun* OE.

lust-house /ˈlʌsthaʊs/ *noun.* Now *rare.* L16.
[ORIGIN Dutch *lusthuis*, German *Lusthaus*, from *Lust* pleasure + *Haus* HOUSE *noun*[1].]
A German or Dutch country house.

†**lustick** *adjective & adverb.* Also **-ig**. E17.
[ORIGIN Dutch *lustig.*]
▸ **A** *adjective.* Merry. E–M17.
▸ **B** *adverb.* Merrily. Only in 17.

lustihead /ˈlʌstɪhɛd/ *noun. arch.* LME.
[ORIGIN from LUSTY + -HEAD[1].]
= LUSTINESS.

lustihood /ˈlʌstɪhʊd/ *noun. arch.* L16.
[ORIGIN from LUSTY + -HOOD.]
Lustiness, vigour.

lustily /ˈlʌstɪli/ *adverb.* ME.
[ORIGIN from LUSTY + -LY[2].]
†**1** With pleasure or delight. ME–M16.
2 With vigour or energy; heartily. ME.

J. B. MORTON The twelve dwarfs cheered lustily, waving their nondescript hats in the air. B. REID I learned to sing.. lustily enough for both of us, because he was too shy.

†**3** With lust or sexual desire; carnally. LME–L16.

lustiness /ˈlʌstɪnɪs/ *noun.* ME.
[ORIGIN from LUSTY + -NESS.]
1 Vigour; liveliness. ME.
†**2** Pleasure, delight. LME–M16.
†**3** Sexual desire, lustfulness. LME–E17.

lustless /ˈlʌs(t)lɪs/ *adjective.* ME.
[ORIGIN from LUST *noun* + -LESS.]
†**1** Without vigour or energy. ME–E17.
†**2** Without pleasure or delight. Only in 16.
3 Without lust or sexual desire. Now chiefly *joc.* L16.

lustly /ˈlʌstli/ *adjective.* Now *rare* or *obsolete.* ME.
[ORIGIN from LUST *noun* + -LY[1].]
1 Pleasant, delightful. ME.
†**2** Lustful; carnal. ME–E17.

lustra *noun pl.* see LUSTRUM.

lustral /ˈlʌstr(ə)l/ *adjective.* M16.
[ORIGIN Latin *lustralis*, formed as LUSTRUM + -AL[1].]
1 Pertaining to, of the nature of, or used in purification rites; purificatory. M16.
2 Occurring every five years; quinquennial. L18.

L

lustrate /ˈlʌstreɪt/ *verb*. **E17.**
[**ORIGIN** Latin *lustrat-* pa. ppl stem of *lustrare* purify by lustral rites, go round, etc., formed as **LUSTRUM**: see **-ATE**³.]
†**1** *verb trans.* View, survey. **E–M17.**
†**2** *verb intrans. & trans.* Pass or go *through* or through (a place). **M17–E18.**
3 *verb trans.* Purify by expiatory sacrifice, ceremonial washing, or other religious rite. **M17.**
■ **lustrative** *adjective* of or pertaining to ritual purification **L19.** **lustratory** /ˈlʌstrət(ə)ri/ *adjective* (*rare*) lustral, expiatory **M18.**

lustration /lʌˈstreɪʃ(ə)n/ *noun*. **E17.**
[**ORIGIN** Latin *lustratio(n-)*, formed as **LUSTRATE**: see **-ATION**.]
1 The action or an act of lustrating something or someone. **E17.** ▸**b** *fig.* Spiritual or moral purification. **M17.** ▸**c** *gen.* Washing. Chiefly *joc.* **E19.**
2 The action or an act of viewing or surveying a place, an army, etc. **E17.**

lustre /ˈlʌstə/ *noun*¹. Also ***luster**. **E16.**
[**ORIGIN** French from Italian *lustro*, from *lustrare* from Latin = illuminate, from **LUSTRUM**.]
1 The quality or condition of shining by reflected light; a sheen, a gloss. Also occas., a glint. Freq. with qualifying adjective. **E16.** ▸**b** A substance used to impart a sheen or gloss to an object. **E18.** ▸**c** An iridescent metallic decorative surface on ceramics; the glaze used to produce this; *gen.* any shining or reflective finish (as on a photograph etc.). **E19.** ▸**d** In full *lustreware*. Pottery or porcelain with an iridescent metallic glaze. **E19.**

> C. DARWIN A coating of a hard glossy substance with a pearly lustre. W. H. G. KINGSTON The wool appeared very long, soft, fine, and of a silky lustre. N. FREELING Even the gilt picture frames had lost all their lustre.

c moonlight lustre: see **MOONLIGHT** *noun & adjective*. **VITREOUS** *lustre*.
2 Luminosity, brilliance, bright light. **M16.** ▸**b** A shining object. **M18.**

> DICKENS The sun was shining with uncommon lustre.

3 *fig.* Brilliance, splendour, glory, distinction, (of character, achievement, etc.); radiance, splendid appearance. **M16.** ▸†**b** Something giving glory or splendour. **E–M17.**

> H. JAMES He had never been dazzled by his sister's intellectual lustre. R. GRAVES Restore the old lustre to the Roman military name. K. CLARK The men through whose greatness . . our own lives have received some occasional lustre.

4 Any of a decorative group of prismatic glass pendants attached to a chandelier or other ornament; a cut-glass chandelier or candelabrum. **L17.**

> B. MASON The roar was . . deafening, and all the lustres in the big chandelier were tinkling.

5 A thin dress fabric with a fine cotton (formerly also silk or mohair) warp and worsted weft, and a glossy surface; any fabric with a sheen or gloss. **M19.**
■ **lustreful** *adjective* lustrous **M19.** **lustreless** *adjective* **E19.**

lustre /ˈlʌstə/ *noun*². Also ***luster**. **LME.**
[**ORIGIN** Anglicized from **LUSTRUM**.]
A period of five years.

lustre /ˈlʌstə/ *verb*. Also ***luster**. **L16.**
[**ORIGIN** from **LUSTRE** *noun*¹.]
†**1** *verb trans.* Make illustrious; make attractive. **L16–M17.**
2 *verb intrans.* Be or become lustrous. Now *rare*. **L16.**
3 *verb trans.* Give a lustre to (cloth, pottery, etc.). **L19.**

lustred /ˈlʌstəd/ *adjective*. Also ***lustered**. **L16.**
[**ORIGIN** from **LUSTRE** *noun*¹, *verb*: see **-ED**², **-ED**¹.]
Esp. of cloth or pottery: having a lustre.

†**lustrifical** *adjective*. **M17–M18.**
[**ORIGIN** from Latin *lustrificus* (formed as **LUSTRUM** + **-FIC**) + **-AL**¹.]
Purificatory.

lustring /ˈlʌstrɪŋ/ *noun*¹ & *adjective*. *arch.* Also **-trine** /-triːn/. **L17.**
[**ORIGIN** from French *lustrine* or its source Italian *lustrino*, from *lustro* lustre, with assim. to **-ING**³. Cf. earlier **LUTESTRING** *noun*¹ & *adjective*.]
▸ **A** *noun.* A glossy silk dress fabric. Also, a similar satin-weave fabric made of silk, wool, or rayon, or a combination of these. **L17.**
▸ **B** *adjective.* Made of lustring. **E20.**

lustring /ˈlʌstrɪŋ/ *noun*². Also ***luster-**. **L19.**
[**ORIGIN** from **LUSTRE** *verb* + **-ING**¹.]
The action of **LUSTRE** *verb*; the manner in which something is lustred.

†**lustrious** *adjective*. *rare*. **M17–M18.**
[**ORIGIN** from **LUSTRE** *noun*¹ after *illustrious*.]
Splendid, lustrous.

lustrous /ˈlʌstrəs/ *adjective*. **E17.**
[**ORIGIN** from **LUSTRE** *noun*¹ + **-OUS**.]
Having a lustre or a sheen; shining; *fig.* splendid.
■ **lustrously** *adverb* **M19.** **lustrousness** *noun* **M19.**

lustrum /ˈlʌstrəm/ *noun*. Pl. **-tra** /-trə/, **-trums**. **L16.**
[**ORIGIN** Latin, orig., a purificatory sacrifice after a quinquennial census, later also, a period of five years: ult. origin unknown.]
A period of five years.

lusty /ˈlʌsti/ *adjective*. **ME.**
[**ORIGIN** from **LUST** *noun* + **-Y**¹.]
1 Of singing, a festivity, etc., (formerly also of a person): merry, cheerful, lively. Now *arch. & dial.* **ME.**

> SIR W. SCOTT The lusty banqueting with sweetmeats and comfits.

†**2** Pleasing, pleasant, agreeable; attractive. **ME–E17.**
†**3** Full of desire, desirous, (*to, to do, for*); *spec.* full of lust or sexual desire, lustful. **ME–L17.**
4 Healthy, strong, physically vigorous. **LME.** ▸†**b** Of an inanimate agency: very effective, strong, powerful. **L16–L17.**

> R. CROMPTON Singing 'Christians Awake!' at the top of his lusty young voice. *News on Sunday* She was delivered of a lusty black-haired boy.

†**5** Insolent, arrogant. **E16–L17.**
6 Of a physical action, esp. one involving effort: energetic, vigorous. Of a meal etc.: hearty, abundant. **M17.**

> S. W. BAKER She gave her a maternal welcome . . bestowing lusty blows on her back.

†**7** Of a thing: massive, large. **M17–M19.**
8 Of a person: massively built; stout, fat. *arch.* **L18.**

lusus /ˈluːsəs, ˈljuː-/ *noun*. Pl. same /-suːs/, **-suses**. **E17.**
[**ORIGIN** Latin *lusus naturae* sport of nature.]
In full ***lusus naturae*** /nəˈtjʊəriː, -rʌɪ/. A freak of nature, an abnormal formation, a natural curiosity.

lutaceous /luːˈteɪʃəs, ljuː-/ *adjective*. **E20.**
[**ORIGIN** from Latin *lutum* mud + **-ACEOUS**.]
GEOLOGY. Of sedimentary rock: of the nature of a lutite, of argillaceous composition.

lutanist *noun* var. of **LUTENIST**.

lute /luːt, ljuːt/ *noun*¹. **ME.**
[**ORIGIN** Old French *leüt*, *lut* (mod. *luth*), prob. from Provençal *laüt*, from Arabic *al-ʿūd* wood (prob. repr. a Hispano-Arabic or N. African pronunc.): see **AL-**². Cf. **LAUD** *noun*², **OUD**.]
1 A musical instrument having a body with rounded pear-shaped back and a neck, and having six to thirteen pairs of strings which are plucked (much used from the 14th to the 17th cents.). Also, any of a large class of stringed musical instruments having a body with a neck, including the classic lute and also bowed and flat-backed instruments. **ME.**
2 A stop in some types of harpsichord. **ME.**
– **COMB.:** **lute harpsichord** *hist.* = **LAUTENCLAVICYMBEL**; **lute-pin** each of the pegs or screws for tuning the strings of a lute.

lute /luːt, ˈljuːt/ *noun*². **LME.**
[**ORIGIN** Old French & mod. French *lut* or medieval Latin *lutum*, spec. use of Latin *lutum* mud, potter's clay.]
1 Clay or cement used to stop a hole, make a joint airtight, coat a crucible, protect a graft, etc.; a particular kind of this substance. **LME.**
†**2** Mud. **L17–M18.**
3 An airtight rubber seal or washer for a jar etc. **L19.**

lute /luːt, ljuːt/ *noun*³. In sense 1 also **loot**. **L19.**
[**ORIGIN** Dutch *loet*.]
1 A ladle or skimmer used in the production of salt to remove scum from a brine pan. *dial.* **L19.**
2 A straight-edged piece of wood for removing excess clay from a brick mould. *US.* **L19.**

lute /luːt, ljuːt/ *verb*¹. Now *rare*. **LME.**
[**ORIGIN** from **LUTE** *noun*¹.]
1 *verb intrans.* Play the lute. **LME.**
2 *verb trans.* Play (a tune) on the lute. **LME.**

lute /luːt, ljuːt/ *verb*² *trans.* **LME.**
[**ORIGIN** Latin *lutare* daub with mud, from *lutum* **LUTE** *noun*².]
1 Coat or cover with lute; seal or stop (as) with lute. **LME.**
2 Fasten, fix, cement (as) with lute. Freq. with adverbs, as *down, on, together*, etc. **LME.**

luteal /ˈluːtɪəl, ˈljuː-/ *adjective*. **E20.**
[**ORIGIN** from Latin *luteus* yellow + **-AL**¹.]
PHYSIOLOGY. Of or pertaining to the corpus luteum.

lutecium *noun* see **LUTETIUM**.

lutefisk /ˈluːt(ə)fɪsk/ *noun*. **E20.**
[**ORIGIN** Norwegian, from *lute* steep in lye (from *lut* lye) + *fisk* fish.]
A Scandinavian dish prepared by soaking dried cod in lye to tenderize it, then skinning, boning, and boiling the fish to a gelatinous consistency.

lutein /ˈluːtɪɪn, ˈljuː-/ *noun*. **M19.**
[**ORIGIN** from Latin *luteum* egg yolk (use as noun of neut. of *luteus* yellow) + **-IN**¹.]
BIOCHEMISTRY. A yellow xanthophyll pigment present in the leaves of plants, in egg yolk, and in the corpus luteum.

luteinize /ˈluːtɪnʌɪz/ *verb trans.* Also **-ise**. **E20.**
[**ORIGIN** from **LUTEIN** + **-IZE**.]
PHYSIOLOGY. Cause to produce lutein; cause to form a corpus luteum. Chiefly as ***luteinized***, ***luteinizing*** *ppl adjectives*. **luteinizing hormone**: secreted by the adenohypophysis and (in females) promoting ovulation and the formation of the corpus luteum, (in males) promoting secretion of androgens.
■ **luteiniˈzation** *noun* the formation of the corpus luteum from the cells that remain of the Graafian follicle after expulsion of the ovum, with accompanying production of lutein **E20.**

lutenist /ˈluːt(ə)nɪst, ˈljuː-/ *noun*. Also **lutanist**. **E17.**
[**ORIGIN** medieval Latin *lutanista*, from *lutana* lute: see **-IST**.]
A person who plays the lute.

luteo- /ˈluːtɪəʊ, ˈljuː-/ *combining form* of Latin *luteus* (neut. *luteum*) yellow, esp. with the sense 'of the corpus luteum': see **-O-**.
■ **luteolysis** /-ˈɒlɪsɪs/ *noun* degeneration of the corpus luteum, as when a discharged ovum is not fertilized **M20.** **luteoˈlytic** *adjective* relating to or effecting luteolysis **M20.**

luteotrophic /ˌluːtɪə(ʊ)ˈtrəʊfɪk, -ˈtrɒfɪk; ˌljuː-/ *adjective*. Also **-tropic** /-ˈtrəʊpɪk, -ˈtrɒpɪk/. **M20.**
[**ORIGIN** from **LUTEO-** + **-TROPHIC**.]
PHYSIOLOGY. Acting to maintain the corpus luteum during pregnancy.
■ **luteotrophin** /-ˈtrəʊfɪn/ *noun* a luteotrophic hormone **M20.**

luteous /ˈluːtɪəs, ˈljuː-/ *adjective*¹. **M17.**
[**ORIGIN** from Latin *luteus* yellow + **-OUS**.]
Chiefly *BOTANY & ZOOLOGY.* Of a deep orange-yellow colour.

†**luteous** *adjective*². **M17–M18.**
[**ORIGIN** from Latin *luteus*, from *lutum* mud: see **-OUS**.]
Of or pertaining to mud.

luter /ˈluːtə, ˈljuː-/ *noun*. Now *rare*. **ME.**
[**ORIGIN** from **LUTE** *verb*¹ + **-ER**¹.]
A lutenist.

lutescent /luːˈtɛs(ə)nt, ljuː-/ *adjective*. **E19.**
[**ORIGIN** from Latin *luteus* yellow + **-ESCENT**.]
Chiefly *BOTANY & ZOOLOGY.* Inclining to yellow; yellowish.

lutestring /ˈluːtstrɪŋ, ˈljuː-/ *noun*¹ & *adjective*. **M17.**
[**ORIGIN** Alt. formed as **LUSTRING** *noun*¹ after **LUTE STRING**.]
▸ **A** *noun.* A glossy silk fabric; a ribbon made of this fabric. **M17.**
▸ **B** *adjective.* Made of lutestring. **E18.**

lutestring *noun*² see **LUTE STRING**.

lute string /ˈluːtstrɪŋ, ljuː-/ *noun*. Also (esp. in sense 2) **lutestring**. **L15.**
[**ORIGIN** from **LUTE** *noun*¹ + **STRING** *noun*.]
1 A string of or for a lute. **L15.**
2 Any of several noctuid moths, esp. of the genus *Tethea*, having lines resembling the strings of a lute on their wings. **E19.**
POPLAR lutestring.

Lutetian /luːˈtiːʃ(ə)n, ljuː-/ *adjective & noun*. **M18.**
[**ORIGIN** from Latin *Lutetia* (see below) + **-AN**.]
▸ **A** *adjective.* **1** Of or pertaining to Lutetia, an ancient city on the site of modern Paris, France; of or pertaining to Paris. **M18.**
2 *GEOLOGY.* Designating or pertaining to a stage of the middle Eocene typified by formations in the Paris basin. **L19.**
▸ **B** *noun. GEOLOGY.* The Lutetian stage of the Eocene. **E20.**

lutetium /luːˈtiːʃɪəm, -sɪəm, ljuː-/ *noun*. Also (earlier, now *rare*) **-cium**. **E20.**
[**ORIGIN** French *lutécium*, from *Lutèce*, Latin *Lutetia*: see **LUTETIAN**, **-IUM**.]
A metallic chemical element, atomic no. 71, that is the heaviest member of the lanthanide series (symbol Lu).

luth /luːθ/ *noun*. **L19.**
[**ORIGIN** French, perh. = *luth* **LUTE** *noun*¹.]
The leatherback turtle, *Dermochelys coriacea*.

Lutheran /ˈluːθ(ə)r(ə)n, ˈljuː-/ *noun & adjective*. **E16.**
[**ORIGIN** from *Luther* (see below) + **-AN**.]
▸ **A** *noun.* A follower of the German Protestant theologian Martin Luther (1483–1546) or his doctrines; *spec.* a member of any of the (chiefly German and Scandinavian) Churches founded on the doctrines of Luther, which accept the Augsburg Confession of 1530, with justification by faith alone as a cardinal doctrine. **E16.**
▸ **B** *adjective.* Of or pertaining to Luther or his theology; adhering to the doctrines of Luther. **M16.**
■ **Lutheranize** *verb trans. & intrans.* make or become Lutheran **M19.**

Lutheranism /ˈluːθ(ə)r(ə)nɪz(ə)m, ˈljuː-/ *noun*. **M16.**
[**ORIGIN** from **LUTHERAN** + **-ISM**.]
The body of doctrine taught by Luther and his followers; adherence to Lutheran doctrines.

Lutherism /ˈluːθərɪz(ə)m, ˈljuː-/ *noun*. **L17.**
[**ORIGIN** formed as **LUTHERANISM** + **-ISM**.]
= **LUTHERANISM**.
■ **Lutherist** *noun* **L19.**

luthern /ˈluːθ(ə)n, ˈljuː-/ *noun*. **M17.**
[**ORIGIN** Perh. alt. of **LUCARNE**.]
More fully ***luthern-window***. A dormer window.

luthier /ˈluːtɪə, ˈljuː-/ *noun*. **L19.**
[**ORIGIN** French, from *luth* **LUTE** *noun*¹: see **-IER**.]
A maker of stringed instruments, *spec.* of the violin family.

lutidine /ˈluːtɪdiːn, ˈljuː-/ *noun*. **M19.**
[**ORIGIN** Partial anagram of **TOLUIDINE**, a similar substance.]
CHEMISTRY. Any of a number of isomeric bases having the formula $C_6H_3(CH_3)_2NH_2$, which are dimethyl derivatives of aniline, and some of which occur in coal tar.

L

luting /ˈluːtɪŋ, ˈljuː-/ *noun*. E16.
[ORIGIN from LUTE *verb*² + -ING¹.]
1 = LUTE *noun*² 1. E16.
2 The action of LUTE *verb*². E17.
3 A seal for closing an aperture, keeping out air or water, etc. E19.

lutino /luːˈtiːnəʊ/ *noun & adjective*. Pl. of noun **-os**. E20.
[ORIGIN from Latin *luteus* yellow, after ALBINO.]
(A bird, usu. a cage bird) having more yellow in its plumage than is usual for the species.

lutist /ˈluːtɪst, ljuː-/ *noun*. E17.
[ORIGIN from LUTE *noun*¹ + -IST.]
A lutenist. Also, a luthier.

lutite /ˈluːtʌɪt, ˈljuː-/ *noun*. E20.
[ORIGIN from Latin *lutum* mud + -ITE¹.]
GEOLOGY. A shale, mudstone, or other sedimentary rock made up very largely of argillaceous sediment.

Lutomer /ˈluːtəmə, ˈljuː-/ *noun & adjective*. M20.
[ORIGIN *Ljutomer* (see below).]
(Designating) any of various white wines, esp. Riesling, produced in Ljutomer, a region in Slovenia, SE Europe.

luton /ˈluːt(ə)n/ *noun*. Also **L-**. L20.
[ORIGIN A town in Bedfordshire, England, where such vehicles are made.]
1 A part of the container of a lorry, van, horsebox, etc., which projects forwards over the cab. Also more fully ***luton roof***. L20.
2 A vehicle with this type of container. Also more fully ***luton van***. L20.

lutrine /ˈluːtrʌɪn, ˈljuː-/ *adjective*. L19.
[ORIGIN from Latin *lutra* otter: see -INE¹.]
ZOOLOGY. Of, pertaining to, or designating the mustelid subfamily Lutrinae, which comprises the otters.

lutulent /ˈluːtjʊl(ə)nt, ˈljuː-/ *adjective*. *literary*. Now *rare*. L16.
[ORIGIN Latin *lutulentus*, from *lutum* mud: see -ULENT.]
Muddy, turbid.
■ **lutulence** *noun* (*rare*) E18.

Lutyenesque /lʌtjənˈɛsk/ *adjective*. M20.
[ORIGIN from *Lutyens* (see below) + -ESQUE.]
Resembling or characteristic of the style of the English architect Sir Edwin Lutyens (1869–1944).

lutz /lʊts/ *noun*. M20.
[ORIGIN Prob. named after the Austrian skater Alois *Lutz* (1899–1918).]
A jump in ice skating in which the skater takes off from the outside back edge of one skate and lands, after a complete rotation in the air, on the outside back edge of the opposite skate.

luv /lʌv, lʊv/ *noun & verb*. *non-standard*. M19.
[ORIGIN Respelling to suggest a dial. or colloq. pronunc.]
▸ **A** *noun*. = LOVE *noun*; *esp*. = LOVE *noun* 6 (freq. as a form of address). M19.
▸ **B** *verb trans. & intrans*. Infl. **-vv-**. = LOVE *verb*. M19.

luvvy /ˈlʌvi/ *noun*. *colloq*. Also **luvvie**. M20.
[ORIGIN from LUV + -Y⁶.]
1 = LOVEY. M20.
B. ANDERSON 'And how are you, luvvie?' asked her sister fondly.
2 An actor or actress, *esp*. one who is considered particularly effusive or affected; someone actively involved with entertainment or the arts. Often *derog*. L20.
J. BURCHILL They were just being Luvvies, pouting for the camera. *attrib*.: A. BARNETT Those involved were pilloried as luvvy members of the 'chattering classes'.

Luwian /ˈluːvɪən, ˈluːɪən/ *noun & adjective*. Also **Luvian**. E20.
[ORIGIN from *Luvia*, *Luwia* a part of Asia Minor + -AN.]
▸ **A** *noun*. A member of an ancient Anatolian people contemporary with the Hittites, known from cuneiform inscriptions; the language of this people. E20.
▸ **B** *adjective*. Of or pertaining to the Luwians or their language. M20.

lux /lʌks/ *noun*. Pl. **lux**. L19.
[ORIGIN Latin = light.]
PHYSICS. The SI unit of illumination, equal to the illumination of a surface all of which is one metre from a uniform point source of light of unit intensity (now one candela), i.e. (as now defined) one lumen per square metre. (Symbol lx.)
■ **luxmeter** *noun* an instrument for measuring the brightness or illumination of a surface E20.

†**lux** *verb trans*. Only in 18.
[ORIGIN French *luxer* or Latin *luxare*: see LUXATE.]
= LUXATE.

luxate /ˈlʌkseɪt/ *verb trans*. Now *rare*. E17.
[ORIGIN Latin *luxat-* pa. ppl stem of *luxare*, from *luxus* dislocated: see -ATE³.]
MEDICINE. Dislocate, put out of joint.

luxation /lʌkˈseɪʃ(ə)n/ *noun*. M16.
[ORIGIN Latin *luxatio(n-)*, formed as LUXATE: see -ATION.]
MEDICINE. (A) dislocation.

luxe /lʌks, lʊks/ *noun*. M16.
[ORIGIN French from Latin *luxus*: see LUXURY.]
(A) luxury. Cf. DE LUXE.

Luxembourgeois /ˈlʌks(ə)mbʊəʒwɑː/ *adjective & noun*. E20.
[ORIGIN French, from *Luxembourg* (see LUXEMBOURGER) + *-ois* -ESE.]
▸ **A** *adjective*. Of or pertaining to Luxembourg or its inhabitants. E20.
▸ **B** *noun*. Pl. same. A native or inhabitant of Luxembourg, = LUXEMBOURGER. M20.

Luxembourger /ˈlʌks(ə)mbɔːgə/ *noun*. Also **-burger**. E20.
[ORIGIN from *Luxembourg* (see below) + -ER¹. Cf. German *Luxemburger*.]
A native or inhabitant of the state of Luxembourg, which lies between Belgium, Germany, and France.

Luxemburgish /lʌks(ə)mˈbɔːgɪʃ/ *noun & adjective*. Also **-isch**. M20.
[ORIGIN German *Luxemburgisch*, from *Luxemburg* Luxembourg + *-isch* -ISH¹.]
(Of) the Franconian dialect spoken by natives of Luxembourg. Also called ***Letzeburgesch***.

luxullyanite /lʌkˈsʌlɪənʌɪt/ *noun*. L19.
[ORIGIN from *Luxullian* (*Luxulyan*), a village in Cornwall + -ITE¹.]
PETROGRAPHY. A porphyritic granite containing tourmaline in radiating clusters of needle-shaped crystals.

luxuriant /lʌgˈʒʊərɪənt, lʌgˈzjʊə-, lʌkˈsjʊə-/ *adjective*. M16.
[ORIGIN Latin *luxuriant-* pres. ppl stem of *luxuriare* grow rank, from *luxuria*: see LUXURY, -ANT¹.]
1 Producing abundantly, prolific. Now *rare*. M16.
2 Of invention, genius, etc.: exuberantly productive. Of speech, style, etc.: florid, richly ornate. E17. ▸†**b** Excessively prosperous. M17–M18.
A. BAIN A luxuriant imagination implies the facility of retaining scenes of every description.
3 Of a plant, hair, etc.: growing profusely; lush. M17.
F. KING Her once luxuriant black hair had gone thin and grey. *Holiday Which?* The steep slopes are covered with luxuriant vegetation, . . a profusion of vines, . . and brilliantly coloured flowers.
4 Luxurious. L17.
C. GIBBON It was a splendid apartment, . . luxuriant to a degree.
■ **luxuriance** *noun* E18. **luxuriancy** *noun* (now *rare*) M17. **luxuriantly** *adverb* E18.

luxuriate /lʌgˈʒʊərɪeɪt, lʌgˈzjʊə-, lʌkˈsjʊə-/ *verb intrans*. E17.
[ORIGIN Latin *luxuriat-* pa. ppl stem of *luxuriare*: see LUXURIANT, -ATE³.]
1 Of a plant, hair, etc.: grow profusely. Formerly also, (of a writer) be exuberantly productive. E17. ▸†**b** *fig*. Grow or develop exuberantly *into*. M17–E19.
SCOTT FITZGERALD Two fine growths of hair which luxuriated in either nostril.
2 Revel *in*, take self-indulgent delight *in*; take one's ease, relax in comfort. E17.
E. FITZGERALD I had a long letter from Morton . . —he is still luxuriating at Venice. R. MACAULAY Mrs Cox told her the story . . . luxuriating in the tragic tale. C. MILNE I lay there luxuriating in the comfort.
■ **luxuriˈation** *noun* M19.

luxurious /lʌgˈʒʊərɪəs, lʌgˈzjʊə-, lʌkˈsjʊə-/ *adjective*. ME.
[ORIGIN Old French *luxurios* (mod. *-rieux*) from Latin *luxuriosus*, from *luxuria*: see LUXURY, -OUS.]
†**1** Lascivious, lecherous. ME–L17.
†**2** Outrageous, excessive. LME–M17.
3 Fond of luxury, self-indulgent, voluptuous. E17.
GLADSTONE A wealthy country, with a large leisured class, in a luxurious age. V. S. NAIPAUL Someone who felt her beauty entitled her to luxurious sensations.
4 Characterized by luxury; of the nature of a luxury; sumptuously comfortable; supplied with luxuries. M17.
A. WEST The polished mahogany . . seemed wonderfully luxurious to me. P. FITZGERALD A luxurious home was maintained in Hendon. JULIETTE HUXLEY Shops flaunted luxurious temptations after the austere essentials of wartime.
5 = LUXURIANT 3. Now *rare*. M17.
G. GISSING March rains had brought the vegetation into luxurious life.
■ **luxuriously** *adverb* M16. **luxuriousness** *noun* M16.

luxurist /ˈlʌkʃərɪst/ *noun*. *rare*. L17.
[ORIGIN from LUXURY + -IST.]
A person addicted to luxury.

luxury /ˈlʌkʃəri/ *noun & adjective*. ME.
[ORIGIN Old French *luxurie* var. of (also mod.) *luxure* from Latin *luxuria*, from *luxus* abundance, sumptuous enjoyment: see -Y³.]
▸ **A** *noun*. †**1** Lechery, lust. ME–E19.
†**2** Luxuriance. Only in 17.
3 (Habitual indulgence in) choice or costly surroundings, possessions, food, etc.; luxuriousness. M17.
A. S. DALE He had grown up in upper-class luxury—taught by governesses. *Kuwait Times* People today want . . luxury and they want comfort.
in the lap of luxury: see LAP *noun*¹.
4 A means or source of luxurious enjoyment; *spec*. something desirable for comfort or enjoyment, but not indispensable. E18.
C. S. LEWIS Luxuries . . such as first-class railway carriages and sleeping-cars. J. KRANTZ Valentine lay . . revelling in the luxury of putting her feet up. J. RULE Her expensive sports car, her one luxury always. P. TOYNBEE The guilty luxury of a day in bed.
▸ **B** *adjective*. Providing great comfort; expensive. E20.
R. P. JHABVALA We took suites of rooms on one floor of a high, huge luxury hotel. *Holiday Which?* It's not worth paying luxury prices to stay here.

LV *abbreviation*.
Luncheon voucher.

LVO *abbreviation*.
Lieutenant of the Royal Victorian Order.

Lw *symbol*.
CHEMISTRY, now *hist*. Lawrencium (cf. LR).

lwei /ləˈweɪ/ *noun*. L20.
[ORIGIN Angolan name.]
A monetary unit of Angola equal to one-hundredth of a kwanza.

LWM *abbreviation*.
Low-water mark.

lx *abbreviation*.
Lux.

ly *abbreviation*.
PHYSICS. Langley(s).

-ly /lɪ/ *suffix*¹.
[ORIGIN Old English *-lić* = Old Frisian, Old Saxon *-līk*, Old High German *-līh* (Dutch *-lijk*, German *-lich*), Old Norse *-ligr*, *-legr*, Gothic *-leiks*, from Germanic, from base also of LICH.]
Forming adjectives usu. from nouns with the senses (*a*) having the qualities of, characteristic of, befitting, as ***beastly***, ***cowardly***, ***knightly***, ***queenly***, ***rascally***, ***scholarly***, ***womanly***; †(*b*) of or pertaining to, as (in early sense) ***manly***; (*c*) recurring at intervals of, as ***daily***, ***hourly***, ***weekly***, ***yearly***.

-ly /lɪ/ *suffix*².
[ORIGIN Old English *līce* = Old Frisian *-like*, Old Saxon *-līko*, Old High German *-līhho* (Dutch *-lijk*, German *-lich*), Old Norse *-liga*, Gothic *-leikō*, from Germanic base of -LY¹ + adverb-forming suffix.]
Forming adverbs (*a*) from adjectives with the senses 'in a — manner' or 'to a — degree', as ***amusingly***, ***deservedly***, ***firstly***, ***fully***, ***greatly***, ***happily***, ***hourly***, ***truly***; (*b*) from ordinal numerals, denoting serial order, as ***firstly***, ***secondly***; (*c*) (now *rare*) from adjectives ending in *-ly*, as ***godlily***, ***livelily***.

Lyaeus /lʌɪˈiːəs/ *noun*. *literary*. *rare*. E17.
[ORIGIN Latin from Greek *Luaios* a surname of the god Bacchus.]
Wine.

lyam /ˈlʌɪəm/ *noun*. *obsolete* exc. *hist*. & *dial*. Also **lyme** /lʌɪm/. LME.
[ORIGIN Old French *liem* (mod. LIEN), from Latin *ligamen* bond, from *ligare* to tie. Cf. LIMER *noun*¹.]
1 A leash for a dog; HERALDRY a charge representing this. LME.
2 More fully ***lyam-hound***. A bloodhound. L15.

lyart /ˈlʌɪət/ *noun & adjective*. *obsolete* exc. *dial*. Also **-ard** /-əd/. ME.
[ORIGIN Old French *liart* or medieval Latin *liardus*.]
▸ **A** *noun*. (A name for) a horse spotted with white or grey, a dapple grey. Long *rare*. ME.
▸ **B** *adjective*. Of a horse: spotted with white or grey; dapple grey. Of hair: grey. LME.

lyase /ˈlʌɪeɪz/ *noun*. M20.
[ORIGIN from LY(SIS + -ASE.]
BIOCHEMISTRY. An enzyme which promotes a reaction in which a double bond is created by removal of substituents, or in which substituents are added to a double bond.

lycaenid /lʌɪˈsiːnɪd/ *noun & adjective*. L19.
[ORIGIN mod. Latin *Lycaenidae* (see below), from *Lycaena* genus name, app. from Greek *lukaina* she-wolf: see -ID³.]
▸ **A** *noun*. A butterfly of the family Lycaenidae, which includes the blues and the hairstreaks. L19.
▸ **B** *adjective*. Of, pertaining to, or designating this family. E20.

lycanthrope /ˈlʌɪk(ə)nθrəʊp/ *noun*. E17.
[ORIGIN mod. Latin *lycanthropus* from Greek *lukanthrōpos*: see LYCANTHROPY.]
1 A person with lycanthropy. E17.
2 A werewolf. M19.

lycanthropy /lʌɪˈkanθrəpi/ *noun*. L16.
[ORIGIN mod. Latin *lycanthropia* from Greek *lukanthrōpia*, from *lukanthrōpos*, from *lukos* wolf + *anthrōpos* man: see -Y³.]
1 A form of madness in which a person believes himself or herself to be an animal (esp. a wolf) and behaves accordingly. L16.
2 The mythical transformation of a person into a wolf. Also called ***werewolfery***, ***werewolfism***. M19.

L

■ **lycan'thropic** *adjective* of or pertaining to lycanthropy; affected with lycanthropy: **E19. lycanthropist** *noun* = LYCANTHROPE **E18.**

lycaon /lɪˈkeɪɒn/ *noun.* **E19.**
[ORIGIN mod. Latin genus name from Greek *lukaōn*, Latin *lycaon* wolflike animal.]
= ***hunting dog*** (b) s.v. HUNTING *noun.*

Lycaonian /lɪkeɪˈəʊnɪən/ *adjective & noun.* **L16.**
[ORIGIN from Latin *Lycaonia*, Greek *Lukaonia* (see below) + -AN.]
▸ **A** *adjective.* Of or pertaining to Lycaonia, an ancient region in southern Asia Minor, its inhabitants, or the language used there. **L16.**
▸ **B** *noun.* **1** The language of Lycaonia. **L19.**
2 A native or inhabitant of Lycaonia. **E20.**

lycée /lise (*pl. same*), ˈliːseɪ/ *noun.* **M19.**
[ORIGIN French from Latin LYCEUM.]
A state secondary school in France.
■ ***lycéen*** /liseɛ̃ (*pl. same*)/ *noun* a pupil at a *lycée* **L19.**

Lyceum /lʌɪˈsiːəm/ *noun.* **L16.**
[ORIGIN Latin from Greek *Lukeion* (sc. *gumnasion* GYMNASIUM) neut. of *Lukeios* epithet of Apollo (from whose neighbouring temple the Lyceum was named).]
1 The garden at Athens in which Aristotle taught his philosophy; Aristotelian philosophy and its adherents. **L16.**
2 = LYCÉE. **E19.**
3 *US HISTORY.* (**l-**.) An institution in which popular lectures were delivered on literary and scientific subjects. **E19.**
4 *THEATRICAL.* [A theatre near the Strand in London, England.] Used *attrib.* to denote a melodramatic performance or style, formerly characteristic of this theatre. **L19.**

lych *noun* var. of LICH.

lychee /ˈlʌɪtʃiː, ˈlɪ-/ *noun.* Also **lichee**, **litchi** /ˈlɪ-/. **L16.**
[ORIGIN Chinese *lìzhī*.]
The fruit of the Chinese tree *Litchi chinensis* (family Sapindaceae), a large berry with a rough brown skin, sweet white pulp, and a single smooth stone, eaten fresh or preserved; the tree itself, widely cultivated in tropical countries.

lychgate /ˈlɪtʃgeɪt/ *noun.* Also **lichgate**. **L15.**
[ORIGIN from LICH + GATE *noun*¹.]
A roofed gateway to a churchyard, formerly used for sheltering a coffin until the clergyman's arrival for a burial.

lychnis /ˈlɪknɪs/ *noun.* **E17.**
[ORIGIN Latin from Greek *lukhnis* a red flower, from *lukhnos* lamp.]
Any of various plants of the genus *Lychnis*, of the pink family, including ragged robin (*L. flos-cuculi*) and some campions. Also (with specifying word), any of certain similar plants.
evening lychnis *N. Amer.* the Old World white campion, *Silene alba*, introduced in N. America. **scarlet lychnis** *N. Amer.* a red-flowered Russian lychnis, *L. chalcedonica*, introduced in N. America.

lychnoscope /ˈlɪknəskəʊp/ *noun.* **M19.**
[ORIGIN from Greek *lukhnos* lamp + -SCOPE (so called from its supposed purpose to allow lepers to see the altar lights).]
ARCHITECTURE. A low side window.
■ **lychnoscopic** *adjective* **M19.**

Lycian /ˈlɪsɪən/ *noun & adjective.* **L16.**
[ORIGIN from Latin *Lycia*, Greek *Lukia* Lycia (see below) + -AN.]
▸ **A** *noun.* **1** A native or inhabitant of Lycia, an ancient region in SW Asia Minor. **L16.**
2 The language of Lycia. **M19.**
▸ **B** *adjective.* Of or pertaining to Lycia, its inhabitants, or language. **E17.**

lycid /ˈlɪsɪd/ *noun & adjective.* **M20.**
[ORIGIN mod. Latin *Lycidae* (see below), from *Lycus* genus name, from Greek personal name *Lukos*, Latin *Lycus*: see -ID³.]
▸ **A** *noun.* Any of various beetles, often conspicuously coloured, of the family Lycidae. **M20.**
▸ **B** *adjective.* Of, pertaining to, or designating this family. **M20.**

lycium /ˈlɪsɪəm/ *noun.* **M16.**
[ORIGIN Late Latin from Greek *lukion*, orig. neut. sing. of *Lukios* Lycian.]
A boxthorn (genus *Lycium*). Formerly also, a juice extracted from a boxthorn.

lycopene /ˈlʌɪkəpiːn/ *noun.* **M20.**
[ORIGIN from LYCOPIN + -ENE.]
CHEMISTRY. A polyunsaturated hydrocarbon, $C_{40}H_{56}$, which is a red carotenoid pigment present in tomatoes and many berries and fruits.

lycoperdon /lʌɪkəˈpəːdən/ *noun.* **M18.**
[ORIGIN mod. Latin (see sense 1 below), irreg. from Greek *lukos* wolf + *perdesthai* break wind.]
1 A puffball fungus of the genus *Lycoperdon*. Now chiefly as mod. Latin genus name. **M18.**
2 ***lycoperdon nut***, = DEER-*ball*. **M19.**

lycopin /ˈlʌɪkəpɪn/ *noun.* **E20.**
[ORIGIN from mod. Latin *Lycop(ersicon*, a genus including the tomato, from Greek *lukos* wolf + *persikos* peach: see -IN¹.]
CHEMISTRY. = LYCOPENE.

lycopod /ˈlʌɪkəpɒd/ *noun.* **M19.**
[ORIGIN from LYCOPODIUM.]
BOTANY. A pteridophyte of the family Lycopodiaceae; a clubmoss.
■ **lycopodi'aceous** *adjective* of or pertaining to the family Lycopodiaceae **M19.**

lycopodium /lʌɪkəˈpəʊdɪəm/ *noun.* **E18.**
[ORIGIN mod. Latin (see below), from Greek *lukos* wolf + *pod-*, *pous* foot, -POD (from the clawlike root of *Lycopodium clavatum*).]
1 A clubmoss of the genus *Lycopodium*, orig. spec. *L. clavatum*. **E18.**
2 In full ***lycopodium powder***, ***lycopodium dust***. A fine flammable powder consisting of ripe spores of *Lycopodium clavatum* or other species, formerly used as a surgical absorbent and in fireworks etc. **M19.**

Lycra /ˈlʌɪkrə/ *noun.* Also **l-**. **M20.**
[ORIGIN Unknown.]
(Proprietary name for) an elastic polyurethane fibre and fabric used esp. for hosiery, underwear, and close-fitting sports clothing.

lyctus /ˈlɪktəs/ *noun.* **E20.**
[ORIGIN mod. Latin (see below) from Greek *Luktos*, Latin *Lyctus* a city in Crete.]
In full ***lyctus beetle***. A wood-boring beetle of the genus *Lyctus*; a powder-post beetle.
■ **lyctid** *noun & adjective* (**a**) *noun* a beetle of the family Lyctidae, which includes powder-post beetles; (**b**) *adjective* of, pertaining to, or designating this family: **M20.**

Lycurgan /lʌɪˈkəːg(ə)n/ *adjective.* **M20.**
[ORIGIN from Latin *Lycurgus* (see below), Greek *Lukourgos* + -AN.]
Of, pertaining to, or characteristic of Lycurgus, the reputed founder of the ancient Spartan constitution (prob. about the end of the 9th cent. BC) or the constitutional innovations attributed to him; harsh, severe.
■ **Lycurgean** *adjective* = LYCURGAN **M19. Lycurgian** *noun* (*rare*) an adherent of Lycurgus or his methods **L16.**

lyddite /ˈlɪdʌɪt/ *noun.* **L19.**
[ORIGIN from *Lydd* a town in Kent, SE England, where the explosive was tested + -ITE¹.]
Chiefly *hist.* A high explosive consisting chiefly of picric acid, much used by the British in the First World War.

Lydian /ˈlɪdɪən/ *adjective & noun.* **L15.**
[ORIGIN from Latin *Lydius*, Greek *Ludios* Lydia (see below) + -AN.]
▸ **A** *noun.* A native or inhabitant of Lydia, an ancient country in Asia Minor. Also, the language used there. **L15.**
▸ **B** *adjective.* **1** Of or pertaining to Lydia, its inhabitants, or language. **L16.**
Lydian stone a black variety of jasper (basanite), formerly used as a touchstone for gold.
2 *MUSIC.* Designating or pertaining to an ancient Greek mode, characterized as soft and effeminate. Also (since the Middle Ages), designating or pertaining to the scale whose notes are at intervals as represented by F–F on the white notes of a piano. **L16.**

lydite /ˈlɪdʌɪt/ *noun.* **E19.**
[ORIGIN from LYDIAN + -ITE¹.]
= ***Lydian stone*** s.v. LYDIAN *adjective* 1.

lye /lʌɪ/ *noun*¹ *& verb.*
[ORIGIN Old English *lēag* = Middle Dutch *lōghe* (Dutch *loog*), Old High German *louga* (German *Lauge*) lye, Old Norse *laug* hot bath, from Germanic base repr. also by LATHER *noun*¹, from Indo-European.]
▸ **A** *noun.* **1** Water made alkaline, esp. by the lixiviation of vegetable ashes; any strong alkaline solution for washing etc. **OE.** ▸**b** Any detergent material. Long *rare*. **ME.**
2 The fluid which forms in a blister etc. or collects in the body in dropsy. Long *dial.* **E17.**
3 Water impregnated with salts by decoction or lixiviation. Now *rare*. **M17.**
– COMB.: **lye corn**: steeped in weak lye to remove the husk.
▸ **B** *verb trans.* Treat with lye. **L18.**

lye *noun*² see LIE *noun*².

lygaeid /lʌɪˈdʒiːɪd, -ˈgʌɪɪd/ *noun & adjective.* **L19.**
[ORIGIN mod. Latin *Lygaeidae* (see below), from *Lygaeus* genus name, from Greek *lugaios* shadowy, gloomy: see -ID³.]
ENTOMOLOGY. ▸**A** *noun.* Any of various dark or brightly coloured heteropteran bugs of the family Lygaeidae, some of which are agricultural pests. **L19.**
▸ **B** *adjective.* Of, pertaining to, or designating this family. **E20.**

lygus /ˈlʌɪgəs/ *noun.* Pl. same. **E20.**
[ORIGIN mod. Latin (see below) from Greek *lugos* chaste tree, withy.]
ENTOMOLOGY. Any of various plant-sucking mirid bugs of the genus *Lygus*, some of which transmit plant diseases. Also ***lygus bug***.

lying /ˈlʌɪɪŋ/ *noun.* **ME.**
[ORIGIN from LIE *verb*¹ + -ING¹.]
1 The action of LIE *verb*¹. **ME.** ▸**b** ***lying-in***, confinement in childbirth. **LME.**

K. AMIS Just lying in the sun and no more, strikes me as a terrible thing to do.

2 A place to lie. Usu. with qualifying adjective. **M19.**

J. T. NETTLESHIP A poet from his birth, nursed in Nature's softest lying.

– COMB.: **lying-in-state** the display of the body of a public figure for public tribute before burial or cremation.

lying /ˈlʌɪɪŋ/ *adjective*¹. **OE.**
[ORIGIN from LIE *verb*¹ + -ING².]
1 That lies (in a more or less horizontal position, etc.); that remains or rests. **OE.**

J. BUCHAN The frost had gone, and the lying snow was as soft as butter.

2 *spec.* Of money, goods, etc.: put by. *Scot.* **E18.**

lying /ˈlʌɪɪŋ/ *adjective*². **ME.**
[ORIGIN from LIE *verb*² + -ING².]
That tells lies; untruthful, deceitful.

E. PIZZEY She'd go . . potty waiting for your next lying 'phone call.

■ **lyingly** *adverb* **LME.**

lying *verb*¹, *verb*² *pres. pple* of LIE *verb*¹, *verb*².

lyke *noun* var. of LICH.

lyke wake /ˈlʌɪkweɪk/ *noun.* Also **lykewake**. **LME.**
[ORIGIN from *lyke* var. of LICH + WAKE *noun*¹. See also LATE WAKE.]
A watch kept at night over a dead body.

Lyle gun /ˈlʌɪl gʌn/ *noun phr.* **L19.**
[ORIGIN D. A. *Lyle* (d. 1937), US army officer and engineer.]
A cannon designed to project a rope to a stranded ship to facilitate salvaging and rescue operations.

Lylian /ˈlɪlɪən/ *adjective.* **E20.**
[ORIGIN from John *Lyly* (c 1554–1606), English dramatist and novelist + -AN.]
Of, pertaining to, or characteristic of John Lyly or his works; euphuistic.

Lyman series /ˈlʌɪmən sɪəriːz/ *noun phr.* **E20.**
[ORIGIN Theodore *Lyman* (1874–1954), US physicist.]
PHYSICS. A series of lines in the ultraviolet spectrum of atomic hydrogen, between 122 and 91 nanometres.

Lyme /lʌɪm/ *noun*¹. **L20.**
[ORIGIN A town in Connecticut, USA, where an outbreak occurred.]
MEDICINE. ***Lyme disease***, ***Lyme arthritis***, a form of arthritis which mainly affects the large joints and is preceded by an erythematous rash, caused by a spirochaete bacterium transmitted by ticks.

lyme *noun*² var. of LYAM.

lyme grass /ˈlʌɪmgrɑːs/ *noun.* **L18.**
[ORIGIN Perh. from LIME *noun*¹: see GRASS *noun*.]
1 A blue-green grass of sandy coasts, *Leymus* (formerly *Elymus*) *arenarius*, often planted to stabilize dunes. **L18.**
2 A noctuid moth, *Photedes elymi*, the caterpillars of which feed on lyme grass. **M19.**

†lymo(u)r *noun* see LIMBER *noun*¹.

lymph /lɪmf/ *noun.* Also in Latin form **†lympha**. **L16.**
[ORIGIN French *lymphe* or Latin *lympha* water nymph, water, prob. dissimilated form of *nympha*, Greek *numphē* nymph.]
1 (Pure) water. Also, a stream. *poet.* **L16.**
†2 *BOTANY.* A colourless fluid in plants; sap. **L17–M19.**
3 A colourless alkaline fluid, resembling blood but lacking red cells, which bathes various tissues and organs of the body and drains into the bloodstream through a network of vessels (the lymphatic system). **L17.**
4 The exudation from an inflamed tissue, a sore, etc.; *spec.* a vaccine obtained from diseased tissue. **E19.**
– PHRASES & COMB.: **lymph gland**, **lymph node** any of several small masses of tissue situated on the lymphatic vessels, responsible for removing foreign bodies from the lymph and for producing lymphocytes and antibodies. ***plastic lymph***: see PLASTIC *adjective* 5.

lymph- *combining form* see LYMPHO-.

†lympha *noun* see LYMPH.

lymphad /ˈlɪmfad/ *noun. obsolete* exc. *hist.* & *HERALDRY.* Also (earlier) **†langfad**. **M16.**
[ORIGIN Gaelic *longfhada*, from *long* ship + *fhada* long.]
A one-masted galley propelled by oars.

†lymphaeduct *noun.* **M17–M18.**
[ORIGIN mod. Latin *lymphaeductus*, from Latin *lymphae* genit. of *lympha* LYMPH + *ductus* DUCT *noun*.]
A lymphatic vessel.

lymphangiectasis /ˌlɪmfandʒɪˈɛktəsɪs/ *noun.* Pl. **-ases** /-əsiːz/. **M19.**
[ORIGIN from LYMPHO- + ANGIO- + mod. Latin ECTASIS.]
MEDICINE. Dilatation of the lymphatic vessels.

lymphangiography /ˌlɪmfandʒɪˈɒgrəfi/ *noun.* **M19.**
[ORIGIN from LYMPHO- + ANGIOGRAPHY.]
MEDICINE. **†1** A description of the lymphatic vessels. *rare* (Dicts.). Only in **M19.**
2 Radiography of the lymphatic vessels, carried out after introduction of a radio-opaque substance. **M20.**
■ **lym'phangiogram** *noun* a radiograph made by lymphangiography **M20. lymphangio'graphic** *adjective* **M20. lymphangio'graphically** *adverb* **M20.**

lymphangioma /lɪmfandʒɪˈəʊmə/ *noun*. Pl. **-mas**, **-mata** /-mətə/. L19.
[ORIGIN from LYMPHO- + ANGIOMA.]
MEDICINE. A tumour-like mass resulting from a proliferation of lymphatic vessels.
■ **lymphangiomatous** *adjective* of the nature of or characterized by a lymphangioma L19.

lymphangiosarcoma /lɪmˌfandʒɪəʊsɑːˈkəʊmə/ *noun*. Pl. **-mas**, **-mata** /-mətə/. E20.
[ORIGIN formed as LYMPHANGITIS + SARCOMA.]
MEDICINE. A sarcoma of the lymphatic vessels.

lymphangitis /lɪmfanˈdʒʌɪtɪs/ *noun*. M19.
[ORIGIN from LYMPHO- + ANGIO- + -ITIS.]
MEDICINE. Inflammation of the walls of lymphatic vessels.

†**lymphate** *verb trans. rare*. Pa. pple & ppl adjective **-ated**, (earlier) **-ate**. LME.
[ORIGIN Orig. pa. pple, from Latin *lymphatus* pa. pple of *lymphare*, from *lympha*: see LYMPH, -ATE[2], -ATE[3].]
1 Dilute with water. LME–L16.
2 Drive mad. Chiefly as ***lymphated*** *ppl adjective*. E17–E18.
■ †**lymphation** *noun* E17–E18.

lymphatic /lɪmˈfatɪk/ *adjective & noun*. M17.
[ORIGIN Latin *lymphaticus* mad (formed as LYMPH: see -ATIC), after Greek *nympholēptos* seized by nymphs.]
▸ **A** *adjective*. †**1** Frenzied, mad. M17–E19.
2 Of or pertaining to lymph; involved in the secretion or conveyance of lymph. M17. ▸†**b** *BOTANY*. Containing or conveying sap. L17–M19.
lymphatic system the network of vessels conveying lymph.
3 Sluggish, flabby, (formerly supposed to be as a result of an excess of lymph in the system). L18.
▸ **B** *noun*. **1** Any of the network of vessels which convey lymph. Formerly also (*BOTANY*), a sap vessel in a plant. Usu. in *pl*. M17.
†**2** An insane person. E–M18.
■ †**lymphatical** *adjective* frenzied E17–E18.

lymphedema *noun* see LYMPHOEDEMA.

lympho- /ˈlɪmfəʊ/ *combining form* of LYMPH: see -O-. Before a vowel **lymph-**. Chiefly *MEDICINE*.
■ **lymphadeˈnectomy** *noun* (an instance of) surgical removal of lymph nodes M20. **lymphadeˈnitis** *noun* inflammation of one or more lymph nodes L19. **lymphadenopathy** /ˌlɪmfadɪˈnɒpəθi/ *noun* diseased condition of lymph nodes E20. **lymphoblast** *noun* an abnormal cell, resembling a large lymphocyte, produced in large numbers in a form of leukaemia E20. **lymphoˈblastic** *adjective* of the nature of or pertaining to lymphoblasts; (of leukaemia) in which lymphoblasts are produced: E20. **lymphoˈgenic** *adjective* = LYMPHOGENOUS E20. **lymphogenous** /lɪmˈfɒdʒɪnəs/ *adjective* (**a**) producing lymph or lymphocytes; (**b**) arising in, produced by, or disseminated via the lymphatic system: L19. **lymphokine** *noun* [Greek *kinein* move] any of various soluble substances released by lymphocytes which are thought to be involved in cell-mediated immunity but to lack the antigen-specificity of antibodies M20. **lymphoˈpenia** *noun* a decrease in the number of lymphocytes in the blood E20. **lymphopoiesis** /ˌlɪmfəʊpɔɪˈiːsɪs/ *noun* the formation of lymphocytes E20. **lymphopoietic** /ˌlɪmfəʊpɔɪˈɛtɪk/ *adjective* of or pertaining to lymphopoiesis E20. **lymphoreˈticular** *adjective* = RETICULOENDOTHELIAL M20. **lymphoˈrrhagia** *noun* the discharge of lymph from a damaged lymphatic vessel L19. **lymphosarˈcoma** *noun*, pl. **-mas**, **-mata** /-mətə/, a sarcoma of lymphoid tissue L19. **lymphotropic** /-ˈtrəʊpɪk, -ˈtrɒpɪk/ *adjective* affecting the lymphatic system L20.

lymphocyte /ˈlɪmfə(ʊ)sʌɪt/ *noun*. L19.
[ORIGIN from LYMPHO- + -CYTE.]
PHYSIOLOGY. A kind of small leucocyte which has a single round nucleus and little or no granulation in the cytoplasm, constitutes about a quarter of the total leucocytes, and is found in large numbers in the lymph nodes etc.
■ **lymphocytic** /-ˈsɪtɪk/ *adjective* of or pertaining to, or characterized by the presence of lymphocytes L19. **lymphocyˈtosis** *noun*, pl. **-toses** /-ˈtəʊsiːz/, an abnormal increase in the number of lymphocytes L19. **lymphocytoˈtoxic** *adjective* (**a**) toxic towards lymphocytes; (**b**) pertaining to or involving lymphocytotoxins: M20. **lymphocytotoˈxicity** *noun* M20. **lymphocytoˈtoxin** *noun* a substance toxic towards lymphocytes E20.

lymphoedema /lɪmfɪˈdiːmə/ *noun*. Also *-**phed-**. L19.
[ORIGIN from LYMPHO- + OEDEMA.]
MEDICINE. Oedema resulting from obstruction of lymph vessels or lymph nodes.
■ **lymphoeˈdematous** *adjective* M20.

lymphogranuloma /ˌlɪmfəʊgranjʊˈləʊmə/ *noun*. Pl. **-mas**, **-mata** /-mətə/. E20.
[ORIGIN from LYMPHO- + GRANULOMA.]
MEDICINE. Any of several diseases involving swelling or inflammation of lymph nodes, *spec*. (**a**) (in full ***lymphogranuloma inguinale*** /ɪŋgwɪˈnɑːli/, also ***lymphogranuloma venereum*** /vɪˈnɪərɪəm/) a venereal disease, esp. of the tropics, caused by chlamydial infection and resulting in destructive inflammation of lymph nodes and lymph vessels, particularly in the inguinal region; (**b**) Hodgkin's disease; (**c**) sarcoidosis.
■ Also **lymphogranulomaˈtosis** *noun*, pl. **-toses** /-ˈtəʊsiːz/, E20.

lymphography /lɪmˈfɒgrəfi/ *noun*. E19.
[ORIGIN from LYMPHO- + -GRAPHY.]
†**1** A description of the lymphatic system. *rare* (Dicts.). Only in E19.
2 = LYMPHANGIOGRAPHY. M20.

lymphoid /ˈlɪmfɔɪd/ *adjective*. M19.
[ORIGIN from LYMPH + -OID.]
PHYSIOLOGY & MEDICINE. Of or pertaining to lymph or the lymphatic system; *esp*. (of tissue) that produces lymphocytes.

lymphoma /lɪmˈfəʊmə/ *noun*. Pl. **-mas**, **-mata** /-mətə/. L19.
[ORIGIN from LYMPH + -OMA.]
MEDICINE. Any of several malignant disorders involving lymphoid tissue.
■ **lymphomaˈtosis** *noun*, pl. **-toses** /-ˈtəʊsiːz/, any of various diffuse neoplastic or hyperplastic disorders originating in lymphoid tissue E20. **lymphomatous** *adjective* of the nature of or characterized by a lymphoma L19.

lymphous /ˈlɪmfəs/ *adjective*. *rare*. L17.
[ORIGIN from LYMPH + -OUS.]
†**1** Of sap: watery. Only in L17.
2 *PHYSIOLOGY & MEDICINE*. Of the nature of or resembling lymph. L19.

lymphy /ˈlɪmfi/ *adjective*. Now *rare*. M19.
[ORIGIN from LYMPH + -Y[1].]
PHYSIOLOGY & MEDICINE. = LYMPHOUS 2.

lyncean /lɪnˈsiːən/ *adjective*. E17.
[ORIGIN from Latin *lynceus* (from Greek *lugkeios*, from *lugx* LYNX) + -AN.]
Lynx-eyed, keen-sighted.

> D. DELILLO Precision was one of the raptures he allowed himself, the lyncean skill for selection and detail.

lynch /lɪn(t)ʃ/ *noun*[1] & *verb*. Orig. *US*. E19.
[ORIGIN from Capt. William *Lynch* (1742–1820), head of a self-constituted judicial tribunal first organized in 1780 in Virginia, USA.]
▸ **A** *noun*. ***lynch law***, (in early use also) ***Lynch's law***, the practice of summary punishment and esp. execution of an alleged offender carried out by a self-constituted illegal court. E19.
▸ **B** *verb trans*. Of a mob or group of people: condemn and put (a person) to death (esp. by hanging) for an alleged offence without a legal trial. M19.

> D. FRANCIS If you don't win they will likely lynch you. J. WAIN The white American was ready first to enslave and later to lynch.

– COMB.: **lynch mob**: intent on lynching someone.
■ **lyncher** *noun* M19. **lynching** *noun* the action of the verb; an execution, esp. a hanging, without a legal trial: M19.

lynch *noun*[2] var. of LINCH *noun*[2].

lynchet /ˈlɪn(t)ʃɪt/ *noun*. L17.
[ORIGIN Prob. from LINCH *noun*[2].]
1 An unploughed strip as a boundary between two fields. L17.
2 A slope or terrace along the face of a chalk down; *spec*. (*ARCHAEOLOGY*) a cultivation terrace. L18.
■ **lynchetted**, **-eted** *adjective* (of land) cultivated by using terraces E20.

lynchpin *noun* var. of LINCHPIN.

Lyngby /ˈlɪŋbi/ *noun & adjective*. E20.
[ORIGIN *Norre-Lyngby* in Denmark, where first discovered.]
(Designating or pertaining to) a Mesolithic culture of the Baltic area.

lyngorm *noun* var. of LINGWORM.

lynx /lɪŋks/ *noun*. ME.
[ORIGIN Latin from Greek *lugx* rel. to Old English *lox*, Old High German *luhs* (German *Luchs*), Old Swedish *lō*.]
1 Any of various small to medium-sized members of the cat family typically having a short tail, tufted ears, and mottled or spotted fur; spec. *Felis lynx* (or *Lynx lynx*), which inhabits forest in NW Europe and northern Asia, and (more fully ***Canadian lynx***) the larger *L. canadensis* of northern N. America. Formerly esp. = CARACAL. ME. ▸**b** The fur of the lynx. M19.
2 (Usu. **L-**.) (The name of) a constellation of the northern hemisphere between Ursa Major and Gemini. Also ***the Lynx***. E18.
– COMB.: **lynx-eye** a keen eye; **lynx-eyed** *adjective* keen-sighted.
■ **lynx-like** *adjective* L16.

lyocell /ˈlʌɪ(ʊ)sɛl/ *noun*. L20.
[ORIGIN Prob. from Greek *luein* loosen + *cell* as in CELLULOSE.]
An artificial fibre spun from a solution made by dissolving wood pulp; a fabric made from such fibre.
– NOTE: Proprietary name in the US.

Lyon /ˈlʌɪən/ *noun*. LME.
[ORIGIN Archaic var. of LION: named from the lion on the royal shield.]
In full ***Lord Lyon*** or ***Lyon King of Arms***. (The title of) the chief herald in Scotland.
– COMB.: **Lyon Court** the court over which the Lyon King of Arms presides.

Lyonese *adjective & noun* var. of LYONNESE.

lyonization /lʌɪənʌɪˈzeɪʃ(ə)n/ *noun*. Also **-isation**. M20.
[ORIGIN from Mary F. *Lyon* (b. 1925), English biologist + -IZATION.]
GENETICS. The inactivation of one of the two X chromosomes in each cell of a developing female mammalian embryo.

Lyonnais /liːəˈneɪ, *foreign* ljɔnɛ/ *adjective & noun*. Fem. **-aise** /-eɪz, *foreign* -ɛːz/. E19.
[ORIGIN French, formed as LYONS. Cf. LYONNESE.]
▸ **A** *adjective*. Of, pertaining to, or characteristic of the city of Lyons (Lyon) or the former province of Lyonnais, in SE France; *spec*. (**-*aise***) in *COOKERY*, designating food, esp. sliced potatoes, cooked with onions or with white wine and onion sauce. E19.
▸ **B** *noun*. Pl. **-ais**, fem. **-aises**, (pronounced as sing.).
1 A native or inhabitant of Lyons. M20.
2 The French dialect of the area of Lyons. M20.
■ **Lyonnois** /liːəˈnwɑː/, fem. **-oise** /-wɑːz/ *noun* (now *rare* or *obsolete*), pl. **-ois**, **-oises**, (pronounced same), = LYONNAIS *noun* 1 M17.

Lyonnese /liːəˈniːz/ *adjective & noun*. Also **Lyonese**. E19.
[ORIGIN formed as LYONS + -ESE.]
▸ **A** *adjective*. Of or pertaining to Lyons, Lyonnais. E19.
▸ **B** *noun*. Pl. same. = LYONNAIS *noun* 1. M19.

Lyons /ˈliːɔ̃ː, ˈlʌɪənz/ *adjective*. M18.
[ORIGIN French *Lyon* a city in SE France.]
Designating various products, esp. fabrics, made in or associated with Lyons.

> ARNOLD BENNETT She bought . . coffee, Lyons sausage, dried prunes. P. WENTWORTH Great ladies . . had bought changeable silks there, and fine Lyons velvet.

lyophile /ˈlʌɪəfʌɪl/ *adjective*. In sense 2 also **-phil** /-fɪl/. E20.
[ORIGIN from Greek *luein* loosen + -PHIL, -PHILE.]
1 *PHYSICAL CHEMISTRY*. = LYOPHILIC *adjective*. E20.
2 *BIOLOGY & MEDICINE*. Of, pertaining to, or employing freeze-drying; freeze-dried. M20.
■ **lyophiliˈzation** *noun* freeze-drying M20. **lyophilize** *verb trans*. freeze-dry M20.

lyophilic /lʌɪə(ʊ)ˈfɪlɪk/ *adjective*. E20.
[ORIGIN formed as LYOPHILE + -IC.]
PHYSICAL CHEMISTRY. Of a colloid: having an affinity for the dispersion medium, and not readily precipitated out by small quantities of electrolyte. Of a sol: containing such a phase, and generally having lower surface tension and a higher viscosity than the dispersion medium, and giving a gel on evaporation or cooling. Cf. LYOPHOBIC.

lyophobic /lʌɪə(ʊ)ˈfəʊbɪk/ *adjective*. E20.
[ORIGIN from Greek *luein* loosen + -O- + -PHOBIA + -IC.]
PHYSICAL CHEMISTRY. Of a colloid: not having an affinity for the dispersion medium, and readily precipitated out by small quantities of electrolyte. Of a sol: containing such a phase, and generally having a similar surface tension and viscosity to the dispersion medium, and on evaporation or cooling giving a solid which cannot readily be reconverted into a sol. Cf. LYOPHILIC.
■ Also **lyophobe** *adjective* E20.

lyotropic /lʌɪə(ʊ)ˈtrəʊpɪk, -ˈtrɒpɪk/ *adjective*. E20.
[ORIGIN from Greek *luein* loosen + -O- + -TROPIC.]
PHYSICAL CHEMISTRY. **1** Associated with the change of internal pressure in a solvent caused by addition of a solute. E20.
lyotropic series: in which ions are arranged in order of their lyotropic effects, esp. their ability to cause precipitation of a lyophilic sol.
2 Designating or pertaining to a mesophase which has its phase transitions readily effected by a change of concentration. M20.

lyra /ˈlʌɪrə/ *noun*. LME.
[ORIGIN Latin from Greek *lura*.]
1 A lyre. Also, any of various other musical instruments descended from or resembling the lyre. LME.
bell lyra: see BELL *noun*[1].
2 (**L-**.) (The name of) a small constellation of the northern hemisphere, lying on the edge of the Milky Way between Hercules and Cygnus; the Lyre. M16.
†**3** A gurnard, the piper *Trigla lyra*. E18–M19.
4 *ANATOMY*. The triangular portion of the undersurface of the corpus callosum lying between the crura of the fornix. M18.
– COMB.: ***lyra glockenspiel***: see GLOCKENSPIEL 2; **lyra viol** a bass viol tuned and played according to a system of tablature; also called ***viola bastarda***.

lyrate /ˈlʌɪreɪt/ *adjective*. M18.
[ORIGIN from Latin LYRA + -ATE[2].]
Chiefly *BOTANY & ZOOLOGY*. Shaped like a lyre.
■ **lyrated** *adjective* = LYRATE M18. **lyrately** *adverb* in a lyrate form L18.

lyre /ˈlʌɪə/ *noun*. ME.
[ORIGIN Old French *lire* (mod. *lyre*) from Latin LYRA.]
1 A plucked stringed musical instrument having strings fixed between a crossbar supported by two arms; *spec*. such an ancient Greek instrument with outwardly curved arms, usu. played with a plectrum and used to accompany song and recitation. ME.
2 (Usu. **L-**.) (The name of) *the* constellation Lyra. M19.
– COMB.: **lyrebird** either of two mainly ground-dwelling Australian birds forming the family Menuridae, *Menura novaehollandiae* and *M. alberti*, which have a lyre-shaped tail; **lyre flower** the plant bleeding heart, *Dicentra spectabilis*; **lyre-shaped** *adjective* shaped like a lyre with outwardly curved arms; **lyretail** any of a number of cyprinodont fishes with coloured tails suggesting lyres.

L

lyric /ˈlɪrɪk/ *adjective & noun*. L16.
[ORIGIN Old French & mod. French *lyrique* or Latin *lyricus* from Greek *lurikos*, from *lura* lyre: see -IC.]
▸ **A** *adjective*. **1** Of or pertaining to the lyre; pertaining to or characteristic of song, meant to be sung; *spec*. (**a**) (of poetry, whether or not intended to be sung) expressing the writer's emotions, usu. briefly and in stanzas or strophes, (of a poet) writing such poems; (**b**) (of a singing voice) using a light register. L16.

V. LEE Poetry which is lyric in spirit as well as in metre. F. FERGUSSON His great speech, 'O wealth and power', is a far more lyric utterance than the ordered exposition. *Opera Now* The American tenor . . is not quite the lyric tenor for the role.

lyric drama opera. **lyric stage** the production or performance of opera.
2 Given to song; singing. Chiefly *poet*. M17.
▸ **B** *noun*. **1** *the lyric*, lyric poetry. L16.
†**2** A lyric poet. L16–M19.
3 A lyric poem; a song; in *pl*., lyric verses. L16.

N. FRYE The poet can express himself in a lyric only by dramatizing the mental state or mood.

4 *sing*. & (usu.) in *pl*. The words of a song (or songs). L19.

M. ANGELOU A joy about the tune that changed the meaning of its sad lyrics. P. B. CLARKE Not all the lyrics and melodies used by Rastas are their own.

†**lyric** *verb trans. rare*. Infl. **-ck-**. L17–E18.
[ORIGIN from the adjective.]
Sing (*over*) in a lyrical manner.

lyrical /ˈlɪrɪk(ə)l/ *adjective*. E16.
[ORIGIN formed as LYRIC *adjective & noun* + -AL[1].]
1 = LYRIC *adjective* 1. E16.
2 Characteristic of, expressed in, or using language appropriate to lyric poetry. E19.

M. TIPPETT The search for lyrical simplicity was . . the hardest thing of all. D. MURPHY A thousand-word lyrical description of the landscape, the birds and the ever-changing . . sky.

3 Excitedly effusive; highly enthusiastic. Freq. in ***wax lyrical***. *colloq*. M20.

Washington Post Exley . . will wax lyrical on the subject, sharing . . remembrances which only great literature imparts.

■ **lyrically** *adverb* E19. **lyricalness** *noun* L19.

†**lyrichord** *noun*. M18–L19.
[ORIGIN from LYRE after *harpsichord*.]
A kind of harpsichord with wire and catgut strings sounded by rotating wheels.

lyricise *verb* var. of LYRICIZE.

lyricism /ˈlɪrɪsɪz(ə)m/ *noun*. M18.
[ORIGIN from LYRIC *noun & adjective* + -ISM.]
Lyric character or style; a lyrical expression; high-flown sentiments or enthusiasm.

lyricist /ˈlɪrɪsɪst/ *noun*. L19.
[ORIGIN from LYRIC *adjective & noun* + -IST.]
1 A person skilled in lyric composition. L19.
2 A person who writes the words of songs. E20.

lyricize /ˈlɪrɪsʌɪz/ *verb*. *rare*. Also **-ise**. M19.
[ORIGIN from LYRIC *adjective & noun* + -IZE.]
1 *verb intrans*. Sing lyrics. M19.
2 *verb trans*. Express or depict lyrically. M19.

Lyrid /ˈlʌɪrɪd/ *adjective & noun*. L19.
[ORIGIN from LYRA 2 + -ID[3].]
ASTRONOMY. (Designating) any of a shower of meteors seeming to radiate from the constellation Lyra in April.

lyriform /ˈlʌɪrɪfɔːm/ *adjective*. M19.
[ORIGIN from LYRE + -I- + -FORM.]
Lyre-shaped.

lyrism /ˈlʌɪərɪz(ə)m, ˈlɪrɪz(ə)m/ *noun*. M19.
[ORIGIN French *lyrisme* or Greek *lurismos* playing on the lyre, from *lura* lyre: see -ISM.]
= LYRICISM. Also (*rare*), a lyrical performance.

lyrist /ˈlɪrɪst/ *noun*. M17.
[ORIGIN Latin *lyrista* from Greek *luristēs*, from *lura* lyre: see -IST.]
1 A person who plays on the lyre. M17.
2 A lyric poet. E19.

lysarden /ˈlɪzəd(ə)n/ *noun*. Also **lyz-**. E17.
[ORIGIN from LIZARD, from its shape.]
EARLY MUSIC. A wind instrument of the cornett family, predating the serpent.

lysate /ˈlʌɪzeɪt/ *noun*. E20.
[ORIGIN from LYSIS + -ATE[2].]
BIOLOGY. A solution or preparation containing the products of lysis of cells.

lyse /lʌɪz/ *verb*. E20.
[ORIGIN Back-form. from LYSIS after *analysis*, *analyse*, etc.]
BIOLOGY. **1** *verb trans*. Bring about lysis of (a cell etc.). E20.
2 *verb intrans*. Undergo lysis. M20.

Lysenkoism /lʌɪˈsɛŋkəʊɪz(ə)m/ *noun*. M20.
[ORIGIN from *Lysenko* (see below) + -ISM.]
Belief in or advocacy of the views of the Russian agronomist T. D. Lysenko (1898–1976), who opposed modern genetics and advocated neo-Lamarckian views and for a time exerted great influence in Soviet Russia.
■ **Lysenkoist** *noun & adjective* (**a**) *noun* an adherent of Lysenkoism; (**b**) *adjective* of or pertaining to Lysenkoists or Lysenkoism: M20.

lysergic /lʌɪˈsəːdʒɪk/ *adjective*. M20.
[ORIGIN from *lys* (in HYDROLYSIS) + ERG(OT + -IC.]
1 CHEMISTRY. ***lysergic acid***, a crystalline tetracyclic compound, $C_{16}H_{16}N_2O_2$, orig. produced by the hydrolysis of ergot alkaloids, which contains the indole nucleus, and of which the hallucinogenic drug LSD is a derivative. M20.
2 *ellipt*. LSD. M20.
lysergic acid diethylamide = LSD.

lysigenous /lʌɪˈsɪdʒɪnəs/ *adjective*. L19.
[ORIGIN from Greek *lusis* loosening + -GENOUS.]
BOTANY. Esp. of intercellular spaces: produced by the breaking down of adjoining cells. Cf. SCHIZOGENOUS.

lysimachia /lʌɪsɪˈmeɪkɪə/ *noun*. L16.
[ORIGIN Latin from Greek *lusimakhion*, from *Lusimakhos* Lysimachus: see LOOSESTRIFE, -IA[1].]
A plant of the genus *Lysimachia* (family Primulaceae); loosestrife.

lysimeter /lʌɪˈsɪmɪtə/ *noun*. L19.
[ORIGIN from Greek *lusis* loosening + -METER.]
An apparatus for measuring mass changes due to leaching, evaporation, etc., undergone by a body of soil.

lysin /ˈlʌɪsɪn/ *noun*. E20.
[ORIGIN from LYSIS + -IN[1].]
BIOLOGY. A substance capable of lysing cells; *spec*. an antibody with this ability.

lysine /ˈlʌɪsiːn/ *noun*. L19.
[ORIGIN German *Lysin*, ult. from Greek *lusis* loosening: see -INE[5].]
BIOCHEMISTRY. A basic amino acid which occurs in proteins and is essential in the human diet; 2,6-diaminohexanoic acid, $COOH{\cdot}CH(NH_2)(CH_2)_3CH_2NH_2$.

lysis /ˈlʌɪsɪs/ *noun*. Pl. **lyses** /ˈlʌɪsiːz/. M16.
[ORIGIN Latin from Greek *lusis* loosening. In sense 2 prob. from ending of HAEMOLYSIS etc.: cf. -LYSIS.]
1 MEDICINE. A gradual resolution of a disease without apparent phenomena (opp. ***crisis***). Now *rare* or *obsolete*. M16.
2 BIOLOGY. The disintegration or dissolution of cells or cell organelles; *esp*. the dissolution of bacterial cells brought about by bacteriophages. E20.

-lysis /lɪsɪs/ *suffix*. Pl. **-lyses** /lɪsiːz/.
[ORIGIN formed as LYSIS.]
Forming nouns (esp. in BIOLOGY, MEDICINE, & CHEMISTRY) with the sense 'decomposition, disintegration, dissolution', the first elem. indicating the agent (***electrolysis***, ***hydrolysis***), the substance or object affected (***glycolysis***, ***haemolysis***, ***frontolysis***), or some other characteristic of the process (***autolysis***, ***heterolysis***).

lyso- /ˈlʌɪsəʊ/ *combining form* of LYSIS: see -O-.
■ **lysoˈsomal** *adjective* (BIOLOGY) of or pertaining to a lysosome or lysosomes M20. **lysosome** *noun* (BIOLOGY) a cytoplasmic cell organelle containing hydrolytic enzymes enclosed in a membrane M20. **lysozyme** *noun* (BIOCHEMISTRY) a low-molecular-weight enzyme capable of hydrolysing a particular mucopolysaccharide found in the cell walls of certain Gram-positive bacteria and hence of lysing such bacteria E20.

lysogenic /lʌɪsəˈdʒɛnɪk/ *adjective*. L19.
[ORIGIN from LYSO- + -GENIC.]
BIOLOGY. Of or pertaining to lysis; capable of producing or undergoing lysis; *spec*. (of a bacterium) capable, without being attacked by a phage, of lysing and liberating a phage normally integrated with the bacterial genome.
■ **lysogenicity** /-ˈnɪsɪti/ *noun* = LYSOGENY M20. **lysogeniˈzation** *noun* the process of lysogenizing a bacterium M20. **lyˈsogenize** *verb trans*. (of a phage) become stably integrated into the genome of (a bacterium) M20. **lyˈsogeny** *noun* the property of being lysogenic; the lysis of a lysogenic bacterium with the subsequent release of phage: M20.

Lysol /ˈlʌɪsɒl/ *noun*. Also **l-**. L19.
[ORIGIN from Greek *lusis* loosening + -OL.]
(Proprietary name for) a solution of coal tar oil in soap.

lysopine /ˈlʌɪsəpiːn/ *noun*. M20.
[ORIGIN from LYS(INE + OCT)OPINE *noun*.]
BIOCHEMISTRY. An opine, $C_9H_{18}N_2O_4$, related to octopine and of similar origin. Cf. NOPALINE.

lyssa /ˈlɪsə/ *noun*. *rare*. E18.
[ORIGIN mod. Latin from Greek *lussa*: cf. LYTTA.]
MEDICINE. Rabies, hydrophobia.

lythe /lʌɪð/ *noun*. *Scot. & Irish*. E16.
[ORIGIN Perh. from Old Norse *lýr* pike.]
The pollack.

lytic /ˈlɪtɪk/ *adjective*. L19.
[ORIGIN Greek *lutikos* able to loose: see -IC.]
1 MEDICINE. Of, pertaining to, or causing gradual resolution of a disease (cf. LYSIS 1). Now *rare* or *obsolete*. L19.
2 BIOLOGY. Of, pertaining to, or causing lysis of a bacterium etc. E20.
■ **lytically** *adverb* M20.

-lytic /ˈlɪtɪk/ *suffix*.
[ORIGIN from or after Greek *-lutikos*: cf. -IC.]
Forming adjectives corresp. to nouns in *-lysis*, as ***analytic***, ***catalytic***, ***haemolytic***.

lytta /ˈlɪtə/ *noun*. E17.
[ORIGIN mod. Latin from Greek *lutta* Attic form of *lussa* LYSSA (with allus. to its formerly supposed connection with liability to rabies).]
A small ligament in a dog's tongue. Cf. WORM *noun* 11.

lyxose /ˈlɪksəʊz, -s/ *noun*. L19.
[ORIGIN from XYLOSE by reversal of 2nd syll.]
CHEMISTRY. A crystalline pentose sugar isomeric with xylose and rare in nature.

lyzarden *noun* var. of LYSARDEN.

LZ *abbreviation*.
Landing zone.

Mm

M, m /ɛm/.
The thirteenth letter of the modern English alphabet and the twelfth of the ancient Roman one, corresp. to Greek *mū*, Semitic *mēm*. The sound normally represented by the letter is a bilabial nasal consonant, usu. voiced, though with an unvoiced ending when followed by an unvoiced consonant, and able to be used syllabically (/-(ə)m/), particularly after /ð/ and /z/ at the end of words (of Greek etymology), as ***rhythm***, ***spasm***, ***schism***, and the suffix ***-ism***. The letter can be silent initially before *n* in Greek derivatives, as ***mnemonic***. Pl. **M's**, **Ms**. See also EM.
▸ **I 1** The letter and its sound.
2 The shape of the letter.
M-roof: formed from two ordinary gable roofs with a valley between them, the section resembling the letter M.
3 *TYPOGRAPHY*. = EM 2.
▸ **II** Symbolical uses.
4 Used to denote serial order; applied e.g. to the thirteenth (or often the twelfth, either I or J being omitted) group or section, sheet of a book, etc.
5 The roman numeral for a thousand.
6 *PHYSICS*. **a** (Cap. M.) Designating the series of X-ray emission lines of an excited atom of longer wavelength than the L-series (cf. L, L 5b), arising from electron transitions to the atomic orbit of third lowest energy, with principal quantum number 3; hence ***M-shell***, this orbit; ***M-electrons***, electrons in this shell; ***M-capture***, the capture by an atomic nucleus of one of the M-electrons. ▸**b** Denoting magnetic quantum numbers (*m* for a single particle, *M* for an assemblage of particles), corresponding to the component of an angular momentum (often indicated by a subscript) in some physically distinguished direction.
▸ **III 7** Abbrevs.: **M.** = Master (now only in academic degrees, = Latin *magister*); †***carry an M under one's girdle***, use a respectful prefix (Mr, Mrs) when addressing someone; Member (of); [French] *Monsieur*. **M** = medium; (as *prefix*) mega-; (*ASTRONOMY*) Messier (number); (of paper quality) middling; million(s); (*CHEMISTRY*) molar; (*ECONOMICS*) money (with following numeral, in measures of money supply); morphine; (in road numbers) motorway. **m.** = (*CRICKET*) maiden (over); male; mare; married; masculine; mile(s); minute(s). **m** = mark(s) (as monetary unit); mass; metre(s); (*MUSIC*) (as *prefix*) mezzo; (as *prefix*) milli-; million(s). **m-** (*CHEMISTRY*) = meta-.

m' *possess. adjective* see MY *possess. adjective*.

'm *noun* see MA'AM *noun*.

m- /em/ *prefix*.
Designating commercial activity conducted electronically by means of mobile phones, as *m-commerce*.

MA *abbreviation*.
1 Massachusetts.
2 Master of Arts.

ma /mɑː/ *noun*. *colloq*. E19.
[ORIGIN Abbreviation of MAMMA *noun*[2].]
Mother. Also, Mrs; used as a form of address to a middle-aged or elderly woman other than one's mother.

P. G. WODEHOUSE Did Ma Purkiss make a speech? A. CARTER They all scattered in fright, bawling for their mas. R. BARNARD Cheery cries of 'Come on, Ma' to elderly ladies.

– COMB.: **ma-in-law**, pl. **mas-in-law**, = *mother-in-law* s.v. MOTHER *noun*[1].

ma. /meɪ/ *abbreviation*.
In some schools: major (elder of two namesakes).

maa /mɑː/ *verb intrans*. E18.
[ORIGIN Imit. Cf. BAA.]
Esp. of a sheep: bleat.

ma'am /mɑːm, mam, *unstressed* məm/ *noun* & *verb*. L17.
[ORIGIN Contr. See also MARM, MAUM, MUM *noun*[4].]
▸ **A** *noun*. Also (*colloq*.) **'m** /(ə)m/.
1 Madam. Chiefly as a respectful form of address: now usu. to a member of royalty or to a superior officer in the women's armed forces, but formerly used more generally to any (esp. married) equal or superior. L17.

DICKENS 'Mrs Sparsit ma'am', said Mr. Bounderby. 'I am going to astonish you.'

THANK-YOU-ma'am.
†**2** A person addressed as 'ma'am'. M–L18.
▸ **B** *verb trans*. Address as 'ma'am'. E19.

G. R. SIMS Don't ma'am me—I'm a miss.

maar /mɑː/ *noun*. Pl. **maars**, **maare** /ˈmɑːrə/. E19.
[ORIGIN German dial.]
1 (Usu. **M-**.) A crater lake in the Eifel district of Germany. E19.
2 *GEOLOGY*. A broad low-rimmed usu. lake-filled volcanic crater of a kind exemplified by the Eifel Maars, formed by an explosive event with little lava. L19.

maas /mɑːs/ *noun*. *S. Afr*. Also in Zulu form **amasi** /əˈmɑːsi/. L19.
[ORIGIN Afrikaans from Zulu (pl.) *amasi* curdled milk.]
Thick sour milk.

Maasai *noun* var. of MASAI.

maasbanker /masˈbaŋkə, mɒsˈbɒŋkə/ *noun*. *S. Afr*. M19.
[ORIGIN Afrikaans from Dutch *marsbanker*. Cf. MOSSBUNKER.]
The scad, *Trachurus trachurus*.

Maastricht /ˈmɑːstrɪxt/ *noun*. L20.
[ORIGIN A city in the south of the Netherlands.]
More fully ***Maastricht agreement***, ***Maastricht treaty***. An agreement reached between European Community leaders at a summit held at Maastricht in December 1991 concerning progress towards European economic, monetary, and political union, also containing a protocol regarding social and employment policy in member states.

mab /mab/ *noun*. Long *obsolete* exc. *dial*. M16.
[ORIGIN Perh. from the female forename *Mab*, abbreviation of *Mabel*. Cf. MOB *noun*[2].]
A disreputable or promiscuous woman.

mabele /məˈbiːli/ *noun*. *S. Afr*. E19.
[ORIGIN Bantu: cf. Zulu, Xhosa *ibele*, pl. *amabele*.]
Kaffir corn, *Sorghum bicolor* var. *caffrorum*; meal or porridge made from this.

Mac /mak/ *noun*[1]. Also (earlier) †**Mack**. E16.
[ORIGIN *Mac-* (also written *Mc-*) patronymic prefix in many Scot. & Irish names = Irish, Gaelic *mac* son.]
1 A person whose name contains the prefix *Mac-*; *gen*. a Scotsman, (formerly also) an Irishman of Celtic origin. E16.
2 Used as a familiar form of address to a (male) stranger. *colloq*. (chiefly *N. Amer*.). E20.

J. WAINWRIGHT The bouncer . . tapped him on the shoulder and said: 'Hey, mac'.

Mac /mak/ *noun*[2]. L20.
[ORIGIN Shortened from *Macintosh*, the name for a range of computers produced by the US company Apple Computer Inc. and named after a variety of apple (see MCINTOSH).]
(Proprietary name for) a personal computer produced by Apple.

mac /mak/ *noun*[3]. *colloq*. Also **mack**. E20.
[ORIGIN Abbreviation.]
= MACKINTOSH 1.

macabre /məˈkɑːbr(ə), *foreign* makɑːbr/ *noun* & *adjective*. LME.
[ORIGIN from Old French *macabré* adjective (mod. *macabre*), perh. alt. of *Macabé* Maccabaeus, Maccabee, with ref. to a miracle play containing the slaughter of the Maccabees. In early use perh. regarded as a proper name.]
▸ **A** *noun*. **1** ***dance of macabre***, = DANSE MACABRE. Long *obsolete* exc. *hist*. LME.
2 A macabre happening. *rare*. E20.
▸ **B** *adjective*. Grim, gruesome. Orig. in ***dance macabre***. Cf. DANSE MACABRE. M19.

H. ACTON With macabre humour—somewhat sinister in retrospect—Nancy wrote . . about her tomb and burial. GODFREY SMITH The macabre pull of the Chamber of Horrors still exercises its malevolent thrall.

■ **macabrely** *adverb* M20.

macaco /məˈkeɪkəʊ/ *noun*[1]. Now *rare* or *obsolete*. Pl. **-os**. L18.
[ORIGIN Portuguese: see MACAQUE. Cf. MACAUCO.]
A macaque; a monkey resembling a macaque.

macaco *noun*[2] var. of MACAUCO.

macadam /məˈkadəm/ *adjective* & *noun*. E19.
[ORIGIN John Loudon *McAdam* (1756–1836), Brit. surveyor.]
▸ **A** *adjective*. Of a roadway: of the kind laid down by McAdam; macadamized. See also TARMACADAM. E19.
▸ **B** *noun*. The material of which a macadamized road is made. E19.

macadamia /makəˈdeɪmɪə/ *noun*. M19.
[ORIGIN mod. Latin (see below), from John *Macadam* (1827–65), Scottish-born chemist.]
Any of various Australian evergreen trees of the genus *Macadamia* (family Proteaceae), esp. *M. integrifolia* and *M. tetraphylla* (both also called ***Queensland nut***) which yield edible nuts (also ***macadamia nut***, ***macadamia tree***); the nut of any of these trees.

macadamize /məˈkadəmʌɪz/ *verb trans*. Also **-ise**. E19.
[ORIGIN from MACADAM + -IZE.]
1 Make or repair (a road) by laying down successive layers of broken stone of nearly uniform size, each layer being consolidated by pressure before the next is laid. Freq. as ***macadamized ppl adjective***. E19. ▸**b** *fig*. Make level or even; raze. Now *rare*. E19.
2 Convert into road metal; break up into pieces. Now *rare* or *obsolete*. E19.
■ **macadamiˈzation** *noun* the action of macadamizing a road; the process, practice, or system of making macadamized roads: E19. **macadamizer** *noun* (*a*) a person who makes macadamized roads; †(*b*) a person who rides on roads when hunting: E19.

macana /məˈkɑːnə/ *noun*. M16.
[ORIGIN Spanish, Portuguese *macaná* from Taino.]
An ironwood club used by some indigenous S. American peoples.

Macanese /makəˈniːz/ *noun* & *adjective*. Also (earlier) **Macaoese** /makaʊˈiːz/, **Macaonese** /makaʊˈniːz/. E20.
[ORIGIN from *Macao* (see below), Portuguese *Macau*, after *Japanese* etc.: see -ESE.]
▸ **A** *noun*. Pl. same.
1 A native or inhabitant of Macao, a former Portuguese dependency on the south coast of China, *esp*. one of mixed Chinese and Portuguese descent. E20.
2 The Portuguese creole language used in Macao. M20.
▸ **B** *adjective*. Of or pertaining to Macao or the Macanese. E20.

macao /məˈkaʊ/ *noun*[1]. Also †**macco**. L18.
[ORIGIN formed as MACANESE.]
A game related to baccarat, in which each player receives only one card.

†**macao** *noun*[2] see MACAW *noun*[1].

Macaoese, **Macaonese** *nouns* & *adjectives* see MACANESE.

macaque /məˈkɑːk, -ˈkak/ *noun*. L17.
[ORIGIN French from Portuguese *macaco* from Bantu *makaku* some monkeys, from *ma* numerical sign + *kaku* monkey. Cf. MACACO *noun*[1], MACAUCO.]
†**1** A kind of monkey native to Brazil. Only in L17.
2 Any of numerous monkeys of the Old World genus *Macaca*, including the rhesus monkey, *M. mulatta*, and the Barbary ape, *M. sylvanus*. M18.
JAPANESE ***macaque***. ***pigtailed macaque***: see PIGTAILED (a). ***rhesus macaque***: see RHESUS 1.

Macarena /ˌmakəˈraɪnə/ *noun*. L20.
[ORIGIN Title of a song by the Spanish duo Los del Rio (1993).]
A dance consisting of set movements performed to a fast Latin rhythm.

Macaronesian /ˌmakərə(ʊ)ˈniːzjən, -ʒ(ə)n/ *adjective*. E20.
[ORIGIN from *Macaronesia* (see below), from Greek *makarōn nēsoi* Islands of the Blessed (mythical islands later identified with the Canaries etc.), from *makar* blessed or happy man + *nēsos* island, after *Polynesia* etc.: see -IAN.]
Chiefly *BOTANY*. Of or pertaining to Macaronesia, a biogeographical region which embraces islands in the eastern N. Atlantic (principally the Azores, Madeira, Canary Islands, and Cape Verde Islands).

macaroni /makəˈrəʊni/ *noun*. Pl. **-ies**. E17.
[ORIGIN Italian †*mac(c)aroni*, later *maccheroni*, pl. of †*mac(c)a-*, *maccherone* from late Greek *makaria* barley food.]
1 Pasta in the form of tubes; an Italian dish consisting largely of this and usu. a sauce. E17.
2 A fop, a dandy; *spec*. one belonging to an 18th-cent. group who imitated extravagant Continental fashions. *obsolete* exc. *hist*. M18.
3 *hist*. A West Indian coin worth a quarter of a dollar or (later) one shilling. E19.
4 In full ***macaroni penguin***. A penguin, *Eudyptes chrysolophus*, apparently so called from its orange crest. M19.
5 An Italian. *slang*. *derog*. M19.
6 Nonsense, meaningless talk. *slang* (chiefly *Austral*.). E20.
– COMB.: **macaroni cheese** a savoury dish consisting of macaroni baked or served with a cheese sauce; **macaroni tool** a square-cutting wood-carving chisel used for finishing recesses.
■ †**macaronian** *adjective* = MACARONIC *adjective*: only in 18. **macaronism** *noun* (now *rare* or *obsolete*) behaviour characteristic of a macaroni; dandyism: L18.

macaronic /makəˈrɒnɪk/ *adjective* & *noun*. E17.
[ORIGIN mod. Latin *macaronicus* from Italian †*macaronico*, later *maccheronico*, joc. from *macaroni*: see MACARONI, -IC.]
▸ **A** *adjective*. †**1** Of the nature of a jumble or medley. E17–E19.

2 (Of verse) of a burlesque form in which vernacular words are introduced into the context of another language, esp. Latin, with appropriate inflections etc.; resembling the mixed jargon of such poetry. **M17**.
†**3** Pertaining to a macaroni; foppish, conceited. *rare*. Only in **E19**.
▸ **B** *noun*. †**1** A jumble, a medley. Only in **E17**.
2 Macaronic language or composition; in *pl.*, macaronic verses. **M17**.
■ **macaronically** *adverb* **E19**.

macaroon /makəˈruːn/ *noun*. **ME**.
[ORIGIN French *macaron* from Italian *maccarone*: see MACARONI, -OON.]
†**1** = MACARONI 1. **ME–M18**.
2 A small cake or biscuit consisting chiefly of ground almonds, white of egg, and sugar; the mixture used to bake this. **E17**.
3 A buffoon, a dolt. Also (*dial.*), a fop. *slang* (now *rare*). **M17**.

Macartney /məˈkɑːtni/ *noun*. **E19**.
[ORIGIN George, Earl *Macartney* (1737–1806), Brit. ambassador to China.]
1 ***Macartney rose***, an evergreen white-flowered climbing rose, *Rosa bracteata*, native to China. **E19**.
2 In full ***Macartney pheasant***. A fireback pheasant, esp. *Lophura ignita*. Now *rare* or *obsolete*. **M19**.

Macassar /məˈkasə/ *adjective & noun*. With ref. to people or language now usu. **Makasar**. **M17**.
[ORIGIN Earlier form of *Makasar*: see below.]
▸ **A** *adjective*. Obtained from or associated with Makasar (now Ujung Pandang), a district of the island of Sulawesi, Indonesia. Also = MAKASARESE *adjective*. **M17**.
Macassar ebony a form of ebony from Sulawesi and neighbouring islands. **Macassar oil** a kind of oil for the hair, orig. represented as consisting of ingredients obtained from Makasar.
▸ **B** *noun*. **1** = MAKASARESE *noun*. **M17**.
2 Macassar oil. Cf. ANTIMACASSAR *noun*. **E19**.

Macassarese *noun & adjective* see MAKASARESE.

macauco /məˈkɔːkəʊ/ *noun*. Now *rare* or *obsolete*. Also **macaco** /məˈkeɪkəʊ/. Pl. **-os**. **M18**.
[ORIGIN French *mococo*, perh. ult. from Malagasy *maka*, *maki* lemur. Cf. MACACO *noun*[1], MACAQUE.]
A lemur.

Macaulayesque /məkɔːlɪˈɛsk/ *adjective*. **M19**.
[ORIGIN from *Macaulay* (see below) + -ESQUE.]
Characteristic of or resembling the historical method or (esp.) literary style of Thomas Babington, Lord Macaulay (1800–59), English historian.

macaw /məˈkɔː/ *noun*[1]. Also (earlier) †**macao**. **E17**.
[ORIGIN Portuguese *macao*, of unknown origin.]
Any of various large long-tailed parrots belonging to the genus *Ara* and other genera, native to tropical and subtropical America.
scarlet macaw: see SCARLET *adjective*.

macaw *noun*[2] see MACCA.

Macc. *abbreviation*.
Maccabees (Apocrypha).

macca /ˈmakə/ *noun*. Also (earlier) **macaw** /məˈkɔː/. **M17**.
[ORIGIN Carib: cf. Arawak *mocoya*, *macoya*.]
A spiny West Indian palm tree, *Acrocomia aculeata*, the nuts of which yield a fragrant oil; *gen.* any prickly shrub; prickles.
– COMB.: **macca-fat (tree)** an oil-bearing palm, esp. *Acrocomia aculeata* or the oil palm, *Elaeis guineensis*.

Maccabee /ˈmakəbiː/ *noun*. **LME**.
[ORIGIN Latin *Maccabaeus*, Greek *Makkabaios*, epithet of Judas (see below), perh. from Hebrew *maqqeḇeṯ* hammer.]
JEWISH HISTORY. Any of a Jewish family (or their supporters), members of which (esp. Judas Maccabaeus) led a religious revolt in Judaea against the Syrian Seleucid king Antiochus IV, in 165 BC. Usu. in *pl.*
Books of the Maccabees, **the Maccabees** four books of Jewish history and theology, of which the first two are included in the Apocrypha.
■ **Maccaˈbean** *adjective & noun* (**a**) *adjective* of or pertaining to Judas Maccabaeus or the Maccabees; (**b**) *noun* = MACCABEE: **M17**.

macchia /ˈmɑːkɪə/ *noun*. **E20**.
[ORIGIN Corsican Italian from Latin *macula* spot.]
= MAQUIS 1.

macchiato /makɪˈɑːtəʊ/ *noun*. Pl. **-os**. **L20**.
[ORIGIN Italian *macchiàto*, lit. 'stained'.]
A drink of caffè macchiato.

†**macco** *noun* var. of MACAO *noun*[1].

maccoboy /ˈmakəbɔɪ/ *noun*. Also †**-baw**, **macouba** /məˈkuːbə/, & other vars. **M18**.
[ORIGIN *Macouba*, a district in Martinique.]
A kind of snuff, usu. scented with attar of roses.

mace /meɪs/ *noun*[1]. **ME**.
[ORIGIN Old French *masse*, *mace* (mod. *masse* large hammer etc.) from Proto-Romance.]
1 *hist.* A weapon consisting of a heavy staff or club, either entirely of metal or having a metal head, often spiked. Formerly also *gen.*, a club. **ME**. ▸†**b** The trident of Neptune. **L16–L18**.

fig.: LONGFELLOW The loud and ponderous mace of Time knocks at the golden portals of the day.

2 A sceptre or staff of office, resembling the weapon of war, which is carried before (or was formerly carried by) certain officials; *spec.* that which lies on the table in the House of Commons when the Speaker is in the chair, viewed as a symbol of the authority of the House. **LME**. ▸**b** A mace-bearer. **M17**.
Sergeant-at-mace: see SERGEANT.
3 A stick with a flat square head, used for propelling the ball in bagatelle or (formerly) billiards. **E18**.
– COMB.: **mace-bearer** a person who carries a mace, esp. as a symbol of authority ceremonially preceding a high dignitary.

mace /meɪs/ *noun*[2]. **ME**.
[ORIGIN Anglo-Norman *macis* or Old French & mod. French *macis*, from Latin *macir* red spicy bark from India: *mace* formed as sing. of *macis*, erron. taken as pl.]
A spice consisting of the dried fleshy aril surrounding the seed (nutmeg) of the fruit of the nutmeg tree.

mace /meɪs/ *noun*[3]. **L16**.
[ORIGIN Malay *mās* prob. from Sanskrit *māṣa* weight of about 17 grains or 1.1 grams.]
hist. **1** In Malay countries: a small gold coin weighing 9 grains or 0.6 gram. **L16**.
2 A monetary unit of China equal to one-tenth of a silver liang or tael. **E17**.

mace /meɪs/ *noun*[4]. *slang*. **M18**.
[ORIGIN Unknown.]
Swindling, robbery by fraud.
on mace on credit.

Mace /meɪs/ *noun*[5]. Also **m-**. **M20**.
[ORIGIN Prob. use of MACE *noun*[1].]
▸ **A** *noun*. (Proprietary name for) an irritant chemical preparation used in aerosol form as a disabling weapon. **M20**.
▸ **B** *verb trans.* Spray (a person) with Mace. **M20**.

mace /meɪs/ *verb*[1] *trans. rare*. **M17**.
[ORIGIN from MACE *noun*[1].]
Strike (as) with a mace.

mace /meɪs/ *verb*[2] *trans. & intrans. slang*. **L18**.
[ORIGIN from MACE *noun*[4].]
Swindle, cheat.

Macedo- /ˈmasɪdəʊ/ *combining form*. **M19**.
[ORIGIN from MACEDONIAN *adjective*[1].]
Forming names of dialects spoken in Macedonia, as ***Macedo-Bulgarian***, ***Macedo-Romanian***, etc.

macédoine /ˈmasɪdwɑːn/ *noun*. **E19**.
[ORIGIN French from *Macédoine* Macedonia, with ref. to the diversity of peoples in the Macedonian empire of Alexander the Great.]
Mixed fruit or vegetables cut up into small pieces; *fig.* a medley, a mixture.

Macedon /ˈmasɪdɒn/ *noun & adjective*. Now *arch.* or *hist.* **ME**.
[ORIGIN Latin *Macedon-*, *Macedo*, Greek *Makedōn*, *-don-* Macedonia.]
▸ **A** *noun*. **1** Ancient Macedonia. **ME**.
2 A Macedonian; ***the Macedon***, Alexander the Great. **LME**.
▸ †**B** *adjective*. Macedonian. **LME–E18**.

Macedonian /masɪˈdəʊnɪən/ *noun*[1] *& adjective*[1]. **ME**.
[ORIGIN from Latin *Macedonius*, Greek *Makedonios*, formed as MACEDON: see -AN.]
▸ **A** *noun*. **1** A native of Macedonia, in ancient times a country corresponding to parts of northern Greece, Bulgaria, and present-day Macedonia; a native of present-day Macedonia, north of Greece. **ME**.
2 a The language of ancient Macedonia, usu. regarded as a variety of Greek. **M16**. ▸**b** The Slavonic language of present-day Macedonia and adjacent areas of Bulgaria and Greece. **M20**.
▸ **B** *adjective*. Of or pertaining to (ancient or present-day) Macedonia or Macedonian. **M16**.

Macedonian /masɪˈdəʊnɪən/ *noun*[2] *& adjective*[2]. **ME**.
[ORIGIN ecclesiastical Latin *Macedonianus* adjective, from *Macedonius* (see below): see -AN.]
ECCLESIASTICAL HISTORY. ▸ **A** *noun*. A follower of the Pneumatomachian doctrine attributed to Macedonius, a bishop of Constantinople in the 4th cent. AD. **ME**.
▸ **B** *adjective*. Of or pertaining to Macedonians or their beliefs. **L16**.

macer /ˈmeɪsə/ *noun*[1]. **ME**.
[ORIGIN Old French *maissier*, *massier*, from *masse* MACE *noun*[1]: see -ER[2].]
A mace-bearer; *spec.* in Scotland, an official who keeps order in courts of law.

macer /ˈmeɪsə/ *noun*[2]. *slang*. **E19**.
[ORIGIN from MACE *verb*[2] + -ER[1].]
A swindler, a cheat.

†**macerable** *adjective*. *rare*. **M17–M18**.
[ORIGIN formed as MACERAL + -ABLE.]
Able to be macerated.

maceral /ˈmas(ə)r(ə)l/ *noun*. **M20**.
[ORIGIN from Latin *macerare* MACERATE *verb* + -AL[1], after *mineral*.]
GEOLOGY. Any of the microscopic structural constituents of coal.

macerate /ˈmasəreɪt/ *noun*. **M20**.
[ORIGIN from the verb, after *filtrate* etc.]
A product obtained by maceration.

macerate /ˈmasəreɪt/ *verb*. **M16**.
[ORIGIN Latin *macerat-* pa. ppl stem of *macerare*, prob. cogn. with Greek *massein* knead: see -ATE[3].]
1 *verb trans.* Soften by steeping in a liquid, with or without heat; wear *away* or separate the soft parts of, by steeping. **M16**. ▸**b** *verb intrans.* Undergo maceration in a liquid. **E17**.

R. B. TODD More complete mastication is performed after the food has been long macerated in the paunch.

2 *verb trans.* Cause to grow thinner or to waste away, esp. by fasting. **M16**.

I. D'ISRAELI Her frame was macerated by her secret sorrows.

†**3** *verb trans.* Fret, vex, worry. **L16–M18**.

L. STERNE A city so macerated with expectation.

■ **macerator** *noun* a person who or thing which macerates something; *esp.* a vessel or machine used for macerating a substance: **L19**.

maceration /masəˈreɪʃ(ə)n/ *noun*. **L15**.
[ORIGIN Latin *maceratio(n-)*, formed as MACERATE *verb*: see -ATION.]
1 The process of wasting away through fasting etc.; mortification of the flesh; an instance of this; the condition so produced. **L15**.
2 The action or process of softening by steeping in a liquid; the state of being subjected to this process; an instance of this. **M16**.
†**3** Fretting, vexation, worry; an instance of this. **E–M17**.

macfarlane /məkˈfɑːlən/ *noun*. **E20**.
[ORIGIN Prob. from the surname *Macfarlane*.]
A kind of caped overcoat with slits in the sides to allow access to pockets in the clothing underneath.

Mach /mɑːk, mak, *foreign* maːx/ *noun*. **E20**.
[ORIGIN Ernst *Mach* (1838–1916), Austrian physicist and philosopher.]
1 ***Mach's principle***, the hypothesis that a body's inertial mass results from its interaction with the rest of the matter in the universe. **E20**.
2 ***Mach number***, the ratio of the speed of a body to the speed of sound in the surrounding medium; ***Mach one***, ***Mach two***, or ***Mach 1***, ***Mach 2***, etc., a speed corresponding to a Mach number of one, two, etc. **M20**.
3 ***Mach bands***, ***Mach's bands***, illusory bright or dark bands perceived where the spatial rate of variation of surface brightness abruptly increases or decreases (as at the edge of an indistinct shadow). **M20**.
– COMB.: **Machmeter** an airspeed indicator that reads directly in Mach numbers.
■ **Machian** *adjective & noun* (**a**) *adjective* of, pertaining to, or characteristic of Ernst Mach or his philosophical ideas, in which the principles of mechanics were based on an extreme sensationalist empiricism; (**b**) *noun* a follower or adherent of Mach: **E20**. **Machism** *noun* the theories of Ernst Mach, *esp.* his concept of empirio-criticism **E20**.

machaerdont *noun & adjective* var. of MACHAIRODONT.

machair /ˈmakə, -x-/ *noun*. **E18**.
[ORIGIN Gaelic.]
In Scotland: a flat or low-lying coastal strip of arable or grassland; land of this nature.

machairodont /məˈkʌɪrədɒnt/ *noun & adjective*. Also **-chaer-**. **L19**.
[ORIGIN from Greek *makhaira* sword, sabre + -ODONT.]
PALAEONTOLOGY. ▸ **A** *noun*. An extinct sabre-toothed felid of the subfamily Machairodontinae. **L19**.
▸ **B** *adjective*. Of or pertaining to this subfamily; sabre-toothed. **L19**.
■ **machairodus** *noun* a machairodont of the genus *Machairodus* **M19**.

machan /mʌˈtʃɑːn/ *noun*. **M19**.
[ORIGIN Hindi *macān* from Sanskrit *mañca*.]
In the Indian subcontinent: an elevated platform, esp. for use in hunting.

Machangana *noun pl.* see SHANGAAN *noun*.

mache /mɑːʃ/ *noun*. Orig. only in *pl.* as †***maches***. **L17**.
[ORIGIN French *mâche*.]
Lamb's lettuce, corn salad.

†**machecole** *verb trans.* **ME–E16**.
[ORIGIN Old French *machecoller*, *machicoler*: see MACHICOLATE.]
= MACHICOLATE.

macher /ˈmaxə/ *noun*. *US colloq.* (freq. *derog.*). **E20**.
[ORIGIN Yiddish from German = maker, doer.]
A man of importance, a bigwig; a braggart.

machete /məˈtʃɛti, -ˈʃɛti/ *noun*. Also anglicized as **matchet** /ˈmatʃɪt/. **L16**.
[ORIGIN Spanish, from *macho* hammer from Latin *marcus*.]
A broad and heavy knife or cutlass, used, esp. in Central America and the W. Indies, as a tool or a weapon.

Machiavel /ˈmakɪəvɛl/ *noun*. **L16**.
[ORIGIN Anglicized from *Machiavelli*: see MACHIAVELLIAN.]
A person who acts on the principles of Machiavelli; an unscrupulous schemer.

■ **machia'vellic** *adjective* (now *rare*) = MACHIAVELLIAN *adjective* **M19**. **machia'vellism** *noun* (now *rare*) = MACHIAVELLIANISM **L16**. †**machiavellist** *noun* = MACHIAVELLIAN *noun* **M16–E19**.

Machiavellian /ˌmakɪə'vɛlɪən/ *noun & adjective*. **M16**.
[ORIGIN from Niccolò dei *Machiavelli* (1469–1527), Florentine statesman (see below) + -IAN.]
▸ **A** *noun*. A person who adopts the principles recommended by Machiavelli in his treatise on statecraft; a person preferring expediency to morality. **M16**.
▸ **B** *adjective*. Of, pertaining to, or characteristic of Machiavelli or his principles; adopting unscrupulous methods; duplicitous, deceitful; cunning, scheming. **L16**.

F. FYFIELD Securing further promotion was a Machiavellian exercise demanding paroxysms of sycophancy.

■ **Machiavellianism** *noun* the principles and practice of Machiavelli; (an instance of) cunning or duplicity in behaviour: **E17**. **Machiavellianly** *adverb* (*rare*) in a Machiavellian manner **L16**.

machicolate /mə'tʃɪkəleɪt/ *verb trans*. **L18**.
[ORIGIN Anglo-Latin *machicollare*, from Old French *machicoler*, ult. from Provençal *machacol*, from *macar* beat, crush + *col* neck: see -ATE[3]. Cf. earlier MACHECOLE.]
ARCHITECTURE. Provide with machicolations. Chiefly as ***machicolated*** *ppl adjective*.

machicolation /mətʃɪkə'leɪʃ(ə)n/ *noun*. **L18**.
[ORIGIN from MACHICOLATE + -ATION.]
ARCHITECTURE. An opening between the corbels which support a projecting parapet, or in the vault of a portal, through which combustibles, molten lead, stones, etc., could be dropped on assailants below. Also, a projecting structure containing a range of such openings.

machicoulis /mɑːtʃɪ'kuːli/ *noun*. Now *rare* or *obsolete*. **L18**.
[ORIGIN French *mâchecoulis*, *mâchi-* from Old French *maschecoulis* rel. to Provençal *machacol*: see MACHICOLATE.]
= MACHICOLATION.

machila /mə'ʃiːlə/ *noun*. Also **-ll-**. **M19**.
[ORIGIN Portuguese formed as MUNCHEEL.]
A kind of litter resembling a hammock, used in Africa.

machinable /mə'ʃiːnəb(ə)l/ *adjective*. **E20**.
[ORIGIN from MACHINE *verb* + -ABLE.]
1 Able to be cut by machine tools. **E20**.
2 Able to be processed by a computer or other machine. **M20**.
■ **machina'bility** *noun* **E20**.

machinal /'makɪn(ə)l/ *adjective*. Now *arch. rare*. **L17**.
[ORIGIN Latin *machinalis*, from *machina* MACHINE *noun*: see -AL[1].]
Of or pertaining to a machine or machines; mechanical.

machinate /'makɪneɪt, 'maʃ-/ *verb*. Pa. pple **-ated**, (earlier) †**-ate**. **M16**.
[ORIGIN Latin *machinat-* pa. ppl stem of *machinari*, from *machina* MACHINE *noun*: see -ATE[3].]
†**1** *verb trans*. Contrive, plan, plot (usu. in a bad sense). **M16–E19**.
2 *verb intrans*. Lay plots; intrigue, scheme. **E17**.
■ **machinating** *ppl adjective* that machinates; given to scheming: **M18**. **machinator** *noun* a person who machinates; an intriguer, a plotter, a schemer: **E17**.

machination /makɪ'neɪʃ(ə)n, maʃ-/ *noun*. **L15**.
[ORIGIN Old French & mod. French, or Latin *machinatio(n-)*, formed as MACHINATE: see -ATION.]
1 An instance of plotting or contrivance; an intrigue, a plot, a scheme. **L15**.

W. RAEPER Through the machinations of the evil Fairy . . the level of the lake begins to subside. M. FORSTER All the machinations of the complicated plot.

2 The action or process of contriving or planning; intrigue, plotting. Now *rare*. **M16**.

G. GISSING A schemer endeavouring to encompass vulgar ends by machination.

†**3** Something contrived or constructed; a machine (esp. of war), a framework, an apparatus. Only in **17**.
†**4** The use or construction of machinery. **M17–E18**.

machine /mə'ʃiːn/ *noun*. **M16**.
[ORIGIN Old French & mod. French from Latin *machina* device, contrivance, engine from Greek *makhana* (Doric), *mēkhanē*, from *mēkhos* contrivance, ult. from Germanic base of MAY *verb*[1].]
1 A structure of any kind, material or abstract; something constructed. Now *rare*. **M16**. ▸†**b** A scheme, a plot. **L16–E18**. ▸†**c** A ship, a boat. **M17–E19**. ▸**d** A vehicle, a (wheeled) conveyance; formerly *esp*. a stagecoach, a mail coach; *ellipt*. = BATHING ***machine***. *obsolete* exc. *hist*. **L17**.

BROWNING To each mortal peradventure earth becomes a new machine. **d** BURKE Your very kind letter . . I received by the machine.

2 The human and animal frame. Chiefly *fig*.: cf. sense 5 below. **E17**.

ADDISON Cheerfulness is . . the best Promoter of Health. Repinings . . wear out the machine insensibly.

3 [Latin *machina*] ▸**a** A military engine or siege tower. *obsolete* exc. *hist*. **M17**. ▸**b** THEATRICAL. A contrivance for the production of stage effects; in *pl*., stage machinery. *obsolete* exc. *hist*. **M17**. ▸**c** In literature etc.: a contrivance for the sake of effect; a supernatural agency, personage, or incident introduced into a narrative; the interposition of one of these. **L17**.

c ADDISON The changing of the Trojan fleet into Water-Nymphs . . is the most violent Machine of the whole Aeneid.

b ***god from the machine***: see GOD *noun*.
4 An apparatus, an appliance; a device for applying mechanical power and having a number of interconnected parts, each with a definite function, *esp*. one that does not utilize human strength; an apparatus of a particular (specified or understood) kind; a bicycle, a motor vehicle; an aircraft; a computer; a typewriter. **M17**. ▸**b** MECHANICS. Any instrument that transmits force or directs its application. **E18**. ▸**c** The penis. Also, a condom. *slang*. **M18**.

W. THOMSON Windmills as hitherto made are very costly machines. J. K. JEROME We were riding our machines . . in the company of many other cyclists. O. DOPPING A company which changes computers normally changes to a machine which is considerably faster. D. ROWE We no longer send five-year-olds into the factory to tend the machines. *Bella* Machines can measure the amount of stress you are under. **b** G. D. CAMPBELL A man's arm is a machine. **c** J. CLELAND With that formidable machine of his, he lets the fury loose.

answering machine, ***flying machine***, ***gaming machine***, ***sewing machine***, ***vending machine***, ***washing machine***, etc. ***rotary machine***, ***spindle machine***, etc. ***Turing machine*** etc. ***infernal machine***: see INFERNAL *adjective*. **b compound machine**: the efficiency of which depends on the combined action of two or more parts. **simple machine**: in which there is no combination of parts, e.g. a lever.

5 *fig*. A thing regarded as a combination of parts moving mechanically, often as contrasted with a being exercising free will; a person who acts mechanically or without thought, or with unfailing regularity. **L17**. ▸**b** The controlling organization of a political party or similar body; a well-organized group acting with (ruthless) efficiency. **M19**.

A. HAMILTON The nearer the soldiers approach to machines, perhaps the better. COLERIDGE To what purpose was he made a spirit of reason . . not a machine of instinct? *fig*.: P. BOWLES The vast beautiful machine of which the air and the mountainside were parts. **b** I. MCEWAN People with connections in the Party machine.

– COMB.: **machine age** an era notable for its extensive use of mechanical devices; esp. *the* present era so considered; **machine code** COMPUTING = ***machine language*** below; **machine finish** a moderately smooth finish given to paper by the machine on which it is made; **machine head** a head for a guitar etc. having worms and pinions, instead of pegs, for tightening the strings; **machine instruction** COMPUTING an instruction in a machine language; **machine language** COMPUTING a language that a particular computer can handle or act on directly, without further translation; **machine-pistol** a sub-machine gun; **machine-readable** *adjective* in a form that a computer can process; **machine room** a room in which machines, *spec*. printing presses, are operated; **machine screw** a threaded bolt having a socket in its head which allows it to be turned with a screwdriver; **machine shop** a workshop for making or repairing machines or parts of machines; **machine tool** a mechanically operated tool for cutting or shaping wood, metals, etc.; **machine translation**: by a computer; **machine-wash** *verb trans*. wash in a washing machine; ***machine word***: see WORD *noun* 12c.
■ **machineless** *adjective* that does not use or require a machine or machines **E20**. **machine-like** *adjective & adverb* (*a*) *adjective* resembling (that of) a machine, esp. in smoothness or independence of operation; (*b*) *adverb* in the manner of a machine: **E18**. **machiner** *noun* †(*a*) a horse employed to draw a stagecoach or other 'machine' (see MACHINE *noun* 1d); (*b*) a person who operates a machine: **L18**.

machine /mə'ʃiːn/ *verb*. **LME**.
[ORIGIN In branch I from Old French & mod. French *machiner* from Latin *machinari* MACHINATE; in branch II from the noun.]
▸†**I 1** *verb trans. & intrans*. Contrive, plot. **LME–L17**.
▸**II 2** *verb trans*. Form, make, or operate on by means of a machine; cut, engrave, shape, print, or sew (something) by means of a machine. **M19**.

Arena Rather than mould the cap and barrel . . we machine them . . from a solid block.

3 *verb intrans*. Operate a machine. *rare*. **L19**.
4 *verb intrans*. Undergo shaping etc. by machine (in a specified way). **M20**.

Practical Woodworking Some woods do machine better than others.

machine gun /mə'ʃiːngʌn/ *noun, adjective, & verb*. As adjective & verb usu. **machine-gun**. **M19**.
[ORIGIN from MACHINE *noun* + GUN *noun*.]
▸ **A** *noun*. A (mounted or portable) gun which is mechanically loaded and fired, and is capable of continuous fire. **M19**.
Lewis machine gun, ***Maxim machine gun***, ***sub-machine gun***, etc.
▸ **B** *attrib*. or as *adjective*. Like (that of) a machine gun, esp. in rapidly (and noisily) repeated action. **E20**.

H. J. LASKI They cross-examined me with machine-gun rapidity. M. PUZO That machine-gun typing.

▸ **C** *verb trans*. (With hyphen.) Infl. **-nn-**. Fire at with a machine gun; hit with machine-gun fire. **E20**.
■ **machine-gunner** *noun* **E20**.

machinery /mə'ʃiːn(ə)ri/ *noun*. **L17**.
[ORIGIN from MACHINE *noun* + -ERY.]
1 The assemblage of contrivances employed for effect in literary work; supernatural personages and incidents, or other contrivances for effect, introduced in a narrative. **L17**.

HANNAH MORE Those who . . deny the immortality of the soul . . introduce the machinery of ghosts. ALDOUS HUXLEY Entangled in a novel I can't quite find a satisfactory machinery for.

2 Machines, or the constituent parts of a machine, taken collectively; the mechanism of a machine or machines. Freq. *transf. & fig*., functional equipment; means or procedures available for action (foll. by *for*, *of*). **M18**.

LD MACAULAY The whole machinery of government was out of joint. J. W. KRUTCH Nuclear weapons and all the machinery of war. *Guardian* The machinery for salary-fixing in the universities is complicated. H. WILSON The industries producing plant and machinery cannot meet the orders. J. GARDAM Then away went the horses and in came the machinery.

3 A system or kind of machinery. **M19**.

E. M. FORSTER All these tubes and buttons and machineries.

machinist /mə'ʃiːnɪst/ *noun*. **E18**.
[ORIGIN French *machiniste*, from *machine*; later directly from MACHINE *noun* + -IST.]
1 A person who invents, makes, or controls machines or machinery; an engineer. **E18**.
2 *spec*. A person who constructs or manages the stage machinery in a theatre. Now *rare*. **M18**.
3 A person who operates a machine, esp. a sewing machine or machine tool. **L19**.

machinofacture /məˌʃiːnə(ʊ)'faktʃə/ *noun*. **E20**.
[ORIGIN from MACHINE *noun* + -O- + FACTURE, after *manufacture*.]
The making of articles by machine; mechanization.

machismo /mə'tʃɪzməʊ, -'kɪz-/ *noun*. **M20**.
[ORIGIN Mexican Spanish, formed as MACHO + *-ismo* -ISM.]
The quality of being macho; male virility, masculine pride; a show of this.

A. CAMPBELL They kissed the bride, and mangled my hand, as if to prove their superior machismo. *Newsweek* The Japanese . . have taken culinary machismo to a new level: scarfing down live seafood.

macho /'matʃəʊ/ *noun*[1] *& adjective*. Orig. *US*. **E20**.
[ORIGIN Mexican Spanish = male animal or plant, (as adjective) masculine, vigorous.]
▸ **A** *noun*. Pl. **-os**.
1 A man; *spec*. an assertively vigorous man, a 'tough guy'. **E20**.

Sunday Express The machos and poseurs drink their lager straight out of the can now.

2 = MACHISMO. **M20**.
▸ **B** *adjective*. Ostentatiously or notably manly and virile. **E20**.

B. T. BRADFORD The glamorous macho Hollywood movie star. P. D. JAMES A macho enthusiasm for selective violence.

MACHO /'matʃəʊ/ *noun*[2]. **L20**.
[ORIGIN Acronym, from Massive (Astrophysical) Compact Halo Object.]
ASTRONOMY. A relatively dark, dense object, such as a brown dwarf, a low-mass star, or a black hole, of a kind believed (in some astronomical theories) to occur in a halo around a galaxy and to contain a significant proportion of the galaxy's mass.

machree /mə'kriː/ *noun*. *Irish*. **L17**.
[ORIGIN Irish *mo chroidhe* (of) my heart.]
As a form of address: my dear, darling.

Machtpolitik /'maxtpolitiːk/ *noun*. **E20**.
[ORIGIN German, from *Macht* power, strength + *Politik* policy, politics.]
Power politics; strength as a potential factor to use in gaining a desired result.

Machupo /mə'tʃuːpəʊ/ *noun*. **M20**.
[ORIGIN from the name of the River *Machupo* in Bolivia, where the disease was first recognized.]
Used *attrib*. to designate a South American arenavirus carried by rodents, which causes a rare form of haemorrhagic fever in humans.

-machy /məki/ *suffix*.
[ORIGIN Greek *-makhia*, from *-makhos* that fights, from base of *makhē* battle: see -Y[3].]
Used, with medial **-o-**, in adoptions of Greek words and analogous English formations with the sense 'fighting, warfare', as ***iconomachy***, ***logomachy***.

Machzor /'mɑːkzɔː, -x-/ *noun*. Pl. **-im** /-ɪm/. **M18**.
[ORIGIN Hebrew *maḥzōr* cycle.]
A Jewish prayer book for use at festivals. Cf. SIDDUR.

macilent /'masɪl(ə)nt/ *adjective*. Now *rare*. **LME**.
[ORIGIN Latin *macilentus*, from *macer* thin, MEAGRE *adjective*: see -LENT.]
Lean, shrivelled, thin; *fig*. jejune.
■ **macilence** *noun* **LME**. **macilency** *noun* **M17**.

MacIntosh *noun* var. of MCINTOSH.

M

mack /mak/ *noun*[1]. *slang*. **L19.**
[**ORIGIN** Abbreviation of **MACKEREL** *noun*[2].]
A pimp.

†**Mack** *noun*[2] see **MAC** *noun*[1].

mack *noun*[3] var. of **MAC** *noun*[3].

Mackay *noun* var. of **McCOY**.

Mackem /ˈmakəm/ *noun*. *colloq.* **L20.**
[**ORIGIN** Prob. with allusion to the phrase *mack 'em and tack 'em* ('make them and take them'), said to refer to the shipbuilding industry of the region.]
A native or inhabitant of Sunderland in NE England.

mackerel /ˈmak(ə)r(ə)l/ *noun*[1]. Pl. **-s**, same. **ME.**
[**ORIGIN** Anglo-Norman *makerel*, Old French *maquerel* (mod. *maquereau*), of unknown origin (cf. **-EL**[2]). Cf. medieval Latin (Flanders) *macarellus* (12).]
1 Any of various swift-swimming pelagic fishes of the family Scombridae, of which several are commercially important as food fishes; esp. *Scomber scombrus*, of the N. Atlantic and Mediterranean, which approaches the shore in shoals in summer for spawning; (with specifying word) any of certain other fishes resembling these. Also, the flesh of any of these fishes as food. **ME.**
a sprat to catch a mackerel: see **SPRAT** *noun*[1]. **FRIGATE** ***mackerel***. ***holy mackerel***: see **HOLY** *adjective* 5. ***horse mackerel***: see **HORSE** *noun*. ***Monterey mackerel***, ***Monterey Spanish mackerel***: see **MONTEREY** 3. ***snake mackerel***: see **SNAKE** *noun*. ***Spanish mackerel***: see **SPANISH** *adjective*.
2 *ANGLING*. (An artificial fly imitating) a kind of mayfly. Also ***mackerel fly***. Now *rare* or *obsolete*. **L18.**
– **COMB.**: **mackerel-back**, **mackerel-backed** *adjectives* †(*a*) *slang* long-backed; (*b*) ***mackerel-back sky***, ***mackerel-backed sky***, = ***mackerel sky*** below; **mackerel boat**: for mackerel fishing; **mackerel breeze**, **mackerel gale** a breeze that ruffles the water, said to favour the catching of mackerel; **mackerel clouds**: in a mackerel sky; ***mackerel fly***: see sense 2 above; ***mackerel gale***: see ***mackerel breeze*** above; **mackerel gull** *N. Amer.* a tern; **mackerel shark** a shark of the family Lamnidae, esp. the porbeagle, *Lamna nasus*, or the mako, *Isurus oxyrinchus*; **mackerel sky** a sky dappled with rows of small white fleecy clouds, resembling the pattern on a mackerel's back.
▪ **mackereling** *noun* (*a*) fishing for mackerel; (*b*) a patterned effect like that of a mackerel sky or mackerel's back: **M19.**

mackerel /ˈmak(ə)r(ə)l/ *noun*[2]. *slang*. **LME.**
[**ORIGIN** Old French *maquerel* (mod. **MAQUEREAU**, *-elle*), from Middle Dutch *makelaer* (Dutch *-aar*) broker, whence also Old French *makelare*.]
A procurer or procuress; a pimp.

Mackinaw /ˈmakınɔː/ *noun*. **E19.**
[**ORIGIN** *Mackinaw* City, Michigan, USA, formerly an important trading post.]
1 In full ***Mackinaw boat***, ***Mackinaw skiff***. A large flat-bottomed sharp-ended boat, used on the Great Lakes of N. America. **E19.**
2 In full ***Mackinaw blanket***. A thick blanket, such as used to be distributed to Indians of the North West by the US government. **E19.**
3 A heavy woollen cloth, now usu. with a plaid design; a garment made of this; *esp.* (also ***Mackinaw coat***, ***Mackinaw jacket***) a thick double-breasted jacket. **M19.**
4 ***Mackinaw trout***, the N. American lake trout, *Salvelinus namaycush*. **M19.**

mackintosh /ˈmakıntɒʃ/ *noun*. In sense 1 also †**M-**. **M19.**
[**ORIGIN** Charles *Macintosh* (1766–1843), Scot. inventor.]
1 Orig. (also ***Mackintosh coat*** etc.), a coat, cloak, etc., made of waterproof material consisting of two or more layers of cloth stuck together with rubber. Now, a rain-proof coat made of this or any other material. Cf. **MAC** *noun*[3]. **M19.**
2 Cloth made waterproof by a layer of rubber. **L19.**
▪ **mackintoshed** *adjective* wearing a mackintosh **M19.**

mackle /ˈmak(ə)l/ *noun*. Also **macle**. **E18.**
[**ORIGIN** French *macule* from Latin *macula* spot. Cf. **MACKLE** *verb*, **MACULE** *noun*.]
A blurred impression in printing. Also, a blurred sheet.

mackle /ˈmak(ə)l/ *verb*. Now *rare*. Also **macle**. **L16.**
[**ORIGIN** Prob. from the noun (although recorded earlier). Cf. **MACULE** *verb*.]
†**1** *verb intrans.* Of a page: become blurred. Only in **L16.**
2 *verb trans.* Orig., blur or spot (a sheet of paper). Now only *spec.*, print (a page) blurred or double. **E18.**

Maclaurin /məˈklɒrın/ *noun*. **E19.**
[**ORIGIN** C. *Maclaurin* (1698–1746), Scot. mathematician.]
MATH. **1** ***Maclaurin theorem***, ***Maclaurin's theorem***, Taylor's theorem in the special case of a function whose argument is zero. **E19.**
2 ***Maclaurin series***, ***Maclaurin's series***, a representation of a function *f*(*x*) as a Taylor series about the origin. **E20.**

macle /ˈmak(ə)l/ *noun*[1]. **M18.**
[**ORIGIN** French from Latin *macula* spot, mesh.]
1 *HERALDRY*. = **MASCLE**. *rare*. **L15.**
2 *CRYSTALLOGRAPHY*. A twinned crystal. **L18.**
3 *MINERALOGY*. **a** = **CHIASTOLITE**. **E19.** ▸**b** *MINERALOGY*. A darker inclusion in a mineral. **M19.**
▪ **macled** *adjective* (of a crystal) twinned **E19.**

macle *noun*[2], *verb* vars. of **MACKLE** *noun*, *verb*.

maclura /məˈkl(j)ʊərə/ *noun*. **E19.**
[**ORIGIN** mod. Latin (see below), from William *Maclure* (1763–1840), US geologist.]
A N. American deciduous tree, *Maclura pomifera* (family Moraceae), bearing an inedible fruit resembling an orange. Also called ***Osage orange***.

macock /ˈmeıkɒk/ *noun*. *US* (now *hist.*). Also **maycock**. **L16.**
[**ORIGIN** Algonquian *mahcawq*.]
An inferior kind of melon, formerly cultivated by some N. American Indians.

Mâcon /ˈmakɔ̃ː/ *noun*. **M19.**
[**ORIGIN** See below.]
A red or white burgundy, produced in the district around Mâcon, a city in eastern France.

Maconochie /məˈkɒnəki/ *noun*. *military slang*. **E20.**
[**ORIGIN** *Maconochie* Brothers of London, makers of such food.]
Meat stewed with vegetables and tinned, esp. as supplied to soldiers on active service. Also, the stomach.

macouba *noun* var. of **MACCOBOY**.

macr- *combining form* see **MACRO-**.

macramé /məˈkrɑːm, -meı/ *noun & adjective*. **M19.**
[**ORIGIN** Turkish *makrama* handkerchief, tablecloth, towel from Arabic *miqrama* bedcover, bedspread.]
▸ **A** *noun*. A fringe, trimming, or lace of knotted thread or cord; knotted work; the art of making this. **M19.**
▸ **B** *attrib.* or as *adjective*. Made of or by macramé. **L19.**

macrauchenia /makrɔːˈkiːnıə/ *noun*. **M19.**
[**ORIGIN** mod. Latin (see below), from Greek *makraukhēn* long-necked, from *makros* long + *aukhēn* neck: see **-IA**[1].]
PALAEONTOLOGY. A long-necked litoptern of the genus *Macrauchenia*, known from fossil remains. Now only as mod. Latin genus name.

macro /ˈmakrəʊ/ *noun & adjective*. **M20.**
[**ORIGIN** Independent use of **MACRO-**.]
▸ **A** *noun*. Pl. **-os**.
1 *COMPUTING*. An instruction in a programming or source language which is equivalent to a specified set of ordinary instructions in an object language (which may be the source language or machine language); a macro-instruction. **M20.**
2 *PHOTOGRAPHY*. Macrophotography; a macro lens. **M20.**
▸ **B** *adjective*. Macroscopic, large-scale; overall, comprehensive; *CHEMISTRY* of macroanalysis; *PHOTOGRAPHY* pertaining to or used in macrophotography; *ECONOMICS* pertaining to macroeconomics. Freq. contrasted with ***micro***. **M20.**

D. WILSON The logic for the individual programs is expressed in terms of macro and micro block-diagrams. *Language* His attention is primarily focused on sociolinguistic research on a fairly macro level.

macro lens: suitable for taking photographs unusually close to the subject.

macro- /ˈmakrəʊ/ *combining form*. Before a vowel also **macr-**.
[**ORIGIN** Greek *makro-*, from *makros* long, large: see **-O-**.]
Used in words adopted from Greek and in English words modelled on these, and as a freely productive prefix, with the senses 'long, large, large-scale, comprehensive', *MEDICINE* 'abnormally enlarged or elongated'. Freq. contrasted with ***micro-***.
▪ **macroˈbenthic** *adjective* of or pertaining to the macrobenthos **M20.** **macroˈbenthos** *noun* the macrofauna of the benthos **M20.** **macroclimate** *noun* the general climate of a relatively large area **M20.** **macrocliˈmatic** *adjective* of or pertaining to a macroclimate or macroclimates **M20.** **macrocyst** *noun* an unusually large cyst **L19.** **macrodiˈagonal** *noun & adjective* (pertaining to or designating) the longer of the diagonals of a rhombic prism **M19.** **macro-engiˈneering** *noun* the design and construction of very large-scale engineering projects **M20.** **macro-evoˈlution** *noun* major evolutionary change, usu. over a long period; the evolution of genera or higher taxa: **M20.** **macro-evoˈlutionary** *adjective* of or pertaining to macro-evolution **M20.** **macrofauna** *noun* (*BIOLOGY*) (a) fauna made up of animals visible to the naked eye; (a) fauna not confined to a microhabitat: **E20.** **macrofossil** *noun* a fossil large enough to be discerned by the naked eye **M20.** **macrogamete** *noun* the larger (female) sex cell of a protozoan **L19.** **macroˈglobulin** *noun* (*BIOCHEMISTRY*) any immunoglobulin of very high molecular weight (about 1,000,000 or more) **M20.** **macroglobuliˈnaemia** *noun* an excess of macroglobulins in the blood **M20.** **macroˈglossia** *noun* abnormal enlargement of the tongue **M19.** **macroˈgnathic**, **macroˈgnathous** *adjectives* having one or both jaws long or protruding **M19.** **macro-instruction** *noun* (*COMPUTING*) = **MACRO** *noun* 1. **M20.** **macrolinˈguistic** *adjective* of or pertaining to macrolinguistics **M20.** **macrolinˈguistics** *noun* the branch of linguistics that deals with language and all its related aspects as a whole **M20.** **macromere** *noun* [Greek *meros* part] *BIOLOGY* a large cell formed by unequal division of an ovum or embryo, e.g. in sea urchins, and appearing at the vegetative pole **L19.** **macroˈmeric** *adjective* (*BIOLOGY*) of or pertaining to a macromere or macromeres **L19.** **macroˈnodular** *adjective* (*MEDICINE*) (of cirrhosis) characterized by the presence of large nodules **M20.** **macroˈnucleus** *noun*, pl. **-nuclei**, *ZOOLOGY* the larger of two nuclei in ciliated protozoans, concerned esp. with feeding **L19.** **macroˈnutrient** *noun* any of the chemical elements (as potassium, nitrogen, calcium, sulphur, phosphorus, or magnesium) which are normally taken up by plants as inorganic salts and are required for growth and development in relatively large amounts (rather than trace amounts) **M20.** **macrophagous** /maˈkrɒfəgəs/ *adjective* (*ZOOLOGY*) feeding on relatively large pieces of food **M20.** **macroˈphallic** *adjective* having a large phallus **M19.** **macroˈphysical** *adjective* of or pertaining to macrophysics **E20.** **macrophysics** *noun* the part of physics that deals with bodies and phenomena on a macroscopic scale **E20.** **macrophyte** *noun* any plant, esp. any aquatic plant, large enough to be discerned by the naked eye **E20.** **macrophytic** /-ˈfıtık/ *adjective* of the nature of a macrophyte; of or pertaining to macrophytes: **E20.** **maˈcropterous** *adjective* long-winged **M19.** **macro-scale** *noun* a large or macroscopic scale; *CHEMISTRY* the scale of macroanalysis: **M20.** **macrosegment** *noun* (*LINGUISTICS*) a continuous unit of speech between two pauses, with a single intonation **M20.** **macroseism** /-sʌız(ə)m/ *noun* orig., a major earthquake; now, any earthquake, as opp. to a microseism: **E20.** **macroˈseismic** *adjective* of, pertaining to, or of the nature of a macroseism; (of data) obtained other than with a seismometer: **E20.** **macrosocioˈlogical** *adjective* of or pertaining to macrosociology **M20.** **macrosociˈology** *noun* the part of sociology that deals with large social groups and large-scale features of human society **M20.** **macrospore** *noun* (*BOTANY*) = **MEGASPORE** **M19.** **macrotrichium** /-ˈtrıkıəm/ *noun*, pl. **-chia** /-kıə/, [Greek *trikh-*, *thrix* hair] any of the larger hairs on the body of certain insects **M20.**

macroanalysis /ˌmakrəʊəˈnalısıs/ *noun*. **M20.**
[**ORIGIN** from **MACRO-** + **ANALYSIS**.]
CHEMISTRY. Quantitative analysis of samples of the size for which the older chemical techniques were usually developed, commonly 0.1–1 gram.

macrobian /məˈkrəʊbıən/ *adjective*. *rare*. **L17.**
[**ORIGIN** from Greek *makrobios*, formed as **MACRO-** + *bios* life: see **-AN**.]
Long-lived.

macrobiotic /ˌmakrə(ʊ)bʌıˈɒtık/ *adjective & noun*. **L18.**
[**ORIGIN** from Greek *makrobiotos*, formed as **MACRO-** + *biotos* life: see **-IC**.]
▸ **A** *adjective*. **1** Inclined or tending to prolong life; relating to the prolongation of life. **L18.**
2 Of or pertaining to a Zen Buddhist dietary system intended to prolong life, comprising pure vegetable foods, brown rice, etc.; advocating or following such a system. **M20.**
▸ **B** *noun*. An advocate or follower of such a dietary system. **L20.**
▪ **macrobiotics** *noun* (*a*) *rare* the science of prolonging life; (*b*) the use or theory of a macrobiotic diet: **M19.**

macrocarpa /makrə(ʊ)ˈkɑːpə/ *noun*. **M19.**
[**ORIGIN** mod. Latin (see below), formed as **MACRO-** + *karpos* fruit.]
A cypress, *Cupressus macrocarpa*, native to the Monterey peninsula of California and widely cultivated elsewhere, esp. as a fast-growing hedge or windbreak. Also called ***Monterey cypress***.

macrocephalic /ˌmakrə(ʊ)sıˈfalık, -kɛˈfalık/ *adjective*. **M19.**
[**ORIGIN** from **MACRO-** + **CEPHALIC**.]
(Of a person) having a long or large head; (of a head or skull) relatively long or large.
▪ **macroceˈphalia** *noun* = **MACROCEPHALY** **L19.** **macroˈcephalous** *adjective* = **MACROCEPHALIC** **M19.** **macroˈcephaly** *noun* macrocephalic condition; abnormal length or size of the head: **L19.**

macrocosm /ˈmakrə(ʊ)kɒz(ə)m/ *noun*. **E17.**
[**ORIGIN** medieval Latin *macrocosmus*, formed as **MACRO-** + Greek *kosmos* world.]
1 The universe; the world of all nature. **E17.**
2 A complex structure or whole, *esp.* one considered to be epitomized by some constituent portion or microcosm. **M19.**
▪ **macroˈcosmic** *adjective* of or pertaining to the macrocosm; of the nature of a macrocosm: **M19.** †**macrocosmical** *adjective* = **MACROCOSMIC** **E17–M19.** **macroˈcosmically** *adverb* **L19.**

macrocyclic /makrə(ʊ)ˈsʌıklık, ˈ-sık-/ *adjective*. **E20.**
[**ORIGIN** from **MACRO-** + **CYCLIC**.]
1 *BOTANY*. Of a rust fungus: having a long life cycle. **E20.**
2 *CHEMISTRY*. Containing or being a ring composed of a relatively large number of atoms. **M20.**
▪ **ˈmacrocycle** *noun* (*CHEMISTRY*) a macrocyclic compound or molecule **M20.**

macrocyte /ˈmakrə(ʊ)sʌıt/ *noun*. **L19.**
[**ORIGIN** from **MACRO-** + **-CYTE**.]
MEDICINE. An abnormally large red blood cell found in some forms of anaemia.
▪ **macrocytic** /-ˈsıtık/ *adjective* of the nature of, pertaining to, or characteristic of a macrocyte; characterized by the presence of macrocytes: **M20.** **macrocytosis** /-sʌıˈtəʊsıs/ *noun* the presence of macrocytes in the blood **L19.**

macroeconomics /ˌmakrəʊiːkəˈnɒmıks, -ɛk-/ *noun*. **M20.**
[**ORIGIN** from **MACRO-** + **ECONOMICS**.]
The branch of economics that deals with large-scale economic factors; the economics of a national economy as a whole. Cf. **MICROECONOMICS**.
▪ **macroeconomic** *adjective* **M20.** **macroeˈconomist** *noun* **M20.** **macroeˈconomy** *noun* a large-scale economic system **M20.**

Macrolepidoptera /ˌmakrəʊlɛpıˈdɒpt(ə)rə/ *noun pl.* **L19.**
[**ORIGIN** from **MACRO-** + **LEPIDOPTERA**.]
The butterflies and moths which are large enough to be of interest to collectors. Cf. **MICROLEPIDOPTERA**.

macrolide /ˈmakrə(ʊ)lʌıd/ *noun*. **M20.**
[**ORIGIN** from **MACRO-** + **L**(**ACTONE** + **-IDE**.]
PHARMACOLOGY. Any of a class of antibiotics containing macrocyclic lactone rings. Also ***macrolide antibiotic***.

M

macrology /maˈkrɒlədʒi/ *noun*. Now *rare* or *obsolete*. Also (earlier) in Latin form †**-logia**. M16.
[ORIGIN Late Latin *macrologia* from Greek *makrologia*, formed as MACRO- + -LOGY.]
In *RHETORIC*, the use of redundant words or phrases; *gen.* prolixity of speech.

macromolecule /makrə(ʊ)ˈmɒlɪkjuːl/ *noun*. L19.
[ORIGIN from MACRO- + MOLECULE.]
CHEMISTRY. †**1** A group of molecules in a crystal bound together in a characteristic shape, supposed to account for the symmetry of the crystal. Only in L19.
2 A molecule composed of a very large number of atoms and having a high molecular weight (e.g. a molecule of a polymer, protein, or nucleic acid). E20.
■ **macromoˈlecular** *adjective* of, pertaining to, or consisting of a macromolecule or macromolecules M20.

macron /ˈmakrɒn/ *noun*. M19.
[ORIGIN Greek *makron* neut. of *makros* long.]
A straight horizontal line ¯ written or printed over a vowel to indicate length or stress.

macrophage /ˈmakrə(ʊ)feɪdʒ/ *noun*. L19.
[ORIGIN from MACRO- + Greek *phagein* eat.]
PHYSIOLOGY. A large phagocytic cell, present in many organs and tissues in both stationary and mobile forms.
■ **macroˈphagic** *adjective* E20.

macrophotography /ˌmakrə(ʊ)fəˈtɒgrəfi/ *noun*. L19.
[ORIGIN from MACRO- + PHOTOGRAPHY.]
Photography in which objects are reproduced larger than or at their actual size but without the degree of magnification that use of a microscope would give. Also called ***photomacrography***.
■ **macroˈphotograph** *noun* a photograph produced by macrophotography E20.

macropodid /məˈkrɒpədɪd/ *noun & adjective*. L19.
[ORIGIN mod. Latin *Macropodidae* (see below), from *Macropus* genus name from Greek *makropous* large foot, formed as MACRO- + *pous* foot: see -POD, -ID[3].]
ZOOLOGY. ▸**A** *noun*. A marsupial of the family Macropodidae, which includes the kangaroos and wallabies. L19.
▸**B** *adjective*. Of, pertaining to, or designating this family. M20.
■ **ˈmacropod** *noun & adjective* = MACROPODID L19.

macropsia /maˈkrɒpsɪə/ *noun*. L19.
[ORIGIN from MACRO- + Greek *-opsia* seeing.]
OPHTHALMOLOGY. A condition of the eyes in which objects appear enlarged.

macroscopic /makrə(ʊ)ˈskɒpɪk/ *adjective*. L19.
[ORIGIN from MACRO- after *microscopic*.]
Visible to the naked eye, as opp. to ***microscopic***; using the naked eye; *fig.* general, comprehensive, concerned with large units.

> G. DANIEL A straight old-fashioned archaeologist . . trained in the macroscopic examination of artifacts.

■ **macroscopical** *adjective* = MACROSCOPIC L19. **macroscopically** *adverb* L19.

macrosmatic /makrɒzˈmatɪk/ *adjective*. L19.
[ORIGIN from MACRO- + Greek *osmē* smell + -ATIC.]
ZOOLOGY. Having well-developed olfactory organs.

macrostructure /ˈmakrə(ʊ)strʌktʃə/ *noun*. E20.
[ORIGIN from MACRO- + STRUCTURE *noun*.]
1 Large-scale or overall structure; structure visible to the naked eye or under low magnification. E20.
2 A thing having such structure. M20.
■ **macroˈstructural** *adjective* L19.

macrurous /məˈkrʊərəs/ *adjective*. E19.
[ORIGIN from mod. Latin *Macrura* former suborder name, from Greek *makros* long + *oura* tail: see -OUS.]
ZOOLOGY. Of, pertaining to, or designating a group of decapod crustaceans having a relatively long abdomen, including the lobsters and crayfish.
■ **macruran** *noun & adjective* (**a**) *noun* a macrurous crustacean; (**b**) *adjective* = MACRUROUS: M19.

mactation /makˈteɪʃ(ə)n/ *noun*. M16.
[ORIGIN Late Latin *mactatio(n-)*, from Latin *mactat-* pa. ppl stem of *mactare* slay: see -ATION.]
(A) sacrificial killing.

macula /ˈmakjʊlə/ *noun*. Pl. **-lae** /-liː/, **-las**. LME.
[ORIGIN Latin.]
1 Chiefly *SCIENCE*. A spot, a stain; *MEDICINE* a permanent spot or stain in the skin. LME.
2 *ANATOMY*. Any of various structures which have the appearance of a spot. M19.
macula lutea /ˈluːtɪə/, pl. **maculae luteae** /ˈluːtiːiː/, [Latin *luteus* yellow] an oval yellowish area surrounding the fovea near the centre of the retina, where visual acuity is most pronounced; also called ***yellow spot***.
■ **macular** *adjective* of or pertaining to maculae; characterized by the presence of maculae; *spec.* of or pertaining to the macula lutea: E19.

maculate /ˈmakjʊlət/ *adjective*. L15.
[ORIGIN Latin *maculatus* pa. pple, formed as MACULATE *verb*: see -ATE[2].]
Spotted, stained; *fig.* defiled, polluted. Now chiefly *literary*, in expressed or implied antithesis to ***immaculate***.

> H. FERGUSSON Her long black hair . . now hung wet and maculate with clay and sand.

maculate /ˈmakjʊleɪt/ *verb trans*. Now *rare*. Pa. pple **-ated**, †**-ate**. L15.
[ORIGIN Latin *maculat-* pa. ppl stem of *maculare*, from *macula* spot: see -ATE[3].]
Spot, stain, soil; *fig.* defile, pollute.
■ **maculated** *adjective* (**a**) = MACULATE *adjective*; (**b**) marked with maculae: M17.

maculation /makjʊˈleɪʃ(ə)n/ *noun*. L15.
[ORIGIN Latin *maculatio(n-)*, formed as MACULATE *verb*: see -ATION.]
1 The action of spotting or defiling; the condition of being spotted or defiled. L15.
2 The state of being marked with maculae; a particular arrangement or pattern of maculae. E19.

maculature /ˈmakjʊlətʃə/ *noun*. M17.
[ORIGIN formed as MACULATE *verb* + -URE.]
†**1** A sheet of waste or blotting paper. *rare* (only in Dicts.). M17–E18.
2 A print taken from a block or print without re-inking, to remove traces of ink from it. E20.

macule /ˈmakjuːl/ *noun*. L15.
[ORIGIN French, or its source Latin *macula* spot.]
1 A blemish, a spot; *esp.* (*MEDICINE*) a macula on the skin. L15.
2 *PRINTING*. = MACKLE *noun*. M19.

macule /ˈmakjuːl/ *verb trans*. *rare*. L15.
[ORIGIN French *maculer*, formed as MACULE *noun*.]
Spot, stain; *PRINTING* = MACKLE *verb* 2.

maculopapule /ˌmakjʊlə(ʊ)ˈpapjuːl/ *noun*. E20.
[ORIGIN from MACULA + -O- + PAPULE.]
MEDICINE. A lesion having characteristics of both a macule and a papule.
■ **maculopapular** *adjective* E20.

maculose /ˈmakjʊləʊs/ *adjective*. E18.
[ORIGIN Latin *maculosus*, from *macula* spot: see -OSE[1].]
Full of spots; spotted.
■ Also **maculous** *adjective* (*rare*) LME.

macumba /məˈkʊmbə/ *noun*. M20.
[ORIGIN Portuguese.]
A black religious cult practised in Brazil, characterized by sorcery, ritual dancing, and the use of fetishes.

macushla /məˈkʊʃlə/ *noun*. *Irish*. L19.
[ORIGIN from Irish *mo* my + *cuisle* pulse: see ACUSHLA. Cf. CUSHLA-MACHREE.]
As a form of address: my dear, darling.

MAD *abbreviation*.
1 Magnetic anomaly detection or detector.
2 Mutual assured destruction.

mad /mad/ *noun*. E18.
[ORIGIN Absol. use of MAD *adjective*.]
1 *pl. The* people who are mad. E18.
2 Madness, fury, anger; a fit of anger. *dial.* & *US slang*. M19.

mad /mad/ *adjective*. Compar. & superl. **-dd-**.
[ORIGIN Old English *ġemǣd(d*, *ġemǣded*, pa. pple of verb meaning 'make insane', from *ġemād* insane = Old Saxon *gimēd* foolish, Old High German *gameit* foolish, vain, boastful, Gothic *gamaiþs* crippled, from Germanic.]
1 Insane; suffering from a psychotic illness. Now also, maniacal, frenzied. OE. ▸†**b** Causing madness. *rare*. M16–L17.

> TENNYSON And then to hear a dead man chatter Is enough to drive one mad.

mad as a hatter, ***mad as a March hare***, etc.
2 Foolish, unwise. Now *spec.* extravagantly or wildly foolish; ruinously imprudent. OE.

> LD MACAULAY The chief justice . . was not mad enough to risk a quarrel on such a subject.

3 Carried away by enthusiasm or desire; wildly excited; infatuated. Foll. by *about*, *for*, *on*, etc. ME. ▸**b** Wildly desirous *to do* something. Now *rare*. E17.

> H. JACOBSON Despite myself I was mad about her. She was so good at what she did.

music-mad, ***poetry-mad***, ***sex-mad***, etc.
4 Beside oneself with anger; moved to uncontrollable rage; furious. Now also, annoyed, exasperated. (Foll. by *at*, *with*, etc.) Chiefly *colloq.* ME.

> C. BROWN I was mad . . I was going to beat both of their asses. J. J. HENNESSY I was so mad with her . . that I walked out of the room.

5 Of an animal: abnormally furious, rabid; *spec.* suffering from rabies. ME.
6 Uncontrolled by reason; (wildly) irrational in demeanour or conduct. LME. ▸**b** Of a storm or wind: wild, violent. L16.

> D. DELILLO Has my life been a mad dash for pleasure?

– PHRASES: **go mad** become insane; become wildly or frenziedly abnormal. **like mad** furiously, with excessive violence or enthusiasm. **run mad** = ***go mad*** above. ***staring mad***: see STARING *adjective* 1.
– SPECIAL COLLOCATIONS & COMB.: **mad-apple** *arch.* [translating Latin *malum insanum*, alt. of an oriental word] an aubergine. **mad-brain** *noun & adjective* (**a**) *noun* a mad-brained person, a scatterbrain; (**b**) *adjective* mad-brained. **mad-brained** *adjective* hot-headed, uncontrolled; scatterbrained. **mad cow disease** *colloq.* = ***bovine spongiform encephalopathy*** s.v. BOVINE *adjective* 1. **mad-doctor** *arch.*: who treats the insane. ***mad Greek***: see GREEK *noun* 5. **madhead** (*obsolete* exc. *dial.*) an insane or wildly foolish person. **mad-headed** *adjective* = ***mad-brained*** above. **madhouse** (**a**) (*arch.* or *colloq.*) a mental home or hospital; (**b**) *colloq.* a scene of extreme confusion or uproar. **mad keen** *adjective* (*slang*) extremely eager. **madman** an insane or wildly foolish man. ***mad mick***: see MICK *noun*[1]. **mad minute** *military slang* a short period of rapid rifle fire or frenzied bayonet practice. **mad money** *colloq.* money for use in an emergency. **mad scientist** an eccentric or dangerously insane scientist (a stock figure of melodramatic horror stories). **madstone** *US* a stone supposedly having the power to counteract the effect of the bite of a rabid animal. **madtom** any catfish of the N. American freshwater genus *Noturus*, comprising small forms resembling tadpoles and with poisonous pectoral fins. **madwoman** an insane or wildly foolish woman.
■ **maddish** *adjective* †(**a**) of or pertaining to a mad person; resembling a mad person in behaviour; (**b**) somewhat mad: L16. **madling** *noun* (now *rare*) a mad person; a person who acts insanely or foolishly: M17.

mad /mad/ *verb*. Infl. **-dd-**. ME.
[ORIGIN from the adjective.]
1 *verb intrans.* Be or become mad; act like a mad person, rage, behave furiously. *arch.* ME.
2 *verb trans.* Make mad; madden, make insane; infuriate, enrage. Now chiefly *US colloq.*, exasperate. LME.

Madagascan /madəˈgask(ə)n/ *adjective & noun*. L19.
[ORIGIN Irreg. from MADAGASCAR + -AN. Cf. MALAGASH, MALAGASY.]
▸**A** *adjective*. Of or pertaining to Madagascar. L19.
▸**B** *noun*. A native or inhabitant of Madagascar. L19.

Madagascar /madəˈgaskə/ *noun*. E17.
[ORIGIN A large island off the east coast of Africa.]
†**1** An inhabitant of Madagascar. E17–M19.
2 Used *attrib.* to designate things found in or associated with Madagascar. E18.
Madagascar jasmine = STEPHANOTIS 1. ***Madagascar periwinkle***: see PERIWINKLE *noun*[1] 1.

Madagascarian /madəgaˈskɛːrɪən/ *noun & adjective*. As noun also **-gascrian** /-ˈgaskrɪən/. L17.
[ORIGIN from MADAGASCAR + -IAN.]
= MADAGASCAN *adjective & noun*.

Madagass /ˈmadəgas/ *noun*. *arch.* E18.
[ORIGIN Var. of MALAGASH.]
A Madagascan.

madal /məˈdɑːl/ *noun*. E20.
[ORIGIN Nepali, Assamese, Bengali *mādal* from Sanskrit *mardala*.]
A double-headed drum used in Nepal and the eastern Indian subcontinent. Cf. MRIDANGAM.

madam /ˈmadəm/ *noun*. Also **madame**. See also MADAME. ME.
[ORIGIN Old French *ma dame* (mod. *madame*) lit. 'my lady'.]
▸**I 1** Used as a form of respectful or polite address or mode of reference, orig. by a servant to or of his or her mistress, or by any person addressing a lady of rank; later used more widely to address or refer to a woman of any rank or position, *spec.* by a sales assistant to or of a female customer or (more fully ***dear madam***) at the beginning of a letter to a woman. Corresp. to ***sir***. ME.

> HENRY FIELDING 'If you will have patience, madam', answered Mrs. Miller, 'I will acquaint you who I am'. *Vogue* Madam comes to look . . . She is so astonished at the absurdly low prices. *Woman's Journal* Shall I have Madame's tray?

2 As a title: ▸**a** Used preceding a woman's forename. *arch.* LME. ▸**b** Used preceding a woman's surname, a woman's designation of rank or (occas.) office, or (formerly) playfully or derisively preceding any noun personified as a woman. E17.

> **b** SHAKES. *Meas. for M.* Behold, behold, where Madam Mitigation comes! GOLDSMITH Good people all, with one accord Lament for Madam Blaize.

3 A woman usually addressed or referred to as 'madam', e.g. a lady of rank, the mistress of a house, etc. M16. ▸**b** An affected fine lady. *derog.* L16. ▸**c** A conceited or precocious girl or young woman. *colloq.* E19. ▸**d** A female brothel-keeper. L19.

> **b** M. CHARLTON What should I care what those fine Madams says of me! **c** M. BINCHY She was a proper little madam that one.

4 Nonsense, humbug. *slang*. M20.
▸**II** See MADAME.
– COMB.: **madam shop** a small shop selling upmarket women's clothing.

madam /ˈmadəm/ *verb trans*. E17.
[ORIGIN from the noun.]
Address as 'madam'.

madame /məˈdɑːm, ˈmadəm, *foreign* madam/ *noun*. Also **madam**. See also MADAM *noun*. Pl. **mesdames** /ˈmeɪdam, *foreign* medam, mɛ-/ (see also MESDAMES). ME.
[ORIGIN Old French: see MADAM *noun*. Partly var. of MADAM *noun*.]
▸**I 1** See MADAM *noun*. ME.
▸**II 2** *FRENCH HISTORY*. (A title of) a female member of the French royal family, *spec.* the eldest daughter of the French king or the dauphin (cf. MADEMOISELLE 3). L16.

M

3 Used as a title (preceding the surname) of or as a respectful form of address to a French married woman or (more widely) a married woman of any non-British nationality (corresp. to English ***Mrs***, ***Lady***, etc.), or in literal renderings of French speech. Abbreviated to *Mme*. E17. ▸**b** Used as a title (preceding a name) by a businesswoman, fortune-teller, etc., esp. to imply skill and sophistication, or foreign origin. Abbreviated to *Mme*. M19.

b JOYCE The window of Madame Doyle, court dress milliner, stopped him. N. COWARD Don't you think, Madame Arcati, that perhaps we've had enough seances?

†**4** A woman usually addressed or referred to as 'Madame'; a French married woman; a Frenchman's wife. E17–M18.

madapollam /madəˈpɒləm/ *noun*. L17.
[ORIGIN *Madapollam*, a suburb of Narsapur in Andhra Pradesh, India.]
A kind of cotton cloth, orig. manufactured at Madapollam.

madar *noun* var. of MUDAR.

madarosis /madəˈrəʊsɪs/ *noun*. Pl. **-oses** /-ˈrəʊsiːz/. L17.
[ORIGIN mod. Latin, from Greek *madarōsis*, from *madaros* bald: see -OSIS.]
MEDICINE. Congenital deficiency or loss of the eyelashes (and eyebrows).
– NOTE: Only in Dicts. before 20.

madcap /ˈmadkap/ *noun & adjective*. L16.
[ORIGIN from MAD *adjective* + CAP *noun*[1].]
▸ **A** *noun*. †**1** A madman; a maniac. *rare*. L16–E17.
2 A person who acts like a maniac; a reckless, wildly impulsive person. Now also, a lively and impulsive young woman. L16.

MABEL COLLINS On the boards she was the merriest, gayest, madcap in the world.

▸ **B** *attrib.* or as *adjective*. Mad, crazy; reckless, wildly impulsive. L16.

R. DEACON A madcap project in Kenya for creating a disease in the sacred baobab trees.

madden /ˈmad(ə)n/ *verb*. E18.
[ORIGIN from MAD *adjective* + -EN[5].]
1 *verb trans.* Make mad; infuriate, excite to frenzy. Also, greatly irritate or annoy. E18.

M

Times The result was one of those baffling reversals of form that madden tipsters.

2 *verb intrans.* Become mad. M18.
■ **maddening** *adjective* that makes a person mad; irritating, vexing: M18. **maddeningly** *adverb* M19.

madder /ˈmadə/ *noun, verb, & adjective*.
[ORIGIN Old English *mædere*, corresp. to Old High German *matara*, Old Norse *maðra* in place names (Swedish *madra*, Norwegian *modra, maure*), obscurely rel. to synon. West Frisian *miede*, Middle Low German, Middle Dutch *mēde* (Dutch *mede, mee*).]
▸ **A** *noun*. **1** A climbing plant, *Rubia tinctorum* (family Rubiaceae), with rough stems, rough whorled leaves, and panicles of small yellowish flowers, formerly cultivated for the reddish-purple dye obtained from the root. Also (with specifying word), any of several related plants. OE.
field madder: see FIELD *noun*. **Indian madder** a dye plant of the Indian subcontinent, *Rubia cordifolia*.
2 The root of *Rubia tinctorum*, employed medicinally or as a source of colouring matter; the dyestuff or pigment prepared from this. ME.
3 A reddish-purple colour, *esp.* one produced by madder dyes or pigments. L19.
rose madder: see ROSE *noun*. ***Rubens madder***: see RUBENS 2b.
▸ **B** *verb trans.* Treat or dye with madder. LME.
▸ **C** *adjective*. Of the colour produced by madder dyes; reddish-purple. M19.
madder brown, madder red, etc.

madding /ˈmadɪŋ/ *ppl adjective*. Now *poet. & rhet.* L16.
[ORIGIN from MAD *verb* + -ING[2].]
1 Becoming mad; acting madly; frenzied. Now chiefly in ***far from the madding crowd***, (of a place) secluded, removed from public notice. L16.

T. GRAY Far from the madding crowd's ignoble strife.

2 That makes a person mad; maddening. L16.

maddle /ˈmad(ə)l/ *verb*. *obsolete* exc. *dial.* M16.
[ORIGIN from MAD *adjective* + -LE[3].]
1 *verb intrans.* Be or become mad; be confused in mind; be dotingly fond *of*. M16.
2 *verb trans.* Make mad; confuse in mind, bewilder. E19.

maddock /ˈmadək/ *noun*. Now *dial.* ME.
[ORIGIN Corresp. to Old Norse *maðkr* (Danish *madike*, Swedish *mask*), Middle Low German *medeke*, dim. of base of MATHE: see -OCK. Cf. MAGGOT, MAWK.]
A maggot or (formerly) an earthworm.

made /meɪd/ *ppl adjective*. LME.
[ORIGIN pa. pple of MAKE *verb*. Earlier (ME) in UNMADE *adjective*.]
▸ **I** *gen.* **1** That has been made. Also ***made-out, made-over***, etc. LME.
home-made, man-made, self-made, etc. ***made to measure***: see MEASURE *noun*.
▸ **II** *spec.* †**2** (Of a story) invented, fictitious; (of a word) coined; (of an errand) invented for a pretext; made-up. LME–M19.
3 Artificially constructed or produced; contrived, arranged. LME.
4 That has undergone a process of manufacture; (of a person) having success in life assured. LME.
5 Of a horse, hound, etc.: fully trained. L15.
6 Foll. by *up*: that has been made up; *spec.* †(***a***) consummate, accomplished; (***b***) put together; composed of parts from various sources; (***c***) artificially contrived or prepared, invented, fabricated; (of a book) made good by the insertion of a leaf etc. from another copy; (***d***) ready-made, not made to measure; (***e***) wearing cosmetics or make-up. E17.

Chicago Tribune Klingon is a tough-to-learn, totally made-up language.

7 Foll. by *up*: *Irish* (of a person) assured of success, lucky; *Irish & N. English* very pleased, delighted. M20.

C. GLAZEBROOK Mickey, that's brilliant! Ee, I'm made up for you.

– SPECIAL COLLOCATIONS: **made dish** a dish of food composed of several separate foods. **made man**, **made guy** a man whose success in life is assured; *slang* a member of the Mafia. **made mast** a ship's mast composed of several pieces of timber. **made-up tie** a tie, esp. a bow tie, with a fixed bow or knot. **made wine** *arch.* a home-made esp. fruit wine.

made *verb pa. t. & pple* of MAKE *verb*.

madefaction /madɪˈfakʃ(ə)n/ *noun*. Long *rare* or *obsolete*. L16.
[ORIGIN French *madéfaction* from Latin *madefactio(n-)*, from *madefact-* pa. ppl stem of *madefacere*, from *madere* be wet: see -FACTION.]
The action or process of making wet or moist; a wetting.

Madeira /məˈdɪərə/ *noun*[1]. L16.
[ORIGIN An island in the Atlantic Ocean (from Portuguese *madeira* timber from Spanish *madera* from Latin *materia* MATTER *noun*, so called because formerly thickly wooded).]
1 A fortified wine made in Madeira. L16.
2 Used *attrib.* to designate things found in, made in, or associated with Madeira. M17.
Madeira cake a kind of plain sponge cake. **Madeira embroidery** broderie anglaise. **Madeira nut** *US* the walnut, *Juglans regia*. **Madeira sauce** a rich brown sauce made with Madeira and served with braised or roast meats. **Madeira wine** = sense 1 above.
■ **Madeiran** *adjective & noun* E19.

madeira /məˈdɪərə/ *noun*[2]. Also (earlier) †**madera**. M17.
[ORIGIN Spanish *madera* timber: see MADEIRA *noun*[1]. Spelling assim. to MADEIRA *noun*[1].]
The Cuban mahogany, *Swietenia mahagoni*. Also ***madeira wood***.

madeleine /ˈmadleɪn/ *noun*. M19.
[ORIGIN French, prob. from *Madeleine* Paulmier, 19th-cent. French pastry cook.]
A (kind of) small rich cake, in French cookery baked in a fluted tin, and in English cookery usu. baked in a dariole mould and decorated with coconut and jam.

Madelung /ˈmad(ə)lʊŋ/ *noun*. M20.
[ORIGIN Erwin *Madelung* (1881–1972), German physicist.]
PHYSICAL CHEMISTRY. **1** ***Madelung constant***, a value associated with an ionic crystalline solid and representing the sum of the potential energy of electrostatic attraction between all the ions of the lattice. M20.
2 ***Madelung potential***, the potential at any point in an ionic lattice due to the combined electric field of all the ions in the lattice. M20.

mademoiselle /madəmwəˈzɛl, *foreign* madmwazɛl/ *noun*. Pl. **mesdemoiselles** /meɪdəmwəˈzɛl, *foreign* medmwazɛl, mɛdmwazɛl/, **mademoiselles** /madəmwəˈzɛlz, *foreign* madmwazɛl/. LME.
[ORIGIN Old French: see MADAM *noun*, DEMOISELLE.]
1 Used as a title (preceding a name) of or as a respectful form of address to an unmarried Frenchwoman or (more widely) an unmarried woman of any non-British nationality (corresp. to English ***Miss***), or in literal renderings of French speech. Also used as a respectful form of address to a French governess or a female French teacher in an English-speaking school. Abbreviated to *Mlle*. LME.
2 A woman usu. addressed or referred to as 'Mademoiselle'; an unmarried Frenchwoman; a French governess. M17.
3 FRENCH HISTORY. (A title of) the eldest daughter of the eldest brother (known as 'Monsieur') of the French king. Later, (a title of) the French king's eldest daughter or (if he had no daughter) the unmarried princess most closely related to him (cf. MADAME 2). L17.
4 A croaker (fish), *Bairdiella chrysoura*, of the southern US. Also called ***silver perch, yellowtail***. *US*. L19.

†**madera** *noun* see MADEIRA *noun*[2].

maderisation *noun* var. of MADERIZATION.

madérisé /maderize/ *adjective*. M20.
[ORIGIN French, pa. pple of *madériser*: see MADERIZATION.]
Of wine: affected with maderization.

maderization /madərʌɪˈzeɪʃ(ə)n/ *noun*. Also **-isation**. M20.
[ORIGIN French *madérisation*, from *madériser*, from *Madère* MADEIRA *noun*[1]: see -IZATION.]
A brown discoloration in white wines, often appearing after overlong or unsuitable storage.
■ ˈ**maderize** *verb intrans.* [French *madériser*: see -IZE] (of wine) be or become *madérisé* M20.

madge /madʒ/ *noun*. L16.
[ORIGIN Prob. from *Madge*, pet form of female forename *Margaret*.]
1 The barn owl. Also ***madge-owl***. Now *rare*. L16.
2 The magpie. Cf. MARGARET 3. E19.

madia /ˈmeɪdɪə/ *noun*. E19.
[ORIGIN mod. Latin (see below), from Chilean Spanish *madi* from Mapuche.]
A coarse hairy Chilean plant, *Madia sativa*, allied to the sunflower, which is cultivated for its oil-rich seeds.

madid /ˈmadɪd/ *adjective*. Now *rare*. E17.
[ORIGIN Latin *madidus*, from *madere* be wet: see -ID[1].]
Wet, moist.

Madison /ˈmadɪs(ə)n/ *noun*[1]. M20.
[ORIGIN Presumably from the personal name or place name *Madison*.]
A dance popular in the early 1960s.

madison /ˈmadɪs(ə)n/ *noun*[2]. E20.
[ORIGIN Named after *Madison* Square Garden, New York, the site of the first such race in 1892.]
A cycle relay race for teams of (usu.) two riders, traditionally lasting for six days, but freq. of much shorter duration.

Madison Avenue /ˌmadɪs(ə)n ˈavənjuː/ *noun phr.* M20.
[ORIGIN A street in New York City, centre of the American advertising business.]
(American) advertising, the (American) advertising business; American advertising agents collectively.

madly /ˈmadli/ *adverb*. ME.
[ORIGIN from MAD *adjective* + -LY[2].]
1 In a mad, insane, or foolish manner. ME.
2 Passionately, fervently; extremely, very. *colloq.* M18.

B. REID I fell madly in love with him. N. MARSH She's madly keen on criminology.

madness /ˈmadnɪs/ *noun*. LME.
[ORIGIN from MAD *adjective* + -NESS.]
1 Mental illness, insanity; *esp.* insanity characterized by wild frenzy, mania. Also, (in an animal) rabies. LME.
canine madness: see CANINE *adjective* 1.
2 Imprudence or (wild) foolishness resembling insanity. LME.

RACHEL ANDERSON It seemed madness to spend . . money paying . . to go where I didn't want to be.

METHOD in one's madness.
3 Wild excitement or enthusiasm; ecstasy. L16.
4 Uncontrollable anger, rage, or fury. M17.

transf.: W. C. SMITH Then I see . . the waves lashed into madness.

5 An instance or spell of madness; a mad act. E18.

mado /ˈmɑːdəʊ/ *noun*. *Austral.* Pl. **-os**. L19.
[ORIGIN Perh. from an Australian Aboriginal language of New South Wales.]
A small marine percoid fish, *Atypichthys mado* (family Kyphosidae), found off eastern Australia and New Zealand.

Madonna /məˈdɒnə/ *noun*. Also **m-**. L16.
[ORIGIN Italian, from *ma* old unstressed form of *mia* my (from Latin *mea*) + *donna* lady (from Latin *domina*): cf. MADAM *noun*.]
1 a Used as a respectful form of address to an Italian woman, or in literal renderings of Italian speech. L16. ▸**b** An Italian woman. *rare*. E17.

a Y. CARTER 'Take my advice and do it now'. He . . shook his head. 'In a minute, Madonna'.

2 The or *the* Virgin Mary; a picture or statue of the Virgin Mary. M17.

R. WEST A single picture hung between two doors . . a Madonna and child painted in flat bright colours.

3 More fully ***Madonna braid***. A hairstyle in which the hair is parted in the centre and arranged smoothly on either side of the face, as in Italian representations of the Madonna. M19.
– COMB.: **Madonna blue** *noun & adjective* (of) a shade of deep blue; ***Madonna braid***: see sense 3 above; **Madonna lily** a white-flowered lily, *Lilium candidum*, traditionally regarded as a symbol of purity and often shown with the Madonna in pictures.
■ **Madonnaish** *adjective* resembling a Madonna E19.

madoqua /ˈmadəʊkwə/ *noun*. *rare*. L18.
[ORIGIN Amharic.]
A dik-dik, esp. *Madoqua satiana* of Ethiopia.

Madras /məˈdrɑːs, -ˈdras/ *noun & adjective*. L17.
[ORIGIN A seaport (since 1995 officially called Chennai) on the east coast of India, capital of Tamil Nadu (formerly also the name of a province).]
▸ **A** *noun*. **1** Used *attrib.* to designate things made in or associated with Madras. L17. ▸**b** *ellipt.* A Madras handkerchief; a Madras curry. M19.

Madras handkerchief a brightly coloured handkerchief of silk and cotton, formerly often worn as a turban in the W. Indies. **Madras curry** a hot curry usu. containing chicken or beef.
2 A cotton fabric with brightly coloured or white stripes, checks, etc., orig. produced in Madras. L19.

madrasah /mə'drasə/ *noun*. Also **madrasa**, **medrese** /mɛ'drɛseɪ/, & other vars. E17.
[ORIGIN Arabic *madrasa*, noun of place from *darasa* to study.]
A Muslim college.

Madrasi /mə'drasi/ *adjective & noun*. Also **-ss-**. M19.
[ORIGIN from *Madras* MADRAS + -I².]
▸ **A** *adjective*. Of or pertaining to Madras (now Chennai) in India. M19.
▸ **B** *noun*. A native or inhabitant of Madras. M19.

madre /'madre/ *noun*. E19.
[ORIGIN Spanish.]
Mother. Chiefly in exclamatory phrs., as ***madre de dios*** /de 'dios/ [lit. 'mother of God'], ***madre mia*** /'mia/ [lit. 'mother mine'], etc.

madreporarian /ˌmadrɪpɔː'rɛːrɪən/ *adjective & noun*. L19.
[ORIGIN from mod. Latin *Madreporaria* former taxonomic name, formed as MADREPORE: see -IAN.]
ZOOLOGY. ▸**A** *adjective*. Of, pertaining to, designating, or characteristic of a stony or true coral (order Scleractinia). L19.
▸ **B** *noun*. A stony coral. L19.

madrepore /'madrɪpɔː/ *noun*. M18.
[ORIGIN French *madrépore* or mod. Latin *Madrepora* (see below) from Italian *madrepora*, presumably from *madre* mother (perh. with allus. to the prolific growth of the coral) + *poro* from Latin *porus* PORE *noun* or Latin *porus* from Greek *pōros* calcareous stone, stalactite.]
1 A stony coral, *esp.* one of the genus *Madrepora* or a related genus. M18. ▸**b** The polyp of a madreporarian coral. M19.
2 = MADREPORITE 1. E19.

madreporic /madrɪ'pɒrɪk/ *adjective*. E19.
[ORIGIN from MADREPORE + -IC.]
1 GEOLOGY. Produced by madrepores; consisting of madreporarian coral. Now *rare*. E19.
2 ZOOLOGY. Pertaining to or designating the madreporite of echinoderms, or structures associated with it or resembling it. M19.

madreporite /madrɪ'pɔːrʌɪt/ *noun*. E19.
[ORIGIN from MADREPORE + -ITE¹ (in sense 2 with ref. to the resemblance to madreporarian coral).]
1 GEOLOGY. A columnar calcareous rock with a radiating prismatic structure, resembling coralline limestone. E19. ▸**b** PALAEONTOLOGY. Fossil madreporarian coral. *rare*. E19.
2 ZOOLOGY. In echinoderms, the pore or perforated plate by which seawater enters the stone canal of the water-vascular system. L19.

madrich /ma'drix, 'madrɪx/ *noun*. Pl. ***-im*** /-ɪm/. M20.
[ORIGIN Hebrew *maḏrīḵ*.]
A group leader, a supervisor, esp. on a kibbutz.

madrier /madrije/ *noun*. Pl. pronounced same. E18.
[ORIGIN French.]
A thick wooden plank used as a support in fortification work, or along with a petard to breach a gate etc.

madrigal /'madrɪg(ə)l/ *noun*. L16.
[ORIGIN Italian from medieval Latin *matricalis* mother: cf. medieval Latin *ecclesia matrix* mother church, MATRIX *noun*.]
1 A short lyrical love poem. L16.
2 MUSIC. A part song for several voices, *spec.* one of a 16th- or 17th-cent. Italian style, arranged in elaborate counterpoint, and sung without instrumental accompaniment. Also, a 14th-cent. Italian pastoral song of several stanzas. L16.

> C. BURNEY The most chearful species of secular Music . . was that of madrigals.

3 *gen.* A song, a ditty. L16.

> J. CLARE Thrushes chant their madrigals.

■ **madriga'lesque** *adjective* having the features or characteristics of a madrigal E20. **madrigalian** /-'geɪlɪən/ *adjective* pertaining to, consisting or characteristic of, or dealing with madrigals M19. **madri'galianism** *noun* = MADRIGALISM M20. **madrigalism** *noun* a musical feature characteristic of a madrigal, *esp.* the illustration of lyrics through vocal composition M20. **madrigalist** *noun* a writer or composer of madrigals L18.

madrilene /madrɪ'liːn, -'lɛn/ *noun*. M20.
[ORIGIN French (*consommé à la*) *madrilène*, formed as MADRILENIAN.]
A clear soup usually served cold.

Madrilenian /madrɪ'leɪnɪən/ *noun & adjective*. E19.
[ORIGIN from Spanish *madrileño*, (fem.) *-leña* of Madrid (see below) + -IAN.]
▸ **A** *noun*. A native or inhabitant of Madrid, the capital of Spain. E19.
▸ **B** *adjective*. Of or pertaining to Madrid. M19.

Madrileño /madrɪ'lenjəʊ, *foreign* madri'leɲo/ *noun*. Pl. **-os** /-əʊz, *foreign* -os/. Fem. **-ña** /-njə, *foreign* -ɲa/. M19.
[ORIGIN Spanish: see MADRILENIAN.]
= MADRILENIAN *noun*.

madroño /mə'drəʊnjəʊ/ *noun*. Pl. **-os**. Also **-na** /-nə/. M19.
[ORIGIN Spanish.]
An evergreen tree of the heath family, *Arbutus menziesii*, of western N. America, with glossy leaves, white flowers, and orange or red berries.

Madura foot /'madʊrə fʊt/ *noun phr*. M19.
[ORIGIN from *Madura*, a city in southern India, now called Madurai.]
MEDICINE. Maduromycosis of the foot.

Madurese /madjʊ'riːz/ *noun & adjective*. E19.
[ORIGIN from *Madura* (see below) + -ESE.]
▸ **A** *noun*. Pl. same.
1 A native or inhabitant of Madura, an island off the north-east coast of Java. E19.
2 The Austronesian language of Madura. E19.
▸ **B** *adjective*. Of or pertaining to Madura or its language. L19.
■ **Maduran** *noun* = MADURESE *noun* M19.

maduro /mə'duːrəʊ/ *noun*. Pl. **-os**. L19.
[ORIGIN Spanish = ripe, mature.]
A dark-coloured cigar.

maduromycosis /ˌmadʊrəʊmʌɪ'kəʊsɪs/ *noun*. Pl. **-coses** /-'kəʊsiːz/. E20.
[ORIGIN from *Madura(i)* (see MADURA FOOT) + -O- + MYCOSIS.]
MEDICINE. A chronic destructive fungal infection of the foot (rarely of other parts). Cf. MADURA FOOT.

madwort /'madwəːt/ *noun*. LME.
[ORIGIN App. from MAD *adjective* + WORT *noun*¹, translating mod. Latin ALYSSUM.]
†**1** Deadly nightshade. Only in LME.
2 Orig., any of several plants said to cure the bites of mad dogs, esp. the crucifer *Alyssum alyssoides*. Now (more fully ***German madwort***), a procumbent blue-flowered plant of the borage family, *Asperugo procumbens*, found as an alien in Britain. L16.

maeander *noun & verb* see MEANDER.

maeandrine *adjective* see MEANDRINE.

maeandrous *adjective* see MEANDROUS.

Maecenas /mʌɪ'siːnəs/ *noun*. M16.
[ORIGIN Gaius *Maecenas* (d. 8 BC), Roman friend of Augustus, statesman, and patron of Horace and Virgil.]
A generous patron of literature or art. Formerly also, any patron.
■ **Maecenatism** *noun* (long *rare*) patronage E17.

maedi /'meɪdi/ *noun*. M20.
[ORIGIN Icelandic *mæði* lit. 'shortness of breath'.]
VETERINARY MEDICINE. A slowly progressive form of interstitial pneumonia in sheep and goats, caused by the maedi-visna virus. Cf. VISNA.
– COMB.: **maedi-visna** *noun & adjective* (*a*) *noun* maedi; visna; (*b*) *adjective* designating the lentivirus that causes both these diseases.

maelstrom /'meɪlstrəm/ *noun*. M17.
[ORIGIN Early mod. Dutch (now *maalstroom*), from *maalen* grind, whirl round + *stroom* STREAM *noun*, whence the Scandinavian forms (e.g. Swedish *malström*, Danish *malstrøm*).]
1 A great whirlpool, orig. one in the Arctic Ocean off the west coast of Norway, formerly supposed to suck in and destroy all vessels within a long radius. M17.

> *American Poetry Review* They have pulled oars while caught in maelstroms.

2 *fig.* A state of turbulence or confusion. M19.

> L. CODY Simon . . succeeded in penetrating the maelstrom round the bar. *Times* The meeting . . is taking place amid a maelstrom of rumours about imminent changes.

Maelzel's metronome /'mɛlts(ə)lz 'mɛtrənəʊm/ *noun phr*. L19.
[ORIGIN Johann N. *Maelzel* (Mälzel) (d. 1838), the inventor.]
A metronome (as invented and designed by Maelzel).

maenad /'miːnad/ *noun*. Also **menad**, **M-**. L16.
[ORIGIN Latin *Maenad-*, *Maenas* from Greek *Mainad-*, *Mainas*, from *mainesthai* rave.]
A Bacchante; *gen.* a frenzied woman.
■ **mae'nadic** *adjective* characteristic of or resembling a maenad; frenzied: M19. **maenadism** *noun* wild or frenzied behaviour L19.

maestoso /mʌɪ'stəʊzəʊ/ *adverb, adjective, & noun*. E18.
[ORIGIN Italian = majestic, from *maestà* from Latin *majestas*, *-tat-* MAJESTY + *-oso* -OUS.]
MUSIC. ▸**A** *adverb & adjective*. A direction: majestic(ally). E18.
▸ **B** *noun*. Pl. **-os**. A majestic piece or movement. L18.

maestrale /mʌɪ'straːleɪ/ *noun*. E19.
[ORIGIN Italian from Latin *magistralis* (sc. *ventus* wind): see MAGISTRAL. Cf. MISTRAL.]
Any of several mainly north-westerly winds which blow in the Mediterranean, esp. a summer wind in the Adriatic, and a winter wind, milder than a mistral, in the west.

maestri *noun pl.* see MAESTRO.

maestria /mʌɪ'striːə/ *noun*. L19.
[ORIGIN Italian from Latin *magisterium*, from *magister* MASTER *noun*¹.]
Skill, mastery.

maestro /'mʌɪstrəʊ, *foreign* ma'ɛstro/ *noun*. Pl. **maestri** /'mʌɪstriː, *foreign* ma'ɛstri/, **maestros**. E17.
[ORIGIN Italian, from Latin *magister* MASTER *noun*¹.]
1 Orig., a form of address for someone eminent in a skill or profession, esp. music. Now, an expert in music; a great musical composer, teacher, or conductor. E17. ▸**b** A great performer or leader in any art, profession, etc. M20.

> E. HEATH Toscanini was conducting, but I could not afford the cost of a seat to hear the maestro. **b** T. H. WHITE He was a better fencer than his maestro.

maestro di cappella /diː kə'pɛlə, *foreign* di kap'pɛlla/ [lit. 'of the chapel'] a choirmaster; a musical director, a conductor.
2 = MAESTRALE. E20.

Maeterlinckian /meɪtə'lɪŋkɪən, 'mɑːtə-/ *adjective*. L19.
[ORIGIN from *Maeterlinck* (see below) + -IAN.]
Of, pertaining to, or characteristic of the Belgian author Maurice Maeterlinck (1862–1949), or his writings.

Mae West /meɪ 'wɛst/ *noun*. *slang*. M20.
[ORIGIN The professional name of an American film actress and entertainer (1892–1980), noted for her large breasts.]
An inflatable life jacket, orig. one issued to Royal Air Force men in the Second World War.

mafeesh /mə'fiːʃ/ *interjection & adjective*. *colloq.* M19.
[ORIGIN Colloq. Arabic *mā fī-š* there are none.]
▸ **A** *interjection*. Expressing rejection: nothing doing! M19.
▸ **B** *adjective*. Finished, done. E20.

MAFF /maf/ *abbreviation*. *hist.*
Ministry of Agriculture, Fisheries, and Food.

Maffia *noun* var. of MAFIA.

maffick /'mafɪk/ *verb intrans. arch.* E20.
[ORIGIN from *Mafeking* (see below), treated joc. as a pres. pple, whence other parts of the verb.]
Celebrate uproariously, rejoice extravagantly, esp. on an occasion of national celebration (orig. the relief of the British garrison besieged in Mafeking, South Africa, in May 1900).

Maffiosa, **Maffioso** *nouns* see MAFIOSO.

maffle /'maf(ə)l/ *verb*. *obsolete* exc. *dial.* LME.
[ORIGIN Cf. early mod. Dutch *maffelen* move the jaws.]
1 *verb intrans.* Stammer; speak indistinctly, mumble. LME.
2 *verb intrans.* Blunder, bungle; delay, waste time. L18.
3 *verb trans.* Confuse, bewilder, muddle. E19.

M

Mafia /'mafɪə/ *noun*. Also **m-**, **-ff-**. M19.
[ORIGIN Sicilian Italian = bragging, spec. hostility towards the law and its upholders, freq. as manifested in vindictive crimes.]
1 ***the Mafia***, an organized secret society of criminals, originating in Sicily but now operating internationally, esp. in the US. Cf. UNIONE SICILIANA. M19.

> A. CHRISTIE One of these secret societies, the Mafia, or the Camorra . . is on their track. A. HAILEY The game is Mafia-controlled, demonstrably crooked.

2 *gen.* Any group regarded as exerting a secret and often sinister influence. M20.

> *New Society* The scientific Mafia got to work as soon as Immanuel Velikovsky's book . . was announced.

mafic /'mafɪk/ *adjective*. E20.
[ORIGIN Contr. of MAGNESIUM and FERRIC.]
PETROGRAPHY. Of, pertaining to, or designating a group of dark-coloured, mainly ferromagnesian minerals; (of a rock) containing a high proportion of such minerals. Cf. FELSIC.

Mafioso /mafɪ'əʊsəʊ/ *noun*. Pl. **-si** /-si/, **-sos**. Fem. **-sa** /-sə/. Also **m-**, **-ff-**. L19.
[ORIGIN Italian, formed as MAFIA.]
A member or supporter of the Mafia.

ma foi /ma fwa/ *interjection*. LME.
[ORIGIN French, lit. 'my faith'.]
Heavens! Goodness!

mafoo /'maːfuː/ *noun*. M19.
[ORIGIN Chinese *mǎ-fū*, from *mǎ* horse + *fū* servant, labourer.]
A Chinese groom, stable boy, or coachman.

Mag /mag/ *noun*¹. *colloq. & dial.* E19.
[ORIGIN Pet form of female forename *Margaret*.]
A magpie. Also ***long-tailed Mag*** (*rare*), the long-tailed tit.

mag /mag/ *noun*² *& verb*. *colloq.* (now chiefly *Austral.*). L18.
[ORIGIN from MAGPIE.]
▸ **A** *noun*. **1** Chatter, talk; (a) chat. L18.
2 A chatterbox. L19.
▸ **B** *verb intrans.* Infl. **-gg-**. Chatter (*away*). E19.

> E. LANGLEY Hurry up! Don't be magging there all day!

mag /mag/ *noun*³. *arch. slang.* L18.
[ORIGIN Unknown. Cf. MAKE *noun*³.]
A halfpenny.

mag /mag/ *noun*⁴. *colloq.* E19.
[ORIGIN Abbreviation.]
= MAGAZINE *noun* 5.

A. BROOKNER Pink harem pants . . as they say in the fashion mags.

mag /mag/ *noun*[5]. Pl. same, **-s**. M19.
[ORIGIN Abbreviation.]
ASTRONOMY. = MAGNITUDE 4. Usu. with preceding numeral.

mag /mag/ *noun*[6]. *colloq.* E20.
[ORIGIN Abbreviation.]
= MAGNETO.

mag /mag/ *noun*[7]. *colloq.* M20.
[ORIGIN Abbreviation.]
Magnesium; magnesium alloy.
– COMB.: **mag wheel** *N. Amer.* a lightweight motor-vehicle wheel made from magnesium steel.

Maga /ˈmagə/ *noun. colloq.* Now *rare* or *obsolete*. Also **m-**. E19.
[ORIGIN Abbreviation.]
A magazine, a periodical; *spec.* Blackwood's Magazine.

magadis /ˈmagədɪs/ *noun*. E18.
[ORIGIN Greek.]
An ancient Greek stringed musical instrument.

magadize /ˈmagədʌɪz/ *verb intrans.* Also **-ise**. L18.
[ORIGIN Greek *magadizein*, formed as MAGADIS + -IZE.]
1 Play or sing in octaves. *rare*. L18.
2 *hist.* Play on the magadis. L19.

magalogue /ˈmagəlɒg/ *noun*. L20.
[ORIGIN from MAG(AZINE *noun* + CAT)ALOGUE.]
A promotional catalogue or sales brochure designed to resemble a high-quality magazine.

Magar /ˈmɑːgɑː/ *noun & adjective*. E19.
[ORIGIN Magar.]
▸ **A** *noun*. A member of a people of central Nepal; the Tibeto-Burman language of this people. E19.
▸ **B** *attrib.* or as *adjective*. Of or pertaining to the Magars or their language. E19.

magatama /ˈmɑːgətɑːmə/ *noun*. L19.
[ORIGIN Japanese, from *maga* curved + *tama* bead.]
A curved ornament or jewel forming part of the Japanese imperial regalia.

magazine /magəˈziːn/ *noun*. L16.
[ORIGIN French *magasin* from Italian *magazzino* from Arabic *makzan*, *-in* storehouse, from *kazana* store up.]
1 A place where goods are kept in store; a storehouse for merchandise; a warehouse, a depot; *transf.* a country or district rich in natural products, a centre of commerce. Now *rare*. L16. ▸**b** A portable receptacle for articles of value. Now *rare*. M18.

BURKE No magazine, from the warehouses of the East India Company to the . . baker's shop, possesses the smallest degree of safety.

2 *MILITARY*. A building for the storage of arms, ammunition, and provisions for use in war; *spec.* a store for large quantities of explosives. L16.

N. NYE A barrell of the best powder in the Magazine.

3 a *MILITARY*. The contents of a magazine; a store (*of*). Formerly also *sing.* & in *pl.*, stores, provisions, equipment. L16. ▸**b** *gen.* A store of provisions, materials, etc. E17.

a GIBBON He used . . a large magazine of darts and arrows. **b** T. BEWICK Each Beaver forms its bed of moss, and each family lays in its magazine of winter provisions.

†**4** A book providing information on a specified subject or for a specified group of people. (Freq. as part of the title.) M17–E19.

5 A periodical publication with articles by various writers; *esp.* one with stories, articles on general subjects, etc., and usu. illustrated with pictures or photographs. M18. ▸**b** More fully ***magazine programme***. A regular television or radio broadcast comprising a variety of entertainment or news items. M20.

DAY LEWIS Short stories . . she had written for parish magazines. A. JUDD They emerged with a bundle of old pornographic magazines. **b** *Listener* The extended Saturday magazine called Sport on 2.

little magazine: see LITTLE *adjective*.

6 A compartment for holding essential supplies in an apparatus; *spec.* a chamber in a repeating rifle, machine gun, etc., containing a supply of cartridges which are fed automatically to the breech; a similar device in a camera, slide projector, etc. M18.

– COMB.: **magazine cover** the (usu. pictorial) cover of a magazine; ***magazine programme***: see sense 5b above; **magazine rights**: of publishing matter in a magazine; **magazine section** a section in a newspaper the contents of which resemble a magazine.
■ **magazinedom** *noun* the world or sphere of magazines M19. **magaziner** *noun* (*rare*) a person who writes articles for magazines M18. **magazinery** *noun* (*rare*) the profession of a writer for magazines; material of the nature of or suitable for a magazine: M19. **magazinish** *adjective* = MAGAZINY L18. **magazinist** *noun* = MAGAZINER E19. **magaziny** *adjective* of the nature of or suitable for a magazine L19.

†**magazine** *verb trans.* M17–M18.
[ORIGIN from the noun.]
Store up (goods) as in a magazine or storehouse. Also foll. by *up*.

magcon /ˈmagkɒn/ *noun*. L20.
[ORIGIN from *magnetic concentration*.]
ASTRONOMY. Any of several regions of the moon's surface having an anomalously high magnetic field strength.

magdalen /ˈmagdəlɪn/ *noun*. Also (esp. in sense 1) **M-**, **-lene** /-liːn/. ME.
[ORIGIN ecclesiastical Latin (*Maria*) *Magdalena*, *-lene* from Greek (*Mariaē*) *Magdalēnē* (Mary) of *Magdala*, a town in ancient Palestine. Cf. MAUDLIN *noun*.]
1 *CHRISTIAN CHURCH*. ***the Magdalen***, ***Mary Magdalen***, a follower of Jesus to whom he appeared after his resurrection (*John* 20:1–18), in the West commonly identified with the sinner of *Luke* 7:37 and represented in hagiology as a reformed prostitute elevated to sanctity by repentance and faith. Cf. MAUDLIN *noun* 1. ME. ▸**b** A representation of Mary Magdalen in art. L17.
2 *transf.* A repentant female sinner; *esp.* a reformed prostitute. M16. ▸**b** *hist.* A home for the refuge and reformation of prostitutes. Also ***magdalen home***, ***magdalen hospital***, etc. Cf. MAUDLIN *noun* 3. M18.
3 An old variety of peach. Cf. MAUDLIN *noun* 4. Long *rare*. L17.
■ **magdalenism** *noun* prostitution M19.

Magdalenian /magdəˈliːnɪən/ *adjective & noun*. L19.
[ORIGIN French *Magdalénien*, from La *Madeleine* (see below) + -IAN.]
ARCHAEOLOGY. ▸**A** *adjective*. Designating or pertaining to a culture of the late upper Palaeolithic period in Europe characterized by fine bone and antler artefacts and a strong artistic tradition, named after a site at La Madeleine in the Dordogne, France. L19.
▸ **B** *noun*. (A person of) this culture. E20.

†**magdaleon** *noun*. LME–L19.
[ORIGIN medieval Latin *magdaleo(n-)* from Greek *magdalia* dough, breadcrumb.]
A cylindrical roll of plaster, salve, or other medicinal substance.

Magdeburg hemisphere /ˈmagdəbəːg ˈhɛmɪsfɪə/ *noun phr.* E19.
[ORIGIN from *Magdeburg*, a city in Germany, home of the inventor, Otto von Guericke (1602–86).]
Either of a pair of brass hemispheres exhausted of air to show atmospheric pressure by their cohesion.

mage /meɪdʒ/ *noun*. Now *arch.* & *literary*. LME.
[ORIGIN Anglicized from MAGUS. Cf. Old French & mod. French *mage*.]
1 A magician; a person of exceptional wisdom and learning. LME.

J. I. M. STEWART I might be in the presence of a mage or wizard in disguise.

2 *spec.* = MAGUS 1. LME.

Magellan /məˈgɛlən/ *noun*. L16.
[ORIGIN Anglicized from Fernão de *Magalhães* (Spanish *Magallanes*), Portuguese explorer (d. 1521).]
Used *attrib.* and in *possess.* = MAGELLANIC.

Magellanic /madʒɪˈlanɪk, magɪ-/ *adjective*. E17.
[ORIGIN from MAGELLAN + -IC.]
Pertaining to or named after Magellan (see MAGELLAN).
Magellanic Cloud *ASTRONOMY* either of two small galaxies (***large Magellanic Cloud***, ***small Magellanic Cloud***) associated with the Milky Way and visible at night in the southern hemisphere as cloudy spots.

Magen David /mɑːˈgɛn dɑːˈviːd/ *noun phr.* L19.
[ORIGIN Hebrew, lit. 'shield of David' (king of Israel from c 1000 BC).]
= ***Star of David*** s.v. STAR *noun*[1] & *adjective*.

magenta /məˈdʒɛntə/ *noun & adjective*. M19.
[ORIGIN *Magenta* in northern Italy, site of a battle (1859) shortly before the dye was discovered.]
▸ **A** *noun*. A brilliant purple-pink aniline dye, fuchsine; the colour of this dye. M19.
▸ **B** *adjective*. Of the colour of magenta. L19.

magg /mag/ *verb trans. Scot.* M18.
[ORIGIN Perh. from MAG *noun*[1], MAGPIE.]
Pilfer, steal.

magged /magd/ *adjective*. M19.
[ORIGIN Unknown.]
1 *NAUTICAL*. Of rope etc.: worn, frayed. M19.
2 Irritated; exhausted, jaded. *dial.* M19.

Maggid /ˈmɑːgɪd/ *noun*. Pl. **-im** /-ɪm/. L19.
[ORIGIN Hebrew *maggīd* narrator.]
An itinerant Jewish preacher.

maggie /ˈmagi/ *noun*. Also **M-**. See also MOGGY. E17.
[ORIGIN *Maggie*, formed as MAG *noun*[1]: see -IE.]
1 A girl. *Scot.* E17.
2 a A magpie. *dial.*, *Austral.* & *NZ*. E19. ▸**b** A common guillemot. *Scot.* L19.
3 In full ***Maggie Ann***. Margarine. *slang*. M20.
4 [*Margaret* Thatcher, Brit. Prime Minister 1979–1990.] A pound coin. *slang*. L20.
– PHRASES: **Maggie's drawers** *US military slang* [said to refer to a song entitled *Those Old Red Flannel Drawers That Maggie Wore*] a red flag used to indicate a miss in target practice.

maggot /ˈmagət/ *noun*. L15.
[ORIGIN Perh. from Anglo-Norman alt. of MADDOCK.]
1 Any soft-bodied limbless larva, esp. of a housefly, blowfly, or other dipteran fly, typically found in decaying organic matter. L15.
2 A whimsical or perverse fancy. E17.
3 A whimsical or capricious person. L17.
■ **maggotry** *noun* (*rare*) †(**a**) folly, absurdity; (**b**) a place where maggots live and are reared: E18.

maggot-pie /ˈmagətpʌɪ/ *noun. obsolete* exc. *dial.* L16.
[ORIGIN from French *Margot*, pet form of female forename *Marguerite* Margaret + PIE *noun*[1].]
A magpie.

maggoty /ˈmagəti/ *adjective*. M17.
[ORIGIN from MAGGOT + -Y[1].]
1 Full of whims and foolish fancies; capricious. M17.
2 Full of maggots. E18.
3 Angry, bad-tempered. Freq. in ***go maggoty***, lose one's temper. *slang* (chiefly *Austral.* & *NZ*). E20.
■ **maggotiness** *noun* E18.

maghemite /magˈhiːmʌɪt/ *noun*. E20.
[ORIGIN from MAG(NETITE + H(A)EM(ATITE + -ITE[1].]
MINERALOGY. A highly ferromagnetic mineral of the spinel group which is a form of ferric oxide, Fe_2O_3, formed principally by alteration of magnetite and crystallizing in the cubic system.

Maghreb *adjective*, **Maghrebi** *noun & adjective* vars. of MAGHRIB, MAGHRIBI.

Maghrebin /magrəˈbɪn/ *adjective*. E20.
[ORIGIN French *Maghrébine*, from Arabic *Maḡribīn* pl. of *Maḡribī*: see MAGHRIBI. Cf. MAUGRABIN.]
= MAGHRIBI *adjective*.

Maghrib /maˈgriːb/ *noun & adjective*. Also **Maghreb**. E17.
[ORIGIN Arabic *Maḡrib* time or place of sunset, west, NW Africa, from *ḡaraba* go away, depart, (of the sun) set. Cf. MAGHRIBI.]
▸ **A** *noun*. (**m-**.) In Islam: one of the five obligatory daily times of prayer, lasting from sunset to dusk; the prayers said at this time. E17.
▸ **B** *adjective*. Of or pertaining to the Maghrib or the Maghribi. M20.

Maghribi /maˈgrɪbiː/ *noun & adjective*. Also **Maghrebi**. E18.
[ORIGIN Arabic *Maḡribī* from *Maḡrib* MAGHRIB + -ī -I[2].]
▸ **A** *noun*. Pl. same. A native or inhabitant of the Maghrib, a region of NW Africa including Morocco, Algeria, and Tunisia; the variety of Arabic spoken in this region. E18.
▸ **B** *attrib.* or as *adjective*. Of or pertaining to the Maghribi or their language. M18.

Maghzen *noun* var. of MAKHZAN.

magi *noun pl.* of MAGUS.

magian /ˈmeɪdʒɪən/ *noun & adjective*. Also **M-**. M16.
[ORIGIN from Latin MAGUS + -IAN.]
▸ **A** *noun*. A magus; *spec.* each of the three Magi. M16.
▸ **B** *adjective*. Of or pertaining to the Magi or magi. E18.
■ **magianism** *noun* the doctrine of the magi E18.

magic /ˈmadʒɪk/ *noun*. Also (*arch.*) **-ck**. LME.
[ORIGIN Old French *magique* (mod. *magie*) from late Latin *magica* from Greek *magikē* use as noun (sc. *tekhnē* art) of *magikos*, from *magos* MAGUS: see -IC.]
1 The supposed art of influencing the course of events and of producing extraordinary physical phenomena by the occult control of nature or of spirits; sorcery, witchcraft. Also, the practice of this art. LME. ▸†**b** A magical procedure or rite; a magical object, a charm. LME–E19.

GIBBON The arts of magic and divination were strictly prohibited. P. LOMAS The Greek army . . would never defeat the Trojans without the help of . . magic.

2 *fig.* An inexplicable and remarkable influence producing surprising results. Also, an enchanting quality; *colloq.* exceptional skill or talent. E17.

DISRAELI What mourner has not felt the magic of time? E. A. FREEMAN Won over by the magic of his personal presence. P. NICHOLS I want to bring back the magic to our marriage. *Soccer* The Italians . . could not . . live with that special brand of Brazilian magic.

3 The art of producing (by sleight of hand, optical illusion, etc.) apparently inexplicable phenomena; conjuring. M19.

R. DAVIES To teach me magic, . . a few things with cards and coins.

– PHRASES: **black magic** [French *magie noire*] magic involving the supposed invocation of evil spirits, harmful or malevolent magic. **like magic** without any apparent explanation; with incredible rapidity. **natural magic** magic involving no invocation of spirits. ***sympathetic magic***: see SYMPATHETIC *adjective*. **white magic** [French *magie blanche*] magic involving the supposed invocation of good spirits, beneficent or harmless magic.

magic /ˈmadʒɪk/ *adjective*. Also (*arch.*) **-ck**. LME.
[ORIGIN Old French & mod. French *magique* from Latin *magicus* from Greek *magikos*: see MAGIC *noun*.]
1 *attrib.* **a** Of or pertaining to magic; working or produced by magic. LME. ▸**b** Of a material object: used or usable in magic rites, endued with supernatural powers. L17.

SHAKES. *1 Hen. VI* Sorcerers.. By magic verses have contriv'd his end. I. MURDOCH He murmured her name like a magic charm to protect.. himself. **b** R. BURNS Where Pleasure is the Magic-wand That, wielded right, Maks Hours like Minutes.

2 Producing surprising results, like those attributed to magic. Also, having a quality of enchantment. **L17.**

JOYCE Timidity and inexperience would fall from him in that magic moment. R. DAHL The summer holidays! Those magic words! C. ACHEBE He never failed once in anything. Had the magic touch.

3 *NUCLEAR PHYSICS.* (Of each of a set of numbers) corresponding to the number of protons or neutrons in nuclei of exceptional stability (the set now taken to be 2, 8, 20, 28, 50, 82, 126, and perhaps 184); (of a nucleus) containing such a number of protons or neutrons, or (***doubly magic***) such a number of each. **M20.**
4 Superlatively good, excellent, fantastic. *colloq.* **M20.**

Weekend Television I found myself agreeing with our producer's favourite comment: magic.

– SPECIAL COLLOCATIONS: **magic bullet** *colloq.* any (usu. undiscovered) highly specific therapeutic agent. **magic carpet** a mythical carpet able to transport a person on it to any desired place. **magic chain stitch**, **magic stitch**: worked with two colours in one needle. **magic circle** (**a**) an arrangement of numbers in concentric circles, with properties similar to the magic square; (**b**) a circle used in magic as a protection against evil; (**c**) (with cap. initials) a society of conjurors; (**d**) a small group of people privileged to receive confidential information, make important decisions, etc. **magic eye** (**a**) (also with cap. initials) (*US* proprietary name for) a miniature cathode-ray tube used esp. to indicate the strength of an electrical signal; (**b**) a photoelectric cell or similar electrical device used for identification, detection, or measurement. **magic glass**, **magic mirror**: in which future events or distant scenes are supposedly displayed. **magic lantern** a simple optical device using slides to display a magnified image on a white screen, wall, etc., in a darkened room. **magic-lanterned** *adjective* (of an image etc.) displayed using a magic lantern. **Magic Marker** (proprietary name for) an indelible marker pen. ***magic mirror***: see ***magic glass*** above. **magic mushroom** a mushroom with hallucinogenic properties, *esp.* one (e.g. the liberty cap) containing psilocybin. **magic realism** a literary or artistic genre in which realism and narrative are combined with surreal, fantastic, dreamlike, or mythological elements. **magic realist** *noun & adjective* (**a**) *noun* an exponent of magic realism; (**b**) *adjective* of or pertaining to magic realists or magic realism. **magic square** a square array of numbers with the property that the sum of those in each vertical, horizontal, or diagonal row is always the same. ***magic stitch***: see ***magic chain stitch*** above. ***magic wand***: see WAND *noun* 7.

magic /ˈmadʒɪk/ *verb trans.* Also (*arch.*) **-ck**. Infl. **-ck-**. **E20.**
[ORIGIN from the noun.]
Change, make, or produce (as if) by magic.

D. FRANCIS He magicked some huge open sandwiches. *Photography* Your.. brief allows you to magic vices into virtues.

magic away cause to disappear (as if) by magic.

magical /ˈmadʒɪk(ə)l/ *adjective.* **M16.**
[ORIGIN from MAGIC *noun* + -AL[1].]
1 Of or pertaining to magic; = MAGIC *adjective* 1a. **M16.** ▸**†b** = MAGIC *adjective* 1b. **E17–M18.**

J. A. FROUDE The service of God was.. of the mind and heart, and not a magical superstition. E. GELLNER Nothing magical is being offered—no mysterious transformation of reality.

2 Resembling magic in action or effect; produced as if by magic. Also, having an enchanting quality. **E17.**

W. BLACK The magical disappearance of about fifty or sixty rabbits. A. CARTER 'Enter these enchanted woods..' Who could resist such a magical invitation?

– SPECIAL COLLOCATIONS: **magical realism** = ***magic realism*** s.v. MAGIC *adjective*. **magical realist** *noun & adjective* = ***magic realist*** s.v. MAGIC *adjective*.
■ **magiˈcality** *noun* magical power or quality **E20.** **magically** *adverb* in a magical manner; (as if) by magic: **L16.**

magician /məˈdʒɪʃ(ə)n/ *noun.* **LME.**
[ORIGIN Old French & mod. French *magicien*, from late Latin *magica* MAGIC *noun*: see -ICIAN.]
1 A person skilled in or practising magic or sorcery. Also, a conjuror. **LME.**

BYRON A wise magician who has bound the devil. A. MASON Her magician had astonished the townspeople by floating.. from the roof of a high building.

2 *fig.* A person who exercises an influence like that of magic; a person of exceptional skill. **E19.**

J. BERMAN The myth of the psychiatrist as a modern magician.. in the psychic landscape of life.

magico- /ˈmadʒɪkəʊ/ *combining form.* **E20.**
[ORIGIN from MAGICAL *adjective*: see -O-.]
Forming adjectives with the sense 'magical and —', as ***magico-erotic***, ***magico-religious***, etc.

magilp *noun* var. of MEGILP.

Maginot Line /ˈmadʒɪnəʊ lʌɪn/ *noun phr.* **M20.**
[ORIGIN from André *Maginot* (1877–1932), French minister of war + LINE *noun*[2], a line of fortifications along the NE border of France, begun in 1920 as a defence against German invasion but overrun in 1940.]
A line of defence on which one relies excessively or blindly.

magister /məˈdʒɪstə/ *noun.* Also **M-**. **LME.**
[ORIGIN Latin: see MASTER *noun*[1].]
Chiefly *hist.* Used as a title of respect preceding the name of a man of academic rank; master.

magisterial /madʒɪˈstɪərɪəl/ *noun & adjective.* **E17.**
[ORIGIN medieval Latin *magisterialis*, from late Latin *magisterius*, from Latin *magister* MASTER *noun*[1]: see -IAL.]
▸ **†A** *noun.* = MAGISTERY 3a. **E–M17.**
▸ **B** *adjective.* **1** Of, pertaining to, or befitting a master, teacher, or someone qualified to speak with authority; authoritative; dictatorial; (of a person) invested with authority. **M17.**

GODFREY SMITH Jeeves is.. naturally magisterial (he takes the chair at.. the.. club for gentlemen's gentlemen). B. CHATWIN These researches.. had culminated in his magisterial paper 'The Mammoth and His Parasites'.

†2 Of, pertaining to, or displaying the skill of a master artist. **M–L17.**
3 Of, pertaining to, or befitting a magistrate or magistrates; (of a person) holding the office of a magistrate; (of an inquiry) conducted by a magistrate or magistrates. **M17.**

Times He announced the setting up of a magisterial inquiry.

†4 Pertaining to a magistery (*ALCHEMY*). Also (*PHARMACOLOGY*) = MAGISTRAL *adjective* 2a. **M17–E18.**
■ **magisterially** *adverb* **E17.** **†magisterialness** *noun* **M17–E18.**

magisterium /madʒɪˈstɪərɪəm/ *noun.* **L16.**
[ORIGIN formed as MAGISTERY.]
1 *ALCHEMY.* = MAGISTERY 3a. Long *obsolete* exc. *hist.* **L16.**
2 *ROMAN CATHOLIC CHURCH.* The teaching function of the Church. **M19.**

magistery /ˈmadʒɪst(ə)ri/ *noun. obsolete* exc. *hist.* **L15.**
[ORIGIN Latin *magisterium* office of master, (in medieval Latin) philosopher's stone, formed as MAGISTER: see -ERY.]
†1 The quality, position, or function of a master; authority. **L15–E18.**
†2 The office or position of a magistrate; magistrates collectively. **M–L16.**
3 *ALCHEMY & MEDICINE.* **a** A master principle of nature; a potent transmuting or curative quality or agency; a substance, such as the philosopher's stone, capable of changing the nature of other substances. Also, a product of such transmutation. **L16.** ▸**b** A precipitate, esp. from an acid solution. **E17.** ▸**c** The concentrated essence of a substance. **M17.** ▸**d** A specially prepared medicine. **M17.**
4 = MAGISTERIUM 2. **L19.**

magistracy /ˈmadʒɪstrəsi/ *noun.* **L16.**
[ORIGIN from MAGISTRATE: see -ACY.]
†1 The existence of magisterial power; the state of being a magistrate. **L16–L17.**
2 The position or office of magistrate; magisterial power or dignity. Now *rare.* **L16.**

LD MACAULAY Literature and science were, in the academical system of England.. armed with magistracy.

3 *spec.* The office, dignity, and function of a particular type of magistrate identified contextually. **E17.**
4 Magistrates collectively; a body of magistrates. **E17.**

P. COLQUHOUN Checks established under the control of a vigilant magistracy.

5 A district under the government of a magistrate; a magistrate's residence. **L19.**

magistral /ˈmadʒɪstr(ə)l, məˈdʒɪstr(ə)l/ *adjective & noun.* **L16.**
[ORIGIN French *magistral* or Latin *magistralis*, from *magister* MASTER *noun*[1] + -AL[1].]
▸ **A** *adjective* **1** **†a** Of a problem or a point of instruction: handed down from the masters of a branch of knowledge; forming part of the accepted course of teaching. **L16–M17.** ▸**b** Of, pertaining to, or befitting a master; authoritative, dogmatic. Now *rare.* **E17.**
2 *MEDICINE.* **a** Of a remedy etc.: devised by a physician for a particular case; not included in the pharmacopoeia. Cf. OFFICINAL *adjective.* **L16.** ▸**†b** Sovereign, supremely effective. **L16–L17.**
3 *FORTIFICATION.* Leading, principal; *spec.* designating a principal line in fieldworks which determines the direction and position of other lines. **E19.**
4 Having the title of 'Master'; of or pertaining to a particular master or masters contextually identified. **M19.**
▸ **B** *noun.* **†1** *PHARMACOLOGY.* A magistral preparation. Only in 17.
2 *FORTIFICATION.* A magistral line. **M19.**

magistrand /ˈmadʒɪstrand/ *noun. Scot.* **E17.**
[ORIGIN medieval Latin *magistrandus* gerundive of *magistrari* become a Master (of Arts): see -AND.]
An undergraduate, orig. *spec.* in an Arts faculty, in the fourth or final year at a Scottish University (now only St Andrews).

magistrate /ˈmadʒɪstrət, -streɪt/ *noun.* **LME.**
[ORIGIN Latin *magistratus*, formed as *magister* MASTER *noun*[1] + -ATE[1].]
†1 The office or dignity of a magistrate. **LME–L16.**
2 *gen.* A civil officer administering the law, a member of the executive government. **LME.**

D. HUME The king was too eminent a magistrate to be trusted with discretionary powers.

3 *spec.* A person conducting a court of summary jurisdiction (see ***magistrates' court*** below); a Justice of the Peace; (freq. with specifying word) a salaried official carrying out such duties. In *pl.* also, the provost and councillors of a Scottish burgh, as forming a court for police jurisdiction and the granting of licences. **L17.**

B. EMECHETA She imagined herself at a court and the magistrate sending her to jail.

4 In full ***Glasgow magistrate***. A herring. *Scot. slang.* **M19.**
– COMB.: **magistrate judge** *US Law* a subordinate judicial officer of a district court, *spec.* one who assists a district judge in preparing cases for trial but who may adjudicate certain civil and criminal trials when both litigant parties agree. **magistrates' court**: conducted by a magistrate and dealing with minor cases and preliminary hearings. ***metropolitan magistrate***: see METROPOLITAN *adjective*. ***resident magistrate***: see RESIDENT *adjective*. ***stipendiary magistrate***: see STIPENDIARY *adjective*.
■ **magistrateship** *noun* the dignity, function, or (term of) office of a magistrate **L16.** **magisˈtratical** *adjective* of, pertaining to, or befitting a magistrate or magistrates **M17.** **magisˈtratically** *adverb* **M17.**

magistrature /ˈmadʒɪstrətʃə/ *noun.* **L17.**
[ORIGIN French, from *magistrat*, formed as MAGISTRATE + -URE.]
1 The dignity or office of a magistrate; *sing.* & in *pl.*, the office of a particular magistrate identified contextually. **L17.** ▸**b** A magistrate's term of office. **E18.**
2 Magistrates collectively; a body of magistrates. **L17.**

Maglemose /magləˈməʊsə/ *adjective.* **E20.**
[ORIGIN formed as MAGLEMOSIAN.]
= MAGLEMOSIAN *adjective.*

Maglemosian /magləˈməʊsɪən/ *adjective & noun.* **E20.**
[ORIGIN from *Maglemose* near Mullerup on the west coast of Denmark: see -IAN.]
▸ **A** *adjective.* Designating or pertaining to a Mesolithic culture of Europe represented by bone and stone implements found at Maglemose. **E20.**
▸ **B** *noun.* (A person of) the Maglemosian culture. **E20.**

maglev /ˈmaglɛv/ *noun.* **L20.**
[ORIGIN from *magnetic levitation.*]
The use of magnetic repulsion to support a train above the rail(s) on which it runs. Usu. *attrib.*

magma /ˈmagmə/ *noun.* **LME.**
[ORIGIN Latin from Greek, from base of *massein* knead.]
†1 The dregs remaining after a semi-liquid substance has been pressed or evaporated. **LME–M19.**
2 A mixture of mineral or organic substances having the consistency of paste; a viscous suspension. Now *rare.* **L17.**
3 *GEOLOGY.* A hot fluid or semi-fluid material beneath the crust of the earth or other planet, from which igneous rocks are formed by cooling and which erupts as lava. **M19.**

fig.: H. G. WELLS The social magma that arose out of this dissolution.

– COMB.: **magma chamber** a reservoir of magma within the planetary crust, esp. below a volcano.
■ **magˈmatic** *adjective* (*GEOLOGY*) of or pertaining to magma **L19.** **magˈmatically** *adverb* (*GEOLOGY*) as regards magma; from or by means of magma: **M20.** **magmatism** *noun* (*GEOLOGY*) (**a**) the theory advocated by magmatists; (**b**) motion or solidification of magma; magmatic activity: **M20.** **magmatist** *noun* (*GEOLOGY*) a person who holds that most plutonic rocks, esp. granites, were formed from magma rather than by metamorphic granitization **M20.**

Magna Carta /magnə ˈkɑːtə/ *noun phr.* Also **Magna Charta**. **L15.**
[ORIGIN medieval Latin, lit. 'great charter'.]
The charter of English personal and political liberty obtained from King John in 1215; *transf.* any similar document establishing rights.

H. G. WELLS Nationalisation will be the Magna Carta of the twentieth century. LD DENNING The delay of justice is a denial of justice. Magna Carta will have none of it.

magna cum laude /magnə kʌm ˈlɔːdiː, ˌmagnɑː kʊm ˈlaʊdeɪ/ *adverbial & adjectival phr.* Chiefly *N. Amer.* **L19.**
[ORIGIN Latin, lit. 'with great praise'.]
With or of great distinction; *spec.* (of a degree, diploma, etc.) of a higher standard than the average (though not the highest). Cf. ***CUM laude***, SUMMA CUM LAUDE.

magnae matres *noun phr.* pl. of MAGNA MATER.

Magnaflux /ˈmagnəflʌks/ *noun & verb.* Also **m-**. **M20.**
[ORIGIN from MAGN(ETIC *adjective* + -*a*- + FLUX *noun*.]
▸ **A** *noun.* (Proprietary name for) a method of testing metal parts for defects by magnetizing them and applying a magnetic powder which adheres to regions of flux leakage; the magnetic powder so used. **M20.**
▸ **B** *verb trans.* Test (a part) by the Magnaflux method. **M20.**

magna mater /magnə ˈmeɪtə, ˈmɑːtə/ *noun phr.* Pl. ***magnae matres*** /magniː ˈmeɪtriːz, magnʌɪ ˈmɑːtreɪz/. **E18.**
[ORIGIN Latin, lit. 'great mother'.]
A mother goddess; a fertility goddess.

magnanerie /maɲanri/ *noun.* Pl. pronounced same. **M19.**
[ORIGIN French, from *magnan* silkworm + -*erie* -ERY.]
A place for keeping or breeding silkworms.

M

magnanimity /magnəˈnɪmɪti/ *noun*. ME.
[ORIGIN Old French & mod. French *magnanimité* from Latin *magnanimitas*, from *magnanimus*: see MAGNANIMOUS, -ITY.]
1 Well-founded high regard for oneself manifesting as generosity of spirit and equanimity in the face of trouble etc.; loftiness of thought or purpose; grandeur or nobility of designs or ambition. Now *rare*. ME.
> D. HUME The queen's magnanimity in forming such extensive projects was the more remarkable.

†**2** Great courage; fortitude. LME–E19.
> A. WILLET In courage and magnanimitie superior to Hercules.

3 Superiority to petty resentment or jealousy, generous disregard of slights; an instance of this. M17.
> V. SACKVILLE-WEST 'You have no notion of my generosity.' .. He began to see himself .. full of magnanimity. D. LESSING A largeness in them, a magnanimity, a .. sweep of understanding.

magnanimous /magˈnanɪməs/ *adjective*. M16.
[ORIGIN from Latin *magnanimus*, from *magnus* great + *animus* mind: see -OUS.]
1 Showing magnanimity; generous in feeling or conduct; not petty; *arch*. nobly ambitious. M16.
> LD MACAULAY The magnanimous frankness of a man .. who could well afford to acknowledge some deficiencies. M. WEST His holiness was relieved enough to be magnanimous.

†**2** Of great courage; nobly valiant; (of a quality, action, etc.) proceeding from or manifesting high courage. L16–M19.
> D. HUME When she saw an evident necessity she braved danger with magnanimous courage.

■ **magnanimously** *adverb* E17. **magnanimousness** *noun* (*rare*) E17.

magna opera *noun phr. pl.* see MAGNUM OPUS.

magnate /ˈmagneɪt/ *noun*. LME.
[ORIGIN Late Latin *magnat-*, *magnas*, from Latin *magnus* great, perh. infl. in 18 by French *magnat*: see -ATE[1].]
1 A great or noble person. Now *esp*. a wealthy and influential person, esp. in business (freq. with specifying word). LME.
> BYRON Born of high lineage .. He mingled with the Magnates of his land. *Sunday Times* The Italian television magnate who has three channels in Italy.

2 *hist*. In Hungary and Poland, a member of the Upper House in the Diet. L18.
– NOTE: Rare before L18.
■ **magnateship** *noun* the dignity or position of a magnate E20.

†**magnes** *noun*. LME–M18.
[ORIGIN Latin from Greek *Magnēs*, *-ētos* (*lithos*) (stone) of Magnesia: see MAGNESIA.]
In full ***magnes stone***. A magnet, a lodestone.

magnesia /magˈniːʒə, -zjə, -ʃə/ *noun*. LME.
[ORIGIN medieval Latin from Greek *magnēsia* mineral from Magnesia in Asia Minor.]
†**1** ALCHEMY. A mineral supposed to be one of the ingredients of the philosopher's stone. LME–M17.
†**2** = MANGANESE 1. Also ***black magnesia***. L17–L18.
3 Orig., & still in non-*techn*. use, hydrated magnesium carbonate, a white earthy powder (†***white magnesia***) used as an antacid and laxative. Now also (chiefly CHEMISTRY), magnesium oxide, MgO, a white heat-resistant solid used in ceramics etc. M18.
Milk of Magnesia: see MILK *noun*.

magnesian /magˈniːʒ(ə)n, -zjən/ *adjective*. L18.
[ORIGIN from MAGNESIA + -AN.]
1 Chiefly GEOLOGY. Of, pertaining to, or containing magnesium salts. L18.
2 MINERALOGY. Having a constituent element partly replaced by magnesium. M20.

magnesic /magˈniːzɪk/ *adjective*. *rare*. M19.
[ORIGIN from MAGNESIA + -IC.]
Containing magnesium salts; (of a salt) containing magnesium.

magnesiochromite /magˌniːzɪəʊˈkrəʊmʌɪt/ *noun*. L19.
[ORIGIN from MAGNESIUM + -O- + CHROMITE.]
MINERALOGY. Orig., a mineral analogous to chromite with magnesium replacing much of the iron. Now usu., any spinel of the general formula (Mg, Fe)(Cr, Al)$_2$O$_4$, *spec*. the endmember picrochromite.

magnesite /ˈmagnɪsʌɪt/ *noun*. E19.
[ORIGIN from MAGNESIA + -ITE[1].]
MINERALOGY. Magnesium carbonate, crystallizing in the trigonal system and usu. occurring as compact white microcrystalline masses.

magnesium /magˈniːzɪəm/ *noun*. L18.
[ORIGIN from MAGNESIA + -IUM.]
CHEMISTRY. †**1** The element manganese. L18–E19.
2 A light silvery metallic chemical element of the alkaline earth group, atomic no. 12, which burns with an intense white light and is a major constituent of rock-forming minerals (symbol Mg). E19.

magnet /ˈmagnɪt/ *noun*. LME.
[ORIGIN Old French *magnete* or its source Latin *magneta* accus. of MAGNES.]
1 MINERALOGY. A rock that is naturally magnetic; magnetite; = LODESTONE 1. *arch*. LME.
> MILTON In midst of this white City stands a Castle built of Magnet.

2 Orig., a piece of iron, steel, alloy, ore, etc., which has the properties of attracting iron and of aligning roughly north–south when freely suspended. Now also, any object which has been given these properties; an object that produces a magnetic field. E17.
> D. FRANCIS Three powerful .. magnets distorting the programs on the tapes.

bar magnet: in the form of a straight bar. **horseshoe magnet**: in the shape of a bar bent until the ends nearly meet. ***permanent magnet***: see PERMANENT *adjective*.
3 *fig*. A thing which attracts. M17.
> *Resurgence* Any new institution .. critical of the existing order .. became a magnet for the disaffected. S. QUINN The Berlin Institute acted as a magnet for a great array of people.

– COMB.: **magnet school** a school designed to attract pupils from various areas or groups, esp. one offering specialist tuition in a particular subject.
■ **magnetician** /-ˈtɪʃ(ə)n/ *noun* an expert in magnetism M19. †**magnetify** *verb trans*. magnetize M17–L18.

magnetar /ˈmagnɪtɑː/ *noun*. L20.
[ORIGIN from MAGNETIC + *-ar* as in *pulsar* and *quasar*.]
ASTRONOMY. A neutron star with a much stronger magnetic field than ordinary neutron stars.

magnetic /magˈnɛtɪk/ *adjective & noun*. E17.
[ORIGIN Late Latin *magneticus*, from Latin *magneta* MAGNET: see -IC.]
▸ **A** *adjective*. **1** Having powers of attraction; very attractive or alluring. E17.
> L. DUNCAN There was something almost magnetic about those eyes. A. LURIE As if drawn by a magnetic force, Polly crossed the floor.

2 a Having the properties of a magnet; pertaining to a magnet or to magnetism; producing, caused by, or operating by means of magnetism. M17. ▸**b** NAUTICAL & AERONAUTICS. Of a bearing: measured relative to magnetic north. Freq. *postpositive*. L18. ▸**c** Capable of acquiring the properties of or of being attracted by a magnet; capable of undergoing an alignment of electron spins. M19.
> **c** H. E. ROSCOE The ferrous salts are magnetic.

†**3** = MAGNETICAL 2. M–L17.
4 Pertaining to animal magnetism; mesmeric. *arch*. E19.
> DICKENS As if he had been in a magnetic slumber.

– SPECIAL COLLOCATIONS: **magnetic anomaly** a local deviation from the general pattern of a magnetic field, esp. that of the earth. **magnetic bottle** a magnetic field that confines a plasma to a restricted region within it. ***magnetic bubble***: see BUBBLE *noun* 7. **magnetic compass** a ship's compass card with magnets attached for reading bearings and courses relative to magnetic north. ***magnetic drum***: see DRUM *noun*[1] 7c. ***magnetic equator***: see EQUATOR 3b. **magnetic field** a field of force produced by a magnetic object or particle or by a changing electric field. ***magnetic flux***: see FLUX *noun* 7b. **magnetic lens** (a device producing) a magnetic field capable of focusing a beam of charged particles. **magnetic memory** (**a**) a dependence of the magnetic state of a body on its previous magnetic history; (**b**) COMPUTING a memory that employs the magnetic properties of its components. ***magnetic meridian***: see MERIDIAN *noun*. **magnetic mine** a submarine mine detonated by the magnetic field of an approaching ship. **magnetic mirror** a magnetic field that causes approaching charged particles to be reflected. **magnetic moment** the property of an object or particle by virtue of which it experiences a torque in an applied magnetic field. ***magnetic needle***: see NEEDLE *noun* 2. ***magnetic north***. ***magnetic permeability***: see PERMEABILITY 2. ***magnetic pole***: see POLE *noun*[2]. **magnetic resonance** = RESONANCE 1i (***magnetic resonance imaging***, an imaging technique used in medicine that employs nuclear magnetic resonance of protons in the body; abbreviation ***MRI***). ***magnetic Reynolds number***: see REYNOLDS 1. **magnetic storm** a large-scale disturbance of the magnetic field of the earth (or of a star or planet). ***magnetic stripe***: see STRIPE *noun*[2] 1c. ***magnetic susceptibility***. ***magnetic tape***: see TAPE *noun* 4. **magnetic termite** an Australian termite, *Amitermes meridionalis*, which builds mounds aligned north–south.
▸ **B** *noun*. †**1** A magnet (*lit*. & *fig*.). M–L17.
2 In *pl*. The branch of knowledge that deals with magnetism. L18.
3 In *pl*. Magnetic devices or materials. M20.
4 In *pl*. Magnetic properties or phenomena collectively. L20.

magnetical /magˈnɛtɪk(ə)l/ *adjective*. Now *rare*. L16.
[ORIGIN formed as MAGNETIC: see -ICAL.]
1 = MAGNETIC *adjective* 2a. L16.
†**2** Designating a remedy for which a magical or occult virtue was claimed. E17–E18.
3 = MAGNETIC *adjective* 1. M17.
4 = MAGNETIC *adjective* 4. *arch*. L18.

magnetically /magˈnɛtɪk(ə)li/ *adverb*. E17.
[ORIGIN from MAGNETIC *adjective* or MAGNETICAL: see -ICALLY.]
In a magnetic manner; by means or in respect of magnetism.

magnetics *noun pl.* see MAGNETIC *noun*.

magnetisable *adjective*, **magnetisation** *noun*, **magnetise** *verb* vars. of MAGNETIZABLE, MAGNETIZATION, MAGNETIZE.

magnetism /ˈmagnɪtɪz(ə)m/ *noun*. E17.
[ORIGIN mod. Latin *magnetismus*, from Latin *magneta*: see MAGNET, -ISM.]
1 The characteristic properties of a magnet; magnetic phenomena, esp. attraction; the property of matter producing these. Cf. FERROMAGNETISM. E17.
> J. TYNDALL A blue flame .. being usually bent by the earth's magnetism.

permanent magnetism: see PERMANENT *adjective*. **terrestrial magnetism** the magnetic properties of the earth as a whole.
2 *fig*. (An) attractive power or influence, *esp*. personal charm. M17.
> R. P. JHABVALA She felt drawn to him by a strength, a magnetism. M. SEYMOUR Fullerton .. whose magnetism was at odds with his modest appearance.

3 The branch of knowledge that deals with magnetic phenomena. M18.
4 = ANIMAL ***magnetism***, MESMERISM. *arch*. L18.
■ **magnetist** *noun* an expert in magnetism M18.

magnetite /ˈmagnɪtʌɪt/ *noun*. M19.
[ORIGIN from MAGNET + -ITE[1].]
MINERALOGY. An oxide of ferrous and ferric iron, Fe$_3$O$_4$, which occurs as grey-black crystals of the cubic system, is strongly magnetic, and is an important ore of iron. Cf. LODESTONE.

magnetization /ˌmagnɪtʌɪˈzeɪʃ(ə)n/ *noun*. Also **-isation**. E19.
[ORIGIN from MAGNETIZE + -ATION.]
The action of magnetizing; the condition of being magnetized.
– COMB.: **magnetization curve** a graph of magnetic induction against magnetic field strength in the same region.

magnetize /ˈmagnɪtʌɪz/ *verb trans*. Also **-ise**. L18.
[ORIGIN from MAGNET + -IZE.]
1 Influence by animal magnetism; mesmerize. *arch*. L18.
> E. B. BROWNING Her own maid magnetizes her twice a day— .. the learned say .. she will recover.

2 Make magnetic; induce magnetism in. E19.
> *Discovery* A natural ore which exists in a magnetized state.

3 Attract as a magnet does (*lit*. & *fig*.). M19.
> E. BOWEN Bligh, as though magnetized, could not help glancing back .. again at the cottage.

■ **magnetizable** *adjective* able to be magnetized L18. **magnetiza'bility** *noun* ability to be magnetized L19. **magnetizer** *noun* L18.

magneto /magˈniːtəʊ/ *noun*. Pl. **-os**. L19.
[ORIGIN Abbreviation of *magneto-electric machine*.]
A small electric generator which uses permanent magnets; *spec*. one used for ignition in an internal-combustion engine.

magneto- /magˈniːtəʊ/ *combining form*.
[ORIGIN from MAGNET, MAGNETIC, MAGNETISM: see -O-.]
Forming words designating processes, devices, phenomena, etc., involving (the use of) magnetism.
■ **magneto'caloric** *adjective* designating or pertaining to the reversible change of temperature that accompanies a change in the magnetization of a paramagnetic or ferromagnetic material E20. **magneto'cardiogram** *noun* (MEDICINE) a chart or record produced by a magnetocardiograph M20. **magneto'cardiograph** *noun* (MEDICINE) an instrument that records or displays the variations in the body's magnetic field resulting from the activity of the heart M20. **magnetocardio'graphic** *adjective* (MEDICINE) involving or pertaining to magnetocardiography L20. **magnetocardi'ography** *noun* (MEDICINE) the practice or technique of using a magnetocardiograph or magnetocardiograms M20. **magneto'chemical** *adjective* of or pertaining to magnetochemistry E20. **magneto'chemistry** *noun* the branch of science that deals with the interrelation of magnetism and chemical phenomena, structure, etc. E20. **magnetograph** *noun* a recording magnetometer M19. **magneto'graphic** *adjective* of or pertaining to a magnetograph L19. **magneto-i'onic** *adjective* of or pertaining to the joint effect of a magnetic field and ionized gas (e.g. in the ionosphere) on the propagation of radio waves E20. **magneto-me'chanical** *adjective* pertaining to the interrelation of magnetic and mechanical properties; *spec*. = MAGNETOGYRIC 2: E20. **magneto-'optical** *adjective* of or pertaining to magneto-optics M19. **magneto-'optics** *noun* the branch of physics that deals with the optical effects of magnetic fields E20. **magnetopause** *noun* the outer limit of a magnetosphere M20. **magnetore'sistance** *noun* dependence of the electrical resistance of a body on an external magnetic field M20. **magnetore'sistive** *adjective* relating to or exhibiting magnetoresistance M20. **magnetosphere** *noun* the region (not necessarily spherical) surrounding the earth or another astronomical body in which its magnetic field is effective and prevails over other magnetic fields M20. **magneto'spheric** *adjective* of or pertaining to a magnetosphere M20. **magneto'static** *adjective* of or pertaining to an unchanging magnetic field L19. **magneto'statics** *noun* the branch of physics that deals with unchanging magnetic fields L19. **magneto'striction** *noun* a dependence of the state of strain of a body (and hence its dimensions) on its state of magnetization L19. **magneto'strictive** *adjective* of, exhibiting, or using magnetostriction E20. **magnetotail** *noun* the broad elongated extension of the earth's

magnetosphere on the side away from the sun L20. **magnetote'lluric** *adjective* pertaining to or designating a technique for investigating the electrical conductivity of the earth by measuring simultaneously fluctuations in its magnetic and electric fields at the surface M20. **magnetote'llurics** *noun* the branch of geophysics that deals with magnetotelluric investigation M20.

magneto-electric /mag,niːtəʊɪ'lɛktrɪk/ *adjective*. M19.
[ORIGIN from MAGNETO- + ELECTRIC.]
Of, pertaining to, or involving electric currents induced in a conducting material by its motion in a magnetic field.
magneto-electric machine *hist.* = MAGNETO.
■ **magneto-electrical** *adjective* magneto-electric L18. **magneto-elec'tricity** *noun* electricity generated by the movement of electrical conductors in a magnetic field M19.

magnetogyric /mag,niːtə(ʊ)'dʒʌɪrɪk/ *adjective*. E20.
[ORIGIN from MAGNETO- + Greek *guros* ring, circle + -IC.]
PHYSICS. **1** Pertaining to or exhibiting the Faraday effect. E20.
2 Designating the ratio of the magnetic moment of an atom or particle to its angular momentum. M20.

magnetohydrodynamic
/mag,niːtəʊhʌɪdrə(ʊ)dʌɪ'namɪk/ *adjective*. M20.
[ORIGIN from MAGNETO- + HYDRO- + DYNAMIC.]
Of, pertaining to, or involving an electrically conducting fluid (as a plasma or molten metal) acted on by a magnetic field; hydromagnetic.
■ **magnetohydrodynamical** *adjective* M20. **magnetohydrodynamics** *noun* the branch of physics that deals with magnetohydrodynamic phenomena (also called ***hydromagnetics***) M20.

magnetoid /mag'niːtɔɪd/ *adjective & noun*. M19.
[ORIGIN from MAGNET + -OID.]
▸ **A** *adjective*. Having properties like those of a magnet. *rare*. M19.
▸ **B** *noun*. A magnetoid body; *spec.* (ASTRONOMY) a massive rotating body of magnetized plasma, postulated to account for the energy emission of quasars. M20.

magnetometer /magnɪ'tɒmɪtə/ *noun*. E19.
[ORIGIN from MAGNETO- + -METER.]
An instrument for measuring magnetic forces, esp. the strength of terrestrial magnetism.
■ **magnetometric** /mag,niːtə(ʊ)'mɛtrɪk/ *adjective* of, pertaining to, or measured by a magnetometer M19. **magnetometry** *noun* L19.

magnetomotive /mag,niːtə(ʊ)'məʊtɪv/ *adjective*. L19.
[ORIGIN from MAGNETO- after *electromotive*.]
Pertaining to or producing magnetic flux.
magnetomotive force a scalar quantity representing the line integral of the magnetic field intensity around a closed line.

magneton /'magnɪtɒn/ *noun*. E20.
[ORIGIN from MAGNETIC *adjective* + -ON.]
PHYSICS. Any of several units of magnetic moment (see below).
Bohr magneton a unit equal to $eh/4\pi m$ (where e and m are the charge and mass of the electron, and h is Planck's constant, in SI units), i.e. about 9.27×10^{-24} joule per tesla. **nuclear magneton** a unit of nuclear magnetic moment, analogous to the Bohr magneton with the mass of the proton replacing that of the electron, equal to about 5.05×10^{-27} joule per tesla.

magnetophone /mag'niːtə(ʊ)fəʊn/ *noun*. In sense 3 also in German form **-phon** /-fɒn/. L19.
[ORIGIN from MAGNETO- + -PHONE.]
†**1** An instrument for producing musical tones by means of a perforated disc that is rotated between a magnet and an induction coil connected to a telephone receiver. Only in L19.
2 An early form of moving-coil microphone. E20.
3 A tape recorder (chiefly with ref. to early German machines). M20.

magnetron /'magnɪtrɒn/ *noun*. E20.
[ORIGIN from MAGNETIC *adjective* + -TRON.]
ELECTRONICS. A diode with a cylindrical anode surrounding a coaxial cathode in which the current is controlled by a magnetic field applied parallel to the axis, now usu. designed to produce microwave pulses of high power.

magnific /mag'nɪfɪk/ *adjective*. *arch.* L15.
[ORIGIN Old French & mod. French *magnifique* or Latin *magnificus*, from *magnus* great: see -FIC.]
†**1** Renowned, glorious. L15–M17.
2 Sumptuous, splendid. L15.
3 Imposing by vastness or dignity; (of language etc.) exalted, sublime; *derog.* pompous, grandiloquent. M16.
†**4** Of a title, expression, etc.: serving to magnify or extol; highly honorific or eulogistic. M16–E18.
†**5** Nobly lavish or munificent. L16–M17.

magnifical /mag'nɪfɪk(ə)l/ *adjective*. *arch.* M16.
[ORIGIN formed as MAGNIFIC + -AL[1].]
†**1** = MAGNIFIC 1. M–L16.
2 = MAGNIFIC 2. M16.
3 Exalted, sublime; honorific, eulogistic. M16.
†**4** = MAGNIFIC 5. L16–E17.

magnifically /mag'nɪfɪk(ə)li/ *adverb*. *arch.* M16.
[ORIGIN from MAGNIFIC or MAGNIFICAL: see -ICALLY.]
Magnificently, splendidly; in eulogistic terms.

magnificat /mag'nɪfɪkat/ *noun*. OE.
[ORIGIN Latin, 2nd person sing. pres. indic. of *magnificare* MAGNIFY: see below.]
1 (**M-**.) A canticle forming part of the Christian liturgy at evensong and vespers, and comprising the hymn of the Virgin Mary in *Luke* 1:46–55 (in the Vulgate beginning *Magnificat anima mea Dominum*). Also, the music to which this is set. OE.
2 *transf.* A song of praise; a paean. E17.

magnification /,magnɪfɪ'keɪʃ(ə)n/ *noun*. LME.
[ORIGIN Partly from ecclesiastical Latin *magnificatio(n-)*, from Latin *magnificat-* pa. ppl stem of *magnificare* MAGNIFY (see -ATION); partly directly from MAGNIFY (see -FICATION).]
1 *gen.* The action or an act of magnifying; the condition of being magnified; the result of magnifying. LME.

> A. C. CLARKE He . . expanded the image as far as the screen magnification would allow. *Which Micro?* 32 sprites in two sizes and two magnifications allowing . . '3D' graphics.

2 A magnified reproduction. M19.

magnificence /mag'nɪfɪs(ə)ns/ *noun*. ME.
[ORIGIN Old French & mod. French, or Latin *magnificentia*, from *magnificent-*: see MAGNIFICENT, -ENCE.]
1 In Aristotelian and scholastic ethics, liberality of expenditure combined with good taste. ME.
†**2** Supreme bounty or munificence. LME–M17.
†**3** Glory; greatness of nature or reputation. LME–M17.
4 Sumptuousness or splendour of surroundings or adornments. Formerly also, an instance or particular display of this. LME.

> G. HARRIS O-grak swirled round to display the full magnificence of his cloak.

5 Grandeur or imposing beauty of appearance. Formerly also (in *pl.*), features constituting this. LME.

> *Sunday Express* The . . scene is dominated by the . . magnificence of Kilimanjaro.

6 With possess. adjective (as ***your magnificence*** etc.): a title of respect given to a monarch or other distinguished person. *obsolete* exc. *hist.* and as repr. a foreign title. LME.

magnificency /mag'nɪfɪs(ə)nsi/ *noun*. Long *arch.* M16.
[ORIGIN Latin *magnificentia*: see MAGNIFICENCE, -ENCY.]
1 Magnificence. M16.
2 A magnificent object, ceremony, etc. L16.

magnificent /mag'nɪfɪs(ə)nt/ *adjective*. LME.
[ORIGIN Old French & mod. French, or Latin *magnificent-* stem (in compar. and superl.) of *magnificus* MAGNIFIC: see -ENT.]
1 Of an abstract thing: exalted, sublime. LME.

> W. COWPER The song magnificent—the theme a worm!

2 Characterized by greatness of achievement or by conduct befitting high position. *obsolete* exc. *hist.* in ***the Magnificent***, used postpositively to designate a particular distinguished ruler etc. E16.
Lorenzo the Magnificent, ***Suleiman the Magnificent***, etc.
3 Of a state of existence: characterized by grandeur or stateliness. Of a person: characterized by display of wealth and ceremonial pomp. M16.

> LD MACAULAY The magnificent king who . . represented France.

4 Sumptuously constructed or decorated; imposingly beautiful, splendid. M16.

> S. LEWIS Our magnificent new hotels . . and the paintings . . in their lobbies.

5 Characterized by expenditure or munificence on a grand scale. Now *rare*. L16.

> T. FULLER Hampton Court was built by . . Cardinal Wolsey; once so magnificent in his expenses.

6 Excellent, splendid, fine. Now chiefly *colloq.* E18.

> R. LYND A magnificent attack was beaten by a still more magnificent defence.

7 In names of animals, esp. birds: having an imposing or splendid appearance. L18.
magnificent frigate bird a very large frigate bird, *Fregata magnificens*, found in the tropical Atlantic and eastern Pacific. **magnificent fruit dove** = WOMPOO. ***magnificent*** RIFLE BIRD.
■ **magnificently** *adverb* LME.

magnifico /mag'nɪfɪkəʊ/ *noun*. Pl. **-o(e)s**. L16.
[ORIGIN Italian (adjective) = magnificent.]
A magnate (orig. a Venetian one); a grandee.

> P. ZIEGLER Three rear-admirals made a respectable tally of naval magnificos.

magnify /'magnɪfʌɪ/ *verb*. LME.
[ORIGIN Old French & mod. French *magnifier* or Latin *magnificare*, from *magnificus*: see MAGNIFIC, -FY.]
1 *verb trans.* Praise highly; glorify, extol; *esp.* render honour to (God). *arch.* LME.

> AV *Luke* 1:46 And Marie said, My soule doth magnifie the Lord.

2 *verb trans.* Make greater in size, status, importance, etc.; enlarge, augment. Now *rare*. LME.

> W. COWPER Her head, adorned with lappets . . And magnified beyond all human size.

3 *verb trans.* Increase the apparent size of (a thing) as with a lens or microscope. M17.

> W. WITHERING When magnified they appear like ill-formed warts. JAYNE PHILLIPS Her glasses magnified her eyes.

magnifying glass (a device with) a convex lens used to increase the apparent size of an object viewed through it.
4 *verb intrans.* Have effect; signify. Now *dial.* E18.
5 *verb trans.* Represent (a thing) as greater than in reality; exaggerate, intensify. (Now freq. assoc. with sense 3 above.) M18.

> G. GREENE Every lie I would magnify into a betrayal. R. THOMAS Isolation magnified feelings that she would have dismissed outside.

■ **magnifier** *noun* M16.

magniloquent /mag'nɪləkwənt/ *adjective*. M17.
[ORIGIN from Latin *magniloquus* (from *magnus* great + *-loquus* speaking) + -ENT.]
Lofty or ambitious in expression, grandiloquent. Also, boastful.

> T. R. LOUNSBURY To describe so slight a performance in so magniloquent a manner. F. DONALDSON Psmith . . is elegant in appearance, imperturbable by nature, a magniloquent tease.

■ **magniloquence** *noun* the quality of being magniloquent E17. **magniloquently** *adverb* M19. **magniloquy** *noun* (*rare*) [Latin *magniloquium*] magniloquence M17.

magnipotent /mag'nɪpət(ə)nt/ *adjective*. Long *rare* or *obsolete*. L16.
[ORIGIN from Latin *magnus* great + POTENT *adjective*[2], after *omnipotent*.]
Possessing great power.
■ **magnipotence** *noun* M19.

magnitude /'magnɪtjuːd/ *noun*. LME.
[ORIGIN Latin *magnitudo*, from *magnus* great, large, rel. to Greek *megas* and Germanic base also of MUCH: see -TUDE.]
†**1** Greatness of character, rank, or position. LME–M17.
2 Great size or extent; great degree or importance. LME.

> J. TYNDALL As our eye ranged over . . the mountain . . the conception of its magnitude grew. C. HAYFORD I cannot see the magnitude of the offence. J. BARZUN We can never forget the magnitude of the difficulties.

3 Size; geometrical measure or extent. LME. ▸**b** A quantity, an amount. L16. ▸**c** The intrinsic size of an earthquake or underground explosion (as distinct from its local intensity), usu. expressed by a logarithmic function of the peak seismometric deflection, adjusted for distance. M20.

> D. BREWSTER The creations of the material world, whether they be of colossal or atomic magnitude.

4 ASTRONOMY. Each of a set of classes into which stars are arranged according to their brilliance, stars of the first magnitude being the most brilliant, those of the sixth barely visible to the naked eye. Now regarded as a value on a continuous scale representing the negative logarithm of the brightness, such that a decrease of one magnitude represents an increase in brightness of 2.512 times. M17.
– PHRASES: **absolute magnitude**: of a star as from a standard distance of 10 parsecs. **apparent magnitude**: of a star as seen from the earth. BOLOMETRIC ***magnitude***. **of the first magnitude**: of the utmost importance. ***order of magnitude***: see ORDER *noun*.

magnitudinous /magnɪ'tjuːdɪnəs/ *adjective*. E19.
[ORIGIN from MAGNITUDE after *platitudinous* etc.]
Characterized by magnitude.

magnolia /mag'nəʊlɪə/ *noun & adjective*. M18.
[ORIGIN mod. Latin (see below), from Pierre Magnol (1638–1715), French botanist: see -IA[1].]
▸ **A** *noun*. **1** Any of various usu. large Asian and N. American trees of the genus *Magnolia* (family Magnoliaceae), much cultivated for their showy cup-shaped flowers produced in spring before the leaves. M18.
2 The colour of some magnolia blossom, a pale pinkish white. M20.
– COMB.: **Magnolia State** *US* the state of Mississippi.
▸ **B** *adjective*. Of the colour of some magnolia blossom; pale pinkish-white. M20.

magnolious /mag'nəʊlɪəs/ *adjective*. *slang*. M19.
[ORIGIN from MAGNOLIA + -OUS.]
Magnificent, splendid, large.

magnon /'magnɒn/ *noun*. M20.
[ORIGIN from MAGN(ETIC + -ON.]
PHYSICS. A quantum or quasiparticle associated with a spin wave in a magnetic material.

magnoperate /mag'nɒpəreɪt/ *verb*. *rare*. E17.
[ORIGIN Partly from Latin *magnopere* greatly (contr. of *magno opere*), partly from Latin *magnus* great + *oper-*, *opus* work, after *operate*: see -ATE[3].]
†**1** *verb trans.* Make greater. Only in E17.
†**2** *verb intrans.* Work at a magnum opus. Only in E19.
3 *verb intrans.* Act in a grand manner. E20.

Magnox /'magnɒks/ *noun*. M20.
[ORIGIN from *magnesium no oxidation*.]
Any of various magnesium-based alloys containing a small proportion of aluminium, developed for the fuel containers of nuclear reactors. Freq. *attrib.*

magnum /ˈmagnəm/ *noun & adjective.* L18.
[ORIGIN Latin, use as noun of neut. sing. of *magnus* large.]
▸ **A** *noun.* **1** A bottle for wine, spirits, etc., twice the standard size, now usu. containing 1½ litres; the quantity of liquor held by such a bottle. L18.

J. GLASSCO There was a magnum of bad champagne waiting in an ice bucket.

2 (Also **M-**.) A Magnum revolver or cartridge (see sense B. below). M20.
3 ZOOLOGY. The section of a bird's oviduct which secretes albumen. M20.
▸ **B** *attrib.* or as *adjective.* (Also **M-**.) Of a cartridge: adapted so as to be more powerful than its calibre suggests. Of a gun: designed to fire such cartridges. M20.
– NOTE: Proprietary name in the US in senses A.2, B.

magnum bonum /magnəm ˈbəʊnəm, ˈbɒnəm/ *noun phr.* E18.
[ORIGIN formed as MAGNUM + use as noun of neut. sing. of Latin *bonus* good.]
1 A variety of large yellow cooking plum. Also ***magnum bonum plum***. E18. ▸**b** A variety of potato, or of several other fruits and vegetables. L19
†**2** = MAGNUM *noun* 1. *Scot.* M–L18.
3 A large-barrelled steel pen. M19.

magnum opus /magnəm ˈəʊpəs, ˈɒpəs/ *noun phr.* Pl. **magnum opuses**, **magna opera** /magnə ˈəʊpərə, ˈɒpərə/. L18.
[ORIGIN Latin = great work.]
A great and usu. large work of art, literature, etc.; *spec.* the most important work of an artist, writer, etc. Cf. ***opus magnum*** s.v. OPUS *noun*.

Magnus effect /ˈmagnəs ɪˌfɛkt/ *noun phr.* E20.
[ORIGIN Heinrich G. *Magnus* (1802–70), German scientist.]
The effect of rapid spinning on a cylinder or sphere moving through a fluid in a direction at an angle to the axis of spin, which results in a sideways force at right angles to both the direction of motion and the axis of spin.

Magosian /maˈgəʊsɪən/ *adjective & noun.* M20.
[ORIGIN from *Magosi* in Uganda + -AN.]
ARCHAEOLOGY. ▸**A** *adjective.* Designating or pertaining to a Stone Age culture in sub-Saharan Africa, thought to be represented by certain finds made in Uganda. M20.
▸ **B** *noun.* The Magosian culture. M20.

M

magot /ˈmagət, *foreign* mago (*pl. same*)/ *noun.* E17.
[ORIGIN French.]
1 The Barbary ape. E17.
2 A small grotesque Chinese or Japanese figurine of porcelain, ivory, wood, etc. M19.

magpie /ˈmagpʌɪ/ *noun & adjective.* L16.
[ORIGIN from MAG *noun*[1] + PIE *noun*[1].]
▸ **A** *noun* **1 a** A common bird of the northern hemisphere, *Pica pica* of the crow family, with a long pointed tail, black and white plumage, and a noisy chattering call, proverbial for its habit of taking and hoarding bright objects. Also (with specifying word), any of several other long-tailed birds of the crow family. L16. ▸**b** More fully ***Australian magpie***. Any of several black and white Australian birds of the butcher-bird family Cracticidae, esp. *Gymnorrhina tibicen*. L18.
a green magpie: of the SE Asian genus *Cissa*.
2 *transf.* An idle or impertinent chatterer; a petty pilferer; a person who collects and hoards objects, information, etc. M17.
3 Orig., an Anglican bishop (from the ceremonial episcopal costume of black chimere and white rochet). Now only, the episcopal costume consisting of these vestments. Chiefly *joc.* or *derog.* E18.
4 A fancy coloured breed of pigeon. M19.
5 A halfpenny. *arch. slang.* M19.
6 A shot from a rifle which strikes the outermost division but one of a target, and is signalled by a black and white flag. *military slang.* L19.
▸ **B** *attrib.* or as *adjective.* Of black and white colouring; two-colour. M17.

Daily Telegraph Ermine that imparts the fashionable magpie effect.

– COMB.: **magpie diver**, **magpie duck** (*a*) the goldeneye, *Bucephala clangula*; (*b*) the smew, *Mergus albellus*; (*c*) the tufted duck, *Aythya fuligula*; **magpie goose** a long-legged, black and white gooselike bird, *Anseranas semipalmata*, of New Guinea and N. Australia; also called ***pied goose***; **magpie lark** any of several Australian birds of the family Grallinidae, *esp.* the common black and white, stilt-legged *Grallina cyanoleuca*; **magpie moth** a white geometrid moth with black and some yellow spots, *Abraxas grossulariata*, whose caterpillars attack fruit bushes; **magpie-robin** (*a*) a long-tailed black and white bird of the thrush family, *Copsychus saularis*, of the Indian subcontinent and SE Asia; also called ***dial-bird***; (*b*) either of two similar birds, *Copsychus sechellarum* of the Seychelles, and *C. albospecularis* of Madagascar.

magret /ˈmagreɪ/ *noun.* L20.
[ORIGIN French (Gascon dial.), dimin. of *magre* lean (in standard French *maigre*).]
A fillet of meat cut from a duck breast.

magslip /ˈmagslɪp/ *noun.* M20.
[ORIGIN App. from *magnetic slip-ring*.]
Chiefly NAUTICAL. An electric motor designed to receive and transmit data concerning the angular position of mechanical equipment by means of the position of its rotor. Cf. SELSYN, SYNCHRO.

magsman /ˈmagzmən/ *noun. slang.* Pl. **-men**. E19.
[ORIGIN from MAG *noun*[2] + -'S[1] + MAN *noun*.]
1 A street swindler, a confidence man. E19.
2 A storyteller, a raconteur. *Austral.* M20.

magtig /ˈmaxtɪx/ *interjection. S. Afr.* L19.
[ORIGIN Afrikaans abbreviation of *allemagtig* almighty.]
Expr. astonishment, awe, etc.

maguari /məˈgwɑːri/ *noun.* L17.
[ORIGIN Portuguese from Tupi *mauári*.]
More fully ***maguari stork***. A S. American stork, *Ciconia maguari*, with a forked tail.

maguey /ˈmagweɪ, *foreign* maˈgej/ *noun.* M16.
[ORIGIN Spanish from Taino.]
Any of various fleshy-leaved agaves; *esp.* the American aloe, *Agave americana*.

magus /ˈmeɪgəs/ *noun.* Also **M-**. Pl. **magi** /ˈmeɪdʒʌɪ/. ME.
[ORIGIN Latin from Greek *magos* from Old Persian *maguš*. Cf. MAGE.]
1 A member of an ancient Persian priestly caste (*hist.*); *transf.* a magician, a sorcerer. ME.
2 ***the Magi***, ***the three Magi***, the three 'wise men' from the East who brought gifts to the infant Jesus (*Matthew* 2:1), a representation of these. LME.

Magyar /ˈmagjɑː/ *noun & adjective.* L18.
[ORIGIN Hungarian.]
▸ **A** *noun.* **1** A member of a people now forming the predominant section of the inhabitants of Hungary. L18.
2 The language of this people; Hungarian. E19.
3 A garment in the Magyar style (see sense B.2 below). E20.
▸ **B** *attrib.* or as *adjective.* **1** Of or pertaining to the Magyars or their language. E19.
2 Designating a style of blouse, bodice, etc., in which the sleeves are cut in one piece with the main part of the garment. E20.
■ **Magyarization** *noun* the action of Magyarizing; the state of being Magyarized: L19. **Magyarize** *verb trans.* make Magyar in form or character L19.

mah /mɑː, *unstressed* mə/ *possess. adjective. black English.* L19.
[ORIGIN Repr. a pronunc.]
= MY *possess. adjective*.

†**Maha** *noun & adjective* see OMAHA.

mahaila /məˈhʌɪlə/ *noun.* E20.
[ORIGIN Iraqi Arabic *muhayla*.]
A kind of large river sailing boat used in Iraq.

mahal /məˈhɑːl, ˈmah(ə)l/ *noun.* E17.
[ORIGIN In sense 1 and 2 from Persian & Urdu *maḥall* from Arabic *maḥall* stopping place, abode, from *ḥall* alight, take up residence; in sense 3 transf. use of Persian *maḥall*.]
1 In the Indian subcontinent: a house or palace for use in summer; also, private apartments. E17.
2 In the Indian subcontinent: a territorial division; a ward of a town; also, a division of an estate or tract of land forming a unit let out for farming, hunting, etc. L18.
3 (**M-**.) A type of coarse-woven carpet made near Arak in Iran. E20.

mahaleb /ˈmɑːhəlɛb/ *noun.* M16.
[ORIGIN French *macaleb* (now *mahaleb*) from Arabic *maḥlab*: later assim. to Arabic.]
A Eurasian cherry, *Prunus mahaleb*, with a hard scented wood (also called ***St Lucie cherry***). Also, the fragrant kernels of its fruits, used in perfumery.

Mahamad /ˈmahəmad/ *noun.* Also **m-**. M19.
[ORIGIN Hebrew *ma'ămad*, from *'āmad* to stand.]
The body of trustees ruling a Sephardic synagogue. Freq. in ***gentlemen of the Mahamad***.

mahant /məˈhʌnt/ *noun.* E19.
[ORIGIN Hindi *mahanta* from Sanskrit *mahāntaḥ*, pl. of *mahat* great.]
In the Indian subcontinent: a religious superior.

maharaja /mɑː(h)əˈrɑːdʒə, məhɑː-/ *noun.* Also **-ah**, **maharaj** /-ˈrɑːdʒ/, **M-**. L17.
[ORIGIN Sanskrit *mahārāja*, from *mahā* great + *rājan* RAJA *noun*[1].]
(The title of) an Indian prince of high rank.

maharana /mɑː(h)əˈrɑːnə, məhɑː-/ *noun. hist.* Also **M-**. E19.
[ORIGIN Hindi *mahārāṇā*, from Sanskrit *mahā-* great + Hindi *rāṇā* RANA.]
(The title of) the ruler of Udaipur, a state in India until 1947, when it became part of Rajasthan.

maharani /mɑː(h)əˈrɑːni, məhɑːˈrɑːni/ *noun.* Also **-nee**, **M-**. M19.
[ORIGIN Hindi *mahārānī*, from Sanskrit *mahā-* great + *rājñī* RANI.]
(The title of) the wife or widow of a maharaja.

Maharashtri /mɑː(h)əˈrɑːʃtri/ *noun & adjective.* L19.
[ORIGIN Sanskrit *Māhārāṣṭrī*, from *Mahārāṣṭra* Maharashtra (see MAHARASHTRIAN), lit. 'great kingdom'. Cf. MARATHA.]
(Of) the Prakrit language of Maharashtra (see MAHARASHTRIAN), the ancestor of Marathi.

Maharashtrian /mɑː(h)əˈrɑːʃtrɪən/ *adjective & noun.* M20.
[ORIGIN from *Maharashtra* (see below) + -IAN. Cf. MAHARASHTRI.]
▸ **A** *adjective.* Of, pertaining to, or characteristic of Maharashtra, a region of central and SW India, since 1960 a state of India. M20.
▸ **B** *noun.* A native or inhabitant of Maharashtra. M20.

maharishi /mɑː(h)əˈrɪʃi/ *noun.* Also **M-**. L18.
[ORIGIN Sanskrit *maharṣi*, from *mahā* great + *ṛṣi* RISHI.]
(The title of) a Hindu sage or holy man; *gen.* (the title of) a popular leader of spiritual thought. Cf. GURU.

K. PLATT Testimonials of faith and gratitude to Guru Maharishi Viparina.

mahatma /məˈhatmə, məˈhɑːt-/ *noun.* L19.
[ORIGIN Sanskrit *mahātman*, from *mahā* great + *ātman* soul.]
1 In the Esoteric Buddhism of members of the Theosophical Society: any of a class of people with preternatural powers, supposed to exist in the Indian subcontinent and Tibet; *transf.* a sage, an adept. L19.
2 (**M-**.) In the Indian subcontinent, (the title of) a revered person regarded with love and respect. M20.
the Mahatma, **Mahatma Gandhi**: Mohandas Karamchand Gandhi (1869–1948).

Mahayana /mɑː(h)əˈjɑːnə, məhɑː-/ *noun.* M19.
[ORIGIN Sanskrit *mahāyāna*, from *mahā* great + *yāna* vehicle.]
A form of Buddhism with syncretistic features, practised in China, Japan, and Tibet. Also ***Mahayana Buddhism***. Cf. THERAVADA.

Mahdi /ˈmɑːdi/ *noun.* E17.
[ORIGIN Arabic (*al-*)*mahdī* lit. 'he who is rightly guided', from pass. pple of *hadā* lead on the right way.]
In Muslim belief: the restorer of religion and justice who will rule before the end of the world; a claimant of this title, *esp.* (*hist.*) Muhammad Ahmad of Dongola in Sudan, who proclaimed himself such in 1881 and launched a political and revolutionary movement which overthrew the Turco-Egyptian regime.
■ **Mahdism** *noun* belief in or adherence to the Mahdi or a Mahdi L19. **Mahdist** *noun* a believer in or adherent of the Mahdi or a Mahdi L19.

Mahican /ˈmahɪk(ə)n/ *noun & adjective.* E17.
[ORIGIN Mahican *Muhhekunneyuk* lit. 'people of the tidal waters'.]
▸ **A** *noun.* A member of an Algonquian people formerly inhabiting parts of Connecticut, Massachusetts, and New York State; the language of this people. Also called MOHICAN. E17.
▸ **B** *attrib.* or as *adjective.* Of or pertaining to the Mahicans or their language. L18.

mahimahi /ˈmɑːhɪˌmɑːhi/ *noun. N. Amer.* E20.
[ORIGIN Hawaiian.]
= DORADO 1.

mah-jong /mɑːˈdʒɒŋ/ *noun & verb.* Also **-ngg**. E20.
[ORIGIN Chinese dial. *ma jiang* sparrows.]
▸ **A** *noun.* A game (orig. Chinese) for four, played with 136 or 144 pieces called tiles, divided into five or six suits. E20.
▸ **B** *verb intrans.* Complete one's hand at mah-jong; win a game of mah-jong. E20.

Mahlerian /mɑːˈlɪərɪən/ *adjective & noun.* M20.
[ORIGIN from *Mahler* (see below) + -IAN.]
▸ **A** *adjective.* Of, pertaining to, or characteristic of the Austrian composer Gustav Mahler (1860–1911) or his music. M20.
▸ **B** *noun.* An interpreter, student, or admirer of Mahler or his music. M20.

mahmudi /mɑːˈmuːdiː/ *noun.* Pl. same. E17.
[ORIGIN Persian *maḥmūdī*, from the name of Shah *Maḥmūd*.]
hist. A Persian silver coin. Also, an Indian gold coin.

mahoe /məˈhəʊ/ *noun*[1]. M17.
[ORIGIN French *mahot* from Carib *mahou*.]
Any of various tropical trees and shrubs, chiefly of the mallow family, with a fibrous bast; *esp. Hibiscus tiliaceus*, widespread in the tropics, and (more fully ***blue mahoe***) the W. Indian *H. elatus*, whose wood is shot with blue. Also, the wood or fibre of such a tree. Cf. PURAU.

mahoe /məˈhəʊi/ *noun*[2]. M19.
[ORIGIN Maori.]
A small bushy New Zealand tree, *Melicytus ramiflorus*, of the violet family, with whitish bark and clusters of small greenish flowers.

mahogany /məˈhɒgəni/ *noun & adjective.* M17.
[ORIGIN Unknown.]
▸ **A** *noun* **1 a** The hard, fine-grained, chiefly reddish-brown wood of any of various trees of the W. Indian and Central American genus *Swietenia* (now chiefly *S. mahagoni*) or related African genus *Khaya* (family Meliaceae), often used for furniture. Also, the colour of this wood when polished; a rich reddish brown. M17. ▸**b** The tree itself. M18.
2 A Cornish drink made of gin and treacle; *slang* a strong mixture of brandy and water. Now *rare*. L18.
3 *transf.* Any of various trees, esp. (*Austral.*) eucalypts, with hard reddish-brown timber like mahogany; *spec.* (*Austral.*) the jarrah, *Eucalyptus marginata*. Also, the wood of these trees. Usu. with specifying word. L18.

African mahogany, forest mahogany, Natal mahogany, swamp mahogany, etc.

4 a A table, *esp.* a dining table. *arch. colloq.* **M19.** ▸**b** The bar in a public house. *colloq.* **M20.**

– **COMB.**: **mahogany birch** *US* = ***mountain mahogany*** (a) s.v. **MOUNTAIN** *noun*.

▸ **B** *adjective*. **1** Made of mahogany. **M18.**

2 Of the colour of polished mahogany; rich reddish-brown. **M18.**

mahoitre /mə'hɔɪtə/ *noun*. Long *obsolete* exc. *hist.* **M19.**
[**ORIGIN** Old French.]
A pad placed in the upper part of a sleeve to give added breadth to the shoulders.

Mahomet /mə'hɒmɪt/ *noun*. *arch.* **ME.**
[**ORIGIN** Old French & mod. French *Mahomet*, †*Mach-* from medieval Latin *Ma(c)hometus* **MUHAMMAD**. Cf. **MAUMET**.]
1 = **MUHAMMAD**. Formerly also, an idol. **ME.**
†**2** A Muslim. **E16–M18.**
3 A breed of pigeon. Now *rare* or *obsolete*. **M18.**
■ †**Mahometical** *adjective* Muslim **M16–E18.** †**Mahometism** *noun* the Muslim religion, Islam **L16–M19.**

Mahometan /mə'hɒmɪt(ə)n/ *noun* & *adjective*. *arch.* (regarded as *offensive* by Muslims). **E16.**
[**ORIGIN** medieval Latin *Ma(c)hometanus*, from *Ma(c)hometus*: see **MAHOMET**, **-AN**.]
▸ **A** *noun*. = **MUSLIM** *noun*. **E16.**
▸ **B** *adjective*. = **MUSLIM** *adjective*. **E17.**
■ **Mahometanism** *noun* (*arch.*) the Muslim religion, Islam (regarded as *offensive* by Muslims) **E17.**

Mahometry /mə'hɒmɪtri/ *noun*. Now *arch. rare*. **L15.**
[**ORIGIN** from **MAHOMET** + **-RY**. Cf. **MAUMETRY**.]
The Muslim religion, Islam. Formerly also, idolatry.

†**mahone** *noun*. **L16–M19.**
[**ORIGIN** French *mahonne*, Spanish *mahona*, Italian *maona*, Turkish *mavuna*, *mavna*, prob. from Arabic *ma'ūna* provisions.]
A flat-bottomed Turkish sailing vessel.

mahonia /mə'həʊnɪə/ *noun*. **E19.**
[**ORIGIN** mod. Latin (see below), from Bernard Mc*Mahon* (*c* 1775–1816), US botanist + **-IA**[1].]
Any of various freq. cultivated Asian and N. American shrubs of the genus *Mahonia*, of the barberry family, with yellow flowers and prickly pinnate leaves; *esp.* the Oregon grape, *M. aquifolium*.

mahorka /mə'hɔːkə/ *noun*. **M19.**
[**ORIGIN** Russian *makhórka*.]
A kind of coarse Russian tobacco.

Mahound /mə'huːnd, mə'haʊnd/ *noun*. **ME.**
[**ORIGIN** Old French *Mahun*, *-um* contr. of **MAHOMET**. Cf. **MAUMET**.]
†**1** A god imagined in the Middle Ages to be worshipped by Muslims. **ME–M19.**
†**2** A monster; a hideous creature. **LME–L16.**
3 The Devil. Chiefly *Scot.* Now *rare* or *obsolete*. **LME.**

mahout /mə'haʊt/ *noun*. **M17.**
[**ORIGIN** Hindi *mahāut*, *mahāvat* from Sanskrit *mahāmātra* high official, elephant-keeper, from *mahā-* great + *mātra* measure.]
In the Indian subcontinent: an elephant-driver.

Mahratta *noun* & *adjective* var. of **MARATHA**.

Mahratti *noun* var. of **MARATHI**.

mahseer /'mɑːsɪə/ *noun*. **M19.**
[**ORIGIN** Hindi *mahāser*, from Sanskrit *mahā-* great + *śaphara* carp.]
Any of various large Indian freshwater cyprinoid fishes, esp. *Barbus tor*, which resembles the barbel.

Mahsud /'mɑːsuːd/ *noun* & *adjective*. **L19.**
[**ORIGIN** Persian *Maḥsūd*, from Arabic *Maḥsūd* envied.]
▸ **A** *noun*. A member of a Pathan people of Waziristan in NW Pakistan. **L19.**
▸ **B** *adjective*. Of or pertaining to this people. **L19.**

†**Mahu** *noun*. Only in **E17.**
[**ORIGIN** Perh. rel. to **MAHOUND**.]
A devil.

mahua /'mʌhʊə/ *noun*. Also **mahwa(h)**, **mohwa** /'məʊwə/, & other vars. **E17.**
[**ORIGIN** Hindi *mahūā*, *moā*, Bihari *mahuar*, Gujarati *mahuṛo*, *mauṛo*, from Sanskrit *madhūka* from *madhu* sweet.]
Any of several Indo-Malayan trees of the genus *Madhuca* (family Sapotaceae), esp. *M. latifolia*, with sweet fleshy edible flowers and oily seeds. Also ***mahua tree***.

mahurat /mə'huːrət/ *noun*. *Indian*. **L20.**
[**ORIGIN** Hindi *mahūrat*, from Sanskrit *muhūrta* a division of time (approximately 48 minutes).]
An auspicious time for an enterprise to begin or for a ceremony to take place, *esp.* an action which marks the beginning of the making of a film.

mai /mʌɪ/ *noun*. *NZ*. **M19.**
[**ORIGIN** Contr.]
= **MATAI** *noun*[1].

maid /meɪd/ *noun*. **ME.**
[**ORIGIN** Abbreviation of **MAIDEN** *noun*. For similar loss of *n* cf. *clew*, *game*, *eve*.]
1 A girl; a young (unmarried) woman. Now *arch.*, *poet.*, & *dial.* **ME.**

> **COLERIDGE** Sweet maid.. Thy sire and I will crush the snake! **P. S. BUCK** The seeking of a maid who might be his son's wife.

2 a A virgin; *spec.* the Virgin Mary. *arch.* **ME.** ▸†**b** A man who has not had sexual intercourse. **ME–E18.**

> **b JONSON** Two noble Maids Of either sexe, to Union sacrificed.

3 A female servant (esp. for indoor work) or attendant. Freq. with specifying word. **ME.**

> **C. ISHERWOOD** She.. kept a maid to do the housework. **J. BARTH** Jane reappeared.. and behind her came the maid with our cocktails.

barmaid, ***chambermaid***, ***dairymaid***, ***housemaid***, ***nursemaid***, etc. ***waiting-maid***: see **WAITING** *ppl adjective* 1.

4 A young skate or thornback. Also, a twaite shad. **L16.**

5 An unmarried woman, a spinster. Now chiefly in **OLD MAID**. **E17.**

> **SIR W. SCOTT** Miss Lucy St. Aubin lived and died a maid for his sake.

6 Any of various objects or contrivances; *spec.* (***a***) = **MAIDEN** *noun* 5; (***b***) = **MAIDEN** *noun* 7a; (***c***) = **MAIDEN** *noun* 6. **L17.**

– **PHRASES**: ***French maid***: see **FRENCH** *adjective*. **Maid Marian** a female character in the traditional morris dance, in later tradition the companion of Robin Hood. **maid of all work** a female servant doing general housework; *fig.* a person doing many jobs. **maid of honour** (***a***) an unmarried lady attending a queen or princess; (***b***) a kind of custard tartlet; (***c***) *N. Amer.* a principal bridesmaid. **OLD MAID**. **the Maid (of Orleans)** [translating French *la Pucelle*] Joan of Arc. ***universal maid***: see **UNIVERSAL** *adjective*.

– **COMB.**: †**maid-child** a female child; **maid-fish** = sense 4 above; **maidservant** = sense 3 above.

■ **maidhood** *noun* maidenhood **ME.** **maidish** *adjective* maidenish **E19.** **maidkin** *noun* (long *rare* or *obsolete*) a young or small maid **LME.** **maidless** *adjective* **M19.** **maidling** *noun* (*rare*) a young or small maid **M19.** **maidy** *noun* (*dial.*) a young or small maid **L19.**

maid /meɪd/ *verb*. **L19.**
[**ORIGIN** from the noun.]
1 *verb trans.* = **MAIDEN** *verb* 2. *dial.* **L19.**
2 *verb intrans.* Do maids' work; act as a maid. **E20.**

> **M. MITCHELL** My Prissy been maidin' fo' Miss India fo' a year now.

3 *verb trans.* Wait on (a person) as a maid. **E20.**

> **A. CHRISTIE** Susanne.. used to look after my clothes and maid me.

maidan /mʌɪ'dɑːn/ *noun*. **M16.**
[**ORIGIN** Persian & Urdu *maidān* from Arabic *maydān*.]
In the Indian subcontinent: an open space in or near a town, used as a parade ground or for public events.

maiden /'meɪd(ə)n/ *noun* & *adjective*.
[**ORIGIN** Old English *mægden* = Old High German *magatīn* from Germanic dim. = maid, virgin, repr. also by Old English *mæg(e)þ*, Old Saxon *magaþ*, Old High German *magad* (German *Magd*, whence dim. *Magdchen*, now *Mädchen* girl), Gothic *magaþs*, and rel. to Germanic from Indo-European base also of Old English, Old Saxon *magu*, Old Norse *mǫgr*, Gothic *magus* son, young man, Old Irish *mug* boy, servant: see **-EN**[1]. Cf. **MAC** *noun*[1], **MAY** *noun*[1].]
▸ **A** *noun*. **1** = **MAID** *noun* 1. **OE.**
2 a = **MAID** *noun* 2a. **OE.** ▸**b** = **MAID** *noun* 2b. Now *dial.* **ME.**

> **a A. DUGGAN** I have never.. seduced a virtuous woman.. the wife I have married.. came to me a maiden. **G. GREENE** The definition of a maiden in common use.. is an unbroken hymen.

3 A maidservant, a female attendant. (Cf. **MAID** *noun* 3.) Now *arch.* & *dial.* **OE.**

> **AV** *Ps.* 123:2 As the eyes of a maiden [looke] vnto the hand of her mistresse.

4 = **MAID** *noun* 5. Long *obsolete* exc. *dial.* **LME.**
5 *hist.* A kind of guillotine, *esp.* one used for executions in Edinburgh. **M16.**
6 An apparatus or instrument used in washing clothes, a dolly. Also, a clothes horse. Chiefly *dial.* **M18.**
7 a The last handful of corn cut in a harvest field, often roughly shaped into the figure of a girl and decorated with ribbons. Also ***harvest maiden***. **L18.** ▸**b** The harvest home and the feast with which it was celebrated. *Scot.* **E19.**
8 a *ellipt.* A maiden horse, a maiden race, a maiden over, a maiden tree. **E19.** ▸**b** A strawberry plant bearing its first crop. **E20.**

– **PHRASES**: ***iron maiden***: see **IRON** *noun* & *adjective*. ***Rhine maiden***: see **RHINE** *adjective*. **the answer to a maiden's prayer** an eligible bachelor.

▸ **B** *attrib.* or as *adjective*. **I 1** Unmarried; virgin. Formerly also, (of a child) female. **ME.**

> **D. ROCK** The girl-like maiden-mother bowed down before the crib. **V. S. PRITCHETT** There are three maiden aunts—an extinct genus now.

2 Of or pertaining to a maiden or maidenhood; suitable for a maiden, having the qualities of a maiden. **L16.**

> **SHAKES.** *Mids. N. D.* And the imperial vot'ress passed on, In maiden meditation fancy-free. **DISRAELI** Not.. a word that could call forth a maiden blush.

3 Of a female animal: unmated. **M19.**

▸ **II 4** That is the first of its kind; made, used, etc., for the first time. Freq. in ***maiden speech*** below. **M16.**

> **J. J. HENNESSY** Other westerners in the party were making their maiden voyages.

5 That has yielded no results. ▸**a** (Of a game) in which no points are scored; *spec.* in **CRICKET** (of an over) in which no runs are scored. **L16.** ▸**b** Of an assize, circuit, or session: orig., at which no capital conviction occurred; now, at which there are no cases for trial. **L17.** ▸**c** Of a horse etc.: that has never won a prize. Of a race: open to a horse etc. that has never won a prize. **M18.** ▸**d** **FOUNDING**. Of a bell: that needs little or no tuning after it has been cast. **E20.**

6 a Of a town, fortress, etc.: that has never been captured. **L16.** ▸**b** Of a soldier, sword, etc.: untried. **L16.** ▸**c** Of soil, metal, etc.: that has never been disturbed; unworked. **E17.** ▸**d** Of a plant or tree: grown from seed as opp. to a stock; not pruned or transplanted. **M17.**

> **a WORDSWORTH** She was a maiden City, bright and free. **b L. RITCHIE** He had not as yet fleshed his maiden sword.

– **SPECIAL COLLOCATIONS & COMB.**: **maiden name** the surname of a girl or woman before marriage. **maiden pink** a wild pink, *Dianthus deltoides*, of gravelly pastures. **maiden plum (tree)** any of various W. Indian trees of the genus *Comocladia* (family Anacardiaceae). **maiden-servant** (long *rare* or *obsolete*) = sense A.3 above. **maiden speech** the first speech delivered in the House of Commons by a Member of Parliament. **maiden's wreath** an ornamental pink- or white-flowered plant, *Francoa sonchifolia*, of the saxifrage family; = ***bridal wreath*** s.v. **BRIDAL** *adjective*. **maiden thought** *poet.* the stage of human development after infancy; a period of innocent untarnished hope. †**maiden-widowed** *adjective* (*rare*, Shakes.) widowed while still a maiden.

■ **maidenhood** *noun* (***a***) the condition or period of being a maiden; †(***b***) = **MAIDENHEAD** *noun*[1]: **OE.** **maidenish** *adjective* (chiefly *derog.*) resembling a maiden, characteristic of a maiden **M18.** **maidenlike** *adjective* & *adverb* (***a***) *adjective* resembling (that of) a maiden, suitable for a maiden; (***b***) *adverb* (*rare*) in the manner of a maiden: **M16.** **maidenship** *noun* (with possess. adjective, as ***your maidenship*** etc.) a playful title of respect given to a maiden **E17.**

maiden /'meɪd(ə)n/ *verb trans.* *obsolete* exc. *dial.* **L16.**
[**ORIGIN** from the noun.]
†**1** Foll. by *it*: act like a maiden; be coy. Only in **L16.**
2 Wash clothes with a maiden or dolly. **M19.**
maidening pot, **maidening tub** a washtub.

maidenhair /'meɪd(ə)nhɛː/ *noun*. **LME.**
[**ORIGIN** from **MAIDEN** *noun* + **HAIR** *noun*.]
1 Any of various ferns of the genus *Adiantum*, of warmer regions of the world, with delicate pale green fan-shaped pinnules; *esp.* (orig. more fully ***black maidenhair***, ***true maidenhair***) *A. capillus-veneris*, a rare British native of sheltered sea cliffs, frequently cultivated. Also ***maidenhair fern***. **LME.**
2 Either of two spleenworts, ferns of the genus *Asplenium*, (***a***) (more fully ***English maidenhair***) *A. trichomanes*, with simply pinnate fronds, frequent on old walls and rocks; (***b***) ***white maidenhair***, wall rue, *A. ruta-muraria*. Now *rare* or *obsolete*. **LME.**
3 ***golden maidenhair***, a fine-leaved moss, *Polytrichum commune*. **L16.**

– **COMB.**: **maidenhair-spleenwort** any of several ferns of the genus *Asplenium*; *spec.* = ***English maidenhair*** (see sense 2(a) above); **maidenhair tree** the ginkgo, the leaves of which resemble the segments of an *Adiantum*.

maidenhead /'meɪd(ə)nhɛd/ *noun*[1]. *arch.* **ME.**
[**ORIGIN** from **MAIDEN** *noun* + **-HEAD**[1].]
The state or condition of a maiden; virginity. Also, the hymen.

maidenhead /'meɪd(ə)nhɛd/ *noun*[2]. **LME.**
[**ORIGIN** from **MAIDEN** *noun* + **HEAD** *noun*.]
A representation of the head or head and shoulders of the Virgin Mary, *spec.* (***a***) as an ornamental finish to the handle of a spoon (occas., a spoon with such a handle); (***b***) **HERALDRY** as a charge on a shield etc.

maidenly /'meɪd(ə)nli/ *adjective*. **LME.**
[**ORIGIN** from **MAIDEN** *noun* + **-LY**[1].]
1 Of or pertaining to a maiden; virginal. **LME.**

> **R. ELLIS** Her maidenly bloom fresh-glowing.

2 Of a person: like a maiden in behaviour or appearance; gentle, modest, shy. **E16.** ▸**b** Of a quality, action, etc.: regarded as appropriate to or characteristic of a maiden. **M16.**

> **MARVELL** Our author is very maidenly, and condescends to his Bookseller not without some reluctance. **b L. GORDON** Maidenly innocence, sweetness, chastity.. might suffer if women were allowed to read Latin and Greek.

■ **maidenliness** *noun* **M16.**

maidenly /'meɪd(ə)nli/ *adverb*. **L16.**
[**ORIGIN** formed as **MAIDENLY** *adjective* + **-LY**[2].]
After the fashion of a maiden; in a maidenly manner.

> **HUGH WALPOLE** He stopped by Jeremy, who was maidenly conscious of his nudity.

maiden's blush /meɪd(ə)nz 'blʌʃ/ *noun phr.* **L16.**
[**ORIGIN** from **MAIDEN** *noun* + **-'S**[1] + **BLUSH** *noun*.]
1 A delicate pink colour. Also (in full ***maiden's blush rose***), a rose of this colour, one of the *Rosa* × *alba* group. **L16.**
2 A small geometrid moth, *Cyclophora punctaria*. **M19.**
3 Either of two Australian trees with pinkish wood, *Sloanea australis* (family Elaeocarpaceae) and *Euroschinus falcatus* (family Anacardiaceae). **L19.**

M

maieutic /meɪˈjuːtɪk/ *adjective.* M17.
[ORIGIN Greek *maieutikos*, from *maieuesthai* act as midwife, from *maia* midwife: see -IC.]
Of a mode of inquiry: Socratic, serving to bring out a person's latent ideas into clear consciousness.

maieutics /meɪˈjuːtɪks/ *noun.* L19.
[ORIGIN formed as MAIEUTIC: see -ICS.]
The maieutic method.

maigre *noun* var. of MEAGRE *noun*[1].

maigre /ˈmeɪɡə, *foreign* mɛɡr/ *adjective.* M16.
[ORIGIN Old French & mod. French: see MEAGRE *adjective*.]
▸ **I** †**1** = MEAGRE *adjective* I. M16–L17.
▸ **II** ROMAN CATHOLIC CHURCH. **2** Designating a day on which abstinence from meat is ordered. L17.
†**3** ***eat maigre***, ***keep maigre***, ***live maigre***, live on a maigre diet. M18–L19.
4 Of food, esp. soup: not containing meat; suitable for eating on maigre days. M18.

maihem *noun & verb* var. of MAYHEM.

maiko /ˈmʌɪkəʊ, *foreign* ˈmaiko/ *noun.* Pl. same, **-os**. L19.
[ORIGIN Japanese, from *mai* dancing + *ko* child.]
A girl who is being trained to become a geisha.

mail /meɪl/ *noun*[1]. Now only *Scot.*
[ORIGIN Old English *mæl*, prob. contr. of Old English *mæþel* meeting, discussion, Old Saxon, Old High German *mahal* assembly, judgement, treaty, Gothic *maþl* meeting place, repl. by forms from Old Norse *mál* speech, agreement. In sense corresp. to Old Norse *máli* stipulation, stipulated pay. Cf. BLACKMAIL.]
†**1** Speech. Only in OE.
2 (A) payment, (a) tax, (a) tribute, (a) rent. OE.
mails and duties the rents of an estate. **silver mail** rent paid in money.
▪ **mailing** *noun* (*a*) a rented farm; (*b*) the rent paid for a farm: LME.

mail /meɪl/ *noun*[2]. ME.
[ORIGIN Old French & mod. French *maille* from Latin *macula* spot, mesh.]
†**1** Any of the metal rings or plates composing mail armour. ME–E18.
2 Armour composed of interlaced rings or chains or of overlapping plates fastened on some material. ME. ▸†**b** A piece of such armour. Only in E17. ▸**c** The protective shell or scales of certain animals. E18.

MILTON Mangl'd with gastly wounds through Plate and Maile. W. MORRIS Through the glimmering thicket the linked mail rang out. *fig.*: G. MACDONALD She was clad in the mail of endurance. **b** SHAKES. *Tr. & Cr.* To hang Quite out of fashion, like a rusty mail. **c** M. ARNOLD The sea-snakes coil and twine, Dry their mail and bask in the brine.

chainmail. ***coat of mail***: see COAT *noun*. ***frock of mail***: see FROCK *noun*. ***shirt of mail***: see SHIRT *noun*.
3 †**a** A small hole for a lace, clasp, or other fastening of a garment to pass through; an eyelet hole, an eye. LME–M17. ▸**b** WEAVING. A ring in a loom through which the warp thread passes. M18.
4 A film over the eye; a defect in vision. Long *obsolete* exc. *dial.* LME.
5 FALCONRY. The breast feathers of a hawk collectively, when the feathers are full-grown. Also, the plumage of certain other birds. L15.
6 A section of interlinked pieces of metal used in rope making for rubbing loose hemp off cordage. M18.
– ATTRIB. & COMB.: In the senses 'made of mail', 'in mail', as ***mail armour***, ***mail shirt***, ***mail-clad*** *adjective*, etc.
▪ **mailless** /-l-l-/ *adjective* E19.

mail /meɪl/ *noun*[3]. ME.
[ORIGIN Old French *male* (mod. *malle* bag, trunk) from Germanic (cf. Old High German *mal(a)ha* wallet, bag, Middle Dutch *male*, Dutch *maal*).]
1 Orig., a bag, a pack, a wallet; a travelling bag. Now (*Scot.* & *US*) in *pl.*, baggage. ME.

R. L. STEVENSON He . . emptied out his mails upon the floor that I might have a change of clothes.

2 A bag or packet of letters for conveyance by post; the postal matter so conveyed; all that is so conveyed on one occasion. Also, the letters etc. delivered at one place or to one person on one occasion. Freq. in titles of newspapers. M17.

D. HAMMETT When I got the mail this morning there was a letter for him. M. DE LA ROCHE They watched the mails and no letter came from her. Z. TOMIN I sent it out with the diplomatic mail.

Daily Mail, ***Oxford Mail***, etc.
3 A person or vehicle to carry postal matter; *ellipt.* a mail boat, a mail train, etc. Also, the system of conveyance of letters etc. by post; the official conveyance or dispatch of postal matter; the post. M17.

L. T. C. ROLT The night mail from Paddington. P. GROSSKURTH The mail was good in those days. Alix Strachey received the letter on Jan. 1 1925.

airmail, ***sea mail***, ***surface mail***, etc. CERTIFIED ***mail***. ***direct mail***: see DIRECT *adjective*.
4 Email; voicemail. Also, a facility for exchanging or recording email or voicemail messages. L20.
– ATTRIB. & COMB.: Designating people and vehicles employed to carry mail, as ***mail boat***, ***mail ship***, ***mail train***, etc. Special combs., as **mailbag** a large bag for mail; **mailbox** (*a*) *hist.* a box in which the mailbags were placed on a mail coach; (*b*) *N. Amer.* a box for delivery of mail; (*c*) a computer file in which a user's email messages are stored; **mail car** (*a*) a railway carriage in which mail is carried; (*b*) IRISH HISTORY a jaunting car used for the conveyance of mail; (*c*) *Austral.* & *NZ* a motor vehicle used for the conveyance of mail (and also sometimes of passengers); **mail carrier** *US* a postman or postwoman; **mail cart** (*a*) a cart for carrying mail by road; (*b*) a light vehicle for carrying children, made with shafts so as to be drawn or pushed by hand; **mail coach** (*a*) *hist.* a stagecoach used primarily for the conveyance of mail; *spec.* a coach used by the Post Office for carrying parcels by road; (*b*) = ***mail car*** (a) above; **mail cover** *US* the monitoring of all mail sent to a specified address; **mail-day** *US* the day on which mail is dispatched or received; **mail drop** *N. Amer.* a place where mail may be left to be collected by another person; **mailman** *N. Amer.* a postman; **mail order** (orig. *US*) an order for goods to be sent by post; ***mail-order firm***, ***mail-order business***, etc., a firm, business, etc., operating mainly by this system; **mail-rider** US HISTORY a mail carrier; **mailroom** a room where mail is collected, sorted, or otherwise dealt with; **mailshot** material posted to potential customers as part of an advertising campaign; **mail slot** *N. Amer.* a letterbox.

mail /meɪl/ *noun*[4]. *obsolete* exc. *hist.* Also **maille**. ME.
[ORIGIN Anglo-Norman *mayle*, Old French *m(e)aille* (whence Middle Dutch *mealge*), from late Latin: see MEDAL *noun*.]
A coin; *spec.* a halfpenny.
maille noble a gold coin of the reign of Edward III; a half-noble.

mail /maːj/ *noun*[5]. Now *rare* or *obsolete*. Pl. pronounced same. M17.
[ORIGIN Old French from Latin *malleus* hammer. Cf. MAUL *noun*, MALL *noun*.]
Orig., the game of pall-mall; a place where the game was played. Later (from the *Mail* in Paris), a public promenade bordered by trees.
the Mail = ***the Mall*** s.v. MALL *noun*[3a].

mail /meɪl/ *verb*[1] *trans.* ME.
[ORIGIN Prob. from MAIL *noun*[3].]
†**1** Tie (*up*), wrap up (goods, a parcel, etc.); envelop. ME–L17.
2 FALCONRY. Cover (a hawk) with a cloth to promote tameness or to ensure passivity during an operation. L16.

mail /meɪl/ *verb*[2] *trans.* *arch.* LME.
[ORIGIN Partly from MAIL *noun*[2], partly back-form. from MAILED *adjective*.]
†**1** Make (a piece of armour) out of mail (*lit.* & *fig.*). Only in LME.
2 Clothe or arm (as) with mail. L18.

†**mail** *verb*[3] *trans.* Also **meal**. L17–E19.
[ORIGIN formed as MOLE *noun*[1].]
Spot, stain.

mail /meɪl/ *verb*[4] *trans.* Orig. *US*. E19.
[ORIGIN from MAIL *noun*[3].]
Send (letters etc.) by post, post.

L. HELLMAN I . . never had an answer to the letter I had mailed from New Orleans. J. WILCOX I want to mail out personalized appeals.

– COMB.: **mail-in** *noun & adjective* (*a*) *noun* an item, as a promotion brochure, postal vote, etc., sent out or returned by post; (*b*) *adjective* (of an item, as a promotion brochure, postal vote, etc.) that is or can be sent through the post; (of a ballot, survey, etc.) conducted by post; **mail-out** *adjective & noun* (*a*) *adjective* = ***mail-in*** *adjective* above; (*b*) *noun* the action of sending out a number of items such as promotion brochures etc. at one time.
▪ **mailaˈbility** *noun* the condition of being mailable L19. **mailable** *adjective* acceptable for conveyance by post M19. **mailer** *noun* (*a*) *US* a person or thing which dispatches (letters etc.) by mail; (*b*) a mail boat; (*c*) *S. Afr.* a middleman who buys liquor legitimately and resells it to an illicit liquor dealer or shebeen keeper; (*d*) a container for the conveyance of items by post; (*e*) an advertising pamphlet, brochure, etc., sent out by post; freq. in ***self-mailer***; (*f*) COMPUTING a program that sends electronic mail messages: M19.

mailed /meɪld/ *adjective.* LME.
[ORIGIN from MAIL *noun*[2] + -ED[2].]
1 Covered with or composed of mail or plates of metal. LME.

JOYCE With his mailed gauntlet he brushed away a furtive tear.

2 Armed with mail, mail-clad; (of a ship) ironclad. LME.

T. WOOLNER With charge of mailèd horse and showers Of steel. *fig.*: *Guardian* Accused . . of being the silk glove that masks the mailed fist.

3 Of a hawk: having mail or breast feathers (of a specified colour). Formerly also, (of a bird's plumage etc.) speckled, spotted. LME.

J. JOSSELYN The Osprey, which in this Country is white mail'd.

4 Of an animal etc.: having a skin or protective covering resembling mail armour. LME.

R. OWEN The ball-proof character of the skin of the largest of these mailed examples.

mailgram /ˈmeɪlɡram/ *noun.* *US*. Also **M-**. M20.
[ORIGIN from MAIL *noun*[3] or *verb*[4] + -GRAM.]
A message transmitted electronically from one post office to another and then delivered by ordinary post; the service providing this form of transmission.

mailing /ˈmeɪlɪŋ/ *noun.* Orig. *US*. M19.
[ORIGIN from MAIL *verb*[4] + -ING[1].]
1 The action of sending something by mail; posting. M19.
direct mailing: see DIRECT *adjective*.
2 Something sent by mail; *spec.* a number of items posted at one time, esp. as part of a publicity campaign, a survey, etc. E20.
– COMB.: **mailing list**: of people to whom advertising matter etc. is to be posted; **mailing shot** = ***mailshot*** s.v. MAIL *noun*[3].

maille *noun* var. of MAIL *noun*[4].

maillot /majo/ *noun.* Pl. pronounced same. L19.
[ORIGIN French.]
1 Tights. L19.
2 A tight-fitting, usu. one-piece, swimsuit. E20.
3 A jersey, a top. M20.

Mailmerge /ˈmeɪlməːdʒ/ *noun.* Also **m-**. L20.
[ORIGIN from MAIL *noun*[3] + MERGE *verb*.]
COMPUTING. (Proprietary name for) a program that draws on a file of names and addresses and a text file to produce multiple copies of a letter each addressed to different recipients.

maim /meɪm/ *noun*[1]. Long *arch.* ME.
[ORIGIN Old French *mayhem*, *mahaing*, *main(e*, from *mahaignier*, *mayner*: see MAIM *verb*. Cf. MAYHEM.]
1 Orig., a serious loss or permanent bodily hurt or disfigurement. Later, loss or permanent disablement of a limb etc.; an injury to the body causing this; a mutilation. ME.

T. FULLER They are so eminent . . that their omission would make a maim in history. G. BANCROFT A crowd gathered round the scaffold when Prynne and Bastwick and Burton were to suffer maim. T. H. WHITE Oh, defend us from death and horrible maims.

2 The loss of an essential part, a grave defect or blemish. L15.

maim /meɪm/ *adjective & noun*[2]. Long *rare*. L15.
[ORIGIN Prob. rel. to MAIM *noun*[1]. Cf. Old French *mehaigne*, mod. French dial. *mécaigne*.]
▸ **A** *noun collect. pl.* *The* class of maimed people. Orig., a maimed person. L15.

Granta We thrashed these representatives of the maim, the halt and the blind.

▸ **B** *adjective.* Maimed. M17.

R. L. STEVENSON His own life being maim, some of them are not admitted in his theory.

maim /meɪm/ *verb trans.* ME.
[ORIGIN Old French *mahaignier*, *mayner* from Proto-Romance: ult. origin unknown. Cf. MAIM *noun*[1].]
Orig., disable, wound, cause bodily hurt or disfigurement to. Now, deprive of (the use of) a limb etc.; mutilate, cripple; *fig.* render powerless or essentially incomplete.

BURKE Pulling down hedges, . . firing barns, maiming cattle. P. WARNER Most were maimed for life by having a hand or foot cut off. J. WYNDHAM To deprive a gregarious creature of companionship is to maim it, to outrage its nature.

▪ **maimer** *noun* M16.

maimai /ˈmʌɪmʌɪ/ *noun.* *NZ*. M19.
[ORIGIN Alt. of MIA-MIA.]
A makeshift shelter of sticks, grass, etc. Now usu., a hide or stand for a person shooting ducks.

maimed /meɪmd/ *adjective & noun.* ME.
[ORIGIN from MAIM *verb* + -ED[1].]
▸ **A** *adjective.* That has been maimed (*lit.* & *fig.*). ME.

J. GARDNER He'd end up maimed, a brace on one boot, no arm in one sleeve.

▸ **B** *noun collect. pl.* *The* class of maimed people. ME.

A. B. JAMESON The sick and maimed who are healed by her intercession.

▪ **maimedly** /ˈmeɪmɪdli/ *adverb* (long *rare* or *obsolete*) L16. **maimedness** /ˈmeɪmɪdnɪs/ *noun* E17.

Maimonidean /mʌɪˌmɒnɪˈdiːən, mʌɪməʊˈnɪdɪən/ *adjective & noun.* Also **-ian**. E19.
[ORIGIN from Latin *Maimonides* (see below): see -AN, -EAN, -IAN.]
▸ **A** *adjective.* Of or pertaining to the Jewish philosopher and theologian Maimonides (Moses ben Maimon, 1135–1204), or his teaching. E19.
▸ **B** *noun.* An adherent or student of Maimonides or his teaching. L19.

main /meɪn/ *noun*[1].
[ORIGIN Old English *mægen* = Old Saxon *megin*, Old High German *magan*, *megin*, Old Norse *magn*, *meg(i)n*, from Germanic base meaning 'have power': cf. MAY *verb*[1]. In branch II from MAIN *adjective*.]
▸ **I** **1** Physical strength, force, or power. Now only in ***with might and main*** s.v. MIGHT *noun*[1]. OE.
†**2** A host of soldiers etc.; a (military) force. OE–ME.
▸ **II** **3** **a** The mainland. Now *arch.* & *poet.* M16. ▸**b** (**M-**.) *hist.* = ***Spanish Main*** s.v. SPANISH *adjective*. L19.

a C. THIRLWALL The island . . was separated from the main by a channel. **b** J. CLAVELL He wanted to go . . south along the Main then back across the Atlantic.

4 A mainsail; a mainmast. **M16.**

SMALL Practical Boat Owner Her main and jib gave us 194 square feet of sail.

5 a The high seas, the open ocean. Now *poet.* **M16.** ▸†**b** A broad expanse. **L16–M17.**

a GOLDSMITH To traverse climes beyond the western main. **b** SHAKES. *Sonn.* Nativity, once in the main of light, Crawls to maturity.

6 a The chief or principal part *of* a whole; the important or essential point *of. arch.* exc. in ***in the main*** below. **L16.** ▸**b** The most important part of some business, subject, argument, etc.; the chief matter or principal thing in hand. **E17.**

a S. JOHNSON The main of life is composed of small incidents. **b** A. COWLEY Frugal, and grave, and careful of the main.

†**7** The object aimed at; a particular end or purpose. **E–M17.**

J. WEBSTER 'Tis the very main of my ambition.

8 A principal channel, duct, or conductor for conveying water, sewage, gas, or (usu. in *pl.*) for the supply of electricity. Also, in *pl.*, the public supply of water, electricity, etc., collectively. **E17.**

G. ORWELL The lights would be switched off at the main. *Listener* There were lights—not from the mains, but from a generator. *attrib.*: *Soviet Weekly* You rent a cottage with mains water and a gas cooker.

9 A principal seam of coal; a coalmine. Also, a main line of a railway. **M19.**

– PHRASES: **in the main** for the most part; in all essential points; mainly. ***rising main***: see RISING *adjective*. ***Spanish Main***: see SPANISH *adjective*. ***with might and main***: see MIGHT *noun*[1].

main /meɪn/ *noun*[2]. *Scot. & N. English.* **LME.**

[ORIGIN Aphet. from DOMAIN.]

sing. (*obsolete*) & in *pl.* treated as *sing.* or (usu.) *pl.* The farm attached to a mansion house; a home farm; a demesne. Freq. in ***the Mains of*** — as the name of a farm.

main /meɪn/ *noun*[3]. **M16.**

[ORIGIN Prob. from ***main chance*** s.v. MAIN *adjective*.]

1 †**a** A principal object or undertaking. **M16–L18.** ▸**b** In the game of hazard, a number (5, 6, 7, 8, or 9) called by a player before throwing the dice. **L16.**

a SHAKES. *1 Hen. IV* To set so rich a main On the nice hazard of one doubtful hour. G. TOWERSON Recreations . . must consequently be . . used as things on the by and not as the main.

†**2** A match (at archery, boxing, bowls, etc.). **L16–L19.**

3 A match between fighting cocks; occas., a number of fighting cocks engaged in a match. **M18.**

Welsh main a series of cockfighting matches organized as a knockout competition.

main /meɪn/ *adjective*. **ME.**

[ORIGIN Partly repr. MAIN *noun*[1] in comb., partly from Old Norse *megenn*, *megn* (in comb. *megin*) strong, powerful.]

1 Of a material object, an animal, etc.: of great size or bulk. *obsolete* exc. *dial.* **ME.** ▸**b** Of a quantity or amount: large. *obsolete* exc. *dial.* **E17.**

MILTON Themselves invaded next, and on their heads Main Promontories flung.

2 †**a** Of an action etc.: manifesting or requiring great force or energy. **LME–L17.** ▸**b** Strong, potent; *esp.* (of a sound) loud. Long *arch. rare.* **LME.** ▸**c** Of strength etc.: exerted to the full, sheer. Now chiefly in ***by main force***. **M16.** ▸†**d** Of motion etc.: swift, speedy, rapid. **M16–M17.**

a H. FOULIS She also gave a main stroke against Cecchino. **b** JOYCE And he answered with a main cry: *Abba! Adonai!* **c** SIR W. SCOTT Yet with main strength his strokes he drew. **d** J. FLETCHER Making with all maine speed to th' port.

†**3** (Of an army) large, powerful; *esp.* designating a complete and fully equipped force as opp. to a small or irregular one. Also, designating a pitched battle as opp. to a skirmish. **LME–E17.**

R. CAREW To withstand any great Navie or maigne invasion. T. SHELTON This Giant . . would pass with a main power into my Land.

4 Esp. of an action, a quality, etc.: very great in degree, value, etc.; highly remarkable for a specified quality; very great or considerable of its kind. (Occas. with *compar. & superl.*) *obsolete* exc. *dial.* **LME.** ▸**b** Of a person or agent: great, remarkable, or pre-eminent for the quality or characteristics indicated. *obsolete* exc. *dial.* **M16.**

D. FEATLEY This is one of our mainest exceptions against the Roman Church. R. L. STEVENSON It [an island] were a main place for pirates once. **b** R. B. SHERIDAN I am a main bungler at a long story.

5 Chief or principal in size or extent. **L15.** ▸**b** Greater or more important than others of the same kind; pre-eminent; leading. **E16.** ▸**c** Constituting the bulk or principal part; designating the chief part of the thing specified. **L16.** ▸†**d** Referring or pertaining to all or the majority; general. **E17–M17.**

W. IRVING After turning from the main road up a narrow lane. *Encycl. Brit.* A rate of fall of 1 in 120 . . is desirable . . for a main sewer. **b** H. ROGERS I went carefully over all the main points of the argument. E. A. FREEMAN The statements may be grouped under two main heads. **c** WELLINGTON The main body of the allied army. **d** SHAKES. *Hen. VIII* By the main assent Of all these learned men, she was divorced.

6 NAUTICAL. Pertaining to, connected with, or near the mainmast or mainsail. **L15.**

JOHN ROSS The main and fore hatchway.

7 Designating a considerable, uninterrupted stretch of water, land, or space. **M16.** ▸†**b** Of earth, rock: forming the principal or entire mass; solid. **M16–M17.**

SHAKES. *Merch. V.* And bid the main flood bate his usual height. MILTON Over all the face of Earth Main Ocean flow'd.

†**8** Of a person: powerful, high in rank or position. **M16–E17.** ▸**b** Of an affair, event, etc.: highly important; having great results or important consequences; momentous. **L16–L17.**

J. FLETCHER So main a person, A man of so much Noble note and honour. **b** MILTON All commit the care And management of this main enterprise To him their great Dictator.

– PHRASES: **main and** — *dial.* = MAIN *adverb*. **the Main Plot** *hist.* the more important of two plots against the government of James I (opp. ***the Bye Plot***).

– SPECIAL COLLOCATIONS & COMB.: **main beam** (*a*) a principal beam which transmits a load directly to a column; (*b*) the undipped beam of the headlights of a motor vehicle. **mainboard** = ***motherboard*** s.v. MOTHER *noun*[1]. **main body** the body of troops forming the chief part of an army or armed force, occupying the space between the vanguard and the rear. **main brace** *noun*[1] [BRACE *noun*[2]] NAUTICAL the brace attached to the main yard; ***splice the main brace*** (*hist.*), serve an extra rum ration. **main brace** *noun*[2] [BRACE *noun*[1]] a principal brace; MECHANICS in a system of braces, the one that takes the principal strain. **main breadth** NAUTICAL the broadest part of a ship at a particular timber or frame. **main chance** †(*a*) = MAIN *noun*[3] 1b; chiefly *fig.*, the likely outcome, the most important point risked or at stake; (*b*) something which is of principal importance, *esp.* the opportunity of enriching or otherwise benefiting oneself; ***an eye to the main chance***, consideration for one's own interests. **main chancer** an opportunist, a person who has an eye to the main chance. **main couple** the principal truss in a roof. **main course** (*a*) any of a number of substantial dishes in a large menu; the principal dish of a meal; (*b*) NAUTICAL (now *rare* or *obsolete*) a mainsail. **main crop** the chief crop, excluding the early and late varieties or sections. **maincrop** *adjective* of or pertaining to the main crop. **main deck** NAUTICAL (*a*) the deck next below the spar deck in a man-of-war; (*b*) the upper deck between the poop and the forecastle in a merchantman. **main dish** = ***main course*** (a) above. ***main drag***: see DRAG *noun* 11. **mainframe** COMPUTING orig., the central processing unit of a computer; now usu., any large or general-purpose computer, *esp.* one supporting numerous peripherals etc. **main guard** *hist.* (*a*) FORTIFICATION the keep of a castle; the part of the building in which the main guard (sense (b) below) is lodged; (*b*) a body of troops constituting a guard, *esp.* a body of cavalry posted on the wings of a camp towards the enemy; a guard in a fortress taking custody of disturbers of the peace etc. **main half-breadth** NAUTICAL a section of the broadest part of a ship. **main line** (*a*) a chief railway line; (*b*) a principal route, a connection, conduit, etc.; (*c*) *slang* a principal vein, esp. as a site for (illicit) drug injection; (the action or habit of making) such an injection (cf. MAINLINE); (*d*) *US* a chief road or street. **main-line** *adjective* of or pertaining to a main line. **main man** (*a*) (*colloq.*, chiefly *US*) a favourite male friend; a man admired for his achievements; (*b*) a principal male figure in an organization, team, etc. **mainmast** the principal mast in a ship. **mainplane** AERONAUTICS a principal supporting surface of an aircraft (as distinguished from a tailplane). **main range** *Austral. & NZ* the principal ridge of a chain of mountains. **mainsail** NAUTICAL the principal sail of a ship; *esp.* the lowest sail on the mainmast in a square-rigged vessel; the sail set on the after part of the mainmast in a fore-and-aft rigged vessel. **main sea** *arch.* the high sea; = MAIN *noun*[1] 5a. **main sequence** ASTRONOMY a series of star types represented on a Hertzsprung-Russell diagram as a continuous band extending from the upper left (hot bright stars) to the lower right (cool dim stars), to which most stars belong (cf. DWARF *noun* 3). **mainsheet** (*a*) NAUTICAL the rope which controls the boom of the mainsail when set; (*b*) *slang* in Jamaica, a drink of rum and water. **mainspring** (*a*) the principal spring in a piece of mechanism, esp. in a watch, clock, etc.; (*b*) *fig.* the chief motive power, the main incentive. **main squeeze** *N. Amer. slang* (*a*) an important person; (*b*) a person's principal friend of the opposite sex. **mainstay** (*a*) NAUTICAL the stay which extends from the maintop to the foot of the foremast; ***mainstay sail***, a storm sail set on the mainstay; (*b*) *fig.* a chief support. **main stem** (*a*) the principal stem (*lit.* & *fig.*); (*b*) *US slang* the main street of a town etc. **mainstream** *noun, adjective, & verb* (*a*) *noun* the principal stream or river etc.; the prevailing trend of opinion, fashion, etc.; EDUCATION the stream or class for those without special needs; (*b*) *adjective* of or pertaining to the mainstream; (of jazz) neither traditional nor modern; belonging to or characteristic of an established field of activity; (*c*) *verb trans. & intrans.* incorporate *into* the mainstream; *spec.* in EDUCATION, place (a pupil) in a class for those without special needs. **main street** (as a name also with cap. initials) the principal street of a town; *fig.* (after Sinclair Lewis's novel *Main Street*, 1920) the mediocrity, parochialism, or materialism regarded as typical of small-town life. **mainstreeting** *N. Amer.* political campaigning in main streets to win electoral support. **maintop** NAUTICAL the top of a mainmast; the platform above the head of the lower mainmast. **main-topgallant** *adjective* (NAUTICAL) designating the mast, sail, yard, etc., above the maintopmast and maintopsail. **maintopmast** NAUTICAL the mast above the lower mainmast. **maintopsail** NAUTICAL the sail above the mainsail. **main-ward** (*a*) the main body of an army; (*b*) the principal ward of a lock. **mainway** the gangway or principal passage in a mine. **main-yard** NAUTICAL the yard on which the mainsail is extended.

main /meɪn/ *verb trans. & intrans.* **E20.**

[ORIGIN from MAIN *adjective*.]

1 *verb trans.* Convert (a road) into a main road. **E20.**

2 *verb trans. & intrans.* = MAINLINE. *slang.* **L20.**

main /meɪn/ *adverb*. Long chiefly *dial.* **M17.**

[ORIGIN from MAIN *adjective*. Cf. MIGHTY *adverb*.]

Very, exceedingly.

W. GODWIN It is main foolish of me to talk to you thus.

Maine /meɪn/ *noun*. **M19.**

[ORIGIN A state in the north-eastern US.]

1 US HISTORY. ***Maine Law***, a law forbidding the manufacture or sale of intoxicating liquors; *spec.* the prohibitory law passed in Maine in 1851. **M19.**

2 ***Maine Coon*** (***cat***), (earlier) ***Maine cat***, a domestic cat of a large, long-haired breed, orig. from America. **E20.**

■ **Mainer** *noun* a native or inhabitant of the state of Maine **L19.** **Mainite** *noun* **M19.**

mainferre /ˈmeɪnfəː/ *noun*. *obsolete* exc. *hist.* **LME.**

[ORIGIN Perh. repr. French *main ferrée* ironclad hand or *main-de-fer* hand of iron.]

A piece of medieval armour; *esp.* a gauntlet for the left arm.

mainland /ˈmeɪnlənd, -land/ *noun*. **LME.**

[ORIGIN from MAIN *adjective* + LAND *noun*[1].]

1 A large continuous extent of land, including the greater part of a country or territory and excluding outlying islands, peninsulas, etc. Formerly also, land as opp. to sea, *terra firma*; *poet.* great extent of country, wide territory. **LME.**

T. H. HUXLEY Pillars of chalk have . . been separated from the mainland. V. S. NAIPAUL Venezuelans flew over from the mainland to shop.

2 (**M-.**) ▸**a** The largest island in Orkney and in Shetland. **M16.** ▸**b** The South Island of New Zealand. *NZ colloq.* **M20.**

– COMB.: **Mainland China** the People's Republic of China, as opp. to Taiwan.

■ **mainlander** *noun* a native or inhabitant of the mainland **M19.**

mainline /ˈmeɪnlʌɪn/ *verb trans. & intrans. slang* (orig. *US*). **M20.**

[ORIGIN from ***main line*** s.v. MAIN *adjective*.]

Inject (heroin or another narcotic drug) intravenously, esp. illicitly.

W. DEVERELL I've seen kids cut those little blue ovals with toot and mainline it. J. UPDIKE You seem like you've snorted or swallowed or mainlined something.

■ **mainliner** *noun* **M20.**

M

mainly /ˈmeɪnli/ *adverb*. **ME.**

[ORIGIN from MAIN *adjective* + -LY[2].]

†**1** With force; vigorously, violently. **ME–M17.** ▸**b** In a loud voice, loudly. **ME–L19.** ▸†**c** Vehemently, strongly; earnestly, eagerly. **LME–E17.**

2 †**a** In a great degree; greatly, considerably, very much, a great deal. Also, entirely, perfectly. **LME–E19.** ▸**b** Very, exceedingly. Cf. MAIN *adverb*. *obsolete* exc. *dial.* **L17.**

a SHAKES. *Haml.* As by your safety, wisdom, all things else, You mainly were stirr'd up. C. LAMB I think we should suit one another mainly. **b** SMOLLETT The captain was mainly wroth, and would . . have done him a mischief.

3 For the most part; in the main; as the chief thing, chiefly, principally. **M17.**

E. SAINTSBURY Then, cottages were mainly of stone. S. PLATH Blackberries on either side, though on the right mainly.

mainmortable /meɪnˈmɔːtəb(ə)l/ *adjective & noun*. *hist.* **E18.**

[ORIGIN French, from *mainmorte* dead hand: see -ABLE. Cf. MORTMAIN.]

▸**A** *adjective*. Of, pertaining to, or designating (the possessions of) serfs childless at death, who under French feudal law were not at liberty to alienate their possessions. **E18.**

▸**B** *noun*. A mainmortable serf. **L18.**

mainour /ˈmeɪnə/ *noun*. Now *arch.* or *hist.* Also **manner** /ˈmanə/. **LME.**

[ORIGIN Anglo-Norman *mainoure*, *meinoure*, *main oevere*, Old French *manuevre*: see MANOEUVRE *noun*.]

LAW. A stolen object found in the possession of a thief when arrested. Chiefly in ***taken with the mainour***, ***found with the mainour***.

in the mainour in the act of doing something unlawful, *in flagrante delicto*.

mainpast /ˈmeɪnpɑːst, -past/ *noun*. **M19.**

[ORIGIN Anglo-Norman *meynpast* from medieval Latin *manupastus*, from *manu* abl. of *manus* hand + *pastus* pa. pple of *pascere* feed (cf. PASTURE *noun*).]

LAW (now *hist.*).

1 A person's household. **M19.**

2 A domestic; a dependant. **L19.**

mainpernor /ˈmeɪnpɔːnə/ *noun*. Now *arch.* or *hist.* **ME.**

[ORIGIN Anglo-Norman *mainpernour* (for *-prenour*), from *mainprendre*, from *main* hand + *prendre* take, equiv. of medieval Latin *manucapere* take in the hand, assume responsibility for.]

LAW. A surety for a prisoner's appearance in court on a specified day; a person who stands surety for another. Cf. MAINPRIZE.

■ †**mainpernable** *adjective* able to be stood surety for **L15–L18.**

mainprize /ˈmeɪnprʌɪz/ *noun & verb. obsolete exc. hist.* **ME.**
[**ORIGIN** Anglo-Norman, Old French *mainprise*, *mein-*, from *mainprendre*: see **MAINPERNOR**.]
▸ **A** *noun.* **1** The action of making oneself legally responsible for the fulfilment of a contract or undertaking by another person; suretyship; *spec.* the action of procuring the release of a prisoner by standing surety for his or her appearance in court at a specified time. **ME.**
2 A person who stands surety for another. **LME.**
▸ **B** *verb trans.* Also **-ise**. Procure or grant the release of (a prisoner) by mainprize; accept a surety for the appearance of. **ME.**

maint /meɪnt/ *adjective. pseudo-arch. rare.* **E18.**
[**ORIGIN** French.]
Many, numerous.

maintain /meɪnˈteɪn, mənˈteɪn/ *verb.* **ME.**
[**ORIGIN** Repr. tonic stem of Old French & mod. French *maintenir* (Anglo-Norman *maintener*) from Proto-Romance, from Latin *manu* abl. of *manus* hand + *tenere* hold.]
†**1** *verb trans.* Practise habitually (a good, bad, etc., action); observe (a rule, a custom). **ME–E17.**

AV *Titus* 3:14 Let ours also learne to maintaine good workes . . that they be not unfruitfull.

2 *verb trans.* **a** Carry on or prosecute (a war, siege, etc.). Also, have ground for sustaining (an action at law). **ME.** ▸†**b** *gen.* Go on with, continue, persevere in (an undertaking); (occas.) go on with the use of (something). **LME–M16.** ▸**c** Preserve or retain (friendly relations, correspondence, a particular attitude, etc.). **E17.**

a DRYDEN Long the doubtful Combat they maintain. *Law Times* To maintain an action of deceit there must be moral delinquency . . of the person proceeded against. W. S. CHURCHILL Britain had found herself alone against Napoleon and for two years . . maintained the struggle single-handed. **c** DISRAELI Lady Annabel for some time maintained complete silence. W. CATHER Even after their misfortunes . . she had maintained her old reserve.

3 *verb trans.* Cause to continue (a state of affairs, a condition, an activity, etc.); keep vigorous, effective, or unimpaired; guard from loss or deterioration. **ME.**

N. CHOMSKY Prince Sihanouk managed to maintain neutrality. *Christian Aid News* The . . soldiers have maintained their reputation and discipline.

M

4 *verb trans.* Orig., secure the continuance of (a possession) *to* a person; secure (a person) *in* continued possession of property. Later, cause to continue in a specified state, relation, or position. **ME.**

W. B. CARPENTER The limb was maintained in this state of tension for several seconds.

5 *verb trans.* Give one's support to, defend, uphold, (a cause, something established, one's side or interest, etc.). **ME.**

MILTON Who single hast maintaind Against revolted multitudes the Cause Of Truth. BURKE The king swears he will maintain . . 'the laws of God'.

6 *verb trans.* **a** Uphold, stand by, support the cause of, (a person, party, etc.); defend, protect, assist; support or uphold *in* (an action, a course of behaviour). Also foll. by †*to do. arch.* **ME.** ▸**b** *LAW* (now *hist.*). Give support to (a party in litigation) without lawful cause. **E18.**

a SHAKES. *2 Hen. VI* Jesu maintain your royal excellence! S. R. GARDINER James was still ready to maintain Somerset against his ill-willers in public.

7 *verb trans.* Hold, keep, defend (a place, a position, a possession, oneself) against hostility or attack, actual or threatened. **ME.**

T. GRAY An Iron race the mountain cliffs maintain. L. GRIFFIN Our . . support . . enabled Abdur Rahman Khan to maintain himself against his many enemies.

8 *verb trans.* Support or uphold in speech or argument; defend (an opinion, statement, etc.); assert the truth or validity of. Also, affirm, assert, or contend (*that*); assert (something *to be*). **ME.**

HOBBES The doctrines maintained by so many Preachers. B. JOWETT Pleasure and pain I maintain to be the first perceptions of children. G. VIDAL Constantius maintained that there was a plot against his life.

9 *verb trans.* **a** Support (one's state in life) by expenditure etc. Also, sustain (life) by nourishment. **ME.** ▸†**b** Bear the expense of, afford. **LME–E17.**

a C. COTTERELL The narrowness of his fortune could not maintain the greatness of his Birth. B. C. BRODIE Food is required because life cannot be maintained without it. **b** SHAKES. *Tam. Shr.* What 'cerns it you if I wear pearl and gold? . . I am able to maintain it.

†**10** *verb trans.* Keep in good order, rule, (a people, a country); preserve *in* a state of peace, etc. **LME–M17.**

COVERDALE *Ecclus* 38:32 Without these maye not the cities be manteyned.

†**11** *verb refl.* Bear or conduct oneself in a specified manner. Also, continue *in* an action or state; keep oneself in a specified state. **LME–E17.**

BACON Great men . . were better to maintaine themselves indifferent and neutrall.

12 *verb trans.* **a** Provide (oneself, one's family, etc.) with means of subsistence or the necessaries of life; bear the living, educational, etc., expenses of (a person). **LME.** ▸†**b** Provide for the keep of (an animal). **L16–L17.** ▸**c** Give a drug to (an individual, esp. a drug addict) in periodic doses sufficient to sustain its effect on the body. **M20.**

a HENRY FIELDING I believe you bred the young man up, and maintained him at the university. G. P. R. JAMES Sufficient to maintain me in comfort and independence as a gentleman. **c** *Science* A program . . to maintain at least 20,000 addicts on methadone.

13 *verb trans.* **a** Pay for the upkeep of; provide means for the equipment of (a garrison etc.); keep (a road, a building, etc.) in repair; take action to preserve (a machine etc.) in working order. **LME.** ▸**b** Provide the means for conducting (a suit or action at law). Cf. senses 2a, 6b above. **M16.**

a AV *1 Esd.* 4:52 Tenne talents yeerely, to maintaine the burnt offerings vpon the Altar every day. DEFOE Strong forts erected . . and strong garrisons maintained in them. E. ROOSEVELT Historic houses that the owners could no longer afford to maintain.

†**14** *verb trans.* Stand for, represent. *rare.* Only in **L16.**

SHAKES. *L.L.L.* This side is Hiems, Winter, . . maintained by the Owl.

■ **maintained** *adjective* that has been maintained; ***maintained school***, a school supported from public funds: **L16.** **maintainment** *noun* (long *rare* or *obsolete*) **E16.**

maintainable /meɪnˈteɪnəb(ə)l, mən-/ *adjective.* **LME.**
[**ORIGIN** from **MAINTAIN** + **-ABLE**.]
1 (Able) to be maintained. **LME.**

Accountant This action is not maintainable.

†**2** Affording a livelihood. *rare.* Only in **L16.**
■ **maintainaˈbility** *noun* **M20.** **maintainableness** *noun* **E18.**

maintainer /meɪnˈteɪnə, mən-/ *noun.* Also (esp. in sense 2) **-or**. **ME.**
[**ORIGIN** formed as **MAINTAINABLE** + **-ER**[1], **-OR**.]
1 *gen.* A person who or thing which maintains someone or something. **ME.**
2 *LAW* (now *hist.*). A person who unlawfully supports a suit in which he or she is not concerned. **LME.**

maintenance /ˈmeɪnt(ə)nəns, -tɪn-/ *noun.* **ME.**
[**ORIGIN** Old French & mod. French, from *maintenir* **MAINTAIN** + **-ANCE**.]
1 *LAW.* The offence of aiding a party in litigation without lawful cause. **ME.**

T. H. WHITE The lawyers were as busy as bees, issuing writs for . . maintenance.

†**2** The action of giving aid, countenance, or support to a person in a course of action. **LME–L16.**
†**3** Bearing, deportment, demeanour, behaviour. **LME–L16.**

SHAKES. *1 Hen. IV* I saw him hold Lord Percy at the point With lustier maintenance than I did look for.

4 The action of upholding or preserving a cause, state of affairs, etc.; the state or fact of being upheld or sustained. **LME.**

Book of Common Prayer The maintenaunce of Goddes true religion and vertue.

5 The action of keeping something in working order, in repair, etc.; the keeping up of a building, garrison, etc., by providing means for equipment etc.; the state or fact of being so kept up; means or provision for upkeep. **LME.**

BURKE They had acted legally . . in their grants of money, and their maintenance of troops. *Cornwall Review* The equipment is simplicity itself, requiring no maintenance. *attrib.*: *Listener* Maintenance engineers at London Airport.

6 **a** The action of providing oneself, one's family, etc., with means of subsistence or the necessaries of life; the fact or state of being so provided. Also, enough to support life; means of subsistence; the amount provided for a person's livelihood. **LME.** ▸**b** In full ***separate maintenance***. An allowance made to a woman (occas. to a man) by a (former) spouse or partner after divorce or separation. Cf. **ALIMONY** 2. **E18.**

a W. LAW The parish allowance to such people, is very seldom a comfortable maintenance. LD MACAULAY The civil servants were clearly entitled to a maintenance out of the revenue. **b** R. MACAULAY All those poor unmarried fathers, ruined by maintenance. P. MORTIMER I suppose your previous husbands pay a bit of maintenance and so on?

7 The act of supporting or upholding in speech or argument; assertion of the truth or validity of an opinion, a tenet, etc. **M16.**

H. R. REYNOLDS He . . appealed . . to the authority of Paul in maintenance of his own peculiar opinions.

– **PHRASES ETC.**: ***cap of maintenance***: see **CAP** *noun*[1]. ***care-and-maintenance***: see **CARE** *noun.* ***RESALE price maintenance***. ***retail price maintenance***: see **RETAIL** *noun* 1. ***separate maintenance***: see sense 6b above.

– **COMB.**: **maintenance dose** a periodic dose of a drug sufficient to sustain its effect on the body; **maintenance order** a court order directing payment of a regular fixed sum for maintenance (sense 6b above) to be paid; **maintenance worker**: employed to keep equipment etc. in repair.

Maintenon /ˈmantənɒn, *foreign* mɛ̃tnɔ̃/ *noun.* **L17.**
[**ORIGIN** French, from the Marquise de *Maintenon*, secretly married to Louis XIV in 1685.]
Used *attrib.* to designate things called after the Marquise de Maintenon.
Maintenon chop, **Maintenon cutlet** a chop, cutlet, prepared with a savoury sauce containing ham and shallots. **Maintenon cross** a cross having a diamond at the end of each limb and worn as an ornament.

maintien /mɛ̃tjɛ̃/ *noun.* **E19.**
[**ORIGIN** French.]
Bearing, deportment.

Maioli /mɑːˈjɒli/ *noun.* **L19.**
[**ORIGIN** from *Maiolus*, Latinized form of the name of Thomas *Mahieu* (fl. 1549–72), French book collector and secretary to Catherine de Medici.]
A French style of bookbinding with elaborate gold tooling, used for some of the books in the library of Thomas Mahieu. Freq. *attrib.*

maiolica *noun* var. of **MAJOLICA**.

mair *noun* see **MAYOR**.

maire /mɛːr/ *noun*[1]. Pl. pronounced same. **L18.**
[**ORIGIN** French: see **MAYOR**.]
A (French) mayor; the chief municipal officer of a French town or of one of the *arrondissements* or districts of Paris.

maire /ˈmʌɪri/ *noun*[2]. **M19.**
[**ORIGIN** Maori.]
Any of several New Zealand trees with heavy close-grained wood: *esp.* (***a***) (more fully ***black maire***) *Nestegis cunninghamii* and (more fully ***white maire***) *N. lanceolata*, both of the olive family; (***b***) *Mida salicifolia*, of the family Santalaceae, with leathery leaves; (***c***) *Syzygium maire*, of the family Myrtaceae, with edible red berries.

mairie /mɛri/ *noun.* Pl. pronounced same. **M19.**
[**ORIGIN** French.]
In France, a town hall; a public building housing the municipal offices of a town or *arrondissement* and often also serving as the official residence of the mayor.

maison /mɛzɔ̃/ *noun.* Pl. pronounced same. **M16.**
[**ORIGIN** French.]
†**1** A house. *Scot.* **M16–M17.**
2 A business (esp. a fashion) house or firm. **E20.**
– **PHRASES & COMB.**: ***maison close*** /kloz/ [lit. 'closed house'] a brothel. ***maison de couture*** /də kutyːr/ a fashion house. ***maison de passe*** /də pas/ [lit. 'house of passage'] a house to which prostitutes can take clients. ***maison de santé*** /də sɑ̃te/ [lit. 'house of health'] a nursing home; *esp.* one for the mentally sick. ***maison tolérée*** /tɔlere/ [lit. 'tolerated house'] a licensed brothel. ***PÂTÉ maison***.

maisonette /meɪzəˈnɛt/ *noun.* **L18.**
[**ORIGIN** French *maisonnette* dim. of *maison* house: see **-ETTE**.]
1 A small house. **L18.**
2 A part of a residential building which is occupied separately, usu. on more than one floor. **E20.**

maistry /ˈmeɪstri/ *noun.* **L18.**
[**ORIGIN** Portuguese *mestre* master.]
In the Indian subcontinent: a master workman, a foreman. Also, a skilled workman, a cook, a tailor, etc.

mai tai /ˈmʌɪ tʌɪ/ *noun.* **M20.**
[**ORIGIN** Prob. from Tahitian *maitai* good, nice, pleasant.]
A cocktail based on light rum, with added curaçao and fruit juices.

Maithili /ˈmʌɪtɪli/ *noun & adjective.* **E19.**
[**ORIGIN** Sanskrit *maithilī* adjective, from *Mithilā*, a place in northern Bihar.]
(Of) one of the Bihari group of dialects; (of) the script used for this language.

Maitrank /ˈmʌɪtraŋk/ *noun.* **M19.**
[**ORIGIN** German, from *Mai* May + *Trank* drink, beverage.]
Wine flavoured with sugar and woodruff.

maître /mɛːtr(ə)/ *noun.* Pl. pronounced same. **E19.**
[**ORIGIN** French, lit. 'master'.]
1 **a** ***maître de ballet*** /də balɛ/, orig., the composer of a ballet who superintended its production and performance; now, a trainer of ballet dancers. **E19.** ▸**b** ***maître d'armes*** /darm/ [lit. 'master of arms'], a fencing instructor. **L19.**
2 The title of or form of address to a French lawyer. **L19.**

maître d' /mɛːtrə də; meɪtrə ˈdə, ˈdiː/ *noun phr. colloq.* Also ***maître de*** /ˈdə/. Pl. ***maîtres d'***, ***maîtres de***, (pronounced same). **M20.**
[**ORIGIN** Abbreviation.]
= **MAÎTRE D'HÔTEL** 2.

maître d'hôtel /mɛːtrə dotɛl, meɪtrə dəʊˈtɛl/ *noun phr.* Pl. ***maîtres d'hôtel*** (pronounced same). **M16.**
[**ORIGIN** French, lit. 'master of house'.]
1 A major-domo, a steward, a butler. **M16.**
2 A hotel manager. Now usu. the manager of a hotel dining room, a head waiter. **L19.**

maîtres d', maîtres de, maîtres d'hôtel *noun phrs. pl.* see MAÎTRE D' etc.

maîtresse /mɛtrɛs/ *noun.* Pl. pronounced same. M19.
[ORIGIN French, formed as MAÎTRE: see -ESS[1].]
1 *maîtresse en titre* /ɑ̃ titr/ [lit. 'mistress in name'], an official or acknowledged mistress. M19.
2 *maîtresse femme* /fam/, a strong-willed or domineering woman. M19.

Maitreya /mʌɪˈtreɪjə/ *noun.* L19.
[ORIGIN Sanskrit, from *mitra* friend, friendship.]
BUDDHISM. The Buddha who will appear in the future; a representation of this Buddha.

maize /meɪz/ *noun & adjective.* M16.
[ORIGIN French *maïs*, †*mahis*, or its source Spanish *maíz*, †*mahiz*, *-is*, †*mayz*, from Taino *mahiz*.]
▸ **A** *noun.* **1** A cereal grass of Central American origin, *Zea mays*, having a terminal male inflorescence and axillary female ears, the grains being embedded in a wooden core (the cob); the grain produced by this grass. Also called ***Indian corn*** and (esp. *N. Amer.*) ***corn***. M16.
2 A pale yellow colour like that of maize. M19.
– COMB.: **maize bird** *US* any of various New World blackbirds, *esp.* the red-winged blackbird, *Agelaius phoeniceus*; **maize smut** a destructive fungus, *Ustilago maydis*, attacking the maize plant; **maize thief** = *maize bird* above; **maize yellow** (of) a pale yellow colour like that of maize.
▸ **B** *adjective.* Of a pale yellow colour like maize. M19.

maizena /meɪˈziːnə/ *noun.* M19.
[ORIGIN Arbitrary expansion of MAIZE.]
(Proprietary name for) maize starch prepared for use as food.

Maj. *abbreviation.*
Major.

maja /ˈmaxa/ *noun.* M19.
[ORIGIN Spanish, fem. of MAJO *noun*[1].]
In Spain and Spanish-speaking countries: a woman who dresses gaily.

†**majestatic** *adjective.* M17–M18.
[ORIGIN medieval Latin *majestaticus*, from *majestat-*: see MAJESTY, -IC.]
Pertaining to the majesty of God. Cf. MAJESTICAL 2.

majestic /məˈdʒɛstɪk/ *adjective & noun.* E17.
[ORIGIN from MAJESTY + -IC.]
▸ **A** *adjective.* Possessing or characterized by majesty; of imposing dignity or grandeur; stately. E17.

> DEFOE He was grave and majestic, and carried it something like a king. V. WOOLF London lies before me . . . Not Rome herself looks more majestic. N. GORDIMER The bar counter was central and majestic as a fine altar in a church.

▸ **B** *noun.* (**M-**.) A variety of potato producing light-skinned kidney-shaped tubers. E20.

majestical /məˈdʒɛstɪk(ə)l/ *adjective.* Now chiefly *poet.* L16.
[ORIGIN from MAJESTIC *adjective* + -ICAL.]
1 = MAJESTIC *adjective.* L16.
†**2** = MAJESTATIC. L16–L17.
■ **majesticalness** *noun* (now *rare* or *obsolete*) majesty E17.

majestically /məˈdʒɛstɪk(ə)li/ *adverb.* L16.
[ORIGIN from MAJESTIC or MAJESTICAL: see -ICALLY.]
In a majestic manner; with majesty, with imposing dignity or grandeur.

> R. K. NARAYAN He stepped out of a first-class compartment majestically. R. ELLMANN Lady Wilde replied majestically, 'I really took no interest in the matter.'

majestuous /məˈdʒɛstjʊəs/ *adjective. rare.* L17.
[ORIGIN French *majestueux*, from *majesté* MAJESTY after *voluptueux* VOLUPTUOUS.]
Majestic.

majesty /ˈmadʒɪsti/ *noun.* ME.
[ORIGIN Old French & mod. French *majesté* (earlier *maesté*) from Latin *majestas*, *-tat-*, from var. of *majus*, *major-* MAJOR *adjective*: see -TY[1].]
1 a *spec.* The greatness and glory of God. ME. ▸**b** The dignity or greatness of a monarch; sovereign power, sovereignty. Also, the person or personality of a monarch. LME. ▸**c** ROMAN HISTORY. The sovereign power and dignity of the Roman people, esp. considered with reference to offences against it. (Cf. LESE-MAJESTY.) M16.

> **a** MILTON That far-beaming blaze of Majesty. B. F. WESTCOTT The incomprehensible majesty of God and His infinite love. **b** N. TINDAL She was a sovereign queen and would do nothing prejudicial to Royal Majesty. LD MACAULAY Daily seen at the palace, and . . known to have free access to majesty. *transf.*: F. MUIR I have no recourse but to face the full majesty of the law.

2 (**M-**.) With possess. adjective (as ***your majesty*** etc.): an honorific title given to a royal etc. person of sovereign rank. ME.

> W. S. CHURCHILL We, your Majesty's most dutiful and loyal subjects.

at Her Majesty's pleasure, at His Majesty's pleasure: see PLEASURE *noun*. ***enjoy Her Majesty's hospitality, enjoy His Majesty's hospitality***: see HOSPITALITY 1. ***Her BRITANNIC Majesty. Her Majesty's servants***: see SERVANT *noun*. ***His BRITANNIC Majesty. His Majesty's servants***: see SERVANT *noun*. ***Imperial Majesty. On Her Majesty's service, On His Majesty's service***: see SERVICE *noun*[1].
3 Kingly or queenly dignity of look, appearance, etc.; impressive stateliness of demeanour, character, expression, etc. LME.

> COLERIDGE Imposing only by the majesty of plain dealing. BYRON Your rugged majesty of rocks And toppling trees. D. CUSACK She moves out with the majesty of a queen leaving a levee.

4 A representation of God or Jesus enthroned within an aureole. LME.
†**5** The external magnificence suitable for a monarch. LME–M17.

> MILTON Heav'ns all-ruling Sire . . with the Majesty of darkness round Covers his Throne.

6 A canopy over a hearse. *obsolete* exc. *hist.* L15.

majlis /madʒˈlɪs/ *noun.* L17.
[ORIGIN Arabic = place of session, from *jalasa* be seated.]
An assembly for discussion, a council; *spec.* the Parliament of any of various N. African or Middle Eastern countries, esp. Iran. Also, a reception room.

majo /ˈmaxo/ *noun*[1]. Pl. **-os** /-ɔs/. M19.
[ORIGIN Spanish.]
In Spain and Spanish-speaking countries: a man who dresses gaily, a dandy.

majo /ˈmeɪdʒəʊ/ *noun*[2]. Pl. **-os**. Also **majoe**. E18.
[ORIGIN Prob. of W. African origin.]
More fully ***majo bitter***. A W. Indian shrub, *Picramnia antidesma* (family Simaroubaceae), used as a medicinal herb.

majolica /məˈjɒlɪkə, -ˈdʒɒl-/ *noun & adjective.* Also **maiolica** /məˈjɒlɪkə/. L16.
[ORIGIN Italian, from the former name of the island of *Majorca*.]
▸ **A** *noun.* A fine kind of Renaissance Italian earthenware with coloured decoration on an opaque white glaze; any of various other kinds of glazed Italian ware. Also, a modern imitation of this. L16.
▸ **B** *attrib.* or as *adjective.* Made of majolica. M19.

major /ˈmeɪdʒə/ *noun*[1]. L16.
[ORIGIN French, short for *sergent-major* SERGEANT MAJOR, orig. a high rank, formed as MAJOR *adjective & noun*[2].]
1 An officer in the army ranking below a lieutenant colonel and above a captain. Also (with specifying word), an officer in charge of a section of band instruments. L16. ▸**b** An officer in the Salvation Army ranking next above a captain. L19. ▸**c** = SERGEANT MAJOR. *military slang.* E20.
drum major. **Major Mitchell** *Austral.* the pink cockatoo, *Cacatua leadbeateri*.
2 More fully ***major wig***. A full wig tied back in one curl. *obsolete* exc. *hist.* M18.
■ **majorship** *noun* (**a**) the rank or office of a major; majority; (**b**) (with possess. adjective, as ***your majorship*** etc.) a mock title of respect given to a major: E18.

major /ˈmeɪdʒə/ *adjective & noun*[2]. ME.
[ORIGIN Latin, compar. of *magnus* great. Perh. also infl. by French *majeur*, †*maiour*, learned var. of Old French *maour*, accus. of *maire* MAYOR.]
▸ **A** *adjective.* **1** Designating the greater or relatively greater of or *of* two things, classes, etc.; opp. ***minor***. Also, unusually important, serious, or significant; (of an operation) life-threatening. ME. ▸**b** *spec.* Designating someone or something greater or more senior within a particular group; *spec.* designating the elder of two pupils with the same surname, or the first to enter a school. M16.

> R. K. NARAYAN He kept us in his charge for the major part of the day. C. HAMPTON It's been a day of major catastrophes. B. REID It's a very young cast, with only two really major adult parts.

2 LOGIC. Of a term: occurring as the predicate of the conclusion of a syllogism. Of a premiss: that contains the major term of a syllogism. M16.

> J. MORLEY A man of genius is at liberty to assume all his major premisses.

†**3** Of full age; out of one's minority. Chiefly *Scot.* E17–L19.
†**4** Paramount to all other claims. *rare* (Shakes.). Only in E17.

> SHAKES. *Tr. & Cr.* My major vow lies here, this I'll obey.

5 MUSIC. Of an interval: normal or perfect, greater by a semitone than the correlative minor interval. Of a key: in which the scale has a major third. Of a scale: with semitones above the third and seventh notes. M17.

> K. AMIS The key is G major, and . . we find the F sharp we expect.

– SPECIAL COLLOCATIONS & PHRASES: ***Friars Major***: see FRIAR. **major axis** GEOMETRY the axis (of a conic section, esp. an ellipse) which passes through the foci; the principal or transverse axis. ***major circle***: see CIRCLE *noun*. **major league** *N. Amer.* the highest-ranking baseball etc. league; *fig.* a top group. **major piece** CHESS a queen, a rook. ***major planet***: see PLANET *noun*[1]. ***Major Prophet***: see PROPHET. **major suit** BRIDGE the suit of spades or hearts. ***major TRANQUILLIZER. PSOAS major. quart major***: see QUART *noun*[2] 2. ***quint major***: see QUINT *noun*[2]. ***TERES major. tierce major***: see TIERCE *noun*[1] 4. ***tonic major***: see TONIC *adjective* 4. ***URSA Major. VARIOLA major.*** See also SERGEANT MAJOR.
▸ **B** *noun.* **1** LOGIC. A major term or premiss. M16.
2 A major individual of a specified class. Now also *spec.*, a major company or organization. E17.

> *Economist* America's independent oil companies make a living by scooping up what the majors leave behind.

†**3** A person of full age. E17–M19.
4 MUSIC. A major interval, key, scale, etc. M17.
5 In a university, college, etc.: a student's special subject or course. Also, a student specializing in a particular subject. *N. Amer.* L19.

> P. THEROUX His major was recreational leadership, but his summer job was waiting on tables. *Popular Science Monthly* He spent two years in the late '80s as an aimless physics major.

6 In Australian Rules football: a goal. M16.
■ **majorly** *adverb* (*colloq.*) very; extremely; largely: M20.

major /ˈmeɪdʒə/ *verb.* E19.
[ORIGIN from MAJOR *noun*[1], *noun*[2].]
1 *verb intrans.* Walk with an important air; strut. Also foll. by *about*. Chiefly *Scot.* E19.
2 *verb trans.* Bully, domineer over. *rare.* E19.
3 *verb intrans.* Foll. by *in*: study or qualify in as a special subject at a university, college, etc. Orig. *US*. E20.

Majorana /majɔːˈrɑːnə/ *noun.* M20.
[ORIGIN Ettore *Majorana* (1906–38), Italian physicist.]
PHYSICS. Used ***attrib.*** with ref. to concepts arising out of Majorana's work.
Majorana effect birefringence to light travelling in a direction at right angles to an applied magnetic field, observed in some liquid and crystalline materials. **Majorana force** the exchange force between two nucleons, in which charge and spin are both exchanged. **Majorana particle** a particle of spin ½ which is its own antiparticle.

majorat /maʒɔra/ *noun.* Pl. pronounced same. E19.
[ORIGIN French from medieval Latin *majoratus* right of primogeniture, (in late Latin) leading position, from Latin *major* MAJOR *adjective*: see -ATE[1].]
LAW. In Spain, Italy, and other countries: the right of primogeniture; an estate attached to the right of primogeniture.

Majorcan /məˈdʒɔːk(ə)n, məˈjɔː-/ *adjective & noun.* E17.
[ORIGIN from *Majorca* (see below) + -AN.]
▸ **A** *adjective.* Of or pertaining to Majorca. E17.
▸ **B** *noun.* A native or inhabitant of Majorca, one of the Balearic Islands in the western Mediterranean. M17.

major-domo /meɪdʒəˈdəʊməʊ/ *noun.* Pl. **-os**. L16.
[ORIGIN (Partly through French *majordome*) from Spanish *mayordomo*, Italian *maggiordomo* from medieval Latin *major domus* highest official of the household, the 'mayor of the palace' under the Merovingian kings.]
1 The chief official of an Italian or Spanish princely household. Also, the head servant of a wealthy household; a house steward, a butler. L16.
†**2** The master of the house. M17–E18.
3 In states of the south-western US, an overseer on a farm or ranch. Also, an official in charge of irrigation in New Mexico. *US*. M19.
■ **major-domoship** *noun* the office of major-domo L17.

majorette /meɪdʒəˈrɛt/ *noun.* Orig. *US*. M20.
[ORIGIN from MAJOR *noun*[1] + -ETTE.]
= ***drum majorette*** s.v. DRUM *noun*[1].

major-general /meɪdʒəˈdʒɛn(ə)r(ə)l/ *noun.* M17.
[ORIGIN French *major général*, formed as *major* MAJOR *noun*[1] + *général* GENERAL *adjective*.]
MILITARY. **1** An officer of general rank, ranking below a lieutenant general. M17.
2 *hist.* Any of the officers placed in command of the twelve administrative districts into which England was divided in Cromwell's system of military government (1655–1657). M17.
■ **major-generalcy** *noun* the office or rank of a major-general M19. **major-generalship** *noun* (**a**) *hist.* the district commanded by a major-general; (**b**) the office or rank of a major-general: L17.

Majorism /ˈmeɪdʒərɪz(ə)m/ *noun.* M19.
[ORIGIN from Georg *Major* (see below) + -ISM.]
ECCLESIASTICAL HISTORY. The opinions held by Georg Major (1502–74), a German Protestant, who maintained that good works are necessary for salvation.
■ **Majorist** *noun* a follower of Georg Major M17. **Majoˈristic** *adjective* pertaining to Majorism or to the Majorists M19.

majoritarian /məˌdʒɒrɪˈtɛːrɪən/ *adjective & noun.* E20.
[ORIGIN from MAJORITY + -ARIAN.]
(A person) governed by or believing in decision by a majority; (a person) supporting the majority party.
■ **majoritarianism** *noun* belief in, or the existence of, rule or decisions by a majority M20.

majority /məˈdʒɒrɪti/ *noun.* M16.
[ORIGIN French *majorité*, in branch I from medieval Latin *majoritas*, formed as MAJOR *adjective*, in branch II formed as MAJOR *noun*[1]: see -ITY.]
▸ **I** †**1** The state or fact of being greater; superiority; preeminence. M16–E18.
2 The state of being of full age; the age at which a person is legally a full adult, usu. either 18 or 21. M16.

> L. STRACHEY A few days before her eighteenth birthday—the date of her majority. *Listener* It is sad that, as it approaches its majority, this organisation should have run into deep waters.

M

3 The greater number or part; a number which is more than half the whole number; *spec.* the larger party voting together in a deliberative assembly or electoral body. **L17.**

BYRON The majority In council were against you. F. H. A. SCRIVENER Nor in the vast majority of instances does it exist. N. CHOMSKY The large majority of its population . . is Khmer . . but there are substantial Chinese and Vietnamese minorities. J. NAGENDA These friends, the majority of whom had been at school with him.

4 The number by which the votes cast for one party or candidate exceed those for the next in rank; *US* the number by which votes for one party etc. are more than those for all others together. **M18.**

J. MCCARTHY A majority of forty-six was given for the resolution. V. BRITTAIN Mr. Harris won the election with a comfortable majority.

▸ **II 5** The rank or office of a major. **L18.**

R. CAPELL This redoubtable sapper, risen from the ranks to a majority, is a type such as makes empires.

– PHRASES: ***absolute majority***: see ABSOLUTE *adjective* 8. **in the majority** belonging to or constituting the majority. ***silent majority***: see SILENT *adjective*. ***the great majority***: see GREAT *adjective*. **the majority** *spec.* the dead; ***join the majority***, die. ***the vast majority***: see VAST *adjective* 5.

– COMB.: **majority carrier** ELECTRONICS in a semiconductor, a charge carrier (electron or hole) of the kind carrying the greater proportion of the current; **majority rule** the principle that the greater number should exercise greater power; **majority verdict** ENGLISH LAW a verdict in a criminal trial agreed by all but one or two of the members of a jury.

majoun /mə'dʒuːn/ *noun*. **L18.**
[ORIGIN Persian & Urdu *ma'jūn*, Turkish *macun*, from Arabic *ma'jūn*, use as noun of pass. pple of *'ajana* knead.]
An intoxicating sweet made of cannabis leaves mixed with poppy seed, nux vomica, ghee, honey, etc.

majuscule /'madʒəskjuːl/ *adjective & noun*. **E18.**
[ORIGIN French, from Latin *majuscula* (*littera*) dim. of *major*: see MAJOR *adjective*, -CULE.]
▸ **A** *adjective*. **1** TYPOGRAPHY. Of a letter: capital. *rare*. **E18.**
2 PALAEOGRAPHY. Of a letter: large (whether capital or uncial); written in large lettering; designating or pertaining to a script having every letter bounded by the same two (imaginary) lines. **E18.**
▸ **B** *noun*. **1** PALAEOGRAPHY. A large letter, whether capital or uncial; (a manuscript in) large lettering or majuscule script. **E18.**
2 TYPOGRAPHY. A capital letter. *rare*. **E19.**
■ **majuscular** /mə'dʒʌskjʊlə/ *adjective* †(**a**) *gen.* large; (**b**) of the nature of a majuscule; written in majuscules: **E19.**

makable /'meɪkəb(ə)l/ *adjective*. Also **makeable**. **LME.**
[ORIGIN from MAKE *verb* + -ABLE.]
That can be made.

makai /mə'kʌɪ/ *adverb & adjective*. **L19.**
[ORIGIN Hawaiian, from *ma* towards + *kai* the sea.]
In Hawaii: in the direction of the sea, seaward.

makan /'makan/ *noun*. **E20.**
[ORIGIN Cf. Malay *makan* to eat, *makanan* food.]
In Malaysia, food.

makar /'makə/ *noun*. *Scot.* **ME.**
[ORIGIN Var. of MAKER.]
= MAKER. Now only, a poet writing in Scots.

makara /'mʌkərə/ *noun*. **L19.**
[ORIGIN Sanskrit: cf. MUGGER *noun*².]
A crocodile, variously represented in Indian art; the equivalent of Capricorn in the signs of the zodiac.

Makasar *adjective & noun* see MACASSAR.

Makasarese /məkasə'riːz/ *noun & adjective*. Also (*arch.*) **Macassar-**. **L19.**
[ORIGIN from *Makasar* (see MACASSAR) + -ESE.]
▸ **A** *noun*. Pl. same. A member of a Malay people of Makasar (now Ujung Pandang) in the island of Sulawesi, Indonesia. Also, the language of this people. **L19.**
▸ **B** *adjective*. Of or pertaining to the Makasarese or their language. **M20.**

make /meɪk/ *noun*¹. *obsolete* exc. *dial.*
[ORIGIN Old English *ġemaca* corresp. to Old Saxon *gimaco* fellow, equal, Old High German *gimahho*, from West Germanic: rel. to MATCH *noun*¹.]
1 An (or one's) equal, a match; (one's) like. **OE.**
2 An animal's, esp. a bird's, breeding partner, a mate; a person's husband or wife, a person's lover or mistress. **OE.**
3 A companion. **ME.**

make /meɪk/ *noun*². **ME.**
[ORIGIN from the verb.]
1 The manner in which a thing (natural or manufactured) is made; style of construction, kind of composition; build of body; (particular) origin or type of manufacture, a brand. **ME.** ▸**b** Of an abstract thing: form, fashion; sort, character, nature; *dial.* a kind, a sort, a species. **M17.** ▸**c** Mental or moral constitution, disposition, or character. **L17.**

H. MARTINEAU Look at his delicate hands and slight make. J. CARY He was crowned by a helmet of French make. E. BRUTON A stone which is near the ideal is said to be of good make or fine make. *Motor Sport* They confine their purchases to one make of car or commercial vehicle.

†**2** Doing, action; *esp.* (*Scot.*) manner of action or behaviour. **LME–M16.**
3 a The action or process of making or manufacture. Now *rare*. **M18.** ▸**b** An amount manufactured; the quantity produced. **M19.**
4 The action of making profit or of advancing oneself. Only in ***on the make*** below. *slang*. **M19.**
5 The act of making electrical contact; the position or condition in which contact is made. **L19.**
6 BRIDGE. A declaration. **E20.**
7 A (sexual) conquest. *slang*. **M20.**
8 An identification or profile of, or information about, a person or thing from police records, fingerprints, etc. *slang*. **M20.**

N. THORNBURG Let me give you a short make on our witness here. N. MAILER 'What's your make on Pangborn?' 'Corporate lawyer. Sharp.'

– PHRASES: **make and mend** the action of making and repairing clothes; NAUTICAL a period set apart for repairing clothes, a period of leisure, a half holiday. **on the make** *slang* (**a**) intent on profit or advancement; (**b**) intent on winning someone's affections, seeking sexual pleasure; (**c**) improving, advancing, getting better. **put the make on** *N. Amer. slang* make sexual advances towards.

make /meɪk/ *noun*³. *slang & dial. arch.* **M16.**
[ORIGIN Unknown. Cf. MAG *noun*³.]
A halfpenny.

make /meɪk/ *verb*. Pa. t. & pple **made** /meɪd/.
[ORIGIN Old English *macian* = Old Frisian *makia*, Old Saxon *makon* (Dutch *maken*), Old High German *mahhōn* (German *machen*), from West Germanic, from Germanic base meaning 'fitting'. Rel. to MATCH *noun*¹.]
▸ **I 1** *verb trans.* Produce by combination of parts or ingredients, by giving a certain form to matter, by extraction, or by modification of some other substance; construct, frame, fashion. (Foll. by *of*, *out of*, *with*.) **OE.** ▸**b** *verb trans. spec.* Produce (an article of food or drink) by culinary or other operations; put together and set alight materials for (a fire); set apart and prepare the site for (a garden, park, road, etc.). **OE.** ▸**c** *verb trans. & †intrans.* Compose, write as the author (a book, a poem, verses, etc., †a letter, †a work of a specified title); draw up (a legal document, esp. one's will). **ME.** ▸**d** *verb intrans.* Produce an article (*for*). Freq. in ***make or mend***. **M19.**

R. PECOCK God that made the world and alle thingis that ben in it. GOLDSMITH As birds sometimes are seen to make their nests. A. URE The patent plan of Mr William Onions of making cast steel. P. MORTIMER The factory made many things beside rope mats. **b** L. HELLMAN That night I was making her saffron rice. S. HARVESTER Who can make tea with a bloody bag like a lavendar sachet? **c** C. C. F. GREVILLE In 1810 the king made another will. P. KAVANAGH I make a lot of ballads. *Punch* He has made only a couple of dozen short stories.

2 *verb trans.* Cause the material or physical existence of; produce by action, bring about (a condition of things, a state of feeling); inflict (a wound); produce (a hole, a mark, a sound, etc.); create or take part in the creation of (a sound recording, film, etc.). **OE.** ▸†**b** Foll. by double obj. (orig. dat. of the person) or *to*, *unto*: cause to happen to or fall to the lot of; cause to experience. **OE–E18.** ▸**c** GRAMMAR. Of a word: form (a certain case, tense, etc.) in a specified manner; change into (a specified form) when inflected. **OE.** ▸**d** Establish (a rule, an ordinance); enact (a law); impose (a rate). Formerly also, found, institute (a religious order etc.); arrange, fix the time and place for (a match), institute (games). **OE.** ▸**e** Prepare or provide (a meal, a feast) for guests; give (a dinner etc.). *arch.* **OE.** ▸**f** Give rise to; have as a result or consequence; be the cause of. **ME.** ▸**g** Bring (a crop etc.) to maturity, grow. *US*. **E18.** ▸**h** ELECTRICITY. Complete or close (a circuit). Opp. ***break***. **M19.**

R. H. MOTTRAM The shell had fallen . . and made a hole the size of the midden at home. J. RHYS They made a hell of a row for a week. G. PRIESTLAND The car was sold to make room in the garage for rabbits. R. ELLMANN Miles . . made a small sketch of Wilde. **f** V. WOOLF One word of affection . . would have made all the difference. DAY LEWIS It made a stanza in my poem, 'The Innocent'. I. MURDOCH He would have liked a coal-fire now, only it made so much work.

a make a commotion, make a fuss, make an impression, make a noise, make a sensation, make a stir, etc.

3 *verb trans.* **a** Create by election, appointment, or ordination; appoint (an officer), ordain (a priest etc.). **OE.** ▸**b** *gen.* Cause a person or persons to become (what is specified by the object). **ME.** ▸**c** Fix (a price). Now only COMMERCE. **LME.** ▸†**d** Translate, render. **E16–E17.** ▸**e** NAUTICAL. Promote in rank. **L18.**

b LD MACAULAY He . . tried . . to make as few enemies as possible. JULIETTE HUXLEY Oxford, where we had so naturally made many friends.

4 *verb trans.* Form by collection of individuals, get together (in early use *spec.* a party, a force, troops). **ME.**

5 *verb trans.* Foll. by *of* or (esp. in physical sense) *out of*: cause what is denoted by the object of the preposition to become what is denoted by the object of the verb; create (one thing) *of* or *out of* another; regard what is denoted by the object of the preposition as being what is denoted by the object of the verb, arrive at (a particular amount or quantity) as the result of calculation or estimation, assign (a meaning) to a statement, expression, representation, etc., or (a cause, motive, or reason) for actions or phenomena, (freq. with interrog. or indef. pronoun as object). **ME.** ▸†**b** *verb intrans.* Foll. by *of*: (**a**) esteem (*well*, *ill*); (**b**) value highly, treat with great consideration. **LME–E19.**

H. JAMES I didn't know at first quite what to make of it. D. H. LAWRENCE Of her own kerchief she made a pad for the wound. M. BRADBURY For the mass of men . . you can't make a silk purse out of a sow's ear. M. WARNOCK Jean Smith who made sense of my manuscript. T. TANNER Too much has perhaps been made of the notion that the English novel is obsessed with . . class.

make a habit of, make a practice of, etc. ***make an example of, make an exhibition of oneself, make a fool of*** (***oneself***), etc.

6 *verb trans.* Produce from one's body or organically (now *spec.* urine, water, formerly also fruit, blossom); (now *dial.*) give birth to, beget. **ME.**

S. T. WARNER Small proud boys making water against notices that say they're not to. L. NIVEN How many children do you expect to die before they grow to make children?

7 *verb trans.* Amount to; (of the latest item in an enumeration) bring up the sum to (a certain amount); be sufficient to constitute, be the essential criterion of, (in proverbial or quasi-proverbial uses, mainly in neg. contexts); avail (now *rare*) or signify (much, little, nothing, etc.). **ME.** ▸†**b** *verb trans. & intrans.* Of arguments or evidence: avail (much, little, etc.) *for*, *against* (an opinion or a disputant). **L16–E18.**

SHAKES. *Ant. & Cl.* The policy of that purpose made more in the marriage than the love of the parties. R. LOVELACE Stone walls doe not a prison make, Nor iron bars a cage. DEFOE All which did not make thirty thousand men. L. GRIFFITHS Because you are an instinctive entrepreneur you know that two plus two makes whatever you want.

8 *verb trans.* **a** Gain, acquire, or earn (money, reputation, etc.) by labour, business, etc. (foll. by *of*, *out of*); *slang & dial.* steal, acquire, manage to get; be sold for or fetch (a certain price). **ME.** ▸**b** In CARDS, win or take (a trick), play to advantage (a certain card), win the number of tricks that fulfils (a contract). **M16.** ▸**c** In various games, secure a score of, score (a point, a run, etc.); (passing into sense 2f) play so as to enable another to score (a goal etc.). **M16.**

a H. ROTH He has a very good job and he makes good money. G. MILLAR Potatoes and onions I had 'made' from the food-dumps round Alexandria. C. CHAPLIN With my bonus I was making two hundred dollars a week. J. GARDAM I'd say the lad took off somewhere and made his fortune. F. WYNDHAM He made quite a name for himself as an amateur jockey. **c** *Rebound* He made 47 and 41 points in the semi-final and final. *Cricketer* In the first 15 minutes of his innings, they made only four.

9 *verb trans.* Form within the mind; give conceptual existence or recognition to; entertain (a doubt, scruple, question, etc.) in the mind; formulate mentally. **LME.** ▸**b** Formulate and set out (a case, a legal title, etc.). **M19.**
10 *verb trans.* Count as, have the position of, form, (a part or unit in an aggregate, a particular member in a series). **LME.**

DICKENS To see that sort of people together, and to make one of 'em.

11 *verb trans.* Be the material or components of, constitute, be made or converted into, serve for; admit of being made into; (of a person) become by development or training, (with obj. a noun qualified by *good*, *bad*, etc.) perform (*well*, *ill*, etc.) the part or function of. **LME.**

W. BECKFORD They [frogs] make a good soup, and not a bad fricassée. J. CONRAD The ridge of his backbone made a chain of small hills. ANTHONY SMITH The last two quotations make particularly pertinent reading. M. AMIS I was nice, extremely friendly, and would make a fine husband.

12 *verb trans.* NAUTICAL. Descry or discern (as) from the top of a mast or tower; come in sight of. **M16.**
▸ **II** †**13** *verb trans.* Handle, manage, deal with in a particular way; bring *to* a specified condition, reduce *to*. **OE–L17.**
14 *verb trans.* Prepare (a bed) for sleeping in, arrange bedclothes on (a bed) for future use. Orig. branch I, as the noun meant not a permanent article of furniture, but a prepared place for rest, which does not exist until 'made'. **ME.**
15 *verb trans.* Shut, close, bar (a door). Long *arch. & dial.* **ME.**
†**16** *verb refl.* Get ready *to do*; prepare *for*. Chiefly *Scot.* **LME–M17.**
17 *verb trans.* **a** Hew or shape (timber); cut up (wood) into faggots or for firewood. *dial.* **LME.** ▸**b** Prepare (fish) by curing or packing. **E16.** ▸**c** Shuffle (cards) for dealing. **L19.**
18 *verb trans.* Effect or secure the success or advancement of; *esp.* endow (a person) with fortune or prosperity; render independent, set up (usu. in *pass.*). **LME.**

G. BERKELEY What one man loses another gets . . as many are made as ruined. O. MANNING His voice is the very voice of Pandarus. He could make my production. S. BELLOW A piece of research that made his reputation decades ago.

19 *verb* †*refl. & intrans.* Prepare to go or proceed in a specified direction. LME.

Shetland Times We made towards her and when we got close we saw smoke and flames coming from the galley.

20 *verb trans.* Turn over and expose (hay or another crop) to the sun. LME.

21 Train (a hawk, a dog, a horse, *for*). LME.

▸ **III 22** *verb trans.* Cause (another person, oneself, a thing) to be or become. As compl. noun, adjective, pa. pple (now chiefly *known, acquainted, felt, heard, understood*), †pred. phr. OE. ▸**b** *verb trans. spec.* With noun as compl.: appoint to the office of, raise to the dignity of; *arch.* transform, transmute, or fashion into (usu. in *pass.*); determine (a thing, occas. a person) to be, establish or set down as (a law, penalty, etc.), take as (one's business, abode, object, etc.). ME. ▸**c** *verb intrans.* With adjective as compl.: cause oneself or another or something to be. ME.

I. MURDOCH Please don't mention this . . not till it's officially made public. A. S. DALE The fact that Scott is an uneven writer does not make him a bad one. J. NAGENDA The grandmother started shrieking and it was impossible to make yourself heard. J. BERMAN She usually remains silent, making it difficult . . to determine the extent of her knowledge. **b** J. WAIN If Ned had known . . he'd have made it his business to help you. J. RATHBONE After the battle of Talavera, Wellesley was made Viscount Wellington.

23 *verb trans.* Regard (another person, †oneself, a thing) as, consider or compute to be; describe or represent as; cause to appear as. As compl. noun, adjective, †pa. pple, †prep. phr. ME.

DICKENS What time may you make it, Mr Twemlow? M. J. GUEST Macbeth is not half so bad as the play makes him. E. BLISHEN What do you make the answer to Number 10, Johnson? A. HALEY He was only seventeen when he had won the bird. That would make him around fifty-six or fifty-seven now. JANET MORGAN Agatha made Hercule Poirot a retired Belgian police officer.

24 *verb trans.* Foll. by *into*: convert into something else; work on (materials) so as to produce something; arrange, divide, or combine so as to form. L16.

G. GISSING The shopman put them aside, to be made into a parcel. E. JENKS The wife and daughters of the shepherd . . make the milk of the herds into butter and cheese. *Observer* Lambeth Palace is rather difficult to make into a home.

▸ **IV 25** *verb trans.* Bring it about *that*. *arch.* OE.

26 *verb trans.* Cause or compel (a person or thing) to do something (foll. by *do* (now usu. only when both *make* and the dependent verb are in the active voice), *to do* (now usu. only when *make* is in the passive voice)); cause (a thing) *to be done*. ME. ▸**b** Compel or force (a person or thing). *colloq.* M17.

E. POUND The snow makyth me to remember her. SCOTT FITZGERALD Wind . . blew the wires and made the lights go off and on again. S. CHITTY Gwen had . . often made her carry the heavy sack of equipment. C. PETERS He wanted to be made to write. **b** *Times* The enemy will not play the game . . and there are none to make him.

27 *verb trans.* †**a** Show or allege *that*. M–L16. ▸**b** Consider, represent, or allege (a person or thing) *to be, (to) do*. L16.

b E. A. FREEMAN Most of the Chronicles make Richard die in 1026.

28 *verb trans.* Recognize, identify. *US criminals' slang.* E20.

▸ **V** Do, perform, accomplish: chiefly idiomatically with nouns of action.

29 *verb trans.* †**a** Work (a miracle); commit (a sin, a crime, a fault), tell (a lie); do (justice, mercy); give (alms). OE–E18. ▸**b** Wage (war). Formerly also, do (battle), join (a fight), take part in (a campaign). ME. ▸**c** Enter into or conclude (a bargain, contract); (now LAW) enter into a contract of (marriage). ME. ▸**d** Go on (a journey etc.). ME. ▸**e** Perform or execute (a bodily movement or gesture, e.g. one expressive of respect or of contempt); deliver orally (a speech). ME.

d ***make an excursion, make a tour, make a trip, make a voyage,*** etc. **e** ***make a bow, make a curtsy, make a leg,*** etc.

30 *verb trans.* In questions introduced by an objective *what*: have as one's business or purpose, do (as ***what make you here?***); (by inversion, as ***what makes you here?***) cause to be or do. *arch.* ME.

31 *verb trans.* With nouns expressing the action of verbs (whether etymologically cognate or not) forming innumerable phrases approximately equivalent in sense to those verbs: see examples below and the nouns. ME.

make an acknowledgement, make an acquisition, make an advance, make an allegation, make (an) allowance, make (an) answer, make an appeal, make an appearance, make one's appearance, make (an) application, make an ascent, make an assault, make an assertion, make (an) assurance, make atonement, make an attack, make an attempt, make (an) avowal, make an award, make a beginning, make a bid, make a blunder, make a calculation, make a call, make a change, make (a) claim, make a climb, make a comment, make a comparison, make a complaint, make conversation, make a dash, make a defence, make delay, make a discovery, make a donation, make an endeavour, make an entrance, make an error, make (an) exception, make (an) excuse, make an experiment, make a find, make a gift, make a grant, make haste, make an incision, make (an) inquiry, make intercession, make a joke, make mention, make a mistake, make a move, make (an) objection, make an observation, make an offer, make (a) pretence, make (a) proclamation, make (a) profession, make progress, make a promise, make proof, make a proposal, make a protest, make provision, make a recovery, make a remark, make (a) reply, make (a) request, make resistance, make restitution, make (a) retreat, make a sacrifice, make a sale, make (a) search, make a shot, make a stand, make a start, make a surrender, make a transition, make a translation, make (a) trial, make use, make a venture, make a vow, etc.

32 *verb trans.* Offer, present, render, (now esp. amends, LAW (chiefly US) a decision or judgement). Formerly *spec.*, do (homage, fealty); pay (some mark of respect); render (support, aid); present (a person's compliments); propound (a question); give (an instance, notice, a reason, warning). Foll. by *to* or indirect obj. ME.

†**33** *verb trans.* Entertain or manifest (a specified emotion). ME–L16.

34 *verb trans.* Exert (an effort). LME.

35 *verb trans.* Incur or suffer (something undesirable). Formerly also (chiefly *Scot.*) defray, provide for (expenses, costs). *arch.* LME.

36 *verb trans.* Eat (a meal). M16.

37 *verb trans.* Accomplish (a distance, a speed) by travelling etc.; reach (a place) in travelling, come to, arrive at; *colloq.* catch (a train etc.), manage (an appointment, date, etc.); achieve, accomplish, reach; (chiefly *N. Amer.*) attain the rank of. M16. ▸**b** Be successful in sexual advances to; win the affection of; *spec.* persuade (a person) to consent to sexual intercourse, seduce. *slang* (orig. *US*). E20.

A. LOVELL When the Wind blew so hard, that we made nine or ten Miles an hour. W. FAULKNER He graduated . . with the highest marks ever made at the Academy. J. BARTH I made the bus with two minutes to spare, and was soon off to Baltimore. T. ROETHKE I could still make the deadline, if I get my manuscript off today. N. MONSARRAT It took the ship another five hours to make the last forty miles. *Observer* Ferrari believes he has the talent ultimately to make the top. K. AMIS They can't make Boxing Day. They'll be down with us. *Ships Monthly* I managed to make the upturned dinghy . . and . . clambered in. S. RUSHDIE The murders barely made the newspapers; they were not reported on the radio.

▸ **VI** †**38** *verb trans.* ***make it*** (with adverb or adverbial phr. of manner or with adjective): act, behave. OE–E17.

39 *verb intrans.* In early use (with adverb or adverbial phr. of manner), behave, act, (now only as in sense 40 below). Later (with adjective), be (now chiefly in ***make bold, make free***). OE.

40 *verb intrans.* Behave or act *as if, as though*, (*colloq.*) *like*. LME. ▸**b** Act as if with the intention *to do*. L19.

AV *Josh.* 8:15 And Ioshua and all Israel made as if they were beaten before them, and fled. M. WOODHOUSE You aren't making much noise . . . For a guy who was making like an avalanche an hour back. **b** S. PHILLIPS He makes to follow, then stops.

41 *verb intrans.* Have to do *with*; interfere *in*. Chiefly in collocation with *meddle*. *dial.* M16.

42 *verb intrans.* NAUTICAL. Of a tide: begin to flow or ebb, rise, flow in a specified direction. M17.

43 *verb intrans.* †**a** NAUTICAL. Have a certain form or appearance; look *like*. M–L18. ▸**b** Of land, landscape, etc.: extend in a certain direction. *US & Austral.* L18.

44 *verb intrans.* Of ice: form. *N. Amer.* L18.

45 *verb intrans.* Of an argument, evidence, influence, etc.: be effective, tell (on one side or the other). L19.

– PHRASES: (A selection of cross-refs. only is included: see esp. other nouns.) **as — as they make them** *colloq.* as — as possible, thoroughly —. **be made** (*a*) be naturally fitted or destined (*for, to do*); ***be made for each other, be made for one another***, form an ideal combination, be ideally suited; (*b*) have been fashioned out *of*, consist *of*, be composed *of*; ***be made of money*** (*colloq.*), be extremely rich; (*c*) (of a person) be built in a specified manner (*well* etc.), have a bodily build of a specified kind. **have got it made, have it made** *colloq.* be sure of success, have it easy, have no more obstacles to overcome. **make a bag** kill a number of game on a shooting expedition. **make a book** arrange a series of bets referring to one and the same race or event. **make a day of it, make a night of it**, etc., continue doing something, esp. enjoying oneself, throughout the day, night, etc. ***make a habit of***: see HABIT *noun*. ***make a hash of***: see HASH *noun*[1]. ***make a head***: see HEAD *noun*. ***make a House***: see HOUSE *noun*[1]. ***make a meal of***: see MEAL *noun*[2] 2. ***make a mock of, make mock of***: see MOCK *noun*. ***make a monkey of, make a monkey out of***: see MONKEY *noun*. ***make a mountain of a molehill, make a mountain out of a molehill***: see MOLEHILL. ***make a night of it***: see ***make a day of it*** above. **make a person's day, make a person's evening**, etc., be the essential factor in the pleasure of a day etc., redeem a day etc. from routine, dullness, or banality. ***make a work***: see WORK *noun*. ***make beautiful music (together)***: see MUSIC *noun*. **make believe** pretend *that, to do*, esp. (of a child in play, etc.) for enjoyment. ***make both ends meet***: see END *noun*. ***make certain***: see CERTAIN *adjective*. ***make default***: see DEFAULT *noun*. **make do** manage with or *with* what is available, esp. as an inferior or temporary substitute; ***make do and mend***, repair for continued use, proceed by expedients. ***make ends meet***: see END *noun*. ***make eyes at***: see EYE *noun*. ***make friends***: see FRIEND *noun*. ***make fun of***: see FUN *noun*. ***make game of***: see GAME *noun*. ***make good***: see GOOD *adjective*. **make good time** accomplish a distance in a short time, keep to or ahead of a schedule on a journey etc. ***make hay***: see HAY *noun*[1]. ***make head or tail of***: see HEAD *noun*. ***make heavy weather of***: see WEATHER *noun*. ***make history***: see HISTORY *noun*. **make in one's way** *arch.* direct one's journey so as to pass by or through (a place). **make it** †(*a*) see sense 38 above; (*b*) succeed in covering an intended distance or reaching an intended place; achieve a desired object; be successful (***make it big*** (*slang*), be very successful, become very prominent); *slang* achieve sexual intercourse (*with*); (*c*) (with compl.) in *imper.*, select or provide (a particular drink, time, place, etc.) from the possibilities. ***make its way***: see WAY *noun*. ***make light of***: see LIGHT *adjective*[1]. ***make light work of***: see LIGHT *adjective*[1]. ***make love***: see LOVE *noun*. ***make merry***: see MERRY *adjective*. ***make mischief***: see MISCHIEF *noun*. ***make money***: see MONEY *noun*. **make much of, make little of**, etc., (*a*) have a high, low, etc., opinion of; treat with much, no, etc., consideration or affection; (*b*) derive much, little, etc., advantage from; make much, little, etc., effort to mark (an occasion etc.). ***make no bones about***: see BONE *noun*. ***make no mistake***: see MISTAKE *noun*. **make nothing of** (*a*) have a very low opinion of, rate or treat as valueless; (*b*) derive no advantage from; make no effort to mark (an occasion etc.); (*c*) find no difficulty in *doing*, feel no scruples at *doing*. ***make oneself scarce***: see SCARCE *adjective*. ***make one's mark***: see MARK *noun*[1]. **make one's soul** (orig. *Irish*) devote one's efforts to the saving of one's soul; repent and be converted. ***make one's way***: see WAY *noun*. **make or break, make or mar** cause either the complete success or the ruin of (a person or thing). ***make peace***: see PEACE *noun*. ***make room***: see ROOM *noun*[1]. **make sail** (*a*) spread a sail or sails; start on a voyage, set sail; (*b*) spread additional sails in order to increase a ship's speed. **make something of** derive some advantage from; make an effort to mark (an occasion etc.); make important or useful; improve or raise in some way. ***make sure***: see SURE *adjective*. **make the bag** contribute most to the total of game killed on a shooting expedition. ***make the worst of***: see WORST *adjective, adverb, & noun*. **make time** (*a*) find an occasion when time is available (*for, to do*); (*b*) *N. Amer. slang* (foll. by *with*) make sexual advances to; be successful in sexual advances to; court or flirt with. ***make to measure***: see MEASURE *noun*. ***make use of***: see USE *noun*. ***make war***: see WAR *noun*[1]. ***make water***: see WATER *noun*. ***make waves***: see WAVE *noun*. ***make way***: see WAY *noun*. ***make welcome***: see WELCOME *adjective*. ***make wing***: see WING *noun*.

– WITH PREPOSITIONS IN SPECIALIZED SENSES: **make after —** *arch.* go in pursuit of, follow. **make against —** be unfavourable to; militate or tell against. **make at —** *arch.* approach (as if) to attack or seize. **make for —** (*a*) operate in favour of, conduce to; tend to the advancement or progress of; confirm (a view etc.); (*b*) proceed or direct one's course towards; go in the direction of; (*c*) assail, make to attack. †**make to —**, †**make unto —** (*a*) = ***make for*** — above; (*b*) be pertinent or applicable to. **make upon —** *arch.* = ***make at*** — above. **make with —** †(*a*) side with, make common cause with; (of a thing) tell in favour of; (*b*) *slang.* [partly translating Yiddish *mach mit*] bring into operation; use, affect; concern oneself with.

– WITH ADVERBS IN SPECIALIZED SENSES: **make away** †(*a*) = ***make away with*** below; (*b*) *arch.* go away suddenly or hastily, make off. **make away with** (*a*) put out of the way; kill; (*b*) remove from its rightful place or ownership; get rid of; dissipate, squander; destroy fraudulently. **make down** (*a*) (chiefly *Scot.*) fold down the sheets etc. on (a bed) to make it ready for use; (*b*) *colloq.* refashion so as to fit a smaller wearer. **make in** go in towards a particular point; intervene in an action; join in a fray. **make off** (*a*) fatten (lambs etc.) for the market; (*b*) depart or leave a place suddenly or hastily, run away, decamp (*with* something in one's possession). **make on** (*a*) *dial.* put together and set alight materials for (a fire); (*b*) go or hasten forward, proceed. **make out** (*a*) draw up (a list, a document, etc.); make a draft of; write out (a bill, cheque, etc., *to* or *in favour of* a person); (*b*) succeed in accomplishing, effect, achieve, (now *Scot.*); ***make it out*** (*slang*), achieve sexual intercourse (*with*); (*c*) *colloq.* manage, make shift, (*to do*), get along, fare, succeed, thrive, get on (well, badly, etc.); *slang* achieve sexual intercourse (*with*); †(*d*) compensate for (a defect etc.); supply the lack or the deficiencies of; (*e*) make complete; get together with difficulty or by degrees; †(*f*) fill up or while away (the time) with some occupation; (*g*) (now only in ART) represent or delineate clearly or in detail; (*h*) establish by evidence, argument, or investigation; demonstrate, prove; claim to have proved, try to prove (a thing, a thing to be, *that*); represent *as*, pretend *to be*; (*i*) find out the meaning of; arrive at an understanding of; decipher; succeed in reading; understand the character or behaviour of (a person); (*j*) discern, discover, find out; distinguish by sight or hearing; (*k*) (now only *dial.*) start, set out, sally forth; get away, escape. **make over** (*a*) hand over (by a formal agreement); transfer the possession of (a thing) from oneself *to* another; (*b*) remake, refashion (a garment etc.); refurbish, reorganize. **make up** †(*a*) erect; build up (a bank etc.); (*b*) serve or act to overcome or supply (a deficiency); make complete; raise (a sum) *to* a larger sum; make good, compensate for; ***make it up to***, compensate (a person *for*); also, compensate *for*, atone *for*; (*c*) (now chiefly *dial.*) fill up (an opening or gap); stop up (a hole or passage); shut or fasten up (a door, a house); (*d*) wrap up (an article); put together into a parcel or package; (*e*) put together, construct, compound, by combination of parts or ingredients; sew together the parts of (a garment etc.), fit together (pieces of material) to form a garment etc., make (cloth) into clothing; get together, collect (a company, a sum of money), provide by contributions from different sources; TYPOGRAPHY arrange into columns or pages; add fuel to (a fire) to keep it burning; also, admit of being made up into a garment etc.; (*f*) compose, compile, draw up (a list, document, etc.); concoct, invent, fabricate (a story, a lie); compose (verses etc.) impromptu, improvise; (*g*) (of component parts) constitute or compose (a whole, (now *rare*) a total), (freq. in *pass.*, foll. by *of* the parts); (*h*) prepare (a person, esp. oneself) for a theatrical performance or other public appearance by means of an appropriate costume, false hair, cosmetics, etc., apply cosmetics to (the face, a facial feature), (chiefly *refl.* or in *pass.*); (now *US*) get (a horse etc.) into good condition for selling; fatten; put in order (a bed, a room, etc.) for a particular occasion; (*i*) set out the items of (an account) in order; add up and balance (an account); (*j*) ***make up one's mind***, come to a decision or conclusion, resolve, (*that, to do*); (*k*) arrange (a marriage etc.), conclude (a treaty); settle (a dispute etc.), end (a quarrel) by reconciliation (freq. ***make it up***); also, be reconciled after a dispute or quarrel, become friends

M

again (also in ***kiss and make up***); (**l**) advance in a certain direction; now only foll. by *to*: draw near to, approach, make advances to (a person), court, curry favour with.

makeable *adjective* var. of MAKABLE.

make-and-break /ˈmeɪk(ə)ndˈbreɪk/ *adjective & noun.* M19.
[ORIGIN from MAKE *verb* + AND *conjunction*[1] + BREAK *verb* (sc. *contact*).]
▸ **A** *adjective.* That alternately makes and breaks electrical contact. M19.
▸ **B** *noun.* **1** The alternate making and breaking of electrical contact. E20.
2 An apparatus for automatically making and breaking electrical contact. E20.

makebate /ˈmeɪkbeɪt/ *noun. arch.* E16.
[ORIGIN from MAKE *verb* + BATE *noun*[1].]
A person who or (occas.) thing which creates contention or discord; a fomenter of strife.

make-belief /ˈmeɪkbɪliːf/ *noun.* M19.
[ORIGIN from MAKE *verb* + BELIEF *noun*.]
Make-believe.

make-believe /ˈmeɪkbɪliːv/ *noun & adjective.* L18.
[ORIGIN from ***make believe*** s.v. MAKE *verb*.]
▸ **A** *noun.* **1** The action of making believe; pretence. L18.
†**2** A person who makes believe or pretends. *rare.* Only in M19.
▸ **B** *adjective.* Of the nature of make-believe, pretended. E19.

Philadelphia Inquirer They polish reading, writing and math skills by running a make-believe record label.

make-do /meɪkˈduː/ *noun & adjective.* L19.
[ORIGIN from ***make do*** s.v. MAKE *verb*.]
▸ **A** *noun.* Pl. **-dos**, **-do's**. A makeshift; a temporary expedient. Also ***make-do-and-mend***. L19.
▸ **B** *adjective.* Characterized by makeshift methods. E20.

†**make-game** *noun.* M18–E19.
[ORIGIN from ***make game (of)*** s.v. GAME *noun*.]
A source of amusement; a laughing stock.

make-hawk /ˈmeɪkhɔːk/ *noun.* L16.
[ORIGIN from MAKE *verb* + HAWK *noun*[1].]
FALCONRY. A hawk employed to teach young ones.

makeless /ˈmeɪklɪs/ *adjective. obsolete* exc. *dial.* ME.
[ORIGIN from MAKE *noun*[1] + -LESS.]
1 Without an equal; matchless, peerless. ME.
M **2** Without a mate; wifeless, husbandless, widowed. LME.

makeover /ˈmeɪkəʊvə/ *noun.* Orig. *N. Amer.* E20.
[ORIGIN from ***make over*** s.v. MAKE *verb*.]
A reorganization, a reshaping; *esp.* (***a***) a thorough refashioning of a person's appearance by beauty treatment; (***b***) a deliberate alteration of the public image of an organization.

Cosmopolitan My makeover starts from scratch and covers everything from skincare to make-up. *Daily Telegraph* Girobank . . is to lose its famous but dated name in a branding makeover.

make-peace /ˈmeɪkpiːs/ *noun & adjective. arch.* E16.
[ORIGIN from ***make peace*** s.v. PEACE *noun*.]
(That is) a peacemaker.

maker /ˈmeɪkə/ *noun.* See also MAKAR. ME.
[ORIGIN from MAKE *verb* + -ER[1].]
1 A person who makes something; a creator or producer (*of*). ME.

AV *Isa.* 45:16 They shall goe to confusion together that are makers of idoles. I. MURDOCH The maker and breaker of many a film career. A. BRIEN Recorders of trivia can become makers of history. *Which?* No guarantee that the name of a maker is a . . guide to the car's . . origin.

clockmaker, ***mapmaker***, ***shoemaker***, etc. **one's Maker**, **the Maker** God (***meet one's Maker***, die).

2 A poet. Cf. MAKAR. *arch.* LME.
3 ***maker-up***, a person who makes something or someone up; *esp.* a person who makes up garments. M16.

makeready /ˈmeɪkrɛdi/ *noun.* M19.
[ORIGIN from ***make ready*** s.v. READY *adjective*.]
1 A position of being ready to fire a gun etc. M19.
2 PRINTING. The final preparation and adjustment for printing; material used in making ready; a sheet on which overlays are pasted for printing a particular forme of type. L19.

makeshift /ˈmeɪkʃɪft/ *noun & adjective.* M16.
[ORIGIN from ***make shift*** s.v. SHIFT *noun*.]
▸ **A** *noun.* †**1** A deceitful or dishonest person. M16–M19.
2 A temporary substitute, esp. of an inferior kind, an expedient. E19.

C. LAMB The cottage was a sorry antediluvian make-shift of a building. A. WEST Quinbury wouldn't do, even as a temporary makeshift.

3 The action of making shift; the state of being a temporary substitute, expediency. L19.

J. GALSWORTHY His marriage with herself but domestic makeshift. D. WELCH The air of poverty and makeshift which hangs round expensive private schools in England.

▸ **B** *adjective.* †**1** Deceitful, dishonest. Only in L16.
2 Of the nature of a makeshift, serving as a temporary substitute, esp. of an inferior kind; formed haphazardly; characterized by makeshifts. L17.

W. S. CHURCHILL A makeshift administration . . struggled ineptly with the situation. F. ASTAIRE There were makeshift repairs with temporary fences and holes covered over with boards. H. CARPENTER Temporary offices . . had been found . . and things were very makeshift there. G. LORD She'd made a makeshift stretcher out of the blanket.

■ **makeshifty** *adjective* M19.

make-up /ˈmeɪkʌp/ *noun.* E19.
[ORIGIN from ***make up*** s.v. MAKE *verb*.]
1 The manner in which something is made up, put together, or composed; composition, constitution; a person's character or temperament. E19.

H. SPENCER Something in the pattern or make-up of their clothes. J. ARCHER Roy Jenkins had announced the make-up of his shadow team.

2 a An appearance of face, dress, etc., adopted for a theatrical performance or other public appearance; the action or process of making up with cosmetics etc. M19. ▸**b** Cosmetics (as lipstick, powder, etc.) used in making up the face etc. L19. ▸**c** In a television studio, on a film set, etc.: the place where performers etc. are made up; (the work of) the people who make up performers etc. *colloq.* M20.

a GEO. ELIOT The Zouaves, with their wondrous make-ups as women. **b** R. JARRELL Her lips were painted a purplish maroon; she had put on no other make-up.

3 PRINTING. The arrangement of text and other matter on a printed page; matter so made up; (preparation of) the layout of a page. Also, an editor's selection of articles to form a number of a periodical. M19.
4 A made-up story; an invention, a fiction. M19.

N. MARSH I'm quite sure it's all a make-up. They think it's true.

5 Something (esp. food) made up from odds and ends. *colloq. & dial.* M19.
6 Replacement of water lost from a boiler etc. by evaporation, leakage, etc.; water added for this purpose. M20.
7 The adding up and balancing of accounts at the end of a certain period. M20.
8 A resit. *US.* M20.

makeweight /ˈmeɪkweɪt/ *noun.* Also **make-weight**. L17.
[ORIGIN from MAKE *verb* + WEIGHT *noun*.]
1 A comparatively small quantity added to make up a certain weight. Formerly *spec.*, a small candle. L17.
2 *fig.* A person or thing of insignificant value thrown in to make up a deficiency or fill a gap. L18.
3 A counterbalancing weight, a counterpoise. L18.

make-work /ˈmeɪkwəːk/ *noun.* Orig. *US.* E20.
[ORIGIN from MAKE *verb* + WORK *noun*.]
Work or activity of little or no value devised mainly to keep someone busy.

makhani /məˈkɑːni/ *adjective.* L20.
[ORIGIN Hindi, from *makkhan* butter.]
Designating an Indian dish cooked in a rich sauce made with butter or ghee, onions, tomatoes, and cream. Usu. *postpositive*.

Makhzan /ˈmɑːgz(ə)n, *foreign* ˈmɑːx-/ *noun.* Also **Maghzen**. M19.
[ORIGIN Arabic *makzan*, *-in* treasury (see MAGAZINE *noun*).]
1 *hist.* A body of Algerian horsemen in the service of France. M19.
2 (The seat of) the Moroccan government; the dominant official class in Morocco. L19.

maki *noun* see MAKI ZUSHI.

makimono /makiˈmoːno, makɪˈməʊnəʊ/ *noun.* Pl. same, **-os**. L19.
[ORIGIN Japanese, from *maki* roll up + *mono* thing.]
A Japanese scroll containing a narrative, usu. in pictures with explanatory writing, designed to be examined progressively from right to left as it is unrolled. Cf. EMAKIMONO.

making /ˈmeɪkɪŋ/ *noun.* OE.
[ORIGIN from MAKE *verb* + -ING[1].]
1 The action of MAKE *verb*; production, preparation, appointment, doing, performance (of a specified action), conversion into something. Freq. with possess., attributing responsibility to a specified agent. Also ***making-up*** etc. OE.

CARLYLE Any making-up of his mind. TENNYSON Since the making of the world. *Conservation News* Mutual sacrifice and making do . . outweigh the hardships and problems. V. S. NAIPAUL I was involved in the slow making of this story. A. N. WILSON A spiritual wilderness of his own making.

bookmaking, ***haymaking***, ***merry-making***, etc.

†**2** Poetical composition; versifying. Also in *pl.*, poetical compositions, poems. ME–E17.
3 Something that has been made; a product of manufacture; (formerly) a creature. Also, the quantity made at one time. ME. ▸**b** In *pl.* Earnings, profits. *colloq.* M19.
4 Advancement, success. Now only in ***be the making of***, be what ensures the success or favourable development of. LME.
†**5** The way in which a thing or person is made; conformation, form, shape, build. LME–M17.
6 The material out of which something may be made; the potentiality of becoming something. Chiefly in ***have the makings (of)***, ***be the makings (of)***. E17. ▸**b** In *pl.* The materials or ingredients for making something; *spec.* paper and tobacco for rolling a cigarette. *N. Amer., Austral., & NZ colloq.* L19.

D. FRANCIS He's too young really. But he's got the makings. A. WEST She obviously had the makings of a successful writer. A. PRICE He's a good copper. With the makings of a very good one.

– PHRASES: ***be the making of***: see sense 4 above. **in the making** *postpositive adjectival phr.* in the course of being developed or formed.

making /ˈmeɪkɪŋ/ *ppl adjective.* LME.
[ORIGIN from MAKE *verb* + -ING[2].]
That makes something or someone. Now chiefly as 2nd elem. of comb., as ***sick-making***.

maki zushi /ˌmaki ˈzuːʃi/ *noun phr.* Also **maki**. E20.
[ORIGIN from Japanese *maki-* (combining stem of *maku* roll up) + *-zushi* SUSHI.]
A Japanese dish consisting of sushi and raw vegetables wrapped in a sheet of seaweed.

mako /ˈmɑːkəʊ/ *noun*[1]. Pl. same, **-os**. M19.
[ORIGIN Maori.]
In full ***mako shark***. A large blue mackerel shark, *Isurus oxyrinchus*, of tropical and temperate oceans worldwide. Also called ***blue pointer***.

mako /ˈmɑːkəʊ/ *noun*[2]. *NZ.* Also **makomako** /ˌmɑːkəʊˈmɑːkəʊ/. Pl. same, **-os**. M19.
[ORIGIN Maori.]
A small New Zealand tree, *Aristotelia serrata* (family Elaeocarpaceae), bearing clusters of small pink flowers and dark red berries.

Makololo /makəˈləʊləʊ/ *noun & adjective.* M19.
[ORIGIN Bantu.]
▸ **A** *noun.* Pl. same, **-os**. A member of an African people now living in Zambia near the junction of the Zambezi and Kafue rivers. M19.
▸ **B** *adjective.* Of or pertaining to this people. M19.

makomako /mɑːkəʊˈmɑːkəʊ/ *noun*[1]. *NZ.* Pl. same, **-os**. M19.
[ORIGIN Maori.]
= KORIMAKO.

makomako *noun*[2] var. of MAKO *noun*[2].

Makonde /məˈkəʊndi/ *noun & adjective.* L19.
[ORIGIN Bantu.]
▸ **A** *noun.* Pl. same, **-s**. A member of a people inhabiting the border area of Tanzania and Mozambique; the Bantu language of this people. L19.
▸ **B** *adjective.* Of or pertaining to this people or their language. L19.

makoré /makəˈreɪ/ *noun.* E20.
[ORIGIN App. W. African.]
A large W. African tree, *Tieghemella heckelii* (family Sapotaceae); the dark red-brown wood of this tree.

makuta *noun* pl. of LIKUTA.

makutu /məˈkuːtuː/ *verb & noun. NZ.* E19.
[ORIGIN Maori.]
▸ **A** *verb trans.* Put a spell on, bewitch. *rare.* E19.
▸ **B** *noun.* Sorcery, witchcraft; a magic spell. M19.

mal- /mal/ *prefix.* Also †**male-**.
[ORIGIN French *mal* adverb from Latin *male* ill, badly, or (occas.) Old French *mal* adjective from Latin *malus* bad.]
In senses 'bad(ly), wrong(ly), improper(ly)', as ***malformation***, ***malodorous***, ***malpractice***, ***maltreat***, and 'not', as ***maladroit***, ***malcontent***.

Mal. *abbreviation.*
Malachi (in the Bible).

Malabar /ˈmaləbɑː/ *noun & adjective.* L16.
[ORIGIN A coastal district of SW India.]
▸ **A** *noun.* Chiefly *hist.*
1 A native or inhabitant of the Malabar coast, SW India. Also, a Tamil. L16.
2 The language of the Malabar coast, Malayalam. Also, Tamil. E19.
3 A brightly coloured cotton handkerchief. L19.
▸ **B** *attrib.* or as *adjective.* Of or pertaining to the Malabar coast; Tamil. M17.
Malabar nightshade: see NIGHTSHADE. **Malabar plum** (the fruit of) the rose apple, *Syzygium jambos*. **Malabar spinach** = ***Malabar nightshade*** s.v. NIGHTSHADE.
■ **Malabaric** /maləˈbɑːrɪk/ *adjective & noun* (now *rare*) (**a**) *adjective* = MALABAR *adjective*; (**b**) *noun* = MALABAR *noun* 2: L17.

malabathrum /maləˈbaθrəm/ *noun.* M16.
[ORIGIN Latin *malabathrum*, *malo-*, *-on* from Greek *malabathron*, *malo-* from Sanskrit *tamālapattram* cinnamon leaf, from *tamāla* a kind of tree + *pattra* leaf, feather.]
hist. (A perfumed ointment prepared from) an aromatic leaf mentioned by ancient writers.

malabsorption /maləb'zɔːpʃ(ə)n/ *noun*. **M20**.
[ORIGIN from MAL- + ABSORPTION.]
MEDICINE. Imperfect absorption of nutrients from the intestines.

Malacca /mə'lakə/ *noun*. **L16**.
[ORIGIN A town and district on the Malay peninsula, SE Asia.]
1 Used *attrib.* to designate things, esp. plants and vegetable products, found in or obtained from Malacca. **L16**.
Malacca cane a walking cane of a rich brown colour, often clouded or mottled, usu. made from a stem of the palm *Calamus scipionum*.
2 *ellipt.* A Malacca cane. **L19**.

malachite /'maləkʌɪt/ *noun & adjective*. **LME**.
[ORIGIN Old French *melochite* (mod. *malachite*) from Latin *molochites* from Greek *molokhitis*, from *molokhē* var. of *malakhē* MALLOW.]
▸ **A** *noun*. **1** A monoclinic basic copper carbonate, usu. occurring as bright-green masses or fibrous aggregates, which is used ornamentally and as an ore of copper. **LME**.
2 A bright green colour like that of malachite. **E20**.
▸ **B** *attrib.* or as *adjective*. Made of or resembling malachite; of the colour of malachite, bright green. **E20**.
– SPECIAL COLLOCATIONS & COMB.: **malachite-green** (**a**) a dye of the colour of malachite; (**b**) = sense A.2 above. **malachite kingfisher** a small blue, green, and red kingfisher, *Alcedo cristata*, found in sub-Saharan Africa.

malacia /mə'leɪʃə/ *noun*. *rare*. **M17**.
[ORIGIN Latin = Greek *malakia* softness, from *malakos* soft.]
MEDICINE. **1** Abnormal craving for particular kinds of food. Now *rare* or *obsolete*. **M17**.
2 Abnormal softening of a tissue or part. **E18**.

malaco- /'maləkəʊ/ *combining form* of Greek *malakos* soft: see **-O-**.
■ **malacopterygian** /ˌmaləkɒptə'rɪdʒɪən/ *adjective & noun* [Greek *pterugion* fin, dim. of *pterux* wing] (ICHTHYOLOGY) (designating) a soft-finned fish, i.e. a bony fish that is not an acanthopterygian **M19**.

malacology /malə'kɒlədʒi/ *noun*. **M19**.
[ORIGIN from MALACO- + -LOGY.]
The branch of zoology that deals with molluscs.
■ **malaco'logical** *adjective* **L19**. **malacologist** *noun* **M19**.

malacon /'malək(ə)n/ *noun*. **M19**.
[ORIGIN German *Malakon* from Greek *malakon* neut. of *malakos* soft.]
MINERALOGY. A soft brown altered form of zircon.

malacostracan /malə'kɒstrək(ə)n/ *noun & adjective*. **M19**.
[ORIGIN from mod. Latin *Malacostraca* (see below), Greek *malakostraka*, from *malakos* soft + *ostrakon* shell: see -AN.]
▸ **A** *noun*. Any crustacean of the class Malacostraca, which includes shrimps, crabs, lobsters, isopods, and amphipods. **M19**.
▸ **B** *adjective*. Of or pertaining to the class Malacostraca. **M19**.
■ **malacostracous** *adjective* = MALACOSTRACAN *adjective* **M19**.

†**malactic** *adjective & noun*. **M16**.
[ORIGIN Greek *malaktikos*, from *malak-* stem of *malassein* soften: see -IC.]
▸ **A** *adjective*. Adapted to soften; emollient. **M16–L19**.
▸ **B** *noun*. An emollient medicine. **M–L17**.

maladaptation /ˌmaladap'teɪʃ(ə)n/ *noun*. **L19**.
[ORIGIN from MAL- + ADAPTATION.]
Faulty or imperfect adaptation; an instance of this.
■ **mala'dapted** *adjective* **E20**.

maladaptive /malə'daptɪv/ *adjective*. **M20**.
[ORIGIN from MAL- + ADAPTIVE.]
Faultily or imperfectly adaptive; not characterized by or given to adaptation.
■ **maladaptively** *adverb* **M20**.

malade imaginaire /malad imaʒinɛːr/ *noun phr*. Pl. **-s -s** (pronounced same). **E18**.
[ORIGIN French, after the title of a play by Molière (1673).]
A person with an imaginary illness.

maladif /maladif/ *adjective*. **L15**.
[ORIGIN French, from *malade* (see MALADY) + *-if* -IVE.]
= MALADIVE.

maladive /'malədɪv/ *adjective*. **E17**.
[ORIGIN formed as MALADIF.]
Of, pertaining to, or affected with sickness, sickly. Cf. MALADIF.

maladjusted /malə'dʒʌstɪd/ *adjective*. **L19**.
[ORIGIN from MAL- + *adjusted* pa. pple of ADJUST.]
Inadequately adjusted; exhibiting or characterized by psychological maladjustment.

maladjustment /malə'dʒʌs(t)m(ə)nt/ *noun*. **M19**.
[ORIGIN from MAL- + ADJUSTMENT.]
Faulty or imperfect adjustment; *spec.* unsuccessful or unsatisfactory adaptation to one's social environment; an instance of this.

maladminister /maləd'mɪnɪstə/ *verb trans*. **M17**.
[ORIGIN from MAL- + ADMINISTER.]
Administer, execute, or manage inefficiently or badly.

maladministration /ˌmalədmɪnɪ'streɪʃ(ə)n/ *noun*. **M17**.
[ORIGIN from MAL- + ADMINISTRATION.]
Faulty or imperfect administration; inefficient or improper management of (esp. public) affairs.
■ **maladministrator** *noun* a person who is guilty of maladministration **M19**.

maladresse /maladrɛs, malə'drɛs/ *noun*. **E19**.
[ORIGIN French, formed as MALADROIT after *adroit*, *adresse*.]
Lack of dexterity or tact; awkwardness.

maladroit /'malədrɔɪt/ *adjective*. **L17**.
[ORIGIN French, formed as MAL- + ADROIT.]
Lacking in adroitness or dexterity; awkward, bungling, clumsy.

F. WYNDHAM The self-consciousness which made her so socially maladroit. *Sunday Express* His maladroit fumbling had been honed to a streamlined accuracy.

■ **maladroitly** *adverb* **L17**. **maladroitness** *noun* **L18**.

†**maladventure** *noun*. **LME–E19**.
[ORIGIN from MAL- + ADVENTURE *noun*.]
A lawless proceeding, an escapade; an unlucky undertaking, a misadventure, misfortune.

malady /'malədi/ *noun*. **ME**.
[ORIGIN Old French & mod. French *maladie*, from *malade* sick, ill, from Proto-Romance, from Latin *male* badly + *habitus* pa. pple of *habere* have, hold.]
1 An ailment, a disease. Formerly also, ill health, disease. **ME**.

D. JACOBSON He was suffering from a malady neither he nor his doctors could explain. ANTHONY SMITH It is not known . . how the malady should be managed.

2 *fig.* A bad quality, habit, or disposition; a condition that calls for a remedy. **LME**.

CARLYLE Our spiritual maladies are but of Opinion.

mala fide /meɪlə 'fʌɪdiː, malə 'fiːdeɪ/ *adverbial & adjectival phr*. **E17**.
[ORIGIN Latin = with bad faith (abl. of MALA FIDES).]
(Acting or done) in bad faith; insincere(ly), not genuine(ly).

mala fides /meɪlə 'fʌɪdiːz, malə 'fiːdeɪz/ *noun phr*. **L17**.
[ORIGIN Latin = bad faith.]
Chiefly *LAW*. Bad faith, intent to deceive.

Malaga /'maləgə/ *noun*. **E17**.
[ORIGIN *Málaga* (see below).]
A white or (now usu.) red fortified wine from Málaga, a seaport in southern Spain. Also ***Malaga wine***.

malagas /malə'gas/ *noun*. *S. Afr.* Also **malgas** /mal'gas, *foreign* -x-/. **M18**.
[ORIGIN Dutch *mallegas* from Portuguese *mangas(-de-velludo)* lit. 'velvet sleeves', the wandering albatross.]
The Cape gannet, *Morus capensis*.

Malagash /'maləgaʃ/ *noun & adjective*. Now *rare* or *obsolete*. **E18**.
[ORIGIN formed as MALAGASY. Cf. MADAGASS.]
▸ **A** *noun*. Pl. same, **-es**. A native or inhabitant of Madagascar. **E18**.
▸ **B** *adjective*. Of or pertaining to Madagascar. **L18**.

Malagasy /malə'gasi/ *adjective & noun*. **M19**.
[ORIGIN Var. of MADAGASCAR. Cf. MADAGASCAN.]
▸ **A** *adjective*. Of or pertaining to Madagascar, its inhabitants, or its language. **M19**.
▸ **B** *noun*. Pl. **-sies**, same.
1 A native or inhabitant of Madagascar. **M19**.
2 The Austronesian language of Madagascar. **M19**.

†**malagma** *noun*. Pl. **-gmata**. **M16–E19**.
[ORIGIN Late Latin from Greek, from *malassein* assuage.]
MEDICINE. An emollient plaster.

Malagueña /malə'geɪnjə/ *noun*. In sense 2 also **m-**. **M19**.
[ORIGIN Spanish, formed as MALAGA.]
1 A woman or girl of Málaga in S. Spain. **M19**.
2 A Spanish dance resembling the fandango. Also, an emotional Spanish Gypsy song. **L19**.

malagueta /malə'gɛtə/ *noun*. Also **-tta**, **melegueta**. **M16**.
[ORIGIN French *maniguette*, †*-guete* alt. of *malaguette* from Spanish *malagueta*: cf. medieval Latin *melegeta*, perh. dim. of Italian *melica* millet.]
= ***grains of Paradise*** s.v. GRAIN *noun*[1] 3a.

mala in se *noun phr*. pl. of MALUM IN SE.

malaise /ma'leɪz/ *noun*. **M18**.
[ORIGIN French, from Old French *mal* bad, ill (from Latin *malus*) + *aise* EASE *noun*. Cf. earlier MALEASE.]
A condition of bodily discomfort, *esp.* one without the development of specific disease; a feeling of uneasiness.

J. HERSEY Suddenly ill with a general malaise, weariness, and feverishness. R. ELLMANN His spiritual malaise which involved anxiety over his future.

malalignment /malə'lʌɪnm(ə)nt/ *noun*. **M20**.
[ORIGIN from MAL- + ALIGNMENT.]
Misalignment; an instance of this.

malambo /mə'lambəʊ/ *noun*. **E19**.
[ORIGIN Amer. Spanish, perh. of African origin.]
The aromatic bark of *Croton malambo*, a shrub (family Euphorbiaceae) of northern S. America, used in medicine and perfumery. Also ***malambo bark***.

malamute /'maləmjuːt/ *noun*. Also **male-**. **M19**.
[ORIGIN Inupiaq (Inuit) *malimiut*, a people of the Kolzebue Sound, Alaska, who developed the breed.]
(A dog of) a spitz breed developed in Alaska, with a thick grey or black and white coat, pointed ears, and a plumed tail curling over the back.

malander(s) *nouns* see MALLENDERS.

malanga /mə'laŋgə/ *noun*. **M19**.
[ORIGIN Amer. Spanish, prob. from Kikongo, pl. of *elanga* water lily.]
Any of several plants grown in the Caribbean and in Central and S. America for their edible tubers.

malapert /'maləpəːt/ *adjective & noun*. *arch*. **ME**.
[ORIGIN Old French, from *mal-* (indicating the opposite) + *apert* var. of *espert* EXPERT *adjective*, but taken as if from MAL- improperly + *apert* bold, pert.]
(A person who is) presumptuous or impudent.
■ **malapertly** *adverb* **LME**. **malapertness** *noun* **LME**.

malapportionment /malə'pɔːʃ(ə)nm(ə)nt/ *noun*. Chiefly *US*. **M20**.
[ORIGIN from MAL- + APPORTIONMENT.]
Bad or inequitable apportionment, *spec.* of representation in a political assembly.
■ **malapportioned** *adjective* **M20**.

malappropriate /malə'prəʊprɪət/ *adjective*. **M19**.
[ORIGIN from MAL- + APPROPRIATE *adjective*.]
Ill-suited, inappropriate.

malappropriate /malə'prəʊprɪeɪt/ *verb trans*. **M19**.
[ORIGIN from MAL- + APPROPRIATE *verb*.]
Misapply.
■ **malappropri'ation** *noun* **M19**.

mala praxis /meɪlə 'praksɪs/ *noun phr*. **M18**.
[ORIGIN mod. Latin, from Latin *mala* fem. of *malus* bad + PRAXIS. Cf. MALPRAXIS.]
LAW. Medical malpractice.

malaprop /'maləprɒp/ *noun & adjective*. **E19**.
[ORIGIN from Mrs *Malaprop* (after MALAPROPOS) in Sheridan's play *The Rivals* (1775).]
▸ **A** *noun*. = MALAPROPISM. **E19**.
▸ **B** *adjective*. = MALAPROPIAN. **E19**.

malapropian /malə'prɒpɪən, -'prəʊpɪən/ *adjective*. **M19**.
[ORIGIN from (the same root as) MALAPROP + -IAN.]
Of the nature of a malapropism; given to malapropisms.

malapropism /'maləprɒpɪz(ə)m/ *noun*. **M19**.
[ORIGIN formed as MALAPROPIAN + -ISM.]
Ludicrous misuse of words, esp. in mistaking a word for another resembling it; an instance of this.
■ **malapro'pistic** *adjective* of the nature of a malapropism **L20**.

malapropos /ˌmalaprə'pəʊ/ *adverb, adjective, & noun*. Also **mal-à-propos** & other vars. **M17**.
[ORIGIN French *mal à propos*, from *mal* ill + *à* to + *propos* purpose: see MAL-, APROPOS.]
▸ **A** *adverb*. In an inopportune or awkward manner; at an inopportune or awkward time; inappropriately. **M17**.
▸ **B** *adjective*. Inopportune, inappropriate. **E18**.
▸ **C** *noun*. Pl. same. An inopportune or inappropriate thing. **M19**.

malar /'meɪlə/ *adjective & noun*. **L18**.
[ORIGIN mod. Latin *malaris*, from Latin *mala* jaw, cheekbone: see -AR[1].]
ANATOMY. ▸ **A** *adjective*. Of or pertaining to the cheek. **L18**.
▸ **B** *noun*. = ***cheekbone*** (a) s.v. CHEEK *noun*. **M19**.

malaria /mə'lɛːrɪə/ *noun*. **M18**.
[ORIGIN Italian *mal' aria* = *mala aria* bad air.]
Orig., an unwholesome condition of the atmosphere in hot countries due to the exhalations of marshes, to which fevers were ascribed. Now (also ***malaria fever***), any of a class of intermittent and remittent febrile diseases formerly supposed to result from this cause, but now known to be due to infection with parasitic protozoans of the genus *Plasmodium*, transmitted by the bite of a mosquito of the genus *Anopheles*.

fig.: T. C. GRATTAN A sort of moral malaria pervading society and carrying off many victims.

quartan malaria: see QUARTAN *adjective*. ***tertian malaria***: see TERTIAN *adjective* 1.
– COMB.: ***malaria fever***: see above; **malaria parasite** a parasitic protozoan of the genus *Plasmodium*, causing malaria.

malarial /mə'lɛːrɪəl/ *adjective*. **M19**.
[ORIGIN from MALARIA + -AL[1].]
1 Infected with malaria; infested with malaria-bearing mosquitoes. **M19**.
2 Of, pertaining to, or of the nature of malaria. **M19**.
■ **malarian** *adjective* pertaining to or causing malaria; malarial: **M19**.

malariology /məlɛːrɪ'ɒlədʒi/ *noun*. **E20**.
[ORIGIN from MALARIA + -OLOGY.]
The scientific study of malaria.
■ **malariologist** *noun* **E20**.

malarious /mə'lɛːrɪəs/ *adjective*. **M19**.
[ORIGIN from MALARIA + -OUS.]
= MALARIAL.

M

malarkey /mə'lɑːki/ *noun. slang.* E20.
[ORIGIN Unknown.]
Humbug, nonsense, foolishness.

malarrangement /malə'reɪn(d)ʒm(ə)nt/ *noun.* M19.
[ORIGIN from MAL- + ARRANGEMENT.]
Faulty or imperfect arrangement.

malassimilation /ˌmalәsɪmɪ'leɪʃ(ə)n/ *noun.* M19.
[ORIGIN from MAL- + ASSIMILATION.]
Imperfect assimilation; *esp.* (MEDICINE) = MALABSORPTION.

malate /'meɪleɪt/ *noun.* L18.
[ORIGIN from MALIC + -ATE[1].]
CHEMISTRY. A salt or ester of malic acid.

malathion /malə'θʌɪən/ *noun.* M20.
[ORIGIN from MAL(EATE + -*a*- + THIO- + -*on*.]
An organophosphorus insecticide, with relatively low toxicity to plants and animals.

Malawi /mə'lɑːwi/ *adjective & noun.* M20.
[ORIGIN See below.]
(A native or inhabitant) of Malawi, a country in south central Africa (formerly Nyasaland).
■ **Malawian** *noun & adjective* M20.

†**malax** *verb trans.* LME.
[ORIGIN Latin *malaxare*: see MALAXATE.]
1 Rub or knead (a plaster etc.) to softness. LME–M18.
2 Of a material agent: soften. M17–M18.

malaxate /'malәkseɪt/ *verb trans.* M17.
[ORIGIN Latin *malaxat-* pa. ppl stem of *malaxare* from Greek *malassein* make soft: see -ATE[3].]
Knead to softness; make soft by mixing or rubbing.
■ **mala'xation** *noun* the action of reducing to a soft mass by kneading or rolling; a form of kneading in massage: M17.

Malay /mə'leɪ/ *noun & adjective.* L16.
[ORIGIN Malay †*Malayu* (now *Me-*).]
▸ **A** *noun.* **1** **a** A member of a people inhabiting Malaysia, Brunei, parts of Indonesia, and other areas. L16. ▸**b** In South Africa, a member of the Muslim community of Cape Town and adjoining districts (chiefly descendants of slaves and immigrants from Malaysia etc.). Also ***Cape Malay***. M18.
2 The Austronesian language of the Malays of Malaysia etc., the official language of the Federation of Malaysia. L16.
3 *ellipt.* A Malay fowl. E19.
▸ **B** *adjective.* **1** Of, pertaining to, or characteristic of the Malays or parts of Malaysia and Indonesia inhabited by them. E17.
Malay apple (the edible fruit of) a tree of the myrtle family, *Syzygium malaccense*, native to the Malay peninsula. **Malay fowl** (a bird of) a large variety of domestic fowl introduced from the Malay peninsula. **Malay peninsula** a peninsula of SE Asia, forming (in the south) the continental part of Malaysia and (in the north) part of Thailand. **Malay tapir** = ***Malayan tapir*** s.v. MALAYAN *adjective*.
2 Of, pertaining to, or characteristic of the Cape Malays. E19.
■ **Malayic** *adjective* (*rare*) = MALAY *adjective* 1 E18.

Malayalam /malə'jɑːləm/ *noun & adjective.* E19.
[ORIGIN Malayalam *Malayāḷam*, from *mala* (Tamil *malai*) mountain + *āḷ* person.]
(Of) a Dravidian language, closely related to Tamil, spoken in the state of Kerala and adjacent parts of SW India.

Malayali /malə'jɑːli/ *noun & adjective.* Also (*arch.*) **-lee**. M19.
[ORIGIN Irreg. from MALAYALAM + -I[2].]
A member of, of or pertaining to, a Malayalam-speaking people chiefly inhabiting the state of Kerala in SW India.

Malayan /mə'leɪən/ *noun & adjective.* L16.
[ORIGIN from MALAY or (in sense 1b) *Malaya* + -AN.]
▸ **A** *noun* **1** **a** = MALAY *noun* 1a. L16. ▸**b** During the existence of the Federation of Malaya (from 1948 until 1963), a native or inhabitant of Malaya (regardless of race or creed). M20.
2 = MALAY *noun* 2. Now *rare.* E17.
▸ **B** *adjective.* = MALAY *adjective* 1. Also, of or pertaining to Malaya (see sense A.1b above). L16.
Malayan tapir a black and white tapir, *Tapirus indicus*, native to SE Asia and Sumatra.
■ **Malayani'zation** *noun* the action or process of Malayanizing something, as by introducing Malayan personnel M20. **Malayanize** *verb trans.* make Malayan in character or composition, employ Malayans in M20.

Malayo- /mə'leɪəʊ/ *combining form* of MALAY: see -O-.
■ **Malayo-Polynesian** *adjective & noun* (**a**) *adjective* of or pertaining to the Malays and the Polynesians; *spec.* of or pertaining to the family of agglutinative languages including Malay and Polynesian languages, Austronesian; (**b**) *noun* the Malayo-Polynesian family of languages, Austronesian: M19.

Malaysian /mə'leɪzɪən, -ʒ(ə)n/ *noun & adjective.* E17.
[ORIGIN from *Malaysia* a name for the Malay archipelago, from root of Malay *Melayu* after *Asia* etc.: see -AN.]
▸ **A** *noun.* A native or inhabitant of the Malay archipelago in SE Asia or *spec.* (now) of the Federation of Malaysia (formed in 1963 from the states of Malaya, Sabah, Sarawak, and the now independent state of Singapore). E17.
▸ **B** *adjective.* Of, pertaining to, or characteristic of the Malay archipelago or (now) Malaysia. E17.
■ **Malaysiani'zation** *noun* the action or process of Malaysianizing something, as by introducing Malaysian personnel L20. **Malaysianize** *verb trans.* make Malaysian in character or composition, employ Malaysians in L20.

malaysianite /mə'leɪzɪənʌɪt, -ʒənʌɪt/ *noun.* M20.
[ORIGIN from MALAYSIAN + -ITE[1].]
GEOLOGY. A tektite from the strewn field of the Malay peninsula.

Malbec /'malbɛk, 'mɒlbɛk/ *noun.* M19.
[ORIGIN French *malbec*, *malbeck*, of unknown origin.]
A variety of dark wine grape native to the Bordeaux region of France; a red wine made from this grape.

†**malbehaviour** *noun.* Also †**male-**. E–M18.
[ORIGIN from MAL- + BEHAVIOUR.]
Bad or improper behaviour.

malcoha *noun* var. of MALKOHA.

malconduct /mal'kɒndʌkt/ *noun.* Also †**male-**. L17.
[ORIGIN from MAL- + CONDUCT *noun*[1].]
Improper conduct; *esp.* improper or dishonest administration of a public office, business, etc.

malconformation /ˌmalkɒnfɔ'meɪʃ(ə)n/ *noun.* L18.
[ORIGIN from MAL- + CONFORMATION.]
Faulty or imperfect conformation; an instance of this.

malconstruction /malkən'strʌkʃ(ə)n/ *noun.* E19.
[ORIGIN from MAL- + CONSTRUCTION.]
Faulty or imperfect construction.

malcontent /'malkəntɛnt/ *adjective & noun.* Also †**male-**. L16.
[ORIGIN Old French & mod. French, formed as MAL- + CONTENT *pred. adjective & noun*[3]. In sense B.2 from MAL- + CONTENT *noun*[2].]
▸ **A** *adjective.* Discontented, dissatisfied; inclined to rebellion or mutiny; restless and disaffected. L16.
▸ **B** *noun.* **1** A malcontent person. L16.

> A. N. WILSON There was every reason for Russian dissidents and malcontents to rejoice.

†**2** A state of discontentment. L16–L17.

malcontented /malkən'tɛntɪd/ *adjective.* Now *rare.* Also †**male-**. L16.
[ORIGIN from MAL- + CONTENTED.]
= MALCONTENT *adjective*.

> J. UPDIKE A group of suspect liberals and malcontented expatriates.

■ **malcontentedly** *adverb* M17. **malcontentedness** *noun* L16.

mal de mer /mal də mɛːr/ *noun phr.* L18.
[ORIGIN French.]
Seasickness.

maldescended /maldɪ'sɛndɪd/ *adjective.* E20.
[ORIGIN from MAL- + *descended* pa. pple of DESCEND.]
MEDICINE. Of a testis: not having descended all the way into the scrotum from the abdominal cavity during development of the fetus, or having descended ectopically.
■ **maldescent** *noun* the state of being maldescended; incomplete or ectopic descent of a testis: E20.

maldevelopment /maldɪ'vɛləpm(ə)nt/ *noun.* L19.
[ORIGIN from MAL- + DEVELOPMENT.]
Faulty or imperfect development.

maldistribution /ˌmaldɪstrɪ'bjuːʃ(ə)n/ *noun.* L19.
[ORIGIN from MAL- + DISTRIBUTION.]
Faulty or imperfect distribution.
■ **maldi'stributed** *ppl adjective* M20.

Maldivian /mɒl'dɪvɪən, mɔːl-/ *noun & adjective.* L18.
[ORIGIN from *Maldives* or *Maldive* islands (see below) + -IAN.]
▸ **A** *noun.* A native or inhabitant of the Maldives, a country consisting of a chain of islands in the Indian Ocean; the form of the Sinhalese language used in the Maldives. L18.
▸ **B** *adjective.* Of or pertaining to the Maldives or the Sinhalese language used there. M19.

maldonite /'mɔːld(ə)nʌɪt/ *noun.* M19.
[ORIGIN from *Maldon*, a place in Victoria, Australia + -ITE[1].]
MINERALOGY. A native alloy of gold and bismuth, crystallizing in the cubic system.

mal du pays /mal dy pe(j)i/ *noun phr.* L18.
[ORIGIN French.]
†**1** A country's or region's prevalent illness. *rare.* Only in L18.
2 Homesickness. E19.

mal du siècle /mal dy sjɛkl/ *noun phr.* E20.
[ORIGIN French.]
World-weariness, weariness of life, deep melancholy because of the condition of the world.

male /meɪl/ *adjective & noun.* LME.
[ORIGIN Old French *ma(s)le* (mod. *mâle*) from Latin *masculus*, from *mas* male (person). Cf. MASCULINE.]
▸ **A** *adjective.* **1** Of, pertaining to, or designating the sex which can beget offspring; in organisms which undergo sexual reproduction, designating, pertaining to, or producing gametes (as spermatozoa) that can fertilize female gametes (ova). LME. ▸**b** Of a plant, flower, etc.: bearing stamens but lacking functional pistils. LME.

> W. CRUISE An estate in tail male was vested in Edmund Hicks, as heir male of . . Launcelot Hicks. F. WELDON Men visitors were only allowed . . if they described themselves as close male relatives. R. K. NARAYAN A male tiger hardly ever lives with the family. C. SIMMONS The male nurse arrived with a wheelchair.

2 Of a plant, mineral, or other object: having a colour or other property associated with maleness, esp. as being superior to a corresponding female property etc. Now *rare* exc. in certain collocations (see below). LME.
3 Of, pertaining to, or characteristic of men or boys or male animals or plants. E17.

> C. DARWIN The common drake . . after the breeding season is well known to lose his male plumage. R. WEST Through the thudding of the engines came the sound of Chris' great male voice. *Rage* Concerned with . . male bonding and buddy movies.

4 Composed or consisting of men or boys or of male animals or plants. L17.
5 Of a mechanical instrument etc.: adapted to penetrate or fill a corresponding female part. L18.
▸ **B** *noun.* **1** A male person, animal, or plant; (the member(s) of) the male sex; a man or boy as distinguished from a woman or girl. LME.

> N. TINBERGEN Such an aggressive bird is always a male. D. FRANCIS About two thirds of the best seats in the Members' stands were reserved for males. P. LOMAS The traditional role of the male has not . . included empathetic caring.

†**2** A male precious stone (cf. sense A.2 above). LME–M18.
– SPECIAL COLLOCATIONS & COMB.: **male chauvinism** prejudice against women, inconsiderate treatment of women. **male chauvinist** a man who is prejudiced against or inconsiderate of women (freq. in ***male chauvinist pig***). **male-chauvinistic** *adjective* characteristic of a male chauvinist, of the nature of male chauvinism. **male fern** a common woodland fern, *Dryopteris filix-mas*. **male gauge** the outer gauge or screw of a printing press. **male impersonator** a female performer dressed and acting as a man. †**male incense** a superior quality of incense, frankincense. ***male* MENOPAUSE**. ***male organ***: see ORGAN *noun*[1] 4d. **male pill** a contraceptive pill for men. **male rhyme** = ***masculine rhyme*** s.v. MASCULINE *adjective*. ***male screw***: see SCREW *noun*[1] 1. ***tail male***: see TAIL *noun*[2] 4.
■ **maleness** *noun* M17.

†**male-** *prefix* var. of MAL-.

malease /ma'liːz/ *noun.* ME.
[ORIGIN formed as MALAISE. In mod. use from MAL- + EASE *noun*.]
1 Absence of ease; uneasiness, discomfort; inconvenience, annoyance; distress, trouble. ME.
†**2** Disease, sickness. ME–E16.
– NOTE: Not recorded between E16 and E20.

maleate /mə'liːeɪt/ *noun.* M19.
[ORIGIN from MALEIC + -ATE[1].]
CHEMISTRY. A salt or ester of maleic acid.

†**malebehaviour** *noun* var. of MALBEHAVIOUR.

malebolge /malɪ'bɒldʒeɪ, *foreign* male'boldʒe/ *noun. literary.* M19.
[ORIGIN Italian *Malebolge*, from *male* fem. pl. of *malo* evil + †*bolge* pl. of *bolgia* lit. 'sack, bag', the name given in Dante's *Inferno* to the eighth circle in hell, consisting of ten rock-bound concentric circular trenches, esp. with allus. to Canto xviii.]
A pool of filth; a hellish place or condition.

Malecite *noun & adjective* var. of MALISEET.

†**maleconduct** *noun*, **malecontent** *adjective & noun*, etc., vars. of MALCONDUCT etc.

†**maledicent** *adjective.* L16–M19.
[ORIGIN Latin *maledicent-* pres. ppl stem of *maledicere*: see MALEDICTION, -ENT.]
Given to speaking evil. Of an utterance: slanderous.

†**maledict** *adjective & noun.* ME–M19.
[ORIGIN Latin *maledictus* pa. pple, formed as MALEDICT *verb*.]
(A person who is) accursed.

maledict /'malɪdɪkt/ *verb trans.* E17.
[ORIGIN Latin *maledict-*: see MALEDICTION.]
1 = BACKBITE. *rare.* E17.
2 Address with maledictions, curse, execrate. E18.

malediction /malɪ'dɪkʃ(ə)n/ *noun.* LME.
[ORIGIN Latin *maledictio(n-)*, from *maledict-* pa. ppl stem of *maledicere* speak evil of, from *male* ill, badly + *dicere* say: see -ION. Cf. French *malédiction*.]
1 (The utterance of) a curse; the condition of being under a ban or curse. LME.

> D. MORTMAN Because she knew she would not challenge the law, they ignored her malediction. D. LESSING A certain liberal white farmer (but the word liberal is a malediction) on Liberation called his workforce to him.

2 Reviling, slander; the condition of being reviled or slandered. M16.

maledictive /malɪ'dɪktɪv/ *adjective.* M19.
[ORIGIN from Latin *maledict-* (see MALEDICTION) + -IVE.]
Characterized by cursing or curses; uttering maledictions.

maledictory /malɪˈdɪkt(ə)ri/ *adjective*. E19.
[ORIGIN formed as MALEDICTIVE + -ORY[2].]
Of the nature of or resembling a malediction.

maleducation /ˌmalɛdjʊˈkeɪʃ(ə)n/ *noun*. M19.
[ORIGIN from MAL- + EDUCATION.]
Imperfect or misdirected education.

malefaction /malɪˈfakʃ(ə)n/ *noun*. E17.
[ORIGIN medieval Latin *malefactio(n-)*, from *male facere* do evil (to), after *benefactio(n-)* BENEFACTION; partly from MALEFACTOR: see -FACTION.]
(An instance of) evildoing, a criminal act.

malefactor /ˈmalɪfaktə/ *noun*. LME.
[ORIGIN Latin, from *male facere*: see MALEFACTION, -OR. Partly through Old French *malfaicteur*.]
1 A person guilty of a heinous offence against the law; a felon, a criminal. LME.
2 An evildoer; a person who behaves badly or wickedly towards another. LME.
■ **malefactress** *noun* a female malefactor M17.

maleffect /malɪˈfɛkt/ *noun*. *rare*. L17.
[ORIGIN from MAL- + EFFECT *noun*.]
A bad or harmful effect.

malefic /məˈlɛfɪk/ *adjective*. M17.
[ORIGIN Latin *maleficus*, from *male* ill, badly: see -FIC.]
Esp. of a stellar influence or magical art or practice: productive of disaster or evil, harmful; baleful in effect or purpose.
■ †**malefical** *adjective* (*rare*) E–M17. **malefically** *adverb* M17.

malefice /ˈmalɪfɪs/ *noun*. *arch*. LME.
[ORIGIN Latin *maleficium* evil deed, sorcery, formed as MALEFIC.]
1 A wicked enchantment; sorcery. LME.
2 An evil deed; mischief. L16.

maleficence /məˈlɛfɪs(ə)ns/ *noun*. M16.
[ORIGIN Latin *maleficentia*, formed as MALEFIC: see -ENCE.]
1 Evildoing; *rare* an evil act. M16.
2 Malefic character; harmfulness. L18.

maleficent /məˈlɛfɪs(ə)nt/ *adjective*. L17.
[ORIGIN from MALEFICENCE: see -ENT.]
1 Harmful, malefic (*to*). L17.
2 Criminal. M18.

maleficial /malɪˈfɪʃ(ə)l/ *adjective*. Now *rare*. E17.
[ORIGIN from (the same root as) MALEFICE: see -IAL. In later use after BENEFICIAL.]
Malefic, maleficent.

maleic /məˈliːɪk/ *adjective*. M19.
[ORIGIN French *maléique* alt. of *malique* MALIC.]
CHEMISTRY. **1** ***maleic acid***, a crystalline unsaturated dibasic acid, *cis*-HOOC·CH=CH·COOH, which is isomeric with fumaric acid and is obtained in the dry distillation of malic acid; *cis*-butenedioic acid. M19.
2 ***maleic anhydride***, the anhydride, $C_4H_2O_3$, of maleic acid, used in synthesis to form addition compounds with substances containing conjugated carbon–carbon double bonds. M20.

mal élevé /mal el(ə)ve/ *adjectival phr*. Fem. ***-ée***. L19.
[ORIGIN French = badly brought up.]
Bad-mannered, ill-bred.

malemute *noun* var. of MALAMUTE.

malengin /ˈmalɛndʒɪn/ *noun*. Long *arch*. Also **-engine**. LME.
[ORIGIN Old French & mod. French (obsolete), from *mal* evil + *engin* contrivance, ENGINE *noun*.]
Evil machination, ill intent; fraud, deceit, guile.

mal-entendu /malɑ̃tɑ̃dy/ *adjective & noun*. E17.
[ORIGIN French, from *mal* ill + *entendu* pa. pple of *entendre* hear, understand.]
► †**A** *adjective*. Mistaken, misapprehended. Only in E17.
► **B** *noun*. Pl. pronounced same. A misunderstanding. L18.

maleo /ˈmalɪəʊ/ *noun*. Pl. **-os**. M19.
[ORIGIN Moluccan Malay.]
More fully ***maleo fowl***. A megapode bird, *Macrocephalon maleo*, inhabiting Sulawesi.

Maler /ˈmɑːlə/ *noun & adjective*. E19.
[ORIGIN Maler = hillmen, ult. from Dravidian *mala* mountain.]
► **A** *noun*. Pl. **-s**, same. A member of a Dravidian people of the Rajmahal hills of northern India; the language of this people (also called ***Malto***, ***Rajmahali***). E19.
► **B** *attrib*. or as *adjective*. Of or pertaining to the Maler or their language. E19.

malerisch /ˈmaːlərɪʃ/ *adjective*. M20.
[ORIGIN German = painterly, from *Maler* painter + *-isch* -ISH[1].]
(Of painting) characterized more by the merging of colours than by a formal linear style; painterly.

malesh /ˈmɑːliːʃ/ *interjection & noun*. Also **maleesh**. E20.
[ORIGIN Colloq. Arabic *ma ʿalay-š* never mind.]
► **A** *interjection*. No matter! never mind! E20.
► **B** *noun*. Indifference, slackness. M20.

†**maletolt** *noun*. ME–E20.
[ORIGIN Anglo-Norman *maletoute*, Old French *maletote*, *maltolte*, *maletoute* (mod. *maltôte*), repr. medieval Latin *mala tolta* bad tax.]
LAW. An unjust or burdensome tax.

malevolence /məˈlɛv(ə)l(ə)ns/ *noun*. LME.
[ORIGIN Old French *malivolence*, *male-* from Latin *malevolentia*, from *malevolent-*: see MALEVOLENT, -ENCE.]
The quality of being malevolent; the wishing or the disposition to wish evil to others; ill will.
■ Also **malevolency** *noun* M17.

malevolent /məˈlɛv(ə)l(ə)nt/ *adjective & noun*. E16.
[ORIGIN Old French *malivolent* or Latin *malevolent-*, from *male* ill, badly + *volent-* pres. ppl stem of *velle* will, wish: see -ENT.]
► **A** *adjective*. **1** Desirous of evil to others; feeling that arises from, or is indicative of ill will; disposed or addicted to ill will. E16.

I. MURDOCH That she's completely malevolent, that she enjoys destroying things? C. BLACKWOOD She was eerie; she was evil; her intentions were entirely malevolent.

2 ASTROLOGY. Exercising an evil or baleful influence. L16.
► †**B** *noun*. A malevolent person. L16–L17.
■ **malevolently** *adverb* E17.

†**malevolous** *adjective*. M16–E18.
[ORIGIN from Latin *malevolus*, from *male* ill, badly + *vol-*, *velle* wish, will + -OUS.]
Malevolent.

malexecution /ˌmalɛksɪˈkjuːʃ(ə)n/ *noun*. L17.
[ORIGIN from MAL- + EXECUTION.]
Bad execution or administration.

malfatti /malˈfati/ *noun pl*. L20.
[ORIGIN from Italian *malfatto* badly made (because the ingredients are typically used to fill ravioli, but in this case are served without being encased in dough).]
Dumplings or gnocchi made with spinach and ricotta.

malfeasance /malˈfiːz(ə)ns/ *noun*. M17.
[ORIGIN Anglo-Norman *malfaisance*, from *mal-* MAL- + Old French & mod. French *faisance*: see FEASANCE. Cf. MISFEASANCE.]
LAW. Evildoing, illegal action; an illegal act; *spec*. official misconduct by a public servant.

malfeasant /malˈfiːz(ə)nt/ *noun*. L19.
[ORIGIN French *malfaisant*, from *mal-* MAL- + *faisant* pres. pple of *faire* do: see -ANT[1].]
An evildoer, a criminal.

malformation /malfɔːˈmeɪʃ(ə)n/ *noun*. E19.
[ORIGIN from MAL- + FORMATION.]
Faulty or anomalous formation or structure of parts; *esp*. congenital abnormality of a part of the body; an instance of this.

malformed /malˈfɔːmd/ *adjective*. E19.
[ORIGIN from MAL- + *formed* pa. pple of FORM *verb*[1].]
Badly formed; marked or characterized by malformation.

malfunction /malˈfʌŋ(k)ʃ(ə)n/ *noun*. M20.
[ORIGIN from MAL- + FUNCTION *noun*.]
Bad or faulty functioning; an instance of this.

malfunction /malˈfʌŋ(k)ʃ(ə)n/ *verb intrans*. M20.
[ORIGIN from MAL- + FUNCTION *verb*.]
Function badly or faultily.

malgas *noun* var. of MALAGAS.

malgovernment /malˈgʌv(ə)nm(ə)nt, -v(ə)m(ə)nt/ *noun*. M17.
[ORIGIN from MAL- + GOVERNMENT.]
Bad government.

malgrace /malˈgreɪs/ *noun*. ME.
[ORIGIN Orig. two words, from Old French *male grace* lit. 'evil grace'.]
†**1** Disfavour. ME–E18.
2 Something unbecoming. *pseudo-arch*. *rare*. L19.

malgré /malgre/ *preposition*. M18.
[ORIGIN French: see MAUGRE.]
In spite of, notwithstanding.
malgré lui /lɥi/ in spite of himself or herself. ***malgré tout*** /tu/ despite everything.

†**malheur** *noun*. L15–M19.
[ORIGIN French (earlier *maleur*), from *mal* evil + *eur* fortune.]
Misfortune.

mali /ˈmɑːliː/ *noun*[1]. M18.
[ORIGIN Hindi *mālī* from Sanskrit *mālin* from *mālā* garland, wreath.]
A member of a caste in the Indian subcontinent whose traditional occupation is gardening; any non-European gardener.

Mali /ˈmɑːli/ *adjective & noun*[2]. E20.
[ORIGIN See below.]
► **A** *adjective*. Of or pertaining to Mali, an ancient empire (of the 13th and 14th cents.) and a modern republic (founded in 1960) in W. Africa. E20.
► **B** *noun*. A native or inhabitant of modern Mali. M20.
■ Also **Malian** *adjective & noun* M20.

Malibu /ˈmalɪbuː/ *noun*. Chiefly *Austral*. & *NZ*. Also **m-**. M20.
[ORIGIN *Malibu* beach, California, USA; prob. a Chumash name.]
In full ***Malibu surfboard***, ***Malibu board***. A long surfboard with a rounded front end.

malic /ˈmalɪk, ˈmeɪlɪk/ *adjective*. L18.
[ORIGIN from Latin *malum* apple + -IC.]
CHEMISTRY. **1** ***malic acid***, a colourless crystalline acid, $HOOC{\cdot}CH_2CH(OH){\cdot}COOH$, present in apples, berries of the mountain ash, and many other fruits. L18.
2 Of an enzyme: that acts on malic acid. M20.

malice /ˈmalɪs/ *noun & verb*. ME.
[ORIGIN Old French & mod. French from Latin *malitia*, from *malus* bad: see -ICE[1].]
► **A** *noun*. †**1** Badness; *esp*. wickedness. ME–M17.
2 The desire to injure another person; active ill will or hatred. In later use also, the desire to tease. ME.

Catholic Herald There isn't an ounce of malice in her.

bear malice feel ill will, now usu. on account of some injury (foll. by *against*, *to*, *toward(s)*).
†**3** Malicious conduct; a malicious act or device. ME–M17.
†**4** Power to harm, harmful action or effect, malignancy; ASTROLOGY the baleful influence of certain stars. LME–L17.
5 LAW. Wrongful intention, esp. as aggravating guilt in certain offences. M16.
malice* AFORETHOUGHT. *malice prepense: see PREPENSE *adjective* 1. ***malice prepensed***: see PREPENSE *verb*. ***stand mute of malice***: see MUTE *adjective* 2.
► **B** *verb trans*. †**1** Speak maliciously of, malign. E16–L17.
2 Bear malice towards. Long *arch*. & *dial*. M16.
■ **maliceful** *adjective* (chiefly *dial*.) malicious E16.

malicho *noun* var. of MALLECHO.

malicious /məˈlɪʃəs/ *adjective & noun*. ME.
[ORIGIN Old French *malicius* (mod. *malicieux*) from Latin *malitiosus*, from *malitia*: see MALICE, -OUS.]
► **A** *adjective*. **1** Given to, arising from, or characterized by malice. ME. ►†**b** Wicked. ME–L15. ►**c** LAW. Characterized by malice aforethought. LME.

MILTON Thou knowst.. what malicious Foe.. seeks to work us woe and shame. E. M. FORSTER Mr Vyse.. took a malicious pleasure in thwarting people. V. BROME Clearly.. a great deal of gossip, backbiting and malicious talk went on. **c** *Daily Telegraph* Guilty verdicts.. for causing an affray and malicious wounding were unsafe and unsatisfactory.

†**2** Harmful, malignant. LME–E18.
†**3** Clever, artful. LME–L16.
► **B** *noun*. A malicious person. *rare*. M16.
■ **maliciously** *adverb* LME. **maliciousness** *noun* LME.

maliferous /məˈlɪf(ə)rəs/ *adjective*. Now *rare*. E18.
[ORIGIN from Latin *malus* bad: see -FEROUS.]
Bringing or producing evil; unwholesome, insalubrious.

malign /məˈlʌɪn/ *adjective*. ME.
[ORIGIN Old French & mod. French *maligne* fem. of Old French & mod. French *malin* or its source Latin *malignus*, from *malus* bad.]
1 Of a thing: evil in nature and effects; baleful, gravely harmful; (chiefly ASTROLOGY) having an evil influence or effect. Formerly also, of sin: heinous. ME.

LONGFELLOW A poison malign Is such Borgia wine.

2 Characterized by ill will; desiring or rejoicing in the suffering of others; malevolent. LME.

A. STORR To discover that the person one believed was on one's side is actually malign.

3 Of a disease etc.: malignant. Now *rare*. LME.
■ **malignly** *adverb* M16.

malign /məˈlʌɪn/ *verb*. LME.
[ORIGIN Old French *malignier* from late Latin *malignare* contrive maliciously, from *malignus*: see MALIGN *adjective*.]
†**1** *verb intrans*. Speak ill, inveigh; plot, contrive. (Foll. by *against*.) LME–E17.
†**2** *verb intrans*. Feel malice or ill will. Foll. by *against*, *at*. LME–M17.
†**3** *verb trans*. Regard with hatred or envy. Also, resent, take amiss. L15–E18.
4 *verb trans*. Speak ill or wrongly of, traduce, slander. M16.

G. GREENE He sounded professional, and I wondered whether perhaps I had maligned him. L. CODY You're maligning all my varied professions.

■ **maligner** *noun* LME.

malignance /məˈlɪgnəns/ *noun*. E17.
[ORIGIN formed as MALIGNANCY: see -ANCE.]
= MALIGNANCY.

malignancy /məˈlɪgnənsi/ *noun*. E17.
[ORIGIN from MALIGNANT: see -ANCY.]
1 Malign or baleful character; great harmfulness. E17.
2 Disaffection to constituted authority; *obsolete* exc. *hist*. (*derog*.) sympathy with the royalist cause during the English Civil War. M17.
3 Malignant or intensely malevolent disposition; envenomed hostility; desire to inflict injury or suffering. M17.
4 An instance of malignancy; a malignant quality. M17.
5 MEDICINE. Malignant quality, now esp. of a cancer or tumour (cf. MALIGNANT *adjective* 2). L17. ►**b** A malignant tumour. M20.

M

malignant /mə'lɪɡnənt/ *adjective & noun.* **M16.**
[ORIGIN Late Latin *malignant-* pres. ppl stem of *malignare*: see MALIGN *verb*, -ANT[1].]
▸ **A** *adjective.* **1** Disposed to rebel against God or against constituted authority; disaffected. Now only *hist.* (*derog.*), sympathetic to the royalist cause during the English Civil War. **M16.**
2 Orig., (of a disease) liable to become progressively more severe; extremely virulent; very infectious. Now chiefly of a cancer or tumour: tending to spread to other parts of the body, or to recur after removal; cancerous. **M16.** ***malignant pustule***: see PUSTULE 1.
3 Chiefly ASTROLOGY. Having an evil influence or effect. **L16.**
4 Characterized by intense ill will; keenly desirous of the suffering or misfortune of others. **L16.**
▸ **B** *noun.* A person who is disaffected towards constituted authority or (in early use) an accepted true religion; a malcontent; *hist.* (*derog.*) a supporter of the royalist cause during the English Civil War. **L16.**
■ **malignantly** *adverb* **M16.**

malignation /malɪɡ'neɪʃ(ə)n/ *noun.* **L15.**
[ORIGIN from late Latin *malignat-* pa. ppl stem of *malignare*: see MALIGN *verb*, -ATION.]
†**1** Feeling of dislike or ill will. **L15–M16.**
†**2** A malefic incantation. Only in **M17.**
3 The action of maligning or slandering. *rare.* **M19.**

†**malignify** *verb trans.* **E17–E19.**
[ORIGIN from Latin *malignus* MALIGN *adjective*: see -I-, -FY.]
Make malign.

malignity /mə'lɪɡnɪti/ *noun.* **LME.**
[ORIGIN Old French *malignité* or Latin *malignitas*, from *malignus* MALIGN *adjective*: see -ITY.]
1 Wicked and deep-rooted ill will or hatred; intense and persistent desire to cause suffering to another person; propensity to this feeling. **LME.** ▸**b** In *pl.* Malignant feelings or actions. **E16.**
2 Wickedness, heinousness. *arch.* **M16.**
3 Noxiousness, deleteriousness. *arch.* **E17.**
4 MEDICINE. = MALIGNANCY 5. **M17.**

malihini /mɑːlɪ'hiːni/ *noun.* **E20.**
[ORIGIN Hawaiian.]
In Hawaii: a stranger, a newcomer; a beginner, a novice.

malik /'malɪk/ *noun.* **M17.**
[ORIGIN Urdu from Arabic, use as noun of active pple of *malaka* possess, rule.]
The chief or headman of a village or other community in parts of the Indian subcontinent and the Middle East.

Maliki /'malɪki/ *noun & adjective.* **L17.**
[ORIGIN Arabic *mālikī*, from *Malik* (see below).]
A follower of, of or pertaining to, one of the four schools of Sunni Muslims, following the rite of the jurist Malik ibn Anas (713–795) and now found mainly in western and northern Africa.
■ Also **Malikite** *noun & adjective* **M19.**

malimbe /mə'lɪmbi/ *noun.* **M20.**
[ORIGIN from the name of the town of *Malimbe* in Angola.]
Any of several weaver birds of the genus *Malimbus*, found in west and central Africa.

Malines /ma'liːn/ *noun & adjective.* Also **m-.** **M19.**
[ORIGIN French name of *Mechelen* in Belgium: see MECHLIN.]
1 (Designating or made of) bobbin lace of a type or floral pattern produced at Mechelen. **M19.**
2 (Designating or made of) a net for millinery or veils. **L19.**
3 (Of or designating) a Belgian breed of the domestic fowl. **E20.**

malinfluence /mal'ɪnflʊəns/ *noun.* **L18.**
[ORIGIN from MAL- + INFLUENCE *noun.*]
Evil influence.

malinger /mə'lɪŋɡə/ *verb intrans.* **E19.**
[ORIGIN Back-form. from MALINGERER.]
Pretend or exaggerate illness in order to escape duty or work.

malingerer /mə'lɪŋɡ(ə)rə/ *noun.* **L18.**
[ORIGIN App. from Old French & mod. French *malingre*, perh. formed as MAL- + *haingre* weak, thin, prob. of Germanic origin.]
A person who malingers.

Malinke /mə'lɪŋkeɪ/ *noun & adjective.* **L19.**
[ORIGIN Malinke.]
▸ **A** *noun.* Pl. same, **-s.** A member of a people of W. Africa; the Mande language of this people. Also called ***Mandinka***. Cf. also MANDING. **L19.**
▸ **B** *attrib.* or as *adjective.* Of or pertaining to the Malinke or their language. **L20.**

Malinowskian /malɪ'nɒfskɪən/ *adjective.* **M20.**
[ORIGIN from *Malinowski* (see below) + -AN.]
Of, pertaining to, or characteristic of the Polish-born anthropologist Bronislaw K. Malinowski (1884–1942) or his works.

malintegration /ˌmalɪntɪ'ɡreɪʃ(ə)n/ *noun.* **M20.**
[ORIGIN from MAL- + INTEGRATION.]
Bad or faulty integration, esp. into society.

Maliseet /'maləsiːt/ *noun & adjective.* Also **Malecite.** **M19.**
[ORIGIN French *Malécite* from Micmac *mali:sit* lit. 'person who speaks poorly or incomprehensibly'.]
▸ **A** *noun.* Pl. same, **-s.**
1 A member of an Algonquian people of New Brunswick and Maine, nearly identical in language and culture to the Passamaquoddy. **M18.**
2 The language of this people. **E20.**
▸ **B** *adjective.* Of or pertaining to the Maliseet or their language. **L18.**

malism /'meɪlɪz(ə)m/ *noun.* **L19.**
[ORIGIN from Latin *malus* bad + -ISM.]
The doctrine that this world is an evil one.

malison /'malɪz(ə)n, -s-/ *noun.* Now *arch. & dial.* **ME.**
[ORIGIN Old French, formed as MALEDICTION.]
A curse, a malediction.

malist /'meɪlɪst/ *noun.* **L19.**
[ORIGIN from Latin *malus* bad + -IST.]
A person who holds the doctrine of malism.
■ **ma'listic** /mə'lɪstɪk/ *adjective* pertaining to or holding the doctrine of malism **L19.**

malkin /'mɔːlkɪn/ *noun. obsolete* exc. *dial.* Also **mawkin.** **ME.**
[ORIGIN Dim. of *Malde* early form of female forenames Maud or Matilda: see -KIN. Cf. MAUX, MERKIN.]
1 (Formerly used as a typical name of) a lower-class or untidy woman, esp. a servant or country girl. **ME.**
†**2** (A name for) a female spectre or demon. (In later use app. associated with sense 5a.) **ME–E17.**
3 A mop; a bundle of rags fastened to the end of a stick, esp. for cleaning out a baker's oven. **LME.**
4 A scarecrow; a ragged puppet, a grotesque effigy. **M16.**
5 a (A name for) a cat. Cf. earlier GRIMALKIN. **L17.** ▸**b** (A name for) a hare. *Scot. & N. English.* **E18.**

malkoha /'malkəʊə/ *noun.* Also **-coha.** **M18.**
[ORIGIN Sinhalese *mal-kohā* lit. 'flower cuckoo', ult. from Sanskrit *mālā* garland + *kokila* cuckoo.]
Any of several long-tailed cuckoos of the genus *Rhopodytes* and related genera, found in SE Asia and the Indian subcontinent.

mall /mal, mɔːl/ *noun.* **ME.**
[ORIGIN Earlier form of MAUL *noun*. In branch II cf. PALL-MALL.]
▸ **I 1** See MAUL *noun.* **ME.**
▸ **II 2** *hist.* ▸**a** A mallet used in the game pall-mall. **M17.** ▸**b** The game pall-mall. **M17.** ▸**c** An alley for the game of pall-mall. **M17.**
3 a A sheltered walk serving as a promenade. Orig. in ***the Mall***, a walk bordered by trees in St James's Park, London, orig. a mall in sense 2c. **L17.** ▸**b** A shopping precinct closed to vehicles; a large shopping centre. Also more fully ***shopping mall***. Chiefly *N. Amer.* **M20.**

> **b** R. KENAN She had originally intended to stop by the mall on the way home.

– COMB.: **mall rat** *slang* a young person who frequents a shopping mall for social purposes, usu. in a large group or gang.
■ **malling** *noun* (*N. Amer.*) (**a**) the development of shopping malls; (**b**) the action or activity of passing time in a shopping mall: **L20.**

†**mall** *verb* var. of MAUL *verb.*

Mallaby-Deeley /maləbɪ'diːli/ *noun. arch. slang.* **E20.**
[ORIGIN Harry *Mallaby-Deeley* (1863–1937), English clothing manufacturer.]
A cheap suit of clothes.

mallam /'maləm/ *noun.* **M19.**
[ORIGIN Hausa *mālam(i).*]
In Nigeria and other parts of Africa, a learned man, a scribe, a teacher.

mallard /'malɑːd, -ləd/ *noun.* Pl. **-s**, same. **ME.**
[ORIGIN Old French *mallard*, (also mod.) *malart* mallard drake, prob. formed as MALE *adjective & noun* + -ARD.]
1 The male of the common holarctic wild duck *Anas platyrhynchos*. Now also, the male or female of this duck. **ME.**
2 The flesh of this duck as food. **LME.**

mallardite /'malədʌɪt/ *noun.* **L19.**
[ORIGIN from Ernest *Mallard* (1833–94), French crystallographer + -ITE[1].]
MINERALOGY. A monoclinic hydrated sulphate of manganese, usu. occurring as rose-coloured fibrous masses.

malleable /'malɪəb(ə)l/ *adjective.* **LME.**
[ORIGIN Old French from medieval Latin *malleabilis*, from Latin *malleare* to hammer, formed as MALLEUS + -ABLE.]
1 Esp. of a metal: able to be hammered or pressed out of shape without a tendency to return to the original shape or to fracture. **LME.**
malleable cast iron, **malleable iron** cast iron which has been decarburized by oxidation under prolonged heat and made somewhat malleable.
2 *transf. & fig.* Able to be fashioned or adapted; adaptable, pliable. **E17.**

> JOHN BROOKE He saw the Prince as undeveloped and malleable and he tried to shape his character. V. BROME Neither the media universe nor the events of everyday life were malleable to his will.

■ **mallea'bility** *noun* **M17.** **malleableize** *verb trans.* make malleable **M19.** **malleableness** *noun* (now *rare*) **M17.**

malleate /'malɪət/ *adjective.* **L19.**
[ORIGIN from MALLEUS + -ATE[2].]
ZOOLOGY. Having a malleus or mallei.

malleate /'malɪeɪt/ *verb trans.* Now *rare.* **L16.**
[ORIGIN Latin *malleat-* pa. ppl stem of *malleare*: see MALLEABLE, -ATE[3].]
Beat with a hammer; *spec.* beat (metal) thin or flat.

malleation /malɪ'eɪʃ(ə)n/ *noun.* Now *rare.* **L15.**
[ORIGIN medieval Latin *malleatio(n-)*, formed as MALLEATE *verb*: see -ATION.]
1 The action of beating something with a hammer; the condition of being beaten with a hammer. **L15.**
2 MEDICINE. A convulsive hammering of one part of the body against another, as a symptom of mental illness. **E19.**

mallecho /'malɪkəʊ/ *noun. rare.* Also **malicho.** **E17.**
[ORIGIN Uncertain: perh. from Spanish *malhecho* misdeed.]
Mischief. Only in ***miching mallecho*** (in and after Shakes.).

> SHAKES. *Haml.* Marry, this is miching mallecho; it means mischief.

– NOTE: The meaning and origin of the phr. are uncertain: it is usu. taken to mean 'skulking (= MITCH *verb*) mischief'.

mallee /'maliː/ *noun.* **M19.**
[ORIGIN Wemba-wemba *mali.*]
Any of various low-growing eucalypts which have many slender stems rising from a large underground stock; scrub or thicket formed by such trees, typical of some arid parts of Australia.
– COMB.: **mallee bird**, **mallee fowl**, **mallee hen** an Australian megapode, *Leipoa ocellata*, inhabiting mallee scrub.

mallei *noun* pl. of MALLEUS.

malleiform /'maliːɪfɔːm/ *adjective.* **M19.**
[ORIGIN formed as MALLEUS + -I- + -FORM.]
Having the form of a hammer.

mallemuck *noun* var. of MOLLYMAWK.

mallenders /'mal(ə)ndəz/ *noun.* Also (earlier) †**-der**, **malan-.** **LME.**
[ORIGIN Old French & mod. French *malandre* from Latin *malandria* pl., pustules on the neck.]
VETERINARY MEDICINE. A dry scabby eruption behind the knee in horses. Cf. SALLENDERS.

malleo- /'malɪəʊ/ *combining form.*
[ORIGIN from MALLEUS: see -O-.]
Forming nouns and adjectives with the sense 'of the bone of the ear'.
■ **malleo-in'cudal** *adjective* (ANATOMY) pertaining jointly to the malleus and the incus of the ear **L19.**

malleolus /ma'liːələs/ *noun.* Pl. **-li** /-lʌɪ, -liː/. **E17.**
[ORIGIN Latin, dim. of MALLEUS.]
†**1** ANTIQUITIES. A kind of burning dart. **E17–L18.**
2 ANATOMY. A protuberance of the tibia (in full ***internal malleolus***, ***medial malleolus***) or of the fibula (in full ***external malleolus***, ***lateral malleolus***) at the side of the ankle. **L17.**
■ **malleolar** /ma'liːələ, 'malɪələ/ *adjective* **E19.**

†**maller** *noun* var. of MAULER.

mallet /'malɪt/ *noun*[1]. **LME.**
[ORIGIN Old French & mod. French *maillet*, from *mailler* to hammer, from *mail* hammer, MAUL *noun*: see -ET[1].]
1 A kind of hammer, usu. with a relatively large head and of wood, used for various purposes, as driving a chisel etc. **LME.**
†**2** A heavy club, a mace. **L15–E16.**
†**3** *fig.* A person or agency that hits, beats down, or crushes. **E16–E19.**
4 ANATOMY. The malleus of the ear. *rare.* **L16.**
5 A long-handled implement like a hammer used for striking the balls in croquet, (formerly) pall-mall, or polo. **M19.**
6 MUSIC. A light padded hammer used for playing the vibraphone, xylophone, or drums. **M20.**
– COMB.: **mallet finger** MEDICINE (the condition of having) a finger permanently flexed at the distal joint; **mallet-shoot** a hammer-shaped slip of a tree or shrub for planting.

†**mallet** *noun*[2]. *rare.* Only in **E17.**
[ORIGIN Spanish *maleta* = French *mallette* dim. of *maille* MAIL *noun*[3]: see -ET[1].]
A little bag or portmanteau.

mallet /'malɪt/ *noun*[3]. **M19.**
[ORIGIN Nyungar *malard.*]
(The timber of) any of various eucalypts with tannin-rich bark, *esp.* yate, *E. cornuta*.

mallet /'malɪt/ *verb trans.* **L16.**
[ORIGIN from MALLET *noun*[1].]
Beat or hammer (as) with a mallet.

malleus /'malɪəs/ *noun.* Pl. **mallei** /'malɪʌɪ/. **M17.**
[ORIGIN Latin = hammer (from its shape).]
1 ANATOMY & ZOOLOGY. The outermost of the three small bones which conduct sound through the mammalian ear, transmitting the vibrations of the tympanum to the incus. Cf. INCUS, STAPES. **M17.**

2 *ZOOLOGY*. In rotifers, either of two parts of the chitinous mouth apparatus, which masticate food by working on the incus. **M19.**

Malling /ˈmɔːlɪŋ/ *noun*. **E20.**
[**ORIGIN** Two villages, East and West *Malling*, in Kent, England.]
1 Used *attrib.* to designate a rootstock for fruit trees developed at the East Malling Research Station. **E20.**
2 Used *attrib.* to designate (articles, esp. tin-enamelled jugs, of) a type of English stoneware of the late 16th cent. **M20.**

Mallorcan /məˈlɔːk(ə)n, məˈljɔː-/ *noun & adjective*. **M19.**
[**ORIGIN** from *Mallorca* Majorca + -**AN**. Cf. **MALLORQUIN**.]
= **MALLORQUIN**.

Mallorquin /məˈlɔːkɪn, məˈljɔː-/ *noun & adjective*. **M19.**
[**ORIGIN** Spanish *Mallorquín*, from *Mallorca* Majorca: see **MAJORCAN**. Cf. **MALLORCAN**.]
▶ **A** *noun*. **1** A Majorcan. **M19.**
2 The Catalan dialect of Majorca. **M19.**
▶ **B** *adjective*. Majorcan. **M19.**

mallow /ˈmaləʊ/ *noun*. Also †**mallows**. **OE.**
[**ORIGIN** Latin *malva* rel. to Greek *malakhē*, *molokhē*. Cf. **MAUVE**.]
Any of various plants of the family Malvaceae and esp. of the genus *Malva*, typically with hairy stems and leaves and deeply cleft purple flowers; spec. *Malva sylvestris* (also ***common mallow***, ***field mallow***, ***wild mallow***).
curled mallow, **curled-leaved mallow** a variety of *Malva verticillata*, grown as a salad plant. **dwarf mallow** a low-growing Eurasian mallow, *Malva neglecta*, common in waste ground. ***glade mallow***: see **GLADE** *noun*[2]. ***Indian mallow***: see **INDIAN** *adjective*. ***Jew's mallow***: see **JEW** *noun*. **MARSHMALLOW**. ***musk mallow***: see **MUSK** *noun*. **rose mallow** = **HIBISCUS**. ***tree mallow***: see **TREE** *noun*.

†**mallowe** *noun* see **MULLOWAY**.

†**mallows** *noun* var. of **MALLOW**.

malm /mɑːm/ *noun & verb*.
[**ORIGIN** Old English *mealm-* (in *mealmstān*) = Old Norse *malr* ore, metal, Gothic *malma* sand, from Germanic base also of **MEAL** *noun*[1].]
▶ **A** *noun*. **1** (More fully ***malm rock***, ***malmstone***) a soft friable rock consisting largely of chalky material; light loamy soil formed by the disintegration of this rock. **OE.**
2 More fully ***malm brick***. A fine-quality brick made orig. from malm, marl, or similar chalky clay. **E19.**
▶ †**B** *verb trans*. **1** Treat (land) with malm. Only in **E17.**
2 Convert (clay) into artificial malm for brick-making; cover (brick earth) with artificial malm. **M–L19.**
■ **malmy** *adjective* of a loamy character **L17.**

Malmaison /malˈmeɪzɒn/ *noun*. **L19.**
[**ORIGIN** Short for French *Souvenirs de Malmaison* recollections of Malmaison (chateau of the French empress Josephine), name of a variety of rose which the carnation was held to resemble.]
HORTICULTURE. In full ***Malmaison carnation***. A kind of carnation variety with a sturdy, large-flowered habit.

malmsey /ˈmɑːmzi/ *noun*. Also **M-**. **LME.**
[**ORIGIN** Middle Dutch, Middle Low German *malmesie*, *-eye*, in medieval Latin *malmasia* from Greek place name *Monemvasia* in the Peloponnese. Cf. **MALVASIA**, **MALVOISIE**.]
1 A strong (now fortified) sweet wine, orig. from around Monemvasia in the Peloponnese, Greece, now also from Spain, the Azores, the Canary Islands, and (esp.) Madeira. Also ***malmsey wine***. **LME.**
2 A kind of grape, orig. from the eastern Mediterranean, from which malmsey was originally made. **E16.**
– **COMB.**: †**malmsey-face** a face inflamed by alcoholic drink; **malmsey madeira** malmsey from Madeira; †**malmsey-nose** a nose inflamed by alcoholic drink; ***malmsey wine***: see sense 1 above.

malnourished /malˈnʌrɪʃt/ *adjective*. **E20.**
[**ORIGIN** from **MAL-** + *nourished* pa. pple of **NOURISH**.]
Suffering from malnutrition; not provided with adequate nourishment.

malnourishment /malˈnʌrɪʃm(ə)nt/ *noun*. **M20.**
[**ORIGIN** from **MAL-** + **NOURISHMENT**.]
= **MALNUTRITION**.

malnutrition /malnjʊˈtrɪʃ(ə)n/ *noun*. **M19.**
[**ORIGIN** from **MAL-** + **NUTRITION**.]
Nutrition which is not adequate to maintain good health, whether through insufficient quantity of food, lack of essential dietary components, unbalanced diet, or malabsorption; the condition of poor health resulting from this.

malobservance /maləbˈzəːv(ə)ns/ *noun*. **E19.**
[**ORIGIN** from **MAL-** + **OBSERVANCE**.]
Observance of a wrong kind.

malobservation /ˌmalɒbzəˈveɪʃ(ə)n/ *noun*. **M19.**
[**ORIGIN** from **MAL-** + **OBSERVATION**.]
Faulty or imperfect observation.

maloca /məˈləʊkə/ *noun*. **M19.**
[**ORIGIN** Portuguese = large hut from Amer. Spanish (raid, attack), from Mapuche *malocan* to fight.]
A large hut in certain Indian settlements in S. America.

malocclusion /maləˈkluːʒ(ə)n/ *noun*. **L19.**
[**ORIGIN** from **MAL-** + **OCCLUSION**.]
DENTISTRY. Faulty or imperfect occlusion of the teeth.

malodorous /malˈəʊd(ə)rəs/ *adjective*. **M19.**
[**ORIGIN** from **MAL-** + **ODOROUS**.]
Evil-smelling (*lit.* & *fig.*).

> **ROSEMARY MANNING** A strong whiff of these malodorous views hung in the air.

■ **malodorously** *adverb* **E20.** **malodorousness** *noun* **L19.**

malodour /malˈəʊdə/ *noun*. **E19.**
[**ORIGIN** from **MAL-** + **ODOUR** *noun*.]
An evil smell, a stench.

malolactic /maləʊ)ˈlaktɪk/ *adjective*. **E20.**
[**ORIGIN** from **MAL(IC** + **-O-** + **LACTIC**.]
Designating bacterial fermentation which converts malic acid (in wine) to lactic acid.

malonic /məˈlɒnɪk/ *adjective*. **M19.**
[**ORIGIN** French *malonique* alt. of *malique* **MALIC**.]
CHEMISTRY. **1** ***malonic acid***, a crystalline acid, $CH_2(COOH)_2$, obtained by the oxidation of malic acid. **M19.**
2 ***malonic ester***, the liquid diethyl ester, $CH_2(COOC_2H_5)_2$, of malonic acid, widely used in a method for synthesizing carboxylic acids. **L19.**
■ **malonate** /ˈmalәneɪt/ *noun* a salt or ester of malonic acid **M19.** ˈ**malonyl** *noun* the divalent radical $\cdot COCH_2CO\cdot$ derived from malonic acid **L19.**

maloperation /ˌmalɒpəˈreɪʃ(ə)n/ *noun*. **E19.**
[**ORIGIN** from **MAL-** + **OPERATION**.]
Faulty or imperfect operation.

malorganization /ˌmalɔːgənʌɪˈzeɪʃ(ə)n/ *noun*. Also **-isation**. **M19.**
[**ORIGIN** from **MAL-** + **ORGANIZATION**.]
Faulty or imperfect organization.

Malorian /məˈlɔːrɪən/ *adjective*. Also **Maloryan**. **E20.**
[**ORIGIN** from *Malory* (see below) + **-AN**.]
Of, pertaining to, or in the manner of the English writer Sir Thomas Malory (d. 1471) or his translations of Arthurian legend.

Malo-Russian /mɑːləʊˈrʌʃ(ə)n/ *noun & adjective*. *arch.* **E19.**
[**ORIGIN** from Russian *Malorossiya* lit. 'Little Russia', Ukraine or *Malorossiyánin* a 'Little Russian', a Ukrainian: see **-AN**.]
= **UKRAINIAN**.

Maloryan *adjective* var. of **MALORIAN**.

maloti *noun* pl. of **LOTI**.

Malozi *noun pl.* see **LOZI**.

malpais /malpɑːˈiːs/ *noun*. *US*. **M19.**
[**ORIGIN** Spanish, from *malo* bad + *país* country, region.]
Rugged or difficult country of volcanic origin.

malperformance /malpəˈfɔːməns/ *noun*. **M20.**
[**ORIGIN** from **MAL-** + **PERFORMANCE**.]
Faulty or imperfect performance.

Malpighian /malˈpɪgɪən/ *adjective*. **M19.**
[**ORIGIN** from Marcello *Malpighi* (1628–94), Italian physician + **-AN**.]
Designating certain anatomical structures discovered by Malpighi or connected with structures discovered by him.
Malpighian body, **Malpighian corpuscle** *ANATOMY* (***a***) a glomerulus of the kidney together with the Bowman's capsule surrounding it; (***b***) any of the lymphoid follicles of the spleen. **Malpighian layer** *ANATOMY* the innermost layer of the epidermis, in which cell division occurs. ***Malpighian pyramid***: see **PYRAMID** *noun* 7. **Malpighian tubule** *ZOOLOGY* a tubular excretory organ, numbers of which open into the gut in certain insects and other arthropods.

malposition /malpəˈzɪʃ(ə)n/ *noun*. **M19.**
[**ORIGIN** from **MAL-** + **POSITION** *noun*.]
Misplacement; the condition of being wrongly placed; *MEDICINE* faulty position of a part or organ, esp. of a fetus in the uterus.

malpractice /malˈpraktɪs/ *noun*. **L17.**
[**ORIGIN** from **MAL-** + **PRACTICE** *noun*.]
1 *LAW*. Improper treatment or culpable neglect of a patient by a physician or of a client by a lawyer. **L17.**
2 *gen.* A criminal or illegal action; wrongdoing, misconduct. **M18.**

malpraxis /malˈpraksɪs/ *noun*. **M19.**
[**ORIGIN** from **MAL-** + Latin **PRAXIS**. Cf. **MALA PRAXIS**.]
LAW. = **MALPRACTICE** 1.

malpresentation /ˌmalprɛz(ə)nˈteɪʃ(ə)n/ *noun*. **M19.**
[**ORIGIN** from **MAL-** + **PRESENTATION**.]
MEDICINE. Abnormal presentation at parturition.

malt /mɒlt, mɔːlt/ *noun*[1] *& adjective*.
[**ORIGIN** Old English *malt* (*mealt*) = Old Saxon *malt* (Dutch *mout*), Old & mod. High German *malz*, Old Norse *malt*, from Germanic, rel. to base of **MELT** *verb*.]
▶ **A** *noun*. **1** Barley or other grain prepared for brewing or distilling or vinegar-making, esp. by steeping, germinating, and drying. **OE.**
brown malt: see **BROWN** *adjective*.
2 Malt liquor; (now *esp.*) malt whisky; an example or drink of this. **E18.** ▸**b** A drink made from dried milk and a malt preparation. *US*. **M20.**
single malt: see **SINGLE** *adjective & adverb*.
▶ **B** *attrib.* or as *adjective*. Prepared or distilled from malt. **OE.**
single malt whisky: see **SINGLE** *adjective & adverb*.
– **COMB. & SPECIAL COLLOCATIONS**: **malt-comb(s)** (now *dial.*) = **COMB** *noun*[2]; **malt distiller** a distiller of malt spirits; **malt distillery** †(***a***) the action or art of the malt distiller; (***b***) a place where malt spirits are distilled; **maltdust** refuse falling from grain in the process of malting; **malt extract** a sweet sticky substance obtained from wort; **malt floor** a floor upon which barley etc. is spread to germinate; †**malt-horse** *arch.* a heavy kind of horse used by maltsters (used occas. as a term of abuse); **malthouse** a building for preparing and storing malt, a malting; **malt kiln** a kiln in which barley etc. is dried after steeping and germinating; **malt liquor** liquor made from malt by fermentation as opp. to distillation, as ale, beer, stout, etc.; **malt-maker** (now *rare*) a maltster; **maltman** a maltster; **malt shop** *N. Amer.* a shop where malted milk is sold; **malt spirits** spirits distilled from malt; **malt sugar** = **MALTOSE**; **malt-tax** *hist.* a tax on malt, imposed by Parliament in 1697, repealed in 1880; **malt vinegar** vinegar made from the fermentation of malt; **malt whisky**: made only from malted barley; cf. ***grain whisky*** s.v. **GRAIN** *noun*[1]; **maltworm** †(***a***) a weevil infesting malt; (***b***) *arch.* a lover of malt liquor, a heavy drinker; **maltwort** (now *rare*) = **WORT** *noun*[2].

Malt /mɒlt, mɔːlt/ *noun*[2]. *slang* (usu. *derog.*). **M20.**
[**ORIGIN** Abbreviation.]
A Maltese.

malt /mɒlt, mɔːlt/ *verb*. **LME.**
[**ORIGIN** from **MALT** *noun*[1].]
1 *verb trans. & intrans.* Convert (barley or other grain) into malt. **LME.**
2 *verb trans.* Make (liquor) with malt; combine with malt. Chiefly as **MALTED** *ppl adjective*. **E17.**
3 *verb intrans.* Admit of being malted. **M18.**
4 *verb trans.* in *pass.* & *intrans.* Of seeds: become malt owing to germination being checked by drought. **M18.**
5 *verb intrans.* Drink malt liquor. *colloq.* Now *rare*. **E19.**
■ **malter** *noun* (*obsolete* exc. *dial.*) a maltster **ME.**

Malta /ˈmɒltə, mɔːltə/ *noun*. **E17.**
[**ORIGIN** An island in the central Mediterranean, given to the Knights Hospitaller in the 16th cent., later a dependency of Great Britain, now an independent republic.]
Used *attrib.* to designate things found in or associated with Malta.
†**Malta cross** a Maltese cross. **Malta fever** *MEDICINE* undulant fever caused by *Brucella melitensis*, as formerly prevalent in Malta and other places in the Mediterranean.

maltalent /ˈmaltal(ə)nt/ *noun & adjective*. **ME.**
[**ORIGIN** Old French, from *mal* evil + *talent* disposition, temper (see **TALENT** *noun*[1]).]
▶ **A** *noun*. †**1** Ill will, malevolence. **ME–E19.**
2 A bad-tempered person. *rare*. **M20.**
▶ †**B** *adjective*. Bad-tempered. Only in **L16.**

maltase /ˈmɒlteɪz, ˈmɔːlt-/ *noun*. **L19.**
[**ORIGIN** from **MALT** *noun*[1] + **-ASE**.]
BIOCHEMISTRY. An enzyme which hydrolyses maltose and similar glycosides, forming glucose.

malted /ˈmɒltɪd, ˈmɔːlt-/ *ppl adjective & noun*. **L17.**
[**ORIGIN** from **MALT** *verb* + **-ED**[1]. Earlier in **UNMALTED**.]
▶ **A** *ppl adjective*. **1** Converted into malt. **L17.**
2 Esp. of (powdered) milk: combined with malt. **L19.**
▶ **B** *noun*. A drink of malted milk. **E20.**

Maltese /mɒlˈtiːz, mɔːl-/ *noun & adjective*. **E17.**
[**ORIGIN** from **MALTA** + **-ESE**.]
▶ **A** *noun*. Pl. same.
1 A native or inhabitant of Malta, an island in the central Mediterranean. Formerly also, a member of the Knights Hospitaller (with headquarters in Malta). **L16.**
2 The Semitic language of Malta, much influenced by Italian. **E19.**
3 A breed of white toy dog; a dog of this breed. **M19.**
4 *ellipt.* Maltese lace. **M19.**
▶ **B** *adjective*. Of or pertaining to Malta or its inhabitants. **M18.**
Maltese cat (an animal of) a bluish-grey short-haired breed of cat. **Maltese cross** (***a***) a cross with the limbs broadened outwards and often indented at the ends (as worn by Knights Hospitaller); (***b***) *PHILATELY* a cross-shaped postmark used on British stamps from their introduction in 1840 until 1844; (***c***) a Geneva mechanism in a cinematographic projector. **Maltese dog** = sense A.3 above. **Maltese lace** a fine bobbin lace associated with Malta. **Maltese terrier** = sense A.3 above.

maltha /ˈmalθə/ *noun*. Now *rare*. **LME.**
[**ORIGIN** Latin from Greek.]
1 A kind of cement made by mixing pitch and wax, or lime and sand, with other ingredients. **LME.**
2 A viscid form of natural asphalt. Also called ***mineral tar***. **E17.**

Malthoid /ˈmalθɔɪd/ *noun*. *Austral. & NZ*. Also **m-**. **M20.**
[**ORIGIN** from **MALTHA** + **-OID**.]
(Proprietary name for) a bituminous material made from wood fibre and used esp. as a roof covering or flooring material.

Malthusian /malˈθjuːzɪən/ *adjective & noun*. **E19.**
[**ORIGIN** from *Malthus* (see below) + **-IAN**.]
▶ **A** *adjective*. Of, pertaining to, or characteristic of the English clergyman and economist Thomas Robert Malthus (1766–1834), the population control advocated by him (see **MALTHUSIANISM**), or his followers. **E19.**
▶ **B** *noun*. An adherent of Malthus in his views on population. **E19.**

M

Malthusianism /mal'θju:zɪənɪz(ə)m/ *noun.* M19.
[ORIGIN from MALTHUSIAN + -ISM.]
The doctrine of T. R. Malthus and his followers that the rate of increase of the population tends to be out of proportion to the increase of its means of subsistence and therefore should be checked, mainly by sexual restraint.

malting /'mɒltɪŋ, 'mɔ:lt-/ *noun.* ME.
[ORIGIN from MALT *verb* + -ING[1].]
1 The action of MALT *verb*. ME.
2 A malthouse. E18.

Malto /'maltəʊ/ *noun & adjective.* L19.
[ORIGIN Maler (Malto) = language of the Maler.]
(Of) the Dravidian language of the Maler, also called ***Maler, Rajmahali***.

maltodextrin /mɒltəʊ'dɛkstrɪn, mɔ:lt-/ *noun.* L19.
[ORIGIN from MALTO(SE + DEXTRIN.]
CHEMISTRY. A dextrin containing maltose, used as a food additive.

maltol /'mɒltɒl, mɔ:lt-/ *noun.* L19.
[ORIGIN from MALT *noun*[1] + -OL.]
CHEMISTRY. A crystalline pyranone derivative, $C_6H_6O_3$, present in larch bark and chicory and prepared by roasting malt.

maltose /'mɒltəʊz, -s, mɔ:lt-/ *noun.* M19.
[ORIGIN from MALT *noun*[1] + -OSE[2].]
CHEMISTRY. A disaccharide consisting of two glucose residues, produced by the hydrolysis of starch under the action of malt, saliva, etc.

maltreat /mal'tri:t/ *verb trans.* E18.
[ORIGIN French *maltraiter*, formed as MAL- + TREAT *verb*.]
Abuse, ill-use; handle roughly or rudely; ill-treat.
■ **maltreater** *noun* E20.

maltreatment /mal'tri:tm(ə)nt/ *noun.* E18.
[ORIGIN French *maltraitement*, formed as MALTREAT: see -MENT.]
The action of maltreating someone or something; the state of being maltreated.

maltster /'mɒltstə, mɔ:lt-/ *noun.* ME.
[ORIGIN from MALT *noun*[1] + -STER.]
A person whose occupation it is to make malt.

malty /'mɒlti, 'mɔ:lti/ *adjective.* E18.
[ORIGIN from MALT *noun*[1] + -Y[1].]
1 Of the nature of or resembling malt. E18.
2 Fond of or affected by malt liquor. *joc. arch.* E19.
■ **maltiness** *noun* M20.

M

malum in se /malәm ɪn 'si:, 'seɪ/ *noun & adjectival phr.* Pl. of noun ***mala in se*** /'malə/. E17.
[ORIGIN medieval Latin = bad in itself.]
(A thing) intrinsically evil or wicked.

malvaceous /mal'veɪʃəs/ *adjective.* L17.
[ORIGIN from Latin *malvaceus*, from *malva* MALLOW: see -ACEOUS.]
BOTANY. Like mallow; of or pertaining to the family Malvaceae to which the mallows belong.

Malvasia /malvə'si:ə, -z-/ *noun.* M17.
[ORIGIN Italian form of *Monemvasia*: see MALMSEY. Cf. MALVOISIE.]
= MALMSEY.

Malvern /'mɒlv(ə)n, 'mɔ:l-/ *noun.* M18.
[ORIGIN A town in Worcestershire, England: cf. MALVERNIAN.]
In full ***Malvern water***. A mineral water from springs near Malvern.

Malvernian /mɒl'və:nɪən, mɔ:l-/ *adjective.* L19.
[ORIGIN from *Malvern* Hills, a range of hills in Worcestershire, England: see -IAN. Cf. MALVERN.]
Chiefly GEOLOGY. Of, pertaining to, or characteristic of the Malvern Hills; *spec.* designating (***a***) a Precambrian series of plutonic rocks forming most of the hills; (***b***) a north-south orientation like that of the hills.

malversate /mal'və:seɪt/ *verb trans.* L19.
[ORIGIN Back-form. from MALVERSATION.]
Use (funds) for an improper purpose, misappropriate.

malversation /malvə'seɪʃ(ə)n/ *noun.* M16.
[ORIGIN French, from *malverser* from Latin *male versari* behave badly: see -ATION.]
1 Corrupt behaviour in a commission, office, employment, or position of trust; an instance of this. M16.
2 Corrupt administration *of* (public money etc.). E18.

†**malverse** *verb intrans.* Chiefly *Scot.* M17–M18.
[ORIGIN French *malverser*: see MALVERSATION.]
Act corruptly in a position of trust.

Malvi /'ma:lvi/ *noun & adjective.* L19.
[ORIGIN Rajasthani.]
(Of) a Rajasthani dialect of NW Madhya Pradesh, India.

malvoisie /'malvɔɪzi, malvɔɪ'zi:/ *noun. arch.* Also **M-**. LME.
[ORIGIN French form of *Monemvasia*: see MALMSEY. Cf. MALVASIA.]
= MALMSEY.

mal vu /mal vy/ *adjectival phr.* E20.
[ORIGIN French, lit. 'badly seen'.]
Held in low esteem, looked down on.

malware /'malwɛ:/ *noun.* L20.
[ORIGIN Shortened from *malicious software*.]
COMPUTING. Software, such as a virus, which is specifically designed to disrupt or damage a computer system.

mam /mam/ *noun. colloq. & dial.* M16.
[ORIGIN Perh. imit. of infants' first speech: see MAMMA *noun*[2]. Cf. MUM *noun*[3].]
Mother.

mama *noun* var. of MAMMA *noun*[2].

mamaliga /mɑmə'li:gə/ *noun.* E19.
[ORIGIN Romanian *mămăligă*.]
Polenta, maize porridge, as a staple food in Romania.

mamaloi /'mam(ə)lwɑ:/ *noun.* Pl. **-s**, same. L19.
[ORIGIN Haitian creole *mamalwa*, from *mama* mother + *lwa* LOA *noun*[2].]
A voodoo priestess. Cf. PAPALOI.

†**Mamamouchi** *noun.* L17–M18.
[ORIGIN Pseudo-Turkish, title pretended to have been conferred by the Sultan upon M. Jourdain, in Molière's play *Le bourgeois gentilhomme*.]
A pompous-sounding title. Also, a person assuming such a title, a ridiculous pretender to elevated dignity.

mama-san /'mamәsan/ *noun.* Pl. **-s**, same. E20.
[ORIGIN Japanese, from *mama* mother + *san* SAN *noun*[3].]
In Japan and the Far East: a woman in a position of authority, *spec.* one in charge of a geisha house; the mistress of a bar.

mamba /'mambə/ *noun.* M19.
[ORIGIN Zulu *imamba*.]
Any of several large venomous semi-arboreal elapid snakes of the tropical African genus *Dendroaspis*; esp. *D. angusticeps*, which occurs in green and black colour phases (***green mamba***, ***black mamba***).

mambo /'mambəʊ/ *noun & verb.* M20.
[ORIGIN Amer. Spanish, prob. from Haitian creole, from Yoruba, lit. 'to talk'.]
▸ **A** *noun.* Pl. **-os**.
1 A kind of rumba, a ballroom dance of Latin American origin; a piece of music for this dance. M20.
2 A voodoo priestess. M20.
▸ **B** *verb intrans.* Dance the mambo. M20.

mambu /'mambu:/ *noun.* L16.
[ORIGIN Portuguese: see BAMBOO.]
= BAMBOO 1.

mamelière /mamɛljɛ:r/ *noun.* Pl. pronounced same. E19.
[ORIGIN French, formed as MAMELLE.]
hist. A piece of armour consisting of a circular plate of metal covering either breast.

mamelle /ma'mɛl/ *noun.* LME.
[ORIGIN Old French & mod. French from Latin MAMILLA: see -EL[1].]
†**1** A woman's breast. LME–L15.
2 A rounded hill, esp. as one of a pair. *N. Amer.* L18.

mamelon /'mamɪlən/ *noun.* M19.
[ORIGIN French = nipple, formed as MAMELLE.]
1 A small rounded eminence or hillock. M19.
2 ZOOLOGY. A small rounded structure, *esp.* the central knob of an echinoid tubercle. L19.
■ **mamelonated** *adjective* covered with rounded protuberances M19.

mameluco /mamə'lu:kəʊ/ *noun.* Pl. **-os**. M19.
[ORIGIN Portuguese, prob. from Arabic *mamlūk*: see MAMELUKE.]
A person with one white and one Brazilian Indian parent; a Brazilian mestizo.

Mameluke /'maməlu:k/ *noun & adjective. obsolete* exc. *hist.* Also **Mamluk** /'maml(j)u:k/. E16.
[ORIGIN French *mameluk* from Arabic *mamlūk* object of possession, slave, use as noun of pass. pple of *malaka* possess.]
▸ **A** *noun.* **1** A member of a regime established and maintained by (emancipated) white military slaves (orig. Kipchaks, later Circassians) which ruled Egypt as a sultanate from 1250 until 1517, continuing as a ruling military caste under Ottoman sovereignty until 1812, and in Syria from 1260 to 1516. E16.
2 A slave in a Muslim country. E16.
3 A member of any military body of slaves; a slavish champion or supporter. M16.
▸ **B** *attrib.* or as *adjective*. Of or pertaining to the Mamelukes. L18.

mamenchisaurus /məmɛntʃɪ'sɔ:rəs/ *noun.* Pl. **-ri** /-rʌɪ/, **-ruses**. M20.
[ORIGIN mod. Latin (see below), from *Mamenchi*, a place in Szechuan province, China, where fossil remains were found + Greek *sauros* lizard.]
A large Jurassic dinosaur of the genus *Mamenchisaurus*, related to the diplodocus and having an extremely long neck.
■ Also **ma'menchisaur** *noun* L20.

mamey *noun* var. of MAMMEE.

mamilla /ma'mɪlə/ *noun.* Also ***-mm-**. Pl. **-llae** /-li:/, **-llas**. L17.
[ORIGIN Latin, dim. of *mamma* breast, teat.]
1 ANATOMY & ZOOLOGY. The nipple of the mamma or mammary gland. L17.
2 *transf.* (ANATOMY, BOTANY, etc.) Any nipple-shaped organ or protuberance; a papilla. E19.

mamillar, **mamillary** *adjectives* see MAMMILLAR, MAMMILLARY.

mamillate *adjective* var. of MAMMILLATE.

mamillated *adjective* see MAMMILLATED.

mamillation *noun*, **mamilliferous**, **mamilliform** *adjectives* vars. of MAMMILLATION etc.

Mamluk *noun & adjective* var. of MAMELUKE.

mamma /'mamə/ *noun*[1]. Pl. **mammae** /'mami:/. OE.
[ORIGIN Latin.]
ANATOMY & ZOOLOGY. The milk-secreting organ of the female in humans and other mammals; the breast; the mammary gland. Also, the corresponding vestigial structure in males.

mamma /mə'mɑ:, 'mamə/ *noun*[2]. Also **mama**. M16.
[ORIGIN Redupl. of *ma* in infants' natural first speech. See also MAMMY *noun*[1], MOMMA, MUMMY *noun*[2]. Cf. MA, MAUMA, MOMMA.]
1 Mother. Used also, chiefly among black people, as a form of address to a mature or older woman. M16.
Mamma mia! /mamә 'mi:ә/ [Italian = mother mine]: expr. surprise or astonishment. **mamma's boy** = ***mother's boy*** s.v. MOTHER *noun*[1].
2 A wife or girlfriend; a sexually attractive (esp. mature) woman. *slang* (chiefly *US*). E20.
sweet mamma: see SWEET *adjective & adverb*.

mammae *noun* pl. of MAMMA *noun*[1].

mammal /'mam(ə)l/ *noun.* E19.
[ORIGIN First used in pl. as an anglicized form of MAMMALIA.]
A furred, warm-blooded, amniote animal of the vertebrate class Mammalia, members of which are characterized by the possession of mammary glands in the female (from which the young are fed) and a four-chambered heart, are typically viviparous (but see MONOTREME; cf. also MARSUPIAL, PLACENTAL), and include humans, rodents, bats, whales, ungulates, carnivores, etc.
■ **mamma'liferous** *adjective* (PALAEONTOLOGY) containing mammalian remains M19. **mammal-like** *adjective* resembling (that of) a mammal; ***mammal-like reptile***, spec. = SYNAPSID *noun*: M20.

Mammalia /mə'meɪlɪə/ *noun pl.* Also **m-**. L18.
[ORIGIN mod. Latin, use as noun of neut. pl. of late Latin *mammalis* adjective, from *mamma*: see MAMMA *noun*[1], -IA[2].]
ZOOLOGY. A class of vertebrate animals comprising the mammals; mammals collectively.

mammalian /mə'meɪlɪən/ *adjective & noun.* E19.
[ORIGIN from MAMMALIA + -AN.]
▸ **A** *adjective.* Of, belonging to, or characteristic of the Mammalia; of, pertaining to, or the nature of a mammal or mammals. E19.
▸ **B** *noun.* A mammal. *rare.* M19.

mammalogy /mə'malədʒi/ *noun.* M19.
[ORIGIN Irreg. from MAMMAL + -LOGY.]
The scientific study of mammals.
■ **mamma'logical** *adjective* of or pertaining to mammalogy M19. **mammalogist** *noun* M19.

mammaplasty /'maməplasti/ *noun.* Also **mammo-**. M20.
[ORIGIN from MAMMA *noun*[1] + -PLASTY.]
Alteration of the shape or size of a breast by plastic surgery; an instance of this.

mammary /'maməri/ *adjective & noun.* E17.
[ORIGIN from MAMMA *noun*[1] + -ARY[1].]
▸ **A** *adjective.* **1** Of or pertaining to the mamma or breast. E17.
mammary gland the milk-secreting gland in the mamma of a female mammal.
†**2** Of a tumour: resembling a mammary gland in structure. Only in 19.
▸ **B** *noun.* **1** A mammary artery, gland, etc. L17.
2 A woman's breast. Usu. in *pl. colloq.* M20.

FHM Mammaries are seen as the essence of femininity.

mammee /ma'mi:/ *noun.* Also **mamey**. L16.
[ORIGIN Spanish *mamei* (whence French *mamey*) from Taino.]
1 More fully ***mammee apple***. A large tropical American tree, *Mammea americana* (family Guttiferae); its edible fruit, which has a sweet yellow aromatic flesh. L16.
2 In full ***mammee sapota***. A Central American tree, *Pouteria sapota* (family Sapotaceae); the oval russet edible fruit of this tree, which has a spicy red flesh (also called ***marmalade plum***, ***zapote***). M17.

mammer /'mamə/ *verb intrans. obsolete* exc. *dial.* LME.
[ORIGIN Imit., with frequentative suffix -ER[5].]
Stammer, mutter. Also, vacillate, waver, be undecided.
■ **mammering** *noun* (***a***) the action of the verb; (***b***) a state of doubt, hesitation, or perplexity: LME.

mammet, **mammetry** *nouns* see MAUMET, MAUMETRY.

mammiferous /ma'mɪf(ə)rəs/ *adjective.* Now *rare.* E19.
[ORIGIN from MAMMA *noun*[1] + -I- + -FEROUS.]
1 = MAMMALIAN *adjective*. E19.
2 ANATOMY. Of a part of the body: bearing the mammae. L19.
■ **mammifer** /'mamɪfə/ *noun* (now *rare*) = MAMMAL *noun* E19.

mammiform /'mamɪfɔ:m/ *adjective.* L17.
[ORIGIN formed as MAMMIFEROUS + -I- + -FORM.]
Breast-shaped; having the form of a dome or rounded cone.

mammilla *noun* see MAMILLA.

mammillar /ˈmamɪlə/ *adjective*. Also **mamill-**. LME.
[ORIGIN formed as MAMMILLARY: see -AR[1].]
= MAMMILLARY 1.

mammillary /ˈmamɪləri/ *adjective*. Also **mamillary**. E17.
[ORIGIN formed as MAMILLA + -ARY[2]: alt. to *-mm-* by assim. to MAMMARY.]
1 Breast-shaped; of the form of a dome or rounded cone; mammiform. E17. ▸**b** Chiefly *MINERALOGY*. Having several smoothly rounded convex surfaces; botryoidal. E19.
mammillary body [Latin *corpus mamillare*] either of a pair of small rounded structures on the ventral surface of the hypothalamus in vertebrates.
2 Of or pertaining to the nipple or (formerly) the breast. M17.

mammillate /ˈmamɪleɪt/ *adjective*. Also **mamill-**. E19.
[ORIGIN formed as MAMMILLARY + -ATE[2].]
Mammillated; mammiform.

mammillated /ˈmamɪleɪtɪd/ *adjective*. Also (earlier) **mamill-**. M18.
[ORIGIN formed as MAMMILLARY + -ED[2].]
1 Characterized by or covered with rounded mounds or lumps; now chiefly *GEOLOGY*, (of a glaciated landform) worn into smooth convexities. Also (*MINERALOGY*), = MAMMILLARY 1b. M18.
2 *BOTANY & ZOOLOGY*. Having a nipple-shaped process or part. M19.

mammillation /mamɪˈleɪʃ(ə)n/ *noun*. Also **mamill-**. M19.
[ORIGIN formed as MAMMILLARY + -ATION.]
1 The condition of being mammillated. M19.
2 A rounded protuberance. M19.

mammilliferous /mamɪˈlɪf(ə)rəs/ *adjective*. Also **mamill-**. M19.
[ORIGIN formed as MAMMILLARY + -I- + -FEROUS.]
Chiefly *ZOOLOGY*. Having or bearing mamillae.

mammilliform /maˈmɪlɪfɔːm/ *adjective*. Also **mamill-**. M19.
[ORIGIN formed as MAMMILLARY + -I- + -FORM.]
ANATOMY & ZOOLOGY. Shaped like or resembling a mamilla; nipple-shaped.

mammitis /maˈmʌɪtɪs/ *noun*. L19.
[ORIGIN from MAMMA *noun*[1] + -ITIS.]
MEDICINE. Inflammation of a mammary gland.

mammo- /ˈmaməʊ/ *combining form* of MAMMA *noun*[1]: see -O-.
▪ **mammogen** *noun* any substance having (supposed) mammogenic activity M20. **mammoˈgenesis** *noun* the stimulation of the growth of the breasts, esp. at puberty M20. **mammoˈgenic** *adjective* of, pertaining to, or causing mammogenesis M20. **mammogram**, **mammograph** *nouns* (*MEDICINE*) a radiograph taken by mammography M20. **mammoˈgraphic** *adjective* of or pertaining to mammography M20. **mammoˈgraphically** *adverb* by means of mammography L20. **maˈmmography** *noun* a technique or procedure for diagnosing and locating abnormalities of the breasts using X-rays; an examination by this technique: M20.

mammock /ˈmamək/ *noun & verb*. Now *arch. & dial.* E16.
[ORIGIN from unkn. 1st elem. + -OCK.]
▸ **A** *noun*. A scrap, a shred, a broken or torn piece. E16.
▸ **B** *verb trans.* Break, cut, or tear into fragments or shreds. E17.

Mammon /ˈmamən/ *noun*. OE.
[ORIGIN Late Latin *mam(m)ona*, *mam(m)on* from New Testament Greek *mam(m)ōnas* (*Matthew* 6:24, *Luke* 16:9, 11, 13) from Hebrew *māmōn* money, wealth.]
In early use, (the proper name of) the devil of covetousness. Later (usu. with more or less personification), wealth regarded as an idol or as an evil influence.

A. N. WILSON The worship of Mammon blatantly overrode any questions of justice, fairness or human kindness.

the Mammon of unrighteousness wealth ill-used or ill-gained.
▪ **Mammondom** *noun* the realm or domain of Mammon E19. **Mammonish** *adjective* influenced by or devoted to Mammon M17. **Mammonism** *noun* devotion to the pursuit of riches M19. **Mammonist** *noun* a worshipper of Mammon, a person devoted to the pursuit of riches M16. **Mammoˈnistic** *adjective* of or pertaining to Mammonists or Mammonism L19. **Mammonite** *noun* = MAMMONIST E18. **Mammonitish** *adjective* resembling Mammon; characteristic of a Mammonist: E17.

mammoplasty *noun* var. of MAMMAPLASTY.

mammoth /ˈmaməθ/ *noun & adjective*. E18.
[ORIGIN Russian *mámo(n)t*, prob. of Siberian origin.]
▸ **A** *noun*. **1** Pl. **-s**, same. Any of several very large extinct mammals of the Pleistocene genus *Mammuthus*, related to the elephants and known from fossil and mummified remains in northern Eurasia and N. America. E18. ▸**b** A mastodon. *US*. E19.
imperial mammoth, ***Siberian mammoth***, ***woolly mammoth***.
2 A thing of huge size. L19.
▸ **B** *adjective*. Comparable to the mammoth in size; huge, gigantic. E19.

LYNDON B. JOHNSON The mammoth task of preparing a $100 billion budget.

mammoth tree the wellingtonia, *Sequoiadendron giganteum*.

mammotrophic /maməʊ)ˈtrəʊfɪk, -ˈtrɒf-/ *adjective*. Also **-tropic** /-ˈtrəʊpɪk, -ˈtrɒp-/. M20.
[ORIGIN from MAMMO- + -TROPHIC, -TROPIC.]
PHYSIOLOGY. Of a hormone or its activity: regulating the growth or milk secretion of the breasts.
▪ **ˈmammotroph** /-trəʊf/ *noun* a cell of the mammalian adenohypophysis which secretes prolactin M20. **mammotrophin**, **mammotropin** *nouns* = PROLACTIN M20.

mammy /ˈmami/ *noun*[1]. E16.
[ORIGIN from (the same root as) MAM + -Y[6]. Cf. MOMMY, MUMMY *noun*[2].]
1 Mother. *colloq. & dial.* E16.
2 In the southern US, esp. before the abolition of slavery, a black woman having the care of white children (cf. earlier MOMMA 1); *gen.* (*offensive*) a black woman. Cf. MAUMA. M19.
– COMB.: **mammy-sick** *adjective* (*arch.*, *derog.*) distressed at being separated from one's mother.

mammy /ˈmami/ *noun*[2]. *W. Afr.* E20.
[ORIGIN W. African use of MAMMY *noun*[1] or MAMMA *noun*[2] as a word for any woman.]
1 ***mammy boat***, ***mammy chair***, a basket or chair used on ships for conveying people to and from boats. E20.
2 ***mammy cloth***, a cotton cloth or robe wrapped around the body. M20.
3 ***mammy lorry***, ***mammy wagon***, a small open-sided vehicle for transporting passengers or goods. M20.
4 ***mammy trader***, a female market trader. M20.

mamo /ˈmeɪməʊ/ *noun*. Pl. **-os**. L19.
[ORIGIN Hawaiian.]
Either of two Hawaiian honeycreepers, the black and yellow *Drepanis pacifica* and (more fully ***black mamo***) the black *D. funerea*, both extinct since the early 20th cent.

mamoty /ˈmaməti/ *noun*. Also **mamootie**. L18.
[ORIGIN Tamil *mammaṭṭi* alt. of *maṉveṭṭi*, from *maṉ* earth + *veṭṭi* spade.]
A digging tool shaped like a hoe with the blade at an acute angle to the handle, used mainly in India.

mampus /ˈmampəs/ *noun*. *dial.* M18.
[ORIGIN Perh. from English dial. *mump* a lump or heap.]
A great number, a crowd.

mam'selle /mamˈzɛl/ *noun*. *colloq.* L18.
[ORIGIN French, contr.]
= MADEMOISELLE.

mamur /maˈmuːr/ *noun*. M19.
[ORIGIN Arabic *ma'mūr* use as noun of past pple of *amara* to order; cf. AMIR.]
An Egyptian official governing a district.

mamzer /ˈmʌmzə/ *noun*. Also **momser**, **momzer**, /ˈmɒmzə/. Pl. **-rim** /-rɪm/, **-ers**. M16.
[ORIGIN Late Latin from Hebrew *mamzēr*.]
A person conceived in a forbidden sexual union, esp. as defined by rabbinical tradition. Also used as a term of abuse or familiarity.

man /man/ *noun*. Pl. **men** /mɛn/.
[ORIGIN Old English *man(n)*, *mon(n)* corresp. to Old Frisian *man*, *mon*, Old Saxon *man*, Old High German *man* (Dutch *man*, German *Mann*), Old Norse *maðr*, Gothic *manna*, from Germanic bases rel. to Sanskrit *manu* man, mankind.]
▸ **I** **1** A human being (formerly explicitly irrespective of sex or age), a person. Now chiefly in general or indefinite applications, as in ***every man***, ***any man***, ***no man***, (in pl.) ***all men***, ***some men***, ***many men***, etc. OE.

D. HUME There is in all men, both male and female, a desire and power of generation. TENNYSON For men may come and men may go, but I go on for ever. J. PLAMENATZ A man, in order to be a man, must know that he is one. *Proverb*: When the wind is in the east, 'tis neither good for man nor beast.

2 (Also **M-**.) (Without article.) The human race or species, humankind, mankind; *ZOOLOGY* the human race viewed as a genus (*Homo*) or species (*H. sapiens*) of animal. OE.

CARLYLE Man is not only a working but a talking animal. M. ESSLIN Winnie's cheerfulness in the face of death . . is an expression of man's courage. *Cornwall Review* Bodmin Moor bears traces of very early man.

▸ **II** **3** An adult male person, as opp. to a woman or boy or both; (non-contrastively, passing into sense 1) an individual (male) person. OE. ▸**b** An adult male eminently endowed with manly qualities. Also, a (male) person of importance. ME. ▸**c** As *voc.* introducing a remark or parenthetically, now sometimes implying contempt or impatience, or as a form of address to both men and women (esp. among black people, among rock and jazz musicians, and *S. Afr. colloq.*), as a meaningless expletive, or as *interjection* expr. surprise, delight, deep emotion, etc. LME.

SHAKES. *Temp.* Misery acquaints a man with strange bedfellows. WORDSWORTH The Child is father to the Man. T. S. ELIOT Mr Simpkins is a man who knows his own mind. B. RUBENS He had seen old men cry, and little boys, but never a man. **c** C. BROWN He said, 'Man, you Claude Brown?' 'Yeah, man, like, I'm the one.' J. NAGENDA He had to leave in a hurry. But . . man, what an achievement!

man of feeling, ***man of honour***, ***man of peace***, ***man of property***, ***man of wisdom***, etc.

4 A member of a fighting force; now *esp.* a rank-and-file soldier or sailor as distinguished from an officer. Usu. in *pl.* OE.
5 *hist.* A vassal, a liegeman. OE.
6 a A manservant; a valet; a workman as distinguished from his employer (usu. in *pl.*). ME. ▸**b** At a university or public school, an undergraduate or student, as distinguished from a graduate or don. *arch.* E19.
7 a A husband. Exc. in ***man and wife***, now chiefly *Scot.*, *dial.*, *S. Afr.*, *& black English*. ME. ▸**b** A lover, a suitor. Long *dial.* ME.
†**8** A non-human being likened to or a thing personified as a male human, e.g. God, the Devil, death. E16–E18.
9 (Without article.) The male human being. L16.
▸ **III** *transf.* **10** Any of the pieces used in playing chess, draughts, backgammon, etc. LME.
11 (A cairn or pile of stones marking) a summit or prominent point of a mountain. *N. English*. LME.
†**12** The obverse of a coin used in tossing (as the side of a penny having the king's head as opp. to Britannia). Cf. WOMAN *noun* 6. E19–M19.
▸ **IV** As 2nd elem. of comb. (in many with pronunc. /mən/).
13 A person, esp. a male, having a specified nationality, place of origin, abode, or education, profession, occupation, or interest; a person, esp. a male, using or skilled in the use of a specified implement; a person, esp. a male, associated with something specified or described as something specified. OE. ▸**b** (An individual of) a prehistoric type of man named from the specified place where remains were found. M19.
axeman, ***badman***, ***barman***, ***bondsman***, ***brakeman***, ***chairman***, ***churchman***, ***clergyman***, ***coalman***, ***countryman***, ***craftsman***, ***Englishman***, ***exciseman***, ***freeman***, ***Frenchman***, ***gentleman***, ***Harvard man***, ***highwayman***, ***journeyman***, ***layman***, ***liegeman***, ***middleman***, ***milkman***, ***Oxford man***, ***penman***, ***postman***, ***rag-and-bone man***, ***Renaissance man***, ***salesman***, ***swordsman***, ***trencherman***, ***university man***, etc. **b** ***Cro-Magnon man***, ***Java man***, ***Neanderthal man***, ***Peking man***, ***Piltdown man***, etc.
14 A piece used in playing a specified game. L15.
chessman, ***draughtsman***, etc.
15 A ship of a specified type. Cf. MAN-OF-WAR. L15.
Indiaman, ***merchantman***, etc.
– PHRASES & COMB.: (A selection of cross-refs. only is included: see esp. other nouns.) Appositional (pl. *men*) with the sense 'male', esp. in names of professions etc. more usually pursued by women, as ***man cook***, ***man nurse***, etc. **a man and a brother** a fellow human being. **as a man** (considered) in respect of his personal character, as distinguished e.g. from his achievements, wealth, etc. **as one man** in unison, unanimously, with one accord. **be a man** be manly, not show fear. **become man**, **be made man** assume human nature. **be man** have human nature. ***be one's own man***: see OWN *adjective*. ***best man***: see BEST *adjective*, *noun*, *& adverb*. ***every man jack***: see JACK *noun*[1]. ***good man!***: see GOOD *adjective*. ***grand old man***: see GRAND *adjective*[1]. ***high men***: see HIGH *adjective*. ***in-and-out man***: see IN AND OUT. ***inner man***: see INNER *adjective & noun*. ***little green man***: see LITTLE *adjective*. ***little man***: see LITTLE *adjective*. ***low men***: see LOW *adjective & noun*[4]. ***man about town***: see TOWN *noun*. ***man alive!***: see ALIVE. **man and boy** *adverb* throughout life from boyhood. **man-ape** an extinct primate intermediate between apes and humans; an australopithecine. ***man-at-arms***: see ARM *noun*[2]. **manbag** a man's handbag or shoulder bag. **man-bites-dog** *adjective* designating a situation in which the usual sufferer is the aggressor. **manbote** (*obsolete exc. hist.*) a fine paid to an overlord for the loss of a man. **man-boy** a youth, an immature man. **man-child**, pl. **men-children**, *arch.* a male child. **man-crazy** *adjective* = ***man-mad*** below. **man-day** a day of work etc. by one person, as a unit of measure. **man-eater** (*a*) a person who eats human flesh, a cannibal; (*b*) an animal, esp. a shark or tiger, that eats or has a propensity for eating human flesh; (*c*) *colloq.* a woman who has many men as lovers. **man-eating** *adjective* (*a*) that eats or has a propensity for eating human flesh; (*b*) (of a woman) having many men as lovers. **man-for-man** = ***man-to-man*** (b) below. ***Man Friday***: see FRIDAY *noun* 1. **man-god** a being (*spec.* Jesus) who is both man and God; a being who is both a man and a god. **man-hater** a hater of humankind, a misanthrope; a hater of the male sex. **man-haul** *verb trans.* haul or draw along (a sledge etc.) by human exertion rather than by dog etc. **manhole** a hole or opening in a floor, pavement, boiler, etc., through which a person may pass; a shaft, usu. with a cover, giving access to a sewer etc. for inspection or repair. **man-hour** an hour of work etc. by one person, as a unit of measure. **manhunt** an organized search for a person, esp. a criminal. **manhunter** a hunter of men; a cannibal, a slave dealer, a brigand. **man in motion** *AMER. FOOTBALL* an offensive back allowed to move during a scrimmage before the ball is put in play. **man-keen** *adjective* (now *dial.*) (*a*) (of an animal) inclined to attack people, fierce, savage; (*b*) (of a woman) very fond of men. **man-killer** a killer of humans; a homicide. **man-mad** *adjective* madly desirous of a man or men. **man-made** *adjective & noun* (*a*) *adjective* made or devised by human effort, not existing in nature; artificially made; (of a fibre) manufactured (from regenerated or synthetic polymer); (*b*) *noun* a man-made fibre or fabric. **man-midwife** (now *rare*) a male midwife, an obstetrician. **man-milliner** (*a*) a male milliner; (*b*) *arch.* a man who busies himself with trifling occupations. **man-mountain** an enormously large person; now *esp.* a large wrestler. **man of action** a man whose life is characterized by physical activity or deeds rather than by thoughts and ideas. **man-of-all-work** a male servant who does all kinds of domestic work. **man of blood** *arch.* [a Hebraism] a man who has been responsible for murder or death. **man of destiny** a man looked upon as an instrument of destiny; *spec.* Napoleon I. **man of distinction** a man distinguished in looks, manners, and bearing. ***man of fortune***: see FORTUNE *noun*. ***man of his hands***: see HAND *noun*. **man of God** a man devoted to the service of God, a saint, an ecclesiastic. ***man of ideas***: see IDEA *noun*. **man of law** *arch.* a lawyer. ***man of leisure***: see

LEISURE *noun*. ***man of letters***: see LETTER *noun*[1]. **man of men** a man of supreme excellence. ***man of SCIENCE***. ***man of sense***: see SENSE *noun*. ***man of straw***: see STRAW *noun*. **man of the cloth** a clergyman, an ecclesiastic. **man of the house** the chief male of a household. **man of the match** the player adjudged to have played best in a particular game of football, cricket, etc. **man of the people** a man who comes from or identifies himself with ordinary people; a working-class man. **man of the world** (***a***) a secular person; a worldly or irreligious person; (***b***) a man experienced in the ways of the world and prepared to accept its conventions, a practical tolerant man with experience of life and society. **man-of-the-worldish**, **man-of-the-worldly** *adjectives* pertaining to or characteristic of a man of the world. ***man of virtu***: see VIRTU 1. ***man of wax***: see WAX *noun*[1]. **man orchid** a rare British orchid of chalk grassland, *Aceras anthropophorum*, the labellum of which resembles a dangling greenish-yellow human figure. **manpack** a compact package containing equipment or supplies, designed to be carried easily by one man. **manqueller** (long *arch.*) a murderer. **man-rate** *verb trans.* make (a rocket, spaceship, etc.) suitable for manned flight; certify as safe for manned flight. **man-rem** a unit of radiation exposure equal to one rem incident on one person. **man-riding** the vehicular transport of miners underground. **manrope** NAUTICAL a rope on the side of a gangway or ladder, held in ascending and descending a ship's side, etc. **man's best friend** *spec.* the dog. ***man's estate***: see ESTATE *noun* 1b. **man-shift** (the amount of work done in) a single shift worked by one man. **man-size**, **man-sized** *adjectives* of the size of a man; large, full-size; large enough to occupy, suit, or satisfy a man. **manslayer** *arch.* a murderer; occas., a manslaughterer. **manslaying** *arch.* murder. **man's man** a man who is popular with or who prefers the company of other men. **man's woman** a woman who is popular with or who prefers the company of men. **man-tailored** *adjective* (of a woman's garment) tailored after the fashion of a man's garment. **man-tiger** (***a***) a man resembling a tiger in ferocity; (***b***) a person believed to transform into a tiger. **man to man**, **man-to-man** *adjective & adverb* (***a***) straightforward(ly), frank(ly); (***b***) *attrib.* designating a type of defensive strategy in a team ball game in which each player is responsible for marking one member of the opposing team. **man-trade** *hist.* the slave trade. **mantrap** *noun & verb* (***a***) *noun* a trap for catching people, esp. trespassers; (***b***) *verb trans.* beset with a mantrap or mantraps. **manway** a small passage used by miners etc. **man-week** a week of work etc. by one person, as a unit of measure. **man-woman** (***a***) a hermaphrodite; (***b***) a mannish woman. **man-year** a year of work etc. by one person, as a unit of measure. **menfolk**, (chiefly *US colloq.*) **-folks** men in general; the men of a family or in a company. **menkind** (now *rare*) men in general. **men-only** *adjective* restricted for the use of men. **men's liberation**, **men's lib** (a movement aimed at) the freeing of men from traditional views of their character and role in society. **men's room** a lavatory for males. **menswear**, **men's wear** clothes for men. **my man**, **my good man**: used as a patronizing form of address. ***new man***: see NEW *adjective*. OLD MAN. **one's man** the person who can fulfil one's requirements or with whom one can deal; *spec.* one's representative or envoy *in* a particular place. **play the man** act in a manly fashion, not show fear. **rights of man** human rights. **separate the men from the boys**, **sort out the men from the boys** *colloq.* distinguish which people in a group are truly mature, manly, or competent. ***strong man***: see STRONG *adjective*. **the man** (***a***) the person in his human (as distinguished from his professional, etc.) capacity or character; (***b***) (also ***the Man***) a person in authority; such persons collectively; a prison governor; a policeman, a detective; the police; one's employer or boss; *black slang* a white man; white people collectively; *US slang* a drug dealer; (***c***) (also ***the very man***) the man most suitable *for* some office, work, or need; the kind of man qualified or likely *to do* something. **the man for me**, (*colloq.*) **the man for my money** the man whom I should choose to employ or support. **the man in the boat** *slang* the clitoris. **the man in the moon** the semblance of a human face seen in the full moon (also as the type of an imaginary person). **the man in the street**, (*US*) **the man on the street** the ordinary person, esp. as opp. to an expert. ***the man on the CLAPHAM omnibus***. **the man who** he who, the person who. **the man X** the man previously known or mentioned as bearing the specified name. **the men's** the men's lavatory. **to a man** without exception. ***utility man***: see UTILITY *adjective*. ***waiting man***: see WAITING *ppl adjective* 1. ***White man***: see WHITE *adjective*. ***write oneself man***: see WRITE *verb*. ***yesterday's man***: see YESTERDAY *noun*. ***young man***: see YOUNG *adjective*.

– NOTE: Despite the original use (see sense 1), in M20 the generic sense 'human beings in general' came to be regarded by some as old-fashioned or sexist. Alternatives such as *the human race* or *humankind* are sometimes preferred, but there are no obvious substitutes for many compound forms, e.g. *manpower* or *man-made*.

■ **manness** /-n-n-/ *noun* (*rare*) †(***a***) human nature; (***b***) maleness: ME. **manward** *adverb & adjective* (***a***) *adverb* [orig. †*to manward*] towards man, in the direction of man; in relation to man; (***b***) *adjective* tending or directed towards man: LME. **manwise** *adverb & pred. adjective* in the fashion or way of men; in respect of a man; concerning individual men: E20.

man /man/ *verb trans.* Infl. **-nn-**.

[ORIGIN Late Old English (*ge*)*mannian*, with corresp. forms in other Germanic langs., formed as the noun.]

▸ **I 1** Act as or provide the person(s) required to serve or defend (a fort, ship, etc.), be ready for action at or in (a particular position or place), undertake (an industrial enterprise, etc.), fulfil the function or work of (a job etc.). LOE. ▸†**b** Equip and send (a boat, occas. an army) *out, forth, after*, etc. L15–L18.

> J. CONRAD The ship of which I knew nothing, manned by men of whom I knew very little. J. K. GALBRAITH The greatest industrial enterprises . . were manned principally by men who could speak no English. D. M. FRAME Well fortified and manned, the town held out stoutly. *Country Quest* A cousin of mine volunteered to man a machine-gun post.

man up provide with the full complement of people, esp. workers, required.

†**2 a** Supply with inhabitants; people. LME–L16. ▸†**b** Fill up with men. *rare* (Spenser). Only in L16.

†**3 a** Provide with followers or attendants; escort (a person, esp. a woman). LME–M18. ▸**b** Provide (a horse) with a rider. M16–M17.

▸ **II 4** †**a** *refl.* Put on a show of manliness. Only in ME. ▸**b** Make (esp. oneself) manly or courageous; brace (oneself or another) *up*; fortify the spirits or courage of (esp. oneself). E17.

5 Be the master of; manage, rule. *obsolete* exc. *dial.* ME.

6 Invest with manly qualities or appearance; make manlike or (formerly, of God) into a man. Now *rare*. L16.

▸ **III 7** Accustom (a hawk or other bird) to human presence or handling; *gen.* make tame or tractable. L16.

■ **manned** *ppl adjective* staffed or guarded by humans; now *esp.* designating or pertaining to aviation or space travel with a human crew: E17.

Man. *abbreviation*.

Manitoba.

mana /ˈmɑːnə/ *noun*[1]. M19.

[ORIGIN Maori.]

Power, authority, prestige (chiefly *NZ*); ANTHROPOLOGY an impersonal supernatural power which can be associated with people or with objects and which can be transmitted or inherited.

†**mana** *noun*[2] var. of MAUND *noun*[2].

manacle /ˈmanək(ə)l/ *noun & verb*. ME.

[ORIGIN Old French & mod. French *manicle* handcuff, (as in mod. French) gauntlet from Latin *manicula* dim. of *manus* hand.]

▸ **A** *noun*. **1** A fetter for the hand; a handcuff; *fig.* a bond, a restraint. Usu. in *pl.* ME.

†**2** A tether or shackle for a horse. M16–E17.

▸ **B** *verb trans.* Fetter or confine (the hands); fetter with handcuffs; *fig.* bind, restrain. ME.

manage /ˈmanɪdʒ/ *noun*. *arch.* L16.

[ORIGIN Italian *maneggio* (whence French MANÈGE), formed as MANAGE *verb*.]

1 a = MANÈGE 2. L16. ▸**b** = MANÈGE 1. M17.

†**2** The action or manner of managing; management. L16–M18.

3 The skilful handling *of* (a weapon etc.). E17.

manage /ˈmanɪdʒ/ *verb*. M16.

[ORIGIN Italian *maneggiare* from Proto-Romance, from Latin *manus* hand.]

▸ **I** *verb trans.* **1** Handle, train, or direct (a horse) in its paces; put through the exercises of the manège. *obsolete* exc. as passing into sense 4. M16.

2 Handle, wield, make use of (a weapon, tool, implement, etc.); control the sailing of (a ship or boat). L16.

> R. L. STEVENSON He carried a crutch, which he managed with wonderful dexterity. G. A. BIRMINGHAM Like a man who might make a wreck of a boat through incapacity to manage her.

3 Conduct or carry on (a war, a business, an undertaking, an operation); control the course of (affairs) by one's own action; control and direct the affairs of (a household, institution, state, etc.); be the manager of (a team etc.); take charge of, attend to (cattle, etc.). L16. ▸**b** Work out in literary treatment. L17.

> D. LESSING The liquor shop that Mr and Mrs Danderlea had been managing for . . twenty years. *Economist* Fulham are managed by an elderly asthmatic who foresaw football's slump. *Washington Post* The saxophonist's career has been managed by his wife. T. BENN If we are to have a managed economy . . 'In whose interests is it to be managed?' H. R. LANDON As Grand Duke of Tuscany he had managed his Duchy wisely. **b** DRYDEN How a tragedy should be contrived and managed, in better verse . . than I could teach others.

4 Cause (a person, animal, etc.) to submit to one's rule or direction. L16.

> G. STEIN This daughter who was always a hard child to manage.

5 Administer, regulate the use or expenditure of (finances, provisions, etc.); (now *rare*) deal with or treat carefully, use sparingly or with judgement, husband (one's health, life, money, etc.). L16. ▸†**b** Treat with indulgence or consideration. Only in E18.

6 Control the use or exploitation of (land etc.); manipulate for a purpose. Formerly also, till. M17.

> *Bird Watching* Heather moorlands, still managed for grouse shooting.

7 Bring (a person) to consent to one's wishes by artifice, flattery, or judicious suggestion of motives. L17.

> GEO. ELIOT Managing one's husband is some pleasure.

8 Bring about by contrivance; succeed in accomplishing or acquiring; find a way *to do*; (freq. *iron.*) be so unskilful or unlucky as *to do*. E18.

> G. VIDAL I was miserable, wondering in what I had managed to offend him. D. ATHILL I struggled to get the sails up, but I managed it. G. HARRIS Huddled in the narrow aisle, Gidjabolgo and Gwerath did manage a little sleep.

9 With *can* or *be able*: cope with the difficulties of; succeed in using, dealing with, etc. E19.

> C. LAMB I had more time on my hands than I could ever manage.

▸ **II** *verb intrans.* †**10** Of a horse: perform the exercises of the manège. L16–E18.

11 Conduct affairs; act as a manager. Formerly also, plot, scheme, intrigue. E17.

> F. NIGHTINGALE As impossible in a book to teach a person . . how to manage, as . . to teach her how to nurse.

12 Succeed (under disadvantages) in one's aim; cope with one's life or situation; contrive to get on *with* (esp. what is hardly adequate). *colloq.* M19.

> A. CARNEGIE I have a good . . wife who manages well. We . . buy our supplies wholesale . . and save one third. G. CLARE She walked slowly and always used a stick, but she managed quite well. R. DAHL They simply amputated . . and . . my father had to manage with one arm.

■ **mana'gee** *noun* (*rare*) the person who is managed (correl. to *manager*) M19.

manageable /ˈmanɪdʒəb(ə)l/ *adjective*. L16.

[ORIGIN from MANAGE *verb* + -ABLE.]

That can be managed; amenable to control or guidance, tractable; admitting of being wielded, manipulated, or administered, workable; able to be accomplished by contrivance.

■ **managea'bility** *noun* L18. **manageableness** *noun* M17. **manageably** *adverb* M19.

managed /ˈmanɪdʒd/ *ppl adjective*. L16.

[ORIGIN formed as MANAGEABLE + -ED[1].]

1 Trained to the manège. *arch.* L16.

2 Controlled, conducted, administered. E17.

well-managed, ***ill-managed***, etc. **managed care** *US* a system of health care emphasizing preventative medicine and home treatment. **managed currency** a currency system which is not tied to the gold standard but is regulated by the government of the country concerned. **managed economy** an economy in which the framework and general policies are regulated or controlled by the government. **managed fund** FINANCE a unit-linked investment plan in which a client's premium is converted into a combination of fixed-interest and property investments, which may be adjusted at the discretion of the fund's managers.

3 Of demeanour, expressions, etc.: nicely restrained, measured. Now *rare*. L18.

management /ˈmanɪdʒm(ə)nt/ *noun*. L16.

[ORIGIN formed as MANAGEABLE + -MENT.]

1 The action of managing; the manner of managing; the application of skill or care in the manipulation, use, treatment, or control of things or persons, or in the conduct of an enterprise, operation, etc.; the administration of (a group within) an organization or commercial enterprise; MEDICINE the technique of treating all the manifestations of a disease etc. L16. ▸†**b** An instance of managing; an administrative act. Only in 17.

> LD MACAULAY In the management of the heroic couplet Dryden has never been equalled. W. S. MAUGHAM She had never been used to the management of money. H. I. ANSOFF Management of a business firm is a very large complex of activities. J. ARGENTI Management by Exception . ., 'don't tell someone if everything is O.K.—only . . if something has gone wrong'. N. SEDAKA Leba began to help with the management of my career.

2 The use of contrivance, prudence, ingenuity, or (esp.) deceit or trickery for effecting some purpose. M17. ▸†**b** A contrivance, a device; a piece of trickery. Only in M18.

> B. JOWETT We rely not upon management or trickery, but upon our own hearts and hands.

†**3** A negotiation. Only in E18.

†**4** Indulgence or consideration shown towards a person; politic moderation in the conduct of a case; an instance of this. E18–E19.

5 *collect.* A governing body of an organization or business, as a board of directors; that group of employees administering and controlling an organization, business, etc.; the group or class of managers. M18.

> J. PLAMENATZ Powerful workers' organizations make demands that neither managements nor governments can ignore. *Broadcast* Management decided it could not afford to replace him.

middle management: see MIDDLE *adjective*.

– COMB.: **management accounting** the provision of financial data and advice to a company for use in the organization and development of its business; **management company** a company which is set up to manage a group of properties, a unit trust, an investment fund, etc.

■ **manage'mental** *adjective* L19.

manager /ˈmanɪdʒə/ *noun*. L16.

[ORIGIN formed as MANAGEABLE + -ER[1].]

1 A person who manages something. Now *rare* in *gen.* sense. L16.

2 A member of a committee in the Houses of Parliament and the US Senate appointed by one House to confer with a similar committee of the other House. M17.

3 A person skilled in managing household affairs, money, etc. Chiefly with qualifying adjective as *good*, *poor*, etc. L17.

4 A person who manages an organization, business establishment, or public institution, or part of one; a person with a primarily executive or supervisory function within an organization etc. E18. ▸**b** A person controlling the

activities of a person or team in sports, entertainment, etc. **M19.**
bank manager, factory manager, floor manager, hotel manager, personnel manager, stage manager, theatre manager, etc. ***middle manager***: see MIDDLE *adjective*. **b** ***football manager, team manager,*** etc.
5 *LAW.* A person appointed to control and account for a business for the benefit of creditors etc. **L18.**
■ **managership** *noun* the office or position of a manager; managerial control; (a) management: **E19.**

manageress /ˌmanɪdʒəˈrɛs, ˈmanɪdʒərɪs/ *noun.* **L18.**
[ORIGIN from MANAGER + -ESS[1].]
A woman manager; *esp.* a woman who has charge of a shop, hotel, canteen, etc.

managerial /manɪˈdʒɪərɪəl/ *adjective.* **M18.**
[ORIGIN formed as MANAGERESS + -IAL.]
Of, pertaining to, or characteristic of a manager, *esp.* a professional manager of or within an organization, business, establishment, etc.
■ **managerialism** *noun* (belief in) the use of professional managers in conducting or planning business or other enterprises **M20.** **managerialist** *noun & adjective* (**a**) *noun* an adherent of managerialism; (**b**) *adjective* of or pertaining to managerialists or managerialism: **M20.** **managerially** *adverb* **M19.**

†**managery** *noun.* **L16.**
[ORIGIN from MANAGE *noun, verb* + -ERY, infl. by French *ménagerie*.]
1 Management; administration; economy. **L16–M18.**
2 = MANÈGE. **L17–L18.**

managing /ˈmanɪdʒɪŋ/ *ppl adjective.* **E18.**
[ORIGIN from MANAGE *verb* + -ING[2].]
That manages; *spec.* (**a**) having executive control or authority; (**b**) fond of scheming or assuming the direction of affairs; (**c**) *arch.* skilful and diligent in management, economical.
managing director, managing editor, etc.

manaia /məˈnʌɪə/ *noun.* **L19.**
[ORIGIN Maori.]
A motif in Maori carving with a birdlike head and a human body.

manakin /ˈmanəkɪn/ *noun.* **E17.**
[ORIGIN Var. of MANIKIN *noun*.]
1 = MANIKIN *noun* 1, 2. *rare.* **E17.**
2 Any of various small fruit-eating passerine birds of the tropical American family Pipridae, the males of which are brightly coloured and have complex courtship displays. Cf. MANIKIN *noun* 3. **M18.**

mañana /maˈɲana, manˈjɑːnə/ *adverb & noun.* **M19.**
[ORIGIN Spanish = morning, tomorrow (in this sense from Old Spanish *cras mañana* lit. 'tomorrow early') ult. from Latin *mane* in the morning.]
Tomorrow, (on) the day after today; (in) the indefinite future (from the supposed easy-going procrastination of Spain and Spanish-speaking countries).

mananose *noun* var. of MANINOSE.

manat /ˈmanat/ *noun.* Pl. same. **L20.**
[ORIGIN Azerbaijani & Turkmen.]
The basic monetary unit of Azerbaijan and Turkmenistan, equal to 100 gopik in Azerbaijan and 100 tenesi in Turkmenistan.

manatee /ˈmanətiː/ *noun.* Also **-ti**. **M16.**
[ORIGIN Spanish *manatí* from Carib *manáti*.]
A sirenian mammal; *spec.* any of several tropical sirenians of the genus *Trichechus*, inhabiting Atlantic coasts and adjacent rivers.
– COMB.: **manatee-grass** *W. Indian* a flowering plant, *Cymodocea manatorum* (family Cymodoceaceae), which grows submerged in the sea.

†**manation** *noun. rare.* **LME–E19.**
[ORIGIN Latin *manatio(n-)*, from *manat-* pa. ppl stem of *manare* flow: see -ATION.]
A flowing out.

manatoka /manəˈtəʊkə/ *noun.* Also **manitoka** /manɪ-/. *S. Afr.* **L19.**
[ORIGIN App. alt. of *Monotoca*, the name of a genus of evergreen Australian shrubs and small trees, applied in error.]
A tall Australian evergreen white-flowered shrub, *Myoporum insulare* (family Myoporaceae), used in South Africa for hedges.

manavilins /məˈnavɪlɪnz/ *noun pl. slang.* Now *rare.* **M19.**
[ORIGIN Unknown.]
Small matters, odds and ends; extra articles.

Manc /maŋk/ *noun & adjective. colloq.* **M20.**
[ORIGIN Abbreviation.]
= MANCUNIAN.

mancala /manˈkɑːlə/ *noun.* **L17.**
[ORIGIN Colloq. Arabic *manqala*, from *naqala* remove, take away.]
A board game for two players, originally Arabic but now common throughout Africa and Asia, played on a special board with rows of holes or hollows, and having as its object the capture of the opponent's pieces.

mancando /manˈkando, manˈkandəʊ/ *adjective & adverb.* **L18.**
[ORIGIN Italian = lacking, failing.]
MUSIC. (A direction:) becoming even softer, dying away.

manche *noun* var. of MAUNCH.

Manchegan /manˈtʃeɪɡ(ə)n/ *adjective & noun.* **E17.**
[ORIGIN from Spanish *manchego, -ga*, from *La Mancha* (see below): see -AN.]
(A native or inhabitant) of La Mancha, a region (formerly a province) of central Spain.

Manchego /manˈtʃeɪɡəʊ/ *noun.* Pl. **-os**. **L18.**
[ORIGIN Spanish *manchego* (see MANCHEGAN).]
1 A native or inhabitant of La Mancha, a Manchegan. **L18.**
2 A firm Spanish cheese traditionally made with sheep's milk. **M20.**

Manchester /ˈmantʃɪstə/ *noun.* **M16.**
[ORIGIN A large city in (Lancashire) NW England, historically the chief centre of cotton manufacture.]
Used *attrib.* to designate things from or associated with Manchester, esp. cotton goods.
Manchester cotton: see COTTON *noun*[2]. **Manchester goods** cotton textiles. **Manchester School** *hist.* a body of politicians (meeting in Manchester) who advocated the principles of free trade and laissez-faire in the mid 19th cent. **Manchester terrier** (a dog of) a breed of small, short-coated, black and tan terrier. **Manchester warehouse** *arch.* a warehouse for cotton textiles. **Manchester warehouseman** *arch.* a storer of cotton textiles. **Manchester wares** = ***Manchester goods*** above.
■ **Manchesterian** /mantʃɪˈstɪərɪən/ *adjective & noun* = MANCUNIAN **L18.** **Manchesterism** *noun* (*hist.*) the principles advocated by or attributed to the Manchester School **L19.** **Manchesteriˈzation** *noun* the action or process of Manchesterizing **M20.** **Manchesterize** *verb trans.* make representative or typical of Manchester **E20.**

manchet /ˈmantʃɪt/ *noun.* **LME.**
[ORIGIN Perh. from elem. of Anglo-Norman *pain demeine, demaine*, medieval Latin *panus dominicus* lit. 'lord's bread' + CHEAT *noun*[2].]
1 (A small loaf or roll of) the finest kind of wheaten bread. *obsolete* exc. *dial. & hist.* **LME.**
2 *HERALDRY.* A small circular loaf or manchet used as a charge. **M17.**

manchette /mɑ̃ʃɛt/ *noun.* Pl. pronounced same. **M19.**
[ORIGIN French, dim. of *manche*: see MAUNCH, -ETTE.]
hist. A kind of trimming worn round the lower part of the sleeve of a woman's dress.

manchineel /man(t)ʃɪˈniːl/ *noun.* **E17.**
[ORIGIN French *mancenille* from Spanish *manzanilla* dim. of *manzana* apple, alt. form of Old Spanish *mazana* from Latin *matiana* (neut. pl., sc. *poma, mala*) a kind of apple.]
1 A poisonous W. Indian tree, *Hippomane mancinella*, of the spurge family, with a highly caustic latex and an acrid fruit. Also ***manchineel tree***. **E17.**
2 a The wood of this tree. **L17.** ▸**b** Poison from this tree. **L19.**

Manchu /manˈtʃuː/ *noun & adjective.* **L17.**
[ORIGIN Manchu = pure.]
▸ **A** *noun.* **1** A member or descendant of a non-Chinese people of Manchuria, who conquered China and formed the last imperial dynasty (1644–1912). **L17.**
2 The language of the Manchus, a member of the Tungusic group in the Altaic language family. **E19.**
▸ **B** *attrib.* or as *adjective.* Of or pertaining to the Manchus or their language. **M18.**
– COMB.: **Manchu-Tungus** *noun & adjective* (of) the language family comprising Manchu and Tungus.

Manchurian /manˈtʃʊərɪən/ *adjective.* **E18.**
[ORIGIN from *Manchuria* (see below) + -AN.]
Of or pertaining to Manchuria, a region forming the north-eastern portion of China (formerly a separate country).
Manchurian crane a crane of eastern Asia, *Grus japonensis*, black and white with a red crown. **Manchurian tiger** the Siberian tiger.

mancia /ˈmantʃə/ *noun.* **L18.**
[ORIGIN Italian.]
A gratuity, a tip.

mancipable /ˈmansɪpəb(ə)l/ *adjective. rare.* **L19.**
[ORIGIN from MANCIPATE + -ABLE.]
ROMAN LAW. That may be conveyed or transferred by mancipation.

†**mancipate** *verb trans.* Pa. pple & ppl adjective **-ated**, (earlier) †**-ate**. **L15.**
[ORIGIN Latin *mancipat-* pa. ppl stem of *mancipare*, from *manceps* purchaser, from *manus* hand + base of *capere* take: see -ATE[3].]
1 Make subject, enslave (*lit. & fig.*). Chiefly foll. by *to, unto*. **L15–E19.**
2 *ROMAN LAW.* Convey or transfer by the formality of mancipation. **M17–L19.**
3 Devote or consecrate *to*. **E18–E19.**

mancipation /mansɪˈpeɪʃ(ə)n/ *noun.* **L16.**
[ORIGIN Latin *mancipatio(n-)*, formed as MANCIPATE: see -ATION.]
1 The action of enslaving; the state of being enslaved. **L16.**
2 *ROMAN LAW.* A ceremonial process by which certain kinds of property were transferred, children emancipated, etc. **M17.**

mancipatory /ˈmansɪpət(ə)ri/ *adjective. rare.* **M19.**
[ORIGIN from MANCIPATE + -ORY[2].]
ROMAN LAW. Pertaining to or involving mancipation.

manciple /ˈmansɪp(ə)l/ *noun.* **ME.**
[ORIGIN Anglo-Norman & Old French var. of *mancipe* from Latin *mancipium* purchase, slave, from *manceps*: see MANCIPATE.]
1 An officer or servant responsible for purchasing provisions for a college, an Inn of Court, a monastery, etc. **ME.**
†**2** A bondslave, a servant. **LME–L16.**

Mancunian /maŋˈkjuːnɪən/ *noun & adjective.* **E20.**
[ORIGIN from Latin *Mancunium* Manchester + -AN.]
(A native or inhabitant) of the city of Manchester in NW England.

mancus /ˈmaŋkəs/ *noun. obsolete* exc. *hist.*
[ORIGIN Old English *mancus* = Old Saxon *mancus*, Old High German (accus. pl.) *manchussa* from medieval Latin *mancusus* from Arabic *manqūš* use as noun (sc. *dīnār* DINAR) of pass. pple of *naqaša* engrave, inscribe.]
An Anglo-Saxon monetary unit of the value of thirty pence.

-mancy /mansi/ *suffix.*
[ORIGIN Repr. Old French *-mancie*, late Latin *-mantia*, Greek *manteia* divination, from *manteuesthai* prophesy, from *mantis* prophet, diviner: see -CY.]
Forming nouns with the sense 'divination by', as ***chiromancy, geomancy, hydromancy, necromancy***, etc.

Mandaean /manˈdiːən/ *adjective & noun.* Also **-dean**. **L17.**
[ORIGIN from Mandaean Aramaic *mandaia*, from *manda* knowledge, + -AN.]
▸ **A** *adjective.* Designating or pertaining to a Mesopotamian Gnostic sect (now Iraqi) regarding St John the Baptist as the Messiah, or the Aramaic dialect in which the sect's sacred books are written. **L17.**
▸ **B** *noun.* A member of the Mandaean sect; the Aramaic dialect of the Mandaean sect. **M18.**
■ Also **Mandaite** /ˈmandeɪʌɪt/ *adjective & noun* **M19.**

mandala /ˈmandələ, ˈmʌn-/ *noun.* **M19.**
[ORIGIN Sanskrit *maṇḍala* disc, circle.]
A symbolic circular figure, usu. with symmetrical divisions and figures of deities, etc., in the centre, used in Buddhism and other religions as a representation of the universe; *JUNGIAN PSYCHOLOGY* an archetype of a similar circle, held to symbolize a striving for unity of self and completeness.
■ **mandalic** /manˈdalɪk, mʌn-/ *adjective* **M20.**

mandamus /manˈdeɪməs/ *noun & verb.* **M16.**
[ORIGIN Latin = we command.]
LAW. ▸**A** *noun.* Orig., any of a number of writs, mandates, etc., issued by the monarch, directing the performance of a certain act. Later, a judicial writ or order issued in the name of the Crown or the government directing an inferior court, a corporation, an officer, etc., to perform a public or statutory duty. **M16.**
▸ **B** *verb trans.* Serve with a mandamus. **E19.**

Mandan /ˈmand(ə)n/ *noun & adjective.* **L18.**
[ORIGIN N. Amer. French *Mandane*, prob. from Dakota *mawátąna*.]
▸ **A** *noun.* Pl. **-s**, same. A member of a Siouan people of North Dakota; the language of this people. **L18.**
▸ **B** *adjective.* Designating or pertaining to this people or their language. **L18.**

mandant /ˈmand(ə)nt/ *adjective & noun.* **M16.**
[ORIGIN Latin *mandant-* pres. ppl stem of *mandare*: see MANDATE *noun*, -ANT[1].]
▸ †**A** *adjective. PHYSIOLOGY.* Of an organ, esp. the brain: that is the source of impulse. **M16–L17.**
▸ **B** *noun. LAW* = MANDATOR. Now *rare* or *obsolete.* **L17.**

mandapa /ˈmʌndəpə/ *noun.* Also **mandap** /ˈmʌndəp/. **E19.**
[ORIGIN Sanskrit *maṇḍapa*.]
In southern India: a temple. Also, a temporary platform set up for weddings and religious ceremonies; a pavilion.

mandarin /ˈmand(ə)rɪn/ *noun*[1] *& adjective.* Also †**-ine**; (esp. in sense A.2) **M-**. **L16.**
[ORIGIN Portuguese *mandarim* alt. of Malay *menteri* from Sanskrit *mantrī, mantrin* counsellor, minister. Cf. MANTRI, MENTRI.]
▸ **A** *noun* **1 a** *hist.* A member of each of the nine grades of Chinese officials under the Empire, selected by examination. Formerly also, any of various other Asian officials. **L16.** ▸**b** A toy figure in Chinese costume, so contrived as to continue nodding for a long time after being shaken. **L18.** ▸**c** A person of much importance; *esp.* a leading government official or politician, a reactionary or secretive bureaucrat. **E20.**

c *Mail on Sunday* Civil servants dropping into private . . jobs with salaries . . three times what they earned as Whitehall mandarins.

2 (**M-**.) The form of the Chinese language formerly used by officials and educated people generally; any of the varieties of this used as a standard language in China, *spec.* the northern variety. **E18.** ▸**b** Obscure or esoteric language. **M20.**
3 *ellipt.* = ***mandarin duck*** below. **M19.**
▸ **B** *attrib.* or as *adjective.* **1** Of or pertaining to mandarins or a Mandarin. **E17.**

P. GOODMAN A mandarin bureaucracy is valuable . . because of the vastness of the underlying population.

2 Esoteric, consciously superior, (of style) affectedly ornate or complex. **E20.**

M

Listener The conventionally acceptable accents and Mandarin prose we learn at school.

– SPECIAL COLLOCATIONS & COMB.: **mandarin coat** a loose silk coat with a mandarin collar. **mandarin collar** a narrow collar standing up from a close-fitting neckline and not quite meeting in front. **mandarin duck** a duck with bright and variegated plumage, *Aix galericulata*, native to eastern Asia and naturalized in Britain. **mandarin jacket**: with a mandarin collar. **mandarin porcelain** Chinese and Japanese porcelain decorated with figures of mandarins. **mandarin sleeve** a wide loose sleeve. **mandarin vase** a vase of mandarin porcelain.

■ **mandarinism** *noun* (*a*) the mandarin system, government by mandarins; (*b*) (an example of) pedantry, highbrow or esoteric study: M19. **mandarinship** *noun* the position, office, or rank of a mandarin L17.

mandarin /ˈmand(ə)rɪn/ *noun*². Also **-ine** /-iːn/. L18.
[ORIGIN French *mandarine* (sc. *orange*: cf. Spanish *naranja mandarina*) fem. of *mandarin*, prob. formed as MANDARIN *noun*¹ & *adjective* after the yellow of mandarins' costume.]
1 More fully ***mandarin orange***. A citrus fruit resembling a small flattened orange, but with sweet pulp and easily detached peel; *esp.* one with yellow or pale orange peel. Also, the tree bearing this fruit, *Citrus reticulata*, widely grown in subtropical regions. Cf. SATSUMA, TANGERINE. L18.
2 An orange colour. Also ***mandarin-orange***. L19.
3 A mandarin-flavoured liqueur. L19.

mandarinate /ˈmand(ə)rɪneɪt/ *noun*. E18.
[ORIGIN from MANDARIN *noun*¹ + -ATE¹.]
The position or office of a mandarin; the body of mandarins, mandarins collectively; government by mandarins.

F. FITZGERALD Their aristocracy sent its sons to compete for the mandarinate in the regional examinations. *Citizen (Ottawa)* The upper mandarinate where access to such information ahead of the rest of the world is a status symbol.

†**mandarine** *noun*¹ & *adjective* var. of MANDARIN *noun*¹ & *adjective*.

mandarine *noun*² var. of MANDARIN *noun*².

mandat /mɑ̃da (*pl. same*), ˈmandat/ *noun*. M19.
[ORIGIN French formed as MANDATE *noun*.]
1 *hist.* A paper money issued by the revolutionary government of France from 1796 to 1797. Cf. ASSIGNAT. M19.
2 In France, a money order. L19.

M

mandatary /ˈmandət(ə)ri/ *noun*. LME.
[ORIGIN Latin *mandatarius*, formed as MANDATE *noun*: see -ARY¹.]
1 Chiefly LAW. A person to whom a mandate is given; *hist.* a state receiving a mandate from the League of Nations. LME.
†**2** A person appointed to a benefice by a papal mandate. E17–E18.

mandate /ˈmandeɪt/ *noun*. E16.
[ORIGIN Latin *mandatum* use as noun of neut. pa. pple of *mandare* command, send out, enjoin, commit, from *manus* hand + base of *dare* give: see -ATE¹.]
1 *gen.* A command, an order, an injunction. Now *literary*. E16.
2 a A judicial or legal command from a superior to an inferior; in early English law, a command of the monarch to a court relating to a private suit; in US law, a document conveying a decision of a court of appeal to a court below for the enactment of judgement. E16. ▸**b** A papal rescript, esp. with reference to preferment to a benefice. E17. ▸**c** *hist.* A command from the monarch to elect a fellow of a college or to confer a degree. E17. ▸†**d** A pastoral letter. M18–E19.
3 a SCOTS LAW. A contract by which a person undertakes to act gratuitously for another. L17. ▸**b** ROMAN LAW. A commission by which one person (the mandator) requests another (the mandatary) to perform gratuitously some service, undertaking to indemnify the mandatary for expenses. M18. ▸**c** A contract of bailment by which a mandatary undertakes to perform gratuitously some service in respect of a thing committed to his or her keeping by the mandator. L18.
4 a The commission as to policy supposed to be given by the electors to their elected representatives; support for a policy or measure regarded by a victorious party, candidate, etc., as derived from the wishes of the people in an election; *gen.* a commission. L18. ▸**b** *hist.* A commission issued by the League of Nations (1919–1946) authorizing a selected power to administer, control, and develop a territory for a specified purpose; the territory so allocated. E20.

a *Tucson Magazine* It's all right to screw the people as long as you were given a large mandate in the previous election.

a doctor's mandate a mandate from the people empowering the government to take extreme measures in the national interest.

mandate /manˈdeɪt/ *verb trans*. E17.
[ORIGIN Latin *mandat-* pa. ppl stem of *mandare*: see MANDATE *noun*, -ATE³.]
1 Command, require by mandate; necessitate. (*rare* before L20.) Now chiefly *US*. E17.
2 Commit (one's sermon) to memory. *Scot.* E18.
3 *hist.* Assign (territory) under a mandate of the League of Nations. E20.
4 Give a mandate to, delegate authority to (a representative, group, organization, etc.). Freq. as ***mandated*** *ppl adjective*. M20.

mandative /ˈmandətɪv/ *adjective*. L16.
[ORIGIN Late Latin *mandativus*, formed as MANDATE *verb*: see -IVE.]
†**1** Of or pertaining to command. L16–M17.
2 GRAMMAR Conveying a command; imperative. M19.

mandator /manˈdeɪtə/ *noun*. L17.
[ORIGIN Latin, formed as MANDATE *verb*: see -OR.]
Chiefly LAW. A person who gives a mandate.

mandatory /ˈmandət(ə)ri/ *adjective & noun*. L15.
[ORIGIN Late Latin *mandatorius* (adjective), formed as MANDATE *verb*: see -ORY². As noun from medieval Latin: see -ORY¹.]
▸ **A** *adjective*. **1** Of the nature of, pertaining to, or conveying a command or mandate. L15.
2 Of an action: obligatory in consequence of a command, compulsory. (Foll. by *upon*.) E19.
3 *hist.* Designating a power or state in receipt of a mandate from the League of Nations, or the system of rule by mandate. E20.
▸ **B** *noun*. **1** A person to whom a mandate is given; = MANDATARY. M17.
2 *hist.* A power or state in receipt of a mandate from the League of Nations to administer and develop a territory. E20.
■ **mandatorily** *adverb* M19.

Mande /ˈmɑːndeɪ/ *noun & adjective*. L19.
[ORIGIN Mande.]
▸ **A** *noun*. Pl. **-s**, same. A member of a large group of peoples of W. Africa; the group of Niger-Congo languages of these peoples. Also called ***Mandingo***. L19.
▸ **B** *attrib.* or as *adjective*. Of or pertaining to these peoples or their group of languages. L19.

Mandean *adjective & noun* var. of MANDAEAN.

Mandelbrot set /ˈmand(ə)lbrɒt sɛt/ *noun phr.* L20.
[ORIGIN Benoit B. *Mandelbrot* (b. 1924), Polish-born US mathematician.]
MATH. The set of all complex numbers c such that under repeated application of the mapping $z \to z^2 + c$ any complex variable z remains within a bounded region of the complex plane.

mandelic /manˈdɛlɪk/ *adjective*. M19.
[ORIGIN from German *Mandel* almond + -IC.]
CHEMISTRY. ***mandelic acid***, a colourless crystalline acid, $C_6H_5CH(OH)COOH$, obtainable from amygdalin and used to treat bacterial infection; α-phenylhydroxyacetic acid.
■ **mandeloˈnitrile** *noun* a yellow oily liquid which is the nitrile of mandelic acid and of which amygdalin is a glycoside L19.

mandevilla /mandəˈvɪlə/ *noun*. M19.
[ORIGIN mod. Latin (see below), from John Henry *Mandeville* (1773–1861), Brit. minister in Buenos Aires.]
Any of various woody climbing plants of the S. American genus *Mandevilla* (family Apocynaceae), with fragrant white, pink, or red flowers, grown for ornament esp. in tropical and subtropical regions; *esp.* Chilean jasmine, *M. laxa*.

mandible /ˈmandɪb(ə)l/ *noun*. Also in Latin form **mandibula** /manˈdɪbjʊlə/, pl. **-lae** /-liː/. LME.
[ORIGIN Old French, or directly from late Latin *mandibula*, from *mandere* chew.]
Now only ANATOMY & ZOOLOGY. **1** A jaw, a jawbone; *esp.* the lower jaw or jawbone in mammals and fishes. Cf. MAXILLA. LME.
2 In birds, either of the two parts, upper and lower, of the beak. L17.
3 In insects and other arthropods, either of the appendages forming the main or anterior mouthparts. Also, in other invertebrates, any of various parts functioning as or resembling jaws. E19.

mandibular /manˈdɪbjʊlə/ *adjective*. M17.
[ORIGIN from Latin *mandibula*: see MANDIBLE, -AR¹.]
ANATOMY & ZOOLOGY. Belonging to, connected with, or forming part of a mandible.
■ Also **mandibulary** *adjective* (*rare*) M17.

mandibulate /manˈdɪbjʊleɪt/ *adjective*. E19.
[ORIGIN formed as MANDIBULAR: see -ATE².]
ZOOLOGY. **1** Esp. of an arthropod: having a mouth adapted for mastication (rather than for sucking), or provided with mandibles (rather than a haustellum or chelicerae). E19.
2 Of a mouth or mouthparts: adapted for mastication; formed as mandibles. M19.
■ **mandibulated** *adjective* = MANDIBULATE *adjective* 1 M19.

mandibulo- /manˈdɪbjʊləʊ/ *combining form*. L19.
[ORIGIN formed as MANDIBULAR: see -O-.]
Forming adjectives with the sense 'pertaining to the mandible', as ***mandibulo-hyoid***, ***mandibulo-maxillary***, etc.

†**mandil** *noun*. M17–M19.
[ORIGIN (Spanish from) Arabic & Persian *mandīl* sash, turban, cloth, handkerchief, from medieval Greek *mantēlion* from Latin *mantelium*, *mantelum*: see MANTLE *noun*.]
A turban.

mandilion /manˈdɪlɪən/ *noun*. *obsolete* exc. *hist.* L16.
[ORIGIN Obsolete French, dim. of *mandil* (now *mandille*), formed as MANDIL.]
A loose coat or cassock, in later times sleeveless, worn by soldiers and menservants as a kind of overcoat.

Manding /ˈmandɪŋ/ *noun & adjective*. M19.
[ORIGIN Mande: cf. MANDINGO.]
▸ **A** *noun*. Pl. same, **-s**.
1 A member of a group of West African peoples speaking closely related dialects of the largest language of the Mande subfamily. M19.
2 A language spoken over a large part of West Africa, traditionally known under the names of its various dialects, including Malinke and Mandinka. M20.
▸ **B** *attrib.* or as *adjective*. Of or pertaining to Manding or its speakers. M20.

Mandingo /manˈdɪŋgəʊ/ *noun & adjective*. E17.
[ORIGIN Mande: cf. MANDING.]
▸ **A** *noun*. Pl. same, **-o(e)s**. = MANDE *noun*. E17.
▸ **B** *adjective*. = MANDE *adjective*. M18.

Mandinka /mənˈdɪŋkə/ *noun & adjective*. Pl. of noun **-s**, same. M20.
[ORIGIN Mande.]
= MALINKE.

mandola /manˈdəʊlə/ *noun*. Also **-dora** /-ˈdɔːrə/. M18.
[ORIGIN Italian. Cf. MANDORE.]
A large early form of mandolin.

mandolin /ˈmandəlɪn/ *noun*. Also (the usual form in sense 2) **-ine**. E18.
[ORIGIN French *mandoline* from Italian *mandolino* dim. of MANDOLA: see -INE¹.]
1 A musical instrument of the lute kind having from four to six paired metal strings stretched on a deeply rounded body, usu. played with a plectrum. E18.
2 A kitchen utensil fitted with cutting blades and used for slicing vegetables. M20.
■ **mandolinist** *noun* a performer on the mandolin L19.

mandor /ˈmandɔː/ *noun*. L19.
[ORIGIN Malay from Portuguese *mandador* a person who gives orders.]
A foreman or overseer in Malaysia or Indonesia.

mandora *noun* var. of MANDOLA.

mandore /manˈdɔː/ *noun*. M17.
[ORIGIN French formed as MANDOLA.]
= MANDOLA.

mandorla /manˈdɔːlə/ *noun*. L19.
[ORIGIN Italian = almond.]
An almond-shaped panel or decorative space in religious art.

mandragora /manˈdragərə/ *noun*. Also anglicized as **-dragore** /-drəˈgɔː/. OE.
[ORIGIN (Old French & mod. French *mandragore* from) medieval Latin *mandragora*, classical Latin *-as* from Greek *mandragoras*, prob. of pre-Hellenic origin.]
= MANDRAKE 1 (*arch.*). Now only (BOTANY), any of the various plants of the genus *Mandragora*.

fig.: J. GALT Earnest employment is the best mandragora for an aching heart.

mandrake /ˈmandreɪk/ *noun*. ME.
[ORIGIN Prob. from Middle Dutch *mandrag(r)e* from medieval Latin MANDRAGORA, assoc. with MAN *noun* (with allus. to the shape of the root) and DRAKE *noun*¹.]
1 A poisonous and narcotic Mediterranean plant of the nightshade family, *Mandragora officinarum*, with a very short stem and solitary purple or whitish flowers, which was formerly credited with magical and medicinal properties because of the supposedly human shape of its forked fleshy root, and reputed to shriek when taken from the ground. ME. ▸†**b** *fig.* Something or someone unpleasant or unwanted; something to be rooted up, a pestilential growth. E16–M17.
2 The May apple, *Podophyllum peltatum*. *US*. E19.

Mandrax /ˈmandraks/ *noun*. M20.
[ORIGIN After MANDRAKE or MANDRAGORA, with arbitrary ending.]
PHARMACOLOGY. (Proprietary name for) a sedative containing methaqualone and diphenhydramine hydrochloride; a tablet of this. Cf. MANDY.

mandrel /ˈmandr(ə)l/ *noun*. Also **-dril** /-drɪl/. E16.
[ORIGIN medieval Latin *maundrellus*, of uncertain origin.]
1 A miner's pick. E16.
2 A cylindrical rod round which metal or other material is forged or shaped. M16.
3 A shaft or spindle to which work is secured while being turned in a lathe. M17.

mandrill /ˈmandrɪl/ *noun*. M18.
[ORIGIN App. from MAN *noun* + DRILL *noun*³.]
†**1** = CHIMPANZEE. Only in M18.
2 A large W. African forest baboon, *Mandrillus sphinx*, the adult of which has a bright red and blue face and blue buttocks. L18.

mandritta /manˈdrɪtə/ *noun. hist.* L16.
[ORIGIN Italian *mandritto* from *mandritta* right hand.]
FENCING. A cut from right to left.

manducable /ˈmandjʊkəb(ə)l/ *adjective. literary.* Now *rare.* E17.
[ORIGIN Late Latin *manducabilis*, from *manducare*: see MANDUCATE, -ABLE.]
Edible; chewable.

manducate /ˈmandjʊkeɪt/ *verb trans. literary.* E17.
[ORIGIN Latin *manducat-* pa. ppl stem of *manducare* chew: see -ATE³.]
Chew, eat.

manducation /mandjʊˈkeɪʃ(ə)n/ *noun. literary.* E16.
[ORIGIN Latin *manducatio(n-)*, formed as MANDUCATE: see -ATION.]
The action of eating or chewing; *spec.* participation in the Eucharist.

manducatory /ˈmandjʊkət(ə)ri/ *adjective.* E19.
[ORIGIN formed as MANDUCATE: see -ORY².]
Chiefly ZOOLOGY. Pertaining to or concerned with eating or chewing.

M and V *abbreviation. military slang.*
Meat and vegetable(s).

mandy /ˈmandi/ *noun. slang.* Also **M-**. L20.
[ORIGIN Abbreviation.]
A tablet of the sedative Mandrax.

mane /meɪn/ *noun.*
[ORIGIN Old English *manu* = Old Frisian *mana*, Middle Dutch *mane* (Dutch *manen* pl.), Old High German *mana* (German *Mähne*), Old Norse *mǫn*, from Germanic.]
1 A growth of long hair on the back of the neck and the shoulders, characteristic of various animals, esp. the horse and lion. OE.
2 A person's long hair. LME.
3 A ridge or tuft of grass or stubble, left by mowers. Now *dial.* E16.
†4 The hackles on the neck of a gamecock. E17–E18.
■ **maneless** *adjective* E19.

-mane /meɪn/ *suffix.*
[ORIGIN French. Cf. -MANIAC.]
In or (occas.) after words from French in sense 'a person who has a mania for (something)', as ***balletomane***, ***bibliomane***, etc.

maneaba /maˈneɪəbə/ *noun.* M20.
[ORIGIN Micronesian.]
In Kiribati and Tuvalu (formerly the Gilbert and Ellice Islands): a meeting house.

maneb /ˈmanɛb/ *noun.* M20.
[ORIGIN from MAN(GANESE + E(THYLENE + BIS-, elems. of systematic name (see below).]
A cyclic organosulphur compound used as a fungicidal powder on vegetables and fruit; manganese ethylene bisdithiocarbamate, $C_4H_6MnN_2S_4$.

maned /meɪnd/ *adjective.* ME.
[ORIGIN from MANE + -ED².]
Having a mane.
maned wolf a wild dog, *Chrysocyon brachyurus*, of S. American grasslands, resembling a shaggy long-legged fox.

manège /maˈneɪʒ/ *noun.* Also **manege**. E17.
[ORIGIN French formed as MANAGE *noun.*]
1 A riding school. E17.
2 The movements in which a horse is trained in a riding school; the art or practice of training and managing horses; horsemanship. L18.

maneh /ˈmɑːneɪ/ *noun.* E17.
[ORIGIN Hebrew *mānēh* prob. from Akkadian (cf. MAUND *noun²*), whence also MINA *noun¹*.]
ANTIQUITIES. A Hebrew coin and weight of between 50 and 60 shekels.

manerial /məˈnɪərɪəl/ *adjective.* Now *rare.* M18.
[ORIGIN medieval Latin *manerialis*, from *manerium* MANOR: see -AL¹.]
= MANORIAL.

manes /ˈmɑːneɪz, ˈmeɪniːz/ *noun.* LME.
[ORIGIN Latin.]
1 *pl.* The deified souls of dead ancestors (as beneficent spirits). LME.
2 *sing.* The spirit or shade of a dead person, considered as an object of reverence or as demanding to be propitiated. L17.

maness /ˈmanɛs/ *noun. rare.* L16.
[ORIGIN from MAN *noun* + -ESS¹.]
Woman as the feminine of man.

maneton /ˈmanɪt(ə)n/ *noun.* E20.
[ORIGIN French = crankpin.]
AERONAUTICS. In a rotary or radial engine, the detachable short end of the crankshaft.

Manetti /maˈnɛti/ *noun.* M19.
[ORIGIN Xavier *Manetti* (1723–84), Italian botanist.]
In full ***Manetti rose***. A dwarf variety of rose much used as a stock.

maneuver *noun, verb* see MANOEUVRE *noun, verb.*

maneuverable *adjective* see MANOEUVRABLE.

manful /ˈmanfʊl, -f(ə)l/ *adjective.* LME.
[ORIGIN from MAN *noun* + -FUL.]
Characterized by manly courage and resolution; brave, resolute.
■ **manfully** *adverb* LME. **manfulness** *noun* LME.

manga /ˈmaŋgə/ *noun¹.* E19.
[ORIGIN Spanish, lit. 'sleeve', from Latin *manica*: see MAUNCH.]
A Mexican and Spanish-American cloak or poncho.

manga /ˈmaŋgə/ *noun².* M20.
[ORIGIN Japanese, from *man-* aimless, involuntary + *-ga* picture.]
A Japanese genre of cartoons, comic books, and animated films, typically with a science-fiction or fantasy theme and sometimes including violent or sexually explicit material.

†**manga** *noun³* see MANGO.

mangabey /ˈmaŋgəbeɪ/ *noun.* L18.
[ORIGIN A region in Madagascar (erroneously applied).]
Any of several small long-tailed forest-dwelling monkeys of the genus *Cercocebus*, of central and West Africa.
sooty mangabey: see SOOTY *adjective*.

mangal /maŋˈgal/ *noun.* E19.
[ORIGIN Ottoman Turkish from Arabic *manqal*.]
A kind of Turkish brazier.

mangan- /ˈmaŋg(ə)n/ *combining form.*
[ORIGIN German *Mangan* MANGANESE.]
MINERALOGY. Forming names of minerals or mineral varieties containing (a large amount of) manganese, as ***manganbrucite***, ***manganhedenbergite***, etc. Cf. MANGANO-.
■ **manganˈapatite** *noun* a fluorescent yellow variety of apatite containing up to 10.5 per cent manganese replacing calcium L19.

manganate /ˈmaŋgənət, -neɪt/ *noun.* M19.
[ORIGIN from MANGANESE + -ATE¹.]
CHEMISTRY. A salt containing oxyanions of manganese; *spec.* a salt of the anion MnO_4^{2-}. Cf. PERMANGANATE.

†**manganeous** *adjective* see MANGANOUS.

manganese /ˈmaŋgəniːz/ *noun.* M17.
[ORIGIN French *manganèse* from Italian *manganese*, unexpl. alt. of medieval Latin *magnesia*, *mangnesia* MAGNESIA.]
1 A black mineral substance consisting largely of the dioxide of manganese (sense 2), used from ancient times in glass-making, and now in many industrial processes. Also ***black manganese***. M17.
2 A hard grey brittle chemical element, atomic no. 25, which is one of the transition metals and is used in steels and magnetic alloys (symbol Mn). L18.
– COMB. & PHRASES: ***black manganese***: see sense 1 above; **grey manganese** = MANGANITE 1; **manganese bronze** an alloy of copper and zinc with manganese; **manganese nodule** a small friable concretion of manganese and iron oxides, found on or in sediments on the ocean floor worldwide; **manganese purple** = ***manganese violet*** below; **manganese spar** (*a*) = RHODONITE; (*b*) = RHODOCHROSITE; **manganese steel** any of various hard steels containing manganese; **manganese violet** a purple manganese-containing phosphate pigment used in the decoration of ceramics.
■ **manganesian** /maŋgəˈniːzjən, -ʒ(ə)n/ *adjective* (chiefly MINERALOGY) of or containing manganese L18.

†**manganesium** *noun.* Also **-sum**. L18–L19.
[ORIGIN from MANGANESE + -IUM.]
CHEMISTRY. = MANGANESE 2.

mangani- /ˈmaŋgəni/ *combining form.*
[ORIGIN from MANGANESE, MANGANIC: see -I-.]
CHEMISTRY. Forming names of compounds (chiefly cyanides) containing trivalent manganese. Cf. MANGANO- 2.

manganic /maŋˈganɪk/ *adjective.* L18.
[ORIGIN from MANGANESE + -IC.]
CHEMISTRY. Of or containing manganese in a higher valency. Cf. MANGANOUS.
manganic acid a (hypothetical) parent acid of manganates.

manganiferous /maŋgəˈnɪf(ə)rəs/ *adjective.* M19.
[ORIGIN formed as MANGANIC + -FEROUS.]
GEOLOGY & MINERALOGY. Containing or yielding manganese.

manganin /ˈmaŋgənɪn/ *noun.* L19.
[ORIGIN formed as MANGANIC + -IN¹.]
METALLURGY. (Proprietary name for) an alloy of copper, manganese, and nickel, used esp. in electrical apparatus.

manganite /ˈmaŋgənʌɪt/ *noun.* E19.
[ORIGIN formed as MANGANIC + -ITE¹.]
1 MINERALOGY. Basic manganese(II) oxide, MnO(OH), occurring massive or as grey or black striated prismatic crystals of the monoclinic system. E19.
2 CHEMISTRY. An oxide of manganese and another metal. M19.
■ **mangaˈnitic** *adjective* containing manganite L19.

Manganja /mənˈgandʒə/ *noun & adjective.* M19.
[ORIGIN Bantu.]
▸ **A** *noun.* Pl. same, **-s**. A member of a people inhabiting southern Malawi; the Bantu language of this people. M19.
▸ **B** *attrib.* or as *adjective.* Of or pertaining to the Manganja or their language. M19.

mangano- /ˈmaŋgənəʊ/ *combining form.*
[ORIGIN from MANGANESE, MANGANOUS: see -O-.]
1 MINERALOGY. Forming names of minerals or mineral varieties containing (a large amount of) manganese, as ***manganocolumbite***, ***manganotantalite***, etc. Cf. MANGAN-.
2 CHEMISTRY. Forming names of compounds (chiefly cyanides) containing divalent manganese. Cf. MANGANI-.

manganoan /maŋgəˈnəʊən/ *adjective.* M20.
[ORIGIN from MANGANO- + -AN: cf. FERROAN.]
MINERALOGY. Having a constituent element partly replaced by divalent manganese.

manganolite /ˈmaŋgənəlʌɪt/ *noun.* L19.
[ORIGIN from MANGANO- + -LITE.]
1 MINERALOGY. = RHODONITE. Now *rare* or *obsolete.* L19.
2 GEOLOGY. Any rock composed predominantly of manganese minerals. L19.

manganous /ˈmaŋgənəs/ *adjective.* Also (earlier) †**-eous**. E19.
[ORIGIN from MANGANESE + -OUS.]
Chiefly CHEMISTRY. Of or containing manganese, *spec.* in the divalent state.

mange /meɪndʒ/ *noun.* LME.
[ORIGIN Old French *manjue*, *mangeue* itch, from *manju-* pres. indic. sing. stem of *mangier* (mod. *manger*) eat from Latin *manducare*: see MANDUCATE.]
1 Any of various itching cutaneous diseases of hairy and woolly animals, and also poultry, caused by parasitic mites which burrow into the skin. Also *loosely*, scabies in humans. LME.
†2 *fig.* A restless desire. M17–L18.
– COMB.: **mange mite** any parasitic mite which causes mange.

mangeao /ˈmaŋɪəʊ/ *noun.* Pl. same, **-os**. M19.
[ORIGIN Maori.]
A New Zealand tree, *Litsea calicaris*, of the laurel family, with tough, light brown wood.

mangel /ˈmaŋg(ə)l/ *noun.* Also **-gold** /-g(ə)ld/. M19.
[ORIGIN Abbreviation.]
= MANGEL-WURZEL.
– COMB.: **mangel beetle** a small blue-black beetle, *Aclypea opaca*, whose larvae feed on the root of the beet; **mangel-fly** a small dipteran fly, *Pegomya hyoscyami*, whose larvae feed on beet leaves.

M

mangel-wurzel /ˈmaŋg(ə)lˌwəːz(ə)l/ *noun.* Also **mangold-wurzel** /ˈmaŋg(ə)ld-/. L18.
[ORIGIN German *Mangoldwurzel*, from *Mangold* beet + *Wurzel* root.]
A variety of beet with a root larger than that of the garden beet, cultivated as food for cattle.
– COMB.: **mangel-wurzel fly** = ***MANGEL-fly***.

manger /ˈmeɪndʒə/ *noun.* ME.
[ORIGIN Old French & mod. French *mangeoire*, from *mangeure* from Proto-Romance, from Latin *manducat-*: see MANDUCATE.]
1 A long open box or trough in a stable, barn, etc., for horses and cattle to eat out of. ME.
at heck and manger: see HECK *noun¹*. ***at rack and manger***: see RACK *noun²*. ***dog in the manger***: see DOG *noun*.
2 NAUTICAL (chiefly *hist.*). A small space in the bows of a ship enclosed by a low board or coaming, intended to keep the water entering the hawse holes from flooding the deck. E17.
■ **mangerful** *noun* E17.

mangetout /ˈmɑ̃ʒtuː, mɑ̃ʒˈtuː/ *noun.* Pl. same, **-s** (pronounced same). E19.
[ORIGIN French *mange-tout* lit. 'eat-all'.]
A variety of pea, *Pisum sativum* var. *macrocarpon*, of which the pods are eaten whole with the seeds they contain. Also ***mangetout pea***. Also called ***sugar pea***.

mangey *adjective* var. of MANGY.

mangle /ˈmaŋg(ə)l/ *noun¹.* E17.
[ORIGIN Spanish: see MANGROVE.]
= MANGROVE.

mangle /ˈmaŋg(ə)l/ *noun².* L17.
[ORIGIN Dutch *mangel* abbreviation of synon. *mangelstok*, from *mangelen* to mangle + *stok* staff, roller, STOCK *noun¹*, ult. from Greek *magganon*: see MANGONEL.]
1 A machine for squeezing water from and pressing linen, clothing, etc., after washing, latterly consisting of two or more cylinders working on each other, formerly of a heavy chest on two cylinders, worked backwards and forwards over wet clothing etc. spread on a table; a wringer. L17.
2 A bicycle. *Austral. & NZ slang.* M20.

mangle /ˈmaŋg(ə)l/ *verb¹ trans.* L15.
[ORIGIN Anglo-Norman *mangler* (cf. medieval Latin *mangulare*) prob. frequentative of *mahaignier* MAIM *verb*: see -LE³.]
Hack, cut, lacerate, or mutilate by repeated blows; cut or hack roughly so as to damage and disfigure; reduce to a more or less unrecognizable condition; spoil (esp. a text) by gross blundering or falsification; make (words) almost unrecognizable by mispronunciation.

T. CAPOTE On his left hand . . what remained of a finger once mangled by a piece of farm machinery. A. CARTER She fell beneath . . a brewer's dray and was mangled to pulp. G. NAYLOR She threw it on the floor and tried to mangle the pictures with her heels. JULIAN GLOAG It was torture to listen to her mangling the language.

■ **mangler** *noun*[1] M16.

mangle /ˈmaŋg(ə)l/ *verb*[2] *trans.* L18.
[ORIGIN from MANGLE *noun*[2].]
Press (linen, clothing, etc.) in a mangle.
■ **mangler** *noun*[2] M19.

mango /ˈmaŋgəʊ/ *noun.* Pl. **mango(e)s**. Also (earlier) †**manga**. L16.
[ORIGIN Portuguese *manga* from Malay *mangga* from Tamil *māṅkāy*, from *mā* mango tree + *kāy* fruit.]
1 The sweet orange-fleshed fruit of an Indian and Myanmar (Burmese) tree, *Mangifera indica* (family Anacardiaceae), which is eaten as dessert or used in its unripe state to make chutney or jam. L16.
2 The tree producing this fruit, widely cultivated in tropical countries. L17.
3 A pickle, esp. of melons or cucumbers, resembling that made of green mangoes. Now *rare*. L17.
4 In full ***mango-bird***, ***mango-hummingbird***. Any of several hummingbirds of the genus *Anthracothorax*, of tropical America and the Caribbean. M18.
– COMB.: **mango-bird** (*a*) in the Indian subcontinent, a golden oriole; (*b*) see sense 4 above; **mango-fish** = TUPSEE; **mango-fly** (*a*) = *TUMBU* ***fly***; (*b*) any of various African tabanid flies of the genus *Chrysops*, which are carriers of loiasis; **mango-ginger** (the pungent root of) an Indian plant, *Curcuma amada*, closely related to turmeric; ***mango-hummingbird***: see sense 4 above.

mangold(-wurzel) *nouns* vars. of MANGEL, MANGEL-WURZEL.

mangonel /ˈmaŋgən(ə)l/ *noun. obsolete* exc. *hist.* ME.
[ORIGIN Old French *mangonel(le)* (mod. *mangonneau*) from medieval Latin *manganellus*, *-gon-* dim. of late Latin *manganum* from Greek *magganon* engine of war, axis of a pulley.]
A military engine for throwing stones and other missiles.

mangosteen /ˈmaŋgəstiːn/ *noun.* L16.
[ORIGIN Orig. from Malay *manggustan* dial. var. of *manggis*.]
1 The fruit of a Malaysian tree, *Garcinia mangostana* (family Guttiferae), with a thick reddish-brown rind enclosing a sweet white juicy pulp; the tree producing this fruit. L16.
2 In the W. Indies, a kind of jujube tree, *Ziziphus mauritiana*. M18.

M

mangrove /ˈmaŋgrəʊv/ *noun.* E17.
[ORIGIN Prob. ult. from Portuguese *mangue*, Spanish *mangle*, from Taino, with 2nd elem. assim. to GROVE.]
1 Any of various tropical trees or shrubs of the genera *Rhizophora* and *Bruguiera* (family Rhizophoraceae) with interlacing aerial roots, which form dense thickets in muddy swamps subject to tidal inundation; *esp.* (in full ***common mangrove***, ***red mangrove***) *Rhizophora mangle*. E17.
2 Any of various other tropical trees or shrubs of similar habit and appearance, esp. of the genus *Avicennia* (of the verbena family). L17.
black mangrove (*a*) *Avicennia marina*, of Florida and the W. Indies; (*b*) *Aegiceras majus*, a similar and related Australian mangrove. **white mangrove** (*a*) W. African and tropical American mangrove, *Laguncularia racemosa* (family Combretaceae); (*b*) a mangrove of the Pacific region, *Avicennia officinalis*, with leaves white beneath.
– COMB.: **mangrove crab** any of various small grapsoid crabs of tropical American mangrove swamps; **mangrove cuckoo** a cuckoo, *Coccyzus minor*, of Florida and the W. Indies; **mangrove fly** a W. African tabanid fly, esp. *Chrysops dimidiatus*; **mangrove-hen** (in Jamaica) the clapper rail, *Rallus longirostris*; **mangrove jack** an edible Indo-Pacific snapper fish, *Lutjanus argentimaculatus*, which frequents mangrove swamps; **mangrove oyster** a small edible Caribbean oyster, *Ostrea frons*, which grows on submerged mangrove roots; **mangrove snapper** the grey snapper, *Lutjanus griseus*, which frequents mangrove swamps.

mangy /ˈmeɪndʒi/ *adjective.* Also **-ey**. LME.
[ORIGIN from MANGE + -Y[1].]
1 Having the mange; of the nature of or caused by the mange. Formerly also, scabby. LME.

E. BLYTON A dreadful animal . . all sort of mangy and moth-eaten.

2 Squalid, poverty-stricken, shabby; contemptible. E16.

R. CROMPTON A mangy fur rug was tied round his arms. J. RABAN That would be a mangy compromise unfair . . even to George.

■ **mangily** *adverb* M17. **manginess** *noun* LME.

manhandle /ˈmanhand(ə)l/ *verb trans.* LME.
[ORIGIN from MAN *noun* + HANDLE *verb*[1].]
†**1** Handle or wield (a tool). Only in LME.
2 †**a** Attack (an enemy). Only in LME. ▸**b** Handle (a person) roughly; pull or hustle about. M19.

b S. KING A drunk had manhandled one of the deputies. J. SMILEY Jess manhandled Harold into the kitchen.

3 Move by human effort alone; move slowly or with difficulty. M19.

manhattan /manˈhat(ə)n/ *noun.* Also **M-**. L19.
[ORIGIN formed as MANHATTANESE.]
A cocktail made with vermouth and a spirit, as whisky or brandy, sometimes with a dash of bitters.

Manhattanese /man,hatəˈniːz/ *noun & adjective.* E19.
[ORIGIN from *Manhattan* (see below) + -ESE.]
▸ **A** *noun.* Pl. same.
1 A native or inhabitant of Manhattan, (the borough including) the island on which the older part of New York City is built, or (*loosely*) New York City. E19.
2 The English dialect of Manhattan or New York City. E20.
▸ **B** *adjective.* Of or pertaining to Manhattan or New York City. M19.

Manhattanite /manˈhat(ə)nʌɪt/ *noun.* L19.
[ORIGIN formed as MANHATTANESE + -ITE[1].]
A native or inhabitant of Manhattan or (*loosely*) New York City.

manhood /ˈmanhʊd/ *noun.* ME.
[ORIGIN from MAN *noun* + -HOOD.]
▸ **I 1** The state or condition of being human; human nature. ME.
†**2** Humaneness. ME–L16.
▸ **II 3** The state of being a man, as opposed to a boy or a woman, or both. LME.
4 Manliness, courage; (now *esp.*) virility, male sexual potency. LME. ▸**b** The male external genitals; the penis. M20.

R. KENAN They jostle me about, making rude comments about my size, manhood, and intelligence. **b** *Mirror* Only 33 per cent of men think their manhood is 'bigger than average'.

5 Men collectively; the adult male members of a population, country, etc. L16.

mani /ˈmɑːni/ *noun*[1]. E17.
[ORIGIN Spanish *maní* from Taino.]
In S. America: the groundnut, *Arachis hypogaea*.

mani /ˈmɑːni/ *noun*[2]. E19.
[ORIGIN Tibetan *mani* from Sanskrit = precious stone.]
Any of various Tibetan Buddhist sacred objects or aids to prayer, *esp.* a wall of stones with religious inscriptions. Also ***mani wall***. Cf. MENDANG.

mania /ˈmeɪnɪə/ *noun.* LME.
[ORIGIN Late Latin from Greek, rel. to *mainesthai* be mad, ult. from Indo-European base of MIND *noun*[1]: see -IA[1].]
1 PSYCHIATRY. Mental disturbance characterized by great excitement or elation, extravagant delusions, and overactivity. LME.
2 Excessive excitement or enthusiasm; (usu.) an excessive enthusiasm or passion (*for*), a temporary enthusiasm or craze (*for*). L17.

M. BRADBURY Building mania or, as it was put, an Edifice Complex. JANET MORGAN It was as well that the house was spacious, since Frederick had a mania for collecting.

-mania /ˈmeɪnɪə/ *suffix.*
[ORIGIN formed as MANIA.]
Forming nouns with the sense 'a particular kind of mania', as ***Anglomania***, ***bibliomania***, ***kleptomania***, ***megalomania***, ***nymphomania***, etc.

†**maniable** *adjective.* L15.
[ORIGIN Old French & mod. French, from *manier* to handle, ult. from Latin *manus* hand: see -ABLE.]
1 Easy to handle or work; flexible, pliable; (of a person etc.) manageable, tractable. L15–E18.
2 That may be handled or felt, palpable. L15–L17.

maniac /ˈmeɪnɪak/ *adjective & noun.* E16.
[ORIGIN Late Latin *maniacus* from late Greek *maniakos*, from Greek MANIA: see -AC.]
▸ **A** *adjective.* **1** Of, pertaining to, or characterized by mania or excessive enthusiasm. E16.
2 Affected with mania; raving mad. L16.

C. GLAZEBROOK There's no way I want to spend time with my maniac mum.

▸ **B** *noun.* A person affected with mania, a mad person; a person with a mania for something. M18.

A. MACLEAN I had a momentary vision of some maniac placing a stick of gelignite under the tractor. R. BRADBURY My mother, a maniac for silent movies, toted me to the cinema.

-maniac /ˈmeɪnɪak/ *suffix.*
[ORIGIN formed as MANIAC. Cf. -MANE.]
Forming adjectives and nouns with the sense '(a person) affected by a particular kind of mania', as ***kleptomaniac***, ***nymphomaniac***, etc.

maniacal /məˈnʌɪək(ə)l/ *adjective.* L17.
[ORIGIN from MANIAC + -AL[1].]
1 = MANIAC *adjective* 1. L17.
2 = MANIAC *adjective* 2. E18.
■ **maniacally** *adverb* M19.

manic /ˈmanɪk/ *adjective.* E19.
[ORIGIN from MANIA + -IC.]
1 Of, pertaining to, or resembling mania; affected with or characteristic of mania. E19.
2 Showing wild, apparently deranged, excitement and energy. Also, frantically busy, hectic. M20.

A. N. WILSON He was a legendary pantomime dame—hurling himself into the parts with . . manic energy. *FHM* Round at Natalie's house it's manic, with Nat's three sisters and me yakking non-stop.

– COMB.: **manic depression** the condition of manic-depressive illness, bipolar disorder; **manic-depressive** *adjective & noun* (*a*) *adjective* characterized by or affected with alternating periods of elation and mental depression; bipolar; (*b*) *noun* a manic-depressive person.
■ **manically** *adverb* M20.

Manichaean /manɪˈkiːən/ *noun & adjective.* Also **-chean**. M16.
[ORIGIN formed as MANICHAEISM + -AN.]
▸ **A** *noun.* An adherent of Manichaeism; *transf.* a dualist. M16.
▸ **B** *adjective.* Of, pertaining to, or characteristic of Manichaeism or its adherents; *transf.* of or pertaining to dualism, dualistic. L16.

Manichaeism /manɪˈkiːɪz(ə)m/ *noun.* Also **-cheism**. E17.
[ORIGIN from late Latin *Manichaeus* (late Greek *Manikhaios*), from *Mani*, *Manes* (*c* 216–76), Persian founder of the system: see -ISM.]
A religious system with Christian, Gnostic, and pagan elements, founded in the 3rd cent. AD and widespread in the Roman Empire and Asia until the 5th (surviving until the 13th), based on a supposed primeval conflict between light and darkness, and representing Satan as coeternal with God; *transf.* dualism.
■ **Manichaeˈistic** *adjective* of, pertaining to, or of the nature of Manichaeism E20.

Manichean *noun & adjective* var. of MANICHAEAN.

Manichee /ˈmanɪkiː/ *noun.* LME.
[ORIGIN formed as MANICHAEISM.]
= MANICHAEAN *noun*.

Manicheism *noun* var. of MANICHAEISM.

manichord /ˈmanɪkɔːd/ *noun. obsolete* exc. *hist.* Also (earlier) †**-dion**. E17.
[ORIGIN French *manichordion*, †*manicorde* from medieval Latin *monochordium* from late Greek *monokhordion*, classical Greek *-khordon* MONOCHORD, assoc. with Latin *manus* hand.]
= CLAVICHORD.

manicotti /manɪˈkɒti/ *noun pl.* M20.
[ORIGIN Italian, pl. of *manicotto* sleeve, muff.]
Large tubular pasta shells; an Italian dish consisting largely of these and usu. a sauce.

manicou /ˈmanɪkuː/ *noun.* M20.
[ORIGIN French, from Portuguese *manicu* from Tupi *maníku*.]
Any of various small opossums of the genus *Marmosa*, of Central and S. America. Also called ***mouse opossum***.

manicure /ˈmanɪkjʊə/ *noun & verb.* L19.
[ORIGIN French, from Latin *manus* hand + *cura* care.]
▸ **A** *noun.* **1** = MANICURIST. Now *rare*. L19.
2 The cosmetic treatment and care of the hands and fingernails, by shaping the nails, removing cuticles, etc.; an instance of such treatment, esp. by a manicurist. L19.

R. DAHL His hairdresser trimmed his hair . . and he always took a manicure at the same time. *attrib.*: A. J. CRONIN She took her manicure set and began to do her nails.

▸ **B** *verb trans.* **1** Apply manicure treatment to (the nails, a person, etc.). L19.
2 *transf.* & *fig.* Trim or cut neatly. E20.

J. BRAINE Big houses with drives . . and manicured hedges.

manicurist /ˈmanɪkjʊərɪst/ *noun.* L19.
[ORIGIN from MANICURE + -IST.]
A person who gives manicure treatment, esp. professionally.

†**manier** *adjective* see MANY.

maniéré /manjere/ *adjective.* M18.
[ORIGIN French.]
Affected or characterized by mannerism, mannered.

manière criblée /manjɛːr krible/ *noun phr.* E20.
[ORIGIN French: see MANNER *noun*[1], CRIBLÉ.]
Criblé engraving.

†**maniest** *adjective* see MANY.

manifest /ˈmanɪfɛst/ *noun.* M16.
[ORIGIN Italian MANIFESTO.]
1 A manifestation, an indication. Now *rare*. M16.

A. MILLER She swears that she never saw . . apparitions, nor any manifest of the Devil.

2 A public proclamation or declaration; a manifesto. Now *rare*. E17.
3 A list of a ship's cargo for the information and use of Customs officers; a list of freight or passengers carried by a train or aeroplane; *gen.* an inventory. E18. ▸**b** A fast freight train. Also ***manifest train***. Chiefly *N. Amer.* E20.

manifest /ˈmanɪfɛst/ *adjective.* ME.
[ORIGIN Old French & mod. French *manifeste* or Latin *manifestus*, earlier *manufestus*, from *manus* hand + *festus* struck (only in compounds, as *infestus* dangerous), from base of *defendere* DEFEND, *offendere* OFFEND.]
1 Clearly revealed to the eye, mind, or judgement; open to view or comprehension; obvious. ME.

manifest destiny (the doctrine of) the (supposed) inevitability of the supremacy or expansion of power of a people or state, orig. esp. of the US or of those of European origin in or over the entire Western hemisphere.

†**2** Having evident signs *of*; evidently possessed *of* or guilty *of*. *literary*. L17–E18.

■ **manifestly** *adverb* (*a*) (now *rare*) in a manifest manner; (*b*) (qualifying a statement) as is manifest, evidently, unmistakably: L15. **manifestness** *noun* L16.

manifest /ˈmanɪfɛst/ *verb*. LME.

[ORIGIN Old French & mod. French *manifester* or Latin *manifestare*, from *manifestus*: see MANIFEST *adjective*.]

1 *verb trans.* Make evident to the eye or to the understanding; show plainly, reveal; display (a quality, condition, feeling, etc.) by action or behaviour; evince; be evidence of, prove, attest. LME.

SHAKES. *2 Hen. IV* Thy life did manifest thou lov'dst me not. M. MEAD The Balinese manifest less fatigue than any people of whom we have a record. E. H. GOMBRICH Royal patronage, to manifest the interest which the King took in the arts. D. FRANCIS Guilt and remorse can manifest themselves in excess of mourning. A. SILLITOE If God manifested Himself . . He would be quickly disowned.

†**2** *verb trans.* Expound, unfold, clear up (a matter). M16–M17.

3 *verb trans.* Record or enumerate in a manifest. M16.

4 *verb intrans.* SPIRITUALISM. Of a ghost or spirit: make an appearance. L19.

5 *verb intrans.* = DEMONSTRATE *verb* 6. Now *rare*. L19.

■ **maniˈfestable** *adjective* (now *rare*) E16. **maniˈfestant** *noun* (now *rare*) = DEMONSTRATOR 3 L19. **manifester** *noun* L15. **manifestive** *adjective* (*rare*) M19.

manifestation /ˌmanɪfɛˈsteɪʃ(ə)n/ *noun*. LME.

[ORIGIN Late Latin *manifestatio(n-)*, from *manifestat-* pa. ppl stem of *manifestare*: see MANIFEST *verb*, -ATION.]

1 The action of manifesting; the fact of being manifested; the demonstration, revelation, or display of the existence, presence, qualities, or nature of some person or thing. LME.

2 An instance of this; a means or thing by which something is manifested. L18. ▸**b** *spec.* = DEMONSTRATION 6. Now *rare*. L19.

3 SPIRITUALISM. A phenomenon or number of phenomena by which the presence of a spirit is supposed to be rendered perceptible. M19.

■ **manifestational** *adjective* (*rare*) L19. **manifestationist** *noun* (*rare*) a believer in manifestation M19.

manifestative /manɪˈfɛstətɪv/ *adjective*. M17.

[ORIGIN medieval Latin *manifestativus*, from *manifestat-*: see MANIFESTATION, -IVE.]

Having the function or quality of manifesting something.

■ **manifestatively** *adverb* in a manifestative manner; in respect of manifestation: M17.

manifesto /manɪˈfɛstəʊ/ *noun & verb*. E17.

[ORIGIN Italian, from *manifestare* from Latin: see MANIFEST *verb*.]

▸**A** *noun*. Pl. **-o(e)s**.

1 A public declaration or proclamation; *esp.* a printed declaration or explanation of policy (past, present, or future) issued by a monarch, state, political party or candidate, or any other individual or body of individuals of public relevance. E17.

P. B. CLARKE The Association's main aims as expressed in the manifesto. M. FOOT She knew what . . the party manifesto committed her to achieve. J. UGLOW A manifesto for a literalism in art and a commitment to describing the mundanities of life.

†**2** A proof, a piece of evidence. M–L17.

▸**B** *verb intrans.* Issue a manifesto or manifestos. *rare*. M18.

manifold /ˈmanɪfəʊld/ *adjective, adverb, & noun*.

[ORIGIN Old English *maniġfeald* = Old Frisian *manichfald*, Old High German *managfalt* (German *mannigfalt*), Gothic *managfalþs*, from Germanic, formed as MANY + -FOLD. Cf. MANYFOLD.]

▸**A** *adjective*. Now chiefly *literary*.

1 Varied or diverse in appearance, form, or character; having various forms, features, component parts, relations, applications, etc.; performing several functions at once. OE. ▸**b** That is the specified thing in many ways or in many relations; entitled to the specified name on many grounds. Now *rare*. ME.

LD MACAULAY A manifold hatred, theological and political, hereditary and personal. W. G. PALGRAVE Coffee though one in name is manifold in fact. **b** W. CONGREVE Secure that manifold villain.

2 Numerous and varied; of many kinds or varieties. Formerly simply, numerous, many. OE.

H. READ This belief that behind manifold appearances there is one enduring reality. O. SITWELL The Bowes Museum is vast, its exhibits are manifold.

†**3** MATH. = MULTIPLE *adjective* 3. ME–M17.

manifold to a multiple of.

▸†**B** *adverb*. **1** In many ways or degrees. ME–L16.

2 In the proportion of many to one. Cf. MANYFOLD. Only in E17.

▸**C** *noun*. †**1** **by manifold**, (occas.) **on manifold**, many times over, in the proportion of many to one. ME–L16.

2 That which is manifold; *spec.* in KANTIAN PHILOSOPHY, the sum of the particulars provided by sense before they have been unified by the synthesis of the understanding. M19.

3 MATH. A topological space each point of which has a neighbourhood homoeomorphic to the interior of a sphere in a Euclidean space of given dimension. L19.

4 = *manifold paper* below. L19.

5 ENGINEERING. A pipe or chamber that has a number of branches, or inlets or outlets; *spec.* (in an internal-combustion engine) that which delivers air and fuel from the carburettor to the cylinders (in full ***inlet manifold***, ***intake manifold***), and that leading from the cylinders to the exhaust pipe (in full ***exhaust manifold***). L19.

– COMB.: **manifold paper** lightweight paper for making carbon copies, copying paper; **manifold writer** (chiefly *hist.*) a machine with carbon paper for multiplying copies of a document etc.

■ **manifoldly** *adverb* (now *literary*) (*a*) in manifold ways; †(*b*) in the proportion of many to one: OE. **manifoldness** *noun* OE.

manifold /ˈmanɪfəʊld/ *verb trans*. OE.

[ORIGIN from the adjective.]

1 Make manifold, multiply. *rare* in *gen.* sense. OE.

2 *spec.* Multiply impressions or copies of, esp. mechanically. *arch.* M19.

– NOTE: Became obsolete in ME. Re-formed in 18.

■ **manifolding** *noun* (*a*) the action of the verb; (*b*) = MANIFOLD *noun* 5: L19. **manifolder** *noun* E20.

maniform /ˈmanɪfɔːm/ *adjective*[1]. *rare*. E19.

[ORIGIN from Latin *manus* hand + -I- + -FORM.]

Having the form of a hand; ENTOMOLOGY chelate.

maniform /ˈmanɪfɔːm/ *adjective*[2]. E19.

[ORIGIN from MANY + -FORM, after *manifold*.]

Multiform.

manify /ˈmanɪfʌɪ/ *verb trans*. *rare*. L18.

[ORIGIN from MAN *noun* + -I- + -FY.]

Make manlike.

manihot *noun* see MANIOC.

manikin /ˈmanɪkɪn/ *noun & adjective*. Also (the only form in sense A.3b) **-nn-**. See also MANAKIN. M16.

[ORIGIN Dutch *manneken* dim. of *man* MAN *noun*: see -KIN. Cf. MANNEQUIN.]

▸**A** *noun*. **1** A little man (freq. *derog.*); a dwarf, a pygmy. M16.

2 A small figure or statue of a man; *spec.* (*a*) an artist's lay figure; (*b*) a model of the human body used for exhibiting the anatomical structure or for demonstrating surgical operations. M16.

3 **a** = MANAKIN 2. L18. ▸**b** Any of various small finchlike birds of the genus *Lonchura* (family Estrildidae), which are found in Africa, Asia, and Australasia and are popular as cage birds. M20.

▸**B** *attrib.* or as *adjective*. Diminutive, dwarf; puny. M19.

Manila /məˈnɪlə/ *adjective & noun*. Also **-ll-**, **m-**. L17.

[ORIGIN The capital and chief port of the Philippines.]

▸**A** *adjective*. **1** *attrib.* Designating things produced in or associated with Manila or the Philippines. L17.

Manila cheroot, **Manila cigar**: of a kind manufactured in Manila. ***Manila*** ELEMI. **Manila hemp** the fibres of the pseudostem of the plant *Musa textilis* (family Musaceae), used to make ropes, matting, paper, etc. **manila paper**: of a light yellow-brown colour made from Manila hemp or other material, used esp. as wrapping paper. ***Manila tamarind***: see TAMARIND 3.

2 Made from Manila hemp or manila paper; of the light yellow-brown colour of manila paper. M19.

P. HIGHSMITH He put on old Manila trousers. D. LODGE The brown Manila envelope . . already . . used twice for the circulation of internal mail.

▸**B** *noun*. **1** Manila hemp; Manila rope; manila paper. M19.

2 A Manila cheroot or cigar. M19.

manilla /məˈnɪlə/ *noun*[1]. L16.

[ORIGIN Spanish, prob. dim. of *mano* hand from Latin *manus*.]

A ring of metal worn on the arm or wrist by some African peoples and used as a medium of exchange.

Manilla *adjective & noun*[2] var. of MANILA.

manille /məˈnɪl/ *noun*. L17.

[ORIGIN French from Spanish *malilla* dim. of *mala* fem. (sc. *carta* card) of *malo* bad.]

CARDS. In quadrille and ombre, the second best trump or honour (being the two of a black suit or the seven of a red suit). Also, a French card game in which the ten or manille is the highest card in each suit.

maninose /ˈmanɪnəʊz/ *noun*. *US*. Also **mananose** & other vars. L17.

[ORIGIN Prob. from Nanticoke.]

The soft-shelled clam, *Mya arenaria*.

manioc /ˈmanɪɒk/ *noun*. Also (earlier) **manihot** /ˈmanɪhɒt/. M16.

[ORIGIN Ult. from Tupi *manioka*.]

The cassava plant, *Manihot esculenta*. Also, the meal made from its starchy root.

maniple /ˈmanɪp(ə)l/ *noun*. ME.

[ORIGIN Old French (mod. *manipule*) or Latin *manipulus* handful, troop of soldiers, from *manus* hand + elem. of unknown origin.]

1 ECCLESIASTICAL. In the Western Church, one of the Eucharistic vestments, consisting now of a strip worn suspended from the left arm near the wrist. Also called ***fanon***. ME.

2 ROMAN HISTORY. A subdivision of the Roman legion, of which a cohort contained three, numbering 120 or 60 men. M16. ▸†**b** *transf.* A small band of soldiers of more or less definite number. L16–M17.

†**3** A handful. L16–E19.

4 A hand. *joc.* E19.

manipulable /məˈnɪpjʊləb(ə)l/ *adjective*. L19.

[ORIGIN from MANIPUL(ATE + -ABLE. Cf. MANIPULATABLE.]

Able to be manipulated.

■ **manipulaˈbility** *noun* M20.

manipulandum /mənɪpjʊˈlandəm/ *noun*. Pl. **-da** /-də/. M20.

[ORIGIN from MANIPUL(ATE + Latin *-andum*: see -AND.]

A thing (to be) manipulated, esp. in a psychological test or experiment.

manipular /məˈnɪpjʊlə/ *adjective & noun*. E17.

[ORIGIN Latin *manipularis*, from *manipulus*: see MANIPLE, -AR[1]. In sense A.2 assoc. with MANIPULATE.]

▸**A** *adjective*. **1** ROMAN HISTORY. Of or pertaining to a maniple of a legion. E17.

2 Of or pertaining to manipulation or handling. E19.

▸**B** *noun*. ROMAN HISTORY. A soldier of a maniple. M19.

manipulatable /məˈnɪpjʊleɪtəb(ə)l/ *adjective*. M20.

[ORIGIN from MANIPULATE + -ABLE.]

= MANIPULABLE.

manipulate /məˈnɪpjʊleɪt/ *verb trans*. E19.

[ORIGIN Back-form. from MANIPULATION, after French *manipuler*: see -ATE[3].]

Handle, esp. with (physical or mental) dexterity; manage, work, or treat by manual or mechanical means; manage by (esp. unfair) dexterous contrivance or influence; stimulate sexually with the hand(s); MEDICINE treat (part of the body, a fracture, etc.) by manual action; COMPUTING carry out operations on (numbers, text, etc.).

E. FERBER Old Eusebio . . was manipulating four cooking vessels at once. JOHN BROOKE A stupid man, manipulated by minds sharper and cleverer than his own. C. TOMALIN She manipulates her . . friends and admirers, using the devotion she inspires for her own ends. *Which?* The burglar usually forced or manipulated the window catch.

manipulation /mənɪpjʊˈleɪʃ(ə)n/ *noun*. E18.

[ORIGIN French, from Latin *manipulus*: see MANIPLE, -ATION.]

†**1** The method of digging silver ore. Only in Dicts. E18–E19.

2 CHEMISTRY. Experimental procedure or technique. *arch.* L18.

3 *gen.* The action or an act of manipulating something or somebody; manual management or action, *spec.* (MEDICINE) the manual treatment of a part of the body; management by (esp. unfair) contrivance or influence. E19.

H. B. STOWE In . . her manipulations, the young disciple had contrived to snatch . . gloves and a ribbon. *Nation* Manipulation signifies a common . . design . . to raise or depress values in order to get other people's money. A. E. STEVENSON Evidence of the distortion and manipulation of the news. *Annabel* Expert advice on caring for your spine, exercise, physiotherapy, and manipulation . . are all available.

manipulative /məˈnɪpjʊlətɪv/ *adjective*. M19.

[ORIGIN from MANIPULATE: see -ATIVE.]

1 Of, pertaining to, or involving manual action or dexterity. M19.

S. SMILES Workmen . . executing machinery requiring manipulative skill.

2 Tending to exercise unscrupulous control or influence over a person or situation. L19.

Glasgow Herald Manipulative television has little to do with informing, educating or entertaining. M. M. R. KHAN Benjamin, even though manipulative, rarely lied.

■ **manipulatively** *adverb* E20. **manipulativeness** *noun* M20.

manipulator /məˈnɪpjʊleɪtə/ *noun*. M19.

[ORIGIN formed as MANIPULATIVE: see -ATOR.]

1 A person who manipulates something or someone. M19.

2 A device used for or in manipulation, as a remote-controlled device for handling radioactive material behind a protective shield. M19.

manipulatory /məˈnɪpjʊlət(ə)ri/ *adjective*. E19.

[ORIGIN formed as MANIPULATIVE + -ORY[2].]

Pertaining to or involving manipulation.

Manipuri /mʌnɪˈpʊəri/ *adjective & noun*. M19.

[ORIGIN from *Manipur* (see below) + -I[2].]

▸**A** *adjective*. Of or pertaining to Manipur, a state in the region of Assam in NE India. M19.

▸**B** *noun*. Pl. **-s**, same.

1 A member of the people of Manipur. M19.

2 The Tibeto-Burman language of the Manipuri. E20.

manis /ˈmeɪnɪs/ *noun*. M18.

[ORIGIN mod. Latin, perh. a spurious sing. of MANES.]

ZOOLOGY. = PANGOLIN. Now only as mod. Latin genus name.

M

ma nishtana /ma nɪʃˈtana/ *noun phr.* E20.
[ORIGIN Hebrew = how different (*sc.* from all other nights!), the opening words.]
JUDAISM. The four questions in the Passover Haggadah, traditionally asked by the youngest member of a Jewish household on Seder Night; this part of the Passover celebrations.

manism /ˈmɑːnɪz(ə)m, ˈmeɪ-/ *noun.* E20.
[ORIGIN from MANES + -ISM.]
The worship of the manes or shades of the dead; ancestor worship.
■ **maˈnistic** *adjective* M20.

Manit. *abbreviation.*
Manitoba.

manito *noun* var. of MANITOU.

manitoka *noun* var. of MANATOTA.

manitou /ˈmanɪtuː/ *noun.* Also **-tu**; **-to**, pl. **-tos**. L17.
[ORIGIN Pidgin Delaware *Manétto* god, spirit, from Delaware (Unami) *manə́tːu* and Delaware (Munsee) *manə́toːw* supernatural being.]
Among some N. American Indians, a spirit (of good or evil) which is an object of religious awe or reverence; anything regarded as having supernatural power, as a fetish.

manjak /ˈmandʒak/ *noun.* Orig. *W. Indian.* Also (earlier) †**mountjack**. M17.
[ORIGIN Perh. ult. from Arawak.]
GEOLOGY. A form of asphalt which occurs in Barbados.

manjee /ˈmɑːndʒi/ *noun.* L17.
[ORIGIN Hindi *mā̃jhī*.]
In the Indian subcontinent: the captain or steersman of a boat.

†**mank** *adjective.* Chiefly *Scot.* E16–M19.
[ORIGIN Old French *manc*, *manque* from Latin *mancus* maimed.]
Maimed, mutilated, defective.

mank /maŋk/ *verb trans. obsolete* exc. *Scot.* ME.
[ORIGIN Late Latin (chiefly Frankish) *mancare*, from *mancus*: see MANK *adjective*.]
Maim, mangle, mutilate.

mankin /ˈmankɪn/ *noun.* M16.
[ORIGIN from MAN *noun* + -KIN.]
A diminutive or puny man; a manikin.

mankind /manˈkʌɪnd, *in sense A.3* ˈmankʌɪnd/ *noun & adjective.* ME.
[ORIGIN from MAN *noun* + KIND *noun*.]
▸ **A** *noun.* **1** The human species; human beings in general. ME.
†**2** Human nature; human feeling, humanity. ME–E17.
3 The male sex; men or male people in general. LME.
▸ †**B** *adjective.* **1** Human. Only in L16.
2 Of a woman: masculine. L16–M17.
3 Male. Only in M17.
– NOTE: Alternatives such as *the human race* or *humankind* are sometimes preferred: see note s.v. MAN *noun*.

manky /ˈmaŋki/ *adjective. dial. & colloq.* M20.
[ORIGIN Prob. from MANK *adjective* + -Y[1], perh. infl. by French *manqué*.]
Bad, inferior, defective; dirty.

M. SYAL Sitting on a manky bus seat, getting discarded bubblegum on his pristine trousers.

manless /ˈmanlɪs/ *adjective.* OE.
[ORIGIN from MAN *noun* + -LESS.]
1 a Having no men; having no human beings. OE. ▸**b** Of a woman: lacking the company of men, *spec.* having no husband or lover. E20.
†**2** Unmanly, effeminate. E16–M17.
■ **manlessness** *noun* †(*a*) cowardice; (*b*) the state or condition of being manless: M17.

manlike /ˈmanlʌɪk/ *adjective & adverb.* L15.
[ORIGIN from MAN *noun* + -LIKE.]
▸ **A** *adjective.* **1** Having (good or bad) qualities or characteristics associated with men as distinguished from women or children; (of a woman) mannish. L15. ▸†**b** Having the qualities or characteristics of humans as distinguished from God, angels, etc.; mortal. L15–L19.
2 Of an animal: resembling a man or human being. L16.
▸ **B** *adverb.* Manfully. L16.
■ **manlikely** *adverb* (*rare*) E16. **manlikeness** *noun* (*rare*) M18.

manling /ˈmanlɪŋ/ *noun. rare.* L16.
[ORIGIN from MAN *noun* + -LING[1].]
A little man.

manly /ˈmanli/ *adjective.* ME.
[ORIGIN from MAN *noun* + -LY[1].]
†**1** Belonging to human beings; human. ME–E17.
2 Having good qualities or characteristics associated with men as distinguished from women or children; *esp.* courageous, independent in spirit, frank, upright. ME. ▸**b** Of a woman: mannish. E16.

T. O. ECHEWA He stored his grief and prided himself in his manly ability to store it.

3 Of a thing, quality, etc.: befitting or belonging to a man; masculine. LME.

L. F. BAUM His manly beauty was so great that Gayelette loved him dearly. A. N. WILSON His silk display handkerchiefs, his manly striped ties.

†**4** Adult, mature. L16–L17.
■ **manlihood** *noun* (*rare*) manliness L16. **manlily** *adverb* LME. **manliness** *noun* LME.

manly /ˈmanli/ *adverb. arch.* OE.
[ORIGIN from MAN *noun* + -LY[2].]
1 In a manly manner; like a man; manfully, courageously. OE.
†**2** Like a human being. OE–M16.
†**3** Excellently. Only in E17.

manna /ˈmanə/ *noun.* OE.
[ORIGIN Late Latin from Hellenistic Greek from Aramaic *mannā* from Hebrew *mān* corresp. to Arabic *mann* exudation of the tamarisk *Tamarix mannifera*.]
▸ **I 1** The edible substance described as miraculously supplied to the Israelites in the wilderness (*Exodus* 16). OE.
2 Spiritual nourishment, *esp.* the Eucharist; something beneficial provided unexpectedly (freq. ***manna from heaven***). ME.
▸ **II 3** A sweet hardened flaky exudation obtained from the manna ash (see below), rich in mannitol and used as a mild laxative. Also, a similar exudation from other plants (e.g. a Middle Eastern tamarisk, *Tamarix mannifera*, a Middle Eastern legume, *Alhagi maurorum*, and the larch) and certain insects. LME.
TREHALA ***manna***.
†**4** (A grain of) frankincense. LME–M18.
†**5** CHEMISTRY. A fine white precipitate. L17–E18.
6 In full ***Polish manna***. The seeds of the floating sweetgrass, *Glyceria fluitans*, used as food. L18.
– COMB.: **manna ash** a white-flowered ash, *Fraxinus ornus*, of southern Europe; **manna-grass** floating sweetgrass, *Glyceria fluitans*; **manna-gum** *Austral.* a manna-yielding eucalyptus, *Eucalyptus viminalis*; **manna-lichen** any of several edible lichens of the genus *Sphaerothallia* (esp. *S. esculenta*) sometimes identified with the manna of the Bible; **manna sugar** = MANNITOL; **manna tree** = ***manna ash*** above.

mannan /ˈmanan/ *noun.* L19.
[ORIGIN from MANNOSE + -AN.]
CHEMISTRY. Any of a group of polysaccharides composed chiefly of mannose residues, occurring widely in plants esp. as reserve foods.

mannequin /ˈmanɪkɪn, -kwɪn/ *noun.* M18.
[ORIGIN French, formed as MANIKIN.]
1 A model of a human figure; an artist's lay figure; a dummy for the display of clothes etc. M18.
2 A woman (or occas. a man) employed by a dressmaker, costumier, etc., to display clothes by wearing them; a model. E20.

manner /ˈmanə/ *noun*[1]. ME.
[ORIGIN Anglo-Norman *manere*, Old French & mod. French *manière*, from Proto-Romance use as noun of fem. of Latin *manuarius* pertaining to the hand, from *manus* hand: see -ER[2].]
1 The way in which something is done or happens; a method of action; a mode of procedure. ME.

New Yorker Not to dispose of these documents or destroy them in any manner. A. BLEASDALE Driving in a manner likely to cause an accident. A. DESAI She leant against the door in the theatrical manner that came naturally to her.

†**2** The state, character, disposition, or nature *of*. ME–M17.
3 Customary mode of acting or behaviour; habitual practice; usage, custom, fashion. Now *literary.* ME.

B. JOWETT Here Ctesippus, as his manner was, burst into a roar of laughter. W. TREVOR Culture is the byword in our villa, but otherwise we live in the local manner. P. B. CLARKE West Indian Pentecostal congregations are distinguishable by their manner of worship.

4 In *pl.* ▸†**a** A person's habitual behaviour or conduct; morals; conduct in its moral aspect; morality. ME–L18. ▸**b** The prevailing modes of life, the customary rules of behaviour, the conditions of society. Sometimes *spec.* good customs or social conditions. ME. ▸†**c** An animal's habits. LME–L18. ▸†**d** The distinctive varieties of disposition and temperament portrayed in a work of literature. L17–L18.

a S. JOHNSON A change of fortune causes a change of manners. GIBBON Divorces were prohibited by manners rather than by laws. **b** SHAKES. *1 Hen. IV* Defect of manners, want of government. J. E. T. ROGERS Contemporary novels are good evidence of manners. **d** ADDISON This is Aristotle's Method of considering, first the Fable, and secondly the Manners.

5 Outward bearing, deportment; a person's characteristic style of attitude, gesture, or utterance. ME. ▸**b** A distinguished or fashionable air. *arch.* L17.

A. LURIE She had developed a special effusive manner. M. FITZHERBERT His sheltered life had led to a singularity of manner. C. SIMMONS What it was in my speech, actions, or manner that provoked these feelings. **b** GOLDSMITH Who can have a manner, who has never seen . . such places where the nobility chiefly resort?

6 In *pl.* & †*sing.* ▸**a** External social behaviour, estimated according to its degree of politeness or of conformity to the accepted standards of behaviour or propriety; (of an animal) trained behaviour, action. ME. ▸**b** Polite social behaviour or deportment; habits indicative of good breeding; (*obsolete* exc. *dial.*) forms of politeness or respect (now only in ***do one's manners***, ***make one's manners***, curtsy, bow, etc.). LME.

D. EDEN Don't you know it's very bad manners to read other people's letters? M. SPARK Trevor threw half a crown backwards on to the counter. 'Manners,' the barmaid said. M. FOOT Sometimes Gaitskell refers self-mockingly to his immaculate Wykehamist manners. **b** Q. CRISP Manners . . are a means of getting what we want without appearing to be absolute swine.

7 A species, kind, or sort *of*; qualified by *all*, *many*, *these*, or a numeral as *pl.*, kinds or sorts *of*. (Formerly often with ellipsis of *of*.) Now only in ***all manner of***, (*arch.*) ***what manner of?*** ME.

SHAKES. *Wint. T.* What manner of fellow was he that robb'd you? L. APPIGNANESI All manner of food and basic commodities were in short supply.

8 A method or style of execution in art, literature, etc.; style. LME. ▸**b** Mannerism. E18.

N. MITFORD An oil painting . . by Boy or Lady Montdore . . . It was in their early manner. P. MEDAWAR People more affected by manner than by matter. M. GIROUARD Nesfield designed his first known building in a post-Gothic manner.

†**9** Measure, moderation. LME–E16.
– PHRASES: **adverb of manner**: which answers or asks the question *how?* ***by all manner of means***, ***by any manner of means***, ***by no manner of means***: see MEAN *noun*[1]. ***comedy of manners***. ***do one's manners***: see sense 6b above. **in a manner** (*a*) in some way, in some degree, so to speak, as it were; †(*b*) to a considerable degree, almost entirely, very nearly. **in a manner of speaking** in some sense, to some extent, so to speak. **in like manner** in a similar way, similarly. **in the manner of** after the style or fashion of, in the guise of, in the same way as. ***make one's manners***: see sense 6b above. ***manner of articulation***: see ARTICULATION *noun* 5. **no manner of —** *arch.* no — whatever. **to the manner born** [Shakes. *Haml.*] destined by birth to be subject to some custom; *colloq.* naturally fitted for some position or employment.

manner *noun*[2] var. of MAINOUR.

mannerable /ˈman(ə)rəb(ə)l/ *adjective. obsolete* exc. *dial.* L15.
[ORIGIN from MANNER *noun*[1] + -ABLE.]
Well-mannered, polite.

mannered /ˈmanəd/ *adjective.* LME.
[ORIGIN from MANNER *noun*[1] + -ED[2].]
1 Having manners of a specified kind (indicated by an adverbial phr., or by a prefixed adjective or adverb). LME. ▸**b** Well-behaved, well-mannered. Long *dial. rare.* LME.
ill-mannered, ***rough-mannered***, ***well-mannered***, etc.
2 Characterized by or given to mannerism. E19.

H. R. HAWEIS That Spohr was too doctrinaire and mannered, . . most musicians will allow. M. FORSTER She began . . to drop the rather mannered style of her first letters.

mannerise *verb* var. of MANNERIZE.

mannerism /ˈmanərɪz(ə)m/ *noun.* E19.
[ORIGIN from MANNER *noun*[1] + -ISM.]
1 Excessive or affected adoption of a distinctive manner or method of treatment, esp. in art and literature; *spec.* (freq. **M-**) a style of art which originated in Italy and preceded the baroque, characterized by stylistic exaggeration and distortion of figures etc. E19.
2 A habitual peculiarity of style or manner; a trick or gesture of speech or action, esp. of an actor. E19. ▸**b** PSYCHIATRY. An ordinary gesture or expression that becomes abnormal through exaggeration or repetition, usu. as a symptom of mental disorder. E20.

Times He has abandoned his mannerisms and been content to make a beautiful picture. N. GORDIMER She fell again into the mannerism of holding her head to one side. P. ACKROYD I detest the critical mannerism that professes to find good in everything.

mannerist /ˈmanərɪst/ *noun & adjective.* L17.
[ORIGIN from MANNER *noun*[1] + -IST, orig. after French *maniériste*.]
▸ **A** *noun.* A person who adopts or adheres to mannerism; *spec.* an exponent or adherent of Mannerism in art. L17.
▸ **B** *adjective.* Of or pertaining to mannerism or mannerists. M20.
■ **manneˈristic** *adjective* characterized by mannerism M19. **manneˈristical** *adjective* M19.

mannerize /ˈmanərʌɪz/ *verb trans. rare.* Also **-ise**. L19.
[ORIGIN from MANNER *noun*[1] + -IZE.]
Make manneristic.

mannerless /ˈmanəlɪs/ *adjective.* L15.
[ORIGIN from MANNER *noun*[1] + -LESS.]
Without manners; ill-mannered, unmannerly.
■ **mannerlessness** *noun* M20.

mannerly /ˈmanəli/ *adjective.* LME.
[ORIGIN from MANNER *noun*[1] + -LY[1].]
1 Characterized by good manners; well-mannered; polite. Formerly also, seemly, decent, respectable, modest. LME.
†**2** Moral, well-conducted. LME–M16.
■ **mannerliness** *noun* L15.

mannerly /ˈmanəli/ *adverb.* LME.
[ORIGIN from MANNER *noun*[1] + -LY[2]. Earlier in UNMANNERLY *adverb.*]
With good manners; politely, courteously. Formerly also, in a seemly manner, decently, becomingly.

Mannesmann /ˈmanɪsmən/ *noun.* E20.
[ORIGIN Reinhard M. *Mannesmann* (1856–1922), German industrialist and inventor.]
Used *attrib.* to designate a method of making thick-walled seamless metal tubes by drawing a heated cylinder of metal lengthwise on to a pointed mandrel.

mannie /ˈmani/ *noun.* Orig. & chiefly *Scot.* Also **manny**. L17.
[ORIGIN from MAN *noun* + -IE, -Y[6].]
A little man. Freq. as a term of endearment to a little boy.

mannikin *noun & adjective* see MANIKIN.

mannish /ˈmanɪʃ/ *adjective.*
[ORIGIN Old English *mennisc*, formed as MAN *noun* + -ISH[1]. Later re-formed on or infl. by MAN *noun.*]
1 Of, pertaining to, or characteristic of the human species. Long *rare*. OE.
2 Of a woman, a woman's attributes, etc.: resembling (those of) a man, masculine. Chiefly *derog.* LME.
3 Of, pertaining to, or characteristic of an adult male person, as opp. to a boy or woman or both. M16.
■ **mannishly** *adverb* M19. **mannishness** *noun* OE.

mannite /ˈmanʌɪt/ *noun.* E19.
[ORIGIN from MANNA + -ITE[1].]
CHEMISTRY. = MANNITOL.
■ **mannitic** /maˈnɪtɪk/ *adjective* derived from mannite M19.

mannitol /ˈmanɪtɒl/ *noun.* L19.
[ORIGIN from MANNITE + -OL.]
CHEMISTRY. A colourless sweet-tasting crystalline alcohol, $CH_2OH(CHOH)_4CH_2OH$, which is found in many plants and is used in various foods and medical products. Also called ***manna sugar***, ***mannite***.

Mannlicher /ˈmanlɪkə, *foreign* ˈmanlɪçər/ *noun.* L19.
[ORIGIN Ferdinand Ritter von *Mannlicher* (1848–1904), Austrian inventor.]
A type of sporting rifle. Also more fully ***Mannlicher rifle***.

mannose /ˈmanəʊz, -s/ *noun.* L19.
[ORIGIN from MANNITE + -OSE[2].]
CHEMISTRY. A hexose sugar which occurs as a component of many natural polysaccharides, esp. mannans.

Mann–Whitney /manˈwɪtni/ *noun.* M20.
[ORIGIN from Henry Berthold *Mann* (1905–2000), Austrian-born US mathematician + Donald Ransom *Whitney* (b. 1915), US statistician.]
STATISTICS. Used *attrib.* with ref. to a method of comparing samples from two unmatched groups of subjects, based on the rank ordering. Chiefly in ***Mann–Whitney test***, ***Mann–Whitney U test***.

manny *noun* var. of MANNIE.

mano /ˈmano, ˈmɑːnəʊ/ *noun.* Pl. **-os** /-ɔs, -əʊz/. E20.
[ORIGIN Spanish = hand.]
ANTHROPOLOGY. A primitive hand-held stone implement, used in the Americas for grinding cereals etc.

mano a mano /ˌmɑːnəʊ ə ˈmɑːnəʊ, *foreign* ˌmano a ˈmano/ *noun, adjectival, & adverbial phr.* Also **mano-a-mano**. M20.
[ORIGIN Spanish = hand to hand.]
▸ **A** *noun phr.* A confrontation, a duel. M20.

> *Vanity Fair* It became clear that a real courtroom mano a mano had begun.

▸ **B** *adjectival & adverbial phr.* Hand to hand; one to one; face to face. M20.

> N. DEMILLE They want to settle this *mano a mano*.

manoao /ˈmanəʊˌaʊ/ *noun.* Also **mon-** /ˈmɒn-/. Pl. same, **-os**. M19.
[ORIGIN Maori.]
A New Zealand coniferous tree, *Halocarpus kirkii* (family Podocarpaceae).

Manoeline *adjective* var. of MANUELINE.

manoeuvrable /məˈnuːvrəb(ə)l/ *adjective.* Also ***maneuver-**. E20.
[ORIGIN from MANOEUVRE *verb* + -ABLE.]
Able to be manoeuvred, (esp. of an aircraft or motor vehicle) easily manoeuvred.
■ **manoeuvraˈbility** *noun* E20.

manoeuvre /məˈnuːvə/ *noun.* Also ***maneuver**. L15.
[ORIGIN French *manœuvre* (Old French *manuevre*), formed as MANOEUVRE *verb.*]
†**1** Work using the hands. *rare*. Only in L15.
2 (A) planned or regulated movement of one or more military, naval, etc., units; (a) tactical or strategic movement or change of position. Now often in *pl.*, large-scale tactical exercises involving various fighting units. M18.

> B. JOWETT The manoeuvres suited to fast-sailing vessels . . cannot be practised in a narrow space. D. FRASER In any siege manoeuvre ceases. M. FITZHERBERT He left . . to go on manoeuvres with the Japanese Army.

3 *gen.* (A) deliberate movement, esp. to deceive or elude; a move or act of control requiring some skill; an ingenious expedient or artifice. L18.

> H. MACMILLAN The Chancellor was at first inclined to regard my visit as . . an election manoeuvre. D. FRANCIS The furniture had been pushed back . . to give the fat man clear space for manoeuvre. K. M. E. MURRAY To dismount . . by falling sideways, a manoeuvre apt to take by surprise any unwary cyclist following.

Valsalva manoeuvre, ***Valsalva's manoeuvre***: see VALSALVA 1.

manoeuvre /məˈnuːvə/ *verb trans. & intrans.* Also ***maneuver**. L18.
[ORIGIN French *manœuvrer* from medieval Latin *man(u)operare* for Latin *manu operari* work with the hand, from *manus* hand.]
(Cause to) perform a manoeuvre or manoeuvres; move or steer by an act of control requiring some skill; employ or effect by stratagem or artifice; act or manipulate schemingly or adroitly. (Foll. by *into, out of*, etc.)

> C. STEAD She manoeuvred the car round a tricky corner. J. C. OATES They maneuver him into the foyer and into the elevator. J. RABAN A scallop boat manoeuvered alongside. R. K. NARAYAN Rann was manoeuvring to elope with the girl. M. FLANAGAN You get what you want. You manoeuvre everyone. J. DISKI He had manoeuvered the conversation from the general to a personal confrontation.

■ **manoeuvrer** *noun* E19. **manoeuvring** *noun* the action of the verb; an instance of this, a manoeuvre: L18.

man-of-war /manəvˈwɔː/ *noun.* Also **man o'war** /man əˈwɔː/. Pl. **men-** /mɛn-/. LME.
[ORIGIN In sense 1 app. after French *homme de guerre*; in sense 2 cf. MAN *noun* 15.]
1 A fighting man; a soldier, a warrior. Now *arch.* or *joc.* LME.
2 A vessel equipped for warfare; a warship belonging to the recognized navy of a country. Now chiefly *hist.* L15.
3 A sailor serving on a man-of-war. More usu. ***man-of-war's-man***. Now chiefly *hist.* L16.
4 More fully ***man-of-war bird***. A large seabird; *spec.* a frigate bird. M17.
5 In full ***Portuguese man-of-war***. A large pelagic siphonophore of the genus *Physalia*, with a float like a sail and numerous stinging tentacles. E18.
6 *hist.* Used *attrib.* to designate a boy's garment resembling that worn by a sailor. L19.
– COMB.: **man-of-war fish** any of various tropical marine fishes of the family Nomeidae, esp. *Nomeus gronovii*, which is often found among the tentacles of Portuguese men-of-war.

manoir /manwɑːr/ *noun.* Pl. pronounced same. M19.
[ORIGIN French: see MANOR.]
A French manor house, or a country house built in the style of one.

manoletina /ˌmanoleˈtina, ˌmanə(ʊ)ləˈtiːnə/ *noun.* Pl. **-as** /-as, -əz/. M20.
[ORIGIN Spanish, from *Manolete* professional name of the Spanish bullfighter Manuel L. R. Sánchez (1917–47) + *-ina* -INE[4].]
BULLFIGHTING. A decorative pass in which the muleta is held behind the back in the left hand. Also called ***orteguina***.

manometer /məˈnɒmɪtə/ *noun.* M18.
[ORIGIN French *manomètre*, from Greek *manos* thin, rare: see -METER.]
An instrument for measuring the pressure in a fluid; *esp.* one consisting of a U-tube containing mercury or other liquid, a difference in the pressures acting on the two ends of the liquid column being indicated by a difference in the levels reached by the liquid in the two arms of the U-tube.
■ **manoˈmetric** *adjective* of or pertaining to a manometer or manometers; made with a manometer: L19. **manoˈmetrical** *adjective* = MANOMETRIC L18. **manoˈmetrically** *adverb* by means of a manometer L19. **manometry** *noun* the use of manometers E20.

ma non troppo /mɑː ˌnɒn ˈtrɒpəʊ/ *adverbial phr.* E20.
[ORIGIN Italian.]
MUSIC. In directions (after an Italian term): but not too much.
allegro ma non troppo etc.

manool /maˈnəʊɒl/ *noun.* Also **manoöl**. M20.
[ORIGIN from MANOAO + -OL.]
CHEMISTRY. A bicyclic diterpenoid alcohol, which occurs in the oil of manoao wood and is used as a base for perfumes.

manor /ˈmanə/ *noun.* ME.
[ORIGIN Anglo-Norman *maner*, Old French *maneir*, (also mod.) *manoir* dwelling, habitation, use as noun of inf. *maneir* dwell from Latin *manere* remain.]
1 A mansion, a house; the principal house of an estate. Also, such a house with the land belonging to it; a landed possession. Now *hist.* exc. in names of or with ref. to specific (ancient) manor houses and in ***lady of the manor*** s.v. LADY *noun & adjective*, ***lord of the manor*** s.v. LORD *noun*. ME.
▸†**b** *fig.* An abode, a resting place. LME–L16.
steward of the manor: see STEWARD *noun.*
2 A unit of English territorial organization, orig. of the nature of a feudal lordship, now consisting of a lord's demesne and lands from whose holders the lord may extract certain fees etc. M16.
3 *N. AMER. HISTORY.* An estate held in fee farm, *esp.* one granted by royal charter in a British colony or by the Dutch governors of what is now New York State. M17.
4 A police district; a local unit of police administration; *transf.* one's home ground, one's own particular territory. *slang.* E20.

> B. FORBES His own Chief Constable . . deeply resented any intrusion into his manor. M. SYAL Which is just one of the rumours I've had to put up with round this manor.

– COMB.: **manor house**, (*arch.*) **manor-place** the mansion of the lord of a manor.
■ **manorship** *noun* = MANOR 2 L18.

manorial /məˈnɔːrɪəl/ *adjective.* L18.
[ORIGIN from MANOR + -IAL. Cf. MANERIAL.]
Of or pertaining to a manor or manors; incidental to a manor.
■ **manorialiˈzation** *noun* the process of making or becoming manorial E20. **manorialize** *verb trans.* make manorial L19.

†**manoscope** *noun. rare.* M18–L19.
[ORIGIN from *mano-* as in MANOMETER + -SCOPE.]
= MANOMETER.

manostat /ˈmanəstat/ *noun.* E20.
[ORIGIN formed as MANOSCOPE + -STAT.]
A device for automatically maintaining a constant pressure in an enclosed space.
■ **manoˈstatic** *adjective* M20.

man o'war *noun phr.* var. of MAN-OF-WAR.

manpower /ˈmanpaʊə/ *noun & verb.* M19.
[ORIGIN from MAN *noun* + POWER *noun.*]
▸ **A** *noun.* **1** The power or agency of people in work; (power as measured in terms of) a unit of rate of performing work, approximately equal to one-tenth of a horsepower. M19.

> G. CLARK The mere transport of these by manpower would have involved 100,000 levies.

2 The body of people available or needed for military service, work, or other purpose; workers viewed as a quantifiable resource, labour. E20.

> A. J. TOYNBEE The invaders found the entire manpower of Macedon arrayed against them. *London Daily News* The company has reduced manpower in glass by 30%. *attrib.*: A. MILLER You would think . . that with the manpower shortage they'd economize on personnel.

▸ **B** *verb trans.* **1** Move (something) by human effort. *US dial.* E20.
2 Provide or run (a business, factory, etc.) with human labour. M20.
3 Conscript for non-military service as part of the war effort. *Austral. & NZ colloq.* (*hist.*). M20.

M

manque /mɑ̃ːk/ *noun.* M19.
[ORIGIN French, from *manquer* fall short (of), lack, fail (from the numbers' failing to be higher).]
In roulette, that section of the cloth covering the numbers 1 to 18; a bet placed on this section.

manqué /ˈmɒŋkeɪ, *foreign* mɑ̃ke/ *adjective.* Fem. also **-ée**. L18.
[ORIGIN French, pa. ppl adjective of *manquer*: see MANQUE.]
1 *postpositive*. That might have been but is not, that has missed being. L18.

> *Saturday Review* 'The History of Anthony Waring' is a poem manqué. G. VIDAL He chose to be a dentist, that last resort of the rabbi manqué.

2 *pred.* Defective, spoilt, missing, lacking. L18.

mansard /ˈmansɑːd, -səd/ *noun.* Also (esp. in sense 2) **-de**. M18.
[ORIGIN French *mansarde* (*toit en mansarde*), from François *Mansard* (1598–1666), French architect.]
1 More fully ***mansard roof***. A roof in which each face has two slopes, the lower one steeper than the upper, a curb roof. M18.
2 A storey or apartment under a mansard roof. L19.
■ **mansarded** *adjective* E20.

manse /mans/ *noun.* L15.
[ORIGIN medieval Latin *mansus*, *-sa*, *-sum*, from *mans-*: see MANSION.]
†**1** The principal house of an estate. L15–L18.
2 An ecclesiastical residence; a house allocated to or occupied by a minister, esp. in the Church of Scotland. M16.
child of the manse, **daughter of the manse**, **son of the manse**, etc., the child etc. of a Protestant minister, esp. in the Church of Scotland.
3 A measure of land regarded as sufficient for the support of a family, *spec.* as an ecclesiastical endowment. *obsolete* exc. *hist.* L16.

manservant /ˈmansəːv(ə)nt/ *noun.* Pl. **menservants** /ˈmɛnsəːv(ə)nts/. LME.
[ORIGIN from MAN *noun* + SERVANT *noun.*]
A male servant.

manship /ˈmanʃɪp/ *noun.* Long *rare*. OE.
[ORIGIN from MAN *noun* + -SHIP.]
†**1** Humanity, kindness; courtesy. OE–LME.
†**2** Homage; honour. Only in ME.
3 Manly courage, manliness. Long *obsolete* exc. *dial.* ME.
4 The condition of being a man. ME.

-manship /mən'ʃɪp/ *suffix*.
[ORIGIN from MAN *noun* + -SHIP, after *churchmanship*, *craftsmanship*, etc. In mod. spec. sense orig. in GAMESMANSHIP.]
Forming nouns denoting skill in a subject or activity; *spec.* skill so deployed as to disconcert a rival or opponent, as ***brinkmanship***, ***gamesmanship***, ***oneupmanship***, etc.

mansion /'manʃ(ə)n/ *noun*. ME.
[ORIGIN Old French & mod. French from Latin *mansio(n-)* stay, station, quarters (whence French *maison* house), from *mans-* pa. ppl stem of *manere* remain, stay. In sense 6 rendering medieval Latin *mansus*, *-sa*: cf. MANSE.]
†**1** The action of remaining, living, or staying in a place. Also, continuance in a position or state. ME–E18.

H. SYDENHAM Sitting presupposes stabilitie and mansion.

2 A place in which to live or lodge, a place of abode; in *pl.* formerly *spec.*, in a larger house or delimited area. *arch.* ME.

TINDALE *John* 14:2 In my fathers housse are many mansions. S. JOHNSON Oxford, the mansion of the liberal arts.

3 A structure or building serving as a place in which to live or lodge. Now only *spec.* a manor house, a large and stately residence. ME. ▸**b** In *pl.* (treated as *sing.*). A large building divided into flats. Chiefly in proper names. L19.

W. VAN T. CLARK He'd built a white wooden mansion . . like a Southern plantation home. *Sunday Express* Plas Mawr . . is a fascinating Elizabethan mansion.

†**4** A stopping place in a journey; the distance between two stopping places; a stage. LME–M18.
5 *ASTROLOGY*. = HOUSE *noun*[1] 9b. Also, each of the twenty-eight divisions of the ecliptic, occupied by the moon on successive days. LME.
6 *hist.* A hide of land. LME.
– PHRASES: **have one's mansion**, **keep one's mansion**, **take one's mansion** have one's dwelling place, reside.
– COMB.: **mansion house** (*a*) *gen.* a dwelling house; (*b*) an official residence; formerly *esp.* that belonging to the benefice of an ecclesiastic; now *spec.* (***the Mansion House***) the official residence of the Lord Mayor of London; (*c*) the house of the lord of a manor, the chief residence of a landed proprietor; (now *US*) a large house of good appearance; †**mansion-seat** (*a*) a place of abode; (*b*) the chief residence of a landed proprietor.
■ **mansionry** *noun* (*rare*) mansions collectively E17.

M

mansionary /'manʃ(ə)n(ə)ri/ *adjective* & *noun*. *rare*. LME.
[ORIGIN medieval Latin *mansionarius*, from Latin *mansio(n-)*: see MANSION, -ARY[1].]
▸ †**A** *adjective*. Living or lodging in a place, resident. LME–E18.
▸ **B** *noun*. †**1** A resident. Only in L15.
†**2** *ECCLESIASTICAL*. An endowment for a chantry priest. Only in M17.
3 A custodian of a church. E18.

manslaughter /'manslɔːtə/ *noun* & *verb*. ME.
[ORIGIN from MAN *noun* + SLAUGHTER *noun*.]
▸ **A** *noun*. †**1** The killing of a human being by a human being; (esp. criminal) homicide, murder. ME–E17.
2 The slaughtering of human beings; destruction of human life. ME.
3 *LAW*. The crime of unlawfully killing a human being in circumstances not amounting to murder, either because the accused lacked the intention necessary to justify a murder conviction or because a specific defence (such as diminished responsibility) is available. ME.
▸ **B** *verb*. **1** *verb intrans.* Slaughter human beings. Chiefly as ***manslaughtering*** *ppl adjective* & *verbal noun*. M19.
2 *verb trans.* Kill (a person) without malice aforethought. *colloq.* E20.
■ **manslaughterer** *noun* (*a*) a person who slaughters human beings; (*b*) a person who commits manslaughter: M19. **manslaughterous** *adjective* M19.
– NOTE: In Scotland the term corresponding to *manslaughter* is 'culpable homicide'. In US law *manslaughter* is generally the lowest degree of criminal homicide, and in many states denotes the causing of death by culpable recklessness or negligence.

manso /'manso/ *noun* & *adjective*. Pl. **-os** /-ɔs/. M19.
[ORIGIN Spanish.]
(A person who or animal which is) meek, tame, or cowardly.

mansonia /man'səʊnɪə/ *noun*. E20.
[ORIGIN mod. Latin (see below), from F. B. *Manson* (fl. 1905), forester in Burma (Myanmar): see -IA[1].]
Any of several large trees of the genus *Mansonia* (family Sterculiaceae), esp. the W. African *M. altissima*; the hardwood obtained from such a tree.

mansuete /man'swiːt, 'manswiːt/ *adjective*. Now *arch.* *rare*. LME.
[ORIGIN Latin *mansuetus*, from *manus* hand + *suetus* accustomed.]
Gentle, mild; tame, not wild or fierce.

mansuetude /'manswɪtjuːd/ *noun*. *arch.* LME.
[ORIGIN Old French & mod. French *mansuétude* or Latin *mansuetudo*, formed as MANSUETE: see -TUDE.]
Gentleness, meekness, docility.

manswear /'manswɛː/ *verb*. Long *obsolete* exc. *Scot.* & *N. English*. Pa. t. **-swore** /-swɔː/; pa. pple **-sworn** /-swɔːn/.
[ORIGIN Old English *mānswerian*, from *mān* wickedness (= Old Frisian, Old Saxon *mēn*, Old High German *mein* (surviving in German *Meineid* perjury), Old Norse *mein*) + *swerian* SWEAR *verb*.]
1 *verb intrans.* Swear falsely. OE.
2 *verb trans.* **a** As ***mansworn*** *ppl adjective*. Perjured. ME. ▸**b** *refl.* Perjure oneself. LME.
†**3** *verb trans.* Swear falsely by (a god etc.); take (a god's name etc.) in vain. LME–M16.
†**4** *verb trans.* Renounce on oath, forswear. LME–M17.

mant /mant/ *noun*. *hist.* L16.
[ORIGIN Sense 1 from Spanish MANTO; sense 2 from French *mante*, ult. from late Latin *mantus*: see MANTLE *noun*.]
1 A fabric of a type originally made in Mantua. L16.
2 = MANTEAU. L17.

manta /'mantə/ *noun*. L17.
[ORIGIN Spanish = blanket.]
1 In Spain and Spanish-speaking countries: a wrap, a cloak. L17.
2 More fully ***manta ray***. A very large tropical ray of the genus *Manta* or the family Mobulidae. Also called ***devilfish***. M18.

manteau /'mantəʊ/ *noun*. M17.
[ORIGIN French: see MANTLE *noun*. Cf. MANTUA.]
1 A loose gown or robe worn by women in the 17th and 18th cents. Also, a cloak. M17.
2 A long loose coat or overshirt worn by some Muslim women. L20.
– COMB.: **manteau-maker** a maker of women's robes; a dress-maker.

manteca /man'tɛkə/ *noun*. *obsolete* exc. *US dial.* E17.
[ORIGIN Spanish, of unknown origin.]
Butter, lard, or fat.

manteel /man'tiːl/ *noun*. Now *rare* or *obsolete*. L15.
[ORIGIN App. from French *mantille* from Spanish MANTILLA. Cf. MANTLE *noun*.]
A cloak or similar garment; a cape or mantle.

mantel /'mant(ə)l/ *noun*. Also **mantle**. LME.
[ORIGIN Specialized use of MANTLE *noun*.]
†**1** A beam across the opening of a fireplace, supporting the masonry above; a manteltree. LME–E19.
2 A mantelpiece. M16. ▸**b** A mantelshelf. M18.
– COMB.: **mantel clock** a clock designed to sit on a mantelpiece; **mantelplace** *dial.* = MANTELPIECE 1.

mantelet /'mantlɪt/ *noun*. Also **mantlet**. LME.
[ORIGIN Old French, dim. of *mantel* MANTLE *noun*: see -ET[1].]
1 A kind of short loose sleeveless cape, cloak, or mantle. LME. ▸†**b** A woollen covering for a horse. LME–M16. ▸†**c** = MANTELLETTA. E17–E18.
2 *MILITARY*. A movable shelter or protective screen, *esp.* (*hist.*) one used to cover the approach of soldiers when besieging a fortified place. Cf. earlier MANTEL 1. E16.

mantelletta /mantɪ'lɛtə/ *noun*. Pl. **-ttas**, **-tte** /-ti/. M19.
[ORIGIN Italian, prob. from medieval Latin *mantelletum* from Latin *mantellum* MANTLE *noun*.]
ROMAN CATHOLIC CHURCH. A sleeveless vestment reaching to the knees, worn by cardinals, bishops, and other high-ranking ecclesiastics.

mantelpiece /'mant(ə)lpiːs/ *noun*. Also **mantle-**. M17.
[ORIGIN from MANTEL + PIECE *noun*.]
1 The ornamental structure of wood, marble, etc., above and around a fireplace; the manteltree of a fireplace with its supports. M17.
2 = MANTELSHELF 1. M18.

mantelshelf /'mant(ə)lʃɛlf/ *noun*. Also **mantle-**. Pl. **-shelves** /-ʃɛlvz/. E19.
[ORIGIN from MANTEL + SHELF *noun*[1].]
1 A projecting part of a mantelpiece serving as a shelf. E19.
2 *MOUNTAINEERING & ROCK-CLIMBING*. A projecting shelf of rock. L19.
– COMB.: **mantelshelf technique** *MOUNTAINEERING & ROCK-CLIMBING* a technique for climbing on to a ledge using the heels of the hands.

manteltree /'mant(ə)ltriː/ *noun*. Also **mantle-**. LME.
[ORIGIN from MANTEL + TREE *noun*.]
1 A beam across the opening of a fireplace, supporting the masonry above. In later use, a stone or arch serving the same purpose. LME.
2 = MANTELPIECE. M17.

mantic /'mantɪk/ *adjective*. M19.
[ORIGIN Greek *mantikos*, from *mantis* prophet, from *man-* as in MANIA: see -IC.]
Of or pertaining to divination or prophecy.
■ †**mantical** *adjective* = MANTIC L16–M17. **mantically** *adverb* E20. **manticism** /-sɪz(ə)m/ *noun* the practice of divination M19.

-mantic /'mantɪk/ *suffix*.
[ORIGIN formed as MANTIC.]
Forming adjectives corresponding to nouns in -MANCY, as ***geomantic*** etc.

manticore /'mantɪkɔː/ *noun*. Also **-cora** /-kɔːrə/, **-ger** /-gə/. ME.
[ORIGIN Latin *manticora* repr. Greek *mantikhōras*, corrupt reading in Aristotle for *martikhoras*, from an Old Persian word for 'man-eater'.]
1 A fabulous monster having the body of a lion, the head of a man, porcupine's quills, and the tail or sting of a scorpion. ME.
2 *HERALDRY*. A monster represented with the body of a beast of prey, the head of a man, sometimes with spiral or curved horns, and sometimes the feet of a dragon. L15.

mantid /'mantɪd/ *noun*. L19.
[ORIGIN from MANTIS + -ID[3].]
A mantis; an insect of the family Mantidae.

mantiger *noun* var. of MANTICORE.

mantilla /man'tɪlə/ *noun*. E18.
[ORIGIN Spanish, dim. of *manta* MANTLE *noun*.]
1 A light scarf, freq. of black lace, worn over the head and shoulders, esp. by Spanish women. E18.
2 A small cape or mantle. M19.

Mantinean /mantɪ'niːən/ *noun* & *adjective*. M16.
[ORIGIN from Greek *Mantineia*, Latin *Mantinea* (see below) + -AN.]
(A native or inhabitant) of the ancient city of Mantinea in Arcadia, Greece.

mantis /'mantɪs/ *noun*. Pl. **-ises**, same. M17.
[ORIGIN mod. Latin from Greek, lit. 'prophet': see MANTIC.]
Any of various predatory insects of the family Mantidae, usu. slender and cryptically coloured, with a mobile triangular head and large raptorial forelimbs held raised and folded like hands in prayer. Also ***praying mantis***.
– COMB.: **mantis shrimp** any of various predatory marine crustaceans of the order Stomatopoda (Hoplocarida), having a pair of large spined raptorial front legs resembling those of a mantis.

mantissa /man'tɪsə/ *noun*. M17.
[ORIGIN Latin *mantis(s)a* makeweight, perh. from Etruscan.]
†**1** An addition of comparatively small importance, esp. to a text or discourse. M–L17.
2 *MATH.* **a** The part of a logarithm after the decimal point. M19. ▸**b** The number or quantity to which an exponent is appended; *spec.* in *COMPUTING*, a number (usu. of a fixed number of digits) which is multiplied by a specified power of a base to represent any number by floating-point representation. M20.

mantle /'mant(ə)l/ *noun*. See also MANTEL. OE.
[ORIGIN Latin *mantellum* var. of *mantelum* rel. to *mantelium*, *-ele*, *-til-* towel, napkin, tablecloth, whence also late Latin *mantus*, medieval Latin *mantum* short cloak. Replaced in Middle English by forms from Old French *mantel* (mod. *manteau*) from Latin.]
1 A loose sleeveless cloak, now usu. one worn by a woman. Now freq. *fig.*, repr. responsibility, authority, etc., handed down (from the passing of Elijah's mantle to Elisha (2 *Kings* 2:13)). OE. ▸**b** More fully ***Irish mantle***. A kind of blanket or plaid worn until the 17th cent. by the rustic Irish. Now *rare* or *obsolete*. L15. ▸**c** *HERALDRY*. = MANTLING *noun* 3. Also, an unslashed robe of estate borne behind an achievement. L16. ▸**d** *transf.* With qualifying colour adjective A person, *spec.* a herald, wearing a mantle of the specified colour. E17.

R. DAHL He had taken upon himself the mantle of Health Officer. V. BROME Since Freud's death the mantle had mutually descended on Anna Freud and Ernest Jones.

d ***Bluemantle*** etc.
†**2** **a** A blanket, a cover. ME–L18. ▸**b** A measure of quantity of furs, containing from 30 to 100 skins. LME–M17.
3 *transf.* & *fig.* A thing that enfolds, enwraps, or encloses; a covering. ME.

SHAKES. *Lear* Poor Tom; that . . drinks the green mantle of the standing pool. MILTON The Moon . . unvaild her peerless light And o're the dark her Silver Mantle threw. J. CONRAD Ribs of grey rock under the dank mantle of matted leafage.

4 *ZOOLOGY*. In molluscs, cirripedes, and brachiopods, the layer of epidermal tissue which encloses the body and secretes the shell. Also, any of various similar enclosing structures, as the body wall of an ascidian. LME.
5 The plumage of the back and folded wings of a bird, esp. if distinct in colour. M19.
6 A fragile lacelike covering fixed over a gas jet to give an incandescent light when heated. Also ***gas mantle***. L19.
7 *BOTANY*. The outer layer of cells in an apical meristem. L19.
8 *ANATOMY & ZOOLOGY*. = PALLIUM 3b. L19.
9 *GEOLOGY*. The layer in the interior of the earth which extends between the crust and the core, and is physically and chemically distinct from each. Formerly *gen.*, that part of the earth outside the core. M20.
– PHRASES & COMB.: ***lady's mantle***: see LADY *noun* & *adjective*. **mantle cavity** the space enclosed between the mantle and the body of a mollusc, brachiopod, etc., containing respiratory organs. **mantle fibre** *CYTOLOGY* any spindle fibre which is attached to a chromosome. ***mantlepiece***: see MANTELPIECE. ***mantleshelf***: see MANTELSHELF. ***mantletree***: see MANTELTREE. ***WATTEAU mantle***.
■ **mantlewise** *adverb* in the manner of a cloak or mantle M16.

mantle /'mant(ə)l/ *verb*. ME.
[ORIGIN Partly from the noun, partly from Old French *manteler*.]
1 *verb trans.* Clothe or wrap in or as in a mantle; cover, conceal; obscure; enfold, embrace; encircle, surround; envelop. ME.

M. ARNOLD The mourning-stole no more Mantled her form. M. AMIS This frenzy of solitude which mantles me now. R. CARVER Clouds mantled the white hills.

2 *verb intrans.* & †*refl.* Of a perched bird of prey: spread the wings over the outstretched legs, spread the wings and tail so as to cover food. **L15.**
3 *verb intrans.* Of a liquid: be or become covered with a coating or scum; form a head. **L16.**
4 *verb intrans.* Form a mantle or covering; spread or be extended over a surface. **M17.**

SIR W. SCOTT Seldom o'er a breast so fair, Mantled a plaid with modest care.

5 *verb intrans.* & *trans.* Suffuse (the cheeks, the face) with a blush; (of a blush etc.) suffuse the cheeks; flush. **E18.**

DISRAELI Her rich face mantling with emotion. W. S. CHURCHILL The blood mantled his cheek.

mantled /ˈmant(ə)ld/ *adjective.* **LME.**
[ORIGIN from MANTLE *noun, verb*: see -ED[2], -ED[1].]
1 Wearing a mantle; covered (as) with a mantle. **LME.** **2** HERALDRY. Having the outside of mantling of a specified tincture. **L16.**

mantlepiece *noun* var. of MANTELPIECE.

mantleshelf *noun* var. of MANTELSHELF.

mantlet *noun* var. of MANTELET.

mantletree *noun* var. of MANTELTREE.

mantling /ˈmantlɪŋ/ *noun.* **E16.**
[ORIGIN from MANTLE *noun, verb* + -ING[1].]
1 †**a** The action of making a mantle. Only in **E16.** ▸**b** The action of MANTLE *verb*. **E17.**
2 Orig., a kind of cloth. Later, material for making mantles. Now *rare*. **M16.**
3 HERALDRY. An ornamental accessory of slashed drapery issuing from a helmet and sometimes resembling acanthus leaves flowing from the helmet; a lambrequin. **L16.**
4 A mantle; a protective or ornamental covering. Now *rare*. **M17.**
5 A blush or suffusion of colour produced by emotion. **M18.**

manto /ˈmantəʊ/ *noun.* Pl. **-os.** **L17.**
[ORIGIN Italian & Spanish from late Latin *mantus*, medieval Latin *mantum*: see MANTLE *noun*.]
A (Spanish etc.) cloak or mantle.

†**mantoa** *noun* var. of MANTUA.

†**Mantoan** *noun & adjective* var. of MANTUAN.

mantology /manˈtɒlədʒi/ *noun. rare.* **L18.**
[ORIGIN Irreg. from Greek *mantis* (see MANTIC) + -OLOGY.]
The art or practice of divination.

Manton /ˈmant(ə)n/ *noun.* **E19.**
[ORIGIN See below.]
hist. More fully ***Joe Manton***. A fowling piece or other firearm made by the London gunsmith Joseph Manton.

man-t'ou /ˈmantəʊ/ *noun.* Also ***mantou***. **M20.**
[ORIGIN Chinese *mántou*.]
Steamed bread, as eaten in N. China.

Mantoux /ˈmɑ̃ːtuː, ˈmantuː/ *noun.* **M20.**
[ORIGIN Charles *Mantoux* (1877–1947), French physician.]
MEDICINE. Used *attrib.* to designate a type of intradermal tuberculin test.

mantra /ˈmantrə/ *noun.* Also (*rare*) **-tram** /-trəm/. **L18.**
[ORIGIN Sanskrit, lit. 'thought', from *man* think.]
A sacred Hindu text or passage, *esp.* one from the Vedas used as a prayer or incantation; in Hinduism and Buddhism, a holy name or word, for inward meditation; *transf.* & *fig.* a repeated phrase or sentence, a formula, a refrain.

mantri /ˈmantri/ *noun.* **L18.**
[ORIGIN Sanskrit *mantrī*: see MANDARIN *noun*[1].]
1 In India etc.: a minister, a counsellor. **L18.**
2 In Indonesia (including the former Netherlands East Indies): a minor official or subordinate functionary vested with some authority. **E19.**

mantric /ˈmantrɪk/ *adjective.* **E20.**
[ORIGIN from MANTRA + -IC.]
Of, pertaining to, or of the nature of a mantra.

mantua /ˈmantjʊə/ *noun.* Also **M-**, †**-toa**. **M16.**
[ORIGIN See sense 1. In sense 2 alt. of MANTEAU after this.]
1 (**M-**.) Used *attrib.* to designate things made in or associated with the city of Mantua in northern Italy. **M16.**
2 *hist.* = MANTEAU. **L17.**
†**3** A material of a type made in Mantua. Only in **18.**
– COMB.: **mantua-maker** *hist.* a person who makes mantuas, a dressmaker; **mantua-making** *hist.* the making of mantuas, dressmaking.
■ **Mantuan** *noun & adjective* (a native or inhabitant) of Mantua **LME.**

Manu /ˈmanuː/ *noun.* **L18.**
[ORIGIN Sanskrit *Manu*: see MAN *noun*.]
In Hindu cosmology: the first man; any of the series of cosmic deities and progenitors of humankind presiding over a distinct period of time or manvantara.

manual /ˈmanjʊ(ə)l/ *adjective & noun.* **LME.**
[ORIGIN Old French & mod. French *manuel* from Latin *manualis*, from *manus* hand: see -AL[1]. Later assim. to Latin.]
► **A** *adjective.* **1** Of or pertaining to the hand or hands; done or performed with the hands, involving physical rather than mental effort; worked by hand, not by automatic equipment or with electronic etc. assistance. **LME.** ▸**b** Of a signature etc.: autograph. Chiefly in SIGN-MANUAL. **LME.**

E. B. TYLOR I expressed my ideas by manual signs. M. MEYER Ibsen hated seeing his wife doing anything manual such as knitting. *Farm Machinery* A manual over-ride to allow the driver to guide the machine into the crop.

manual alphabet the finger alphabet. **manual exercise** MILITARY exercise or drill in handling a rifle or musket.

2 LAW. Of occupation, possession: actual, in one's own hands, not merely prospective. **M16.**
3 That works with the hands; engaged in labour involving physical rather than mental effort. **M17.**

G. GREENE Do you believe . . that a manual labourer should be paid less than a man who works with his brains?

► **B** *noun.* **1** A small book for handy use; a concise treatise, an abridgement, a handbook, a textbook; a book of instructions for operating a machine, learning a subject, etc.; ECCLESIASTICAL HISTORY a book containing the forms to be observed by priests in the administration of the sacraments etc. **LME.**

B. TRAPIDO Roger had duly acquired us an antiquated sex manual. P. ROSE A great number of domestic manuals about women's place appeared in the 1830s. *Practical Motorist* The manual is very comprehensive and is in three volumes.

2 *ellipt.* Anything distinguished by manual operation, as (a vehicle with) a manual gearbox, a manual typewriter, etc. **L17.**
3 MILITARY. = ***manual exercise*** above. **M18.**
4 An organ keyboard played with the hands, as opp. to one operated by the feet. **M19.**
■ **manualism** *noun* (*rare*) the action or process of teaching by means of the manual alphabet **L19.** **manualist** *noun* †(*a*) a person who works or labours with the hands; (*b*) a user or advocate of the manual alphabet: **L16.** **manually** *adverb* **L15.**

†**manuary** *noun & adjective.* **M16.**
[ORIGIN Latin *manuarius*, from *manus* hand: see -ARY[1].]
► **A** *noun.* **1** An indulgence given for touching a sacred relic. Only in **M16.**
2 A manual worker. **L16–M17.**
► **B** *adjective.* Of or pertaining to the hand; performed by or with the hands; manual. **L16–M19.**

manubrium /məˈn(j)uːbrɪəm/ *noun.* Pl. **-ia** /-ɪə/, **-iums.** **M17.**
[ORIGIN Latin.]
†**1** A handle, a haft. *rare*. Only in **M17.**
2 ANATOMY & ZOOLOGY. A projection like a handle, esp. (*a*) on the malleus of the mammalian ear; (*b*) in some birds, on the keel of the sternum; (*c*) in rotifers, forming the lower part of the malleus; (*d*) in coelenterates, forming the tube which bears the mouth. **M19.** ▸**b** The broad upper part of the sternum of mammals, with which the clavicles and first ribs articulate. **M19.**
■ **manubrial** *adjective* **M19.**

manucaption /manjʊˈkapʃ(ə)n/ *noun. obsolete* exc. *hist.* **L16.**
[ORIGIN medieval Latin *manucaptio(n-)*, from *manucapt-* pa. ppl stem of *manucapere* lit. 'take by the hand': see -ION.]
LAW. **1** = MAINPRIZE *noun* 1. **L16.**
2 A writ directing the bringing in of a person charged with a felony. **L16.**
■ **manucaptor** *noun* = MAINPERNOR **E16.**

manucode /ˈmanjʊkəʊd/ *noun.* **M19.**
[ORIGIN French from mod. Latin *manucodiata* from Malay *manuk dewata* bird of the gods. Cf. MANUCODIATA.]
A bird of paradise; *spec.* any of several blue-black birds of the genus *Manucodia*, of New Guinea, *esp.* the trumpet bird (also found in Queensland, Australia).

†**manucodiata** *noun.* **M16–M18.**
[ORIGIN mod. Latin: see MANUCODE.]
A bird of paradise.

manuduction /manjʊˈdʌkʃ(ə)n/ *noun.* **E16.**
[ORIGIN medieval Latin *manuductio(n-)*, from *manu ducere* lead by the hand, guide: see -ION.]
1 The action or an act of leading, guiding, or introducing. **E16.**
2 A means or instrument of guidance or introduction. Now *rare*. **E17.**

†**manuductor** *noun.* **M17–M19.**
[ORIGIN from Latin *manu* by the hand + Latin DUCTOR leader.]
A guide, a director; *spec.* the conductor of a band or choir.

†**manuductory** *adjective.* **L17–M19.**
[ORIGIN formed as MANUDUCTOR: see -ORY[2].]
Leading (as) by the hand; that leads up to or towards something; introductory.

Manueline /ˈmanjʊəlʌɪn/ *adjective.* Also **Manoel-** /ˈmanəʊəl-/. **E20.**
[ORIGIN from *Manuel* I, king of Portugal + -INE[1].]
Of, pertaining to, or designating a style of Portuguese architecture developed during the reign of Manuel I (1495–1521) and characterized by ornate elaborations of Gothic and Renaissance styles.

†**manufaction** *noun.* **E17–M18.**
[ORIGIN from Latin *manu* by hand + *factio(n-)* making, FACTION *noun*[1].]
Manufacture.

†**manufactor** *noun.* **M17–E19.**
[ORIGIN from Latin *manu* by hand + *factor* maker, FACTOR *noun*.]
A manufacturer, an artificer.

manufactory /manjʊˈfakt(ə)ri/ *noun. arch.* **M16.**
[ORIGIN Alt. of MANUFACTURE *noun, verb* after FACTORY: see -ORY[1].]
1 The production of manufactured goods. **M16.**
2 A place where a product is manufactured; a factory or workshop. **M17.**
3 A product of labour, a manufactured article. **M17–E19.**

manufactory /manjʊˈfakt(ə)ri/ *adjective. arch.* **M17.**
[ORIGIN formed as MANUFACTOR: see -ORY[2].]
†**1** Of a person: engaged in manufacture. Only in **M17.**
2 Pertaining to or of the nature of manufacture; engaged in manufacture. **E18.**

manufacture /manjʊˈfaktʃə/ *noun.* **M16.**
[ORIGIN French from Italian *manifattura* with refashioning after Latin *manu factum* made by hand: see FACT, -URE.]
1 †**a** An article made by hand; a person's handiwork. **M16–E18.** ▸**b** An article or material produced by physical labour or machinery, now *spec.* one produced on a large scale. **E17.** ▸**c** *derog.* A product of mere mechanical labour; an article produced merely to supply the demand of the market. **L19.**
2 †**a** The action or process of making something by hand. Only in **E17.** ▸**b** The action or process of making articles or material by physical labour or machinery, now *spec.* on a large scale. **E17.** ▸**c** A particular branch or form of productive industry. **L17.** ▸**d** *derog.* Production involving mere mechanical labour, as contrasted with that requiring intellect or imagination. Also, deliberate fabrication of false statements etc. on a large scale. **E19.**
b of home manufacture, **of foreign manufacture**, **of English manufacture**, etc., manufactured at home, abroad, etc. **c *linen manufacture***, ***woollen manufacture***, etc.
†**3** Working with the hands; a manual occupation, handicraft. Only in **17.**
4 A manufacturing establishment or business; a factory. Long *rare*. **M17.**
■ **manufactural** *adjective* of or pertaining to manufacture **M18.**

manufacture /manjʊˈfaktʃə/ *verb trans.* **M17.**
[ORIGIN from the noun.]
1 Make or fabricate from material; produce by physical labour or machinery, now *spec.* on a large scale. **M17.**
2 Bring (material) into a form suitable for use. **L17.** ▸**b** Produce by natural agency. **M19.**

R. CROMPTON Throwing paper pellets at her (manufactured previously for the purpose). E. LANGLEY Dried tea leaves from which he manufactured reconditioned tea. C. THUBRON China . . still manufactures steam engines. **b** ANTHONY HUXLEY Unique characteristic of plants is their capacity to manufacture energy from light.

3 *derog.* Invent fictitiously, deliberately fabricate. Also, produce by mere mechanical labour rather than by intellect or imagination. **M18.**

D. MACDONALD His books seem to have been manufactured rather than composed. R. DEACON Attempts to manufacture evidence against . . Western politicians.

■ **manufactura'bility** *noun* ability to be manufactured **L20.** **manufacturable** *adjective* able to be manufactured **L18.**

manufacturer /manjʊˈfaktʃ(ə)rə/ *noun.* **L17.**
[ORIGIN from MANUFACTURE *verb* + -ER[1].]
1 An artisan or craftsperson; a worker in a factory or workshop. *arch.* **L17.**
2 An employer of workers for manufacturing; a factory owner; a manufacturing company or group. **L17.**
3 *derog.* A producer of something by mere mechanical labour. Also, a deliberate fabricator of false statements. **M18.**

manuka /ˈmɑːnʊkə, məˈnuːkə/ *noun.* **E19.**
[ORIGIN Maori.]
Any of several Australasian trees and shrubs of the genus *Leptospermum*, of the myrtle family, with a hard dark close-grained wood and an aromatic leaf used as a substitute for tea; esp. *L. scoparium*, of New Zealand and Tasmania.

manul /ˈmɑːnʊl/ *noun.* **L18.**
[ORIGIN App. from Kyrgyz.]
A small wild cat, *Felis manul*, of the mountains and steppes of central Asia. Also called ***Pallas's cat***.

manumise /ˈmanjʊmʌɪz/ *verb trans.* Now *rare*. Also **-miss** /-mɪs/, **-ize.** **E16.**
[ORIGIN Latin *manumiss-*: see MANUMISSION. Form in *-ise* after *promise* etc., in *-ize* after *-ise*, *-ize* variation.]
Chiefly *hist.* = MANUMIT.

M

manumission /manjʊˈmɪʃ(ə)n/ *noun*. LME.
[ORIGIN Old French & mod. French, or Latin *manumissio(n-)*, from *manumiss-* pa. ppl stem of *manumittere* MANUMIT.]
Chiefly *hist.* The action of manumitting, the fact of being manumitted; formal release from slavery or servitude; an act or instance of this.

manumit /manjʊˈmɪt/ *verb trans.* Infl. **-tt-**. LME.
[ORIGIN Latin *manumittere*, pre-classical Latin *manu emittere* lit. 'send out from one's hand'.]
Chiefly *hist.* Release from slavery; release from bondage or servitude; set free.

M. MITCHELL Old Angus had never manumitted a single slave. S. HEANEY Subjugated yearly under arches, Manumitted by parchments and degrees.

■ **manumitter** *noun* L18.

manumize *verb* var. of MANUMISE.

manumotive /manjʊˈməʊtɪv/ *adjective*. E19.
[ORIGIN from Latin *manu* by hand + MOTIVE *adjective*.]
Of a vehicle: propelled by a mechanism worked by hand.

manurable /məˈnjʊərəb(ə)l/ *adjective*. E17.
[ORIGIN from MANURE *verb* + -ABLE.]
†**1** LAW. Admitting of being held in corporeal possession. E17–M18.
2 Of land: that can be worked or cultivated. Long *rare*. M17.
3 Able to be manured or fertilized. E19.

†**manurage** *noun*. *rare*. L16–L18.
[ORIGIN from MANURE *verb* + -AGE.]
Occupation or cultivation of land.

manurance /məˈnjʊər(ə)ns/ *noun*. Now *rare*. LME.
[ORIGIN from MANURE *verb* + -ANCE.]
†**1** Tenure, occupation (of land or other property); control, management. LME–E18.
2 Formerly, cultivation (of land), tillage. Later, manuring. L16. ▸†**b** *fig.* Cultivation or training of the character or faculties. L16–E17.

manure /məˈnjʊə/ *noun*. M16.
[ORIGIN from the verb.]
1 Dung or compost (to be) spread over or mixed with soil to fertilize it. Also, (an) artificial fertilizer. M16.
green manure: see GREEN *adjective*. ***liquid manure***: see LIQUID *adjective & noun*. ***long manure***: see LONG *adjective*¹. ***short manure***: see SHORT *adjective*.
†**2** The action of MANURE *verb*; cultivation. M16–L17.
– COMB.: **manure heap** a heap of manure and sometimes other organic refuse kept for fertilizer.
■ **manurey, -ry** *adjective* splashed or littered with manure L19.

manure /məˈnjʊə/ *verb*. LME.
[ORIGIN Anglo-Norman *mainoverer*, Old French *mano(u)vrer* (mod. *manœuvrer*): see MANOEUVRE *verb*. Assim. to -URE.]
†**1** *verb trans.* Hold or occupy (land, property); have the tenure of; administer, manage. LME–M17. ▸†**b** *verb trans. & intrans.* Live in or *in* (a place). L16–L17.
2 *verb trans.* Orig., till, cultivate (land). Later *spec.*, enrich (land) with manure; apply manure to; supply with fertilizing material. LME. ▸†**b** Improve or develop (the body, mind, etc.) by training. M16–L18. ▸†**c** Promote the growth of, cultivate (a plant). L16–M18. ▸**d** *verb intrans.* Apply manure. M19.
†**3** *verb trans.* Work on with the hands; handle. LME–L16.
■ †**manurement** *noun* cultivation (*lit. & fig.*) M17–E18. **manurer** *noun* E16.

manurial /məˈnjʊərɪəl/ *adjective*. M19.
[ORIGIN Irreg. from MANURE *noun* + -IAL.]
Of, pertaining to, or of the nature of manure.

manus /ˈmeɪnəs/ *noun*. Pl. same /-nuːs/. E16.
[ORIGIN Latin = hand.]
†**1** ***manus Christi*** [lit. 'hand of Christ'], sugar boiled in rose water, as a drink for invalids. E16–E18.
2 The hand, or an analogous part of an animal's body. *literary* or ZOOLOGY. L16.
3 ROMAN LAW. The power or authority which certain husbands had over their wives. M19.

†**manuscribe** *verb trans. rare.* M17–E19.
[ORIGIN from Latin *manu* by hand + *scribere* write.]
Write with one's (own) hand.

manuscript /ˈmanjʊskrɪpt/ *adjective & noun*. L16.
[ORIGIN medieval Latin *manuscriptus*, from Latin *manu* by hand + *scriptus* pa. pple of *scribere* write. Cf. medieval Latin *manuscriptum* document in a person's own hand.]
▸ **A** *adjective*. Written by hand, not printed; (of paper) printed with staves for writing music by hand. L16.
▸ **B** *noun*. **1** A book, document, etc., written by hand; a book, document, etc., written before the general adoption of printing in a country; a written composition which has not been printed, an author's written or typed copy of a work for printing and publication. Abbreviation *MS*, pl. *MSS*. E17.

M. COWLEY Sheets of typewritten manuscript, with words crossed out. K. CLARK Only three or four antique manuscripts of the Latin authors are still in existence. J. BERMAN Freud usually destroyed all the . . original manuscripts after a work was published.

2 A person's (style of) handwriting. M19.
3 The state of being in written form; writing as opp. to print. L19.

H. CARPENTER Strong did not recommend that '*Outlines*' . . be published, and the book remained in manuscript.

– COMB.: **manuscript paper** paper ruled for writing music on.
■ **manuscriptal** *adjective* (*rare*) L17. **manuˈscriptural** *adjective* (*rare*) [after SCRIPTURAL] E19.

manvantara /manˈvantərə/ *noun*. M19.
[ORIGIN Sanskrit, formed as MANU + *antara* interval.]
In Hindu cosmology: any of the fourteen periods, each presided over by a special Manu or cosmic god, which make up a *kalpa*.

Manx /maŋks/ *adjective & noun*. E16.
[ORIGIN Old Norse, assumed metath. alt. of *Man-* (nom. *Mǫn*) from Old Irish *Manu* Isle of Man + *-skr* -ISH¹.]
▸ **A** *adjective*. Of or pertaining to (the inhabitants or language of) the Isle of Man in the Irish Sea. E16.
▸ **B** *noun*. **1** The Celtic language of the Isle of Man, not now learned as a first language but still in use for ceremonial purposes. M17.
2 As *pl. The* people of the Isle of Man. L17.
3 A Manx cat. L19.
– SPECIAL COLLOCATIONS & COMB.: **Manx cat** a tailless variety of the domestic cat, originating in the Isle of Man. ***Manx*** LOGHTAN. **Manxman** a (male) native of the Isle of Man. **Manx shearwater** a shearwater of Atlantic and Mediterranean waters, *Puffinus puffinus*, which is brownish black with white underparts. **Manxwoman** a female native of the Isle of Man.

many /ˈmɛni/ *adjective* (in mod. usage also classed as a *determiner*), *pronoun*, & *noun*. Compar. †**manier** (now served by MORE *adjective* etc.), †**maniest** (now served by MOST).
[ORIGIN Old English *manig*, *monig*, later *mænig*, corresp. to Old Frisian *man(i)ch*, *monich*, *menich*, Old Saxon *manag*, Middle Dutch *menech* (Dutch *menig*), Old High German *manag*, *menig* (German *manch*), Old Swedish *mangher*, Gothic *manags*, from Germanic.]
▸ **A** *adjective*. **1** A great (indefinite) number of. Preceding *noun sing.* with the indef. article *a(n)* or *another* (now *literary* or *rhet.*), *noun sing.* without article (long *obsolete* exc. *Scot.*), *noun pl.* (†and any determiners); following *noun pl.* (*poet. & arch.*). OE.

SHAKES. *Ant. & Cl.* Letters . . of many our contriving friends. DICKENS We must drink many happy returns to her. R. ELLIS Many a wistful boy, and maidens . . desire it. BROWNING In its hope that for many and many a year we may have your very self among us. A. WILSON She dearly loved . . a gentleman at her feet, and many a one . . she'd had. R. GORDON It's going to be many a long day before I get involved. M. L. KING Errands to be run, phone calls to be made, typing, so many things. C. JACKSON There weren't many Cadillacs around in those days. *comb.*: SHELLEY Like a dome of many-coloured glass. A. N. WHITEHEAD And space is many-dimensional.

2 As subj. or compl. of *be*: (indefinitely) great in number. Treated as *sing.* (only in ***many is the*** —, ***many was the*** —, etc., esp. ***many is the time*** etc.) or *pl.* Now *literary* or *rhet.* ME.

E. BOWEN Though they were still many, the lamps were fewer. *Encounter* Many were the times we went out to hunt. J. NAGENDA Many's the time I've asked myself, 'Why me?'

3 *A* great number of; (now usu.) *a good*, *great*, etc., number of. L16.
▸ **B** *pronoun & noun*. **1** *absol.* Many people or things understood contextually; many people; a great number *of*, a lot *of*. OE.

J. MORLEY Many of his ideas . . did not belong to him peculiarly. T. HARDY When . . the audience withdrew, many chose to find their way out. O. MANNING He was only one knave of many. G. GREENE Many served very gallantly in the Red Cross.

2 *The* great body of persons or things (specified or understood); *the* majority. E16.

COLERIDGE The . . foolish self-opinion of the half-instructed many.

3 *A* great number (*of*); (now usu.) *a good*, *great*, etc., number (*of*). E16.

THACKERAY Catholic gentry, of whom there were a pretty many in the country. JULIETTE HUXLEY A good many were separated at birth from their mothers.

†**4** [App. by confusion with MEINIE.] A company, a host, a flock (*of*); one's retinue or following. L16–E18.
– PHRASES: **as many** the same number of, that number of. **as many again** the same number additionally. †**as many as** all who. ***have many strings to one's bow***: see STRING *noun*. ***how many***: see HOW *adverb*. ***in so many words***: see WORD *noun*. ***many a time***, ***many a time and oft***, ***many a time and often***, ***many's the time***: see TIME *noun*. ***of many words***: see WORD *noun*. **one too many** something not wanted, something repeated to excess. **the one and the many** PHILOSOPHY unity and plurality. **too many for** more than a match for.
– COMB.: **many-body** *adjective* pertaining to or involving three or more bodies or particles, *spec.* with ref. to the problem of predicting their future positions and motions given their present states and manner of interacting; **many-headed** *adjective* having many heads; ***the many-headed***, ***the many-headed beast***, ***the many-headed monster***, the people, the populace; **many–many** *adjective* designating or pertaining to a correspondence or relation between two sets such that each member of either set is associated with or related to two or more members of the other; **many–one** *adjective* designating or pertaining to a correspondence or relation such that two or more members of one set are associated with or related to each member of a second set; **many-sided** *adjective* having many sides, aspects, bearings, capacities, or possibilities; **many-sidedness** the condition of being many-sided; **many-splendoured** *adjective* full of wonders or marvels; **many-valued** *adjective* (MATH.) having more than one value for some or all of its argument(s); that maps to more than one point, number, etc.; **many-where** *adverb* (*rare*) in many places.
■ **manyness** *noun* (*rare*) †(**a**) a great number; (**b**) plurality, numerousness: LME.

manyatta /manˈjatə/ *noun*. E20.
[ORIGIN Masai.]
Among certain African peoples, esp. the Masai: a group of huts forming a unit within a common fence.

manyfold /ˈmɛnɪfəʊld/ *adverb*. M17.
[ORIGIN from MANY + -FOLD. Cf. MANIFOLD *adverb*.]
In the proportion of many to one.

manyogana /manjəˈɡɑːnə/ *noun*. Also **-kana** /-ˈkɑːnə/. M19.
[ORIGIN Japanese *man'yōgana*, from *Man'yōshū* lit. 'collection of a myriad leaves', an 8th-cent. poetry anthology in which the system is found + KANA.]
A system of writing in use in Japan in the 8th cent. in which Chinese characters represented Japanese sounds.

manyplies /ˈmɛnɪplʌɪz/ *noun*. Chiefly *dial.* E18.
[ORIGIN from MANY + *plies* pl. of PLY *noun* (from its many folds).]
†**1** A complex or tortuous argument. *Scot.* E18–E19.
2 The omasum or third stomach of a ruminant. Also (*joc.*), a person's stomach. L18.

manzanilla /manzəˈnɪlə, -ˈniːljə; *foreign* manθaˈniʎa/ *noun*. M19.
[ORIGIN Spanish, lit. 'camomile'.]
1 A kind of pale very dry sherry; a drink or glass of this. M19.
2 A variety of olive, distinguished by small thin-skinned fruit. E20.

manzanita /manzəˈniːtə, *foreign* manθaˈnita/ *noun*. M19.
[ORIGIN Spanish, dim. of *manzana* apple.]
(The fruit of) any of various bearberries of the south-western US.

manzello /manˈzɛləʊ/ *noun*. Pl. **-os**. M20.
[ORIGIN Coined by the American saxophonist Roland Kirk (1936–77).]
A musical instrument resembling a soprano saxophone.

manzil /ˈmʌnzɪl/ *noun*. Also **men-** /ˈmɛn-/. E17.
[ORIGIN Arabic, from *nazala* descend, alight.]
In the Middle East: a stopping place; the distance between two stopping places, a stage.

MAO *abbreviation*.
Monoamine oxidase.

Mao /maʊ/ *adjective*. M20.
[ORIGIN from *Mao* Zedong: see MAOISM.]
Designating a garment or article of clothing characterized by a simplicity of style based on dress formerly worn in Communist China.

J. MITCHELL Mao boiler suit to show he was one of the righteous.

Maoism /ˈmaʊɪz(ə)m/ *noun*. M20.
[ORIGIN from *Mao* Zedong (Tse-Tung) (1893–1976), Chairman of the Central Committee of the Chinese Communist Party + -ISM.]
The Marxist-Leninist theories of Mao Zedong developed and formerly practised in China.
■ **Maoist** *noun & adjective* (**a**) *noun* a follower of Mao or his theories; (**b**) *adjective* of or pertaining to Maoism or Maoists: M20.

maomao /ˈmaʊmaʊ/ *noun*. *NZ*. PL. same, **-os**. L19.
[ORIGIN Maori.]
An edible blue marine fish, *Scorpis aequipinnis* (family Kyphosidae), of New Zealand and Australian waters. Also ***blue maomao***.

Maori /ˈmaʊri, ˈmɑː(ə)ri/ *noun & adjective*. E19.
[ORIGIN Maori.]
▸ **A** *noun*. Pl. same, **-s**.
1 A member of the Polynesian aboriginal people of New Zealand. Also, the language of this people. E19.
2 (Also **m-**.) Each of three brightly coloured wrasses, *Ophthalmolepsis lineolatus*, of the S. Australian coast, and *Cheilinus undulatus* and *C. fasciatus* of the tropical Indian and Pacific Oceans. Also ***Maori wrasse***. L19.
▸ **B** *attrib.* or as *adjective*. Of or pertaining to the Maori or their language. M19.
– SPECIAL COLLOCATIONS, PHRASES, & COMB.: KOPA MAORI. **Maori bug** *NZ* a large cockroach, *Platyzosteria novaeseelandiae*, which emits an unpleasant smell when disturbed. **Maori dog** *NZ* a dog of Polynesian origin first introduced to New Zealand by the Maori and now extinct. **Maori hen** = WEKA. **Maoriland** (*colloq.*, chiefly *Austral.*) New Zealand; **Maorilander** (*colloq.*, chiefly *Austral.*) a New Zealander; **Maori oven** = HANGI. **Maori PT** *NZ slang* (*offensive*) taking it easy and doing nothing. ***Maori wrasse***: see sense A.2 above.
– NOTE: In New Zealand the pl. form *Maori* is preferred to *Maoris*.
■ **Maoridom** *noun* the Maori world; Maori culture: M19.

Maoritanga /maʊrɪˈtaŋə/ *noun*. M19.
[ORIGIN Maori.]
The culture, traditions, and heritage of the Maori people; the fact of being a Maori.

M

maormor *noun* var. of MORMAOR.

Mao-tai /maʊˈtʌɪ/ *noun*. M20.
[ORIGIN A town in SW China.]
A strong sorghum-based liquor distilled in SW China.

map /map/ *noun*[1]. E16.
[ORIGIN medieval Latin *mappa (mundi)* lit. 'sheet (of the world)', from Latin *mappa* tablecloth, napkin + *mundi* genit. of *mundus* world.]
1 A (flat) representation of the earth's surface or a part of it, showing physical, geographical, or political features, as mountains, roads, relative rainfall, territorial divisions, etc.; a similar representation of the sky showing the relative positions of stars etc., or of the surface of a planet etc. Also, a diagrammatic representation of a route etc. E16. ▸**b** A diagram representing the spatial distribution of anything or the relative positions of its components; *spec.* (GENETICS) a diagram which represents the linear order and relative distance apart of the known genes of (part of) a chromosome (also ***linkage map***). M19.

A. FRASER The King had to be shown where Tangier was on the map. J. RABAN Finding Qatar . . on a map of Arabia requires . . perseverance. R. B. PARKER The Holiday Inn . . had a map of downtown Portland in its lobby. *Sunday Times* A small, bearded Armenian whose face is a map of worry lines. **b** W. L. BRAGG Electron density map of the phthalocyanine molecule.

2 A representation or account of a state of things (now *rare* or *obsolete*); the embodiment *of* a quality etc.; the very picture or image *of*. Now *rare*. L16.

BURKE I don't know the map of their situation.

3 A person's face. *slang*. E20.
4 MATH. = MAPPING 2. M20.
– PHRASES: CONTOUR ***map***. KARNAUGH ***map***. ***linkage map***: see sense 1b above. ***moving map***: see MOVING *adjective*. **off the map** into (or in) oblivion or an insignificant position; of no account. **on the map** in an important or prominent position; of some account or importance; freq. in ***put on the map***. ***video map***: see VIDEO *adjective & noun*.
– COMB.: **map butterfly** a small nymphalid butterfly, *Araschnia levana*, with prominent white veins on the underside of the wings; **map-fire** artillery fire in which maps are used for laying the guns; **map lichen** a lichen, *Lecidea geographica*, whose thallus has markings resembling a map; **map-maker** a person who makes maps, a cartographer; **map-making** the making of maps, cartography; **map-measurer**, **map-meter** an instrument for measuring distances on maps; **map-net** = GRATICULE 1; **map projection** a geometrical or cartographic method of representing on a flat surface (part of) the earth's surface; **map-read** *verb intrans.* consult and interpret a map (chiefly as ***map-reading*** *verbal noun*); **map reference** a set of numbers or letters specifying a location as represented on a map; **map turtle** any of several freshwater turtles of the genus *Graptemys* (family Emydidae), which have prominent markings on the head and shell; esp. *G. geographica*, of the central US and the Great Lakes.
■ **mapless** *adjective* M17. **mappy** *adjective* like a map M19.

†**map** *noun*[2] see MOP *noun*[3].

map /map/ *verb*. Infl. **-pp-**. L16.
[ORIGIN from MAP *noun*[1].]
1 *verb trans.* Make a map of; represent or delineate (as) on a map; establish the relative positions, or the spatial relations or distribution, of (an object or its components). L16. ▸**b** Associate with each element of (a set) one or more elements of another set in accordance with a mapping; associate (an element) with one or more others in this way; COMPUTING associate (an item of data) with a specified location in memory; associate (a memory location) with a data item; LINGUISTICS convert *into* by the application of a rule. Foll. by *to, into, onto*. M20.

P. CAREY Cartographers were still able to map the questionable parts of the nether regions. W. BRONK To explore / and map a surrounding country. **b** N. CHOMSKY The transformational rules map deep structures into surface structures.

2 *verb trans.* Foll. by *out*: ▸**a** Orig., record in detail. Later, plan; envisage; outline. E17. ▸**b** Represent in detail on a map. M17. ▸**c** Divide into districts, as by lines on a map. M19.

a H. CARPENTER He mapped out the imaginative territory . . he would explore in closer detail. *Daily Express* Robson maps out plan for 1990.

3 *verb intrans.* Fall into place on a map or plan; *spec.* have a specified position on a genetic map. L19.
■ **mappable** *adjective* that may be represented on or by a map E20. **mapper** *noun* a map-maker M17. **mappery** *noun* (*derog.*) map-making E17. **mappist** *noun* (*rare*) = MAPPER E17.

mapau /ˈmɑːpaʊ/ *noun*. *NZ*. Also **mapou**. M19.
[ORIGIN Maori.]
Any of several New Zealand trees; esp. *Myrsine australis* (family Myrsinaceae), an evergreen tree with reddish twigs and clusters of small white flowers (also called ***red matipo***).

mape /ˈmɑːpeɪ/ *noun*. Also **mapé**. L19.
[ORIGIN Polynesian.]
= IVI.

Mapharsen /maˈfɑːs(ə)n/ *noun*. M20.
[ORIGIN from *meta-amino para-hydroxyl* + ARSEN(IC *noun & adjective*[1].]
An organic arsenical drug formerly used to treat syphilis.

maple /ˈmeɪp(ə)l/ *noun & adjective*.
[ORIGIN Old English *mapel-* (in *mapeltrēow*, *mapulder* corresp. to Old Saxon *mapulder*, Middle Low German *mapeldorn*). Simple form recorded from ME.]
▸ **A** *noun*. **1** A Eurasian tree, *Acer campestre* (family Aceraceae), with fruit in the form of two winged samaras joined together and palmately lobed leaves (more fully ***common maple***, ***hedge maple***). Also (with specifying word), any of numerous similar trees of this or other genera. Also ***maple tree***. OE.
Japanese maple, ***mountain maple***, ***Norway maple***, ***soft maple***, etc.
2 The wood of these trees. Also ***maple wood***. LME. ▸**b** The colour of maple wood, a light brown. M19.
3 In full ***maple pea***. A variety of field pea with mottled seeds. E18.
▸ **B** *attrib.* or as *adjective*. Made of or resembling maple wood; of the colour of maple wood, light brown. M17.
– SPECIAL COLLOCATIONS & COMB.: **maple beer** an alcoholic drink made from maple sap. **maple bush** a shrubby maple, *Acer spicatum*, of mountains in N. America (also called ***mountain maple***). **maple candy** a sweet made from maple sap. **maple-honey** *US* the uncrystallized part of the sap of the sugar maple. **maple key** the fruit of a maple. **maple leaf** (*a*) the leaf of the maple, used as an emblem of Canada; (*b*) a Canadian gold coin traded as an item for collectors and investors. **maple molasses** *US* = ***maple syrup*** below. ***maple pea***: see sense A.3 above. **maple sugar** *N. Amer.* sugar obtained by evaporation from the sap of certain maples, *esp.* the sugar maple. **maple syrup** a syrup obtained by evaporating maple sap or dissolving maple sugar; ***maple syrup disease***, ***maple syrup urine disease***, a rare metabolic disorder leading to diminished intelligence and usu. fatal at a very early age, in which the urine has a characteristic smell of maple syrup owing to the presence of certain amino acids. ***maple tree***: see sense A.1 above. ***maple wood***: see sense A.2 above.

mapou *noun* var. of MAPAU.

†**mapp** *noun* see MOP *noun*[3].

mappemonde /mapˈməʊnd/ *noun*. LME.
[ORIGIN Old French & mod. French from medieval Latin *mappa mundi*: see MAP *noun*[1].]
hist. A map of the world. Formerly also, the world itself.

mapping /ˈmapɪŋ/ *noun*. E18.
[ORIGIN from MAP *verb* + -ING[1].]
1 The action of MAP *verb*. E18.
mapping pen a pen, esp. a dip pen, with a very fine nib. ***video mapping***: see VIDEO *adjective & noun*.
2 MATH. & LINGUISTICS etc. A correspondence by which each element of a given set has associated with it one or more elements of a second set; a transformation; *spec.* a continuous transformation. Cf. MAP *noun*[1] 4. E20.

maprotiline /məˈprəʊtɪliːn/ *noun*. L20.
[ORIGIN from unidentified 1st elem. + alt. of *-tyline* after AMITRIPTYLINE etc.]
PHARMACOLOGY. A tetracyclic antidepressant.

Mapuche /maˈpʊtʃi/ *noun & adjective*. Pl. of noun same, **-s**. L19.
[ORIGIN Mapuche, from *mapu* country + *che* people.]
▸ **A** *noun*. A member of a S. American Indian people of central Chile and adjacent parts of Argentina; their language. Also called ***Araucanian***. L19.
▸ **B** *adjective*. Of or pertaining to this people or their language. M20.

maquereau /makro/ *noun*. Pl. ***-eaux*** /-o/. L19.
[ORIGIN French.]
= MACKEREL *noun*[2].

maquette /maˈkɛt/ *noun*. L19.
[ORIGIN French from Italian *macchietta* speck, little spot, dim. of *macchia* spot, from *macchiare* to spot, stain, from Latin *maculare* MACULATE *verb*.]
A small preliminary sketch or wax or clay model from which a sculpture is elaborated.

maqui /mɑːˈkiː/ *noun*. E18.
[ORIGIN Spanish *maquí* from Mapuche.]
A Chilean evergreen shrub, *Aristotelia chilensis* (family Elaeocarpaceae), whose berries are sometimes used to adulterate wine.

maquiladora /makijaˈdora/ *noun*. L20.
[ORIGIN Mexican Spanish, from *maquilar* assemble.]
A factory in Mexico run by a foreign company and exporting its products to the country of that company.

maquillage /makijaʒ/ *noun*. L19.
[ORIGIN French, from *maquiller* make up one's face, from Old French *masquiller* to stain, alt. of *mascurer* darken: see -AGE.]
Make-up, cosmetics; the application of this.
■ ***maquillé(e)*** /makije/ *adjective* wearing cosmetics, made up L19.

maquis /ˈmɑːkiː/ *noun*. Pl. same. E19.
[ORIGIN French formed as MACCHIA.]
1 The dense scrub characteristic of certain Mediterranean coastal regions, esp. in Corsica. E19.
2 (Usu. **M-**.) A member of the French resistance movement during the German occupation (1940–5). M20. ▸**b** A member of any resistance group or army. M20.
■ **maquisard** /mɑːkiːˈzɑː/ *noun* a member of the Maquis M20.

mar /mɑː/ *noun*[1]. ME.
[ORIGIN from the verb.]
1 A hindrance, an obstruction; a speech impediment. *obsolete* exc. *Scot*. ME.
2 A thing which mars or impairs something, a drawback *to*. Formerly also, a fault. M16.

P. S. BUCK Almost a mar to his beauty were his two black brows, too heavy . . for his young, pale face.

Mar /mɑː/ *noun*[2]. E17.
[ORIGIN Aramaic.]
An honorific title for a saint or a member of the higher clergy, chiefly in the Nestorian and Jacobite Churches.

mar /mɑː/ *verb*. Infl. **-rr-**.
[ORIGIN Old English *merran*, (West Saxon) *mierran* = Old Frisian *meria*, Old Saxon *merrian* hinder (Dutch *marren* fasten, tie up, loiter), Old High German *marren*, *merren* hinder, Old Norse *merja* bruise, crush, Gothic *marzjan* cause to stumble (translating Greek *skandalizein*).]
1 *verb trans.* Hinder, interrupt, or stop (a person, event, etc.). *obsolete* exc. *Scot*. OE.
2 *verb trans.* Damage so as to render useless, ruin, impair the quality. Now chiefly, detract from or impair the perfection of, disfigure. OE. ▸†**b** *verb intrans.* Deteriorate, spoil. ME–E17.

R. W. HAMILTON The vessel is so marred that it cannot be repaired. W. S. MAUGHAM Not a wrinkle marred the smoothness of her skin. D. LODGE She led a busy, enjoyable life, only slightly marred by occasional twinges of anxiety. D. FRASER Brooke, complete with a streaming cold which had marred the week-end. P. LOMAS His interesting ideas are rather marred by a self-indulgent . . style.

make or mar: see MAKE *verb*.
3 †**a** *verb intrans.* Be or become bewildered or confused. OE–E16. ▸**b** *verb trans.* Confuse, bewilder; trouble; annoy. Long *obsolete* exc. *Scot*. ME.
4 *verb trans.* **a** Do bodily harm to. *arch.* ME. ▸**b** *fig.* Ruin (a person, a person's fortunes, etc.); ruin morally, corrupt. Now only (*dial.*), spoil (a child) by indulgence. ME.
– COMB.: **mar resistance**, **mar-resistant** *adjective* resistance, resistant, to loss of gloss by abrasion.

Mar. *abbreviation*.
March.

mara /ˈmɑːrə/ *noun*[1]. M19.
[ORIGIN Amer. Spanish *mará* from Mapuche.]
= ***Patagonian cavy*** s.v. PATAGONIAN *adjective*.

Mara /ˈmɑːrə/ *noun*[2]. L19.
[ORIGIN Sanskrit *Māra* slaughter, death, from *mṛ-* die.]
BUDDHISM. The personification of evil.

marabou /ˈmarəbuː/ *noun & adjective*. Also **mari-** /ˈmarɪ-/, **-bout**. E19.
[ORIGIN French from Arabic *murābiṭ* holy man (see MARABOUT *noun*[1]), the stork being regarded as holy.]
▸ **A** *noun*. **1** A tropical African stork, *Leptoptilos crumeniferus*, which has an inflatable pendent pouch on the neck and feeds on carrion. Also ***marabou stork***. E19.
2 A tuft of soft white down from the wings or tail of this stork, used for trimming hats etc.; *collect.* trimming made of this down. E19.
3 An exceptionally white kind of raw silk which can be dyed without first removing the natural gum and is used in crêpe weaving. M19.
▸ **B** *adjective*. Made of marabou. E19.

marabout /ˈmarəbuːt/ *noun*[1]. E17.
[ORIGIN French from Portuguese *marabuto* from Arabic *murābiṭ*, from *ribāṭ* frontier station, where merit could be acquired by combat against the infidel. Cf. MARAVEDI.]
1 A Muslim holy man or mystic, esp. in N. Africa. E17.
2 A shrine marking the burial place of a marabout. M19.

marabout *noun*[2] & *adjective* var. of MARABOU.

marabunta /marəˈbʌntə/ *noun*. M19.
[ORIGIN Guyanese name.]
In Guyana and the Caribbean islands, a social wasp.

†**marabuto** *noun*. E17–M19.
[ORIGIN Spanish.]
NAUTICAL. A jib sail.

maraca /məˈrakə/ *noun*. Also **-cc-**. L16.
[ORIGIN Portuguese *maracá* from Tupi *mbara'ká* from *marâ* tumult, noise + *akâ* chief, or from Guarani *mbaracá*.]
A Latin American percussion instrument made from a hollow gourd or gourd-shaped container filled with beans etc., and usu. shaken in pairs. Usu. in *pl.*

maracock /ˈmarəkɒk/ *noun*. *obsolete* exc. *hist*. E17.
[ORIGIN Perh. from Virginia Algonquian.]
(The fruit of) any of certain American passion flowers, esp. the May-pop, *Passiflora incarnata*, of the southern US.

marae /məˈrʌɪ/ *noun*. M18.
[ORIGIN Polynesian.]
Orig. (now *hist.*), a Polynesian sacrificial altar or sacred enclosure. Now, the courtyard of a Maori meeting house, esp. as a forum or centre for ceremonies and social functions.

M

marage /ˈmɑːreɪdʒ/ *verb trans.* **M20.**
[ORIGIN from MAR(TENSITE + AGE *verb*.]
METALLURGY. Strengthen (a steel alloy) by a process of slow cooling involving the transformation of austenite to martensite and subsequent age hardening.
maraging steel: suitable for or hardened by maraging, usu. containing up to 25 per cent nickel and smaller amounts of other metals.

marah /ˈmɑːrə/ *noun & adjective.* **LME.**
[ORIGIN Hebrew *mārāh* (fem. of *mar* bitter) used as a proper name in *Exodus* 15:23 and *Ruth* 1:20.]
In biblical allusions: bitter(ness).

maral /ˈmɑːr(ə)l/ *noun.* **M19.**
[ORIGIN Turkic.]
A red deer, *Cervus elaphus*, of the Caspian subspecies.

Maranao /ˈmarənaʊ/ *noun & adjective.* **M20.**
[ORIGIN Maranao *Maranáw*, from *ranaw* lake.]
▸ **A** *noun.* Pl. same.
1 A member of a Moro people inhabiting the province of Lanao del Sur and parts of central Cotabato province on the island of Mindanao in the Philippines, and some areas of northern Borneo. **M20.**
2 The Austronesian language of this people. **M20.**
▸ **B** *attrib.* or as *adjective*. Of or pertaining to the Maranao or their language. **M20.**

maranatha /marəˈnaθə/ *adverb, noun, & interjection.* Also **M-**. **LME.**
[ORIGIN Greek, from Aramaic *māran ʾeṯā* our Lord has come, or *māranā ṯā* O Lord, come.]
▸ **A** *adverb.* In translations of *1 Corinthians* 16:22.: at the coming of the Lord. **LME.**
▸ **B** *noun.* [By a misunderstanding of *1 Corinthians* 16:22.] More fully ***anathema maranatha***. A portentously intensified anathema; a terrible curse. **M17.**
▸ **C** *interjection.* In the early Church: expr. a deep longing for the coming of the Lord. **L19.**

Marangoni /maraŋˈgəʊni/ *noun.* **M20.**
[ORIGIN Carlo G. M. *Marangoni* (1840–1925), Italian physicist.]
PHYSICS. **1** ***Marangoni effect***, small-scale turbulence at a liquid interface owing to local variations in surface tension. Hence ***Marangoni instability***, instability in a liquid interface associated with such variations. **M20.**
2 ***Marangoni number***, a dimensionless number equal to the ratio of the surface tension gradient in a liquid to the product of viscous drag and the rate of heat diffusion. **M20.**

maranta /məˈrantə/ *noun.* **M18.**
[ORIGIN mod. Latin (see below) from Bartollomeo *Maranta*, 16th-cent. Italian herbalist.]
Any of various tropical American monocotyledonous plants of the genus *Maranta* (family Marantaceae), which includes the arrowroot; *esp.* the prayer plant, *M. leuconeura*, of Brazil, which has variegated leaves, and is grown as a house plant.

marantic /məˈrantɪk/ *adjective.* **L19.**
[ORIGIN Greek *marantikos*, from *marainein* waste away: see -IC.]
MEDICINE. Pertaining to or of the nature of marasmus.

marasca /məˈraskə/ *noun.* **M19.**
[ORIGIN Italian, aphet. from *amarasca*, from *amaro* bitter.]
A small black Dalmatian cherry, a variety of morello cherry grown for the distilling of maraschino. Also ***marasca cherry***.

maraschino /marəˈskiːnəʊ/ *noun.* Pl. **-os. L18.**
[ORIGIN Italian, formed as MARASCA + *-ino* -INE[1].]
A strong sweet liqueur distilled from the marasca cherry.
– COMB.: **maraschino cherry**: preserved in real or imitation maraschino and used esp. to decorate cocktails etc.

†**marasme** *noun.* **E17–E18.**
[ORIGIN French.]
= MARASMUS.

marasmic /məˈrazmɪk/ *adjective.* **L19.**
[ORIGIN from MARASMUS + -IC.]
Pertaining to or arising from marasmus; affected with marasmus.

marasmus /məˈrazməs/ *noun.* **M16.**
[ORIGIN mod. Latin from Greek *marasmos*, from *marainein* waste away.]
Severe loss of weight in a person, esp. an undernourished child; MEDICINE the condition in a child of having a weight less than 60 per cent of the normal for his or her age.

Maratha /məˈratə/ *noun & adjective.* Also **Mahratta. M18.**
[ORIGIN Marathi *Marāṭhā*, Hindi *Marhaṭṭā* from Sanskrit *Māhārāṣṭra* great kingdom. Cf. MAHARASHTRI.]
Chiefly *hist.* ▸**A** *noun.* A member of the princely and military classes of the former Hindu kingdom of Maharashtra in central India (now the modern Indian state of Maharashtra). **M18.**
▸ **B** *attrib.* or as *adjective*. Of or pertaining to the Marathas. **M18.**

Marathi /məˈrati/ *noun & adjective.* Also **Mahratti. L17.**
[ORIGIN formed as MARATHA: see -I[2].]
(Of or pertaining to) the Indo-Aryan language of the Marathas, now the official language of the Indian state of Maharashtra.

marathon /ˈmarəθ(ə)n/ *noun & adjective.* **L19.**
[ORIGIN *Marathōn* in Greece, site of an Athenian victory over an invading Persian army in 490 BC, news of the victory traditionally being said to have been announced in Athens by a messenger who ran all the way from the battlefield and fell dead on arrival.]
▸ **A** *noun.* **1** A long-distance running race, usu. of 26 miles 385 yards (42.195 km). **L19.**

> JOHN HOPKINS British runners are to be found among the leaders in almost every international Marathon.

2 Any race, competition, or activity of long distance or duration requiring endurance. **E20.**

> G. PRIESTLAND The gradual conversion of Christmas . . into a TV-watching marathon. *Packet (Camborne)* Leukaemia sufferer Louise . . will benefit from a 72 hour sponsored CB marathon.

▸ **B** *attrib.* or as *adjective*. Of, pertaining to, or designating a marathon or marathons; of long distance or duration. **E20.**

> F. WILT Regarded as one of the world's premier marathon runners. *Christian Aid News* Agriculture Ministers . . emerged from 90-hour, marathon talks in Brussels.

■ **marathoner** *noun* a person who competes in a marathon **E20.**

Marathonian /marəˈθəʊnɪən/ *adjective.* **E17.**
[ORIGIN from Latin *Marathonius*, formed as MARATHON + -IAN.]
Of or pertaining to Marathon or the battle of Marathon.

maraud /məˈrɔːd/ *noun. rare.* **E19.**
[ORIGIN French *maraude*, formed as MARAUD *verb*.]
The action of raiding or plundering.

maraud /məˈrɔːd/ *verb.* **L17.**
[ORIGIN French *marauder*, from *maraud* rogue, vagabond, scoundrel.]
1 *verb intrans.* Make a plundering raid (*on*); plunder; raid. Also, pilfer systematically. **L17.**

> P. S. BUCK Robbers who . . marauded . . . Many houses they had burned and women . . carried away. E. FIGES Perched in the bottom branch of a tree to escape marauding tigers.

2 *verb trans.* Plunder (a place). **E19.**
■ **marauder** *noun* **L17.**

maravedi /marəˈveɪdi/ *noun.* **M16.**
[ORIGIN Spanish *maravedí* from Arabic *murābiṭīn* (oblique case pl. of *murābiṭ*: see MARABOUT *noun*[1]) name of the N. African Berber rulers of Muslim Spain from the late 11th cent. to 1145.]
A small medieval Spanish coin and monetary unit. Also, a former Spanish and Portuguese gold coin.

marble /ˈmɑːb(ə)l/ *noun & adjective.* Orig. also †**marbre. ME.**
[ORIGIN Old French, dissimilated form of Old French & mod. French *marbre* from Latin *marmor* from Greek *marmaros* shining stone, orig. (block of) stone, but later assoc. with *marmairein* shine.]
▸ **A** *noun.* **1** Limestone that has been recrystallized by metamorphism and is capable of taking a polish; *esp.* one that is pure white or has a mottled surface. Also, a kind or variety of this. **ME.** ▸**b** *fig.* As a type of something hard, inflexible, or durable. **L16.**

> **b** M. E. BRADDON Clarice had made up her mind . . , and she was marble.

Connemara marble, ***forest marble***, ***landscape marble***, ***statuary marble***, etc.
2 A piece, block, or slab of marble; a marble monument. **ME.** ▸†**b** *spec.* A tomb or tombstone made of marble. **ME–M18.** ▸**c** The stone as a material used for making tombs and tombstones. *poet.* **E17.** ▸**d** ANTIQUITIES. In *pl.* A collection of sculpture made of marble. Freq. with specifying word. **M17.** ▸**e** A slab of marble on which to grind paints etc. **L17.**
d ***Oxford marbles***, ***Elgin marbles***, etc.
†**3 a** A mottled or dappled colour resembling that of variegated marble; a cloth of such a colour. **LME–E18.** ▸**b** The marbled pattern or paper used in ornamenting books. **L17–E19.**
4 A small ball orig. made of marble, now usu. of glass, clay, etc., used in a game played esp. by children (also ***playing marble***); in *pl.*, the game itself. **L17.** ▸**b** [translating French *meubles*.] In *pl.* Furniture, movables, personal effects. *slang.* **M19.** ▸**c** In *pl.* Mental faculties; brains; common sense. *slang.* **E20.**

> HARPER LEE Children were playing marbles in Tom's front yard. DENNIS POTTER Its eyeballs changed colour and fell at my feet like squashy marbles. **c** *Daily Telegraph* At 91, Mr. Schotz not only has all his marbles, he is gifted with concentration.

– PHRASES: **make one's marble good** *Austral.* & *NZ slang* make a good impression on a person, ingratiate oneself. ***pass in one's marble***: see PASS *verb*.
▸ **B** *adjective.* **1** Made of or consisting of marble. **LME.**

> G. GREENE The beer slopped over on to the marble top of the table.

2 Of a variegated or mottled colour; marbled. **LME.**
3 *fig.* Hard, cold, or rigid like marble; enduring as marble; smooth as marble. **M16.**

> SHAKES. *3 Hen. VI* Her tears will pierce into a marble heart.

– SPECIAL COLLOCATIONS & COMB.: **marble bone** (*a*) *sing.* & in *pl.* = OSTEOPETROSIS; (*b*) a bone affected by osteopetrosis. **marble cake** (orig. *US*) a cake with a mottled appearance like that of marble. **marble gall** a hard, dark brown gall formed on the common oak by the gall wasp *Andricus kollari*. **marble orchard** *US slang* a cemetery. **marble-paper** paper coloured in imitation of marble. **marble-stone** (*obsolete* exc. *dial.*) = senses A.1, 2 above. **marble-wood** any of various trees with mottled or banded wood, esp. *Diospyros marmorata* (family Ebenaceae) of the Andaman Islands, and the native olive, *Olea paniculata*, of Australia; the timber of such a tree.

marble /ˈmɑːb(ə)l/ *verb trans.* **L16.**
[ORIGIN from the noun.]
†**1** Cause to become marble, or to resemble marble in whiteness or hardness. *rare.* **L16–L19.**
2 Stain or colour (paper, the edge of a book, etc.) to look like variegated marble. **L17.**

marbled /ˈmɑːb(ə)ld/ *adjective.* **L16.**
[ORIGIN from MARBLE *noun*, *verb*: see -ED[2], -ED[1]. Cf. MARL *noun*[3].]
1 Made of marble; portrayed in marble; decorated with marble. **L16.**

> M. CHABON The marbled steps of the library.

2 (Of paper, the edge of a book, soap, etc.) coloured or stained with a variegated pattern; mottled, dappled. **E17.** ▸**b** *spec.* Of meat: having the lean streaked with thin layers of fat. **L18.**

> *Art & Craft* The children used . . marbled paper to represent the water. A. LURIE Wiping the worn marbled vinyl with a wet wadded paper towel.

marbled beauty a noctuid moth, *Cryphia domestica*, with white wings mottled with grey. **marbled green** a noctuid moth, *Cryphia muralis*, with wings of varying colours. **marbled newt** a large green newt, *Triturus marmoratus*, with black blotches, found in SW Europe. **marbled white (butterfly)** a satyrid butterfly, *Melanargia galathea*, with creamy wings with black markings.

marbleize /ˈmɑːb(ə)lʌɪz/ *verb trans.* Orig. *US*. Also **-ise. M19.**
[ORIGIN from MARBLE *noun* + -IZE.]
Stain or colour to look like variegated marble; give a variegated appearance to, esp. by an artificial process. Chiefly as ***marbleized*** *ppl adjective*.

marbler /ˈmɑːblə/ *noun.* **ME.**
[ORIGIN from MARBLE *noun*, *verb* + -ER[1].]
1 A person who quarries or carves marble. Now *rare* or *obsolete*. **ME.**
2 A person who marbles paper etc. Also, an instrument for marbling paper. **M19.**

marblet /ˈmɑːblɪt/ *noun.* **M19.**
[ORIGIN from MARBLE *noun* + -ET[1], after French *marbré* pa. pple of *marbrer* to marble.]
A S. American iguanid lizard, *Polychrus marmoratus*.

marbling /ˈmɑːblɪŋ/ *noun.* **L17.**
[ORIGIN from MARBLE *noun*, *verb* + -ING[1].]
1 The action of MARBLE *verb*. **L17.**
2 Colouring or marking resembling that of marble. **E18.** ▸**b** *spec.* In meat, the quality or state of being streaked with thin layers of fat. **E20.**

marbly /ˈmɑːbli/ *adjective.* **LME.**
[ORIGIN from MARBLE *noun* + -Y[1].]
Resembling marble; rigid or cold like marble.

†**marbre** *noun & adjective* see MARBLE *noun & adjective*.

Marburg /ˈmɑːbəːg/ *noun.* **M20.**
[ORIGIN A city in Germany.]
Used *attrib.* to designate (the virus causing) an acute, often fatal, haemorrhagic febrile disease.

marc /mɑːk/ *noun.* **E17.**
[ORIGIN French, formed as MARCH *verb*[2]. Cf. MURK *noun*[2].]
1 The refuse of processed grapes etc. **E17.**
2 A brandy made from this. Also ***marc brandy***. **M19.**

Marcan /ˈmɑːk(ə)n/ *adjective.* **E20.**
[ORIGIN from Latin *Marcus* Mark + -AN.]
CHRISTIAN CHURCH. Of, pertaining to, or characteristic of the evangelist St Mark or the Gospel attributed to him.

†**marcantant** *noun. rare* (Shakes.). Only in **E17.**
[ORIGIN Repr. Italian *mercatante*.]
A merchant.

marcasite /ˈmɑːkəsʌɪt, -ziːt/ *noun & adjective.* **LME.**
[ORIGIN medieval Latin *marcasita* from Arabic *marqašīṯā* from Syriac *marqašīṯā*.]
▸ **A** *noun.* **1** Orig., a metallic sulphide (as pyrites) or similar compound, *esp.* one which resembled the metal which it was (often erroneously) believed to contain. Now, iron pyrites, esp. as used in jewellery; MINERALOGY the orthorhombic form of iron pyrites, occurring as bronze-yellow crystals with a metallic lustre. **LME.**
2 A piece of marcasite, esp. as used in jewellery; an ornament made of marcasite. **LME.**
▸ **B** *attrib.* or as *adjective*. Made or consisting of marcasite; set or ornamented with a marcasite or marcasites. **L16.**
■ **marcaˈsitical** *adjective* pertaining to or containing marcasite **L17.**

marcassin /mɑːˈkasɪn/ *noun.* Now *rare* or *obsolete*. **E18.**
[ORIGIN French.]
HERALDRY. A young wild boar with a limp tail, as a charge.

marcato /mɑːˈkɑːtəʊ/ *adverb & adjective.* M19.
[ORIGIN Italian, pa. pple of *marcare* mark, accent, of Germanic origin.]
MUSIC. (With each note) emphasized.

marcel /mɑːˈsɛl/ *noun & verb.* L19.
[ORIGIN François *Marcel* Grateau (1852–1936), French hairdresser.]
▸ **A** *noun.* Also **M-**. In full ***marcel wave***. A deep artificial wave in the hair produced by heated curling tongs. L19.
▸ **B** *verb trans.* Infl. **-ll-**, *-l-. Wave (hair) in this way. E20.

marcella /mɑːˈsɛlə/ *noun & adjective.* L18.
[ORIGIN Repr. a pronunc. of MARSEILLES.]
(Made of) an imitation of Marseilles quilting, used for coverlets, petticoats, etc.

marcescent /mɑːˈsɛs(ə)nt/ *adjective.* E18.
[ORIGIN Latin *marcescent-* pres. ppl stem of *marcescere* inceptive of *marcere* wither, be faint: see -ESCENT.]
BOTANY. Withering but not falling off.
▪ **marcescence** *noun* marcescent condition M19.

March /mɑːtʃ/ *noun*[1]. OE.
[ORIGIN Old French *march(e)* north-eastern var. of *marz*, (also mod.) *mars* from Latin *Martius* (*mensis*) (month) of Mars.]
The third month of the year in the Gregorian calendar.

Proverb: March comes in like a lion and goes out like a lamb.

– COMB.: **March brown** *ANGLING* (an artificial fly) imitating a kind of large brown mayfly; **March court**, **March meeting** *US* a court or town meeting held in March, being the principal one of the year; **March fly** (*a*) any dark-coloured hairy fly of the family Bibionidae; (*b*) *Austral.* any bloodsucking tabanid horsefly; **March hare** a hare in the breeding season, characterized by much leaping, chasing, etc.; freq. in ***mad as a March hare***; ***March meeting***: see ***March court*** above; **March moth** a drab geometrid moth, *Alsophila aescularia*, whose larvae feed on plum and cherry trees.

march /mɑːtʃ/ *noun*[2]. ME.
[ORIGIN Old French & mod. French *marche* from Proto-Romance (cf. MARQUIS), medieval Latin *marca* from Old Frankish, from Germanic base of MARK *noun*[1]. Cf. MERCIAN.]
1 Chiefly *hist.* The border or frontier of a country; *sing.* & (now usu.) in *pl.*, a tract of land on the border of a country, a disputed tract separating one country from another. ME. ▸**b** The boundary of an estate. Chiefly *Scot.* LME. ▸**c** A boundary mark, a landmark. Long *obsolete* exc. *dial.* L15.
the Marches the parts of England along the border with Wales (and formerly Scotland).
†**2** A country, a territory. ME–L15.
3 *hist.* [German *Mark*, Italian *marca*.] Any of various (specified) German or Italian territories or principalities. Cf. MARK *noun*[1] 2. E18.
– COMB.: **march-land** (chiefly *hist.*) land comprising the marches of a country; a border district; **march-man** *hist.* an inhabitant of the marches or borders; **march stone** (chiefly *Scot.* & *N. English*) a stone marking the boundary of an estate.

march /mɑːtʃ/ *noun*[3]. M16.
[ORIGIN Old French & mod. French *marche*, from *marcher* MARCH *verb*[2], or from MARCH *verb*[2].]
†**1** An intention; the tendency or drift of thought. Only in M16.
2 The action or an act of marching; the regular forward movement together of a body of troops; the similar orderly forward movement of an exploring party, a procession, etc.; the distance covered by marching for a (specified) period. L16. ▸**b** The regular and uniform step of a body of troops etc. Freq. with specifying adjective. M17. ▸**c** A long difficult walk. L17. ▸**d** A journey of any kind, *esp.* one made by canoe or dog sledge. *Canad.* E20.

SHAKES. *1 Hen. VI* Two mightier troops . . Which join'd with him and made their march for Bordeaux. W. IRVING A march of three or four days . . brought Captain Bonneville . . to Jackson's Hole. J. G. FARRELL Relief comes nearer . . as much as twenty miles nearer with every day's march.

b ***quick march***, ***slow march***, etc.
†**3** A move of a chess piece. L16–M19.
4 A tune or composition of marked rhythm and esp. characterized by rhythmical drum beats, designed to accompany the marching of troops etc.; any composition of similar character and form. L16. ▸**b** A beating of a drum in a particular rhythm as an accompaniment to the marching of troops. E17.
5 Advance, forward movement, progress. Also, the course or direction of advance. E17.

A. WEST I was a problem for her . . in the course of her march towards some goal. J. K. GALBRAITH The enemy of the conventional is not ideas but the march of events. H. JACOBSON Harry's quick sketch of the march of history.

6 *CARDS.* In euchre, the winning of all five tricks by one side. M19.
7 A procession organized as a protest or demonstration. Also ***protest march***. E20.

J. MORTIMER Newspapers had ridiculed . . supporters of C.N.D. for not turning out on the march. *Lilith* Feminism . . isn't a part-time practice that happens only at meetings or marches.

– PHRASES & COMB.: ***dead march***: see DEAD *adjective* etc. **gain a march on**, **get a march on** get ahead of to the extent of a march; gain an advantage over. **line of march** the direction or route of marching. ***Long March***: see LONG *adjective*[1]. **march fracture** *MEDICINE* a stress fracture of the metatarsal. **march past** the marching of troops past a saluting point at a review. **steal a march on** get ahead of by stealth; gain an (unnoticed) advantage over.

march /mɑːtʃ/ *verb*[1]. ME.
[ORIGIN Old French *marchir*, formed as MARCH *noun*[2].]
1 *verb intrans. & trans.* Border (*on*); have a common frontier or boundary with or *with*. ME.

Times The frontiers of Dakota, Montana and Washington march with the Canadian dominion. M. BORWICK The Ainsty country proper which marches the Branham Moors on the western end.

†**2** *verb trans.* Fix or mark the boundaries of with landmarks. *Scot.* LME–L17.

march /mɑːtʃ/ *verb*[2]. LME.
[ORIGIN Old French & mod. French *marcher* walk, (orig. tread, trample) from Proto-Gallo-Romance, from late Latin *marcus* hammer.]
1 *verb intrans.* Walk in a military manner with a regular and measured tread; (of a body of troops) walk in step and in time with a regular and uniform movement. Also, start on a march. Also with adverbs. LME. ▸**b** Take part in a protest march. M20.

R. MACAULAY Near to where . . the Ten Thousand marched down from the mountains. P. F. BOLLER He had difficulty keeping step when his company . . marched to music. **b** *Freedomways* Civil rights workers . . face screaming mobs . . as they peacefully march to end housing discrimination. G. GREENE No one has protested, no one has marched.

2 *verb intrans.* Walk or proceed in a steady or deliberate manner. Also with adverbs, as *off*, *on*, *out*, etc. M16.

C. RAYNER She . . marched away down the corridor . . with what shreds of dignity she could. *Stamps* March along to your local dealer for further details.

3 *verb trans.* Cause to march or walk in a military manner. Now also *gen.*, cause (a person) to walk or go; force to go, conduct. Freq. with adverbs L16.

D. H. LAWRENCE The officer spoke two words, they saluted and marched off their prisoner. J. M. COETZEE They march me out of the yard.

†**4** *verb intrans.* Have a specific position in a series; rank *with*, *after*, etc. E–M17.
5 *verb intrans.* Advance, make progress; continue unrelentingly. M17.
6 *verb trans.* Traverse (a distance or area) in marching. E19.
– PHRASES: ***march in a net***: see NET *noun*[1]. **marching band** a band which plays on the march in parades etc. **marching girl** *Austral.* & *NZ* a member of a team of girls who march in formation in parades etc.

marchantia /mɑːˈkantɪə/ *noun.* M18.
[ORIGIN mod. Latin (see below), from N. *Marchant* (d. 1678), French botanist: see -IA[1].]
Any of various liverworts of the genus *Marchantia*; esp. *M. polymorpha*, one of the most representative liverworts and the one to which the name liverwort was first applied.

Märchen /ˈmɛːrçən/ *noun.* Pl. same. Also **m-**. L19.
[ORIGIN German = fairy tale from Middle High German *merechyn* short verse narrative, from Middle High German *mære* (Old High German *mārī*) news, famous, ult. from Germanic, + *-chin*, -KIN dim. suffix.]
A folk tale or fairy tale.

marcher /ˈmɑːtʃə/ *noun*[1]. ME.
[ORIGIN from MARCH *noun*[2] + -ER[1].]
hist. †**1** A person with territory adjoining that of another. Only in ME.
2 An inhabitant or a lord of a march or border district. LME.
†**3** A border territory or march. LME–L15.
– PHRASES: **Lord Marcher**, pl. **-s -s**, a lord who enjoyed royal liberties and had exclusive jurisdiction over territory in the marches obtained by border warfare.
▪ **marchership** *noun* the position or office of a Lord Marcher M19.

marcher /ˈmɑːtʃə/ *noun*[2]. L16.
[ORIGIN from MARCH *verb*[2] + -ER[1].]
1 A person who marches or walks. L16.
2 *spec.* A person who takes part in a protest or demonstration march. E20.

marchesa /marˈkeːza/ *noun.* Pl. **-se** /-ze/. L18.
[ORIGIN Italian, fem. of MARCHESE *noun*[1].]
In Italy, a marchioness.

marchese /marˈkeːze/ *noun*[1]. Pl. **-si** /-zi/. E16.
[ORIGIN Italian.]
In Italy, a marquis.

marchese *noun*[2] pl. of MARCHESA.

marchesi *noun* pl. of MARCHESE *noun*[1].

marching /ˈmɑːtʃɪŋ/ *noun.* M16.
[ORIGIN from MARCH *verb*[2] + -ING[1].]
1 The action of MARCH *verb*[2]; an instance of this. M16. ▸**b** ***marching past***, the action of performing a march past. M19.
†**2** The move of a chess piece. *rare.* Only in M16.
– COMB.: **marching order** (*a*) equipment or a formation for marching; (*b*) in *pl.*, the direction for troops to depart for war etc.; *fig.* a dismissal (freq. in ***get one's marching orders***).

marchioness /ˈmɑːʃ(ə)nɪs/ *noun.* L16.
[ORIGIN medieval Latin *marchionissa*, from *marchio(n-)* captain of the marches, from *marca* MARK *noun*[1], MARCH *noun*[2]: see -ESS[1].]
1 The wife or widow of a marquess; a woman holding the rank of marquess in her own right. L16. ▸**b** A maid of all work. *joc.* L19.
2 A variety of pear. E18.

marchpane *noun & adjective* see MARZIPAN.

marcid /ˈmɑːsɪd/ *adjective.* Now *rare.* LME.
[ORIGIN Latin *marcidus* withered, from *marcere* wither: see -ID[1].]
Withered, wasted; weak, feeble.

Marcionist /ˈmɑːʃ(ə)nɪst, -ʃɪən-/ *noun.* LME.
[ORIGIN Late Latin *Marcionista*, late Greek *Markiōnistēs*, from *Marcion*: see MARCIONITE, -IST.]
ECCLESIASTICAL HISTORY. = MARCIONITE.

Marcionite /ˈmɑːʃ(ə)nʌɪt, -ʃɪən-/ *noun & adjective.* M16.
[ORIGIN ecclesiastical Latin *Marcionita*, from *Marcion*: see below, -ITE[1]. Cf. MARCIONIST.]
ECCLESIASTICAL HISTORY. ▸**A** *noun.* An adherent of the rigorously ascetic sect founded in Rome in the 2nd cent. AD by Marcion of Sinope, who rejected the authority of the Old Testament. M16.
▸ **B** *attrib.* or as *adjective.* Of or pertaining to the Marcionites. M18.
▪ **Marcionitism** *noun* the doctrines of the Marcionites L19.

Marcomanni /ˈmɑːkə(ʊ)maniː/ *noun pl.* L16.
[ORIGIN Latin, of Germanic origin: cf. MARK *noun*[1], MARCH *noun*[2], MAN *noun*.]
An ancient Germanic people of the Suevian group who lived in central Europe north of the Danube until the 4th cent. AD.

Marconi /mɑːˈkəʊni/ *noun.* L19.
[ORIGIN Guglielmo, Marchese *Marconi* (1874–1937), Italian physicist.]
1 *hist.* Used *attrib.* to designate (things connected with) the system of radio-telegraphy invented by Marconi. L19.
2 *NAUTICAL.* Used *attrib.* to designate (a part of) a type of rig, so called after its resemblance to a radio mast. E20.
▪ **marconigram** *noun* (*hist.*) a radio-telegram E20. **marconigraph** *noun & verb* (*hist.*) (*a*) *noun* an apparatus used for transmitting radio-telegrams; (*b*) *verb trans. & intrans.* send (a message) by radio-telegraphy: E20. **marcoˈnigraphy** *noun* (*hist.*) radio-telegraphy E20. **Marconist** *noun* (*hist.*) an operator of a Marconi system E20.

marcor /ˈmɑːkɔː/ *noun.* Long *rare* or *obsolete.* M17.
[ORIGIN Latin, from *marcere* waste away.]
Orig., decay. Later *spec.*, emaciation.

M

marcot /ˈmɑːkɒt/ *noun & verb.* E20.
[ORIGIN Back-form. from MARCOTTAGE.]
HORTICULTURE. ▸**A** *noun.* A plant propagated by marcottage. E20.
▸ **B** *verb intrans.* Infl. **-tt-**. Propagate by marcottage. E20.

marcottage /mɑːkɒˈtɑːʒ, mɑːˈkɒtɪdʒ/ *noun.* E20.
[ORIGIN French = layering.]
HORTICULTURE. A method of propagating plants in which an incision is made below a joint or node and covered with a thick layer of moss etc., into which new roots grow.

Marcusian /mɑːˈk(j)uːzɪən/ *adjective & noun.* M20.
[ORIGIN from *Marcuse* (see below) + -IAN.]
▸ **A** *adjective.* Of or pertaining to Herbert Marcuse (1898–1979), US philosopher and writer, or his political views. M20.
▸ **B** *noun.* A supporter of the political views of Marcuse. M20.

mard /mɑːd/ *adjective. dial.* E20.
[ORIGIN Repr. pronunc. of *marred* pa. pple of MAR *verb*. Cf. MARD *verb*.]
Of a child: spoilt; peevish.

mard /mɑːd/ *verb trans. dial.* L19.
[ORIGIN Cf. MARD *adjective*, MAR *verb*.]
Spoil (a child) by indulgence.

Mardi gras /mɑːdɪ ˈgrɑː/ *noun phr.* L17.
[ORIGIN French, lit. 'fat Tuesday'.]
Shrove Tuesday, celebrated in some traditionally Roman Catholic communities with a carnival; the last day of a carnival etc., esp. in France; *Austral.* a carnival or fair at any time.

mardy /ˈmɑːdi/ *adjective. dial.* E20.
[ORIGIN from MARD *adjective* + -Y[1].]
(Esp. of a child) spoilt, sulky, whining.

mare /mɛː/ *noun*[1].
[ORIGIN Old English *mearh* = Old Frisian, Middle Low German, Middle Dutch *mer(r)ie*, Old High German *mar(i)ha*, Dutch *merrie*, German *Mähre*, Old Norse *merr*, from Germanic, from base repr. also by Gaelic *marc*, Welsh *march* stallion, Cornish *margh*.]
1 In early use, the horse. Later, the female of a horse, ass, zebra, or other equid; *esp.* the female of a horse. OE.
2 A woman. Usu. *derog.* ME.
†**3** A see-saw. Also = HORSE *noun* 5(a). Also ***wild mare***. L16–E19.
4 A kind of trestle used by masons. M17.
– PHRASES: ***flying mare***: see FLYING *ppl adjective*. ***grey mare***: see GREY *adjective*. **mare's nest** a (wonderful) discovery which proves or will prove to be illusory. **mare's tail** (*a*) an aquatic plant, *Hippuris vulgaris* (family Hippuridaceae), having an erect stem with leaves

in whorls and small greenish axillary flowers; (*b*) in *pl.*, long straight streaks of cirrus cloud, often believed to herald stormy weather. ***Shanks' mare***, ***Shanks's mare***: see SHANK *noun*. †**two-legged mare**, †**three-legged mare** the gallows. ***wild mare***: see sense 3 above.

mare /mɛː/ *noun*[2]. Long *obsolete* exc. *dial.* & in NIGHTMARE *noun & adjective, verb*
[ORIGIN Old English *mære*, corresp. to Middle Low German *mar*, Middle Dutch *mare*, *maer*, Old High German *mara* (German *Mahr*), Old Norse *mara*, from Germanic.]
1 = NIGHTMARE *noun* 1, 2. OE. ▸†**b** The blues, melancholy. E16–E17.
†**2** A spectre, a hag. LME–E16.

mare /ˈmɑːreɪ, -ri/ *noun*[3]. Pl. **-ria** /-rɪə/, (occas.) **-res** /-reɪz, -riːz/. M19.
[ORIGIN Latin = sea.]
ASTRONOMY. Any of the extensive areas of flat terrain ('seas') on the surface of the moon, which appear dark and were once thought to be seas; a similar area on Mars etc.
– NOTE: From 17 in mod. Latin proper names, as *Mare Imbrium*, *Mare Tranquillitatis*, etc.

marechal /mareɪˈʃal/ *noun*. *hist.* Also **-ale**; (earlier) **marshal**. L17.
[ORIGIN App. formed as MARÉCHAL.]
A scented powder made from various flowers, a perfume; a hair powder scented with this.

maréchal /mareʃal/ *noun*. Pl. ***-chaux*** /-ʃo/. M19.
[ORIGIN French: see MARSHAL *noun*[1].]
A French marshal or field marshal.

Maréchal Niel /ˌmareɪʃ(ə)l ˈniːl/ *noun phr.* M19.
[ORIGIN French, formed as MARÉCHAL + Adolphe *Niel* (1802–69), Marshal of France.]
A climbing noisette rose of a variety bearing large well-formed fragrant yellow flowers.

maréchaussée /mareʃose/ *noun*. Also ***M-***. Pl. pronounced same. L18.
[ORIGIN French from Old French *mareschaucie*: see MARSHALCY.]
A French military force under the command of a marshal (*hist.*). Also (*joc. & colloq.*), the French police, the gendarmerie.

maréchaux *noun* pl. of MARÉCHAL.

mare clausum /mɑːreɪ ˈklaʊsʊm, mɛːrɪ ˈklɔːzəm/ *noun phr.* Pl. **maria clausa** /mɑːrɪə ˈklaʊsə, mɛːrɪə ˈklɔːzə/. M17.
[ORIGIN Latin = closed sea, title of a work by John Selden (1584–1654), English jurist, written in answer to Grotius (see MARE LIBERUM).]
A sea under the jurisdiction of a particular country. Cf. MARE LIBERUM.

Maree *noun & adjective* var. of MARIA.

Marek's disease /ˈmarɛks dɪˌziːz/ *noun phr.* M20.
[ORIGIN Josef *Marek* (d. 1952), Hungarian veterinary surgeon.]
VETERINARY MEDICINE. An infectious disease of poultry caused by a herpesvirus, which attacks nerves, causing paralysis, or initiates widespread tumour formation.

mare liberum /mɑːreɪ ˈliːbərʊm, mɛːrɪ ˈlʌɪbərəm/ *noun phr.* Pl. **maria libera** /mɑːrɪə ˈliːbərə, mɛːrɪə ˈlʌɪbərə/. M17.
[ORIGIN Latin = free sea, title of a treatise by Hugo Grotius (1583–1645), Dutch jurist.]
A sea open to all nations. Cf. MARE CLAUSUM.

maremma /məˈrɛmə/ *noun*. Pl. **-me** /-mi/. E19.
[ORIGIN Italian from Latin *maritima* fem. of *maritimus* MARITIME.]
In Italy: low marshy land near the seashore; an area of this.
– COMB.: **maremma sheepdog** an Italian breed of sheepdog; a dog of this breed.

Marengo /məˈrɛŋgəʊ/ *noun*. M19.
[ORIGIN A village in northern Italy, scene of Napoleon's victory over the Austrians in 1800, after which the dish is said to have been served to him.]
COOKERY. ***chicken Marengo***, ***chicken à la Marengo***, chicken sautéed in oil, served with a tomato sauce, and traditionally garnished with eggs and crayfish.

mareogram /ˈmarɪə(ʊ)gram/ *noun*. E20.
[ORIGIN from Latin *mare* sea + -O- + -GRAM.]
A graphical record of variations in sea level.
■ **mareograph** *noun* = MARIGRAPH L19. **mareoˈgraphic** *adjective* pertaining to or concerned with the (automatic) recording of variations in sea level L19.

Mareva /məˈreɪvə, məˈriːvə/ *noun*. L20.
[ORIGIN *Mareva*, name of a shipping company which was the first plaintiff to be granted such an injunction (1975).]
ENGLISH LAW (now *hist.*). In full ***Mareva injunction***. A court order freezing a debtor's assets to prevent them being taken abroad.

Marfan's syndrome /ˈmɑːfã(ŋ)z ˌsɪndrəʊm/ *noun phr.* Also **Marfan syndrome**. M20.
[ORIGIN A. B. J. *Marfan* (1858–1942), French paediatrician.]
MEDICINE. A hereditary disorder of connective tissue resulting in abnormally long and thin digits and frequently in optical and cardiovascular defects.

marg *noun* var. of MARGE *noun*[2].

Margaret /ˈmɑːg(ə)rɪt/ *noun*. LME.
[ORIGIN Female forename.]
1 A daisy. Cf. MARGUERITE. *obsolete* exc. *dial.* LME.
†**2** A variety of apple. L16–M19.
3 A magpie. Cf. MADGE 2, MAG *noun*[1] 2. *dial.* M19.

margaric /mɑːˈgarɪk/ *adjective*. E19.
[ORIGIN French *margarique*, from Greek *margaron* pearl, in ref. to the pearly lustre of the crystals: see -IC.]
CHEMISTRY. ***margaric acid***: orig., a fatty acid obtained from animal fat, now known to be a mixture of palmitic and stearic acids; now, a crystalline fatty acid, $C_{17}H_{35}COOH$; also called ***heptadecanoic acid***.
■ ˈ**margarate** *noun* a salt or ester of margaric acid E19.

†**margarin** *noun*. E–L19.
[ORIGIN from MARGARIC + -IN[1].]
CHEMISTRY. A glyceryl ester of margaric acid.

margarine /mɑːdʒəˈriːn, ˈmɑːgəriːn/ *noun & verb*. L19.
[ORIGIN French, misapplication of *margarine* = MARGARIN.]
▸ **A** *noun*. A substance made by emulsifying vegetable oils or animal fats with water, milk, etc., and used as a substitute for butter. L19.
▸ **B** *verb trans.* Spread (esp. bread) with margarine. E20.

margarita /mɑːgəˈriːtə/ *noun*. Also **M-**. E20.
[ORIGIN Spanish equiv. of female forename Margaret.]
1 A kind of Spanish wine. Now *rare*. E20.
2 A cocktail made with tequila and citrus fruit juice. M20.

margaritaceous /mɑːg(ə)rɪˈteɪʃəs/ *adjective*. E19.
[ORIGIN from Latin *margarita* (see MARGARITE) + -ACEOUS.]
ZOOLOGY. Pearly.

margarite /ˈmɑːgərʌɪt/ *noun*. ME.
[ORIGIN In branch I from Old French (mod. *marguerite*) from Latin *margarita* from Greek *margaritēs* from *margaron* pearl, *margaros* pearl-oyster, in branch II from Greek *margaron* pearl: see -ITE[1].]
▸ **I 1** A pearl. Long *arch.* ME.
▸ **II 2** MINERALOGY. A calcium aluminosilicate of the mica group, usu. occurring as scales having a pearly lustre. E19.
3 PETROGRAPHY. A line of globulites resembling a string of pearls. L19.

margaritiferous /mɑːg(ə)rɪˈtɪf(ə)rəs/ *adjective*. M17.
[ORIGIN from Latin *margaritifer*, from *margarita*: see MARGARITE, -I-, -FEROUS.]
Producing pearls.

margate /ˈmɑːgɪt/ *noun*. M18.
[ORIGIN Perh. from *Margate*, a coastal town in Kent.]
In full ***margate fish***. A grunt, *Haemulon album*, largely grey in colour, found in the western Atlantic, important as a food fish.

margay /ˈmɑːgeɪ/ *noun*. L18.
[ORIGIN French, from Portuguese *maracajá* from Tupi *mbaraka'ya* cat.]
A Central and S. American felid, *Felis wiedii*.

marge /mɑːdʒ/ *noun*[1]. Now *poet.* M16.
[ORIGIN Old French & mod. French, formed as MARGIN *noun*.]
A margin; *esp.* the edge of a body of water.

marge /mɑːdʒ/ *noun*[2]. *colloq.* Also **marg**. E20.
[ORIGIN Abbreviation.]
= MARGARINE *noun*.

†**margeline** *noun*. L16–L18.
[ORIGIN French *morgeline*.]
Scarlet pimpernel, *Anagallis arvensis*.

margent /ˈmɑːdʒ(ə)nt/ *noun*. Now *arch. & poet.* L15.
[ORIGIN Alt. of MARGIN *noun* as in *ancient*, *pageant*, etc.]
= MARGIN *noun* 1, 2.

margin /ˈmɑːdʒɪn/ *noun*. LME.
[ORIGIN Latin *margin-*, *margo* rel. to MARK *noun*[1]. Cf. MARGENT.]
1 That part of a surface which lies immediately within its boundary, esp. when in some way distinguished from the rest of the surface; *esp.* the space immediately adjacent to a river or piece of water; an edge, a border, a brink. LME. ▸**b** BOTANY & ZOOLOGY. A contour or boundary line of a body, or a distinct border differing in texture etc. from the main body. M18.

> SOUTHEY Between the mountain-base And the green margin of the waters. R. C. HUTCHINSON Here the road was rough, its margins indistinct. *fig.*: P. FITZGERALD The margin between alarm and fascination was soon crossed. **b** D. MORRIS A sharp margin between the lips and the surrounding face.

2 The space on a page between the extreme edge and the main body of written or printed matter, sometimes containing notes, references, illuminations, etc.; *esp.* the border at either side of the page as distinguished from the head and foot. Also, an annotation made in such a border; a ruled line marking off such a border. LME.

> J. IRVING Both sides of the page . . were . . filled. Dr Larch was not a man for leaving margins.

3 CARPENTRY. The flat part of the stiles and rails of framed work. E19.
4 a A condition near the limit below or beyond which something ceases to be possible or desirable. M19. ▸**b** An amount of space, time, money, material, etc., by which something exceeds or falls short of what is required; *spec.* = ***profit margin*** s.v. PROFIT *noun*. M19. ▸**c** STOCK EXCHANGE. A sum deposited by a speculative seller or buyer with a broker to cover the risk of loss on a transaction on account. M19. ▸**d** An addition to a person's wage or salary for extra skill or responsibility. *Austral. & NZ.* M20.

> **a** J. BUCHAN The working classes . . being nearer the margin of subsistence . . are . . likely to be content with what meets their immediate needs. **b** A. LURIE He realizes by what a narrow margin he has been saved. P. AUSTER All investigations of this sort must make allowances for a certain margin of error.

– PHRASES: **margin of safety** an allowance made for safety; *spec.* a number equal to the factor of safety minus one.
– COMB.: **margin call** a demand by a broker that an investor deposit further cash or securities to guarantee the margin on an investment; **margin release** a mechanism on a typewriter which allows typing in the margin previously set; the key operating this.
■ **marginless** *adjective* M19.

margin /ˈmɑːdʒɪn/ *verb*. L16.
[ORIGIN from the noun.]
†**1** *verb trans.* Provide with marginal notes; annotate in the margin. Also, specify in the margin of a page. L16–L19.
2 *verb trans.* Provide with a margin, edge, or border. Usu. in *pass.* E18.
3 STOCK EXCHANGE. **a** *verb trans.* Deposit a margin on (an account etc.). L19. ▸**b** *verb intrans.* Foll. by *up*: provide additional margin when what has been paid is insufficient. *US.* L19.

marginal /ˈmɑːdʒɪn(ə)l/ *adjective, noun, & verb*. L16.
[ORIGIN medieval Latin *marginalis*, formed as MARGIN *noun*: see -AL[1].]
▸ **A** *adjective*. **1** Written or printed in the margin of a page. L16.

> J. HUTCHINSON The earliest books left spaces for . . marginal decorations.

2 Pertaining to an edge, border, or boundary; situated at or affecting the extreme edge of an area, body, etc.; not central. M17.

> W. BLACK A marginal growth of willow and flag. C. LLOYD If its leaves start marginal browning . . I'm in trouble.

3 a That is on or close to the margin below or beyond which something ceases to be possible or desirable; *esp.* of or pertaining to goods produced and marketed at a small margin of profit. L19. ▸**b** Of land, ore, etc.: barely worth developing. Of a farmer etc.: working such land. E20. ▸**c** SOCIOLOGY. Of an individual or group: partly belonging to two differing societies or cultures but not fully integrated into either. E20. ▸**d** Of minor importance, small, having little effect. (Foll. by *to*.) E20. ▸**e** Of a constituency etc.: held by a very small majority, in which an election is likely to be very closely contested. M20.

> **b** *Which?* Large areas of marginal land . . have been ploughed up. **d** P. ZWEIG His reputation was at best that of a marginal poet. K. ISHIGURO Our contribution was always marginal. No-one cares . . what the likes of you and me once did. **e** *Times* Redistribution can make a safe seat marginal.

a marginal benefit the additional benefit arising from a unit increase in a particular activity. **marginal cost** the cost added by making one extra item of a product.
4 STOCK EXCHANGE. Of or pertaining to margins; of the nature of a margin. L19.
▸ **B** *noun*. **1** A marginal note, reference, or decoration. Now *rare*. E17.
2 ORNITHOLOGY. A feather on the edge of a bird's wing. L19.
3 A marginal constituency or seat. M20.
4 BOTANY. A plant that requires constantly wet soil, and typically grows in shallow water at the edge of a pond etc. L20.
▸ †**C** *verb trans.* Enter in the margin of a book; add marginal notes to. E17–L18.
■ **marginalism** *noun* economic analysis which gives prominence to marginal factors in the economy E20. **marginalist** *noun & adjective* (*a*) *noun* an adherent or practitioner of marginalism; (*b*) *adjective* of or pertaining to marginalists or marginalism: E20. **margiˈnality** *noun* E20. **marginally** *adverb* (*a*) in the margin of a page; as a marginal note; (*b*) at, in, or towards the margin or edge; (*c*) by a small margin, slightly: E17.

marginalia /mɑːdʒɪˈneɪlɪə/ *noun pl.* M19.
[ORIGIN medieval Latin, neut. pl. of *marginalis*: see MARGINAL, -IA[2].]
Marginal or incidental notes.

marginalize /ˈmɑːdʒɪn(ə)lʌɪz/ *verb*. Also **-ise**. M19.
[ORIGIN from MARGINAL + -IZE.]
1 *verb trans. & intrans.* Make marginal notes (on). *rare*. M19.
2 *verb trans.* Make marginal; remove from the centre; *esp.* move to the margin of a sphere of activity, make economically marginal, impoverish. L20. ▸**b** Treat as marginal; depreciate, undervalue. L20.
■ **marginaliˈzation** *noun* M20.

marginate /ˈmɑːdʒɪnət/ *adjective*. L18.
[ORIGIN Latin *marginatus*, from *marginat-* (see MARGINATE *verb*) + -ATE[2].]
Chiefly BOTANY & ZOOLOGY. Having a distinct margin.

marginate /ˈmɑːdʒɪneɪt/ *verb trans.* E17.
[ORIGIN Sense 1 from Latin *marginat-* pa. ppl stem of *marginare*, formed as MARGIN *noun*. Senses 2, 3 directly from MARGIN *noun*: see -ATE[3].]

M

1 Chiefly *BOTANY & ZOOLOGY*. Provide with a margin or border. Chiefly as ***marginated*** *ppl adjective*. **E17.**
2 Annotate with marginal notes. *rare*. **E17.**
3 = MARGINALIZE *verb* 2. **M20.**
■ **margiˈnation** *noun* (***a***) a marginated appearance or marking; (***b***) *rare* annotation with marginal notes: **M19.**

margined /ˈmɑːdʒɪnd/ *adjective*. **L18.**
[**ORIGIN** from MARGIN *noun, verb*: see -ED[2], -ED[1].]
Chiefly *BOTANY & ZOOLOGY*. Having a margin, esp. of a specified kind; marginate.

margo /ˈmɑːɡəʊ/ *noun*. Pl. **-os**. **M20.**
[**ORIGIN** Latin = MARGIN *noun*.]
BOTANY. The network of cellulose strands surrounding the torus of the pit membrane in a bordered pit of a gymnosperm.

margosa /mɑːˈɡəʊsə/ *noun*. **E19.**
[**ORIGIN** Portuguese *amargosa* fem. of *amargoso* bitter.]
= NEEM.

margrave /ˈmɑːɡreɪv/ *noun*. Also (esp. in titles) **M-**. **M16.**
[**ORIGIN** Middle Dutch *markgrave* = Old High German *marcgrāvo* (German *Markgraf*), from *marca* MARK *noun*[1] + *grāve* GRAVE *noun*[2].]
hist. Orig., a military governor of a German border province. Later, a hereditary prince in any of certain states of the Holy Roman Empire.
■ **margravate** *noun* = MARGRAVIATE **L18.** **marˈgravial** *adjective* of or pertaining to a margrave **M18.** **marˈgraviate** *noun* the territory ruled by a margrave **E18.**

margravine /ˈmɑːɡrəviːn/ *noun*. Also (esp. in titles) **M-**. **L17.**
[**ORIGIN** Dutch *markgravin* fem. of *markgraaf* MARGRAVE.]
hist. The wife of a margrave; the female ruler of a margraviate.

marguerite /mɑːɡəˈriːt/ *noun*. **E17.**
[**ORIGIN** French equiv. of female forename *Margaret*.]
Orig. (*rare*), the common daisy. Now, (a flower or flowering stem of) any of various (cultivated) plants with flowers like those of the daisy; *esp*. (***a***) the ox-eye daisy, *Leucanthemum vulgare*; (***b***) the Paris daisy, *Chrysanthemum frutescens*.
blue marguerite a blue-flowered plant of the composite family, *Felicia amelloides*, native to southern Africa.

Marheshvan /mɑːˈhɛʃvən/ *noun*. Also **-ches-** /-ˈxɛs-/, **-chesh-** /-ˈxɛʃ-/. **M17.**
[**ORIGIN** Hebrew: see HESVAN.]
hist. = HESVAN.

Mari /ˈmɑːri/ *noun*. Pl. same, **-s**. **E20.**
[**ORIGIN** Cheremiss (Russian *mariets*, pl. *-itsy*).]
= CHEREMISS.

Maria /ˈmarɪə/ *noun*[1] *& adjective*. Also **Maree** /ˈmari/. **E19.**
[**ORIGIN** Gond *maṛia*.]
▸ **A** *noun*. Pl. **-s**, same. A member of a jungle-dwelling Dravidian people of central India; the Dravidian language of this people. **E19.**
▸ **B** *attrib*. or as *adjective*. Of or pertaining to the Marias or their language. **L19.**

maria *noun*[2] *pl*. see MARE *noun*[3].

mariachi /marɪˈɑːtʃi/ *noun*. **E20.**
[**ORIGIN** Mexican Spanish *mariache, -chi*.]
An itinerant Mexican folk band (also ***mariachi band***); a member of such a band.

maria clausa *noun phr*. pl. of MARE CLAUSUM.

mariage blanc /marjaʒ blɑ̃/ *noun phr*. Pl. **-s -s** (pronounced same). **E20.**
[**ORIGIN** French, lit. 'white marriage'.]
An unconsummated marriage.

mariage de convenance /marjaʒ də kɔ̃vnɑ̃s/ *noun phr*. Pl. ***mariages de convenance*** (pronounced same). **M19.**
[**ORIGIN** French.]
A marriage of convenience.

mariages blancs, ***mariages de convenance*** *noun phrs*. pls. of MARIAGE BLANC, MARIAGE DE CONVENANCE.

Marial /ˈmɛːrɪəl/ *adjective*. **E20.**
[**ORIGIN** French.]
= MARIAN *adjective*[2] 2.

maria libera *noun phr*. pl. of MARE LIBERUM.

marialite /ˈmarɪəlʌɪt, məˈriːəl-, məˈrʌɪəl-/ *noun*. **M19.**
[**ORIGIN** German *Marialit*, from *Marie* wife of Gerhard vom Rath, 19th-cent. German mineralogist + *-lit* -LITE.]
MINERALOGY. An aluminosilicate mineral, the sodium- and chloride-rich end member of the scapolite series. Cf. MEIONITE.

Marian /ˈmɛːrɪən/ *noun*[1] *& adjective*[1]. **M16.**
[**ORIGIN** Latin *Marianus*, from *Marius*: see below, -AN.]
▸ **A** *noun*. An adherent or supporter of the Roman general Gaius Marius (d. 86 BC). **M16.**
▸ **B** *adjective*. Of or pertaining to Marius or his party. **E17.**

Marian /ˈmɛːrɪən/ *adjective*[2] *& noun*[2]. **E17.**
[**ORIGIN** from Latin *Maria* MARY + -AN.]
▸ **A** *adjective* **1 a** Of or pertaining to Mary Queen of England (1516–58), or her reign (1553–8). **E17.** ▸**b** Of or pertaining to Mary, Queen of Scots (1542–87). **E20.**
2 *CHRISTIAN CHURCH*. Of or pertaining to the Virgin Mary; characterized by special veneration for her. **E18.**
▸ **B** *noun*. **1** A person who has a special veneration for the Virgin Mary. **M17.**
2 *hist*. A supporter of Mary Queen of England; an English Catholic during her reign. **M19.**
3 *hist*. A supporter of Mary, Queen of Scots. **L19.**

Marianism /ˈmɛːrɪənɪz(ə)m/ *noun*. **M19.**
[**ORIGIN** from MARIAN *adjective*[2] + -ISM.]
Particular or excessive veneration of the Virgin Mary; *rare* (*derog*.) a religious system based on this.

Marianist /ˈmɛːrɪənɪst/ *noun*. **L19.**
[**ORIGIN** formed as MARIANISM + -IST.]
ROMAN CATHOLIC CHURCH. **1** *hist*. A member of the Knights of the Holy Virgin, founded at Bologna in 1233 and devoted to protecting the helpless in the religious troubles between the Guelphs and Ghibellines. **L19.**
2 A member of the Society of Mary, founded in Bordeaux in 1817 by W. J. Chaminade and devoted to missionary work and the veneration of the Virgin Mary. Cf. MARIST. **E20.**

Mariavite /ˈmɛːrɪəvʌɪt/ *noun & adjective*. **E20.**
[**ORIGIN** Polish *Mariawita*, from Latin *qui Mariae vitam imitantur* who copy the life of Mary.]
▸ **A** *noun*. A member of a Polish Christian sect founded in 1906. **E20.**
▸ **B** *adjective*. Of or pertaining to this sect. **E20.**

maribou(t) *noun & adjective* var. of MARABOU.

mari complaisant /mari kɔ̃plɛzɑ̃/ *noun phr*. Pl. **-s -s** (pronounced same). **L19.**
[**ORIGIN** French.]
A husband tolerant of his wife's adultery.

mariculture /ˈmarɪkʌltʃə/ *noun*. **M19.**
[**ORIGIN** from Latin *mari-*, *mare* sea + CULTURE *noun*.]
The cultivation of the resources of the sea; *esp*. the cultivation of fish for food.
■ **mariˈcultural** *adjective* **E20.** **mariˈculturist** *noun* a person engaged in or specializing in mariculture **M20.**

marid /ˈmarɪd/ *noun*. **M19.**
[**ORIGIN** Arabic *mārid* active pple of *marada* to rebel.]
A very powerful wicked jinn in Arabian stories and Muslim mythology.

marie /ˈmɑːri/ *noun*. **L19.**
[**ORIGIN** French equiv. of female forename *Mary*.]
More fully ***marie biscuit***. A type of plain sweet biscuit.

Marie Celeste /ˌmarɪ sɪˈlɛst/ *noun*. **M20.**
[**ORIGIN** Alt. of *Mary Celeste*, a ship found in the N. Atlantic in 1872, in perfect condition but abandoned.]
A building, vessel, etc., suddenly and inexplicably deserted.

Marie Louise /ˌmarɪ luːˈiːz/ *noun*. **E19.**
[**ORIGIN** *Marie Louise* of Austria (1791–1847), second wife of Napoleon.]
A variety of yellow-skinned pear.

Marie Rose /ˌmarɪ ˈrəʊz/ *noun*. **L20.**
[**ORIGIN** Prob. from the female forename *Marie Rose*, perh. with allus. to the pink colour of the sauce.]
Marie Rose sauce, a cold sauce made from mayonnaise and tomato purée and served with seafood, esp. prawns.

marigenous /məˈrɪdʒɪnəs/ *adjective*. **L16.**
[**ORIGIN** from Latin *mari-*, *mare* sea + -GENOUS.]
Produced in or by the sea.

marigold /ˈmarɪɡəʊld/ *noun & adjective*. **ME.**
[**ORIGIN** from female forename *Mary* (prob. with ref. to the Virgin Mary) + GOLD *noun*[2].]
▸ **A** *noun*. **1** A common garden flower, *Calendula officinalis*, of the composite family, with large orange-yellow daisy-like flowers (also ***pot marigold***); a flowering stem of this plant. Also, (a flowering stem of) either of two related garden plants, *Tagetes patula* (more fully ***French marigold***) and *T. erecta* (more fully ***African marigold***), with feathery leaves and flowers in various shades of yellow, maroon, etc. **ME.** ▸**b** Any of various other related or similar plants. Freq. with specifying word. **L16.**
b ***Cape marigold***, ***corn marigold***, ***marsh marigold***, etc.
2 A variety of cider apple, with a striped skin. Also ***marigold apple***. Long *rare* or *obsolete*. **L16.**
3 The colour of a marigold flower, bright orange-yellow. **M19.**
– **COMB.**: ***marigold apple***: see sense 2 above; **marigold window** *ARCHITECTURE* a rose window.
▸ **B** *adjective*. Of the colour of a marigold flower, bright orange-yellow. **L19.**

marigot /ˈmarɪɡɒt/ *noun*. Pl. pronounced same. **M18.**
[**ORIGIN** French.]
In W. Africa, a side channel of a river.

marigraph /ˈmarɪɡrɑːf/ *noun*. **M19.**
[**ORIGIN** from Latin *mari-*, *mare* sea + -GRAPH.]
A gauge for measuring the tide.

marijuana /marɪˈhwɑːnə, marjʊˈɑːnə/ *noun*. Also **-huana**. **L19.**
[**ORIGIN** Mexican Spanish *mariguana*. Cf. JU-JU *noun*[1].]
1 = CANNABIS 2, *esp*. cannabis in a form for smoking. **L19.**
2 = CANNABIS 1. **E20.**

marikina /marɪˈkiːnə/ *noun*. **L18.**
[**ORIGIN** French from Tupi *murikina* (cf. Portuguese *mariquiná*).]
= ***golden lion tamarin*** s.v. LION *noun*.

marimba /məˈrɪmbə/ *noun*. **E18.**
[**ORIGIN** Congolese.]
A kind of deep-toned xylophone, originating in Africa and consisting of wooden keys on a frame with a tuned resonator beneath each key.

marimbaphone /məˈrɪmbəfəʊn/ *noun*. **E20.**
[**ORIGIN** from MARIMBA + -PHONE.]
= MARIMBA.

marimonda /marɪˈmɒndə/ *noun*. *rare*. **M18.**
[**ORIGIN** Amer. Spanish, prob. from a local name.]
The long-haired spider monkey, *Ateles belzebuth*.

marina /məˈriːnə/ *noun*. **L18.**
[**ORIGIN** Italian & Spanish fem. of *marino* from Latin *marinus* MARINE *adjective*.]
1 A harbour or seaside area. Now *rare*. **L18.**
2 A specially designed harbour with moorings for pleasure yachts and small boats. **M20.**

> *Holiday Which?* A sandy beach with watersports, a marina full of smart yachts, and a lido.

marinade /marɪˈneɪd/ *noun*. **E18.**
[**ORIGIN** French from Spanish *marinada*, from *marinar* to pickle in brine (= Italian *marinare*, French *mariner*), from *marino* (see MARINA). Cf. MARINATE *adjective, verb*.]
A mixture of oil, wine, spices, or similar ingredients in which meat, fish, or other food is soaked before cooking in order to flavour or soften it; the meat, fish, etc. thus soaked.

marinade /ˈmarɪneɪd/ *verb trans. & intrans.* **E18.**
[**ORIGIN** formed as MARINADE *noun*.]
Soak in a marinade.

marinara /mɑːrɪˈnɑːrə, ˈmar-/ *adjective*. **M20.**
[**ORIGIN** Italian *alla marinara* sailor-fashion, from fem. of *marinero* seafaring.]
Designating a sauce made from tomatoes, onions, herbs, etc., usu. served with pasta.

marinate /ˈmarɪneɪt/ *adjective*. **M17.**
[**ORIGIN** Italian *marinato* pa. pple of *marinare* = Spanish *marinar*: see MARINADE *noun*, -ATE[2].]
Marinaded.

marinate /ˈmarɪneɪt/ *verb*. **M17.**
[**ORIGIN** Italian *marinare* or French *mariner* = Spanish *marinar*: see MARINADE *noun*, -ATE[3].]
1 *verb trans. & intrans.* = MARINADE *verb*. **M17.**
†**2** *verb trans.* Prepare (poultry) by a certain method of stuffing. **E18–E19.**
■ **mariˈnation** *noun* **M20.**

marine /məˈriːn/ *noun & adjective*. **ME.**
[**ORIGIN** Old French & mod. French, fem. of *marin* from Latin *marinus*, from *mari-*, *mare* sea: see -INE[1].]
▸ **A** *noun*. †**1** The coast or shore by the sea; a harbour. **ME–E18.**
2 A soldier trained to serve at sea, or on shore under specified circumstances; in *pl*., a body of such soldiers. Formerly also *gen*., a sailor. **L16.** ▸**b** More fully ***dead marine***. An empty bottle. *slang* (chiefly *Austral. & NZ*). **M19.**

> W. CRUISE A commission in the marines. D. A. THOMAS The destroyer *Anthony* landed 50 marines.

Royal Marine: see ROYAL *adjective*. **tell that to the marines** *colloq*.: indicating incredulity (cf. ***tell that to the horse-marines*** s.v. HORSE-MARINE 1).
3 The collective shipping, fleet, or navy of a country; seagoing vessels collectively, esp. with reference to nationality or class. **M17.**

> G. BORROW To this inconsiderable number of vessels is the present war marine of Spain reduced.

mercantile marine: see MERCANTILE *adjective* 1. ***merchant marine***: see MERCHANT *noun & adjective*.
4 The department concerned with the navy in the French and some other foreign governments. **L18.**
5 A seascape. **M19.**
▸ **B** *adjective*. **1** Of, pertaining to, found in, or produced by the sea; inhabiting or originating in the sea. **LME.** ▸†**b** *CHEMISTRY*. Of a substance: obtainable from the sea. **E17–E19.** ▸**c** Of an artist etc.: that depicts sea subjects. **L19.**

> F. HOYLE Marine waters are in general deeper than freshwater systems. A. LURIE Umbrellas bobbed and dodged like multicolored marine plants.

2 Of or pertaining to shipping, a navy, or naval matters. **M16.**

> J. MARRYAT The petitioners pray that they may have the privilege of . . effecting marine insurance as a company. *Sunday Express* According to marine records, 20,000 vessels foundered in this century alone.

3 Of, pertaining to, or situated on the coast. **M17.**

> I. MURDOCH I see you in a cosy marine bungalow on the sea front.

4 Of or pertaining to the marines; trained to serve at sea. **L17.**

marine barracks, ***marine captain***, ***marine officer***, ***marine regiment***, etc.

5 Esp. of an instrument: used or adapted for use at sea. **E18.**

– SPECIAL COLLOCATIONS & COMB.: **†marine acid** hydrochloric acid. ***marine architecture***: see ARCHITECTURE *noun* 1. **marine band** GEOLOGY a thin bed containing marine fossils, situated between non-marine strata. **marine-biological** *adjective* of or pertaining to marine biology. **marine biologist** a person engaged or expert in marine biology. **marine biology** the biology of plants and animals living in the sea. **marine blue** [from the colour of the Royal Marines' uniform] (of) a dark blue. **marine glue** an adhesive mixture of shellac and rubber used in ship carpentry. **marine iguana** a large marine lizard, *Amblyrhynchus cristatus*, of the Galapagos Islands. **marineland** a zoo designed to exhibit and preserve marine animals. **marine railway** a slipway to facilitate the handling of boats for repair etc. **†marine salt** common salt, sodium chloride, (later) any chloride. **marine science** the science of the sea and the life, minerals, etc., contained in it; any of the individual disciplines involved in this. **marine scientific** *adjective* of or pertaining to marine science. **marine scientist** a person engaged or expert in marine science. **marine soap** a soap which lathers well with seawater. **marine store** (*a*) in *pl.*, new or old ships' materials etc. sold as merchandise; (*b*) a shop selling these. **marine toad** = *cane toad* s.v. CANE *noun*[1]. ***marine trumpet***: see TRUMPET *noun*.

marined /məˈriːnd/ *adjective*. Now *rare* or *obsolete*. **E19.**
[ORIGIN from MARINE *adjective* + -ED[1].]
HERALDRY. Designating an animal whose lower body is represented as a fishtail.

mariner /ˈmarɪnə/ *noun*. **ME.**
[ORIGIN Anglo-Norman, or Old French & mod. French *marinier* from medieval Latin *marinarius*, from Latin *marinus*: see MARINE, -ER[2].]
1 A person who navigates or assists in navigating a ship; a sailor; LAW any person employed on a ship. **ME.**
master mariner (*a*) the commander of a ship; (*b*) *spec.* the captain of a merchant vessel.
†2 *spec.* A fighting man on board ship. **M–L17.**
– COMB.: ***mariner portage***: see PORTAGE *noun*[1] 3; **mariner's compass** (*a*) a compass showing magnetic or true north and the bearings from it; (*b*) *the* southern constellation Pyxis Nautica; ***mariner's portage***: see PORTAGE *noun*[1] 3.
■ **†marinership** *noun* the skill or art of a mariner **M16–E17.**

marinera /mariˈnera/ *noun*. **E20.**
[ORIGIN Spanish, fem. of *marinero* marine, seafaring.]
= CUECA.

marinescape /məˈriːnskeɪp/ *noun*. **E20.**
[ORIGIN from MARINE *adjective* + -SCAPE *noun*[3], after *landscape*.]
A picturesque view of the sea, a seascape.

M

marinise *verb* var. of MARINIZE.

Marinism /məˈriːnɪz(ə)m/ *noun*. **M19.**
[ORIGIN from *Marini* (see below) + -ISM.]
The affected style of writing characteristic of the Italian poet Giovanni Battista Marini (d. 1625).
■ **Marinist** *noun* an imitator of Marini **M19.**

marinize /məˈriːnʌɪz/ *verb trans.* Also **-ise**. **M20.**
[ORIGIN from MARINE *adjective* + -IZE.]
Modify, convert, or adapt for marine use. Chiefly as ***marinized*** *ppl adjective*.

Mariolatry /mɛːrɪˈɒlətri/ *noun*. *derog.* **E17.**
[ORIGIN from Latin *Maria* MARY + -OLATRY.]
Excessive reverence for the Virgin Mary.
■ **Mariolater** *noun* a person who practises Mariolatry **M19.** **Mariolatrous** *adjective* characterized by Mariolatry **M19.**

Mariology /mɛːrɪˈɒlədʒi/ *noun*. **M19.**
[ORIGIN formed as MARIOLATRY + -OLOGY.]
That part of Christian theology dealing with Mary as the virgin mother of Jesus.
■ **Marioˈlogical** *adjective* **M20.**

marionette /ˌmarɪəˈnɛt/ *noun*. **M17.**
[ORIGIN French *marionnette*, from *Marion* dim. of *Marie* MARY: see -ETTE.]
1 A puppet with jointed limbs operated by strings. **M17.**
2 The bufflehead (duck), *Bucephala albeola*. Now *rare* or *obsolete*. *US*. **M19.**
■ **marionettish** *adjective* **E20.** **marionettist** *noun* a person who operates marionettes **E20.**

Mariotte /ˈmarɪɒt/ *noun*. **M19.**
[ORIGIN Edme *Mariotte* (c 1620–84), French physicist.]
1 ***Mariotte bottle***, ***Mariotte flask***, ***Mariotte's bottle***, ***Mariotte's flask***, a bottle with an outlet near the bottom and an adjustable tube passing through a cork in the neck, which if filled above the bottom of the tube gives a flow of constant head equal to the height of the bottom of the tube above the outlet. **M19.**
2 ***Mariotte's law***, = BOYLE'S LAW. **M19.**
3 ***Mariotte's tube***, a U-tube with one arm short and sealed and the other long and open to the air. **M19.**

mariposa /marɪˈpəʊsə, *in sense 2 also foreign* mariˈposa/ *noun*. **M19.**
[ORIGIN Spanish, lit. 'butterfly'.]
1 In full ***mariposa lily***, ***mariposa tulip***. Any plant of the genus *Calochortus*, of the lily family, the members of which have brightly coloured flowers and are native to western N. America; *spec.* any with large cup-shaped flowers. **M19.**
2 BULLFIGHTING. A movement in which the bullfighter draws the bull by flapping the cape behind his or her back. **M20.**

mariposite /marɪˈpəʊzʌɪt, -sʌɪt/ *noun*. **M19.**
[ORIGIN from *Mariposa* County, California + -ITE[1].]
MINERALOGY. A green or greenish-yellow variety of muscovite, containing a relatively high proportion of silica and up to 1 per cent chromic oxide.

mariscal /məˈrɪsk(ə)l/ *adjective*. Now *rare* or *obsolete*. **E19.**
[ORIGIN from mod. Latin *marisca* haemorrhoids (from Latin, lit. 'coarse fig': cf. FIG *noun*[1] 2a) + -AL[1].]
MEDICINE. Of the nature of haemorrhoids.

maris complaisants *noun phr.* pl. of MARI COMPLAISANT.

marish /ˈmarɪʃ/ *noun & adjective*[1]. Now *arch.* & *dial.* **ME.**
[ORIGIN Old French & mod. French *marais*, †*mareis* from medieval Latin *mariscus* MARSH *noun*[1].]
▸ **A** *noun*. = MARSH *noun*[1]. **ME.**
▸ **B** *adjective*. Marshy; found or produced in a marsh. **M16.**
■ **†marishy** *adjective* = MARISH *adjective*[1] **E17–E18.**

marish /ˈmɛːrɪʃ/ *adjective*[2]. *rare*. **L17.**
[ORIGIN from MARE *noun*[1] + -ISH[1].]
Characteristic of a mare.

marismas /maˈrismǝz/ *noun pl.* **L19.**
[ORIGIN Spanish, pl. of *marisma* marsh, mudflat.]
The marshy waste lands near the Guadalquivir river in southern Spain.

Maris Piper /ˌmarɪs ˈpʌɪpə/ *noun*. **M20.**
[ORIGIN Named after *Maris* Lane, Cambridge, original site of the institute where the variety was developed; *Piper* was chosen arbitrarily as a word beginning with *p-* for *potato*.]
A variety of potato with creamy flesh and smooth oval tubers.

Marist /ˈmɛːrɪst/ *noun & adjective*. **L19.**
[ORIGIN French *Mariste*, from *Marie* MARY: see -IST.]
(A member) of any of various Roman Catholic missionary and teaching orders, esp. the Society of Mary founded in Lyons in the early 19th cent. Cf. MARIANIST.

marital /ˈmarɪt(ə)l/ *adjective*. **L15.**
[ORIGIN Latin *maritalis*, from *maritus* husband: see -AL[1].]
1 Of or pertaining to marriage or the relations between (people living as) husband and wife. **L15.**

> R. INGALLS Isabelle gave no hint as to the marital status of the next four people. R. P. JHABVALA Our parents were having marital squabbles. R. DINNAGE My husband was feeling very threatened . . so we went to marital therapy together.

2 Of or characteristic of a husband. **E17.**
– SPECIAL COLLOCATIONS: **marital rape** sexual intercourse forced on a woman by her husband, knowingly against her will.
■ **mariˈtality** *noun* (*rare*) excessive affection of a wife for her husband **E19.** **maritally** *adverb* as if married, as a married person **M19.**

maritime /ˈmarɪtʌɪm/ *adjective & noun*. **M16.**
[ORIGIN (French from) Latin *maritimus*, from *mari-*, *mare* sea + *-timus*, as in *finitimus* neighbouring etc.]
▸ **A** *adjective*. **1** Living or found near the sea; (of a country, district, etc.) bordering on the sea. **M16.**

> *Bird Watching* More maritime than the common tern, it is less inclined to nest away from the coast. *Sunday Express* Rock gardens include many maritime plants like thrift.

maritime pine a southern European pine, *Pinus pinaster*, distinguished by its clustered cones and often planted in coastal areas to bind the sand. **Maritime Provinces** = sense B.2 below.
2 Of a fighting force: intended for service at sea. **M16.**
3 Connected with the sea in relation to navigation, commerce, etc. **L16.**

> GIBBON Britain . . already assumed its natural and respectable station of a maritime power. JOHN BRIGHT Maritime law . . consists of opinions and precedents for the most part. E. HEATH Hundreds of ships . . loading and unloading; where else . . can one see maritime trade on that scale?

4 Of, pertaining to, arising from, or existing in the sea. Now *rare* or *obsolete*. **E17.**

> JOHN ROSS An interesting maritime landscape.

5 Characteristic of a sailor; nautical. **M18.**
6 Of climate: moist and temperate owing to the influence of the sea. **M20.**
▸ **B** *noun*. **†1** The sea coast; a region adjoining the sea. **L16–M17.**
2 (**M-**.) In *pl.* *The* eastern provinces of Canada adjoining the Atlantic Ocean (Nova Scotia, New Brunswick, and Prince Edward Island). **E20.**
■ **Maritimer** *noun* a native or inhabitant of the Maritimes **M20.**

Marivaudage /marivodaʒ/ *noun*. **M18.**
[ORIGIN French, from P. C. de *Marivaux* (1688–1763), French novelist and dramatist.]
Exaggeratedly sentimental or affected style, language, etc., characteristic of Marivaux.

marjoram /ˈmɑːdʒ(ə)rəm/ *noun*. **LME.**
[ORIGIN Old French *marjorane* (mod. *marjolaine*) = Provençal, Spanish, Italian *majorana*, Romanian *măgheran* from medieval Latin *majorana*, of unknown origin.]
Any of various labiate plants of the genus *Origanum*, aromatic herbs much used in cooking; esp. *O. vulgare* (more fully ***wild marjoram***), native on chalk and limestone and the source of oregano, and the less pungent *O. majorana* (more fully ***sweet marjoram***, ***knotted marjoram***), and *O. onites* (more fully ***pot marjoram***). Also, the leaves of such a plant as used to flavour meat dishes etc.

mark /mɑːk/ *noun*[1].
[ORIGIN Old English (Anglian) *merc*, (West Saxon) *mearc* = Old Frisian *merke*, Old Saxon *marka* (Dutch *mark*), Old High German *marc(h)a* (German *Mark*), Old Norse *mǫrk*, Gothic *marka*, from Germanic noun rel. to Latin *margo* MARGIN *noun*. In branch IV from MARK *verb*. Cf. MARCH *noun*[2].]
▸ **I** A boundary.
1 A boundary, a frontier, a limit. Now only *arch.* & *poet.* **OE.**
2 [German *Mark*, Italian *marca*.] Any of various (specified) German or Italian territories or principalities. Cf. MARCH *noun*[2] 3. Now *arch.* or *hist.* **E18.**
3 A communal tract of land held by a Germanic or medieval German village community. **M19.**
▸ **II** Something indicating a boundary, position, etc.
†4 A standard, a banner. **OE–ME.**
5 A stone or other monument serving as a memorial or as a guide. Long *spec.*, an object on shore or at sea whose position serves to guide or warn a passing traveller. **OE.** ▸**b** A fishing ground. **M20.**

> HOBBES Men that have past by a Rock at Sea, set up some mark, thereby to remember their former danger, and avoid it.

†6 A post, stone, fence, etc., indicating a boundary; = LANDMARK *noun* 1. **ME–M18.**
7 A target, butt, or other object to be aimed at with a missile or projectile; *slang* an intended victim of a swindler etc. **ME.** ▸**†b** The quarry of a hawk etc. **L16–L17.** ▸**c** The jack in bowls. Also, a position allowed for this resulting from the initial delivery. **M17.** ▸**d** BOXING. The pit of the stomach. **M18.**

> G. ORWELL Perched on the hill-tops . . we should have made lovely marks for artillery. T. H. WHITE Shooting one arrow each at any agreed mark. *fig.*: G. J. WHYTE-MELVILLE Gilbert's efforts to amuse her often fell short of the mark.

8 An object indicating the terminal point of a race. Chiefly *fig.*, an object desired or striven for, a goal, a standard for attainment. **ME.**

> T. NORTON Let this be our perpetual marke, to aide all men faithfully.

9 A line, notch, post, attached object, etc., intended to record or indicate position, esp. for measurement. **ME.** ▸**b** *fig.* A fixed or recognized standard; (preceded by a numeral) (an approximation of) a limit or total. **M18.** ▸**c** The height or distance achieved by an athlete's throw, jump, etc.; the measurement representing this; *transf.* a best performance, a record. **E20.**

> M. BRIDGMAN She slips the letter in her novel for a mark. *Daily Chronicle* The floods . . call attention to the little interest . . taken by local authorities as regards erecting flood-marks. **b** F. W. ROBINSON He made the sum come pretty near the mark. J. I. M. STEWART Mr. Gender is asking whether we can borrow a sum somewhere near the million mark. S. KNIGHT Only by the criticism . . of an Opposition can a government be kept up to the mark. **c** *Sun (Baltimore)* The victor's time was one of the best marks of the meeting.

10 *spec.* ▸**a** NAUTICAL. A piece of material or a knot used to indicate a position on a sounding line. **M18.** ▸**b** In rugby football, a heel mark on the ground made by a player who has caught the ball direct from a kick or knock-on or throw-forward by an opponent. In Australian Rules football, the catching of a ball direct from a kick of at least fifteen metres; the spot from which the subsequent kick is taken. **M19.** ▸**c** ATHLETICS. A competitor's starting point in a race; a line drawn to indicate this. **L19.** ▸**d** With following numeral: a specific setting used for measuring the temperature of a gas oven. **E20.**

> **c** G. MITCHELL 'On your marks,' said the starter. The swimmers were poised and ready. **d** N. LAWSON Preheat the oven to gas mark 6.

▸ **III** A sign, a token, an indication.
11 An appearance, action, etc., indicating something; a sign, a token. **OE.** ▸**†b** A vestige, a trace. **ME–L16.** ▸**c** A characteristic property, a distinctive feature. **ME.** ▸**d** *spec.* A depression in each of a horse's incisor teeth, which by its appearance and gradual disappearance gives some indication of the animal's age; the age when this is apparent. Freq. in ***mark of mouth***. **LME.**

> R. GRAVES The broad-headed halberd and the long sword are marks of high rank. A. GRAY All . . bowed their heads as a mark of respect. R. K. NARAYAN I could invite him to have a group photo with me as a mark of friendship. **c** R. CROMPTON That disregard for consequences which is the mark of youth.

12 a A written character, as an asterisk etc.; *spec.* such a character, usu. a cross, made in place of a signature by an illiterate person. **OE.** ▸**b** A stamp, seal, label, inscription, etc., on an article, identifying it or indicating its ownership, origin, good quality, etc. **ME.** ▸**c** A visible sign, as a badge, brand, etc., identifying a person's occupation, status, etc. **ME.** ▸**d** HERALDRY. A small charge added to a coat of arms as a sign of distinction, esp. cadency. **E17.** ▸**e** A point awarded for a pupil's correct answer etc.; *esp.* a written symbol or a numeral representing the number of such points gained, esp. out of a given possible total, awarded as an assessment of proficiency or conduct. **E19.**

a H. SWEET The stress-marks are put before the element on which the stress begins. JOYCE He visited the chief factory . . and signed his mark in the visitors' book. ***exclamation mark***, ***question mark***, etc. **b** J. FRYER The Company's Mark upon all their Goods. **e** *Nature* No marks out of 10. JULIETTE HUXLEY My highest mark was for composition for which the Director commended me. *fig.*: H. JAMES Sculpture . . uninjured as if . . under glass. One good mark for the French Revolution!

b ***earmark***, ***hallmark***, ***trademark***, etc.

13 A visible trace or impression on a surface, produced by nature, accident, or design, as a stain, blemish, scar, fleck, stroke, dot, etc. ME. ▸**b** *spec.* In *pl.* The footprints or tracks of an otter. Cf. MARCH *noun*[3] 1. Long *dial.* ME. ▸**c** *TELECOMMUNICATIONS.* Each of a succession of strokes, dots, etc., on or holes in a paper strip whose relative duration and separation convey telegraphic information; any signal that conveys information by its intermittent presence rather than by its magnitude. Opp. ***space***. M19.

R. K. NARAYAN She . . renewed the vermilion mark on her forehead. W. TREVOR There was a dark mark, a smudge or a bruise, on her left cheek. J. GARDAM You can probably pick out their spade marks.

†**14** A flock of swans marked with the same identifying brand. LME–M16.

†**15** A particular type or class of person. LME–M16.

16 A particular brand, make, or design of an article; *esp.* (freq. **M-** and followed by a numeral) a manufactured product (as a car, aeroplane, etc.) as represented at a particular stage in its design and development. M17.

J. WAMBAUGH Philo was peeking up over the hood of a red Mark V when Tutu saw him.

17 That which suits or pleases one particularly. *colloq.* M18.

T. PARKER This cottage was going, so I took it . . . It's just about my mark this is.

18 A die or stamp for impressing on goods a symbol identifying the manufacturer. L18.

▸**IV** †**19** Attention, notice, heed. ME–E19.

SIR W. SCOTT Little matter worthy of mark occurred.

20 Importance, note. Chiefly in ***of mark***. L16.

R. WEST This French tutor was a man of mark . . who had . . held a lectureship in Paris.

– PHRASES: **be quick off the mark** lose no time in starting. **beside the mark** = *wide of the mark* below. **be slow off the mark** waste time in starting. ***black mark***: see BLACK *adjective*. **bless the mark** *interjection* = *God save the mark* below. ***full marks***: see FULL *adjective*. **get off the mark** start. **God save the mark**, **God bless the mark** *interjections* (freq. *iron.*) apologizing for or disagreeing with a preceding word or phrase. ***high-water mark***: see HIGH *adjective* etc. ***late mark***: see LATE *adjective* & *noun*[2]. ***leading mark***: see LEADING *adjective*. **leave a mark**, **make a mark** leave or make a permanent, important, or obvious impression. ***long mark***: see LONG *adjective*[1]. ***low-water mark***: see LOW *adjective* & *noun*[4]. ***make a mark***: see *leave a mark* above. **make one's mark** attain distinction. ***mark twain***: see TWAIN *noun* 1b. ***mason's mark***: see MASON *noun*. **overshoot the mark**, **overstep the mark** *fig.* go beyond a fixed or accepted standard or limit; behave improperly. **save the mark** *interjection God save the mark* above. ***short mark***: see SHORT *adjective*. ***the mark of the Beast***: see BEAST *noun*. ***wide of the mark***: see WIDE *adjective*.

– COMB.: **mark-boat** a boat moored at a particular spot and serving as a guide; **mark man**, **mark mason**, **mark master** a Freemason holding a certain rank; **mark-to-market** *adjective* (*FINANCE*) denoting or pertaining to a system of valuing assets by the most recent market price; **mark-vessel** = *mark-boat* above.

■ **markless** *adjective* E19.

mark /mɑːk/ *noun*[2].

[ORIGIN Old English *marc* corresp. to Old Frisian *merk*, Middle Dutch *marc*, (Dutch *mark*), Middle High German *marke* (German *Mark*), Old Norse *mǫrk*, prob. all from medieval Latin *marcus*, *marca* (whence also French, Provençal *marc*, Spanish *marco*, Italian *marco*, *-a*): perh. ult. identical with MARK *noun*[1].]

1 A measure of weight, chiefly for gold and silver, formerly used throughout western Europe and usu. equal to 8 ounces (226.8 grams). Now only, any of various similar foreign measures of weight. OE.

2 A monetary unit, orig. representing the value of a mark weight of pure silver, equal to thirteen shillings and fourpence in the (English and Scottish) currency of the day. *obsolete* exc. *hist.* OE. ▸**b** A Scottish coin of this value. *obsolete* exc. *hist.* ME.

3 Any of various foreign monetary units (*obsolete* exc. *hist.*). Now *spec.* the basic monetary unit of Germany until the introduction of the euro in 2002, equal to 100 pfennigs; (see also DEUTSCHMARK, OSTMARK). ME.

4 In Orkney and Shetland: a division of land originally representing the value of one Scottish mark. Also ***markland***. *obsolete* exc. *hist.* L15.

mark /mɑːk/ *verb*.

[ORIGIN Old English *mearcian* = Old Frisian *merkia*, Old Saxon *(gi)markon* appoint, observe (Dutch *marken*), Old High German *marchōn* plan, Old Norse *marka* mark, observe, from West Germanic, from Germanic base of MARK *noun*[1].]

▸**I** Put a mark on.

1 *verb trans.* Trace out boundaries for; plot or plan out. Now usu. foll. by *out*. OE. ▸†**b** Fashion, frame. *poet.* Only in LME.

BROWNING All that time stood Rosamund Page . . on the turf marked out for the party's firing-place. A. CHRISTIE William is the gardener. He keeps the paths and marks the tennis courts.

2 *verb trans.* Make a mark or marks on (a thing or person) by drawing, stamping, cutting, hitting, etc.; form or represent by making marks. OE. ▸**b** Orig., embroider. Now *spec.* put a person's initials or other identifying mark on (clothing, linen, etc.) by means of embroidery, ink, etc. ME. ▸**c** In *pass.* Have or bear natural marks. LME. ▸**d** Attach a price to (an article or goods). M19. ▸**e** Draw or cut lines on (an object) to act as a guide during subsequent machining, cutting, aligning, etc. Foll. by *off*. L19. ▸**f** Earmark (a lamb or calf); castrate (a lamb). *Austral.* & *NZ.* L19.

W. TREVOR Throwing her fork down, marking the white tablecloth. Z. TOMIN She scratched me, the stupid cow has marked me for life. *fig.*: E. FEINSTEIN Those pains of childhood never leave us. We are marked by them for ever. **b** J. PAYN We are marking the house linen. **c** W. S. DALLAS The species of the genus *Argynnis* . . are elegantly marked with silvery spots.

3 *verb trans. fig.* ▸**a** Designate as if by placing a mark on; characterize; destine. Foll. by *as*, *down*, *for*, *out*, (now *rare*) *to do*. OE. ▸†**b** Mete out, allot. *poet.* ME–L15. ▸**c** Separate *from* something else as by drawing a boundary line or imposing a distinctive mark. Usu. foll. by *off*, *out*. E18.

a R. H. MOTTRAM Only the boots and the hatless head marked her for a follower of the continental tradition. J. BETJEMAN Pedestrians and dogs and cats—we mark them down for slaughter. M. BRAGG His boots, his cap, his heavy flapping jacket all marked him out as a miner. **c** T. E. HARVEY Her son's serious ways, by which he was marked out from his . . brothers and sisters. A. BULLOCK This was an attitude . . which marked him off from Morrison.

4 **a** *verb trans.* Note down, indicate in writing (long *obsolete* exc. *Scot.*); indicate or represent by a mark, symbol, or marker. OE. ▸**b** *verb intrans.* Of a horse: indicate its age by its mark of mouth (MARK *noun*[1] 11d). M18. ▸**c** *verb trans.* & *intrans.* Record (points) in a game. E19. ▸**d** *verb trans.* & *intrans.* Award marks to or grade (an examination, pupil, etc.). L19. ▸**e** *verb trans.* *STOCK EXCHANGE.* Record the price at the making of (a bargain or transaction). E20.

a R. MACAULAY Some of the rivers and small lakes that I saw marked on the map. A. MOOREHEAD Mark your routes as permanently as possible, by leaving records, sowing seeds, building cairns. R. K. NARAYAN They made Jaggu return to the starting point, marked it with white paint. **d** G. GREENE He marked him 100% for Classics. *Today* The anguished expression of a man who has marked too many misspelt exam papers.

†**5** *verb trans.* Make (the sign of the cross) with the hand. ME–L16.

6 *verb trans.* Be a distinguishing mark of, characterize; be a noteworthy feature or attendant circumstance of. Freq. in *pass.* M17. ▸**b** Indicate the position or course of; be an indication of. L17. ▸**c** In *pass.* Of a feature etc.: be (more or less) strikingly noticeable. E19.

W. S. MAUGHAM He came towards her with the springy gait which marked his eager vitality. S. UNWIN The official end of the Congress was marked by a Dinner. A. BRIEN Mother does nothing to mark the occasion. **b** J. C. POWYS They had been planted to mark the spot where the Vikings had landed. D. STOREY The grave was marked by a small round-headed stone. M. ESSLIN This homecoming marked the beginning of the most productive period in Beckett's life.

7 *verb trans.* Show or manifest (one's approval, displeasure, etc.) by some significant action. L18.

E. GASKELL Sitting down herself on a . . stool to mark her sense of the difference in their conditions.

8 *verb trans. MILITARY.* Indicate (the pivots, formations, etc.) in military evolutions. L18.

▸**II** Direct one's course or aim.

†**9** *verb trans.* & *intrans.* Direct or continue on (one's way). ME–L16.

10 †**a** *verb trans.* Aim a blow or missile at; strike, hit. ME–E16. ▸**b** *verb intrans.* Take aim, aim a blow. (Foll. by *to*.) Long *obsolete* exc. *Scot.* ME.

▸**III** Notice, observe.

11 *verb trans.* Notice; observe, watch. ME.

DISRAELI I looked up, I marked the tumultuous waving of many torches. F. HERBERT She marked how he fingered his beard.

12 *verb trans.* & *intrans.* Consider; give one's attention (to); take notice (of). LME.

K. WATERHOUSE There is, mark you, no guarantee. R. WEST Mark my words, he'll come back.

13 *verb trans.* Note the place of going to cover of (game) after it has been put up. Also foll. by *down*. LME.

14 *verb trans.* & *intrans. SPORT.* Keep close to and so hamper (a player in an opposing team). L19. ▸**b** *AUSTRAL. RULES FOOTBALL.* Catch (the ball). L19.

– PHRASES, & WITH ADVERBS IN SPECIALIZED SENSES: ***mark a person's card***: see CARD *noun*[2] 3b. **mark down** (**a**) reduce the price of; (**b**) make a written note of; (see also sense 3 above). **mark time** (**a**) *MILITARY* march on the spot, without moving forward; (**b**) act routinely; go through the motions; (**c**) await an opportunity to advance. **mark up** (**a**) correct or annotate (copy or proofs) for typesetting, printing, etc.; (**b**) raise the price of. ***mark with a white stone***: see WHITE *adjective*.

– COMB.: **markdown** a reduction in price; **markup** (**a**) the amount added to the cost price of goods to cover overheads and provide profit; (**b**) the process or result of marking up copy or proofs; (**c**) *COMPUTING* the process of assigning tags to elements of a text to indicate their relation to the structure of the text; the tags so assigned.

■ **markable** *adjective* (*rare*) †(**a**) remarkable; (**b**) able to receive a mark or imprint: LME.

marked /mɑːkt/ *adjective*. OE.

[ORIGIN from MARK *noun*[1], *verb*: see -ED[2], -ED[1].]

1 Having a visible mark; *spec.* (of a playing card) having a distinctive mark on the back to enable or facilitate cheating or conjuring. OE.

2 Clearly defined, clearly noticeable; evident. L18.

D. BREWSTER We slightly resented a piece of marked incivility. M. DRABBLE The resemblance between mother and daughter was marked. S. KITZINGER Fear of miscarriage also has a marked effect on the physical expression of sexual feelings.

3 *LINGUISTICS.* Of a form, entity, etc., in a binary pair: carrying or distinguished by a (specified) distinctive feature; less frequent or usual of the two. M20.

– SPECIAL COLLOCATIONS: **marked cheque**: whose value is guaranteed by a bank. **marked man** (**a**) a person whose conduct is watched with suspicion or hostility; a person on whom vengeance will be taken; (**b**) a person destined to succeed. **marked price** the price of an article for sale indicated by an attached label etc.

■ **markedly** /ˈmɑːkɪdli/ *adverb* E19. **markedness** /ˈmɑːkɪdnɪs/ *noun* M19.

marker /ˈmɑːkə/ *noun*. OE.

[ORIGIN from MARK *verb* + -ER[1].]

†**1** A secretary, clerk, or scribe. Only in OE.

2 **a** A person who marks boundaries. *rare.* LME. ▸**b** A person who marks game. *rare.* L15. ▸**c** A person who records the score in a game or at target practice; a scorer. Also, a scoreboard or card etc. to record a score. M16. ▸**d** A person who puts a mark, stamp, etc., on something. M16. ▸**e** *MILITARY.* A person placed as a formation mark in military evolutions. L18.

3 An implement, tool, or device for making a mark or marks. E18. ▸**b** *spec.* More fully ***marker pen***. A broad-tipped felt pen used esp. for highlighting or for marking indelibly. M20.

b ***Magic Marker***: see MAGIC *adjective*.

4 **a** A bookmark. M19. ▸**b** An object acting as a guide to direction or indicating a route, boundary, etc.; *spec.* a flare dropped from an aircraft to illuminate or mark a target. M19. ▸**c** A distinctive feature, characteristic, etc., *esp.* one aiding recognition. E20. ▸**d** A monument, memorial stone, etc., marking a place of special interest. E20.

a M. R. MITFORD I had no marker, and the richly bound volume closed. **b** J. ARCHER As they approach the six-furlong marker—Rosalie and Crown Princess come up on the stand side. *attrib.*: C. BONINGTON Marker flags are essential . . to ensure that sherpas follow the selected route safely. **c** *Gainesville Daily Sun* We added a number of plants that were very good markers of wetlands.

5 Something worthy to be compared. Usu. in neg. contexts. *US colloq.* L19.

W. HUNT The early days of Montana were not a marker to what I have gone through.

6 A promissory note; an IOU. *US slang.* L19.

7 *SPORT.* A player whose function is to mark or guard a player of the opposing team. E20.

8 *LINGUISTICS.* A word, affix, etc., which distinguishes or determines the class or function of the form, construction, etc., with which it is used. M20.

9 *GENETICS.* An allele used to identify a chromosome or to locate other genes on a genetic map. M20.

– COMB.: **marker crude** a grade of (usu. light) crude oil whose price, fixed by agreement between oil producers, is used as a guideline for other oil prices; ***marker pen***: see sense 3b above.

market /ˈmɑːkɪt/ *noun*.

[ORIGIN Late Old English *-markett* in *ġēarmarkett* year market (cf. Old English *ġēares ċēping* year's market) from Old Saxon *iārmarket* = Old High German *iārmarchāt*, 2nd elem. of which is from Latin *mercatus* (whence (through Proto-Romance) Old French *marchiet* (mod. *marché*), Old Provençal *mercat* (mod. *marcatz*)), from *mercārī* buy, from *merc-*, *merx* merchandise. Cf. MART *noun*[1].]

1 A meeting or gathering together of people for the purchase and sale of provisions or livestock, publicly displayed, at a fixed time and place; the occasion or time of this. Also, a company of people so gathered. LOE. ▸**b** *LAW* (now *hist.*). The right granted to the lord of a manor, a municipality, etc., to establish such a meeting. LOE. ▸**c** *The* stock market. L19.

DAY LEWIS The rest of the flat cart was filled with hens for the market. C. THUBRON Markets spilling over the pavements with sacks of bananas, improvised stalls piled with cheap clothes. **c** *Sunday Times* The market's initial reaction to the Benlox bid was incredulous.

2 An open space or covered building in which provisions, livestock, etc., are displayed for sale. Now also, a supermarket. ME.

M. L. KING The largest cattle market east of Fort Worth.

M

3 The action or business of buying and selling; an instance of this, a commercial transaction; a (*good* or *bad*) bargain. *obsolete* exc. *dial.* & in phrs. ME. ▸†**b** The marketing or selling *of* a commodity. Only in 17.
4 The rate of purchase and sale of a commodity, share, etc.; market value. Also, a share performing in a specified way in the stock market. M16.

T. HARDY Just when I sold the markets went lower. P. KAVANAGH The market rose sixpence after I had sold first time. *Times* Bulmer shares have certainly been a strong market in recent weeks.

5 An opportunity for buying or selling. Chiefly in phrs. below. Now *rare* or *obsolete*. L16.
6 A place or group with a demand for a commodity or service. E17.

D. MACDONALD The important change was the replacement of the individual patron by the market. M. EDWARDES The United States of America—our major sports car market.

7 Sale as controlled by supply and demand; *esp.* a demand *for* a commodity or service. L17.

Times Lit. Suppl. A market surely exists for an esoteric study of Wittgenstein's notoriously recondite ideas.

8 *The* trade in a specified commodity. L17.
– PHRASES: **be in the market for** wish to buy. ***black market***: see BLACK *adjective*. **bring to market** offer for sale (***bring one's pigs to market***: see PIG *noun*¹). ***buyer's market***, ***buyers' market***: see BUYER 1. ***Common Market***: see COMMON *adjective*. ***drive one's pigs to market***: see PIG *noun*¹. ***free market***: see FREE *adjective*. **go to market** *colloq.* (*a*) make an attempt; (*b*) *Austral.* & *NZ* behave in an angry manner, become angry. ***grey market***: see GREY *adjective*. ***idols of the market***: see IDOL *noun*. **lose one's market** miss one's chance of doing business. **make a market** *STOCK EXCHANGE* induce active dealing in a stock or share by being both a buyer and a seller of it. **make a market of**, **make one's market of** make a profit out of. †**make market** trade. ***make one's market of***: see ***make a market of*** above. **market overt** *LAW* (now *hist.*) (offering for sale goods in) an open and legally constituted market. ***mass market***: see MASS *noun*² & *adjective*. ***milk the market***: see MILK *verb*. ***open market***: see OPEN *adjective*. ***parallel market***: see PARALLEL *adjective*. ***play the market***: see PLAY *verb*. ***price out of the market***: see PRICE *verb* 1. ***rig the market***: see RIG *verb*⁴. ***seller's market***, ***sellers' market***: see SELLER. ***single market***: see SINGLE *adjective* & *adverb*. ***stand the market***: see STAND *verb*. ***straddle the market***: see STRADDLE *verb*. ***vertical market***: see VERTICAL *adjective*.
– COMB.: **market basket** a large basket usu. with a lid, used to carry provisions etc.; **market cross**: erected in a marketplace; **market day**: on which a market is regularly held, usu. weekly; **market economy** an economy subject to and determined by free competition; **market garden** a piece of land on which fruit and vegetables are grown to be sold at a market; **market gardener** a person who owns or is employed in a market garden; **market house** a building in which a market is held; **market hunter** a person who hunts game to sell at a market; **market leader** the company selling the largest quantity of a particular type of product; the most popular brand; **market-maker** a member of a stock exchange who buys and sells continuously within prescribed regulations; **market man** (*a*) a man who buys or sells in a market; (*b*) a man who works in a stock exchange; **market-peace** *hist.* a peace or truce prevailing in a market on market days; **marketplace** (*a*) an open space in a town where a market is held; (*b*) the world of commerce or trade; *fig.* any place or environment where ideas etc. are exchanged; **market potential** the estimated potential demand for and sales of a commodity or service; **market price**, **market rate** the current price which a commodity or service fetches in the market; **market research** the study of consumers' needs and preferences, esp. for a particular commodity or service; **market researcher** a person engaged in market research; **market share** the portion of a market secured by a particular company or product; **market shooter** a person who shoots game to sell at a market; **market socialism** an economic system in which a country's resources are publicly owned but production is determined by the private customer; **marketspace** (*a*) a place or area where commercial dealing takes place, a market; (*b*) commerce carried out by electronic means, esp. via the Internet; **market square** an open square in which a town market is held; **market stall** a trader's stand or booth in a market; **marketstead** *arch.* = ***marketplace*** above; **market town**: where a market is held regularly; **market value** the current or saleable value of a commodity or service; **market woman**: who buys or sells in a market.

market /ˈmɑːkɪt/ *verb*. LME.
[ORIGIN from the noun.]
1 *verb trans.* Sell in a market; bring or send to a market. LME.
2 *verb intrans.* Deal in a market, buy and sell; purchase provisions, shop. M17.

R. CHANDLER Then I have to go uptown and market.

3 *verb trans.* Promote and distribute (a product etc.) for sale. E20.

Lancaster Guardian It is . . important that the resort continues to be marketed as a seaside holiday destination.

marketable /ˈmɑːkɪtəb(ə)l/ *adjective*. L16.
[ORIGIN from MARKET *verb* + -ABLE.]
1 Able to be marketed; that finds a ready market; saleable. L16.
2 Of or pertaining to trade; *spec.* (of price, value) that may be obtained in buying or selling. E17.
■ **marketaˈbility** *noun* L19. **marketableness** *noun* E19. **marketably** *adverb* M19.

marketeer /mɑːkɪˈtɪə/ *noun*. M17.
[ORIGIN from MARKET *noun* + -EER.]
1 A person who sells in a market. M17.
2 *hist.* A supporter of Britain's entry into the Common Market. M20.
3 A specialist in marketing. L20.

marketer /ˈmɑːkɪtə/ *noun*. Chiefly *US*. L18.
[ORIGIN from MARKET *verb* + -ER¹.]
1 A person who buys or sells in a market. L18.
2 A person who promotes and distributes a product for sale. M20.

marketing /ˈmɑːkɪtɪŋ/ *noun*. M16.
[ORIGIN from MARKET *verb* + -ING¹.]
1 The action of MARKET *verb*; an instance of this. M16. ▸**b** *spec.* The action, business, or process of promoting and selling a product etc., including market research, choice of product, advertising, and distribution. L19.

b P. PARISH Many over-the-counter preparations contain vitamins and these are the subject of intense marketing.

2 a Something bought at a market; a purchase. *rare*. E18. ▸**b** Produce to be sold at market. *rare*. L19.
– COMB.: **marketing mix** the combination of factors that can be controlled by a company to influence consumers to purchase a product; **marketing research** the study of the factors involved in marketing a product.

marketization /ˌmɑːkɪtʌɪˈzeɪʃ(ə)n/ *noun*. Also **-isation**. M20.
[ORIGIN from MARKET *noun* + -IZATION.]
Exposure of an economy, industry, etc., to market forces; *spec.* conversion of a national economy from a planned to a market economy.
■ ˈ**marketize** *verb* M20.

markhor /ˈmɑːkɔː/ *noun*. Also **-ore**. M19.
[ORIGIN Persian *mār-ḵwār* lit. 'serpent-eater'.]
A large wild goat, *Capra falconeri*, with a slate-grey coat and long spiral horns, found in mountain woodlands in central Asia.

marking /ˈmɑːkɪŋ/ *noun*. OE.
[ORIGIN from MARK *verb* + -ING¹.]
1 The action of MARK *verb*; an instance of this. OE.
2 a A letter, character, symbol, etc.; a system of notation. OE. ▸**b** A mark or pattern of marks, esp. on an animal. Freq. in *pl.* ME.

a C. PHILLIPS Despite the markings on their tickets people just took whatever cabin they could find. **b** R. DAHL The shape and colour and markings of perhaps several hundred different but very similar dogs.

†**3** Notice, consideration. LME–E17.
– COMB.: **marking board** (*a*) a scoreboard; (*b*) a board in a stock exchange for registering transactions; **marking cotton** coloured cotton thread for marking linen etc.; **marking ink** indelible ink for marking linen etc.; †**marking iron** (*a*) a branding iron; (*b*) a device for making patterns on pastry; **marking nut** the fruit of a tropical Asiatic tree, *Semecarpus anacardium* (family Anacardiaceae), the juice of which is used to mark linen; **marking stitch** a stitch used in marking linen etc.

markka /ˈmɑːkɑː/ *noun*. Pl. **markkaa**, **markkas**. L19.
[ORIGIN Finnish.]
The basic monetary unit of Finland until the introduction of the euro in 2002, equal to 100 penniä.

markman /ˈmɑːkmən/ *noun*. Pl. **-men**. M16.
[ORIGIN from MARK *noun*¹ + MAN *noun*.]
†**1** = MARKSMAN 1. M16–M17.
2 *hist.* A person living in a mark (MARK *noun*¹ 3). M19.

Markov /ˈmɑːkɒf/ *noun*. Also **-off**. M20.
[ORIGIN A. A. *Markov* (1856–1922), Russian mathematician.]
MATH. Used *attrib.* to designate (the characteristic property of) any stochastic process for which the probabilities of the different future states depend only on the existing state and not on how that state was arrived at.
Markov chain a Markov process in which there are a denumerable number of possible states or in which transitions between states occur at discrete time intervals (freq. with constant transition probabilities).
■ **Markovian** /mɑːˈkəʊvɪən/ *adjective* pertaining to or of the nature of a Markov process M20.

marksman /ˈmɑːksmən/ *noun*. Pl. **-men**. M17.
[ORIGIN from MARK *noun*¹ + -S¹ + MAN *noun*.]
1 A person skilled or practised in shooting or aiming at a mark or target; *spec.* a person who attains a certain standard of proficiency in rifle practice. Cf. earlier MARKMAN 1. M17.
2 A person who makes a mark in place of a signature. L18.
3 A person who ranges competitors in a race. L19.
■ **marksmanship** *noun* the skill or art of a marksman M19.

markswoman /ˈmɑːkswʊm(ə)n/ *noun*. Pl. **-women**. E19.
[ORIGIN formed as MARKSMAN + WOMAN *noun*.]
A woman skilled or practised in shooting or aiming at a mark or target.

markworthy /ˈmɑːkwəːði/ *adjective*. L18.
[ORIGIN from MARK *noun*¹ + -WORTHY, after German *merkwürdig*.]
Worthy of note, notable.

marl /mɑːl/ *noun*¹. ME.
[ORIGIN Old French *marle* (mod. *marne*, dial. *marle*) from medieval Latin *margila* from Latin *marga* (after *argilla* white clay).]
1 Soil consisting principally of clay mixed with calcium carbonate and forming a loose unconsolidated mass, valuable as a fertilizer. ME.
burning marl [after Milton *Paradise Lost*] the torments of hell.
2 Earth, soil. *poet.* L16.
3 A brick made from marl. E19.
– COMB.: **marl-pit**: from which marl is dug; **marl slate** *GEOLOGY* fissile, usu. calcareous, shale; **marlstone** *GEOLOGY* argillaceous and ferruginous limestone such as lies between the Upper and Lower Lias of England.

marl /mɑːl/ *noun*². *obsolete* exc. *dial.* E17.
[ORIGIN Contr.]
= MARVEL *noun*¹.

marl /mɑːl/ *noun*³ & *adjective*. L19.
[ORIGIN Contr. of MARBLED.]
▸ **A** *noun*. A mottled yarn made from two or more differently coloured threads twisted together; fabric produced from this yarn. L19.
▸ **B** *attrib.* or as *adjective*. Made or consisting of marl. E20.

marl /mɑːl/ *verb*¹ *trans.* ME.
[ORIGIN from MARL *noun*¹.]
Apply marl to (land); fertilize (as) with marl; *fig.* (*arch.*) enrich.
■ **marler** *noun* now *dial.* a person who digs or spreads marl ME.

marl /mɑːl/ *verb*² *trans.* LME.
[ORIGIN Dutch *marlen*: see MARLINE.]
†**1** Tie, noose. Only in LME.
2 *NAUTICAL.* Fasten with marline or other light rope; secure *together* by a succession of half hitches; wind serving round (a parcelled rope), securing it with a half hitch at each turn. E18.

marl /mɑːl/ *verb*³. *obsolete* exc. *dial.* L16.
[ORIGIN Contr.]
= MARVEL *verb*.

marlberry /ˈmɑːlb(ə)ri/ *noun*. *US*. L19.
[ORIGIN Prob. from dial. var. of MARBLE *noun* + BERRY *noun*¹.]
An evergreen shrub or small tree, *Ardisia escallonoides* (family Myrsinaceae), with white flowers and black berries, found in the W. Indies and Central America.

marled /mɑːld/ *adjective*. Orig. *Scot.* Also **merled**, **mirled**, /məːld/. E16.
[ORIGIN Perh. from Old French *merelé*, from *merelle* counter, game played with counters (mod. *marelle* hopscotch): see -ED². Cf. MARLY *adjective*².]
Mottled, variegated, streaked.

†**marlet** *noun*. M16–L17.
[ORIGIN Old French & mod. French *merlette* martlet, app. dim. of *merle* blackbird: see MERLE *noun*¹, -ET¹.]
A martin; *HERALDRY* a martlet.

marlin /ˈmɑːlɪn/ *noun*¹. *US*. M19.
[ORIGIN Prob. from *marl*, contr. of MARBLE *noun*.]
A godwit, *esp.* the great marbled godwit, *Limosa fedoa*.

marlin /ˈmɑːlɪn/ *noun*². E20.
[ORIGIN App. from MARLIN(SPIKE).]
Any of several large marine game fishes and food fishes of the genera *Makaira* and *Tetrapterus* with the upper jaw elongated to form a pointed snout.

marline /ˈmɑːlɪn/ *noun*. LME.
[ORIGIN Dutch *marlijn* (from *marren* to bind + *lijn* LINE *noun*¹) & *marling* (from *marlen* frequentative of Middle Dutch *marren* + *-ing* -ING¹).]
NAUTICAL. Light rope of two strands.

marlinspike /ˈmɑːlɪnspʌɪk/ *noun*. Also **-line-**. Orig. (now *rare*) **marling-** /ˈmɑːlɪŋ-/. M16.
[ORIGIN App. from *marling* pres. pple of MARL *verb*² + SPIKE *noun*², the 1st elem. being later interpreted as MARLINE. Cf. MARLIN *noun*².]
NAUTICAL. A pointed iron tool used to lift the strands of rope in splicing, as a lever in marling, etc.

marlion *noun* var. of MERLION.

marlite /ˈmɑːlʌɪt/ *noun*. L18.
[ORIGIN from MARL *noun*¹ + -ITE¹.]
A variety of marl which resists the decomposing action of air.

marloes /ˈmɑːləʊz/ *noun*. Chiefly *dial.* E19.
[ORIGIN Perh. from MAR(BLE *noun* + arbitrary *-loes*.]
The game of marbles.

Marlovian /mɑːˈləʊvɪən/ *adjective* & *noun*. L19.
[ORIGIN from mod. Latin *Marlovia* Marlowe (see below) + -IAN.]
▸ **A** *adjective*. Pertaining to or characteristic of the English dramatist Christopher Marlowe (1564–93). L19.
▸ **B** *noun*. An admirer or student of Marlowe or his writing. L19.

marly /ˈmɑːli/ *adjective*¹. ME.
[ORIGIN from MARL *noun*¹ + -Y¹.]
Resembling marl; composed of marl; having much marl.

marly /ˈmɑːli/ *adjective*². *Scot.* & *dial.* E18.
[ORIGIN Rel. to MARLED: see -Y¹.]
= MARLED.

marm /mɑːm, mam/ *noun*. Chiefly *US*. E19.
[ORIGIN Respelling of MA'AM. Cf. MAUM.]
1 = MA'AM. E19.
2 Mother (also as a form of address). M19.

marmalade /ˈmɑːməleɪd/ *noun, adjective, & verb*. L15.
[ORIGIN French *marmelade* from Portuguese *marmelada*, from *marmelo* quince, dissimilated form of Latin *melimelum* from Greek *melimēlon* kind of apple grafted on a quince, from *meli* honey + *mēlon* apple.]
▸ **A** *noun*. **1** A preserve made by boiling fruits (orig. quinces, now citrus fruit, *spec.* oranges) with sugar to form a consistent mass. L15.
OXFORD *marmalade*.
2 (The fruit of) the marmalade tree. Also ***natural marmalade***. L18.
– COMB.: **marmalade box** (the fruit of) the genipapo tree, *Genipa americana*; **marmalade plum** (the fruit of) the marmalade tree; **marmalade tree** the mammee sapota tree, *Pouteria sapota*.
▸ **B** *adjective*. †**1** Sweet. Only in E17.
2 Made with or consisting of marmalade. L19.
3 Of the colour of marmalade; orange, ginger. E20.
S. T. WARNER Jim was . . a mottled marmalade cat.
▸ **C** *verb trans*. Spread with marmalade. M20.
■ **marmalady** *adjective* resembling marmalade esp. in sweetness, stickiness or colour E17.

marmalize /ˈmɑːməlʌɪz/ *verb trans. colloq.* Also **-ise**. M20.
[ORIGIN Of uncertain origin; perh. humorously from *marmal-* (in MARMALADE) + -IZE (perh. after *pulverize*).]
Beat (someone) up; defeat heavily.
J. GASH They are real aggro men who'll marmalize anybody for a few quid.

marmem /ˈmɑːmɛm/ *noun*. L20.
[ORIGIN from MAR(TENSITE + MEM(ORY.]
METALLURGY. = ***shape memory*** s.v. SHAPE *noun*[1].

marmennill /mɑːˈmɛnɪl/ *noun*. *rare*. E19.
[ORIGIN Icelandic, dim. of *mar* sea + *mann-*, *maður* man.]
A merman.

marmite /ˈmɑːmʌɪt; *in sense 1 also foreign* marmit (*pl. same*)/ *noun*. L16.
[ORIGIN French.]
1 An earthenware cooking vessel. L16.
petite marmite: see PETITE *adjective* 2.
2 (Also **M-**.) (Proprietary name for) a savoury extract made from fresh brewer's yeast, used esp. in sandwiches and for flavouring. E20.

marmiton /marmitɔ̃/ *noun*. Pl. pronounced same. *rare*. M18.
[ORIGIN French, formed as MARMITE.]
A servant in a kitchen doing menial work.

marmolite /ˈmɑːm(ə)lʌɪt/ *noun*. E19.
[ORIGIN from Greek *marmairein* to shine + -O- + -LITE.]
PETROGRAPHY. A pale green laminated serpentine with a pearly lustre.

marmoraceous /mɑːməˈreɪʃəs/ *adjective*. *rare*. E19.
[ORIGIN from Latin *marmor* MARBLE *noun* + -ACEOUS.]
Pertaining to or resembling marble.

†**marmorate** *adjective*. M16.
[ORIGIN Latin *marmoratus* pa. pple of *marmorare* overlay with marble, from *marmor* MARBLE *noun*: see -ATE[2].]
†**1** Overlaid with or enclosed in marble. Only in M16.
2 BOTANY & ZOOLOGY. Variegated or veined like marble. E–M19.

marmoreal /mɑːˈmɔːrɪəl/ *adjective*. Chiefly *poet. & rhet.* L18.
[ORIGIN from Latin *marmoreus*, from *marmor* MARBLE *noun*: see -AL[1].]
1 Resembling marble or a marble statue; cold, smooth, white, etc., like marble. L18.
2 Made or composed of marble. E19.
■ **marmoreally** *adverb* M19.

marmorean /mɑːˈmɔːrɪən/ *adjective*. *poet. & rhet.* M17.
[ORIGIN formed as MARMOREAL + -AN.]
= MARMOREAL.

marmoset /ˈmɑːməzɛt/ *noun*. LME.
[ORIGIN Old French & mod. French *marmouset* grotesque image, young boy, (dial.) ape, of unknown origin.]
†**1** A grotesque figure; an idol; a gargoyle. LME–M18.
2 Orig., any small monkey. Now, any of several small neotropical monkeys with fine silky coats and long bushy tails which together with tamarins constitute the family Callitricidae; *spec.* any of the genus *Callithrix*. LME.
SILVERY ***marmoset***.
†**3** **a** A man one despises. L15–E19. ▸**b** A woman, a child, (used as a term of endearment or playful reproach). E16–M18.

marmot /ˈmɑːmət/ *noun*. E17.
[ORIGIN French *marmotte*, prob. alt. of Romansch *murmont* from Proto-Romance word meaning 'mountain mouse'.]
Any of several burrowing colonial rodents of the genus *Marmota*, belonging to the same family (Sciuridae) as squirrels and found on high grassland in Europe, Asia, and N. America. Also (with specifying word), any of various similar mammals.
hoary marmot: see HOARY 4. **Polish marmot** = BOBAC. PRAIRIE ***marmot***. ***whistling marmot***: see WHISTLING *ppl adjective*.

maro /ˈmaraʊ/ *noun*. Pl. **-os**. M18.
[ORIGIN Polynesian.]
A loincloth worn by certain South Sea Islanders.

marocain /marəˈkeɪn/ *noun & adjective*. E20.
[ORIGIN French, from *Maroc* (see MOROCCO) + *-ain* -AN. Cf. MAROQUIN.]
▸ **A** *noun*. (A garment made from) a crêpe fabric of silk or wool or both. E20.
▸ **B** *adjective*. Made of marocain. L20.

maroela *noun* var. of MARULA.

Maronite /ˈmarənʌɪt/ *noun & adjective*. E16.
[ORIGIN medieval Latin *Maronita*, from *Maron* reputed 5th-cent. founder of the sect: see -ITE[1].]
▸ **A** *noun*. A member of a sect of Syrian Christians living chiefly in Lebanon and now in communion with the Roman Catholic Church. E16.
▸ **B** *adjective*. Of or pertaining to the Maronites. E17.

maroodi *noun* var. of MARUDI.

maroon /məˈruːn/ *noun*[1] *& adjective*. L16.
[ORIGIN French *marron* from Italian *marrone* from medieval Greek *maraon*. Cf. MARRON *noun*[1].]
▸ **A** *noun*. †**1** = MARRON *noun*[1] 1. L16–M19.
2 A firework intended to imitate the noise of a cannon, used esp. as a warning. M18.
3 A brownish-crimson or claret colour. L18.
▸ **B** *adjective*. Of the colour maroon. L18.

maroon /məˈruːn/ *noun*[2]. M17.
[ORIGIN French *marron*, †*maron* from Spanish *cimarrón*: see CIMARRON, -OON.]
1 (Also **M-**.) Any of the black people in the mountains and forests of Suriname and the W. Indies who are descended from runaway slaves. M17.
2 In full ***maroon party***, †***maroon frolic***. A pleasure party, *esp.* a hunting or fishing trip of the nature of a picnic but of longer duration. *Southern US*. L18.
3 A person who is marooned. L19.

maroon /məˈruːn/ *verb*. L17.
[ORIGIN from MAROON *noun*[2].]
†**1** *verb trans*. As ***marooned*** *ppl adjective*. Lost in the wilds. Only in L17.
2 *verb trans*. Put (a person) ashore and leave on a desolate island or coast (as was done by buccaneers and pirates) by way of punishment. Freq. as ***marooned*** *ppl adjective*. E18. ▸**b** Cause (a person) to be unable to leave a place. Freq. as ***marooned*** *ppl adjective*. E20.
b F. ASTAIRE We ran into a snow bank and were marooned for twenty-four hours.
3 *verb intrans*. Camp out for several days on a pleasure party. *Southern US*. L18.
4 *verb intrans*. Idle, loiter. E19.
■ **marooner** *noun* (*a*) a buccaneer, a pirate; (*b*) a person who maroons someone: M17.

maroquin /ˈmarəkɪn/ *adjective & noun*. E16.
[ORIGIN French, from alt. (prob. after Spanish *marroquín*) of *Maroc* (see MOROCCO) + *-in* -INE[1]. Cf. MAROCAIN.]
▸ **A** *adjective*. = MOROCCO *adjective* 1, 2. E16.
▸ †**B** *noun*. = MOROCCO *noun*. M16–E19.

maror /mɑːˈrɔː/ *noun*. L19.
[ORIGIN Hebrew *mārōr*.]
Bitter herbs eaten at the Passover Seder service as a reminder of the bitterness of the Israelites' captivity in Egypt.

marotte /marɔt/ *noun*. Pl. pronounced same. E17.
[ORIGIN French.]
A fool's bauble.

marouflage /maruflaʒ/ *noun*. Pl. pronounced same. L19.
[ORIGIN French, from *maroufler* attach (canvas) to a wall, from *maroufle* (layer of) adhesive used for the purpose.]
ART. **1** The act or process of pasting a painted canvas to a wall, traditionally using an adhesive made of white lead ground in oil. L19.
2 A piece of leather or other material used as a backing to show off decorative ironwork. M20.

Marplan /ˈmɑːplan/ *noun*. M20.
[ORIGIN Uncertain: perh. rel. to MARSILID.]
PHARMACOLOGY. (Proprietary name for) the drug isocarboxazid.

marplot /ˈmɑːplɒt/ *noun*. E18.
[ORIGIN from MAR *verb* + PLOT *noun*.]
A person who spoils a plot or hinders the success of any undertaking.

marque /mɑːk/ *noun*[1]. LME.
[ORIGIN French from Provençal *marca*, from *marcar* seize as a pledge, perh. ult. from Germanic base of MARK *noun*[1]. Cf. MART *noun*[3].]
hist. Reprisals. Long only as below.
letter of marque (*a*) (in full ***letter of marque and reprisal***) orig., a licence granted by a monarch authorizing a subject to take reprisals on the subjects of a hostile state; later, legal authority to fit out an armed vessel and use it in the capture of enemy merchant shipping and to commit acts which would otherwise have constituted piracy; usu. in *pl.*; (*b*) a ship carrying letters of marque; a privateer.

marque /mɑːk/ *noun*[2]. E20.
[ORIGIN French, back-form. from *marquer* to mark or brand, alt. of Old French *merchier*, from *merc* limit, of Scandinavian origin (cf. Old High German *marc(h)a* MARK *noun*[1]).]
A make or brand of something, esp. a motor vehicle.
Autosport Lancia won the day in Madeira, when examples of their marque filled the first six places.

marquee /mɑːˈkiː/ *noun & adjective*. L17.
[ORIGIN from MARQUISE, taken as a pl. & assim. to -EE[1].]
▸ **A** *noun*. **1** A tent large enough to hold many people, used esp. for social or commercial functions. L17.
2 = MARQUISE 3b. *N. Amer.* M20.
▸ **B** *attrib.* or as *adjective*. [from the practice of billing the name of an entertainer on the *marquee* (i.e. awning) over the entrance to a theatre.] Famous; outstanding, pre-eminent. Orig. & chiefly *US*. M20.
D. HALBERSTAM Their [the Yankees'] marquee names . . still inspired awe and fear among opponents.

marquench /ˈmɑːkwɛn(t)ʃ/ *verb trans*. M20.
[ORIGIN from MAR(TENSITE + QUENCH *verb*.]
METALLURGY. Temper (steel) by martempering, esp. with the constant-temperature stage too short to allow the austenite/martensite transformation to be isothermal. Chiefly as ***marquenching*** *verbal noun*.

marquesa /marˈkesa, mɑːˈkeɪzə/ *noun*. M19.
[ORIGIN Spanish, fem. of *marqués* MARQUIS.]
A Spanish marchioness.

Marquesan /mɑːˈkeɪs(ə)n, -z-/ *noun & adjective*. L18.
[ORIGIN from *Marquesas* (see below) + -AN.]
▸ **A** *noun*. A native or inhabitant of the Marquesas Islands in the S. Pacific; *spec.* a member of the aboriginal Polynesian people of these islands. Also, the Polynesian language of this people. L18.
▸ **B** *adjective*. Of or pertaining to the Marquesans or their language. E19.

marquess, **marquessate** *nouns* see MARQUIS etc.

marquetry /ˈmɑːkɪtri/ *noun*. M16.
[ORIGIN French *marqueterie*, from *marqueter* variegate, formed as MARQUE *noun*[2]: see -ERY.]
Inlaid work in wood, ivory, etc., esp. as used for the decoration of furniture.

marquis /ˈmɑːkwɪs/ *noun*. Also **marquess**, (esp. in titles) **M-**. ME.
[ORIGIN Old French *marchis* (later altered to *marquis* after Provençal *marques*, Spanish *marqués*) from Proto-Romance base of MARCH *noun*[2].]
1 In some Continental countries: orig. (now *hist.*), a ruler of certain territories (originally marches or frontier districts); later, a nobleman (or, in the 16th and 17th cents., a noblewoman) ranking below a duke and above a count. ME.
2 (Now usu. **marquess**.) A British or Irish hereditary nobleman of the second rank of the peerage, below a duke and above an earl. LME.

marquisate /ˈmɑːkwɪsət/ *noun*. Also (now usual in sense 1) **-quess-**. M16.
[ORIGIN from MARQUIS + -ATE[1], after French *marquisat*, Italian *marchesato*, etc.]
1 In some Continental European countries: the territorial lordship or possessions of a marquis or margrave. M16.
2 The rank or dignity of a marquess. Formerly also, a place from which a marquess takes his title. L16.

marquise /mɑːˈkiːz, *foreign* markiz (*pl. same*)/ *noun*. M17.
[ORIGIN French, fem. of *marquis*: see MARQUIS.]
1 (The title of) a marchioness in Continental Europe or (formerly) Britain. M17.
†**2** A variety of pear. E18–L19.
3 †**a** = MARQUEE 1. M18–M19. ▸**b** A permanent canopy projecting over the entrance to a hotel, theatre, etc. Cf. MARQUEE 2. L19.
4 A ring set with a pointed oval gem or cluster of gems. Also more fully ***marquise ring***. L19.

marquisette /mɑːkɪˈzɛt/ *noun & adjective*. E20.
[ORIGIN French, dim. of *marquise*: see MARQUISE, -ETTE.]
(Of) a plain gauze dress fabric orig. made from silk, later from cotton.

marquois scale /ˈmɑːkwɔɪz skeɪl/ *noun phr.* L18.
[ORIGIN from alt. of French *marquoir* ruler used by tailors, from *marquer* (see MARQUE *noun*[2]) + *-oir* -ORY[1], + SCALE *noun*[4].]
An apparatus for drawing equidistant parallel lines.

marra *noun & adjective* var. of MARROW *noun*[2] *& adjective*.

marram /ˈmarəm/ *noun*. M17.
[ORIGIN Old Norse *marálmr*, from *marr* sea + *hálmr* HAULM.]
1 A coastal grass, *Ammophila arenaria*, with long dense spikes and far-creeping roots, often planted in order to bind sand. Also ***marram grass***. M17.

M

2 A sandhill grown over with this grass. *local*. **M19.**

Marrano /mə'rɑːnəʊ/ *noun*. Pl. **-os**. **M16.**
[ORIGIN Spanish, of unknown origin.]
In medieval Spain: a christianized Jew or Moor, *esp.* one who merely professed conversion in order to avoid persecution.
■ **Marranism** *noun* the practice of Marranos of professing Christianity to avoid persecution **M18.**

marrer /'mɑːrə/ *noun*. **L15.**
[ORIGIN from MAR *verb* + -ER[1].]
A person who mars something.

marri /'mari/ *noun*. **M19.**
[ORIGIN Nyungar.]
(The timber of) a western Australian red gum tree, *Eucalyptus calophylla*.

marriable /'marɪəb(ə)l/ *adjective*. Now *rare*. **LME.**
[ORIGIN Old French & mod. French *mariable*, from *marier* MARRY *verb*: see -ABLE.]
Able to be married; marriageable.

marriage /'marɪdʒ/ *noun*. **ME.**
[ORIGIN Old French & mod. French *mariage*, from *marier* MARRY *verb*: see -AGE.]
1 Legally recognized personal union entered into by a man and a woman usu. with the intention of living together and having sexual relations, and entailing property and inheritance rights; the condition of being a husband or wife; the relation between persons married to each other. **ME.**

D. ROWE Most of us enter into marriage with romantic ideas.

2 The action or an act of getting married; the ceremony or procedure by which two persons are made husband and wife. **ME.** ▸**b** This ceremony together with the accompanying festivities; a wedding. *arch*. **LME.**
†**3** A dowry. **ME–L16.**
4 An intimate union. **LME.**

Dance Theatre Journal The marriage of art and industry is back in fashion.

5 *hist*. The right of a feudal superior (in England *spec*. the monarch) to exact a fine for the marriage of a vassal; the sum of money so acquired. **LME.**
6 A particular union between a husband and wife. **LME.**

S. KITZINGER The marriage started to crack under the impact of . . 'appalling rows'. *Woman & Home* She had a son and a daughter by her first marriage.

†**7** A person viewed as a prospective husband or wife; a (good or bad) match. **LME–E17.**
8 In bezique, pinochle, and similar card games, the declaration of a king and queen of the same suit. In patience, two consecutive cards of the same suit. **M19.**
9 A married antique. **M20.**
– PHRASES: ***arranged marriage***: see ARRANGE *verb* 3. ***civil marriage***: see CIVIL *adjective*. ***common-law marriage***: see COMMON LAW. **communal marriage** the system in some cultures by which, in a small community, all the men are regarded as married to all the women, and vice versa. ***fleet marriage***: see FLEET *noun*[2]. **group marriage** = *communal marriage* above. **in marriage** (*a*) in the matrimonial state, in wedlock; (*b*) as husband or wife (freq. in ***give in marriage***, ***take in marriage***). ***in the way of marriage***: see WAY *noun*. ***jactitation of marriage***: see JACTITATION 1. ***left-hand marriage***: see LEFT HAND *adjectival phr*. ***marriage of convenience***: see CONVENIENCE *noun*. ***MIXED marriage***. ***open marriage***: see OPEN *adjective*. **plural marriage** polygamy. ***propose marriage***: see PROPOSE *verb* 4a. ***PUTATIVE marriage***. ***secondary marriage***: see SECONDARY *adjective*. ***SHOTGUN marriage***. ***steal a marriage***: see STEAL *verb*.
– COMB.: **Marriage Act** any of the Acts of Parliament regulating marriages; **marriage articles** an antenuptial agreement about rights of property and succession; **marriage bed** (the rights and duties of) the sexual relationship of a husband and wife; **marriage broker** (*a*) *derog*. a matchmaker; (*b*) in a culture in which arranged marriages are the norm, a person who arranges marriages for a fee; **marriage bureau** an agency which arranges introductions for people wishing to marry; **marriage certificate** a copy of the record of a legal marriage which is given to the persons concerned, with details of names, date, etc.; **marriage counselling**, **marriage guidance** the counselling of married people who are having problems in their relationship; **marriage licence** (*a*) a document giving official permission to marry; (*b*) a marriage certificate; **marriage lines** *colloq*. one's marriage certificate; **marriage market** the supply of and demand for eligible partners for marriage; **marriage payment** ANTHROPOLOGY = ***bride price*** s.v. BRIDE *noun*[1]; **marriage portion** a portion or dowry given to a bride at her marriage; **marriage-ring** a wedding ring; **marriage settlement** a legal arrangement securing certain property for an intended wife and sometimes also for any children of the marriage; **marriage-song** = EPITHALAMIUM.

marriageable /'marɪdʒəb(ə)l/ *adjective*. **L16.**
[ORIGIN from MARRIAGE + -ABLE.]
Able to be married, *esp*. old or rich enough for marriage, eligible; suitable for marriage.
■ **marriagea'bility** *noun* **M19.**

married /'marɪd/ *adjective & noun*. **LME.**
[ORIGIN from MARRY *verb* + -ED[1]. Earlier in UNMARRIED.]
▸**A** *adjective*. **1** United to another person in marriage. **LME.**
2 Pertaining to or characteristic of married people or marriage. **L16.**
married bliss, ***married life***, ***married quarters***, etc.
3 Of an antique: put together from parts of two or more different articles, sometimes of different dates. **M20.**
– SPECIAL COLLOCATIONS: **married print** CINEMATOGRAPHY a positive film carrying both pictures and a soundtrack.
▸**B** *noun*. A married person; *collect. pl.*, *the* class of married people collectively. Freq. in ***young marrieds***. **L16.**

marrier /'marɪə/ *noun*. **L16.**
[ORIGIN from MARRY *verb* + -ER[1].]
A person who marries someone or something.

Marrism /'mɑːrɪz(ə)m/ *noun*. **M20.**
[ORIGIN from *Marr* (see below) + -ISM.]
(Advocacy of) the linguistic theories advocated by the Russian linguist and archaeologist N. Y. Marr (1865–1934), in which language is regarded as a phenomenon of social class rather than of nationality.
■ **Marrist** *adjective* **M20.**

marron /'marɒn; *foreign* marɔ̃, ma-/ *noun*[1]. **L19.**
[ORIGIN French: see MAROON *noun*[1] & *adjective*.]
A large and particularly sweet kind of chestnut. Now chiefly in ***marron glacé*** below.
marron glacé /'glaseɪ, *foreign* glase/, pl. **-s -s** (pronounced same), a chestnut preserved in and coated with sugar or syrup, as a sweet.

marron /'mar(ə)n/ *noun*[2]. **M20.**
[ORIGIN Nyungar *marran*.]
A large freshwater crayfish, *Cherax tencrimanus*, of western Australia.

marrot /'marət/ *noun*. Chiefly *Scot*. **M17.**
[ORIGIN Prob. imit. of the bird's call; cf. MURRE.]
An auk; *esp*. the guillemot.

marrow /'marəʊ/ *noun*[1].
[ORIGIN Old English *mærh*, *mærg* (West Saxon) *mearh*, *mearg*, corresp. to Old Frisian *merg*, *merch*, Old Saxon *marg* (Dutch *merg*), Old High German *mar(a)g* (German *Mark*), Old Norse *mergr*, from Germanic.]
1 The soft vascular fatty substance in the cavities of bones (also ***bone marrow***); this as the type of vitality and strength or (freq. with biblical allusion) of rich and nutritious food. **OE.**
†**2** The pith of a plant; the pulp of a fruit. **OE–L18.**
3 The substance of the spinal cord. Now always ***spinal marrow***. **LME.**
4 The vital or essential part, = GOODNESS 4; the inmost or central part. Freq. with *the*. **LME.**
5 In full ***vegetable marrow***. The long cylindrical green, white, or striped fruit of a kind of gourd, *Cucurbita pepo*, eaten as a vegetable; the plant producing this, a trailing annual with deep yellow flowers. **E19.**
– PHRASES: **to the marrow** right through, to the centre of one's being.
– COMB.: **marrow pudding**: made with beef or vegetable marrow; **marrow squash** *N. Amer*. a vegetable marrow; **marrow-stem (kale)** a coarse kind of kale grown esp. in Australia and New Zealand as fodder.
■ **marrowed** *adjective* full of marrow **ME. marrowy** *adjective* full of marrow; of the nature of marrow: **LME.**

marrow /'marəʊ/ *noun*[2] & *adjective*. Now *dial*. Also **marra** /'marə/. **LME.**
[ORIGIN Prob. from Old Norse *margr* many, (fig.) friendly, communicative.]
▸**A** *noun*. **1** A companion, a fellow worker, a partner. **LME.**
2 A thing which makes a pair with another, a counterpart. **E16.**
3 One's equal or like; a match. Formerly also, an opponent. **M16.**
4 A husband or wife. **L16.**
▸**B** *adjective*. Similar, corresponding. **L16.**

marrow /'marəʊ/ *verb*. *Scot. & N. English*. **LME.**
[ORIGIN from MARROW *noun*[2].]
1 a *verb trans*. Join, associate; pair. **LME.** ▸**b** *verb intrans*. Be a partner or fellow worker (*with*). **M16.**
†**2** *verb trans*. Be a companion to; marry. **E16–L18.**
3 *verb trans*. Resemble, be equal to; produce something equal to, match. **M16.**

marrowbone /'marə(ʊ)bəʊn/ *noun*. **ME.**
[ORIGIN from MARROW *noun*[1] + BONE *noun*.]
1 A bone containing edible marrow. **ME.**
2 *sing*. & (usu.) in *pl*. The knees. *joc*. **M16.**
3 In *pl*. Fists as weapons. *slang*. **E17.**
4 In *pl*. Crossbones. **M19.**

marrowfat /'marə(ʊ)fat/ *noun*. **E18.**
[ORIGIN from MARROW *noun*[1] + FAT *noun*[2].]
1 A substance like tallow prepared by boiling down marrow. *N. Amer*. **E18.**
2 In full ***marrowfat pea***. A kind of large rich pea. **M18.**

marrowless /'marə(ʊ)lɪs/ *adjective*[1]. **E17.**
[ORIGIN from MARROW *noun*[1] + -LESS.]
Having no marrow.

marrowless /'marə(ʊ)lɪs/ *adjective*[2]. Now *dial*. **M17.**
[ORIGIN from MARROW *noun*[2] + -LESS.]
Companionless; unmarried; unequalled; lacking the other member of the pair.

marrowsky /mə'raʊski/ *noun*. **M19.**
[ORIGIN Perh. a personal name.]
A variety of slang, or a slip in speaking, characterized by transposition of initial letters, syllables, or parts of two words; an instance of this, a spoonerism.
■ **marrowskying** *noun* the transposition of initial letters etc. **M19.**

Marrucinian /maruː'sɪnɪən/ *noun & adjective*. **M19.**
[ORIGIN from Latin *Marrucini* Marrucinians + -AN.]
▸**A** *noun*. **1** A member of an ancient Oscan-Umbrian people of eastern Italy. **M19.**
2 The language of this people. **M20.**
▸**B** *adjective*. Designating, of, or pertaining to this people. **M19.**
■ **Ma'rrucian** *noun* (long *rare* or *obsolete*) = MARRUCINIAN *noun* 1 **L16. Ma'rrucine** *noun* (long *rare* or *obsolete*) = MARRUCINIAN *noun* 1 **E17.**

marry /'mari/ *verb*. **ME.**
[ORIGIN Old French & mod. French *marier* from Latin *maritare*, from *maritus* married, (as noun) husband, prob. from Indo-European.]
▸**I** *verb trans*. **1** Join (two persons, one person *to* another) in marriage; constitute as husband and wife according to law or custom. **ME.**

SHAKES. *A.Y.L.* You shall be the priest, and marry us. A. LIVINGSTONE She became engaged to him and the following June they were married.

2 Of a parent or guardian: give in marriage, cause to be married. **ME.**

R. PLAYER Her parents married her to . . a wealthy landowner.

†**3** *verb refl*. = sense 6 below. **ME–E19.**
4 Take as one's husband or wife. **LME.** ▸**b** Obtain (something) by getting married. Freq. in ***marry money***. **M19.**

F. HUME He had added to his crime by marrying a pretty girl.

5 *transf. & fig*. **a** Unite intimately, join closely or permanently; correlate. **LME.** ▸**b** NAUTICAL. Splice (two ropes) together without increasing girth. Also, bring together (two ropes) so as to haul them together equally. **E19.** ▸**c** In *pass*. Of the king or queen in certain card games: be declared as held in the same hand with the queen or king of the same suit. **M19.** ▸**d** STOCK EXCHANGE. Set (one transaction) against another transaction. **M20.**

a G. SAINTSBURY This hybrid and bizarre vocabulary is . . admirably married to the substance of the writing. *Annabel* Some men found it difficult to marry their objective views with their own situations.

▸**II** *verb intrans*. **6** Enter into marriage, get married; take a husband or wife. Also foll. by *on* (*Scot.*), *with* (now *US*). **ME.** ▸**b** *transf. & fig*. Enter into intimate union; join, so as to form one; (of wine etc.) mature. **E16.**
7 Of a minister etc.: conduct a marriage ceremony. **M16.**
– PHRASES, & WITH ADVERBS & PREPOSITIONS IN SPECIALIZED SENSES: **marry above oneself** marry a person of higher social position. ***marry a fortune***: see FORTUNE *noun*. **marry below oneself**, **marry beneath oneself** marry a person of lower social position. **marry into** become a member of (a family) as a result of marrying one of its members. ***marry into money***, ***marry money***: see MONEY *noun*. **marry off** (of a parent or guardian) find a husband or wife for (a child or ward). **marry out** marry a person of a different clan, group, religion, etc. ***marry over the broomstick***: see **broomstick** s.v. BROOM. **marry up** (*a*) *colloq*. tie up or preoccupy in marriage; (*b*) join or link up *with*. **marry well** have or make a successful marriage in terms of harmony, material gain, or social standing. ***marry with the left hand***: see LEFT HAND *noun phr*. 1.

marry /'mari/ *interjection*. Now *arch*. **LME.**
[ORIGIN Alt. of (the Virgin) MARY.]
Expr. assertion, surprise, indignation, etc., esp. in response to a question. Cf. MARY 1.
marry come up: expr. indignant or amused surprise or contempt.

Mars /mɑːz/ *noun*. **OE.**
[ORIGIN Latin *Mars*, *Mart-* (reduced form of *Mavors*, *Mavort-*) the Roman god of war (see below). Cf. MAVORS.]
1 The god of war of the ancient Romans, ranking in importance next to Jupiter and identified from an early period with the Greek Ares. Also *fig*. (*arch.*), warfare, warlike prowess, fortune in war. **OE.** ▸†**b** A great warrior. **M16–M19.**
2 The fourth planet in order of distance from the sun, whose orbit lies between those of the earth and Jupiter. **ME.** ▸†**b** A great warrior. **M16–M19.**
3 ALCHEMY. The metal iron. *obsolete* exc. *hist*. **LME.**
4 HERALDRY. The tincture gules in the fanciful blazon of arms of sovereign princes. *obsolete* exc. *hist*. **L16.**
– COMB.: **marsquake** [after *earthquake*] a tremor or violent shaking of part of the surface of the planet Mars.

Marsala /mɑː'sɑːlə/ *noun*. **E19.**
[ORIGIN See below.]
In full ***Marsala wine***. A white wine resembling a light sherry that is exported from Marsala, a town on the west coast of Sicily.

Marsanne /mɑː'san/ *noun*. **E19.**
[ORIGIN The name of a town in southern France.]
A variety of white wine grape originating in the northern Rhône area of France.

Marse *noun* see MAS *noun*[1].

Marseillais /mɑːseɪˈjeɪ, *foreign* marsɛjɛ/ *adjective & noun*. L17.
[ORIGIN French, from *Marseille* (see MARSEILLES) + *-ais* -ESE.]
▸ **A** *adjective*. Belonging or pertaining to Marseilles, a port in SE France. L17.
▸ **B** *noun*. Pl. same. A native or inhabitant of Marseilles. L18.

Marseillaise /mɑːseɪˈjeɪz, -s(ə)ˈleɪz, *foreign* marsɛjɛːz/ *noun*. L18.
[ORIGIN French, from fem. adjective of MARSEILLAIS.]
The national anthem of France, composed in 1792 on the declaration of war against Austria and first sung in Paris by Marseilles patriots. Also more fully ***Marseillaise hymn***.

Marseilles /mɑːˈseɪlz/ *noun*. E18.
[ORIGIN Anglicized from *Marseille*, a port in SE France.]
Used *attrib.* with ref. to things native to or associated with Marseilles.
Marseilles quilting a stiff cotton fabric, similar to piqué. **Marseilles ware** a type of pottery produced in Marseilles during the 17th and 18th cents.

marsh /mɑːʃ/ *noun*[1].
[ORIGIN Old English *mersć*, *merisć* = Middle Low German *mersch*, *marsch*, Middle Dutch *mersch(e*, from West Germanic base also of Latin *mariscus*. Cf. MARISH *noun & adjective*[1].]
1 (A tract of) low-lying land that is flooded in wet weather and usually more or less watery at all times. OE.
J. BUCHAN Out of the marshes a fog crept. P. DICKINSON The awkward sploshing of his paddle . . had been the loudest sounds in the marsh.
2 A meadow; a stretch of grassland near a river or the sea. *local*. L18.
– COMB.: **Marsh Arab**: from the marsh area of southern Iraq; ***marsh arrowgrass***: see ***arrowgrass*** s.v. ARROW *noun*; **marshbird** (*a*) either of two streaked warblers of the genus *Megalurus* (family Sylviidae) found in Australia, New Guinea, and Indonesia, *M. timoriensis* and *M. gramineus*; (*b*) either of two small birds of the genus *Pseudoleistes* (family Icteridae), having yellow and brown plumage and found in S. American swamps and marshes; **marsh blackbird** the American red-winged blackbird, *Agelaius phoeniceus*; **marshbuck** = SITATUNGA; **marsh elder** (*a*) (now *dial.*) the guelder rose, *Viburnum opulus*; (*b*) any of various plants of the genus *Iva*, of the composite family, native to salt marshes in N. America; **marsh fern** a delicate fern of fens, *Thelypteris palustris*; **marsh fever** malaria; **marsh fritillary** a tawny nymphalid butterfly, *Eurodryas aurinia*; **marsh frog** a large frog, *Rana ridibunda*, with a loud chuckling call, native to SW and eastern Europe; **marsh gas** gas, mainly methane, generated by decaying matter in marshes; **marsh grass** any of various grasses growing in marshy ground or salt marshes; *spec.* (*US*) a cordgrass, *Spartina patens*; **marsh harrier** a large harrier, *Circus aeruginosus*, of Old World wetlands; **marsh hawk** *US* = ***hen harrier*** s.v. HEN *noun*; **marsh hay**: made from marsh grasses; **marshman** a person who lives in marshy country; **marsh marigold** a plant of wet places, *Caltha palustris*, of the buttercup family, bearing yellow flowers; **marsh orchid** any of a group of European orchids of the genus *Dactylorhiza* (esp. *D. praetermissa* and *D. incarnata*) which have unspotted leaves and purple or pink flowers and occur in damp and marshy ground; ***marsh pennywort***: see ***pennywort*** (b) s.v. PENNY; **marsh pink** = SABBATIA; **marsh quail** *US* a meadow lark; **marsh samphire** = ***glasswort*** (a) s.v. GLASS *noun & adjective*; **marsh spot** a deficiency disease of garden peas, caused by a lack of manganese; **marsh tacky** *US* a small pony bred in marshy districts; **marsh tern** the gull-billed tern, *Gelochelidon nilotica*; **marsh tit**, **marsh titmouse** a tit, *Parus palustris*, of deciduous woods and hedges in Europe and the Far East; **marsh treader** *US* a water bug of the family Hydrometridae; **marsh trefoil** = BUCKBEAN; **marsh violet** a violet of wet acid peaty places, *Viola palustris* (also called ***bog violet***); **marsh warbler** a Eurasian warbler, *Acrocephalus palustris*, with plain brown plumage and a song involving much mimicry of other birds; **marsh worm** a kind of worm used as a bait in angling; **marshwort** any of several creeping aquatic umbelliferous plants of the genus *Apium*; *esp.* fool's watercress, *A. nodiflorum*; **marsh wren** a N. American wren, *Cistothorus palustris*, which frequents marshes and swamps.

Marsh /mɑːʃ/ *noun*[2]. M19.
[ORIGIN James *Marsh* (1794–1846), Brit. chemist.]
Used in *possess.* and *attrib.* to designate a test for the presence of arsenic in which nascent hydrogen is used to reduce any arsenic present to the gas arsine, which is then converted into a dark stain of metallic arsenic by heat.

marshal /ˈmɑːʃ(ə)l/ *noun*[1]. OE.
[ORIGIN Old French *mareschal* (mod. MARÉCHAL) from Frankish Latin *mariscalcus* from Germanic (whence also Old High German *marahscalh*, German †*Marschalk*, *Marschall*), from two words meaning 'horse' (repr. by MARE *noun*[1]) and 'servant' (repr. by Old English *scealc*).]
†**1** A person who tends horses; a smith; *esp.* a person who treats diseases of horses, a farrier. OE–E18.
2 A chief official of a royal household or court (in the Middle Ages usually entrusted with the military affairs of the monarch); a high officer of state. Formerly *spec.* (now *hist.*) = ***Earl Marshal*** s.v. EARL. ME.
3 An officer of a court of law responsible for the custody of prisoners and for the keeping of order, and frequently entrusted with the keeping of a prison. Also ***Marshal of the Exchequer***, ***Marshal of the King's Bench***, ***Marshal of the Queen's Bench***. *obsolete* exc. *hist.* ME. ▸**b** An official (now usually a barrister) who accompanies a judge on circuit to act as secretary and personal assistant. Also ***judge's marshal***. M19.
4 A person responsible for arranging ceremonies or controlling people at a race, banquet, etc. ME. ▸**b** In full ***City marshal***. An officer of the corporation of the City of London. M17.
Bike Events Marshals along the route . . to guide the way and help you to get there.
5 a Orig., any senior army officer; a commander, a general. Later (esp. in ***marshal of the field***, ***marshal of the camp***), a (senior) officer of a definite rank, which varied according to period and country. Now *obsolete* exc. in ***Field Marshal*** s.v. FIELD *noun & adjective*. LME. ▸**b** An officer of the highest rank in any of various armies. L15. ▸**c** An officer of any of several high ranks in the Royal Air Force. E20.
6 a Orig., an official with certain police duties. Now (*US*), a police officer or sheriff with responsibility for a designated area; the administrative head of a police or fire department. L16. ▸**b** A legal officer in each judicial district responsible for executing court precepts. *US*. L18.
7 The chief of the proctors' attendants at Oxford University; either of two officials appointed by the Vice-Chancellor of Cambridge University to act as his messengers, to summon meetings, etc. E19.
– PHRASES: ***Air Chief Marshal***, ***Air Marshal***: see AIR *noun*[1]. ***City marshal***: see sense 4b above. ***Earl Marshal***: see EARL *noun*. ***judge's marshal***: see sense 3b above. **knight marshal** †(*a*) a military officer acting as a quartermaster; (*b*) *hist.* an officer in the royal household with judicial functions (see MARSHALSEA). **Marshal of the Admiralty (Court)** an officer of the Court of Admiralty concerned with executing warrants issued by the court etc. ***Marshal of the Exchequer***, ***Marshal of the King's Bench***, ***Marshal of the Queen's Bench***: see sense 3 above. **Marshal of the Royal Air Force** the highest rank in the Royal Air Force, equivalent to Field Marshal and Admiral of the Fleet.
– COMB.: **marshal-man** any of a number of men (formerly under the orders of the knight marshal) belonging to the royal household, and going before the British monarch in processions to clear the way; a similar officer under the orders of the marshal of the City of London.
■ **marshaˈless** *noun* the wife of a marshal L18. **marshalship** *noun* = MARSHALCY 1 M16.

†**marshal** *noun*[2] see MARECHAL.

marshal /ˈmɑːʃ(ə)l/ *verb*. Infl. **-ll-**, ***-l-**. LME.
[ORIGIN from MARSHAL *noun*[1].]
†**1** *verb trans.* Tend (a horse) as a farrier. Also, fake up (a horse) for sale. LME–E16.
2 *verb trans.* Arrange, place, or rank in order at a banquet, table, etc. LME. ▸†**b** Arrange (a banquet). Also foll. by *up*. L16–E17.
3 *verb trans.* Arrange or draw up (armed forces) in order for fighting, exercise, or review; arrange in a body or procession; arrange (competitors) for a race etc. LME. ▸**b** *verb refl.* & *intrans.* Take up positions in a due arrangement. L17.
D. A. THOMAS Jan Evertsen and Cornelis Tromp marshalled the Dutch fleet into a controlled withdrawal.
4 *verb trans.* Dispose, arrange, or set (things, material or abstract) in methodical order. LME. ▸**b** FINANCE. Arrange (assets or securities) according to availability to meet various kinds of claims. L18.
Law Times Clients . . need to be represented by those who are adepts in marshalling facts and handling witnesses.
marshalling yard an area of branching and interconnected railway lines where trains can be assembled from individual trucks etc.
5 *verb trans.* Usher or guide (a person) on his or her way; conduct ceremoniously. L16.
R. CROMPTON Eglantine saw a hedge with a gate in it and marshalled her party through that.
6 *verb trans.* HERALDRY. Combine (two or more coats of arms) in one escutcheon to form a single composition; associate (accessories) with a coat of arms to form a complete achievement. L16.
■ **marshaller** *noun* E17.

Marshalate /ˈmɑːʃ(ə)leɪt/ *noun*. L19.
[ORIGIN from MARSHAL *noun*[1] + -ATE[1].]
1 *hist.* The period of the rule of Marshal MacMahon as President of the French Republic (1873–9). L19.
2 The position or rank of Marshal in the French army. M20.
3 (**m-**.) The position or rank of a marshal. *US*. M20.

marshalcy /ˈmɑːʃ(ə)lsi/ *noun*. ME.
[ORIGIN Anglo-Norman *mareschalcie*, Old French *mareschaucie* from Frankish Latin *mariscalcia* (Anglo-Latin *marescalcia*), from *mariscalcus* MARSHAL *noun*[1] + *-ia* -Y[3]. Cf. MARSHALSEA, MARÉCHAUSSÉE.]
1 The position or rank of marshal. ME.
†**2** A military force under the command of a marshal. Chiefly as translating French *maréchaussée*. LME–M18.
†**3** Farriery. LME–E18.

Marshall /ˈmɑːʃ(ə)l/ *noun*. M20.
[ORIGIN See below.]
Used *attrib.* to designate (aid provided under) a plan initiated in 1947 by George C. Marshall (1880–1959), US Secretary of State, to supply financial assistance to certain western European countries to further their recovery after the Second World War.

Marshallese /mɑːʃəˈliːz/ *noun & adjective*. M20.
[ORIGIN from *Marshall* (see below) + -ESE.]
▸ **A** *noun*. Pl. same.
1 The Micronesian language of the Marshall Islands, a group of islands in the NW Pacific administered by the US under trusteeship of the United Nations. M20.
2 A native or inhabitant of the Marshall Islands. L20.
▸ **B** *adjective*. Of or pertaining to the Marshall Islands or Marshallese. M20.

Marshallian /mɑːˈʃalɪən/ *adjective*. L19.
[ORIGIN from *Marshall* (see below) + -IAN.]
Of or pertaining to the English political economist Alfred Marshall (1842–1924) or his work, esp. his concepts of marginal utility and elasticity of demand.

marshalsea /ˈmɑːʃ(ə)lsiː/ *noun*. LME.
[ORIGIN formed as MARSHALCY, with assim. to SEA *noun*.]
hist. **1** A court formerly held before the steward and the knight marshal of the royal household of England (latterly before a barrister appointed by the knight marshal), orig. to hear cases between the monarch's servants, but afterwards with wider jurisdiction. LME.
2 (**M-**.) A former prison in Southwark, London, under the control of the knight marshal. LME.

marshland /ˈmɑːʃlənd/ *noun*. OE.
[ORIGIN from MARSH *noun*[1] + LAND *noun*[1].]
Land consisting of marshes; marshy country.
■ **marshlander** *noun* a person or animal that lives on marshland L18.

marshmallow /mɑːʃˈmaləʊ/ *noun*. OE.
[ORIGIN from MARSH *noun*[1] + MALLOW.]
1 A shrubby herb, *Althaea officinalis*, of the mallow family, which grows in brackish ditches and has ovate leaves, pale pink flowers, and a mucilaginous root. OE.
2 A soft sweet confection made orig. from the root of this plant, but now from albumen, gelatin, sugar, etc.; a small cake of this. Also (*fig.*), something or someone that is soft at the centre; a sentimental person. L19.
– COMB.: **marshmallow roast** a party at which marshmallows are roasted and served.
■ **marshmallowy** *adjective* sentimental, cloying E20.

marshy /ˈmɑːʃi/ *adjective*. LME.
[ORIGIN from MARSH *noun*[1] + -Y[1].]
1 Pertaining to or of the nature of a marsh; consisting of or containing marshes. LME.
2 Produced in or characteristic of marshland. L17.
■ **marshiness** *noun* E18.

Marsi /ˈmɑːsiː/ *noun pl.* L16.
[ORIGIN Latin.]
hist. A Sabine people who lived near the Fucine Lake in ancient central Italy.

Marsian /ˈmɑːsɪən/ *noun & adjective*. *hist.* L16.
[ORIGIN from MARSI + -IAN.]
▸**A** *noun*. **1** A member of the Marsi. L16.
2 The language of the Marsi. M19.
▸ **B** *adjective*. Of or pertaining to the Marsi or their language. E17.
■ Also **Marsic** *adjective* E17.

†**marsilian** *noun*. M17–M19.
[ORIGIN Italian *marsigliana*, from *Marsiglia* Marseilles.]
A square-sterned Venetian ship.

Marsilid /ˈmɑːsɪlɪd/ *noun*. M20.
[ORIGIN Unknown.]
(Proprietary name for) the drug iproniazid phosphate.

marsipobranch /ˈmɑːsɪpəbraŋk/ *noun & adjective*. L19.
[ORIGIN mod. Latin *Marsipobranchii* (alternative name for the class Agnatha), from Greek *marsipos* (see MARSUPIUM) + *bragkhia* gills.]
ZOOLOGY. = AGNATHAN.
■ Also **marsipoˈbranchiate** *noun & adjective* L19.

marsouin /marswɛ̃/ *noun*. Pl. pronounced same. M16.
[ORIGIN French from Old High German *meriswin* cognate with English *mereswine* s.v. MERE *noun*[1].]
Any of various cetaceans of the family Delphinidae, *esp.* a beluga or (formerly) a porpoise.

marsupial /mɑːˈsuːpɪəl/ *adjective & noun*. L17.
[ORIGIN mod. Latin *marsupialis*, formed as MARSUPIUM: see -AL[1].]
▸ **A** *adjective*. **1** Pertaining to or resembling a marsupium or pouch. L17.
2 Designating, of, or pertaining to a marsupial or the order Marsupialia. E19. ▸**b** Of or pertaining to the pouch of a marsupial. E19.
marsupial mole: see MOLE *noun*[2] 1. **marsupial mouse** any of numerous mouselike carnivorous marsupials of Australia and New Guinea, members of the family Dasyuridae. **b marsupial bone** an epipubic bone.
▸ **B** *noun*. A mammal (e.g. a kangaroo or an opossum) of the order Marsupialia, characterized by young that are born imperfectly developed and are usu. carried after birth in a pouch on the mother's belly, over the mammilae. M19.
■ **marsupialiˈzation** *noun* (MEDICINE) the action of marsupializing a cyst etc.; the surgical formation of a pouch: L19. **marsupialize** *verb trans.* (MEDICINE) surgically convert (a cyst etc.) into a pouch by making a permanent wide opening to the exterior L19. **marsupian**, **marsupiate** *adjectives & nouns* = MARSUPIAL M19.

M

marsupite /ˈmɑːsjʊpʌɪt/ *noun*. E19.
[ORIGIN mod. Latin *marsupites*, formed as MARSUPIUM: see -ITE¹.]
PALAEONTOLOGY. A fossil crinoid whose shell resembles a purse.

marsupium /mɑːˈsuːpɪəm/ *noun*. Pl. **-ia** /-ɪə/. M17.
[ORIGIN Latin (also *-pp-*) from Greek *marsupion*, *-sipion* dim. of *marsipos* purse.]
ZOOLOGY & MEDICINE. A structure resembling a bag or pouch; *spec*. (**a**) the pouch of a female marsupial; †(**b**) the pecten of a bird's eye.

mart /mɑːt/ *noun*¹. ME.
[ORIGIN Dutch †*mart* var. of *markt* MARKET *noun*.]
1 A periodical gathering of people for the purpose of buying and selling, esp. (in early use) in the Low Countries; a market. ME.
> M. BINCHY He went to Mass on a Sunday as regularly as . . to the marts to buy sheep.

†**2** Buying and selling; trade. Also, a bargain. M16–M17.
3 An auction room; a tradesman's shop or stall; (now *poet*. & *rhet*.) any public place for buying and selling. L16.
> D. H. LAWRENCE She puts me away like a saleswoman whose mart is Endangered by the pilferer.

4 A city, region, or locality where things are bought and sold; a centre of trade. E17.

mart /mɑːt/ *noun*². *Scot. & N. English*. ME.
[ORIGIN Gaelic & Irish.]
1 An ox or cow fattened for slaughter. ME.
†**2** A carcass, a slaughtered animal. Only in LME.

mart /mart/ *noun*³. *hist*. L16.
[ORIGIN Alt., app. infl. by MART *noun*¹.]
= MARQUE *noun*¹.

mart /mɑːt/ *noun*⁴. Chiefly *dial*. E18.
[ORIGIN Back-form. from FOUMART.]
A marten; *esp*. (also ***sweet-mart***) the pine marten. Cf. FOUMART.

†**mart** *verb*. L16–L18.
[ORIGIN from MART *noun*¹.]
1 *verb trans*. Make merchandise of, deal in. L16–L18.
2 *verb intrans*. Do business at a mart; bargain. Only in E17.

Martaban /ˈmɑːtəban/ *noun*. Also **-bani** /-ˈbani/. L16.
[ORIGIN See below.]
(Designating) a kind of glazed pottery, used esp. for jars or pots, made at Martaban, a town in the district of Pegu in Myanmar (Burma).

M

martagon /ˈmɑːtəg(ə)n/ *noun*. LME.
[ORIGIN French from Turkish *marṭağān* form of turban worn by Sultan Mehmed I.]
More fully ***martagon lily***. A Eurasian lily, *Lilium martagon*, bearing dull purplish-red nodding flowers with reflexed perianth segments (also called ***Turk's-cap lily***). Also, any of several similar lilies.

martel /ˈmɑːt(ə)l/ *noun & verb*. ME.
[ORIGIN Old French (mod. *marteau*) from medieval Latin *martellus* from Latin *martulus* var. of *marculus* small hammer: see -EL².]
▸ **A** *noun*. *hist*. A hammer, *esp*. one used in war. ME.
▸ †**B** *verb intrans*. Infl. **-ll-**. Rain blows *on*. *rare* (Spenser). Only in L16.

martelé /ˈmɑːt(ə)leɪ/ *adjective, adverb, & noun*. L19.
[ORIGIN French, pa. pple of *marteler* to hammer.]
MUSIC. With ref. to bowed stringed instruments: = MARTELLATO.

martellato /mɑːtɪˈlɑːtəʊ/ *adjective, adverb, & noun*. L19.
[ORIGIN Italian, pa. pple of *martellare* to hammer.]
MUSIC. ▸**A** *adjective & adverb*. (Played) with notes heavily accented and left before their full time has expired. L19.
▸ **B** *noun*. Martellato playing. M20.

Martello /mɑːˈtɛləʊ/ *noun*. Pl. **-os**. E19.
[ORIGIN Alt. (by assoc. with Italian *martello* hammer) of Cape *Mortella* in Corsica, where such a tower proved difficult for the English to capture in 1794.]
In full ***Martello tower***. A small circular fort with very thick walls, *esp*. any of those erected in Britain as a coastal defence during the Napoleonic Wars.

martemper /ˈmɑːtɛmpə/ *verb trans*. M20.
[ORIGIN from MAR(TENSITE + TEMPER *verb*¹.]
METALLURGY. Temper (steel) by quenching rapidly to a temperature just above that at which martensite begins to form, allowing the temperature to stabilize, and then cooling slowly, esp. so that the austenite/martensite transformation is isothermal. Chiefly as ***martempering*** *verbal noun*.

marten /ˈmɑːtɪn/ *noun*. ME.
[ORIGIN Middle Dutch *martren* from Old French *martrine* use as noun (sc. *peau* skin) of *martrin*, from *martre* from West Germanic (whence also Old High German *mardar*, German *Marder*), extended form of Germanic base of Old English *mearþ*, Old Norse *mǫrðr*. Cf. MARTER.]
1 The fur or dressed skin of a marten. Formerly freq. in *pl*. ME.
2 Any of several bushy-tailed arboreal mustelid mammals of the genus *Martes*, found in forests of Eurasia and N. America. Also †***marten cat***. LME.
pine marten: see PINE *noun*². ***stone marten***: see STONE *noun, adjective, & adverb*.

Martenot /ˈmɑːt(ə)nəʊ/ *noun*. Pl. same, **-s**. M20.
[ORIGIN from *Martinot*: see ONDES MARTENOT.]
= ONDES MARTENOT.

martensite /ˈmɑːtɪnzʌɪt/ *noun*. L19.
[ORIGIN from A. *Martens* (1850–1914), German metallurgist + -ITE¹.]
METALLURGY. A hard, very brittle solid solution of carbon in iron, formed from austenite when steel is quenched very rapidly.
▪ **martensitic** /mɑːtɪnˈzɪtɪk/ *adjective* pertaining to or containing martensite; involving the formation of martensite (from austenite): E20. **marten'sitically** *adverb* L20.

†**marter** *noun*. ME–L16.
[ORIGIN French *martre*: see MARTEN.]
(The fur or dressed skin of) a marten.

Martha /ˈmɑːθə/ *noun*. ME.
[ORIGIN Female forename, with allus. to *Luke* 10:38–42.]
An active or busy woman, much concerned with domestic affairs; in Christian allegory, used as a symbol of the active life. Opp. MARY 4.

Martha Gunn /mɑːθə ˈgʌn/ *noun*. E20.
[ORIGIN *Martha Gunn* (1727–1815), a female bathing attendant celebrated for having dipped the Prince of Wales in the sea at Brighton.]
A jug in the form of a woman, analogous to a toby jug. Also ***Martha Gunn jug***.

martial /ˈmɑːʃ(ə)l/ *adjective*. LME.
[ORIGIN Old French & mod. French, or Latin *martialis*, from *Mart-*, MARS: see -AL¹, -IAL.]
1 a Of or pertaining to war or battle; (of music) appropriate to warfare. LME. ▸**b** Of sports, exercises, etc.: serving as training for warfare. LME.
2 Warlike; brave, valiant; fond of fighting. LME.
3 Of or pertaining to the army or the military profession; military rather than civil. *obsolete* exc. in COURT MARTIAL. L15.
4 Characteristic of or suitable for a warrior. L16.
†**5** Of, pertaining to, or characteristic of the Roman god Mars. *rare* (Shakes.). Only in E17.
6 (Usu. **M-**.) Of or pertaining to the planet Mars, Martian; *ASTROLOGY* influenced by Mars; (of an animal or plant) poisonous, stinging. Now *rare* or *obsolete*. E17.
†**7** *CHEMISTRY*. Of or pertaining to iron; containing iron. L17–L19.
– SPECIAL COLLOCATIONS: **martial art** any of various sports or skills, mainly of Japanese origin, which originated as forms of self-defence or attack, such as judo, karate, and kendo (usu. in *pl*.). **martial eagle** a large crested eagle, *Polemaetus bellicosus*, of central and southern Africa. **martial law** (**a**) government of a country or district by military authority, with ordinary civil laws suspended; †(**b**) military law.
▪ **martialism** *noun* warlike quality E17. **martialist** *noun* (**a**) a person skilled in war; a military man; †(**b**) *ASTROLOGY* a person born under the influence of Mars: M16. **marti'ality** *noun* martial quality or state M17. **martialize** *verb trans*. (*rare*) make martial E17. **martially** *adverb* L16. **martialness** *noun* E18.

Martian /ˈmɑːʃ(ə)n/ *adjective & noun*. LME.
[ORIGIN Old French *martien* or Latin *Martianus*, from *Marti-*, MARS: see -IAN.]
▸ **A** *adjective*. †**1** Of or pertaining to war or battle. LME–L16.
2 Of or pertaining to the month of March. E17.
3 Of or pertaining to the planet Mars or its (imagined) inhabitants. L19.
▸ **B** *noun*. An (imagined) inhabitant of Mars. L19.

martin /ˈmɑːtɪn/ *noun*¹. E16.
[ORIGIN Male forename, prob. a use of the name of St *Martin* of Tours: see MARTINMAS. Cf. MARTIN *noun*².]
1 Any of various typically short-tailed birds belonging to the swallow family Hirundinidae or (*dial*.) otherwise resembling the swallow. E16.
bank martin, ***bee-martin***, ***fairy martin***, ***house martin***, ***sand martin***, etc.
†**2** A dupe. L16–E17.
– COMB.: **martin-box** *US* a box or coop for martins to build in; **martin bug** a bloodsucking bug, *Oeciacus hirundinis*, whose principal host is the house martin; **martin-house** *US* = ***martin-box*** above.

Martin /ˈmɑːtɪn/ *noun*². M17.
[ORIGIN from St *Martin*: see MARTINMAS. Cf. MARTIN *noun*¹.]
Orig. more fully †***dry Martin***, †***Martin dry***. A variety of pear, so called from being ripe at Martinmas.

martinet *noun*¹. /ˈmɑːtɪnɪt/ LME.
[ORIGIN French, dim. of male forename *Martin*: see -ET¹. Cf. MARTLET *noun*¹.]
†**1** A martin; a swift. LME–M19.
2 A student at the medieval University of Paris who did not belong to a college. *hist*. M19.

martinet /ˈmɑːtɪnɪt/ *noun*². L15.
[ORIGIN Old French & mod. French in various unconnected senses, perh. belonging to etymologically distinct words.]
†**1** A watermill for an iron forge. Only in L15.
†**2** A small cart. Only in L15.
3 A military engine for throwing large stones. *obsolete* exc. *hist*. E16.

martinet /mɑːtɪˈnɛt/ *noun*³. L17.
[ORIGIN *Martinet* (see below).]
†**1** The system of drill invented by J. Martinet, 17th-cent. French drill master. Only in L17.
2 A military or naval officer who is a stickler for strictness of discipline; a rigid disciplinarian. M18.
▪ **martinetism** *noun* the spirit or action characteristic of a martinet E19.

martineta /mɑːtɪˈneɪtə/ *noun*. L19.
[ORIGIN Amer. Spanish prob. from Spanish *martinete* night heron.]
A tinamou, *Eudromia elegans*, of S. Argentina.

martinettish /mɑːtɪˈnɛtɪʃ/ *adjective*. Also **-etish**. M19.
[ORIGIN from MARTINET *noun*³ + -ISH¹.]
Having the characteristics of a martinet.

martingale /ˈmɑːtɪŋgeɪl/ *noun & verb*. L16.
[ORIGIN French, in *chausse à la martingale* kind of hose fastening at the back, perh. from mod. Provençal *marte(n)galo* fem. of *marte(n)gal* inhabitant of Martigues in Provence.]
▸ **A** *noun*. **1** A strap or arrangement of straps fastened at one end to the noseband, bit, or reins of a horse and at the other to its girth, to prevent it from rearing or throwing back its head and to strengthen the action of the bit. L16.
Irish martingale, ***running martingale***, ***standing martingale***, etc.
2 *NAUTICAL*. A stay which holds down the jib boom of a square-rigged ship, running from the boom to the dolphin-striker (also ***martingale-stay***); a dolphin-striker. Also, in a dinghy, a rope running from the boom to the foot of the mast, to prevent the boom from rising when it swings outwards. L18.
3 A gambling system in which a player who is losing repeatedly doubles the stake in the hope of eventual recoupment. E19.
▸ **B** *verb*. †**1** *verb trans*. Restrain (a horse) with a martingale. Only in E17.
2 *verb intrans*. Gamble according to a martingale. E19.
3 *verb trans*. *NAUTICAL*. Secure with a martingale or guy. L19.

martingana /mɑːtɪŋˈgɑːnə/ *noun*. E19.
[ORIGIN Sicilian Italian.]
A kind of boat used in Sicily.

Martini /mɑːˈtiːni/ *noun*¹. L19.
[ORIGIN See below.]
In full ***Martini rifle*** (also ***Martini–Henry*** (***rifle***) [see HENRY *noun*¹]). A rifle used in the British army from 1871 to 1891, combining a breech mechanism invented by Friedrich von Martini with a .45-calibre barrel devised by Benjamin Tyler Henry.

Martini /mɑːˈtiːni/ *noun*². Also **m-**. L19.
[ORIGIN *Martini* & Rossi, Italian firm selling vermouth; as cocktail perh. of different origin.]
(Proprietary name for) a type of vermouth. Also, a cocktail consisting of gin and dry vermouth, sometimes with the addition of orange bitters.
dry Martini *spec*. a Martini containing more gin than vermouth.

Martiniquan /mɑːtɪˈniːk(ə)n/ *noun & adjective*. Also **-ican**. L19.
[ORIGIN from *Martinique* (see below) + -AN.]
▸ **A** *noun*. A native or inhabitant of Martinique, an island in the W. Indies. L19.
▸ **B** *adjective*. Of or pertaining to Martinique or the Martiniquans. E20.
▪ **Martiniquais** /mɑːtɪˈniːkeɪ/ *noun & adjective* (**a**) *noun* (pl. same) = MARTINIQUAN *noun*; (**b**) *adjective* = MARTINIQUAN *adjective*: L19.

Martinist /ˈmɑːtɪnɪst/ *noun*. L16.
[ORIGIN from *Martin* (see below) + -IST.]
1 *hist*. A supporter of 'Martin Marprelate', the writer or writers of certain controversial tracts published in 1588–9. L16.
2 A member of a school of mystics founded by L. C. de Saint-Martin (1743–1803). L19.
▪ **Martinism** *noun* (**a**) *hist*. the tenets of 'Martin Marprelate'; (**b**) the system of L. C. de Saint-Martin: L16.

Martinmas /ˈmɑːtɪnməs/ *noun*. ME.
[ORIGIN from St *Martin* (see sense 1) + MASS *noun*¹.]
1 (The date, 11 November, of) the feast of St Martin, 4th-cent. Bishop of Tours and patron saint of France, formerly the usual time in England for hiring servants and slaughtering cattle to be salted for the winter and still one of the Scottish quarter days. ME.
†**2** A person one despises. *rare* (Shakes.). Only in L16.
– COMB.: †**Martinmas beef**, †**Martinmas flesh**, †**Martinmas meat** the meat of an ox salted at Martinmas.

Martinware /ˈmɑːtɪnwɛː/ *noun*. L19.
[ORIGIN from *Martin* (see below) + WARE *noun*².]
A type of brown, salt-glazed, freq. elaborately modelled pottery made by the Martin brothers in Southall, now part of London, in the late 19th and early 20th cents.

martlet /ˈmɑːtlɪt/ *noun*¹. LME.
[ORIGIN French *martelet* alt. of *martinet*: see MARTINET *noun*¹.]
1 A swift; a swallow, a house martin. *arch*. LME.
2 *HERALDRY*. A bird with tufts of feathers for legs and no feet, borne as a charge. LME.

†**martlet** *noun*². LME–L19.
[ORIGIN Alt. of MARTRET.]
(The fur or dressed skin of) a marten.

†**martly** *adverb.* E17–E18.
[ORIGIN from MART *noun*[1] + -LY[2].]
At the time of each mart or fair.

†**martret** *noun.* Only in LME.
[ORIGIN from MARTER + -ET[1].]
A polecat.

martynia /mɑːˈtɪnɪə/ *noun.* M18.
[ORIGIN mod. Latin (see below), from John *Martyn* (1699–1768), English botanist: see -IA[1].]
A Mexican plant, *Martynia annua* (family Pedaliaceae), with viscid hairy stems, campanulate corollas, and long-beaked fruits which are sometimes pickled.

martyr /ˈmɑːtə/ *noun & verb.*
[ORIGIN Old English *martir* = Old Frisian, Old Saxon, Old High German *martir*, from ecclesiastical Latin *martyr* from Greek *martur*.]
▶ **A** *noun.* **1** A person who voluntarily undergoes the death penalty for refusing to renounce the Christian faith or a Christian doctrine, for persevering in a Christian virtue, or for obeying a law of the Church. OE.
2 A person who undergoes death or great suffering on behalf of any religious or other cause, or as a consequence of devotion to some object. (Foll. by *to*.) OE.
3 A person who suffers tortures comparable to those described in the legends of martyrs; a constant sufferer. (Foll. by *to* an ailment, etc.) M16. ▸**b** A person who dies a victim *to* something. L18.

Law Times The deceased . . had been a martyr for years to rheumatic gout.

4 A person who displays or exaggerates their discomfort or distress in order to obtain sympathy. L19.

R. CROMPTON She broke off with the sigh of a patient martyr as William came in.

– PHRASES: **make a martyr of** (now freq. *joc.*) subject to hardship or inconvenience.
▶ **B** *verb trans.* **1** Put to death as a martyr; make a martyr of. OE.
†**2** Kill, esp. by a cruel death. ME–L18.
3 Inflict severe suffering or pain on; torment. ME.
4 a Spoil; bespatter; bungle, mismanage. Long *obsolete* exc. *Scot. & dial.* LME. ▸†**b** Inflict wounds or disfiguring blows on; mutilate; disfigure. M16–M17.
■ **martyred** *adjective* that has been martyred, made to suffer martyrdom; expressive of martyrdom: M16. **martyrial** /mɑːˈtɪrɪəl/ *adjective* (*rare*) befitting a martyr L17. **martyrish** *adjective* having the air of a martyr L19.

martyrdom /ˈmɑːtədəm/ *noun.* OE.
[ORIGIN from MARTYR + -DOM.]
1 The sufferings and death of a martyr; the act of becoming or the condition of being a martyr. OE.

J. A. FROUDE Encouraging catholics to persevere to martyrdom for their faith. B. GELDOF 'That's what I'm giving up,' I said with an expression of insufferable martyrdom.

†**2** Slaughter. Esp. in ***make martyrdom***. ME–L15.
3 Severe pain or suffering; torment. ME.

martyrion /mɑːˈtɪrɪən/ *noun.* Also in Latin form **-ium** /-ɪəm/. Pl. of both **-ia** /-ɪə/. M17.
[ORIGIN Greek.]
A shrine, oratory, or church built in memory of a martyr; a building marking the place of a martyrdom or the site of a martyr's relics.

martyrize /ˈmɑːtərʌɪz/ *verb.* Also **-ise**. LME.
[ORIGIN Late Latin *martyrizare*, from ecclesiastical Latin *martyr*: see MARTYR, -IZE.]
1 *verb trans.* = MARTYR *verb* 1. Now *rare.* LME.
2 *verb intrans.* Be or become a martyr. *rare.* LME.
3 *verb trans.* = MARTYR *verb* 3. M17.

E. BOWEN He looked at me and said: 'Go!' . . I saw that my presence martyrised him.

†**4** *verb trans.* = MARTYR *verb* 4b. M17–E18.
5 *verb trans.* Cause to suffer hardship on behalf of a cause. M19.

A. MORRISON She proceeded to martyrize herself by a show of 'setting to rights' in the room.

■ **martyriˈzation** *noun* the action of making a martyr of someone L15.

martyrly /ˈmɑːtəli/ *adjective. rare.* M17.
[ORIGIN from MARTYR + -LY[1].]
Resembling or characteristic of a martyr.

martyrly /ˈmɑːtəli/ *adverb. rare.* E19.
[ORIGIN from MARTYR + -LY[2].]
In a manner befitting a martyr.

martyrolatry /mɑːtəˈrɒlətri/ *noun.* L19.
[ORIGIN from MARTYR + -O- + -LATRY.]
Excessive reverence for martyrs.

martyrology /mɑːtəˈrɒlədʒi/ *noun.* L16.
[ORIGIN In sense 1 from medieval Latin *martyrologium* from ecclesiastical Greek *marturologion*, from *martur* (see MARTYR) + *logos* discourse: see -LOGY. In sense 2 from MARTYR + -OLOGY.]
1 A list or account of martyrs; *spec.* a book listing Christian martyrs and other saints in the order of their commemoration, with a description of their lives and sufferings. L16.
2 The branch of history or literature that deals with the lives of martyrs; histories of martyrs collectively. E19.
■ **martyrologe** *noun* (*rare*) [French] = MARTYROLOGY E16. **martyroˈlogical** *adjective* M17. **martyrologist** *noun* L17.

martyry /ˈmɑːtəri/ *noun.* ME.
[ORIGIN medieval Latin *martyrium* from Greek *marturion* witness, martyrdom, from *martur*: see MARTYR, -Y[4].]
†**1** Martyrdom; suffering, torment. ME–L17.
2 = MARTYRION. E18.

marudi /məˈruːdi/ *noun.* Also **-oodi**. M18.
[ORIGIN Arawak *marodi*.]
In Guyana, a guan (bird).

marula /məˈruːlə/ *noun.* Also **maroela**, **merula**, & other vars. M19.
[ORIGIN Afrikaans from Setswana, Sesotho *morula*.]
A central and southern African tree, *Sclerocarya birrea* subsp. *caffra* (family Anacardiaceae), bearing an oval yellow fruit used locally to make beer; the fruit of this tree.

marum /ˈmɛːrəm/ *noun. arch.* M17.
[ORIGIN Latin from Greek *maron*.]
Either of two aromatic labiate plants of the Iberian peninsula, *Thymus mastichina* (see MASTIC *noun* 3) and *Teucrium marum*, formerly used in medicine to induce sneezing.

marv /mɑːv/ *adjective. slang.* M20.
[ORIGIN Abbreviation.]
Marvellous.

marvel /ˈmɑːv(ə)l/ *noun*[1]. ME.
[ORIGIN Old French & mod. French *merveille* from Proto-Romance use as sing. noun of Latin *mirabilia* neut. pl. of *mirabilis* wonderful, from *mirari* wonder at. Cf. MARL *noun*[2].]
1 A wonderful or astonishing thing; a cause of surprise, admiration, or wonder. ME.

G. HARRIS The blind singer who spoke so vividly of the marvels of the north. R. INGALLS She's a marvel at discipline.

†**2** A wonderful story or legend. ME–L15.
3 Wonder, astonishment, surprise, admiration. *arch.* ME.
†**4** A miracle. ME–L16.
– PHRASES: **marvel of Peru** a tropical American plant, *Mirabilis jalapa* (family Nyctaginaceae), with funnel-shaped flowers of various colours which open at dusk; also called ***false jalap***, ***four o'clock flower***, ***pretty-by-night***.

marvel /ˈmɑːv(ə)l/ *noun*[2]. Chiefly *dial.* M18.
[ORIGIN Alt.]
A marble.

marvel /ˈmɑːv(ə)l/ *verb.* Infl. **-ll-**, ***-l-**. LME.
[ORIGIN Old French & mod. French *merveiller*, formed as MARVEL *noun*[1]. Cf. MARL *verb*[3].]
1 *verb intrans.* & †*trans.* (*refl.* & in *pass.*) Be filled with wonder or astonishment; be struck with surprise. (Foll. by *at*, *that*, *to do*.) LME.

G. HARRIS Kerish marvelled to find this ancient custom . . still kept. M. FORSTER Elizabeth . . marvelled at his self-control.

2 *verb intrans.* & †*trans.* (*refl.* & in *pass.*) Feel astonished curiosity; ask oneself wonderingly. Foll. by interrog. clause. LME.
†**3** *verb trans.* Wonder or be astonished at. Freq. in *pass.* with clause attached. LME–M19.
4 *verb trans.* Cause to wonder; astonish. Now *rare.* LME.
■ **marveller** *noun* a person given to marvelling M16. **marvellingly** *adverb* in a marvelling manner, with wonder or astonishment L19.

marvellous /ˈmɑːv(ə)ləs/ *adjective, adverb, & noun.* Also ***marvelous**. ME.
[ORIGIN Old French *merveillos* (mod. *merveilleux*), from *merveille*: see MARVEL *noun*[1], -OUS.]
▶ **A** *adjective.* **1** Such as to excite wonder or astonishment; wonderful, astonishing; excellent. ME.

A. GERAS Yasha looks like a child opening a marvellous gift. E. O'NEILL The play was such a marvelous success!

2 Of poetry etc.: concerned with the supernatural. E18.
– SPECIAL COLLOCATIONS: **marvellous apple** = ***balsam apple*** s.v. BALSAM *noun*.
▶ **B** *adverb.* Marvellously; excellently. *arch.* ME.
▶ **C** *noun.* ***the marvellous***, that which is marvellous; *esp.* the prodigious or extravagantly improbable. *arch.* M18.
■ **marvellously** *adverb* ME. **marvellousness** *noun* M16.

marver /ˈmɑːvə/ *noun & verb.* M19.
[ORIGIN French *marbre* MARBLE *noun*.]
▶ **A** *noun.* A polished slab of marble or iron on which glass-blowers roll and shape hot glass under the blowpipe. M19.
▶ **B** *verb trans.* Roll (glass) on a marver. M19.

Marwari /mɑːˈwɑːri/ *noun & adjective.* E19.
[ORIGIN Marathi *Mārvāṛī* from Sanskrit *maru* desert, wilderness.]
▶ **A** *noun.* Pl. **-s**, same.
1 A native or inhabitant of Marwar, a region now part of the state of Rajasthan in NW India. E19.
2 The dialect of Rajasthani used in Marwar. L19.
▶ **B** *adjective.* Of or pertaining to Marwar. M19.

Marxian /ˈmɑːksɪən/ *adjective*[1] *& noun*[1]. L19.
[ORIGIN from *Marx* (see MARXISM *noun*[1]) + -IAN.]
▶ **A** *adjective.* Of or pertaining to the political and economic theories of Karl Marx. L19.
▶ **B** *noun.* A follower or adherent of the political and economic theories of Karl Marx. L19.
■ **Marxianism** *noun* adherence to Marxian doctrines or theories L19.

Marxian /ˈmɑːksɪən/ *adjective*[2] *& noun*[2]. M20.
[ORIGIN from *Marx* (see below) + -IAN.]
▶ **A** *adjective.* Of, pertaining to, or characteristic of the Marx Brothers (Chico, Harpo, Groucho, and Zeppo), 20th-cent. US comedians. M20.
▶ **B** *noun.* An admirer or student of the Marx Brothers or their films. M20.

Marxisant /marksizɑ̃/ *adjective.* Also **m-**. M20.
[ORIGIN French, from *Marxiste* MARXIST *noun*[1] & *adjective*[1] + *-ant* -ANT[1].]
Having Marxist leanings.

Marxise *verb* var. of MARXIZE.

Marxism /ˈmɑːksɪz(ə)m/ *noun*[1]. L19.
[ORIGIN from *Marx* (see below) + -ISM, perh. through French *Marxisme*, German *Marxismus*.]
The political and economic theories of the German-born writer Karl Marx (1818–83), esp. that, as labour is basic to wealth, historical development must lead to the violent overthrow of the capitalist class and the taking over of the means of production by the proletariat, in accordance with scientific laws determined by dialectical materialism.
– COMB.: **Marxism–Leninism** the doctrines of Marx as interpreted and put into effect by Lenin; Leninism; official Communist interpretation of the doctrines of Marx as implemented by Lenin, developed as a set of principles to guide policy and behaviour.

Marxism /ˈmɑːksɪz(ə)m/ *noun*[2]. M20.
[ORIGIN formed as MARXIAN *adjective*[2] & *noun*[2] + -ISM.]
The type of comedy performed by the Marx Brothers; a witticism typical of the Marx Brothers.

Marxist /ˈmɑːksɪst/ *noun*[1] *& adjective*[1]. L19.
[ORIGIN formed as MARXISM *noun*[1] + -IST.]
▶ **A** *noun.* A follower of Karl Marx's political and economic theories; a member of a political organization, with international affiliations, based on Marxism. L19.
▶ **B** *adjective.* Of or pertaining to Marxism or Marxists; advocating Marxism. L19.
– COMB.: **Marxist–Leninism** = ***Marxism–Leninism*** s.v. MARXISM *noun*[1]; **Marxist–Leninist** *adjective* of, pertaining to, or characteristic of Marxism–Leninism.
■ **Marˈxistically** *adverb* M20.

Marxist /ˈmɑːksɪst/ *noun*[2] *& adjective*[2]. M20.
[ORIGIN formed as MARXIAN *adjective*[2] & *noun*[2] + -IST.]
= MARXIAN *adjective*[2] & *noun*[2].

Marxite /ˈmɑːksʌɪt/ *adjective & noun.* Now *rare.* L19.
[ORIGIN formed as MARXISM *noun*[1] + -ITE[1].]
= MARXIST *noun*[1] & *adjective*[1].

Marxize /ˈmɑːksʌɪz/ *verb.* Also **-ise**. M20.
[ORIGIN formed as MARXITE + -IZE.]
1 *verb trans.* Form or adapt in accordance with the doctrines of Karl Marx; give a Marxist character to. M20.
2 *verb intrans.* Follow or advocate Marxism. M20.

Mary /ˈmɛːri/ *noun.* Pl. **Marys**. OE.
[ORIGIN Female forename from ecclesiastical Latin *Maria* (partly through Old French & mod. French *Marie*) from Greek *Maria*, *Mariam* from Hebrew *miryām* Miriam.]
1 The name of the mother of Jesus, also called the (Blessed) Virgin Mary, or Saint Mary, used in oaths. Cf. MARRY *interjection*. OE.
Holy Mary!, ***by Saint Mary!***, etc.
2 [With allus. to *Luke* 10:38–42.] A contemplative or intellectual woman; in Christian allegory, used as a symbol of the contemplative life. Opp. MARTHA. ME.
3 A woman, *esp.* an Aboriginal woman. *Austral. slang.* M19.
4 A homosexual man. *slang.* E20.
– COMB. & PHRASES: ***Joseph and Mary***: see JOSEPH *noun* 1(b); ***Little Mary***: see LITTLE *adjective*; **Mary Ann** (**a**) *slang* a taximeter; (**b**) *slang* marijuana; (**c**) see sense 4 above; †**Mary-bud** the bud of a marigold; **Mary Jane** *slang* marijuana; **Mary lily** the Madonna lily, *Lilium candidum*; **Mary Queen of Scots cap** a Mary Stuart cap; **Mary Warner** *slang* marijuana; ***muscle Mary***: see MUSCLE *noun*[1]; ***Queen Mary***: see QUEEN *noun*; ***Typhoid Mary***: see TYPHOID *adjective*; ***Virgin Mary***: see VIRGIN *noun*.

Maryland /ˈmɛːrɪland/ *noun.* E18.
[ORIGIN from MARY (after Henrietta *Maria* (1609–69) Queen Consort of King Charles I) + LAND *noun*[1].]
Used ***attrib.*** to designate things found in or associated with Maryland, a state of the eastern US.
Maryland chicken (also **chicken Maryland**, **chicken à la Maryland**) a piece of chicken covered in breadcrumbs and fried, and served with sweetcorn and bacon. ***Maryland yellowthroat***: see ***yellowthroat*** s.v. YELLOW *adjective*.
■ **Marylander** *noun* a native or inhabitant of Maryland M17.

Marymass /ˈmarɪmas, ˈmɛːrɪ-/ *noun.* Now *Scot. dial.* ME.
[ORIGIN from MARY + MASS *noun*[1].]
CHRISTIAN CHURCH. **1** A festival of the Virgin Mary, *esp.* the Assumption, 15 August, or (formerly) Candlemas, 2 February. ME.

M

2 A mass in honour of the Virgin Mary. Chiefly in the oath ***by the Marymass***. *hist.* **M16.**

Marys *noun* pl. of **MARY.**

Mary Stuart /mɛːrɪ ˈstjuːət/ *noun & adjective.* **M19.**
[**ORIGIN** See below.]
(Designating) a style of clothes, hair, etc., similar to those worn by Mary Stuart, Queen of Scots (1542–87), *spec.* head-gear with a central dip or peak over the forehead.

marzacotto /mɑːtsəˈkɒtəʊ, mɑːz-/ *noun.* Pl. **-os. L19.**
[**ORIGIN** Italian.]
A transparent glaze used by Italian majolica workers.

marzipan /ˈmɑːzɪpan, mɑːzɪˈpan/ *noun & adjective.* Also (*arch.*) **marchpane** /ˈmɑːtʃpeɪn/. **M16.**
[**ORIGIN** German, earlier *marcipan* alt. (as if from Latin *Marci panis* Mark's bread) of *marczapan* from Italian *marzapane*.]
▸ **A** *noun.* A paste of ground almonds, sugar, etc., made up into small cakes or used as a coating on large cakes; a cake or shaped piece of this. **M16.**
▸ †**B** *adjective.* Dainty, delicate. **E–L17.**
– **COMB.:** **marzipan layer** *FINANCE* (*slang*) the (tier of) executives ranking immediately below the partners in a firm.
■ **marzipanned** *adjective* covered with marzipan **L20.**

Mas /mas/ *noun*[1]. Also **Mas'**, (esp. repr. *black English*) **Marse** /mɑːs/. **L16.**
[**ORIGIN** Abbreviation of **MASTER** *noun*[1].]
Master; mister.
– **COMB.:** **Mas John** *joc. & derog., arch.* a Scottish Presbyterian minister, in contrast to an Anglican or Roman Catholic one.

mas /mɑs/ *noun*[2]. Pl. same. **E20.**
[**ORIGIN** Provençal.]
A farm, house, or cottage in the south of France.

mas /mɑːs/ *noun*[3]. *W. Indian.* **M20.**
[**ORIGIN** Abbreviation of **MASQUERADE.**]
(A) carnival, (a) festival; a procession, a parade.

Mas' *noun* see **MAS** *noun*[1].

masa /ˈmasa/ *noun.* **E20.**
[**ORIGIN** Spanish.]
In Central and S. American cuisine, a type of dough made from cornmeal and used to make tortillas etc.

Masai /ˈmɑːsʌɪ, məˈsʌɪ, mɑːˈsʌɪ/ *noun & adjective.* Also **Maas-. M19.**
[**ORIGIN** Masai.]
▸ **A** *noun.* Pl. same.
1 A member of a pastoral people inhabiting parts of Kenya and Tanzania. **M19.**
2 The Nilotic language of this people. **M19.**
▸ **B** *attrib.* or as *adjective.* Of or pertaining to the Masai or their language. **M19.**

masala /məˈsɑːlə/ *noun.* **L18.**
[**ORIGIN** Urdu *masālā*, var. of *maṣāliḥ* from Persian *maṣāliḥ* from Arabic *maṣāliḥ*, pl. of *maṣlaḥa* source of improvement.]
1 Any of various spice mixtures ground into a paste or powder for use in Indian cookery; a dish flavoured with this. Cf. **GARAM MASALA. L18.**
2 *fig.* A person or thing that comprises a varied mixture of elements. **L20.**

masalchi *noun* var. of **MUSSALCHEE.**

Masarwa /məˈsɑːwə/ *noun & adjective. S. Afr.* **M19.**
[**ORIGIN** African name.]
▸ **A** *noun.* Pl. same. A member of a Bushman people inhabiting the N. Kalahari desert. **M19.**
▸ **B** *adjective.* Of or pertaining to this people. **L19.**

mascara /maˈskɑːrə/ *noun & verb.* **L19.**
[**ORIGIN** Italian *mascara*, *maschera* **MASK** *noun*[2].]
▸ **A** *noun.* A cosmetic for darkening and colouring the eyelashes. **L19.**
▸ **B** *verb trans.* Put mascara on. **M20.**

mascaret /maskare/ *noun.* Pl. pronounced same. **M17.**
[**ORIGIN** French from Gascon dial. = spotted cow, from *mascara* (cf. Provençal *mascarar*, Old French *mascurer*, French *mâchurer* daub, black the face), app. with allus. to the bore's resemblance to the movement of running cattle.]
In France, a tidal bore.

mascaron /maskarɔ̃ (*pl. same*), ˈmaskər(ə)n/ *noun.* **M17.**
[**ORIGIN** French from Italian *mascherone*, from *maschera* **MASK** *noun*[2].]
In decorative art, a grotesque face or mask.

mascarpone /maskəˈpəʊneɪ, -ˈpəʊni/ *noun.* **E20.**
[**ORIGIN** Italian.]
A soft mild Italian cream cheese.

mascle /ˈmɑːsk(ə)l/ *noun.* **ME.**
[**ORIGIN** Anglo-Norman from Anglo-Latin *ma(s)cula* alt. of Latin *macula* **MAIL** *noun*[2] by assoc. with **MASK** *noun*[1].]
†**1** A spot, a speck. Only in **ME.**
†**2** The mesh of a net. **ME–L17.**
3 *HERALDRY.* A charge in the form of a lozenge with a lozenge-shaped opening through which the field appears. **LME.**
4 *hist.* Any of the perforated lozenge-shaped plates of metal fastened to the outer surface of 13th-cent. military tunics. **E19.**
■ **mascled** *adjective* covered with mascles **LME.**

mascon /ˈmaskɒn/ *noun.* **M20.**
[**ORIGIN** from *mass concentration*.]
ASTRONOMY. Any of the concentrations of denser material thought to exist under some lunar maria; a similar thing on another planet.

mascot /ˈmaskɒt/ *noun.* **L19.**
[**ORIGIN** French *mascotte* from mod. Provençal *mascotto* fem. of *mascot* dim. of *masco* witch: see **-OT**[1].]
A thing, animal, or person supposed to bring luck.
■ **mascotry** *noun* attachment to or belief in mascots; the use of mascots: **E20.**

masculate /ˈmaskjʊleɪt/ *verb trans. rare.* **E17.**
[**ORIGIN** from Latin *masculus* **MALE** *adjective* + **-ATE**[3].]
Make masculine.

masculine /ˈmaskjʊlɪn/ *adjective & noun.* **ME.**
[**ORIGIN** Old French & mod. French *masculin*, fem. *-ine* from Latin *masculinus*, *-ina*, from *masculus* **MALE** *adjective*: see **-INE**[1].]
▸ **A** *adjective.* **1** *GRAMMAR.* Designating the gender to which belong words classified as male on the basis of sex or some arbitrary distinction, such as form; (of a word) belonging to this gender; (of a suffix, inflection, etc.) used with or to form words of this gender. **ME.**
2 Of a person or animal: male. Now *rare.* **LME.**
3 †**a** Of an object to which sex was attributed: male. **LME–E19.** ▸**b** Designating a variety of apricot. **E17.**
4 Of or pertaining to men; peculiar to or assigned to men; characteristic or regarded as characteristic of men; manly, virile; vigorous, powerful. **L16.** ▸†**b** Of a material thing or physical quality: powerful in action, strong. **M17–E18.**

W. COWPER Or if in masculine debate he shared. L. DUNCAN 'Hello, Sue?' a masculine voice said . . . 'This is David Ruggles.' S. WEINTRAUB Her interest in masculine good looks remained undiminished.

5 Of a woman or a woman's qualities or attributes: having capacities, manners, appearance, or tastes regarded as characteristic of or appropriate to men. **E17.**
– **SPECIAL COLLOCATIONS:** **masculine protest** in Adlerian psychology, the adoption of overtly masculine behaviour by a person of either sex in (unconscious) reaction to the stereotypical association of femininity and submissiveness. **masculine rhyme**: between lines ending in stressed syllables.
▸ **B** *noun.* **1** A man. Formerly also, man, men. Now *rare.* **LME.**
2 *GRAMMAR.* A masculine word, form, etc.; the masculine gender. **M16.**
■ **masculinely** *adverb* **E17.** **masculineness** *noun* **M17.**

masculinise *verb* var. of **MASCULINIZE.**

masculinism /ˈmaskjʊlɪnɪz(ə)m/ *noun.* **E20.**
[**ORIGIN** from **MASCULINE** + **-ISM.**]
Advocacy of the rights of men; anti-feminism, machismo.

masculinist /ˈmaskjʊlɪnɪst/ *noun & adjective.* **E20.**
[**ORIGIN** formed as **MASCULINISM** + **-IST.**]
▸ **A** *noun.* An advocate of the rights of men. **E20.**
▸ **B** *adjective.* Of or pertaining to the advocacy of the rights of men; characterized by or designating attitudes, values, etc., held to be typical of men. **E20.**

masculinity /maskjʊˈlɪnɪti/ *noun.* **M18.**
[**ORIGIN** French *masculinité*, formed as **MASCULINE**: see **-ITY.**]
The state or fact of being masculine; the characteristic quality or qualities of men; manliness.

M. MOORCOCK The occasional intrusion of his masculinity into a world predominantly filled by women and children. E. SHOWALTER The public image of the Great War was one of strong unreflective masculinity.

masculinize /ˈmaskjʊlɪnʌɪz/ *verb trans.* Also **-ise. M19.**
[**ORIGIN** from **MASCULINE** + **-IZE.**]
1 Make masculine or more masculine. **M19.**
2 Induce male physiological characteristics in. **E20.**
■ **masculiniˈzation** *noun* **L19.**

masculinoid /ˈmaskjʊlɪnɔɪd/ *adjective.* **E20.**
[**ORIGIN** formed as **MASCULINIZE** + **-OID.**]
Masculine (but not male); of male form or appearance.

masculist /ˈmaskjʊlɪst/ *noun & adjective.* **L20.**
[**ORIGIN** formed as **MASCULINIZE** + **-IST**, after **FEMINIST.**]
= **MASCULINIST.**

masculy /ˈmaskjʊli/ *adjective.* **M16.**
[**ORIGIN** from **MASCLE** + **-Y**[5].]
HERALDRY. Covered with mascles.

mase /meɪz/ *verb intrans.* **M20.**
[**ORIGIN** Back-form. from **MASER**, as though this were an agent noun in **-ER**[1].]
= **LASE**; *esp.* lase in the microwave part of the spectrum.

maser /ˈmeɪzə/ *noun.* **M20.**
[**ORIGIN** Acronym, from *microwave amplification by stimulated emission of radiation*. Cf. **LASER** *noun*[2].]
A laser; *spec.* one that emits microwaves. Also (*ASTRONOMY*), an interstellar gas cloud which emits microwaves naturally by stimulated emission.

mash /maʃ/ *noun*[1]. Also †**mask.**
[**ORIGIN** Old English *māsc* = Middle Low German *mēsch*, *mäsch*, Middle High German *meisch* crushed grapes (German *Maisch*), from West Germanic, perh. ult. rel. to Old English *miscian* mix. Cf. **MUSH** *noun*[1].]
▸ **I 1** *BREWING.* Malt mixed with hot water to form wort. **OE.**
2 A mixture of boiled grain, bran, etc., given as a warm food to animals. **E16.**

Field Most horses have a mixture of nuts and oats with a bran mash at weekends.

3 Anything reduced to a soft pulpy consistency, by beating or crushing, by mixing with or steeping in water, etc. **L16.** ▸**b** *fig.* A confused mixture; a muddle. Cf. **MISHMASH. L16.** ▸**c** The state of being mashed or reduced to a soft mass. **M17.**

SMOLLETT One of his great toes was crushed into a mash. **b** G. W. THORNBURY His will is an extraordinary mash of grammar. **c** W. SOYINKA A pawpaw turned to red mash.

4 Mashed potatoes, esp. as served with sausages. *colloq.* **E20.**

M. DICKENS The chap had bought him tea and bangers and mash.

▸ **II** [from **MASH** *verb*[2] II.]
5 a The action of **MASH** *verb*[2]; an infatuation, a crush. *arch. slang.* **L19.** ▸**b** A person who is the object of infatuation. *arch. slang.* **L19.**
– **COMB.:** **mash note** *arch. slang* a love letter; **mash-roll**, **mash-staff** an instrument used to stir the malt in a mash tub; **mash tub**, **mash tun**, **mash vat**: in which malt is mashed.
– **NOTE:** Not recorded before **E16** exc. in combinations.

mash /maʃ/ *noun*[2]. *Scot. & N. English.* **L17.**
[**ORIGIN** from **MASH** *verb*[2] or French *masse* **MACE** *noun*[1].]
A heavy hammer for breaking stone.

†**mash** *noun*[3] & *verb*[1] var. of **MESH** *noun & verb.*

mash /maʃ/ *verb*[2] *trans.* Also (*Scot. & N. English*) **mask** /mask/. **ME.**
[**ORIGIN** from **MASH** *noun*[1]. In branch II back-form. from **MASHER.**]
▸ **I 1 a** *BREWING.* Mix (malt) with hot water to form wort. **ME.** ▸**b** Brew (beer etc.). Now only *fig.* in ***be masking***, (of a storm etc.) be brewing. *obsolete* exc. *dial.* **M16.** ▸**c** Infuse (tea). *dial.* **L18.**

c B. HINES There's some tea mashed if you want a cup.

2 Beat into a soft mass; crush, pound, or smash to a pulp. Also foll. by *up*. **ME.** ▸**b** *spec.* Reduce (food) to a homogeneous mass by crushing, beating, or stirring. **E17.** ▸†**c** Make a hash of. **M17–M18.**

S. O'FAOLÁIN The sound of feet mashing the gravel outside. S. BRILL He mashed his cigar out on the man's desk. G. KEILLOR The front of the car was mashed in back to the engine block. **b** A. TYLER I mashed my peas with my spoon. M. ANGELOU The Irish accent was as palpable as mashed potatoes. *fig.*: SIR W. SCOTT I can clear the ground better now by mashing up my old work . . with new matter.

3 Mix, mingle. **LME.**
4 Feed with a mash. *rare.* **M19.**
▸ **II 5** Excite sentimental admiration in (a person of the opposite sex); ***be mashed on***, be infatuated with, have a crush on. *arch. slang.* **L19.**
– **COMB.:** **mash-up** a mixture or fusion of disparate elements; *esp.* a musical track comprising the vocals of one recording placed over the instrumental backing of another.
■ **mashed** *noun* (*colloq.*) mashed potatoes; = **MASH** *noun*[1] 4: **E20.**

mash /maʃ/ *verb*[3] *trans. W. Indian.* **E20.**
[**ORIGIN** Prob. var. of **SMASH** *verb*[1].]
Foll. by *up*: spoil, damage, or destroy by violence. Also, cause trouble for (a person), esp. by careless talk.

masha /ˈmaʃə/ *noun.* **M19.**
[**ORIGIN** Hindi *māṣā* from Sanskrit *māsa*.]
In the Indian subcontinent: a unit of weight equal to about 0.97 gram.

mashallah /maˈʃalə, mɑːʃɑːˈlɑː/ *interjection.* **E19.**
[**ORIGIN** Arabic *mā šāʾa llāh* from *mā* whatever + *šāʾa* to wish + *Allāh* God.]
(This is) what God wills (as an expression of praise or resignation).

masher /ˈmaʃə/ *noun.* **L16.**
[**ORIGIN** from **MASH** *verb*[2] + **-ER**[1].]
†**1** A person who mashes malt or mixes wine. **L16–E17.**
2 A machine, vessel, or utensil for mashing malt, fruit, vegetables, etc. **M19.**

R. CROMPTON A rusty potato masher of ancient design.

3 A fashionable young man of the late Victorian or Edwardian era, a dandy. *arch. slang.* **L19.** ▸**b** A man who makes unwelcome sexual advances to women. *N. Amer. slang.* **E20.**

Sunday Australian Brighton's West Pier, once the trysting place for Edwardian mashers and their ladyloves.

mashie /ˈmaʃi/ *noun*. L19.
[ORIGIN Uncertain: perh. from French *massue* club.]
GOLF (now chiefly *hist.*). An iron-headed club used for lofting or for medium distances.

attrib.: A. BLOND We work in rooms not a mashie shot from Gray's Inn.

– COMB.: **mashie-niblick** a club combining the features of mashie and niblick, now called a number 7 iron.

mashlum *noun* see MASLIN *noun*[2].

Mashona /məˈʃɒnə, -ˈʃəʊ-/ *noun & adjective*. M19.
[ORIGIN Bantu. Cf. SHONA.]
▸ **A** *noun*. Pl. **-s**, same. A member of the Shona people. M19.
▸ **B** *attrib.* or as *adjective*. Of or pertaining to this people. L19.

mashrabiyya /maʃrəˈbɪə/ *noun*. Also ***moucharaby*** /muːˈʃarəbi/. M19.
[ORIGIN French *moucharaby* from Arabic *mašrabiyya*, from *mašraba* pitcher, from *šariba* to drink.]
Orig., a stone balcony with a parapet and machicolations. Now, in N. Africa, a balcony enclosed with latticework.

masjid /ˈmʌsdʒɪd, ˈmas-/ *noun*. L16.
[ORIGIN Arabic, lit. 'place of prostration' from *sajada* bow down in worship: see MOSQUE.]
A mosque.

mask /mɑːsk/ *noun*[1]. Long *obsolete* exc. *dial.*
[ORIGIN Old English *max*, perh. metath. alt. of MESH *noun*, or from cognate Old Norse *mǫskve*.]
In early use, a net. Later, a mesh.

mask /mɑːsk/ *noun*[2]. Also †**masque**. See also MASQUE *noun*. E16.
[ORIGIN French *masque* from Italian *maschera*, perh. from Arabic *maskara* buffoon, from *sakira* ridicule.]
▸ †**I 1** See MASQUE *noun*. E16.
▸ **II 2 a** A covering worn to conceal the face or the upper part of it, as a disguise at balls etc.; a grotesque or comical representation of a face worn at carnivals, parties, etc. M16. ▸**b** A covering worn on the face for protection; *esp.* a screen of wire, gauze, etc., to protect the face from injury, e.g. in fencing; a face covering worn by a surgeon, dentist, etc., to prevent infection. L16. ▸**c** CLASSICAL ANTIQUITIES. A hollow figure of a human head worn by actors, to identify the character represented and to amplify the voice. E17. ▸**d** A respirator used to filter inhaled air or to supply gas for inhalation. L19.

a DEFOE I had no Mask but I ruffled my Hoods . . about my face. **b** P. PARISH Doctors . . nurses and anyone who handles the drug frequently should wear masks and rubber gloves.

a in mask disguised behind a mask. ***iron mask***: see IRON *noun & adjective*. ***loo mask***: see LOO *noun*[2]. ***vizard-mask***: see VIZARD 1, 2. **b *gas mask***: see GAS *noun*[1].

3 *fig.* **a** A disguise, a pretence; a pretended appearance or expression. L16. ▸**b** A thing which covers something or hides something from view. L16.

a GOLDSMITH A base, ungenerous wretch who under the mask of friendship has undone me. J. BUCHAN He hadn't a face, only a hundred masks that he could assume when he pleased. **b** KEATS The new soft-fallen mask Of snow upon the mountains.

4 a A stone representation of a face, used in panels, keystones, etc. M18. ▸**b** A likeness of a person's face in clay, wax, etc.; *esp.* one made by taking a mould from the face itself. L18. ▸**c** A person's face regarded as resembling a mask, esp. through having set into a particular expression. L18. ▸**d** The face or head of an animal; *esp.* that of a fox (displayed as a hunting trophy). E19. ▸**e** A cosmetic preparation spread on the face, a face pack. M20.
b DEATH-*mask*.
5 ENTOMOLOGY. The enlarged labium of a dragonfly larva, which can be extended to seize prey. L18.
6 a FORTIFICATION. A screen to protect men engaged in constructing a work, to conceal a battery, etc. E19. ▸**b** PHOTOGRAPHY. A screen used to cover any part of an image which it is desired to exclude. L19. ▸**c** ELECTRONICS. In the manufacture of microcircuits, a thin surface layer that is removed in parts allowing selective modification of the underlying material. M20.
– COMB.: **mask jug** a jug with a lip or front shaped like a face.

†**mask** *noun*[3] var. of MASH *noun*[1].

mask /mɑːsk/ *verb*[1] *trans.* Long *obsolete* exc. *dial.* LME.
[ORIGIN from MASK *noun*[1].]
Mesh, enmesh (*lit.* & *fig.*).

mask /mɑːsk/ *verb*[2]. Also †**masque**. M16.
[ORIGIN from MASK *noun*[2].]
1 *verb intrans.* Take part in a masque or masquerade. M16.
†**2** *verb intrans.* Be or go in disguise; hide one's real nature under an outward show. L16–M17.
3 *verb trans.* Cover or provide with a facial mask. Freq. in *pass.*, wear or be disguised with a mask. L16.

SHAKES. *Lucr.* I have no one to blush with me . . To mask their brows and hide their infamy. TENNYSON A rout of saucy boys Brake on us . . Mask'd like our maids.

4 *verb trans.* Conceal from view by interposing something, cover. L16. ▸**b** MILITARY. Conceal (a battery, force, etc.) from the view of the enemy; hinder (a force) from action. E18. ▸**c** PHOTOGRAPHY etc. Cover, shade, or mount with a mask. L19. ▸**d** Of a sound or other object of perception: diminish or prevent the perception of (another stimulus). E20. ▸**e** CHEMISTRY. Prevent (a substance) from taking part in a certain reaction by causing it to undergo another preliminary reaction. M20. ▸**f** Provide or shield with a covering, such as masking tape. M20.

A. WEST His eyebrows almost masked his eyes. A. CARTER No paint nor powder . . can mask that red mark on my forehead. **c** R. K. NARAYAN Don't worry that you may also be in the picture—I'll mask you. **d** *Encycl. Brit.* The substantially greater intensity of one odour may mask another.

f masking tape adhesive tape used in painting to cover areas on which paint is not wanted.
5 *verb trans. fig.* Disguise (feelings etc.) under an assumed outward show; conceal (intentionally or otherwise) the real nature, intent, or meaning of. L16.

R. B. SHERIDAN He has been obliged to mask his pretensions. R. BUSH A world-renowned writer whose celebrity masked a ruined marriage and a barren pen. *Independent* The figures mask an erratic progress. R. CHRISTIANSEN Her depression set in . . masked from friends and acquaintances, but painfully communicated to Shelley.

▪ **masked** *adjective* (**a**) having, wearing, or provided with a mask; (**b**) concealed or disguised with a mask or by a masking process; (**c**) ZOOLOGY having facial markings or features suggesting a mask (***masked owl***, any of several Australasian and Indonesian barn owls of the genus *Tyto*); (**d**) ***masked ball***, a ball at which masks are worn: M16.

mask *verb*[3] see MASH *verb*[2].

maskelynite /ˈmask(ə)lɪnʌɪt/ *noun*. L19.
[ORIGIN from Neville Story-*Maskelyne* (1823–1911), English mineralogist + -ITE[1].]
MINERALOGY. A colourless aluminosilicate glass which occurs in some meteorites and in rocks subjected to intense shock.

masker *noun* var. of MASQUER.

masker /ˈmɑːskə/ *verb trans.* Long *obsolete* exc. *dial.*
[ORIGIN Old English (in *malscrung* verbal noun), app. with isolated Germanic cognates.]
Bewilder. Usu. in *pass.*

maskinonge /ˈmaskɪnɒn(d)ʒ/ *noun*. *N. Amer.* Also **muskellunge** /ˈmʌsk(ə)lʌn(d)ʒ/ & other vars. Pl. **-s**, same. L18.
[ORIGIN Ult. from Ojibwa *ma:škino:še:* from *ma:š* ill-formed + *kino:še:* northern pike.]
A large pike, *Esox masquinongy*, of the Great Lakes of N. America, valued as a game fish. Also called ***musky***.

maslin /ˈmazlɪn/ *noun*[1]. *obsolete* exc. *dial.*
[ORIGIN Old English *mæstling*, *mæslen*, prob. rel. to Middle High German *mess(e* brass (early mod. & dial. German *mess*, *mesch*, *möss*, *mösch*) and cognates with suffixes, Middle Dutch, Middle High German *messinc*, *missinc* (Dutch, German *Messing*).]
1 A kind of brass. Now only *attrib.* in ***maslin kettle***, a large pan for boiling fruit for preserve. OE.
2 A vessel made of this brass; *spec.* = ***maslin kettle*** above. OE.

maslin /ˈmazlɪn/ *noun*[2]. Now *dial.* Also (*Scot.*) **mashlum** /ˈmaʃləm/, & other vars. ME.
[ORIGIN Old French *mesteillon* from Proto-Romance from Latin *mistus* pa. pple of *miscere* MIX *verb*: Cf. Middle Dutch *mastelūn* (Dutch *masteluin*).]
1 Mixed grain, *esp.* rye mixed with wheat. Also, bread made from this. ME.
†**2** *fig.* A mixture, a medley. L16–M19.

masochism /ˈmasəkɪz(ə)m/ *noun*. L19.
[ORIGIN from Leopold von Sacher-*Masoch* (1835–95), Austrian novelist, who described the practice + -ISM.]
The condition or state of deriving (esp. sexual) gratification from one's own pain or humiliation; *colloq.* enthusiasm for doing what appears to be painful or tiresome. Cf. SADISM, SADOMASOCHISM.

masochist /ˈmasəkɪst/ *noun*. L19.
[ORIGIN formed as MASOCHISM + -IST.]
A person who exhibits or is given to masochism.
▪ **masoˈchistic** *adjective* of, pertaining to, resembling, or characterized by masochism L19. **masoˈchistically** *adverb* M20.

mason /ˈmeɪs(ə)n/ *noun*. ME.
[ORIGIN Old Northern French *machun* or (later) Old French *masson* (later *maçon*) from Proto-Romance, prob. from Germanic (whence also Old High German (*stein*) *mezzo*, German *Steinmetz* stonemason), perh. rel. to MATTOCK.]
1 A builder and worker in stone; a worker who dresses and lays stone in building. ME.
MONUMENTAL ***mason***.
2 (Usu. **M-**.) = FREEMASON. L15.
– COMB.: **mason-bee**, **mason-wasp** any of numerous solitary bees and wasps belonging to the family Megachilidae or subfamily Eumeninae respectively, which lay eggs in hard cells made out of clay, earth, etc.; **mason's mark** a distinctive device carved on stone by the mason who dressed the stone; ***mason-wasp***: see ***mason-bee*** above; **mason-work** stonework, masonry.

mason /ˈmeɪs(ə)n/ *verb trans.* LME.
[ORIGIN Old French *maçoner* (mod. *maçonner*), from *maçon*: see MASON *noun*.]
1 Build of masonry; strengthen with masonry. LME.
†**2** Build *in(to)* a wall. Only in 16.
3 HERALDRY. As ***masoned*** pa. pple: marked with lines representing the joints in masonry. L17.
▪ **masoner** *noun* (*obsolete* exc. *dial.*) a mason, a bricklayer L15.

Mason–Dixon line /meɪs(ə)nˈdɪks(ə)n lʌɪn/ *noun phr.* Also (earlier) **Mason and Dixon('s) line**. L18.
[ORIGIN Charles *Mason* & Jeremiah *Dixon*, English astronomers, who surveyed the line in 1763–7.]
The boundary between Maryland and Pennsylvania, taken as the northern limit of the slave-owning states before the abolition of slavery in the US.

masonic /məˈsɒnɪk/ *adjective*. L18.
[ORIGIN from MASON *noun* + -IC.]
1 (Usu. **M-**.) Of, pertaining to, or characteristic of Freemasons or Freemasonry. L18.
2 Of or pertaining to stonemasons or stonemasonry. *rare*. E19.

Masonite /ˈmeɪs(ə)nʌɪt/ *noun*. Also **m-**. E20.
[ORIGIN from *Mason* Fibre Co., Laurel, Mississippi, US + -ITE[1].]
(Proprietary name for) fibreboard made from wood fibre pulped under steam at high pressure.

Mason jar /ˈmeɪs(ə)n dʒɑː/ *noun phr.* Orig. *US*. L19.
[ORIGIN John *Mason* (fl. 1858), US inventor.]
A wide-mouthed glass jar with an airtight screw top, used in home bottling.

masonry /ˈmeɪs(ə)nri/ *noun*. LME.
[ORIGIN Old French *maçonerie* (mod. *-nn-*), from *maçon*: see MASON *noun*, -ERY.]
1 The art, skill, or occupation of a mason; the art or work of building in stone. Now *rare*. LME.
2 Work executed by a mason; stonework. LME.

J. BUCHAN By the use of out-jutting stones and gaps in the masonry . . I got to the top. *attrib.*: *New York Times* A 14-story masonry and glass building.

3 (Usu. **M-**.) = FREEMASONRY. L17.
▪ **masonried** *adjective* built or strengthened with masonry M19.

masoor /mʌˈsʊə/ *noun*. Also **masoor dal** /dɑːl/. L20.
[ORIGIN Hindi *masūr*.]
Lentils of a small orange-red variety.

Masorah /masəˈrɑː, məˈsɔːrə/ *noun*. Also **-ss-**, **-ra**. M17.
[ORIGIN Hebrew var. of *māsōreṯ* bond (*Ezekiel* 20:37), from *ʾāsar* bind (later interpreted as 'tradition' as if from *māsar* hand down).]
The body of traditional information and comment relating to the text of the Hebrew Scriptures, compiled by Jewish scholars in the 10th cent. and earlier; the collection of critical notes in which this information is preserved.

M

Masorete /ˈmasəriːt/ *noun*. Also **-ss-**. M17.
[ORIGIN French *Massoret* & mod. Latin *Massoreta*, orig. misuse of Hebrew *māsōreṯ* (see MASORAH), with subsequent assim. of the ending to Latin *-eta*, Greek *-ētēs*.]
Any of the Jewish scholars who contributed to the formation of the Masorah.
▪ **Masoretic** /masəˈrɛtɪk/ *adjective* of, pertaining to, or proceeding from the Masoretes L17. **Masoˈretical** *adjective* (now *rare*) = MASORETIC L17. **Masorite** *noun* (now *rare*) = MASORETE E17.

masque /mɑːsk/ *noun*. Also †**mask**. See also MASK *noun*[2]. E16.
[ORIGIN formed as MASK *noun*[2].]
▸ **I 1** A masquerade, a masked ball. Now *rare*. E16. ▸†**b** A set of masquers. L16–E17.
2 A form of amateur dramatic entertainment, popular at Court and amongst the nobility in 16th- and 17th-cent. England, consisting of dancing and acting performed by masked players, orig. in dumbshow, later with metrical dialogue. E16. ▸**b** A dramatic composition intended for this. E17.
▸ **II** See MASK *noun*[2].

†**masque** *verb* var. of MASK *verb*[2].

masquer /ˈmɑːskə/ *noun*. Also **masker**. M16.
[ORIGIN from *masque* MASK *verb*[2] + -ER[1].]
A person who takes part in a masquerade or a masque; a person in masquerade.

masquerade /mɑːskəˈreɪd, mas-/ *noun & verb*. L16.
[ORIGIN French *mascarade* (whence Spanish *mascarada*) from Italian *mascherata*, from *maschera* MASK *noun*[2]: see -ADE.]
▸ **A** *noun*. **1** A ball at which the guests wear masks and other disguises (often of a rich or fantastic kind); a masked ball. L16. ▸**b** *transf.* & *fig.* A gathering or procession of fantastic or ill-assorted characters. L16.

b POPE Visits to ev'ry Church we daily paid, And march'd in ev'ry holy Masquerade.

2 a Disguise worn at or suitable for a masquerade; *gen.* disguise; *fig.* pretended outward appearance. Chiefly in ***in masquerade***. M17. ▸**b** A false outward show, a pretence; the action of masquerading. M19.

a BYRON And, after all, what is a lie? 'Tis but The truth in masquerade. **b** S. BRETT His masquerade of pretending that the phone was being answered . . by . . a horde of underlings.

†**3** A masquer. M17–E18.
†**4** A kind of textile fabric. L17–M19.

▸ **B** *verb.* **1** *verb intrans.* Appear or go about in disguise; have or assume a false appearance. Usu. foll. by *as.* **L17.**

C. JACKSON I feel fifty-five when I look at that sophomoric adolescent masquerading as a man. A. BRIEN Paris is a huge fairground or amusement park masquerading as a capital city.

2 *verb trans.* Disguise the appearance of. *rare.* **L17.**

■ **masquerader** *noun* a person who takes part in a masquerade; a person who masquerades or assumes disguise: **L17.**

mass /mas, mɑːs/ *noun*[1]. Also **M-**.

[**ORIGIN** Old English *mæsse*, *messe*, corresp. to Old Frisian, Old Saxon *missa*, Old High German *messa*, *missa* (German *Messe*), Old Norse *messa*, from ecclesiastical Latin *missa* verbal noun (whence Old French & mod. French *messe*, Italian *messa*, Spanish *misa*), from *missa*. ppl stem of *mittere* send (away), perh. from the formula of dismissal (*Ite, missa est*) at the end of the service.]

1 (Freq. **M-**.) The Eucharist, *esp.* (in post-Reformation use) that of the Roman Catholic Church, or as administered and doctrinally viewed by Roman Catholics; a particular celebration of this. **OE.**

B. MOORE Where every Catholic went to Mass of a Sunday. P. TOYNBEE His priest at Cwmbran celebrated mass. D. CUPITT It was important to assist souls in purgatory with Masses, indulgences and prayers. M. SPARK Wanda had been to the one o'clock Polish mass at Brompton Oratory.

2 A feast day or festival of a specified saint etc. Long *obsolete* exc. as 2nd elem. of comb. (***Candlemas***, ***Christmas***, ***Lammas***, etc.). **OE.**

3 A rite used in a celebration of the Eucharist, esp. in the Roman Catholic Church. **LME.**

4 A musical setting of those invariable parts of the Mass which are commonly sung (the Kyrie, Gloria, Credo, Sanctus, Benedictus, and Agnus Dei). **L16.**

– **PHRASES**: ***Black Mass***: see **BLACK** *adjective*. **by the mass**: expr. assertion, imprecation, outrage, etc. **dry mass** *hist.* an abbreviated form of mass without either consecration or communion. **high mass** (a) mass celebrated with the assistance of a deacon and subdeacon, with incense and music. **low mass** (a) mass said without music and with the minimum of ceremony. ***mass of requiem***: see **REQUIEM** *noun*[1] 1. ***Mass of the Presanctified***: see **PRESANCTIFY**. ***midnight mass***. ***nuptial mass***: see **NUPTIAL** *adjective* 1. ***pontifical mass***: see **PONTIFICAL** *adjective* 1. ***red mass***: see **RED** *adjective*. ***sacring of mass***, ***sacring of the mass***: see **SACRING** 1. **solemn mass** = ***high mass*** above. ***votive mass***: see **VOTIVE** *adjective* 1.

– **COMB.**: **mass book** a missal; **mass day** *arch.* a saint's feast day; **mass-house** *derog.* (*obsolete* exc. *hist.*) a Roman Catholic place of worship; **mass-monger** *derog.* (*arch.*) a Roman Catholic; **mass-penny** *arch.* an offering of money made at mass; **mass-priest** *arch.* a priest whose function is to celebrate mass, *esp.* (*derog.*) a Roman Catholic priest.

mass /mas/ *noun*[2] & *adjective*. **LME.**

[**ORIGIN** Old French & mod. French *masse* from Latin *massa* from Greek *maza* barley-cake, perh. rel. to *massein* knead.]

▸ **A** *noun.* **1** A coherent body of fusible or plastic material (as dough or clay), not yet fashioned into objects of definite shape; a lump of raw material for moulding, casting, etc. *obsolete* exc. as passing into sense 2. **LME.** ▸†**b** A kind of matter able to be fashioned or moulded. **L15–E18.** ▸**c** An amorphous quantity of material used in or remaining after a chemical or pharmaceutical operation. **M16.**

2 A coherent body of matter of unspecified shape, often one of relatively large bulk; a solid physical object; *MEDICINE* a tumour or growth that is palpable or visible. **LME.** ▸†**b** *MEDICINE*. The whole quantity *of* blood in an animal body. **E17–M18.**

W. R. GROVE When the magnet as a mass is in motion. J. TYNDALL Adjacent to us rose the mighty mass of the Finsteraarhorn.

3 A dense aggregation of objects apparently forming a continuous body; a large quantity, amount, or number (of material or abstract things); an oppressively or bewilderingly large amount. Freq. in *pl.* **L15.** ▸†**b** *spec.* A large sum *of* money, treasure, etc.; *ellipt.* a stock, a fund. **M16–E18.** ▸**c** Foll. by *of*: a person or thing viewed (hyperbolically) as consisting of a large number of the things specified. **E17.** ▸**d** An extensive unbroken expanse of colour, light, shadow, etc.; any of the several main portions each having some unity in colour, lighting etc., which the eye distinguishes in a painting etc. **M17.** ▸**e** A volume or body of sound; *MUSIC* the effect of a large number of instruments or voices of the same character. **L19.**

LD MACAULAY They removed a vast mass of evil. J. IRVING The mass of logs . . moved swiftly downstream. S. BELLOW Uncle knew masses of stuff about plants. **b** T. FULLER Keeping their money for them till it amounted to a mass. **c** S. SMILES The Church itself was seen to be a mass of abuses. L. CODY This shoulder's going to be . . a mass of bruises in the morning. **d** I. ZANGWILL The occasional fineness of line, the masterly distribution of masses.

4 a Solid bulk, massiveness. **E17.** ▸**b** *PHYSICS*. The quantity of matter which a body contains, as measured by its acceleration under a given force or by the force exerted on it by a gravitational field. **E18.**

a SHAKES. *Haml.* This army of such mass and charge. **b** E. RUTHERFORD The helium nucleus has a mass nearly four times that of hydrogen.

5 A large number of people collected closely together or viewed as forming an aggregate in which their individuality is lost; *the* generality of humankind, *the* main body of a nation, people, etc.; (usu. in *pl.*) *the* ordinary people. **E18.**

C. CONNOLLY What illness performs for the individual, war accomplishes for the mass. J. HIGGINS Cussane liked seaside towns, especially the ones that catered for the masses. M. FOOT Some hours later he stood on tiptoe amid a heaving, breathless mass.

– **PHRASES**: ***atomic mass***. ***centre of mass***: see **CENTRE** *noun*. ***critical mass***. ***gravitational mass***. **in mass** en masse, bodily, all at once. **in the mass** without distinction of component parts or individuals. ***levy in mass***: see **LEVY** *noun*[1] 2. ***missing mass***. ***relative atomic mass***, ***relative molecular mass***: see **RELATIVE** *adjective*. ***solar mass***: see **SOLAR** *adjective*[1]. **the mass of**, **the great mass of** the greater part or majority of.

▸ **B** *attrib.* or as *adjective.* Relating to, done by, or affecting large numbers of people or things; large-scale. **M18.**

D. DELILLO A brief pause before the mass wailing recommenced. E. LONGFORD George V had had to support his Prime Minister . . with a mass creation of Liberal peers. *City Limits* You can't blame the communities for not coping with mass unemployment.

– **COMB. & SPECIAL COLLOCATIONS**: **mass action** (*a*) ***law of mass action*** (*CHEMISTRY*), the principle that the rate of a chemical reaction is proportional to the masses of the reacting substances; (*b*) the action of a mass of people; **mass defect** *PHYSICS* the sum of the masses of the constituent particles of an atomic nucleus, as free individuals, minus the mass of the nucleus (a quantity which effectively represents the binding energy of the nucleus); **mass effect** (*a*) *METALLURGY* the effect of size and shape in causing different rates of cooling in different parts of an object following heat treatment; (*b*) *sing.* & (usu.) in *pl.*, a total or grand effect; (*c*) an effect due to or dependent on mass; **mass-energy** *PHYSICS* mass and energy regarded as interconvertible manifestations of the same phenomenon, according to the laws of relativity; the mass of a body regarded relativistically as energy; **mass man** a hypothetical average man; *esp.* one regarded as lacking individuality and being dominated by the mass media; **mass market** the market for mass-produced goods; **mass-market** *verb trans.* market (a product) on a large scale; **mass medium** a medium of communication (such as radio, television, newspapers) that reaches a large number of people; usu. in *pl.*, such media collectively; **mass meeting** a meeting of a large body of people; *esp.* a meeting of all or most of the members of a workforce etc.; **mass noun** *GRAMMAR* a noun denoting something (as a substance or quality) which cannot be counted, in English usu. a noun which in common usage lacks a plural and is not used with an indefinite article (opp. ***count noun***); **mass number** *NUCLEAR PHYSICS* the total number of protons and neutrons in an atomic nucleus; **mass observation** (chiefly *hist.*) the study and recording of the social habits and opinions of ordinary people; **mass-point** *PHYSICS* an entity conceived as having mass but (like a geometrical point) lacking spatial extension; **mass-produce** *verb trans.* manufacture by mass production; **mass production** the production of manufactured articles in large quantities by a standardized process; **mass radiography** radiography of the chests of large numbers of people by a quick routine method; **mass-ratio** the ratio of the mass of a fully fuelled rocket to that of the same rocket without fuel; **mass society**: in which the population is largely homogeneous and is strongly influenced by the mass media; **mass spectrograph** a mass spectrometer which employs photographic detection of the deflected ions; **mass spectrometer**, **mass spectroscope** an apparatus for measuring the masses of isotopes, molecules, and molecular fragments by ionizing them and determining their trajectories in electric and magnetic fields; **mass spectrometry**, **mass spectroscopy** the use of the mass spectrometer to analyse substances; **mass spectrum** a record obtained with a mass spectrometer, in which ions from a sample are represented as dispersed according to their mass-to-charge ratio; **mass transit** the provision of an extensive, coordinated system of public transport in a city, urban area, etc.

mass /mas/ *verb*[1] *intrans.* Now *rare* or *obsolete*. **OE.**

[**ORIGIN** from **MASS** *noun*[1].]

Celebrate mass; say or sing mass.

mass /mas/ *verb*[2]. **LME.**

[**ORIGIN** Old French & mod. French *masser*, from *masse* **MASS** *noun*[2].]

1 *verb trans.* Form or gather into a mass; bring together in masses; *esp.* concentrate (troops etc.) in a particular place. Also (now *rare*) foll. by *up*. **LME.**

J. RUSKIN But all these virtues mass themselves in the Greek mind into the two main ones. *Boston Sunday Herald* A nationwide movement designed to mass anti-war support.

2 *verb intrans.* Collect, assemble, or come together in masses. **M19.**

DAY LEWIS The compulsive force of waters that have stealthily massed behind a dam. A. BULLOCK The German forces were massing for the invasion of the United Kingdom.

mass /mas/ *verb*[3] *trans. rare.* **L18.**

[**ORIGIN** French *masser*: see **MASSAGE**.]

Massage.

■ **masser** *noun* a masseur, a masseuse **L18.**

Mass. *abbreviation.*

Massachusetts.

Massa /ˈmasə/ *noun.* **M18.**

[**ORIGIN** Repr. a pronunc.]

In representations of black speech: master.

Massachusett /ˌmasəˈtʃuːsɪt/ *noun* & *adjective.* **E17.**

[**ORIGIN** Massachusett *Massachusêuck*.]

▸ **A** *noun.* **1** A member of an Algonquian people formerly inhabiting the eastern part of Massachusetts. **E17.**

2 The extinct language of the Massachusetts. **M20.**

▸ **B** *adjective.* Of or pertaining to the Massachusetts or their language. **E17.**

massacre /ˈmasəkə/ *noun.* **L16.**

[**ORIGIN** Old French & mod. French (also †*maçacre* etc.) shambles, butchery, of unknown origin.]

1 A general slaughter of people or (less usu.) animals; carnage. **L16.** ▸**b** *fig.* A great destruction or downfall. Now *esp.* (*colloq.*), a crushing defeat in sport. **L16.**

SHAKES. *Tit. A.* For I must talk of murders, rapes, and massacres. G. BORROW Plunder and massacre had been expected.

†**2** A cruel or atrocious murder. **L16–E17.**

massacre /ˈmasəkə/ *verb trans.* **L16.**

[**ORIGIN** Old French & mod. French *massacrer*, formed as **MASSACRE** *noun*.]

1 Cruelly or violently kill (people, less usu. animals) in numbers; make a general slaughter of. **L16.**

P. WARNER He marched them out bound . . and massacred them with sword and spear.

2 Mutilate, mangle. Long *obsolete* exc. *dial.* **L16.**

3 Murder (one person) cruelly or violently. **E17.**

G. P. R. JAMES He would be massacred the moment he showed his face amongst the infuriated mob.

4 *fig.* Perform (a piece of music, a play, etc.) very ineptly. *colloq.* **E19.** ▸**b** Defeat heavily, esp. in a sporting event; trounce. *colloq.* **M20.**

C. WILLIS The carillon was massacring 'In the Bleak Midwinter', which also seemed fitting. **b** *Scotsman* Ipswich . . should massacre Norwich on Wednesday at home in the East Anglian derby.

■ **massacrer** *noun* **L16.**

massage /ˈmasɑːʒ, məˈsɑːʒ, -dʒ/ *noun* & *verb.* **M19.**

[**ORIGIN** French, from *masser* apply massage to, perh. from Portuguese *amassar* knead.]

▸ **A** *noun.* **1** The application (usu. with the hands) of pressure and strain on the muscles and joints of the body by rubbing, kneading, etc., in order to stimulate their action and increase their suppleness; an instance or spell of such manipulation. **M19.**

Swedish massage: see **SWEDISH** *adjective*.

2 *euphem.* The services of prostitutes. Chiefly in ***massage parlour*** below. **E20.**

– **COMB.**: **massage parlour** an establishment providing massage; *euphem.* a brothel operating under the guise of providing massage.

▸ **B** *verb trans.* **1** Apply massage to; treat by means of massage. **L19.** ▸**b** Rub (lotion etc.) *into* by means of massage. **L20.**

I. MCEWAN Mary massaged his back . . with convergent movements of her thumbs. *fig.*: P. D. JAMES He wasn't looking for a female subordinate to massage his ego. **b** L. CODY She massaged some warmth into her cramped fingers.

2 Manipulate (data, figures, etc.), esp. in order to give a more acceptable result. **M20.**

■ **massager** *noun* (*a*) a masseur, a masseuse; (*b*) a machine used for massaging: **L19.** **massagist** *noun* a masseur, a masseuse **L19.**

Massagetae /masəˈgiːtʌɪ/ *noun pl.* **LME.**

[**ORIGIN** Latin from Greek *Massagetai*, perh. from Scythian name *Masakata* Great Sakas.]

An ancient Scythian people who lived to the east of the Caspian Sea.

Massalian *noun* & *adjective* var. of **MESSALIAN**.

Massaliot /məˈsalɪət/ *noun* & *adjective.* Also **-ssil-** /-ˈsɪl-/. **M19.**

[**ORIGIN** from Greek *Massalia*, Latin *Massilia* (see below), after *Cypriot* etc. Cf. earlier **MASSILIAN**.]

▸ **A** *noun.* A native or inhabitant of Massalia (or Massilia, mod. Marseilles), a Greek colony founded *c* 600 **BC** to the east of the mouth of the Rhône on the Mediterranean coast of southern France. **M19.**

▸ **B** *adjective.* Of or pertaining to Massalia or its inhabitants. **M19.**

massasauga /masəˈsɔːgə/ *noun.* **M19.**

[**ORIGIN** Alt. of **MISSISSAUGA**.]

A small spotted venomous N. American rattlesnake, *Sistrurus catenatus*. Also ***massasauga rattler***.

massé /ˈmaseɪ/ *adjective* & *noun.* **L19.**

[**ORIGIN** French, pa. pple of *masser* play a massé stroke, from *masse* **MACE** *noun*[1].]

BILLIARDS etc. (Designating) a stroke made with the cue more or less vertical, so as to impart extra swerve to the cue ball.

massecuite /masˈkwiːt/ *noun.* **L19.**

[**ORIGIN** French, lit. 'cooked mass'.]

The juice of sugar cane after concentration by boiling.

massed /mast/ *ppl adjective.* **M19.**

[**ORIGIN** from **MASS** *verb*[2] + **-ED**[1].]

1 Gathered into a mass; assembled in a mass. **M19.**

O. MANNING There was shade from the massed foliage of palms, sycamores, banyans and mangoes. A. LIVELY The serried ranks of young girls, and the massed drums that drove them on.

2 Of an inscription: having the words arranged to form a solid column of lettering. **E20.**

M

3 *PSYCHOLOGY.* Designating conditioning or training in which practice is concentrated with very short intervals between repetitions. M20.

masseter /ma'siːtə/ *noun.* L16.
[ORIGIN Greek *masētēr*, from *masasthai* chew.]
ANATOMY. More fully ***masseter muscle***. Either of a pair of muscles passing from the maxilla and zygomatic arch on each side of the head to the ramus of the mandible, and used in mastication.
■ **masse'teric** *adjective* E19.

masseur /ma'səː/ *noun.* Fem. **masseuse** /ma'səːz/. L19.
[ORIGIN French, from *masser* (see MASSAGE) + *-eur* -OR.]
A person who provides massage (professionally).
Swedish masseur: see SWEDISH *adjective*.

Massic /'masɪk/ *adjective & noun.* E17.
[ORIGIN Latin *Massicus* a mountain in Campania.]
(Designating) a wine produced in Campania, Italy, in classical times.

massicot /'masɪkɒt/ *noun.* L15.
[ORIGIN French (also †*masticot*), obscurely rel. to Italian *marzacotto* unguent, Spanish *mazacote* kali, mortar, prob. through medieval Latin from Arabic.]
Yellow lead monoxide or litharge used as a pigment.

massif /'masɪf, ma'siːf, *foreign* masif (*pl. same*)/ *noun.* E16.
[ORIGIN French, use as noun of *massif* MASSIVE.]
1 A block of building. Passing into *fig.* use of sense 2. E16.
> *Times* There must, dear God, be something between slums and concrete massifs.

2 A large mountain mass; a compact group of mountain heights. L19.
> A. N. WILSON The Russians made inroads into the main Caucasus *massif. transf.*: T. KENEALLY Her path took her over the sandstone under the cliffs . . massifs taller than she.

3 *HORTICULTURE.* A mass or clump of plants. L19.

massify /'masɪfʌɪ/ *verb trans.* M20.
[ORIGIN from MASS *noun*[2] + -I- + -FY.]
Form into a mass society.
■ **massifi'cation** *noun* M20.

Massilian /mə'sɪlɪən/ *noun & adjective.* M16.
[ORIGIN from Latin *Massilia* (see MASSALIOT) + -AN.]
= MASSALIOT.

Massiliot *noun & adjective* var. of MASSALIOT.

Massim /'masɪm/ *noun & adjective.* L19.
[ORIGIN Alt. of *Misima*, offshore island of Papua New Guinea.]
▸ **A** *noun.* Pl. same. A member of a people of SE Papua New Guinea. L19.
▸ **B** *adjective.* Of or pertaining to this people. L19.

massive /'masɪv/ *adjective & noun.* LME.
[ORIGIN French *massif*, *-ive* alt. of Old French *massiz* MASSY *adjective*: see -IVE.]
▸ **A** *adjective.* **1** Forming or consisting of a large mass; having great size and weight or solidity; large in scale physically. LME. ▸**b** Of (an article of) gold or silver: solid, not hollow or plated. LME. ▸**c** Of architectural or artistic style: presenting great masses, solid. M19.
> J. A. MICHENER They had built a massive wall nine feet high and four feet thick. W. S. BURROUGHS She is a massive woman with arms like a wrestler. O. MANNING The wall enclosed a row of palms from which hung massive bunches of red dates.

2 Forming a solid or continuous mass; compact, dense, uniform; existing in compact continuous masses. Now *esp.* (**a**) (of a mineral) not definitely crystalline; (**b**) (of a rock formation) lacking structural divisions. M16.
3 (Of an abstract thing) solid, substantial; impressive, great or imposing in scale. Now freq. in weakened sense: very large, great, far-reaching. L16. ▸**b** Particularly successful or influential; famous. *colloq.* L20.
> L. STEPHEN Scott was a man of more massive and less impulsive character. *Word* He died suddenly of a massive heart attack. B. GELDOF Slotted between the news and *Top of the Pops*—giving us a massive captive audience. M. BRETT America runs a massive trade deficit. **b** *Unity* The new . . album . . is due out in June and will be massive.

4 Of or pertaining to masses (as distinct from molecules). *rare.* L19.
5 *PHYSICS.* Of a particle: having non-zero mass, not massless. M20.
▸ **B** *noun.* A group or gang of young people; *esp.* the followers of a particular kind of music such as hip hop or jungle. *slang*, orig. *black English*. L20.
> *M8* DJs from England and abroad . . became firm favourites amongst the Scottish massive.

■ **massiveness** *noun* M16. **ma'ssivity** *noun* E20.

massively /'masɪvli/ *adverb.* M16.
[ORIGIN from MASSIVE *adjective* + -LY[2].]
In a massive way; to a massive extent.
> K. TYNAN The plane was massively overloaded when it took off.

massively parallel (of a computer) consisting of a great many parallel processing units, and so able to execute many different parts of a program at the same time.

massless /'maslɪs/ *adjective.* L19.
[ORIGIN from MASS *noun*[2] + -LESS.]
Having no mass.
■ **masslessness** *noun* M20.

Massorah *noun* see MASORAH.

Massorete *noun* var. of MASORETE.

massoy /'masɔɪ/ *noun.* E19.
[ORIGIN Malay *mesui*.]
The bark of a tree, *Cryptocarya aromatica* (family Lauraceae), native to New Guinea. Also ***massoy-bark***.

massula /'masjʊlə/ *noun.* Pl. **-lae** /-liː/. M19.
[ORIGIN mod. Latin, dim. of Latin *massa* MASS *noun*[2].]
BOTANY. **1** In certain orchids, a cluster of pollen grains developed from a single cell. M19.
2 In certain heterosporous ferns, the tissue surrounding the maturing microspores. L19.

massy /'masi/ *noun. dial.* (chiefly *US*). E19.
[ORIGIN Repr. a pronunc.]
In interjections: mercy.

massy /'masi/ *adjective.* Exc. in sense 5, now *literary* or *arch.* LME.
[ORIGIN Perh. orig. from Old French *massiz* (whence *massif* MASSIVE) from popular Latin from Latin *massa* MASS *noun*[2], or directly from MASS *noun*[2]: see -Y[1].]
1 Solid and weighty; heavy as consisting of compact matter; (esp. of precious metals) occurring in mass, solid, not hollow or alloyed. LME. ▸†**b** Compact, dense. E16–E19. ▸†**c** Solid, having three dimensions. M16–M17.
> M. TWAIN Its furniture was all of massy gold.

2 Consisting of a large mass or masses of heavy material; of great size and weight; (of a building) consisting of great blocks of masonry. LME. ▸**b** Of architectural or artistic style: presenting great masses. E19.
> LD MACAULAY The massy remains of the old Norman castle. **b** *Modern Painters* This predilection for massy stability of form is present in Moore's earliest life-drawings.

3 Of large size; voluminous, bulky; spreading in a mass or in masses. LME.
> J. UPDIKE Brick pinnacles and massy trees.

4 Of an abstract thing: great, substantial, impressive. L16.
5 *PHYSICS.* = MASSIVE *adjective* 5. M20.
■ **massily** *adverb* (long *rare*) massively LME. **massiness** *noun* massiveness M16.

mast /mɑːst/ *noun*[1].
[ORIGIN Old English *mæst* = Middle & mod. Low German, Middle Dutch & mod. Dutch, Old & mod. High German *mast*, from West Germanic (Old Norse *mastr* etc. being from Middle Low German) from Indo-European, whence perh. Latin *malus* mast, Old Irish *maite*, *matán* club.]
1 A long pole or spar, often one of a number, set up more or less vertically on the keel of a sailing vessel to support its sails. OE. ▸**b** *NAUTICAL.* A piece of timber suitable for use as a mast. L15.
> LYTTON Afar off you saw the tall masts of the fleet. G. BENNETT The funnels and masts of warships.

foremast, ***mainmast***, ***mizzenmast***, ***royal mast***, ***topmast***, etc. **before the mast**, **afore the mast** *NAUTICAL* as an ordinary seaman (quartered in the forecastle). ***dolphin of the mast***: see DOLPHIN 4b. ***made mast***: see MADE *ppl adjective*. ***nail one's colours to the mast***: see COLOUR *noun*.

2 *gen.* A pole; a tall pole or other slender structure set upright for any purpose; *esp.* (**a**) a flagpole; (**b**) a post or latticework upright supporting a radio or television aerial; (**c**) (in full ***mooring mast***) a strong steel tower to the top of which an airship can be moored. E16.
> J. WYNDHAM The tower was flying two flags on one mast. S. HYLAND The enormous meccano structure of the television mast on top of Sydenham Hill.

— COMB.: **mast coat** *NAUTICAL* a covering of painted canvas round the foot of a mast and secured to the deck, to prevent ingress of water; **mastman** (chiefly *US*) a sailor whose duty is to oversee the working of halyards etc. in sailing; **mast-step** *NAUTICAL* a block fixed to the keelson in which a mast is set.
■ **mastless** *adjective* L16.

mast /mɑːst/ *noun*[2].
[ORIGIN Old English *mæst* = Middle Low German, Middle Dutch, Old High German *mast*, from West Germanic, prob. from base of MEAT *noun*.]
collect. & (*rare*) in *pl.* The fruit of beech, oak, chestnut, and other woodland trees, esp. when fallen, as food for pigs etc.
> A. HIGGINS He could see the beech tree . . and the pheasants rooting in the beech mast.

— COMB.: **mast cell** [German *Mast* = fattening, feeding] *PHYSIOLOGY* a cell filled with basophil granules, found in numbers in the connective tissue and releasing histamine and other substances in inflammatory and allergic reactions; **mast year**: in which woodland trees produce a good crop of mast.

†**mast** *noun*[3]. M18–L19.
[ORIGIN Alt. of French *masse* MACE *noun*[1] by confusion with MAST *noun*[1].]
A heavy billiard cue, of which the broad end was used for striking.

mast /mɑːst/ *verb trans.* E16.
[ORIGIN from MAST *noun*[1].]
Provide with masts.

mastaba /'mastəbə/ *noun.* Also **-ah**. E17.
[ORIGIN Arabic *maṣṭaba*, of unknown origin.]
1 In Islamic countries: a (stone) bench or seat attached to a house. E17.
2 *ARCHAEOLOGY.* An ancient Egyptian flat-topped tomb, rectangular or square in plan and with sides sloping outward to the base. Also ***mastaba tomb***. L19.

mastage /'mɑːstɪdʒ/ *noun. obsolete* exc. *hist.* M16.
[ORIGIN from MAST *noun*[2] + -AGE.]
The mast of trees; the right of feeding animals on mast.

mastalgia /ma'staldʒə/ *noun.* M19.
[ORIGIN from Greek *mastos* breast + -ALGIA.]
MEDICINE. Pain in the breast.

mastax /'mastaks/ *noun.* M19.
[ORIGIN Greek = mouth.]
ZOOLOGY. The muscular pharynx of a rotifer, containing the masticatory jaws.

mastectomy /ma'stɛktəmi/ *noun.* E20.
[ORIGIN from Greek *mastos* breast + -ECTOMY.]
Surgical removal of a breast; an instance of this.

masted /'mɑːstɪd/ *adjective.* E17.
[ORIGIN from MAST *noun*[1], *verb*: see -ED[2], -ED[1].]
1 Provided with a mast or masts. Freq. as 2nd elem. of comb., as ***two-masted*** etc. E17.
2 Of a harbour etc.: thronged with masts. *rare.* M18.

master /'mɑːstə/ *noun*[1] *& adjective.* Also (esp. in titles) **M-**.
[ORIGIN Old English *mæġister*, *maġister* (corresp. to Old Frisian *māster*, (also Old Saxon) *mēster*, Old & mod. High German *meister*, Old Norse *meistari*), a Germanic adoption from Latin; reinforced by Old French *maistre* (mod. *maître*) from Latin *magister*, *magistr-*, usu. referred to *magis* adverb = more.]
▸ **A** *noun.* **I** A person (orig. & usu. a man) having control or authority.
1 *gen.* A man having direction or control over the action of another or others; a director, a leader, a chief, a commander; a ruler, a governor. *obsolete* exc. as below. OE.
> SHAKES. *Tit. A.* Like stinging bees . . Led by their master to the flow'red fields.

2 a The captain of a merchant vessel (also ***master mariner***). Orig. also (in *pl.*), the officers, the crew. ME. ▸**b** *hist.* A naval officer (ranking next below a lieutenant) responsible for the navigation and sailing of a warship during warlike operations. See also ***master and commander*** below. L16.
3 A person who employs another; one's superior in a business, hierarchy, etc.; a monarch in relation to a minister etc.; the owner of a slave. ME. ▸**b** The owner of an animal; the person whom an animal is accustomed to obey; (more fully ***master of foxhounds***, ***master of hounds***, ***master of beagles***, etc.) the person who owns or controls a pack of foxhounds, beagles, etc.; a member of a hunt who supervises the kennels and hunting arrangements generally. LME. ▸**c** A device or component which directly controls another. Opp. ***slave***. Cf. sense B.2b below. M20.
> G. BORROW I have lived in many houses and served many masters. A. WILSON The manservant . . was as old as his master. **b** M. MAETERLINCK The dog who meets with a good master is the happier of the two.

4 a The male head of a house or household; with *possess.* (now *joc.* exc. *dial.*) a woman's husband. ME. ▸**b** The head or presiding officer of a society, institution, etc., e.g. of certain colleges (in Oxford, Cambridge, and elsewhere), guilds, livery companies, Masonic lodges, etc. LME. ▸**c** In titles of various officials; *spec.* in *LAW* a subordinate judge of the Chancery and Queen's Bench Divisions of the High Court, dealing primarily with procedural and preliminary matters. LME.
> **a** DICKENS I'm a-watching for my master. R. K. NARAYAN The master of the house rose to his feet. **b** *Times* The first woman to hold office as Master of the United College.

5 The possessor or owner of something (now usu. of a quality, skill, etc.); a person highly accomplished in a particular activity (foll. by *of*). ME.
> J. TRUSLER I was master of more than twenty pounds. W. CRUISE Judgement and discretion, which an infant was not master of. J. AGATE Barrie was a master of plot and invention.

6 A person having the power to control, use, or dispose of something at will. Chiefly *pred.*, foll. by *of*. ME.
> JOSEPH HALL An honest man's word must be his master. J. R. GREEN To secure a landing at all, the Spaniards had to be masters of the Channel.

M

7 A person who overcomes another, a victor; a person who gets the upper hand. ME. ▸**b** *BRIDGE.* = ***master card*** (a) below. M20.

TENNYSON If they quarrell'd, Enoch stronger-made Was master.

8 The jack in bowls. Long *rare*. M16.
9 A thing from which a number of copies are made; the original copy of a sound recording, film, data file, etc. E20.

Melody Maker Band requires record company/label to release high quality master.

▸ **II** A teacher; a person qualified to teach.
10 A male tutor or teacher; *esp.* one in a school, a schoolmaster. OE.

E. BLISHEN Mr. Oakes, the P. T. master, was our captain. D. STOREY A master came from the school to talk of Richard's university chances.

11 A man of whom one is a disciple; a revered male teacher in religion, philosophy, etc.; the (male) teacher from whom one has chiefly learned, or whose doctrines one accepts. ME.

G. BORROW Why should I be ashamed of their company when my Master mingled with publicans and thieves? G. SAINTSBURY John Keats . . and his master Leigh Hunt.

12 A skilled workman, orig. one qualified by training and experience to teach apprentices; a workman who is in business on his own account. ME.

R. H. TAWNEY Gilds . . appear to have included 5,000 masters, who employed not more than 6,000 to 7,000 journeymen.

13 A holder of a specific degree of a university or other academic institution, orig. of a level which conveyed authority to teach in the university. LME. ▸**b** In *possess.*: = ***master's degree*** below. *N. Amer. colloq.* M20.
14 An artist of great skill, one regarded as a model of excellence; a work of painting or sculpture by such an artist (chiefly in ***old master*** s.v. OLD *adjective*). LME.

T. GRAY With a Master's hand, and Prophet's fire. K. CLARK When one compares the figures by the master himself . . with those of his assistants.

15 a *CHESS.* A player of proved ability at international or national level. Cf. GRAND MASTER 3. M19. ▸**b** In *pl.* In some sports, a class for competitors over the usual age for the highest level of competition. Usu. *attrib.* L20.

M

▸ **III** As a title of rank or compliment.
16 As *voc.* (*obsolete* exc. *dial.*): sir. Also (now *arch.* & *rhet.*) in *pl.*, often with *my*: sirs, gentlemen (freq. *iron.*). ME.

SHAKES. *Haml.* You are welcome, masters; welcome, all. N. GORDIMER they had tried to train him to drop the 'master' for the ubiquitously respectful 'sir'.

17 Used preceding the name or designation of a man of high social rank or of learning, accomplishment, etc. *arch.* ME. ▸†**b** Used preceding a title of office or profession, etc. ME–M17.

M. PATTISON Two allegorical pieces by Master Hans Holbein.

18 (*Master of* —.) As a courtesy title of the heir apparent to a Scottish baron, viscount, or (formerly) earl. L15.

D. DUNNETT When her husband died . . the elder boy . . became third Baron Culter, and . . his brother received the heir's title of Master of Culter.

19 Used preceding the name of a boy not old enough to be called *Mr.* Hence (freq. as a form of address), a boy; also ***young master***, ***little master***. L16. ▸**b** Used, with disparaging implication, preceding the name of an adult. L19.

SWIFT Maids, misses, and little master . . in a third [coach]. DICKENS Wait a bit Master Davy, and I'll—I'll tell you something.

— PHRASES: **be one's own master** be independent or free to do as one wishes. GRAND MASTER. †**great master** = GRAND MASTER 1, 2. ***little master***: see sense 19 above. ***little Masters***: see LITTLE *adjective*. ***lord and master***: see LORD *noun*. **make oneself master of** acquire a thorough knowledge of or facility of. **master and commander** (until 1814) the full title of the rank of Commander in the Royal Navy. ***master-at-arms***: see ARM *noun*[2]. ***Master in Lunacy***: see LUNACY 1. ***Master of Arts***: see ART *noun*[1]. ***master of beagles***: see sense 3b above. ***master of ceremonies***: see CEREMONY *noun*. ***master of foxhounds***, ***master of hounds***: see sense 3b above. ***Master of Misrule***: see MISRULE *noun*. ***Master of Request(s)***: see REQUEST *noun*. ***Master of Science***: see SCIENCE. **Master of the Horse** (the title of) the third official of the British royal household, attending the monarch on state occasions. ***Master of the King's Music***, ***Master of the Queen's Music***: see MUSIC *noun* 4. ***Master of the Request(s)***: see REQUEST *noun*. ***master of the revels***: see REVEL *noun*[1] 2. ***Master of the Rolls***: see ROLL *noun*[1]. **master's degree** a degree of Master of Arts, Master of Science, etc. **master's mate** *hist.* a petty officer rated as an assistant to the master of a warship. ***old master***: see OLD *adjective*. ***young master***: see sense 19 above.

▸ **B** *attrib.* or as *adjective*. **1** That is a master; chief, leading, commanding; great, powerful. ME. ▸**b** Chiefly *hist.* Designating an official with authority over others of the same kind. ME. ▸**c** Designating a workman who is a master as distinguished from an apprentice or journeyman, or who employs others. ME. ▸**d** Supremely or consummately skilled; accomplished, expert. ME. ▸**e** *CHESS.* Of the standard of master (cf. sense A.15 above). L19.

SHAKES. *Jul. Caes.* The choice and master spirits of this age. POPE The master Ram at last approach'd the gate. **c** C. KINGSLEY He would be a man and a master-sweep. M. MOORCOCK A master baker, he had written for the trade journals. **d** TENNYSON And last the master-bowman, he, Would cleave the mark. T. S. ELIOT He's the master criminal who can defy the Law. L. DEIGHTON Champion was some kind of master spy.

2 Of a (material or abstract) thing: main, principal; controlling, supreme. ME. ▸**b** *spec.* Designating a device or component which directly controls the action of others. Opp. ***slave***. E20. ▸**c** Designating the copy of a tape, disc, file, etc., which is the authoritative source for copies. E20.

POPE One master Passion in the breast, Like Aaron's serpent, swallows up the rest. **c** A. MILLER It all goes into the master file in the governor's office.

3 Of, pertaining to, or characteristic of a master. E17.
— COMB. & SPECIAL COLLOCATIONS: **Master Aircrew** a Royal Air Force rank equivalent to warrant officer; **masterbatch** a concentrated mixture used in the production of synthetic rubbers and plastics; **master-builder** (*a*) a skilled builder or architect; (*b*) a builder who employs other workmen; **master card** (*a*) *BRIDGE* a card that cannot be beaten unless trumped; (*b*) a record card which summarizes the information recorded on a number of other cards; **master-class** (*a*) the most powerful or influential class in society; (*b*) a class receiving instruction from a distinguished musician etc.; an advanced class given by a distinguished musician etc.; **master clock** a clock which transmits regular pulses of electricity for controlling other devices; **master-craftsman** a craftsman who is a master; an expert worker; ***Master Gunner***: see GUNNER 1; **master-hand** (*a*) the hand or agency of a master; (*b*) a highly skilled worker; **master key** a key that will open a number of different locks, each of which has its own key that will not open any of the rest; **master-man** †(*a*) (chiefly *Scot.*) a chief, a leader; (*b*) a master with apprentices or employees; ***master MARINER***; **master mason** (*a*) a skilled mason; a mason who employs other workers; (*b*) (***Master Mason***) a fully qualified Freemason, who has passed the third degree; **master oscillator** *ELECTRONICS*: used to produce a constant frequency, esp. the carrier frequency of a radio etc. transmitter; **master race** a race of people considered or claiming to be pre-eminent; *spec.* (in Nazi Germany) the 'Aryans' regarded as a superior people; **master-singer** = MEISTERSINGER; **master-spring** (now *rare* or *obsolete*) a mainspring (chiefly *fig.*); **master stroke** an act or touch worthy of a master; an outstandingly skilful act of policy etc.; one's cleverest move; **master-touch** a touch worthy of a master; a masterly manner of dealing with something; **master-work** (*a*) a masterpiece; (*b*) an action of chief importance; †(*c*) a main drainage or irrigation channel.
■ **masterhood** *noun* LME.

master /ˈmɑːstə/ *noun*[2]. E19.

[ORIGIN from MAST *noun*[1] + -ER[1].]

With numeral prefixed: a vessel having the specified number of masts.

three-master, ***seven-master***, etc.

master /ˈmɑːstə/ *verb trans.* ME.

[ORIGIN from MASTER *noun*[1] & *adjective*. Cf. Old French *maistrier*.]

1 Get the better of in a contest or struggle; overcome, defeat. ME.

J. BERESFORD Lord Edward was mastered, brought to the Castle, and committed to Newgate. G. P. R. JAMES Deep grief masters me.

2 Reduce to subjection, compel to obey; break, tame. ME.

GOLDSMITH The Zebra . . could never be entirely mastered. GEO. ELIOT A woman who would have liked to master him.

3 Temper, season; modify. *obsolete* exc. *DYEING*, season or age (dyestuffs); in *TANNING*, subject (skins) to the action of an astringent lye. LME.
†**4** Have at one's disposal; own, possess. L16–M17.

SHAKES. *Merch. V.* The wealth That the world masters.

5 †**a** Execute with skill. Only in E17. ▸**b** Make oneself master of (an art, science, etc.); acquire complete knowledge or understanding of, acquire complete facility in using. L17.

b R. G. COLLINGWOOD I have never been able to master the piano. K. WATERHOUSE We had mastered the mysteries of foreplay, contraception, climax. A. MACLEAN Captain Imrie had long mastered the art of dining gracefully at sea.

6 Act the part of master towards; rule as a master; be the master of (a school etc.). E17.
7 Record the master disc or tape for (a sound recording); make a recording of (a performance) from which a master can be created. M20.
■ **masterer** *noun* (*rare*) E17. **mastering** *noun* (*a*) the action of the verb; (*b*) *TANNING* a kind of lye made of lime etc. (cf. MASTER *verb* 3): L15.

masterate /ˈmɑːstərət/ *noun*. E20.

[ORIGIN from MASTER *noun*[1] & *adjective* + -ATE[1].]

The status or dignity of a person holding a master's degree.

masterdom /ˈmɑːstədəm/ *noun*. OE.

[ORIGIN from MASTER *noun*[1] & *adjective* + -DOM.]

†**1** The position or office of master or teacher; the degree of master. *rare*. OE–LME.
2 The position of being master; dominion, absolute control, supremacy. LME. ▸†**b** Masterful behaviour. *rare* (Spenser). Only in L16.
†**3** With *possess.*: = MASTERSHIP 3. L16–E17.

masterful /ˈmɑːstəfʊl, -f(ə)l/ *adjective*. LME.

[ORIGIN from MASTER *noun*[1] & *adjective* + -FUL.]

1 Given to acting the part of master; accustomed to insist on having one's own way; imperious, overbearing; (of an action) high-handed, despotic, arbitrary. LME. ▸†**b** *LAW* (chiefly *Scot.*). Of (the action of) a robber etc.: using violence or threats. LME–E19. ▸†**c** Of natural agency: violent, overwhelming. E16–M17.

HUGH WALPOLE Mrs. Moy-Thompson . . had long ago been crushed into a miserable negligibility by her masterful husband. P. GAY Freud knew what he wanted, and his masterful impetuosity carried her with him.

2 Having the capacities of a master; commanding; powerful and vigorous in rule; (in weakened sense) self-confident, assured, assertive. Also, indicative of authority, command, or confidence. LME.

J. HUTCHINSON This masterful disregard of logical thought. V. SACKVILLE-WEST He was . . growing more . . masterful, and arranged his life as it pleased him. DENNIS POTTER Her change of tone allowed him to play the smoothly masterful role which pleased him most.

3 Characterized by the skill that constitutes a master; masterly. Freq. with some admixture of sense 2. E17.

Aviation Week The Arabs did a masterful job of concealing their true intentions.

■ **masterfully** *adverb* LME. **masterfulness** *noun* L16.

masterless /ˈmɑːstəlɪs/ *adjective*. LME.

[ORIGIN from MASTER *noun*[1] & *adjective* + -LESS.]

1 Having no master. Of an animal: deprived of a controlling hand. LME. ▸**b** Having no reputable means of living; vagrant. Long *obsolete* exc. *hist.* L15. ▸**c** Of unknown authorship or provenance. L19.
†**2** Unable to be mastered; ungovernable. E17–M18.
■ **masterlessness** *noun* M19.

masterly /ˈmɑːstəli/ *adjective*. M16.

[ORIGIN from MASTER *noun*[1] & *adjective* + -LY[1].]

†**1** Belonging to, characteristic of, or resembling a master or lord; arbitrary, despotic, imperious, domineering. M16–M18.

DRYDEN You are a saucy, masterly companion; and so I leave you.

2 Resembling, characteristic of, or worthy of a master or skilled workman; skilfully exercised or performed. M16.

J. M. MURRY Time and again he marshals the evidence, in his masterly fashion, so that the conclusion . . appears inevitable. H. ACTON Wilson Steer painted a masterly portrait of her in her heyday.

3 *MINING.* ***masterly lode***, a main lode. L19.
■ **masterliness** *noun* E18.

masterly /ˈmɑːstəli/ *adverb*. Now *rare*. LME.

[ORIGIN from MASTER *noun*[1] & *adjective* + -LY[2].]

In a masterly manner.

SHAKES. *Wint. T.* Masterly done! The very life seems warm upon her lip.

mastermind /ˈmɑːstəmʌɪnd/ *noun* & *verb*. L17.

[ORIGIN from MASTER *noun*[1] & *adjective* + MIND *noun*[1].]

▸ **A** *noun*. **1** (A person with) an outstanding or commanding intellect. L17.

P. G. WODEHOUSE You can't expect two master-minds like us to pig it in that room downstairs. E. JENKINS Hers was one of the earliest master-minds in advertising.

2 The person (or other body) directing an intricate, esp. criminal, enterprise. L19.

A. TROLLOPE The police thought that I had been the master-mind among the thieves.

▸ **B** *verb trans.* Be the mastermind behind (an enterprise, a crime, etc.); plan and direct. M20.

S. BRILL Sammy Pro was indicted for masterminding a counterfeiting operation. A. BRIGGS Sweeping changes in the power . . of the Church masterminded by Thomas Cromwell were effected.

masterpiece /ˈmɑːstəpiːs/ *noun*. E17.

[ORIGIN from MASTER *noun*[1] & *adjective* + PIECE *noun*, after Dutch *meesterstuk*, German *Meisterstück*.]

1 A work of outstanding artistry or skill; a masterly production; a consummate example *of* some skill or other kind of excellence; (with *possess.*) a person's best piece of work. E17. ▸**b** A remarkable or singular person or thing. *colloq.* E20.

SHAKES. *Macb.* Confusion now hath made his masterpiece. F. QUARLES Man is heav'n's Master-piece. K. CLARK It is . . a masterpiece of Gothic architecture. A. LURIE A dealer can't always fill his gallery with masterpieces. *fig.*: JONSON Here, we must rest; this is our maister-piece; We cannot thinke to goe beyond this.

†**2** The most important feature, or the chief excellence, of a person or thing. Only in 17.

mastership /ˈmɑːstəʃɪp/ *noun*. LME.

[ORIGIN from MASTER *noun*[1] & *adjective* + -SHIP.]

1 The condition of being a master or ruler; dominion, rule, ascendancy, control. LME. ▸**b** Mastery, the upper

hand. Now *rare* or *obsolete*. **LME.** ▸**c** The authority of a master or teacher. **L16.**
2 The function, office, or dignity of a master, esp. a schoolmaster; the term of office of a master. **LME.**
†**3** With possess. adjective (as ***your mastership*** etc.): a title of respect given to a master. **LME–E17.**
4 The skill or knowledge of a master; mastery, thorough knowledge *of* a subject. **E17.** ▸**b** The status of a recognized master in a craft; the holding of a master's degree. **L17.**
5 The existence of masters or employers in industrial organization. **M19.**

masterwort /ˈmɑːstəwəːt/ *noun.* **E16.**
[ORIGIN from MASTER *noun*[1] & *adjective* + WORT *noun*[1].]
Any of various umbellifers used as pot herbs or medicinally; *spec.* (***a***) any of the genus *Astrantia*, comprising perennial plants of woods and damp meadows in Europe and western Asia; (***b***) *Peucedanum ostruthium*, a perennial native to southern Europe and naturalized in moist places elsewhere.

mastery /ˈmɑːst(ə)ri/ *noun.* **ME.**
[ORIGIN Old French *maistrie*, from *maistre* MASTER *noun*[1] & *adjective*: see -Y[3].]
1 The state or condition of being master, controller, or ruler; authority, dominion; an instance of this. **ME.** ▸†**b** Predominance; prevailing character. **L15–M17.**
J. R. GREEN Edward's aim . . was . . to save English commerce by securing the mastery of the Channel. A. TOFFLER Science first gave man a sense of mastery over his environment.
2 Superiority or ascendancy in competition or strife; the upper hand; victory (leading to domination). **ME.**
S. AUSTIN He . . always gained the mastery in the end. K. LINES There were many battles between the two armies . . yet neither side gained mastery.
†**3** Superior force or power. **ME–E19.**
4 Masterly skill or knowledge; supreme talent; skilful use or intellectual command *of* a technique, subject, instrument, etc. **ME.** ▸**b** The action of mastering a subject etc. **L18.**
H. KELLER I am surprised at the mastery of language which your letter shows. K. AMIS After half an hour of further attempts . . he considered he had a fair mastery of the weapon. M. FOOT Lloyd George returned to the platform with all his old mastery and relish. **b** SIR W. SCOTT It is matter beyond my mastery.
†**5** An action demonstrating skill or power; a feat, a trick; a test of strength or skill. **ME–L17.**
†**great mastery**, †**little mastery** a great, little, etc., achievement, a matter of great, little, etc., difficulty. †**try masteries** engage in a trial of skill, strength, etc. (*with*).

masthead /ˈmɑːsthɛd/ *noun & verb.* **L15.**
[ORIGIN from MAST *noun*[1] + HEAD *noun*.]
▸ **A** *noun.* **1** The head or highest part of a mast; *esp.* that of the lower mast as a place of observation or punishment, or of the whole mast as the place for flying flags etc. **L15.** ▸**b** A person stationed at the masthead. **M19.**
fig.: R. L. STEVENSON He was . . enjoying to the mast-head the modest pleasures of admiration.
2 The title, colophon, motto, etc., of a newspaper or journal, printed conspicuously esp. above the editorial or at the top of the first page. Orig. *US*. **M19.**
Oxford Art Journal Another of his designs . . was the masthead of a . . theatrical column in a magazine.
▸ **B** *verb trans.* **1** Send (a sailor) to the masthead as a punishment. **E19.**
2 Raise (a yard, sail, etc.) to its position on the mast or at the masthead. **M19.**

†**mast-holm** *noun.* **L16–E18.**
[ORIGIN from MAST *noun*[2] + HOLM *noun*[2].]
The holm oak.

mastic /ˈmastɪk/ *noun & adjective.* **LME.**
[ORIGIN Old French & mod. French from late Latin *mastichum*, *masticha*, vars. of *mastiche* from Greek *mastikhē*, presumed to be from *mastikhan*: see MASTICATE.]
▸ **A** *noun.* **1** A gum or resin which exudes from the bark of mastic trees (see sense 2), used in making varnish and (formerly) medicinally. Also ***mastic gum***, ***gum mastic***. **LME.**
2 In full ***mastic tree***. An evergreen shrub, *Pistacia lentiscus* (family Anacardiaceae), yielding mastic gum, native to the Mediterranean region. Also, any of certain related trees and shrubs yielding similar gums, *esp.* (more fully ***American mastic***) *Schinus molle*, native to tropical America. **LME.** ▸**b** A timber tree of the W. Indies and Florida, *Sideroxylon foetidissimum* (family Sapotaceae). **M17.**
†**3** In full ***herb mastic***. A labiate shrub, *Thymus mastichina*, native to Iberia and N. Africa. Cf. MARUM. **L16–M19.**
4 Orig., a kind of resinous or bituminous cement. Now, any waterproof, plastic, putty-like substance used as a filler, sealant, etc. **E18.**
5 A liquor flavoured with mastic gum; = MASTIKA. **L19.**
6 The colour of mastic; a shade of pale yellow. **L19.**
▸ **B** *attrib.* or as *adjective.* **1** Of a cement, adhesive, etc.: of the nature or consisting of mastic (sense A.4 above). **E19.**
2 Of the colour of mastic; pale yellow. **L19.**

masticable /ˈmastɪkəb(ə)l/ *adjective. rare.* **E19.**
[ORIGIN from MASTICATE + -ABLE.]
Able to be masticated.
■ **mastica'bility** *noun* **M19.**

masticate /ˈmastɪkeɪt/ *verb trans.* **M16.**
[ORIGIN Late Latin *masticat-* pa. ppl stem of *masticare* from Greek *mastikhan* grind the teeth, rel. to *masasthai* chew and perh. to synon. Latin *mandere*: see -ATE[3].]
1 Grind (food) to a pulp in the mouth; grind with the teeth, chew. **M16.**
2 Mechanically reduce (rubber etc.) to a pulp. **M19.**

mastication /mastɪˈkeɪʃ(ə)n/ *noun.* **LME.**
[ORIGIN Late Latin *masticatio(n-)*, formed as MASTICATE: see -ATION.]
The action or process of masticating something.

masticator /ˈmastɪkeɪtə/ *noun.* **L17.**
[ORIGIN from MASTICATION + -OR.]
1 In *pl.* The teeth, the jaws. *joc.* **L17.**
2 A person or animal that chews. **E19.**
3 A machine for grinding or pulping. **M19.**

masticatory /ˈmastɪkət(ə)ri/ *noun & adjective.* **L16.**
[ORIGIN mod. Latin *masticatorius*, *-um*, from *masticare*: see MASTICATE, -ORY[1], -ORY[2].]
▸ **A** *noun.* A substance, *esp.* a medicinal one, that is to be chewed. **L16.**
▸ **B** *adjective.* **1** Of, pertaining to, or concerned with mastication. **E17.**
2 *MEDICINE.* Affecting the organs of mastication. **M19.**

mastiff /ˈmastɪf, ˈmɑː-/ *noun.* **ME.**
[ORIGIN Obscurely repr. Old French *mastin* (mod. *mâtin*) from Proto-Romance from Latin *mansuetus* (earlier *mansues*) tamed, tame: see MANSUETE.]
A breed of large strong dog with a large head, drooping ears, and pendulous lips, used as a watchdog; a dog of this breed. Also ***mastiff dog***.
bull-mastiff: see BULL *noun*[1] & *adjective*. ***Tibetan mastiff***: see TIBETAN *adjective*.
– COMB.: **mastiff bat** any of numerous heavily built bats with a broad muzzle that belong to the family Molossidae and occur in warmer parts of the world; *esp.* an American bat of the genus *Molossus* or the genus *Eumops*.

†**mastiff** *adjective.* **LME.**
[ORIGIN Alt. of MASTY by assoc. with MASTIFF *noun* and *massive*.]
1 Of a swine: fattened. Only in **LME.**
2 Massive, solid, bulky; burly. **L15–M18.**

mastigoneme /ˈmastɪɡəniːm/ *noun.* **M20.**
[ORIGIN from Greek *mastig-*, *mastix* whip + *nēma* thread.]
BIOLOGY. Any of the hairlike structures situated, usu. in rows, on the flagellum of some unicellular eukaryotes.

mastigophore /ˈmastɪɡəfɔː/ *noun.* **M17.**
[ORIGIN formed as MASTIGOPHOROUS: see -PHORE.]
†**1** *GREEK HISTORY.* An usher carrying a whip for dispersing crowds. *rare* (Dicts.). Only in **M17.**
2 *ZOOLOGY.* = FLAGELLATE *noun.* **L19.**

mastigophorous /mastɪˈɡɒf(ə)rəs/ *adjective.* **E19.**
[ORIGIN from Greek *mastigophoros*, from *mastig-*, *mastix* whip: see -PHOROUS.]
1 That carries a scourge. *joc.* **E19.**
2 *ZOOLOGY.* Having flagella; flagellate. **L19.**
■ Also **mastigo'phoric** *adjective* **E19.**

mastigure /ˈmastɪɡjʊə/ *noun.* **M19.**
[ORIGIN mod. Latin *mastigura*, *-urus*, from Greek *mastig-*, *mastix* whip + *oura* tail.]
A N. African agamid lizard of the genus *Uromastix*, with a spiny tail.

mastika /maˈstiːkə/ *noun.* **L19.**
[ORIGIN mod. Greek *mastikha*.]
A liquor flavoured with mastic gum; = MASTIC *noun* 5.

masting /ˈmɑːstɪŋ/ *noun.* **E17.**
[ORIGIN from MAST *noun*[1], *verb* + -ING[1].]
1 The action or process of fitting a ship etc. with masts. **E17.**
2 Masts collectively. **E18.**
3 The action of felling trees for masts. *N. Amer.* **E18.**

mastitis /maˈstʌɪtɪs/ *noun.* **E19.**
[ORIGIN from Greek *mastos* breast + -ITIS.]
MEDICINE. Inflammation of the mammary gland in people or animals.
summer mastitis: see SUMMER *noun*[1].

-mastix /ˈmastɪks/ *suffix.*
[ORIGIN from Greek *mastix* scourge, after *Homeromastix* scourge of Homer (the name given to the grammarian Zoïlus on account of the severity of his censure of the Homeric poems).]
Used esp. in the 17th cent. to form quasi-Greek combs. designating persons or books etc. violently hostile to some person, class, institution, etc., as ***Puritano-mastix***, ***Satiromastix***, etc.

masto- /ˈmastəʊ/ *combining form.*
[ORIGIN In sense 1 from MASTOID; in sense 2 from Greek *mastos* breast: see -O-.]
1 Pertaining jointly to the mastoid process or bone and some other part of the skull, as ***masto-parietal*** etc.
2 Affecting or involving the mammary gland.
■ **masto'dynia** *noun* (MEDICINE) neuralgia of the female breast **E19.** **ma'stopathy** *noun* any disease or dysfunction of the female breast **M19.**

mastodon /ˈmastədɒn/ *noun.* **E19.**
[ORIGIN from Greek *mastos* breast + -ODON.]
PALAEONTOLOGY. A large extinct mammal of the genus *Mammut*, resembling the elephant but having nipple-shaped tubercles in pairs on the crowns of the molar teeth.
■ **masto'donic** *adjective* (*rare*) = MASTODONTIC **M19.** **masto'dontic** *adjective* of or pertaining to a mastodon; resembling the mastodon: **M19.**

mastoid /ˈmastɔɪd/ *adjective & noun.* **M18.**
[ORIGIN French *mastoïde* or mod. Latin *mastoides* from Greek *mastoeidēs*, from *mastos* breast: see -OID.]
▸ **A** *adjective.* Chiefly *ANATOMY & ZOOLOGY.* Shaped like a female breast. Also, of or pertaining to the mastoid process or bone. **M18.**
mastoid bone (***a***) the mastoid process; (***b***) in fishes and reptiles, a bone of the skull homologous with this. **mastoid process** a conical prominence of the temporal bone behind the ear.
▸ **B** *noun.* **1** *ANATOMY.* = ***mastoid process***, ***mastoid bone*** above. **M19.**
2 = MASTOIDITIS. *colloq.* **M20.**
■ **ma'stoidal** *adjective* of or pertaining to the mastoid process **M19.** **mastoi'dectomy** *noun* (an instance of) surgical incision of the mastoid process, in order to relieve infection within its cavities **L19.** **mastoi'ditis** *noun* inflammation of (the cavities of) the mastoid process **L19.**

†**mastuprate** *verb intrans.* **E–M17.**
[ORIGIN Alt. of Latin *masturbat-* (see MASTURBATE) as if from Latin *manus* hand + *stuprare* defile: see -ATE[3].]
= MASTURBATE.
■ **mastupration** *noun* (long *rare*) **E17.**

masturbate /ˈmastəbeɪt/ *verb.* **M19.**
[ORIGIN Latin *masturbat-* pa. ppl stem of *masturbari*, of unknown origin: see -ATE[3]. Cf. MASTUPRATE.]
1 *verb trans.* Manually stimulate the genitals of (oneself or another person) for sexual pleasure. **M19.**
2 *verb intrans.* Stimulate one's own genitals for sexual pleasure. **L19.**
■ **masturbator** *noun* a person who masturbates **E18.** **masturbatory** *adjective* of, pertaining to, or involving masturbation **M19.**

masturbation /mastəˈbeɪʃ(ə)n/ *noun.* **E17.**
[ORIGIN Latin *masturbatio(n-)*, formed as MASTURBATE: see -ATION. Cf. MASTUPRATION.]
The action or practice of masturbating; manual stimulation of the genitals for sexual pleasure.
mutual masturbation manual stimulation of each other's genitals by two people for sexual pleasure.

masty /ˈmɑːsti/ *adjective.* Long *obsolete* exc. *dial.* **LME.**
[ORIGIN from MAST *noun*[2] + -Y[1]. Cf. MASTIFF *adjective*.]
1 †**a** Of a pig: fattened. **LME–M16.** ▸**b** Burly, big-bodied. **M16.**
†**2** Producing mast. **L16–M17.**

masula /məˈsuːlə/ *noun. obsolete* exc. *hist.* Also **-ah.** **L17.**
[ORIGIN Perh. from Marathi *māsḷī* or Konkani *māsḷī* fish.]
A large surf boat used on the Coromandel coast of India. Also ***massoola boat***.

†**masures** *noun pl. rare.* **E17–L18.**
[ORIGIN French.]
Ruins (of buildings); ramshackle habitations.

masurium /məˈz(j)ʊərɪəm/ *noun.* **E20.**
[ORIGIN from German *Masuren*, a region of NE Poland + -IUM.]
HISTORY OF SCIENCE. The element of atomic no. 43 (later named ***technetium***), mistakenly claimed to have been discovered spectroscopically.

mat /mat/ *noun*[1]. Also †**-tt.**
[ORIGIN Old English *matt*, *meatt(e)*, corresp. to Middle Dutch *matte*, Old High German *matta* (Dutch *mat*, German *Matte*), from West Germanic from late Latin *matta*.]
1 A piece of a coarse material, usu. woven or plaited, used for lying, sitting, or kneeling on, or as a protective covering for floors, walls, etc. Also, a small rug. **OE.** ▸**b** *spec.* An article of this kind, or of material such as rubber or cork, placed on the floor near a door for people entering to wipe their shoes on. Cf. ***doormat*** s.v. DOOR. **M17.** ▸**c** *BOWLS.* = FOOTER *noun*[1] 2. **L19.** ▸**d** A piece of padded material, canvas, etc., on which wrestling bouts, gymnastic displays, etc., take place. **E20.**
S. PEPYS A very fine African mat, to lay upon the ground under a bed of state. C. ACHEBE Joy was now having her hair done, seated on a mat on the floor. **b** *Independent* The excitement . . on seeing an envelope, the address handwritten, on the mat.
bath mat, ***prayer mat***, etc. **on the mat** *colloq.* in trouble with some authority; = ***on the carpet*** (b) s.v. CARPET *noun*. **d go to the mat** contend in wrestling etc. (*with*); *fig.* argue or struggle (*with*).
2 A coarse piece of sacking on which a feather bed is laid. Also, a bed covering, a quilt. Now *dial.* **ME.**
3 *NAUTICAL.* A thick web of rope yarn used to protect standing rigging from the friction of other ropes. **ME.**
4 **a** Material of which mats are made; plaited or woven rushes, straw, etc.; matting. *obsolete* exc. *attrib.* **E16.** ▸**b** A bag made of matting. **L17.**
5 A thin flat article (orig. of plaited straw, but now usu. of cork, plastic, etc., and often ornamental) to be placed

M

under a dish, plate, etc., in order to protect the surface beneath from heat, moisture, etc. E19.
beer mat, drip mat, place mat, table mat, etc.
6 *transf.* A thick tangled mass of hair, vegetation, etc., esp. forming a layer. E19. ▸**b** ENGINEERING. A flat interwoven or lattice structure used as a foundation or support. L19.

A. DESAI His chin sank down into the mat of black hair on his chest.

7 A type of cloak or cape worn by the Maori; hence, *the* Maori way of life. *NZ.* E19.
KOROWAI ***mat***.
8 The closely worked part of a lace design. M19.
– COMB.: **mat-grass** a wiry grass of moorland and mountainside, *Nardus stricta*; **mat-man** *slang* a wrestler; **matweed** any of various rushlike grasses, as marram; **mat-work** (*a*) matting; a structure like a mat; (*b*) physical exercises performed on a mat.

mat /mat/ *noun*[2]. M18.
[ORIGIN Abbreviation.]
CARDS. = MATADOR 2.

mat /mat/ *noun*[3]. *colloq.* E20.
[ORIGIN Abbreviation.]
= MATINÉE 1.

mat /mat/ *noun*[4]. E20.
[ORIGIN Abbreviation.]
= MATRIX *noun* 3a.

mat *noun*[5] var. of MATT *noun*[1].

mat *adjective* var. of MATT *adjective*.

mat /mat/ *verb*[1]. Infl. **-tt-**. LME.
[ORIGIN from MAT *noun*[1].]
†**1** *verb intrans.* Make mats. *rare.* Only in LME.
2 *verb trans.* Cover or provide with mats or matting. M16.
3 *verb trans.* Cover with something resembling a mat; cover with an entangled or hardened mass. L16.

F. W. ROBERTSON A temple . . matted with ivy. A. MASON Clods of earth still matted the hair.

4 *verb trans.* Form into a mat; entangle or entwine (*together*) in a thick mass. L16. ▸**b** Make by interlacing, form into a mat. E19.

A. TUCKER To . . disentangle the boughs where they had matted themselves together.

5 *verb intrans.* Become entangled (*together*), form tangled masses. M18.
6 *verb trans.* Put 'on the mat'; reprimand; = CARPET *verb* 2. *colloq.* M20.

mat *verb*[2] var. of MATT *verb*.

-mat /mat/ *suffix*.
[ORIGIN Abbreviation of -MATIC.]
Forming names (freq. proprietary) of equipment that works automatically, or establishments operating such equipment, as ***Laundromat***.

Matabele /matə'bi:li, -'beɪli/ *noun & adjective*. E19.
[ORIGIN from Bantu *ma-* tribal prefix + Sesotho (*le*)*tebele*: see NDEBELE.]
▸ **A** *noun*. Pl. **-s**, same. A Ndebele, esp. in Zimbabwe. E19.
▸ **B** *attrib.* or as *adjective*. Of or pertaining to the Indebele, esp. in Zimbabwe. M19.
Matabele ant a large black stinging ant, *Megaponera foetens*, found in Zimbabwe.

matachin /matə'ʃi:n/ *noun*. *obsolete* exc. *hist.* L16.
[ORIGIN French (now *matassin*) from Spanish *matachin* or Italian *mattaccino*, of unknown origin.]
1 A kind of sword dancer in an extravagantly fanciful costume. L16.
†**2** A masked dance performed by matachins (usu. three). L16–L17.

matador /'matədɔ:/ *noun*. Also (esp. senses 2, 3) **-ore**. L17.
[ORIGIN Spanish, from *matar* kill.]
1 A bullfighter whose task is to kill the bull. L17.
2 In some card games (as quadrille, ombre, solo): any of the highest trumps so designated by the rules of the game. L17.
3 A domino game in which halves are matched so as to make a total of seven; any of the dominoes which have seven spots altogether, together with the double blank. M19.
– COMB.: **matador pants** = *TOREADOR* ***pants***.
■ **mata'dora** *noun* a female matador M20.

mataeology /matɪ'ɒlədʒi/ *noun*. *rare*. M17.
[ORIGIN from Greek *mataios* vain + -O- + -LOGY.]
Vain or unprofitable discourse.

matagouri /matə'gʊəri, -'gaʊri/ *noun*. *NZ*. Also **-gauri** /-'gaʊri/. M19.
[ORIGIN Alt. of Maori TUMATAKURU.]
A thorny New Zealand shrub, *Discaria toumatou* (family Rhamnaceae). Also called ***Irishman***, ***wild Irishman***, ***tumatakuru***.

Mata Hari /mɑ:tə 'hɑ:ri/ *noun*. M20.
[ORIGIN Name taken by Margaretha Gertruida Zelle (1876–1917), Dutch courtesan and spy who lived in the Dutch East Indies from 1897 to 1902, from Malay *matahari* sun, from *mata* eye + *hari* day.]
A beautiful and seductive female spy.

matai /'matʌɪ/ *noun*[1]. M19.
[ORIGIN Maori.]
A New Zealand coniferous tree, *Prumnopitys taxifolia* (also called ***black pine***); the light-coloured wood of this tree.

matai /mə'tʌɪ/ *noun*[2]. E20.
[ORIGIN Samoan.]
In a Samoan extended family, the person who is chosen to succeed to a chief's or orator's title and honoured as the head of the family.

matamata /matə'matə/ *noun*. M19.
[ORIGIN Brazilian Portuguese *matamatá* from Tupi *matamatá*.]
A S. American turtle, *Chelus fimbriatus*, with a lumpy carapace, long neck, and broad flat head.

matapi /'matəpi:/ *noun*. Also **-pee**. L18.
[ORIGIN Arawak.]
A pliable basket used in Guyana for expressing the poisonous juice from the root of the cassava or manioc.

Matara diamond /'mɑ:tərə ˌdʌɪəmənd/ *noun phr.* Also (earlier) **Matu-**. E19.
[ORIGIN A town in Sri Lanka.]
A colourless or smoky variety of zircon used as a gem; = JARGON *noun*[2].

matata /'matətə/ *noun*. *NZ*. M19.
[ORIGIN Maori.]
= ***fernbird*** s.v. FERN *noun*.

match /matʃ/ *noun*[1].
[ORIGIN Old English *gemæćća* from Germanic, rel. to base of *gemaca* MAKE *noun*[1].]
†**1** A husband, a wife, a partner, a lover. Also, an animal's mate. OE–M17.
†**2** An equal in age, rank, position, etc.; a fellow, a companion. OE–L16.
3 a A person (occas. a number of persons or a thing) able to contend with another as an equal. ME. ▸†**b** An opponent, a rival. LME–L16.

a K. ISHIGURO Sometimes, even Father's no match for Mother.

4 a A person, thing, action, etc., equal to another in some quality. LME. ▸**b** A person or thing that exactly corresponds to or resembles another, or that forms a matching pair with another. E16. ▸**c** A more or less matching pair; two persons, things, or sets each the counterpart of the other. M16. ▸**d** COMPUTING. A record or string that matches the requirements of a search or is identical with a given record etc. M20.

a E. GASKELL I don't believe there is his match anywhere for goodness. **b** J. PALMER You've got two nice creatures, they are right elegant matches.

†**5** A matching of adversaries against each other; a contest viewed with regard to the equality or inequality of the parties. LME–E17.
6 A contest or competitive trial of skill in some sport, exercise, or operation, in which two or more people or teams compete against each other; an engagement or arrangement for such a contest. Also, a contest in which animals are made to compete. M16.

Economist In the cricket match, the 'Windies' scraped home in a nail-biting finish.

ploughing match, return match, slanging match, test match, etc.
†**7** An agreement, a bargain. M16–E18.
8 a A marriage, a marriage agreement, *esp.* one viewed as more or less advantageous with regard to wealth or status. L16. ▸†**b** The action of marrying; relationship by marriage. L16–M17. ▸**c** A person viewed with regard to his or her eligibility for marriage, esp. on the grounds of wealth or rank. L16. ▸**d** A heraldic representation of a marriage. Long *rare*. E17.

a H. ALLEN Although Don Luis was . . older than his bride . . the match seemed a fortunate one. **c** G. MEREDITH He's the great match of the county.

9 ELECTRICITY. An equality of impedance between two coupled devices. M20.
– PHRASES: **be a match for** be equal to. **find one's match**, **meet one's match** encounter or come up against one's equal, esp. in strength or ability. ***game, set, and match***: see GAME *noun*. ***hatches, matches, and dispatches***: see HATCH *noun*[2]. **make a match** bring about a marriage. ***man of the match***: see MAN *noun*. ***meet one's match***: see ***find one's match*** above. **more than a match for** superior to in strength, ability, etc. ***steal a match***: see STEAL *verb*. ***varsity match***: see VARSITY *adjective*.
– COMB.: **match ball** (*a*) in cricket etc., a ball of the standard specified by the laws of the game; (*b*) in tennis, a ball that may decide a match; **match book** (*a*) a book containing dates and details of horse races; (*b*) CRICKET a book containing the scores etc. of matches played by a club or an eleven; **match-card** CRICKET a card summarizing the score and listing the players in batting order, a scorecard; **match-fit** *adjective* in good physical condition for a match, sufficiently fit to play in a match; **match play** (*a*) the play in a match; (*b*) GOLF play in which the score is reckoned by counting the holes gained on each side; **match point** (*a*) the state of a game when one side or player needs only one point to win the match; this point; (*b*) BRIDGE a unit of scoring in tournament play; **match race** orig., a race run between two horses; more widely, a race run as a competition; **match-rifle** a rifle used in shooting competitions; **match-winner** a person who contributes to or brings about victory in a match; **match-winning** *adjective* contributing to or bringing about victory in a match.

match /matʃ/ *noun*[2]. LME.
[ORIGIN Old French *meiche*, *mesche* (mod. *mèche*) corresp. to Spanish, Portuguese *mecha*, Italian *miccia*, which have been referred to Latin *myxa* (from Greek *muxa*) nozzle of a lamp, (in medieval Latin) lamp-wick.]
†**1** The wick of a candle or lamp. LME–M17.
2 A piece of wick, cord, etc., designed to burn steadily when lit at the end, and used to fire a cannon, ignite a trail of gunpowder etc. M16. ▸**b** The material of which this is made; cord etc. prepared for ignition. L16.
3 A piece of cord, cloth, paper, etc., dipped in melted sulphur so as to be readily ignited with a tinderbox, and used to light a candle or lamp, or to set fire to fuel. *obsolete* exc. *hist.* M16. ▸**b** A similar object used for fumigation. E18.
4 A short slender piece of wood, wax, etc., tipped with a composition which bursts into flame when rubbed on a rough or specially prepared surface or, formerly, when brought into contact with a chemical reagent. M19.

M. LOWRY Three cigarettes were lit on one match. P. BOWLES Give me a match . . My candle's gone out.

Congreve match, lucifer match, safety match, slow match, etc.
– PHRASES: **put a match to** set fire to.
– COMB.: **matchbook** a book (BOOK *noun* 8) containing matches; **match-head** the mass of flammable composition forming the tip of a match; **match-safe** *US* a container for holding matches and keeping them dry or preventing accidental ignition.

match /matʃ/ *adjective*. *obsolete* exc. *techn.* L15.
[ORIGIN from attrib. & appositive uses of MATCH *noun*[1].]
That matches; corresponding.
match dissolve CINEMATOGRAPHY & TELEVISION a fade from one picture to another in which a similar or identical object appears in the same place in each picture. **match-plane** either of two planes used respectively to form the groove and tongue in grooving and tonguing boards.

match /matʃ/ *verb*[1]. LME.
[ORIGIN from MATCH *noun*[1].]
1 a *verb trans.* Encounter with equal power, be a match for; equal, rival. Formerly also, encounter as an adversary. LME. ▸†**b** *verb intrans.* Meet in combat, fight (*with*). LME–L16.

a K. ISHIGURO We are now a mighty nation, capable of matching any of the Western nations.

2 *verb trans.* Place in opposition or conflict *against* or *with*. Also, place in competition or comparison *with*. LME.

SHAKES. *Rom. & Jul.* That fair . . With tender Juliet match'd, is now not fair. W. S. MAUGHAM The prospect of matching his wits with such an antagonist excited him.

3 *verb trans.* **a** Arrange (persons or things) according to fitness or equality; place in a suitable or equal pair or set; provide with an adversary or competitor of equal power. Also foll. by *up*. Usu. in *pass.*, esp. in ***ill-matched***, ***well-matched***. LME. ▸**b** Proportion, make to correspond *to* or *with*. L17. ▸**c** CARPENTRY. Provide (a board) with a tongue and a groove on opposite edges, to allow interlocking with other boards. M19. ▸**d** ELECTRICITY. Equalize (two coupled impedances) so as to bring about the maximum transfer of power from one to the other; make (a device) equal in effective impedance *to*. E20.

b M. ARNOLD God doth match His gifts to man's believing.

4 a *verb trans.* Join in marriage (esp. with ref. to the suitability or otherwise of the partnership); procure a match for; connect (a family) by marriage. Also foll. by *to*, *with*. *arch.* LME. ▸**b** *verb intrans.* Join oneself in marriage, marry. Foll. by *into*, *with*. Now *rare* exc. *dial.* M16.

a J. TIPPER I am heartily glad your dear Sister is so happily match'd to Mr. Stevens.

†**5** *verb trans.* Associate, join in companionship or cooperation; put together so as to form a pair or set *with* another person or thing. L15–M17.
6 a *verb intrans.* Be equal *with*; be suitably coupled (*with*); correspond, harmonize, go. M16. ▸**b** *verb trans.* Be equal to; correspond to, go with, be the match or counterpart of. L16.

a OED These patterns do not match. **b** A. C. BOULT His knowledge of Westminster Abbey was exceeded by none and matched by few. W. TREVOR She put on her red and black dress, with a hat that perfectly matched it.

†**7** *verb trans.* Regard, treat, or speak of as equal. L16–E17.
8 *verb trans.* **a** Find or produce an equal to. Also, find (a person or thing) suitable for another. L16. ▸**b** Provide with a suitable addition or counterpart; *spec.* (seek to) find material, a garment, etc., that complements or accords with (another). E17.

a J. PORY Excellent wines, and sugars which cannot be matched. **b** J. HAWTHORNE As if it were a question of matching knitting-yarns.

†**9** *verb trans.* Procure as a match. *rare* (Shakes.). Only in L16.
– PHRASES: ***ill-matched***: see ILL *adjective & adverb*. **matched orders** COMMERCE systems of manipulation on a stock exchange involving artificial treatment of orders to buy and sell shares etc. **match up to** attain the standard of, equal. ***mix and match***: see MIX *verb*.

to match corresponding in a particular respect with something already mentioned. *well-matched*: see WELL *adverb*.
– COMB.: **match-up** the action of pairing or setting in opposition, esp. in sport or politics, two suited or equal persons or things (cf. sense 3 above); a pair so matched; a contest between such a pair.
■ **matcher** *noun* E17.

match /matʃ/ *verb*² *trans.* Now *rare*. M17.
[ORIGIN from MATCH *noun*².]
Fumigate (wine, liquor, or casks) by burning sulphur matches (MATCH *noun*² 3).

matchable /ˈmatʃəb(ə)l/ *adjective*. M16.
[ORIGIN from MATCH *verb*¹ + -ABLE. Earlier in UNMATCHABLE.]
1 Able to be matched, equalled, or rivalled. M16.
†2 Comparable, equal, similar. Foll. by *to*, *with*. L16–L17.
†3 Suitable, accordant. E17–E19.
■ **matchableness** *noun* E17.

matchboard /ˈmatʃbɔːd/ *noun* & *verb*. M19.
[ORIGIN from MATCH *adjective* + BOARD *noun*.]
CARPENTRY. ▸**A** *noun*. A board which has a tongue along one edge and a groove in the opposite edge, so that it interlocks with other similar boards. M19.
▸**B** *verb trans.* Cover or provide with matchboards. L19.
■ **matchboarding** *noun* matchboards fitted together to form a building material M19.

matchbox /ˈmatʃbɒks/ *noun*. L18.
[ORIGIN from MATCH *noun*² + BOX *noun*².]
†1 MILITARY. A metal tube full of small holes, in which a soldier carried a lighted match (MATCH *noun*² 2). Only in L18.
2 A box for holding matches. M19.
3 Something very small, *esp.* a very small house or flat. E20.

JOYCE Got notice to quit this match-box and am . . looking for a flat.

– COMB.: **matchbox bean** *Austral.* a leguminous climbing plant, *Entada phaseoloides*; the seed pod of this, used to make matchboxes.

matchcoat /ˈmatʃkəʊt/ *noun*. *obsolete* exc. *hist.* Orig. †**matchco** (pl. **-os**). E17.
[ORIGIN Virginia Algonquian *matchkore* deerskin robe, alt. by folk etym. as if from MATCH *noun*¹, *verb*¹ + COAT *noun*.]
A kind of mantle formerly worn by American Indians, orig. made of fur skins and later of coarse woollen cloth; the cloth used for this.

matchet *noun* see MACHETE.

matchless /ˈmatʃlɪs/ *adjective*. M16.
[ORIGIN from MATCH *noun*¹ + -LESS.]
1 Having no match, without an equal, incomparable. M16.

H. AINSWORTH There she stood before him, in all her matchless beauty.

†2 That are not a match or pair. *rare* (Spenser). Only in L16.
†3 Unmarried. E–M17.

matchlock /ˈmatʃlɒk/ *noun*. M17.
[ORIGIN from MATCH *noun*² + LOCK *noun*².]
hist. A gunlock in which a match (MATCH *noun*² 2) is placed to ignite the powder; a gun having such a lock.

matchmake /ˈmatʃmeɪk/ *verb intrans.* Pa. t. & pple (*rare*) **-made** /-meɪd/. E17.
[ORIGIN Back-form. from MATCHMAKER *noun*.]
Scheme or contrive to bring about a marriage. Chiefly as *matchmaking verbal noun & ppl adjective*.

matchmaker /ˈmatʃmeɪkə/ *noun*. M17.
[ORIGIN from MATCH *noun*¹ + MAKER.]
1 A person who schemes or enjoys scheming to bring about a match or marriage. M17.

Woman & Home The Princess of Wales, reportedly an incorrigible matchmaker during Sarah's and Andrew's courtship.

2 A person who arranges a boxing match or other sporting contest. E18.

match-maker /ˈmatʃmeɪkə/ *noun*. M17.
[ORIGIN from MATCH *noun*² + MAKER.]
A person who makes matches (MATCH *noun*²).

matchstick /ˈmatʃstɪk/ *noun* & *adjective*. L18.
[ORIGIN from MATCH *noun*² + STICK *noun*¹.]
▸**A** *noun*. 1 (The stick of) a wooden match. L18.

E. PIZZEY She . . looked down at her legs. 'They're not like matchsticks any more.'

2 A thin person. *slang*. M20.
▸**B** *attrib.* or as *adjective*. Very thin, skeletal. Also, (of a drawing, a drawn figure, etc.) executed with short straight lines. M20.

Guardian Matchstick men—taught by adults, copied by infants—can be death to child art.

matchwood /ˈmatʃwʊd/ *noun*. L16.
[ORIGIN from MATCH *noun*² + WOOD *noun*¹.]
†1 Touchwood. Only in L16.
2 Wood suitable for matchsticks. L16.
into matchwood into minute pieces (after verbs like *break*).

mate /meɪt/ *noun*¹. ME.
[ORIGIN Old French & mod. French *mat* in *eschec mat* CHECKMATE.]
CHESS. = CHECKMATE.
fool's mate: see FOOL *noun*¹. *scholar's mate*: see SCHOLAR *noun*. See also SELFMATE, STALEMATE.

mate /meɪt/ *noun*². ME.
[ORIGIN Middle Low German *mate*, *gemate* (Flemish *gemaat*, Dutch *maat*) = Old High German *gimmazzo*, from West Germanic bases of Y- (denoting association), MEAT *noun*, the lit. sense being 'messmate'.]
1 †**a** A creature, a fellow, a chap. Freq. *derog.* ME–E17. ▸**b** A companion, a fellow, a comrade, a friend; a fellow worker. LME. ▸**c** (With specifying word.) A person with whom one shares accommodation. M17. ▸**d** A helper or assistant to a more skilled worker. L19.

b P. BARKER She expected to see two of his mates but no, the men were strangers. *New Society* I was with my mate, John's brother.

b *playmate*, *running mate*, *schoolmate*, etc. **be mates with**, **go mates with** be an associate or partner of. **c** *cabin-mate*, *cell-mate*, *flat-mate*, *room-mate*, etc.
2 Used as a form of address to an equal. *colloq.* LME.

S. L. ELLIOTT Well, well—pleased to meet you mate. *Listener* Look, mate, we *live* here.

3 NAUTICAL. **a** The rank of officer on a merchant ship next below that of master, divided into *first mate*, *second mate*, *third mate*, etc., according to seniority; an officer of this rank. L15. ▸**b** An assistant to an officer on board ship. L15. ▸**c** An assistant to a warrant officer in the US navy. L19.

a W. H. GRAY An old scholar, who was first mate on board a ship.

b *BOATSWAIN's mate*. *master's mate*: see MASTER *noun*¹.
4 A suitable associate or (formerly) adversary; an equal, a match. *arch.* M16.
5 **a** A partner in marriage. Formerly also (*rare*), a lover. M16. ▸**b** Either of a pair of animals. L16.

b B. GILROY Like a bird calling for its mate she called and called for Danny.

6 Either of a pair of things; a counterpart, a parallel; *spec.* a solid or fixed point on a railway line which pairs or mates with the movable tongue or switch on the other rail. L16.

N. MARSH The glove is Mrs. Wilde's . . . She wore the mate yesterday.

■ **matehood** *noun* = MATESHIP 1 E20. **mateless** *adjective* L16.

mate *noun*³ var. of MATY *noun*.

†**mate** *adjective*. ME.
[ORIGIN Old French & mod. French *mat* mated at chess from Persian *māt* in phr. (used in chess) *šāh māt*: see CHECKMATE, MATE *noun*¹.]
1 Overcome, vanquished; exhausted, worn out. ME–M16.
2 Dejected, downcast; alarmed, distraught. ME–M16.
3 Mated in chess. LME–L16.

mate /meɪt/ *verb*¹. ME.
[ORIGIN French *mater*, formed as MATE *adjective*.]
1 CHESS. **a** *verb trans.* Checkmate. ME. ▸†**b** *verb intrans.* Be checkmated. LME–L16.

a G. ORWELL It was like trying to make a move at chess when you were already mated.

†2 *verb trans.* Overcome, defeat, subdue. ME–E17.
3 *verb trans.* Nonplus, confound; make powerless or worthless. *obsolete* exc. *dial.* ME.
†4 *verb trans.* Put out of countenance; make helpless; daunt, abash; stupefy. LME–E19.
5 *verb trans.* Exhaust, weary; dull (passion). *obsolete* exc. *Scot. dial.* LME.

mate /meɪt/ *verb*². E16.
[ORIGIN from MATE *noun*².]
1 **a** *verb trans.* Be a match for; equal, rival. Now *poet.* E16. ▸**b** *verb intrans.* Claim equality *with*. *arch.* L17.

a SIR W. SCOTT In speed His galley mates the flying steed.

2 *verb intrans.* & *trans.* = MATCH *verb*¹ 4. L16.

LYTTON I fear that the king will be teased into mating my sister with the Count of Charolois.

3 *verb trans.* Join suitably *with*; associate, treat as comparable *with*. L16.
4 **a** *verb trans.* Pair (animals) for breeding. Also foll. by *up*. E17. ▸**b** *verb intrans.* Of animals: come together for breeding; copulate (*with*). M19.

a *Oban Times* The first common seal in Scotland to give birth in captivity . . was mated last April. **b** D. H. LAWRENCE Dark, like a lair where strong beasts had lurked and mated.

5 **a** *verb intrans.* Associate or keep company *with*. M19. ▸**b** *verb trans.* Accompany suitably. *rare*. L19.

a G. NAYLOR Contempt mates well with pity.

6 MECHANICS. **a** *verb intrans.* Of a part: make a good or proper fit *with*. E20. ▸**b** *verb trans.* Fit or join (a part) *with* or *to*. M20.

b *Time* The orbiter will be 'mated' to a carrier plane.

– PHRASES: **mating call** a characteristic call used by an animal during the mating season, esp. by males to attract potential mates. **mating season** a period of the year during which members of an animal species mate, often adopting a special coloration and characteristic behaviour.

maté /ˈmateɪ/ *noun*. E18.
[ORIGIN Spanish *mate* from Quechua *mati*.]
1 A gourd, calabash, etc., in which the leaves of the shrub maté are infused. Also *maté-cup*. E18.
2 (An infusion of) the leaves of a S. American shrub, *Ilex paraguariensis* (family Aquifoliaceae); the shrub itself. Also more fully *YERBA maté*. M18.

matelassé /mat(ə)ˈlaseɪ, *foreign* matlase (*pl. same*)/ *noun* & *adjective*. Also **-lasse**. L19.
[ORIGIN French, pa. pple of *matelasser* to quilt, from *matelas* MATTRESS.]
▸**A** *noun*. A silk or wool fabric with a raised design. L19.
▸**B** *adjective*. Having a raised design like quilting. L19.

matelot /ˈmatləʊ/ *noun*. M19.
[ORIGIN French = sailor. Cf. MATLOW.]
1 A sailor. *nautical slang*. M19.
2 A deep shade of blue. Now *rare*. E20.

matelote /ˈmat(ə)ləʊt, *foreign* matlɔt (*pl. same*)/ *noun*. E18.
[ORIGIN French, formed as MATELOT.]
A dish of fish etc. served in a sauce of wine, onions, etc.

mater /ˈmeɪtə/ *noun*. LME.
[ORIGIN Latin, lit. 'mother'.]
†1 The womb. LME–L15.
2 The thickest plate of an astrolabe. *obsolete* exc. *hist.* L16.
3 Mother. Cf. PATER. Chiefly *joc.* & *school slang*. M19.

†**materas** *noun* var. of MATRASS *noun*¹.

Mater Dolorosa /ˌmeɪtə dɒləˈrəʊsə/ *noun phr.* Pl. **Matres Dolorosae** /ˌmeɪtriːz dɒləˈrəʊsiː/. E19.
[ORIGIN medieval Latin, lit. 'sorrowful mother'.]
(A title of) the Virgin Mary, as having a role in the Passion of Christ; a representation, in painting or sculpture, of the Virgin Mary sorrowing; *transf.* a woman resembling the sorrowful Virgin in appearance, manner, etc.

materfamilias /meɪtəfəˈmɪlɪas/ *noun*. M18.
[ORIGIN Latin, from MATER + *familias* old genit. of *familia* FAMILY.]
The female head of a family or household.

material /məˈtɪərɪəl/ *adjective* & *noun*. ME.
[ORIGIN Old French & mod. French *matériel*, †*-ial* from late Latin *materialis*, from Latin *materia* matter: see -AL¹.]
▸**A** *adjective*. 1 Of or pertaining to matter or substance; formed or consisting of matter; corporeal. ME. ▸†**b** Forming the material or substance of a thing. *rare* (Shakes.). Only in E17.

a J. BUTLER The material world appears to be . . boundless and immense. *Annabel* The accumulation of material things has never been of great significance to me.

2 **a** PHILOSOPHY. Of or pertaining to matter as opp. to form. LME. ▸**b** LOGIC. Concerned with the matter, not the form, of reasoning. E17. ▸**c** PHILOSOPHY & THEOLOGY. That is so by conduct or matter, rather than by motive or form. M17.
3 **a** Serious, important; of consequence. L15. ▸**b** Pertinent, relevant; essential *to*; LAW having a logical connection with the facts at issue. L15. ▸**c** Chiefly LAW. Of evidence or a fact: significant, influential, esp. to the extent of determining a cause, affecting a judgement, etc. L16. ▸†**d** Full of sense or sound information. Only in 17.

a G. GROTE The Athenians had a material interest in the quarrel. **b** SIR W. SCOTT Certain passages material to his understanding the rest of this important narrative.

4 Of conduct, a point of view, etc.: not elevated or spiritual. L16.

C. BRONTË What I saw struck me . . as grossly material, not poetically spiritual.

5 Concerned with or involving matter or the use of matter; relating to the physical, as opp. to the intellectual or spiritual, aspect of things; concerned with physical progress, bodily comfort, etc. M17.

M. MCCARTHY No nation with any sense of material well-being would endure the food we eat.

†6 Physically bulky, massive, or solid. M17–M18.
– SPECIAL COLLOCATIONS & COMB.: *material cause*: see CAUSE *noun*. *material culture*: see CULTURE *noun*. **material girl** *colloq.* [title of a song (1984) by the US singer and actress Madonna] a worldly or materialistic woman or girl. **material implication** LOGIC a relationship which always holds between two propositions except when the first is true and the second false. **material noun** GRAMMAR = *mass noun* s.v. MASS *noun*² & *adjective*. **material object** PHILOSOPHY an object regarded as having a physical existence independent of consciousness. **material-objectness** PHILOSOPHY the state of existing as a material object. **material thing** = *material object* above. **material witness** US LAW a witness whose evidence is likely to be sufficiently important to influence the outcome of a trial.
▸**B** *noun*. 1 *sing.* & in *pl.* **a** The matter of which a thing is or may be made. LME. ▸**b** The constituent parts of something. M17.

a SWIFT A palace may be built . . of materials so durable as to last for ever. K. CLARK The new material that was going to transform the art of building—iron.

a raw material unmanufactured material, material from which something is or may be made.

M

2 *sing.* & in *pl.* Information, evidence, ideas, etc., for use in writing a book or script, drawing a conclusion, etc. LME.

H. MOORE A painter . . must be continually gathering material from his experience of things seen. E. KUZWAYO I returned to Thabu' Nehu to seek out material for my book.

3 In *pl.* Items needed for an activity. L16. ***building materials, cleaning materials, writing materials***, etc.

4 Cloth, fabric. M19.

S. PLATH The girls had pocket-book covers made out of the same material as their dresses.

5 With specifying word: a person or thing suitable for a specific role or purpose. L19. ***academic material, officer material***.

– COMB.: **material clerk, materials clerk**: who controls the supply of materials in a business; **material control, materials control**: of working materials in relation to production plans; **material handling, materials handling** the movement and storage of materials in a factory; **material man, materials man** a man responsible for the materials required in building or manufacturing; **material science, materials science** the branch of science that deals with the structure and properties of materials, esp. with relation to their (potential) usefulness.

materialise *verb* var. of MATERIALIZE.

materialism /məˈtɪərɪəlɪz(ə)m/ *noun*. E18.
[ORIGIN from MATERIAL + -ISM.]
1 PHILOSOPHY. The doctrine that nothing exists except matter and its movements and modifications. Also, the doctrine that consciousness and will are wholly due to the operation of material agencies. E18. ***dialectical materialism***: see DIALECTICAL *adjective* 2.
2 A tendency to prefer material possessions and physical comfort to spiritual values; a way of life based on material interests. L18. ▸**b** CHRISTIAN CHURCH. An excessive emphasis on the material aspects of the sacraments at the expense of the spiritual. *derog.* E19.

New York Review of Books They were mostly from poor rural districts and hated the sinful materialism of the wicked city.

3 ART. A tendency to lay stress on the material aspect of the objects represented. M19.

materialist /məˈtɪərɪəlɪst/ *noun & adjective*. M17.
[ORIGIN formed as MATERIALISM + -IST.]
▸ **A** *noun*. **1** PHILOSOPHY. An adherent of materialism. M17.

M

D. HUME The materialists, who conjoin all thought with extension.

2 A person who takes a material view of things or who favours material possessions and physical comfort. M19.

P. MORTIMER My mother's family, stern materialists who believed devoutly in success.

▸ **B** *attrib.* or as *adjective*. Materialistic. M19.

materialistic /məˌtɪərɪəˈlɪstɪk/ *adjective*. M19.
[ORIGIN from MATERIALIST + -IC.]
Pertaining to, characterized by, or devoted to materialism.

P. B. CLARKE A highly industrialized, materialistic society like Britain.

■ **materialistically** *adverb* M19.

materiality /mətɪərɪˈalɪti/ *noun*. E16.
[ORIGIN Orig. from medieval Latin *materialitas* material quality or embodiment. Later from MATERIAL + -ITY.]
1 That which constitutes the matter or material of something. Long *rare*. E16.
2 a The quality of being composed of matter. L16. ▸**b** That which is material; in *pl.*, material things. E19.

a G. ADAMS The decomposition of the rays of light proves their materiality.

3 Material aspect or character. L16.

DENNIS POTTER It . . cannot release the smallest breath of life out of the suffocatingly dead materiality of things.

4 Now chiefly LAW. The quality of being relevant or significant. M17.

materialize /məˈtɪərɪəlʌɪz/ *verb*. Also **-ise**. E18.
[ORIGIN from MATERIAL *adjective* + -IZE.]
1 *verb trans.* Make material; represent in material form. Also, make materialistic. E18.

N. HAWTHORNE I had the glimmering of an idea, and endeavoured to materialize it in words.

2 SPIRITUALISM. **a** *verb trans.* Cause (a spirit etc.) to appear in bodily form. M19. ▸**b** *verb intrans.* Of a spirit etc.: appear in bodily form. L19.

a A. MASON He had astonished thousands by materializing objects out of nothing.

3 *verb intrans.* Come into perceptible existence; become actual fact. Also (*colloq.*), arrive or be present when expected. L19.

HENRY MILLER I was always being promised things which never materialized. W. TREVOR Words formed on her lips but did not materialize.

■ **materiaIiˈzation** *noun* M19. **materializer** *noun* (*rare*) E19.

materially /məˈtɪərɪəli/ *adverb*. LME.
[ORIGIN from MATERIAL *adjective* + -LY².]
1 Chiefly LOGIC & PHILOSOPHY. With regard to matter as opp. to form. LME.
2 In respect of matter or material substance. L16.

L. HOWELL As he created all Men out of the same matter, they are materially equal.

†**3** Of speaking or writing: with an appropriate use of matter; soundly; pertinently. E17–M18.
4 In a material degree; substantially, considerably. Also, in respect of material interests. M17.

G. GROTE Tribes differing materially in habits and civilization. H. JAMES She . . had even contributed materially to the funds required.

materialness /məˈtɪərɪəlnɪs/ *noun*. L16.
[ORIGIN from MATERIAL *adjective* + -NESS.]
The quality of being material.

materia medica /məˈtɪərɪə ˈmɛdɪkə/ *noun phr. pl.* M17.
[ORIGIN mod. Latin translating Greek *hulē iatrikē* healing material.]
The remedial substances used in the practice of medicine; (treated as *sing.*) the branch of medicine that deals with their origins and properties.

materia prima /məˈtɪərɪə ˈprʌɪmə/ *noun phr.* M16.
[ORIGIN Latin.]
= ***first matter*** s.v. MATTER *noun*.

†**materiate** *verb trans.* L17–E19.
[ORIGIN Latin *materiat-* pa. ppl stem of *materiare* (in classical Latin construct of wood, in scholastic use, as in sense 2 below), from *materia* MATTER *noun*.]
SCHOLASTIC PHILOSOPHY. **1** Supply or be the matter or material part of. Only in L17.
2 Make (a form) inherent in a particular matter. Only in E19.

matériel /materjɛl, mətɪərɪˈɛl/ *noun*. E19.
[ORIGIN French, use as noun of adjective: see MATERIAL.]
1 Available means or resources. Also (*rare*), technique. E19.
2 The equipment, supplies, etc., used in an army, navy, or business. Opp. ***personnel***. E19.

Time The U.S. tacitly backed the rebellion, encouraging the Shah to supply the Kurds with arms and matériel.

mater lectionis /ˌmeɪtə lɛktɪˈəʊnɪs/ *noun phr.* Pl. ***matres lectionis*** /ˌmeɪtriːz lɛktɪˈəʊnɪs/. M17.
[ORIGIN mod. Latin, lit. 'mother of reading'.]
A letter which has the function of a diacritical mark; *spec.* in Hebrew writing, a sign indicating a vowel sound.

maternal /məˈtəːn(ə)l/ *adjective*. L15.
[ORIGIN Old French & mod. French *maternel* or from Latin *maternus*, from *mater* MOTHER *noun*¹: see -AL¹.]
1 Of or pertaining to a mother or mothers; motherly. L15. ▸**b** Having the instincts of motherhood. L18. ▸**c** *spec.* Of or pertaining to the mother in pregnancy and childbirth; uterine (as opp. ***fetal***). E19.

J. ROSENBERG Mothers . . tired from their exhausting maternal duties. **b** G. F. ATHERTON She is not maternal . . I never saw a baby held so awkwardly. **c** A. S. NEILL Who can say what effect . . maternal rigidity has on the newborn baby?

2 That is a mother. Now *rare*. E16.
3 Belonging to a mother. E17.

DICKENS Interposed Lavvy, over the maternal shoulder.

4 Inherited from or related through a mother or the mother's side. M17.

H. BAILEY Vera's maternal grandfather . . was Welsh.

– SPECIAL COLLOCATIONS: **maternal language, maternal tongue** (now *rare*) a mother tongue, one's native language.
■ **maternalism** *noun* maternal instincts; the characteristics or state of motherhood: E20. **maternaˈlistic** *adjective* motherly, maternal M20. **maternally** *adverb* M17.

maternity /məˈtəːnɪti/ *noun & adjective*. E17.
[ORIGIN French *maternité* from medieval Latin *maternitas*, from Latin *maternus*: see -ITY.]
▸ **A** *noun*. **1** The quality or condition of being a mother; motherhood. E17.

S. KITZINGER She feels tied down by maternity and domesticity.

2 The qualities or conduct characteristic of a mother; motherliness. Now *rare*. E19.

H. DRUMMOND The tender maternity of the bird.

3 A maternity ward or hospital. L19.
▸ **B** *attrib. adjective*. **1** For a woman during and just after childbirth. L19. ***maternity benefit, maternity hospital, maternity leave***, etc.
2 Of a garment etc.: suitable for a pregnant woman. L19. ***maternity dress, maternity wear***, etc.

mateship /ˈmeɪtʃɪp/ *noun*. L16.
[ORIGIN from MATE *noun*² + -SHIP.]
1 The condition of being a mate; companionship, fellowship. Formerly also, equality. Now chiefly *Austral. & NZ*. L16.
2 ZOOLOGY. Pairing of one animal with another. E20.

matey /ˈmeɪti/ *noun*. *colloq.* L18.
[ORIGIN Dim. of MATE *noun*²: see -Y⁶.]
A companion, a mate. DOCKYARD ***matey***.

matey /ˈmeɪti/ *adjective*. Also **maty**. E20.
[ORIGIN from MATE *noun*² + -Y¹.]
Like a mate or mates; friendly, familiar, sociable.

mateyness /ˈmeɪtɪnɪs/ *noun*. Also **matiness**. E20.
[ORIGIN from MATEY *adjective* + -NESS.]
Friendliness, sociableness.

matfellon /ˈmatfɛl(ə)n/ *noun*. *obsolete* exc. *dial.* ME.
[ORIGIN Old French *matefelon*, app. from *mater* MATE *verb*¹ + *felon* FELON *noun*².]
Knapweed.

math /mɑːθ, maθ/ *noun*¹. *obsolete* exc. *dial.* and in AFTERMATH, LATTERMATH.
[ORIGIN Old English *mǣþ* corresp. to Middle High German *māt*, *mād-* (German *Mahd*), from Germanic base also of MOW *verb*¹: see -TH¹.]
A mowing; the amount of a crop mowed.

math /mʌt/ *noun*². E19.
[ORIGIN Hindi *maṭh* from Sanskrit *maṭha* hut, cell.]
In the Indian subcontinent, a Hindu convent of celibate mendicants.

math /maθ/ *noun*³. *N. Amer. colloq.* M19.
[ORIGIN Abbreviation.]
= MATHEMATICS. Cf. MATHS.
new math: see NEW *adjective*.

mathe /meɪð/ *noun*. Long *rare* or *obsolete* exc. *Scot.*
[ORIGIN Old English *maþa*, *maþu*, cogn. with Old Saxon *maþo*, Old High German *mado* (Dutch, German *Made*), Old Norse *maðkr* (see MADDOCK), Gothic *maþa*, from Germanic: ult. origin unknown.]
A maggot, grub, or worm.

mathematic /maθ(ə)ˈmatɪk/ *noun & adjective*. LME.
[ORIGIN Old French & mod. French *mathématique* or Latin *mathematicus* from Greek *mathēmatikos*, from *mathēma(t-)* something learned, science, from base of *manthanein* learn. As noun repr. ellipt. uses of the fem. adjectives (*sc.* Latin *ars*, *disciplina*, Greek *tekhnē*, *theōria*).]
▸ **A** *noun*. See also MATHEMATICS.
1 = MATHEMATICS. *obsolete* exc. *hist.* LME.
†**2** A mathematician; an astrologer. M16–L17.
†**3** In *pl.* Dice which roll true. L17–E18.
▸ **B** *adjective*. = MATHEMATICAL *adjective*. Now *rare*. LME.
– NOTE: Gradually superseded as noun between 16 and 18 by MATHEMATICS in the modern sense.

mathematical /maθ(ə)ˈmatɪk(ə)l/ *adjective & noun*. L15.
[ORIGIN formed as MATHEMATIC: see -ICAL.]
▸ **A** *adjective* **1 a** Of, pertaining to, or of the nature of mathematics. L15. ▸**b** Of a person: expert in mathematics; studying or teaching mathematics. E16. ▸**c** Of a concept, object, etc.: as understood or defined in mathematics. M16.
†**2 a** Astrological. M16–L17. ▸**b** Mechanical. Only in M16.
3 *transf.* **a** Rigorously exact. E17. ▸**b** Exactly regular. L18.

a COLERIDGE A theory conducted throughout with mathematical precision. **b** J. HAWTHORNE Straight paths and mathematical grass-plots.

– SPECIAL COLLOCATIONS: ***mathematical*** GEOGRAPHY. ***mathematical induction***: see INDUCTION 1c. **mathematical instrument** an instrument used in drawing geometrical figures (usu. in *pl.*). **mathematical linguist** an expert in or student of mathematical linguistics. **mathematical linguistics** a branch of linguistics that deals with the application of mathematical models and procedures to the analysis of linguistic structure. **mathematical logic** logic that is mathematical in its method, manipulating symbols according to definite and explicit rules of derivation; symbolic logic. **mathematical logician** an expert in or student of mathematical logic. **mathematical philosophy** the branch of philosophy that deals with the nature of mathematics. **mathematical point**: having a position but no extension in any dimension. **mathematical table** a table of the values of a mathematical function (e.g. logarithms) for different values of the variable.
▸ **B** *noun*. In *pl.* Mathematical objects or entities. *obsolete* exc. *hist.* M16.

mathematically /maθ(ə)ˈmatɪk(ə)li/ *adverb*. M16.
[ORIGIN from MATHEMATIC *adjective* or MATHEMATICAL: see -ICALLY.]
1 With mathematical accuracy or exactness. M16.
2 By mathematical methods; according to mathematical principles; in terms of mathematics. L16.

mathematician /maθ(ə)məˈtɪʃ(ə)n/ *noun*. L15.
[ORIGIN Old French & mod. French *mathématicien*, from Latin *mathematicus* MATHEMATIC: see -IAN.]
1 An expert in or student of mathematics. L15.
†**2** An astrologer. L16–E18.

mathematicise *verb* var. of MATHEMATICIZE.

mathematicism /maθ(ə)ˈmatɪsɪz(ə)m/ *noun*. E20.
[ORIGIN from MATHEMATIC *adjective* + -ISM.]
PHILOSOPHY. The opinion that everything can be described ultimately in mathematical terms, or that the universe is fundamentally mathematical.

mathematicize /maθ(ə)ˈmatɪsʌɪz/ *verb*. Also **-ise**. M19.
[ORIGIN from MATHEMATIC *adjective* + -IZE.]
1 *verb intrans.* = MATHEMATIZE 1. *rare*. M19.
2 *verb trans.* Consider or treat (a subject) in mathematical terms; reduce to mathematics. Chiefly as ***mathematicized, mathematicizing*** *ppl adjectives*. M19.
■ **mathematiciˈzation** *noun* the action of mathematicizing; the state of being mathematicized: M20.

mathematico- /maθ(ə)ˈmatɪkəʊ/ *combining form*.
[ORIGIN from MATHEMATICAL, MATHEMATICS: see -O-.]
Partly mathematical and partly —, as ***mathematico-logical***.

mathematics /maθ(ə)ˈmatɪks/ *noun pl.* M16.
[ORIGIN Pl. of MATHEMATIC *noun*, prob. after French (*les*) *mathématiques*, repr. Latin *mathematica* neut. pl., Greek (*ta*) *mathēmatika*: see -ICS.]
Orig. (treated as *pl.*, freq. with *the*), the sciences or disciplines of the quadrivium collectively; later, these and optics, architecture, navigation, etc. Now (treated as *sing.*), the abstract deductive science of space, number, quantity, and arrangement, including geometry, arithmetic, algebra, etc., studied in its own right (more fully ***pure mathematics***), or as applied to various branches of physics and other sciences (more fully ***applied mathematics***). Colloq. abbreviation **maths**, (*N. Amer.*) ***math***.
higher mathematics: see HIGH *adjective, adverb, & noun*. ***new mathematics***: see NEW *adjective*.

mathematize /ˈmaθ(ə)mətʌɪz/ *verb*. Also **-ise**. E18.
[ORIGIN from MATHEMAT(IC + -IZE.]
1 *verb intrans.* Reason mathematically; perform mathematical calculations. E18.
2 *verb trans.* Regard or treat (a problem, object, etc.) in mathematical terms; mathematicize. L19.
■ **mathematiˈzation** *noun* E20.

mathemeg /ˈmaθəmɛg/ *noun*. L18.
[ORIGIN Woods Cree *ma:θame:k*. Cf. TITTYMEG.]
A catfish of the genus *Ictalurus*, of N. American lakes.

mathern *noun* var. of MAYTHEN.

mathesis /məˈθiːsɪs/ *noun*. *arch.* L15.
[ORIGIN Late Latin from Greek *mathēsis*, from base of *manthanein* learn.]
Mental discipline; learning or science, *esp.* mathematical science. Also, the personification of this.
■ **mathetic** /məˈθɛtɪk/ *adjective* E19.

maths /maθs/ *noun*. *colloq.* E20.
[ORIGIN Abbreviation.]
= MATHEMATICS. Cf. MATH *noun*³.
new maths: see NEW *adjective*.

Mathurin /ˈmaθjʊrɪn/ *adjective & noun*. E17.
[ORIGIN The chapel of St *Mathurin* in Paris.]
ECCLESIASTICAL HISTORY. ▸**A** *adjective*. Of or pertaining to an order of regular canons (officially called Trinitarians) founded in 1198 by St John of Matha for the redemption of Christian captives. E17.
▸**B** *noun*. A Mathurin canon. L17.

-matic /ˈmatɪk/ *suffix*. M20.
[ORIGIN from AUTO)MATIC *adjective*.]
Forming nouns (usu. proprietary names) with the sense 'a device which works automatically or mechanically', as ***Instamatic***.

matico /məˈtiːkəʊ, *foreign* maˈtiko/ *noun*. M19.
[ORIGIN Spanish *yerba Matico*, from *yerba* herb + *Matico* dim. of *Mateo* Matthew: reputedly named after a soldier who discovered its medicinal properties.]
A Peruvian wild pepper, *Piper angustifolium*; the dried leaves of this plant, formerly used as a styptic.

matie /ˈmeɪti/ *noun*. Chiefly *Scot.* Also **mattie** /ˈmati/ & other vars. E18.
[ORIGIN Dutch *maatjes* (*haring* herring), earlier *maetgens-*, *maeghdekins-*, from *maagd* maid (cf. MAIDEN *noun*) + *-ken* -KIN. See also MATJE.]
A herring in the condition considered best for food, when the roe or milt is not fully developed.

matier, **matiest** *adjectives* see MATEY *adjective*.

matière /matjɛːr/ *noun*. E20.
[ORIGIN French.]
The quality an artist gives to the pigment used.

Matilda /məˈtɪldə/ *noun*. L19.
[ORIGIN Female forename.]
1 A bushman's bundle, a swag. *Austral. & NZ slang*. L19.
waltz Matilda, **walk Matilda** carry a swag.
2 A British tank in use in the Second World War. M20.

matily /ˈmeɪtɪli/ *adverb*. M20.
[ORIGIN from MATEY *adjective* + -LY².]
In a friendly, familiar, or sociable fashion.

matin /ˈmatɪn/ *noun*. Pl. **matins**, **mattins** (treated as *sing.* or *pl.*). ME.
[ORIGIN Old French & mod. French *matines* pl. (sing. *matin*) from ecclesiastical Latin *matutinas* use as noun of fem. accus. pl. (prob. sc. *vigilias* watches) of *matutinus* MATUTINE.]
▸**I** In *pl.*
1 ECCLESIASTICAL. **a** (The canonical hour of) an office appointed in the breviary, properly a night office, but also said at daybreak (with the following office, lauds) or on the previous evening. ME. ▸**b** The entire public service preceding the first mass on Sunday. Long *obsolete* exc. *hist.* ME. ▸**c** An Anglican service held in the morning with a set form similar to that of evensong, based on the earlier matins with elements from lauds and prime. M16.
†**2** More fully ***devil's matins***. A service of devil worship attributed to witches; *transf.* an uproar. E17–E19.
3 A morning duty, occupation, or performance. *arch.* M17.
▸**II** In *pl. & sing.*
4 The morning song of birds. *poet.* M16.
▸†**III** *sing.* **5** A morning. *rare*. E17–M19.
– PHRASES: ***Parisian matins***: see PARISIAN *adjective*.

matin /ˈmatɪn/ *adjective*. *literary*. M17.
[ORIGIN from MATIN *noun*.]
Belonging to the early morning; = MATINAL *adjective*.

mâtin /mɑtɛ̃/ *noun*. Pl. pronounced same. L16.
[ORIGIN French: see MASTIFF *noun*.]
A watchdog; a mastiff.

matinal /ˈmatɪn(ə)l/ *adjective*. Now *rare*. E19.
[ORIGIN Old French & mod. French, from *matin*: see MATIN *noun*, -AL¹.]
Belonging to or taking place in the morning; early. Also, early-rising.

matinée /ˈmatɪneɪ, *foreign* matine (*pl. same*)/ *noun*. Also **-nee**. M19.
[ORIGIN French = morning, what occupies a morning, from *matin*: see MATIN *noun*, -EE¹.]
1 An afternoon performance at a theatre, cinema, or concert hall. Abbreviation MAT *noun*³. M19.
2 A woman's lingerie jacket. L19.
– COMB.: **matinée coat** a baby's short outer garment; **matinée idol** a handsome actor of a type supposed to be admired chiefly by women; **matinée jacket** = ***matinée coat*** above.

matiness *noun* var. of MATEYNESS.

matipo /ˈmatɪpəʊ/ *noun*. Pl. **-os**. M19.
[ORIGIN Maori.]
Either of two New Zealand evergreen trees, *Pittosporum tenuifolium* (family Pittosporaceae), which bears clusters of purple flowers (also ***black matipo***), and *Myrsine australis*, the mapau (also ***red matipo***).

matje /ˈmatjə/ *noun*. Also **-jes** /-jəs/. L19.
[ORIGIN formed as MATIE, reintroduced from Dutch.]
More fully ***matje herring***. A young herring, esp. salted or pickled.

matless /ˈmatlɪs/ *adjective*. M19.
[ORIGIN from MAT *noun*¹ + -LESS.]
Not provided with a mat or mats.

matlow /ˈmatləʊ/ *noun*. *slang*. E20.
[ORIGIN Repr. a pronunc. of MATELOT.]
A sailor.

matoke /maˈtəʊkeɪ/ *noun*. M20.
[ORIGIN Bantu.]
A preparation of the flesh of bananas, used as food in Uganda; bananas.

matra /ˈmɑːtrə/ *noun*. L19.
[ORIGIN Sanskrit *mātrā*.]
In Indian music, a beat or a subdivision of a beat within a rhythmic phrase.

matraca /məˈtrɑːkə/ *noun*. L19.
[ORIGIN Spanish.]
In Spain, a mechanical wooden rattle used instead of church bells on Good Friday.

matrass /ˈmatrəs/ *noun*¹. Orig. †**materas**. LME.
[ORIGIN Old French *materas*, *matelas* (later *matras*) from late Latin *mattaris* from classical Latin *mataris*, of Gaulish origin.]
A quarrel or bolt for a crossbow.

matrass /ˈmatrəs/ *noun*². L16.
[ORIGIN French *matras*, perh. from MATRASS *noun*¹ (with allus. to the shape), infl. by Arabic *maṭara* leather bottle, or ult. from Greek *metrētēs* a liquid measure.]
A glass vessel with a round or oval body and a long neck, formerly used in distillation.

Matres Dolorosae *noun phr.* pl. of MATER DOLOROSA.

matres lectionis *noun phr.* pl. of MATER LECTIONIS.

matri- /ˈmatri, ˈmeɪtri/ *combining form*.
[ORIGIN from Latin *matr-*, *mater* MOTHER *noun*¹ + -I-.]
Forming nouns and adjectives, esp. in ANTHROPOLOGY & SOCIOLOGY, with the sense '(of or pertaining to) relationship through a female line'.
■ **matriˈcentred**, **matriˈcentric** *adjectives* centred on the mother, having a mother as the head of the family or household M20. **maˈtriclan** *noun* a matrilineal clan M20. **matriˈfocal** *adjective* matricentric M20. **matriˈlateral** *adjective* (esp. of marriage between cousins) pertaining to or designating a relationship in which a mother and one of her siblings or other relatives are both involved as parents M20.

matriarch /ˈmeɪtrɪɑːk/ *noun*. E17.
[ORIGIN formed as MATRI- on false analogy of *patriarch*: see -ARCH.]
A woman who is the head of a family or tribe, or who dominates an organization; an elderly woman who is highly respected.

> L. WOOLF Mrs. Eckhard was one of those immensely energetic, dominating Jewish matriarchs.

matriarchal /meɪtrɪˈɑːk(ə)l/ *adjective*. M19.
[ORIGIN formed as MATRI- + -AL¹, after *patriarchal*.]
Of or pertaining to a matriarch or maternal rule; pertaining to, of the nature of, or based on matriarchy; ANTHROPOLOGY designating or exhibiting a form of social organization characterized by matriarchy.

> B. JOWETT They . . are getting too old for the matriarchal form of government. E. B. TYLOR The Indian tribes further south are largely matriarchal.

■ **matriarchalism** *noun* the condition or state of having a matriarchal organization or rule L19.

matriarchate /meɪtrɪˈɑːkət/ *noun & adjective*. L19.
[ORIGIN formed as MATRI- + -ATE¹, after *patriarchate*.]
ANTHROPOLOGY. ▸**A** *noun*. A matriarchal community; a matriarchal form of social organization. L19.
▸**B** *adjective*. Matriarchal. L19.

matriarchy /ˈmeɪtrɪɑːki/ *noun*. L19.
[ORIGIN formed as MATRI- + -Y³, after *patriarchy*.]
A form of social organization in which the mother is the head of the family and descent and relationship are reckoned through the female line; a society, organization, etc., governed by a woman or women; government by a woman or women.

Matric /məˈtrɪk/ *noun*. *colloq.* Also **m-**. L19.
[ORIGIN Abbreviation.]
Matriculation.

matric /ˈmeɪtrɪk/ *adjective*. E20.
[ORIGIN from MATR(IX *noun* + -IC.]
MATH. Of or pertaining to a matrix or matrices.

matrical /ˈmatrɪk(ə)l, məˈtrʌɪk(ə)l/ *adjective*. *rare*. E17.
[ORIGIN Late Latin *matricalis*, formed as MATRIX *noun*: see -AL¹.]
Pertaining to a matrix or womb.

matricaria /matrɪˈkɛːrɪə/ *noun*. L16.
[ORIGIN medieval Latin *matricaria*, from Latin *matric-* MATRIX *noun* + *-aria* -ARY¹.]
Orig., feverfew, *Tanacetum parthenium*. Later (BOTANY), any of various plants of the composite family belonging or formerly belonging to the genus *Matricaria*, which originally included feverfew.

†**matrice** *noun* var. of MATRIX *noun*.

matrices *noun pl.* see MATRIX *noun*.

matricide /ˈmatrɪsʌɪd, ˈmeɪtrɪ-/ *noun*. L16.
[ORIGIN In sense 1 from Latin *matricidium*, in sense 2 from Latin *matricida*, both from *matr-*, *mater* mother: see -CIDE.]
1 The action of killing one's mother. L16.
2 A person who kills his or her mother. M17.
■ **matriˈcidal** *adjective* E19.

matricula /məˈtrɪkjʊlə/ *noun*. *obsolete* exc. *hist.* Pl. **-lae** /-liː/. M16.
[ORIGIN Late Latin, dim. of Latin MATRIX *noun*: see -CULE.]
A list or register of people belonging to an order, society, etc.; a certificate of enrolment in such a register.

matriculability /məˌtrɪkjʊləˈbɪlɪti/ *noun*. E20.
[ORIGIN from MATRICUL(ATE *verb* + -ABILITY.]
Ability or fitness to matriculate.

matriculae *noun* pl. of MATRICULA.

matriculant /məˈtrɪkjʊl(ə)nt/ *noun*. M19.
[ORIGIN medieval Latin *matriculant-* pres. ppl stem of *matriculare*: see MATRICULATE *verb*, -ANT¹.]
A person who matriculates; a candidate for matriculation.

matricular /məˈtrɪkjʊlə/ *adjective & noun*. L16.
[ORIGIN medieval Latin *matricularius*, *-aris*, formed as MATRICULA: see -AR¹, -AR². In branch A.II also infl. by MATRIX *noun*.]
▸**A** *adjective* **I 1** Pertaining to or of the nature of a matricula, esp. (*hist.*) the one listing the contributions that member states were required to make to the Holy Roman (later the German) Empire. L16.
▸**II** †**2** Of a language: original; from which others are derived. Only in L18.
3 Of or belonging to the womb. L19.
▸†**B** *noun*. = MATRICULA. Only in E17.

matriculate /məˈtrɪkjʊlət/ *adjective & noun*. L15.
[ORIGIN medieval Latin *matriculatus* pa. pple of *matriculare*: see MATRICULATE *verb*, -ATE².]
▸†**A** *adjective*. Matriculated. L15–E18.
▸**B** *noun*. A person who has matriculated. Now chiefly *Indian*. E18.

matriculate /məˈtrɪkjʊleɪt/ *verb*. M16.
[ORIGIN medieval Latin *matriculat-* pa. ppl stem of medieval Latin *matriculare*, formed as MATRICULA: see -ATE³.]
1 a *verb trans.* Enter (a name) in the register of a university, college, or polytechnic; admit as a member of a university, college, or polytechnic. M16. ▸**b** *verb intrans.* Be admitted as a member of a university, college, or polytechnic. M17.
†**2** *verb trans.* Insert (a name) in a register or official list; admit or incorporate into a society etc. by this means; enrol (a soldier). L16–E18.

M

3 *verb trans.* *HERALDRY* (chiefly *Scot.*). Record (arms) in an official register. **L16.**

matriculation /mətrɪkjʊˈleɪʃ(ə)n/ *noun.* **M16.**
[ORIGIN medieval Latin *matriculatio(n-)*, formed as MATRICULATE *verb*: see -ATION.]
1 The action or an act of matriculating; *esp.* formal admission into a university, college, or polytechnic. Also, an examination to qualify for this. **M16.**
2 *HERALDRY* (chiefly *Scot.*). A registration of armorial bearings. **E19.**

matrilineal /matrɪˈlɪnɪəl/ *adjective.* **E20.**
[ORIGIN from MATRI- + LINEAL *adjective*.]
Of, pertaining to, or based on (kinship with) the mother or the female line; recognizing kinship with and descent through females.
■ **ˈmatriline** /-lʌɪn/ *noun* a matrilineal line of descent **M20.** **matrilineage** *noun* matrilineal lineage **M20.** **matrilineˈality** *noun* **M20.** **matrilineally** *adverb* **E20.** **matrilinear** *adjective* = MATRILINEAL **E20.** **ˈmatriliny** *noun* the observance of matrilineal descent and kinship **E20.**

matrilocal /matrɪˈləʊk(ə)l/ *adjective.* **E20.**
[ORIGIN from MATRI- + LOCAL *adjective*.]
Designating or pertaining to a pattern of marriage in which a married couple settles in the wife's home or community.
■ **matriloˈcality** *noun* the custom of matrilocal residence **M20.** **matrilocally** *adverb* **M20.**

matrimonial /matrɪˈməʊnɪəl/ *adjective & noun.* **LME.**
[ORIGIN Old French & mod. French, or Latin *matrimonialis*, from *matrimonium*: see MATRIMONY, -AL[1].]
▸ **A** *adjective.* **1** Of or pertaining to marriage. **LME.**

T. HARDY There were hardly two houses in Little Hintock unrelated by some matrimonial tie. A. KENNY My parents sold their matrimonial home and made a formal agreement of separation.

2 Derived from marriage. **M16.**

J. H. BURTON Conferring on the Dauphin the 'crown matrimonial'.

3 Tending or calculated to promote marriage; inclining towards marriage. **M18.**

HENRY FIELDING She had matrimonial charms in great abundance.

– SPECIAL COLLOCATIONS: **matrimonial agency**, **matrimonial bureau** a marriage bureau. **matrimonial agent** a person who works in a matrimonial agency.
▸ **B** *noun* **1** †**a** A marriage, a wedding. Only in **L15.** ▸**b** In *pl.* Marriage celebrations, nuptials. **L20.**
2 In *pl.* ▸**a** Matrimonial matters or prospects. *rare.* **M19.** ▸**b** *US Law.* Legal practice involving marital or domestic cases. **L20.**
■ **matrimonially** *adverb* (**a**) according to the manner or laws of marriage; (**b**) by right of marriage; (**c**) as regards the married state: **E17.** †**matrimonious** *adjective* = MATRIMONIAL *adjective* **M17–M19.**

matrimony /ˈmatrɪməni/ *noun.* **ME.**
[ORIGIN Anglo-Norman *matrimonie* = Old French *matremoi(g)ne* from Latin *matrimonium*, from *matr-*, *mater* MOTHER *noun*[1]: see -MONY.]
1 The rite or institution of marriage; the action of marrying. **ME.** ▸†**b** A marriage; an alliance by marriage. **LME–M18.** ▸†**c** The marriage service. Only in **E18.**
2 The state of being married; the relation between married persons. **ME.**
†**3** A husband, a wife. Only in **17.**
4 *CARDS.* An obsolete game played with a full pack of cards and resembling Newmarket. Also, the marriage of a king and queen. **E19.**
5 A mixture of two different items of food or drink. *slang & dial.* **E19.**
– COMB.: **matrimony vine** either of two kinds of boxthorn, *Lycium barbarum* and *L. chinense*, shrubs of the nightshade family sometimes grown in gardens.

matrioshka *noun* var. of MATRYOSHKA.

matriotism /ˈmeɪtrɪətɪz(ə)m/ *noun.* **M19.**
[ORIGIN Alt. of PATRIOTISM after Latin *matr-*, *mater* MOTHER *noun*[1].]
Love of one's mother country, university, school, etc.

matrist /ˈmatrɪst/ *noun & adjective.* **M20.**
[ORIGIN from MATRI- + -IST, after *patrist*.]
PSYCHOLOGY. ▸**A** *noun.* A person whose behaviour or attitude is influenced or dominated by the mother. **M20.**
▸ **B** *attrib.* or as *adjective.* Of or pertaining to such influence or domination. **M20.**

matrix /ˈmeɪtrɪks/ *noun.* Also †**matrice**. Pl. **-trixes**, **-trices** /-trɪsiːz/. **LME.**
[ORIGIN Latin = breeding female, register, (in late Latin) womb, from *matr-*, *mater* MOTHER *noun*[1]: see -TRIX.]
1 The uterus, the womb. *arch.* **LME.**
2 A place or medium in which something is bred, produced, or developed; a setting or environment in which a particular activity or process occurs or develops; a place or point of origin and growth. **M16.** ▸**b** *ANATOMY & ZOOLOGY.* The formative tissue from which a tooth, hair, feather, nail, etc., arises. **M19.** ▸**c** *BOTANY.* The substrate on which a fungus or a lichen grows. **M19.**

H. E. MANNING The root and matrix of the Catholic Church. H. GEORGE This is the matrix in which mind unfolds. A. W. READ The family is the matrix in which we see the bubbling up of linguistic experimentation.

3 a A mould in which something is cast or shaped; *PRINTING* a metal block in which a character is stamped or engraved so as to form a mould for casting a type; an engraved die used to strike a coin or medal. **L16.** ▸**b** The bed or hollowed place in a slab in which a monumental brass is fixed. **M19.** ▸**c** A (positive or negative) copy of an original disc recording that is used in the making of other copies. **E20.** ▸**d** *PHOTOGRAPHY.* A dyed print in relief used for transferring colour to a final colour print. **M20.**

a *Archaeological Journal* Matrix of the seal of William Picard.

4 a The rock material in which a fossil, gem, etc., is embedded. **M17.** ▸**b** Any relatively fine or homogeneous substance in which coarser or larger particles are embedded; *spec.* in *BUILDING*, lime, fine cement. **M19.**

b J. E. GORDON The function of the matrix is simply to glue together a number of strong fibres.

5 *MATH.* An array of symbols or mathematical expressions arranged in a rectangle of rows and columns, treated as a single entity and now usu. written within round brackets. **M19.** ▸**b** *transf.* A rectangular arrangement or tabulation of words, data, etc.; *spec.* in *LOGIC*, (a part of) a truth table, a set of basic truth tables. **E20.** ▸**c** *LOGIC.* An expression that would become a statement if its variables were replaced by constants (i.e. by names of individuals, classes, or statements, as appropriate). **E20.** ▸**d** *COMPUTING.* An interconnected array of elements that has a number of inputs and outputs and resembles a lattice in its design. **M20.** ▸**e** *TELEVISION & BROADCASTING.* A circuit designed to produce outputs that are linear combinations, in different proportions, of a number of inputs. Freq. *attrib.* **M20.** ▸**f** An organizational structure in which two or more lines of command, responsibility, or communication may run through the same individual. **M20.** ▸**g** *COMPUTING.* A rectangular array of potential image points. Chiefly in ***dot matrix*** s.v. DOT *noun*[1], ***matrix printer*** below. **M20.**
diagonal matrix, ***row matrix***, ***unitary matrix***, etc. **b** *PAY-OFF matrix*. ***progressive matrices***: see PROGRESSIVE *adjective*.
6 *DENTISTRY.* A plate of metal or composition to serve as a temporary wall for a cavity of a tooth during filling. **L19.**
– COMB.: **matrix isolation** *CHEMISTRY* a technique for preparing free radicals or other unstable species by trapping them in a very cold inert substrate (such as solid argon) so that they can be studied spectroscopically; **matrix mechanics** *PHYSICS* a form of quantum mechanics in which the operators corresponding to physical coordinates (position, momenta, etc.) are represented by matrices with time-dependent elements; **matrix number** a number assigned by a record company to a matrix in the manufacture of records; **matrix printer** a printer in which each printed character is made up of a pattern of tiny dots; **matrix sentence** *LINGUISTICS* in transformational grammar, a sentence into which subordinate sentences are introduced.

matrix /ˈmeɪtrɪks/ *verb trans.* **M20.**
[ORIGIN from the noun.]
Combine (signals) in different proportions so as to obtain one or more linear combinations of them.

matroclinous /matrəˈklʌɪnəs/ *adjective.* **E20.**
[ORIGIN from Latin *matr-*, *mater* MOTHER *noun*[1] + -O- + Greek *klinein* to lean, slope + -OUS.]
GENETICS. Resembling the female more closely than the male parent; involving or possessing a tendency to inherit a character or characters from the female parent only.
■ **ˈmatrocliny** *noun* matroclinous inheritance **E20.**

matron /ˈmeɪtr(ə)n/ *noun.* Also (esp. as a title) **M-**. **LME.**
[ORIGIN Old French & mod. French *matrone* from Latin *matrona*, from *matr-*, *mater* MOTHER *noun*[1].]
1 A married woman, *esp.* one characterized by dignity, staid discreet behaviour, and plump motherly appearance. **LME.**

R. K. NARAYAN She would grow into a bulky matron. R. CHRISTIANSEN A Roman matron, exerting influence from the family hearth by force of her incorruptible virtue. *transf.*: SHAKES. *Rom. & Jul.* Come, civil night, Thou sober-suited matron, all in black.

matron of honour a married woman who attends the bride at a wedding.
2 *spec.* A married woman considered as having expert knowledge in matters of childbirth, pregnancy, etc. Now only (*hist.*) in ***jury of matrons*** s.v. JURY *noun*. **LME.**
3 a Orig., a woman in charge of the domestic arrangements of a public institution. Later, a woman (occas. a man) in charge of the nurses in a hospital (now also called ***senior nursing officer***); a woman managing the domestic arrangements of a school etc., esp. the care of the sick. **M16.** ▸**b** A female prison warder. *US.* **M20.**

a *Beano* Now I shall visit matron and get my sore finger bandaged. ROSEMARY MANNING She obtained a post at Great Ormond Street Hospital . . . She would have ended up as matron.

4 A female dog or horse used for breeding. **M20.**
■ **matronage** *noun* (**a**) a body of matrons; matrons collectively; (**b**) guardianship by a matron; (**c**) matronhood: **L16.** **matronhood** *noun* the condition of being a matron **M19.** **matronism** *noun* (*rare*) (**a**) qualities regarded as befitting a matron; (**b**) guardianship by a matron: **E17.** **matronlike** *adjective* resembling or regarded as befitting a matron; matronly: **L16.** **matronship** *noun* (**a**) (with possess. adjective, as ***your matronship*** etc.) *joc.* a mock title of respect given to a matron; (**b**) matronhood; (**c**) the position or office of matron: **M16.**

matronal /ˈmeɪtr(ə)n(ə)l/ *adjective.* **E17.**
[ORIGIN French from Latin *matronalis*, from *matrona*: see MATRON, -AL[1].]
1 Of or pertaining to a matron; regarded as befitting a matron. **E17.**
2 Having the characteristics of a matron. **M18.**

Matronalia /matrəˈneɪlɪə/ *noun* (treated as *sing.* or *pl.*). **L16.**
[ORIGIN Latin, use as noun of neut. pl. of *matronalis*: see MATRONAL.]
ROMAN HISTORY. A festival in honour of the goddess Juno and her son Mars, celebrated by married women.

matronize /ˈmeɪtr(ə)nʌɪz/ *verb.* Also **-ise**. **L16.**
[ORIGIN from MATRON + -IZE.]
1 *verb intrans.* Act as a matron. **L16.**
†**2** *verb trans.* Make into a matron. **M18–M19.**
3 *verb trans.* **a** Act as a female chaperone to. **E19.** ▸**b** *US.* Preside as a matron over, act as hostess to (a party etc.). **L19.**
4 *verb trans.* Of a woman: patronize. *joc.* **M19.**

matronly /ˈmeɪtr(ə)nli/ *adjective.* **M17.**
[ORIGIN formed as MATRONIZE + -LY[1].]
Like a matron; characteristic of or regarded as befitting a matron.

M. R. MITFORD She was making a handsome matronly cap. W. WHARTON The nursing supervisor . . . A big matronly type.

■ **matronliness** *noun* **M19.**

†**matronly** *adverb.* **L16–E19.**
[ORIGIN formed as MATRONIZE + -LY[2].]
In the manner of a matron.

matronymic /matrəˈnɪmɪk/ *noun & adjective.* **L18.**
[ORIGIN from Latin *matr-*, *mater* MOTHER *noun*[1], after *patronymic*.]
▸ **A** *noun.* A metronymic; a metronymic suffix. **L18.**
▸ **B** *adjective.* = METRONYMIC *adjective*. **L19.**

matross /məˈtrɒs/ *noun.* **M17.**
[ORIGIN Dutch *matroos* from French *matelots* pl. of *matelot* sailor.]
MILITARY HISTORY. An artillery soldier next in rank below a gunner.

matryoshka /matrɪˈɒʃkə/ *noun.* Also **matri-**. Pl. **-oshki** /-ˈɒʃki/. **M20.**
[ORIGIN Russian *matrëshka*, lit. 'little matron'.]
More fully ***matryoshka doll***. Any of a set of traditional Russian wooden dolls of differing sizes, each somewhat resembling a skittle in shape and designed to nest inside the next largest.

matsu /ˈmatsuː/ *noun.* **E18.**
[ORIGIN Japanese.]
Any of several Japanese pine trees, *esp.* the Japanese red pine, *Pinus densiflora*, and the black pine, *P. thunbergii*.

matsuri /matˈsuːri/ *noun.* **E18.**
[ORIGIN Japanese.]
A solemn festival celebrated periodically at Shinto shrines in Japan.

matt /mat/ *noun*[1]. Also **mat**. **M19.**
[ORIGIN French *mat* use as noun of *mat* MATT *adjective*.]
1 In gilding, (the appearance of) unburnished gold; a dull lustreless appearance. **M19.**
2 A border of dull gold round a picture. Also, a sheet of cardboard placed on the back of a print etc. and covered by a mount forming a margin round the print; the mount itself. **M19.**
3 In glass-painting, a layer of colour matted on the glass (see MATT *verb* 2). **L19.**
4 A punch for producing a matt finish on metal. **L19.**

†**matt** *noun*[2] var. of MAT *noun*[1].

matt /mat/ *adjective.* Also **mat**, **matte**. **M17.**
[ORIGIN French *mat*, sometimes identified with Old French & mod. French *mat* MATE *adjective*.]
Of a colour, surface, etc.: without lustre, dull.

matt /mat/ *verb trans.* Also **mat** (infl. **-tt-**). **E17.**
[ORIGIN In senses 1 and 2 from French *mater*, from *mat* MATT *adjective*. In sense 3 from MATT *noun*[1].]
1 Make (colours etc.) dull; give a matt appearance to; frost (glass). **E17.**
2 In glass-painting, cover (glass) with a layer of colour smoothed over with a soft brush. **L19.**
3 Mount (a print etc.) on a cardboard backing; provide (a print etc.) with a border. Chiefly as ***matted*** *ppl adjective*, ***matting*** *verbal noun*. **M20.**

Matt. *abbreviation.*
Matthew (esp. New Testament).

mattamore /ˈmatəmɔː/ *noun.* **L17.**
[ORIGIN French *matamore* from Arabic *maṭmūra*, from *ṭamara* put underground, bury.]
In N. Africa, an underground storehouse, granary, or habitation (esp. a prison).

mattar /ˈmatə/ *noun*. L19.
[ORIGIN Hindi *matar*, Punjabi *mattar*.]
1 The grass pea, *Lathyrus sativus*. *Indian*. L19.
2 A variety of pea from the Indian subcontinent. Also, peas collectively. E20.

matte /mat/ *noun*. E19.
[ORIGIN French, use as noun of fem. of *mat* MATT *adjective*.]
1 METALLURGY. A molten mixture of impure metal sulphides produced during the smelting of sulphide ores of copper, nickel, etc. E19.
2 CINEMATOGRAPHY. A mask used to obscure or shade an image or part of one. M20.

matte *adjective* var. of MATT *adjective*.

matted /ˈmatɪd/ *adjective*. M16.
[ORIGIN from MAT *noun*¹, *verb*¹: see -ED², -ED¹.]
1 Laid or spread with matting or mats. M16. ▸**b** Made of plaited rushes; (of a chair etc.) rush-bottomed. L16. ▸**c** Formed of mats as a covering. E18.

Daily Telegraph The bedrooms have traditional matted floors. **b** J. A. MICHENER Rushes from the wadi . . to be woven into a tightly matted roof. **c** DEFOE We pitched our matted tents.

2 Esp. of plants, hair, etc.: tangled and interlaced; covered with a tangled layer; compressed into the semblance of a mat. L16. ▸**b** Covered with a dense growth. L18.

T. ROETHKE The briary hedge, the tangle of matted underbrush. R. P. JHABVALA He had long hair, all tangled and matted. *Florist's Journal* The roots are very apt to get matted in the pots. **b** E. DARWIN By thee the plowshare rends the matted plain.

3 Enclosed or wrapped in matting. M17.
■ **mattedly** *adverb* (*rare*) L19.

matter /ˈmatə/ *noun*. ME.
[ORIGIN Anglo-Norman *mater(i)e*, Old French & mod. French *matière* from Latin *materia* (also *materies*) timber, stuff of which a thing is made, subject of discourse.]
▸ **I 1** The substance or the substances collectively of which a physical object consists; constituent material, esp. of a particular kind. *obsolete* exc. as passing into senses 3, 4. ME.

T. ELYOT He vsed no golde but pure beryll and christall, and other like mattier to drinke in.

2 A substance used or acted on in a physical operation. *obsolete* exc. as passing into sense 3. LME.

J. PALSGRAVE I make the printe of a thyng in any mater or stuffe.

3 A physical substance. Freq. with specifying adjective. LME.

P. ABRAHAMS Jacob recognized the familiar farming community smells of animal dung, vegetable matter.

colouring matter, ***faecal matter***, etc.

4 That which has mass and occupies space; physical substance as distinct from spirit, mind, qualities, etc. LME.

Scientific American It explodes when it drags matter from a companion star.

5 Pus. LME.

HUGH MILLER My injured foot . . discharged great quantities of blood and matter.

▸ **II 6** †**a** In scholastic philosophy: the result of the first act of creation, substance without form. ME–E17. ▸**b** In Aristotelian and scholastic philosophy, the component of a thing which has bare existence but requires an essential determinant (*form*) to make it a thing of a determinate kind. LME. ▸**c** In Kantian philosophy: the element of knowledge supplied by feeling, as distinct from that (*form*) supplied by the mind. M19.
7 THEOLOGY. The essential substance employed in a sacrament, as water in baptism, the bread and wine in the Eucharist, as distinct from the required words of the rite. ME.
8 LOGIC. The particular content of a proposition or syllogism as distinct from its form. L17.

F. BOWEN In respect to their Matter, both the Premises and the Conclusion may be false.

▸ **III 9** Material for expression; fact or thought as material for a book, speech, etc. ME.

STEELE Whether they have Matter to talk of or not.

†**10** The subject of a book, speech, etc.; a theme, a topic. ME–E18.

SPENSER Thee, O Queene! the matter of my song.

†**11** That with which a branch of knowledge deals; what belongs to a subject of study. ME–L16.
12 Orig., ground, reason, or cause for doing or being something. Later, what is or may be the occasion *of* or *for* a specified feeling. ME.

MILTON This is the matter why Interpreters . . will not consent it to be a true story. A. E. HOUSMAN 'Tis sure small matter for wonder If sorrow is with one still.

13 a The substance of a book, speech, etc.; the contents of a composition in respect of the facts or ideas expressed, as distinct from the form of words used to express them. ME. ▸†**b** Sense, substance, as distinct from nonsense. *rare* (Shakes.). L16–E17.

a DRYDEN Though I cannot much commend the style . . there is somewhat in the matter. **b** SHAKES. *Much Ado* I was born to speak all mirth and no matter.

14 a An event, circumstance, question, etc., which is or may be an object of consideration or practical concern; in *pl.*, events, circumstances, etc., generally. Formerly with *possess.*, an event etc. of concern to the person specified, (one's) affair. ME. ▸**b** In *pl.* Physical objects. Now *rare* or *obsolete*. E18.

a J. BARTH There was one final matter to be settled before I could call myself really free. W. ABISH Lunch, a serious matter. W. TREVOR I have been thinking about many of the matters we discussed.

15 A thing or things collectively of a particular kind or related to a particular thing. Usu. foll. by *for* or *of*, or with specifying word. LME. ▸**b** A subject of contention, dispute, etc.; LAW a thing which is to be tried or proved; statements or allegations which come under the consideration of a court; a case. LME.

SHAKES. *Merry W.* I will make a Star Chamber matter of it. N. WANLEY Mens Consciences are not to be forced in matters of Religion. J. DORAN This new-fangled scholarism was a very sad matter indeed. **b** E. L. LINTON They rarely met without crossing swords on one matter if not another.

hanging matter, ***money matters***, etc.

†**16** Material cause; elements of which something consists or out of which it arises. L16–E19.

BACON The matter of seditions is of two kindes, Much povertye and much discontent.

17 A quantity or amount (*of*). Usu. with specifying adjective, esp. *small*. Now *rare* or *obsolete*. M17.

M. NEEDHAM At first an easie matter was demanded by the King of Denmark. HENRY FIELDING I . . sent a small matter to his wife.

18 Things printed or written, or to be printed or written (freq. with specifying word); TYPOGRAPHY the body of a printed work as distinct from the titles, headings, etc. L17.

J. CARLYLE We have printed half the matter. M. LEITCH Under the cushioned seat he knew there would be reading matter.

printed matter, ***written matter***, etc.

– PHRASES: ***a matter***: see ***a small matter*** below. **a matter of** (*a*) approximately; (*b*) a circumstance that involves, a circumstance depending (*only*) etc. on. **a matter of fact** (*a*) what pertains to the realm of fact (as distinct from probability, opinions, etc.); ***as a matter of fact***: see FACT *noun*; (*b*) LAW the part of a judicial inquiry concerned with the truth of the alleged facts (as distinct from ***a matter of law*** below). ***a matter of form***: see FORM *noun*. **a matter of law** the part of a judicial inquiry concerned with the correctness of the legal procedure (as distinct from ***a matter of fact*** above). ***a matter of life and death***: see LIFE *noun*. ***a matter of opinion***: see OPINION *noun*. ***a matter of record***: see RECORD *noun*. **a small matter**, **a matter** *adverb* (*arch.*) somewhat, slightly. ***be of no matter***: see ***no matter*** below. ***dark matter***: see DARK *adjective*. ***dry matter***: see DRY *adjective*. **first matter** a formless primordial substance considered as the original material of the universe. **for that matter**, (*arch.*) **for the matter of that** (*a*) so far as that is concerned; (*b*) and indeed also (something further). ***front matter***: see FRONT *noun* & *adjective*. ***grey matter***: see GREY *adjective*. **in the matter of** [Law Latin *in re*] (chiefly LAW) in relation to, with regard to. ***make no matter***: see ***no matter*** below. †**matter in it** some importance attaching to it. ***matter of breviary***: see BREVIARY 1. ***matter of course***: see COURSE *noun*¹. ***matter of record***: see RECORD *noun*. ***matter subject***: see SUBJECT *adjective*. ***mend matters***: see MEND *verb*. ***mince matters***, ***mince the matter***: see MINCE *verb*. ***mind over matter***: see MIND *noun*¹. ***no laughing matter***: see LAUGHING *verbal noun*. **no matter** (*a*) ***make no matter***, ***be of no matter***, be of no consequence or importance; (*b*) *colloq.* it is of no consequence or importance, never mind. **the matter** (*a*) the circumstance or state of things involving or concerning a person or thing, *esp.* one calling for remedy or explanation (freq. in ***what is the matter?***); ***what is the matter with?*** (*colloq.*) what is troubling, what is wrong with?, *joc.* what is the objection to, what is there to complain of in?; †(*b*) something contemplated, intended, or desired; ***to the matter***, to the point, relevant(ly); ***from the matter***, irrelevant(ly); †(*c*) ***on the matter***, ***on the whole matter***, taking the thing as a whole, speaking generally, for all practical purposes. **what matter?** that need not disquiet us. ***white matter***: see WHITE *adjective*.

– COMB.: **matter-of-fact** *adjective* pertaining to, having regard to, or depending on actual fact as distinct from what is speculative or fanciful; unimaginative; prosaic; **matter-of-factly** *adverb* in a matter-of-fact manner; **matter-of-factness** matter-of-fact quality or character; **matter wave** PHYSICS a particle considered in terms of its wavelike properties, a de Broglie wave.

■ **matterful** *adjective* (esp. of a book etc.) full of matter or substance E19. †**matterish** *adjective* of the nature of pus, mattery M16–E18. **mattery** *adjective* (*a*) full of, forming, or discharging pus; purulent; †(*b*) full of sense or meaning: L15.

matter /ˈmatə/ *verb*. M16.
[ORIGIN from the noun.]
1 *verb intrans.* Secrete or discharge pus; suppurate. *obsolete* exc. *dial.* M16.
2 *verb intrans.* & (*poet.*, *rare*) *trans.* with dat. obj. Be of importance (*to*), signify. Usu. in neg. & interrog. contexts. M16. ▸**b** Of a person: be important, have influence. M19.

V. BROME He was still unpersuaded that his own fate mattered very much. R. INGALLS She hadn't brought her glasses with her; not that it really mattered. **b** L. WOOLF He knew everyone who mattered.

3 a *verb trans.* Be concerned about, care for, regard, mind; approve of, like. *obsolete* exc. *dial.* M17. ▸**b** *verb intrans.* Care, mind. Now *rare* or *obsolete*. L17.

†**matterative** *adjective*. L15–E18.
[ORIGIN Irreg. from MATTER *noun* or *verb* after *maturative*: see -ATIVE.]
Of the nature of or containing pus.

matterless /ˈmatəlɪs/ *adjective*. LME.
[ORIGIN from MATTER *noun* + -LESS.]
†**1** Without materials. *rare*. Only in LME.
2 Having no matter; not embodied in matter. Now *rare*. LME.
†**3** Devoid of sense or meaning. E17–M18.
4 Of no concern or importance; immaterial. Now *arch.* & *dial.* M17. ▸**b** Of a person: of no consequence; incompetent, shiftless, helpless. *dial.* L18.

Matthean /maˈθiːən/ *adjective*. Also **-aean**. L19.
[ORIGIN from Latin *Matthaeus* Matthew + -AN, -EAN.]
CHRISTIAN CHURCH. Of, pertaining to, or characteristic of the evangelist St Matthew or the Gospel attributed to him.

Matthew principle /ˈmaθjuː ˌprɪnsɪp(ə)l/ *noun phr.* L20.
[ORIGIN St *Matthew* (see MATTHEAN).]
The principle that more will be given to those who already have (with ref. to *Matthew* 25:29).

Matthew Walker /maθjuː ˈwɔːkə/ *noun*. M19.
[ORIGIN Personal name.]
NAUTICAL. More fully ***Matthew Walker knot***. A knot tied in the separated strands of the end of a rope.

mattie *noun* var. of MATIE.

mattify /ˈmatɪfʌɪ/ *verb trans.* L20.
[ORIGIN from MATT *adjective* + -IFY.]
Of a cosmetic: reduce the shine or oiliness of (the complexion).

matting /ˈmatɪŋ/ *noun*¹ & *adjective*. M16.
[ORIGIN from MATT *verb*, *noun*¹ + -ING¹.]
▸ **A** *noun*. **1** The covering of a floor etc. with mats or matted fabric; the process of making mats or material for mats. M16.
2 Material for mats, mats collectively. E17.

JAN MORRIS The windows are covered with loose matting to keep the sun out.

3 A thing that has become matted; the action of becoming matted; the state of being matted. E17.

P. H. GOSSE The matting of the vegetation, impeding the flow of the water.

▸ **B** *attrib.* or as *adjective*. Covered with or made of matting. E19.

matting /ˈmatɪŋ/ *noun*². L17.
[ORIGIN from MATT *verb* + -ING¹.]
1 (The production of) a matt surface. L17.
2 The action of providing a print etc. with a matt as a backing or border; such a matt. M19.

mattins *noun pl.* see MATIN *noun*.

mattock /ˈmatək/ *noun* & *verb*. OE.
[ORIGIN from unkn. 1st elem. + -OCK.]
▸ **A** *noun*. A tool similar to a pick but with one arm of the head curved like an adze and the other ending in a chisel edge or a point, used for breaking up hard ground, grubbing up trees, etc. OE.
▸ **B** *verb trans.* Dig *up* (as) with a mattock. M17.

mattoid /ˈmatɔɪd/ *adjective* & *noun*. *rare*. L19.
[ORIGIN Italian *mattoide*, from *matto* insane: see -OID.]
PSYCHOLOGY. (Designating) a person of erratic behaviour, approaching the psychotic.

mattress /ˈmatrɪs/ *noun*. ME.
[ORIGIN Old French *materas* (mod. *matelas*) cogn. with or from Italian *materasso*, parallel with Old Catalan *almatratzt*, Old Portuguese *almatrá* (mod. *almadraque*), Old Spanish *almatraque* (mod. *almadraque*), from Arabic *matrah* place where something is thrown, carpet, cushion, seat, bed, from *taraha* throw.]
1 A large case of strong fabric for sleeping on, with a soft or firm filling, or filled with air or water; any of various devices used similarly and containing or consisting of springs. ME.
air mattress, ***flock-mattress***, ***hair mattress***, ***spring mattress***, ***wire mattress***, etc.
†**2** A protective covering, *esp.* one for plants; a mat. M17–E18.
3 A place where sugar cane is grown or stored. *US*. E19.
4 ENGINEERING. A strong mat consisting of pieces of brushwood fastened together, used in the construction of dykes, piers, etc., and placed on riverbanks to prevent scour. L19.

Matura diamond *noun phr.* see MATARA DIAMOND.

M

maturant /ˈmatjʊr(ə)nt/ *noun & adjective*. Now *rare* or *obsolete*. M17.
[ORIGIN Latin *maturant-* pres. ppl stem of *maturare*: see MATURATE, -ANT[1].]
▸ **A** *noun*. = MATURATIVE *noun*. M17.
▸ **B** *adjective*. = MATURATIVE *adjective*. M19.

maturase /ˈmatjʊreɪz/ *noun*. L20.
[ORIGIN from MATURE *adjective* or *verb* + -ASE.]
BIOCHEMISTRY. Any of a group of enzymes which catalyse the excision of introns from mitochondrial mRNA, and may themselves be coded for by intronic sequences.

maturate /ˈmatjʊreɪt/ *verb*. M16.
[ORIGIN Latin *maturat-* pa. ppl stem of *maturare*, formed as MATURE *adjective*: see -ATE[3].]
1 *verb trans*. Mature, ripen; *esp*. cause (a boil, abscess, etc.) to come to a head. Now *rare* or *obsolete*. M16.
†**2** *verb trans*. METALLURGY & ALCHEMY. Purify (esp. a metal); change by purification *into*; convert (an ore) *into* pure metal; *spec*. convert (base metal) into gold. M17–M18.
3 *verb intrans*. Esp. of a boil or abscess: undergo maturation; mature, ripen. M17.

maturation /matjʊˈreɪʃ(ə)n/ *noun*. LME.
[ORIGIN Old French & mod. French, or medieval Latin *maturatio(n-)*, formed as MATURATE: see -ATION.]
1 MEDICINE. The formation or encapsulation of pus; suppuration; the process of causing this. LME.
†**2** The forwarding of a business, enterprise, etc. L16–M17.
†**3** ALCHEMY. Purification; *esp*. conversion of a base metal into gold. Only in 17.
4 The action of becoming or making ripe or matured; an instance of this. E17.

W. JAMES A flaw in white wines caused by their absorption of too much oxygen during . . maturation.

5 The process of coming to full growth or development; the completing or perfecting of a plan, work, etc. M17.

W. O. WEIGLE Acquired early in life before maturation of the immune mechanisms.

†**6** PHYSICS. The (supposed) natural ripening or development of material substances by the operation of heat and motion. M17–M18.
– COMB.: **maturation division** BIOLOGY either of the two divisions of meiosis.
■ **maturational** *adjective* E20.

M

maturative /məˈtjʊərətɪv/ *adjective & noun*. Now *rare* or *obsolete*. LME.
[ORIGIN Old French & mod. French *maturatif, -ive* or medieval Latin *maturativus*, formed as MATURATE *verb*: see -ATIVE.]
▸ **A** *adjective*. **1** MEDICINE. Causing the formation of pus; suppurative. LME.
†**2** Having the power or function of ripening fruit etc.; of or pertaining to maturation. M–L17.
▸ **B** *noun*. MEDICINE. A maturative remedy. LME.

mature /məˈtjʊə/ *adjective*. LME.
[ORIGIN Latin *maturus* ripe, timely, early, perh. rel. to *mane* early, in the morning. Cf. MATUTINE.]
1 Of thought or deliberation: suitably careful and adequate. Of a plan, conclusion, etc.: formed after adequate deliberation. LME.

BURKE On a full and mature view and comparison of the historical matter. LYTTON The interval . . allowed no time for mature and careful reflection.

2 Complete in natural development or growth; fully developed, fully grown; (of wine, cheese, etc.) ready for consumption; (of fruit) ripe (now *rare*). LME. ▸†**b** *fig*. Ripe or ready *for*. E–M17.

Christian Science Monitor Use a mature Cheddar with a lot of taste. *Natural World* The loss of mature oak and beech.

3 a Having the powers of body and mind fully developed, adult; (of personal qualities etc.) fully developed. Also foll. by *in*. E16. ▸**b** Of or pertaining to maturity or manhood. *rare*. E17.

a H. A. L. FISHER A society more . . mature than the western Europe of the early middle ages. H. GUNTRIP A relationship between two fully mature adult persons. L. CODY The hair was young, but the style was mature.

†**4** That takes place early; prompt. (Cf. earlier & later MATURELY *adverb* 2.) Only in 17.

MARVELL Carrying things on with the maturest expedition.

†**5** Of an event: occurring at the fitting time. Of time: due. E–M17.
6 MEDICINE. (Of a boil or abscess) that has come to a head; (of a progressive cataract) completely opaque. E19.
7 Of a bill etc.: due for payment. L19.
8 Designating or pertaining to an economy that has developed to a point at which further expansion no longer occurs; (of a product) no longer subject to substantial development or investment. E20. **mature student**: who undertakes a course of study at a later age than normal.
■ **matureness** *noun* the state of being mature, maturity M17.

mature /məˈtjʊə/ *verb*. LME.
[ORIGIN Latin *maturare*, formed as MATURE *adjective*.]
1 *verb trans*. & *intrans*. Bring to or reach a mature state; develop fully; ripen. LME.

J. LUBBOCK In some cases the stigma has matured before the anthers are ripe. A. TOFFLER Our children mature physically more rapidly than we did. *Country Living* The ancient practice of maturing wines in oak casks.

2 *verb trans*. *fig*. Make ready; perfect, bring to full development (a plan, a course of action, etc.); develop *into*. M17.
3 *verb intrans*. *fig*. Ripen or develop *into* or *to*. E19.
4 *verb intrans*. Of a bill etc.: reach the time fixed for payment; become due. M19.

What Mortgage When the policy matures, it will pay off your loan.

maturely /məˈtjʊəli/ *adverb*. L15.
[ORIGIN from MATURE *adjective* + -LY[2].]
1 With full deliberation, after mature consideration. L15.
†**2** Promptly; in good time; not too late; early. M16–L18.
3 With complete natural development or growth; in a manner indicative of maturity. M19.

maturity /məˈtjʊərɪti/ *noun*. LME.
[ORIGIN Latin *maturitas*, formed as MATURE *adjective*: see -ITY.]
†**1** Deliberateness of action; mature consideration, due deliberation. LME–M18.
2 The state of being mature; fullness or perfection of natural development or growth; ripeness. LME.

T. S. ELIOT I do not mean the impressionable period of adolescence, but the period of full maturity.

†**3** Due promptness. M16–L17.
4 The state of being complete, perfect, or ready. M16.

H. H. WILSON Measures which . . were nearly brought to maturity.

5 The state of being due for payment; the time at which a bill etc. becomes due; a bill etc. due at a specified time. Also, the time when an insurance policy, security, etc., matures. E19.

Moneypaper The stocks . . run the range of maturities from a few months time to well into the next century.

matutinal /matjʊˈtʌɪn(ə)l, məˈtjuːtɪn(ə)l/ *adjective*. M16.
[ORIGIN Late Latin *matutinalis*, formed as MATUTINE: see -AL[1].]
Of or pertaining to the morning, occurring or performed in the morning, early.

matutine /ˈmatjʊtʌɪn, -tɪn/ *adjective*. L15.
[ORIGIN Latin *matutinus*, from *Matuta* goddess of the dawn, rel. to *maturus* MATURE *adjective*: see -INE[1]. Cf. MATIN *adjective*.]
1 = MATUTINAL L15.
2 Of a celestial object: that rises above the horizon before sunrise. M16.

maty /ˈmeɪti/ *noun*. Also **mate** /meɪt/. E19.
[ORIGIN Perh. from Malayalam *mēṭṭi* house servant, Tamil *mēṭṭi*, Telugu *mēṭi* under-servant, menial.]
In the Indian subcontinent: a servant, *esp*. an assistant or subordinate one.

maty *adjective* var. of MATEY *adjective*.

matzo /ˈmʌtsə, ˈmatsəʊ/ *noun*. Pl. **-os**, **-oth** /-əʊt/. Also **matzah** /ˈmʌtsə, ˈma-/. M17.
[ORIGIN Yiddish *matse* from Hebrew *maṣṣāh*.]
(A wafer of) unleavened bread for Passover.
– COMB.: **matzo ball** a small dumpling made of seasoned matzo meal bound together with egg and chicken fat, typically served in chicken soup; **matzo meal** meal made from ground matzos.

mauby /ˈməʊbi/ *noun*. *W. Indian*. L18.
[ORIGIN formed as MOBBIE.]
A drink made from the bark of trees of the genus *Colubrina* or related plants of the buckthorn family.

maud /mɔːd/ *noun*. M17.
[ORIGIN Perh. from *maldy* dial. var. of MEDLEY.]
A grey striped plaid worn by shepherds in Scotland, esp. in the south. Also, a travelling rug, a wrap.

maudit /modi/ *adjective*. M20.
[ORIGIN French, lit. 'cursed', from *maudire* to curse. Cf. POÈTE MAUDIT.]
Of an artist etc.: insufficiently appreciated by their contemporaries, esp. as being outside the bounds of decency or good taste. Usu. *postpositive*.

Times Lit. Suppl. As fits an artist maudit, there is no exact record of his birth.

maudle /ˈmɔːd(ə)l/ *verb*. *rare*. E18.
[ORIGIN Back-form. from MAUDLIN *adjective*.]
1 *verb trans*. Make maudlin. E18.
2 *verb intrans*. Talk in a maudlin way. E19.

maudlin /ˈmɔːdlɪn/ *noun*. In branch I also **M-**. ME.
[ORIGIN Old French & mod. French *Madeleine* from ecclesiastical Latin *Magdalena*: see MAGDALEN. In branch II from the adjective.]
▸ **I** †**1** = MAGDALEN 1. ME–L16. ▸**b** A penitent resembling Mary Magdalen. Cf. MAGDALEN 2. E–M17.
2 (More fully ***sweet maudlin***) the plant sweet yarrow, *Achillea ageratum*. Formerly also, costmary, *Tanacetum balsamita*. LME.
†**3** = MAGDALEN 2b. Only in E17.
†**4** An old variety of peach, = MAGDALEN 3. Also, an old variety of pear. M17–E18.
▸ **II 5** Weak or mawkish sentiment. M19.
– COMB.: **maudlin tide** the period of some days around 22 July, the feast of St Mary Magdalen.

maudlin /ˈmɔːdlɪn/ *adjective*. E17.
[ORIGIN from the noun, with allus. to pictures of the Magdalen weeping.]
1 Given to tears, lachrymose; weeping, tearful. *arch*. E17.
2 Tearful and emotional as a result of drink. (Earliest in ***maudlin-drunk*** below.) E17.

G. VIDAL Wine made him maudlin, affectionate, confused.

3 Characterized by tearful sentimentality; mawkishly emotional; weakly sentimental. M17.

J. A. MICHENER 'I have the best wife in the world,' he said with maudlin sentiment.

– COMB.: **maudlin-drunk** in the maudlin stage of intoxication.
■ **maudlinism** *noun* the state of being maudlin-drunk M19. **maudlinly** *adverb* M19.

Maugrabee /ˈmɔːɡrəbiː/ *noun*. *literary*. E18.
[ORIGIN formed as MAGHRIBI.]
An African Moor.

Maugrabin /ˈmɔːɡrəbɪn/ *noun & adjective*. *arch*. E19.
[ORIGIN Arabic *Maġribīn* pl. of *Maġribī*: see MAGHRIBI. Cf. MAGHREBIN.]
= MAGHRIBI.

maugre /ˈmɔːɡə/ *noun, preposition, & adverb*. ME.
[ORIGIN Old French & mod. French *maugré* (mod. *malgré* preposition), from *mal* from Latin *malum* bad, evil + *gré* pleasure from Latin *gratum* use as noun of neut. of *gratus* pleasing.]
▸ **A** *noun*. †**1** Ill will, displeasure, spite. ME–M16.
†**2** The state of being regarded with ill will; an instance of this. ME–M16.
3 ***in maugre of***, ***in the maugre of***, in spite of, notwithstanding the power of. Long *rare* or *obsolete* exc. *Scot*. LME.
▸ **B** *preposition*. In spite of, notwithstanding the power of. *arch*. ME.

HUGH MILLER I continued my rounds, maugre the suspicion.

▸ †**C** *adverb*. Notwithstanding. LME–E17.

maul /mɔːl/ *noun*. Also (earlier) †**mall**. See also MALL *noun*. ME.
[ORIGIN Old French & mod. French *mail* from Latin MALLEUS. Cf. MAIL *noun*[5], MALLET *noun*[1], MELL *noun*[1]. In senses 3, 4 from MAUL *verb*.]
▸ **I 1** *hist*. = MACE *noun*[1] 1. Also, a wooden club. ME.
2 Orig. *gen*., a massive hammer. Now, any of various special kinds of heavy hammer or beetle used in pile-driving, shipbuilding, mining, etc. LME. ▸†**b** *fig*. A person regarded as the irresistible enemy or terrible oppressor of a particular class, institution, etc. LME–E18.
†**3** A heavy blow, as struck with a hammer. Only in M17.
4 In RUGBY LEAGUE, an act of mauling or tackling a player. In RUGBY UNION, a loose scrum in which the ball is off the ground (opp. ***ruck***). M19.
▸ **II** See MALL *noun*.

maul /mɔːl/ *verb*. Also †**mall**. ME.
[ORIGIN from the noun In sense 7 perh. a different word.]
†**1** *verb trans*. Strike with a heavy weapon; knock *down*. ME–M17. ▸**b** *verb intrans*. Hammer. LME–E17. ▸**c** *verb trans*. Split (rails) with a maul and wedge. *US*. L17–L19.
2 *verb trans*. Subject to damaging criticism, injure by criticizing. L16.

I. HAMILTON The book received a mauling from the critics.

3 *verb trans*. Beat and bruise (a person); maltreat, knock about. E17.

J. DORAN Thrashing the bishop and terribly mauling his body of followers.

4 *verb trans*. Damage seriously, shatter, mangle; *esp*. (of an animal) tear and mutilate (a prey etc.). L17.

V. WOOLF They worried him, they mauled him with their great yellow teeth.

5 *verb trans*. Handle roughly or carelessly (usu. foll. by *about*); damage by rough handling. Also *dial*., lift *down*. M18.
6 *verb intrans*. Toil, work hard. *dial*. E19.
7 *verb trans*. & *intrans*. RUGBY. Orig., tackle. Now usu., take part in a maul. M19.

Maulana /maʊˈlɑːnə/ *noun*. M19.
[ORIGIN Arabic *mawlānā* our master.]
(A title given to) a Muslim man revered for his religious learning or piety.

mauler /ˈmɔːlə/ *noun*. Also †**maller**. ME.
[ORIGIN from MAUL *verb* + -ER[1].]
1 Orig., a massive hammer. Later, a person who mauls something. Also = MAUL *noun* 2b. ME.
2 A hand, a fist. Cf. MAULEY. *slang*. E19.

mauley /ˈmɔːli/ *noun*. *slang*. L18.
[ORIGIN Uncertain, perh. from MAULER, perh. from Shelta *malya* (itself perh. from transposition of Gaelic *lámh* hand).]
A hand, a fist.

maul oak /ˈmɔːl əʊk/ *noun phr.* **L19.**
[ORIGIN Perh. from Spanish *maula* sham + OAK.]
An evergreen oak, *Quercus chrysolepis*, of the south-western US.

maulstick /ˈmɔːlstɪk/ *noun.* **M17.**
[ORIGIN Dutch *maalstok*, from *malen* to paint + *stok* stick.]
A light stick with a padded leather ball at one end, held by a painter in one hand as a support for the hand used for painting.

maulvi /ˈmaʊlvi/ *noun.* Also **moulvi** /ˈmuːlvi/. **L18.**
[ORIGIN Urdu *maulvī* from Arabic *mawlawī* judicial (used as noun), from *mawlā* MULLAH.]
A Muslim doctor of the law, an imam; *gen.* (esp. in the Indian subcontinent, used as a form of address to) a learned person or teacher.

maum /mɔːm/ *noun. US colloq. & dial.* Also **mawm.** **M19.**
[ORIGIN Var. of MA'AM or MAM. Cf. MARM.]
A title of respect prefixed to the first name of a black woman who looks after white children.

mauma /ˈmɔːmə/ *noun.* **M19.**
[ORIGIN Var. of MAMMA *noun*[2]. Cf. MAMMY *noun*[1].]
= MAMMY *noun*[1] 2.

mau-mau /ˈmaʊmaʊ/ *verb trans. US slang.* **L20.**
[ORIGIN from MAUMA.]
Terrorize, threaten.

Mau Mau /ˈmaʊmaʊ/ *noun & adjective.* **M20.**
[ORIGIN Kikuyu.]
▸ **A** *noun.* Pl. **-s**, same. An African secret society originating among the Kikuyu and active in the 1950s, having as its aim the expulsion of European settlers and the ending of British rule in Kenya; (treated as *pl.*) members of this society. **M20.**
▸ **B** *attrib.* or as *adjective.* Of or pertaining to (a member of) the Mau Mau. **M20.**

maumet /ˈmɔːmɪt/ *noun.* Now *arch. & dial.* Also **mamm-** /ˈmam-/, **momm-** /mɒm-/, & other vars., and with cap. initial. **ME.**
[ORIGIN Old French *mahomet* idol, MAHOMET.]
†**1** A false god, an idol. Cf. MAHOMET 1. **ME–M17.**
2 a A dressed-up figure; a doll, a puppet. Also, a person of grotesque appearance, esp. in dress. **LME.** ▸**b** *fig.* A person who is the tool of another. **LME.** ▸**c** A baby, a child. **M20.**
3 A contemptible or hateful person. **E16.**
†**4** = MAHOMET 3. Now *rare* or *obsolete.* **L17.**
■ **maumetry** *noun* (*a*) idolatry; heathenism; †(*b*) in *pl.*, idolatrous beliefs or practices; †(*c*) idols collectively; (*d*) = MAHOMETRY: **ME.**

maun /mɒn, mɔːn/ *aux. verb. Scot.* **LME.**
[ORIGIN Old Norse *man* pres. t. of *munu* MUN *verb.*]
= MUST *verb*[1] II, III, IV, MUN *verb.*

maunch /mɑːn(t)ʃ, mɔːn(t)ʃ/ *noun.* Also **manche** /mɑːn(t)ʃ/. **L15.**
[ORIGIN Old French & mod. French *manche* from Latin *manica*, from *manus* hand.]
A sleeve. Now only *hist.* & HERALDRY, a loose straight hanging sleeve of a kind worn in the late Middle Ages.

maund /mɔːnd/ *noun*[1]. *obsolete* exc. *dial.*
[ORIGIN Old English *mand*, partly Old French & mod. French *mande* from Middle Low German, Middle Dutch (Dutch *mand*): ult. origin unknown.]
1 A woven basket with a handle or handles. **OE.**
2 A measure of capacity. **ME.**
3 A utensil for moving grapes or hops. **M19.**
■ **maundful** *noun* as much as a maund will hold, a basketful **E19.**

maund /mɔːnd/ *noun*[2]. **L16.**
[ORIGIN Arabic *mann* from Akkadian *mana* (whence Greek *mna*, Latin *mina*): cf. Hebrew *māneh* MANEH.]
A unit of weight in the Indian subcontinent and western Asia, varying greatly in value according to locality.

†**maund** *noun*[3]. *slang.* **E17–L18.**
[ORIGIN from MAUND *verb.*]
Begging.

†**maund** *verb trans. & intrans. slang.* **M16–M19.**
[ORIGIN Perh. from Old French & mod. French *mendier* beg, from Latin *mendicare*: see MENDICANT.]
Beg.

†**maunder** *noun*[1]. *slang.* **E17–L19.**
[ORIGIN from MAUND *verb* + -ER[1].]
A beggar.

maunder /ˈmɔːndə/ *noun*[2]. **M19.**
[ORIGIN from MAUNDER *verb.*]
(A piece of) idle incoherent talk or writing.

maunder /ˈmɔːndə/ *verb.* **E17.**
[ORIGIN Perh. frequentative of MAUND *verb*: see -ER[5].]
†**1** *verb intrans.* Grumble, mutter, growl. **E17–M19.**
2 *verb intrans.* Move or act in a dreamy, idle, or inconsequent manner; dawdle. **M18.** ▸**b** *verb trans.* Fritter *away* (one's time, life, etc.). **M19.**
3 *verb intrans. & trans.* Say (something) in a dreamy and rambling manner. **M19.**

> A. TROLLOPE Men . . had heard the old Major maunder on for years past.

■ **maunderer** *noun* **M17.** **maundering** *noun* the action of the verb; an instance of this; rambling or drivelling talk; dotage: **E17.** **maunderingly** *adverb* in a maundering manner; inconsequently: **E20.**

Maunder minimum /ˈmɔːndə ˈmɪnɪməm/ *noun phr.* **L20.**
[ORIGIN E. W. *Maunder* (1851–1928), English astronomer.]
A prolonged minimum in sunspot activity on the sun between about 1645 and 1715, which coincided with the Little Ice Age in the northern hemisphere.

†**maunding** *noun. slang.* **E17–E19.**
[ORIGIN from MAUND *verb* + -ING[1].]
The action or an act of begging; an abusive demand.

†**maunding** *adjective. slang.* **E17–E18.**
[ORIGIN from MAUND *verb* + -ING[2].]
Mendicant.

Maundy /ˈmɔːndi/ *noun.* Also **m-.** **ME.**
[ORIGIN Old French *mandé* from Latin *mandatum* commandment, MANDATE *noun*, in *mandatum novum* a new commandment (with ref. to *John* 13:34), the opening of the first antiphon sung at the Maundy ceremony (see below).]
1 Orig., the ceremony of washing the feet of a number of poor people, performed by royal or other eminent people or by ecclesiastics, on the Thursday before Easter, and commonly followed by the distribution of clothing, food, or money. Now, the distribution by the British monarch of specially minted silver coins (***Maundy money*** below) to a number of chosen recipients. **ME.** ▸†**b** *fig.* Almsgiving, bounty, largesse. **L16–M17.** ▸**c** The money distributed by the British monarch at the Maundy ceremony. Also ***Royal Maundy***. **M19.**
†**2** The Last Supper. Also (*rare*), the Eucharist. **LME–M17.**
– COMB.: **Maundy coin** a specially minted coin given as Maundy money; **Maundy dish**, **Maundy purse**: used to hold the money to be distributed at a Maundy ceremony; **Maundy money** silver money distributed by the British monarch on Maundy Thursday; ***Maundy purse***: see ***maundy dish*** above; **Maundy Thursday** the Thursday before Good Friday.

Mauretanian *adjective & noun* see MAURITANIAN.

Maurist /ˈmɔːrɪst/ *adjective & noun. hist.* **M18.**
[ORIGIN from St *Maur* (see below) + -IST.]
▸**A** *adjective.* Of or pertaining to the French Benedictine congregation founded in 1621 by St Maur, a disciple of St Benedict, and famous for its scholarship. **M18.**
▸ **B** *noun.* A member of this congregation. **L19.**

Mauritanian /mɒrɪˈteɪnɪən/ *adjective & noun.* Also (now usu. in senses A.1, B.1) **Mauretanian.** **M16.**
[ORIGIN Partly from *Mauretania*, from Latin *Maurus* (see MOOR *noun*[2]), partly from *Mauritania*: see below, -IAN.]
▸ **A** *adjective.* **1** Of or pertaining to the ancient region of Mauretania in N. Africa, corresponding to parts of present-day Morocco and Algeria. **M16.**
2 Of or pertaining to the modern state of Mauritania on the west coast of Africa. **M20.**
▸ **B** *noun.* **1** A native or inhabitant of ancient Mauretania. *rare.* **E17.**
2 A native or inhabitant of the modern state of Mauritania. **M20.**

Mauritian /məˈrɪʃ(ə)n/ *adjective & noun.* **L18.**
[ORIGIN from *Mauritius* (see below) + -AN.]
▸ **A** *adjective.* Of or pertaining to the island of Mauritius in the Indian Ocean. **L18.**
▸ **B** *noun.* A native or inhabitant of Mauritius. **M19.**

mauryah *interjection* var. of MOYA.

Mauryan /ˈmaʊrɪən/ *adjective.* **L19.**
[ORIGIN from *Maurya* (see below) + -AN.]
hist. Of or pertaining to the dynasty founded by Candragupta Maurya, which ruled northern India from 321 to *c* 184 BC.

Mauser /ˈmaʊzə/ *noun.* **L19.**
[ORIGIN Paul von *Mauser* (1838–1914), German inventor.]
(Proprietary name for) any of various firearms, *esp.* a repeating rifle.
– COMB.: **Mauser action** a strong bolt action of the type invented by Mauser.

mausoleum /mɔːsəˈlɪəm/ *noun.* Pl. **-lea** /-ˈlɪə/, **-leums.** **L15.**
[ORIGIN Latin from Greek *Mausōleion*, from *Mausōlos* Mausolos (see below).]
1 M-. The magnificent tomb of Mausolus, King of Caria, erected in the 4th cent. BC at Halicarnassus by his queen Artemisia. **L15.**
2 A large and stately tomb or place of burial. **L15.**

> *fig.*: H. BROOKE O! London, London! thou mausoleum of dead souls!

†**3** = CATAFALQUE 1. **L17–E18.**
■ **mausolean** *adjective* **M16.**

mauther *noun* var. of MAWTHER.

mauvais /mɔvɛ/ *adjective.* Fem. ***-aise*** /-ɛz/. **E18.**
[ORIGIN French.]
Bad. Only in French phrs.
mauvais coucheur /kuʃœːr/, pl. ***mauvais coucheurs*** (pronounced same), [*coucheur* bedfellow] a difficult, uncooperative, or unsociable person. ***mauvaise honte*** /ɔ̃t/ [lit. 'ill shame'] false shame; painful diffidence. ***mauvaise langue*** /lɑ̃g/, pl. ***mauvaises langues*** (pronounced same), [*langue* tongue] an evil tongue; a vituperative gossip, a scandalmonger. ***mauvais pas*** /pɑ/, pl. same, [*pas* step] MOUNTAINEERING a place that is difficult or dangerous to negotiate. ***mauvais quart d'heure*** /kar dœːr/, pl. ***mauvais quarts d'heure*** (pronounced same), [lit. 'bad quarter of an hour'] a brief but unpleasant period of time. ***mauvais sujet*** /syʒɛ/, pl. ***mauvais sujets*** (pronounced same), [*sujet* subject] a worthless person, a bad lot. ***mauvais ton*** /tɔ̃/ [*ton* taste] (now *rare*) what is disapproved of by good society; bad form.

mauve /məʊv/ *noun & adjective.* **M19.**
[ORIGIN French from Latin *malva* MALLOW.]
▸ **A** *noun.* **1** *hist.* A bright but delicate purple aniline dye that was one of the earliest synthetic dyes. Also called ***mauveine***, ***Perkin's mauve***, etc. (see PERKIN 1). **M19.**
2 The colour of this dye; any of a range of dull shades of purple between lilac and maroon. **M19.**
▸ **B** *adjective.* Of the colour mauve. **M19.**
■ **mauvish** *adjective* somewhat mauve **L19.**

mauveine /ˈməʊviːn/ *noun.* Also **-in** /-ɪn/. **M19.**
[ORIGIN from MAUVE + -INE[5], -IN[1].]
CHEMISTRY. = MAUVE *noun* 1.

maux /mɔːks/ *noun. obsolete* exc. *dial.* Pl. **-es**, same. **L16.**
[ORIGIN Perh. rel. to MALKIN *noun.*]
An untidy or unkempt woman. Formerly also, a prostitute.

maven /ˈmeɪv(ə)n/ *noun. N. Amer.* **M20.**
[ORIGIN Hebrew *mēḇīn* understanding.]
An expert, a connoisseur.

maverick /ˈmav(ə)rɪk/ *noun, adjective, & verb.* **M19.**
[ORIGIN Samuel A. *Maverick* (1803–70), Texas engineer who owned but did not brand cattle.]
▸ **A** *noun.* **1** An unbranded calf or yearling. *N. Amer.* **M19.**
2 An unorthodox or independent-minded person; an individualist; *US* a politician who will not affiliate with a regular political party. **L19.**

> A. HAILEY He was an original thinker, a maverick who would not be silenced. M. SARTON Minna . . had always been a maverick, the odd one out in a solid, conservative family.

▸ **B** *attrib.* or as *adjective.* That is a maverick; unorthodox, independent-minded. **L19.**

> CLIVE JAMES A maverick scientist who treats science as an art. B. GELDOF It was the kind of maverick scheme which a single permanent charity could not have afforded.

▸ **C** *verb.* **1** *verb trans.* Seize or brand (an animal) as a maverick. Also, take possession of without any legal claim; steal. **L19.**
2 *verb intrans.* Stray or wander like a maverick. **E20.**

mavis /ˈmeɪvɪs/ *noun.* Now *poet. & dial.* **LME.**
[ORIGIN Old French & mod. French *mauvis.*]
A song thrush.
red mavis: see RED *adjective.*

Mavors /ˈmeɪvɔːz/ *noun. literary.* **M16.**
[ORIGIN Latin: see MARS.]
= MARS 2.

mavourneen /məˈvʊəniːn/ *noun. Irish.* **E19.**
[ORIGIN Irish *mo mhuirnín*, from *mo* my + *muirnín* dim. of *muirn* affection: see -EEN[2].]
My darling.

mavrodaphne /mavrəˈdafni/ *noun.* **E20.**
[ORIGIN mod. Greek from late Greek *mauros* dark (Greek *amauros*) + *daphnē* laurel.]
A dark-red sweet Greek wine; the grape from which this is made.

mavrone /məˈvrəʊn/ *interjection. Irish.* **E19.**
[ORIGIN Irish *mo bhrón*, from *mo* my + *brón* grief.]
Expr. sorrow.

maw /mɔː/ *noun*[1].
[ORIGIN Old English *maga* corresp. to Old Frisian *maga*, Middle Dutch *maghe* (Dutch *maag*), Old High German *mago* (German *Magen*), Old Norse *magi*, from Germanic.]
1 The stomach of an animal or (now *joc.*) a person; the cavity of the stomach. Formerly *spec.*, the abomasum or fourth stomach of a ruminant. **OE.**

> N. HAWTHORNE Destined to glut the ravenous maw of that detestable man-brute.

2 †**a** Any of various internal organs, as (*a*) the abdominal cavity as a whole; the belly; (*b*) the womb; (*c*) the liver. **ME–E16.** ▸**b** The swim bladder of a fish. **LME.**
3 The throat, the gullet; *esp.* the jaws or mouth of a voracious mammal or fish. **LME.**

> *Trout & Salmon* It stuck its head up out of the river . . and it opened its great maw wide. K. LETTE She tossed a fistful of crisps into her maw with alarming savagery. *transf.*: K. KESEY We'll face the terrible maw of a muzzle-loading shotgun.

†**4** Appetite, inclination, liking. **L16–E18.**

> C. CIBBER I have no great Maw to that Business, methinks.

maw /mɔː/ *noun*[2]. Long *obsolete* exc. *Scot. & N. English.* **LME.**
[ORIGIN Reduced form of MALLOW.]
sing. & (usu.) in *pl.* (treated as *sing.*). A mallow.

maw /mɔː/ *noun*[3]. *obsolete* exc. *dial.* **LME.**
[ORIGIN Old Norse *már* = Old English *mǣw*: see MEW *noun*[1].]
A gull, *esp.* the common gull, *Larus canus.*

M

maw /mɔː/ *noun*[4]. *obsolete* exc. *hist.* M16.
[ORIGIN Perh. from Irish *mámh* trump.]
A Gaelic card game from which the game twenty-five developed.

maw /mɔː/ *noun*[5]. *colloq. & dial.* (chiefly *US*). E19.
[ORIGIN Repr. a pronunc. of MA *noun*: cf. PAW *noun*[2].]
= MA *noun*.

mawashi /mə'waːʃi/ *noun.* M20.
[ORIGIN Japanese, from *mawasu* to put round.]
A type of loincloth worn by a sumo wrestler.

mawk /mɔːk/ *noun. obsolete* exc. *dial.* LME.
[ORIGIN Old Norse *maðkr*: see MADDOCK.]
A maggot.

mawkin *noun* var. of MALKIN.

mawkish /'mɔːkɪʃ/ *adjective.* M17.
[ORIGIN from MAWK + -ISH[1].]
1 Inclined to sickness; without appetite. *obsolete* exc. *dial.* M17.
2 Having a nauseating, sickly, or insipid taste. L17.

P. V. WHITE She reached out for the . . barley water . . and tried to find comfort in . . that mawkish stuff.

3 Feebly sentimental; imbued with sickly or false sentiment. E18.

C. P. SNOW Dickens made a mawkish cult of Mary Hogarth, and idolised her.

■ **mawkishly** *adverb* M18. **mawkishness** *noun* E18.

mawky /'mɔːki/ *adjective. obsolete* exc. *dial.* M18.
[ORIGIN from MAWK + -Y[1].]
1 = MAWKISH 2, 3. M18.
2 Maggoty (*lit. & fig.*). L18.

mawm *noun* see MAUM.

†**mawmish** *adjective.* L16–M19.
[ORIGIN from base of MALM *noun* + -ISH[1].]
= MAWKISH 2, 3.

mawseed /'mɔːsiːd/ *noun. arch.* E18.
[ORIGIN Partial translation of German dial. *Mahsaat*, *Mohsamen*, from *Mah*, *Moh* poppy (German *Mohn*) + *Saat*, *Samen* seed.]
The seed of the opium poppy, *Papaver somniferum*.

mawther /'mɔːðə/ *noun.* Now *dial.* Also **mauther**. LME.
[ORIGIN Perh. a var. of MOTHER *noun*[1]; cf. Norwegian use of *mor* mother as an address for young girls.]
A young girl.

M

Mawworm /'mɔːwɔːm/ *noun.* Now *rare.* E19.
[ORIGIN *Mawworm*, a character in Isaac Bickerstaffe's play *The Hypocrite*, 1769.]
A hypocritical pretender to sanctity.

maw-worm /'mɔːwɔːm/ *noun.* Now *rare* or *obsolete.* L16.
[ORIGIN from MAW *noun*[1] + WORM *noun*.]
A parasitic worm, esp. a nematode, infesting the gut of humans and other mammals.

max /max/ *noun*[1]. *slang.* Now *rare* or *obsolete.* E18.
[ORIGIN Perh. shortened from MAXIMUM *noun*, in ref. to the strength of the drink.]
Gin.

max /maks/ *noun*[2] *& adjective. N. Amer. colloq.* M19.
[ORIGIN Abbreviation of MAXIMUM.]
▸ **A** *noun.* **1** A maximum figure, achievement, etc. M19.

Independent We should pursue our dreams, never settle for second best, live life to the max.

2 A maximum security prison. M20.

J. WELCH He had learned to live in an eight-by-ten cell in the new max.

▸ **B** *attrib.* or as *adjective*. Maximum. L19.

C. GLAZEBROOK I leave a suitable pause for max dramatic effect.

max q AERONAUTICS the maximum dynamic pressure exerted on an aircraft or spacecraft in the course of its flight; the part of a flight during which the highest aerodynamic pressures are encountered.

max /maks/ *verb. US colloq.* L19.
[ORIGIN from MAX *noun*[2] *& adjective*.]
1 *verb trans. & intrans.* (usu. foll. by *out*). Do (a thing) well; perform to the limit of one's capacity, endurance, etc. L19.
2 *verb intrans.* Complete a maximum prison sentence. L20.

max /maks/ *adverb. US colloq.* L20.
[ORIGIN formed as MAX *verb*.]
At the maximum, at the most.

max. *abbreviation.*
Maximum.

maxi /'maksi/ *noun. colloq.* M20.
[ORIGIN from MAXI-.]
A thing that is large or long of its kind; *spec.* (**a**) a maxi-skirt; (**b**) *Austral. & NZ* a maxi-yacht.

maxi- /'maksi/ *combining form.* M20.
[ORIGIN from MAXI(MUM: cf. MINI-.]
Forming chiefly nouns denoting a thing that is large or long of its kind, esp. a garment or (*Austral. & NZ*) a racing yacht, as ***maxi-coat***, ***maxi-skirt***, etc.

maxilla /mak'sɪlə/ *noun.* Pl. **-llae** /-liː/. LME.
[ORIGIN Latin = jaw.]
1 A jaw, a jawbone; *spec.* either of a pair of bones forming (part of) the upper jaw in vertebrates. Cf. MANDIBLE. LME.
2 In insects and other arthropods, either of a pair of mouthparts posterior to and accessory to the mandibles. L18.
■ **maxillar** *adjective & noun* (a) maxillary M17. **maxillary** *adjective & noun* (**a**) *adjective* of, pertaining to, or designating a maxilla; forming part of a maxilla; (**b**) *noun* a maxillary bone; a maxilla: E17.

maxilliped /mak'sɪlɪpɛd/ *noun.* Also **-pede** /-piːd/. M19.
[ORIGIN from MAXILLA + -I- + Latin *ped-*, *pes* foot.]
ZOOLOGY. In crustaceans, an appendage modified for feeding and occurring in pairs behind the maxillae.

maxillo- /mak'sɪləʊ, 'maksɪləʊ/ *combining form.*
[ORIGIN from MAXILLA: see -O-.]
Forming adjectives with the sense 'pertaining to the maxilla and —', as ***maxillo-facial***, ***maxillo-mandibular***, etc., and nouns etc. derived from them.

maxim /'maksɪm/ *noun*[1]. LME.
[ORIGIN French *maxime* or its source medieval Latin *maxima* use as noun (sc. *propositio* proposition) of fem. of *maximus*: see MAXIMUM. Cf. MAXIMA *noun*[1].]
†**1** A self-evident proposition assumed as a premiss in mathematical or dialectical reasoning. LME–L17.

R. BENTLEY It is urged as an universal Maxim, That Nothing can procede from Nothing.

2 A proposition, esp. a pithily worded one, expressing a general truth drawn from science, law, or experience. Cf. earlier MAXIMUM 1. L16.

Weekly Notes He considered at length the meaning of the maxim, 'a man's house is his castle.' J. BERMAN She acts out the psychoanalytic maxim that wishes and fears are often inextricably related.

3 A rule or principle of conduct; a pithily expressed precept of morality or prudence. L16.

D. M. FRAME The maxim 'Know thyself' was on the temple of Apollo at Delphi.

■ **maximist** *noun* a person who makes or coins maxims M19.

Maxim /'maksɪm/ *noun*[2]. L19.
[ORIGIN Sir Hiram S. *Maxim* (1840–1916), US-born Brit. inventor.]
In full ***Maxim gun***, ***Maxim machine gun***. A single-barrelled quick-firing machine gun with a barrel surrounded by an outer casing filled with water to keep the parts cool.

†**maxima** *noun*[1]. M16.
[ORIGIN medieval Latin: see MAXIM *noun*[1].]
1 = MAXIM *noun*[1]. M–L16.
2 MUSIC. = LARGE *noun* 4. M18–E19.

maxima *noun*[2] pl. of MAXIMUM *noun*.

maximal /'maksɪm(ə)l/ *adjective.* L19.
[ORIGIN from MAXIMUM + -AL[1].]
Consisting of or relating to a maximum; of the greatest possible size, duration, or capacity.
■ **maxi'mality** *noun* the property of being maximal M20. **maximally** *adverb* L19.

maximalist /'maksɪm(ə)lɪst/ *noun & adjective.* E20.
[ORIGIN from MAXIMAL + -IST, after Russian *maksimalist*. Cf. BOLSHEVIK.]
▸ **A** *noun.* A person who holds out for the maximum of his or her demands and rejects compromises; *spec.* (*hist.*) a member of the part of the Russian Social Democratic Party which favoured extreme methods; a member of any similar group outside the former USSR. E20.
▸ **B** *attrib.* or as *adjective*. Of, pertaining to, or characteristic of maximalists or maximalism. E20.
■ **maximalism** *noun* the beliefs or practices of maximalists E20.

maximand /'maksɪmand/ *noun.* M20.
[ORIGIN from MAXIM(IZE *verb* + -AND.]
A thing which is to be maximized.

maximin /'maksɪmɪn/ *noun & adjective.* M20.
[ORIGIN from MAXI(MUM + MIN(IMUM, after *minimax*.]
MATH. ▸ **A** *noun.* The largest of a set of minima. M20.
▸ **B** *attrib.* or as *adjective*. Of, pertaining to, or of the nature of a maximin; *spec.* in GAME THEORY, designating a strategy that maximizes the smallest gain that can be relied on by a participant in a game or other situation of conflict. Cf. MINIMAX *noun & adjective*. M20.

maximize /'maksɪmʌɪz/ *verb.* Also **-ise**. E19.
[ORIGIN from Latin *maximus* (see MAXIMUM) + -IZE.]
1 *verb trans.* Increase to the highest possible degree; enhance to the utmost. E19.

A. S. DALE He . . went to his father for advice on how to maximize his income.

2 *verb intrans.* Chiefly THEOLOGY. Maintain the most rigorous or comprehensive interpretation possible of a doctrine or an obligation. L19.

W. S. LILLY I am far from wishing to maximize upon this matter.

3 *verb intrans.* Reach a maximum value. L20.

Globe & Mail (Toronto) If emissions were curtailed now, the resultant ozone destruction would maximize around 1990.

■ **maximi'zation** *noun* E19. **maximizer** *noun* M19.

maximum /'maksɪməm/ *noun & adjective.* M16.
[ORIGIN (French from) mod. Latin use as noun of neut. of Latin *maximus* superl. of *magnus* great.]
▸ **A** *noun.* Pl. **-ima** /-ɪmə/, **-imums**.
▸ †**I 1** = MAXIM *noun*[1] 2. Only in M16.
▸ **II 2** The highest possible magnitude or quantity of something attained, attainable, or customary; an upper limit of magnitude or quantity. Formerly also, the largest portion in which matter can exist. M17. ▸**b** The highest amount (esp. of temperature, barometric pressure, etc.) attained or recorded within a particular period. E19.

T. M. LINDSAY A strange compound of minimum of fact and maximum of theory. A. STORR Dependence is at its maximum at birth, when the human infant is most helpless.

3 MATH. The greatest value which a variable may have; the largest element in a set; a point at which a continuously varying quantity ceases to increase and begins to decrease. M18.
4 A superior limit imposed by authority; *esp.* in FRENCH HISTORY, a limit of price for corn. E19.
– COMB.: **maximum thermometer**: which records the highest temperature attained since it was last set.
▸ **B** *attrib.* or as *adjective*. Of or pertaining to a maximum, that is a maximum. E19.

Z. TOMIN It was a game requiring maximum concentration.

maximum price: that may not by law etc. be exceeded.

maxina /'maksɪnə/ *noun.* E20.
[ORIGIN Perh. from MAXIXE.]
A kind of ballroom dance in common time.

maxixe /mak'siːks, *foreign* mə'ʃiʃə/ *noun.* E20.
[ORIGIN Portuguese.]
A dance for couples, of Brazilian origin, resembling the polka and the local tango.

Maxwell /'makswɛl/ *noun.* L19.
[ORIGIN James Clerk *Maxwell* (1831–79), Scot. physicist.]
PHYSICS. **1** Used in *possess.* and *attrib.* to designate concepts originated by Maxwell. L19.
Maxwell demon, **Maxwell's demon** a device (or imaginary being) conceived as allowing only fast-moving molecules to pass through a hole in one direction and only slow-moving ones in the other direction, so that if the hole is in a partition dividing a gas-filled vessel into two parts, one side becomes warmer and the other cooler, in violation of the second law of thermodynamics. **Maxwell distribution**, **Maxwell's distribution** (a formula describing) the distribution of molecular velocities predicted by Maxwell's law, the number with a velocity between v and $v + dv$ being proportional to $\exp(-\frac{1}{2}mv^2/kT)v^2\,dv$ (where m is the mass of a molecule, k is Boltzmann's constant, and T is the absolute temperature). **Maxwell equation**, **Maxwell's equation** each of a set of four linear partial differential equations which summarize the classical properties of the electromagnetic field and relate space and time derivatives of the electric and magnetic field vectors, the electric displacement vector, and the magnetic induction vector, and also involve the electric current and charge densities. **Maxwell law**, **Maxwell's law** a law in classical physics giving the probabilities of different velocities for the molecules of a gas in equilibrium.
2 (**m-**.) A unit of magnetic flux in the cgs system, equal to the flux through an area of one square centimetre normal to a uniform induction of one gauss, and equivalent to 10^{-8} weber. E20.
■ **Maxwellian** /maks'wɛlɪən/ *adjective* of, pertaining to, or originated by J. C. Maxwell; in accordance with Maxwell's law or equations: L19.

Maxwell–Boltzmann /makswɛl'bəʊltsmən/ *noun.* E20.
[ORIGIN from MAXWELL + BOLTZMANN.]
PHYSICS. Used *attrib.* to designate certain concepts in the kinetic theory of gases.
Maxwell–Boltzmann distribution = ***Maxwell distribution*** s.v. MAXWELL 1, ***BOLTZMANN distribution***.

Maxwell's duiker /'makswɛlz 'dʌɪkə/ *noun phr.* E20.
[ORIGIN Charles *Maxwell*, 19th-cent. English soldier and explorer.]
A small grey or brown duiker, *Cephalophus maxwelli*, of W. African forests.

may /meɪ/ *noun*[1]. *poet. arch.*
[ORIGIN Old English *mǣg* reinforced or replaced in Middle English by forms from Old Norse *mær* (genit. *meyjar*) maid = Gothic *mawi*, from Germanic fem. of base of Gothic *magus* boy. Cf. MAIDEN *noun*.]
A maiden, a virgin.

May /meɪ/ *noun*[2]. In sense 2 also **m-**. LOE.
[ORIGIN Old French & mod. French *mai* from Latin *Maius* (sc. *mensis* month) pertaining to the Italic goddess *Maia*.]
1 The fifth month of the year in the Gregorian calendar. Also *fig.*, with allus. to May's position at the beginning of summer in the northern hemisphere; *poet.* one's bloom, one's prime, the heyday. LOE. ▸**b** The festivities of May Day. L15.
2 Hawthorn blossom; (occas.) the hawthorn tree. LME.
3 At Cambridge University: an examination or (in *pl.*) examinations held in May; in *pl.*, boat races held during May Week (see below). M19.
– PHRASES: **May and January** a young woman and an old man as husband and wife. ***nuts in May***: see NUT *noun*. **Queen of the**

May, †**Queen of May** a girl chosen to be queen of games on May Day, usu. being gaily dressed and crowned with flowers.
– COMB.: **May apple** a N. American plant, *Podophyllum peltatum*, of the barberry family, with a solitary waxy flower; the yellowish egg-shaped fruit of this plant, produced in May; **May beetle** = *May-bug* below; **May-bird** a whimbrel; **May-blob** marsh marigold, *Caltha palustris*; **May-bug** any of various beetles of the scarab family which appear in late spring, *esp.* (in Europe) the cockchafer, (in N. America) the June bug, *Phyllophaga*; **May-bush** (a branch of) hawthorn; †**May butter** unsalted butter preserved in the month of May for medicinal use; **May-cherry** (*a*) a small early kind of cherry; (*b*) *US* (the fruit of) any of various shrubs of the genus *Amelanchier*; = *juneberry* s.v. JUNE *noun*; **May Day** 1 May, esp. as marked by festivities or as an international holiday in honour of workers; **mayday** [repr. pronunc. of French *m'aider* help me] an international radio distress signal; *transf.* a call for help; **May dew** dew gathered in the month of May, esp. on 1 May, popularly supposed to have medicinal and cosmetic properties; **mayduke** an early-ripening variety of duke cherry; **mayfish** (*a*) the twaite shad; (*b*) *US* the striped killifish, *Fundulus majalis*, of the Atlantic coast of N. America; **mayflower** (*a*) *dial.* any of various plants flowering in May, *esp.* the cowslip, *Primula veris*, and lady's smock, *Cardamine pratensis*; (*b*) *N. Amer.* the trailing arbutus, *Epigaea repens*; **May game** (*a*) in *pl.*, the merrymaking and sports associated with 1 May; (*b*) a performance or entertainment in May Day festivities; *gen.* a frolic, an entertainment; a foolish or extravagant action or performance; (*c*) *arch.* an object of sport, jest, or ridicule, a laughing stock; **May lady** (*obsolete* exc. *hist.*) a Queen of the May; **May lily** orig., lily of the valley; now, a rare allied woodland plant, *Maianthemum bifolium*; **May morn** (*poet.*), **May morning** the morning of 1 May; **May-pop** *US* (the fruit of) the passion flower, *Passiflora incarnata*; **May queen** the Queen of the May; **May rose** any of various roses flowering in May; **May Week** at Cambridge University, a week in late May or early June when intercollegiate boat races are held. See also MAYFLY.

may /meɪ/ *noun*³. M19.
[ORIGIN from MAY *verb*¹.]
An instance of what is expressed by the auxiliary verb ***may***; a possibility.

may /meɪ/ *verb*¹. Pres.: 1, 2, 3, sing. & pl. **may**; 2, sing. (*arch.*) **mayst** /meɪst/, **mayest** /ˈmeɪəst/. Pa.: 1, 2, 3, sing. & pl. **might** /mʌɪt/, (now *dial.*) **mought** /mɔːt/; 2, sing. (*arch.*) **mightest** /ˈmʌɪtɪst/. Neg. **may not**, (*colloq.*) **mayn't** /meɪnt/; **might not**, (*colloq.*) **mightn't** /ˈmʌɪt(ə)nt/. No other parts used.
[ORIGIN Old English *mæg* (1st person sing.) = Old Frisian *mei*, Old Saxon, Old High German *mag* (Dutch, German *mag*), Old Norse *má*, Gothic *mag*: a Germanic preterite-present verb with primary meaning 'have power'.]
▶ **I** As full verb.
†**1** *verb intrans.* Be strong; have power or influence; prevail (*over*). OE–LME. ▸**b** *verb trans.* With cognate obj.: have (might, power). ME–L15.
▶ **II** As auxiliary verb (often *ellipt.* with verb understood or supplied from the context).
2 Have ability or power to; = CAN *verb*¹ 4. *arch.* OE.

M. DRAYTON Thy mighty strokes who may withstand. M. ARNOLD We.. have endured Sunshine and rain as we might.

3 As ***may*** or (rejecting or qualifying a hypothesis etc. or implying improbability) in pa. form ***might***: have the possibility, opportunity, or suitable conditions to; be likely to; (***may be***, ***may do***, perhaps is, will, or does; ***may have been***, ***may have done***, (now *rare*) ***might be***, ***might do***, perhaps was or did, perhaps has been or done, perhaps can or could). (Pa. indic. now *rare* as tending to be interpreted as subjunct.) OE. ▸**b** In pa. form ***might***: used to. *poet.* E19. ▸**c** In pa. form ***might*** (subjunct.) with perf. inf.: would not have found it difficult to (perform an omitted act of duty or kindness). In pa. form ***might*** with pres. inf.: ought not find it difficult to (perform a similar omitted act). *colloq.* M19.

STEELE The Improvement of our Understandings may, or may not, be of Service to us, according as it is managed. SIR W. SCOTT He joyed to see the cheerful light, And he said Ave Mary, as well he might. B. JOWETT I dare say.. that you may be right. SCOTT FITZGERALD I thought you might want to know. *Times Lit. Suppl.* Twenty years ago you might hear a sixpence described as a 'Lord'. S. SASSOON She had hoped and prayed that I might get a home-service job. *Atlantic Monthly* Any outside disturbance .. may well bring disaster to the whole region. *National Observer (US)* One theory.. was that frozen plumbing may have caused .. a contamination of the water system. P. THEROUX It might have been sisal, but more likely was the tequila plant. P. NIESEWAND A flypast might be nice. How about some sky-divers? **c** G. B. SHAW Really,.. you might at least join your flats. W. CATHER You might have told me there was a snake behind me!

4 As ***may*** or (rejecting or qualifying a hypothesis etc. or implying improbability) in pa. form ***might***: be allowed by authority, law, rule, morality, reason, etc., to. OE. ▸**b** *LAW.* In the interpretation of some statutes: shall, must. E18.

THACKERAY May we take your coach to town? A. E. HOUSMAN 'Twill do no harm to take my arm. 'You may, young man, you may'.

5 In pa. form ***might*** as subjunct. in conditional sentences: were or would be or have been able to, were or would be or have been allowed to, were or would perhaps. OE.

BYRON Oh! might I kiss those eyes of fire, A million scarce would quench desire. E. RICKERT One might see in her withered.. face the wreckage of a great beauty. *Times* If a grave crisis were ever to arise on the western borders of Russia, the isolationists might be swept off their feet. E. A. CARLSON If Weldon had stopped here he might have won the battle. N. GORDIMER If we'd still been children, I might have been throwing stones at him in a tantrum.

6 In clauses of purpose or result: as part of a periphrastic subjunct. expressing virtually the same meaning as the subjunct. of the principal verb, which this combination has largely superseded. OE.

S. JOHNSON Lest my appearance might draw too many compliments. LD MACAULAY It was not easy to devise any expedient which might avert the danger.

7 In exclamations: expr. a wish (usu. ***may***; ***might*** also when its realization is thought hardly possible). LME.

DICKENS May the present moment.. be the worst of our lives!

8 In questions: ***may*** with inf. is sometimes substituted for the indic. of the principal verb to render the question less abrupt or pointed. E16.

WORDSWORTH Sisters and brothers, little maid, How many may you be?

– PHRASES ETC.: **be that as it may** irrespective of the situation regarding that, that may well be so (but there are other considerations). ***may I have the pleasure?***: see PLEASURE *noun*. ***may it please you***. ***may your shadow never grow less!***: see SHADOW *noun*. **that is as may be** the truth of that is not yet determined, that may well be so (but it is not a significant consideration).

may /meɪ/ *verb*² *intrans. arch.* L15.
[ORIGIN from MAY *noun*².]
Take part in the festivities of May Day or in the pleasures of the month of May; gather flowers in May. Chiefly as ***maying*** *verbal noun*.
■ **mayer** *noun* L16.

maya /ˈmɑːjə/ *noun*¹. L18.
[ORIGIN Sanskrit *māyā*, from *mā* create.]
In *HINDUISM*, illusion, magic, the supernatural power wielded by gods and demons. In *HINDUISM & BUDDHISM*, the power by which the universe becomes manifest, the illusion or appearance of the phenomenal world.

Maya /ˈmʌɪ(j)ə, ˈmeɪ(j)ə/ *adjective & noun*². Also (earlier) †**Maye**. Pl. of noun **-s**, same. E19.
[ORIGIN Spanish from Maya.]
▶ **A** *adjective*. Of or pertaining to an American Indian people of Yucatan and Central America whose ancient civilization was at its peak between the 4th and the 8th cents; Mayan. E19.
▶ **B** *noun*. **1** A member of this people, a Mayan. M19.
2 The group of languages spoken by this people. M19.

Mayan /ˈmʌɪ(j)ən, ˈmeɪ(j)ən/ *adjective & noun*. M19.
[ORIGIN from MAYA *noun*² & *adjective* + -AN.]
▶ **A** *adjective*. Of or pertaining to the Mayas or their group of languages. M19.
▶ **B** *noun*. **1** = MAYA *noun*² 1. E20.
2 = MAYA *noun*² 2. M20.
■ **Mayanist** *noun* an expert in or student of Mayan culture M20.

maybe /ˈmeɪbiː, -bi/ *adverb & noun*. Also (*colloq. & dial.*) **mebbe** /ˈmɛbi/. LME.
[ORIGIN from *it may be*. Cf. MAYHAP.]
▶ **A** *adverb*. Possibly, perhaps. LME.

JOYCE I'll make it worth while. And I don't mean may-be. *New Yorker* I wanted to think maybe she was different now.

▶ **B** *noun*. What may be; a possibility. Now *rare*. L16.

maycock *noun* var. of MACOCK.

†**Maye** *noun & adjective* see MAYA *noun*² & *adjective*.

mayest *verb* see MAY *verb*¹.

Mayfair /ˈmeɪfɛː/ *noun & adjective*. E18.
[ORIGIN from MAY *noun*² + FAIR *noun*¹.]
▶ **A** *noun*. A fair held in May, *esp.* (*hist.*) that held annually in the 17th and 18th cents. in Brook fields near Hyde Park Corner in London; the fashionable and opulent district in the West End of London occupying the site of the old fairground. E18.
▶ **B** *attrib.* or as *adjective*. Of, pertaining to, or characteristic of Mayfair. M19.
■ **Mayfairish** *adjective* M20.

mayfly /ˈmeɪflʌɪ/ *noun*. Pl. **-flies**, same. E17.
[ORIGIN from MAY *noun*² + FLY *noun*¹.]
†**1** A dragonfly, alderfly, or caddis fly. E17–E19.
2 Any of various insects of the order Ephemeroptera, having aquatic larvae and short-lived adults with three long abdominal cerci and a characteristic bobbing mating flight; an ephemerid; *spec.* in *ANGLING*, (an artificial fly imitating) an adult of the genus *Ephemera*. M17.

mayhap /meɪˈhap, ˈmeɪhap/ *adverb*. Now *arch. & dial.* M16.
[ORIGIN from *it may hap* (HAP *verb*¹). Cf. MAYBE.]
Perhaps, possibly.
■ Also **mayhappen** *adverb* M16.

mayhem /ˈmeɪhɛm/ *noun & verb*. Also †**maihem**. LME.
[ORIGIN Anglo-Norman *mahem*, Old French *mahaing* MAIM *noun*¹.]
▶ **A** *noun*. **1** *LAW*. Malicious injury to or maiming of a person, orig. so as to impair or destroy the victim's capacity for self-defence. *hist.* LME. ▸**b** Violent behaviour, *esp.* physical assault. Orig. *US*. L19.
2 Violent and damaging action; violent disorder, rowdy confusion, chaos. L19.

H. CARPENTER The ability to work at his desk in the middle of domestic mayhem. *Daily Express* It was mayhem on the motorway.

▶ **B** *verb trans.* Infl. **-m-**, ***-mm-**. Injure or maim maliciously. Now *rare*. M18.

mayn't *verb* see MAY *verb*¹.

mayo /ˈmeɪəʊ/ *noun*. *colloq.* M20.
[ORIGIN Abbreviation.]
Mayonnaise.

mayonnaise /meɪəˈneɪz/ *noun*. E19.
[ORIGIN French, also *magnonaise*, *mahonnaise*, perh. fem. of *mahonnais* adjective, from *Mahon* capital of Minorca.]
A thick sauce consisting of yolk of egg beaten up with oil and vinegar and seasoned with salt etc., used as a dressing esp. for salad, eggs, cold meat, or fish; a dish (of meat etc.) having this sauce as a dressing.
■ **mayonnaised** *adjective* dressed with mayonnaise M20.

mayor /mɛː/ *noun*. In sense 2 usu. **mair**. ME.
[ORIGIN Old French & mod. French *maire* from Latin MAJOR *adjective*, used as noun in late Latin.]
1 The head or chief officer of the municipal corporation of a city or borough in England, Wales, Ireland, parts of the British Commonwealth, the US, and formerly in Scotland (where now ***provost***); in England and Wales now also, the head of a district council with the status of a borough. Occas., a French *maire* or (formerly) a similar municipal officer in other European towns; any of various administrative officers in other European countries, as the Netherlands and Switzerland. ME.
2 *hist.* In Scotland, any of various officers with delegated jurisdiction or executive functions under the monarch or under some judicial authority. ME.
– PHRASES: ***Lord Mayor***: see LORD *noun*. **mayor of the palace** [French *maire du palais* translating medieval Latin *major domus*] *hist.* (orig. under the later Merovingian kings) a nominal subordinate wielding the power of his titular superior.
■ **mayordom** *noun* (*obsolete* exc. *hist.*) = MAYORALTY 1 M16.
mayorlet *noun* (*rare*) a petty mayor M19.

mayoral /mɑːjəˈrɑːl, *foreign* majoˈral/ *noun*. L16.
[ORIGIN Spanish, from *mayor* greater from Latin MAJOR *adjective*.]
In Spain and Spanish-speaking countries, a conductor in charge of a train of animals or group of people.

mayoral /ˈmɛːr(ə)l/ *adjective*. L17.
[ORIGIN from MAYOR + -AL¹.]
Of or pertaining to a mayor or mayoralty.

mayoralty /ˈmɛːr(ə)lti/ *noun*. LME.
[ORIGIN Old French *mairalté*, from *maire* MAYOR: see -TY¹.]
1 The status or office of a mayor. LME.
2 The period during which a mayor holds office. LME.

mayoress /ˈmɛːrɪs/ *noun*. LME.
[ORIGIN from MAYOR + -ESS¹.]
1 The wife of a mayor; a woman fulfilling the ceremonial duties of a mayor's wife. LME.
Lady Mayoress: see LADY *noun* 5b.
2 A woman holding the office of mayor. L19.

mayorship /ˈmɛːʃɪp/ *noun*. L15.
[ORIGIN from MAYOR + -SHIP.]
= MAYORALTY 1.

mayory /ˈmɛːri/ *noun*. Now *rare*. L17.
[ORIGIN from MAYOR + -Y⁵, after French *mairie* etc.]
The district over which a (Continental) mayor has jurisdiction; the place of business of a mayor.

maypole /ˈmeɪpəʊl/ *noun*. E16.
[ORIGIN from MAY *noun*² + POLE *noun*¹.]
1 A high pole, traditionally painted with spiral stripes and decorated with flowers, set up on a green or other open space, around which people dance on May Day holding long ribbons attached to the top. M16.
2 A tall object or (esp.) person. *joc.* L16.

mayst *verb* see MAY *verb*¹.

maythe /meɪð/ *noun*. *arch.* Also **maythes** /meɪðz/.
[ORIGIN Old English *magoþe* weak fem., *maegþa* weak masc., of unknown origin.]
1 Any of various kinds of mayweed or camomile; *esp.* stinking camomile, *Anthemis cotula*. OE.
†**2** ***red maythe***, pheasant's eye, *Adonis annua*. L16–E18.

maythen /ˈmeɪð(ə)n/ *noun*. *obsolete* exc. *dial.* Also **mathern**. ME.
[ORIGIN Repr. Old English *mæg(e)þan*, *magoþan*, oblique cases and pl. of *mægeþa*, *magoþa*: see MAYTHE.]
= MAYTHE 1.

maythes *noun* var. of MAYTHE.

M

mayweed /ˈmeɪwiːd/ *noun*. **M16**.
[ORIGIN from MAYTHE, MAYTHEN + WEED *noun*[1].]
Any of various kinds of wild camomile found as weeds of cultivated ground; *esp.* (more fully ***scentless mayweed***) *Tripleurospermum inodorum* and (more fully ***stinking mayweed***) *Anthemis cotula*.

mazagan /ˈmazəgan/ *noun*. **M18**.
[ORIGIN *Mazagan* in Morocco, where it grows wild.]
In full ***mazagan bean***. A small early variety of the broad bean, *Vicia faba*.

Mazahua /məˈzɑːwə/ *noun & adjective*. **L18**.
[ORIGIN Mazahua.]
▸ **A** *noun*. Pl. **-s**, same.
1 A member of an American Indian people of Mexico. **L18**.
2 The language of this people. **M20**.
▸ **B** *adjective*. Of or pertaining to this people or their language. **M20**.

mazame /məˈzeɪm, məˈzɑːmeɪ/ *noun*. **L18**.
[ORIGIN French, from Nahuatl *maçame* pl. of *maçatl* deer, mistaken for sing.]
Any of various American deer; *spec.* = BROCKET 2. Also (occas.), a Rocky Mountain goat.

mazar /məˈzɑː/ *noun*. **M19**.
[ORIGIN Arabic *mazār* place visited, from *zāra* to visit.]
A Muslim tomb revered as a shrine.

mazard /ˈmazəd/ *noun*[1]. Also **-zz-**. **L16**.
[ORIGIN Alt. of MAZER by assoc. of *-er* with -ARD. Perh. earlier as MAZZARD *noun*[1].]
†**1** A cup, a bowl, a drinking vessel. Also ***mazard bowl***. **L16–L17**.
2 The head; the face. *joc.* (*arch.*). **L16**.

mazard *noun*[2] var. of MAZZARD *noun*[1].

mazarine /mazəˈriːn, ˈmazəriːn/ *noun & adjective*. Also **mazarin** /ˈmazərɪn/. **L17**.
[ORIGIN Perh. from Cardinal Jules *Mazarin* (1602–61) or the Duchesse de *Mazarin* (d. 1699). In sense A.1 perh. a different word.]
▸ **A** *noun*. **1** *hist.* A deep plate, usually of metal, *esp.* one placed as a strainer inside a serving dish. Formerly also ***mazarine dish***, ***mazarine plate***. **L17**.
2 (A fabric or garment of) a deep rich blue. Now *rare*. **L17**.
3 In full ***mazarine blue***. A Eurasian blue (lycaenid) butterfly, *Cyaniris semiargus*. **E19**.
▸ **B** *adjective*. Of a deep rich blue colour. Now *rare*. **L17**.

Mazatec /ˈmazətɛk/ *adjective & noun*. Also **Mazateco** /mazəˈtɛkəʊ/. **L19**.
[ORIGIN Spanish *Mazateca* from Nahuatl *masa:te:ka* from *masa:* deer + *te:ka*, suffix denoting 'inhabitant of the place of'.]
▸ **A** *attrib.* or as *adjective*. Of or pertaining to an American Indian people of southern Mexico. **L19**.
▸ **B** *noun*. Pl. **-s**, same.
1 A member of this people. **E20**.
2 The language of this people. **M20**.

Mazdaean /ˈmazdɪən/ *adjective & noun*. Also **-dean**. **M19**.
[ORIGIN formed as MAZDAISM + -EAN.]
▸ **A** *adjective*. Zoroastrian. **M19**.
▸ **B** *noun*. A Zoroastrian. **L19**.

Mazdaism /ˈmazdə-ɪz(ə)m/ *noun*. Also **Mazde-**. **L19**.
[ORIGIN from Avestan *mazdā*, the supreme god (Ahura Mazdā, Ormuzd) of ancient Persian religion + -ISM.]
Zoroastrianism.
■ **Mazdaist** *noun* a Zoroastrian **E20**.

Mazdean *adjective & noun* var. of MAZDAEAN.

Mazdeism *noun* var. of MAZDAISM.

maze /meɪz/ *noun*[1]. **ME**.
[ORIGIN from MAZE *verb*.]
†**1** ***the maze***, delirium, delusion, disappointment. Only in **ME**.
†**2** A delusive fancy; a trick, a deception. Only in **LME**.
3 A state of bewilderment. *obsolete* exc. *dial.* **LME**.
4 A structure consisting of a network of winding and intercommunicating paths and passages arranged in bewildering complexity (freq. with a correct path concealed by blind alleys), esp. formed by hedges in a garden or represented on paper by a pattern of lines, and designed as a puzzle or as a device to study intelligence and learning. Also, a structure with a single winding path much greater in distance from beginning to end than the direct line. **LME**.
5 *transf.* & *fig.* Any confusing or complex network, route, or mass. **M16**. ▸**b** A winding movement, esp. in a dance. Now *dial.* **E17**.

E. MUIR And all the roads ran in a maze Hither and thither, like a web. A. BLOND In a maze of back alleys, we finally climbed a fire escape. *Guns & Weapons* The average bloke is put through a maze of paperwork.

■ **mazeful** *adjective* (*arch.*) bewildering, confusing **L16**. **mazelike** *adjective* resembling (that of) a maze **L16**.

maze *noun*[2] var. of MEASE.

maze /meɪz/ *verb*. **ME**.
[ORIGIN Aphet. from AMAZE *verb*.]
1 *verb trans.* Stupefy, daze. Formerly also, craze, infatuate. Usu. in *pass.* Now *arch.* & *dial.* **ME**. ▸†**b** *verb intrans.* Be stupefied or delirious. **LME–M16**.
2 *verb trans.* Bewilder, perplex, confuse. **ME**.
3 *verb intrans.* Move in a mazelike course, wander (as) in a maze. **L16**.
■ **mazedly** *adverb* in a bewildered, confused, or stupefied manner **ME**. **mazedness** *noun* the state of being bewildered, confused, or stupefied **LME**.

mazel tov /ˈmaz(ə)l tɔːv, tɒf/ *interjection*. **L17**.
[ORIGIN mod. Hebrew *mazzāl ṭōḇ* lit. 'good star', from Hebrew *mazzāl* star, formed as MOZZLE.]
Among Jews: good luck, congratulations.

mazement /ˈmeɪzm(ə)nt/ *noun*. **L16**.
[ORIGIN Partly from MAZE *verb* + -MENT, partly aphet. from AMAZEMENT.]
A state of stupor or trance. Now usu., amazement.

mazer /ˈmeɪzə/ *noun*. *obsolete* exc. *hist.* **ME**.
[ORIGIN Old French *masere* of Germanic origin, perh. reinforced from Middle Dutch *maeser* maple.]
1 A hardwood, esp. maple, used as a material for drinking cups. Also ***mazer wood***. **ME**. ▸**b** The tree yielding this wood; a maple. Also ***mazer tree***. Long *rare*. **ME**.
2 A bowl, drinking cup, or goblet without a foot, orig. one made of mazer wood. Also ***mazer bowl***, ***mazer cup***. **ME**.
†**3** The head. **L16–M17**.

mazey *adjective* var. of MAZY.

Mazhabi /ˈmʌzhəbiː/ *noun*. **M19**.
[ORIGIN Persian & Urdu *maḏhabī* way of thinking, persuasion, from Arabic *maḏhabī* denominational, sectarian.]
In the Indian subcontinent, esp. the Punjab: a Sikh.

mazout *noun* var. of MAZUT.

mazuma /məˈzuːmə/ *noun*. *US & Austral. slang*. **E20**.
[ORIGIN Yiddish, from Hebrew *mĕzummān*, from *zimmēn* prepare.]
Money, cash; *esp.* betting money.

mazurka /məˈzəːkə, məˈzʊəkə/ *noun*. **E19**.
[ORIGIN French, or from German *Masurka* from Polish *mazurka* woman of the province Mazovia.]
1 A Polish dance in triple time, usu. with a slide and hop. **E19**.
2 A piece of music for this dance or composed in its rhythm, usu. with accentuation of the second or third beat. **M19**.

mazut /məˈzuːt/ *noun*. Also **mazout**. **L19**.
[ORIGIN Russian.]
A viscous liquid left as residue after the distillation of petroleum, used in Russia as a fuel oil and coarse lubricant.

mazy /ˈmeɪzi/ *adjective*. Also **-ey**. **E16**.
[ORIGIN from MAZE *noun*[1] + -Y[1].]
1 Giddy, dizzy, confused in the head. *dial.* **E16**.
2 Resembling or of the nature of a maze; full of windings and turnings. **L16**.
3 Moving in a mazelike course, twisting and turning. **E18**.
■ **mazily** *adverb* **M19**. **maziness** *noun* **E18**.

mazzard /ˈmazəd/ *noun*[1]. *dial.* & *US*. Also **mazard**. **L16**.
[ORIGIN Perh. a use of MAZARD *noun*[1].]
More fully ***mazzard cherry***. The wild form of the sweet cherry, *Prunus avium*, esp. when used as a stock for grafting; the small black or dark red fruit of this tree.

mazzard *noun*[2] var. of MAZARD *noun*[1].

Mazzinian /matˈsiːnɪən/ *adjective & noun*. **M19**.
[ORIGIN from *Mazzini* (see below) + -AN.]
▸ **A** *adjective*. Of or pertaining to the Italian patriot and revolutionary Giuseppe Mazzini (1805–72) or his policies, esp. advocacy of a united republican Italy. **M19**.
▸ **B** *noun*. An adherent of Mazzini. **M19**.

MB *abbreviation*.
1 Latin *Medicinae Baccalaureus* Bachelor of Medicine.
2 COMPUTING. Megabyte.

MBA *abbreviation*.
Master of Business Administration.

mbalax /(ə)mˈbalaks/ *noun*. **L20**.
[ORIGIN Wolof, lit. 'rhythm'.]
A type of Senegalese popular music derived from a combination of traditional Wolof drumming patterns and Cuban popular music.

mbaqanga /(ə)mbəˈkaŋgə/ *noun*. **M20**.
[ORIGIN Zulu *umbaqanga*, lit. 'steamed maize bread'.]
A rhythmical popular music style of southern Africa.

MBE *abbreviation*.
Member of (the Order of) the British Empire.

mbira /(ə)mˈbɪərə/ *noun*. **L19**.
[ORIGIN Shona, prob. an alt. of *rimba* a note.]
A musical instrument of southern Africa consisting of a set of keys or tongues attached to a resonator, which are plucked with the thumb and forefingers. Also called ***sansa***.

MBO *abbreviation*.
Management buyout.

mbongo /(ə)mˈbɒŋgəʊ/ *noun*. *S. Afr. slang*. Pl. **-os**. **E20**.
[ORIGIN Alt. of IMBONGI.]
A political stooge or apologist, a 'yes-man'.

Mbps *abbreviation*.
COMPUTING. Megabits per second.

Mbuti /(ə)mˈbuːti/ *noun & adjective*. **M20**.
[ORIGIN Mbuti.]
▸ **A** *noun*. Pl. **-s**, same. A member of a pygmy people of western Uganda and adjacent areas of the Democratic Republic of Congo (Zaire); a language of this people. **M20**.
▸ **B** *attrib.* or as *adjective*. Of or pertaining to the Mbutis or their languages. **M20**.

Mbyte *abbreviation*.
Megabyte(s).

MC *abbreviation*[1].
1 Member of Congress.
2 Military Cross.
3 Music cassette.

Mc *abbreviation*[2].
Megacycle(s); megacycles per second.

MC /ɛmˈsiː/ *noun & verb*. **L18**.
[ORIGIN Abbreviation of *master of ceremonies*.]
▸ **A** *noun*. **1** A master of ceremonies. **L18**.
2 A person who provides entertainment by instructing the DJ and performing rap music. See also EMCEE. **L20**.
▸ **B** *verb intrans.* Pa. t. & pple **MC'd**. Act or perform as a master of ceremonies or an MC. **M20**.

MCB *abbreviation*.
Miniature circuit-breaker.

McBurney's point /məkbəːnɪz ˈpɔɪnt/ *noun phr.* **L19**.
[ORIGIN Charles *McBurney* (1845–1913), US surgeon.]
MEDICINE. The point on the surface of the abdomen which lies on a line from the tip of the right hip bone to the navel and one-third of the way along it, which is the point of maximum tenderness in appendicitis.

MCC *abbreviation*.
Marylebone Cricket Club (formerly, the governing body of English cricket and the official title of touring teams representing England).

McCarthyism /məˈkɑːθɪɪz(ə)m/ *noun*. **M20**.
[ORIGIN from *McCarthy* (see below) + -ISM.]
The policy of hunting out (suspected) Communists and removing them from Government departments or other positions, *spec.* as pursued by Senator Joseph R. McCarthy (1908–57) in the US in the 1950s.
■ **McCarthyite** *noun & adjective* (**a**) *noun* a supporter of this policy; (**b**) *adjective* of McCarthy or McCarthyism: **M20**.

McCoy /məˈkɔɪ/ *noun*. *colloq.* Also **Mackay** /məˈkʌɪ/. **M19**.
[ORIGIN Of uncertain origin: earliest in the phr. *the real Mackay*, in which *real* may be a corruption of the name of the *Reay* branch of the Scottish Mackay family; the form *McCoy* appears to be of US origin.]
the real McCoy, the genuine article, the real thing.

J. TORRINGTON 'How d'you know the armour's real?' 'Oh, I'm sure it's the real McCoy.'

mcg *abbreviation*.
Microgram(s).

McGuffin /məˈgʌfɪn/ *noun*. Also **Mac-**. **M20**.
[ORIGIN A Scottish surname, used in this sense by the Brit. film director Sir Alfred Hitchcock, and allegedly adopted from a humorous story involving such an object.]
An object or event in a film or book which initially appears to be of great significance but which actually serves merely to advance the plot.

M.Chir. *abbreviation*.
Latin *Magister Chirurgiae* Master of Surgery.

mCi *abbreviation*.
Millicurie(s).

McIntosh /ˈmakɪntɒʃ/ *noun*. Also **MacIntosh**. **L19**.
[ORIGIN John *McIntosh* (1777–c 1846), Canad. farmer.]
In full ***McIntosh Red***. A red-skinned variety of eating apple.

McJob /məkˈdʒɒb/ *noun*. *colloq. derog.* **L20**.
[ORIGIN from *Mc-* (in the name of the *McDonald's* chain of fast-food restaurants, popularly regarded as a source of such employment) + JOB *noun*[1].]
An unstimulating, low-paid job with few prospects, *esp.* one created by the expansion of the service sector.

McKenzie /məˈkɛnzi/ *noun*. **L20**.
[ORIGIN Name of the litigants in the case (*McKenzie* v. *McKenzie*) in which the English Court of Appeal ruled that any party in a trial is entitled to non-professional assistance in court.]
LAW. A non-professional person who attends a trial as a helper or adviser of one of the parties. Also ***McKenzie friend***, ***McKenzie man***, etc.

McLuhanism /məˈkluːənɪz(ə)m/ *noun*. **M20**.
[ORIGIN from *McLuhan* (see below) + -ISM.]
The social ideas of the Canadian writer H. Marshall McLuhan (1911–80), such as that the effect of the intro-

duction of the mass media is to deaden the critical faculties of individuals.
■ **McLuha'nesque** *adjective* resembling or characteristic of McLuhan or his ideas **M20**.

McMansion /mək'manʃ(ə)n/ *noun*. *US colloq., derog.* **L20**.
[**ORIGIN** from *Mc-* (as in **MCJOB**) + **MANSION**.]
A modern house built on a large and imposing scale, but regarded as ostentatious and lacking in architectural integrity.

McNaughten rules /mək'nɔːt(ə)n ruːlz/ *noun phr. pl.* Also **McNaghten rules**, **M'Naughten rules**. **L19**.
[**ORIGIN** Daniel *M'Naghten*, acquitted of murder in 1843: the rules arose out of the consideration of his case by the House of Lords.]
The British rules or criteria for judging criminal responsibility where there is a question of insanity.

M.Com. *abbreviation*.
Master of Commerce.

m-commerce /ɛm'kɒməːs/ *noun*. **L20**.
[**ORIGIN** from **M**(**OBILE** *adjective* + **COMMERCE** *noun*.]
Commercial activity conducted through mobile electronic media, such as mobile phones.

MCP *abbreviation*.
Male chauvinist pig.

MCR *abbreviation*.
Middle common room.

Mc/s *abbreviation*.
Megacycles per second.

McTimoney /mək'tɪməni/ *noun*. **L20**.
[**ORIGIN** John *McTimoney* (1914–80), Brit. chiropractor.]
Used *attrib.* to designate a gentle form of chiropractic treatment involving very light and swift movements of the practitioner's hands.

MD *abbreviation*.
1 Latin *Medicinae Doctor* Doctor of Medicine.
2 Managing Director.
3 Maryland.
4 Mentally deficient.
5 Mini Disc.
6 Musical Director.

Md *symbol*.
CHEMISTRY. Mendelevium.

Md. *abbreviation*.
Maryland.

MDA *abbreviation*.
PHARMACOLOGY. 3,4-methylenedioxyamphetamine, a synthetic hallucinogenic drug.

MDF *abbreviation*.
Medium-density fibreboard.

MDMA *abbreviation*.
PHARMACOLOGY. 3,4-methylenedioxymethamphetamine, a derivative of amphetamine that causes euphoria and hallucinations, orig. produced as an appetite suppressant; also called ***ecstasy***.

MDT *abbreviation*. *N. Amer.*
Mountain Daylight Time.

ME *abbreviation*.
1 Maine.
2 Middle English.
3 Myalgic encephalomyelitis (or encephalopathy).

me *noun*[1] var. of **MI** *noun*.

me /miː, *unstressed* mɪ/ *pers. pronoun, 1 sing. objective (accus. & dat.), noun*[2], *& possess. adjective*.
[**ORIGIN** Old English *mē̆* (i) accus. corresp. to Old Frisian *mi*, Old Saxon *mī*, *mē* (Dutch *mij*) & further to Latin *me*, Greek (*e*)*me*, Old Irish *mé* (Irish *mí*, *mi*), Welsh *mi*, Sanskrit *mā*, (ii) dat. corresp. to Old Frisian *mi(r)*, Old Saxon *mī* (Dutch *mij*), Old & mod. High German *mir*, Old Norse *mér*, Gothic *mis*, from Indo-European base (in all Indo-European langs.). As adjective prob. from unstressed var. of **MY** *adjective*.]
▸ **A** *pronoun*. **1** Objective (direct & indirect) of **I** *pronoun*: the speaker or writer himself or herself. **OE**. ▸**b** Myself. Now *arch. & poet.* exc. *N. Amer. colloq.* **OE**.

SHAKES. *Per.* And make a conquest of unhappy me. C. LAMB He enters me his name in the book. T. HARDY Can I ask you to do me one kindness? SCOTT FITZGERALD There aren't any caddies here except me. I. MCEWAN Why did you take that picture of me? J. SIMMS So he reluctantly gave me absolution of my sins. M. AMIS My flat is small and also costs me a lot of money. **b** I. MURDOCH I should steadfastly hold me in the Faith. P. GRACE I've got me a job down at the timber yard.

See also **MESEEMS**, **METHINKS**.
2 Subjective: I. In standard use esp. pred. after *be* & after *as*, *than*. Now *colloq.* **LME**.

BYRON Lord Delawarr is considerably younger than me. E. WAUGH Edith and Olive and me have talked it over.

3 With less definite syntactical relation to the context. (Chiefly exclamatory.) **L16**.

MILTON Me miserable! which way shall I flie Infinite wrauth. F. BURNEY 'Don't you dance?' he said. 'Me?' cried she, embarrassed. M. EDGEWORTH Which would be hard on us and me a widow. A. S. NEILL 'I'm going to start to-day to learn to read.' 'Me too,' said Donald. D. BARNES Jed would say North, and Jod would say South, and me sitting between them going mad. *Listener* Me, I like fighting too.

– **PHRASES**: ***ay me!***: see **AY** *interjection*[2]. ***be me*** *colloq.* be suited to me, represent my real self. ***dear me!***: see **DEAR** *interjection*. ***mighty me!***: see **MIGHTY** *adjective*. ***riddle me a riddle***: see **RIDDLE** *verb*[1] 2. ***search me***: see **SEARCH** *verb*[1]. ***stone me***: see **STONE** *verb*. ***the laugh is on me***: see **LAUGH** *noun*.
– **COMB.**: **me-and-you** *slang* a menu; **me generation** a generation of people that are concerned chiefly with themselves, especially in being selfishly materialistic; *spec.* the generation of affluent young adults in the US and other Western countries in the 1970s and 1980s; **me-too** *adjective & verb* (**a**) *adjective* designating or pertaining to views, policies, etc., adopted from, or products etc. copied from, an opponent or rival; (**b**) *verb trans.* adopt or appropriate (a policy etc.) from an opponent or rival; **me-tooer** a person who adopts or appropriates a policy etc. from an opponent or rival; **me-tooism** the adoption or appropriation of a policy etc. from an opponent or rival.
▸ **B** *noun*. One's personality, the ego. **E19**.
▸ **C** *adjective*. My. *colloq. & dial.* **M19**.
■ **me-ward(s)** *adverb* towards me **ME**.

Me. *abbreviation*.
1 Maine.
2 French *Maître* Advocate.

meacock /'miːkɒk/ *noun & adjective*. Now *arch. rare*. **E16**.
[**ORIGIN** Perh. orig. the name of some bird.]
▸ **A** *noun*. An effeminate person; a coward, a weakling. **E16**.
▸ †**B** *adjective*. Effeminate, cowardly, weak. **L16–M17**.

mea culpa /meɪə 'kʊlpə, miːə 'kʌlpə/ *interjection & noun phr.* **ME**.
[**ORIGIN** Latin, lit. '(through) my own fault': from the prayer of confession in the Latin liturgy of the Church.]
▸ **A** *interjection*. Acknowledging one's guilt or responsibility for an error. **ME**.
▸ **B** *noun phr.* An utterance of 'mea culpa'; an acknowledgement of one's guilt or responsibility for an error. **E19**.

mead /miːd/ *noun*[1].
[**ORIGIN** Old English *medu*, *meodu* = Old Frisian, Middle Low German (Dutch) *mede*, Old High German *metu*, *mitu* (German *Met*), Old Norse *mjǫðr*, from Germanic from Indo-European base also of Greek *methu* wine, Sanskrit *madhu* honey, sweet drink.]
Alcoholic liquor produced by fermenting a mixture of honey and water.
– **COMB.**: **mead-bench** *ANTIQUITIES* a seat at a Germanic feast when mead was drunk; **mead-hall** *ANTIQUITIES* a Germanic banqueting hall.

mead /miːd/ *noun*[2]. Now *poet. & dial.*
[**ORIGIN** Old English *mǣd*: see **MEADOW**.]
1 = **MEADOW** 1. **OE**.
†**2** = **MEADOW** 2. **ME–L17**.

meadow /'mɛdəʊ/ *noun & verb*.
[**ORIGIN** Old English *mǣdwe* etc., oblique cases of *mǣd*, from Germanic, from base also of **MOW** *verb*[1].]
▸ **A** *noun*. **1** Orig., a piece of land permanently covered with grass to be mown for use as hay; later, any piece of cultivated grassland. Also, a tract of low well-watered ground, esp. near a river. **OE**.
water meadow: see **WATER** *noun*.
2 Land used for the cultivation of grass, esp. for hay. **OE**.
3 ***beaver meadow***, a fertile tract of land left dry above a demolished beaver dam. *N. Amer.* **M17**.
4 A low level tract of uncultivated grassland, esp. along a river or in a marshy region near the sea. *N. Amer.* **L17**.
5 A feeding ground of fish. **M19**.
– **COMB.**: **meadow beauty** any of several N. American plants of the genus *Rhexia* (family Melastomataceae), with four-petalled pink flowers; **meadow bird** = **BOBOLINK**; **meadow brown** a common brown and orange satyrid butterfly, *Maniola jurtina*; **meadow buttercup** a Eurasian buttercup, *Ranunculus acris*, common in grassland; **meadow cat's tail** = **TIMOTHY**; **meadow crake** = **CORNCRAKE**; **meadow fescue** a tall Eurasian fescue with flat leaves, *Festuca pratensis*, which is grown for pasture in Europe and N. America; **meadow foam** *US* the poached-egg flower, *Limnanthes douglasii*; **meadow frog** = ***leopard frog*** s.v. **LEOPARD** *noun*; **meadow grass** a grass of the genus *Poa*; **meadow ground** a piece of ground used for the cultivation of grass, esp. for hay; **meadowland** (a stretch of) land used for the cultivation of grass, esp. for hay; **meadowlark** *N. Amer.* any of several American songbirds of the genus *Sturnella*, speckled brown with yellow underparts, *esp.* (more fully ***eastern meadowlark***) *S. magna* and (more fully ***western meadowlark***) *S. neglecta*; **meadow mouse** = ***meadow vole*** below; **meadow mushroom** an edible fungus, *Agaricus campestris*; **meadow parsnip** a yellow-flowered umbelliferous plant, *Thaspium trifoliatum*, of the US; **meadow pipit** a common European pipit, *Anthus pratensis*, inhabiting open country, heath, and moorland; also called ***titlark***; **meadow rue** any of various plants constituting the genus *Thalictrum*, of the buttercup family, having leaves like those of rue and apetalous flowers; *spec.* (more fully ***common meadow rue***) *Thalictrum flavum*, a plant of riversides; **meadow saffron** a plant of the lily family, *Colchicum autumnale*, producing pale purple flowers like crocuses in autumn and broad leaves the following spring; also called ***naked ladies***; ***meadow soft-grass***: see ***soft-grass*** s.v. **SOFT** *adjective*; ***meadow* VETCHLING**; **meadow vole** a N. American vole, *Microtus pennsylvanicus*.
▸ **B** *verb trans.* Devote (land) to the production of grass, esp. for hay; use as meadow. **M18**.
■ **meadowed** *adjective* (**a**) provided with meadows (chiefly as 2nd elem. of comb., as ***well-meadowed***); (**b**) devoted to the production of grass, esp. for hay; used as meadow: **M17**. **meadowing** *noun* (**a**) land used or suitable for the cultivation of grass; (**b**) the action of the verb: **M16**. **meadowless** *adjective* **L19**. **meadowy** *adjective* resembling a meadow **L16**.

meadowsweet /'mɛdəʊswiːt/ *noun*. **M16**.
[**ORIGIN** from **MEADOW** + **SWEET** *adjective*.]
A plant of the rose family, *Filipendula ulmaria*, of wet meadows and stream banks, with panicles of creamy-white fragrant flowers; *US* any of several shrubs of the allied genus *Spiraea*.

meadstead *noun* var. of **MIDSTEAD**.

†**meadsweet** *noun*. **LME–L18**.
[**ORIGIN** from **MEAD** *noun*[2], *noun*[1] (cf. **MEADWORT**) + **SWEET** *adjective*.]
Meadowsweet, *Filipendula ulmaria*.

†**meadwort** *noun*. **OE–L18**.
[**ORIGIN** from **MEAD** *noun*[1] + **WORT** *noun*[1]: perh. the flowers were used for flavouring mead. Later assoc. with **MEAD** *noun*[2].]
= **MEADSWEET**.

meager *adjective, noun, & verb* see **MEAGRE** *adjective, noun*[2], *& verb*.

meagre /'miːgə/ *noun*[1]. Also (earlier) **maigre** /'meɪgə/. **L16**.
[**ORIGIN** French *maigre*: see **MEAGRE** *adjective, noun*[2], *& verb*.]
A large edible carnivorous sciaenid fish, *Argyrosomus regius*, of the Mediterranean, the E. Atlantic, and the SW Indian Ocean.

meagre /'miːgə/ *adjective, noun*[2], *& verb*. Also ***meager**. **LME**.
[**ORIGIN** Anglo-Norman *megre*, Old French & mod. French *maigre*, from Latin *macer*, *macr-* rel. to Greek *makros* long, *makethnos* tall, slender, *mēkos* length. See also **MAIGRE** *adjective*.]
▸ **A** *adjective* **I 1** Of a person, animal, limb, etc.: having little flesh; lean, thin, emaciated. **LME**.

W. COWPER He calls for Famine, and the meagre fiend Blows mildew from between his shrivelled teeth. SIR W. SCOTT The meagre condition of his horse. W. IRVING A meagre wiry old fellow.

2 Deficient or inferior in quantity, size, or quality; lacking fullness, richness, or elaboration; poor, scanty; inadequate, unsatisfying. **M16**.

E. K. KANE The meagre allowance of two pounds of raw flesh every other day. K. AMIS The . . notes of a recorder playing a meagre air were distantly audible. D. HALBERSTAM Gas had ignited the building because Otis took such meager and inadequate safety precautions. L. AUCHINCLOSS A pompous beaux-arts facade much too grand for the meager, three-window frontage. E. KUZWAYO It augmented my meagre income.

▸ **II 3** = **MAIGRE** *adjective* II. **E18**.
▸ **B** *absol.* as *noun*. †**1** Leanness, emaciation. **LME–M16**.
2 Maigre diet. Now *rare*. **L18**.
▸ †**C** *verb trans.* Make meagre or lean. **L16–E19**.
■ **meagrely** *adverb* **L16**. **meagreness** *noun* **LME**.

M

meal /miːl/ *noun*[1].
[**ORIGIN** Old English *melu* = Old Frisian *mel*, Old Saxon *melo* (Dutch *meel*), Old High German *melo* (German *Mehl*), Old Norse *mjǫl*, from Germanic, from Indo-European base also of Latin *molere* grind.]
1 The edible part of any grain or pulse, now usu. other than wheat, ground to a powder. Also (*spec.*), in Scotland and Ireland, oatmeal, in the US, maize flour. Cf. **FLOUR** *noun*. **OE**. ▸†**b** The finer part of ground grain, in contrast with ***bran***. **L16–E17**.
Indian meal: see **INDIAN** *adjective*. **OATMEAL**. ***round meal***: see **ROUND** *adjective*. ***wholemeal***: see **WHOLE** *adjective*.
2 *transf.* A powder produced by grinding; a powdery substance resembling flour; *BOTANY* the powder covering the surface of the leaves etc. of certain plants. **M16**.
bonemeal etc.
– **COMB.**: **meal beetle** any beetle of the family Tenebrionidae whose larval or adult forms infest granaries etc.; **mealberry** the bearberry, *Arctostaphylos uva-ursi*; **mealman** a dealer in meal; **meal moth** any of several moths which infest mills, granaries, etc., esp. *Pyralis farinalis*; **meal worm** the larva of a meal beetle; ***meal-worm beetle*** = ***meal beetle*** above.

meal /miːl/ *noun*[2]. Also †**mele**.
[**ORIGIN** Old English *mǣl* corresp. to Old Frisian *mēl*, *māl*, Old Saxon *-māl* sign, measure (Dutch *maal*), Old High German *māl* time (German *Mal* time, *Mahl* meal), Old Norse *mál* point or portion of time, mealtime, Gothic *mēl* time, from Germanic, from Indo-European base meaning 'to measure'.]
1 A measure. Long *obsolete* exc. as **-MEAL**. **OE**.
2 An occasion of taking food, *esp.* a customary one at a more or less fixed time of day; the food eaten at or provided for such an occasion. **OE**.
make a meal of (**a**) consume as a meal, devour; (**b**) treat in an excessively fussy manner, make (a task etc.) seem unduly laborious.
3 The quantity of milk given by a cow at one milking; the time of milking. Now *dial.* **E17**.
– **COMB.**: **meal-pennant**: displayed during mealtimes in the US navy and on yachts; a red pennant; **meals-on-wheels** *noun & adjective* (designating) a service, usually provided by a women's voluntary organization, whereby meals are delivered to old people, invalids, etc.; **meal ticket** a ticket entitling a person to a meal, esp. at a specified place for a reduced cost; *fig.* a source of income or livelihood, *esp.* a husband or wife regarded merely as such; **mealtide** (*obsolete* exc. *Scot.*) mealtime; one's food; **mealtime** the (usual) time for eating a meal.
■ **mealless** /-l-l-/ *adjective* **M19**.

meal /miːl/ *verb*[1]. L15.
[ORIGIN from MEAL *noun*[1].]
1 *verb intrans.* Make a meal; eat meals. L15.
2 *verb trans.* Provide sustenance for, feed. M17.

meal /miːl/ *verb*[2]. Chiefly *Scot.* E17.
[ORIGIN from MEAL *noun*[1].]
1 *verb trans.* Cover with meal; powder with meal; add meal to. E17.
2 *verb trans.* Grind into meal; reduce to meal or fine powder. L17.
3 *verb intrans.* Yield or be plentiful in meal. L18.
■ **mealable** *adjective* E19.

†**meal** *verb*[3] var. of MAIL *verb*[3].

-meal /miːl/ *suffix.*
[ORIGIN Old English *mǣlum* instr. pl. of *mǣl* MEAL *noun*[2].]
Forming adverbs from nouns with the sense 'measure, quantity taken at one time', as ***flockmeal***, ***inchmeal***, ***piecemeal***.

mealer /ˈmiːlə/ *noun.* M19.
[ORIGIN from MEAL *noun*[2], *verb*[2] + -ER[1].]
1 As 2nd elem. of comb.: a person who eats a specified number of meals a day. M19.
2 A person who takes meals at one place and lodges at another. *US colloq.* L19.

mealie /ˈmiːli/ *noun. S. Afr.* Also **mielie**. E19.
[ORIGIN Afrikaans *mielie* from Portuguese *milho* maize, millet, from Latin *milium*.]
Maize; a corncob (usu. in *pl.*).
green mealie a corncob gathered and cooked while it is still green. ***stamped mealies***: see STAMP *verb*.
– COMB.: **mealie-cob** a corncob; ***mealie-cob worm***, the caterpillar of the corn earworm, *Heliothis armigera*, a noctuid moth; **mealie meal** coarse meal of maize (a staple food); **mealiepap** [Afrikaans *pap* porridge] mealie meal porridge; **mealie rice** finely stamped grains of maize used instead of rice.

mealy /ˈmiːli/ *adjective.* M16.
[ORIGIN from MEAL *noun*[1] + -Y[1].]
1 Resembling meal, having the qualities of meal or flour, powdery; (of boiled potatoes) dry and powdery. M16.
2 Covered with or as with meal, flour, or any fine dust or powder. M16. ▸**b** Of colour, a horse: spotty, interspersed with whitish specks. L17. ▸**c** Of complexion: pale. M19.
3 Containing meal or flour; farinaceous. L16.
4 Not outspoken, afraid to speak plainly; mealy-mouthed. L16.
– SPECIAL COLLOCATIONS & COMB.: **mealy bug** any of various scale insects of the family Pseudococcidae, which are covered with a waxy powder. **mealy-mouth** *noun & verb* (**a**) *noun* a mouth which never speaks plainly; a soft, indirect, or reticent manner of speaking; a mealy-mouthed person; (**b**) *verb trans. & intrans.* avoid speaking plainly (about), be mealy-mouthed (about). **mealy-mouthed** *adjective* not outspoken, afraid to speak one's mind or to use plain terms; soft-spoken. **mealy-mouthedly** *adverb* in a mealy-mouthed manner. **mealy-mouthedness** the quality of being mealy-mouthed. **mealy pudding** = ***white pudding*** s.v. WHITE *adjective*. ***mealy redpoll***: see REDPOLL *noun*[1]. **mealy tree** = ***wayfaring tree*** s.v. WAYFARING *noun*.
■ **mealiness** *noun* E17.

M

mean /miːn/ *noun*[1]. ME.
[ORIGIN Partly from MEAN *adjective*[2], partly from Old French *meien*, *moien* use as noun of adjective: see MEAN *adjective*[2].]
▸ **I** That which is in the middle.
1 *MUSIC.* A middle or intermediate part in a harmonized composition or performance, *esp.* the tenor and alto. Also, a person performing such a part; an instrument on which such a part is played. *obsolete* exc. *hist.* ME.
2 That which is intermediate; a condition, quality, disposition, or course of action, that is equally removed from two opposite (esp. blameable) extremes; a medium. Freq. with laudatory adjective, as ***golden mean***. LME. ▸†**b** Absence of extremes; moderation. M16–E18.

> P. TILLICH Aristotle's doctrine of courage as the right mean between cowardice and temerity. N. GORDIMER The climate of each day the same cool mean, neither summer nor winter.

†**3** The middle (of something). LME–L17.
†**4** Something interposed or intervening. LME–L16.
5 a *MATH.* A term intermediate in position between the first and last terms of a progression; a term such that performing an operation on it *n* times is equivalent to operating similarly on a set of *n* items; a mean value, an average; *spec.* = ***arithmetic mean*** s.v. ARITHMETIC *adjective*. L15. ▸**b** An average amount or value; the mean pressure, temperature, etc. E19.

> *Nature* Englishmen are normally distributed in height with a mean of 5 feet 8 inches.

▸ **II** An intermediary agent or instrument.
†**6** A mediator, an intermediary, a negotiator, an ambassador, an intercessor. LME–E17. ▸**b** *sing.* & in *pl.* Mediation, intercession; instigation. LME–M17.
7 *sing.* (*arch.*) & in *pl.* (usu. treated as *sing.*). An instrument, agency, method, or course of action, by which some object is or may be attained, or some result is or may be brought about. Formerly also, a condition permitting or conducing to something, an opportunity. LME. ▸†**b** In *pl.* Stratagem, trickery. LME–E17.

> W. SCLATER Vncharitable is that sentence . . that Baptisme is necessarie as a meane to saluation. T. OVERBURY In warre, there is no meane to erre twice. G. ORWELL Power is not a means, it is an end. DAY LEWIS How deeply the loss impoverished my growing years . . there is no means of telling. G. GREENE Try other means first. B. CHATWIN A solitary gas-ring was her only means of cooking.

8 In *pl.* The resources available for effecting some object; *spec.* financial resources, esp. in relation to requirements or habits of expenditure. Also, money, wealth. M16.

> C. P. SNOW There was plenty of money . . . Proust could draw on substantial private means. R. ELLMANN He declined . . to live within his means.

– PHRASES: ***arithmetic mean***: see ARITHMETIC *adjective*. **by all means**, **by all manner of means** (**a**) in every possible way; (**b**) at any cost, without fail; (**c**) (emphasizing a permission, request, or injunction) certainly. **by any means**, **by any manner of means** in any way, at all. ***by fair means or foul***: see FAIR *adjective*. **by means of**, †**by mean of** (**a**) by the agency or instrumentality of (a person or thing, *doing*); †(**b**) in consequence of, by reason of, owing to. **by no means**, **by no manner of means** (**a**) in no way, not at all; (**b**) on no account. **by that means**, †**by that mean** by means of that, in that way, thus. **by this means**, †**by this mean** by means of this, in this way, thus. **find means**, **find the means**, †**find mean**, †**find the mean** find out a way (*to do*), contrive or manage (*to do*). ***geometric mean***: see GEOMETRIC 1. ***golden mean***: see GOLDEN *adjective*. †**in the mean** in the meantime. **man of means**, **person of means**, **woman of means**: having a substantial income, being wealthy. ***means and ways***: see WAY *noun*. **means of grace** *CHRISTIAN THEOLOGY* the sacraments and other religious agencies viewed as the means by which divine grace is imparted to the soul, or by which growth in grace is promoted. ***private means***: see PRIVATE *adjective*. ***regression to the mean***: see REGRESSION 4b. ***ways and means***: see WAY *noun*.
– COMB.: **means-end(s)** *attrib. adjectives* of or pertaining to the ways of achieving a result considered together with the result; **means test** an official inquiry into an applicant's private resources, determining or limiting a grant or allowance of money from public funds; **means-test** *verb trans.* subject (a person) to a means test, assess (a grant etc.) by a means test; **means-testable** *adjective* subject to a means test.

mean /miːn/ *noun*[2]. *obsolete* exc. *SCOT. dial.* ME.
[ORIGIN from MEAN *verb*[2].]
A lament, a complaint.

mean /miːn/ *adjective*[1] & *adverb*[1].
[ORIGIN Old English *mǣne* (rare) for *gemǣne* = Old Frisian *gemēne*, Old Saxon *gimēni* (Dutch *gemeen*), Old High German *gimeini* (German *gemein*), Gothic *gamains*, from Germanic, formed as Y- + base repr. also by antecedent form of Latin *communis* COMMON *adjective*.]
▸ **A** *adjective* **I 1** Common to two or more persons or things; possessed jointly. Long *obsolete* exc. *dial.* OE.
▸ **II** Inferior.
2 Of a person, rank, etc.: low in the social hierarchy, not noble or gentle. Also, poor, badly off. *obsolete* exc. as passing into sense 4. OE.

> BUNYAN Thou shalt not steal, though thou be very mean.

3 Inferior in ability, learning, or perception; having or exhibiting little mental power. Now chiefly in ***the meanest understanding***, ***the meanest capacity***, etc. LME.
4 Poor in quality or condition; of little value, contemptible; comparatively worthless. Now chiefly *N. Amer. colloq.* LME. ▸**b** In low spirits, in poor health, not quite well. *US colloq.* M19.

> C. M. KIRKLAND You've had a pretty mean time.

5 Undignified, low; not elevated or sublime. LME.

> MARVELL He nothing common did or mean, Upon that memorable scene.

6 Not imposing in appearance, shabby; characterized by poverty. E17.

> E. A. FREEMAN The robes . . made all that France . . had beheld of the same kind seem mean by comparison. E. JOLLEY Very different from the mean dirty streets they had come from.

7 Lacking moral dignity, ignoble, small-minded; uncooperative, unkind, or unfair; *colloq.* (orig. *N. Amer.*) vicious, nasty, difficult to handle or deal with, unpleasant. Also (*colloq.*), ashamed of one's conduct. M17.

> I. D'ISRAELI Charles . . was mean enough to suspend her pension. R. T. COOKE It would be awful mean of me to leave you here alone. *Motocross Rider* Sittendorf . . is a mean, treacherous course mixing . . steep climbs, and menacing rocks.

8 Niggardly, not generous or liberal, stingy. M18.

> A. MASSIE She was kept short of money, for Willy . . was mean.

9 Remarkably clever or adroit; excellent; formidable. *slang* (orig. *US*). E20.

> *Golf* Many of the women . . play a mean game of golf.

– SPECIAL COLLOCATIONS & PHRASES: **mean streets** (**a**) streets where the poor live or work; (**b**) streets noted for violence and crime. **mean white** (chiefly *US, derog.*) (of) a poor and landless Southern white person, = ***poor white*** s.v. POOR *adjective*. **no mean** — a very good —, a not inconsiderable —.
▸ **B** *adverb.* Meanly. Now *non-standard*. E17.

mean /miːn/ *adjective*[2] & *adverb*[2]. ME.
[ORIGIN Anglo-Norman *me(e)n*, Old French *meien*, *moien* (mod. *moyen*) from Latin *medianus* MEDIAN *adjective*.]
▸ **A** *adjective* †**1 a** Occupying a middle or an intermediate place in sequential order or spatial position. ME–E19. ▸**b** *MUSIC.* Designating the tenor and alto parts and the tenor clef, as intermediate between the bass and treble. L16–E18.
2 Intermediate in kind, quality, or degree. Now *rare*. ME.
3 Intermediate in time; coming between two points of time or two events; intervening. Now only in MEANTIME, MEANWHILE. LME.
4 *LAW.* = MESNE *adjective*. LME.
†**5** Used as an intermediary; serving as a means or instrument; intervening as part of a process. LME–E17.
6 Not far above or below the average; moderate, mediocre, middling. Later only disparagingly and so coincident with MEAN *adjective*[1]. LME.
7 *MATH.* Of a value: so related to a given set of values that the sum of their differences from it is zero; that is an arithmetic mean; average. LME.
– SPECIAL COLLOCATIONS & PHRASES: ***extreme and mean ratio***: see EXTREME *adjective* 2. **mean free path** *PHYSICS* the mean distance travelled by a particle between interactions (e.g. by a gas molecule between collisions). **mean moon** a hypothetical moon assumed to move uniformly in the ecliptic in the same time as the actual moon. **mean proportional** a quantity related to two given quantities in such a way that dividing it by the smaller gives the same result as dividing the larger by it; the geometric mean of the quantities. **mean solar day** *ASTRONOMY* the time between successive passages of the mean sun across the meridian. **mean solar time**: as calculated by the motion of the mean sun (i.e. as shown by an ordinary clock). **mean square** the (arithmetic) mean of the squares of a set of numbers; ***mean-square deviation***, ***mean-square error***, the mean of the squares of the differences between a set of values and some fixed value. **mean sun** a hypothetical sun conceived as moving uniformly through the sky throughout the year, used in calculating time. MEANTIME. **mean time** = ***mean solar time*** above (GREENWICH ***Mean Time***); **mean tone** *MUSIC* the averaged or standard interval (halfway between a greater and less major second) used as a basis for tuning keyboard instruments before the adoption of equal temperament.
▸ †**B** *adverb.* **1** Moderately; comparatively less. LME–E17.
2 Intermediately. LME–M17.

mean /miːn/ *verb*[1]. Pa. t. & pple **meant** /mɛnt/, †**meaned**.
[ORIGIN Old English *mǣnan* = Old Frisian *mēna* signify, Old Saxon *mēnian* intend, make known (Dutch *meenen*), Old & mod. High German *meinen* (now usu. 'have an opinion'), from West Germanic, from Indo-European base of MIND *noun*[1].]
1 a *verb trans.* Have as one's purpose or intention, have in mind, (esp. *to do*). OE. ▸†**b** *verb trans.* Aim at, direct one's way to. *rare*. LME–E18. ▸**c** *verb trans.* Design (a thing) for a definite purpose, intend (a person or thing) to have a particular future, nature, or use, destine to a fate, (foll. by *for, to be, to do*, †*to*); expect or require *to be, to do*. Freq. in *pass.* LME. ▸**d** *verb intrans.* Be *well* (occas. *ill* etc.) intentioned or disposed. (Foll. by *to, towards, by*, or indirect obj.) LME. ▸**e** *verb trans.* Intend (a remark, allusion, etc.) to have a particular reference. Foll. by †*at*, †*by, for, of*, †*to*. Now *rare*. E16.

> **a** M. TWAIN I didn't know I was doing any harm; I didn't *mean* to do any harm. S. T. WARNER I have been meaning . . to write and thank you. T. CONNOR For much he never got round to doing, but meant to, when the weather bucked up. G. VIDAL She had meant to speak . . humorously but somehow the words had come out all wrong. **c** R. KIPLING Roads were meant to be walked upon. G. B. SHAW All progress means war with Society. T. S. ELIOT I am not Prince Hamlet, nor was meant to be. M. BARING His plays are meant for drawing rooms. A. D. HOPE They begot me in their bed Meaning me to be a boy. *New Yorker* The worst . . is that I'm meant to give a speech. **d** RIDER HAGGARD I do not think that your cousin means kindly by you. S. B. JACKMAN He means well . . and you can't say worse than that about anyone. **e** H. STURGIS There is a young don in the story, and . . someone . . decided it was meant for me.

2 *verb trans.* Intend to indicate (a certain object), convey (a certain sense) or refer to (a certain person or thing) when using some word, sentence, significant action, etc., (in interrog. contexts) have as a motive or justification, (now freq. foll. by *by* a thing, *doing*); (in emphatic contexts) be sincere or serious in saying. OE.

> W. COBBETT And what is meaned by 'The fear of the Lord'? MRS H. WARD No top-coat in such weather! What do you mean by that, sir? L. M. MONTGOMERY When I tell you to come in at a certain time I mean that time. E. WAUGH When Lady Metroland said half past one she meant ten minutes to two. I. MURDOCH By freedom we mean absence of external restraint. E. BOWEN 'You're not coming in?' asked Henry, meaning, into the vicarage.

3 *verb trans.* Have as signification; signify, import; have as an equivalent in another language; entail, necessitate, involve; portend. OE. ▸**b** Be of a specified degree of account or importance *to* (a person), esp. as a source of benefit or as an object of regard or affection; matter (a lot, nothing, etc., *to*). L19.

> J. BUCHAN Autumn meant the thick, close odour of rotting leaves. P. KAVANAGH The wind's over Brannagan's, now that means rain. V. SCANNELL You wouldn't know what the word beautiful means. G. GREENE A suicide always means an inquest. R. ELLMANN He was prizeman . . which meant he was excused from the annual examinations. **b** C. P. SNOW She meant much to me, much more than any other human being. J. RHYS It means a lot, a friendly word just now.

4 †**a** *verb trans. & intrans.* foll. by *of*. Say, tell, mention. OE–L18. ▸†**b** *verb intrans. & trans.* Think, imagine. ME–M17.

▸**c** *verb trans.* In *pass.* Be reputed or reported *to be*, *to do*. M20.

†**5** *verb trans. & intrans.* foll. by *of*, *on*, *upon*. Have in mind, remember. ME–E16.

– PHRASES ETC.: **do you mean to say that —?**, **do you mean to tell me that —?** *colloq.* are you sincere or serious in saying etc. that —?, will you confirm that it is indeed true that —? **(if) you know what I mean**, **(if) you see what I mean**, **(if) you understand what I mean**, etc. *colloq.*: expr. a hope that one has been understood in spite of not having expressed oneself clearly. **I mean** *colloq.*: used as a mere conversational filler. ***mean business***. **mean it** be sincere or serious, not be joking or exaggerating. ***mean mischief***: see MISCHIEF *noun*. **you don't mean to say that —?**, **you don't mean to tell me that —?** *colloq.* you are surely not sincere or serious in saying etc. that —?, it is surely not true that —?

■ †**meanless** *adjective* meaningless M18–M19.

mean /miːn/ *verb*². Long *obsolete* exc. *Scot.*

[ORIGIN Old English *mǣnan* rel. to MOAN *noun*.]

1 *verb trans.* Complain of, lament for; pity. OE.

2 *verb intrans. & †refl.* Lament, mourn; complain. OE.

†**3** *verb trans.* State as a grievance; represent by way of formal complaint or petition. L15–M18.

mean /miːn/ *verb*³ *trans.* L19.

[ORIGIN from MEAN *noun*¹.]

Calculate the arithmetic mean of; average. Also foll. by *up*.

meander /mɪˈandə, miː-/ *noun & verb*. Also (now *rare*) **maeander**. L16.

[ORIGIN (French *méandre* from) Latin *maeander* from Greek *maiandros* transf. use of name of a winding river in Phrygia.]

▸ **A** *noun*. **1** Any of the curves or bends in the course of a winding river etc.; any of the crooked or winding paths of a maze or passages of a labyrinth; a convolution. Usu. in *pl.* L16.

W. BECKFORD Springs whose frequent meanders gave .. the appearance of a vast green carpet shot with silver. *Natural History* The *Jorge Carlos* rounds a meander of the Amazon River and the Peruvian city of Iquitos comes into view. *fig.*: J. ARBUTHNOT Ten long years did Hocus steer his Cause through all the meanders of the law.

†**2** A labyrinth, a maze. L16–L18.

3 A circuitous journey or movement; a deviation. Usu. in *pl.* M17.

4 An ornamental pattern of lines winding in and out with rectangular turnings, or crossing one another at right angles. E18.

▸ **B** *verb*. **1** *verb intrans.* (Of a river, stream, etc.) flow in meanders; take a winding course, wind about. E17. ▸†**b** *verb trans.* Pass or travel deviously along or through (a river etc.). *US*. E–M19.

G. E. HUTCHINSON Any river flowing in an easily eroded flood plain is .. apt to meander. *Sunday Express* The road .. meanders along the lush Conwy valley.

2 *verb intrans.* Of a person: wander deviously or aimlessly. M19.

K. GRAHAME He thought his happiness was complete .. as he meandered aimlessly along. K. WATERHOUSE I meandered around the outside of the library building.

■ **meandered** *adjective* (now *rare*) winding, labyrinthine E17. **meandering** *noun* (*a*) the action of the verb; (*b*) a meander (usu. in *pl.*): M17.

meandrine /mɪˈandrɪn, miː-/ *adjective*. Also (now *rare*) **maean-**. M19.

[ORIGIN from MEANDER *noun* + -INE¹.]

Characterized by convolutions; *esp.* designating or describing brain corals.

meandrous /mɪˈandrəs, miː-/ *adjective*. Also (now *rare*) **maean-**. M17.

[ORIGIN formed as MEANDRINE + -OUS.]

Full of or characterized by meanders; winding.

meaner /ˈmiːnə/ *noun*. M16.

[ORIGIN from MEAN *verb*¹ + -ER¹.]

A person who means, intends, or purposes. Chiefly with qualifying adverb (as ***well-meaner***) or (formerly) adjective.

meanie /ˈmiːni/ *noun*. *colloq.* Also **meany**. E20.

[ORIGIN from MEAN *adjective*¹ + -IE, -Y⁶.]

A mean-minded or stingy person.

meaning /ˈmiːnɪŋ/ *noun*. ME.

[ORIGIN from MEAN *verb*¹ + -ING¹.]

1 That which is or is intended to be expressed or indicated by a sentence, word, dream, symbol, action, etc.; a signification, a sense; an equivalent in another language; (in interrog. contexts) a motive, a justification. ME. ▸**b** Significance, importance. L17.

AV *Dan.* 8:15 When I .. had seene the vision, and sought for the meaning. T. HARDY What's the meaning of this disgraceful performance? R. K. NARAYAN Will you kindly make your meaning clearer? J. GARDNER Simon seemed unable to make sense of the words, but then their meaning came through. J. GARDAM First meaning of row with us seems to be quarrel. P. GROSSKURTH Whenever Melanie asked .. the meaning of a French .. expression, he never had to consult a dictionary. **b** R. P. GRAVES There is no God, and therefore there is no meaning or purpose in life.

double meaning: see DOUBLE *adjective & adverb*. ***grammatical meaning***. ***lexical meaning***: see LEXICAL 1.

†**2** Remembrance; a commemoration, a memorial. ME–E16.

3 An intention, a purpose. *arch.* LME.

meaning /ˈmiːnɪŋ/ *adjective*. L15.

[ORIGIN from MEAN *verb*¹ + -ING².]

1 Having an intention or purpose. Chiefly with qualifying adverb (as ***well-meaning***). L15.

2 Conveying or expressing meaning or thought; expressive, meaningful, significant; suggestive. E18.

R. HOGGART She gave me a meaning look. R. DAVIES Willard .. gently stroked my left buttock. Gave it a meaning squeeze.

■ **meaningly** *adverb* LME. **meaningness** *noun* M18.

meaningful /ˈmiːnɪŋfʊl, -f(ə)l/ *adjective*. M19.

[ORIGIN from MEANING *noun* + -FUL.]

Full of meaning or expression; significant; amenable to interpretation; having a recognizable function in a language or sign system; able to function as a term in such a system.

Physics Bulletin The phoneme is the smallest meaningful unit of sound a listener can perceive. J. J. HENNESSY Chris and Jayne turned to each other with raised eyebrows and meaningful looks. G. JOSIPOVICI There were no precious objects that had been particularly meaningful to him.

■ **meaningfully** *adverb* L19. **meaningfulness** *noun* E20.

meaningless /ˈmiːnɪŋlɪs/ *adjective*. L18.

[ORIGIN formed as MEANINGFUL + -LESS.]

Without meaning or signification; devoid of expression; without purpose. Also, having no recognizable function in a language or sign system, unable to function as a term in such a system.

L. NKOSI The girl spoke a language that was meaningless to me. *Independent* The law is meaningless if it is not implemented.

■ **meaninglessly** *adverb* E19. **meaninglessness** *noun* M19.

meanly /ˈmiːnli/ *adverb*¹. LME.

[ORIGIN from MEAN *adjective*¹ + -LY².]

†**1** Insignificantly, pettily. Only in LME.

2 Humbly, basely. L15.

3 Indifferently, poorly, badly. M16. ▸**4** Sordidly, selfishly, stingily. E17.

†**meanly** *adverb*². LME–M18.

[ORIGIN from MEAN *adjective*² + -LY².]

In a middling degree or manner; intermediately; tolerably; fairly; (only) moderately.

meanness /ˈmiːnnɪs/ *noun*. M16.

[ORIGIN from MEAN *adjective*¹ + -NESS.]

1 The state or quality of being mean; inferiority; slightness, smallness; lowness or humbleness of rank, birth, etc.; insignificance; lack of dignity or grandeur; poorness of appearance or equipment, shabbiness; pettiness; niggardliness, stinginess. M16.

2 An instance of meanness, a deficiency; a mean act. Usu. in *pl.* E18.

meant *verb pa. t. & pple* of MEAN *verb*¹.

meantime /ˈmiːntʌɪm/ *noun & adverb*. Also **mean time**. ME.

[ORIGIN from MEAN *adjective*² 3 + TIME *noun*. Cf. MEANWHILE.]

▸ **A** *noun*. The time intervening between one particular period or event and another: in ***for the meantime***, so long as the interval lasts, intended to serve for the interim; ***in the meantime***, †***in meantime***, †***the meantime***, (*a*) = MEANWHILE *adverb* 1, †(*b*) = MEANWHILE *adverb* 2. ME.

D. EDEN In the meantime that hundred pounds must be sent. H. ACTON Other books on the same subject are liable to be published in the meantime. *Which?* The telephone will .. redial the number, even if you've hung up in the meantime.

▸ **B** *adverb*. **1** = MEANWHILE *adverb* 1. L16.

Times Lit. Suppl. Meantime .. the numbers of people .. increased immensely.

†**2** = MEANWHILE *adverb* 2. L16–L17.

meanwhile /ˈmiːnwʌɪl/ *noun & adverb*. Also **mean while**. LME.

[ORIGIN from MEAN *adjective*² 3 + WHILE *noun*. Cf. MEANTIME.]

▸ **A** *noun*. The time intervening between one particular period or event and another: in ***the meanwhile***, †***in meanwhile***, (arch.) ***the meanwhile***, (*a*) = sense B.1 below; (*b*) (now *rare* or *obsolete*) = sense B.2 below. LME.

Daily Telegraph In the meanwhile, the Government is effectively admitting that state spending is out of control.

▸ **B** *adverb*. **1** During or within the time intervening between one particular period or event and another; while a particular thing is going on, at the same time; for the present. LME.

S. BEDFORD Meanwhile, she had seen that they were given everything. E. WAUGH I shall be saying a few words after dinner. Meanwhile I expect you can all do with a drink. JULIETTE HUXLEY My mother meanwhile arrived from Neuchâtel.

2 Nevertheless, still. L16.

L. STEPHEN Meanwhile, however, one characteristic .. must be noticed.

meany *noun* var. of MEANIE.

mear *noun & verb* var. of MERE *noun*² & *verb*.

mearing *noun* var. of MERING.

mease /miːz/ *noun*. *dial.* Also **maze** /meɪz/. ME.

[ORIGIN Old French *meise*, *maise* barrel for herrings, of Germanic origin: cf. Middle High German *meise*, Middle Low German, Middle Dutch *mēse*.]

A measure for herrings, equal to five hundreds, esp. long hundreds.

measle *noun* see MEASLES.

†**measle** *adjective* see MESEL *adjective & noun*.

measle /ˈmiːz(ə)l/ *verb trans.* E17.

[ORIGIN from MEASLE(S).]

1 Infect with measles. E17.

2 Cover (a part of the body etc.) with blotches or spots. M17.

measled /ˈmiːz(ə)ld/ *adjective*. ME.

[ORIGIN from MEASLE(S, MEASLE *verb*: see -ED², -ED¹.]

1 Infected with measles. ME.

2 Blotchy, spotted. Now *rare*. M17.

measles /ˈmiːz(ə)lz/ *noun pl.*, also used as *sing.* Also (in some senses) in sing. form **measle**. ME.

[ORIGIN Prob. from Middle Low German *masele*, Middle Dutch *masel* pustule, spot on the skin (Dutch *mazelen* measles) = Old High German *masala* blood-blister, from Germanic: see -S¹.]

1 *pl.* (now usu. treated as *sing.*) & (now *joc.*) as *sing.*, ***measle***. An infectious viral disease characterized by a blotchy pink rash preceded and accompanied by catarrh and fever, freq. occurring in epidemics. ME. ▸**b** *pl.* The inflamed spots characteristic of this disease. Formerly also, the pustules of any eruptive disease. LME.

German measles: see GERMAN *adjective*¹.

2 a *pl.* (treated as *sing.*) & †as *sing.* ***measle***. A disease of pigs caused by invasion of muscle tissue by the scolex of the tapeworm; a similar disease of cattle etc. L16. ▸**b** (***measle***.) The scolex or cysticercus which causes this disease. M19.

3 Orig. (as *sing.*, ***measle***), a blister or excrescence on a tree. Later (*pl.*), a disease of certain trees which causes the bark to become rough and irregular. Now *rare* or *obsolete*. E17.

measly /ˈmiːzli/ *adjective*. L16.

[ORIGIN from MEASLES + -Y¹.]

1 Infected with measles, suffering from measles. L16.

Woman's Realm The measly child .. needs .. tender, loving care.

2 Of or pertaining to measles; resembling measles. L18. ▸**b** Blotchy, spotty. L19.

b F. RAPHAEL A mauve Mini, measly with rust, drew his attention.

3 Inferior, contemptible, of little value. *slang*. M19.

Sunday Telegraph They have mastered only a measly five batting points all season.

measurable /ˈmɛʒ(ə)rəb(ə)l/ *adjective*. ME.

[ORIGIN Old French & mod. French *mesurable* from late Latin *mensurabilis* MENSURABLE.]

1 Able to be measured or perceived; susceptible of measurement or computation; MATH. (of a set) having a defined measure. Formerly also, of moderate size, dimensions, quantity, duration, or speed. ME.

within a measurable distance of near to (some undesirable condition or event).

†**2** Of a person, action, etc.: characterized by moderation; moderate, temperate. ME–E18.

†**3** Uniform in movement; metrical, rhythmical; MUSIC in strict time. M16–L17.

■ **measuraˈbility** *noun* L17. **measurableness** *noun* LME.

measurably /ˈmɛʒ(ə)rəbli/ *adverb*. LME.

[ORIGIN from MEASURABLE + -LY².]

†**1** Moderately, in moderation. LME–L19.

2 In due measure or proportion; proportionably. Now *rare*. LME.

3 In some measure, to some extent. *US*. M18.

4 To a measurable extent. M19.

measurage /ˈmɛʒ(ə)rɪdʒ/ *noun*. Long *hist.* LME.

[ORIGIN Old French & mod. French *mesurage*, formed as MEASURE *verb*: see -AGE.]

1 A duty payable on the cargo of a ship. LME.

†**2** A measurement; an act of measuring. LME–M17.

measure /ˈmɛʒə/ *noun*. ME.

[ORIGIN Old French & mod. French *mesure* from Latin *mensura*, from *mens-* pa. ppl stem of *metiri* to measure: see -URE.]

▸ **I 1** Size or quantity as ascertained or ascertainable by measuring (now chiefly in ***made to measure*** below); *spec.* (*a*) FENCING the distance of one fencer from another as determined by the length of his or her reach when lunging or thrusting; (*b*) the width of a full line of type or print, esp. as measured in picas; (*c*) the width of an organ pipe. ME. ▸**b** *fig.* State, character, or ability as assessed or assessable by judgement or observation, what is estimated to be expected (chiefly in ***get the measure of***, ***take the measure of*** below). Formerly also, an estimate, an opinion, a notion. M17. ▸†**c** Duration. M17–E18.

M

fig.: SHAKES. *Two Gent.* Come not within the measure of my wrath.

2 An instrument for measuring; *spec.* (**a**) a vessel of standard capacity used for separating and dealing out fixed quantities of various substances, as grain, liquids, coal, etc.; (**b**) a graduated rod, line, tape, etc., for taking measurements. ME.
tape measure, yard-measure, etc.
3 A unit or denomination of measurement; the quantity indicated by any such unit. Also, (the quantity indicated by) any of various specific units of capacity (formerly also of length) understood from context or usage, as a bushel. ME.

W. C. BRYANT These Brought wine, a thousand measures. A. C. CLARKE A furlong is an obsolete measure of length.

4 A quantity, degree, or proportion (of something), esp. as granted to or bestowed on a person; an extent, an amount. LME.

P. GALLICO He was shocked by the measure of .. hatred of him he caught in her expression. A. BULLOCK Attlee found a surprising measure of agreement with Truman.

5 A method of measuring; *esp.* a system of standard denominations or units of length, surface, or volume. Usu. with specifying word. LME.
linear measure, liquid measure, etc.
6 The action or process of measuring, measurement. Now *rare*. LME.
7 That by which something is computed, estimated, judged, or regulated, or with which something is compared in respect of quantity or quality; a criterion, a test. Chiefly in ***be the measure of***. L16.

BACON Time is the measure of businesse, as money is of wares. G. M. TREVELYAN The busy life of the rivers was a measure of the badness of the roads. C. MILNE Customers such as this .. whose measure of a book lay in how much they had paid for it.

8 MATH. **a** = DIVISOR 2. L16. ▸**b** A number assigned to a set under a specified rule such that the number assigned to the union of non-overlapping sets is equal to the sum of the numbers assigned to each of the sets; the rule itself. E20.
9 A stratum or bed of mineral. Now only in *pl.* M17.
coal measures, Culm Measures.
▸**II** †**10** That which is commensurate or adequate; satisfaction. ME–E17.
11 Moderation, temperance. Also, an extent not to be exceeded, a limit. Now only in certain phrs. (see below). ME.
12 †**a** Proportion; due proportion, symmetry. LME–M17. ▸**b** ***in measure as*** [after French *à mesure que*], in proportion as. L18.
13 Treatment handed out to a person, esp. by way of punishment or retribution. *arch.* L16.

W. COWPER Such hard and arbitrary measure here.

▸**III 14** (A kind of) poetical rhythm, metre; a metrical group or unit, as of a dactyl or two iambuses, trochees, spondees, etc.; a metre. LME.
15 An air, a tune, a melody. Now *poet.* LME.

LYTTON Strange wild measures, on his violin.

16 (A step of) a dance; *esp.* a grave or stately dance. *arch.* LME.

SIR W. SCOTT Now tread we a measure!

17 The quantitative relation between notes determining the kind of rhythm (duple, triple, etc.) of a piece of music; the time of a piece of music; a bar of music. L16.
18 Rhythmical motion, esp. as regulated by music; the rhythm of a movement. L16.
▸**IV 19** A plan or course of action intended to attain some object, a suitable action; *spec.* a legislative enactment proposed or adopted. L17.

W. S. CHURCHILL His second measure, a Land Act to prevent uncompensated eviction, had been passed in 1870. R. K. NARAYAN We are only trying some new measures to meet the competition. H. MACMILLAN The increase in the Bank Rate as a short-term measure.

– PHRASES: **above measure** = ***beyond measure*** below. **a measure of** some degree of. ***apothecaries' measure***: see APOTHECARY 1. **beyond measure** excessively, extremely. ***BINARY measure***. **by measure** as determined by measuring (as opp. to weighing or counting). ***COAL measures***. ***Culm Measures***: see CULM *noun*[1] 4. **fill up the measure of** *arch.* complete the sum of, add what is lacking to the completeness of. **for good measure** as something beyond the minimum, as a finishing touch. ***full measure***: see FULL *adjective*. **get the measure of** = ***take the measure of*** (b) below. **have the measure of** have an (accurate) opinion of the abilities or character of, have taken the measure of. **in a great measure**, **in a large measure**, **in large measure** to a considerable extent or degree, largely. **in a measure** to a certain extent, to some degree, somewhat. ***in large measure***: see ***in a great measure*** above. **in measure** *arch.* to a limited extent, in part. ***in measure as***: see sense 12b above. **in some measure** to a certain extent, in some degree, somewhat. **in the same measure** to the same extent. **keep measure** (**a**) observe strict time; (**b**) (also †***keep measures***) be moderate or restrained in action (usu. in neg. contexts). ***long measure***: see LONG *adjective*[1]. **made to measure** (of a garment etc.) made in accordance with measurements taken, as opp. to ready-made; *transf.* & *fig.* fashioned to fulfil specified requirements, appropriate for a particular purpose. ***optic measure***: see OPTIC *adjective*. **out of all measure** *arch.* excessively, extremely. ***POULTER'S measure***. **set measures to** limit. ***short measure***: see SHORT *adjective*. ***square measure***: see SQUARE *adjective*. **take the measure of**, †**take measure of** (**a**) measure (a person) for clothes etc.; (**b**) form an estimate of; *esp.* weigh or gauge the abilities or character of, assess what to expect from (a person). ***tread a measure***: see TREAD *verb*. ***Winchester measure***: see WINCHESTER 1.

measure /ˈmɛʒə/ *verb*. ME.
[ORIGIN Old French & mod. French *mesurer* from Latin *mensurare*, from *mensura*: see MEASURE *noun*.]
▸**I** *verb trans.* †**1** Regulate, moderate, restrain. ME–L16.
2 Apportion by measure, deal *out*, now esp. to some known capacity or in some fixed unit. ME.

L. STEPHEN Sermons were measured out with no grudging hand. G. GREENE She had carefully measured out a quadruple whisky.

3 Ascertain or determine the spatial magnitude or quantity of (something), ascertain or determine (a spatial magnitude or quantity), by the application of some object of known size or capacity or by comparison with some fixed unit. ME. ▸†**b** Form of, raise or reduce to, certain dimensions or proportions. ME–E16. ▸**c** Mark off or *off* (a line of definite length) in a certain direction. M19.

GOLDSMITH Instruments called anemometers .. made to measure the velocity of the wind. G. ORWELL He could walk three kilometres, measured by pacing the cell. A. GRAY The doctor measured this with a pocket ruler.

4 Estimate the amount, duration, value, etc., of (an abstract thing) by comparison with some standard; judge or estimate the greatness or value of (a person, a quality, etc.) by a certain standard or rule; appraise by comparison with something else. ME.

W. COWPER Measure life By its true worth, the comfort it affords. R. LYND It is, of course, extremely difficult to measure the happiness of any animal.

5 Travel over, traverse (a certain distance, a tract of country). Chiefly *poet.* LME.

SHAKES. *Merch. V.* For we must measure twenty miles to-day.

†**6** Encircle, encompass. LME–L17.
7 Mark the boundary or course of; delimit. Usu. foll. by *out*. *poet.* E16.
8 a Be the measure of, be a means of measuring. L16. ▸**b** MATH. Of a quantity: be a factor or divisor of (another quantity). Formerly also *refl.*, be exactly divisible *by*. Now *rare* or *obsolete*. L16.

a J. N. LOCKYER For common purposes, time is measured by the Sun.

9 a Adjust (something) *to* an object or *by* a standard. *arch.* L16. ▸†**b** Be commensurate with. L16–M17.

a JER. TAYLOR You must measure your desires by your fortune .. not your fortunes by your desires.

†**10** Turn into metre. L16–L18.
11 Have a measurement of (so much). L17.

J. C. LOUDON Each shutter measuring four feet six inches.

12 Bring into competition, opposition, or comparison *with*; *refl.* try one's strength *against*. E18.
13 Take the measure of (a person, *for* clothes etc.); form an estimate of; look (a person) up and down. M18.

A. E. HOUSMAN In many an eye that measures me. R. P. JHABVALA The little tailor .. measured me right there .. in his open shop.

▸**II** *verb intrans.* **14** Take measurements; use a measuring instrument. E17.

B. JOWETT The young carpenter should be taught to measure and use the rule.

15 a Vie in measurement *with*; be comparable *with*. E18. ▸**b** Foll. by *up*: be equal in ability etc., have the necessary qualifications, meet the required standard, (foll. by *to*). E20.

b S. I. LANDAU A free-lancer who does not measure up is easily dismissed.

16 Admit of measurement. M18.
– PHRASES: †**measure back** retrace (one's steps, the road). **measure one's length**, †**measure out one's length** fall flat on the ground (accidentally). **measure swords** (of duellists) ascertain that the swords being used are of equal length (*hist.*); meet in a contest or battle, try one's strength *with*.

measured /ˈmɛʒəd/ *adjective*. LME.
[ORIGIN from MEASURE *noun*, *verb*: see -ED[2], -ED[1].]
†**1** Moderate, temperate. LME–L15.
2 That has been measured to determine spatial magnitude or quantity; apportioned or dealt out by measure; (of work) paid according to the amount done. LME. ▸**b** Accurately regulated, correctly proportioned. E17. **measured mile** a distance of one mile carefully measured, esp. for determining the speed of a ship.
3 Written in metre; metrical. L16. ▸**b** Having a marked or fixed rhythm; rhythmical; regular in movement. E17.

b CARLYLE I heard a measured tread; and then .. advanced on me eight soldiers.

4 Esp. of language: carefully weighed or calculated; deliberate and restrained. E19.

R. GITTINGS The measured, objective tone of these critical pronouncements.

▪ **measuredly** *adverb* E19. **measuredness** *noun* M19.

measureless /ˈmɛʒəlɪs/ *adjective*. LME.
[ORIGIN from MEASURE *noun* + -LESS.]
Having no bounds or limits; unlimited, immeasurable, infinite.
▪ **measurelessly** *adverb* M19. **measurelessness** *noun* M19.

†**measurely** *adverb*. L16–M19.
[ORIGIN from MEASURE *noun* + -LY[2].]
Moderately.

measurement /ˈmɛʒəm(ə)nt/ *noun*. E17.
[ORIGIN from MEASURE *verb* + -MENT.]
†**1** = ADMEASUREMENT 1. Only in E17.
2 The action or an act of measuring; mensuration. M18.
3 A dimension ascertained by measuring; a size, quantity, or extent measured by a standard. M18.

J. GASKELL Her bust measurement must be all of 34 inches. *Which?* Our rating includes measurements for sharpness, .. sound frequency range.

4 A system of measuring or of measures. M19.
– COMB.: **measurement cargo**, **measurement freight**, **measurement goods**: on which freight is charged by measurement of bulk rather than by weight.

measurer /ˈmɛʒ(ə)rə/ *noun*. LME.
[ORIGIN from MEASURE *verb* + -ER[1].]
1 A person who measures or takes measurements; *esp.* a person whose duty or office it is to see that goods or commodities are of the proper measure. LME.
2 An instrument used for measuring. M18.

measuring /ˈmɛʒ(ə)rɪŋ/ *noun*. ME.
[ORIGIN from MEASURE *verb* + -ING[1].]
1 The action of MEASURE *verb*; the process of taking measurements; measurement, mensuration. ME.
†**2** A dimension. Only in 16.
– ATTRIB. & COMB.: Designating vessels or instruments used for measuring, esp. with graduations, as ***measuring cup***, ***measuring jug***, ***measuring rod***, ***measuring spoon***, ***measuring tape***, ***measuring yard***, etc. Special combs., as **measuring cast** (now *rare* or *obsolete*) a competitive throw so nearly equal to another that measurement is required to decide the superiority; *fig.* a subtle question, a difficult point, a doubtful matter.

measuring /ˈmɛʒ(ə)rɪŋ/ *adjective*. L16.
[ORIGIN from MEASURE *verb* + -ING[2].]
1 That measures. L16.
2 ***measuring worm***, the larva of a geometrid moth. M19.

meat /miːt/ *noun*.
[ORIGIN Old English *mete* = Old Frisian *met(e*, Old Saxon *meti*, Old Norse *matr*, Gothic *mats*, from Germanic, from base of METE *verb*.]
▸**I 1** Food; nourishment for people or animals; *esp.* solid food, as opp. to drink. Now *arch.* & *dial.* OE.

S. JOHNSON The horses could not travel all day without rest or meat. SHELLEY He had .. meat and drink enough. *Proverb*: One man's meat is another man's poison.

2 A kind of food, an article of food. *obsolete* exc. in ***sweetmeat***. OE.
bake-meat, ***milkmeat***, etc.
3 A meal; (occas.) the principal meal of a day, dinner. *obsolete* exc. in ***after meat***, ***at meat***, ***before meat*** (*arch.*), after, at, before, a meal, after, in the process of, before, eating. ME.
4 The flesh of animals used as food, now esp. excluding fish and poultry; (usu. with specifying word) the edible soft part of a shellfish; *US dial.* bacon; animal flesh prepared for eating. ME. ▸**b** *collect.* Living animals such as are killed for food; game animals; *US* one's quarry or prey. E16.

b N. GORDIMER The third one had gone off, early, to shoot some meat—a family of wart-hogs.

butcher meat, ***carcass meat***, ***crabmeat***, ***horsemeat***, ***mincemeat***, ***pigmeat***, etc. ***duck's meat***, ***duckmeat***: see DUCK *noun*[1].
5 The edible part of a fruit, nut, or egg; the pulp, kernel, yolk and white, etc., as opp. to the rind, peel, or shell. Now chiefly *US*. LME.

SHAKES. *Rom. & Jul.* Thy head is as full of quarrels as an egg is full of meat. D. JOHNSON Belinda ate coconut meat off the shell.

6 A kind of meat. Usu. in *pl.* L17.

W. TREVOR There was .. ham and pork and other meats.

▸**II** *transf.* & *fig.* **7** *sing.* & *collect. pl.* The penis; the female genitals; the human body regarded as an instrument of sexual pleasure. *coarse slang*. L16.

SHAKES. *2 Hen. IV* Away, you mouldy rogue, away! I am meat for your master. G. DAVIS I kept Maxine's .. younger brothers outside while Teddy slipped the meat to her in the bedroom.

8 Human flesh; the human body regarded as large or powerful; muscle or fat on a person. *colloq.* M19.

F. O'CONNOR He liked women with meat on them, so you didn't feel .. their old bones.

9 Something enjoyable or advantageous; matter of importance or substance; the gist or main part (of a story, situation, etc.). L19.

M. McLuhan Send the enclosed article to Al . . . It is full of meat. *Rally Sport* The meat of the rally was in seven stages in Kielder Forest.

10 The centre of a cricket bat, of the head of a golf club, etc. Esp. in ***hit on the meat, hit with the meat***. *slang*. E20.

– PHRASES: ***after meat, at meat***: see sense 3 above. **beat the meat** *coarse slang* (of a male) masturbate. ***before meat***: see sense 3 above. **be meat and drink to** be a source of intense enjoyment to. ***butcher's meat***: see BUTCHER *noun*. ***cold meat***: see COLD *adjective*. ***cry roast meat***: see ROAST *adjective*. ***cuckoo's meat***: see CUCKOO *noun*. ***duck's meat***: see DUCK *noun*[1]. ***easy meat***: see EASY *adjective*. **green meat** grass or green vegetables used as food or fodder. **make meat of** kill. **meat and potatoes** *fig.* basics, ordinary but fundamental things. **meat and two veg** (*a*) *colloq.* plain English cooking; (*b*) *slang* the male genitals. **piece of meat** *slang* a person regarded as a purely physical specimen; a woman regarded as an instrument of sexual pleasure. ***plates of meat***: see PLATE *noun* 25c. ***pounded meat***: see POUND *verb*[1]. ***red meat***: see RED *adjective*. ***strong meat***: see STRONG *adjective*. ***white meat***: see WHITE *adjective*.

– COMB.: **meat-ant** *Austral.* any of several ants of the genus *Iridomyrmex*, *esp.* the large reddish-purple *I. purpureus*; **meat-axe** a butcher's cleaver; **meatball** (*a*) a ball of minced or chopped meat; (*b*) *slang* an unintelligent or boring person; **meat breakfast** a breakfast that includes a meat dish; **meat cube** a small cube of concentrated meat extract; **meat fly** a fly that breeds in meat, a bluebottle; **meat grinder** a mincing machine; *fig.* a destructive action or process; **meathead** *slang* a stupid person; **meat-headed** *adjective* (*slang*) stupid; **meathook** (*a*) a hook on which to hang meat carcasses etc.; (*b*) *slang* an arm, a hand; **meat-house** (*a*) a building in which to hang meat; (*b*) *slang* a brothel; **meat jelly** a jelly prepared from meat; **meat loaf** a loaf of minced or chopped meat; **meatman** †(*a*) a person who provides food, a caterer; †(*b*) a person who eats meat; (*c*) a person who sells or supplies meat; a butcher; **meat market** †(*a*) a market where food of any kind is sold; (*b*) a market for butcher's meat; (*c*) *slang* a rendezvous for people seeking sexual encounters; **meat-offering** in biblical translations, a sacrifice consisting of food; **meat-packer** a meat-packing business; **meat-packing** the business of processing and packing meat and distributing it to retailers; **meat poisoning** food poisoning caused by meat; **meat rack** *slang* = *meat market* (c) above; **meat rail** a rail for supporting meat in a larder, refrigerated container, etc.; **meat safe** a ventilated cupboard for storing meat, usu. made of wire gauze or perforated zinc; **meatspace** *slang* the physical world, as opposed to cyberspace or a virtual environment; **meat tea** a tea at which meat is served, a high tea; **meat ticket** *military slang* an identity disc; **meat wagon** *slang* (chiefly *N. Amer.*) an ambulance; a police van; a hearse; **meat works** (chiefly *Austral.* & *NZ*) (*a*) an establishment where meat is processed and packed; (*b*) a slaughterhouse.

■ **meatless** *adjective* (*a*) *arch.* having no food; (*b*) without meat; (of prepared food) containing no meat: OE. **meatlessness** *noun* E20.

meat /miːt/ *verb*. *obsolete* exc. *dial.* OE.
[ORIGIN from the noun.]
1 *verb trans.* Feed, supply with food. OE.
well-meated *adjective* (of an animal) well fed, having plenty of flesh.
2 *verb intrans.* Eat, partake of food. L16.

meato- /mɪˈeɪtəʊ/ *combining form* of MEATUS: see -O-.
■ **meatotomy** /miːəˈtɒtəmi/ *noun* (an instance of) surgical incision into the urethral meatus L19.

meatus /mɪˈeɪtəs/ *noun*. Pl. **-es**, same /mɪˈeɪtjuːs/. LME.
[ORIGIN Latin, lit. 'passage, course', from *meare* go, pass.]
†**1** A channel, a passage. LME–L17.
2 *spec.* in ANATOMY. A tubular passage in the body, *esp.* the external auditory meatus. Usu. with specifying word. LME.
auditory meatus, **external auditory meatus** the channel leading into the ear. **nasal meatus**, **olfactory meatus** a deep groove in the nasal cavity. **urethral meatus**, **urinary meatus** the external orifice of the urethra.
■ **meatal** *adjective* M19.

meaty /ˈmiːti/ *adjective*. L18.
[ORIGIN from MEAT *noun* + -Y[1].]
1 a Full of meat; fleshy. L18. ▸**b** *fig.* Full of substance. L19.

a J. T. Farrell A girl whose slim, tall but meaty figure. B. Bryson He thrust a meaty hand at me and introduced himself. **b** J. Irving There were good heroes and their meaty adventures. *Times* The star of countless comic films plays a meatier role in . . *Long Day's Journey Into Night*.

2 Of or pertaining to meat; like meat. M19.
■ **meatiness** *noun* L19.

mebbe *adverb* & *noun* see MAYBE.

mebos /ˈmiːbɒs, *foreign* ˈmeːbɔs/ *noun*. *S. Afr.* L18.
[ORIGIN Afrikaans, prob. from Japanese *umeboshi* dried and salted apricots.]
A confection made from dried flattened apricots, preserved in salt and sugar.

Mebyon Kernow /mɛbjɒn ˈkɔːnəʊ/ *noun phr.* (treated as *sing.* or *pl.*). M20.
[ORIGIN Cornish, lit. 'Sons of Cornwall'.]
A Cornish nationalist party.

mecamylamine /mɛkəˈmʌɪləmiːn, -ˈmɪl-/ *noun*. M20.
[ORIGIN from ME(THYL + CAM(PHOR *noun* + -YL + AMINE.]
PHARMACOLOGY. A ganglionic blocking agent used to treat extreme hypertension.

mecate /meɪˈkɑːteɪ/ *noun*. Chiefly *US*. M19.
[ORIGIN Mexican Spanish from Nahuatl *mecatl*.]
A rope made of horsehair or of maguey fibre, used esp. to tether or lead a horse.

Mecca /ˈmɛkə/ *noun*. E18.
[ORIGIN Arabic *Makka*, birthplace of Muhammad in Saudi Arabia, and place of pilgrimage for Muslims (cf. KAABA).]
1 ***Mecca balm***, ***Mecca balsam***, = ***balm of Gilead*** s.v. BALM *noun*[1]. Chiefly *hist.* E18.
2 A place regarded as supremely sacred or valuable, or where a faith, policy, etc., originated. Now usu., a place which attracts people of a particular group or with a particular interest. M19.

W. Golding The airfield was a Mecca for children. C. Chaplin Hollywood was fast becoming the Mecca of writers, actors and intellectuals.

■ **Meccan** *adjective* & *noun* (*a*) *noun* a native or inhabitant of Mecca; (*b*) *adjective* of or pertaining to Mecca: E17.

Meccano /mɪˈkɑːnəʊ/ *noun*. Also **m-**. E20.
[ORIGIN Invented word, after *mechanic* etc.]
(Proprietary name for) a system for constructing model machines, vehicles, etc., from reusable metal components, and for components of this.

mech /mɛk/ *noun*. *slang*. E20.
[ORIGIN Abbreviation.]
A mechanic.

mechanic /mɪˈkanɪk/ *adjective* & *noun*. LME.
[ORIGIN (Old French & mod. French *mécanique* from) Latin *mechanicus*, from Greek *mēkhanikos* from *mēkhanē* MACHINE *noun*: see -IC.]
▸ **A** *adjective*. **1** Pertaining to or involving manual labour or skill. Now *rare* or *obsolete*. LME.
2 Of a person: having a manual occupation; working at a trade. Also, low in the social scale; vulgar, coarse. *arch.* M16.
3 Pertaining to or of the nature of a machine or machines; worked by machinery. *arch.* E17.
4 = MECHANICAL *adjective* 6. Now *rare* or *obsolete*. M17.
5 Worked or working like a machine; automatic, unthinking. *arch.* L17.
▸ **B** *noun*. See also MECHANICS.
1 A manual worker; an artisan. *arch.* E16. ▸†**b** A person of low birth or status. L17–M18.
mechanics' institute, **mechanics' institution** *hist.* any of various societies providing education for working people.
†**2** A manual trade or craft. Only in 17.
3 A skilled manual worker, *esp.* one who makes, uses, or repairs machinery. M17.

A. MacLean The overalled mechanic was still at work on the helicopter's engine.

DENTAL *mechanic*.
4 A person who cheats at gambling games, esp. cards; a card sharp. *US* & *Austral. slang*. L19.
5 A hired assassin. *slang*. L20.

mechanical /mɪˈkanɪk(ə)l/ *adjective* & *noun*. LME.
[ORIGIN formed as MECHANIC: see -ICAL.]
▸ **A** *adjective*. **1** Involving manual work; of the nature of handicraft or craftsmanship. Now *rare*. LME.
2 Concerned with or involving machinery or tools; acting, worked, or produced by a machine or mechanism. L15.

R. Ingalls A story about a girl who danced with a mechanical robot. F. Hoyle James Croll calculated these results without the aid of any mechanical or electronic calculator. *Daily Telegraph* Three . . jets were grounded by mechanical faults and an accident.

†**3** Concerned with or involving material objects or physical conditions, practical. L16–E19.
4 Employed in manual work; lower-class. Now *rare*. L16.

A. S. Neill When invention is left out, dancing becomes mechanical and dull. M. Esslin The mechanical exchange of platitudes that might as well be spoken into the wind.

5 Performing or performed without thought; lacking spontaneity or originality; machine-like; automatic, routine. E17.
6 Physical; of, pertaining to, or caused by physical properties, forces, agents, etc. Now freq. opp. ***chemical***. L16. ▸**b** Pertaining to mechanics as a science. Now *rare*. M17.

J. E. Gordon Almost anything . . added to a metal will affect its mechanical properties. B. W. Sparks It is convenient to differentiate between physical, or mechanical, weathering and chemical weathering.

7 Of a theory, an advocate of a theory: explaining phenomena in terms of physical properties only. Now *hist.* M17.
8 MATH. Of a curve: (drawable but) not expressible by an equation of finite and rational algebraical form. L17.

– SPECIAL COLLOCATIONS: **mechanical advantage** the ratio of the force produced by a machine to the force applied to it. **mechanical construction** GEOMETRY: of a curve as a whole, without the calculation of individual points. **mechanical drawing**: performed with the help of instruments, as compasses, rulers, etc. **mechanical engineer** an expert in mechanical engineering. **mechanical engineering** the branch of engineering that deals with the design, construction, and maintenance of machines. ***mechanical equivalent of heat***: see EQUIVALENT *noun*. ***mechanical mixture***: see MIXTURE 4. **mechanical pencil** *N. Amer.* a propelling pencil. ***mechanical power***: see POWER *noun* 13. **mechanical pulp**: prepared without chemical degradation. ***mechanical stoker***: see STOKER 1. **mechanical twin** METALLURGY a twinned crystal produced by mechanical deformation. **mechanical zero** the state or position in which a measuring instrument remains when the quantity which it measures is absent.
▸ **B** *noun*. **1** A manual worker; an artisan. *arch.* E17.

Shakes. *Mids. N. D.* A crew of patches, rude Mechanicals, That worke for bread, vpon Athenian stalles.

2 In *pl.* ▸†**a** The science relating to the construction of machines. Only in E17. ▸**b** Mechanical parts, esp. of a vehicle. E19.
3 PRINTING. A completed assembly of artwork and copy. M20.
■ **mechaniˈcality** *noun* the quality of being mechanical or like a machine L18. **mechanicaliˈzation** *noun* L19. **mechanicalize** *verb trans.* make mechanical E17. **mechanically** *adverb* L16. **mechanicalness** *noun* E17.

mechanicalism /mɪˈkanɪk(ə)lɪz(ə)m/ *noun*. L19.
[ORIGIN from MECHANICAL + -ISM.]
1 PHILOSOPHY. The doctrine that all natural phenomena are produced by mechanical forces; = MECHANISM 4. L19.
2 Machine-like procedure; routine. E20.
■ **mechanicalist** *noun* an adherent of the doctrine of mechanicalism L19.

mechanician /mɛkəˈnɪʃ(ə)n/ *noun*. L16.
[ORIGIN from MECHANIC + -IAN.]
A person skilled in a manual occupation, an artisan. Now also, a person skilled in the construction of machinery, a mechanic.

mechanicism /mɪˈkanɪsɪz(ə)m/ *noun*. E18.
[ORIGIN formed as MECHANICIAN + -ISM.]
= MECHANICALISM 2.

mechanicist /mɪˈkanɪsɪst/ *noun*. L19.
[ORIGIN formed as MECHANICIAN + -IST.]
PHILOSOPHY. An adherent of the doctrine of mechanicalism, a mechanicalist.

mechanico- /mɪˈkanɪkəʊ/ *combining form*.
[ORIGIN from Latin *mechanicus* MECHANIC: see -O-.]
Mechanical and —.
■ **mechanico-ˈchemical** *adjective* pertaining partly to mechanics and partly to chemistry M19. **mechanico-corˈpuscular** *adjective* designating a doctrine viewing all phenomena as explicable by the movement of atoms according to mechanical laws E19. **mechanico-ˈmorphic** *adjective* = MECHANOMORPHIC M20. **mechanico-ˈmorphism** *noun* = MECHANOMORPHISM M20. **mechanico-ˈphysical** *adjective* of or pertaining to the philosophy which explains all phenomena as the outcome of the motions and interactions of matter in accordance with physical laws L19.

M

mechanics /mɪˈkanɪks/ *noun*. E17.
[ORIGIN Pl. of MECHANIC: see -ICS.]
1 Treated as *sing.* or (occas.) *pl.* ▸**a** The body of theoretical and practical knowledge concerned with the invention and construction of machines, the explanation of their operation, and the calculation of their efficiency; mechanical engineering. E17. ▸**b** The branch of applied mathematics that deals with the motion and equilibrium of bodies and the action of forces, and includes statics, dynamics, and kinematics. Now distinguished as ***classical mechanics*** (as opp. to ***quantum mechanics*** s.v. QUANTUM *adjective*). L17.
b ***celestial mechanics***, ***fluid mechanics***, ***statistical mechanics***, ***wave mechanics***, etc.
2 *pl.* The working parts of a machine. Also, the technical or procedural details, the practicalities, (*of* something). M19.

Punch It is a pity the mechanics of the story take up so much of the time. *Which?* We explain the mechanics of buying and selling.

mechanise *verb* var. of MECHANIZE.

mechanism /ˈmɛk(ə)nɪz(ə)m/ *noun*. M17.
[ORIGIN mod. Latin *mechanismus*, from Greek *mēkhanē* MACHINE *noun*: see -ISM.]
1 The structure or way of working of the parts in a machine or natural system; the mode of operation of a process. M17.
2 A system of mutually adapted parts working together (as) in a machine; a piece of machinery; a means by which a particular effect is produced. Also (*collect.*), machinery, mechanical appliances. L17. ▸**b** PSYCHOLOGY. An unconscious, structured set of mental processes underlying a person's behaviour or responses. L19.

J. Imison The part of the mechanism of a watch which shows the hour. P. Bowles A part of the mechanism that held his being together. *Physics Bulletin* Some mechanism must be found for judging the quality of the work.

†**3** Mechanical action; action according to the laws of mechanics. L17–L18.
4 PHILOSOPHY. The doctrine that all natural (esp. biological or mental) phenomena are produced by mechanical forces. Cf. MECHANICALISM 1. L17.
5 In painting, sculpture, music, etc.: the mechanical or physical execution of a work of art, technique. M19.

– PHRASES: ***defence mechanism***: see DEFENCE *noun*. ***isolating mechanism***. ***tilt mechanism***: see TILT *noun*[2] 7.

mechanist /ˈmɛk(ə)nɪst/ *noun.* **E17.**
[**ORIGIN** from MECHANIC + -IST.]
1 A person skilled in constructing machinery. Formerly also, an artisan. **E17.**
2 *PHILOSOPHY.* An adherent of the doctrine of mechanicalism. **M17.**
3 An expert in or student of mechanics. **E18.**
▪ **mechaˈnistic** *adjective* (**a**) of, pertaining to, or connected with mechanics or mechanism; (**b**) pertaining to or holding mechanical theories: **L19.** **mechaˈnistically** *adverb* in a mechanistic manner; on mechanistic principles: **E20.**

mechanize /ˈmɛk(ə)nʌɪz/ *verb.* Also **-ise.** **E18.**
[**ORIGIN** formed as MECHANIST + -IZE.]
1 *verb trans.* Make mechanical, give a mechanical character to. **E18.**
2 *verb trans.* **a** Introduce machinery in or into (a factory, process, industry, etc.). Freq. as ***mechanized*** *ppl adjective.* **E19.** ▸**b** Equip (an army or force) with mechanical weapons and vehicles. **E20.**

a W. GOLDING A sweet factory which was small enough not to be mechanized. **b** *Encycl. Brit.* The Germans had broken abruptly with the past by mechanizing their artillery.

3 *verb intrans.* Work as a mechanic. Also, move mechanically. *rare.* **L19.**
▪ **mechaniˈzation** *noun* **M19.** **mechanizer** *noun* (**a**) a person who mechanizes; (**b**) = MECHANICIST: **M19.**

mechano- /ˈmɛk(ə)nəʊ/ *combining form.*
[**ORIGIN** Greek *mēkhano-* combining form of *mēkhanē* MACHINE *noun*: see -O-.]
Of or pertaining to machines or mechanical phenomena, properties, etc.
▪ **mechanoˈcaloric** *adjective* (*PHYSICS*) designating a phenomenon by which a linear flow of superfluid liquid helium (helium II) generates a temperature difference between its ends **M20.** **mechanoˈchemical** *adjective* of or pertaining to mechanochemistry **M20.** **mechanoˈchemically** *adverb* in accordance with the laws of mechanochemistry **M20.** **mechanoˈchemistry** *noun* the branch of science that deals with the relation between mechanical and chemical phenomena and the interconversion of these forms of energy **E20.** **mechano-eˈlectric, mechano-eˈlectrical** *adjectives* pertaining to or producing a conversion of mechanical movement into corresponding electrical effects **M20.** **mechaˈnology** *noun* (*rare*) the science or a treatise that deals with machines or mechanisms **M19.** **mechanoreˈception** *noun* (*BIOLOGY*) (the mechanism of) the detection of a mechanical stimulus by means of mechanoreceptors; sensitivity to mechanical stimuli: **M20.** **mechanoreˈceptive** *adjective* (*BIOLOGY*) capable of performing mechanoreception; sensitive to mechanical stimuli: **M20.** **mechanoreˈceptor** *noun* (*BIOLOGY*) a sensory receptor that responds to mechanical stimuli, such as pressure changes resulting from touch or sound **E20.** **mechanoˈsensitive** *adjective* (*BIOLOGY*) mechanoreceptive **M20.** **mechanoˈtherapy** *noun* (*MEDICINE*) physiotherapy; *esp.* that involving the use of mechanical apparatus, e.g. to provide exercise: **L19.**

mechanomorphic /mɛk(ə)nə(ʊ)ˈmɔːfɪk/ *adjective.* **L19.**
[**ORIGIN** formed as MECHANO- + Greek *morphē* form + -IC.]
Having the form or qualities of a machine or mechanism; of the nature of mechanomorphism.
▪ **mechanomorphism** *noun* the concept or conceiving of something, esp. a god, as mechanomorphic **E20.**

méchant /meʃɑ̃/ *adjective.* Fem. ***-ante*** /-ɑ̃ːt/. **E19.**
[**ORIGIN** French.]
Malicious, spiteful.

mechatronics /mɛkəˈtrɒnɪks/ *noun.* **L20.**
[**ORIGIN** from MECHA(NICS + ELEC)TRONICS.]
The branch of technology which combines mechanical engineering with electronics.

Mechlin /ˈmɛklɪn/ *noun & adjective.* **L15.**
[**ORIGIN** Former name of *Mechelen* (or Malines) in Belgium. Cf. MALINES.]
(Designating or made of) a lace or other fine fabric orig. produced at Mechelen.

mechoacan /mɛˈtʃəʊək(ə)n/ *noun.* Also **M-.** **L16.**
[**ORIGIN** *Mechoacan*, a Mexican province.]
1 Any of several plants related to morning glory which have purgative roots, esp. *Ipomoea pandurata* of the southern US; the root of such a plant. **L16.**
†**2** A purgative drug obtained from the roots of the mechoacan. **E17–M18.**

mecholyl /ˈmɛkəlʌɪl, -lɪl/ *noun.* **M20.**
[**ORIGIN** from ME(THYL + CHOL(INE + -YL.]
PHARMACOLOGY. = METHACHOLINE.

Meckel /ˈmɛk(ə)l/ *noun.* **M19.**
[**ORIGIN** J. F. *Meckel* (1714–74), or his grandson J. F. *Meckel* (1781–1833), German anatomists.]
ANATOMY & MEDICINE. **1** ***Meckel's diverticulum***, a sacciform appendage of the ileum in some individuals; a pathological condition in which gastric acid is secreted by cells associated with this. **M19.**
2 ***Meckel's cartilage***, a cartilaginous rod or bar in the mandibular region of a vertebrate embryo, around which the malleus and parts of the jaw arise. **L19.**

meclozine /ˈmɛkləzɪn, -iːn/ *noun.* Also ***meclizine.** **M20.**
[**ORIGIN** from ME(THYL + C(H)LO(RINE *noun* + PIPERA)ZINE.]
PHARMACOLOGY. An antihistamine drug derived from piperazine which is taken mainly as an anti-emetic, esp. to prevent motion sickness.

M.Econ. *abbreviation.*
Master of Economics.

meconin /ˈmiːkənɪn/ *noun.* Also **-ine** /-iːn/. **M19.**
[**ORIGIN** from Greek *mēkōn* poppy + -IN[1], -INE[5].]
CHEMISTRY. A crystalline aromatic lactone which is one of the alkaloid components of opium.

meconium /mɪˈkəʊnɪəm/ *noun.* **E17.**
[**ORIGIN** Latin from Greek *mēkōnion*, from *mēkōn* poppy.]
†**1** (Thickened) juice from the opium poppy; opium. **E17–E19.**
2 A dark, greenish, sticky substance found in the intestine of a fetus in the later part of gestation and forming the first faeces of a newborn infant. **E18.** ▸**b** *ENTOMOLOGY.* The first faeces of an insect newly emerged from the pupa. **L18.**

meconopsis /miːkəˈnɒpsɪs/ *noun.* Pl. same, **-nopses** /-ˈnɒpsiːz/. **E19.**
[**ORIGIN** mod. Latin *Meconopsis* (see below), from Greek *mēkōn* poppy + *opsis* appearance.]
Any of various ornamental plants of the genus *Meconopsis*, of the poppy family, which includes the Welsh poppy, *M. cambrica*, and the blue poppies, *M. betonicifolia* etc., of China and the Himalayas.

Mec Vannin /mɛk ˈvanɪn/ *noun phr.* (treated as *sing.* or *pl.*). **M20.**
[**ORIGIN** Manx, lit. 'Sons of (the Isle of) Man'.]
A Manx nationalist party.

med /mɛd/ *noun*[1] *& adjective. colloq.* **M19.**
[**ORIGIN** Abbreviation.]
▸ **A** *noun.* **1** = MEDIC *noun*[1], MEDICAL *noun* 1. **M19.**
2 = MEDICINE *noun*[1]. **M20.**
▸ **B** *adjective.* = MEDICAL *adjective.* **M20.**

Med /mɛd/ *noun*[2]. *colloq.* **M20.**
[**ORIGIN** Abbreviation.]
The Mediterranean Sea.

med. *abbreviation.*
Medium.

M.Ed. *abbreviation.*
Master of Education.

médaillon /medajɔ̃/ *noun.* Pl. pronounced same. **E20.**
[**ORIGIN** French: see MEDALLION.]
A small, flat, round or oval cut of meat or fish.

medaka /məˈdɑːkə/ *noun.* **E20.**
[**ORIGIN** Japanese, from *me(y)* eye + *-daka* high.]
Any of several small Asian freshwater fishes of the genus *Oryzias* (family Oryziatidae), commonly found in paddy fields and popular in aquaria.

medal /ˈmɛd(ə)l/ *noun.* **L16.**
[**ORIGIN** French *médaille* from Italian *medaglia* = Old French *m(e)aille*, Spanish *medalla*, ult. from popular Latin *medialia* small coin.]
1 A metal disc bearing a figure or an inscription, used as a charm or trinket or as a religious symbol. **L16.**

JOYCE A pious medal he had that saved him.

2 A piece of metal, usu. in the form of a coin, struck or cast with an inscription or image, *spec.* (**a**) to commemorate a person, action, or event, (**b**) to recognize the bravery or service of a soldier etc., (**c**) to reward merit, proficiency, or excellence in any art or subject. **L16.**

Field The Mayor . . presented the cup and medals to the winning team.

bronze medal, George Medal, gold medal, Military Medal, etc.
– **PHRASES:** ***the reverse of the medal***: see REVERSE *noun.*
– **COMB.:** **medal chief** *N. AMER. HISTORY* an Indian chief who received a medal from the colonial or US authorities; **medal play** *GOLF* play in which the score is reckoned by counting the number of strokes taken to complete a round by each side (opp. ***match play*** s.v. MATCH *noun*[1]); **medal ribbon** a ribbon of specific colours and design for attaching a particular medal or for wearing without a medal; **medal round** *GOLF* a round of medal play.
▪ **medalet** *noun* a small medal **L18.** **meˈdallic** *adjective* of, pertaining to, or resembling a medal; represented on a medal: **E18.**

medal /ˈmɛd(ə)l/ *verb trans.* Infl. **-ll-**, ***-l-.** **E19.**
[**ORIGIN** from the noun.]
Decorate or honour with a medal. Usu. in *pass.*

New Yorker He was eulogized . . renowned and medalled for his war record.

▪ **medalled** *adjective* decorated with a medal; (of a picture etc.) for which a medal has been awarded: **M19.**

medalist *noun* see MEDALLIST.

medalize *verb* see MEDALLIZE.

medallion /mɪˈdaljən/ *noun & verb.* **M17.**
[**ORIGIN** French *médaillon* from Italian *medaglione* augmentation of *medaglia* MEDAL *noun.*]
▸ **A** *noun.* **1** A large medal. Also, a piece of jewellery in the shape of a medal, worn as a pendant. **M17.**
2 A round or oval tablet or panel, usu. decorated in relief; a round or oval portrait, design, etc. **M18.**
3 = MÉDAILLON. **E20.**
4 A permit licensing a taxi. *US colloq.* **M20.**
– **COMB.:** **medallion man** *slang* a flashily dressed, overconfident man characterized as wearing a shirt open to reveal a medallion.
▸ **B** *verb trans.* Ornament with a medallion or medallions. **E19.**
▪ **medallionist** *noun* (*rare*) a maker of medallions **L19.**

medallise *verb* var. of MEDALLIZE.

medallist /ˈmɛd(ə)lɪst/ *noun.* Also ***medalist.** **L17.**
[**ORIGIN** from MEDAL *noun* + -IST.]
1 A person who is knowledgeable about or interested in medals. **L17.**
2 An engraver, designer, or maker of medals. **M18.**
3 A recipient of a (specified) medal awarded for merit. **L18.** ***bronze medallist, gold medallist***, etc.

medallize /ˈmɛd(ə)lʌɪz/ *verb trans. rare.* Also **-ise**, ***medalize.** **E18.**
[**ORIGIN** from MEDAL *noun* + -IZE.]
Represent or illustrate on a medal.

medano /ˈmɛdənəʊ/ *noun. rare.* Pl. **-os.** **M19.**
[**ORIGIN** Spanish *médano.*]
A shifting crescent-shaped sand dune, a barchan.

meddle /ˈmɛd(ə)l/ *verb.* **ME.**
[**ORIGIN** Old French *medler, mesdler* vars. of *mesler* (mod. *mêler*) from Proto-Romance from Latin *miscere* mix. Cf. MELL *verb.*]
†**1** *verb trans.* Mix, mingle, combine, (esp. *with, together*). **ME–M17.** ▸**b** Mix (goods) fraudulently. **LME–E17.**
†**2** *verb intrans.* Of things: mingle, combine. **ME–E17.**
†**3** *verb intrans.* Have sexual intercourse (*with*). **ME–M17.**
†**4** *verb intrans.* Engage in conflict, fight, (*with*). **ME–E17.**
†**5** *verb refl.* Concern or busy oneself (*with*). **ME–M16.**
†**6** *verb intrans.* Mingle or associate *with.* **LME–L16.**
7 *verb intrans.* Orig., concern oneself or deal *with*, take part *in*. Now, concern oneself unduly (*with*), interfere (*in*). **LME.**

A. CARY She had better attend her own affairs, and I will tell her so if she comes here meddling. J. P. DONLEAVY Who's been meddling with the dresser? J. RULE I don't want you to think I'm meddling in your private affairs.

▪ **meddler** *noun* **LME.** **meddlesome** *adjective* given to meddling or interfering **E17.** **meddlesomely** *adverb* **M19.** **meddlesomeness** *noun* **L17.** **meddlingly** *adverb* in a meddling manner **M18.**

Mede /miːd/ *noun.* **OE.**
[**ORIGIN** Latin *Medi* pl. = Greek *Mēdoi.*]
A member of an ancient Indo-European people who established an empire in Media, south-west of the Caspian Sea and including most of Persia (now Iran), in the 7th cent. BC. Cf. MEDIAN *noun*[1].
law of the Medes and Persians: see LAW *noun*[1].

medevac /ˈmɛdɪvak/ *noun & verb. US.* Also **medi-.** **M20.**
[**ORIGIN** from MED(ICAL *adjective* + EVAC(UATION.]
▸ **A** *noun.* A military helicopter for transporting wounded soldiers etc. to hospital. **M20.**
▸ **B** *verb trans.* Infl. **-ck-.** Transport by medevac. **M20.**

medfly /ˈmɛdflʌɪ/ *noun.* Chiefly *US.* Also **M-.** **M20.**
[**ORIGIN** from MED *noun*[2] + FLY *noun*[1].]
AGRICULTURE & HORTICULTURE. = ***Mediterranean fruit fly*** s.v. MEDITERRANEAN *adjective* 1b.

media /ˈmiːdɪə/ *noun*[1]. Pl. **-iae** /-ɪiː/, same. **M19.**
[**ORIGIN** Latin, fem. of *medius* MID *adjective*, used ellipt.]
1 *PHONETICS.* A voiced stop in Greek; a (voiced) unaspirated stop. **M19.**
2 *ANATOMY.* An intermediate layer in the wall of a blood vessel or lymphatic vessel; = ***TUNICA media.*** **L19.**

media /ˈmiːdɪə/ *noun*[2]. **E20.**
[**ORIGIN** Pl. of MEDIUM *noun.*]
pl. & collect. sing. The main means of mass communication (also ***mass media***), esp. newspapers, radio, and television; the reporters, journalists, etc., working for organizations engaged in such communication; *sing.* (*non-standard*) a means of mass communication, a medium.

Survey The media of today . . are quite incapable of presenting sustained argument. *Daily Mirror* His idea that the media is responsible for society's ills. *attrib.*: *Times* He . . became a considerable media personality.

MIXED media, trial by the media: see TRIAL *noun.*
– **COMB.:** **media event** an event intended to attract publicity; **mediascape** (**a**) communications media as a whole; (**b**) the world as perceived or presented by the media.
– **NOTE:** As *media* is the pl. of *medium*, the sing. uses are traditionally regarded as erroneous; however, use as a collective pl. with a sing. verb (like e.g. *government*) is now generally accepted. Cf. notes at AGENDA, DATA.
▪ **mediagenic** *adjective* (*colloq.*, chiefly *US*) apt to convey a favourable impression when reported by the media, esp. by television **L20.**

media *noun*[3] *pl.* see MEDIUM *noun.*

mediacy /ˈmiːdɪəsi/ *noun.* **LME.**
[**ORIGIN** from MEDIATE *adjective*: see -ACY.]
†**1** Intercession. Only in **LME.**
2 The quality of being mediate; indirect or intermediate agency, intermediacy. **M19.**

mediaeval *adjective & noun* var. of MEDIEVAL.

medial /ˈmiːdɪəl/ *adjective & noun.* **L16.**
[**ORIGIN** Late Latin *medialis*, from *medius* MID *adjective*: see -AL[1].]
▸ **A** *adjective.* **1** *MATH.* Pertaining to or designating a mathematical mean, or a line or area which is a mean proportional. **L16.**

M

2 Situated in the middle, intermediate, (foll. by *to*); (of a letter etc.) occurring in the middle of a word or between words. **E18.** ▸**b** ANATOMY & ZOOLOGY. Situated in or relating to the median plane of the body or the midline of an organ; towards the median plane. (Foll. by *to*.) Opp. ***lateral***. **E19.**
3 Of average or ordinary dimensions, average. **L18.**
– SPECIAL COLLOCATIONS: **medial cadence** MUSIC a cadence in which the leading chord is inverted. ***medial malleolus***: see MALLEOLUS 2.
▸ **B** *noun*. **1** A medial letter; a form of a letter used in the middle of a word. **L18.**
2 PHONETICS. = MEDIA *noun*[1] 1. **M19.**
■ **medially** *adverb* in or towards a medial or central position **M19.**

Median /ˈmiːdɪən/ *noun*[1] & *adjective*[1]. **LME.**
[ORIGIN from *Media* + -AN or MEDE + -IAN.]
▸ **A** *noun*. = MEDE. Also, the language of the Medes, related to Old Persian. **LME.**
▸ **B** *adjective*. Of or pertaining to the Medes or their language. **L16.**

median /ˈmiːdɪən/ *noun*[2] & *adjective*[2]. **LME.**
[ORIGIN French *(veine) médiane* or medieval Latin *medianus* (in *mediana vena*) from Latin, from *medius* MID *adjective*: see -AN.]
▸ **A** *noun*. **1** ANATOMY. A median vein or nerve. Formerly *spec.*, the antecubital vein. Now *rare* or *obsolete*. **LME.**
2 GEOMETRY. A line drawn from a vertex of a triangle to the midpoint of the opposite side. **L19.**
3 STATISTICS. A median quantity, term, or value. Cf. MEAN *noun*[1] 5a, MODE *noun* 11. **E20.**
4 = ***median strip*** below. **M20.**
▸ **B** *adjective*. **1** ANATOMY, BOTANY, & ZOOLOGY. Of, pertaining to, or designating the plane which divides a body, organ, or limb into (roughly) symmetrical (e.g. right and left) halves; sagittal; situated in or directed towards this plane, medial. Formerly also, designating certain structures in the arm, as the antecubital vein. **L16.**
median fin ZOOLOGY in fishes, an unpaired fin on the median line (dorsal, caudal, or anal).
2 *gen.* (Situated in the) middle; intermediate, central. **M17.**
median strip *N. Amer.* a strip of ground, paved or landscaped, dividing a street or highway.
3 STATISTICS. Designating or pertaining to the midpoint of a frequency distribution, such that the variable has an equal probability of falling above or below it; designating the middle term of a discrete series arranged in order of magnitude, or if there is no middle term, the mean of the middle two terms. **L19.**
■ **medianly** *adverb* in a median direction or position **L19.**

mediant /ˈmiːdɪənt/ *noun*. **E18.**
[ORIGIN French *médiante* from Italian *mediante*, from *mediare* come between from late Latin *mediare* be in the middle, from *medius* MID *adjective*.]
MUSIC. The third note of a diatonic scale. Also, one of the regular modulations of a church mode.

mediant /ˈmiːdɪənt/ *adjective*. *rare*. **M19.**
[ORIGIN Late Latin *mediant-* pres. ppl stem of *mediare*: see MEDIANT *noun*, -ANT[1].]
Intervening.

mediastinum /ˌmiːdɪəˈstʌɪnəm/ *noun*. Pl. **-na** /-nə/. Orig. also anglicized as †**mediastine**. **LME.**
[ORIGIN Neut. of medieval Latin *mediastinus* medial, from Latin = a low class of slave, from *medius* MID *adjective*.]
ANATOMY. A partition between two body cavities or two parts of an organ; *esp.* that dividing the thorax, separating the right and left pleural cavities. Also, the space in the thorax between the pleural sacs, containing the heart, aorta, trachea, oesophagus, thymus, etc.
■ **mediastinal** *adjective* **E19.** **mediastiˈnitis** *noun* inflammation of the mediastinum of the thorax **M19.**

mediate /ˈmiːdɪət/ *adjective*. **LME.**
[ORIGIN Latin *mediatus* pa. pple of *mediare*: see MEDIATE *verb*, -ATE[2].]
1 Intermediate or intervening *between* in state, position, time, etc. Now *rare*. **LME.**
2 a *spec.* (*hist.*) (Of a feudal lord or tenant) related through an intermediary; (of a feudal relationship between lord and tenant) effected through an intermediary. **LME.** ▸**b** *gen.* Dependent on or involving an intermediate person, thing, or action; (of a person or thing in relation to another) connected indirectly through another. **L16.**
b mediate inference: arrived at through a middle term. **mediate knowledge**: obtained by means of inference or testimony rather than by intuition or perception.
3 MEDICINE. Of auscultation or percussion: performed with some object or instrument placed against the body. **E19.**
■ **mediately** *adverb* with an intermediary agency, with a person or thing intervening, indirectly **LME.** **mediateness** *noun* **E18.**

mediate /ˈmiːdɪeɪt/ *verb*. **M16.**
[ORIGIN Latin *mediat-* pa. ppl stem of *mediare*, from *medius* MID *adjective*. Partly back-form. from MEDIATION.]
†**1** *verb trans.* Divide (a thing) into two equal parts. **M16–E17.**
2 *verb trans.* **a** Settle or soothe (a dispute etc.) by mediation. **M16.** ▸**b** Bring about or obtain (an agreement etc.) by acting as mediator. **L16.**
3 *verb intrans.* †**a** Take a moderate position, avoid extremes. *rare*. Only in **E17.** ▸**b** Occupy an intermediate position, be *between*; form a connecting link *between* one thing and another. **M17.**
4 *verb intrans.* Act as a mediator; intervene (*between* parties in dispute) to produce agreement or reconciliation. **E17.**

L. NAMIER As for the King's advisers, he considered it their task to mediate between . . King and Parliament.

5 *verb trans.* Act as an intermediary in facilitating (a result) or conveying (a gift etc.); in *pass.*, be imparted mediately; PSYCHOLOGY bring about by acting as an intermediate stage between stimulus and response, or an intention and its realization; act as or make use of a mediator. **M17.**

H. JOHNSON The United States pledged to mediate Guatemala's claim to British Honduras territory. R. D. LAING My experience of you is always mediated through your behaviour.

■ **mediated** *adjective* interposed, intervening; PSYCHOLOGY involving or arrived at by mediation: **M19.** **mediative** *adjective* (*rare*) that mediates, pertaining to mediation or a mediator **E19.**

mediation /miːdɪˈeɪʃ(ə)n/ *noun*. **LME.**
[ORIGIN Late Latin *mediatio(n-)* (formed as MEDIATE *verb*) or from MEDIATOR: see -ATION.]
1 Mediative action; the process or action of mediating between parties in dispute to produce agreement or reconciliation; intercession on behalf of another. **LME.**

H. KISSINGER They . . offered their mediation to break the . . deadlock.

2 a The state or fact of serving as an intermediary; means, agency, medium. **LME.** ▸**b** PSYCHOLOGY. The interposition of stages or processes between stimulus and result, or intention and realization. **E20.**

a A. BROOKNER A will to overcome . . translated, without the mediation of her mind, into excellent bodily health.

†**3** Division by two, halving, bisection. **LME–E18.**
4 MUSIC. The part of a plainsong or Anglican chant which lies between the two reciting notes. **M19.**
■ **mediational** *adjective* **E20.**

mediatize /ˈmiːdɪətʌɪz/ *verb trans.* Also **-ise**. **E19.**
[ORIGIN French *médiatiser*, from *médiat* from Latin *mediatus*: see MEDIATE *adjective*, -IZE.]
Annex (a state), leaving the former government or ruler a title and (usu.) some authority.
■ **mediatiˈzation** *noun* the action of mediatizing a state; the state of being mediatized: **E19.**

mediator /ˈmiːdɪeɪtə/ *noun*. **ME.**
[ORIGIN Old French & mod. French *médiateur*, †-*our* from Christian Latin *mediator*, from Latin *mediare* (see MEDIATE *verb*) or directly from *medius* MID *adjective* after Greek *mesitēs* as used in the New Testament: see -OR.]
1 CHRISTIAN THEOLOGY. A person, esp. Jesus, who mediates between God and humanity. **ME.**
2 A person who intervenes between two parties, esp. to effect reconciliation; an intercessor; a person who brings about (an agreement) or settles (a dispute) by mediation. **LME.**

D. ROWE She had to act as a mediator between her mother and father whenever they quarrelled.

†**3** A go-between; a messenger, an agent. **LME–L17.**
4 A thing which effects a transition between one stage and another; *spec.* in PSYCHOLOGY, an agent in mediation, an intermediate stage. **M20.**
■ **mediaˈtorial** *adjective* of, pertaining to, or characteristic of a mediator or mediation **M17.** **mediatorship** *noun* the office or position of a mediator **L16.** **mediatory** /ˈmiːdɪət(ə)ri/ *adjective* having the function of mediating; pertaining to or of the nature of mediation: **E17.**

mediatrix /miːdɪˈeɪtrɪks/ *noun*. Now *rare*. Pl. **-trices** /-trɪsiːz/, **-trixes**. **L15.**
[ORIGIN Late Latin, fem. of *mediator*: see MEDIATOR, -TRIX.]
A female mediator.
■ Also **ˈmediatress** *noun* **E17.** **ˈmediatrice** *noun* **LME.**

media vuelta /ˈmedja ˈvwelta/ *noun phr.* **M20.**
[ORIGIN Spanish, lit. 'half-turn'.]
BULLFIGHTING. A method of killing a bull by approaching and stabbing it from behind.

medic /ˈmɛdɪk/ *noun*[1] & *adjective*[1]. **E17.**
[ORIGIN Latin *medicus*, from *mederi* heal (noun perh. infl. by Old French *médique* physician): see -IC. Partly also abbreviation of MEDICAL.]
▸ **A** *noun*. A physician, a medical practitioner; a medical student. Now *colloq.* **E17.**

K. BOYLE Our medics are up there shooting the people full of inoculations.

▸ **B** *adjective*. = MEDICAL *adjective*. *poet.* **E18.**

Medic /ˈmiːdɪk/ *noun*[2] & *adjective*[2]. **L19.**
[ORIGIN Latin *Medicus* from Greek *Mēdikos* Median: see -IC.]
= MEDIAN *noun*[1] & *adjective*[1].

medica /ˈmiːdɪkə/ *noun*. Now *rare*. **LME.**
[ORIGIN Latin: see MEDICK.]
= MEDICK.

medicable /ˈmɛdɪkəb(ə)l/ *adjective*. **L16.**
[ORIGIN Latin *medicabilis*, from *medicare*, -*ari*: see MEDICATE, -ABLE.]
†**1** Possessing medicinal properties. **L16–M17.**
2 Able to be treated or cured medically. **E17.**

J. ARMSTRONG For want of timely care Millions have died of medicable wounds.

Medicaid /ˈmɛdɪkeɪd/ *noun*. Also **m-**. **M20.**
[ORIGIN from MEDIC(AL *adjective* + AID *noun*.]
In the US, a scheme providing state and Federal funds for people needing assistance with medical expenses. Cf. MEDICARE.

medical /ˈmɛdɪk(ə)l/ *adjective* & *noun*. **M17.**
[ORIGIN French *médical* or medieval Latin *medicalis*, from Latin *medicus* physician, from *mederi* heal: see -AL[1]. Cf. MEDIC *noun*[1] & *adjective*[1].]
▸ **A** *adjective*. **1** Of or pertaining to the science or practice of medicine in general; of or pertaining to medicine as opp. to surgery. **M17.** ▸**b** Of or pertaining to conditions requiring medical (esp. as opp. to surgical) treatment or diagnosis. **L19.**

R. INGALLS He isn't the kind to go flipping through medical dictionaries. *Daily Telegraph* The drug epidemiology unit of Boston University Medical Centre. **b** E. KUZWAYO And this sudden new medical condition—was it caused by prison conditions?

2 Curative; medicinal. *rare*. **M17.**
– SPECIAL COLLOCATIONS: **medical board** a body of medical experts responsible for the medical examination of soldiers, the maintenance of public health, etc. **medical certificate** a certificate from a doctor giving the state of a person's health. **medical examiner** (**a**) a doctor who carries out an examination for physical health or fitness; (**b**) *US* a medically qualified public officer who investigates unusual or suspicious deaths, performs postmortems, and initiates inquests. **medical garden** (an area of) a garden devoted to the cultivation of medicinal plants. **medical hall** in Ireland, a pharmacy, a chemist's shop. **medical jurisprudence** the law as it relates to the practice of medicine. **medical officer** a doctor appointed by a company or public authority to attend to matters relating to health. **medical practitioner** a person who practises medicine; *esp.* (in Britain) one who has a registered qualification in medicine. **medical register** a register of all doctors legally in practice. **medical school** (a school or faculty of) a college or university in which medicine is studied.
▸ **B** *noun*. **1** A student or practitioner of medicine. *colloq.* **E19.**
2 An examination to determine the state of a person's physical health or fitness. **E20.**

A. MCCOWEN I didn't pass the Medical owing to my bad sight.

■ **medically** *adverb* in a medical manner; with respect to medical science or practice or the medical profession: **M17.**

medicalize /ˈmɛdɪk(ə)lʌɪz/ *verb trans.* Also **-ise**. **L20.**
[ORIGIN from MEDICAL + -IZE. Cf. French *médicaliser*.]
Give a medical character to; involve medicine in, view in medical terms, esp. unwarrantedly.
■ **medicaliˈzation** *noun* **L20.**

M

medicament /mɪˈdɪkəm(ə)nt, ˈmɛdɪk-/ *noun* & *verb*. **LME.**
[ORIGIN French *médicament* or Latin *medicamentum*, from *medicari*: see MEDICATE, -MENT.]
▸ **A** *noun*. A substance used for medical treatment; a medicine, a remedy. **LME.**

MORTIMER COLLINS There are few medicaments equal to walking at your fastest pace.

▸ **B** *verb trans.* Administer medicaments to. *rare*. **M19.**
■ **medicaˈmental** *adjective* (long *rare*) of the nature of a medicament, medicinal **M17.** **medicaˈmentally** *adverb* (now *rare*) **M17.** **medicaˈmentary** *adjective* (long *rare*) of the nature of or pertaining to a medicament or medicaments **L16.**

Medicare /ˈmɛdɪkɛː/ *noun*. Also **m-**. **M20.**
[ORIGIN from MEDI(CAL *adjective* + CARE *noun*.]
In the US, a health insurance scheme for people over 65 years of age; in Canada and Australia, a national health care scheme financed by taxation. Cf. MEDICAID, DENTICARE.

medicaster /ˈmɛdɪkastə/ *noun*. Now *rare*. **M17.**
[ORIGIN French *médicastre* or its source Italian *medicastro*, ult. from Latin *medicus*: see MEDIC *noun*[1] & *adjective*[1], -ASTER.]
A pretender to medical skill, a quack.

medicate /ˈmɛdɪkeɪt/ *verb trans.* **E17.**
[ORIGIN Latin *medicat-* pa. ppl stem of *medicari* administer remedies to, from *medicus*: see MEDIC *noun*[1] & *adjective*[1], -ATE[3].]
1 Treat medically; administer remedies to, heal, cure. **E17.**
2 a Impregnate *with* a medicinal substance. Freq. as ***medicated ppl adjective***. **E17.** ▸†**b** Treat or mix (a thing) *with* drugs or other substances; adulterate (food etc.). **M17–M19.**

a *Lancet* The soap is pleasantly medicated with . . eucalyptus. *Trade Marks Journal* A medicated preparation in tablet form for human use as a sedative and hypnotic.

■ **medicative** *adjective* (now *rare*) curative, healing **M17.**

medication /mɛdɪˈkeɪʃ(ə)n/ *noun*. **LME.**
[ORIGIN Latin *medicatio(n-)*, formed as MEDICATE: see -ATION. Cf. French *médication*.]
1 The action of treating medically; treatment with a medicinal substance. **LME.**
2 The action of impregnating with a medicinal substance. **M18.**
3 A drug or drugs prescribed or given as medical treatment. **M20.**

D. W. GOODWIN Nor is there evidence that antidepressant medications are useful in the treatment of alcoholism. B. SPOCK The doctor can prescribe medication to relieve the symptoms.

Medicean /mɛdɪˈtʃiːən, -siːən, mɛˈdiːtʃɪən/ *adjective*. **M17.**
[**ORIGIN** mod. Latin *Mediceus*, from Italian *Medici* (see below) + **-AN**.]
Of or pertaining to the Medici family, rulers of Florence during the 15th cent.

Medici /ˈmɛdɪtʃi, mɛˈdiːtʃi/ *adjective*. **M19.**
[**ORIGIN** See **MEDICEAN**.]
Of, pertaining to, or associated with the Medici family.
Medici collar a large pleated fan-shaped collar standing upright at the rear and sloping to meet a low neckline at the front. **Medici lace** a type of fine intricately worked lace, scalloped on one edge.

medicinable /ˈmɛdsɪnəb(ə)l, ˈmɛdɪsɪn-/ *adjective*. Now *arch.* or *poet.* **LME.**
[**ORIGIN** Old French *medecinable*, from *medeciner*: see **MEDICINE** *verb*, **-ABLE**.]
= **MEDICINAL** *adjective* 1.

medicinal /məˈdɪsɪn(ə)l/ *adjective & noun*. **LME.**
[**ORIGIN** Old French & mod. French *médicinal* from Latin *medicinalis*, from *medecina*: see **MEDICINE** *noun*[1], **-AL**[1].]
▸ **A** *adjective*. **1** Having healing or curative properties or attributes; therapeutic. **LME.**

J. BETJEMAN Your medicinal springs where their wives took the waters. JULIAN GLOAG A glass of Burgundy to go with it—purely for medicinal purposes, of course.

medicinal leech a leech, *Hirudo medicinalis*, used (now infrequently) for blood-letting.
2 Of or pertaining to the science or the practice of medicine. **LME.** ▸**b** Resembling (that of) medicine or a medicine. **E19.**
▸ **B** *noun*. A medicinal substance. **M17.**
■ **medicinally** *adverb* **LME.**

medicine /ˈmɛds(ə)n; ˈmɛdɪsɪn/ *noun*[1]. **ME.**
[**ORIGIN** Old French *medecine*, *-icine* (mod. *médecine*) from Latin *medicina*, from *medicus*: see **MEDIC** *noun*[1] & *adjective*[1], **-INE**[4].]
1 The science or practice of the diagnosis and treatment of illness and injury and the preservation of health; *spec.* the science or practice of restoring and preserving health by drugs and the regulation of diet, habits, etc., rather than by surgical methods. **ME.**

J. T. FLEXNER Morgan apprenticed himself to an experienced doctor; there was no other way of studying medicine. J. RABAN Traditional Arab medicine—the herbal remedies which were now banned in the new hospitals.

2 A substance or preparation used in the treatment of illness; a medicament, a drug; *esp.* one taken orally. Also, such substances generally. **ME.** ▸**b** *fig.* A remedy, *esp.* one which is necessary but disagreeable or unwelcome. **ME.**

J. WESLEY One of the mistresses . . near death . . found no help from all the medicines she had taken. **b** M. R. MITFORD He finds in constant employment a medicine for great grief.

†**3** A drug used for other than remedial purposes, as a cosmetic, poison, potion, etc. **LME–E17.**
4 Among N. American Indians, (an object or practice thought to possess) magical, esp. healing or protective, power. **E19.** ▸**b** = ***medicine man*** below. **E19.**
5 Alcoholic drink. Now also, narcotic, esp. addictive, drugs. *slang*. **M19.**
– **PHRASES**: **a dose of one's own medicine**, **a taste of one's own medicine**, etc., repayment or retaliation in kind, tit for tat. **bad medicine** (*a*) among N. American Indians, bad luck (regarded as able to be inherited or acquired); (*b*) *slang* a thing or person regarded as being sinister or ill-omened. ***clinical medicine***: see **CLINICAL** 1. ***forensic medicine***: see **FORENSIC** *adjective*. ***fringe medicine***: see **FRINGE** *adjective*. ***nuclear medicine***: see **NUCLEAR** *adjective*. ***patent medicine***: see **PATENT** *adjective*. ***preventive medicine***: see **PREVENTIVE** *adjective*. ***social medicine***: see **SOCIAL** *adjective*. ***socialized medicine***: see **SOCIALIZE** *verb* 2. **take one's medicine** submit to or endure something necessary or deserved but disagreeable; learn a lesson.
– **COMB.**: **medicine ball** a large heavy stuffed usu. leather ball thrown and caught for exercise; **medicine chest** a box containing medicines, items for first aid, etc.; **medicine glass** a small drinking glass graduated for use in measuring medicines; **medicine line** (now *rare*) among N. American Indians, the border between Canada and the US; **medicine lodge** a structure used for religious ceremonies by certain N. American Indian peoples; a religious society among these peoples; **medicine man** (*a*) a healer or shaman among N. American Indians and other peoples; (*b*) *colloq.* a doctor; **medicine murder** murder committed to obtain parts of the body for medicine; ritual murder; **medicine seal** *ARCHAEOLOGY* a small cubical or oblong stone with inscriptions in intaglio, apparently used by Roman physicians for marking their drugs; **medicine show** *N. Amer.* a travelling show in which entertainers attract customers to whom medicine can be sold; **medicine stamp** = ***medicine seal*** above; **medicine tree** the horseradish tree; **medicine wheel** a stone circle built by N. American Indians; **medicine wolf** *US* = **COYOTE**; **medicine woman** a N. American Indian female healer or shaman.

†**medicine** *noun*[2]. **LME–M17.**
[**ORIGIN** Old French & mod. French *médecin* or its source medieval Latin *medicinus* physician, use as noun of Latin *medicinus* adjective, from *medicus*: see **MEDICINE** *noun*[1].]
A medical practitioner.

medicine /ˈmɛds(ə)n; ˈmɛdɪsɪn/ *verb trans. arch.* **LME.**
[**ORIGIN** Old French & mod. French *médeciner*, formed as **MEDICINE** *noun*[1].]
1 Treat or cure by means of medicine; give medicine to. **LME.**
†**2** Bring *to* a certain state by medicinal means. *rare*. **E17–E19.**

SHAKES. *Oth.* Not poppy, nor mandragora . . Shall ever medicine thee to that sweet sleep.

mediciner /mɪˈdɪsɪnə, ˈmɛdsɪnə/ *noun. arch.* (orig. *Scot.*). **LME.**
[**ORIGIN** from **MEDICINE** *noun*[1], *verb* + **-ER**[1]. Cf. Old French *medecineur*.]
A physician, a healer.

medick /ˈmiːdɪk/ *noun*. **LME.**
[**ORIGIN** Latin *medica* from Greek *Mēdikē* (*poa*) lit. 'Median (grass)'.]
Any of various leguminous plants of the genus *Medicago*, sometimes grown as fodder; *esp.* (*a*) (more fully ***purple medick***) lucerne, *M. sativa*; (*b*) (more fully ***black medick***) *M. lupulina*.

medico /ˈmɛdɪkəʊ/ *noun*. Now *slang* or *joc.* Pl. **-o(e)s**. **L17.**
[**ORIGIN** Italian from Latin *medicus* **MEDIC** *noun*[1].]
A medical practitioner; a medical student.

medico- /ˈmɛdɪkəʊ/ *combining form*. **M17.**
[**ORIGIN** from Latin *medicus* **MEDIC** *noun*[1] + **-O-**.]
Forming chiefly adjectives with the sense 'designating or pertaining to medicine and —', as ***medico-botanical***, ***medico-legal***, ***medico-social***, etc.

mediety /mɪˈdʌɪɪti/ *noun*. **LME.**
[**ORIGIN** Late Latin *medietas* half (in classical Latin middle), from Latin *medius* **MID** *adjective*: see **-ITY**. Cf. **MOIETY**.]
1 †**a** A half. **LME–L17.** ▸**b** *LAW*. Either of two parts into which something (esp. an ecclesiastical benefice) is divided, a moiety. **E17.**
†**2** A middle or intermediate state, position, or quality. **L16–M17.**
†**3** *MATH*. (The quality of being) a mean. **L16–L17.**

medieval /mɛdɪˈiːv(ə)l, miː-/ *adjective & noun*. Also **mediaeval**. **E19.**
[**ORIGIN** from mod. Latin *medium aevum* middle age + **-AL**[1]. Cf. earlier **MIDDLE AGE** *noun* 2, **MIDDLE-AGED** 2.]
▸ **A** *adjective*. Of, pertaining to, or characteristic of the Middle Ages. Also (*colloq.*), old-fashioned, archaic, primitive; *spec.* barbarous, cruel. **E19.**

Edinburgh Review The economic difference between ancient, medieval and modern society. J. GATHORNE-HARDY It was a medieval farmhouse, and it hadn't been modernised. M. MCCARTHY It was medieval of Macy's to fire her because she'd had a breakdown.

Medieval Greek, ***Medieval history***, ***Medieval Latin***, etc.
▸ **B** *noun*. A person who lived in the Middle Ages. **M19.**
■ **medievalism** *noun* (*a*) belief and practice characteristic of the Middle Ages; medieval thought, religion, art, etc.; (*b*) adherence to or interest in medieval ideals or styles; an instance of this: **M19.** **medievalist** *noun* (*a*) a person who lived in the Middle Ages; (*b*) an expert in or student of medieval history, culture, etc.; a person practising medievalism in art, religion, etc.: **M19.** **medievalize** *verb* (*a*) *verb trans.* make medieval in character; (*b*) *verb intrans.* favour medieval ideas or styles: **M19.** **medievally** *adverb* **M19.**

medimnus /mɪˈdɪmnəs/ *noun*. Pl. **-ni** /-nʌɪ/. Also anglicized as **medimn(e)** /mɪˈdɪm/. **L16.**
[**ORIGIN** Latin from Greek *medimnos*. Cf. French *médimne*.]
An ancient Greek unit of capacity equivalent to approx. 55 litres, or 12 gallons.

medin /mɛˈdiːn/ *noun*. Also **-ine**. **L16.**
[**ORIGIN** French *médin*, Italian *medino* from colloq. Arabic *maydī* from the Sultan al-*Mu'ayyad* Šayk, who first issued it in the 15th cent.: see **-INE**[1].]
A coin of low denomination, orig. of silver and later of bronze, formerly used in Egypt and corresponding to the Turkish para.

medina /mɪˈdiːnə/ *noun*. Also **M-**. **E20.**
[**ORIGIN** Arabic *madīna* town, city.]
The old Arab or non-European quarter of a N. African town.

Medinal /ˈmɛdɪn(ə)l/ *noun*. Also **m-**. **E20.**
[**ORIGIN** Perh. from **MEDI(CAL** + *Na* sodium + **-AL**[2].]
PHARMACOLOGY. (Proprietary name for) the drug barbitone sodium.

medio /ˈmɛdɪəʊ/ *noun*. Pl. **-os**. **E19.**
[**ORIGIN** Spanish = half.]
hist. A coin of low denomination used in Mexico and Cuba.

medio- /ˈmiːdɪəʊ/ *combining form*. **M19.**
[**ORIGIN** from Latin *medius* **MID** *adjective* + **-O-**.]
Of or relating to the middle (of an organ or part), as ***mediodorsal***, ***medio-occipital***, ***mediopassive***.

mediocre /miːdɪˈəʊkə/ *adjective*. Also †**médiocre**. **L16.**
[**ORIGIN** (French *médiocre* from) Latin *mediocris* of middle height or degree, from *medius* **MID** *adjective* + *ocris* rugged mountain.]
Of middling quality, neither bad nor good, average; indifferent, of poor quality, second-rate.

Observer Television—all it has ever done is to teach people how to tolerate mediocre entertainment. D. ROWE You cannot bear the thought of being mediocre and ordinary. *absol.*: *Law Times* The mediocre . . always form numerically the largest portion of every profession.

■ **mediocracy** *noun* (a group or state having) rule by mediocre people; a ruling body consisting of mediocre people: **L19.** ˈ**mediocrist** *noun* (now *rare*) a person of mediocre talents or ability **L18.**

mediocrity /miːdɪˈɒkrɪti/ *noun*. **LME.**
[**ORIGIN** Old French & mod. French *médiocrité* from Latin *mediocritas*, from *mediocris*: see **MEDIOCRE**, **-ITY**.]
†**1** Moderate fortune or condition in life. **LME–E19.**
2 The quality or condition of being intermediate between two extremes. Formerly also, a thing equally removed from two opposite extremes; a mean. **M16.**
†**3** A middle course of action; moderation, temperance. **M16–L18.**
†**4** The possession of attributes in a medium or moderate degree; moderate degree, quality, or amount. **L16–E19.**
5 The quality or condition of being mediocre. **L16.**

D. PARKER There are certain things . . beside which even distinguished, searching, passionate novels pale to mediocrity.

6 A person of mediocre talents or ability. **L17.**

C. C. TRENCH A worthy mediocrity of great application and dignity, but no talent save for time-serving.

■ **medi͵ocritiˈzation** *noun* (orig. *US*) the action or process of making mediocre; reduction to a common level of mediocrity: **L20.** **mediocritize** *verb trans.* make mediocre, reduce to a common level of mediocrity. **L20.**

mediopalatal /͵miːdɪəʊˈpalət(ə)l/ *adjective*. **E20.**
[**ORIGIN** from **MEDIO-** + **PALATAL** *adjective*.]
PHONETICS. Articulated with the tongue against the middle part of the hard palate; designating this part of the palate.

mediopassive /͵miːdɪəʊˈpasɪv/ *adjective & noun*. **L19.**
[**ORIGIN** from **MEDIO-** + **PASSIVE**.]
GRAMMAR. (Pertaining to or designating) the middle voice of a verb or a voice equivalent to the middle and passive voices.

Medise *verb* var. of **MEDIZE**.

Medism /ˈmiːdɪz(ə)m/ *noun*. **M19.**
[**ORIGIN** Greek *mēdismos*, from *Mēdizein* **MEDIZE**.]
1 *GREEK HISTORY*. Sympathy with or favouring of the Medes or Persians, enemies of Greece in the 6th and 5th cents. BC, on the part of a Greek. **M19.**
2 A word or idiom belonging to the language of the Medes. **M19.**

meditate /ˈmɛdɪteɪt/ *verb*. **M16.**
[**ORIGIN** Latin *meditat-* pa. ppl stem of *meditari* frequentative from Indo-European stem meaning 'measure': see **-ATE**[3]. Cf. **METE** *verb*, **MODE**.]
1 *verb intrans.* Exercise the mental faculties in (esp. religious or spiritual) thought or contemplation. (Foll. by *on*, *upon*, *over*.) **M16.**

R. K. NARAYAN He has renounced the world; he does nothing but meditate. J. R. ACKERLEY My study was understood to be private ground where the Great Mind could meditate undisturbed. A. BELL He frequently meditated on the moral qualities of sound diet.

2 *verb trans.* Muse over, reflect on; consider, study, ponder. Also, plan by turning over in the mind, conceive mentally, (a thing, †*to do*). **L16.** ▸**b** Fix one's attention on; observe intently or with interest. **E18.**

G. SARTON We ought to meditate the immortal words of Pericles. J. CONRAD The cat . . seemed to meditate a leap. W. S. CHURCHILL The British had remained at Halifax awaiting reinforcements . . and meditating their strategy.

■ **meditant** *adjective & noun* (*rare*) (*a*) *adjective* meditating; (*b*) *noun* a person who meditates: **M17.** **meditater** *noun* = **MEDITATOR M19.** **meditatingly** *adverb* meditatively **M18.** **meditator** *noun* a person who meditates **E17.**

meditation /mɛdɪˈteɪʃ(ə)n/ *noun*. **ME.**
[**ORIGIN** Old French & mod. French *méditation* from Latin *meditatio(n-)*, formed as **MEDITATE**: see **-ATION**.]
1 a The action or practice of profound spiritual or religious reflection or mental contemplation. **ME.** ▸**b** Continuous thought on one subject; (a period of) serious and sustained reflection or mental contemplation. **LME.**

a J. HEWITT Buddhist meditation utilizes Yoga . . which lays emphasis on the trance. J. DISKI I imagine myself walking silent cloisters, my head bent in meditation. **b** K. J. DOVER Philosophy . . was not the product of solitary meditation, to be communicated by a spell-binding orator.

a *Transcendental Meditation*: see **TRANSCENDENTAL**.
2 A written or spoken discourse, freq. on a religious subject, arising from considered thought. **ME.**

Sunday Express These ideas are often meditations on a theme, rather than jokes or anecdotes.

meditative /ˈmɛdɪtətɪv, -teɪtɪv/ *adjective & noun*. **E17.**
[**ORIGIN** from **MEDITATE** + **-IVE**; partly from Old French & mod. French *méditatif*, *-ive* (noun from late Latin *meditativus*).]
▸ **A** *adjective*. **1** Inclined or accustomed to meditation. Also, engaged in the meditation *of*. **E17.**

J. R. GREEN The melancholy and meditative Jaques.

2 Accompanied by or indicative of meditation; pertaining to meditation. **M18.**
†**3** *GRAMMAR*. = **DESIDERATIVE** *adjective* 1. Only in **M18.**

▸ †**B** *noun.* GRAMMAR = DESIDERATIVE *noun.* E17–M19.
▪ **meditatively** *adverb* E19. **meditativeness** *noun* M19.

Mediterranean /ˌmɛdɪtəˈreɪnɪən/ *adjective & noun.* Also **m-**. M16.
[ORIGIN Latin *mediterraneus* inland, from *medius* MID *adjective* + *terra* land, earth; in late Latin applied to the Mediterranean Sea, *Mare Mediterraneum*: see -AN, -EAN.]
▸ **A** *adjective* **1 a** ***Mediterranean Sea***, the almost land-locked sea separating southern Europe from Africa, connected with the Atlantic Ocean by the Strait of Gibraltar, with the Black Sea by the Bosphorus, and (now) with the Red Sea by the Suez Canal. M16. ▸**b** Of, pertaining to, or characteristic of the Mediterranean Sea; of, pertaining to, or characteristic of countries bordering the Mediterranean Sea or their inhabitants. M16.
b Mediterranean climate the climate of countries around the Mediterranean Sea, characterized by hot dry summers and mild wet winters; any similar climate elsewhere. **Mediterranean fruit fly** a tephritid fruit fly, *Ceratitis capitata*, whose maggots burrow into citrus and other fruits; also called ***medfly***.
2 (Of water) nearly or entirely surrounded by land, land-locked; (of land) inland, remote from the coast. E17.
▸ **B** *noun.* **1** *The* Mediterranean Sea. Also, an inland sea or lake, a body of water nearly or entirely surrounded by dry land. E17.
2 A human physical type found especially in countries bordering the Mediterranean Sea, characteristically dark-complexioned and not tall; a person of this physical type. L19.
▪ **Mediterraneanize** *verb trans.* make Mediterranean in character or attributes E20.

meditullium /mɛdɪˈtʌlɪəm/ *noun.* Now *rare* or *obsolete.* E17.
[ORIGIN Latin, from *medius* MID *adjective* + 2nd elem. perh. cogn. with *tellus* earth.]
A middle part or substance; *spec.* †(***a***) ANATOMY = DIPLOE; (***b***) BOTANY an inner layer in a leaf, root, etc.

medium /ˈmiːdɪəm/ *noun & adjective.* Pl. of noun **-ia** /-ɪə/, **-iums**. See also MEDIA *noun*². L16.
[ORIGIN Latin, lit. 'middle, midst', (in medieval Latin) 'means', use as noun of *medius* MID *adjective.* Cf. French *médium.*]
▸ **A** *noun.* **1** A middle quality, degree, or condition; something intermediate in nature or degree. L16. ▸†**b** Moderation. L17–L18.

I. MILNER Is there no medium between going to Court, and going a hunting?

†**2** LOGIC. The middle term of a syllogism; a ground of proof or inference. L16–E19.
3 a An intervening substance through which a force acts on objects at a distance or through which impressions are conveyed to the senses, as air, water, etc. L16. ▸**b** A pervading or enveloping substance; the substance in which an organism lives or is cultured; *fig.* one's environment, one's usual social setting. M17.

a *fig.*: H. JAMES The intensely habitual stillness offered a submissive medium to the sound of a distant church bell. D. JACOBSON What a strange medium time is: transparent when you look back.. opaque when you.. look forward. **b** G. GROTE You cannot thus abstract any man from the social medium by which he is surrounded. A. HARDY The shape of a fish is.. all-important in a fluid medium.

†**4** A (geometric or arithmetic) mean; an average. E17–E19.
5 An intermediate agency, instrument, or channel; a means; *spec.* a channel of mass communication, as newspapers, radio, television, etc. See also MEDIA *noun*². E17.

SLOAN WILSON Television is developing into the greatest medium for mass education and entertainment. H. READ If we have ideas to express, the proper medium is Language.

6 a A person acting as an intermediary, a mediator. *rare.* E19. ▸**b** (Pl. **-iums**.) A person thought to be in contact with the spirits of the dead and to communicate between the living and the dead. M19.
7 A liquid substance with which a pigment is mixed for use in painting. Also, anything used as a raw material by an artist etc.; a style or variety of art, as determined by the materials or artistic form used. M19. ▸**b** PHOTOGRAPHY. A varnish used as a material in retouching. L19.

H. BELLOC Four pictures were set in the walls.. mosaics, they seemed—but he did not examine their medium closely. *Sunday Express* Water colour is his medium. ROSEMARY MANNING Despite my occasional wish that I had been a painter.. words are my medium.

8 THEATRICAL. A screen fixed in front of a light source in order to throw a coloured light on a stage. M19.
9 COMMERCE. A medium-dated security. M20.
– PHRASES: ***circulating medium***: see CIRCULATE. ***contrast medium***: see CONTRAST *noun.* ***happy medium***: see HAPPY *adjective.* ***mass medium***: see MASS *noun*² & *adjective.* **medium of circulation**, **medium of exchange** a thing serving as the instrument of commercial transactions, as coin, notes, etc. ***TYRODE's medium***.
▸ **B** *adjective.* †**1** Average, mean. L17–E19.
2 Intermediate between two or more degrees in size, character, amount, quality, etc.; *spec.* (***a***) (of paper) between royal and demy in size, usu. 600 × 470 mm; (***b***) (of wine etc.) having a flavour midway between dry and sweet; (***c***) (of meat) cooked between well done and rare. E18.

A. JUDD He was of medium height, slightly built. T. BERGER You don't want a violent boil; just.. firm and medium, a little higher than a simmer.

– SPECIAL COLLOCATIONS & COMB.: **medium bowler** CRICKET a bowler who bowls at a medium pace. **medium bowling** CRICKET: in which the ball travels at a medium speed. **medium close-up** a cinematic or television shot intermediate between a medium shot and a close-up. **medium-dated** *adjective* (COMMERCE) (of a security) having between five and fifteen years until expiry. **medium frequency** an intermediate frequency (of oscillation); *spec.* a frequency of a medium wave, between 300 and 3000 kilohertz. **medium-pacer** *colloq.* (CRICKET) = ***medium bowler*** above. **medium-range** *adjective* (of an aircraft etc.) able to travel a medium distance. **medium rare** (of meat) cooked between medium and rare. **medium shot** a cinematic or television shot intermediate between a close-up and a long shot. **medium wave** TELECOMMUNICATIONS a radio wave with wavelength between a hundred metres and a kilometre.
▪ **mediumism** *noun* the practices or profession of a spiritualistic medium M19. **mediuˈmistic** *adjective* of, pertaining to, or having the characteristics of a spiritualistic medium M19. **mediumly** *adverb* moderately, to a medium or average extent E20. **mediumship** *noun* (***a***) the state or condition of being or acting as a spiritualistic medium; (***b***) intervening agency, intermediation: M19.

medius /ˈmiːdɪəs/ *noun.* Long *rare.* M16.
[ORIGIN Latin, lit. 'middle'.]
MUSIC. = MEAN *noun*¹ 1.

medivac *noun* var. of MEDEVAC.

Medize /ˈmiːdʌɪz/ *verb intrans.* Also **-ise**, **m-**. E17.
[ORIGIN Greek *Mēdizein*, from *Mēdoi* Medes: see MEDE, -IZE.]
GREEK HISTORY. Of a Greek: sympathize with or favour the interests of the Medes or Persians, enemies of Greece in the 6th and 5th cents. BC. Cf. MEDISM.

medjidie /mɛˈdʒiːdɪeɪ/ *noun.* M19.
[ORIGIN Turkish *mecidiye* silver coins, from *Mejid* (see below).]
1 *the Medjidie*, a Turkish order or decoration instituted by the Sultan Abdul-Mejid (1823–61). M19.
2 A Turkish silver coin first minted by the Sultan Abdul-Mejid, equal to 20 piastres. L19.

medlar /ˈmɛdlə/ *noun.* LME.
[ORIGIN Old French *medler* from var. of *mesle* from Latin *mespila, -us, -um* from Greek *mespilē, mespilon*: for the ending cf. *cedar, poplar.*]
1 The tree *Mespilus germanica*, of the rose family, grown for its fruit (also ***medlar tree***). Also (with specifying word), any of several related trees. LME.
Japanese medlar: see JAPANESE *adjective.* **Neapolitan medlar**, **oriental medlar** the azarole, *Crataegus azarolus*.
2 The fruit of the medlar tree, like a small brown-skinned apple with a large cup-shaped 'eye' between the persistent calyx lobes, which is eaten when half-rotten. LME.

medley /ˈmɛdli/ *noun, adjective, & verb.* ME.
[ORIGIN Old French *medlee* var. of *meslee* MÊLÉE from Proto-Romance use as noun of fem. pa. pple of medieval Latin *misculare* mix. Cf. MEDDLE.]
▸ **A** *noun.* **1** Combat, conflict; fighting, esp. hand-to-hand. *arch.* ME.
2 A combination, a mixture, a collection, now *esp.* a heterogeneous one, a miscellany; *spec.* (***a***) a cloth woven with wools of different colours or shades; (***b***) a musical composition consisting of parts or subjects of a diverse or incongruous nature; a group of (parts of) songs or instrumental pieces performed together as a continuous whole; (***c***) a literary miscellany or collection; (***d***) a relay race in which team members swim sections in different strokes, run distances of unequal length, etc. ME.

M. DE LA ROCHE A strange medley of bowls, vases, and boxes—Eastern and English, ancient and Victorian. R. MACAULAY A medley of harsh.. voices, raised in dispute. R. P. JHABVALA The string quartet had struck up a medley of old Broadway show tunes.

▸ **B** *adjective.* †**1** Of a mixed colour; variegated, motley. ME–L17.
2 Composed of diverse or incongruous parts or elements; mixed, motley. LME.
▸ **C** *verb trans.* Pa. t. & pple **medleyed**, **medlied**. Make a mixture of; intermix. Usu. in *pass.* LME.

Medo- /ˈmiːdəʊ/ *combining form.* M18.
[ORIGIN from Latin *Medus* from Greek *Mēdos*, from *Medoi*: see MEDE, -O-.]
Forming nouns and adjectives in the sense 'Median and —', as ***Medo-Persian***.

Médoc /meɪˈdɒk, *foreign* medɔk (*pl. same*)/ *noun.* Also **Medoc**. M19.
[ORIGIN French: see below.]
A red wine produced in Médoc, an area in SW France.

medrese *noun* var. of MADRASAH.

medrinaque /mɛdrɪˈnaki, *foreign* medriˈɲake/ *noun.* Now *rare* or *obsolete.* E18.
[ORIGIN Spanish *medriñaque*, of unknown origin.]
Fibre from the sago palm and other trees of the Philippines; cloth made from this fibre.

medulla /mɛˈdʌlə/ *noun.* LME.
[ORIGIN Latin = pith, marrow, perh. from *medius* MID *adjective.*]
BIOLOGY. **1** ANATOMY. ▸**a** The (inner) substance of the brain and spinal cord. Now *rare* or *obsolete.* LME. ▸**b** ANATOMY & ZOOLOGY. The marrow of a bone. Also, the central part or substance of various organs or structures where distinguishable from a cortex, e.g. of a kidney, adrenal gland, hair, or feather; pith. LME. ▸**c** In full ***medulla oblongata*** /ɒblɒŋˈɡɑːtə/ [Latin, lit. 'prolonged marrow']. The continuation of the spinal cord within the cranium, forming the hindmost part of the brain and containing regulatory centres for the heart, lungs, swallowing reflex, etc. L17. ▸**d** The myelin sheath of a nerve. Now *rare.* M19.
b ADRENAL ***medulla***.
2 BOTANY. The pith or soft internal tissue of a plant. M17.
†**3** *fig.* The essential or central matter of a subject. Also, a compendium, a summary. M17–M18.

medullar /mɪˈdʌlə/ *adjective.* Now *rare* or *obsolete.* M16.
[ORIGIN Late Latin *medullaris*, formed as MEDULLA: see -AR¹.]
= MEDULLARY.

medullary /mɛˈdʌl(ə)ri, ˈmɛd(ə)l-/ *adjective.* E17.
[ORIGIN formed as MEDULLA: see -ARY².]
1 †**a** Of or pertaining to the soft pulp of a fruit. E17–E19. ▸**b** BOTANY. Of, pertaining to, or designating the pith of a plant. M19.
b medullary ray each of the sheets of tissue in the stem of a dicotyledonous plant that extend radially from the pith to the cortex between the vascular bundles. **medullary sheath** in some higher plants, a layer of cells surrounding the pith of the stem.
2 *transf. & fig.* Pertaining to the inner part of anything. Long *rare.* M17.
3 ANATOMY & ZOOLOGY. Pertaining to or designating the medulla of an organ or structure or the medulla oblongata. L17.
medullary plate EMBRYOLOGY = ***neural plate*** s.v. NEURAL *adjective.*
4 MEDICINE. = ENCEPHALOID. E19.
▪ **medullated** /ˈmɛd(ə)leɪtɪd, mɛˈdʌl-/ *adjective* (of a nerve or nerve fibre) myelinated M19.

medulloblastoma /mɛˌdʌləʊblaˈstəʊmə/ *noun.* Pl. **-mas**, **-mata** /-mətə/. E20.
[ORIGIN from MEDULLA + -O- + BLASTO- + -OMA.]
MEDICINE. A malignant brain tumour in children.

medusa /mɪˈdjuːzə, -sə/ *noun.* Pl. **-sae** /-ziː, -siː/, **-sas**. LME.
[ORIGIN Latin from Greek *Medousa* the only mortal one of the three Gorgons in Greek mythol., with snakes for hair and a gaze which turned any beholder to stone: in sense 2 orig. as mod. Latin genus name.]
1 (Usu. **M-**.) A terrifying or ugly woman, a gorgon. LME.
2 A jellyfish; *spec.* in ZOOLOGY, a coelenterate in the medusoid stage of its life cycle. M18.
– COMB.: **medusa fish** the stromateoid fish *Icichthys lockingtoni* (family Centrolophidae) of the N. Pacific, the young of which often swim close to jellyfishes.
▪ **medusal** *adjective* = MEDUSAN *adjective* M19. **medusan** *adjective & noun* (***a***) *adjective* of, pertaining to, or resembling a medusa, or (occas.) the Gorgon Medusa; (***b***) *noun* a medusoid coelenterate: L18.

Medusa's head /mɪˌdjuːzəz ˈhɛd, -səz/ *noun phr.* M16.
[ORIGIN from MEDUSA + -'S¹ + HEAD *noun.*]
1 ASTRONOMY. A cluster of stars including the bright star Algol, in the constellation Perseus. M16.
2 a A succulent southern African spurge, *Euphorbia caput-Medusae*, with many long drooping branches. M18. ▸**b** A Malayan orchid, *Bulbophyllum medusae*, with lateral sepals prolonged into threadlike processes. M19.
3 Any of various brittlestars with long, flexible, freq. branched arms; a basket fish. L18.

medusiform /mɪˈdjuːsɪfɔːm/ *adjective.* M19.
[ORIGIN from MEDUSA'S HEAD + -I- + -FORM.]
ZOOLOGY. = MEDUSOID *adjective.*

medusoid /mɪˈdjuːsɔɪd/ *adjective & noun.* M19.
[ORIGIN from MEDUSA + -OID.]
ZOOLOGY. ▸**A** *adjective.* Resembling a jellyfish or medusa; designating or pertaining to the reproductive, usu. free-swimming, stage of many coelenterates, in which the animal has a more or less domed shape with a central, downward-facing mouth and one or more rings of tentacles. M19.
▸ **B** *noun.* A medusoid coelenterate; in some hydrozoans, a medusoid reproductive bud. Cf. HYDROID. M19.

mee /miː/ *noun.* M20.
[ORIGIN Chinese *miàn* (Wade–Giles *mien*) flour.]
A Chinese dish made with noodles and other ingredients, popular in Malaysia.

meech /miːtʃ/ *verb intrans.* Now chiefly *US.* E17.
[ORIGIN Dial. var. of MITCH *verb.*]
Retire from view; slink *off*; skulk *around*. Chiefly as ***meeching*** *ppl adjective.*

meed /miːd/ *noun.*
[ORIGIN Old English *mēd* = Old Frisian *mēde*, Old Saxon *mēda, mieda*, Old High German *mēta, mieta* (German *Miete*), from West Germanic, rel. to Old English *meord*, Gothic *mizdō* (from Germanic), Greek *misthos* reward.]
1 Orig., something given in return for labour or service, or for (good or ill) desert; recompense, reward. Later, a reward or prize given for excellence or achievement; one's merited portion *of* praise, honour, etc. Now *arch. & literary.* OE. ▸†**b** A gift. *rare.* Only in E17.

M

B. M. CROKER All the . . senior ladies, had received their due meed of attention. **b** SHAKES. *Timon* No meed but he repays Sevenfold above itself.

†**2** Reward dishonestly offered or accepted; bribery. ME–E19.
†**3** Merit, excellence, worth. LME–L18.

SHAKES. *3 Hen. VI* My meed hath got me fame.

4 A fair share or proportion *of*. E20.

Daily Telegraph The Golden Age had its meed of tin goods.

■ **meedless** *adjective* LME.

meeja /ˈmiːdʒə/ *noun*. *slang*. Also **-jer**. L20.
[ORIGIN Repr. a pronunc.]
= MEDIA *noun*² 1.

meek /miːk/ *adjective & adverb*. ME.
[ORIGIN Old Norse *mjúkr* soft, pliant, gentle, rel. to Gothic form attested in *mūkamōdei* meekness.]
▸ **A** *adjective* **1** †**a** Courteous, kind; merciful, indulgent. ME–E17. ▸**b** Not proud or self-willed; piously gentle in nature; humble, submissive. Also (now freq. *derog.*), inclined to submit tamely to oppression or injury, easily imposed on. ME.

a SHAKES. *Jul. Caes.* I am meek and gentle with these butchers! **b** J. WAINWRIGHT He was no longer the meek, apologetic Barker of a few months ago. A. T. ELLIS 'He'll think you're dying.' I was too meek to tell her that I wished I was. *absol.*: AV *Matt.* 5:5 Blessed are the meeke: for they shall inherit the earth.

b as meek as a lamb, **as meek as Moses**, etc., very meek.
†**2** Of an animal: tame, gentle, not fierce. ME–M16.
3 Not violent or strong; mild. *arch.* ME.

S. E. FERRIER A meek, gray, autumnal day.

▸ †**B** *adverb*. Meekly. *rare*. ME–E17.

SHAKES. *Macb.* This Duncan Hath borne his faculties so meek.

■ **meekly** *adverb* ME. **meekness** *noun* ME.

meek /miːk/ *verb*. Long *rare* or *obsolete*. ME.
[ORIGIN from MEEK *adjective & adverb*.]
1 *verb trans.* Make meek. ME.
†**2** *verb intrans.* Be or become meek. Only in ME.

meeken /ˈmiːk(ə)n/ *verb*. Now *rare*. ME.
[ORIGIN from MEEK *adjective* + -EN⁵.]
1 *verb trans.* Make meek; humble, tame; lessen the violence of; abase. ME.
2 *verb intrans.* Become meek or submissive; submit meekly (*to*). L15.

M

meemie /ˈmiːmi/ *noun*. *slang* (orig. *US*). In sense 2 also **mimi**. E20.
[ORIGIN Uncertain; in sense 2 prob. from the female forename *Mimi*, after MOANING *minnie*.]
1 Orig., a state of drunkenness, delirium tremens. Later, hysterics; a hysterical person. Freq. in ***the meemies***, ***the screaming meemies***. E20.
2 *hist.* ***screaming meemie***, a German rocket mortar in use in the Second World War. M20.

meerkat /ˈmɪəkat/ *noun*. L15.
[ORIGIN Dutch from Middle Low German *meerkatte* (Old High German *merikazza*, German *Meerkatze*) lit. 'sea cat', perh. orig. alt. of an oriental name: cf. Hindi *markaṭ*, Sanskrit *markaṭa* ape.]
†**1** A monkey. L15–M16.
2 Any of several mongooses of southern Africa, *esp.* the suricate or grey meerkat (see below). E19.
grey meerkat (*a*) a gregarious diurnal mongoose, *Suricata suricatta*, sometimes kept as a pet (also called ***suricate***, ***zenick***); (*b*) a solitary nocturnal mongoose, *Paracynictis selousi*. **red meerkat** a diurnal mongoose, *Cynictis penicillata*, with a tan coat. **slender-tailed meerkat** = ***grey meerkat*** (a) above.

meerschaum /ˈmɪəʃɔːm, -ʃəm/ *noun*. L18.
[ORIGIN German, from *Meer* sea (see MERE *noun*¹) + *Schaum* foam (see SCUM), translating Persian *kef-i-daryā* foam of sea, with ref. to its frothiness.]
1 Hydrated magnesium silicate occurring as a soft white or yellowish claylike mineral; sepiolite. L18.
2 A tobacco pipe with a bowl made from this. L18.

meese /miːz/ *noun*. *obsolete* exc. *dial.* Also **mese**.
[ORIGIN Old English *mēos* = Flemish *mies*, Old High German *mios*, Old Norse *mýrr* (see MIRE *noun*¹), from Germanic, whence also Old Norse *mosi* MOSS *noun*.]
Moss.

meet /miːt/ *noun*. E19.
[ORIGIN from MEET *verb*.]
1 A meeting; an assignation or appointment. E19. ▸**b** A meeting of criminals or with an illicit supplier of drugs. Also, a meeting place, *esp.* one used by thieves. *slang*. M19.
2 A meeting of hounds and people for a hunt. Also, an organized event at which a number of races or other athletic contests are held. M19.

Horse & Hound The Clifton Foot arrived with . . their hounds to join . . the Ilminster pack at a joint meet.

3 MATH. **a** A point, line, or surface of intersection. L19. ▸**b** The intersection of two or more sets; the infimum of two or more elements of a lattice. M20.

meet /miːt/ *adjective & adverb*. *arch.*
[ORIGIN Old English (West Saxon) *gemǣte* = Old High German *gamāzi* (German *gemäss*), formed as Y- + METE *verb*.]
▸ **A** *adjective*. †**1** Commensurate. Only in OE.
2 Having the proper dimensions; made to fit. Also, close-fitting, barely large enough. Long *rare* or *obsolete* exc. *Scot.* ME.
3 Suitable, fit, proper (*for, to do*). Also, (usu. *pred.*, of an action) fitting, becoming, proper. ME.

AV *Mark* 7:27 It is not meet to take the childrens bread, and to cast it vnto the dogges. V. SACKVILLE-WEST I should never suggest coming to tea. It would not be meet. S. DONALDSON They could not accept gifts without making meet return.

†**4** Equal (*to*), on the same level. Only in LME. ▸**b** ***be meet with***, be even with, be revenged on. L16–L17.
▸ **B** *adverb*. In a meet, fit, or proper manner; sufficiently. Also, exactly. Long *obsolete* exc. *dial.* ME.
■ **meetly** *adverb* fittingly, suitably; moderately: ME. **meetness** *noun* fitness, suitability; moderation: ME.

meet /miːt/ *verb*. Pa. t. & pple **met** /mɛt/.
[ORIGIN Old English *mētan*, (Northumbrian) *mœ̄ta*, *gemētan* (see Y-) = Old Frisian *mēta*, Old Saxon *mōtian* (Dutch *moeten*), Old Norse *mœta*, Gothic *gamotjan*, from Germanic base also of MOOT *noun*¹.]
▸ **I** *verb trans.* **1** Come on, come across, fall in with, find. Now *dial.* exc. as passing into sense 4 or as ***meet with*** (a) below. OE.
2 a Come face to face with (a person) from the opposite or a different direction. OE. ▸**b** Arrive intentionally in the presence of (an approaching person etc.) from the opposite or a different direction (freq. in ***go to meet***, ***run to meet***, etc.). Also, go somewhere to be present at the arrival of and welcome etc. (a person, a train, etc.). ME. ▸**c** Of an object: come into contact or association with (a person or thing moving on a different course). Also, (of a line, road, etc.) reach a point of contact or intersection with (another line, road, etc.). ME. ▸**d** Of an object of attention: present itself to, come to the notice of, (the hearing, sight, etc.). M17. ▸**e** NAUTICAL. Control the sheer of (a ship) by putting the helm towards the opposite side. L18.

a JAS. HOGG They perceived the two youths coming, as to meet them, on the same path. **b** OED An omnibus from the hotel meets all trains. G. GREENE I will arrange that he shall meet you here tomorrow. **c** LD MACAULAY The gibbet was set up where King Street meets Cheapside. H. ROTH The raw night air met him at the . . doorway. **d** G. M. TREVELYAN All that met his ear or eye. R. H. MOTTRAM The first object that met the gaze of the little party . . was Leon's garden ladder.

3 Encounter, experience, suffer (one's death, a certain fate or treatment, etc.). Now *rare* or *poet.*, exc. as in ***meet with*** below. OE.

M. PATTISON This generous appeal met no response. A. S. BYATT The awesome Flamborough Head, where so many have met terrible deaths.

4 Confront or oppose in battle, a contest, etc.; fight a duel with. OE. ▸**b** *fig.* Oppose or grapple with (an objection, difficulty, evil, etc.). M18.

LD MACAULAY The king did not then wish to meet them. F. E. SMEDLEY I should be forced to meet him . . if he were to challenge me. **b** J. R. GREEN The threats of Charles were met by Offa with defiance. D. ROWE We struggle on, meeting . . an endless stream of difficulties.

5 Come accidentally or intentionally into the company of or into personal relations with (a person); come across (a person) in the course of social or business dealings. ME.

S. HASTINGS She loved meeting new people.

6 Come into conformity with (a person, a person's wishes or opinions). L17.

LD MACAULAY The Estates . . would go as far as their consciences would allow to meet His Majesty's wishes.

7 Satisfy (a demand or need); satisfy the requirements of (a particular case); be able or sufficient to discharge (a financial obligation). L18.

H. MACMILLAN We received generous help to meet our urgent needs. K. M. E. MURRAY He had . . more demands on him than he could possibly meet. *Which?* All radial car tyres in this country must meet . . regulation standards.

▸ **II** *verb intrans.* **8** (Of things) come into contact, come together so as to occupy the same place; (of a line, road, etc.) reach a point of contact or intersection with another; (of a person's gaze, eyes, etc.) encounter the gaze, eyes, etc., of another. ME. ▸**b** Of qualities etc.: unite in the same person. L16. ▸†**c** Agree, tally. *rare*. L16–E19.

R. KIPLING East is East, and West is West, and never the twain shall meet. V. WOOLF Their eyes met for a second. E. BOWEN Plaits were strained round her skull to meet at the top. P. LARKIN Where sky and Lincolnshire and water meet. **b** J. T. FOWLER The nobility of two races met in the child.

9 Of two or more people: come from opposite or different directions to the same place or so as to be in each other's presence, either accidentally or intentionally; come face to face. Also foll. by *together*. LME. ▸†**b** Come to or be present at a meeting; keep an appointment. LME–E18. ▸**c** Of the members of a society, group, etc.: assemble for purposes of conference, business, etc. LME. ▸**d** Arrive at or be in mutual agreement. L18.

J. GAY We only part to meet again. E. PEACOCK They had not met for years. G. VIDAL She came towards him and they met beneath a portrait of her. **b** SHAKES. *Coriol.* The people . . are summon'd To meet anon, upon your approbation. **c** J. COLVILLE The House met, and . . Hore-Belisha rose to make his resignation speech.

10 Come together as rivals in a battle, fight. ME. ▸**b** Of two competitors or teams: compete in a sporting contest. L19.

J. BURKE He led an army of some 18,000 to meet the Scots at Pinkie. **b** *Time Out* Extended lunch breaks ahoy on June 7 when England meet Argentina at 12.30pm.

11 Of two or more people: become acquainted with each other for the first time. M17.

DICKENS I told him how we had first met.

— PHRASES & COMB.: ***hail-fellow-well-met***: see HAIL *interjection*. ***make both ends meet***, ***make ends meet***: see END *noun*. **meet-and-greet** *colloq.* an organized event during which a celebrity meets and talks with members of the public. **meet a person's eye**, **meet a person's gaze** etc. (*a*) see that a person is looking at one; (*b*) reciprocate a person's look without turning away. **meet halfway** †(*a*) forestall, anticipate; (*b*) respond to the friendly advances of; (*c*) come to a compromise with. ***meet one's Maker***: see MAKER 1. ***meet one's match***: see MATCH *noun*¹. ***meet on one's own ground***: see GROUND *noun*. **meet the case** be adequate. **meet the ear** be audible. **meet the eye** be visible. **meet-the-people** *adjective* (orig. *US*) designating a tour etc. made by a public personage, esp. a politician, to meet members of the general public. **meet trouble halfway** distress oneself needlessly about what may happen. **more than meets the eye** hidden qualities or complications. ***well met***: see WELL *adverb*.
— WITH ADVERBS & PREPOSITIONS IN SPECIALIZED SENSES: **meet in with** *Scot.* meet, encounter. **meet up** (*a*) happen to meet; (*b*) ***meet up with*** (*colloq.*), overtake or fall in with; meet, encounter; become acquainted with. **meet with** (*a*) come on, come across, fall in with, find; †(*b*) = senses 2a, b above; †(*c*) = senses 4, 4b above; †(*d*) come into or be in physical contact with; (of a garment) extend to (a certain point); (*e*) experience, receive, suffer (one's death, a certain fate, etc.); (*f*) have a business etc. meeting with. ***pleased to meet you***: see PLEASE.
■ **meeter** *noun* (*a*) a person who attends or takes part in a meeting, *esp.* a participant in a meeting of the Society of Friends; (*b*) a person who meets someone: M17.

meeten /ˈmiːt(ə)n/ *verb trans.* *arch. rare*. E19.
[ORIGIN from MEET *adjective* + -EN⁵.]
Make meet or fit (*for*).

meeterly /ˈmiːtəli/ *adverb*. Chiefly *N. English*. L16.
[ORIGIN Perh. rel. to MEET *adjective*: see -LY².]
Tolerably, moderately; handsomely, agreeably.

meeting /ˈmiːtɪŋ/ *noun*.
[ORIGIN Old English *gemēting*, re-formed in Middle English from MEET *verb* + -ING¹.]
1 A private or (now often) public gathering or assembly of people for entertainment, discussion, legislation, etc.; an assembly of people, esp. the Society of Friends, for worship; a Nonconformist congregation, esp. of the Society of Friends. Also, the people attending a meeting, collectively. OE. ▸**b** = ***race meeting*** s.v. RACE *noun*¹. L17.

L. R. BANKS We had a meeting . . to decide what to do. *Friends' Quarterly* We do require that the prospective member attend our Meetings. M. SPARK Turning up once a month for a directors' meeting. **b** R. DAHL Amber Flash nearly beat him on three legs last meeting.

2 The action of MEET *verb*; the action or an act of coming together, encountering, assembling, etc. ME.

H. P. BROUGHAM The peoples' right of Meeting in large bodies. H. CARPENTER At a first meeting he would talk as if he had known you for years.

3 A duel. Formerly also, a fight, a battle. ME.
4 a The junction, intersection, confluence, etc., of two or more things. LME. ▸**b** A joint in carpentry or masonry. M17.

a T. MOORE The Meeting of the Waters.

5 = ***meeting place*** below. *poet.* L16.

SHAKES. *1 Hen. IV* On Thursday we ourselves will march. Our meeting Is Bridgenorth.

— PHRASES: **go to meeting** attend a Nonconformist assembly for worship, esp. one of the Society of Friends. ***mass meeting***: see MASS *noun*² & *adjective*. ***mothers' meeting***: see MOTHER *noun*¹ & *adjective*. ***parents' meeting***: see PARENT *noun*. ***preparative meeting***: see PREPARATIVE *adjective*. ***protracted meeting***: see PROTRACT *verb* 2. ***statutory meeting***. ***take the sense of the meeting***: see SENSE *noun*. ***Yearly Meeting***: see YEARLY *adjective* 2.
— COMB.: **meeting house** †(*a*) a (private) house used for a meeting; (*b*) a place of worship (*US* or *derog.* exc. as used for meetings of the Society of Friends); (*c*) in Polynesia, a public hall; **meeting place** (*a*) a place at which a meeting occurs; †(*b*) = ***meeting house*** (b) above.
■ **meetinger** *noun* (*arch. derog.*) a member of a Nonconformist congregation E19.

mefenamic /mɛfəˈnamɪk/ *adjective*. M20.
[ORIGIN from ME(THYL + -*fen*- alt. of PHEN(YL + AM(INO- + BENZO)IC.]
PHARMACOLOGY. ***mefenamic acid***, a drug which inhibits prostaglandin synthesis and is used as an anti-inflammatory agent and analgesic, *N*-2,3-xylylanthranilic acid.

méfiance /mefjɑ̃s/ *noun*. **L19.**
[**ORIGIN** French.]
Mistrust.

mefloquine /ˈmɛfləkwiːn/ *noun*. **L20.**
[**ORIGIN** from **ME(THYL** + **FL(UOR)O-** + **QUIN(OLIN)E.**]
PHARMACOLOGY. A fluorinated derivative of quinoline used as an antimalarial drug.

Meg /mɛg/ *noun*[1]. Now *dial*. **M16.**
[**ORIGIN** Pet form of female forename *Margaret*.]
1 (A name for) an unruly or coarse girl or woman. **M16.**
Meg Dorts: see **DORT** *noun*.
2 ***Meg's diversion***, a foolish action, foolish behaviour. **E19.**

meg /mɛg/ *noun*[2]. *slang & dial.* **L17.**
[**ORIGIN** Unknown.]
†**1** A guinea. **L17–M18.**
2 Any of various coins of low value. **M18.**

meg /mɛg/ *noun*[3]. Pl. same, **-s. L20.**
[**ORIGIN** Abbreviation.]
1 *ELECTRICITY*. A megohm. **L20.**
2 *COMPUTING*. A megabyte. **L20.**

mega /ˈmɛgə/ *adjective & adverb*. *colloq*. (orig. *US*). **M20.**
[**ORIGIN** Independent use of **MEGA-.**]
▸ **A** *adjective*. Large, great. Also, brilliant, excellent. **M20.**

Smash Hits His mega transfer deal to ITV, rumoured to be worth a cool £500,000. J. **GOODWIN** I was sorry I'd missed it, cos it sounded mega.

▸ **B** *adverb*. Extremely, very. **M20.**

K. **LETTE** I raved on about how hard it must have been growing up with mega rich oldies.

mega- /ˈmɛgə/ *combining form*. Before a vowel also **meg-**.
[**ORIGIN** Greek, combining form of *megas* great. Cf. **MEGALO-.**]
1 Used in words adopted from Greek, in English words modelled on these, and as a freely productive prefix, with the sense 'very large'. ▸**b** *MEDICINE*. Involving gross dilatation or hypertrophy of a part, as ***megacolon***, ***megaureter***.
2 Used in names of units of measurement etc. to denote a factor of one million (10^6), as ***megahertz***, ***megawatt***, also (in *COMPUTING*) a factor of 2^{20} (1,048,576), as ***megabyte***. Abbreviation M.
■ **megabit** *noun* (*COMPUTING*) one million (or 1,048,576) bits, as a unit of data size or memory capacity **M20. megabuck** *noun* (*colloq.*) a million dollars, in *pl.*, very large sums of money **M20. megabyte** *noun* (*COMPUTING*) one million (or 1,048,576) bytes, as a unit of data size or memory capacity **M20. megacity** *noun* a very large city, *esp.* one with a population of over 10 million people **M20. megacycle** *noun* one million cycles (of an oscillatory or periodic phenomenon); *esp.* one million cycles per second, a megahertz: **E20. megadeath** *noun* the death of a million people, esp. as a unit in estimating the possible effects of nuclear war **M20. megadont** *adjective* (*ANTHROPOLOGY*) having or designating teeth of a large size, esp. as measured by a recognized dental index **L19. megadose** *noun* a very large dose of a vitamin, drug, etc., *spec.* one which is at least ten times the recommended daily intake **L20. megafauna** *noun* (*BIOLOGY*) the large or macroscopic animals or animal life, esp. the large vertebrates, of a given area, habitat, or epoch **E20. megaˈgamete** *noun* (*BIOLOGY*) the larger (usu. female) gamete in an organism where the male and female gametes differ in size **L19. megagaˈmetophyte** *noun* (*BOTANY*) a gametophyte that develops from a megaspore, a female gametophyte **E20. megamachine** *noun* a social system dominated by technology and functioning without regard for specifically human needs **M20.** †**megameter** *noun* an instrument for taking large measurements, esp. for calculating longitude from the position of the stars **M18–L19. megamillioˈnaire** *noun* a multimillionaire **M20. megaˈnucleus** *noun* (*ZOOLOGY*) the larger of two nuclei in ciliated protozoa, concerned with vegetative processes **L19. megaphyll** *noun* (*BOTANY*) a usu. large type of leaf (esp. the frond of a fern) marked by branching veins and usu. associated with leaf gaps in the stele **E20. meˈgaphyllous** *adjective* (*BOTANY*) having megaphylls **E20. megaripple** *noun* (*PHYSICAL GEOGRAPHY*) an extensive undulation in a sandy beach or seabed, usu. of the order of tens of metres from crest to crest and tens of centimetres in height **M20. megashear** *noun* (*GEOLOGY*) a transcurrent fault in which the displacement is greater than the thickness of the crust **M20. megastar** *noun* a very famous person, esp. in the world of entertainment **L20. megastardom** *noun* the condition of being a megastar; the world of megastars: **L20. megastore** *noun* a large store selling wares from its own factory to the customer **L20. megaˈstructural** *adjective* of or pertaining to a megastructure **M20. megastructure** *noun* a massively large construction or complex, *esp.* one consisting of many buildings **M20. megaunit** *noun* (*BIOLOGY & MEDICINE*) a million international units **E20. megaˈvitamin** *adjective* (*MEDICINE*) designating or pertaining to therapy based on the taking of large doses of vitamins **L20.**

megacephalic /mɛgəsɪˈfalɪk, -kɛˈfalɪk/ *adjective*. **M19.**
[**ORIGIN** from **MEGA-** + **-CEPHALIC.**]
= **MACROCEPHALIC.**
■ Also **megacephalous** *adjective* **M19.**

megachiropteran /mɛgəkʌɪ(ə)rˈɒpt(ə)rən/ *adjective & noun*. **L19.**
[**ORIGIN** from mod. Latin *Megachiroptera* (see below), formed as **MEGA-** + *Chiroptera*: see **CHIROPTERAN.**]
ZOOLOGY. ▸**A** *adjective*. Of or pertaining to the chiropteran suborder Megachiroptera, which includes flying foxes and other fruit bats. **L19.**
▸ **B** *noun*. A megachiropteran bat. **L19.**

†**megacosm** *noun*. **E17–M19.**
[**ORIGIN** from **MEGA-** after *microcosm*.]
= **MACROCOSM.**

megaflop /ˈmɛgəflɒp/ *noun*. **L20.**
[**ORIGIN** from **MEGA-** + acronym from *floating-point* operations per second (with *-s* taken as pl. suffix **-S**[1]).]
COMPUTING. A unit of computing speed equal to one million or 2^{20} floating-point operations per second.

megakaryocyte /mɛgəˈkarɪəsʌɪt/ *noun*. **L19.**
[**ORIGIN** from **MEGA-** + **KARYO-** + **-CYTE.**]
PHYSIOLOGY. A giant cell of the bone marrow, which has a large irregularly lobed nucleus and from which blood platelets are formed.
■ **megakaryoblast** *noun* a cell which develops into a megakaryocyte **M20.** ˌ**megakaryoˈcytic** *adjective* **E20.** ˌ**megakaryocytopoiˈesis** *noun* production of megakaryocytes **L20.**

megalith /ˈmɛgəlɪθ/ *noun*. **M19.**
[**ORIGIN** Back-form. from **MEGALITHIC**: see **-LITH.**]
ARCHAEOLOGY. A large stone, *esp.* one forming (part of) a prehistoric monument; a megalithic monument.

megalithic /mɛgəˈlɪθɪk/ *adjective*. **M19.**
[**ORIGIN** from **MEGA-** + **-LITHIC.**]
ARCHAEOLOGY. Designating prehistoric monuments constructed of large stones; designating or pertaining to a culture, people, etc., characterized by the erection of such monuments.

megalo- /ˈmɛgələʊ/ *combining form*. Before a vowel also **megal-**.
[**ORIGIN** Greek, combining form of *megas* great: see **-O-**. Cf. **MEGA-.**]
= **MEGA-** 1.
■ **megaloblast** *noun* (*MEDICINE*) a large abnormally developed erythroblast typical of certain forms of anaemia **L19. megaloˈblastic** *adjective* (of anaemia) characterized by megaloblasts **E20.** †**megaloˈcardia** *noun* (*MEDICINE*) abnormal enlargement of the heart: only in **M19. megalocyte** *noun* (*MEDICINE*) a macrocyte **L19. megalopod** *adjective & noun* (a person or creature) having large feet **E20. megalosphere** *noun* (*ZOOLOGY*) the initial chamber of a megalospheric foraminifer **L19. megaloˈspheric** *adjective* (*ZOOLOGY*) designating certain foraminifera having a large initial chamber and a single large nucleus **L19.**

megalocephalic /ˌmɛg(ə)lə(ʊ)sɪˈfalɪk, -kɛˈfalɪk/ *adjective*. **L19.**
[**ORIGIN** from **MEGALO-** + **-CEPHALIC.**]
= **MACROCEPHALIC.**
■ **megaloˈcephalous** *adjective* = **MEGALOCEPHALIC L19. megaloˈcephaly** *noun* macrocephalic condition **L19.**

megalomania /mɛg(ə)lə(ʊ)ˈmeɪnɪə/ *noun*. **L19.**
[**ORIGIN** from **MEGALO-** + **-MANIA.**]
Delusions of grandeur or self-importance, esp. resulting from mental illness; a passion for grandiose schemes; lust for power.
■ **megalomaniac** *adjective & noun* (*a*) *adjective* affected by or characteristic of megalomania; (*b*) *noun* a megalomaniac person: **L19. megalomaniacal** /-məˈnʌɪək(ə)l/ *adjective* megalomaniac **L19. megalomanic** /-ˈmanɪk/ *adjective* megalomaniac **L20.**

megalomartyr /mɛg(ə)lə(ʊ)ˈmɑːtə/ *noun*. **L18.**
[**ORIGIN** Late Greek *megalomartur*, formed as **MEGALO-** + Greek *martur* **MARTYR** *noun*.]
In the Orthodox Church, a martyr to whom particular veneration is given.

megalopa /mɛgəˈləʊpə/ *noun*. **E19.**
[**ORIGIN** mod. Latin (orig. as genus name), from Greek *megalōpos* large-eyed, or from Latin **MEGALO-** + *ops* eye.]
ZOOLOGY. A larval stage in the development of crabs, following the nauplius stage and having the adult number of trunk segments and legs; a crab in this stage. Also called ***megalops***. Freq. *attrib.*

megalopolis /mɛgəˈlɒp(ə)lɪs/ *noun*. **E19.**
[**ORIGIN** from **MEGALO-** + **-POLIS.**]
A very large city or urban complex.

megalopolitan /mɛg(ə)lə(ʊ)ˈpɒlɪt(ə)n/ *adjective & noun*. **E20.**
[**ORIGIN** formed as **MEGALOPOLIS** + Greek *politēs* citizen: see **-AN.**]
▸ **A** *adjective*. Of or pertaining to (the way of life characteristic of) a megalopolis. **E20.**
▸ **B** *noun*. A native or inhabitant of a megalopolis. **M20.**

megalops /ˈmɛgəlɒps/ *noun*. **M19.**
[**ORIGIN** mod. Latin (orig. as genus name), alt. of **MEGALOPA.**]
ZOOLOGY. = **MEGALOPA.** Freq. *attrib.*

megalosaurus /mɛg(ə)lə(ʊ)ˈsɔːrəs/ *noun*. Pl. **-ri** /-rʌɪ/. Also anglicized as **megalosaur** /ˈmɛg(ə)lə(ʊ)sɔː/. **E19.**
[**ORIGIN** mod. Latin, from **MEGALO-** + Greek *sauros* **-SAUR.**]
A large bipedal carnivorous theropod dinosaur of the genus *Megalosaurus*, of the Eurasian Jurassic and Cretaceous.
■ **megaloˈsaurian** *adjective & noun* (*a*) *adjective* of, pertaining to, or resembling (that of) a megalosaurus; (*b*) *noun* a megalosaurus; an animal resembling a megalosaurus: **M19.**

megamouth /ˈmɛgəmaʊθ/ *noun*. **L20.**
[**ORIGIN** from **MEGA-** + **MOUTH** *noun*.]
A shark, *Megachasma pelagios*, with a very large wide mouth, first captured in 1976 off the Hawaiian Islands. Also ***megamouth shark***.

megaphone /ˈmɛgəfəʊn/ *noun & verb*. **L19.**
[**ORIGIN** from **MEGA-** + **-PHONE.**]
▸ **A** *noun*. A large funnel-shaped device for amplifying the voice and directing it over a distance. **L19.**
▸ **B** *verb intrans. & trans.* Speak or utter (as) through a megaphone. **E20.**
■ **megaphonic** /-ˈfɒnɪk/ *adjective* **L19. megaphonist** *noun* a person who speaks through a megaphone **E20.**

megapixel /ˈmɛgəpɪks(ə)l/ *noun*. **L20.**
[**ORIGIN** from **MEGA-** + **PIXEL.**]
COMPUTING. A unit of graphic resolution equivalent to 2^{20} or (strictly) 1,048,576 pixels.

megapode /ˈmɛgəpəʊd/ *noun*. Also **-pod** /-pɒd/. **M19.**
[**ORIGIN** mod. Latin *Megapodius* genus name, from **MEGA-** + **-POD.**]
Any of various brown or black gallinaceous birds of the Australasian family Megapodiidae, which have large strong feet and incubate their eggs in mounds of sand, leaves, etc.

megapolis /məˈgap(ə)lɪs/ *noun*. **M17.**
[**ORIGIN** from **MEGA-** + **-POLIS.**]
A major city.

Megarian /mɛˈgɛːrɪən/ *noun & adjective*. Also **-ean. M16.**
[**ORIGIN** Partly from Latin, Greek *Megara* a city in Greece, partly from Latin *Megareus* of Megara: see **-IAN, -EAN.**]
▸ **A** *noun*. An inhabitant of the ancient Greek city of Megara; *spec.* a member or adherent of the school of philosophy founded *c* 400 **BC** by Euclides of Megara. **M16.**
▸ **B** *adjective*. **1** Of or pertaining to the Megarian school of philosophy. **E17.**
2 Designating a type of bowl of the Hellenistic period, usu. hemispherical with relief ornament. **E20.**

Megaric /mɛˈgarɪk/ *adjective & noun*. **M17.**
[**ORIGIN** Greek *Megarikos* of or belonging to Megara: see **MEGARIAN, -IC.**]
▸ **A** *adjective*. = **MEGARIAN** *adjective* 1. **M17.**
▸ **B** *noun*. = **MEGARIAN** *noun*. **M19.**

megaron /ˈmɛgər(ə)n/ *noun*. **L19.**
[**ORIGIN** Greek.]
In ancient Greece, the great central hall of a type of house characteristic esp. of the Mycenaean period.

megascope /ˈmɛgəskəʊp/ *noun*. **M19.**
[**ORIGIN** from **MEGA-** + **-SCOPE.**]
A modification of the camera obscura or magic lantern which throws a reflected magnified image of an object upon a screen.
■ **megascopic** /-ˈskɒpɪk/ *adjective* (*a*) visible to the naked eye, macroscopic; (*b*) of or pertaining to a megascope or its use; (*c*) *spec.* (of a photographic image etc.) enlarged, magnified: **M19. megascopically** /-ˈskɒp-/ *adverb* **L19.**

megasea /mɛˈgasɪə/ *noun*. **L19.**
[**ORIGIN** mod. Latin *Megasea* (see below), from Greek *megas* large, with ref. to the size of the leaves.]
Any of various ornamental plants of the former genus *Megasea*, now called *Bergenia*; a bergenia.

megaspore /ˈmɛgəspɔː/ *noun*. **M19.**
[**ORIGIN** from **MEGA-** + **SPORE.**]
BOTANY. The larger of the two kinds of spores in heterosporous cryptogams, which develop into female gametophytes; the analogous structure (the immature embryo sac) in seed plants.
■ **megaspoˈrangium** *noun*, pl. **-gia**, a sporangium containing megaspores **L19. megaˈsporophyll** *noun* a leaf or modified leaf which bears megasporangia **E20.**

megass /məˈgas/ *noun*. **M19.**
[**ORIGIN** from **BAGASSE** or its root, French *bagasse*.]
The fibrous residue left after the extraction of sugar from sugar cane.

megatherium /mɛgəˈθɪərɪəm/ *noun*. Pl. **-ria** /-rɪə/. Also anglicized as **megathere** /ˈmɛgəθɪə/. **E19.**
[**ORIGIN** mod. Latin, as if Greek *mega thērion* great animal: see **MEGA-.**]
PALAEONTOLOGY. **1** Any of several large extinct edentate mammals (ground sloths) of the genus *Megatherium* and related genera of the Upper Tertiary of S. America. **E19.**
2 *transf. & fig.* A thing of huge or ungainly proportions. **M19.**
■ **megatherial** *adjective* resembling a megatherium, ponderous, unwieldy **L19. megatherian** *adjective & noun* (of, pertaining to, resembling, or designating) a megatherium **M19. megatherioid** *adjective & noun* (resembling or pertaining to) a megatherium or similar extinct edentate mammal **M19.**

megaton /ˈmɛgətʌn/ *noun & adjective*. **M20.**
[**ORIGIN** from **MEGA-** + **TON** *noun*[1].]
▸ **A** *noun*. A unit of explosive power, equal to that of one million tons of TNT. **M20.**
▸ **B** *attrib.* or as *adjective*. Of or pertaining to a megaton; of the size or power of a megaton. **M20.**

City Limits A single aircraft armed with binary warheads would kill as many civilians as a single megaton nuclear bomb. *fig.*: *Daily Telegraph* Another British spy scandal of 'megaton proportions' was forecast yesterday.

■ **megatonnage** *noun* explosive power of nuclear weapons, as expressed in megatons **M20.**

Megger /ˈmɛɡə/ *noun*. Also **m-**. **E20**.
[**ORIGIN** Uncertain: perh. from **MEGOHM**.]
(Proprietary name for) an instrument designed mainly for measuring electrical insulation resistance.

Megillah /məˈɡɪlə/ *noun*. Also **m-**. **M17**.
[**ORIGIN** Hebrew *mĕgillāh* lit. 'roll, scroll'.]
1 Each of five books of the Hebrew Scriptures (the Song of Solomon, Ruth, Lamentations, Ecclesiastes, and Esther) appointed to be read on certain Jewish notable days; *esp.* the Book of Esther, read at the festival of Purim. Also, a copy of all, or any, of these books. **M17**.
2 A long, tedious, or complicated story. Freq. in ***a whole Megillah***, ***the whole Megillah***. *slang*. **M20**.

High Times Drooped leading edges, cupped wingtips, . . the whole Megillah. S. BELLOW He tried to brief me . . the main part of what he said was a regular Megillah.

megilp /məˈɡɪlp/ *noun*. Also **magilp** & other vars. **M18**.
[**ORIGIN** Unknown.]
A mixture, usu. of linseed oil with turpentine or mastic varnish, used as a vehicle for oil colours.

megimide /ˈmɛɡɪmʌɪd/ *noun*. **M20**.
[**ORIGIN** App. from **ME(THYL** + **G(LUTARIC** + **IMIDE**.]
PHARMACOLOGY. A cyclic organic compound which acts as a medullary respiratory stimulant and has been used to counteract the effects of barbiturates; 3-ethyl-3-methylglutarimide.

megohm /ˈmɛɡəʊm/ *noun*. **M19**.
[**ORIGIN** from **MEGA-** + **OHM**.]
ELECTRICITY. A million ohms.

megrim /ˈmiːɡrɪm/ *noun*[1]. *arch*. **LME**.
[**ORIGIN** Var. of **MIGRAINE**.]
1 Migraine. **LME**.
2 Vertigo. **L16**.
3 A whim, a fancy, a fad. **L16**.
4 In *pl*. Low spirits; depression. **M17**.

G. R. SIMS Having as many dislikes as a fashionable lady with the megrims. S. KING He was . . talking mostly to keep the megrims away.

5 In *pl*. The staggers in horses etc. **M17**.

megrim /ˈmiːɡrɪm/ *noun*[2]. **M19**.
[**ORIGIN** Perh. from **MEAGRE** *noun*[1].]
Either of two flatfishes of European waters, the scaldfish, *Arnoglossus laterna*, and the sail-fluke, *Lepidorhombus whiffiagonis*.

M

mehari /məˈhɑːri/ *noun*. **M18**.
[**ORIGIN** French *méhari*, pl. *méhara* from Arabic *mahrī* (pl. *mahārī*, *mahārā*), use as noun of adjective = of Mahra (a region of southern Arabia).]
In N. Africa and the Middle East: a dromedary, a riding camel.

mehendi *noun* var. of **MEHNDI**.

mehmandar /ˈmeɪmændɑː/ *noun*. *hist*. **E17**.
[**ORIGIN** Persian *mihmāndār*, from *mihmān* guest.]
In Persian-speaking countries and the Indian subcontinent: an official appointed to act as courier to an important traveller.

mehndi /ˈmɛndi/ *noun*. Chiefly *Indian*. Also **mehendi**. **E19**.
[**ORIGIN** Hindi *mehndī* from Sanskrit *mendhikā*.]
1 The henna plant, *Lawsonia inermis*. **E19**.
2 The art or practice of applying temporary henna tattoos, *spec.* as part of a bride or groom's preparations for a wedding; such a tattoo. **M19**.

mehtar /ˈmeɪtə/ *noun*. **M17**.
[**ORIGIN** Persian & Urdu *mihtar* headman, prince, occurring esp. in titles, compar. of *mih* great.]
1 Orig., (the title of) any of several important officers of the Persian royal household. Later, a groom or a stable boy in Persia (Iran). **M17**.
2 In the Indian subcontinent: a house sweeper, a scavenger; the lowest-ranking house servant. **E19**.
3 *hist*. (The title of) the ruler of Chitral (in NW Pakistan). **L19**.

meibomian /mʌɪˈbəʊmɪən/ *adjective*. **E19**.
[**ORIGIN** from H. *Meibom* (1638–1700), German anatomist: see **-IAN**.]
ANATOMY. Pertaining to or designating various large sebaceous glands of the human eyelid, whose infection results in chalazia.
meibomian cyst = **CHALAZION**.

Meiji /ˈmeɪdʒi/ *noun & adjective*. **L19**.
[**ORIGIN** Japanese, lit. 'enlightened government', from *mei* shining light + *ji* peace, rule.]
▸ **A** *noun*. The period of the rule of the Japanese emperor Mutsuhito (1868–1912), marked by the modernization and westernization of Japan. **L19**.
▸ **B** *adjective*. Of, pertaining to, or characteristic of this period. **L19**.

mein Gott /maɪn ˈɡɒt/ *interjection*. **L18**.
[**ORIGIN** German.]
= ***my God*** s.v. **GOD** *noun* 5(c).

mein Herr /maɪn ˈhɛr/ *noun phr*. **L18**.
[**ORIGIN** German, from *mein* my + **HERR**.]
Used as a German form of address to a man; a German man.

meinie /ˈmeɪni/ *noun*. Now chiefly *arch*. **ME**.
[**ORIGIN** Old French & mod. French *meinée*, *mesnée* = Provençal *mesnada* from Proto-Romance, from Latin *mansio(n-)* **MANSION**: see **-Y**[5]; later also infl. by **MANY** *noun*.]
1 A family, a household. *obsolete* exc. *Scot*. **ME**.
2 A body of retainers or followers; a retinue. **ME**.
†**3** A body of people employed together or united by a common purpose; an army, a ship's crew, a congregation, etc. **ME–L16**.
4 A crowd of people; *derog*. a crew, a set. **LME**.
5 A number or collection of things. *obsolete* exc. *Scot*. **LME**.
†**6** A herd or flock of animals. **L15–M16**.

meio- /ˈmʌɪəʊ/ *combining form* of Greek *meiōn* less, smaller: see **-O-**.
▪ **meioˈbenthic** *adjective* (*BIOLOGY*) of or pertaining to the meiobenthos **M20**. **meioˈbenthos** *noun* (*BIOLOGY*) the section of the benthos that includes animals of intermediate or meiofaunal size **M20**. **meiofauna** *noun* (*BIOLOGY*) the medium-sized (esp. the small but not microscopic) animals or animal life of a given area, habitat, or epoch **M20**. **meioˈfaunal** *adjective* (*BIOLOGY*) of or pertaining to meiofauna **M20**. **meionite** *noun* (*MINERALOGY*) an aluminosilicate mineral, the calcium- and carbonate-rich end member of the scapolite series; cf. **MARIALITE**: **E19**. **meiophylly** *noun* [Greek *phullon* leaf] *BOTANY* the suppression of one or more leaves in a whorl **M19**. **meiotaxy** *noun* (*BOTANY*) the suppression of an entire whorl of floral organs **M19**.

meiosis /mʌɪˈəʊsɪs/ *noun*. Pl. **-oses** /-ˈəʊsiːz/. **M16**.
[**ORIGIN** mod. Latin from Greek *meiōsis*, from *meioun* lessen, from *meiōn* less: see **-OSIS**.]
1 *RHETORIC*. **a** A figure of speech by which something is intentionally presented as smaller, less important, etc., than it really is. Now *rare*. **M16**. ▸**b** = **LITOTES**. **M17**.
2 *BIOLOGY*. The division of a diploid cell nucleus into four haploid nuclei; this division together with the accompanying cell division giving rise to gametes (or in some organisms, a haploid generation), the diploid chromosome number being regained at a subsequent fertilization. Cf. **MITOSIS**. **E20**.
meiosis I the first of the two divisions of meiosis, in which homologous chromosomes pair, exchange material, and separate, one of each pair going to each daughter nucleus. **meiosis II** the second division of meiosis, in which each nucleus divides as in mitosis, without pairing of chromosomes.

meiotic /mʌɪˈɒtɪk/ *adjective*. **E20**.
[**ORIGIN** Greek *meiōtikos* diminishing, from *meioun* lessen.]
1 *BIOLOGY*. Of, pertaining to, or occurring during meiosis. **E20**.
2 *RHETORIC*. Characterized by meiosis. **E20**.
▪ **meiotically** *adverb* **L17**.

mei ping /meɪ ˈpɪŋ/ *noun phr*. **E20**.
[**ORIGIN** Chinese *méi píng* prunus vase from *méi* plum + *píng* vase.]
A kind of Chinese porcelain vase with a narrow neck designed to hold a single spray of flowers.

meisie /ˈmeɪsi/ *noun*. *S. Afr*. **M19**.
[**ORIGIN** Afrikaans, from Dutch *meisje*.]
A girl or young woman.

Z. MDA They said Greek boys had no right to smooch with Afrikaner meisies.

Meissen /ˈmʌɪs(ə)n/ *noun*. **M19**.
[**ORIGIN** A town in Germany near Dresden.]
More fully **Meissen china**. Dresden china.

J. WADE Her face . . had the smooth, pleased prettiness of Meissen.

Meissner /ˈmʌɪsnə/ *noun*. **L19**.
[**ORIGIN** Georg *Meissner* (1829–1905), German anatomist.]
ANATOMY. **1** ***Meissner's corpuscle***, a mechanoreceptive sensory nerve ending found in the dermis in various parts of the body. **L19**.
2 ***Meissner's plexus***, a network of parasympathetic nerve fibres serving the muscles and mucous membranes in the wall of the gut. **L19**.

Meissner effect /ˈmʌɪsnər ɪˌfɛkt/ *noun phr*. **M20**.
[**ORIGIN** F. W. *Meissner* (1882–1974), German physicist.]
PHYSICS. The existence of zero, or very low, magnetic induction in a superconducting material even in the presence of a magnetic field; *esp.* the expulsion of magnetic flux when a material becomes superconducting in a magnetic field.

-meister /ˈmʌɪstə/ *suffix*. *colloq*.
[**ORIGIN** German *Meister* **MASTER** *noun*[1].]
Forming nouns denoting persons regarded as skilled or prominent in a specified area of activity, as ***schlockmeister***, ***spinmeister***, etc.

Meistersinger /ˈmʌɪstəzɪŋə, -sɪŋ-/ *noun*. Pl. same, **-s**. **M19**.
[**ORIGIN** German, from *Meister* **MASTER** *noun*[1] + *Singer* **SINGER** *noun*[1].]
A member of any of the German guilds for lyric poets and musicians in the 14th to 16th cents.

meith /miːθ/ *noun*. *Scot*. **LME**.
[**ORIGIN** App. from Old Norse *mið* mark, but assoc. with Latin *meta* **METE** *noun*[1].]
1 A landmark or sea mark; a boundary, a goal. **LME**.
2 A measurement. **E18**.

meitnerium /mʌɪtˈnɪərɪəm/ *noun*. **L20**.
[**ORIGIN** from Lise *Meitner* (1878–1968), German physicist + **-IUM**.]
A very unstable radioactive chemical element (atomic no. 109), produced artificially (symbol Mt).

Mekhitarist /ˈmɛkɪtɑːrɪst/ *noun & adjective*. **M19**.
[**ORIGIN** from *Mekhitar* (see below) + **-IST**.]
▸ **A** *noun*. A member of a congregation of Roman Catholic Armenian monks originally founded at Constantinople in 1701 by Mekhitar, an Armenian, and finally established by him in 1717 in the island of San Lazzaro, south of Venice. **M19**.
▸ **B** *adjective*. Of or pertaining to the Mekhitarists. **L19**.

mekometer /mɪˈkɒmɪtə/ *noun*. **L19**.
[**ORIGIN** from Greek *mēkos* length + **-OMETER**.]
1 *MILITARY*. An instrument for finding the range for infantry fire. **L19**.
2 A device for the accurate measurement of distance in which light polarized at a microwave frequency is beamed at a reflector and the polarization of the reflected light analysed. **M20**.

mel /mɛl/ *noun*. **M20**.
[**ORIGIN** from **MEL(ODY**.]
ACOUSTICS. A unit of subjective pitch, defined so that the number of mels is proportional to the pitch of a sound, and the pitch of a 1000-hertz note is 1000 mels.

mela /ˈmeɪlɑː, -lə/ *noun*. **E19**.
[**ORIGIN** Hindi *melā* from Sanskrit *melāka* assembly, from *mil-* to meet.]
A Hindu festival and assembly.

melaena /mɪˈliːnə/ *noun*. Also *-**lena**. **E19**.
[**ORIGIN** mod. Latin from Greek *melaina* fem. of *melas* black.]
MEDICINE. Dark sticky faeces containing partly digested blood; (a condition characterized by) the production of such faeces, following internal bleeding or the swallowing of blood.

melaleuca /mɛləˈl(j)uːkə/ *noun*. **L18**.
[**ORIGIN** mod. Latin (see below), from Greek *melas* black + *leukos* white.]
Any of numerous mostly Australian shrubs and trees of the genus *Melaleuca*, of the myrtle family, with bundles of protruding brightly coloured stamens. Also called ***honey-myrtle***.

melam /ˈmɛlam/ *noun*. Now *rare*. **M19**.
[**ORIGIN** German, of arbitrary formation.]
CHEMISTRY. A buff, insoluble amorphous organic substance obtained by distilling ammonium thiocyanate.

melamed /mɪˈlɑːməd/ *noun*. **L19**.
[**ORIGIN** Hebrew *mĕlammēḏ*.]
A teacher of elementary Hebrew.

melamine /ˈmɛləmiːn/ *noun*. In sense 2 also **M-**. **M19**.
[**ORIGIN** from **MELAM** + **AMINE**.]
1 *CHEMISTRY*. A crystalline heterocyclic compound made esp. by heating cyanamide; 2,4,6-triamino-1,3,5-triazine, $(CNH_2)_3N_3$. **M19**.
2 A melamine resin, or a plastic derived from one. **M20**.
– **COMB.**: **melamine resin** any of various thermosetting resins made by condensing melamine with aldehydes, used for moulded items, adhesives in laminates, and coatings for textiles and paper.

melampode /ˈmɛləmpəʊd/ *noun*. *arch*. Also in Latin form **melampodium** /mɛləmˈpəʊdɪəm/. **L16**.
[**ORIGIN** Latin *melampodium* from Greek *melampodion*, from *melan-*, *melas* black + *pod-*, *pous* foot.]
Black hellebore, *Helleborus orientalis*.

melan- *combining form* see **MELANO-**.

melanaemia /mɛləˈniːmɪə/ *noun*. Also *-**nemia**. **M19**.
[**ORIGIN** from **MELANO-** + **-AEMIA**.]
MEDICINE. A condition in which the blood contains melanin or other dark pigment, as in haemochromatosis.
▪ **melanaemic** *adjective* **M19**.

melancholia /mɛlənˈkəʊlɪə/ *noun*. **LME**.
[**ORIGIN** Late Latin: see **MELANCHOLY** *noun*.]
†**1** Black bile; = **CHOLER ADUST**. Only in **LME**.
2 Orig., severe or clinical depression. Now, a feeling of deep sadness, gloom, melancholy. **E17**.

J. LEES-MILNE There is still a strong streak of melancholia in the Lyttleton family.

▪ **melancholiac** *adjective & noun* (a person) affected with melancholia **M19**.

melancholic /mɛlənˈkɒlɪk/ *adjective & noun*. **LME**.
[**ORIGIN** Old French & mod. French *mélancolique* from Latin *melancholicus* from Greek *melankholikhos*, from *melankholia* **MELANCHOLY** *noun*: see **-IC**.]
▸ **A** *adjective*. †**1** Of or pertaining to choler adust, one of the cardinal humours; attributed to or believed to contain this humour. **LME–L19**.
2 Characterized by or liable to melancholy. **LME**.

L. STRACHEY Melancholic by temperament, he could yet be lively on occasion.

3 Causing or expressing sadness and depression; saddening, melancholy. **L16**.

E. GRIFFITH I wrote a long, and of course, a melancholic letter to you.

▶ **B** *noun*. A person affected with melancholy; a melancholiac. LME.

■ **melancholically** *adverb* L19.

melancholious /mɛlənˈkəʊlɪəs/ *adjective*. Now *rare*. LME.
[ORIGIN Old French *melancolieus*, from *mélancolie* MELANCHOLY *noun*: see -IOUS.]
1 = MELANCHOLIC *adjective* 2, 3. LME.
†**2** = MELANCHOLIC *adjective* 1. LME–M16.

melancholise *verb* var. of MELANCHOLIZE.

melancholist /ˈmɛlənk(ə)lɪst/ *noun*. Now *rare* or *obsolete*. L16.
[ORIGIN from MELANCHOLY *noun* + -IST.]
A person liable to melancholy, a melancholiac.

melancholize /ˈmɛlənk(ə)lʌɪz/ *verb*. Now *rare* or *obsolete*. Also **-ise**. L16.
[ORIGIN formed as MELANCHOLIST + -IZE.]
1 *verb intrans. & refl.* Be or become melancholy. L16.
2 *verb trans.* Make melancholy. M17.

melancholy /ˈmɛlənk(ə)li/ *noun*. ME.
[ORIGIN Old French & mod. French *mélancolie* from late Latin *melancholia* from Greek *melankholia*, from *melan-*, *melas* black + *kholē* bile: see -Y³.]
1 MEDICINE. Orig. (*obsolete* exc. *hist.*), a pathological condition attributed to a supposed excess of choler adust, one of the cardinal humours, and distinguished esp. by sullenness, irascibility, and sadness. Later, (now *rare*) pathological depression, melancholia. ME. ▸**b** *hist.* = ***choler adust*** s.v. CHOLER 2. LME.

H. LYTE The disseases called choler or melancholy. W. H. O. SANKEY Cases of melancholy which are accompanied by great restlessness.

†**2** Irascibility, anger, sullenness. LME–L16.

personified: SHAKES. *John* If that surly spirit, melancholy, Hath bak'd thy blood.

3 Sadness, dejection, depression; *esp.* pensive or meditative sadness. Also, inclination or tendency to this. LME. ▸**b** An annoyance, a vexation. Now chiefly *literary*. L15. ▸**c** A state, episode, or mood of (pensive or meditative) sadness etc. L16.

M. W. MONTAGU It gives me too much melancholy to see so agreeable a young creature buried alive. E. L. DOCTOROW Melancholy had taken the will out of her muscles. S. HASTINGS The autumnal countryside induced in her a pervasive feeling of melancholy. **b** H. JAMES These melancholies haven't prevented the London season from roaring and elbowing along. **c** BURKE In spite of all my efforts, I fall into a melancholy which is inexpressible.

melancholy /ˈmɛlənk(ə)li/ *adjective*. LME.
[ORIGIN from the noun.]
1 Affected with or characterized by melancholy; liable to melancholy. Now *esp.* (inclined to be) sadly thoughtful or meditative. LME. ▸†**b** = MELANCHOLIC *adjective* 1. E–M17.

J. THOMSON A certain music, never known before, Here soothed the pensive, melancholy mind. R. HUGHES He felt acutely melancholy, not very far from tears.

†**2** Irascible, angry; sullen. LME–E17.
3 Suggestive of or expressing sadness; depressing, dismal. L16.

W. LITHGOW Padua is the most melancholy City of Europe. H. JACOBSON They cannot read a word of the melancholy poems.

melancholy thistle a thistle of upland pastures, *Cirsium helenioides*, with a thornless stem and a single drooping head.

4 Of a fact, event, etc.: lamentable, deplorable. E18.

L. STERNE Melancholy! to see such sprightliness the prey of sorrow.

■ **melancholily** *adverb* M16. **melancholiness** *noun* E16. †**melancholish** *adjective* (*a*) causing melancholy; (*b*) somewhat melancholy: M16–M19.

†**melancholy** *verb trans.* L15–E19.
[ORIGIN Old French *melancolier*, formed as MELANCHOLY *noun*.]
Make melancholy.

Melanchthonian /mɛlaŋkˈθəʊnɪən/ *noun & adjective*. L17.
[ORIGIN from *Melanchthon* Graecized form of surname of Philipp Schwarzerd (lit. 'black earth') + -IAN.]
▶ **A** *noun*. An adherent or student of the German Protestant reformer Philipp Melanchthon (1497–1560). L17.
▶ **B** *adjective*. Of or pertaining to (the beliefs of) Melanchthon. M18.

melanemia *noun* see MELANAEMIA.

Melanesian /mɛləˈniːzjən, -ʒ(ə)n/ *noun & adjective*. M19.
[ORIGIN from *Melanesia* (see below), from Greek *melas* black + *nēsos* island + -IA¹, after *Polynesia*: see -AN.]
▶ **A** *noun*. A native or inhabitant of Melanesia, an island group in the SW Pacific including the Solomon Islands, the Bismarck archipelago, Santa Cruz, Vanuatu, New Caledonia and Fiji; *spec.* a member of the dominant people of Melanesia. Also, the group of Austronesian languages spoken in Melanesia. M19.
▶ **B** *adjective*. Of or pertaining to Melanesia, the Melanesians, or their group of languages. M19.

Melanesoid /mɛləˈniːzɔɪd/ *adjective*. M20.
[ORIGIN formed as MELANESIAN: see -OID.]
Similar in physical type to a Melanesian; resembling a Melanesian.

mélange /melɑ̃ːʒ (*pl. same*), meɪˈlɒ̃ʒ/ *noun*. M17.
[ORIGIN French, from *mêler* mix: see MELL *verb*.]
1 A mixture; a collection of heterogeneous items or elements, a medley. M17.
2 Yarn, esp. woollen yarn, to which dye has been applied unevenly so as to leave some areas undyed; a fabric of such a yarn. L19.
3 Coffee made with sugar and whipped cream; a drink of this. E20.

Melanian /mɪˈleɪnɪən/ *adjective*. M19.
[ORIGIN French *mélanien*, from Greek *melan-*, *melas* black: see -IAN.]
ANTHROPOLOGY. Orig. = NEGRITO. Later (of a person), black.

melanic /mɪˈlanɪk/ *adjective & noun*. E19.
[ORIGIN from Greek *melan-*, *melas* black + -IC.]
▶ **A** *adjective*. **1** ANTHROPOLOGY. Having black hair and a black or dark complexion. E19.
2 a Of or pertaining to melanin; containing melanin. M19. ▸**b** Of a variety of animal: characterized by (esp. industrial) melanism. L19.

b *Nature* The murk of nineteenth century Manchester fostered the melanic form . . of the peppered moth.

▶ **B** *noun*. A melanic variety of an animal. E20.

melanin /ˈmɛlənɪn/ *noun*. M19.
[ORIGIN formed as MELANIC + -IN¹.]
BIOCHEMISTRY. Any of various dark brown or black pigments present in the hair, skin, eyes, etc., of people and animals, derived from tyrosine by polymerization and produced in increased amounts during tanning and in certain diseases.

melanism /ˈmɛlənɪz(ə)m/ *noun*. M19.
[ORIGIN formed as MELANIC + -ISM.]
1 ZOOLOGY & PHYSIOLOGY. Darkness of colour, hereditary or (less commonly) pathological, resulting from an excess of melanin in the skin, fur, feathers, scales, etc. Cf. MELANOSIS. M19.

industrial melanism the prevalence of dark-coloured varieties of animals (esp. moths) in industrial areas where they are better camouflaged against predators than paler forms.

2 Chiefly ORNITHOLOGY. A melanic variety of a bird etc. M19.
■ **melaˈnistic** *adjective* characterized by melanism L19. **melaniˈzation** *noun* the process or result of developing melanism; the development of melanin: E20. **melanized** *adjective* having undergone melanization L19.

melanite /ˈmɛlənʌɪt/ *noun*. E19.
[ORIGIN from Greek *melan-*, *melas* black + -ITE¹.]
MINERALOGY. A velvet-black variety of andradite garnet.

melano /ˈmɛlənəʊ/ *noun*. *rare*. Pl. **-os**. E20.
[ORIGIN from MELANISM after *albino*.]
= MELANIC *noun*.

melano- /ˈmɛlənəʊ/ *combining form*. Before a vowel also **melan-**.
[ORIGIN from Greek *melan-*, *melas* black; in many scientific terms, from MELANIN: see -O-.]
Dark-coloured; *spec.* of or pertaining to melanin.
■ **melanoblast** *noun* (ANATOMY & ZOOLOGY) (a cell that develops into) a melanocyte E20. **melanoˈcratic** *adjective* (PETROGRAPHY) (of a rock) dark-coloured, rich in dark-coloured minerals E20. **melanoderm** *noun & adjective* (a person who is) dark-skinned E20. **melanoˈderma** *noun* (MEDICINE) melanosis; chloasma: M19. **melanoˈdermia** *noun* (MEDICINE) melanoderma L19. **melanoˈdermic** *adjective* (*a*) pertaining to or exhibiting melanoderma; (*b*) (naturally) dark-skinned: L19. **melanoˈgenesis** *noun* (PHYSIOLOGY) the formation of melanin E20. **melanophore** *noun* (ZOOLOGY) a cell containing melanin, *esp.* such a cell in the lower vertebrates which is contractile and confers the ability to change the depth of colour E20. **melanosome** *noun* (PHYSIOLOGY) a particle in the cytoplasm of melanocytes in which melanin is thought to be formed M20. **melanoˈvanadite** *noun* (MINERALOGY) a black opaque monoclinic oxide of calcium and vanadium occurring as bunches of needle-like crystals E20.

†**melanocomous** *adjective*. Only in M19.
[ORIGIN from Greek *melanokomēs*, formed as MELANO- + *komē* hair + -OUS.]
ANTHROPOLOGY. Black-haired.

melanocyte /ˈmɛlənə(ʊ)sʌɪt, mɪˈlanə(ʊ)-/ *noun*. L19.
[ORIGIN from MELANO- + -CYTE.]
ANATOMY & ZOOLOGY. A mature melanin-forming cell, esp. in the skin. Also, a melanophore.
– COMB.: **melanocyte-stimulating hormone** a hormone that stimulates melanocytes or melanophores and causes darkening of the skin; abbreviation ***MSH***.

melanoid /ˈmɛlənɔɪd/ *adjective*. M19.
[ORIGIN from MELANO- + -OID.]
MEDICINE. Resembling melanin; resembling or of the nature of melanosis.

melanoma /mɛləˈnəʊmə/ *noun*. Pl. **-mas**, **-mata** /-mətə/. M19.
[ORIGIN from MELANO- + -OMA.]
MEDICINE. A melanotic growth; *esp.* a tumour which contains or produces melanin, a tumour of melanocytes (in its malignant form associated with skin cancer). Also, the condition of having a melanoma or melanomas.

melanophlogite /mɛləˈnɒflədʒʌɪt/ *noun*. L19.
[ORIGIN from MELANO- + Greek *phlog-*, *phlox* flame (with ref. to the mineral's turning black when heated) + -ITE¹.]
MINERALOGY. A form of silica containing organic impurities, occurring in minute cubes on sulphur and formerly thought to be a polymorph of quartz.

melanose /ˈmɛlənəʊs/ *noun*. E19.
[ORIGIN French *mélanose* MELANOSIS.]
†**1** = MELANOSIS *noun* 1. Only in E19.
2 A disease of grapes, citrus fruit, etc., caused by the fungus *Septoria ampelina*. L19.

melanose /ˈmɛlənəʊs/ *adjective*. Now *rare*. E19.
[ORIGIN formed as MELANIC + -OSE¹.]
MEDICINE. = MELANIC 2a.

melanosis /mɛləˈnəʊsɪs/ *noun*. Pl. **-noses** /-ˈnəʊsiːz/. E19.
[ORIGIN mod. Latin, from Greek *melan-*, *melas* black + -OSIS.]
MEDICINE. **1** Abnormal or excessive development of melanin in the skin or other tissue; a discoloration due to this. E19.
2 = MELANOMA. M19.

melanotic /mɛləˈnɒtɪk/ *adjective*. E19.
[ORIGIN from MELANOSIS + -OTIC.]
1 MEDICINE. Characterized by or of the nature of melanosis. E19.
2 ZOOLOGY. = MELANISTIC. L19.

melanous /ˈmɛlənəs/ *adjective*. Now *rare*. M19.
[ORIGIN from Greek *melan-*, *melas* black + -OUS.]
ANTHROPOLOGY. Having or designating dark or blackish hair and complexion.

melanterite /mɪˈlantərʌɪt/ *noun*. E19.
[ORIGIN from Greek *melantēria* black metallic dye or ink, from *melan-*, *melas* black: see -ITE¹.]
MINERALOGY. Ferrous sulphate heptahydrate occurring as a colourless or blue-green monoclinic mineral, freq. with marcasite; native copperas.

melanuria /mɛləˈnjʊərɪə/ *noun*. L19.
[ORIGIN from MELANO- + -URIA.]
MEDICINE. The production of urine which contains dark pigments such as melanin, or which darkens on standing.
■ **melanuric** *adjective* of, pertaining to, or characterized by melanuria; ***melanuric fever***, blackwater fever: L19.

melaphyre /ˈmɛləfʌɪə/ *noun*. Now *rare*. E19.
[ORIGIN French *mélaphyre*, from Greek *melas* black + PORPHYRY.]
GEOLOGY. Any of various dark-coloured porphyritic (esp. basaltic) rocks.

melasma /mɪˈlazmə/ *noun*. Pl. **-mata** /-mətə/. M16.
[ORIGIN mod. Latin from Greek ult. from *melas* black.]
= CHLOASMA.

†**melasses** *noun* see MOLASSES.

melastoma /mɪˈlastəmə/ *noun*. Pl. **-mae** /-miː/, **-mas**. M18.
[ORIGIN mod. Latin (see below), from Greek *melas* black + *stoma* mouth, because the fruit of some species blackens the mouth.]
Any of various shrubs of the genus *Melastoma* (family Melastomataceae) of SE Asia, with white or purple flowers and sweet edible berries.

melatonin /mɛləˈtəʊnɪn/ *noun*. M20.
[ORIGIN from MELA(NO- + SERO)TONIN.]
BIOCHEMISTRY. An indole derivative formed in the pineal gland of various mammals (principally from serotonin), which inhibits melanin formation and is thought to be concerned with regulating the reproductive cycle.

Melba /ˈmɛlbə/ *noun*. Also **m-**. E20.
[ORIGIN Nellie *Melba* (formed as MELBURNIAN) stage name of the Austral. operatic soprano Helen Mitchell (1861–1931).]
1 ***peach Melba***, ***pêche Melba***, ***pêches Melba*** /pɛʃ/, a confection of ice cream and peaches flavoured with raspberry sauce. E20.
2 ***Melba sauce***, a raspberry sauce for desserts. E20.
3 ***Melba toast***, ***toast Melba***, thinly sliced bread toasted or baked to crispness. E20.

Melburnian /mɛlˈbəːnɪən/ *noun*. Also **-bournian**. M19.
[ORIGIN from (Latinized alt. of) *Melbourne* (see below) + -IAN.]
A native or inhabitant of Melbourne, the capital city of Victoria, Australia.

melch *adjective* var. of MELSH.

Melchite /ˈmɛlkʌɪt/ *noun*. Also **Melkite**. E17.
[ORIGIN ecclesiastical Latin *Melchitae* (pl.) from Byzantine Greek *Melkhitai* repr. Syriac *malkāyā* royalist (in agreement with the Byzantine Emperor: see below), from *malkā* king: see -ITE¹.]
ECCLESIASTICAL. Orig., an Eastern Christian adhering to the Orthodox faith as defined by the councils of Ephesus (AD 431) and Chalcedon (AD 451) and as accepted by the Byzantine Emperor. Now, an Orthodox or Uniate Christian belonging to the patriarchates of Antioch, Jerusalem, or Alexandria.

meld /mɛld/ *verb*¹ & *noun*¹. L19.
[ORIGIN German *melden* announce, declare (at cards).]
CARDS. ▶ **A** *verb trans. & intrans.* Declare (a combination of cards) in pinochle, canasta, rummy, and other card games. L19.
▶ **B** *noun*. A combination of cards to be declared in pinochle, canasta, rummy, and other card games. L19.

M

meld /mɛld/ *verb*² *& noun*². Orig. *US*. M20.
[ORIGIN Perh. from MELT *verb* + WELD *verb*.]
► **A** *verb trans. & intrans.* Merge, blend together. M20.

Time He has plans to meld his eleven departments into five. *National Geographic* Then cloud and grey sea melded and a steady rain slanted across . . the island.

► **B** *noun.* A thing formed by merging or blending. L20.

Black World A spectacular meld of rock music, drama, film, poetry and song.

melded /ˈmɛldɪd/ *adjective.* M20.
[ORIGIN Blend of MELT *verb* and WELDED *adjective*: cf. MELD *verb*² *& noun*².]
Formed from or using man-made fibres that have an outer sheath which has been melted to bind the fibres together into a fabric.

melder /ˈmɛldə/ *noun. Scot.* L15.
[ORIGIN Old Norse *meldr* from base of *mala* to grind.]
1 A quantity of meal ground at one time. L15.
†**2** An occasion of taking corn to be ground. L18–E19.

†**mele** *noun* var. of MEAL *noun*².

mêlée /ˈmɛleɪ/ *noun.* Also **melée**, **melee**. M17.
[ORIGIN French from Old French *meslée* pa. ppl adjective of *mesler* var. of *mesler* MEDDLE *verb*. Sense 2 prob. a different word. Cf. MEDLEY, MELLAY.]
1 A battle at close quarters, a hand-to-hand fight; a confused struggle or skirmish, esp. involving many people; a crush, turmoil; a muddle. M17.
2 *collect.* Small diamonds less than about a carat in weight. E20.

melegueta *noun* var. of MELAGUETA.

melena *noun* var. of MELAENA.

melezitose /mɪˈlɛzɪtəʊz, -s/ *noun.* Also **-liz-** /-ˈlɪz-/. M19.
[ORIGIN from French *mélèze* larch, after *melitose*.]
BIOCHEMISTRY. A trisaccharide sugar, containing one fructose and two glucose units, originally isolated from the sap of larches.

Melian /ˈmiːlɪən/ *noun & adjective.* M16.
[ORIGIN from Greek *Mēlos* Melos (see below) + -IAN.]
► **A** *noun.* A native or inhabitant of Melos, the most south-easterly of the Cycladic islands in the Aegean Sea. M16.
► **B** *adjective.* Of or pertaining to the island of Melos. L17.

M

melianthus /mɛlɪˈanθəs/ *noun.* M18.
[ORIGIN mod. Latin (see below), from Greek *meli* honey + *anthos* flower.]
A plant of the genus *Melianthus* (family Melianthaceae, but orig. including members of other families); now *spec.* = ***honey flower*** (a) s.v. HONEY *noun*.

melibiose /mɛlɪˈbʌɪəʊz, -s/ *noun.* L19.
[ORIGIN from Greek *meli* honey + BI- + -OSE².]
CHEMISTRY. A disaccharide sugar, $C_{12}H_{22}O_{11}$, composed of a glucose and a galactose unit, obtainable by partial hydrolysis of raffinose.
■ **melibiase** *noun* an enzyme which hydrolyses melibiose L19.

Meliboean /mɛlɪˈbiːən/ *adjective. rare* (Milton). M17.
[ORIGIN from Latin *Meliboeus* (designating a purple dye) + -AN.]
Of or pertaining to Meliboea, an island forming part of ancient Syria, colonized from Thessaly, and famous for its purple dye.

melic *noun*¹ var. of MELICK.

melic /ˈmɛlɪk/ *adjective & noun*². L17.
[ORIGIN Latin *melicus* from Greek *melikos*, from *melos* song: see -IC.]
► **A** *adjective.* (Of poetry) intended to be sung; of or pertaining to strophic Greek lyric verse. L17.
► **B** *noun.* Melic poetry. L19.

meliceris /mɛlɪˈsɪərɪs/ *noun.* Now *rare* or *obsolete*. Pl. **-cerides** /-ˈsɛrɪdiːz/. M16.
[ORIGIN mod. Latin from Greek *melikēris* some eruptive disease, from *meli* honey + *kēros* wax.]
MEDICINE. A cyst containing matter which resembles honey; such matter.

melick /ˈmɛlɪk/ *noun.* Also **melic**. M18.
[ORIGIN mod. Latin *melica* (see below), perh. from Italian *melica*, *meliga* sorghum.]
Any of several grasses of the genus *Melica*; *esp.* either of two woodland grasses, *M. uniflora* and *M. nutans*, with racemes or panicles of plump purplish spikelets. Also ***melick grass***.

†**melicrate** *noun.* LME–L18.
[ORIGIN Late Latin *melicratum* from Greek *melikraton*, from *meli* honey + *karannunai*, *ker-* mix.]
A drink made with honey and water.

melilite /ˈmɛlɪlʌɪt/ *noun.* Also **mell-**. E19.
[ORIGIN from Greek *meli* honey + -LITE.]
MINERALOGY. A tetragonal calcium aluminosilicate, also containing magnesium, found in igneous and metamorphic rocks and in slags.

melilot /ˈmɛlɪlɒt/ *noun.* LME.
[ORIGIN Old French & mod. French *mélilot* from Latin *melilotos* from Greek *melilōtos*, from *meli* honey + *lōtos* LOTUS.]
Any of various leguminous plants of the genus *Melilotus*, which smell of newly mown hay when dry and have trifoliate leaves and long racemes of small yellow or white flowers.

meline /ˈmiːlʌɪn/ *adjective.* L19.
[ORIGIN mod. Latin *Melinae* (see below), from Latin *meles* marten, badger (in mod. Latin genus name of the Eurasian badger): see -INE¹.]
ZOOLOGY. Of, pertaining to, or designating the mustelid subfamily Melinae, which includes the badgers; resembling or characteristic of a badger.

melinite /ˈmɛlɪnʌɪt/ *noun.* M19.
[ORIGIN from Greek *mēlinos* (of the colour) of quince, from *mēlon* quince, apple: see -ITE¹. In sense 2 from French *mélinite*.]
1 MINERALOGY. A clay resembling yellow ochre. M19.
2 A high explosive based on picric acid; lyddite. L19.

melioidosis /ˌmɛlɪɔɪˈdəʊsɪs/ *noun.* Pl. **-doses** /-ˈdəʊsiːz/. E20.
[ORIGIN from Greek *mēlis* a disease of asses (prob. glanders) + -OID + -OSIS.]
MEDICINE. An infectious disease of (chiefly tropical) rodents, similar to glanders, caused by the bacterium *Pseudomonas pseudomallei* and occasionally transmitted to people (in whom it is often fatal) and animals.

meliorate /ˈmiːlɪəreɪt/ *verb.* M16.
[ORIGIN Late Latin *meliorat-* pa. ppl stem of *meliorare* improve, from Latin *melior* better: see -ATE³.]
1 *verb trans.* = AMELIORATE *verb* 1. Also, mitigate (suffering etc.). M16.
2 *verb intrans.* = AMELIORATE *verb* 2. M17.
3 *verb intrans.* SCOTS LAW. Make meliorations. M19.
■ **meliorator** *noun* L18.

melioration /ˌmiːlɪəˈreɪʃ(ə)n/ *noun.* LME.
[ORIGIN formed as MELIORATE: see -ATION.]
1 Amelioration, improvement; LINGUISTICS development of a more favourable meaning or connotation (opp. ***pejoration***). LME.
2 A change for the better; a thing or an action by which something is made better; an improvement. M17. ▸**b** SCOTS LAW. In *pl.* Improvements made on rented property, esp. by the tenant. Now *rare*. M18.

meliorative /ˈmiːlɪərətɪv/ *adjective & noun.* E19.
[ORIGIN formed as MELIORATE: see -ATIVE.]
► **A** *adjective.* Ameliorating, improving; LINGUISTICS giving or acquiring a more favourable meaning or connotation (opp. ***pejorative***). E19.
► **B** *noun.* LINGUISTICS. A meliorative word, affix, etc. M20.

meliorism /ˈmiːlɪərɪz(ə)m/ *noun.* L19.
[ORIGIN from Latin *melior* better + -ISM.]
The doctrine that the world may be made significantly better by human effort.
■ **meliorist** *noun & adjective* (*a*) *noun* an adherent of meliorism; (*b*) *adjective* of or pertaining to meliorists or meliorism: M19.

†**meliority** *noun.* L16–M19.
[ORIGIN Old French *meliorité* or medieval Latin *melioritas*, formed as MELIORISM: see -ITY.]
The quality or condition of being better; superiority.

meliphagine /mɛˈlɪfədʒʌɪn/ *adjective.* L19.
[ORIGIN from mod. Latin *Meliphaga* genus name, formed as MELIPHAGOUS: see -INE¹.]
ORNITHOLOGY. Of, pertaining to, or designating the family Meliphagidae or the subfamily Meliphaginae of honey-eaters.

meliphagous /mɛˈlɪfəgəs/ *adjective.* E19.
[ORIGIN from Greek *meli* honey + *phagos* eater + -OUS.]
Mellivorous; ORNITHOLOGY meliphagine.

melisma /mɪˈlɪzmə/ *noun.* Pl. **-mata** /-mətə/, **-mas**. L19.
[ORIGIN Greek, lit. 'song'.]
MUSIC. Orig., a melodic tune or melodic music. Now, in singing, the prolongation of one syllable over a number of notes.
■ **melismatic** /-ˈmatɪk/ *adjective* of, pertaining to, or characteristic of melisma L19.

melissa /mɪˈlɪsə/ *noun.* LME.
[ORIGIN Greek = bee.]
Lemon balm, *Melissa officinalis*, esp. as a source of a volatile oil.

melissic /mɪˈlɪsɪk/ *adjective.* M19.
[ORIGIN from MELISSIN + -IC.]
CHEMISTRY. ***melissic acid***, a straight-chain fatty acid, $CH_3(CH_2)_{28}COOH$, found in various plant and animal waxes.

melissin /mɪˈlɪsɪn/ *noun.* M19.
[ORIGIN formed as MELISSA + -IN¹.]
CHEMISTRY. Melissyl alcohol.

melissyl /mɪˈlɪsʌɪl, -sɪl/ *noun.* M19.
[ORIGIN formed as MELISSIN + -YL.]
CHEMISTRY. The straight-chain hydrocarbon radical $C_{30}H_{60}$·, found in various compounds derived from waxes. Usu. in *comb*.
– COMB.: **melissyl alcohol** a straight-chain alcohol, $CH_3(CH_2)_{28}CH_2OH$, obtained from beeswax and other waxes; also called ***melissin***.

melitose /ˈmɛlɪtəʊz, -s/ *noun.* Now *rare* or *obsolete*. M19.
[ORIGIN from Greek *melit-*, *meli* honey + -OSE².]
CHEMISTRY. = RAFFINOSE.

melittin /mɪˈlɪtɪn/ *noun.* M20.
[ORIGIN from Greek *melitta* bee + -IN¹.]
BIOCHEMISTRY & PHARMACOLOGY. A polypeptide present in bee venom and used against penicillin-resistant bacteria and in the treatment of rheumatism.

melituria /mɛlɪˈtjʊərɪə/ *noun.* Now *rare* or *obsolete*. M19.
[ORIGIN from Greek *melit-*, *meli* honey + -URIA.]
MEDICINE. Glycosuria.

melizitose *noun* var. of MELEZITOSE.

melkbos /ˈmɛlkbɒs/ *noun. S. Afr.* Also **-bosch** /-bɒʃ/. M19.
[ORIGIN Afrikaans *melkbosch*, from *melk* milk + *bosch* bush.]
Any of several shrubs or small trees with milky latex; *esp.* (*a*) the Transvaal rubber tree, *Diplorhynchus condylocarpon* (family Apocynaceae); (*b*) any of various shrubby or tree-sized spurges, esp. *Euphorbia mauritanica*.

Melkite *noun* var. of MELCHITE.

melktert /ˈmɛlktɛːt/ *noun. S. Afr.* M20.
[ORIGIN Afrikaans, from *melk* milk + *tert* tart, pie.]
A kind of open tart with a custard filling sprinkled with cinnamon.

mell /mɛl/ *noun*¹. Now only *Scot. & N. English*. ME.
[ORIGIN Var. of MAUL *noun*.]
Orig., a mace, a club. Later, a heavy hammer or beetle (= MAUL *noun* 2), esp. as a token given to the loser of a competition; a gavel.

†**mell** *noun*². LME–M19.
[ORIGIN Latin *mel*, *mell-* = Greek *meli*, *melit-*.]
Honey.

mell /mɛl/ *verb.* Now chiefly *arch. & dial.* ME.
[ORIGIN Old French *meller*: see MÊLÉE. Cf. MEDDLE.]
1 *verb trans. &* †*intrans.* Mix, mingle, combine. Also foll. by *together*, *with*. ME.
2 *verb intrans.* Associate, have dealings *with*. ME.
3 *verb intrans.* Come together, mingle, in combat. ME.
4 *verb refl.* Concern or busy oneself. *arch.* ME.
†**5** *verb intrans.* Copulate. LME–M17.
6 *verb intrans.* Concern, busy, oneself; deal *with*, treat; interfere, meddle. LME.

mellaginous /mɛˈladʒɪnəs/ *adjective.* L17.
[ORIGIN from mod. Latin *mellagin-*, *mellago* a preparation resembling honey, from *mell-*, *mel* honey: see -OUS.]
Pertaining to or of the nature of honey.

mellah /ˈmɛlə/ *noun.* E19.
[ORIGIN Moroccan Arab. *mallāh* Jewish quarter, from *al-Mallāh* (lit. 'the salty area'), the name of the district into which the Jewish community of Fez were compelled to move in 1438.]
A Jewish quarter in a Moroccan or Turkish city.

mellay /ˈmɛleɪ/ *noun.* Now *rare*. ME.
[ORIGIN Old French *mellée*: see MÊLÉE, -Y⁵. Cf. MEDLEY.]
†**1** A cloth of a mixture of colours or shades of colour. ME–L16.
2 Orig., a battle or quarrel. Later, a mêlée, a confused hand-to-hand fight. LME.

†**melleous** *adjective.* M17–M18.
[ORIGIN from Latin *melleus*, from *mell-*, *mel* honey: see -EOUS.]
Of the nature of, resembling, or containing honey.

melliferous /mɛˈlɪf(ə)rəs/ *adjective.* M17.
[ORIGIN from Latin *mellifer*, from *mell(i)-*, *mel* honey: see -FEROUS.]
Yielding or producing honey.

mellification /ˌmɛlɪfɪˈkeɪʃ(ə)n/ *noun.* Long *rare*. M17.
[ORIGIN Latin *mellificatio(n-)*, from *mellificat-* pa. ppl stem of *mellificare*, from *mellificus*, from *mell(i)-*, *mel* honey: see -FICATION.]
The action or process of making honey.

mellifluence /mɛˈlɪflʊəns/ *noun.* M17.
[ORIGIN formed as MELLIFLUENT + -ENCE.]
The state or quality of being mellifluent.

mellifluent /mɛˈlɪflʊənt/ *adjective.* E17.
[ORIGIN Late Latin *mellifluent-*, from Latin *mell(i)-*, *mel* honey + *fluent-*: see FLUENT.]
= MELLIFLUOUS.

mellifluous /mɛˈlɪflʊəs/ *adjective.* L15.
[ORIGIN from Old French *melliflue* or its source late Latin *mellifluus*, from Latin *mell(i)-*, *mel* honey + *-fluus* flowing, from *fluere* flow: see -OUS.]
1 Flowing with honey; sweetened (as) with honey. Now *rare*. L15.

THACKERAY No one lacked . . of raspberry open-tarts, nor of mellifluous bull's-eyes.

2 Pleasingly smooth and musical to hear, flowing. L15.

Vanity Fair I grew up around people who had wonderful, mellifluous voices.

■ **mellifluously** *adverb* M18. **mellifluousness** *noun* E19.

mellilite *noun* var. of MELILITE.

mellisonant /mɛˈlɪsənənt/ *adjective. arch.* M17.
[ORIGIN from Latin *mell(i)-*, *mel* honey + *sonant-*, pres. ppl stem of *sonare* to sound: see -ANT¹.]
Sweet-sounding.

mellite /ˈmɛlʌɪt/ *noun*. E19.
[ORIGIN mod. Latin *mellites*, from Latin *mell-*, *mel* honey: see -ITE[1].]
MINERALOGY. Aluminium mellitate, a tetragonal mineral occurring naturally as honey-yellow crystals, esp. in lignite; honeystone.

mellitic /mɛˈlɪtɪk/ *adjective*. E19.
[ORIGIN from MELLITE + -IC.]
CHEMISTRY. ***mellitic acid***, a soluble crystalline acid, $C_6(COOH)_6$, obtainable from mellite or by oxidizing carbon with nitric acid; benzenehexacarboxylic acid.
■ **ˈmellitate** *noun* a salt or ester of mellitic acid E19.

mellivorous /mɛˈlɪv(ə)rəs/ *adjective*. E19.
[ORIGIN from mod. Latin *mellivorus*, from Latin *mell(i)-*, *mel* honey: see -VOROUS.]
Of an animal: feeding naturally on honey.

mellophone /ˈmɛləfəʊn/ *noun*. Chiefly US. E20.
[ORIGIN from MELLO(W *adjective* + -PHONE.]
A type of brass instrument similar to the orchestral horn; an alto or tenor horn. Cf. MÉLOPHONE.

mellotron /ˈmɛlətrɒn/ *noun*. M20.
[ORIGIN from MELLO(W *adjective* + ELEC)TRON(IC.]
MUSIC. An electronic device simulating the sounds of orchestral instruments.

mellow /ˈmɛləʊ/ *adjective* & *noun*. LME.
[ORIGIN Perh. from attrib. use of Old English *melu* (*melw-*) MEAL *noun*[1].]
▸ **A** *adjective*. **1** Of fruit: soft, sweet, and juicy with ripeness. Now chiefly *literary*. LME. ▸**b** Rich, soft, and suggestive of ripeness; (of wine) well-matured, smooth; (of sound, colour, light, etc.) full and pure without harshness. M16. ▸**c** Of soil: soft, rich, and loamy. M16. ▸**d** Soft and smooth to the touch. L18.

SHAKES. *Coriol.* As Hercules Did shake down mellow fruit. SIR W. SCOTT Mellow nuts have hardest rind. **b** KEATS Season of mists and mellow fruitfulness. TOECKEY JONES A mellow voice said 'Rhonda, this is Joel speaking'. R. P. JHABVALA In a mellow evening light, the scene was dignified. **c** DRYDEN Hoary Frosts . . will rot the Mellow Soil.

2 *fig.* Mature, ripe in age; (esp. of a person's character) softened by age, experience, etc.; having the gentleness or dignity of maturity. L16.

SMOLLETT In florid youth or mellow age. M. ARNOLD The mellow glory of the Attic stage. C. CONNOLLY A raw and intolerant nation eager to destroy the tolerant and mellow.

3 Affected by liquor, esp. pleasantly; slightly drunk. E17.

W. S. MAUGHAM Bartolomeo . . was, if not drunk, at least mellow.

4 a Good-humoured, genial, jovial; relaxed, easy. E18. ▸**b** Satisfying; attractive; skilful; pleasant. *US slang*. M20.

a ADDISON In all thy Humours, whether grave or mellow. R. SILVERBERG He was . . always wondrously relaxed: truly the mellow man.

▸ **B** *noun*. A state of relaxation or comfort. *US colloq.* L20.
harsh someone's mellow *US slang* ruin someone's relaxed mood.
■ **mellowly** *adverb* M18. **mellowness** *noun* M16. **mellowspeak** *noun* (*US slang*) [-SPEAK] bland or euphemistic language L20. **mellowy** *adjective* (*arch. rare*) mellow LME.

mellow /ˈmɛləʊ/ *verb*. L16.
[ORIGIN from the adjective.]
1 *verb trans.* Make mellow. L16.

S. ROGERS Its colours mellow'd, not impair'd, by time. LYTTON The year . . had mellowed the fruits of the earth. TENNYSON There he mellow'd all his heart with ale. E. BOWEN Age may have mellowed him, for he . . made a benevolent grandfather. F. FORSYTH The sun was blistering, but mellowed by a light wind. C. THUBRON It was a brutal city, and its past did nothing to mellow it.

2 *verb intrans.* Become mellow. L16. ▸**b** Foll. by *out*: relax, become less intense. *N. Amer. colloq.* L20.

SHAKES. *Rich. III* So now prosperity begins to mellow And drop into the rotten mouth of death. EVELYN Those which attain not their full ripeness . . but must be laid up to mellow in the House. A. E. W. MASON The sunlight mellowed and reddened. *My Weekly* She has mellowed and finds being a good wife and mother . . important. P. D. JAMES High summer was browning and mellowing into autumn.

melo /ˈmɛləʊ/ *noun*. *colloq.* Pl. **-os**. L19.
[ORIGIN Abbreviation.]
= MELODRAMA.

melocactus /mɛlə(ʊ)ˈkaktəs/ *noun*. Pl. **-ti** /-tʌɪ/, **-tuses**. M18.
[ORIGIN mod. Latin (see below), from late Latin *melo* MELON *noun*[1] + CACTUS.]
BOTANY. Any of various cacti of the genus *Melocactus*, native to Central and S. America. Also called ***melon-cactus***, ***melon-thistle***.

melocoton /ˈmɛlə(ʊ)kɒt(ə)n/ *noun*. *obsolete* exc. *hist.* E17.
[ORIGIN Spanish *melocotón* from Italian *melocotogno* quince from medieval Latin *melum cotoneum* (= late Latin *malum cotoneum*): see QUINCE.]
A late-ripening, thickly downy variety of peach. Also ***melocoton peach***.

melodeon /mɪˈləʊdɪən/ *noun*. Also **-ion**. M19.
[ORIGIN Alt. of MELODIUM; in sense 3 perh. from MELODY after *accordion*.]
1 A wind instrument with a keyboard, the bellows being moved by means of pedals worked by the performer's feet (an earlier form of the American organ). M19.
2 (Also **M-**.) A music hall. *arch. US*. M19.
3 A kind of accordion. L19.

melodia /mɪˈləʊdɪə/ *noun*. M19.
[ORIGIN Late Latin: see MELODY.]
A kind of organ stop with a flutelike tone.

melodial /mɪˈləʊdɪəl/ *adjective*. L16.
[ORIGIN from MELODY + -AL[1].]
Of or pertaining to melody.
■ **melodially** *adverb* E19.

melodic /mɪˈlɒdɪk/ *adjective*. E19.
[ORIGIN French *mélodique* from late Latin *melodicus* from Greek *melōidikos*, from *melōidia* MELODY: see -IC.]
Of or pertaining to melody; having or producing melody.
melodic minor MUSIC a scale with a major sixth and seventh ascending and a minor sixth and seventh descending.
■ **melodically** *adverb* in a melodic manner, with regard to melody L19.

melodica /mɪˈlɒdɪkə/ *noun*. L19.
[ORIGIN from MELOD(Y + HARMON)ICA.]
1 A small pipe organ, invented by J. A. Stein of Vienna. Now *hist.* L19.
2 A wind instrument with a small keyboard controlling a row of reeds, and a mouthpiece at one end. M20.

melodion *noun* var. of MELODEON.

melodious /mɪˈləʊdɪəs/ *adjective*. LME.
[ORIGIN Old French *melodieus* (mod. *mélodieux*) = medieval Latin *melodiosus*, from Latin *melodia* MELODY: see -IOUS.]
1 Characterized by melody; sweet-sounding, tuneful. LME.

DRYDEN A music more melodious than the spheres. I. MCEWAN Her voice was melodious.

2 Producing melody; singing sweetly. L16.

SHAKES. *Tit. A.* Where like a sweet melodious bird it sang.

†**3** Susceptible to melody. L16–E17.
4 Having a melody; pertaining to or of the nature of melody. E18.
■ **melodiously** *adverb* LME. **melodiousness** *noun* M16.

melodise *verb* var. of MELODIZE.

melodist /ˈmɛlədɪst/ *noun*. L18.
[ORIGIN from MELODY + -IST.]
1 A singer. L18.
2 A composer of melodies; a person skilled in melody. E19.

melodium /mɪˈləʊdɪəm/ *noun*. M19.
[ORIGIN from MELODY after *harmonium*.]
= MELODEON 1.

melodize /ˈmɛlədʌɪz/ *verb*. Also **-ise**. M17.
[ORIGIN from MELODY + -IZE.]
1 *verb intrans.* Make melody, produce sweet music; *poet.* blend melodiously *with*. M17.
2 *verb trans.* Make melodious. M18.
3 *verb trans.* Compose a melody for (a song). L19.

melodrama /ˈmɛlə(ʊ)drɑːmə/ *noun*. L18.
[ORIGIN Alt. of MELODRAME after *drama*.]
1 Orig., a (usu. romantic and sensational) play interspersed with songs and accompanied by orchestral music. Now, a sensational dramatic piece with crude appeals to the emotions and usu. a happy ending; the genre of drama of this type. L18.
2 A story, occurrence, series of incidents, etc. resembling the plot of a melodrama; behaviour or events that resemble melodrama. E19.

New York Times Our family has a tendency to make melodrama out of molehills.

melodramatic /mɛlə(ʊ)drəˈmatɪk/ *adjective*. L18.
[ORIGIN from MELODRAMA after *dramatic*.]
Of or pertaining to melodrama; characteristic of melodrama, esp. in being exaggerated or overemotional.

New Yorker The story is turgid, melodramatic nonsense.

■ **melodramatically** *adverb* M19.

melodramatics /mɛlə(ʊ)drəˈmatɪks/ *noun pl.* L19.
[ORIGIN from MELODRAMATIC: see -ICS.]
Melodramatic behaviour, action, or writing.

melodramatise *verb* var. of MELODRAMATIZE.

melodramatist /mɛlə(ʊ)ˈdramətɪst/ *noun*. E19.
[ORIGIN from MELODRAMA after *dramatist*.]
A writer of melodramas.

melodramatize /mɛlə(ʊ)ˈdramətʌɪz/ *verb trans.* Also **-ise**. E19.
[ORIGIN formed as MELODRAMATIST, after *dramatize*.]
Make melodramatic; adapt (a novel etc.) into a melodrama.

melodrame /ˈmɛlə(ʊ)dram/ *noun*. Now *rare* or *obsolete*. L18.
[ORIGIN French *mélodrame*, from Greek *melos* song, music + French *drame* DRAMA.]
A melodrama.

melody /ˈmɛlədi/ *noun* & *verb*. ME.
[ORIGIN Old French & mod. French *mélodie* from late Latin *melodia* from Greek *melōidia* singing, choral song, from *melōidos* musical, from *melos* song, music + *ōidē* ODE: see -Y[3].]
▸ **A** *noun*. **1** Sweet music, either vocal or instrumental; beautiful arrangement of musical sounds; tunefulness. ME.

SHAKES. *Mids. N. D.* Philomel with melody, Sing in our sweet lullaby. SHELLEY Whilst all the winds with melody are ringing.

†**2** A song or other musical performance. ME–M16.
3 a A series of single notes arranged in musically expressive succession; an air. E17. ▸**b** A poem, song, etc., written to be sung to a particular arrangement of single notes in expressive succession. E19. ▸**c** The principal part in a harmonized piece of music. L19.

a DAY LEWIS From childhood I could pick up a melody by ear. S. RUSHDIE A glade filled with the gentle melodies of song-birds. **b** W. CARLETON The touching and inimitable Melodies of my countryman Thomas Moore. **c** W. S. ROCKSTRO Arrangements with the melody, as usual, in the Tenor.

4 MUSIC. (The branch of music that deals with) the arrangement of single notes in expressive succession. Cf. HARMONY 3. E18.

F. BURNEY Melody and Harmony . . had been cultivated for the use of the church.

▸ **B** *verb intrans.* Make melody; sing. *rare*. L16.

meloe /ˈmɛləʊiː/ *noun*. M17.
[ORIGIN mod. Latin *Meloe*, *Meloë*, perh. connected with Latin *mel* honey.]
ENTOMOLOGY. Any of various oil beetles mainly of the genus *Meloe*, several of which spend the larval stage within the brood cells of wild bees. Now chiefly as mod. Latin genus name.

meloid /ˈmɛlɔɪd, -əʊɪd/ *noun* & *adjective*. L19.
[ORIGIN mod. Latin *Meloidae* (see below), formed as MELOE: see -ID[3].]
ENTOMOLOGY. ▸**A** *noun*. A beetle of the family Meloidae, which includes oil beetles and blister beetles. L19.
▸ **B** *adjective*. Of, pertaining to, or designating this family. L19.

M

melologue /ˈmɛlə(ʊ)lɒg/ *noun*. E19.
[ORIGIN from Greek *melos* song, music + -LOGUE.]
A musical composition of verses in which some are sung and others recited.

melomane /ˈmɛlə(ʊ)meɪn/ *noun*. M19.
[ORIGIN French *mélomane*, from Greek *melos* song, music: see -MANE.]
A person who is very enthusiastic about music.

melomania /mɛlə(ʊ)ˈmeɪnɪə/ *noun*. L19.
[ORIGIN French *mélomanie*, from Greek *melos* song, music: see -MANIA.]
An enthusiasm, passion, or craze for music.
■ **melomaniac** *noun* a passionate or obsessive enthusiast for music L19. **melomanic** /-ˈmanɪk/ *adjective* (now *rare* or *obsolete*) characterized by melomania E19.

melon /ˈmɛlən/ *noun*[1]. LME.
[ORIGIN Old French & mod. French from late Latin *melon-*, *melo* contr. of Latin *melopepo* MELOPEPON.]
1 The fruit of a gourd, *Cucumis melo*, with sweet green, yellowish-pink, etc., flesh; the plant bearing this. Also, a watermelon. LME. ▸**b** *fig.* A large profit to be divided among a number of people. *slang*. E20.
cantaloupe melon, ***honeydew melon***, ***musk melon***, etc.
2 ZOOLOGY. In many toothed whales, a mass of waxy material in the head, thought to focus acoustic signals; the dome this forms on the forehead. L19.
3 In *pl.* Large breasts. *slang*. M20.
– COMB.: **melon-cactus** = MELOCACTUS; **melon-caterpillar** = *melonworm* below; **melon-oil** oil from the melon of a cetacean; **melon pink** (of) a yellowish-pink colour; **melon-seed** a seed from a melon; ***melon-seed body*** (MEDICINE), a small loose rounded mass found in the cavities of inflamed joints and in certain types of cyst (usu. in *pl.*); **melon-shell** (the shell of) any of various very large smooth-shelled volutes of the tropical Indo-Pacific, *esp.* one of the genus *Melo*; **melon-thistle** = MELOCACTUS; **melon-wood** a yellow Mexican wood resembling sandalwood, used for furniture; **melonworm** the greenish caterpillar of an American pyralid moth, *Diaphania hyalinata*, which is a pest of pumpkins, melons, and other cucurbits.
■ †**meloniere** *noun* [French *melonnièr*] a melonry M17–E18. †**melonist** *noun* a person who cultivates melons M17–E18. **melonry** *noun* a place for the cultivation of melons E18.

melon /ˈmɛlən/ *noun*[2]. *Austral.* M19.
[ORIGIN Abbreviation.]
= PADEMELON.
– COMB.: **melon-hole** = GILGAI.

melongena /mɛlənˈdʒiːnə/ *noun*. L18.
[ORIGIN mod. Latin, formed as MELONGENE.]
(The fruit of) the aubergine, *Solanum melongena*.

melongene /ˈmɛləndʒiːn/ *noun*. *W. Indian*. M19.
[ORIGIN French *mélongène*, ult. formed as AUBERGINE.]
= MELONGENA.

†**melopepon** *noun.* M16–E18.
[ORIGIN Latin *melopepon-*, *melopepo* from Greek *mēlopepōn*, from *mēlon* apple + *pepōn* a kind of gourd.]
A kind of pumpkin.

mélophone /ˈmɛlə(ʊ)fəʊn; *foreign* melɔfɔn (*pl. same*)/ *noun.* Also **mel-** /ˈmɛl-/. M19.
[ORIGIN French from Greek *melos* song, music: see -PHONE.]
A kind of portable reed organ with a hand bellows and keys, shaped like a guitar or a hurdy-gurdy. Cf. MELLOPHONE.

meloplasty /ˈmɛlə(ʊ)plasti/ *noun. rare.* L19.
[ORIGIN from Greek *mēlon* apple, (poet.) cheek + -PLASTY.]
Surgical repair of a cheek by grafting and plastic surgery; an instance of this.
■ **melo'plastic** *adjective* M19.

melopoeia /mɛlə(ʊ)ˈpiːə/ *noun.* E18.
[ORIGIN Greek *melopoiia*, from *melopoios* maker of songs, from *melos* song, music + *poiein* make.]
†**1** The art of composing melodies; the branch of dramatic art that deals with music. E18–L19.
2 The musical and rhythmic qualities of poetic language. E20.
■ **melopoeic** *adjective* E20.

melos /ˈmɛlɒs, ˈmiːlɒs/ *noun.* M18.
[ORIGIN Greek = song, music.]
MUSIC. Song, melody; *spec.* the succession of tones considered apart from rhythm; an uninterrupted flow of melody.

melo-tragedy /mɛlə(ʊ)ˈtradʒədi/ *noun. rare.* E19.
[ORIGIN from Greek *melos* song, music + -O- + TRAGEDY.]
A tragic play in which songs occur; an operatic tragedy.

melphalan /ˈmɛlfəlan/ *noun.* M20.
[ORIGIN Arbitrary formation, partly from L-*phenylalanine*.]
PHARMACOLOGY. A nitrogen mustard used intravenously to treat cancers, esp. myelomatosis; 4-bis(2-chloroethyl)amino-L-phenylalanine, $C_{13}H_{18}N_2O_2Cl_2$.

melpomenish /mɛlˈpɒmɪnɪʃ/ *adjective. literary. rare.* E19.
[ORIGIN from Greek *Melpomenē* (lit. 'singer') the Muse of tragedy + -ISH[1].]
Tragic.

melsh /mɛlʃ/ *adjective. Long dial.* Also **melch** /mɛltʃ/.
[ORIGIN Old English *mel(i)sć*, *mylsć*, from base also of Middle High German *molwic*, German *mollig*, *mollecht*, *molsch*, *mulsch* soft, Old High German *molawēn* be soft, cogn. with Latin *mollis* tender: see -ISH[1]. Cf. MULSH.]
Mellow, soft, tender; (of weather) mild.

M

melt /mɛlt/ *noun*[1]. M19.
[ORIGIN from MELT *verb*.]
1 Metal etc. in a melted condition. M19.
2 A quantity of metal etc. melted at one operation. L19.
3 The process of melting. Freq. in ***on the melt***. L19.
4 A sandwich, hamburger, or other dish containing or topped with melted cheese. Usu. with modifying word, as ***tuna melt***. Orig. *N. Amer.* M20.
– COMB.: **melt-spin** *verb trans.* prepare by melt-spinning (freq. as ***melt-spun*** *ppl adjective*); **melt spinning** the extrusion of a heat-softened substance (esp. a polymer) through a spinneret to form a fibre; **melt water** water resulting from the melting of ice or snow, esp. that of a glacier.

melt *noun*[2] var. of MILT *noun*.

melt /mɛlt/ *verb.* Pa. t. **melted**; pa. pple **melted**, **molten** /ˈməʊlt(ə)n/.
[ORIGIN Old English (i) strong verb *meltan*, (ii) (Anglian) weak verb *meltan*, (West Saxon) *mieltan* = Old Norse *melta*, from base also of MALT *noun*, repr. Indo-European base also of Greek *meldein* melt, Latin *mollis*, Sanskrit *mṛdu* soft. Cf. MILD, SMELT *verb*[1].]
▸ **I** *verb intrans.* **1** Become liquefied by heat; (foll. by *away*) be destroyed by liquefaction; (foll. by *down*) become liquid and lose structure. OE. ▸**b** Of a person: perspire excessively, suffer extreme heat. *colloq.* L18.

E. WAUGH The frost broke; the snow melted away. I. MCEWAN He stared ahead at the large flakes melting on contact with the windscreen. *Scientific American* There would be no possibility that the fuel core would melt down.

2 a Orig., (of food) be digested. Later, become disintegrated, liquefied, or softened, esp. by the agency of moisture; dissolve. OE. ▸**b** Of clouds etc.: be dispersed; break *into* rain. LME. ▸**c** Vanish, disappear; (foll. by *away*) depart unobtrusively. E17.

b W. BLACK The clouds had melted into a small and chilling rain. **c** A. THIRKELL David . . melted from the room. E. WAUGH Popotakis's old clients melted away to other . . resorts. M. UNDERWOOD He didn't hang around afterwards . . he melted away.

3 †**a** Be overwhelmed with dismay or grief. OE–E17. ▸**b** Become softened by pity, love, etc.; yield to entreaty; dissolve *into* tears or laughter. ME. ▸**c** Foll. by *away*: become ecstatic. *rare.* E18.

a AV *Josh.* 2:11 Our hearts did melt, neither did there remaine any more courage in any man. **b** STEELE She melted into a Flood of Tears. J. W. BURGON At sight of the dusty . . urchins, his heart evidently melted. **c** WILLIAM COLLINS There let me oft, retir'd by day In dreams of passion melt away.

4 Waste *away*, become gradually smaller; dwindle *down to* a particular point or condition. ME.

SHAKES. *Ant. & Cl.* Authority melts from me. LD MACAULAY The host which had been the terror of Scotland melted away. M. TWAIN When one . . sees his resources melt down to a two-months' supply.

5 Filter in, become absorbed *into*. LME.

SHELLEY Like fiery dews that melt Into the bosom of a frozen bud.

6 Of sound: be soft and liquid. E17.

S. ROGERS The enchanting serenade . . melts along the moonlight-glade.

7 Pass by imperceptible degrees *into* another form. L18.

W. COWPER Downs . . That melt and fade into the distant sky. HUGH WALPOLE Cool brown colours melting into the blue or grey of the sky.

▸ **II** *verb trans.* **8 a** Liquefy by heat; (foll. by *away*) cause to disappear by liquefaction; (foll. by *down*) change (coin, plate, etc.) by heat into liquid metal for use as raw material; (foll. by *up*) fashion (an object) from molten metal. OE. ▸†**b** Liquefy by heat and refashion (an object) *into* another shape; form (an image etc.) out of molten material. LME–E17. ▸**c** Cause (a person) to perspire excessively, subject to extreme heat. *colloq.* L17.

a J. TYNDALL A sun or planet once molten, would continue for ever molten. G. GREENE I am melting down some old family silver. F. HOYLE If all that ice were melted, the resulting water would raise sea level by perhaps 80 metres. *Holiday Which?* Workshops contain furnaces for melting the blister steel. **b** AV *Isa.* 40:19 The workeman melteth a grauen image, and the goldsmith spreadeth it ouer with golde.

a melted butter: see BUTTER *noun*[1] 1.

9 a Orig., digest. Later, dissolve, make a solution of. OE. ▸†**b** Disintegrate, loosen (soil). E17–E18.

a P. BARROUGH A Syrupe is of medicines a juyce with Sugar or Hony molten therin.

10 Disperse, cause to disappear. Also foll. by *away*. ME.

F. PARKMAN Cold, disease, famine, thirst, and the fury of the waves melted them away.

11 a Foll. by *away*: cause to become ecstatic. *rare.* ME. ▸**b** Soften (a person, the feelings, etc.) by appealing to pity, love, etc.; touch. Freq. as ***melted*** *ppl adjective*. LME.

a ADDISON Alas, thy Story melts away my Soul. **b** R. K. NARAYAN The thought of her melted him. M. FITZHERBERT His heart was melted.

†**12** Weaken, enervate. Also, foll. by *down*. L16–E18.

SHAKES. *Much Ado* Manhood is melted into curtsies, valour into compliment.

13 Spend, squander (money). Also, cash (a cheque etc.). Chiefly *arch. slang.* E17.
14 Blend (individual components) *into* one mass of colour, sound, etc. L18.

W. BLACK Mist . . melted whole mountains into a soft dull grey.

■ **melta'bility** *noun* (*rare*) ability to be melted M19. **meltable** *adjective* able to be melted E17. **melty** *adjective* melting E20.

meltdown /ˈmɛltdaʊn/ *noun.* M20.
[ORIGIN from MELT *verb* + DOWN *adverb*.]
1 The action or process of melting; *spec.* the melting of part of a nuclear reactor, esp. the core or its metal shielding. M20. ▸**b** An uncontrolled and usu. disastrous incident with far-reaching repercussions; COMMERCE a sudden rapid drop in the value of a currency, shares, etc., a crash. L20.
2 A mass of melted-down material. L20.

meltemi /mɛlˈtɛmi/ *noun.* M19.
[ORIGIN mod. Greek *meltémi*, Turkish *meltem*.]
A dry north-westerly wind which blows during the summer in the eastern Mediterranean; = ETESIAN *noun*.

melter /ˈmɛltə/ *noun.* E16.
[ORIGIN from MELT *verb* + -ER[1].]
1 A person who or thing which melts something; *spec.* a person whose employment involves the melting of metals, esp. in a factory, a mint, etc. E16.
2 = FREESTONE 2. M18.

melting /ˈmɛltɪŋ/ *noun.* OE.
[ORIGIN from MELT *verb* + -ING[1].]
1 The action of MELT *verb*; an instance of this. OE.
2 In *pl.* Melted material; a substance produced by melting. M16.
– COMB.: **melting house** a building for the process of melting, esp. at a mint; **melting point** the temperature at which a solid melts; **melting pot** a vessel for melting metals etc.; *fig.* a place of reconstruction or vigorous mixing (freq. in ***in the melting pot***).

melting /ˈmɛltɪŋ/ *adjective.* OE.
[ORIGIN from MELT *verb* + -ING[2].]
That melts or is in the process of melting (*lit. & fig.*); *esp.* (of a person, a mood, etc.) feeling or showing pity, love, etc., yielding to emotion; (of food) that dissolves easily in the mouth; (of fruit) sweet and tender.

SHAKES. *Oth.* Albeit unused to the melting mood. MILTON The melting voice through mazes running. R. DAHL The heavy rich smell of melting chocolate!

■ **meltingly** *adverb* L16. **meltingness** *noun* E17.

melton /ˈmɛlt(ə)n/ *noun.* Also **M-**. E19.
[ORIGIN *Melton* Mowbray, a town in central England.]
1 In full ***Melton jacket***, ***Melton coat***, etc. A jacket, coat, etc., made of melton cloth. E19.
2 More fully ***melton cloth***. A kind of cloth with a close-cut nap used esp. for jackets, coats, etc. M19.
3 ***Melton pie***, ***Melton Mowbray pie***, a kind of raised meat pie. L19.

melty /ˈmɛlti/ *adjective.* E20.
[ORIGIN from MELT *verb* + -Y[1].]
Apt to melt.

Melungeon /mɪˈlʌndʒ(ə)n/ *noun. US.* E19.
[ORIGIN Perh. from alt. of MÉLANGE.]
A member of a people of mixed black, white, and Amerindian descent inhabiting the southern Appalachian mountains in the eastern US.

melusine /mɛl(j)ʊˈsiːn/ *noun.* E20.
[ORIGIN French *mélusine*, perh. connected with *Mélusine*, a fairy in French folklore.]
A silky long-haired felt, used for making hats.

melvie /ˈmɛlvi/ *verb trans. Scot. Long rare or obsolete.* L18.
[ORIGIN Prob. ult. from MEAL *noun*[1].]
Cover with meal.

Melvillian /mɛlˈvɪlj(ə)n/ *adjective.* M20.
[ORIGIN from *Melville* (see below) + -IAN.]
Of, pertaining to, or characteristic of the US novelist and poet Herman Melville (1819–91), or his work.
■ Also **Melvillean** *adjective* M20.

mem /mɛm/ *noun*[2]. L19.
[ORIGIN Abbreviation.]
= MEMSAHIB.

mem /mɛm/ *adjective & noun*[1]. Also **mem.** (point). L15.
[ORIGIN Abbreviation: cf. MEMO.]
▸ **A** *adjective.* = MEMORANDUM. L15.
▸ **B** *noun.* A memorandum. E19.

member /ˈmɛmbə/ *noun.* ME.
[ORIGIN Old French & mod. French *membre* from Latin *membrum* limb.]
1 A part or organ of the body; *esp.* a limb or other separable portion. ME. ▸**b** *spec.* In *pl.*, the genitals; *sing.* the penis. ME. ▸**c** BIOLOGY. Any part of a plant or animal viewed with regard to its form and position. L19.

D. MORRIS Vultures, who plunge their heads and necks into gory carcasses, have lost their feathers from these members. S. BELLOW Leprosy—you lose a toe now and then; none of the main members have to be affected. *fig.*: ADDISON The Body of the Law is no less encumbered with superfluous Members. **b** J. HELLER The first time I laid eyes on Abigail . . my member grew hard as hickory.

2 Each of the individuals, countries, etc., belonging to or forming a society or assembly; *spec.* (**a**) (usu. **M-**, more fully ***Member of Parliament***, ***Member of Congress***, etc.) a person who has been formally elected to take part in the proceedings of a parliament; (**b**) a person admitted to the lowest grade of an order, as the 5th class of the Order of the British Empire. Formerly also, a native or inhabitant (of a country or city). ME. ▸**b** *ellipt.* A member of the community, a person. Now *slang & dial.* E16. ▸†**c** A participant. M16–E17. ▸**d** A black person. *US slang.* M20.

THACKERAY Captain Raff, the honourable member for Epsom. W. S. CHURCHILL Austria was still a member of the German Confederation. C. IVES The action of a mob does not necessarily mean that a majority of its members are stupid. *Daily Mirror* Members of our swimming club were involved in rescuing three people. R. GUY All the members of the Maldoon family were assembled.

3 Each of the constituent portions of a complex structure. LME. ▸**b** ARCHITECTURE. Each of the parts of a building, each of the mouldings in a collection of mouldings, as in a cornice, capital, base, etc. L17.
4 A component part or branch of a political body or, formerly, of a trade, art, profession, etc. LME.
5 A section or district, esp. an outlying part, of an estate, manor, parish, port, etc. LME.
6 A division or clause of a sentence; a branch of a disjunctive proposition. M16.
7 MATH. A group of figures or symbols forming part of a numerical expression or formula; either of the sides of an equation. E17.
8 Each of the items forming a series. E18.
– PHRASES: **carnal member** *arch.* = sense 1b above. ***private member***: see PRIVATE *adjective*. **privy member(s)** *arch.* = sense 1b above. ***secret members***: see SECRET *adjective & noun*. ***sitting member***: see SITTING *ppl adjective* 4. ***unofficial member***: see UNOFFICIAL *adjective* 2. **unruly member** [after *James* 3:5–8] the tongue. **virile member** *arch.* the penis.
– COMB.: Esp. in the sense 'that is a member of a society, assembly, (esp.) international organization, etc.', as ***member country***, ***member society***, ***member state***, etc. **member bank** *US* a bank which holds shares in, and has representation on the board of directors of, a Federal Reserve Bank.
■ **memberess** *noun* (*rare*) a female member, *spec.* a female Member of Parliament L18. **memberless** *adjective* E17.

member /ˈmɛmbə/ *verb trans. colloq.* Also **'member**. E19.
[ORIGIN Aphet.]
Remember.

membered /ˈmɛmbəd/ *adjective*. LME.
[ORIGIN from MEMBER *noun* + -ED².]
1 Having members, esp. a specified kind or number; divided into members. LME.
2 *HERALDRY*. Of a bird: having legs of a different tincture from the body. M16.

membership /ˈmɛmbəʃɪp/ *noun*. M17.
[ORIGIN from MEMBER *noun* + -SHIP.]
1 The condition or status of a member of a society, assembly, or other (organized) body. (Foll. by *of*, (now esp. US) *in*.) M17.
P. GROSSKURTH Klein was elected to full membership in the Berlin Society.
church membership etc.
2 The number of members in a particular body; the body of members. M19.
Brownie Our Pack has a membership of 20 keen Brownies. *Times Educ. Suppl.* Teachers' leaders, who . . were out of touch with their membership.

membra disjecta /mɛmbrə dɪsˈjɛktə/ *noun phr. pl.* E19.
[ORIGIN Alternative word order.]
= DISJECTA MEMBRA.

membral /ˈmɛmbr(ə)l/ *adjective*. E17.
[ORIGIN from MEMBER *noun* + -AL¹.]
Pertaining to or characteristic of a member or members. Now chiefly *ANATOMY & ZOOLOGY*, appendicular.

membranaceous /mɛmbrəˈneɪʃəs/ *adjective*. L17.
[ORIGIN from late Latin *membranaceus*, from *membrana* MEMBRANE: see -ACEOUS.]
BIOLOGY. Resembling or of the nature of a membrane; membranous.

membranate /ˈmɛmbrənət/ *adjective*. *rare*. L18.
[ORIGIN from MEMBRANE + -ATE².]
Having a membrane or membranes; of the nature of a membrane.

membrane /ˈmɛmbreɪn/ *noun*. LME.
[ORIGIN (French *membrane* from) Latin *membrana* skin covering part of the body, use as noun of fem. adjective (sc. *cutis* skin) from *membrum* limb, MEMBER *noun*.]
1 a *ANATOMY & BIOLOGY*. Any thin, pliable, usu. fibrous sheet or layer of tissue, freq. serving to separate other structures or to line a part or organ; the tissue of which this is formed. LME. ▸**b** *MEDICINE*. A thin sheetlike structure formed as a result of disease. M18. ▸**c** *CYTOLOGY*. Any of various thin, fluid, semipermeable lipid bilayers with included proteins which form structures within living cells, *esp.* more fully (*cell membrane*) that which bounds the cell. L19.
a basement membrane, *mucous membrane*, *pit membrane*, etc. **c** *PLASMA membrane*.
2 Orig., parchment. Now, each of the parts of a parchment roll. LME.
3 Any thin extended sheetlike barrier of material. L19.
P. DAVIES The surface of a balloon . . is a membrane of rubber.
– COMB.: **membrane bone** a bone which develops from membranous connective tissue, not cartilage; **membrane filter**: made of cellulosic material and capable of retaining objects as small as bacteria, used in microbiology and water purification; **membrane filtration**: by means of a membrane filter.
■ **membraneless** *adjective* L19. **membranoid** *adjective* resembling or consisting of membrane M19.

membranella /mɛmbrəˈnɛlə/ *noun*. Pl. **-llae** /-liː/. Also anglicized as **-nelle** /-ˈnɛl/. L19.
[ORIGIN mod. Latin, dim. of Latin *membrana* MEMBRANE.]
ZOOLOGY. In some ciliates, a long flattened locomotory organ formed from fused cilia.

membraneous /mɛmˈbreɪnɪəs/ *adjective*. L16.
[ORIGIN from late Latin *membraneus*, from Latin *membrana* MEMBRANE: see -OUS.]
= MEMBRANOUS.

membraniform /mɛmˈbreɪnɪfɔːm/ *adjective*. E19.
[ORIGIN from MEMBRANE + -I- + -FORM.]
Having the character or structure of a membrane.

membrano- /ˈmɛmbrənəʊ/ *combining form* of MEMBRANE: see -O-.
■ **membranoˈgenic** *adjective* producing (a) membrane L19. **membraˈnology** *noun* the branch of science that deals with membranes (now esp. cell membranes) L18. **membranophone** *noun* a musical instrument which employs a stretched membrane to produce the sound M20.

membranous /ˈmɛmbrənəs/ *adjective*. L16.
[ORIGIN French *membraneux*, formed as MEMBRANE: see -OUS.]
1 Consisting of, resembling, or of the nature of (a) membrane; membranaceous; *esp.* in *BOTANY*, thin and more or less translucent. L16.
membranous labyrinth the soft structures of the inner ear, including the cochlea, utricle, saccule, and semicircular canals.
2 *MEDICINE*. Of a disease: involving the formation or expulsion of (a) membrane. L19.

membranula /mɛmˈbreɪnjʊlə/ *noun*. Pl. **-lae** /-liː/, **-las**. Also anglicized as **-ule** /-juːl/. E19.
[ORIGIN Latin, dim. of *membrana* MEMBRANE: see -ULE.]
BIOLOGY. Any of various small membranes or membranous structures; *spec.* in *ENTOMOLOGY*, a small opaque region at the base of the forewing in some dragonflies.

membrification /ˌmɛmbrɪfɪˈkeɪʃ(ə)n/ *noun*. *rare*. L17.
[ORIGIN from Latin *membrum* MEMBER *noun*: see -FICATION.]
Formation of members or limbs.

membrillo /mɛmˈbriʎo, mɛmˈbriːljəʊ/ *noun*. E20.
[ORIGIN Spanish = quince.]
A Spanish preserve of quinces.

membrum virile /mɛmbrəm vɪˈrʌɪli, vɪˈriːli/ *noun phr.* L17.
[ORIGIN Latin = male member.]
The penis.

meme /miːm/ *noun*. L20.
[ORIGIN from Greek *mimēma* that which is imitated, after GENE.]
BIOLOGY. An element of a culture or system of behaviour that may be considered to be passed from one individual to another by non-genetic means, esp. imitation.
■ **memetic** /mɪˈmɛtɪk/ *adjective* L20.

memento /mɪˈmɛntəʊ/ *noun*. Pl. **-o(e)s**. LME.
[ORIGIN Latin, imper. of *meminisse* remember, ult. redupl. of base of MIND *noun*¹.]
1 *CHRISTIAN CHURCH*. Either of the two prayers (beginning with *Memento*) in the canon of the Mass, in which the living and the dead are respectively commemorated; the commemoration of the living or the dead in these prayers. LME.
2 A reminder, warning, or hint as to future conduct or events. Now *esp.* an object serving as such a reminder or warning. L16.
3 A reminder of a past event or condition, of an absent person, or something that once existed. Now *esp.* an object kept as a memorial of some person or event, a souvenir. M18.
– PHRASES: ***memento mori*** /ˈmɔːrʌɪ, ˈmɔːri/ [Latin = remember that you have to die] a warning or reminder of death, *esp.* a skull or other symbolical object. ***memento vivere*** /ˈviːvəri/ [Latin = remember that you have to live, after *memento mori*] a reminder of life; a reminder of the pleasure of living.

Memnonian /mɛmˈnəʊnɪən/ *adjective*. *literary*. E17.
[ORIGIN from Latin *Memnonius* (from Greek *Memnoneios*, from *Memnōn* Memnon) + -AN.]
Of or pertaining to Memnon, a mythical demigod said to have erected the citadel or palace at the ancient city of Susa in SW Iran (also thought to be represented by a statue at Thebes in Egypt believed to give out a musical sound when touched by the dawn); Persian, Iranian.

memo /ˈmɛməʊ/ *adjective*, *noun*, & *verb*. E18.
[ORIGIN Abbreviation. Cf. MEM *adjective* & *noun*¹.]
▸ **A** *adjective*. = MEMORANDUM *adjective*. E18.
▸ **B** *noun*. Pl. **-os**. = MEMORANDUM *noun* 1, esp. 1e. E18.
M. BRADBURY Can I draw the chair's attention to the departmental memo, circulated this very morning. S. QUINN The Department of State issued a memo in response to Horney's renewed application for a passport.
▸ **C** *verb trans*. Send a memo to. M20.

memoir /ˈmɛmwɑː/ *noun*. L15.
[ORIGIN French *mémoire* (masc.) specific use of fem. noun = MEMORY.]
1 A note, a memorandum, a record, now *spec.* an official one. L15.
2 *sing.* & in *pl.* A record of events or history from personal knowledge or from special sources of information; an autobiographical or (occas.) biographical record. M17.
J. FOWLES Gosse was . . immortalized half a century later in his son Edmund's famous and exquisite memoir. E. PAWEL His memoirs, though . . based on notes made at the time, were never submitted for publication.
3 An essay or dissertation on a learned subject specially studied by the writer. In *pl.* also, (the record of) the proceedings or transactions of a learned society. L17.
■ **memoirist** *noun* a writer of memoirs or of a memoir M18.

memomotion /ˈmɛməʊməʊʃ(ə)n/ *noun*. M20.
[ORIGIN Alt. of MICROMOTION, perh. after Latin *memor* mindful & related words.]
Movement of the body recorded by time-lapse photography for purposes of work study. Usu. *attrib*.

memorabilia /mɛm(ə)rəˈbɪlɪə/ *noun pl.* L18.
[ORIGIN Latin, neut. pl. of *memorabilis*: see MEMORABLE, -IA².]
1 Memorable or noteworthy things. L18.
2 Souvenirs. L19.

memorable /ˈmɛm(ə)rəb(ə)l/ *adjective* & *noun*. L15.
[ORIGIN French *mémorable* or Latin *memorabilis*, from *memorare*: see MEMORANDUM, -ABLE.]
▸ **A** *adjective*. Worthy of remembrance or note, worth remembering, not to be forgotten; able to be remembered, easy to remember. L15.
R. SCRUTON Our century is memorable for nothing so much as its violence. E. FEINSTEIN Was there anything special about you? I don't remember a single memorable thing.
▸ **B** *noun*. In *pl.* = MEMORABILIA 1. Now *rare*. E17.
■ **memoraˈbility** *noun* M17. **memorableness** *noun* E18. **memorably** *adverb* E17.

†**memorand** *adjective* & *noun*. ME.
[ORIGIN Latin *memorandus*: see MEMORANDUM.]
▸ **A** *adjective*. Serving as a memorial. Only in ME.
▸ **B** *noun*. **1** A memorial. Only in ME.
2 = MEMORANDUM *noun*. L17–E18.

memorandum /mɛməˈrandəm/ *adjective*, *noun*, & *verb*. LME.
[ORIGIN Latin, neut. sing. of *memorandus* gerundive of *memorare* bring to mind, from *memor* mindful. Cf. MEM *noun*¹, MEMO.]
▸ **A** *adjective*. To be remembered: placed at the beginning of a note of something to be remembered or a record (for future reference) of something done. Now only *LAW*. LME.
▸ **B** *noun*. Pl. **-da** /-də/, **-dums**.
1 a A note to help the memory, a record of events or of observations on a particular subject, esp. for future consideration or use. L15. ▸**b** *LAW*. A writing or document summarizing or embodying the terms of a transaction, contract, agreement, establishment of a company etc. In maritime insurance, a clause in a policy enumerating the articles in respect of which underwriters have no liability. L16. ▸**c** A record of a money transaction. L16. ▸**d** An informal diplomatic message, esp. summarizing the state of a question or justifying a decision. M17. ▸**e** An informal written communication of a kind conventionally not requiring a signature, as within a business or organization, usu. written on paper headed 'Memorandum'. L19.
b *memorandum of ASSOCIATION*.
†**2** An injunction to remember something. L16–M17.
3 A reminder; a memento, a souvenir. *obsolete* exc. *Scot. dial.* L16.
▸ **C** *verb trans*. Now *rare*. Make a memorandum of. L18.

memorate /ˈmɛməreɪt/ *verb trans*. Long *rare*. E17.
[ORIGIN Latin *memorat-* pa. ppl stem of *memorare*: see MEMORANDUM, -ATE³.]
Bring to mind; mention; remember.

memorative /ˈmɛm(ə)rətɪv/ *adjective* & *noun*. Now *rare*. LME.
[ORIGIN Old French & mod. French *mémoratif*, *-ive* or late Latin *memorativus*, formed as MEMORATE: see -IVE.]
▸ **A** *adjective*. **1** Preserving or reviving the memory of some person or thing; commemorative. LME.
2 Of or pertaining to memory. LME.
†**3** Having a good memory; retentive. L15–L17.
▸ †**B** *noun*. A memorial. L15–L17.

memorial /mɪˈmɔːrɪəl/ *adjective* & *noun*. LME.
[ORIGIN Old French & mod. French *mémorial* or Latin *memorialis* adjective (late Latin *memoriale* noun, sign of remembrance, memorial, monument), from *memoria* MEMORY: see -AL¹.]
▸ **A** *adjective*. **1** Preserving or intended to preserve the memory of a person or thing; commemorative. LME.
Times A memorial service for General Grant will be held in Westminster Abbey. *Morning Star* The memorial reunion of resistance fighters.
†**2** Remembered; worthy to be remembered, memorable. LME–M17.
3 Of or pertaining to memory. Formerly also, intended to assist the memory, mnemonic. LME.
F. BOWERS A memorial lapse, but not a misreading, must be posited.
▸ **B** *noun*. †**1** Remembrance, recollection; (a person's) memory or power of recollection. LME–L18.
2 A memorial act; an act of commemoration; *spec.* = COMMEMORATION 1b. LME.
3 A thing, as a monument, a custom, etc., by which the memory of a person, thing, or event is preserved. LME.
4 A record, a chronicle; esp. in *pl.*, memoirs. LME.
†**5** A note, a memorandum. E16–E19.
6 Any of various informal diplomatic papers. M16.
7 A statement of facts forming the basis of or expressed in the form of a petition or remonstrance to a person in authority, a government, etc. L17.
8 *LAW*. **a** *SCOTS LAW*. A statement of facts drawn up to be submitted for counsel's opinion. Also, an advocate's brief. E18. ▸**b** An abstract of the particulars of a deed etc. serving for registration. E19.
– COMB.: **Memorial Day** any of various days set aside for the commemoration of those who died in war; *spec.* in the US, 30 May, or the last Monday in May, set aside for the commemoration of those who died on active service and observed as a public holiday in many states.

memorial /mɪˈmɔːrɪəl/ *verb*. M18.
[ORIGIN from the noun.]
1 *verb trans*. Address a memorial to (a person); memorialize. M18.
2 *verb intrans*. Draw up a memorial; petition *for*. M18.

memorialise *verb* var. of MEMORIALIZE.

memorialist /mɪˈmɔːrɪəlɪst/ *noun*. E18.
[ORIGIN from MEMORIAL *noun* + -IST.]
1 A person who gives a memorial address or presents a memorial. E18.
2 A writer of biographical or historical memorials, a memoirist. M18.

memorialize /mɪˈmɔːrɪəlʌɪz/ *verb trans*. Also **-ise**. L18.
[ORIGIN formed as MEMORIALIST + -IZE.]
1 Preserve the memory of; be or supply a memorial of; commemorate. L18.
2 Address or present a memorial to. L18.
■ **memorialiˈzation** *noun* L19. **memorializer** *noun* M19.

M

memorially /mɪˈmɔːrɪəli/ *adverb*. M17.
[ORIGIN from MEMORIAL *adjective* + -LY².]
1 By heart, from memory. M17.
2 As a memorial; so as to preserve a memory. *rare*. L19.

memoria technica /mɪˌmɔːrɪə ˈtɛknɪkə/ *noun phr*. M18.
[ORIGIN mod. Latin (= technical memory) repr. Greek *to mnēmonikon tekhnēma*.]
A method of assisting the memory by artificial contrivances; a system of mnemonics, a mnemonic aid.

memoried /ˈmɛmərɪd/ *adjective*. L16.
[ORIGIN from MEMORY + -ED², -ED¹.]
1 Having a memory, esp. of a specified kind, as ***long-memoried, short-memoried***. L16.
2 Full of or fraught with memories. M19.

memorious /mɪˈmɔːrɪəs/ *adjective*. Now *rare*. E16.
[ORIGIN from Old French *memorieux* from medieval Latin *memoriosus*, from *memoria*: see MEMORY, -OUS.]
Having or showing a good memory.

memorise *verb* var. of MEMORIZE.

memorist /ˈmɛm(ə)rɪst/ *noun*. *rare*. L17.
[ORIGIN from MEMORY or MEMORIZE: see -IST.]
†**1** A person who prompts the memory. Only in L17.
2 A person who memorizes things; a person with a retentive memory. L19.

memoriter /mɪˈmɒrɪtə/ *adverb & adjective*. E17.
[ORIGIN Latin, from *memor* mindful.]
▸ **A** *adverb*. From memory, by heart. E17.
▸ **B** *adjective*. Spoken or speaking from memory. E19.

memorize /ˈmɛmərʌɪz/ *verb*. Also **-ise**. L16.
[ORIGIN from MEMORY + -IZE.]
1 *verb trans.* Keep alive the memory or recollection of; cause to be remembered, make memorable. Now *rare*. L16.
2 *verb trans.* Perpetuate the memory of in writing; relate, record, mention. Now *rare*. L16.
3 *verb trans.* Commit to memory, learn by heart. M19.

B. PYM Groping for the light switch, whose position he had not yet memorized perfectly. G. NAYLOR The great slave poet, Jupiter Hammon, who memorized thousands of verses.

4 *verb intrans.* Learn things by heart. L19.
■ **memorizable** *adjective* L19. **memoriˈzation** *noun* L19. **memorizer** *noun* M19.

M

memory /ˈmɛm(ə)ri/ *noun*. ME.
[ORIGIN Old French *memorie*, (also mod.) *mémoire* from Latin *memoria*, from *memor* mindful: see -Y³.]
1 The faculty by which things are remembered; the capacity for retaining, perpetuating, or reviving the thought of things past; an individual's faculty for remembering things. ME. ▸**b** The capacity of a body or substance for manifesting effects of its previous state, behaviour, or treatment, or for returning to a previous state when the cause of the transition from that state is removed; such effects, such a state. L19. ▸**c** A device (usu. part of a computer) in which data or program instructions may be stored and from which they may be retrieved when required; capacity for storing data etc. in this way. M20.

H. B. STOWE Topsy had an uncommon verbal memory. F. GALTON One favourite expedient was to associate the sight memory with the muscular memory. O. HENRY 'I've seen that fellow somewhere,' said Littlefield, who had a memory for faces. T. CAPOTE The prisoner . . proud of . . a brilliant memory, recited the names and addresses. W. TREVOR Memory fails me when I think about the men of the mill. **c** C. STOLL Other computer folks measure size in megabytes of memory.

2 The fact or condition of being remembered; remembrance, commemoration. Now only in ***in memory of*** below. ME. ▸**b** CHRISTIAN CHURCH. A commemoration, esp. of the dead. *obsolete* exc. *hist*. LME.
3 The perpetuated knowledge or recollection (*of* something); what is remembered *of* a person, object, or event; (good or bad) posthumous reputation. ME.

SWIFT His late Majesty King William the Third, of ever glorious and immortal Memory. E. M. FORSTER I have my children and the memory of my dear wife to consider. JONATHAN MILLER Acute head injuries . . can rob the patient of any memory of the events . . leading up to the accident.

4 The knowledge which a person can recover or has recovered by mental effort; the function of the mind regarded as a store for this. LME. ▸**b** An act or instance of remembering; a representation in the memory; a person or thing as remembered; a recollection. E19.

G. GROTE A considerable portion of the Greeks of Olbia could repeat the Iliad from memory. R. HARLING Perhaps . . it has slipped your memory. F. WYNDHAM A grim experience, which I later managed to blot out almost completely from my memory. C. SIMMONS I searched my memory for an instance of parental betrayal. **b** G. ORWELL His mother's memory tore at his heart because she had died loving him. E. FEINSTEIN My earliest memories turn around a room with a huge wooden table.

†**5** A memorial account or record; a history. LME–M18.
6 A memorial object or act; a memento; a monument. Long *obsolete* exc. *Canad. dial.*, an embroidered memorial wall hanging. LME.
7 The length of time over which the recollection of a person or a number of persons extends. M16.

– PHRASES: ***commit to memory***: see COMMIT *verb* 1. **in memory of** so as to keep alive the remembrance of; as a record of. ***legal memory***: see LEGAL *adjective*. ***living memory***: see LIVING *adjective*. ***long memory***: see LONG *adjective*¹. ***magnetic memory***: see MAGNETIC *adjective*. ***PHOTOGRAPHIC memory***. **the Immortal Memory**: a toast to the Scottish poet Robert Burns (1759–96). †**to the memory of** = *in memory of* above.

– COMB.: **memory bank** the memory device of a computer; *fig.* the human memory; **memory-belief** a memory implicitly believed in though probably unverifiable; **memory board** (*a*) a board on which is fixed or written something which is to be remembered; (*b*) THEATRICAL a programmable console for the semi-automatic control of stage lighting; (*c*) COMPUTING a flat, freq. detachable, array of memory devices in a computer; **memory book** *US* a blank book in which cuttings from newspapers etc. are pasted for preservation; a scrapbook; an autograph album; **memory cell** (*a*) a single unit of memory storage in a device or (*fig.*) the brain; (*b*) PHYSIOLOGY a long-lived lymphocyte capable of responding to a particular antigen even when the antigen is reintroduced long after the initial exposure that produced the lymphocyte; **memory cycle** COMPUTING (the time taken by) the process of replacing one unit of data in a memory by another; **memory drug** a drug supposed to improve the memory; **memory drum** (*a*) PSYCHOLOGY a revolving device on which items to be learned are successively presented; (*b*) a drum-shaped memory device in a computer; **memory effect** an effect in a body or substance arising from memory; **memory lane** *fig.* a succession of sentimental memories deliberately pursued (chiefly in ***down memory lane***); **memory span** PSYCHOLOGY the maximum number of items that can be recalled in the correct order immediately after a single presentation of them; **memory trace** PSYCHOLOGY a hypothetical trace left in the nervous system by the act of memorizing, an engram.
■ **memoryless** *adjective* M19.

Memphian /ˈmɛmfɪən/ *noun & adjective*. E17.
[ORIGIN from *Memphis* (see below) + -AN.]
▸ **A** *noun*. **1** A native or inhabitant of the ancient Egyptian city of Memphis; *literary* an Egyptian. E17.
2 A native or inhabitant of Memphis, Tennessee. M19.
▸ **B** *adjective*. **1** Of or pertaining to Memphis in Egypt; *literary* Egyptian. E17.
2 Of or pertaining to Memphis, Tennessee. M19.

Memphitic /mɛmˈfɪtɪk/ *adjective*. LME.
[ORIGIN Latin *Memphiticus* from Greek *Memphitikos*, from *Memphitēs* inhabitant of Memphis: see -ITE¹, -IC.]
Of or pertaining to the ancient Egyptian city of Memphis or the dialect of Coptic spoken there.

memsahib /ˈmɛmsɑːɪb/ *noun*. *Indian*. M19.
[ORIGIN from *mem* var. of MA'AM + SAHIB.]
A European married woman as spoken of or to by Indians.

men *noun* pl. of MAN *noun*.

menaccanite /məˈnakənʌɪt/ *noun*. L18.
[ORIGIN Irreg. from *Manaccan*, a village in Cornwall + -ITE¹.]
MINERALOGY. A ferrian variety of ilmenite.

menace /ˈmɛnəs/ *noun*. ME.
[ORIGIN Latin *minacia* (pl. in classical Latin), from *minac-*, *minax* threatening, from base of *minari* threaten.]
1 A declaration or indication of hostile intention, or of a probable evil or catastrophe; a threat; the action of threatening. Now *literary*. ME.

J. A. FROUDE The fierce menace was delivered amidst frowning groups of . . nobles. J. NAGENDA The voice . . had menace and the contempt which the power of the gun gave its owner.

2 A thing threatening danger or catastrophe; a dangerous or obnoxious thing or person; a great inconvenience. M19.

J. R. GREEN The old social discontent . . remained a perpetual menace to public order. A. SILLITOE They said I was a menace to honest lads like Mike.

public menace: see PUBLIC *adjective & noun*. ***red menace***: see RED *adjective*.
■ **menaceful** *adjective* threatening M18.

menace /ˈmɛnəs/ *verb*. ME.
[ORIGIN Anglo-Norman *manasser*, Old French *menacier* (mod. *menacer*) from Proto-Romance, formed as MENACE *noun*.]
1 *verb trans.* Utter menaces against; threaten. ME.

E. L. RICE Maurrant . . menaces the man with his revolver. A. STORR We are menaced by the possibility of a nuclear holocaust.

2 *verb intrans.* Utter menaces; be threatening. ME.

BURKE Earth below shook; heaven above menaced.

3 *verb trans.* Hold out as a punishment, penalty, or danger; threaten to inflict. ME.

H. H. MILMAN No threatened excommunication is now menaced. J. MARTINE The solitary dissentient was menacing to leave the meeting-house.

■ †**menacement** *noun* menacing, threatening E17–E19. **menacer** *noun* E17. **menacing** *noun* (now *rare*) (*a*) the action of the verb; (*b*) a threat, a menace: ME. **menacing** *ppl adjective* that menaces or threatens, threatening LME. **menacingly** *adverb* L16.

menad *noun* var. of MAENAD.

menadione /mɛnəˈdʌɪəʊn/ *noun*. Orig. *US*. M20.
[ORIGIN from ME(THYL + NA(PHTHALENE + -DIONE.]
PHARMACOLOGY. A synthetic yellow derivative of naphthoquinone used to treat haemorrhage by stimulating prothrombin production; 2-methyl-1,4-naphthoquinone, $C_{11}H_8O_2$. Also called ***menaphthone***, ***vitamin K***$_3$. Cf. MENAQUINONE.

ménage /meɪˈnɑːʒ; *foreign* menaːʒ (*pl. same*)/ *noun*. Also **menage**. ME.
[ORIGIN Old French *menaige*, *man-* (mod. *ménage*) from Proto-Romance, from Latin *mansio(n-)*: see MANSION, -AGE.]
1 A domestic establishment, a household. Formerly also, the members of a household. ME. ▸**b** A sexual relationship; an affair. M20.
ménage à deux /a dø, ɑː ˈdɜː/ [= of two] an arrangement or relationship of two people living together. ***ménage à quatre*** /a katr, ɑː ˈkɑːtrə/ [= of four] an arrangement or relationship of four people living together. ***ménage à trois*** /a trwa, ɑː ˈtrwɑː/ [= of three] an arrangement or relationship in which three people live together, usually consisting of a husband, and wife, and the lover of one of these.
2 The management of a household, housekeeping. E19.
3 A benefit society or savings club of which every member pays in a fixed sum weekly; an arrangement for paying for goods by instalments. *Scot. & N. English*. E19.

menagerie /məˈnadʒ(ə)ri/ *noun*. L17.
[ORIGIN French *ménagerie*, from *ménage*: see MÉNAGE, -ERY.]
1 A collection of wild animals in cages or enclosures, *esp.* one kept for exhibition; a place or building in which such a collection is kept. L17. ▸**b** A collection of strange or outlandish people. M19.
†**2** An aviary. M18–M19.
■ **menagerist** *noun* a keeper of a menagerie M19.

menald /ˈmɛn(ə)ld/ *adjective*. Now *rare*. Also **mennal** /ˈmɛn(ə)l/. E17.
[ORIGIN Unknown.]
Of an animal: spotted, speckled; (of a deer) of a dappled chestnut colour.

menalty /ˈmɛn(ə)lti/ *noun*. *rare*. M16.
[ORIGIN from MEAN *adjective*² + -AL¹ + -TY¹.]
The middle class.

W. H. AUDEN Sons of the menalty Divining their future from plum stones.

menaphthone /məˈnafθəʊn/ *noun*. M20.
[ORIGIN from ME(THYL + NAPHTH(ALENE + -ONE.]
PHARMACOLOGY. = MENADIONE.

Menapian /mɪˈnapɪən/ *adjective & noun*. M20.
[ORIGIN from Latin *Menapii* a people of northern Gaul in Roman times + -IAN.]
GEOLOGY. (Designating or pertaining to) a middle Pleistocene glaciation in northern Europe preceding the Elster and Saale glaciations, and possibly corresponding to the Günz of the Alps.

menaquinone /mɛnəˈkwɪnəʊn/ *noun*. M20.
[ORIGIN from ME(THYL + NA(PHTHALENE + QUINONE.]
BIOCHEMISTRY. An isoprenoid derivative of menadione synthesized in the body by (esp. intestinal) bacteria and essential for blood clotting. Also called ***vitamin K***$_2$.

menarche /məˈnɑːki/ *noun*. E20.
[ORIGIN from Greek *mēn* month + *arkhē* beginning.]
The first appearance of menstruation; the age at which this occurs.
■ **menarcheal** *adjective* M20.

menazon /ˈmɛnəz(ə)n/ *noun*. M20.
[ORIGIN from ME(THYL + AMI)N(O- + AZ(O- + THI)ON(ATE.]
An organic compound containing sulphur, phosphorus, and a triazine ring, used as an insecticide and acaricide.

mench *verb* var. of MENSH.

mend /mɛnd/ *noun*. ME.
[ORIGIN Partly aphet. from AMEND *noun*, partly from the verb. Cf. MENDS.]
†**1** Reparation, restoration, recompense. ME–M17.
2 ***on the mend***, recovering from sickness, improving in health or condition. E19.
3 An act of mending, a repair; a repaired hole etc. in a fabric. L19.
make and mend: see MAKE *noun*².

mend /mɛnd/ *verb*. ME.
[ORIGIN Anglo-Norman *mender* aphet. from *amender* AMEND *verb*. Partly directly aphet. from AMEND *verb*.]
▸ **I** With reference to defects.
1 a *verb trans.* Free (a person, character, habits) from sin or fault; improve morally; reform. Now *arch. & dial.* exc. in ***mend one's manners***, ***mend one's ways***. ME. ▸**b** *verb intrans.* Reform. Now *rare* exc. in proverb *it is never too late to mend*. ME.
2 a *verb trans.* Remove the defects of (a thing); improve by correction or alteration. *obsolete* exc. as passing into sense 5. ME. ▸**b** *verb intrans.* Become less faulty. Of conditions: become less unfavourable, improve. LME.
3 a *verb trans.* Rectify, remedy, remove (an evil); correct, put right (a fault, something wrong). ME. ▸**b** *verb intrans.* Of a fault: undergo rectification. E18.

a SHELLEY Poverty, the which I sought to mend By holding a poor office in the state. R. K. NARAYAN He tried to mend his previous statement.

4 *verb trans.* Make amends or reparation for, atone for (a misdeed, an injury). *obsolete* exc. in proverb ***least said, soonest mended***. ME.

5 *verb trans.* **a** Restore to a complete or sound condition (something broken, decayed, worn, torn, etc.); repair or make good (a defective part); add fuel to (a fire). **ME.** ▸**b** Adjust, set right. *obsolete* exc. *NAUTICAL.* **E16.** ▸**c** Repair the garments of (a person). *arch. colloq.* **L19.**

a STEELE A blind Beggar . . with a Needle and thread thriftily mending his Stockings. KEATS A vile old pen . . . The fault is in the Quill: I have mended it. DAY LEWIS He mended his nets. S. CHITTY The stove would not work and she was too miserable to get it mended. **c** W. S. GILBERT She will tend him, nurse him, mend him.

6 a *verb trans.* Restore to health, cure, heal. *arch.* **ME.** ▸**b** *verb intrans.* Regain health, recover from sickness, heal. **E16.**

b H. WILLIAMSON No bones broken . . but he has some way to go to mend. R. D. LAING Even broken hearts have been known to mend.

▸ **II** Without distinct reference to defects.

7 *verb trans.* Improve the condition or fortune of. Now *rare* or *obsolete*. **ME.**

8 *verb trans.* Improve on, surpass, better. Now *rare*. **ME.**

9 *verb trans. & intrans.* Improve physically, fatten. *obsolete* exc. *Scot. & N. Irish.* **LME.**

†**10 a** *verb trans.* Improve by additions; supplement. **LME–E18.** ▸**b** *verb intrans.* Improve in amount or price. **E17–E19.**

11 *verb* †*intrans. & trans.* Improve in quality. Now *rare*. **M16.**

– PHRASES: **end or mend** = *mend or end* below. *LEAST said, soonest mended.* ***make or mend***: see MAKE *verb*. **mend matters** rectify or improve the state of affairs. **mend one's pace** walk more quickly, travel faster. **mend or end** either improve or (if that is impossible) put an end to.

■ **mendable** *adjective* **M16.** **mender** *noun* **LME.**

mendacious /mɛnˈdeɪʃəs/ *adjective.* **E17.**

[ORIGIN from Latin *mendac-*, *mendax* prob. orig. speaking incorrectly or falsely, from *mendum* defect, fault + -OUS.]

Lying; untruthful; false.

■ **mendaciously** *adverb* **E17.** **mendaciousness** *noun* mendacity **M19.**

mendacity /mɛnˈdasɪti/ *noun.* **M17.**

[ORIGIN ecclesiastical Latin *mendacitas*, *-tat-*, formed as MENDACIOUS: see -ACITY.]

1 The quality of being mendacious; habitual lying or deceiving. **M17.**

2 An instance of this; a lie, a falsehood. **M17.**

mendang /mɛnˈdaŋ/ *noun.* Also **-dong** /-ˈdɒŋ/, **-dung** /-ˈdʌŋ/. **M19.**

[ORIGIN Tibetan.]

A Tibetan sacred wall composed of flat stones with religious inscriptions. Cf. MANI *noun*[2].

Mende /ˈmɛndi/ *noun & adjective.* Also **-di.** **L19.**

[ORIGIN Mende.]

▸ **A** *noun.* Pl. **-s**, same.

1 A member of a people inhabiting Sierra Leone in W. Africa. **L19.**

2 The Mande language of the Mende. **E20.**

▸ **B** *attrib.* or as *adjective.* Of or pertaining to the Mende or their language. **L19.**

mendelevium /mɛndəˈliːvɪəm, -ˈleɪvɪəm/ *noun.* **M20.**

[ORIGIN from Dmitri Ivanovich *Mendeleev* (1834–1907), Russian chemist + -IUM.]

A radioactive metallic chemical element of the actinide series, atomic no. 101, which is produced artificially (symbol Md).

Mendelian /mɛnˈdiːlɪən/ *adjective & noun.* Also **m-.** **E20.**

[ORIGIN from Gregor Johann *Mendel* (1822–84), Moravian monk & botanist + -IAN.]

BIOLOGY. ▸**A** *adjective.* Pertaining to or designating the theory of heredity first propounded by Mendel; following the laws or principles of Mendelism. **E20.**

▸ **B** *noun.* A person who accepts or advocates Mendel's principles of heredity. **E20.**

■ **Mendelianism** *noun* = MENDELISM **E20.**

Mendelism /ˈmɛnd(ə)lɪz(ə)m/ *noun.* **E20.**

[ORIGIN from *Mendel* (see MENDELIAN) + -ISM.]

BIOLOGY. The theory that the inheritance of any particular character is controlled by the inheritance of discrete units (now called genes) which occur in pairs in somatic cells and separate (largely) independently of each other at meiosis; (Mendelian) genetics.

■ **Mendelist** *noun* (*rare*) = MENDELIAN *noun* **E20.** **Mendelize** *verb intrans.* behave or be inherited in accordance with Mendelian principles **E20.**

Mendelssohnian /mɛnd(ə)lˈsəʊnɪən/ *adjective.* **M19.**

[ORIGIN from *Mendelssohn* (see below) + -IAN.]

Of, pertaining to, or characteristic of the German composer Felix Mendelssohn-Bartholdy (1809–47) or his music, esp. its quality of being expressive and picturesque without passion.

■ Also **Mendelssohnic** *adjective* **L19.**

Mendi *noun & adjective* var. of MENDE.

mendicancy /ˈmɛndɪk(ə)nsi/ *noun.* **E18.**

[ORIGIN from MENDICANT: see -ANCY.]

The state or condition of being a mendicant or beggar; the habit or practice of begging.

mendicant /ˈmɛndɪk(ə)nt/ *noun & adjective.* **LME.**

[ORIGIN Latin *mendicant-* pres. ppl stem of *mendicare* beg, from *mendicus* beggar, from *mendum* defect, fault: see -ANT[1].]

▸ **A** *noun.* **1** A mendicant friar (see sense B.1 below). **LME.**

2 A beggar; a person who lives by begging. **L15.**

▸ **B** *adjective.* **1** Designating or belonging to any of the religious orders whose members (known as friars) lived solely on alms. **L15.**

2 Begging; given to or characterized by begging. Also, characteristic of a beggar. **E17.**

†**mendicate** *verb trans. & intrans.* **E17–M19.**

[ORIGIN Latin *mendicat-* pa. ppl stem of *mendicare*: see MENDICANT, -ATE[3].]

Beg or ask (for) like a beggar.

■ †**mendiˈcation** *noun* begging **M17–M19.**

mendicity /mɛnˈdɪsɪti/ *noun.* **LME.**

[ORIGIN Old French & mod. French *mendicité* from Latin *mendicitas*, *-tat-*, from *mendicus*: see MENDICANT, -ITY.]

1 The state or condition of a mendicant or beggar, beggary. Also, the existence or numbers of mendicants. **LME.**

2 The practice or habit of begging. **E19.**

mending /ˈmɛndɪŋ/ *noun.* **ME.**

[ORIGIN from MEND *verb* + -ING[1].]

1 The action of MEND *verb.* **ME.**

invisible mending: see INVISIBLE *adjective.*

2 a In *pl.* Articles to be repaired. *rare.* **M19.** ▸**b** Clothing requiring or in the process of repair. **L19.**

mendipite /ˈmɛndɪpʌɪt/ *noun.* **M19.**

[ORIGIN from the *Mendip* Hills, Somerset + -ITE[1].]

MINERALOGY. Native lead oxychloride, an orthorhombic mineral usu. occurring as massed white crystals.

mendment /ˈmɛndm(ə)nt/ *noun.* **ME.**

[ORIGIN Aphet. from AMENDMENT.]

1 Amendment, improvement, reparation, correction, reformation. Now *rare.* **ME.**

2 *spec.* Improvement of the soil; fertilizer, manure; = AMENDMENT 3b. *obsolete* exc. *dial.* **M17.**

mendong *noun* var. of MENDANG.

mends /mɛndz/ *noun. obsolete* exc. *Scot.* **ME.**

[ORIGIN Aphet. from AMENDS. Cf. MEND *noun.*]

1 Amends; recompense, reparation. **ME.**

†**2** Means of obtaining restoration or reparation; a remedy; a cure. **LME–M17.**

mendung *noun* var. of MENDANG.

meneer *noun* see MYNHEER.

meneghinite /mɛnɪˈgiːnʌɪt, mɛˈnɛgɪn-/ *noun.* **M19.**

[ORIGIN from G. G. A. *Meneghini* (1811–89), Italian mineralogist + -ITE[1].]

MINERALOGY. A monoclinic sulphide and antimonide of lead and copper, usu. occurring as greyish-black prisms and in fibrous masses.

Menevian /məˈniːvɪən/ *adjective & noun.* **M19.**

[ORIGIN from *Menevia*, medieval Latin name of St David's, S. Wales + -AN.]

GEOLOGY. ▸**A** *adjective.* Of, pertaining to, or designating a group of fossiliferous rocks of Cambrian age found in Wales. **M19.**

▸ **B** *noun.* The Menevian formation. **L19.**

meng /mɛŋ, mɛn(d)ʒ/ *verb trans. & intrans.* Long *obsolete* exc. *dial.*

[ORIGIN Old English *mengan* = Old Frisian *menza*, Old Saxon *mengian*, Old High German *mengen* (Dutch, German *mengen*), Old Norse *menga*, from Germanic, from base repr. also in AMONG.]

Mix, mingle, blend.

M.Eng. *abbreviation.*

Master of Engineering.

mengkuang /mɛŋˈkwaŋ/ *noun.* **E20.**

[ORIGIN Malay.]

Any of various large SE Asian trees of the genus *Pandanus* (family Pandanaceae), providing leaves that can be woven into matting, etc.; (matting made from) such leaves.

mengkulang /ˈmɛŋkuːlaŋ/ *noun.* **M20.**

[ORIGIN Malay.]

Any of various Malayan timber trees of the genus *Heritiera* (family Sterculiaceae), esp. *H. simplicifolia*; the wood of these trees.

mengovirus /ˈmɛŋgəvʌɪrəs/ *noun.* Also **Mengo virus.** **M20.**

[ORIGIN from *Mengo* district, Uganda + VIRUS.]

BIOLOGY. A picornavirus originally found in monkeys but capable of infecting other species and causing encephalomyelitis in humans.

menhaden /mɛnˈheɪd(ə)n/ *noun.* **L18.**

[ORIGIN Narragansett *munnawhatteaûg*.]

A fish of the herring family, *Brevoortia tyrannus*, of the Atlantic coast of N. America, an important source of fish guano and oil.

menhir /ˈmɛnhɪə/ *noun.* **M19.**

[ORIGIN Breton *maen-hir* (*maen* stone, *hir* long) = Welsh *maen hir*, Cornish *mênhere*.]

ARCHAEOLOGY. A single tall upright monumental stone, esp. of prehistoric times.

menial /ˈmiːnɪəl/ *adjective & noun.* **LME.**

[ORIGIN Anglo-Norman *menial*, *meignial*, from *meinie* MEINIE: see -AL[1].]

▸ **A** *adjective.* **1** Pertaining to the household, domestic. *obsolete* in *gen.* sense. **LME.**

2 Of a servant: forming one of the household, domestic, latterly *spec.* with implication of employment for show rather than use. **LME.**

3 Proper to or performed by a menial or domestic servant; now *spec.* of the nature of drudgery, servile, degrading. **L17.**

S. SPENDER His nature was so menial that he was unhappy without dust-pan and brush. B. PYM He could hardly ask her to do such menial work.

▸ **B** *noun.* A domestic servant; latterly *esp.* a liveried manservant employed for show rather than use, a pompous or arrogant servant. **LME.**

■ **menially** *adverb* **M19.**

Ménière /mɛnˈjɛː/ *noun.* Also **Menière, -iere.** **L19.**

[ORIGIN Prosper *Ménière* (1799–1862), French physician.]

MEDICINE. ***Ménière's disease***, ***Ménière's syndrome***, a disease of the membranous labyrinth of the ear associated with tinnitus, progressive deafness, and intermittent vertigo.

meninges /mɪˈnɪndʒiːz/ *noun pl.* Also (*rare*) in sing. **meninx** /ˈmiːnɪŋks/. **M16.**

[ORIGIN mod. Latin from Greek *mēnigx*, *mēnigg-* membrane.]

The three membranes enveloping the brain and spinal cord: the dura mater, arachnoid, and pia mater.

■ **meningeal** *adjective* of or pertaining to the meninges **L18.** **meningic** *adjective* (*rare*) = MENINGEAL **E19.**

meningioma /mɪˌnɪndʒɪˈəʊmə/ *noun.* Pl. **-mas, -mata** /-mətə/. **E20.**

[ORIGIN from MENING(O- + ENDOTHEL)IOMA.]

MEDICINE. A tumour, usu. benign, arising from meningeal tissue (usu. that of the brain).

meningism /mɪˈnɪndʒɪz(ə)m, ˈmɛnɪn-/ *noun.* **E20.**

[ORIGIN from MENINGITIS + -ISM.]

MEDICINE. Stiffness of the neck, esp. in fevers of children, resembling that caused by meningitis.

meningitis /mɛnɪnˈdʒʌɪtɪs/ *noun.* Pl. **meningitides** /-tɪdiːz/. **E19.**

[ORIGIN formed as MENINGES + -ITIS.]

MEDICINE. (An) inflammation of the meninges of the brain or spinal cord.

■ **meningitic** /-ˈdʒɪtɪk/ *adjective* **M19.**

meningo- /mɪˈnɪŋgəʊ, mɪˈnɪndʒəʊ/ *combining form.*

[ORIGIN from MENINGES + -O-.]

MEDICINE. Of or involving the meninges.

■ **meningocele** *noun* a protrusion of the meninges through a gap in the spine due to a congenital defect **M19.** **meningoˈcoccal** *adjective* of, pertaining to, involving, or caused by a meningococcus **E20.** **meningoˈcoccus** *noun*, pl. **-cocci** /-ˈkɒk(s)ʌɪ, -iː/, a bacterium, *Neisseria meningitidis*, involved in cerebrospinal fever and meningitis **L19.** **meningoencephaˈlitis** *noun* inflammation of the membranes of the brain and the adjoining cerebral tissue **L19.** **meningoenˈcephalocele** *noun* = CEPHALOCELE **L19.** **meningomyeˈlitis** *noun* inflammation of the spinal cord and its membranes **L19.** **meningoˈmyelocele** *noun* = MYELOMENINGOCELE **L19.**

meninx *noun* sing. of MENINGES.

Menippean /mɪˈnɪpɪən/ *adjective.* **L17.**

[ORIGIN from *Menippus* (see below) + -EAN.]

Characteristic of or resembling the satirical style of the Greek philosopher Menippus (fl. 3rd cent. BC).

meniscal /mɪˈnɪsk(ə)l/ *adjective. rare.* **M19.**

[ORIGIN from MENISCUS + -AL[1].]

Of the nature of or resembling a meniscus.

■ Also **meniscate** *adjective* **M19.**

menisci *noun* pl. of MENISCUS.

meniscoid /mɪˈnɪskɔɪd/ *adjective.* **E19.**

[ORIGIN from MENISCUS + -OID.]

BOTANY. Resembling a meniscus in form; thin, domed, and thickest in the middle.

■ Also **meniˈscoidal** *adjective* **L19.**

meniscus /mɪˈnɪskəs/ *noun.* Pl. **-sci** /-sʌɪ/. **L17.**

[ORIGIN mod. Latin from Greek *mēniskos* crescent, dim. of *mēnē* moon.]

1 A lens convex on one side and concave on the other; *esp.* a convexo-concave lens (i.e. one thickest in the middle, with a crescent-shaped section). **L17.**

2 A crescent moon. *rare.* **E18.**

3 The convex or concave upper surface of a column of liquid in a tube, caused by surface tension or capillarity. **E19.**

4 *ANATOMY.* A disclike interarticular fibrocartilage situated between the articular surfaces of certain joints, as those of the wrist and knee. **M19.**

5 A figure in the form of a crescent. **L19.**

■ **meniscectomy** /mɛnɪˈsɛktəmi/ *noun* (an instance of) surgical removal of a meniscus, esp. that of the knee **E20.**

mennal *adjective* var. of MENALD.

Mennecy /ˈmɛnəsi/ *adjective & noun*. M19.
[ORIGIN A town near Paris, France.]
(Designating) a soft-paste porcelain made at Mennecy.

†**Mennist** *noun & adjective*. *US*. M18–L19.
[ORIGIN formed as MENNONITE.]
= MENNONITE.

Mennonist /ˈmɛnənɪst/ *noun*. M17.
[ORIGIN formed as MENNONITE + -IST.]
= MENNONITE *noun*.

Mennonite /ˈmɛnənʌɪt/ *noun & adjective*. M16.
[ORIGIN from *Menno* Simons (1496–1561), their early leader + -ITE[1].]
▸ **A** *noun*. A member of a Christian sect which arose in Friesland in the 16th cent. maintaining such principles as opposition to infant baptism, the taking of oaths, military service, and the holding of civic offices. M16.
▸ **B** *attrib*. or as *adjective*. Of or pertaining to the Mennonites. M18.

meno /ˈmɛnəʊ, ˈmeɪnəʊ/ *adverb*. E18.
[ORIGIN Italian.]
MUSIC. Less: used in directions, as ***meno mosso***.

meno- /ˈmɛnəʊ/ *combining form*. Before a vowel **men-**.
[ORIGIN from Greek *mēn*, *mēnos* month: see -O-.]
Forming nouns with the sense 'menstruation, menses', as ***menorrhoea***.

men-of-war *noun* pl. of MAN-OF-WAR.

menologia *noun pl.* see MENOLOGY.

menologist /mɪˈnɒlədʒɪst/ *noun*. L18.
[ORIGIN formed as MENOLOGY.]
A compiler of a menology.

menology /mɪˈnɒlədʒi/ *noun*. Also in Latin form **menologium** /mɛnə(ʊ)ˈləʊdʒɪəm/, pl. **-ia** /-ɪə/, **-iums**. E17.
[ORIGIN mod. Latin *menologium* from ecclesiastical Greek *mēnologion*, from *mēn* month + LOGOS account.]
An ecclesiastical calendar of the months; *spec.* a calendar of the Greek Orthodox Church containing biographies of the saints in the order of the dates on which they are commemorated.

Menominee /mɪˈnɒmɪniː/ *noun & adjective*. Also **-ni**. E18.
[ORIGIN Ojibwa *mano:mini:* lit. 'wild-rice person'.]
▸ **A** *noun*. Pl. same, **-s**.
1 A member of an Algonquian people of Michigan and Wisconsin. E18.
2 The language (formerly) spoken by this people. L19.
3 In full ***Menominee whitefish***. A whitefish, *Prosopium cylindraceum*, of lakes in northern N. America. L19.
▸ **B** *attrib*. or as *adjective*. Of or pertaining to the Menominee or their language. E19.

M

menopausal /mɛnə(ʊ)ˈpɔːz(ə)l/ *adjective*. E20.
[ORIGIN from MENOPAUSE + -AL[1].]
Of, pertaining to, or characteristic of the menopause; undergoing the menopause.

> M. WEST Lotte was at the low point of one of her menopausal depressions. *Which?* The typical shoplifter is not the muddled, middle-aged, menopausal woman many would have us believe.

menopause /ˈmɛnə(ʊ)pɔːz/ *noun*. L19.
[ORIGIN from MENO- + *pausis* cessation, PAUSE *noun*.]
The final cessation of the menstrual cycle; the period of a woman's life when this occurs, usu. between the ages of 40 and 50. Also (in full ***male menopause***), a supposedly corresponding stage in a man's life; a crisis of identity, confidence, etc., experienced by a middle-aged man.
■ **menopausic** *adjective* (*rare*) = MENOPAUSAL L19.

menorah /mɪˈnɔːrə/ *noun*. L19.
[ORIGIN Hebrew *mĕnōrāh* candlestick.]
A holy candelabrum with seven branches that was used in the temple in Jerusalem; a candelabrum having any number of branches, but usually eight, used in Jewish worship, esp. during Hanukkah; a representation of either as a symbol of Judaism.

menorrhagia /mɛnəˈreɪdʒɪə/ *noun*. L18.
[ORIGIN mod. Latin, from MENO- + -RRHAGIA.]
MEDICINE. Excessively heavy bleeding at menstruation.
■ **menorrhagic** /-ˈradʒɪk/ *adjective* pertaining to or suffering from menorrhagia M19.

menorrhoea /mɛnəˈriːə/ *noun*. Also ***-rrhea**. M19.
[ORIGIN Back-form. from AMENORRHOEA.]
MEDICINE. Normal bleeding at menstruation. Also, menorrhagia.

mensa /ˈmɛnsə/ *noun*. L17.
[ORIGIN Latin = table.]
1 The grinding surface of a molar tooth. *rare*. L17.
2 ECCLESIASTICAL. The upper surface, esp. the top slab, of an altar; an altar table. M19.
3 (**M-**.) (The name of) an inconspicuous constellation of the southern hemisphere, lying between Dorado and the South Pole; the Table. M19.
4 (**M-**.) (The name of) an organization of people with high intelligence quotients. M20.

†**mensal** *noun*[1] & *adjective*[1]. L15.
[ORIGIN from Latin *mensis* month + -AL[1].]
▸ **A** *noun*. A monthly account. L15–E16.
▸ **B** *adjective*. Monthly. M–L19.

mensal /ˈmɛns(ə)l/ *adjective*[2] & *noun*[2]. LME.
[ORIGIN Late Latin *mensalis*, from *mensa* table: see -AL[1].]
▸ **A** *adjective*. **1** Of, pertaining to, or used at the table. LME.
2 a *Irish & SCOTTISH hist.* Designating land set aside to provide food for the royal table. E17. ▸**b** Designating a church, benefice, etc., appropriated to defray some of the expenses of a (Roman Catholic) bishop or other cleric, *spec.* in Ireland and in Scotland before the Reformation. E17.
▸ **B** *noun*. A mensal church or benefice. E17.

mensch /mɛnʃ/ *noun*. M20.
[ORIGIN Yiddish from German = person.]
A person of integrity or rectitude; a just, honest, or honourable person.

mense /mɛns/ *noun & verb*. *obsolete* exc. *Scot. & N. English*. Orig. †**mensk**. E16.
[ORIGIN Old Norse *mennska* humanity, corresp. to Old Saxon, Old High German *menniskī*, from Germanic base of MANNISH. Later form repr. Scot. pronunc.]
▸ **A** *noun*. **1** Humanity, kindness; courtesy, hospitality; propriety, decorum. E16.
2 Honour, credit. M16.
†**3** A reward or recompense. L16–E19. ▸**4** Neatness, tidiness; newness, gloss. *N. English*. M19.
▸ **B** *verb trans*. **1** Grace; adorn, decorate; be a credit to, do honour to. E17.
2 Put in order, tidy. *N. English*. M19.
■ **menseful** *adjective* proper, decorous, discreet M17. **menseless** *adjective* without propriety, decorum, or seemliness M16.

menservants *noun* pl. of MANSERVANT.

menses /ˈmɛnsiːz/ *noun pl*. L16.
[ORIGIN Latin, pl. of *mensis* month.]
The menstrual discharge. Also, the time of menstruation.

mensh /mɛnʃ/ *verb intrans*. *colloq*. Also **-ch**. E20.
[ORIGIN Abbreviation of MENTION *verb*.]
Mention something.

Menshevik /ˈmɛnʃɪvɪk/ *noun & adjective*. *hist*. E20.
[ORIGIN Russian *men'shevik* = member of the minority, from *men'shiĭ* less, compar. of *malyĭ* little.]
▸**A** *noun*. A member of a minority faction of the Russian Social Democratic Party who opposed the Bolshevik policy of non-cooperation with other opponents of the tsarist regime and violent revolutionary action by a small political elite. Cf. BOLSHEVIK *noun* 1. E20.
▸ **B** *attrib*. or as *adjective*. Of or pertaining to Mensheviks or Menshevism. E20.
■ **Menshevism** *noun* the doctrine and practices of the Mensheviks E20. **Menshevist** *noun & adjective* = MENSHEVIK E20.

†**mensk** *noun & verb* see MENSE.

mens rea /mɛnz ˈriːə/ *noun phr*. M19.
[ORIGIN Latin = guilty mind.]
LAW. The state of mind which makes an illegal act a crime; criminal state of mind.

mens sana in corpore sano /mɛns ˈsɑːnə ɪn ˌkɔːpərə ˈsɑːnəʊ/ *noun phr*. E17.
[ORIGIN Latin (Juvenal).]
A sound mind in a sound body, esp. regarded as the ideal of education. Also *ellipt.* as ***mens sana***.

menstrua *noun pl.* see MENSTRUUM.

menstrual /ˈmɛnstrʊəl/ *adjective*. LME.
[ORIGIN Latin *menstrualis*, from *menstruus* monthly, from *mensis* month: see -AL[1].]
1 Of or pertaining to menstruation. LME.
menstrual cycle the process of ovulation and menstruation in sexually mature women and female primates.
2 Monthly; happening once a month, varying in monthly periods. Now *rare* or *obsolete*. L16.

menstruant /ˈmɛnstrʊənt/ *adjective & noun*. *rare*. M17.
[ORIGIN Late Latin *menstruant-* pres. ppl stem of *menstruare*: see MENSTRUATE, -ANT[1].]
(A woman who is) menstruating.

menstruate /ˈmɛnstrʊeɪt/ *verb*. M17.
[ORIGIN Late Latin *menstruat-* pa. ppl stem. of *menstruare*, from Latin *menstrua*: see MENSTRUUM, -ATE[3].]
†**1** *verb trans*. Soil as with menstrual blood. Only in M17.
2 *verb intrans*. Undergo menstruation; undergo the menstrual cycle. E19.

menstruation /mɛnstrʊˈeɪʃ(ə)n/ *noun*. M18.
[ORIGIN from MENSTRUATE + -ATION.]
The process of discharging blood and other material from the lining of the uterus through the vagina, which occurs in sexually mature women (except during and for a time after pregnancy) normally at intervals of about one lunar month, until the menopause.

menstruous /ˈmɛnstrʊəs/ *adjective*. LME.
[ORIGIN Old French *menstrueus* or late Latin *menstruosus*, from Latin *menstrua*: see MENSTRUUM, -OUS.]
1 Undergoing menstruation. LME.
2 Of or pertaining to menstruation; = MENSTRUAL 1. LME.
†**3** Soiled (as) with menstrual blood; horribly filthy or polluted. LME–L17.
†**4** = MENSTRUAL 2. *rare*. M17–M19.

menstruum /ˈmɛnstrʊəm/ *noun*. Pl. **-strua** /-strʊə/, **-struums**. LME.
[ORIGIN Latin, use as noun of *menstruus* monthly, from *mensis* month. In classical Latin (in sense 1) only as pl. *menstrua*.]
1 *sing.* & in *pl.* Menses. Now *rare*. LME.
2 CHEMISTRY & PHARMACOLOGY. A solvent; a liquid medium. *arch*. E17.

mensual /ˈmɛnsjʊəl, -ʃʊəl/ *adjective*. E17.
[ORIGIN Late Latin *mensualis*, irreg. from Latin *mensis* month after *annualis* annual: see -AL[1].]
Of or relating to a month; monthly.

Mensur /mɛnˈzuːr, mɛnˈsʊə/ *noun*. Pl. ***-ren*** /-rən/, **-rs**. M17.
[ORIGIN German, lit. 'measure'.]
†**1** The distance between two duellers. Only in M17.
2 In Germany, a fencing duel between students fought with partially blunted weapons. M19.

mensurable /ˈmɛnʃ(ə)rəb(ə)l, -sjə-/ *adjective*. LME.
[ORIGIN French, or late Latin *mensurabilis*, from *mensurare*: see MENSURATE, -ABLE.]
†**1 a** Moderate. Only in LME. ▸**b** Just, fair. Only in M17.
2 Able to be measured; having assigned limits. L16.
3 MUSIC. Having fixed rhythm with notes and rests indicating a definite duration, *spec.* as characterizing the style succeeding simple plainsong. L18.
■ **mensuraˈbility** *noun* (*rare*) L17.

mensural /ˈmɛnʃ(ə)r(ə)l, -sjə-/ *adjective*. L16.
[ORIGIN Latin *mensuralis*, from *mensura* MEASURE *noun*: see -AL[1].]
1 MUSIC. = MENSURABLE 3. L16.
2 Of or pertaining to measuring. M17.
■ **mensuralist** *noun & adjective* (**a**) *noun* a composer or advocate of mensurable music, *spec.* plainsong; (**b**) *adjective* of or pertaining to mensurable music or mensuralists: E20.

mensurate /ˈmɛnʃəreɪt, -sjə-/ *verb trans*. M17.
[ORIGIN Late Latin *mensurat-* pa. ppl stem of *mensurare*, from Latin *mensura* MEASURE *noun*: see -ATE[3].]
Measure; ascertain the size, extent, or quantity of.
■ **mensurative** *adjective* capable of measuring; adapted for taking measurements: M19. **mensurator** *noun* a means of or apparatus for measuring M17.

mensuration /mɛnʃəˈreɪʃ(ə)n, -sjə-/ *noun*. L16.
[ORIGIN Late Latin *mensuratio(n-)*, formed as MENSURATE: see -ATION.]
1 The action or an act of measuring. L16.
2 MATH. The part of geometry that deals with the measurement of lengths, areas, and volumes. E18.
■ **mensurational** *adjective* L19.

Mensuren *noun pl.* see MENSUR.

-ment /m(ə)nt/ *suffix*.
[ORIGIN Repr. French *-ment* or (its source) Latin *-mentum*.]
Used in nouns adopted from French or Latin and in English formations modelled on these and as a productive suffix, expr. the result, product, or means of an action, usu. from verbs and verb stems, as ***abridgement***, ***accomplishment***, ***banishment***, ***bereavement***, ***commencement***, ***embodiment***, ***enhancement***, ***excitement***, ***fragment***, ***garment***, ***implement***, ***ligament***, ***ornament***, ***treatment***, ***wonderment***, etc., but also from adjectives, as ***betterment***, ***merriment***, ***oddment***.

mental /ˈmɛnt(ə)l/ *adjective*[1] & *noun*. LME.
[ORIGIN Old French & mod. French, or late Latin *mentalis*, from *ment-*, *mens* mind: see -AL[1].]
▸ **A** *adjective*. **1** *gen*. Of or pertaining to the mind. LME.

> R. C. HUTCHINSON One whose mental growth had stunted the physical. M. WARNOCK Memory is a mental phenomenon.

2 Carried on or performed by the mind; taking place in the mind. E16.

> *Listener* Hearing it I could not help directing a mental kick at all those other . . plays. K. WATERHOUSE His mental calculations . . seemed to be giving him trouble.

mental restriction: see RESTRICTION 5.
3 Of or pertaining to the mind as an object of study; concerned with the phenomena of mind. E19.
4 Characterized by the possession of mind, intellectual. *rare*. M19.

> J. JONES This young man is also very mental His being is riddled with theory and hypothesis.

5 Of or pertaining to disorders or illnesses of the mind. L19. ▸**b** Mentally ill or mentally disabled (now regarded as *offensive*). Now also, irrational, uncontrolled, very eccentric. *colloq*. E20.
mental asylum, ***mental hospital***, ***mental nurse***, ***mental patient***, etc. **b go mental** *colloq*. become mentally unbalanced; lose one's self-control; become very angry.
– SPECIAL COLLOCATIONS: **mental age** the degree of mental development of a person, expressed as the age at which a similar level is attained by an average person. **mental arithmetic**: performed without the use of written figures or other visible symbols. ***mental block***: see BLOCK *noun* 10c. **mental cruelty** conduct which inflicts suffering on the mind of another person, esp. (*US*) as constituting grounds for legal separation or divorce. ***mental defective***: see DEFECTIVE *noun* 2. ***mental deficiency***: see DEFICIENCY 1. **mental disability** the condition of being of such low intelligence, or having the intellectual capacities so underdeveloped, as to inhibit normal social functioning; an instance of this. **mental handicap** mental disability. **mental healer** a practitioner of mental healing. **mental healing** healing effected by

mental effort. ***mental health***: see HEALTH 5. **mental hygiene** (measures directed towards the preservation or improvement of) mental health. ***mental note***: see NOTE *noun*[2] 14. **mental ratio** = INTELLIGENCE ***quotient***. **mental set** the set or predisposition of the mind which governs reactions to stimuli. **mental test** = INTELLIGENCE ***test***. **mental year** the average mental attainment of each year of growth, used as a unit of measurement of mental development.

▸ **B** *noun*. †**1** An intellectual faculty. *rare*. Only in L17.

†**2** A mental reservation. *rare*. Only in E18.

3 A mentally ill person; a mental patient. *colloq.* (now *offensive*). E20.

— NOTE: Use of the adjective in sense 5 was widespread L19–M20. It is now regarded as old-fashioned or offensive and has been largely replaced by *psychiatric*.

▪ **mentalize** *verb trans.* develop or cultivate mentally; give a mental quality to: E19.

mental /ˈmɛnt(ə)l/ *adjective*[2]. E18.

[ORIGIN French, from Latin *mentum* chin: see -AL[1].]

1 Of or pertaining to the chin. E18.

2 BIOLOGY. Of, pertaining to, or situated on the mentum. M19.

mentalism /ˈmɛnt(ə)lɪz(ə)m/ *noun*. L19.

[ORIGIN from MENTAL *adjective*[1] + -ISM.]

1 A mental process. *rare*. L19.

2 The theory that physical events are ultimately explicable only as aspects or functions of the mind; belief in the primacy of mind. L19.

mentalist /ˈmɛnt(ə)lɪst/ *noun & adjective*. M17.

[ORIGIN formed as MENTALISM + -IST.]

▸ **A** *noun* **1 a** A person who conceals his or her real thoughts. *rare*. M17. ▸**b** A magician who apparently demonstrates extraordinary mental powers, such as telepathy, precognition, etc. E20.

2 An adherent of mentalism. L19.

3 An eccentric or mad person. *colloq.* L20.

Marie Claire I thought you were snoggable, but now I think you're a mentalist.

▸ **B** *attrib.* or as *adjective*. Of or pertaining to mentalists or mentalism. M20.

▪ **mentaˈlistic** *adjective* of, pertaining to, or of the nature of mentalism L19. **mentaˈlistically** *adverb* M20.

mentality /mɛnˈtalɪti/ *noun*. L17.

[ORIGIN formed as MENTALISM + -ITY.]

1 A mental action. *rare*. L17.

2 Mental ability; intellectual quality, intellectuality. M19.

3 Mental character or disposition; (an) outlook; a kind or degree of intelligence. L19.

R. MACAULAY We should not be at all friendly with a government so little liberal in mentality. U. LE GUIN These Port managers . . tended to acquire the bureaucratic mentality: they said No automatically. J. BAYLEY Hardy and D. H. Lawrence . . use the story . . as a kind of safety-valve, for things in their mentalities which demanded direct . . expression.

mentally /ˈmɛnt(ə)li/ *adverb*. LME.

[ORIGIN formed as MENTALISM + -LY[2].]

In the mind, by a mental operation; as regards the mind.

M. KLINE Leonardo da Vinci . . . Incredibly endowed both physically and mentally. A. HUTSCHNECKER People who commit suicide are mentally sick people. D. MADDEN Mentally, she recited a fragment of poetry.

mentally defective: see DEFECTIVE *adjective* 1C. ***mentally deficient***: see DEFICIENT *adjective* 3. **mentally handicapped** having a mental disability.

mentation /mɛnˈteɪʃ(ə)n/ *noun*. M19.

[ORIGIN from Latin *ment-*, *mens* mind + -ATION.]

Mental activity; an instance or product of this.

menthol /ˈmɛnθɒl, -θ(ə)l/ *noun*. M19.

[ORIGIN from Latin *mentha* mint + -OL.]

A crystalline terpenoid alcohol with a characteristic cooling odour and taste, obtainable from peppermint and other oils, or by hydrogenation of thymol, and used in medicines (esp. decongestants), perfumes, etc.; 2-isopropyl-5-methylcyclohexanol, $C_{10}H_{19}OH$.

▪ **mentholated** *adjective* treated or impregnated with menthol; containing menthol: M20.

menthone /ˈmɛnθəʊn/ *noun*. L19.

[ORIGIN from MENTHOL + -ONE.]

CHEMISTRY. An optically active cyclic ketone which is a colourless oily liquid occurring in peppermint and other oils; 2-isopropyl-5-methylcyclohexanone, $C_{10}H_{18}O$.

menticide /ˈmɛntɪsʌɪd/ *noun*. M20.

[ORIGIN from Latin *menti-*, *mens* mind + -CIDE.]

The (esp. institutionalized) undermining or destruction of the mind or will.

menticulture /ˈmɛntɪkʌltʃə/ *noun*. *rare*. M19.

[ORIGIN from Latin *menti-*, *mens* mind + -CULTURE.]

The cultivation of the mind.

▪ **mentiˈcultural** *adjective* M19.

mention /ˈmɛnʃ(ə)n/ *noun*. ME.

[ORIGIN Old French & mod. French from Latin *mentio(n-)*, from base of *meminisse* remember, ult. redupl. of base of MIND *noun*[1]: see -ION.]

1 The action or an act of referring to, remarking on, or introducing the name of a person or thing, now *spec.* incidentally, as not obviously essential to the context (foll. by *of*). Orig. in ***make mention of*** below. ME. ▸**b** [abbreviation of *honourable mention*, *mention in dispatches*, etc.] A formal or official commendatory reference, as in a military dispatch. L19.

R. L. STEVENSON The mention of his name leads me on to speak of our ship's cook. E. KUZWAYO There is no mention of the circumstances which preceded my ill-health. S. HASTINGS He distinguished himself by winning a mention in despatches for valour at Sedan.

HONOURABLE ***mention***. **make mention of** refer to, introduce the name of, (in general use now usu. in neg. contexts, as ***make no mention of***).

2 An indication, a vestige, a trace, a remnant. *obsolete* exc. *Scot.* M16.

mention /ˈmɛnʃ(ə)n/ *verb*. M16.

[ORIGIN French *mentionner*, formed as MENTION *noun*.]

1 *verb trans.* Refer to or remark on incidentally; specify by name or otherwise; state incidentally *that*. M16.

J. OSBORNE Letters in which I'm not mentioned at all. P. O'DONNELL I wouldn't mind a drink, though, now you mention it. R. ELLMANN He forebore to mention that he planned to stop in Rome.

don't mention it *colloq.*: indicating that one considers offered thanks or apology to be inappropriate or excessive. ***mentioned in dispatches***: see DISPATCH *noun*. **not to mention**: introducing a fact or making a reference of primary importance.

†**2** *verb intrans.* Foll. by *of*: refer to, speak of. M16–L18.

▪ **mentionable** *adjective* that can or may be mentioned, worthy of mention, (earlier & more usual in ***unmentionable***) M19. **mentioned** *ppl adjective* of which mention has been made (now chiefly as 2nd elem. of comb., as ***before-mentioned***, ***undermentioned***, etc.) M16. **mentioner** *noun* (now *rare*) E17.

mento /ˈmɛntəʊ/ *noun*. Pl. **-os**. E20.

[ORIGIN Perh. of African origin, or from Spanish *mentar* to mention, presumably with ref. to the conversational nature of songs in this style.]

A Jamaican style of popular music and dance; a song or dance in this style.

mento- /ˈmɛntəʊ/ *combining form* of Latin *mentum* chin: see -O-.

▪ **mento-Meckelian** /-mɛˈkiːlɪən/ *adjective & noun* (ANATOMY) (designating) a bone in the jaw formed in part by the ossification of Meckel's cartilage L19. **mento-ˈvertical** *adjective & noun* (designating or pertaining to) the diameter of the head from the menton to the highest point of the vertex E20.

menton /ˈmɛnt(ə)n/ *noun*. E20.

[ORIGIN French, formed as MENTUM.]

ANATOMY. = GNATHION.

mentor /ˈmɛntɔː/ *noun & verb*. M18.

[ORIGIN French from Latin *Mentor* from Greek *Mentōr* the guide and adviser of Odysseus' son Telemachus (prob. chosen as a name in reference to base meaning 'remember, think, counsel').]

▸ **A** *noun*. An experienced and trusted adviser or guide; a teacher, a tutor; *spec.* an experienced person in a company, college, etc. who trains and counsels new employees or students. M18.

▸ **B** *verb trans.* Advise or train (esp. a younger colleague). Freq. as ***mentoring*** *verbal noun*. L20.

▪ **mentee** *noun* a person who is advised, trained, or counselled by a mentor M20. **mentorial** /mɛnˈtɔːrɪəl/ *adjective* of or pertaining to a mentor, containing advice E19.

mentri /ˈmɛntri/ *noun*. L19.

[ORIGIN Malay *menteri* from Sanskrit *mantrī* MANTRI.]

In Malaysia and Indonesia: a government minister.

mentri besar /bɪˈsɑː/ a chief minister.

mentum /ˈmɛntəm/ *noun*. L17.

[ORIGIN Latin = chin.]

1 ANATOMY. The chin. L17.

2 ENTOMOLOGY. A part of the base of the labium in some insects. E19.

3 BOTANY. A projection formed by the sepals and the base of the column in some orchids. M19.

menu /ˈmɛnjuː/ *noun*. M17.

[ORIGIN French = detailed list, use as noun of adjective = small from Latin *minutus* MINUTE *adjective*. In branch I short for *menu peuple*.]

▸ †**I 1** The common people. *rare*. Only in M17.

▸ **II 2** A list of the dishes to be served at a banquet or meal or available at a restaurant etc.; a card etc. on which a menu is written or printed. Also, the food served or available. M19.

Journal of Home Economics Exactly the same menu was served in a large college dining room and at the cafeteria. D. JOHNSON The waiter brought me a menu.

3 *transf.* A list of things available or for completion. L19. ▸**b** COMPUTING. A computer-generated list of available commands, facilities, or other options, usu. displayed onscreen, for selection by the operator. M20.

H. G. WELLS All the intelligent ones feel baffled at the menu of these degree courses.

— COMB.: **menu bar** COMPUTING a horizontal bar, typically located at the top of the screen below the title bar, containing drop-down menus; **menu card** a card on which a menu is written or printed; **menu-driven** *adjective* (of a program or computer) operated by making selections from menus.

menudo /mɪˈnuːdəʊ/ *noun*. E20.

[ORIGIN Mexican Spanish, use as noun of adjective = small from Latin *minutus* MINUTE *adjective*.]

A spicy Mexican soup made from tripe.

menuet *noun & verb* var. of MINUET.

menura /mɪˈn(j)ʊərə/ *noun*. Chiefly *Austral.* E19.

[ORIGIN mod. Latin (see below), from Greek *mēnē* crescent moon + *oura* tail (from the crescent-shaped spots on the tail).]

A bird of the genus *Menura*; a lyrebird.

menus plaisirs /məny plɛziːr/ *noun phr. pl.* L17.

[ORIGIN French = small pleasures.]

Simple pleasures; small personal expenses or gratifications; fanciful or trifling objects bought with pocket money.

menzil *noun* var. of MANZIL.

Meo /ˈmeɪəʊ/ *noun*[1] & *adjective*[1]. M19.

[ORIGIN Rajasthani.]

▸ **A** *noun*. Pl. **-os**, same. A member of a people of the Mewat region in NW India (now called Alwar and part of Rajasthan) and neighbouring areas; a Mewati; *spec.* one professing Hinduism. M19.

▸ **B** *attrib.* or as *adjective*. Of or pertaining to this people. L19.

Meo *noun*[2] & *adjective*[2] var. of MIAO.

meow *noun*, *verb*, & *interjection* var. of MIAOW.

MEP *abbreviation*.

Member of the European Parliament.

mepacrine /ˈmɛpəkrɪn, -iːn/ *noun*. M20.

[ORIGIN from ME(THOXY- + -*p*- (perh. from PENTANE) + ACR(ID)INE.]

PHARMACOLOGY. A tricyclic base derived from acridine, used as an anthelmintic and antimalarial drug. Also called ***quinacrine***, (proprietary) ***Atebrin***.

meperidine /məˈpɛrɪdɪn, -iːn/ *noun*. Chiefly *US*. M20.

[ORIGIN from ME(THYL + PI)PERIDINE.]

PHARMACOLOGY. = PETHIDINE.

mephenesin /məˈfɛnəsɪn/ *noun*. M20.

[ORIGIN from ME(THYL + PHEN(YL + CR)ES(OL + -IN[1].]

PHARMACOLOGY. A phenoxy compound, $CH_3{\cdot}C_6H_4O{\cdot}CH_2CH(OH)CH_2OH$, used as a muscle relaxant and tranquillizer.

Mephistophelean /ˌmɛfɪstəˈfiːlɪən/ *adjective*. Also **-ian**. M19.

[ORIGIN formed as MEPHISTOPHELES + -AN, -IAN.]

Of, pertaining to, or resembling Mephistopheles; fiendish; fatally tempting.

Mephistopheles /mɛfɪˈstɒfɪliːz/ *noun*. Also (earlier) †**Mephostophilis**, †**Mephostophilus**. L16.

[ORIGIN The evil spirit to whom Faust in German legend sold his soul, esp. as represented in Marlowe's *Doctor Faustus* (c 1590) and Goethe's *Faust* (1808–32).]

A fiendish person, a person who entraps another to destruction, a fatal tempter.

mephitic /mɪˈfɪtɪk/ *adjective*. E17.

[ORIGIN Late Latin *mephiticus*, formed as MEPHITIS: see -IC.]

Offensive to the smell; (of a vapour or exhalation) pestilential, noxious, poisonous.

▪ Also **mephitical** *adjective* E18.

mephitis /mɪˈfʌɪtɪs/ *noun*. M17.

[ORIGIN Latin.]

A noxious or pestilential emanation, esp. from the earth; an obnoxious or poisonous stench.

▪ **mephitism** *noun* (*arch.*) evil-smelling poisoning of the air E19.

†**Mephostophilis**, **Mephostophilus** *nouns* see MEPHISTOPHELES.

meprobamate /mɪˈprəʊbəmeɪt/ *noun*. M20.

[ORIGIN from ME(THYL + PRO(PYL + CAR)BAMATE.]

PHARMACOLOGY. A bitter-tasting carbamate, $CH_3CH_2CH_2{\cdot}C(CH_2O{\cdot}CO{\cdot}NH_2)_2CH_3$, used as a mild tranquillizer. Proprietary name ***Miltown***.

mepyramine /mɪˈpɪrəmiːn/ *noun*. M20.

[ORIGIN from ME(THYL + PYR(IDINE + AMINE.]

PHARMACOLOGY. A polycyclic substituted amine with antihistamine properties, used to treat allergic conditions.

mer /məː/ *noun*. M20.

[ORIGIN Back-form. from POLYMER. Cf. -MER.]

CHEMISTRY. The repeating unit in a polymeric molecule.

mer- /məː/ *prefix*.

[ORIGIN After MERMAID.]

Of the mermaid kind, as ***merbaby***, ***merchild***, ***merman***, ***merwoman***, etc.

-mer /mə/ *suffix*.

[ORIGIN Repr. Greek *meros* part, after *isomer*, *polymer*.]

Forming nouns chiefly denoting particular kinds of polymer, as ***dimer***, ***elastomer***, or isomer, as ***epimer***, ***tautomer***. Also used with prefixed numeral to denote polymers of a given number of units, as ***9-mer***, ***16-mer***.

meranti /məˈranti/ *noun*. L18.

[ORIGIN Malay.]

(The hardwood timber of) any of various trees of the genus *Shorea* (family Dipterocarpaceae), native to Indonesia and parts of Malaysia.

M

merbau /ˈməːbaʊ/ *noun*. **L18**.
[ORIGIN Malay.]
(The hardwood timber of) either of two leguminous trees, *Intsia bijuga* and *I. palembanica*, native to Malaysia and Indonesia.

merbromin /məˈbrəʊmɪn/ *noun*. **M20**.
[ORIGIN from MER(CURIC + BROM(O- + -IN¹.]
PHARMACOLOGY. A fluorescein derivative containing bromine and mercury, obtained as greenish iridescent scales which dissolve in water to give a red solution used as an antiseptic. US proprietary name ***Mercurochrome***.

merc /məːk/ *noun*. *colloq*. **M20**.
[ORIGIN Abbreviation of MERCENARY.]
A mercenary soldier.

mercado /məːˈkɑːdəʊ, *foreign* merˈkaðo/ *noun*. Pl. **-os** /-əʊz, *foreign* -ɔs/. **M19**.
[ORIGIN Spanish from Latin *mercatus* MARKET *noun*.]
A market in Spain and Spanish-speaking countries.

Mercalli scale /məːˈkalɪ skeɪl/ *noun phr*. **E20**.
[ORIGIN Giuseppe *Mercalli* (1850–1914), Italian geologist.]
GEOLOGY. An arbitrary 12-point scale for expressing the intensity of an earthquake at any place.

mercantile /ˈməːk(ə)ntʌɪl/ *adjective*. **M17**.
[ORIGIN French from Italian, from *mercante* MERCHANT *noun*: see -ILE.]
1 Of or pertaining to merchants or their trade; concerned with the exchange of merchandise; of or pertaining to trade or commerce; commercial. **M17**.

J. ARBUTHNOT The Expedition of the Argonauts . . was partly mercantile, partly military. G. CRABBE A bill That was not drawn with true mercantile skill. G. J. GOSCHEN Putting aside . . the . . currency altogether, and confining ourselves to the more mercantile part of the question. G. STEINER The new mercantile society . . followed hard on the decay of feudalism.

mercantile marine the shipping employed in commerce as opp. to war, the merchant navy.

2 Having payment or gain as the motive; mercenary; fond of bargaining. **M18**.
mercantile system *hist*.: based on the principles of mercantilism.
■ **mercantilely** *adverb* from a mercantile point of view; with regard to business transactions: **E19**.

mercantilism /ˈməːk(ə)ntʌɪlɪz(ə)m/ *noun*. **M19**.
[ORIGIN from MERCANTILE + -ISM.]
1 Belief in the benefits of trade; the principles or practice characteristic of merchants; commercialism. **M19**.
2 *hist*. The economic theory that trade generates wealth and is stimulated by the accumulation of bullion, which a government should encourage by promoting exports and restricting imports. **L19**.
■ **mercantilist** *noun & adjective* (*hist*.) (**a**) *noun* an advocate of mercantilism; (**b**) *adjective* of or pertaining to mercantilism or mercantilists: **M19**. **mercantiˈlistic** *adjective* of the nature of mercantilism **L19**.

mercaptan /məˈkapt(ə)n/ *noun*. **M19**.
[ORIGIN from mod. Latin (*corpus*) *mercurium captans* lit. 'seizing mercury'.]
CHEMISTRY. Any of a series of organic compounds containing a sulphydryl group, ·SH, many of which have a strong, unpleasant odour; a thio-alcohol, a thiol.
■ **mercaptide** *noun* a salt of a mercaptan, containing the anion RS⁻ where R is an alkyl or aryl group **M19**.

mercapto- /məˈkaptəʊ/ *combining form*. Before a vowel also **mercapt-**. Also as attrib. adjective **mercapto**.
[ORIGIN from MERCAPTAN + -O-.]
CHEMISTRY. Designating or containing the radical ·SH (or a substituted form of this).
■ **mercaptoˈpurine** *noun* (*PHARMACOLOGY*) any of various mercapto derivatives of purine; *spec*. 6-mercaptopurine, $C_5H_4N_4S$, a yellow cytotoxic agent used esp. to treat leukaemia in children: **M20**. **mercapturic** /məːkapˈtjʊərɪk/ *adjective*: ***mercapturic acid***, any of various acids of formula $RSCH_2CH(NH{\cdot}CO{\cdot}CH_3)COOH$ (where R is an aryl group), some of which are excreted in the urine as detoxication products of aromatic compounds **L19**.

Mercator /məːˈkeɪtə/ *noun*. **L16**.
[ORIGIN Gerhardus *Mercator*, Latinized name of Gerhard Kremer (1512–94), Flemish cartographer.]
1 Used *attrib*. and in *possess*. with ref. to a cylindrical map projection in which meridians are represented by equidistant straight lines at right angles to the equator and any course that follows a constant compass bearing is represented by a straight line. **L16**.

R. HINKS The great distortion in the north and south makes Mercator's projection . . unsuitable for a land map.

transverse Mercator: see TRANSVERSE *adjective*.
2 (A map drawn on) Mercator's projection. **E18**.

mercatorial /məːkəˈtɔːrɪəl/ *adjective*¹. Now *rare*. **M17**.
[ORIGIN from Latin *mercatorius*, from *mercator*, from *mercari* to trade + -AL¹.]
Of or pertaining to merchants or merchandise; mercantile.

Mercatorial /məːkəˈtɔːrɪəl/ *adjective*². **L19**.
[ORIGIN from MERCATOR + -IAL.]
Of, pertaining to, or derived from Mercator or Mercator's projection.

mercatory /ˈməːkət(ə)ri/ *adjective*. *rare*. **M17**.
[ORIGIN formed as MERCATORIAL *adjective*¹: see -ORY².]
= MERCATORIAL *adjective*¹.

mercement /ˈməːsm(ə)nt/ *noun*. Long *obsolete* exc. *Scot*. Also **merci-** /ˈməːsɪ-/, †**mercia-**. **ME**.
[ORIGIN Aphet. from AMERCEMENT, AMERCIAMENT.]
= AMERCEMENT. Also, judgement, mercy.

mercenary /ˈməːsɪn(ə)ri/ *noun & adjective*. **LME**.
[ORIGIN Latin *mercenarius*, earlier *-nn-*, from *merces*, *merced-* reward, wages: see MERCY, -ARY¹.]
▸ **A** *noun*. **1** A person who works merely for money or other material reward; a hireling, a mercenary person. Now *rare* or *obsolete*. **LME**.
2 A person who receives payment for his or her services; *spec*. a professional soldier serving a foreign power. **E16**.
▸ **B** *adjective*. **1** Working or done merely for money or other material reward; actuated or characterized by self-interest; motivated by desire for money or other material reward. **M16**.

H. JAMES I might improve my fortune by some other means than by making a mercenary marriage. A. E. HOUSMAN These . . Followed their mercenary calling, And took their wages and are dead. A. WEST The activities of mercenary and unscrupulous journalists.

2 Hired, serving for wages or hire, now *spec*. as a soldier for a foreign power. **L16**.

JOHN BROOKE As the British could not raise their own army they had to use mercenary troops.

†**3** Salaried, stipendiary. **M17–L18**.
■ **mercenarian** /məːsɪˈnɛːrɪən/ *adjective & noun* (*rare*) †(**a**) *noun* a mercenary, a hired soldier; (**b**) *adjective* of or pertaining to mercenaries: **L16**. **mercenarily** *adverb* **E17**. **mercenariness** *noun* **E17**.

mercer /ˈməːsə/ *noun*. **ME**.
[ORIGIN Anglo-Norman *mercer*, Old French & mod. French *mercier* from Proto-Romance, from Latin *merc-*, *merx* merchandise: see -ER².]
A dealer in textile fabrics, esp. silks, velvets, and other costly materials.

mercerize /ˈməːsərʌɪz/ *verb trans*. Also **-ise**. **M19**.
[ORIGIN from John *Mercer* (d. 1866) of Accrington, NW England, said to have discovered the process in 1844 + -IZE.]
Treat (cotton fabric or thread) under tension with a solution usu. of sodium or potassium hydroxide to give greater strength and impart lustre.
■ **merceriˈzation** *noun* **M19**.

mercery /ˈməːs(ə)ri/ *noun*. **ME**.
[ORIGIN Old French & mod. French *mercerie*, from *mercier*: see MERCER, -Y³.]
1 *collect*. The wares sold by a mercer. **ME**.
†**2** ***the Mercery***, the Mercers' Company; the trade in mercery; the part of a city where this is carried on. **LME–M17**.
3 A mercer's shop. **L19**.

merchandise /ˈməːtʃ(ə)ndʌɪz/ *noun*. **ME**.
[ORIGIN Old French & mod. French *marchandise*, from *marchand* MERCHANT *noun*: see -ISE².]
1 The action of buying and selling goods or commodities for profit; the business of a merchant; commerce, trading. *arch*. **ME**.
2 *sing*. & †*pl*. The commodities of commerce; goods to be bought and sold. **ME**. ▸†**b** A kind of merchandise; a saleable commodity. **LME–M19**.
– PHRASES: **make a merchandise of**, **make merchandise of** *arch*. deal or traffic in, esp. inappropriately in something which should not be the subject of trade.

merchandise /ˈməːtʃ(ə)ndʌɪz/ *verb*. **LME**.
[ORIGIN from the noun.]
1 *verb intrans*. Trade, traffic; engage in the business of a merchant. *arch*. **LME**.
2 *verb trans*. Buy and sell; barter; traffic in. *arch*. **M16**.
3 *verb trans*. Put on the market, promote the sale of (goods etc.); *transf*. advertise (an idea or person), publicize. **E20**.

A. E. STEVENSON That you can merchandise candidates . . like breakfast cereal . . is . . the ultimate indignity to the democratic process.

■ **merchandisable** *adjective* = MERCHANTABLE (*rare* before **20**) **L15**. **merchandiser** *noun* (**a**) a person who merchandises something or someone; (**b**) a display stand for merchandise: **L16**.

merchandry /ˈməːtʃ(ə)ndri/ *noun*. Long *arch*. **LME**.
[ORIGIN Old French & mod. French *march(ë)anderie*, from *marchand* MERCHANT *noun*: see -RY.]
Trade, commerce; the business of a merchant.

merchant /ˈməːtʃ(ə)nt/ *noun & adjective*. **ME**.
[ORIGIN Old French *march(ë)ant*, later (also mod.) *marchand*, from Proto-Romance pres. ppl stem of verb from Latin *mercari* to trade, from *merc-*, *merx* merchandise: see -ANT¹.]
▸ **A** *noun*. **1** A person whose occupation is the purchase and sale of goods or commodities for profit; (without specifying word usu.) a wholesale trader, esp. dealing with foreign countries; (esp. *Scot*., *N. English*, & *US*, & as 2nd elem. of comb.) a retail trader, a shopkeeper. **ME**. ▸**b** A buyer, a customer. *Scot*. **L17**.
coal merchant, ***corn merchant***, ***wine merchant***, etc.
2 A fellow, a person. Now usu. with specifying word, a person with an interest in or partiality for the thing specified. *slang*. **M16**.

G. F. SIMS Sorry to be such a gloom merchant.

speed merchant etc.
3 A trading vessel, a merchantman. **L16**.
†**4** A supercargo. Only in **17**.
– PHRASES: **merchant of death** a person who makes a profession of war; *spec*. (**a**) a dealer in armaments; (**b**) a mercenary soldier.
▸ **B** *adjective* (*attrib*. & *postpositive*). **1** Connected with merchandise; relating to trade or commerce. Chiefly in ***law-merchant***, ***statute-merchant***. **LME**.
2 (Of a ship) serving for the transport of merchandise; of or pertaining to the mercantile marine. **LME**.
3 (Of a town) occupied in commerce, commercial; consisting of merchants. **LME**.
– SPECIAL COLLOCATIONS & COMB.: **merchant-adventurer** *hist*. a merchant engaged in the organization and dispatch of trading expeditions overseas and the establishment of factories and trading stations in foreign countries; a member of an association of such merchants incorporated by royal charter or other lawful authority. **merchant bank** a bank whose main business is the providing of long-term credit and the support and financing of commercial enterprises. **merchant banker** a person engaged in merchant banking; in *pl*. also, a merchant bank as a firm. **merchant banking** the activity of a merchant bank; the provision of commercial loans and financing. **merchant-bar** a bar of merchant iron. **merchant fleet** a fleet of merchant ships, a merchant navy. **merchant guild** a (medieval) guild of merchants. **merchant iron** iron in finished bars, ready for sale. **merchantman** (**a**) *arch*. a merchant, a trader; (**b**) a ship conveying merchandise, a vessel of the mercantile marine. **merchant marine** (chiefly *US*) the merchant navy, the mercantile marine. †**merchant mill** *US* a mill engaged in the grinding of grain for wholesale selling. **merchant navy** a fleet or number of ships used in trade and not for purposes of war, a country's mercantile marine. **merchant prince** a merchant of princely wealth and munificence. **merchant-princely** *adjective* characteristic of a merchant prince. **merchant seaman**: serving in a merchant ship or merchant navy. **merchant service** the merchant navy, the mercantile marine. ***merchant stapler***: see STAPLER *noun*¹ 1. †**merchant-stranger** a merchant from another country; a foreign trader. **merchant-tailor** *hist*. a tailor who supplies the materials of which his goods are made; a member of the company of such tailors. **merchant-venturer** *hist*. = ***merchant-adventurer*** above.
■ **merchanthood** *noun* (*rare*) **M19**. **merchantlike** *adjective & adverb* (**a**) *adjective* resembling or befitting a merchant; formerly also, of or pertaining to merchants or commerce, mercantile; (**b**) *adverb* after the manner of a merchant: **LME**. **merchantly** *adjective* pertaining to or characteristic of a merchant **L16**. **merchantry** *noun* (**a**) the business of a merchant; trade, commercial dealings; (**b**) merchants collectively: **L18**.

merchant /ˈməːtʃ(ə)nt/ *verb*. **LME**.
[ORIGIN Old French *march(ë)ander* (mod. *marchander*), formed as MERCHANT *noun & adjective*.]
1 *verb intrans*. Trade as a merchant. Formerly also, bargain, haggle. Now chiefly as ***merchanting*** *verbal noun & ppl adjective*. **LME**.
2 *verb trans*. Trade or deal in; buy and sell. Now *rare*. **E16**.

merchantable /ˈməːtʃ(ə)ntəb(ə)l/ *adjective*. **L15**.
[ORIGIN from MERCHANT *verb* + -ABLE.]
1 Suitable or prepared for purchase or sale; that may or can be bought or sold; saleable; marketable. **L15**.
†**2** Of or pertaining to trade; commercial. **E–M17**.
■ **merchantaˈbility** *noun* **L19**. **merchantableness** *noun* **M18**.

merchet /ˈməːtʃɪt/ *noun*. *obsolete* exc. *hist*. **ME**.
[ORIGIN Anglo-Norman = Old Northern French MARKET *noun*.]
A fine paid by a tenant or bondsman to his overlord for liberty to give his daughter in marriage.

merciable /ˈməːsɪəb(ə)l/ *adjective*. Long *arch*. *rare*. **ME**.
[ORIGIN Old French, formed as MERCY: see -ABLE.]
Merciful, compassionate.

†**merciament** *noun* see MERCEMENT.

Mercian /ˈməːsɪən, ˈməːʃ(ə)n/ *noun & adjective*. **E16**.
[ORIGIN from medieval Latin *Mercia* from Old English *Merċe*, *Mierċe* (pl.) lit. 'borderers', from Germanic base of MARCH *noun*², MARK *noun*¹: see -AN.]
▸ **A** *noun*. **1** A native or inhabitant of the Anglo-Saxon kingdom of Mercia in central England. **E16**.
2 The (Anglian) dialect of Old English spoken in Mercia. **M19**.
▸ **B** *adjective*. Of or pertaining to Mercia or its dialect. **M16**.

merciful /ˈməːsɪfʊl, -f(ə)l/ *adjective*. **ME**.
[ORIGIN from MERCY + -FUL.]
Having, feeling, or exercising mercy; characterized by mercy; compassionate; affording relief from misery etc.

DRYDEN God is infinitely merciful. G. K. CHESTERTON The world was growing more merciful and therefore no one would ever desire to kill. E. PIZZEY When you get to my age, death really is a merciful release. J. MORTIMER There was a merciful gap in Leslie's speech, into which the Chairman hurried to pour oil.

■ **mercifully** *adverb* (**a**) in a merciful manner; as a mercy, through (God's) mercy; (**b**) *colloq*. (modifying a sentence) it is a mercy (that), fortunately: **ME**. **mercifulness** *noun* **LME**.

†**mercify** *verb trans*. *rare*. **L16–E19**.
[ORIGIN from MERCY + -FY.]
Pity, extend mercy to.

merciless /ˈməːsɪlɪs/ *adjective & adverb*. LME.
[ORIGIN from MERCY + -LESS.]
▸ **A** *adjective*. **1** Without mercy; showing no mercy; pitiless, unrelenting. LME.

L. STEPHEN A doggrel epitaph . . turned his fine phrases into merciless ridicule. A. HUTSCHNECKER The merciless demands of reality. U. BENTLEY A merciless creature, glorying in the heartache of her rivals.

†**2** Obtaining no mercy. LME–M16.
▸ †**B** *adverb*. Mercilessly. LME–M16.
■ **mercilessly** *adverb* L16. **mercilessness** *noun* L16.

merciment *noun* see MERCEMENT.

Merckani *noun* var. of AMERICANI.

mercurate /ˈməːkjʊreɪt/ *verb trans*. E20.
[ORIGIN from MERCURY + -ATE[3].]
CHEMISTRY. Convert into a mercury derivative; introduce mercury into as a substituent, esp. in an aromatic ring.
■ **mercuˈration** *noun* the process of mercurating or of becoming mercurated E20.

mercurial /məːˈkjʊərɪəl/ *noun & adjective*. Also (now chiefly in senses B.1, 2) **M-**. ME.
[ORIGIN Old French & mod. French *mercuriel* or (in sense B.1) *mercurial* or Latin *mercurialis*, from *Mercurius*: see MERCURY, -AL[1].]
▸ **A** *noun*. †**1** Any of the plants called mercury (see MERCURY 6). ME–M17.
2 A person born under the planet Mercury or having the qualities supposed to result from such a birth; a lively, ready-witted, or volatile person. M16.
3 Any compound, esp. a drug or medicine, that contains mercury. L17.
▸ **B** *adjective*. **1** Of or pertaining to the planet Mercury; ASTROLOGY influenced by Mercury, proceeding from the influence of Mercury. LME.
2 Of or pertaining to the god Mercury. Now *rare*. L15.
3 Of or pertaining to the metal mercury; consisting of or containing mercury; MEDICINE (now *rare*, of a disease, a symptom) produced by the presence of mercury; ALCHEMY pertaining to or consisting of mercury, the elementary principle. M16.
4 Born under the planet Mercury, or having the qualities supposed to result from such a birth; subject to sudden changes of mood, volatile, lively and unpredictable. L16.

A. MACLEAN Changes her mind a bit quick, doesn't she? Mercurial, you'd say? I. PATTISON She knew only too well how mercurial Father's moods could be.

■ **mercurialism** *noun* (MEDICINE) (chronic) mercury poisoning E19. **mercurialist** *noun* †(**a**) = MERCURIAL *noun* 2; (**b**) (*obsolete* exc. *hist.*) a medical practitioner who advocated the use of drugs containing mercury, esp. in the treatment of syphilis: M16. **mercuriˈality** *noun* †(**a**) that part of something consisting of or containing mercury; (**b**) liveliness, volatility: M16. **mercurialiˈzation** *noun* (now *rare*) the action of treating something with mercury; the condition of being mercurialized: E19. **mercurialize** *verb* (now *rare*) †(**a**) *verb intrans. & trans.* (with *it*) behave in a mercurial manner; (**b**) *verb trans.* subject to the action of mercury; treat with mercury: E17. **mercurially** *adverb* M17. **mercurialness** *noun* (*rare*) E19.

Mercurian /məːˈkjʊərɪən/ *adjective & noun*. Also **m-**. L16.
[ORIGIN from MERCURY + -AN.]
▸ **A** *adjective*. †**1** = MERCURIAL *adjective* 3. L16–L17.
2 Of or pertaining to the god Mercury; = MERCURIAL *adjective* 2. E18.
3 ASTRONOMY. Of or pertaining to the planet Mercury. Cf. MERCURIAL *adjective* 1. L19.
▸ **B** *noun*. **1** A person born under the planet Mercury. L16.
2 An (imagined) inhabitant of the planet Mercury. M19.

mercuric /məːˈkjʊərɪk/ *adjective*. L18.
[ORIGIN from MERCURY + -IC.]
†**1** Containing mercury. L18–E19.
2 CHEMISTRY. Of or containing mercury in the divalent state. M19.

mercurification /məːˌkjʊrɪfɪˈkeɪʃ(ə)n, məːˌkjʊə-/ *noun*. Now *rare* or *obsolete*. L17.
[ORIGIN from MERCURY + -FICATION.]
1 Orig. (ALCHEMY), the action or process of obtaining the mercurial principle of a metal. Later, the extraction of metallic mercury from its ore. L17.
2 Treatment with mercury. M19.
■ †**mercurified** *adjective* that has undergone mercurification L17–L18.

Mercurochrome /məːˈkjʊərəkrəʊm/ *noun*. Chiefly *N. Amer.* Also **m-**. E20.
[ORIGIN from MERCURY + -O- + Greek *khrōma* colour.]
PHARMACOLOGY. (US proprietary name for) the drug merbromin.

mercurous /ˈməːkjʊrəs/ *adjective*. M19.
[ORIGIN from MERCURY + -OUS.]
CHEMISTRY. Of or containing mercury in the monovalent state.

mercury /ˈməːkjʊri/ *noun*. In branches I, IV usu. **M-**. OE.
[ORIGIN Latin *Mercurius* (from *merc-*, *merx* merchandise), a Roman god, identified from an early period with the Greek Hermes, the god of eloquence and dexterity, protector of traders and thieves, presider over roads, messenger of the gods, etc.]
▸ **I 1** The planet which is the nearest of the major planets to the sun. OE.
2 HERALDRY. The tincture purpure in the fanciful blazon of arms of sovereign houses. *obsolete* exc. *hist.* M16.
▸ **II 3** A heavy silvery-white metallic chemical element, atomic no. 80, which is liquid at room temperature, dissolves other metals to form amalgams, and is used in thermometers and barometers (symbol Hg). Also called ***quicksilver***. LME. ▸**b** This element or one of its compounds prepared for medicinal use. L16. ▸**c** The column of mercury in a barometer or thermometer; atmospheric pressure or temperature indicated by this, esp. as rising or falling. M17.
4 ALCHEMY. One of the elementary principles of which all substances were supposed to be compounded. LME.
†**5** Spirit, liveliness; volatility of temperament, unpredictability; wittiness. M17–L18.
▸ **III 6 a** The pot herb Good King Henry. LME. ▸**b** Either of two plants of the spurge family, with inconspicuous greenish flowers and opposite toothed leaves, *Mercurialis perennis* (in full ***dog's mercury***), a perennial woodland plant, and *Mercurialis annua* (in full ***annual mercury***), a garden weed. LME.
▸ **IV 7** A statue or image of the god Mercury, usu. represented as a young man with winged sandals and hat, bearing a caduceus. Formerly *spec.*, = HERM. L16.
8 a A messenger, a bringer of news. Also, a go-between. L16. ▸†**b** A guide or conductor on the road. L16–M17. ▸†**c** A nimble person; a dexterous thief. E–M17. ▸**d** A hawker or distributor of pamphlets or news-sheets, *esp.* a female one. *hist.* M17.
9 A newspaper. Freq. (now only) in titles. M17.
– COMB.: **mercury arc** (**a**) an electric discharge through mercury vapour; (**b**) = ***mercury vapour lamp*** below; **mercury gilding**: using an amalgam of gold and mercury from which the mercury is driven off by heat; **mercury lamp** = ***mercury vapour lamp*** below; **mercury pool** a mass of liquid mercury, esp. used as an electrode; ***mercury sublimate***: see SUBLIMATE *noun* 1; **mercury tilt switch** an electric switch in which the circuit is made by mercury flowing into a gap when the device tilts; **mercury vapour** a vapour of mercury atoms or ions above liquid mercury or at low pressure; ***mercury vapour lamp***, a lamp in which bluish light (rich in ultraviolet) is produced by an electrical discharge through a mercury arc; ***mercury vapour pump***, a pump for producing high vacuums by entraining molecules of the gas to be evacuated in a jet of mercury vapour.

mercy /ˈməːsi/ *noun & adjective*. ME.
[ORIGIN Old French & mod. French *merci* from Latin *merces*, *merced-* reward, wages, revenue, in Christian Latin used for *misericordia* pity.]
▸ **A** *noun*. **1** Forbearance and compassion shown to a powerless person, esp. an offender, or to one with no claim to receive kindness; kind and compassionate treatment in a case where severity is merited or expected. ME. ▸**b** *spec.* God's forbearance and forgiveness of sins. ME. ▸**c** *spec.* Clemency or forbearance shown by a conqueror or absolute ruler. ME.

BURKE Their enemies will fall upon them . . and show them no mercy.

2 Disposition to forgive or show compassion; compassionateness, mercifulness. ME.

D. HAMMETT I've thrown myself on your mercy, told you that without your help I'm utterly lost. *Times* The process of sovietization has been applied to the Baltic States without mercy.

3 As *interjection*. Asking for mercy or (also ***mercy me!***, ***mercy on us!***, ***for mercy's sake!***, ***God-a-mercy!***, ***lord-a-mercy!***) expr. surprise, fear, etc. ME.
4 An act of mercy; an event or circumstance calling for special thankfulness; a blessing, a relief. ME.

C. BRONTË What a mercy you are shod with velvet, Jane! JOYCE Its a mercy we werent all drowned.

5 = AMERCEMENT. *obsolete* exc. *hist.* ME.
– PHRASES & COMB.: †**at mercy** absolutely in the power of a victor or superior; liable to punishment or hurt at the hands of another; on sufferance. **at the mercy of** wholly in the power of, at the discretion or disposal of; liable to danger or harm from. †**cry a person mercy** beg the pardon or forgiveness of a person. †**deed of mercy** = ***work of mercy*** below. ERRAND ***of mercy***. **have mercy on**, **have mercy upon** show mercy to. †**in mercy** absolutely in one's power as the victor or superior. **leave to the mercy of** leave at the mercy of, expose to probable danger or harm from. ***Lord have mercy (on us)***: see LORD *noun*. **mercy sakes!** *US* (expr. surprise, fear, etc.) for mercy's sake! **mercy seat** the golden covering placed upon the Ark of the Covenant, regarded as the resting place of God; the throne of God in Heaven. ***prerogative of mercy***: see PREROGATIVE *noun* 1. ***sin one's mercies***: see SIN *verb* 2. **Sister of Mercy** a member of a Roman Catholic sisterhood dedicated to works of mercy; *popularly* a member of any nursing sisterhood. **small mercy** a minor piece of good fortune (usu. in *pl.*). ***tender mercies***: see TENDER *adjective* & *noun*[3]. ***thankful for small mercies***: see THANKFUL 1. **work of mercy** an act of compassion towards a suffering fellow creature, *spec.* each of seven spiritual and seven corporal works enumerated in medieval theology.
▸ **B** *attrib.* or as *adjective*. Administered or performed out of mercy or desire to relieve suffering; motivated by compassion. E20.

Sun A mercy flight bringing 68 seriously-wounded refugees from Bosnia arrived in Britain last night.

mercy killing the killing of a patient suffering from an incurable and painful disease, typically by the administration of large doses of painkilling drugs.

merd /məːd/ *noun*. L15.
[ORIGIN formed as MERDE.]
A piece or ball of excrement.

merde /mɛrd/ *noun*. E20.
[ORIGIN French from Latin *merda*.]
Excrement, dung. Also (*slang*) as *interjection*, expr. annoyance, exasperation, surprise, etc.

merdeka /məːˈdeɪkə/ *noun*. M20.
[ORIGIN Malay from Sanskrit *mahardhika*, lit. 'of great prosperity' from *maha* great + *rdhi* prosperity + *-ka* adjectival suffix.]
In Malaysia and Indonesia: freedom, independence.

merdivorous /məːˈdɪv(ə)rəs/ *adjective*. *rare*. M19.
[ORIGIN from Latin *merda* excrement + -VOROUS.]
Chiefly ENTOMOLOGY. Coprophagous.

mere /mɪə/ *noun*[1].
[ORIGIN Old English *mere* corresp. to Old Saxon *meri* sea (Dutch *meer* sea, pool), Old High German *mari*, *meri* (German *Meer*), Old Norse *marr* sea, Gothic *mari-*, from Germanic from Indo-European base also of Old Church Slavonic *morje* (Russian *more*), Latin *mare*.]
1 The sea. Long *obsolete* exc. in *comb.* (cf. MER-). OE. ▸†**b** An arm of the sea. L16–L17.
2 A sheet of standing water; a lake, a pond. Now chiefly *dial.* & *literary*. OE.
3 A marsh, a fen. *obsolete* exc. *dial.* E17.
– COMB. (cf. MER-): †**mereswine** a dolphin, a porpoise.

mere /mɪə/ *noun*[2] & *verb*. Now chiefly *dial.* Also **mear**.
[ORIGIN Old English *(ge)mǣre* = Middle Dutch *mēre*, Old Norse *(landa)mæri* landmark, from Germanic, perh. rel. to Latin *murus* wall.]
▸ **A** *noun*. A boundary; an object indicating a boundary, a landmark; *spec.* a ridge of uncultivated land or a road serving as a boundary. OE.
– COMB.: **meresman** a person appointed to find out the exact boundaries of a parish etc.; **merestone** a stone set up as a landmark.
▸ **B** *verb*. **1** *verb trans*. Mark *out* boundaries on (land). Now usu., record the position of (a boundary) by specifying its relation to or *to* a visible feature on the ground. OE.
2 †**a** *verb intrans*. Abut *upon*; be bounded *by*. L16–E18. ▸**b** *verb trans*. Adjoin, border on. *Irish dialect*. L19.

mere /ˈmɛri/ *noun*[3]. E19.
[ORIGIN Maori.]
A Maori war club, *esp.* one made of greenstone.

mere /mɪə/ *adjective & adverb*. OE.
[ORIGIN Anglo-Norman *meer* (in legal uses), Old French *mier* or its source Latin *merus*.]
▸ **A** *adjective*. †**1** Pure, unmixed; undiluted. OE–M19.
2 Done, performed, or exercised without help; sole. Now only LAW. LME.
†**3** That is what it is in the full sense of the term; absolute, sheer, downright. LME–L18.
4 Having no greater extent, range, value, power, or importance than the designation implies; that is barely or only what it is said to be; (chiefly *pred.*) insignificant, ordinary, foolish, inept. M16.

J. M. MURRY The mere remembering of great works is not knowledge of them. M. DICKENS Sissons, who didn't count, because she was the Junior and mere. C. MILNE A tiny push, the merest fraction of my full weight. J. BARNES The great Gothic cathedrals . . had the power to convert by their mere presence.

– SPECIAL COLLOCATIONS: **mere right** LAW a right to property with no right to possession.
▸ †**B** *adverb*. Merely. L15–M17.
■ **mereness** *noun* (*rare*) †(**a**) purity; (**b**) the state or quality of being merely something or of being small or insignificant: M17.

-mere /mɪə/ *suffix*.
[ORIGIN Repr. Greek *meros* part.]
Chiefly BIOLOGY. Forming nouns with the sense 'part, segment', as ***blastomere***, ***centromere***, ***metamere***.

mère /mɛːr, mɛː/ *noun*. M19.
[ORIGIN French = mother.]
The mother, elder: appended to a name to distinguish between a mother and daughter of the same name.

M. LOWRY Taskerson mère had taken a fancy to the French boy.

Meredithian /mɛrɪˈdɪθɪən/ *adjective & noun*. Also **-ean**. L19.
[ORIGIN from *Meredith* (see below) + -IAN, -EAN.]
▸ **A** *adjective*. Of, pertaining to, or characteristic of the English novelist and poet George Meredith (1828–1909) or his work. L19.
▸ **B** *noun*. An admirer or student of Meredith or his work. L19.

mereing *noun* var. of MERING.

merel /ˈmɛr(ə)l/ *noun*. Also **merril**, **merrill**. LME.
[ORIGIN Old French (mod. *méreau*) token, coin, counter, from Proto-Romance.]
1 In *pl.* A game played on a board between two players, each with an equal number of pebbles, discs of wood or metal, pegs, or pins. Also called ***nine men's morris***, ***morris***. LME.
2 Each of the counters or pieces used in this game. LME.

M

merely /ˈmɪəli/ *adverb*. LME.
[ORIGIN from MERE *adjective* + -LY².]
†**1** Without admixture or qualification; purely; without the help of others. LME–M17.
†**2** Absolutely, entirely; quite, altogether. E16–L18. ▸**b** As a matter of fact, actually. L16–E17.

SHAKES. *Haml.* Things rank and gross in nature Possess it merely.

3 Without any other quality, reason, purpose, view, etc.; only (what is referred to) and nothing more. Often preceded by *not*. L16.

C. P. SNOW The interests I have been describing merely add glow and savour to . . a pleasant time. D. FRANCIS The contents looked merely like ordinary files. Z. TOMIN I am . . shivering and . . not merely because the weather has changed. D. ATHILL Some of his activities had a purpose beyond that of merely passing the time. M. BRETT This process constituted . . theft rather than merely . . market custom.

merengue /məˈrɛŋgeɪ/ *noun*. Also **meringue** /məˈraŋ/. L19.
[ORIGIN Amer. Spanish from Haitian creole *méringue* lit. 'meringue' from French.]
A dance of Dominican and Haitian origin, with alternating long and short stiff-legged steps; a piece of music for this dance, usu. in duple and triple time.

mereology /mɛrɪˈɒlədʒi/ *noun*. M20.
[ORIGIN French, irreg. from Greek *meros* part + -OLOGY.]
PHILOSOPHY. The abstract study of the relations between parts and wholes.
■ **mereoˈlogical** *adjective* M20.

merese /məˈriːz/ *noun*. E20.
[ORIGIN Unknown.]
A rib, flange, or collar on the stem of a glass vessel.

merestead *noun* see MIDSTEAD.

meretrices *noun pl.* see MERETRIX.

meretrician /mɛrɪˈtrɪʃ(ə)n/ *noun & adjective*. *rare*. M17.
[ORIGIN formed as MERETRICIOUS + -AN.]
▸ **A** *noun*. A prostitute. M17.
▸ †**B** *adjective*. = MERETRICIOUS 1. Only in E18.

meretricious /mɛrɪˈtrɪʃəs/ *adjective*. E17.
[ORIGIN from Latin *meretricius* (from *meretric-*, MERETRIX) + -OUS.]
1 Of, pertaining to, characteristic of, or befitting a prostitute; having the character of a prostitute. E17.
2 Showily but falsely attractive. M17.

ROSEMARY MANNING It is possible to be sentimental, meretricious and even downright dishonest in painting or in music. A. LURIE Like a stage set after the lights have been turned off, Key West had lost its meretricious charm.

■ **meretriciously** *adverb* M18. **meretriciousness** *noun* E18.

meretrix /ˈmɛrɪtrɪks/ *noun*. *arch*. Pl. **-trices** /-trɪsiːz/, **-trixes**. OE.
[ORIGIN Latin, from *mereri* serve for hire: see MERIT *noun*, -TRIX.]
A prostitute.

merganser /məːˈganzə, -s-/ *noun*. M17.
[ORIGIN mod. Latin, from *mergus* diver + *anser* goose.]
Any of a group of large holarctic diving ducks of the genus *Mergus*, with long narrow serrated bills hooked at the tip. Cf. ***sawbill*** s.v. SAW *noun*¹.
common merganser = GOOSANDER. **hooded merganser** a crested N. American merganser, *Mergus cucullatus*. **red-breasted merganser** a crested merganser, *Mergus serrator*, of N. America and northern Eurasia. **white merganser** = SMEW.

merge /məːdʒ/ *verb & noun*. M17.
[ORIGIN Latin *mergere* dip, plunge; in legal senses through Anglo-Norman *merger*.]
▸ **A** *verb*. †**1** *verb trans*. Immerse (esp. oneself). Foll. by *in*. M17–M19.
2 *verb trans*. In LAW, incorporate or embody (an estate, title, etc.) in a greater or superior one; *gen*. cause (something) to be absorbed into something else, so as to lose its own character or identity; join or blend, esp. gradually; combine, amalgamate. Foll. by *in*, (occas.) *into*, *with*. E18.

COLERIDGE The patriotism of the citizen ennobles, but does not merge, the individual energy of the man. W. S. CHURCHILL The war between Britain and Spain . . was soon merged in a general European struggle. B. BAINBRIDGE His face was a mess. The stings and constellations of pimples were merged. B. PYM As if trying to merge herself with the rows of books behind her. *Independent* Bromley Council wants to merge the school with nearby Ramsden Boys'.

3 *verb intrans*. In LAW, be incorporated or embodied in a greater title, estate, etc.; *gen*. be absorbed and disappear, lose character or identity by absorption into something else; join or blend, esp. gradually; combine, amalgamate. Foll. by *in*, *into*, *with*. E18.

M. RENAULT The next few evenings all merged for him later into a common memory. M. BRADBURY The groups that began as separate and compartmentalized begin to merge and mix. H. WILSON The two departments merged in November . . and, inevitably, it became a virtual takeover. T. K. WOLFE So he took that street, but it quickly merged with a narrow side street.

▸ **B** *noun*. An act or instance or merging, a merger. E19.
■ **merˈgee** *noun* a participant in a merger M20. **mergence** *noun* the action of merging, the condition of being merged M19.

merger /ˈməːdʒə/ *noun*. E18.
[ORIGIN Anglo-Norman use as noun of inf.: see MERGE, -ER⁴.]
1 LAW. Incorporation or embodiment of a right, estate, contract, action, etc., in another. E18.
2 The combination or consolidation of two commercial companies, organizations, institutions, etc., into one. M19.
3 *gen*. An act of merging; the fact of being merged. L19.

merguez /məːˈgɛz/ *noun*. L20.
[ORIGIN French, from Arabic *mirkās*, *mirqās*, of uncertain origin.]
A spicy beef and lamb sausage coloured with red peppers, orig. made in parts of North Africa.

mericarp /ˈmɛrɪkɑːp/ *noun*. M19.
[ORIGIN French *méricarpe*, irreg. from Greek *meros* part + *karpos* fruit.]
BOTANY. A portion of a fruit which divides to form a perfect fruit; *esp*. either of the two one-seeded carpels which together constitute the fruit in umbelliferous plants.

meridian /məˈrɪdɪən/ *noun*. LME.
[ORIGIN Old French & mod. French *méridien* or Latin *meridianum* noon, the south, medieval Latin *meridiana* noon, siesta, uses as noun of Latin *meridianus*: see MERIDIAN *adjective*. In sense 5 ult. for Latin *circulus meridianus* meridian circle, translating Greek *kuklos mesēmbrinos*.]
1 Midday, noon. Long *rare*. LME.
2 a A midday rest, a siesta. *obsolete* exc. *hist*. LME. ▸**b** A midday drink. *Scot. obsolete* exc. *hist*. L18.
3 The point at which the sun or a star attains its highest altitude; the zenith. *arch*. LME. ▸**b** *fig*. The point or period of highest development or perfection; full splendour; one's prime of life. L16.
†**4** The south. LME–E17.
5 ASTRONOMY & GEOGRAPHY. A great circle of the celestial sphere which passes through the celestial poles and the zenith of a given place on the earth's surface, or the great circle of the earth which lies in the same plane; that half of the latter circle which extends from pole to pole through a place, corresponding to a line of longitude. Also, a line (on a map, globe, etc.) representing one of these. LME. ▸**b** A graduated ring or half-ring within which an artificial globe is suspended. M17. ▸**c** GEOMETRY. Any great circle of a sphere that passes through the poles; any line on a surface of revolution that is in a plane with its axis. E18.
6 *transf*. & *fig*. A distinctive locality, situation, or character; *the* tastes, habits, capacities, etc., *of* a particular set of people etc. L16.
7 ACUPUNCTURE. Any of the pathways in the body along which energy is said to flow, *esp*. each of a set of twelve associated with specific organs. M20.
– PHRASES: ***Greenwich meridian***. ***inferior meridian***: see INFERIOR *adjective*. **magnetic meridian** the great circle of the earth that passes through a given point on its surface and the magnetic poles. ***prime meridian***: see PRIME *adjective*.
– COMB.: **meridian circle** a telescope fitted with a graduated circle, by which the right ascension and declination of a star may be determined; **meridian-mark** a mark fixed due north or south of an astronomical instrument, by which it is aligned in the meridian.

meridian /məˈrɪdɪən/ *adjective*. LME.
[ORIGIN Old French & mod. French *méridien* or Latin *meridianus*, from *meridies* midday, south, from (by dissimilation) *medius* middle + *dies* day: see -AN.]
1 Of or pertaining to midday or noon. Now *literary*. LME.
2 Of or pertaining to the position, strength, etc., of the sun at midday. LME. ▸†**b** Of supreme excellence; consummate. M17–M18. ▸**c** *fig*. Pertaining to or characteristic of the point or period of highest development or splendour (of a person, institution, etc.). L17.
3 Of, pertaining to, or of the nature of a meridian. LME.
meridian altitude the angle between the horizon and a celestial object as it crosses the meridian. **meridian circle**, **meridian line** = MERIDIAN *noun* 5.
4 Southern, meridional. *rare*. LME.

meridional /məˈrɪdɪən(ə)l/ *adjective & noun*. Also **-dia-**. LME.
[ORIGIN Old French & mod. French *méridional* from late Latin *meridionalis*, irreg. from *meridies* (see MERIDIAN *adjective*) after *septentrionalis* SEPTENTRIONAL.]
▸ **A** *adjective*. **1** Of or pertaining to the south; situated in the south; southern, southerly. LME. ▸**b** *spec*. Pertaining to or characteristic of the inhabitants of southern Europe. M19.
†**2** Of or pertaining to the position of the sun at midday; pertaining to or characteristic of midday. LME–M19.
3 Of, pertaining to, or aligned with a meridian. M16.
4 Of a marking or structure on a roundish body: lying in a plane with the axis of the body. Cf. MERIDIAN *noun* 5C. M17.
▸ **B** *noun*. †**1** The south. Only in M16.
2 A native or inhabitant of the south. Now *spec*. a native or inhabitant of the south of France. E17.
■ **meridioˈnality** *noun* the state of being on the meridian, or aligned along a meridian M17. **meridionally** *adverb* in or along a meridian or meridians; north and south; in the direction of the poles (of a magnet): L16.

mering /ˈmɪərɪŋ/ *noun*. Now chiefly *dial*. Also **mear-**, **mere-**. M16.
[ORIGIN from MERE *verb* + -ING¹.]
= MERE *noun*².

meringue /məˈraŋ; *foreign* mərɛ̃g (*pl. same*)/ *noun*¹. E18.
[ORIGIN French, of unknown origin.]
A confection made chiefly of sugar and whites of eggs whipped together and baked crisp; a small cake or shell of this, usu. decorated or filled with cream.
meringue à la Chantilly, **meringue Chantilly** a meringue filled with sweetened whipped cream.

meringue *noun*² var. of MERENGUE.

merino /məˈriːnəʊ/ *noun & adjective*. Pl. of noun **-os**. L18.
[ORIGIN Spanish, of unknown origin.]
1 (Designating or pertaining to) a breed of sheep prized for the fineness of its wool, originating in Spain; (designating) a sheep of this breed. L18. ▸**b** ***pure merino***, (**a**) an early immigrant to Australia with no convict origins, a member of a leading family in Australian society, a person of fine breeding or good character; (**b**) *attrib*. first-class, well-bred, excellent. *Austral. slang*. E19.
2 (Of) a soft fine material resembling cashmere, made of wool (orig. merino wool) or wool and cotton. E19. ▸**b** A garment, esp. a dress or shawl, made of this; *W. Indian* a vest. M19.
3 (Of) a fine woollen yarn used in the manufacture of hosiery and knitwear. L19.

merise /məˈriːz/ *noun*. L17.
[ORIGIN French, perh. blend of *amer* bitter, *cerise* cherry. Cf. earlier MERRY *noun*.]
A kind of small black cherry; the tree that bears this.

merisis /ˈmɛrɪsɪs/ *noun*. M20.
[ORIGIN from Greek *meris* (also *meros*) part, after *auxesis*.]
BIOLOGY. Growth by cellular multiplication.

merismatic /mɛrɪzˈmatɪk/ *adjective*. M19.
[ORIGIN from Greek *merismat-*, *merisma* separated part, from *merizein* divide into parts, from *meros* part: see -ATIC.]
BIOLOGY. Of, pertaining to, exhibiting, or designating division into portions by the formation of internal partitions.

merismoid /məˈrɪzmɔɪd/ *adjective*. M19.
[ORIGIN from Greek *merisma* (see MERISMATIC) + -OID.]
BOTANY. Of a sporophore, esp. an agaric: having a branched or laciniate pileus.

merispore /ˈmɛrɪspɔː/ *noun*. L19.
[ORIGIN Irreg. from Greek *meros* part + SPORE.]
MYCOLOGY. A spore cell in a compound spore.

merissa /məˈrɪsə/ *noun*. M19.
[ORIGIN Arabic *marisa*, from *marasa* to soak.]
A Sudanese drink made from fermented maize.

meristele /mɛrɪˈstiːl, -ˈstiːli/ *noun*. L19.
[ORIGIN from Greek *meris* (also *meros*) part + STELE.]
BOTANY. A strand of vascular tissue made up of xylem surrounded by phloem.
■ **meristelic** *adjective* E20.

meristem /ˈmɛrɪstɛm/ *noun*. L19.
[ORIGIN Irreg. from Greek *meristos* divided, divisible, from *merizein* divide into parts, from *meros* part, with ending after *phloem*, *xylem*.]
BOTANY. A tissue which continues to undergo cell division and differentiation throughout the life of a plant, found esp. in root and shoot apices and in the cambium; merismatic tissue.
■ **meristeˈmatic** *adjective* of, pertaining to, or of the nature of meristem L19. **meristeˈmatically** *adverb* after the manner of meristem L19.

meristic /məˈrɪstɪk/ *adjective*. L19.
[ORIGIN from Greek *meris* (also *meros*) part + -ISTIC.]
BIOLOGY. Of or relating to the presence or number of similar units, parts, or segments making up a structure.
■ **meristically** *adverb* L19.

merit /ˈmɛrɪt/ *noun*. ME.
[ORIGIN Old French & mod. French *mérite* from Latin *meritum* price, value, service rendered, use as noun of neut. pa. pple of *merere*, *-ri* earn, deserve, rel. to Greek *meiresthai* obtain as a share, *moira* share, fate, *meros* part.]
†**1** Deserved reward or punishment. ME–E18.
2 The quality of deserving well or of being entitled to reward or gratitude; claim or title to commendation or esteem; excellence, worth; *spec*. (**a**) CHRISTIAN THEOLOGY the quality, in actions or persons, of being entitled to future reward from God; (**b**) BUDDHISM & JAINISM the quality of actions in one of a person's states of existence which helps determine a better succeeding state. ME. ▸**b** Claim to gratitude, the honour or credit of bringing about (something). Foll. by *of*. Now *rare*. E18.

C. ACHEBE I had had scholarships . . without any godfather's help but purely on my own merit. C. MILNE A single book, one that we feel to have some special merit, not an obvious bestseller but one . . deserving our support.

Order of Merit an order whose members are admitted for distinguished achievement.
3 *sing*. & in *pl*. The condition or fact of deserving, deserts. Now *rare*. LME.

A. G. MORTIMER His superabundant merits, which are laid up as a rich treasure for His Church.

4 A thing entitling a person to reward or gratitude. Usu. in *pl*., *spec*. in CHRISTIAN THEOLOGY, good works viewed as entitling a person to future reward from God. LME.

M

5 A point of intrinsic quality; a commendable quality, an excellence, a good point. Earliest in *pl.*, the intrinsic rights and wrongs *of* a matter, esp. a legal case, the intrinsic excellences or defects of something. M16.

R. K. NARAYAN Talking about the picture, its merits and demerits. M. N. COX Each case must be judged on its merits. *Observer* It at least has the merit of a certain rough honesty.

make a merit of account or represent (some action of one's own) as meritorious.

– COMB.: **merit good** ECONOMICS a commodity or service, such as education, that is regarded by society or government as deserving public finance; **merit increase** an increase in pay for personal ability or achievement; **merit money** money awarded as a merit increase; **merit monger** *arch. (derog.)* a person who seeks to merit salvation or eternal reward by good works; **merit pay** pay awarded as a merit increase; **merit rating** the assessment of an employee's ability to do his or her job; a measurement of this ability; **merit system** the system of giving (promotion in) public office according to the competence of the candidates rather than because of their political affiliations etc.

■ **meritless** *adjective* L16.

merit /ˈmɛrɪt/ *verb*. L15.

[ORIGIN Old French & mod. French *mériter*, formed as MERIT *noun*.]

†**1** *verb trans.* Reward, recompense. *rare*. L15–E17.

2 *verb trans.* Be or become entitled to or worthy of, deserve, (a thing, *to do*); earn by merit. E16.

R. HOOKER Did they think that men doe merit rewards in heaven by the workes they performe on earth? R. DAHL I asked whether the story was really interesting enough to merit being put on paper. A. HARDING He had been harsh . . to Peter, who had surely done nothing to merit such treatment. *Which?* This iron doesn't merit a recommendation.

3 *verb intrans.* Acquire merit; become entitled to reward, gratitude, or commendation. Now *rare*. E16.

4 *verb intrans.* Deserve, esp. *well* (*of* a person). L16.

■ **meritable** *adjective* meritorious LME. **meritedly** *adverb* deservedly M17. †**meriting** *ppl adjective* deserving, meritorious: E17–M18.

meritocracy /mɛrɪˈtɒkrəsi/ *noun*. M20.

[ORIGIN from MERIT *noun* + -O- + -CRACY.]

Government or the holding of power by people selected on the basis of merit, *spec.* in a competitive educational system; a society governed by such people or in which such people hold power; a ruling or influential class of educated people.

■ **ˈmeritocrat** *noun & adjective* (*a*) *noun* an adherent of meritocracy, a member of a meritocracy; (*b*) *adjective* belonging to a meritocracy: M20. **meritoˈcratic** *adjective* characterized by meritocracy; of or pertaining to meritocrats or meritocracy: M20.

meritorious /mɛrɪˈtɔːrɪəs/ *adjective*. LME.

[ORIGIN from Latin *meritorius*, from *merere*, *-ri* (see MERIT *noun*) + *-orius* -ORY[2]: see -OUS.]

1 Entitling a person to reward, *spec.* in CHRISTIAN THEOLOGY future reward from God; deserving reward or gratitude; well-deserving, meriting commendation, having merit (freq. with implication, though of a limited kind). LME.

B. JOWETT Well-conducted and meritorious citizens. E. F. BENSON This performance, very meritorious in itself, for he played well, had been quite sufficient for him. R. A. KNOX The good works done by the heathen were good works done without the grace of Christ; they could not, therefore, be meritorious.

†**2** Earning or deserving some specified good or evil. Foll. by *of*. M16–M18.

†**3** Given in accordance with merit; merited. L16–M17.

4 LAW. Of an action or claim: likely to succeed on the merits of the case. L20.

W. A. BOGART Meritorious claims and defences are encouraged; unfounded ones are chilled.

– SPECIAL COLLOCATIONS: **meritorious cause** CHRISTIAN THEOLOGY an action or agent that causes some good or evil result by meriting it.

■ **meritoriously** *adverb* (*a*) in a meritorious manner; so as to deserve commendation; †(*b*) so as to acquire merit; †(*c*) deservedly: L15. **meritoriousness** *noun* M17.

Merkani *noun* var. of AMERICANI.

merkin /ˈməːkɪn/ *noun*. E17.

[ORIGIN App. var. of MALKIN.]

1 An artificial covering of hair for the pubes. Also, an artificial vagina. E17.

2 The female external genitals. M17.

merle /məːl/ *noun*[1]. *poet.*, orig. *Scot.* L15.

[ORIGIN Old French & mod. French from Latin *merula*, (post-classical) *-ulus*.]

The blackbird, *Turdus merula*.

merle /məːl/ *adjective & noun*[2]. E20.

[ORIGIN from *merled*, *mirled* vars. of MARLED *adjective*.]

(A dog, esp. a collie) having blue-grey fur speckled or streaked with black.

merled *adjective* var. of MARLED.

merlin /ˈməːlɪn/ *noun*. ME.

[ORIGIN Anglo-Norman *merilun* aphet. from Old French *esmirillon* (mod. *émerillon*) augm. of *esmiril* from Frankish word corresp. to Old High German *smerlo*, *smiril* (German *Schmerl*).]

A small falcon, *Falco columbarius*, of N. America and northern Eurasia, with pale brown streaked underparts, a barred tail, and (in the male) a slate-blue and (in the female) a deep brown back.

Merlin chair /ˈməːlɪn tʃɛː/ *noun phr.* L18.

[ORIGIN from J. J. *Merlin* (1735–1803), its inventor.]

hist. A type of wheelchair.

merling /ˈməːlɪŋ/ *noun*. Now *rare*. ME.

[ORIGIN Old French *merlenc* (mod. *merlan*) from Latin *merula* a kind of fish: see -ING[3].]

A (European) whiting.

merlion /ˈməːlɪən/ *noun*. Also **mar-** /ˈmɑː-/. L15.

[ORIGIN Prob. var. of MERLIN.]

HERALDRY. A bird with either no feet (identical with the heraldic martlet) or neither feet nor beak.

merlon /ˈməːlən/ *noun*. E18.

[ORIGIN French from Italian *merlone* augm. of *merlo* battlement.]

A part of an embattled parapet between two embrasures; a similar structure on a battleship.

Merlot /ˈməːləʊ, -lɒt, *foreign* mɛrlo/ *noun*. E19.

[ORIGIN French.]

(The vine bearing) a black grape used in wine making; red wine made from these grapes.

mermaid /ˈməːmeɪd/ *noun*. ME.

[ORIGIN from MERE *noun*[1] + MAID *noun*.]

1 An imaginary partly human sea creature with the head and trunk of a woman and the tail of a fish or cetacean (in early use often identified with the siren of classical mythology); a representation of such a creature, esp. (HERALDRY) depicted with long flowing golden hair and a comb in the left hand and a mirror in the right. ME.

2 †**a** A sweet singer, a siren. Also, a prostitute. L16–E17. ▸**b** A woman who is at home in water. *joc.* L19.

– COMB.: **mermaid's glove(s)** a marine organism somewhat resembling a glove; *esp.* a sponge, *Halichondria palmata*; **mermaid's hair** a dark green filamentous seaweed, *Lyngbya majuscula*; **mermaid's purse** the horny egg case of a skate, ray, or shark; a sea purse; **mermaid-weed** any of various N. American aquatic plants of the genus *Proserpinaca* (family Haloragaceae), having leaves toothed like a comb.

■ Also **mermaiden** *noun* (now *rare*) LME.

merman /ˈməːman/ *noun*. Pl. **-men** /-mɛn/. E17.

[ORIGIN from MER- + MAN *noun*, after MERMAID.]

A male of the mermaid kind, an imaginary partly human sea creature with the head and trunk of a man and the tail of a fish or cetacean; a representation of such a creature, esp. (HERALDRY) depicted with a trident in the right hand and a conch-shell trumpet in the left.

mermithid /məːˈmɪθɪd/ *noun & adjective*. L19.

[ORIGIN from mod. Latin *Mermithoidea*, from *Mermis* (see below): see -ID[3].]

ZOOLOGY. ▸**A** *noun*. Any of various nematode worms of the genus *Mermis* or the order Mermithoidea, whose larvae are parasites of insects. L19.

▸**B** *adjective*. Of, pertaining to, or designating such worms. L19.

mero /ˈmɛːrəʊ/ *noun*. Pl. **-os**. Also **merou** /ˈmɛruː/. M18.

[ORIGIN Spanish *mero*, French *mérou*.]

Any of various groupers; *esp.* the dark brown *Epinephelus guaza*, of the Mediterranean and E. Atlantic (also called ***dusky perch***).

mero- /ˈmɛrəʊ/ *combining form*[1]. Before a vowel also **mer-**.

[ORIGIN from Greek *meros* part, fraction: see -O-.]

Part, partly. Freq. opp. HOLO-.

■ **meroˈblastic** *adjective* (BIOLOGY) (of an ovum) undergoing partial cleavage, usu. on the surface of a large yolk L19. **merocrine** *adjective* (PHYSIOLOGY) of, pertaining to, or designating a gland in which cytoplasm is not lost during secretion E20. **meroˈcyanine** *adjective & noun* (CHEMISTRY) (designating) any of a class of neutral dyes (many used as photographic sensitizers) in which a nitrogen atom and a carbonyl group (both usu. parts of heterocycles) are linked by a conjugated chain of carbon atoms M20. **meroˈdiploid** *adjective & noun* (BACTERIOLOGY) (*a*) *adjective* (made up of cells) having second copies of part of the normal chromosome complement; (*b*) *noun* a merodiploid organism: M20. **merogamete** *noun* (BIOLOGY) a gamete formed by fission of a vegetative cell in some protists and usu. smaller than an ordinary individual E20. **meˈrogamy** *noun* (BIOLOGY) a mode of reproduction in some protists involving the fusion of merogametes E20. **meroˈgonic** *adjective* (BIOLOGY) of, pertaining to, or of the nature of merogony L19. **meˈrogony** *noun* (BIOLOGY) (*a*) the production of an embryo from a portion of an ovum; (*b*) = SCHIZOGONY: L19. **meroˈhedral** *adjective* (of a crystal or crystal form) less symmetrical than is possible for its crystal class L19. **meroˈistic** *adjective* [Greek *ōion* egg] BIOLOGY (of an ovariole) having nurse cells L19. **meroˈmictic** *adjective* (of a lake) in which water below a certain depth does not circulate with the upper layers, usu. as a result of high salt concentration M20. **meroˈmorphic** *adjective* (MATH.) (of a complex function) analytic in a given domain except for a finite number of poles L19. **meroˈmyosin** *noun* (BIOCHEMISTRY) either of the two components of myosin which correspond roughly to the rod-shaped and globular parts of the molecule M20. **meroˈplankton** *noun* (BIOLOGY) meroplanktonic organisms L19. **meroplankˈtonic** *adjective* (BIOLOGY) (of an aquatic organism) passing only part of its life cycle as plankton L19. **merosyˈmmetrical** *adjective* = MEROHEDRAL L19. **meroˈsymmetry** *noun* the condition or quality of being merohedral L19. **merosysteˈmatic** *adjective* = MEROHEDRAL L19. **meroˈzoite** *noun* (ZOOLOGY) any of the cells produced by multiple fission (schizogony) of a schizont E20. **meroˈzygote** *noun* = MERODIPLOID *noun* M20.

mero- /ˈmɪərəʊ/ *combining form*[2].

[ORIGIN from Greek *mēros* thigh: see -O-.]

ANATOMY & ZOOLOGY. Forming nouns and adjectives with the sense 'of the thigh or an analogous structure'.

■ **merocele** *noun* (now *rare* or *obsolete*) a femoral hernia E19.

Meroitic /mɛrəʊˈɪtɪk/ *adjective & noun*. M19.

[ORIGIN from *Meroë* (see below) + -ITIC.]

▸**A** *adjective*. Of or pertaining to the ancient Nubian kingdom of Meroë in NE Africa or its language. M19.

▸**B** *noun*. The language of this kingdom, of uncertain affiliation. M19.

■ **Meroite** /ˈmɛrəʊʌɪt/ *noun & adjective* (*a*) *noun* a native or inhabitant of Meroë; (*b*) *adjective* = MEROITIC *adjective*: M19.

meronym /ˈmɛrənɪm/ *noun*. L20.

[ORIGIN from MERO- + -NYM.]

LINGUISTICS. A word denoting an object which forms part of another object (such as *sleeve* in relation to *coat*, *shirt*, etc.).

■ **meronymy** /məˈrɒnəmi/ *noun* L20.

merops /ˈmɛrɒps/ *noun*. L17.

[ORIGIN Latin from Greek.]

The bee-eater, *Merops apiaster*. Now only as mod. Latin genus name.

meros *noun* var. of MERUS.

merostome /ˈmɛrəstəʊm/ *noun*. L19.

[ORIGIN from mod. Latin *Merostomata* (see below), formed as MERO-[1] + Greek *stomat-*, *stoma* mouth.]

ZOOLOGY. Any arthropod of the class Merostomata; a horseshoe crab.

merou *noun* var. of MERO.

-merous /mərəs/ *suffix*. L19.

[ORIGIN Extracted from DIMEROUS etc.]

Chiefly BOTANY. Forming adjectives in sense 'having (a specified number of) parts', as ***pentamerous***, ***tetramerous***. Also used with prefixed numeral, as ***2-merous***, ***five-merous***.

Merovingian /mɛrəˈvɪndʒɪən/ *noun & adjective*. L17.

[ORIGIN French *mérovingien*, from medieval Latin *Merovingi* (pl.), from Latin *Meroveus* their reputed founder: see -ING[3], -IAN.]

▸**A** *noun*. A member of the first dynasty of Frankish kings founded by Clovis and reigning in Gaul and Germany from about 500 to 751–2. Also, the style of handwriting developed from Roman cursive during this period and characteristic of it. L17.

▸**B** *adjective*. Designating or pertaining to this dynasty or the style of handwriting characteristic of the period of its rule. L17.

merrie *adjective & adverb* see MERRY *adjective & adverb*.

merril, **merrill** *nouns* vars. of MEREL.

merrily /ˈmɛrɪli/ *adverb*. OE.

[ORIGIN from MERRY *adjective* + -LY[2].]

1 In early use, pleasantly, agreeably, cheerfully, happily. In later use, with exuberant gaiety, joyously, mirthfully. OE.

†**2** Jocularly, facetiously, wittily, in jest. LME–E18.

3 With alacrity; briskly. LME.

merriment /ˈmɛrɪm(ə)nt/ *noun*. L16.

[ORIGIN from MERRY *adjective* + -MENT.]

†**1** A thing that contributes to mirth; a jest; a brief comic dramatic entertainment; a humorous or scurrilous publication. L16–E19.

2 The action of making merry; animated enjoyment or jocularity; mirth, fun. L16.

†**3** Entertainment, amusement. Only in L16.

merriness /ˈmɛrɪnɪs/ *noun*. OE.

[ORIGIN from MERRY *adjective* + -NESS.]

The quality or condition of being merry.

merry /ˈmɛri/ *noun*. Now chiefly *dial.* L16.

[ORIGIN formed as MERISE.]

The wild cherry tree, *Prunus avium* (also ***merry-tree***); the small black fruit of this tree.

merry /ˈmɛri/ *adjective & adverb*. Also (now *pseudo-arch.*) **merrie**.

[ORIGIN Old English *myr(i)ġe* from Germanic base also of MIRTH.]

▸**A** *adjective*. **1** Of a thing: pleasing, agreeable, delightful. *obsolete* exc. as passing into senses 3, 5. OE.

2 Of looks, appearance: (orig.) pleasant, agreeable, bright; (later) expressive of cheerfulness, mirthful. *obsolete* exc. as passing into sense 3. OE.

3 Of a person, action, attribute, etc.: full of animated enjoyment (in early use chiefly with reference to feasting or sport); full of laughter or gaiety; joyous, mirthful; (of general disposition) given to joyousness or mirth. OE. ▸†**b** Happy. LME–M17. ▸**c** Slightly tipsy. *colloq.* L16. ▸**d** Pleasantly amused; being facetious. Foll. by *with*, *on*, *upon* (a person). *arch.* E17.

W. IRVING His memory was always cherished as that of a merry companion. J. L. WATEN From within came the sound of merry voices. *Proverb*: The more the merrier. **c** N. HINTON They'd finished the champagne and started on the wine so they were all a bit merry.

4 Of a saying, jest, etc.: amusing, diverting, funny. Passing into sense 5. *arch.* LME.

M

R. K. NARAYAN The men . . made a few merry jokes.

5 Designating or pertaining to a time, season, etc., characterized by festivity or rejoicing. **M16.**

M. WEBB It was a merry scene, with the bright holly and mistletoe.

– PHRASES ETC.: ***lead a person a merry dance***: see DANCE *noun*. **make merry** be festive or jovial; indulge in feasting and jollity. **make merry over**, †**make merry with** make fun of, ridicule. **merry Andrew** a comic entertainer; a buffoon, a clown, a mountebank's assistant. **merry Christmas!**: a conventional salutation just before or at Christmas. ***merry dancers***: see DANCER 3. **merry England**, (esp. *iron.*) **merrie England** England characterized by (orig.) pleasant landscape etc. or (later, freq. *iron.*) the cheerfulness or animation of its people. †**merry-go-down** *slang* strong ale. **merry-go-round** *noun & adjective* (*a*) *noun* a revolving machine on which people ride round and round for amusement, as one with horses, cars, etc., at a fair or one in a playground; a roundabout; *fig.* a cycle of bustling activity, a pointless circular course; (*b*) *adjective* designating or pertaining to a railway system whereby a train of coal hoppers runs perpetually on a circular route between consignor and consignee. ***merry Greek***: see GREEK *noun*. ***merry hell***: see HELL *noun*. **merrymake** *noun & verb* (*a*) *noun* (*arch.*) (a) merrymaking; (*b*) *verb intrans.* make merry, be festive, revel. **merrymaker** a person who makes merry, a participant in festivities, a reveller. **merrymaking** (*a*) the action of making merry, revelling; conviviality; (*b*) an occasion of festivity, a convivial entertainment. **merryman** a jester, a buffoon. **merry-meeting** (now *arch. & dial.*) a festive or convivial gathering. **merry men** the companions in arms or followers of a knight, an outlaw chief, etc.; *joc.* a person's followers or assistants. **merry thought** the forked bone between the neck and breast of a bird, the wishbone; the portion of a bird when carved that includes this. **Merry Widow** [the English name of Franz Lehár's operetta *Die Lustige Witwe*] an amorous or designing widow; ***Merry Widow hat***, a type of ornate wide-brimmed hat. ***play merry hell*** (***with***): see HELL *noun*. **the Merry Monarch**: Charles II.

▸ **B** *adverb*. Merrily. Now *rare*. **OE.**

merry /ˈmɛri/ *verb*. Long *rare*.
[ORIGIN Old English *myrgan*, from Germanic base of MERRY *adjective*; later directly from MERRY *adjective*.]
1 *verb intrans.* Be merry; act or play merrily. **OE.**
†**2** *verb trans.* Make (a person etc.) merry. **ME–E17.**

mersalyl /ˈməːsəlɪl/ *noun*. **M20.**
[ORIGIN from MER(CURY + SAL(IC)YL.]
PHARMACOLOGY. An organomercury compound, $C_{13}H_{16}NO_6$-HgNa, which is a powerful diuretic formerly used to treat oedema.

M

Mersenne /məːˈsɛn, *foreign* mɛrsɛn/ *noun*. **L19.**
[ORIGIN Marin *Mersenne* (1588–1648), French mathematician and musician.]
MATH. Used *attrib.* and in *possess.* to designate numbers of the form $2^p - 1$ (where *p* is a prime number).

†**mersion** *noun*. **M17–L19.**
[ORIGIN Late Latin *mersio(n-)*, from Latin *mers-* pa. ppl stem of *mergere* dip, MERGE *verb*: see -ION.]
Immersion, in early use *spec.* in baptism.

Mertensian /məːˈtɛnzɪən/ *adjective*. Also **m-**. **M20.**
[ORIGIN from R. *Mertens* (1894–1975), German zoologist + -IAN.]
ZOOLOGY. ***Mertensian mimicry***, a form of mimicry in which a mildly noxious animal is imitated by both harmless Batesian and poisonous Müllerian mimics.

Merthiolate /məːˈθʌɪəleɪt/ *noun*. Also **m-**. **E20.**
[ORIGIN from MER(CURY + THIO- + SALICY)LATE.]
PHARMACOLOGY. (US proprietary name for) thiomersal.

Mertonian /məːˈtəʊnɪən/ *adjective & noun*. **L17.**
[ORIGIN from *Merton* College (named from its founder Walter de Merton) + -IAN.]
▸ **A** *adjective*. Of or pertaining to Merton College or its members; *spec.* designating or pertaining to a school of mathematics and astronomy that existed there in the 14th cent. **L17.**
▸ **B** *noun*. A member of Merton College, Oxford. **L19.**

Meru /ˈmɛruː/ *noun & adjective*. **E20.**
[ORIGIN A town and district in central Kenya.]
▸ **A** *noun*. Pl. same, **-s**.
1 A member of a people inhabiting the Meru region of Kenya. **E20.**
2 The Bantu language of this people. **E20.**
▸ **B** *attrib.* or as *adjective*. Of or pertaining to the Meru or their language. **E20.**

merula *noun* var. of MARULA.

merus /ˈmɪərəs/ *noun*. Also **-os**. **L18.**
[ORIGIN Greek *mēros* thigh.]
1 †**a** ANATOMY. The thigh. **L18–L19.** ▸**b** ZOOLOGY. One of the joints of a maxilliped. **M19.**
2 ARCHITECTURE. The plane surface between the grooves of a triglyph. **E19.**

merveille du jour /mɛːˌveɪ dʊ ˈʒʊə/ *noun phr*. **L19.**
[ORIGIN French = wonder of the day.]
A noctuid moth, *Dichonia aprilina*, with pale green and black wings.

merwoman /ˈməːwʊmən/ *noun*. Pl. **-women** /-wɪmɪn/. **E19.**
[ORIGIN from MER- + WOMAN *noun*, after MERMAID.]
A mermaid when older or married.

merycism /ˈmɛrɪsɪz(ə)m/ *noun*. **M19.**
[ORIGIN mod. Latin *merycismus* from Greek *mērukismos* rumination, from *mērukizein* ruminate: see -ISM.]
MEDICINE. A rare condition in which food is returned to the mouth after a short period in the stomach. Cf. RUMINATION 2.

mesa /ˈmeɪsə/ *noun*. **M18.**
[ORIGIN Spanish = table from Latin *mensa*.]
1 A high rocky tableland or plateau; a flat-topped hill with precipitous sides. Earliest in names of particular plateaux or hills. Orig. *US*. **M18.**
2 ELECTRONICS. A raised flat-topped portion of *n*- or *p*-type semiconductor in a transistor or diode surrounded by an area in which the underlying *p*- or *n*-type material (respectively) has been exposed by etching. Usu. *attrib.*, as ***mesa diode***, ***mesa transistor***. **M20.**

mesad /ˈmɛsad/ *adverb*. **L19.**
[ORIGIN from Greek *mesos* middle + -AD[3].]
ANATOMY. = MESIAD.

mésalliance /mezaljɑ̃s (*pl. same*), mɛˈzalɪəns/ *noun*. **L18.**
[ORIGIN French, from *més-* MIS-[1] 2 + *alliance* ALLIANCE. Cf. MISALLIANCE.]
A marriage with a person thought to be of inferior social position; an unsuitable union.

Q. BELL When . . Julia's relations did make a really disastrous *mésalliance* the young couple were firmly . . removed to the colonies.

mes ami(e)s *noun phr. pl.* see MON AMI.

mesangium /mɪˈsandʒɪəm/ *noun*. **M20.**
[ORIGIN formed as MESO- + Greek *aggeion* vessel + -IUM.]
ANATOMY. The part of a renal glomerulus where the afferent and efferent arterioles are closest together.
■ **mesangial** *adjective* of or pertaining to the mesangium; *spec.* pertaining to or designating cells of the glomerulus between the capillary endothelium and the basement membrane: **M20.**

mesaortitis /ˌmɛseɪɔːˈtʌɪtɪs, ˌmiːz-/ *noun*. **E20.**
[ORIGIN from MESO- + AORTA + -ITIS.]
MEDICINE. Mesarteritis of the aorta.

†**mesaraic** *adjective & noun*. Also **-ser-**. **LME–M19.**
[ORIGIN medieval Latin *mesaraïcus* from Greek *mesaraïkos*, from *mesaraion*, from *meson* middle + *araia* flank, belly: see -IC.]
ANATOMY. ▸**A** *adjective*. = MESENTERIC. **LME–L19.**
▸ **B** *noun*. A mesenteric vein. Usu. in *pl.* **LME–M19.**

mesarch /ˈmɛzɑːk, ˈmiːz-, -s-/ *adjective*. **L19.**
[ORIGIN from MESO- + Greek *arkhē* beginning, origin.]
1 BOTANY. Of primary xylem: developing both from the centre of the stem and the periphery. **L19.**
2 ECOLOGY. Of a succession of plant communities: originating in a mesic or moderately moist habitat. **E20.**

mesarteritis /ˌmɛsɑːtəˈrʌɪtɪs, ˌmiːz-/ *noun*. **M19.**
[ORIGIN from MESO- + ARTERITIS.]
MEDICINE. Inflammation of the middle layer (tunica media) of the wall of an artery.
■ **mesarteritic** /-ˈrɪtɪk/ *adjective* **L19.**

mesati- /ˈmɛsəti, ˈmiːz-/ *combining form*.
[ORIGIN from Greek *mesatos* midmost (superl. of *mesos* middle): see -I-.]
Chiefly ANATOMY. Intermediate. Cf. MESO-.
■ **mesaticeˈphalic** *adjective* = MESOCEPHALIC **L19.** **mesatiˈpellic** *adjective* [Greek *pella* bowl] having or designating a pelvis of a proportion intermediate between dolichopellic and platypellic **L19.**

mesaxon /mɛˈsaks(ə)n/ *noun*. **M20.**
[ORIGIN from MES(ENTERY + AXON.]
ANATOMY. A membranous structure linking the outside of a Schwann cell to the central axon, in myelinated nerve fibres having a spiral cross-section and forming the myelin sheath.

mesaxonic /miːzakˈsɒnɪk, mɛz-/ *adjective*. **L19.**
[ORIGIN from MESO- + Greek *axōn* axis + -IC.]
ZOOLOGY. Of a foot (of an ungulate): having the axis running through the central toe.

mescal /ˈmɛskal, mɛˈskal/ *noun*. **E18.**
[ORIGIN Spanish *mezcal* from Nahuatl *mexcalli*.]
1 Any of several plants of the genus *Agave* found in Mexico and the south-western US, used as sources of fermented liquor, food, or fibre; *esp.* the American aloe, *Agave americana*. **E18.** ▸**b** The cooked root, head, or other parts of such a plant eaten as food. **M18.**
2 A strong intoxicating spirit distilled from the fermented sap of the American aloe or allied species. Cf. TEQUILA. **E19.**
3 A small desert cactus, *Lophophora williamsii*, of Mexico and Texas, having a soft segmented body a few inches high in the form of a flattened globe; a preparation of this used as a hallucinogenic drug. Cf. MESCALINE, PEYOTE. **L19.**
– COMB.: **mescal button** the dried disc-shaped crown of the cactus *Lophophora williamsii*, consumed for its hallucinogenic effects; this plant.
■ **ˈmescalism** *noun* the practice of consuming mescal buttons or mescaline; intoxication resulting from this: **E20.**

Mescalero /mɛskəˈlɛːrəʊ/ *noun & adjective*. **M19.**
[ORIGIN Amer. Spanish, lit. '(person) of the mescal', alluding to the people's traditional use of the mescal plant as a staple food.]
▸ **A** *noun*. Pl. same, **-os**.
1 A member of an Apache people now resident in New Mexico. **M19.**
2 The Athabaskan language spoken by the Mescalero, closely related to Navajo. **M20.**
▸ **B** *adjective*. Of or pertaining to this people or their language. **M19.**

mescaline /ˈmɛskəlɪn, -iːn/ *noun*. Also **-in** /-ɪn/. **L19.**
[ORIGIN German *Mezcalin*, *Mesc-*, formed as MESCAL: see -IN[1], -INE[5].]
An alkaloid derived from mescal buttons, having intoxicating and hallucinogenic properties similar to but milder than those of LSD; 3,4,5-trimethoxyphenethylamine, $(CH_3O)_3 \cdot C_6H_2 \cdot CH_2CH_2NH_2$.

mesclun /ˈmɛsklən/ *noun*. **L20.**
[ORIGIN French (also *mesclum*) from Provençal, lit. 'mixture'.]
A Provençal green salad made from a selection of lettuces with other edible leaves and flowers.

mesdames /meɪˈdam, *foreign* medam/ *noun pl.* **M16.**
[ORIGIN French, pl. of MADAME.]
1 Pl. of MADAME. **M16.**
2 Used as pl. of MRS. **M18.**

mesdemoiselles *noun* pl. of MADEMOISELLE.

†**mese** *noun*[1]. **LME–E18.**
[ORIGIN Old French, fem. of *mes* from late Latin *mansum*, *-us*: see MANSE. Cf. MIDSTEAD.]
= MESSUAGE.

mese /ˈmɛsiː/ *noun*[2]. **E17.**
[ORIGIN Greek *mesē* (sc. *khordē* string) fem. of *mesos* middle.]
In ancient Greek music, the fixed note which is the highest note of a lower tetrachord or lower pair of tetrachords, and in some scales is identical with the lowest note of a higher tetrachord (cf. PARAMESE), sometimes regarded as the keynote of a scale or system.

mese *noun*[3] var. of MEESE.

meseems /mɪˈsiːmz/ *verb intrans. impers. arch.* Also **meseemeth** /mɪˈsiːmɪθ/. Pa. t. **meseemed**. **LME.**
[ORIGIN Orig. two words, ME *pronoun* (*dat.*) & 3rd person sing. of SEEM *verb*. Cf. METHINKS.]
It seems to me. (With noun clause, with or without *that*.)

CARLYLE Meseems I could discover fitter objects of piety!

†**mesel** *adjective & noun*. In sense A2 also **measle**. **ME.**
[ORIGIN Old French from medieval Latin *misellus*, *mis-* from Latin *misellus* wretched, wretch, dim. of *miser* wretched: see -EL[2]. Assoc. with MEASLES.]
▸ **A** *adjective*. **1** Afflicted with leprosy or a similar disease; leprous. **ME–E17.**
2 Of an animal, esp. a fish: diseased. **LME–M16.**
▸ **B** *noun*. **1** A leper. **ME–M16.** ▸**b** *fig.* A foul person. **LME–M18.**
2 Leprosy or a similar disease; *transf.* any affliction. **LME–M16.**

meself *pronoun* see MYSELF.

mesembryanthemum /mɪˌzɛmbrɪˈanθɪməm/ *noun*. **M18.**
[ORIGIN mod. Latin (see below), from (ult.) Greek *mesēmbria* noon + *anthemon* flower, with subsequent misspelling.]
Any of numerous chiefly southern African succulent plants of or formerly included in the genus *Mesembryanthemum* (family Aizoaceae), freq. cultivated for their colourful daisy-like flowers which open only in bright sunshine.

mesencephalon /mɛsɛnˈsɛf(ə)lɒn, miːz-, -ˈkɛf-/ *noun*. **M19.**
[ORIGIN from MESO- + ENCEPHALON.]
ANATOMY & ZOOLOGY. The midbrain.
■ **mesencephal** *noun* = MESENCEPHALON **M19.** **mesencephalic** /-sɪˈfalɪk/ *adjective* **M19.**

mesenchyme /ˈmɛsəŋkʌɪm, ˈmiːz-/ *noun*. Also **mesenchyma** /mɪˈsɛŋkɪmə/. **L19.**
[ORIGIN from Greek *mesos* middle + *egkhuma* infusion.]
ANATOMY & ZOOLOGY. A loosely organized, mainly mesodermal embryonic tissue which develops into connective and skeletal tissues, blood, etc.
■ **mesenchymal** /mɪˈsɛŋkɪm(ə)l/, **mesenchymatous** /mɪsɛnˈkɪmətəs, -ˈkʌɪm-, miːz-/ *adjectives* **L19.**

mesenteron /mɪˈsɛntərɒn/ *noun*. **L19.**
[ORIGIN from Greek *mesos* middle + *enteron* intestine.]
ANATOMY & ZOOLOGY. The midgut.

mesentery /ˈmɛs(ə)nt(ə)ri/ *noun*. **LME.**
[ORIGIN mod. Latin *mesenterium* from Greek *mesenterion*, from *mesos* middle + *enteron* intestine: see -Y[3].]
1 ANATOMY. A fold of peritoneal tissue which attaches an organ, esp. the small intestine, to the posterior wall of the abdomen. **LME.**
2 ZOOLOGY. Any of various animal structures which serve to attach organs, esp. the gut, to the body wall; *esp.* each of the longitudinal sheets of tissue which divide the body cavity of many coelenterates. **M19.**
■ **mesenterial** /mɛs(ə)nˈtɪərɪəl/ *adjective* **E17.** **mesenteric** /mɛs(ə)nˈtɛrɪk/ *adjective* **M17.** **mesenteritis** /mɪˌsɛntəˈrʌɪtɪs/ *noun* (MEDICINE) inflammation of the mesentery **L18.**

†**meseraic** *adjective & noun* var. of MESARAIC.

†**mesestead** *noun* see MIDSTEAD.

meseta /meˈseta/ *noun*. E20.
[ORIGIN Spanish, dim. of MESA.]
In Spain and Spanish-speaking countries: a plateau; spec. *the* high plateau of central Spain.

mesethmoid /mɛˈsɛθmɔɪd/ *adjective & noun*. L19.
[ORIGIN from MESO- + ETHMOID.]
ANATOMY. (Of, pertaining to, or designating) the ethmoid bone or the cartilage from which this develops.

mesh /mɛʃ/ *noun & verb*. Also †**mash**. LME.
[ORIGIN Prob. from Middle Dutch *maesche*, *masche* (Dutch *maas*) from Germanic.]
▸ **A** *noun*. **1** Any of the open spaces or interstices between the strands of a net, sieve, etc. LME. ▸**b** In *pl.*, the strands between the interstices of a net etc.; *collect.* netting. E17. ▸**c** *ELECTRICITY*. A closed loop in a network. L19. ▸**d** The coarseness or spacing of the strands of a grid, net, or screen; (with preceding numeral) a measure of this (representing the number of openings per unit length) or of the size of particles which will (just) pass through such a grid etc. M20.

A. HARDY Birds . . swoop down to peck at the fish through the meshes of the net. **b** *fig.*: JULIETTE HUXLEY Ottoline and Bertie remained, bound still in the meshes of their great love affair.

2 An interlaced fabric or structure, a network, netting; a grid, a framework; *fig.* a thing or situation which holds or constrains; an entanglement, a snare. M16 ▸**b** *BUILDING*. A steel network used as reinforcement in concrete. E20. ▸**c** *COMPUTING*. A set of finite elements used to represent a geometric object for modelling or analysis. M20. ▸**d** *COMPUTING*. A computer network in which each computer or processor is connected to a number of others, esp. as an *n*-dimensional lattice. L20.

F. NORRIS He was entangled; already his foot was caught in the mesh that was being spun. T. CAPOTE The cell windows are . . not only barred but covered with a wire mesh. M. BRADBURY Fitting her toes into the light, stretchable mesh of the tights. C. THUBRON Roads sliced through the mesh of alleys and courtyards.

3 *ENGINEERING*. A state of engagement between (the teeth of) gearwheels, toothed racks, etc. Chiefly in ***in mesh***, ***out of mesh***, ***into mesh***. L19.
– COMB.: **meshwork** meshes collectively; structure consisting of meshes; a network.
▸ **B** *verb* **I 1** *verb trans.* Catch (a thing or person) in the meshes of a net; *fig.* entangle, involve inextricably. M16.
2 *verb refl. & intrans.* Become enmeshed or entangled. L16.
3 *verb intrans.* Of the teeth of a wheel etc.: be engaged *with* another piece of machinery. M19.
4 *verb trans.* Cause (gears, esp. those of a motor vehicle) to become engaged; put into mesh. L19.
5 *verb intrans.* Fit in, be harmonious; combine. (Foll. by *together*, *with*.) M20.

E. BLISHEN Our strange young lives so uneasily failing to mesh with the lives of our teachers. *Women's Review* Historical meanings in practice often mesh together in a way which may confuse modern viewers.

6 *verb trans.* Bring *together*; harmonize, reconcile. M20.
▸ **II 7** *verb trans.* Construct the meshes of (a net, snare, etc.). Chiefly *Canad. dial.* E17.
■ **meshed** *adjective* having the form or appearance of mesh; tangled, intricate: E17. **meshing** *noun* (*a*) the action of the verb, *spec.* the making of meshes in a net; (*b*) a meshed structure, meshwork: E17. **meshy** *adjective* consisting of meshes, resembling mesh E17.

meshuga /mɪˈʃʊɡə/ *adjective*. *slang*. Also **-gga(h)** & other vars. L19.
[ORIGIN Yiddish *meshuge* from Hebrew *mĕšuggāʻ*. Cf. German *meschugge* crazy.]
Mad, crazy; stupid. Chiefly *pred.* (cf. MESHUGENER).

meshugaas /mɪˈʃʊɡɑːs/ *noun*. *slang*. Also **mishugas** & other vars. L19.
[ORIGIN Yiddish from Hebrew *mĕšuggāʻ*: see MESHUGA.]
Madness, craziness; nonsense, foolishness.

meshugener /mɪˈʃʊɡənə/ *attrib. adjective & noun*. *slang*. Also **-gg-**, **-nah**, & other vars. L19.
[ORIGIN Positional var. of MESHUGA.]
(A person who is) mad, crazy, or stupid.

meshugga, meshuggah *adjectives* vars. of MESHUGA.

meshuggenah, **meshuggener** *nouns* vars. of MESHUGENER.

meshumad /mɪˈʃʊmad/ *noun*. Also **-mm-**. Pl. **-im** /-ɪm/. L19.
[ORIGIN Yiddish from Hebrew *mĕšummād* lit. 'a person who is destroyed', or *mĕšu'mād* baptized, from Aramaic *'mad* be baptized.]
An apostate from Judaism.

mesia /ˈmiːzɪə/ *noun*. M19.
[ORIGIN mod. Latin *Mesia* (former genus name), of unknown origin.]
In full ***silver-eared mesia***. A songbird, *Leiothrix argentauris* (family Timaliidae), of SE Asia, the male of which has red and yellow plumage with a black and white head.

mesiad /ˈmiːzɪad, ˈmɛsɪad/ *adverb*. E19.
[ORIGIN from MESIAL + -AD[3].]
ANATOMY. Towards the median line of a body.

mesial /ˈmiːzɪəl, ˈmɛsɪəl/ *adjective*. E19.
[ORIGIN Irreg. from Greek *mesos* middle + -IAL.]
Chiefly *ANATOMY*. Pertaining to, situated in, or directed towards the middle line of a body; median. Also, situated mesially with respect *to*.
■ **mesially** *adverb* in a mesial position or direction M19.

mesic /ˈmiːzɪk, ˈmɛzɪk/ *adjective*[1]. E20.
[ORIGIN from Greek *mesos* middle + -IC.]
ECOLOGY. Of a habitat: containing a moderate amount of moisture.

mesic /ˈmiːzɪk, ˈmɛzɪk/ *adjective*[2]. M20.
[ORIGIN from MESON *noun*[3] + -IC.]
PARTICLE PHYSICS. Of, pertaining to, or of the nature of a meson; *spec.* designating a system analogous to an atom in which a meson takes the place of either an orbital electron or the nucleus.

†**mesite** *noun*[1]. M–L19.
[ORIGIN French *mésite* from Greek *mesitēs* go-between (as being intermediate between alcohol and ether): see -ITE[1].]
Acetone.

mesite /ˈmeɪziːt/ *noun*[2]. L20.
[ORIGIN French *mésite*, from Malagasy.]
Any of a number of endangered ground-dwelling birds of the family Mesitornithidae, found in Madagascar, which resemble thrushes but are related to the button-quails.

mesityl /ˈmɛsɪtʌɪl, -tɪl/ *noun*. M19.
[ORIGIN from MESITE[1] + -YL.]
CHEMISTRY. A hypothetical radical derived from acetone.
– COMB.: **mesityl oxide** a colourless oily flammable ketone, $CH_3CO{\cdot}CH{:}C(CH_3)_2$, used as a solvent; 4-methyl-3-penten-2-one.
■ **mesitylene** /mɪˈsɪtɪliːn/ *noun* a colourless liquid hydrocarbon, 1,3,5-trimethylbenzene, obtainable from petroleum M19.

meslé /ˈmɛzleɪ/ *adjective*. Long *rare* or *obsolete*. Fem. **-ée**. M17.
[ORIGIN Old French, pa. ppl adjective of *mesler* (mod. *mêler*) mix.]
HERALDRY. Of a field: composed equally of a metal and a colour.

mesmerian /mɛzˈmɪərɪən/ *noun & adjective*. *rare*. E19.
[ORIGIN formed as MESMERISM + -IAN. Cf. French *mesmérien*.]
▸ †**A** *noun*. A follower of the Austrian physician Mesmer; a mesmerist. Only in E19.
▸ **B** *adjective*. Pertaining to mesmerism. E19.

mesmeric /mɛzˈmɛrɪk/ *adjective*. E19.
[ORIGIN formed as MESMERISM + -IC.]
Pertaining to, characteristic of, producing, or produced by mesmerism; hypnotic, fascinating.

O. MANNING Odd experiences, induced perhaps by the mesmeric dazzle of the light.

■ **mesmerical** *adjective* (*rare*) M19. **mesmerically** *adverb* M19.

mesmerise *verb* var. of MESMERIZE.

mesmerism /ˈmɛzmərɪz(ə)m/ *noun*. L18.
[ORIGIN from F. A. *Mesmer*, Austrian physician (1734–1815) + -ISM.]
The process or practice of inducing a hypnotic state, usu. accompanied by insensibility to pain and muscular rigidity, by the influence of an operator over the will of a patient (orig. with ref. to the system of F. A. Mesmer), hypnotism; the state so induced, hypnosis; *fig.* fascination. Also, belief in this process; an influence producing such a state. Formerly also called ***animal magnetism***, ***magnetism***.
■ **mesmerist** *noun* a person who practises mesmerism; (occas.) a believer in mesmerism: L18.

mesmerize /ˈmɛzmərʌɪz/ *verb trans.* Also **-ise**. E19.
[ORIGIN formed as MESMERISM + -IZE.]
Subject to the influence of mesmerism, hypnotize; lead *into* something as if by mesmerism; *fig.* fascinate, hold spellbound. Freq. as ***mesmerized*** *ppl adjective*.

I. COMPTON-BURNETT I am mesmerized into silence; Dulcia fascinates me like a snake. P. PEARCE They stood at the window . . watching the snow . . mesmerized by it.

■ **mesmerizaˈbility** *noun* the extent to which a person may be mesmerized M19. **mesmerizable** *adjective* able to be mesmerized M19. **mesmeriˈzation** *noun* E19. **mesmerizer** *noun* E19.

†**mesnalty** *noun*. M16–M18.
[ORIGIN Law French *mesnalte*, from *mesne* (see MESNE) after *comunalte* COMMONALTY.]
LAW. The estate of a mesne lord; the condition of being a mesne lord.

mesne /miːn/ *noun & adjective*. LME.
[ORIGIN Law French, var. of Anglo-Norman *meen* MEAN *adjective*[2]: for the unetymological *s* cf. DEMESNE.]
▸ †**A** *noun*. **1** = MEAN *noun*[1] 2, 7. LME–E19.
2 In full ***writ of mesne***. A writ by which a tenant could recover damages from a mesne lord whose failure to perform services owed to a superior lord had led the latter to distrain chattels on the tenant's land. E16–E19.
3 = ***mesne lord*** below. M16–E18.
▸ **B** *adjective*. †**1** ***in the mesne time***, in the meantime. Only in LME.
2 Occurring or performed at a time intermediate between two dates. *obsolete* exc. *LAW*. M16.
mesne process *hist.* any writ or process issued between the primary and the final process. **mesne profits** the profits of an estate received by a tenant in wrongful possession and recoverable by the landlord.
3 *LAW* (now *hist.*). Of a person: intermediate, intervening. E19.
mesne lord a lord holding an estate from a superior feudal lord.

meso- /ˈmɛsəʊ, ˈmɛzəʊ, ˈmiːsəʊ, ˈmiːzəʊ/ *combining form*. In sense 1, before a vowel also **mes-**. In sense 2 also as attrib. adjective **meso**.
[ORIGIN from Greek *mesos* middle (in some anat. terms extracted from MESENTERY): see -O-.]
1 Forming chiefly scientific terms, with the sense 'middle, intermediate'.
2 *CHEMISTRY*. (As prefix usu. italicized.) Designating an isomer which has one or more pairs of enantiomorphic structural units so arranged that the molecule as a whole is optically inactive.
■ **meso-aˈppendix** *noun* (*ANATOMY*) the mesentery of the appendix L19. **mesoblast** *noun* (*EMBRYOLOGY*) the mesoderm, esp. in the earliest stages M19. **mesoˈblastic** *adjective* (*EMBRYOLOGY*) of or pertaining to the mesoblast L19. **mesocarp** *noun* (*BOTANY*) the middle layer of the pericarp of a fruit, between the endocarp and the exocarp E19. **mesocolic** /-ˈkɒlɪk/ *adjective* (*ANATOMY*) of or relating to the mesocolon E19. **mesocolon** *noun* (*ANATOMY*) a fold of peritoneum which supports the colon L17. **mesoconch** /-kɒŋk/, **mesoˈconchic** *adjectives* (*ANTHROPOLOGY*) in which the orbit of the eye is of moderate height in relation to its width E20. **mesoˈconchous** *adjective* (*ANTHROPOLOGY*) = MESOCONCHIC L19. **mesoconchy** *noun* the condition of being mesoconchic E20. **mesocyclone** *noun* (*METEOROLOGY*) a rotating column of rising air, associated with a small area of low pressure, which may develop into a tornado M20. **mesoˈdorsal** *adjective* (*ZOOLOGY*) situated on the middle of the back L19. **mesofauna** *noun* (*ECOLOGY*) animals of intermediate size, esp. those found in soil (such as earthworms, arthropods, nematodes, and molluscs) M20. **mesoform** *noun* (*PHYSICAL CHEMISTRY*) = MESOPHASE M20. **mesogaster** *noun* (*ANATOMY*) the mesentery which supports the stomach E19. **mesogloea**, *-**glea** /-ˈɡliːə/ *noun* [Greek *gloia* glue] *ZOOLOGY* a gelatinous layer between the endoderm and ectoderm of a coelenterate M19. **mesoˈgloeal**, *-**gleal** *adjective* (*ZOOLOGY*) of, pertaining to, or of the nature of (a) mesogloea L19. **mesoˈgnathic** *adjective* (*ANTHROPOLOGY*) = MESOGNATHOUS L19. **mesognathism** /mɪˈsɒɡnəθɪz(ə)m/ *noun* (*ANTHROPOLOGY*) = MESOGNATHY L19. **mesoˈgnathous** *adjective* (*ANTHROPOLOGY*) having or designating an intermediate facial profile, neither prognathous nor orthognathous L19. **mesognathy** /mɪˈsɒɡnəθi/ *noun* (*ANTHROPOLOGY*) mesognathous condition L19. **meso-iˈnositol** *noun* (*BIOCHEMISTRY*) = MYO-INOSITOL M20. **mesoˈkurtic** *adjective* [Greek *kurtos* bulging] *STATISTICS* of, pertaining to, or designating a frequency distribution having the same kurtosis as the normal distribution E20. **mesokurˈtosis** *noun* (*STATISTICS*) the property of being mesokurtic E20. **mesolect** *noun* [-LECT] *LINGUISTICS* the dialect or variety of any language with an intermediate level of prestige; an intermediate form between the acrolect and the basilect: L20. **mesoˈlectal** *adjective* (*LINGUISTICS*) of, pertaining to, or of the nature of a mesolect L20. **mesoˈlimbic** *adjective* (*ANATOMY*) situated in or pertaining to the middle of the limbic system of the brain L20. **mesomere** *noun* (*EMBRYOLOGY*) a medium-sized cell produced by some forms of embryonic cleavage L19. **mesomeˈtritis** *noun* (*MEDICINE*) inflammation of the mesometrium L19. **mesometrium** /-ˈmiːt-/ *noun* [Greek *mētra* womb] *ANATOMY & ZOOLOGY* the fold of peritoneum which supports the uterus or (in birds) the oviduct M19. **mesoˈnotum** *noun* (*ENTOMOLOGY*) the dorsal portion of the mesothorax of an insect M19. **mesopause** *noun* (*METEOROLOGY*) the upper boundary of the mesosphere, at an altitude of about 80 km (50 miles), where the temperature begins to increase with height M20. **mesopeˈlagic** *adjective* pertaining to or inhabiting the intermediate depths of the sea, *spec.* those between 200 and 1000 metres (approx. 660 and 3280 ft) down M20. **mesophase** *noun* (*PHYSICAL CHEMISTRY*) a mesomorphic phase, a liquid crystal E20. **mesophile** *noun* (*BIOLOGY*) a mesophilic organism E20. **mesoˈphilic** *adjective* (*BIOLOGY*) (of an organism, esp. a bacterium) flourishing at moderate temperatures L19. **mesoˈplankton** *noun* (*a*) plankton in the region between about 200 metres (approx. 660 ft) from the sea floor and 200 metres from the surface; (*b*) relatively large microplankton: L19. **mesoplankˈtonic** *adjective* of, pertaining to, or of the nature of mesoplankton L19. **mesopodium** /-ˈpəʊdɪəm/ *noun*, pl. **-ia**, *ZOOLOGY* the middle lobe of the foot of a mollusc M19. **mesorrhine** /-ˈrʌɪn/ *adjective* [Greek *rhin-*, *rhis* nose] *ANTHROPOLOGY* (of the nose) moderately long and wide; having such a nose: L19. **mesoˈsalpinx** *noun*, pl. **-salpinges** /-salˈpɪndʒiːz/, [Greek *salpinx*: cf. SALPINGO-] *ANATOMY* a peritoneal fold above the mesovarium which encloses the Fallopian tubes L19. **mesoˈsaprobe**, **mesosaˈprobic** *adjectives* (of running water) partially polluted E20. **mesoscale** *noun* (*METEOROLOGY*) an intermediate scale, between that of weather systems and that of microclimates, on which such phenomena as storms occur M20. **mesoscaphe**, **-scaph** *noun* a bathyscaphe designed for use at moderate depths M20. **mesoˈscopic** *adjective* on a medium scale; *spec.* in *GEOLOGY*, large enough for examination with the naked eye but not too large to allow inspection of the whole: M20. **mesoˈseismal** *adjective* pertaining to or designating the region near the epicentre of an earthquake L19. **mesospore** *noun* (*BOTANY*) the middle layer of a spore L19. **mesostasis** /mɪˈsɒstəsɪs/ *noun* (*PETROGRAPHY*) the most recently formed interstitial substance in an igneous rock L19. **mesoˈsternal** *adjective* (*ENTOMOLOGY & ANATOMY*) of, pertaining to, or of the nature of a mesosternum E19. **mesoˈsternum** *noun*, pl. **-na**, **-nums** (*a*) *ENTOMOLOGY* the sternum of the mesothorax of an insect; (*b*) *ANATOMY* the part of the breastbone between the manubrium and the xiphisternum: E19. **mesosuchian** /-ˈsjuːkɪən/ *adjective & noun* [Greek *soukhos* crocodile] *PALAEONTOLOGY* (*a*) *adjective* of, pertaining to, or designating the extinct suborder Mesosuchia of Jurassic and Cretaceous crocodiles; (*b*) *noun* a crocodile of this suborder: L19. **mesoˈtherapy** *noun* (in cosmetic surgery) a procedure in which multiple tiny injections of pharmaceuticals, vitamins, etc. are delivered into the mesodermal layer of tissue under the skin, to promote the loss of fat or cellulite L20. **mesotherm** *noun* (*BOTANY*) a plant requiring a moderate temperature L19. **mesoˈthermal** *adjective* (*PETROGRAPHY*) of, pertaining to, or designating mineral and ore deposits formed by hydrothermal action at intermediate temperature

M

and pressure E20. **meso'thermic** *adjective* (BOTANY) of, pertaining to, or of the nature of a mesotherm E20. **mesotho'racic** *adjective* (ENTOMOLOGY) of, pertaining to, or of the nature of a mesothorax M19. **meso'thorax** *noun* (ENTOMOLOGY) the middle segment of the thorax of an insect E19. **meso'tonic** *adjective* (MUSIC) designating or pertaining to the mean tone M19. **meso'varium** *noun* (ANATOMY) a peritoneal fold above the mesometrium which supports the ovaries L19.

Meso-American /ˌmɛsəʊə'mɛrɪk(ə)n, ˌmɛz-, ˌmiːs-, ˌmiːz-/ *adjective & noun*. Also **Mesoamerican**. M20.
[ORIGIN from *Meso-America* (see below, MESO-, AMERICAN) + -AN.]
▸ **A** *adjective*. Of or pertaining to Meso-America, the region of America from central Mexico to Nicaragua, or any of several advanced pre-Columbian cultures which flourished there; *loosely*, Central American. M20.
▸ **B** *noun*. A member of a Meso-American people. M20.

mesocephalic /ˌmɛsə(ʊ)sɪ'falɪk, ˌmɛz-, ˌmiːs-, ˌmiːz-, -kɛ'falɪk/ *adjective*. M19.
[ORIGIN from MESO- + -CEPHALIC.]
Having a medium-sized head; *spec*. having a cranial index between 75 and 80.
■ **'mesocephal** *noun*, pl. **-s**, [back-form. from mod. Latin pl.] a mesocephalic person L19. **meso'cephali** *noun pl.* (now *rare* or *obsolete*) [mod. Latin] mesocephals M19. **meso'cephalism**, **meso'cephaly** *nouns* mesocephalic condition L19.

mesocracy /mɛ'sɒkrəsi/ *noun*. *rare*. L19.
[ORIGIN from MESO- + -CRACY.]
Government or the holding of power by the middle classes; a society governed by the middle classes, or in which the middle classes hold power.

mesocratic /mɛsə(ʊ)'kratɪk, mɛz-, miːs-, miːz-/ *adjective*. M19.
[ORIGIN from MESO- + *-cratic* as in *democratic* etc.]
1 Of or pertaining to the middle classes. *rare*. M19.
2 PETROGRAPHY. Of a rock: intermediate in composition between leucocratic and melanocratic rock. E20.

mesode /'mɛsəʊd/ *noun*. M19.
[ORIGIN Greek *mesōdos*, formed as MESO- + *ōdē* ODE.]
A part of a Greek choral ode coming between the strophe and antistrophe.
■ **me'sodic** *adjective* pertaining to or of the nature of a mesode L19.

mesoderm /'mɛsə(ʊ)dəːm, 'mɛz-, 'miːs-, 'miːz-/ *noun*. M19.
[ORIGIN from MESO- + Greek *derma* skin.]
BIOLOGY. The middle germ layer of the embryo in early development, between endoderm and ectoderm; cells or tissues derived from this.
■ **meso'dermal**, **meso'dermic** *adjectives* of, pertaining to, or derived from the mesoderm L19.

mesogastrium /mɛsə(ʊ)'gastrɪəm, mɛz-, miːs-, miːz-/ *noun*. E19.
[ORIGIN mod. Latin, formed as MESO- + Greek *gastr-*, *gastēr* stomach: see -IUM.]
1 ANATOMY & ZOOLOGY. The mesentery of the stomach in the embryo; (orig. also) any of various structures that develop from this. E19.
2 MEDICINE & SURGERY. The middle region of the abdomen between the epigastrium and the hypogastrium. M19.
■ **mesogastric** *adjective* M19.

mesolabe /'mɛsə(ʊ)leɪb, 'mɛz-, 'miːs-, 'miːz-/ *noun*. *obsolete* exc. *hist*. L16.
[ORIGIN Latin *mesolabium*, from Greek *mesolabos*, *-on*, from *mesos* middle + *lab-* base of *lambanein* take: cf. ASTROLABE.]
An instrument used to find mean proportional lines.

Mesolithic /mɛsə(ʊ)'lɪθɪk, mɛz-, miːs-, miːz-/ *adjective & noun*. M19.
[ORIGIN from MESO- + -LITHIC.]
ARCHAEOLOGY. ▸**A** *adjective*. Designating or pertaining to part of the Stone Age intermediate between the Palaeolithic and the Neolithic periods. M19.
▸ **B** *noun*. *The* Mesolithic period. M20.

R. BRADLEY In Ireland.. microliths do not occur in the late Mesolithic.

mesomerism /mɪ'sɒmərɪz(ə)m, mɪ'zɒm-/ *noun*. E20.
[ORIGIN from MESO- after *tautomerism*.]
CHEMISTRY. The property exhibited by certain molecules of having a structure which cannot adequately be represented by a single structural formula but is intermediate between two or more graphical structures which differ in the distribution of electrons. Also called ***resonance***.
■ **meso'meric** *adjective* of, pertaining to, exhibiting, or arising from mesomerism L19.

mesomorph /'mɛsə(ʊ)mɔːf, 'mɛz-, 'miːs-, 'miːz-/ *noun*. E20.
[ORIGIN from MESO- + -MORPH.]
1 A person whose build is powerful, compact, and muscular (with noticeable development of tissue derived from embryonic mesoderm, as bones, muscles, and connective tissue). E20.
2 PHYSICAL CHEMISTRY. A mesophase or liquid crystal. *rare*. M20.
■ **mesomorphy** *noun* the state or property of being a mesomorph M20.

mesomorphic /mɛsə(ʊ)'mɔːfɪk, mɛz-, miːs-, miːz-/ *adjective*. E20.
[ORIGIN formed as MESOMORPH + -IC.]
1 PHYSICAL CHEMISTRY. Of, pertaining to, or of the nature of a liquid crystal, intermediate between the ordered state of matter in crystals and the disordered state in ordinary liquids. E20.
2 Having the bodily build of a mesomorph; of, pertaining to, or characteristic of a mesomorph. M20.
■ **mesomorphism** *noun* (PHYSICAL CHEMISTRY) the state or property of being mesomorphic M20. **mesomorphous** *adjective* (PHYSICAL CHEMISTRY) = MESOMORPHIC 1 E20.

meson /me'sɒn/ *noun*[1]. E19.
[ORIGIN Spanish *mesón*.]
An inn or lodging house in Mexico or the south-western US.

meson /'mɛsɒn/ *noun*[2]. L19.
[ORIGIN Use as noun of neut. of Greek *mesos* middle.]
ANATOMY. The median plane, which divides a body into two roughly symmetrical halves.

meson /'miːzɒn, 'mɛzɒn/ *noun*[3]. M20.
[ORIGIN from MESO- + -ON.]
PARTICLE PHYSICS. Orig., any of a group of subatomic particles intermediate in mass between an electron and a proton. Now *spec*. any such particle that has zero or integral spin and can take part in the strong interaction.
mu-meson, ***omega meson***, ***phi meson***, etc.
– COMB.: **meson factory** *colloq.* an establishment with a high-energy accelerator etc. for producing and experimenting with an intense beam of mesons.

mesonephros /mɛsə(ʊ)'nɛfrɒs, mɛz-, miːs-, miːz-/ *noun*. Pl. **-nephroi** /-'nɛfrɔɪ/. Also (now *rare*) **-nephron** /-'nɛfrɒn/, pl. **-nephra** /-'nɛfrə/. L19.
[ORIGIN from MESO- + Greek *nephros* kidney.]
ANATOMY & ZOOLOGY. The second of the three segments of the embryonic kidney in vertebrates, which becomes the adult kidney of fishes and amphibians and survives in humans and other amniotes as the epididymis (in males) and the epoophoron (in females). Also called ***Wolffian body***. Cf. METANEPHROS, PRONEPHROS.
■ **mesonephric** *adjective* L19.

mesonic /miː'zɒnɪk, mɛ-/ *adjective*. M20.
[ORIGIN from MESON *noun*[3] + -IC.]
PARTICLE PHYSICS. = MESIC *adjective*[2].

mesophyll /'mɛsə(ʊ)fɪl, 'mɛz-, 'miːs-, 'miːz-/ *noun*. M19.
[ORIGIN from Greek *mesos* middle + *phullon* leaf.]
BOTANY. The parenchyma of a leaf, between the upper and lower layers of epidermis.
■ **meso'phyllic** *adjective* L19.

mesophyte /'mɛsə(ʊ)fʌɪt, 'mɛz-, 'miːs-, 'miːz-/ *noun*. L19.
[ORIGIN from MESO- + -PHYTE.]
BOTANY. A plant of a group intermediate between hydrophytes and xerophytes, i.e. one avoiding extremes of moisture and dryness.
■ **mesophytic** /-'fɪtɪk, mɛz-, miːs-, miːz-/ *adjective* L19.

Mesopotamia /mɛsəpə'teɪmɪə/ *noun*. M19.
[ORIGIN Greek (sc. *khōra* country), from *mesos* middle + *potamos* river: see MESOPOTAMIAN.]
(A name for) an area between two rivers.

Mesopotamian /mɛsəpə'teɪmɪən/ *noun & adjective*. M16.
[ORIGIN from *Mesopotamia* (see below) + -AN.]
▸ **A** *noun*. A native or inhabitant of Mesopotamia, a region in SW Asia between the Tigris and the Euphrates rivers, site of the ancient civilizations of Sumer, Babylon, and Assyria, and now in Iraq. M16.
▸ **B** *adjective*. Of or pertaining to Mesopotamia. L18.

mesosaur /'mɛsəsɔː/ *noun*. L19.
[ORIGIN mod. Latin *Mesosaurus* (see below), from Greek *mesos* middle + *sauros* lizard.]
PALAEONTOLOGY. A small aquatic reptile of the genus *Mesosaurus*, of the early Permian period, with an elongated body, flattened tail, and a long narrow snout with many needle-like teeth.

mesosiderite /mɛsə(ʊ)'sɪdərʌɪt, mɛz-, miːs-, miːz-, -sʌɪ'dɪərʌɪt/ *noun*. M19.
[ORIGIN from MESO- + SIDERITE.]
GEOLOGY. A stony-iron meteorite in which the principal silicates are pyroxene and plagioclase.

mesosome /'mɛsəsəʊm, 'mɛz-, 'miːs-, 'miːz-/ *noun*. In sense 1 also **-soma** /mɛsə'səʊmə/, pl. **-mata** /-mətə/. L19.
[ORIGIN from MESO- + Greek *sōma* body.]
1 ZOOLOGY. The middle region or segment of the body of various invertebrates (as scorpions, lophophorates). L19.
2 BACTERIOLOGY. A membranous structure in many bacteria that is associated with respiratory and photosynthetic activity. M20.

mesosphere /'mɛsə(ʊ)sfɪə, 'mɛz-, 'miːs-, 'miːz-/ *noun*. M20.
[ORIGIN from MESO- + -SPHERE.]
1 METEOROLOGY. The layer of the earth's atmosphere above the stratopause and below the mesopause, in which temperature decreases with height. M20.
2 GEOLOGY. The lower layer of the earth's mantle, which is resistant to plastic flow and not involved in tectonic processes. M20.
■ **mesospheric** /mɛsə(ʊ)'sfɛrɪk, mɛz-, miːs-, miːz-/ *adjective* of, pertaining to, or occurring in the mesosphere M20.

mesothelia *noun* pl. of MESOTHELIUM.

mesothelioma /ˌmɛsə(ʊ)θiːlɪ'əʊmə, ˌmɛz-, ˌmiːs-, ˌmiːz-/ *noun*. Pl. **-mas**, **-mata** /-mətə/. E20.
[ORIGIN from MESOTHELIUM + -OMA.]
MEDICINE. A tumour of mesothelial tissue, associated esp. with exposure to asbestos.

mesothelium /mɛsə(ʊ)'θiːlɪəm, mɛz-, miːs-, miːz-/ *noun*. Pl. **-lia** /-lɪə/. L19.
[ORIGIN from MESO- + EPI)THELIUM.]
ANATOMY. Epithelium that forms the surface layer of the mesoderm and lines the embryonic body cavity; (a body of) tissue derived from this, which lines the pleurae, peritoneum, and pericardium.
■ **mesothelial** *adjective* L19.

mesothorium /mɛsə(ʊ)'θɔːrɪəm, mɛz-, miːs-, miːz-/ *noun*. E20.
[ORIGIN from MESO- + THORIUM.]
NUCLEAR PHYSICS. Either of two radioactive nuclides produced during the decay of thorium, radium 228 (***mesothorium I***), produced by α-decay of thorium 232, and actinium 228 (***mesothorium II***), produced by β-decay of mesothorium I.

mesotron /'miːzətrɒn, 'mɛz-, 'miːs-, 'mɛs-/ *noun*. *obsolete* exc. *hist*. M20.
[ORIGIN from MESO- + *-tron*, after *electron*, *neutron*.]
PARTICLE PHYSICS. = MESON *noun*[3].

mesozoan /mɛsə'zəʊən, miːz-/ *adjective & noun*. E20.
[ORIGIN from MESOZOON + -AN.]
ZOOLOGY. ▸**A** *adjective*. Of or pertaining to mesozoa or the phylum Mesozoa. E20.
▸ **B** *noun*. A member of the phylum Mesozoa, comprising minute animals with no organs or body cavity which are parasitic on marine invertebrates. M20.

Mesozoic /mɛsə(ʊ)'zəʊɪk, mɛz-, miːs-, miːz-/ *adjective & noun*. M19.
[ORIGIN from MESO- + -ZOIC.]
GEOLOGY. ▸**A** *adjective*. Designating or pertaining to the second era of the Phanerozoic eon, following the Palaeozoic and preceding the Cenozoic, and comprising the Triassic, Jurassic, and Cretaceous periods. M19.
▸ **B** *noun*. The Mesozoic era; the rocks collectively dating from this time. L19.

mesozoon /mɛsə(ʊ)'zəʊən, mɛz-, miːs-, miːz-/ *noun*. Pl. **-zoa** /-'zəʊə/. L19.
[ORIGIN mod. Latin *Mesozoa* pl., from Greek MESO- + *zōia* pl. of *zōion* animal.]
ZOOLOGY. Orig., an animal intermediate in structure between protozoans and metazoans. Now *spec*. = MESOZOAN *noun*. Usu. in *pl.*

mespilus /'mɛspɪləs/ *noun*. M16.
[ORIGIN mod. Latin (see below) from Latin: see MEDLAR.]
Any of various trees and shrubs now or formerly belonging to the genus *Mespilus*, of the rose family, e.g. the medlar, *M. germanica*.
snowy mespilus a kind of juneberry, *Amelanchier lamarckii*.

mesquin /mɛskɛ̃/ *adjective*. Now *rare*. E18.
[ORIGIN French.]
Mean, sordid, shabby.

mesquite /'mɛskiːt, mɛ'skiːt/ *noun*. Also **-it**. M18.
[ORIGIN Mexican Spanish *mezquite* from Nahuatl *mizquitl*.]
1 Any of various thorny pinnate-leaved leguminous shrubs and small trees of the genus *Prosopis*, of arid regions of Mexico, the south-western US, etc., esp. *P. glandulosa*; vegetation or terrain in which these plants predominate. M18.
2 = ***mesquite-grass*** below. M19.
– COMB.: **mesquite bean** the pod of the mesquite, used as fodder; **mesquite-grass** any of various grasses, esp. of the genus *Bouteloua*, that grow in association with the mesquite.

mess /mɛs/ *noun*. ME.
[ORIGIN Old French *mes* portion of food, mod. *mets* (infl. by *mettre* place) from late Latin *missus* course of a meal, from Latin *miss-* pa. ppl stem of *mittere* send (out). See also MUSS *noun*[2].]
▸**I 1 a** A serving of food; a course of a meal; a prepared dish (of a specified kind of food). *arch*. ME. ▸**b** A quantity (of food) sufficient to make a dish; the quantity of milk given by a cow at one milking. Now *dial. & US*. E16. ▸**c** A (large) quantity or number *of* something. *N. Amer. colloq.* M19.

A. UTTLEY Beautiful copper saucepans filled with savoury messes which they put on the stove.

2 A portion or kind of liquid, partly liquid, or pulpy food; a quantity of this for an animal, esp. a hound. LME. ▸**b** An unappealing concoction or pulp, esp. of foodstuffs. E19.
3 a A state or situation of confusion or muddle; a condition of embarrassment or trouble. E19. ▸**b** A dirty or untidy state of things or of a place; a thing or collection of things causing such a state; dirty or misplaced things collectively. M19. ▸**c** Excrement, esp. of a domestic animal or a child. *colloq.* E20. ▸**d** A person whose life or

affairs are confused; a dirty or untidy person. Also, an objectionable, ineffectual, or stupid person. *colloq.* M20.

a M. WEST With the world in such a mess.. you were wise to retire from it. W. GOLDING Anyone.. after a month.. in a boat will know what a mess we were in. **b** D. FRANCIS The overturned mess of paints and easel which the young man had left. J. CANNAN Oh, the mess they leave on our little common.. in spite of the litter baskets. **d** T. K. WOLFE His hair felt like a bird's nest. He was a mess.

▸**II 4 a** Orig., each of the groups, usu. of four people, into which the guests at a banquet were commonly divided. Now, a company of esp. legal professional people who regularly take meals together. LME. ▸**b** In the armed forces, each of the groups into which a regiment etc. is divided and whose members take meals together. Also, the place where meals are taken in such groups, a place for communal recreation for the members of a mess. M16. ▸**c** (Without article.) The taking of a meal in such a group. L18.

b B. REID Lance bombardiers couldn't drink in the officers' mess.

†**5** *gen.* A company or group of four persons or things. E16–L19.

– PHRASES: **lose the number of one's mess** *military slang* die, be killed. **make a mess** (*a*) put things into a disorderly, untidy, or dirty state; (*b*) (esp. of a domestic animal or a child) defecate. **make a mess of** (*a*) mishandle (an undertaking), spoil or botch (a job of work); (*b*) make disorderly, untidy, or dirty. **mess of pottage** [*Genesis* 25:29–34] a material or trivial comfort gained at the expense of something more important.

– COMB.: **mess-boy** NAUTICAL a man or boy who waits at table in a mess; **mess jacket** a short tailless jacket reaching just below the waistline, worn esp. at a mess; **mess kit** (*a*) a soldier's cooking and eating utensils; (*b*) (military) uniform designed to be worn at meals; **mess room** a dining or recreation room for the members of a mess; **mess tin** a small oval bucket, part of a mess kit. See also MESSMATE.

mess /mɛs/ *verb.* LME.

[ORIGIN from the noun.]

1 *verb trans.* Serve up (food); divide (food) into portions. *obsolete* exc. *dial.* LME.

†**2** *verb trans.* Divide (a ship's company) into messes. Only in 17.

3 *verb intrans.* Take one's meals, esp. as a member of a mess; share accommodation or facilities. E18.

4 *verb trans.* Provide with food in a mess, supply with food. E19.

5 *verb intrans.* Mix or associate *with*. Only in ***mess or mell***, ***mess and mell***. *Scot.* E19.

6 *verb intrans.* **a** Busy oneself in an untidy or desultory way, act with no definite purpose or result, dabble, (usu. foll. by *about*, *around*). Also, make a mess, put things into a disorderly or untidy state; (esp. of a domestic animal or a child) defecate. *colloq.* M19. ▸**b** Foll. by *with*: interfere or get involved with; make a mess of; trouble, annoy. *N. Amer. colloq.* E20. ▸**c** Foll. by *up*: make a mess of a situation; get into trouble. *N. Amer. colloq.* M20.

a K. GRAHAME What boy has ever passed a bit of water without messing in it? R. K. NARAYAN A guest would mean a great deal of messing about with oil and frying-pan. E. BLYTON The children messed about that day, doing nothing at all. N. HINTON And don't go messing round with drugs. **b** J. MALCOLM He was playing with fire when he messed with you.

7 *verb trans.* **a** Make a mess of; disorder, make dirty or untidy; mishandle (an undertaking); spoil, ruin. (Foll. by *up*.) M19. ▸**b** Handle roughly or interferingly; treat unfairly or inconsistently; inconvenience, annoy. Usu. foll. by *about*, *around*. *colloq.* L19.

a T. HILLERMAN Tell me more about how these sand paintings got messed up. P. LOMAS I would have had to behave in a very silly way to have messed up the interview. A. GERAS The wind tears at your hair and messes your clothes. **b** *Essex Weekly News* Defendant.. had never been messed about by policemen before. *Jackie* He's been messing her about for ages.

– COMB.: **mess-up** a mess, a muddle; a confused situation.

■ **messing** *noun* (*a*) the action of the verb; (*b*) participation in a mess or common meal; (*c*) the food served to an individual in a mess: ME.

messa di voce /ˈmessa di ˈvotʃe, ˈmɛsə dɪ ˈvəʊtʃi/ *noun phr.* Pl. ***messe di voce*** /ˈmesse, ˈmɛseɪ/. L18.

[ORIGIN Italian, lit. 'placing of the voice'.]

In singing, a gradual crescendo and diminuendo on a long-held note.

message /ˈmɛsɪdʒ/ *noun & verb.* ME.

[ORIGIN Old French & mod. French from Proto-Romance from Latin *missus* pa. pple of *mittere* send: see -AGE.]

▸**A** *noun.* **1** A usu. brief communication transmitted through a messenger or other agency; an oral, written, or recorded communication sent from one person or group to another. ME. ▸**b** A communication by a prophet or preacher or from God. M16. ▸**c** An official or formal communication, as between a ruler or parliament and a lower authority or the public. M16. ▸**d** A television or radio advertisement. *US.* E20. ▸**e** An electronic communication generated automatically by a computer program. M20. ▸**f** An item of electronic mail. L20.

J. VAN DRUTEN I left a message at my hotel telling him to come.. and pick me up. R. K. NARAYAN He remembered the message he had been entrusted with. S. BELLOW I.. left a haughty message on the answering machine. **b** J. LOGAN His oracles of truth proclaim the message brought to man. **c** LD MACAULAY A royal message authorizing the Commons to elect another Speaker.

2 The carrying of a communication; a mission, an errand. ME. ▸**b** In *pl.* Articles bought on an errand, shopping. Chiefly *Scot. & Irish.* E20.

3 The central import of something; an implicit esp. polemical meaning in an artistic work etc. E19.

Times His real gifts for story-telling and satirical observation are.. obscured by too heavy an insistence on the 'message' implicit in the plot.

– PHRASES: **get the message** *colloq.* understand a position stated or implied. **off-message** inconsistent with or not conveying the intended message; esp. (POLITICS) deviating from the official party line; †**of message** carrying a communication, doing an errand. **on-message** †(*a*) = ***of message*** above; (*b*) consistent with or conveying the intended message; esp. (POLITICS) in accordance with the official party line.

– COMB.: **message boy** *Scot.* an errand boy; **message card** a card on which a message may be written; *hist.* a card of invitation to a reception or entertainment; **message stick** a wooden stick carved with significant marks and used as a means of communication or identification among Australian Aborigines; **message switching** (COMPUTING & TELECOMMUNICATIONS) a mode of data transmission in which a message is sent as a complete unit and routed via a number of intermediate nodes at which it is stored and then forwarded.

▸**B** *verb trans.* Send or communicate as a message; transmit (a plan etc.) by signalling etc. Also, send a message to. L16.

Sun (Baltimore) General MacArthur messaged them by radio: 'Thanks for a grand ride.' J. H. VANCE Lindbergh.. messaged that he would visit.

■ **messaging** *noun* the sending of a message or messages, esp. electronically M19. **messageless** *adjective* E20.

messagerie /mesaʒri/ *noun.* Pl. pronounced same. L18.

[ORIGIN French: see MESSAGERY.]

The transportation or delivery of goods, messages, or people; a conveyance for these. In *pl.* also, goods, messages, or people for transportation or delivery.

messagery /ˈmɛsɪdʒ(ə)ri/ *noun.* Long *arch. rare.* LME.

[ORIGIN French *messagerie*, from *messager* MESSENGER + *-erie* -ERY.]

The occupation or function of a messenger; the carrying of a message or errand.

Messalian /mɛˈseɪlɪən/ *noun & adjective.* Also **Ma-** /ma-/. M16.

[ORIGIN Late Greek *Messalianos*, *Mass-* from Syriac *mṣalyānā* person who prays, from *ṣallī* pray.]

ECCLESIASTICAL HISTORY. ▸**A** *noun.* = EUCHITE. Formerly also = HESYCHAST. L16.

▸**B** *adjective.* Of or pertaining to the Messalians. M16.

Messalina /mɛsəˈliːnə/ *noun.* L16.

[ORIGIN Valeria *Messalina*, third wife of the Roman Emperor Claudius.]

A licentious and scheming woman.

messaline /ˈmɛsəliːn/ *noun & adjective.* E20.

[ORIGIN French, formed as MESSALINA.]

(Made of) a soft lightweight and lustrous silk or rayon fabric.

messan /ˈmɛs(ə)n/ *noun. Scot.* Also **-in**. L15.

[ORIGIN Gaelic *measan* = Irish *measán*, Middle Irish *mesán*.]

A small pet dog, a lapdog. Also ***messan-dog***.

Messapian /məˈseɪpɪən/ *adjective & noun. hist.* E17.

[ORIGIN from Latin *Messapius*, from *Messapia* (see below) + -AN.]

▸**A** *adjective.* Of or pertaining to the ancient district of Messapia, in southern Italy (now Apulia and Calabria), its inhabitants, or their language. E17.

▸**B** *noun.* **1** A native or inhabitant of Messapia. L18.

2 The language of the Messapians. L19.

■ **Messapic** *noun & adjective* (of) the language of the Messapians M20.

messe di voce *noun phr.* pl. of MESSA DI VOCE.

Messeigneurs *noun* pl. of MONSEIGNEUR.

messenger /ˈmɛsɪndʒə/ *noun & verb.* ME.

[ORIGIN Old French & mod. French *messager*, formed as MESSAGE: see -ER². For the intrusive *n* cf. *passenger*, *scavenger*, etc.]

▸**A** *noun.* **1** A person who carries a message or goes on an errand for another; a person employed to carry messages. ME. ▸**b** A bearer *of* (a specified message). ME. ▸**c** BIOLOGY. A molecule or substance that carries (esp. genetic) information. Freq. *attrib.* M20.

D. CARKEET You can't shoot the messenger for bringing bad news. M. FLANAGAN Jason asked for a cheque to be sent round by messenger.

2 A person sent forward to prepare the way; a herald, a precursor, a harbinger. *arch.* ME.

fig.: SHAKES. *Jul. Caes.* Yon grey lines That fret the clouds are messengers of day.

3 A government official employed to carry dispatches and formerly to apprehend state prisoners; a courier. LME.

4 a Esp. NAUTICAL. An endless rope, cable, or chain used with a capstan to haul a cable or to drive a powered winch etc. Also, a light line used to haul or support a larger cable. M17. ▸**b** A device able to be sent down a line, esp. in order to trip a mechanism. M18.

– PHRASES: ***express messenger***: see EXPRESS *adjective*. **King's Messenger**, **Queen's Messenger** a courier employed by the British Government to carry important official papers within Britain and abroad. ***second messenger***: see SECOND *adjective*.

– COMB.: **messenger-at-arms** *Scot.* an official employed to execute writs from the Court of Session and the High Court of Justiciary; **messenger cable** a cable used to support a power cable or other conductor of electricity; a suspension cable or wire; **messenger RNA** BIOLOGY RNA which is synthesized in a cell nucleus with a nucleotide sequence complementary to the coding sequence of a gene (transcription), and passes from the nucleus to a ribosome, where its nucleotide sequence determines the amino-acid sequence of a protein synthesized there (translation); abbreviation ***mRNA***; **messenger wire** = ***messenger cable*** above.

▸**B** *verb trans.* Send by messenger. (*rare* before L20.) E19.

■ **messengership** *noun* the position or function of a messenger E17.

Messenian /mɛˈsiːnɪən/ *noun & adjective.* E16.

[ORIGIN from Latin *Messenius* from Greek *Messēnios* of Messenia (see below) + -AN.]

▸**A** *noun.* **1** A native or inhabitant of (esp. ancient) Messenia, a region in the SW Peloponnese in Greece. E16.

2 The dialect of ancient Greek spoken in Messenia. E20.

▸**B** *adjective.* Of or pertaining to Messenia, the (ancient) Messenians, or their dialect. E17.

messer /ˈmɛsə/ *noun*¹. M17.

[ORIGIN from MESS *verb* + -ER¹.]

†**1** A supplier of meat to ships. M17–M18.

2 A person who makes a mess; a muddler, a bungler. *colloq.* E20.

Messer /ˈmɛsə/ *noun*². M16.

[ORIGIN Italian *messere*.]

Used as a title preceding the name of an Italian man: = MR.

Messiah /mɪˈsʌɪə/ *noun.* Also (earlier) †**-ias**. OE.

[ORIGIN Old French & mod. French *Messie* from popular Latin *Messias* from Greek *Messias* from Aramaic *mᵉšīḥā*, Hebrew *māšīaḥ* anointed, from *māšaḥ* anoint. Mod. form *Messiah* created by the Geneva translators of 1560 as looking more Hebraic than *Messias*.]

1 The promised deliverer of the Jewish nation prophesied in the Hebrew Scriptures; Jesus regarded as the saviour of humankind. OE.

2 An actual or expected liberator of an oppressed people or country etc.; a leader or saviour of a specified group, cause, etc. M17.

Guardian Howard Jarvis.. the Messiah of taxpayers. P. B. CLARKE Haile Selassie, former emperor of Ethiopia and the Rastafarian Messiah.

■ **Messiahship** *noun* the character or position of the Messiah or of a Messiah; the fact of being the Messiah: E17.

messianic /mɛsɪˈanɪk/ *adjective.* Also **M-**. M19.

[ORIGIN French *messianique*, from *Messie* MESSIAH after *rabbinique* RABBINIC: see -IC.]

1 Of, pertaining to, or characteristic of the Messiah or a Messiah; inspired by hope of or belief in the Messiah or a Messiah. E19.

A. S. DALE Fanatics who wanted to lead Messianic cults to replace Christianity.

2 Fervent or passionate. M20.

New Yorker Not everyone responded to the messianic intensity of Morrison's stage persona. *Daily Telegraph* Ewa Pascoe is messianic about encouraging women on to the Internet.

■ **messianically** *adverb* M19. **meˈssianism** *noun* belief in a coming Messiah M19.

Messidor /ˈmɛsɪdɔː, *foreign* mesidɔːr/ *noun.* L18.

[ORIGIN French, from Latin *messis* harvest + Greek *dōron* gift: see -OR.]

The tenth month of the French Republican calendar (introduced 1793), extending from 19 June to 18 July.

Messier /ˈmɛsɪə/ *noun.* M19.

[ORIGIN Charles *Messier* (1730–1817), French astronomer.]

ASTRONOMY. Used *attrib.* to designate a catalogue of 109 non-stellar objects visible in the northern sky, first published in 1774, and (usu. with an identifying numeral) objects listed in the catalogue.

Listener The Great Nebula (Messier 31).

messieurs *noun* pl. of MONSIEUR.

messin *noun* var. of MESSAN.

messire /mesiːr/ *noun.* Now *arch.* or *hist.* L15.

[ORIGIN Old French, from *mes* my (from Latin *meus*) + SIRE *noun*. Cf. MONSIEUR.]

Used *voc.* or preceding the name of a high-ranking French noble or any important man: my lord, sir.

messmate /ˈmɛsmeɪt/ *noun.* M17.

[ORIGIN from MESS *noun* + MATE *noun*².]

1 A regular companion at meals; a member of a mess, esp. in the armed forces. M17.

2 (The wood of) any of several rough-barked eucalypts, esp. *Eucalyptus cloeziana* and *E. obliqua*. *Austral.* M19.

M

Messrs /ˈmɛsəz/ *noun pl.* Also **Messrs.** (point). **M18.**
[**ORIGIN** Abbreviation.]
Messieurs. Now usu. as pl. of **MR** and in addressing a private firm or company by name.

J. SMEATON I returned with Messrs. Jessop and Richardson to Plymouth. J. H. MAPLESON Messrs. Steinway now . . undertook to supply each leading member of the Company with pianos.

messuage /ˈmɛswɪdʒ/ *noun.* **LME.**
[**ORIGIN** Anglo-Norman *mes(s)uage*, prob. orig. misreading of *mesnage* **MÉNAGE**: see **-AGE**.]
Orig., the portion of land intended to be or actually occupied as a site for a dwelling house and its appurtenances. Later (*LAW*), a dwelling house with its outbuildings and the adjacent land assigned to its use.

messy /ˈmɛsi/ *adjective.* **E17.**
[**ORIGIN** from **MESS** *noun* + **-Y**[1].]
1 Of the nature of a mess; involving, accompanied by, or causing mess or disorder; untidy, dirty. **E17.**

J. B. PRIESTLEY A messy, dribbling, pie-faced urchin. B. BRYSON I walked on into Christchurch by way of a long, messy street.

2 Difficult to deal with, full of awkward complications; immoral, unethical. *colloq.* **E20.**

J. DISKI How do they fit in? Messy old emotions. *Daily Mirror* She finally buckled under the weight of a messy divorce.

■ **messily** *adverb* **E20. messiness** *noun* **M19.**

mestee *noun* var. of **MUSTEE**.

†**mesteque** *noun.* **M17–M19.**
[**ORIGIN** Unknown.]
A kind of fine cochineal.

mesterolone /mɛˈstɛrələʊn/ *noun.* **M20.**
[**ORIGIN** from **ME(THYL** + **STEROL** + **-ONE**.]
PHARMACOLOGY. A synthetic androgen used to treat male hypogonadism.

mestizo /mɛˈstiːzəʊ/ *noun & adjective.* Pl. of noun **-os**. Fem. **-za** /-zə/. **L16.**
[**ORIGIN** Spanish from Proto-Romance from Latin *mixtus* pa. pple of *miscere* mix.]
▸ **A** *noun.* A Spanish or Portuguese person with parents of different races, *spec.* one with a Spaniard as one parent and an American Indian as the other; *gen.* any person of mixed blood. Also, a Central or S. American Indian who has adopted European culture. **L16.**
▸ **B** *attrib.* or as *adjective.* That is a mestizo or mestiza. **E17.**

J. A. MICHENER He was one of the first of Mexico's mestizo children, half Spanish, half Indian.

M

mesto /ˈmɛstəʊ/ *adverb & adjective.* **E19.**
[**ORIGIN** Italian from Latin *maestus* sad.]
MUSIC. A direction: sad(ly), mournful(ly).

mestome /ˈmɛstəʊm/ *noun.* Also **mestom** /ˈmɛstəm/. **L19.**
[**ORIGIN** from Greek *mestōma* filling up, from *mestoun* fill up, from *mestos* full.]
BOTANY. The conducting part of a fibrovascular bundle. Now only in ***mestome sheath***, the inner thick-walled sheath which surrounds the vascular tissue in some grasses. Cf. **STEREOME 1**.

mestranol /ˈmɛstrənɒl/ *noun.* **M20.**
[**ORIGIN** from **ME(THYL** + **O)ESTRA(DIOL** + *-n-* + **-OL**.]
PHARMACOLOGY. A synthetic oestrogen, the 3-methyl ether of ethynyloestradiol, which is more potent than oestradiol and is commonly used in oral contraceptives.

met /mɛt/ *noun*[1]. *obsolete* exc. *dial.*
[**ORIGIN** Old English *gemet* = Old Saxon *gimet*, Old High German *gamez*, Old Norse *mét* (neut. pl.) weight of a balance, from Germanic base also of **MEET** *adjective*, **METE** *verb*.]
†**1** Size, dimension, or quantity as determinable by measurement. **OE–E16.**
2 = **MEASURE** *noun* 3. **OE.**
3 = **MEASURE** *noun* 2. **OE.**
†**4** = **MEASURE** *noun* 11. **OE–LME.**
†**5** The action of measuring. Only in **ME.**
†**6** = **MEASURE** *noun* 5. **ME–E17.**

met /mɛt/ *noun*[2]. *colloq.* Also **met.**, **M-**. **L19.**
[**ORIGIN** Abbreviation.]
1 *The* Metropolitan Line or (*hist.*) Railway in London, *the* Metropolitan Opera House in New York, *the* Metropolitan Police in London. **L19.**
2 *The* Meteorological Office. **M20.**

met /mɛt/ *adjective. colloq.* Also **met.**, **M-**. **M20.**
[**ORIGIN** Abbreviation.]
1 Meteorological. Esp. in ***the Met Office***. **M20.**
2 Metropolitan. **M20.**

met *verb pa. t. & pple* of **MEET** *verb.*

met- *prefix* var. of **META-**.

meta /ˈmiːtə/ *noun*[1]. Pl. **-tae** /-tiː/. **L16.**
[**ORIGIN** Latin.]
ROMAN ANTIQUITIES. A conical column placed at each end of a racetrack to mark the turning place; a boundary marker.

Meta /ˈmɛtə/ *noun*[2]. Also **m-**. **E20.**
[**ORIGIN** Abbreviation.]
(Proprietary name for) metaldehyde, esp. as used in block form.

meta /ˈmɛtə/ *adjective & adverb.* Freq. italicized. **L19.**
[**ORIGIN** from **META-**.]
▸ **A** *adjective.* **1** *CHEMISTRY.* Characterized by or relating to (substitution at) two carbon atoms separated by one other in a benzene ring; at a position next but one *to* some (specified) substituent in a benzene ring. **L19.**
2 Of a creative work: referring to itself or to the conventions of its genre, self-referential. *US.* **L20.**
– SPECIAL COLLOCATIONS: **meta key** *COMPUTING* a key which activates a particular function when held down simultaneously with another key.
▸ **B** *adverb. CHEMISTRY.* So as to form meta-substituted compounds. **M20.**

meta- /ˈmɛtə/ *prefix.* Before a vowel or *h* also **met-**.
[**ORIGIN** Greek *met(a)-* (*meth-*), occurring separately as the preposition *meta* with, after. In sense 1 after **METAPHYSICS**.]
1 Denoting a nature of a higher order or more fundamental kind, as ***metalanguage***, ***metatheory***.
2 Chiefly *ANATOMY & ZOOLOGY.* Denoting position behind, at the back, or after.
3 *BIOLOGY.* Denoting occurrence or development at a later stage or time.
4 *CHEMISTRY.* **a** Denoting derivation from, metamerism with, or resemblance to a given compound; *spec.* in names of salts and acids containing fewer molecules of water. ▸**b** (Freq. italicized.) Denoting substitution in a benzene ring at carbon atoms separated by one carbon atom. Cf. **ORTHO-** 2b, **PARA-**[1] 3.
5 *GEOLOGY.* Denoting metamorphism.
6 Denoting change, alteration, or effect generally.
■ **meˈtabasis** *noun*, pl. **-ases** /-əsiːz/, a transition, *spec.* (**a**) *RHETORIC* from one subject or point to another; (**b**) *MEDICINE* from one remedy etc. to another: **M16. metabioˈlogical** *adjective* of or pertaining to metabiology **E20. metabiˈology** *noun* a hypothetical science supposed to deal with phenomena of living organisms in a manner beyond the scope of conventional biology **E20. metaˈchrosis** *noun* [Greek *khrōsis* colouring] *ZOOLOGY* ability to change colour **L19. metaˈcinnabar** *noun* (*MINERALOGY*) mercuric sulphide, occurring as a black mineral crystallizing in the cubic system, dimorphous with cinnabar **L19. metacogˈnition** *noun* (*PSYCHOLOGY*) awareness and understanding of one's own thought processes, esp. regarded as having a role in directing those processes **L20. metacommuniˈcation** *noun* communication taking place with or underlying a more obvious form of communication; *sing.* & in *pl.* principles or theories about communication derived from the study of communication: **M20. metacommuniˈcational**, **metacoˈmmunicative** *adjectives* concerned with or pertaining to metacommunication **M20. metaˈconal** *adjective* (*ZOOLOGY*) of, pertaining to, or of the nature of a metacone **L19. metacone** *noun* (*ZOOLOGY*) a cusp on the posterior buccal corner of the tribosphenic upper molar tooth **L19. metaˈconid** *noun* (*ZOOLOGY*) a cusp on the posterior lingual corner of the trigonid of the tribosphenic lower molar tooth **L19. metaˈcontrast** *noun* (*PSYCHOLOGY*) a change, esp. a diminution, in the after-effect of a visual stimulus as a result of a rapidly succeeding second stimulus **M20. metaconule** /-ˈkaʊnjuːl/ *noun* (*ZOOLOGY*) an intermediate cusp between the hypocone and the metacone of a mammalian upper molar tooth **L19. metacryst** *noun* (*PETROGRAPHY*) a large crystal formed in a metamorphic rock by recrystallization **E20. metadata** *noun* (*COMPUTING*) a set of data that describes and gives information about other data **L20. meta-ˈethical** *adjective* of or pertaining to meta-ethics **M20. meta-ˈethics** *noun* the branch of knowledge that deals with the foundations of ethics, esp. of ethical statements **M20. metafiction** *noun* (a work of) fiction which does not rely on traditional ideas of realism or does not conform to experience of the world **M20. metaˈfictional** *adjective* pertaining to or of the nature of metafiction **L20. metafile** *noun* (*COMPUTING*) (a graphics file stored in) a device-independent format that can be exchanged between different systems or software **L20. metagaˈlactic** *adjective* (*ASTRONOMY*) of, pertaining to, or designating the (or a) metagalaxy **M20. metaˈgalaxy** *noun* (*ASTRONOMY*) the entire system of galaxies and other bodies which makes up the universe; a cluster or group of galaxies: **M20. metageoˈmetrical** *adjective* of or pertaining to metageometry **L19. metageˈometry** *noun* non-Euclidean geometry **L19. metagnathism** /mɛˈtagnəθɪz(ə)m/ *noun* (*ORNITHOLOGY*) metagnathous condition **L19. metagnathous** /mɛˈtagnəθəs/ *adjective* (*ORNITHOLOGY*) having or designating a beak with crossed tips **L19. metalaw** *noun* a hypothetical legal code based on the principles underlying existing legal codes and designed to provide a framework of agreement between diverse legal systems **M20. metaˈlegal** *adjective* of or pertaining to (the principles of) metalaw **M20. metamessage** *noun* an ulterior or underlying message, an innuendo; *ADVERTISING* a statement that relies on implication rather than exhortation, a message conveyed in this way: **M20. metamict** *adjective* [Greek *miktos* mixed] (of a mineral) made amorphous through the radioactive decay of atoms contained in it **E20. metamictiˈzation** *noun* the process of becoming metamict; the state of being metamict: **M20. metamictness** *noun* metamict character **M20. metaneˈphridial** *adjective* (*ZOOLOGY*) of or pertaining to a metanephridium **M20. metaneˈphridium** *noun*, pl. **-dia**, *ZOOLOGY* a nephridium whose inner end opens into a coelom, as in many worms **M20. metaˈnotum** *noun* (*ENTOMOLOGY*) the dorsal part of the metathorax of an insect **M19. metaphone** *noun* (*LINGUISTICS*) each of two or more equally acceptable variants of a phoneme (e.g. the first vowel /ʌɪ/ or /iː/ of *either*) **M20. metaˈphonic** *adjective* (*PHILOLOGY*) affected by or involving metaphony **E20. meˈtaphonized** *adjective* (*PHILOLOGY*) affected by metaphony **L19. meˈtaphony** *noun* (*PHILOLOGY*) umlaut (the vowel change) **L19. metaˈpodial** *noun* (*ANATOMY & ZOOLOGY*) a metacarpal or metatarsal bone **L19. metaˈpodium** *noun* (*ZOOLOGY*) the posterior lobe of the foot of a mollusc **M19. metarhoˈdopsin** *noun* (*BIOCHEMISTRY*) either of two interconvertible intermediates (the orange ***metarhodopsin I*** and the yellow ***metarhodopsin II***) that are formed from lumirhodopsin when rhodopsin is bleached by light and undergo spontaneous hydrolysis to retinal and opsin **M20. metarule** *noun* a convention or universal rule in a symbolic system, esp. a linguistic system **M20. metascience** *noun* the branch of philosophy that has science as its subject **M20. metascienˈtific** *adjective* of or pertaining to metascience **M20. metascienˈtifically** *adverb* in a metascientific manner **M20. metaˈsternal** *adjective* (*ENTOMOLOGY & ANATOMY*) of, pertaining to, or of the nature of a metasternum **E19. metaˈsternum** *noun*, pl. **-na**, **-nums** (**a**) *ENTOMOLOGY* the ventral piece of the metathorax of an insect; (**b**) *ANATOMY* = **XIPHISTERNUM**: **E19. meta-talk** *noun* talk in which there are hidden meanings **M20. methaˈthoracic** *adjective* (*ENTOMOLOGY*) of, pertaining to, or of the nature of a metathorax **M19. metaˈthorax** *noun* (*ENTOMOLOGY*) the third, posterior segment of the thorax of an insect **E19. metavolˈcanic** *noun & adjective* (*GEOLOGY*) (designating) a volcanic rock that has been subjected to metamorphosis **M20. metaxylem** /mɛtəˈzʌɪləm/ *noun* (*BOTANY*) the later-formed part of the primary xylem, maturing after elongation of the plant tissue is complete **L19.**

metabiosis /mɛtəbʌɪˈəʊsɪs/ *noun.* **L19.**
[**ORIGIN** from **METABOLIC** after *symbiosis*, *symbiotic*.]
BIOLOGY. A form of ecological dependence in which one organism must modify the environment before the second is able to live in it.
■ **metabiotic** /-ˈɒtɪk/ *adjective* of, pertaining to, or of the nature of metabiosis **L19.**

metabolic /mɛtəˈbɒlɪk/ *adjective.* **M18.**
[**ORIGIN** Greek *metabolikos* changeable, formed as **METABOLISM**: see **-IC**.]
1 Pertaining to or involving transition. *rare.* **M18.**
2 *BIOLOGY & BIOCHEMISTRY.* Pertaining to, involving, or produced by metabolism. **M19.**
metabolic pathway any sequence of chemical, usu. enzyme-catalysed reactions undergone by a compound within a living cell or organism.
3 *BIOLOGY.* Pertaining to, of the nature of, or exhibiting metaboly. **E20.**
■ **metabolically** *adverb* as regards or by means of metabolism **E20.**

metabolise *verb* var. of **METABOLIZE**.

metabolism /mɛˈtabəlɪz(ə)m/ *noun.* **L19.**
[**ORIGIN** from Greek *metabolē* change, from *metaballein* to change, formed as **META-** + *ballein* throw + **-ISM**.]
BIOLOGY & BIOCHEMISTRY. The sum of the chemical processes, in a cell or organism, by which complex substances are synthesized and broken down, and growth and energy production sustained; anabolism and catabolism considered together; the overall rate at which these processes occur; the sum of the chemical changes undergone in the body by any particular substance.
basal metabolism: see **BASAL** *adjective* 1.
■ **metabolite** *noun* any substance produced during or necessary to metabolism **L19.**

metabolize /mɛˈtabəlʌɪz/ *verb.* Also **-ise**. **M19.**
[**ORIGIN** from Greek *metabolē* change (see **METABOLISM**) + **-IZE**.]
†**1** *verb trans.* Change or edit (a text). Only in **M19.**
2 *BIOLOGY & BIOCHEMISTRY.* **a** *verb trans.* Cause (a substance) to undergo metabolism; process by metabolism. **L19.** ▸**b** *verb intrans.* Perform or undergo metabolism. **L19.**
■ **metabolizaˈbility** *noun* ability to be metabolized **E20. metabolizable** *adjective* (**a**) (of a substance) able to be processed in metabolism; (**b**) (of energy) that can be made available or produced by metabolic processes: **E20. metabolizer** *noun* **L20.**

metaboly /mɛˈtabəli/ *noun.* **L19.**
[**ORIGIN** from Greek *metabolē* change (see **METABOLISM**) + **-Y**[3].]
BIOLOGY. The changes of shape characteristic of protists with a firm but flexible pellicle; euglenoid movement.

†**metacarp** *noun* see **METACARPUS**.

metacarpal /mɛtəˈkɑːp(ə)l/ *adjective & noun.* **M18.**
[**ORIGIN** from **METACARPUS** + **-AL**[1].]
ANATOMY. ▸**A** *adjective.* Of or pertaining to the metacarpus. **M18.**
▸ **B** *noun.* A metacarpal bone. **M19.**

metacarpi *noun* pl. of **METACARPUS**.

metacarpo- /mɛtəˈkɑːpəʊ/ *combining form* of next: see **-O-**.
■ **metacarpophalanˈgeal** *adjective* (*ANATOMY*) of, pertaining to, or (esp.) connecting the metacarpus and the phalanges **M19.**

metacarpus /mɛtəˈkɑːpəs/ *noun.* Pl. **-pi** /-pʌɪ, -piː/. Formerly also anglicized as †**metacarp**. **LME.**
[**ORIGIN** mod. Latin, alt. of Greek *metakarpion* after **CARPUS**: see **META-**.]
ANATOMY & ZOOLOGY. The part of the skeleton between the carpus or wrist and the phalanges, consisting of e.g. the five long bones of the hand in humans, and the cannon bone of the foreleg in horses and other quadrupeds.

metacentre /ˈmɛtəsɛntə/ *noun.* Also ***-center**. **M18.**
[**ORIGIN** French *métacentre*, formed as **META-** + **CENTRE** *noun*.]
The point of intersection between an imaginary line drawn vertically through the centre of buoyancy of a floating vessel when it is upright and a corresponding line through the new centre of buoyancy when the vessel is tilted. Also called ***shifting centre***.

metacentric /mɛtəˈsɛntrɪk/ *adjective & noun.* **L18.**
[**ORIGIN** formed as **METACENTRE** + **-IC**.]
▸ **A** *adjective.* **1** *PHYSICS & SHIPBUILDING.* Of or pertaining to the metacentre of a ship etc. **L18.**

metacentric height the height of the metacentre of a floating body above the centre of gravity.
2 *CYTOLOGY.* Of a chromosome: having the centromere at or near the centre. **M20.**
▸ **B** *noun.* A metacentric chromosome. **M20.**

metacercaria /mɛtəsəːˈkɛːrɪə/ *noun.* Pl. **-iae** /-ɪiː/. **E20.**
[**ORIGIN** from **META-** + **CERCARIA.**]
ZOOLOGY. A parasitic trematode in encysted form.

metacetone /mɛˈtasɪtəʊn/ *noun.* **M19.**
[**ORIGIN** from **MET(A-** + **ACETONE.**]
CHEMISTRY. A colourless flammable liquid ketone, $(C_2H_5)_2CO$, obtained by distillation of sugar in excess lime; pentan-3-one.

metachromasia /mɛtəkrəˈmeɪzɪə/ *noun.* **L19.**
[**ORIGIN** formed as **METACHROMATIC**: see **-CHROMASIA.**]
BIOLOGY. The property of certain biological materials of staining a different colour from that of the stain solution used; the property of certain stains of changing colour in the presence of certain biological materials.
■ Also **metachromasy** /-ˈkrəʊməsi/ *noun* **E20.**

metachromatic /mɛtəkrəˈmatɪk/ *adjective.* **L19.**
[**ORIGIN** from **META-** + Greek *khrōmat-*, *khrōma* colour + **-IC.**]
1 Of or pertaining to metachromatism. **L19.**
2 *BIOLOGY.* Of, pertaining to, exhibiting, or involving metachromasia. Cf. **ORTHOCHROMATIC** 2. **L19.**
■ **metachromatically** *adverb* **E20.**

metachromatism /mɛtəˈkrəʊmətɪz(ə)m/ *noun.* **L19.**
[**ORIGIN** formed as **METACHROMATIC** + **-ISM.**]
1 Change or variation of colour. **L19.**
2 *BIOLOGY.* = **METACHROMASIA. L19.**

metachrome /ˈmɛtəkrəʊm/ *noun & adjective.* **L19.**
[**ORIGIN** from **META-** + Greek *khrōma* colour.]
CHEMISTRY. ▸**A** *noun.* A body or substance that changes colour. *rare.* **L19.**
▸ **B** *adjective.* (Of a mordant dye) able to be applied simultaneously with the mordant in the same bath; pertaining to or involving dyes of this kind. **E20.**

metachromism /mɛtəˈkrəʊmɪz(ə)m/ *noun. rare.* **L19.**
[**ORIGIN** formed as **METACHROME** + **-ISM.**]
CHEMISTRY. Change of colour.

metachronism /mɛˈtakrənɪz(ə)m/ *noun.* **E17.**
[**ORIGIN** medieval Latin *metachronismus*, from Greek *metakhron(i)os* happening later, formed as **META-** + *khronos* time: see **-ISM.**]
1 An error in chronology consisting in placing an event later than its real date (opp. **PROCHRONISM**). Cf. **PARACHRONISM.** Long *rare.* **E17.**
2 *BIOLOGY.* The coordination of the movement of cilia or similar parts into a progressive wave. **E20.**
■ **metachronal** /mɛˈtakrən(ə)l/ *adjective* (*BIOLOGY*) exhibiting or characteristic of metachronism **E20. metaˈchronally** *adverb* **E20.**

metacism /ˈmɛtəsɪz(ə)m/ *noun. rare.* **M17.**
[**ORIGIN** Late Latin *metacismus* from late Greek *mutakismos* fondness for the letter m, from *mu*, name of the letter: see **-ISM.**]
The placing of a word with final *m* before a word beginning with a vowel, regarded as a fault in Latin prose composition. Also, the pronouncing of a final *m* which ought to be elided before a following vowel.

metacyclic /mɛtəˈsʌɪklɪk, -ˈsɪk-/ *adjective & noun.* **L19.**
[**ORIGIN** from **META-** + **CYCLIC.**]
▸ **A** *adjective.* **1** *MATH.* Of or pertaining to the permutation of a set of elements in a cycle. **L19.**
2 *BIOLOGY & MEDICINE.* Designating the form that some trypanosomes assume in the intermediate (invertebrate) host, in which they are infective for the vertebrate host. **E20.**
▸ **B** *noun. BIOLOGY & MEDICINE.* A metacyclic trypanosome. **M20.**

metadyne /ˈmɛtədʌɪn/ *noun.* **M20.**
[**ORIGIN** from **META-** + Greek *dunamis* force, power.]
ELECTRICITY. A rotary direct-current generator in which the output voltage can be varied by a control field perpendicular to the main field, used in position or speed control systems.

metae *noun* pl. of **META** *noun*[1].

metage /ˈmiːtɪdʒ/ *noun.* **E16.**
[**ORIGIN** from **METE** *verb* + **-AGE.**]
The action of measuring officially the content or weight of a load of grain, coal, etc.; the duty paid for such measuring (cf. **MEASURAGE**).

metagenesis /mɛtəˈdʒɛnɪsɪs/ *noun.* **M19.**
[**ORIGIN** from **META-** + **-GENESIS.**]
BIOLOGY. Alternation between sexual and asexual reproduction; alternation of generations.
■ **metageˈnetic** *adjective* pertaining to, characterized by, or involving metagenesis **M19. metageˈnetically** *adverb* **M19.**

metagnomy /mɛˈtagnəmi/ *noun.* **E20.**
[**ORIGIN** French *métagnomie*, formed as **META-** + Greek *gnōmē* thought.]
The supposed acquisition of information by supernormal means; divination, clairvoyance. Also, the power of acquiring information in this way.
■ **ˈmetagnome** *noun* a person having the power of metagnomy, a medium **M20. metagˈnomic** *adjective* of or pertaining to metagnomy **E20.**

metagram /ˈmɛtəgram/ *noun.* **E19.**
[**ORIGIN** from Greek **META-** + **-GRAM**, after *anagram*.]
A kind of puzzle in which a word is changed by replacing some of its letters.

metagrobolize /mɛtəˈgrɒbəlʌɪz/ *verb trans. joc.* Now *rare.* Also **-ise. M17.**
[**ORIGIN** French †*metagraboulizer*.]
Puzzle, mystify; puzzle out.

métairie /meteri/ *noun.* Pl. pronounced same. **L18.**
[**ORIGIN** French, formed as **MÉTAYER.**]
A farm held on the *métayage* system.

metake /ˈmɛtəkeɪ/ *noun.* **L19.**
[**ORIGIN** Japanese *medake*, from *me-* female + *take* bamboo.]
A tall slender Japanese bamboo, *Pseudosasa japonica*. Also called ***arrow bamboo***.

metakinesis /mɛtəkʌɪˈniːsɪs, -kɪ-/ *noun.* Pl. **-neses** /-ˈniːsiːz/. **L19.**
[**ORIGIN** from **META-** + **KINESIS.**]
1 *CYTOLOGY.* **a** The separation of chromatids during anaphase. **L19.** ▸**b** The process of alignment of chromosomes on the equator of the spindle. **M20.**
2 A manifestation of consciousness or mental phenomena. *rare.* **L19.**
■ **metakinetic** /-kɪˈnɛtɪk/ *adjective* **L19.**

metal /ˈmɛt(ə)l/ *noun & adjective.* Also †**mettle**. See also **METTLE. ME.**
[**ORIGIN** Old French & mod. French *métal*, †*metail* or its source Latin *metallum* mine, quarry, metal from synon. Greek *metallon*.]
▸ **A** *noun* **I 1** Any of the class of substances including the elements gold, silver, copper, iron, lead, and tin, and certain alloys (as brass and bronze), characteristically lustrous, ductile, fusible, malleable solids that are good conductors of heat and electricity; *CHEMISTRY* an element that readily forms positive ions. **ME.** ▸**b** Material of this nature; *spec.* (**a**) as that of arms and armour; (**b**) cast iron. **ME.** ▸†**c** Precious metal, gold. *rare* (Shakes.). **L16–E17.**

> ADAM SMITH The durableness of metals is the foundation of this steadiness of price. **b** SHAKES. *John* That I must draw this metal from my side To be a widow-maker! RACHEL ANDERSON We heard the metal click as the latch on the big gate was lifted. M. BRETT A contract for delivery of a ton of metal.

base metal: see **BASE** *adjective*. ***precious metal***: see **PRECIOUS** *adjective*. **b *Britannia metal***, ***gunmetal***, ***Wood's metal***, etc.
2 Ore. **ME.**
3 †**a** An object made of metal; *spec.* (**a**) a medal, a coin; (**b**) a metal reflector of a telescope. **LME–L18.** ▸**b** In *pl.* The rails of a railway or tramway. **M19.**

> **b** N. WOOLER Oil gas . . remained in use right up until the 1960s, particularly on London Midland metals.

4 *HERALDRY.* Either of the tinctures or and argent. **LME.**
5 Material, matter, substance; *esp.* earthy matter. **M16.**
6 Molten glass before it is blown or cast. **L16.**
7 The metal composing the barrel of a gun; (also ***line of metal***) a gunner's line of sight (chiefly in ***under metal***, ***over metal***); the guns or firepower of a warship etc. (chiefly in ***weight of metal***). **L16.**
8 A specific alloy used in any particular craft or trade. Freq. with preceding adjective or noun. **E18.**
9 Hardened clay, shale; rock met with in the course of mining; in *pl.*, strata containing minerals. Chiefly *Scot.* **E18.**
10 Broken stone for use in making roads (also ***road metal***) or as ballast for railway lines. **L18.**
11 Heavy metal or similar rock music. **L20.**
▸ †**II** See **METTLE** *noun*.
▸ **B** *attrib.* or as *adjective*. Made or consisting of metal; metallic. **LME.**

> M. S. POWER She washed him in the big metal tub in front of the fire.

— **COMB. & SPECIAL COLLOCATIONS: metal age** a period when weapons and tools were commonly made of copper, bronze, or iron; **metal arc welding** arc welding in which the melting of a metal electrode provides the joining material; **metal detector** an instrument for detecting metallic objects under the ground from their magnetic effects above ground; ***metal fatigue***: see **FATIGUE** *noun* 2b; **Metalflake** (proprietary name for) a protective metallic paint, varnish, etc., containing coloured chips of laminated or metallized film; **metalmark** any butterfly of the predominantly S. American family Riodinidae, many members of which have brilliant metallic markings on the wings; **metal thread** = *METALLIC thread*; **metalware** utensils or other articles made of metal; **metalwork** (**a**) work, esp. artistic work, in metal; the art of working in metal; (**b**) in *pl.*, a factory where metal is produced; **metalworker** a worker in metal, a craftsman or -woman who works in metal.

metal /mɛt(ə)l/ *verb trans.* Infl. **-ll-**, ***-l-**. **L16.**
[**ORIGIN** from the noun.]
†**1** In *pass.* Be made of a specified substance or in a specified way. **L16–E17.**
2 Provide or fit with metal. **E17.**
3 Make or mend (a road) with road metal. **E19.**

metalanguage /ˈmɛtəlaŋgwɪdʒ/ *noun.* **M20.**
[**ORIGIN** from **META-** + **LANGUAGE** *noun*[1].]
A language used for the description or analysis of another language; a system of propositions about other propositions.

metalation /mɛtəˈleɪʃ(ə)n/ *noun.* **M20.**
[**ORIGIN** from **METAL** *noun* + **-ATION.**]
CHEMISTRY. The introduction into an organic compound of a metal atom in place of a hydrogen atom.
■ **ˈmetalate** *verb trans.* bring about metalation in **M20.**

metalaxyl /mɛtəˈlaksɪl/ *noun.* **L20.**
[**ORIGIN** from **META-** + **A)LA(NINE** + **XYL(ENE.**]
A fungicide that is effective against mildew on some crops.

metaldehyde /mɪˈtaldɪhʌɪd/ *noun.* **M19.**
[**ORIGIN** from **META-** + **ALDEHYDE.**]
CHEMISTRY. A solid that is a low polymer of acetaldehyde and is used to kill slugs and snails and as a fuel for cooking and heating. Cf. **META** *noun*[2].

metaled *adjective* see **METALLED.**

metalepsis /mɛtəˈlɛpsɪs/ *noun.* **M16.**
[**ORIGIN** Latin from Greek *metalēpsis*, from *metalambanein* to substitute, formed as **META-** + *lambanein* take.]
A rhetorical figure consisting in the metonymical substitution of one word for another which is itself figurative.
■ **metaleptic** *adjective* **M17.**

metalik /mɛˈtalɪk/ *noun.* **L19.**
[**ORIGIN** Turkish, prob. from mod. Greek *metallikos* **METALLIC.**]
hist. A former Turkish coin worth 10 paras.

metalimnion /mɛtəˈlɪmnɪən/ *noun.* Pl. **-nia** /-nɪə/. **M20.**
[**ORIGIN** from **META-** + Greek *limnion* dim. of *limnē* lake.]
The layer of water in a stratified lake beneath the epilimnion and above the hypolimnion, in which the temperature decreases rapidly with depth.
■ **metalimnetic** /-lɪmˈnɛtɪk/ *adjective* of or within a metalimnion **M20.**

metaling *noun* see **METALLING.**

metalingual /mɛtəˈlɪŋgw(ə)l/ *adjective.* **M20.**
[**ORIGIN** from **META-** + **LINGUAL.**]
= **METALINGUISTIC.**

metalinguistic /mɛtəlɪŋˈgwɪstɪk/ *adjective.* **M20.**
[**ORIGIN** from **META-** + **LINGUISTIC.**]
Of or pertaining to a metalanguage or metalinguistics.
■ **metaˈlinguist** *noun* **M20. metalinguistically** *adverb* from the point of view of metalinguistics **M20. metalinguistics** *noun* (**a**) the branch of linguistics that deals with metalanguages; (**b**) *rare* the branch of linguistics that deals with the relation of language to the other elements of a culture: **M20.**

metalist *noun* see **METALLIST.**

metalize *verb* see **METALLIZE.**

metalled /ˈmɛt(ə)ld/ *adjective.* Also ***metaled. L16.**
[**ORIGIN** from **METAL** *noun, verb*: see **-ED**[2], **-ED**[1].]
1 †**a** Made or consisting of metal; containing metal. **L16–M17.** ▸**b** Having a covering or fittings of metal. **E19.**
2 Of a road: made with road metal; having a specially made hard surface. **E19.**

†**metalleity** *noun.* **M18–M19.**
[**ORIGIN** French *métalléité*, from Latin *metalleus* of the nature of metal, from *metallum* **METAL** *noun*: see **-ITY.**]
The quality of being metallic; metallic qualities collectively.

metallic /mɪˈtalɪk/ *adjective & noun.* **LME.**
[**ORIGIN** Latin *metallicus* from Greek *metallikos*, from *metallon* **METAL** *noun*: see **-IC.**]
▸ **A** *adjective.* **1** Pertaining to, consisting of, or containing a metal or metals; of the nature of or resembling a metal. **LME.** ▸**b** Involving or consisting of coin as distinguished from paper money. **L18.**

> *Scientific American* Metallurgists were able to make a number of accurate predictions about metallic behaviour. Z. TOMIN A large metallic sign rattled incessantly on a swaying post.

†**2** Connected with mining or metallurgy. **M17–M19.**
3 Yielding metal, metalliferous. **L17.**

> R. KIRWAN Metallic veins are never found in beds of lava.

4 Having the form or outward characters of a metal; (of a metal) uncombined with other substances. **M18.**

> R. RAYMOND The ore is . . free from base metals, and carries metallic silver. F. HOYLE At high temperatures, iron condenses in its metallic form.

5 a Resembling a metal in appearance; *esp.* having or designating the peculiar sheen characteristic of metals; iridescent, glossy. **L18.** ▸**b** Of taste: suggestive of metal. **E19.** ▸**c** Of sound: resembling that produced by metal when struck; (esp. of the voice or a cry) harsh and unmusical. **M19.**

> **a** I. MURDOCH Her reddish brown hair, to which a . . scattering of grey gave a metallic patina. *Practical Motorist* The En Vogue has metallic blue paintwork.

— **SPECIAL COLLOCATIONS: metallic arc welding** = ***metal arc welding*** s.v. **METAL** *noun*. **metallic bond** *CHEMISTRY* the kind of bond that exists between the atoms in a metal, with electrons delocalized throughout the crystal lattice rather than shared. **metallic circuit** a telegraphic circuit in which the return is through a wire rather than the earth. **metallic soap** any of a class of soaps (containing an alkaline earth or heavy metal instead of an alkali metal) which are soluble in organic solvents but not in water and are used in waterproofing and in making antioxidants, lubricants, and fungicides. **metallic thread**: made from metal or a

M

synthetic material resembling metal. ***metallic tractors***: see TRACTOR 1. **metallic yarn** = ***metallic thread*** above.

▸ **B** *noun*. **1** An article or substance made of or containing metal. Usu. in *pl.* M16.

2 A metallic paint or colour. L20.

■ **metallically** *adverb* by means of a metal or metals; in the manner of a metal or metals: M19. **metallicity** /mɛtəˈlɪsɪti/ *noun* (***a***) the quality of being metallic; (***b***) *ASTRONOMY* the proportion of the material of a star that is an element other than hydrogen or helium: M19.

metallide /ˈmɛt(ə)lʌɪd/ *verb trans.* M20.
[ORIGIN from METAL *noun* & *adjective* + -IDE.]
Deposit as an electroplated metal coating by a method involving immersion in a bath of molten fluoride salts, so that the metal forms a surface layer whose composition varies from the surface inwards. Chiefly as ***metalliding*** *verbal noun*.

metalliferous /mɛtəˈlɪf(ə)rəs/ *adjective*. M17.
[ORIGIN from Latin *metallifer*, from *metallum* METAL *noun*: see -FEROUS.]
Containing or yielding metal.

metalline /ˈmɛtəlʌɪn/ *adjective*. LME.
[ORIGIN Old French *metalin* (mod. *métallin*), from *métal*: see METAL *noun*, -INE[1].]
1 = METALLIC *adjective* 1. LME.
2 Made of metal. L16.
3 Resembling metal in appearance, lustre, etc. L16.
4 Impregnated with metallic substances; (of vapour) arising from or produced by metal. E17.
5 Metalliferous. E17.

metalling /ˈmɛt(ə)lɪŋ/ *noun*. Also ***metaling**. E19.
[ORIGIN from METAL *verb* + -ING[1].]
1 Road metal. E19.
2 The action of METAL *verb*. L19.

metallise *verb* var. of METALLIZE.

metallist /ˈmɛt(ə)lɪst/ *noun*. Also ***metalist**. E17.
[ORIGIN from METAL *noun* + -IST.]
†**1** A metallurgist. E17–M18.
2 An advocate of the use of a particular metal as currency or of metal as the principal or sole currency. *hist.* L19.

metallize /ˈmɛt(ə)lʌɪz/ *verb trans.* Also **-ise**, ***metalize**. L16.
[ORIGIN from METAL *noun* + -IZE.]
1 Make metallic; give a metallic form or appearance to. L16.
2 Coat or cover with metal. E20.
■ **metalliˈzation** *noun* M17. **metallizer** *noun* a machine or plant for metallizing something; a person or organization involved in metallizing something: M20.

metallo- /mɪˈtaləʊ, ˈmɛt(ə)ləʊ/ *combining form* of Greek *metallon* METAL *noun*: see -O-.
■ **metalloˈcarborane** *noun* (*CHEMISTRY*) a compound consisting of metal ions complexed with ligands containing carbon, boron, and hydrogen M20. **meˈtallocene** *noun* (*CHEMISTRY*) any of a group of organometallic compounds, freq. with a sandwich structure, typified by ferrocene M20. **ˈmetallochrome** *noun* a prismatic tinting imparted to polished steel plates by depositing a film of lead oxide on them M19. **meˈtallochromy** *noun* the application of metallochromes for decorative purposes M19. **meˈtalloenzyme** *noun* (*BIOCHEMISTRY*) an enzyme which is a metalloprotein M20. **metalloˈgenesis** *noun* = METALLOGENY E20. **metallogeˈnetic** *adjective* of or pertaining to metallogeny E20. **metallogeˈnetically** *adverb* as regards metallogeny E20. ˌ**metalloˈgenic** *adjective* (***a***) (of an element) occurring in ores or as the native metal, rather than in rocks; (***b***) = METALLOGENETIC: E20. **metaˈllogeny** *noun* the origin of mineral deposits, esp. as related to petrographic and tectonic features; the branch of geology that deals with this: E20. ˌ**metallo-orˈganic** *adjective* (*CHEMISTRY*) = ORGANOMETALLIC *adjective* L19. **meˈtallophone** *noun* a musical instrument in which the sound is produced by striking metal bars of varying pitches L19. **metalloprotein** *noun* (*BIOCHEMISTRY*) a protein whose molecule contains a metal atom M20. **metallothionein** /mɪˌtaləʊˈθʌɪəniːn/ *noun* (*BIOCHEMISTRY*) any of a group of proteins in some organisms which bind toxic heavy metals such as cadmium and mercury and so provide protection against these metals M20.

metallography /mɛtəˈlɒɡrəfi/ *noun*. L17.
[ORIGIN from METALLO- + -GRAPHY. Cf. French *métallographie*.]
†**1** A treatise or description of metals. L17–M19.
2 The branch of science that deals with the structure of metals, esp. on a microscopic scale; the metallographic features of something. L19.
■ **metallographer** *noun* E20. **metalloˈgraphic** *adjective* (***a***) of or pertaining to metallography; (***b***) of or pertaining to the description of coins: M19. **metalloˈgraphical** *adjective* = METALLOGRAPHIC (a) E20. **metalloˈgraphically** *adverb* M20.

metalloid /ˈmɛt(ə)lɔɪd/ *noun* & *adjective*. E19.
[ORIGIN from METAL *noun* + -OID.]
CHEMISTRY. ▸**A** *noun*. Orig., (***a***) a solid non-metallic element; (***b***) an alkali metal or an alkaline earth metal. Now, an element intermediate in its properties between a typical metal and a typical non-metal (e.g. boron, silicon, germanium). E19.
▸ **B** *attrib.* or as *adjective*. Of, pertaining to, or of the nature of a metalloid. M19.
■ **metaˈlloidal** *adjective* E19.

metallurgical /mɛtəˈləːdʒɪk(ə)l/ *adjective*. L18.
[ORIGIN from METALLURGY + -ICAL.]
Of or pertaining to metallurgy; concerned with metallurgy.
■ **metallurgic** *adjective* = METALLURGICAL M18. **metallurgically** *adverb* M19.

metallurgy /mɪˈtalədʒi, ˈmɛt(ə)ləːdʒi/ *noun*. M17.
[ORIGIN from Greek *metallon* METAL *noun* + *-ourgia* work, working (as in *kheirourgia* SURGERY).]
The art of working metals, comprising the separation of them from other substances in the ore, smelting, and refining; *spec.* the process of extracting metals from their ores. Also, the branch of science that deals with the structure, properties, and behaviour of metals.
■ **metallurgist** *noun* an expert in or student of metallurgy; a worker in metal: L17.

metally /ˈmɛt(ə)li/ *adjective*. LME.
[ORIGIN from METAL *noun* & *adjective* + -Y[1].]
1 Metallic, metalline. *obsolete* exc. *poet.* LME.
2 Mixed with shale. *dial.* L19.

metalogic /mɛtəˈlɒdʒɪk/ *noun*. M19.
[ORIGIN from META- + LOGIC.]
1 The part of metaphysics which relates to the foundations of logic. Now *rare*. M19.
2 The field of study that deals with the processes and structures of logic. M20.
■ **metalogical** *adjective* (***a***) of or pertaining to metalogic; (***b***) that is outside the province of logic: M19. **metalogically** *adverb* in terms of or by means of metalogic M20. **metalogician** /-ˈdʒɪʃ(ə)n/ *noun* an expert in or student of metalogic E20.

metamathematics /ˌmɛtəmaθ(ə)ˈmatɪks/ *noun*. L19.
[ORIGIN from META- + MATHEMATICS.]
The field of study that deals with the structure and formal properties of mathematics and similar formal systems.
■ **metamathematical** *adjective* (***a***) of or pertaining to metamathematics; (***b***) *rare* that is outside the province of mathematics: M19. **metamathematically** *adverb* by means of metamathematics; from the point of view of metamathematics: M20. ˌ**metamatheˈmatician** /-ˈtɪʃ(ə)n/ *noun* an expert in or student of metamathematics M20.

metamer /ˈmɛtəmə/ *noun*. L19.
[ORIGIN Back-form. from METAMERIC.]
CHEMISTRY. A compound which exhibits metamerism; a compound metameric with another.
■ Also **meˈtameride** *noun* (now *rare* or *obsolete*) M19.

metamere /ˈmɛtəmɪə/ *noun*. L19.
[ORIGIN from META- + Greek *meros* part.]
ZOOLOGY. A body segment of a metameric organism; = SOMITE.

metameric /mɛtəˈmɛrɪk/ *adjective*. M19.
[ORIGIN formed as METAMERE + -IC.]
1 *CHEMISTRY*. Characterized by metamerism. M19.
2 *ZOOLOGY*. (Of an organism) having a body consisting of several similar segments or metameres; of, pertaining to, or characterized by metamerism. L19.
■ **metamerically** *adverb* with metameric segmentation L19.

metamerism /mɪˈtamərɪz(ə)m/ *noun*. M19.
[ORIGIN formed as METAMERE + -ISM.]
1 *CHEMISTRY*. Orig., the relationship of two or more compounds that have the same molecular formula but different properties (i.e. isomerism). Later, the relationship between organic compounds that have similar molecular structures and differ only in the alkyl groups or other substituents they contain. M19.
2 *ZOOLOGY*. The condition of consisting of several similar segments or metameres; metameric segmentation; an instance of this. L19.

metamerous /mɪˈtam(ə)rəs/ *adjective*. L19.
[ORIGIN from METAMERE + -OUS.]
ZOOLOGY. = METAMERIC 2.

meta-metalanguage /mɛtəˈmɛtəlaŋɡwɪdʒ/ *noun*. M20.
[ORIGIN from META- + METALANGUAGE.]
A language used in the description of another language which is itself a metalanguage; the universal linguistic or symbolic system from which a particular metalanguage derives.

metamorphic /mɛtəˈmɔːfɪk/ *adjective* & *noun*. E19.
[ORIGIN from META- + Greek *morphē* a form + -IC, after METAMORPHOSIS.]
▸ **A** *adjective*. **1** Characterized by or exhibiting metamorphosis. E19.
2 *GEOLOGY*. Pertaining to, characterized by, or formed by metamorphism; (of rock) that has undergone transformation by means of heat, pressure, or other natural agencies. M19.
3 That causes metamorphism or metamorphosis. M19.

> *Scientific American* Metamorphic water plays a major role in the genesis of ores.

▸ **B** *noun*. A metamorphic rock. Usu. in *pl.* L19.

metamorphise *verb* var. of METAMORPHIZE.

metamorphism /mɛtəˈmɔːfɪz(ə)m/ *noun*. M19.
[ORIGIN formed as METAMORPHIC + -ISM.]
GEOLOGY. Alteration of the composition or structure of a rock by heat, pressure, or other natural agencies.
dynamic metamorphism: see DYNAMIC *adjective*. ***progressive metamorphism***: see PROGRESSIVE *adjective*. ***regional metamorphism***: see REGIONAL *adjective*.

metamorphize /mɛtəˈmɔːfʌɪz/ *verb trans.* Also **-ise**. L16.
[ORIGIN formed as METAMORPHIC + -IZE.]
= METAMORPHOSE *verb* 1, 2, 3.

metamorphopsia /mɛtəmɔːˈfɒpsɪə/ *noun*. E19.
[ORIGIN from METAMORPH(OSIS + Greek *-opsia* seeing, from *opsis* sight: see -IA[1].]
OPHTHALMOLOGY. A defect of vision characterized by distortion of things seen.

†**metamorphose** *noun*. E17–L19.
[ORIGIN Anglicization.]
= METAMORPHOSIS.

metamorphose /mɛtəˈmɔːfəʊz/ *verb*. L16.
[ORIGIN French *métamorphoser*, from *métamorphose* (noun) formed as METAMORPHOSIS.]
1 *verb trans.* Change *into* or *to* something else by supernatural means. L16.

> GEO. ELIOT Perhaps they metamorphose themselves into a tawny squirrel.

2 *verb trans.* Change the form or character of; alter the nature or disposition of; transform. Foll. by *into*, *to*. L16.

> T. HARDY The waves rolled in furiously . . and were metamorphosed into foam.

3 *verb trans.* Subject to metamorphosis or metamorphism. M17.

> A. H. GREEN The rocks . . are highly metamorphosed Lower Silurian beds.

4 *verb intrans.* Undergo metamorphosis or metamorphism; change. (Foll. by *into*.) E19.

> P. NORMAN Photographs of the grown up men into whom these two . . little boys have metamorphosed. J. MAY The monster scorpion metamorphosed into a handsome young ogre. S. RUSHDIE She sees the Parsee ayah metamorphosing, becoming liquid, flowing outwards until she fills the room.

■ **metamorphoser** *noun* L16.

metamorphosis /mɛtəˈmɔːfəsɪs, mɛtəmɔːˈfəʊsɪs/ *noun*. Pl. **-phoses** /-fəsiːz, -ˈfəʊsiːz/. LME.
[ORIGIN Latin from Greek *metamorphōsis*, from *metamorphoun* transform, formed as META- + *morphē* a form: see -OSIS.]
1 The action or process of changing in form, shape, or substance; *esp.* transformation by supernatural means. LME. ▸†**b** A metamorphosed form. L16–M19.
2 A complete change in appearance, circumstances, condition, or character. M16.

> *Independent* The seaside town of Blackpool announced bold plans for its metamorphosis yesterday.

3 *BIOLOGY*. Normal change of form of a living organism, part, or tissue; *spec.* the transformation that some animals undergo in the course of becoming adult (e.g. from tadpole to frog, or pupa to adult insect), in which there is a complete alteration of form and habit. M17. ▸**b** *CHEMISTRY*. The change of a compound to a new form, esp. by catalytic action. Now *rare*. M19.
■ **metamorphosic** *adjective* L18.

metamorphosize /mɛtəˈmɔːfəsʌɪz/ *verb trans.* & *intrans.* Also **-ise**. L19.
[ORIGIN from METAMORPHOSIS + -IZE.]
= METAMORPHOSE *verb*.

†**metamorphostical** *adjective*. *rare*. E18–L19.
[ORIGIN formed as METAMORPHOSIZE after Greek words in *-ostikos*: see -ICAL.]
Of or pertaining to metamorphosis.

metamorphotic /mɛtəmɔːˈfɒtɪk/ *adjective*. E19.
[ORIGIN formed as METAMORPHOSIZE + -OTIC.]
Pertaining to or based on metamorphosis; causing metamorphosis.

metanalysis /mɛtəˈnalɪsɪs/ *noun*. E20.
[ORIGIN from META- + ANALYSIS.]
PHILOLOGY. Reinterpretation of the division between words or syntactic units (e.g. of *a naddre* as *an addre* in Middle English to give mod. *adder*).
■ **meˈtanalyse** *verb trans.* subject to or alter by metanalysis M20.

metanephros /mɛtəˈnɛfrɒs/ *noun*. Pl. **-nephroi** /-ˈnɛfrɔɪ/. Also (now *rare*) **-nephron** /-ˈnɛfrɒn/, pl. **-nephra** /-ˈnɛfrə/. L19.
[ORIGIN from META- + Greek *nephros* kidney.]
ZOOLOGY & ANATOMY. The third of the three segments of the embryonic kidney in vertebrates, which develops into the kidney and ureter in adult reptiles, birds, and mammals but disappears in lower animals. Cf. MESONEPHROS, PRONEPHROS.
■ **metanephric** *adjective* L19.

metanoia /mɛtəˈnɔɪə/ *noun*. L16.
[ORIGIN Greek, from *metanoein* change one's mind, repent.]
Penitence; reorientation of one's way of life, spiritual conversion.

metaphase /ˈmɛtəfeɪz/ *noun*. L19.
[ORIGIN German, formed as META- + Greek PHASIS.]
BIOLOGY. The stage of mitotic or meiotic nuclear division when the chromosomes become attached to the spindle fibres; a dividing nucleus at this stage.

M

– COMB.: **metaphase plate** the equatorial plane of a spindle during metaphase, with the centromeres of the chromosomes on or near the plane.

metaphor /ˈmɛtəfə, -fɔː/ *noun*. L15.
[ORIGIN Old French & mod. French *métaphore* or Latin *metaphora* from Greek, from *metapherein* transfer, formed as META- + *pherein* to bear.]
1 A figure of speech in which a name or descriptive word or phrase is transferred to an object or action different from, but analogous to, that to which it is literally applicable; an instance of this, a metaphorical expression. L15.
R. A. KNOX It is a metaphor if you describe Oxford as a hive of industry.
MIXED *metaphor*.
2 A thing considered as representative of some other (usu. abstract) thing; a symbol. M19.
■ **metaphoric** /mɛtəˈfɒrɪk/ *adjective* = METAPHORICAL L16. **metaphorical** /mɛtəˈfɒrɪk(ə)l/ *adjective* characterized by the use of metaphor; of the nature of metaphor; used metaphorically; not literal, figurative: M16. **metaphorically** /mɛtəˈfɒrɪk(ə)li/ *adverb* in a metaphorical sense; by the use of metaphor: L16. **metaphorist** *noun* (*rare*) a person who uses metaphors E18. **metaphorize** *verb trans.* (*a*) change metaphorically *into*; (*b*) ply with metaphor: M17.

metaphosphoric /mɛtəfɒsˈfɒrɪk/ *adjective*. M19.
[ORIGIN from META- + PHOSPHORIC.]
CHEMISTRY. ***metaphosphoric acid***, a glassy deliquescent solid, $(HPO_3)_n$, obtained by heating orthophosphoric acid.
■ **metaˈphosphate** *noun* a salt of metaphosphoric acid M19.

metaphrase /ˈmɛtəfreɪz/ *noun & verb*. As noun also (earlier) in Latin form †-**phrasis**. M16.
[ORIGIN mod. Latin *metaphrasis* from Greek, from *metaphrazein* translate, formed as META- + *phrazein* tell.]
▸ **A** *noun*. †**1** A metrical translation. M16–M18.
2 (A) translation. Now *spec.* (a) word-for-word translation as opp. to (a) paraphrase. M17.
▸ **B** *verb trans.* †**1** Translate, esp. in verse. E–M17.
2 Alter the phrasing or language of; reword. M19.

metaphrast /ˈmɛtəfrast/ *noun*. E17.
[ORIGIN Greek *metaphrastēs*, *metaphrazein*, formed as METAPHRASE.]
A person who puts a composition into a different literary form, e.g. by turning prose into verse or one metre into another. Formerly also, a translator.
■ **metaˈphrastic** *adjective* [Greek *metaphrastikos*] of the nature of (a) metaphrase L18. **metaˈphrastically** *adverb* by way of a metaphrase L16.

metaphysic /mɛtəˈfɪzɪk/ *noun*[1] *sing*. LME.
[ORIGIN Old French & mod. French *métaphysique* from medieval Latin *metaphysica* fem. sing., for earlier neut. pl. repr. by METAPHYSICS.]
1 = METAPHYSICS 1. LME.
2 = METAPHYSICS 2. M19.

metaphysic /mɛtəˈfɪzɪk/ *adjective & noun*[2]. Now *rare*. E16.
[ORIGIN medieval Latin *metaphysicus* adjective, from *metaphysica* noun pl.: see METAPHYSICS.]
▸ **A** *adjective*. Metaphysical. E16.
▸ †**B** *noun*. A metaphysician. L16–E17.

metaphysical /mɛtəˈfɪzɪk(ə)l/ *adjective & noun*. LME.
[ORIGIN from METAPHYSIC *noun*[1] + -AL[1].]
▸ **A** *adjective* **1 a** Of, belonging to, or of the nature of metaphysics; such as is recognized by metaphysics. LME. ▸**b** Excessively subtle or abstract. Long *rare*. M17. ▸**c** Not empirically verifiable. M19.
a A. KOESTLER Traversed the frontier between metaphysical speculation and empirical science. D. ROWE As metaphysical . . as believing that death is a doorway to another life. **c** A. J. AYER The metaphysical thesis that philosophy affords us knowledge of a reality transcending the world of science.
a *metaphysical philosophy*: see PHILOSOPHY *noun* 2c.
2 a Abstract, incorporeal, supersensible; supernatural. L16. ▸**b** CHRISTIAN SCIENCE. That transcends matter or the physical. Esp. in ***metaphysical healing***. L19.
3 Fond of or suited to the study of metaphysics. E17.
4 Based on abstract general reasoning or a priori principles. M17.
SIR W. SCOTT Wars have been waged for points of metaphysical right.
5 Fanciful, imaginary. E18.
6 Of certain 17th-cent. poets: exhibiting subtlety of thought and complex imagery. Of poetry: typical of the metaphysical poets; expressing emotion within an intellectual context. M18.
▸ **B** *noun*. †**1** In *pl.* Metaphysics. Only in M16.
2 A metaphysical poet. Freq. in *pl.* L19.
■ **metaphysiˈcality** *noun* the quality of being metaphysical E20. **metaphysically** *adverb* (*a*) in a metaphysical manner or sense; according to the principles of metaphysics; from a metaphysical point of view; †(*b*) supernaturally; preternaturally: L16.

metaphysician /mɛtəfɪˈzɪʃ(ə)n/ *noun*. LME.
[ORIGIN Prob. from METAPHYSIC *noun*[1] after *physic*, *physician*. Cf. Old French *methafisicien*.]
An expert in or student of metaphysics.

metaphysicize /mɛtəˈfɪzɪsʌɪz/ *verb intrans*. Also **-ise**. L18.
[ORIGIN from METAPHYSICS + -IZE.]
Indulge in metaphysical speculation; think, talk, or write metaphysically.

metaphysico- /mɛtəˈfɪzɪkəʊ/ *combining form*. M18.
[ORIGIN from METAPHYSIC *adjective & noun*[2], METAPHYSIC(AL *adjective* + -O-.]
Metaphysical and —, as ***metaphysico-ethical***, ***metaphysico-theological***, etc.

metaphysics /mɛtəˈfɪzɪks/ *noun pl.* (treated as *sing.* or *pl.*). M16.
[ORIGIN Pl. of METAPHYSIC *noun*[1], repr. medieval Latin *metaphysica* neut. pl., medieval Greek (*ta*) *metaphusika* for earlier *ta meta ta phusika* 'the (works of Aristotle) after the Physics'.]
1 The branch of philosophy that deals with the first principles of things, including such concepts as being, substance, essence, time, space, cause, and identity; theoretical philosophy as the ultimate science of being and knowing. M16.
2 The theoretical principles or higher philosophical rationale of a particular branch of knowledge. M19.
3 The philosophy of mind. M19.
4 Abstract or subtle talk; mere theory. L20.

metaphysis /mɪˈtafɪsɪs/ *noun*. Pl. **-physes** /-fɪsiːz/. M18.
[ORIGIN mod. Latin, from Greek *metaphuesthai* become by change, formed as META- + *phu-* grow; in sense 2 after DIAPHYSIS, EPIPHYSIS.]
†**1** Transformation; metamorphosis. *rare*. Only in M18.
2 ANATOMY. The site of advancing ossification at one or both ends of a growing long bone, between the diaphysis and the epiphysial cartilage. E20.
■ **metaphyseal** /mɛtəˈfɪzɪəl, mɛtəfɪˈziːəl/ *adjective* E20. **metaphysial** /mɛtəˈfɪzɪəl, mɛtəfɪˈziːəl/ *adjective* E20.

metaplasia /mɛtəˈpleɪzɪə/ *noun*. L19.
[ORIGIN from Greek *metaplassein* mould into a new form, formed as META- + *plassein* to mould: see -PLASIA.]
BIOLOGY & MEDICINE. Transformation of one kind of differentiated adult tissue into another.
■ **metaplastic** /-ˈplastɪk/ *adjective* pertaining to or characterized by metaplasia L19.

metaplasm /ˈmɛtəplaz(ə)m/ *noun*. OE.
[ORIGIN In sense 1 from Latin *metaplasmus*, Greek *metaplasmos*, from *metaplassein*: see METAPLASIA. In sense 2 from META- + PROTO)PLASM.]
1 In RHETORIC, the transposition of words from their usual or natural order; in GRAMMAR, the alteration of a word by addition, removal, or transposition of letters or syllables. OE.
2 BIOLOGY. The non-living constituents of cytoplasm, such as pigment granules. L19.

metapolitical /mɛtəpəˈlɪtɪk(ə)l/ *adjective*. M17.
[ORIGIN from META- + POLITICAL.]
1 Lying outside the sphere of politics. M17.
2 Relating to metapolitics; given to the study of metapolitics. E19.

metapolitics /mɛtəˈpɒlɪtɪks/ *noun*. Also (*rare*) **-ic**. L18.
[ORIGIN from META- + POLITICS *noun* pl.]
Abstract political science; *derog.* unpractical political theorizing.
■ **metapolitician** /ˌmɛtəpɒlɪˈtɪʃ(ə)n/ *noun* a person who holds or advocates theories of metapolitics E19.

metapsychics /mɛtəˈsʌɪkɪks/ *noun*. E20.
[ORIGIN from META- + PSYCHIC *noun* + -S[1], after METAPHYSICS.]
The field of study that deals with phenomena beyond the scope of orthodox psychology.
■ **metapsychic**, **metapsychical** *adjectives* E20. **metapsychist** *noun* an expert in or student of metapsychics E20.

metapsychology /mɛtəsʌɪˈkɒlədʒi/ *noun*. M19.
[ORIGIN from META- + PSYCHOLOGY.]
Speculative inquiry regarding the ultimate nature of the mind and its functions which cannot be studied experimentally. Also, the field of study that deals with the theories and practice of psychology.
■ **ˌmetapsychoˈlogical** *adjective* E20.

metapsychosis /mɛtəsʌɪˈkəʊsɪs/ *noun*. *rare*. Pl. **-choses** /-ˈkəʊsiːz/. L19.
[ORIGIN from META- + PSYCHOSIS.]
The supposed psychic action of one mind on another.

metasequoia /mɛtəsɪˈkwɔɪə, -ˈkɔɪə/ *noun*. M20.
[ORIGIN mod. Latin, from META- + SEQUOIA.]
A Chinese deciduous coniferous tree, *Metasequoia glyptostroboides*, belonging to a genus known at first only from fossil remains. Also called ***dawn redwood***.

metasoma /mɛtəˈsəʊmə/ *noun*. L19.
[ORIGIN from META- + Greek *sōma* body.]
ZOOLOGY. **1** The hinder portion of the abdomen of an arachnid or other arthropod. L19.
2 The posterior portion of the body of a cephalopod, enveloped in the mantle. L19.

metasomatic /mɛtəsəˈmatɪk/ *adjective*. L19.
[ORIGIN from METASOMA & METASOMATISM + -IC.]
1 ZOOLOGY. Pertaining to the metasoma. L19.
2 GEOLOGY. Pertaining to or of the nature of metasomatism. L19.
■ **metasomatically** *adverb* E20.

metasomatism /mɛtəˈsəʊmətɪz(ə)m/ *noun*. L19.
[ORIGIN from META- + Greek *sōma(t-)* body + -ISM.]
GEOLOGY. Change in the composition of a rock as a result of the introduction or removal of chemical constituents.
■ **metasomatize** *verb trans.* change as a result of metasomatism M20.

metastable /mɛtəˈsteɪb(ə)l/ *adjective*. L19.
[ORIGIN from META- + STABLE *adjective*.]
PHYSICS etc. **1** (Of equilibrium) stable only under small disturbances and capable of changing to a more stable state; of, pertaining to, or existing in such equilibrium. L19.
2 Of an excited state of an atom, nucleus, etc.: having an exceptionally long lifetime; passing to another state so slowly as to appear stable. E20.
■ **metastaˈbility** *noun* E20. **metastably** *adverb* M20.

metastases *noun* pl. of METASTASIS.

Metastasian /mɛtəˈsteɪsɪən, -zɪən/ *adjective*. M20.
[ORIGIN from *Metastasio* (see below) + -AN.]
Of, pertaining to, or characteristic of the Italian poet and librettist Pietro Metastasio (1698–1782).

metastasis /mɪˈtastəsɪs/ *noun*. Pl. **-ases** /-əsiːz/. L16.
[ORIGIN Late Latin from Greek = removal, change, from *methistanai* remove, change.]
1 RHETORIC. A rapid transition from one point to another. Long *rare*. L16.
2 a MEDICINE. The transference of a bodily function, pain, or disease, or of diseased matter, from one site to another; *spec.* the occurrence or development of secondary foci of disease at a distance from the primary site, as in many cancers. M17. ▸**b** BIOLOGY. Metabolism. *rare*. L19.
3 *gen.* Transformation; change from one condition to another. *rare*. M19.
■ **metastasize** *verb intrans.* (of a disease, esp. a tumour) undergo metastasis, spread to other sites in the body E20. **metaˈstatic** *adjective* (MEDICINE) pertaining to, characterized by, or produced by metastasis E19.

metasyncrisis /mɛtəˈsɪŋkrɪsɪs/ *noun*. Now *rare*. M16.
[ORIGIN mod. Latin from Greek *metasugkrisis*, from *metasugkrinein* use diaphoretics, formed as META- + *sugkrinein* compare.]
MEDICINE. The evacuation of diseased matter, esp. through the pores of the skin.
■ **metasynˈcritic** *adjective* of the nature of, pertaining to, or producing metasyncrisis M19. **metasynˈcritical** *adjective* (long *rare* or obsolete) = METASYNCRITIC M17.

metatarsal /mɛtəˈtɑːs(ə)l/ *adjective & noun*. E18.
[ORIGIN from METATARSUS + -AL[1].]
ANATOMY. ▸**A** *adjective*. Of or pertaining to the metatarsus. E18.
▸ **B** *noun*. A metatarsal bone. M19.

metatarsi *noun* pl. of METATARSUS.

metatarso- /mɛtəˈtɑːsəʊ/ *combining form* of next: see -O-.
■ **metatarsophalanˈgeal** *adjective* (ANATOMY) of, pertaining to, or (esp.) connecting the metatarsus and the phalanges M19.

metatarsus /mɛtəˈtɑːsəs/ *noun*. Pl. **-tarsi** /-ˈtɑːsʌɪ, -siː/. LME.
[ORIGIN mod. Latin, formed as META- + TARSUS.]
1 ANATOMY & ZOOLOGY. The group of five long bones of the human foot (and of the hind foot of quadrupeds) between the tarsus and the phalanges or toes; the tarsometatarsus of a bird. LME.
2 ENTOMOLOGY. The basal joint of the tarsus, esp. when much developed. E19.
■ **ˌmetatarˈsalgia** *noun* (MEDICINE) pain in the metatarsus L19.

metate /məˈtɑːteɪ/ *noun*. E17.
[ORIGIN Mexican Spanish from Nahuatl *metatl*.]
In Central America, a flat or somewhat hollowed oblong stone on which grain, cocoa, etc., are ground by means of a smaller stone. Also ***metate-stone***.

metatherian /mɛtəˈθɪərɪən/ *adjective & noun*. L19.
[ORIGIN from mod. Latin *Metatheria* (see below), formed as META- + Greek *thēria* pl. of *thērion* wild animal: see -AN.]
▸ **A** *adjective*. Of, pertaining to, or designating the mammalian infraclass Metatheria, comprising the single order Marsupialia (the marsupials). L19.
▸ **B** *noun*. A metatherian mammal, a marsupial. L19.

metathesis /mɛˈtaθɪsɪs, mɪ-/ *noun*. Pl. **-theses** /-θɪsiːz/. M16.
[ORIGIN Late Latin from Greek, from *metatithenai* transpose, change, formed as META- + *tithenai* put, place.]
1 LINGUISTICS. The transposition of sounds or letters in a word; the result of such a transposition. Formerly also, the transposition of words. M16.
†**2** MEDICINE. Spread of a disease within the body, metastasis; movement of diseased matter to another part of the body. L17–M19.
3 *gen.* Change or reversal of condition. E18.
4 CHEMISTRY. (An) interchange of an atom or atoms between two different molecules; *esp.* double decomposition. L19.
■ **metathesize** *verb intrans. & trans.* (LINGUISTICS) undergo or subject to metathesis M20. **metathetic** /mɛtəˈθɛtɪk/, **metathetical** /-ˈθɛtɪk(ə)l/ *adjectives* characterized by or involving metathesis M19.

metatony /mɪˈtatəni/ *noun*. M20.
[ORIGIN French *métatonie*, formed as META- + Greek *tonos* sound, TONE *noun*: see -Y[3].]
PHILOLOGY. In Baltic and Slavonic languages, any of certain kinds of substitution of one distinctive intonation for

M

another in a given syllable; these substitutions collectively.
■ **meta'tonic** *adjective* M20.

Metatron /mɪˈtatrɒn/ *noun*. M19.
[ORIGIN Hebrew *mĕṭaṭrōn*, of uncertain origin.]
In Jewish mystical theology, a supreme angelic being, usually identified with either Michael or Enoch.

metatrophic /mɛtəˈtrəʊfɪk, -ˈtrɒf-/ *adjective*. L19.
[ORIGIN from META- + -TROPHIC.]
BIOLOGY. †**1** Designating a change in form or proportion of parts of an organism during its lifetime. Only in L19.
2 Of an organism: dependent on the presence of organic substances for nutrition. E20.

Metawileh /mɛˈtɑːwɪleɪ/ *noun*. L18.
[ORIGIN Arabic *matāwila* pl. of *mutawālī*.]
A sect of Shiite Muslims in Lebanon and Syria.

Metaxa /mɪˈtaksə/ *noun*. M20.
[ORIGIN Greek surname and company name.]
(Proprietary name for) a dark Greek brandy; a drink or glass of this brandy.

métayer /metɛje/ *noun*. Pl. pronounced same. L18.
[ORIGIN French from medieval Latin *medietarius*, from *medietas* half: see MOIETY.]
A farmer who holds land on the *métayage* system.
■ ***métayage*** /metɛjaːʒ/ (*pl. same*) *noun* a system of land tenure in western Europe and the US, in which the farmer pays a certain proportion (generally half) of the produce to the owner as rent, and the owner generally provides stock and seed L19.

metazoan /mɛtəˈzəʊən/ *noun & adjective*. L19.
[ORIGIN mod. Latin *Metazoa* (see below), from META- + Greek *zōia* pl. of *zōion* animal: see -AN.]
ZOOLOGY. ▶**A** *noun*. An animal of the group Metazoa (comprising all animals except protozoa and sponges), members of which have bodies composed of more than one cell and display differentiation of tissue. L19.
▶**B** *adjective*. Of, pertaining to, or designating this group of animals. L19.
■ **metazoic** *adjective* = METAZOAN *adjective* L19. **metazoon** *noun*, pl. **-zoa**, = METAZOAN *noun* (usu. in *pl.*) L19.

mete /miːt/ *noun*[1]. LME.
[ORIGIN Old French from Latin *meta*: see META *noun*[1].]
†**1** A goal, a destination. LME–L15.
M **2** A boundary, a limit, (material or abstract); a boundary stone or mark. Freq. (esp. LAW) in ***metes and bounds***. L15.

mete /miːt/ *noun*[2]. *arch.* M18.
[ORIGIN from METE *verb*.]
Size, quality, character, etc., as ascertainable by measuring; measure.

mete /miːt/ *verb*.
[ORIGIN Old English *metan* = Old Frisian *meta*, Old Saxon *metan*, Old High German *mezzan* (Dutch *meten*, German *messen*), Old Norse *meta*, Gothic *mitan*, from Germanic, from Indo-European base repr. also by Latin *meditari* MEDITATE, Greek *medesthai* care for.]
1 *verb trans.* Ascertain or determine the dimensions or quantity of, measure. Now *poet. & dial.* exc. in allus. to *Matthew* 7:2. Cf. MEASURE *verb* 3. OE. ▸†**b** Complete the full measure or amount of. Also foll. by *forth*, *out*. E17–L18.

> AV *Matt.* 7:2 With what measure ye mete, it shall be measured to you againe.

†**2** *verb trans.* Mark (*out*) the boundary or course of; = MEASURE *verb* 7. OE–E19.
3 *verb trans.* Estimate the greatness or value of. Cf. MEASURE *verb* 4. *arch.* OE.
†**4** *verb trans. & intrans.* Travel or go (a distance). Cf. MEASURE *verb* 5. OE–L17.
5 *verb trans.* Apportion by measure, allot; *esp.* allot (punishment, praise, reward, etc.). Usu. foll. by *out*. Now *literary*. OE.

> T. COLLINS I meted out half a pint of water to him. S. NAIPAUL Blakey described the punishments meted out to refractory children.

†**6** *verb intrans.* Take measurements; measure distances *for* shooting at a mark; aim *at*. LME–M17.

†**metecious** *adjective* see METOECIOUS.

metel /ˈmiːt(ə)l/ *noun*. Also †**methel**. E16.
[ORIGIN mod. Latin *methel*, from Arabic *jawz* (= nut) *māṯil*.]
†**1** ***metel nut***, ***nut metel***, a narcotic fruit covered with small spines, prob. that of the thorn apple, *Datura stramonium*. Only in 16.
2 (The fruit of) the hairy thorn apple, *Datura metel*. M18.

metempiric /mɛtɛmˈpɪrɪk/ *noun*. Now *rare* or *obsolete*. In sense 1 also **-ics**. L19.
[ORIGIN from META- 1 + EMPIRIC.]
1 The branch of philosophy that deals with things outside the sphere of knowledge derived from experience. L19.
2 A metempiricist. L19.
■ **metempirical** *adjective* pertaining to matters outside the sphere of knowledge derived from experience L19. **metempirically** *adverb* L19. **metempiricism** /-sɪz(ə)m/ *noun* L19. **metempiricist** /-sɪst/ *noun* L19.

metempsychosis /ˌmɛtɛmsʌɪˈkəʊsɪs/ *noun*. Pl. **-choses** /-ˈkəʊsiːz/. L16.
[ORIGIN Late Latin, from Greek *metempsukhōsis*, formed as META- + *en* in + *psukhē* soul: see -OSIS.]
Transmigration of the soul; *esp.* the passage of the soul of a person or animal at or after death into a new body of the same or a different species (a tenet of the Pythagoreans and certain Eastern religions).
■ **metempsychose** *noun & verb* †(*a*) *noun* [French *métempsycose*] = METEMPSYCHOSIS; (*b*) *verb trans.* transfer (a soul) from one body to another: L16. **metempsychosic** *adjective* E20. †**metempsychosical** *adjective*: only in E17. **metempsychosist** *noun* a person who believes in metempsychosis M19.

metencephalon /mɛtɛnˈsɛfəlɒn, -ˈkɛf-/ *noun*. M19.
[ORIGIN from META- + ENCEPHALON.]
ANATOMY. The part of the hindbrain comprising the cerebellum and the pons, between the myelencephalon and the mesencephalon; the part of the embryonic brain that develops into this.
■ ˌ**metence'phalic** *adjective* L19.

met-enkephalin /mɛtɛnˈkɛfəlɪn/ *noun*. L20.
[ORIGIN from MET(HIONINE + ENKEPHALIN.]
BIOCHEMISTRY. The enkephalin whose peptide chain ends with a methionine unit.

metensomatosis /ˌmɛtɛnsəʊməˈtəʊsɪs/ *noun*. M17.
[ORIGIN Late Latin from Greek *metensōmatōsis*, formed as META- + *en* in + *sōma(t-)* body: see -OSIS.]
Re-embodiment of the soul.

meteor /ˈmiːtɪə, -tɪɔː/ *noun & adjective*. L15.
[ORIGIN mod. Latin *meteorum* from Greek *meteōron* use as noun of neut. of *meteōros* raised up, lofty, formed as META- + alt. of base of *aeirein* raise.]
▶**A** *noun*. **1** Any atmospheric phenomenon. Now *techn.* L15.
2 A small mass of rock or metal that enters the earth's atmosphere and as a result of friction with it becomes sufficiently incandescent to be visible; a shooting star. Formerly also, a comet. L16. ▸**b** Any of various other luminous atmospheric appearances, as the aurora borealis, the ignis fatuus, etc. Now *poet.* L16. ▸**c** A meteoroid. L18.
†**3** In *pl.* A treatise on atmospheric phenomena. L16–M17.
– COMB.: **meteor shower** a group of meteors that seem to come from the same point in the sky, appearing when the earth passes through a meteor swarm; **meteor swarm** a group of meteoroids moving together in the same orbit; **meteor trail** a bright streak of ionized gas formed by a meteor passing through the upper atmosphere, which can provide a reflector for radio communication.
▶**B** *attrib.* or as *adjective*. Blazing or flashing like a meteor; of short duration, transient. Chiefly *poet.* E18.
■ †**meteorize** *verb* (*a*) *verb intrans. & trans.* vaporize; (*b*) *verb intrans.* flash or sparkle like a meteor: M17–E19.

meteoric /miːtɪˈɒrɪk/ *adjective*. E17.
[ORIGIN Partly from medieval Latin *meteoricus* from Greek *meteōros* (see METEOR), partly from METEOR: see -IC.]
†**1** Relating to or combining the earth and the heavens. Only in E17.
2 Of, pertaining to, or derived from meteors; consisting of meteors. L18.

> C. OLLIER The water emitted by hot springs is usually of meteoric origin.

3 a (Of a plant) dependent on atmospheric conditions; (esp. of water) produced by or derived from the atmosphere. Now *rare* or *obsolete*. L18. ▸**b** Pertaining to the atmosphere; GEOLOGY designating water derived from the atmosphere by precipitation or condensation. E19.
4 Transiently or irregularly brilliant; sudden and rapid. E19.

> C. CHAPLIN Maurice had a meteoric rise as a theatrical entrepreneur. A. C. BOULT The years 1931 to 1939 saw a meteoric development in broadcasting.

■ **meteorically** *adverb* (*a*) in accordance with atmospheric conditions; (*b*) with the suddenness and speed of a meteor: M19.

meteorism /ˈmiːtɪərɪz(ə)m/ *noun*. Now *rare*. Also in mod. Latin form **meteorismus** /miːtɪəˈrɪzməs/. M19.
[ORIGIN Greek *meteōrismos* elevation, from *meteōrizein*: see METEORIZE, -ISM.]
MEDICINE. Flatulent distension of the abdomen with gas in the alimentary canal.
■ **meteo'ristic** *adjective* pertaining to or affected by meteorism L19.

meteorite /ˈmiːtɪərʌɪt/ *noun*. E19.
[ORIGIN from METEOR + -ITE[1].]
A fallen meteor; a mass of rock or metal that has fallen to the earth from beyond the atmosphere. Cf. AEROLITE, SIDERITE.
■ **meteoritic** /miːtɪəˈrɪtɪk/ *adjective* of or pertaining to meteorites; of the nature of a meteorite: M19. **meteo'ritical** *adjective* M20. **meteo'ritically** *adverb* E20. **meteo'riticist** /-sɪst/ *noun* an expert in or student of meteoritics M20. **meteo'ritics** *noun* the branch of science that deals with meteors and meteorites E20.

meteorograph /ˈmiːtɪərəɡrɑːf/ *noun*. L18.
[ORIGIN French *météorographe*, from Greek *meteōron*: see METEOR, -O-, -GRAPH.]
An apparatus for automatically recording several different kinds of meteorological phenomena at the same time.
■ **meteorogram** *noun* a chart or record produced by a meteorograph L19.

meteoroid /ˈmiːtɪərɔɪd/ *noun*. M19.
[ORIGIN from METEOR + -OID.]
A small body of rock or metal moving through space, of the same nature as those which become visible as meteors when they pass through the atmosphere.
■ **meteo'roidal** *adjective* L19.

†**meteorolite** *noun*. E–L19.
[ORIGIN French *météorolithe*, from Greek *meteōron*: see METEOR, -O-, -LITE.]
A meteorite.
■ †**meteorolitic** *adjective* E–L19.

meteorology /miːtɪəˈrɒlədʒi/ *noun*. M16.
[ORIGIN Greek *meteōrologia*, from *meteōron*: see METEOR, -OLOGY.]
1 The branch of science that deals with phenomena and processes of the atmosphere, esp. with a view to forecasting the weather. M16.
2 The character of a particular region as regards weather, atmospheric changes, etc. L17.
■ **meteoro'logic** *adjective* meteorological M17. **meteoro'logical** *adjective* [Greek *meteōrologikos*] of or pertaining to meteorology or atmospheric phenomena L16. **meteoro'logically** *adverb* L17. **meteorologist** *noun* M17.

†**meteoroscopy** *noun*. M17–L19.
[ORIGIN from METEOR + -O- + -SCOPY, or from METEOROSCOPE + -Y[3].]
Observation of celestial objects. Also, observation of the weather.
■ †**meteoroscope** *noun* [Greek *meteōroskopion*] an instrument for taking observations of celestial objects E17–L19.

†**meteorous** *adjective*. M17–L19.
[ORIGIN from Greek *meteōros*: see METEOR, -OUS.]
= METEORIC.

meter /ˈmiːtə/ *noun*[1]. ME.
[ORIGIN from METE *verb* + -ER[1].]
A person who measures; a measurer; *esp.* a person responsible for seeing that commodities are of the proper measure.

meter /ˈmiːtə/ *noun*[2]. E19.
[ORIGIN First in *gas meter*: perh. a use of METER *noun*[1] suggested by GASOMETER (L18).]
1 An instrument for automatically measuring or indicating the quantity, degree, or rate of something (e.g. electricity consumed or flowing, speed of travel, fuel remaining); *spec.* (identified contextually) a taximeter. E19. ▸**b** A parking meter. M20.

> J. H. GOODIER The gloss meter works on the principle of directing a beam of light on to a painted panel. *Sunday Express* The taxi's meter ticked away expensively.

exposure meter, ***frequency meter***, ***gas meter***, ***moisture meter***, ***tuning meter***, ***water meter***, ***wet meter***, etc.
2 A 25-cent coin. *US slang*. M20.
– COMB.: **meter-feeder** a motorist who usu. or habitually illicitly extends his or her parking time by putting more money in the meter instead of moving away; **meter maid** (orig. *US*) a female traffic warden; **meter-reader** a person responsible for reading gas or electricity meters.
■ **meterless** *adjective* having no meter; done without the use of a meter: L20.

meter *noun*[3], *noun*[4] see METRE *noun*[1], *noun*[2].

meter /ˈmiːtə/ *verb*[1]. L19.
[ORIGIN from METER *noun*[2].]
1 a *verb trans. & intrans.* Measure by means of a meter; supply through a meter. L19. ▸**b** *verb trans.* Regulate the flow of; deliver (fluid) in regulated amounts *to*. M20.

> **a** *Practical Photography* Meter from the highlights so that the shadow detail is underexposed. **b** *Scientific American* The water is metered to each plant through the drip-irrigation installation.

2 *verb trans.* Provide with a meter or meters. M20.

> M. BRADBURY The terrace has been metered for parking. *Liverpool Echo* TV lounge, colour TV, metered fires in bedrooms.

meter *verb*[2] see METRE *verb*.

-meter /ˈmɪtə/ *suffix*.
[ORIGIN Greek *metron* measure.]
1 PROSODY. Forming nouns denoting a line of poetry with a specified number of measures, as ***hexameter***, ***pentameter***.
2 Forming nouns denoting measuring instruments: orig. (as in ***barometer***, ***hydrometer***, ***hygrometer***, ***thermometer***) repr. mod. Latin forms in ***-metrum***, with the ending intended to represent the Greek *metron* measure (see METRE *noun*[1]); later in words with the same ending ***-ometer*** formed on Greek bases, as ***anemometer***, ***chronometer***, and in hybrid formations, some imitating the form of Greek compounds, as ***gasometer***, ***galvanometer***, ***pedometer***, others with the combining vowel *i* of the Latin first elem., as ***calorimeter***, ***gravimeter***. In some late formations ***-meter*** is appended to mod. words without any attempt to assimilate the form of the first elem. to that of a Greek or Latin combining form, as in ***voltameter***, ***ammeter***.

metestrus *noun* see METOESTRUS.

metethereal /mɛtɪˈθɪərɪəl/ *adjective*. E20.
[ORIGIN from META- + ETHEREAL.]
Spiritual, transcendental.

metewand /ˈmiːtwɒnd/ *noun*. LME.
[ORIGIN from METE *verb* or MET *noun*[1] + WAND *noun*.]
†**1** A measuring rod. LME–L19.
2 A standard of measurement or estimation. *arch.* M16.
■ Also †**meteyard** *noun* OE–L19.

metformin /mɛtˈfɔːmɪn/ *noun*. M20.
[ORIGIN from METH(YL + FORM(ALDEHYDE + IM)IN(O-.]
PHARMACOLOGY. A biguanide derivative, $C_4H_{11}N_5$, used in the oral treatment of diabetes.

meth /mɛθ/ *noun*[1]. Also **crystal meth**. *slang*. M20.
[ORIGIN Abbreviation.]
(A tablet of) the drug methamphetamine.

meth *noun*[2] var. of METHS.

meth- /mɛθ, miːθ/ *combining form*.
[ORIGIN from METHYL.]
Used in forming names of substances, esp. drugs, containing methyl groups.

methacholine /mɛθəˈkəʊliːn/ *noun*. M20.
[ORIGIN from METH- + *-a-* + CHOLINE.]
PHARMACOLOGY. A parasympathomimetic agent with effects similar to those of histamine, used to treat some heart arrhythmias.

methacrylic /mɛθəˈkrɪlɪk/ *adjective*. M19.
[ORIGIN from METH- + ACRYLIC.]
CHEMISTRY. ***methacrylic acid***, 1-methylacrylic acid, $CH_2{:}C(CH_3)COOH$, a colourless compound melting at 15°C, which polymerizes when distilled and is used in the manufacture of methacrylate resins.
■ **methacrylate** /mɪˈθakrɪlət/ *noun* a salt or ester of methacrylic acid, *esp.* any of the esters of methacrylic acid used in making resins by polymerization; *POLYMETHYL* ***methacrylate***: M19.

methadone /ˈmɛθədəʊn/ *noun*. M20.
[ORIGIN from METH- + A(MINO- + DI-[2] + -ONE, elems. of the systematic name.]
PHARMACOLOGY. A powerful synthetic analgesic which is similar to morphine in its effects but less sedative and is used as a substitute drug in the treatment of morphine and heroin addiction. Proprietary name ***Physeptone***.

methaemoglobin /ˌmɛθiːməˈɡləʊbɪn, -θiː-/ *noun*. Also ***-hem-**. L19.
[ORIGIN from META- + HAEMOGLOBIN.]
BIOCHEMISTRY. A stable oxide of haemoglobin in which the iron of the haem group is in a ferric rather than a ferrous state, and so unable to combine with oxygen.
■ **methaemoglobiˈnaemia** *noun* (MEDICINE) presence of methaemoglobin in the blood L19. **methaemoglobiˈnuria** *noun* (MEDICINE) presence of methaemoglobin in the urine L19.

methamphetamine /mɛθamˈfɛtəmiːn, -ɪn/ *noun*. M20.
[ORIGIN from METH- + AMPHETAMINE.]
PHARMACOLOGY. A methyl derivative of amphetamine with effects that are more rapid in onset and longer lasting, used as a stimulant of the central nervous system. Cf. METHEDRINE.

methanal /ˈmɛθənal/ *noun*. L19.
[ORIGIN from METHANE + -AL[2].]
CHEMISTRY. = FORMALDEHYDE.

methanation /mɛθəˈneɪʃ(ə)n/ *noun*. M20.
[ORIGIN from METHAN(E + -ATION.]
Conversion (esp. of carbon monoxide and hydrogen) into methane.
■ ˈ**methanate** *verb trans.* [back-form.] convert into methane, subject to methanation M20.

methane /ˈmiːθeɪn, ˈmɛθeɪn/ *noun*. M19.
[ORIGIN from METH- + -ANE.]
CHEMISTRY. A colourless odourless flammable gas, CH_4, the simplest of the alkanes, which occurs in natural gas, coal gas, and decaying organic matter, forms an explosive mixture with air, and is used as a fuel. Cf. ***firedamp*** s.v. FIRE *noun*.

methano- /ˈmɛθənəʊ, mɛˈθanəʊ/ *combining form* of prec.: see -O-.
■ **meˈthanogen** *noun* a methanogenic bacterium L20. **methanoˈgenesis** *noun* the production of methane by living organisms, esp. bacteria M20. **methanoˈgenic** *adjective* producing methane; pertaining to or involving methanogenesis; *spec.* designating archaebacteria etc. which reduce carbon dioxide to methane: M20. **methanometer** /mɛθəˈnɒmɪtə/ *noun* an instrument for measuring the concentration of methane, esp. in mines L19. **methanotroph** /-trəʊf/ *noun* a micro-organism that derives its carbon and energy from methane L20.

methanoic /mɛθəˈnəʊɪk/ *adjective*. L19.
[ORIGIN from METHANE + -OIC.]
CHEMISTRY. = FORMIC 1.

methanol /ˈmɛθənɒl/ *noun*. L19.
[ORIGIN formed as METHANOIC + -OL.]
CHEMISTRY. A colourless volatile flammable liquid alcohol, CH_3OH, used as an intermediate in the synthesis of formaldehyde, as a solvent, and as a denaturant for ethyl alcohol; methyl alcohol.
■ **methaˈnolic** *adjective* in or of methanol M20.

methapyrilene /mɛθəˈpɪrɪliːn/ *noun*. M20.
[ORIGIN from METH- + *-a-* + alt. of PYR(ID)YL + -ENE.]
PHARMACOLOGY. An antihistamine agent also used to induce sleep.

methaqualone /mɛˈθakwələʊn/ *noun*. M20.
[ORIGIN from METH- + *-a-* + QU(ININE + A(ZO- + -O)L + -ONE, elems. of the systematic name.]
PHARMACOLOGY. A hypnotic and sedative drug derived from quinazoline. Proprietary name ***Quaalude***; cf. also MANDRAX.

Methedrine /ˈmɛθədrɪn, -iːn/ *noun*. M20.
[ORIGIN from METH- + BENZ)EDRINE.]
PHARMACOLOGY. (Proprietary name for) the drug methamphetamine.

metheglin /mɪˈθɛɡlɪn, ˈmɛθəɡlɪn/ *noun*. Chiefly *hist.* LME.
[ORIGIN Welsh *meddyglyn*, from *meddyg* medicinal (from Latin *medicus*: see MEDIC *noun*[1] & *adjective*[1]) + *llyn* liquor (= Irish *lionn*, Gaelic *leann*).]
A spiced or medicated variety of mead, associated particularly with Wales.

methel *noun* var. of METEL.

methemoglobin *noun* see METHAEMOGLOBIN.

methenamine /mɛˈθiːnəmiːn, -ˈθɛn-/ *noun*. Chiefly *US*. E20.
[ORIGIN from METHENE + AMINE.]
CHEMISTRY. = HEXAMETHYLENETETRAMINE.

methene /ˈmɛθiːn/ *noun*. M19.
[ORIGIN from METH- + -ENE.]
CHEMISTRY. = METHYLENE.

methi /ˈmeɪti/ *noun*. *Indian*. M19.
[ORIGIN Sanskrit, Hindi *methī*, from Dravidian.]
Fenugreek.

methicillin /mɛθɪˈsɪlɪn/ *noun*. M20.
[ORIGIN from METH- + PEN)ICILLIN.]
PHARMACOLOGY. A semi-synthetic penicillin used against staphylococci which produce penicillinase.

methide /ˈmɛθʌɪd, ˈmiːθ-/ *noun*. M19.
[ORIGIN from METH- + -IDE.]
CHEMISTRY. A binary compound of methyl, esp. with a metal.

methimazole /mɛˈθɪməzəʊl/ *noun*. M20.
[ORIGIN from METH- + IM(ID)AZOLE.]
PHARMACOLOGY. An imidazole derivative with antithyroid properties, used to treat hyperthyroidism.

methinks /mɪˈθɪŋks/ *verb intrans. impers.* Now *arch., poet., & joc.* Also **methinketh** /mɪˈθɪŋkəθ/. Pa. t. **methought** /mɪˈθɔːt/. OE.
[ORIGIN Orig. two words, ME *pronoun (dat.)* + 3rd person sing. of THINK *verb*[1]. Cf. MESEEMS.]
It seems to me. (With noun clause, with or without *that*.)

> TENNYSON At last methought that I had wander'd far In an old wood. *Times* Someone will, methinks, have to invent low-alcohol champagne.

methiocarb /mɪˈθʌɪəkɑːb/ *noun*. M20.
[ORIGIN from METH- + THIO- + CARB(AMATE.]
CHEMISTRY. A carbamate used as an insecticide, molluscicide, and acaricide, common in garden preparations.

methionine /mɪˈθʌɪəniːn/ *noun*. E20.
[ORIGIN from METH- + THION- + -INE[5].]
BIOCHEMISTRY. A hydrophobic sulphur-containing amino acid, $CH_3S(CH_2)_2CH(NH_2)COOH$, which occurs in proteins and is essential in the human diet; 2-amino-4-(methylthio)butyric acid.

methisazone /mɪˈθɪsəzəʊn/ *noun*. M20.
[ORIGIN from METH- + IS(ATIN + SEMICARB)AZONE.]
PHARMACOLOGY. A thiosemicarbazone, $C_{10}H_{10}N_4OS$, with prophylactic activity against smallpox.

metho /ˈmɛθəʊ/ *noun*[1]. *Austral. & NZ colloq.* Pl. **-os**. M20.
[ORIGIN from ***methylated spirits*** s.v. METHYLATE *verb* + -O.]
1 Methylated spirits. M20.
2 A person addicted to drinking methylated spirits. M20.

Metho /ˈmɛθəʊ/ *noun*[2] & *adjective*. *Austral. colloq.* M20.
[ORIGIN Abbreviation.]
▸ **A** *noun*. Pl. **-os**. = METHODIST *noun* 4. M20.
▸ **B** *adjective*. = METHODIST *adjective*. M20.

method /ˈmɛθəd/ *noun*. LME.
[ORIGIN Latin *methodus* from Greek *methodos* pursuit of knowledge, mode of investigation, from *meta* (see META-) + *hodos* way.]
▸ **I** Procedure for attaining an object.
1 The recommended or prescribed medical treatment for a specific disease. *obsolete* exc. as in sense 2 below. LME. ▸**b** *hist.* (**M-**.) The system of medicine practised by the ancient school of Methodists. LME.
2 A mode of procedure; a (defined or systematic) way of doing a thing, *esp.* (with specifying word or words) in accordance with a particular theory or as associated with a particular person. L16. ▸**b** Any of various ordered sets of changes in bell-ringing. M17. ▸**c** THEATRICAL. An acting theory and technique in which an actor aspires to complete emotional identification with a part. Freq. *attrib.* E20.

> B. JOWETT The theses of Parmenides are expressly said to follow the method of Zeno. ISAIAH BERLIN Some believe in coercion, others in gentler methods. W. S. CHURCHILL New methods of smelting brought a tenfold increase in the output of iron. W. RAEPER MacDonald followed the usual Congregational method of delivering his sermons extempore. **c** *attrib.*: F. HOWERD Although George may only have been playing a eunuch, I nearly turned him into a method actor. K. WILLIAMS 'I suppose it's all instinct with me.' 'That is better than method acting,' said Alfred.

▸ **II** Systematic arrangement, order.
3 The branch of logic that deals with the description and arrangement of arguments or propositions for the investigation or exposition of a truth. M16.
4 Order in thinking or expressing thoughts; the orderly arrangement of ideas; *gen.* orderliness, regularity, or planning in doing anything. M16.

> V. S. NAIPAUL That briefcase suggested method, steadiness, many commissions.

5 The order and arrangement of a literary work, speech, etc.; an author's design or plan. Long *rare* or *obsolete*. L16. ▸†**b** A written systematically ordered collection of rules, observations, etc., on a particular subject. L16–E19. ▸†**c** The summary of the contents of a book, esp. as a list. E–M17. ▸†**d** BOTANY & ZOOLOGY. A scheme of classification. E–M19.
†**6** A particular orderly arrangement according to a regular plan or design. M17–M18.

> ADDISON I would have all the knives and forks . . laid in a method.

– PHRASES: ***direct method***: see DIRECT *adjective*. **method in one's madness** sense or reason in what appears to be foolish or abnormal behaviour. ***method of exclusion(s)***: see EXCLUSION. ***method of least squares***: see SQUARE *noun*. ***ORGANIZATION and methods***. ***scientific method***: see SCIENTIFIC *adjective*.
– COMB.: **methods engineer** a person whose occupation is methods engineering; **methods engineering** the organization or improvement of business and management methods by method study; **method study**, **methods study** the systematic study of business and management methods with a view to increasing efficiency.
■ **methodless** *adjective* E17.

méthode champenoise /metɔd ʃɑ̃pənwɑːz/ *noun phr.* E20.
[ORIGIN French, lit. 'champagne method'.]
The method of introducing a sparkle into wine by allowing the last stage of fermentation to take place in the bottle; a sparkling wine made in this way.

Methodenstreit /meˈtoːdənʃtraɪt/ *noun*. Pl. ***-e*** /-ə/. L19.
[ORIGIN German, lit. 'methods struggle'.]
(A) discussion or dispute concerning the methodology of a field of study.

methodic /mɪˈθɒdɪk/ *adjective* & *noun*. M16.
[ORIGIN Late Latin *methodicus* from Greek *methodikos*, from *methodos* METHOD: see -IC.]
▸ **A** *adjective*. †**1** (**M-**.) = METHODICAL 1. M16–M19.
2 = METHODICAL 2. E17.
▸ †**B** *noun*. (**M-**.) = METHODIST *noun* 1. M16–M19.

methodical /mɪˈθɒdɪk(ə)l/ *adjective*. L16.
[ORIGIN formed as METHODIC + -ICAL.]
1 *hist.* (**M-**.) Of, pertaining to, or designating the ancient school of Methodists. L16.
2 Characterized by method or order; (of a person) acting with or observant of method or order. L16. ▸**b** Of a material thing: arranged in a neat or orderly manner. *rare*. M17.

> V. WOOLF Painters live lives of methodical absorption, adding stroke to stroke. SLOAN WILSON They had been methodical, they had done things According to Plan.

■ **methodicalness** *noun* L17.

methodically /mɪˈθɒdɪk(ə)li/ *adverb*. L16.
[ORIGIN from METHODIC *adjective* or METHODICAL: see -ICALLY.]
In a methodical manner.

> R. K. NARAYAN She was steadily, definitely, methodically working herself up into a breakdown. D. FRANCIS I went methodically round the house . . locking and bolting all the outside doors.

methodise *verb* var. of METHODIZE.

Methodism /ˈmɛθədɪz(ə)m/ *noun*. In sense 2 **m-**. M18.
[ORIGIN from METHOD + -ISM.]
1 The system, faith, and practice of the Methodist Churches. M18.
2 Adherence to or excessive regard for fixed methods. M19.
3 *hist.* The doctrine and practice of the ancient school of Methodists. L19.

Methodist /ˈmɛθədɪst/ *noun* & *adjective*. In sense 2 **m-**. L16.
[ORIGIN mod. Latin *methodista*, from Latin *methodus* METHOD: see -IST.]
▸ **A** *noun*. **1** *hist.* A physician of an ancient school of medical thought that attributed disease either to narrowing or relaxation of the body's internal 'pores'. L16.
2 An advocate or follower of the use of a (particular or specified) method. L16. ▸**b** BOTANY & ZOOLOGY. A person who classifies or arranges according to a particular (esp. artificial) method or scheme. *obsolete* exc. *hist.* M18.

M

3 *hist.* A member of a 17th-cent. group of Roman Catholic apologists. L17.

4 A member of any of several Protestant denominations (now chiefly united) originating in the 18th-cent. evangelistic movement founded by John and Charles Wesley and George Whitefield. M18. ▸**b** A person of strict religious views. *derog.* Now *rare* or *obsolete*. M18.

> G. GORER The most sizable Protestant group after the Church of England are the Methodists. S. PLATH My mother had been a Catholic before she was a Methodist.

Primitive Methodist: see PRIMITIVE *adjective*. ***Wesleyan Methodist***: see WESLEYAN *adjective*.

▸ **B** *adjective*. Of or pertaining to (the denomination of) the Methodists. M18.

> *Harper's Magazine* Judson Noth, a local Methodist preacher. E. P. THOMPSON The evangelical revival resulted in the distinct Methodist Church.

■ **Metho'distic** *adjective* of, pertaining to, or characteristic of the Methodists or their doctrines, methods, or appearance L18. **Metho'distical** *adjective* = METHODISTIC M18. **Methodistically** *adverb* in accordance with the principles or practice of Methodists L18.

methodize /ˈmɛθədʌɪz/ *verb trans.* Also **-ise**. L16.
[ORIGIN from METHOD + -IZE.]
1 Reduce to method or order; arrange (ideas etc.) in an orderly manner. L16. ▸**b** Make (a person) orderly or methodical. L18.
2 Convert to Methodism. *rare*. M19.
■ **methodi'zation** *noun* the action or process of reducing to method or order; the state of being methodized or ordered: E19. **methodizer** *noun* L17.

methodology /mɛθəˈdɒlədʒi/ *noun*. E19.
[ORIGIN mod. Latin *methodologia* or French *méthodologie*, formed as METHOD + -OLOGY.]
1 The branch of knowledge that deals with method and its application in a particular field. Also, the study of empirical research or the techniques employed in it. E19.
2 A body of methods used in a particular branch of study or activity. M19.
■ **methodo'logical** *adjective* M19. **methodo'logically** *adverb* in a methodological manner or respect L19. **methodologist** *noun* M19.

Methody /ˈmɛθədi/ *noun & adjective*. *colloq. & dial.* M18.
[ORIGIN from METHOD(IST + -Y[6].]
▸ **A** *noun*. = METHODIST *noun* 4. M18.
▸ **B** *adjective*. = METHODIST *adjective*. L18.

M

methohexitone /mɛθəˈhɛksɪtəʊn/ *noun*. M20.
[ORIGIN from METH- + -O- + HEX(A- + BARB)IT(URIC + -ONE.]
PHARMACOLOGY. A derivative of barbituric acid, given intravenously as an anaesthetic.
■ Also **methohexital** *noun* (chiefly *US*) M20.

†**methomania** *noun*. M–L19.
[ORIGIN from Greek *methē* strong drink + -O- + -MANIA.]
Alcoholism, dipsomania.

methonium /mɪˈθəʊnɪəm/ *noun*. M20.
[ORIGIN from METH- + -ONIUM.]
PHARMACOLOGY. Any of various (salts of) polymethylene bistrimethylammonium cations, $[(CH_3)_3N(CH_2)_x{=}N(CH_3)_3]^{2+}$, some of which are ganglionic blocking agents used to treat hypertension. Chiefly in ***methonium compound***.

methoprene /ˈmɛθəpriːn/ *noun*. L20.
[ORIGIN from METH- + IS)OPRENE.]
A derivative of an isoprene polymer, $C_{19}H_{34}O_3$, which causes arrest of development in various insects and is used as an insecticide.

methotrexate /mɛθəˈtrɛkseɪt, miːθə-/ *noun*. M20.
[ORIGIN from METH- + elems. of unknown origin.]
PHARMACOLOGY. A cytotoxic orange-brown powder which is a folic acid antagonist used to treat certain cancers; 4-amino-10-methylfolic acid.

methought *verb pa. t.* of METHINKS.

methoxide /mɪˈθɒksʌɪd/ *noun*. L19.
[ORIGIN from METHOXY- + -IDE.]
CHEMISTRY. A salt or simple compound containing the methoxyl radical, as ***sodium methoxide***, $NaOCH_3$.

methoxy- /mɪˈθɒksi/ *combining form*. Also as attrib. adjective **methoxy**.
[ORIGIN from METH- + OXY-.]
CHEMISTRY. Designating or containing a methoxyl group.
■ **methoxychlor** *noun* a crystalline compound, $(C_6H_4{\cdot}OCH_3)_2CHCCl_3$, related to DDT and used as an insecticide, esp. for veterinary hygiene M20.

methoxyl /mɪˈθɒksʌɪl, -sɪl/ *noun*. M19.
[ORIGIN formed as METHOXY- + -YL.]
CHEMISTRY. The radical $CH_3O{\cdot}$, derived from methanol. Usu. in *comb.*

meths /mɛθs/ *noun*. *colloq.* Also **meth** /mɛθ/. M20.
[ORIGIN Abbreviation.]
= ***methylated spirits*** s.v. METHYLATE *verb*.

> *attrib.*: M. TRIPP I'd seen a meths drinker spewing blood the night before.

Methuen /ˈmɛθjʊɪn/ *noun*. *arch. rare*. M18.
[ORIGIN Paul *Methuen* (1672–1757), English diplomat who negotiated a commercial treaty between England and Portugal in 1703.]
Portuguese wine.

Methuselah /mɪˈθ(j)uːz(ə)lə/ *noun*. Also **-alem** /-ələm/. E17.
[ORIGIN Hebrew *mĕṯūšelah*, a pre-Noachian patriarch, stated to have lived 969 years (*Genesis* 5:27).]
1 A very old person or thing, esp. as a type or representation of extreme longevity. E17.
2 (Usu. **m-**.) A very large wine bottle, equivalent to eight ordinary bottles. M20.

methyl /ˈmiːθʌɪl, ˈmɛθ-, -θɪl/ *noun*. M19.
[ORIGIN French *méthyle*, German *Methyl*, back-form. from French *méthylène*, German *Methylen* METHYLENE.]
CHEMISTRY. The radical $CH_3{\cdot}$ derived from methane, present in methanol, methanoic (formic) acid, etc. Usu. in *comb.*
– COMB.: **methyl alcohol** = METHANOL; **methylbenzene** = TOLUENE; **methylcellulose** any of a range of white, tasteless compounds produced by etherifying cellulose and used as thickening, emulsifying, and stabilizing agents, esp. in foods, laxatives, and adhesives; **methyldopa** *PHARMACOLOGY* a whitish powder, $C_{10}H_{13}NO_4$, used as a hypotensive agent; **methyl ethyl ketone** a colourless volatile liquid, $CH_3COCH_2CH_3$, used as a solvent for organic materials; butanone; **methyl green** a green dye used in microscopy to stain chromatin; **methyl isobutyl ketone** a liquid ketone, $(CH_3)_2CHCH_2COCH_3$, used as a solvent; hexone, 4-methylpentan-2-one; **methyl isocyanate** a toxic gas, CH_3NCO, used in making certain pesticides; **methyl methacrylate** a volatile colourless liquid, $CH_2{=}C(CH_3)COOCH_3$, that readily polymerizes to form resinous glassy materials such as Perspex and Plexiglas; such a polymeric material; **methyl orange** an orange crystalline compound which is the sodium salt of a sulphur-containing azo dye, chiefly used in solution as an acid–base indicator, giving a pink colour at pH 3 and yellow at pH 4.4; **methylphenidate** a sympathomimetic drug used as a CNS stimulant to treat various depressive and lethargic conditions; **methyl red** a red crystalline acidic azo dye, $(CH_3)_2N{\cdot}C_6H_4{\cdot}N{:}N{\cdot}C_6H_4{\cdot}COOH$, used in solution as an acid–base indicator, giving a red colour at pH 4.4 and yellow at pH 6; **methyl rubber** an early synthetic rubber made by polymerizing dimethylbutadiene; **methyl salicylate** a colourless or pale yellow liquid, $C_6H_4(OH)CO{\cdot}OCH_3$, the chief constituent of oil of wintergreen and sweet birch oil, which is used as a flavouring, in perfumery, and in analgesic liniments and ointments; **methyltestosterone** *PHARMACOLOGY* any of the methyl derivatives of testosterone; *esp.* (more fully ***17-methyltestosterone***) a synthetic androgen used to treat hormonal imbalances and certain cancers; **methylthiouracil** a drug which inhibits thyroid activity and is used to control thyrotoxicosis; 6-methyl-2-thiouracil; **methyl violet** gentian violet.

methylal /ˈmɛθɪlal/ *noun*. M19.
[ORIGIN from METHYL + -AL[2].]
CHEMISTRY. A colourless volatile fragrant liquid, $(CH_3O)_2CH_2$, used as a solvent and formerly as an anaesthetic.

methylate /ˈmɛθɪleɪt/ *noun*. M19.
[ORIGIN formed as METHYLATE *verb* + -ATE[1].]
CHEMISTRY. = METHOXIDE.

methylate /ˈmɛθɪleɪt/ *verb trans.* M19.
[ORIGIN from METHYL + -ATE[3].]
CHEMISTRY. Introduce one or more methyl groups into (a compound or group). Also, adulterate with methanol. Chiefly as ***methylated*** *ppl adjective*.
methylated spirit(s) ethyl alcohol containing methanol; *esp.* that sold for general use, being made unfit for drinking by addition of about ten per cent methanol, and usu. also some pyridine and a violet dye.
■ **methy'lation** *noun* the process of methylating (esp. alcohol) M19. **methylator** *noun* a person who methylates alcohol L19.

methylene /ˈmɛθɪliːn/ *noun*. M19.
[ORIGIN French *méthylène*, irreg. from Greek *methu* wine + *hulē* wood (see -YL, -ENE).]
CHEMISTRY. The radical $\cdot CH_2\cdot$, which is the basic unit of hydrocarbon chains. Also ***methylene group***.
– COMB.: **methylene blue** a green crystalline compound, blue in aqueous solution, used in dyeing, as an antiseptic, and as a microscopic stain for bacteria.

methylic /mɛˈθɪlɪk/ *adjective*. Now *rare* or *obsolete*. M19.
[ORIGIN from METHYL + -IC.]
CHEMISTRY. Of, pertaining to, or including methyl.

methysergide /mɛθɪˈsəːdʒʌɪd/ *noun*. M20.
[ORIGIN from METH- + L)YSERG(IC + AM)IDE.]
PHARMACOLOGY. A lysergic acid derivative with serotonin-blocking properties, used as a preventive drug for recurrent migraine.

metic /ˈmɛtɪk/ *noun*. E19.
[ORIGIN Irreg. from Greek *metoikos*, formed as META- + *-oikos* dwelling, from *oikein* dwell: see -IC.]
hist. A resident alien in a Greek city with some of the privileges of citizenship.

metical /mɛtɪˈkal/ *noun*. L20.
[ORIGIN Portuguese, formed as MITHQAL.]
The basic monetary unit of Mozambique, equal to 100 centavos.

meticulous /mɪˈtɪkjʊləs/ *adjective*. M16.
[ORIGIN from Latin *meticulosus*, from *metus* fear: see -ULOUS.]
†**1** Fearful, timid. M16–L17.
2 Overcareful about minute details. Now also simply, careful, precise. E19.

> R. LEHMANN A letter written in a minute and meticulous hand.

■ **meticu'losity** *noun* M17. **meticulously** *adverb* L17. **meticulousness** *noun* E20.

métier /ˈmeɪtɪeɪ, *foreign* metje/ *noun*. L18.
[ORIGIN French, from Proto-Romance alt. of Latin *ministerium* service, MINISTRY, prob. infl. by *mysterium* MYSTERY *noun*[1].]
One's occupation or department of activity. Now usu., a field in which one has special skill or ability; one's forte.

> W. A. PERCY Power? I knew nothing about it and it certainly wasn't my métier.

†**metif** *noun*. E–L19.
[ORIGIN French *métif* alt. of *métis*: see METIS.]
A person with one white and one quarter black parent.

metis /meɪˈtiːs; *Canad.* meɪˈtiː, ˈmeɪti/ *noun*. Pl. same /meɪˈtiː(s), ˈmeɪti, ˈmeɪtɪz/). Also (fem.) **métisse** /meɪˈtiːs, *Canad. also* ˈmeɪtɪːs/, pl. **-s**. E19.
[ORIGIN French *métis* from Old French *mestis* from Proto-Romance, from Latin *mixtus*: see MESTIZO.]
A person of mixed descent; *esp.* (in Canada) a person with one white and one American Indian parent.

metoclopramide /mɛtəˈkləʊprəmʌɪd/ *noun*. M20.
[ORIGIN from MET(H)O(XY)- + C(H)L(OR)O-[2] + PR(OCAIN)AMIDE.]
PHARMACOLOGY. An amide with dopamine-receptor blocking properties, used to treat hypothyroidism and as an anti-emetic.

†**metoecious** *adjective*. Also ***metec-**. Only in L19.
[ORIGIN from META- + Greek *oikia* house: see -IOUS.]
BOTANY. = HETEROECIOUS.
■ †**metoecism** *noun* = HETEROECISM: only in L19.

metoestrus /meˈtiːstrəs/ *noun*. Also ***metest-**. E20.
[ORIGIN from META- + OESTRUS.]
BIOLOGY. The short period following oestrus in many mammals during which sexual activity subsides.
■ **metoestrous** *adjective* E20.

metol /ˈmɛtɒl/ *noun*. L19.
[ORIGIN Arbitrary.]
PHOTOGRAPHY. A soluble white crystalline compound, the sulphate of *p*-methylaminophenol, used as a photographic developer. Also, the free base, *p*-methylaminophenol.

Metonic /mɪˈtɒnɪk/ *adjective*. M17.
[ORIGIN from Greek *Metōn* Athenian astronomer + -IC.]
Metonic cycle, ***Metonic period***, †***Metonic year***, the cycle of 19 Julian years in which the moon returns (nearly) to the same apparent position with regard to the sun, so that the new and full moons occur at the same dates in the corresponding year of each cycle.

metonym /ˈmɛtənɪm/ *noun*. E17.
[ORIGIN Back-form. from METONYMY: see -NYM.]
A word used metonymically. Formerly also, metonymy.

metonymy /mɪˈtɒnɪmi/ *noun*. M16.
[ORIGIN Late Latin *metonymia* from Greek *metōnumia* lit. 'change of name', formed as META- + *onuma* name: see -NYM, -Y[3].]
1 The substitution of a word denoting an attribute or adjunct of a thing for the word denoting the thing itself; an instance of this. M16.

> *Athenaeum* 'Stokes', the name of the inventor . . has, by metonymy, come to mean the trench mortar gun itself.

2 A thing used or regarded as a substitute for or symbol of something else. M20.
■ **meto'nymic** *adjective* of, involving, or used in metonymy L18. **meto'nymical** *adjective* = METONYMIC M16. **meto'nymically** *adverb* L16.

metope /ˈmɛtəʊp, ˈmɛtəpi/ *noun*. M16.
[ORIGIN Latin *metopa* from Greek *metopē*, from *meta* between + *opē* hole in a frieze for a beam end.]
ARCHITECTURE. A square space between triglyphs in a Doric frieze.

metopic /mɪˈtɒpɪk/ *adjective*. L19.
[ORIGIN from Greek *metōpon* forehead + -IC.]
Of or pertaining to the forehead; frontal; (of a skull) exhibiting metopism.
■ **'metopism** *noun* continued presence in the skull of an open frontal suture beyond infancy L19.

metoposcopy /mɛtəˈpɒskəpi/ *noun*. M16.
[ORIGIN French *métoposcopie* from Latin *metoposcopus* from Greek *metōposkopos*, from *metōpon* forehead: see -SCOPY.]
1 The art of judging character or telling a person's fortune from the forehead or face. M16.
†**2** The appearance or physical features of a person's forehead. M17–L19.
■ †**metoposcopist** *noun* a person skilled in metoposcopy L16–L19.

metoprolol /mɪˈtɒprəlɒl/ *noun*. L20.
[ORIGIN from MET(H- + -O- + PRO(PRANO)LOL.]
PHARMACOLOGY. A beta blocker used to treat hypertension and angina.

Metran /ˈmɛtran/ *noun*. M19.
[ORIGIN Ethiopic.]
= ABUNA.

metre /ˈmiːtə/ *noun*[1]. Also ***meter**. OE.
[ORIGIN (Old French & mod. French *mètre* from) Latin *metrum* from Greek *metron* measure, from Indo-European base + instr. suffix.]
1 *PROSODY*. Poetic rhythm or scheme as determined by the number and length of the feet in a line; a (specified) form of this. OE.

W. EMPSON The demands of metre allow the poet to say something which is not normal colloquial English. G. S. FRASER The metre of Michael Alexander's rendering is . . easy and pleasant to read.

2 Poetic composition, verse. Formerly also, a verse, a poem. ME.
3 *PROSODY*. A metrical group or measure. L19.
4 The basic pattern of beats in a piece of music. L19.
– PHRASES: ***common metre***: see COMMON *adjective*. ***long metre***: see LONG *adjective*[1]. ***short metre***: see SHORT *adjective*.
– COMB.: **metre psalm** = ***metric psalm*** s.v. METRIC *adjective*[1].
■ **metreless** *adjective* L19.

metre /ˈmiːtə/ *noun*[2]. Also ***meter**. L18.
[ORIGIN French *mètre* formed as METRE *noun*[1].]
The fundamental unit of length in the metric system, approximately equal to 39.37 inches, and now, as an SI unit, defined as equal to the distance travelled by light in free space in 1/299,792,458 second. (Symbol m.)
superficial metre: see SUPERFICIAL *adjective* 1.
– COMB.: **metre-angle** *OPHTHALMOLOGY* a unit of convergence equal to the angle between the line of sight of either eye and the median line passing between the eyes when fixating a point on the median line one metre away; **metre-candle** = LUX *noun*; **metre-kilogram-second** *adjective* designating or pertaining to a system of measurement in which these three elements form the basic units of length, mass, and time respectively.
– NOTE: Orig. intended to represent one ten-millionth of the length of a quadrant of the meridian, and defined by reference to a platinum-iridium standard kept in Paris; later defined in terms of the wavelength (605.8 nanometres) of a particular orange line in the spectrum of krypton 86.

metre /ˈmiːtə/ *verb*. Also ***meter**. LME.
[ORIGIN from METRE *noun*[1].]
1 *verb trans.* Compose in or put into metre. LME.
2 *verb intrans.* Versify. Now *rare* or *obsolete*. LME.

metrete /mɪˈtriːt/ *noun*. ME.
[ORIGIN Latin *metreta* from Greek *metrētēs*, from *metrein* to measure, from *metron* METRE *noun*[1].]
An ancient Greek liquid measure equivalent to approx. 41 litres, or 9 gallons.

metric /ˈmɛtrɪk/ *noun*[1] & *adjective*[1]. L15.
[ORIGIN Latin *metricus* from Greek *metrikos*, from *metron* METRE *noun*[1]: see -IC, -ICS.]
▸ **A** *noun*. **1** In *pl.* (treated as *sing.*) or (now *rare*) *sing.* The branch of study that deals with metre. L15.
2 *PROSODY*. = METRE *noun*[1] 1. M20.
▸ **B** *adjective*. Pertaining to or composed in a poetic metre. M17.
– SPECIAL COLLOCATIONS: **metric psalm** a biblical psalm translated into verse.

metric /ˈmɛtrɪk/ *adjective*[2] & *noun*[2]. M19.
[ORIGIN French *métrique*, from *mètre* METRE *noun*[2]: see -IC.]
▸ **A** *adjective*. **1** Of, pertaining to, or based on the metre; *spec.* designating the decimal measuring system having the metre, litre, and gram (or kilogram) as its respective units of length, volume, and mass. M19.
metric HUNDREDWEIGHT. ***metric ton***: see TON *noun*[1] 4.
2 *MATH. & PHYSICS*. Pertaining to, involving, or defining distance (or an abstract quantity analogous to distance). M19.
3 Having the metric system as the principal system of weights and measures. E20.

D. FRANCIS The Australians had already gone metric, to the confusion of my mental arithmetic.

▸ **B** *noun*. **1** *MATH. & PHYSICS*. A metric function. E20.
2 The metric system of measurement. M20.
3 Esp. *PSYCHOLOGY & LINGUISTICS*. A system or standard of measurement. M20.
4 In *pl.* A set of figures or statistics that measure results, esp. in business. L20.
– SPECIAL COLLOCATIONS: **metric space** *MATH.* a set together with a metric defined for all pairs of elements of the set.

-metric /ˈmɛtrɪk/ *suffix*.
[ORIGIN from or after French *-métrique* from (the same root as) Latin *metricus* METRIC *noun*[1] & *adjective*[1].]
Forming adjectives corresp. to nouns in ***-meter*** or ***-metry***, as ***barometric***, ***gravimetric***.

metrical /ˈmɛtrɪk(ə)l/ *adjective*[1]. L15.
[ORIGIN formed as METRIC *noun*[1] & *adjective*[1]: see -ICAL.]
1 *PROSODY*. Of, pertaining to, or composed in metre. L15.
2 Of, involving, or determined by measurement. M17.

metrical /ˈmɛtrɪk(ə)l/ *adjective*[2]. Now *rare*. L18.
[ORIGIN French *métrique* METRIC *adjective*[2] & *noun*[2] + -AL[1].]
= METRIC *adjective*[2] 1.

metrically /ˈmɛtrɪk(ə)li/ *adverb*[1]. M17.
[ORIGIN from METRIC *adjective*[1] or METRICAL *adjective*[1] + -ICALLY.]
PROSODY. With regard to metre; (translated) into metre.

metrically /ˈmɛtrɪk(ə)li/ *adverb*[2]. M20.
[ORIGIN from METRIC *adjective*[2] or METRICAL *adjective*[2] + -ICALLY.]
In or with the metric system of weights and measures.

metricate /ˈmɛtrɪkeɪt/ *verb*. M20.
[ORIGIN Back-form. from METRICATION.]
1 *verb intrans.* Change to or adopt the metric system of weights and measures. M20.
2 *verb trans.* Convert or adapt to the metric system. L20.

metrication /mɛtrɪˈkeɪʃ(ə)n/ *noun*. M20.
[ORIGIN from METRIC *adjective*[2] + -ATION.]
Conversion to the metric system of weights and measures; the adoption of the metric system.

metrician /mɪˈtrɪʃ(ə)n/ *noun*. L15.
[ORIGIN formed as METRIC *noun*[1] & *adjective*[1] + -ICIAN.]
PROSODY. †**1** A person writing in metre. L15–M16.
2 An expert in or student of metre. M19.

metrification /ˌmɛtrɪfɪˈkeɪʃ(ə)n/ *noun*. LME.
[ORIGIN In sense 1 from medieval Latin *metrificatio(n-)*, from Latin *metrificat-* pa. ppl stem of *metrificare*: see METRIFY, -ATION. In sense 2 from METRI(C *adjective*[2] + -FICATION.]
1 *PROSODY*. Metrical composition or structure. LME.
2 = METRICATION. M20.

†**metrify** *verb trans.* L15–L19.
[ORIGIN Old French *metrifier* or medieval Latin *metrificare*, from Latin *metrum* METRE *noun*[1]: see -FY.]
Put into metre, make a metrical version of.

metrisable *adjective* var. of METRIZABLE.

metrisation *noun* var. of METRIZATION.

metrist /ˈmɛtrɪst/ *noun*. M16.
[ORIGIN medieval Latin *metrista*, from Latin *metrum* METRE *noun*[1]: see -IST.]
A person who writes or composes (esp. skilfully) in metre.

metritis /mɪˈtrʌɪtɪs/ *noun*. E19.
[ORIGIN from Greek *mētra* womb + -ITIS.]
MEDICINE. Inflammation of the uterus.
■ **metritic** /mɪˈtrɪtɪk/ *adjective* M19.

metrizable /mɪˈtrʌɪzəb(ə)l/ *adjective*. Also **-isable**. E20.
[ORIGIN formed as METRIZATION + -ABLE.]
MATH. Of a topological space: able to be assigned a metric which makes it a metric space whose topology is identical to that of the original space.
■ **metrizaˈbility** *noun* E20.

metrization /mɛtrʌɪˈzeɪʃ(ə)n/ *noun*. Also **-isation**. E20.
[ORIGIN from METRIC *noun*[1] + -IZATION.]
MATH. The process of assigning a metric to a metrizable topological space.

metro /ˈmɛtrəʊ, ˈmeɪ-/ *noun*[1]. *colloq.* Also **M-**. Pl. **-os**. E20.
[ORIGIN French *métro* abbreviation of (*Chemin de Fer*) *Métropolitain* Metropolitan (Railway).]
An underground railway system in a city, esp. Paris.

metro /ˈmɛtrəʊ/ *adjective* & *noun*[2]. M20.
[ORIGIN Abbreviation of METROPOLITAN *adjective*.]
▸ **A** *adjective*. = METROPOLITAN *adjective* 2a, b. M20.

Economist The metro counties are Labour's territory.

▸ **B** *noun*. Pl. **-os**. The metropolitan area of a city. *Canad.* L20.

metrocracy /mɪˈtrɒkrəsi/ *noun*. L19.
[ORIGIN from Greek *mētr-*, *mētēr* mother: see -CRACY.]
= MATRIARCHY.

metroland /ˈmɛtrə(ʊ)land/ *noun*. Also **M-**. E20.
[ORIGIN from METRO(POLITAN *adjective* + LAND *noun*[1].]
The area surrounding a metropolis, *spec.* that around London, esp. to the north-west, served by the underground railway.
■ **metrolander** *noun* E20.

Metroliner /ˈmɛtrəʊlʌɪnə/ *noun*. Also **metro-liner**. M20.
[ORIGIN from METRO(POLITAN *adjective* + LINER *noun*[2].]
A high-speed intercity train in the US.

metrology /mɛˈtrɒlədʒi/ *noun*. E19.
[ORIGIN from Greek *metron* METRE *noun*[1] + -OLOGY.]
The branch of science that deals with measurement.
■ **metroˈlogical** *adjective* M19. **metrologist** *noun* M19.

†**metromania** *noun*. M18–L19.
[ORIGIN from Greek *metron* METRE *noun*[1] + -MANIA.]
A mania for writing poetry.
■ †**metromaniac** *noun* & *adjective* M–L19.

metronidazole /mɛtrəˈnʌɪdəzəʊl/ *noun*. M20.
[ORIGIN from ME(THYL + NITRO- + IM)IDAZOLE, elems. of the systematic name (see below).]
PHARMACOLOGY. An imidazole derivative used to treat infection by some anaerobic organisms, esp. trichomoniasis; 2-(2-methyl-5-nitroimidazol-1-yl)ethanol, $C_6H_9N_3O_3$.

metronome /ˈmɛtrənəʊm/ *noun*. E19.
[ORIGIN from Greek *metron* METRE *noun*[1] + *nomos* law, rule.]
MUSIC. A device for marking time which emits a regular tick at a selected rate, esp. by means of an oscillating rod or pendulum.
■ **metroˈnomic** *adjective* of or pertaining to a metronome; *fig.* resembling the action of a metronome: L19. **metroˈnomically** *adverb* in a metronomic way; according to a metronome: E19.

metronymic /mɛtrəˈnɪmɪk/ *noun* & *adjective*. M19.
[ORIGIN from Greek *mētr-*, *mētēr* mother, after PATRONYMIC.]
▸ **A** *noun*. A name derived from that of a mother or maternal ancestor, esp. by addition of an affix indicating such descent. M19.
▸ **B** *adjective*. Designating such a name or such an affix; (of a group or culture) using such names. L19.
■ **meˈtronymy** *noun* the practice of using metronymics L19.

metrop /mɪˈtrɒp/ *noun*. *colloq.* L19.
[ORIGIN Abbreviation.]
= METROPOLIS 3a.

metroplex /ˈmɛtrəʊplɛks/ *noun*. Chiefly *N. Amer.* M20.
[ORIGIN from METRO(POLITAN *adjective* + COM)PLEX *noun*.]
A very large metropolitan area, *spec.* one which is an aggregation of two or more cities.

Times The whole metroplex of Houston ranks as an enterprise zone.

metropole /ˈmɛtrəpəʊl/ *noun*. L15.
[ORIGIN Old French & mod. French *métropol* formed as METROPOLIS.]
1 a A chief town or city. Now *rare*. L15. ▸**b** The parent state of a colony. Cf. METROPOLIS 2. E19.

b *Survey* No longer were all the colonies economically indebted to the metropoles.

†**2** = METROPOLIS 1. M–L19.
3 A luxury hotel. L19.

metropolis /mɪˈtrɒp(ə)lɪs/ *noun*. Pl. **-lises**, **-li** /-lʌɪ, -liː/. M16.
[ORIGIN Late Latin from Greek *mētropolis*, from *mētēr*, *mētr-* mother + *polis* city.]
1 *ECCLESIASTICAL*. The see of a metropolitan bishop. M16.
2 The mother city or parent state of a colony, *spec.* an ancient Greek one. M16.

J. A. ROEBUCK The best means of making the wants of the colonies known to . . the metropolis which founds them.

3 The chief city of a country, a capital; any large busy city; ***the metropolis***, such a city, (esp., in Britain, London) as distinct from its surrounding rural or provincial areas. L16. ▸**b** A city as the centre of some specified activity. Usu. foll. by *of*. L17. ▸**c** *BOTANY & ZOOLOGY*. The district in which a species, group, etc., is most represented. *rare*. E19.

P. THEROUX The border town of Tecún Umán was so small it made Tapachula seem a metropolis. **b** J. BRYCE Rome is the metropolis of religion.

metropolitan /mɛtrəˈpɒlɪt(ə)n/ *noun* & *adjective*. LME.
[ORIGIN Late Latin *metropolitanus*, from Greek *mētropolitēs*, from *mētropolis*: see METROPOLIS, -AN.]
▸ **A** *noun*. **1** *ECCLESIASTICAL*. (The title of) a bishop having the oversight of the bishops of a province, in the Western Church now approximately coextensive with archbishop, in the Orthodox Church ranking above an archbishop and below a patriarch. LME.
2 A chief town, a metropolis. Now *rare*. LME.
†**3** = METROPOLIS 3b. E17–E18.
4 A native or inhabitant of a metropolis; a person who has metropolitan or urbane ideas, manners, etc. L18.

A. BRIEN These sophisticated metropolitans, all of them Petersburg graduates.

▸ **B** *adjective*. **1** *ECCLESIASTICAL*. Belonging to an ecclesiastical metropolis. Also, pertaining to or characteristic of a metropolitan. LME.
2 Of, pertaining to, or constituting a metropolis or large city. Later also, (of a person, lifestyle, etc.) urbane, sophisticated, exciting. M16. ▸**b** Designating or pertaining to a city underground railway system. M19. ▸**c** Designating a type of early English pottery found in or near London. L19.

V. S. NAIPAUL The metropolitan excitements of London. J. GOODWIN They pile on the bus on Friday night and head for . . the heart of metropolitan glamour.

3 Of, pertaining to, or designating the parent state of a colony. E19.
– SPECIAL COLLOCATIONS: **metropolitan bishop** = sense A.1 above. **metropolitan county** each of six units of English local government centred on a large urban area (in existence from 1974 to 1986). **metropolitan district** an English administrative unit consisting of a town or city and a borough. **metropolitan magistrate** a paid professional magistrate in London (cf. STIPENDIARY).
■ **metropolitanate** *noun* = METROPOLITANSHIP M19. **metropolitanism** *noun* metropolitan spirit, ideas, or institutions M19. **metropolitaniˈzation** *noun* the process of giving a metropolitan character to a person or area M20. **metropolitanize** *verb trans.* make metropolitan; convert into a metropolis: M19. **metropolitanship** *noun* the office or see of a metropolitan bishop M17.

†**metropolite** *noun*. L16–L19.
[ORIGIN Late Latin *metropolita* from Greek *mētropolitēs*, from *mētropolis* METROPOLIS: see -ITE[1].]
1 *ECCLESIASTICAL*. = METROPOLITAN *noun* 1. L16–L19.
†**2** = METROPOLIS 3. L16–M17.

metropolitical /mɛtrəpəˈlɪtɪk(ə)l/ *adjective*. M16.
[ORIGIN from medieval Latin *metropoliticus*, formed as METROPOLITE: see -AL[1].]
1 *ECCLESIASTICAL*. = METROPOLITAN *adjective* 1. M16.
2 = METROPOLITAN *adjective* 2a, 3. E17.
■ **metropolitically** *adverb* M17.

M

metrorrhagia /miːtrəˈreɪdʒɪə/ *noun.* L18.
[ORIGIN from Greek *mētra* womb + -O- + -RRHAGIA.]
MEDICINE. Abnormal uterine haemorrhage.
■ **metrorrhagic** *adjective* M19.

metrosexual /ˌmɛtrə(ʊ)ˈsɛkʃʊəl/ *noun & adjective. colloq.* L20.
[ORIGIN from METRO(POLITAN *adjective* + SEXUAL.]
▶ **A** *noun.* A heterosexual urban man who enjoys shopping, fashion, and similar interests traditionally associated with women or homosexual men.
Washington Post Girls like to see guys well groomed, but please, no metrosexuals.
▶ **B** *adjective.* Designating or pertaining to metrosexuals.

metrostaxis /miːtrəˈstaksɪs/ *noun.* L19.
[ORIGIN from Greek *mētra* womb + *-staxis*, from *stazein* drip.]
MEDICINE. Slight continuous uterine haemorrhage.

-metry /mɪtri/ *suffix.*
[ORIGIN Repr. Greek *-metria*, from *-metrēs* measurer, from *metron* METRE *noun*¹: see -Y³.]
Used in words adopted from Greek and in English words modelled on these, usu. denoting the action, process, or science of measuring something (as ***alkalimetry***, ***chronometry***, ***gasometry***), *spec.* (corresp. to nouns in ***-meter***) by means of a particular instrument (as ***barometry***).

metteur en scène /mɛtœːr ɑ̃ sɛn/ *noun phr.* Pl. ***metteurs en scène*** (pronounced same). L19.
[ORIGIN French, lit. 'a person who puts on the stage'.]
A producer of a play; a director of a film.

mettle /ˈmɛt(ə)l/ *noun & adjective.* Also †**metal**. E16.
[ORIGIN Var. of METAL *noun & adjective.*]
▶ **A** *noun* **I 1** The quality of a person's disposition or temperament. E16.
J. CHEEVER We think we know each other's mettle intimately.
2 A person's spirit or courage. L16.
JULIETTE HUXLEY I feared . . I had not the mettle to cope with this whirlwind.
3 The natural vigour or spirit of an animal, esp. a horse. L16.
J. MARTINEAU They have horses of best descent and mettle.
▶ †**II** See METAL *noun.*
– PHRASES: **on one's mettle** inspired to do one's best. †**put a person off his or her mettle** undermine a person's courage. **put a person on his or her mettle** test a person's powers of endurance or resistance. **show one's mettle** reveal or demonstrate one's courage. **try a person's mettle** = *put a person on his or her metal* above.
▶ **B** *adjective.* **1** Of spirited temperament. *obsolete* exc. *Scot.* L16.
R. L. STEVENSON He is an honest and a mettle gentleman.
2 See METAL *adjective.*
■ **mettled** *adjective* (*a*) = METTLESOME; (*b*) having a temperament of a specified kind: L16. **mettlesome** *adjective* full of mettle; spirited: M17.

Mettwurst /ˈmɛtvʊrst/ *noun.* M19.
[ORIGIN German.]
A type of smoked German sausage.

meu /mjuː/ *noun.* E16.
[ORIGIN Irreg. formed as MEUM *noun*².]
= MEUM *noun*².

meubles /mœbl/ *noun pl.* ME.
[ORIGIN Old French *mo(e)bles*, *muebles*, use as noun (pl.) of adjective, from Latin *mobilis* MOBILE *adjective.* Reintroduced from French in 18 in sense 2.]
†**1** Movable property or goods; *spec.* (SCOTS LAW) movable as opp. to heritable property; = MOVABLE *noun* 2. ME–L16.
2 (Items of) household furniture. L18.

meum /ˈmiːəm, ˈmeɪəm/ *noun*¹. *arch.* L16.
[ORIGIN Latin, neut. of *meus* mine.]
The principle that a person has sole rights to his or her own property and no rights to another's. Chiefly in ***meum and tuum***, (the distinction between) what is mine or one's own and what is yours or another's.

meum /ˈmiːəm/ *noun*². M16.
[ORIGIN Latin from Greek *mēon*.]
= SPIGNEL.

meunière /məːˈnjɛː, *foreign* mønjɛːr/ *adjective.* E20.
[ORIGIN French (*à la*) *meunière* lit. '(in the manner of) a miller's wife'.]
COOKERY. Esp. of fish: cooked or served in lightly browned butter with lemon juice and parsley. Usu. *postpositive.*

Meursault /məːˈsəʊ, ˈməː-, *foreign* mœrso (*pl. same*)/ *noun.* M19.
[ORIGIN A commune in the Côte d'Or, France.]
A (usu. white) burgundy wine produced near Beaune.

meuse /mjuːs, -z/ *noun & verb.* Now *dial.* Also **muse**. E16.
[ORIGIN Old French *musse*, *m(o)uce* (mod. dial. *muche*) hiding place, from *musser*, *muchier* to hide (whence MITCH *verb*). Cf. MUSET.]
▶ **A** *noun.* **1** A gap in a hedge or fence through which hares, rabbits, etc., pass, esp. as a means of escape; *fig.* a way out of a difficulty. E16.
2 The form (lair) of a hare. E17.
▶ **B** *verb intrans.* Go through a meuse. L17.

MeV *abbreviation.*
Mega-electronvolt(s).

mevalonic /mɛvəˈlɒnɪk/ *adjective.* M20.
[ORIGIN from ME(THYL + VAL(ERIC *adjective* + LACT)ON(E + -IC.]
BIOCHEMISTRY. ***mevalonic acid***, a crystalline compound, $C_6H_{12}O_4$, which is a growth factor for some lactobacilli and a precursor of cholesterol in animals and carotenoids in plants; 3,5-dihydroxy-3-methylpentanoic acid.
■ **mevalonate** /mɪˈvalənеɪt/ *noun* a salt or ester of mevalonic acid; *loosely* the acid itself or its anion: M20.

mew /mjuː/ *noun*¹.
[ORIGIN Old English *mǣw*, corresp. to Old Saxon *mēu* (Middle Low German, Middle Dutch *mēwe*, Dutch *meeuw*), from Germanic, whence also Old High German *mēh*, Old Norse *már* (pl. *mávar*, *máfar*).]
A gull. Also called ***seamew***.
– COMB.: **mew gull** (chiefly *N. Amer.*) the common gull, *Larus canus.*

mew /mjuː/ *noun*². ME.
[ORIGIN Old French & mod. French *mue*, from *muer*: see MEW *verb*¹.]
1 A cage for hawks, esp. while moulting; in *pl.*, the building(s) housing a set of these. ME.
2 †**a** A cage for confining animals, esp. poultry, for fattening. LME–M19. ▸**b** A breeding cage. Now *dial.* LME.
3 †**a** A place of confinement. LME–E17. ▸**b** A secret place; a den. Now *rare.* LME.
– PHRASES: **in mew** (*a*) (of a hawk) in the process of moulting; †(*b*) (of a person) in hiding or confinement.

mew /mjuː/ *noun*³ *& interjection.* E17.
[ORIGIN Imit.: rel. to MEW *verb*². Cf. MIAOW *noun.*]
†**1** (A sound) expr. derision. Only in E17.
2 (Repr.) the characteristic cry of a cat, seabird, etc. L18.
transf.: DENNIS POTTER The sounds of his weeping grew from a pathetic little mew into a violent sob.

mew /mjuː/ *verb*¹. LME.
[ORIGIN In branch I from Old French & mod. French *muer*, from Latin *mutare*: see MUTATION *noun*; in branch II from MEW *noun*².]
▶ **I 1** *verb trans. & intrans.* Of a bird, esp. a hawk: moult, shed (feathers). LME. ▸†**b** Of a stag: cast (its antlers). LME–L18.
†**2** *verb trans. & intrans. fig.* Change or remove (clothing). LME–M17.
▶ **II** †**3** *verb trans.* Coop *up* (poultry etc.) for fattening. *rare.* LME–M17.
4 *verb trans.* Confine, enclose; conceal. Now usu. foll. by *up.* LME.
5 *verb trans.* Put (a hawk) in a cage at moulting time. M16.

mew /mjuː/ *verb*² *intrans.* ME.
[ORIGIN Imit.: rel. to MEW *noun*³. Cf. MIAOW.]
1 Of a cat, seabird, etc.: make its characteristic cry. ME.
D. M. THOMAS A little black cat at her feet, mewing up at her pathetically.
2 *transf.* Of a person: utter a similar sound esp. in distress or (formerly) derision; *fig.* whimper, whine. E17.
B. BRYSON I mewed some pitiful apology.

Mewari /mɛˈwɑːri/ *noun & adjective.* L19.
[ORIGIN from *Mewar* (see below) + -I².]
▶ **A** *noun.* The language spoken in Udaipur (formerly Mewar), a former state in NW India, now part of Rajasthan. L19.
▶ **B** *adjective.* Of or pertaining to Udaipur (Mewar) or its inhabitants. E20.

Mewati /mɛˈwɑːti/ *noun & adjective.* L18.
[ORIGIN Hindi *mevātī*, formed as MEO *noun*¹ *& adjective*¹.]
▶ **A** *noun.* Pl. same, **-s**.
1 A member of a people of the Mewat region in NW India (now called Alwar and part of Rajasthan) and neighbouring areas; a Meo; *spec.* one professing Islam. L18.
2 The Rajasthani dialect of this people. E20.
▶ **B** *attrib.* or as *adjective.* Of or pertaining to the Mewati or their dialect. M19.

mewl /mjuːl/ *verb & noun.* M16.
[ORIGIN Imit. Cf. MIAUL.]
▶ **A** *verb intrans.* **1** Esp. of an infant: cry feebly, whimper. M16.
2 = MEW *verb*² 1. E17.
▶ **B** *noun.* A thin cry, a whimper. M19.

mews /mjuːz/ *noun.* LME.
[ORIGIN Pl. of MEW *noun*².]
1 Orig., the royal stables at Charing Cross in London, built on the former site of the royal hawk mews. Later *gen.*, any set of stable buildings grouped round an open yard or alley. Treated as *sing.* or *pl.* LME.
2 Such a set of buildings converted into accommodation for people. Also, (a dwelling in) a row of town houses built in the style of a mews. E19.

mewt /mjuːt/ *verb intrans. obsolete* exc. *dial.* ME.
[ORIGIN Imit.]
= MEW *verb*².

Mex /mɛks/ *adjective & noun. US slang.* M19.
[ORIGIN Abbreviation.]
▶ **A** *adjective.* = MEXICAN *adjective.* M19.
▶ **B** *noun.* Pl. same. = MEXICAN *noun*; *spec.* = ***MEXICAN dollar***. M19.

Mexican /ˈmɛksɪk(ə)n/ *noun & adjective.* L16.
[ORIGIN Spanish *mexicano* (now *mej-*), from *Mexico*, from Nahuatl *Mexitli* one of the names of the Aztec god of war: see -AN.]
▶ **A** *noun.* **1** A native or inhabitant of Mexico. L16.
2 Nahuatl. Also = ***Mexican Spanish*** below. L18.
3 = ***Mexican dollar*** below. E19.
▶ **B** *adjective.* Of or pertaining to Mexico or its inhabitants. L16.
– SPECIAL COLLOCATIONS & COMB.: **Mexican-American** *adjective & noun* (designating or pertaining to) a person of Mexican descent in the US. **Mexican brown** *slang* crude heroin. **Mexican dollar** the Mexican peso; a coin of this value. **Mexican embroidery** a kind of embroidery characterized by brightly coloured floral or geometric designs. **Mexican fruit fly** a Central American dipteran insect, *Anastrepha ludens*, a pest of mangoes and citrus fruit. **Mexican hairless (dog)** (an animal of) a breed of small dog, lacking hair except for tufts on the head and tail. **Mexican-Indian** *adjective & noun* (designating or pertaining to) a member of any of the aboriginal peoples of Mexico. **Mexican orange** a Mexican shrub, *Choisya ternata*, of the rue family, grown for its fragrant white flowers. **Mexican overdrive** *US slang* (the neutral gear position used when) coasting downhill in a motor vehicle. **Mexican poppy** a prickly-leaved poppy, *Argemone mexicana*, a weed in many warm countries. ***Mexican* SCAMMONY**. **Mexican shilling** *hist.* a silver coin formerly current in some states of the US. **Mexican Spanish** (of) the variety of Spanish used in Mexico. **Mexican stand-off** (orig. in poker) a situation in which there is no clear winner; an impasse. **Mexican tea** a strong-scented goosefoot, *Chenopodium ambrosioides*, used as a flavouring in Mexico and medicinally. **Mexican thistle** = ***Mexican poppy*** above. **Mexican War** the war of 1846–8 between the US and Mexico. ***Mexican wave***: see WAVE *noun* 5e.
■ **Mexicaniˈzation** *noun* the action of Mexicanizing L19. **Mexicanize** *verb trans. & intrans.* make or become Mexican in character, manners, ideas, etc. M19.

Mexicano /mɛksɪˈkɑːnəʊ/ *noun & adjective.* L19.
[ORIGIN Spanish: see MEXICAN.]
▶ **A** *noun.* Pl. **-os**. Fem. **-a** /-ə/. A native or inhabitant of Mexico; a person of Mexican descent, *esp.* a Mexican-American. L19.
▶ **B** *attrib.* or as *adjective.* Pertaining to or designating a Mexicano. L19.

mexiletine /mɛkˈsʌɪlətiːn/ *noun.* L20.
[ORIGIN from ME(TH- + *xil-* alt. of XYL(ENE + ET(H + -INE⁵.]
PHARMACOLOGY. A cyclic derivative of propanol used to treat ventricular arrhythmia; 1-(2,6-dimethylphenoxy)-2-propanamine, $C_6H_3(CH_3)_2OCH_2CH(CH_3)NH_2$.

Meyerbeerian /mʌɪəˈbɪərɪən/ *adjective.* L19.
[ORIGIN from *Meyerbeer* (see below) + -IAN.]
Characteristic of or resembling the work of the German operatic composer Giacomo Meyerbeer (1791–1864), noted esp. for long grand operas dealing with epic subjects in a spectacular way.

mézair /meɪˈzɛː, *foreign* mezɛːr (*pl. same*)/ *noun.* M18.
[ORIGIN French, from Italian *mezzaria* middle gait.]
HORSEMANSHIP. A movement involving a series of levades with a short step between each.

meze /ˈmeɪzeɪ/ *noun.* Pl. same, **-s**. E20.
[ORIGIN Turkish = snack, appetizer, from Persian *maza* to taste, relish.]
(Any of) a selection of hot and cold dishes served as a starter in the Middle East and eastern Mediterranean region.

Mezentian /mɪˈzɛnʃ(ə)n/ *adjective.* L18.
[ORIGIN from *Mezentius* (see below) + -AN.]
Of a union: comparable to that of Mezentius, a mythical Etruscan king who had living people bound to corpses and left to starve; cruelly binding.
SYD. SMITH That fatal and Mezentian oath which binds the Irish to the English Church.

mezereon /mɪˈzɪərɪən/ *noun.* Also **-eum** /-ɪəm/. L15.
[ORIGIN medieval Latin from Arabic *māzariyūn*.]
A Eurasian early-flowering woodland shrub, *Daphne mezereum* (family Thymelaeaceae), with fragrant purplish or rose-coloured flowers; the dried bark of the root of this, formerly used in liniments.

mezuza /məˈzuːzə/ *noun.* Also **-ah**. Pl. **-zoth** /-zəʊt/. M17.
[ORIGIN Hebrew *mĕzūzāh* lit. 'doorpost' (*Deuteronomy* 6:9).]
A piece of parchment inscribed with Pentateuchal texts enclosed in a case and attached to the doorpost of a Jewish house in fulfilment of religious law.

mezz /mɛz/ *noun. slang.* M20.
[ORIGIN *Mezz* Mezzrow (1899–1972), US jazz clarinettist and drug user.]
Marijuana.
– COMB.: **mezzroll** a marijuana cigarette.

mezzadria /meddzaˈdriːa/ *noun.* Also ***mezzeria*** /meddzeˈriːa/. L19.
[ORIGIN Italian.]
hist. A system of feudal land tenure in Italy whereby a farmer paid the landowner a proportion (orig. half) of the farm's produce as rent.

M

■ *mezzadro* /med'dzadro/ *noun*, pl. *-ri* /-ri/, a tenant farmer of this system L19.

mezzaluna /mɛtsəˈluːnə/ *noun*. M20.
[ORIGIN Italian, lit. 'half moon'.]
A crescent-shaped cutting utensil comprising a semicircular blade with a handle on top or at either end, used with a rocking motion for chopping food.

mezza-majolica /mɛtsəməˈjɒlɪkə, -ˈdʒɒlɪkə/ *noun*. M19.
[ORIGIN Italian, from *mezza* fem. of *mezzo* (see MEZZO *adverb*) + MAJOLICA.]
A kind of Italian decorative pottery made between the 15th and 17th cents., less elaborate than true majolica.

mezzani /mɛdˈzɑːni/ *noun*. L19.
[ORIGIN Italian, pl. of *mezzano*: see MEZZANINE.]
Pasta in the form of medium-sized tubes; an Italian dish consisting largely of this and usu. a sauce.

mezzanine /ˈmɛzəniːn/ *noun & adjective*. E18.
[ORIGIN French from Italian *mezzanino* dim. of *mezzano* middle, medium, from Latin *medianus* MEDIAN.]
▸ **A** *noun*. **1** A low storey between two others in a building, usu. between the ground floor and the floor above. E18. ▸**b** The lowest gallery in a theatre or cinema; a dress circle. *N. Amer.* E20.
2 THEATRICAL. A floor beneath the stage, from which the traps are worked. M19.
▸ **B** *adjective*. **1** Designating an intermediate floor, storey, etc. E19.
2 COMMERCE. Designating unsecured, higher-yielding loans that are subordinate to bank loans and secured loans but rank above equity. L20.

> *Observer* Potential raiders looked to venture capitalists . . to provide mezzanine finance.

mezza voce /mɛtsə ˈvɒtʃi/ *adverbial, noun, & adjectival phr.* L18.
[ORIGIN Italian *mezza* fem. of MEZZO *adverb* + *voce* voice.]
MUSIC. (With) half of the possible vocal or instrumental power; restrained.

mezzeria *noun* var. of MEZZADRIA.

mezzo /ˈmɛtsəʊ/ *noun & adjective*. Pl. of noun **-os**. M19.
[ORIGIN Abbreviation.]
= MEZZO-SOPRANO.

> *Times* Irina Arkipovna has been singing leading mezzo roles at the Bolshoi for almost 20 years.

mezzo /ˈmɛtsəʊ/ *adverb*. M18.
[ORIGIN Italian = middle, half, from Latin *medius* MEDIUM.]
MUSIC. Qualifying a direction: half, moderately, fairly. **mezzo forte** moderately loud. **mezzo piano** moderately soft.

Mezzofanti /mɛtsəʊˈfanti, mɛdz-/ *noun*. Long *rare*. M19.
[ORIGIN Giuseppe *Mezzofanti* (1774–1849), Italian cardinal who mastered over fifty languages.]
A person of exceptional linguistic ability.

> G. M. HOPKINS We have a . . young sucking Mezzofanti among us who could have written in seven languages.

■ **mezzofantic** *adjective* E20.

Mezzogiorno /mɛtsəʊˈdʒɔːnəʊ/ *noun*. M20.
[ORIGIN Italian, from MEZZO *adverb* + *giorno* day.]
The southern part of Italy, including Sicily and Sardinia.

mezzo-relievo /ˌmɛtsəʊrɪˈliːvəʊ/ *noun*. Also **-rilievo** /-rɪˈljeɪvəʊ/. Pl. **-os**. L16.
[ORIGIN Italian: see MEZZO *adverb*, RELIEVO *noun*[1].]
(A sculpture, moulding, carving, etc., in) half relief (see RELIEF *noun*[2]).

mezzo-soprano /ˌmɛtsəʊsəˈprɑːnəʊ/ *noun & adjective*. M18.
[ORIGIN Italian: see MEZZO *adverb*, SOPRANO. Cf. MEZZO *noun & adjective*.]
MUSIC. ▸**A** *noun*. Pl. **-os**. A female voice intermediate in compass between soprano and contralto; a singer with such a voice; a part written for such a voice. M18.
▸ **B** *adjective*. Designating, pertaining to, or intended for a mezzo-soprano. L18.

mezzo termine /mɛttso ˈtɛrmine/ *noun phr.* Pl. ***mezzo termini*** /ˈtɛrmini/. M18.
[ORIGIN Italian: see MEZZO *adverb*.]
A middle term, measure, or period.

> C. M. YONGE In writing up to that *mezzo termine* of our lives, I have been living it over again.

mezzotint /ˈmɛtsəʊtɪnt, ˈmɛzəʊ-/ *noun & verb*. M18.
[ORIGIN Anglicized from MEZZOTINTO.]
▸ **A** *noun*. **1** A half-tint. Now *rare* or *obsolete*. M18.
2 A method of engraving a copper or steel plate by roughening it and then partially scraping the surface away so that it produces tones and halftones. Also, a print produced by this process. E19.

> M. R. JAMES An indifferent mezzotint is, perhaps, the worst form of engraving known.

– COMB.: **mezzotint rocker** = CRADLE *noun* 9.
▸ **B** *verb trans*. Engrave in mezzotint. E19.
■ **mezzotinter** *noun* M18.

mezzotinto /mɛttsoˈtinto/ *noun*. Now *rare*. M17.
[ORIGIN Italian, lit. 'half-tint': see MEZZO *adverb*.]
†**1** = MEZZOTINT *noun* 1. M17–L18.
2 = MEZZOTINT *noun* 2. M17.

MF *abbreviation*[1].
Medium frequency.

mf *abbreviation*[2].
MUSIC. Mezzo forte.

MFA *abbreviation*.
Multi-Fibre Agreement (or Arrangement).

MFH *abbreviation*.
Master of Foxhounds.

MFN *abbreviation*.
Most favoured nation (see FAVOURED *adjective*[2]).

MG *abbreviation*[1].
Machine gun.

mg *abbreviation*[2].
Milligram(s).

Mg *symbol*.
CHEMISTRY. Magnesium.

mganga /(ə)mˈgaŋgə/ *noun*. Pl. ***mgangas***, ***waganga*** /wəˈgaŋgə/. M19.
[ORIGIN Bantu.]
In Tanzania and other parts of E. Africa: an indigenous African doctor, a witch doctor.

MGB *abbreviation*. *hist*.
Russian *Ministérstvo Gosudárstvennoĭ Bezopásnosti* Ministry of State Security.

MGM *abbreviation*.
Metro-Goldwyn-Mayer (film company).

Mgr *abbreviation*.
1 Manager.
2 French *Monseigneur*.
3 Monsignor.

MH *abbreviation*.
Medal of Honor.

MHC *abbreviation*.
BIOCHEMISTRY. Major histocompatibility complex (of proteins involved in immunity).

MHD *abbreviation*.
Magnetohydrodynamic(s).

MHK *abbreviation*.
Member of the House of Keys (in the Isle of Man).

mho /məʊ/ *noun*. Pl. **mhos**. L19.
[ORIGIN OHM spelled backwards.]
ELECTRICITY. The cgs unit of conductance, equal to the conductance of a body whose resistance is one ohm. Cf. SIEMENS 2b.

MHR *abbreviation*.
Member of the House of Representatives (in the US and Australia).

MHz *abbreviation*.
Megahertz.

MI *abbreviation*.
1 Michigan.
2 Military Intelligence (***MI5***, ***MI6***, respectively British security service and espionage departments, until 1964).
3 Mounted Infantry.

mi /miː/ *noun*. Also **me**. LME.
[ORIGIN from Latin *mi(ra)*: see UT and cf. ALAMIRE, BEMI.]
MUSIC. The third note of a scale in a movable-doh system; the note E in the fixed-doh system.

mi /mʌɪ/ *adjective*[1]. *colloq*. L18.
[ORIGIN Abbreviation.]
= MINOR *adjective* 1b.

mi *adjective*[2] see MY *adjective*.

mi. *abbreviation*.
Mile(s).

MIA *abbreviation*.
Missing in action.

miacid /ˈmʌɪəsɪd/ *adjective & noun*. E20.
[ORIGIN mod. Latin *Miacidae* (see below), from *Miacis* genus name: see -ID[3].]
PALAEONTOLOGY. ▸**A** *adjective*. Of, pertaining to, or designating the extinct family Miacidae of small carnivorous mammals, known from N. American Palaeocene and Eocene fossils. E20.
▸ **B** *noun*. An animal of this family. M20.

miai /ˈmiai/ *noun*. L19.
[ORIGIN Japanese, from *mi* seeing + *ai* mutually.]
The first formal meeting of the prospective partners in a Japanese arranged marriage.

mia-mia /ˈmʌɪəmʌɪə/ *noun*. *Austral*. M19.
[ORIGIN Uncertain; perh. either from Nyungar *maya-maya* or Wathawurung and Wuywurung *miam miam*. See also MAIMAI.]
An Aboriginal hut or shelter; *transf*. a temporary shelter built by a traveller.

mianserin /mʌɪˈansərɪn/ *noun*. L20.
[ORIGIN Uncertain: includes SER(OTON)IN.]
PHARMACOLOGY. A tetracyclic compound, $C_{18}H_{20}N_2$, with sedative effects, used to treat depression.

Miao /mɪˈaʊ/ *adjective & noun*. Also **Meo** /mɪˈəʊ/. M19.
[ORIGIN Chinese *Miáo*.]
= HMONG.
■ Also **Miaotse** /mɪˈaʊtsi/ *noun & adjective* (pl. of noun same) E19.

miaow /mɪˈaʊ/ *noun, interjection, & verb*. Also **meow**, **miaouw**. M17.
[ORIGIN Imit. Cf. MEW *noun*[3] & *interjection*, MIAUL, & French *miaou*.]
▸ **A** *noun & interjection*. (Repr.) the characteristic cry of a cat; *fig*. (a sound) implying spite or maliciousness in the person addressed (cf. CAT *noun*[1] 2). M17.

> E. BRADFORD 'He's always . . where the bar is.' She leaned forward. 'Miaouw!'

▸ **B** *verb intrans*. Make this sound. M17.

miargyrite /mʌɪˈɑːdʒɪrʌɪt/ *noun*. M19.
[ORIGIN from Greek *meiōn* less + *arguros* silver + -ITE[1].]
MINERALOGY. A monoclinic sulphide of silver and antimony, a minor ore of silver usu. occurring as small black prisms.

miarolitic /miːərəˈlɪtɪk/ *adjective*. L19.
[ORIGIN from Italian (dial.) *miarolo* a variety of granite: see -LITE, -IC.]
PETROGRAPHY. Characterized by or designating irregular cavities in igneous rocks into which crystals project.

mias /ˈmʌɪəs/ *noun*. Now *rare* or *obsolete*. Pl. same. M19.
[ORIGIN Dayak *maias*.]
An orang-utan.

miasm /ˈmʌɪaz(ə)m/ *noun*. M17.
[ORIGIN In sense 1 from French *miasme*, in sense 2 from German *Miasm*, both formed as MIASMA.]
1 = MIASMA. M17.
2 HOMEOPATHY. A supposed predisposition to a particular disease, which a person either inherits or acquires. M19.

miasma /mɪˈazmə, mʌɪ-/ *noun*. Pl. **-mas**, **-mata** /-mətə/. M17.
[ORIGIN Greek *miasma(t-)* defilement, pollution, rel. to *miainein* pollute.]
1 (An) infectious or noxious vapour, esp. from putrescent organic matter, which pollutes the atmosphere. M17.

> R. WEST Open ditches exhaling miasma. J. G. FARRELL Fever-bearing mists and miasmas hung everywhere.

2 *fig*. A polluting, oppressive, or foreboding atmosphere; a polluting or oppressive influence. M19.

> M. PUZO The swampy miasma of Southern religiosity. E. PAWEL Kafka . . felt himself once again drowning in academic miasma.

■ **miasmal** *adjective* = MIASMATIC 1 M19. **miasmic** *adjective* = MIASMATIC 1 E19. **miasmically** *adverb* M20.

miasmatic /mɪəzˈmatɪk, mʌɪ-/ *adjective*. M19.
[ORIGIN formed as MIASMA + -IC.]
1 Of, pertaining to, caused by, or having the nature of a miasma. M19.
2 HOMEOPATHY. Of, pertaining to, or caused by a miasm. L20.

miaul /mɪˈɔːl/ *verb*. M17.
[ORIGIN French *miauler*, of imit. origin.]
1 *verb intrans*. Of a cat: miaow, mew, yowl. Of a person: cry or yowl like a cat. M17.

> *Punch* Like the bursting of atomic bombs, Cats call to cats and Toms miaul to Toms.

2 *verb trans*. Sing (a song etc.) in a manner derisively likened to the cry of a cat. M19.

> G. MEREDITH The boy . . concluded by miauling 'Amalia' in the triumph of contempt.

Mic *abbreviation*.
Micah (in the Bible).

mic /mʌɪk/ *noun*. *colloq*. Also **mic.** (point). M20.
[ORIGIN Abbreviation.]
= MICROPHONE. Cf. MIKE *noun*[3].

mica /ˈmʌɪkə/ *noun*. Pl. **micas**, (in sense 1) †**micae**. L17.
[ORIGIN Latin = grain, crumb, perh. extended in use by assoc. with *micare* shine.]
MINERALOGY. †**1** A small plate of talc, selenite, or other glistening crystalline substance found in the structure of a rock. L17–E19.
2 Any of a group of monoclinic minerals composed of hydrous aluminosilicates of sodium, potassium, magnesium, etc., which occur in minute glittering plates or scales in granite and other rocks, and in crystals separable into thin, transparent, usu. flexible laminae, and are used as thermal or electric insulators. L18.
common mica muscovite. **water mica** clear colourless mica. ***white mica***: see WHITE *adjective*.
– COMB.: **mica flap** the flap of a mica valve; **mica-schist**, **mica-slate** a slaty metamorphic rock composed of quartz and mica; **mica valve** a device consisting of a flap of mica hinged at the top, used (esp. in ventilator shafts etc.) to allow air to flow in one direction only.
■ **micaceous** /mʌɪˈkeɪʃəs/ *adjective* containing or resembling mica; pertaining to or of the nature of mica: L18.

Micawber /mɪˈkɔːbə/ *noun*. M19.
[ORIGIN Wilkins *Micawber*, a character in Dickens's novel *David Copperfield*.]
An idle optimist; a person who trusts in the future to provide.

M

A. TROLLOPE It may be that after all the hopes of the West-Australian Micawbers will be realized. *attrib.*: *Guardian* The Green Paper's hope that growth will provide comes dangerously near the Micawber tradition.

■ **Micawberish** *adjective* resembling or characteristic of Micawber; idly optimistic, irresponsible: L19. **Micawberism** *noun* an attitude or the attitudes characteristic of Micawber; idle optimism: L19.

MICE *abbreviation.*
Member of the Institution of Civil Engineers.

mice *noun pl.* see MOUSE *noun.*

micelle /mɪˈsɛl, mʌɪˈsɛl/ *noun.* Also **-lla** /-lə/, pl. **-llae** /-liː/. L19.
[ORIGIN German *Micell*, formed as dim. of Latin *mica* crumb.]
CHEMISTRY. **1** Each of the minute ordered aggregates within the microfibrils of a crystal-like polymer; = CRYSTALLITE 2C. L19.
2 An aggregate of molecules in a colloidal solution, such as those formed by detergents. E20.
■ **micellar** *adjective* of, pertaining to, or composed of micelles L19. **micelliˈzation** *noun* the formation of micelles M20.

Mich. *abbreviation.*
1 Michaelmas.
2 Michigan.

Michael /ˈmʌɪk(ə)l/ *noun.* M16.
[ORIGIN Male forename. In sense 3 substitution for MICKEY *noun* interpreted as the name.]
1 = MICHAELMAS. *obsolete* exc. *Scot.* M16.
2 = MICKEY FINN. *US slang.* M20.
3 ***take the Michael*** (***out of***), = ***take the mickey*** (***out of***) s.v. MICKEY *noun. slang.* M20.

Michaelangelesque *adjective* var. of MICHELANGELESQUE.

Michaelis constant /mɪˈkeɪlɪs ˈkɒnst(ə)nt/ *noun phr.* M20.
[ORIGIN Leonor *Michaelis* (1875–1949), German-born US chemist.]
BIOCHEMISTRY. That concentration of a given substrate which catalyses the associated reaction at half the maximum rate.

Michaelmas /ˈmɪk(ə)lməs/ *noun.* ME.
[ORIGIN Contr. of *St Michael's mass.*]
(The date, 29 September, of) the feast of St Michael, one of the quarter days in England, Wales, and Ireland.
– COMB.: **Michaelmas daisy** (a flowering stem of) any of various late-flowering garden asters, forms and hybrids of *Aster novi-belgii*, *A. novae-angliae*, and other N. American species, with long panicles of lilac, white, crimson, etc., blooms; **Michaelmas sitting**(**s**) = *Michaelmas term* (b) below; **Michaelmas term** (*a*) a term in some universities beginning soon after Michaelmas; (*b*) the first of the terms or sessions of the High Court in England; **Michaelmas tide** the season of Michaelmas.

†**miche** *noun*, *verb* vars. of MITCH *noun*, *verb*.

Michelangelesque /ˌmʌɪkəlandʒəˈlɛsk/ *adjective.* Also **Michael-**. E19.
[ORIGIN from *Michelangelo* (see below) + -ESQUE.]
Of, pertaining to, or after the manner of the Florentine sculptor, painter, architect, and poet Michelangelo Buonarroti (1475–1564).

Michelin man /ˈmɪtʃəlɪn ˌman/ *noun.* L20.
[ORIGIN from the brothers André and Édouard *Michelin*, who founded the Michelin Tyre Company in 1888 and introduced a series of travel guides and road maps in 1900.]
A cartoon character whose body and limbs are composed of pneumatic tyres; *colloq.* a fat person.

Michelsberg /ˈmɪk(ə)lzbəːɡ/ *adjective.* E20.
[ORIGIN See below.]
ARCHAEOLOGY. Designating or pertaining to a Neolithic culture of Belgium, Germany, northern France, and Switzerland, illustrated esp. by pottery remains found at Michelsberg in Baden, Germany.

Michelson /ˈmʌɪk(ə)ls(ə)n/ *noun.* L19.
[ORIGIN A. A. *Michelson* (1852–1931), German-born US physicist.]
PHYSICS. Used *attrib.* and in *possess.* to designate (*a*) the Michelson–Morley experiment (see MICHELSON–MORLEY); (*b*) an interferometer of the type used in this experiment.

Michelson–Morley /ˌmʌɪk(ə)ls(ə)nˈmɔːli/ *noun.* L19.
[ORIGIN from MICHELSON + E. W. *Morley* (1838–1923), US chemist and physicist.]
PHYSICS. Used *attrib.* to designate an experiment performed in 1887 in which a beam of light was divided and made to travel over two paths, parallel and perpendicular to the earth's motion, before being recombined, the behaviour of the resulting interference fringes showing that the speed of light was the same in both directions, contrary to the notion that the earth moves through an ether.

micher /ˈmɪtʃə/ *noun. obsolete* exc. *dial.* ME.
[ORIGIN App. from Old French agent noun, formed as MITCH *verb*: see -ER².]
†**1** A secret or petty thief. ME–E19.
†**2** A person who skulks about with dishonest intent; a pander, a go-between. LME–M17.
3 A truant. M16.
■ **michery** *noun* pilfering, cheating LME.

Michigan /ˈmɪʃɪɡ(ə)n/ *noun.* E19.
[ORIGIN A state in the north-western US.]
1 Used *attrib.* to designate things from or associated with Michigan. E19.
2 A card game similar to Newmarket. *US.* E20.
■ **Michigander** /mɪʃɪˈɡandə/ *noun* a native or inhabitant of Michigan M19. **Michiganian** /mɪʃɪˈɡeɪnɪən/ *noun* = MICHIGANDER E19.

Michurinism /mɪˈtʃʊərɪnɪz(ə)m/ *noun.* M20.
[ORIGIN from *Michurin* (see below) + -ISM.]
Belief in or advocacy of the views of the Russian horticulturist I. V. Michurin (1855–1935); Lysenkoism.
■ **Michurinist** *noun & adjective* (*a*) *noun* an advocate of or believer in Michurinism; (*b*) *adjective* of or pertaining to Michurinism or Michurinists: M20.

mick /mɪk/ *noun*¹ *& adjective. slang.* Also **M-**. M19.
[ORIGIN Pet form of male forename *Michael*. Cf. MICKEY *noun*, MIKE *noun*².]
► **A** *noun.* **1** An Irishman. Usu. *offensive.* M19.
2 A Roman Catholic. *offensive.* E20.
3 ***mad mick***, a pick (for breaking up hard ground, rock, etc.). E20.
► **B** *attrib.* or as *adjective.* Irish; Roman Catholic. Usu. *offensive.* L19.

mick /mɪk/ *noun*². *Austral. slang.* E20.
[ORIGIN Unknown.]
In the game of two-up, the reverse side of a coin.

mickery /ˈmɪkəri/ *noun. Austral.* Also **mickerie**. L19.
[ORIGIN Wangganguru (an Australian Aboriginal language of northern South Australia) *migiri*.]
A waterhole or excavated well, esp. in a dry riverbed; marshy ground.

mickey /ˈmɪki/ *noun.* Also **micky**. M19.
[ORIGIN Familiar form of the given name *Michael*: cf. MICK *noun*¹, MIKE *noun*². In sense 7 perh. after *Mickey Bliss*, rhyming slang for *piss*; sense 8 substitution for MIKE *noun*¹ interpreted as the name *Mike*.]
1 (**M-**). A Roman Catholic. *slang* (*offensive*). M19.
2 (**M-**). An Irishman. *US slang* (*offensive*). M19.
3 A (usu. unbranded) bull calf. *Austral. slang.* L19.
4 The penis. *Irish slang.* E20.
5 = ***noisy miner*** s.v. NOISY *adjective* 1. *Austral. colloq.* E20.
6 A small bottle of liquor. Chiefly *Canad. colloq.* E20.
7 ***take the mickey*** (***out of***), act in a satirical or teasing manner (towards). Cf. MICHAEL 3, MIKE *noun*² 3. *colloq.* M20.

B. GELDOF The boarders would laugh and take the mickey because I was a day boy.

8 ***do a micky***, go away, escape. *slang.* M20.
– COMB.: **mickey-take** *verb & noun colloq.* (*a*) *verb intrans.* tease, mock; (*b*) *noun* an instance of mickey-taking.

Mickey Finn /mɪki ˈfɪn/ *noun & verb. slang* (orig. *US*). E20.
[ORIGIN App. a personal name, of unknown origin.]
► **A** *noun.* A strong alcoholic drink, now *esp.* one deliberately adulterated with a sleep-inducing drug or a laxative; a drug or laxative used as such an adulterant. E20.
► **B** *verb trans.* (With hyphen.) Adulterate or drug with a Mickey Finn. M20.

Mickey Mouse /mɪki ˈmaʊs/ *adjective. colloq.* M20.
[ORIGIN A mouselike cartoon character created by the American cartoonist Walt Disney (1901–66).]
Of inferior quality; ridiculous, trivial; (of music, art, etc.) trite, brash.

Citizen (*Ottawa*) There is absolutely nothing Mickey Mouse about tractor-pulling—it's a serious and well-organized sport.

Mickey-mousing /mɪkiˈmaʊsɪŋ/ *noun.* M20.
[ORIGIN formed as MICKEY MOUSE + -ING¹.]
CINEMATOGRAPHY. The matching of a film's action with appropriate simultaneous music.

mickle *adjective* etc., var. of MUCKLE.

micklemote /ˈmɪk(ə)lməʊt/ *noun.* Also **-gemote** /-ɡɪməʊt/. LOE.
[ORIGIN from *mickle* var. of MUCKLE *adjective* + MOOT *noun*¹.]
hist. The great council or parliamentary assembly under the Anglo-Saxon kings.

micky *noun* var. of MICKEY.

micky-mick *noun* see MINGIMINGI.

Micmac /ˈmɪkmak/ *noun & adjective.* M18.
[ORIGIN French from Micmac *mi:kəmax* pl. (*mi:kəmaw* sing.).]
► **A** *noun.* Pl. same, **-s**. A member of an Algonquian people of the Maritime Provinces and Newfoundland in Canada; the language of this people. M18.
► **B** *attrib.* or as *adjective.* Of or pertaining to this people or their language. M18.

†**mico** *noun.* Pl. **-os**. E17–M19.
[ORIGIN Spanish from Tupi *micó*.]
A small S. American marmoset, *esp.* one of the genus *Callithrix*.

Micoquian /mɪˈkəʊkɪən/ *adjective & noun.* E20.
[ORIGIN French *Micoquien*, from La *Micoque*, a place in the Dordogne, France: see -IAN.]
ARCHAEOLOGY. ► **A** *adjective.* Designating or pertaining to a stage of the Acheulian culture in central and western Europe, characterized by fine pointed hand axes. E20.
► **B** *noun.* The Micoquian culture. E20.

micrencephaly /mʌɪkrɛnˈsɛf(ə)li, -ˈkɛf-/ *noun.* L19.
[ORIGIN from MICRO- + Greek *egkephalos* brain + -Y³.]
MEDICINE. The condition of having a small brain. Also, microcephaly.

†**micrify** *verb trans.* Only in M19.
[ORIGIN from MICRO- after MAGNIFY.]
Make small; render insignificant.

micrite /ˈmɪkrʌɪt/ *noun.* M20.
[ORIGIN from MICR(OCRYSTALLINE + -ITE¹.]
PETROGRAPHY. Microcrystalline calcite present as an interstitial constituent or matrix material in some kinds of limestone; a limestone consisting chiefly of this.
■ **micritic** /mɪˈkrɪtɪk/ *adjective* containing a high proportion of micrite M20.

micro /ˈmʌɪkrəʊ/ *noun & adjective. colloq.* M19.
[ORIGIN Independent use of MICRO-.]
► **A** *noun.* Pl. **-os**.
1 ENTOMOLOGY. A moth belonging to the Microlepidoptera. M19.
2 A microskirt. M20.
3 A microcomputer; a microprocessor. L20.
4 A microwave oven. Chiefly *US.* L20.
► **B** *adjective.* **1** Microscopic; very small; small-scale; CHEMISTRY of microanalysis. Freq. contrasted with ***macro***. E20.
2 Microeconomic. M20.

micro- /ˈmʌɪkrəʊ, *esp.* MEDICINE ˈmɪkrəʊ/ *combining form.*
Before a vowel also **micr-**.
[ORIGIN Greek *mikro-* from *mikros* small: see -O-.]
1 Used in words adopted from Greek and in English words modelled on these, and as a freely productive prefix, with the senses: (*a*) small, reduced in size, (of a garment) very short, as ***microprocessor***, ***microskirt***; MEDICINE involving arrested development or underdevelopment of a part, as ***microcephaly***; (*b*) (in names of instruments, techniques, and disciplines) dealing with small effects or small quantities, involving the use of a microscope, revealed by a microscope, as ***microanalyser***, ***micro-electronic***; (*c*) containing or pertaining to something in minute form, quantity, or degree, as ***microphagous***, ***microvascular***; (*d*) pertaining to or obtained by microphotography, microphotographically reduced in size, as ***microbook***, ***microtext***; (*e*) CHEMISTRY of or pertaining to microanalysis, as ***micro-scale***.
2 Used in names of units of measurement to denote a factor of one-millionth (10^{-6}), as ***microgram***, ***microinch***; also redupl. to denote a factor of 10^{-12} (cf. PICO-), as ***micromicrofarad***. (Symbol μ.)
■ **microˈaerophil(e)** *adjective & noun* (*a*) *adjective* = MICROAEROPHILIC; (*b*) *noun* a microaerophilic organism: E20. **microaeroˈphilic** *adjective* (of a micro-organism) requiring little free oxygen, or oxygen at a lower partial pressure than that of atmospheric oxygen E20. **microˈammeter** *noun* an ammeter for measuring currents of the strength of a few microamperes E20. **microamp** *noun* = MICROAMPERE E20. **microampere** *noun* one millionth of an ampere L19. **microaˈnatomist** *noun* an expert in or student of microanatomy M20. **microaˈnatomy** *noun* the anatomy of very small structures; histology; the histology *of* a thing: L19. **microˈaneurysm** *noun* (MEDICINE) a very small aneurysm M20. **microangiˈopathy** *noun* (a) disease of the small blood vessels M20. **microarray** GENETICS a set of DNA sequences representing the entire set of genes of an organism, arranged in a grid pattern for use in genetic testing M20. **microatoll** *noun* a circular growth of coral a few metres in diameter with a central depression, such as is found in intertidal areas in warm seas and on the flats inside a coral reef M20. **microbalance** *noun* a balance for weighing masses of a fraction of a gram E20. **Microballoon** *noun* (proprietary name in US for) an artificial hollow microsphere M20. **microˈbarograph** *noun* an instrument for measuring very small changes in atmospheric pressure, such as those resulting from a distant explosion E20. **microˈbarom** *noun* a minute oscillation of atmospheric pressure with a period of the order of 5 seconds M20. **microbeam** *noun* a very narrow beam of radiation M20. **microˈbenthic** *adjective* of or belonging to the microbenthos M20. **microbenthos** *noun* the microfauna of the benthos, *spec.* bottom-dwelling marine organisms less than 0.1 mm long M20. **microbiota** *noun* the micro-organisms of an area, site, or object collectively E20. **microblade** *noun* (ARCHAEOLOGY) a small blade of flint or other stone struck from a prepared core M20. **microbody** *noun* (CYTOLOGY) a very small organelle, *esp.* a peroxisome M20. **microbore** *adjective* designating (a heating system with) a central-heating pipe with a very narrow bore M20. **microbrew** *noun* (chiefly *N. Amer.*) (a variety of) beer produced in a microbrewery L20. **microbrewery** *noun* (chiefly *N. Amer.*) a brewery which produces limited quantities of beer, often for consumption locally or on its own premises L20. **microbrowser** COMPUTING an Internet browser for use with mobile phones and other hand-held devices with small screens L20. **microˈburin** *noun* (ARCHAEOLOGY) the piece of stone that is snapped off a notched blade as waste when making a microlith M20. **microburst** *noun* a sudden strong air current produced by the impact with the ground of a fast localized downdraught M20. **microbus** *noun* a small passenger vehicle with seats fitted as in a bus M20. **microcaloˈrimeter** *noun* an instrument for measuring very small amounts of heat E20. **microcaloriˈmetric** *adjective* of or pertaining to microcalorimetry E20. **microcaloˈrimetry** *noun* the use of a microcalorimeter; measurement of very small amounts of heat: E20. **microcapsule** *noun* a minute capsule used to contain drugs, dyes, etc. and render them temporarily inactive M20. **microcar** *noun* a small and fuel-efficient car L20. **Microcard** *noun* (US proprietary name for) an opaque card bearing microphotographs of a number of pages of a book, periodical, etc. M20. **microcard** *verb trans.* reproduce on Microcards M20. **microˈcellular** *adjective* (esp. of synthetic substances) containing

or characterized by minute cells or pores E20. **microˈchemical** *adjective* of or pertaining to microchemistry M19. **microchemist** *noun* an expert in or student of microchemistry E20. **microˈchemistry** *noun* the branch of chemistry that deals with the reactions and properties of substances in minute quantities, e.g. in living tissue M19. **microcinematoˈgraphic** *adjective* of, pertaining to, or involving microcinematography E20. **microcinemaˈtography** *noun* the cinematography of very small objects with the aid of a microscope E20. **microcircuit** *noun* a minute electric circuit, *esp.* an integrated circuit M20. **microcircuitry** *noun* microcircuits collectively; the branch of electronics that deals with microcircuits: M20. **microcirculation** *noun* circulation of the blood in the smallest blood vessels M20. **microˈclastic** *adjective* (GEOLOGY) minutely clastic L19. **microˈcoccal** *adjective* caused by, of, or pertaining to a micrococcus or micrococci L19. **microˈcoccus** *noun*, pl. **-cocci** /-ˈkɒk(s)ʌɪ, -k(s)iː/, a bacterium of the family Micrococcaceae of Gram-positive spherical organisms L19. **microcode** *noun & verb* (COMPUTING) (***a***) *noun* microinstructions collectively; a single microinstruction; each of the bit patterns of which a microinstruction is composed; (***b***) *verb trans.* = MICROPROGRAM *verb*: M20. **microcolony** *noun* a group of animals or plants, esp. bacteria, found in a microhabitat; a very small group of cells in culture: E20. **microcontinent** *noun* (GEOLOGY) an oceanic, often submarine, plateau that is thought to be an isolated fragment of continental material M20. **microcontiˈnental** *adjective* (GEOLOGY) of, pertaining to, or of the nature of a microcontinent M20. **microcontroller** COMPUTING a control device which incorporates a microprocessor L20. **microcook** *verb trans. & intrans.* (*US*) = MICROWAVE *verb* L20. **microcopy** *noun & verb* (***a***) *noun* a copy of a text that has been reduced in size by the use of microphotography; microcopied form (chiefly in ***in microcopy***); (***b***) *verb trans. & intrans.* make a microcopy (of): M20. **microcrack** *noun* a very small or fine crack M20. **microcracking** *noun* microcracks collectively; the occurrence or formation of microcracks: M20. **microcredit** *noun* the lending of small amounts of money at low interest to new businesses in the developing world L20. **microcyst** *noun* a bacterial or myxamoeboid resting cell, *esp.* one with a thick cell wall L19. **microdegree** *noun* a millionth of a degree centigrade (kelvin) M20. **microdensiˈtometer** *noun* a densitometer for measuring the density of very small areas of a photographic image M20. **microdensitoˈmetric** *adjective* of, pertaining to, or involving microdensitometry M20. **microdensiˈtometry** *noun* the use of a microdensitometer; measurement of the density of very small areas of a photographic image: M20. **microdermabrasion** *noun* a cosmetic treatment in which the face is sprayed with exfoliant crystals to remove dead epidermal cells L20. **microˈdiorite** *noun* (GEOLOGY) a rock similar to diorite but fine-grained E20. **micro-eˈlectrode** *noun* an electrode with a very fine tip, e.g. for investigating the electrical properties of individual cells E20. **micro-electrophoˈresis** *noun* electrophoresis in which the migration of individual particles or cells is observed using a microscope M20. **micro-electrophoˈretic** *adjective* of, pertaining to, or involving micro-electrophoresis M20. **micro-enˈcapsulate** *verb trans.* enclose in a microcapsule M20. **micro-encapsuˈlation** *noun* the process of enclosing in microcapsules M20. **micro-engiˈneering** *noun* engineering on a very small scale, esp. combined with micro-electronics M20. **micro-ˈenterprise** *noun* (a) business operating on a small scale, esp. one supported by a programme of assistance in an economically deprived area or developing country L20. **micro-environment** *noun* (chiefly BIOLOGY) the immediate small-scale environment of a thing, esp. as a distinct part of a larger environment M20. **micro-environˈmental** *adjective* (chiefly BIOLOGY) of, pertaining to, or of the nature of a micro-environment M20. **micro-evolution** *noun* evolutionary change within a species or smaller group of plants or animals, usu. over a short period E20. **micro-evoˈlutionary** *adjective* of or pertaining to micro-evolution M20. **microfarad** *noun* one millionth of a farad L19. **microfauna** *noun* (BIOLOGY) (a) fauna made up of minute animals; (a) fauna found in a microhabitat: L19. **microˈfaunal** *adjective* (BIOLOGY) of or pertaining to microfauna M20. **microfelˈsitic** *adjective* (GEOLOGY) cryptocrystalline L19. **microfibre** *noun* an extremely fine fibre; *spec.* (a fabric made from) a very fine synthetic yarn: M20; **microfibril** *noun* (BIOLOGY) a small fibril visible only under an electron microscope, *esp.* each of a group that together make up a fibril (such as a cellulose fibril in the wall of a plant cell) M20. **microˈfibrillar** *adjective* (BIOLOGY) composed of microfibrils M20. **microfilament** *noun* (CYTOLOGY) any of the small rodlike structures, about 4–7 nanometres in diameter, that are present in the cytoplasm of many eukaryotic cells and are thought to have a structural function and to be involved with cell motility M20. **microfilaˈmentous** *adjective* (CYTOLOGY) of or pertaining to a microfilament or microfilaments L20. **microfiˈlaria** *noun* (ZOOLOGY) the minute larval form of a filaria L19. **microfinance** *noun* = MICROCREDIT L20. **microfloppy** *noun & adjective* (COMPUTING) (designating) a floppy disk with a diameter less than 5¼ inches, 13.3 cm (usu. 3½ inches, 8.9 cm) L20. **microflora** *noun* (BIOLOGY) (a) flora made up of minute plants; (a) flora found in a microhabitat: E20. **microfossil** *noun* a fossil or fossil fragment that can only be seen with a microscope E20. **microfracture** *noun* a very small or fine fracture in a material M20. **microˈfracturing** *noun* the state of having microfractures; the formation of microfractures: M20. **microfungus** *noun* a fungus in which no sexual process has been observed or in which the reproductive organs are microscopic L19. **microgamete** *noun* (BIOLOGY) the smaller (usu. male) gamete in an organism where the male and female gametes differ in size L19. **microgaˈmetocyte** *noun* (BIOLOGY) a gametocyte that gives rise to microgametes E20. **microgaˈmetophyte** *noun* (BOTANY) a gametophyte that develops from a microspore; a male gametophyte: E20. **microgram** *noun* a millionth of a gram L19. **microgranite** *noun* (a) granite rock that is recognizable as crystalline only under a microscope L19. **micrograˈnitic** *adjective* of, pertaining to, or of the nature of microgranite L19. **microˈgravity** *noun* very weak gravity, such as that in a spacecraft L20. **microgroove** *noun* a very narrow groove on a gramophone record M20. **microˈgyria** *noun* (MEDICINE) abnormal smallness of the gyri of the brain L19. **microhabitat** *noun* (ECOLOGY) a habitat which is of small or limited extent and which differs in character from some surrounding more extensive habitat M20. **microhardness** *noun* the hardness of a very small area of a sample, as measured by an indenter E20. **microimage** *noun* an image so small that it cannot be read etc. unaided M20. **microinch** *noun* a millionth of an inch M20. **microinˈject** *verb trans.* (chiefly BIOLOGY) inject *into* a microscopic object such as an individual cell; inject something into (such an object): M20. **microinˈjection** *noun* (BIOLOGY & MEDICINE) injection on a microscopic scale, esp. into an individual cell or part of a cell E20. **microkernel** *noun* (COMPUTING) (in an operating system) a kernel which has only the most basic in-built functions and can be configured to suit different systems by the addition of software modules L20. **microlending** *noun* = MICROCREDIT L20. **microlevel** *noun* the most detailed or elementary level of a hierarchy M20. **microlinˈguistic** *adjective* of or pertaining to microlinguistics M20. **microlinˈguistics** *noun* the branch of linguistics that deals with the analysis of specific linguistic data, as contrasted with prelinguistics and metalinguistics M20. **microlitre** *noun* a millionth of a litre L19. **micro-machining** *noun* the process or technique of shaping objects on a very small scale esp. using laser or particle beams M20. **micromanage** *verb trans.* manage every part, however small, of (an enterprise or activity), esp. with undesirable avoidance of delegation L20. **microˈmanagement** *noun* the action of micromanaging an enterprise or activity L20. **microˈmanager** *noun* a person who (esp. habitually) micromanages an enterprise or activity L20. **microˈmania** *noun* (a) persistent or exaggerated tendency to belittle oneself L19. **microˈmaniac** *noun* a person with micromania E20. **micromaˈnipulate** *verb trans.* manipulate on a microscopic scale or with a micromanipulator M20. **micromanipuˈlation** *noun* the performance of extremely delicate operations (e.g. the isolation of single cells) under a microscope, esp. using a micromanipulator; an operation so performed: E20. **micromaˈnipulator** *noun* an instrument used to perform micromanipulations, allowing a micropipette etc. to be operated in the field of view of a microscope E20. **microˈmastia** *noun* [Greek *mastos* breast] the condition in a post-pubertal woman of having an abnormally small breast E20. **microˈmazia** *noun* [Greek *mazos* breast] = MICROMASTIA L19. **micromere** *noun* [Greek *meros* part] BIOLOGY a small cell formed by unequal division of an ovum or embryo, e.g. in sea urchins, and appearing at the animal pole L19. **micromesh** *noun* material (esp. nylon) consisting of a very fine mesh M20. **microˈmillimetre** *noun* (***a***) a millionth of a millimetre, a nanometre; †(***b***) a thousandth of a millimetre, a micrometre: L19. **micromodule** *noun* (ELECTRONICS) a miniaturized module consisting of a stack of interconnected micro-elements M20. **microˈmolar** *adjective* (CHEMISTRY) designating or involving amounts of the order of a micromole or concentrations of the order of one micromole per litre M20. **micromole** *noun* (CHEMISTRY) one millionth of a mole M20. **microˈnodular** *adjective* (MEDICINE) (esp. of a form of cirrhosis) characterized by the presence of small nodules M20. **microˈnuclear** *adjective* (ZOOLOGY) of or pertaining to a micronucleus L19. **microˈnucleus** *noun* (ZOOLOGY) the smaller of two nuclei in ciliated protozoa, concerned esp. with reproduction L19. **microˈnutrient** *noun* (BIOLOGY) any of the chemical elements which are required in trace amounts by organisms for normal growth and development M20. **micro-oˈpaque** *noun & adjective* (designating) a type of microform produced on card or paper instead of film M20. **micro-oven** *noun* a microwave oven M20. **micropayment** *noun* a very small payment made each time a user accesses an Internet page or service L20. **microˈperthite** *noun* (MINERALOGY) a form of perthite in which the lamellae are microscopic L19. **microperˈthitic** *adjective* (MINERALOGY) of, pertaining to, or of the nature of microperthite L19. **microphage** *noun* [Greek *phagein* eat] PHYSIOLOGY a small phagocytic leucocyte L19. **microphagous** /mʌɪˈkrɒfəgəs/ *adjective* [Greek *phagein* eat] BIOLOGY feeding on minute particles or micro-organisms E20. **microphoˈtometer** *noun* an instrument for making photometric measurements of very small areas L19. **microphotoˈmetric** *adjective* of, pertaining to, or involving microphotometry M20. **microphoˈtometry** *noun* the use of microphotometers M20. **microphyll** *noun* (BOTANY) a very short leaf, as in a clubmoss, with a single unbranched vein and no leaf gaps in the stele M20. **microˈphyllous** *adjective* having small leaves or (*spec.*) microphylls M19. **micropipette** *noun* a very fine pipette for measuring, transferring, or injecting very small quantities of liquid E20. **microplankton** *noun* plankton of small size, *spec.* between 50 micrometres and 0.5 millimetre E20. **micropore** *noun* a very small pore L19. **micropoˈrosity** *noun* microporous condition M20. **microˈporous** *adjective* containing or characterized by micropores; microcellular: L19. **micropower** *adjective* generating, using, or pertaining to small amounts of power M20. **microprism** *noun* (PHOTOGRAPHY) an area of the focusing screen of some reflex cameras which is covered with a grid of tiny prisms and splits up the image when the subject is not in focus M20. **microprobe** *noun & verb trans.* (examine using) a microanalyser M20. **microproˈjection** *noun* the process of projecting an enlarged image of a microscopic specimen E20. **microproˈjector** *noun* an apparatus for microprojection M20. **micropropaˌgation** *noun* the propagation of plants by growing plantlets in tissue culture and then planting them out L20. **microˈpterous** /mʌɪˈkrɒpt(ə)rəs/ *adjective* [Greek *pteron* wing] ENTOMOLOGY having small wings E19. **micropublication** *noun* (a) publication in microform L20. **micropublish** *verb trans.* publish in microform (freq. as ***micropublishing*** *verbal noun*) M20. **micropulsation** *noun* a small oscillation in the strength of the earth's magnetic field M20. **microreader** *noun* an apparatus for producing an enlarged readable image from a microfilm or microprint M20. **microrecord** *noun* a documentary record in micrographically reduced form M20. **microˈsatellite** (***a***) GENETICS a set of short repeated DNA sequences at a particular locus on a chromosome, which vary in number in different individuals and so can be used for genetic fingerprinting; (***b***) a very small space satellite: M20. **micro-scale** *noun* a small or microscopic scale; CHEMISTRY the scale of microanalysis: M20. **microscooter** *noun* a small, lightweight, two-wheeled foldable scooter, for either children or adults L20. **microsecond** *noun* one millionth of a second E20. **microsection** *noun* a very thin section of a specimen that can be mounted on a slide for microscopic examination L19. **microsegment** *noun* (PHONETICS) a unit of sound enclosed between two open junctures M20. **microseism** *noun* †(***a***) a minor earthquake; (***b***) an imperceptible disturbance of the earth's crust detectable by a seismometer but not caused by an earthquake: L19. **microˈseismic** *adjective* of, pertaining to, or of the nature of a microseism; (of data) obtained with a seismometer: L19. **microsite** *noun* (***a***) ECOLOGY a small, distinct area or habitat within a particular ecosytem; (***b***) COMPUTING a small auxiliary website designed to function as a supplement to a primary website: M20. **microsleep** *noun* a transitory state of sleep, esp. in a person deprived of normal sleep; a period or occasion of such sleep: M20. **microslide** *noun* a slide prepared for microscopic examination E20. **microspecies** *noun* (TAXONOMY) a species differing only in minor characters from others of its group, often one of limited geographical range forming part of an aggregate species L19. **microspectrophoˈtometer** *noun* an instrument for the spectrophotometric investigation of individual cells or particles M20. **microˌspectrophotoˈmetric** *adjective* of, pertaining to, or involving microspectrophotometry M20. **microspectrophoˈtometry** *noun* the use of microspectrophotometers M20. **microsphere** *noun* a minute sphere; *spec.* one obtained by cooling a solution of a proteinoid: L19. **microˈspheric** *adjective* of, pertaining to, or of the nature of a microsphere L19. **microstate** *noun* a very small country M20. **microstrip** *noun* (ELECTRICITY) a transmission line for microwaves that consists of dielectric material coated on one side with a metallic film forming a conducting strip and on the other with a metallic coating that serves as an earth; material of this kind: M20. **microstylous** *adjective* (BOTANY) having a short style in association with long filaments L19. **microswitch** *noun* a switch which can be operated rapidly by a small movement M20. **microteaching** *noun* (*US*) the teaching of a small group for a short time as part of a training or refresher course for teachers M20. **microtechnique** *noun* a technique for handling, preparing, or investigating very small amounts of something L19. **microtechˈnology** *noun* technology that uses or is concerned with microelectronics or with components whose size is measured in microns M20. **microtext** *noun* (a) text that is micrographically reduced in size M20. **microtopoˈgraphic**, **microtopoˈgraphical** *adjectives* of or pertaining to microtopography M20. **microtoˈpography** *noun* surface features on a small or microscopic scale M20. **microtraˈbecula** *noun*, pl. **-lae**, CYTOLOGY a filament of the microtrabecular lattice L20. **microtraˈbecular** *adjective* (CYTOLOGY) pertaining to or designating a lattice of protein filaments in the cytoplasm of cells which is concerned with the transport of molecules in the cell L20. **microtron** *noun* (PHYSICS) a variant of the cyclotron in which electrons are accelerated by microwaves M20. **microˈtubular** *adjective* (CYTOLOGY) of, pertaining to, or of the nature of a microtubule M20. **ˈmicrotubule** *noun* (CYTOLOGY) a small, relatively rigid tubule, present in numbers in the cytoplasm of many cells, thought to have a structural function and to be involved with cell motility M20. **microunit** *noun* (MEDICINE) a millionth part of a unit, esp. of an international unit (e.g. of insulin) E20. **microˈvascular** *adjective* of or pertaining to the smallest blood vessels E20. **microˈvillar** *adjective* (CYTOLOGY) of, pertaining to, or involving a microvillus or microvilli M20. **microˈvillous** *adjective* (CYTOLOGY) = MICROVILLAR M20. **ˈmicrovillus** *noun* (CYTOLOGY) any of a number of minute projections from the surface of some cells; a process similar to a villus but smaller: M20. **microwatt** *noun* one millionth of a watt E20. **microweld** *verb trans.* join by a very small weld M20.

microanalyser /mʌɪkrəʊˈanəlʌɪzə/ *noun*. Also ***-lyzer**. M20.
[ORIGIN from MICRO- + ANALYSER.]
An instrument in which a beam of radiation (usu. electrons) is focused on to a minute area of a sample and the resulting secondary radiation (usu. X-ray fluorescence) is analysed to yield chemical information.

microanalysis /ˌmʌɪkrəʊəˈnalɪsɪs/ *noun*. M19.
[ORIGIN from MICRO- + ANALYSIS.]
CHEMISTRY. Orig., the analysis of very small samples, or very small areas of an object. Now *spec.* the quantitative analysis of samples weighing only a few milligrams.
■ **microˈanalyst** *noun* E20. **microanaˈlytical** *adjective* E20.

microbe /ˈmʌɪkrəʊb/ *noun*. L19.
[ORIGIN French, formed as MICRO- + Greek *bios* life.]
An extremely minute living organism, a micro-organism; *esp.* a bacterium that causes disease or fermentation.
■ **miˈcrobial** *adjective* of, pertaining to, or caused by microbes L19. **miˈcrobially** *adverb* by or with microbes M20. **miˈcrobian** *adjective* (now *rare*) = MICROBIAL L19. **miˈcrobic** *adjective* = MICROBIAL L19. **miˌcrobiˈcidal** *adjective* that kills microbes; of or pertaining to a microbicide or its action: L19. **miˈcrobicide** *noun & adjective* (***a***) *noun* a microbicidal agent; (***b***) *adjective* (now *rare*) microbicidal: L19.

microbiology /ˌmʌɪkrə(ʊ)bʌɪˈɒlədʒi/ *noun*. L19.
[ORIGIN from MICRO- + BIOLOGY.]
The branch of science that deals with micro-organisms.
■ **microbioˈlogic** *adjective* E20. **microbioˈlogical** *adjective* L19. **microbioˈlogically** *adverb* E20. **microbiologist** *noun* L19.

microcephalic /mʌɪkrə(ʊ)sɪˈfalɪk, -kɛˈfalɪk/ *adjective & noun*. M19.
[ORIGIN from MICRO- + -CEPHALIC.]
Chiefly MEDICINE & ANTHROPOLOGY. ▸**A** *adjective*. Having an abnormally small head or skull. M19.
▸**B** *noun*. A microcephalic person. L19.
■ **microˈcephalism** *noun* = MICROCEPHALY M19. **microˈcephalous** *adjective* = MICROCEPHALIC *adjective* M19. **microˈcephalus** *noun*, pl. **-li** /-lʌɪ, -liː/, (***a***) = MICROCEPHALIC *noun*; (***b***) = MICROCEPHALY: M19. **microˈcephaly** *noun* microcephalic condition M19.

microchip /ˈmʌɪkrə(ʊ)tʃɪp/ *noun & verb*. M20.
[ORIGIN from MICRO- + CHIP *noun*.]
▸**A** *noun*. A semiconductor chip, an integrated circuit, *esp.* one in which large-scale integration is employed. M20.
▸**B** *verb trans*. Implant a microchip under the skin of (a domestic animal) as a means of identification. L20.

microchiropteran /ˌmʌɪkrəʊkʌɪˈrɒpt(ə)rən/ *adjective & noun*. L19.
[ORIGIN from mod. Latin *Microchiroptera* (see below), formed as MICRO- + *Chiroptera*: see CHIROPTERAN.]
▸**A** *adjective*. Of or pertaining to the chiropteran suborder Microchiroptera, which comprises all bats other than megachiropterans, most of them insectivorous. L19.

▸ **B** *noun*. A microchiropteran bat. **L19.**

microclimate /ˈmʌɪkrə(ʊ)ˌklʌɪmət/ *noun*. **E20.**
[**ORIGIN** from **MICRO-** + **CLIMATE**.]
The climate of a very small or restricted area, or of the immediate surroundings of an object, esp. where this differs from the climate generally.

F. POHL Outside . . the microclimate of my little garden . . the air was too thin and too dry.

▪ **microcliˈmatic** *adjective* **E20.** **microcliˈmatically** *adverb* **M20.**

microclimatology /ˌmʌɪkrə(ʊ)klʌɪməˈtɒlədʒi/ *noun*. **M20.**
[**ORIGIN** from **MICRO-** + **CLIMATOLOGY**.]
The branch of science that deals with microclimates.
▪ **microclimatoˈlogical** *adjective* **M20.** **microclimatologist** *noun* **M20.**

microcline /ˈmʌɪkrə(ʊ)klʌɪn/ *noun*. **M19.**
[**ORIGIN** German *Mikroklin*, formed as **MICRO-** + Greek *klinein* to lean, slope (from its angle of cleavage differing only slightly from 90 degrees).]
MINERALOGY. A triclinic potassium feldspar characteristic of granites and pegmatites, similar to orthoclase but forming large translucent crystals of a green, pink, or brown colour.

microcomputer /ˈmʌɪkrə(ʊ)kəmˌpjuːtə/ *noun*. **M20.**
[**ORIGIN** from **MICRO-** + **COMPUTER**.]
A small computer or computer system, usu. one built around a single microprocessor; a home or personal computer. Also, a microprocessor.
▪ **microcomputing** *noun* computing using a microcomputer **L20.**

microcosm /ˈmʌɪkrə(ʊ)kɒz(ə)m/ *noun*. Also in quasi-Greek form **microcosmos** /mʌɪkrə(ʊ)ˈkɒzmɒs/. **ME.**
[**ORIGIN** French *microcosme* or medieval Latin *micro(s)cosmus* from Greek *mikros kosmos* little world.]
1 The world of human nature (as opp. to all nature); humanity viewed as an epitome of the universe. **ME.**

R. SCRUTON To step down from the world of national politics, into the microcosm of ordinary human relations.

2 A community or other complex unity regarded as presenting an epitome of the world, or as constituting a world in itself. **M16.**

S. RUSHDIE The street was his microcosm and afforded him all his delights and pains.

M

3 A miniature representation (*of*). **E17.**

G. A. SHEEHAN Like many sports, the marathon is a microcosm of life.

microcosmic /mʌɪkrə(ʊ)ˈkɒzmɪk/ *adjective*. **L18.**
[**ORIGIN** from **MICROCOSM** + **-IC**.]
Of or pertaining to a microcosm; of the nature of a microcosm.
microcosmic salt hydrated sodium ammonium hydrogen phosphate, $HNaNH_4PO_4 \cdot 4H_2O$, a crystalline compound originally obtained from human urine.
▪ **microcosmical** *adjective* (now *rare*) microcosmic **L16.** **microcosmically** *adverb* **M19.**

microcrystal /ˈmʌɪkrə(ʊ)krɪst(ə)l/ *noun*. **L19.**
[**ORIGIN** from **MICRO-** + **CRYSTAL** *noun*.]
A crystal visible only under a microscope.

microcrystalline /mʌɪkrə(ʊ)ˈkrɪstəlʌɪn/ *adjective*. **L19.**
[**ORIGIN** from **MICRO-** + **CRYSTALLINE**.]
Formed of microscopic crystals.
microcrystalline wax a high-molecular-weight hydrocarbon wax obtained from the residual lubricating fraction of crude oil, used in making waxed paper, adhesives, and polishes.
▪ **microcrystaˈllinity** *noun* **M20.**

microcyclic /mʌɪkrə(ʊ)ˈsʌɪklɪk, -ˈsɪk-/ *adjective*. **E20.**
[**ORIGIN** from **MICRO-** + **CYCLIC**.]
BOTANY. Of a rust fungus: having a short life cycle.

microcyte /ˈmʌɪkrə(ʊ)sʌɪt, ˈmɪ-/ *noun*. **L19.**
[**ORIGIN** from **MICRO-** + **-CYTE**.]
MEDICINE. An unusually small red blood cell.
▪ **microcytic** /mʌɪkrə(ʊ)ˈsɪtɪk/ *adjective* of the nature of, pertaining to, or characteristic of a microcyte; characterized by the presence of microcytes: **E20.** **microcyˈtosis** *noun* the presence of microcytes in the blood **L19.**

microdot /ˈmʌɪkrə(ʊ)dɒt/ *noun & verb*. **M20.**
[**ORIGIN** from **MICRO-** + **DOT** *noun*[1].]
▸ **A** *noun*. **1** A photograph, esp. of printed or written matter, reduced to the size of a dot. **M20.**
2 A tiny capsule or tablet of LSD. **L20.**
▸ **B** *verb trans*. Infl. **-tt-**. Make a microdot or microdots of. **M20.**

microdrive /ˈmʌɪkrə(ʊ)drʌɪv/ *noun*. **M20.**
[**ORIGIN** from **MICRO-** + **DRIVE** *noun*.]
1 A small stepping motor or motor-driven apparatus for manipulating micro-electrodes. **M20.**
2 *COMPUTING*. A peripheral storage device for holding a cartridge similar to a microfloppy but containing a continuous loop of tape. **L20.**

microeconomics /ˌmʌɪkrəʊiːkəˈnɒmɪks, -ɛk-/ *noun*. **M20.**
[**ORIGIN** from **MICRO-** + **ECONOMICS**.]
The branch of economics that deals with small-scale economic factors; the economics of the individual firm, product, consumer, etc., rather than the aggregate. Cf. **MACROECONOMICS**.
▪ **microeconomic** *adjective* **M20.** **microeˈconomist** *noun* **M20.** **microeˈconomy** *noun* a small-scale economic system **M20.**

micro-electronics /ˌmʌɪkrəʊɪlɛkˈtrɒnɪks, -ɛl-/ *noun*. **M20.**
[**ORIGIN** from **MICRO-** + **ELECTRONICS**.]
The branch of technology that deals with the design, manufacture, and use of microcircuits. Also, micro-electronic devices or circuits.
▪ **micro-electronic** *adjective* **M20.**

micro-element /ˈmʌɪkrəʊˌɛlɪm(ə)nt/ *noun*. **M20.**
[**ORIGIN** from **MICRO-** + **ELEMENT** *noun*.]
1 *BOTANY*. = **MICRONUTRIENT**. **M20.**
2 *ELECTRONICS*. A thin flat miniaturized circuit made with standardized length and width for assembly into a micromodule. **M20.**

microfiche /ˈmʌɪkrə(ʊ)fiːʃ/ *noun*. Pl. same, **-s**. **M20.**
[**ORIGIN** from **MICRO-** + French *fiche* slip of paper, index card.]
A flat piece of film, usually the size of a standard catalogue card, containing microphotographs of the pages of a book, periodical, etc. Cf. **FICHE** *noun*[2].
– **COMB.**: **microfiche reader** a device for projecting a readable image of a microfiche on to a screen.

microfilm /ˈmʌɪkrə(ʊ)fɪlm/ *noun & verb*. **E20.**
[**ORIGIN** from **MICRO-** + **FILM** *noun*.]
▸ **A** *noun*. (A length of) photographic film containing microphotographs of the pages of a book, periodical, etc. **E20.**
– **COMB.**: **microfilm reader** a device for projecting a readable image on to a screen from microfilm.
▸ **B** *verb trans*. Record on microfilm. **M20.**
▪ **microfilmer** *noun* (**a**) a camera for producing images on microfilm; (**b**) a person who operates such a camera: **M20.**

microform /ˈmʌɪkrə(ʊ)fɔːm/ *noun*. **E20.**
[**ORIGIN** from **MICRO-** + **FORM** *noun*.]
Microphotographic form; a microphotographic reproduction on film or paper of a book, periodical, etc., requiring magnification to produce a readable image.

microglia /mʌɪkrə(ʊ)ˈglʌɪə, mɪ-/ *noun* (usu. treated as *pl*.). **E20.**
[**ORIGIN** from **MICRO-** + **GLIA**.]
ANATOMY. **1** *pl*. Glial cells derived from mesoderm that function as macrophages (scavengers) in the central nervous system and form part of the reticuloendothelial system. **E20.**
2 *sing*. Tissue composed of such cells. **M20.**
▪ **microglial** *adjective* **E20.**

micrograph /ˈmʌɪkrə(ʊ)grɑːf/ *noun*. **M19.**
[**ORIGIN** from **MICRO-** + **-GRAPH**.]
An enlarged image of an object as seen through a microscope, obtained either by hand drawing or (now usu.) photographically.

micrography /mʌɪˈkrɒgrəfi/ *noun*. **M17.**
[**ORIGIN** from **MICRO-** + **-GRAPHY**.]
1 The description or delineation of objects visible only under a microscope. **M17.**
2 The technique of producing micrographs or of studying objects by means of them. **E20.**
▪ **micrographer** *noun* a person who produces micrographs **M19.** **microˈgraphic** *adjective* **M19.** **microˈgraphically** *adverb* by means of micrography or a micrograph **L19.** **microˈgraphics** *noun* the production of photographically reduced texts **M20.**

microinstruction /ˈmʌɪkrəʊɪnˌstrʌkʃ(ə)n/ *noun*. **M20.**
[**ORIGIN** from **MICRO-** + **INSTRUCTION**.]
COMPUTING. Each of a sequence of instructions executed in response to a more comprehensive instruction; *spec*. one that corresponds to one of the smallest, most elementary operations in a computer and is produced in accordance with a microprogram.

Microlepidoptera /ˌmʌɪkrə(ʊ)lɛpɪˈdɒpt(ə)rə/ *noun pl*. **M19.**
[**ORIGIN** from **MICRO-** + **LEPIDOPTERA**.]
The numerous moths which are mostly smaller than those of interest to collectors. Cf. **MACROLEPIDOPTERA**.
▪ **microlepidopterist** *noun* an expert in or student of Microlepidoptera **M19.** **microlepidopterous** *adjective* **M19.**

microlight /ˈmʌɪkrə(ʊ)lʌɪt/ *adjective & noun*. **L20.**
[**ORIGIN** from **MICRO-** + **LIGHT** *adjective*[1].]
(Of, pertaining to, or designating) a small low-speed lightweight one- or two-seater aircraft of open construction, used for recreation and racing.
▪ **microlighting** *noun* flying a microlight as a pastime or hobby **L20.**

microlite /ˈmʌɪkrə(ʊ)lʌɪt/ *noun*. **M19.**
[**ORIGIN** from **MICRO-** + **-LITE**.]
1 *MINERALOGY*. A complex oxide of tantalum and niobium with sodium and calcium, crystallizing in the cubic system as yellow, brownish, or blackish translucent crystals. **M19.**
2 *PETROGRAPHY*. = **MICROLITH 1**. **L19.**
▪ **microlitic** /mʌɪkrə(ʊ)ˈlɪtɪk/ *adjective* (*PETROGRAPHY*) of or pertaining to microlites; characterized by the presence of microlites: **L19.**

microlith /ˈmʌɪkrə(ʊ)lɪθ/ *noun*. **L19.**
[**ORIGIN** from **MICRO-** + **-LITH**.]
1 *PETROGRAPHY*. A microscopic acicular crystal with determinable optical properties, such as occurs in the groundmass of some rocks. **L19.**
2 *ARCHAEOLOGY*. A small shaped stone tool with a sharpened edge that was used with a haft, characteristic of Mesolithic cultures. **E20.**
▪ **microˈlithic** *adjective* of or pertaining to microliths; *PETROGRAPHY* characterized by the presence of microliths; *ARCHAEOLOGY* characterized by the use of microliths: **L19.**

micrologic /ˈmʌɪkrə(ʊ)ˌlɒdʒɪk/ *noun*. **L19.**
[**ORIGIN** from **MICRO-** + **LOGIC** *noun*.]
Micro-electronic logic.

micrology /mʌɪˈkrɒlədʒi/ *noun*. **M17.**
[**ORIGIN** Sense 1 from Greek *mikrologia*, formed as **MICRO-** + *-logia* **-LOGY**; sense 2 from **MICRO-** + **-LOGY**.]
1 The discussion or investigation of trivial things or petty affairs; hair-splitting. **M17.**
2 The branch of science which depends on the use of a microscope. Also, a treatise on microscopic organisms. **M19.**
▪ **microˈlogical** *adjective* **M19.** **micrologist** *noun* an expert in or student of the examination and description of microscopic objects **M19.**

micrometeoroid /mʌɪkrəʊˈmiːtɪərɔɪd/ *noun*. **M20.**
[**ORIGIN** from **MICRO-** + **METEOROID**.]
A microscopic particle in space or of extraterrestrial origin which is small enough not to suffer ablation in the earth's atmosphere.
▪ **micrometeor** *noun* = **MICROMETEOROID** **M20.** **micrometeˈoric** *adjective* micrometeoroidal **M20.** **micrometeorite** *noun* a micrometeoroid, *spec*. one that has entered the earth's atmosphere **M20.** **micrometeoˈritic** *adjective* of the nature of a micrometeorite; pertaining to or produced by micrometeorites: **M20.** **micrometeoˈroidal** *adjective* of the nature of a micrometeoroid; pertaining to or produced by micrometeoroids: **L20.**

micrometeorology /ˌmʌɪkrə(ʊ)miːtɪəˈrɒlədʒi/ *noun*. **M20.**
[**ORIGIN** from **MICRO-** + **METEOROLOGY**.]
The branch of science that deals with the meteorological characteristics of a small area and with small-scale meteorological phenomena.
▪ **micrometeoroˈlogical** *adjective* **M20.** **micrometeorologist** *noun* **M20.**

micrometer /mʌɪˈkrɒmɪtə/ *noun*[1]. **E18.**
[**ORIGIN** French *micromètre*, formed as **MICRO-**: see **-METER**.]
An instrument or gauge for measuring very small objects or differences in size; *esp*. one in which linear movement is produced by turning a screw of fine pitch whose angular position is read as linear position.

micrometer *noun*[2] see **MICROMETRE**.

micrometre /ˈmʌɪkrə(ʊ)ˌmiːtə/ *noun*. Also ***-meter**. **L19.**
[**ORIGIN** from **MICRO-** + **METRE** *noun*[2].]
A millionth of a metre; = **MICRON**. (Symbol μ.)

micrometrical /mʌɪkrə(ʊ)ˈmɛtrɪk(ə)l/ *adjective*. **E18.**
[**ORIGIN** from **MICROMETER** *noun*[1] after *metre*, *metric*: see **-METRIC**, **-AL**[1].]
Pertaining to or of the nature of a micrometer; obtained by the use of a micrometer.
▪ **micrometric** *adjective* = **MICROMETRICAL** **M19.** **micrometrically** *adverb* by means of a micrometer **M19.** **micrometry** /-ˈkrɒmɪtri/ *noun* the measurement of very small objects; the use of a micrometer: **M19.**

microminiature /mʌɪkrə(ʊ)ˈmɪnɪtʃə/ *adjective*. **M20.**
[**ORIGIN** from **MICRO-** + **MINIATURE** *noun & adjective*.]
Much reduced in size, as a result of microminiaturization; even smaller than a size regarded as miniature.
▪ **microminiaturiˈzation** *noun* extreme miniaturization; *spec*. the development or use of techniques for making electronic components and devices of greatly reduced size: **M20.** **microminiaturize** *verb trans*. produce in a very much smaller version **M20.**

micromotion /ˈmʌɪkrə(ʊ)ˌməʊʃ(ə)n/ *noun*. **E20.**
[**ORIGIN** from **MICRO-** + **MOTION**.]
Small movements of the body recorded cinematographically for purposes of work study etc. Usu. *attrib*.

micron /ˈmʌɪkrɒn/ *noun*. **L19.**
[**ORIGIN** Greek *mikron* neut. of *mikros* small.]
= **MICROMETRE**.

Micronesian /mʌɪkrə(ʊ)ˈniːzjən, -ʒ(ə)n/ *noun & adjective*. **M19.**
[**ORIGIN** from *Micronesia* (see below), intended to mean 'region of small islands', from **MICRO-** + Greek *nēsos* island + **-IA**[1], after *Polynesia*: see **-AN**.]
▸ **A** *noun*. A native or inhabitant of Micronesia, a group of small islands in the western region of the N. Pacific which includes the Caroline, Mariana, Marshall, and Gilbert Islands. Also, the group of Austronesian languages spoken in Micronesia. **M19.**
▸ **B** *adjective*. Of or pertaining to Micronesia, the Micronesians, or their group of languages. **M19.**

micronize /ˈmʌɪkrənʌɪz/ *verb trans*. Also **-ise**. **M20.**
[**ORIGIN** from **MICRON** + **-IZE**, or back-form. from *Micronizer* (proprietary name in the US).]
Break up into very fine particles.

■ **microni'zation** *noun* M20.

micro-organism /mʌɪkrəʊ'ɔːg(ə)nɪz(ə)m/ *noun*. Also **microorganism**. L19.
[ORIGIN from MICRO- + ORGANISM.]
An organism too small to be seen except with the aid of a microscope, e.g. a bacterium or virus.

microphone /'mʌɪkrəfəʊn/ *noun*. L17.
[ORIGIN from MICRO- + -PHONE.]
1 An instrument by which quiet sounds can be made louder. Now *rare*. L17.
2 An instrument for converting sound waves impinging on it into variations in electric voltage or current, which may then be amplified or transmitted for reconversion into sound (as in broadcasting and the telephone) or recorded; *esp*. one made as an independent unit. L19.

B. MOORE Some with cameras, some with microphones and sound equipment.

■ **microphoned** *adjective* (*a*) containing or equipped with a microphone; (*b*) *rare* picked up and transmitted by a microphone: E20.

microphonic /mʌɪkrə'fɒnɪk/ *noun & adjective*. M19.
[ORIGIN from MICROPHONE + -IC.]
▸ **A** *noun*. **1** In *pl*. The branch of science that deals with the amplification of sound. *rare*. M19.
2 a ELECTRONICS. An undesired signal or modulation produced (e.g. in a valve) by mechanical vibration. Usu. in *pl*. E20. ▸**b** PHYSIOLOGY. A microphonic signal generated in the cochlea of the ear. M20.
▸ **B** *adjective*. **1** Of or pertaining to a microphone or the use of microphones. L19.
2 Characterized by or pertaining to the production of variations in electrical potential in response to sound waves or vibrations; (of an electrical signal) produced by sound waves or vibrations. L19.
■ **mi'crophony**, **mi'crophonism** *nouns* (ELECTRONICS) the production of microphonics M20.

microphoto /'mʌɪkrə(ʊ),fəʊtəʊ/ *noun*. *colloq*. Pl. **-os**. L19.
[ORIGIN Abbreviation.]
= MICROPHOTOGRAPH 2.

microphotograph /mʌɪkrə(ʊ)'fəʊtəgrɑːf/ *noun*. M19.
[ORIGIN from MICRO- + PHOTOGRAPH.]
1 A photograph reduced to microscopic size. M19.
2 A photograph of a microscopic object on a magnified scale; = PHOTOMICROGRAPH. M19.
■ **microphoto'graphic** *adjective* M19. **microphoto'graphically** *adverb* by means of microphotography L19. **micropho'tography** *noun* the art or practice of making microphotographs M19.

microphthalmos /mʌɪkrɒf'θalmɒs/ *noun*. M19.
[ORIGIN from MICRO- + Greek *ophthalmos* eye.]
MEDICINE. Abnormal smallness of one or both eyes.
■ **microphthalmia** *noun* = MICROPHTHALMOS L19. **microphthalmic** *adjective* pertaining to or characterized by microphthalmos M19.

microphysics /'mʌɪkrə(ʊ),fɪzɪks/ *noun*. L19.
[ORIGIN from MICRO- + PHYSICS.]
The branch of physics that deals with bodies and phenomena on a microscopic or smaller scale, esp. with molecules, atoms, and subatomic particles.
■ **micro'physical** *adjective* L19.

microphyte /'mʌɪkrə(ʊ)fʌɪt/ *noun*. M19.
[ORIGIN from MICRO- + -PHYTE.]
A microscopic plant, *esp*. a bacterium.
■ **micro'phytal**, **microphytic** /-'fɪtɪk/ *adjectives* M19.

microprint /'mʌɪkrə(ʊ)prɪnt/ *noun*. M20.
[ORIGIN from MICRO- + PRINT *noun*.]
A photographic print of text reduced by microphotography; printed matter so reduced.
■ **microprinting** *noun* the production of microprint M20.

microprocessor /mʌɪkrə(ʊ)'prəʊsɛsə/ *noun*. M20.
[ORIGIN from MICRO- + PROCESSOR.]
A device that can function as the central processing unit of a computer and consists of one or more occas. more integrated circuits or chips.

microprogram /'mʌɪkrə(ʊ),prəʊgram/ *noun & verb*. M20.
[ORIGIN from MICRO- + PROGRAM *noun*.]
COMPUTING. ▸**A** *noun*. A program that causes any machine instruction to be transformed into a sequence of microinstructions. M20.
▸ **B** *verb trans*. Infl. **-mm-**. Use microprogramming with (a computer); bring about by means of a microprogram. M20.
■ **micro'programmable** *adjective* able to be microprogrammed M20. **micro'programmer** *noun* a person who writes microprograms or is a specialist in microprogramming M20. **micro'programming** *noun* the technique of making machine instructions generate sequences of microinstructions in accordance with a microprogram rather than initiate the desired operations directly, so that by changing the microprogram the set of possible machine instructions can be varied M20.

micropsia /mʌɪ'krɒpsɪə/ *noun*. L19.
[ORIGIN from MICRO- + Greek *-opsia* seeing.]
OPHTHALMOLOGY. A condition of the eyes in which objects appear smaller than normal.

micropyle /'mʌɪkrə(ʊ)pʌɪl/ *noun*. E19.
[ORIGIN French, formed as MICRO- + Greek *pulē* gate.]
1 BOTANY. The opening in the integument of an ovule, through which the pollen tube penetrates to the embryo sac. Also, the small pore in the ripe seed which represents this opening. E19.
2 ZOOLOGY. A small opening in the egg of some animals, esp. insects, through which spermatozoa can enter. M19.
■ **micropylar** *adjective* M19.

microradiography /,mʌɪkrə(ʊ)reɪdɪ'ɒgrəfi/ *noun*. E20.
[ORIGIN from MICRO- + RADIOGRAPHY.]
Radiography of the fine structure of an object.
■ **micro'radiogram** *noun* the original image obtained on a sensitive plate or film in microradiography E20. **micro'radiograph** *noun* a photographic enlargement of a microradiogram M20. **microradio'graphic** *adjective* of or obtained by microradiography M20.

microscope /'mʌɪkrəskəʊp/ *noun & verb*. M17.
[ORIGIN mod. Latin *microscopium*, formed as MICRO- + -SCOPE.]
▸ **A** *noun*. **1** An optical instrument, consisting of a lens or combination of lenses, which produces a magnified image of an object close to it so as to reveal details invisible to the naked eye (also called ***light microscope***, ***optical microscope***). Also, an instrument analogous to this in function but employing radiation other than visible light (e.g. electrons or X-rays). M17.

fig.: *Economist* American motor insurance is now to be put under the microscope.

electron microscope: see ELECTRON *noun*[2].
2 (Usu. **M-**.) *The* constellation Microscopium. M19.
– COMB.: ***microscope slide***: see SLIDE *noun* 7(b).
▸ **B** *verb trans*. Magnify; *fig*. scrutinize minutely. *rare*. M19.
■ **microscopist** /mʌɪ'krɒskəpɪst, 'mʌɪkrəskəʊpɪst/ *noun* a person who habitually uses a microscope or who is skilled in its use M19. **microscopy** /mʌɪ'krɒskəpi/ *noun* the use of a microscope. M17.

microscopic /mʌɪkrə'skɒpɪk/ *adjective*. L17.
[ORIGIN from MICROSCOPE + -IC.]
1 Having the function or power of a microscope. L17.

POPE Why has not Man a microscopic eye?

2 So small as to be invisible or indeterminate without the use of a microscope; extremely small (*lit*. & *fig*.). M18.

ANTHONY HUXLEY Water and soil teem with microscopic plants. *Daily Telegraph* Although the Foreign Ministers sat for two hours and 20 minutes . . progress was microscopic.

3 = MICROSCOPICAL 1. Now chiefly *fig*., regarded in terms of small units, concerned with minute detail (opp. ***macroscopic***). L18.

D. CECIL The microscopic concentration of a scientist conducting an important experiment.

microscopical /mʌɪkrə'skɒpɪk(ə)l/ *adjective*. M17.
[ORIGIN formed as MICROSCOPIC + -ICAL.]
1 Of or pertaining to the microscope or its use. M17.

F. RUTLEY The present state of microscopical knowledge. B. UNSWORTH Microscopical and chemical analysis of paint samples.

2 = MICROSCOPIC 2. Now *rare*. M18.
■ **microscopically** *adverb* by means of a microscope; so minutely as to be visible only with a microscope; as seen under a microscope: L17.

Microscopium /mʌɪkrə'skəʊpɪəm/ *noun*. E19.
[ORIGIN mod. Latin, formed as MICROSCOPE.]
(The name of) an inconspicuous constellation of the southern hemisphere, between Piscis Austrinus and Sagittarius; the Microscope.

microscreen /'mʌɪkrə(ʊ)skriːn/ *noun*. M20.
[ORIGIN from MICRO- + SCREEN *noun*[1].]
1 A screen with a fine mesh. M20.
2 A small screen for displaying an image; *spec*. a liquid crystal display in the keyboard of a microcomputer. L20.

microsmatic /mʌɪkrɒz'matɪk/ *adjective*. L19.
[ORIGIN from MICRO- + Greek *osmē* smell + -ATIC.]
ZOOLOGY. Having poorly developed olfactory organs.

microsome /'mʌɪkrəsəʊm/ *noun*. L19.
[ORIGIN from MICRO- + -SOME[3].]
CYTOLOGY. Orig., a small granule in the cytoplasm of a cell. Now, a cytoplasmic particle consisting of a fragment of endoplasmic reticulum and attached ribosomes from a cell disrupted by ultracentrifugation; a ribosome in an intact cell.
■ **micro'somal** *adjective* L19.

microsporangium /,mʌɪkrəʊspə'randʒɪəm/ *noun*. Pl. **-ia** /-ɪə/. M19.
[ORIGIN from MICRO- + SPORANGIUM.]
BOTANY. A sporangium containing microspores.

microspore /'mʌɪkrə(ʊ)spɔː/ *noun*. M19.
[ORIGIN from MICRO- + SPORE.]
BOTANY. The smaller of the two kinds of spores in heterosporous cryptogams, which develop into male gametophytes; the analogous structure (the immature pollen grain) in seed plants.
■ **micro'sporocyte** *noun* a mother cell that divides into four microspores E20. **microsporo'genesis** *noun* the development of microspores E20. **microsporoge'netic** *adjective* of or pertaining to microsporogenesis L20. **microsporous** *adjective* having small seeds; resembling or derived from a microspore: M19.

microsporidian /,mʌɪkrəʊspə'rɪdɪən/ *adjective & noun*. E20.
[ORIGIN from mod. Latin *Microsporidia* (see below), from MICRO- + SPORE + Greek *-idion* dim. suffix: see -AN.]
ZOOLOGY. ▸**A** *adjective*. Of, pertaining to, or designating the sporozoan phylum Microspora or (formerly) the class Microsporidia, comprising protozoan parasites of arthropods and fishes. E20.
▸ **B** *noun*. A protozoan of this phylum. E20.
■ **microsporidi'osis** *noun* nosema disease of bees E20.

microstructure /'mʌɪkrə(ʊ),strʌktʃə/ *noun*. L19.
[ORIGIN from MICRO- + STRUCTURE *noun*.]
Structure on a microscopic or very small scale; fine structure.
■ **micro'structural** *adjective* L19. **micro'structurally** *adverb* as regards microstructure M20.

microsurgery /mʌɪkrə(ʊ)'səːdʒ(ə)ri/ *noun*. E20.
[ORIGIN from MICRO- + SURGERY.]
Manipulation (as by injection, dissection, etc.) of individual cells with the aid of microscopy; surgery of such intricacy as to necessitate being performed using microscopy.
■ **micro'surgical** *adjective* M20.

microtherm /'mʌɪkrə(ʊ)θəːm/ *noun*. L19.
[ORIGIN from MICRO- + Greek *thermē* heat.]
BOTANY. A plant requiring a cold habitat and low mean temperatures for successful growth.

microtine /'mʌɪkrə(ʊ)tʌɪn/ *noun & adjective*. L19.
[ORIGIN mod. Latin *Microtinae* (see below), from *Microtus* genus name, formed as MICRO- + Greek *ōt-*, *ous* ear: see -INE[1].]
▸ **A** *noun*. A rodent of the subfamily Microtinae (family Muridae), which includes voles and lemmings. L19.
▸ **B** *adjective*. Of, pertaining to, or designating this subfamily. E20.

microtome /'mʌɪkrə(ʊ)təʊm/ *noun & verb*. M19.
[ORIGIN from MICRO- + -TOME.]
▸ **A** *noun*. An instrument for cutting extremely thin sections for microscopic work. M19.
▸ **B** *verb trans*. Cut in sections with a microtome. L19.

microtone /'mʌɪkrə(ʊ)təʊn/ *noun*. E20.
[ORIGIN from MICRO- + TONE *noun*.]
A musical interval smaller than a semitone.
■ **micro'tonal** *adjective* of or pertaining to a microtone or microtones; employing or producing microtones: M20. **microto'nality** *noun* the use of microtones M20. **microtonally** *adverb* M20.

M

microwave /'mʌɪkrə(ʊ)weɪv/ *noun & verb*. M20.
[ORIGIN from MICRO- + WAVE *noun*.]
▸ **A** *noun*. **1** A short electromagnetic wave; now *spec*. one with a wavelength between about one millimetre and 30 centimetres (corresponding to a frequency between 300 GHz and 1 GHz), or one whose length is such that it is convenient to use hollow waveguides for its transmission. M20.
2 *ellipt*. A microwave oven; microwave cookery. L20.
▸ **B** *attrib*. or as *adjective*. Of or pertaining to microwaves, employing microwaves; (of food) heated or cooked in a microwave oven, suitable for microwave cooking. M20.

Television As the USSR covers such a vast area microwave links are used for TV and other communications. S. TOWNSEND My father . . went to the pub and had a microwave mince and onion pie.

microwave oven an oven in which food is heated by passing microwaves through it, the resulting generation of heat inside the food facilitating rapid cooking.
▸ **C** *verb trans*. **1** Transmit (signals, information, etc.) using microwave radiation. M20.
2 Heat or cook in a microwave oven. L20.
■ **microwavable** *adjective* suitable for cooking or heating in a microwave oven L20.

micrurgy /'mʌɪkrəːdʒi/ *noun*. E20.
[ORIGIN from MICRO- + *-urgy* after *metallurgy*.]
The performance of delicate manipulations under a microscope, esp. on biological material such as individual cells.
■ **mi'crurgical** *adjective* E20.

mictic /'mɪktɪk/ *adjective*. E20.
[ORIGIN from Greek *miktos* mixed + -IC.]
BIOLOGY. Of, pertaining to, or produced by mixis; of mixed parentage or descent.

micturate /'mɪktjʊreɪt/ *verb intrans*. M19.
[ORIGIN Back-form. from MICTURITION: see -ATE[3].]
Urinate.

micturition /mɪktjʊ'rɪʃ(ə)n/ *noun*. E18.
[ORIGIN from Latin *micturire*, from *mi(n)ct-* pa. ppl stem of *meiere* urinate: see -ITION.]
Urination.

mid /mɪd/ *noun*[1]. OE.
[ORIGIN Absol. use of MID *adjective*.]
1 The middle. Now *dial*. OE.
2 Something in the middle, *esp*. a middle note or tone. M20.

mid /mɪd/ *noun*[2]. *slang*. **M18.**
[**ORIGIN** Abbreviation.]
= **MIDSHIPMAN.**

mid /mɪd/ *attrib. adjective & adverb.* Superl. **MIDMOST**, (*arch.*) **middest.**
[**ORIGIN** Old English *midd* (recorded only in oblique forms *midde*, *middes*, etc.), corresp. to Old Frisian *midde*, Old Saxon *middi*, Old High German *mitti*, Old Norse *miðr*, Gothic *midjis*, from Germanic, from Indo-European base (whence also Latin *medius*, Greek *mesos* **MESO-**).]
▸ **A** *adjective*. (Freq. with hyphen.)
1 That is the part or point in the middle of. Now chiefly of a period of time and in special collocations & *comb.* Freq. in phrs. after *in*. **OE.** ▸**b** Introducing an adverbial phr. In the middle of. **M16.**

F. W. L. ADAMS From mid-June to mid-October. W. D. HOWELLS The wind rises, and by mid-afternoon, blows half a gale. H. D. LLOYD The gas-company suspended its operations in mid-course. *Which?* This had a mid position allowing flow both to the radiators and hot water supply. J. NAGENDA She rushed off . . leaving Roger in mid-joke. M. BRETT Many pension funds were showing surpluses in the mid 1980s. **b** G. MEREDITH Light that Caught him mid-gallop, blazed him home.

2 Being in or occupying a middle position. **LME.**

KEATS In the mid-days of autumn.

3 *spec.* ▸**a** *PHONETICS*. Of a sound: produced with (part of) the tongue in a middle position between high and low. **M19.** ▸**b** Of a colour: occupying a middle position in a range of shades. **E20.**
– **SPECIAL COLLOCATIONS & COMB.**: **mid-age** middle age. **mid-aged** *adjective* middle-aged. **mid-Atlantic** *noun & adjective* (*a*) *noun* the middle of the Atlantic Ocean; (*b*) *adjective* having characteristics of or features appealing to people both of Britain and of America. **midbrain** the part of the brainstem which joins the forebrain to the hindbrain; = **MESENCEPHALON. mid-brow** *noun & adjective* = *middlebrow* s.v. **MIDDLE** *adjective*. **mid-calf** *adjective & noun* (reaching to) the point halfway down the calf of the leg. **mid-circle** *GEOMETRY* †(*a*) the great circle equidistant from the poles of a sphere; (*b*) the circle passing through the midpoints of the sides of a triangle. **midcrop** a crop harvested between the main crops. **midcult** *colloq.* middlebrow culture. **mid-cycle** *adjective & noun* (*PHYSIOLOGY*) (occurring during) the middle of the menstrual cycle. **mid-earth** *arch. rare* (*a*) the middle of the earth; (*b*) = *middle earth* (a) s.v. **MIDDLE** *adjective*. **Mideast** (chiefly *US*) = *Middle East* s.v. **MIDDLE** *adjective*. **mid-engined** *adjective* (of a car) having the engine located centrally between the front and rear axles. **mid-European** *adjective & noun* = *Middle-European* s.v. **MIDDLE** *adjective*. **mid-feather** a thin structure dividing or partitioning the interior of a furnace, flue, etc. **midgut** *ANATOMY & ZOOLOGY* the middle part of the gut, in vertebrates including the small intestine. **mid-heaven** (*a*) *ASTRONOMY & ASTROLOGY* the meridian, or middle line of the heavens; *esp.* the point where the ecliptic meets the meridian; (*b*) the middle of the sky. **midiron** *GOLF* (*a*) an iron with a medium degree of loft; (*b*) a number 2 iron. **midline** *ANATOMY & ZOOLOGY* a median line; the median plane or plane of bilateral symmetry. **midlittoral** *adjective & noun* (*ECOLOGY*) (designating) the zone on the seashore which is both covered and uncovered by the neap tides. †**mid man** (*a*) a mediator, an umpire; (*b*) a male midwife. **mid-ocean** *noun & adjective* (*a*) *noun* the middle of an ocean; (*b*) *adjective* situated or occurring in the middle of an ocean (***mid-ocean ridge***, a long mountainous seismically active ridge, freq. with a central rift, rising from the abyssal plain in the middle of an ocean basin and marking the site of magmatic upwelling associated with sea-floor spreading). **mid-oceanic** *adjective* situated in, occurring in, or pertaining to the middle of an ocean. **midpoint** the middle point. **midrib** (*a*) *BOTANY* a large, usu. strengthened, vein along the midline of a leaf; (*b*) *ARCHAEOLOGY* a central ridge on the blade of a weapon. **midsagittal** *adjective* (*ANATOMY*) designating or situated in an anteroposterior median plane. **mid-sea** *noun & adjective* (*literary*) (situated or occurring in) the open sea. **midsection** (*a*) the middle part of something; (*b*) a person's midriff. **mid-shot** *CINEMATOGRAPHY* a medium shot. **mid-sky** *poet.* the middle of the sky. **midsole** a layer of material between the inner and outer soles of a shoe, for absorbing shock. **mid-spoon** *GOLF* a wooden-headed club of medium size. **mid-square** *adjective* (*MATH.*) designating a method of generating a pseudorandom sequence of digits by squaring an arbitrary large number, taking the middle digits of the result and using these as the first digits of the series and as the number to be squared to provide the next digits, and so on. **midterm** *noun & adjective* (occurring in) the middle of a period of office, an academic term, a pregnancy, etc. **midtown** *noun & adjective* (chiefly *US*) (situated or occurring in) the middle of a town, esp. when forming a distinct area. **mid-Victorian** *adjective & noun* (*a*) *adjective* pertaining to or characteristic of the middle of the Victorian period; (*b*) *noun* a person of the mid-Victorian period. **mid-water** the part of a body of water near neither the bottom nor the surface. **midweek** *noun & adjective* (occurring in) the middle of the week. **Midwest** the middle of the western part of the US, the region adjoining the northern Mississippi. **Midwestern** *adjective* of or pertaining to the Midwest. **Midwesterner** a native or inhabitant of the Midwest. **midwicket** *CRICKET* (the position of) a fielder placed between mid-on and square leg on a line bisecting the line joining the wickets. **mid-wing** *adjective* (*AERONAUTICS*) designating an aircraft having the main wings placed approximately halfway between the top and bottom of the fuselage.
▸ **B** *adverb*. In the middle. Long *obsolete* exc. in *comb.*, as ***mid-mounted*** *adjective*. **OE.**

†**mid** *preposition*[1]. **OE–LME.**
[**ORIGIN** Old English *mid*, (Northumbrian) *miþ*, corresp. to Old Frisian *mith*, Old Saxon *mid* (Dutch *met*), German *mit*, Old Norse *með*, Gothic *miþ*, cogn. with Greek *meta* (see **META-**).]
With.
– **NOTE**: Prob. survives in **MIDWIFE** *noun*.

mid /mɪd/ *preposition*[2]. Now *poet.* Also **'mid. LME.**
[**ORIGIN** Aphet.]
= **AMID.**
– **NOTE**: Rare before **19.**

mid-air /*as noun* mɪd'ɛː, *as adjective* 'mɪdɛː/ *noun & adjective*. **E17.**
[**ORIGIN** from **MID** *adjective* + **AIR** *noun*[1].]
▸ **A** *noun*. Some part or section of the air above ground level or above another surface. Chiefly in ***in mid-air***. **E17.**

S. HILL The humming birds hovered, whirring softly in mid-air.

▸ **B** *attrib.* or as *adjective*. Situated or occurring in mid-air. **L18.**

Guardian If something is not done soon about these near misses, there is bound to be a mid-air collision.

Midas /'mʌɪdəs/ *noun*. **M16.**
[**ORIGIN** Latin & Greek, a king of Phrygia whose touch was said to turn all things to gold, and to whom also Apollo gave asses' ears as a punishment for not appreciating his music.]
1 A person incapable of appreciating something; ***Midas ear(s)***, ***Midas-eared***, (having) an incapacity to appreciate something. **M16.**
2 A person whose actions always bring financial reward; ***Midas touch***, the ability to turn one's actions to financial advantage. **L18.**

midas fly *noun phr.* see **MYDAS FLY.**

midday /*as noun* mɪd'deɪ, *as adjective* 'mɪddeɪ/ *noun & adjective*. **OE.**
[**ORIGIN** from **MID** *adjective* + **DAY** *noun*.]
▸ **A** *noun*. **1** The middle of the day, when the sun is at its highest point; noon. **OE.** ▸†**b** *ECCLESIASTICAL*. = **SEXT** 1. **OE–LME.**

E. TEMPLETON He never ate more than one course at midday when he was working.

†**2** [Cf. French *midi*.] The south. **LME–E17.**
▸ **B** *attrib.* or as *adjective*. Of or pertaining to midday; occurring at midday, (of a train etc.) leaving or arriving at midday. **ME.**

P. BOWLES Narrow alleys, where the shade was a blessing after the midday sun. E. KUZWAYO We had our mid-day meal together daily. *Scotsman* To catch the midday flight to Jersey.

midden /'mɪd(ə)n/ *noun*. **ME.**
[**ORIGIN** Of Scandinavian origin: cf. Danish *Mødding*, earlier *møgdyng*, from *møg* **MUCK** *noun*[1] + *dynge* heap (cf. **DUNG** *noun*), Norwegian dial. *mykjardunge*, *mitting*.]
1 A dunghill, a manure heap; a refuse heap. **ME.**

fig.: *Expression!* My own enthusiasm for the arts, then, grew up in the fertilising midden of unselfconsciousness.

2 *ARCHAEOLOGY*. A prehistoric refuse heap of shells and bones and often also discarded artefacts; *spec.* = ***KITCHEN midden***. **M19.**
3 A receptacle for refuse, a dustbin; the place where dustbins are kept. *Scot. colloq.* **L19.**
– **COMB.**: **midden cock** = ***DUNGHILL cock***; **midden fowl** = ***DUNGHILL fowl***; **middenstead** *arch. & dial.* the place where a midden or dunghill is formed.

midder /'mɪdə/ *noun*. *slang*. **E20.**
[**ORIGIN** from **MID(WIFERY** + **-ER**[6].]
Midwifery; a midwifery case.

middest *adjective* see **MID** *adjective*.

middie *noun* var. of **MIDDY** *noun*[1].

middle /'mɪd(ə)l/ *attrib. adjective & noun*.
[**ORIGIN** Old English *middel* = Old Frisian *middel*, Old Saxon *middil* (Dutch *middel*), Old High German *mittil* (German *mittel*), from West Germanic, from Germanic base of **MID** *adjective*: see **-LE**[1].]
▸ **A** *adjective*. **1** Designating that member of a group or series or that part of a whole situated so as to have the same number of members or parts on each side; equidistant from the ends or boundaries of a thing; situated at the centre. **OE.** ▸†**b** Average, mean. **L17–L18.**

GOLDSMITH He was at that middle time of life which is happily tempered with the warmth of youth. W. M. CRAIG In the same way you will get the middle line of the mouth. J. TYNDALL The middle portion of the glacier. *Punch* My middle sister, Emily.

2 = **MID** *adjective* 1. Now *rare*. **ME.**

J. MACCULLOCH The two months of middle summer.

3 Of size, rank, quality, or (now rarely) position in space or time: intermediate; medium. Of a course of action, an opinion, etc.: mediating. Of a colour: = **MID** *adjective* 3b. **LME.** ▸**b** Middle-sized (now *rare*); (of wool) having medium-length staple. **LME.** ▸**c** Of or pertaining to the middle classes. **L18.**

N. ROWE The middle Space, a Valley low depress'd. BURKE An Administration, that having no scheme of their own, took a middle line. T. D. ACLAND The want of better education, accessible to the middle ranks on easy terms. E. PACE The immaturity that plagued middle-level intelligence officials. D. FRANCIS A man . . of middle height . . and middling grey hair.

4 *GRAMMAR*. Of or designating (the voice of) a verb (esp. in Greek) which expresses reflexive or reciprocal action. **M18.**
5 Designating a language at an intermediate stage in its history, between the old and modern forms. **M19.**
6 *GEOLOGY*. Designating a subdivision of a formation or period intermediate between two others (upper and lower). **M19.**
– **SPECIAL COLLOCATIONS & COMB.**: *Middle Academy*: see **ACADEMY** 2. **Middle America** (*a*) the region comprising Central America, Mexico, and the Antilles; (*b*) the middle class in the US, esp. as a conservative political force. **Middle American** *adjective & noun* (a native or inhabitant) of Middle America. **Middle Atlantic States** the states of New York, New Jersey, and Pennsylvania. **Middle Britain** the middle class in Britain, esp. as a conservative political force. **middlebrow** *noun & adjective* (a person) claiming to be or regarded as only moderately intellectual or cultured. **middle C** *MUSIC* the C near the middle of the piano keyboard, the note between the treble and bass staves, at about 260 hertz frequency. **middle common room** a common room in a university college for the use of graduate students who are not fellows; graduate students collectively. **middle course** a compromise between two extremes (***steer a middle course***: see **STEER** *verb*[1]). **middle deck** a ship's deck between the upper deck and the lower deck. **middle distance** (*a*) the part of a (painted or actual) landscape between the foreground and the background; (*b*) a race distance intermediate between that of a sprint and a long-distance race, now usu. 800 or 1500 metres and their imperial equivalents (880 yards etc.). **middle distillate** a petroleum fraction that distils at intermediate temperatures (about 180 to 340 degrees C), from which is obtained paraffin, diesel oil, and heating oil. ***middle ear***: see **EAR** *noun*[1]. **middle earth** (*a*) *arch.* the earth, as situated between heaven and hell or as supposedly occupying the centre of the universe; (*b*) the real world as distinct from fairyland; †(*c*) the middle of the earth. **Middle East** the area around the eastern Mediterranean, *esp.* those countries from Egypt to Iran inclusive. **Middle Eastern** *adjective* of, pertaining to, situated in, or occurring in the Middle East. **middle eight** *colloq.* the eight bars in the middle of a conventionally structured popular tune, often of a different character from the other parts of the tune. **Middle England** (*a*) central England; (*b*) the middle class in England, esp. as a conservative political force. ***Middle English***: see **ENGLISH** *adjective & noun*. **Middle-European** *adjective* of, pertaining to, or characteristic of central Europe or its people. **middle finger**: between the index finger and the third finger. **middle game** the central phase of a chess game when strategies are developed. **middle genus** *LOGIC* a genus which is itself a species of a higher genus. **middle ground** (*a*) *NAUTICAL* a shallow place, as a bank or bar, esp. as a navigational obstruction; (*b*) = ***middle distance*** (a) above; (*c*) an area of moderation or compromise. **middle guard** (*a*) *CRICKET* the position occupied by a batsman defending the middle stump with the bat; (*b*) *AMER. FOOTBALL* a defensive lineman who plays between the defensive tackles. **middle income** an average income. **Middle Kingdom** (*a*) *hist.* China, *spec.* its eighteen inner provinces; (*b*) *the* eleventh and twelfth Dynasties, which ruled Egypt from the 22nd to the 18th cents. BC. **middle lamella** *BOTANY* the thin layer between two adjacent plant cell walls. **middle leg** *slang* the penis. **middle-length** *adjective* of medium length. **middle life** (*a*) the middle of a person's life, middle age; (*b*) middle-class life. **middle linebacker** *AMER. FOOTBALL*: who plays behind the middle of the defensive line. **middle management** the middle level of management in a business or company, esp. comprising departmental managers. **middle manager** a manager at the level of middle management. **middle name** (*a*) a name between a person's first name and surname; (*b*) *fig.* the outstanding characteristic of a person. **middle passage** *hist.* the middle part of a slave's transportation from Africa to America, the sea passage. **middle period** the middle phase of a culture, artist's work, etc. **middle piece** the part of a horse's body between the forelegs and the hind legs. **Middle Pointed** *ARCHITECTURE* (now *hist.*) decorated Gothic. **middle price** *STOCK EXCHANGE* the average of the bid and offer prices of a particular stock. **middle rail** the rail of a door level with the hand, on which the lock is usually fixed. **middle-rank** *adjective* of intermediate status or value. **middle-rate** *adjective* mediocre. **middle rib** a cut of beef consisting of the ribs between the fore ribs and the chuck ribs. **middle-road** *adjective* = ***middle-of-the-road*** below. **middle school** (*a*) a secondary school for children between the ages of 9 and 13; (*b*) the middle (esp. third and fourth) forms in a secondary school. **middle-sized** *adjective* of medium size. ***middle spotted woodpecker***: see ***SPOTTED woodpecker***. **Middle States** = ***Middle Atlantic States*** above. **middlestead** *dial.* the central part of a barn where threshing formerly took place. ***Middle Temple***: see **TEMPLE** *noun*[1] 6. ***middle term***: see **TERM** *noun*. **middle-tone** = ***halftone*** (c) s.v. **HALF-**. †**middle wall** a partition wall. **middle watch** the watch from midnight to 4 a.m.; the members of a ship's crew on deck duty during this. **middleware** *COMPUTING* software that occupies a position in a hierarchy between the operating system and the applications, and whose task is to ensure that software from a variety of sources will work together correctly. **middle-water** *adjective* designating or pertaining to fishing carried out at a medium distance from land. **middle way** (*a*) = ***middle course*** above; (*b*) the eightfold path of Buddhism between indulgence and asceticism. **Middle West** = ***Midwest*** s.v. **MID** *adjective*. **Middle Western** *adjective* = ***Midwestern*** s.v. **MID** *adjective*. **Middle White** (an animal of) a medium-sized white (orig. Yorkshire) breed of pig with prick ears. **middle wicket** = ***midwicket*** s.v. **MID** *adjective*. **middle world** *arch.* = ***middle earth*** (a) above. **middle years** the years in the middle of a person's life, middle age. **middle youth** the time of life between early adulthood and middle age.
▸ **B** *noun*. **1** The middle point, part, or position. (Foll. by *of*.) **OE.** ▸**b** A strip of unplanted ground between two rows of a planted crop. Usu. in *pl. US.* **E19.**

R. K. NARAYAN I noticed her sitting erect in the middle of the road. C. ANGIER Mr Peterman demanded to know why she had walked out in the middle of her act. T. PARKS There was just one . . polished-wood table in the middle and then cupboards about the walls. L. CODY It could have been the middle of the night. Z. TOMIN Make sure this story has a happy beginning, middle and end.

†**2** The position of being among or surrounded by a group of people or within a town etc. Chiefly in ***in the middle of***, in the midst of. OE–M18.

H. BROOKE [He] is come to rob me in broad day, and in the middle of my own people.

3 a A person's waist. OE. ▸**b** The part of a side of bacon between the fore-end and the gammon cuts. L19.

G. BORROW He has got it buckled round his middle beneath his pantaloons.

4 A mean; a point of moderation or compromise. Now *rare*. ME.

DEFOE To keep the safe middle between these extremes.

†**5** An intermediate cause or agency. *rare*. ME–L17.
6 NAUTICAL. = ***middle ground*** (a) above. E18.
7 GRAMMAR. The middle voice of a verb; a middle verb. M18.
8 CRICKET. = ***middle guard*** (a) above. M19.
9 A brief essay of a literary kind esp. in a weekly journal, usu. placed between the leading articles and the reviews. M19.
10 A middle-class person. *colloq*. M20.

– PHRASES & COMB.: **in the middle** *slang* in a difficult or dangerous position, in trouble. **in the middle of** †(*a*) see sense B.2 above; (*b*) in the process of *doing*. ***knock into the middle of next week***: see KNOCK *verb*. ***law of excluded middle***, ***law of excluded third***: see EXCLUDE 5. **middle-of-the-road** *adjective* (of a person, course of action, music, etc.) avoiding extremes, unadventurous. ***pig in the middle***: see PIG *noun*[1]. ***piggy in the middle***: see PIGGY *noun*. ***play both ends against the middle***: see PLAY *verb*. ***principle of excluded middle***, ***principle of excluded third***: see EXCLUDE 5. ***turn sides to middle***: see SIDE *noun*. ***undistributed middle***.

▪ **middleness** *noun* (*rare*) the fact or condition of being of middle rank or quality E20.

middle /ˈmɪd(ə)l/ *verb*. LME.
[ORIGIN from MIDDLE *noun*.]
†**1** *verb intrans*. Be at the middle point. Only in LME.
†**2** *verb trans*. with *it*. Take a middle course. Only in M17.
3 *verb trans*. Bisect. *rare*. E18.
4 *verb trans*. NAUTICAL. Fold or double in the middle. M19.
5 *verb trans*. Place in the middle. L19.
6 *verb trans*. & *intrans*. FOOTBALL. Pass (the ball) from one of the wings to midfield in front of the goal. L19.
7 *verb trans*. Strike (a ball) with the middle of the bat or racket. M20.

middle age /mɪd(ə)l ˈeɪdʒ/ *noun phr*. & *adjective*. As adjective usu. **middle-age**. LME.
[ORIGIN from MIDDLE *adjective* + AGE *noun*.]
▸**A** *noun phr*. **1** The age between youth and old age, now regarded as between about 45 and 60. LME.
2 ***the Middle Ages***, (now *rare*) ***the Middle Age***, the period of European history from the fall of the Roman Empire in the West (*c* 500) to the fall of Constantinople (1453), or (usu.) from *c* 1000 to *c* 1453. E17.
▸**B** *attrib*. or as *adjective*. **1** Of or pertaining to the Middle Ages, medieval. Now *rare*. M18.
2 Of or pertaining to middle age. L19.
middle-age spread an increase in bodily girth, often associated with middle age.
▪ **middle-ˈageing** *adjective* becoming middle-aged L19. **middle-ˈager** *noun* (chiefly *US*) a middle-aged person M20.

middle-aged /mɪd(ə)lˈeɪdʒd/ *adjective*. M16.
[ORIGIN from MIDDLE AGE + -ED[2].]
1 In middle age, (now) aged between about 45 and 60. M16. ▸**b** Characteristic of or considered appropriate to a person in middle age. M19.
b ***middle-aged spread*** = ***middle-age spread*** s.v. MIDDLE AGE.
†**2** Of or pertaining to the Middle Ages; medieval. E17–M19.

middle class /mɪd(ə)l ˈklɑːs/ *noun phr*. & *adjective*. As adjective usu. **middle-class**. M18.
[ORIGIN from MIDDLE *adjective* + CLASS *noun*.]
▸**A** *noun*. A class of society between an upper and lower or working class, including professional and business workers and their families; *sing*. & in *pl*., the members of such a class. M18.
upper middle class: see UPPER *adjective*.
▸**B** *adjective*. Of, pertaining to, or characteristic of the middle class; conservative. M19.

I. HISLOP Twee, prim and dull . . . Even her voice sounded middle-class. D. ROWE The prejudice that middle-class people can hold about the working class.

▪ **middle-classdom** *noun* (the characteristics of) the middle classes as a whole M20. **middle-classness** *noun* the quality or state of being middle-class. L19.

middleman /ˈmɪd(ə)lman/ *noun*. Pl. **-men** /-mɛn/. LME.
[ORIGIN from MIDDLE *adjective* + MAN *noun*.]
†**1** A workman employed in the making of iron wire. Only in LME.
†**2** A soldier in the fifth or sixth rank in a file of ten deep. Only in 17.
3 A person who takes a middle course. M18.
4 a A person who paddles or rows in the middle of a boat. *N. Amer*. M18. ▸**b** The middle climber of a mountaineering team. L19. ▸**c** Chiefly *hist*. A man in the middle of a line of blackface minstrels who led the dialogue between songs. *US*. L19.
5 A person standing in an intermediate relation to two parties; *spec*. (*a*) a trader who handles a commodity between its producer and its consumer; (*b*) an intermediary. M18. ▸**b** *hist*. In Ireland, a person who leased land and sublet it at a higher rate. L18.
▪ **middlemanship** *noun* the system of employing middlemen M19.

middlemost /ˈmɪd(ə)lməʊst/ *adjective*. Now *rare*. ME.
[ORIGIN from MIDDLE *adjective* + -MOST.]
That is in the very middle or nearest the middle. (Now only of position.)

middler /ˈmɪd(ə)lə/ *noun*. M16.
[ORIGIN from MIDDLE *adjective* + -ER[1].]
†**1** An intermediary, a mediator. M16–L17.
2 A worker who performs the middle one of three operations in the preparation of flax. M19.

middlescent /mɪdəˈlɛs(ə)nt/ *adjective* & *noun*. M20.
[ORIGIN from MIDDLE *adjective* after *adolescent*.]
▸**A** *adjective*. Of or pertaining to middle age, middle-aged. M20.
▸**B** *noun*. A middle-aged person. M20.
▪ **middlescence** *noun* middle age M20.

middleveld /ˈmɪd(ə)lvɛlt, -f-/ *noun*. L19.
[ORIGIN Partial translation of Afrikaans *middelveld*.]
(A region of) veld situated at an intermediate altitude; *spec*. the region in Transvaal, South Africa, between 900 and 1200 m (3000 and 4000 ft) above sea level.

middleweight /ˈmɪd(ə)lweɪt/ *noun* & *adjective*. M19.
[ORIGIN from MIDDLE *adjective* + WEIGHT *noun*.]
▸**A** *noun*. A weight at which boxing etc. matches are made, intermediate between welterweight and heavyweight, in the amateur boxing scale now being between 71 and 75 kg, though differing for professionals, wrestlers, and weightlifters, and according to time and place; a boxer etc. of this weight. M19.
▸**B** *adjective*. (Of a boxer etc.) that is a middleweight; of or pertaining to middleweights. L19.
– PHRASES: **junior middleweight** (of) a weight in professional boxing of between 66.7 and 69.8 kg; (designating) a boxer of this weight. **light middleweight** (of) a weight in amateur boxing of between 67 and 71 kg; (designating) a boxer of this weight.

middling /ˈmɪd(ə)lɪŋ/ *noun*. OE.
[ORIGIN Prob. orig. from MID *adjective* + -LING[1]; later, the adjective used absol.]
1 A middle or intermediate part or thing. OE. ▸**b** A mediocre or average person or thing. Freq. in ***among the middlings***, of a mediocre class. Chiefly *dial*. E19.
2 In *pl*. ▸**a** Things of intermediate size or quality, *esp*. goods of the second of three grades. M16. ▸**b** People of mediocre talent, qualities, etc., or of moderate means. M18.

middling /ˈmɪd(ə)lɪŋ/ *adjective* & *adverb*. Orig. *Scot*. ME.
[ORIGIN Prob. from MID *adjective* + -LING[2].]
▸**A** *adjective*. **1** Of medium or moderate size; moderately large. Now (*colloq*.) passing into sense 4. ME.

J. RATHBONE He was a man of middling height.

2 †**a** Intermediate between two things; moderate. LME–M18. ▸**b** Middle-aged. *rare*. E17.
3 Designating the second of three grades into which certain goods are sorted according to quality. M16.
4 Moderately good; mediocre, second-rate. M17.

D. FRANCIS Etty gave him middling horses to ride.

fair-to-middling: see FAIR *adjective*.
5 Designating or pertaining to the middle class. Now *rare*. L17.
▸**B** *adverb*. **1** Moderately, fairly. *colloq*. E18.
2 Fairly well (esp. in health). *colloq*. E19.
▪ **middlingly** *adverb* M18. **middlingness** *noun* M19.

Middx. *abbreviation*.
Middlesex.

middy /ˈmɪdi/ *noun*[1]. *colloq*. Also **middie**. E19.
[ORIGIN from MID *noun*[2] + -Y[6].]
1 A midshipman. E19.
2 More fully ***middy blouse***. A kind of loose blouse with a sailor collar. E20.

middy /ˈmɪdi/ *noun*[2]. *Austral*. *slang*. M20.
[ORIGIN from MID *noun*[1] + -Y[6].]
A medium-sized measure of beer or other liquor; a glass holding this quantity.

midear /mɪˈdɪə/ *noun*. E20.
[ORIGIN from MY *adjective* + DEAR *noun*, repr. an informal or dial. pronunc.]
As a form of address: my dear.

midfield /*as noun & adverb* mɪdˈfiːld, *as adjective* ˈmɪdfiːld/ *noun*, *adjective*, & *adverb*. LME.
[ORIGIN from MID *adjective* + FIELD *noun*.]
▸**A** *noun*. **1** The middle of a field. LME.
2 SPORT. The middle of the field of play (freq. in ***in midfield***); the players positioned in midfield collectively. L19.

Times Poland's goal came after Norman Hunter . . lost possession in midfield.

▸**B** *attrib*. or as *adjective*. Of or pertaining to the midfield, positioned in midfield. L19.

Sunday Telegraph The demands on a midfield player are burdensome.

▸**C** *adverb*. In midfield. L19.
▪ **midfielder** *noun* a player positioned in midfield M20.

midge /mɪdʒ/ *noun*.
[ORIGIN Old English *myċġ(e)*, corresp. to Old Saxon *muggia* (Dutch *mug*), Old High German *mucca* (German *Mücke*), Old Norse *mý* (Swedish *mygg*, *mygga*), from Germanic, rel. to Latin *musca* fly, Greek *muia*.]
1 A small insect resembling a gnat; *spec*. in ENTOMOLOGY, any of numerous small slender dipterans of the family Chironomidae, common in swarms near water, or (more fully ***biting midge***) of the family Ceratopogonidae. OE. ▸**b** A small or insignificant person. Chiefly *Scot*. & *N. English*. M18.
fungus midge, ***gall midge***, ***pear midge***, etc.
2 *hist*. A kind of small one-horse fly (carriage). Cf. FLY *noun*[2] 3b. M19.

midgern /ˈmɪdʒ(ə)n/ *noun*. Long *obsolete* exc. *dial*. Also **-erum** /-ərəm/.
[ORIGIN Old English *miċġern* = Old Saxon *midgarni*, Old High German *mittigarni*, from Germanic base of MID *adjective* + base of Old Norse *gorn* bowel, gut: see YARN.]
1 Orig., the fat surrounding the entrails of an animal. Later, leaf fat. OE.
2 = MIDRIFF 1. *rare*. LME.

midget /ˈmɪdʒɪt/ *noun* & *adjective*. E19.
[ORIGIN from MIDGE + -ET[1].]
▸**A** *noun*. **1** A very small thing; *spec*. a small vehicle. E19.
2 An extremely small person. M19.
▸**B** *attrib*. or as *adjective*. Very small, small-scale, tiny. M19.

Midi /miːˈdiː, *foreign* midi/ *noun*[1] & *adjective*. M19.
[ORIGIN French.]
▸**A** *noun*. *The* south of France. M19.
▸**B** *attrib*. or as *adjective*. Of or pertaining to the south of France. M20.

midi /ˈmɪdi/ *noun*[2]. M20.
[ORIGIN from MIDI-.]
A garment of medium length, *esp*. a skirt or coat reaching to mid-calf.

MIDI /ˈmɪdi/ *noun*[3]. Also **midi**. L20.
[ORIGIN Acronym, from *m*usical *i*nstrument *d*igital *i*nterface.]
An electronic device by means of which electronic musical instruments, synthesizers, and computers can be interconnected and used simultaneously. Usu. *attrib*.

midi- /ˈmɪdi/ *combining form*. M20.
[ORIGIN from MID *adjective*, MIDDLE *adjective*, after MAXI-, MINI-.]
Forming chiefly nouns denoting something of medium size or length, esp. a garment reaching to mid-calf, as ***midi-coat***, ***midiskirt***.
midibus a medium-sized bus, seating about 25 passengers. **midi-system** a set of compact stacking hi-fi equipment components.

midinette /mɪdɪˈnɛt, *foreign* midinɛt (*pl. same*)/ *noun*. E20.
[ORIGIN French, from *midi* midday + *dînette* light dinner.]
A French, esp. a Parisian, female shop assistant; *esp*. a milliner's assistant.

Midland /ˈmɪdlənd/ *adjective* & *noun*. In gen. senses also **m-**. L15.
[ORIGIN from MID *adjective* + LAND *noun*[1].]
▸**A** *adjective*. **1** Situated in the middle of a country; central and inland; remote from the sea. L15. ▸**b** *spec*. Of or pertaining to the midland counties of England. L15. ▸**c** Of or pertaining to the midland area of the US or the regional type of American English spoken there. L19.
b ***Midland*** HAWTHORN.
2 Designating or pertaining to the Mediterranean Sea. Now *literary*. L16.
▸**B** *noun*. †**1** The middle part of the land in a holding. *Scot*. Only in L15.
2 In *pl*. & †*sing*. The middle part of a country, *spec*. (***the Midlands***), the inland counties of central England; (***Midland*** or ***the Midlands***), the central area of the US, esp. as regarded as a dialectal area of American English. M16.

Daily Telegraph The Prime Minister will visit the Midlands as he launches a nationwide roadshow.

▪ **Midlander** *noun* a native or inhabitant of the English Midlands or the Midland of the US E17.

mid-leg /mɪdˈlɛg/ *noun* & *adverb*. M16.
[ORIGIN from MID *adjective* + LEG *noun*.]
▸**A** *noun*. **1** The middle of the leg. M16.
2 ENTOMOLOGY. Each of the intermediate or second pair of legs of an insect. E19.
▸**B** *adverb*. To the middle of the leg. E19.

mid-life /*as noun* mɪdˈlʌɪf, *as adjective* ˈmɪdlʌɪf/ *noun* & *adjective*. Orig. *US*. E19.
[ORIGIN from MID *adjective* + LIFE *noun*.]
▸**A** *noun*. Middle age; the period between youth and old age. E19.
▸**B** *attrib*. or as *adjective*. Existing or occurring in mid-life; middle-aged. M19.

M

mid-life crisis a crisis of confidence or identity occurring in mid-life, characterized by the feeling that one is growing old or that life is passing one by.

midmost /ˈmɪdməʊst/ *adjective, noun, adverb, & preposition.*
[ORIGIN Old English *midmest* from Germanic, from base repr. by Old High German *in mittamen* in the middle + -EST[1]. Later alt. by assoc. with -MOST: cf. FOREMOST.]
▸ **A** *adjective.* That is in the very middle, with regard to position, age, etc. OE.
▸ **B** *absol.* as *noun.* The midmost part, the middle. Now *arch. & poet.* LME.
▸ **C** *adverb.* In the middle or midst. *poet.* E18.
▸ †**D** *preposition.* In the middle or midst of. M–L19.

midnight /ˈmɪdnʌɪt/ *noun & adjective.* OE.
[ORIGIN from MID *adjective* + NIGHT *noun.*]
▸ **A** *noun.* **1** The middle of the night; 12 o'clock at night. OE.
2 (A period of) intense darkness; deep gloom. L16.
R. KIPLING This is the midnight—let no star Delude us—dawn is very far. M. L. KING A tragic breakdown of . . standards, and the midnight of moral degeneration deepens.
▸ **B** *attrib.* or as *adjective.* Of, occurring at, or pertaining to midnight. LME.
– SPECIAL COLLOCATIONS & PHRASES: ***burn midnight oil, burn the midnight oil***: see OIL *noun.* **midnight blue** (of) a very dark shade of blue. **midnight feast**: held at midnight, esp. secretly by children. **midnight mass**: celebrated at or shortly before midnight, esp. on Christmas Eve. **midnight sun** the sun as seen in the polar regions at midnight during summer (***land of the midnight sun***: see LAND *noun*[1]).
■ **midnightly** *adverb (rare)* at midnight, every midnight M19.

midnoon /mɪdˈnuːn, ˈmɪdnuːn/ *noun.* L16.
[ORIGIN from MID *adjective* + NOON *noun.*]
Midday; noon.
fig.: LYTTON A man of your years. At the midnoon of manhood.

mid-off /mɪdˈɒf/ *noun.* M19.
[ORIGIN from MID *adjective* + OFF *adjective.*]
CRICKET. (The position occupied by) a fielder near the bowler on the off side.

mid-on /mɪdˈɒn/ *noun.* L19.
[ORIGIN from MID *adjective* + ON *adjective.*]
CRICKET. (The position occupied by) a fielder near the bowler on the on side.

M

mid-range /mɪdˈreɪn(d)ʒ/ *noun & adjective.* M19.
[ORIGIN from MID *adjective* + RANGE *noun*[1].]
▸ **A** *noun.* A central or halfway point, an approximate midpoint, *spec.*: (***a***) STATISTICS the arithmetic mean of the largest and the smallest values in a sample or other group; (***b***) the middle part of the range of audible frequencies; a loudspeaker designed to reproduce such frequencies with fidelity. M19.
▸ **B** *adjective.* Existing in or functioning at the middle part of a range; *spec.* in the middle of a range of products with regard to size, quality, or price. E20

Midrash /ˈmɪdraʃ, -rʌʃ/ *noun.* Pl. **Midrashim** /mɪˈdraʃɪm, mɪdraˈʃɪm; mɪdrʌˈʃɪm/. E17.
[ORIGIN Hebrew *midrāš* commentary, from *dāraš* study, expound.]
An ancient homiletic commentary on a text from the Hebrew scriptures, characterized by non-literal interpretation and legendary illustration. Also, the mode of exegesis characteristic of such a commentary. Cf. HAGGADAH 2.
■ **Miˈdrashic** *adjective* of or pertaining to a Midrash or Midrashim M19.

midriff /ˈmɪdrɪf/ *noun.*
[ORIGIN Old English *midhrif* (= Old Frisian *midref*), formed as MID *adjective* + *hrif* belly (= Old Frisian *hrif, href*, Old High German *href*), of unknown origin.]
1 The diaphragm. OE. ▸†**b** *transf.* A partition. M17–M18.
shake the midriff, tickle the midriff cause laughter.
2 The area of the front of the body between the chest and the waist; the part of a garment which covers this area. M20.
JAN MORRIS They seem to have gone badly to seed, having . . heavy haunches and protruding midriffs.

mids /mɪdz/ *noun & preposition.* Long *obsolete* exc. *Scot.* ME.
[ORIGIN from MID *noun*[1] + -S[3], in adverbial phrs. after *in* etc.: cf. MIDST.]
▸ **A** *noun.* **1** The middle, the midst. Chiefly in ***in mids (of)***, ***in the mids (of)***. ME.
†**2** A means. E16–E18.
3 A mean between two extremes; a middle course, a compromise. M16.
▸ †**B** *preposition.* In the middle of, among. LME–E17.

mid-season /*as noun* mɪdˈsiːz(ə)n, *as adjective* ˈmɪdsiːz(ə)n/ *noun & adjective.* E17.
[ORIGIN from MID *adjective* + SEASON *noun.*]
▸ **A** *noun.* †**1** The time in the middle of the day; noon. *rare* (Shakes.). Only in E17.
2 The middle of the season. L19.
▸ **B** *attrib.* or as *adjective.* Of or pertaining to the middle of the season; occurring in the middle of the season. L19.

midship /ˈmɪdʃɪp/ *noun.* L15.
[ORIGIN from MID *adjective* + SHIP *noun.*]
The middle part of a ship or boat.
– COMB.: **midship beam** the longest beam in a ship, lodged in the midship frame; **midship frame** the timber or frame in a ship having the greatest breadth.

midshipman /ˈmɪdʃɪpmən/ *noun.* Earlier †**midships-**. Pl. **-men**. E17.
[ORIGIN from MIDSHIP or (earlier) MIDSHIPS + MAN *noun.*]
In the British navy, an officer ranking above a naval cadet and below a sub-lieutenant; in the US navy, a naval cadet.
■ **midshipmanship** *noun* the position or office of midshipman L18.

midshipmite /ˈmɪdʃɪpmʌɪt/ *noun. nautical slang.* M19.
[ORIGIN Alt., after MITE *noun*[2].]
= MIDSHIPMAN.

midships /ˈmɪdʃɪps/ *noun & adverb.* E17.
[ORIGIN Prob. of Low German origin (Dutch *midscheeps*, from *mid* MID *adjective* + *scheeps* genit. of *schip* SHIP *noun*): cf. German *Mittschiffs*. As adverb aphet. from AMIDSHIPS.]
▸ **A** *noun.* = MIDSHIP. E17.
▸ **B** *adverb.* = AMIDSHIPS. L18.

†**midshipsman** *noun* see MIDSHIPMAN.

midst /mɪdst/ *noun, preposition, & adverb.* LME.
[ORIGIN formed as MIDS + *t* as in *against, amongst*, etc.: cf. AMIDST.]
▸ **A** *noun.* **1** The middle point or part; the middle *of*; the position of being involved in or surrounded by something, or a number of people etc. Now chiefly in ***in the midst of, in our midst, in their midst***, etc. LME.
J. WAIN The tiny station was in the midst of its . . half-hour of alertness. A. JUDD Philip noticed Edward standing in the midst of a group. J. DISKI Men from the local village . . would drop in to join the . . strangers in their midst. P. LOMAS In the midst of war a general . . presents himself . . as being more certain.
†**2** = MIDS *noun* 3. *Scot.* E17–L18.
▸ **B** *preposition.* In the middle of; among. *arch.* L16.
SHELLEY Midst others of less note, came one frail Form, A phantom among men.
▸ **C** *adverb.* **1** In the middle place. Only in ***first, last, and midst*** & vars. (after Milton). M17.
MILTON On Earth joyn all yee Creatures to extoll Him first, him last, him midst.
2 In the midst (*of*). *poet.* L17.

midstead /ˈmɪdstɛd/ *noun.* Long *obsolete* exc. *dial.* Also **mead-, mere-**, (earliest) †**mese-**, & other vars. M16.
[ORIGIN from MESE *noun*[1] + STEAD *noun*, alt. after MEAD *noun*[2], MERE *noun*[2], etc.]
= MESSUAGE.

midstream /*as noun & adverb* mɪdˈstriːm, *as adjective* ˈmɪdstriːm/ *noun, adjective, & adverb.* ME.
[ORIGIN from MID *adjective* + STREAM *noun.*]
▸ **A** *noun.* The middle of a stream. ME.
change horses in midstream, swap horses in midstream: see HORSE *noun.*
▸ **B** *attrib.* or as *adjective.* **1** Pertaining to, situated in, or occurring in the middle of a stream. L19.
2 MEDICINE. Designating urine other than that first or last passed in an act of urinating. M20.
▸ **C** *adverb.* In the middle of a stream. L19.

midsummer /*as noun* mɪdˈsʌmə, *as adjective* ˈmɪdsʌmə/ *noun & adjective.* OE.
[ORIGIN from MID *adjective* + SUMMER *noun*[1].]
▸ **A** *noun.* The middle of summer; *spec.* the period about the summer solstice. OE.
▸ **B** *attrib.* or as *adjective.* Of or pertaining to midsummer; occurring in midsummer. ME.
– SPECIAL COLLOCATIONS & COMB.: **Midsummer Day, Midsummer's Day** 24 June, one of the quarter days in England, Wales, and Ireland. **midsummer madness** extreme folly or madness. ***Midsummer's Day***: see ***Midsummer Day*** above.
■ **midsummery** *adjective* M19.

midward /ˈmɪdwəd/ *adjective, noun, & preposition.* Long *arch.* OE.
[ORIGIN from MID *adjective* + -WARD.]
▸ **A** *adjective.* †**1** The middle of. OE–M16.
2 Occupying the middle. LME.
▸ **B** *noun.* The middle (part). OE.
▸ †**C** *preposition.* In the middle of. LME–E19.

midwater /mɪdˈwɔːtə/ *noun & adjective.* L16.
[ORIGIN from MID *adjective* + WATER *noun.*]
▸ **A** *noun.* Water between the surface and the bottom; water distant from the shore or bank. L16.
▸ **B** *attrib.* or as *adjective.* Situated or occurring in midwater. M19.

midway /ˈmɪdweɪ, mɪdˈweɪ/ *noun, adverb, adjective, & preposition.* OE.
[ORIGIN from MID *adjective* + WAY *noun.*]
▸ **A** *noun.* **1** The middle of the way or distance, the halfway point. Now *poet.* OE.
†**2** A middle course, a medium. LME–L19.
3 A central avenue at an exhibition, fair, etc., along which the chief exhibits or amusements are placed. Also (*colloq.*), any cheap place of amusement. *N. Amer.* L19.
▸ **B** *adverb.* In the middle of the way or distance; halfway. Also (*US*) foll. by *of*. ME.
▸ **C** *adjective.* †**1** Medium, moderate. L16–L17.
2 Situated in the middle of the way, occupying the middle. Chiefly *poet.* E17.
▸ **D** *preposition.* In the middle of, halfway down, along, etc. *rare.* L18.

midwife /ˈmɪdwʌɪf/ *noun.* Pl. **-wives** /-wʌɪvz/. ME.
[ORIGIN Prob. from MID *preposition*[1] + WIFE *noun.*]
1 A person, esp. a woman, with experience or training in assisting women in labour and childbirth, now *spec.* a nurse holding additional qualifications for this task. ME.
2 *fig.* A person who or thing which helps to bring something into being. L16.
– COMB.: **midwife toad** a European toad, *Alytes obstetricans*, the male of which carries the eggs on his hind legs until the young hatch.
■ **midwifely** *adjective (rare)* of, pertaining to, or characteristic of a midwife E17.

midwife /ˈmɪdwʌɪf/ *verb.* Pa. t. & pple **-wifed** or **-wived**. M16.
[ORIGIN from the noun.]
1 *verb trans. & intrans.* Act as a midwife for a mother at the birth of a baby. M16.
2 *verb trans.* Help to bring into being. M17.
New Yorker: *Le Monde* was born . . as an independent paper, and was midwifed by de Gaulle himself.

midwifery /ˈmɪdwɪfri, mɪdˈwɪf(ə)ri/ *noun.* L15.
[ORIGIN from MIDWIFE *verb* + -ERY.]
The work or profession of a midwife; the branch of medicine that deals with this; obstetrics.

midwinter /*as noun* mɪdˈwɪntə, *as attrib. adjective* ˈmɪdwɪntə/ *noun & adjective.* OE.
[ORIGIN from MID *adjective* + WINTER *noun.*]
▸ **A** *noun.* The middle of winter; *spec.* the period about the winter solstice. OE.
▸ **B** *attrib.* or as *adjective.* **1** Of, pertaining to, or occurring in midwinter. OE.
2 Cold as midwinter. *poet.* L19.

midwives *noun* pl. of MIDWIFE *noun.*

MIEE *abbreviation.*
Member of the Institution of Electrical Engineers.

Miehle /ˈmiːlə/ *noun.* L19.
[ORIGIN from Robert *Miehle* (d. 1932), US printer.]
(Proprietary name for) a flatbed cylinder printing press.

mielie *noun* var. of MEALIE.

mien /miːn/ *noun*[1]. *literary.* E16.
[ORIGIN Prob. aphet. from DEMEAN *noun*, later assim. to French *mine* look, aspect.]
1 The look or bearing of a person, as showing character, mood, etc. E16.
A. POWELL Tall, stately . . she possessed a very aristocratic mien.
2 ***make a mien, make mien***, pretend *to do*, make a show *of doing*. E18.

mien /miːn/ *noun*[2]. L19.
[ORIGIN Chinese *miàn* (Wade-Giles *mien*) wheat flour, noodles. Cf. earlier CHOW MEIN.]
Wheat flour noodles.

Miesian /ˈmiːzɪən/ *adjective & noun.* M20.
[ORIGIN from *Mies* (see below) + -IAN.]
▸ **A** *adjective.* Of, pertaining to, or characteristic of the style of the German-American architect Ludwig Mies van der Rohe (1886–1969). M20.
▸ **B** *noun.* A devotee or follower of this style. M20.

mietjie /ˈmiːki, -tʃi/ *noun. S. Afr.* M19.
[ORIGIN Afrikaans, of imit. origin.]
= KLAAS'S CUCKOO.

mifepristone /mɪfɪˈprɪstəʊn/ *noun.* L20.
[ORIGIN Prob. from *mife-* (repr. *aminophenol*) + PR(OPYL + *ist-* (repr. *oestradiol*) + -ONE, elems. of the systematic name.]
PHARMACOLOGY. A synthetic steroid, $C_{29}H_{35}NO_2$, that inhibits the action of progesterone and is administered in early pregnancy to induce abortion.

miff /mɪf/ *noun & verb. colloq.* E17.
[ORIGIN Perh. imit.: cf. early mod. German *muff* interjection & noun, expr. disgust.]
▸ **A** *noun.* A fit of pique, a huff; a petty quarrel, a tiff. E17.
▸ **B** *verb.* **1** *verb intrans.* Take offence. Foll. by *at, with. rare.* L18.
2 *verb trans.* Put out of humour; offend, irritate. Chiefly as ***miffed*** *ppl adjective.* E19.
J. CARROLL They were miffed because they couldn't go to the match.
3 *verb intrans.* Foll. by *off*: (of a plant) deteriorate, fade. L19.
■ **miffish** *adjective* = MIFFY L18.

miffy /ˈmɪfi/ *adjective. colloq.* E19.
[ORIGIN from MIFF + -Y[1].]
1 Easily offended or irritated. E19.
2 Of a plant: delicate, not robust. M19.

mig /mɪɡ/ *noun*[1]. Long *obsolete* exc. *dial.*
[ORIGIN Old English *miċġe* (fem.), *migga* (masc.), rel. to Old Norse *míga*, late Latin *mingere* urinate.]
Urine; the drainings from manure.

MiG /mɪɡ/ *noun*[2] *& adjective*. M20.
[ORIGIN Russian *MIG*, from A. I. Mikoyan + *i* and + M. I. Gurevich, Russian aircraft designers.]
(Designating) a type of Russian fighter aircraft.

might /mʌɪt/ *noun*[1].
[ORIGIN Old English *miht*, (non-West Saxon) *mæht* = Old Frisian *mecht*, *macht*, Old Saxon, Old High German *maht* (German *Macht*), Gothic *mahts*, from Germanic, from base also of MAY *verb*[1]: see -T[1].]
1 Ability, (effective) power (*to do*); efficacy. *obsolete* exc. *poet.* OE. ▸†**b** In *pl.* The active powers of feeling, thinking, etc. OE–L16.

SHAKES. *Tr. & Cr.* To be wise and love Exceeds man's might. SHELLEY Liquors .. whose healthful might Could medicine the sick soul to happy sleep.

2 Bodily strength (great or small). Now chiefly *rhet.* OE.

A. P. HERBERT She had lifted three paddles .. heaving with all her small might.

3 Great strength, imposing power; mightiness. Now chiefly *rhet.* OE. ▸**b** Superior force or power to enforce one's will. Usu. contrasted with *right*. ME.

WORDSWORTH The might Of the whole world's good wishes with him goes. S. QUINN: Wilhelm III ascended to power with the determination to consolidate Prussian might. **b** B. JOWETT They went to war, preferring might to right.

†**4** = PRINCIPALITY 5. OE–M17.
5 A considerable quantity or amount *of*. *dial.* M19.
– PHRASES: **with all one's might**, **with might and main** with all one's strength, to the utmost of one's ability.
■ **mightful** *adjective* (*arch.*) mighty, powerful OE. **mightless** *adjective* (*arch.*) powerless, impotent OE. †**mightly** *adverb* = MIGHTILY OE–L19.

might /mʌɪt/ *noun*[2]. M19.
[ORIGIN from *might* pa. of MAY *verb*[1].]
An instance of what is expressed by the auxiliary verb *might*; a possibility.

might *verb* see MAY *verb*[1].

might-be /ˈmʌɪtbi/ *noun & adjective*. M17.
[ORIGIN from *might* pa. of MAY *verb*[1] + BE.]
▸ **A** *noun*. What might be; a (remote) possibility. M17.
▸ **B** *adjective*. That might be; (remotely) possible. M20.

mightest *verb* see MAY *verb*[1].

might-have-been /ˈmʌɪt(h)əvbiːn/ *noun*. M19.
[ORIGIN from *might* pa. of MAY *verb*[1] + HAVE *verb* + *been* pa. pple of BE.]
What might have been; a thing or event which might have occurred; a person who might have been greater or more eminent.

E. H. GOMBRICH The historian has little use for questions of might-have-been. *Listener* It was instructive to have the opportunity of hearing this gifted might-have-been.

mightily /ˈmʌɪtɪli/ *adverb*. OE.
[ORIGIN from MIGHTY *adjective* + -LY[2].]
1 In a mighty manner; powerfully, strongly; with great effort. OE.

AV *Jonah* 3:8 Let man and beast .. cry mightily vnto God. DOUGLAS STUART Her mother and father had worked mightily, with the pick and shovel. J. WINTERSON The Lord is working mightily.

2 To a high degree; greatly, very much. Now *colloq.* LME.

W. OWEN Graves was mightily impressed.

mightiness /ˈmʌɪtɪnɪs/ *noun*. ME.
[ORIGIN from MIGHTY *adjective* + -NESS.]
1 The state or condition of being mighty, powerfulness, great strength. ME.
2 With possess. adjective (as ***your mightiness*** etc.): a title of respect given to a personage of exalted rank. Now only in ***High Mightiness***, (***a***) *hist.* an honorific designation of a member of the States General of the Netherlands; (***b***) *iron.* a form of address or mode of reference to a person considered to be high and mighty. L16.

mightn't *verb* see MAY *verb*[1].

mighty /ˈmʌɪti/ *adjective & adverb*.
[ORIGIN Old English *mihtiġ* = Old Frisian *mechtig*, *machtig*, Old Saxon *mahtig*, Old High German *mahtīg* (German *mächtig*), from Germanic base of MIGHT *noun*[1]: see -Y[1].]
▸ **A** *adjective*. **1** Possessing might or power; powerful, potent, strong. Freq. *rhet.*, possessing a transcendent or imposing degree of power. OE.

DRYDEN Mighty Caesar, thund'ring from afar, Seeks on Euphrates' Banks the Spoils of War. W. COWPER On every mind some mighty spell she cast. WORDSWORTH And hear the mighty waters rolling evermore. LONGFELLOW The smith, a mighty man is he, With large and sinewy hands. M. FOOT So mighty a figure as Lloyd George, who had taken command of No. 10 Downing Street in war and peace.

2 Huge, massive, bulky. ME.

H. JAMES Flying buttresses thrown forth like an array of mighty oars.

3 a Considerable; very great in amount, extent, or degree. Now *colloq.* L16. ▸**b** *attrib.* Thoroughgoing; being or having the quality of the noun indicated to a high degree. L17.

Beano Don't disturb me .. I've a mighty lot of studying to do. **b** G. BORROW He is a mighty liberal.

– PHRASES: ***high and mighty***: see HIGH *adjective*, *adverb* & *noun*. **mighty (me)!** *Scot. & dial.* expr. surprise or mild exasperation.
▸ **B** *noun collect. pl.* *The* class of mighty people. OE.

AV 2 *Sam.* 1:19 How are the mightie fallen!

▸ **C** *adverb*. Very; greatly, extremely. Now *colloq.* ME.

P. MANN I've got a mighty important announcement to make.

migma /ˈmɪɡmə/ *noun*. M20.
[ORIGIN Greek = mixture.]
GEOLOGY. (A) magma containing solid material.

migmatite /ˈmɪɡmətʌɪt/ *noun*. E20.
[ORIGIN from Greek *migmat-*, MIGMA: see -ITE[1].]
GEOLOGY. A rock composed of two intermingled but distinguishable components, usu. a granitic rock within a metamorphic host rock.
■ **mig'matic** *adjective* composed of migmatite E20. **migmatitic** /-ˈtɪtɪk/ *adjective* = MIGMATIC M20. **migmati'zation** *noun* the process by which a migmatite is formed M20. **migmatized** *adjective* converted into a migmatite M20.

mignardise /miɲardiːz (*pl. same*), mɪnjədʌɪz/ *noun*. E17.
[ORIGIN French, from *mignard* delicate, dainty, rel. to MIGNON: see -ISE[1].]
1 Affected delicacy of behaviour or appearance; an affectation. E17.
2 A variety of crochet formed by working fine ribbon or braid into the design. L19.

mignon /ˈmiːnjɒn, *foreign* miɲɔ̃/ *adjective*. Fem. **-onne** /-ɒn, *foreign* -ɔn/. L17.
[ORIGIN French: see MINION *noun*[1] *& adjective*.]
Delicately formed; prettily small or delicate.
filet mignon: see FILET *noun*[1] 1.

mignonette /mɪnjəˈnɛt/ *noun*. E18.
[ORIGIN French *mignonnette* dim. of MIGNON: see -ETTE.]
1 A kind of light fine narrow pillow lace. Also ***mignonette lace***. E18.
2 Any of several plants of the genus *Reseda* (family Resedaceae), with small greenish or whitish flowers in spikelike racemes; spec. *R. odorata*, cultivated for its fragrant flowers. Also (more fully ***wild mignonette***), a related plant of chalky ground, *R. lutea*. L18. ▸**b** A colour resembling that of the flowers of the mignonette; greyish green or greenish white. L19. ▸**c** A perfume derived from or resembling that of the flowers of the mignonette. L19.

mignonne *adjective & noun* see MIGNON.

migod /mɪˈɡɒd/ *interjection*. E19.
[ORIGIN from MY *adjective* + GOD *noun*, repr. an informal pronunc. Cf. OMIGOD.]
Expr. astonishment or shock, pain, or anger: my God!

migraine /ˈmiːɡreɪn, ˈmʌɪ-/ *noun*. See also MEGRIM *noun*[1]. LME.
[ORIGIN Old French & mod. French from late Latin *hemicrania* from Greek *hēmikrania*, from *hēmi-* half, HEMI- + *kranion* skull.]
A recurrent throbbing headache, usu. affecting one side of the head, often accompanied by nausea or disturbed vision; the illness or condition characterized by such headaches.
■ **migraineur** /miːɡreɪˈnəː/ *noun* a person subject to attacks of migraine L20. **migrainous** *adjective* pertaining to or of the nature of migraine; subject to attacks of migraine: L19.

migrant /ˈmʌɪɡr(ə)nt/ *adjective & noun*. L17.
[ORIGIN Latin *migrant-* pres. ppl stem of *migrare* MIGRATE: see -ANT[1].]
▸ **A** *adjective*. That migrates. L17.
▸ **B** *noun*. **1** A person who or animal which migrates. M18. ▸**b** An immigrant; a new settler in Australia. *Austral.* E20.
2 BOTANY. A plant whose distribution has changed or extended. E20.

migrate /mʌɪˈɡreɪt, ˈmʌɪɡreɪt/ *verb*. E17.
[ORIGIN Latin *migrat-* pa. ppl stem of *migrare*: see -ATE[3].]
1 *verb intrans.* Move from one place to another. Now *rare* in *gen.* sense. E17.
2 *verb intrans.* BIOLOGY. Of an animal, flock, etc.: go from one region or habitat to another; *esp.* pass regularly between habitats according to the seasons, or as part of the life cycle. E18. ▸**b** Of a plant: undergo a change in or extension of its distribution. L19.

A. C. CLARKE Whales migrate north from the polar feeding grounds to have their calves in the tropics.

3 *verb intrans.* Of a person, a people, etc.: move from one country or place of residence to settle in another. L18.

B. C. BRODIE The agricultural labourer is tempted .. to migrate to a manufacturing town.

4 *verb intrans.* Chiefly BIOLOGY & CHEMISTRY. Of a cell, atom, molecule, etc.: move from one position or region to another, or in a particular direction, esp. in a non-random manner. L19.

H. DOWNEY The monocytes migrate into inflamed tissues. J. C. WARE Ions .. migrate independently in a solution and at different rates.

5 *verb intrans. & trans.* COMPUTING. Move from the use of one kind of computer or program to another. L20.
■ **migrative** /ˈmʌɪɡrətɪv/ *adjective* migratory E19. **migrator** *noun* a person who migrates; an animal, esp. a bird, which migrates: M18.

migration /mʌɪˈɡreɪʃ(ə)n/ *noun*. E16.
[ORIGIN Latin *migratio(n-)*, formed as MIGRATE: see -ATION.]
1 The migrating of a person, a people, etc., from one country or place of residence to settle in another; an instance of this. E16.
2 The action, phenomenon, or an instance of animals, birds, etc., migrating. M17. ▸**b** BOTANY. Change in or extension of the distribution of a plant. E20.
3 Chiefly BIOLOGY & CHEMISTRY. The non-random movement from one place to another of a cell, atom, molecule, etc. L19.
■ **migrational** *adjective* L19.

migratory /ˈmʌɪɡrət(ə)ri, mʌɪˈɡreɪt(ə)ri/ *adjective*. E18.
[ORIGIN from MIGRATE + -ORY[2].]
1 Characterized by or given to (esp. periodical or seasonal) migration. E18.

J. A. HAMMERTON A migratory fish which comes to the islands in autumn. W. LIPPMANN The inevitable and desirable human resistance to a migratory existence.

migratory locust any of various locusts which periodically increase suddenly in numbers, undergo mass migrations, and devastate vegetation; spec. *Locusta migratoria*, widespread in the Old World tropics.
2 Of or pertaining to migration. M18.

Bird Watching The staggering migratory feats of the Arctic tern.

■ **migratorial** /mʌɪɡrəˈtɔːrɪəl/ *adjective* (*rare*) migratory M19.

mihrab /ˈmiːrɑːb/ *noun*. L17.
[ORIGIN Arabic *miḥrāb*.]
1 A niche, chamber, or slab in a mosque, indicating the direction of Mecca. L17.
2 A niche motif on a prayer rug, resembling the shape of a mihrab in a mosque. M19.

mijnheer *noun* var. of MYNHEER.

Mikado /mɪˈkɑːdəʊ/ *noun*. Pl. **-os**. E18.
[ORIGIN Japanese, lit. 'exalted gate', from *mi-* , honorific prefix + *kado* gate: cf. ***the Sublime Porte***.]
1 *hist.* The emperor of Japan. E18.
2 In full ***Mikado pheasant***. A rare pheasant of the mountains of Taiwan, *Syrmaticus mikado*, having deep purple plumage with white markings. E20.

mikan /ˈmɪkɑːn/ *noun*. E17.
[ORIGIN Japanese, from *mi-* (in *mitsu*) honey + *-kan* citrus.]
In Japan: a satsuma.

mike /mʌɪk/ *noun*[1] *& verb*[1]. *slang*. E19.
[ORIGIN Unknown.]
▸ **A** *noun*. A rest; a period of idleness; an act of shirking. E19.
do a mike, **have a mike** be idle, escape from or evade work.
▸ **B** *verb intrans.* Shirk work; idle away one's time; go *off* to avoid a task. M19.

mike /mʌɪk/ *noun*[2]. In senses 1, 2 **M-**. M19.
[ORIGIN Pet form of male forename *Michael*: cf. MICK *noun*[1], MICKEY *noun*. In sense 3 substitution for MICKEY *noun* interpreted as the name *Mick(e)y*.]
1 (A name for) an Irishman. *rare*. M19.
2 ***for the love of Mike!***: expr. exasperation or surprise. *colloq.* E20.
3 ***take the mike*** (***out of***) = ***take the mickey*** (***out of***) s.v. MICKEY *noun*. *slang*. M20.

mike /mʌɪk/ *noun*[3] *& verb*[2]. *colloq.* E20.
[ORIGIN Abbreviation.]
▸ **A** *noun*. A microphone. E20.
▸ **B** *verb trans.* Place a microphone in (a place) or close to (a person, instrument, or amplifier). Also foll. by *up*. M20.

mike /mʌɪk/ *noun*[4]. *slang*. M20.
[ORIGIN Abbreviation.]
A microgram, *spec.* of lysergic acid diethylamide (LSD).

Mikimoto pearl /mɪkɪˈməʊtəʊ ˈpəːl/ *noun phr.* M20.
[ORIGIN See below.]
A pearl cultured by means of a technique perfected by the Japanese pearl-farmer Kokichi Mikimoto (1858–1954).

mikva /ˈmɪkvə/ *noun*. Also **-vah**, **-veh**. M19.
[ORIGIN Yiddish *mikve* from Hebrew *miqweh* lit. 'collection, mass, esp. of water'.]
A bath in which certain Jewish ritual purifications are performed; the action of taking such a bath.

mil /mɪl/ *noun*. In branch I also (earlier) **mille**. L17.
[ORIGIN In branch I from Latin *mille* thousand; in branch II formed as MILL *noun*[2]; in branch III abbreviation (cf. MILL *noun*[3]).]
▸ **I 1** See PER MIL. L17.
▸ **II 2** *hist.* ▸**a** A proposed coin of the value of one thousandth of a pound sterling. M19. ▸**b** In Cyprus, Hong

M

Kong, Palestine, and Egypt, a coin with a value equivalent to one thousandth of the basic monetary unit. E20. **3** A unit of length equal to one thousandth of an inch, used esp. in measuring the diameter of wire. L19. **4** Either of two units of angular measure: (**a**) 1/1600 of a right angle (3.375 minutes of arc); (**b**) 1/1000 of a radian (approx. 3.438 minutes of arc). E20.
▸ **III 5** Chiefly PHARMACOLOGY. = MILLILITRE. E20. **6** = MILLIMETRE. L20.

Milad /ˈmiːlɑːd/ *noun*. L20.
[ORIGIN from Arabic *mīlād al-nabīy* birthday of the prophet.]
The annual celebration of the prophet Muhammad's birthday.

milady /mɪˈleɪdi/ *noun*. L18.
[ORIGIN French, from English *my lady*: cf. MILORD.]
(A form of address used in speaking to) an English noblewoman or great lady.

milage *noun* var. of MILEAGE.

Milan /mɪˈlan/ *adjective*. LME.
[ORIGIN Italian *Milano*.]
Designating any of various products, esp. textile fabrics and steelwork, made or originating in Milan, the chief city of Lombardy in northern Italy; Milanese.

Milanese /mɪləˈniːz/ *noun & adjective*. L15.
[ORIGIN formed as MILAN + -ESE.]
▸ **A** *noun*. Pl. same.
1 A native or inhabitant of the Italian city of Milan. L15. **2** The dialect of Italian spoken in Milan. M17. **3** *The* territory of the old duchy of Milan. *obsolete* exc. *hist.* E18. **4** = *Milanese silk* below. E20.
▸ **B** *adjective*. Of or pertaining to Milan, its inhabitants, or its dialect. M16.
Milanese silk a fine warp-knit fabric with interlocking stitches, made from silk or (now) rayon etc.

milch /mɪltʃ/ *adjective & verb*. ME.
[ORIGIN Repr. 2nd elem. of Old English *þrimilce* May (when cows could be milked thrice daily), from Germanic base of MILK *noun*.]
▸ **A** *adjective*. **1** Of a mammal: giving or kept for milk. ME.
milch cow (**a**) a cow giving or kept for milk; (**b**) *fig.* (*colloq.*) a ready source of regular income or profit; *spec.* a person from whom money is easily drawn.
†**2** Of a woman, esp. a wet nurse: lactating. ME–E18. †**3** Milky. LME–E17.

fig.: SHAKES. *Haml.* The instant burst of clamour that she made . . Would have made milch the burning eyes of heaven.

▸ **B** *verb trans*. Milk. L16.
■ **milcher** *noun* an animal that yields milk E18.

mild /mʌɪld/ *adjective, adverb, & noun*.
[ORIGIN Old English *milde* = Old Frisian *milde*, Old Saxon *mildi*, Old High German *milti* (Dutch, German *mild*), Old Norse *mildr*, Gothic *-mildeis*, *milds*, from Germanic, from Indo-European base also of Latin *mollis*, Greek *malakos* soft.]
▸ **A** *adjective* **1 a** Of a person having power, as a ruler: gracious, merciful, kind, indulgent; not harsh or severe. *arch.* OE. ▸**b** Of a rule, regime, punishment, etc.: not strict or severe. L16.

a JOHN ROGERS It teaches us . . to adore him as a mild and merciful Being. J. A. HERAUD This mild prince . . is deservedly popular. **b** ADAM SMITH The penalties imposed by this milder statute. H. ADAMS The rule of the Benedictines was always mild.

2 Of a person: gentle in character, manners, behaviour, etc.; not easily provoked. Of behaviour, language, etc.: conciliatory, inoffensive. OE. ▸**b** Of an animal: tame, gentle; not wild or fierce. Now *rare* or *obsolete*. ME. ▸**c** Of physical exercise, a fight, etc.: not (very) violent. Of amusement or recreation: moderate, gentle, not boisterous. M19. ▸**d** Of a person or action: feeble; lacking in energy, vigour, etc. L19.

R. ELLMANN Though mild in disposition, John Wilde was strenuous in argument. E. WILSON The stories of Turgenev, which seem mild enough . . today. **c** A. BAIN There should also be social amusements of a mild character. C. ACHEBE A mild scuffle began right in front of me.

3 Of weather, etc.: not rough or stormy, not sharp or severe; calm, fine; moderately warm. Of a climate: temperate. LME. **4 a** Of a medicine: operating gently; not producing violent effects. Of food, tobacco, etc.: not sharp, strong, or too hot in taste; not pungent. LME. ▸**b** Of (an attack of) an illness: not severe or acute. M18. **5** Of light, or a luminous body: shining softly. M17. **6** Of soil, wood, etc.: soft, easy to work. *dial.* M19.
– SPECIAL COLLOCATIONS & COMB.: **mild beer** beer not strongly flavoured with hops (opp. *bitter*). **mild-hearted** *adjective* tender-hearted, gentle, merciful. **mild steel**: containing only a small percentage of carbon, of great strength and toughness, but not readily tempered or hardened.
▸ **B** *adverb*. Mildly. *poet.* OE.

C. WESLEY Mild he lays his Glory by, Born—that Man no more may die.

▸ **C** *noun*. (A drink of) mild beer. E18.
■ **mildish** *adjective* E19. **mildness** *noun* OE.

milden /ˈmʌɪld(ə)n/ *verb*. E17.
[ORIGIN from MILD + -EN⁵.]
1 *verb trans.* Make mild or milder. E17. **2** *verb intrans.* Become mild or milder. M19.

mildew /ˈmɪldjuː/ *noun & verb*.
[ORIGIN Old English *mildēaw*, *meledēaw* = Old Saxon *milidou* (Dutch *meeldauw*), Old High German *militou* (German, with assim. to *Mehl* MEAL *noun*¹, *Mehltau*), from Germanic, from base also of Latin *mel*, Greek *meli* honey, + base of DEW *noun*.]
▸ **A** *noun*. †**1** = HONEYDEW 1, 2. OE–M17. **2** A destructive growth on plants consisting of minute fungi and usu. appearing as a thin whitish coating; a similar growth on paper, leather, wood, etc., when exposed to damp. Also, an attack or form of the disease. ME.
POWDERY **mildew**.
▸ **B** *verb*. **1** *verb trans.* Taint with mildew. E17. **2** *verb intrans.* Become tainted with mildew. M17.
■ **mildewy** *adjective* resembling, of the nature of, or tainted with mildew M19.

mildly /ˈmʌɪldli/ *adverb*. OE.
[ORIGIN from MILD *adjective* + -LY².]
In a mild manner. Also (modifying an adjective), somewhat, slightly.

Spectator A mildly mixed-up little boy.

to put it mildly without any exaggeration (freq. *iron.*, implying understatement).

milds /mʌɪldz/ *noun*. Now *Scot. & N. English*. Also **miles** /mʌɪlz/.
[ORIGIN Old English *melde* weak fem., cogn. with Old High German *melda*, *melde* (mod. German *Melde*), also with different ablaut grades *malta*, *molto*, Middle Low German, Dutch *melde*.]
Any of several weeds of the goosefoot family; *esp.* fat hen, *Chenopodium album*.

mile /mʌɪl/ *noun*.
[ORIGIN Old English *mīl* (fem.) = Middle Dutch *mīle* (Dutch *mijl*), Old High German *mīl(l)a* (German *Meile*), from West Germanic, from Latin *mil(l)ia* pl. of *mil(l)e* thousand.]
1 Orig., the Roman unit of distance of 1,000 paces, equal to approx. 1,618 yards; also, a unit of distance (varying widely according to period and locality) derived from this. Now (also ***statute mile***), a standard unit of length and distance equal to 1,760 yards (approx. 1.609 kilometres). OE. ▸**b** *loosely & hyperbol.* A great distance, amount, or interval. Freq. in *pl.* (adverbial), by a great distance, amount, or interval. L16. ▸**c** A race over a distance of one mile. E20.

b E. M. DELAFIELD I should have thought he'd be miles better than no one. J. PORTER She *was* on the scrounge . . . You could spot it a mile off. *Independent* People will run a mile when faced with an . . American wanting to talk.

†**2** The time it might take to travel a mile. ME–L16.
– PHRASES: ***GEOGRAPHICAL* mile**. ***measured* mile**: see MEASURED 2. ***NAUTICAL* mile**. ***not a hundred miles from***: see HUNDRED *adjective*. ***Roman mile***: see ROMAN *adjective*. ***run a mile***: see RUN *verb*. **stick out a mile** be extremely obvious. **the mile-high club** *humorous* an imaginary association of people who have had sexual intercourse on an aircraft.
– COMB.: **mile-a-minute** any of several rapidly climbing plants, *esp.* (usu. as ***mile-a-minute vine*** or ***mile-a-minute plant***) the Russian vine, *Fallopia baldschuanica*, or the kudzu vine, *Pueraria lobata*; **milecastle** any of a series of forts erected by the Romans at intervals along a military wall, esp. Hadrian's Wall across northern England; **mile-eater** *colloq.* a fast driver or traveller; **mile mark** a milestone or other object placed to indicate the distance of a mile from a given point; **milepost** a post or stone serving as a mile mark.

mileage /ˈmʌɪlɪdʒ/ *noun*. Also **milage**. E18.
[ORIGIN from MILE + -AGE.]
1 a A travel allowance at a fixed rate per mile. E18. ▸**b** A rate per mile charged for the use of railway vehicles carrying goods or passengers over another company's line. M19.

a *Guardian* The newspaper . . declined to pay mileage for the use of cars on the firm's business.

2 a A distance in miles; *spec.* (**a**) the number of miles of road made, used, or travelled; (**b**) the number of miles a vehicle can travel per litre, gallon, etc., of fuel. M19. ▸**b** *fig.* Benefit, profit, advantage; scope for investigation. M19.

a *Time* Taxes . . on the purchase of cars with poor gas mileage. *Lancaster Guardian* Austin Montego . . has 34,097 mileage. **b** B. T. BRADFORD He's such an opportunist he'll find a way to get mileage out of this. *Notes & Queries* There is still plenty of mileage in Hassett's approach, as her book proves.

miler /ˈmʌɪlə/ *noun*. E19.
[ORIGIN from MILE *noun* + -ER¹.]
1 As 2nd elem. of comb.: a walk or journey of a specified number of miles. *colloq.* E19. **2** An athlete or horse specializing or competing in races over a distance of one mile. L19.

miles *noun* var. of MILDS.

miles gloriosus /ˌmiːleɪz glɔːrɪˈəʊsəs, ˌmʌɪliːz/ *noun*. *literary*. Pl. ***milites gloriosi*** /ˌmiːlɪteɪz glɔːrɪˈəʊsiː, ˌmʌɪlɪtiːz glɔːrɪˈəʊsʌɪ/. L16.
[ORIGIN The title of a Latin comedy by Plautus (*c* 250–184 BC).]
A boastful soldier.

Milesian /mʌɪˈliːʃɪən, -ʃ(ə)n, mɪ-/ *noun*¹ *& adjective*¹. M16.
[ORIGIN from Latin *Milesius* from Greek *Milēsios*: see -AN.]
▸ **A** *noun*. A native or inhabitant of ancient Miletus, a city in Asia Minor. M16.
▸ **B** *adjective*. Of or pertaining to Miletus or its inhabitants. L16.

Milesian /mʌɪˈliːʃɪən, -ʃ(ə)n, mɪ-/ *adjective*² *& noun*². L16.
[ORIGIN from *Milesius* (see below) + -AN.]
▸ **A** *adjective*. Of or pertaining to Milesius, a mythical Spanish king whose sons were said to have conquered the ancient kingdom of Ireland about 1300 BC, or his people; Irish. L16.
▸ **B** *noun*. A member of the people descended from the companions of Milesius; an Irish person. L17.

milestone /ˈmʌɪlstəʊn/ *noun & verb*. M17.
[ORIGIN from MILE *noun* + STONE *noun*.]
▸ **A** *noun*. A stone or pillar set up by a road to mark a distance in miles; *fig.* an event marking a significant stage in a life, history, etc. M17.

Art & Artists This exhibition represents a milestone in a young artist's career.

▸ **B** *verb trans*. Mark (stages etc.) as if by milestones. M19.

milfoil /ˈmɪlfɔɪl/ *noun*. ME.
[ORIGIN Old French *milfoil* (mod. MILLEFEUILLE) from Latin *milefolium*, *millef-*, from Latin *mile*, *mille* a thousand + *folium* leaf (see FOIL *noun*¹), after Greek *muriophullon* (from *murios* myriad + *phullon* leaf).]
1 Any of various plants of the genus *Achillea*, of the composite family, with feathery finely divided leaves; *esp.* yarrow, *A. millefolium*. ME. **2** In full ***water milfoil***. Any of various aquatic plants constituting the genus *Myriophyllum* (family Haloragaceae), which have whorled finely pinnate leaves and spikes of inconspicuous flowers. L16.

milia *noun* pl. of MILIUM *noun*¹.

miliaceous /mɪlɪˈeɪʃəs/ *adjective*. *rare*. L17.
[ORIGIN from MILIUM *noun*¹ + -ACEOUS.]
MEDICINE. Miliary.

†**miliad** *noun*. *rare*. E17–L19.
[ORIGIN Irreg. from Latin *milia* pl. of *mille* thousand: see -AD¹.]
A group of one thousand; a period of one thousand years.

miliaria /mɪlɪˈɛːrɪə/ *noun*. E19.
[ORIGIN mod. Latin, formed as MILIARY *adjective*².]
MEDICINE. A papular or vesicular rash of the skin accompanying profuse sweating, caused by obstruction of the sweat ducts; *esp.* (more fully ***miliaria rubra*** /ˈruːbrə/ [= red]) prickly heat.

miliary *adjective*¹ *& noun* var. of MILLIARY.

miliary /ˈmɪlɪəri/ *adjective*². L17.
[ORIGIN Latin *miliarius* pertaining to millet, from MILIUM millet: see -ARY¹.]
1 Resembling a millet seed, or an aggregation of millet seeds; granular. L17. **2** MEDICINE. Characterized by spots or lesions resembling millet seeds. M18.
†**miliary fever** a form of miliaria. **miliary tuberculosis** acute generalized tuberculosis.

Milice /milis/ *noun*. Also **m-**. Pl. pronounced same. M17.
[ORIGIN French from Latin *militia* warfare.]
†**1** Military service. *rare*. Only in M17. **2** In France: a militia or army. L17. ▸**b** A force employed by the Vichy government of 1940–4 to repress internal dissent. M20.
■ ***milicien*** /milisjɛ̃ (*pl. same*)/ *noun* a member of the Milice M20.

miliciano /miliˈθjano/ *noun*. Pl. **-os** /-ɔs/. Fem. **-na** /-na/. M20.
[ORIGIN Spanish.]
hist. A member of an irregular Republican force formed during the Spanish Civil War of 1936–9.

milieu /ˈmiːljəː, mɪˈljəː, *foreign* miljø/ *noun*. Pl. **-ieus**, **-ieux** /-əːz, *foreign* -ø/. M19.
[ORIGIN French, from *mi* (from Latin *medius* MID *adjective*) + LIEU place.]
1 An environment; (esp. social) surroundings. M19.

DYLAN THOMAS Will an artistic milieu make his writing any better.

2 *transf.* A group of people with a shared (cultural) outlook; a social class or set. M20. ▸**b** (Also **M-**.) In France: (a group or organization belonging to) the criminal underworld. L20.

P. BOWLES The American milieu in Tangier was peculiarly hermetic. **b** *Times* They have to keep an eye on . . the serious underworld, the *milieu*.

– COMB.: **milieu therapy** PSYCHOLOGY a form of group psychotherapy which relies on the social environment evolved by the staff and patients in the treatment unit.

miling /ˈmʌɪlɪŋ/ *noun*. E20.
[ORIGIN from MILE *noun* + -ING¹.]
The action of running a mile (as an athletic event).

milioline /ˈmɪlɪəlʌɪn/ *adjective & noun*. **L19.**
[ORIGIN from mod. Latin *Miliola* (see below), dim. of Latin *milium* millet: see -INE[1].]
ZOOLOGY & PALAEONTOLOGY. ▸**A** *adjective*. Of, pertaining to, or designating the foraminiferan genus *Miliola* or to the suborder Miliolina. **L19.**
▸**B** *noun*. A milioline foraminifer. **L19.**

miliolite /ˈmɪlɪəlʌɪt/ *noun*. **M19.**
[ORIGIN formed as MILIOLINE + -ITE[1].]
GEOLOGY & PALAEONTOLOGY. A fossil milioline foraminifer; (in full ***miliolite limestone***) a fine-grained limestone consisting largely of these.

militaire /militɛːr/ *noun*. Pl. pronounced same. **M18.**
[ORIGIN French.]
In France, a soldier.

militancy /ˈmɪlɪt(ə)nsi/ *noun*. **M17.**
[ORIGIN from MILITANT: see -ENCY.]
The condition or fact of being militant, esp. in pursuing a political or social end.

> C. PANKHURST Those of you who can express your militancy by going to the House of Commons and refusing to leave without satisfaction.

▪ **militance** *noun* †(*a*) combat, warfare; (*b*) militancy: **LME.**

militant /ˈmɪlɪt(ə)nt/ *adjective & noun*. **LME.**
[ORIGIN Old French & mod. French, or Latin *militant-* pres. ppl stem of *militare*: see MILITATE *verb*, -ANT[1].]
▸**A** *adjective*. **1** Engaged in warfare. **LME.**

> E. YOUNG This is a militant state, nor must man unbuckle his armour, till he puts on his shroud.

the Church militant: see CHURCH *noun* 3.
†**2** Of a banner, standard, etc.: military. **L15–E17.**
3 Combative. **E17.**

> E. BOWEN Her weariness and distraction brought the partisan in him to its most militant. J. L. ESPOSITO A militant reformist movement.

4 Aggressively active in pursuing a political or social end. **E20.**
▸**B** *noun*. **1** A person engaged in warfare. **E17.**
2 A person who is militant in pursuing a political or social end. **E20.**
▪ **militantly** *adverb* **E17.**

militaria /mɪlɪˈtɛːrɪə/ *noun pl.* **M20.**
[ORIGIN from MILITARY *adjective & noun* + -IA[2].]
Military articles of historical interest.

militarise *verb* var. of MILITARIZE *verb*.

militarism /ˈmɪlɪtərɪz(ə)m/ *noun*. **M19.**
[ORIGIN French *militarisme*, from *militaire*: see MILITARY, -ISM.]
Military attitudes or ideals; the attachment of (undue) importance to military values and military strength; the policy of maintaining a strong military capability.

> T. PARKER The high calling of professional militarism. *Sanity* We don't want militarism . . because we experienced one of the bloodiest battles of the Second World War.

militarist /ˈmɪlɪt(ə)rɪst/ *noun & adjective*. **E17.**
[ORIGIN from MILITARY + -IST.]
▸**A** *noun*. A soldier, a warrior; a person who studies military science; a person having military or militaristic attitudes and ideals. **E17.**
▸**B** *adjective*. Characterized by militarism. **L19.**

> A. E. STEVENSON Much of the world has come to think of us as militarist and . . a menace to peace.

▪ **milita'ristic** *adjective* characterized by militarism **L19.** **milita'ristically** *adverb* **M20.**

militarize /ˈmɪlɪt(ə)rʌɪz/ *verb trans.* Also **-ise**. **M19.**
[ORIGIN from MILITARY + -IZE.]
Make military or warlike; equip with military resources; imbue with militarism.
▪ **militari'zation** *noun* **L19.**

military /ˈmɪlɪt(ə)ri/ *adjective & noun*. **LME.**
[ORIGIN Old French & mod. French *militaire* or Latin *militaris*, from *milit-*, *miles* soldier + *-aris* -ARY[1].]
▸**A** *adjective*. **1** Of, pertaining to, or characteristic of a soldier or soldiers or armed forces; used, performed, or brought about by a soldier or soldiers or armed forces; appropriate to a soldier or armed forces. **LME.**

> J. STEINBECK Cyrus developed an excellent military mind. C. S. FORESTER Phillips was in uniform . . but that was the only thing that was military about him. A. STORR Military organization is based upon a strict rank order and absolute obedience. W. BOYD It was not a civil but a military matter. *Today* The Band of the Welsh Guards . . usually plays stirring military marches.

2 *spec.* Living as a soldier; belonging to an army or one of the other armed services. **L16.**

> *Trailer Life* During World War II American military men were able to foil the enemy by resorting to American vernacular.

– SPECIAL COLLOCATIONS: **military academy** an institution for training army cadets. **military age** the age at which a person becomes liable for military service. **military attaché** an army officer serving with an embassy or attached as an observer to a foreign army. **military band** a band of musicians attached to a military unit. **military braid** a broad braid such as is worn on soldiers' uniforms. **military brush** = *military hairbrush* below. **military chest** an army's treasury. **military college** = *military academy* above. **Military Cross** a decoration instituted in 1915 and awarded to officers for gallantry in combat; abbreviation *MC*. **military drum** a side or snare drum. **military engineering**: dealing with the construction of bridges, fortifications, etc., and the laying and destruction of mines. **military hairbrush** a hairbrush without a handle. ***military honours***: see HONOUR *noun*. **military hospital**: for the treatment of soldiers, esp. in the field. **military-industrial complex** a country's military establishment and those industries producing arms or other military materials, regarded as a powerful vested interest. **military law** (an ordinance or rule forming part of) the law governing an army. **Military Medal** a decoration of similar distinction to the Military Cross, instituted in 1916 for enlisted soldiers; abbreviation *MM*. **military orchid**, **military orchis** a European orchid, *Orchis militaris*, with pinkish-grey, helmet-shaped flowers, now very rare in Britain. **military police** a corps responsible for police and disciplinary duties in the armed forces. **military policeman**, **military police officer**: belonging to the military police. **military school** = *military academy* above. **Military Secretary** an army staff officer who acts as personal and confidential secretary to the commander-in-chief or certain other specified officers. **military service** (*a*) *hist.* the service in war due from a vassal to his feudal superior; (*b*) service in the armed forces. **military tenure** *hist.* a feudal tenure under which a vassal owed his superior certain defined services in war. ***military tribune***: see TRIBUNE *noun*[1] 1. **military two-step** *DANCING* a variation of the two-step, with military gestures such as saluting.
▸**B** *noun*. **1** A military man, *esp.* an army officer. *rare*. **E18.**
2 The armed forces; soldiers generally. Treated as *sing.* or *pl.* **M18.**

> A. S. NEILL People whose houses were occupied by the military. LADY BIRD JOHNSON A lot more understanding of what the military puts up with.

▪ **militarily** *adverb* (*a*) in a military or warlike manner; (*b*) from a military point of view: **M17.** **militariness** *noun* **L16.** **militaryism** *noun* militarism **M19.**

militate /ˈmɪlɪteɪt/ *verb*. **L16.**
[ORIGIN Latin *militat-* pa. ppl stem of *militare* serve as a soldier, from *milit-*, *miles* soldier: see -ATE[3].]
1 *verb intrans.* Of evidence, a fact, a circumstance: have force or effect *against* (rarely †*for*, *in favour of*). **L16.** ▸†**b** Conflict, be inconsistent *with*. **M18–M19.**

> P. BOWLES It's crude. I don't think that militates against its success.

2 *verb intrans.* **a** Serve as a soldier; take part in warfare. Now *rare*. **E17.** ▸†**b** Contend, strive. **M17–M19.** ▸**c** Advocate or employ militant action in pursuit of a political or social end. **M20.**

> **a** BURKE The supply of her armies militating in so many distant countries. **b** GIBBON The invisible powers of heaven . . seemed to militate on the side of the pious emperor. **c** V. WOOLF Tell me all about Mrs Pankhurst and the suffrage. Why did you militate?

3 *verb trans.* Dispute, debate (a question). Now *rare*. **M18.**

†**militation** *noun*. **LME–L18.**
[ORIGIN medieval Latin *militatio(n-)*, formed as MILITATE: see -ATION.]
Strife, conflict.

milites gloriosi *noun phr.* pl. of MILES GLORIOSUS.

militia /mɪˈlɪʃə/ *noun*. **L16.**
[ORIGIN Latin = military service, warfare, war, from *milit-*, *miles* soldier.]
†**1** A system of military discipline, organization, and tactics; a manner or means of conducting warfare. **L16–L17.**
2 A military force, a body of soldiers; *spec.* a military force raised from the civilian population, as distinguished from mercenaries or professional soldiers; an auxiliary military force drawn from the civilian population in order to supplement the regular forces in an emergency; *collect.* the members of such a militia. **L16.**

> C. MERIVALE A genuine militia, chosen from the citizens themselves. *Westminster Gazette* The Militia must in future be 'more soldierly'. D. JACOBSON The call-up of new recruits and reservists into the militia. *Times* They feared reprisals from left-wing militias. *attrib.*: MERLE COLLINS Come out, militia members, this is the time to defend your country.

3 The body of people, usu. men, legally liable to military service, without enlistment. *US*. **L18.**
– COMB.: **militiaman** a member of a militia; **militiawoman** a female member of a militia.

milium /ˈmɪlɪəm/ *noun*[1]. Pl. **milia** /ˈmɪlɪə/. **LME.**
[ORIGIN Latin = millet.]
1 = MILLET *noun*[1]. Now only as mod. Latin genus name. **LME.**
2 *MEDICINE*. A condition of the sebaceous glands in which small, hard, pale keratinous nodules are formed on the skin. Also, such a nodule. **M19.**

Milium /ˈmɪlɪəm/ *noun*[2]. **M20.**
[ORIGIN Prob. from *Mil-* (in the name of the Deering *Milliken* Company, who developed the fabric) + -IUM.]
(Proprietary name for) a type of insulating fabric.

milk /mɪlk/ *noun & adjective*.
[ORIGIN Old English (Anglian) *milc*, (West Saxon) *meol(o)c* = Old Frisian *melok*, Old Saxon *miluk* (Dutch *melk*), Old High German *miluh* (German *Milch*), Old Norse *mjólk*, Gothic *miluks*, from Germanic, from Indo-European base also of Latin *mulgere* (see EMULSION), Greek *amelgein*.]
▸**A** *noun*. **1** An opaque white fluid secreted by the mammary glands of female mammals for nourishing their young. Also, the milk of cows, goats, sheep, etc., used as food for humans. **OE.** ▸†**b** Lactation; the milk-yielding condition induced by childbirth. **E16–L17.**

> P. S. BUCK Out of the woman's great brown breast the milk gushed forth for the child. M. PYKE Milk is an excellent food for man, and . . an equally good food for bacteria. L. CODY One cup of coffee, milk and no sugar.

buttermilk, ***certified milk***, ***condensed milk***, ***dried milk***, ***evaporated milk***, ***scald milk***, ***skimmed milk***, ***whole milk***, etc.
2 A milky juice or latex secreted by certain plants, e.g. coconut milk. **LOE.**
3 *fig.* **a** [esp. with allus. to *1 Corinthians* 3:2, *Hebrews* 5:12] Nourishment appropriate to the earliest stages of development; something easy and pleasant to learn. Freq. in ***milk for babes***. **LME.** ▸**b** Something pleasant and (supposedly) nourishing. **LME.**

> **a** A. WILSON The undiluted milk of the Nazarene gospel. A. MASON All knowledge, all speculation, all endeavour, were reduced to this children's milk.

4 A culinary, pharmaceutical, cosmetic, or other preparation of herbs, drugs, etc., resembling milk. **LME.**
cleansing milk, ***virgin's milk***, etc.
†**5** The milt of a fish. **LME–E18.**
6 *ellipt.* A milkman. *colloq.* **L19.**
– PHRASES ETC.: *ALMOND* **milk**. ***bread and milk***: see BREAD *noun*[1]. **Bristol milk** †(*a*) *slang* sherry; (*b*) *spec.* a style of medium sherry. *CERTIFIED* **milk**. *COCONUT* **milk**. **come home with the milk**, **go home with the milk** arrive home early in the morning. **cry over spilt milk** lament an irrecoverable loss or irreparable error. ***devil's milk***: see DEVIL *noun*. ***go home with the milk***: see *come home with the milk* above. ***in-milk***: see IN-[1]. **in the milk** (of grain) having a milky consistency due to incomplete development. **milk and honey** [with allus. to the biblical description of the promised land] abundance, comfort, prosperity. **milk and water** (*a*) milk diluted with water; †(*b*) the colour of this, a bluish white; also, a kind of cloth of this colour; (*c*) *fig.* feeble, insipid, or mawkish discourse, thought, sentiment, etc. **milk-and-water** *adjective* (*a*) resembling milk diluted with water; (*b*) feeble, insipid, mawkish. ***milk for babes***: see sense 3a above; **milk of human kindness** [with allus. to Shakespeare's *Macb.*] compassion, humanity. **milk of almonds** = *ALMOND* ***milk***. **Milk of Magnesia** (proprietary name for) a white suspension of magnesium hydroxide in water, taken as an antacid or a laxative. **milk of sulphur** a suspension of amorphous powdered sulphur in water; precipitated sulphur obtained from this. ***moose milk***: see MOOSE *noun*[1]. **mother's milk** (*a*) the milk of a particular child's own mother; (*b*) *fig.* something wholesome or nourishing; something proper or appropriate to a person; (*c*) *slang* any of various alcoholic drinks. **out of the milk** (of grain) beginning to mature. ***pigeon's milk***: see PIGEON *noun*[1]. **pure milk** something of the purest or finest quality. ***rice milk***: see RICE *noun*[2]. ***sugar of milk***: see SUGAR *noun & adjective*. **the milk in the coconut** *colloq.* a puzzling fact or circumstance. ***tiger milk***: see TIGER *noun*. ***top of the milk***: see TOP *noun*[1].
– COMB.: **milk bank**: storing human milk; **milk bar** (*a*) a snack bar selling milk drinks and other refreshments; (*b*) *Austral.* a corner shop; **milk-blooded** *adjective* (*arch.*) cowardly, spiritless; **milk bush** any of various shrubs and trees with a milky sap, *esp.* (*a*) *Austral.* = **caustic bush** s.v. CAUSTIC *adjective*; (*b*) *S. Afr.* = MELKBOS (b); **milk cap** any of various fungi of the genus *Lactarius*, which yield a milky latex when broken (***saffron milk cap***: see SAFFRON *adjective*); **milk chocolate** †(*a*) a drink made from chocolate and milk; (*b*) chocolate for eating, made with milk; **milk coffee** coffee made with milk, white coffee; **milk cow** (now *dial.*) a cow yielding milk or kept for milking; **milk drop** a small delicate grey or white toadstool of leaf litter, *Mycena galopus*, which yields a latex when broken; **milk duct** *ANATOMY* any of several ducts which convey milk from the mammary glands through the nipple to the exterior; **milkfish** a large fork-tailed silver marine fish, *Chanos chanos*, cultured for food in SE Asia and the Philippines; **milk float** a low-bodied (now usu. electric) vehicle for delivering milk; **milk glass** a semi-translucent glass, whitened by the addition of various ingredients; also called *opaline*; **milk-house** a dairy, a place for storing or selling milk; **milk-leg** a painful swelling, usu. of the legs, which may occur after childbirth; **milk line** *EMBRYOLOGY* (the line occupied by) a ridge of thickened ectoderm along either side of a mammalian embryo, on which, in females, the mammary glands later form; **milk-livered** *adjective* (*arch.*) cowardly; **milk-loaf** a loaf of bread made with milk; **milkmaid** (*a*) a girl or woman who milks cows etc., or is employed in a dairy; (*b*) *dial.* (in *pl.*) any of several plants; *esp.* lady's smock, *Cardamine pratensis*; **milkman** a man who sells or delivers milk; **milk name** a name given to a Chinese child at one month old, later superseded by more formal names but occasionally used, esp. as an endearment; **milk-parsley** a tall umbelliferous plant of fens, *Peucedanum palustre*, having a milky juice when young; **milk powder** a preparation of dehydrated milk; **milk pudding**: made with rice, sago, tapioca, etc., baked with milk in a dish; **milk punch** a drink made of spirits mixed with milk and occas. other ingredients; **milk purslane** any of several small N. American spurges, esp. *Euphorbia maculata*; **milk ridge** *EMBRYOLOGY* = ***milk line*** above; **milk room** a room in a house or dairy in which milk is stored; **milk round**, (*N. Amer.*) **milk route**, **milk run** (*a*) a route on which milk is regularly collected from farmers or delivered to customers; (*b*) *transf.* a regular trip or tour involving calls at several places; **milk shake** a frothy drink made from milk, flavouring, etc., mixed by shaking or whisking etc.; **milk-sick** *adjective* affected with milk-sickness; **milk-sickness** *US* a disease of cattle and sheep in the western US, caused by ingestion of certain plants and sometimes communicated to humans in meat or dairy produce; **milk snake** a harmless, usu. brightly marked N. American colubrid snake, *Lampropeltis triangulum*, formerly supposed to suck milk from cows; **milkstone** (*a*) (now *rare* or *obsolete*) any of various white stones, e.g. flint pebbles; (*b*) a hard deposit formed in or on dairy equipment by precipitation

from milk; **milk stout** a kind of sweet stout made with lactose; **milk sugar** lactose; **milk thistle** (*a*) a thistle with white-veined leaves, *Silybum marianum*; (*b*) [from the milky juice] = ***sowthistle*** s.v. SOW *noun*[1]; **milk-toast** *US* toast softened in milk; **milk tooth** a temporary tooth in a young mammal; **milk train** a train chiefly transporting milk, usu. very early in the morning; **milk-tree** any of several trees having a milky juice; *esp.* the cow tree, *Brosimum utile*; **milk-tube**, **milk vessel** BOTANY a laticiferous tube; **milk-vetch** = ASTRAGALUS; *esp.* = ***liquorice vetch*** s.v. LIQUORICE 3; **milk-walk** (*a*) a milkman's regular round for the sale of milk; (*b*) a dairy business; **milk-warm** *adjective* approximately as warm as milk newly drawn from the cow; **milkwood (tree)** any of several trees having a milky sap; *spec.* (*a*) *Austral.* any of several trees of the family Apocynaceae, esp. *Alstonia scholaris*; (*b*) *S. Afr.* any of several trees of the family Sapotaceae; *esp.* (more fully ***white milkwood***) *Sideroxylon inerme* and (more fully ***red milkwood***) *Mimusops obovata*.

▸ **B** *adjective*. Milk-white. *rare*. L15.

▪ **milken** *adjective* (now *rare*) (*a*) consisting of or having much milk; (*b*) resembling milk, esp. in colour; †(*c*) *fig.* mild, gentle: OE. **milkful** *adjective* (*obsolete* exc. *dial.*) containing much milk, replete with milk L16. **milkless** *adjective* M17. **milkness** *noun* (*obsolete* exc. *Scot.*) (*a*) the yield of milk from an animal or herd; (*b*) *gen.* dairy produce: L15.

milk /mɪlk/ *verb*.
[ORIGIN Old English *milcian*, formed as MILK *noun & adjective*.]

▸ **I 1** *verb trans.* Draw milk from (a mammal, esp. a cow, a goat, a sheep, etc.). OE. ▸**b** Extract or draw (milk). Usu. in *pass.* Now *rare*. LME. ▸†**c** Obtain milk from by sucking. *rare* (Shakes.). Only in E17.

> *Medical & Physical Journal* This cow being troublesome . . he had . . milked her himself. R. SUTCLIFF The goats were led from door to door to be milked into jugs.

2 *verb intrans.* Secrete or yield milk. Formerly of women, now only of cows, goats, sheep, etc. OE.

†**3** *verb trans.* Suckle. LME–L16.

4 *verb trans.* Put milk into or on to. *colloq.* L19.

> J. WAINWRIGHT She milked and sugared both mugs of tea.

▸ **II** *transf. & fig.* †**5** *verb trans.* Create. *rare*. Only in LME.

6 *verb trans.* Deprive or defraud of money etc.; exploit, turn into a source of (freq. illicit) profit, advantage, information, etc.; extract all possible advantage from. E16.

> M. RICHLER He's pulled in for milking pay phones. *Daily Telegraph* A former Lloyd's underwriter . . deliberately milked the company . . of more than £40,000.

7 *verb trans.* Elicit, draw *out*; drain *away*, *out of*; extract or extort (money, advantage, information, etc.) from a person, a business, etc. E17.

> J. WAINWRIGHT The parents and guardians—the people from whom he milked money. G. SWIFT An almost successful embezzler . . being discovered after years milking the company funds. C. MCCULLOUGH All they care about is what they can milk out of him.

8 *verb trans.* Extract sap, venom, etc., from. M18.

9 *verb trans.* Intercept (a telegram, telephone message, etc.); tap (a telephone or telegraph wire, etc.). *slang*. L19.

10 *verb trans.* THEATRICAL. Exploit (a scene, a situation, a line, etc.) to elicit an extreme or extended reaction; contrive to elicit an extreme or extended reaction from (an audience). E20.

> K. TYNAN The same dead desire to milk laughs from lines which have ceased to be funny. *Daily Telegraph* A . . versatile comedienne, who can milk the last drop of comedy out of any situation.

– PHRASES: **milk dry** *fig.* completely drain away the resources of (a person or thing). **milk the bull**, **milk the ram** *fig.* engage in an enterprise doomed to failure.

▪ **milker** *noun* (*a*) a person who or thing which milks a cow etc.; (*b*) an animal, esp. a cow, yielding milk or kept for milking: L15.

milkie *noun* var. of MILKY *noun*.

milking /ˈmɪlkɪŋ/ *noun*. OE.
[ORIGIN from MILK *verb* + -ING[1].]

1 The action of MILK *verb*. OE.
deep-milking: see DEEP *adverb*.

2 The quantity of milk drawn from a cow etc., or from a dairy, at one time. M16.

– COMB.: **milking machine** a device for the automatic milking of cows, using intermittent suction via a cup on each teat; **milking parlour** a shed specially equipped for milking cows; **milking shorthorn** (an animal of) a breed of shorthorn developed specially for producing milk.

milko /ˈmɪlkəʊ/ *interjection & noun*. M19.
[ORIGIN from MILK *noun* + O *interjection*, -O.]

▸ **A** *interjection*. (A milkman's call) indicating that milk is available. M19.

▸ **B** *noun*. Pl. **-os**. A milkman. *slang*. E20.

milksop /ˈmɪlksɒp/ *noun*. LME.
[ORIGIN from MILK *noun* + SOP *noun*[1].]

†**1** *sing.* & in *pl.* Bread and milk; milky food. LME–E17.

†**2** An infant still on a milk diet. Only in LME.

3 A spiritless man or youth. LME.

▪ **milksoppy** *adjective* spiritless, insipid L19.

milkweed /ˈmɪlkwiːd/ *noun*. L16.
[ORIGIN from MILK *noun* + WEED *noun*[1].]

1 Any of certain plants with milky juice, *esp.* sowthistle, *Sonchus oleraceus*, and sun spurge, *Euphorbia helioscopia*. Now *dial.* L16.

2 Any of various N. American plants of the genus *Asclepias* (family Asclepiadaceae), which have a copious milky juice and seeds plumed with long silky hairs; esp. *A. syriaca*. E19.

3 In full ***milkweed butterfly***: = MONARCH *noun* 3. L19.

– COMB.: **milkweed beetle** any of several red and black N. American beetles of the genus *Tetraopes*; **milkweed bug** either of two red and black N. American bugs of the family Lygaeidae, *Oncopeltus fasciatus* and *Lygaeus kalmi*; ***milkweed butterfly***: see sense 3 above.

milk-white /ˈmɪlkwʌɪt/ *noun & adjective*. OE.
[ORIGIN from MILK *noun* + WHITE *noun*, *adjective*.]
(Of) pure white; white like milk.

milkwort /ˈmɪlkwəːt/ *noun*. ME.
[ORIGIN from MILK *noun* + WORT *noun*[1].]

†**1** A kind of lettuce. ME–LME.

2 Any of several small plants of the genus *Polygala* (family Polygalaceae), having racemes of small irregular blue, pink, or white flowers, and formerly supposed to increase the milk of nursing mothers; *esp.* (more fully ***common milkwort***) *P. vulgaris* and (more fully ***heath milkwort***) *P. serpyllifolia*. L16.

3 In full ***sea milkwort***. A plant of brackish turf, *Glaux maritima*, of the primrose family, with small pink axillary flowers. L16.

4 = SPURGE *noun*. Now *dial.* M17.

milky /ˈmɪlki/ *noun*. *slang*. Also **milkie**. L19.
[ORIGIN from MILK *noun* + -Y[6].]
A milkman.

milky /ˈmɪlki/ *adjective*. LME.
[ORIGIN from MILK *noun* + -Y[1].]

1 Resembling milk, esp. in colour. Also, (of a gem, glass, liquid, etc.) cloudy, resembling milk in water. LME.

> T. H. HUXLEY The liquid becomes milky as the carbonic gas . . bubbles through. R. WEST The . . bowl of blue and white porcelain shone with the proper clean milky radiance.

2 a Of or consisting of milk. *rare*. LME. ▸**b** Containing or mixed with milk; having much milk; *poet.* yielding milk. M17. ▸**c** BOTANY. Full of white or pale-coloured juice. M18.

> **b** W. C. BRYANT Argos, richly stocked In milky kine.

3 *transf. & fig.* **a** Of a person, a person's action, a personal attribute, etc.: mild, gentle; timorous, weak, compliant; *slang* cowardly. E17. ▸**b** Of a sound: soft, pleasant. *poet.* E20.

> **a** BYRON They made . . me (the milkiest of men) a satirist. G. GREENE I'm not milky . . I just don't want another killing.

▪ **milkily** *adverb* (*rare*) L19. **milkiness** *noun* (*a*) the state or condition of resembling milk; (*b*) cloudy whiteness of the sky etc.; nebulosity; (*c*) *fig.* mildness, gentleness; weakness: E17.

Milky Way /mɪlkɪ ˈweɪ/ *noun phr.* LME.
[ORIGIN from MILKY *adjective* + WAY *noun*, translating Latin *via lactea*.]

1 *The* faintly luminous band encircling the heavens and containing the countless stars of the main disc of the galaxy to which the earth belongs. LME. ▸**b** A galaxy, spec. *the* galaxy to which the earth belongs. M19.

2 *fig.* †**a** The region of a woman's breast. *poet.* E17–E18. ▸**b** A path etc. brilliant in appearance, or leading to heaven. M17.

mill /mɪl/ *noun*[1].
[ORIGIN Old English *mylen* from West Germanic from late Latin *molinum*, *-ina*, from Latin *mola* grindstone, mill, rel. to *molere* grind (see MEAL *noun*[1]). For loss of final *n* cf. ELL *noun*[1].]

1 a A building designed and fitted with machinery for grinding corn into flour, orig. chiefly worked by wind or water power. OE. ▸**b** An apparatus for grinding corn. M16.

> **b** P. S. BUCK With this ox tied to his mill he could grind the grain.

a flouring mill, ***grist mill***, etc. ***floating mill***, ***horse mill***, ***watermill***, ***windmill***, etc.

2 A machine working in the manner of a corn mill, not necessarily used for grinding; a machine performing a specified operation on a material in the process of manufacture. Also, a building fitted with such machinery; a building etc. where a specified industrial or manufacturing process is carried out. LME. ▸**b** *spec.* An apparatus or a machine for grinding or reducing a solid substance to powder, shreds, pulp, etc. Also, a building fitted with machinery for this purpose. M16. ▸**c** A machine which performs its work by rotary motion, *esp.* a lapidary's machine for cutting, polishing, or engraving gems. E17. ▸**d** A machine for stamping gold and silver coins. M17. ▸**e** An apparatus for juicing or expressing the liquid from fruit, vegetables, plants, etc., by grinding or crushing. L17.

> R. K. NARAYAN Years ago there were two weaving mills at the end of the street. I. MCEWAN Back again on Monday to toil in the mills, factories, timber yards and quaysides of London. **b** H. BELLOC Black pepper . . ground large . . in fresh granules from a proper wooden mill.

cotton mill, ***reversing mill***, ***silk mill***, ***steel mill***, etc. **b** ***coffee mill***, ***pepper mill***, ***salt mill***, etc.

3 A fist fight; a boxing match. *slang*. E19.

4 a A treadmill. M19. ▸**b** A prison, a guardhouse. *slang*. M19.

5 A circling movement of cattle. *US*. L19.

> E. HOUGH He did all he could to break the 'mill' and get the cattle headed properly.

6 MINING. An excavation in rock, transverse to the workings, supplying filler. L19.

7 A typewriter. *US slang*. E20.

8 The engine of an aircraft or motor vehicle. *slang*. E20.

> *Custom Car* The basic set-up is a 302 Mustang mill with early Jag suspension.

– PHRASES: ***gastric mill***. ***glacier mill***. **go through the mill** experience difficulty, hardship, suffering, etc. ***grist for the mill***, ***grist to the mill***: see GRIST *noun*[1] 2. **pass through the mill** = ***go through the mill*** above. **put through the mill** cause to experience difficulty, hardship, suffering, etc. ***run of the mill***: see RUN *noun*. ***trouble at t' mill*** etc.: see TROUBLE *noun*.

– COMB.: **mill band** a continuous belt for the wheels of mill machinery; **mill bill** a steel adze fixed in a wooden handle, used for dressing and cracking millstones; **mill-clack** a clapper in a mill; a heraldic representation of this; **mill dam** (*a*) a dam built across a stream to interrupt the flow and raise the level of the water so as to make it available for turning a wheel; (*b*) the area covered by water held in check by such a dam; **mill-dog** *Canad.* a kind of clamp for securing logs in a sawmill; **mill-dust** fine floury dust thrown out during the grinding of corn; **mill finish** the finish of paper not subjected to any extra processing after manufacture; **mill-hand** a worker in a mill or factory; **mill-head** a reservoir of pent-up water which, when released, turns a watermill; **mill-hopper** a hopper for corn ready for grinding; **mill-horse**: used for turning or working a mill; **mill-house** a building in which milling is carried on; **mill-ink** = ***mill rind*** below; **mill-lands** *hist.*: attached or appertaining to a corn mill, esp. in Scotland; **millman** a man in charge of or employed in a mill; **mill-pick** an iron tool for producing a corrugated surface on a millstone; a heraldic representation of this; **mill-post** (*a*) *hist.* a post supporting a windmill; (*b*) in *pl.* (*joc.*), thick or fat legs; **mill-power** (a unit for measuring) water power for driving a mill; **mill privilege**, **mill right** *US* the privilege or right of using water for driving a mill; **mill rind** the iron supporting the upper millstone of a corn mill and carrying the eye which rests on the end of the mill spindle; a heraldic representation of this; **mill-ring** (*a*) the space in a mill between the runner and the frame surrounding it; (*b*) the meal scattered around a millstone, regarded as a perquisite of the miller; **mill-run** (*a*) a (standard) period of operation of a mill; (*b*) timber sawn to standard specifications; **mill-sail** a sail on a windmill; **mill-scale** METALLURGY iron oxide deposited on iron or steel during hot working; **mill seat** a site suitable for a watermill; **mill-shaft** (*a*) a metal shaft used for driving machinery in a mill; (*b*) a tall chimney on a manufacturing mill; **mill site** *US* = ***mill seat*** above; **mill stream** a mill race; **mill tail** the water downstream from a mill which has passed through the mill wheel; †**mill-tooth** a grinding or molar tooth; **mill town**: characterized by the presence of a manufacturing mill or mills; **mill weir** = ***mill dam*** above; **mill wheel** a wheel, esp. a water wheel, used to drive a mill; a heraldic representation of this; **mill-work** (the designing or construction of) machinery used in a mill or factory.

mill /mɪl/ *noun*[2]. L18.
[ORIGIN Abbreviation of Latin *millesimum* thousandth part, after CENT *noun*[1]. Cf. MIL.]

1 One-thousandth of a dollar, a money of account in N. America. L18.

2 One-thousandth of a pound, proposed as a coin in Great Britain, and employed in Cyprus and Egypt. L19.

▪ **millage** *noun* (*US*) [-AGE] the rate of taxation in mills per dollar to which a given area, group, etc., is liable L19.

mill /mɪl/ *noun*[3]. *colloq.* L19.
[ORIGIN Abbreviation: cf. MIL 6.]
Chiefly PHOTOGRAPHY. = MILLIMETRE.

> *Practical Photography* Good old thirty-five mill. It's a great film format to work with.

mill /mɪl/ *noun*[4]. *colloq.* Also **mill.** (point). Pl. same. M20.
[ORIGIN Abbreviation.]
= MILLION.

> J. ARCHER How do you imagine I felt when we were overdrawn seven mill.

mill /mɪl/ *verb*[1]. M16.
[ORIGIN from MILL *noun*[1]. Cf. MULL *verb*[1].]

▸ **I 1** *verb trans.* Thicken (cloth etc.) in a fulling mill. M16.

2 *verb trans.* Grind (corn) in a mill; produce (flour) by grinding. Usu. in *pass.* L16. ▸**b** Pound or grind to powder; crush to fragments. L18. ▸**c** Hull (seeds) in a mill. M19. ▸**d** Cut (butter, curd, soap, etc.) into small shreds for mixing or blending. M20.

> DELIA SMITH Rye is more commonly milled into various grades of flour for bread-making.

3 *verb trans.* Beat or whip (chocolate, cream, etc.) to a froth. Also foll. by *up*. M17.

> DICKENS A second milled and frothed the chocolate.

4 *verb trans.* Beat, strike; fight, overcome. Also, smash, break. *slang*. L17. ▸**b** *verb intrans.* Fight, box. *slang*. M19.

> **b** *London Daily News* An ageing journeyman boxer who had spent years milling in small halls.

5 *verb trans.* †**a** Stamp (coins) by means of a mill. *rare*. Only in L17. ▸**b** Flute the edge of (a coin or any piece of flat metal); produce regular grooves or similar markings on the edge of (a coin). E18.

6 *verb trans.* Subject to a manufacturing process in a mill; saw in a sawmill; cut (metal) with a rotating tool. L17.

▸ **II 7** *verb intrans.* Of a whale: turn around, reverse direction. M19.

8 *verb intrans.* Move continuously round, *spec.* in a circular mass, in or among a crowd, or aimlessly or confusedly. Also foll. by *about, around.* L19.

> O. HENRY The aroused cattle milled around the . . corral in a plunging mass. R. PARK They lost their bearings and milled aimlessly around. B. MOORE A hundred invited guests milling on the lawn.

9 *verb trans.* Turn (an idea) *over* in one's mind. E20.

▪ **millable** *adjective* suitable for milling M19.

†**mill** *verb*² *trans. slang.* M16–E19.
[ORIGIN Perh. a use of MILL *verb*¹.]
Rob (a house, shop, etc.). Also, steal.

millboard /ˈmɪlbɔːd/ *noun.* E18.
[ORIGIN Alt. of *milled board* s.v. MILLED *adjective.*]
1 A kind of strong pasteboard, orig. made of a pulp of old rope, sacking, paper, and other coarse matter milled or rolled with high pressure, used for bookbinding etc.; a piece of this. E18.
2 A specially prepared board for sketching. M19.

mille *noun* see MIL *noun.*

†**millecuple** *adjective.* M17–M18.
[ORIGIN Irreg. from Latin *mille* thousand, after DECUPLE *adjective.*]
Thousandfold.

milled /mɪld/ *adjective.* E17.
[ORIGIN from MILL *verb*¹ + -ED¹.]
†**1** Polished by some mechanical process. *rare.* Only in E17.
2 a Of a coin: (*a*) struck in a mill; (*b*) having the edge fluted or grooved by milling. M17. ▸†**b** Of knitwear: ribbed. L17–E19. ▸**c** Marked with transverse grooves or ribs; *esp.* (of the head of a screw etc.) serrated to afford a hold for adjustment. E18.
3 Pressed, fulled. M17.
4 Flattened by rolling or beating. L17.
milled board = MILLBOARD.
5 Whipped or beaten to a froth. M18.
6 Ground, hulled, juiced, powdered, pressed, shredded, etc., in a mill. E19.

millefeuille /miːlˈfəːj, *foreign* milfœːj/ *noun.* Pl. pronounced same. L19.
[ORIGIN French, lit. 'thousand leaves'.]
A rich confection of thin layers of puff pastry and a filling of jam, cream, etc.

millefiore /ˌmiːlɪfɪˈɔːri/ *noun.* M19.
[ORIGIN Italian, from *mille* thousand + *fiore* flowers.]
A kind of ornamental glass made by fusing together a number of glass rods of different sizes and colours and cutting the mass into sections which exhibit ornamental figures of varying pattern, usually embedded in colourless transparent glass to make paperweights etc. Also ***millefiore glass***.

mille-fleurs /milflœːr/ *noun.* L18.
[ORIGIN French, lit. 'a thousand flowers'.]
1 A perfume distilled from flowers of different kinds. L18.
2 A pattern of flowers and leaves used in tapestry, on porcelain, etc. Usu. *attrib.* E20.

millegrain /ˈmɪlɪgreɪn/ *noun & adjective.* Also **milli-**. E20.
[ORIGIN from French *mille* thousand + GRAIN *noun*¹.]
(Designating) a gem setting of beaded or crenellated metal.

millenarian /mɪlɪˈnɛːrɪən/ *adjective & noun.* E17.
[ORIGIN from late Latin *millenarius*: see MILLENARY, -ARIAN.]
▸ **A** *adjective.* Of or pertaining to the millennium; believing in a millennium marking an era of radical change or the beginning of a Utopian period, esp. (CHRISTIAN CHURCH) a thousand-year age of peace and righteousness associated with the Second Coming of Christ. E17.
▸ **B** *noun.* A person who believes in a millennium, *esp.* one who believes that Christ will reign on earth in person for a thousand years. M17.
▪ **millenarianism** *noun* = MILLENARISM E19.

millenarism /ˈmɪlɪnərɪz(ə)m/ *noun.* M17.
[ORIGIN from MILLENARY + -ISM.]
CHRISTIAN CHURCH. The doctrine of or belief in the coming of the millennium.

millenarist /ˈmɪlɪnərɪst/ *noun & adjective.* M17.
[ORIGIN from MILLENARY + -IST.]
CHRISTIAN CHURCH. ▸**A** *noun.* = MILLENARY *noun* 2. M17.
▸ **B** *adjective.* = MILLENARY *adjective* 1. L19.

millenary /mɪˈlɛnəri, ˈmɪlɪnəri/ *noun & adjective.* M16.
[ORIGIN from late Latin *millenarius* consisting of a thousand, commander of a thousand, from *milleni* a thousand each, from *mille* a thousand: see -ARY¹. In sense A.2 from ecclesiastical Latin *millenarii* millenarian heretics.]
▸ **A** *noun.* **1** A total sum of one thousand; *esp.* a continuous period of one thousand years. M16. ▸**b** (A celebration of) a thousandth anniversary. L19.
sabbatical millenary: see SABBATICAL *adjective.*
2 CHRISTIAN CHURCH. A believer in the millennium. M16.
▸ **B** *adjective.* **1** CHRISTIAN CHURCH. Of or pertaining to the millennium, or believers in the millennium. L16.
2 Consisting of or pertaining to a thousand, esp. a thousand years. E17.
millenary petition *hist.* a petition presented by Puritan ministers (represented as one thousand) to James I in 1603, requesting changes in ecclesiastical ceremony etc.

millenism *noun* var. of MILLENNISM.

millenium *noun* see MILLENNIUM.

millennia *noun pl.* see MILLENNIUM.

millennial /mɪˈlɛnɪəl/ *adjective & noun.* M17.
[ORIGIN from MILLENNIUM + -AL¹.]
▸ **A** *adjective.* **1** CHRISTIAN CHURCH. Of or pertaining to the millennium. M17.
2 Consisting of or pertaining to a thousand years. E19.
▸ **B** *noun.* (A celebration of) a thousandth anniversary. L19.
▪ **millennialism** *noun* = MILLENARISM E20. **millennialist** *noun & adjective* (*a*) *noun* = MILLENARY *noun* 2; (*b*) *adjective* = MILLENARY *adjective* 1: M19.

millennian /mɪˈlɛnɪən/ *noun & adjective.* L17.
[ORIGIN from MILLENNIUM + -AN.]
▸ **A** *noun.* CHRISTIAN CHURCH. A believer in the millennium. L17.
▸ **B** *adjective.* **1** CHRISTIAN CHURCH. Of or pertaining to the millennium. L18.
2 Pertaining to or characteristic of a period in which one millennium ends and another begins. L19.

millennism /ˈmɪlənɪzm/ *noun. rare.* Also **millenism**. L17.
[ORIGIN from MILLENNIUM + -ISM.]
CHRISTIAN CHURCH. = MILLENARISM.
▪ **millennist** *noun* = MILLENARY *noun* 2 M17.

millennium /mɪˈlɛnɪəm/ *noun.* Also (now *non-standard*) **millenium**. Pl. **-iums**, **-ia** /-ɪə/. M17.
[ORIGIN mod. Latin, from Latin *mille* thousand, after *biennium* (see BIENNIAL).]
1 A period of one thousand years. Also, a thousandth anniversary. M17.

> *Scientific American* The millenniums preceding the 17th century. *Sunday Times* The distilled wisdom of millennia of human experience.

sabbatical millennium: see SABBATICAL *adjective.*
2 CHRISTIAN CHURCH. *The* period of one thousand years during which (according to one interpretation of *Revelation* 20:1–5) Christ will reign in person on earth. M17.
3 A period of peace, happiness, prosperity, and ideal government. E19.

> A. STORR If only society were better organized . . , men would live in peace . . and the millenium would be at last realised. *Marxism Today* Who . . will draft this constitution? And with what in mind? To usher in a socialist millennium?

– COMB.: **millennium bug** a problem with some computers in which the software was unable to deal correctly with dates of 1 January 2000 or later, arising from the misinterpretation of a two-digit number used to represent the year.
– NOTE: Spelling *millenium*, formed by analogy with e.g. *millenarian* and *millenary*, was used from L17 but is now regarded as erroneous.

millepede *noun* var. of MILLIPEDE.

millepore /ˈmɪlɪpɔː/ *noun.* M18.
[ORIGIN mod. Latin *Millepora* (see below), from Latin *mille* thousand + *porus* passage, PORE *noun.*]
ZOOLOGY. Any of a group or order (Milleporina) of colonial hydrozoans which secrete coral-like calcareous skeletons covered with minute pores through which the polyps protrude; *esp.* a hydrozoan of the genus *Millepora.*

miller /ˈmɪlə/ *noun*¹. OE.
[ORIGIN Prob. (with assim. to MILL *noun*¹) from Middle Low German, Middle Dutch *molner, mulner* (Dutch *molnaar, mulder*) = Old Saxon *mulineri*, corresp. to Old High German *mulināri* (German *Müller*), Old Norse *mylnari*, from late Latin *molinarius*, from *molina* MILL *noun*¹: see -ER¹.]
1 A person who grinds corn in a mill; the proprietor or tenant of a corn mill. Cf. MILLWARD. OE. ▸**b** A person who operates a milling machine. Freq. with specifying word. M19. ▸**c** A milling machine; a rotating cutting tool. M19.
b *cloth-miller, saw-miller*, etc.
†**2** A boxer. Also, a murderer. *slang.* E17–M19.
†**3** A kind of ray (fish). *rare.* E17–M19.
4 Any of various white or white-powdered insects; *esp.* (also ***miller-moth***) a noctuid moth, *spec.* a pale grey and white noctuid, *Acronicta leporina.* M17.
5 Any of various birds with distinctive white plumage or markings, as (*a*) a male hen harrier; (*b*) a whitethroat. Chiefly *dial.* L19.
– COMB. & PHRASES: ***floury miller***; ***miller-moth***: see sense 4 above; **miller's soul** = ***miller-moth*** above; **miller's thumb** (*a*) any of various small freshwater sculpins of the genus *Cottus*, *esp.* the European bullhead, *C. gobio*; (*b*) *dial.* any of various small birds, as the goldcrest and the long-tailed tit.
▪ **millering** *noun* the work or trade of a miller M18.

Miller /ˈmɪlə/ *noun*². L19.
[ORIGIN W. H. *Miller* (1801–80), English scientist.]
CRYSTALLOGRAPHY. Used *attrib.* with ref. to a method for specifying the position and orientation of a crystal plane or face in terms of the reciprocals of its intercepts with the three crystal axes.
Miller index each of the three integers which together specify a crystal plane in this method.
▪ **Millerian** /mɪˈlɪərɪən/ *adjective* of, pertaining to, or designating Miller's method for specifying crystal planes L19.

Miller effect /ˈmɪlər ɪˌfɛkt/ *noun phr.* M20.
[ORIGIN from J. M. *Miller* (1882–1962), US physicist.]
ELECTRONICS. The feedback effect whereby capacitance in the output of a valve or transistor increases its input impedance.

Millerite /ˈmɪlərʌɪt/ *noun*¹. *US.* M19.
[ORIGIN from William *Miller* (see below) + -ITE¹.]
A believer in the doctrines of William Miller (d. 1849), an American preacher who interpreted the Scriptures as foretelling the imminent coming of Christ and the end of the world.
▪ **Millerism** *noun* the doctrines of William Miller M19.

millerite /ˈmɪlərʌɪt/ *noun*². M19.
[ORIGIN formed as MILLER *noun*² + -ITE¹.]
MINERALOGY. Native nickel sulphide, crystallizing in the hexagonal system usu. as brassy or bronze crystals.

millesimal /mɪˈlɛsɪm(ə)l/ *adjective & noun.* L17.
[ORIGIN from Latin *millesimus* thousandth + -AL¹.]
▸ **A** *adjective.* Thousandth; consisting of thousandth parts. L17.
▸ **B** *noun.* A thousandth (part). E18.

millet /ˈmɪlɪt/ *noun*¹. LME.
[ORIGIN Old French & mod. French, dim. of (dial.) *mil* from Latin *milium.*]
A cereal grass, *Panicum miliaceum*, widely grown in warm countries, with small spikelets arranged in a loose panicle; the grain of this plant. Also (with specifying word), any of various other drought-resistant usu. small-seeded cereal grasses grown esp. in warm countries of the world.
bulrush millet, foxtail millet, Hungarian millet, wood millet, etc.
– COMB.: **millet-grass** = ***wood millet*** above; **millet seed** *noun & adjective* (*a*) *noun* the seed or grain of millet; (*b*) *adjective* (of grains of sand) almost spherical as a result of abrasion by the wind.

millet /ˈmɪlɛt/ *noun*². E20.
[ORIGIN Turkish = nation, group of co-religionists, from Arabic *milla(t)* religion.]
hist. A part of the population of the Ottoman Empire that owed allegiance to a particular religious leader, esp. a non-Muslim one.

milli- /ˈmɪli/ *combining form.*
[ORIGIN from Latin *mille* thousand + -I-.]
Used in names of units of measurement to denote a factor of one-thousandth (10^{-3}), as ***millicurie, millimole, milliwatt***; also occas. combined with *micro-* to denote a factor of 10^{-9} (corresp. to NANO-), as ***millimicroampere, millimicromole***. Abbreviation **m**.
▪ **millibar** *noun* (METEOROLOGY) the usual unit of barometric pressure, equal to a thousandth of a bar (100 pascals) E20. **milliosmole** /mɪlɪˈɒzməʊl/ *noun* (PHYSICAL CHEMISTRY) an amount of an osmotically effective ion in solution equal to a milligram divided by the atomic mass of the ion M20.

milliammeter /mɪlɪˈamɪtə/ *noun.* E20.
[ORIGIN from MILLI- + AMMETER.]
An instrument for measuring electric currents of the order of milliamperes.

milliamp /ˈmɪlɪamp/ *noun. colloq.* E20.
[ORIGIN Abbreviation.]
= MILLIAMPERE.

milliampere /mɪlɪˈampɛː/ *noun.* L19.
[ORIGIN from MILLI- + AMPERE.]
ELECTRICITY. One-thousandth of an ampere.
▪ **milliamperage** *noun* current expressed in or of the order of milliamperes E20.

Millian /ˈmɪlɪən/ *adjective & noun.* M19.
[ORIGIN from *Mill* (see below) + -IAN. Cf. MILLITE.]
▸ **A** *adjective.* Of or pertaining to the English utilitarian philosopher and political theorist John Stuart Mill (1806–73) or his theories. M19.
▸ **B** *noun.* A follower of Mill or his theories. M20.

milliard /ˈmɪlɪɑːd/ *noun.* L18.
[ORIGIN French, from *mille* thousand.]
A thousand million.
▪ **milliar'daire** *noun* (now *rare*) [after MILLIONAIRE] a person possessing a thousand million pounds, dollars, etc. L19.

milliary /ˈmɪlɪəri/ *adjective & noun.* Also **miliary**. LME.
[ORIGIN Latin *milliarius*, from *mille* thousand: see MILE, -ARY¹.]
▸ **A** *adjective.* **1** ROMAN HISTORY. Designating a unit of one thousand soldiers. LME.
2 Of or pertaining to the ancient Roman mile of a thousand paces; marking a mile. M17.
▸ **B** *noun.* A stone or mark set up by the ancient Romans as a point of departure in measuring distances of a thousand paces; a milestone. E17.

millieme /ˈmɪljɛm/ *noun.* In sense 1 **-ième**. M19.
[ORIGIN French *millième* thousandth.]
†**1** A unit of weight equal to one-thousandth of a gram, esp. as a measure of the fineness of gold and silver. M–L19.
2 A monetary unit of Egypt and Sudan, equal to one-thousandth of a pound. Cf. MILLIME. E20.

M

milligram /ˈmɪlɪgram/ *noun*. Also **-gramme**. L18.
[ORIGIN from MILLI- + GRAM *noun*².]
One-thousandth of a gram.

millilitre /ˈmɪlɪliːtə/ *noun*. Also *-**liter**. E19.
[ORIGIN from MILLI- + LITRE.]
A thousandth of a litre, a cubic centimetre.

millime /ˈmɪlɪm/ *noun*. E20.
[ORIGIN French *millième* MILLIEME.]
A monetary unit of Tunisia, equal to one-thousandth of a dinar.

millimetre /ˈmɪlɪmiːtə/ *noun*. Also *-**meter**. L18.
[ORIGIN from MILLI- + METRE *noun*².]
A thousandth of a metre, equal to 0.03937 inch.

Daily Telegraph Solidarity is indispensable and without it we won't move a millimetre forward.

millimetre of mercury = TORR.
▪ **millimetric** /mɪlɪˈmɛtrɪk/ *adjective* (*a*) of the order of a millimetre in (wave)length; pertaining to or involving electromagnetic radiation having a wavelength of 1 to 10 millimetres; (*b*) minute: L19.

milliner /ˈmɪlɪnə/ *noun & verb*. LME.
[ORIGIN from MILAN + -ER¹.]
▸ **A** *noun*. †**1** (**M-**.) A native or inhabitant of the Italian city of Milan. LME–L19.
2 Orig., a seller of fancy wares and accessories, esp. such as were originally made in Milan. Now, a person who makes or sells women's hats. M16.
▸ **B** *verb intrans*. Make women's hats. Chiefly as ***millinering*** *verbal noun*. M19.
▪ **millinerial** /mɪlɪˈnɪərɪəl/ *adjective* of or pertaining to a milliner or millinery M19. **millinery** *noun* (*a*) articles made or sold by a milliner; (*b*) the trade or business of a milliner: L17.

milling /ˈmɪlɪŋ/ *noun*. LME.
[ORIGIN from MILL *verb*¹ + -ING¹.]
1 The action of MILL *verb*¹. LME.
2 The series of grooves on the edge of a coin, the grooved edge of a coin. E19.
– COMB.: **milling machine** *spec*. a machine in which an object fixed to a carriage is subjected to the action of a rotating tool.

million /ˈmɪljən/ *noun & adjective* (in mod. usage also classed as a ***determiner***), **(*cardinal numeral*)**. LME.
[ORIGIN Old French & mod. French, prob. from Old Italian & mod. Italian †*millione* (now *milione*), from *mille* thousand + augm. suffix *-one* -OON.]
▸ **A** *noun*. **I** Pl. now usu. same after a numeral and often after a quantifier, otherwise **-s**; as *sing*. usu. preceded by *a*, or in emphatic use *one*.
1 A thousand times a thousand units *of* a specified category or group (now almost always definite, as ***a million of the***, ***a million of those***, etc., ***one million of its***, ***one million of his mother's***, etc.); a thousand times a thousand persons or things identified contextually, as pounds or dollars, years in dates, chances (in giving odds), units in oil production, etc.; *pl*. after a quantifier, multiples of a thousand times a thousand such persons or things. Usu. treated as *pl*. LME. ▸**b** In *pl*. without specifying word: several million; *hyperbol*. very large numbers. (Foll. by *of*.) LME. ▸**c** A quantity equal to this, a very large amount. Now chiefly in ***a million of money***. LME. ▸**d** *The* multitude, *the* bulk of the population. E17.

R. P. WARD By loans . . and other speculations, he achieved his million. *Manchester Examiner* He could count his soldiers by the million. D. H. LAWRENCE In the world beyond, how easily we might spare a million or two of humans. W. FAULKNER The whole million of them we have lost. W. S. CHURCHILL More than a million of the Local Defence Volunteers. F. FORSYTH Six million of his fellow Jews. I. MCEWAN Tens of millions have been saved in social security payments. **b** A. BULLOCK He persisted in regarding Molotov . . as responsible for the murder of millions. S. BELLOW A huge tree . . old, arthritic . . but still capable of putting forth millions of leaves.

a million to one chance a very low probability. **a — in a million**, **one in a million** a very valuable or unusual person or thing (of the type specified or understood). **gone a million** *Austral. & NZ colloq*. completely lost, in a hopeless state. ***one in a million***: see ***a — in a million*** above.
2 A thousand times a thousand as an abstract number, the symbol(s) or figure(s) representing this (1,000,000 in arabic numerals); in *pl*. after a numeral, that number of multiples of a thousand times a thousand as an abstract number, the symbol(s) or figure(s) representing any such number (as 5,000,000). LME.
▸ **II 3** In *pl*. (treated as *sing*.) = GUPPY *noun*¹. Also ***millions fish***. E20.
▸ **B** *adjective*. After an article, possessive, etc.: a thousand times a thousand (a cardinal numeral represented by 1,000,000 in arabic numerals); *hyperbol*. a very great many. After a numeral or quantifier: multiples of a thousand times a thousand. LME.

A. S. NEILL A million men say grace before meals . . and probably 999,999 men say it mechanically. M. ANGELOU A heckler had asked why sixteen million Africans allowed three million whites to control them. S. RUSHDIE She would never marry Haroun Harappa, no, not in a million years. *Scotsman* My Dad's car goes a *million* times faster than your Dad's car.

like a million dollars, **a million dollars** excellent, splendid, magnificent.
– COMB.: Forming compound numerals (cardinal or ordinal) with numerals below a million, as **1,600,000** (read ***one million six hundred thousand***), **1,000,080** (read ***one million and eighty***). Special combs., as **million-dollar** *adjective* worth or costing a million dollars; *fig*. expensive-looking, splendid, attractive; **million-seller** a record, book, etc., of which a million copies have been sold; ***millions fish***: see sense A.3 above.
▪ **millionism** *noun* (*rare*) millionairedom M19. **millionist** *noun* (*rare*) a millionaire M19.

millionaire /mɪljəˈnɛː/ *noun & adjective*. E19.
[ORIGIN French *millionnaire*, formed as MILLION. Cf. MILLIONARY.]
▸ **A** *noun*. A person whose assets are worth at least a million pounds, dollars, etc.; a person of great wealth. E19.
Millionaires' Row (a name for) a street containing the residences of very rich people.
▸ **B** *attrib*. or as *adjective*. **1** Having assets worth at least a million pounds, dollars, etc. M19.
2 GEOGRAPHY. Designating a city with a population of more than a million. M20.
▪ **millionairedom** *noun* the condition of being a millionaire L19. **millionaireship** *noun* the position or state of a millionaire E20. **millionairess** *noun* a female millionaire L19. **millionairish** *adjective* characteristic of a millionaire L19.

millionary /ˈmɪljənəri/ *noun & adjective*. Now *rare*. L18.
[ORIGIN from MILLION + -ARY¹, after French *millionnaire*: see MILLIONAIRE.]
▸ †**A** *noun*. = MILLIONAIRE *noun*. L18–L19.
▸ **B** *adjective*. = MILLIONAIRE *adjective* 1. E19.

millioned /ˈmɪljənd/ *adjective*. Now *rare*. E17.
[ORIGIN from MILLION + -ED².]
1 Numbering a million. E17.
2 Possessing millions of pounds, dollars, etc. M18.

millionfold /ˈmɪljənfəʊld/ *noun & adjective*. L16.
[ORIGIN from MILLION + -FOLD.]
▸ **A** *noun*. Pl. same. A million times the number or quantity: used adverbially. L16.

O. SACKS A very bitter substance such as strychnine could be diluted a millionfold and still be tasted.

▸ **B** *adjective*. A million times as many or as much. M19.

millionth /ˈmɪljənθ/ *adjective & noun*. L17.
[ORIGIN from MILLION + -TH², after HUNDREDTH.]
1 *adjective & noun*. (The person or thing) that is number one million in a series. L17.

J. WAIN For the millionth time . . I can easily see why . . she had ideas once about going on the stage.

millionth part = sense 2 below.
2 *noun*. Each of a million equal parts into which something is or may be divided, a fraction which when multiplied by one million gives one. M19.

J. C. MAXWELL Your sum of Vital energy is not the millionth of an erg.

millipede /ˈmɪlɪpiːd/ *noun*. Also **mille-**. E17.
[ORIGIN Latin *millepeda* woodlouse, from *mille* thousand + *ped-*, *pes* foot.]
1 Any of numerous herbivorous terrestrial arthropods of the class Diplopoda, having an elongated body with many segments, most of which bear two pairs of legs. E17.
2 A terrestrial isopod; a woodlouse. Now *rare*. M17.
3 = CENTIPEDE. *rare*. E18.

milliprobe /ˈmɪlɪprəʊb/ *noun*. M20.
[ORIGIN from MILLI- + PROBE *noun*.]
An instrument for analysing small amounts of material; *spec*. a form of spectrophotometer used esp. to study fragile or precious objects, in which a narrow beam of accelerated particles (usu. protons) is directed at the specimen and the resulting fluorescence analysed.

millisecond /ˈmɪlɪsɛk(ə)nd/ *noun*. E20.
[ORIGIN from MILLI- + SECOND *noun*¹.]
A thousandth of a second.

Millite /ˈmɪlʌɪt/ *noun & adjective*. M19.
[ORIGIN formed as MILLIAN + -ITE¹.]
= MILLIAN.

millivolt /ˈmɪlɪvəʊlt, -vɒlt/ *noun*. M19.
[ORIGIN from MILLI- + VOLT *noun*¹.]
ELECTRICITY. One-thousandth of a volt.
▪ **milliˈvoltmeter** *noun* an instrument for measuring voltages of the order of millivolts E20.

mill-ken /ˈmɪlkɛn/ *noun*. *slang*. *obsolete* exc. *hist*. M17.
[ORIGIN from MILL *verb*² + KEN *noun*².]
A thief, a housebreaker.

mill-mountain /ˈmɪlmaʊntɪn/ *noun*. Now *rare* or *obsolete*. M17.
[ORIGIN Unknown.]
Fairy flax, *Linum catharticum*.

millocracy /mɪˈlɒkrəsi/ *noun*. Now *hist*. or *joc*. M19.
[ORIGIN from MILL *noun*¹: see -CRACY.]
The body of mill-owners regarded as a dominant or ruling class.
▪ **ˈmillocrat** *noun* M19.

Millon /ˈmɪlən/ *noun*. L19.
[ORIGIN A. N. E. *Millon* (1812–67), French chemist.]
CHEMISTRY. **1** ***Millon's base***, a yellow powder, $Hg_2NOH{\cdot}2H_2O$, which is a mercury-substituted derivative of ammonia. L19.
2 a ***Millon's reagent***, a clear solution of mercuric nitrate containing some nitrous acid, used in Millon's test. L19. ▸**b** ***Millon's test***, ***Millon's reaction***, ***Millon test***, ***Millon reaction***, an analytical test for phenolic compounds (e.g. oestrogens and (esp.) proteins containing tyrosine), which give a pink or reddish precipitate with Millon's reagent. L19.

millpond /ˈmɪlpɒnd/ *noun*. LME.
[ORIGIN from MILL *noun*¹ + POND *noun*.]
1 A pool of water retained by a mill dam for driving a watermill. LME.
like a millpond (of a stretch of water) very calm.
2 The Atlantic Ocean, esp. as separating Britain and N. America. *joc*. E19.

mill pool /ˈmɪl puːl/ *noun phr*. OE.
[ORIGIN from MILL *noun*¹ + POOL *noun*¹.]
A millpond.

mill race /ˈmɪl reɪs/ *noun phr*. L15.
[ORIGIN from MILL *noun*¹ + RACE *noun*¹.]
The current of water that drives a mill wheel; a channel in which water runs to a watermill.

Mills /mɪlz/ *noun*. E20.
[ORIGIN Sir William *Mills* (1856–1932), English engineer.]
Mills bomb, ***Mills grenade***, a type of hand grenade serrated on the outside to form shrapnel on explosion.

Mills & Boon /mɪlz (ə)nd ˈbuːn/ *noun & adjectival phr*. E20.
[ORIGIN See below.]
(Proprietary name for) light and formulaic romantic fiction published by Mills & Boon Limited; idealized and sentimental romantic situations associated with this type of literature. Also ***attrib***. or as ***adjective***.

Observer I know this sounds a bit Mills & Boon, but Penny and I are an item.

Mill's Methods /mɪlz ˈmɛθədz/ *noun phr. pl*. L19.
[ORIGIN J. S. *Mill*: see MILLIAN.]
LOGIC. The five canons of inductive inquiry for discovering and establishing the validity of causal relations between phenomena.

millstone /ˈmɪlstəʊn/ *noun*. OE.
[ORIGIN from MILL *noun*¹ + STONE *noun*.]
1 Either of a pair of circular stones which grind corn by the rotation of the upper stone on the lower one. OE. ▸**b** HERALDRY. A charge representing a millstone. LME.
NETHER ***millstone***. **see far into a millstone** (usu. *iron*.) be extraordinarily acute.
2 *fig*. A heavy burden; an oppressive force. E18.

F. WELDON 109 Holden Road was a millstone rather than an asset. B. GELDOF The problems of Ethiopia and its hapless peoples, caught between the millstones of natural disaster and international politics.

– COMB.: **millstone grit** GEOLOGY any hard siliceous rock suitable for making millstones; *spec*. (freq. **M- G-**) a coarse sandstone of the British Carboniferous, lying immediately below the coal measures.

millward /ˈmɪl(w)əd/ *noun*. Now *dial*. OE.
[ORIGIN from MILL *noun*¹ + WARD *noun*.]
Orig., the keeper of a (manorial) mill. Later, a miller.

millwright /ˈmɪlrʌɪt/ *noun*. LME.
[ORIGIN from MILL *noun*¹ + WRIGHT *noun*.]
A person who designs or builds mills or mill machinery.
▪ **millwrighting** *noun* the trade of a millwright E19.

milo /ˈmʌɪləʊ/ *noun*. L19.
[ORIGIN Sesotho *maili*.]
A drought-resistant variety of sorghum grown esp. in the central US. Also ***milo maize***.

milometer /mʌɪˈlɒmɪtə/ *noun*. M20.
[ORIGIN from MILE *noun* + -OMETER.]
An instrument for measuring the number of miles travelled by a vehicle.

milord /mɪˈlɔːd; *foreign* milɔːr (*pl. same*)/ *noun*. Also †**milor**. E17.
[ORIGIN French, from English *my lord*; cf. MILADY, MILORDO.]
An English nobleman in Europe; an Englishman travelling in Europe in aristocratic style; a wealthy Englishman.

milordo /mɪˈlɔːdəʊ/ *noun*. Pl. **-di** /-di/. M18.
[ORIGIN Italian, formed as MILORD.]
An English nobleman in Italy; a wealthy Englishman travelling in Italy.

Milori /mɪˈlɔːri/ *noun*. Also **m-**. L19.
[ORIGIN A. *Milori*, 19th-cent. French dye manufacturer.]
1 ***Milori green***, chrome green. L19.
2 ***Milori blue***, a very pure Prussian blue. L19.

milpa /ˈmɪlpə/ *noun*. M17.
[ORIGIN Mexican Spanish from Nahuatl *milpan*.]
In Central America and Mexico, a small cultivated field, usu. of corn or maize.

– COMB.: **milpa system** a system of cultivation involving cyclic burning off, forest re-establishment, and cultivation.

Milquetoast /ˈmɪlktəʊst/ *noun & adjective*. Chiefly *N. Amer.* Also **m-**. M20.
[ORIGIN Caspar *Milquetoast*, a cartoon character created by H. T. Webster in 1924.]
(A person who is) timid or unforthcoming.

milreis /ˈmɪlreɪs/ *noun*. Pl. same. L16.
[ORIGIN Portuguese, from *mil* thousand + REI *noun* + -S[1].]
hist. A former monetary unit of Portugal and Brazil equal to 1,000 reis, replaced in Portugal by the escudo in 1911 and in Brazil by the cruzeiro in 1942.

Milroy's disease /ˈmɪlrɔɪz dɪˌziːz/ *noun phr.* E20.
[ORIGIN W. F. *Milroy* (1855–1942), US physician.]
MEDICINE. A hereditary condition characterized by lymphoedema of the extremities, usu. the lower legs.

milt /mɪlt/ *noun & verb*. As noun also **melt** /mɛlt/.
[ORIGIN Old English *milt(e*, corresp. to Old Frisian, Middle Dutch *milte* (Dutch *milt*), Old High German *milzi* (German *Milz*), Old Norse *milti*, from Germanic, perh. rel. to base of MELT *verb*.]
▸ **A** *noun*. **1** The spleen (now chiefly, that of a domestic animal). OE.
2 The semen of a male fish; the testes of a male fish. L15.
– COMB.: **miltwaste** (now *rare* or *obsolete*) the rustyback fern, *Ceterach officinarum*.
▸ **B** *verb trans. & intrans.* Of a male fish: fertilize with or emit milt. *rare*. L17.
■ **milter** *noun* a male fish, esp. in spawning time E17.

Milton /ˈmɪlt(ə)n/ *noun*. M18.
[ORIGIN See MILTONIC.]
A person whose great innate ability is frustrated by lack of opportunity. Chiefly in ***mute inglorious Milton***.
– NOTE: After a line in T. Gray's *Elegy Written in a Country Churchyard*.

miltonia /mɪlˈtəʊnɪə/ *noun*. M19.
[ORIGIN mod. Latin (see below), from Charles Fitzwilliam, Viscount *Milton* (1786–1857), English politician and horticulturist + -IA[1].]
Any of various epiphytic orchids of the tropical S. American genus *Miltonia*, bearing large brilliantly coloured flowers.

Miltonian /mɪlˈtəʊnɪən/ *adjective & noun*. E18.
[ORIGIN formed as MILTONIC + -IAN.]
▸ **A** *adjective*. = MILTONIC *adjective*. E18.
▸ **B** *noun*. An admirer, student, or imitator of Milton. M18.

Miltonic /mɪlˈtɒnɪk/ *adjective & noun*. E18.
[ORIGIN from *Milton* (see below) + -IC.]
▸ **A** *adjective*. Of, pertaining to, or characteristic of the English poet John Milton (1608–74) or his (esp. epic) style, language, or imagery. E18.
▸ **B** *noun*. †**1** Miltonic language. *rare*. Only in E18.
2 In *pl.* Verses by or (usu.) typical of Milton. L18.
■ **Miltonically** *adverb* M19.

Miltonise *verb* var. of MILTONIZE.

Miltonism /ˈmɪlt(ə)nɪz(ə)m/ *noun*. E19.
[ORIGIN formed as MILTONIC + -ISM.]
A Miltonic mode of expression; Miltonic language or style.

Miltonist /ˈmɪlt(ə)nɪst/ *noun*. M17.
[ORIGIN formed as MILTONIC + -IST.]
An admirer or student of the English poet John Milton (1608–74) or his writing.

Miltonize /ˈmɪlt(ə)nʌɪz/ *verb*. Also **-ise**. L18.
[ORIGIN formed as MILTONIC + -IZE.]
1 *verb trans.* Give a Miltonic character to. *rare*. L18.
2 *verb intrans.* Imitate the literary style of Milton. E20.

Miltown /ˈmɪltaʊn/ *noun*. M20.
[ORIGIN Perh. from the name of *Milltown*, New Jersey, a town situated close to the laboratories manufacturing the product.]
PHARMACOLOGY. (Proprietary name for) the drug meprobamate.

miltsiekte /ˈmɪltsɪktə/ *noun*. *S. Afr.* M19.
[ORIGIN Afrikaans, from *milt* spleen + *siekte* sickness.]
Anthrax in livestock.

miltz /mɪlts/ *noun*. E20.
[ORIGIN German *Milz* MILT *noun*.]
In Jewish cookery, the spleen of an animal.

milwell /ˈmɪlwəl/ *noun*. Long *dial.* or *hist.* Also **milwel**, **melwel**, & other vars. ME.
[ORIGIN Anglo-Norman *muluelle* (Latinized as *mulvellus*), Old French *muluel*, prob. alt. of. *moruel* dim. of *morue*, medieval Latin *morua* cod.]
The cod (fish).

mim /mɪm/ *adjective*. Chiefly *Scot. & dial.* L16.
[ORIGIN Imit. of the pursing of the mouth. Cf. MIMP.]
Affectedly modest or demure; primly silent or quiet.
– COMB.: **mim-mouthed** *adjective* affectedly reticent.

Mimamsa /mɪˈmɑːmsə/ *noun*. L18.
[ORIGIN Sanskrit *mīmāṃsā* investigation, critical evaluation, from *man-* think.]
One of the six systems of Hindu philosophy, based on the interpretation of Vedic ritual and text.

mimbar *noun* var. of MINBAR.

mime /mʌɪm/ *noun & verb*. E17.
[ORIGIN Latin *mimus* from Greek *mimos*.]
▸ **A** *noun*. **1** A mimic; a jester. Now chiefly *spec.*, a practitioner of the technique of mime (see sense 3 below), a mime artist. E17.

C. J. CORNISH Those . . famous mimes, the Indian mynahs. *New Yorker* The chalkfaced mime Jousts with the crowd.

2 CLASSICAL HISTORY. A simple farcical drama characterized by mimicry and the ludicrous representation of familiar types of character. Also, a performer in a mime. E17.
3 The art or technique of expressing or conveying action, character, or emotion without words and using only gestures, movement, etc., or (*spec.* in BALLET) using a fixed set of these; an expression of action etc. or a performance using such means. M20.

Westworld (Vancouver) Within minutes, each group presented a mime, so well performed that they could have been practising for hours.

▸ **B** *verb*. **1** *verb trans.* Imitate, mimic. E18.
2 *verb trans. & intrans.* Use mime to express or convey (action, character, or emotion) or in the acting of (a play or part). M19. ▸**b** Of a singer: mouth the words of (a song etc.) along with a soundtrack. M20.

J. CLAVELL She . . put her hand to her head pretending pain, mimed being drunk and sleeping like a stone. A. CARTER She rubbed her stomach, pointed to her mouth . . clearly miming an invitation to supper.

■ **mimer** *noun* a mime or mimic, a buffoon, a jester; a person who mimes: M18.

mimeo /ˈmɪmɪəʊ/ *noun & verb*. M20.
[ORIGIN Abbreviation of MIMEOGRAPH *noun*.]
▸ **A** *noun*. Pl. **-os**. A copy of a document, newspaper, etc., reproduced by means of a mimeograph. M20.
▸ **B** *verb trans.* = MIMEOGRAPH *verb*. M20.

mimeograph /ˈmɪmɪəɡrɑːf/ *noun & verb*. L19.
[ORIGIN Irreg. from Greek *mimeomai* I imitate + -GRAPH.]
▸ **A** *noun*. A duplicating machine for producing copies from a stencil; a copy produced in this way. L19.
▸ **B** *verb trans.* Reproduce (text or diagrams) by means of a mimeograph. L19.

mimesis /mɪˈmiːsɪs, -mʌɪ-/ *noun*. M16.
[ORIGIN Greek *mimēsis*, from *mimeisthai*: see MIMETIC.]
1 Chiefly RHETORIC. Imitation of another person's words or actions. M16. ▸**b** The representation of the real world in art, poetry, etc. M20.
2 BIOLOGY. = MIMICRY 2. Now *rare*. M19.
3 SOCIOLOGY. The deliberate imitation of the behaviour of one group of people by another as a factor in social change. M20.

mimester /ˈmʌɪmstə/ *noun*. *rare*. M19.
[ORIGIN from MIME *verb* + -STER.]
A practitioner of mime, a mime artist.

mimetic /mɪˈmɛtɪk/ *adjective*. M17.
[ORIGIN Greek *mimētikos*, from *mimeisthai* imitate, from *mimos* MIME *noun*: see -IC.]
1 Having an aptitude for mimicry or imitation, habitually practising mimicry or imitation. M17.
2 Pertaining to, characterized by, or of the nature of imitation; *spec.* representing the real world in art, literature, etc.; of or pertaining to mimesis. M17.
3 = MIMIC *adjective* 3. M18.
4 a BIOLOGY. Characterized by or of the nature of mimicry. M19. ▸**b** MEDICINE. Of a disease: resembling another disease. *rare*. M19. ▸**c** CRYSTALLOGRAPHY. Of a crystal: having a high degree of apparent symmetry due to twinning or malformation. L19.
■ **mimetical** *adjective* (*rare*) = MIMETIC 1 E17. **mimetically** *adverb* M17.

mimetism /ˈmɪmɪtɪz(ə)m/ *noun*. *rare*. L19.
[ORIGIN Irreg. from MIMETIC + -ISM.]
= MIMICRY.

mimetite /ˈmɪmɪtʌɪt, ˈmʌɪ-/ *noun*. M19.
[ORIGIN from Greek *mimētēs* imitator + -ITE[1].]
MINERALOGY. Lead chloroarsenate, a hexagonal mineral resembling pyromorphite and usu. found as yellow to brown crusts or needle-like crystals.

mimi *noun* see MEEMIE.

mimiambi /mɪmɪˈambʌɪ, mʌɪ-/ *noun pl.* E18.
[ORIGIN Latin from Greek *mimiamboi* pl., from *mimos* MIME *noun* + *iambos* IAMBUS.]
CLASSICAL PROSODY. Mimes written in iambic or scazontic verse.

†**mimiambic** *adjective & noun*. E18.
[ORIGIN mod. Latin *mimiambicus*, formed as MIMIAMBI: see -IC.]
CLASSICAL PROSODY. ▸**A** *adjective*. Of or pertaining to mimiambi; (of a poet) writing mimiambi. E18–M19.
▸ **B** *noun*. In *pl.* = MIMIAMBI. M–L19.

mimic /ˈmɪmɪk/ *adjective & noun*. L16.
[ORIGIN Latin *mimicus* from Greek *mimikos*, from *mimos* MIME *noun*: see -IC.]
▸ **A** *adjective*. **1** Tending to practise or having an aptitude for mimicry or imitation. Formerly also, being or resembling a mime or jester. L16.

W. COWPER 'Sweet Poll!' his doting mistress cries, 'Sweet Poll!' the mimic bird replies.

2 Of, pertaining to, or of the nature of mimicry or imitation. E17.
3 *attrib.* That is a copy of; having an (esp. amusing or ludicrous) imitative resemblance to. E17.

G. ORWELL At the international level sport is frankly mimic warfare.

▸ **B** *noun*. **1** A person practising or skilled in mimicry or imitation, esp. of another's manner, voice, etc., in order to amuse. E17. ▸**b** A poor or feeble imitation. Now *rare*. E17.

M. FOOT A marvellous mimic; he could have made another career as a music-hall comedian.

2 Mimicry; imitation. *rare*. M17.

W. GASS She would throw her head back in the mimic of gargantuan guffaws, soundless and shaking.

3 BIOLOGY. An animal or plant which exhibits mimicry. M19. ▸**b** ENTOMOLOGY. = VICEROY. M20.
■ **mimical** *adjective* = MIMIC *adjective* E17. **mimically** *adverb* E17.

mimic /ˈmɪmɪk/ *verb trans.* Infl. **-ck-**. L17.
[ORIGIN from MIMIC *noun*.]
1 Imitate or copy (a person, gesture, action, etc.), esp. to amuse or ridicule; imitate or copy minutely or servilely. Also, represent in mime. L17.

DEFOE The devil is known to mimic the methods, as well as the actions of his maker. L. STEPHEN The absurdity of mimicking a man who was his junior. R. KIPLING 'This is disgraceful,' said Maisie, mimicking Mrs. Jennett's tone. TOLKIEN You should have been the king's jester and earned your bread, and stripes too, by mimicking his counsellors. G. GREENE The purser mimicked the action of a man drinking and pointed towards me.

2 Of a thing: have a close resemblance to; have the appearance of; *spec.* in MEDICINE, (of a drug) produce an effect very similar to (the effect of another substance or agency). M18.
3 BIOLOGY. Have a mimetic resemblance to (something else) in form or colour. M19.
Müllerian mimic: see MÜLLERIAN *adjective*[2].
■ **mimicker** *noun* L17.

mimicry /ˈmɪmɪkri/ *noun*. L17.
[ORIGIN from MIMIC *noun* + -RY.]
1 The action, practice, or art of mimicking; an act, instance, or example of this. L17.

BARONESS ORCZY The mimicry was so perfect, the tone of the voice so accurately produced. DENNIS POTTER When she told them what the wicked old witch said . . her own face twisted and snarled in chilling mimicry. D. FRASER With his gift of mimicry, he also caught the great man's manner perfectly.

in mimicry of in imitation of.
2 BIOLOGY. A close external resemblance which (part of) one living creature (or occas. a nest or other structure) bears to (part of) another, or to some inanimate object. E19.

R. DAWKINS A remarkable perfection of mimicry on the part of the cuckoo eggs.

MERTENSIAN ***mimicry***. ***Müllerian mimicry***: see MÜLLERIAN *adjective*[2].

miminy-piminy /ˌmɪmɪnɪˈpɪmɪni/ *adjective*. *arch.* E19.
[ORIGIN Fanciful formation: cf. MIM, NIMINY-PIMINY.]
Ridiculously affected or over-refined; finical.

mimographer /mʌɪˈmɒɡrəfə/ *noun*. M17.
[ORIGIN from Latin *mimographus* from Greek *mimographos*, from *mimos* MIME *noun*: see -GRAPHER.]
CLASSICAL HISTORY. A writer or composer of mimes.

mimosa /mɪˈməʊzə, -sə/ *noun & adjective*. M18.
[ORIGIN mod. Latin (see below), app. from Latin *mimus* MIME *noun* + *-osa* fem. of *-osus* -OSE[1] (named from its being as sensitive as an animal).]
▸ **A** *noun*. **1** Any of various tropical or subtropical leguminous shrubs, trees, lianas, etc., of the genus *Mimosa*, chiefly with bipinnate leaves and small pink or white flowers in ball-like clusters; *esp.* the sensitive plant, *Mimosa pudica*. Also, any of certain, chiefly Australian, trees of the related genus *Acacia*; *esp.* (the blossom of) the silver wattle, *A. dealbata*. Also ***mimosa tree***. M18.
2 In full ***mimosa-bark***. The bark of various Australian acacias, used in tanning. Also called ***wattle-bark***. M19.
3 A bright yellow colour resembling that of the flowers of the silver wattle. E20.
4 A cocktail consisting of orange juice and champagne. M20.
▸ **B** *adjective*. Of the colour mimosa, bright yellow. E20.

mimp /mɪmp/ *verb & noun*. Chiefly *Scot. & dial.* E17.
[ORIGIN Imit. Cf. MIM.]
▸ †**A** *noun*. **1** A prim or affectedly modest woman. Only in E17.
2 A pursing of the lips. L18–E19.
▸ **B** *verb intrans.* Speak or act in an affected manner. L17.

mimsy /ˈmɪmzi/ *adjective*. Also **mimsey**. M19.
[ORIGIN In sense 1, nonsense word invented by Lewis Carroll. In sense 2, from MIM: cf. *clumsy*, *flimsy*.]
1 Unhappy. M19.

M

L. CARROLL All mimsy were the borogoves.

2 Prim, affected. **L19.**

J. CANNAN The lawns.. torn up and replaced by a mimsy pseudo-Elizabethan rose-garden. S. FRY He was one of a long line of mimsy and embittered middle-class sensitives.

mimulus /ˈmɪmjʊləs/ *noun*. **M18.**
[ORIGIN mod. Latin (see below), app. dim. of Latin *mimus* MIME *noun*.]
Any of various moisture-loving plants of the chiefly American genus *Mimulus*, of the figwort family, with chiefly bright yellow, sometimes red-blotched flowers like those of antirrhinums; *esp.* the monkey flower, *M. guttatus*.

min /mɪn/ *noun*[1]. **M16.**
[ORIGIN Abbreviation.]
A minute.

Min /mɪn/ *adjective & noun*[2]. **E20.**
[ORIGIN See below.]
▸ **A** *adjective*. Of or pertaining to the district of Min in Fukien province, SE China, or to the group of Chinese dialects spoken there. **E20.**
▸ **B** *noun*. The Min group of Chinese dialects. **M20.**

Min. *abbreviation*[1].
1 Minister.
2 Ministry.

min. *abbreviation*[2].
1 Minim.
2 Minimum.
3 Minute(s).

mina /ˈmʌɪnə/ *noun*[1]. Pl. **-nae** /-niː/, **-nas**. **L15.**
[ORIGIN Latin from Greek *mna*, prob. ult. from Akkadian.]
1 An ancient monetary unit formerly used in Greece and Greek-speaking countries, equal to 100 drachmas. **L15.**
2 An ancient unit of weight formerly used in Western Asia, Greece, and Egypt, approx. equal to 1 lb (0.4536 kg). Also = MANEH. **L16.**

mina *noun*[2] see MYNAH.

minable *adjective* var. of MINEABLE.

minacious /mɪˈneɪʃəs/ *adjective*. **M17.**
[ORIGIN from Latin *minac-*, *-ax* (from *minari* threaten) + -OUS.]
Menacing, threatening.
■ **minaciously** *adverb* L17. **minaciousness** *noun* M19.

M

minacity /mɪˈnasɪti/ *noun*. **L16.**
[ORIGIN from (the same root as) MINACIOUS + -ITY, after *tenacious*, *tenacity*.]
(A) tendency to use threats; menace.

minae *noun pl.* see MINA *noun*[1].

Minaean /mɪˈniːən/ *noun & adjective*. Also **Minean**. **E17.**
[ORIGIN from Latin *Minaeus*, from Arabic *Ma'īn* + -AN.]
▸ **A** *noun*. **1** A native or inhabitant of Ma'īn, an ancient kingdom of southern Arabia. **E17.**
2 The Semitic language of the Minaeans. **M20.**
▸ **B** *adjective*. Of or pertaining to the Minaeans or their language. **M19.**
■ **Minaic** *adjective & noun* = MINAEAN L19.

Minamata disease /mɪnəˈmɑːtə dɪˌziːz/ *noun phr.* **M20.**
[ORIGIN *Minamata*, a town in Japan.]
MEDICINE. Chronic poisoning by alkyl mercury compounds (from industrial waste), characterized by (usu. permanent) impairment of brain functions such as speech, sight, and muscular coordination.

minar /mɪˈnɑː/ *noun*. **M17.**
[ORIGIN Persian & Urdu *mīnār* from Arabic *manār*: see MINARET.]
In India and the Far East: a lighthouse; a tower, a turret.

minaret /ˈmɪnərɛt, mɪnəˈrɛt/ *noun*. **L17.**
[ORIGIN French, or Spanish *minarete*, Italian *minaretto*, from Ottoman Turkish *menāre* from Arabic *manāra(h)* lighthouse, minaret, from *nāra* to shine.]
1 A tall tower or turret connected with a mosque and surrounded by one or more projecting balconies from which a muezzin calls at hours of prayer. **L17.**
2 *transf.* An object or structure shaped like this. **M19.**
■ **minareted** *adjective* having or characterized by minarets M19.

minargent /mɪˈnɑːdʒ(ə)nt/ *noun*. **M19.**
[ORIGIN from ALU)MIN(IUM + French *argent* silver.]
A silver-coloured alloy consisting of cupro-nickel with some tungsten and aluminium, used in jewellery.

minarichi *noun* var. of MINNERICHI.

minatory /ˈmɪnət(ə)ri/ *adjective & noun*. **M16.**
[ORIGIN Late Latin *minatorius*, from Latin *minat-* pa. ppl stem of *minari* threaten: see -ORY[2].]
▸ **A** *adjective*. Expressing or conveying a threat; threatening, menacing. **M16.**

G. VIDAL Letitia gave a laugh.. not unlike the minatory rattle of a leper's bell. P. ACKROYD He talks in minatory terms to the ghost of the.. boy he had once been, and berates him.

▸ †**B** *noun*. A threat, a menace. *rare*. **L16–L17.**
■ **minatorily** *adverb* M17. **minatoriness** *noun* M20.

minauderie /mɪˈnəʊdəri, *foreign* minodri (*pl. same*)/ *noun*. *arch.* **M18.**
[ORIGIN French, from *minauder* simper, flirt, from *mine* MIEN *noun*[1].]
Coquetry, flirtation; a coquettish manner or air.

minaudière /minodjɛːr/ *noun*. Pl. pronounced same. **E18.**
[ORIGIN French: cf. MINAUDERIE.]
†**1** A coquettish woman. **E18–E19.**
2 A small handbag without a handle, a clutch bag. **M20.**

†**minaway** *noun*. Chiefly *Scot.* **L17–E19.**
[ORIGIN French *menuet*.]
= MINUET *noun*.

minbar /ˈmɪnbɑː/ *noun*. Also **mim-** /mɪm-/. **E19.**
[ORIGIN Arabic = pulpit, from *nabara* raise.]
A small set of steps in a mosque from which the *khutba* is delivered.

mince /mɪns/ *verb & noun*. Also (now *dial.*) **minch** /mɪn(t)ʃ/. **LME.**
[ORIGIN Old French *mincier* (dial. *minchier*) from Proto-Romance, from Latin MINUTIA.]
▸ **A** *verb*. **1** *verb trans.* Cut up or grind (esp. meat) into very small pieces. **LME.** ▸†**b** Carve (a plover). **L15–M19.** ▸**c** Cut (a person) up into small pieces. **E17.**

Country Living Mince the rest of the meat with the.. pork.

2 *verb trans.* Subdivide (*up*) minutely. **LME.**
†**3** *verb trans.* Diminish, take away from. Chiefly *Scot.* **L15–L19.**
4 **a** *verb trans. & †intrans.* Lessen or diminish (something) in representation; minimize. Now *rare*. **M16.** ▸**b** *verb trans.* Restrain (one's words etc.) within the bounds of politeness or decorum. Usu. in neg. contexts. **L16.**

b T. S. ELIOT I didn't mince my words, I said to her myself.

5 *verb trans. & intrans.* Utter or speak in an affectedly refined or precise manner. **M16.**
6 *verb intrans.* Walk with short steps and an affected preciseness or daintiness. **M16.** ▸**b** *verb trans.* Perform or enact in an affectedly precise or dainty manner. **E17.**

V. WOOLF Three white pigeons.. minced with tiny steps on their little pink feet. DENNIS POTTER He minces out with an ogling smile.

– COMB. & PHRASES: **minced meat** (*a*) meat cut up or ground into very small pieces; (*b*) *rare* = MINCEMEAT 3; **minced pie** = *mince pie* (a) below; **mince matters** = *mince the matter* (b) below; **mince pie** (*a*) a usu. small round pie containing mincemeat, traditionally eaten esp. at Christmas; (*b*) *rhyming slang* an eye (usu. in *pl.*); **mince the matter** †(*a*) make light of the matter in question; (*b*) use polite expressions to indicate disapproval etc. (usu. in neg. contexts).

▸ **B** *noun*. **1** Minced meat. **E19.**
2 An instance of mincing speech; a mincing walk. **E20.**
3 = ***mince pie*** (b) above. Usu. in *pl. rhyming slang*. **M20.**
■ **mincer** *noun* (*a*) a machine which or (*rare*) a person who minces meat etc.; (*b*) a person who speaks or walks in an affectedly dainty manner: L16. **mincing** *adjective* that minces; affectedly refined or precise in speech or movement: M16. **mincingly** *adverb* L16. **mincingness** *noun* M19.

mincemeat /ˈmɪnsmiːt/ *noun*. **M17.**
[ORIGIN Alt. of ***minced meat*** s.v. MINCE *verb*.]
1 ***make mincemeat of***, defeat decisively or easily. **M17.**
†**2** = ***minced meat*** (a) s.v. MINCE *verb*. **E–M18.**
3 A mixture of currants, raisins, sugar, suet, chopped apples, candied peel, spices, etc. **M19.**

Mincha /ˈmɪnxɑː/ *noun*. Also ***-ah***. **M17.**
[ORIGIN Hebrew *minḥāh* lit. 'gift, offering'.]
The Jewish daily afternoon worship.

†**minchen** *noun*. **OE–E19.**
[ORIGIN Old English *mynecenu* fem. of *munuc* MONK *noun*[1].]
A nun.
■ †**minchery** *noun* a nunnery M17–L19.

minchiate /mɪnˈkjɑːteɪ/ *noun*. **M18.**
[ORIGIN Italian.]
hist. A card game derived from tarot, formerly played in Tuscany, western Italy.

mind /mʌɪnd/ *noun*[1].
[ORIGIN Old English *gemynd* corresp. to Old High German *gimunt*, Gothic *gamunds* memory, from Germanic, from base of Y- + weak grade of ablaut series from Indo-European base meaning 'revolve in the mind, think'.]
▸ **I** Memory.
†**1** The faculty of memory. **OE–LME.**
2 Remembrance, recollection, memory. Chiefly in phrs. **OE.**

AUSTIN CLARKE Hard to hold the difference in mind. *Times Lit. Suppl.* Poets must flick in and out of mind As if we had no other kind Of knowing. *Proverb*: Out of sight, out of mind.

3 That which is remembered *of* a person or thing; the memory *of*. Long *obsolete* exc. *Scot.* **OE.**
4 †**a** The action of commemorating; (a) commemoration; a memorial. **OE–L15.** ▸**b** *spec.* (chiefly ROMAN CATHOLIC CHURCH). The commemoration of a deceased person by a requiem mass or (later more widely) special prayers held on the day of the death or funeral in any month or year following. *obsolete* exc. in ***month's mind***, ***year's mind***. *arch.* **OE.**
†**5** Mention, record. Chiefly in ***make mind of***, ***make mind that***. Only in **ME.**

▸ **II** Thought; purpose, intention.
6 †**a** The action or state of thinking about something; the thought *of*. Chiefly in ***have mind of***, think of, give heed to. **OE–L16.** ▸**b** Attention, heed. Usu. in neg. contexts with *pay*. *N. Amer. colloq.* **E20.**

b P. HIGHSMITH Clara, knowing its harmlessness, paid it no mind. K. KESEY McMurphy didn't pay the guy any mind and went on arguing.

7 **a** Purpose, intention. *obsolete* exc. in phrs. **ME.** ▸**b** An inclination, a wish; a liking. Freq. in phrs. **LME.**

b D. DU MAURIER Entertained when he had the mind to do so. J. MAY We buried the furnace so we can.. make more iron when we've a mind to. J. NAGENDA We could all do it if we were of a mind to.

8 The direction of a person's thoughts, desires, inclinations, or energies. Freq. in phrs. **ME.**

D. EDEN At first her mind had not been on Fergus. R. LARDNER I'll stop talking.. and keep my mind on the game. J. WAIN Took his mind off the two things he wanted.. to forget. E. KUZWAYO My mind would drift back to Thaba'Nchu.

9 A person's opinion, judgement, or view. Chiefly in phrs. **LME.**

POPE Pray let me know your mind in this. M. W. MONTAGU I don't doubt you'll be of my mind.

10 A (usu. specified) disposition, character, or way of thinking and feeling. **LME.** ▸†**b** A particular feeling or attitude towards something. **L15–E17.**

SHAKES. *Two Gent.* Fear not; he bears an honourable mind And will not use a woman lawlessly. R. G. COLLINGWOOD The philosophy of craft.. was one of the greatest.. achievements of the Greek mind. **b** AV *Acts* 12:20 Herode bare an hostile mind intending warre.

11 The state of a person's thoughts and feelings. **E16.**

W. SHENSTONE How, with one trivial glance, Might she ruin the peace of my mind! J. WAIN That ought to set Ned's mind at ease.

▸ **III** Mental or psychic faculty.
12 **a** The seat of awareness, thought, volition, and feeling; cognitive and emotional phenomena and powers as constituting a controlling system, *spec.* as opp. ***matter***; the spiritual as distinguished from the bodily part of a human being. **ME.** ▸**b** A person or a group of people collectively as the embodiment of mental faculties. **L16.** ▸**c** A controlling or directing spiritual being or agency. **E17.**

a C. WORDSWORTH His mind was filled with gloomy forebodings. J. GALSWORTHY His lively, twisting mind.. had recorded with amusement the confusion. G. F. KENNAN The example of the Russian revolution.. was in everybody's mind. P. PARISH The effects of L.S.D. on the mind are unpredictable. C. ANGIER She had built up an idea of England in her mind. A. ARONSON Rembrandt's interest in.. men's and women's minds in moments of uncontrolled passion. **b** W. J. MICKLE The same ungenerous minds.. who advised the rejection of Columbus. *Daily Telegraph* This cleavage of the European mind.

13 *spec.* The intellect, intellectual powers, esp. as distinguished from the will and emotions. **ME.**

W. COWPER Possessor of a soul refined, An upright heart, and cultivated mind.

14 The healthy or normal condition of the mental faculties. Freq. in phrs. **LME.**

LD MACAULAY He was drunk.. or out of his mind. J. WAIN No one in his right mind will refuse.. if it is free.

– PHRASES: ***a load off a person's mind***: see LOAD *noun*. ***at the back of one's mind***: see BACK *noun*[1]. ***balance of mind***: see BALANCE *noun*. ***bear in mind***: see BEAR *verb*[1]. **be in two minds** be undecided. ***blow a person's mind***: see BLOW *verb*[1]. ***bring to mind***: see BRING *verb*. ***call to mind***: see CALL *verb*. **cast one's mind back** think back *to*; recall an earlier time. **change of mind** a change or alteration of one's opinion, plans, etc. **change one's mind** change or alter one's purpose, opinion, plans, etc. **close one's mind (to)**, **shut one's mind (to)** refuse to consider (changes, new ideas, etc.), be unreceptive (to). **come to mind** (of a thought, idea, etc.) suggest itself. ***cross one's mind***: see CROSS *verb*. ***enter one's mind***: see ENTER *verb* 1b. **give a bit of one's mind to**, **give a piece of one's mind to** scold, reproach. **give one's mind to** apply oneself to, concentrate on. **have a mind**, **have a good mind** (*a*) be strongly inclined or tempted (*to*, *to do*); (*b*) (*arch.*) foll. by *to*: have a liking for. **have a mind of one's own** be capable of independent opinions. **have half a mind** = *have a mind* above. **have in mind** plan, intend. ***have mind of***: see sense 6 above. ***hearts and minds***: see HEART *noun*. †**in mind (to do)** = ***in the mind (to do)*** below. **in my mind** = *to my mind* (a) below. †**in the mind (to do)** disposed or inclined (*to do*). **know one's own mind** form and adhere to a decision or purpose without vacillating; be decisive. **lose one's mind** become insane. ***make up one's mind***: see ***make up*** (j) s.v. MAKE *verb*. **mind over matter** the power of the mind asserted over the physical universe. **month's mind** (*a*) see sense 4b above; (*b*) (*obsolete* exc. *dial.*) an inclination, a fancy. ***mortal mind***: see MORTAL *adjective* 2. †**of mind (to do)** = ***in the mind (to do)*** above. **of one mind** in agreement, of the same opinion. †**of the mind (to do)** = ***in the mind (to do)*** above. ***one's mind's eye***: see EYE *noun*. **on one's mind** occupying or esp. troubling one's thoughts. ***open mind***: see OPEN *adjective*. **open one's mind (to)** consider readily (changes, new ideas, etc.), be receptive (to). ***PRESENCE of mind***. **put in mind** remind (a person) *of*. **put out of one's mind** deliberately forget. **read a person's mind** discern a person's thoughts. ***shut one's mind (to)***: see ***close one's mind (to)*** above. **speak one's mind** give one's candid opinion. ***split mind***: see SPLIT *ppl adjective*. ***the life of the mind***: see LIFE *noun*. ***the mind's eye***: see EYE *noun*. ***things of the mind***: see THING *noun*[1]. ***time out of mind***: see TIME *noun*. ***tiny mind***: see TINY *adjective*. **to my mind, to her mind**, etc., (**a**) in my etc. opinion; (**b**) to my etc. liking.

– COMB.: **mind-bender** *slang* a person who or thing which influences or alters one's mood; *spec.* a hallucinogenic drug; **mind-bending** *adjective* (*slang*) (esp. of a drug) influencing or altering the mind; **mind-bendingly** *adverb* (*slang*) in a mind-bending manner; **mind-blowing** *adjective* (*slang*) (**a**) (of a drug etc.) inducing hallucinations; (**b**) confusing; shattering; **mind-blowingly** *adverb* (*slang*) in a mind-blowing manner; **mind-boggling** *adjective* overwhelming, startling; **mind-bogglingly** *adverb* in a mind-boggling manner, to a mind-boggling extent; **mind-cure** the supposed curing of a disease by the mental powers of the healer; **mind-curer**, **mind-curist** a person who practises mind-cure; **mind-expanding** *adjective* psychedelic; **mind-game** a game designed to test or exercise the intellect; **mind-healer** = ***mind-curer*** above; **mind-healing** = ***mind-cure*** above; **mind-meld** (in science fiction) a supposed technique for the psychic fusion of two or more minds, permitting unrestricted communication or deep understanding (orig. from the US television series *Star Trek*); **mind-read** *verb trans.* apparently discern the thoughts of (another person); **mind-reader** a person capable of mind-reading; **mind-set** (**a**) habits of mind formed by previous events or an earlier environment; (**b**) *loosely* a frame of mind, a mental attitude; **mindshare** consumer awareness of a particular product or brand, esp. compared to the profile enjoyed by competitors' products; **mind-transference** telepathy.

mind /mɪnd/ *noun*[2]. Now *rare*. M19.
[ORIGIN Middle Irish, mod. *mionn*.]
ARCHAEOLOGY. An Irish lunula.

mind /mʌɪnd/ *verb*. ME.
[ORIGIN from MIND *noun*[1].]
1 *verb trans.* Remind (*of*, *that*, *to do*). Now *rare* exc. *Scot.* ME. ▸†**b** Serve as a reminder of. L16–E17.

R. BURNS There's not a bonie bird that sings, But minds me o' my Jean. TENNYSON They mind us of the time When we made bricks in Egypt.

2 *verb trans.* Remember, recollect. Also with refl. pronoun as indirect obj. Now *arch.* & *dial.* exc. *Scot.* LME. ▸**b** *verb intrans.* & *refl.* Foll. by *of*: remember, recollect. Now *arch.* & *dial.* L17.

MRS H. WOOD I mind me that something was said about that paper. C. MACKENZIE Nobody in the islands could mind such a storm of rain. **b** THACKERAY I mind me of a time that's gone.

3 *verb trans.* †**a** Mention, record. LME–M16. ▸**b** Remember or mention in one's prayers, pray for. Long *obsolete* exc. *Scot. dial.* LME.
4 *verb trans.* Bear in mind; take care to remember, make certain, *that*. Usu. in *imper.* LME.

T. HARDY Mind you make a good impression upon him.

5 *verb trans.* Apply oneself to, concern oneself diligently with, (business, one's affairs, etc.). LME. ▸†**b** Care for, like, value. M17–M18.

G. BERKELEY If some certain persons minded piety more than politics. **b** SMOLLETT His heir . . minded nothing but fox-hunting.

6 *verb trans.* Perceive, notice, be aware of. *obsolete* exc. *dial.* L15.
7 *verb trans.* Plan, contemplate, intend, (†an action etc., †*that*, *to do*). *obsolete* exc. *dial.* E16.
8 a *verb trans.* Attend to, heed, esp. with the intention of obeying. Now chiefly *N. Amer.* M16. ▸**b** *verb intrans.* Pay attention; take note. Usu. in *imper.* with emphatic force or qualifying a statement. *colloq.* E19.

a A. LURIE Her little brothers always ganged up on her . . and wouldn't mind what she said. **b** E. WAUGH Suppose you were just a crook . . . I don't say you are, mind, but supposing. J. BRAINE They bought it from a bankrupt woolman . . Mind you, they don't use half of it. M. SPARK Foreigners always talk like that, mind you.

9 *verb trans.* & *intrans.* Object (to), be annoyed (by); be troubled or concerned (by). Usu. in neg. & interrog. contexts. E17.

J. PORTER 'Tea, Mr Dover?' 'I don't mind if I do' said Dover, passing his cup. D. ATHILL I greatly minded making a fool of myself. C. P. SNOW I don't mind him having a look.

10 a *verb trans.* Be careful or attentive about; be wary concerning, be on one's guard against (now usu. in *imper.*). L17. ▸**b** *verb intrans.* Look out, be careful. Usu. foll. by *out*. Usu. in *imper. colloq.* L17.

a MRS H. WARD 'Mind what you're about,' cried Purcell, angrily. J. BETJEMAN And mind the terrier when you call. **b** H. JAMES Take care . . they'll see you, if you don't mind. *American Speech* Children whizzing around on bicycles . . shouting 'Mind out!'.

11 *verb trans.* Take charge of or look after (esp. a child, shop, etc.) temporarily. Also, guard, protect. L17.

T. HARDY A boy who was minding a gingerbread stall. C. STEAD They were being minded by Louisa.

– PHRASES ETC.: **don't mind me**, **don't mind us**, etc., *iron.* don't worry about me, us, etc.; do as you please. **do you mind?** *ellipt.* do you mind not doing that?, please do not do that. **mind one's eye** be on one's guard. ***mind one's hits***: see HIT *noun* 3. ***mind one's own business***: see BUSINESS. ***mind one's Ps and Qs***: see P, P 1. ***mind one's step***: see STEP *noun*[1]. **mind the shop** [cf. sense 11 above] have temporary charge of affairs. **mind-your-own-business** a dwarf creeping plant of the nettle family, *Soleirolia soleirolii*, cultivated in greenhouses and as a house plant. ***never mind***, ***never you mind***: see NEVER.

minded /ˈmʌɪndɪd/ *adjective*. L15.
[ORIGIN from MIND *noun*[1] + -ED[2].]
1 Intending, disposed, inclined, (*to do*). L15.

R. L. STEVENSON He . . can speak like a book when so minded. M. SPARK I wasn't minded to take on a girl of twenty-two. P. PULLMAN I must be blunt. They're not minded to renew your grant.

†**2** Having a specified disposition towards a person or thing. E16–L17.
3 As 2nd elem. of comb.: ▸**a** Having a specified kind of mind. E16. ▸**b** Inclined or well able to think in a specified way. E17. ▸**c** Interested in or enthusiastic about a specified thing. E20.

b *Daily Chronicle* Monotonous even to the most . . statistically-minded. **c** *Guardian* A bowling-green for the sports-minded customer.

a absent-minded, ***bloody-minded***, ***feeble-minded***, ***high-minded***, etc.

Mindel /ˈmɪnd(ə)l/ *adjective* & *noun*. E20.
[ORIGIN A river in southern Germany.]
GEOLOGY. (Designating or pertaining to) a Pleistocene glaciation in the Alps preceding the Riss, possibly corresponding to the Elsterian of northern Europe.

minder /ˈmʌɪndə/ *noun*. LME.
[ORIGIN from MIND *noun*[1], *verb* + -ER[1].]
†**1** A person with a good memory. *rare*. Only in LME.
2 A person employed to have charge of or look after a specified thing; *spec.* a person employed to look after a child outside the home (as at a crèche) for a fixed part of the day. Chiefly as 2nd elem. of comb. LME. ▸**b** A child who is looked after at a crèche etc. *rare*. M19.

R. DINNAGE The children had been dumped with various minders.

child-minder, ***dog-minder***, ***machine-minder***, etc.

3 In early use (*slang*), a person employed to protect a criminal; a thief's assistant. Later *gen.*, a person employed to protect anyone, esp. a famous person or an inexperienced political candidate in an election campaign. E20.

L. GRIFFITHS If there's a threat of physical violence you have to call on your minder. *Independent* Living in luxury, surrounded by minders and assistants.

Mindererus /mɪndəˈrɪərəs/ *noun*. Now *rare* or *obsolete*. Also **m-**. L18.
[ORIGIN Latinized form of the name of R. M. *Minderer* (d. 1621), German physician.]
PHARMACOLOGY. ***spirit of Mindererus***, ***spirits of Mindererus***, a solution of ammonium acetate, formerly used as a febrifuge.

mindful /ˈmʌɪn(d)fʊl, -f(ə)l/ *adjective*. ME.
[ORIGIN from MIND *noun*[1] + -FUL.]
1 Taking heed or care; being conscious or aware. Freq. foll. by *of*, *that*, *to do*. ME.
2 Inclined or intending *to do*. *formal*. M16.
▪ **mindfully** *adverb* LME. **mindfulness** *noun* M16.

mindless /ˈmʌɪndlɪs/ *adjective*. OE.
[ORIGIN from MIND *noun*[1] + -LESS.]
1 Unintelligent, stupid; (of an activity etc.) not requiring thought or skill. OE.
2 Thoughtless, heedless, careless, (*of*). LME.
▪ **mindlessly** *adverb* M19. **mindlessness** *noun* M17.

mindly /ˈmʌɪndli/ *adjective*. *rare*. LME.
[ORIGIN from MIND *noun*[1] + -LY[1].]
Of or pertaining to the mind; mental.

mine /mʌɪn/ *noun*. ME.
[ORIGIN Old French & mod. French (perh. from *miner* MINE *verb*) or directly from MINE *verb*.]
1 An excavation or a system of excavations in the earth for the extraction of metal, metallic ore, coal, salt, etc. ME. ▸**b** *fig.* An abundant source or supply. M16. ▸†**c** *transf.* A subterranean cavity. Only in E17.

B. BYARS Friends were working the mine, digging out turquoise. B. MOORE The great moonlit slag heaps of the Gorodok mines. **b** D. H. LAWRENCE The courage of our own feelings . . becomes a mine of practical truth. B. GILROY They . . found her a mine of information.

coalmine, ***diamond mine***, ***salt mine***, ***tin mine***, etc.

2 A mineral; ore. Now only *spec.*, iron ore. ME.
3 MILITARY. **a** A subterranean passage dug under an enemy position (esp. the wall of a besieged fortress) in order to gain entrance or (later esp. with the use of an explosive) to collapse a wall or fortification. Also, the explosive charge placed in such a passage. LME. ▸**b** A receptacle containing explosive placed in or on the ground or in the water with the purpose of destroying enemy personnel, ships, etc. Freq. with specifying word. LME.

b B. MASON His jeep passed over a mine; wreckage was strewn over a wide area.

b *limpet mine*, ***magnetic mine***, ***pressure mine***, etc.

4 A firework propelling crackers into the air. Now *rare*. M18.
5 A tunnel or network of tunnels made in the interior of a leaf by an insect larva. M19.

– COMB.: **mine-car** a wheeled container used in a mine for the underground transport of coal etc.; **mine-detector** an instrument for detecting the presence of explosive mines; **mine-dump** *S. Afr.* a large mound or hill of mining waste at the surface of a mine, esp. a gold mine, or former mine; **minefield** (**a**) an area laid with explosive mines; (**b**) *fig.* a situation or subject presenting unseen hazards; **mine-hunt** *verb intrans.* hunt or sweep for mines; **mine-hunter** = ***minesweeper*** below; **mine-iron** = ***mine-pig*** below; **minelayer** a ship or aircraft equipped to lay explosive mines; **mine-laying** *noun* & *adjective* (**a**) *noun* the operation of laying explosive mines; (**b**) *adjective* that lays explosive mines; **mine-pig** pig iron made from mine or ore; **mine-pit** a pit or shaft in a mine; **mine shaft**: giving access to a mine; **mine-sinker** a device for keeping a mine submerged; **mine-stone** ore, *esp.* iron ore; **minesweeper** a ship for clearing away floating and submarine mines; **mine-sweeping** *noun* & *adjective* (**a**) *noun* the operation of clearing away floating or submarine mines; (**b**) *adjective* that clears away floating or submarine mines; **mine tin**: worked out of the lode; **mine-town** = ***mining town*** s.v. MINING *verbal noun*; **mine-work** = sense 1 above.

mine /mʌɪn/ *possess. adjective* (in mod. usage also classed as a *determiner*) & *pronoun*, *1 sing.*
[ORIGIN Old English *mīn* = Old Frisian, Old Saxon, Old High German *mīn*. (Dutch *mijn*, German *mein*), Old Norse *minn*, Gothic *meins*, from Germanic, from Indo-European locative form of base of ME *pronoun* + adjectival suffix.]
▸ **A** *adjective*. = MY *adjective*. Used *attrib.* before a vowel or *h* (*arch.*) or as the first of two or more possess. adjectives qualifying the same following noun. Also (*arch.*) used with emphatic force following any noun. Cf. THINE *adjective*. OE.

SWIFT A little below the level of mine eyes. C. A. BRISTED There, reader mine! Is that last page grave . . enough for you? J. CONRAD I venture to ask that mine and Mr Razumov's intervention should not become public. P. G. WODEHOUSE I entered the saloon bar and requested mine host to start pouring.

▸ **B** *pronoun*. [absol. use of the adjective: cf. THINE *pronoun*.]
1 My one(s), that or those belonging or pertaining to me. Formerly also *spec.*, my property; my affair. OE.

J. RHYS Talking about cats you don't know how I miss mine. I. MURDOCH It is our duty, yours and mine. J. SIMMS The frog had been given to me: it was mine. B. GILROY 'Life is sweet' . . 'Not mine. It's not worth a single cent.'

2 *of mine*, belonging or pertaining to me. LME.

mine /mʌɪn/ *verb*. ME.
[ORIGIN Old French & mod. French *miner*, perh. orig. Proto-Gallo-Romance deriv. of Celtic word repr. by Irish *méin*, Gaelic *mèinn* ore, mine, Welsh *mwyn* ore, †mine. Cf. MINERAL *noun*.]
1 *verb intrans.* **a** Dig in the earth. Also, make subterranean passages. Long *rare* or *obsolete*. ME. ▸**b** *verb trans.* Dig or burrow in (the earth); make (a hole, passage, one's way) underground by digging; *transf.* make a hollow or groove in. LME. ▸**c** *verb trans.* In *pass.* Provided with subterranean passages. E19.

b SIR W. SCOTT Condemned to mine a channell'd way, O'er solid sheets of marble grey.

2 a *verb trans.* & *intrans.* Chiefly in ancient warfare: dig a passage under the foundations of (a wall, fort, etc.), esp. in order to cause collapse or gain entrance. Now *rare* or *obsolete*. ME. ▸**b** *verb trans.* Lay explosive mines under or in. M17.

b K. DOUGLAS The verges . . in the road were mined with anti-personnel . . mines. O. MANNING We started mining Norwegian waters.

3 *verb trans. fig.* Ruin or destroy slowly, undermine. LME.
4 *verb trans.* Extract (metals, ore, coal, etc.) from a mine. LME ▸**b** *fig.* Extract (information, an idea, etc.) from an abundant source or supply. M20. ▸**c** Analyse (a database) to generate new information. L20.

A. MOOREHEAD Gold had to be mined by machinery. *Scientific American* Oil left in the ground after pumping can be mined.

deep-mined: see DEEP *adverb*.

5 *verb trans.* & *intrans.* Dig in (the earth, a place, etc.) for metal, ore, coal, etc. Freq. foll. by *for*. LME. ▸**b** *fig.* Delve into or *into* (an abundant source or supply) to extract information, an idea, etc. L19.

SIR W. SCOTT Nature had assigned to him . . a serf, to mine for the gold. W. W. SMYTH The . . rich coalfield . . mined as early as 1302. **b** G. GREENE By mining into layers of personality hitherto untouched. *Lochaber News* The . . cast mined every rich seam of comedy.

6 *verb trans.* Exhaust (soil or land) by excessive cultivation. M20.

mineable /ˈmʌɪnəb(ə)l/ *adjective*. Also **minable**. L16.
[ORIGIN from MINE *verb* + -ABLE.]
Able to be mined.

Minean *noun* & *adjective* var. of MINAEAN.

Minenwerfer /ˈmiːnənvɛrfər, -wəːfə/ *noun*. Also **m-**. E20.
[ORIGIN German, from *Minen* (pl.) mines + *Werfer* lit. 'thrower', from *werfen* to throw.]
hist. A German trench mortar of the First World War.

M

miner /ˈmʌɪnə/ *noun*. ME.
[ORIGIN Old French *minëor*, *minour* (mod. *mineur*), from *miner*: see MINE *verb*, -ER[2], -OR. In sense 4, alt. of MYNAH.]
1 A person who works in a mine. ME.
2 A person who excavates subterranean passages in order to destroy an enemy position, esp. with the aid of an explosive charge. Freq. in ***sappers and miners*** (cf. ***Royal Sappers and Miners*** s.v. SAPPER). ME.
3 A burrowing insect or larva; *esp*. = ***leaf miner*** s.v. LEAF *noun*[1]. E19.
4 a Any of various Australian honeyeaters of the genus *Manorina*. M19. ▸**b** Any of various small S. American ovenbirds of the genus *Geositta*, which excavate a long burrow for breeding. E20.
– PHRASES: ***bell miner***: see BELL *noun*[1]. ***miner's disease*** = ***miner's lung*** below. ***miner's inch***: see INCH *noun*[1] 1c. **miner's lettuce** a kind of spring beauty, *Montia perfoliata*, sometimes eaten as a salad. **miner's lung** pneumoconiosis due to inhalation of coal dust. **miner's right** *Austral*. & *NZ* a licence to dig for gold etc. on private or public land. ***noisy miner***: see NOISY *adjective* 1.

minera /mɪˈnɪərə/ *noun*. *hist. rare*. M17.
[ORIGIN medieval Latin from Old French *min(i)ere*: see MINERAL *noun*.]
The matrix in which a metal or precious stone was supposed to grow. Also, the ore of a metal.

mineragraphy /mɪnəˈrɑgrəfi/ *noun*. E20.
[ORIGIN from MINERA(L *noun* + -GRAPHY.]
= MINERALOGRAPHY.
■ **minera'graphic** *adjective* E20.

mineral /ˈmɪn(ə)r(ə)l/ *noun*. LME.
[ORIGIN Old French, or medieval Latin *minerale* use as noun of neut. sing. of *mineralis*, from *minera* ore from Old French *min(i)ere* mine, perh. ult. from Proto-Gallo-Romance deriv. whence perh. also MINE *noun*, *verb*: see -AL[1].]
1 A substance obtained by mining; *esp*. one other than a native metal, an ore. LME. ▸†**b** The art or industry of mining. L15–L16. ▸†**c** A mine. L16–E17.
2 A (naturally occurring) substance that is neither animal nor vegetable; an inorganic substance (now freq., one required in the diet). LME. ▸†**b** An inorganic substance used as a drug. M16–M18.
3 A solid, usu. naturally occurring, inorganic substance of homogeneous composition and distinctive chemical and physical properties. E19.
4 An artificial mineral water or other effervescent drink. Usu. in *pl*. L19.
– COMB.: **mineral dressing** treatment of ore so as to remove gangue and concentrate the valuable constituents; **mineral rod** a divining rod for finding mineral veins.

mineral /ˈmɪn(ə)r(ə)l/ *adjective*. LME.
[ORIGIN Old French, or medieval Latin *mineralis*: see MINERAL *noun*, -AL[1].]
1 Of a material substance: neither animal nor vegetable in origin; inorganic. LME.
2 a Of the nature of a mineral; obtained or obtainable by mining. L16. ▸**b** Impregnated with minerals. Formerly also, (of colour) indicating such impregnation. M17.
†**3** Of or pertaining to mines or mining. Of a person: skilled in mining. L16–E18.
– SPECIAL COLLOCATIONS: **mineral black** a black pigment made from graphite or slate. **mineral blue** a Prussian blue made lighter by the addition of alumina. **mineral brown** a brown pigment coloured with iron oxide. ***mineral chameleon***: see CHAMELEON *noun* 5. **mineral charcoal** a fibrous substance like charcoal found between layers of coal; = FUSAIN 2. **mineral coal** †(*a*) a variety of coal in which there are no traces of vegetable structure; (*b*) native coal (as distinct from charcoal). **mineral green** Scheele's green, copper arsenite. **mineral grey** a pale blue-grey pigment obtained in the making of ultramarine from lapis lazuli. **mineral jelly** petroleum jelly. **mineral oil** petroleum; a distillation product of petroleum. **mineral pitch** asphalt. **mineral purple** (*a*) a dark red pigment containing iron oxide; (*b*) purple of Cassius. **mineral soil**: in which the organic constituents are small in proportion to the inorganic ones. ***mineral tallow***: see TALLOW *noun* 2. **mineral tar** = MALTHA 2. **mineral violet** = *MANGANESE* ***violet***. **mineral water** (*a*) water found in nature with some dissolved mineral salts present; a kind of such water; (*b*) an artificial (esp. effervescent) imitation of this, *esp*. soda water; (*c*) any effervescent non-alcoholic drink. **mineral wax** a fossil resin, *esp*. ozocerite. **mineral wool** a fine matted fibrous substance made from inorganic material, used for packing, insulation, etc. **mineral yellow** any of various inorganic yellow pigments; *esp*. a lead oxychloride.

mineralise *verb* var. of MINERALIZE.

mineralist /ˈmɪn(ə)r(ə)lɪst/ *noun*. E17.
[ORIGIN from MINERAL *noun* + -IST.]
†**1** A follower of Paracelsus in his use of minerals in medicines. Only in E17.
2 A mineralogist. M17.

mineralize /ˈmɪn(ə)r(ə)lʌɪz/ *verb*. Also **-ise**. M17.
[ORIGIN from MINERAL *noun*, *adjective* + -IZE.]
1 *verb trans*. Change wholly or partly into a mineral substance; change (a metal) into an ore. Chiefly as ***mineralized*** *ppl adjective*. M17. ▸**b** *verb intrans*. Undergo such a change. *rare*. M19.
2 *verb trans*. Add a mineral or minerals to; impregnate with inorganic substances; make into mineral water. Chiefly as ***mineralized*** *ppl adjective*. L18.
3 *verb intrans*. Seek for or study minerals. Now *rare*. L18.
4 *verb trans*. In *pass*. Of a vein, deposit, etc.: contain ore or minerals to a specified extent. L19.
■ **mineralizable** *adjective* L19. **minerali'zation** *noun* the process or action of mineralizing something; the state of being mineralized: M18. **mineralizer** *noun* (chiefly GEOLOGY) (*a*) a substance that combines with a metal to form an ore, as oxygen, sulphur, arsenic, etc.; (*b*) a volatile constituent which controls or promotes the formation of minerals from a magma; a substance which promotes the artificial synthesis of a mineral: L18.

mineralocorticoid /mɪn(ə)rələˈkɔːtɪkɔɪd/ *noun*. M20.
[ORIGIN from MINERAL *noun* + -O- + CORTICOID.]
BIOCHEMISTRY. Any of various corticosteroids (e.g. aldosterone) which are involved esp. with maintaining the salt balance in the body.

mineralography /mɪn(ə)rəˈlɒgrəfi/ *noun*. E20.
[ORIGIN from MINERAL *noun* + -OGRAPHY.]
MINERALOGY. The branch of science that deals with the physical and chemical microstructure of minerals, esp. of polished sections as studied with a reflecting microscope.
■ **mineralo'graphic** *adjective* of or using mineralography E20.

mineralogy /mɪnəˈralədʒi/ *noun*. L17.
[ORIGIN from MINERAL *noun* + -LOGY.]
1 The branch of science that deals with minerals. L17.
2 (A description of) the distribution of minerals in a region, or within a (type of) rock. L18.
■ **minera'logic** *adjective* (now chiefly *US*) = MINERALOGICAL E19. **minera'logical** *adjective* of, pertaining to, or used in mineralogy L18. **minera'logically** *adverb* as regards mineralogy E19. **mineralogist** *noun* M17.

mineraloid /ˈmɪn(ə)rəlɔɪd/ *noun*. E20.
[ORIGIN from MINERAL *noun* + -OID.]
MINERALOGY. A mineral which has an amorphous rather than crystalline structure.

minerval /mɪˈnəːv(ə)l/ *noun*. E17.
[ORIGIN Latin, from *Minerva* (earlier *Men-*) the Roman goddess of handicrafts, wisdom (cf. Sanskrit *manasvin* wise), and later also of war from earlier form rel. to Sanskrit *manas* mind, Greek *menos* courage, fury, from base of MIND *noun*[1].]
A gift given in gratitude by a pupil to a teacher.

Minervois /minɛːˈvwɑː/ *noun*. E20.
[ORIGIN See below.]
A wine produced in the district of Minervois, in the department of Aude in southern France.

minery /ˈmʌɪnəri/ *noun*. Now *rare* or *obsolete*. M16.
[ORIGIN medieval Latin *mineria*, *-aria*, from *minare* to mine.]
1 A place where mining is carried out, a mine. M16. ▸†**b** Materials for mining. Only in L17.
†**2** The art or industry of mining. Only in L18.

minestra /mɪˈnɛstrə/ *noun*. Pl. **-stre** /-stri/. L17.
[ORIGIN Italian.]
In Italy: (a) soup, *esp*. minestrone.

minestrone /mɪnɪˈstrəʊni/ *noun*. L19.
[ORIGIN Italian.]
A thick soup containing vegetables, beans, and pasta.

minette /mɪˈnɛt/ *noun*. L19.
[ORIGIN French.]
GEOLOGY. **1** A dark porphyritic igneous rock consisting chiefly of biotite and alkaline feldspars. L19.
2 In full ***minette ore***. A low-grade oolitic iron ore found mainly in Luxembourg and Lorraine. E20.

minever *noun* var. of MINIVER.

Ming /mɪŋ/ *noun* & *adjective*. L18.
[ORIGIN Chinese *Ming* lit. 'bright, clear'.]
1 (Designating or pertaining to) a dynasty ruling in China from the 14th to the 17th cent., between the Mongol and the Manchu dynasties. L18.
2 (Designating) porcelain ware made in China during this period, characterized by elaborate designs and vivid colours. L19.
3 (Designating or being of) any of various colours, esp. green or blue, characteristic of this porcelain. E20.

ming /mɪŋ/ *verb*. *obsolete* exc. *dial*.
[ORIGIN Late Old English *(ge)myn(e)gian* from West Germanic (cf. Old High German *bi-munigōn*), from Germanic.]
1 *verb trans*. Remind (a person); warn. Foll. by *of*, *on*, *that*, *to do*. LOE.
2 *verb trans*. Bring into remembrance; commemorate; mention. Formerly also simply, remember. LOE.
†**3** *verb intrans*. Give an account; relate. Only in LME.

minge /mɪn(d)ʒ/ *noun*. *dial*. & *coarse slang*. E20.
[ORIGIN Romany, of uncertain origin.]
The female genitals. Also, women regarded collectively as a means of sexual gratification.

mingei /mɪŋˈgeɪ/ *noun*. M20.
[ORIGIN Japanese, from *min* people + *gei* arts.]
Japanese folk art; traditional Japanese handicraft.

mingimingi /ˈmɪŋɪˌmɪŋi/ *noun*. Also (*dial*.) **micky-mick** /ˈmɪkɪmɪk/. M19.
[ORIGIN Maori.]
Any of several New Zealand evergreen shrubs belonging to or formerly included in the genus *Cyathodes* (family Epacridaceae); esp. *C. juniperina* and *C. fasciculata*, with tiny green flowers and red or white berries.

minging /ˈmɪŋɪŋ/ *adjective*. *slang* (orig. *Scot*.). L20.
[ORIGIN Perh. from Scots dial. *ming* excrement + -ING[2].]
Foul-smelling; very bad or unpleasant.
■ **minger** *noun* an ugly or unattractive person, esp. a woman L20.

mingle /ˈmɪŋg(ə)l/ *verb* & *noun*. Also (earlier) †**mengle**. L15.
[ORIGIN Frequentative of MENG: see -LE[3].]
▸ **A** *verb*. **1** *verb trans*. & *intrans*. Mix, blend, combine in a mixture. Freq. foll. by *with*. L15. ▸†**b** *verb trans*. Join in (conversation, friendship, etc.) *with* another person. L16–E17. ▸†**c** *verb trans*. *fig*. Put together so as to make one. *rare* (Shakes.). Only in E17.

W. STYRON Blood mingled with the water, turning it a muddy crimson. M. PUZO He found a bundle of newly washed clothes . . and mingled his own clothes with these. M. MEYER Applause . . was mingled with hissing. A. BROOKNER A look in which superiority mingled with forbearance.

mingle eyes: see EYE *noun*.
†**2** *verb trans*. **a** Mix up so as to confuse. M16–E18. ▸**b** Form or make up by mixing various ingredients. E17–L19.
3 *verb intrans*. Of a person: move about at a social function, talking with others; circulate, mix; associate *with*. Also, join or participate *in*. E17.

Law Times He is very anxious to avoid any appearance of mingling in party disputes. J. C. OATES She must mingle, must ease into a conversation. A. T. ELLIS Women who . . prefer to mingle only with those . . as attractive as themselves.

▸ **B** *noun*. The action of mingling; the state of being mingled; a mingled mass, a mixture. Now *rare*. M16.

SWIFT To represent persons . . without any mingle of my own interest. T. BOSTON A mingle of many different seeds.

– COMB.: **mingle-mangle** a mixture, *esp*. a confused one.
■ **minglement** *noun* the action of mingling; (a) mixture: E17. **mingler** *noun* L16.

Mingrelian /mɪŋˈgriːlɪən/ *noun* & *adjective*. E17.
[ORIGIN from *Mingrelia* (see below) + -AN.]
▸ **A** *noun*. **1** A member of a people inhabiting Mingrelia, an area of the Kutais region of the Caucasus. E17.
2 The S. Caucasian language of this people. M17.
▸ **B** *adjective*. Of or pertaining to this people. L18.

mingy /ˈmɪndʒi/ *adjective*. *colloq*. E20.
[ORIGIN Perh. from M(EAN *adjective*[1] + ST)INGY *adjective*[2].]
Mean, stingy, niggardly; depressingly small.
■ **mingily** *adverb* M20.

minhag /mɪnˈhag/ *noun*. Pl. same, **-hagim** /-ˈhagɪm/. M19.
[ORIGIN Hebrew *minhāg* custom, usage, conduct, from *nāhag* to drive or lead.]
JUDAISM. A custom or practice, *esp*. one which has taken on the force of law. Also, the form of liturgy used by a particular Jewish community.

mini /ˈmɪni/ *noun*. M20.
[ORIGIN Abbreviation: cf. MINI-.]
1 A small car; a minicab; *spec*. (**M-**) (proprietary name for) a distinctive small car first made in Britain in 1959. M20.
2 A miniskirt; a minidress. M20.
3 A minicomputer. L20.

mini /ˈmɪni/ *adjective*. *colloq*. M20.
[ORIGIN Abbreviation of MINIATURE *adjective*: cf. MINI-.]
Very small, tiny.

Delaware Today Stretch your weekend into a mini summer vacation.

Mini Disc a recordable magneto-optical disc resembling a small compact disc (cf. **minidisk** s.v. MINI-).

mini- /ˈmɪni/ *combining form*. M19.
[ORIGIN from MINI(ATURE *adjective* (reinforced by MINIMUM): cf. MAXI-.]
Forming chiefly nouns denoting something small, short, or minor of its kind.
minibar (a cabinet containing) a selection of mostly alcoholic drinks placed in a hotel room for the use of a guest, a charge being added to the room bill for those used. **minibeast** *colloq*. a small invertebrate animal such as an insect or spider. **mini-break** a very short vacation. **mini-budget** a small usu. interim budget. **minibus** a bus for a relatively small number of passengers. **minicab** a car like a taxi but available only by phone. **minicam** a hand-held video camera. **minicamp** *N. Amer*. a place where a particular professional sports team carries out trials of potential new players, or training for a particular set of players, prior to its main pre-season training; the sessions held at such a place. **minicell** BIOLOGY a miniature cell, without nuclear material, produced by cell division in a particular strain of the bacterium *Escherichia coli*. **mini-coat** a short coat. **minicomputer** a computer of size and storage capacity greater than a microcomputer but smaller than a mainframe (usu. housed in one or a few cabinets). **minidisk** COMPUTING a small data-storage disk (cf. DISKETTE, ***Mini Disc*** s.v. MINI *adjective*). **minidress** a very short dress. **minifloppy (disk)** COMPUTING a small floppy disk 5¼ inches (13.3 cm) in diameter. **minigene** BIOLOGY a short (usu. coding) sequence of DNA. **minigolf** = ***miniature golf*** s.v. MINIATURE *adjective*. **minihole** ASTRONOMY a very small black hole. **mini-mall** a small shopping mall, esp. one with access to each shop from the outside rather than from an interior hallway. **minimart** *N. Amer*. a convenience store. **mini-me** *colloq*. a person closely resembling a smaller or younger version of another. ***Mini-Moke***: see MOKE *noun*[2]. **Minipiano**, **m-** (proprietary name for) a small piano. **minipill** a contraceptive pill containing a progestogen alone (not oestrogen). **mini-roundabout** a small traffic roundabout, indicated by road markings or a very low island. **mini-rugby** a simplified version of rugby with only nine players in a team.

miniseries (orig. *US*) a usu. short television series dealing with a single complete theme or plot. **miniskirt** a very short skirt. **mini-summit** an interim meeting of heads of government, usu. on a particular issue. **minitower** a small, free-standing, vertical module containing a computer's central processing unit, disk drive, etc. **minitrack** *noun* a system for tracking the position of a satellite by the phase difference between radio signals received by two aerials on the ground (usu. *attrib.*). **minivan**, (proprietary) **Mini Van** a small van; (also) a van fitted with seats in the back for transporting passengers.

miniaceous /mɪnɪˈeɪʃəs/ *adjective*. Now *rare* or *obsolete*. L17.
[ORIGIN from Latin *miniaceus*, from MINIUM: see -ACEOUS.]
Of the colour of cinnabar; vermilion.

miniate /ˈmɪnɪeɪt/ *verb trans.* M17.
[ORIGIN Latin *miniat-* pa. ppl stem of *miniare* rubricate, illuminate, from MINIUM: see -ATE³.]
Colour or paint with vermilion; rubricate, illuminate, (a manuscript).

miniature /ˈmɪnɪtʃə/ *noun & adjective*. L16.
[ORIGIN Italian *miniatura* from medieval Latin, from *miniare* MINIATE: see -URE. Cf. MINI-.]
▸ **A** *noun*. **1** An image or representation on a small scale. Also occas., a minutely finished production. L16. ▸**b** A thing that is much smaller or briefer than usual; *spec.* (*a*) CHESS a problem involving seven or fewer pieces; a game decided in a small number of moves; (*b*) a very small bottle of spirits; (*c*) a short piece of music. E20.

DRYDEN Tragedy is the miniature of human life. **b** P. CUTTING Ben and I crept up to my room to share a miniature of cherry brandy. J. MARQUAND A miniature of a man, as small as . . the dwarfed trees.

2 The art or action, orig. that of a medieval illuminator, of painting portraits on a small scale and with minute finish, usu. on ivory or vellum; a portrait of this kind. M17.

HUGH WALPOLE Painters in Enamel and Miniature. N. PEVSNER Miniatures painted minutely on parchment. A. LURIE He was tall and thin, with a short pointed beard like a man in an Elizabethan miniature.

3 The rubrication or illumination of a manuscript; a picture in an illuminated manuscript; (an) illuminated design. M17.
– PHRASES: **in miniature** on a small scale; in a brief or abridged form.
▸ **B** *adjective*. Represented, designed, etc., on a small scale; much smaller than normal; tiny. E18.

SCOTT FITZGERALD A miniature picture theatre with four rows of overstuffed chairs.

miniature camera, ***miniature poodle***, ***miniature railway***, etc. **miniature golf** a game in which a club is used to putt a small ball into a succession of holes on a green etc.
■ **miniaturist** *noun* an illuminator of manuscripts; a painter of miniatures: M19.

miniature /ˈmɪnɪtʃə/ *verb trans.* L17.
[ORIGIN from MINIATURE *noun & adjective*.]
Represent or describe in miniature; reduce to miniature dimensions.

miniaturize /ˈmɪnɪtʃərʌɪz/ *verb trans.* Also **-ise**. M20.
[ORIGIN from MINIATURE *noun & adjective* + -IZE.]
Produce in a smaller version; make small.
■ **miniaturiˈzation** *noun* the process or an instance of miniaturizing something M20.

minicom /ˈmɪnɪkɒm/ *noun*. L20.
[ORIGIN from MINI- + *com* in COMMUNICATION, after *telecom*.]
A small electronic typewriter and screen linked to a telephone system to enable people with impaired hearing or speech to send and receive messages; a communications system using such a device.
– NOTE: Proprietary name in the US.

Minié /ˈmɪnɪeɪ/ *noun & adjective*. M19.
[ORIGIN Claude-Étienne *Minié* (1804–79), French army officer.]
MILITARY HISTORY. (Designating) an elongated bullet designed by Minié or a rifle adapted for firing this bullet.

minifundium /mɪnɪˈfʌndɪəm/ *noun*. Pl. **-ia** /-ɪə/. Also **-io** /-ɪəʊ/, pl. **-ios**. M20.
[ORIGIN mod. Latin, or Spanish *minifundio* smallholding: cf. LATIFUNDIUM.]
In Latin America: a small farm or property, *esp.* one that is too small to support a single family. Usu. in *pl.*
■ **minifunˈdist**, **-sta** *noun* a person who owns or works on a minifundium M20.

minify /ˈmɪnɪfʌɪ/ *verb trans.* L17.
[ORIGIN Irreg. from Latin *minor* less, *minimus* least, after MAGNIFY.]
1 Underestimate the size or importance of. L17.
2 Reduce or lessen in size or importance. M19.
■ **minifiˈcation** *noun* L19.

minikin /ˈmɪnɪkɪn/ *noun & adjective*. M16.
[ORIGIN Dutch *minneken*, from *minne* love + *-ken* -KIN.]
▸ **A** *noun*. **1** A small or insignificant person or thing. Also *spec.*, (a term of endearment for) a slight young girl or woman (now *dial.*). M16.
2 A thin string of gut used for the treble string of a lute or viol. Also ***minikin string***. Long *rare*. M16.
3 A kind of small pin. Also ***minikin pin***. E18.
▸ **B** *adjective*. **1** Orig., dainty, elegant, sprightly. Now (*derog.*), affected, mincing. M16.
2 Of a thing: diminutive; miniature; tiny. L16.
†**3** Of a voice: shrill. Only in E17.
†**4** Designating a kind of baize. E17–E18.
– SPECIAL COLLOCATIONS: **minikin pin** = sense A.3 above. **minikin string** = sense A.2 above.

minim /ˈmɪnɪm/ *noun & adjective*. LME.
[ORIGIN As noun, repr. various ellipt. uses in medieval Latin of Latin *minimus* least, smallest, superl. of *parvus* small (see MINOR *adjective & noun*). As adjective directly from Latin *minimus*.]
▸ **A** *noun*. **1** MUSIC. A symbol for a note with the time value of half a semibreve or two crotchets, having a hollow head and a straight stem; a note of this length. LME.
2 (**M-**.) A friar belonging to the mendicant order founded by St Francis of Paola (1416–1507). M16.
3 The least possible portion (*of*). Formerly also, an atom, a minute particle. L16.
4 A person, animal, or thing of the smallest size or importance. Usu. *derog.* L16.
5 A single downstroke of a pen. L16.
6 A unit of liquid capacity in apothecaries' measure, equal to about one drop of liquid; the sixtieth part of a fluid drachm. E19.
7 A very small (usu. bronze) Roman coin. L19.
▸ **B** *adjective*. Smallest, extremely small. L17.

minima *noun* pl. of MINIMUM *noun*.

minimal /ˈmɪnɪm(ə)l/ *adjective*. M17.
[ORIGIN from Latin *minimus* (see MINIM) + -AL¹.]
1 Extremely small; of a minimum amount, quantity, or degree; very slight, negligible. M17.

A. DAVIS News media . . following a conscious policy of minimal or no coverage.

2 LINGUISTICS. Of a set or (usu.) pair of forms: distinguished by only one feature. M20.

H. A. GLEASON Calling *bill* and *pill* a minimal pair we assume that they differ by only one phoneme.

3 ART. Characterized by the use of simple or primary forms, structures, etc., often geometric and massive. M20. ▸**b** Characterized by simplicity and lack of adornment. M20.

Listener Creating huge, minimal forms with the palette knife in a few colours. **b** *Independent* A series of minimal, simple evening dresses in luxurious fabrics.

4 MUSIC. Characterized by the repetition of short phrases which change very gradually as the music proceeds. L20.
– SPECIAL COLLOCATIONS: **minimal free form** LINGUISTICS the smallest form which can be used by itself as an utterance. **minimal pair** LINGUISTICS a pair of words distinguished by a single phoneme.
■ **miniˈmality** *noun* (LINGUISTICS) the quality or character of being minimal M20. **minimalize** *verb trans.* = MINIMIZE L20. **minimally** *adverb* E20.

minimalist /ˈmɪnɪm(ə)lɪst/ *noun & adjective*. E20.
[ORIGIN from MINIMAL + -IST, or (in senses A.1, B.1) from French *minimaliste*, translating Russian *men'shevik* MENSHEVIK.]
▸ **A** *noun*. **1** (Also **M-**.) Orig. (*hist.*), a Menshevik. Later also, any person advocating small or moderate reforms or policies. E20.
2 An advocate or practitioner of minimal art; a composer of minimal music. M20.
3 An advocate or proponent of minimalism; a person who rejects superfluity or excess. L20.

J. HOLMS Her years of carrying all she owned on her back had made her something of a minimalist.

▸ **B** *adjective*. **1** Orig. (*hist.*), Menshevik. Later also, advocating moderate policies. E20.
2 Of or pertaining to minimal art or music. M20.
3 Lacking adornment; basic, simple. L20.

Zest Swedish minimalist style: polished wooden floorboards; lots of space, and pristine white walls.

■ **minimalism** *noun* (*a*) minimal art or music; (*b*) deliberate lack of decoration or adornment in style or design: E20. **minimaˈlistic** *adjective* of or pertaining to minimalism, minimalist M20.

minimax /ˈmɪnɪmaks/ *noun & adjective*. E20.
[ORIGIN from MINI(MUM + MAX(IMUM.]
MATH. ▸**A** *noun*. **1** A point in a topological space at which a function defined on the space is stationary and which has a local maximum in one direction and a local minimum in another. E20.
2 The smallest of a set of maxima. M20.
▸ **B** *attrib.* or as *adjective*. Of, pertaining to, or of the nature of a minimax; *spec.* in GAME THEORY, designating (*a*) a strategy that minimizes the greatest loss or risk to which a participant in a game etc. will be liable; (*b*) the theorem that for a finite zero-sum game with two players, the smallest maximum loss that a player can choose to risk is equal to the greatest minimum guaranteed gain. Cf. MAXIMIN. E20.

minimax /ˈmɪnɪmaks/ *verb*. M20.
[ORIGIN from MINIMAX *noun & adjective*.]
MATH. **1** *verb trans.* Make equal to a minimax value. M20.
2 *verb intrans.* Adopt or employ a minimax strategy. M20.

minimi *noun* pl. of MINIMUS *noun*.

minimise *verb* var. of MINIMIZE.

minimism /ˈmɪnɪmɪz(ə)m/ *noun*. E19.
[ORIGIN formed as MINIM *noun* + -ISM.]
1 Absorption in minute details. Now *rare* or *obsolete*. E19.
2 THEOLOGY. The policy or practice of minimizing the substance of a dogma, esp. that of papal infallibility. L19.

minimize /ˈmɪnɪmʌɪz/ *verb*. Also **-ise**. E19.
[ORIGIN from Latin *minimus* (see MINIM) + -IZE.]
1 *verb trans.* Reduce to the smallest possible amount, extent, or degree. E19.

Which? There's more than one . . layout for the carpet to minimise wastage.

2 *verb trans. & intrans.* Estimate (a thing) at the lowest possible amount, value, significance, etc.; underestimate or play down (a problem, dogma, etc.); treat (a thing) as negligible. L19.

Christian World Let no one think . . Jesus ever minimised the . . sinfulness of sin. A. HUTSCHNECKER Pride made him minimize his inner terror.

3 *verb intrans.* Attain a minimum value. L20.
■ **minimiˈzation** *noun* M19. **minimizer** *noun* M19.

minimum /ˈmɪnɪməm/ *noun & adjective*. M17.
[ORIGIN Latin, use as noun of neut. of *minimus*: see MINIM *noun & adjective*.]
▸ **A** *noun*. Pl. **-ima** /-ɪmə/, **-imums**.
†**1** The smallest portion into which matter is divisible; an atom. Also, the hypothetical smallest possible portion of time or space. M17–M18.
2 The smallest amount or quantity possible, usual, attainable, etc. L17. ▸**b** The lowest amount of a varying quantity (e.g. temperature, pressure, etc.) attained or recorded within a particular period. E19.

C. BEATON In general, L. is very business-like with a minimum of jokes and interruptions. R. K. NARAYAN Peace reigned at home, with speech reduced to a minimum.

3 MATH. The least value which a variable or a function may have; the smallest element in a set; a point at which a continuously varying quantity ceases to decrease and begins to increase; the value of a quantity at such a point. M18.
– COMB.: **minimum thermometer**: which records the lowest temperature attained since it was last set.
▸ **B** *adjective*. That is a minimum; that is the lowest possible, usual, attainable, etc. E19.

Which? Gold and platinum cards may have a minimum income level for applicants.

– SPECIAL COLLOCATIONS: ***minimum free form*** LINGUISTICS = ***MINIMAL free form***. **minimum lending rate** ECONOMICS the minimum percentage at which a central bank will discount bills (abolished in Britain in 1981).

minimus /ˈmɪnɪməs/ *noun & adjective*. L16.
[ORIGIN Latin: see MINIM.]
▸ **A** *noun*. Pl. **-mi** /-mʌɪ/.
†**1** A very small or insignificant creature. L16–L19.
2 = MINIM 7. M19.
3 ANATOMY & ZOOLOGY. The smallest finger or toe. L19.
▸ **B** *adjective*. Designating the youngest of several pupils with the same surname or the last to enter a school. (Appended to a surname and used esp. in public schools.) Cf. MINOR *adjective* 1b. L18.

mining /ˈmʌɪnɪŋ/ *verbal noun*. ME.
[ORIGIN from MINE *verb* + -ING¹.]
The action of MINE *verb*; *esp.* the art or industry of extracting metals, coal, etc., from a mine.
coal mining, ***gold mining***, ***hydraulic mining***, etc.
– COMB.: **mining hole** a hole bored to receive a blasting charge in mining; **mining town** a town in which mining is the dominant industry.

mining /ˈmʌɪnɪŋ/ *ppl adjective*. M16.
[ORIGIN from MINE *verb* + -ING².]
That mines.
mining bee any of various solitary bees of the family Andrenidae, many of which nest in tunnels in the ground, sometimes grouped in colonies.

minion /ˈmɪnjən/ *noun¹ & adjective*. E16.
[ORIGIN French *mignon* repl. Old French *mignot*: cf. MIGNON.]
▸ **A** *noun*. **1** Orig., a favourite of a monarch, prince, or other powerful person. Now, a follower or underling of a powerful person, *esp.* a servile or unimportant one. E16. ▸†**b** A lover or mistress. Chiefly *derog.* M16–L19. ▸**c** A favourite child, servant, animal, etc. Now *derog.* M16.

Q Joking genially with pressmen while his minions fawn around him.

2 A small kind of ordnance. *hist.* E16.
3 A size of type between nonpareil and brevier. M17.
†**4** A kind of peach. Also more fully ***minion peach***. L17–M19.
▸ †**B** *adjective*. **1** Dainty, elegant, fine. E16–M19.
2 Dearly loved, favourite, pet. E16–M19.

†**minion** *noun²*. E17.
[ORIGIN French from Latin MINIUM.]
1 = MINIUM. E–M17.
2 Calcined iron ore used in cement or mortar. L18–L19.

M

miniscule *noun & adjective* see MINUSCULE.

minish /ˈmɪnɪʃ/ *verb. arch.* ME.
[ORIGIN Old French *menu(i)sier*, ult. from Latin MINUTIA: cf. MINCE *verb & noun.*]
▸ **I** *verb trans.* **1** = DIMINISH 1, 2. ME. ▸**b** Break up *into* (parts etc.). *rare.* LME.
2 Disparage, belittle. *rare.* LME.
3 Take away, remove. L15.
▸ **II** *verb intrans.* **4** = DIMINISH 6. ME.
†**5** Take something away. LME–E16.

minister /ˈmɪnɪstə/ *noun.* ME.
[ORIGIN Old French & mod. French *ministre* from Latin *minister*, from *minus* less, adverb corresp. to *minor* MINOR *adjective*, parallel in formation to correl. *magister* MASTER *noun*[1].]
1 a A person acting under the authority or as an agent of another; *spec.* †(**a**) a law officer; †(**b**) a subordinate officer, an underling. Now *rare.* ME. ▸**b** A person or thing employed or used to achieve a purpose or intention, convey a gift, etc. Foll. by *of*. Now *rare* exc. as passing into sense 2. LME.

a S. JOHNSON The community, of which the magistrate is only the minister. **b** H. P. LIDDON The Angels are ministers of the Divine Will.

2 ECCLESIASTICAL. **a** A person, esp. an ordained one, with a certain liturgical ministry or function; a member of the clergy, esp. in a Protestant Church, responsible for leading or coordinating preaching, public worship, and pastoral care in a particular church, chapel, community, etc.; a pastor. ME. ▸**b** A functionary or official of a religion other than Christianity. Long *rare.* LME. ▸**c** ROMAN CATHOLIC CHURCH. (The title of) the superior of certain religious orders. Also ***minister general***. LME.

a GEO. ELIOT Something between the Catholic priest and the dissenting minister. L. M. MONTGOMERY That's the way the ministers say it in church. R. A. KNOX You will want human ministers to dispense the sacraments.

a minister of religion (esp. in official use) a member of the clergy of any denomination.

3 †**a** A servant, an attendant. LME–L18. ▸**b** A person who ministers to the wants of another. *arch.* E19.
4 POLITICS. (Also **M-**.) **a** A person appointed to act for a head of state etc. in a particular government department; a person in charge of a government department; a Secretary of State. E17. ▸**b** A diplomatic agent officially representing a state or sovereign in a foreign country, *esp.* one ranking below an ambassador. E18.

a M. E. G. DUFF The King . . immediately dismissed his Ministers. *Daily Mirror* At a Cabinet meeting some Ministers . . complained that the Chancellor had got it all wrong.

a Foreign Minister: see FOREIGN. **Minister of State** a minister in the British Government, *esp.* one holding a rank below that of a head of department. **Minister of the Crown** a minister or head of a department in the British Government. ***minister premier***: see PREMIER *adjective* 1. **Minister without Portfolio** a minister in the British Government, with Cabinet rank but not in charge of a specific department. ***premier minister***: see PREMIER *adjective* 1. ***Prime Minister***: see PRIME *adjective*.

5 A fish: = ***horn pout*** s.v. HORN *noun & adjective*. US. M19.
▪ **ministership** *noun* the office or position of a minister M16. †**ministral** *adjective* (*rare*) pertaining to a minister or agent E18–M19.

minister /ˈmɪnɪstə/ *verb.* ME.
[ORIGIN Old French & mod. French *ministrer* from Latin *ministrare*, from *minister*: see MINISTER *noun.*]
1 *verb intrans.* CHRISTIAN CHURCH. Serve or officiate at a service; act as a minister. ME.
2 *verb intrans.* Serve, esp. at table; attend to or *to* the needs of another; assist, be useful, (*to* a person, cause, etc.); be conducive or contribute *to* something. LME.
ministering angel a kind-hearted person, esp. a woman, who nurses or comforts others.
3 *verb trans.* Provide, supply, impart, (something necessary or helpful). Formerly also, administer (justice, a sacrament, etc.). *arch.* LME.

A. P. STANLEY The story . . was able to minister true consolation.

ministerial /mɪnɪˈstɪərɪəl/ *adjective & noun.* M16.
[ORIGIN French *ministériel* or late Latin *ministerialis*, from Latin *ministerium* MINISTRY, but app. interpreted as deriv. of MINISTER *noun*: see -IAL.]
▸ **A** *adjective.* **1** Pertaining to the office, function, or character of a minister of religion. M16.
2 Pertaining to or entrusted with the execution of the law or the commands of a superior. L16.
3 Subsidiary or instrumental in achieving a purpose etc. E17.

DE QUINCEY We may admit arts of style and ornamental composition as the ministerial part of rhetoric.

4 Of or pertaining to a Minister of State or a government department; supporting the Government against the Opposition. M17.

Economist Too many MPs dream only of ministerial office.

▸ **B** *noun.* †**1** In *pl.* Subsidiary provisions. Only in M17.
2 *hist.* An executive household officer under the feudal system. E19.
▪ **ministerialism** *noun* support for the Government E19. **ministerialist** *noun* a supporter of the Government L18. **ministerially** *adverb* in the manner or capacity of a minister E17.

ministrable /ˈmɪnɪstrəb(ə)l/ *adjective & noun.* E20.
[ORIGIN French, formed as MINISTER *verb*: see -ABLE.]
POLITICS. (A person who is) likely or expected to become a minister.

ministrant /ˈmɪnɪstr(ə)nt/ *adjective & noun.* M16.
[ORIGIN Latin *ministrant-* pres. ppl stem of *ministrare*: see MINISTER *verb*, -ANT[1].]
▸ **A** *adjective.* That ministers. M16.
▸ **B** *noun.* A person who ministers. E19.

ministrate /ˈmɪnɪstreɪt/ *verb trans.* Long *rare.* L15.
[ORIGIN Latin *ministrat-*: see MINISTRATION, -ATE[3].]
Administer.

ministration /mɪnɪˈstreɪʃ(ə)n/ *noun.* ME.
[ORIGIN Old French, or Latin *ministratio(n-)*, from *ministrat-* pa. ppl stem of *ministrare* MINISTER *verb*: see -ATION.]
1 The action or an act of serving or ministering, esp. in religious matters; in *pl.*, the services of a minister of religion etc. ME.
†**2** The action of administering a sacrament, justice, an estate, etc.; administration. ME–L16.
†**3** Agency, instrumentality. LME–M16.
4 The action of supplying, providing, or giving something. Foll. by *of*. L15.

†**ministrative** *adjective.* M–L19.
[ORIGIN App. from MINISTER *verb* + -ATIVE.]
Pertaining to or of the nature of ministration; affording service or assistance.

ministrator /ˈmɪnɪstreɪtə/ *noun. rare.* LME.
[ORIGIN Latin, from *ministrare*: see MINISTER *verb*, -ATOR.]
A person who ministers or administers. Formerly also, the executor of a will.

†**ministrer** *noun.* LME–M19.
[ORIGIN from MINISTER *verb* + -ER[1].]
A person who ministers or serves.

ministress /ˈmɪnɪstrɪs/ *noun.* L15.
[ORIGIN from MINISTER *noun* + -ESS[1].]
A female minister. Chiefly *fig.*

M. AKENSIDE Beauty sent from heaven, The lovely ministress of truth and good.

ministry /ˈmɪnɪstri/ *noun.* ME.
[ORIGIN Latin *ministerium*, from MINISTER *noun.*]
1 The functions or a particular function of a minister, priest, etc.; the action or an act of religious ministration. ME. ▸**b** *collect.* The clergy; the ministers of a Church, esp. the Established Church. Now *rare.* M16. ▸**c** The period of tenure of a particular minister. M16. ▸**d** *The* clerical profession or calling; the office of minister of a church or congregation. M16.

J. SWAN A certain Priest . . was suspended from his ministry. **c** *Church Times* He continued to serve the college throughout his ministry. **d** D. CUPITT Being intended for the ministry he entered Strasburg University to study theology.

2 The action of ministering; ministration. Now *rare.* LME. ▸†**b** A particular kind of ministration; a function, an office. LME–M17. ▸†**c** The condition or fact of being an agent or instrument; agency, instrumentality. L16–L19.

TENNYSON My idea of heaven is the perpetual ministry of one soul to another. **c** A. PHELPS Heroic believers become such by the ministry of heroic pains.

3 *collect.* The body of executive officers responsible for the functions of government or the law; now *spec.* the ministers responsible for the administration of a country or state. E18. ▸**b** The period of office of a government or a government minister. E19.

b M. DRABBLE The novel also records the history of the duke of Omnium's ministry.

4 (Also **M-**.) A government department headed by a minister; the building occupied by a government department. M19.

C. BROOKS Pickthorn was furious—but furious!—with Churchill about the reconstruction of the Ministry.

Ministry of Agriculture, ***Ministry of Defence***, ***Ministry of the Interior***, etc.

minium /ˈmɪnɪəm/ *noun.* LME.
[ORIGIN Latin.]
1 Cinnabar, esp. as a red pigment; vermilion. *obsolete* exc. *hist.* LME.
2 Any red earth. Long *rare* or *obsolete*. E17.
3 = ***red lead*** s.v. RED *adjective*. M17.

miniver /ˈmɪnɪvə/ *noun.* Also **-nev-**. ME.
[ORIGIN Anglo-Norman *menuver* from Old French & mod. French *menu vair*, from *menu* little (see MENU) + VAIR.]
1 A kind of fur (now plain white) used as a lining and trimming in ceremonial dress. L16.
2 Orig., the animal from which this fur was (supposedly) obtained. Now only (*dial.*), a stoat or ermine in its white winter coat. E17.

minivet /ˈmɪnɪvɪt/ *noun.* M19.
[ORIGIN Perh. alt. of Latin *miniat-* (see MINIATE), with ref. to the typical red and black plumage of the male.]
Any of various brightly coloured cuckoo shrikes of the genus *Pericrocotus*, of tropical Asia.

mink /mɪŋk/ *noun & adjective.* LME.
[ORIGIN Uncertain: rel. to Swedish *menk*, *mänk*: cf. Low German *mink* otter.]
▸ **A** *noun.* **1** The skins or dark brown fur of the mink (see sense 2 below); a garment made of this fur. LME.
2 Either of two semi-aquatic mammals of the genus *Mustela* that resemble stoats, *M. vison*, native to N. America and farmed for its fur, and the European *M. lutreola*. E17.
3 A dark brown colour. M20.
▸ **B** *attrib.* or as *adjective*. Made of the fur of the mink. Also, of the colour mink. M19.

minke /ˈmɪŋkə, -ki/ *noun.* M20.
[ORIGIN Norwegian, perh. from *Meincke* a 19th-cent. whaling gunner, who mistook it for the larger blue whale.]
In full ***minke whale***. A small baleen whale, *Balaenoptera acutorostrata*. Also called ***piked whale***, ***lesser rorqual***.

Minkowski /mɪŋˈkɒfski/ *noun.* E20.
[ORIGIN Hermann *Minkowski* (1864–1909), Russian-born German mathematician.]
PHYSICS. Used *attrib.* with ref. to various concepts occurring in or arising from the work of Minkowski, esp. his theory that the universe has four orthogonal dimensions (the three spatial dimensions and time).

Minn. *abbreviation.*
Minnesota.

minnarichi *noun* var. of MINNERICHI.

Minnelied /ˈmɪnəliːt/ *noun.* Pl. ***-lieder*** /-liːdə(r)/. E19.
[ORIGIN German, from *Minne* love + *Lied* song.]
A love song written by a Minnesinger, or in the style of the Minnesingers.

minneola /mɪnɪˈəʊlə/ *noun.* M20.
[ORIGIN *Minneola*, a town in Florida, USA.]
A thin-skinned, deep reddish variety of tangelo.

minnerichi /mɪnəˈrɪtʃi/ *noun. Austral.* Also **mi(n)na-**. E20.
[ORIGIN Australian Aboriginal language of South Australia.]
The red mulga, *Acacia cyperophylla*.

Minnesinger /ˈmɪnəsɪŋə/ *noun.* Also **m-**. E19.
[ORIGIN German, from *Minne* love + †*Singer* (mod. *Sänger*) singer.]
A German lyric poet or singer of the 12th to 14th cents.

Minnesong /ˈmɪnəsɒŋ/ *noun.* M19.
[ORIGIN German *Minnesang*, from *Minne* love + *Sang* song.]
A song of a Minnesinger; the corpus of such songs. Cf. MINNELIED.

Minnesota /mɪnɪˈsəʊtə/ *noun.* M20.
[ORIGIN formed as MINNESOTAN.]
Minnesota Multiphasic Personality Inventory, a personality test made up of over 500 items, the responses to which are graded for various personality traits. Abbreviation ***MMPI***.

Minnesotan /mɪnɪˈsəʊtən/ *noun & adjective.* M19.
[ORIGIN from *Minnesota* (see below) + -AN.]
(A native or inhabitant) of Minnesota, a state in the north central US.

minnie /ˈmɪni/ *noun*[1]. M16.
[ORIGIN Uncertain: perh. childish alt. of *mammy*.]
1 One's mother. *Scot. & N. English.* M16.
2 In Orkney and Shetland: one's grandmother; an old woman. L19.

Minnie /ˈmɪni/ *noun*[2]. *slang.* Also **m-**. E20.
[ORIGIN Abbreviation of MINENWERFER.]
MILITARY HISTORY. (A bomb discharged by) a German trench mortar in the First World War.
moaning Minnie: see MOANING *ppl adjective*.

minnow /ˈmɪnəʊ/ *noun.* LME.
[ORIGIN Perh. repr. Old English word cogn. with Old High German *muniwa* (translating Latin *capito* a large-headed fish) but infl. by Old French *menuise*, from Proto-Romance word meaning 'small objects': cf. MINUTIA.]
1 A small freshwater cyprinid fish, *Phoxinus phoxinus*, common in streams, lakes, and ponds in Europe. Also *loosely*, any small (esp. cyprinid) fish; *dial.* a stickleback. LME. ▸**b** A small or insignificant person or thing. L16.

b *Sunday Times* The airline is still a minnow by the standards of the big flag carriers.

2 ANGLING. A minnow attached to a hook for use as bait; an artificial bait resembling this. E17.
– COMB.: **minnow-fisher** a person who fishes for minnows or with minnows as bait.

Minoan /mɪˈnəʊən/ *adjective & noun.* L19.
[ORIGIN from (Latin) *Minōs*, Greek *Minōs*, legendary king of Crete to whom a palace excavated at Knossos was attributed + -AN.]
▸ **A** *adjective.* Of or pertaining to the Bronze Age civilization of Crete (*c* 3000–1100 BC) or its people, culture, or language. L19.

▸ **B** *noun*. **1** A native or inhabitant of the Minoan world. **E20.**
2 The language or scripts associated with the Minoan civilization. **M20.**

Min of Ag /mɪn əv ˈag/ *noun phr. colloq.* **M20.**
[**ORIGIN** Abbreviation.]
The Ministry of Agriculture, Fisheries, and Food in the British Government.

minol /ˈmʌɪnɒl/ *noun*. **M20.**
[**ORIGIN** Prob. from **MINE** *noun* + **-OL**.]
An explosive consisting of a mixture of ammonium nitrate, TNT, and aluminium powder.

minor /ˈmʌɪnə/ *adjective & noun*. **ME.**
[**ORIGIN** Latin, compar. of *parvus* small, rel. to *minuere* lessen. Of Franciscan friars from Old French *menour* in *freres menours* lit. 'lesser brothers', medieval Latin *fratres minores*.]
▸ **A** *adjective*. **1** Lesser; designating or pertaining to the lesser or relatively lesser of or *of* two things, classes, etc.; opp. ***major***. Also, comparatively unimportant or insignificant; (of an operation) relatively simple or small scale. In earliest use (**M-**), designating a Franciscan friar. **ME.** ▸**b** Designating the younger of two pupils with the same surname or the second to enter a school. (Appended to a surname and used esp. in public schools.) Cf. **MINIMUS** *adjective*. **L18.**

D. CARNEGIE He praised my work, assured me that he only wanted a minor change. F. ASTAIRE Harriet had a prominent role, but . . Betty and Lucille were still playing minor parts.

2 Of less than full age; below the age of majority. Now *rare*. **L15.**
3 *LOGIC*. (Of a term) functioning as the subject of the conclusion in a syllogism; (of a premiss) containing the minor term of a syllogism. **L16.**
4 That constitutes the minority. **M17.**
5 *MUSIC*. (Of an interval) smaller by a semitone than the correlative major interval; (of a scale) with semitones above the second, fifth, and seventh notes; (of a key) based on a minor scale, tending to produce a melancholy effect. **L17.**
▸ **B** *noun*. **1** (**M-**.) *ellipt*. A Franciscan friar. **ME.**
2 *LOGIC*. A minor term or premiss. **LME.**
3 A person who has not yet attained his or her majority. Cf. **INFANT** *noun*[1] 2. **E17.**

L. DUNCAN We're minors, aren't we? Not one of us is eighteen yet.

4 A minor interval, key, scale, etc. (*MUSIC*); a minor theatre, a minor work; a minor company or organization. **L18.**
5 Any of various noctuid moths chiefly of the genus *Oligia*. Usu. with specifying word. **M19.**
6 In a university etc.: (a qualification in) a subject or course secondary to one's main subject or course. **L19.**
7 *BRIDGE*. (A card in) a minor suit. **E20.**
– **SPECIAL COLLOCATIONS & PHRASES**: ***harmonic minor***: see **HARMONIC** *adjective*. **in a minor key** (of a novel, life, etc.) understated, uneventful. ***MELODIC minor***. **minor axis** *GEOMETRY* the axis of an ellipse which passes through the centre at right angles to the major axis. ***minor canon***: see **CANON** *noun*[2] 2. **minor determinant** *MATH*. a determinant whose matrix is formed from that of another determinant by deleting one or more rows and columns. **minor league** *N. Amer.* a league of professional clubs in baseball, football, etc., below the level of the major leagues. **minor orders** *CHRISTIAN CHURCH* the degrees of the ordained ministry below those of bishop, priest, deacon, and (formerly, in the West) subdeacon. **minor piece** *CHESS* a knight, a bishop. ***minor planet***: see **PLANET** *noun*[1]. ***Minor Prophet***: see **PROPHET**. **minor suit** *BRIDGE* the suit of diamonds or clubs. ***minor TRANQUILLIZER***. ***quint minor***: see **QUINT** *noun*[2]. ***TERES minor***. ***tierce minor***: see **TIERCE** *noun*[1] 4. ***tonic minor***: see **TONIC** *adjective* 4. ***URSA Minor***. ***VARIOLA minor***.

minor /ˈmʌɪnə/ *verb intrans*. Chiefly *N. Amer.* **M20.**
[**ORIGIN** from **MINOR** *adjective & noun*.]
Foll. by *in*: study or qualify in as a subsidiary subject at a university, college, etc.

minorate /ˈmʌɪnəreɪt/ *verb trans*. Pa. pple & ppl adjective **-ated**, (earlier) †**-ate**. **LME.**
[**ORIGIN** medieval Latin *minorat-* pa. ppl stem of *minorare* diminish, from **MINOR** *adjective & noun*: see **-ATE**[3].]
Diminish, lessen, reduce.
■ **minoration** *noun* **LME.** †**minorative** *adjective & noun* (**a**) *adjective* that diminishes or lessens, gently laxative; (**b**) *noun* a gentle laxative: **M16–E19.**

Minorca /mɪˈnɔːkə/ *noun*. **M19.**
[**ORIGIN** formed as **MINORCAN**.]
A variety of the domestic fowl with black, white, or blue glossy plumage.

Minorcan /mɪˈnɔːk(ə)n/ *adjective & noun*. **M18.**
[**ORIGIN** from *Minorca*, Spanish *Menorca* (see below) + **-AN**.]
▸ **A** *adjective*. Of or pertaining to Minorca, the easternmost of the Balearic Islands in the western Mediterranean. **M18.**
▸ **B** *noun*. A native or inhabitant of Minorca. **M19.**

Minoress /ˈmʌɪnərɪs/ *noun*. *obsolete* exc. *hist.* **LME.**
[**ORIGIN** Old French *menouresse*, from *menour*: see **MINOR** *adjective & noun*, **-ESS**[1].]
A Franciscan nun of the second order, a Poor Clare.

Minorite /ˈmʌɪnərʌɪt/ *adjective & noun*. *arch.* **M16.**
[**ORIGIN** from **MINOR** *adjective & noun* + **-ITE**[1].]
▸ **A** *adjective*. Of the order of Friars Minor, Franciscan. **M16.**
▸ **B** *noun*. **1** A Friar Minor, a Franciscan. **M16.**
†**2** A person of minor rank or concerned with minor matters. **M17–E19.**

minority /mʌɪˈnɒrɪti, mɪ-/ *noun & adjective*. **L15.**
[**ORIGIN** French *minorité* or medieval Latin *minoritas*, from **MINOR** *adjective & noun*: see **-ITY**.]
▸ **A** *noun*. **1** The state of being a minor; the period of a person's life prior to attaining full age. **L15.** ▸†**b** The condition or fact of being smaller, inferior, or subordinate. **M16–E18.**

J. R. GREEN The long minority of Henry the Sixth who was a boy . . at his father's death.

2 The smaller number or part; a number which is less than half the whole number. Also *spec.*, (the number of votes cast for or by) the smaller party voting together in a deliberative assembly or electoral body. **M18.**

H. WILSON The right of a minority to differ from the majority. D. FRANCIS He was one of the minority of men in morning suits.

3 A small group of people differing from the rest of a community in ethnic origin, religion, language, or culture; a member of such a group. **E20.**

Equals A campaign against racial hatred and the discrimination . . facing ethnic minorities. I. MURDOCH You're so keen on the rights of minorities, underprivileged groups or whatever jargon you use.

national minority: see **NATIONAL** *adjective*.
▸ **B** *attrib.* or as *adjective*. Of, for, composed of, or appealing to a minority of people. **L18.**

Language The lack of trained personnel . . qualified to work with minority children. R. DAWKINS Zoology is still a minority subject in universities.

– **COMB.**: **minority carrier** *ELECTRONICS* in a semiconductor, a charge carrier (electron or hole) of the kind carrying the smaller proportion of the electric current; **minority debt**: incurred by a person while underage; **minority government**: in which the governing party has most seats but still less than half the total; **minority movement** a movement to secure justice or proper representation for minorities; **minority report** a separate report presented by members of a committee etc. who disagree with the majority.

minot /mino/ *noun*. *obsolete* exc. *hist.* Pl. pronounced same. **L16.**
[**ORIGIN** French, from *mine* a measure of 6 bushels.]
A former French unit of capacity, normally equal to 3 French bushels (approx. 39.36 litres, 8.66 gallons).

Minotaur /ˈmʌɪnətɔː/ *noun*. **OE.**
[**ORIGIN** Old French (mod. *Minotaure*) from Latin *Minotaurus* from Greek *minōtauros*, from *Minōs* (see **MINOAN**) + *tauros* bull.]
GREEK MYTHOLOGY. A monster with the body of a man and the head of a bull, which was kept in a Cretan labyrinth and fed with human flesh.
– **COMB.**: **minotaur beetle** a black Eurasian dung beetle, *Typhaeus typhoeus*, with three horns on the thorax.

minoxidil /mɪˈnɒksɪdɪl/ *noun*. **L20.**
[**ORIGIN** from **A)MINO-** + **OX(IDE** + *-il*, of unknown origin.]
PHARMACOLOGY. A pyrimidine derivative used to treat hypertension which can also promote hair growth when applied topically; 2, 6-diamino-4-piperidinopyridine-1-oxide, $C_9H_{15}N_5O$.

minster /ˈmɪnstə/ *noun*.
[**ORIGIN** Old English *mynster* = Old High German *munistri* (German *Münster*), Middle Dutch *monster*, Old Norse *mustari* rel. to ecclesiastical Latin *monasterium* **MONASTERY**.]
†**1** A monastery; a Christian religious house. **OE–E16.**
2 The church of a monastery; a church originating in a monastic establishment. Also, any large or important church, *esp.* a collegiate church or former collegiate church. Also ***minster church***. **OE.** ▸†**b** *transf.* A temple. **ME–L16.**
Beverley Minster, ***York Minster***, etc.

minstrel /ˈmɪnstr(ə)l/ *noun*. **ME.**
[**ORIGIN** Old French *menestral*, *-(e)rel*, *mini-* entertainer, handicraftsman, servant from Provençal *menest(ai)ral* officer, attendant, employee, musician from late Latin *ministerialis* official, officer, from Latin *ministerium*: see **MINISTRY**, **-AL**[1].]
†**1** A servant with a special function. *rare*. Only in **ME.**
2 Orig., a person employed by a patron to entertain with singing, storytelling, buffoonery, etc.; a jester. Now (*hist.*), a medieval singer or musician, *esp.* one singing or reciting heroic or lyric poetry and providing musical accompaniment. **ME.**
3 *transf.* Any musician, singer, or poet. *poet. & rhet.* **E18.**
4 *hist.* A member of a band of entertainers with blacked faces, performing songs and music ostensibly of black origin. Usu. in *pl.* **M19.**
blackface minstrel, ***Negro minstrel***.
■ †**minstrelship** *noun* minstrelsy, the performance of music **L15–E19.**

minstrelsy /ˈmɪnstr(ə)lsi/ *noun*. **ME.**
[**ORIGIN** Old French *menestralsie*, from *menestrel*: see **MINSTREL**.]
1 The art or occupation of a minstrel; the practice of playing and singing. *arch.* **ME.**
2 A group or gathering of minstrels; *collect.* musicians, singers. **ME.**
†**3** Musical instruments collectively; a musical instrument. **LME–E16.**
4 Minstrel poetry. **E19.**

mint /mɪnt/ *noun*[1].
[**ORIGIN** Old English *mynet*, corresp. (with variation of gender) to Old Frisian *menote*, *munte*, Old Saxon *munita* (Dutch *munt*), Old High German *munizza*, *muniz* (German *Münze*), from Germanic, from Latin *moneta*: see **MONEY** *noun*.]
1 A coin; money. Now *rare* or *obsolete*. **OE.**
2 A place where money is coined, usu. under the authority and direction of the state. **LME.** ▸**b** *fig.* A place where something originates or is generated; a source, a fount, (*of*). **M16.**

b H. SACHEVERELL The Pulpit, and the Press, those Mints of Atheism. TENNYSON But thou and I are one in kind, As moulded like in Nature's mint.

†**3** Coinage. **L15–E17.**
4 A set of machines for coining. **L16.**
5 A vast sum of or *of* money. **M17.**

M. M. R. KHAN How elegantly she dresses . . . Must have cost her husbands a mint.

– **COMB.**: **mint-bill** *hist.* a bill or promissory note given by an officer of the mint to an importer of bullion deposited for coining; **mint condition** the condition of a freshly minted coin, as-new condition; chiefly in ***in mint condition***; **mint-mark** a mark on a coin indicating the mint at which it was struck; **mint par**, **mint parity** (more fully ***mint par of exchange***, ***mint parity of exchange***) (**a**) the ratio between the gold equivalent of the currency units of two countries; (**b**) the rate of currency exchange between two countries based on this ratio; **mint master** (**a**) the superintendent of coinage at a mint; (**b**) a person who coins new ideas, words, etc.; **mint price** the standard price of bullion as recognized at a mint; **mint state** = ***mint condition*** above.

mint /mɪnt/ *noun*[2] *& adjective*[1].
[**ORIGIN** Old English *minte* = Old High German *minza* (German *Minze*), from West Germanic, from Latin *ment(h)a* from Greek *minthē*, *minthos*, prob. of Mediterranean origin.]
▸ **A** *noun*. **1** (The leaves of) any of various aromatic labiate plants of the genus *Mentha*, which bear lilac flowers and include spearmint, peppermint, and other culinary herbs; *spec.* spearmint, *Mentha spicata*, or another cultivated form. Formerly freq. in *pl.* in collect. sense. **OE.** ▸**b** With specifying word: any of various plants of allied genera, e.g. *Clinopodium* and (in N. America) *Pycnanthemum* and *Monarda*. **ME.**
bergamot mint: see **BERGAMOT** *noun*[2] 3. ***horsemint***: see **HORSE** *noun*. **PEPPERMINT**. **SPEARMINT**. **b** ***catmint***: see **CAT** *noun*[1].
2 A sweet or chocolate flavoured with an extract of such a plant, esp. peppermint. **L19.**
3 Mint-green colour. **M20.**
▸ **B** *attrib.* or as *adjective*. Flavoured with, or containing mint; of the colour of mint. **E19.**
– **SPECIAL COLLOCATIONS & COMB.**: **mint cake** (**a**) a very thin sweet cake flavoured with chopped fresh mint; (**b**) a peppermint-flavoured sweet. **mint-green** *adjective & noun* (of) a pale green colour like that of mint. **mint julep** (chiefly *US*) an iced alcoholic drink flavoured with fresh mint. **mint sauce** (**a**) finely chopped mint in vinegar and sugar, usu. eaten with roast lamb; (**b**) *slang* money, cash. **mint-sling** *US* an alcoholic drink flavoured with mint. **mint tea**, **mint-water** a cordial distilled from mint.

mint /mɪnt/ *noun*[3]. Long *obsolete* exc. *dial.* **LME.**
[**ORIGIN** Uncertain: perh. contr. of **MINUTE** *noun*.]
A small insect, a mite, a weevil.

mint /mɪnt/ *adjective*[2]. **E20.**
[**ORIGIN** Ellipt. for *in mint condition*: see **MINT** *noun*[1].]
In mint condition, as new.

L. O'KEEFFE As conspicuously new as a pair of mint Levis.

mint /mɪnt/ *verb*[1]. Now *arch. & dial.*
[**ORIGIN** Old English *myntan*, prob. ult. from Indo-European base of **MIND** *noun*[1].]
†**1** *verb intrans. & trans.* Think. **OE–ME.**
2 *verb intrans. & trans.* Intend; try; venture (*to do*). **OE.**
3 *verb trans.* Attempt, aim, (a blow). **OE.**
4 *verb intrans.* Aim a blow; take aim in shooting; make a threatening movement. (Foll. by *at*, *to*.) **ME.** ▸†**b** Make a movement to seize something. Foll. by *to*. **E17–E19.**
5 *verb intrans.* Make an attempt; aim *at*, aspire *to*. **ME.**
6 *verb trans.* Mention, speak of. Long *rare*. **LME.**

mint /mɪnt/ *verb*[2] *trans*. **OE.**
[**ORIGIN** from **MINT** *noun*[1].]
1 Make (coin) by stamping metal. **OE.** ▸**b** Produce or invent (a word, phrase, idea, etc.) for the first time. Cf. **COIN** *verb*[1]. **M17.**

b COLERIDGE To mint a more appropriate term. *fig.*: F. POPCORN A newly minted female college graduate.

†**2** Convert (bullion) into coin; *fig.* impress with a stamp or character. **M16–M18.**

H. BROOKE To have his soul melted and minted as mine has been.

mintage /ˈmɪntɪdʒ/ *noun*. **L16.**
[**ORIGIN** from **MINT** *noun*[1] or *verb*[2] + **-AGE**.]
1 The action or process of minting money; *fig.* the coining of a new word, idea, etc. **L16.**

H. J. S. MAINE Few literary theories of modern mintage have more to recommend them.

2 The product of a mint; a coin or coins originating from a specified source. Freq. *fig.* **M17.**
3 The cost of or duty paid for minting. **M17.**
4 *fig.* A stamp, an impression. **M17.**

minted /ˈmɪntɪd/ *adjective*[1]. **L19.**
[ORIGIN from **MINT** *noun*[2] + **-ED**[2].]
Flavoured with mint.

minted /ˈmɪntɪd/ *adjective*[2]. *slang.* **L20.**
[ORIGIN from **MINT** *verb*[2] + **-ED**[1].]
Having plenty of money, rich.

minter /ˈmɪntə/ *noun.*
[ORIGIN Old English *mynetere* = Old Saxon *muniteri* (Middle Dutch, Dutch *munter*), Old High German *munizzāri*, from late Latin *monetarius*, from *moneta*: see **MONEY** *noun*, **-ARY**[1].]
†**1** A money-changer. **OE–ME.**
2 A person who coins or stamps money. **OE.**

Minton /ˈmɪntən/ *noun & adjective.* **M19.**
[ORIGIN See below.]
(Designating) pottery made at Stoke-on-Trent, Staffordshire, England, from 1793 onwards, by Thomas Minton (1766–1836) and his successors.

minty /ˈmɪnti/ *adjective*[1]. **M19.**
[ORIGIN from **MINT** *noun*[2] + **-Y**[1].]
Containing or full of mint; having the flavour of mint.

minty /ˈmɪnti/ *noun & adjective*[2]. *US slang.* **M20.**
[ORIGIN Unknown.]
▸ **A** *noun.* A homosexual man or woman. **M20.**
▸ **B** *adjective.* Homosexual; (of a man) conspicuously affecting female mannerisms, effeminate. **M20.**

minuend /ˈmɪnjʊɛnd/ *noun.* **E18.**
[ORIGIN Latin *minuendus* (sc. *numerus* number) gerundive of *minuere* diminish: see **-END**.]
MATH. The number from which another number (the subtrahend) is to be subtracted.

minuet /mɪnjʊˈɛt/ *noun & verb.* Also **men-** /mɛn-/. **L17.**
[ORIGIN French *menuet* use as noun of adjective *menuet* small, fine, delicate, dim. of *menu* small: see **MENU**, **-ET**[1].]
▸ **A** *noun.* **1** A slow stately dance for two in triple time, fashionable in the 18th cent. **L17.**
2 A piece of music for this dance or in its rhythm, often forming a movement in a suite, sonata, or symphony. **L17.**
▸ **B** *verb intrans.* Dance a minuet. **M19.**

minuetto /minuˈetto, mɪnjʊˈɛtəʊ/ *noun.* Pl. ***-tti*** /-t(t)i/, ***-ttos*** /-təʊz/. **E18.**
[ORIGIN Italian.]
= **MINUET** *noun.*

minus /ˈmʌɪnəs/ *preposition, noun, adverb, & adjective.* **L15.**
[ORIGIN Latin, use as adverb of neut. of *minor* adjective: see **MINOR** *adjective & noun.*]
▸ **A** *preposition* **I 1** Made less by, reduced by, with the subtraction or deduction of, (a specified number, amount, or proportion); below zero by (a specified amount). Also (*colloq.*), lacking, deprived of, without. **L15.**

J. MARQUAND His left hand was . . minus three fingers. R. HOLMES A snowy night with a temperature of minus eighteen degrees. *Which?* The cost of replacing the items . . minus a deduction.

▸ **II 2** As the name of the mathematical symbol −, signifying a negative quantity, quality, or grade, or something subtracted. **L16.**

P. WILSON I had given her a C minus in the freshman course.

alpha minus, ***beta minus***, ***gamma minus***: see **ALPHA** etc. ***omega minus***: see **OMEGA** 2.
▸ **B** *noun.* **1** The mathematical symbol −. Also ***minus sign***. **L16.**
2 A quantity subtracted; a negative quantity; a loss, a deficiency, a disadvantage. **E18.**

Daily Telegraph The current account had been in deficit with a minus of £75 million. *American Speech* For almost every minus, there is a compensating plus.

▸ **C** *adverb.* (Charged) negatively. **M18.**
▸ **D** *adjective.* **1** Of a quantity: negative, preceded by the minus sign; of the nature of a negative quantity or a deficit. Also (*colloq.*), lacking; insignificant; non-existent, absent. **L18.**

Moneypaper A tendency to exaggerate plus and minus points.

2 Negatively charged. **L18.**
3 *PRINTING & PHOTOGRAPHY.* Designating a complementary colour, i.e. that of white light from which a specified colour has been removed. **E20.**

minuscule /ˈmɪnəskjuːl/ *noun & adjective.* Also (*non-standard*) **mini-** /ˈmɪnɪ-/. **E18.**
[ORIGIN French from Latin *minuscula* (sc. *littera* letter) fem. of *minusculus* rather less, dim. of **MINOR** *adjective & noun*: see **-CULE**.]
▸ **A** *noun.* In *PALAEOGRAPHY*: a small letter, as opp. to a capital or uncial; (a manuscript in) a small cursive script developed from early Roman hands and written as between four notional lines (with ascenders and descenders). Formerly also (*TYPOGRAPHY*), a small or lower-case letter. **E18.**
▸ **B** *adjective.* **1 a** *TYPOGRAPHY.* Of a letter: small, lower-case. Now *rare* or *obsolete*. **E18.** ▸**b** *PALAEOGRAPHY.* Of a letter: small, not capital or uncial; of, written in, or concerning minuscules. **M19.**

b *Bodleian Library Record* An elegant minuscule script of about the mid-twelfth century.

2 Extremely small, tiny; very insignificant or unimportant. **L19.**

New York Times Such concentration on minuscule . . matters is a waste of time. W. STYRON Alcohol in minuscule amounts . . caused me nausea.

— NOTE: Spelling *miniscule*, formed by assoc. with **MINI-**, is very common but regarded as erroneous.
■ **minuscular** /mɪˈnʌskjʊlə/ *adjective* (*PALAEOGRAPHY*) of the nature of a minuscule, composed of minuscules **M18.**

minute /ˈmɪnɪt/ *noun & verb.* **LME.**
[ORIGIN Old French & mod. French from late Latin use as noun of Latin *minuta* fem. of *minutus*: see **MINUTE** *adjective*. In senses 1 and 2 of noun from medieval Latin *pars minuta prima* first minute part, the 1/60 of a unit in a system of sexagesimal fractions. In sense 4 of noun perh. from medieval Latin *minuta scriptura* a draft in small writing.]
▸ **A** *noun.* **1** The sixtieth part of an hour. Also, any of the sixty lines or marks on the face of a clock etc., marking intervals of one minute. **LME.** ▸**b** A short space of time; an instant; a (specified) moment. **LME.** ▸**c** The distance one can travel in a minute by a stated or implied means. **L19.**

P. BARKER Rivers had a few minutes before his next appointment. **b** N. BAKER I lost sight of her for a minute.

2 The sixtieth part of a degree of angular measurement. Also ***minute of arc***. **LME.**
3 †**a** A coin of very small value; a mite. **LME–L16.** ▸**b** A small particular, a detail; a very small or unimportant thing. *obsolete* exc. *dial.* **L15.**
4 a A rough draft; a note or memorandum giving instructions to an agent etc., or serving as a reminder or record of a transaction etc. Also (in *pl.*), a brief summary of the proceedings at a meeting. **LME.** ▸**b** An official memorandum authorizing or recommending a course of action. **M16.** ▸**c** *SCOTS LAW.* A memorandum relating to matters of procedure or evidence presented to a court by a party to a suit. **M19.**

a R. WRIGHT The minutes and transcripts of conferences involving the Six Nations.

— PHRASES: ***arc minute***: see **ARC** *noun*. **at the minute** at the present time. **just a minute** *interjection* (**a**) requesting someone to wait a short time; (**b**) as a prelude to a query or objection. ***last minute***, ***last-minute***: see **LAST** *adjective*. ***mad minute***: see **MAD** *adjective*. **the minute (that)** as soon as. ***up to the minute***: see **UP** *adverb*[1]. **wait a minute** *imper. & interjection* = ***just a minute*** above.
— COMB.: **minute bell**: tolled at intervals of a minute, esp. as a sign of mourning or distress; **minute book**: containing systematic records of the transactions of a society, court, etc.; **minute glass** a sand glass that runs for a minute; **minute gun**: fired at intervals of a minute, esp. at a funeral; **minute hand** the long hand of a clock or watch, which indicates minutes; †**minute-jack** a fickle or changeable person; **minute steak** a thin slice of steak to be cooked quickly; **minute wheel**: that moves the minute hand of a clock or watch.
▸ **B** *verb trans.* **1 a** Draft (a document, a scheme); record in a minute or the minutes; make a minute of the contents of (a document). **E17.** ▸**b** Inform (someone) by means of a minute or memorandum; send minutes to (a person). **E20.**
2 Time to the nearest minute; time accurately. **E17.**
■ **minuter** *noun* a person who writes minutes or notes proceedings **E19.**

minute /mʌɪˈnjuːt/ *adjective.* **LME.**
[ORIGIN Latin *minutus* pa. pple of *minuere* make small, diminish.]
†**1** Chopped small. *rare*. Only in **LME.**
†**2** Of an impost, tithe, etc.: lesser. **L15–L17.**
3 Very small; insignificant, petty. **E17.**

R. K. NARAYAN Such minute type that you would have to search for it with a magnifying glass.

4 Of an investigation, record, inquirer, etc.: characterized by attention to detail; very precise, particular, or accurate. **L17.**

L. STRACHEY A minute and detailed analysis . . followed, filling several pages.

■ **minuteness** *noun* **M17.**

minutely /ˈmɪnɪtli/ *adjective.* **E17.**
[ORIGIN from **MINUTE** *noun* + **-LY**[1].]
Occurring, performed, etc., every minute.

minutely /ˈmɪnɪtli/ *adverb*[1]. **L16.**
[ORIGIN formed as **MINUTELY** *adjective* + **-LY**[2].]
Every minute, minute by minute.

minutely /mʌɪˈnjuːtli/ *adverb*[2]. **L16.**
[ORIGIN from **MINUTE** *adjective* + **-LY**[2].]
1 Orig., into small pieces. Now, on a minute scale. **L16.**
2 In a minute manner, kind, or degree; with great precision or exactness. **E18.**

minuteman /ˈmɪnɪtman/ *noun.* Chiefly *US*. Pl. **-men**. **L18.**
[ORIGIN from **MINUTE** *noun* + **MAN** *noun*.]
1 *hist.* A member of a class of militiamen of the American revolutionary period, who held themselves ready for instant military service. **L18.** ▸**b** *transf. & fig.* In the US, a political watchdog or activist; a member of an organization concerned with specific political issues. **E20.**
2 (**M-**.) A type of US three-stage intercontinental ballistic missile. **M20.**

minuterie /mɪˈnjuːt(ə)ri/ *noun.* **M20.**
[ORIGIN French = clockwork, timing mechanism, from **MINUTE** *noun*: see **-ERY**.]
(An electric light controlled by) a light switch incorporating a timing mechanism to turn it off automatically after a short time.

minutia /mɪˈnjuːʃɪə, mʌɪ-/ *noun.* Pl. **-tiae** /-ʃiː, -ʃɪʌɪ/. **L18.**
[ORIGIN Latin = smallness (in pl., trifles), from *minutus* **MINUTE** *adjective*.]
A precise detail; a small or trivial matter or object. Usu. in *pl.*
■ **minutiose** /-ʃɪəʊs/ *adjective* dealing with minutiae **M19.** **minutious** *adjective* characterized by attention to minutiae **L18.**

minutial /mɪˈnjuːʃɪəl/ *adjective.* *arch.* **E17.**
[ORIGIN formed as **MINUTIA** + **-AL**[1].]
Of the nature of minutiae; pertaining to details.

minx /mɪŋks/ *noun.* **M16.**
[ORIGIN Perh. alt. of **MINIKIN**.]
†**1** A pet dog. **M16–E17.**
2 An impudent, cunning, or boldly flirtatious young woman. Formerly also, a prostitute. **L16.**

Z. GREY The little minx was giving Cal's hand a sly squeeze.

■ **minxish** *adjective* having the character of a minx **L19.** **minxishly** *adverb* **E20.** **minxy** *adjective* **M20.**

miny /ˈmʌɪni/ *adjective.* *rare.* **E17.**
[ORIGIN from **MINE** *noun* + **-Y**[1].]
Of or pertaining to a mine or mines; mineral.

Minyan /ˈmɪnɪən/ *noun*[1] *& adjective.* **M16.**
[ORIGIN from Latin *Minyae*, Greek *Minuai* Minyans (see below) + **-AN**.]
▸ **A** *noun.* A member of an ancient people said to have inhabited parts of central Greece, with whom the legends about Jason and the Argonauts are associated. **M16.**
▸ **B** *adjective.* **1** Of or pertaining to the Minyans. **L16.**
2 Designating a type of very smooth grey pottery first found at Orchomenus in Boeotia and orig. attributed to the Minyans. **E20.**

minyan /ˈmɪnjən/ *noun*[2]. Pl. **-im** /-ɪm/. **M18.**
[ORIGIN Hebrew *minyān* lit. 'count, reckoning'.]
The quorum of ten males over thirteen years of age required for traditional Jewish public worship.

minyanim *noun* pl. of **MINYAN** *noun*[2].

Miocene /ˈmʌɪəsiːn/ *adjective & noun.* **M19.**
[ORIGIN Irreg. from Greek *meiōn* less + *kainos* new, recent (as containing remains of fewer modern species than the Pliocene).]
GEOLOGY. ▸**A** *adjective.* Designating or pertaining to the fourth epoch of the Tertiary period or sub-era, after the Oligocene and before the Pliocene. **M19.**
▸ **B** *noun.* The Miocene epoch; the series of rocks dating from this time, containing fossil evidence of numerous mammals and the first hominids. **M19.**
■ **Mioˈcenic** *adjective* **M19.**

miogeocline /mʌɪəˈdʒiːəklʌɪn/ *noun.* **M20.**
[ORIGIN from **MIOGEOSYNCLINE**.]
GEOLOGY. = **MIOGEOSYNCLINE**.
■ **miogeoˈclinal** *adjective* **L20.**

miogeosyncline /ˌmʌɪə(ʊ)dʒiːəˈsɪŋklʌɪn/ *noun.* **M20.**
[ORIGIN from Greek *meiōn* less + **GEOSYNCLINE**.]
GEOLOGY. A geosyncline containing little or no volcanic rock; *esp.* one situated between a larger, volcanic geosyncline (eugeosyncline) and a stable area of the crust (craton).
■ **miogeosynˈclinal** *adjective* of, pertaining to, or of the nature of a miogeosyncline **M20.**

miombo /mɪˈɒmbəʊ/ *noun.* Pl. **-os**. **M19.**
[ORIGIN Bantu.]
Any of several tropical African leguminous trees of the genus *Brachystegia*; open woodland dominated by such trees, esp. in Tanzania.

miosis /mʌɪˈəʊsɪs/ *noun.* Also (earlier) **my-**. **E19.**
[ORIGIN from Greek *muein* shut the eyes + **-OSIS**.]
MEDICINE. (Abnormal or excessive) contraction of the pupil of the eye.

miotic /mʌɪˈɒtɪk/ *adjective & noun.* Also (earlier) **my-**. **M19.**
[ORIGIN from **MIOSIS** + **-OTIC**.]
▸ **A** *adjective.* Pertaining to, causing, or exhibiting miosis. **M19.**
▸ **B** *noun.* An agent which produces miosis. **M19.**

mi-parti /miparti/ *adjective & adverb.* **E17.**
[ORIGIN French, pa. pple of *mipartir* divide in half, from *mi-* (from Latin *medium* middle) + *partir* divide.]
HERALDRY. (Divided) per pale.

Mipolam /ˈmɪpəlam/ *noun*. Also **m-**. **M20**.
[ORIGIN Arbitrary.]
(Proprietary name for) plastic composed of polyvinyl chloride, used for chemically resistant piping and containers.

MIPS /mɪps/ *abbreviation*.
COMPUTING. Million instructions per second.

Miquelet /ˈmɪkəlɪt/ *noun*. **L17**.
[ORIGIN French from Spanish *miquelete*, *migue-*, from Catalan *Miquel*, Spanish *Miguel* Michael.]
Orig., a member of a body of Catalonian bandits active in the Pyrenees in the 17th cent.; a Spanish guerrilla soldier during the Peninsular War. Later also, a soldier of any of various local regiments of Spanish infantry, chiefly performing escort duties.
– COMB.: **Miquelet lock** a type of flintlock developed in Spain.

Mir /mɪə/ *noun*[1]. **E17**.
[ORIGIN Persian & Urdu *mīr* leader, commander, from Arabic *amīr*: see AMIR.]
= AMIR, EMIR.

mir /mɪə/ *noun*[2]. **M19**.
[ORIGIN Russian.]
A village community in pre-revolutionary Russia.

Mir /mɪə/ *noun*[3] *& adjective*. **E20**.
[ORIGIN from *Mirabad* a town in the Sarawan district of Iran.]
(Designating) a rare and fine quality Saraband rug woven in Mirabad.

mirabelle /mɪrəˈbɛl/ *noun*. **E18**.
[ORIGIN French.]
1 (A fruit from) a European variety of plum tree. **E18**.
2 (A) liqueur distilled from mirabelles, esp. those grown in Alsace, France. **M20**.

mirabile dictu /mɪˌrɑːbɪleɪ ˈdɪktuː/ *adverbial phr.* **E19**.
[ORIGIN Latin *mirabile* neut. of *mirabilis* (see MIRABLE) + *dictu* supine of *dicere* say.]
Wonderful to relate.

> S. KING For once, *mirabile dictu*, they all seem to be getting along.

mirabilia /mɪrəˈbɪlɪə/ *noun pl.* **E19**.
[ORIGIN Latin, use as noun of neut. pl. of *mirabilis*: see MIRABLE, -IA[2].]
Wonders, marvels, miracles.

mirabilite /mɪˈrabɪlʌɪt/ *noun*. **M19**.
[ORIGIN from *(sal) mirabilis* s.v. SAL *noun*[1], formed as MIRABLE: see -ITE[1].]
MINERALOGY. Native hydrated sodium sulphate (Glauber's salt), a monoclinic mineral found usu. as colourless prisms or massive deposits, esp. near salt springs or lakes, and in caves.

†**mirable** *adjective & noun*. **L15**.
[ORIGIN Latin *mirabilis* wonderful, from *mirari* to wonder: see MIRACLE, -ABLE.]
▸ **A** *adjective*. Wonderful, marvellous. **L15–E17**.

> SHAKES. *Tr. & Cr.* Not Neoptolemus so mirable . . could promise to himself A thought of added honour torn from Hector.

▸ **B** *noun*. A marvel, a wonder. **M17–M19**.

miracidium /mʌɪrəˈsɪdɪəm/ *noun*. Pl. **-dia** /-dɪə/. **L19**.
[ORIGIN from Greek *meirakidion* dim. of *meirakion* boy, stripling: see -IDIUM.]
ZOOLOGY. A digenean trematode (fluke) in the ciliated free-swimming larval stage, in which form it passes from the definitive to the (first) intermediate host, forming a sporocyst. Cf. CERCARIA.
■ **miracidial** *adjective* **M20**.

miracle /ˈmɪrək(ə)l/ *noun & verb*. **ME**.
[ORIGIN Old French & mod. French from Latin *miraculum* object of wonder, from *mirari*, *-are* look at, wonder, from *mirus* wonderful.]
▸ **A** *noun*. **1** A marvellous event not ascribable to human or natural agency, and therefore attributed to the intervention of a supernatural agent, esp. (in Christian belief) God; *spec.* an act demonstrating control over nature, serving as evidence that the agent is either divine or divinely favoured. **ME**.

> G. GREENE There were miracles too; a virgin wept salt tears and a candle . . burnt inexplicably for one week. B. MOORE Without a miracle, Christ did not rise from His tomb and ascend into heaven.

2 Now more fully ***miracle play***. A medieval dramatic representation based on the life of Jesus or the legends of the saints. **ME**.
3 *transf.* A remarkable or marvellous phenomenon or event. Also (with specifying word), a remarkable development in a specified area. Freq. *hyperbol.* **ME**. ▸**b** A person or thing of more than natural excellence; a surpassing specimen or example *of*. **LME**.

> F. L. WHIPPLE To overcome gravity and carry men out into space . . is to me a true miracle. *London Daily News* The compact disc miracle could prove to be a very short-lived one. *attrib.*: *Times* The discoverer of the 'miracle' rice and wheat strains . . was awarded the Nobel Peace Prize. **b** J. LAWSON The Humming-Bird is the Miracle of all our wing'd Animals.

– PHRASES: **to a miracle** marvellously well.
– COMB.: **miracle cure** (a drug, treatment, etc., said to effect) a remarkable or extraordinary cure; **miracle drug** a drug treating or curing previously untreatable or incurable illnesses and representing a breakthrough in medical science; **miracle fruit** (the fruit of) a W. African tree, *Synsepalum dulcificum* (family Sapotaceae), whose berries have the property of making sour or salt things taste sweet; **miracle man**: who performs miracles; ***miracle play***: see sense 2 above.
▸ **B** *verb*. †**1** *verb refl.* Be revealed by a miracle. *rare* (Shakes.). Only in **E17**.
2 *verb intrans. & trans.* Work miracles (on, for). *rare*. **M17**.
■ †**miracular** *adjective* miraculous **E18–M19**. **miˈraculist** *noun* a believer in miracles **E19**.

miraculize /mɪˈrakjʊlʌɪz/ *verb trans.* Also **-ise**. **E18**.
[ORIGIN from Latin *miraculum* (see MIRACLE) + -IZE.]
Make miraculous; consider as miraculous.

miraculous /mɪˈrakjʊləs/ *adjective*. **LME**.
[ORIGIN Old French & mod. French *miraculeux* or medieval Latin *miraculosus*, from Latin *miraculum*: see MIRACLE, -ULOUS.]
1 Of the nature of a miracle; supernatural; produced or effected by a miracle. **LME**. ▸†**b** Of or pertaining to a miracle or miracles. **M16–M19**.

> R. INGALLS Vision . . had always struck her as miraculous.

2 *transf.* Resembling a miracle; extraordinary, remarkable; astonishing. **L16**. ▸**b** Intoxicated, very drunk. *dial.* **L19**.

> J. F. LEHMANN All problems which we discussed in our letters seemed to settle themselves with miraculous ease. J. DISKI One of those miraculous London autumns that made winter seem improbable.

3 Of a thing or (formerly) a person: having the power to work miracles. **L16**.

> A. B. JAMESON The miraculous oil which flowed under her shrine.

miraculous berry = ***miracle fruit*** s.v. MIRACLE *noun*. **miraculous fruit** the fruit of a tropical African plant, *Thaumatococcus danielli* (family Marantaceae), with similar properties to the miracle fruit.
■ **miraculously** *adverb* in a miraculous manner; (as) by a miracle; in a miraculous degree: **LME**. **miraculousness** *noun* **L16**.

mirador /miraˈdɔr/ *noun*. **L17**.
[ORIGIN Spanish, from *mirar* look, observe.]
In Spain: a watchtower. Also, a turret or belvedere on the top of a Spanish house.

mirage /ˈmɪrɑːʒ, mɪˈrɑːʒ/ *noun*. **E19**.
[ORIGIN French, from *se mirer* be reflected or mirrored, from Latin *mirare*: see MIRACLE, -AGE.]
1 An optical illusion caused by atmospheric conditions (usu. the refraction of light in heated air); *esp.* the false appearance of a distant sheet of water in a desert or on a hot road. Also, the appearance in the sky of a reflected image of a distant object, a wavelike appearance of warmed air just above the ground. **E19**.

> R. RENDELL It was a mirage he had seen in that river village, a trick of the heat and light.

2 *fig.* An illusion, a fantasy. **E19**.

> M. HOLROYD Such promised happiness is only a mirage. *Sunday Times* Iraq's military might was all a mirage, a smokescreen that gulled everyone.

3 Any of various pale fashion colours; *esp.* pale blue, grey, or turquoise. **E20**.
■ **miragy** *adjective* of, pertaining to, or of the nature of a mirage **L19**.

Miranda /mɪˈrandə/ *adjective*. **M20**.
[ORIGIN from *Miranda* versus Arizona, the 1966 case that led to the Supreme Court ruling on the matter.]
US LAW. Designating or pertaining to the duty of the police to inform a person taken into custody of his or her right to legal counsel and the right to remain silent under questioning.
■ **Mirandize** *verb trans.* inform (an arrested person) of his or her legal rights, in accordance with the Miranda ruling **L20**.

MIRAS /ˈmʌɪrəs/ *abbreviation*.
Mortgage interest relief at source.

mirbane /ˈməːbeɪn/ *noun*. **M19**.
[ORIGIN French, of unknown origin.]
essence of mirbane, ***oil of mirbane***, nitrobenzene as used in perfumery.

Mirditë /ˈməːdɪtə/ *noun & adjective*. Pl. same. Also (*sing.*) **-ita**, **-ite** /-ʌɪt/. **M19**.
[ORIGIN See below.]
▸ **A** *noun*. A member of a people inhabiting Mirditë, a region around the river Drin in Albania. **E19**.
▸ **B** *adjective*. Of or pertaining to the Mirditë. **M19**.

mire /ˈmʌɪə/ *noun*[1]. **ME**.
[ORIGIN Old Norse *mýrr*, ult. from Germanic base of MOSS *noun*.]
1 A wet swampy area of land; a boggy place; *gen.* swampy ground, bog. **ME**. ▸**b** ECOLOGY. An ecosystem in which wet peat is the substrate for vegetation. **M20**.

> S. NAIPAUL The track . . was a mire, impassable even for four-wheel drive vehicles.

2 Wet or soft mud; slush; dirt. **ME**.
3 *fig.* An undesirable state or condition (formerly esp. of sin) from which it is difficult to extricate oneself. **LME**.

> P. TOYNBEE Still floundering and foundering in the same old mire of complexities and contradictions.

■ †**mirish** *adjective* **M17–E18**.

†**mire** *noun*[2]. **ME–L15**.
[ORIGIN Perh. from Old English word corresp. to Middle Dutch *miere* (Dutch *mier*), Middle Low German *mīre*.]
An ant.
– NOTE: Survives as 2nd elem. of PISMIRE.

mire /ˈmʌɪə/ *verb*. **LME**.
[ORIGIN from MIRE *noun*[1].]
1 *verb trans.* Cause to be stuck or embedded in a mire; *fig.* involve in difficulties. **LME**. ▸**b** Of bog, mud, etc.: hold fast, entangle. **L19**.

> J. HELLER No turbulent . . hailstorms or thunderstorms to mire or discomfit them. *New Yorker* The milk cow was mired in a bog hole. **b** R. ADAMS A wide marsh that mired them to the knees.

2 *verb trans.* Bespatter or soil with mire or filth; *fig.* defile. **L15**.

> M. ARNOLD Her palfrey's flanks were mired and bathed in sweat.

3 *verb intrans.* Sink in (a) mire; be bogged *down*. **E17**.

> W. SEWALL The roads being soft . . I mired down.

mired /ˈmʌɪrɛd/ *noun*. **M20**.
[ORIGIN Contr. of *micro reciprocal degree*.]
PHOTOGRAPHY. A unit expressing the reciprocal of colour temperature, defined as 10^{-6} per kelvin.

mirepoix /mɪrpwa/ *noun*. Pl. same. **L19**.
[ORIGIN French, from the Duc de *Mirepoix* (1699–1757), French diplomat and general.]
COOKERY. A mixture of sautéed diced vegetables used in sauces etc. or served as a separate dish.

mirex /ˈmʌɪrɛks/ *noun*. Orig. *US*. **M20**.
[ORIGIN Unknown.]
An organochlorine insecticide used esp. against ants.

mirid /ˈmɪrɪd, ˈmʌɪ-/ *noun & adjective*. **E20**.
[ORIGIN mod. Latin *Miridae*, the family formerly called Capsidae, from *Miris* genus name, from Latin *mirus* wonderful, extraordinary: see -ID[3].]
▸ **A** *noun*. Any bug of the heteropteran family Miridae, which includes numerous plant pests; a plant bug. **E20**.
▸ **B** *adjective*. Of, pertaining to, or designating this family. **M20**.

mirific /mʌɪˈrɪfɪk/ *adjective*. Chiefly *joc.* (now *rare*). **L15**.
[ORIGIN French *mirifique* from Latin *mirificus*, from *mirus* wonderful: see -FIC.]
Doing wonders; exciting wonder or astonishment; marvellous.
■ **mirifical** *adjective* **L16**. **mirifically** *adverb* **L19**.

mirin /ˈmɪrɪn/ *noun*. **L19**.
[ORIGIN Japanese, from *mi-* taste + *rin* remove astringency.]
A sweet rice wine used as a flavouring in Japanese cookery.

mirk *noun, adjective, verb* arch. vars. of MURK *noun*[1], *adjective*, *verb*.

mirky *adjective* arch. var. of MURKY.

mirl /məːl/ *verb*[1]. *Scot.* **M19**.
[ORIGIN Alt. of MIRR.]
Move briskly; turn round, twirl.

mirl *verb*[2] var. of MURL.

mirligoes /ˈməːlɪgəʊz, ˈmɛrl-/ *noun pl. Scot.* **L18**.
[ORIGIN Fanciful formation from MIRL *verb*[1], after *vertigo*.]
Dizziness, vertigo.

mirliton /ˈməːlɪtɒn/ *noun*. **E19**.
[ORIGIN French = reed pipe, of imit. origin.]
1 A musical instrument resembling a kazoo; any instrument in which a sound is given a nasal quality by means of a vibrating membrane. **E19**.
2 A chayote. *US*. **E20**.

miro /ˈmɪərəʊ/ *noun*[1]. Pl. same, **-os**. **E19**.
[ORIGIN Maori.]
(The wood of) a New Zealand evergreen coniferous tree, *Prumnopitys ferruginea* (family Podocarpaceae), with large reddish-purple arils. Also ***miro tree***.

miro /ˈmɪərəʊ/ *noun*[2]. *NZ*. Also **miro-miro** /mɪərəʊˈmɪərəʊ/. Pl. same, **-os**. **M19**.
[ORIGIN Maori.]
A New Zealand songbird of the genus *Petroica* (family Eopsaltridae), the New Zealand tomtit, *P. macrocephala*; also occas. the New Zealand robin, *P.* (formerly *Miro*) *australis*.

miroton /mirotɔ̃/ *noun*. Pl. pronounced same. **E18**.
[ORIGIN French.]
A dish of small thin slices of meat, esp. made into ragout.

M

mirr /mɜː/ *verb intrans. Scot.* M19.
[ORIGIN Norwegian *mirra*.]
Tingle, quiver, tremble.

mirrnyong /ˈmɜːnjɒŋ/ *noun. Austral.* Also **myrnyong**. L19.
[ORIGIN Prob. from an Australian Aboriginal language of Victoria.]
A mound of shells, ashes, and other debris accumulated in a place used for cooking by Australian Aborigines; an Aboriginal kitchen midden.

mirror /ˈmɪrə/ *noun & verb*. ME.
[ORIGIN Old French *mirour* (mod. *miroir*, from var. *mirēoir*) from Proto-Romance from Latin *mirat-* pa. ppl stem of *mirari*: see MIRACLE, -OR.]
▸ **A** *noun*. **I** *lit*. **1** A smooth surface, formerly of polished metal, now usu. (exc. in some scientific instruments) of glass coated on one side with aluminium or silver, which reflects light rays to form an image; a looking glass. ME.

T. IRELAND She tried to catch her reflection in the mirror on the wall.

2 A glass or crystal used in magic. *arch*. ME.
▸ **II** *fig*. **3** A person or thing embodying a feature or characteristic deserving of imitation; a pattern, an exemplar; a model of excellence; a paragon. Freq. foll. by *of*. Now *rare*. ME. ▸†**b** A person or thing embodying something to be avoided; a deterrent, a warning. *rare*. LME–M17.

L. STRACHEY In the eyes of Victoria he was the mirror of manly beauty.

4 A thing or (*poet*.) a person regarded as giving a faithful reflection or true description of something. LME.

R. CHRISTIANSEN The Poet's mind was no longer a mirror reflecting Nature.

▸ **III** *transf*. **5** Something which reflects an image, *esp*. water. Usu. *poet*. LME.
6 ARCHITECTURE. A small round or oval ornament with a border. M19.
7 ORNITHOLOGY. A white spot on the black wing tip of a gull. E20.
– PHRASES: **by mirrors** (as if) by magic. ***long mirror***: see LONG *adjective*[1]. ***magic mirror***: see MAGIC *adjective*. ***magnetic mirror***: see MAGNETIC *adjective*. **with mirrors** = *by mirrors* above.
– COMB.: **mirrorball** a revolving ball covered with small mirrored facets, used to provide lighting effects at discos or dances; **mirror carp** an abnormal variety of the carp having just two or three rows of enlarged scales; **mirror embroidery** = *mirrorwork* below; **mirror finish** a reflective surface; **mirror fugue** MUSIC a fugue that can be played reversed or inverted; **mirror glass** (glass used in) a mirror; **mirror image** an image etc. identical to its original but with the structure reversed; *loosely* an identical image, copy, etc.; **mirror nucleus**, **mirror nuclide** NUCLEAR PHYSICS either of two nuclides of the same atomic mass, each having as many protons as the other has neutrons; **mirror-plate** (*a*) a plate of glass suitable for a mirror; (*b*) a metal plate used for fixing a mirror etc. to a wall or base; **mirror scale** a graduated scale provided with an adjacent mirror so as to avoid parallax errors when taking readings; **mirror site** COMPUTING a site on a network which exactly replicates another site, usu. created to provide faster access for users in a distant part of the world by enabling them to use a server geographically closer to them; **mirror stage** PSYCHOLOGY a stage in a child's development considered to be typified by its reacting to its reflection as if it were a real person; **mirror symmetry**: as of an object and its reflection; **mirrorwork** small round pieces of mirror appliquéd on fabric; **mirror-writer** a person who practises mirror writing; **mirror writing** reversed writing (esp. characteristic of aphasia), like ordinary writing reflected in a mirror.
▸ **B** *verb trans*. †**1** Be a model for in behaviour. Only in LME.
2 Reflect as in a mirror. L16.

W. GOLDING The clear water mirrored the clear sky.

3 Imitate, reproduce, represent. E19.

O. WILDE The gracious and comely form he had so skilfully mirrored in his art. SCOTT FITZGERALD Tom glanced around to see if we mirrored his unbelief.

4 COMPUTING. **a** Maintain a copy of (a network site) at a mirror site. L20. ▸**b** Store copies of data on (two or more hard disks) as a method of protecting it. L20.
■ **mirrored** *adjective* (*a*) fitted with a mirror or mirrors; (*b*) having a reflective surface; (*c*) reflected (as) by a mirror: L18. **mirrorize** *verb trans*. reflect (as) in a mirror L16. **mirror-like** *adjective* E19. **mirrory** *adjective* M19.

mirth /mɜːθ/ *noun*.
[ORIGIN Old English *myriġþ*, from Germanic base also of MERRY *adjective*: see -TH[1].]
†**1** Pleasurable feeling, enjoyment, gratification; happiness; (religious) joy. OE–L17. ▸**b** A cause of joy. OE–LME.
2 Rejoicing; merrymaking; jollity, gaiety. ME.

W. IRVING The genial festival of Christmas, which . . lights up the . . home with mirth and jollity.

3 A thing affording pleasure or amusement; a diversion, an (esp. musical) entertainment. Now *rare*. ME.
4 Merriment, hilarity, laughter. Formerly also, jocularity; ridicule. ME. ▸†**b** A cause of hilarity. ME–E18.

D. H. LAWRENCE Blue eyes . . swimming over with laughter-tears, their clear cheeks were flushed crimson with mirth. S. BELLOW Leventhal was smiling also, but without much mirth.

– COMB.: **mirthquake** *colloq*. an extremely funny play, film, etc.
■ **mirthsome** *adjective* mirthful, joyous L18.

mirthful /ˈmɜːθfʊl, -f(ə)l/ *adjective*. ME.
[ORIGIN from MIRTH + -FUL.]
1 Of a person, mood, etc.: joyful, full of merriment; characterized by or exhibiting mirth. ME.
2 Of a thing: amusing. ME.
■ **mirthfully** *adverb* E16. **mirthfulness** *noun* M18.

mirthless /ˈmɜːθlɪs/ *adjective*. LME.
[ORIGIN formed as MIRTHFUL + -LESS.]
Joyless; sad, dismal.
■ **mirthlessly** *adverb* L19. **mirthlessness** *noun* E18.

MIRV /mɜːv/ *noun & verb*. M20.
[ORIGIN Acronym, from multiple independently-targeted re-entry vehicle.]
▸ **A** *noun*. A missile containing several independently guided warheads; a warhead carried by such a missile. M20.
▸ **B** *verb trans*. Equip (a rocket, missile system, etc.) with a MIRV or MIRVs. M20.

miry /ˈmʌɪ(ə)ri/ *adjective*. LME.
[ORIGIN from MIRE *noun*[1] + -Y[1].]
1 Resembling or containing mire; swampy; muddy. LME.
2 a Covered or bespattered with mire. L15. ▸**b** *fig*. Dirty, defiled; despicable. L15.
■ **miriness** *noun* E17.

mirza /ˈmɪːzɑː/ *noun*. M16.
[ORIGIN Persian *mīrzā*, from *mīr* leader (from Arabic *'amīr* AMIR) + *zād* son.]
In Iran: a royal prince (*hist*.); a common honorific title for an official or a man of learning, or (*postpositively*, *hist*.) a royal prince.

Mirzapur /ˈmɜːzəpʊə/ *noun & adjective*. L19.
[ORIGIN A town in the state of Uttar Pradesh in northern India.]
(Designating) a type of carpet manufactured in Mirzapur.

MIS *abbreviation*.
COMPUTING. Management information systems.

mis /mɪz/ *adjective*. *colloq*. E20.
[ORIGIN Abbreviation.]
Miserable.

mis- /mɪs/ *prefix*[1].
[ORIGIN Old English *mis-* = Old Frisian, Old Saxon *mis-*, Old High German *missa-*, *missi-* (Dutch *mis-*, German *miss-*), Old Norse *mis-*, Gothic *missa-*, from Germanic.]
1 Prefixed to verbs & verbal derivs. with the sense 'amiss, badly, wrongly, mistakenly', as ***misdirect***, ***misguided***, ***misleading***, ***misguidedly***, ***misleadingly***.
2 Prefixed to nouns of action, condition, and quality in the sense 'bad, wrong, faulty, perverse, misdirected', as ***misalignment***, ***mispronunciation***.
3 Prefixed to agent nouns to form nouns with the sense 'a person who or thing which mis—s', as ***misuser***.
4 Prefixed to adjectives & derived adverbs with the sense 'wrongly, erroneously, perversely', as ***misrepresentative***.
5 Expr. negation (of something good or desirable); = ***dis-***, ***in-***, ***un-***.
6 Prefixed as an intensive to words denoting something wrong or bad.
■ **misˈact** *verb trans*. (long *rare*) act badly E17. **misaˈddress** *verb trans*. address (a letter etc.) wrongly; address (remarks etc.) inappropriately or impertinently: M17. **misaˈdjustment** *noun* (a) lack of adjustment E18. **misaˈffection** *noun* (now *rare* or *obsolete*) (*a*) = DISAFFECTION 1; (*b*) a disease, a disorder: E17. **misaˈgree** *verb intrans*. (now *dial*.) disagree M16. **misˈaim** *verb trans*. (*rare*) aim amiss E19. **misalloˈcation** *noun* (*a*) failure to allocate efficiently or fairly M20. **misaˈlly** *verb trans*. (*rare*) ally or join inappropriately L17. **misappeˈllation** *noun* the using or a use of a wrong word in referring to something E19. **misaˈppreciate** *verb trans*. fail to appreciate rightly E19. **misappreciˈation** *noun* (an) erroneous appreciation or valuation M19. **misaˈrranged** *adjective* wrongly arranged M19. **misaˈrrangement** *noun* (a) bad or wrong arrangement M18. **misarticuˈlation** *noun* faulty articulation M19. **misaˈscription** *noun* (a) false ascription E20. **misaˈssign** *verb trans*. (*rare*) assign erroneously E17. **misaˈward** *verb trans*. (*rare*) award wrongly L19. **misbeˈgin** *verb trans*. (*rare*) begin amiss or badly L16. **misbeˈstow** *verb trans*. bestow wrongly or improperly M16. **misˈbode** *verb trans*. (*rare*) forebode (something evil); chiefly as ***misboding*** *verbal noun & ppl adjective*: E17. **misˈbound** *adjective* (of a book) badly or wrongly bound E19. **misˈcasualty** *noun* (long *obsolete* exc. *dial*.) a mischance, a mishap L16. **misˈcatalogued** *adjective* wrongly catalogued E20. **mischaracteriˈzation** *noun* the action or an instance of mischaracterizing something M20. **misˈcharacterize** *verb trans*. characterize wrongly L18. **misˈcharge** *verb trans*. (now *rare*) charge wrongly or falsely L15. **misˈchoice** *noun* (a) wrong or improper choice L16. **misˈchoose** *verb trans. & intrans*. make a wrong choice (of) ME. **misˈchristen** *verb trans*. (*rare*) misname M17. **mis-ˈcipher** *verb trans*. (*rare*) express wrongly in cipher M17. **mis-ciˈtation** *noun* (an) incorrect citation, (a) misquotation M17. **mis-ˈcite** *verb trans*. cite incorrectly, misquote E17. **misclassifiˈcation** *noun* (an) incorrect classification E19. **misˈclassify** *verb trans*. classify incorrectly E20. **misˈclosure** *noun* the deviation of the final surveyed position of a point from the initial one after a traverse has been carried out starting at the point and leading back to it M20. **misˈcode** *verb trans*. code incorrectly M20. **misˈcolour** *verb trans*. (*a*) give a wrong or improper colour to; (*b*) misrepresent, misinterpret, (a fact etc.): LME. **miscoˈmmunicate** *verb trans*. communicate incorrectly or imperfectly M17. **miscommuniˈcation** *noun* (an instance of) incorrect or imperfect communication M20. **miscompreˈhend** *verb trans*. fail to understand; misunderstand E19. **miscompreˈhension** *noun* misunderstanding M19. **miscomˈpuˈtation** *noun* a wrong or faulty computation M17. **miscomˈpute** *verb intrans*. miscalculate M17. **misconˈfigure** *verb trans*. (COMPUTING) configure incorrectly L20. **misconˈjecture** *noun* (*rare*) (an) erroneous conjecture M17. **misconˈjunction** *noun* a wrong conjunction M19. **miscoˈnnection** *noun* a wrong connection L18. **misˈconsecrated** *adjective* (*a*) consecrated to a wrong purpose; (*b*) improperly consecrated: L18. **misconˈvey** *verb refl*. convey a wrong impression of one's meaning M19. **misˈcook** *verb trans*. (chiefly *Scot*.) cook badly; spoil in cooking; *fig*. mismanage: E16. **misˈcounsel** *verb trans*. counsel or advise wrongly LME. **misˈcreed** *noun* (*poet*., *rare*) a mistaken creed E19. **misdeˈcide** *verb intrans*. (*rare*) make a wrong decision E19. **misdeˈcision** *noun* (*rare*) wrong decision or judgement E19. **misdeclaˈration** *noun* (an) incorrect declaration, esp. in an official context E20. **misdeˈliver** *verb trans*. (*a*) deliver to the wrong person or at the wrong place; (*b*) hand down improperly: M19. **misdeˈlivery** *noun* wrong delivery L17. **misdeˈrive** *verb trans*. (*a*) misdirect; (*b*) assign a wrong derivation to: M17. †**misdeˈsert** *noun* the condition of being undeserving L16–L19. †**misdeˈserve** *verb* (*a*) *verb intrans*. deserve ill; (*b*) *verb trans*. fail to deserve: L17–M19. **misdeˈvoted** *adjective* (*rare*) improperly devoted; devoted to a wrong object: E17. †**misdiet** *verb & noun* (*a*) *verb trans*. feed a wrong diet to; (*b*) *noun* wrong diet, improper feeding: L15–E18. †**misdight** *adjective* ill-clothed; badly prepared or provided; ill-treated: ME–E17. **misdistriˈbution** *noun* wrong or faulty distribution L19. †**misdread** *noun* (*rare*, Shakes.) dread of evil: only in E17. **misˈdrive** *verb trans*. †(*a*) *rare* commit (a wrong); (*b*) drive in a wrong direction: ME. **misˈemphasis** *noun* incorrect emphasis L19. **misˈentry** *noun* (now *rare* or *obsolete*) an erroneous entry L16. **misˈexecute** *verb trans*. execute or carry out improperly E18. **misexeˈcution** *noun* improper execution M16. **misexplain** /mɪsɪkˈspleɪn/ *verb trans*. explain incorrectly L17. **misˈfaith** *noun* (*rare*) disbelief; mistrust: LME. **misˈfame** *verb trans*. (*rare*) spread a false report concerning, defame LME. **misˈfeature** *noun* a distorted feature; a bad feature or trait: E19. **misfeed** *noun* an instance of faulty feeding of something (esp. paper) through a machine M20. **misˈfile** *verb trans*. file wrongly M20. **misforˈmation** *noun* malformation E19. **misˈformed** *adjective* malformed, misshapen L16. **misˈfunction** *noun* = DYSFUNCTION M20. †**misgraffed** *adjective* (*rare*, Shakes.) badly grafted, badly matched: only in E17. **misˈgrounded** *adjective* falsely grounded; ill-founded: E17. **misˈgrown** *adjective* grown out of shape; misshapen: LME. **misˈgrowth** *noun* a distorted or abortive growth M17. **misˈhook** *verb & noun* (CRICKET) (*a*) *verb trans*. hook (a ball) badly; (*b*) *noun* a bad hook: M20. **misimˈpression** *noun* a wrong impression L17. **misinˈfer** *verb trans*. (long *rare*) (*a*) infer wrongly; (*b*) draw a wrong inference from: L16. **misˈkey** *verb trans. & intrans*. type (a character, word, etc.) wrongly on a keyboard, keypad, etc. L20. **misˈlabel** *verb trans*. label incorrectly M19. **misˈlearn** *verb trans*. learn badly or incorrectly L17. **misˈliver** *noun* (now *rare* or *obsolete*) a person who leads an evil life LME. **misˈliving** *noun* evil living ME. **misˈlodge** *verb trans*. †(*a*) mislay; (*b*) lodge in a wrong place: E17. **misˈluck** *noun & verb intrans*. (chiefly *Scot*.) (meet with) misfortune M16. **misˈmade** *adjective* †(*a*) misshapen; (*b*) badly or wrongly made: L15. **misˈmake** *verb trans*. (*obsolete* exc. *Scot*.) (*a*) make bad or badly; (*b*) *refl*. trouble oneself, put oneself out: ME. **misˈmark** *verb trans*. (now *rare*) (*a*) *refl*. guess wrongly; (*b*) mark wrongly: LME. **misˈmarriage** *noun* an unsuitable marriage E19. **misˈmetre** *verb trans*. spoil the metre of (verse etc.) LME. **misˈnumber** *verb trans*. number incorrectly E17. **misobˈservance** *noun* (*rare*) failure to observe rules or conditions properly LME. **misˈoccupy** *verb trans*. (*rare*) occupy or employ wrongly M16. **misperˈform** *verb trans*. perform improperly M17. **misperˈformance** *noun* (an) improper performance L17. **misperˈsuade** *verb trans*. (now *rare* or *obsolete*) persuade wrongly or into error L16. **misperˈsuasion** *noun* (now *rare* or *obsolete*) a misconception; a wrong conviction: L16. **misˈpleading** *noun* (now *rare*) wrong pleading; a mistake in pleading: M16. **misˈpointing** *noun* †(*a*) pointing with the wrong finger; (*b*) (now *rare*) (an instance of) incorrect punctuation: M16. **misˈpraise** *verb trans*. (now *rare*) (*a*) dispraise, blame; (*b*) praise wrongly: ME. **misˈprisal** *noun* (*rare*) contempt, disdain, scorn E17. **misˈproud** *adjective* (*arch*.) wrongly or wickedly proud; arrogant: ME. **misˈrate** *verb trans*. (now *rare*) estimate wrongly E17. **misˈrecognize** *verb trans*. incorrectly identify while apparently recognizing M20. †**misregard** *noun* lack of regard or care; neglect, contempt: M16–L17. **misreˈlate** *verb trans*. relate or recount incorrectly E17. **misˈrender** *verb trans*. render or interpret incorrectly M17. **misreˈpeat** *verb trans*. (now *rare* or *obsolete*) repeat incorrectly E17. **misreˈsemblance** *noun* (long *rare*) (*a*) a lack of resemblance; (*b*) a bad likeness or portrait: E17. **misˈroute** *verb trans*. divert or re-route to the wrong destination or by a longer or more expensive route M20. **misˈscript** *noun* an error in writing M19. **misˈsee** *verb trans*. see imperfectly, take a wrong view of L15. **misˈsell** *verb trans*. sell badly or wrongly; *spec*. sell (a financial product such as a pension) to a customer on the basis of wrong, misleading, or incomplete advice: (*rare* before L20) LME. **misˈsend** *verb trans*. send to a wrong place or person; chiefly as ***missent*** *ppl adjective*: LME. **misˈserve** *verb trans*. (now *rare*) serve badly or unfaithfully ME. **misˈset** *verb trans*. (*a*) misplace; (*b*) *Scot*. put in a bad mood: ME. **misˈstyle** *verb trans*. (*rare*) style or term incorrectly E17. **misˈsuit** *verb trans*. suit badly E17. **misˈsworn** *adjective* (chiefly *Scot*.) perjured, forsworn E16. **misˈterm** *verb trans*. apply a wrong term or name to L16. **misˈtutored** *adjective* badly instructed or brought up M18. **misˈvalue** *verb trans*. value wrongly E17. **misvocaliˈzation** *noun* (an instance of) the insertion of incorrect vowel-signs in forms of writing consisting mainly or entirely of consonants M20.

mis- /mɪs/ *prefix*[2].
[ORIGIN Old French *mes-* (mod. *més-*, *mes-*, *mé-*) from Proto-Romance, ult. from Latin *minus* (see MINUS): assim. to MIS-[1].]
Occurring with the sense 'bad(ly), wrong(ly)' and with neg. force in a few words adopted from French, as ***misadventure***, ***mischief***, ***misnomer***.

mis- *prefix*[3] (*combining form*) see MISO-.

misadventure /mɪsədˈvɛntʃə/ *noun*. ME.
[ORIGIN Old French *mesaventure*, from *mesavenir* turn out badly (from *mes-* MIS-[2] + *avenir* from Latin *advenire*: see ADVENT), after *aventure* ADVENTURE *noun*.]
1 Bad luck; a piece of bad luck; a mishap, a misfortune. ME.

M

M. FITZHERBERT After some misadventures . . Lloyd and Aubrey decided to abandon their projected ride.

2 *ENGLISH LAW.* Homicide committed accidentally by a person in doing a lawful act, without any intention of hurt. Now chiefly in ***death by misadventure, homicide by misadventure.*** **E16.**

misadventured /ˌmɪsədˈvɛntʃəd/ *adjective. arch.* **L16.**
[ORIGIN from MISADVENTURE + -ED[2].]
Unfortunate.

misadventurous /mɪsədˈvɛntʃ(ə)rəs/ *adjective.* Now *rare.* **LME.**
[ORIGIN Orig. from Old French *mesaventureux*, from *mesaventure*: see MISADVENTURE, -OUS. Later from MISADVENTURE + -OUS.]
Unfortunate, unlucky.

misadvice /mɪsədˈvʌɪs/ *noun.* Long *rare.* **M17.**
[ORIGIN from MIS-[1] 2 + ADVICE.]
Wrong advice.

misadvise /mɪsədˈvʌɪz/ *verb trans.* **LME.**
[ORIGIN from MIS-[1] 1 + ADVISE.]
†**1** *refl.* Take bad advice; act unadvisedly. **LME–E17.**
2 Give incorrect advice to. **M16.**

W. HUNT Shipping companies had misadvised them on the practicability of the glacial route.

■ **misadvised** *adjective* ill-advised, imprudent; wrongly advised: **LME.**

misalign /mɪsəˈlʌɪn/ *verb trans.* **M20.**
[ORIGIN from MIS-[1] 1 + ALIGN.]
Give a wrong or imperfect alignment to.
■ **misalignment** *noun* **E20.**

misalliance /mɪsəˈlʌɪəns/ *noun.* **M18.**
[ORIGIN from MIS-[1] 2 + ALLIANCE *noun*, after French MÉSALLIANCE.]
An improper alliance, association, or union; *esp.* an unsuitable marriage.

misandry /mɪˈsandri/ *noun.* **E20.**
[ORIGIN from MIS-[3] + ANDR(O- + -Y[3].]
The hatred of men (i.e. the male sex specifically).
■ **misandrist** *noun* a person, esp. a woman, who hates men, a man-hater **L20.**

misanter *noun* var. of MISAUNTER.

misanthrope /ˈmɪz(ə)nθrəʊp, mɪs-/ *noun & adjective.* Also (earlier) in Greek & Latin forms †**misanthropos**, pl. **-poi**, †**-pus**, pl. **-pi**. **E17.**
[ORIGIN French from mod. Latin *misanthropus* from Greek *misanthrōpos*, formed as MIS-[3] + *anthrōpos* man.]
▸ **A** *noun.* A hater of humankind; a person who distrusts people and avoids their company. **E17.**
▸ **B** *adjective.* Misanthropic. **M18.**
■ **misanˈthropic** *adjective* pertaining to, resembling, or characteristic of a misanthrope; characterized by misanthropy: **M18.** **misanˈthropical** *adjective* misanthropic **E17.** **misanˈthropically** *adverb* **L18.** **miˈsanthropist** *noun* a misanthrope **M17.** **miˈsanthropize** *verb intrans.* be a misanthrope **M19.**

misanthropy /mɪsˈanθrəpi, mɪˈzan-/ *noun.* **M17.**
[ORIGIN Greek *misanthrōpia*, formed as MIS-[3] + *anthrōpos* man: see -IA[1].]
Hatred of humankind; the character, nature, or condition of a misanthrope.

misapply /mɪsəˈplʌɪ/ *verb trans.* **L16.**
[ORIGIN from MIS-[1] 1 + APPLY.]
Apply to a wrong person or object; make a wrong application of.
■ **misappliˈcation** *noun* the action or an act of misapplying something, esp. money **E17.**

misapprehend /ˌmɪsaprɪˈhɛnd/ *verb trans.* **E17.**
[ORIGIN from MIS-[1] 1 + APPREHEND.]
Apprehend wrongly; fail to understand rightly, misunderstand.

misapprehension /ˌmɪsaprɪˈhɛnʃ(ə)n/ *noun.* **E17.**
[ORIGIN from MIS-[1] 2 + APPREHENSION.]
The action or an act of misapprehending something; an erroneous belief, a mistaken assumption.

J. TYNDALL An opinion, founded on a grave misapprehension. L. CODY It's a common misapprehension . . that the elderly lose their memories.

■ **misapprehensive** *adjective* apt to misapprehend **M17.** **misapprehensively** *adverb* **M19.** **misapprehensiveness** *noun* **M19.**

misappropriate /mɪsəˈprəʊprɪət/ *adjective. rare.* **L19.**
[ORIGIN from MIS-[1] 5 + APPROPRIATE *adjective.*]
Inappropriate.

misappropriate /mɪsəˈprəʊprɪeɪt/ *verb trans.* **E19.**
[ORIGIN from MIS-[1] 1 + APPROPRIATE *verb.*]
Apply or assign to a wrong use; *spec.* apply (money belonging to another) dishonestly to one's own use, embezzle.

W. PLOMER He had misappropriated the funds entrusted to him.

■ **ˌmisappropriˈation** *noun* **L18.**

misattribution /ˌmɪsatrɪˈbjuːʃ(ə)n/ *noun.* **L19.**
[ORIGIN from MIS-[1] 2 + ATTRIBUTION.]
(An) attribution, esp. of a work of art or literature, to the wrong person.

New York Review of Books Such activities as sifting out fakes and correcting misattributions.

■ **misaˈttribute** *verb trans.* attribute wrongly **E20.**

misaunter /mɪsˈɔːntə/ *noun.* Long *obsolete* exc. *Scot. & N. English.* Also **misanter** /mɪsˈantə/. See also MISHANTER. **ME.**
[ORIGIN Contr.]
= MISADVENTURE.

misbecome /mɪsbɪˈkʌm/ *verb trans.* Pa. t. **-became** /-bɪˈkeɪm/; pa. pple **-become**. **M16.**
[ORIGIN from MIS-[1] 1 + BECOME.]
Be unsuitable for, be unbecoming to.

misbecoming /ˌmɪsbɪˈkʌmɪŋ/ *adjective.* **L16.**
[ORIGIN from MIS-[1] 1 + BECOMING *adjective*, or from MISBECOME + -ING[2].]
Unsuitable, unbecoming.

SIR W. SCOTT A paroxysm of laughter has seized him at a misbecoming time and place.

■ **misbecomingly** *adverb* **E17.** **misbecomingness** *noun* **M17.**

misbeget /mɪsbɪˈgɛt/ *verb trans. rare.* Infl. as BEGET; pa. t. **-got** /-ˈgɒt/, (*arch.*) **-gat** /-ˈgat/, pa. pple **-gotten** /-ˈgɒt(ə)n/. **ME.**
[ORIGIN from MIS-[1] 1 + BEGET.]
Beget unlawfully.

misbegotten /mɪsbɪˈgɒt(ə)n/ *adjective.* **M16.**
[ORIGIN from MIS-[1] 1 + *begotten* pa. pple of BEGET.]
Unlawfully begotten; illegitimate; *fig.* ill-conceived; contemptible. Also used as a term of abuse.

misbehave /mɪsbɪˈheɪv/ *verb intrans.* & (now *rare*) *refl.* **L15.**
[ORIGIN from MIS-[1] 1 + BEHAVE.]
1 Behave badly; conduct oneself improperly. **L15.**

M. WARNOCK Having misbehaved, I was shut in the night nursery as a punishment.

2 Of a machine etc.: fail to function correctly. **M19.**
■ **misbehaviour** *noun* **L15.**

misbeholden /mɪsbɪˈhəʊld(ə)n/ *adjective.* Long *obsolete* exc. *Scot. & N. English.* **L16.**
[ORIGIN from MIS-[1] 1 + *beholden* pa. pple of BEHOLD.]
Unbecoming, indiscreet. Chiefly in ***misbeholden word.***

misbelief /mɪsbɪˈliːf/ *noun.* **ME.**
[ORIGIN from MIS-[1] 2, 5 + BELIEF.]
1 Erroneous or unorthodox religious belief; heresy. **ME.** ▸**b** *gen.* (An) erroneous belief; (a) false opinion or notion. **LME.**
†**2** Lack of belief; disbelief, incredulity. **ME–M17.**

misbelieve /mɪsbɪˈliːv/ *verb.* **ME.**
[ORIGIN from MIS-[1] 1, 5 + BELIEVE.]
1 *verb intrans.* Believe falsely; hold an erroneous or unorthodox belief. Now chiefly as ***misbelieving*** *ppl adjective* and in MISBELIEVER. **ME.**
2 *verb trans.* Not believe; distrust (a person); disbelieve (a thing). *obsolete* exc. *Scot.* **LME.**

misbeliever /mɪsbɪˈliːvə/ *noun.* **LME.**
[ORIGIN from MIS-[1] 3 + BELIEVER.]
A person who holds an erroneous or unorthodox belief; a heretic, an infidel.

misbeseem /mɪsbɪˈsiːm/ *verb trans. arch.* **L16.**
[ORIGIN from MIS-[1] 1 + BESEEM.]
= MISBECOME.

misbirth /mɪsˈbəːθ/ *noun. rare.* **M17.**
[ORIGIN from MIS-[1] 2 + BIRTH *noun*[1].]
A stillbirth; a premature birth with loss of the fetus.

misborn /mɪsˈbɔːn/ *adjective.* Long *rare* or *obsolete.* **OE.**
[ORIGIN from MIS-[1] 1 + BORN *adjective.*]
1 Prematurely born; abortive; born deformed. **OE.**
2 Born illegitimately; baseborn. **L16.**

misc. *abbreviation.*
Miscellaneous.

miscalculate /mɪsˈkalkjʊleɪt/ *verb intrans. & trans.* **L17.**
[ORIGIN from MIS-[1] 1 + CALCULATE.]
Calculate or reckon wrongly; misjudge.

LD MACAULAY The conspirators found that they had miscalculated. E. WAUGH They never contemplated . . military conquest . . and entirely miscalculated the spirit of the people.

■ **miscalcuˈlation** *noun* (a) wrong or faulty calculation; a misjudgement: **E18.** **miscalculator** *noun* a person who miscalculates **M19.**

miscall /mɪsˈkɔːl/ *verb trans.* **LME.**
[ORIGIN from MIS-[1] 1 + CALL *verb.*]
1 Call by a wrong or inappropriate name; misname. Freq. with compl. **LME.** ▸**b** Misread, mispronounce. *dial.* **M19.**

R. ELLMANN What Wilde carelessly miscalled in print the *Sonata Impassionata.*

2 Call by a bad name; call (a person) names; abuse, malign. Now *arch. & dial.* **LME.**

miscarriage /mɪsˈkarɪdʒ, ˈmɪskarɪdʒ/ *noun.* **L16.**
[ORIGIN from MISCARRY + -AGE.]
†**1 a** Misconduct, misbehaviour. **L16–L17.** ▸**b** A misdemeanour, a misdeed. **M17–E19.**
2 Mismanagement, maladministration; failure (of an enterprise etc.); a blunder, a mistake. Now *rare* exc. in ***miscarriage of justice*** below. **E17.** ▸†**b** Mishap, disaster. Only in **18.**
miscarriage of justice a failure of the judicial system to attain the ends of justice.
3 The action of giving birth with loss of the fetus, esp. in the period before a live birth is possible; an instance of this; *spec.* a spontaneous abortion. **M17.**

A. N. WILSON Bessie became pregnant again . . but had a miscarriage.

4 The failure of a letter, freight, etc., to reach its destination. **M17.**

miscarry /mɪsˈkari/ *verb.* **ME.**
[ORIGIN Old French *mescarier*, formed as MIS-[1], CARRY *verb.*]
†**1** *verb intrans. & trans.* in *pass.* Come to harm, misfortune, or destruction; (of a person) meet one's end; (of an inanimate object) be lost or destroyed. **ME–M18.**

SHAKES. *Lear* Our sister's man is certainly miscarried.

2 *verb intrans. & refl.* Go wrong or astray; do wrong, misbehave. Long *rare.* **ME.**
†**3** *verb trans.* Cause (a person) to go wrong; mislead, delude, seduce. **LME–L17.**
4 *verb intrans.* **a** Have a miscarriage. Also (now *rare*) foll. by *of* the fetus. **E16.** ▸**b** Of a fetus: be born dead in a miscarriage. **L16.**

Daily Telegraph In most other abnormalities associated with late motherhood, the woman miscarries.

5 *verb intrans.* †**a** Of a plant, seed, etc.: be abortive or unproductive; fail. **L16–M18.** ▸**b** Of a plan, business, etc.: go wrong; come to nothing; be unsuccessful. **E17.** ▸**c** Of a person: fail in one's purpose or object; be unsuccessful. **E17.**

b H. HALLAM A similar proposition in the session . . seems to have miscarried in the Commons. **c** R. W. EMERSON If our young men miscarry in their first enterprises, they lose all heart.

6 *verb intrans. &* †*trans.* in *pass.* Of a letter etc.: fail to reach its proper destination; get into wrong hands. **E17.**

miscast /mɪsˈkɑːst/ *verb.* Pa. t. & pple **-cast**. **LME.**
[ORIGIN from MIS-[1] 1 + CAST *verb.*]
†**1** *verb trans.* Cast (one's eye) with evil intent. Only in **LME.**
2 *verb trans. & intrans.* Miscalculate. Exc. *dial.* now only as ***miscasting*** *verbal noun.* **M16.**
3 *verb trans.* Give an unsuitable role to (an actor); allot the roles in (a play or film) to unsuitable actors. Usu. in *pass.* **E20.**

miscegenation /ˌmɪsɪdʒɪˈneɪʃ(ə)n/ *noun.* **M19.**
[ORIGIN Irreg. from Latin *miscere* MIX *verb* + *genus* race + -ATION.]
The mixing of people considered to be of different racial types; *esp.* the interbreeding of whites and non-whites.
■ **ˈmiscegenated** *adjective* produced by miscegenation; of mixed descent: **M19.**

miscellanea /mɪsəˈleɪnɪə/ *noun.* **L16.**
[ORIGIN Latin, neut. pl. of Latin *miscellaneus*: see MISCELLANEOUS.]
As *pl.*, miscellaneous items, esp. literary compositions, collected together. As *sing.*, a miscellaneous collection, esp. of literary compositions; a miscellany.

†**miscellaneal** *adjective.* **M17–E18.**
[ORIGIN from Latin *miscellaneus*: see MISCELLANEOUS, -AL[1].]
Miscellaneous.

miscellaneous /mɪsəˈleɪnɪəs/ *adjective.* **E17.**
[ORIGIN from Latin *miscellaneus*, from *miscellus* mixed, from *miscere* MIX *verb*: see -EOUS.]
1 (With a sing. noun) consisting of members or elements of different kinds, of mixed composition or character; (with a pl. noun) of various kinds. **E17.**

DICKENS He was a sort of town-traveller for a number of miscellaneous houses. R. K. NARAYAN I received a miscellaneous collection of mail-catalogues, programmes . . and what not.

2 Of a person: having various qualities or aspects; many-sided. **M17.**
■ **miscellaneously** *adverb* with variety or diversity; in various ways, on miscellaneous subjects: **M17.** **miscellaneousness** *noun* **E18.**

miscellany /mɪˈsɛləni/ *noun.* **E17.**
[ORIGIN (French *miscellanées* fem. pl. from) Latin MISCELLANEA, with assim. to -Y[3].]
1 A mixture, a medley. **E17.**

R. MACAULAY A miscellany of assorted amusements—Greek plays, . . playing cards, a chessboard, bottles and glasses.

2 In *pl.* Separate articles or studies on a subject, or compositions of various kinds, collected into one volume. (Freq. in titles of books.) Long *rare* or *obsolete.* **E17.**
3 A literary work or production containing miscellaneous pieces on various subjects. **M17.**

Times Lit. Suppl. The variety of the contents of this military miscellany.

■ **miscellanist** *noun* a writer of miscellanies **E19.**

†**miscellany** *adjective.* **E17–L18.**
[ORIGIN formed as MISCELLANEOUS, perh. after MISCELLANY *noun.*]
Miscellaneous.

M

mischance /mɪsˈtʃɑːns/ *noun*. ME.
[ORIGIN Old French *mesch(e)ance*, from *mescheoir*, from *mes-* MIS-² + *cheoir* befall: see CHANCE *noun*.]
1 Bad luck. Formerly also, disaster, calamity. ME.
2 A piece of bad luck; a mishap, an unlucky accident. Formerly also, an accidental injury or mutilation; a state of unhappiness, an evil fate. ME.
– PHRASES: **by mischance**, **by some mischance** by an unlucky accident, by misfortune.
▪ **mischanceful** *adjective* (*arch.*) unfortunate ME. **mischancy** *adjective* (chiefly *Scot.*) unfortunate E16.

mischance /mɪsˈtʃɑːns/ *verb*. Long *rare*. M16.
[ORIGIN from MIS-¹ 1 + CHANCE *verb*.]
1 *verb intrans.* Happen unfortunately. M16.
†**2** *verb trans.* in *pass.* Be unfortunate; have bad luck. M–L16.

mischanter *noun* var. of MISHANTER.

mischief /ˈmɪstʃɪf/ *noun*. ME.
[ORIGIN Old French *mesch(i)ef* (mod. *méchef*), from *meschever*, from *mes-* MIS-² + *chever* come to an end (of), from *chef* head.]
1 Evil plight or condition; misfortune; trouble, distress. Formerly also, need, want, poverty. Long *obsolete* exc. *Scot.* ME. ▸†**b** A misfortune, a calamity. ME–M17.
†**2** Wickedness. ME–E17.
3 An injury inflicted by a person or other agent; an evil arising out of or existing in certain conditions; an evil consequence. Now only in *pl.* exc. in ***do a mischief to*** below. LME.

S. SMILES The social mischiefs . . from a neglect of the purifying influence of women.

4 Harm or evil considered as attributable to a particular agent or cause. L15.

SIR W. SCOTT It was hardly possible two such . . rascals should colleague together without mischief.

5 A pathological condition. Formerly, a disease, an illness. M16.
6 A cause or source of harm or evil; *spec.* a person whose conduct or influence is harmful, or who causes petty annoyance or acts in a vexatious manner. L16.

L. M. MONTGOMERY She was a dreadful mischief when she was a girl.

7 ***the mischief***, the devil: in exclamatory and imprecatory phrs. (cf. DEVIL *noun* 1). L16.

R. KIPLING You 'eathen, where the mischief 'ave you been? J. M. SYNGE I am coughing away like the mischief to-day.

8 *LAW.* A wrong or hardship which it is the object of a statute to remove or for which the common law affords a remedy. E17.
9 Formerly, harmful character, influence, or intent. Now, playful or teasing mischievousness, playful malice. M17. ▸**b** *The* most unfortunate aspect or vexatious circumstance (*of* an affair). M17.

SWIFT But Cupid, full of mischief, longs To vindicate his mother's wrongs. A. MENEN Suddenly his eyes looked mischief again.

10 Vexatious or annoying action or conduct; behaviour, esp. in a child, which is troublesome but not malicious, except in a playful or teasing way. L18.

B. POTTER Now run along, and don't get into any mischief.

– PHRASES: **do a mischief to** wound, injure or kill (oneself, another). **make mischief** create or promote discord, esp. by gossip. **mean mischief** intend to create or promote trouble or discord.
– COMB.: **mischief-maker** a person who makes mischief; **mischief night** an evening, orig. 30 April, now 4 November or 31 October (Halloween), on which children traditionally indulge in mischievous pranks.
▪ **mischiefful** *adjective* (now *dial.*) †(**a**) unfortunate, disastrous; (**b**) mischievous: ME.

mischief /ˈmɪstʃɪf/ *verb trans. arch.* LME.
[ORIGIN from the noun. Cf. MISCHIEVE.]
Do harm to; inflict harm or physical injury on.

mischieve /mɪsˈtʃiːv/ *verb*. ME.
[ORIGIN Old French *meschever*: see MISCHIEF *noun*.]
†**1** *verb intrans.* Suffer injury; meet with misfortune. ME–E17.
2 *verb trans.* Afflict or overwhelm with misfortune; destroy, ruin. *arch.* LME.
3 *verb trans.* Do physical harm to, wound, hurt; injure, damage. Now *Scot.* LME.
†**4** *verb trans.* Abuse, slander. M17–M18.

mischievous /ˈmɪstʃɪvəs/ *adjective*. ME.
[ORIGIN Anglo-Norman *meschevous* from Old French *meschever*: see MISCHIEF *noun*, -OUS.]
†**1** Unfortunate, calamitous, disastrous; (of a person) miserable, needy, poverty-stricken. ME–M17.
2 Having harmful effects or results; inflicting damage or injury; having a harmful influence or intent. Now chiefly *Scot.* LME.
3 Disposed to or full of mischief; playfully troublesome or teasing; (of behaviour) of the nature of mischief. L17.

Beano Two mischievous little bear cubs are always landing in some sort of pickle. G. VIDAL Darius gave me a great, mischievous smile. V. S. NAIPAUL An unlikely bond between the two men was a mischievous sense of humour.

▪ **mischievously** *adverb* †(**a**) unfortunately, disastrously; (**b**) with harmful effect, result, or intent; (**c**) playfully, teasingly: ME. **mischievousness** *noun* M16.

misch metal /mɪʃ ˈmɛt(ə)l/ *noun phr.* E20.
[ORIGIN German *Mischmetall*, from *mischen* to mix + *Metall* metal.]
An alloy of cerium, lanthanum, and other rare earth metals, used as an additive in various alloys, e.g. in making flints for cigarette lighters.

Mischsprache /ˈmɪʃʃpraːxə/ *noun*. Pl. ***-en*** /-ən/. M20.
[ORIGIN German.]
= MIXED ***language***.

mischty /ˈmɪstʃi/ *noun*. *dial.* Also **-chy**. L19.
[ORIGIN Alt.]
Mischief.

miscible /ˈmɪsɪb(ə)l/ *adjective & noun*. L16.
[ORIGIN medieval Latin *miscibilis*, from Latin *miscere* MIX *verb*: see -IBLE.]
▸ **A** *adjective*. Able to be mixed (*with* something); *spec.* (of a liquid) capable of forming a true solution *with* another liquid, (of liquids) mutually soluble. L16.

T. THOMSON Alcohol has a strong affinity for water, and is miscible with it. *Armed Forces* A mono-propellant . . may comprise . . a combination of miscible liquids such as hydrazine, hydrazine nitrate and water.

▸ **B** *noun*. A miscible substance. *rare*. M17.
▪ **misciˈbility** *noun* M18.

misconceit /mɪskənˈsiːt/ *noun*. *arch.* LME.
[ORIGIN from MIS-¹ 2 + CONCEIT *noun*.]
= MISCONCEPTION.

misconceit /mɪskənˈsiːt/ *verb trans. arch.* L16.
[ORIGIN from MIS-¹ 1 + CONCEIT *verb*.]
= MISCONCEIVE 2.

misconceive /mɪskənˈsiːv/ *verb*. LME.
[ORIGIN from MIS-¹ 1 + CONCEIVE.]
1 *verb intrans.* Have a false conception, entertain wrong notions, (*of*). LME.
2 *verb trans.* Form a false conception of; fail to understand rightly; devise or plan badly. L16.

Times His Lordship said that the action was obviously completely misconceived. *Shetland Times* Public apprehension about the health effects of radiation was misconceived.

▪ **misconceiver** *noun* E17.

misconception /mɪskənˈsɛpʃ(ə)n/ *noun*. M17.
[ORIGIN from MIS-¹ 2 + CONCEPTION.]
A false view or opinion (*about*); the action or an act of misconceiving something.

Which? Some of their answers showed misconceptions about what drugs do.

misconduct /mɪsˈkɒndʌkt/ *noun*. L17.
[ORIGIN from MIS-¹ 2 + CONDUCT *noun*¹.]
1 Improper or wrong behaviour; (in *pl.*) instances of improper or wrong behaviour. L17.

A. PRYCE-JONES His misery was said to be due to the misconduct . . of his wife.

2 Bad management, mismanagement; *esp.* culpable neglect of duties. E18.

BURKE Whenever in any matter of money there is concealment, you must presume misconduct.

3 *ICE HOCKEY.* A penalty assessed against a player for abusive conduct or other misbehaviour. In full ***misconduct penalty***. M20.

misconduct /mɪskənˈdʌkt/ *verb trans.* M18.
[ORIGIN from MIS-¹ 1 + CONDUCT *verb*.]
1 Mismanage. M18.
2 *refl.* Misbehave. L19.

Daily Telegraph It is a criminal offence to misconduct yourself at the polls.

misconstruct /mɪskənˈstrʌkt/ *verb trans.* L16.
[ORIGIN from MIS-¹ + CONSTRUCT *verb*.]
1 Misconstrue. Chiefly *Scot.* L16.
2 Construct badly. E19.

misconstruction /mɪskənˈstrʌkʃ(ə)n/ *noun*. E16.
[ORIGIN from MIS-¹ 2 + CONSTRUCTION.]
1 The action or an act of misconstruing something or someone. E16.
2 Faulty or bad construction. *rare*. E19.

misconstrue /mɪskənˈstruː/ *verb trans.* LME.
[ORIGIN from MIS-¹ 1 + CONSTRUE *verb*.]
1 Put a wrong construction on (a word, an action, etc.); mistake the meaning of (a person); take in a wrong sense. LME.

E. BOWEN He had misjudged her attitude, misconstrued her motives.

2 Infer wrongly. *rare*. E19.

miscontent /mɪskənˈtɛnt/ *noun*. Long *rare*. L16.
[ORIGIN from MIS-¹ 2 + CONTENT *noun*².]
Discontent.

miscontent /mɪskənˈtɛnt/ *adjective*. Now *arch. & dial.* E16.
[ORIGIN from MIS-¹ 4, 5 + CONTENT *pred. adjective*.]
Not content, dissatisfied.

miscontent /mɪskənˈtɛnt/ *verb trans.* E16.
[ORIGIN from MIS-¹ 1, 5 + CONTENT *verb*.]
Dissatisfy, displease.
▪ **miscontentment** *noun* (*arch.*) M16.

miscopy /mɪsˈkɒpi, *as noun also* ˈmɪskɒpi/ *verb & noun*. M19.
[ORIGIN from MIS-¹ 1 + COPY *verb*¹.]
▸ **A** *verb trans.* Copy incorrectly. M19.
▸ **B** *noun*. An error in copying. M19.

miscount /mɪsˈkaʊnt, ˈmɪskaʊnt/ *noun*. M16.
[ORIGIN from MIS-¹ 2 + COUNT *noun*¹. Cf. Old French *mesconte(e)*.]
A wrong count or reckoning; a miscalculation.

miscount /mɪsˈkaʊnt/ *verb*. LME.
[ORIGIN from MIS-¹ 1 + COUNT *verb*. Cf. Old French *mesconter* (mod. (*se*) *mécompter*).]
1 *verb intrans.* Make a wrong calculation. LME.
2 *verb trans.* Miscalculate, misreckon. M16.

SIR W. SCOTT After twice miscounting the sum, he threw the whole to his daughter.

miscreance /ˈmɪskrɪəns/ *noun*. *arch.* LME.
[ORIGIN Old French *mescreance* (mod. *mécréance*), from *mes-* MIS-² + CREANCE.]
False belief or faith; misbelief.

miscreancy /ˈmɪskrɪənsi/ *noun*. E17.
[ORIGIN from MISCREANCE: see -ANCY.]
1 = MISCREANCE. *arch.* E17.
2 Villainy, depravity. E19.

miscreant /ˈmɪskrɪənt/ *adjective & noun*. ME.
[ORIGIN Old French *mescreant* (mod. *mécréant*) misbelieving, unbelieving, pres. pple of *mescroire* (mod. *mécroire*) disbelieve, from *mes-* MIS-² + *croire* from Latin *credere* believe: see -ANT¹.]
▸ **A** *adjective*. **1** Misbelieving, heretical. *arch.* ME.
2 Depraved, villainous, base; rebellious, reprobate. L16.

POPE All the miscreant race of human kind.

▸ **B** *noun*. **1** A misbeliever, a heretic. *arch.* LME.
2 A villain, a criminal; a reprehensible man. L16.

LYTTON He belongs to a horrible gang of miscreants, sworn against all order and peace.

†**miscreate** *ppl adjective*. M16–L19.
[ORIGIN from MIS-¹ 1 + CREATE *adjective*.]
Miscreated.

miscreate /mɪskrɪˈeɪt/ *verb trans. rare*. E17.
[ORIGIN from MIS-¹ 1 + CREATE *verb*.]
Create wrongly or badly.
▪ **miscreation** *noun* (**a**) the action of the verb; (**b**) a miscreated or misshapen thing: M19. **miscreative** *adjective* creating or forming wrongly or badly E19.

miscreated /mɪskrɪˈeɪtɪd/ *ppl adjective*. L16.
[ORIGIN from MIS-¹ 1 + *created* pa. pple of CREATE *verb*: see -ED¹.]
Created or formed improperly or unnaturally; misshapen, deformed.

miscue /mɪsˈkjuː/ *noun*¹ *& verb*¹. M19.
[ORIGIN from MIS-¹ 2 (or stem of MISS *verb*¹) + CUE *noun*³.]
▸ **A** *noun*. **1** *BILLIARDS & SNOOKER* etc. A failure to strike the ball properly with the cue. M19.
2 *transf. & fig.* An error resulting in some kind of failure. L19.
▸ **B** *verb intrans.* Make a miscue. L19.

miscue /mɪsˈkjuː/ *noun*² *& verb*². E20.
[ORIGIN from MIS-¹ 2 + CUE *noun*².]
▸ **A** *noun*. An unexpected response or failure to respond to a phonetic or contextual cue in reading; an error, a slip. E20.
▸ **B** *verb*. **1** *verb trans. & intrans.* Misread or misinterpret (a cue); cause (a cue) to be misread. E20.
2 *verb intrans.* Make an error in reading. M20.

misdate /mɪsˈdeɪt, *as noun also* ˈmɪsdeɪt/ *verb & noun*. L16.
[ORIGIN from MIS-¹ 1 + DATE *verb*.]
▸ **A** *verb trans. & intrans.* Assign or affix a wrong date (to); date wrongly. L16.
▸ **B** *noun*. An instance of misdating; a wrong date. E18.

misdeal /mɪsˈdiːl, *as noun also* ˈmɪsdiːl/ *verb & noun*. L15.
[ORIGIN from MIS-¹ 1 + DEAL *verb*.]
▸ **A** *verb*. Pa. t. & pple **-dealt** /-ˈdɛlt/.
†**1** *verb intrans.* Distribute unfairly. Only in L15.
2 *verb intrans.* Deal or act improperly. M16.
3 *verb intrans. & trans.* Make a mistake in dealing (cards). M19.
▸ **B** *noun*. A mistake in dealing cards; a misdealt hand. L18.

misdeed /mɪsˈdiːd/ *noun*.
[ORIGIN Old English *misdǣd* = Old High German *missitāt*, Gothic *missadeþs*, from Germanic base of MIS-¹, DEED *noun*.]
An evil deed; a wrongdoing; a crime.

R. K. NARAYAN He catalogued our sins and misdeeds.

misdeem /mɪsˈdiːm/ *verb*. Now chiefly *arch. & poet.* ME.
[ORIGIN from MIS-¹ 1 + DEEM *verb*.]
1 *verb intrans.* Form a wrong judgement (*of*); hold a mistaken opinion. ME.

H. F. CARY Farther on, If I misdeem not, Soldanieri bides.

2 *verb trans.* Have a mistaken opinion or view of. LME. ▸**b** Suppose mistakenly *that*. L16. ▸**c** Wrongly suppose (a person or thing) to be something else; mistake (a thing) *for* another. M17.

J. R. LOWELL If ever with distempered voice or pen We have misdeemed thee, here we take it back.

†**3** *verb intrans. & trans.* Form an unfavourable judgement (of), think ill (of or *of*). LME–M18.

†**4 a** *verb intrans.* Suspect evil. LME–L16. ▸**b** *verb trans.* Have a suspicion of; suspect (some evil). L15–E17.

misdemean /mɪsdɪˈmiːn/ *verb intrans. & refl.* E16.
[ORIGIN from MIS-¹ 1 + DEMEAN *verb*¹.]
Misbehave, misconduct oneself.

misdemeanant /mɪsdɪˈmiːnənt/ *noun.* E19.
[ORIGIN from MISDEMEAN + -ANT¹.]
A person convicted of a misdemeanour; *transf.* a person guilty of misconduct.

misdemeanour /mɪsdɪˈmiːnə/ *noun.* Also ***-or**. E16.
[ORIGIN from MIS-¹ 2 + DEMEANOUR.]
1 LAW (now chiefly *hist.* exc. in *US*). A criminal offence which, in common law, is distinguished from and less heinous than a felony or treason. E16.
2 Bad behaviour, misconduct; an instance of this; a misdeed, an offence. E16.

H. JAMES He had been guilty of a misdemeanour in succumbing to the attractions of the admirable girl. I. MURDOCH A criminal who asks for other misdemeanours to be taken into account.

misdescribe /mɪsdɪˈskrʌɪb/ *verb trans.* E19.
[ORIGIN from MIS-¹ 1 + DESCRIBE.]
Describe inaccurately.
■ **misdescription** *noun* (an) inaccurate description M19. **misdescriptive** *adjective* giving an inaccurate description (*of*) E20.

misdiagnose /mɪsˈdʌɪəgnəʊz/ *verb trans.* E20.
[ORIGIN from MIS-¹ 1 + DIAGNOSE.]
Diagnose wrongly (a condition, an individual suffering from a condition).

misdiagnosis /ˌmɪsdʌɪəgˈnəʊsɪs/ *noun.* Pl. **-noses** /-ˈnəʊsiːz/. M20.
[ORIGIN from MIS-¹ 2 + DIAGNOSIS.]
(A) wrong diagnosis.

misdial /mɪsˈdʌɪəl/ *verb intrans. & trans.* Infl. **-ll-**, ***-l-**. M20.
[ORIGIN from MIS-¹ 1 + DIAL *verb*.]
Dial (a telephone number) wrongly.

misdid *verb pa. t.*: see MISDO.

misdirect /mɪsdʌɪˈrɛkt, -dɪ-/ *verb trans.* E17.
[ORIGIN from MIS-¹ 1 + DIRECT *verb*.]
Direct wrongly; give a wrong direction to; *spec.* send (a person, letter, etc.) to a wrong address.

ROSEMARY MANNING Talents are too often misdirected or not fully developed. M. WESLEY She had come to the wrong house, had been misdirected.

misdirection /mɪsdʌɪˈrɛkʃ(ə)n, -dɪ-/ *noun.* M18.
[ORIGIN from MIS-¹ 2 + DIRECTION.]
1 a Wrong direction or guidance; direction to a wrong address. M18. ▸**b** Distraction, diversion of a person's attention, esp. by a conjuror or thief. M20.
2 A wrong direction, line, or course. M19.

misdivision /mɪsdɪˈvɪʒ(ə)n/ *noun.* L19.
[ORIGIN from MIS-¹ 2 + DIVISION.]
1 (An instance of) incorrect division. L19.
2 *spec.* in CYTOLOGY. (An) abnormal (esp. transverse instead of longitudinal) division of a chromosome at meiosis or mitosis. M20.

misdo /mɪsˈduː/ *verb.* Infl. as DO *verb*; pa. t. usu. **-did** /-ˈdɪd/, pa. pple **-done** /-ˈdʌn/.
[ORIGIN Old English *misdōn*, from Germanic base of MIS-¹, DO *verb*.]
1 *verb intrans.* Do evil or wrong; do harm or injury. Now *rare* or *obsolete*. OE.

DRYDEN I have misdone; and I endure the Smart.

2 *verb trans.* **a** Do in error, make a mistake in doing. Now *rare* or *obsolete*. OE. ▸**b** Do badly or improperly. M19.

a T. KYD O poore Horatio, what hadst thou misdone.

3 *verb trans.* Harm, injure, wrong. Long *rare*. ME.
†**4** *verb trans.* Destroy, do away with. ME–E17.
■ **misdoer** *noun* (now *rare*) a wrongdoer, a malefactor ME. **misdoing** *noun* (**a**) the action of the verb; (**b**) a misdeed: ME.

misdoubt /mɪsˈdaʊt/ *noun.* Now chiefly *Scot. & dial.* M16.
[ORIGIN from MIS-¹ 6 + DOUBT *noun*.]
Apprehension of evil; mistrust, suspicion; a misgiving, doubt, or suspicion.
■ **misdoubtful** *adjective* (*rare*) suspicious L16. **misdoubtfully** *adverb* (*rare*) L16.

misdoubt /mɪsˈdaʊt/ *verb.* Now chiefly *Scot. & dial.* M16.
[ORIGIN from MIS-¹ 6 + DOUBT *verb*.]
1 *verb trans.* Have doubts as to the existence, truth, or reality of (a thing). Also foll. by (*but*) *that*. Earliest as ***misdoubting*** *verbal noun*. M16.
2 *verb trans.* Fear, suspect; be suspicious about. M16. ▸**b** *verb refl. & intrans.* Suspect; be suspicious *of*. *obsolete* or *arch.* M17.

M. DRAYTON Warn'd by Danger to misdoubt the worst. *Harper's Magazine* I misdoubt the ladies won't like it.

3 *verb trans.* Have doubts about the character, honesty, etc., of (a person); mistrust. L16.
4 *verb trans.* Have misgivings or forebodings with regard to. L16.

DICKENS I much misdoubt an amateur artist's success in this vast place.

misdraw /mɪsˈdrɔː/ *verb.* Pa. t. **-drew** /-druː/; pa. pple **-drawn** /-drɔːn/. ME.
[ORIGIN from MIS-¹ 1 + DRAW *verb*.]
†**1** *verb intrans.* Go astray. Only in ME.
2 *verb trans.* Draw or draw up incorrectly. LME.
†**3** *verb trans.* Entice, allure, mislead. LME–L16.
■ **misdrawing** *noun* a faulty drawing LME.

mise /miːz, mʌɪz/ *noun.* LME.
[ORIGIN Old French = action of setting, expenses, wages, arbitration, from *mis* pa. pple of *mettre* place, set, from Latin *mittere* send, (later) put, place.]
†**1** LAW. The issue in a writ of right. LME–M19.
†**2** In *pl.* Expenses, costs. LME–L15.
†**3** A grant, payment, or tribute made to secure a liberty or immunity. L15–M19.
4 A settlement by agreement. Chiefly *hist.* E18.

misease /mɪsˈiːz/ *noun. arch.* ME.
[ORIGIN Old French *mesaise*, from *mes-* MIS-² + *aise* EASE *noun*.]
1 Distress, trouble, misery; extreme suffering or discomfort. ME.
2 Lack of the means of living; poverty, need, want. ME.
3 Uneasiness, disquiet. E20.

mise au point /miːz o pwɛ̃/ *noun phr.* Pl. ***mises au point*** (pronounced same). E20.
[ORIGIN French.]
A focusing or clarification of an obscure subject or problem.

miseducate /mɪsˈɛdjʊkeɪt/ *verb trans.* M17.
[ORIGIN from MIS-¹ 1 + EDUCATE.]
Educate wrongly or badly.
■ **miseduˈcation** *noun* E17.

mise-en-page /miːzɑ̃paːʒ/ *noun.* Pl. ***mises-en-page*** (pronounced same). E20.
[ORIGIN French *mise en pages* page-setting, imposition.]
The design of a printed page etc., including the layout of text and illustrations. Also, the composition of a picture.

mise en place /miz ɑ̃ plas/ *noun phr.* M20.
[ORIGIN French, lit. 'putting in place'.]
In a professional kitchen: the initial preparation of equipment and ingredients carried out before the commencement of cooking.

mise en scène /miːz ɑ̃ sɛn/ *noun phr.* Also ***mise-en-scène***. Pl. ***mises en scène*** (pronounced same). M19.
[ORIGIN French.]
1 The staging of a play; the scenery and properties of a stage production. M19.
2 The setting or surroundings of an event or action. L19.

misemploy /mɪsɪmˈplɔɪ, -ɛm-/ *verb trans.* E17.
[ORIGIN from MIS-¹ 1 + EMPLOY *verb*.]
Employ or use wrongly or improperly.
■ **misemployment** *noun* L16.

miser /ˈmʌɪzə/ *adjective, noun, & verb.* L15.
[ORIGIN Latin = wretched, unfortunate.]
▸ †**A** *adjective.* **1** Miserly, niggardly. L15–M19.
2 Miserable, wretched. M16–E17.
▸ **B** *noun.* †**1** A miserable or wretched person; a wretch. M16–M19.
2 A person who hoards wealth and lives miserably in order to do so. Also, an avaricious grasping person, a niggard. M16.

GOLDSMITH As some lone miser, visiting his store, Bends at his treasure, counts, recounts it o'er. V. WOOLF Like a miser, she has hoarded her feelings within her own breast.

▸ **C** *verb trans.* Hoard *up* in a miserly way. *rare.* L19.
■ **miserhood** *noun* (*rare*) miserliness M19.

miserabilism /ˈmɪz(ə)rəbɪlɪz(ə)m/ *noun.* L19.
[ORIGIN mod. Latin *miserabilismus*, from Latin *miserabilis* MISERABLE: see -ISM.]
Pessimism, gloomy negativity.
■ **miserabilist** *noun & adjective* (**a**) *noun* an advocate or adherent of miserabilism; (**b**) *adjective* of or pertaining to miserabilism or miserabilists: E20.

miserable /ˈmɪz(ə)rəb(ə)l/ *adjective & noun.* LME.
[ORIGIN Old French & mod. French *misérable* from Latin *miserabilis* pitiable, from *miserari* be pitiful, from *miser*: see MISER *adjective*, -ABLE.]
▸ **A** *adjective.* **I** Of a person.
1 Existing in a state of external discomfort or distress; needy, poverty-stricken, wretchedly poor. Now *rare.* LME.
2 Miserly, mean, stingy. Now chiefly *Scot., Austral., & NZ.* L15.
3 Full of mental misery; wretchedly unhappy or uncomfortable. L16.

C. ANGIER She was miserable and agitated and quarrelling with everyone.

▸ **II 4** Of a thing: pitiable, deplorable. Now *rare.* LME.
5 Of a condition, an event, etc.: full of misery; causing wretchedness or extreme discomfort. L15.

V. BRITTAIN Three miserable weeks of disappointment . . and anxiety, and depression. A. WESKER A cold, miserable, two-roomed flat, all on your own. D. FRANCIS It was an uncomfortable, miserable, thought.

6 Unworthy, inadequate; contemptible, mean. E16.

New Republic The miserable pensions that are being paid to the widows of fallen soldiers. G. ORWELL The miserable little threepenny-bit.

▸ **B** *noun.* A miserable person; a person who is extremely unhappy or wretched. M16.
■ **miseraˈbility** *noun* (*rare*) M16. **miserableness** *noun* E16. **miserably** *adverb* LME.

misère /mɪˈzɛː(r), *foreign* mizɛr (*pl. same*)/ *noun.* L18.
[ORIGIN French = poverty, misery.]
1 Misery; a miserable condition or circumstance. L18.
misère ouverte /uːˈvɛːt/ [French *ouvert* open] (in solo whist) a declaration by which the caller undertakes to win no tricks, playing with all his or her cards exposed on the table.
2 CARDS. A declaration by which the caller undertakes not to win any tricks. E19.

misereatur /mɪˌzɛrɪˈeɪtə/ *noun.* L15.
[ORIGIN Latin (= may (God) have mercy), 3rd person sing. pres. subjunct. of *misereri* (see MISERERE): its first word.]
ECCLESIASTICAL. In the Western Church: = ABSOLUTION 1b.

miserere /mɪzəˈrɪəri, -ˈrɛː-/ *noun.* ME.
[ORIGIN Latin, imper. sing. of *misereri* have pity, have mercy, from *miser* MISER *adjective*.]
1 a Psalm 51 (50 in the Vulgate), beginning *Miserere mei Deus* 'Have mercy upon me, O God', one of the penitential psalms. ME. ▸**b** A musical setting of this psalm. L18.
2 *transf.* A cry for mercy; a prayer in which mercy is sought. E17.
†**3** In full ***miserere mei*** [= on me]. Severe colic; ileus. E17–L18.
4 = MISERICORD 4. L18.

misericord /mɪˈzɛrɪkɔːd/ *noun.* ME.
[ORIGIN Old French & mod. French *miséricorde* from Latin *misericordia*, from *misericors* pitiful, from *miser*, stem of *misereri* (see MISERERE) + *cord-*, *cor* heart.]
1 Compassion, pity, mercy. Also as *interjection. arch.* ME.
2 A dagger for dealing a death stroke. ME.
3 *hist.* An apartment in a monastery in which certain relaxations of the rule were permitted. LME.
4 A shelving projection on the underside of a hinged seat in a choir stall, which, when turned up, gives support to someone standing. E16.

M

miserly /ˈmʌɪzəli/ *adjective.* L16.
[ORIGIN from MISER *noun* + -LY¹.]
1 Of, pertaining to, or characteristic of a miser; niggardly, stingy. L16.

V. S. NAIPAUL A miserly and cruel man who counted every biscuit in the tin.

2 Of a quantity: paltry, meagre. M20.
■ **miserliness** *noun* M17.

misery /ˈmɪz(ə)ri/ *noun.* LME.
[ORIGIN from Anglo-Norman var. of Old French & mod. French *misère* or from Latin *miseria* from *miser*: see MISER *adjective*, -Y³.]
1 The state of being in external discomfort or distress; wretchedness of outward circumstances. LME.

J. RUSKIN The misery of unaided poverty.

2 a A distressing condition or circumstance; a cause or source of wretchedness. Now only in *pl.* LME. ▸**b** A wretched person or place. L18. ▸**c** A gloomy self-pitying person; a killjoy. *colloq.* E20.

a H. CARPENTER He's one of those people who really feels the miseries of the world. **c** WILLY RUSSELL You can be a real misery sometimes, can't y'?

3 The state of being wretchedly or profoundly unhappy; extreme sorrow or distress. E16.

J. HERSEY The general blur of misery through which they moved.

†**4** Miserliness, niggardliness. M16–E17.
5 Bodily pain. *dial.* E19.
6 CARDS. = MISÈRE 2. *colloq.* M19.
– PHRASES: **misery me!** expr. self-pity, distress, or general wretchedness. **put out of one's misery** release from suffering or suspense. **the miseries** *colloq.* a fit of peevishness or depression.
– COMB.: **misery guts** *colloq.* = sense 2c above.

mises au point, ***mises-en-page***, ***mises en scène*** *noun phrs.* pls. of MISE AU POINT etc.

misesteem /mɪsɪˈstiːm/ *noun.* M19.
[ORIGIN from MIS-¹ 2 + ESTEEM *noun*.]
Want of esteem or respect; disrespect.

misesteem /mɪsɪˈstiːm/ *verb trans. arch.* L16.
[ORIGIN from MIS-¹ 1 + ESTEEM *verb*.]
= MISESTIMATE *verb*.

misestimate /mɪsˈɛstɪmət/ *noun.* M19.
[ORIGIN from MIS-¹ 2 + ESTIMATE *noun*.]
A wrong estimate or valuation.

misestimate /mɪsˈɛstɪmeɪt/ *verb trans.* M19.
[ORIGIN from MIS-¹ 1 + ESTIMATE *verb*.]
Estimate wrongly, have a false estimate of.

misestimation /ˌmɪsɛstɪˈmeɪʃ(ə)n/ *noun.* E19.
[ORIGIN from MIS-¹ 2 + ESTIMATION.]
(A) wrong or false estimation.

misexpress /mɪsɪkˈsprɛs, -ɛk-/ *verb refl.* E18.
[ORIGIN from MIS-¹ 1 + EXPRESS *verb*¹.]
Express oneself wrongly or badly.
■ **misexpression** *noun* M17. **misexpressive** *adjective* E19.

misfall /mɪsˈfɔːl/ *verb intrans.* Long *obsolete* exc. *Scot.* Pa. t. **-fell** /-ˈfɛl/; pa. pple **-fallen** /-ˈfɔːl(ə)n/. ME.
[ORIGIN from MIS-¹ 1 + FALL *verb.* Cf. Middle Low German, Middle Dutch, Dutch *misvallen*, Middle High German *missevallen*, German *missfallen*.]
†**1** Suffer misfortune, come to grief. Only in ME.
2 Of an event, chance, etc.: happen unfortunately, turn out badly. ME.

misfare /mɪsˈfɛː/ *noun.* Long *rare.* ME.
[ORIGIN from MIS-¹ 2 + FARE *noun*¹.]
A mishap; misfortune.

misfare /mɪsˈfɛː/ *verb intrans.* Long *obsolete* exc. *Scot.*
[ORIGIN Old English *misfaran* = Old Frisian *misfara*, Middle High German *missevarn*, Old Norse *misfara*, from Germanic base of MIS-¹, FARE *verb.*]
1 Fare badly, come to grief. OE.
†**2** Go wrong, transgress. OE–L16.

misfeasance /mɪsˈfiːz(ə)ns/ *noun.* L16.
[ORIGIN Old French *mesfaisance*, from pres. pple of *mesfaire* (mod. *méfaire*), from *mes-* MIS-² + *faire* do: see -ANCE. Cf. MALFEASANCE.]
LAW. (A) transgression, (a) trespass; *spec.* (a) wrongful exercise of authority, *spec.* in the management of a company or the performance of a public office.
■ **misfeasor** *noun* a person who commits a misfeasance M17.

†**misfeign** *verb intrans. rare* (Spenser). Only in L16.
[ORIGIN from MIS-¹ 1 + FEIGN *verb.*]
Feign with an intention to do wrong.

misfell *verb pa. t.* of MISFALL.

misfield /mɪsˈfiːld, *as noun also* ˈmɪsfiːld/ *verb & noun.* L19.
[ORIGIN from MIS-¹ 1 + FIELD *verb.*]
CRICKET & RUGBY etc. ▸**A** *verb trans. & intrans.* Field (a ball) badly. L19.
▸**B** *noun.* An instance of bad fielding of a ball. E20.

M

†**misfigure** *noun.* L15–M19.
[ORIGIN from MIS-¹ 2 + FIGURE *noun.*]
Disfigurement, deformity.

misfigure /mɪsˈfɪɡə/ *verb trans. obsolete* exc. *dial.* M16.
[ORIGIN from MIS-¹ 1 + FIGURE *verb.*]
Disfigure, distort; disguise.

misfire /mɪsˈfʌɪə, *as noun also* ˈmɪsfʌɪə/ *verb & noun.* M18.
[ORIGIN from MIS-¹ 1 + FIRE *verb.* Cf. *miss fire* s.v. MISS *verb*¹.]
▸**A** *verb intrans.* **1** Of a gun, a gun's charge: fail to discharge or explode. M18.
2 Of an internal-combustion engine: suffer failure of the fuel to ignite (correctly or at all). E20.

Classic Racer The engine started misfiring during the fifth lap.

3 Fail to have an intended effect; go wrong. M20.

A. N. WILSON Either it was a mistake . . or . . a nasty practical joke which had hideously misfired.

▸**B** *noun.* **1** A failure to discharge or explode; *fig.* a failure of intention. Cf. MISS-FIRE. L18.
2 The action or an instance of misfiring. E20.

Rally Sport After a lead came off the distributor . . they had to contend with a misfire.

misfit /ˈmɪsfɪt/ *noun & adjective.* E19.
[ORIGIN from MIS-¹ 2 + FIT *noun*³.]
▸**A** *noun.* **1** A garment etc. which does not fit the person for whom it is meant. *arch.* E19.

G. B. SHAW Clothed in a seedy misfit which made him look lamentably down on his luck.

2 A person who is unsuited to his or her environment, work, etc. M19.

M. DRABBLE Forever desiring, . . never achieving, an eternal misfit.

3 PHYSICAL GEOGRAPHY. A misfit stream (see sense B.3 below). E20.
▸**B** *attrib.* or as *adjective.* **1** Not fitting properly. L19.
2 Pertaining to or designating social misfits. E20.
3 PHYSICAL GEOGRAPHY. Designating or pertaining to a stream which, on the basis of its present-day flow, would have eroded a larger or a smaller valley than it has done. Cf. OVERFIT, UNDERFIT. M20.

misfit /mɪsˈfɪt/ *verb trans. & intrans.* Infl. **-tt-**. M19.
[ORIGIN from MIS-¹ 1 + FIT *verb*¹, or from MISFIT *noun & adjective.*]
Fail to fit, fit badly.

misfortunate /mɪsˈfɔːtʃ(ə)nət/ *adjective.* Now chiefly *Scot.* & *US.* E16.
[ORIGIN from MIS-¹ 4 + FORTUNATE *adjective.*]
Unfortunate.

misfortune /mɪsˈfɔːtʃuːn, -tʃ(ə)n/ *noun.* LME.
[ORIGIN from MIS-¹ 2 + FORTUNE *noun.*]
1 Bad fortune, ill luck; an instance of this. LME.

J. B. MOZLEY Misfortune, adversity, soften the human heart. M. FLANAGAN You have had your own misfortunes, even disasters.

2 A pregnancy or birth outside marriage; an illegitimate child. Chiefly in ***have a misfortune***, ***meet with a misfortune***, have an illegitimate child. *dial.* & *colloq.* E19.
■ **misfortuned** *adjective* (now *rare*) affected by misfortune, unfortunate L15. †**misfortuner** *noun* an unfortunate person: only in L18.

misgive /mɪsˈɡɪv/ *verb.* Pa. t. **-gave** /-ɡeɪv/; pa. pple **-given** /-ˈɡɪv(ə)n/. E16.
[ORIGIN from MIS-¹ 1, 5 + GIVE *verb.*]
1 *verb trans.* Of a person's mind, heart, etc.: incline (the person) to doubt or apprehension, fill with suspicion or foreboding, (*about*); cause to fear *that.* E16. ▸**b** *verb intrans.* Of the mind, (*rare*) a person, etc.: have misgivings. E17.

V. ACKLAND We were to set out on a honeymoon. My heart misgave me.

2 *verb intrans.* Fail, go wrong; *spec.* (of a gun) misfire. Chiefly *Scot.* L16.
3 *verb trans.* Give wrongly. Now *rare.* E17.

J. RUSKIN His swift correction of my misgiven Wordsworth's line.

■ **misgiver** *noun* (*rare*) a person who has misgivings E17.

misgiving /mɪsˈɡɪvɪŋ/ *noun.* L16.
[ORIGIN from MISGIVE *verb* + -ING¹.]
The action of MISGIVE *verb*; a feeling of mistrust, apprehension, or loss of confidence, (freq. in *pl.*).

R. K. NARAYAN They still had many misgivings about the expedition. C. THUBRON This religion of materialism filled me with misgiving.

misgo /mɪsˈɡəʊ/ *verb intrans. obsolete* exc. *dial.* Infl. as GO *verb*; pa. t. usu. **-went** /-ˈwɛnt/, pa. pple usu. **-gone** /-ˈɡɒn/. ME.
[ORIGIN from MIS-¹ 1 + GO *verb.*]
1 Go astray; go the wrong way. ME.
2 Go wrong in conduct or action; make a mistake; miscarry. ME.

misgotten /mɪsˈɡɒt(ə)n/ *adjective.* LME.
[ORIGIN from MIS-¹ 1 + GOTTEN *ppl adjective.*]
1 Wrongly obtained; ill-gotten. LME.
2 = MISBEGOTTEN. LME.

misgovern /mɪsˈɡʌv(ə)n/ *verb trans.* LME.
[ORIGIN from MIS-¹ 1 + GOVERN.]
Govern wrongly or badly; mismanage, misdirect. Now *spec.* direct and control the affairs of (a state etc.) wrongly or badly, mismanage the government of.
■ **misgovernor** *noun* LME.

misgovernance /mɪsˈɡʌv(ə)nəns/ *noun.* Now *rare* or *obsolete.* LME.
[ORIGIN from MIS-¹ 2 + GOVERNANCE.]
†**1** Misconduct, misbehaviour. LME–E17.
†**2** Mismanagement, misuse. LME–L17.
3 Misgovernment. LME.

misgoverned /mɪsˈɡʌv(ə)nd/ *adjective.* LME.
[ORIGIN from MISGOVERN + -ED¹.]
†**1** Characterized by misconduct; immoral. LME–E17.
†**2** Unruly; misdirected. L16–M17.
3 Badly ruled; mismanaged. M19.

misgovernment /mɪsˈɡʌv(ə)nm(ə)nt, -vəm(ə)nt/ *noun.* LME.
[ORIGIN from MIS-¹ 2 + GOVERNMENT.]
†**1** Unruly behaviour; misconduct. LME–M17.
2 Bad government of a country or state; maladministration. Also, disorder, anarchy. L16.
†**3** *gen.* Mismanagement. E17–L18.

misguidance /mɪsˈɡʌɪd(ə)ns/ *noun.* E17.
[ORIGIN from MIS-¹ 2 + GUIDANCE.]
Misdirection.

misguide /mɪsˈɡʌɪd/ *verb.* LME.
[ORIGIN from MIS-¹ 1 + GUIDE *verb.*]
†**1** *verb refl.* Go astray; conduct oneself or one's affairs badly. LME–M17.
2 *verb trans.* Mismanage, misgovern. Also, treat badly; injure, spoil. *obsolete* exc. *Scot.* L15.
3 *verb trans. & intrans.* Misdirect, mislead. L15.

GOLDSMITH Vanity is more apt to misguide men than false reasoning.

■ **misguider** *noun* (now *rare*) L16.

misguided /mɪsˈɡʌɪdɪd/ *adjective.* E16.
[ORIGIN from MISGUIDE + -ED¹.]
1 Guided in a wrong direction; *spec.* misdirected or mistaken in action or thought. E16.

M. MEYER A . . tragedy of a lonely, misguided and tormented spirit. *Private Eye* The country has been brought to a halt by the . . misguided actions of . . malcontents.

†**2** Badly behaved, immoral. E16–L17.

■ **misguidedly** *adverb* M19. **misguidedness** *noun* E19.

mishandle /mɪsˈhand(ə)l/ *verb trans.* L15.
[ORIGIN from MIS-¹ 1 + HANDLE *verb*¹.]
Handle or treat badly, wrongly, or roughly. Also, manage or deal with wrongly or ineffectively.

S. WEYMAN Solomon is old, and they may mishandle him. E. PIZZEY He mishandled the cork. The champagne exploded over the table. *Daily Mail* Senior officials mishandled the sale and development of a hospital site.

mishanter /mɪˈʃantə/ *noun. Scot.* & *N. English.* Also **mischanter** /mɪsˈtʃantə/. M18.
[ORIGIN Var. of MISAUNTER. Formed with *-sch-* app. after *mischance*.]
Misadventure, a mishap.

mishap /ˈmɪshap/ *noun.* ME.
[ORIGIN from MIS-¹ 2 + HAP *noun.*]
1 Bad luck, misfortune (now *rare*); harm, injury. ME.

Independent She skated impressively without mishap.

2 An unlucky accident. ME.

Publishers Weekly Miss Read begins her summer holiday with a mishap, a fall that nets her a broken arm and an injured ankle.

mishappen /mɪsˈhap(ə)n/ *verb intrans.* Now *rare.* ME.
[ORIGIN from MIS-¹ 1 + HAPPEN *verb.*]
(Of a person) meet with mishap or misfortune; (of an event etc.) happen unfortunately.

mishear /mɪsˈhɪə/ *verb.* Pa. t. & pple **-heard** /-hɔːd/. OE.
[ORIGIN from MIS-¹ 1 + HEAR.]
†**1** *verb trans.* Disobey. Only in OE.
2 *verb trans. & intrans.* Hear incorrectly or imperfectly. OE.

mishit /mɪsˈhɪt, ˈmɪshɪt/ *noun.* L19.
[ORIGIN from MIS-¹ 2 + HIT *noun.*]
In various sports: a faulty or bad hit of a ball.

mishit /mɪsˈhɪt/ *verb trans.* Infl. **-tt-**. Pa. t. & pple **-hit**. E20.
[ORIGIN from MIS-¹ 1 + HIT *verb.*]
In various sports: hit (a ball) badly, strike a ball from (an opponent) badly.

mishla /ˈmɪʃlɔː/ *noun.* Also **mush-** /ˈmʌʃ-/, **-law**. L17.
[ORIGIN Miskito *mushla*.]
A fermented liquor from plantain, cassava, maize, etc., made in eastern Central America.

mishmash /ˈmɪʃmaʃ/ *noun & verb.* Also **mish-mash**. L15.
[ORIGIN Redupl. of MASH *noun*¹.]
▸**A** *noun.* A confused mixture; a medley, a hodgepodge, a jumble. L15.

C. THUBRON He began to reminisce in a mishmash of German and English. J. IRVING It was a . . mishmash of the parts that were still serviceable.

▸**B** *verb trans.* Make a mishmash of; throw into confusion. L17.

Mishnah /ˈmɪʃnə/ *noun.* Also **-a**. E17.
[ORIGIN Post-biblical Hebrew *mišnāh* repetition, instruction.]
The collection of precepts and customs which form the basis of the Talmud and is held to embody the contents of Jewish Oral Law. Also, a paragraph of this.
■ **Mishnaic** /mɪʃˈneɪɪk/ *adjective* E18. **Mishnic** *adjective* E18. †**Mishnical** *adjective* E18–M19.

misidentify /mɪsʌɪˈdɛntɪfʌɪ/ *verb trans.* L19.
[ORIGIN from MIS-¹ 1 + IDENTIFY.]
Identify erroneously.
■ **misidentifiˈcation** *noun* E20.

†**misimprove** *verb trans.* M17.
[ORIGIN from MIS-¹ 5 + IMPROVE *verb*².]
1 Use wrongly or badly; abuse. Latterly chiefly *US.* M17–L19.
2 Make worse in attempting to improve. Only in M19.
■ †**misimˈprovement** *noun* M17–L19.

misinclined /mɪsɪnˈklʌɪnd/ *adjective. rare.* E17.
[ORIGIN from MIS-¹ 1 + INCLINE *verb.*]
†**1** Wrongly inclined. Only in E17.
2 Disinclined. M19.

misinform /mɪsɪnˈfɔːm/ *verb trans.* LME.
[ORIGIN from MIS-¹ 1 + INFORM *verb.*]
Give wrong or misleading information to.
■ **misinformant** *noun* a person who gives wrong or misleading information M19. **misinforˈmation** *noun* (*a*) the action of misinforming someone; the condition of being misinformed; (*b*) wrong or misleading information: L16. **misinformative** *adjective* giving wrong or misleading information E20. **misinformer** *noun* a misinformant L16.

misinstruct /mɪsɪnˈstrʌkt/ *verb trans.* M16.
[ORIGIN from MIS-¹ 1 + INSTRUCT.]
Instruct wrongly or badly.
■ **misinstruction** *noun* (an instance of) wrong or bad instruction M17.

misintelligence /mɪsɪnˈtɛlɪdʒ(ə)ns/ *noun.* Now *rare.* M17.
[ORIGIN from MIS-¹ 2 + INTELLIGENCE *noun.*]
†**1** Misunderstanding; disagreement, discord. M17–M18.
2 Wrong impression as to meaning or facts. L18.
3 Misinformation. E19.
4 Lack of intellect. M19.

misinterpret /mɪsɪnˈtəːprɪt/ *verb trans.* M16.
[ORIGIN from MIS-¹ 1 + INTERPRET.]
Interpret wrongly; draw a wrong inference from.
■ **misinterpretable** *adjective* E17. **misinterpreˈtation** *noun* L16. **misinterpreter** *noun* L16.

misjoin /mɪsˈdʒɔɪn/ *verb trans.* M16.
[ORIGIN from MIS-¹ 1 + JOIN *verb*.]
Join or connect wrongly or unsuitably.

misjoinder /mɪsˈdʒɔɪndə/ *noun.* L18.
[ORIGIN from MIS-¹ 2 + JOINDER.]
LAW. Improper joinder of parties in an action; improper joinder of offences in a criminal prosecution.

misjudge /mɪsˈdʒʌdʒ/ *verb trans. & intrans.* LME.
[ORIGIN from MIS-¹ 1 + JUDGE *verb*.]
Judge or assess wrongly; have or form a wrong opinion (of).
Bella How easy it is to misjudge from appearances. F. WELDON Sandy misjudged the speed of the incoming traffic.
■ **misjudgement** *noun* E16. **misjudger** *noun* (*rare*) M16.

miskal *noun* var. of MITHQAL.

misken /mɪsˈkɛn/ *verb trans. Scot. & N. English.* L15.
[ORIGIN from MIS-¹ 1, 5 + KEN *verb*.]
= MISKNOW.

miskick /mɪsˈkɪk, *as noun also* ˈmɪskɪk/ *verb & noun.* L19.
[ORIGIN from MIS-¹ 1 + KICK *verb*¹.]
▸ **A** *verb trans. & intrans.* Kick (a ball etc.) badly or wrongly. L19.
▸ **B** *noun.* An instance of miskicking, a bad kick. L19.

Miskito /mɪˈskiːtəʊ/ *adjective & noun.* Also **Mosquito** /mɒ-/. Pl. **-os**. L18.
[ORIGIN Spanish *Mosquito* and its etymon Miskito.]
▸ **A** *adjective.* Designating or pertaining to an American Indian people living on the Atlantic coast of Nicaragua and Honduras, or their language. L17.
▸ **B** *noun.* A member of this people; their language. L17.

misknow /mɪsˈnəʊ/ *verb trans.* Pa. t. **-knew** /-njuː/; pa. pple **-known** /-nəʊn/. ME.
[ORIGIN from MIS-¹ 1, 5 + KNOW *verb*.]
1 Refuse to recognize or notice; affect ignorance of; disown. ME.
2 Not know or be aware of; be ignorant of. *obsolete* exc. *Scot.* LME.
3 Fail to recognize; mistake the identity of. LME.
4 Have a wrong idea of; misapprehend, misunderstand. M16. ▸†**b** *refl.* Have false ideas about oneself, one's position, etc. Chiefly *Scot.* M16–E17.
■ **misknowledge** *noun* †(*a*) failure to recognize or acknowledge; (*b*) lack of understanding: L15.

mislay /mɪsˈleɪ/ *verb trans.* Pa. t. & pple **mislaid** /mɪsˈleɪd/. LME.
[ORIGIN from MIS-¹ 1 + LAY *verb*¹.]
1 Place or set wrongly; err in placing (a thing). Now *rare.* LME.
2 Accidentally put (a thing) in a place where it cannot readily be found; *euphem.* lose. E17.
N. MITFORD Cedric went . . to buy *Vogue*, having mislaid his own copy.

mislead /mɪsˈliːd/ *verb trans.* Pa. t. & pple **misled** /mɪsˈlɛd/.
[ORIGIN Old English *mislǣdan*, from MIS-¹ 1 + LEAD *verb*¹.]
1 Lead astray in action or conduct; cause to have an incorrect impression or belief. OE.
M. FITZHERBERT His optimistic reports misled the politicians. *Daily Mail* British Coal bosses accused Mr. Scargill of deliberately misleading his members.
†**2** Mismanage. ME–L15.
3 Lead or guide in the wrong direction. L16.
■ **misleader** *noun* LME.

misleading /mɪsˈliːdɪŋ/ *adjective.* L16.
[ORIGIN from MISLEAD + -ING².]
That leads someone astray, that causes error; imprecise, confusing, deceptive.
W. TREVOR My delicate appearance was misleading. *Which?* The Act will make it illegal to make misleading statements about ticket prices.
■ **misleadingly** *adverb* M19. **misleadingness** *noun* M19.

mislear /mɪsˈlɪə/ *verb trans.* Long *obsolete* exc. *dial.* Also **-lere**.
[ORIGIN Old English *mislǣran*, from MIS-¹ 1 + LERE *verb*.]
Misteach; mislead, misguide.

misleared /mɪsˈlɪəd/ *adjective. Scot. & N. English.* Also **-lered**. L16.
[ORIGIN from MISLEAR + -ED¹.]
Bad-mannered, rude.

misled *verb pa. t. & pple* of MISLEAD.

mislike /mɪsˈlʌɪk/ *verb & noun. arch.*
[ORIGIN Old English *mislīcian*, from MIS-¹ 1 + LIKE *verb*¹.]
▸ **A** *verb.* **1** *verb trans.* Be displeasing to; displease, offend. OE.
†**2** *verb intrans.* Be displeased. Also, be troubled or uneasy. ME–M17.
†**3** *verb intrans.* Grow sickly or unhealthy; waste away. LME–E17.
4 *verb trans.* Be displeased at; disapprove of; dislike. E16.
GLADSTONE They mistrust and mislike the centralisation of power.
▸ **B** *noun.* †**1** Discomfort, trouble, unhappiness. Only in ME.
2 Distaste for, dislike *of*. Also, a dislike. M16.
†**3** Wasting away; sickliness, disease. M16–E17.
†**4** Disaffection, dissension. L16–M17.
■ **misliker** *noun* M16. **misliking** *noun* = MISLIKE *noun* ME.

mislippen /mɪsˈlɪp(ə)n/ *verb trans. Scot. & N. English.* M16.
[ORIGIN from MIS-¹ 1 + LIPPEN *verb*.]
1 Deceive; disappoint. M16.
2 Neglect, overlook. L16.
3 Suspect. E19.

mislocate /mɪsləʊˈkeɪt/ *verb trans.* E19.
[ORIGIN from MIS-¹ 1 + LOCATE *verb*.]
Assign an incorrect location or position to.
■ **mislocation** *noun* M17.

mismanage /mɪsˈmanɪdʒ/ *verb trans. & intrans.* L17.
[ORIGIN from MIS-¹ 1 + MANAGE *verb*.]
Manage badly or wrongly.
M. MEYER Hansen was frequently drunk and mismanaged the estate.
■ **mismanagement** *noun* M17. **mismanager** *noun* a bad manager L17.

mismatch /mɪsˈmatʃ, ˈmɪsmatʃ/ *noun.* E17.
[ORIGIN Partly from MIS-¹ 2 + MATCH *noun*¹, partly from the verb.]
A bad match; a discrepancy. Also, an unequal or unfair sporting contest.
Christian Science Monitor A basic mismatch between the capability of the utilities and a very demanding technology.

mismatch /mɪsˈmatʃ/ *verb trans.* L16.
[ORIGIN from MIS-¹ 1 + MATCH *verb*¹.]
Match badly, unsuitably, or incorrectly.

mismate /mɪsˈmeɪt/ *verb trans.* E19.
[ORIGIN from MIS-¹ 1 + MATE *verb*².]
Mismatch, mate badly or unsuitably. Chiefly as ***mismated*** *ppl adjective.*

mismeasure /mɪsˈmɛʒə/ *verb trans.* M18.
[ORIGIN from MIS-¹ 1 + MEASURE *verb*.]
Measure or estimate incorrectly.
■ **mismeasurement** *noun* M19.

mismove /mɪsˈmuːv/ *noun. US.* L19.
[ORIGIN from MIS-¹ 2 + MOVE *noun*.]
A wrong or faulty move.

misname /mɪsˈneɪm/ *verb trans.* E16.
[ORIGIN from MIS-¹ 1 + NAME *verb*.]
†**1** Call by an abusive name; insult. E16–L19.
2 Call by a wrong name; name wrongly or unsuitably. M16.
Contemporary Review The now misnamed Pacific Ocean.

misnome /mɪsˈnəʊm/ *verb trans. rare.* E19.
[ORIGIN Back-form. from MISNOMER.]
Misname.

misnomer /mɪsˈnəʊmə/ *noun & verb.* LME.
[ORIGIN Anglo-Norman, use as noun of Old French *mesnom(m)er*, from *mes-* MIS-² + *nommer* from Latin *nominare*, from *nomen* name: see -ER⁴.]
▸ **A** *noun.* **1** A wrong name or designation. LME.
S. BRETT Hickton's rehearsal schedule (probably a misnomer for a process that was continuous).
2 The use of a wrong name; a misapplication of a term. M17.
B. GELDOF To call the place a camp would have been a misnomer.
▸ **B** *verb trans.* Misname, apply a misnomer to. Chiefly as ***misnomered*** *ppl adjective.* M18.

miso /ˈmiːsəʊ/ *noun.* E17.
[ORIGIN Japanese, prob. ult. from a northern Korean language.]
Paste made from fermented soya beans and barley or rice malt, used in Japanese cookery.

miso- /ˈmɪsəʊ, ˈmʌɪsəʊ/ *combining form.* Before a vowel also **mis-**.
[ORIGIN Greek, from base of *misein* to hate, *misos* hatred: see -O-.]
Forming nouns and adjectives with the sense 'hating, hatred of, a hater of'. Cf. PHILO-.
■ **miˈsologist** *noun* a hater of reason or discussion L19. **miˈsology** *noun* hatred of reason or discussion; hatred of learning or knowledge: M19. **misoˈneism** *noun* [Greek *neos* new] hatred of novelty L19. **misoˈneist** *noun* a hater of novelty L19. **miˈsosophy** *noun* hatred of wisdom M19.

misogamy /mɪˈsɒɡəmi, mʌɪ-/ *noun.* M17.
[ORIGIN mod. Latin *misogamia*, from Greek *misogamos* hating marriage, formed as MISO- + -GAMY.]
Hatred of marriage.
■ **misogamist** *noun* a hater of marriage E18.

misogynist /mɪˈsɒdʒ(ə)nɪst, mʌɪ-/ *noun.* E17.
[ORIGIN from Greek *misogunēs*, formed as MISO- + *gunē* woman: see -IST.]
A hater of women.
M. MEYER He did not flirt, but was certainly no misogynist.
■ **misogyˈnistic** *adjective* pertaining to or characteristic of misogynists or misogyny; misogynous: E19.

misogyny /mɪˈsɒdʒ(ə)ni, mʌɪ-/ *noun.* M17.
[ORIGIN mod. Latin *misogynia* from Greek *misogunia*, formed as MISOGYNIST: see -Y³.]
Hatred of women.
■ **ˈmisogyne** *noun* (now *rare*) = MISOGYNIST E19. **misoˈgynic** *adjective* = MISOGYNOUS E19. **misogynism** *noun* = MISOGYNY M19. **misogynous** *adjective* having a hatred of women; characterized by misogyny: L19.

misorder /mɪsˈɔːdə/ *noun.* Now *rare.* E16.
[ORIGIN from MIS-¹ 2 + ORDER *noun*.]
1 Lack or breach of order; confusion, disorder, misbehaviour. E16. ▸†**b** A commotion, a riot. M16–L19.
†**2** Bad or wrong order. M16–M17.

misorder /mɪsˈɔːdə/ *verb trans.* Now *rare* or *obsolete.* LME.
[ORIGIN from MIS-¹ 1 + ORDER *verb*.]
†**1** *refl.* Misbehave oneself; be disorderly or ill-behaved. LME–M18.
2 Put into disorder; confuse, disturb. L15.

misorient /mɪsˈɔːrɪɛnt, -ˈɒr-/ *verb trans.* M20.
[ORIGIN from MIS-¹ 1 + ORIENT *verb*.]
Orient differently or variably; orient badly.
■ **misorienˈtation** *noun* M20.

misorientate /mɪsˈɔːrɪɛnteɪt, -ˈɒr-/ *verb trans.* M20.
[ORIGIN from MIS-¹ 1 + ORIENTATE.]
= MISORIENT.

misperceive /mɪspəˈsiːv/ *verb trans.* E20.
[ORIGIN from MIS-¹ 1 + PERCEIVE *verb*.]
Perceive wrongly or incorrectly; mistake.
■ **misperception** *noun* (a) wrong or incorrect perception E18.

mispickel /ˈmɪspɪk(ə)l/ *noun.* L17.
[ORIGIN German.]
MINERALOGY. Arsenopyrite.

misplace /mɪsˈpleɪs/ *verb.* M16.
[ORIGIN from MIS-¹ 1 + PLACE *verb*.]
▸ **I** *verb trans.* **1** Assign a wrong position to. Now *rare.* M16.
2 Put in the wrong place; mislay, lose. Also, put in the wrong hands. L16.
W. COWPER The globe and sceptre in such hands misplaced. *Femina* The . . form had been misplaced by the company.
3 Bestow (one's affections etc.) on a wrong or inappropriate object; place (one's confidence etc.) misguidedly. Freq. as ***misplaced*** *ppl adjective.* M17.
H. JACOBSON I am prepared to accept your . . misplaced enthusiasm.
▸ †**II** *verb intrans.* **4** Use wrong or unsuitable words. *rare* (Shakes.). Only in E17.
■ **misplacement** *noun* M17.

misplay /mɪsˈpleɪ, ˈmɪspleɪ/ *noun.* Chiefly *US.* M19.
[ORIGIN from MIS-¹ 2 + PLAY *noun*.]
A bad or forbidden play or move in a game; bad or wrong play.

misplay /mɪsˈpleɪ/ *verb trans.* Chiefly *US.* L18.
[ORIGIN from MIS-¹ 1 + PLAY *verb*.]
Play wrongly, badly, or in contravention of the rules.

misprint /*as verb* mɪsˈprɪnt, *as noun* ˈmɪsprɪnt/ *verb & noun.* E16.
[ORIGIN from MIS-¹ 1 + PRINT *verb*.]
▸ **A** *verb.* **1** *verb trans.* Print incorrectly, print by mistake. E16.
2 *verb intrans.* Of a deer: leave footprints in a pattern different from the usual one. E20.
▸ **B** *noun.* A mistake in printing or in a printed work. E19.
A. PRICE The same story, only . . with more misprints, in the *Guardian.*

misprision /mɪsˈprɪʒ(ə)n/ *noun*¹. LME.
[ORIGIN Anglo-Norman *mesprisioun* = Old French *mesprison* error, wrong action or speech, from *mesprendre* (mod. *méprendre*), from *mes-* MIS-² + *prendre* take. Cf. MISPRIZE *verb*².]
1 LAW. A wrongful act or omission; *spec.* a misdemeanour or failure of duty by a public official. Now *rare.* LME.
2 LAW (now *hist.*). In full ***misprision of treason*** or ***felony***. Orig., an offence similar to, but less serious than, treason or felony. Subsequently, the crime of (deliberately) concealing one's knowledge of a treasonable act or a felony. M16.
3 The mistaking of one thing for another; a misunderstanding, a mistake. L16.

misprision /mɪsˈprɪʒ(ə)n/ *noun*². *arch.* L16.
[ORIGIN from MISPRIZE *verb*¹, after MISPRISION *noun*¹.]
Contempt, scorn. Also, failure to appreciate or recognize the value of something (usu. foll. by *of*).

misprize /mɪsˈprʌɪz/ *verb*¹ & *noun*¹. L15.
[ORIGIN Old French *mesprisier* (mod. *mépriser*), from *mes-* MIS-² + *priser*, from *pris-*: see PRIZE *verb*¹.]
▸ **A** *verb trans.* Despise, scorn. Also, fail to appreciate the value or good qualities of. L15.
▸ **B** *noun.* = MISPRISION *noun*². *rare.* L16.
■ **misprizer** *noun* (*rare*) L16.

M

misprize /mɪsˈprʌɪz/ *verb*[2] & *noun*[2]. Long *rare*. L15.
[ORIGIN Old French *mespris* pa. pple of *mesprendre* commit a crime (mod. *se méprendre* be mistaken): see MISPRISION *noun*[1].]
▸ **A** *verb trans.* Mistake, misunderstand. L15.
▸ †**B** *noun.* Mistake, error. *rare* (Spenser). Only in L16.

mispronounce /mɪsprəˈnaʊns/ *verb trans.* L16.
[ORIGIN from MIS-[1] 1 + PRONOUNCE *verb*.]
Pronounce incorrectly.
■ **ˌmispronunciˈation** *noun* M16.

misproportioned /mɪsprəˈpɔːʃ(ə)nd/ *adjective.* M16.
[ORIGIN from MIS-[1] 1 + PROPORTIONED.]
Badly or wrongly proportioned.
■ **misproportion** *noun* (a) lack of proportion L16.

mispunctuate /mɪsˈpʌŋ(k)tʃʊeɪt, -tjʊ-/ *verb trans. & intrans.* M19.
[ORIGIN from MIS-[1] 1 + PUNCTUATE *verb*.]
Punctuate incorrectly.
■ **mispunctuˈation** *noun* E19.

misquote /mɪsˈkwəʊt/ *noun.* M19.
[ORIGIN from MIS-[1] 2 + QUOTE *noun*[2].]
An incorrect quotation, a misquotation.

misquote /mɪsˈkwəʊt/ *verb trans.* L16.
[ORIGIN from MIS-[1] 1 + QUOTE *verb*.]
Quote incorrectly.
■ **misquoˈtation** *noun* (*a*) inaccuracy in quoting; (*b*) an incorrect quotation: E17. **misquoter** *noun* M19.

misread /mɪsˈriːd/ *verb trans.* Pa. t. & pple **misread** /mɪsˈrɛd/. M17.
[ORIGIN from MIS-[1] 1 + READ *verb*.]
Read or interpret (a text, a situation, etc.) wrongly.
■ **misreader** *noun* M19. **misreading** *noun* an incorrect reading, a misinterpretation M19.

misrecite /mɪsrɪˈsʌɪt/ *verb trans.* Now *rare*. L16.
[ORIGIN from MIS-[1] 1 + RECITE *verb*.]
Recite, relate, or describe incorrectly.
■ **misrecital** *noun* M16.

misreckon /mɪsˈrɛk(ə)n/ *verb.* E16.
[ORIGIN from MIS-[1] 1 + RECKON *verb*.]
1 *verb trans.* Reckon or calculate (an amount) incorrectly; make a wrong calculation in respect of (a certain number). E16.
†**2** *verb trans.* Charge (a person) wrongly, *esp.* overcharge. M16–M17.
3 *verb intrans.* Make a wrong calculation; be out in one's reckoning. E17.

M

misrecollect /ˌmɪsrɛkəˈlɛkt/ *verb trans. & intrans.* L18.
[ORIGIN from MIS-[1] 1 + RECOLLECT *verb*.]
Recollect wrongly or imperfectly.
■ **misrecollection** *noun* E19.

misregister /mɪsˈrɛdʒɪstə/ *noun.* M20.
[ORIGIN from MIS-[1] 2 + REGISTER *noun*[1].]
PRINTING. The inaccurate positioning of printed matter on a sheet, *esp.* the misalignment of two or more colours in relation to each other.

misregistration /ˌmɪsrɛdʒɪˈstreɪʃ(ə)n/ *noun.* M20.
[ORIGIN from MIS-[1] 2 + REGISTRATION.]
Misalignment or faulty registration of images, esp. of the three fields that compose a colour television picture.

misremember /mɪsrɪˈmɛmbə/ *verb trans. & intrans.* M16.
[ORIGIN from MIS-[1] 1 + REMEMBER *verb*.]
Remember wrongly or imperfectly; *dial.* forget.
■ **misremembrance** *noun* (*rare*) M16.

misreport /mɪsrɪˈpɔːt/ *noun.* LME.
[ORIGIN from MIS-[1] 2 + REPORT *noun*.]
†**1** Unfavourable repute. LME–L17.
2 A false or incorrect report. M16.

A. LANG If they are all misreports . . what is the value of anthropological evidence?

3 False or inaccurate reporting. Now *rare*. M16.

Times Lit. Suppl. Hepburn has cleared away a huge clutter of accumulated legend and misreport.

misreport /mɪsrɪˈpɔːt/ *verb.* LME.
[ORIGIN from MIS-[1] 1 + REPORT *verb*.]
1 *verb trans.* Report incorrectly; give a false account of. LME.

H. LATIMER Christ himselfe was misreported, & falsely accused. DE QUINCEY His behaviour . . scandalously misreported by Bennet.

†**2** *verb intrans.* Give a false report (*of*). E16–E17.
†**3** *verb trans.* Speak ill of; slander. M16–E17.
■ **misreporter** *noun* (now *rare*) M16.

misrepresent /ˌmɪsrɛprɪˈzɛnt/ *verb trans.* M17.
[ORIGIN from MIS-[1] 1 + REPRESENT *verb*.]
1 Represent wrongly or imperfectly; give a false representation or account of. M17.

H. JAMES I'm not at all keen about marrying—your son misrepresented me.

2 Represent badly as an agent or representative, fail in acting as a representative of. *rare*. M19.
■ **ˌmisrepresenˈtation** *noun* the action of the verb; (a) wrong or incorrect representation: M17. **misrepreˈsentative** *noun* a person who fails to represent others, a bad representative L18. **misrepreˈsentative** *adjective* not (properly) representative (*of*) M18. **misrepresenter** *noun* a person who misrepresents L17.

misrule /mɪsˈruːl/ *noun.* LME.
[ORIGIN from MIS-[1] 2 + RULE *noun*.]
†**1** Disorderly conduct; ill-regulated living; excess. LME–E17.
2 Bad rule or government; misgovernment. Also, disorder, anarchy. LME.
– PHRASES: **Lord of Misrule**, **Master of Misrule** (*a*) (*hist.*) a person presiding over Christmas games and revelry in a wealthy household; (*b*) *transf.* a person, emotion, etc., that causes disorderly conduct; a ringleader.

misrule /mɪsˈruːl/ *verb trans.* LME.
[ORIGIN from MIS-[1] 1 + RULE *verb*.]
†**1** Manage or control badly. LME–E19.
2 Rule or govern badly. LME.
■ **misruler** *noun* (*rare*) †(*a*) a disorderly person; (*b*) a bad ruler: LME.

miss /mɪs/ *noun*[1].
[ORIGIN Old English *miss*, corresp. to Middle Low German, Middle High German *misse* (Dutch *mis*), Old Norse *missa*, *missir*.]
1 Deprivation or loss of or *of* a person or thing. Now *rare*. OE. ▸†**b** Observable lack. L17–E18.

C. H. SPURGEON Temporal blessings are not trifles, for the miss of them would be a dire calamity. **b** DEFOE There was no miss of the usual Throng of People in the Streets.

2 (A feeling of) disadvantage or regret caused by the loss or absence *of* a person or thing. Chiefly in ***have miss of***, ***have a miss of***, ***find a great miss of***, ***find great miss of***, ***feel the miss of***, etc. Now *dial.* & *colloq.* ME.
†**3** Wrong, wrongdoing, offence; a wrong, a misdeed. Latterly *Scot.* ME–E19.

G. CHAPMAN Some other way I might repair this shameful miss.

4 A failure to hit something aimed at. M16. ▸**b** BILLIARDS etc. A failure to hit the object ball, on account of which the opponent scores; *esp.* a deliberate failure which leaves the cue ball in a safe position. M19. ▸**c** An unsuccessful gramophone record. M20.

RIDER HAGGARD He has just killed half a dozen . . partridges without a miss. *Proverb*: A miss is as good as a mile.

near miss: see NEAR *adjective*. **b give a miss (in baulk)** deliberately fail to hit the object ball (in baulk). **score a miss** receive points from a miss by one's opponent.

5 A failure to obtain or achieve something. Now *rare*. E17.

R. L'ESTRANGE Aërius turn'd Heretique upon the misse of a Bishoprick.

6 A failure to do or attend something: in ***give (a thing) a miss***, omit to do or attend (something), avoid, leave alone. *colloq.* E20.

J. CANNAN I'm afraid I've given church a miss this morning.

miss /mɪs/ *noun*[2]. Also (esp. in titles) **M-**. E17.
[ORIGIN Abbreviation of MISTRESS *noun*.]
1 A kept woman, a mistress; a prostitute. *obsolete* exc. *dial.* E17.

M. CHARLTON I would rather chuse to see this child . . the wife of an honest man, than the Miss of a Nobleman.

2 (**M-**.) Used as a title preceding the name of an unmarried woman or girl without a higher or honorific or professional title, or a married woman's maiden name retained for professional or other reasons. M17. ▸**b** Used preceding the name of a country, group, etc. as a title of a young woman representing it, esp. in a beauty contest. E20.

W. F. HARVEY Saxon was introduced . . to Parke and Mrs. Parke and Miss Cornelius. J. BETJEMAN Now I'm engaged to Miss Joan Hunter Dunn. *Times* Miss Ure . . was found collapsed by her husband, Mr. Robert Shaw, the actor.

b ***Miss America***, ***Miss World***, etc.

3 A young unmarried woman; a girl, *esp.* one at school or who has lately left school. Now usu. *derog.*, with implication of silliness or wilfulness. M17. ▸**b** In *pl.* (with ref. to sizes or styles of articles of clothing): girls of from about 10 to 17 years of age; garments or garment sizes suitable for girls of this age. L19.

A. P. HERBERT Closing her blue eyes dreamily like some Victorian miss. M. ALLINGHAM A sulky little miss if ever I saw one. **b** *Vogue* We pass through the Baby Linen on our way to the Misses.

4 (Without proper name or article.) Used without ref. to married status as a conventional form of address or reference to a (young) woman, e.g. a shop assistant or waitress, (among children) a female teacher (corresp. to *sir*), or (orig.) the daughter of the house. M17.

BYRON Is it miss or the cash of mamma you pursue? J. B. PRIESTLEY 'Let's have coffee, shall we? Miss! Miss!' M. GEE Miss who was kind and taught drama.

5 = MRS. *dial.* (chiefly *US*). L18.
– PHRASES: ***junior miss***: see JUNIOR *adjective*. **Miss Ann(e)**, **Miss Annie** *US black slang*, *derog.* (a name for) a young white woman, esp. the daughter of a landowner. ***Miss Lonelyhearts***: see LONELY *adjective*. **Miss Milligan** a kind of patience played with two packs of cards. ***Miss Molly***: see MOLLY *noun*[1] 2. **Miss Nancy** *dial.* & *colloq.* (a name for) an unheroic or effeminate male. **Miss Right** the young woman who would make the ideal wife for a particular person, one's destined wife. **miss sahib** *Indian* the daughter of a memsahib, a European girl. **Miss Willmott's ghost** [Ellen Ann Willmott (1860–1934), English horticulturist] a large ornamental sea holly, *Eryngium giganteum*, which turns white after it has flowered.

miss /mɪs/ *noun*[3]. M18.
[ORIGIN Perh. a use of MISS *noun*[2], or of MISS *noun*[1].]
CARDS. In loo: an extra hand for which any of the players may discard his or her own.

miss /mɪs/ *noun*[4]. *colloq.* L19.
[ORIGIN Abbreviation.]
= MISCARRIAGE 3.

miss /mɪs/ *verb*[1].
[ORIGIN Old English *missan* = Old Frisian *missa*, Middle & mod. Low German, Middle Dutch & mod. Dutch *missen*, Old & mod. High German *missen*, Old Norse *missa*, from Germanic: see MIS-[1].]
▸ **I** *verb trans.* & (*arch.*) *intrans.* foll. by *of*. Fail to hit, meet, etc.
1 Fail to hit or strike (esp. a target). OE.

D. FRANCIS Thanked the fates that the destructive lump of metal had missed my heart. F. CHICHESTER The compass showed that I was fifty-five degrees off course, headed to miss even Tasmania. C. SIMMONS Mr. Margin put the phone down hard, missing the cradle. *fig.*: J. R. GREEN Cromwell . . in his later years felt bitterly that Puritanism had missed its aim.

2 Fail to obtain, receive, or attain to. ME. ▸**b** Fail to capture or catch. L16.

LD MACAULAY A project which . . had very narrowly missed of success. J. CONRAD He missed a larger fame only by the chances of the service. **b** J. G. WHITTIER They had missed of the old chief, but had captured his son. *Daily Chronicle* Jackson was missed off a 'balloon' in the long field.

3 a Fail to achieve or accomplish. ME. ▸**b** Fail *to do*; (now *Scot.* & *dial.*) have no success in *doing*. LME.

a DEFOE If he miss'd of his Business outward bound, he was to go up to China. **b** KEATS I was in pain, Lest I should miss to bid thee a good morrow. A. C. SWINBURNE With what excellent care . . this has been done, no one can miss of seeing.

4 a Lose or fail to hit on (the right path). Chiefly in ***miss one's way***. LME. ▸**b** Fail to obtain footing on (a step, plank, etc.). M16.

b J. JACKSON Till wee misse the bridge and fall into the ditch.

5 Fail to observe, hear, or perceive intellectually. L15.

K. WATERHOUSE She was missing the whole . . point. J. WILCOX Mr. Pickens missed the turn off Flat Avenue. V. GORNICK Although my mother never seemed to be listening . . she missed nothing.

6 Escape, avoid. Now *dial.* exc. with specification of a margin, as *just*, *narrowly*, etc. E16.

J. BUCHAN A stranger who had just missed death by an ace. E. WAUGH He narrowly missed being run down by a large . . car.

7 Fail to make possible or intended contact with (a person). M16.

V. BRITTAIN In the crowd . . we had somehow missed each other.

8 a Fail to take advantage of (an opportunity etc.). E17. ▸**b** Not be able or fortunate enough to witness, experience, etc.; be too late to catch (a train etc.) or to watch (an event, broadcast programme, etc.). E17.

a T. M. LINDSAY Better to be imposed upon . . than to miss the chance of entertaining a brother Christian. C. THUBRON Beneath the city's surface, I felt, a vivid life was going on and I was missing it. Z. TOMIN I slept heavily, missing the early dusk. B. CONACHER I wouldn't have missed playing in the best league in the world. **b** M. SARTON You'd better go and pack now, or you'll miss that plane. J. HOWKER Because of them sitting there nattering . . we missed the six o'clock news.

▸ **II** *verb intrans.* Fail.
†**9** Go wrong, make a mistake. Orig. ***impers.*** OE–M18.

R. ASCHAM If a childe misse . . in forgetting a worde, or in chaunging a good with a worse.

10 Fail to hit the target; fail to take a catch. ME.

A. LOVELL In cutting off Heads, they . . never miss.

†**11** Come to an end, give out. ME–E16.
†**12** Be lacking. Foll. by indirect obj., *to*. LME–E19.
13 Fail to happen, come, etc. *obsolete* exc. *Scot.* LME.
14 Of a person, a plan, etc.: be unsuccessful. Now *rare* or *obsolete*. L16.

DRYDEN The bank above must fail before the venture miss.

15 a Of a crop etc.: be unproductive, fail. *dial.* E17. ▸**b** Of a woman: fail to menstruate at the normal time, miss a period. M20. ▸**c** Of an animal: fail to conceive after mating. M20.
16 Of a motor vehicle or engine: undergo failure of ignition in one or more cylinders. E20.
▸ **III** *verb trans.* Be without.
17 Be without, lack; cease to have, lose. Also, do without. Now only (*colloq.*) in ***be missing***, have lost, be without. ME. ▸†**b** In *pass.* Be missing or absent. LME–L16.

O. FELTHAM He hath good Materials for a foundation: but misseth wherewith to rear the walls. G. NAYLOR Dr. Buzzard's truck is missing both fenders.

18 Notice the absence or loss of. ME.

S. Raven By the time Nancy had missed him . . it would be too late.

19 Perceive with regret the absence or loss of; feel the lack of. ME.

R. P. Jhabvala He is lonely and misses his family very much.

▸ **IV** *verb trans.* Omit.

20 Omit, leave out (esp. part of what one is reading, writing, etc.). Also foll. by *out*. ME.

G. Vidal Burden's heart missed a beat. M. S. Power He creeps up the stairs, missing the fifth and ninth which creak. K. Gibbons The only one that can read is Starletta and she misses words.

21 Omit the performance of (a customary or expected action); fail to keep (an appointment); fail to attend (church, school, etc., a given spectacle, ceremony, etc.). M16.

Henry Fielding She . . rarely missed a ball, or any other public assembly. A. Lively Tommy has grown impatient with me for missing rehearsals.

– PHRASES ETC.: ***hit-and-miss***: see HIT *verb*. **miss a trick** *colloq.* fail to take advantage of an opportunity or notice something important (usu. in neg. contexts). **missed abortion** the retention of a fetus in the womb for a period after it has died. **missed approach** AERONAUTICS an approach that is discontinued for any reason. **miss fire** (of a firearm) fail to go off, misfire; *fig.* be unsuccessful. ***miss one's guess***: see GUESS *noun*. ***miss one's tip***: see TIP *noun*[4]. ***miss plant***: see PLANT *noun* 7. **miss stays** NAUTICAL fail in an attempt to go about from one tack to another. **miss the boat**, **miss the bus** *colloq.* lose an opportunity.

– WITH ADVERBS IN SPECIALIZED SENSES: **miss out** *colloq.* miss or be deprived of an experience (foll. by *on*); (see also sense 20 above).

■ **missable** *adjective* (*a*) GOLF (of a stroke, esp. a putt) capable of missing the hole (opp. ***holeable***); (*b*) able to be missed (more usual in ***unmissable***): E20.

miss /mɪs/ *verb*[2] *trans.* E19.
[ORIGIN from MISS *noun*[2].]
Address as 'miss'.

Miss. *abbreviation.*
Mississippi.

missaid *verb pa. t. & pple* of MISSAY.

missal /ˈmɪs(ə)l/ *noun & adjective.* ME.
[ORIGIN ecclesiastical Latin *missale* neut. sing. of *missalis* adjective, from *missa* MASS *noun*[1]. Adjective from *missalis*.]
▸ **A** *noun.* A book containing the service of the Mass for the whole year; *loosely* a Roman Catholic book of prayers, esp. when illuminated. Also more fully ***missal book***. ME.
▸ **†B** *adjective.* Of or pertaining to the Mass. LME–M17.

missay /mɪsˈseɪ/ *verb. arch.* Pa. t. & pple **missaid** /mɪsˈsɛd/. ME.
[ORIGIN from MIS-[1] 1 + SAY *verb*[1].]
1 *verb trans.* Speak ill of (a person); abuse, slander. ME.

T. Heywood Is she such a Saint, None can missay her?

†2 *verb trans.* Say with abusive or slanderous intent. ME–E17.
†3 *verb intrans.* Speak abusively or slanderously (*of*). ME–L16.

Spenser Her tongue . . brought forth speeches myld when she would have missayd.

4 *verb trans.* Say wrongly or incorrectly. Now *rare*. ME.
5 *verb intrans.* Say what is not right or correct, tell an untruth. LME.

Byron Some of mosque, and some of church, And some, or I missay, of neither.

misseem /mɪsˈsiːm/ *verb.* Now *rare*. L15.
[ORIGIN from MIS-[1] 1 + SEEM *verb*.]
1 *verb trans.* Be unbecoming or unbefitting to. L15.
†2 *verb intrans.* Give a false appearance. *rare* (Spenser). Only in L16.

missel *noun* var. of MISTLE.

missense /ˈmɪs-sɛns/ *adjective.* M20.
[ORIGIN from MIS-[1] 2 + SENSE *noun*.]
GENETICS. Of, pertaining to, or designating a mutation which causes the substitution of one amino acid for another at a particular point in a polypeptide or protein molecule.

miss-fire /mɪsˈfʌɪə, ˈmɪsfʌɪə/ *noun.* E19.
[ORIGIN from ***miss fire*** s.v. MISS *verb*[1]. Cf. MISFIRE *noun*.]
A failure to discharge or explode.

misshape /mɪsˈʃeɪp/ *noun.* Now *rare*. LME.
[ORIGIN from MIS-[1] 2 + SHAPE *noun*.]
A physical deformity; a misshapen body or person.

misshape /mɪsˈʃeɪp/ *verb trans.* Pa. t. & pple **-shaped**, (*arch.*) **-shapen** /-ˈʃeɪp(ə)n/. LME.
[ORIGIN from MIS-[1] 1 + SHAPE *verb*.]
Give a bad, ugly, or wrong shape to; deform.
■ **misshaped** *adjective* misshapen, deformed L15. †**misshapedness** *noun* (*rare*) E17–E18.

misshapen /mɪsˈʃeɪp(ə)n/ *adjective.* LME.
[ORIGIN from MIS-[1] 1 + *shapen* pa. pple of SHAPE *verb*.]
Having a bad, ugly, or wrong shape; deformed, monstrous; distorted (*lit. & fig.*). Formerly also, morally monstrous or ugly.

J. Steinbeck She was misshapen; her belly, tight . . and distended. *New York Review of Books* Some federal courts have developed misshapen theories of a conspiracy.

■ **misshapenly** *adverb* E17. **misshapenness** /-n-n-/ *noun* L16.

†misshapen *verb trans. rare*. LME–L18.
[ORIGIN Prob. from pa. pple of MISSHAPE *verb*: see -EN[6]. Perh. partly from MIS-[1] 1 + SHAPEN *verb*[1].]
Distort, make misshapen.

missie *noun* var. of MISSY *noun*.

missikin /ˈmɪsɪkɪn/ *noun. joc.* E19.
[ORIGIN from MISSY *noun* + -KIN.]
A girl or young woman.

missile /ˈmɪsʌɪl/ *adjective & noun.* E17.
[ORIGIN Latin *missilis* (adjective), from *miss-* pa. ppl stem of *mittere* send (out); sense B.2 from *missile* use as noun of neut. sing. of adjective: see -ILE.]
▸ **A** *adjective.* **1** Of a projectile etc.: suitable for throwing at a target or for discharge from a machine. E17.
2 Of a weapon: that discharges arrows, bullets, etc. *rare*. E19.
▸ **B** *noun.* **†1** In *pl.* [= Latin *missilia*]. Sweets, perfumes, etc., thrown as largesse by Roman emperors. *rare*. E–M17.
2 A weapon or other object suitable for throwing at a target or discharging from a machine. M17. ▸**b** A destructive projectile that is self-propelling and directed by remote control or automatically. M20.

R. P. Jhabvala The children . . often threw stones and other missiles.

b cruise missile, ***Exocet missile***, ***Pershing missile***, etc. ***ballistic missile***. ***guided missile***: see GUIDE *verb*.

– COMB.: **missileman** a person engaged in the construction, design, flying, or operation of a missile.

■ **missilery** *noun* (*N. Amer.*) missiles collectively, a collection of missiles M19.

missing /ˈmɪsɪŋ/ *adjective.* LME.
[ORIGIN from MISS *verb*[1] + -ING[2].]
1 Not present, not to be found; absent, lost. LME.

R. C. Hutchinson A protracted wrangle with the laundry about a missing shirt.

missing link something lacking to complete a series; *spec.* a hypothetical animal assumed to be an evolutionary link between humans and the anthropoid apes. **missing mass** the amount by which an observed or measured mass falls short of an expected or inferred mass; *esp.* in ASTRONOMY, the difference between the calculated mass of the universe, a cluster of galaxies, etc., and the sum of the masses of the observed objects in the system.

2 Of a person: absent from a place, esp. their home, and not having traced or confirmed to be alive; (of a soldier, sailor, etc.) not present after an action but not definitely known to have been killed, wounded, or taken prisoner. M19.

R. K. Narayan He was busy searching for a missing son.

be among the missing *US colloq.* be away from home.

■ †**missingly** *adverb* (*rare*, Shakes.) with a sense of loss: only in E17.

missiology /mɪsɪˈɒlədʒi/ *noun.* M20.
[ORIGIN Irreg. from MISSION *noun* + -OLOGY.]
The branch of knowledge that deals with the methods, purpose, etc., of religious missions.
■ **missioˈlogical** *adjective* M20. **missiologist** *noun* M20.

mission /ˈmɪʃ(ə)n/ *noun.* M16.
[ORIGIN French, or Latin *missio(n-)*, from *miss-* pa. ppl stem of *mittere* send (out): see -ION.]
1 An act or instance of sending someone or (formerly, *rare*) something, or an instance of being sent, esp. to perform some function or service; *spec.* of (***a***) *hist.* Jesuits to seminaries abroad; (***b***) members of a religious organization to do missionary work abroad; (***c***) THEOLOGY the second or third person of the Trinity by the first, or the third person by the second, in a form manifest to humankind; (***d***) people with authority to preach the Christian faith and administer the sacraments; (***e***) a body of people to a foreign country to conduct negotiations, establish political or commercial relations, etc. M16.
2 A body of people sent abroad to spread a religious faith; a body of missionaries; *gen.* a delegation of people sent abroad to perform an important assignment. E17. ▸**b** A body of people established to do work similar to missionary work in their own country, esp. among the poor or disadvantaged. Also ***home mission***, ***city mission***, etc. E19.

Daily Telegraph A joint mission from Northern Ireland to America to promote industrial investment.

3 The purpose for which such a body is sent or established; an important task or assignment; in *pl.*, organized missionary activities; *gen.* an important task. L17. ▸**b** A strongly felt aim, ambition, or calling; a person's vocation or work in life. E19.

J. Conrad To escort that . . lady back . . as a personal mission of the highest honour. **b** G. B. Shaw I believe we have a sacred mission to spread British ideas. P. Carey Mrs Dalton was a woman with a mission . . to demystify the treatment of mental illness.

4 A permanent establishment of missionaries in a country; a missionary post or station; a mission house. M18. ▸**b** A religious centre established in a district for missionary, evangelical, or humanitarian work. L18.

Southey They . . To the nearest mission sped and ask'd the Jesuit's aid.

5 An intensive course of preaching, services, etc. organized to stimulate interest in the work of a parish or in the Christian faith. L18.

F. Wyndham She . . continued on her measured, purposeful mission to the umbrella shop.

6 A journey with a purpose, *spec.* to preach and extend the Christian faith. L18.
7 A military or scientific operation or expedition, *esp.* an operational flight carried out by an aircraft. E20. ▸**b** An expedition into space. M20.

J. Coe He flew a top-secret mission over Berlin. **b** *Scientific American* The lunar samples returned to the earth by the Apollo missions.

– COMB.: **mission-critical** *adjective* (chiefly with ref. to computers) vital to the functioning of an organization or completion of a task; **mission control** a group or organization responsible for directing a spacecraft and its crew; **mission creep** a gradual shift in objectives during the course of a military campaign, often resulting in an unplanned long-term commitment; **mission furniture** *US* a plain, solid style of furniture modelled originally on the furniture of Spanish missions in N. America; **mission house** a building where a Christian mission is conducted; **mission impossible** [*Mission: Impossible*, US TV series first shown in 1966] a very demanding or hopeless assignment; **mission oak** *US* mission furniture made of oak; **mission statement** a formal summary of the aims and values of a company, organization, or individual; **mission stiff** *US slang* a person who frequents missions; *esp.* a tramp who pretends to be religious so as to get free food and lodging.

■ **missional** *adjective* (*rare*) missionary E20. **missionate** *verb intrans.* (*US*) conduct a mission, do missionary work E19. **missionist** *noun* a person who does missionary work E20. **missionize** *verb trans. & intrans.* conduct a mission (to), do missionary work (among) E19.

mission /ˈmɪʃ(ə)n/ *verb.* L17.
[ORIGIN from the noun.]
1 *verb trans.* Send on a mission; give (a person) a mission to perform. Usu. in *pass.* L17.
2 *verb trans.* Conduct a religious mission among (a people) or in (a district). L18.
3 *verb intrans.* Conduct a mission. L19.

missionary /ˈmɪʃ(ə)n(ə)ri/ *noun & adjective.* E17.
[ORIGIN mod. Latin *missionarius* (whence also French *missionnaire*), from Latin *missio(n-)*: see MISSION *noun*, -ARY[1].]
▸ **A** *noun.* **1** A person sent on or engaged in a religious mission, *esp.* in a foreign country; a person engaged in missionary work. E17.

M. Angelou If more Africans had eaten more missionaries, the Continent would be in better shape. *transf.*: *Listener* The latest missionary for F. R. Leavis's organic community.

home missionary, ***city missionary***, etc.

†2 An agent, an emissary; *esp.* a person sent on a political mission. L17–E19.
†3 A missionary body or establishment. E–M18.
4 The sweet briar, *Rosa rubiginosa*, introduced to New Zealand by missionaries and now an invasive weed. *NZ*. L19.
▸ **B** *adjective.* **1** Of or pertaining to religious missions; sent on or engaged in a mission; characteristic of a person sent on or engaged in a religious mission. M17.

Max-Müller The three missionary religions, Buddhism, Mohammedanism, and Christianity. *Company* He obviously has a missionary zeal to clean and tidy up other people's lives.

†2 Sent out. L17–M19.

S. Dobell The night . . calling By missionary winds and twilight birds.

– COMB. & SPECIAL COLLOCATIONS: **missionary box**: for the reception of contributions to the funds of a missionary society; **missionary position** *colloq.* the position for sexual intercourse in which the woman lies underneath the man and facing him.

■ **missionarize** *verb intrans.* do missionary work M19. **missionaryship** *noun* M19.

missionary /ˈmɪʃ(ə)n(ə)ri/ *verb trans. & intrans. rare*. M19.
[ORIGIN from the noun.]
Preach to (a person) as or in the manner of a missionary.

missioned /ˈmɪʃ(ə)nd/ *adjective.* Chiefly *poet.* L18.
[ORIGIN from MISSION *noun*, *verb*: see -ED[2], -ED[1].]
Having a mission; sent on a mission or errand.

missioner /ˈmɪʃ(ə)nə/ *noun.* M17.
[ORIGIN from MISSION *noun* + -ER[1].]
A person sent on a mission, a missionary; *esp.* a Jesuit missionary. Now chiefly, a person who leads a parochial mission (in some dioceses, a permanent clerical officer).

missis *noun* var. of MISSUS.

missish /ˈmɪsɪʃ/ *adjective.* Chiefly *derog.* L18.
[ORIGIN from MISS *noun*[2] + -ISH[1].]
Resembling or characteristic of a miss, young lady, or schoolgirl; affectedly demure, squeamish, or sentimental.
■ **missishness** *noun* M19.

M

Mississauga /mɪsɪˈsɔːɡə/ *noun & adjective*. **E18.**
[**ORIGIN** Ult. from Ojibwa *misiza:gi:*, lit. 'people of the large river outlet' (Mississagi River in Ontario, Canada).]
▸ **A** *noun*. Pl. same, **-s**.
1 A member of an Algonquian people of Canada. **E18.**
2 (**m-**.) = MASSASAUGA. **M19.**
▸ **B** *adjective*. Of or pertaining to the Mississauga. **M18.**

mississippi /mɪsɪˈsɪpi/ *noun*. **E18.**
[**ORIGIN** Fanciful application of *Mississippi*, a N. American river.]
A game similar to bagatelle, in which balls are driven against cushions at the side of the table so as to go through arches at the end of the table.

Mississippian /mɪsɪˈsɪpɪən/ *noun & adjective*. **L18.**
[**ORIGIN** from *Mississippi* (see below) + -AN.]
▸ **A** *noun*. **1** A native or inhabitant of Mississippi, a state of the US on the Gulf of Mexico. **L18.**
2 *GEOLOGY*. The Mississippian period; the system of rocks dating from this time. **E20.**
▸ **B** *adjective*. **1** Of or pertaining to the state of Mississippi. **E19.**
2 *GEOLOGY*. Designating or pertaining to the period of the Palaeozoic era in N. America, following the Devonian and preceding the Pennsylvanian, and corresponding to the Lower Carboniferous in Europe. **L19.**
3 *ARCHAEOLOGY*. Designating or relating to a settled N. American Indian culture of the south-eastern US, dated to about AD 800–1300. **M20.**

missive /ˈmɪsɪv/ *adjective & noun*. **LME.**
[**ORIGIN** medieval Latin *missivus* (in *litterae missivae*), from Latin *miss-*: see MISSION *noun*, -IVE.]
▸ **A** *adjective*. **1** ***letter missive***, ***letters missive***, ***missive letter***, a letter or epistle sent from one person or body to another; *spec.* (***a***) a letter from a superior authority, esp. the monarch, conveying a command, recommendation, or permission; now chiefly, in the Church of England, a letter from the monarch to a dean and chapter nominating the person whom they are to elect bishop; (***b***) *SCOTS LAW* = sense B.2 below; (***c***) *US* (among Congregationalists) an official letter inviting churches to send delegates to a council. **LME.**
†**2** = MISSILE *adjective*. **M16–E19.**
†**3** Sent on an errand or as a message. **E17–M19.**
▸ **B** *noun*. **1** A written message, a letter; *spec.* = ***missive letter*** above. Now usu., a letter that is official or (*joc.*) long or serious. Orig. chiefly *Scot.* **E16.**

Private Eye These congratulatory missives can prove tedious to plough through.

2 *SCOTS LAW*. A document in the form of a letter interchanged by the parties to a contract (usu. one to do with property). Also ***missive of lease***. **E16.**
conclude missives *SCOTS LAW* sign a contract with the vendor of a property or piece of land to signify change of ownership.
†**3** A messenger. *rare*. **E–M17.**
†**4** An object hurled or thrown; a missile. **M17–E19.**

missort /mɪsˈsɔːt, *as noun also* ˈmɪs-sɔːt/ *verb & noun*. **L16.**
[**ORIGIN** from MIS-[1] 1 + SORT *verb*.]
▸ **A** *verb trans*. Sort (esp. letters) badly; allot to a wrong place in sorting. **L16.**
▸ **B** *noun*. An instance of missorting; a letter etc. missorted. **L19.**

missound /mɪsˈsaʊnd/ *verb*. *rare*. **LME.**
[**ORIGIN** from MIS-[1] 1 + SOUND *verb*[1].]
†**1** *verb intrans*. Be discordant; be incompatible, disagree. **LME–L15.**
2 *verb trans*. Mispronounce. **M16.**

Missouri /mɪˈzʊəri, -s-/ *noun & adjective*. **E18.**
[**ORIGIN** A river and state in the US.]
▸ **A** *noun*. A member of a Siouan people, first encountered by Europeans near the Missouri River; the language of this people. **E18.**
▸ **B** *attrib.* or as *adjective*. Of or pertaining to the Missouris or their language. **M18.**

Missourian /mɪˈzʊərɪən, -s-/ *adjective & noun*. **M18.**
[**ORIGIN** formed as MISSOURI + -AN.]
▸ **A** *adjective*. Of or pertaining to Missouri. **M18.**
▸ **B** *noun*. A native or inhabitant of the state of Missouri in the US. **E19.**

missourite /mɪˈzʊərʌɪt, -s-/ *noun*. **L19.**
[**ORIGIN** formed as MISSOURI + -ITE[1].]
GEOLOGY. A grey granular igneous rock composed mainly of pyroxene, leucite, and sometimes olivine.

miss-out /ˈmɪsaʊt/ *noun*. *slang*. **E20.**
[**ORIGIN** from ***miss out*** s.v. MISS *verb*[1].]
1 In *pl.* In gambling: loaded dice. **E20.**
2 A losing throw in craps. **M20.**

misspeak /mɪsˈspiːk/ *verb*. Infl. as SPEAK *verb*; pa. t. usu. **-spoke** /-ˈspəʊk/, pa. ple usu. **-spoken** /-ˈspəʊk(ə)n/. **OE.**
[**ORIGIN** from MIS-[1] 1 + SPEAK *verb*.]
†**1** *verb intrans*. Mutter, grumble. Only in **OE.**
2 *verb intrans*. Speak wrongly or improperly; speak disrespectfully *of*. **ME–E17.**
3 *verb trans*. Mispronounce. *rare*. **L16.**
4 *verb refl. & intrans*. Speak unclearly or misleadingly; fail to convey one's intended meaning. Chiefly *US*. **L19.**

misspeech /mɪsˈspiːtʃ/ *noun*. **LME.**
[**ORIGIN** from MIS-[1] 2 + SPEECH *noun*.]
†**1** Malicious speaking. **LME–L15.**
2 Incorrect speaking, mispronunciation. *rare*. **L19.**

misspell /mɪsˈspɛl; *as noun also* ˈmɪs-spɛl/ *verb & noun*. **M17.**
[**ORIGIN** from MIS-[1] 1 + SPELL *verb*[2].]
▸ **A** *verb trans*. Pa. t. & pple **-spelled**, **-spelt**. Spell incorrectly. **M17.**
▸ **B** *noun*. A misspelling. *rare*. **L19.**
■ **misspelling** *noun* (an instance of) bad spelling **L16.**

†**misspence** *noun* var. of MISSPENSE.

misspend /mɪsˈspɛnd/ *verb trans*. Pa. t. & pple **-spent** /-spɛnt/. **LME.**
[**ORIGIN** from MIS-[1] 1 + SPEND *verb*.]
Spend wrongly, badly, or wastefully. Now chiefly as ***misspent*** *ppl adjective*.

Time He has posted in his apartment an old obituary of Orsen Welles, the patron saint of misspent genius.

■ **misspender** *noun* **L16.**

†**misspense** *noun*. Also **-ce**. **L16–L18.**
[**ORIGIN** from MIS-[1] 2 + SPENSE.]
Improper or wasteful expenditure.

misspent *verb pa. t. & pple* of MISSPEND.

misspoke, **misspoken** *verbs* see MISSPEAK.

miss-stay *verb* var. of MISSTAY.

misstate /mɪsˈsteɪt/ *verb trans*. **M17.**
[**ORIGIN** from MIS-[1] 1 + STATE *verb*.]
State erroneously; make wrong statements about.
■ **misstatement** *noun* a wrong or erroneous statement **L18.**

misstay /mɪsˈsteɪ/ *verb intrans*. Also **miss-stay**. **E19.**
[**ORIGIN** App. from ***miss stays*** s.v. MISS *verb*[1].]
Of a ship: miss stays.

misstep /mɪsˈstɛp/ *noun*. **L18.**
[**ORIGIN** from MIS-[1] 2 + STEP *noun*[1].]
A wrong step, a slip. Chiefly *fig.*

A. LURIE A misstep, an error in tact or tone, which would have hurt our friendship. *Scientific American* For a mountain goat one misstep could be fatal.

misstep /mɪsˈstɛp/ *verb intrans*. Infl. **-pp-**. **ME.**
[**ORIGIN** from MIS-[1] 1 + STEP *verb*.]
Take a wrong step; go astray.

missus /ˈmɪsɪs, -ɪz/ *noun*. *dial.* & *colloq.* Also **missis**. **L18.**
[**ORIGIN** Repr. an informal pronunc. of MISTRESS *noun*: cf. MRS.]
1 The mistress of a household; (in former British colonies) a white female employer, *loosely* any white woman. Chiefly as a form of address. **L18.**

P. ABRAHAMS I work for old missus when I was a child.

2 The wife of the person speaking, addressed, or referred to. Cf. MISTER *noun*[2] 3. **E19.**

DENNIS POTTER We haven't got to the stage of interviewing the candidate's missis yet.

3 Used as a form of address to an older woman, esp. one who is a stranger. **M19.**

G. B. SHAW He won't get no cab until half-past eleven, missus.

missy /ˈmɪsi/ *noun*. Also **missie**. **L17.**
[**ORIGIN** from MISS *noun*[2] + -Y[6].]
(An affectionate or playful or (occas.) contemptuous form of address to) a young girl, a miss.
■ **missyish** *adjective* = MISSISH **E19.**

missy /ˈmɪsi/ *adjective*. Usu. *derog.* **E19.**
[**ORIGIN** from MISS *noun*[2] + -Y[1].]
= MISSISH.

mist /mɪst/ *noun*[1].
[**ORIGIN** Old English *mist* = Middle & mod. Low German, Middle Dutch & mod. Dutch *mist*, Icelandic *mistur*, Norwegian dial., Swedish *mist*, from Germanic, from Indo-European base repr. also by Greek *omikhlē* mist, fog.]
1 A diffuse cloud of minute water droplets suspended in the atmosphere on or near the ground, so as to limit visibility (but to a lesser degree than fog); the obscurity produced by this. Also, any condensed vapour that settles in fine droplets on a surface and obscures glass etc. **OE.** ▸**b** A diffuse cloud of small particles; a haze or haziness produced by distance or (*fig.*) time etc. **L18.** ▸**c** A grey colour suggestive of mist. **E20.**

G. GREENE The mist from his breath obscured the pane. H. CARPENTER Often the view was blurred by a slight mist, for the weather was generally damp. **b** W. COWPER The rustling straw sends up a frequent mist Of atoms. *Tarzan Monthly* Treasure from a civilization that has been lost in the mists of time for centuries.

Scotch mist: see SCOTCH *adjective*.
2 Dimness of eyesight; a haze or film before the eyes caused by illness, the shedding of tears, etc. **OE.**

C. LAMB A juggler, who threw mists before your eyes. TENNYSON She did not weep But o'er her meek eyes came a happy mist.

3 Any of various abstract things conceived as obscuring a person's mental vision or outlook, or as veiling the real character or blurring the outlines of a thing. **OE.**

J. BARZUN To glimpse . . truth through the mists of adolescent incoherence.

†**4** A state of obscurity or uncertainty; an atmosphere of doubt. **M16–E18.**

G. BURNET In this mist matters must be left till the great revelation of all secrets.

– **COMB.**: **mist-blower** a device for spraying insecticide into the tops of trees; **mistbow** = ***fogbow*** s.v. FOG *noun*[2]; **mist-flower** a blue-flowered hemp agrimony, *Eupatorium caelestinum*, of the eastern US; **mist net** *noun & verb* (***a***) *noun* a net made of very fine threads, used to trap birds etc. for ringing or examination; (***b***) *verb trans.* trap in a mist net; **mist propagation** a method of rooting plant cuttings in which high humidity is maintained in a greenhouse by an automatic system of watering with fine spray at regular intervals; **mist propagator** an installation for mist propagation.
■ **mistful** *adjective* full of mist; obscured (as if) with mist: **M18.** **mistless** *adjective* free from mist **M19.** **mistlike** *adjective & adverb* like a mist **L16.**

†**mist** *noun*[2]. **LME–M17.**
[**ORIGIN** Perh. a use of MIST *noun*[1], infl. by *mystery*, *mystic* etc.]
= MYSTERY *noun*[1] 1.

mist /mɪst/ *verb*. **OE.**
[**ORIGIN** from MIST *noun*[1].]
1 *verb intrans*. Be or become misty; gather or appear in the form of a mist; (of the eyes, outlines, etc.) become dim or blurred. Now freq. foll. by *over*, *up*. **OE.**

E. BOWEN Fluctuations in temperature . . make polish mist over. B. MOORE The room misted like a steam bath. T. HEALD 'Oh, Simon', she said, her eyes misting with tears.

2 *verb trans*. Cover or obscure (as) with mist; envelop in mist; make (the eyes) dim with tears. Also foll. by *over*, *up*. **LME.** ▸**b** Spray (a plant) with vaporized moisture. **M20.**

W. GOLDING Rage misted my spectacles. R. INGALLS A fog had begun to mist over the landscape.

mistake /mɪˈsteɪk/ *noun*. **E17.**
[**ORIGIN** from the verb.]
1 A misconception about the meaning of something; a thing incorrectly done or thought; an error of judgement. **E17.** ▸**b** An instance of a woman's becoming pregnant unintentionally; an unplanned baby. *colloq.* **M20.**

J. T. MICKLETHWAITE It is a great mistake to think that a building looks better for being empty. F. CHICHESTER I . . was worried to find silly mistakes creeping into my calculations, mistakes like writing down a number wrongly.

2 Error, the condition of being mistaken or incorrectly done. Chiefly in ***by mistake***, ***in mistake for*** below. **L17.**

SHELLEY Falsehood, mistake, and lust.

– **PHRASES**: †**a mistake of** a misconception as to. **and no mistake** *colloq.* without any doubt. **by mistake** erroneously, mistakenly. **in mistake for** in error for. **make no mistake** have no doubt (*about*). †**under a mistake** under a misapprehension.

mistake /mɪˈsteɪk/ *verb*. Pa. t. **mistook** /mɪˈstʊk/; pa. pple **mistaken** /mɪˈsteɪk(ə)n/, (*dial. & non-standard*) **mistook**. **ME.**
[**ORIGIN** Old Norse *mistaka* take in error, (refl.) miscarry (Swedish *misstaga* be mistaken), formed as MIS-[1] + *taka* TAKE *verb*. Cf. Old French *mesprendre* (see MISPRIZE *verb*[2]), which has prob. influenced the meaning.]
1 *verb intrans*. Transgress, do wrong. *obsolete* exc. *Scot.* **ME.**
†**2** *verb trans*. Take improperly or in error. **LME–M17.**
3 *verb trans*. Make an error in the choice of (one's route, target, etc.). Formerly also, make an error regarding (a date, number, etc.); perform (an action) at a wrong time. *arch.* **LME.**

E. YOUNG When blind ambition quite mistakes her road.

4 *verb trans*. Attach a wrong meaning to the words or actions of (a person); misunderstand. **LME.** ▸†**b** Have a wrong view of the character of (a person). **L16–L17.**

R. K. NARAYAN I was only trying to suggest . . . So please don't mistake me.

5 *verb trans*. Have a misconception regarding (an opinion, statement, action, purpose, etc.); attach an erroneous meaning to. **L15.**

A. J. AYER My reasoning on this point was not in itself incorrect, but . . I mistook its purport.

†**6** *verb trans*. Suppose erroneously to be or *to be*. **L15–M18.**

T. FULLER Vincent of Coventrie was . . bred a Franciscan (though Learned Leland mistakes him a Carmelite).

7 *verb trans*. **a** Be under a misconception about the identity of; take to be somebody or something else; estimate wrongly. Now chiefly in phrs. below. **L16.** ▸**b** Foll. by *for*: identify wrongly as (some other person or thing). **E17.**

b R. DAHL The doctor . . was so drunk that he mistook the fractured elbow for a dislocated shoulder.

a there's no mistaking it is impossible not to recognize (a person or thing). **mistake one's man** judge wrongly or underestimate the character or capabilities of the person one is dealing with.

8 *verb intrans.* (*arch.*), & *trans.* in *pass.* as **be mistaken** & (now *Scot.*) *refl.* Make a mistake; be in error, be under a misapprehension. **L16.**

T. HARDY A.. greatcoat, which, if he mistook not, was the very same garment as.. had adorned the chair. D. L. SAYERS You may think that the prisoner was mistaken.. about the time he left the flat.

■ **mistakable** *adjective* able to be mistaken or misunderstood **M17.** **mistaker** *noun* **M16.** **mistakingly** *adverb* erroneously, mistakenly **M17.**

mistaken /mɪˈsteɪk(ə)n/ *adjective.* **M16.**
[ORIGIN pa. pple of MISTAKE *verb*.]

1 Based on or resulting from a mistake, erroneous. **M16.**

E. A. FREEMAN A mistaken feeling of loyalty hindered him. *American Speech* 'Ten gallon' has been arrived at by a mistaken translation of a Spanish word.

mistaken identity: see IDENTITY 1.

2 Having a wrong opinion or judgement, being under a misapprehension. **E17.**

W. S. JEVONS There ought not to be so many mistaken people vainly acting in opposition to his lessons.

■ **mistakenly** *adverb* **M17.** **mistakenness** /-n-n-/ *noun* **M19.**

misteach /mɪsˈtiːtʃ/ *verb trans.* Pa. t. & pple **-taught** /-tɔːt/. **LOE.**
[ORIGIN from MIS-¹ 1 + TEACH *verb*.]
Teach badly, wrongly, or incorrectly.

misted /ˈmɪstɪd/ *adjective.* **LME.**
[ORIGIN from MIST *noun*¹, *verb*: see -ED², -ED¹.]
Obscured by or hidden in mist; dulled, blurred.

mistell /mɪsˈtɛl/ *verb trans.* Pa. t. & pple **-told** /-təʊld/. **L15.**
[ORIGIN from MIS-¹ 1 + TELL *verb*.]
†**1** Number incorrectly; miscount. **L15–M17.**
2 Relate or recount incorrectly; (now *Scot.*) misinform. **M16.**

†**mistemper** *verb trans.* **L15.**
[ORIGIN from MIS-¹ 1 + TEMPER *verb*¹.]
Chiefly as ***mistempered*** *ppl adjective.*
1 Disturb or disorder. **L15–L19.**
2 Mix badly or unsuitably. **E16–M17.**
3 Temper (a weapon) for an evil purpose. Only in **L16.**

mister /ˈmɪstə/ *noun*¹. Now *arch.* & *dial.* **ME.**
[ORIGIN Anglo-Norman *mester*, Old French *mestier* (mod. MÉTIER), from Proto-Romance contr. of Latin *ministerium*: see MYSTERY *noun*².]
▸ **I** †**1** A trade; a profession, a craft. **ME–E17.**
†**2** A person's office or function; an employment, an occupation; a practice. **ME–L16.**
†**3** Skill in a profession. **LME–L16.**
▸ **II 4** Need (†*of*), necessity; a state of difficulty or distress, *esp.* a lack of means. Long *obsolete* exc. *Scot.* **ME.** ▸†**b** A need, a lack. *Scot.* **E16–E19.**
†**5** A necessity; in *pl.* necessary articles, fittings, etc. Chiefly *Scot.* **L15–E19.**
– COMB.: **mister man** (long *arch.*) †(*a*) a craftsman, a man having a particular occupation; (*b*) (by misanalysis) a kind or class of man; **mister wight** (long *arch.*) (*a*) a kind or class of person or creature; (*b*) (by misunderstanding) a particular person or creature.

mister /ˈmɪstə/ *noun*². Also (esp. in titles) **M-**. **E16.**
[ORIGIN Weakened form of MASTER *noun*¹ originating from reduced stress in use before a name. Cf. MISTRESS *noun*.]
1 Used as a title preceding the name of a man without a higher or honorific or professional title, or preceding any of various designations of office. Now usu. written MR exc. when used humorously or ironically. **E16.** ▸**b** The word 'mister' (Mr) as a title; a person addressed as 'Mr', a man without a title of nobility etc. **M18.**

A. PRICE The sergeant's '*Mister* Audley' and his slight disdain. **b** S. FOOTE Has his majesty dubb'd me a Knight for you to make me a Mister? P. MOYES We're all good friends.. We don't use no Mister and Missus.

2 (Without proper name.) Used as a form of address to an adult male stranger, *esp.* one of superior status. Now *non-standard.* **M18.** ▸**b** NAUTICAL. Used as a form of address to a ship's mate. **L19.**

E. LEONARD Mister, gimme a dollar.

3 The husband of the person speaking, addressed, or referred to. *colloq.* **M20.**

†**mister** *verb*¹. Chiefly *Scot.* **LME.**
[ORIGIN from MISTER *noun*¹.]
1 *verb intrans.* **a** *impers.* in (*it*) ***misters*** etc., it is necessary or needful etc. (*to do*). **LME–E19.** ▸**b** Find it necessary (*to do*). **LME–L16.**
2 *verb intrans.* Of a thing: be necessary or requisite. **LME–E16.**
3 *verb trans.* & *intrans.* Have need of or *of*, require. **LME–E18.**

mister /ˈmɪstə/ *verb*² *trans.* **M18.**
[ORIGIN from MISTER *noun*².]
Address as 'Mr'.

mistery *noun* var. of MYSTERY *noun*².

†**misthink** *verb.* Pa. t. & pple **-thought**. **ME.**
[ORIGIN from MIS-¹ 1 + THINK *verb*².]
1 *verb intrans.* Have sinful thoughts. **ME–E17.**
2 *verb intrans.* & *trans.* Have mistaken thoughts; think mistakenly *that*. **M16–L17.**
3 *verb trans.* & *intrans.* with *of*. Have an unfavourable opinion of; think (a thought) to a person's detriment. **E17–M19.**

misthought /mɪsˈθɔːt/ *noun.* **ME.**
[ORIGIN from MIS-¹ 2 + THOUGHT *noun*¹.]
Mistaken thought or opinion.

misthrive /mɪsˈθrʌɪv/ *verb intrans.* Now *rare.* Pa. t. **-throve** /-ˈθrəʊv/, **-thrived**; pa. pple **-thriven** /-ˈθrɪv(ə)n/, **-thrived**. **M16.**
[ORIGIN from MIS-¹ 1 + THRIVE *verb*.]
Be unsuccessful; fail to thrive.

mistico /ˈmɪstɪkəʊ/ *noun.* Pl. **-o(e)s**. **E19.**
[ORIGIN Uncertain: perh. ult. from Arabic *musaṭṭah* armed vessel.]
A coasting vessel with three masts, formerly used in the Mediterranean.

†**mistified** *adjective.* Also †**myst-**. Only in **M19.**
[ORIGIN from MIST *noun*¹ or MISTY *adjective*: see -FY, -ED¹.]
Misty, fogged.

mistigris /ˈmɪstɪgrɪs/ *noun.* **L19.**
[ORIGIN French *mistigri* jack of clubs.]
A joker or other card played as a wild card in some versions of poker etc.; the highest trump in certain trick games. Also, a game in which such a card is used.

mistime /mɪsˈtʌɪm/ *verb.* **LOE.**
[ORIGIN formed as MIS-¹ 1 + TIME *verb*.]
†**1** *verb intrans.* Of an event: cause misfortune. Of a person: suffer misfortune. **LOE–LME.**
2 *verb trans.* Do or say (something) at a bad or inappropriate moment. Also, miscalculate or misstate the time of. **LME.**

C. THUBRON The SS *Dzhurma* mistimed her sailing and was locked in pack-ice for nine months.

■ **mistimed** *adjective* †(*a*) unfortunate; (*b*) badly timed, unseasonable; (*c*) *dial.* keeping irregular hours: **L15.**

mistitle /mɪsˈtʌɪt(ə)l/ *verb trans.* **E17.**
[ORIGIN from MIS-¹ 1 + TITLE *verb*.]
Give a wrong title or name to.

mistle /ˈmɪs(ə)l/ *noun.* Also **missel**.
[ORIGIN Old English *mistel* = Old High German *mistil* (German *Mistel*), Dutch *mistel*, Old Norse *mistil-*: ult. origin unknown.]
†**1** Mistletoe. Also, basil. **OE–L17.**
2 In full ***mistle thrush***, (dial.) ***mistle bird***. A large greyish Eurasian thrush, *Turdus viscivorus*, noted for eating the berries of mistletoe and other plants. **E17.**

mistletoe /ˈmɪs(ə)ltəʊ/ *noun.*
[ORIGIN Old English *misteltān* (= Old Norse *mistilteinn*), formed as MISTLE + *tān* twig (= Dutch *teen* withe, Old High German *zein* rod, Old Norse *teinn* twig, spit).]
A European plant, *Viscum album* (family Viscaceae), which is parasitic on various trees (esp. apple and poplar), bears white glutinous berries, and is used in Christmas decorations. Also (in full ***American mistletoe***), any of several N. American parasitic plants of the related genus *Phoradendron*, esp. *P. serotinum*.

W. IRVING The mistle-toe is still hung up in farm-houses.. at Christmas.

– COMB.: **mistletoe bird** *Austral.* a small black, white, and crimson flowerpecker, *Dicaeum hirundinaceum*; **mistletoe cactus** any of various cacti of the mainly tropical American genus *Rhipsalis*, esp. *R. baccifera*, with white fruits resembling those of mistletoe.

mistook *verb* see MISTAKE *verb*.

mistral /ˈmɪstr(ə)l, mɪˈstrɑːl/ *noun.* **E17.**
[ORIGIN French from Provençal from Latin *magistralis* (sc. *ventus* wind): see MAGISTRAL. Cf. MAESTRALE.]
A strong cold north-west wind which blows through the Rhône valley and southern France into the Mediterranean, mainly in winter.

mistranslate /mɪstransˈleɪt, -trɑːns-/ *verb trans.* **M16.**
[ORIGIN from MIS-¹ 1 + TRANSLATE *verb*.]
Translate incorrectly.
■ **mistranslation** *noun* **L17.**

†**mistreading** *noun.* **L16–M18.**
[ORIGIN from MIS-¹ 1 + TREADING *noun*.]
A misdeed, a transgression.

mistreat /mɪsˈtriːt/ *verb trans.* **LME.**
[ORIGIN from MIS-¹ 1 + TREAT *verb*.]
Treat badly or wrongly.

A. HUTSCHNECKER How can I forgive her for abandoning me at age three and mistreating me physically?

■ **mistreatment** *noun* **E18.**

mistress /ˈmɪstrɪs/ *noun* & *adjective.* **ME.**
[ORIGIN Old French *maistresse* (mod. *maîtresse*), from *maistre* MASTER *noun*¹ + *-esse* -ESS¹, with subsequent shortening of first vowel (cf. MISTER *noun*²). See also MRS.]
▸ **A** *noun* **I 1** †**a** A woman who has charge of a child or young person; a governess. Only in **ME.** ▸**b** A female tutor or teacher, *esp.* one in a school; a woman who teaches a particular subject. **ME.**

b POPE When I was at School, my Mistress did ever extol me above the rest.

b SCHOOLMISTRESS. ***French mistress***, ***music mistress***, ***sewing mistress***, etc.

2 A woman who employs others in her service; a woman in relation to her servants or slaves. Also, the female owner of an animal (cf. sense 11 below), a woman or girl whom an animal is accustomed to obey. **LME.**

J. M. SLOAN Jane Welsh was among the best of mistresses to her servants.

3 The female head of a household, family, or other establishment; the female principal of a college. **LME.** ▸**b** The wife of a farmer (in relation to his tenants), a minister, etc. Chiefly *Scot.* **L17.**

J. M. BARRIE Her mother's death made her mistress of the house and mother to her little brother.

Mistress of the Robes (in the English royal household) a lady of high rank, charged with the care of the Queen's wardrobe. ***Mistress of Girton College*** etc.

4 A woman having the power to control, use, or dispose of something at will. Chiefly *pred.*, foll. by *of*. **LME.**

A. POWELL She was perfectly calm, mistress, as ever, of the situation.

5 †**a** The female governor of a territory, state, or people. **LME–L18.** ▸**b** A country, state, etc., which has supremacy or control over other countries etc. **LME.** ▸†**c** The chief, the first. **L15–E17.**

b W. S. CHURCHILL At sea and on land England was mistress of the outer world.

†**6** A woman, goddess, or thing personified as female that has control over a person or is regarded as a guiding influence. **LME–L17.**

SHAKES. *Lear* Mumbling of wicked charms, conjuring the moon To stand's auspicious mistress.

†**7** A female patron or inspirer. **LME–E18.**

S. CENTLIVRE Want, the mistress of invention.

8 A woman loved and courted by a man; a sweetheart. Now *arch.* & *dial.* **LME.**

T. HARDY They were yet mere lover and mistress.

9 A woman (other than a wife) with whom a man has a long-standing sexual relationship. **LME.**

LD MACAULAY His Protestant mistresses gave less scandal than his Popish wife.

10 A woman proficient in an art, study, or other branch of knowledge. Now *rare.* **LME.**

ADDISON I would advise all young Wives to make themselves Mistresses of Wingate's Arithmetick. D. LESSING Our Mrs. Van is a mistress of rules and regulations.

11 A female possessor or owner (*of*). Now *rare* or *obsolete* exc. as passing into senses 2, 10. **M16.**

G. WASHINGTON Without a considerable reinforcement, Frederick county will not be mistress of fifteen families. J. AUSTEN Elinor.. more anxious to be alone than to be mistress of the subject.

▸ **II** Used as a title or preceding a name.
12 Used *voc.* as a respectful form of address; madam, ma'am. Now *arch.* & *W. Indian.* **LME.**

SHAKES. *L.L.L.* Studies my lady? Mistress, look on me.

13 a Used as a title preceding the first name or surname of an unmarried woman or girl; = MISS *noun*² 2. *obsolete* exc. *dial.* **LME.** ▸**b** Used as a title preceding the surname (orig. also the first name) of a married woman; = MRS. Now *dial.* & *W. Indian.* **L15.**

b D. DUNNETT Are ye there, Mistress Rossi?

▸ **III** *techn.* **14** The jack in bowls. Cf. MASTER *noun*¹ 8. **L16.**
15 A lantern used in coalmines. **M19.**
▸ **B** *attrib.* or as *adjective.* That is a mistress; (of a thing personified as female or (formerly) with a noun grammatically fem. in Latin or French) chief, leading, commanding, great, powerful. **L16.**

T. JACKSON Rome.. the Mistresse-citie of the world.

– COMB.: **mistresspiece** (long *rare*) [after MASTERPIECE] an outstanding example of female beauty or accomplishment.
■ **mistresshood** *noun* the condition or status of a mistress (of a household) **L19.** †**mistressing** *verbal noun* the action of courting or having an affair with a mistress **M17–M19.** **mistressless** *adjective* **L19.**

mistress /ˈmɪstrɪs/ *verb trans.* **L16.**
[ORIGIN from the noun.]
1 Provide with a mistress. **L16.**
2 Call or address as 'mistress'. **E19.**
3 Become mistress of (an art). *rare.* **M19.**
4 Dominate as a mistress. **E20.**
– PHRASES: **mistress it** play the part of a mistress.

M

mistressly /ˈmɪstrɪsli/ *adjective*. M18.
[ORIGIN from MISTRESS *noun* + -LY[1].]
1 Belonging to the mistress of a household. *rare*. M18.
2 Resembling or characteristic of a woman proficient in an art. Cf. MASTERLY *adjective* 2. Now *rare*. L18.

mistress-ship /ˈmɪstrɪsʃɪp/ *noun*. LME.
[ORIGIN from MISTRESS *noun* + -SHIP.]
†**1** The status of a woman to whom the title of mistress was used. Only in ***your mistress-ship***. LME–M17.
2 The condition or status of mistress or head of a household etc.; the authority of a woman in the position of a mistress. L16.
3 Pre-eminent skill in an art etc. shown by a woman. Now *rare* or *obsolete*. E19.
4 The post of mistress in a school. L19.

mistrial /mɪsˈtrʌɪəl, ˈmɪstrʌɪəl/ *noun*. E17.
[ORIGIN from MIS-[2] 2 + TRIAL *noun*.]
1 A trial rendered invalid by some error, as a disqualification in a judge or juror. E17.
2 An inconclusive trial, as where the jury cannot agree. *US*. L19.

mistrust /mɪsˈtrʌst/ *noun*. LME.
[ORIGIN from MIS-[2] 2 + TRUST *noun*.]
Lack of trust or confidence, suspicion, distrust, (foll. by *of*, *in*). Formerly also, doubt as to the truth or probability *of* a thing.

SHAKES. *Jul. Caes.* Mistrust of good success hath done this deed. A. STORR Beethoven's deafness increased his mistrust of other human beings.

mistrust /mɪsˈtrʌst/ *verb*. LME.
[ORIGIN from MIS-[1] 1, 5 + TRUST *verb*, prob. after Old French *mesfier* (mod. *méfier*).]
1 *verb trans.* Have no confidence in, be suspicious of; doubt the truth, validity, or genuineness of. LME.

E. M. FORSTER I rather mistrust young men who slip into life gracefully. J. KLEIN I would tend to mistrust my own abilities.

2 *verb trans.* **a** Suspect *that*. Now *dial.* & *US*. LME. ▸**b** Suspect the existence of or future occurrence of (harm etc.). Now *rare* or *obsolete*. M16.

a O. W. HOLMES I mistrusted he didn't mean to come. **b** J. FLORIO They were all asleepe mistrusting no harme.

3 *verb intrans.* Be distrustful, suspicious, or without confidence. LME.
▪ **mistruster** *noun* LME.

mistrustful /mɪsˈtrʌstfʊl, -f(ə)l/ *adjective*. E16.
[ORIGIN from MISTRUST *noun* + -FUL.]
1 Lacking in trust or confidence; distrustful, suspicious, (*of*). E16.
†**2** Causing mistrust or suspicion. *rare* (Shakes.). Only in L16.
▪ **mistrustfully** *adverb* E17. **mistrustfulness** *noun* M16.

mistrusting /mɪsˈtrʌstɪŋ/ *adjective*. M16.
[ORIGIN from MISTRUST *verb* + -ING[2].]
Suspicious, mistrustful.
▪ **mistrustingly** *adverb* M16.

mistrustless /mɪsˈtrʌs(t)lɪs/ *adjective*. Now *rare*. L16.
[ORIGIN from MISTRUST *noun* + -LESS.]
Free from mistrust or suspicion; unsuspecting (*of*).

mistry /mɪsˈtrʌɪ/ *verb trans*. M17.
[ORIGIN from MIS-[1] 1 + TRY *verb*.]
Try (a person or case) wrongly or badly, subject to a wrong or badly conducted trial.

mistryst /mɪsˈtrʌɪst, -ˈtrɪst/ *verb*. *Scot.* & *N. English*. M17.
[ORIGIN from MIS-[1] 1 + TRYST *verb*.]
1 *verb trans.* & *intrans.* (with *with*). Fail to keep an engagement with. M17.
2 *verb trans.* In *pass.* Be perplexed, confused, or frightened. E19.

mistune /mɪsˈtjuːn/ *verb*. LME.
[ORIGIN from MIS-[1] 1 + TUNE *verb*.]
†**1** *verb intrans.* Be out of tune. Only in LME.
2 *verb trans.* Tune wrongly; put out of tune, make discordant; perform (music) out of tune. E16.

misty /ˈmɪsti/ *adjective*.
[ORIGIN Old English *mistig*, formed as MIST *noun*[1] + -ig -Y[1].]
1 Clouded, obscured, or accompanied by mist; consisting of mist. OE. ▸**b** Clouded with fine particles resembling mist. M19. ▸**c** Of the eyes: blurred with tears. Of a person: having misty eyes. M19.

c C. POTOK My father's eyes were misty . . and I cried a little. T. K. WOLFE You would even see engineers . . getting misty about those old days.

2 *fig.* **a** Obscure, unintelligible; vague, indistinct; confused. LME. ▸**b** Not illuminated by reason, truth, etc. Formerly also, marked by or causing ignorance. E16.

a C. GROSS The jurists had not yet shrouded the notion in misty complexity. M. S. POWER He became one of her sweet, misty memories.

▪ **mistily** *adverb* ME. **mistiness** *noun* (*a*) misty condition; (*b*) vapour, haze, mist: LME.

mistype /mɪsˈtʌɪp/ *verb*. M20.
[ORIGIN from MIS-[1] 1 + TYPE *verb*[1].]
1 *verb trans.* & *intrans.* Type (a letter, words, etc.) incorrectly. M20.
2 *verb trans.* Wrongly assign to a particular type; misclassify. L20.

misunderstand /ˌmɪsʌndəˈstand/ *verb*. Pa. t. & pple **-stood** /-ˈstʊd/. ME.
[ORIGIN from MIS-[1] 1 + UNDERSTAND.]
1 *verb trans.* Fail to understand rightly (words, a statement, etc.), take in a wrong sense. ME.

J. BRIGGS They had misunderstood the phrase 'washed raisins' and washed the raisins in soap.

2 *verb trans.* Misinterpret the words or actions of (a person). ME.

DENNIS POTTER Please do not misunderstand me, ladies and gentlemen. E. KUZWAYO Very offhand, even to the point where she could easily be misunderstood as unkind or uncaring.

3 *verb intrans.* Fail to understand. LME.

R. K. NARAYAN They might misunderstand if I said anything contrary to their views.

▪ **misunderstandable** *adjective* M19. **misunderstander** *noun* E16.

misunderstanding /ˌmɪsʌndəˈstandɪŋ/ *noun*. LME.
[ORIGIN from MISUNDERSTAND *verb* + -ING[1].]
1 Failure to understand; mistake of the meaning; an instance of this, a misconception, a misinterpretation. LME.
2 An interruption of harmonious relations; dissension, disagreement; a slight disagreement or quarrel. M17.

misunderstood *verb pa. t.* & *pple* of MISUNDERSTAND.

misusage /mɪsˈjuːsɪdʒ/ *noun*. Now *rare*. M16.
[ORIGIN from MIS-[2] 2 + USAGE.]
†**1** Misconduct; corrupt practice, abuse. M–L16.
2 Ill usage; mistreatment. Formerly also in *pl.*, instances of this. M16.
3 Bad or wrong use, misuse. M16.

misuse /mɪsˈjuːs/ *noun*. LME.
[ORIGIN from MIS-[2] 2 + USE *noun*.]
1 Wrong or improper use, misapplication; *spec.* non-therapeutic use of a drug; an instance of this. LME.

Q The word 'classic' is prone to wild misuse. P. LOMAS The misuse of power that can occur in the psychoanalyst's office.

†**2** (An instance of) misconduct. E16–E17.
3 Ill treatment. *rare*. L16.

misuse /mɪsˈjuːz/ *verb trans*. LME.
[ORIGIN from MIS-[1] 1 + USE *verb*.]
1 Use wrongly or improperly, apply to a wrong purpose; *spec.* take (a drug) for non-therapeutic purposes. LME.

R. DEACON The Chinese experienced his treachery when . . he had . . misused their funds.

2 †**a** Violate, abuse sexually. LME–M16. ▸**b** Subject to ill treatment; maltreat. M16.

b J. GALSWORTHY Relating . . the innumerable occasions on which Fortune had misused her.

†**3** Deceive, delude. LME–E17.
†**4** *refl.* Misbehave. M16–E17.
†**5** Speak evil of; abuse, deride. L16–M17.

ROBERT BURTON Socrates was brought upon the stage by Aristophanes, and misused to his face.

†**6** Speak falsely of, misrepresent. *rare* (Shakes.). Only in L16.

SHAKES. *Sonn.* All my vows are oaths but to misuse thee.

misuser /mɪsˈjuːzə/ *noun*[1]. M16.
[ORIGIN from MISUSE *verb* + -ER[1].]
A person who misuses something or someone.

misuser /mɪsˈjuːzə/ *noun*[2]. E17.
[ORIGIN Old French *mesuser*, inf. used as noun: see -ER[4].]
LAW. Unlawful use of a liberty or benefit such as may lead to its forfeiture.

misventure /mɪsˈvɛntʃə/ *noun*. *arch.* M16.
[ORIGIN from MIS-[2] 2 + VENTURE *noun*.]
A mischance, a misfortune. Also, a foolish or ill-starred venture.

†**miswandered** *adjective*. L16–E17.
[ORIGIN from MIS-[1] 1 + *wandered* pa. pple of WANDER *verb*.]
In which one has gone astray.

SPENSER His late miswandred wayes now to remeasure right.

†**misween** *verb*. ME.
[ORIGIN from MIS-[1] 1 + WEEN.]
1 *verb intrans.* Have a wrong opinion (*that*). ME–M17.
2 *verb trans.* Think wrongly of, misjudge. E17–M18.
▪ †**misweening** *noun* false belief; misjudgement; mistrust: L15–L16.

†**miswend** *verb*. Pa. t. & pple **-went**. OE.
[ORIGIN from MIS-[1] 1 + WEND *verb*[1].]
1 *verb trans.* (in *pass.*) & *intrans.* Go astray (*lit.* & *fig.*); come to grief. OE–E18.

P. SIDNEY What? is thy Bagpipe broke, or are thy lambes miswent?

2 *verb trans.* Turn in a wrong direction; misapply; lead astray; pervert. ME–L15.

miswent *verb pa. t.* & *pple*: see MISGO, MISWEND.

misword /mɪsˈwəːd/ *noun*. Now *dial.* ME.
[ORIGIN from MIS-[2] 2 + WORD *noun*.]
A harsh, angry, or cross word.

L. P. HARTLEY Together they had got on very well—not a 'misword' between them.

misword /mɪsˈwəːd/ *verb trans*. L17.
[ORIGIN from MIS-[1] 1 + WORD *verb*.]
Word or express incorrectly.

miswrite /mɪsˈrʌɪt/ *verb trans*. Pa. t. **-wrote** /-ˈrəʊt/; pa. pple **-written** /-ˈrɪt(ə)n/. LOE.
[ORIGIN from MIS-[1] 1 + WRITE *verb*.]
Write incorrectly or by mistake.
▪ **miswriting** *noun* an error in writing LME.

misy /ˈmɪsi/ *noun*. *obsolete* exc. *hist.* M16.
[ORIGIN Latin from Greek *misu*.]
In translations or echoes of Pliny: a yellow crystalline mineral, often identified as copiapite.

misyoke /mɪsˈjəʊk/ *verb intrans.* & *trans*. M17.
[ORIGIN from MIS-[1] 1 + YOKE *verb*.]
Join or be joined in marriage unsuitably.

MIT *abbreviation*.
Massachusetts Institute of Technology.

mit *noun* var. of MITT.

mit /mɪt/ *preposition* & *adverb*. *joc.* & *colloq.* L18.
[ORIGIN German = with.]
With (me, us, etc.).

W. JAMES I . . suppose Mrs. Godkin will come *mit*.

mita /ˈmita/ *noun*. E18.
[ORIGIN Amer. Spanish from Quechua *mit'a* turn, successive or alternate order.]
hist. A group of Peruvian Indians used by the Spaniards in S. America as forced labour.

Mitanni /mɪˈtani/ *adjective* & *noun*. L19.
[ORIGIN Mitannian or Hurrian.]
▸ **A** *attrib.* or as *adjective*. Of or pertaining to Mitanni, a kingdom which flourished in northern Mesopotamia during the 15th–14th cents. BC, thought to have had a Hurrian population but Indo-Iranian rulers. L19.
▸ **B** *noun*. Pl. same.
1 A member of the predominant people of Mitanni. E20.
2 The language of this people, Mitannian. M20.

Mitannian /mɪˈtanɪən/ *adjective* & *noun*. L19.
[ORIGIN formed as MITANNI + -AN.]
▸ **A** *adjective*. = MITANNI *adjective*. L19.
▸ **B** *noun*. **1** A member of the Mitanni. E20.
2 The language of the Mitanni. E20.

Mitbestimmung /ˈmɪtbəʃtɪmʊŋ/ *noun*. M20.
[ORIGIN German = co-determination.]
In Germany, the policy in industry of involving both workers and management in decision-making.

mitch /mɪtʃ/ *noun*. Now *Scot. dial.* Also †**miche**. L15.
[ORIGIN Perh. rel. to German *Micke* fork of a branch, Dutch *mik* forked stick.]
A support for a piece of machinery or equipment, esp. a gun.

mitch /mɪtʃ/ *verb*. *obsolete* exc. *dial.* Also †**miche**. LME.
[ORIGIN App. from Old French *muchier* hide, lurk. Cf. MEECH, MOOCH *verb*.]
†**1** *verb trans.* Pilfer. LME–L16.
2 *verb intrans.* **a** Retire from view; lurk out of sight; skulk. M16. ▸**b** Play truant. L16.

mitch-board /ˈmɪtʃbɔːd/ *noun*. L19.
[ORIGIN Perh. from MITCH *noun* + BOARD *noun*.]
NAUTICAL. A support for a boom, yard, etc., when not in use.

mitchel /ˈmɪtʃ(ə)l/ *noun*. Now *rare* or *obsolete*. E17.
[ORIGIN Perh. from the name of Humfrey *Michell*, clerk or surveyor of the works at Windsor Castle in the reign of Queen Elizabeth I.]
A usu. square paving stone, varying in size from fifteen inches (approx. 38 cm) to two feet (approx. 61 cm).

mitchella /mɪˈtʃɛlə/ *noun*. L18.
[ORIGIN mod. Latin (see below), from John *Mitchell* (d. 1768), English-born Amer. botanist.]
A N. American trailing evergreen plant, *Mitchella repens*, of the madder family. Also called ***partridgeberry***.

Mitchell grass /ˈmɪtʃ(ə)l ɡrɑːs/ *noun phr*. L19.
[ORIGIN Sir Thomas Livingstone *Mitchell* (1792–1855), Scottish-born explorer.]
Any of various Australian fodder grasses of the genus *Astrebla*.

mite /mʌɪt/ *noun*[1].
[ORIGIN Old English *mīte* = Middle Low German, Middle Dutch *mīte* (Dutch *mijt*), Old High German *mīza* gnat, from Germanic.]
Orig., any minute insect or arachnid, esp. a small parasite infesting hawks. Now, any small free-living often

parasitic arachnid of the order Acari, which also includes ticks.
cheese mite, *harvest mite*, *itch mite*, *mange mite*, etc.
– COMB.: **mite-borne typhus**, **mite typhus** = *scrub typhus* s.v. SCRUB *noun*[1].
▪ **miticide** *noun* a substance used to kill mites M20. **mity** *adjective* full of or containing many mites M17.

mite /mʌɪt/ *noun*[2]. LME.
[ORIGIN Middle Low German, Middle Dutch *mīte* from Germanic, prob. identical with MITE *noun*[1].]
1 *hist.* Orig., a Flemish copper coin of very small value. Later, any very small unit of currency; *spec.* half a farthing. LME. ▸**b** *one's mite*, *widow's mite* (with allus. to *Mark* 12:42) a person's modest contribution to a cause, charity, etc., *esp.* the most the giver can manage, the best one can do. M17.

AV *Mark* 12:42 A certaine poore widow.. threw in two mites, which make a farthing. **b** R. K. NARAYAN You must contribute your mite for the economic and political salvation of our country.

†**2** A very small weight; *spec.* the twentieth part of a grain. LME–E18.
3 A tiny amount, a little bit, a fragment; *fig.* (chiefly *a mite*, *one mite*) a jot, a whit, (adverbial) somewhat, slightly, a little. Now *colloq.* LME.

J. RAY The Ants.. drop upon them a small Mite of their stinging Liquor. M. ANGELOU His left hand was only a mite bigger than Bailey's. J. CARROLL Colman withdrew a mite, holding his smile down. *New Health* Turning back now seemed a mite unadventurous.

4 A very small object or living creature, *esp.* a tiny child. L16.

A. WEST The poor mite does all he can to keep out of your way.

– COMB.: **mite society** *hist.* a 19th-cent. society which collected funds for charity by small contributions.

mitella /mɪˈtɛlə/ *noun*. M17.
[ORIGIN Latin, orig. = headband, dim of *mitra*: see MITRE *noun*[1].]
†**1** MEDICINE. A sling for the arm. M17–M19.
2 A plant of the genus *Mitella*; = *mitrewort* s.v. MITRE *noun*[1]. M18.

miter *noun*, *verb* see MITRE *noun*[1], *noun*[2], *verb*[1], *verb*[2].

mitered *adjective* see MITRED.

mithan /ˈmɪθ(ə)n/ *noun*. M19.
[ORIGIN Khasi *mythun* (whence Assamese *methon*).]
In the Indian subcontinent: = GAYAL.

mither *verb* var. of MOIDER.

mithqal /mɪθˈkɑːl/ *noun*. Also ***miskal***, (earlier) †***mitigal***. M16.
[ORIGIN (Portuguese *matical*, Spanish *mitical* from) Arabic *mitqāl*, from *taqala* weigh.]
An Arabian unit of weight equal to about 4½ grams or ⅙ ounce.

Mithraeum /mɪˈθriːəm/ *noun*. Pl. **-aea** /-iːə/. L19.
[ORIGIN mod. Latin, from Latin *Mithras*: see MITHRAIC.]
ANTIQUITIES. A sanctuary of the god Mithras; a chapel for the worship of Mithras.

Mithraic /mɪˈθreɪɪk/ *adjective*. L17.
[ORIGIN (from Latin *Mithras*, *Mithres* from Greek *Mithras* from) Old Persian, Avestan *Mithra* = Sanskrit *Mitra*, one of the gods of the Vedic pantheon: see -IC.]
Of or pertaining to Mithras, an ancient Persian god worshipped in much of northern and western Europe in the time of the Roman Empire, and later often identified with the sun.
▪ **Mithraicism** /-sɪz(ə)m/ *noun* = MITHRAISM M19.

Mithraism /ˈmɪθrə-ɪz(ə)m/ *noun*. E19.
[ORIGIN formed as MITHRAIC + -ISM.]
The worship of the god Mithras, the religion or cult of followers of Mithras.
▪ **Mithraist** *noun* a worshipper of or believer in Mithras L19. **Mithraˈistic** *adjective* = MITHRAIC *adjective* E20.

mithridate /ˈmɪθrɪdeɪt/ *noun*. E16.
[ORIGIN medieval Latin *mithridatum*, alt. of late Latin *mithridatium*, orig. neut. of *Mithridatius* adjective, pertaining to Mithridates: see MITHRIDATIC, -ATE[1].]
1 *hist.* (A medicine claimed to be) a universal antidote or preservative against poison and disease. E16.

fig.: SOUTHEY A drop of the true elixir, no mithridate so effectual against the infection of vice.

2 *mithridate mustard*, pennycress, *Thlaspi arvense*. L16.

Mithridatic /mɪθrɪˈdatɪk/ *adjective*. In sense 2 also **m-**. M17.
[ORIGIN Latin *mithridaticus* from Greek *Mithridatikos*, from *Mithridatēs*: see below, -IC.]
1 Of, pertaining to, or resembling Mithridates VI, king of Pontus (d. 63 BC), who reputedly made himself immune to poisons by constantly using antidotes. M17.
2 Pertaining to or of the nature of mithridatism. M19.

mithridatism /ˈmɪθrɪdeɪtɪz(ə)m, mɪˈθrɪdətɪz(ə)m/ *noun*. M19.
[ORIGIN from *Mithridates* (see MITHRIDATIC) + -ISM.]
Immunity to a poison induced by administering gradually increased doses of the poison.
▪ **miˈthridatize** *verb trans.* make proof against a poison by the administration of gradually increasing doses of it M19.

MITI *abbreviation*.
Ministry of International Trade and Industry (in Japan).

mitigable /ˈmɪtɪgəb(ə)l/ *adjective*. L17.
[ORIGIN medieval Latin *mitigabilis*, from *mitigare*: see MITIGATE, -ABLE.]
Able to be mitigated.

†**mitigal** *noun* see MITHQAL.

mitigant /ˈmɪtɪg(ə)nt/ *adjective* & *noun*. *rare*. M16.
[ORIGIN Latin *mitigant-* pres. ppl stem of *mitigare*: see MITIGATE, -ANT[1].]
▸ **A** *adjective*. Mitigating, soothing. M16.
▸ **B** *noun*. A soothing medicine; a lenitive. M19.

mitigate /ˈmɪtɪgeɪt/ *verb*. LME.
[ORIGIN Latin *mitigat-* pa. ppl stem of *mitigare*, from *mitis* mild, gentle: see -ATE[3].]
1 *verb trans.* Make milder in manner or attitude, make less hostile; mollify. Now *rare*. LME.
2 *verb trans.* Give relief from (pain, suffering, etc.); lessen the suffering or trouble caused by (an evil or difficulty of any kind). LME.

E. WAUGH I have to endure these sufferings.. and your presence will mitigate them. A. FRASER The King's eventual course of action did nothing to mitigate the conspirators' difficulties. JULIETTE HUXLEY The depths of obsessive despair which he so often tried to mitigate.

3 *verb trans.* Make (anger, hatred, etc.) less fierce or violent. L15.

W. H. PRESCOTT The envoys.. interposed to mitigate the king's anger.

4 *verb trans.* Lessen the rigour or severity of (a law), make less oppressive; reduce the severity of (a punishment); make (a custom) more humane. M16. ▸**b** Lessen the gravity of (an offence); palliate, extenuate. E18.

Irish Press Two fines of £100, mitigated to £2 each, were imposed. **b** LD MACAULAY He could see no mitigating circumstances, no redeeming merit.

5 *verb trans.* Moderate (the severity, rigour, etc., *of* something). Also, make (heat, cold, light, etc.) more bearable. L16.

A. BEVAN Even successful rebellion could not serve to mitigate the rigours of toil. A. BURGESS The sun, its heat mitigated by the strong sea-wind.

6 *verb intrans.* Become mitigated; grow milder or less severe. *rare*. M17.
▪ **mitigator** *noun* L16. **mitigatory** *adjective* & *noun* (**a**) *adjective* that mitigates something; alleviating, palliative; (**b**) *noun* a mitigatory thing; a soothing remedy; a plea in extenuation: L16.

mitigation /mɪtɪˈgeɪʃ(ə)n/ *noun*. LME.
[ORIGIN Old French & mod. French, or Latin *mitigatio(n-)*, formed as MITIGATE: see -ATION.]
1 The action of mitigating something; the fact or condition of being mitigated. LME. ▸**b** A mitigating circumstance or provision. E18.

A. BRIEN He was found guilty. I refused to make any statement in mitigation. R. ELLMANN They decided to ask for mitigation of his sentence on medical grounds. **b** J. BUTLER Mitigations and reliefs are provided.. for most of the afflictions in human life.

†**2** Softening, qualification, esp. of wording. L16–E18.

Mitnagged /mɪtˈnagɛd/ *noun*. Pl. **-im** /-ɪm/. E20.
[ORIGIN Hebrew *miṯnaggēḏ* opponent.]
A religious opponent of the Hasidim; any Jew who is not a Hasid.

mitochondrion /mʌɪtəˈkɒndrɪən/ *noun*. Pl. **-dria** /-drɪə/. E20.
[ORIGIN from Greek *mitos* thread + *khondrion*, dim. of *khondros* granule, lump (of salt).]
BIOLOGY. An organelle that primarily functions to store and release energy through the Krebs cycle and is present (usu. in great numbers) in the cytoplasm of most cells.
▪ **mitochondrial** *adjective* of or pertaining to a mitochondrion or mitochondria E20. **mitochondrially** *adverb* by, in, or through mitochondria M20.

mitogen /ˈmʌɪtədʒ(ə)n/ *noun*. M20.
[ORIGIN from MITOSIS + -GEN.]
BIOLOGY. A substance or agent that induces or stimulates mitosis.
▪ **mitogeˈnetic**, **mitoˈgenic** *adjectives* inducing or stimulating mitosis E20.

mitosis /mʌɪˈtəʊsɪs/ *noun*. Pl. **-toses** /-ˈtəʊsiːz/. L19.
[ORIGIN from Greek *mitos* thread of a warp + -OSIS.]
CYTOLOGY. The process of division by which a cell nucleus gives rise to two daughter nuclei identical to the parent in number and size of chromosomes; an instance of this. Cf. MEIOSIS.

mitotic /mʌɪˈtɒtɪk/ *adjective*. L19.
[ORIGIN from MITOSIS + -OTIC.]
CYTOLOGY. Of, pertaining to, characterized by, or exhibiting mitosis.
▪ **mitotically** *adverb* by mitosis L19.

mitraille /mitrɑːj, mɪˈtreɪl/ *noun*. L18.
[ORIGIN Old French & mod. French = small money, pieces of metal, alt. of Old French *mitaille*, from *mite* rel. to MITE *noun*[2].]
Cannon shot consisting of masses of small missiles from a cannon; *spec.* small shot fired from a *mitrailleuse*.

mitrailleur /mitrajœːr/ *noun*. Pl. pronounced same. M19.
[ORIGIN French, from *mitrailler* fire mitraille, formed as MITRAILLE, + *-eur* -OR.]
= MITRAILLEUSE.

mitrailleuse /mitrajøːz/ *noun*. Pl. pronounced same. M19.
[ORIGIN French, fem. of MITRAILLEUR.]
A breech-loading machine gun with several barrels that can discharge small missiles rapidly and simultaneously in large quantities or singly in quick succession.

mitral /ˈmʌɪtr(ə)l/ *adjective* & *noun*. E17.
[ORIGIN mod. Latin *mitralis*, from Latin *mitra* MITRE *noun*[1]: see -AL[1].]
▸ **A** *adjective*. **1** Of, pertaining to, or resembling a mitre. E17.
2 ANATOMY & MEDICINE. Designating or pertaining to the left auriculo-ventricular valve of the heart, so called from its shape. Also called *bicuspid valve*. L17.
▸ **B** *ellipt.* as *noun*. The mitral valve. M19.

mitre /ˈmʌɪtə/ *noun*[1]. Also ***miter**. ME.
[ORIGIN Old French from Latin *mitra* from Greek *mitra* belt, turban, perh. of Asian origin.]
1 ECCLESIASTICAL. A tall deeply cleft headdress worn by a bishop or abbot, esp. as a symbol of episcopal office, forming in outline the shape of a pointed arch, and often made of embroidered white linen or satin. ME. ▸**b** *The* episcopal office or dignity. LME. ▸**c** *hist.* A kind of headdress resembling a bishop's mitre, worn by women in medieval times. L19.

b LD MACAULAY Baxter.. refused the mitre of Hereford.

2 a ANTIQUITIES. A headband worn by women in ancient Greece. Also, an Asian headdress, regarded by the Romans as effeminate when worn by men. LME. ▸†**b** A kind of turban worn by Asian peoples. L16–M17.
3 HEBREW ANTIQUITIES. The ceremonial turban of a high priest. Also (*rare*), the headdress of an ordinary priest. LME.
4 Any of numerous marine gastropods, esp. of the genus *Mitra*, with a shell resembling a mitre in shape. Also *mitre-shell*. M18.
– COMB.: *mitre-shell*: see sense 4 above; **mitrewort** any of various plants of the N. American and Asian genus *Mitella* (family Saxifragaceae) (also called *bishop's cap*) or (*false mitrewort*) the related N. American genus *Tiarella*.

mitre /ˈmʌɪtə/ *noun*[2]. Also ***miter**. M17.
[ORIGIN Perh. transf. use of MITRE *noun*[1].]
1 a In full *mitre joint*. A right-angled joint of wood or some other material, in which the angle made by the joined pieces is bisected by the line of junction. M17. ▸**b** Either of the shaped ends or edges which form such a joint; a 45° angle such as these ends or edges have. E18.
2 In full *mitre square*. A bevel with the blade set at 45°, or with two blades set at 45° to one another, for bevelling mitre joints. L17.
3 In full *mitre wheel*. Either of a pair of bevelled cog-wheels with teeth set at 45° and right-angled axes. M19.
– COMB.: **mitre bevel** = sense 2 above; **mitre block**, **mitre board**, **mitre box** a block or frame of wood with slits for guiding a saw when cutting mitre joints; **mitre cramp**: for securing a glued mitre joint while it is drying; **mitre gear** either of a pair of bevel gears of equal length with right-angled shafts; *mitre joint*: see sense 1 above; **mitre plane**: with an oblique surface for making mitre joints; **mitre shooting board**: used in chamfering the edges of wood; *mitre square*: see sense 2 above; *mitre wheel*: see sense 3 above.

mitre /ˈmʌɪtə/ *verb*[1] *trans.* Also ***miter**. ME.
[ORIGIN from MITRE *noun*[1].]
Confer or bestow a mitre on (a bishop or abbot), raise to a rank to which the dignity of wearing a mitre belongs.

mitre /ˈmʌɪtə/ *verb*[2]. Also ***miter**. M17.
[ORIGIN from MITRE *noun*[2].]
1 *verb trans.* Join with a mitre joint; make a mitre joint in; cut or shape to a mitre. Freq. as *mitred ppl adjective*. M17.

DIY Today They have produced coving corners, thus eliminating the need to mitre pieces of coving together.

2 *verb intrans.* Form a mitre, meet in a mitre joint. M18.

J. S. FOSTER Two parallel slopes with slopes normal to these.. which mitre or intersect.

▪ **mitring** *noun* (**a**) the action of the verb; (**b**) the shaped end of a piece prepared to be mitred with another: M17.

mitred /ˈmʌɪtəd/ *adjective*. Also ***mitered**. LME.
[ORIGIN from MITRE *noun*[1], *verb*[1]: see -ED[2], -ED[1].]
1 Wearing or entitled to wear a mitre. LME.
2 Formed like a mitre. M16.
– SPECIAL COLLOCATIONS: **mitred abbey** *hist.* an abbey ruled by a mitred abbot. **mitred abbot** *hist.* an abbot entitled to wear a mitre (and before the Reformation to be a member of the House of Lords).

mitriform /ˈmʌɪtrɪfɔːm/ *adjective*. E19.
[ORIGIN mod. Latin *mitriformis*, from *mitra* MITRE *noun*[1]: see -FORM.]
BOTANY & ZOOLOGY. Resembling or shaped like a mitre; conical, hollow, and open at the base.

M

mitry /ˈmʌɪtri/ *adjective*. M19.
[ORIGIN from MITRE *noun*[1] + -Y[1].]
HERALDRY. Charged with mitres.

Mitsein /ˈmɪtzʌɪn/ *noun*. M20.
[ORIGIN German, use as noun of inf. *mitsein*, from *mit* with + *sein* be.]
PHILOSOPHY. The concept of a person's being in its relationship with others.

mitsumata /mɪtsʊˈmɑːtə/ *noun*. L19.
[ORIGIN Japanese, lit. 'three-pronged fork', from *mitsu* three (prongs) + *mata* fork.]
A yellow-flowered deciduous shrub, *Edgeworthia papyrifera* (family Thymelaeaceae), native to China and widely cultivated in Japan, where its bast fibre is used to make paper.

mitt /mɪt/ *noun*. Also **mit**. M18.
[ORIGIN Abbreviation of MITTEN.]
1 A knitted or lace covering for the hand, leaving the fingers and thumb exposed; a fingerless glove. M18.
SIR W. SCOTT The black silk gloves, or mitts. *Practical Photography* The . . digits of a market trader jutting . . out of fingerless mitts.
2 = MITTEN 1. E19. ▸**b** BASEBALL. A protective glove worn by the catcher or first baseman. L19.
3 A hand. Usu. in *pl. slang*. L19.
M. LEITCH Young Terry came into the room holding a full mug in his massive mitt.
– PHRASES: **the frozen mitt** *slang* an unfriendly reception; intentionally unfriendly treatment. **the glad mitt** *slang* a warm or friendly reception; = ***the glad hand*** s.v. GLAD *adjective*. **the icy mitt** = ***the frozen mitt*** above. **tip one's mitt**: see TIP *verb*[1].
– COMB.: **mitt camp** *US slang* a palmist's or fortune-teller's establishment, tent, etc.; **mitt joint** *US slang* (*a*) a gambling house; (*b*) = ***mitt camp*** above; **mitt-reader** *US slang* a palmist, a fortune-teller.
■ **mitted** *adjective* provided with or wearing mitts or mittens L19.

Mittagessen /ˈmɪtaːkˌɛsən/ *noun*. Also **m-**. L19.
[ORIGIN German.]
In Germany and Austria: a midday meal, lunch.

Mitteleuropa /ˌmɪt(ə)ljʊˈrəʊpə/ *noun*. E20.
[ORIGIN German.]
Central Europe regarded as a political or cultural entity.
■ **Mittel-Euroˈpean** *adjective & noun* M20.

Mittelschmerz /ˈmɪtəlʃmɛrts/ *noun*. L19.
[ORIGIN German = middle pain.]
MEDICINE. Pain in the lower abdomen regularly experienced by some women midway between successive menstrual periods and often thought to coincide with ovulation.

Mittelstand /ˈmɪtlʃtant, ˈmɪt(ə)lstand/ *noun*. M20.
[ORIGIN German.]
In Germany: the middle class. Now also (ECONOMICS), the medium-sized companies in any country, viewed as an economic unit.

mitten /ˈmɪt(ə)n/ *noun*. ME.
[ORIGIN Old French & mod. French *mitaine* = Provençal *mitana* (cf. medieval Latin *mitan(n)a* from Proto-Romance form with the sense 'skin-lined glove cut off at the middle', from Latin *medietas* half.]
1 A covering for the hand with one section for all four fingers and another for the thumb, worn for warmth or protection. Also (now *dial.*), a thick winter glove. ME.
2 *slang*. **a** Handcuffs. In *pl*. L16. ▸**b** A hand. Usu. in *pl*. E19. ▸**c** A boxing glove. Usu. in *pl*. M19.
3 = MITT 1. M18.
– PHRASES: **get the mitten** *slang* (*a*) (of a lover, partner, etc.) be jilted or rejected; (*b*) be dismissed from office, get the sack. **give (a person) the mitten**, **hand (a person) the mitten** *slang* end a relationship with (a person); jilt, reject.
– COMB.: **mitten crab** a Chinese crab, *Eriocheir sinensis*, with long silky hairs on the pincers of the male, introduced into western European estuaries.
■ **mittened** *adjective* provided with or wearing mittens E19.

mittimus /ˈmɪtɪməs/ *noun & verb*. LME.
[ORIGIN Latin, lit. 'we send', the first word of the writ in Latin.]
▸**A** *noun*. **1** LAW. ▸†**a** A writ to transfer records from one court to another. LME–E18. ▸**b** A warrant committing a person to prison. Now *US*. L16.
2 A dismissal from office; a notice to quit. Chiefly in ***get one's mittimus***, be dismissed. Now *dial*. L16.
†**3** A magistrate. *joc*. M17–L18.
▸†**B** *verb trans*. Commit to prison by a warrant. M18–M19.

Mitty /ˈmɪti/ *noun*. M20.
[ORIGIN from Walter *Mitty*, hero of James Thurber's short story *The Secret Life of Walter Mitty*.]
A person who indulges in daydreams, esp. of a life much more exciting and glamorous than his or her real life.
■ **Mittyˈesque** *adjective* M20.

mitumba /mɪˈtʊmbə/ *noun*. L20.
[ORIGIN Swahili, pl. of *mtumba*, lit. 'bale (of cloth)'.]
In eastern and central Africa: second-hand clothing, esp. that donated by aid agencies in the West.

mitzvah /ˈmɪtsvə/ *noun*. Pl. **-voth** /-vəʊt/. E18.
[ORIGIN Hebrew *miṣwāh* commandment.]
JUDAISM. A precept; a duty, an obligation. Also, a good deed. Cf. BAR MITZVAH, BAT MITZVAH.

mivvy /ˈmɪvi/ *noun*. *slang*. Now *rare*. M19.
[ORIGIN Unknown.]
1 A marble. M19.
2 A woman, *esp*. the landlady of a lodging house. *derog*. L19.
3 A person who is adept at something; a genius, a marvel. E20.

Miwok /ˈmiːwɒk, ˈmʌɪ-/ *noun & adjective*. M19.
[ORIGIN Miwok = people.]
▸**A** *noun*. Pl. **-s**, same. A member of a Penutian people of California; the language of this people. LM19.
▸**B** *attrib*. or as *adjective*. Of or pertaining to the Miwok or their language. E20.

mix /mɪks/ *noun*. L16.
[ORIGIN from the verb.]
1 *gen*. The act or result of mixing; a mixture; the state of being mixed; a number of ingredients mixed together or intended for mixing. L16.
W. D. HOWELLS You'll be ruined. Oh, poor Mr. Welling! Oh, what a fatal, fatal—mix! B. EMECHETA Ezechial was a typical product of this cultural mix.
2 A mix-up, a muddle. *colloq*. L19.
3 A commercially prepared mixture of ingredients from which something, as a cake, concrete, etc. can be made. E20.
B. MACDONALD I could use automatic biscuit mix for the crust.
4 CINEMATOGRAPHY, TELEVISION, & AUDIO etc. The action or process of combining or merging film pictures or soundtracks; a transition between two pictures or sounds in which one fades out as the other fades in, a dissolve. E20. ▸**b** A version of a recording in which the component tracks are mixed in a different way; a recording made by mixing other recordings. L20.
b N. SEDAKA The mixes did not sound particularly Top 40ish.
b ***rough mix***: see ROUGH *adjective*.
5 The proportion or combination of different components that make up a product, plan, policy, or other integrated whole. M20.
Broadcast The editorial mix is likely to include personality pages . . and cartoon strips. *Lancaster Guardian* Without schools, villages lost their mix of age groups.
6 = MIXER 5. M20.

mix /mɪks/ *verb*. Pa. t. & pple **mixed**, †**mixt**. LME.
[ORIGIN Back-form. from MIXED.]
1 *verb trans*. Put together or combine (two or more substances or things) so that the constituents of each are diffused among those of the other or others; mingle, blend; *fig*. combine or blend (different principles, qualities, etc.). LME. ▸**b** Prepare (a compound, cocktail, etc.) by combining various ingredients. L15. ▸†**c** Add as an ingredient, intersperse. (Foll. by *to*.) E17–M18.
M. W. MONTAGU Their own hair . . they mix with a great deal of false. JOHN BAXTER Mix a small quantity of salt with the food. **b** A. CROSS Kate, mixing herself another martini.
2 *verb trans*. **a** Unite (a person, oneself) *with* another in dealings or acquaintance. Formerly also, join in sexual intercourse. Now *rare*. E16. ▸†**b** Unite (the eyes) in an interchange of glances. *rare*. L16–M19. ▸**c** Join and clasp (hands). *rare*. E18.
3 *verb intrans*. **a** Have sexual intercourse *with*. Now *rare*. E17. ▸**b** Move socially *in*, †*among*; keep company *with*, socialize *with*. M17. ▸**c** Be involved (*in*), participate (*in*). E19. ▸**d** Be sociable. E19.
b B. EMECHETA You can keep to yourself, you don't have to mix with them. **d** M. SPARK In no great hurry for the flat, preferring hotel life where one need not mix.
4 *verb intrans*. Be mixed, admit of being mixed; combine, blend together; go (well or badly) *with*. E16.
GOLDSMITH Sending up a part of their substance by evaporation, to mix in this great alembic. R. DEACON Espionage and politics do not mix.
5 *verb trans. & intrans*. Cross in breeding. M18.
6 CINEMATOGRAPHY, TELEVISION, & AUDIO etc. ▸**a** *verb trans*. Blend (two pictures or sounds) temporarily by fading one out as the other is faded in. E20. ▸**b** *verb trans*. Combine (two or more sound signals) into one in a mixer; create (a recording) by combining a number of separate recordings or tracks. E20. ▸**c** *verb intrans*. Pass from one picture or sound to another by fading one out as the other is faded in. (Foll. by *from*, *to*.) M20.
– PHRASES & COMB.: **mix and match** select and combine complementary or coordinating items so as to form a matching collection; (of an item) coordinate with other related items. **mix-and-match** *adjective & noun* (*a*) *adjective* suitable for or selected by mixing and matching, complementary, coordinating, assorted; (*b*) *noun* an instance of mixing and matching. **mix-down** the action or an act of mixing down a multitrack recording; a recording made in this way. **mix it** *slang* start fighting; fight, cause trouble. **mix one's drinks** drink different kinds of alcoholic liquor in close succession; become intoxicated by this means. **mix-up** the state of being mixed up; *spec*. a state of confusion, a muddle, a mess; a misunderstanding; a fight.
– WITH ADVERBS IN SPECIALIZED SENSES: **mix down** convert (a multitrack sound recording or multiple signal) to one consisting of fewer tracks or components. **mix in** join in, take part, be sociable. **mix up** (*a*) mix thoroughly; ***mix it up*** (*slang*), fight vigorously; (*b*) combine unsuitably or confusingly; confuse, mistake; (*c*) in *pass*., be involved *in* or associated *with* (esp. something shady or discreditable).
■ **mixable** *adjective* M19. **mixible** *adjective* (long *rare*) E17. **mixy** *adjective* (*a*) adapted for mixing; (*b*) *colloq*. sociable: E20.

mixed /mɪkst/ *adjective*. Also †**mixt**. LME.
[ORIGIN Old French & mod. French *mixte* (spec. in Anglo-Norman law phr. *accioun mixte* action partly real, partly personal) from Latin *mixtus* pa. pple of *miscere* mingle, mix, rel. to Greek *misgein*, *mignunai*: see -ED[1].]
1 LAW (now *hist*.). Of an action: of the nature of both a real and a personal action. LME.
2 Mingled or blended together; formed by the mingling or combining of different substances, individuals, etc. LME.
E. PIZZEY Get two bunches of mixed summer flowers.
3 Consisting of different or dissimilar elements or qualities; not of one kind, not pure or simple. LME.
L. MACNEICE None of our hearts are pure, we always have mixed motives. A. W. CARDINALL The area . . is peopled by mixed races. *Guardian* Unstreaming, or teaching children in mixed ability groups. *Shetland Times* The new far-reaching controls on fishing activity . . have had a mixed welcome.
4 Containing people from various backgrounds; unrestricted. Also, containing people of doubtful character or status. E17.
S. MIDDLETON 'It's a decent district, isn't it?' 'Yes. A bit mixed at the bottom end.'
5 For, involving, or comprising both sexes. M17.
Times University House . . became the first ever mixed students' hostel.
6 Of a science: involving or dealing with matter, not pure or simply theoretical. Now *rare* or *obsolete*. M17.
7 PHONETICS. = CENTRAL *adjective* 4. M19.
8 Mentally confused, muddled, esp. through drink. *colloq*. L19.
– SPECIAL COLLOCATIONS & COMB.: **mixed angle** (*obsolete* exc. *hist*.): formed by the intersection of a straight line and a curve. **mixed bag** a diverse assortment of people, items, etc. **mixed bathing** simultaneous bathing in the same place by people of both sexes. **mixed bed** a flower bed containing an assortment of plants. **mixed blessing** a thing having advantages but also disadvantages. **mixed blood** (*a*) descent from two or more races; (*b*) a person of mixed descent. **mixed border** a long flower bed containing a wide variety of different plants. **mixed bunch** = ***mixed bag*** above. **mixed company** (*a*) company comprising both sexes; (*b*) company comprising people of different backgrounds or characters. **mixed crystal** PHYSICAL CHEMISTRY a homogeneous crystal formed of more than one crystalline substance. **mixed doubles** a game of doubles in tennis, badminton, etc., in which each pair of players comprises a member of either sex. **mixed economy** an economic system containing both private and state enterprise. **mixed farming** farming which combines the raising of livestock and arable cultivation. **mixed feelings** conflicting emotions; a combination of pleasure and dismay. **mixed grill** a dish consisting of several different grilled items of food. **mixed language** a language made up of a mixture of elements from two or more other languages; a creolized language. **mixed-manned** *adjective* (of a military force) comprising people of more than one nationality. **mixed marriage** a marriage between people of different races or religions. **mixed media** (*a*) the use of a variety of mediums in an entertainment, work of art, etc.; (*b*) = ***mixed technique*** below. **mixed-media** *adjective* = MULTIMEDIA. **mixed metaphor** a combination of two or more inconsistent metaphors. **mixed number** MATH.: consisting of an integer and a fraction. **mixed-pressure** *adjective* (of a steam turbine) powered by both high- and low-pressure steam. **mixed school**: in which girls and boys are taught together. **mixed technique** a technique in painting in which tempera and oils are combined. **mixed-traffic** *adjective* (of a locomotive) suitable for both passenger and freight haulage. **mixed-up** (*a*) involved, intermingled; (*b*) *colloq*. mentally or emotionally confused; socially maladjusted.
■ **mixedly** *adverb* (now *rare*) M16. **mixedness** *noun* M17.

mixen /ˈmɪks(ə)n/ *noun*. Now *arch*. or *dial*.
[ORIGIN Old English from Germanic, rel. to Old Saxon, Old High German, *mist* (German *Mist*), Gothic *maihstus* dung, ult. from Germanic base meaning 'make water' (cf. Old English *miċġe*, *migga* urine, Old English *migan*, Low German *migen*, Old Norse *miga* urinate).]
1 A place where dung and refuse are laid; a dunghill. Also, a heap of dung, compost, etc., used for manure. OE.
2 (A term of abuse or reproach for) a woman or child. *dial*. M18.

mixer /ˈmɪksə/ *noun*. L16.
[ORIGIN from MIX *verb* + -ER[1].]
1 A person who blends or mixes liquids, materials, etc. L16. ▸**b** A person who mixes drinks, a bartender. M19.
2 A machine or device for mixing; *spec*. an electrical appliance for mixing foods. L19. ▸**b** A container for mixing drinks; a cocktail shaker. L19.
3 A person in respect of his or her ability to mix socially with others; a sociable person. L19. ▸**b** A social gathering to enable people to get to know one another. *N. Amer. colloq*. E20.
A. STORR A child who is a poor mixer and cannot stand up for himself. R. DEACON He was a good mixer in all classes of society. **b** *New Yorker* He had married a girl he had met at a mixer.

M

4 a CINEMATOGRAPHY, TELEVISION, & AUDIO etc. A device designed to receive two or more separate signals and combine them in a single output. Also, a person who operates such a device. E20. ▸**b** ELECTRONICS. A device that produces an output signal containing frequencies equal to the sum and the difference of the frequencies of two input signals. M20.
5 A soft drink with which an alcoholic drink is diluted, as soda water etc.; an alcoholic drink used in cocktails. E20.
6 A troublemaker. *slang*. M20.
7 A type of dry pet food which can be mixed with moist tinned food. L20.
– COMB.: **mixer tap** a tap through which both hot and cold water can be drawn at the same time, in any proportion.

Mix-Hellene /mɪkshɛˈliːn/ *noun*. Now *rare*. M19.
[ORIGIN Greek *mixhellēn*, formed as MIXO- + HELLENE.]
CLASSICAL HISTORY. A person of mixed Greek and barbarian descent.

mixing /ˈmɪksɪŋ/ *verbal noun*. E16.
[ORIGIN from MIX *verb* + -ING[1].]
The action of MIX *verb*.
– COMB.: **mixing desk** a console where sound signals are mixed during recording or broadcasting; **mixing valve** a valve in which separate supplies of hot and cold water are mixed together; a mixer tap.

mixis /ˈmɪksɪs/ *noun*. M20.
[ORIGIN Greek = mixing, (sexual) intercourse.]
BIOLOGY. Sexual reproduction, esp. with alternation of different nuclear phases.

mixite /ˈmɪksʌɪt/ *noun*. L19.
[ORIGIN from A. *Mixa*, 19th-cent. Czech mining official + -ITE[1].]
MINERALOGY. A hexagonal hydrated basic arsenate of copper and bismuth, usu. occurring as green fibrous encrustations.

Mixmaster /ˈmɪksmɑːstə/ *noun*. Also **m-**. M20.
[ORIGIN from MIX *verb* + MASTER *noun*[1].]
1 (Proprietary name for) a type of electrical food mixer; *transf.* & *fig.* a machine or device with whirring blades, a thing constantly on the move. M20.
2 (**m-**.) A sound-recording engineer or disc jockey who is an accomplished mixer of music. *colloq.* L20.
– COMB.: **Mixmaster universe** ASTRONOMY a cosmological model in which the universe is made isotropic by continual expansions and contractions along randomly distributed directions.

mixo- /ˈmɪksəʊ/ *combining form*.
[ORIGIN Repr. Greek *mixo-*, from base of *mignunai* to mix (cf. MIX *verb*): see -O-.]
Used in the sense 'mixed'.
■ **mixohaline** /-ˈheɪlʌɪn/ *adjective* [Greek *halinos* of salt] brackish M20. **mixotrophic** /-ˈtrəʊfɪk, -ˈtrɒfɪk/ *adjective* (BIOLOGY) designating, pertaining to, or characterized by a combination of autotrophic and heterotrophic nutrition E20. **mixotrophically** /-ˈtrəʊf-, -ˈtrɒf-/ *adverb* (BIOLOGY) by mixotrophic nutrition L20.

mixolimnion /mɪksəˈlɪmnɪən/ *noun*. Pl. **-nia** /-nɪə/. M20.
[ORIGIN from MIXO- + Greek *limnion* dim. of *limnē* lake.]
The upper, freely circulating layer of a meromictic lake.

mixologist /mɪkˈsɒlədʒɪst/ *noun*. *US slang*. M19.
[ORIGIN from MIX *noun* or *verb* + -OLOGIST.]
A person who is skilled at mixing drinks.

mixolydian /mɪksəˈlɪdɪən/ *adjective*. L16.
[ORIGIN Greek *mixo-ludios* half-Lydian: see MIXO-, LYDIAN.]
MUSIC. Designating that mode which has G for its final and D for its dominant, or which is represented on the piano by the white notes from G to G. Also, designating the highest in pitch of the ancient Greek modes.

mixoploid /ˈmɪksəplɔɪd/ *adjective* & *noun*. M20.
[ORIGIN from MIXO- + -PLOID.]
BIOLOGY. ▸**A** *adjective*. Composed of cells which are of differing ploidy or have differing numbers of chromosomes. M20.
▸**B** *noun*. A mixoploid organism. M20.
■ **mixoploidy** *noun* mixoploid condition M20.

mixt /mɪkst/ *noun*. *arch.* or *hist.* L16.
[ORIGIN Latin *mixtum* neut. of *mixtus* mixed.]
Something consisting of different elements mixed together; *esp.* a chemical compound.

†**mixt** *adjective* var. of MIXED.

†**mixt** *verb* see MIX *verb*.

mixte /mikst/ *adjective* & *noun*. Pl. of noun pronounced same. L20.
[ORIGIN French = mixed.]
(Designating) a bicycle or bicycle frame having no crossbar but instead two thin tubes running from the head of the steering column to either side of the rear axle.

Mixtec /ˈmiːstɛk/ *noun* & *adjective*. Also (earlier) **Mixteca** /miːˈstɛkə/; **Mixteco** /miːˈstɛkəʊ/, pl. **-os**. L18.
[ORIGIN Spanish from Nahuatl *mixtecah* person from a cloudy place.]
▸**A** *noun*. **1** A member of a people of Central America. L18.
2 The language of this people. M19.
▸**B** *attrib.* or as *adjective*. Of or pertaining to the Mixtecs or their language. E20.
■ **Miˈxtecan** *noun* & *adjective* (of or pertaining to) the Mixtec language L18.

mixtie-maxtie *adjective* & *noun* var. of MIXTY-MAXTY.

mixtilinear /mɪkstɪˈlɪnɪə/ *adjective*. E18.
[ORIGIN from Latin *mixtus* MIXED + LINEAR, after *rectilinear*.]
Formed or bounded by both straight and curved lines.

mixtion /ˈmɪkstʃ(ə)n/ *noun*. *arch.* or *hist.* LME.
[ORIGIN Old French & mod. French *mistion* from Latin *mixtio(n-)*, from *mixt-*: see MIXTURE, -ION.]
The action or process of mixing; a mixture.

mixture /ˈmɪkstʃə/ *noun*. LME.
[ORIGIN French, or its source Latin *mixtura*, from *mixt-* pa. ppl stem of *miscere* mix: see -URE.]
1 The action, process, or fact of mixing or combining; an instance of this; a product of mixing; a combination, esp. one in which the component elements are individually distinct. LME. ▸**b** The action or an act of adding an ingredient; the presence of a diverse element in the composition of something. Also, an amount or proportion added; an admixture. E16. ▸**c** A medicinal or other preparation consisting of two or more ingredients mixed together; *spec.* a liquid medicine as opp. to pills, powder, or other solid medicine. M16.

> J. TYNDALL From the intimate mixture of air and water we obtain foam. N. ALGREN The other women regarded her with a strange mixture of admiration and pity. I. FLEMING The usual mixture of tourists and businessmen and local people coming home. P. CUTTING They bombed a mixture of military and civilian targets. **b** B. KEACH Adulterating the Word of God by the Mixture of their own Fancies. A. DICKSON The soil in which there is a great mixture of moss. **c** *Longman's Magazine* I took a sip of the horrid mixture.

c the mixture as before (an instruction on a medicine bottle) the same dose as previously; *fig.* something repeated or already encountered.
†**2** Sexual intercourse. L15–E18.
3 a A variegated fabric, usu. of soft colouring. E18. ▸**b** MUSIC. In full ***mixture stop***. An organ stop with several ranks of pipes. L18. ▸**c** A blend of tea, tobacco, snuff, etc. M19.
a heather mixture, ***Oxford mixture***, etc.
4 CHEMISTRY. The mechanical mixing of two or more substances without chemical change, as opp. to chemical combination; a product of such mixing. Also ***mechanical mixture***. M18.
5 a In an internal-combustion engine, the vaporized or gaseous fuel together with air that forms the explosive charge in the cylinder. L19. ▸**b** A combination of petrol with a small proportion of oil, used as a combined fuel and lubricant in some two-stroke engines. M20.
a lean mixture: see LEAN *adjective*.

mixty-maxty /mɪkstɪˈmaksti/ *adjective* & *noun*. *Scot.* & *dial.* Also **mixtie-maxtie**. L18.
[ORIGIN Varied redupl. of *mixt* MIXED: see -Y[6], -IE.]
▸**A** *adjective*. Incongruously mixed; jumbled together, muddled. L18.
▸**B** *noun*. Something incongruously mixed; a confused mass, a heterogeneous mixture. E19.

miz /mɪz/ *noun*. Pl. **mizzes**. E20.
[ORIGIN Abbreviation of MISTRESS *noun*.]
1 Used as a title preceding a woman's name: Mrs, Miss. *Southern US*. E20.
2 = MS. L20.

mizen *noun* var. of MIZZEN.

mizmaze /ˈmɪzmeɪz/ *noun*. M16.
[ORIGIN Varied redupl. of MAZE *noun*[1].]
1 A labyrinth, a maze. M16.
2 Mystification, bewildering delusion; a state of confusion. Chiefly *dial.* E17.

Mizo /ˈmiːzəʊ/ *noun* & *adjective*. M19.
[ORIGIN Lushai, lit. 'highlander', from *mi* person + *zo* hill.]
▸**A** *noun*. Pl. same, **-os**. A member of a people inhabiting the territory of Mizoram in NE India. M19.
▸**B** *adjective*. Of or pertaining to these people. M19.

Mizpah /ˈmɪzpə/ *adjective*. L19.
[ORIGIN Hebrew *Miṣpāh* place name in ancient Palestine.]
Designating a ring, locket, etc., given as an expression or token of association or remembrance, orig. and esp. one with 'Mizpah' inscribed on it (with allus. to *Genesis* 31:49).

mizuna /mɪˈzuːnə/ *noun*. L20.
[ORIGIN Japanese, from *mizu* water + *na* greens.]
More fully ***mizuna greens***. An oriental rape, *Brassica rapa* var. *nipposinica*, with finely cut leaves that are eaten as a salad vegetable.

mizzen /ˈmɪz(ə)n/ *noun*. Also **mizen**. LME.
[ORIGIN French *misaine* (now foresail, foremast) from Italian *mezzana* use as noun of fem. of *mezzano* middle.]
NAUTICAL. **1** More fully ***mizzensail***. The lowest fore-and-aft sail on the mizzenmast of a full-rigged ship. Formerly also, a similarly shaped principal sail in certain small craft. LME.
2 In full ***mizzenmast***. The mast aft of the mainmast in a ship of three or more masts. LME.
– COMB.: **mizzen top** a platform near the head of the mizzenmast; **mizzen topmast** the mast next above the lower mizzenmast; **mizzen topsail** the sail above the mizzensail, set on the mizzen topmast; **mizzen yard** the yard on which the mizzensail is extended.

mizzle /ˈmɪz(ə)l/ *noun*[1]. L15.
[ORIGIN from MIZZLE *verb*[1].]
Fine rain, drizzle.

mizzle /ˈmɪz(ə)l/ *noun*[2]. *slang*. E20.
[ORIGIN from MIZZLE *verb*[2].]
A disappearance, a vanishing act.
do a mizzle depart suddenly, vanish.

mizzle /ˈmɪz(ə)l/ *verb*[1] *intrans.* LME.
[ORIGIN Prob. from Low German *miseln* = Dutch dial. *miezelen*, Western Flemish *mizzelen*, *mijzelen*, frequentative (see -LE[3]) of the Low German base repr. by Dutch dial. *miesregen* drizzle, *miezig*, Low German *misig* drizzling.]
Rain in very fine drops, drizzle. Usu. *impers.* in ***it mizzles***, ***it is mizzling***, etc.

> M. R. MITFORD It did not absolutely rain, it only mizzled. K. TENNANT A cold wind and a grey, mizzling rain.

mizzle /ˈmɪz(ə)l/ *verb*[2] *intrans.* *slang*. L18.
[ORIGIN Unknown.]
Disappear suddenly; decamp, vanish, take oneself off.
■ **mizzler** *noun* M19.

mizzle /ˈmɪz(ə)l/ *verb*[3] *intrans.* M20.
[ORIGIN Perh. from MOAN *verb* + GRIZZLE *verb*[2].]
Complain, whimper; whine fretfully.

mizzly /ˈmɪzli/ *adjective*. M16.
[ORIGIN from MIZZLE *noun*[1] or *verb*[1] + -Y[1].]
Of the nature of mizzle; marked by mizzling rain; drizzly.

MJI *abbreviation*.
Member of the Institute of Journalists.

M.Juris /ɛm ˈdʒʊərɪs/ *abbreviation*.
Latin *Magister Juris* Master of Law.

Mk *abbreviation*.
1 Mark (I, II, III, etc.).
2 Mark (former German currency).
3 Mark (esp. New Testament).

mks *abbreviation*.
Metre-kilogram-second (system).

Mkt *abbreviation*.
Market.

ml *abbreviation*.
1 Mile(s).
2 Millilitre(s).

MLA *abbreviation*.
1 Member of the Legislative Assembly.
2 Modern Language Association (of America).

MLC *abbreviation*.
Member of the Legislative Council.

MLD *abbreviation*.
Minimum lethal dose.

M.Litt. *abbreviation*.
Latin *Magister Litterarum* Master of Letters.

Mlle *abbreviation*.
Mademoiselle.

Mlles *abbreviation*.
Mesdemoiselles.

MLR *abbreviation*.
Minimum lending rate.

MLRS *abbreviation*.
Multiple launch rocket system.

MM *abbreviation*[1].
1 Maelzel's metronome.
2 Messieurs.
3 Military Medal.

mm *abbreviation*[2].
Millimetre(s).

mm /(ə)m/ *interjection*. Also **m'm**. E20.
[ORIGIN Imit.]
Expr. hesitation or inarticulate interrogation, assent, reflection, or satisfaction. Cf. UM *interjection*.

Mme *abbreviation*.
Madame.

Mmes *abbreviation*.
Mesdames.

m.m.f. *abbreviation*.
Magnetomotive force.

MMP *abbreviation*. *NZ*.
Mixed member proportional (designating the system used in New Zealand general elections since 1996).

MMR *abbreviation*.
Measles, mumps, rubella (vaccine).

MMS *abbreviation*.
Multimedia Messaging Service (for mobile phones).

M.Mus. *abbreviation*.
Master of Music.

MN *abbreviation*.
1 Merchant Navy.
2 Minnesota.

Mn *symbol.*
CHEMISTRY. Manganese.

MNA *abbreviation.*
In Canada: Member of the National Assembly (of Quebec).

mna /mnɑː/ *noun.* Now *rare.* LME.
[ORIGIN Greek.]
= MINA *noun*[1].

M'Naghten rules, M'Naughten rules *noun phrs. pl.*
vars. of MCNAUGHTEN RULES.

mneme /ˈniːmiː/ *noun.* E20.
[ORIGIN Greek *mnēmē* memory.]
PSYCHOLOGY & PHYSIOLOGY. The capacity for retaining after-effects of experience or stimulation. Also = MEMORY *trace.*
■ **mnemic** *adjective* pertaining to, of the nature of, or involving mneme E20. **mnemically** *adverb (rare)* E20. **mnemicness** *noun (rare)* M20.

mnemon /ˈniːmɒn/ *noun. rare.* M20.
[ORIGIN formed as MNEME + -ON.]
PSYCHOLOGY. A unit of memory.

mnemonic /nɪˈmɒnɪk, niː-/ *noun & adjective.* M17.
[ORIGIN medieval Latin *mnemonicus* from Greek *mnēmonikos* from *mnēmōn, mnēmon-* mindful, from *mna-* base of *mnasthai* remember: see -IC.]
▸ **A** *noun.* †**1** = MNEMONICS. M17–M19.
2 A mnemonic device, formula, or code. M19.
▸ **B** *adjective.* **1** Intended or designed to aid the memory; of or pertaining to mnemonics. Also, (of a formula, code, etc.) easy to remember or understand. L18.

J. AUEL His drawing was no more than a mnemonic aid to remind them of a place they knew. *Computing Equipment* Mnemonic option coding (opposed to numeric menus), and on-screen help messages.

2 Of or pertaining to memory. E19.

Gentleman's Magazine The mnemonic power of the late Professor Porson.

■ **mnemonical** *adjective* = MNEMONIC *adjective* 1 M17. **mnemonically** *adverb* M19. **mnemonician** /-ˈnɪʃ(ə)n/ *noun (rare)* = MNEMONIST M19. **ˈmnemonize** *verb trans.* express by a mnemonic formula M19.

mnemonics /nɪˈmɒnɪks, niː-/ *noun pl.* (usu. treated as *sing.*). E18.
[ORIGIN Greek *mnēmonika* neut. pl. of *mnēmonikos*: see MNEMONIC, -IC.]
The art of improving or developing the memory, esp. by artificial aids; a system of precepts and rules intended to aid or improve the memory.

mnemonist /ˈniːmənɪst/ *noun.* M19.
[ORIGIN from MNEMONIC: see -IST.]
An expert in mnemonics; a teacher of memory training and improvement; a person who exhibits his or her powers of memory.

mnemotechny /ˈniːmətɛkni/ *noun.* M19.
[ORIGIN formed as MNEME + Greek *-tekhnia, teknē* art: see -Y[3].]
= MNEMONICS.
■ **mnemotechnic** *adjective* = MNEMONIC *adjective* M19. **mnemotechnics** *noun pl.* = MNEMONICS M19.

MO *abbreviation.*
1 Medical officer.
2 Missouri.
3 CHEMISTRY. Molecular orbital.
4 Money order.

Mo *symbol.*
CHEMISTRY. Molybdenum.

mo /məʊ/ *noun*[1]. *colloq.* Pl. **mos.** L19.
[ORIGIN Abbreviation of MOMENT *noun.*]
A very short time, a moment.

I. WATSON If you'll hang on a mo, I'll take you myself.

mo /məʊ/ *noun*[2]. *Austral. & NZ colloq.* Pl. **mos.** L19.
[ORIGIN Abbreviation.]
= MOUSTACHE.

mo /məʊ/ *adverb, noun*[3], *& adjective. obsolete* exc. *Scot. & N. English.*
[ORIGIN Old English *mā* = Old Frisian *mā(r, mēr*, Old Saxon, Old High German *mēr* (Middle Dutch *mee*, German *mehr*), Old Norse *meir*, Gothic *mais*, from Germanic compar. from Indo-European.]
▸ **A** *adverb.* †**1** In or to a greater degree, extent, or quantity. OE–E16.
2 Longer, further, again, besides. Chiefly in ***any mo***, ***ever mo***, ***never mo***, ***no mo***. OE.
▸ **B** *noun.* †**1** Something in addition; an additional quantity or amount. OE–ME.
2 A greater number; more individuals of the kind specified or implied. (Foll. by *of, than.*) OE.
3 Other individuals of the kind specified; others in addition to those mentioned. OE.
▸ **C** *adjective.* = MORE *adjective.* OE.

Mo. *abbreviation*[1].
Missouri.

mo. *abbreviation*[2].
Month.

m. o. *abbreviation.*
Modus operandi (see MODUS).

-mo /məʊ/ *suffix.*
[ORIGIN The final syllable of terms derived from the abl. sing. masc. of Latin ordinal numerals.]
Forming nouns denoting a book size by the number of leaves into which a sheet of paper has been folded, as ***duodecimo***, ***sextodecimo***, etc., also read or written as ***12mo***, ***16mo***, etc.

moa /ˈməʊə/ *noun.* M19.
[ORIGIN Maori.]
A large flightless bird of the genus *Dinornis*, resembling an ostrich, formerly inhabiting New Zealand and now extinct.
– COMB.: **moa-hunter** a member of an early Maori culture in New Zealand distinguished by the hunting of moas.

Moabite /ˈməʊəbʌɪt/ *adjective & noun.* ME.
[ORIGIN Latin *Moabita* (Greek *Mōabitēs*, repr. Hebrew *mōʼāḇī*), from *Moab*: see below, -ITE[1].]
▸ **A** *adjective.* Of or pertaining to Moab, an ancient region east of the Dead Sea, or its inhabitants. ME.
Moabite stone a monument erected by Mesha king of Moab, *c* 850 BC, which has an early example of an inscription in the Moabite language.
▸ **B** *noun.* A member of a Semitic people living in Moab. LME.
■ **Moabitess** *noun (rare)* a Moabite woman M16. **Moabitish** *adjective* of, pertaining to, or resembling the Moabites E17.

moan /məʊn/ *noun.* ME.
[ORIGIN Ult. from Germanic base (perh. repr. in Old English) whence also MEAN *verb*[2]. Cf. MEAN *noun*[2].]
1 Complaint, lamentation; a complaint, a lament. ME. ▸†**b** A state of grief or lamentation. E16–M17.

TENNYSON And oft I heard the tender dove, In firry woodlands making moan.

2 a A long low mournful sound indicative of physical or mental suffering or physical pleasure. L16. ▸**b** A low plaintive sound made by wind, water, etc. E19.

a I. MURDOCH The rhythmical moan with which the . . sufferer tries to soothe the . . pain. C. JOHNSON I heard the squeaking of mattress springs, . . and at last a venereal moan.

3 A grievance, a grumble; an airing of complaints. E20.

Camera Weekly Another moan has been that the range of lenses . . is . . limited.

moan /məʊn/ *verb.* ME.
[ORIGIN from the noun.]
1 *verb trans.* **a** Lament or bewail one's lot. Now *rare.* ME. ▸†**b** *refl.* Complain of, lament for; bemoan, bewail. LME–L17.

a THACKERAY She . . bitterly moaned the fickleness of her Matilda.

2 *verb intrans.* Lament, grieve. Now chiefly *Scot. & poet.* ME.

G. BRIMLEY Listen to the fierce Achilles moaning for his lost mistress.

3 *verb trans.* Condole with (a person); pity. *obsolete* exc. *Scot.* L16.
4 *verb intrans.* Make a low mournful sound indicative of physical or mental suffering or physical pleasure; utter with a moan or moans. E18. ▸**b** Of wind, water, etc.: make a low plaintive sound. E19.

T. PERROTTA I clutched my stomach and moaned. **b** A. B. DAVIDSON You hear . . the forests moan.

5 *verb intrans. & trans.* Complain or grumble, esp. about something trivial; say or utter complainingly. E20.

A. HUTSCHNECKER He moaned about what a hard day he had had. *Woman's Own* Sitting around moaning has never been her style. *Reader's Digest* 'I had so many things planned for today,' she moaned.

■ **moaner** *noun* E17.

moanful /ˈməʊnfʊl, -f(ə)l/ *adjective.* Now *rare.* M16.
[ORIGIN from MOAN *noun* + -FUL.]
(Of a person, an action, etc.) full of moaning or lamentation; expressing grief; (of a melody, song, etc.) plaintive, mournful.
■ **moanfully** *adverb (long rare)* E17.

moaning /ˈməʊnɪŋ/ *ppl adjective.* LME.
[ORIGIN from MOAN *verb* + -ING[2].]
That moans.
moaning minnie *colloq.* (**a**) a kind of German trench mortar; a bomb from such a mortar; (**b**) an air-raid siren; (**c**) a moaner, a grouser.
■ **moaningly** *adverb* L18.

moar /mɔː/ *noun.* M17.
[ORIGIN Manx = Irish & Gaelic *maor.*]
A government officer in the Isle of Man.

moat /məʊt/ *noun & verb.* Also †**mote.** LME.
[ORIGIN Var. of MOTE *noun*[2].]
▸ **A** *noun.* **1** A deep and wide defensive ditch surrounding a town, castle, etc., and usually filled with water. LME.
2 A pond, a lake. *obsolete* exc. *dial.* LME.
▸ **B** *verb trans.* Surround with or as with a moat, ditch, or trench. LME.

mob /mɒb/ *noun*[1]. L17.
[ORIGIN Abbreviation of MOBILE *noun*[2].]
1 A disorderly or riotous crowd; a rabble. L17.

B. MASON A lawless mob . . looting and defying the police. J. NAGENDA I've just escaped death at the hands of a mob.

2 *The* ordinary people, *the* populace, *the* masses. L17.
†**3** Ordinary or disorderly people forming a crowd. L17–L18.
4 An assemblage of people; a multitude, a crowd, a group. L17. ▸**b** A battalion, a regiment; a military unit. *military slang.* E20.

transf.: E. YOUNG 'Twill not make one amid a mob of thoughts. **b** J. HIGGINS Her husband's a major with your old mob.

5 A flock or herd of animals (orig. representing some sort of threat or problem). *Austral. & NZ.* E19.

B. WANNAN He met a drover leisurely following a mob of sheep.

6 a A gang of thieves or pickpockets working together; a member of such a gang. *slang.* M19. ▸**b** More fully ***the mob***. An organized association of violent criminals; *spec.* (**M-**), a society similar to the Mafia, controlling organized crime in the US and elsewhere. *slang.* E20.

b *Guardian* The Mob from its Chicago headquarters runs the subcontinent. M. ATWOOD It was the mob who put Ellis up to making the bust.

a swell mob: see SWELL *adjective* 2.
– COMB.: **mob-handed** *adjective & adverb (colloq.)* in considerable numbers; **mob law** law imposed and enforced by a mob; **mobsman** a member of a mob; a mobster; **mob rule** rule imposed and enforced by a mob.
■ **mobbism** *noun* mobbish behaviour L18.

mob /mɒb/ *noun*[2]. *obsolete* exc. *hist.* M17.
[ORIGIN Var. of MAB.]
†**1** A prostitute or promiscuous woman. *slang.* M–L17.
†**2** A négligé. M17–E18.
3 More fully ***mob-cap***. A large indoor cap covering all the hair, worn by women in the 18th and early 19th cents. M18.

mob /mɒb/ *verb*[1] *trans.* Now *rare* or *obsolete.* Infl. **-bb-**. M17.
[ORIGIN from MOB *noun*[2]: cf. earlier MOBLE.]
Muffle the head of (a person); dress untidily. Also foll. by *up.*

mob /mɒb/ *verb*[2]. Infl. **-bb-**. L17.
[ORIGIN from MOB *noun*[1].]
1 *verb trans.* Crowd round or press upon (a person) in order to attack or admire; crowd into (a building or place). L17. ▸†**b** Force (a person) *into* an action etc. or drive *from* a place by crowding round and being oppressive. Now *rare.* E18. ▸**c** Of a group of birds: fly noisily and aggressively close to (a predator etc.). E20.

a R. K. NARAYAN You will be mobbed and unable to leave the place.

†**2** *verb intrans. & trans.* (with *it*). Go in disguise to the unfashionable part of a theatre etc. L17–M19.
3 *verb intrans.* Form a mob, congregate in a mob. E18. ▸**b** Of animals, esp. sheep: gather in a mob. *Austral. & NZ.* L19

S. FRY Adrian has seen him mobbing around with his friends as if nothing had happened.

■ **mobbed** *adjective* crowded, packed with people L19. **mobber** *noun* M18. **mobbing** *noun* (**a**) the action of the verb; an instance of this; (**b**) SCOTS LAW violent or riotous action performed with others for a common illegal purpose: E18.

mobbie /ˈmɒbi, ˈməʊbi/ *noun.* Also **mobby.** M17.
[ORIGIN Carib *mabi* (drink made from) sweet potato. See also MAUBY.]
1 A West Indian alcoholic drink made either from sweet potatoes or from sugar, ginger, and other ingredients. M17.
2 The juice from apples and peaches, used in making brandy; apple and peach brandy. *US.* Now *rare.* E18.

mobbish /ˈmɒbɪʃ/ *adjective.* L17.
[ORIGIN from MOB *noun*[1] + -ISH[1].]
Resembling or characteristic of a mob; disorderly, tumultuous. Formerly also, characteristic of or appealing to the mob or the ordinary people; common.
■ **mobbishly** *adverb* E18. **mobbishness** *noun* E20.

mobby *noun* var. of MOBBIE.

mobe /məʊb/ *noun. colloq.* L20.
[ORIGIN Abbreviation.]
A mobile phone.

mobile /ˈməʊbɪl/ *noun*[1]. Now *rare.* L15.
[ORIGIN French (in *premier mobile* etc.) from Latin *mobile* neut. of *mobilis*: see MOBILE *adjective.*]
1 = PRIMUM MOBILE 1. Chiefly with *first, grand, great,* etc. L15.
2 METAPHYSICS. A body in motion or capable of movement. L17.

mobile /ˈməʊbɪliː/ *noun*[2]. *arch.* L16.
[ORIGIN Latin *mobile* (*vulgus*) lit. 'the excitable crowd'.]
In full ***mobile vulgus*** /ˈvʌlɡʌs/. *The* ordinary people, *the* mass of the population, *the* mob.

M

mobile /ˈməʊbʌɪl/ *noun*³. M20.
[ORIGIN from MOBILE *adjective*.]
1 A decorative structure usu. consisting of hanging pieces of metal, plastic, etc., which can each move and turn freely. M20.

> M. GEE She brought me a mobile of . . fishes and hung it . . over my bed.

2 *MUSIC.* A musical composition consisting of separate units which can be arranged in a variety of ways. M20.
3 *ellipt.* **a** A mobile canteen. M20. ▸**b** A mobile police patrol. L20. ▸**c** A mobile phone. L20.

mobile /ˈməʊbʌɪl/ *adjective*. L15.
[ORIGIN Old French & mod. French from Latin *mobilis*, from *movere* MOVE *verb*: see -ILE.]
1 Capable of movement; movable; not fixed or stationary. L15.

> J. G. WOOD The hind toe of each foot is very mobile. T. H. HUXLEY The mobile liquid passes into a compact rigid solid.

2 Characterized by facility or versatility of movement; *spec.* (of facial features) expressive, that can easily change in expression. M19.

> N. HAWTHORNE This idea filled her mobile imagination with agreeable fantasies. J. HIGGINS He was handsome . . with a mobile, intelligent mouth.

3 Of troops, a police patrol, etc.: that may be easily and rapidly moved from place to place. L19.
4 *SOCIOLOGY.* (Of a person) able to move into different social levels or to change environment or field of employment; (of a society) not rigidly stratified, able to accommodate social or professional movement. E20.

> E. GELLNER Whether the rulers are . . able to run a mobile society . . in which rulers and ruled can merge.

downwardly mobile tending to decline in social and professional status. **upwardly mobile** improving or ambitious to improve one's social and professional status.
5 Of a shop, library, or other facility: accommodated in a vehicle so as to be transportable and serve different places. M20.

> *New Statesman* Feeding centres and mobile canteens.

– SPECIAL COLLOCATIONS: **mobile home** a large transportable structure, as a large caravan, set up permanently and used as living accommodation. **mobile phone**, **mobile telephone** a portable telephone using a cellular radio system. **mobile sculpture** a sculpture having moving parts.

-mobile /məbiːl/ *suffix*.
[ORIGIN from AUTO)MOBILE *noun*.]
Forming nouns designating vehicles of a particular type, as ***snowmobile***.

Mobilian /məʊˈbɪlɪən/ *noun & adjective*. M18.
[ORIGIN Perh. from *Mobile* a town in Alabama, USA + -IAN.]
(Designating or pertaining to) a lingua franca or trade language formerly used in south-eastern N. America.

mobiliary /məʊˈbɪlɪəri/ *adjective*. L17.
[ORIGIN French *mobiliaire*, from Latin *mobilis*: see MOBILE *adjective*: see -ARY¹.]
1 Of a court or legal procedure in the Channel Islands: of or pertaining to movable property. L17.
2 Of or pertaining to household furniture. M19.
3 *MILITARY.* Of or pertaining to mobilization. L19.

mobilisation *noun*, **mobilise** *verb* vars. of MOBILIZATION, MOBILIZE.

mobilism /ˈməʊbɪlɪz(ə)m/ *noun*. E20.
[ORIGIN French *mobilisme*, formed as MOBILE *adjective*: see -ISM.]
1 Belief in or tendency towards change; *PHILOSOPHY* the view that nothing is fixed. E20.
2 *GEOLOGY.* (Belief in) the theory that the continents undergo lateral movement and deformation. M20.
■ **mobilist** *noun & adjective* (*a*) *noun* a believer in the theory of continental drift; (*b*) *adjective* of or pertaining to mobilism or mobilists: M20.

mobility /məʊˈbɪlɪti/ *noun*¹. LME.
[ORIGIN Old French & mod. French *mobilité* from Latin *mobilitas*, from *mobilis*: see MOBILE *adjective*, -ITY.]
1 Ability to move or to be moved; ease or freedom of movement. LME.

> J. BERNSTEIN Organs adapted for touching are endowed with the greatest mobility. W. S. CHURCHILL The accident which I suffered . . has greatly decreased my mobility.

2 Ability or tendency to change easily or quickly; changeableness; *spec.* (of facial features) facility of change of expression, expressiveness. M16.

> M. HALE Daily observe in our selves a strange mobility . . in our Imaginative . . Faculty.

3 *SOCIOLOGY.* The ability or potential to move between different social levels, fields of employment, etc. Also ***social mobility***. L18.
upward mobility: see UPWARD *adjective*.
4 *PHYSICS* etc. ▸**a** Freedom of movement of the particles of a fluid. E19. ▸**b** The degree to which a charge carrier moves in a definite direction in response to an electric field, usu. expressed as the average speed (cm/sec) in a field of one volt per cm divided by the net number of charges on the carrier. L19.
– COMB.: **mobility allowance** a social-security benefit payable to a disabled person to assist with the cost of travel.

mobility /məʊˈbɪlɪti/ *noun*². Now *rare*. L17.
[ORIGIN from MOBILE *noun*², MOB *noun*¹, after *nobility*.]
The mob; *the* ordinary people.

mobilization /ˌməʊbɪlʌɪˈzeɪʃ(ə)n/ *noun*. Also **-isation**. L18.
[ORIGIN French *mobilisation*, formed as MOBILIZE: see -ATION.]
The action or process of mobilizing something or someone; the fact of being mobilized.

> *Economist* The task of the planner is the more effective mobilisation of all economic resources. *Armed Forces* A dogfight between Israeli and Syrian aircraft was used as an excuse for Syrian mobilisation.

■ **mobilizational** *adjective* M20.

mobilize /ˈməʊbɪlʌɪz/ *verb*. Also **-ise**. M19.
[ORIGIN French *mobiliser*, formed as MOBILE *adjective*: see -IZE.]
1 *verb trans.* Make movable or capable of movement; bring into circulation. M19. ▸**b** *MEDICINE.* Free or detach surgically. L19. ▸**c** Make (a substance) able to be transported by or as a liquid. L19.
2 *verb trans. & intrans.* Prepare (orig. troops, an army) for action or active service; make or become ready for action. M19.

> W. S. CHURCHILL Would it not be helpful to call up the reserves and mobilize the TA? H. MACMILLAN Israel mobilised and . . invaded the Sinai peninsula. A. HUTSCHNECKER Active hope . . mobilizes an individual's vast energies.

■ **mobilizable** *adjective* L19. **mobilizer** *noun* E20.

Möbius /ˈməːbɪəs/ *noun*. E20.
[ORIGIN August Ferdinand *Möbius* (1790–1868), German mathematician.]
Möbius strip, ***Möbius band***, etc., a surface having only one side and one edge, formed by twisting one end of a rectangular strip through 180 degrees and joining it to the other end.

moble /ˈmɒb(ə)l/ *verb trans.* Now *rare* or *obsolete*. E17.
[ORIGIN Frequentative of MOB *verb*¹ (though recorded earlier): see -LE³.]
Muffle the head or face of (a person). Usu. foll. by *up*.

moblog /ˈmɒblɒg/ *noun*. E21.
[ORIGIN blend of MOBILE *noun*³ and WEBLOG.]
A weblog that consists of pictures and other content posted from a mobile phone.

mobocracy /mɒbˈɒkrəsi/ *noun*. M18.
[ORIGIN from MOB *noun*¹: see -CRACY.]
1 Mob rule, government by a mob. M18.
2 The mob or ordinary people as a ruling body; a ruling mob. M18.
■ **ˈmobocrat** *noun* a person who advocates mobocracy, a demagogue L18. **moboˈcratic** *adjective* L18.

mobster /ˈmɒbstə/ *noun*. M18.
[ORIGIN from MOB *noun*¹ + -STER, after *gangster*.]
†**1** A member of a mob or crowd; a member of the common people. Only in M18.
2 A member of a group of criminals; a gangster. *colloq.* E20.

moc /mɒk/ *noun*. *N. Amer. colloq.* M20.
[ORIGIN Abbreviation.]
= MOCCASIN.

†**Moca** *noun* var. of MOKO *noun*¹.

mocamp /ˈməʊkamp/ *noun*. M20.
[ORIGIN from MO(TOR *noun* + CAMP *noun*².]
A campsite which can accommodate tents, caravans, etc., and has various amenities.

moccasin /ˈmɒkəsɪn/ *noun*. E17.
[ORIGIN Powhatan *mockasins* (pl.), *mawhcasuns* (pl.); cogn. with Massachusett *mokussinash* (pl.), Narragansett *mokússinass* (pl.).]
1 a A kind of soft leather shoe, worn by N. American Indians, trappers, etc. E17. ▸**b** A soft informal shoe resembling this. L19.
2 A venomous N. American crotaline snake of the genus *Agkistrodon*; *spec.* (more fully ***water moccasin***) the semi-aquatic *A. piscivorus* of the southern US (also called ***cotton-mouth (moccasin)***). L18.
– COMB.: **moccasin flower**, **moccasin plant** *N. Amer.* a lady's slipper orchid, esp. the pink-flowered *Cypripedium acaule*; **moccasin snake** = sense 2 above; **moccasin telegraph** *N. Amer.* a rapid and often surreptitious means of transmitting information; a bush telegraph.
■ **moccasined** *adjective* wearing or provided with moccasins E19.

Mocha /ˈmɒkə/ *noun*¹. Also **m-**. L17.
[ORIGIN Prob. formed as MOCHA *noun*² & *adjective*.]
1 In full ***Mocha stone***. Moss agate or a similar form of chalcedony with dendritic markings. L17.
2 (**m-**.) Any of various brown and grey geometrid moths of the genus *Cyclophora*. Also †***Mocha stone***. L18.
3 A type of English pottery, made from the late 18th to the early 20th cent., with coloured patterned bands on a white or cream body. M19.

mocha /ˈmɒkə/ *noun*² & *adjective*. L18.
[ORIGIN *Mocha*, a port in Yemen on the Red Sea.]
▸ **A** *noun*. **1 a** A fine quality coffee, orig. produced in Yemen. Also ***mocha coffee***. L18. ▸**b** A flavouring made from this, often with chocolate added, used in cakes etc. L19. ▸**c** The colour of mocha coffee; a dark brown colour. L19.
2 A soft kind of sheepskin. L19.
▸ **B** *adjective*. Of mocha; *spec.* flavoured with mocha. L19.
mocha brown = sense A.1c above.

mochaccino /mɒkəˈtʃiːnəʊ/ *noun*. Pl. **-os**. L20.
[ORIGIN Blend of MOCHA *noun*² and CAPPUCCINO.]
A cappuccino containing chocolate syrup or chocolate flavouring.

Moche /ˈməʊtʃeɪ/ *noun & adjective*. M20.
[ORIGIN from the *Moche* valley in Peru: see MOCHICA.]
▸ **A** *adjective*. Of or pertaining to a pre-Incan culture of northern Peru which flourished from the 1st to the 7th cent. AD. Cf. MOCHICA. M20.
▸ **B** *noun*. Pl. same. The Moche culture. Also, a person of this culture. L20.

mochi /ˈmɒtʃi/ *noun*. Pl. same. E17.
[ORIGIN Japanese.]
A cake made from glutinous rice, steamed and pounded.

Mochica /məˈtʃiːkə/ *noun & adjective*. Also †**Moxa**. L16.
[ORIGIN Spanish, either from the name of the *Moche* archaeological site and valley on the north-west coast of Peru, or from Mochica *muchik* self-designation.]
▸ **A** *noun*. Pl. same. A member of a pre-Inca people living on the Peruvian coast; their language. Also called YUNCA. L16.
▸ **B** *adjective*. Of or pertaining to this people or their language. L19.
■ **Mochican** *adjective & noun* M20.

mock /mɒk/ *noun*. LME.
[ORIGIN from the verb or (sense 4) the adjective.]
1 a A derisive action or speech. Now *rare*. LME. ▸**b** Derision, mockery. *rare*. M16.
2 A thing to be derided; something deserving scorn. L15.

> G. GREENE He has become the mock of all his contemporaries.

3 The action of mocking or imitating someone or something; an imitation, a sham. Now *rare*. M17.
4 In *pl.* Mock examinations. M20.

> F. MOUNT Emma's done brilliantly in her mocks.

– PHRASES: **make a mock of**, **make mock of** ridicule. **put a mock on**, **put the mock on** *Austral. slang* put a stop to.
– COMB.: **mock-bird** *US* a mockingbird.
■ **mockage** *noun* (now *rare*) mockery, ridicule, derision; the fact or condition of being mocked; an object of mockery: L15.

mock /mɒk/ *attrib. adjective*. M16.
[ORIGIN Partly from the noun, partly from stem of the verb in comb. with an object.]
1 Sham, imitation, esp. without intention to deceive; pretended, fake; *spec.* (of an examination) set to give practice for a specified more serious examination. M16.

> B. PYM It was quite an imposing façade, mock Palladian. ALAN BENNETT He's doing his mock A levels next week. RACHEL ANDERSON Humphrey . . rolled his eyes upward in mock disapproval.

2 In names of plants etc.: = FALSE *adjective* 7. M16.
– SPECIAL COLLOCATIONS: **mock auction** (*a*) a Dutch auction; (*b*) an auction of worthless goods, in which false bids are made in order to elicit genuine bids from others. **mock auctioneer** the auctioneer at a mock auction. ***mock croc***. **mock goose** (now *rare*) leg of pork cooked to resemble goose. **mock lead** = BLENDE. **mock moon** = PARASELENE. **mock-nightingale** *dial.* the blackcap, *Sylvia atricapilla*. **mock olive** any of various Australian trees of the genus *Notelaea*, of the olive family, with succulent fruit and hard wood. **mock orange** (*a*) a philadelphus; (*b*) *Austral.* an evergreen shrub, *Pittosporum undulatum* (family Pittosporaceae), with fragrant flowers. **mock privet** = PHILLYREA. **mock sun** = PARHELION. **mock turtle soup** soup made from a calf's head etc. to resemble turtle soup.

mock /mɒk/ *verb*. LME.
[ORIGIN Old French *mo(c)quer* (mod. *se moquer de* laugh at) deride, jeer, from Proto-Romance base repr. also by Italian dial. *moka*, Spanish *mueca* grimace, Portuguese *moca* derision.]
1 *verb trans.* Hold up to ridicule; deride with scornful words or gestures; scoff at. LME. ▸**b** Defy, flout. Now *rare*. M16.

> T. GRAY These hated walls that seem to mock my shame. J. WILSON A fiend . . Come here to mock . . My dying agony.

2 *verb intrans.* **a** Use ridicule; act or speak so as to show scorn; jeer, scoff. (Foll. by *at*, †*with*.) LME. ▸†**b** Jest, trifle. LME–E17.

> G. HARRIS The jangling of the keys at his waist seemed to mock at him.

3 *verb trans.* Deceive, delude, befool; tantalize, disappoint. LME.
4 *verb trans.* **a** Ridicule by imitation; mimic contemptuously. L16. ▸†**b** Simulate, make a false pretence of. *rare* (Shakes.). L16–E17.

> **a** S. HASTINGS Mocking everything and everybody in her witty . . high-pitched way.

5 *verb trans.* Foll. by *up*: make a mock-up of; imitate, contrive. E20.
■ **mockable** *adjective* E17. **mockingly** *adverb* in a mocking manner M16.

M

mockado /mɒˈkɑːdəʊ/ *noun & adjective. hist.* M16.
[ORIGIN App. alt. of Italian †*mocaiardo* mohair.]
▸ **A** *noun.* Pl. **-o(e)s.** A wool velvet, usu. of inferior quality, formerly used for clothing. M16.
▸ †**B** *attrib.* or as *adjective.* Made of this fabric. Also, Inferior, fraudulent. L16–L17.

mocker /ˈmɒkə/ *noun*[1]. LME.
[ORIGIN from MOCK *verb* + -ER[1].]
1 A person who mocks, derides, or scoffs. LME.

JOSEPH PARKER Even the mocker may find his way into the church. *transf.*: AV *Prov.* 20:1 Wine is a mocker, strong drinke is raging.

2 A person who deceives or deludes. Long *rare* or *obsolete.* M16.
3 A mockingbird. *US.* L18.
4 (A cause of) bad luck; a thing that thwarts a person. Chiefly in ***put the mockers on***, (*a*) bring bad luck to; (*b*) put a stop to. *slang.* E20.
– COMB.: **mockernut** a N. American hickory, *Carya tomentosa* (more fully ***mockernut hickory***); the fruit of this, a large nut with a small kernel.

mocker /ˈmɒkə/ *verb & noun*[2]. *Austral. & NZ slang.* E20.
[ORIGIN Perh. from Arabic *makwa*, from *kawā* to press clothes.]
▸ **A** *verb trans.* Dress *up.* Chiefly as ***mockered up*** *ppl adjective.* E20.
▸ **B** *noun.* Clothing, dress. M20.

mockery /ˈmɒk(ə)ri/ *noun.* LME.
[ORIGIN Old French & mod. French *moquerie*, formed as MOCK *verb*: see -ERY.]
1 Derision, ridicule; a derisive utterance or action. LME. ▸**b** A subject or occasion of derision or ridicule. M16.

V. S. PRITCHETT She laughed . . a high chilling laugh of mockery. **b** G. P. R. JAMES He made a mockery of the very acquirements he boasted of.

2 Mimicry, imitation; a counterfeit or absurdly inadequate representation. L16.
3 (A) ludicrously futile action; something insultingly unfitting. E17.

mocket /ˈmɒkɪt/ *noun.* Long *obsolete* exc. *dial.* M16.
[ORIGIN Shortened alt. of MUCKENDER.]
A bib, a handkerchief.

mock-heroic /mɒkhɪˈrəʊɪk/ *noun & adjective.* M17.
[ORIGIN from MOCK *adjective* + HEROIC.]
▸ **A** *noun.* An imitation in a burlesque manner of heroic literary style or character. Usu. in *pl.* M17.
▸ **B** *adjective.* Imitating the style of heroic literature in order to satirize an unheroic subject. E18.

mockingbird /ˈmɒkɪŋbəːd/ *noun.* L17.
[ORIGIN from *mocking* pres. pple of MOCK *verb* + BIRD *noun.*]
Any of various long-tailed songbirds of the New World family Mimidae, spec. *Mimus polyglottos* of the southern US and Central America, noted for mimicking other birds' calls and other sounds. Also (*local*), any of various other birds with imitative calls.

mockney /ˈmɒkni/ *noun. colloq.* L20.
[ORIGIN Blend of MOCK *adjective* and COCKNEY.]
A form of speech perceived as an affected imitation of cockney in accent and vocabulary.

mockumentary /mɒkjʊˈmɛnt(ə)ri/ *noun.* M20.
[ORIGIN Blend of MOCK *adjective* and DOCUMENTARY.]
A television programme or film which takes the form of a serious documentary in order to satirize its subject.

mock-up /ˈmɒkʌp/ *noun.* E20.
[ORIGIN from MOCK *verb* + UP *adverb*[1].]
1 An experimental model or replica of a proposed aircraft, ship, or other construction. E20.
2 *transf. & fig.* A plan; an imitation. M20.

mocky /ˈmɒki/ *noun & adjective. US slang. offensive.* L19.
[ORIGIN Perh. from Yiddish *makeh* a plague.]
▸ **A** *noun.* A Jew. L19.
▸ **B** *attrib.* or as *adjective.* Jewish. M20.

moco /ˈməʊkəʊ/ *noun.* Pl. **-os.** M19.
[ORIGIN Ult. from Tupi *mocó.*]
The rock cavy, *Kerodon rupestris.*

mocock /məʊˈkɒk/ *noun. N. Amer.* L18.
[ORIGIN Ojibwa *makak* box, birch-bark basket.]
A container like a basket made from birch bark.

moco-moco /məʊkəʊˈməʊkəʊ/ *noun.* Also **mucka-mucka** /ˈmʌkəmʌkə/ & other vars. M18.
[ORIGIN Galibi.]
A tall aroid plant, *Montrichardia arborescens*, of Guyana and other parts of tropical America.

MOD *abbreviation.*
Ministry of Defence.

Mod /mɒd/ *noun*[1]. L19.
[ORIGIN Gaelic *mòd* assembly, court from Old Norse *mót*: see MOOT *noun*[1].]
A Highland meeting for Gaelic literary and musical competitions.

mod /mɒd/ *noun*[2] *& verb. colloq.* M20.
[ORIGIN Abbreviation.]
▸ **A** *noun.* A modification. M20.
▸ **B** *verb trans.* Infl. **-dd-.** Modify. M20.
■ **modder** L20.

mod /mɒd/ *noun*[3] *& adjective.* M20.
[ORIGIN Abbreviation of MODERN or MODERNIST.]
▸ **A** *noun.* (Usu. **M-**.) A young person, esp. in the 1960s, belonging to or associated with a group aiming at stylishness and smart modern dress. Freq. contrasted with ***rocker.*** M20.
▸ **B** *adjective.* Modern, sophisticated, stylish, esp. in dress. Also (**M-**), characteristic of or belonging to Mods. M20.
See also MOD CON.

mod /mɒd, ˈmɒdjʊləʊ/ *preposition.* M19.
[ORIGIN Abbreviation.]
MATH. = **MODULO** *preposition.*

modacrylic /mɒdəˈkrɪlɪk/ *adjective & noun.* M20.
[ORIGIN from *modified* ppl adjective of MODIFY + ACRYLIC.]
(Designating or made of) a man-made fibre consisting of molecules with 35 to 85 per cent by mass of $CH_2CH(CN)$ units (derived from acrylonitrile).

modal /ˈməʊd(ə)l/ *adjective & noun.* M16.
[ORIGIN medieval Latin *modalis*, from Latin *modus*: see MODE, -AL[1].]
▸ **A** *adjective.* **1** LOGIC. Designating or pertaining to a proposition involving the affirmation of possibility, impossibility, necessity, or contingency, or in which the predicate is affirmed or denied of the subject with a qualification; (of an argument) containing a modal proposition as a premiss. M16.
modal logic the branch of logic that deals with modal propositions.
2 LAW. Of a legacy, contract, etc.: containing provisions defining the manner in which it is to take effect. Now *rare.* L16.
3 MUSIC. Of or pertaining to a musical mode; using a mode or modes. L16.
4 Of or pertaining to mode or form as contrasted with substance. E17.
5 GRAMMAR. **a** Of or pertaining to the mood of a verb; (of a verb) used in expressing a mood of another verb. L18. ▸**b** Of a particle: denoting manner. L19.

a E. H. GROUT The modal auxiliaries *may, might, can, could, must, ought*, . . give a cast to the whole sentence.

6 a STATISTICS. Of, pertaining to, or of the nature of a mode; (of a value etc.) that occurs most frequently in a sample or population. L19. ▸**b** Representative, typical. M20.

a *Journal of Genetic Psychology* The modal age of the youngsters was 13. **b** R. K. MERTON The characteristic (modal) pattern for handling a standardized problem.

b modal personality an imaginary personality held to be typical of a particular society or group, esp. through possessing the modal characteristics of the population.
7 PETROGRAPHY. Of or pertaining to the mode of a rock; as indicated by a mode. E20.
▸ **B** *noun.* **1** LOGIC. A modal proposition. L16.
2 GRAMMAR. A modal verb. M20.
■ **modally** *adverb* M17.

modalise *verb* var. of MODALIZE.

modalism /ˈməʊd(ə)lɪz(ə)m/ *noun.* Also **M-.** M19.
[ORIGIN from MODAL + -ISM.]
CHRISTIAN THEOLOGY. The doctrine that the three persons of the Trinity are merely three different modes or aspects of the divine nature; Sabellianism.
■ **modalist** *noun & adjective* (*a*) *noun* a person who holds or professes modalism; (*b*) *adjective* = MODALISTIC: E18. **modaˈlistic** *adjective* of or pertaining to modalism or modalists M19.

modality /məʊˈdalɪti/ *noun.* M16.
[ORIGIN medieval Latin *modalitas*, formed as MODAL *adjective*: see -ITY.]
1 The quality or fact of being modal; a modal quality or circumstance; the modal attributes of something. M16.

J. NORRIS We cannot conceive a circle as being distinct from extension whose modality it is.

2 LOGIC. **a** The fact of being a modal proposition or syllogism. Also, a qualification which makes a proposition modal. E17. ▸**b** The feature of a judgement defined by its classification as problematic, assertoric, or apodictic. M19.
3 PSYCHOLOGY. **a** A category of sensation, a sense (as sight, hearing). Formerly also, a qualitative aspect of a particular category of sensation. L19. ▸**b** An attribute or trait of personality. M20.

a G. HUMPHREY Sensory presentation of various modalities—auditory, kinaesthetic, and so on.

4 GRAMMAR. The property of a verb or verbal form that is represented or distinguished by its mood. E20.
5 a MEDICINE. A method or technique of treatment, *esp.* one not involving drugs. E20. ▸**b** In diplomacy, politics, etc.: a procedure, a method. M20. ▸**c** A mode of action or of behaviour. M20.

a *Muscle & Fitness* Sensible modalities such as the application of ice and heat are what the joint . . needs to heal. **b** G. F. KENNAN The modalities of German unification must flow from the will of the German people.

6 MUSIC. The quality or fact of being modal. M20.

modalize /ˈməʊd(ə)lʌɪz/ *verb trans.* Also **-ise.** M19.
[ORIGIN from MODAL + -IZE.]
Chiefly LOGIC. Make modal.
■ **modaliˈzation** *noun* M20.

mod con /mɒd ˈkɒn/ *noun phr. colloq.* M20.
[ORIGIN Abbreviation of *modern convenience.*]
An amenity, appliance, etc., typical of a well-equipped modern home; any gadget or labour-saving device. Usu. in *pl.*

Leicester Mercury A BMW with electrically-operated windows and other mod-cons.

mode /məʊd/ *noun & adjective.* LME.
[ORIGIN In branch I, from Latin *modus* measure etc., from Indo-European base repr. also by METE *verb.* In branch II, from French *mode* fem. from Latin *modus*, with change of gender due to final *e.* See also MOOD *noun*[2].]
▸ **A** *noun.* **I 1** MUSIC. ▸**a** Orig., a tune, an air. Later, a particular scheme or system of sounds, *spec.* (*a*) each of the ancient Greek scales (Dorian, Phrygian, Lydian, Ionian, etc.) in which music in the diatonic style was composed; any of the scales used in other (e.g. oriental) systems of music; (*b*) (in medieval church music) each of the scales in which plainsong was composed (derived from and named after, but not always corresponding to, the ancient Greek ones), beginning on different notes of the natural scale, and thus having the intervals differently arranged; (*c*) (in modern music) either of the two classes (*major* and *minor*) of keys, having the intervals differently arranged; formerly sometimes = KEY *noun*[1] 6. LME. ▸**b** The proportion (3 or 2) of a long to a large or a breve to a long, determining rhythm. *obsolete* exc. *hist.* M17.
2 GRAMMAR. = MOOD *noun*[2] 2. Now *N. Amer.* LME.
3 LOGIC. **a** = MOOD *noun*[2] 1. M16. ▸**b** The character of a proposition as either necessary, contingent, possible, or impossible; each of the four kinds into which propositions are divided as having one or another of these qualities. M19.
4 A way or manner in which something is done or takes place; a method of procedure; a means. M17. ▸**b** A mode of expression. *rare.* L18. ▸**c** PHYSICS. Any of the distinct kinds or patterns of vibration that an oscillatory system can sustain. M19. ▸**d** Any of a number of distinct ways in which a machine, computer system, etc., operates. M20.

M. MITCHELL With the old horse dead, their one mode of conveyance was gone. D. JACOBSON Such highflown display is now the only mode of self-expression open to her. **d** D. ADAMS The massive computer was now in total active mode.

5 A particular form, manner, or variety (of some quality, process, or condition). Now *rare* exc. in ***mode of life*** and similar uses. M17. ▸**b** PETROGRAPHY. The quantitative mineral (as distinct from chemical) composition of a rock sample. Cf. NORM *noun* 3. E20.

POPE Modes of Self-love the Passions we may call.

6 PHILOSOPHY. A manner or state of being of a thing; a thing considered as possessing certain non-essential attributes. Also (now *rare*), an attribute or quality of a substance. L17.

J. A. FROUDE God is an all-perfect Being . . existence is a mode of perfection, and therefore God exists.

▸ **II 7** A prevailing fashion, custom, or style, esp. of a particular place or period; (*arch.*) *the* fashion in dress, etiquette, etc., prevalent in society at the time. M17. ▸**b** Conventional usage in dress, manners, etc., esp. among people of fashion. L17. ▸†**c** A fashionable person or thing. E18–E19.

W. C. SMITH A sort of dandies in religion, Affecting the last mode. A. LURIE Historians of costume have put forward various explanations for the modes of the 1920s. **b** T. JEFFERSON These sentiments became a matter of mode.

8 A thin light glossy black silk, alamode. *obsolete* exc. *hist.* M18.
9 LACE-MAKING. *sing.* & in *pl.* Fancy stitching or stitches used to fill enclosed spaces in a design. M19.
10 [Short for French *gris mode* fashion grey.] Any of several shades of grey used in women's clothing. Now *rare.* L19.
11 STATISTICS. The value or range of values of the variable which occurs most frequently in a set of data etc. L19.
– PHRASES: **all the mode** enjoying general but usually temporary popularity, fashionable at the time in question. **in the mode** in fashion or customary use, esp. in polite society. †**man of mode** = *man of fashion* s.v. FASHION *noun* 7.
– COMB.: **mode-locked** *adjective* (PHYSICS) subjected to or resulting from mode-locking; **mode-locking** PHYSICS a technique of establishing a fixed phase relationship between the modes of oscillation in a laser, resulting in the emission at nanosecond intervals of short trains of picosecond light pulses.
▸ **B** *adjective.* Made of the silk mode (*obsolete* exc. *hist.*). Also (*rare*), of the grey mode. L18.
■ **modeless** *adjective* †(*a*) unmeasured; (*b*) having no mode: L16.

model /ˈmɒd(ə)l/ *noun & adjective*. L16.

[ORIGIN French †*modelle* (now *modèle*) from Italian *modello* from Proto-Romance alt. of Latin MODULUS.]

▸ **A** *noun*. **I** Representation of structure.

†**1** An architect's set of designs for a projected building; a similar set of drawings representing the proportions and arrangement of an existing building. Also, a plan of a town, garden, etc. L16–E18. ▸†**b** A summary, an abstract. E17–M18.

SHAKES. *2 Hen. IV* When we mean to build, We first survey the plot, then draw the model.

2 a *fig.* A person or thing resembling another, esp. on a smaller scale. Now *dial.* exc. in ***the model of, the very model of***. L16. ▸**b** A three-dimensional representation of an existing person or thing or projected structure, showing the proportions and arrangement of its component parts. E17. ▸**c** An archetypal image or pattern. M18. ▸**d** DENTISTRY. A cast of the teeth or oral cavity, used to construct dental appliances. M19. ▸**e** A simplified description of a system, process, etc., put forward as a basis for theoretical or empirical understanding; a conceptual or mental representation of something. E20. ▸**f** MATH. A set of entities that satisfies all the formulae of a given formal or axiomatic system. M20.

a S. PATRICK These quiet places are . . little models of Heaven. **b** L. DURRELL He had a model of the perfect woman built in rubber. T. PYNCHON Some dainty pasteboard model, a city-planner's city, perfectly detailed. **c** T. REID Every work of art has its model framed in the imagination. **e** *Scientific American* A model designed to forecast next week's weather ignores these variables.

b working model: constructed to imitate the movements of the machine which it represents. **e *Rutherford model***: see RUTHERFORD 1.

†**3** A mould; something that envelops closely. *rare* (Shakes.). Only in L16.

SHAKES. *Hen. V* O England! model to thy inward greatness.

†**4** A small portrait; (by confusion) a medallion. E–M17.

5 An object or figure in clay, wax, etc., for reproduction in a more durable material. Formerly also, a sketch for a painting. L17.

South African Panorama Mr Bhana creates these images by first making a clay model.

6 A plasterer's tool for moulding a cornice, having a pattern in profile which is impressed on the plaster by working the tool backwards and forwards. E19.

▸ **II** Type of design.

7 The design, pattern, or structural type of a material or abstract thing. L16. ▸**b** A garment by a particular designer, of a particular season, etc.; a copy of such a garment. L19. ▸**c** A motor vehicle etc. of a particular design or produced in a specified year; each of a series of varying designs of the same type of object. E20.

F. BROOKE This Town is . . built very stately at the Italian model. J. R. GREEN The new faith . . borrowed from Calvin its model of Church government. **b** *Times* The Valentino collection is untypically small . . . Strikes have dogged the production of the models. **c** J. GRENFELL They got a new car. Well, it's not *new*, 1944 model. *Practical Motorist* Sales of Uno and Panda models rose.

New Model: see NEW *adjective*. **c Model T** an early model of car produced by the American Ford Company; *fig.* a person who or thing which is outmoded, mass-produced, etc.

†**8** Scale of construction; allotted measure; the measure of a person's ability or capacity. Only in 17.

H. HIBBERT Shall any reduce . . the thoughts and wayes of God to their narrow and straitned model?

9 The curvature of the surface of a violin etc. M19.

▸ **III** An object of imitation.

10 A person or work proposed or adopted for imitation; an exemplar. M17. ▸**b** BIOLOGY. An animal or plant to which another bears a mimetic resemblance. L19.

C. ACHEBE A budding dictator might choose models far worse than the English gentleman of leisure.

11 A person employed to pose for an artist, sculptor, photographer, etc. Also, an actual person, place, etc., on which a fictional character, location, etc., is based. L17. ▸**b** A person employed to display clothes by wearing them. E20. ▸**c** *euphem.* A prostitute. M20.

W. S. MAUGHAM He could not afford a model but painted still life. P. AUSTER Alexander Selkirk (thought by some to be the model for Robinson Crusoe). **b** D. G. PHILLIPS The sleek tight-fitting trying-on robe of the professional model. G. BLACK He looked like a male model . . for expensive men's knitwear.

12 An exemplary person or thing; a perfect exemplar *of* some excellence. Also, a representative specimen *of* some quality etc. L18.

E. KUZWAYO She was a perfect model of womanhood. C. TOMALIN Gilbert Cannon, fair-haired, handsome, pipe-smoking, . . the very model of the successful young Georgian man of letters.

13 a = ***model dwelling*** below. Usu. in *pl. colloq.* L19. ▸**b** = ***model lodging house*** below. *Scot. colloq.* L19.

– COMB.: **model-drawing** (the branch of study that deals with) drawing in perspective from solid figures; **model-room** a room for the storage or exhibition of models of machinery etc.; **model theory** the branch of mathematics that deals with the construction and properties of models of formal systems etc.

▸ **B** *attrib.* or as *adjective*. **1** Serving as an example; exemplary, ideally perfect. M19.

R. LARDNER A model young man, sober, industrious and 'solid'. J. IRVING Bees are a model society, a lesson in teamwork!

model dwelling any of a set of (esp.) 19th-cent. working men's flats, supposedly offering unusually comfortable and healthy accommodation at low rents. **model lodging house** (now *Scot.*) a large lodging house or hostel, nominally of superior standards.

2 Designating a small-scale model of the (kind of) object specified. E20.

ARNOLD BENNETT He sailed model yachts for us. E. NESBIT Among his presents he had a model engine.

■ **modelize** *verb trans.* frame or construct according to a model; give a particular shape to; organize: E17.

model /ˈmɒd(ə)l/ *verb*. Infl. **-ll-**, ***-l-**. L16.

[ORIGIN from the noun, after French *modeler*.]

1 *verb trans.* †**a** Draw a plan of; produce a preliminary version of. Also, give an outline or synopsis of. (Foll. by *forth, out*.) L16–L17. ▸**b** Frame a model or miniature replica of. M17.

b LONGFELLOW Many a ship that sailed the main Was modelled o'er and o'er again.

2 *verb trans.* †**a** Foll. by *out*: produce (a facial expression) by studied effort. Only in E17. ▸**b** Form in imitation of a particular model. Now usu. foll. by *(up)on* the model. L17. ▸**c** Assimilate in form *to*. L17. ▸†**d** Bring *into* a specified shape. E18–E19. ▸**e** Give shape to, frame, fashion, (a document, argument, or other abstract object). M18.

b R. G. COLLINGWOOD Alexander's philosophy of nature is even more closely modelled on the *Critique of Pure Reason*. T. IRELAND She'd always modelled herself on her older sister.

3 *verb trans.* Produce (a figure or likeness) as a model in clay, wax, etc. M17. ▸**b** Devise a (usu. mathematical) model or simplified description of (a phenomenon, system, etc.). M20.

R. INGALLS She was modelling a bust in clay. **b** *Nature* The first attempts to model the urban system were made by traffic engineers.

†**4** *verb trans.* Organize (a group of people, a community, a government, etc.). M17–M19.

R. FIDDES God, who founded human society, may model it as he pleases.

†**5** *verb trans.* Train in or mould to a particular mode of life or behaviour. M17–M18.

G. FARQUHAR 'Tis an insupportable toil . . for women . . to model their husbands to good breeding.

6 *verb trans. & intrans.* In drawing, painting, etc.: form with or assume the appearance of natural relief, (cause to) appear three-dimensional. M19.

7 *verb intrans.* Produce or devise a model. M19.

O. W. HOLMES I rough out my thoughts in talk as an artist models in clay.

8 a *verb intrans.* Pose or act as a model; be a fashion or photographic model. E20. ▸**b** *verb trans.* Display (clothes) as a model. E20.

a T. CALLENDER She modelled for him for free. She was a good sitter.

modeler *noun* see MODELLER.

modeliar *noun* see MUDALIYAR.

modeling *noun* see MODELLING.

modelist *noun* see MODELLIST.

modeller /ˈmɒd(ə)lə/ *noun*. Also ***modeler**. L16.

[ORIGIN from MODEL *verb* + -ER[1].]

A person who models something or who makes models; *esp.* a person who forms models in clay, plaster, wax, etc.

financial modeller: see FINANCIAL *adjective*.

modelling /ˈmɒd(ə)lɪŋ/ *noun*. Also ***modeling**. M17.

[ORIGIN from MODEL *verb* + -ING[1].]

1 The action of MODEL *verb*. M17.

2 *spec.* The work of a fashion or photographic model. M20.

3 The devising or use of abstract or mathematical models. M20.

financial modelling: see FINANCIAL *adjective*.

modellist /ˈmɒd(ə)lɪst/ *noun*. Now *rare*. Also ***modelist**. M17.

[ORIGIN from MODEL *noun* or *verb* + -IST.]

A maker of models.

modello /mɒˈdɛləʊ, *foreign* moˈdɛllo/ *noun*. Pl. **-lli** /-(l)li/, **-llos**. M20.

[ORIGIN Italian: see MODEL *noun*.]

A detailed sketch for a larger painting, prepared for a patron's approval. Also, a small model for a larger sculpture.

modem /ˈməʊdɛm/ *noun & verb*. M20.

[ORIGIN from MO(DULATOR + DEM(ODULATOR.]

▸ **A** *noun*. A combined modulator and demodulator, used esp. to connect a computer to a telephone line, for converting digital electrical signals to analogue or audio ones and vice versa. M20.

▸ **B** *verb intrans. & trans.* Infl. **-m(m)-**. Signal or send via a modem. L20.

modena /ˈmɒdɪnə/ *noun & adjective*. Also (esp. sense 2) **M-**. E19.

[ORIGIN *Modena*: see MODENESE.]

1 More fully ***modena red***. (Of) a deep purple colour. E19.

2 (**M-**.) In full ***Modena pigeon***. A stocky variety of the domestic pigeon with red legs. L19.

modenature /məˈdiːnətʃə/ *noun*. M17.

[ORIGIN French *modénature* from Italian *modanatura*, from *modano* moulding: see -URE.]

ARCHITECTURE. (A series of) mouldings decorating a cornice.

Modenese /mɒdɪˈniːz/ *adjective & noun*. E18.

[ORIGIN from *Modena* (see below) + -ESE.]

▸ **A** *adjective*. Of or pertaining to the northern Italian city of Modena or its inhabitants. L17.

▸ **B** *noun*. Pl. same. A native or inhabitant of Modena. E18.

moderacy /ˈmɒd(ə)rəsi/ *noun*. *rare*. E17.

[ORIGIN from MODERATE *adjective* + -CY.]

Moderation; (esp. political) moderateness.

moderant /ˈmɒd(ə)r(ə)nt/ *noun*. *rare*. L19.

[ORIGIN Latin *moderant-* pres. ppl stem of *moderari* MODERATE *verb*: see -ANT[1].]

A moderating thing.

moderantism /ˈmɒd(ə)r(ə)ntɪz(ə)m/ *noun*. L18.

[ORIGIN French *modérantisme*, from *modérant* pres. pple of *modérer* MODERATE *verb*: see -ISM.]

hist. The doctrine and spirit of the moderate Republican Party during and after the French Revolution.

moderate /ˈmɒd(ə)rət/ *adjective & noun*. LME.

[ORIGIN Latin *moderatus* pa. pple, formed as MODERATE *verb*: see -ATE[2].]

▸ **A** *adjective*. **1 a** Avoiding excess or extremes of conduct; observing, exhibiting, or acting with moderation; temperate in conduct or expression. LME. ▸**b** Not extreme in opinion; not strongly partisan; (also **M-**) designating or pertaining to any of various political and ecclesiastical parties avoiding extreme views. M17.

a SHAKES. *Merch. V.* O love, be moderate, allay thy ecstacy. GIBBON In the reformation of religion, his first steps were moderate and cautious. *Graphic* Teetotallers and moderate drinkers will probably be at war on this point. **b** G. GORER The children of police officers regard their fathers' profession with enthusiasm; but . . their wives . . are usually more moderate.

2 a Of medium quantity, quality, size, or extent; fairly large or good; tolerable; *derog.* mediocre, scanty. LME. ▸**b** Of a process, condition, or agency: not intense, violent, or severe; intermediate in strength or degree; *spec.* (of a wind) registering in the low to medium figures on the Beaufort scale. LME. ▸**c** Of a price, charge, etc.: reasonable, low. E20.

E. B. PUSEY The rest are very moderate productions. **b** E. RAFFALD Bake them in a moderate oven. N. PEVSNER It is a moderate climate with no scorching heat nor paralysing cold. M. ANGELOU The record player was on to a moderate volume. **c** H. CARPENTER Unfurnished houses at a moderate rent seemed impossible to find.

▸ **B** *noun*. A person who holds moderate opinions in politics, religion, etc.; FRENCH HISTORY (also **M-**) a Girondist. M17.

Listener 'Moderates' . . are at present containing the extremists and hot-heads.

■ **moderately** *adverb* LME. **moderateness** *noun* L16.

moderate /ˈmɒdəreɪt/ *verb*. Pa. pple **-ated**, †**-ate**. LME.

[ORIGIN Latin *moderat-* pa. ppl stem of *moderari*, *-are* reduce, control: see -ATE[3].]

1 *verb trans.* Make less violent, severe, intense, or rigorous. Formerly also, reduce the amount of (a fine, charge, etc.). LME. ▸**b** *verb intrans.* Become less violent, severe, intense, or rigorous. L17. ▸**c** *verb trans.* NUCLEAR PHYSICS. Slow down (a neutron); slow down neutrons in (a reactor). Cf. MODERATOR 6c. M20.

T. LEDIARD I . . advise you to moderate your demands. T. CAPOTE A short-tempered man who has difficulty moderating his excessive vigour. **b** R. L. STEVENSON Although the wind had not yet moderated, the clouds were all . . blown away.

2 *verb trans.* †**a** Adjust in quantity or proportion. L15–M17. ▸†**b** Exercise a controlling influence over; regulate, control. M16–E19. ▸**c** Review (examination papers, results, candidates, etc.) in relation to an agreed standard so as to ensure consistency of marking. M20.

3 a *verb trans.* In academic and ecclesiastical contexts: preside over (a deliberative body) or at (a debate etc.). L16. ▸**b** *verb intrans.* Act as moderator, preside, now esp. in the Presbyterian Church in Scotland. L16. ▸**c** *verb trans.* Monitor (an Internet bulletin board or chat room) for inappropriate or offensive content. L20.

†**4 a** *verb intrans.* Act as mediator or arbitrator. Also, take a mediating view. L16–M18. ▸**b** *verb trans.* Decide (a question) as an arbitrator. E17–M18.

M

– PHRASES: **moderate a call**, **moderate in a call** *Scot.* (of a presbytery or its leader) preside over the formal invitation to a minister elect.

■ **moderated** *ppl adjective* that has been moderated; *esp.* †(*a*) reasonably restricted and limited; (*b*) NUCLEAR PHYSICS provided with or slowed down by a moderator: L16.

moderation /mɒdəˈreɪʃ(ə)n/ *noun*. LME.

[ORIGIN Old French & mod. French *modération* from Latin *moderatio(n-)*, formed as MODERATE *verb*: see -ATION.]

1 †**a** Limitation, restriction; a restricting proviso or clause. LME–E18. ▸**b** The action of making something less violent, severe, intense, or rigorous. Formerly also, reduction of expenditure etc. Now *rare*. L15. ▸†**c** Control, rule; a system of government. E16–E18. ▸**d** NUCLEAR PHYSICS. The action or process of slowing down neutrons by the use of a moderator. M20. ▸**e** EDUCATION. The action or process of moderating examination papers etc. M20.

2 The quality of being moderate, esp. in conduct, opinion, etc.; avoidance of excess or extremes, temperance. Formerly also, avoidance of severity, clemency. LME.

B. JOWETT He is sensible that moderation is better than total abstinence. O. WILDE Moderation is a fatal thing. Nothing succeeds like excess.

in moderation in a moderate manner or proportion.

3 The action of presiding over a presbytery's formal invitation to a minister elect; a meeting for the purpose of formally inviting a minister elect. *Scot.* E18.

4 (**M-**.) In *pl.* The first public examination in certain faculties for the BA degree at Oxford University. Abbreviation MODS. M19.

■ **moderationist** *noun* an advocate of moderation; *spec.* a person who supports moderate drinking as opp. to total abstinence: L18.

moderatism /ˈmɒd(ə)rətɪz(ə)m/ *noun*. L18.

[ORIGIN from MODERATE *adjective* & *noun* + -ISM.]

The principles or policy of a moderate political or ecclesiastical party; belief in moderation.

■ **moderatist** *noun* E18.

moderato /mɒdəˈrɑːtəʊ/ *adverb* & *noun*. E18.

[ORIGIN Italian = MODERATE *adjective*.]

MUSIC. ▸**A** *adverb*. A direction: at a moderate pace or tempo. E18.

▸**B** *noun*. Pl. **-os**. A movement or piece marked to be performed in such a way. M18.

M

moderator /ˈmɒdəreɪtə/ *noun*. LME.

[ORIGIN Latin, formed as MODERATE *verb*: see -OR.]

†**1** A ruler, a governor. LME–M19.

2 A person who acts as an arbitrator between disputants; an arbiter. Also, a mediator. M16.

3 A Presbyterian minister elected to preside over an ecclesiastical body. M16.

4 *gen.* A person chosen to preside over a meeting or assembly and conduct its business. L16. ▸**b** The chair of a television or radio discussion. *N. Amer.* M20. ▸**c** A person who moderates an Internet bulletin board or chat room. L20.

5 a Orig., a public officer appointed to preside over the disputations or exercises for university degrees. Later, (*a*) at Cambridge, either of two officers responsible for the proper conduct of the mathematical tripos examination; (*b*) at Oxford, an examiner for Moderations. L16. ▸**b** At Dublin University: an honours graduate. M19. ▸**c** An examiner who moderates examination papers etc. M20.

6 A person who or thing which mitigates something or makes something moderate. E17. ▸**b** A regulator to control the flow of oil to the wick of an oil lamp; (also ***moderator lamp***) a lamp equipped with this. M19. ▸**c** A substance that slows down neutrons passing through it; *spec.* one used in a nuclear reactor to control the rate of fission. M20.

■ **modera'torial** *adjective* pertaining to or characteristic of a moderator M19. **moderatorship** *noun* the function or office of moderator M17.

†**moderatrix** *noun*. Pl. **-trices**, **-trixes**. L16–M18.

[ORIGIN Latin, formed as MODERATOR: see -TRIX.]

A female moderator.

■ Earlier †**moderatrice** *noun* [French]: only in M16.

modern /ˈmɒd(ə)n/ *adjective* & *noun*. L15.

[ORIGIN Old French & mod. French *moderne*, or its source late Latin *modernus*, from Latin *modo* just now, after Latin *hodiernus* of today (from *hodie* today).]

▸**A** *adjective*. †**1** Now existing; current, present; currently holding office. L15–M18.

2 Of or pertaining to the present and recent times, as opp. to the remote past. L16.

A. BULLOCK Ernest Bevin owed less to formal education than any Englishman to hold so high an office . . in modern times.

secondary modern school: see SECONDARY *adjective*.

3 Characteristic of the present and recent times; not old-fashioned or obsolete, in current fashion. L16. ▸**b** Of a person: up-to-date in lifestyle, outlook, opinions, etc.; liberal-minded. E18.

E. HEATH Tehran has developed into a modern city. M. M. KAYE It was no old-fashioned musket but a modern precision-made weapon. **b** T. PARKS My father was . . considered . . modern because he had introduced singing with a guitar on the chancel steps.

†**4** Everyday, ordinary, commonplace. L16–E17.

SHAKES. *A.Y.L.* The justice, . . Full of wise saws and modern instances.

5 *spec.* ▸**a** Designating the form of a language currently used, or the form representing the most recent significant stage of development, as opp. to any earlier form. L17. ▸**b** Of a typeface: having straight serifs and marked contrast between the thick and thin parts of the letters. M18. ▸**c** Belonging to a comparatively recent period in the history of the earth. E19. ▸**d** Designating or pertaining to art and architecture marked by a departure from traditional styles and values. E19.

a modern Greek, ***modern Hebrew***, ***modern Irish***, etc.

– SPECIAL COLLOCATIONS: **modern convenience** = MOD CON. **modern dance** a free expressive style of dancing distinct from classical ballet. **modern-day** of or in the present or recent times. ***modern English***: see ENGLISH *adjective* & *noun*. **modern first edition** the first edition of a book published after *c* 1900. **modern Greats** (at Oxford University) the school of philosophy, politics, and economics. **modern history**: *spec.* of the period after the Middle Ages or after the fall of the Western Roman Empire. **modern jazz** jazz as developed in the 1940s and 1950s, *esp.* bebop. **modern languages** European languages (esp. French and German) as a subject of study, as opp. to Latin and Greek. ***modern Latin***: see LATIN *adjective* & *noun*. **modern** PENTATHLON. **modern school** (*a*) in some English public schools, a separately organized division of the school in which Greek and most Latin is excluded from the curriculum; (*b*) *hist.* = ***secondary modern school*** s.v. SECONDARY *adjective*. **modern side** = ***modern school*** (a) above.

▸**B** *noun*. **1** A person or thing belonging to the present time. Usu. in *pl.* L16.

H. ALLEN Few moderns . . can resist . . patronising the past. *Country Life* The Walker Art Centre houses a world-famous collection of moderns.

Danish modern: see DANISH *adjective*. ***secondary modern***: see SECONDARY *adjective*. ***Swedish modern***: see SWEDISH *adjective*.

2 A person with modern tastes or opinions. Usu. in *pl.* L19.

3 = ***modern first edition*** above. E20.

■ **modernly** *adverb* (*a*) (now *rare*) in modern times; (*b*) in a modern manner; after the fashion of modern times: E17. **modernness** /-n-n-/ *noun* M17.

moderne /məˈdɜːn, *foreign* mɔdɛrn/ *adjective* & *noun*. M20.

[ORIGIN French = modern.]

(Designating or characterized by) a popularization of the art deco style marked by bright colours and austere geometric shapes, or (freq. *derog.*) any ultra-modern style.

moderner /ˈmɒd(ə)nə/ *noun*. L16.

[ORIGIN from MODERN *adjective* + -ER¹.]

A modern person.

modernise *verb* var. of MODERNIZE.

modernism /ˈmɒd(ə)nɪz(ə)m/ *noun*. M18.

[ORIGIN from MODERN *adjective* + -ISM.]

1 A usage, mode of expression, peculiarity of style, etc., characteristic of modern times. M18.

2 Modern character or quality of thought, expression, technique, etc.; affinity for what is modern. M19.

3 THEOLOGY. A movement towards modifying traditional beliefs and doctrines in accordance with modern ideas, esp. in the Roman Catholic Church in the late 19th and early 20th cents. E20.

4 The methods, style, or attitude of modern artists, writers, architects, composers, etc.; *spec.* a style of painting etc. rejecting classical and traditional methods of expression. E20.

Modernismus /modɛrˈnɪsmʊs, mɒdəˈnɪzməs/ *noun*. Freq. *derog.* M20.

[ORIGIN German = MODERNISM.]

Modernism in architecture, art, etc.

modernist /ˈmɒd(ə)nɪst/ *noun* & *adjective*. L16.

[ORIGIN from MODERN *adjective* + -IST.]

▸**A** *noun*. †**1** A person who lives in modern times. Only in L16.

2 A supporter or follower of modern ways or methods; an adherent of modernism. E18.

3 *spec.* ▸**a** THEOLOGY. A supporter or advocate of theological modernism. E20. ▸**b** An artist, architect, writer, etc., whose work is characterized by modernism. E20. ▸**c** A person who plays or appreciates modern jazz. M20.

▸**B** *attrib.* or as *adjective*. Of, pertaining to, or characteristic of modernists or modernism. M19.

■ **moder'nistic** *adjective* of, pertaining to, or suggestive of modernism or modernists; having affinity for what is modern: E20. **moder'nistically** *adverb* M20.

modernity /məˈdɜːnɪti/ *noun*. E17.

[ORIGIN formed as MODERNIST + -ITY.]

1 The quality or condition of being modern; modernness of character. M17.

2 A modern thing. M18.

modernize /ˈmɒd(ə)nʌɪz/ *verb trans.* & *intrans.* Also **-ise**. E18.

[ORIGIN French *moderniser*, from *moderne* MODERN *adjective*: see -IZE.]

Make (something) modern; give a modern character or appearance to (something), esp. by installing modern equipment or adopting modern ideas or methods.

HENRY MILLER Even when a town becomes modernized . . there are still vestiges of the old. *Philadelphia Inquirer* Operating costs have shot up as the company was forced to modernize aging cars.

■ **modernizable** *adjective* M20. **moderni'zation** *noun* (*a*) the action or an act of modernizing; the state of being modernized; (*b*) a modernized version: L18. **modernizer** *noun* M18.

modest /ˈmɒdɪst/ *adjective*. M16.

[ORIGIN Old French & mod. French *modeste* from Latin *modestus* keeping due measure, from base of MODERATE *verb* + pa. ppl suffix.]

1 Having a moderate or humble estimate of one's own abilities or merits; unassuming, diffident, bashful; not bold or forward. Of an action, attribute, etc.: proceeding from or indicating such qualities. M16. ▸**b** *fig.* Of a thing: apparently shy of observation, not conspicuous. L18.

J. F. LEHMANN Leonard . . sat in modest silence, with lowered eyes. B. PYM He was too modest to believe that Penelope could have fallen in love with him. **b** R. BURNS Wee, modest, crimson-tipped flow'r.

†**2** Well-conducted, orderly; not harsh or domineering. L16–M17.

3 Decorous in manner and conduct; scrupulously avoiding impropriety or indecency; reserved in sexual matters. L16.

C. C. TRENCH There was nothing modest or delicate in her approach to sex. L. CODY She didn't think she was excessively modest, it was just that there were some things you got used to doing in private.

4 Not excessive, not exaggerated, moderate; limited, restrained, slight; unpretentious in size, quantity, appearance, etc.; undistinguished on the social or economic scale; not lavish or wealthy. E17.

I. MCEWAN These were modest, achievable tasks. K. WATERHOUSE Colchester Place Mansions is an altogether more modest establishment—no more than a converted house. T. K. WOLFE This was a modest sum compared to what other people spent. H. R. LANDON The father had a very modest position as a bass-singer at the Mannheim court.

■ **modestly** *adverb* M16.

modesty /ˈmɒdɪsti/ *noun* & *adjective*. M16.

[ORIGIN Old French & mod. French *modestie* or Latin *modestia*, from *modestus*: see MODEST, -Y³.]

▸**A** *noun*. †**1** Moderation; reasonableness; self-control; mildness of rule. M16–M19.

GIBBON The modesty of Alaric was interpreted . . as a sure evidence of his weakness.

2 The quality of being modest about oneself. M16. ▸†**b** Deferential feeling. L16–M17. ▸**c** The quality of being modest in size, quantity, appearance, etc.; unpretentious character. E20.

P. MEDAWAR 'Just here our capacities fail us,' he says, with a modesty not found in . . his successors. R. DEACON With typical modesty he gave most of the credit . . to a Zulu assistant. **c** *Blackwood's Magazine* The straitness of their surroundings, the modesty of their homes.

3 Modest behaviour, manner, or appearance. M16. ▸**b** = ***modesty piece*** below. *arch.* M18.

E. B. BROWNING He could not think highly of the modesty of any woman who could read Don Juan! *Mail on Sunday* She still has to bow to her Muslim background in modesty of dress.

4 Any of certain inconspicuous plants; *spec.* (*a*) thorow-wax; (*b*) a white-flowered creeping plant, *Whipplea modesta*, of the hydrangea family, native to the western US. M19.

▸**B** *attrib.* or as *adjective*. Serving to prevent immodest exposure of the (female) body. Orig. in ***modesty piece*** below. E18.

modesty piece *arch.* a piece of lace etc. covering the bosom, worn with a low-cut dress. **modesty skirt** a short skirt on a woman's swimming costume.

modi *noun pl.* see MODUS.

modiation /məʊdɪˈeɪʃ(ə)n/ *noun*. Long *obsolete* exc. *hist.* M17.

[ORIGIN Late Latin *modiatio(n-)*, ult. from Latin MODIUS: see -ATION.]

Measurement by volume; a levy assessed by volume.

modicity /məˈdɪsɪti/ *noun*. *rare*. E17.

[ORIGIN French *modicité* from medieval Latin *modicitat-*, from Latin *modicus*: see MODICUM, -ITY.]

Moderateness.

modicum /ˈmɒdɪkəm/ *noun*. LME.

[ORIGIN Latin = little way, short time, neut. sing. of *modicus* moderate, from *modus* MODE.]

1 A small quantity or portion; a limited amount. LME.

A. TROLLOPE With the cup of coffee comes a small modicum of dry toast. L. CODY Slinger, of course, has a modicum of native wit. *Evening Telegraph (Grimsby)* Fleming . . caused more than a modicum of unrest in the Mariners defence whenever he charged forward.

†**2** A person of small stature. *joc.* E–M17.

†**3** The female genitalia. *slang.* M17–M18.

modifiable /ˈmɒdɪfʌɪəb(ə)l/ *adjective.* E17.
[ORIGIN from MODIFY + -ABLE.]
Able to be modified.
■ **modifiaˈbility** *noun* E19. **modifiableness** *noun* L19.

modificable /ˈmɒdɪfɪkəb(ə)l/ *adjective. rare.* E18.
[ORIGIN from Latin *modificare* MODIFY: see -ABLE.]
Modifiable.
■ **modificaˈbility** *noun* M19.

modificand /ˈmɒdɪfɪkand/ *noun. rare.* M19.
[ORIGIN Latin *modificandus*, from *modificare*: see MODIFY, -AND.]
Chiefly GRAMMAR. A word etc. that is (to be) modified.

modification /ˌmɒdɪfɪˈkeɪʃ(ə)n/ *noun.* L15.
[ORIGIN Old French & mod. French, or Latin *modificatio(n-)*, from *modificat-* pa. ppl stem of *modificari*, *-are*: see MODIFY, -FICATION.]
1 SCOTS LAW. The action of assessing or awarding a payment; *esp.* (*hist.*) the fixing of a parish minister's stipend. L15.
†**2** PHILOSOPHY. **a** The bringing of a thing into a particular mode of existence; differentiation into a variety of forms. E16–M19. ▸**b** The form of existence belonging to a particular object; a particular form into which a thing is differentiated; a mode of being. M17–M19.
3 The action or an act of making changes to something without altering its essential nature or character; partial alteration; orig. *spec.* the action of qualifying a statement etc. Also, the state of being so changed. E17. ▸**b** BIOLOGY. The development of non-heritable changes in an organism, as opp. to ***variation***, ***mutation***. L19.

J. TYNDALL It required but a slight modification of our plans. *Which?* Manufacturers are quick to respond with modifications.

4 The result of such alteration; a modified form, a variety. M17. ▸**b** BIOLOGY. The non-heritable changes produced in an organism in response to a particular environment. L19.

W. A. MILLER Stearin may exist in three modifications, each of which has a different fusing point.

5 GRAMMAR. **a** Qualification or limitation of the sense of one word, phrase, etc., by another; an instance or the result of this. E18. ▸**b** (An) alteration of a vowel by umlaut. M19.
■ **modificational** *adjective* of the nature of or arising from modification M19. ˈ**modificative** *noun & adjective* [medieval Latin *modificativus*] (now *rare*) (**a**) GRAMMAR a modifying word or clause; (**b**) *adjective* having the property of modifying: M17. ˈ**modificator** *noun* (*rare*) = MODIFIER L16. ˈ**modificatory** *adjective* modifying; tending to modify: E19.

modifier /ˈmɒdɪfʌɪə/ *noun.* L16.
[ORIGIN from MODIFY + -ER¹.]
1 SCOTS LAW. An official who assesses or awards a payment etc. L16.
2 A person who or thing which modifies or alters something, or produces variation. L17. ▸**b** GRAMMAR. A word, phrase, or clause which modifies another; a phonetic sign or symbol which modifies a character. M19. ▸**c** GENETICS. A gene which modifies the phenotypic expression of a gene at another locus. E20.

modify /ˈmɒdɪfʌɪ/ *verb trans.* LME.
[ORIGIN Old French & mod. French *modifier* from Latin *modificari*, *-are*, from *modus* MODE: see -FY.]
1 SCOTS LAW. Assess or decree the amount of (a payment, *hist.* esp. a parish minister's stipend); award (a payment) *to.* LME.
†**2** Limit, restrain; appease, assuage. LME–M16.
3 Make partial or minor changes to; alter without radical transformation. Orig. *esp.* qualify or moderate (a statement etc.), alter so as to make less severe; now freq., alter so as to improve. LME.

J. LANG There is generally a light breeze to modify the heat. T. H. HUXLEY The agents which are now at work in modifying the crust of the earth. P. FITZGERALD Freddie . . did in fact modify her behaviour. *New York Times* The company has concentrated on modifying cars developed by Renault for the American market. *Which?* One of our tested sets . . can be modified to run off a . . battery.

†**4** PHILOSOPHY. Give (an object) its particular form of being or distinguishing characters; differentiate into a variety of forms. M17–L18.
5 GRAMMAR. **a** Limit or qualify the sense of (a word, phrase, etc.). E18. ▸**b** Change (a vowel) by umlaut. M19.

modii *noun* pl. of MODIUS.

modillion /məˈdɪljən/ *noun.* M16.
[ORIGIN French *modillon*, †*modiglion* from Italian *modiglione* from Proto-Romance, ult. from Latin *mutulus* MUTULE.]
ARCHITECTURE. A projecting bracket placed in series under the corona of the cornice in the Corinthian, composite and Roman Ionic orders; *gen.* an ornamental bracket under eaves etc.
■ **modillioned** *adjective* ornamented with modillions L19.

modiolus /məˈdʌɪələs/ *noun.* Pl. **-li** /-lʌɪ, -liː/, **-luses**. In sense 2 also **-la** /-lə/, pl. **-lae** /-liː/. L17.
[ORIGIN Latin = nave of a wheel, dim. of MODIUS.]
1 SURGERY. The crown of a trepan. Long *rare* or *obsolete*. L17.
2 A horse mussel of the genus *Modiolus* (formerly *Modiola*). Now only as mod. Latin genus name. L18.
3 ANATOMY. The conical axis of the cochlea of the ear. E19.
■ **modiolar** *adjective* (ANATOMY) of or pertaining to the modiolus of the ear M19.

modish /ˈməʊdɪʃ/ *adjective.* M17.
[ORIGIN from MODE + -ISH¹.]
Conforming to or following the mode or prevailing fashion; fashionable.

L. STRACHEY Eugénie, cool and modish, floated in an infinitude of flounces. *Times Lit. Suppl.* Fashionable, even modish, it is competently written. F. RAPHAEL He was always prone to behave as fashion required . . . Modish debauchery never went against his grain.

■ **modishly** *adverb* M17. **modishness** *noun* L17.

Modistae /məˈdɪstʌɪ/ *noun pl.* E20.
[ORIGIN Latin, from *modus* MODE.]
A group of later medieval grammarians who put forward a system of Latin grammar in which Priscian's word categories were integrated into the framework of scholastic philosophy.

modiste /mɒˈdiːst, *foreign* mɔdist (*pl. same*)/ *noun.* M19.
[ORIGIN French, from *mode* fashion, MODE *noun* + *-iste* -IST.]
A person who makes, designs, or deals in articles of fashion; *esp.* a fashionable milliner or dressmaker.

modistic /məˈdɪstɪk/ *adjective*¹. E20.
[ORIGIN from MODISTE + -IC.]
Of or pertaining to fashion(s).

modistic /məˈdɪstɪk/ *adjective*². M20.
[ORIGIN from MODISTAE + -IC.]
Of or pertaining to the Modistae.

modius /ˈməʊdɪəs/ *noun.* Pl. **modii** /ˈməʊdɪʌɪ/. LME.
[ORIGIN Latin.]
1 *hist.* A Roman measure of corn, equal to about a peck; in the Middle Ages, a measure of capacity of varying size, often equated with a bushel. LME.
2 A tall cylindrical headdress with which certain gods are represented in classical art. E19.

Modoc /ˈməʊdɒk/ *noun & adjective.* M19.
[ORIGIN Klamath *mo:wat'a:k*, lit. 'in the extreme south', a name for Tule Lake in the centre of the Madoc territory.]
▸ **A** *noun.* Pl. **-s**, same.
1 A member of a Penutian people of the Oregon–California border. M19.
2 The language of this people, resembling Klamath. L19.
▸ **B** *attrib.* or as *adjective.* Of or pertaining to the Modoc or their language. M19.

modom /ˈmɒdəm/ *noun. colloq.* E20.
[ORIGIN Repr. an affectedly refined pronunc.]
Madam.

Mods /mɒdz/ *noun pl. colloq.* M19.
[ORIGIN Abbreviation.]
The examination Moderations at Oxford University (see MODERATION 4).

modular /ˈmɒdjʊlə/ *adjective & noun.* E19.
[ORIGIN mod. Latin *modularis*, from Latin MODULUS: see -AR¹.]
▸ **A** *adjective.* **1** MATH. Of or pertaining to a modulus or module. E19.
†**2** ARCHITECTURE. Of or pertaining to a module as a unit of length. *rare.* Only in M19.
3 Employing or involving a module or modules as the basis of design, measurement, or construction; (of a facility, service, etc.) provided in a number of discrete stages. M20. ▸**b** Of an educational course: designed as a series of units or discrete sections. M20.
▸ **B** *ellipt.* as *noun.* A thing of modular construction or design. M20.
■ **moduˈlarity** *noun* the property of being modular; use of modules in design or construction: E20. **modulariˈzation** *noun* the action or process of making something modular; construction on modular principles: M20. **modularize** *verb trans.* make modular; construct on modular principles: M20. **modularly** *adverb* on modular principles E20.

modulate /ˈmɒdjʊleɪt/ *verb.* M16.
[ORIGIN Latin *modulat-* pa. ppl stem of *modulari* measure, adjust to rhythm, make melody, from MODULUS: see -ATE³.]
1 *verb trans.* Intone (a song etc.). *rare.* M16.
2 *verb trans.* Regulate, adjust, temper, vary conformably *to*; soften, tone down; *esp.* attune (the voice, sounds, etc.) to a certain pitch or key, vary or inflect in tone; give tune or melody to. E17.

GIBBON The songs of triumph were modulated to psalms and litanies. A. RADCLIFFE She determined to modulate that nature to her own views. G. GREENE She spoke gently . . for it was difficult to modulate her husky voice.

3 *verb trans. & intrans.* MUSIC. (Cause to) change from one key to another. (Foll. by *from*, *to*.) E18.
4 *verb trans.* **a** Vary the amplitude, frequency, or some other characteristic of (an electromagnetic wave or other oscillation, a beam of particles, etc.) in accordance with the variations of a second signal, usu. of lower frequency; vary (a property of a signal) in this way. Also, apply a signal to (a device) so as to vary its output signal; impress (a signal) *on* (*to*) a carrier wave by modulation. E20. ▸**b** *gen.* Exert a modifying or controlling influence on (a physical property, phenomenon, etc.). M20.

a J. H. REYNER The radio transmission of sound . . is usually accomplished by modulating a high-frequency carrier-wave. **b** *Scientific American* The steam flow is modulated by a control valve. *Nature* Speculations on how thunderstorm electrification might modulate rainfall.

5 *verb intrans.* BIOLOGY. Of a cell: undergo modulation *into*. M20.
6 *verb intrans.* Converse on Citizens' Band radio. *US slang.* L20.
■ **modulative** *adjective* (*rare*) serving to modulate something E19. **modulatory** *adjective* pertaining to or serving for modulation L19.

modulation /mɒdjʊˈleɪʃ(ə)n/ *noun.* LME.
[ORIGIN Latin *modulatio(n-)*, formed as MODULATE: see -ATION.]
1 Singing, making music; a tune; in *pl.*, notes, sounds. Now *rare*. LME.
2 The action of modulating something appropriately; variation of line, form, etc., with regard to artistic effect; a tempering or toning down. Formerly also, rhythmical movement. M16.
3 The action of inflecting the voice or an instrument musically; variation of tone or pitch; a particular inflection or intonation. M16.
4 ARCHITECTURE. The proportioning or regulating of the parts of an order by the module. M17.
5 MUSIC. **a** The action or process of passing from one key to another in the course of a piece; (a) change of key. L17. ▸†**b** Composition, performance, or arrangement in a particular mode or key. Also, a chord or succession of notes. Only in 18. ▸**c** *hist.* Any of certain notes in each church mode, on which a phrase of melody had to begin and end. L19.
6 Melodious literary composition; harmonious treatment of language. M18.
7 The process of modulating a wave or beam, esp. in order to impress a signal on it; the extent to which a modulated carrier wave is varied; a waveform or signal so impressed. E20. ▸**b** *gen.* The process of exerting a controlling or modifying influence on a physical property or phenomenon. M20.
AMPLITUDE ***modulation***. FREQUENCY ***modulation***.
8 BIOLOGY. Reversible variation in the activity or form of a cell in response to a changing environment. M20.
– COMB.: **modulation frequency** the frequency of a wave used to modulate another wave; **modulation index** a coefficient representing the degree of modulation of a carrier wave; *spec.* the ratio of the difference between the maximum and minimum frequencies of a frequency-modulated carrier to the frequency of the modulating signal.

modulator /ˈmɒdjʊleɪtə/ *noun.* E16.
[ORIGIN from MODULATE + -OR.]
1 A person who or thing which modulates something; *spec.* (**a**) a device that produces modulation of a wave; (**b**) a regulating mechanism. E16.
2 MUSIC. A chart used in the tonic sol-fa system, showing the relations of tones and scales. M19.

module /ˈmɒdjuːl/ *noun.* L16.
[ORIGIN French, or its source Latin MODULUS: see -ULE.]
†**1** Allotted compass or scale; one's power or capabilities. L16–L17.
†**2** **a** A plan, design, or model of a larger thing. L16–L17. ▸**b** A mere image or counterfeit. *poet.* L16–E17.

b SHAKES. *John* But a clod And module of confounded royalty.

3 A standard or unit for measuring. E17.
4 **a** ARCHITECTURE. In the classic orders, the unit of length by which proportions are expressed, usu. the diameter or semidiameter of the column at the base of the shaft. M17. ▸**b** A length chosen as a basis for the dimensions of parts of a building, items of furniture, etc., so that all lengths are integral multiples of it. M20.

b J. S. FOSTER In Great Britain the accepted module is 100mm.

5 MATH. **a** = MODULUS 2. *rare.* L19. ▸**b** Orig., a set that is a subset of a ring and is closed under addition and subtraction. Now usu., a commutative additive group whose elements may be multiplied by those of a ring, the product being in the group and multiplication being associative and distributive. E20.
6 ENGINEERING. The pitch diameter of a gearwheel (in millimetres) divided by the number of teeth. E20.
7 (Now the predominant sense.) Each of a series of standardized parts or units from which a complex structure, e.g. a building or a piece of furniture, is or can be assembled; *loosely* a more or less independent component part. M20. ▸**b** ASTRONAUTICS. A separable section of a spacecraft that can operate as an independent unit. M20. ▸**c** COMPUTING etc. Any of a number of distinct but interrelated units from which a program may be built up or into which a complex activity may be analysed. M20. ▸**d** Any of a number of distinct units or periods of education or training which can be combined to make up a course. M20.

A. TOFFLER Pressed-steel modules . . hoisted by crane and plugged into building frames. *Good Housekeeping* A . . Habitat sofa which fits together in modules. *fig.*: D. ATTENBOROUGH The basic architectural module on which the echinoderm body is built. **d** *Lilith* Students can take a degree by selecting the modules they want.

b ***lunar excursion module, lunar module***: see LUNAR *adjective*.

moduli *noun pl.* see MODULUS.

modulo /ˈmɒdjʊləʊ/ *preposition*. L19.
[ORIGIN Latin, abl. of MODULUS.]
MATH. With respect to a modulus of (a given value).

modulus /ˈmɒdjʊləs/ *noun*. Pl. **-li** /-lʌɪ, -liː/, **-luses**. M16.
[ORIGIN Latin, dim. of *modus* MODE.]
†**1** *ARCHITECTURE.* = MODULE *noun* 4a. M16–M17.
2 *MATH.* **a** A number by which logarithms to one base must be multiplied in order to obtain the corresponding logarithms to another base. M18. ▸**b** A constant multiplier, coefficient, or parameter. M19. ▸**c** A measure of a quantity which depends on two or more other quantities; *esp.* the absolute value of a complex quantity. M19. ▸**d** A number by which another number may be divided leaving a remainder. Cf. CONGRUENT 2b, RESIDUE 4. M19.
3 *PHYSICS & ENGINEERING.* A numerical quantity representing some property of a substance, and equal to the ratio of the magnitude of a (usu. mechanical) cause to the magnitude of its effect on the substance; *spec.* = ***modulus of elasticity*** below. E19.
bulk modulus: see BULK *noun*[1] *& adjective*. **modulus of elasticity**, **elastic modulus** the ratio of the stress acting on a substance to the strain produced (also YOUNG'S MODULUS). ***modulus of*** RIGIDITY.

modus /ˈməʊdəs/ *noun*. Pl. ***modi*** /ˈməʊdʌɪ/, **moduses**. L16.
[ORIGIN Latin = MODE.]
1 *LAW.* The qualification of the terms of a conveyance etc., or the consideration involved. Long *obsolete* exc. *hist.* L16.
2 A money payment, *spec.* (in full †***modus decimandi*** [Latin = mode of tithing]) one in lieu of tithe. E17.
3 A mode; *esp.* the way in which something is done; a mode or manner of operation. Now chiefly in Latin phrs. (see below) or *ellipt.* = ***modus operandi*** below. M17.
4 *LOGIC.* A mood: in ***modus ponens***, ***modus tollens*** below. M19.
– PHRASES: ***modus decimandi***: see sense 3 above. ***modus operandi*** /ɒpəˈrandiː, -dʌɪ/ [= mode of operating] (***a***) the way in which something operates; (***b***) the way in which a person sets about a task. ***modus ponens*** /ˈpəʊnɛnz/ [= mood that affirms] *LOGIC* (an argument employing) the rule that the consequent *q* may be inferred from the conditional statement *if p then q* and the statement *p*. ***modus tollens*** /ˈtɒlɛnz/ [= mood that denies] *LOGIC* (an argument employing) the rule that the negation of the antecedent *p* (i.e. *not-p*) may be inferred from the conditional statement *if p then q* and the consequence *not-q*. ***modus vivendi*** /vɪˈvɛndiː, -dʌɪ/ [= mode of living] a way of living or coping; *esp.* a working arrangement between parties in dispute or disagreement which enables them to carry on pending a settlement.

†**mody** *adjective*. Only in 18.
[ORIGIN from MODE + -Y[1].]
Fashionable, modish.

moellon /ˈmwɛlɒn/ *noun*. L19.
[ORIGIN French.]
= DEGRAS 1.

moeritherium /mɪərɪˈθɪərɪəm/ *noun*. E20.
[ORIGIN mod. Latin (see below), from Greek *Moiris*, a lake in Egypt near where remains were first discovered + *thērion* wild animal.]
An extinct proboscidean mammal of the genus *Moeritherium*, known from fossil remains of Upper Eocene age.

Moeso-Goth /ˈmiːsəʊgɒθ/ *noun*. E19.
[ORIGIN mod. Latin *Moesogothi* pl., from Latin *Moesi* people of Moesia: see GOTH.]
A member of a Gothic tribe which inhabited Moesia, a region corresponding to modern Bulgaria and Serbia, in the 4th and 5th cents.
■ **Moeso-ˈGothic** *adjective & noun* (***a***) *adjective* of or pertaining to the Moeso-Goths or their language; (***b***) *noun* the language of the Moeso-Goths: M18.

moeurs /mœːrs, mœːr/ *noun pl.* M19.
[ORIGIN French, formed as MORES.]
The behaviour, customs, or habits of a people or a group of people.

mofette /mɒˈfɛt/ *noun*. L18.
[ORIGIN French from Neapolitan Italian *mofetta* = Spanish *mofeta*.]
(An exhalation of gas from) a fissure or fumarole.

moffie /ˈmɒfi/ *noun*. *slang* (chiefly *S. Afr.*). E20.
[ORIGIN Perh. abbreviation and alt. of HERMAPHRODITE.]
An effeminate man; a male homosexual; a male transvestite.

mofo /ˈməʊfəʊ/ *noun*. *US coarse slang*. Pl. **-os**. M20.
[ORIGIN Abbreviation.]
= ***motherfucker*** s.v. MOTHER *noun*.

mofussil /məʊˈfʌsɪl/ *noun & adjective*. *Indian*. L18.
[ORIGIN Urdu *mufaṣṣil* from Persian *mufaṣṣal* from Arabic *mufaṣṣal*, pass. pple of *faṣṣala* divide, classify.]
▸ **A** *noun*. *The* rural localities of a district as distinguished from the chief station or the town. L18.
▸ **B** *attrib.* or as *adjective*. Of the mofussil; remote, provincial. E19.

mog /mɒg/ *noun*. *slang*. E20.
[ORIGIN Abbreviation of MOGGY.]
A cat.

Mogadon /ˈmɒgədɒn/ *noun*. M20.
[ORIGIN Unknown.]
(Proprietary name for) the drug nitrazepam; a tablet of this.

moggy /ˈmɒgi/ *noun*. Also **-ie**. L17.
[ORIGIN Var. of MAGGIE.]
1 A girl or young woman, later *esp.* an untidily dressed one. *dial. & slang*. Now *rare*. L17.
2 A calf or cow. *dial.* E19.
3 A cat. *colloq.* E20.

BBC Wildlife Put cat guards round your trees to stop neighbourhood moggies invading nests.

Moghul *noun & adjective* var. of MOGUL *noun*[1] *& adjective*.

mogo /ˈməʊgəʊ/ *noun*. Pl. **-os**. L18.
[ORIGIN Dharuk *mugu*.]
A stone hatchet used by Australian Aborigines.

†**Mogor** *noun & adjective* var. of MOGUL *noun*[1] *& adjective*.

mogote /məˈgəʊti/ *noun*. L19.
[ORIGIN Spanish = hillock, heap, haystack.]
PHYSICAL GEOGRAPHY. A steep-sided hill of roughly circular cross-section characteristic of karst topography, esp. in Cuba. Cf. HUM *noun*[3].

mogra /ˈməʊgrə/ *noun*. M17.
[ORIGIN Hindi *mogrā* from Sanskrit *mudgara*.]
Arabian jasmine, *Jasminum sambac*.

Mogul /ˈməʊg(ə)l/ *noun*[1] *& adjective*. Also †**Mogor**, **Moghul**, (now preferred for the empire) **Mughal** /ˈmʊg(ə)l, ˈmuː-/, (esp. in sense A.2) **m-**. L16.
[ORIGIN Urdu *muğal* from Persian *muğul* from Mongolian *mongγol* = MONGOL. Var. *-or* prob. after Portuguese.]
▸ **A** *noun*. **1** *hist.* A Mongolian; *spec.* (***a***) a follower of Genghis Khan in the 13th cent.; (***b***) a member of the Muslim dynasty, descended from Tamerlane, which ruled an empire in India, based on Delhi, from the 16th to the 19th cent. L16.
the Mogul, **the Great Mogul** the Mughal emperor at Delhi.
2 An important or influential person; a powerful autocrat. *colloq.* L17.

A. MILLER The son of a Hollywood Mogul.

†**3** = ***Mogul plum*** below. Only in E18.
4 A steam locomotive of 2-6-0 wheel arrangement. L19.
▸ **B** *adjective*. **1** *hist.* Mongolian; *spec.* of or pertaining to the Mughals or their empire in India. E17.
†**2** ***Mogul plum***, a particular variety of large plum. M18–M19.

mogul /ˈməʊg(ə)l/ *noun*[2]. M20.
[ORIGIN Prob. from southern German dial. *Mugel*, *Mugl*.]
A bump on a ski slope.

Moguntine /məˈgʌntʌɪn/ *adjective*. Now *rare* or *obsolete*. L16.
[ORIGIN from Latin *Moguntia* Mainz + -INE[1].]
Of or pertaining to the city of Mainz, Germany, esp. as an early centre of printing.

MOH *abbreviation*.
Medical Officer of Health.

mohair /ˈməʊhɛː/ *noun & adjective*. L16.
[ORIGIN Arabic *mukayyar* lit. 'select, choice', pass. pple of *kayyara* prefer, later assim. to HAIR *noun*: cf. MOIRE.]
▸ **A** *noun*. **1** A fabric, yarn, or mixture made from the hair of the Angora goat or in imitation of this. L16.
2 A garment made of such material. M17.
3 The hair of the Angora goat. M18.
▸ **B** *attrib.* or as *adjective*. Made or consisting of mohair. M17.

Mohammed *noun*, **Mohammedan** *adjective & noun* vars. of MUHAMMAD, MUHAMMADAN.

moharra *noun* var. of MOJARRA.

Moharram *noun* var. of MUHARRAM.

Mohave /məˈhɑːvi/ *noun & adjective*. Also **Mojave**. M19.
[ORIGIN Mohave *hamakhá:v*.]
▸ **A** *noun*. Pl. **-s**, same. A member of a Yuman people living along the Colorado River; the language of this people. M19.
▸ **B** *attrib.* or as *adjective*. Of or pertaining to the Mohaves or their language. M19.

Mohawk /ˈməʊhɔːk/ *noun & adjective*. See also MOHOCK. M17.
[ORIGIN Narragansett *mohowawog* lit. 'man-eaters'.]
▸ **A** *noun*. Pl. **-s**, same.
1 A member of an Iroquois people, one of the five of the original Iroquois confederation, orig. inhabiting parts of upper New York State; the language of this people. M17.
2 *SKATING.* A step from either edge of the skate to the same edge on the other foot in an opposite direction. Cf. CHOCTAW *noun* 2. L19.
3 (Also **m-**.) A Mohican haircut. Chiefly *US*. L20.
▸ **B** *attrib.* or as *adjective*. **1** Of or pertaining to the Mohawks or their language. M18.
2 (Also **m-**.) Designating a Mohican haircut. Chiefly *US*. L20.

Mohegan /məʊˈhiːg(ə)n/ *noun & adjective*. M17.
[ORIGIN Mohegan, lit. 'people of the tidal waters'.]
▸ **A** *noun*. A member of an American Indian people formerly inhabiting the western parts of Connecticut and Massachusetts; the language of this people. Also called MOHICAN. M17.
▸ **B** *attrib.* or as *adjective*. Of or pertaining to the Mohegans or their language. M17.

mohel /ˈməʊ(h)(ə)l/ *noun*. E17.
[ORIGIN Hebrew *mōhēl*.]
A person who performs the Jewish rite of circumcision.

Mohican /məʊˈhiːk(ə)n, ˈməʊɪk(ə)n/ *noun & adjective*. E17.
[ORIGIN Blend of English forms of the self-designations of two Algonquian Indian peoples, the Mahicans and the Mohegans; in modern use chiefly after the novel *The Last of the Mohicans* (1826) by J. Fenimore Cooper.]
▸ **A** *noun*. **1** A member of either the Mahican or Mohegan peoples; the language of these peoples. E17.
last of the Mohicans *the* sole survivor(s) of a noble race or kind.
2 (Also **m-**.) A hairstyle in which the head is shaved except for a strip of hair from the middle of the forehead to the back of the neck. Cf. MOHAWK *noun* 3. L20.
▸ **B** *adjective*. **1** Designating or pertaining to the Mahicans or Mohegans. M17.
2 (Also **m-**.) Designating a Mohican (hairstyle). Cf. MOHAWK *adjective* 2. M20.

Mohiniattam /ˈməʊhɪnɪˌatəm/ *noun*. M20.
[ORIGIN from *Mohini* supreme seductress of Hindu mythology (from Sanskrit *muh-* confuse, bewilder) + Tamil *āṭṭam* dance.]
An Indian dance for women, orig. from Kerala in SW India, noted for its gentle and graceful style.

Moho /ˈməʊhəʊ/ *noun*. Also **m-**. M20.
[ORIGIN Abbreviation.]
GEOLOGY. The Mohorovičić discontinuity.

Mohock /ˈməʊhɒk/ *noun*. *hist.* E17.
[ORIGIN Var. of MOHAWK.]
A member of a band of aristocratic hooligans who roamed the streets of London at night in the early 18th cent.

mohohu /məˈhuːhuː/ *noun*. Now *rare*. M19.
[ORIGIN Setswana.]
In southern Africa: the white rhinoceros, *Ceratotherium simum*.

mohonono /məʊhəˈnəʊnəʊ/ *noun*. Pl. **-os**. M19.
[ORIGIN Silozi *muHonono*.]
An evergreen tree with grey-green leaves, *Terminalia sericea* (family Combretaceae), native to southern Africa.

Mohorovičić discontinuity /məʊhəˈrəʊvɪtʃɪtʃ dɪsˌkɒntɪˈnjuːɪti/ *noun phr.* M20.
[ORIGIN A. *Mohorovičić* (1857–1936), Yugoslav seismologist.]
GEOLOGY. The discontinuity between the earth's crust and the mantle which is believed to exist at a depth of about 10–12 km (6–7½ miles) under the ocean beds and 40–50 km (25–30 miles) under the continents. Abbreviation MOHO.

Mohs /məʊz/ *noun*. M19.
[ORIGIN Friedrich *Mohs* (1773–1839), German mineralogist.]
Used *attrib.* and in *possess.* to designate a hardness scale in which ten reference minerals, ranging from very soft (talc) to very hard (diamond), are assigned values of one to ten in order of increasing hardness.

mohur /ˈməʊhə/ *noun*. E17.
[ORIGIN Persian & Urdu *muhr* seal, cogn. with Sanskrit *mudrā*.]
A gold coin used in India from the 16th cent. onward. Also called *dinar*.

mohwa *noun* var. of MAHUA.

Moi /ˈməʊɪ/ *noun & adjective*. Now considered *derogatory*. E19.
[ORIGIN French, Vietnamese *Moï*, lit. 'savage'.]
= MONTAGNARD *noun* 2, *adjective* 2.

moi /mwa/ *pers. pronoun*. *joc.* M18.
[ORIGIN French = me.]
Me; I, myself.

moider /ˈmɔɪdə/ *verb*. *dial.* Also **mither** /ˈmʌɪðə/, **moither** /ˈmɔɪðə/. L16.
[ORIGIN Perh. from Irish *modartha* dark, murky, morose, of uncertain origin.]
1 *verb trans.* Confuse, perplex, bewilder; worry, bother, fatigue; pester. Usu. in *pass.* L16.

J. O'FAOLAIN 'I'm a bit moidered,' she apologized. N. BAGNALL He was so moithered by the new language . . that he felt he had to use it.

2 *verb intrans.* Work very hard, toil. *rare*. E19.
3 *verb intrans.* Be delirious; babble; wander about aimlessly, ramble. M19.

D. WINSOR That phrase . . kept moithering round my brain.

moidore /ˈmɔɪdɔː/ *noun*. E18.
[ORIGIN Portuguese *moeda d'ouro* coin of gold.]
A Portuguese gold coin current in England in the first half of the 18th cent., then worth about 27 shillings.

moiety /ˈmɔɪɪti/ *noun*. LME.
[ORIGIN Old French *moité*, (also mod.) *moitié* from Latin *medietas*, *-tat-*, from *medius* MID *adjective*: see -ITY. Cf. MEDIETY.]
1 A half, either of two equal parts. LME.

H. MACMILLAN The opportunity of acquiring half the shares in the Regent Oil Company—the other moiety was held by Caltex. *Southern Star (Eire)* Starting the second moiety of the game, Aidan Twomey moved from centre.

2 Either of two (occas. more) parts (not necessarily equal) into which something is or can be divided. Also (now only with qualifying adjective), a small part, a lesser share of something. L16.

SHAKES. *1 Hen. IV* Methinks my moiety, North from Burton here, In quantity equals not one of yours.

†**3** One's wife or (less usu.) husband. *joc.* M18–E19.
4 ANTHROPOLOGY. Either of two primary social divisions of a tribe (esp. of Australian Aborigines). L19.
5 CHEMISTRY. A group of atoms forming part of a molecule. M20.

L. W. BROWDER Nucleotides of ribosomal RNA are also altered by the addition of methyl groups to the ribose moieties.

moil /mɔɪl/ *noun*[1]. Now *arch. & dial.* E17.
[ORIGIN from the verb.]
1 Toil, drudgery. Freq. in ***toil and moil***. E17.
2 Mud, mire. E19.
3 Turmoil, confusion; trouble, vexation. M19.

†**moil** *noun*[2]. M17–E19.
[ORIGIN Perh. alt. of MULE *noun*[1] (in sense 'hybrid').]
(Cider produced from) a variety of apple.

moil /mɔɪl/ *noun*[3]. *dial.* M19.
[ORIGIN from Irish *maol* or Welsh *moel* lit. 'bald'. Cf. earlier MOILED, MOILEY, MULL *noun*[3].]
A hornless cow or bull.

moil /mɔɪl/ *verb*. LME.
[ORIGIN Old French *moillier* wet, moisten, paddle in mud (mod. *mouiller*) from Proto-Romance, from Latin *mollis* soft.]
1 *verb trans.* Wet, moisten; soil, bedaub. Now *arch. & dial.* LME. ▸†**b** *fig.* Defile. *rare.* L16–M17.
2 *verb intrans.* Toil, work hard, drudge. Freq. in ***toil and moil***. M16.
3 *verb trans.* Weary, fatigue; harass, worry. Chiefly *refl.* & in *pass.* Now *rare* or *obsolete*. M16.
4 *verb intrans. & trans.* Burrow (in). Long *obsolete* exc. *dial.* M16.
5 *verb intrans.* Move around in agitation or confusion; swirl, mill about. M20.

moiled /mɔɪld/ *adjective*. *dial.* M19.
[ORIGIN formed as MOIL *noun*[3] + -ED[2].]
Of cattle: hornless.

moiley /ˈmɔɪli/ *noun*. *Scot. & Irish.* E19.
[ORIGIN formed as MOIL *noun*[3] + -Y[6]. Cf. earlier MULEY *noun & adjective*[1].]
= MOIL *noun*[3].

Moine /mɔɪn/ *noun*. L19.
[ORIGIN *the Moine* (Gaelic *A' Mhòine*), an area near Loch Eriboll in NW Scotland.]
GEOLOGY. ***the Moine(s)***, a highly folded series of metamorphic rocks in NW Scotland and western Ireland, believed to have been deposited in Precambrian times and metamorphosed later. Also ***Moine series***.
■ **Moinian** *adjective & noun* (of, pertaining to, or designating) this series M20.

moire /mwɑː/ *noun*. M17.
[ORIGIN French, later form of *mouaire* MOHAIR.]
A watered fabric (orig. mohair, now usu. silk). Also ***moire antique***.

moiré /ˈmwɑːreɪ/ *adjective & noun*. E19.
[ORIGIN French, pa. pple of *moirer* give a watered appearance to, formed as MOIRE.]
▸**A** *adjective*. **1** Of silk: watered. Also, (of metal etc.) having a clouded appearance like watered silk. E19.
2 Designating or pertaining to a pattern of light and dark fringes observed when a pattern of lines, dots, etc., is visually superimposed on another similar pattern, or on an identical one slightly out of alignment with the first. M20.
▸**B** *noun*. **1** A variegated or clouded appearance like that of watered silk, esp. as an ornamental finish applied to metal; a moiré pattern or effect. E19.
2 = MOIRE. M19.

moirette /mwɑːˈrɛt/ *noun*. L19.
[ORIGIN from MOIRE + -ETTE.]
A textile fabric made to imitate moire.

moissanite /ˈmɔɪsənʌɪt, ˈmwas-/ *noun*. E20.
[ORIGIN from H. *Moissan* (1852–1907), French chemist + -ITE[1].]
MINERALOGY. A green (sometimes black or bluish) silicon carbide, which crystallizes in the hexagonal system, is a rare constituent of meteoric iron, and is made artificially as carborundum.

moist /mɔɪst/ *adjective & noun*. LME.
[ORIGIN Old French *moiste* (mod. *moite*), perh. from Proto-Romance from Latin *mucidus* mouldy, alt. by assoc. with *musteus* new, fresh, from *mustum* MUST *noun*[1].]
▸**A** *adjective*. **1** Slightly wet; containing moisture; damp, humid. LME. ▸**b** Of the eyes: wet with tears, ready to shed tears. Formerly also, rheumy (as a sign of old age). LME. ▸**c** *hist.* Designating a quality associated with wetness and regarded in medieval and later times as one of four qualities inherent in all things; having a preponderance of this quality. Cf. ***cold***, ***dry***, ***hot***. LME. ▸**d** Of a season, climate, etc.: rainy, having some or considerable rainfall. L15.

F. NORRIS It had rained copiously, and the soil, still moist, disengaged a pungent aroma. T. KENEALLY He sucked a pebble to keep his mouth moist. I. MURDOCH A full-lipped mouth all moist with . . lipstick and tears. **b** SHAKES. *2 Hen. IV* Have you not a moist eye . . And will you yet call yourself young? A. MASSIE Her eyes grew moist . . with regret for the past. **d** DRYDEN Invoke the Pow'rs who rule the Sky, For a moist Summer.

†**2** Juicy, succulent; fresh, new. LME–E17.
†**3** Bringing rain or moisture; containing water or other liquid. LME–E18.
†**4** Liquid; watery. LME–E17.
5 Associated or connected with liquid; *poet.* accompanied by tears; MEDICINE accompanied by a discharge of phlegm, pus, etc. M16.
– SPECIAL COLLOCATIONS: ***moist gangrene***: see GANGRENE *noun* 1. ***moist scall***: see SCALL *noun*. **moist sugar** (now *rare*) unrefined or partially refined sugar.
▸†**B** *noun*. Moisture; moist quality, moistness. LME–M18.
■ **moistful** *adjective* (*rare*) moist LME. **moistify** *verb trans.* (*rare*) moisten L18. **moistish** *adjective* E17. **moistless** *adjective* (*rare*) free from moisture, dry L16. **moistly** *adverb* †(*a*) drunkenly; (*b*) in a moist manner: L16. **moistness** *noun* (*a*) the quality or state of being moist; †(*b*) moisture: LME.

moist /mɔɪst/ *verb*. ME.
[ORIGIN from (the same root as) the adjective.]
†**1** *verb intrans.* Grow moist. ME–L15.
2 *verb trans.* Moisten. *obsolete* exc. *dial.* LME. ▸†**b** *fig.* Soften (the heart etc.). LME–L16.
3 *verb intrans.* Drizzle. *US rare.* E20.

moisten /ˈmɔɪs(ə)n/ *verb*. M16.
[ORIGIN from MOIST *adjective* + -EN[5].]
†**1** *verb trans.* Nourish or refresh. Also, soften or weaken (the heart). M16–M17.
2 *verb trans.* Make moist; wet superficially or moderately. M16. ▸**b** *spec.* Wet (the lips, throat, etc.) with drink. (Foll. by *with*.) E17.

E. BOWEN The pianist moistened the tips of her fingers to flatten her hair. A. CARTER A little fountain of fresh water that moistened the shingle. **b** SIR W. SCOTT You have been moistening your own throat.

b ***moisten one's clay***: see CLAY *noun* 3.
3 *verb intrans.* Become moist. M19.

G. SWIFT He held Sophie . . and I saw . . his eyes moisten.

■ **moistener** *noun* E17.

moisture /ˈmɔɪstʃə/ *noun*. LME.
[ORIGIN Old French *moistour* (mod. *moiteur*), from *moiste* MOIST *adjective*, with suffix-substitution: see -URE.]
†**1** Moistness; the quality or state of being moist or damp. LME–L18.
2 Water or other liquid diffused in a small quantity as vapour, through a solid, or condensed on a surface. Also, tears moistening the eyes. LME. ▸**b** The liquid part or constituent of a body; the humour or moist property inherent in plants and animals (cf. MOIST *adjective* 1c). Also ***radical moisture***. *obsolete* exc. *hist.* LME.

C. MCCULLOUGH The last drop of moisture had long since evaporated. JAYNE PHILLIPS October, a clean moisture in the air.

†**3** Liquid; drink. LME–M18.
– COMB.: **moisture content** the proportional amount of moisture in any substance; **moisture cream** a cosmetic cream to keep the skin moist; **moisture meter** an instrument for indicating moisture content, esp. by measuring electrical resistivity.
■ **moistureless** *adjective* M16.

moisturize /ˈmɔɪstʃərʌɪz/ *verb trans.* Also **-ise**. M20.
[ORIGIN from MOISTURE + -IZE.]
Make moist; *esp.* (of a cosmetic) make (the skin) less dry. Freq. as ***moisturizing*** *verbal noun & ppl adjective*.
■ **moisturizer** *noun* a cosmetic preparation to keep the skin moist M20.

moisty /ˈmɔɪsti/ *adjective*. LME.
[ORIGIN from MOIST *adjective* + -Y[1]. Cf. MUSTY *adjective*[2].]
Moist, damp. Now chiefly (in collocation with ***misty***) with ref. to weather or climate.

C. M. YONGE It is not doing the place justice to study it on a misty, moisty morning.

moit /mɔɪt/ *noun*. *dial.*, *Austral.*, & *NZ.* M19.
[ORIGIN Alt. of MOTE *noun*[1].]
A particle of wood, stick, etc., caught in the wool of a sheep.

moither *verb* var. of MOIDER.

mojarra /məʊˈharə/ *noun*. Also **moh-**. M17.
[ORIGIN Amer. Spanish.]
Any of various fishes, now *spec.* a small silvery percoid fish of the family Gerreidae, found in neotropical coastal waters.

Mojave *noun & adjective* var. of MOHAVE.

mojito /mə(ʊ)ˈhiːtəʊ/ M20. *noun*.
[ORIGIN Cuban Spanish, from MOJO *noun*[3] + dim. suffix *-ito*.]
A cocktail originating in Cuba and consisting of white rum, lime or lemon juice, sugar, mint, ice, and carbonated or soda water.

mojo /ˈməʊdʒəʊ/ *noun*[1]. *colloq.* (chiefly *US*). Pl. **-os**. E20.
[ORIGIN Prob. of African origin: cf. Gullah *moco* witchcraft, magic, Fulfulde *moco'o* medicine man.]
1 Magic, voodoo; a charm or amulet. E20.

JULIA PHILLIPS Didn't wanna put a mojo on it; didn't wanna tempt the evil eye.

2 Power, force, or influence of any kind (often with sexual connotations). M20.

G. DONALDSON Sharon King is . . working her mojo on the sophomores and freshmen.

mojo /ˈməʊdʒəʊ/ *noun*[2]. *US slang.* M20.
[ORIGIN Uncertain; perh. a spec. sense of MOJO *noun*[1]]
A narcotic drug, *esp.* morphine.

mojo /ˈməʊdʒəʊ, ˈməʊhəʊ/ *noun*[3]. *US.* L20.
[ORIGIN Prob. from Spanish *mojo* wet from *mojar* make wet.]
A sauce or marinade of Cuban origin, containing garlic, olive oil, sour oranges and (freq.) other citrus fruits.

moke /məʊk/ *noun*[1]. *slang & dial.* M19.
[ORIGIN Probably from a personal name.]
1 A donkey. M19. ▸**b** A horse, *esp.* a very poor one. *Austral. & NZ.* M19.
2 A stupid person, a dolt. M19.
3 A black person. *US derog. & offensive.* M19.

Moke /məʊk/ *noun*[2]. M20.
[ORIGIN A use of MOKE *noun*[1] (= donkey); *Mini* from the design of car (see MINI *noun* 1).]
(Proprietary name for) a small, open-sided car used off-road and for leisure purposes. Also ***Mini-Moke***.

moki /ˈməʊki/ *noun*[1]. *NZ.* M19.
[ORIGIN Maori.]
Either of two edible percoid marine fishes, the grey and white *Latridopsis ciliaris* (family Latridae), and (in full ***red moki***) the fish *Cheilodactylus spectabilis* (family Cheilodactylidae), which is reddish-brown with dark brown bars.

moki /ˈməʊki/ *noun*[2]. Also **mokihi**. M19.
[ORIGIN Maori.]
NZ HISTORY. A Maori raft made of bulrushes.

moki-moki *noun* see MOKO-MOKO.

Moko /ˈməʊkəʊ/ *noun*[1]. Pl. **-os**, (in sense 1, also) same. Also (earlier) †**Moca**. L18.
[ORIGIN Yoruba.]
1 A Yoruba-speaking member of a people of southern Nigeria. L18.
2 (**m-**.) ▸**a** A variety of banana grown in Trinidad. E20. ▸**b** A bacterial disease affecting the banana and other plantains. L20.
– COMB.: **moko disease** = sense 2b above; **moko fig** = sense 2a above.

moko /ˈməʊkəʊ/ *noun*[2]. Pl. same, **-os**. M19.
[ORIGIN Maori.]
The system or a pattern of tattooing the face practised by Maori.

moko-moko /məʊkəʊˈməʊkəʊ/ *noun*. *NZ.* Pl. same, **-os**. In sense 1 also **moki-moki** /məʊkɪˈməʊki/ & other vars. L19.
[ORIGIN Maori.]
1 = KORIMAKO. Now *rare.* L19.
2 A lizard of the genus *Lygosoma*. L19.

mokopuna /ˈmɒkɒpʊnə/ *noun*. *NZ.* Pl. same, **-s**. E19.
[ORIGIN Maori.]
In Maori culture: a grandchild; a descendant.

moksha /ˈmɒkʃə/ *noun*. L18.
[ORIGIN Sanskrit *mokṣa*, from *muc* set free, release.]
HINDUISM & JAINISM. The final release of the soul from a cycle of incarnations; the bliss so attained. Also called ***mukti***.

mol *noun* see MOLE *noun*[5].

mola /ˈməʊlə/ *noun*[1]. LME.
[ORIGIN Latin.]
1 MEDICINE. = MOLE *noun*[4]. Now *rare*. LME.
2 A large fish of the family Molidae, *esp.* the sunfish, *Mola mola*. L17.
3 ENTOMOLOGY. = MOLAR *noun* 2. E19.

mola /ˈməʊlə/ *noun*[2]. M20.
[ORIGIN Kuna.]
A square of brightly coloured appliquéd cloth worn as a blouse by Kuna Indian women of the San Blas Islands, Panama.

molal /ˈməʊl(ə)l/ *adjective*. E20.
[ORIGIN from MOLE *noun*[5] + -AL[1].]
PHYSICAL CHEMISTRY. **1** = MOLAR *adjective*[3] 1. E20.
2 Of a solution: containing one mole, or a specified number of moles, of solute per kilogram of solution. Of a concentration: expressed in terms of these quantities. Cf. MOLAR *adjective*[3] 2. E20.
■ **moˈlality** *noun* the molal concentration of a solution E20.

M

Molale /məʊˈlɑːli/ *noun*. **M19.**
[**ORIGIN** Clackamas Chinook *mulálíš* or Tualatin and Santiam Kalapuya *mule*.]
▸ **A** *noun*. Pl. same, **-s**. A member of a Penutian people of Oregon; the language of this people. **M19.**
▸ **B** *attrib.* or as *adjective*. Of or pertaining to the Molale or their language. **M19.**

†**molan** *noun* see **MULLEN** *noun*[1].

molar /ˈməʊlə/ *noun & adjective*[1]. As noun orig. only in Latin pl. form †**molares**. **ME.**
[**ORIGIN** Latin *molaris* adjective = of a mill, noun = grindstone, molar tooth, from *mola* mill: see **-AR**[1].]
▸ **A** *noun*. **1** A grinding tooth at the back of a mammal's mouth; a true molar (see below). **ME.**
false molar a premolar, a molar tooth which has replaced a deciduous tooth. **true molar** a molar tooth which is not preceded by a deciduous tooth.
2 *ENTOMOLOGY.* A molar process. Cf. **MOLA** *noun*[1] 3. **L19.**
▸ **B** *adjective*. **1** Of a tooth: serving to grind; *spec.* designating any of the back teeth of mammals. **E17.** ▸**b** Of or pertaining to a molar tooth. **M19.**
2 *MEDICINE.* Of the nature of a mola or false conception. *rare.* **E19.**
3 *ENTOMOLOGY.* Designating or pertaining to any of the thick internal processes with a grinding surface found on and near the base of the mandibles of many insects. **L19.**
– **NOTE**: As noun not recorded in anglicized form *molar* before 19.

molar /ˈməʊlə/ *adjective*[2]. **M19.**
[**ORIGIN** from Latin *moles* mass + **-AR**[1].]
1 Of or pertaining to mass; acting on or by means of large masses or units. Freq. contrasted with ***molecular***. **M19.**
2 *PSYCHOLOGY.* Of or pertaining to behaviour as a whole, or an integrated set of responses serving a common goal. Cf. **MOLECULAR** *adjective* 4. **E20.**

molar /ˈməʊlə/ *adjective*[3]. **E20.**
[**ORIGIN** from **MOLE** *noun*[5] + **-AR**[1].]
PHYSICAL CHEMISTRY. **1** Of or pertaining to one mole of a substance; = **MOLAL** *adjective* 1. **E20.**
2 Of a solution: containing one mole, or a specified number of moles, of solute per litre of solution. Of a concentration: expressed in terms of these quantities. Cf. **MOLAL** *adjective* 2. **E20.**
▪ **moˈlarity** *noun* the molar concentration of a solution **M20.**

†**molares** *noun pl.* see **MOLAR** *noun & adjective*[1].

M

molariform /məʊˈlarɪfɔːm/ *adjective*. **M19.**
[**ORIGIN** mod. Latin *molariformis*, formed as **MOLAR** *noun & adjective*[1]: see **-FORM**.]
Chiefly *ZOOLOGY.* Having the form of or resembling a molar tooth.

molarization /məʊlərʌɪˈzeɪʃ(ə)n/ *noun*. Also **-isation**. **E20.**
[**ORIGIN** from **MOLAR** *noun & adjective*[1] + **-IZATION**.]
ZOOLOGY. The assumption, during the course of evolution, of the characteristics of a molar tooth by a premolar or other tooth.
▪ **ˈmolarized** *adjective* showing the consequences of molarization **L20.**

†**molary** *adjective*. **L17–L19.**
[**ORIGIN** French *molaire* **MOLAR** *adjective*[1]: see **-ARY**[2].]
Adapted for grinding or pulverizing food; = **MOLAR** *adjective*[1] 1.

†**molass** *noun*. *Scot.* **M16–M19.**
[**ORIGIN** formed as **MOLASSES**.]
A liquor distilled from molasses.

molasse /məˈlas/ *noun*. **L18.**
[**ORIGIN** French formed as **MOLASSES**.]
GEOLOGY. A thickly bedded sedimentary deposit consisting of soft ungraded sandstones, marls, conglomerates, etc. Orig. *spec.* (**M-**) such a deposit of Miocene to Oligocene age in the region between the Alps and the Jura.

molasses /məˈlasɪz/ *noun*. Also (earlier) †**mel-** & other vars. See also earlier **MOLASS**. **L16.**
[**ORIGIN** Portuguese *melaço* from late Latin *mellaceum* must, use as noun of neut. sing. of *mellaceus* of the nature of honey, from Latin *mel*, *mell-* honey.]
Uncrystallized syrup drained from raw sugar in refining; *N. Amer.* golden syrup.

fig.: *New York Times* The mournful molasses of his prose.

▪ **molassed** *adjective* containing much molasses **M20.** **molassied** /məˈlasɪd/ *adjective* (*rare*) **M19.**

molcajete /mɒlkaˈxete, mɒlkəˈheɪteɪ/ *noun*. **E20.**
[**ORIGIN** Mexican Spanish, from Nahuatl *mo:lcaxitl*.]
A mortar for grinding spices and small seeds in.

mold *nouns, verbs* see **MOULD** *nouns, verbs*.

Moldavian /mɒlˈdeɪvɪən/ *noun & adjective*. **E17.**
[**ORIGIN** from *Moldavia* (see below) + **-AN**.]
▸ **A** *noun*. **1** A native or inhabitant of Moldavia (Moldova) in eastern Europe, one of the two principalities from which Romania was formed and later a constituent republic of the USSR, now the independent state of Moldova. **E17.**
2 The Romanian language as spoken and written in Moldavia. **M19.**
▸ **B** *adjective*. Of or pertaining to Moldavia or its inhabitants. **E17.**

moldavite /ˈmɒldəvʌɪt/ *noun*. **L19.**
[**ORIGIN** German *Moldawit*, from *Moldan* the Vltava River in Bohemia: see **-ITE**[1].]
GEOLOGY. Orig., the material (resembling obsidian) of tektites. Now, a tektite from the strewn field in Bohemia and Moravia.

molded *adjectives*, **molder** *noun, verb*, **molding** *nouns* see **MOULDED** *adjectives* etc.

Moldovan /mɒlˈdəʊv(ə)n/ *noun & adjective*. **M19.**
[**ORIGIN** from *Moldova* (see below) + **-AN**.]
▸ **A** *noun*. Orig. = **MOLDAVIAN** *noun* 1. Now *spec.* a native or inhabitant of the republic of Moldova (Moldavia). **M19.**
▸ **B** *adjective*. Of or pertaining to Moldova (Moldavia) or its inhabitants. **L20.**

Moldo-Wallachian /ˌmɒldəʊwəˈleɪkɪən/ *adjective*. **M19.**
[**ORIGIN** from **MOLDAVIAN** + **-O-** + **WALLACHIAN**.]
Of or pertaining to both Moldavia and Wallachia, principalities of Romania united in 1859.

moldy *adjective*[1], *adjective*[2] see **MOULDY** *adjective*[1], *adjective*[2].

mole /məʊl/ *noun*[1].
[**ORIGIN** Old English *māl* corresp. to Middle Low German *mēl*, Old High German *meil*, *meila*, from Germanic, whence also Old English *mǣlan*, Old High German *meilen* to stain.]
†**1** *gen.* A discoloured spot, esp. on cloth, linen, etc. **OE–L19.**
2 A spot or blemish on the human skin; *spec.* a small, often slightly raised patch made dark by an abnormally high concentration of melanin. **LME.**
†**3** *fig.* A blemish, a fault; a distinguishing or identifying mark. **M17–M18.**

mole /məʊl/ *noun*[2] *& adjective*. **ME.**
[**ORIGIN** Prob. from Middle Dutch *mol*, *moll(e)*, Middle & mod. Low German *mol*, *mul*.]
▸ **A** *noun*. **1** Any of various small burrowing mammals (insectivores) of the family Talpidae; *esp.* the Eurasian *Talpa europaea*, with grey velvety fur, very small eyes, and very short strong forelimbs adapted for digging. Also (with specifying word), any of various other animals considered to resemble this. Formerly used as a type of blindness (erron. attributed to the mole in classical and later times). **ME.**
duck-mole: see **DUCK** *noun*[1]. **golden mole** any of various burrowing insectivores of the African family Chrysochloridae. **marsupial mole** a small burrowing Australian marsupial, *Notoryctes typhlops*, with pale yellow fur and no functional eyes. ***star-nosed mole***: see **STAR** *noun*[1] *& adjective*.
2 *fig.* **a** A person who works in darkness. **E17.** ▸†**b** A person with defective (physical or mental) vision. Only in 17. ▸**c** A secret agent who gradually achieves a position deep within the security defences of a country; a trusted person within an organization etc. who betrays confidential information. *colloq.* **L20.**
3 a The borer of a mole plough. **E19.** ▸**b** A remotely operated or automatic machine capable of tunnelling or crawling. **M20.**
4 In *pl.* Moleskin trousers. **L19.**
5 The grey colour of moleskin. **E20.**
– **COMB.**: **mole-cast** a molehill; **mole-catcher** (*a*) a person whose business it is to catch moles; †(*b*) a detested or contemptible person; **mole-coloured** *adjective* = sense B. below; ***mole-cricket***: see **CRICKET** *noun*[1]; **mole drain** a drain made by a mole plough; **mole-drain** *verb trans.* drain (land) using a mole plough; **mole plough** a plough in which a pointed iron shoe attached to an upright support is drawn along beneath the surface, making a hollow (drainage) channel resembling a mole's burrow; **mole rat** any of various subterranean rodents of the African family Bathyergidae and certain other Old World subfamilies; **mole snake** a non-venomous colubrid snake, *Pseudaspis cana*, native to southern and eastern Africa, which feeds on rats and mice.
▸ **B** *adjective*. Of the grey colour of moleskin. **E20.**

mole /məʊl/ *noun*[3]. **LME.**
[**ORIGIN** Sense 1 from Latin *moles* mass; senses 2, 3 from French *môle* from Latin.]
†**1** A great mass, a large piece; bulk, mass. **LME–E18.**
2 A massive structure, esp. of stone, serving as a pier, breakwater, or causeway; the water area contained within such a structure; a man-made harbour, a port. **M16.**
†**3** *ANTIQUITIES.* A Roman form of mausoleum. **M17–M19.**
– **COMB.**: **mole-head** the outward or seaward end of a mole.

mole /məʊl/ *noun*[4]. **LME.**
[**ORIGIN** Latin **MOLA** *noun*[1].]
MEDICINE. An abnormal mass of tissue in the uterus; a false conception.
HYDATIDIFORM ***mole***.

mole /məʊl/ *noun*[5]. Also **mol**. **E20.**
[**ORIGIN** German *Mol*, from *Molekul* molecule.]
PHYSICAL CHEMISTRY. That amount of a given substance or species having a mass in grams numerically the same as its molecular or atomic weight, equivalent (in the International System of Units) to the quantity of specified molecules, ions, electrons, etc., that in number equals the number of atoms in 0.012 kg of the carbon isotope of mass 12.
– **COMB.**: **mole fraction** the ratio of the number of moles of a component in a solution to the total number of moles of all components present.

mole /ˈmoli, ˈməʊli/ *noun*[6]. **M20.**
[**ORIGIN** Mexican Spanish from Nahuatl *mo:lli* sauce, stew.]
A highly spiced Mexican sauce made chiefly from chilli and chocolate, served with meat.

mole /məʊl/ *verb trans.* **L18.**
[**ORIGIN** from **MOLE** *noun*[2].]
1 Free (ground) from molehills or moles. Chiefly as ***moling*** *verbal noun*. **L18.**
2 Burrow or form holes in, as a mole does; bring *out* by burrowing or delving (chiefly *fig.*). **M19.**

W. M. **RAINE** Tait would mole out quite enough evidence against him.

▪ **moling** *verbal noun* the action of the verb; *esp.* the making of mole drains: **L18.**

†**molebat** *noun*. **L16–L19.**
[**ORIGIN** French *molebout*, prob. from dial. *mole* from Latin **MOLA** *noun*[1]; *-bout* rel. to **BUTT** *noun*[1].]
The sunfish, *Mola mola*.

molecula /məˈlɛkjʊlə/ *noun*. *hist.* Pl. **-lae**. **M17.**
[**ORIGIN** mod. Latin: see **MOLECULE**.]
1 A molecule. **M17.**
†**2** A small mass. **E18–E19.**

molecular /məˈlɛkjʊlə/ *adjective*. **L18.**
[**ORIGIN** from **MOLECULE** + **-AR**[1].]
1 Of or pertaining to a molecule or molecules; consisting of molecules; acting or inherent in the molecules of a substance. **L18.** ▸**b** Designating the branch of a science that deals with phenomena at the molecular level. **L19.**
2 *BIOLOGY.* Consisting, or believed to consist, of submicroscopic particles (cf. **MOLECULE** 3); finely granular. Now only in ***molecular layer*** below. **E19.**
3 *PHILOSOPHY.* Of a proposition, sentence, etc.: consisting of or analysable into simpler propositions, sentences, etc., connected by one or more conjunctions. **L19.**
4 Of or pertaining to a small part or detail of a subject, system, etc., rather than to the whole; small-scale; *esp.* (*PSYCHOLOGY*) concerned with or pertaining to an elementary unit of behaviour such as a physiological response (cf. **MOLAR** *adjective*[2] 2). **E20.**
– **SPECIAL COLLOCATIONS**: **molecular biology** the branch of biology that deals with the structure and function of macromolecules essential to life (as nucleic acids, proteins, etc.). **molecular electronics** (*a*) (now *hist.*) = **MICRO-ELECTRONICS**; (*b*) a branch of electronics in which individual molecules perform the same function as micro-electronic devices such as diodes. **molecular gastronomy** the application of scientific principles to food preparation. **molecular heat** the heat capacity of one gram-molecule of a substance. **molecular layer** *ANATOMY* (*a*) either of the two plexiform layers of the retina; (*b*) the outermost layer of the cortex of the cerebellum and cerebrum, containing a mass of nerve fibres with many synapses but relatively few cells. **molecular sieve** a crystalline substance, esp. a zeolite, with pores of molecular dimensions which allow the entry of molecules smaller than a certain size. **molecular weight** = ***relative molecular mass*** s.v. **RELATIVE** *adjective*. ***relative molecular mass***: see **RELATIVE** *adjective*.
▪ **molecuˈlarity** *noun* (*a*) molecular quality; molecular agencies generally; (*b*) *CHEMISTRY* the number of reacting molecules involved in a single step of a chemical reaction: **M19.** **molecularly** *adverb* in a molecular manner; as regards molecules; on a molecular scale: **M19.**

molecule /ˈmɒlɪkjuːl/ *noun*. **L18.**
[**ORIGIN** French *molécule* from mod. Latin *molecula* dim. of Latin *moles* **MOLE** *noun*[3]: see **-CULE**. Cf. earlier **MOLECULA**.]
1 Any of the extremely minute particles of which material substances are thought to consist. Now *spec.* (*CHEMISTRY*), the smallest fundamental unit of a chemical compound that can take part in the chemical reactions characteristic of that compound; a number of atoms chemically joined together. **L18.**
TSCHERMAK'S MOLECULE.
2 *gen.* A very small particle. **L18.**
†**3** *BIOLOGY.* A minute but functional particle of tissue that is invisible or barely visible under a microscope. **E–M19.**

molehill /ˈməʊlhɪl/ *noun*. **LME.**
[**ORIGIN** from **MOLE** *noun*[2] + **HILL** *noun*.]
A small mound of earth thrown up by a mole in burrowing near the surface of the ground.
make a mountain (out) of a molehill attribute great importance to something, esp. a difficulty or grievance, which is really insignificant.
▪ **molehilly** *adjective* **E19.**

molendinar /mɒlənˈdiːnə/ *adjective*. *rare. joc.* **E19.**
[**ORIGIN** medieval Latin *molendinarius*, from *molendinum* mill: see **-AR**[1].]
Of or pertaining to a mill or miller.
– **NOTE**: Chiefly in the writings of Sir Walter Scott.
▪ **molendinary** /məˈlɛndɪn(ə)ri/ *adjective & noun* (belonging to) a mill **E19.**

Moler /ˈməʊlə/ *noun*. Also **m-**. **E20.**
[**ORIGIN** Danish, from dial. *mo* loose chalky soil (= Norwegian, Swedish *mo* sandy heath) + *ler* loam, clay (also Norwegian, Swedish).]
(Proprietary name for) a kind of diatomaceous earth used as a building material.

moleskin /ˈməʊlskɪn/ *noun & adjective*. M17.
[ORIGIN from MOLE *noun*[2] + SKIN *noun*.]
▸ **A** *noun*. **1** The skin of the mole used as fur. Also, another skin sheared so as to resemble this. M17.
2 A strong soft fine-piled cotton fustian the surface of which is shaved before dyeing. E19. ▸**b** In *pl*. Outer garments, esp. trousers, made of this. M19.
▸ **B** *adjective*. Made of moleskin. M19.

molest /məˈlɛst/ *noun*. Long *arch*. ME.
[ORIGIN Old French *moleste* use as noun of Latin *molestus*: see MOLEST *verb*.]
Trouble, hardship; molestation, injury.
■ **molestful** *adjective* troublesome, annoying, painful L16.

molest /məˈlɛst/ *verb trans*. LME.
[ORIGIN Old French *molester* or Latin *molestare*, from *molestus* troublesome, perh. rel. to *moles* MOLE *noun*[3].]
1 Cause trouble to; vex, annoy, inconvenience. Now *rare*. LME. ▸**b** Of disease: afflict, affect. M16–E19.
ADDISON The Colds of Winter, and the Heats of Summer, are equally incapable of molesting you.
2 Interfere or meddle with (a person or (formerly) a thing) harmfully or with hostile intent. LME. ▸**b** *spec*. Sexually assault or abuse (a person, esp. a woman or child). L19.
E. CALDWELL A person was more likely to be mugged or .. otherwise molested in downtown Zephyrfield. **b** A. SILLITOE She would carry a bag of pepper to throw in the face of any man who might try to molest her.
■ **molester** *noun* M16. **molestive** *adjective* tending to cause annoyance; intentionally troublesome or interfering: E20.

molestation /mɒlɛˈsteɪʃ(ə)n, məʊ-/ *noun*. LME.
[ORIGIN Old French & mod. French from medieval Latin *molestatio(n-)*, from Latin *molestat-* pa. ppl stem of *molestare*: see MOLEST *verb*, -ATION.]
1 The action of molesting someone or (now *rare*) something; the condition of being molested; intentional annoyance, harassment. Formerly also, vexation, distress. LME. ▸**b** SCOTS LAW (now *hist*.). The harassing of a person in his or her possession or occupation of lands. LME. ▸**c** Sexual assault or abuse, esp. of a woman or child. M20.
2 An instance of molesting or being molested; a cause of annoyance. Now *rare*. LME.

moletronics /mɒlɪˈtrɒnɪks/ *noun*. M20.
[ORIGIN Shortened from *molecular electronics*.]
= *MOLECULAR electronics*.

moley /ˈməʊli/ *noun*. *slang*. M20.
[ORIGIN Unknown.]
A potato containing embedded razor blades, used as a weapon.

molimen /mə(ʊ)ˈlʌɪmən/ *noun*. Now *rare* or *obsolete*. Pl. **molimina** /mə(ʊ)ˈlɪmɪnə/. M19.
[ORIGIN Latin *molimen*, *-min-* effort, from *moliri* make an effort.]
MEDICINE. An effort by which the system endeavours to perform a natural function, esp. menstruation.

moliminous /mə(ʊ)ˈlɪmɪnəs/ *adjective*. *arch*. M17.
[ORIGIN formed as MOLIMEN + -OUS.]
†**1** Involving great effort or endeavour; laborious. M17–E18.
2 Massive, cumbrous; weighty, momentous. M17.

molinary /ˈməʊlɪn(ə)ri/ *adjective*. *rare*. L18.
[ORIGIN from late Latin *molina* mill + -ARY[1].]
Of or pertaining to the grinding of corn.

molindone /ˈmɒlɪndəʊn/ *noun*. M20.
[ORIGIN from MO(RPHO)L(INE + IND(OLE + -ONE.]
PHARMACOLOGY. An indole derivative, $C_{16}H_{24}N_2O_2$, used in the treatment of schizophrenia and other psychoses.

moline /məˈlʌɪn/ *adjective*. M16.
[ORIGIN Prob. from Anglo-Norman, from *molin* (mod. French *moulin*) mill.]
HERALDRY. Of or resembling the broadened and curved extremities of a mill rind. Chiefly in ***cross moline***, a cross having the end of each limb broadened and curved back in this way.

molinete /moliˈnete, məʊlɪˈneɪti/ *noun*. M20.
[ORIGIN Spanish, lit. '(toy) windmill, little mill'.]
BULLFIGHTING. A kind of decorative pass in which the matador turns away in the direction opposite to that of the bull's charge.

Molinism /ˈmɒlɪnɪz(ə)m/ *noun*[1]. *rare*. M17.
[ORIGIN from Luis de *Molina* (1535–1600), Spanish Jesuit + -ISM.]
THEOLOGY. The doctrine that the efficacy of grace depends simply on the will which freely accepts.
■ **Molinist** *noun*[1] & *adjective*[1] (**a**) *noun* a believer in the doctrine of Molinism; (**b**) *adjective* of or pertaining to Molinism or Molinists: M17.

Molinism /ˈmɒlɪnɪz(ə)m/ *noun*[2]. *rare*. E18.
[ORIGIN from Miguel de *Molinos* (c 1640–96), Spanish priest + -ISM.]
THEOLOGY. Quietism.
■ **Molinist** *noun*[2] & *adjective*[2] (**a**) *noun* a quietist; (**b**) *adjective* of or pertaining to quietism or quietists: M19.

molinology /mɒlɪˈnɒlədʒi/ *noun*. M20.
[ORIGIN from late Latin *molina* mill + -OLOGY.]
The branch of knowledge that deals with mills and milling.
■ **molinoˈlogical** *adjective* L20. **molinologist** *noun* M20.

moll /mɒl/ *noun & verb*. E17.
[ORIGIN Pet form of female forename *Mary*. Cf. MOLLY *noun*[1].]
▸ **A** *noun*. A girl, a woman; *esp*. a prostitute; a female pickpocket or thief; a criminal's female accomplice; the girlfriend of a gangster or criminal. E17.
T. MIDDLETON None of these common Molls neither, but discontented and unfortunate gentlewomen. A. T. ELLIS A cigarette held between her teeth so that she looked like a gangster's moll.
– COMB.: **moll-buzzer** *slang* a pickpocket or thief whose victims are mainly women; **moll-heron** *dial*. a heron; **mollrowing** /-raʊɪŋ/ *slang* (**a**) going out with (disreputable) women; (**b**) (a) caterwauling; **moll-shop** *slang* a brothel; **moll-washer** *dial*. the pied wagtail.
▸ **B** *verb trans*. *slang*.
†**1** ***moll it up with***, go out with (a woman). Only in E19.
2 As ***molled*** *ppl adjective*. Accompanied by or going out with a woman. Also foll. by *up*. M19.

mollescent /mɒˈlɛs(ə)nt/ *adjective*. *rare*. E19.
[ORIGIN Latin *mollescent-* pres. ppl stem of *mollescere* become soft, from *mollis* soft: see -ESCENT.]
Tending to become soft.
■ **mollescence** *noun* E19.

molleton /ˈmɒlɪtɒn/ *noun*. L18.
[ORIGIN French, from *mollet* dim. of *mol* soft.]
Swanskin (flannel).

†**molliable** *adjective*. L17–M18.
[ORIGIN from Latin *mollire* soften + -ABLE.]
Able to be softened.

mollie *noun*[1], *noun*[2], *noun*[3] vars. of MOLLY *noun*[1], *noun*[2], *noun*[3].

mollient /ˈmɒlɪənt/ *noun & adjective*. *rare*. E17.
[ORIGIN Latin *mollient-* pres. ppl stem of *mollire* soften, from *mollis* soft: see -ENT.]
▸ †**A** *noun*. MEDICINE. A softening application, an emollient. Only in E17.
▸ **B** *adjective*. Softening. E18.

†**mollifaction** *noun*. *rare*. L16–E19.
[ORIGIN from MOLLIFY: see -FACTION.]
= MOLLIFICATION.

mollification /ˌmɒlɪfɪˈkeɪʃ(ə)n/ *noun*. LME.
[ORIGIN Latin *mollificatio(n-)*, from *mollificat-* pa. ppl stem of *mollificare*: see MOLLIFY, -ATION.]
The action of mollifying someone or (now *rare*) something; an instance of this; (a) reduction in severity; (an) appeasement.
■ ˈ**mollificative** *adjective & noun* (now *rare*) (**a**) *adjective* that causes mollification or softening; †(**b**) *noun* a medicine that softens: LME.

mollify /ˈmɒlɪfʌɪ/ *verb*. LME.
[ORIGIN French *mollifier* or Latin *mollificare*, from *mollis* soft: see -FY.]
1 *verb trans*. Make soft or supple; make tender. Now *rare*. LME.
2 *verb trans*. Soften in temper or disposition; allay the anger or indignation of; calm, pacify, appease. Freq. in *pass*. LME. ▸†**b** *verb intrans*. Become softened in temper or disposition; relax one's severity, become less angry, relent. E16–E19.
G. SANTAYANA 'Always nagging,' muttered Mrs. Darnley, secretly mollified by feeling her son's arm round her waist. A. GUINNESS The Colonel looked crosser, so I added, 'Sir', which mollified him slightly.
†**3** *verb trans*. Enervate, enfeeble. L15–L16.
4 *verb trans*. Reduce in violence or intensity; reduce in harshness, severity, or rigour; express more favourably. Now *rare*. L15.
DRYDEN Now mince the Sin, And mollifie Damnation with a Phrase. R. TRAVERS Had he mollified his hard nature and softened his savage sentiments.
■ **mollifiable** *adjective* E17. **mollifier** *noun* L16. **mollifyingly** *adverb* in a mollifying manner E20.

mollisol /ˈmɒlɪsɒl/ *noun*. M20.
[ORIGIN from Latin *mollis* soft + -SOL.]
SOIL SCIENCE. A soil of an order comprising temperate grassland soils with a dark, humus-rich surface layer containing high concentrations of calcium and magnesium.

mollities /mɒˈlɪʃiːz/ *noun*. Now *rare*. E17.
[ORIGIN Latin, from *mollis* soft.]
†**1** Effeminacy. Only in E17.
2 MEDICINE. Softening, softness, esp. of the brain or bones. M19.

mollitious /mɒˈlɪʃəs/ *adjective*. *rare*. E17.
[ORIGIN formed as MOLLITIES + -ITIOUS[1].]
Luxurious, sensuous.

mollitude /ˈmɒlɪtjuːd/ *noun*. *rare*. L16.
[ORIGIN Latin *mollitudo*, from *mollis* soft: see -TUDE.]
Softness; effeminacy.

mollock /ˈmɒlək/ *verb intrans*. *slang*. M20.
[ORIGIN Prob. from blend of MOLL, MULLOCK.]
Pursue amorous adventures; copulate. Also, dally, lounge.
S. GIBBONS He's off a-mollocking somewheres in Howling.

mollusc /ˈmɒləsk/ *noun*. Also ***-sk**. L18.
[ORIGIN French *mollusque* from mod. Latin *mollusca* (see below) neut. pl. of Latin *molluscus*, from *mollis* soft.]
ZOOLOGY. Any animal of the phylum Mollusca, members of which (as limpets, snails, cuttlefish, oysters, mussels, etc.) have soft bodies and (usu.) hard shells.
– NOTE: Orig. used more widely (after Linnaeus), including also echinoderms, annelids, and hydroids.
■ **moˈlluscan** *adjective & noun* (**a**) *adjective* of, pertaining to, or characteristic of a mollusc or molluscs; (**b**) *noun* a mollusc: E19.

mollusca *noun pl*. see MOLLUSCUM.

molluscicide /məˈlʌskɪsʌɪd/ *noun*. M20.
[ORIGIN from MOLLUSC + -I- + -CIDE.]
A substance used to kill molluscs.
■ **mollusciˈcidal** *adjective* M20.

molluscoid /məˈlʌskɔɪd/ *adjective*. M19.
[ORIGIN Sense 1 from MOLLUSC; sense 2 from MOLLUSCUM: see -OID.]
1 ZOOLOGY. Resembling a mollusc; like that of a mollusc. M19.
2 MEDICINE. = MOLLUSCOUS 2. *rare*. L19.

molluscous /məˈlʌskəs/ *adjective*. E19.
[ORIGIN formed as MOLLUSCOID + -OUS.]
1 Of or pertaining to molluscs; of the nature of a mollusc. E19. ▸**b** *fig*. Like a mollusc; flabby, invertebrate. L19.
2 MEDICINE. Of, pertaining to, or of the nature of molluscum. M19.

molluscum /məˈlʌskəm/ *noun*. Pl. **-sca** /-skə/. E19.
[ORIGIN mod. Latin, neut. of *molluscus*: see MOLLUSC.]
MEDICINE. **1** Any of various skin disorders characterized by soft rounded swellings or nodules; *esp*. molluscum contagiosum (see below). E19.
molluscum contagiosum /kɒnteɪdʒɪˈəʊsəm/ [Latin = contagious] a viral disorder characterized by groups of small smooth painless pinkish nodules with a central depression, that yield a milky fluid when squeezed. **molluscum sebaceum** /sɪˈbeɪʃəm/ [Latin = sebaceous] = KERATOACANTHOMA.
2 A soft nodule characteristic of such a disorder. M19.
– COMB.: **molluscum body** any of the characteristic ovoid bodies, thought to be degenerate epidermal cells, found in the nodules of molluscum contagiosum; a cytoplasmic inclusion in a degenerating epidermal cell.

mollusk *noun* see MOLLUSC.

Mollweide /ˈmɒlvʌɪdə/ *noun*. E20.
[ORIGIN Karl B. *Mollweide* (d. 1825), German mathematician and astronomer.]
Used in *possess*. and *attrib*. to designate a homalographic map projection in which the surface of the globe is represented by an ellipse, with lines of latitude represented by the major axis and straight lines parallel to it (spaced more closely towards the poles), and meridians represented by the minor axis and equally spaced elliptical curves.

molly /ˈmɒli/ *noun*[1]. Also **mollie**, (in senses 1, 2) **M-**. E18.
[ORIGIN Pet form of female forename *Mary*. Cf. MOLL.]
1 A young woman or girl. Also, a prostitute. *slang & dial*. E18.
2 (A name for) an effeminate or homosexual man. Also ***Miss Molly***. *slang*. E18.
†**3** A large fruit basket. Only in L19.
– COMB.: **mollycot** *dial*. a man who busies himself with domestic duties supposedly the concern of a woman; **molly cottontail** *US* a cottontail.

molly /ˈmɒli/ *noun*[2]. Also **mollie**. M19.
[ORIGIN Perh. abbreviation of MOLLYMAWK.]
NAUTICAL. **1** The fulmar. M19.
2 A meeting of captains held on board one of several whaling ships in company. L19.

molly /ˈmɒli/ *noun*[3]. Also **mollie**. M20.
[ORIGIN Abbreviation of *Mollienesia*, former mod. Latin genus name, irreg. from Count F. N. *Mollien* (1758–1850), French statesman: see -IA[1].]
Any of several small live-bearing freshwater fishes of the genus *Poecilia*, found from the USA to northern S. America; esp. *P. sphenops*, which has been bred into many colour varieties and is popular as an aquarium fish.

molly /ˈmɒli/ *verb trans*. E18.
[ORIGIN Sense 1 from MOLLY *noun*[1]; sense 2 from MOLLYCODDLE *verb*.]
†**1** Of a man: engage in homosexual anal intercourse with. *slang*. E–M18.
2 Mollycoddle. E20.

mollycoddle /ˈmɒlɪkɒd(ə)l/ *verb & noun*. M19.
[ORIGIN from MOLLY *noun*[1] + CODDLE *verb*[2] & *noun*.]
▸ **A** *verb trans*. Coddle, pamper. M19.
R. K. NARAYAN That boy grew up fearlessly .. at an age when other boys were being mollycoddled.
▸ **B** *noun*. A person (usu. male) who is mollycoddled; an effeminate man or boy, a milksop. M19.

M

G. B. SHAW You are a mollycoddle. If you were a real man you would . . delight in beating him.

■ **mollycoddler** *noun* M19.

molly-dooker /ˈmɒlɪduːkə/ *noun. Austral. slang.* M20.
[ORIGIN from MOLLY *noun*[1] or MAULEY + DUKE *noun* + -ER[1].]
A left-handed person.

mollyhawk /ˈmɒlɪhɔːk/ *noun.* L19.
[ORIGIN Alt.]
= MOLLYMAWK.

Molly Maguire /ˌmɒlɪ məˈɡwʌɪə/ *noun.* M19.
[ORIGIN A typical Irish female name: members of the first society disguised themselves as women.]
hist. **1** A member of a secret society formed in Ireland in 1843 for the purpose of resisting eviction for the non-payment of rent. M19.
2 A member of a secret society formed by Pennsylvania miners to resist the mine-owners, suppressed in 1876. M19.

mollymawk /ˈmɒlɪmɔːk/ *noun.* Also **-mauk**, **mallemuck** /ˈmalɪmʌk/, & other vars. L17.
[ORIGIN Dutch *mallemok*, from *mal* foolish + *mok* gull.]
A fulmar, petrel, or similar bird; *spec.* any of the smaller albatrosses of the genus *Diomedea*.

moloch /ˈməʊlɒk/ *noun.* In sense 1 usu. **M-**. E17.
[ORIGIN Late Latin from Greek *Molokh* from Hebrew *mōleḵ*, a Canaanite idol to whom children were sacrificed as burnt offerings (*Leviticus* 18:21), held to be alt. of *meleḵ* king, by substitution of the vowels of *bōšeṯ* shame.]
1 An object to which horrible sacrifices are made. E17.
2 A slow-moving spiny Australian lizard, *Moloch horridus*, of grotesque appearance. Also called ***mountain devil***, ***spiny lizard***, ***thorny devil***. M19.
3 = ***dusky titi*** s.v. DUSKY 1. L19.
– COMB.: **moloch gibbon** = *SILVERY* ***gibbon***.

molossi *noun* pl. of MOLOSSUS.

Molossian /məˈlɒsɪən/ *noun & adjective. hist.* M16.
[ORIGIN from Latin *Molossia* (see below) = Greek *Molossia*, *Molossus*: see -AN.]
▸**A** *noun.* **1** A native or inhabitant of Molossia, a district of Epirus, Greece. M16.
2 A kind of mastiff. L19.
▸**B** *adjective.* Of or pertaining to Molossia; *esp.* designating a kind of mastiff. E17.

molossid /məˈlɒsɪd/ *noun & adjective.* M20.
[ORIGIN mod. Latin *Molossidae* (see below), formed as MOLOSSUS: see -ID[3].]
ZOOLOGY. ▸**A** *noun.* A bat of the family Molossidae, the members of which are heavily built with a tail extending well beyond the tail membrane. Cf. ***free-tailed bat*** s.v. FREE *adjective* etc., ***mastiff bat*** s.v. MASTIFF *noun.* M20.
▸**B** *adjective.* Of, pertaining to, or designating this family. M20.
■ Also †**molossine** *noun & adjective* M–L19.

molossus /məˈlɒsəs/ *noun.* Pl. **-ssi** /-sʌɪ/. L16.
[ORIGIN Latin = Greek *Molossos*: see MOLOSSIAN.]
1 *PROSODY.* A metrical foot consisting of three long syllables. L16.
2 *hist.* More fully ***molossus dog***. A Molossian mastiff. E17.

Molotov /ˈmɒlətɒf/ *noun.* M20.
[ORIGIN Vyacheslav Mikhailovich *Molotov* (1890–1986), Soviet Minister for Foreign Affairs 1939–49.]
1 In full ***Molotov cocktail***. A makeshift incendiary grenade, consisting of a bottle or other breakable container filled with flammable liquid, and a means of ignition. M20.
2 ***Molotov bread basket***, (in the Second World War) a container carrying high explosive and scattering incendiary bombs. M20.

molt *noun, verb* see MOULT *noun, verb*.

molten /ˈməʊlt(ə)n/ *adjective.* ME.
[ORIGIN Strong pa. pple of MELT *verb*.]
†**1** (Of metal etc.) that has been melted and again solidified; (of an object) made of cast metal. ME–E18.
†**2** Dissolved in a liquid; *loosely* partially liquefied. Only in ME.
3 Liquefied by heat; in a state of fusion. Chiefly (connoting a higher temperature than ***melted***) of metal, rock, etc. LME. ▸**b** *fig.* Fiery, passionate; liquid. E19.

N. CALDER A yellow-hot fountain of molten rock. R. THOMAS Nick carried his away . . as if it was a bowl of molten gold. **b** F. HARRISON The molten passion of Burke.

molten *verb pa. pple*: see MELT *verb*.

molter *noun, verb* see MOULTER *noun, verb*[1].

molto /ˈmɒltəʊ/ *adverb.* L18.
[ORIGIN Italian from Latin *multus* much.]
MUSIC. Very. (Modifying adjectives from Italian.)

†**molton** *noun.* L18–M19.
[ORIGIN French *molleton* MOLLETON.]
= MOLLETON.

Molucca /məˈlʌkə/ *noun.* L17.
[ORIGIN *Molucca* Islands, or *Moluccas*, a group of islands in SE Asia, now part of Indonesia.]
Used *attrib.* to designate things found in or associated with the Molucca Islands.
Molucca balm a cultivated labiate plant, *Moluccella laevis*, native to the eastern Mediterranean region. **Molucca bean** the nicker nut. **Molucca crab** the horseshoe crab.
■ **Moluccan** *adjective & noun* (**a**) *adjective* of or pertaining to the Molucca Islands, their inhabitants, or any of the Austronesian languages spoken by them; (**b**) *noun* a native or inhabitant of the Molucca Islands: E18. †**Moluccian** *noun* = MOLUCCAN *noun*: only in E17.

moly /ˈməʊli/ *noun*[1]. M16.
[ORIGIN Latin from Greek *mōlu*, perh. rel. to Sanskrit *mūla* root.]
1 *GREEK MYTHOLOGY.* A magical herb having a white flower and a black root, said by Homer to have been given by Hermes to Odysseus as a charm against the sorceries of Circe. M16.
2 Any of various plants that have been supposed to be identical with the moly of Homer; *spec.* a yellow-flowered southern European allium, ***Allium moly***. L16.

moly /ˈmɒli/ *noun*[2]. *colloq.* M20.
[ORIGIN Abbreviation.]
Molybdenum; *esp.* molybdenum disulphide as an engine lubricant.

molybdate /məˈlɪbdeɪt/ *noun.* L18.
[ORIGIN from MOLYBDIC + -ATE[1].]
CHEMISTRY. A salt containing oxyanions of hexavalent molybdenum; *esp.* a salt of the anion MoO_4^{2-}.

molybdena /mɒlɪbˈdiːnə/ *noun. hist.* M17.
[ORIGIN Latin *molybdaena* from Greek *molubdaina* angler's plummet, from *molubdos* lead.]
Orig., an ore or salt of lead. Later, molybdenite; molybdenum.

molybdenite /məˈlɪbdənʌɪt/ *noun.* L18.
[ORIGIN from MOLYBDENA + -ITE[1].]
A sulphide of molybdenum. Now *spec.* in *MINERALOGY*, molybdenum disulphide as a trigonal mineral usu. occurring as tabular bluish-grey crystals.

molybdenum /məˈlɪbdənəm/ *noun.* L18.
[ORIGIN from MOLYBDENA + *-um* after other chemical elements (usu. in -IUM).]
A brittle silvery-white chemical element, atomic no. 42, which is one of the transition metals and is used in steel to give strength and resistance to corrosion (symbol Mo).
– COMB.: **molybdenum blue** a deep-blue colloidal complex oxide or mixture of oxides of molybdenum produced when an acidic solution of a molybdate is reduced.

molybdic /məˈlɪbdɪk/ *adjective.* L18.
[ORIGIN from MOLYBDENA + -IC.]
CHEMISTRY & MINERALOGY. Containing or derived from molybdenum; of molybdenum, esp. when hexavalent (cf. MOLYBDOUS). Chiefly in ***molybdic acid***, a parent acid of molybdates; a hydrated form of molybdenum trioxide (MoO_3) obtained from acid solutions of molybdates.

molybdite /məˈlɪbdʌɪt/ *noun.* M19.
[ORIGIN formed as MOLYBDIC + -ITE[1].]
MINERALOGY. Molybdenum trioxide, crystallizing in the orthorhombic system and usu. occurring as yellow needles or encrustations.

molybdo- /məˈlɪbdəʊ/ *combining form* of (**a**) Greek *molubdos* lead (now *rare*); (**b**) *CHEMISTRY.* MOLYBDENUM: see -O-.
■ **molybdomancy** *noun* (*rare*) divination by observing motions in molten lead L19.

molybdophyllite /mɒˌlɪbdəˈfɪlʌɪt/ *noun.* E20.
[ORIGIN from MOLYBDO- + Greek *phullon* leaf + -ITE[1].]
MINERALOGY. A colourless or pale green hexagonal hydrated silicate of lead and magnesium.

molybdous /məˈlɪbdəs/ *adjective.* Now *rare.* L18.
[ORIGIN from MOLYBDENA + -OUS.]
CHEMISTRY. Of molybdenum in a lower valency. Cf. MOLYBDIC.

molysite /ˈmɒlɪsʌɪt/ *noun.* M19.
[ORIGIN from Greek *molusis* (for *molusma*) stain, from *molunein* to stain: see -ITE[1].]
MINERALOGY. Ferric chloride as a hexagonal mineral, formed as a yellow to red sublimation product near fumaroles and rapidly hydrated by the air.

mom /mɒm/ *noun. colloq.* (chiefly *N. Amer.*). L19.
[ORIGIN Partly var. of MAM, MUM *noun*[3], partly abbreviation of MOMMA.]
Mother; *spec.* a matriarchal American mother.

J. HELLER The hot dog, the Brooklyn Dodgers, Mom's apple pie. That's what everyone's fighting for.

– COMB.: **mom-and-pop** *attrib. adjective* (*US*) designating a small shop, store, etc., of a type often run by a married couple.

mombin /mɒmˈbiːn/ *noun.* M19.
[ORIGIN Amer. Spanish *mombin* from Caribbean name.]
(The fruit of) a W. Indian tree of the genus *Spondias* (family Anacardiaceae), *esp.* (more fully ***yellow mombin***) *S. mombin* and (more fully ***red mombin***) *S. purpurea*. Cf. ***hog plum*** s.v. HOG *noun*.

mome /məʊm/ *noun*[1]. *arch.* M16.
[ORIGIN Unknown.]
A stupid person, a fool.

mome *noun*[2] var. of MOMME.

moment /ˈməʊm(ə)nt/ *noun.* ME.
[ORIGIN Old French & mod. French from Latin *momentum* (i) movement, moving power, (ii) importance, consequence, (iii) moment of time, particle, from *movere* MOVE *verb*: see -MENT.]
1 A very brief portion or period of time; a point in time, an instant. ME. ▸**b** Usu. with *the* or *possess.*: the instant that is appropriate or decisive for something or someone; the fitting moment; the momentary conjunction of circumstances, esp. as affording an opportunity. L18. ▸**c** A (brief) period of time marked by a particular quality of experience. E20.

R. HUGHES All woke at the same moment as if by clockwork. G. VIDAL He returned, a moment later, breathless. L. DUNCAN The moment he heard his own voice . . he felt like an idiot. **b** A. BULLOCK His moment came in 1944. W. TREVOR Until the moment's right for you to take over. J. NAGENDA Lofty and romantic sentiments such as man and moment meeting. R. ELLMANN The moment had come to issue a book of his poems. **c** G. B. SHAW Why do you select my most tragic moments for your most irresistible strokes of humour.

2 a In medieval measurement of time, the tenth part of a point (see POINT *noun*[1] 2e), the fortieth or fiftieth part of an hour. *obsolete* exc. *hist.* LME. ▸**b** A second of time. Now only *Scot.* M17. ▸**c** *GEOLOGY.* A period of geological time corresponding to a stratigraphical zone. M20.
†**3** A small particle, an infinitesimal amount; a detail. LME–M18.
4 Importance, weight. Now only in ***of moment***, ***of great moment***, ***of little moment***, ***of some moment***, etc. E16.

JO GRIMOND A wheel flew off . . but otherwise nothing of moment happened. A. SCHLEE There are so many things of more moment than how I feel.

†**5** A cause or motive of action; a determining influence or consideration. E17–M18.

SHAKES. *Ant. & Cl.* I have seen her die twenty times upon far poorer moment.

6 A definite stage, period, or turning point in a course of events. (Now distinguished from sense 1.) M17.

C. BIGG Three great moments in that fateful process.

7 *PHYSICS* etc. ▸†**a** Momentum. Only in E18. ▸**b** Any of various functions describing torsional effects, generally having the form of the product of a force and a distance; *spec.* the turning effect produced by a force; the magnitude of this, equal to the product of the force and the perpendicular distance from its line of action to the point about which rotation may occur. M19. ▸**c** *STATISTICS.* Each of a series of quantities (***first moment***, ***second moment***, etc.) that express the average or expected value of the first, second, etc., powers of the deviation of each component of a frequency distribution from some given value, usu. the mean or zero. L19.

b J. S. FOSTER Equilibrium . . is obtained when the . . moments of some forces acting on a member are balanced. *Forestry* A turning moment of 1 Nm is produced by a force of 1 kg acting over a length of 1 m.

8 An element of a complex conceptual entity. M19.
– PHRASES & COMB.: ***at this moment in time***: see TIME *noun*. ***dipole moment***, ***first moment***: see sense 7c above. **for a moment** (**a**) *pred.* destined to last for only a moment; (**b**) *adverbial phr.* during a moment. **for the moment** (**a**) so far as the immediate future is concerned; (**b**) temporarily during the brief space referred to. **have one's moments**, **have its moments** be impressive, successful, happy, etc., on occasions. ***in the heat of the moment***: see HEAT *noun*. ***last moment***: see LAST *adjective*. **live for the moment**, **live in the moment** live without concern for the future. ***magnetic moment***: see MAGNETIC *adjective*. **moment-hand** (*obsolete* exc. *Scot.*) the seconds hand of a watch etc. **moment of inertia** (of a body about an axis) the sum of the products of the mass of each particle of the body and the square of the distance of each particle from the axis. **moment of truth** [Spanish *el momento de la verdad*] (**a**) the time of the final sword thrust in a bullfight; (**b**) a crisis, a turning point; a testing situation. **moment-to-moment** *adjective* immediately and continually experienced, required, considered, etc. **not for a moment**, **not for one moment** emphatically not. **of the moment** of importance at the time in question. **one moment** *ellipt.* wait, listen, etc., for one moment. **on the moment** (now *rare*) immediately, instantly. ***on the spur of the moment***: see SPUR *noun*[1]. ***psychological moment***: see PSYCHOLOGICAL *adjective*. ***quadrupole moment***: see QUADRUPOLE *adjective*. ***sacrament of the present moment***: see SACRAMENT *noun*. ***second moment***: see sense 7c above. **the moment** *ellipt.* at the moment when, as soon as ever. **this moment** (**a**) without a moment's delay, immediately; (**b**) just now, hardly a moment ago. **to the moment** with exact punctuality; for the exact time required. ***weak moment***: see WEAK *adjective*.

momenta *noun* pl. of MOMENTUM.

momental /məˈmɛnt(ə)l/ *adjective.* E17.
[ORIGIN Late Latin *momentalis*, from Latin *momentum*: see MOMENT, -AL[1].]
†**1** Having only the duration of a moment; momentary. E–M17.

†**2** Important; of moment. *rare*. Only in E19.
3 *MATH*. Of or pertaining to momentum. *rare*. L19.

momentaneous /məʊm(ə)nˈteɪnɪəs/ *adjective*. LME.
[ORIGIN from late Latin *momentaneus*, from Latin *momentum* MOMENT: see -OUS.]
1 Lasting for only a moment; momentary. LME.
†**2** Occurring in a moment, instantaneous. M17–L18.
†**3** *MATH*. Infinitesimal. Only in E18.
■ **momentaˈneity** *noun* transitory character; momentariness: E20. **momentaneously** *adverb* M18. **momentaneousness** *noun* E18.

†**momentany** *adjective*. LME–E18.
[ORIGIN French *momentané* formed as MOMENTANEOUS: see -Y[5].]
Pertaining to the moment, momentary; transitory; evanescent.

momentarily /ˈməʊm(ə)nt(ə)rɪli, məʊm(ə)nˈtɛrɪli/ *adverb*. M17.
[ORIGIN from MOMENTARY + -LY[2].]
1 For a moment, fleetingly. M17.

New Yorker He seemed momentarily taken aback by her question.

2 At the moment, instantly. Now *rare*. L18.
3 At every moment; moment by moment. *rare*. E19.
4 At any moment, very soon. *N. Amer*. E20.

W. C. WILLIAMS The husband is still living but his death is momentarily expected.

momentary /ˈməʊm(ə)nt(ə)ri/ *adjective*. LME.
[ORIGIN Latin *momentarius*, from *momentum* MOMENT: see -ARY[1].]
1 Lasting only a moment; of a moment's duration; transitory. LME.

E. WAUGH Hinsley's momentary irritation subsided. A. JUDD Tim's momentary glance did not even show recognition.

2 Of a living being: short-lived, ephemeral. *literary*. L16.

R. LLOYD Born like a momentary fly, To flutter, buzz about, and die.

3 Recurring or operative at every moment. Now *rare*. M18.

T. WARTON The due clock swinging slow . . Measuring time's flight with momentary sound.

†**4** Instant, instantaneous. L18–M19.

DISRAELI If anything occurred which required my momentary attention.

†**5** *MATH*. Infinitesimal. E–M19.
■ **momentariness** *noun* E19.

momently /ˈməʊm(ə)ntli/ *adjective*. *rare*. LME.
[ORIGIN from MOMENT + -LY[1].]
1 Enduring for a moment. LME.
2 Occurring at every moment. M17.

momently /ˈməʊm(ə)ntli/ *adverb*. *arch*. or *literary*. L16.
[ORIGIN from MOMENT + -LY[2].]
1 From moment to moment, continually. L16.
2 At any moment. L18.
3 For a single moment, fleetingly, momentarily. E19.

momentous /mə(ʊ)ˈmɛntəs/ *adjective*. M17.
[ORIGIN from MOMENT + -OUS.]
†**1** Having motive force. Only in M17.
2 **a** Of a thing: of moment; of great consequence or importance; important, weighty. M17. ▸**b** Of a person: influential, important. Now *rare*. M17.

a M. MEAD Never before . . has mankind had such momentous choices placed in his hands. M. MEYER A momentous day for Europe, for it marked the outbreak of the Franco-Prussian War.

■ **momentously** *adverb* M18. **momentousness** *noun* L17.

momentum /məˈmɛntəm/ *noun*. Pl. **-ta** /-tə/. OE.
[ORIGIN Latin: see MOMENT.]
†**1** In medieval reckoning: the fortieth part of an hour. Only in OE.
†**2** A turning motion; *PHYSICS* = MOMENT *noun* 7b. *rare*. E17–M19.
3 **a** *PHYSICS*. The quantity of motion of a moving body, equal to the product of the mass and the velocity of the body. L17. ▸**b** The effect of inertia in the continuance of motion; impetus gained by movement; *fig*. strength or continuity derived from an initial effort. L18.

b J. TYNDALL His momentum rolled him over and over down the incline. R. HAYMAN Tiredness vanished as the narrative gathered momentum. E. PAWEL Teenage friendships tend to develop their own momentum.

a angular momentum: see ANGULAR 2.
†**4** *MATH*. An infinitesimal increment. Only in M18.
†**5** Force of movement. M18–E19.
6 = MOMENT *noun* 8. *rare*. E19.
– COMB.: **momentum space** *PHYSICS* a three-dimensional space in which each particle of a physical system is represented by a point whose three Cartesian coordinates are numerically equal to the components of its momentum in the directions of the three coordinate axes.

Momi *noun* pl. of MOMUS.

momism /ˈmɒmɪz(ə)m/ *noun*. Orig. *US*. Also **M-**. M20.
[ORIGIN from MOM + -ISM.]
Excessive attachment to or domination by one's mother.

momma /ˈmɒmə/ *noun*. E19.
[ORIGIN Alt. of MAMMA *noun*[2]. Cf. MOM, MOMMY.]
1 In the southern US, esp. before the abolition of slavery, a black woman having the care of white children. Cf. MAMMY *noun*[1] 2. E19.
2 Mother (= MAMMA *noun*[2] 1). Also = MAMMA *noun*[2] 2. Chiefly *US*. L19.

momme /mɒm, ˈmɒmeɪ/ *noun*. Also **mome**. Pl. **-s**, same. E18.
[ORIGIN Japanese *monme*.]
A Japanese unit of weight equal to 3.75 grams (about ⅛ ounce).

mommet, **mommetry** *nouns* see MAUMET, MAUMETRY.

mommy /ˈmɒmi/ *noun*. *colloq*. (chiefly *US*). M19.
[ORIGIN Alt. of MAMMY *noun*[1]. Cf. MOM, MUMMY *noun*[2].]
Mother.
– COMB.: **mommy track** an interrupted or delayed career path followed by some women (by choice or out of necessity) as a result of raising a family.

mompe /ˈmɒmpi, ˈmɒmpeɪ/ *noun pl*. Also **mompei**. E20.
[ORIGIN Japanese *monpe*.]
Baggy working trousers worn in Japan esp. by women.

momser *noun* var. of MAMZER.

Momus /ˈməʊməs/ *noun*. *literary*. Pl. **Momuses**, **Momi** /ˈməʊmʌɪ/. M16.
[ORIGIN Latin = Greek *Mōmos* the god of ridicule in Greek mythol.]
A fault-finder, a carping critic.

momzer *noun* var. of MAMZER.

Mon /məːn/ *noun*[1] & *adjective*. L18.
[ORIGIN Mon.]
▸ **A** *noun*. Pl. **-s**, same. A member of an Indo-Chinese people now inhabiting eastern Myanmar (Burma) and western Thailand but having their ancient capital at Pegu in the south of Burma; the Austro-Asiatic language of this people. Also called ***Talaing***. Cf. MON-KHMER, PEGUAN. L18.
▸ **B** *attrib*. or as *adjective*. Of or pertaining to the Mons or their language. E19.

mon /mɒn/ *noun*[2]. Pl. same. L19.
[ORIGIN Japanese.]
A Japanese family crest or badge, often used in decorative design.

mon /mʌn/ *noun*[3]. *colloq*. Also **mun**. L19.
[ORIGIN Abbreviation.]
Money.

mon- *prefix* see MONO-.

Mon. *abbreviation*.
1 Monday.
2 Monmouthshire (a former county in Wales).

mona /ˈməʊnə/ *noun*. L18.
[ORIGIN Spanish, Portuguese *mona*, *-o*, Italian *monna*: see MONKEY *noun*.]
A W. African guenon, *Cercopithecus mona*. Also ***mona guenon***, ***monkey***.

monachal /ˈmɒnək(ə)l/ *adjective*. Also **-cal**. L16.
[ORIGIN Old French & mod. French *monacal* or ecclesiastical Latin *monachalis*, from Latin *monachus* MONK *noun*[1]: see -AL[1].]
Monastic; monkish.

monachise *verb* var. of MONACHIZE.

monachism /ˈmɒnəkɪz(ə)m/ *noun*. L16.
[ORIGIN from Latin *monachus* MONK *noun*[1] + -ISM.]
The mode or rule of life of a monk or nun; the monastic system or principle; monasticism.

monachize /ˈmɒnəkʌɪz/ *verb*. *rare*. Also **-ise**. L19.
[ORIGIN formed as MONACHISM + -IZE.]
1 *verb intrans*. Live as a monk; become a monk. L19.
2 *verb trans*. Cause to become a monk. L19.
■ **monachiˈzation** *noun* E19.

monacid /mɒˈnasɪd/ *adjective*. M19.
[ORIGIN from MONO- + ACID *adjective*.]
CHEMISTRY. Of a base etc.: (composed of molecules) able to combine with one monovalent acid radical.

monack *noun* var. of MOONACK.

monad /ˈmɒnad, ˈməʊ-/ *noun* & *adjective*. In sense 1 also (earlier) in Latin form **-as** /-as/, pl. **-ades** /-ədiːz/. E17.
[ORIGIN French *monade* or its source late Latin *monas*, *monad-* from Greek, from *monos* alone: see -AD[1].]
▸ **A** *noun*. **1** The number one, unity; a unit. In later use with ref. to ancient Greek philosophy, in which the numbers were regarded as being generated from the unitary one. E17. ▸**b** (**M-**.) Used in ref. to God. M17.

b S. ROSEN Unity, or a non-articulated monad, is unspeakable and unthinkable.

2 *PHILOSOPHY*. Esp. in the philosophy of Leibniz: an indivisible unit of being (as a soul, an atom); an absolutely simple entity. L17.

L. MUMFORD A monad that can think and feel is more important than a galaxy of impassive stars.

3 *BIOLOGY*. A hypothetical simple organism, *esp*. one assumed as the first term in the genealogy of living beings, or regarded as associated with others to form an animal or vegetable body. E19.
†**4** *CHEMISTRY*. A monovalent element or group. Only in M19.
▸ **B** *attrib*. or as *adjective*. That is a monad; monadic. M19.
■ **moˈnadiform** *adjective* (*BIOLOGY*) having the form of a monad or simple organism M19.

monadelphous /mɒnəˈdɛlfəs/ *adjective*. E19.
[ORIGIN from MONO- + Greek *adelphos* brother + -OUS.]
BOTANY. Of stamens: united by the filaments so as to form one group. Of a plant: having the stamens so united.

monades *noun pl*. see MONAD.

monadic /mɒˈnadɪk/ *adjective*. L18.
[ORIGIN Greek *monadikos*, from *monad-*, *monas*: see MONAD, -IC.]
1 Composed of monads or units; pertaining to or of the nature of a monad; existing singly. L18. ▸**b** *PHILOSOPHY*. Designating or pertaining to a predicate that is non-relational and applies to only one subject term; (of a proposition, fact, etc.) containing such a predicate. L19.
2 Of or pertaining to monadism. M19.
■ **monadical** *adjective* = MONADIC *adjective* 1 M17. **monadically** *adverb* L18.

monadism /ˈmɒnədɪz(ə)m, ˈməʊ-/ *noun*. M19.
[ORIGIN from MONAD + -ISM.]
PHILOSOPHY. The theory of the monadic nature of matter; the philosophical doctrine of monads, esp. as formulated by Leibniz.
■ **monadist** *noun* L18. **monaˈdistic** *adjective* L19.

monadnock /məˈnadnɒk/ *noun*. L19.
[ORIGIN *Monadnock*, a hill in New Hampshire, USA.]
PHYSICAL GEOGRAPHY. A hill or mountain of erosion-resistant rock rising above a peneplain.

monadology /mɒnəˈdɒlədʒi, məʊ-/ *noun*. M18.
[ORIGIN French *monadologie*, formed as MONAD: see -OLOGY.]
The philosophical doctrine of monads.
■ **monadoˈlogical** *adjective* L19. **monadoˈlogically** *adverb* M20.

monal /mɒˈnɑːl/ *noun*. Also **monaul** /mɒˈnɔːl/. L18.
[ORIGIN Nepali *monāl*, Hindi *munāl*.]
Any of several crested pheasants of the genus *Lophophorus*; *spec*. (also ***Himalayan monal***) the Impeyan pheasant, *L. impeyanus*. Also ***monal pheasant***.

Mona Lisa /məʊnə ˈliːzə/ *noun* & *adjective*. E20.
[ORIGIN A portrait by Leonardo da Vinci: see GIOCONDA.]
▸ **A** *noun*. A woman having an enigmatic smile or expression such as that of the woman in Leonardo's painting *Mona Lisa*; an enigma. M19.
▸ **B** *attrib*. or as *adjective*. Of a smile etc.: enigmatic, reminiscent of the *Mona Lisa*. E20.

Mona marble /məʊnə ˈmɑːb(ə)l/ *noun phr*. E19.
[ORIGIN from *Mona* Roman name for Anglesey (Welsh *Ynys Môn*), island off the north coast of Wales.]
A serpentine limestone from the metamorphic beds of Anglesey.

mon ami /mɔn ami/ *noun phr*. Also (fem.) ***mon amie***. Pl. ***mes amis*** (fem. ***mes amies***) /mez ami/. LME.
[ORIGIN French.]
As a form of address: my friend.

monamide /ˈmɒnəmʌɪd/ *noun*. M19.
[ORIGIN from MONO- + AMIDE.]
CHEMISTRY. A compound whose molecule contains one amino group.

monamine *noun* var. of MONOAMINE.

monandrous /mɒˈnandrəs/ *adjective*. E19.
[ORIGIN from Greek *monandros* having one husband, formed as MONO- + *andr-* male: see -ANDROUS.]
1 *BOTANY*. Having a single stamen. E19.
2 *ZOOLOGY*. Having one male mate. M19.

monandry /mɒˈnandri/ *noun*. Also (earlier) †**monoandry**. M19.
[ORIGIN from MONOGAMY after *polygamy*, *polyandry*.]
1 The practice or custom of mating with only one male, or of having only one husband at a time. M19.
2 *BOTANY*. The condition of having one stamen. E20.

monarch /ˈmɒnək/ *noun* & *verb*. LME.
[ORIGIN Old French & mod. French *monarque* or late Latin *monarcha* from Greek *monarkhēs*, more freq. *monarkhos*, from *monos* alone: see MONO-, -ARCH.]
▸ **A** *noun*. **1** Orig., a sole and absolute ruler of a state. Later also, any ruler bearing the title of king, queen, emperor, empress, or the equivalent. LME.

SHAKES. *Merch. V*. The quality of mercy . . becomes The throned monarch better than his crown. R. SCRUTON In the figure of the monarch there is . . all the majesty of state.

the Merry Monarch: see MERRY *adjective*.
2 *transf*. & *fig*. A person or thing of great power or pre-eminence in a particular sphere. L16.

W. COWPER I am monarch of all I survey. BYRON Mont Blanc is the monarch of mountains.

3 More fully ***monarch butterfly***. A large migratory orange and black danaid butterfly, *Danaus plexippus*, native to the Americas and known as a vagrant in western Europe. Also called ***milkweed butterfly***. L19.
4 = ***monarch flycatcher*** below. M20.

M

– COMB.: *monarch butterfly*: see sense 3 above; **monarch flycatcher** a flycatcher of the Old World family Monarchidae, *esp.* one of the genus *Monarcha*.

▸ **B** *verb intrans. & trans.* (with *it*). Behave like a monarch, act autocratically. *rare.* E17.

▪ **monarchess** *noun* (now *rare*) a female monarch L16.

monarch /ˈmɒnɑːk/ *adjective.* L19.
[ORIGIN from MONO- + Greek *arkhē* beginning, origin.]
BOTANY. Of the primary xylem of the root: arising from one point of origin. Of a root: having such a xylem.

monarchal /məˈnɑːk(ə)l/ *adjective.* L16.
[ORIGIN Old French, or medieval Latin *monarchalis*, from late Latin *monarcha* MONARCH *noun*: see -AL[1].]
1 Of, pertaining to, or characteristic of a monarch; befitting a monarch. L16.
2 = MONARCHICAL 4. L16.
3 = MONARCHICAL 1. L16.
▪ **monarchally** *adverb* E17.

monarchial /məˈnɑːkɪəl/ *adjective.* M16.
[ORIGIN from MONARCH *noun* or MONARCHY: see -IAL, -AL[1].]
†**1** Having the status of a monarch. M16–M17.
2 Of the nature of a monarchy; ruled by a monarch. E17.
3 Of or befitting a monarch. L18.

Monarchian /məˈnɑːkɪən/ *noun & adjective.* M18.
[ORIGIN Late Latin *monarchiani* pl., from *monarchia*: see MONARCHY, -AN.]
ECCLESIASTICAL HISTORY. ▸ **A** *noun.* A heretic in the 2nd and 3rd cents. who denied the doctrine of the Trinity. Cf. PRAXEAN. M18.
▸ **B** *adjective.* Of or pertaining to the Monarchians or their beliefs. M19.
▪ **Monarchianism** *noun* M19.

monarchic /məˈnɑːkɪk/ *adjective.* E17.
[ORIGIN French *monarchique* or medieval Latin *monarchicus* from Greek *monarkhikos*, from *monarkhos*: see MONARCH *noun*, -IC.]
1 = MONARCHICAL 1. E17.
†**2** = MONARCHICAL 3. E17–E19.
3 = MONARCHAL 1. M17.

monarchical /məˈnɑːkɪk(ə)l/ *adjective.* L16.
[ORIGIN formed as MONARCHIC + -ICAL.]
1 Of the nature of or having the characteristics of a monarchy; (of a state) ruled by a monarch; (of government) vested in a monarch. L16.
2 = MONARCHAL 1. L16.
3 Of or pertaining to monarchy; favouring monarchy as a form of government. E17.
4 Having the status, power, or functions of a monarch. Formerly also, autocratic. E17.
▪ **monarchically** *adverb* L16.

M

monarchise *verb* var. of MONARCHIZE.

monarchism /ˈmɒnəkɪz(ə)m/ *noun.* L18.
[ORIGIN French *monarchisme*, formed as MONARCHY: see -ISM.]
The principles of monarchical government; advocacy of monarchy or the monarchical principle.

monarchist /ˈmɒnəkɪst/ *noun & adjective.* M17.
[ORIGIN from MONARCHY + -IST.]
▸ **A** *noun.* **1** An advocate or supporter of monarchy. M17.
†**2** A person believing in one supreme god, esp. among other gods. *rare.* L17–L19.
▸ **B** *adjective.* Advocating or supporting monarchy; of or pertaining to monarchism or monarchists. M19.

monarchize /ˈmɒnəkʌɪz/ *verb.* Also **-ise**. L16.
[ORIGIN from MONARCH *noun* + -IZE.]
1 *verb intrans.* & †*trans.* with *it*. Perform the office of monarch; rule as a monarch; rule absolutely. L16.
2 *verb trans.* †**a** Make subservient to one monarch; rule over as a monarch. Only in E17. ▸**b** Make a monarchy of. M17.

†**Monarcho** *noun.* L16–M17.
[ORIGIN Italian (= *monarca* monarch), title assumed by an insane Italian who fancied himself emperor of the world.]
(A title for) a person generally ridiculed for absurd pretensions.

monarcho-fascist /məˌnɑːkəʊˈfaʃɪst/ *adjective.* M20.
[ORIGIN from MONARCH(IST + -O- + FASCIST.]
In Communist phraseology: designating or pertaining to a Fascist government with a monarch as titular head of state, esp. that established in Greece after the Second World War.

monarchy /ˈmɒnəki/ *noun.* ME.
[ORIGIN Old French & mod. French *monarchie* from late Latin *monarchia* from Greek *monarkhia* from *monarkhos* MONARCH *noun*: see -Y[3].]
1 A state ruled by a monarch. ME. ▸†**b** The territory of a monarch. *rare.* M16–L17.

> A. BULLOCK He was not concerned whether Greece became a monarchy or a republic.

2 Undivided rule by a single person; absolute power; *fig.* pre-eminence, predominance. LME.

> W. CONGREVE Nobody can dispute Your Lordship's Monarchy in Poetry. J. B. MOZLEY Gregory VII . . claimed the monarchy of the world.

3 Rule by a monarch; a form of government with a monarch at the head. E17.

> C. V. WEDGWOOD The conception of monarchy for which King Charles both lived and died.

– PHRASES: *constitutional monarchy*: see CONSTITUTIONAL *adjective* 4. *Fifth Monarchy*: see FIFTH *adjective*.

monarda /məˈnɑːdə/ *noun.* M18.
[ORIGIN mod. Latin (see below), from Nicolas *Monardes* (1493–1588), Spanish physician and botanist.]
Any of various fragrant N. American labiate plants constituting the genus *Monarda*, which bear heads of showy tubular flowers (also called ***bergamot***, ***wild bergamot***); *spec.* one grown for ornament, *esp.* Oswego tea, *Monarda didyma*.

monas *noun* see MONAD.

monaster /mɒˈnastə/ *noun.* L19.
[ORIGIN from MONO- + ASTER.]
CYTOLOGY. = ASTER *noun* 3.

monasterial /mɒnəˈstɪərɪəl/ *adjective.* Now *rare.* LME.
[ORIGIN Late Latin *monasterialis*, from ecclesiastical Latin *monasterium*: see MONASTERY, -AL[1].]
Belonging to or of the nature of a monastery.

monastery /ˈmɒnəst(ə)ri/ *noun.* LME.
[ORIGIN ecclesiastical Latin *monasterium* from ecclesiastical Greek *monastērion*, from Greek *monazein* live alone, from *monos* alone.]
(A place of residence of) a community living under religious vows; a monastic establishment; *esp.* (the residence of) a community of monks living in seclusion.

monastic /məˈnastɪk/ *adjective & noun.* LME.
[ORIGIN Old French & mod. French *monastique* or late Latin *monasticus* from Greek *monastikos*, from *monazein*: see MONASTERY, -IC.]
▸ **A** *adjective.* †**1** Of or pertaining to a hermit; anchoritic. Only in LME.
2 Of or pertaining to people living in seclusion from the world under religious vows, as monks, nuns, friars, etc.; of or pertaining to a monastery or monasteries. M16. ▸**b** Resembling or suggestive of monks or their way of life; (of existence) solitary and celibate. M17.

> H. CARPENTER The bedroom is bare and looks a little like a monastic cell. **b** DONNE He sinkes the deepe Where harmlesse fish monastique silence keepe.

3 *BOOKBINDING.* Designating a method of finishing by tooling without gold. L19.
▸ **B** *noun.* A member of a monastic order; a monk. M17.
▪ **monastical** *adjective* †(**a**) = MONASTIC *adjective* 1; (**b**) = MONASTIC *adjective* 2: LME. **monastically** *adverb* E17. **monasticism** /-sɪz(ə)m/ *noun* the monastic system or mode of life L18. **monasticize** /-sʌɪz/ *verb trans.* make monastic in character; convert to monasticism: M19.

Monastral /mɒˈnastr(ə)l/ *noun.* M20.
[ORIGIN Unknown.]
(Proprietary name for) any of various synthetic pigments of high fastness, of which there are two classes: (**a**) blue and green phthalocyanine derivatives; (**b**) red and violet quinacridone derivatives.

monatomic /mɒnəˈtɒmɪk/ *adjective.* M19.
[ORIGIN from MONO- + ATOMIC.]
CHEMISTRY. Containing one atom; consisting of single atoms rather than molecules. Also, monobasic, monovalent.

monaul *noun* var. of MONAL.

monaural /mɒnˈɔːr(ə)l/ *adjective.* L19.
[ORIGIN from MONO- + AURAL *adjective*[1].]
1 Of or pertaining to the use of one ear only. L19.
2 = MONOPHONIC *adjective* 3. M20.
▪ **monaurally** *adverb* M20.

monaxial /mɒnˈaksɪəl/ *adjective.* L19.
[ORIGIN from MONO- + AXIAL.]
Chiefly *BOTANY & ZOOLOGY.* Having only one axis; developing along a single line.

monazite /ˈmɒnəzʌɪt/ *noun.* M19.
[ORIGIN from Greek *monazein* be solitary (on account of its rarity) + -ITE[1].]
MINERALOGY. A commercially important monoclinic phosphate of cerium, lanthanum, other rare earth elements, and thorium, occurring as small brownish crystals, often in detrital sands associated with granites and gneisses.

Monbazillac /mɒnˈbazɪlak, *foreign* mɔ̃bazijak/ *noun.* Also **Mont-** /mɒnt-/. M19.
[ORIGIN French (see below).]
A sweet, white dessert wine, similar to Sauternes, produced at Monbazillac (Dordogne), in SW France.

mon cher /mɔ̃ ʃɛːr/ *noun phr.* L17.
[ORIGIN French.]
As a form of address to a male: my dear, my dear fellow.

monchiquite /mɒnˈtʃiːkwʌɪt/ *noun.* L19.
[ORIGIN from Serra de *Monchique*, a mountain range in southern Portugal + -ITE[1].]
PETROGRAPHY. A lamprophyre containing small phenocrysts of olivine and augite, and usu. also biotite or an amphibole, in a glassy groundmass containing analcime.

Mond /mɒnd/ *noun.* L19.
[ORIGIN Ludwig *Mond* (1839–1909), German-born Brit. chemist.]
CHEMISTRY. Used *attrib.* to designate (the plant used in and the products of) certain processes devised by Mond, *spec.* (**a**) a method of manufacturing producer gas from coal using air and excess steam, with ammonia as a by-product; (**b**) a process for purifying nickel by thermal decomposition of nickel carbonyl obtained from crude nickel oxide by reduction with hydrogen followed by reaction with carbon monoxide.

mondain /mɔ̃dɛ̃/ *noun & adjective.* Also (fem.) ***mondaine*** /mɔ̃dɛn/. M19.
[ORIGIN French: see MUNDANE.]
▸ **A** *noun.* Pl. pronounced same. A worldly or fashionable person. Cf. DEMI-MONDAINE. M19.
▸ **B** *adjective.* Of the fashionable world; worldly. L19.

Monday /ˈmʌndeɪ, -di/ *noun, adverb, & adjective.*
[ORIGIN Old English *mōnandæg* corresp. to Old Frisian *mōne(n)dei*, Middle Low German, Middle Dutch *mān(en)dach* (Dutch *maandag*), Old High German *mānatag* (German *Montag*), Old Norse *mánadagr*, formed as MOON *noun*[1] + DAY *noun*.]
▸ **A** *noun.* The second day of the week, following Sunday. OE.
Black Monday (**a**) Easter Monday; (**b**) *school slang* the first school day after a vacation; (**c**) *STOCK EXCHANGE.* Monday, 19 October 1987, the day of a worldwide collapse of stock markets. †**Bloody Monday** *school slang* the first day of vacation, a day of punishment for offenders. *Collop Monday*: see COLLOP *noun*[1]. *Easter Monday*: see EASTER *noun*. *Hock Monday*: see HOCK-. **Saint Monday** *arch. slang.* Monday spent in idleness as a consequence of drunkenness on the Sunday. *Shrove Monday*: see SHROVE-. *Yellow Monday*: see YELLOW *adjective*.
▸ **B** *adverb.* On Monday. Now chiefly *N. Amer.* ME.
▸ **C** *attrib.* or as *adjective.* Of Monday; characteristic of Monday; taking place on Monday(s). L16.
Monday Club a right-wing Conservative club that originally held its meetings on Mondays. **Monday-clubber** a member of the Monday Club. **Monday-morning** *attrib. adjective* characterized by or suggestive of lethargy or disinclination after a busy or eventful weekend. *Monday morning quarterback*: see QUARTERBACK *noun* 2.
▪ **Mondayish** *adjective* suffering from or marked by indisposition or lethargy resulting from a busy or eventful weekend (orig. *spec.* of clergymen) E19. **Mondayishness** *noun* M19. **Mondays** *adverb* (*colloq.*) on Mondays, each Monday L20.

monde /mɔ̃ːd, mɔːnd/ *noun.* Earlier in BEAU MONDE. M18.
[ORIGIN French = world.]
The world of fashionable or aristocratic people; such people collectively. Also, a person's particular circle or set.
BEAU MONDE. DEMI-MONDE. *grand monde*: see GRAND *adjective*[2]. HAUT MONDE. *tout le monde*: see TOUT *adjective, noun*[5], *& adverb*.

mondial /ˈmɒndɪəl/ *adjective.* L15.
[ORIGIN French, formed as MONDE.]
†**1** Worldly, temporal. Only in L15.
2 Pertaining to, affecting, or involving the whole world; worldwide, universal. E20.

mon Dieu /mɔ̃ djø/ *interjection.* M17.
[ORIGIN French.]
My God! (cf. GOD *noun* 5).

mondo /ˈmɒndəʊ/ *noun*[1]. Pl. **-os**. M20.
[ORIGIN mod. Latin *Mondo* (former genus name), from Japanese *mondō* (now only in *bakumondō*), from *mon* gate + *-dō* comb. form of *-tō* winter.]
More fully ***mondo grass***. Any of various plants constituting the genus *Ophiopogon*, of the lily family, with short stems and mats of long grasslike leaves; esp. *O. japonicus*, native to Japan and Korea, which is grown as a carpeting plant. Also called ***lily-turf***.

mondo /ˈmɒndəʊ/ *noun*[2]. Pl. **-os**. E20.
[ORIGIN Japanese, from *mon* asking + *dō* answering.]
An instructional technique of Zen Buddhism consisting of rapid dialogue of questions and answers between teacher and pupil.

mondo /ˈmɒndəʊ/ *adjective & adverb. slang.* M20.
[ORIGIN from Italian *Mondo Cane* lit. 'world of a dog', title of a film (1961) showing bizarre behaviour, which inspired a series of imitations.]
▸ **A** *adjective.* **1** Often with a pseudo-Italian noun or adjective: used in ref. to an unexpected, bizarre, or anarchic view of the phenomenon concerned. M20.
2 As an intensifier: considerable, much; huge. M20.
▸ **B** *adverb.* Very, extremely. M20.

> J. BIRMINGHAM The best thing about it was the mondo cool badge on the door.

mondongo /mɒnˈdɒŋgəʊ/ *noun.* Pl. **-os**. E17.
[ORIGIN Spanish = tripe, black pudding: cf. MUNDUNGUS.]
A Latin American or W. Indian dish composed of tripe.

Mondrian /ˈmɒndrɪən/ *noun & adjective.* M20.
[ORIGIN Anglicized form of *Mondriaan* (see below).]
(In or resembling) the geometrical abstract style of the Dutch painter Piet Mondriaan (1872–1944); (of) neo-plasticism.

monecious *adjective* see MONOECIOUS.

Monégasque /mɒnɪˈgask, *foreign* mɔnegask (*pl. same*)/ *noun & adjective*. **L19**.
[**ORIGIN** French.]
▸ **A** *noun*. A native or inhabitant of Monaco, an independent principality forming an enclave on the Mediterranean coast of France. **L19**.
▸ **B** *adjective*. Pertaining to or characteristic of Monaco or its inhabitants. **L19**.

Monel /ˈməʊn(ə)l/ *noun*. Also **m-**. **E20**.
[**ORIGIN** Ambrose *Monell* (d. 1921), US businessman.]
In full ***Monel metal***. Any of a group of alloys composed of about 68 per cent nickel and 30 per cent copper with small amounts of other elements, having a high-tensile strength and good corrosion resistance.

monellin /ˈmɒnəlɪn/ *noun*. **L20**.
[**ORIGIN** from *Monell* Chemical Senses Center, Philadelphia + **-IN**[1].]
CHEMISTRY. A sweet-tasting protein isolated from the berries of the tropical African plant *Dioscoreophyllum cumminsii* (family Menispermaceae).

moneme /ˈmɒniːm/ *noun*. **M20**.
[**ORIGIN** French *monème*, formed as **MONO-**: see **-EME**.]
LINGUISTICS. = **MORPHEME**.

monensin /məˈnɛnsɪn/ *noun*. **M20**.
[**ORIGIN** from mod. Latin *cinna)monens(is* (see below) + **-IN**[1].]
VETERINARY MEDICINE. An antibiotic and ionophore produced by the bacterium *Streptomyces cinnamonensis*, used as a feed additive to increase the meat yield of livestock.

monepiscopacy /mɒnɪˈpɪskəpəsi/ *noun*. **L19**.
[**ORIGIN** from **MONO-** + **EPISCOPACY**.]
Government of the Church by bishops who have sole authority within their dioceses, rather than share it with other bishops.
■ **monepiscopal** *adjective* **L19**.

moneron /məˈnɪərɒn/ *noun*. Pl. **Monera** /məˈnɪərə/, **m-**. Formerly also anglicized as †**moner**. **M19**.
[**ORIGIN** from Greek *monērēs* single.]
BIOLOGY. Orig., a member of a group of protozoa (in Haeckel's scheme) composed of organisms of the simplest form. Now (as pl. *Monera*), a kingdom comprising all prokaryotic single-celled organisms (i.e. bacteria and cyanophytes).
■ **moneran** *adjective & noun* **L19**.

monetarism /ˈmʌnɪt(ə)rɪz(ə)m/ *noun*. **M20**.
[**ORIGIN** from **MONETARY** + **-ISM**.]
The doctrine or theory that economic stabilization is achieved by tight control of the money supply; control of the money supply according to this doctrine.

monetarist /ˈmʌnɪt(ə)rɪst/ *adjective & noun*. **E20**.
[**ORIGIN** from **MONETARY** + **-IST**.]
▸ **A** *adjective*. Monetary; *esp.* in accordance with or advocating monetarism. **E20**.
▸ **B** *noun*. An advocate or practitioner of monetarism. **M20**.
■ **monetaˈristic** *adjective* pertaining to or of the nature of monetarism **L20**.

monetary /ˈmʌnɪt(ə)ri/ *adjective*. **M17**.
[**ORIGIN** French *monétaire* or late Latin *monetarius*, from Latin *moneta* **MINT** *noun*[1]: see **-ARY**[1].]
1 Of or pertaining to coinage or currency. **M17**.
monetary unit the standard unit of value of a country's coinage.
2 Of or pertaining to money with reference to its value or purchasing power; pecuniary, financial. **M19**.
■ **moneˈtarian** *adjective* (*rare*) monetary **E18**. **monetarily** *adverb* **M19**. **monetarize** *verb trans*. = **MONETIZE** **M20**.

monetise *verb* var. of **MONETIZE**.

monetite /ˈməʊnɪtʌɪt/ *noun*. **L19**.
[**ORIGIN** from *Moneta* island near Puerto Rico in the Caribbean + **-ITE**[1].]
MINERALOGY. A triclinic hydrogen phosphate of calcium occurring as translucent, pale yellow crystals.

monetize /ˈmʌnɪtʌɪz/ *verb trans*. Also **-ise**. **M19**.
[**ORIGIN** from Latin *moneta* (see **MONEY** *noun*) + **-IZE**.]
Convert into the form of money; put (metal) into circulation as money; assess in terms of money.
■ **monetiˈzation** *noun* **M19**.

money /ˈmʌni/ *noun*. Pl. **moneys**, **monies**. **ME**.
[**ORIGIN** Old French *moneie* (mod. *monnaie* change) from Latin *moneta* mint (in Rome), money, orig. epithet of Juno, in whose temple the mint was housed.]
1 A current medium of exchange in the form of coins and (in mod. use) banknotes; coins and banknotes collectively. **ME**. ▸**b** Any objects or material serving the same purposes as coin. **LME**. ▸**c** One of the four suits in packs of playing cards in Italy, Spain, and Spanish-speaking countries, and in tarot packs. **L16**.

> AV 1 *Kings* 21:2 I will give thee the worth of it in money. J. RULE Ann watched her counting out her money. E. CALDWELL Opening the purse, he . . dropped the money into it.

2 Property, wealth, possessions, resources, etc., viewed as convertible into coin or banknotes or having value expressible in terms of these. **ME**. ▸**b** (With demonstrative or possess. adjective) a sum applied to a particular purpose or in the possession of a particular person. Also, wages, salary; one's pay; remuneration, profit. **ME**.

> J. GROSS He left Oxford forced to make his own way . . without money or influence. R. ELLMANN Wilde . . was again short of money. N. HINTON They cost a fortune . . . He hasn't got that sort of money. *Proverb*: Time is money. **b** SHAKES. *Com. Err.* The money that you owe me for the chain. R. KIPLING Come back when your money's spent. *Bella* I asked her for the money back. H. GARNER Working for Malloy-Harrison . . the money was better than most. J. WINTERSON There was no money in vermin any more.

b ***beer money***, ***conscience money***, ***danger money***, ***dirt money***, ***earnest money***, ***glove money***, ***hush money***, ***pocket money***, ***protection money***, ***spending money***, etc.
3 (With *pl.*) A particular kind of coin, coinage, or currency. **ME**.
4 In *pl.* Sums of money; a sum of money. Now chiefly in legal and quasi-legal parlance. **LME**.

> *Daily Telegraph* The receivers of a company in liquidation were entitled to keep moneys loaned. P. AUSTER The publisher . . paid all fees, monies and royalties.

– **PHRASES**: ***accept wooden money***: see **WOODEN** *adjective*. ***a good run for one's money***, ***a run for one's money***: see **RUN** *noun*. **at the money** = ***for the money*** below. **be everybody's money** (freq. in neg. contexts) (*a*) *arch.* be what everybody prefers or can afford to buy; (*b*) be to everyone's liking. ***big money***: see **BIG** *adjective*. ***black money***: see **BLACK** *adjective*. ***buy money***: see **BUY** *verb*. ***coin money***: see **COIN** *verb*[1]. ***dirty money***: see **DIRTY** *adjective*. ***easy money***: see **EASY** *adjective*. ***even money***: see **EVEN** *adjective*. ***folding money***: see **FOLDING** *ppl adjective*. **for money** in return or exchange for money. **for my money** (*a*) in my opinion; (*b*) — is my choice (or favourite) (***the man for my money***: see **MAN** *noun*.). **for the money** at the price paid. ***front money***: see **FRONT** *noun, adjective, & adverb*. ***funny money***: see **FUNNY** *adjective*. ***hard money***: see **HARD** *adjective*. ***hot money***: see **HOT** *adjective*. **in the money** among the prizewinners; amply or sufficiently supplied with money; rich. ***mad money***: see **MAD** *adjective*. **make money** acquire or earn money; *esp.* make a profit (*out of*). ***make the money fly***: see **FLY** *verb*. **marry into money**, **marry money** marry a wealthy spouse, marry a person with a wealthy family. **money for jam**, **money for old rope** a profitable return for little or no trouble; a very easy job; someone or something easy to profit from. ***money of account***: see **ACCOUNT** *noun*. ***near money***: see **NEAR** *adjective*. ***new money***: see **NEW** *adjective*. ***not for love or money***: see **LOVE** *noun*. ***old money***: see **OLD** *adjective*. ***paper money***: see **PAPER** *noun & adjective*. ***plastic money***: see **PLASTIC** *adjective*. **put one's money on** bet on (a horse etc.); *fig.* favour or depend on, expect the success of. **put one's money where one's mouth is** produce, bet, or pay out money to support one's statements or opinions. ***ready money***: see **READY** *adjective*. ***real money***: see **REAL** *adjective*[2]. ***see the colour of a person's money***: see **COLOUR** *noun*. ***smart money***: see **SMART** *adjective*. ***spend money like water***: see **WATER** *noun*. ***take wooden money***: see **WOODEN** *adjective*. ***throw good money after bad***: see **THROW** *verb*. **throw money at** try to solve (a problem) by increased expenditure alone, without due consideration. ***value for money***: see **VALUE** *noun*. ***white money***: see **WHITE** *adjective*. **your money or your life**: a formula attributed to highwaymen etc. in obtaining money from their victims.
– **COMB.**: **money-back** *adjective* (of a system, agreement, etc.) providing for the customer's money to be refunded if the goods or service provided are not satisfactory; **money bag** a bag for holding money; **moneybags** *colloq.* (freq. *derog.*) a person chiefly remarkable as a possessor or lover of money; a wealthy person; **money belt** a belt with a purse for carrying money; **money-bill** a bill in Parliament for granting supplies; †**money-bound** *adjective* (*colloq.*) detained for lack of money; **money box** a box in which money is kept; *esp.* a closed box into which money is dropped through a slit; **money-broker** a money-dealer; **money centre** a place of pre-eminent importance in the financial affairs of a region or country; **money-changer** a person whose business it is to change money at a fixed or authorized rate; **money-clause** a clause (in a parliamentary bill) for granting supplies; ***money cowrie***: see **COWRIE** 1; **money crop** *US* = ***cash crop*** s.v. **CASH** *noun*[1]; **money-dealer** a person who deals in money in the way of exchange, banking, lending, etc.; **money flower** honesty, *Lunaria annua*; ***money-grubber***: see **GRUBBER** *noun* 3; **money-grubbing** *noun & adjective* (given to or characterized by) the assiduous amassing of money by contemptible methods; **money illusion**: that money has a fixed value in terms of its purchasing power; **money-jobber**, **money-jobbing** a dealer, dealing, in money or coin; **moneylender** a person whose business is lending money at interest; **moneylending** *noun & adjective* (engaged in) the business of lending money at interest; **moneymaker** †(*a*) a person who coins money; †(*b*) a maker of counterfeit coin; (*c*) a person who gains or earns much money; (*d*) a person skilled in or intent on making money; (*d*) a profitable thing, idea, etc., a money-spinner; **moneymaking** *noun & adjective* (*a*) *noun* the acquiring of wealth; the making of profits; (*b*) *adjective* occupied in or intent on making money; profitable, lucrative; **money-man** *colloq.* a financier; a financial expert; **money market** (*a*) the market in short-term finance between banks and other financial institutions (sometimes including the foreign exchange market and the bullion market); these institutions collectively; (*b*) *US* = ***money centre*** above; **money matters** the financial side of things, financial affairs; **money-monger** *derog.* (*arch.*) a moneylender; **money-mongering** *derog.* (*arch.*) moneylending; **money order** an order for payment of a specified sum issued at a bank or post office and payable at another (in British use not bearing the name of a specified payee); **money-power** (*a*) the power to coin money, regulate its use, etc.; (*b*) the power exercised by money or by wealthy people, firms, etc.; ***money scrivener***: see **SCRIVENER** 3; **money shot** a sequence in a pornographic film that shows ejaculation; *fig.* a crucial or pivotal moment; **money spider** a very small spider supposed to bring good luck in financial matters to the person over whom it crawls; *spec.* a spider of the family Linyphiidae; **money-spinner** (*a*) a money spider; (*b*) a person who or (now more usu.) thing which makes a lot of money; something very profitable; **money-spinning** *adjective* very profitable; **money supply** *ECONOMICS* the total amount of money in circulation or in being in a country (as measured by various criteria); **money tree** *US* a source of easily obtained or unlimited money; **money wages** income expressed in terms of monetary value, with no account taken of purchasing power; **moneywort** = ***CREEPING Jenny***; ***Cornish moneywort***, a creeping plant of the figwort family, *Sibthorpia europaea*, with small pink flowers.
■ **moneyless** *adjective* **LME**.

money /ˈmʌni/ *verb trans*. **LME**.
[**ORIGIN** from the noun or (sense 1) French *monnayer*.]
1 Coin, mint. *rare*. **LME**.
2 Supply with money, give money to; (formerly) bribe. Long *rare*. **LME**.
3 Dispose of for money. *rare*. **E17**.
4 Foll. by *out*: state the price of; give the prices of items in (a tender or estimate). *Scot.* **M19**.

moneyed /ˈmʌnɪd/ *adjective*. Also **monied**. **LME**.
[**ORIGIN** from **MONEY** *noun, verb*: see **-ED**[2], **-ED**[1].]
1 Having or possessing (much) money; wealthy. **LME**. ▸†**b** Supplied (*well* etc.) with money. **L15–L17**.
2 Consisting of money, derived from money. **L18**.
3 Of a corporation etc.: having power to deal in money. *US*. **L19**.

moneyer /ˈmʌnɪə/ *noun*. **LME**.
[**ORIGIN** Old French *mon(n)ier*, *-oier* (mod. *monnayeur*) from late Latin *monetarius*, from Latin *moneta* **MONEY** *noun*: see **-ER**[1].]
†**1 a** A money-changer. Only in **LME**. ▸**b** A banker, a financier. **E18–M19**.
2 Chiefly *hist.* A person who coins money; a coiner, a minter. **LME**.

money's-worth /ˈmʌnɪzwəːθ/ *noun*. **L16**.
[**ORIGIN** from **MONEY** *noun* + **-'S**[1] + **WORTH** *noun*[1].]
1 An equivalent for the sum of money paid or to be paid; full value. Now chiefly with possess. pronoun. **L16**.

> D. CECIL Playgoers expected their moneysworth in those days.

2 A thing that is worth money or is recognized as equivalent to money. Cf. earlier **MONEY-WORTH**. *arch.* **E17**.

> H. J. STEPHEN An obligation to pay money or money's worth.

money-worth /ˈmʌnɪwəːθ/ *noun*. **LME**.
[**ORIGIN** from **MONEY** *noun* + **WORTH** *noun*[1].]
1 = **MONEY'S-WORTH** 2. Now *rare* or *obsolete*. **LME**.
2 Worth in money, value when exchanged for money. **E20**.

mong /mʌŋ/ *noun*[1]. Long *obsolete* exc. *dial.* Also **mung**.
[**ORIGIN** Old English *ġemang*, from Germanic base also of **MENG**. Aphet. early in Middle English.]
1 A mingling, a mixture. Formerly also, commerce. Long *rare*. **OE**.
2 A mixture of different kinds of grain or meal; = **MASLIN** *noun*[2] 1. **ME**.
3 A crowd, an assembly. **ME**.
– **COMB.**: **mongcorn** a mixture of kinds of grain, esp. wheat and rye, sown together.

mong /mʌŋ/ *noun*[2]. *Austral. slang*. **E20**.
[**ORIGIN** Abbreviation of **MONGREL** *noun*.]
A dog.

'mong /mʌŋ/ *preposition*. *poet*. **ME**.
[**ORIGIN** Aphet.]
Among.

mongan /ˈmɒŋg(ə)n/ *noun*. **L19**.
[**ORIGIN** Warrgamay (an Australian Aboriginal language of northern Queensland).]
A ring-tailed possum, *Pseudocheirus herbertensis*, inhabiting the rainforest of NE Queensland.

monger /ˈmʌŋgə/ *noun & verb*.
[**ORIGIN** Old English *mangere* (= Old High German, Old Norse *mangari*), from *mangian* (= Old Saxon *mangon*, Old Norse *manga*) deal, trade, from Germanic, from Latin *mango* dealer, trader: see **-ER**[1].]
▸ **A** *noun*. A dealer or trader (in some specified commodity). Exc. in long-established combs. usu. *derog.*, a person who promotes or carries on a petty or disreputable traffic in something specified. Usu. as 2nd elem. of comb. **OE**.

> C. KINGSLEY My only fear is people will fancy me a verbal-inspiration-monger. V. WOOLF He's a priest, a mystery-monger.

cheesemonger, ***fishmonger***, ***ironmonger***, ***newsmonger***, ***scandalmonger***, ***scaremonger***, ***warmonger***, ***whoremonger***, etc.
▸ **B** *verb trans*. Deal or traffic in. Chiefly as ***mongering*** *verbal noun* (usu. as 2nd elem. of comb.) & *ppl adjective*. **L16**.

Mongo /ˈmɒŋgəʊ/ *noun*[1] & *adjective*. **E20**.
[**ORIGIN** Mongo.]
▸ **A** *noun*. Pl. **-os**, same. A member of a people living in the Democratic Republic of Congo (Zaire); the Bantu language of this people. **E20**.
▸ **B** *attrib*. or as *adjective*. Of or pertaining to the Mongos or their language. **M20**.

mongo /ˈmɒŋgəʊ/ *noun*[2]. Pl. **-os**, same. **M20**.
[**ORIGIN** Mongolian *möngö* silver.]
A monetary unit of Mongolia, equal to one-hundredth of a tugrik.

M

Mongol /ˈmɒŋg(ə)l/ *adjective & noun*. In senses A.2, B.2 also **m-**. L17.
[ORIGIN Mongolian, said to be from *mong* brave. Cf. MOGUL.]
▸ **A** *noun*. **1** A member of an Asian people now chiefly inhabiting Mongolia, but formerly extending more widely; a Mongolian. M18. ▸**b** The principal language of Mongolia, Khalkha. M19.
2 A person with Down's syndrome. Now *offensive*. L19.
▸ **B** *adjective*. **1** Of, pertaining to, or characteristic of Mongolia (see MONGOLIAN), its people, or their language; Mongolian. L17.
2 Pertaining to or affected with Down's syndrome. Now *offensive*. L19.
– NOTE: *Mongol* was adopted in L19 to refer to people with Down's syndrome, owing to the similarity of some of the physical symptoms of the disorder with the normal facial characteristics of East Asian people. This use is now unacceptable, and has been replaced in scientific as well as in most general contexts by *Down's syndrome*.

Mongolian /mɒŋˈgəʊlɪən/ *adjective & noun*. In sense A.3 also **m-**. E18.
[ORIGIN from MONGOL + -IAN.]
▸ **A** *adjective*. **1** Of or pertaining to the central Asian territory or modern republic of Mongolia; of or pertaining to the Mongols or their language. E18.
2 = MONGOLOID *adjective* 1. E19.
3 Affected with Down's syndrome. Now *offensive*. M19.
– SPECIAL COLLOCATIONS: **Mongolian eye**: having an epicanthus. **Mongolian fold** = EPICANTHUS. **Mongolian hotpot** a Mongolian dish consisting of thinly sliced meat, vegetables, etc., cooked in simmering stock at the table. **Mongolian pheasant** a pheasant, *Phasianus colchicus*, of a subspecies with a broken white neck ring, native to southern Russia and Mongolia, and introduced with other races into western Europe and elsewhere; also called *Kyrgyz pheasant*. **Mongolian spot** a bluish or brownish spot which is present in the sacral region of most newborn babies in Asia and usu. disappears in infancy.
▸ **B** *noun*. **1** A native or inhabitant of Mongolia; a Mongol. M18.
2 = MONGOLOID *noun* 1. M19.
3 The language of Mongolia, usu. considered a member of the Altaic family (though its affiliations are now in doubt). M19.

Mongolic /mɒŋˈgɒlɪk/ *adjective & noun*. E19.
[ORIGIN from MONGOL + -IC.]
▸**A** *adjective*. **1** Of, pertaining to, or designating a group of Altaic languages including Mongolian, Kalmyk, and Buryat. E19.
2 Mongolian. M19.
▸ **B** *noun*. The Mongolic language group. E19.

mongolism /ˈmɒŋg(ə)lɪz(ə)m/ *noun*. Now *offensive*. Also **M-**. E20.
[ORIGIN from MONGOL + -ISM.]
MEDICINE. Down's syndrome.

Mongolize /ˈmɒŋg(ə)lʌɪz/ *verb trans. rare*. Also **-ise**. M19.
[ORIGIN from MONGOL + -IZE.]
Make Mongolian in character, customs, etc.
■ **Mongoliˈzation** *noun* L19.

Mongoloid /ˈmɒŋg(ə)lɔɪd/ *adjective & noun*. In senses A.2, B.2 also **m-**. M19.
[ORIGIN from MONGOL + -OID.]
▸ **A** *adjective*. **1** Resembling or having some of the characteristic physical features of Mongolians; *spec.* designating or pertaining to the division of humankind including the indigenous peoples of eastern Asia, SE Asia, and the Arctic region of N. America, and characterized by dark eyes with an epicanthic fold, pale ivory to dark skin, straight dark hair, and little facial and bodily hair. M19.
2 Affected with Down's syndrome. Now *offensive*. L19.
▸ **B** *noun*. **1** A person of Mongoloid physical type. M19.
2 A person affected with Down's syndrome. Now *offensive*. M20.
– NOTE: The terms *Mongoloid*, *Negroid*, *Caucasoid*, and *Australoid* were introduced in 19 by anthropologists attempting to classify human racial types, but are now regarded as having little scientific validity and as potentially offensive.

mongoose /ˈmɒŋguːs/ *noun*. Also †**mungoose**. Pl. **-gooses**. L17.
[ORIGIN Marathi *maṅgūs*, *muṅ-* from Telegu *muṅgisi*, Kannada *muṅgisa*.]
1 Any of various long-tailed short-legged carnivorous mammals of the family Viverridae (which also includes the civets and genets), native to southern Asia and Africa, and noted for the ability to kill venomous snakes. L17.
slender mongoose: see SLENDER *adjective*.
2 A nectar-eating lemur, *Lemur mongoz*, of Madagascar and the Comoro Islands. More fully ***mongoose lemur***. M18.

mongrel /ˈmʌŋgr(ə)l/ *noun & adjective*. LME.
[ORIGIN App. from base meaning 'mix' (cf. MENG, MONG *noun*[1]) + -REL.]
▸ **A** *noun*. **1** A dog whose sire and dam are of different breeds. Chiefly & now only, a dog of no definable breed resulting from various crossings. LME. ▸**b** As a term of abuse: a contemptible person, a cur. Now *Austral. & NZ*. L16.

R. CROMPTON It.. stood eager, alert, friendly, a mongrel unashamed.

2 A person of mixed descent; a person whose parents are of different nationalities or (formerly) differing social status. *offensive*. M16.

J. G. EDGAR Men.. of every race, mongrels almost to a man.

3 †**a** A person of mixed or undefined opinions; a person whose political allegiance etc. varies according to expediency. *derog*. M16–E18. ▸**b** A thing of mixed or intermediate character; a cross, a hybrid. *derog*. E17. ▸**c** An animal or plant resulting from the crossing of different types (usually, different breeds or varieties), esp. other than by design. L17.

b CARLYLE Some cart, or dilapidated mongrel between cart and basket.

▸ **B** *adjective*. **1 a** Of or pertaining to mixed descent; having parents or ancestors of different nationalities. *offensive*. M16. ▸**b** Of mixed origin, nature, or character; not referable to any definite species or type; being neither one thing nor the other. *derog*. L16. ▸**c** Of a word, dialect, etc.: made up of elements from different languages. E17.

a SOUTHEY To learn that law from Norman or from Dane, Saxon .. or whatever name Suit best your mongrel race! **b** P. SIDNEY Neither the admiration and commiseration, nor the right sportfulnes, is by their mungrell Tragy-comedie obtained. **c** E. O. M. DEUTSCH The Aramaic.. had become.. a mongrel idiom.

2 Of a dog: that is a mongrel, of no definable breed. L16. ▸**b** Worthless, contemptible. Now chiefly *Austral. & NZ*. L16. ▸**c** Of an animal or plant: produced by the crossing of different varieties etc. (Cf. sense A.3c above.) M17.

b SHAKES. *Lear* A knave, a rascal.. and the son and heir of a mongrel bitch. **c** BOSWELL Their sheep being of a mongrel race.

■ **mongreldom** *noun* = MONGRELISM L19. **mongrelism** *noun* the condition or quality of being mongrel or hybrid L16. **mongreliˈzation** *noun* M19. **mongrelize** *verb trans.* make mongrel in breed, race, composition, or character E17. **mongrelly** *adjective* resembling a mongrel M19.

ˈmongst /mʌŋst/ *preposition. poet.* M16.
[ORIGIN Aphet.]
Amongst.

monial /ˈməʊnɪəl/ *noun*. ME.
[ORIGIN Old French *moinel* (mod. *meneau*), use as noun of *moi(e)nel* adjective = middle, from *moien*: see MEAN *adjective*[2], -AL[1]. Cf. MUNNION.]
ARCHITECTURE. A mullion in a window.

monic /ˈmɒnɪk/ *adjective*. M20.
[ORIGIN from MONO- + -IC.]
MATH. Of a polynomial: having the coefficient of the term of highest degree equal to one.

monicker *noun* var. of MONIKER.

monied *adjective* var. of MONEYED.

monies *noun pl.* see MONEY *noun*.

moniker /ˈmɒnɪkə/ *noun. slang*. Also **monicker**. M19.
[ORIGIN Unknown.]
A name, a nickname.

monilia /məˈnɪlɪə/ *noun*. Pl. same, **-ias**, **-iae** /-ɪiː/. M18.
[ORIGIN mod. Latin (see below), from Latin *monile* necklace (with allus. to the chains of spores): see -IA[1].]
Any fungus now or formerly belonging to the genus *Monilia*, which formerly included certain pathogenic fungi now assigned to *Candida*.
■ **monilial** *adjective* of, pertaining to, or caused by a monilia or monilias M20. **moniliasis** /mɒnɪˈlʌɪəsɪs/ *noun*, pl. **-ases** /-əsiːz/, MEDICINE = CANDIDIASIS E20.

moniliform /məˈnɪlɪfɔːm/ *adjective*. E19.
[ORIGIN French *moniliforme* or mod. Latin *moniliformis*, from Latin *monile* necklace: see -FORM.]
Chiefly ANATOMY & ZOOLOGY etc. Of the form of or resembling a necklace or string of beads.

monimolimnion /mɒnɪməˈlɪmnɪən/ *noun*. Pl. **-mnia** /-mnɪə/. M20.
[ORIGIN from Greek *monimos* stable + *limnion* dim. of *limnē* lake.]
The lower, denser, non-circulating layer of water in a meromictic lake.

monish /ˈmɒnɪʃ/ *verb trans.* Now *rare*. ME.
[ORIGIN Old French *monester* aphet. from *amonester* ADMONISH.]
1 Admonish; ECCLESIASTICAL = MONITION *verb*. ME.
†**2** Exhort to do; give warning of; call to mind. LME–M16.
■ **monishment** *noun* L15.

monism /ˈmɒnɪz(ə)m, ˈməʊ-/ *noun*. M19.
[ORIGIN mod. Latin *monismus*, from Greek *monos* single: see -ISM.]
A theory or system of thought which recognizes a single ultimate principle, being, force, etc., rather than more than one (cf. DUALISM 1, PLURALISM 2); *spec.* (**a**) a theory that denies the duality of matter and mind; (**b**) the doctrine that there is only one supreme being, as opp. to a belief in good and evil as conflicting powers.
neutral monism: see NEUTRAL *adjective*.

monist /ˈmɒnɪst/ *noun*. M19.
[ORIGIN from Greek *monos* single + -IST.]
A person who holds any of the doctrines of monism.
neutral monist: see NEUTRAL *adjective*.

monistic /məˈnɪstɪk/ *adjective*. M19.
[ORIGIN from MONIST + -IC.]
Of, pertaining to, or of the nature of monism; advocating any of the theories of monism.
■ **monistically** *adverb* L19.

monition /məˈnɪʃ(ə)n/ *noun & verb*. LME.
[ORIGIN Old French & mod. French from Latin *monitio(n-)*, from *monit-* pa. ppl stem of *monere* advise, warn: see -ITION.]
▸ **A** *noun*. **1** = ADMONITION. LME.
2 A warning of the presence or imminence of something (now *spec.* of some impending danger). LME.
3 An official or legal notice, *esp.* one calling on a person to do something specified; *spec.* (ECCLESIASTICAL) a formal notice from a bishop or ecclesiastical court admonishing a person not to commit an offence. LME.
▸ **B** *verb trans.* ECCLESIASTICAL. Warn by a monition. L19.

monitor /ˈmɒnɪtə/ *noun*. E16.
[ORIGIN Latin, from *monit-*: see MONITION, -OR.]
†**1** An official letter conveying an admonition. *Scot.* E–M16.
2 A school pupil or (esp. *US*) college student assigned disciplinary or other special duties (formerly in some cases including teaching). M16.

W. S. MAUGHAM I was going to make you a monitor next term.

3 A person who or thing which admonishes someone or gives advice or a warning as to conduct. E17.

C. MORGAN I am happy to-night, for my monitor tells me.. to be happy. C. THUBRON Once authority had sanctioned violence, no monitor inside him had called a halt.

4 a A reminder, a warning. M17. ▸**b** A person who monitors something; *spec.* a person employed to listen to and report on (esp. foreign) radio broadcasts. E20. ▸**c** A television receiver used in a studio to display the picture from a particular camera; a VDU connected directly to the source of a video signal, esp. one from a computer. Also ***monitor screen*** etc. M20. ▸**d** Any instrument or device for monitoring some process or quantity, as for detecting or measuring radioactivity. M20. ▸**e** A loudspeaker used in a studio for listening to what is being recorded; any large or powerful speaker, *esp.* one used on stage by a band. Also more fully ***monitor speaker***. M20. ▸**f** A computer program which monitors the running of other programs or the operation of a system. M20.

a A. JOLLY Such emblematical rites.. are useful helps and monitors to our weak minds. **c** S. BRETT He caught sight of something on one of the monitors. It was a shot from a camera.. focused nowhere in particular.

†**5** = BACKBOARD *noun* 2(a). L18–M19.
6 More fully ***monitor lizard***. Any of various large tropical Old World lizards constituting the genus *Varanus* and the family Varanidae (so called from being supposed to warn of the vicinity of crocodiles). E19.
Komodo monitor, *Nile monitor*, etc.
7 *hist.* [from the name of an ironclad used in the US Civil War.] A warship having a low freeboard and one or more heavy guns, suitable esp. for shore bombardment. M19.
8 A clerestory in the roof of a railway carriage, building, etc. Freq. *attrib. US*. L19.
9 A jointed nozzle used in hydraulic mining, which may be turned in any direction. L19.
■ **monitorship** *noun* M17. **monitress** *noun* a female monitor M18. **monitrix** *noun* (*rare*) = MONITRESS E17.

monitor /ˈmɒnɪtə/ *verb trans.* E19.
[ORIGIN from the noun.]
†**1** Guide as a monitor. *rare*. Only in E19.
2 a Check or regulate the technical quality of (a radio transmission, television signal, etc.). E20. ▸**b** Listen to and report on (radio broadcasts, telephone conversations, etc.). M20. ▸**c** *gen.* Observe, supervise, keep under review; measure or test at intervals, esp. for the purpose of regulation or control. M20.

b *Times Review of Industry* The output from the analyser can be monitored with headphones. D. HASTON Three weeks in Kleine Scheidegg, monitoring weather forecasts twice a day. **c** *Scientific American* The radius of the mirror was monitored frequently. H. KISSINGER A cease-fire and standstill to be monitored by UN representatives.

monitorial /mɒnɪˈtɔːrɪəl/ *adjective*. E18.
[ORIGIN French, or from Latin *monitorius* MONITORY + -AL[1].]
1 = MONITORY *adjective*. E18.
2 Of, pertaining to, or performed by a monitor or monitors. E19.

monitory /ˈmɒnɪt(ə)ri/ *noun & adjective*. LME.
[ORIGIN Latin *monitorius*, formed as MONITOR *noun*: see -ORY[2].]
▸ **A** *noun*. **1** A letter containing an admonition or warning, *esp.* one issued by a bishop or pope. LME.
†**2** An admonition; a warning. M16–M18.
▸ **B** *adjective*. Giving or conveying a warning; serving to admonish; admonitory. L15.

monk /mʌŋk/ *noun*[1].
[ORIGIN Old English *munuc* = Old Frisian *munek*, Old Saxon *munik* (Dutch *monnik*), Old High German *munih* (German *Mönch*), Old Norse *múnkr*, from Germanic from popular Latin var. of late Latin *monachus* from late Greek *monakhos*, use as noun of adjective = single, solitary, from *monos* alone.]

1 A member of a Christian community of men living apart from the world under vows of poverty, chastity, and obedience, according to the rule of a particular order, and devoted chiefly to religious duties and contemplation. Also, a member of a similar community of adherents of any other religion. OE.
black monk: see BLACK *adjective*. *Pied Monk*: see PIED *adjective*. *white monk*: see WHITE *adjective*.

2 Any of various animals or things whose form suggests the cowled figure of a monk; *spec.* (**a**) (also †*sea-monk*) = *monkfish* below; (**b**) PRINTING a blotch or area of excessive inking (cf. FRIAR 4). E17.

– COMB.: *monk bond*: see BOND *noun*[2] 9; †**monk-craft** *derog.* = MONKERY; **monkfish** (**a**) a bottom-dwelling shark of the genus *Squatina*, with a somewhat flattened body and broad winglike pectoral fins; esp. *S. squatina* of eastern Atlantic and Mediterranean waters; (**b**) an anglerfish; †**monk-house** a monastery; **Monk-Latin** a corrupt form of Latin used by monks; †**monk-monger** *derog.* a favourer of monks or monasticism; **monk's bench** = *monk's table* below; **monk seal** any of various light-bellied seals of the genus *Monachus*, esp. *M. monachus* of the Mediterranean and adjacent seas; **monk-seam**, **monk's-seam** NAUTICAL a seam in which the selvedges of sails are sewn flat one over the other; **monk's gun** a 16th-cent. wheel-lock gun, supposedly invented by the monk Schwarz, the alleged inventor of gunpowder; **monk shoe**, **monk's shoe** a low shoe with a strap passing over the instep, buckled at the side; **monk's rhubarb** a kind of dock, *Rumex pseudoalpinus*, formerly grown as a pot-herb; *monk's-seam*: see *monk-seam* above; *monk's shoe*: see *monk shoe* above; **monk's table** a convertible wooden seat, the back of which is hinged to swing over and rest horizontally on the arms, thus forming a table.

■ **monkdom** *noun* the condition of a monk; monks collectively; the domain of monks: M19. **monkhood** *noun* the state or profession of a monk; the monastic life, monasticism; monks collectively: OE. **monkism** *noun* monasticism E18. **monkship** *noun* the monastic system; monks collectively: E17.

monk /mʌŋk/ *noun*[2]. *slang*. M19.
[ORIGIN Abbreviation.]
A monkey.

monkery /ˈmʌŋkəri/ *noun*. Chiefly *derog.* E16.
[ORIGIN from MONK *noun*[1] + -ERY.]

1 A body or community of monks; a monastery. Also, monks collectively; the monks of a particular place. E16.
2 The state, condition, or profession of monks; monastic life, monasticism. M16.
3 In *pl.* Monkish practices, appurtenances, or paraphernalia. E17.
4 Conduct or practice characteristic of or attributed to (esp. medieval) monks; a monastic way of life marked by corruption and other abuses. M17.
5 The way of life of a tramp; a district frequented by tramps. *arch. slang*. L18.

monkey /ˈmʌŋki/ *noun*. M16.
[ORIGIN Uncertain: perh. from Low German dim. of Proto-Romance word (whence French †*monne*, Italian *monna*, Spanish, Portuguese *mono*, *-a*).]

▸ **I 1** Any of numerous primates of a group including the families Cebidae (capuchins, howler monkeys, etc.), Callitricidae (marmosets, tamarins, etc.), and Cercopithecidae (baboons, macaques, colobuses, etc.), *esp.* any of the long-tailed kinds. M16. ▸**b** The fur of any of certain monkeys. L19.
capuchin monkey, *green monkey*, *New World monkey*, *Old World monkey*, *rhesus monkey*, *spider monkey*, etc.

2 a A person who performs comical antics; a mimic. L16. ▸**b** A mischievous person, esp. a child. E17.

> **b** BYRON A little curly-headed, good-for-nothing, And mischief-making monkey from his birth.

3 A sheep. *Austral.* L19.
4 *the monkey*, a kind of dance performed to rock music. M20.

▸ **II** †**5** A kind of gun or cannon. Only in M17.
6 Any of various appliances; *spec.* a pile-driving machine consisting of a heavy hammer or ram working vertically in a groove (also *monkey engine*); the ram of such a machine. M18.
7 A receptacle for liquor; *esp.* a globular earthenware water vessel with a straight upright neck. M19.
8 Five hundred pounds sterling. *slang*. M19.

– PHRASES (chiefly *colloq.* & *slang*): **a barrel of monkeys**, **a cartload of monkeys**, **a wagonload of monkeys**, etc.: a type of something extremely cunning, mischievous, jolly, or disorderly. **cold enough to freeze the balls off a brass monkey** *coarse slang* extremely cold (see also *brass-monkey(s)* s.v. BRASS *adjective*). *grease monkey*: see GREASE *noun*. **have a monkey on one's back**, **have the monkey on one's back** (*slang*, orig. *US*) be addicted to a drug. **have one's monkey up**, **get one's monkey up** be angry. **make a monkey of**, **make a monkey out of** *colloq.* humiliate by making appear ridiculous. **monkey on a stick** a toy consisting of the figure of a monkey able to slide up and down a stick, used as a type of restlessness or agitation. **monkey's allowance** harsh treatment and little pay. **not give a monkey's (fuck)**, **not care a monkey's (fuck)** & vars., *coarse slang* not care at all; be completely indifferent or unconcerned. **put a person's monkey up** annoy, anger, (a person). *softly softly catchee monkey*: see SOFTLY *adverb* 3. *STUFFED monkey*. **suck the monkey** drink liquor from the bottle, or from a coconut shell, or from a cask using a straw; *gen.* tipple. **three monkeys**, **three wise monkeys** a conventional sculptured group of three monkeys, one with its paws over its mouth ('speak no evil'), one with its paws over its eyes ('see no evil'), and one with its paws over its ears ('hear no evil'); used allusively to refer to people who choose to ignore or keep silent about wrongdoing etc. **where the monkey keeps his nuts**, **where the monkey puts his nuts** *coarse slang* in the anus.

– COMB.: **monkey-apple** (the fruit of) any of various tropical trees and shrubs, esp. (**a**) *Anisophyllea laurina* (family Anisophyllaceae) of W. Africa; (**b**) a neotropical plant of the genus *Annona* (family Annonaceae); **monkey bars** a piece of playground equipment consisting of a ladder mounted horizontally above the ground, for children to swing from; **monkey bike** a small motorcycle designed for use over rough terrain, esp. in motocross racing; **monkey-board** a footboard at the back of a vehicle for a footman etc. to stand on; **monkey-boat** (**a**) a long narrow canal boat; (**b**) a small boat used as a tender; **monkey bread** (the fruit of) the baobab tree; **monkey bridge** NAUTICAL a small raised platform above a bridge, deckhouse, etc., on a ship; **monkey business** *colloq.* mischief, trickery, fooling about; **monkey-chaser** *US slang* (*offensive*) a black person from the W. Indies or other tropical region; **monkey-eating eagle** a very large eagle, *Pithecophaga jefferyi*, native to the Philippines; *monkey engine*: see sense 6 above; **monkey-face** a face like a monkey's; a funny face; *W. Indian colloq.* a grimace; **monkey-faced** *adjective* having a face like a monkey's; *monkey-faced owl* (*US colloq.*), the barn owl; **monkey flower** any of various plants of the genus *Mimulus*, of the figwort family, *esp.* the yellow-flowered N. American *M. guttatus*; **monkey gland** *colloq.* a gland or testicle from a monkey or another primate, grafted on to a man as a possible means of rejuvenation; **monkey-house** a building at a zoo etc. in which monkeys are kept; **monkey island** NAUTICAL = *monkey bridge* above; **monkey-jacket** a short close-fitting jacket worn by sailors etc. or at a mess; **monkey-man** (**a**) *US slang* a weak and servile husband; (**b**) a man resembling a monkey; **monkey nut** a peanut; **monkey orchestra** a group of Meissen or other porcelain figures representing monkeys playing musical instruments; **monkey orchid**, **monkey orchis** a rare orchid, *Orchis simia*, native to Europe and the Mediterranean region, the flower having a purple lip suggesting a monkey in shape; **monkey parade** *slang* a social gathering of young people out of doors; **monkey-pod (tree)** the rain tree or saman, *Albizia saman*; **monkey-pot** any of certain Brazilian trees of the genus *Lecythis* (family Lecythidaceae); the woody seed vessel of such a tree, formerly used as a trap for monkeys; **monkeypox** a virus disease of monkeys (transmissible to humans), similar to smallpox; **monkey-puzzle (tree)**, **monkey-puzzler** a large evergreen pine, *Araucaria araucana*, native to Chile, having whorled branches densely covered with leaves; also called *Chile pine*; **monkey-rope** *S. Afr.* any of various climbing plants, esp. *Secamone alpinii* (family Asclepiadaceae); **monkey's fist** a thick knot made at the end of a rope to give it weight when it is thrown; **monkeyshine** *US slang* = *monkey trick* below (usu. in *pl.*); **monkey suit** *slang* a uniform; a formal dress suit, evening dress; **monkey trial** a trial of a teacher for teaching evolutionary theories, contrary to the laws of certain states of the US; *spec.* that of J. T. Scopes in Tennessee in 1925; **monkey trick** a mischievous, foolish, or underhand trick or act; an antic; (usu. in *pl.*); **monkey wrench** a wrench or spanner having an adjustable jaw; *throw a monkey wrench into the works* (*colloq.*), cause confusion or trouble (cf. *throw a spanner in the works* s.v. SPANNER *noun*[1]).

monkey /ˈmʌŋki/ *verb*. M17.
[ORIGIN from the noun.]

1 *verb trans.* Ape the manners of, mimic; ridicule, mock. M17.
2 *verb intrans.* Play mischievous or foolish tricks; fool or mess *about* or *around*; tamper *with*. *colloq.* (orig. *US*). L19.

> J. HILTON Bryant had been monkeying on Wall Street, and the result had been a warrant for his arrest. *Times* Any departure from tradition . . would be as serious as monkeying about with . . an old school tie.

monkeyfy /ˈmʌŋkɪfʌɪ/ *verb trans.* Now *rare*. E18.
[ORIGIN from MONKEY *noun* + -FY.]
Make to resemble a monkey; make ridiculous-looking.

monkeyish /ˈmʌŋkɪɪʃ/ *adjective*. E17.
[ORIGIN formed as MONKEYFY + -ISH[1].]
Like a monkey; playful, mischievous; imitative.
■ **monkeyishly** *adverb* E20. **monkeyishness** *noun* E19.

monkeyism /ˈmʌŋkɪɪz(ə)m/ *noun*. E19.
[ORIGIN from MONKEY *noun* + -ISM.]
Behaviour like that of a monkey.

Mon-Khmer /ˈmɔːnkmɛː/ *noun & adjective*. L19.
[ORIGIN from MON *noun*[1] & *adjective* + KHMER.]
(Designating or pertaining to) a group of Austro-Asiatic languages spoken in SE Asia, of which the most important are Mon and Khmer.

monkish /ˈmʌŋkɪʃ/ *adjective*. M16.
[ORIGIN from MONK *noun*[1] + -ISH[1].]

1 Of or pertaining to monks; monastic. M16. ▸**b** Used, made, or performed by monks. E17. ▸**c** That is a monk. L17.

> **b** W. DALRYMPLE I hear the quiet rumour of hushed monkish talk . . the purposeful rustle of habits.

2 Resembling a monk; suggestive of a monk or monks. L16.

> ROBERT MANNING A few friends to offer the writer some relief from his monkish isolation in quarters.

3 Characteristic of monks or the monastic system; *esp.* (*derog.*) displaying corruption or other disreputable characteristics attributed to medieval monasticism. L16.
■ **monkishly** *adverb* E18. **monkishness** *noun* E18.

monkly /ˈmʌŋkli/ *adjective*. OE.
[ORIGIN from MONK *noun*[1] + -LY[1].]
Of or pertaining to a monk or monks; monastic.
■ **monkliness** *noun* L19.

monkshood /ˈmʌŋkshʊd/ *noun*. Also **monk's-hood**. L16.
[ORIGIN from MONK *noun*[1] + -'S[1] + HOOD *noun*[1].]

1 Any of numerous highly toxic plants of the genus *Aconitum*; *esp.* the European *A. napellus*, which bears purple flowers with a hood. L16.
2 Larkspur, *Consolida ambigua*. Now *rare* or *obsolete*. L16.
†**3** ANATOMY. The trapezius muscle. Only in 17.

Monmouth cap /ˌmɒnməθ ˈkap/ *noun phr. obsolete* exc. *hist.* L16.
[ORIGIN *Monmouth*, a town in Gwent, Wales.]
A flat round cap formerly worn by soldiers and sailors.

mono /ˈmɒnəʊ/ *noun & adjective*. *colloq.* M20.
[ORIGIN Abbreviation.]

▸ **A** *noun*. Pl. **-os**.
1 (A) monophonic recording or reproduction. M20.
2 = MONONUCLEOSIS. Chiefly *N. Amer.* M20.
3 PHOTOGRAPHY & TELEVISION etc. = MONOCHROME *noun* 1b, 2b. L20.
4 = MONOFILAMENT. L20.

▸ **B** *adjective*. **1** = MONOPHONIC *adjective* 3. M20.
2 PHOTOGRAPHY & TELEVISION etc. = MONOCHROME *adjective* 2. L20.

mono- /ˈmɒnəʊ/ *combining form*. Before a vowel also **mon-**.
[ORIGIN Greek, from *monos* alone, only, single: see -O-.]
Used in words adopted from Greek and in English formations modelled on these, and as a freely productive prefix, with the senses 'one, alone, single', 'having, involving, etc., one'; CHEMISTRY signifying the presence of a single atom, radical, etc., of a particular kind in a molecule etc. Cf. UNI-.

■ **monobrow** *noun* (*colloq.*) a pair of eyebrows that meet above the nose, giving the appearance of a single eyebrow; a person with such eyebrows, *joc.* a stupid person: L20. **monobuoy** *noun* a floating platform anchored in deep water offshore at which oil tankers and other large vessels can moor L20. **mono-cable** *noun & adjective* (designating or involving) an aerial ropeway in which a single endless rope is used to support and move loads E20. **monoˈcarbonate** *noun* (now *rare* or *obsolete*) a salt containing the carbonate anion, CO_3^{2-}; a carbonate (cf. BICARBONATE): M19. **monoˈcausal** *adjective* in terms of or having a sole cause M20. **monoˈcellular** *adjective* (BIOLOGY) = UNICELLULAR M19. **monoˈcentric** *adjective* (BIOLOGY) having a single centre; CYTOLOGY having a single centromere: L19. **monoˈcephalous** *adjective* (BOTANY) (of a plant) having only one head or umbel M19. **monochasial** /-ˈkeɪz-/ *adjective* (BOTANY) (of a cyme) that is a monochasium L19. **monochasium** /-ˈkeɪz-/ *noun*, pl. **-ia**, [Greek *khasis* chasm, separation] BOTANY a cyme in which each flowering branch gives rise to one lateral branch, so that the inflorescence is helicoid or asymmetrical L19. **monochlaˈmydeous** *adjective* [Greek *khlamud-*, *khlamus* cloak] BOTANY having only one floral envelope; having a single perianth: M19. **monoˈchloride** *noun* a salt containing one chloride ion to each combining ion or radical M19. **monoˈchroic** *adjective* (*rare*) = MONOCHROME *adjective* 1 L19. **monociˈstronic** *adjective* (GENETICS) containing as much genetic information as is carried by a single cistron M20. **mono-coloured** *adjective* (*rare*) of only one colour L18. **monoconˈdylian**, **monoconˈdylic** *adjectives* (ZOOLOGY) (of a skull) having one occipital condyle, as that of birds and reptiles (opp. DICONDYLIAN) L19. **monoconsoˈnantal** *adjective* containing a single consonant M20. **monoˈcormic** *adjective* [Greek *kormos* trunk (of a tree)] BOTANY (esp. of a conifer) having a single main axis of growth L19. **monoˈcrotic** *adjective* (MEDICINE) (of the pulse) having a single detectable beat (opp. *dicrotic*) L19. **monocrystal** *noun* a single crystal M20. **monoˈcrystalline** *adjective* consisting of monocrystals; constituting a monocrystal: M20. **monoˈdentate** *adjective* (CHEMISTRY) (of a ligand) having only one point of attachment to a central atom M20. **monodiaˈlectal** *adjective* speaking only one dialect M20. **monodiˈmensional** *adjective* existing in or having only one dimension; linear: E20. **monoˈdisperse** *adjective* (PHYSICAL CHEMISTRY) designating or pertaining to a colloid containing particles of uniform size E20. **monoenerˈgetic** *adjective* (PHYSICS) (consisting of particles) of the same energy; emitting radiation all of one energy: M20. **monoethaˈnolamine** *noun* a viscous high-boiling liquid, $H_2NCH_2CH_2OH$, used in making detergents; 2-aminoethanol: E20. **monofil** *noun & adjective* = MONOFILAMENT E20. **monofilament** *noun & adjective* (made up of) a single strand of man-made fibre M20. **monoˈfunctional** *adjective* (CHEMISTRY) having or corresponding to a single functional group per molecule M20. **monogerm** *adjective* (AGRICULTURE) designating or pertaining to varieties of sugar beet in which each seed ball has its contents reduced to one fruit and so gives rise to only one seedling M20. **monoˈglacial** *adjective* designating a theory postulating only one glacial period during the Pleistocene E20. **monoˈglacialism** *noun* the monoglacial theory M20. **monoˈglacialist** *noun & adjective* (**a**) *noun* a supporter of monoglacialism; (**b**) *adjective* of or pertaining to monoglacialism or monoglacialists: E20. **monoˈglyceride** *noun* (BIOCHEMISTRY) a compound consisting of glycerol esterified at only one of its hydroxyl groups M19. **monoˈhydrate** *noun* (CHEMISTRY) a hydrate containing one mole of water per mole of the compound M19. **monohyˈdrated** *adjective* (CHEMISTRY) hydrated with one molecule of water per molecule of compound M19. **monoˈlobular** *adjective* (MEDICINE) consisting of or affecting a single lobule or lobe L19. **monomeˈniscous** *adjective* (of the eyes of invertebrates) having only one lens L19. **monoˈmictic** *adjective* (of a lake) having only one overturn each year M20. **monomineˈralic** *adjective* (PETROGRAPHY) composed of a single mineral E20. **monomorˈphemic** *adjective* (LINGUISTICS) consisting of a single morpheme M20. **monoˈnucleotide** *noun* (BIOCHEMISTRY) any of the compounds

M

formed from one molecule each of phosphoric acid, a sugar, and a heterocyclic base, that are the units of which nucleic acids are composed; a monomeric nucleotide: E20. **mono'petalous** *adjective* (BOTANY) (**a**) gamopetalous; (**b**) having one petal: L17. **monophone** *noun* (*rare*) PHONETICS a single sound; *esp.* a phoneme having no allophones: L19. **monoph'thalmic** *adjective* one-eyed M19. **mono'phyllous** *adjective* (BOTANY) having or consisting of one leaf M18. **monopro'pellant** *noun & adjective* (employing) a substance used as rocket fuel without an additional oxidizing agent M20. **mo'nopterous** *adjective* (BOTANY) (of a seed) having one wing M19. **monopulse** *adjective* designating (the mode of operation of) radar in which the direction and usu. the range of a target is determined from a single echo pulse M20. **mo'norchid** *noun & adjective* (a person or animal) having only one testicle L19. **mo'norchidism** *noun* absence of one testicle M19. **mo'norchis** *noun*, pl. **monorchides** /-ɪdiːz/, = MONORCHID *noun* E18. **monose'mantic** *adjective* (LINGUISTICS) (of a word or phrase) having only one meaning M20. **mono'sepalous** *adjective* (BOTANY) (**a**) = GAMOSEPALOUS; (**b**) having one sepal: M19. **monospe'cific** *adjective* (BIOLOGY) pertaining to or consisting of only one species; (of an antibody) specific to one antigen: E20. **monospore** *noun & adjective* (**a**) *noun* an undivided spore; (**b**) *adjective* = MONOSPOROUS: L19. **mono'sporous** *adjective* having a single spore; derived from a single spore: M19. **mono'static** *adjective* (of radar) having a single aerial as both transmitter and receiver M20. **monostome** *noun & adjective* (ZOOLOGY) (an animal) having only one mouth or sucker M19. **mono'stylous** *adjective* (BOTANY) having only one style M19. **mono-'substituted** *adjective* (CHEMISTRY) formed by or displaying mono-substitution L19. **mono-substi'tution** *noun* (CHEMISTRY) substitution affecting only one of the atoms or positions in a molecular structure L19. **monosympto'matic** *adjective* exhibiting or concerning a single dominant symptom L19. **monosy'naptic** *adjective* (PHYSIOLOGY) involving a single synapse M20. **monosy'stemic** *adjective* (LINGUISTICS) that establishes a single overall system of language analysis M20. **monotherapy** *noun* the treatment of a disease with a single drug M20. **monothetic** /-'θɛtɪk/ *adjective* (**a**) PHILOSOPHY (*rare*) that postulates a single essential element; (**b**) TAXONOMY (of a classification) having groups formed on the basis of a single characteristic, or a series of single characteristics: L19. **mono'thetically** *adverb* (TAXONOMY) on the basis of a single characteristic or a series of single characteristics M20. **monotower** *noun & adjective* (designating) a crane whose jib is mounted on a single tower M20. **monotrochal** /mə'nɒtrək(ə)l/ *adjective* [Greek *trokhos* wheel, ring] ZOOLOGY having a single band or ring of cilia L19. **monotrophic** /-'trəʊfɪk, -'trɒfɪk/ *adjective* (ECOLOGY) feeding on one kind of food, or one host organism E20. **mono-un'saturated** *adjective* (CHEMISTRY) (of a compound, esp. a fat) saturated except for one multiple bond M20. **mo'novular** *adjective* (BIOLOGY) monozygotic E20. **monoxenous** /mə'nɒksɪnəs/ *adjective* (BIOLOGY) [Greek *xenos* stranger] (of a parasite) restricted to a single host species M20.

M

monoamine /mɒnəʊ'eɪmiːn/ *noun*. Also **monamine** /mɒn'eɪmiːn/. M19.
[ORIGIN from MONO- + AMINE.]
BIOCHEMISTRY. Any compound having a single amine group in its molecule; *spec.* one which is a neurotransmitter (e.g. serotonin, noradrenaline).
– COMB.: **monoamine oxidase** an enzyme which catalyses the oxidation (and hence the inactivation) of monoamine neurotransmitters; ***monoamine oxidase inhibitor***, any of a class of antidepressant drugs which inhibit the activity of monoamine oxidase (so allowing accumulation of serotonin and noradrenaline in the brain).
■ **monoami'nergic** *adjective* releasing or involving a monoamine as a neurotransmitter; (of a diet) rich in monoaminergic substances: M20.

†**mono-andry** *noun* see MONANDRY.

monoao *noun* var. of MANOAO.

monobasic /mɒnə(ʊ)'beɪsɪk/ *adjective*. M19.
[ORIGIN from MONO- + BASIC *adjective*.]
CHEMISTRY. Of an acid: having one replaceable hydrogen atom. Formerly also, monovalent.

monoblastic /mɒnə(ʊ)'blastɪk/ *adjective*. L19.
[ORIGIN from MONO- + Greek *blastos* sprout, bud + -IC.]
1 BOTANY. Having a single germinal layer. L19.
2 PHYSIOLOGY. Of or pertaining to monoblasts. L20.
■ **'monoblast** *noun* (PHYSIOLOGY) a cell which develops into a monocyte E20.

monobloc /'mɒnə(ʊ)blɒk/ *adjective*. E20.
[ORIGIN French, formed as MONO- + *bloc* BLOCK *noun*.]
Made as, contained in, or involving a single casting.

monobrominated /mɒnə(ʊ)'brəʊmɪneɪtɪd/ *adjective*. M19.
[ORIGIN from MONO- + BROMINATE + -ED[1].]
CHEMISTRY. Having one bromine atom added to or substituted in the molecule.

monocarpellary /mɒnə(ʊ)'kɑːpəl(ə)ri/ *adjective*. M19.
[ORIGIN from MONO- + CARPELLARY.]
BOTANY. Having or consisting of a single carpel.

monocarpic /mɒnə(ʊ)'kɑːpɪk/ *adjective*. M19.
[ORIGIN from MONO- + Greek *karpos* fruit + -IC.]
BOTANY. Of a plant: bearing fruit only once during its life cycle.
■ **'monocarp** *noun* a monocarpic plant M19.

monocarpous /mɒnə(ʊ)'kɑːpəs/ *adjective*. M18.
[ORIGIN In sense 1 from MONO- + CARPEL; in sense 2 formed as MONOCARPIC: see -OUS.]
BOTANY. **1** = MONOCARPELLARY. M18.
2 = MONOCARPIC. M19.

monoceros /mə'nɒs(ə)rəs/ *noun*. ME.
[ORIGIN Old French from Latin from Greek *monokerōs*, from *monos* MONO- + *keras* horn.]
†**1** A unicorn. ME–M18.
†**2** A fish having a single hornlike process, as a sawfish. Also, a narwhal. L16–E19.
3 (**M-**.) (The name of) an inconspicuous constellation on the celestial equator lying in the Milky Way between Canis Major and Canis Minor; the Unicorn. L18.

monochlorinated /mɒnə(ʊ)'klɔːrɪneɪtɪd/ *adjective*. M19.
[ORIGIN from MONO- + CHLORINATE + -ED[1].]
CHEMISTRY. Having one chlorine atom added to or substituted in each molecule.

monochord /'mɒnə(ʊ)kɔːd/ *noun*. LME.
[ORIGIN Old French & mod. French *monocorde* from late Latin *monochordon* from Greek *monokhordon* use as noun of *monokhordos* having a single string, formed as MONO- + *khordē* string: see CORD *noun*[1] & *adjective*. In sense 3 from MONO- + CHORD *noun*[1].]
1 A musical instrument consisting of a soundboard with a single string and often a movable bridge, orig. used esp. to teach the intervals of plainsong, now esp. for mathematical determination of musical intervals. LME.
2 *hist.* A medieval musical instrument with several strings and bridges for the production of a combination of sounds. LME.
3 A harmonious combination of sound; *fig.* harmony, concord. Now *rare*. LME.

monochromasy /mɒnə(ʊ)'krəʊməsi/ *noun*. E20.
[ORIGIN from MONO- + -CHROMASY.]
OPHTHALMOLOGY. = MONOCHROMATISM 2.

monochromat /mɒnə(ʊ)'krəʊmat/ *noun*. Also **-ate** /-eɪt/. L19.
[ORIGIN Back-form. from MONOCHROMATIC.]
A person with monochromatism.

monochromate /mɒnə(ʊ)'krəʊmeɪt/ *verb trans*. M20.
[ORIGIN Back-form. from MONOCHROMATOR.]
= MONOCHROMATIZE. Chiefly as ***monochromated***, ***monochromating*** *ppl adjectives*.

monochromatic /mɒnə(ʊ)krə'matɪk/ *adjective*. E19.
[ORIGIN from MONO- + CHROMATIC *adjective*. Cf. MONOCHROME.]
1 Having or producing only one colour; *spec.* (of light) of one wavelength. Also, (of other radiation) of a single wavelength or energy throughout. E19.
2 Executed in monochrome. E19.
3 OPHTHALMOLOGY. Having or designating a form of colour blindness in which all colours appear as shades of one colour. E20.
■ **monochromatically** *adverb* (**a**) in a monochromatic way; (**b**) without regard to colour: L19. **monochromaticity** /-'tɪsɪti/ *noun* monochromatic condition; extent of concentration at one wavelength or frequency: M20.

monochromatise *verb* var. of MONOCHROMATIZE.

monochromatism /mɒnə(ʊ)'krəʊmətɪz(ə)m/ *noun*. M19.
[ORIGIN from MONOCHROMATIC + -ISM.]
1 The quality or fact of being monochromatic. M19.
2 OPHTHALMOLOGY. Complete colour blindness. M20.
■ **monochromatist** *noun* a painter in monochrome E19.

monochromatize /mɒnə(ʊ)'krəʊmətʌɪz/ *verb trans*. Also **-ise**. M20.
[ORIGIN from MONOCHROMATISM + -IZE.]
Make (radiation) monochromatic. Chiefly as ***monochromatized***, ***monochromatizing*** *ppl adjectives*.
■ **monochromati'zation** *noun* M20.

monochromator /'mɒnə(ʊ)krəmeɪtə, mɒnə(ʊ)'krɒmɪtə/ *noun*. E20.
[ORIGIN from MONOCHROMATIC + -OR.]
PHYSICS. A device used to select radiation of (or very close to) a single wavelength or energy.

monochrome /'mɒnəkrəʊm, mɒnə(ʊ)'krəʊm/ *noun & adjective*. M17.
[ORIGIN In sense 1 from medieval Latin *monochroma*; in senses 2, 3, from French from Greek *monokhrōmos*: both ult. from Greek *monokhrōmatos* of one colour, formed as MONO- + *khrōma(t-)* colour.]
▸ **A** *noun*. **1** A painting executed in different shades of one colour. M17. ▸**b** A photograph in shades of one colour; *esp.* a black and white photograph. M20.
2 Representation in one colour (esp. in ***in monochrome***). Also, the state of being in one colour; a tract of one colour. M19. ▸**b** PHOTOGRAPHY & TELEVISION etc. Reproduction in black and white. E20.

J. WAIN The moonlight didn't enable one to see colours, but even in monochrome .. the effect was tasteful. *fig.*: *Listener* A dramatic exaggeration .. inevitably crept into the gentle monochrome.

3 A paint or glaze of a single colour. E20.
▸ **B** *adjective*. **1** Having only one colour; executed in one colour. M19.
2 PHOTOGRAPHY & TELEVISION etc. Reproducing all colours as shades of grey; black and white; of or pertaining to such reproduction. E20.
■ **mono'chromic** *adjective* = MONOCHROME *adjective* 1 M19. **'monochromist** *noun* a painter in monochrome M17. **mono'chromous** *adjective* = MONOCHROME *adjective* 1 M19. **'monochromy** *noun* the art of painting in monochrome M19.

monochronic /mɒnə(ʊ)'krɒnɪk/ *adjective*. M19.
[ORIGIN from Greek *monokhronos* (formed as MONO- + *khronos* time) + -OUS.]
Relating to a single period of time; synchronic.

monocle /'mɒnək(ə)l/ *noun*. L18.
[ORIGIN French (orig. adjective) formed as MONOCULUS.]
A single eyeglass.
■ **monocled** *adjective* wearing a monocle L19.

monoclinal /mɒnə(ʊ)'klʌɪn(ə)l/ *adjective & noun*. M19.
[ORIGIN from MONO- + Greek *klinein* to lean, slope + -AL[1].]
GEOLOGY. ▸**A** *adjective*. **1** Designating or consisting of strata that slope in the same direction, esp. at the same angle. Orig. *US*. M19.
2 Of a fold: consisting of a single slope connecting strata that are parallel but out of line. L19.
▸ **B** *noun*. = MONOCLINE. L19.
■ **monoclinally** *adverb* M19.

monocline /'mɒnə(ʊ)klʌɪn/ *noun*. L19.
[ORIGIN formed as MONOCLINAL: cf. ANTICLINE.]
GEOLOGY. **1** A monoclinal fold. L19.
2 A set of monoclinal strata. E20.

monoclinic /mɒnə(ʊ)'klɪnɪk/ *adjective*. M19.
[ORIGIN formed as MONOCLINAL: see -IC.]
CRYSTALLOGRAPHY. Designating or pertaining to a crystal system referred to three unequal axes, two of which intersect at right angles, the third or principal axis intersecting one of these at right angles and the other obliquely.

monoclinous /mɒnə(ʊ)'klʌɪnəs/ *adjective*. E19.
[ORIGIN from French *monocline* or mod. Latin *monoclinus*, from Greek MONO- + *klinē* bed: see -OUS.]
BOTANY. Of a flower or flowering plant: having stamens and pistils in the same flower, hermaphrodite.

monoclonal /mɒnə(ʊ)'kləʊn(ə)l/ *adjective*. E20.
[ORIGIN from MONO- + CLONAL.]
BIOLOGY. Forming a single clone; derived asexually from a single individual or cell.
monoclonal antibody a pure specific antibody produced in large quantities from a cultured cell line.

monocoque /'mɒnə(ʊ)kɒk/ *noun & adjective*. E20.
[ORIGIN French, from *mono-* MONO- + *coque* eggshell.]
▸ **A** *noun*. **1** An aircraft fuselage or other structure having an outer covering in the form of a rigid load-bearing shell, usu. without longerons or stringers. E20.
2 A motor vehicle underframe and body built as a single rigid structure (or in racing cars as a number of boxlike sections) throughout which the stresses are distributed. M20.
▸ **B** *attrib*. or as *adjective*. Designating or based on a structure of this type. E20.

monocot /'mɒnə(ʊ)kɒt/ *noun*. M19.
[ORIGIN Abbreviation.]
BOTANY. = MONOCOTYLEDON.

monocotyledon /ˌmɒnə(ʊ)kɒtɪ'liːd(ə)n/ *noun*. E18.
[ORIGIN mod. Latin *monocotyledones* pl., formed as MONO- + COTYLEDON.]
BOTANY. A flowering plant having one cotyledon; a member of the group Monocotyledoneae (or Monocotyledones) comprising such plants. Cf. DICOTYLEDON.
■ **monocotyledonous** *adjective* L18.

monocracy /mə'nɒkrəsi/ *noun*. E17.
[ORIGIN from MONO- + -CRACY.]
Government by a single person, autocracy.

monocrat /'mɒnə(ʊ)krat/ *noun*. L18.
[ORIGIN from Greek *monokratēs* ruling alone: see MONO-, -CRAT.]
A partisan of monocracy or monarchy; *spec.* in *US HISTORY*, (Thomas Jefferson's name for) a member of the Federalist party. Also (*rare*), a sole ruler, an autocrat.
■ **mono'cratic** *adjective* (*rare*) M19.

monocular /mə'nɒkjʊlə/ *adjective & noun*. M17.
[ORIGIN from late Latin MONOCULUS + -AR[1].]
▸ **A** *adjective*. **1** Having only one eye. M17.
2 Of or pertaining to one eye only; adapted to or using one eye. Cf. UNIOCULAR 2. M19. ▸**b** Wearing a monocle. *rare*. E20.
▸ **B** *noun*. **1** A one-eyed person. *rare*. L19.
2 A field glass or microscope for use with one eye, usu. as opp. ***binocular(s)***. M20.
■ **monocu'larity** *noun* monocular condition M19. **monocularly** *adverb* with one eye only L19. **'monocule** *noun* (*rare*) = MONOCULUS L18. **monoculist** *noun* (*rare*) a one-eyed person E17.

monoculi *noun* pl. of MONOCULUS.

monoculous /mə'nɒkjʊləs/ *adjective*. M17.
[ORIGIN from late Latin MONOCULUS: see -ULOUS.]
One-eyed.

monoculture /'mɒnə(ʊ)kʌltʃə/ *noun*. E20.
[ORIGIN Irreg. from MONO- + CULTURE *noun*, perh. after French.]
1 The cultivation or exploitation of a single crop, or the maintenance of a single kind of animal, to the exclusion of others. E20.

J. ARDAGH The monoculture of cheap wine was dangerous for the region's economy.

2 An area in which such a practice prevails. M20.

fig.: *Listener* Los Angeles's least endearing characteristic: the tendency to fragment into self-contained, specialised areas—social monocultures.

■ **mono'cultural** *adjective* E20. **mono'culturist** *noun* a person who practises or advocates monoculture L20.

monoculus /mə'nɒkjʊləs/ *noun*. Pl. **-li** /-lʌɪ, -liː/. ME.
[ORIGIN Late Latin, from Greek MONO- + Latin *oculus* eye, after Greek *monophthalmos*.]
1 A one-eyed person or creature. ME.
2 A cyclopoid. M18.
3 A bandage for one eye. *rare*. M19.

monocycle /'mɒnə(ʊ)sʌɪk(ə)l/ *noun*. M19.
[ORIGIN from MONO- + CYCLE *noun*, after *bicycle*, *tricycle*.]
A vehicle having one wheel, turned by pedalling; a unicycle.

monocyclic /mɒnə(ʊ)'sʌɪklɪk, -'sɪk-/ *adjective*. M19.
[ORIGIN from Greek MONO- + *kuklos* circle + -IC.]
1 MATH. Involving, having, or consisting of a single closed curve, circuit, or cycle. Now *rare*. M19.
2 BOTANY. **a** Of a set of floral parts (sepals, stamens, etc.): forming a single whorl. L19. ▸**b** Annual. *rare*. E20.
3 ZOOLOGY. Of an echinoderm: having only a single ring of basal plates, or of tentacles. L19.
4 CHEMISTRY. (Composed of molecules) having a single ring of atoms. E20.
5 GEOLOGY. Having undergone a single cycle of erosion or of mountain building. M20.

monocyst /'mɒnə(ʊ)sɪst/ *noun*. M19.
[ORIGIN from MONO- + CYST.]
MEDICINE. A structure consisting of a single cyst.
■ **mono'cystic** *adjective* (**a**) MEDICINE having or consisting of a single cyst; (**b**) ZOOLOGY designating or pertaining to a group of gregarines without body segmentation: L19. **mono'cystid** *noun & adjective* (ZOOLOGY) (**a**) *noun* a monocystic gregarine; (**b**) *adjective* = MONOCYSTIC (b): L19.

monocyte /'mɒnə(ʊ)sʌɪt/ *noun*. E20.
[ORIGIN from MONO- + -CYTE.]
A large phagocytic white blood cell with a single oval or kidney-shaped nucleus and clear greyish cytoplasm.
■ **monocytic** /-'sɪtɪk/ *adjective* E20. **monocy'tosis** *noun* (MEDICINE & VETERINARY MEDICINE) abnormal increase in the number of monocytes in the blood E20.

monodactyl /mɒnə(ʊ)'daktɪl/ *adjective*. Also **-yle**. E19.
[ORIGIN Greek *monodaktulos*, from MONO- + *daktulos* finger.]
ZOOLOGY. = MONODACTYLOUS.
■ **monodactyly** *noun* monodactylous condition L19.

monodactylous /mɒnə(ʊ)'daktɪləs/ *adjective*. M19.
[ORIGIN from MONODACTYL + -OUS.]
ZOOLOGY. Having only one finger, toe, or claw.

†**monodelph** *noun*. M–L19.
[ORIGIN French *monodelphe* from mod. Latin *monodelphia* pl., from Greek MONO- + *delphus* womb.]
ZOOLOGY. A mammal of the former subclass Monodelphia, a eutherian.
■ †**mono'delphian**, **mono'delphous** *adjectives* M–L19.

monodic /mə'nɒdɪk/ *adjective*. E19.
[ORIGIN Greek *monōdikos*, from *monōdos*: see MONODY, -IC.]
Chiefly MUSIC. Of, pertaining to, or of the nature of monody.
■ †**monodical** *adjective*: only in M17. **monodically** *adverb* L19.

monodist /'mɒnədɪst/ *noun*. M18.
[ORIGIN from MONODY + -IST.]
1 A person who writes or sings a monody. M18.
2 A person who composes in the monodic style. E20.

monodon /'mɒnədɒn/ *noun*. M18.
[ORIGIN mod. Latin (see below), from Greek *monodont-*, *monodous*, from MONO-: see -ODON, -ODONT.]
ZOOLOGY. The narwhal, *Monodon monoceros*. Now chiefly as mod. Latin genus name.

monodont /'mɒnədɒnt/ *adjective*. *rare*. L19.
[ORIGIN Greek *monodont-*: see MONODON, -ODONT.]
ZOOLOGY. Having one persistent tusk or tooth.
■ **mono'dontal** *adjective* M19.

monodrama /'mɒnə(ʊ)drɑːmə, mɒnə(ʊ)'drɑːmə/ *noun*. L18.
[ORIGIN from MONO- + DRAMA.]
A dramatic piece for a single performer. Now *esp.* an opera for one singer.
■ **monodra'matic** *adjective* pertaining to or characteristic of a monodrama E19. **mono'dramatist** *noun* a writer of a monodrama E19.

monodromy /mə'nɒdrəmi/ *noun*. L19.
[ORIGIN from Greek MONO- + *dromos* course + -Y[3].]
MATH. 1 The property that a curve described by rotation through four right angles is closed. L19.
2 The property that if a (complex) variable *z* returns to its original value by any path, the function *f*(*z*) also returns to its original value. E20.
■ **monodromic** /mɒnə(ʊ)'drəʊmɪk/ *adjective* (of a function) having a single value for each value of the variable L19.

monody /'mɒnədi/ *noun*. E17.
[ORIGIN Late Latin *monodia* from Greek *monōdia*, from *monōdos* singing alone, from MONO- + *ōdē* ODE: see -Y[3].]
1 In Greek drama, an ode sung by a single voice, esp. by one of the actors in a tragedy (as distinct from the chorus); a mournful song or dirge. E17.
2 A poem in which a mourner bewails a person's death. M17.
3 Monotonous sound; monotony. M19.
4 MUSIC. = MONOPHONY 1; *spec.* a 17th-cent. style of writing for a solo voice or instrument accompanied by a figured bass. Also, a composition in this style. L19.

monoecious /mə'niːʃəs/ *adjective*. Also ***monec-**. M18.
[ORIGIN from mod. Latin *Monoecia*, a class in Linnaeus's sexual system, formed as MONO- + Greek *oikos* house: see -IOUS.]
1 BOTANY. Having male and female flowers separate but on the same plant. Also, (of a cryptogam) having both male and female organs on the same individual. M18.
2 ZOOLOGY. Hermaphrodite. E19.
■ **monoeciously** *adverb* M19. **monoecism** /-sɪz(ə)m/ *noun* monoecious condition L19. **monoecy** /-si/ *noun* = MONOECISM M20.

monogamic /mɒnə'gamɪk/ *adjective*. M19.
[ORIGIN from (the same root as) MONOGAMY + -IC.]
Of or pertaining to monogamy; practising monogamy, monogamous.
■ **monogamian** /mɒnə(ʊ)'geɪmɪən/ *adjective* (*rare*) = MONOGAMIC L19. **monogamically** *adverb* E20.

monogamist /mə'nɒgəmɪst/ *noun & adjective*. M17.
[ORIGIN from Greek *monogamos* marrying only once, from MONO- + *gamos* marriage: see -IST.]
▸**A** *noun*. 1 A person who by custom or law is debarred from remarrying after the death of the first spouse. Opp. ***digamist***. Now *rare*. M17.
2 A person who has only one living and undivorced spouse. Opp. ***bigamist***, ***polygamist***. M18.
▸**B** *adjective*. = MONOGAMISTIC. L19.
■ **monoga'mistic** *adjective* of or pertaining to monogamists or monogamy; favouring monogamy: L19.

monogamous /mə'nɒgəməs/ *adjective*. L18.
[ORIGIN from (the same root as) MONOGAMY + -OUS.]
1 ZOOLOGY. Of an animal, esp. a bird: pairing with only one mate for the breeding season, or for life. L18.
2 Having or permitted to have only one living and undivorced spouse at one time. Opp. ***bigamous***, ***polygamous***. E19.
3 Refraining or debarred from remarriage after the death of the first spouse. Opp. ***digamous***. Now *rare*. E19.
4 Of or pertaining to monogamy. L19.
■ **monogamously** *adverb* L19. **monogamousness** *noun* M20.

monogamy /mə'nɒgəmi/ *noun*. E17.
[ORIGIN French *monogamie* from ecclesiastical Latin, Greek *monogamia*, from Greek *monogamos*: see MONOGAMIST, -GAMY.]
1 The practice or principle of marrying only once, or of not remarrying after the death of the first spouse. Opp. ***digamy***. Now *rare*. E17.
2 The condition, rule, or custom of being married to only one person at a time. Opp. ***bigamy***, ***polygamy***. E18.
serial monogamy: see SERIAL *adjective*.
3 ZOOLOGY. The habit of animals, esp. birds, of living in pairs, or having only one mate. L18.

monogastric /mɒnə(ʊ)'gastrɪk/ *adjective*. M18.
[ORIGIN from MONO- + GASTRIC.]
1 ANATOMY. Of a muscle: having a single 'belly' or thick fleshy part. M18.
2 ZOOLOGY. Having only one stomach or digestive cavity. E19.

monogenean /ˌmɒnə(ʊ)dʒɪ'niːən, mɒnə(ʊ)'dʒɛnɪən/ *noun & adjective*. M20.
[ORIGIN from mod. Latin *Monogenea* (see below), formed as MONO- + Greek *genea* race, generation: see -AN.]
ZOOLOGY. ▸**A** *noun*. A fluke of the class Monogenea, which comprises chiefly ectoparasitic species restricted to one host, usu. a fish. M20.
▸**B** *adjective*. Of or pertaining to the monogeneans. M20.

monogeneous /mɒnə(ʊ)'dʒiːnɪəs/ *adjective*. *rare*. M19.
[ORIGIN from MONO- + Greek *genē-*, *genos* kind, race + -OUS.]
1 BIOLOGY. = MONOGENOUS 2. M19.
2 ZOOLOGY. = MONOGENEAN *adjective*. L19.

monogenesis /mɒnə(ʊ)'dʒɛnɪsɪs/ *noun*. M19.
[ORIGIN from MONO- + -GENESIS.]
1 BIOLOGY. Generation from a single parent; asexual reproduction. Now *rare* or *obsolete*. M19.
2 BIOLOGY. (A theory proposing) the origin of a species (esp. *Homo sapiens*), or of all organisms, from a single ancestor or ancestral pair; monogeny. L19.
3 LINGUISTICS. (A theory proposing) the common origin of all languages. M20.

monogenetic /mɒnə(ʊ)dʒɪ'nɛtɪk/ *adjective*. M19.
[ORIGIN from MONO- + GENETIC.]
1 Having the same origin or source, derived from one source. M19. ▸**b** GEOLOGY. Resulting from a single process of formation. L19.
2 BIOLOGY. Of or pertaining to monogenesis. L19.
3 ZOOLOGY. Of a parasite: having a life cycle restricted to one host. L19.

monogenic /mɒnə(ʊ)'dʒɛnɪk/ *adjective*. M19.
[ORIGIN from MONO- + -GENIC or (sense 2) GENIC *adjective*.]
1 GEOLOGY. = MONOGENOUS 3. *rare*. M19.
2 BIOLOGY & MEDICINE. Involving or controlled by a single gene. M20.
■ **monogenically** *adverb* M20.

monogenist /mə'nɒdʒɪnɪst/ *noun & adjective*. M19.
[ORIGIN formed as MONOGENY + -IST.]
▸**A** *noun*. 1 A person who believes or maintains the theory of human monogeny. M19.
2 A person who maintains the unity of origin of living beings. M19.
▸**B** *adjective*. Of or pertaining to monogenism or monogenists. M19.
■ **monogenism** *noun* the theory or doctrine of monogeny M19. **monoge'nistic** *adjective* of or pertaining to monogenists or monogenism M19.

monogenous /mə'nɒdʒɪnəs/ *adjective*. Now *rare*. M19.
[ORIGIN formed as MONOGENEOUS.]
1 BOTANY. Endogenous. M19.
2 BIOLOGY. Having a single common origin; monophyletic. M19.
3 GEOLOGY. Of a clastic rock: derived from a single pre-existing rock. L19.
4 BIOLOGY. Designating asexual reproduction involving one parent. L19.

monogeny /mə'nɒdʒəni/ *noun*. M19.
[ORIGIN from MONO- + Greek *genos* kind, race + -Y[3].]
The (theoretical) common origin of the human species, esp. from one pair of ancestors. Also, the theory of such origination, monogenism.

monoglot /'mɒnə(ʊ)glɒt/ *adjective & noun*. M19.
[ORIGIN Greek *monoglōttos*, from MONO- + *glōtta* tongue.]
▸**A** *adjective*. Speaking, writing, or understanding only one language. M19.
▸**B** *noun*. A person who knows only one language. M19.

monogram /'mɒnəgram/ *noun & verb*. E17.
[ORIGIN Sense 1 from Latin *monogrammus*; sense 2 from French *monogramme* from late Latin *monogramma* from Greek, formed as MONO-, -GRAM.]
▸**A** *noun*. †1 A picture drawn in lines without shading or colour; a sketch. E17–M19.
2 A device composed of two or more letters (esp. the initials of a person's name) interwoven together. L17.

R. DAHL Several of the spoons bore the monogram of Christ.

▸**B** *verb trans*. Infl. **-mm-**. Decorate with or reproduce as a monogram. Chiefly as ***monogrammed*** *ppl adjective*, bearing a monogram. M20.

R. CHANDLER Monogrammed towels on a rack. *Sunday Times* Hand-made suits and shoes, HFII monogrammed on every shirt.

■ **monogra'mmatic** *adjective* of, pertaining to, or in the style of a monogram. L18.

monograph /'mɒnəgrɑːf/ *noun & verb*. E19.
[ORIGIN from MONO- + -GRAPH, to replace MONOGRAPHY.]
▸**A** *noun*. 1 A detailed written study on a single specialized topic, orig. in botany or zoology. E19.
†2 = MONOGRAM *noun* 2. *rare*. M–L19.
▸**B** *verb trans*. Produce a monograph on; treat in a monograph. M19.

monographer /mə'nɒgrəfə/ *noun*. L18.
[ORIGIN from mod. Latin *monographus* (see MONOGRAPHY) + -ER[1].]
The author of a monograph.

monographic /mɒnə(ʊ)'grafɪk/ *adjective*. M18.
[ORIGIN In branch I from MONO- + -GRAPHIC; in branch II from MONOGRAPHY or MONOGRAPH + -IC.]
▸**I** †1 Of a picture etc.: consisting of lines without shading or colour. (Cf. MONOGRAM *noun* 1.) M18–M19.
2 Representing a sphere in a single diagram. *rare*. M19.
3 = MONOGRAMMATIC. L19.
▸**II** 4 Of, pertaining to, or of the nature of a monograph. Cf. earlier MONOGRAPHICAL. E19.
5 Of an art gallery or exhibition: showing the works of a single artist. L20.
■ **monographical** *adjective* (*rare*) = MONOGRAPHIC 4 L18. **monographically** *adverb* M19.

monographist /mə'nɒgrəfɪst/ *noun*. E19.
[ORIGIN from MONOGRAPHY or MONOGRAPH + -IST.]
= MONOGRAPHER.

monography /mə'nɒgrəfi/ *noun*. Now *rare* or *obsolete*. L18.
[ORIGIN mod. Latin *monographia*, from *monographus* writer of a specialized treatise, from MONO- + *-graphus*: see -GRAPH, -Y[3].]
= MONOGRAPH *noun* 1.

monogyne /'mɒnədʒʌɪn/ *adjective*. E20.
[ORIGIN formed as MONOGYNY.]
ENTOMOLOGY. Of (a colony of) social insects: having a single queen.

monogynous /mə'nɒdʒɪnəs/ *adjective*. M18.
[ORIGIN formed as MONOGYNY + -OUS.]
1 BOTANY. Of a flower or flowering plant: having only one pistil, style, or stigma. Now *rare*. M18.
2 ZOOLOGY. Pairing with only one female; pertaining to or involving monogyny. L19.

monogyny /mə'nɒdʒɪni/ *noun*. L19.
[ORIGIN from Greek MONO- + *gunē* woman, wife: see -Y[3].]
The practice or custom of mating with only one female, or of having only one wife at a time.
■ **monogynist** *noun* a person who practises or advocates monogyny L19.

M

monohull /ˈmɒnə(ʊ)hʌl/ *noun & adjective.* M20.
[ORIGIN from MONO- + HULL *noun*[2].]
(A boat) having a single hull.

monohybrid /mɒnə(ʊ)ˈhʌɪbrɪd/ *noun & adjective.* E20.
[ORIGIN from MONO- + HYBRID.]
GENETICS. (Designating or pertaining to) a hybrid that is heterozygous with respect to a single gene.
■ **monohybridism** *noun* (*rare*) monohybrid condition E20.

monohydric /mɒnə(ʊ)ˈhʌɪdrɪk/ *adjective.* M19.
[ORIGIN from MONO- + HYDRIC *adjective*[1].]
CHEMISTRY. Containing a single hydroxyl group or (formerly) a single hydrogen atom in the molecule.

monoicous /mɒˈnɔɪkəs/ *adjective.* E19.
[ORIGIN formed as MONOECIOUS: see -OUS.]
BOTANY. Esp. of a cryptogam: monoecious.

monoid /ˈmɒnɔɪd/ *noun.* M19.
[ORIGIN Greek *monoeidēs* uniform, from MONO- + *eidos* form: see -OID.]
MATH. **1** A surface having a conical point of the highest possible $(n-1)$th order. Now *rare.* M19.
2 A semi-group possessing an identity element. M20.

monoideism /ˌmɒnəʊʌɪˈdiːɪz(ə)m/ *noun.* L19.
[ORIGIN from MONO- + IDEA + -ISM.]
(Abnormal or hypnotic) concentration of the mind on one idea.
■ **monoideˈistic** *adjective* E20.

monokaryon /mɒnə(ʊ)ˈkarɪən/ *noun.* M20.
[ORIGIN from MONO- + Greek *karuon* nut.]
BIOLOGY. A mononuclear cell, spore, or mycelium (in higher fungi that have a dikaryotic stage).
■ **monokaryˈotic** *adjective* containing a monokaryon; composed of monokaryons: M20.

monokini /mɒnə(ʊ)ˈkiːni/ *noun.* M20.
[ORIGIN from MONO- after BIKINI (as if from BI-).]
A scanty one-piece beach garment; *esp.* one equivalent to the lower part of a bikini, worn by women and girls.

monolatry /məˈnɒlətri/ *noun.* L19.
[ORIGIN from MONO- + -LATRY.]
The worship of one god, where other gods may be supposed to exist.
■ **monolater**, **monolatrist** *nouns* E20. **monolatrous** *adjective* L19.

M

monolayer /ˈmɒnəleɪə/ *noun.* E20.
[ORIGIN from MONO- + LAYER *noun.*]
1 CHEMISTRY etc. A layer or film one molecule thick. E20.
2 BIOLOGY & MEDICINE. A cell culture consisting of a layer one cell thick. M20.

monolingual /mɒnə(ʊ)ˈlɪŋgw(ə)l/ *adjective & noun.* L19.
[ORIGIN from MONO- + LINGUAL.]
▸ **A** *adjective.* **1** Knowing or using only one language. L19.
2 Written in only one language. M20.
▸ **B** *noun.* A person who knows only one language. M20.
■ **monolingualism** *noun* the state of knowing or using only one language M20.

monolinguist /mɒnə(ʊ)ˈlɪŋgwɪst/ *noun.* E20.
[ORIGIN from MONO- + LINGUIST.]
= MONOLINGUAL *noun.*

monolith /ˈmɒn(ə)lɪθ/ *noun & adjective.* M19.
[ORIGIN French *monolithe* from Greek *monolithos*, from MONO- + *lithos* stone.]
▸ **A** *noun.* **1** A single block of stone, *esp.* a large one shaped into a pillar or monument; ENGINEERING a large block of concrete, brickwork, etc., sunk in water, e.g. in the building of a dock. M19.
2 A person or thing like a monolith, esp. in being massive, immovable, or solidly uniform; a large impersonal political or corporate body. M20.

W. H. AUDEN The monolith Of State. J. WAIN You just wouldn't expect to get a flow of words out of a monolith like that.

▸ **B** *adjective.* Monolithic (*lit. & fig.*). M19.
■ **monolithal** *adjective* (*rare*) monolithic M19. **monolithism** *noun* monolithic quality, esp. of a totalitarian organization E20.

monolithic /mɒnəˈlɪθɪk/ *adjective.* E19.
[ORIGIN from (the same root as) MONOLITH + -IC.]
1 Formed of a single (large) block of stone; of the nature of a monolith. E19.
2 Of, pertaining to, or characterized by monoliths. M19.
3 ARCHITECTURE. Made of a solid unbroken mass (of concrete). L19.
4 *transf. & fig.* Like a monolith; massive; immovable, unwavering, unemotional; solidly uniform; (of an organization) large and autocratic or monopolistic. E20.

A. L. ROWSE The Fourth Symphony of Sibelius, the most monolithic of them all. *Nature* Would not the merging of the research councils create too monolithic a central sponsor? CLIVE JAMES For all its monolithic sense of purpose, the Soviet Union seems hopelessly barren.

5 ELECTRONICS. Of a solid-state circuit: composed of active and passive components formed in a single chip. M20.
■ **monolithically** *adverb* E20.

monolog *noun* see MONOLOGUE.

monological /mɒnəˈlɒdʒɪk(ə)l/ *adjective.* E19.
[ORIGIN from Greek *monologos* MONOLOGUE + -ICAL.]
Of, pertaining to, or of the nature of a monologue. Also, given to monologues.
■ **monologic** *adjective* pertaining to or of the nature of a monologue M19.

monologise *verb* var. of MONOLOGIZE.

monologist /məˈnɒlədʒɪst, ˈmɒn(ə)lɒgɪst/ *noun.* Also **-guist** /-gɪst/. E18.
[ORIGIN from MONOLOGUE + IST.]
1 A person who talks in monologue or soliloquizes. Also, a person who monopolizes conversation. E18.
2 A person who performs monologues. M19.

monologize /məˈnɒlədʒʌɪz, ˈmɒn(ə)lɒgʌɪz/ *verb intrans.* Also **-gu-** /-g-/, **-ise.** E19.
[ORIGIN from MONOLOGUE + -IZE.]
Talk in monologue; deliver a monologue.

monologue /ˈmɒn(ə)lɒg/ *noun & verb.* M16.
[ORIGIN French, formed as MONO- + -LOGUE: cf. late Greek *monologos* speaking alone.]
▸ **A** *noun.* Also ***-log.**
1 A long speech or harangue delivered by one person in company or in conversation; talk or discourse of the nature of a soliloquy. M16.

P. H. GIBBS He . . held everybody spellbound by a brilliant monologue on post-war problems. R. P. JHABVALA They weren't conversations . . they were monologues.

2 A scene in a drama in which one person speaks alone. Also, a dramatic composition for a single performer; a dramatic entertainment performed throughout by one person. M17. ▸**b** The form or style of dramatic scenes or compositions for one person. M17. ▸**c** A literary composition in the form of a soliloquy, *spec.* in Old English verse. L18.

E. HOLMES The opera began with a monologue. B. REID I learned monologues from her, and she saw that I had acting potential. **b** DRYDEN He also gives you an account of himself . . in monologue.

▸ **B** *verb intrans.* = MONOLOGIZE. E19.
■ **monologian** /mɒnəˈləʊdʒɪən/ *noun* (*rare*) = MONOLOGIST E17. **monology** /məˈnɒlədʒi/ *noun* †(**a**) a monologue; (**b**) the habit of monologizing: E17.

monologuise *verb* var. of MONOLOGIZE.

monologuist *noun* var. of MONOLOGIST.

monologuize *verb* var. of MONOLOGIZE.

monomachy /məˈnɒməki/ *noun.* Also in Latin form **monomachia** /mɒnə(ʊ)ˈmakɪə/. L16.
[ORIGIN Late Latin *monomachia* from Greek *monomakhia*, formed as MONO- + -MACHY.]
A combat or contest between two; a single combat, a duel.

monomania /mɒnə(ʊ)ˈmeɪnɪə/ *noun.* E19.
[ORIGIN from MONO- + -MANIA.]
1 A mental illness in which a person is dominated by one irrational set of ideas. E19.
2 An exaggerated enthusiasm for one subject; an obsession, a craze (*for*). M19.
■ **monomaniac** *noun & adjective* (**a**) *noun* a person who has (a) monomania; (**b**) *adjective* = MONOMANIACAL: E19. **monomaniacal** /-məˈnʌɪək(ə)l/ *adjective* pertaining to, characterized by, or exhibiting monomania M19. **monomaniacally** /-məˈnʌɪək(ə)li/ *adverb* M19.

†**monome** *noun & adjective.* M18–M19.
[ORIGIN French, after *binome*: see BINOMIAL. Cf. MONOMIAL.]
MATH. = MONOMIAL *noun* 1.

monomer /ˈmɒnəmə/ *noun.* E20.
[ORIGIN from MONO- + -MER.]
CHEMISTRY. A compound from which a dimer, trimer, polymer, etc., is or might be formed by the linking together of its molecules (with or without those of another compound).
■ **monoˈmeric** *adjective* of the nature of a monomer, consisting of a monomer or monomers L19.

monomerous /məˈnɒm(ə)rəs/ *adjective.* E19.
[ORIGIN formed as MONOMER + -OUS.]
1 ENTOMOLOGY. Consisting of only one segment. E19.
2 BOTANY. Of a flower: having one member in each whorl. L19.

monometallic /mɒnə(ʊ)mɪˈtalɪk/ *adjective.* M19.
[ORIGIN from MONO- + METALLIC, after *bimetallic.*]
1 Consisting of one metal only; CHEMISTRY containing one metal atom in the molecule. M19.
2 Pertaining to, involving, or using a standard of currency based on one metal. Now chiefly *hist.* L19.
■ **monometallism** /-ˈmɛt(ə)lɪz(ə)m/ *noun* the monometallic system or standard of currency L19. **monometallist** /-ˈmɛt(ə)lɪst/ *noun & adjective* (**a**) *noun* an advocate of monometallism; (**b**) *adjective* favouring monometallism: L19.

monometer /məˈnɒmɪtə/ *noun.* E19.
[ORIGIN Late Latin (adjective) from Greek *monometros* adjective, from MONO- + *metron* METRE *noun*[1].]
PROSODY. A line consisting of one metrical foot.

monometric /mɒnə(ʊ)ˈmɛtrɪk/ *adjective.* M19.
[ORIGIN from MONO- + -METRIC.]
1 CRYSTALLOGRAPHY. = CUBIC *adjective* 2b. Now *rare* or *obsolete.* M19.
2 Written in one metre. *rare.* L19.

monomial /məˈnəʊmɪəl/ *noun & adjective.* E18.
[ORIGIN Irreg. from MONO- after *binomial.*]
▸ **A** *noun.* **1** MATH. An expression consisting of one term only. E18.
2 = MONONYM. *rare.* L19.
▸ **B** *adjective.* **1** MATH. Consisting of one term only. E19.
2 Designating or pertaining to a term, esp. a taxonomic name, consisting of one word only; mononymic. L19.

monomino /məˈnɒmɪnəʊ/ *noun.* Pl. **-oes.** M20.
[ORIGIN from MONO- + DOMINO, by deliberate false analogy as though the latter were from DI-[2]. Cf. PENTOMINO.]
MATH. A square considered as a structural unit or as occupying a position in a grid.

monomolecular /ˌmɒnə(ʊ)məˈlɛkjʊlə/ *adjective.* L19.
[ORIGIN from MONO- + MOLECULAR.]
CHEMISTRY. **1** Involving a single molecule; (of a reaction) having a molecularity of one; unimolecular. L19.
2 Of a film or layer: one molecule thick. E20.

monomorphic /mɒnə(ʊ)ˈmɔːfɪk/ *adjective.* M19.
[ORIGIN from MONO- + Greek *morphē* form + -IC.]
Having or existing in only one form; monomorphous; *esp.* in BIOLOGY, (of a population or species) identical or homogeneous as regards morphology or genotype.

monomorphism /mɒnə(ʊ)ˈmɔːfɪz(ə)m/ *noun.* M19.
[ORIGIN formed as MONOMORPHIC + -ISM.]
1 BIOLOGY. Monomorphic condition. M19.
2 MATH. A one-to-one homomorphism. M20.

monomorphous /mɒnə(ʊ)ˈmɔːfəs/ *adjective.* M19.
[ORIGIN formed as MONOMORPHIC + -OUS.]
Chiefly BIOLOGY. Having or characterized by only one form; (of an insect) hemimetabolous.

monomyarian /ˌmɒnə(ʊ)mʌɪˈɛːrɪən/ *adjective & noun.* M19.
[ORIGIN from mod. Latin *Monomyaria* former taxonomic name, formed as MONO- + Greek *mus* muscle: see -ARY[1], -AN.]
▸ **A** *adjective.* Of a bivalve mollusc: having only one (posterior) adductor muscle. M19.
▸ **B** *noun.* A monomyarian mollusc (e.g. an oyster). M19.
■ Also **monoˈmyary** *adjective & noun* M19.

Monongahela /mənɒŋgəˈhiːlə/ *noun. US.* Now *rare.* E19.
[ORIGIN A river in Pennsylvania, USA.]
(American) rye whiskey.

mononuclear /mɒnə(ʊ)ˈnjuːklɪə/ *adjective & noun.* L19.
[ORIGIN from MONO- + NUCLEAR.]
Chiefly BIOLOGY. ▸**A** *adjective.* Having one nucleus. L19.
▸ **B** *noun.* A mononuclear cell; *spec.* a monocyte. E20.

mononucleated /mɒnə(ʊ)ˈnjuːklɪeɪtɪd/ *adjective.* L19.
[ORIGIN from MONO- + NUCLEUS: see -ATE[2], -ED[1].]
= MONONUCLEAR *adjective.*
■ Also **mononucleate** *adjective* E20.

mononucleosis /ˌmɒnə(ʊ)njuːklɪˈəʊsɪs/ *noun.* Pl. **-oses** /-ˈəʊsiːz/. E20.
[ORIGIN from MONONUCLEAR + -OSIS.]
MEDICINE. An abnormally high proportion of mononuclear leucocytes (monocytes or lymphocytes), or of monocytes alone, in the blood; *esp.* (more fully ***infectious mononucleosis***) glandular fever.

mononym /ˈmɒnənɪm/ *noun.* L19.
[ORIGIN from MONO- + -NYM.]
A term consisting of one word only.
■ **monoˈnymic** *adjective* L19.

monoped /ˈmɒnəpɛd/ *noun & adjective.* E19.
[ORIGIN from MONO- + Latin *ped-*, *pes* foot.]
= MONOPOD.

monophagous /məˈnɒfəgəs/ *adjective.* M19.
[ORIGIN from MONO- + -PHAGOUS. Cf. Greek *monophagos* that eats alone.]
That eats only one kind of food.

monophagy /məˈnɒfədʒi/ *noun.* E17.
[ORIGIN Greek *monophagia* eating alone, formed as MONO- + -PHAGY.]
1 The eating of only one kind of food. E17.
2 Eating alone. M17.

monophasic /mɒnə(ʊ)ˈfeɪzɪk/ *adjective.* L19.
[ORIGIN from MONO- + PHASE *noun* + -IC.]
Exhibiting a single phase; *esp.* (PHYSIOLOGY) designating or pertaining to (a record of) a nerve impulse that is of the same sign throughout.
■ **monophasically** *adverb* by a technique yielding a monophasic record E20. **monophasicity** /-ˈzɪsɪti/ *noun* M20.

monophonemic /mɒnə(ʊ)fəˈniːmɪk/ *adjective.* M20.
[ORIGIN from MONO- + PHONEMIC.]
LINGUISTICS. Of or pertaining to a single phoneme; consisting of a single phoneme.
■ **monophoneˈmatic** *adjective* = MONOPHONEMIC *adjective* M20. **monophoneˈmatically** *adverb* M20.

monophonic /mɒnə(ʊ)ˈfɒnɪk/ *adjective*. E19.
[ORIGIN from MONO- + Greek *phōnē* sound + -IC.]
†**1** Of an alphabet: phonetic. Only in E19.
2 *MUSIC*. = HOMOPHONIC 1. Also, having a simple melodic line predominating over other parts. L19.
3 Of sound recording and reproduction: involving only one channel, so that the sound output seems to come from a single source; = MONAURAL *adjective* 2. Opp. STEREOPHONIC. M20.
■ **monophonically** *adverb* M20.

monophonous /məˈnɒf(ə)nəs/ *adjective*. *rare*. M19.
[ORIGIN formed as MONOPHONIC + -OUS.]
1 = HOMOPHONOUS. M19.
2 *MUSIC*. Of a musical instrument: producing only one note at a time. Also, monophonic. L19.

monophony /məˈnɒfəni/ *noun*. L19.
[ORIGIN formed as MONOPHONIC: see -PHONY.]
1 Music in which there is a single melodic line. L19.
2 Monophonic recording or reproduction. M20.

monophthong /ˈmɒnəfθɒŋ/ *noun*. E17.
[ORIGIN Greek *monophthoggos* adjective, from MONO- + *phthoggos* voice, sound.]
PHONETICS. A single vowel sound, a vowel sound without any glide.
■ **monophˈthongal** *adjective* L18. **monophthongiˈzation** *noun* the process or state of being monophthongized L19. **monophthongize** *verb trans. & intrans.* convert, undergo conversion, into a monophthong E20.

monophyletic /ˌmɒnə(ʊ)fʌɪˈlɛtɪk/ *adjective*. L19.
[ORIGIN from MONO- + Greek *phuletikos*, from *phulē* tribe: see -IC.]
BIOLOGY. (Of a group or taxon) descended from a common evolutionary ancestor or ancestral group; (of a classification) employing such taxa. Also *spec.*, holophyletic.
■ ˈ**monophyly** *noun* the state of being monophyletic E20.

monophyodont /mɒnə(ʊ)ˈfʌɪədɒnt/ *noun & adjective*. M19.
[ORIGIN from Greek *monophuēs* single (formed as MONO- + *phuē* growth) + -ODONT.]
ZOOLOGY. (Designating or pertaining to) an animal which grows only one set of teeth. Cf. DIPHYODONT.

Monophysite /məˈnɒfɪsʌɪt/ *noun & adjective*. M17.
[ORIGIN ecclesiastical Latin *Monophysita* from ecclesiastical Greek *monophusitēs*, formed as MONO- + *phusis* nature: see -ITE[1].]
CHRISTIAN THEOLOGY. ▸**A** *noun*. A person who holds that there is only one inseparable nature in the person of Jesus, contrary to a declaration of the council of Chalcedon in AD 451; *loosely* a member of the Coptic, Ethiopian, Armenian, or Jacobite Church. M17.
▸**B** *adjective*. Of or pertaining to the doctrine of the Monophysites or a Church professing this doctrine. L18.
■ **monophysitic** /ˌmɒnə(ʊ)fɪˈsɪtɪk/ *adjective* (*rare*) = MONOPHYSITE *adjective* E19. **monophysitism** *noun* the doctrine of the Monophysites M19.

monopitch /ˈmɒnə(ʊ)pɪtʃ/ *noun & adjective*. M20.
[ORIGIN from MONO- + PITCH *noun*[2].]
▸**A** *noun*. Uniformity of vocal pitch. M20.
▸**B** *adjective*. Of a roof: having a single uniformly sloping surface. Of a building: having such a roof. M20.

monoplane /ˈmɒnəpleɪn/ *noun*. E20.
[ORIGIN from MONO- + PLANE *noun*[4].]
An aeroplane having only one wing across or (now usu.) on either side of the fuselage. Formerly also, the wing of such an aeroplane.

monoplegia /mɒnə(ʊ)ˈpliːdʒə/ *noun*. L19.
[ORIGIN from MONO- + -PLEGIA.]
MEDICINE. Paralysis restricted to one limb or region of the body.
■ **monoplegic** *adjective* pertaining to or affected with monoplegia L19.

monoploid /ˈmɒnə(ʊ)plɔɪd/ *adjective & noun*. E20.
[ORIGIN from MONO- + -PLOID.]
BIOLOGY. = HAPLOID *adjective & noun*.
■ **monoploidy** *noun* = HAPLOIDY M20.

monopod /ˈmɒnə(ʊ)pɒd/ *noun & adjective*. Also **-pode** /-pəʊd/. E19.
[ORIGIN Latin *monopodius* adjective, *-ium* noun from late Greek *monopodios* adjective, *-ion* noun, formed as MONO- + *pod-*, *pous* foot.]
▸**A** *noun*. A creature or structure having only one foot; *spec.* (*a*) (usu. **-pode**) any of a mythical race of beings having only one foot, with which they shaded themselves from the sun; (*b*) a one-legged support for a camera etc. E19.
▸**B** *adjective*. Having only one foot. L19.

monopodium /mɒnə(ʊ)ˈpəʊdɪəm/ *noun*. Pl. **-ia** /-ɪə/. E19.
[ORIGIN formed as MONO- + PODIUM.]
1 A table or stand with a single support. Also, a support for an early 19th-cent. table, sideboard, etc., comprising an animal's head with a single foot. E19.
2 *BOTANY*. A single continuous growth axis which extends at its apex and produces successive lateral shoots. Cf. SYMPODIUM. L19.
■ **monopodial** *adjective* (*BOTANY*) pertaining to or of the nature of a monopodium L19. **monopodially** *adverb* (*BOTANY*) in the manner of a monopodium L19.

monopodous /məˈnɒpədəs/ *adjective*. *rare*. L19.
[ORIGIN from Greek MONO- + *pod-*, *pous* foot + -OUS.]
Having one foot.

monopody /məˈnɒpədi/ *noun*. M19.
[ORIGIN mod. Latin *monopodia* from Greek, formed as MONOPODOUS: see -Y[3].]
PROSODY. A measure consisting of a single metrical foot.

monopolar /mɒnə(ʊ)ˈpəʊlə/ *adjective*. L19.
[ORIGIN from MONO- + POLAR *adjective*.]
Pertaining to or having a single pole; *esp.* designating or pertaining to medical techniques and apparatus involving the use of two electrodes, one of which acts as a neutral or reference electrode.

monopole /ˈmɒnəpəʊl/ *noun*[1]. M16.
[ORIGIN Old French & mod. French, or late Latin *monopolium* MONOPOLY.]
†**1** A monopoly. M16–L17.
†**2** A conspiracy. M–L16.
3 (**M-**.) (The designation of) champagne of a brand exclusive to a particular shipper. L19.

> T. BURKE Two bottles of dry Monopole to be put on the ice.

monopole /ˈmɒnəpəʊl/ *noun*[2]. M20.
[ORIGIN from MONO- + POLE *noun*[2].]
1 A single electric charge or (esp.) magnetic pole (also ***magnetic monopole***), having a spherically symmetric field. M20.
2 A radio aerial consisting of a single conducting rod with an electrical connection at one end. M20.

monopolise *verb* var. of MONOPOLIZE.

monopolist /məˈnɒp(ə)lɪst/ *noun & adjective*. E17.
[ORIGIN from MONOPOLY or MONOPOLE *noun*[1] + -IST.]
▸**A** *noun*. A person who monopolizes something or who possesses a monopoly; a person who favours monopoly. E17.
▸**B** *adjective*. Enjoying or favouring a monopoly. M19.
■ **monopolism** *noun* the system of monopolies; support for a monopoly: M19.

monopolistic /mənɒpəˈlɪstɪk/ *adjective*. M19.
[ORIGIN from MONOPOLIST + -IC.]
Of, pertaining to, or characterized by a monopoly or a system of monopolies; of the nature of a monopoly.
■ **monopolistically** *adverb* E20.

monopolize /məˈnɒpəlʌɪz/ *verb trans*. Also **-ise**. E17.
[ORIGIN from MONOPOLY or MONOPOLE *noun*[1] + -IZE.]
Have or obtain a monopoly of; obtain exclusive possession or control of (a trade, commodity, etc.); get or keep entirely to oneself; dominate or prevent others from sharing in (a conversation, a person's attention, etc.).

> P. G. WODEHOUSE One of those forceful characters which monopolize any stage on which they appear. R. LARDNER We'd better join the ladies or my wife will say I'm monopolizing you.

■ **monopolizable** *adjective* L19. **monopoliˈzation** *noun* the action or process of monopolizing something or someone; the condition of being monopolized: E18. **monopolizer** *noun* E17.

monopoly /məˈnɒp(ə)li/ *noun*. M16.
[ORIGIN Latin *monopolium* from Greek *monopōlion*, *-pōlia*, from MONO- + *pōlein* sell.]
1 Exclusive possession or control of the trade in a commodity, service, etc.; the condition of having no competitor in one's trade or business; *LAW* a situation in which one supplier or producer controls more than a specified fraction of the market. M16. ▸**b** *spec.* An exclusive privilege (conferred by a monarch, state, etc.) of selling some commodity or trading with a particular place or country. L16.

> BURKE You have, in this kingdom, an advantage in Lead, that amounts to a monopoly. **b** J. SINCLAIR The Public Revenue [of Russia] . . is likely to increase, particularly the . . monopoly of brandy.

2 *gen.* Exclusive possession, control, or exercise of something. Foll. by *of*, *on*. E17.

> A. E. STEVENSON We claim no monopoly on the ideals we assert. L. GRIFFITHS For two years I had a monopoly of conkers in the playground.

3 A thing which is the subject of a monopoly. M19.

> M. E. G. DUFF The culture . . of tobacco was made a Crown monopoly.

4 A company etc. which has a monopoly. L19.

> E. BELLAMY The absorption of business by ever larger monopolies continued.

5 (**M-**.) (Proprietary name for) a board game in which the players engage in property dealings, the board representing streets etc. in a large city. M20.

> J. GARDAM The sky darkened during supper and during Monopoly the rain began.

– COMB.: **monopoly capitalism** a capitalist system typified by trade monopolies in the hands of a few people; **Monopoly money** imitation money used in the game of Monopoly; money having no real existence or value; inflated currency; **monopoly value** the value of something that is the subject of a monopoly; extra value arising from the holding of a monopoly.

monopolylogue /mɒnəˈpɒlɪlɒg/ *noun*. *obsolete* exc. *hist*. E19.
[ORIGIN from MONO- + POLY- + -LOGUE.]
An entertainment in which a single performer sustains many characters.

Monoprix /ˈmɒnə(ʊ)priː/ *noun*. M20.
[ORIGIN French, lit. 'one price'.]
Any of a chain of stores in France in which cheap goods are sold (orig. all at the same price). Also ***Monoprix store*** etc.

monops /ˈmɒnɒps/ *adjective & noun*. *rare*. M19.
[ORIGIN from Greek MONO- + *ōps* eye.]
(A being) having one eye.

monopsony /məˈnɒpsəni/ *noun*. M20.
[ORIGIN from MONO- + Greek *opsōnein* buy provisions + -Y[3].]
ECONOMICS. A situation in which there is a sole or predominant consumer for a particular product.
■ **monopsonist** *noun* the consumer in a monopsony M20. **monopsoˈnistic** *adjective* pertaining to or of the nature of a monopsony M20.

monopsychism /mɒnə(ʊ)ˈsʌɪkɪz(ə)m/ *noun*. M19.
[ORIGIN from MONO- + PSYCHE *noun*[1] + -ISM.]
(The theory proposing) the unity of all human souls.

monopteros /məˈnɒptərɒs/ *noun*. Also (earlier) †**-on**, †**monopter**. L17.
[ORIGIN Use as noun of Latin adjective from Greek, = having one wing, from MONO- + *pteron* wing. Earlier forms from Greek & from French *monoptère*.]
CLASSICAL ANTIQUITIES. A temple consisting of a single circle of columns supporting a roof.
■ **monopteral** *adjective* of the construction of a monopteros E19.

monoptic /məˈnɒptɪk/ *adjective*. M17.
[ORIGIN from MONO- + OPTIC *adjective*.]
= MONOCULAR *adjective*.
■ **monoptically** *adverb* M20.

monoptote /ˈmɒnəptəʊt/ *noun*. E17.
[ORIGIN Late Latin *monoptotus* from late Greek *monoptōtos* having one case, from Greek MONO- + *ptōtos* falling, cogn. with *ptōsis* case.]
GRAMMAR. A noun occurring in a single oblique case (as Latin *astu*).

monorail /ˈmɒnə(ʊ)reɪl/ *adjective & noun*. L19.
[ORIGIN from MONO- + RAIL *noun*[2].]
▸**A** *adjective*. Having or using a single rail; designating or pertaining to a railway in which the track is a single rail. L19.
monorail camera a camera mounted on a rail which allows positional adjustment and may support additional components.
▸**B** *noun*. A railway in which the track is a single rail, on or suspended from which vehicles run; a vehicle that runs in this way. E20.

monorheme /ˈmɒnə(ʊ)riːm/ *noun*. M20.
[ORIGIN from MONO- + RHEME.]
LINGUISTICS. A single element or word with a phrasal meaning.

monorhine /ˈmɒnə(ʊ)rʌɪn/ *adjective*. L19.
[ORIGIN from MONO- + Greek *rhin-*, *rhis* nose.]
ZOOLOGY. Having only one nasal passage; *spec.* designating agnathan vertebrates.
■ **monorhinal** *adjective* = MONORHINE L19. **monorhinous** *adjective* = MONORHINE E20.

monorhyme /ˈmɒnə(ʊ)rʌɪm/ *noun & adjective*. Also (*arch.*) **-rime**. M18.
[ORIGIN French *monorime*, formed as MONO- + *rime* RHYME *noun*.]
PROSODY. ▸**A** *noun*. A poem or passage in which all the lines have the same rhyme; in *pl.*, lines having one rhyme. M18.
▸**B** *adjective*. Having a single rhyme. M19.
■ **monorhymed** *adjective* = MONORHYME *adjective* L19.

monosabio /monoˈsabjo, mɒnəʊˈsabɪəʊ/ *noun*. Pl. **-os** /-ɔs, -əʊz/. L19.
[ORIGIN Spanish, from *mono* monkey + *sabio* wise, trained.]
BULLFIGHTING. A picador's assistant in the ring.

monosaccharide /mɒnə(ʊ)ˈsakərʌɪd/ *noun*. L19.
[ORIGIN from MONO- + SACCHARIDE.]
CHEMISTRY. A sugar which cannot be hydrolysed to give simpler sugars.
■ Also **monosaccharose** *noun* E20.

monose /ˈmɒnəʊz, -s/ *noun*. L19.
[ORIGIN from MONO- + -OSE[2].]
BIOCHEMISTRY. = MONOSACCHARIDE.

monosemic /mɒnə(ʊ)ˈsiːmɪk/ *adjective*. L19.
[ORIGIN from Greek *monosēmos*, from MONO- + *sēma* sign, mark: see -IC.]
1 *PROSODY*. Consisting of or equal to a single mora. *rare*. L19.
2 *LINGUISTICS*. Having only one meaning. M20.

monosemy /ˈmɒnə(ʊ)siːmi, məˈnɒsɪmi/ *noun*. M20.
[ORIGIN from MONO- + Greek *sēma* sign, mark + -Y[3], after POLYSEMY.]
LINGUISTICS. The property of having only one meaning.
■ **monosemous** *adjective* L20.

monosexual /mɒnə(ʊ)ˈsɛkʃʊəl/ *adjective*. L19.
[ORIGIN from MONO- + SEXUAL.]
1 Of or pertaining to one sex only. L19.
2 *ZOOLOGY*. Having the male and female reproductive organs in different individuals, dioecious. E20.

M

3 Sexually attracted to individuals of one sex only. **E20.**
■ **monosexu'ality** *noun* **E20.**

monosign /ˈmɒnə(ʊ)sʌɪn/ *noun.* **M20.**
[ORIGIN from MONO- + SIGN *noun*.]
A sign or word used with only one meaning at a time. Opp. PLURISIGN.
■ **mono'signative** *adjective* (of a sign or word) used with only one meaning at a time **M20.**

monosiphonous /mɒnə(ʊ)ˈsʌɪf(ə)nəs/ *adjective.* **M19.**
[ORIGIN from Greek MONO- + *siphōn* tube, pipe + -OUS.]
BOTANY. Of an alga: having fronds composed of a single strand of large elongated cells.
■ Also **monosiphonic** /-sʌɪˈfɒnɪk/ *adjective* **L19.**

monoski /ˈmɒnəskiː/ *noun & verb.* **M20.**
[ORIGIN from MONO- + SKI *noun, verb*.]
▶ **A** *noun.* A single ski on which a person stands with both feet. **M20.**
▶ **B** *verb intrans.* Use a monoski. **M20.**
■ **monoskier** *noun* **M20.**

monosodium /mɒnə(ʊ)ˈsəʊdɪəm/ *adjective.* **M19.**
[ORIGIN from MONO- + SODIUM *noun*.]
CHEMISTRY. Designating compounds, chiefly salts, containing one sodium atom or ion for each combining radical or ion.
monosodium glutamate the white crystalline sodium salt of glutamic acid, used in foods as a flavour enhancer or (esp. in Chinese etc. cuisine) a condiment.

monosome /ˈmɒnəsəʊm/ *noun.* **E20.**
[ORIGIN from MONO- + -SOME[3].]
CYTOLOGY. **1** An unpaired chromosome in a diploid chromosome complement; a diploid individual having such a chromosome. **E20.**
2 A single ribosome attached to a molecule of messenger RNA. **M20.**

monosomic /mɒnə(ʊ)ˈsəʊmɪk/ *adjective & noun.* **E20.**
[ORIGIN from MONOSOME + -IC.]
CYTOLOGY. ▶**A** *adjective.* Having or designating a diploid chromosome complement in which one (occas. more than one) chromosome lacks its homologous partner. **E20.**
▶ **B** *noun.* A monosomic individual or variety. **E20.**
■ **'monosomy** *noun* monosomic character or condition. **M20.**

monospermic /mɒnə(ʊ)ˈspəːmɪk/ *adjective.* **L19.**
[ORIGIN formed as MONOSPERMOUS + -IC.]
1 *BOTANY.* = MONOSPERMOUS. **L19.**
2 *BIOLOGY.* Pertaining to or exhibiting monospermy. **E20.**

monospermous /mɒnə(ʊ)ˈspəːməs/ *adjective.* **L17.**
[ORIGIN from MONO- + Greek *sperma* seed, SPERM + -OUS.]
BOTANY. Producing only one seed.
■ **'monosperm** *noun* (*rare*) a monospermous plant **L19.** **monospermal** *adjective* = MONOSPERMOUS **M19.**

monospermy /ˈmɒnə(ʊ)spəːmi/ *noun.* **E20.**
[ORIGIN formed as MONOSPERMOUS: see -Y[3].]
BIOLOGY. Penetration of an ovum by a single sperm.

monostable /ˈmɒnə(ʊ)steɪb(ə)l/ *adjective.* **M20.**
[ORIGIN from MONO- + STABLE *adjective*.]
Chiefly *ELECTRONICS.* Having only one stable position or state.

monostich /ˈmɒnə(ʊ)stɪk/ *noun.* Also (earlier) in Greek form †**-stichon**. **L16.**
[ORIGIN Late Latin *monostichum*, *-ium* from Greek *monostikhon* use as noun of *monostikhos* adjective, from MONO- + *stikhos* row, line of verse.]
PROSODY. A poem or epigram consisting of only one metrical line.

monostich /ˈmɒnə(ʊ)stɪk/ *adjective.* **M17.**
[ORIGIN Greek *monostikhos*: see MONOSTICH *noun*.]
PROSODY. Consisting of a single line of verse.

†**monostichon** *noun* see MONOSTICH *noun*.

monostichous /məˈnɒstɪkəs, mɒnə(ʊ)ˈstʌɪkəs/ *adjective.* **M19.**
[ORIGIN from Greek *monostikhos* (see MONOSTICH *noun*) + -OUS.]
(Having parts) arranged in or consisting of a single layer or row; *BOTANY* arranged in a single vertical row.

monostrophic /mɒnə(ʊ)ˈstrɒfɪk/ *adjective.* **L17.**
[ORIGIN Greek *monostrophikos*, from *monostrophos* adjective, formed as MONO- + STROPHE: see -IC.]
PROSODY. Consisting of repetitions of the same strophic arrangement.

†**monosyllaba** *noun* pl. of MONOSYLLABON.

monosyllabic /mɒnə(ʊ)sɪˈlabɪk/ *adjective.* **M18.**
[ORIGIN from MONO- + SYLLABIC. Cf. medieval Latin *monosyllabicus*, French *monosyllabique*.]
1 Of a word: consisting of one syllable. **M18.**
2 Consisting of monosyllables or of a monosyllable; *spec.* (of a language, e.g. Chinese) having a vocabulary wholly composed of monosyllables. **M18.**
3 Of a person: uttering only monosyllables. **L19.**
■ †**monosyllabical** *adjective* = MONOSYLLABIC **M17–M19.** **monosyllabically** *adverb* **E19.** **monosyllabicity** /-sɪləˈbɪsɪti/ *noun* **M20.**

monosyllabism /mɒnə(ʊ)ˈsɪləbɪz(ə)m/ *noun.* **E19.**
[ORIGIN from MONOSYLLABLE + -ISM.]
The quality or condition of being monosyllabic; addiction to the use of monosyllables.

monosyllable /ˈmɒnə(ʊ)sɪləb(ə)l/ *noun & adjective.* **M16.**
[ORIGIN from MONO- + SYLLABLE *noun*, prob. after Latin MONOSYLLABON.]
▶ **A** *noun.* A word of one syllable. **M16.**

> A. TROLLOPE 'No.' She pronounced the monosyllable alone.

in monosyllables in monosyllabic words; in simple direct words; curtly, bluntly; saying little but 'yes' or 'no'.
▶ **B** *adjective.* = MONOSYLLABIC *adjective* 1, 2. Now *rare.* **L16.**

†**monosyllabon** *noun.* Pl. **-ba.** **L16–E18.**
[ORIGIN Latin from Greek *monosullabon* neut. of *monosullabos* adjective, from *monos* MONO- + *sullabē* SYLLABLE *noun*.]
A monosyllable.

monosymmetrical /ˌmɒnə(ʊ)sɪˈmɛtrɪk(ə)l/ *adjective.* **L19.**
[ORIGIN from MONO- + SYMMETRICAL.]
1 Chiefly *BOTANY.* Divisible into exactly similar halves in one plane only; zygomorphic. **L19.**
2 *MINERALOGY.* = MONOCLINIC. **L19.**
■ **monosymmetric** *adjective* = MONOSYMMETRICAL **L19.** **monosymmetrically** *adverb* **L19.** **mono'symmetry** *noun* monosymmetrical condition **L19.**

monotechnic /mɒnə(ʊ)ˈtɛknɪk/ *adjective.* **E20.**
[ORIGIN from MONO- after POLYTECHNIC.]
Dealing with or (of a college etc.) providing instruction in a single technical subject.

monotessaron /mɒnə(ʊ)ˈtɛsərən/ *noun.* **M17.**
[ORIGIN Erron. from Greek MONO- after DIATESSARON.]
= DIATESSARON 3.

monothalamic /ˌmɒnə(ʊ)θəˈlamɪk/ *adjective.* **M19.**
[ORIGIN from MONO- + Greek *thalamos* chamber + -IC.]
1 *ZOOLOGY.* = MONOTHALAMOUS. **M19.**
2 *BOTANY.* Of a fruit: formed from a single flower. **L19.**

monothalamous /mɒnə(ʊ)ˈθaləməs/ *adjective.* **E19.**
[ORIGIN formed as MONOTHALAMIC + -OUS.]
ZOOLOGY. Of a shell, hollow organ, etc.: having only one chamber.

monotheism /ˈmɒnə(ʊ)ˌθiːɪz(ə)m/ *noun.* **M17.**
[ORIGIN from Greek MONO- + *theos* god + -ISM.]
The doctrine or belief that there is only one God.

monotheist /ˈmɒnə(ʊ)ˌθiːɪst/ *noun & adjective.* **L17.**
[ORIGIN formed as MONOTHEISM + -IST.]
▶ **A** *noun.* A person who believes in only one God; an adherent of monotheism. **L17.**
▶ **B** *adjective.* = MONOTHEISTIC. **E19.**
■ **monothe'istic** *adjective* of, pertaining to, believing in, or characterized by monotheism **M19.** **monothe'istically** *adverb* **E20.**

Monothelite /məˈnɒθɪlʌɪt/ *noun & adjective.* Also **-lete** /-liːt/. **LME.**
[ORIGIN medieval Latin *monothelita* from late Greek *monothelētēs*, from Greek MONO- + *thelētēs* agent noun from *thelein* to will.]
THEOLOGY. ▶**A** *noun.* A person who holds the (heretical) doctrine (first propounded in the 7th cent.) that Jesus had only one (divine) will. Cf. DYOTHELITE. **LME.**
▶ **B** *adjective.* Of or pertaining to the Monothelites or Monothelitism. **E17.**
■ **Monothelism** *noun* (*rare*) = MONOTHELITISM **L17.** **Monothe'litic** *adjective* = MONOTHELITE *adjective* **E18.** **Monothelitism** *noun* the doctrine of the Monothelites **E18.**

monothematic /ˌmɒnə(ʊ)θɪˈmatɪk/ *adjective.* **L19.**
[ORIGIN from MONO- + THEMATIC.]
Chiefly *MUSIC.* Having a single dominant theme or element.

monotint /ˈmɒnə(ʊ)tɪnt/ *noun.* **L19.**
[ORIGIN from MONO- + TINT *noun*.]
Representation in one colour or tint (chiefly in ***in monotint***). Also, a picture in one colour.

monotocardian /mɒnəʊtəˈkɑːdɪən/ *adjective & noun.* **E20.**
[ORIGIN from mod. Latin *Monotocardia* former taxonomic name, from Greek MONO- + *ōtos*, *ous* auricle + *kardia* heart: see -AN.]
▶ **A** *adjective.* Designating or pertaining to a group of prosobranch molluscs having only one auricle and one gill. **E20.**
▶ **B** *noun.* A monotocardian mollusc. **E20.**

monotocous /məˈnɒtəkəs/ *adjective.* **L19.**
[ORIGIN from Greek *monotokos*, from MONO- + *tok-*, *tiktein* bring forth: see -OUS.]
1 *ZOOLOGY.* Normally bearing only one at a birth; uniparous. **L19.**
2 *BOTANY.* = MONOCARPIC. **L19.**

monotone /ˈmɒnətəʊn/ *noun & adjective.* **M17.**
[ORIGIN mod. Latin *monotonus* adjective from late Greek *monotonos*, from MONO- + *tonos* TONE *noun*.]
▶ **A** *noun.* **1** A continuance or uninterrupted repetition of the same tone; an utterance or other sound continued or repeated without change of pitch. **M17.**

> C. AIKEN On the bare boards.. The rain drummed monotones. M. ANGELOU His replies to questions.. were generally given in a monotone.

2 *fig.* A monotonous continuance or recurrence *of* something. **M19.**

> J. RUSKIN Its [science's] history is a monotone of endurance and destruction.

3 Monotony or sameness of style in writing etc.; something composed in a monotonous style. **L19.**
4 = MONOTINT. **L19.**
▶ **B** *adjective.* **1** Unchanging or repetitious in pitch or tone. **M18.**
2 *MATH.* = MONOTONIC *adjective* 2. **E20.**
■ **monotoned** *adjective* (*rare*) having only one tone **M19.** **monotonely** *adverb* (*MATH.*) = MONOTONICALLY (b) **E20.**

monotone /ˈmɒnətəʊn/ *verb trans.* **M19.**
[ORIGIN from the noun.]
Recite, speak, or sing in a monotone; intone on a single note.

monotonic /mɒnə(ʊ)ˈtɒnɪk/ *adjective.* **L18.**
[ORIGIN formed as MONOTONE *verb* + -IC.]
1 Of or pertaining to a monotone; uttered in a monotone. Also, capable of producing only a single tone. **L18.**
2 *MATH.* Of a function or sequence: varying consistently so that it either never increases or never decreases. **E20.**
■ **monotonically** *adverb* (*a*) in the manner of a monotone; (*b*) *MATH.* in the manner of a monotonic function: **L19.** **monotonicity** /-ˈnɪsɪti/ *noun* **M20.**

monotonous /məˈnɒt(ə)nəs/ *adjective.* **L18.**
[ORIGIN formed as MONOTONE *verb* + -OUS.]
1 (Of sound, utterance, etc.) continuing on the same note; having little or no variation in tone, pitch, or cadence. **L18.**
2 Lacking in variety; uninteresting or tedious through continued sameness. **E19.**

> LD MACAULAY The monotonous smoothness of Byron's versification. A. TOFFLER We are driving along a monotonous turnpike. E. HEATH The food was.. extraordinarily monotonous.

3 *MATH.* = MONOTONIC *adjective* 2. **L19.**
■ **monotonist** *noun* (*rare*) a person who is monotonous or who delights in monotony **M18.** **monotonize** *verb trans.* make monotonous **E19.** **monotonously** *adverb* (*a*) in a monotonous manner; with tiresome uniformity or lack of variation; (*b*) *MATH.* = MONOTONICALLY (b): **L18.** **monotonousness** *noun* **E19.**

monotony /məˈnɒt(ə)ni/ *noun.* **M17.**
[ORIGIN French *monotonie* from late Greek *monotonia*, from *monotonos* MONOTONE *adjective*: see -Y[3].]
1 Sameness of tone or pitch; lack of variety in cadence or inflection. Also, a monotonous sound, a monotone. **M17.**
2 Tedious repetition and routine; lack of interesting variety; dull or tedious routine. **E18.**

> I. BANKS The monotony of this dull waste of grass. R. THOMAS The monotony of domestic life bored her.

monotreme /ˈmɒnə(ʊ)triːm/ *noun & adjective.* **E19.**
[ORIGIN from Greek MONO- + *trēmat-*, *trēma* hole, perforation.]
ZOOLOGY. ▶**A** *noun.* Any of various oviparous mammals of the order Monotremata, having a common opening for the urogenital and digestive systems, now restricted to Australia and New Guinea and comprising the duck-billed platypus and the echidnas. **E19.**
▶ **B** *adjective.* Of or pertaining to this order. **M19.**
■ **mono'tremate** *adjective & noun* (a) monotreme **M19.** **mono'trematous** *adjective* = MONOTREME *adjective* **M19.**

monotriglyph /mɒnə(ʊ)ˈtrʌɪglɪf/ *noun & adjective.* **E18.**
[ORIGIN Latin *monotriglyphus* from Greek *monotrigluphos* adjective, from MONO- + *trigluphos* TRIGLYPH.]
ARCHITECTURE. ▶**A** *noun.* A spacing between columns of the Doric order which allows the use of one triglyph in the frieze, between those over the columns. **E18.**
▶ **B** *adjective.* Having only one triglyph in the space over an intercolumniation. **L18.**
■ **monotri'glyphic** *adjective* = MONOTRIGLYPH *adjective* **M19.**

monotropa /məˈnɒtrəpə/ *noun.* **M18.**
[ORIGIN mod. Latin (see below) from Greek *monotropos* living alone, solitary, from MONO- + *tropos* turn, direction, way, manner.]
A plant of the genus *Monotropa* (family Pyrolaceae); *esp.* = ***INDIAN pipe***.

monotropic /mɒnə(ʊ)ˈtrɒpɪk/ *adjective.* **L19.**
[ORIGIN from MONO- + Greek *tropos* turn + -IC.]
1 *MATH.* = MONODROMIC. *rare.* **L19.**
2 *PHYSICAL CHEMISTRY.* Exhibiting monotropy. **L19.**

monotropy /məˈnɒtrəpi/ *noun.* **E20.**
[ORIGIN from MONO- + Greek *tropē* turning + -Y[3].]
PHYSICAL CHEMISTRY. The existence of two polymorphs of a substance, one of which is stable and the other metastable under all known conditions.
■ Also **monotropism** *noun* **E20.**

monotype /ˈmɒnə(ʊ)tʌɪp/ *noun.* **L19.**
[ORIGIN from MONO- + -TYPE, TYPE *noun*.]
1 *TAXONOMY.* A monotypic genus or other taxon. **L19.**
2 (A process for making) a single print taken from oil colour or printers' ink painted on a sheet of glass or metal. **L19.**
3 (**M-**.) (Proprietary name for) a composing machine consisting of a caster, which produces type in individual characters, and a keyboard, which produces punched tape used to control the caster. Now chiefly *hist.* **L19.**

monotypic /mɒnə(ʊ)ˈtɪpɪk/ *adjective*. M19.
[ORIGIN from mod. Latin *monotypus*, formed as MONO- + -TYPE: see -IC.]
1 Of or having only one type; *spec.* in TAXONOMY, representing or designating a taxon which contains only one taxon of the next subordinate rank, esp. a genus which contains only one species. M19.
2 BIOLOGY. Of evolution: = ANAGENETIC. Now *rare* or *obsolete*. L19.

monotypous /məˈnɒtɪpəs/ *adjective*. Now *rare* or *obsolete*. M19.
[ORIGIN formed as MONOTYPIC: see -OUS.]
= MONOTYPIC 1.

monovalent /mɒnə(ʊ)ˈveɪl(ə)nt/ *adjective*. L19.
[ORIGIN from MONO- + -VALENT.]
1 CHEMISTRY. Having a valency of one. L19.
2 MEDICINE. **a** Being or containing an antigen from a single strain of a micro-organism. M20. **›b** Of an antigen or antibody: having only one site at which attachment to (respectively) antibody or antigen can occur. M20.
■ **monovalence**, **monovalency** *nouns* L19.

monoxide /məˈnɒksʌɪd/ *noun*. M19.
[ORIGIN from MONO- + OXIDE.]
CHEMISTRY. An oxide containing one atom of oxygen in the molecule or empirical formula.

monoxylon /məˈnɒksɪlən/ *noun*. Pl. **-la** /-lə/. Also **monoxyle** /məˈnɒksɪl/, pl. **-s**. M16.
[ORIGIN Greek *monoxulon* neut. of *monoxulos*, from MONO- + *xulon* wood.]
A canoe or boat made from one piece of wood.
■ **monoˈxylic**, **monoˈxylous** *adjectives* (**a**) formed or made out of a single piece of wood; (**b**) using one piece of wood to make a boat, coffin, etc.: M19.

monozygotic /ˌmɒnə(ʊ)zʌɪˈɡɒtɪk/ *adjective & noun*. E20.
[ORIGIN from MONO- + ZYGOTE + -IC.]
▸ **A** *adjective*. Of twins, triplets, etc.: derived from a single ovum, identical. E20.
▸ **B** *noun*. An individual monozygotic twin, triplet, etc. E20.
■ **monozygosity** *noun* the condition of being monozygotic E20. **monoˈzygous** *adjective* = MONOZYGOTIC *adjective* E20.

Monroe doctrine /mənˈrəʊ ˌdɒktrɪn, ˈmʌnrəʊ/ *noun phr.* M19.
[ORIGIN James *Monroe*, US president 1817–25.]
A principle of US foreign policy that any intervention by external powers in the politics of the Americas is a potentially hostile act against the US.
■ **Monroeism**, **Monroism** *noun* adherence to the Monroe doctrine L19.

mons /mɒnz/ *noun*. E17.
[ORIGIN Abbreviation.]
†**1** = MOUNT *noun* 4. E–L17.
2 = MONS PUBIS. M19.

Monseigneur /mɔ̃sɛɲœːr, mɒnsɛˈnjəː/ *noun*. Pl. ***Messeigneurs*** /mesɛɲœːr, mɛsɛnˈjəː/. M16.
[ORIGIN French, from *mon* my + *seigneur* lord.]
1 A French honorific title given to an eminent person, esp. a prince, cardinal, archbishop, or bishop. M16.
†**2** = MONSIGNOR. E–M17.

monsieur /məˈsjəː, *foreign* məsjø/ *noun*. Pl. **messieurs** /mɛˈsjəː, *foreign* mɛsjø/. E16.
[ORIGIN French, from *mon* my + *sieur* lord. See also MOSSOO, MOUNSEER.]
1 Used as a title (preceding the surname or other designation) of or as a respectful form of address to a French or French-speaking man or (more widely) a man of any non-British nationality (corresp. to English ***Mr***), and in literal renderings of French speech. Abbreviated to *M.* E16. **›b** In *pl.* Used as pl. of MR. Now only in abbreviated form MESSRS. L18.

SHAKES. *Mids. N. D.* Mounsieur Cobweb; good mounsieur, get you your weapons in your hand. N. FREELING That is quite correct, Monsieur le Juge. **b** THACKERAY Lady Agnes . . voted the two Messieurs Pendennis most agreeable men.

2 A man usually addressed or referred to as '*Monsieur*'; a Frenchman, orig. one of rank. Now *rare* or *obsolete*. E16. **›†b** The French people. L17–E18.

N. LUTTRELL At last the monsieurs struck, and are brought into Plymouth.

3 *hist.* (A title of) the second son or eldest brother of the King of France. M16.

Monsignor /mɒnˈsiːnjə, mɒnsiːˈnjɔː/ *noun*. Also **-gnore** /-ˈnjɔːreɪ/. Pl. **-gnori** /-ˈnjɔːri/. L16.
[ORIGIN Italian *Monsignor(e)* after French MONSEIGNEUR.]
An honorific title given to a Roman Catholic prelate, officer of the papal court and household, etc.

monsoon /mɒnˈsuːn/ *noun*. L16.
[ORIGIN Early mod. Dutch *monssoen* (mod. *moesson*, infl. by French forms) from Portuguese *monção* (cf. Old Spanish *monzon*) from Arabic *mawsim* season, fixed period, from *wasama* to brand, mark.]
1 A seasonal wind which blows in southern Asia, esp. in the Indian Ocean, approximately from the south-west from April to October (in full ***south-west monsoon***, ***summer monsoon***, ***wet monsoon***, ***rainy monsoon***), and from the north-east from October to April (in full ***north-east monsoon***, ***winter monsoon***, ***dry monsoon***). L16. **›b** The rainfall which accompanies the south-west or summer monsoon; the rainy season. M18.

C. FRANCIS The monsoons regularly bring torrential rain. **b** R. K. NARAYAN When the monsoon set in, in October–November, the circus moved out of Malgudi.

b the change of the monsoon the period of stormy weather between the north-east and the south-west monsoons.
2 Any wind which reverses its direction seasonally, as the temperature varies between two areas, esp. between land and ocean. L17.
– COMB.: **monsoon forest** a deciduous forest in a region of heavy seasonal rainfall.
■ **monsoonal** *adjective* pertaining to or of the nature of a monsoon L19. **monsoonish** *adjective* L19.

mons pubis /mɒnz ˈpjuːbɪs/ *noun phr.* Pl. **montes pubis** /ˌmɒntiːz/. L19.
[ORIGIN Latin = mount of the pubes.]
ANATOMY. The rounded mass of fatty tissue on the lower abdomen, over the joint of the pubic bones; *esp.* that of a female (= MONS VENERIS).

monster /ˈmɒnstə/ *noun & adjective*. ME.
[ORIGIN Old French & mod. French *monstre* from Latin *monstrum*, orig. a divine portent or warning, from *monere* warn.]
▸ **A** *noun*. **1** An animal, plant, or other thing, which deviates markedly from the normal type; *spec.* a congenitally malformed animal, a deformed fetus or neonate. ME.

R. W. EMERSON The members have suffered amputation from the trunk, and strut about so many walking monsters. *Scientific American* If the exceptions are strongly counter to intuition, they are sometimes called monsters.

†**2** Something extraordinary or unnatural; a prodigy, a marvel. LME–E18.
3 An imaginary creature, usu. large and of frightening appearance, and often made up of incongruous elements. LME.

K. CROSSLEY-HOLLAND She was a monster with a hundred heads. *fig.*: N. ROWE Oh thou fell Monster, War.

4 A person of inhuman and horrible cruelty or wickedness; an atrocious example *of* evil, a vice, etc. L15.

E. BAKER He was watching the monster who was now whipping the little girl with a . . rope. S. HASTINGS A monster of selfishness . . 'roaring like a bull because everything is not just as he always has it'. C. ACHEBE The Emperor may be a fool but he isn't a monster.

5 An animal of huge size; anything very large and unwieldy (and freq. also hideous). E16.

TENNYSON The wallowing monster spouted his foam-fountains in the sea. H. BASCOM The large ugly printing press . . . The Editor-in-Chief . . seldom visits this clanging monster.

▸ **B** *attrib.* or as *adjective*. Of extraordinary size or extent; gigantic, huge, monstrous. M19.

R. CROMPTON Their jaws never ceased to move rhythmically around a couple of Monster Humbugs. J. STEINBECK Joe got up . . and ate a monster breakfast. R. INGALLS There you are, caught in a monster machine.

monster truck an extremely large truck; *spec.* a pick-up truck modified for racing, with greatly oversized tyres.

monster /ˈmɒnstə/ *verb trans.* E17.
[ORIGIN from the noun.]
1 Make a monster of. *rare*. E17.
2 Exhibit or point out as something remarkable. *rare*. E17.
3 Depict as monstrous; defame, disparage. Chiefly *Austral.* L20.

monstera /mɒnˈstɪərə/ *noun*. M19.
[ORIGIN mod. Latin (see below), app. from Latin *monstrum* MONSTER *noun*, from the odd appearance of the leaves in some species.]
Any of various climbing aroid plants constituting the tropical American genus *Monstera*, some species of which have perforated leaves; *esp.* the Swiss cheese plant, *M. deliciosa*.

monstrance /ˈmɒnstr(ə)ns/ *noun*. LME.
[ORIGIN medieval Latin *monstrantia*, from Latin *monstrant-* pres. ppl stem of *monstrare* show, from *monstrum*: see MONSTER *noun*, -ANCE.]
†**1** Demonstration, proof. LME–M17.
2 ROMAN CATHOLIC CHURCH. An open or transparent receptacle, usu. of gold or silver, for the exposition of the consecrated Host or (occas.) relics. LME.

monstre sacré /mɔ̃ːstr sakre/ *noun phr.* Pl. **-s -s** (pronounced same). M20.
[ORIGIN French, lit. 'sacred monster'.]
A striking, eccentric, or controversial public figure.

monstriferous /mɒnˈstrɪf(ə)rəs/ *adjective*. Long *rare* or *obsolete*. M16.
[ORIGIN from Latin *monstrum* MONSTER *noun* + -FEROUS.]
Producing or bearing monsters.

monstrosity /mɒnˈstrɒsɪti/ *noun*. M16.
[ORIGIN Late Latin *monstrositas*, from Latin *monstrosus*: see MONSTROUS, -ITY.]
1 An abnormality of growth; a part, organ, or creature that is abnormally developed. M16.

fig.: C. A. BRIGGS The word Jehovah . . is a linguistic monstrosity.

2 A huge (imaginary) creature, a monster. L16. **›b** A hideous or outrageous thing; *esp.* an unsightly building. M19.

SIR T. BROWNE We shall tolerate flying Horses . . Harpies and Satyres: for these are monstrosities . . or else Poeticall fancies. **b** J. C. OATES They have a roomy sprawling house, a late-Victorian monstrosity.

3 The condition or fact of being monstrous. E17.

Sunday Times They can gloss over the monstrosity of their nature with obscene bourgeois good taste.

monstrous /ˈmɒnstrəs/ *adjective & adverb*. LME.
[ORIGIN Old French *monstreux* or Latin *monstrosus*, from *monstrum* MONSTER *noun*: see -OUS.]
▸ **A** *adjective*. †**1** Strange, unnatural; odd in conduct or disposition. LME–M18.

SHAKES. *Mids. N. D.* O monstrous! O strange! We are haunted.

2 (Of a creature) of the nature of a monster; of large size and fearsome appearance; of or pertaining to a monster or monsters. L15. **›b** Containing many monsters. Now *rare* or *obsolete*. M17.

MILTON Nature breeds, Perverse, all monstrous, all prodigious things . . Gorgons and Hydra's, and Chimera's dire. A. MASON A beaked and feathered face whose monstrous features slowly, as he gazed, dissolved into his own.

3 Abnormally formed; congenitally malformed. M16.

EDWARD WHITE A mingling of the law and the gospel; which like all unnatural unions, produced a monstrous birth.

4 Like or befitting a monster of wickedness; atrocious, horrible. M16.

SHAKES. *John* Thou monstrous slanderer of heaven and earth!

5 Outrageously wrong or absurd. M16.

J. I. M. STEWART An error too monstrous for contemplation. M. STOTT It seems monstrous to pay 23p for what used to cost 2d.

6 Unnaturally or extraordinarily large; huge, enormous. M16.

R. L. STEVENSON Laying out vast projects, and planning monstrous foundations. R. DAHL His face was like a monstrous ball of dough.

7 Very great; remarkable in extent, degree, etc. *colloq.* E18.

SWIFT We have a monstrous deal of snow. D. JOHNSON The temperature was monstrous.

▸ **B** *adverb*. Exceedingly, wonderfully, very. *colloq.* (now chiefly *US*). M16.
■ **monstrously** *adverb* L15. **monstrousness** *noun* L16.

†**monstruous** *adjective*. LME–E18.
[ORIGIN from Latin *monstruosus*, irreg. from *monstrum* MONSTER *noun*: see -OUS.]
Monstrous.
■ †**monstruosity** *noun* [French *monstruosité*] LME–L18. †**monstruously** *adverb* M16–E18. †**monstruousness** *noun* M16–M17.

mons Veneris /mɒnz ˈvɛnərɪs/ *noun phr.* Pl. **montes Veneris** /ˌmɒntiːz/. E17.
[ORIGIN Latin = mount of Venus: cf. VENUS.]
1 PALMISTRY. The ball of the thumb. E17.
2 ANATOMY. The rounded mass of fatty tissue on a female's lower abdomen, above the vulva. Cf. MONS PUBIS. L17.

Mont. *abbreviation*.
Montana.

montage /mɒnˈtɑːʒ, ˈmɒntɑːʒ/ *noun*. M20.
[ORIGIN French, from *monter* to mount.]
1 CINEMATOGRAPHY & TELEVISION. The selection and arrangement of separate sections of film as a consecutive whole; the blending (by superimposition) of separate shots to form a single picture; a sequence or picture resulting from such a process. M20.

attrib.: *Listener* A montage sequence from a Russian silent film.

2 *gen.* The process or technique of producing a composite whole by combining several different pictures, pieces of music, or other elements, so that they blend with or into one another; the result of such a process; a miscellany, a pastiche. M20.

Montagnais /ˈmɒntənjeɪ, *foreign* mɔ̃taɲɛ/ *noun & adjective*. Also (earlier) †**-ois**. E18.
[ORIGIN French = mountaineer.]
▸ **A** *noun*. Pl. same. A member of an Algonquian people of eastern Canada; the language of this people. Cf. earlier MOUNTAINER 3, also MOUNTAINEER *noun* 1b. M17.
▸ **B** *attrib.* or as *adjective*. Of or pertaining to the Montagnais or their language. M19.

Montagnard /mɒntəˈnjɑːd, *foreign* mɔ̃taɲaːr (*pl. same*)/ *noun & adjective*. E19.
[ORIGIN French, from *montagne* MOUNTAIN: see -ARD.]
▸ **A** *noun*. **1** A member of 'the Mountain', an extreme democratic party of the French Revolution. E19.
2 A member of an aboriginal people living in the highlands of southern Vietnam. M20.
3 (**m-**.) A native or inhabitant of a mountain region; a highlander. M20.

M

▸ **B** *adjective.* **1** (**m-**.) Inhabiting a mountain region. **M19.**
2 Of or pertaining to the Montagnards of Vietnam. **M20.**

montagne russe /mɔ̃taɲ rys/ *noun phr. Canad.* Pl. **-s -s** (pronounced same). **M19.**
[ORIGIN French, lit. 'Russian mountain'.]
A switchback, a scenic railway, a roller coaster.

†**Montagnois** *noun & adjective* see MONTAGNAIS.

Montagu /ˈmɒntəgjuː/ *noun.* **E19.**
[ORIGIN George *Montagu* (1751–1815), Brit. naturalist.]
Used *attrib.* or in *possess.* to designate various animals described by Montagu.
Montagu's blenny a small blenny, *Coryphoblennius galerita*, of intertidal pools around the Mediterranean and NE Atlantic. **Montagu's harrier** a relatively small migratory Eurasian harrier, *Circus pygargus*. **Montagu shell** (the shell of) any of various small marine bivalves of the family Montacutidae, which live as commensals on echinoderms. **Montagu's sea snail** a small fish of the NE Atlantic, *Liparis montagui*, which feeds on littoral crustaceans.

Montague /ˈmɒntəgjuː/ *noun.* **L19.**
[ORIGIN Personal name, of unknown origin.]
HAIRDRESSING. A flat curl, secured by a hairpin etc., worn at the front of the hair. Also ***Montague curl***. Usu. in *pl.*

montan /ˈmɒnt(ə)n/ *adjective.* **E20.**
[ORIGIN formed as MONTANE.]
montan wax, a hard, brittle substance, consisting mainly of higher fatty acids and their esters, which is extracted from lignite or peat by organic solvents and used in polishes and as an electrical insulator.

Montaña /mɔnˈtaɲa/ *noun.* **M19.**
[ORIGIN Spanish = MOUNTAIN.]
In Spanish-American countries: a forest of considerable extent; *spec.* the forested eastern foothills of the Andes in Peru etc.

Montanan /mɒnˈtanən, -ˈtɑː-/ *noun.* **L19.**
[ORIGIN from *Montana* (see below) + -AN.]
A native or inhabitant of the state of Montana, in the north-western US.
■ Also **Montanian** *noun* **M19.**

montane /ˈmɒnteɪn/ *adjective.* **M19.**
[ORIGIN Latin *montanus*, from *mont-*, *mons* mountain: see MOUNT noun[1], -ANE. See also MONTAN.]
Of, pertaining to, or inhabiting mountainous country; *spec.* designating or pertaining to the belt of upland vegetation below the tree line.

M

Montanism /ˈmɒntənɪz(ə)m/ *noun.* **L16.**
[ORIGIN from *Montanus* (see below) + -ISM.]
ECCLESIASTICAL HISTORY. The tenets of a heretical millenarian and ascetic Christian sect that set great store by prophecy, founded in Phrygia by Montanus in the middle of the 2nd cent.
■ **Montanist** *noun & adjective* (**a**) *noun* an adherent of Montanism; (**b**) *adjective* of or pertaining to Montanism or Montanists: **M16.** **Montaˈnistic** *adjective* **M17.** **Montanize** *verb intrans.* conform to the tenets of Montanism **L16.**

†**montant** *noun.* **LME.**
[ORIGIN French, use as noun of pres. pple of *monter* mount: see -ANT[1]. See also MUNTIN.]
1 = MUNTIN. **LME–M19.**
2 A downright blow or thrust. *rare.* Only in **L16.**

Montbazillac *noun* var. of MONBAZILLAC.

montbretia /mɒn(t)ˈbriːʃə/ *noun.* **M19.**
[ORIGIN mod. Latin *Montbretia* former genus name, from A. F. E. Coquebert de *Montbret* (1780–1801), French botanist: see -IA[1].]
Any of various cultivated hybrid plants of the genus *Crocosmia*, of the iris family, with bright orange-yellow trumpet-shaped flowers.

mont de piété /mɔ̃ də pjete/ *noun phr.* Pl. ***monts de piété*** (pronounced same). **M19.**
[ORIGIN French. Cf. Italian MONTE DI PIETÀ.]
A state pawnbroking organization in France providing loans to the poor at low rates of interest. Cf. MONTE DI PIETÀ, ***mount of piety*** s.v. MOUNT noun[1].

monte /ˈmɒnti/ *noun.* In branch I (esp. sense 2) also **-ty**. **E19.**
[ORIGIN Spanish = mountain, pile of cards left after dealing.]
▸ **I 1** A Spanish and Spanish-American gambling game usu. played with a pack of forty cards. Also (in full ***three-card monte***), a form of three-card trick. **E19.**
2 A certainty; *spec.* a horse considered a safe bet to win a race. *Austral. & NZ colloq.* **L19.**
▸ **II 3** In Spanish-American countries: a small wooded tract; (a region of) chaparral or scrub. **M19.**

Monte Carlo /mɒntɪ ˈkɑːləʊ/ *noun & adjective.* **M20.**
[ORIGIN A town in Monaco, famous for its casino.]
1 (Designating or involving) any of various methods of estimating the solution to numerical problems by the random (or pseudorandom) sampling of numbers in a probabilistic simulation. **M20.**
2 ***Monte Carlo fallacy***, the fallacy that the probability of a particular outcome to one of a series of repeated but independent chance events is inversely dependent on the previous outcomes (e.g., that repeated failure increases the probability of success on the next occasion). **M20.**

monte di pietà /ˌmonte di pjeˈtaː/ *noun phr.* Pl. ***monti di pietà*** /ˌmonti/. **M17.**
[ORIGIN Italian. Cf. French MONT DE PIÉTÉ.]
A state pawnbroking organization in Italy providing loans to the poor at low rates of interest. Cf. MONT DE PIÉTÉ, ***mount of piety*** s.v. MOUNT noun[1].

Montefiascone /ˌmɒntɪfɪəˈskəʊni/ *noun.* **M17.**
[ORIGIN See below.]
A sweet white wine made in the region of Montefiascone, a town in Latium, central Italy. Also ***Montefiascone wine***.

monteith /mɒnˈtiːθ/ *noun.* **L17.**
[ORIGIN from Scot. surname *Monteith*: in sense 1 app. from a 17th-cent. Scotsman who wore a cloak with a scalloped bottom edge; in sense 2 from Henry Monteith, 19th-cent. Scot. dyer.]
1 A large ornamental punchbowl, often silver, with a scalloped rim. **L17.**
2 A cotton handkerchief with a pattern of white spots on a coloured background. *obsolete* exc. *hist.* **L19.**

monte-jus /ˈmɒntəʒuːs, *foreign* mɔ̃tʒys/ *noun.* **M19.**
[ORIGIN French, from *monter* raise + *jus* juice.]
In sugar-refining, an apparatus for raising the level of the liquid by means of air or steam pressure.

montelimar /mɒnˈtɛlɪmɑː/ *noun.* **E20.**
[ORIGIN *Montélimar*, a town in the department of Drôme in SE France.]
A type of nougat orig. made in Montélimar.

Montem /ˈmɒntɛm/ *noun. obsolete* exc. *hist.* **M18.**
[ORIGIN from Latin *ad montem* to the hill (with ref. to a mound near Slough where the event was held).]
A festival celebrated until 1844 by the scholars of Eton College, who processed in fancy dress to raise money for the expenses of the senior colleger at King's College, Cambridge.

Montenegrin /mɒntɪˈniːgrɪn/ *noun & adjective.* Also **-ine**. **L18.**
[ORIGIN from *Montenegro* (see below) + -IN(E[1]).]
▸ **A** *noun.* A native or inhabitant of Montenegro, a republic on the Adriatic coast, formerly part of Yugoslavia. **L18.**
▸ **B** *adjective.* Of or pertaining to Montenegro or its inhabitants. **M19.**

Montepulciano /ˌmɒntɪpʊlˈtʃɑːnəʊ/ *noun.* **L17.**
[ORIGIN See below.]
A red Italian wine made in the region of Montepulciano, a town in Tuscany, western Italy.

montera /mɔnˈtera/ *noun.* Also (now *rare*) **-ro** /-rəʊ/, pl. **-os** /-əʊs/. **E17.**
[ORIGIN Spanish, from *montero* mountaineer, hunter, from *monte* MOUNT noun[1].]
A Spanish cap, orig. worn for hunting, with a spherical crown and flaps able to be drawn over the ears. Now usu. *spec.*, the black hat worn by a bullfighter.

Monterey /mɒntəˈreɪ, ˈmɒntəreɪ/ *noun.* **M19.**
[ORIGIN A city in California, USA.]
1 ***Monterey cypress***, = MACROCARPA. **M19.**
2 ***Monterey pine***, a tall pine, *Pinus radiata*, native to the south-western US, widely planted as an ornamental and timber tree. **M19.**
3 ***Monterey mackerel***, ***Monterey Spanish mackerel***, a mackerel, *Scomberomorus concolor*, found in warm parts of the Pacific. **L19.**
4 ***Monterey Jack (cheese)*** [named after David *Jacks*, a Scotsman who first produced the cheese in the 1890s], a kind of cheese resembling Cheddar. **M20.**

montero *noun* see MONTERA.

montes pubis *noun phr.* pl. of MONS PUBIS.

Montessori /mɒntɪˈsɔːri/ *noun.* **E20.**
[ORIGIN Maria *Montessori* (1870–1952), Italian physician and educationalist.]
Used *attrib.* to designate an educational system, esp. for young children, that seeks to develop natural interests and abilities rather than use formal methods.
■ **Montessorian** *adjective & noun* (**a**) *adjective* of or pertaining to the Montessori educational system; (**b**) *noun* an advocate or follower of this system: **M20.** **Montessorianism** *noun* the Montessori educational system **E20.**

montes Veneris *noun phr.* pl. of MONS VENERIS.

Monteverdian /mɒntɪˈvəːdɪən/ *adjective.* **M20.**
[ORIGIN from *Monteverdi* (see below) + -AN.]
Of or pertaining to the Italian baroque composer Claudio Monteverdi (1567–1643), his music, or his style of composition.

Montezuma's revenge /mɒntɪˌzuːməz rɪˈvɛn(d)ʒ/ *noun phr. slang.* **M20.**
[ORIGIN from *Montezuma* II (1466–1520), last Aztec emperor of Mexico.]
Diarrhoea suffered by visitors to Mexico.

Montgolfier /mɒntˈgɒlfɪə, *foreign* mɔ̃gɔlfje (*pl. same*)/ *noun.* **L18.**
[ORIGIN J. M. & J. E. *Montgolfier*, French brothers, who built the first such balloon which flew in 1783.]
hist. An early form of hot-air balloon. Also ***Montgolfier balloon***.

Montgomery /məntˈgɒm(ə)ri/ *noun.* **L19.**
[ORIGIN William F. *Montgomery* (1797–1859), Irish gynaecologist.]
ANATOMY. **1** ***Montgomery's glands***, ***Montgomery glands***, ***glands of Montgomery***, glands in the areola of a woman's nipple, thought to be accessory mammary glands. **L19.**
2 ***Montgomery's tubercles***, ***Montgomery tubercles***, ***tubercles of Montgomery***, small swellings on the areola which contain the outlets of Montgomery's glands, esp. when enlarged in early pregnancy. **L19.**

month /mʌnθ/ *noun.*
[ORIGIN Old English *mōnaþ* = Old Frisian *mōnath*, *mōn(a)d*, Old Saxon *mānoþ* (Dutch *maand*), Old High German *mānōd* (German *Monat*), Old Norse *mánuðr*, Gothic *mēnōþs*, from Germanic, rel. to MOON noun[1].]
1 A fraction of a year corresponding to the period of revolution of the moon; any of usu. twelve roughly equal periods into which a year is divided; *spec.* each of the twelve (January, February, March, etc.) in the calendar inherited by Western nations from the Romans. **OE.**

> R. K. NARAYAN On the first of the month you were sure of your money. W. TREVOR In the summer months, in June and July and August.

2 ASTRONOMY. A period in which the moon makes a complete revolution relative to some point, either fixed or movable; *esp.* the period from one new moon to the next, equal to 29 days, 12 hours, 44 minutes, 2.7 seconds. **OE.**
3 A space of time either extending between the same dates in successive months of the calendar, or containing four weeks or 28 days; such a period (identified contextually) forming part of a term of imprisonment, leave, notice, etc., or of pregnancy (commonly reckoned to last nine months normally); in *pl.*, a long while. **OE.** ▸**b** A month's pay. *colloq.* **L18.**

> SHELLEY What you in one night squander were enough For months! G. GREENE Remember me . . . I'll see you again in a month or two. *Venue* I only got six months, deferred. Not bad with my form. **b** G. B. SHAW I'll go this very minute. You can keep my month.

†**4** In *pl.* The menstrual discharge; a menstrual period. **L16–L17.**
– PHRASES: ***anomalistic month***. ***calendar month***: see CALENDAR noun. ***draconic month***: see DRACONIC adjective 3. **from month to month** continuously or without interruption from one month to the next. ***lunar month***: see LUNAR adjective. †**month about** during alternate months. **month after month** each month as a sequel to the preceding one, esp. in an unvarying sequence. **month by month** in each successive month, monthly without ceasing. **month of Sundays** an indefinitely long period (usu. in neg. contexts); also, used as a type of dullness. **month's man** a man hired for one month's work during harvest. ***month's mind***: see MIND noun[1] 4b. ***r month***: see R, R 1. ***solar month***: see SOLAR adjective[1]. ***synodic month***: see SYNODIC 2. **this day month** at a time a month after the day indicated. ***tropical month***: see TROPICAL adjective 1.
– COMB.: **month clock**: that goes for a month between windings; **month-long** *adjective & adverb* (lasting) for a whole month.
■ **monther** *noun* (with preceding numeral) a person or thing lasting or aged the specified number of months **L19.**

monthly /ˈmʌnθli/ *adjective & noun.* **OE.**
[ORIGIN from MONTH + -LY[1].]
▸ **A** *adjective.* †**1** Of or pertaining to the moon, lunar. Only in **OE.**
2 Of or pertaining to a month. Also, payable every month. **M16.**

> R. GODDEN Indian servants are required to pour out drinks from a bottle that cost at least half their monthly wages.

monthly nurse a nurse who attends a mother during the first month after labour.
3 Done, recurring, produced, etc., once a month or every month. **L16.**

> LYTTON She saw Evelyn opening the monthly parcel from London. A. N. WILSON *David Copperfield* was published in monthly parts.

monthly rose the China rose, *Rosa chinensis*, formerly believed to flower every month.
4 Continued or enduring for a month. Now *rare* exc. with the notion of recurrence. **L16.**

> R. GREENE Minutes ioyes are monthlie woes. R. WHELAN He had wangled monthly extensions of his visa.

▸ **B** *noun.* **1** *sing.* & (usu.) in *pl.* The menstrual discharge; a menstrual period. *colloq.* **OE.**
2 A magazine etc. published once in each month. **M19.**

monthly /ˈmʌnθli/ *adverb.* **LME.**
[ORIGIN from MONTH + -LY[2].]
Once a month; in each or every month; month by month.

> J. MITCHELL He had to report monthly on birth, deaths, sickness . . and other matters of interest.

monticellite /mɒntɪˈsɛlʌɪt/ *noun*. **M19.**
[ORIGIN from T. *Monticelli* (1758–1846), Italian mineralogist + -ITE¹.]
MINERALOGY. An orthorhombic mineral of the olivine group which is a calcium magnesium silicate and usu. occurs as yellowish crystals.

monticle /ˈmɒntɪk(ə)l/ *noun*. **L15.**
[ORIGIN formed as MONTICULE: see -CLE.]
= MONTICULE 1.

monticule /ˈmɒntɪkjuːl/ *noun*. **L18.**
[ORIGIN French from late Latin *monticulus* dim. of *monti-*, *mons* MOUNT *noun*¹: see -CULE. Cf. earlier MONTICLE.]
1 A small mountain or hill. **L18.** ▸**b** *spec.* A small conical mound produced by a volcanic eruption. **M19.**
2 Chiefly *PALAEONTOLOGY.* A minute swelling or bump, esp. on a fossil shell. **L19.**
■ **monˈticulose** *adjective* (*PALAEONTOLOGY*) covered with minute bumps **M19.**

monti di pietà *noun phr.* pl. of MONTE DI PIETÀ.

Montilla /mɒnˈtɪljə/ *noun*. **L18.**
[ORIGIN A town in S. Spain. Cf. AMONTILLADO.]
A dry fortified Spanish wine resembling sherry, produced in the area around Montilla.

montmorillonite /mɒntməˈrɪlənʌɪt/ *noun*. **M19.**
[ORIGIN from *Montmorillon*, a town in France + -ITE¹.]
MINERALOGY. Orig., a rose-red clay mineral. Now, any montmorillonoid; *spec.* an alumina-rich montmorillonoid containing some sodium and magnesium.
– COMB.: **montmorillonite group** the group of clay minerals comprising the montmorillonoids.
■ **montmorillonitic** /ˌmɒntmərɪləˈnɪtɪk/ *adjective* resembling or containing montmorillonite **M20.**

montmorillonoid /mɒntməˈrɪlənɔɪd/ *noun & adjective*. **M20.**
[ORIGIN from MONTMORILLONITE + -OID.]
MINERALOGY. (Designating or pertaining to) any of a group of clay minerals which undergo reversible expansion on absorbing water and have a characteristic structure in which water molecules are situated between sheets composed of two layers of silicon atoms sandwiching one nominally of aluminium, the silicon and aluminium being variously replaced by other elements.

Montonero /mɒntəˈnɛːrəʊ/ *noun*. Pl. **-os.** **E19.**
[ORIGIN Amer. Spanish, from Spanish *montón* heap, mass, crowd + *-ero* -EER.]
†**1** In Argentina: a peasant rebel against imperial Spain. **E–M19.**
2 A member of a left-wing Peronist guerrilla organization in Argentina. **L20.**

Montpellier /mɒntˈpɛlɪeɪ, *foreign* mɔ̃pɛlje/ *noun*. **L18.**
[ORIGIN A town in the department of Hérault, southern France.]
1 ***Montpellier maple***, a small tree or shrub, *Acer monspessulanum*, native to the Mediterranean region. **L18.**
2 a ***Montpellier yellow***, = ***mineral yellow*** s.v. MINERAL *adjective*. **M19.** ▸**b** ***Montpellier green***, = VERDIGRIS ***green***. **M20.**
3 ***Montpellier butter***, a sauce made with mixed herbs, oil, egg yolks, and butter, served with cold poultry or fish. **L19.**

Montrealer /mɒntrɪˈɔːlə/ *noun*. **L19.**
[ORIGIN from *Montreal* (French *Montréal*) (see below) + -ER¹.]
A native or inhabitant of the city of Montreal in Quebec, Canada.

monts de piété *noun phr.* pl. of MONT DE PIÉTÉ.

Montserratian /mɒn(t)səˈratɪən/ *noun & adjective*. **L19.**
[ORIGIN from *Montserrat* (see below) + -IAN.]
▸ **A** *noun*. A native or inhabitant of Montserrat, one of the Leeward Islands in the W. Indies. **L19.**
▸ **B** *adjective*. Of or pertaining to Montserrat. **L20.**

montuno /mɒnˈtuːnəʊ/ *noun*. Pl. **-os.** **M20.**
[ORIGIN Amer. Spanish = native to mountains, wild, untamed.]
1 A traditional male costume worn in Panama, consisting of white cotton short trousers and an embroidered shirt. **M20.**
2 An improvised passage in a rumba. **M20.**

monture /ˈmɒntʃə/ *noun*. **M18.**
[ORIGIN French, from *monter* MOUNT *verb*: see -URE.]
A mounting, a setting; the manner in which something is set or mounted.

monty /ˈmɒnti/ *noun*¹. *colloq.* **L20.**
[ORIGIN Uncertain: *monty* is perh. short for *Montague Burton*, Brit. men's tailor, *the full monty* apparently meaning 'Sunday-best three-piece suit'; the phr. may also be derived from *Monty*, the nickname of Field Marshal Bernard Law Montgomery (1887–1976), who is said to have insisted on a full English breakfast. Use with ref. to nudity comes from the Brit. film *The Full Monty* (1997), about a group of unemployed men who become strippers.]
the full monty, the full amount expected, desired, or possible; *spec.* (with ref. to striptease) total nudity.

C. GLAZEBROOK They'll be sending a SWAT team round . . armed response units, snipers, helicopters, dogs, the full monty.

monty *noun*² see MONTE *noun*.

monument /ˈmɒnjʊm(ə)nt/ *noun & verb*. **ME.**
[ORIGIN Old French & mod. French from Latin *monumentum*, *moni-*, from *monere* remind: see -MENT.]
▸ **A** *noun*. †**1** A sepulchre, a burial place. **ME–M17.**
2 A written document, a record. Formerly also, a piece of information given in writing. **LME.**

BURKE All our monuments bear a strong evidence to this change [in the laws].

3 A structure or edifice intended to commemorate a notable person, action, or event; a stone or other structure built over a grave or in a church etc. in memory of a dead person. Formerly also, a carved figure, a statue, an effigy. **LME.**

E. LONGFORD Old Tom Picton was given . . a monument . . in St. Paul's Cathedral. W. MCILVANNEY That was a monument they were sittin' beside. To the men from the village.

4 An enduring thing, *esp.* a thing that by its survival commemorates a person, action, period, or event; a structure or edifice surviving from a past age; an outstanding survival of an early literature. Freq. foll. by *of*. **E16.** ▸**b** A thing surviving as a symbol of or witness to a process or activity. Foll. by *to*. **M20.**

W. S. MAUGHAM A painter's monument is his work. G. K. ANDERSON The most important monument of Old English epic literature . . is . . *Beowulf*. *fig.*: *London Review of Books* Brecht . . has become a cultural monument Is it then not time . . to consider blowing him up? **b** D. ROWE Psychiatric hospitals are monuments to the destruction of the human spirit.

ancient monument: see ANCIENT *adjective* 4.
5 †**a** A thing serving for identification; a thing that warns, a portent. **L16–M17.** ▸**b** An indication or token (*of* a fact). Now *rare*. **E17.** ▸**c** *US LAW.* A fixed object referred to in a document as a means of locating a tract of land or its boundaries. **E19.**

a SHAKES. *Tam. Shr.* Wherefore gaze this goodly company As if they saw some wondrous monument? **b** G. MATHESON They came to Aaron to ask a sign—a visible monument of the Divine Presence.

▸ **B** *verb trans.* = MONUMENTALIZE. **E17.**

monumental /mɒnjʊˈmɛnt(ə)l/ *adjective*. **L16.**
[ORIGIN from MONUMENT + -AL¹.]
1 Of, pertaining to, or serving as a monument or monuments. Formerly also, of or pertaining to the tomb, sepulchral. **L16.** ▸†**b** Serving as a memento. *rare*. **E17–M18.**

G. CLARK With Christianity came literacy, coinage and monumental architecture. **b** SHAKES. *All's Well* He hath given her his monumental ring.

2 Having the physical aspect of a monument; (esp. of a work of art) comparable to a monument in size, permanence, etc. **E17.** ▸**b** Historically prominent and significant. Now *rare*. **M19.**

V. S. NAIPAUL The farm buildings (made monumental by the snowfall). **b** M. COREN He quoted from Macaulay's monumental speech.

3 Great in importance, extent, or size; vast, stupendous. **E17.**

V. GLENDINNING She could turn on Wells for his monumental male selfishness.

– SPECIAL COLLOCATIONS: **Monumental City** *US* the city of Baltimore, Maryland. **monumental mason** a maker of tombstones etc.
■ **monumentalism** *noun* a monumental style; building on a grand scale: **L19.** **monumenˈtality** *noun* the quality of being monumental **L19.** **monumentalize** *verb trans.* make a permanent record of (a person, thing, event, etc.), esp. by means of a monument **M19.** **monumentally** *adverb* by way of a monument or memorial; in a monumental way or degree; *loosely* greatly, extremely: **E17.**

mon vieux /mɔ̃ vjø/ *noun phr.* **L19.**
[ORIGIN French.]
Old friend, old man: used as an affectionate form of address.

-mony /məni/ *suffix* (not productive).
Repr. Latin *-monia*, *-monium*, French *-monie*, forming nouns chiefly of action or state from verbal stems, as ***alimony***, ***ceremony***, ***matrimony***, ***parsimony***, ***sanctimony***, ***testimony***.

monzonite /ˈmɒnzənʌɪt/ *noun*. **L19.**
[ORIGIN from Mount *Monzoni* in the Tyrol, Italy + -ITE¹.]
GEOLOGY. A granular igneous rock with a composition intermediate between syenite and diorite, *spec.* one containing approximately equal amounts of orthoclase and plagioclase.
■ **monzonitic** /mɒnzəˈnɪtɪk/ *adjective* pertaining to, of the nature of, or containing monzonite **E20.**

moo /muː/ *noun*¹. *slang*. **M20.**
[ORIGIN Abbreviation.]
= MOOLAH.

moo /muː/ *verb*, *noun*², & *interjection*. **M16.**
[ORIGIN Imit.]
▸ **A** *verb intrans.* Of a bovine animal: make its characteristic deep resonant vocal sound, low. Of a person: make a sound imitative or suggestive of this. **M16.**

J. RHYS The cows here moo at me.

▸ **B** *noun*. **1** (Repr.) the low of a bovine animal; an act of lowing. Also as *interjection*. **L18.**

O. NASH The cow is of the bovine ilk; One end is moo, the other, milk. B. REID When . . she finishes up alone on the stage, going 'Moo, Moo, Moo', you realize . . she will be a success as a cow.

2 A cow. *colloq.* Chiefly *N. Amer. & Austral.* **M20.**
3 A woman. *colloq. derog.* **M20.**

J. SPEIGHT Course it's tax free . . you silly moo.

– COMB.: **moo-cow** a child's word for a cow.

mooch /muːtʃ/ *verb & noun*. Also **mouch**. **LME.**
[ORIGIN Prob. from Old French *muchier* (Norman dial. *mucher*) hide, skulk (whence also MITCH *verb*).]
▸ **A** *verb*. †**1** *verb intrans.* Pretend to be poor. *rare*. Only in **LME.**
2 *verb intrans.* Play truant, esp. to pick blackberries. *dial.* **E17.**
3 *verb intrans.* Skulk, sneak; loiter or loaf *about*. Now *esp.* wander aimlessly, saunter desultorily, (*along*, *around*, *off*). *colloq.* **M19.**

R. LEHMANN The rest of the time I mooch about and go to the pictures. P. KAVANAGH There was Joe Finnegan still mooching around like a man who had lost a shilling in the grass.

4 *verb trans.* Pilfer, steal. *colloq.* **M19.**

Daily Telegraph They . . would hotly assert that they never mooched a penny.

5 *verb trans. & intrans.* Cadge, scrounge. (Foll. by *off*, *on* a person.) *colloq.* (chiefly *N. Amer.*). **M19.**

D. JOHNSON One of the endless train . . here to mooch lunch.

6 *verb intrans.* Fish with light tackle allowed to drift. *N. Amer. dial.* **M20.**

Sun (Vancouver) Most anglers troll, rather than mooch or strip-cast.

▸ **B** *noun*. **1** The action or an act of loafing or scrounging. *colloq.* **M19.**
be on the mooch cadge, scrounge. **do a mooch**, **go for a mooch** loiter, wander.
2 The fruit of the blackberry. *dial.* **M19.**
3 A loiterer, a loafer. *colloq.* **E20.**

moocha *noun* var. of MUCHI.

moocher /ˈmuːtʃə/ *noun*. Chiefly *colloq.* Also **moucher**. **LME.**
[ORIGIN from MOOCH *verb* + -ER¹.]
1 A person who loiters aimlessly. Also, an opportunist poacher or thief. **LME.**
2 A beggar, a scrounger. Chiefly *N. Amer.* **M19.**
3 A person who plays truant, orig. esp. to pick blackberries. *dial.* **L19.**
4 A person who fishes with light tackle allowed to drift. *N. Amer. dial.* **M20.**

moochin /ˈmuːxɪn/ *noun*. *Welsh*. **M20.**
[ORIGIN Anglicized from Welsh *mochyn* pig.]
An objectionable person.

DYLAN THOMAS Up you get, you moochin, or I'll take you home.

mood /muːd/ *noun*¹ & *adjective*.
[ORIGIN Old English *mōd* = Old Frisian, Old Saxon *mōd* (Dutch *moed*), Old High German *muot* (German *Mut*), Old Norse *móðr* anger, grief, Gothic *mōþs*, *mōd-* anger, emotion, from Germanic.]
▸ **A** *noun*. †**1** Mind, heart, thought, feeling. **OE–LME.**
†**2** *spec.* ▸**a** Fierce courage; pride. **OE–L15.** ▸**b** Anger. **ME–E17.** ▸**c** Passionate grief. Only in **ME.**
b ***peck mood***: see PECK *verb*¹ 1.
3 The temporary state of mind or feelings of a person or group. Freq. with specifying word. **OE.** ▸**b** *spec.* A fit of unaccountable bad temper or depression, a bad mood, (usu. in *pl.*); in *pl.* also, changes of mood. **M19.** ▸**c** *transf.* The atmosphere or pervading tone of a place, event, composition, etc.; *esp.* one inducing a certain state of mind or emotion. **E20.**

I. COMPTON-BURNETT Duncan remained silent, and his mood cast a gloom. E. TAYLOR Even if I want to paint again . . I don't want to be in the painting *mood*. W. MAXWELL He was in a cheerful mood. E. KUZWAYO The sudden change of mood among the members. **b** TENNYSON Sir Torre . . being in his moods Left them. *Observer* A creature of moods and temperament. **c** *Outdoor Living (NZ)* You can choose a fence that enhances the general mood of your home. M. FOOT At the 1979 Conference the mood was set.

bad mood, ***good mood***, etc. **in a mood**, **in the mood** disposed, inclined, (*for*, †*of*, *to do*). **in no mood** not disposed, disinclined, (*for*, *to do*). **b be in a mood (with)**, **get into a mood (with)** be, become, peevish or bad-tempered (towards).
– COMB.: **mood-altering** *adjective* (of a drug) capable of inducing changes of mood; **mood drug** a mood-altering drug, *esp.* a stimulant; **mood-elevating** *adjective* (of a drug) having a stimulant or antidepressant effect; **mood swing** *PSYCHOLOGY* an abrupt and unaccountable change of mood.
▸ **B** *attrib.* or as *adjective*. Inducing or suggestive of a particular mood. **L19.**

H. KEMELMAN The organ had been playing mood music, a series of mournful cadenzas in a minor key.

M

mood /muːd/ *noun*². LME.
[ORIGIN Alt. of MODE *noun & adjective* by assoc. with MOOD *noun*¹ & *adjective*.]
1 GRAMMAR. Any of the groups of forms of a verb which indicate whether the action of the verb is represented as fact or in some other manner, as a possibility, command, wish, etc.; the quality of a verb as represented or distinguished by a particular mood. Cf. ASPECT *noun* 9, TENSE *noun* 2. LME.
2 LOGIC. Any of the classes into which each of the four figures of valid categorical syllogism is subdivided according to the quality (affirmative or negative) and quantity (universal or particular) of the constituent propositions. Also, the type of structure to which a syllogism belongs in respect of quality and quantity alone. Cf. MODE *noun* 3a. M16.
imperative mood, ***optative mood***, ***predicative mood***, ***subjunctive mood***, etc.
3 MUSIC. **a** In medieval music, the duration or time value of a note in relation to another in the rhythm of a piece. Cf. MODE *noun* 1b. L16. ▸**b** = MODE *noun* 1a. L16–M19.

moody /ˈmuːdi/ *adjective & noun*.
[ORIGIN Old English *mōdiġ*, formed as MOOD *noun*¹ + -Y¹.]
▸ **A** *adjective*. †**1** Brave, bold, high-spirited. OE–M18.
†**2** Proud, haughty; stubborn, wilful. OE–LME.
†**3** Angry, given to anger. ME–L17.
4 Subject to or indulging in moods of bad temper, depression, etc.; sullen. L16. ▸**b** Inducing or evoking a mood of melancholy or mystery. E19.

> T. SHARPE The Fellows dined in moody silence. D. DELILLO The boy is fourteen, often evasive and moody. **b** *Photo Answers* Grainy film . . gives a soft, moody effect.

5 Counterfeit, false; risky. *slang*. M20.
▸ **B** *noun*. **1** Bluff; nonsense, rubbish. Chiefly in ***old moody, a lot of old moody***. *colloq*. M20.

> R. BUSBY The same old moody he'd heard a thousand times before.

2 A bad mood; in *pl.*, a fit of depression, low spirits. *colloq*. M20.

> *Observer* I can't stand people having the moodies.

■ **moodily** *adverb* OE. **moodiness** *noun* OE.

mooey /ˈmuːɪ/ *noun*. *slang*. M19.
[ORIGIN Romany *mooi*. Cf. MOW *noun*².]
A mouth; a face.

M

Moog /məʊɡ, muːɡ/ *noun*. Also **m-**. M20.
[ORIGIN R. A. *Moog*, (1934–2005), US engineer, the inventor.]
(Proprietary name for) an electronic keyboard instrument producing a variety of different sounds. Also ***Moog synthesizer***.

mook /muːk/ *noun*. *US slang*. M20.
[ORIGIN Perh. from MOKE *noun*¹.]
A stupid or incompetent person.

> SPIKE LEE Who are you gonna listen to, me or that mook?

mool /muːl/ *noun*. *Scot. & N. English*. LME.
[ORIGIN App. var. of MOULD *noun*¹.]
(A clod of) earth; loose soil; *spec.* (the soil for) a grave; in *pl.*, the grave.

moolah /ˈmuːlə/ *noun*. *slang* (orig. *US*). Also **moola**. M20.
[ORIGIN Unknown. See also MOO *noun*¹.]
Money.

mooley *noun & adjective* var. of MULEY *noun & adjective*¹.

mooli /ˈmuːli/ *noun*. Also **muli**. M20.
[ORIGIN Hindi *mūlī* from Sanskrit *mūlikā*, from *mūla* root.]
A long white radish, the root of *Raphanus sativus* var. *longipinnatus*, used in eastern cooking.

Moomba /ˈmuːmbə/ *noun*. *Austral*. M20.
[ORIGIN Wemba-wemba and Wuywurung *mumba*, from *mum* buttocks, anus + *-ba* at, in, on, interpreted as 'let's get together and have fun'.]
An annual pre-Lent festival held in Melbourne.

moon /muːn/ *noun*¹.
[ORIGIN Old English *mōna* = Old Frisian *mōna*, Old Saxon *māno* (Dutch *maan*), Old High German *māno* (German *Mond*), Old Norse *máni*, Gothic *mēna*, from Germanic word rel. to base of MONTH, ult. from Indo-European base repr. also by Latin *metiri* MEASURE *verb*, the moon being used to measure time.]
1 *The* natural satellite of the earth; a secondary planet which orbits around the earth, visible (esp. at night) by the light of the sun which it reflects. (In some contexts regarded as a passive overseer or witness to (the actions of) humankind; in others, a type of something extravagant or unattainable.) OE. ▸**b** A natural satellite of any planet. M17.

> SHAKES. *A.Y.L.* Pray you no more of this; 'tis like the howling of Irish wolves against the moon. *Listener* To . . expect to see what you yourself would choose . . is . . asking for the moon. *New Statesman* Those politicians . . promise the moon. *USA Today* The Class of 2000 won't necessarily go to the moon, but they will do some sub-orbital flying. **b** *Scientific American* Umbriel is the darkest of the major Uranian moons.

2 The moon as visible (chiefly with a specified phase or point reached) during any one lunar month. Also, the moon when visible at any particular time or place. OE. ▸†**b** With ordinal numeral: a specified day after a new moon. *rare*. OE–E18.

> H. NISBET The moon . . bathed everything . . as only Australian moons can do. R. INGALLS The starlight is bright to see by even when the moon isn't out.

crescent moon, ***harvest moon***, ***hunter's moon***, ***quarter-moon***, etc.
3 The period from one new moon to the next; a lunar month; *gen.* a month. Now chiefly *poet.* or *joc.* (esp. in ***many a moon***, ***many moons*** below). LME. ▸**b** = HONEYMOON. E18. ▸**c** (Pl. same, **-s**.) A month's imprisonment. *slang*. M19.

> P. S. BUCK A moon of days passed and the thing was not yet complete. **b** BYRON We are . . to set off by ourselves to Halnaby for the Moon. **c** E. WALLACE Gunner's got three moon for bein' a suspected.

4 The period of time in any one night during which the moon is visible. Long *rare*. LME.
5 = MOONLIGHT *noun* 1. *poet*. LME.
6 A (round or crescent-shaped) representation of the moon; a moon-shaped object. LME. ▸**b** The disc etc. representing the moon in a clock which exhibits its phases. M16. ▸**c** *sing.* & in *pl.* The buttocks. *slang*. M18. ▸**d** A moon-shaped mark or area; *spec.* a small area of greater translucence in porcelain. M19. ▸**e** An act of 'mooning' or exposing the buttocks. *slang*. L20.

> TENNYSON Pure quintessences of precious oils In hollow'd moons of gems. **c** S. BECKETT Placing her hands upon her moons, plump and plain.

†**7** ALCHEMY. The metal silver. L15–M17.
8 = MOONSHINE *noun* 3; *spec.* whiskey. *US colloq*. E20.

> B. KROETSCH Give these gentlemen some of that moon.

– PHRASES: ***bark against the moon***, ***bark at the moon***: see BARK *verb*¹. ***blue moon***: see BLUE *adjective*. ***change of the moon***: see CHANGE *noun* 1b. ***cry for the moon***: see CRY *verb* 2. ***dark of the moon***: see DARK *noun*¹. ***eclipse of the moon***: see ECLIPSE *noun*. ***full moon***: see FULL *adjective*. **many a moon**, **many moons** a very long time. ***mean moon***: see MEAN *adjective*². ***mock moon***: see MOCK *adjective*. ***new moon***: see NEW *adjective*. ***new of the moon***: see NEW *noun*. ***old moon***: see OLD *adjective*. **over the moon** *colloq.* very happy or delighted. **shoot the moon** *colloq.* make a moonlight flit. ***the glimpses of the moon***: see GLIMPSE *noun* 3. ***the man in the moon***: see MAN *noun*. ***the moon's age***: see AGE *noun* 1. ***zodiac of the moon***: see ZODIAC *noun* 1b.
– COMB.: **moonball** *verb & noun* (*slang*) (deliver) a very high lob in tennis; **moonbeam** a ray of moonlight; **moon boot** a thickly padded boot designed for low temperatures; **moon-bounce** the use of the moon as a reflector of (esp. UHF) radio waves from one ground station to another; **moon buggy** a vehicle designed for the use of astronauts on the moon; **moon-cake** a round cake eaten in China during the Moon Festival; **moon-clock** a clock showing the phases of the moon; **moon-curser**, **-cusser** (orig. *dial.*, chiefly *hist.*) = WRECKER *noun*¹ 1; **moon-daisy** the ox-eye daisy, *Leucanthemum vulgare*; **moon-dial** a dial for showing the hours of the night by the moon; **moon-down** *N. Amer.* = **moonset** below; **moon-face** a round, full face; *spec.* in MEDICINE, a rounded swollen face associated with certain hormonal imbalances, e.g. an excess of glucocorticoids; **moon-faced** *adjective* having a moon-face; **Moon Festival** a mid-autumn festival in China; **moonfish** any of various pale or silver-coloured marine fishes with round, usu. thin bodies, *esp.* (*a*) the opah; (*b*) a sunfish, *Mola mola*; (*c*) any of several N. American carangids, as the look-down, *Selene vomer*; (*d*) an Indo-Pacific fish, *Monodactylus argenteus*; **moon flask** ANTIQUITIES a Chinese circular ceramic bottle with a flattened body; **moon-flower** any of several tropical plants with white flowers fragrant at night; esp. *Ipomoea alba*, of the bindweed family; **moongate** a circular Chinese gateway in a wall; **moon-madness** lunacy; **moon-man** †(*a*) a Gypsy; (*b*) an imagined dweller in the moon; (*c*) a lunar astronaut; **moon-month** a lunar month; **moon pool** a shaft through the bottom of a drill ship or oil rig for lowering and raising equipment etc.; **moon probe** ASTRONAUTICS (a vehicle used for) an exploratory unmanned space flight made towards the moon; **moonquake** a tremor of the moon's surface; **moon rat** a gymnure; esp. *Echinosorex gymnurus* of Malaya, Sumatra, and Borneo, which is blackish with white markings; **moonrise** (the time of) the rising of the moon; **moon-rocket** (*a*) a rocket designed for flight to the moon; (*b*) a ride at a funfair imitating this; **moonscape** (a representation of) the surface or landscape of the moon; a wasteland resembling this; **moonseed** a N. American woody climbing plant, *Menispermum canadense* (family Menispermaceae), so called from its crescent-shaped seeds; **moonset** (the time of) the setting of the moon; **moon-shaped** *adjective* shaped like the moon; *esp.* crescent-shaped; **moonshot** a launch of a spacecraft to or towards the moon; **moonstomp** *noun & verb* (perform) a dance to ska music characterized by heavy rhythmic stamping; **moonstruck** *adjective* mentally distracted, dazed through the supposed influence of the moon; *arch.* lunatic; **moon-up** *N. Amer.* = *moonrise* above; **moonwalk** *verb & noun* (*a*) *verb intrans.* walk (as if) on the moon; (*b*) *noun* a walk (as if) on the moon; **moonwalker** a person who moonwalks; **moonwort** a dwarf fern, *Botrychium lunaria*, with sterile fronds divided into crescent-shaped segments; **moon-year** a lunar year.
■ **moonish** *adjective* resembling, characteristic of, or influenced by the moon; *fig.* changeable, fickle: LME. **moonless** *adjective* without a moon; not lit up by the moon: M16. **moonlike** *adjective* resembling or characteristic of the moon LME.

Moon /muːn/ *noun*². M19.
[ORIGIN Dr William *Moon* (1818–94), English inventor.]
In full ***Moon type***, ***Moon's type***. An embossed type used in books for blind people.

Moon /muːn/ *noun*³. E20.
[ORIGIN Henry *Moon* (1845–92), English surgeon.]
MEDICINE. ***Moon's molar***, ***Moon's tooth***, ***Moon's mulberry molar***, ***Moon's mulberry tooth***, = ***mulberry molar*** s.v. MULBERRY *noun*.

moon /muːn/ *verb*. E17.
[ORIGIN from MOON *noun*¹.]
▸ **I 1** *verb trans.* **a** Expose to moonlight. *rare*. E17. ▸**b** Hunt (a possum) by moonlight. *Austral*. L19.
2 *verb trans. & intrans.* Shine (upon) as a moon; give out (light) as a moon. *rare*. M19.
3 *verb intrans. & trans.* Expose one's buttocks (*to*). *slang*. M20.
▸ **II 4** *verb intrans.* Move or look listlessly or aimlessly *about*, *along*, *around*, etc. *colloq*. M19.

> THOMAS HUGHES I mooned up and down the High-street, staring at all the young faces. A. N. WILSON Tennyson mooned about in pubs, worried about whether there was life beyond the grave.

5 a *verb trans.* Pass *away* (a period of time) in an aimless or listless manner. L19. ▸**b** *verb intrans.* Act aimlessly or dreamily from infatuation for a person or thing (foll. by *over*); gaze adoringly *at*. *colloq*. E20.

> **a** W. C. SMITH Why had I mooned away the night? **b** J. JOHNSTON I just couldn't bear . . sitting there all evening looking at you two mooning at each other. P. LIVELY Carrie's in the big greenhouse, mooning over the alpines.

■ **mooner** *noun* †(*a*) a kind of watchdog; (*b*) a person who idles or moons about: L16. **mooningly** *adverb* in a listless or aimless manner L19.

moonack /ˈmuːnak/ *noun*. *US*. Now *rare*. Also **-ax** /-aks/, **mon-** /ˈməʊn-/. M17.
[ORIGIN Delaware (Munsee) *mo:nâhke:w*, lit. 'earth digger'.]
The woodchuck, *Marmota monax*. Formerly also, a similar-looking mythical animal of ill omen.

moon-blind /ˈmuːnblʌɪnd/ *adjective*. L17.
[ORIGIN from MOON *noun*¹ + BLIND *adjective*.]
1 Of a horse: suffering from moon-eye. L17.
2 Of a person: suffering night blindness, supposedly from sleeping exposed to the moon's rays. M19.
■ **moon-blindness** *noun* E18.

mooncalf /ˈmuːnkɑːf/ *noun*. Pl. **-calves** /-kɑːvz/. M16.
[ORIGIN from MOON *noun*¹ + CALF *noun*¹, perh. after German *Mondkalb*.]
1 †**a** A misshapen fetus; a monstrosity. M16–M19. ▸**b** A person with a mental disability. *colloq*. E17.
2 A person who gazes at the moon or idles time away; an absent-minded person. Formerly also, a fickle person. E17.
3 An animal imagined to inhabit the moon. *rare*. E20.

mooned /muːnd, *poet.* ˈmuːnɪd/ *adjective*. M16.
[ORIGIN from MOON *noun*¹, *verb*: see -ED², -ED¹.]
†**1** Lunatic, mad. *rare*. Only in M16.
2 Crescent-shaped; ornamented or marked with (crescent) moons. E17.

> MILTON Th' Angelic Squadron . . sharpning in mooned hornes Thir Phalanx.

3 Accompanied or lit by the moon or moonlight. E17.

> E. BLUNDEN Lingering along the blue stream's mooned curves.

moon-eye /ˈmuːnʌɪ/ *noun*. E17.
[ORIGIN from MOON *noun*¹ + EYE *noun*; in sense 1 translating late Latin *oculus lunaticus*.]
1 An inflammatory disease of horses causing intermittent blindness; an eye affected with this. E17.
2 Any of several freshwater fishes resembling herring, of the family Hiodontidae of eastern N. America, esp. *Hiodon tergisus*. Also, a cisco. M19.

moon-eyed /ˈmuːnʌɪd/ *adjective*. E17.
[ORIGIN from MOON-EYE + -ED².]
1 a Of a horse: affected with moon-eye, moon-blind. E17. ▸**b** Purblind; squint-eyed. *obsolete* exc. *dial*. L17.
†**2** Having eyes adapted for seeing at night. L17–E19.
3 Drunk, intoxicated. *US slang*. M18.
4 Having round wide open eyes. L18.

moonga *noun* var. of MUGA.

moonias /ˈmuːnjas, ˈmuːnɪas/ *noun*. L19.
[ORIGIN Plains Cree *mônîya:s* white person from Southern Algonquian *mo:niya:winini*, from *mo:niya:* Montreal + *-inini* person.]
Among North American Indians in Canada: a newcomer; a white person.

Moonie /ˈmuːni/ *noun*. *slang*. L20.
[ORIGIN from Sun Myung *Moon*, founder of the Unification Church in 1954 + -IE.]
A member of the Unification Church.

moonlet /ˈmuːnlɪt/ *noun*. M19.
[ORIGIN from MOON *noun*¹ + -LET.]
1 A small moon. M19.
2 An artificial satellite. M20.

moonlight /ˈmuːnlʌɪt/ *noun & adjective*. ME.
[ORIGIN from MOON *noun*¹ + LIGHT *noun*.]
▸ **A** *noun*. **1** The light of the moon; this as visible at a particular time or place. ME.

A. NOYES The road was a ribbon of moonlight. E. TAYLOR A misty moonlight furred the grass, like rime. DENNIS POTTER Moonlight filtering behind him made menacing shadows.

moonlight and roses sentimentality, romance.
†2 A painting of a moonlit landscape. M–L18.
3 = MOONSHINE *noun* 3. Now *rare* or *obsolete*. E19.
4 An excursion or raid by moonlight; *spec.* = ***moonlight flit*** below (chiefly in ***do a moonlight***). *colloq.* L19.
▸ **B** *adjective.* Moonlit; taking place or performed by the light of the moon. L16.

J. RULE She took me for a moonlight ride.

– SPECIAL COLLOCATIONS & COMB.: **moonlight flit**, **moonlight flitting** a hurried, usu. nocturnal, removal or change of abode, esp. in order to avoid paying rent. **moonlight lustre** a 19th-cent. porcelain lustre glaze with a marbled effect.

moonlight /ˈmuːnlʌɪt/ *verb intrans.* Pa. t. & pple **-lighted**. L19.
[ORIGIN from MOONLIGHT *noun & adjective.*]
1 Engage by night in a stealthy or illicit activity, esp. a raid. Chiefly as ***moonlighting*** *verbal noun.* L19.
2 Make a moonlight flit. *colloq.* E20.
3 Do paid work, esp. at night, in addition to one's regular employment. Chiefly as ***moonlighting*** *verbal noun.* Cf. SUNLIGHTING 2. *colloq.* M20.

A. S. DALE He began to work days at one job and moonlight at another. D. LESSING At weekends I cooked in a café, underpaid of course, it was moonlighting.

▪ **moonlighter** *noun* M19.

moonlit /ˈmuːnlɪt/ *adjective.* E19.
[ORIGIN from MOON *noun*[1] + LIT *adjective.*]
Lighted by the moon; bathed in moonlight.

moonraker /ˈmuːnreɪkə/ *noun.* L18.
[ORIGIN from MOON *noun*[1] + RAKER *noun*[1].]
1 A native of the county of Wiltshire in SW England. *colloq.* L18.
2 NAUTICAL. A small square sail above the skysail. E19.
▪ **moonraking** *noun* (*arch.*) pursuing idle thoughts M19.

moonshine /ˈmuːnʃʌɪn/ *noun & verb.* LME.
[ORIGIN from MOON *noun*[1] + SHINE *noun.*]
▸ **A** *noun.* **1** = MOONLIGHT *noun* 1. Now chiefly *poet.* & *W. Indian.* LME. ▸**b** (A type of) something insubstantial or unreal (orig. in †***moonshine in the water***). Now *esp.* foolish or visionary talk, ideas, etc. LME.
†2 A month. *rare* (Shakes.). Only in E17.
3 Smuggled spirit; *esp.* (*N. Amer.*) illicitly distilled liquor, esp. whiskey. L18.
▸ **B** *verb.* **1** *verb trans.* Cheat, deceive. Now *rare* or *obsolete.* E19.
2 *verb intrans.* Make liquor, esp. whiskey, illicitly. *N. Amer. colloq.* L19.
▪ **moonshiner** *noun* (*a*) a smuggler; (*b*) *US* a distiller of moonshine: M19. **moonshiny** *adjective* (*a*) moonlit; (*b*) of the colour of moonlight, resembling moonlight; (*c*) vain, unreal: E17.

moonstone /ˈmuːnstəʊn/ *noun.* L15.
[ORIGIN from MOON *noun*[1] + STONE *noun.*]
Any of various milky, pearly, or opalescent varieties of albite and other minerals, used in jewellery; MINERALOGY a lustrous opalescent variety of orthoclase.

moonwards /ˈmuːnwədz/ *adverb.* M19.
[ORIGIN from MOON *noun*[1] + -WARDS, -WARD.]
Towards the moon.
▪ Also **moonward** *adverb* M19.

moony /ˈmuːni/ *adjective.* L16.
[ORIGIN from MOON *noun*[1], *verb* + -Y[1].]
1 Of or pertaining to the moon; resembling or characteristic of the moon. L16.

D. L. SAYERS Shining with a thin, moony radiance.

2 *spec.* ▸**a** Shaped like a crescent moon; lunate. Now *rare.* L16. ▸**b** Shaped like a full moon; (esp. of a face) circular, round. M19.

a F. RAPHAEL He had large hands with moony nails. **b** M. GORDON I looked moony and ridiculous in the mirror.

3 Moonlit. Also, of the colour of moonlight. M17.

YEATS Robed all in raiment moony white. C. MACKENZIE A gratefully warm and moony night.

4 (Of a person) inclined to act in a listless or aimless manner; stupidly dreamy. M19. ▸**b** Slightly drunk. *slang.* Now *rare* or *obsolete.* M19.

STEVIE SMITH Intending to prove his thoughts were not moony With love, or any such stuff.

▪ **moonily** *adverb* M19. **mooniness** *noun* L19.

moop *verb* var. of MOUP.

moor /mʊə, mɔː/ *noun*[1].
[ORIGIN Old English *mōr* = Old Saxon *mōr* marsh, Middle Dutch & mod. Dutch *moer*, Middle & mod. Low German *mōr* (German *Moor*), Old High German *muor*, from Germanic, perh. rel. to MERE *noun*[1].]
1 An open area of uncultivated land; *esp.* such an area covered in heather etc.; a heath. Also, an area of such land preserved for shooting. OE.

J. GARDAM They sped across the moor among the dotted farms. D. AVERST With the 'glorious twelfth' only three days off politicians were deserting Westminster for the grouse moors.

Dartmoor, Exmoor, Otmoor, etc.
2 A marsh, a fen. Now *dial.* & *US.* ME.
3 The soil of which moorland consists; peat. *Scot.* & *dial.* L16.
– PHRASES: **the Moor** *slang.* Dartmoor Prison on Dartmoor, SW England.
– COMB.: **moor-band (pan)** an iron pan found in moorland or below a bog; **moor-bird** a grouse, *esp.* a red grouse; **moorburn** *Scot.* the seasonal burning of heather etc. on a moor to make way for new growth; **moor-coal** a friable variety of lignite; **moorcock** a male red grouse; (occas.) a blackcock; **moor-evil** *dial.* = ***moor-sickness*** below; **moorfowl** = ***moor-bird*** above; **moor game** (red) grouse; **moor grass** (*a*) (more fully ***purple moor grass***) a coarse grass, *Molinia caerulea*, often dominant in moorland and heath; (*b*) ***blue moor grass***, a grass of limestone pasture esp. in northern England, *Sesleria caerulea*; **moor-hag** = ***peat hag*** s.v. PEAT *noun*[1]; **moor-head** the highest part of a moor; **moor-ill** *dial.* = ***moor-sickness*** below; **moorlog** peat, esp. as dredged from the North Sea; **moorman** *noun*[1] (*a*) an official who has charge of a moor; (*b*) a person who lives on a moor; **moor-palm(s)** *dial.* (*a*) the catkins of any of several moorland willows, esp. *Salix repens*; (*b*) the flowering spikelets of cotton grass, *Eriophorum vaginatum*; **moor-pan** = ***moor-band (pan)*** above; **moor-sick** *adjective* (*dial.*) affected with moor-sickness; **moor-sickness** *dial.* [perh. alt. of Old Norse compound from *moðr* exhausted: cf. Norn *mu, mø*] a wasting disease of sheep and cattle, *esp.* liver fluke; **moorsman** a person who lives on moors; a person familiar with moors; **moorstone** (a slab or piece of) a coarse granite found esp. in Cornwall.

Moor /mʊə, mɔː/ *noun*[2]. LME.
[ORIGIN Old French *More* (mod. *Maure*) from Latin *Maurus* (medieval Latin *Morus*) from Greek *Mauros.*]
1 Orig. (now *hist.*), a native or inhabitant of Mauretania, a region of N. Africa corresponding to parts of present-day Morocco and Algeria. Later, a member of a Muslim people of mixed Berber and Arab descent inhabiting NW Africa, esp. present-day Mauritania, who in the 8th cent. conquered Spain. Formerly also *gen.*, a black person (cf. BLACKAMOOR). LME.
2 A Muslim; *spec.* an Indian or Sri Lankan Muslim. Now *arch. rare.* L16.
– COMB.: **Moor macaque** a brownish-black macaque, *Macaca maurus*, of Sulawesi; **Moorman** *noun*[2] (now *arch. rare*) = sense 2 above; †**Moor's-head** (*a*) a horse's head of a darker colour than its body; (*b*) (a heraldic representation of) the head of a Moor; (*c*) a type of vessel lid used in distilling.
▪ **Mooress** *noun* (now *arch. rare*) a female Moor E17.

moor /mʊə, mɔː/ *verb & noun*[3]. LME.
[ORIGIN Prob. from Middle & mod. Low German *mōren*; cf. Old English *mǣrels, mārels* mooring rope, Middle Dutch verbs *māren, mēren, moeren* (Dutch *meren*).]
▸ **A** *verb.* **1** *verb trans.* Secure (a ship, buoy, etc.) in a particular place with a cable or rope fastened to the shore or to an anchor. LME.

P. V. WHITE Judd . . had moored the raft to a tree on the opposite bank.

2 *verb intrans.* & *refl.* Secure one's ship etc. in a particular place; anchor. Also foll. by *up.* E17. ▸**b** *verb intrans.* Of a ship: be made secure in a particular place. L17.

G. ANSON We carried our hawsers . . in order to moor ourselves nearer in shore. A. WEST We slid up the bank and moored for our picnic under a huge alder. **b** J. H. BENNET A . . quay, that enables small vessels to moor close to land.

▸ **B** *noun.* An act of mooring. M18.

moorage /ˈmʊərɪdʒ, ˈmɔː-/ *noun.* M17.
[ORIGIN from MOOR *verb* + -AGE.]
1 The action or process of mooring a ship etc.; the condition of being moored; a place for mooring. M17.
2 Money paid for the use of moorings. L17.

Moorcroft /ˈmʊəkrɒft, ˈmɔː-/ *noun & adjective.* E20.
[ORIGIN William *Moorcroft* (1872–1945), English potter.]
(Designating) a type of pottery produced in Cobridge, Staffordshire, characterized by powdered blue effects and flambé glazes.

moorhen /ˈmʊəhɛn, ˈmɔː-/ *noun.* ME.
[ORIGIN from MOOR *noun*[1] + HEN *noun.*]
1 An aquatic bird of the rail family, *Gallinula chloropus*, with chiefly brownish-black and grey plumage and a reddish bill extended into a plate on the forehead, found on or near fresh water in temperate and tropical regions (also called ***waterhen***, (US) ***common gallinule***). Also, any of various other rails, chiefly of the genus *Gallinula.* ME.
2 A female red grouse. ME.

mooring /ˈmʊərɪŋ, ˈmɔː-/ *noun.* LME.
[ORIGIN from MOOR *verb* + -ING[1].]
1 The action of MOOR *verb*; an instance of this. LME.
2 A rope, anchor, etc., by or to which a ship, buoy, etc. is moored; *spec.* a set of permanent anchors and chains laid down for the mooring of a ship etc. Freq. in *pl.* M18.
3 The place in a river or harbour where a vessel can be moored. Usu. in *pl.* M18.
– COMB.: ***mooring mast***: see MAST *noun*[1] 2; **mooring post** (*a*) a post fixed into the ground for mooring a boat etc. to a landing place; (*b*) a piece of wood in the deck of a large ship to which moorings are fastened; **mooring swivel** a swivel used to shackle two chains together in mooring.

moorish /ˈmʊərɪʃ, ˈmɔː-/ *adjective*[1]. LME.
[ORIGIN from MOOR *noun*[1] + -ISH[1].]
†1 Boggy, swampy; (of water) resembling that found in a bog or swamp; *fig.* spongy, soft. LME–E19.
2 Of, pertaining to, or having the characteristics of a moor; having much moorland. M16.
3 Inhabiting a moor; growing on moorland. E17.

Moorish /ˈmʊərɪʃ, ˈmɔː-/ *adjective*[2]. LME.
[ORIGIN from MOOR *noun*[2] + -ISH[1].]
1 Of or pertaining to the Moors; *spec.* characteristic or in the style of furniture and architecture produced by the Moors in Spain and N. Africa. LME.
2 Muslim. Now *arch. rare.* E17.
– SPECIAL COLLOCATIONS: **Moorish gecko** a harmless gecko, *Tarentola mauritania*, of dry regions around the western Mediterranean; also called **tarentola**. **Moorish idol** a fish of the surgeonfish family, *Zanclus cornutus*, which occurs among coral reefs in the Indian and Pacific Oceans and has a deep body with black and white stripes.

moorland /ˈmʊələnd, ˈmɔː-/ *noun & adjective.* OE.
[ORIGIN from MOOR *noun*[1] + LAND *noun*[1].]
▸ **A** *noun.* Orig., uncultivated land; *esp.* fenland. Now, an extensive area of heath or moor. OE.
▸ **B** *attrib.* or as *adjective.* Of the nature of, pertaining to, or inhabiting moorland. M16.

Moorpark /ˈmʊəpɑːk, ˈmɔː-/ *noun.* L18.
[ORIGIN *Moor Park*, Hertfordshire, southern England, the house of Sir William Temple (1628–99), who cultivated the fruit.]
A large orange-fleshed variety of apricot.

moor-pout /ˈmʊəpaʊt, ˈmɔː-/ *noun.* E16.
[ORIGIN from MOOR *noun*[1] + var. of POULT *noun*[1].]
A young grouse.

moorpunky /ˈmɔːpʌŋki/ *noun.* M18.
[ORIGIN Hindi *mor-pankhī* lit. 'peacock-tailed'.]
In the Indian subcontinent, a pleasure boat with a shape suggestive of a peacock, formerly used on the Ganges.

†**Moors** *adjective & noun. Indian.* M18–L19.
[ORIGIN Perh. from Dutch †*Moorsch* (now *Moors*) MOORISH *adjective*[2].]
= HINDUSTANI *noun* 1, *adjective.*

moory /ˈmʊəri/ *noun.* Also **moree** /ˈmɔːriː/. E17.
[ORIGIN Uncertain: perh. rel. to Portuguese *morim* shirting.]
hist. A kind of Indian cloth.

moory /ˈmʊəri, ˈmɔːri/ *adjective.* OE.
[ORIGIN from MOOR *noun*[1] + -Y[1].]
1 Marshy, fenny; growing in a marsh or fen. OE.
2 = MOORISH *adjective*[1] 2. L18.

moose /muːs/ *noun*[1]. Pl. same. E17.
[ORIGIN Eastern Abnaki *mos.*]
An elk (*Alces alces*), *esp.* a N. American or Siberian elk.
– COMB.: **moose berry** = (the fruit of) the moose bush; **moose-bird** *N. Amer.* the Canada jay; **moose bush** a N. American white-flowered shrub, *Viburnum alnifolium*, of the honeysuckle family; **moose fly** any of several N. American horseflies, *esp.* one of the genus *Chrysops*; **moose milk** *Canad.* (*a*) rum and milk; (*b*) home-made liquor; **moose pasture** *Canad.* land of no value; **moosewood** (*a*) striped maple, *Acer pensylvanicum*; (*b*) leatherwood, *Dirca palustris*; **moose-yard** *N. Amer.* an area in which the snow has been trodden down by moose remaining there during the winter months.

moose /muːs/ *noun*[2]. *US military slang.* M20.
[ORIGIN formed as MOUSMÉ.]
A young Japanese or Korean woman; *esp.* the wife or mistress of a serviceman stationed in Japan or Korea.

moosh *nouns* see MUSH *noun*[1], *noun*[4], *noun*[5].

moo shu /muː ˈʃuː/ *noun phr.* Also **moo shi** /muː ˈʃiː/. M20.
[ORIGIN Chinese *mùxu.*]
A Chinese dish consisting of pork or other meat stir-fried with vegetables and rolled in thin pancakes.

moot /muːt/ *noun*[1]. Also **mote** /məʊt/ (latterly chiefly as 2nd elem. of comb.).
[ORIGIN Old English *mōt* from Germanic, from base also of MEET *verb*: cf. Middle Dutch *moet*, (also mod.) *gemoet*, Middle High German *muoze* meeting, attack, Old Norse *mót*, and MOD *noun*[1]. See also GEMOT.]
1 An assembly of people, *esp.* = GEMOT; a place where a meeting is held. Long *arch.* or *hist.* OE.
burghmote, folkmoot, shiremoot, wardmote, etc.
†2 *gen.* A meeting, an encounter. OE–L15.
†3 Litigation; an action at law; a plea; accusation. OE–E17.
†4 Argument; discussion; talking. ME–L17.
5 The discussion of a hypothetical case by law students for practice; a hypothetical doubtful case that may be used for discussion; a moot court. M16.
– COMB.: **moot court**: at which law students argue imaginary cases for practice; **moot hall** (*a*) (*hist.* exc. as a proper name) a council chamber; a town hall; (*b*) LAW a hall where moot cases are discussed; **moot-hill** *hist.*: on which people gathered for a moot.

†**moot** *noun*[2]. E–L19.
[ORIGIN Unknown: rel. to earlier MOOTER *noun*[2].]
A piece of hard wood hooped with iron at each end, used in block-making. Also, a tool for shaping treenails cylindrically to the desired size.

M

moot /muːt/ *adjective.* M16.
[ORIGIN from attrib. use of MOOT *noun*[1] (in sense 5).]
1 Open to argument; debatable, doubtful. Freq. qualifying *point.* M16.

P. G. WODEHOUSE The point was very moot, and for a moment he hesitated. G. DURRELL Whether he could have bitten us successfully . . was rather a moot point.

2 LAW. Of a case, issue, etc.: of no practical significance or relevance; abstract, academic. M19.
■ **mootness** *noun* (US LAW) E20.

moot /muːt/ *verb*[1].
[ORIGIN Old English *mōtian*, formed as MOOT *noun*[1].]
1 †**a** *verb intrans.* Speak, converse; *Scot.* complain. OE–E17. ▸**b** *verb trans.* Say, utter, mention. *obsolete* exc. *Scot.* LME.
2 a *verb intrans.* Argue, plead, discuss, dispute, esp. in a law case; LAW debate a hypothetical case, take part in a moot. Now only as ***mooting*** *verbal noun.* OE. ▸†**b** *verb trans.* Argue (a point, case, etc.). LME–E19.
3 *verb trans.* Raise or bring forward for discussion. M17.

J. N. ISBISTER Ideas about the possibility of a Zionist state were beginning to be mooted. J. F. LEHMANN As the months went by . . the mooted job . . receded even further into improbability.

■ **mootable** *adjective* M16.

moot /muːt/ *verb*[2] *trans. obsolete* exc. *dial.* E17.
[ORIGIN Unknown.]
Dig up, dig up by the roots; dig out (*spec.* an otter).

†**moot** *verb*[3] *trans.* Only in M19.
[ORIGIN from MOOT *noun*[2]. Cf. earlier MOOTER *noun*[2].]
Shape (a treenail) by means of a moot.

mootah /ˈmuːtə/ *noun. US slang.* Also **mooter**, **mota**. E20.
[ORIGIN Prob. from Mexican Spanish *mota* marijuana.]
Marijuana.

mooter /ˈmuːtə/ *noun*[1]. OE.
[ORIGIN from MOOT *verb*[1] + -ER[1].]
†**1** A speaker; a person who argues; a lawyer who argues cases in a court of justice, a pleader; a person who discusses a hypothetical legal case. OE–E19.
2 A person who raises a matter for discussion. M19.

†**mooter** *noun*[2]. M18.
[ORIGIN Rel. to MOOT *noun*[2], *verb*[3]: see -ER[1].]
1 A person who shaped treenails with a moot. M18–E19.
2 A treenail. Only in M19.

M

mooter *noun*[3] var. of MOOTAH.

†**mop** *noun*[1]. ME.
[ORIGIN Uncertain: perh. rel. to MOPE *noun*, *verb*.]
1 A fool, a simpleton. ME–L15.
2 A baby or toddler. Also, a rag doll. LME–L16.
– NOTE: Survives as 1st elem. of MOPPET, MOPSY.

†**mop** *noun*[2]. LME–M18.
[ORIGIN Unknown.]
A young fish, esp. a whiting or gurnard. Also ***whiting mop***, ***gurnard mop***.

mop /mɒp/ *noun*[3]. Also (earlier) †**map(p)**. L15.
[ORIGIN Uncertain: perh. ult. connected with Latin *mappa* (see MAP *noun*[1]). In branch II from the verb.]
▸**I 1** An implement consisting of a long stick with a bundle of thick loose strings or a piece of foam rubber etc. fastened to one end so as to soak up liquid easily, used in cleaning floors (also ***floor mop***); (in full ***dish mop***), a smaller form of this for washing dishes. L15.

B. REID A lady who was cleaning the floor with a bucket and mop.

2 A thick mass of something, esp. of or *of* hair. E19.

R. CROMPTON Thomas's blue eyes, beneath a mop of curls.

mops and brooms *slang* half-drunk. ***Mrs Mop***: see MRS.
3 Any of various small instruments resembling a mop, as (*a*) a circular pad of cloth used in polishing silver with rouge; (*b*) a surgical instrument with a sponge at the end of a handle, for applying medicated fluids or removing purulent matter. M19.
▸**II 4** ***mop-up***, the action or an act of mopping something up. E20.
5 A rub, wipe, or clean with a mop. L20.
– COMB.: **mop-board** *US* a skirting board; **mophead** (*a*) the head of a mop; (*b*) (a person with) a thick head of hair; **mopstick** the handle of a floor mop; ***mop-up***: see sense 4 above.

mop /mɒp/ *noun*[4]. *arch.* L15.
[ORIGIN Rel. to MOP *verb*[1].]
A grimace, orig. esp. as made by a monkey. Chiefly in ***mops and mows***.

mop /mɒp/ *noun*[5]. L17.
[ORIGIN Perh. from a mop (MOP *noun*[3]) carried by maidservants seeking employment.]
ENGLISH HISTORY. An annual fair at which servants seeking to be hired assembled together. Also ***mop fair***.

mop /mɒp/ *verb*[1] *intrans. arch.* Infl. **-pp-**. M16.
[ORIGIN Rel. to MOP *noun*[4].]
Make a grimace. Chiefly in ***mop and mow***.

mop /mɒp/ *verb*[2] *trans.* Infl. **-pp-**. E18.
[ORIGIN from MOP *noun*[3].]
1 Foll. by *up*: (*a*) wipe up (water etc.) with or as with a mop; absorb; (*b*) *slang* drink or eat greedily; (*c*) *colloq.* appropriate, use up, (profits, cash, etc.); (*d*) *colloq.* make an end of, slaughter, (esp. a straggler or remnant); MILITARY complete the occupation of (a district etc.) by capturing or killing enemy forces left there. E18.

RIDER HAGGARD As he mopped up the streaming blood with a sponge. *Royal Air Force Journal* The enemy was still fighting behind us but they would be mopped up in time. *Sun (Baltimore)* West Virginia communities began mopping-up operations . . after two surging creeks flooded homes. *Lean Living* He . . drifted away into the crowd mopping up a couple of Bloody Mary's as he went. *Country Living* She has mopped up surplus energy by having another son. M. BRETT The charge . . is . . 5 per cent, which will mop up the first year's income.

2 Rub, wipe, or clean with or as with a mop. M18.

Z. TOMIN Joseph, the old barman, was mopping the table.

mop the floor with: see FLOOR *noun*.
3 Wipe (one's face, brow, etc.) to remove perspiration or tears; wipe (perspiration or tears) *from* one's face, brow, etc. M19.

E. M. FORSTER 'Oh, good!' exclaimed Mr. Beebe, mopping his brow. A. SILLITOE He mopped the tears from her eyes.

mopane /mɒˈpɑːni/ *noun. S. Afr.* Also **mopani**. M19.
[ORIGIN Bantu *mo-pane*.]
A leguminous tree, *Colophospermum mopane*, of desert regions in southern Africa, bearing small green flowers and with leaves consisting of a pair of leaflets which fold together during intense heat.
– COMB.: **mopane worm** a black spotted caterpillar which feeds on mopane leaves and is an item of diet.

mope /məʊp/ *noun.* LME.
[ORIGIN Perh. of Scandinavian origin (cf. Old Swedish *mopa* befool, Swedish dial. *mopa* sulk, Danish *maabe* be stupid or unconscious). In senses 2, 3 from the verb. Cf. MOP *noun*[1].]
1 A fool, a simpleton. Now chiefly *US.* LME.
2 A person who mopes. L17.
3 In *pl.* Depression of spirits. Usu. ***the mopes***. M18.

mope /məʊp/ *verb.* M16.
[ORIGIN Rel. to MOPE *noun*.]
1 *verb intrans.* Be in an abstracted or stupefied state; act without conscious thought. Long *obsolete* exc. *dial.* M16.
2 *verb intrans.* Remain in a listless, apathetic condition, without making any effort to rouse oneself; be gloomily dejected; behave sulkily. Also foll. by *about*, *around*, (adverbs & prepositions). L16.

D. WELCH The town seemed full of almost useless men moping at street corners. A. WEST I would mope about the apartment with my hands in my pockets. M. GORDON Get out into the open. Don't mope around.

3 *verb trans.* Make gloomily dejected, cause to mope. Now only *refl.* and in *pass.*, = sense 2 above. E17.

E. GASKELL I've got quite moped and dismal.

– COMB.: †**mope-eyed** *adjective* short-sighted.

moped /ˈməʊpɛd/ *noun.* M20.
[ORIGIN Swedish, from 'trampcykel med motor och pedaler', pedal cycle with engine and pedals.]
Orig., a motorized pedal cycle. Now usu., a light two-wheeled motor vehicle with a small engine, *spec.* one of not more than 50 cc.

moper /ˈməʊpə/ *noun.* E18.
[ORIGIN from MOPE *verb* + -ER[1].]
A person who mopes.

mopery /ˈməʊp(ə)ri/ *noun. colloq.* E20.
[ORIGIN from MOPE *verb* + -ERY.]
1 Mopish behaviour; a fit of moping. E20.
2 Loitering or other petty lawbreaking, esp. when used as an excuse to arrest or harass someone. *US.* E20.

mophrodite /ˈmɒfrədʌɪt/ *noun.* Now *rare* or *obsolete.* E18.
[ORIGIN Alt.]
= HERMAPHRODITE *noun*.

mopish /ˈməʊpɪʃ/ *adjective.* E17.
[ORIGIN from MOPE *verb* + -ISH[1].]
Given to or characterized by moping; causing moping.
■ **mopishly** *adverb* M17. **mopishness** *noun* L16.

Moplah /ˈmɒplə/ *noun.* L18.
[ORIGIN Malayalam *mā-pilla* from *mā* great + *pilla* child.]
Any of the Muslim inhabitants of Malabar, SW India.

mopoke /ˈməʊpəʊk/ *noun. Austral.* Also (chiefly *NZ*) **morepork** /ˈmɔːpɔːk/. E19.
[ORIGIN Imit. of the bird's call.]
1 Any of several nocturnal birds with a distinctive cry; *spec.* (*a*) = BOOBOOK; (*b*) the tawny frogmouth, *Podargus strigoides*. E19.
2 A stupid or boring person. M19.

mopper-up /mɒpərˈʌp/ *noun.* E20.
[ORIGIN from MOP *verb*[2] + -ER[1] + UP *adverb*[1].]
Chiefly MILITARY. A person who mops up things or people; *esp.* a person who mops up an enemy area.

moppet /ˈmɒpɪt/ *noun.* E17.
[ORIGIN from MOP *noun*[1] + -ET[1].]
1 A baby, a girl; a darling, a favourite; (freq. as an affectionate form of address). Also *derog.* a gaily dressed or frivolous woman. E17.
2 *derog.* A man. *arch.* E18.

moppie /ˈmɒpi/ *noun. S. Afr.* M20.
[ORIGIN Afrikaans from Dutch *mopje* ditty.]
A street song of the Cape Malays, usu. of a teasing nature.

moppy /ˈmɒpi/ *adjective.* E18.
[ORIGIN from MOP *noun*[3] + -Y[1].]
Of hair, foliage, etc.: resembling a mop; thick and untidy.

mopsy /ˈmɒpsi/ *noun.* Now *rare* exc. *dial.* L16.
[ORIGIN from MOP *noun*[1] + -SY.]
1 A pretty child, a darling, a sweetheart (esp. as a form of address). L16.
2 An untidy or unkempt woman. L17.

moptop /ˈmɒptɒp/ *noun. colloq.* M20.
[ORIGIN from MOP *noun*[3] + TOP *noun*[1].]
1 A man's hairstyle in the form of a long shaggy bob. M20.
2 A person with such a hairstyle. M20.

S. KING Girls screaming their heads off for the moptops from Liverpool.

mopus /ˈməʊpəs/ *noun*[1]. *arch. slang.* L17.
[ORIGIN Unknown.]
In *pl.*, money. Formerly *sing.*, a halfpenny or farthing.

†**mopus** *noun*[2]. M17–M19.
[ORIGIN from MOPE *noun*.]
A fool, a simpleton.

mopy /ˈməʊpi/ *adjective.* E19.
[ORIGIN from MOPE *verb* + -Y[1].]
= MOPISH.

moquette /mɒˈkɛt/ *noun.* M18.
[ORIGIN French, perh. formed as MOCKADO.]
A heavy piled fabric used for carpets and upholstery.

MOR *abbreviation.*
Middle-of-the-road (music).

mor /mɔː/ *noun.* M20.
[ORIGIN Danish = humus.]
SOIL SCIENCE. Humus forming a discrete layer on top of the soil with little mineral soil mixed with it, characteristic of coniferous forests and generally strongly acid. Cf. MULL *noun*[7].

mora /ˈmɔːrə/ *noun*[1]. Pl. **morae** /ˈmɔːriː/. M16.
[ORIGIN Latin = delay.]
1 SCOTS LAW. Undue delay in the assertion of a claim etc. M16.
†**2** A short space of time; a delay. *rare.* M–L17.
3 a A unit of metrical time equal to the duration of a short syllable. M19. ▸**b** LINGUISTICS. The minimal unit of duration of a speech sound. M20.

mora /ˈmɔːrə/ *noun*[2]. Also **morra** /ˈmɒrə/. M17.
[ORIGIN Italian, of unknown origin.]
An Italian game in which one player guesses the number of fingers being held up by another. Formerly also called ***love***.

mora /ˈmɔːrə/ *noun*[3]. E19.
[ORIGIN Either from Arawak, or shortened from Tupi *moira-tinga* white tree, referring to the blossoms, from *moira* tree + *tinga* white.]
A lofty leguminous tree, *Mora excelsa*, found in Guyana and Trinidad. Also ***mora tree***.

mora /ˈmɔːrə/ *noun*[4]. E19.
[ORIGIN Hindi *moṛhā*, Marathi *moṛā*.]
In the Indian subcontinent: a stool; a wicker chair.

mora /ˈmɔːrə/ *noun*[5]. E19.
[ORIGIN Greek, from *mor-*, *mer-* divide.]
GREEK HISTORY. Each of the (orig. six) divisions of which the Spartan army consisted.

moraine /məˈreɪn/ *noun.* L18.
[ORIGIN French from Savoyard Italian *morena*, from southern French *mor(re)* muzzle, snout, from Proto-Romance word whence also MORION *noun*[1].]
1 An area or bank of debris that a glacier or ice sheet has carried down and deposited; the material forming such a deposit. L18.
end moraine, ***lateral moraine***, ***push moraine***, etc.
2 HORTICULTURE. A bed made largely of stones covered with fine chippings, designed to produce suitable conditions for alpine plants. E20.
■ **morainal** *adjective* morainic L19. **morainic** *adjective* of, pertaining to, or of the nature of a moraine M19.

moral /ˈmɒr(ə)l/ *noun.* LME.
[ORIGIN Use as noun of MORAL *adjective*, infl. also by late Latin *morale* neut. sing., *moralia* neut. pl., French *moral*, *morale* (cf. MORALE).]
1 In *pl.* & †*sing.* Moral matters: the title of various books by classical writers, *spec.* St Gregory the Great's work on the moral exposition of the biblical Book of Job. LME.
2 a The moral teaching or practical lesson of a story, event, etc. L15. ▸**b** An exposition of the moral teaching or practical lesson contained in a literary work; that part

of a work which applies or points the moral meaning. Now *rare*. M16. ▸†**c** Import, significance. L16–M19.

> **a** DICKENS There's a moral in everything. *Scientific American* As a general moral we conclude that war as man wages it finds no counterpart in nature.

3 †**a** A symbolic figure. Only in L16. ▸**b** A counterpart, a likeness. Chiefly in ***the very moral of***. M18.
4 = MORALITY 4b. Long *obsolete* exc. *hist.* L16.
5 In *pl.* & †*sing.* Moral habits, conduct, or (formerly) qualities; habits of life with regard to right and wrong conduct; *spec.* sexual conduct; without qualification, good or right habits or conduct. E17.

> A. BEVAN This may be sound economics. It could not be worse morals. *Weekly News (Cambridge)* He was concerned over the lack of morals . . among the town's young people.

6 In *pl.* (usu. treated as *sing.*). = MORALITY 5a. Now *rare*. M17.
7 A moral certainty. *slang* (now chiefly *Austral. & NZ*). M19.
8 = MORALE 2. Now *rare*. L19.

moral /ˈmɒr(ə)l/ *adjective*. LME.
[ORIGIN Latin *moralis* (rendering Greek *ēthikos* ETHIC *adjective*), from *mor-*, *mos* custom (pl. *mores* manners, morals): see -AL[1].]
1 Of or pertaining to human character or behaviour considered as good or bad; of or pertaining to the distinction between right and wrong, or good and evil, in relation to the actions, volitions, or character of responsible beings; ethical; (of knowledge, judgements, etc.) pertaining to the nature and application of this distinction. LME. ▸**b** Of a feeling: arising from the contemplation of something as good or bad. M18. ▸**c** Of a concept or term: involving ethical praise or blame. M19.

> J. B. MOZLEY Eloquence, imagination, poetical talent, are no more moral goodness than riches are. G. GREENE His books . . represent a moral struggle. M. FLANAGAN It's not my habit to pass moral judgements.

2 Treating of or concerned with right and wrong, or the rules of right conduct, as a subject of study. LME.
moral philosophy, ***moral science***, ***moral theology***, etc.
3 †**a** Of a person, esp. a writer: enunciating moral precepts. LME–M18. ▸**b** Of a literary work, a pictorial or dramatic representation, etc.: dealing with the rightness and wrongness of conduct; having the teaching of morality as a motive; conveying a moral. Formerly also, allegorical, emblematical. LME.

> **b** SHAKES. *Timon* A thousand moral paintings . . That shall demonstrate these quick blows of Fortune's More pregnantly than words.

4 Of persons, habits, conduct, etc.: morally good, conforming to or reflecting accepted standards of conduct. LME. ▸**b** *spec.* Virtuous with regard to sexual conduct. E19.

> D. CECIL Profoundly moral in his outlook he thought that man lived to be virtuous.

5 **a** Of an action: subject to moral law; having the property of being right or wrong. Of rights, obligations, responsibility, etc.: founded on moral law, valid according to principles of morality. L16. ▸**b** Of an agent, an agent's attributes: capable of moral action; capable of choosing between right and wrong. M18.

> **b** W. PALEY The moral and accountable part of his terrestrial creation.

6 Pertaining to, affecting, or operating on the character or conduct, as distinguished from the intellectual or physical nature of human beings; *esp.* designating the incidental effect of an action or event (e.g. a victory or defeat) in producing confidence or discouragement, sympathy or hostility, etc. L16.

> A. ALISON All the moral advantages of a victory were on the side . . of the French. D. J. WEST A paper . . seeking to prove the moral imbecility of habitual criminals.

7 Designating probable evidence that rests on a knowledge of human nature or a person's character; designating any evidence which is merely probable and not demonstrative. Chiefly in ***moral certainty*** below. M17.
8 Qualifying a descriptive noun: that is such metaphorically, relative to moral character or condition. L17.

> GLADSTONE An undenominational system of religion, framed by or under the authority of the State, is a moral monster. A. E. STEVENSON The Bill of Rights is the moral spine of the nation.

9 Of, pertaining to, or concerned with the morals of a person or a community. L18.

> M. L. KING This change in climate was created through the moral leadership of Mahatma Gandhi.

– SPECIAL COLLOCATIONS: **moral certainty** a degree of probability so great as to admit of no reasonable doubt; a practical certainty. **moral courage** the kind of courage which enables a person to encounter odium, disapproval, or contempt rather than depart from the right course. **moral cowardice** unworthy fear of other people's disapproval or hostility. **moral fibre** = *moral courage* above (freq. in ***lack of moral fibre***). **moral hazard** (chiefly with ref. to insurance) lack of incentive to guard against risk where one is protected from its consequences, e.g. by insurance. ***moral*** INSPIRATION. **moral law** the body of requirements to which an action must conform to be right or virtuous; a particular requirement of this kind. **moral majority** (*a*) (with cap. initials) a right-wing movement in the US; (*b*) the majority of people, regarded as favouring firm moral standards. **moral panic** an instance of public anxiety or alarm in response to a problem regarded as threatening the moral standards of society. **moral play** (*obsolete* exc. *hist.*) a morality play. **moral pressure** persuasion in which a person's moral sense is appealed to. **moral psychology**: concerned with the psychological effect on behaviour of rules of conduct, esp. the sense of right and wrong. **moral rights** LAW the rights of an author etc. to protect the integrity and ownership of his or her work. **Moral Re-Armament** (the theories or practice of) the Oxford Group Movement. **moral sciences** (at Cambridge University) former name for philosophy. **moral sense** the ability to distinguish between right and wrong, esp. as a faculty of the human mind. **moral support** support or help the effect of which is psychological rather than physical. **moral turpitude** (an instance of) conduct considered depraved. **moral tutor** a tutor in a university, college, etc., appointed to have a particular concern for the moral welfare of a particular student or particular students. **moral victory** an indecisive result or an actual defeat which it is believed will produce the moral effects of an actual victory.

moral /ˈmɒr(ə)l/ *verb trans. & intrans.* Infl. **-ll-**, ***-l-**. E17.
[ORIGIN from the noun.]
= MORALIZE *verb*
■ †**moraller** *noun* (*rare*, Shakes.) a moralizer: only in E17.

morale /məˈrɑːl/ *noun*. M18.
[ORIGIN French *moral* (formed as MORAL *adjective*), respelt to indicate stress. Cf. LOCALE.]
1 Morality, morals; moral teaching. Now *rare*. M18.
2 The mental and emotional attitude of a person or group with regard to confidence, hope, zeal, willingness, etc.; degree of contentment with one's lot or situation. M19.

> E. ROOSEVELT Sight of a new uniform and . . fresh men at the front would restore their morale. Z. TOMIN She gave me a . . majestic half-smile. It boosted my morale.

– COMB.: **morale-booster** an event, occurrence, or saying which raises morale.

moraled *adjective* see MORALLED.

moralise *verb* var. of MORALIZE.

moralism /ˈmɒr(ə)lɪz(ə)m/ *noun*. L17.
[ORIGIN from MORAL *noun*, *adjective* + -ISM.]
1 Fondness for moralizing; an act of moralizing. L17.
2 The practice of a natural system of morality; religion consisting of or reduced to moral practice. M19.

moralist /ˈmɒr(ə)lɪst/ *noun*. L16.
[ORIGIN from MORAL *noun* + -IST.]
1 A teacher or student of morals; a moral philosopher. L16.
2 A person given to moralizing or making moral judgements. L16.
senior moralist: see SENIOR *adjective*.
3 A person who behaves in a morally commendable way. E17.
†**4** A person who lives by a natural system of ethics, independently of religion. M17–E19.

moralistic /ˌmɒrəˈlɪstɪk/ *adjective*. M19.
[ORIGIN from MORALIST + -IC.]
Pertaining to or characteristic of a moralist; overfond of making moral judgements about others' behaviour, too ready to moralize.

> A. CROSS He was unbearably pompous and moralistic.

■ **moralistically** *adverb* L19.

morality /məˈralɪti/ *noun*. LME.
[ORIGIN (Old French & mod. French *moralité* from) late Latin *moralitas*, from Latin *moralis*: see MORAL *adjective*, -ITY.]
†**1** Ethical wisdom; knowledge of moral science. Only in LME.
2 In *pl.* Moral qualities or endowments. Now *rare*. LME.
3 **a** Moral discourse or instruction, moralizing; a moral lesson or exhortation. LME. ▸†**b** Moral sense or interpretation; the moral of a story, event, etc. LME–E17.
4 †**a** A literary work or artistic representation inculcating a moral lesson; a moralizing commentary; a moral allegory. LME–M17. ▸**b** A morality play. L18.

> **b** HUGH WALPOLE The actors seemed like figures in a Morality.

5 **a** The doctrine or branch of knowledge that deals with right and wrong conduct and with duty and responsibility; moral philosophy, ethics. LME. ▸**b** In *pl.* Points of ethics, moral principles or rules. E17. ▸**c** A particular system of moral philosophy or moral conduct. L17.

> **a** SWIFT The learning of this people . . consisting only in morality, history, poetry, and mathematics. **b** F. NORRIS The trite moralities and ready-made aphorisms of the philanthropists. **c** E. A. FREEMAN The morality of the Gospel had a direct influence upon the politics of the age. C. ACHEBE He has no sense of political morality. J. GLOVER In our society . . morality derived from religious commands and prohibitions is declining, but still powerful.

6 The quality or fact of being moral; the degree of conformity of an idea, practice, etc., to moral law; moral goodness or rightness. L16.

> J. S. MILL The morality of an action depends on its foreseeable consequences. J. M. MCPHERSON Opponents also questioned the expediency, morality, even the theology of the legal tender bill.

7 Moral conduct; *esp.* good moral conduct; behaviour conforming to moral law; moral virtue. L16.

> M. STOTT Concern for one's fellows seems to me the essence of morality.

– COMB.: **morality play** a drama of a kind (popular in the 15th and 16th cents) intended to inculcate a moral or spiritual lesson, the chief characters being personifications of abstract qualities. **morality squad** *Canad.* a police unit dealing with infractions of legislation concerning prostitution, pornography, etc.

moralize /ˈmɒr(ə)lʌɪz/ *verb*. Also **-ise**. LME.
[ORIGIN Old French & mod. French *moraliser* or medieval Latin *moralizare*, from late Latin *moralitas*: see MORALITY, -IZE.]
1 *verb trans.* Interpret morally or symbolically; explain the moral meaning of; make the subject of moral reflection. LME.

> *American Notes & Queries* Medieval . . mythographers normally moralize Narcissus as the man who wastes himself in pursuing worldly goods.

†**2** *verb trans.* Supply (a literary work) with a moral or a subject for moralizing; (of an incident, event, etc.) exemplify the moral of (a story, saying, etc.). L16–E18.
3 *verb trans.* Give a moral quality to. L16.
4 **a** *verb intrans.* Indulge in moral reflection or talk; pass moral judgements (*on*); found a moral *on* an event etc. M17. ▸**b** *verb trans.* Change the condition or aspect of (a person or thing) by moral talk or reflection. Foll. by *into*, *out of*. E18.

> **a** W. IRVING No one can moralize better after a misfortune has taken place. *Evening Times (Glasgow)* No attempt to moralize on a young man I have always found to be pleasant.

5 *verb trans.* Improve the morals of. M17.

> O. CHADWICK Can you moralize them and civilize them without having religion at the bottom of it?

■ **moralizable** *adjective* E20. **moraliˈzation** *noun* [late Latin *moralizatio(n-)*] the action or an act of moralizing; moral interpretation; a moralizing commentary (*on* a text): LME. **moralizer** *noun* L16. **moralizing** *verbal noun* the action of the verb, *esp.* indulgence in moral reflection or talk; an instance of this: LME. **moralizingly** *adverb* in a moralizing manner L18.

moralled /ˈmɒr(ə)ld/ *adjective*. Also ***moraled**. E17.
[ORIGIN from MORAL *noun* + -ED[2].]
Having morals (of a specified kind).

moralless /ˈmɒr(ə)l-lɪs/ *adjective*. M19.
[ORIGIN from MORAL *noun* + -LESS.]
Without a moral or morals.

morally /ˈmɒr(ə)li/ *adverb*. LME.
[ORIGIN from MORAL *adjective* + -LY[2].]
†**1** In a moral sense; with a moral meaning or purpose. *rare*. LME–E16.
2 In respect of moral character or conduct; from the point of view of morality or moral law; with reference to moral responsibility. LME.

> M. SINCLAIR More than ever morally inert. D. OGILVY Morally, I find myself between the rock and the hard place. *Observer* I believe that the possession and use of nuclear weapons can be morally acceptable.

3 In accordance with morality; virtuously. M16.
4 On grounds of moral evidence. M17.

> T. DREISER I am morally certain he uses money to get what he is after.

moralness /ˈmɒr(ə)lnɪs/ *noun*. *rare*. M17.
[ORIGIN from MORAL *adjective* + -NESS.]
The quality or condition of being moral.

moran /ˈmɒr(ə)n/ *noun*. Pl. same. E20.
[ORIGIN Masai.]
A member of the warrior group of the Masai people of E. Africa, which comprises the younger unmarried males.

morass /məˈras/ *noun*. L15.
[ORIGIN Middle Low German *moras* & Dutch *moeras* alt. (by assim. to *moer* MOOR *noun*[1]) of Middle Dutch *maras* from Old French & mod. French *marais*: see MARISH *noun*.]
1 A bog, a marsh, (now *literary*); a very wet or muddy area of ground. L15.

> C. PRIEST The lane . . was an almost impassable morass of deep puddles and squelching mud.

2 *fig.* A complicated or confused situation, place, etc., that it is difficult to escape from or make progress through. M19.

> M. DRABBLE She was aware of an emotional situation of unparalleled density and complexity, of some dark morass of intrigue.

– COMB.: **morass-weed** *W. Indian* a hornwort, *Ceratophyllum demersum*.
■ **morassy** *adjective* L17.

Morasthite /ˈmɒrəsθʌɪt/ *noun*. LME.
[ORIGIN from *Moresheth-Gath* (see below) + -ITE[1].]
In biblical translations and allusions: a native or inhabitant of Moresheth-Gath, a town near the Philistine city of Gath.
the Morasthite: the prophet Micah.

M

morat /ˈmɔːrət/ *noun.* **E19.**
[**ORIGIN** medieval Latin *moratum*, from Latin *morus* mulberry: see **-ATE**¹.]
hist. A drink made of honey and flavoured with mulberries.

†**moration** *noun. rare.* **M17–M19.**
[**ORIGIN** Latin *moratio(n-)*, from *morat-*: see **MORATORIUM**, **-ATION**.]
A delay.

moratorium /mɒrəˈtɔːrɪəm/ *noun.* Pl. **-iums**, **-ia** /-ɪə/. **L19.**
[**ORIGIN** mod. Latin, use as noun of neut. sing. of late Latin *moratorius* that delays, from *morat-* pa. ppl stem of *morari* to delay: see **-ORIUM**.]
1 *LAW.* A legal authorization to a debtor to postpone payment for a certain time; the period of such a postponement. **L19.**
2 A postponement or deliberate temporary suspension of some activity etc. **M20.**

Daily Telegraph Could we not now have a moratorium on Dylan Thomas records? *Nature* A provision calling for a five-year moratorium on the killing of all ocean mammals.

moratory /ˈmɒrət(ə)ri/ *adjective.* **L19.**
[**ORIGIN** Late Latin *moratorius*: see **MORATORIUM**, **-ORY**².]
LAW. Authorizing postponement of payment; of or pertaining to postponement of payment.

moratto /məˈratəʊ/ *noun.* Now *rare* or *obsolete*. Pl. **-os.** **M18.**
[**ORIGIN** Ult. from Spanish.]
A variety of pea. Also ***moratto pea***.

Moravian /məˈreɪvɪən/ *noun*¹ *& adjective*¹. **M16.**
[**ORIGIN** from medieval Latin *Moravia*, from the River *Morava*: see **-AN**.]
▸**A** *noun.* **1** A native or inhabitant of Moravia, a region around the River Morava, now part of the Czech Republic. **M16.**
2 A member or adherent of a Protestant Church holding Hussite doctrines, founded in Saxony in the early 18th cent. by emigrants from Moravia. **M18.**
▸**B** *adjective.* Of or pertaining to Moravia or the Moravians. **E17.**
■ **Moravianism** *noun* the religious system of the Moravians **E19.**

Moravian /məˈreɪvɪən/ *noun*² *& adjective*². *hist.* **L16.**
[**ORIGIN** from medieval Latin *Moravia* Moray (see below) + **-AN**.]
▸**A** *noun.* A native or inhabitant of Moray in NE Scotland (in early use, one of the great divisions of the country, later, a county occupying part of the territory formerly so named). **L16.**
▸**B** *adjective.* Of or pertaining to Moray. **L19.**

M

moray /mɒˈreɪ, ˈmɒreɪ/ *noun.* **E17.**
[**ORIGIN** Portuguese *moréia* from Latin **MURAENA**.]
More fully ***moray eel***. A voracious eel-like fish of the family Muraenidae, inhabiting warm-temperate and tropical coastal waters; spec. *Muraena helena*, a large eel of the Mediterranean and eastern Atlantic.

morbid /ˈmɔːbɪd/ *adjective.* **M17.**
[**ORIGIN** Latin *morbidus*, from *morbus* disease: see **-ID**¹.]
1 Of the nature of or indicative of disease; affected by disease, unhealthy. Formerly also, productive of disease. **M17.**
morbid anatomy the anatomy of diseased organs and tissues.
2 Of a mental state, an idea, etc.: unwholesome, sickly; marked by exaggerated or inappropriate feelings of gloom, apprehension, or suspicion. Of a person: given to morbid feelings or fancies. **M19.**

G. GORDON Morbid lot, they're only happy when their friends have died. W. GOLDING Lewis himself had a deep, and one might think morbid, fear of dead bodies.

■ **morbidly** *adverb* **E19.** **morbidness** *noun* **M17.**

morbidezza /morbiˈdeddza, mɔːbɪˈdetsə/ *noun.* **E17.**
[**ORIGIN** Italian, from *morbido* morbid, formed as **MORBID**.]
1 *PAINTING.* Lifelike delicacy in flesh tints. **E17.**
2 Delicacy, softness, esp. in musical performance; sensibility, smoothness; effeminacy, sickliness. **L19.**

morbidity /mɔːˈbɪdɪti/ *noun.* **E18.**
[**ORIGIN** from **MORBID** + **-ITY**.]
1 The quality or condition of being diseased or ill; a pathological state or symptom; a morbid characteristic or idea. **E18.**

Independent An important cause of both morbidity and mortality in pedal cyclists is major head injury.

2 Prevalence of disease; the extent or degree of prevalence of disease in a district. **L19.**

morbific /mɔːˈbɪfɪk/ *adjective.* **M17.**
[**ORIGIN** (French *morbifique* from) mod. Latin *morbificus*, from *morbus* disease: see **-FIC**.]
1 Causing disease; pathogenic. **M17.**
2 Diseased; pertaining to or caused by disease. **M17.**
■ Also †**morbifical** *adjective*: only in 17.

morbility /mɔːˈbɪlɪti/ *noun.* Now *rare.* **M19.**
[**ORIGIN** German *Morbilität*, from Latin *morbus* disease: see **-ILE**, **-ITY**.]
= **MORBIDITY** 2.

morbilli /mɔːˈbɪlʌɪ/ *noun pl.* **LME.**
[**ORIGIN** medieval Latin, pl. of *morbillus* pustule, spot characteristic of measles, dim. of Latin *morbus* disease.]
MEDICINE. (The spots characteristic of) measles.

morbilliform /mɔːˈbɪlɪfɔːm/ *adjective.* **L19.**
[**ORIGIN** from medieval Latin *morbillus* (see **MORBILLI**) + **-I-** + **-FORM**.]
MEDICINE. Resembling (that of) measles.

morbillivirus /mɔːˈbɪlɪˌvʌɪrəs/ *noun.* **M20.**
[**ORIGIN** formed as **MORBILLIFORM** + **VIRUS**.]
Any of a genus of paramyxoviruses including those of measles, rinderpest, and canine distemper.

morbillous /mɔːˈbɪləs/ *adjective.* **L18.**
[**ORIGIN** from medieval Latin *morbillosus*, from *morbillus*: see **MORBILLI**, **-OUS**.]
MEDICINE. Of or pertaining to measles.

morbleu /mɔrblø/ *interjection.* **M17.**
[**ORIGIN** French, alt. of *mort Dieu* god's death.]
A comic oath, usu. attributed to French speakers.

morbose /ˈmɔːbəʊs/ *adjective.* Long *rare* or *obsolete*. **L17.**
[**ORIGIN** formed as **MORBOUS**: see **-OSE**¹.]
Caused by or causing disease; diseased, unhealthy.

morbous /ˈmɔːbəs/ *adjective.* Long *rare.* **LME.**
[**ORIGIN** from Latin *morbosus*, from *morbus* disease: see **-OUS**.]
Causing disease; of or pertaining to disease, diseased.

morceau /mɔːˈsəʊ, *foreign* mɔrso/ *noun.* Pl. **-eaux** /-əʊz, *foreign* -o/. **M18.**
[**ORIGIN** French: see **MORSEL**.]
A short literary or musical composition.
morceau de salon /də salɔ̃/ [= of the salon] a well-known tune elaborated by variations etc.

morcellate /ˈmɔːsəleɪt/ *verb trans.* **L19.**
[**ORIGIN** from **MORCELLE(MENT** + **-ATE**³.]
Divide into many pieces; *fig.* fragment. Chiefly as ***morcellated*** *ppl adjective*.
■ **morceˈllation** *noun* the action or process of morcellating something; *esp.* (*MEDICINE*) the surgical breaking up of a tumour or other growth into small pieces: **L19.**

morcellement /mɔrsɛlmɑ̃/ *noun.* **M19.**
[**ORIGIN** French, from *morceler* break in pieces, from Old French *morcel* **MORSEL**: see **-MENT**.]
Division into many pieces; *spec.* (*MEDICINE*) morcellation.

mordacious /mɔːˈdeɪʃəs/ *adjective.* Now *rare.* **M17.**
[**ORIGIN** from Latin *mordac-* (see **MORDICANT**) + **-IOUS**.]
1 (Of sarcasm or invective) biting, keen; characterized by or using biting sarcasm or invective. **M17.**
†**2** Of a material substance: pungent; caustic. Only in **L17.**
3 Biting (with teeth or fangs); given to biting. **L18.**

mordacity /mɔːˈdasɪti/ *noun.* **L16.**
[**ORIGIN** French *mordacité* or Latin *mordacitas*, formed as **MORDACIOUS**: see **-ACITY**.]
†**1** Pungency, sharpness. **L16–E19.**
2 Caustic quality, sarcasm, acerbity. **M17.**
†**3** Tendency to bite. **L17–E19.**

mordant /ˈmɔːd(ə)nt/ *noun, adjective, & verb.* **LME.**
[**ORIGIN** Old French & mod. French *mordant* (use as noun of) pres. ppl adjective of *mordre* to bite from Proto-Romance alt. of Latin *mordere*: see **-ANT**¹.]
▸**A** *noun.* †**1** An ornamental metal fastening on a girdle or belt. **LME–E16.**
2 A substance enabling a dye or stain to become fixed in the fabric, tissue, etc., on which it is used, usu. applied beforehand. **L18.**
3 An adhesive compound for fixing gold leaf. **E19.**
4 A corrosive liquid used to etch the lines on a printing plate. **L19.**
▸**B** *adjective.* **1** Of sarcasm etc.: caustic, cutting, biting. **L15.**

O. SACKS His wit had always been sharp, but now became mordant.

†**2** Sharp, keen. Of pain: acute, burning. **L16–L19.**
3 Corrosive. **E17.**
4 a Having the property of a mordant or fixative. **E19.** ▸**b** Of a dye: becoming fixed on the fibre only if a mordant is applied. **E20.**
▸**C** *verb trans.* Impregnate or treat with a mordant. **M19.**
■ **mordancy** *noun* the quality of being biting in speech; sarcastic force; incisiveness: **M17.** **mordantly** *adverb* (**a**) bitingly, sarcastically; (**b**) in the manner of a mordant: **M19.**

†**mordechin** *noun. Indian.* Also **mordisheen** & other vars. **L16–E19.**
[**ORIGIN** Portuguese *mordexim* from Marathi *moḍachī*.]
Cholera.

mordent /ˈmɔːd(ə)nt/ *noun.* **E19.**
[**ORIGIN** German from Italian *mordente* use as noun of verbal adjective from *mordere* to bite from Proto-Romance: see **MORDANT**.]
MUSIC. An ornament consisting of the rapid alternation of the note written with the one immediately below it. Also = **PRALLTRILLER**.

mordicant /ˈmɔːdɪk(ə)nt/ *adjective.* Long *rare.* **LME.**
[**ORIGIN** Late Latin *mordicant-* pres. ppl stem of *mordicare* bite, gripe, from Latin *mordac-*, *mordax* biting, abrasive, from *mordere* to bite: see **-ANT**¹.]
Corrosive, biting, sharp.

mordication /mɔːdɪˈkeɪʃ(ə)n/ *noun.* Now *rare.* **LME.**
[**ORIGIN** (Old French from) late Latin *mordicatio(n-)*, from *mordicat-* pa. ppl stem of *mordicare*: see **MORDICANT**, **-ATION**.]
1 A biting, burning, or pricking sensation. **LME.**
†**2** Corrosiveness. Only in **LME.**

mordida /morˈdida/ *noun.* **M20.**
[**ORIGIN** Central Amer. & Mexican Spanish.]
In Mexico and Central America: a bribe, an illegal exaction.

mordoré /mɔrdɔre/ *noun.* **L18.**
[**ORIGIN** French, formed as **MOOR** *noun*² + **DORÉ**.]
A colour between brown and red; russet.

Mordvin /ˈmɔːdvɪn/ *noun.* Pl. **-vins**, **-va** /-və/, same. **M18.**
[**ORIGIN** Russian.]
1 A member of a people of Finnish descent inhabiting the region of the middle Volga, in western Russia; a native or inhabitant of the Russian republic of Mordvin. **M18.**
2 The Finno-Ugric language of this people. **L19.**
■ **Mordˈvinian** *adjective & noun* (**a**) *adjective* of or pertaining to the Mordvins; (**b**) *noun* = **MORDVIN**: **L19.**

more /mɔː/ *noun*¹. *obsolete* exc. *dial.*
[**ORIGIN** Old English *more*, *moru* = Old Saxon *morha*, Middle Low German *more*, Old High German *mor(a)ha* (Middle High German *mor(h)e*, *mörhe*, German *Möhre*), from Germanic.]
1 The root of a tree or plant; the fibrous roots of a tap root; a tree stump. **OE.** ▸†**b** A plant. *poet. rare* (Spenser). Only in **L16.**
†**2** *fig.* Origin, source. Only in **ME.**

more /ˈmɔːreɪ/ *noun*². **E17.**
[**ORIGIN** Latin, abl. of *mos*: see **MORES**.]
Fashion, custom: only in Latin adverbial phrs.
more hispanico /hɪˈspanɪkəʊ/ in accordance with Spanish custom. ***more majorum*** /məˈdʒɔːrəm/ [genit. pl. of *majores* ancestors] in traditional manner. ***more meo*** /ˈmeɪəʊ/ in my own fashion. ***more suo*** /ˈsuːəʊ/ in his own fashion.

more /mɔː/ *adjective* (in mod. usage also classed as a *determiner*), *noun*³, *adverb*, *& preposition*.
[**ORIGIN** Old English *māra* (fem., neut. *māre*) = Old Frisian *māra*, Old Saxon *mēro* (Middle Dutch *mēre*, mod. Dutch *meer*, *meerder*), Old High German *mēro* (German *mehr*, with compar. suffix *mehrere* several), Old Norse *meire*, Gothic *maiza*, from Germanic deriv. of base of **MO** *adverb*, *noun*³, *& adjective*. Serving as compar. of **MANY**, **MUCH**. Cf. also **MOST**.]
▸**A** *adjective.* **1 a** Greater in size, larger; (of a person or animal) taller, bigger; greater in number, quantity, or amount. Long only in ***the more part***. Now *arch. rare.* **OE.** ▸**b** With nouns of quality, condition, action, etc.: greater in degree or extent. *obsolete* exc. as passing into sense 2 and in ***(the) more's the pity***. **OE.** ▸†**c** *spec.* Designating the greater or superior of two things, places, etc., of the same name. Also, designating the elder of two siblings. **ME–L16.** ▸†**d** Greater in power, authority, or importance. Only in **ME.** ▸**e** Qualifying the designation of a person: entitled to the designation in a greater degree. Long *obsolete* exc. in ***the more fool you***, ***the more fool he***, etc. (passing into adverb). **LME.**

b J. LOUTHIAN And, for the more Verification, I and the said Witnesses have subscribed the same.

2 Additional to the quantity or number specified or implied; an additional amount or number of; further. Now *rare* exc. with preceding or implied indef. or numeral adjective, & in ***without more ado***. **ME.**

T. HARDY It was too dark to arrange more flowers that night. H. H. FINLAYSON Without more ado, the men reach for their spears. G. ORWELL I have three more chapters and an epilogue to do. W. S. CHURCHILL Not to cut any more coal or make any more steel. B. NICHOLS No more wine, George, thank you.

3 Existing in greater quantity, amount, or degree; a greater quantity or amount of. **ME.**

B. JOWETT Ten is two more than eight. *Bookman* Had he but shown a little more firmness.

4 More numerous. *arch.* **M16.**

RV *2 Kings* 6:16 They that be with us are more than they that be with them.

5 A greater number of. **L16.**

G. GREENE For more years than he could remember he had kept a record. G. GORDON He had more teeth filled than she had.

▸**B** *noun.* **1 a** Something that is more; a greater quantity, amount, proportion, or degree. (Foll. by *of*.) **OE.** ▸**b** As compl.: something of greater importance or significance. **OE.**

a MILTON Where more is meant than meets the ear. J. TYNDALL The more I saw of my guide the more I liked him. I. MCEWAN You know more about it than I do. **b** LD MACAULAY Honour and shame were scarcely more to him than light and darkness to the blind.

†**2** Ancestors, elders; people of high rank. **ME–E17.**

SHAKES. *Macb.* Both more and less have given him the revolt.

3 An additional quantity, amount, or number; something else in addition to what is specified. Chiefly with preceding or implied indef. or numeral adjective **ME.** ▸**b** The 'something more' that has been mentioned or implied in the context. *poet. & rhet.* L16.

J. RUSKIN Of this, however, more in another place. V. PALMER Heard any more about that thousand? G. LYALL They'll want to know more. **b** M. ARNOLD Know, man hath all which Nature hath, but more.

4 *pl.* A greater number *of* the class specified; a greater number of people. E17.

A. WILSON I'm glad they've come in. The more the merrier.

► **C** *adverb.* **1** In addition; in repetition or continuance of what has taken place; again, longer; besides, (now only after a designation of quantity or number). OE.

R. BRIDGES Never call me woman more. E. NESBIT There are one or two things more. B. PYM I looked forward to being alone once more.

2 In a greater degree, to a greater extent; *spec.* modifying an adjective or adverb to form the compar. (the normal mode of forming the compar. of adjectives & adverbs with three or more syllables, and of most of those with two syllables; also (now *arch. & dial.*) used pleonastically before the compar. of an adjective or adverb). ME.

TENNYSON But Paris was to me More lovelier than all the world beside. M. ARNOLD I too have wish'd, no woman more, This starting, feverish heart away. H. T. BUCKLE The fine arts are addressed more to the imagination; the sciences to the intellect. G. BORROW 'Are the Welsh.. as clannish as the Highlanders?'.. 'Yes,.. and a good deal more'. E. BLUNDEN The bronze moon was more quiet.. than the morning. R. LEHMANN I wish I saw you more. J. STEINBECK Then it was June, and the sun shone more fiercely. S. BEDFORD My brother has a system too, but yours is more interesting. P. D. JAMES She could hardly have been more wrong. A. BROOKNER The salon was more agreeable than her room would have led her to expect.

3 Being or having something specified to a greater measure or degree *than* another; more correctly said to be the one thing *than* the other. Also foll. by *of* and with ellipsis of the *than* clause. ME.

T. MEDWIN More dead than alive. H. T. BUCKLE The Puritans were more fanatical than superstitious. YEATS *The Shadowy Waters*.. is more of a ritual than a human story. M. AMIS They were enjoying a kiss—well, more of a snog really.

4 Modifying a clause. Further, moreover. LME.

G. W. DASENT He was industrious, and more, he was handsome.

► †**D** *preposition.* = PLUS *preposition.* M16–E18.

– PHRASES (of adjective, noun, & adverb): **and more**: used (chiefly after a statement of quantity or number) to indicate an indefinite or unspecified addition to what has been mentioned. **any more than**: excluding or denying the following clause equally with one just mentioned. ***do more harm than good***: see HARM *noun*. **more and more** in an increasing degree, to an increasing extent. ***more by token***: see TOKEN *adjective*. ***more haste, less speed***: see HASTE *noun*. ***more like***: see LIKE *adjective* etc. ***more often than not***: see OFTEN *adverb*. **more or less** as an estimate, approximately; in a greater or less degree; to a greater or less extent. **more so** to a greater extent (than the other specified). ***more's the pity***: see PITY *noun*. **more than —**: indicating that the word so qualified is (in some obvious respect) inadequate to the intended meaning. ***more than a match for***: see MATCH *noun*[1]. ***more than meets the eye***: see MEET *verb*. ***more than somewhat***: see SOMEWHAT *adverb*. **neither more nor less than** exactly, precisely, (that) and nothing else. ***no more***: see NO *adverb*[2]. ***once more***. **or more**: added to approximate designations of quantity, to indicate that the actual amount is probably greater than that stated. ***the more's the pity***: see PITY *noun*. ***what is more***.

more /mɔː/ *verb. obsolete* exc. *dial.* ME.
[ORIGIN from MORE *noun*[1].]
1 *verb intrans.* Take root, become rooted. Chiefly *fig.* ME.
†**2** *verb trans.* Root, implant; establish. ME–L16.
3 *verb trans.* Uproot, root *up*. ME.

moree *noun* var. of MOORY *noun*.

moreen /mə'riːn/ *noun & adjective.* L17.
[ORIGIN Unknown. Cf. MORELLA *noun*[1], -EEN[1].]
(Made of) a stout woollen or woollen and cotton material used for furnishing.

moreish /'mɔːrɪʃ/ *adjective. colloq.* Also **morish**. M18.
[ORIGIN from MORE *noun*[3] + -ISH[1].]
Pleasant to eat, causing a desire for more.

morel /mə'rɛl/ *noun*[1]. LME.
[ORIGIN Old French *morele*, mod. *-elle* (= medieval Latin *morella*, *maur-*) prob. fem. of *morel* (mod. *moreau*) from medieval Latin *morellus*: see MORELLO. Cf. MOREL *noun*[2].]
Any of various kinds of nightshade; *spec.* = ***petty morel*** (a) below.
petty morel (*a*) black nightshade, *Solanum nigrum*; (*b*) *US*. American spikenard, *Aralia racemosa*.

†**morel** *noun*[2]. E17–E19.
[ORIGIN App. from French †*morelle*, prob. from medieval Latin *morellus*: see MORELLO. Cf. MOREL *noun*[1].]
= MORELLO.

morel /mə'rɛl/ *noun*[3]. Also **morille** /mə'riːj, *foreign* mɔriːj (*pl. same*)/. M17.
[ORIGIN French *morille* from Dutch, rel. to Old High German *morhila* (German *Morchel* fungus).]
Any of various edible cup fungi of the genus *Morchella*, esp. *M. esculenta*, with a honeycombed pale brown and dark brown cap.

†**morella** *noun*[1]. M17–E18.
[ORIGIN Perh. from MOIRE + -ELLA.]
A kind of material formerly used for dresses, curtains, etc.

†**morella** *noun*[2] var. of MORELLO.

Morellian /mə'rɛlɪən/ *adjective & noun.* L19.
[ORIGIN from Giovanni *Morelli* (1816–91), Italian art critic + -IAN.]
► **A** *adjective.* Of, pertaining to, or characteristic of a method of systematic art criticism stressing the study of detail as a guide in the attribution of paintings. L19.
► **B** *noun.* A follower of the Morellian method. E20.
■ **Morellianism** *noun* L19.

morello /mɒ'rɛləʊ/ *noun.* Pl. **-os**. Also †**-lla**. E17.
[ORIGIN App. from Italian *morello* (fem. *-la*) blackish from medieval Latin *morellus*, *maur-* (of a horse) dark brown, dim. of Latin *Maurus* MOOR *noun*[2]: cf. MOREL *noun*[1], *noun*[2].]
A form of the sour cherry, *Prunus cerasus*, with a dark fruit; the fruit of this tree. Also ***morello cherry***.

morena /mɒ'reɪnə/ *noun.* M19.
[ORIGIN Sesotho.]
In Lesotho (formerly Basutoland), southern Africa: (the title of) a chief; also used as a respectful form of address to any person.

moreness /'mɔːnɪs/ *noun. rare.* LME.
[ORIGIN from MORE *adjective* + -NESS.]
1 The condition of being or having more. LME.
†**2** Plurality. Only in 17.

Morenu /mɒ'reɪnuː/ *noun.* M17.
[ORIGIN Hebrew *mōrēnū* lit. 'our teacher'.]
(An honorific title conferred on) a rabbi or Talmudic scholar.

Moreote /'mɔːrɪəʊt/ *adjective & noun.* E19.
[ORIGIN mod. Greek *Moreōtēs*, from *Morea*, a name of the Peloponnese peninsula: see -OTE.]
► **A** *adjective.* Of or pertaining to the Peloponnese peninsula, Greece. E19.
► **B** *noun.* A native or inhabitant of the Peloponnese. M19.

moreover /mɔːr'əʊvə/ *adverb.* Orig. as two words. ME.
[ORIGIN from MORE *adverb* + OVER *adverb*.]
†**1** More, in excess. ME–E16.
2 Besides, further. Used at the beginning of a clause, or parenthetically, to introduce a statement as additional to what has been said. Freq. preceded by *and*. ME.

R. KIPLING There is, moreover, a written paper of the hours of the trains that go south. *Nature* One cannot communicate with the world outside; and moreover, one would inexorably be propelled towards the centre. R. WHELAN Moreover, by the time the attack was scheduled to begin.. it would be light enough to photograph.

†**3** Modifying a clause. In addition to the fact *that*. *rare.* LME–E17.

morepork *noun* see MOPOKE.

mores /'mɔːreɪz, -riːz/ *noun pl.* L19.
[ORIGIN Latin, pl. of *mos* manner, custom.]
1 The acquired customs and moral assumptions which give cohesion to a community or social group. L19.

G. GREER Perhaps the pop revolution.. has had a far-reaching effect on sexual *mores*.

2 ZOOLOGY. The habits, behaviour, etc., of a group of animals of the same kind. E20.

Moresca /mə'rɛskə/ *noun.* M19.
[ORIGIN Italian, fem. of MORESCO. Cf. MORISCA.]
An Italian folk dance related to the English morris dance.

Moresco /mə'rɛskəʊ/ *adjective & noun.* M16.
[ORIGIN Italian, from *Moro* MOOR *noun*[2] + *-esco* -ESQUE. Cf. MORISCO.]
► **A** *adjective.* Of or pertaining to the Moors; Moorish. M16.
► **B** *noun.* Pl. **-o(e)s**.
1 A morris dance or similar dance. M16.
2 A Moor, esp. in Spain. L16.

Moresque /mə'rɛsk/ *adjective & noun.* LME.
[ORIGIN French from Italian *moresco*: see MORESCO, -ESQUE.]
► **A** *noun.* **1** (An example of) Moorish ornamentation. LME.
†**2** A morris dance. E16–E18.
► **B** *adjective.* Moorish in style or ornamental design. E17.

Moreton Bay /mɔːt(ə)n 'beɪ/ *noun phr.* E19.
[ORIGIN See below.]
Used *attrib.* to designate trees first found in the neighbourhood of Moreton Bay, Queensland, Australia.
Moreton Bay chestnut a leguminous tree, *Castanospermum australe*, with racemes of yellow flowers and large woody pods (cf. ***black bean*** (b) s.v. BLACK *adjective*). **Moreton Bay fig** a fig tree, *Ficus macrophylla*, with large glossy leaves, often planted for shade in Australia. **Moreton Bay pine** the hoop pine, *Araucaria cunninghamii*.

†**morfound** *verb & noun.* LME.
[ORIGIN Old French & mod. French *morfondre*, from *morve* mucus + *fondre* melt, FOUND *verb*[2].]
► **A** *verb intrans. & trans.* (*refl.* & in *pass.*). Of a horse or other animal: take a severe chill, be numb with cold. LME–E18.
► **B** *noun.* A disease of animals, resulting from becoming chilled after being too hot. E16–E18.
■ †**morfounder** *verb intrans. & trans.* (*refl.* & in *pass.*) = MORFOUND *verb* E16–M18.

morgan /'mɔːg(ə)n/ *noun*[1]. Now *dial.* M17.
[ORIGIN Perh. rel. to female forename *Margaret*.]
Any of several white-rayed plants of the composite family; *esp.* (*a*) stinking camomile, *Anthemis cotula*; (*b*) the ox-eye daisy, *Leucanthemum vulgare*.

Morgan /'mɔːg(ə)n/ *noun*[2]. M19.
[ORIGIN Justin *Morgan* (1747–98), Amer. teacher and owner of a stallion from which the breed descends.]
A breed of light thickset horse developed in New England; an animal of this breed. Also ***Morgan colt***, ***Morgan horse***, etc.

morgan /'mɔːg(ə)n/ *noun*[3]. E20.
[ORIGIN T. H. *Morgan*: see MORGANISM.]
GENETICS. A unit of the effective distance on a chromosome between two linked genes, defined so that the distance in morgans between two genes is equal to the frequency of crossing over between them when they are close enough together for the effect of multiple crossing over to be negligible.

morganatic /mɔːgə'natɪk/ *adjective.* L16.
[ORIGIN French *morganatique*, German *morganatisch*, or their source medieval Latin *morganaticus*, in *matrimonium ad morganaticam*, in which the last word is prob. from Germanic word (whence German *Morgengabe*) = Old English *morgengifu* (from *morgen* MORN + base of GIVE *verb*), morning gift, the husband's gift to the wife after consummation relieving him of further liability.]
†**1** Designating a morning gift. *rare.* Only in L16.
2 (Of a marriage) between a man (less commonly a woman) of high rank and a woman (or man) of lower rank, the spouse and children having no claim to the possessions or title of the person of higher rank; (of a spouse) married to a person of higher rank in this way. E18.
■ **morganatically** *adverb* M19.

morganise *verb* var. of MORGANIZE.

Morganism /'mɔːg(ə)nɪz(ə)m/ *noun.* M20.
[ORIGIN from *Morgan* (see below) + -IST.]
BIOLOGY (now *hist.*). Mendelian genetics as propounded by Thomas Hunt Morgan (1866–1945), US geneticist and zoologist, incorporating the theory of the gene now generally accepted.
■ **Morganist** *noun* a supporter or advocate of Morganism M20.

morganite /'mɔːg(ə)nʌɪt/ *noun.* E20.
[ORIGIN from J. P. *Morgan* (1837–1913), US financier + -ITE[1].]
MINERALOGY. A pink transparent variety of beryl used as a gemstone.

M

morganize /'mɔːg(ə)nʌɪz/ *verb trans. US.* Also **-ise**. M19.
[ORIGIN from William *Morgan* (d. 1826) of the US, who was alleged to have been murdered by Freemasons.]
Assassinate secretly in order to prevent or punish disclosures.

morgay *noun* var. of MORGY.

morgen /'mɔːg(ə)n/ *noun.* E17.
[ORIGIN Dutch & German (see MORN), app. meaning 'the area of land that can be ploughed in a morning'.]
A measure of land in the Netherlands and South Africa (and hence in parts of the US), equal to about 0.8 hectare or two acres. Also, in Norway, Denmark, and Germany, a measure of land now equal to about 0.3 hectare or two-thirds of an acre.

morgenstern /'mɔːg(ə)nstəːn/ *noun.* M17.
[ORIGIN German, from *Morgen* MORN + *Stern* STAR *noun*[1].]
hist. A weapon consisting of a heavy ball attached either as the head of a club set with spikes or at the end of a chain. Also called ***morning star***.

morgue /mɔrg/ *noun*[1]. Pl. pronounced same. L16.
[ORIGIN French, of unknown origin.]
A haughty demeanour; haughty superiority, pride.

PERRY ANDERSON The famous *morgue* and truculence of Wittgenstein, Namier or Popper, expressed their inner confidence of superiority.

– NOTE: Formerly anglicized.

morgue /mɔːg/ *noun*[2]. E19.
[ORIGIN French, proper name of a Paris mortuary: prob. identical with MORGUE *noun*[1].]
1 A mortuary. E19.

C. THUBRON The dressing room was like a morgue. Exhausted bathers stretched inert under sheets.

2 In a newspaper office, the collection of material assembled for the future obituaries of people still living. Also, repository of cuttings, photographs, and information in a newspaper office, film studio, etc. *slang.* E20.

morgy /'mɔːgeɪ/ *noun. dial.* Also **-gay**. M17.
[ORIGIN Cornish *morgi*, from *mor* sea + *ky*, *kei* dog.]
A dogfish; *esp.* the lesser-spotted dogfish, *Scyliorhinus canicula*.

MORI /'mɒri/ *abbreviation.*
Market & Opinion Research International.

moribund /'mɒrɪbʌnd/ *adjective & noun.* E18.
[ORIGIN Latin *moribundus*, from *mori* die.]
► **A** *adjective.* **1** At the point of death; dying. E18.

J. P. HENNESSY The people they indicated as moribund did in truth die soon afterwards.

2 *fig.* About to come to an end. Also, lacking inspiration, vitality, or vigour. M19.

Spectator We all talk of the Turkish Empire as moribund. C. CONNOLLY A stagnant world and a moribund society.

▸ **B** *absol.* as *noun.* A dying person; *pl.* the dying. M19.

W. H. AUDEN We know no fuss or pain or lying Can stop the moribund from dying.

■ **mori'bundity** *noun* moribund condition M19.

moriche /mɒˈrɪtʃeɪ/ *noun.* M19.
[ORIGIN Amer. Spanish, from Carib *morisi*, perh. related to Tupi *mburiti*.]
A tall S. American palm, *Mauritia flexuosa*, used as a source of sago, fibre, and (from the sap) wine. Also ***moriche palm***.

moriform /ˈmɔːrɪfɔːm/ *adjective. rare.* M19.
[ORIGIN from Latin *morum* mulberry + -I- + -FORM.]
Chiefly MEDICINE. Having the shape or form of a mulberry.

morigerate /məˈrɪdʒ(ə)rət/ *adjective. rare.* LME.
[ORIGIN Latin *morigeratus* pa. pple of *morigerari* comply with, humour, formed as MORIGEROUS: see -ATE[2].]
†**1** Of a (specified) character or nature. Only in LME.
2 Compliant, obedient. M16.

morigeration /mərɪdʒəˈreɪʃ(ə)n/ *noun.* Now *rare.* LME.
[ORIGIN Latin *morigeratio(n-)* compliance, from *morigerat-* pa. ppl stem of *morigerari*: see MORIGERATE, -ATION.]
Obedience, compliance; deference to superiors, obsequiousness.

†**morigerous** *adjective.* E17–E19.
[ORIGIN from Latin *morigerus* (from *mor-*, *mos* custom, humour + *gerere*, after *morem gerere* humour (a person)) + -OUS.]
Obedient, compliant, submissive (*to*).

morille *noun* var. of MOREL *noun*[3].

morillo *noun* var. of MORRILLO.

morillon /mɒˈrɪlən/ *noun*[1]. L17.
[ORIGIN French (Old French *moreillon*), from *mor* dark brown, whence *morel*: see MOREL *noun*[1].]
A variety of vine producing early black grapes; a grape from such a vine.

morillon /mɒˈrɪlən/ *noun*[2]. Now *rare* or *obsolete.* L17.
[ORIGIN French.]
A female or young goldeneye (formerly mistaken for a separate species).

morinda /məˈrɪndə/ *noun.* M18.
[ORIGIN mod. Latin (see below), from Latin *morus* mulberry + *Indus* Indian.]
Any of various small trees of the genus *Morinda*, of the madder family, native esp. to tropical Asia, with roots and bark which yield red and yellow dyes.

morindin /məˈrɪndɪn/ *noun.* M19.
[ORIGIN formed as MORINDA + -IN[1].]
CHEMISTRY. An orange-red glycoside pigment present in the root bark of morindas and other plants. Cf. SOORANJEE.
■ **morindone** *noun* an orange-red anthraquinone derivative which is the aglycone of morindin M19.

moringa /məˈrɪŋgə/ *noun.* L17.
[ORIGIN mod. Latin (see below).]
Any of various African and Asian trees of the genus *Moringa* (family Moringaceae); esp. *M. oleifera*, of NW India, the source of ben nut oil.

morion /ˈmɒrɪən/ *noun*[1]. M16.
[ORIGIN French from Spanish *morrión*, from *morro* round object from Proto-Romance. Cf. MORAINE.]
hist. A kind of helmet, without beaver or visor, worn by soldiers in the 16th and 17th cents.

morion /ˈmɒrɪən/ *noun*[2]. M18.
[ORIGIN French from Latin *morio(n)* error for *mormorion*.]
MINERALOGY. A brown or black variety of quartz.

Moriori /mɒrɪˈɔːri/ *noun.* Pl. same, **-s**. M19.
[ORIGIN Polynesian.]
1 A member of the original Polynesian people inhabiting the Chatham Islands and parts of New Zealand before the Maori conquest in the early 19th cent; a descendant of this people. M19.
2 The language of the Moriori. M19.

Morisca /məˈrɪskə/ *noun.* M20.
[ORIGIN Spanish, fem. of MORISCO. Cf. MORESCA.]
A Spanish folk dance related to the English morris dance.

Morisco /məˈrɪskəʊ/ *adjective & noun.* M16.
[ORIGIN Spanish, from *Moro* MOOR *noun*[2] + *-isco* -ESQUE. Cf. MORESCO.]
▸ **A** *adjective.* Of or pertaining to the Moors; Moorish. M16.
▸ **B** *noun.* Pl. **-o(e)s**.
1 A Moor in Spain, *esp.* one who had accepted Christian baptism. *hist.* M16.
2 A morris dance or other dance with Moorish elements. M16. ▸†**b** A morris dancer. *rare* (Shakes.). Only in L16.
3 Moorish art, ornament, etc. E18.

morish *adjective* var. of MOREISH.

Morisonian /mɒrɪˈsəʊnɪən/ *noun & adjective.* M19.
[ORIGIN from *Morison* (see below) + -IAN.]
CHRISTIAN CHURCH. ▸**A** *noun.* A follower of the Scottish minister James Morison, founder of a sect called the Evangelical Union; a member or adherent of the Evangelical Union. M19.
▸ **B** *adjective.* Holding the doctrines of Morison or of the Evangelical Union. M19.

morkin /ˈmɔːkɪn/ *noun.* Now *rare* or *obsolete.* LME.
[ORIGIN Anglo-Norman *mortekine* alt. (infl. by -KIN) of Old French *mortecine* from late Latin *morticina* carrion, use as noun of neut. pl. of Latin *morticinus* that has died, from *mort-*, *mors* death.]
An animal killed by disease or accident.

Morlacco /mɔːˈlakəʊ/ *noun.* Now *rare.* Pl. **-cchi** /-kiː/. L18.
[ORIGIN Italian: see MORLACH.]
hist. = MORLACH *noun*.
■ **Mor'lacchian** *noun & adjective* = MORLACH E19.

Morlach /ˈmɔːlak/ *noun & adjective.* Also †**-ck**. M17.
[ORIGIN Italian *Morlacco*, pl. *-cchi* (also Croatian *Morlak*, pl. *-laci*) from late Latin *Morovlachus* from Byzantine Greek *Mauroblaxos*, from *mauros* black + *Blaxos* Vlach: cf. VLACH.]
▸**A** *noun.* A member of a Vlach people inhabiting an area formerly called Morlacchia, centred on the Adriatic port of Ragusa (modern Dubrovnik), between the 12th and 15th cents. L18.
▸ **B** *adjective.* Of, pertaining to, or characteristic of Morlacchia. L18.

†**morling** *noun.* LME.
[ORIGIN App. formed after MORKIN by substitution of -LING[1] for -KIN.]
1 Wool taken from the skin of a dead sheep. LME–M19.
2 = MORKIN. M17–M18.

mormal /ˈmɔːm(ə)l/ *noun.* Long *obsolete* exc. *dial.* LME.
[ORIGIN Old French *mortmal*, from *mort* dead + *mal* evil.]
An inflamed sore, esp. on the leg.

mormaor /ˈmɔːmɛː/ *noun.* Also **maormor** /ˈmɛːmɔː/. E19.
[ORIGIN Gaelic *mormaer* (mod. *mórmhaor*), from *mòr* great + *maor* bailiff.]
In ancient Scotland, a high steward of a province.

mormo /ˈmɔːməʊ/ *noun.* Now *rare.* Pl. **-os**. E17.
[ORIGIN Greek *mormō* a hideous female monster.]
A hobgoblin; an imaginary terror.

Mormon /ˈmɔːmən/ *noun & adjective.* M19.
[ORIGIN The prophet reputed to be the author of the Book of Mormon (see below).]
▸ **A** *noun.* A member or adherent of the Church of Jesus Christ of Latter-day Saints, a millenary Christian sect founded in 1830 by Joseph Smith (1805–44) who claimed to have discovered and translated by divine inspiration the 'Book of Mormon', a text accepted by Mormons as Scripture along with the Bible, relating the story of a group of Hebrews who migrated to America *c* 600 BC. M19.
▸ **B** *attrib.* or as *adjective.* Of or pertaining to the Mormons. M19.
Mormon Bible (***a***) a translation of the Bible executed and used by the Mormons; (***b***) the Book of Mormon. **Mormon Church** the Church of Jesus Christ of Latter-day Saints. **Mormon City** Salt Lake City, Utah. **Mormon cricket** a bush cricket, *Anabrus simplex*, of the western US which is destructive to cereal crops. **Mormon State** in the US, a state in which Mormons predominate, *spec.* Utah. **Mormon trail**: followed by Mormon migrants to Utah in 1847. **Mormon war**: *spec.* between Utah Mormons and federal troops in 1857–8.
■ **Mormondom** *noun* (***a***) the Mormons collectively; (***b***) the territory or practices of the Mormons: M19. **Mormo'ness** *noun* a female Mormon M19. **Mormonish** *adjective* pertaining to or characteristic of the Mormons or their beliefs M19. **Mormonism** *noun* the doctrine and practices of the Mormons M19. **Mormonist** *noun* (*rare*) = MORMON *noun* M19. **Mormonite** *noun & adjective* (now *rare*) = MORMON M19.

mormoopid /mɔːməʊˈɒpɪd/ *noun & adjective.* L20.
[ORIGIN mod. Latin *Mormoopidae* (see below), from Greek *mormō* MORMO + *ōps* eye, face: see -ID[3].]
▸ **A** *noun.* Any small insectivorous bat of the family Mormoopidae of central and N. America, in which the nose leaf is reduced or absent but the lips are elaborate and leaf-shaped. L20.
▸ **B** *adjective.* Of, pertaining to, or designating this family. L20.

mormyrid /ˈmɔːmɪrɪd/ *noun & adjective.* L19.
[ORIGIN mod. Latin *Mormyridae* (see below), from *Mormyrus* genus name, from Greek *mormuros*: see -ID[3].]
ZOOLOGY. ▸**A** *noun.* Any of various thick-bodied freshwater fishes of the African family Mormyridae, many of which possess electric organs and some of which have an elongated snout that resembles an elephant's trunk. L19.
▸ **B** *adjective.* Of, pertaining to, or designating this family. E20.
■ **mormyrus** *noun* †(***a***) a distinctively marked sea fish; (***b***) a mormyrid (now only as mod. Latin genus name): E17.

morn /mɔːn/ *noun.*
[ORIGIN Old English *morgen*, *mor(g)n-* = Old Frisian *morgen*, *morn*, Old Saxon, Old High German *morgan* (Dutch *morgen*, German *Morgen*), from Germanic. See also MORROW.]
1 The beginning of the day; dawn, sunrise. *poet.* OE. ▸**b** The east. *poet.* M17.

M. ARNOLD Thy high mountain platforms, Where Morn first appears.

2 The early part of the day; morning. Now chiefly *poet.* OE.

L. G. GIBBON It went on from morn till night.

3 The following morning. Also, the day after today or the day mentioned; = MORROW 2. Now only ***the morn***, tomorrow (as noun & adverb). Now *Scot.* & *N. English.* OE.

J. M. BARRIE The morn's the Sabbath.

– COMB.: **morn star** (*obsolete* exc. *poet.*) = MORNING STAR 1.
■ **mornless** *adjective* (*rare*) L18.

Mornay /ˈmɔːneɪ/ *noun & adjective.* Also **m-**. E20.
[ORIGIN Perh. from Philip de *Mornay* (d. 1623), French Huguenot writer.]
(In full ***Mornay sauce***, ***sauce Mornay***) a rich white sauce flavoured with cheese; (designating) a dish served with this sauce.

morne /mɔːn/ *noun*[1]. L15.
[ORIGIN Old French & mod. French, from *morner* blunt (a lance), from *morne* blunted, dull, ult. from Frankish.]
hist. The blunted head of a tilting lance.

morne /mɔːn/ *noun*[2]. *rare.* L19.
[ORIGIN Amer. French, perh. alt. of Spanish *morón*.]
In the Americas: a small round hill.

morne /mɔːn/ *adjective. literary.* M19.
[ORIGIN Old French & mod. French, from Frankish base also of MORNE *noun*[1].]
Dismal, dreary.

morné /ˈmɔːneɪ/ *adjective.* E18.
[ORIGIN French, pa. pple of *morner* blunt: see MORNE *noun*[1].]
HERALDRY. Of a lion rampant: having no tongue, teeth, or claws.

morning /ˈmɔːnɪŋ/ *noun.* ME.
[ORIGIN from MORN + -ING[1], after EVENING.]
1 The process or fact of the approach of dawn; the time about sunrise. ME. ▸**b** Daybreak; (the light of) dawn. Freq. personified. *poet.* L16.

W. CATHER He wandered about . . all night, till morning put out the fireflies and the stars.

2 The beginning or early part of the day, esp. from sunrise until noon; this time spent in a particular way or characterized by particular weather, conditions, experiences, etc. LME. ▸**b** The part of the day extending to dinner time. Now *obsolete* exc. *hist.* M18.

W. COWPER My morning is engrossed by the garden. *Times Lit. Suppl.* A morning's browsing in a book shop. DENNIS POTTER A hint of steely night . . showed that morning was on its way. J. GARDAM The sun's well up now and I never saw such a morning. E. SEGAL One August morning . . he turned five.

Monday morning, ***Tuesday morning***, etc.

3 *fig.* The beginning or early part of anything compared to a day; the early part *of* one's life etc. L16.

W. H. PRESCOTT A war which hung like a dark cloud on the morning of her reign.

4 a An alcoholic drink taken before breakfast. Chiefly *Scot.* E18. ▸**b** A light meal taken at rising, some time before breakfast. *dial.* E19. ▸**c** *ellipt.* A morning newspaper. *colloq.* M20.

c *Daily Telegraph* The . . 12 mornings printed in major provincial towns and cities.

5 *ellipt.* As *interjection.* Good morning. *colloq.* L19.

– PHRASES: **in a morning** *colloq.* = ***of a morning*** below. **in the morning** (***a***) (following a specified time) between midnight and noon, = ***a.m.***; (***b***) during or in the course of the morning; (***c***) habitually in the morning; (***d***) tomorrow morning. ***last morning***: see LAST *adjective*. **morning after** (***a***) ***the morning after*** (***the night before***), a morning on which a person has a hangover; (***b***) a hangover; *gen.* an unpleasant aftermath of pleasure; (***c***) ***morning-after pill***, a contraceptive pill effective when taken some hours after sexual intercourse. **morning, noon, and night** incessantly, all day. **of a morning** *colloq.* habitually in the morning. ***pride of the morning***: see PRIDE *noun*[1]. **this morning** (during) the morning of today. ***TOMORROW morning***. ***YESTERDAY morning***.

– ATTRIB. & COMB.: In the senses 'of or pertaining to morning', 'existing, taking place, etc., during the morning', '(intended to be) worn or used during the morning', 'operating, acting, or on duty during the morning', as ***morning call***, ***morning flight***, ***morning gown***, ***morning light***, ***morning meal***, ***morning shower***, ***morning train***, etc. Special combs., as **morning coat** a coat having tails, and with the front edge sloping back from the waist down; **morning coffee**: taken at mid-morning or (occas.) at breakfast; **morning dress** a man's morning coat and striped trousers; **morning gift** *hist.* a gift from a husband to his wife on the morning following the consummation of their marriage; **morning glory** (***a***) any of various tropical American climbing plants belonging to the genus *Ipomoea* or related genera of the bindweed family, esp. *I. purpurea* and *I. violacea*, with large trumpet-shaped flowers which fade in the afternoon; (***b***) *US slang* a thing which fails to live up to its promise; ***morning gun***: see GUN *noun*; **morning line** a list of probable betting odds established by the bookmaker prior to a sporting event; **morning paper** a newspaper published for sale during the (early) morning; **morning prayer** (***a***) a prayer said in the morning; (***b***) the Anglican service of matins; the Roman Catholic service of lauds; **morning room** a room used as a sitting room during the morning or early part of the day; **morning sickness** nausea occurring in the morning, esp. early in pregnancy; **morning tea**: taken before rising or at mid-morning; **morningtide** (now

poet.) the morning, the early part of the day; **morning watch** †(*a*) the last of the three or four watches into which the night was divided by the Jews and Romans; (*b*) NAUTICAL (the person or people keeping) the watch between 4 and 8 a.m.
■ **morningless** *adjective* (*poet. rare*) E19.

mornings /ˈmɔːnɪŋz/ *adverb*. Now *colloq. & US*. E17.
[ORIGIN Pl. of MORNING: cf. EVENINGS (earlier uses of -s[3] being identified with -s[1]).]
In the morning, every morning.

morning star /ˈmɔːnɪŋ ˈstɑː/ *noun phr.* M16.
[ORIGIN from MORNING + STAR *noun*[1].]
1 A planet, esp. Venus, when visible in the east before sunrise. M16. ▸**b** *fig.* Jesus Christ. Also, a person regarded as a precursor. M16.
2 *hist.* = MORGENSTERN. L17.

Moro /ˈmɔːrəʊ/ *noun*. Pl. **-os**. L19.
[ORIGIN Spanish = MOOR *noun*[2].]
A Muslim of the Philippines.

Moroccan /məˈrɒk(ə)n/ *adjective & noun*. L17.
[ORIGIN from MOROCCO + -AN.]
▸ **A** *adjective*. Of or pertaining to Morocco, a country in NW Africa. L17.
▸ **B** *noun*. A native or inhabitant of Morocco. L18.

morocco /məˈrɒkəʊ/ *adjective & noun*. Also (the usual spelling in sense A.1) **M-**. E17.
[ORIGIN from *Morocco* (see below); cf. MAROQUIN.]
▸ **A** *attrib.* or as *adjective*. **1** Of, pertaining to, or originating in Morocco, a country in NW Africa; Moroccan. E17.
2 Made of or covered with morocco leather. M18.
▸ **B** *noun*. Pl. **-os**. Fine flexible leather made (orig. in Morocco) from goatskin tanned with sumac, used esp. in bookbinding and shoemaking; leather imitating this, made from sheepskin, lambskin, etc.; a variety or example of such leather. Also ***morocco leather***. M17.
French morocco: see FRENCH *adjective*. ***Levant morocco***: see LEVANT *adjective*[2] 1. ***Niger morocco***: see NIGER *noun*[2] 1. ***Persian morocco***: see PERSIAN *adjective*. ***red morocco***: see RED *adjective*.

morology /məˈrɒlədʒi/ *noun*. E17.
[ORIGIN Greek *mōrologia*, from *mōros* foolish: see -LOGY.]
†**1** Foolish talking. E–M17.
2 The study of fools and folly. *joc.* E20.
■ **moroˈlogical** *adjective* (*joc.*) E17. **morologist** *noun* (*rare*) E18.

moron /ˈmɔːrɒn/ *noun*. E20.
[ORIGIN Greek *mōron* neut. of *mōros* foolish.]
1 MEDICINE. An adult with mild learning difficulties. *arch.* Now regarded as *offensive*. E20.
2 A stupid or slow-witted person; a fool. *colloq.* E20.

> M. S. POWER It's nothing but a bloody waste of .. energy sending that damn moron to school.

■ **moˈronic** *adjective* E20. **moˈronically** *adverb* M20. **moronism** *noun* M20. **moˈronity** *noun* M20.

morose /məˈrəʊs/ *adjective*. M16.
[ORIGIN Late Latin *morosus*, from Latin *mor-*, *mos* manner: see MORAL *adjective*, -OSE[1].]
(Of a person, mood, etc.) sullen, bad-tempered; (of an outlook, philosophy, etc.) pessimistic, gloomy.

> J. A. ALEXANDER Pleasures which a more morose religion would proscribe as dangerous. CONAN DOYLE The moody, morose, brooding creature. A. HUTSCHNECKER The need then was to rouse him out of his morose mood.

■ **morosely** *adverb* M17. **moroseness** *noun* M17. **moˈrosity** *noun* M16.

morosoph /ˈmɔːrəsɒf/ *noun*. M17.
[ORIGIN French *morosophe* from Greek *mōrosophos*, from *mōros* foolish + *sophos* wise.]
Orig., a wise fool, a jester. Now, a foolish pedant or would-be philosopher.
■ Also **moˈrosophist** *noun* (*rare*) E17.

morph /mɔːf/ *noun*[1]. *US slang*. E20.
[ORIGIN Abbreviation.]
= MORPHINE.

morph /mɔːf/ *noun*[2]. M20.
[ORIGIN from MORPH(EME.]
LINGUISTICS. **1** = ALLOMORPH. M20.
2 A phoneme or series of phonemes forming a variant or a number of variants of a morpheme. M20.

morph /mɔːf/ *noun*[3]. M20.
[ORIGIN Greek *morphē* form.]
BIOLOGY. A variant form of an animal or plant produced by genetic differences.

morph /mɔːf/ *verb trans.* L20.
[ORIGIN Extracted from METAMORPHOSIS.]
Alter or animate (a computerized image) by transformation of a digital representation. Chiefly as ***morphing*** *verbal noun*.

-morph /mɔːf/ *suffix*.
[ORIGIN Repr. Greek *morphē* form.]
Forming nouns with the sense 'a thing having a particular form or character', as ***allelomorph***, ***endomorph***, ***isomorph***, ***polymorph***.

morphallaxis /mɔːfəˈlaksɪs/ *noun*. Orig. †**morpholaxis**. L19.
[ORIGIN from Greek *morphē* form + *allaxis* exchange.]
ZOOLOGY. Regeneration by the transformation of existing body tissues. Opp. EPIMORPHOSIS.
■ **morphallactic** *adjective* E20.

morpheme /ˈmɔːfiːm/ *noun*. L19.
[ORIGIN French *morphème* from Greek *morphē* form, after *phonème* PHONEME.]
LINGUISTICS. The smallest morphological unit of language, which cannot be analysed into smaller units. Also (now *rare*), a morphological element considered in its functional relations in a linguistic system.
– COMB.: **morpheme alternant** = ALLOMORPH.

morphemic /mɔːˈfiːmɪk/ *adjective*. M20.
[ORIGIN from MORPHEME + -IC.]
LINGUISTICS. Of or pertaining to morphemes; of the nature of a morpheme.
■ **morphemically** *adverb* M20.

morphemics /mɔːˈfiːmɪks/ *noun*. M20.
[ORIGIN from MORPHEME + -ICS.]
The branch of linguistics that deals with morphemes and word structure.

Morpheus /ˈmɔːfɪəs/ *noun*. LME.
[ORIGIN Latin, name of the god of dreams. See also MURPHY *noun*[1].]
(The god of) dreaming or (*popularly*) sleep.
in the arms of Morpheus asleep.
■ **Morphean** *adjective* (*a*) of or pertaining to Morpheus; (*b*) sleepy, drowsy: M17.

morphew /ˈmɔːfjuː/ *noun*. Now *rare* or *obsolete*. Pl. same. LME.
[ORIGIN medieval Latin *morphea* (mod. Latin *morphoea*) from Italian *morfea*, of unknown origin.]
A blemish or scurf mark on the skin.

morphia /ˈmɔːfɪə/ *noun*. E19.
[ORIGIN formed as MORPHINE + -IA[1].]
= MORPHINE.

morphic /ˈmɔːfɪk/ *adjective*. M19.
[ORIGIN from Greek *morphē* form + -IC.]
BIOLOGY. **1** Of or pertaining to form or anatomical shape; morphological. M19.
morphic resonance the (supposed) cooperative influence of similar entities (living or inanimate) in facilitating the genesis of a new entity of the same kind.
2 Of or pertaining to animal or plant morphs. M20.
■ **morphically** *adverb* in relation to or as regards shape or form; morphologically: L19.

morphine /ˈmɔːfiːn/ *noun*. E19.
[ORIGIN from MORPHEUS + -INE[5].]
CHEMISTRY. An alkaloid narcotic extracted from opium, used in medicine chiefly as a painkiller, and addictive on continued use.
■ **morphinated** /-fɪn-/ *adjective* containing morphine L19. **morphined** *adjective* (*rare*) drugged (as) with morphine L19. **morphinism** /-fɪn-/ *noun* addiction to or dependence on morphine or opium L19. **morphinist** /-fɪn-/ *noun* (now *rare*) a person addicted to morphine L19. **morphinoˈmania** *noun* = MORPHIOMANIA L19. **morphinoˈmaniac** *noun* = MORPHIOMANIAC L19.

morphiomania /mɔːfɪəˈmeɪnɪə/ *noun*. L19.
[ORIGIN from MORPHIA + -O- + -MANIA.]
Craving for morphine, morphine addiction.
■ **morphiomaniac** *noun* a person who craves morphine, a morphine addict L19.

morphism /ˈmɔːfɪz(ə)m/ *noun*. M20.
[ORIGIN from MORPH *noun*[3] + -ISM.]
BIOLOGY. The existence of morphs or variant forms of an animal or plant species.

-morphism /ˈmɔːfɪz(ə)m/ *suffix*.
[ORIGIN formed as MORPH *noun*[3] + -ISM.]
Forming nouns with the senses (*a*) the condition or property of having a particular form or character; (*b*) MATH. 'a transformation or correspondence of a certain kind', as ***heteromorphism***, ***isomorphism***.

morpho /ˈmɔːfəʊ/ *noun*. Pl. **-os**. M19.
[ORIGIN mod. Latin (see below) from Greek *Morphō* an epithet of Aphrodite.]
Any of several large Central and S. American nymphalid butterflies of the genus *Morpho*, esp. one with iridescent blue wings. Also ***morpho butterfly***.

morpho- /ˈmɔːfəʊ/ *combining form*.
[ORIGIN from Greek *morphē* form or from MORPH(EME: see -O-.]
Forming nouns and adjectives with the senses 'of or pertaining to form', 'having a particular form or character', LINGUISTICS 'of or pertaining to morphemes'.
■ **morphograˈphemic** *adjective* (LINGUISTICS) of or pertaining to the written form of words M20. **morphoˈlexical** *adjective* (LINGUISTICS) of or pertaining to lexical form M20. **morphophone** *noun* (LINGUISTICS) a unit representing the phonemes occurring in dialectally different pronunciations of morphemes M20. **morphoˈphonic** *adjective* of or pertaining to morphophones M20. **morphoˈphonics** *noun* = MORPHOPHONOLOGY M20. **morphosynˈtactic** *adjective* (LINGUISTICS) of or pertaining to morphosyntax M20. **morphosynˈtactically** *adverb* (LINGUISTICS) with regard to morphosyntax M20. **morphoˈsyntax** *noun* (LINGUISTICS) a branch of linguistics combining morphology and syntax and their interaction M20. **morphoˈtactic** *adjective* (LINGUISTICS) of or pertaining to morphotactics M20. **morphoˈtactically** *adverb* (LINGUISTICS) with regard to morphotactics M20. **morphoˈtactics** *noun* the branch of linguistics that deals with the sequence of morphemes in a language (cf. LEXOTACTICS, PHONOTACTICS) M20.

morphodite /ˈmɔːfədʌɪt/ *noun*. Now *US dial.* E18.
[ORIGIN Abbreviation & alt.]
Orig., a hermaphrodite. Later, a homosexual or transvestite.

morphoea /mɔːˈfiːə/ *noun*. LME.
[ORIGIN mod. Latin: see MORPHEW.]
Orig. = MORPHEW. Now, localized scleroderma in which the skin is replaced by connective tissue.

morphogen /ˈmɔːfədʒ(ə)n/ *noun*. M20.
[ORIGIN from MORPHO- + -GEN.]
BIOLOGY. A chemical agent able to cause or determine morphogenesis.

morphogenesis /mɔːfə(ʊ)ˈdʒɛnɪsɪs/ *noun*. L19.
[ORIGIN from MORPHO- + -GENESIS.]
1 BIOLOGY. The origination and development of morphological characters; morphogeny. L19.
2 PHYSICAL GEOGRAPHY. The formation of landscapes or landforms. M20.
■ **morphogeˈnetic** *adjective* L19. **morphogeˈnetical** *adjective* L20. **morphogeˈnetically** *adverb* as regards morphogenesis E20.

morphogenic /mɔːfə(ʊ)ˈdʒɛnɪk/ *adjective*. L19.
[ORIGIN from MORPHOGENESIS: see -GENIC.]
BIOLOGY. Of the nature of a morphogen; morphogenetic.

morphogeny /mɔːˈfɒdʒəni/ *noun*. L19.
[ORIGIN from MORPHO- + -GENY.]
1 BIOLOGY. = MORPHOGENESIS 1. L19.
2 PHYSICAL GEOGRAPHY. = MORPHOGENESIS 2. E20.

morphographer /mɔːˈfɒgrəfə/ *noun*. *rare*. L17.
[ORIGIN from MORPHO- + -GRAPHER.]
†**1** A person skilled in the delineation of form. Only in L17.
2 BIOLOGY. A morphologist. L19.

morphography /mɔːˈfɒgrəfi/ *noun*. M19.
[ORIGIN from MORPHO- + -GRAPHY.]
(The scientific description of) external form.
■ **morphoˈgraphical** *adjective* L19.

†**morpholaxis** *noun* see MORPHALLAXIS.

morpholine /ˈmɔːfəliːn/ *noun*. L19.
[ORIGIN from MORPHINE with insertion of -OL.]
CHEMISTRY. A cyclic amine, C_4H_9NO, which is a hygroscopic oil used as a solvent for resins and dyes and whose fatty-acid salts are emulsifying soaps used in floor polishes.

morphology /mɔːˈfɒlədʒi/ *noun*. E19.
[ORIGIN from MORPHO- + -LOGY.]
1 BIOLOGY. The branch of biology that deals with the form of living organisms, and with relationships between their structures. E19.
2 LINGUISTICS. The form (including change, formation, and inflection) of words in a language; the branch of linguistics that deals with this. M19.
3 *gen.* Shape, form, external structure or arrangement, esp. as an object of study or classification. Also, a particular form or structure. M19.
social morphology: see SOCIAL *adjective*.
■ **morphoˈlogic** *adjective* = MORPHOLOGICAL L19. **morphoˈlogical** *adjective* of, pertaining to, or derived from morphology M19. **morphoˈlogically** *adverb* M19. **morphologist** *noun* M19. **morphologiˈzation** *noun* (LINGUISTICS) (*a*) conversion of a phonetic or phonemic feature to a morphological one; (*b*) morphological reinterpretation of a phonological rule or process: L20. **morphologize** *verb trans.* (LINGUISTICS) subject (a feature, rule, or process) to morphologization (usu. in *pass.*) L20.

morphomaniac /mɔːfə(ʊ)ˈmeɪnɪak/ *noun*. L19.
[ORIGIN from MORPH(INE + -O- + -MANIAC.]
= MORPHIOMANIAC.

morphometry /mɔːˈfɒmɪtri/ *noun*. M19.
[ORIGIN from MORPHO- + -METRY.]
The process of measuring the external shape and dimensions of landforms, living organisms, or other objects.
■ **morphoˈmetric** *adjective* of or pertaining to morphometry or morphometrics M20. **morphoˈmetrical** *adjective* = MORPHOMETRIC M19. **morphoˈmetrically** *adverb* M20. **morphoˈmetrics** *noun pl.* (*a*) (treated as *sing.*) morphometry (esp. of living organisms); (*b*) morphometric features or properties: M20.

morphon /ˈmɔːfɒn/ *noun*. L19.
[ORIGIN German, from Greek *morphē* form + *on* being. Cf. -ON.]
1 BIOLOGY. A biological individual distinguished by morphological features. Now *rare* or *obsolete*. L19.
2 LINGUISTICS. In stratificational grammar, = MORPHOPHONEME. M20.
■ **morˈphonic** *adjective* M20.

morphoneme /ˈmɔːfəʊniːm/ *noun*. M20.
[ORIGIN Contr. formed as MORPHOPHONEME.]
LINGUISTICS. = MORPHOPHONEME.
■ **morphoˈnemic** *adjective* M20.

morphonology /mɔːfəˈnɒlədʒi/ *noun*. M20.
[ORIGIN Contr. formed as MORPHOPHONOLOGY.]
LINGUISTICS. = MORPHOPHONOLOGY.
■ **morphonoˈlogic**, **morphonoˈlogical** *adjectives* M20.

M

morphophoneme /mɔːfə(ʊ)ˈfəʊniːm/ *noun.* M20.
[ORIGIN from MORPHO- + PHONEME. Cf. MORPHONEME.]
LINGUISTICS. Any of the variant phonemes representing the same morpheme.
■ **morphophoˈnemic** *adjective* of or pertaining to morphophonemes M20. **morphophoˈnemically** *adverb* as a morphophoneme; with regard to morphophonemics: M20. **morphophoˈnemics** *noun* = MORPHOPHONOLOGY M20.

morphophonology /ˌmɔːfəʊfəˈnɒlədʒi/ *noun.* M20.
[ORIGIN from MORPHO- + PHONOLOGY.]
LINGUISTICS. The branch of linguistics that deals with the phonological representation of morphemes.
■ **morphophonoˈlogical** *adjective* M20.

morphopoiesis /ˌmɔːfəʊpɔɪˈiːsɪs/ *noun.* M20.
[ORIGIN from MORPHO- + POIESIS.]
BIOLOGY. The formation of an organic structure from a limited number of subunits.
■ **morphopoietic** /-pɔɪˈɛtɪk/ *adjective* assisting morphopoiesis; shape-determining: M20.

morphosis /mɔːˈfəʊsɪs/ *noun.* Pl. **-phoses** /-ˈfəʊsiːz/. L17.
[ORIGIN Greek *morphōsis* a shaping, from *morphoun* to shape, from *morphē* form: see -OSIS.]
†**1** Form, figure, configuration. Only in L17.
2 *BOTANY.* The manner of development of an organism, esp. as marked by structural change. M19.

morphotectonic /ˌmɔːfəʊtɛkˈtɒnɪk/ *adjective.* M20.
[ORIGIN formed as MORPHOTECTONICS: see -IC.]
GEOLOGY. Of or pertaining to morphotectonics.

morphotectonics /ˌmɔːfəʊtɛkˈtɒnɪks/ *noun.* M20.
[ORIGIN from MORPHO(LOGY + TECTONICS.]
GEOLOGY. The branch of geomorphology that deals with the tectonic origins of large topographic features of the earth's surface (as continents, mountain ranges, river basins). Also, the morphotectonic character or features of a region.

morphotropism /mɔːfə(ʊ)ˈtrəʊpɪz(ə)m/ *noun.* L19.
[ORIGIN formed as MORPHOTROPY: see -ISM.]
CRYSTALLOGRAPHY. = MORPHOTROPY.

morphotropy /mɔːˈfɒtrəpi/ *noun.* E20.
[ORIGIN from MORPHO- + -TROPY.]
CRYSTALLOGRAPHY. The changes in crystal structure brought about by replacing one kind of atom or radical in a crystal by others; the branch of science that deals with these.
■ **morphotropic** /-ˈtrəʊpɪk, -ˈtrɒpɪk/ *adjective* of, pertaining to, or exhibiting morphotropy L19.

morpion /ˈmɔːpɪən/ *noun. rare.* E17.
[ORIGIN French.]
A crab louse.

morra *noun* var. of MORA *noun*[2].

†**morrice** *adjective, noun, & verb* var. of MORRIS *noun*[2] *& verb.*

morrillo /moˈriʎo, məˈriːljəʊ/ *noun.* Also **mori-**. Pl. **-os** /-ɔs, -əʊz/. M20.
[ORIGIN Spanish = fleshy part of an animal's neck.]
BULLFIGHTING. The muscle at the back of a bull's neck, one of the targets for a bullfighter's lance.

morris /ˈmɒrɪs/ *noun*[1]. E17.
[ORIGIN Alt. of *merels*: see MEREL.]
More fully ***nine men's morris***. The game merels.

morris /ˈmɒrɪs/ *noun*[2] *& verb.* Also †**morrice**. E16.
[ORIGIN Var. of MOORISH *adjective.* Cf. Flemish *mooriske dans*, Dutch *moors dans*.]
▸ **A** *noun.* **1** A traditional English dance by groups of people in fancy costume (usu. representing legendary or symbolic figures) with ribbons and bells or sticks. Also ***morris dance***. E16.
2 A body of morris dancers. E16.
– COMB.: **morris bell** any of the (many) small metal bells attached to the clothing of a morris dancer. **morris dancer** a person who participates in morris dancing. **morris dancing** the action or practice of performing morris dances. **morris-pike** *hist.* a type of pike supposed to be of Moorish origin.
▸ **B** *verb intrans.* **1** Dance; *slang* be hanged. Now *rare.* E18.
2 Move away rapidly; decamp. Also foll. by *off*. *slang.* Now *rare.* M18.

Morris /ˈmɒrɪs/ *adjective.* L19.
[ORIGIN See below.]
Designating a style of simple utilitarian furniture, or richly decorated fabric, wallpaper, etc., characterized by intricate patterns of birds, flowers, and leaves, designed or made by the English poet and craftsman William Morris (1834–96).
Morris chair a type of easy chair with open padded arms and an adjustable back.
■ **Moˈrrisian** *adjective* of, pertaining to, or characteristic of William Morris or his work L19. **Morrisite** *noun* an adherent or student of the principles and practice of William Morris M20.

Morrison shelter /ˈmɒrɪs(ə)n ˌʃɛltə/ *noun phr.* M20.
[ORIGIN Herbert S. *Morrison*, UK Secretary of State for Home Affairs and Home Security (1940–5) when the shelter was adopted.]
hist. A transportable indoor steel table-shaped air-raid shelter.

Morris tube /ˈmɒrɪs tjuːb/ *noun phr.* L19.
[ORIGIN from Richard *Morris* (d. 1891), English inventor.]
A small-bore rifle barrel that can be inserted in a large-bore rifle or shotgun for shooting practice.

morrow /ˈmɒrəʊ/ *noun.* Now *dial. & literary.* LOE.
[ORIGIN Var. of MORN (Old English *morgen*) with *-w-* as reflex of Old English *-g-*.]
1 Morning. Also *ellipt.* as *interjection*, good morrow, good morning. *obsolete* exc. *dial.* LOE.
> R. S. THOMAS Twm went to bed and woke on the grey morrow.

2 (Usu. with *the*.) The following day; ***the morrow*** (adverbial), on the following day. ME.
> B. T. WASHINGTON On the morrow I can begin a *new* day of work.

3 *fig.* The time immediately following a particular event. (Foll. by *of*.) L16.
> A. BULLOCK There was resentment, on the morrow of victory.

– COMB.: **morrow-mass** (*obsolete* exc. *hist.*) the first mass of the day; **morrow-speech** (*obsolete* exc. *hist.*) a periodical assembly of a guild held on the day following a feast.
■ **morrowless** *adjective* (*rare*) not subject to time; without end: L19.

morse /mɔːs/ *noun*[1]. LME.
[ORIGIN Old French & mod. French *mors* from Latin *morsus* bite, catch, from *mors-* pa. ppl stem of *mordere* bite.]
The clasp or fastening of a cope, freq. made of gold or silver and set with precious stones.

morse /mɔːs/ *noun*[2]. Now *rare* or *obsolete.* L15.
[ORIGIN Ult. from Lappish *moršša*, whence Finnish *mursu*, Russian *morzh*.]
A walrus.

Morse /mɔːs/ *noun*[3] *& verb*[1]. M19.
[ORIGIN Samuel F. B. *Morse* (1791–1872), US electrician and inventor of the recording telegraph.]
TELEGRAPHY. ▸ **A** *noun.* **1** Used *attrib.* to designate (things pertaining to) the recording telegraph. M19.
2 In full ***Morse code***. An alphabet or code, devised by Morse for use with the recording telegraph, in which the letters are represented by combinations of long and short light or sound signals. M19.
▸ **B** *verb intrans. & trans.* Signal using Morse code. E20.

morse /mɔːs/ *verb*[2] *trans. Scot. obsolete* exc. *hist.* M16.
[ORIGIN Aphet. from French *amorcer* prime (a gun), prepare for (an operation).]
†**1** Grease (a firearm). Only in M16.
2 Prime (a gun). Chiefly as ***morsing*** *verbal noun.* M16.

morsel /ˈmɔːs(ə)l/ *noun & verb.* ME.
[ORIGIN Old French (mod. MORCEAU), dim. of *mors*: see MORSE *noun*[1], -EL[2].]
▸ **A** *noun.* **1** A small piece, *esp.* one cut or broken from a mass; a fragment. ME.
> S. O'FAOLÁIN Sean.. dropped the.. record bit by bit into the fire, frowning as each morsel melted.

2 A bite; a mouthful; a small piece of food. Now passing into sense 1. ME.
> K. A. PORTER Frau Baumgartner took a morsel of food.

3 A choice dish, a dainty. LME.
> W. C. WILLIAMS Oranges, chocolate, and those precious morsels which his mother could not afford.

4 A small meal; a snack. LME.
5 *fig.* A small person. *joc.* E17.
▸ **B** *verb trans.* Infl. **-ll-**, ***-l-**.
1 Divide into small pieces. L16.
2 Distribute (property etc.) in small quantities. Foll. by *out*. M19.
■ **morseliˈzation** *noun* (*rare*) the action or an act of morselizing something L19. **morselize** *verb trans.* (*rare*) break up into small pieces L19.

Morse taper /mɔːs ˈteɪpə/ *noun phr.* Also **m-**. L19.
[ORIGIN Prob. from *Morse* Twist Drill Co. of Massachusetts, USA.]
A taper on a shank or socket that is one of a standard series having specified dimensions and angles.
– NOTE: *Morse* is a proprietary name in the US.

morsure /ˈmɔːʒə/ *noun.* Now *rare.* LME.
[ORIGIN Old French & mod. French from late Latin *morsura*, from *mors-*: see MORSE *noun*[1], -URE.]
The action or an act of biting; a bite.

mort /mɔːt/ *noun*[1]. ME.
[ORIGIN Old French & mod. French from Latin *mort-*, *mors* death. In sense 4 prob. formed as MORT *adjective*.]
†**1** Death, slaughter. ME–L16.
2 *HUNTING.* The note sounded on a horn at the death of the deer. Chiefly in ***blow a mort***. L15.
†**3** A dead body, a corpse. L15–L19.
4 The skin of a sheep or lamb that has died a natural death. Also ***mort skin***. *dial.* L16.
– COMB.: **mortcloth** (*arch.*, chiefly *Scot.*) (a fee paid for the use of) a funeral pall; ***mort-skin***: see sense 4 above.

mort /mɔːt/ *noun*[2]. L15.
[ORIGIN Unknown.]
A salmon in its third year.

mort /mɔːt/ *noun*[3]. *dial.* L17.
[ORIGIN Perh. from Old Norse *mergð* multitude, from *margr* many, infl. by *mortal* in sense 'excessive(ly)'.]
A large quantity or number, a great deal. Usu. foll. by *of*.

†**mort** *noun*[4] see MOT *noun*[1].

mort /mɔːt/ *adjective.* Long *obsolete* exc. *dial.* LME.
[ORIGIN Old French & mod. French from Latin *mortuus* pa. pple of *mori* die.]
Dead.

mortadella /mɔːtəˈdɛlə/ *noun.* Pl. **-llas**, **-lle** /-li/. E17.
[ORIGIN Italian, irreg. from Latin *murtatum* (sausage) seasoned with myrtle berries.]
A large spiced pork sausage; Bologna sausage.

mortal /ˈmɔːt(ə)l/ *adjective, adverb, & noun.* LME.
[ORIGIN Old French, Latinized var. of Old French & mod. French *mortel*, or directly from Latin *mortalis*, from *mort-*, *mors* death: see -AL[1].]
▸ **A** *adjective.* **1** Subject to death, destined to die. LME. ▸†**b** Doomed to immediate death. E16–E17.
> A. MASON They were banished from the garden and.. became mortal: prey to sickness, destined to old age and death.

2 *transf.* Of or pertaining to humanity as subject to death; of or pertaining to material, temporal or earthly existence; associated with death. LME.
> T. KEIGHTLEY The axe descending, terminated his mortal existence.

mortal mind *CHRISTIAN SCIENCE* the source in humans of all delusion and error, creating the illusion of bodily sensations, pain, and illness. ***this mortal coil***: see COIL *noun*[1].
3 a Causing death; fatal; *hyperbol.* very hurtful or damaging. (Foll. by *to*.) LME. ▸**b** Of pain, grief, fear, etc.: intense; very serious. LME. ▸**c** Pertaining to or accompanying death. LME. ▸**d** Of a period of time or a region: characterized by many deaths. Now *rare* or *obsolete.* M17. ▸**e** Destructive (*to* a thing). L17.
> **a** L. STRACHEY The Duchess of York had been attacked by a mortal disease. A. G. GARDINER I have.. seen a batsman receive a mortal blow from a ball. **b** A. HUTSCHNECKER An hour of mortal dread when.. I was facing a firing squad.

4 *CHRISTIAN THEOLOGY.* Of sin: entailing damnation; depriving the soul of divine grace; = DEADLY *adjective* 4. Opp. ***venial***. LME.
> MERLE COLLINS Missing church on Sundays was a mortal sin.

5 a Of war, a battle, etc.: fought to the death. LME. ▸**b** Of an enemy: relentless, implacable. LME. ▸**c** (Of enmity, hatred, etc.) pursued to the death; unappeasable; having the character of such enmity. L15.
> **b** LD MACAULAY Halifax.. was the constant and mortal enemy of French ascendancy. **c** ADDISON A Tribe of Egoists for whom I have always had a mortal Aversion.

6 Conceivable, imaginable, (after *any*, *every*, *no*, etc.). Cf. EARTHLY *adjective* 4. *colloq.* E17.
> J. GARDAM He knew every mortal thing you did.

7 Extremely great, excessive. *colloq.* E18.
> DICKENS I was a mortal sight younger then.

8 [Ellipt. for ***mortal drunk*** below.] Very drunk. *colloq.* Chiefly *Scot. & N. English.* L18.
9 Long; tedious. *colloq.* E19.
> LYTTON And so on for 940 mortal pages.

▸ **B** *adverb.* Mortally; extremely, excessively. *arch.* Now *dial. & slang.* LME.
mortal drunk very drunk.
▸ **C** *noun.* **1** A being subject to death; a human being, as contrasted with an immortal. L15.
> D. ROWE We are all fallible mortals. We all die.

2 A person, *esp.* one of ordinary strength, skill, etc. E18.
> *Cosmopolitan* Us mere mortals who can't afford a personal trainer or team of beauticians.

no mortal nobody.
■ **mortalism** *noun* (*CHRISTIAN THEOLOGY*) belief in the mortality of the soul M17. **mortalist** *noun* (*CHRISTIAN THEOLOGY*) an adherent of mortalism M17. **mortalize** *verb* †(**a**) *verb intrans.* become mortal; (**b**) *verb trans.* make mortal; consider or represent as mortal: E17.

mortality /mɔːˈtalɪti/ *noun.* ME.
[ORIGIN Old French & mod. French *mortalité* from Latin *mortalitas*, from *mortalis*: see MORTAL, -ITY.]
1 The condition of being mortal or subject to death; mortal nature or existence. ME.
> T. CAPOTE A man insuring his life is not unlike.. a man signing his will; thoughts of mortality.. occur. F. WELDON She did not want to think of herself diluting down through the generations. She craved mortality.

2 Loss of life on a large scale; abnormal frequency of death, as by war or pestilence. LME. ▸†**b** An individual's death or decease. L16–M18. ▸**c** The number of deaths in a given area or period, esp. from a particular cause; the average frequency of death, the death rate, (also ***mortality rate***). M17.
> **c** S. KITZINGER The mortality for breast cancer has not been reduced in the last 40 years.

c bill of mortality: see BILL *noun*[3].
3 Deadliness, power to kill. Now *rare* or *obsolete*. LME.
4 *CHRISTIAN THEOLOGY*. The quality or fact of incurring damnation. M16.

mortally /ˈmɔːt(ə)li/ *adverb*. LME.
[ORIGIN from MORTAL *adjective* + -LY[2].]
1 In such a manner or to such a degree that death or (*CHRISTIAN THEOLOGY*) damnation ensues; so as to cause death or damnation. LME.

R. DAHL Mortally wounded on the deck of his ship. O. SACKS In the last months of his life, when mortally ill.

2 Intensely, bitterly, grievously; *colloq.* extremely, exceedingly, very. LME.

R. L. STEVENSON Looking mortally sheepish. ALDOUS HUXLEY The . . young lady . . would be mortally offended.

3 = HUMANLY 2. *rare*. E17.

J. WAINWRIGHT Faster than seemed mortally possible.

mortar /ˈmɔːtə/ *noun*[1] & *verb*[1]. OE.
[ORIGIN Partly from Anglo-Norman *morter*, Old French & mod. French *mortier* from Latin MORTARIUM (to which the English spelling was finally assim.), partly from Low German. Cf. MORTAR *noun*[2] & *verb*[2].]
▸ **A** *noun*. 1 A vessel of marble, brass, or other hard material, with a cup-shaped cavity in which ingredients for pharmacy, cookery, etc., are pounded with a pestle (cf. PESTLE *noun* 2 for its symbolic use). OE. ▸**b** Any of various mechanical pounding or grinding devices. M18.

E. RUTHERFORD Finely powdered in an agate mortar. P. MATTHIESSEN Women . . pound grain in stone mortars.

†2 A weight or yoke, esp. of wood, worn about the neck as an instrument of punishment. LME–L18.
3 A bowl of wax or oil with a floating wick, used esp. as a night light. Later also, a kind of thick candle. *obsolete* exc. *hist.* LME.
4 A short piece of artillery with a large bore and trunnions on the breech, for firing missiles at high angles. Formerly also †*mortar piece*. M16. ▸**b** *transf.* Any of various devices for firing a lifeline, a firework, etc. M17.

E. BLUNDEN A long-range trench mortar. B. ENGLAND A . . red star shell exploded in the sky. A mortar had been fired.

– COMB.: **mortar-bed** (*a*) the part of a gun carriage on which the gun rests; (*b*) the bed on which the ore is crushed in a stamp mill; *mortar piece*: see sense 3 above.
▸ **B** *verb trans.* Direct mortar fire on to; bombard with mortar bombs. M20.

A. JUDD You have been mortared . . . Your platoon is decimated.

mortar /ˈmɔːtə/ *noun*[2] & *verb*[2]. ME.
[ORIGIN Anglo-Norman *morter* = Old French & mod. French *mortier* (see MORTAR *noun*[1] & *verb*[1]) with transference of meaning from the vessel to the substance produced in it, as already in Latin.]
▸ **A** *noun*. 1 A mixture of lime or cement and sand mixed with water, used in building to bond stone and brick. Also, any of various other materials with the same use. ME.
bricks and mortar: see BRICK *noun*.
2 Plaster etc. used to face brick, stone, wood, etc. LME.
▸ **B** *verb trans.* Fix, join, or plaster with mortar. M16.
■ **mortarless** *adjective* M17. **mortary** *adjective* of the nature of mortar, consisting of mortar E19.

mortarboard /ˈmɔːtəbɔːd/ *noun*. M18.
[ORIGIN from MORTAR *noun*[2] + BOARD *noun*.]
1 A small square board with a handle on the underside, for holding mortar in bricklaying. M18.
2 An academic cap of black cloth with a stiff flat square top. M19.

mortarium /mɔːˈtɛːrɪəm/ *noun*. Pl. **-ia** /-ɪə/. M19.
[ORIGIN Latin: cf. MORTAR *noun*[1].]
ROMAN ANTIQUITIES. A Roman vessel for pounding or grinding.

mort d'ancestor /mɔː ˈdansɪstə/ *noun phr.* ME.
[ORIGIN Anglo-Norman *mordancestre*, *mort d'auncestre* lit. 'ancestor's death'.]
LAW (now *hist.*). An assize brought by the rightful heir against a person who usurped an inheritance.

mortgage /ˈmɔːɡɪdʒ/ *noun* & *verb*. LME.
[ORIGIN Old French, lit. 'dead pledge', from *mort* dead + *gage* GAGE *noun*[1].]
▸ **A** *noun*. 1 A legal agreement by which a bank, building society, etc. lends money at interest in exchange for taking title of the debtor's property, with the condition that the conveyance of title becomes void upon the payment of the debt; a deed effecting this; a debt secured by this; a loan resulting from this. LME.

V. S. PRITCHETT Chekhov borrowed four thousand roubles . . and got a ten-year mortgage. *What Mortgage* A mortgage is a means to . . get and keep a roof over your head.

†**in mortgage** mortgaged. *puisne mortgage*: see PUISNE *adjective* 3. *second mortgage*: see SECOND *adjective*.
2 *fig.* A pledge, a bond. LME.
– COMB.: **mortgage rate** the rate of interest charged on a loan secured by mortgage; freq., a common rate of interest on such loans agreed among building societies etc.
▸ **B** *verb trans.* 1 Make over (property, esp. a house or land) by or through a mortgage. LME.

R. K. NARAYAN He would get his house back from the man to whom he had mortgaged it. J. WILCOX If your house is mortgaged, the bank should have those records.

2 *fig.* Pledge (*to*); make liable; establish a claim to (an income etc.) in advance. Usu. in *pass.* L16.

Economist The hoary argument that Canada is being mortgaged to Wall Street bankers.

■ **mortgageable** *adjective* L17. **mortgaˈgee** *noun* the creditor in a mortgage, now usu. a bank or building society L16. **mortgager** *noun* = MORTGAGOR M17. **mortgagor** /mɔːɡɪˈdʒɔː/ *noun* a person who mortgages property; the debtor in a mortgage: M16.

mortice *noun* & *verb* var. of MORTISE.

mortician /mɔːˈtɪʃ(ə)n/ *noun*. *N. Amer.* L19.
[ORIGIN from Latin *mort-*, *mors* death (cf. MORT *noun*[1]) + -ICIAN.]
An undertaker; a person who arranges funerals.

mortier /mɔrtje/ *noun*. Pl. pronounced same. E18.
[ORIGIN French Cf. MORTAR *noun*[2].]
hist. A cap formerly worn by high officials of France.

mortiferous /mɔːˈtɪf(ə)rəs/ *adjective*. Now *rare*. M16.
[ORIGIN from Latin *mortifer* (from *mort-*, *mors* death) + -OUS.]
Bringing or causing (physical or spiritual) death.

mortific /mɔːˈtɪfɪk/ *adjective*. *rare*. M17.
[ORIGIN ecclesiastical Latin *mortificus*, from Latin *mort-*, *mors* death: see -FIC.]
Deadly.

mortification /ˌmɔːtɪfɪˈkeɪʃ(ə)n/ *noun*. LME.
[ORIGIN Old French & mod. French from ecclesiastical Latin *mortificatio(n-)*, from *mortificat-* pa. ppl stem of *mortificare*: see MORTIFIED, -ATION.]
1 The action or practice of mortifying the flesh or its appetites. LME.

L. CODY There's no virtue in any mortification, either of the flesh or the spirit.

2 *SCOTS LAW*. The action or an act of disposing of property for religious or other charitable purposes; property given for such purposes. Cf. MORTMAIN. LME.
3 Gangrene, necrosis. LME.

J. G. FARRELL The dark hue of mortification had already spread over half the palm.

†4 Deadening or destruction of vitality or activity; devitalization. LME–L18.
†5 Chemical alteration of the external form of a substance; destruction or neutralization of the activity of a chemical substance. E17–E18.
6 (A cause of) deep humiliation; severe disappointment, great vexation. M17.

N. MONSARRAT His mortification and grief at failing in his resolve knew no bounds. N. ANNAN He had the mortification of being ordered to retire from the bench.

mortified /ˈmɔːtɪfʌɪd/ *adjective*. LME.
[ORIGIN from MORTIFY + -ED[1].]
1 Subdued by self-denial, abstinence, or bodily discipline, ascetic. Now *rare*. LME.
2 Gangrenous, necrotic. LME.

O. SACKS There was a horrible smell of mortified tissue and preservative in the air.

3 Deeply humiliated, very embarrassed or ashamed. E18.

H. N. SCHWARZKOPF I'd have been mortified if my friends had found out I was learning ballroom dancing.

■ **mortifiedly** *adverb* L16. **mortifiedness** *noun* M17.

mortify /ˈmɔːtɪfʌɪ/ *verb*. LME.
[ORIGIN Old French & mod. French *mortifier* from ecclesiastical Latin *mortificare* kill, subdue (the flesh), from Latin *mort-*, *mors* death: see -FY.]
†1 *verb trans.* Deprive of life; kill. Also, make insensible. LME–L17.
†2 *verb trans.* Destroy the vitality, vigour, or activity of; neutralize the effect or value of; deaden (pain); dull (colour). LME–E18.
†3 *verb trans.* Chemically alter the external form of; deprive (a chemical substance) of activity. LME–E18.
4 *verb trans.* Subdue, subjugate, (the body, an appetite, a passion) by self-denial, abstinence, or bodily discipline. LME. ▸†**b** *verb intrans.* Practise self-mortification; be an ascetic. M16–M19.

G. SANTAYANA The suffering may be a means of mortifying and outgrowing your sins.

5 *verb trans.* *SCOTS LAW*. Dispose of (property) for religious or other charitable purposes. L15.
†6 *verb trans.* & *intrans.* *COOKERY*. Make or become tender by hanging, keeping, etc. L16–L18.
7 *verb intrans.* Become gangrenous or necrotic. L16.

E. BOWEN A scratch . . in Henry's arm had mortified.

8 *verb trans.* Cause to feel deeply humiliated; wound the feelings of. L17.

P. ROSE It mortified Effie that her husband left her constantly alone.

■ **mortifier** *noun* E17. **mortifying** *adjective* that mortifies someone or something; deeply humiliating: LME. **mortifyingly** *adverb* M18.

mortise /ˈmɔːtɪs/ *noun* & *verb*. Also **-ice**. LME.
[ORIGIN Old French *mortoise* (mod. *mortaise*) = Spanish *mortaja*, perh. from Arabic *murtaj* locked, place of locking.]
▸ **A** *noun*. A cavity or recess in a framework into which the end of some other part is fitted to form a joint; *spec.* in *CARPENTRY*, a (usu. rectangular) recess cut in the surface of a piece of timber etc. to receive a tenon. Also, a groove or slot in or through which to put a rope, an adjustable pin, etc. LME.
mortise and tenon, **tenon and mortise** a joint composed of a mortise and a tenon; the method of joining pieces of wood etc. with a mortise and a tenon.
– COMB.: **mortise lock** a lock recessed into a mortise in the frame of a door, a window, etc.
▸ **B** *verb trans.* 1 Fasten, fix, or join securely; *spec.* in *CARPENTRY*, join with a mortise and tenon; fasten *into* or *to* by means of mortise and tenon. LME.
2 Cut a mortise in; cut *through* with a mortise. E17.
■ **mortiser** *noun* a machine for cutting mortises M19.

Mortlake /ˈmɔːtleɪk/ *noun*. In sense 2 **m-**. L17.
[ORIGIN A town in Surrey, England.]
1 Used *attrib.* to designate a kind of tapestry woven at Mortlake in the first half of the 17th cent. L17.
2 *PHYSICAL GEOGRAPHY*. An oxbow lake. Now *rare*. E20.

mortmain /ˈmɔːtmeɪn/ *noun*. LME.
[ORIGIN Anglo-Norman & Old French *mortemain* from medieval Latin *mortua manus* dead hand, from fem. of Latin *mortuus* dead + *manus* hand, prob. with allus. to impers. ownership.]
LAW (now *hist.*).
1 The condition of lands or tenements held inalienably by an ecclesiastical or other corporation; lands or tenements so held. LME.

fig.: G. GREENE Catholics are always said to be freed in the confessional from the mortmain of the past.

†2 A licence of mortmain, conveying the monarch's permission to vest property in a corporation. M16–M17.
– COMB.: **mortmain act** any of several acts imposing restrictions on the devising of property to charitable use, *esp.* that of 1736.

Morton /ˈmɔːt(ə)n/ *noun*. L19.
[ORIGIN T. G. *Morton* (1835–1903), US surgeon.]
MEDICINE. Used in *possess.* to designate a painful condition of the foot caused by compression of a plantar nerve by a metatarsal.
Morton's foot, *Morton's toe*.

Morton's fork /mɔːt(ə)nz ˈfɔːk/ *noun phr.* M19.
[ORIGIN John *Morton* (c 1420–1500), Archbishop of Canterbury and minister of Henry VII.]
The argument (used by Morton to extract loans) that the obviously rich must have money and the frugal must have savings; *transf.* a situation in which there are two choices or alternatives whose consequences are equally unpleasant.

†**mortrel** *noun*. LME–L18.
[ORIGIN Old French *morterel*, *-uel*.]
A kind of soup.

mortuary /ˈmɔːtjʊəri, -tʃʊ-/ *noun* & *adjective*. LME.
[ORIGIN As noun, from Anglo-Norman *mortuarie* from medieval Latin *mortuarium* neut. sing. of Latin *mortuarius* (whence the English adjective: cf. French *mortuaire*), from *mortuus* dead: see -ARY[1].]
▸ **A** *noun*. 1 *hist.* A customary gift formerly claimed by the incumbent of a parish from the estate of a deceased parishioner. LME. ▸†**b** A fine payable to any of certain ecclesiastical dignitaries on the death of a priest within his jurisdiction. L16–L18.
†2 A funeral. LME–E17.
†3 A burial place, a sepulchre. Only in M17.
4 A place where dead bodies are kept for a time, either for purposes of examination or pending burial or cremation. M19.

Shetland Times Helicopters began lifting the bodies . . taking them ashore to the improvised mortuary.

▸ **B** *adjective*. 1 Of or pertaining to the burial or cremation of the dead. LME.

D. MADDEN They trundled the solid lozenge of pale wood into the hospital's chilly mortuary chapel.

2 Of, pertaining to, or depending on death; relating to or reminiscent of death. M16.

W. GOLDING The craft of the Egyptologist is too often mortuary . . and I think that mummies are . . disgusting.

morucho /moˈrutʃo/ *noun*. Pl. **-os** /-ɔs/. M20.
[ORIGIN Spanish.]
A half-breed bull reared in Spain.

morula /ˈmɔːr(j)ʊlə/ *noun*[1]. Pl. **-lae** /-liː/. E19.
[ORIGIN mod. Latin, dim. of *morum* mulberry.]
†1 *MEDICINE*. A segmented growth such as occurs in yaws; a disease characterized by such growths. E–L19.
2 *BIOLOGY*. A solid cluster of cells formed by repeated division of a fertilized ovum, prior to its development into a blastula. L19.

morula *noun*[2] var. of MARULA.

M

morwong /ˈmɔːwɒŋ/ *noun*. **L19.**
[**ORIGIN** Prob. from an Australian Aboriginal language of coastal New South Wales.]
Any of several marine food fishes of the family Cheilodactylidae and esp. the genus *Nemadactylus*, found off the Australian coast and distinguished by elongated rays in the pectoral fin.

MOS *abbreviation*.
Metal-oxide semiconductor.

mosaic /məʊˈzeɪɪk/ *noun & adjective*[1]. **M16.**
[**ORIGIN** Old French *mosaicq*, *mu-* (mod. *mosaïque*) from Italian *mosaico*, †*mu-* from medieval Latin *mosaicus*, *mu-*, obscurely from late Greek *mouseion*, *-sion* (see MUSEUM), whence late Latin (*opus*) *museum* and *musivum* (see MUSIVE).]
▸**A** *noun*. **1** The process of producing pictures or decorative patterns by cementing together small pieces of stone, glass, or other (usu. hard) material of various colours; pictures or patterns, or a constructive or decorative material, produced in this way. **M16.** ▸**b** A piece of mosaic; a design in mosaic. **M17.**

K. CLARK The floors were of mosaic with figures, like a Roman pavement. S. KITZINGER We shall be able, as if piecing together fragments of mosaic, to learn more and more. **b** J. J. HENNESSY The expenditure of £60,000 on a mosaic outside the council offices.

2 *transf. & fig.* Something resembling mosaic or a mosaic in its diversity of composition; *spec.* a mosaic map or photograph. **M17.**

W. HOGARTH The pine-apple, which nature has . . distinguished by bestowing . . rich mosaic upon it. *Listener* Janacek . . building his structures from a mosaic of ideas. M. GEE Living like animals, the floor . . a mosaic of bottles and coke-cans and girly magazines.

3 BIOLOGY. An individual (commonly an animal) composed of cells of two genetically different types. **E20.**
4 An array of small photoemissive metal plates forming the target plate in a television camera tube; an array of piezoelectric transducers in an ultrasonic detector. **E20.**
5 Mosaic disease of plants. **E20.**
rugose mosaic: see RUGOSE 1.
▸**B** *adjective*. **1** Pertaining to mosaic as a form of art; produced in mosaic. **L16.** ▸**b** *transf. & fig.* Diverse in composition or appearance; resembling the colours or patterns of mosaic. **M17.**

P. CUTTING The bathhouse with its . . bright mosaic floors. **b** *Railway Magazine* The large diagrammatic mosaic control panel gives details of all the power supplies.

M

2 EMBRYOLOGY. Of, pertaining to, or characterized by a mode of development in which regions in an embryo are predetermined by the corresponding regions in that embryo at an earlier stage of development. **L19.**
3 BIOLOGY. Having or composed of cells of two genetically different types. **E20.**
4 Of a composite photograph or map: made up of a number of separate photographs of overlapping areas. **E20.**
5 CRYSTALLOGRAPHY. Of (the structure of) a crystal: made up of small blocks of perfect lattices set at very slight angles to one another. **M20.**
– SPECIAL COLLOCATIONS: **mosaic disease** a virus disease that results in leaf variegation in tobacco, maize, sugar cane, etc. **mosaic gold** (*a*) tin disulphide (stannic sulphide), used as an imitation gold pigment; (*b*) an alloy of copper and zinc used in cheap jewellery and ornamental metalwork. **mosaic work** = sense A.1 above.
▪ **mosaically** *adverb* **M17.**

Mosaic /məʊˈzeɪɪk/ *adjective*[2]. **M17.**
[**ORIGIN** French *mosaïque* or mod. Latin *Mosaicus*, formed as MOSES: see -IC.]
Of or pertaining to Moses, the Hebrew prophet who in the Bible led the Israelites out of slavery in Egypt and passed on to them the Ten Commandments, and to whom the authorship of the Pentateuch was traditionally ascribed; of or pertaining to the writings and institutions attributed to Moses.
Mosaic law the ancient law of the Hebrews contained in the Pentateuch.

mosaic /məʊˈzeɪɪk/ *verb trans*. Infl. **-ck-**. **L18.**
[**ORIGIN** from MOSAIC *noun & adjective*[1].]
1 Decorate or pattern (as) with mosaics. **L18.**
2 Combine as if into a mosaic; produce by such combination. *rare*. **M19.**

Mosaical /məʊˈzeɪɪk(ə)l/ *adjective*. Now *rare*. **M16.**
[**ORIGIN** formed as MOSAIC *adjective*[2]: see -ICAL.]
= MOSAIC *adjective*[2].
†**Mosaical rod** a divining rod.

mosaicism /məʊˈzeɪɪsɪz(ə)m/ *noun*. **E20.**
[**ORIGIN** from MOSAIC *noun & adjective*[1] + -ISM.]
BIOLOGY. The property or state of being composed of cells of two genetically different types. Cf. MOSAIC *noun* 3 & *adjective*[1] 4.

mosaicist /məʊˈzeɪɪsɪst/ *noun*. **M19.**
[**ORIGIN** from MOSAIC *noun & adjective*[1] + -IST.]
A person who makes or deals in mosaic; a worker in mosaic.

Mosaism /ˈməʊzeɪɪz(ə)m/ *noun*. **M19.**
[**ORIGIN** mod. Latin *Mosaismus*, formed as MOSES: see -ISM.]
The religious system, laws, and ceremonies prescribed by Moses; adherence to the Mosaic system or doctrines.

Mosan /ˈməʊs(ə)n/ *noun*. **E20.**
[**ORIGIN** Salish *mús* four + -AN.]
An American Indian language group of the north-western US and western Canada.

Mosan /ˈməʊz(ə)n/ *adjective*. **E20.**
[**ORIGIN** French, from Latin *Mosa* Meuse: see -AN.]
Of or pertaining to a style of decorative art developed in the Meuse valley in western Europe in the 11th to 13th cents.

mosasaur /ˈməʊsəsɔː/ *noun*. **M19.**
[**ORIGIN** mod. Latin *Mosasaurus* genus name, from Latin *Mosa* the River Meuse, near which the first remains were found: see -SAUR.]
Any of a group of large extinct marine lizards of the Cretaceous period.
▪ **mosaˈsaurian** *adjective & noun* (of, pertaining to, or of the nature of) a mosasaur **M19.** **mosaˈsaurus** *noun*, pl. **-ri** /-rʌɪ/, **-ruses**, a mosasaur of the genus *Mosasaurus* **E19.**

moscatello /mɒskəˈtɛləʊ/ *noun*. Also †**-dello**. Pl. **-lli** /-liː/, **-llos**. **E17.**
[**ORIGIN** Italian: see MUSCATEL.]
= MUSCATEL 1, *spec.* from Italy.

moscato /məˈskɑːtəʊ/ *noun*. Pl. **-os**. **E20.**
[**ORIGIN** Italian: see MUSCAT.]
A sweet Italian dessert wine.

moschatel /mɒskəˈtɛl/ *noun*. **M18.**
[**ORIGIN** French *moscatelle* from Italian *moscatella*, from *moscato* musk.]
An inconspicuous plant of shady places, *Adoxa moschatellina* (family Adoxaceae), with ternate leaves and a terminal head of musk-scented green flowers. Also called ***town-hall clock(s)***.

Moscow mule /ˈmɒskəʊ ˈmjuːl/ *noun phr*. **M20.**
[**ORIGIN** from *Moscow*, the capital of Russia + MULE *noun*[1].]
A cocktail based on vodka and ginger beer.

†**mose** *verb intrans. rare* (Shakes.). Only in **E17.**
[**ORIGIN** Unknown.]
Suffer from glanders.

Moselle /mə(ʊ)ˈzɛl/ *noun*. Also **Mosel** /ˈməʊz(ə)l/. **L17.**
[**ORIGIN** See below. *Moselle* is the French, *Mosel* the German name of the river.]
A light dry white wine produced in the valley of the Moselle in Germany. Also more fully ***Moselle wine***.

Moses /ˈməʊzɪz/ *noun*. **E16.**
[**ORIGIN** ecclesiastical Latin *Moses*, *Moyses*, ecclesiastical Greek *Mōsēs*, from Hebrew *Mōšeh*. In sense 4 prob. alt. of MIMOSA.]
1 A person resembling the Hebrew prophet Moses (see MOSAIC *adjective*[2]), esp. in his character as lawgiver or leader. **E16.** ▸**b** Used as an oath or expletive. Also ***holy Moses***. **M19.** ▸**c** A male Jew. *derog.* **M19.**

M. L. KING In nearly every territory . . a courageous Moses pleaded passionately for the freedom of his people.

2 In full ***Moses boat***. A broad flat-bottomed boat used in the W. Indies. Also, a kind of boat used in Massachusetts. *obsolete* exc. *hist.* **E18.**
3 ***prickly Moses***, any of several wattles with needle-like phyllodes, esp. *Acacia ulicifolia* and *A. verticillata*. *Austral.* **L19.**
– COMB.: **Moses basket** a carrycot or small portable cot for a baby, esp. of wickerwork; ***Moses boat***: see sense 2 above.

mosey /ˈməʊzi/ *verb intrans. slang* (orig. *US*). **E19.**
[**ORIGIN** Unknown.]
Orig., go away quickly or promptly; make haste. Now, walk in a leisurely or aimless manner; wander, amble. Freq. foll. by adverb.

M. BRADBURY What say we mosey up to the ranch house? S. BELLOW I . . moseyed around in the lobby.

MOSFET /ˈmɒsfɛt/ *noun*. **M20.**
[**ORIGIN** Acronym, from metal oxide semiconductor *field-effect transistor*.]
ELECTRONICS. A field-effect transistor in which there is a thin layer of silicon oxide between the gate and the channel.

mosh /mɒʃ/ *verb intrans. slang*. **L20.**
[**ORIGIN** Perh. alt. of MASH *verb*[2] or MUSH *verb*[1].]
Dance to rock music in a violent manner involving jumping up and down and deliberately colliding with other dancers.
– COMB.: **mosh pit** the area in front of the stage where such dancing usu. takes place.

moshav /ˈməʊʃɑːv/ *noun*. Pl. **-im** /-ɪm/. **E20.**
[**ORIGIN** mod. Hebrew *mōšāḇ* dwelling, colony.]
In Israel, a group of agricultural smallholdings worked partly on a cooperative and partly on an individual basis.

moskeneer /mɒskəˈnɪə/ *verb trans. slang*. **L19.**
[**ORIGIN** Yiddish from Hebrew *maškōn* a pledge.]
Pawn (an article) for more than the real value.

mosker /ˈmɒskə/ *noun. slang*. **L19.**
[**ORIGIN** from MOSK(ENEER + -ER[1].]
A person who pawns an article for more than its real value.

mosker /ˈmɒskə/ *verb intrans*. Long *obsolete* exc. *dial.* **E17.**
[**ORIGIN** Prob. rel. to Middle Dutch *mosch* marsh, moss.]
Decay, rot; crumble *away*.

moskonfyt /ˈmɒskɒnfeɪt/ *noun. S. Afr.* **L19.**
[**ORIGIN** Afrikaans, from *mos* must + *konfyt* jam.]
A thick syrup prepared from grapes.

Moslem *noun & adjective*, **Moslemin** *noun & adjective* vars. of MUSLIM, MUSLIMIN.

Mosleyite /ˈməʊzlɪʌɪt/ *noun & adjective*. **M20.**
[**ORIGIN** from *Mosley* (see below) + -ITE[1].]
▸**A** *noun*. A follower or adherent of the English politician Sir Oswald Mosley (1896–1980), founder of the British Union of Fascists, or his views. **M20.**
▸**B** *adjective*. Of, pertaining to, or resembling Mosley or his views. **M20.**

Mosotho *noun sing.* see SOTHO.

mosque /mɒsk/ *noun*. **LME.**
[**ORIGIN** French *mosquée* from Italian *moschea* (whence also German *Moschee*), ult. from Arabic *masjid* lit. 'place of prostration'.]
1 A Muslim place of worship. **LME.**
2 *The* body of Muslims collectively; *the* Islamic authorities. *rare*. **L18.**

mosquito /mɒˈskiːtəʊ, mə-/ *noun*[1]. Pl. **-oes**. **L16.**
[**ORIGIN** Spanish, Portuguese, dim. of *mosca* fly from Latin *musca*.]
Any of various slender biting dipteran insects, esp. of the genera *Culex*, *Anopheles*, and *Aedes*, the female of which punctures the skins of animals (including humans) with a long proboscis and sucks blood.

attrib.: R. P. JHABVALA They came back, sunburned and full of mosquito bites.

– COMB.: **mosquito-bar** *US* a kind of mosquito net; **mosquito bee** a very small stingless bee; **mosquito-boat** *US* a motor torpedo boat; **mosquito-boot**: worn to protect the foot from mosquitoes; ***mosquito coil***: see COIL *noun*[2] 4f; **mosquito-curtain** = ***mosquito net*** below; **mosquito fish** a fish that eats mosquito larvae and pupae; *spec.* a small toothcarp, *Gambusia affinis*, native to the eastern and southern US and introduced elsewhere for mosquito control; **mosquito fleet** a fleet of small fast manoeuvrable boats; **mosquito hawk** *N. Amer.* (*a*) the nighthawk *Chordeiles minor*; (*b*) a dragonfly; **mosquito net** a fine net of gauze or lace to keep off mosquitoes; **mosquito netting** a coarse fabric with open meshes, used for mosquito nets.
▪ **mosquital** *adjective* of or pertaining to a mosquito or mosquitoes **L19.** **mosquitoey** *adjective* infested with mosquitoes **M19.**

Mosquito *noun*[2] & *adjective* var. of MISKITO.

moss /mɒs/ *noun*.
[**ORIGIN** Old English *mos* = Middle Low German, Middle Dutch *mos* bog, moss (Dutch *mos*), Old High German *mos* (German *Moos*), from Germanic word rel. to Old Norse *mosi* bog, moss & ult. to Latin *muscus* moss.]
▸**I 1 a** A bog, a swamp; *esp.* a peat bog. *Scot. & N. English*. **OE.** ▸**b** Wet spongy soil. *Scot. & N. English*. **L16.**
2 In full ***moss-crop***. Either of the two common kinds of cotton grass, *Eriophorum vaginatum* and *E. angustifolium*. *Scot. & N. English*. **L15.**
▸**II 3** A plant of the class Musci, comprising small bryophytes with scalelike leaves usu. spirally arranged and the spore capsule usu. opening by a lid, which grow in crowded masses in bogs, on the surface of the ground, on stones, trees, etc.; *collect.* the mass formed by such a plant. Also, any of certain algae, lichens, pteridophytes, or flowering plants resembling moss in habit; *rare* seaweed. **OE.**

R. K. NARAYAN There was still one step . . slippery with moss.

bog-moss, ***Ceylon moss***, ***clubmoss***, ***hair moss***, ***Iceland moss***, ***running moss***, ***sphagnum moss***, etc.
4 a An excrescence or encrustation resembling moss; *esp.* the covering of the calyx and pedicels of the moss rose. **E17.** ▸†**b** A kind of sugar coating. **E18–M19.** ▸**c** Hair. *slang*. **M20.**
5 In full ***moss rose***. A cultivar of the cabbage rose, *Rosa centifolia*, with a mosslike covering of glands on the calyx and freq. also the pedicels. **L18.**
6 *ellipt.* Moss green. **L19.**
– COMB.: **moss agate** a variety of agate containing brown or black mosslike dendritic forms; **moss-bag** *Canad.* a light board with a cloth flap attached to each side, used by Indians to carry a baby with the flaps laced together and a lining of moss; **moss-berry** the cranberry, *Vaccinium oxycoccos*; **moss campion** a pink-flowered, almost stemless campion, *Silene acaulis*, found in mountains and on northern coasts; **moss-cheeper** *dial.* (*a*) the meadow pipit, *Anthus pratensis*; (*b*) the reed bunting, *Emberiza schoeniclus*; ***moss-crop***: see sense 2 above; **moss green** a green colour resembling that of moss; **moss-grown** *adjective* overgrown with moss; *fig.* antiquated; **moss-hag** *Scot.* broken ground or a hole from which peat has been dug; **moss horn** *US* = ***mossy horn***; **moss-house** a garden shelter lined or covered with moss; **moss-oak** ancient oak wood preserved in a blackened state in peat bogs etc.; bog oak; **moss opal** a variety of opal containing dendritic markings like those of moss agate; **moss-peat** peat formed from mosses, esp. those of the genus *Sphagnum*; **moss pink** a low-growing phlox, *Phlox subulata*, of the central US, with pink, violet, etc., flowers; ***moss rose***: see sense 5 above; **moss-stitch** alternation of plain and purl stitches in knitting; **moss-wood** the wood of trees found buried in peat bogs.
▪ **mosslike** *adjective* resembling moss **M17.**

moss /mɒs/ *verb*. LME.
[ORIGIN from the noun.]
1 *verb intrans.* Become mossy. LME.
2 *verb trans.* Cover with moss. L16.

E. B. BROWNING When years had mossed the stone.

†**3** *verb trans.* Remove moss from (trees etc.). L17–E18.
4 *verb intrans.* Gather or collect moss. E18.

Mossad /mɒˈsad, ˈmɒsad/ *noun*. M20.
[ORIGIN Hebrew *mōsāḏ* institution.]
1 *hist.* An underground organization formed in 1938 to bring Jews from Europe to Palestine. M20.
2 The principal intelligence service of Israel. L20.

moss-back /ˈmɒsbak/ *noun*. *N. Amer.* L19.
[ORIGIN from MOSS *noun* + BACK *noun*[1].]
1 A large old fish. L19.
2 *hist.* A person who hid during the American Civil War to avoid conscription for the Southern army. L19.
3 A person attached to antiquated notions; an extreme conservative. *colloq.* L19.
■ **moss-backed** *adjective* (*colloq.*) very old-fashioned; extremely conservative: L19.

Mössbauer /ˈmɔːsbaʊə/ *noun*. M20.
[ORIGIN Rudolf L. *Mössbauer* (b. 1929), German physicist.]
PHYSICS. Used *attrib.* to designate (spectroscopy involving) an effect in which an atomic nucleus bound in a crystal emits a gamma ray of sharply defined frequency which can be used as a probe of energy levels in other nuclei.

mossbunker /ˈmɒsbʌŋkə/ *noun*. L18.
[ORIGIN Dutch *marsbanker*. Cf. MAASBANKER.]
= MENHADEN.

mossed /mɒst/ *adjective*. M18.
[ORIGIN from MOSS *noun, verb*: see -ED[2], -ED[1].]
Covered or overgrown with moss.

mosser /ˈmɒsə/ *noun*. M17.
[ORIGIN from MOSS *noun, verb* + -ER[1].]
1 = MOSS-TROOPER. M17.
2 A person who works in cutting and preparing peats. M19.
3 A collector or gatherer of moss. L19.

Mossi /ˈmɒsi/ *noun & adjective*. E19.
[ORIGIN African name.]
▸ **A** *noun*. Pl. same, **-s**. A member of a people of Burkina Faso in W. Africa; the language of this people. E19.
▸ **B** *adjective*. Of or pertaining to the Mossi. M19.

mossie /ˈmɒsi/ *noun*[1]. *S. Afr.* L19.
[ORIGIN Afrikaans from Dutch *musje* dim. of *mus* sparrow: see -IE.]
= ***Cape sparrow*** s.v. CAPE *noun*[1].

mossie /ˈmɒsi, ˈmɒzi/ *noun*[2]. *slang*. Also **-zz-** /-z-/. M20.
[ORIGIN Abbreviation: see -IE.]
A mosquito.

mosso /ˈmɒsəʊ/ *adverb*. L19.
[ORIGIN Italian, pa. pple of *muovere* move.]
MUSIC. A direction: rapidly, with animation.

mossoo /məˈsuː/ *noun*. *joc. & derog. arch.* E19.
[ORIGIN Repr. an anglicized pronunc. of MONSIEUR. Cf. MOUNSEER.]
A Frenchman.

moss-trooper /ˈmɒstruːpə/ *noun*. M17.
[ORIGIN from MOSS *noun* + TROOPER.]
A pillager or marauder of the Scottish Borders in the middle of the 17th cent.; any bandit or raider.
■ **moss-trooping** *noun* banditry, raiding M19.

mossy /ˈmɒsi/ *adjective*. In sense 1 also (earlier, *obsolete* exc. *dial.*) **mosy** /ˈməʊzi/. LME.
[ORIGIN from MOSS *noun* + -Y[1].]
▸ **I 1** Covered with something like moss; appearing as if covered with moss; resembling moss; downy, velvety; hairy. LME.

J. WILKINS Bearing mossy flowers.

2 Overgrown or covered with moss, having much moss; surrounded by moss. M16.

R. WEST A shed that let in rain through its mossy tiles.

3 †**a** Stupid, dull. *slang*. L16–E17. ▸**b** Extremely conservative or reactionary; old-fashioned, out of date; old. *US slang*. E20.
▸ **II 4** Marshy, boggy; peaty. *Scot. & N. English*. E16.
– SPECIAL COLLOCATIONS & COMB.: **mossy-backed** *adjective* = MOSS-BACKED. **mossy-cup oak** the bur oak, *Quercus macrocarpa*. **mossy cyphel**. **mossy horn** *US* an old steer; an old cowboy. **mossy saxifrage** a white-flowered saxifrage of rocky places, *Saxifraga hypnoides*, with mosslike cushions of leafy shoots.
■ **mossiness** *noun* E17.

most /məʊst/ *adjective* (in mod. usage also classed as a *determiner*), *noun, & adverb*.
[ORIGIN Old English *māst* (late Northumbrian) = Old Frisian *māst*, *maest*, Old Saxon *mēst* (Dutch *meest*), Old & mod. High German *meist*, Old Norse *mestr*, Gothic *maists*, from Germanic, from bases of MO *adverb, noun*[3], *& adjective*, -EST[1]. Serving as superl. of MANY, MUCH. Cf. also MORE *adjective* etc. See also MOSTEST.]
▸ **A** *adjective*. **1 a** Greatest in size, largest; greatest in number, quantity, or amount. Long only in ***the most part***. OE. ▸†**b** With nouns of quality, condition, action, etc.: greatest in degree or extent; utmost; very great. OE–E18. ▸**c** Greatest in power, authority, or importance. Long *obsolete* exc. *Scot.* OE. ▸†**d** Qualifying the designation of a person: entitled to the designation in the highest degree. ME–L17.

a L. A. ECHARD The most imaginable fatigue. **d** W. WALKER He had been a most Mad-man had he stood against them.

2 The greatest number of; the majority of; nearly all of. OE.

J. CONRAD The calm gulf is filled on most days of the year by . . clouds. *Daily Telegraph* I walked (though most people motor) to Salcombe Regis.

3 Existing in the greatest quantity, amount, or degree; the greatest quantity or amount of. LME.

J. RUSKIN The work . . which was begun with most patience.

– PHRASES: **for the most part** (**a**) usually, on the whole, in most cases; (**b**) as regards the greater or greatest part.
▸ **B** *noun*. **1** The greatest quantity, amount, proportion, or degree. (Foll. by *of*.) OE.

E. F. BENSON Some had gone to the writers . . , and some to the College, . . but the most had gone to the fire. C. D. SIMAK 'All my neighbours have lost their leases?' 'The most of them'. N. SEDAKA Mom had to work throughout most of her childhood.

2 *pl.* The greatest or most important people. Usu. in assoc. with *least*. Now only *poet.* in ***most and least***, all without exception. ME.
3 *pl.* The greatest number, the majority, (*of*); *spec.* the majority of people. L15.

BURKE A number of fine portraits, most of them of persons now dead. Z. TOMIN It's the shock—you've had it worse than most.

4 *The* best thing, *the* most exciting thing. Cf. ***the greatest*** s.v. GREAT *noun*. *slang*. M20.
– PHRASES: **at most**, **at the most** as the greatest amount; as the best possible; on the most generous estimate. **make the most of** (**a**) employ to the best advantage; (**b**) treat with the greatest consideration. ***most and least***: see sense B.2 above.
▸ **C** *adverb*. **1** In the greatest degree, to the greatest extent; *spec.* modifying an adjective or adverb to form the superl. (the normal mode of forming the superl. of adjectives & adverbs with three or more syllables, and of most of those with two syllables; also (*arch.*) used pleonastically before the superl. of an adjective or adverb). OE.

SHAKES. *Jul. Caes.* This was the most unkindest cut of all. T. HARDY Of all the phenomena . . those appertaining to comets had excited him most. M. SINCLAIR Just when I expected most to find you. V. WOOLF Humblest, most candid of women! *Washington Post* Who in the world would you most like to dine with? **b** S. JOHNSON I am . . your Lordship's most humble . . servant. SCOTT FITZGERALD 'It most certainly is not.' Dick assured her.

most favoured nation: see FAVOURED *adjective*[2]. ***the Most High***: see HIGH *adjective*. **most significant bit** COMPUTING the bit in a binary number which is of the greatest numerical value. **b *Most Honourable***: see HONOURABLE 3b. ***Most Reverend***: see REVEREND.

2 Mostly; for the most part. Long *obsolete* exc. *Scot.* OE. ▸**b** As an intensive superl. qualifying adjectives and adverbs: in the greatest possible degree, very. E16.
3 Almost, nearly. Now *dial. & US*. L16.

M. TWAIN Punching their fists most into each other's faces.

– COMB.: †**mostwhat** *adverb & adjective* (**a**) *adverb* for the most part; (**b**) *adjective* the greater part of; †**mostwhen** *adverb* most frequently, on most occasions; **mostwhere** *adverb* (*rare*) in most places.

-most /məʊst/ *suffix*.
[ORIGIN Old English *-mest*, from Germanic superl. suffix with *-m-* + base of -EST[1], but long regarded as from MOST *adjective*.]
Forming superlative adjectives and adverbs from words denoting position in space, time, or serial order, viz. (**a**) prepositions, as ***foremost***, ***inmost***, ***utmost***; (**b**) compars. in *-er*, as ***furthermost***, ***innermost***, ***uttermost***; (**c**) positive adjectives, as ***backmost***, ***topmost***.

mostest /ˈməʊstɪst/ *adjective, noun, & adverb*. *dial. & joc.* L19.
[ORIGIN from MOST + -EST[1].]
= MOST.

E. TERRY It's mostest kind to write to me. *Time* Porter Foley, who could get there fustest with the mostest drinks. *Daily Herald* Here's the hostess with the mostest.

mostlings /ˈməʊstlɪŋz/ *adverb*. *dial.* E19.
[ORIGIN from MOST + -LINGS.]
Mostly, usually; almost, nearly.

mostly /ˈməʊstli/ *adverb*. M16.
[ORIGIN from MOST *adjective* + -LY[2].]
1 For the most part; on the whole; usually. M16.

H. JAMES One went through the vain motions, but it was mostly a waste of life. V. WOOLF She talked more about virginity than women mostly do.

†**2** In the greatest degree, to the greatest extent; most. L16–E19.

mosy *adjective* see MOSSY.

MOT *abbreviation*.
1 Ministry of Transport.
2 [ellipt. for *MOT test*.] A compulsory annual test of the roadworthiness of a motor vehicle of above a specified age, or a certificate of passing such a test.

mot /mɒt/ *noun*[1]. *slang* (now *arch.* or *dial.*). Also **mott**, (earlier) †**mort**. M16.
[ORIGIN Unknown.]
1 A girl, a woman. M16.
2 A prostitute or promiscuous woman. M16.

mot /mo, məʊ/, (*pl. same*); *in sense* 1 mɒt/ *noun*[2]. L16.
[ORIGIN French = word, saying from Proto-Gallo-Romance alt. of popular Latin *muttum* rel. to Latin *muttire* to murmur. Cf. MOTTO.]
1 Orig., a motto. Later (now *dial.*) a word, an opinion. L16.
2 A witty saying. E19.

A. POWELL Good talkers . . remembered chiefly for their comparatively elaborate *mots*.

– PHRASES: *BON mot*. ***mot d'ordre*** /mo dɔrdr, məʊ ˈdɔːdrə/, pl. **-s -s** (pronounced same), [French = of command] a political slogan; a statement of policy; an oral directive. ***mot juste*** /mo ʒyst, məʊ ˈʒuːst/, pl. **-s -s** (pronounced same), [French = exact, appropriate] the precisely appropriate expression.
– NOTE: Formerly fully anglicized.

mota *noun* var. of MOOTAH.

motard /mɔtaːr/ *noun*. Pl. pronounced same. M20.
[ORIGIN French, from *moto-* combining form of *moteur* (cf. MOTO-): see -ARD.]
A member of the French motor cycle police.

mote /məʊt/ *noun*[1].
[ORIGIN Old English *mot* = West Frisian, Dutch *mot* sawdust, dust of turf (in Middle Dutch *steenmot*, *turfmot*), of unknown origin.]
1 A particle of dust; *esp.* one seen floating in a sunbeam; an irritating particle in the eye or throat; *fig.* (with allus. to *Matthew* 7:3) a fault observed in another person by a person who ignores a greater fault of his or her own (usu. ***mote in a person's eye*** etc.: cf. ***beam in one's eye*** s.v. BEAM *noun*). OE. ▸**b** A minute particle of foreign matter in food or drink. Now *Scot.* ME. ▸†**c** Any minute particle; something very minute or trivial, a trifle; (in neg. contexts) a jot. ME–E18. ▸†**d** = An atom. L16–E17.

C. AIKEN Where are the human hearts that danced like motes In the sunshafts of your brilliance! L. DEIGHTON Black smoke . . bringing oily smears, motes of soot. L. VAN DER POST The mote in our neighbour's eye is invariably a reflection of the beam in our own.

†**2** A blemish, a flaw. LME–E18.
3 Orig., a tuft of fibre. Now, a seed bearing such a tuft, as an imperfection in wool or cotton. L16.
4 A straw, a stalk of hay; a slender twig. Now *dial.* L16.

mote /məʊt/ *noun*[2]. *obsolete* exc. *hist.* See also MOAT *noun*. ME.
[ORIGIN Old French *mot(t)e* clod, hillock, mound, castle, etc. (mod. French *motte*: see MOTTE *noun*[2]).]
1 A mound, a hill, esp. as the seat of a camp, city, or building; an embankment. Also ***mote-hill***. Cf. MOTTE *noun*[2]. ME.
2 A barrow, a tumulus. E16.

mote /məʊt/ *noun*[3]. *arch.* ME.
[ORIGIN Old French MOT *noun*[2].]
A note of a hunting horn or bugle.

†**mote** *noun*[4]. LME–M19.
[ORIGIN Latin *motus*, from *mot-*: see MOTION.]
Motion (of a celestial object).

mote *noun*[5] see MOOT *noun*[1].

mote /məʊt/ *aux. verb*[1]. Long *arch.* Pres. & pa. (all persons) **mote**.
[ORIGIN Old English *mōt* (see MUST *verb*[1]): a West Germanic and Gothic preterite-pres. verb.]
1 Expr. permission or possibility, or a wish: may. OE. ▸**b** Might, could. LME.

E. FAIRFAX Within the postern stood Argantes stout To rescue her, if ill mote her betide. E. JONG 'The Goddess will do what She will' 'So mote it be, ' said the Grandmaster.

2 Expr. necessity or obligation: must. OE.

mote /məʊt/ *verb*[2]. E16.
[ORIGIN from MOTE *noun*[1].]
†**1** *verb intrans. & trans.* Find fault (with). *rare*. E16–L19.
2 *verb trans.* Remove flecks or specks from (cloth). L17.

mote /məʊt/ *verb*[3] *intrans*. *colloq.* Now *rare*. L19.
[ORIGIN Back-form. from MOTOR *verb*.]
Drive or ride in a car.

moted /ˈməʊtɪd/ *adjective*. E19.
[ORIGIN from MOTE *noun*[1] + -ED[2].]
Full of dust motes.

motel /məʊˈtɛl/ *noun*. E20.
[ORIGIN Blend of MOTOR *noun & adjective* and HOTEL.]
A roadside hotel catering primarily for motorists; *spec.* one comprising self-contained accommodation with adjacent parking space.
■ **motelier** *noun* the manager or owner of a motel M20.

moteless /ˈməʊtlɪs/ *adjective*. LME.
[ORIGIN from MOTE *noun*[1] + -LESS.]
†**1** Without blemish, spotless. LME–M17.
2 Free from dust motes. L19.

M

moteling /ˈməʊtlɪŋ/ *noun. rare.* E17.
[ORIGIN from MOTE noun[1] + -LING[1].]
A little mote; a very small thing.

motet /məʊˈtɛt/ *noun.* LME.
[ORIGIN Old French & mod. French, dim. of MOT noun[2]: see -ET[1]. Cf. medieval Latin *motetus*, *-um*, MOTTETTO.]
A short choral composition, *esp.* one for liturgical use or setting a religious text. Formerly also, a melody, a song.

motey /ˈməʊti/ *adjective.* L16.
[ORIGIN from MOTE noun[1] + -Y[1]. See also MOTTY.]
Full of motes or specks; spotty.

moth /mɒθ/ *noun*[1].
[ORIGIN Old English *moþþe* (also *mohþe*), obscurely rel. to synon. Middle Low German, Middle Dutch *motte* (Dutch *mot*), Middle & mod. High German *motte*, Old Norse *motti*.]
†**1** A worm, a maggot, a woodlouse; any small crawling thing. OE–E19.
2 **a** Orig., the larva of a clothes moth. Later (more fully ***clothes moth***), a small lepidopteran insect (of the genera *Tinea* and *Tineola*) whose larvae are destructive to clothes and other fabrics. OE. ▸**b** Any of the large group of insects (including clothes moths) which together with butterflies constitute the order Lepidoptera and are distinguished from butterflies (in most instances) by nocturnal activity, hairlike or slender antennae that are not clubbed, thicker bodies, the usu. folded position of the wings when at rest, and duller colouring. M17.
b ***codling moth***, ***emerald moth***, ***gypsy moth***, ***hawk moth***, ***silk moth***, etc.
†**3** [translating Latin *tinea*.] A disease of the scalp; ringworm. *rare.* LME–E17.
4 *fig.* A thing that causes gradual destruction or disappearance. Now *rare.* L16.
5 A prostitute. *arch. slang.* L19.
– COMB.: **moth-borer** the larval form of various moths which damage plants by boring into stems or other parts, esp. the sugar cane borer, *Diatraea saccharalis*; **moth fly** an insect of the family Psychodidae of tiny dipteran flies with hairy bodies and wings; an owl midge; **moth mullein** a mullein, *Verbascum blattaria*, with yellow flowers and smooth leaves, reputedly attractive to moths; **moth orchid** any of various freq. epiphytic orchids constituting the genus *Phalaenopsis*, chiefly of the Malay archipelago, with flat spreading petals suggesting a moth; **mothproof** *adjective & verb trans.* (make) resistant to damage by moths; **mothproofer** a substance for mothproofing clothes or textile fibres.
■ **mothlike** *adjective* resembling (that of) a moth L18. **mothy** *adjective* filled with or characterized by moths; reminiscent of a moth: L16.

moth /məʊθ/ *noun*[2]. M19.
[ORIGIN Hindi *moth*, Bihari *moth* from Sanskrit *mukuṣtha*.]
More fully ***moth bean***. A bean, *Phaseolus aconitifolius*, grown esp. in India as a vegetable, for fodder, etc.

moth /mɒθ/ *verb intrans.* E17.
[ORIGIN from MOTH noun[1].]
†**1** Become moth-eaten. *Scot.* Only in 17.
2 Hunt for moths. Chiefly as ***mothing*** *verbal noun.* E19.

mothball /ˈmɒθbɔːl/ *noun & verb.* L19.
[ORIGIN from MOTH noun[1] + BALL noun[1].]
▸ **A** *noun.* **1** A ball of camphor or naphthalene placed among stored fabrics to keep moths away. L19.
2 *fig.* In *pl.* A prolonged state of being in disuse or reserve or out of active service. Chiefly in ***in mothballs***, ***out of mothballs***. E20.

> A. E. STEVENSON Take the Paley Report out of mothballs, and review its recommendations. *Guardian* Apollo hardware put in mothballs . . could be brought out.

▸ **B** *verb trans.* Store among or in mothballs; take out of use or active service; put in storage for an indefinite time. M20.

> *Modern Railways* A passenger service on the mothballed . . line would cost up to £5 million to provide. *New Internationalist* Environmental protests have persuaded the Aquino Government to mothball the Bataan nuclear plant.

moth-eaten /ˈmɒθiːt(ə)n/ *adjective.* LME.
[ORIGIN from MOTH noun[1] + *eaten* pa. pple of EAT *verb*.]
1 Damaged or destroyed by moths; (of a person) shabby. LME.

> L. DEIGHTON Koch was a small moth-eaten man.

2 Antiquated, time-worn. M16.

> *Pilot* The cross runway . . is pretty moth-eaten and is closed.

■ **moth-eat** *verb trans.* (now *rare*) damage or destroy (as) by moths L16.

mothed /mɒθt/ *adjective.* M19.
[ORIGIN from MOTH noun[1] + -ED[2].]
Full of moths, moth-eaten.

mother /ˈmʌðə/ *noun*[1] *& adjective.*
[ORIGIN Old English *mōdor* = Old Frisian, Old Saxon *mōdor* (Dutch *moeder*), Old High German *muotar* (German *Mutter*), Old Norse *móðir*, from Germanic, from Indo-European base also of Latin *mater*, Greek (Doric) *matēr*, (Attic, Ionic) *mētēr*, Old Church Slavonic *mati* (*mater-*), Old Irish *máthir* (Irish *máthair*), Sanskrit *mātṛ*, *mātar-*, Tocharian *mācar*. See also MOTHER noun[2].]
▸ **A** *noun.* **1** A female parent of a human being (used as a form of address by a son or daughter, and sometimes a son- or daughter-in-law, and sometimes also familiarly by the father of a woman's child or children or by any husband); a woman who undertakes the responsibilities of a mother towards a child. Also, a female parent of an animal. OE. ▸**b** As *interjection.* Expr. surprise, dismay, etc. Freq. ***my mother!*** M19.

> TENNYSON Lambs are glad Nosing the mother's udder. A. CHRISTIE Mother and I . . feel it's only neighbourly to do what we can. *Woman's Own* Expectant mothers will be immunized.

adoptive mother, ***biological mother***, ***birth mother***, ***foster-mother***, ***natural mother***, etc.
2 A female ancestor. Long *rare.* OE.
3 *fig.* A quality, institution, place, etc., that is likened to a mother in her aspect of giving birth or exercising protective care, or as an object of affectionate respect; a source; a main stock or stem. OE.

> GOLDSMITH Nature, a mother kind alike to all. B. FRANKLIN The repeal of that mother of mischiefs, the Stamp Act. *South African Panorama* The cow . . is celebrated as mother and rescuer of the Hindu people.

4 Used as a form of address to an elderly woman, esp. of little means or education. Also used (instead of 'Mrs') before the surname of such a person. *arch.* ME.

> A. CHRISTIE 'Don't you take on so, mother' that's what the sergeant said to me.

5 A woman who exercises control like that of a mother, or who is looked up to as a mother; a matron, a housemother. LME. ▸**b** The head or superior of a female religious community. Also used as a form of address. E17. ▸**c** A woman who runs a brothel. *slang.* L18. ▸**d** A female owner of a pet, esp. a dog. *colloq.* E20.

> L. STRACHEY The Queen was hailed . . as the mother of her people. *Guardian* A new school and dormitory for the pages 'with a full-time mother and hot meals'.

†**6** ANATOMY. (In full ***hard mother***) = DURA MATER; (in full ***godly mother***, ***meek mother***, ***mild mother***, ***soft mother***) = PIA MATER. LME–E17.
7 †**a** The womb. LME–E18. ▸**b** Hysteria. *arch.* L15.
8 Womanly or maternal qualities. L16.
†**9** A certain figure in geomancy. L16–L19.
10 Liquid left after a dissolved substance has been crystallized out. E17.
11 In full ***artificial mother***. An apparatus for rearing chickens artificially. E19.
12 A cask or vat used in vinegar-making. M19.
13 A disc with grooves that is made from the plating of an electrotyped master matrix and is used to make a stamper for gramophone records. E20.
14 **a** *ellipt.* = ***motherfucker*** below. *N. Amer. coarse slang.* M20. ▸**b** A thing very big of its kind. Chiefly in ***big mother***. Cf. ***the father of a***, ***the father and mother of a*** s.v. FATHER *noun. N. Amer. colloq.* L20.

> **a** J. UPDIKE You haven't seen the lab! . . We finally got the mother finished, all but some accessory wiring.

– PHRASES: ***artificial mother***: see sense 11 above. **be mother** *colloq.* serve out food or drink; *spec.* be the person who pours the tea. **fits of the mother** *arch.* hysteria. ***hard mother***, ***godly mother***: see sense 6 above. **(just) like mother makes (it)**, **(just) like mother used to make (it)** having the qualities of home cooking; exactly to one's taste. ***meek mother***, ***mild mother***: see sense 6 above. **Mother of God** the Virgin Mary. ***mother of months***: see ***mother of the months*** below. **Mother of Parliaments** (*a*) England; (*b*) the British Parliament. †**mother of the maids** the head of the maids of honour in the royal household. **mother of the months**, **mother of months** the moon. **mother of thyme** wild thyme, *Thymus praecox* subsp. *arcticus*. **mothers and fathers** a game in which children play at being mother and father. ***my sainted mother***: see SAINTED 2. ***Reverend Mother***: see REVEREND. ***soft mother***: see sense 6 above. ***surrogate mother***: see SURROGATE *adjective*. ***the father and mother of a***: see FATHER *noun*. ***wife and mother***: see WIFE *noun*.
▸ **B** *attrib.* or as *adjective.* (Freq. with hyphen.)
1 That is a mother. ME.

> COLERIDGE The mother-falcon hath her nest above it.

2 Inherited or learned from one's mother; native. LME.

> G. BORROW You want two things, brother: mother sense, and gentle Rommany.

– SPECIAL COLLOCATIONS & COMB.: **mother-and-babe** *adjective* = ***mother-in-babe*** below. **mother-and-baby home** a maternity home for unmarried mothers, usu. with prenatal and postnatal services. **motherboard** a printed circuit board containing the principal components of a microcomputer etc., to which daughterboards may be connected. **Mother Bunch** †(*a*) *slang* water; (*b*) *colloq.* a stout or untidy old woman. ***Mother Carey's chicken***: see CHICKEN *noun*[1]. **mother cell** BIOLOGY a cell which undergoes division and gives rise to daughter cells; *spec.* a cell which undergoes meiotic division. ***Mother Church***: see CHURCH *noun.* **mother-city** (*a*) the city from which the founders of a colony came; (*b*) a city regarded as serving as a mother to someone. **mother-clove** the dried fruit of the clove tree, resembling a clove in appearance but less aromatic. **mother coal** mineral charcoal. **mother complex** PSYCHOLOGY a complex about one's mother. **mother country** (*a*) a country in relation to its colonies or dependencies, the country from which the founders of a colony came; (*b*) the country of one's birth. **mother earth** the earth considered as the mother of its inhabitants and productions; the ground; earth, soil. **mother-figure** a person or thing endowed with some of the attributes of a mother; *esp.* an older woman who is seen as a source of nurture, support, etc. **motherfucker** *coarse slang* (chiefly *N. Amer.*), an obnoxious or despicable person; a very unpleasant person or thing. **motherfucking** *adjective* (*coarse slang*, chiefly *N. Amer.*) despicable, obnoxious, very unpleasant. **mother goddess** †(*a*) CLASSICAL MYTHOLOGY a goddess who is the mother of a hero; (*b*) a deity with the attributes of a mother; a fertility goddess. **Mother Goose rhyme** *N. Amer.* a nursery rhyme. **mother-grabbing** *adjective* (*US slang*) = ***mother-fucking*** above. **mother hen** (*a*) a hen with chicks; (*b*) a person who sees to the needs of others, esp. in a fussy or annoying way. **mother-house** the founding house of a religious order. **Mother Hubbard** a kind of cloak; (chiefly *US*) a kind of loose-fitting garment. **mother image**, **mother imago** PSYCHOLOGY the mental image of an idealized or archetypal mother. **mother-in-babe** *adjective* designating a wooden bobbin with a hollow shank which contains another smaller bobbin. **mother-in-law**, pl. **mothers-in-law**, (*a*) the mother of one's spouse; †(*b*) a stepmother; (*c*) ***mother-in-law's tongue***, a W. African plant, *Sansevieria trifasciata*, of the agave family, with long transversely banded leaves, grown as a house plant. **motherland** a person's native country; a country as the source or producer of something. **mother language** = ***mother tongue*** below. **mother liquid**, **mother liquor** = sense A.10 above. **mother-lode** MINING a principal vein of ore; *fig.* a principal or rich source. **mother love**: such as a mother feels for her child. **mother-loving** *adjective* (*a*) that loves one's own mother; (*b*) *coarse slang* = ***mother-fucking*** above. **mother mould** a rigid mould which holds a sculptor's casting material. **mother naked** *adjective* completely naked. ***Mother Nature***: see NATURE *noun.* **mother of thousands** (*a*) any of several creeping plants prolific in flowers; *esp.* ivy-leaved toadflax, *Cymbalaria muralis*; (*b*) mind-your-own-business, *Soleirolia soleirolii*. **mother plane** an aircraft which launches or controls another aircraft. **mother plant** a parent plant from which other plants have been derived. **mother queen** (*a*) a queen mother; (*b*) a queen bee. **mother right** (*a*) matriarchy; (*b*) the custom by which dynastic succession passes only in the female line. **mother's boy**, **mother's darling** a boy or man who is excessively influenced by or attached to his mother. **Mother's Day**, **Mothers' Day** (orig. *US*) a day on which mothers are honoured with cards, gifts, etc.: in N. America, the second Sunday in May; in Britain, Mothering Sunday. **mother's help** a person who helps a mother, mainly by looking after children. **mother ship** (*a*) a ship or airship escorting or having charge of a number of other, usu. smaller, craft; (*b*) an aircraft or rocket from which another aircraft or rocket is launched or controlled. **Mother Shipton** a noctuid moth, *Euclidimera mi*, with a wavy mark on each forewing said to resemble the face of a crone; also called ***shipton moth***. **mother's mark** (now *rare*) a naevus. **mothers' meeting** orig., a meeting (usually weekly) of mothers connected with a parish or congregation, for the purpose of receiving instruction and advice; now usu. *fig.*, a group of people in conversation together, esp. when they should be doing something else. ***mother's milk***: see MILK *noun.* **mother's pet** (*a*) an indulged or spoiled child; (*b*) the youngest child of a family. **mother's ruin** *colloq.* gin. **mother's son** a man (chiefly in ***every mother's son***, every man, everyone). **mother stone** (*a*) the matrix of a mineral; (*b*) a rock from which another is derived by structural or chemical change. **Mothers' Union** an Anglican organization for women with the aim of fostering Christian family life. ***Mother Superior***: see SUPERIOR *adjective.* **mother tincture** HOMEOPATHY a pure undiluted tincture of a drug. **mother-to-be**, pl. **mothers-to-be**, an expectant mother. **mother tongue** (*a*) one's native language; (*b*) a language which has given rise to others. **mother water** = sense 10 above. **mother wit** a person's natural wit; common sense. **motherwort** any of various plants formerly believed valuable in diseases of the womb; *spec.* a labiate herb, *Leonurus cardiaca*.
■ **motherkin(s)** *noun* (an affectionate name for) one's mother L19. **motherling** *noun* = MOTHERKIN(S) M19. **mothership** *noun* (long *rare*) motherhood; the conduct of a mother; motherly care: LME.

mother /ˈmʌðə/ *noun*[2]. L15.
[ORIGIN Prob. a use of MOTHER noun[1]: corresp. in form and sense to Middle Dutch *moeder* (Dutch *moer*), German *Mutter*, and in sense to French *mère (de vinaigre)*, Spanish & Italian *madre*.]
1 Dregs, scum, orig. that of oil, later that rising to the surface of fermenting liquors. *obsolete* exc. in ***mother of grapes*** = MARC *noun* 1. L15.
2 In full ***mother of vinegar***. A ropy mucilaginous substance produced on the surface of alcoholic liquids during acetogenic fermentation, and used to initiate such fermentation in other alcoholic liquids. L17.

mother /ˈmʌðə/ *verb*[1]. LME.
[ORIGIN from MOTHER noun[1].]
1 *verb trans.* Be or become the mother of, give birth to; *fig.* be the source of, give rise to. LME. ▸**b** Take care of or protect as a mother; behave in a motherly way towards. M19.

> *Scientific American* Through normal birth, she has just mothered a normal, contented baby. **b** G. BOURNE If he is wakeful, mother him for a short time.

2 *verb trans.* Foll. by *on*, *upon*: attribute the maternity of (a child) to; *fig.* attribute the authorship of (a work) to; ascribe the origin of (something) to. M16.

> *Blackwood's Magazine* Many venerable repartees were mothered on her.

†**3** *verb trans.* Appear as, or acknowledge oneself as, the mother or source of. M17–L19.
4 **a** *verb trans.* Find a mother for (a lamb or calf); pick out from a flock the mother of (a particular lamb). Also foll. by *up*. M19. ▸**b** *verb intrans.* Of a lamb or calf: attach itself to a ewe or cow as mother. Also foll. by *up*. M20.
■ **motherer** *noun* (*rare*) L19.

mother /ˈmʌðə/ *verb*² *intrans.* L17.
[ORIGIN from MOTHER *noun*².]
†**1** Become full of sediment; become mouldy. L17–L18.
2 Become sticky; adhere. *dial.* L19.

mothercraft /ˈmʌðəkrɑːft/ *noun.* E20.
[ORIGIN from MOTHER *noun*¹ + CRAFT *noun.*]
The business of being a mother; knowledge of and skill in looking after and bringing up children.

mothered /ˈmʌðəd/ *adjective*¹. M17.
[ORIGIN from MOTHER *noun*¹ + -ED².]
Having a mother or mothers (of a specified number or kind).

†**mothered** *adjective*². L17–E18.
[ORIGIN from MOTHER *noun*² + -ED².]
Containing mother.

†**motherhead** *noun.* ME.
[ORIGIN from MOTHER *noun*¹ + -HEAD¹.]
1 The state or condition of being a mother; motherly care. Only in ME.
2 An embodiment of maternal qualities. *rare.* Only in L19.

motherhood /ˈmʌðəhʊd/ *noun & adjective.* LME.
[ORIGIN from MOTHER *noun*¹ + -HOOD.]
▸ **A** *noun.* †**1** With possess. adjective: a title of respect for a mother. LME–L15.
2 The condition or fact of being a mother. L15.
motherhood and apple pie something regarded as so obviously decent and good as to be beyond question or criticism; *esp.* traditional American values or culture.
3 Motherly feeling or love. *rare.* L16.
▸ **B** *attrib.* or as *adjective.* Of an issue, report, etc.: protective, withholding the worst aspects. *N. Amer.* L20.

mothering /ˈmʌð(ə)rɪŋ/ *noun.* M17.
[ORIGIN from MOTHER *noun*¹, *verb*¹ + -ING¹.]
1 The custom of visiting, communicating with, or giving presents to one's mother (formerly, one's parents) on the fourth Sunday in Lent. Now *rare* exc. in ***Mothering Sunday***, that Sunday. M17.
2 The action of MOTHER *verb*¹; motherly care or supervision. M19.

mothering /ˈmʌð(ə)rɪŋ/ *ppl adjective.* M19.
[ORIGIN from MOTHER *noun*¹, *verb*¹ + -ING².]
1 That acts as a mother. M19.
2 [Cf. *mother-fucking* s.v. MOTHER *noun*¹.] Despicable, obnoxious; very unpleasant. *US slang.* M20.

motherless /ˈmʌðəlɪs/ *adjective, noun, & adverb.* LOE.
[ORIGIN from MOTHER *noun*¹ + -LESS.]
▸ **A** *adjective.* Having no mother; having a dead, absent, or unknown mother. LOE.
▸ **B** *noun collect. pl.* *The* class of motherless people or motherless children. *rare.* LME.
▸ **C** *adverb.* Completely. Chiefly in ***motherless broke***, ***stone motherless —***. *Austral. slang.* L19.
■ **motherlessness** *noun* M19.

motherlike /ˈmʌðəlʌɪk/ *adjective & adverb.* M16.
[ORIGIN formed as MOTHERLESS + -LIKE.]
▸ **A** *adjective.* Resembling a mother; having the qualities of a mother. M16.
▸ **B** *adverb.* In a motherlike manner. M16.

motherly /ˈmʌðəli/ *adjective.* OE.
[ORIGIN formed as MOTHERLESS + -LY¹.]
1 Of or pertaining to a mother. *rare.* OE.
2 Befitting or characteristic of a mother. ME.

R. WEST When she picks up facts she kind of gives them a motherly hug.

3 Resembling a mother; having the character, manner, or appearance of a mother. M16.

I. MCEWAN A friendly, motherly woman . . insisted on fastening his seatbelt for him.

■ **motherliness** *noun* M17.

motherly /ˈmʌðəli/ *adverb.* Now *rare.* OE.
[ORIGIN formed as MOTHERLESS + -LY².]
In a motherly manner.

mother-of-pearl /mʌð(ə)rəfˈpəːl/ *noun.* Also (earlier) †**mother-pearl.** L15.
[ORIGIN translating French †*mère perle*, corresp. to Italian, Spanish *madreperla*, Dutch *paarlemoer*, German *Perlmutter.*]
1 A smooth shining iridescent substance forming the inner layer of the shell of a mollusc, esp. an oyster. L15.
2 A shellfish yielding mother-of-pearl. L16.
– COMB.: **mother-of-pearl cloud** a kind of iridescent cloud occurring above the tropopause which is sometimes seen in high latitudes after sunset; **mother-of-pearl work** a kind of embroidery in which pieces of mother-of-pearl are sewn on velvet or silk.

mothery /ˈmʌð(ə)ri/ *adjective.* L17.
[ORIGIN from MOTHER *noun*² + -Y¹.]
Of wine or vinegar: turbid with fermented matter, fetid.

motif /məʊˈtiːf/ *noun.* M19.
[ORIGIN French: see MOTIVE *noun.*]
1 A distinctive, significant, or dominant idea or theme; *spec.* (**a**) ART a distinctive feature, subject, or structural principle in a composition or design; (**b**) in literature or folklore, a particular or recurrent event, situation, theme, character, etc.; (**c**) MUSIC a figure, a leitmotif. M19.

P. TILLICH Another motif of recent Existentialism . . is the escape into authority. M. SWANTON This 'Tree of Life' motif is . . rare in Celtic sculpture. H. CARPENTER The quest-motif . . as a framework for an account of a spiritual journey. *Music Teacher* The Brahmsian characteristics are so clear, the motifs, the harmonic shifts.

2 An ornamental design or piece of decoration; *spec.* (**a**) an ornament of lace, braid, etc., sewn separately on a garment; (**b**) an ornament on a vehicle identifying the maker, model, etc. L19.

Times The banning of dangerous *motifs* mounted where the radiator cap used to be. W. TREVOR The patterned motif was repeated on either side of the hall door.

3 A motivation, a basis, (for an idea etc.). L19.
4 BIOCHEMISTRY. A distinctive section of a protein or DNA molecule, having a specific function. L20.

motile /ˈməʊtʌɪl/ *adjective & noun.* M19.
[ORIGIN from Latin *motus* motion + -ILE, after *mobile.*]
▸ **A** *adjective.* **1** BIOLOGY. Capable of motion; characterized by motion. M19.
2 PSYCHOLOGY. Of, pertaining to, or characterized by responses that involve motor imagery; (of a person) responding to perceptions more readily in terms of motor or kinaesthetic imagery than in auditory or visual terms. L19.
▸ **B** *noun.* PSYCHOLOGY. A motile person. L19.
■ **motility** /məʊˈtɪlɪti/ *noun* E19.

Motilon /məʊtɪˈləʊn/ *adjective & noun.* Also **-lone**. Pl. of noun same, **-lones** /-ˈləʊnz, -ˈləʊnɪz/. E20.
[ORIGIN Spanish *Motilón*, lit. 'shaven-headed one', with ref. to their custom of shaving their hair at the back and sides and leaving only the top to grow.]
Designating or pertaining to, a member of, any of various peoples of Colombia; (of) any of several languages spoken by the Motilon, esp. the Chibchan or Carib languages of the two main groups.

motion /ˈməʊʃ(ə)n/ *noun & verb.* LME.
[ORIGIN Old French & mod. French from Latin *motio(n-)*, from *mot-* pa. ppl stem of *movere* MOVE *verb*: see -ION.]
▸ **A** *noun.* **1** †**a** The action of moving or urging (a person) *to do* something, *that* something be done; a suggestion; an instigation, an instruction. LME–L18. ▸**b** LAW. A formal application made to a court for a ruling or order, esp. an interlocutory injunction. LME. ▸**c** A formal proposition or proposal put before a committee, council, legislature, etc. M16.

c B. MONTGOMERY They . . tabled a motion that . . each zone might act as it thought best. J. D. MACDONALD A motion that we dispense with the reading of the minutes.

†**2** **a** A motive, a reason; a ground or cause of action. LME–M17. ▸**b** An inner prompting or impulse; a desire, an inclination; a stirring of the soul, an emotion. LME–M18.
3 A commotion, (an) agitation; irregular movement, shaking. LME.

T. PERCIVAL The mixtures . . have some little fermentative motion in them. G. CRABBE His groans now told the motions of the cart.

4 The action, process, or condition of moving or being moved; an instance or variety of this. LME. ▸**b** PHILOSOPHY. Any kind of change; becoming. *arch.* exc. as translating Greek *kinēsis*. L17.

A. KOESTLER The moon's motion round the earth. A. TUTUOLA Leaves were bowing . . in slow motion.

5 **a** The action of the body in walking, running, etc.; a manner of walking or stepping; gait, carriage. L16. ▸†**b** The power of locomotion of an animate body; (strenuous) physical exercise. Only in 17.
6 An evacuation of the bowels. Also (*sing.* & in *pl.*), faeces. L16.
†**7** A puppet show; a puppet (*lit.* & *fig.*). L16–L17.
8 **a** A change of posture; a visible bodily movement, a gesture. E17. ▸**b** A step, gesture, or other movement of the body acquired by drill and training; *spec.* (MILITARY) each of the successive actions constituting a prescribed exercise of arms. E17. ▸**c** In *pl.* & †*sing.* Activities performed by a person or body of people in pursuit of a goal; *esp.* the movements of an army in the field. Now *rare* or *obsolete.* L17.

a TENNYSON Her eyes on all my motions with a mute observance hung.

9 A piece of moving mechanism. Formerly also, the movement of a watch. E17.

G. F. FIENNES The axles went . . faster than the wheels, which wasn't so good for the motion.

10 MUSIC. †**a** Movement, tempo. L17–E18. ▸**b** The melodic progression of a single part with reference to the intervals taken by it; the progression of two or more parts with relation to each other. M18.
– PHRASES: **go through the motions** (**a**) simulate by gestures or movements (an act *of*); (**b**) make a pretence, do something perfunctorily or superficially. ***harmonic motion***: see HARMONIC *adjective.* **in motion** moving, not at rest. ***local motion***: see LOCAL *adjective.* ***lost motion***: see LOST *adjective.* **make a motion** (**a**) begin to move (*towards, to do*); (**b**) beckon, gesture to (a person *to do* something). ***man in motion***: see MAN *noun.* ***oblique motion***: see OBLIQUE *adjective.* **of one's own motion** *arch.* of one's own accord. ***perpetual motion***: see PERPETUAL *adjective.* ***proper motion***: see PROPER *adjective.* **put in motion**, **set in motion** set going or working. ***similar motion***: see SIMILAR *adjective* 2. ***slow motion***: see SLOW *adjective & adverb.* ***thermal motion***: see THERMAL *adjective.*
– COMB.: **motion photography** cinematography; **motion picture** a cinema film; **motion sickness** nausea induced by motion, esp. travelling in a vehicle; **motion study**: of the movements involved in the most efficient performance of a task; **motion-work** the mechanism for moving the hands of a watch or clock.
▸ **B** *verb.* †**1** *verb trans.* **a** Approach (a person) with a request; petition or suggest to (a person). L15–M16. ▸**b** Propose, move, (a thing, *to do, that*). E16–M19. ▸**c** Propose or recommend (a person) for employment etc. L16–L17.

b I. NEWTON Thanks . . for motioning to get the experiment . . tried. W. ROW They motioned in the Committee that . . Hamilton should be general-major.

†**2** *verb intrans.* Make a proposal, bring forward a motion, offer a plan. *rare.* E16–M19.
3 *verb intrans.* †**a** Make a motion or movement as if *to do.* M18–E19. ▸**b** Make a gesture for the purpose of directing or guiding a person. L18.

b G. VIDAL Gracefully, he motioned for us to join him. C. GEBLER My uncle motioned with his fat hands.

4 *verb trans.* Direct or guide (a person) by a sign or gesture. L18.

J. BUCHAN I got my door open and motioned him in. J. HIGGINS He . . motioned them to sit on the sofa.

■ **motionable** *adjective* (*rare*) capable of motion M19.

motional /ˈməʊʃ(ə)n(ə)l/ *adjective.* E17.
[ORIGIN from MOTION *noun* + -AL¹.]
Of or pertaining to motion; characterized by (certain) motions; ELECTRICITY (of an impedance) arising from the motion of a conductor in a magnetic field.
■ **motionally** *adverb* as regards motion M20.

motionless /ˈməʊʃ(ə)nlɪs/ *adjective.* L16.
[ORIGIN from MOTION *noun* + -LESS.]
Not moving; incapable of motion.
■ **motionlessly** *adverb* M19. **motionlessness** *noun* E19.

M

motitation /məʊtɪˈteɪʃ(ə)n/ *noun. rare.* M17.
[ORIGIN from Latin *motitat-* pa. ppl stem of *motitare* frequentative of *movere* MOVE *verb*: see -ATION.]
A quivering movement.

motivate /ˈməʊtɪveɪt/ *verb trans.* M19.
[ORIGIN from MOTIVE *noun* + -ATE³, after French *motiver*, German *motivieren.*]
1 Supply or be a motive for (an action); provide (a person etc.) with a motive or incentive (*to do*); stimulate the interest of (a person) in an activity. M19.

M. INNES The action was motivated only by the . . fact that there was nothing else to do with him. *Rugby World* The club coach who has to motivate players. D. LODGE We need to . . motivate more working-class children to go to university.

2 Serve as a reason for, justify, (a decision etc.). L20.

Nature The publisher motivates the slim size of the volumes by claiming it makes them more likely to be read.

■ **motivated** *adjective* that has been motivated; having a motive or motivation: M20. **motivative** *adjective* serving to motivate M20. **motivator** *noun* E20.

motivation /məʊtɪˈveɪʃ(ə)n/ *noun.* L19.
[ORIGIN Partly from MOTIVE *verb*, partly from MOTIVATE: see -ATION.]
1 The action or an act of motivating something or someone. L19.
2 The (conscious or unconscious) stimulus, incentive, motives, etc., for action towards a goal, esp. as resulting from psychological or social factors; the factors giving purpose or direction to behaviour. Also, a motive. E20.

R. S. WOODWORTH The instincts are extraordinarily important in the study of motivation. *Scientific American* Other important motivations for attempting to synthesize speech.

3 The state or condition of being motivated; the degree to which a person is motivated; enthusiasm, drive. M20.

M. N. COX The second basic requirement is adequate motivation to persist. *Woman's Home* It was his background that gave him the motivation to succeed.

4 (A) manner or means of movement. M20.
– COMB.: **motivation research** the psychological or sociological investigation of motives, esp. those influencing the decisions of consumers.
■ **motivational** *adjective* M20. **motivationally** *adverb* M20.

motive /ˈməʊtɪv/ *noun & verb.* LME.
[ORIGIN Old French & mod. French *motif* use as noun of adjective: see MOTIVE *adjective.*]
▸ **A** *noun.* †**1** A matter etc. moved or brought forward; a motion, a proposition. LME–M17. ▸**b** An inward or spiritual prompting or impulse. LME–M17.
2 A factor or circumstance inducing a person to act in a certain way; an emotion, reason, goal, etc., influencing

or tending to influence a person's volition. LME. ▸**b** *spec.* The purpose or aim motivating a person committing a crime. L18.

> *Independent* The main motive is their yearning to look heroic and receive praise. **b** C. FREMLIN The motive for the kidnapping was as yet unclear.

†**3** A moving limb or organ. *rare.* LME–E17.
†**4** An instigator, an inciter. Only in 17.
5 A motif in art, literature, or music. M19.
▸ **B** *verb trans.* = MOTIVATE. M17.

motive /ˈməʊtɪv/ *adjective.* LME.
[ORIGIN Old French & mod. French *motif, -ive* from late Latin *motivus*, from Latin *mot-* pa. ppl stem of *movere* MOVE *verb*: see -IVE.]
1 a Having the quality of causing or initiating movement; productive of or used in the production of physical or mechanical motion. LME. ▸**b** Of nerves: = MOTOR *adjective* 1. *rare.* M17.

> **a** *Nature* Convection in the lower mantle . . provides the motive force for continental drift. *fig.*: M. ARNOLD The French Revolution . . found . . its motive power in the intelligence of men.

a motive power (*a*) power to initiate movement, drive machinery, etc.; (*b*) railway locomotives collectively.
†**2** Capable of movement, mobile; moving. LME–E17.
3 That moves or tends to move a person to a particular course of action; motivating. E16.

> E. H. SEARS Those . . whose motive principles are selfish. DISRAELI Public reputation is a motive power.

motiveless /ˈməʊtɪvlɪs/ *adjective.* E19.
[ORIGIN from MOTIVE *noun* + -LESS.]
Having no motive, irrational.

> M. ALLINGHAM This cruel and . . motiveless crime.

■ **motivelessly** *adverb* L19. **motivelessness** *noun* L19.

motivi *noun* pl. of MOTIVO.

motivic /ˈməʊtɪvɪk/ *adjective.* M20.
[ORIGIN from MOTIVE *noun* + -IC: cf. MOTIF.]
MUSIC. Of or pertaining to a motif or motifs.

motiviert /motiˈviːrt/ *adjective.* E19.
[ORIGIN German.]
Motivated.

M

motivity /məʊˈtɪvɪti/ *noun.* L17.
[ORIGIN from MOTIVE *adjective* + -ITY.]
The power to cause or initiate motion.

motivo /moˈtiːvo/ *noun.* Pl. **-vi** /-vi/. M18.
[ORIGIN Italian: cf. MOTIVE *noun*, MOTIF.]
MUSIC. A motif.

motley /ˈmɒtli/ *adjective, noun, & verb.* LME.
[ORIGIN Uncertain: perh. ult. from MOTE *noun*[1].]
▸ **A** *adjective.* **1** Diversified in colour, multicoloured; variegated. LME.

> SHAKES. *A.Y.L.* O that I were a fool!, I am ambitious for a motley coat.

2 (Composed of elements) of diverse or varying character, form, appearance, etc. L16.

> *Daily Telegraph* A motley crew with no ranks . . and half of them without uniforms. *Sunday Express* A fairytale with . . a motley assortment of evil baddies.

▸ **B** *noun.* †**1** A cloth of mixed colour. LME–E17.
2 A mixture of colours, variegation; an incongruous mixture. LME.

> J. LE CARRÉ A motley of foreign registration stickers covering one door.

3 (The multicoloured costume of) a professional fool or jester. *obsolete* exc. *hist.* L16.
wear motley play the fool.
▸ **C** *verb trans.* Make motley; mix incongruously. LME.
■ **motleyness** *noun* E19.

motmot /ˈmɒtmɒt/ *noun.* E19.
[ORIGIN Amer. Spanish: imit.]
Any of several mainly insectivorous passerine birds of the neotropical family Momotidae, some of which have a double racket-tail.

moto /ˈməʊtəʊ/ *noun*[1]. M18.
[ORIGIN Italian.]
MUSIC. Movement, pace.
CON MOTO. **moto perpetuo** /pəˈpɛtjʊəʊ/, pl. **moti perpetui** /ˌməʊtiː pəˈpɛtjʊiː/ [= perpetual motion] a rapid instrumental composition consisting mainly of notes of equal value (cf. PERPETUUM MOBILE 2).

moto /ˈməʊtəʊ/ *noun*[2]. Pl. **-os.** L20.
[ORIGIN Abbreviation of MOTOCROSS.]
A motocross or BMX race.

moto- /ˈməʊtəʊ/ *combining form.*
[ORIGIN from MOTOR *adjective*: see -O-.]
Motor.
■ **motocross** *noun* cross-country motorcycle racing M20. **motoˈneuron** *noun* (*BIOLOGY*) = **motor neuron** s.v. MOTOR *adjective* E20. **motoˈsensitive** *adjective* (*rare*) composed of motor and sensory nerve fibres M19.

moton /ˈməʊtɒn/ *noun.* Long *hist.* L15.
[ORIGIN Middle French *mouton* (in *épaule de mouton*, lit. 'shoulder of mutton', with reference to the shape of the armour).]
A piece of armour worn over the right arm at tournaments or (in later use) for protecting the armpit.

motor /ˈməʊtə/ *noun & adjective.* LME.
[ORIGIN Latin = mover; later, partly from *mot-* (see MOTIVE *adjective*) + -OR, partly after French *moteur.*]
▸ **A** *noun.* **1** A person who or thing which causes motion. LME.

> G. SARTON God exists, for it is the necessary principle and end of everything, the first motor. *fig.*: H. ARENDT Violence proved an excellent motor to set the mob . . in motion.

2 *ANATOMY.* A muscle which produces the main force of a movement of part of the body. Also, motor nerve. Now *rare.* E19.
3 a A machine for producing motive power from some other form of energy, esp. electrical energy; an engine, *esp.* that of a vehicle. M19. ▸**b** *ellipt.* A car, a motor vehicle. L19.

> **b** *Princeton Alumni Weekly* Many motors early took the highroad.

a phonic motor: see PHONIC *adjective* 1.
4 *PSYCHOLOGY.* = MOTILE *noun.* Now *rare.* L19.
▸ **B** *attrib.* or as *adjective.* **1** *ANATOMY & PHYSIOLOGY.* Designating or pertaining to neurons, nerves, or nerve fibres which initiate or convey impulses resulting in an action, esp. muscular contraction. Opp. SENSORY *adjective.* E19.
2 Of, pertaining to, or involving muscular movement. M19.
3 Causing or producing motion; motive. L19.
4 Of a vehicle, vessel, etc.: driven or powered by a motor. L19.
motor cruiser, motor launch, motor mower, motor yacht, etc.
5 Of, pertaining to, or designed for use in motors, motor vehicles, or motoring. E20.
motor accident, motor garage, motor horn, motor industry, motor insurance, motor mechanic, motor traffic, motor transport, etc.
– SPECIAL COLLOCATIONS & COMB.: **motor area** any part of the central nervous system which has a motor function; esp. = ***motor cortex*** below. **motor bicycle** (*a*) a motorcycle; (*b*) a moped. **motorbike** (*a*) *noun* a motorcycle; (*b*) *verb intrans.* travel on a motorcycle.. **motor boat** a motor-driven boat or launch. **motor-boat** *verb intrans.* (*a*) travel in a motor boat; (*b*) *ELECTRONICS* (of an amplifier) exhibit motor-boating. **motor-boating** (*a*) travel in a motor boat; (*b*) *ELECTRONICS* oscillation in an amplifier of such low frequency that individual cycles may be heard as a characteristic sound, caused by feedback from output to input, often through a common voltage supply. **motor bus** a bus with an engine. **motor-bus** *verb intrans.* travel by (motor) bus. **motor camp** (orig. *US*) a campsite catering for motorists, caravans, etc. **motor car** (*a*) a car; (*b*) *US* a rail car for freight or passengers propelled by its own motors. **motor caravan** a van equipped with beds, cooking facilities, etc., like a caravan. **motor coach** (*a*) = COACH *noun* 1c; (*b*) a passenger coach on an electrified railway equipped with its own motor. **motor-coaster** (*a*) a motorized vessel employed in sailing along a coast; (*b*) a type of big dipper at a funfair. **motor cop** *N. Amer. colloq.* a police officer on a motorcycle. **motor cortex** the part of the cerebral cortex in which originate the nerve impulses that initiate voluntary muscular activity. **motor court** *US* a motel. **motorcycle** a two-wheeled motor-driven road vehicle without pedal propulsion. **motorcyclist** a rider of a motorcycle. **motor-drive** (*a*) a drive or journey in a car; (*b*) driving power provided by a motor or engine. **motor generator** *ELECTRICITY* an apparatus consisting of a mechanically coupled electric motor and generator which may be used to control the voltage, frequency, or phase of a supply. **motor home** *N. Amer.* a very large vehicle equipped as a self-contained home. **motor hotel**, **motor inn**, **motor lodge** a motel. **motorman** a driver of a tram, underground train, etc. **motor mouth** *N. Amer. slang* a person who talks fast or incessantly. **motor nerve**: having a motor function. **motor neuron**: having a motor function; ***motor neuron disease***, a progressive disease characterized by degeneration of motor neurons and wasting and weakness of muscles. **motor-racing** racing of motorized vehicles, esp. cars, as a sport. **motor root** the anterior or ventral root of spinal or certain cranial nerves, containing axons of motor neurons. **motor-sailer** a boat equipped with both sails and an engine. ***motor scooter***: see SCOOTER *noun* 5b. **motor unit** a neuroanatomical unit comprising a single motor neuron and the muscle fibres on which it acts. **motor vehicle** a road vehicle powered by an internal-combustion engine. **motor wind** *PHOTOGRAPHY* a camera winding mechanism driven by a motor.
■ **motored** *adjective* provided or equipped with a motor E20.

motor /ˈməʊtə/ *verb.* L19.
[ORIGIN from the noun.]
1 *verb trans.* **a** Convey (a person or goods) in a motor vehicle. L19. ▸**b** Travel over (a distance) in a motor vehicle. E20.

> **a** J. COLVILLE Philip . . motored me to Trent Park.

2 *verb intrans.* **a** Travel or drive in a motor vehicle. L19. ▸**b** Travel in a motor boat; use an engine in a sailing boat. M20.

> **a** J. BUCHAN Mayot had motored to Cirencester. *fig.*: *Sunday Times* The directors are buying enthusiastically. The shares are starting to motor.

motorable /ˈməʊt(ə)rəb(ə)l/ *adjective.* E20.
[ORIGIN from MOTOR *verb* + -ABLE.]
Of a road or district: suitable for or usable by motor vehicles.

Motorail /ˈməʊtəreɪl/ *noun.* M20.
[ORIGIN Blend of MOTOR *noun* and RAIL *noun*[2].]
A rail service in which cars are transported together with their drivers and passengers.

Motorama /məʊtəˈrɑːmə/ *noun.* M20.
[ORIGIN Blend of MOTOR *noun* and *-orama* after PANORAMA.]
An exhibition of motor vehicles.

motorcade /ˈməʊtəkeɪd/ *noun & verb.* Orig. *US.* E20.
[ORIGIN from MOTOR *noun* + CAVAL)CADE.]
▸ **A** *noun.* A procession of motor vehicles. E20.
▸ **B** *verb intrans.* Travel in a motorcade. M20.

motordom /ˈməʊtədəm/ *noun.* E20.
[ORIGIN from MOTOR *noun* + -DOM.]
The world of motoring; the people who use motor vehicles; motor vehicles collectively.

motorial /məʊˈtɔːrɪəl/ *adjective.* Now *rare* or *obsolete.* M18.
[ORIGIN App. from MOTOR *noun & adjective* + -IAL, after *sensorial.*]
BIOLOGY & PHYSIOLOGY. Of or pertaining to motion; *spec.* of or pertaining to a motor nerve; motor.

motoric /məˈtɔːrɪk/ *adjective.* L19.
[ORIGIN from MOTOR *noun & adjective* + -IC, after German *Motorik* motor functions.]
1 Of, pertaining to, or characterized by muscular movement. L19.
2 (Usu. **motorik.**) Of music: marked by precision or repetitiveness suggestive of mechanized action. M20.

> *Q* The motorik beat—Krautrock's defining, relentless rhythm.

motoring /ˈməʊt(ə)rɪŋ/ *verbal noun.* L19.
[ORIGIN from MOTOR *verb* + -ING[1].]
The action of driving or travelling in a motor vehicle, esp. a car.
– COMB.: **motoring cap**, **motoring goggles**, **motoring veil**, etc.: for wearing in an open car.

motorise *verb* var. of MOTORIZE.

motorism /ˈməʊtərɪz(ə)m/ *noun.* E20.
[ORIGIN from MOTOR *noun* + -ISM.]
The use or prevalence of motor vehicles; the world of motoring.

motorist /ˈməʊt(ə)rɪst/ *noun.* L19.
[ORIGIN from MOTOR *noun* + -IST.]
A person who drives or rides in a car.

motorium /məʊˈtɔːrɪəm/ *noun.* E20.
[ORIGIN mod. Latin, from Latin *motorius* moving, from *mot-* stem of *movere* move: cf. -ORY[1].]
1 *PSYCHOLOGY.* The centres in the brain concerned in the function of voluntary muscle; the system of the body capable of initiating and effecting muscular movement. E20.
2 *ZOOLOGY.* A cytoplasmic structure forming the centre of the neuromotor apparatus of some ciliates. E20.

motorize /ˈməʊtərʌɪz/ *verb trans.* Also **-ise.** E20.
[ORIGIN from MOTOR *noun* + -IZE.]
1 *PSYCHOLOGY.* Apprehend in terms of movements or motor imagery. *rare.* E20.
2 Provide or equip with a motor or with motor vehicles. E20.
■ **motoriˈzation** *noun* (*a*) *PSYCHOLOGY* (*rare*) the process of apprehending something in a motile manner; (*b*) the introduction, use, or possession of motor vehicles; the process of equipping with motor vehicles: E20.

motorless /ˈməʊtəlɪs/ *adjective.* L19.
[ORIGIN from MOTOR *noun* + -LESS.]
1 Not provided with or using a motor. L19.
2 Of a road etc.: having little or no traffic. L20.

motorway /ˈməʊtəweɪ/ *noun.* E20.
[ORIGIN from MOTOR *noun* + WAY *noun.*]
A dual carriageway specially designed for fast long-distance traffic and subject to special regulations concerning its use.

> *Radio Times* A motorway differs from all other types of road in that it has no crossroads, no traffic lights, no pedestrian crossings. *attrib.*: J. MANN She had pulled into the motorway café.

– COMB.: **motorway madness** *colloq.* reckless driving on a motorway, esp. in fog.

motory /ˈməʊtəri/ *adjective.* Now *rare* or *obsolete.* L17.
[ORIGIN Late Latin *motorius*, from Latin MOTOR *adjective*: see -ORY[2].]
= MOTOR *adjective* 2, 3.

motoscafo /motoˈskaːfo/ *noun.* Pl. **-fi** /-fi/. M20.
[ORIGIN Italian.]
In Italy: a motor boat; *esp.* one used to carry passengers on the Venetian canals.

Motown /ˈməʊtaʊn/ *noun & adjective.* M20.
[ORIGIN Contr. of *Motor Town*, nickname of Detroit, Michigan, USA, an important car-manufacturing city.]
(Designating, pertaining to, or in the style of) a kind of music blending soul and pop styles, made popular in the 1960s by black musicians and singers recording for the Motown Record Company. Cf. TAMLA, TAMLA MOTOWN.
– NOTE: Proprietary name.

mott *noun*[1] var. of MOT *noun*[1].

mott *noun*[2] var. of next.

motte /mɒt/ *noun*¹. *US*. Also **mott**. M19.
[ORIGIN Amer. Spanish *mata* grove, plant from Spanish = bush, clump.]
A clump of trees in prairie country.

motte /mɒt/ *noun*². L19.
[ORIGIN French = mound: cf. MOTE *noun*².]
ANTIQUITIES. A large man-made earthen mound with a flattened top, usu. surmounted by a fort, castle, etc.
motte-and-bailey *adjective* designating or pertaining to a kind of castle built in Britain by the Normans, consisting of a fort on a motte surrounded by a bailey.

mottetto /mɒt'tetto, mɒ'tɛtəʊ/ *noun*. Pl. **-tti** /-t(t)i/, **-ttos** /-təʊz/. M17.
[ORIGIN Italian, formed as MOTTO + *-etto* -ET¹. Cf. MOTET.]
A motet, *spec.* an Italian one.

mottle /'mɒt(ə)l/ *noun & adjective*. L17.
[ORIGIN Prob. back-form. from MOTLEY *adjective*.]
▸ **A** *noun*. **1** Any of the spots, patches, or blotches of a mottled surface. L17.
2 An irregular arrangement of spots, patches, or blotches of colour. M19.
▸ **B** *adjective*. = MOTTLED. Chiefly in comb., as ***mottle-faced*** *adjective*. L17.

mottle /'mɒt(ə)l/ *verb trans*. E17.
[ORIGIN Back-form. from MOTTLED.]
Mark or dapple with spots, patches, or blotches. Chiefly as ***mottled*** *ppl adjective*.
S. BELLOW Women's faces . . mottled with crying. S. KING A huge gull with mottled gray wings.
■ **mottler** *noun* M19. **mottling** *noun* (the production of) a mottled appearance M19.

mottled /'mɒt(ə)ld/ *adjective*. L17.
[ORIGIN formed as MOTTLE *noun* + -ED².]
Dappled with spots or blotches; marked with spots, streaks, or patches of different colour.
B. ASHLEY He looked up at the mottled sky.
mottled beauty a geometrid moth, *Alcis repandata*, which occurs in various pale and dark brown forms. **mottled calf** a variegated leather used for bookbinding. **mottled iron** a soft kind of cast iron. **mottled umber** a geometrid moth, *Erannis defoliaria*, of which the female is wingless.

motto /'mɒtəʊ/ *noun & verb*. L16.
[ORIGIN Italian from Proto-Gallo-Romance word whence also MOT *noun*².]
▸ **A** *noun*. Pl. **-o(e)s**.
1 Orig., a sentence or phrase attached to an emblematical design to explain its significance. Later, a sentence or phrase chosen as encapsulating the beliefs or ideals of an individual, family, or institution; a maxim adopted as a rule of conduct. L16. ▸**b** HERALDRY. A significant word or sentence usu. placed on a scroll, either below an achievement of arms or above the crest, usu. expressing a maxim, aspiration, etc. E17. ▸**c** A verse or saying in a paper cracker etc. M19.
W. S. CHURCHILL With the motto 'Trust the People' . . he appealed to the rank and file. S. J. PERELMAN Think in telegrams, that's my motto. U. HOLDEN With a Latin motto on the blazer pocket. **b** O. NEUBECKER Mottoes become an integral part of the coat of arms.
2 A short quotation or epigram placed at the beginning of a book, chapter, etc.; an epigraph. E18.
3 A sweet wrapped in fancy paper together with a saying or scrap of verse. Also ***motto-kiss***. *US*. M19.
4 MUSIC. A recurrent phrase having some symbolical significance. L19.
▸ **B** *verb trans*. Inscribe with a motto. L17.

mottramite /'mɒtrəmʌɪt/ *noun*. L19.
[ORIGIN from *Mottram* St Andrew's, a village in Cheshire + -ITE¹.]
MINERALOGY. An orthorhombic basic vanadate of lead, zinc, and copper, occurring as green or brownish blades or black encrustations and forming a series with descloizite.

motty /'mɒti/ *adjective*. *Scot*. L16.
[ORIGIN formed as MOTEY, repr. pronunc.]
= MOTEY.

Motu /'məʊtuː/ *noun & adjective*. L19.
[ORIGIN Melanesian.]
▸ **A** *noun*. Pl. same. A member of a Melanesian people of Papua New Guinea inhabiting the area of Port Moresby; the language of this people. L19.
▸ **B** *attrib*. or as *adjective*. Of or pertaining to the Motu or their language. L19.
■ Also **Motuan** *adjective & noun* L19.

motuca /mə'tuːkə/ *noun*. Also **-ka**. M19.
[ORIGIN Portuguese from Tupi *mutuca*.]
A Brazilian tabanid horsefly, *Hadrus lepidotus*. Also ***motuca fly***.

motu proprio /məʊtuː 'prəʊprɪəʊ, 'prɒp-/ *adverbial & noun phr*. E17.
[ORIGIN Latin.]
▸ **A** *adverbial phr*. Of one's own volition, on one's own initiative, spontaneously. E17.
▸ **B** *noun phr*. Pl. ***motu proprios***. An edict issued by the Pope personally to the Roman Catholic Church, or to a part of it. E17.

mou /muː/ *noun*. Also **mu**. Pl. same. M19.
[ORIGIN Chinese *mǔ*.]
A Chinese unit of area, varying locally but usu. equal to about 670 square metres.

mouch *verb & noun* var. of MOOCH.

moucharaby *noun* var. of MASHRABIYYA.

mouchard /muʃaːr/ *noun*. Pl. pronounced same. E19.
[ORIGIN French, from fig. use of *mouche* fly: see MOUCHE, -ARD.]
A police spy, *esp*. a French one.

mouche /muːʃ/ *noun*. L17.
[ORIGIN French, lit. 'a fly', from Latin *musca*.]
1 *hist*. A small patch of black plaster worn on the face as an ornament or to conceal a blemish. L17.
2 A natural mark on the face resembling such a patch; a beauty spot. M19.

moucher *noun* var. of MOOCHER.

mouchette /muː'ʃɛt/ *noun*. E20.
[ORIGIN French.]
ARCHITECTURE. A motif in curvilinear tracery shaped like a curved dagger.

mouchoir /muʃwaːr (*pl. same*), 'muːʃwɑː/ *noun*. L17.
[ORIGIN French.]
A handkerchief.

moue /muː/ *noun & verb*. M19.
[ORIGIN French: see MOW *noun*².]
▸ **A** *noun*. A pouting expression, a pout. M19.
M. CHEEK She licked her lips, made a little moue, and said she was sorry.
▸ **B** *verb intrans*. Pout. M20.

mouflon /'muːflɒn/ *noun*. Also **-ff-**. L18.
[ORIGIN French from Italian *muflone* from Proto-Romance.]
1 Either of two wild mountain sheep, *Ovis orientalis*, native to the Middle East and established also in Sardinia, Corsica, and central Europe, and the closely related European species *Ovis musimon* (both now sometimes included in *O. aries*, the domestic sheep). L18.
2 The fur of the mouflon; woollen fabric made from this or a similar fur. E20.

mought *verb* see MAY *verb*¹.

mouillé /muje, 'muːjeɪ/ *adjective*. M19.
[ORIGIN French, pa. pple of *mouiller* wet, moisten.]
PHONETICS. Of a consonant, esp. *l*, *n*, or *r*: palatalized, softened.

moujik *noun* var. of MUZHIK.

moul /məʊl/ *verb*¹. *obsolete* exc. *Scot. & N. English*. ME.
[ORIGIN Ult. from Old Norse verb rel. to *mygla* grow mouldy.]
1 *verb intrans*. Grow or become mouldy. ME.
2 *verb trans*. Make mouldy. LME.

moul /məʊl, muːl/ *verb*² *trans*. Long *dial*. M16.
[ORIGIN Var. of MOULD *verb*¹, perh. after French *mouler* to mould.]
Mould (something). In later use, knead (dough); shape (bread) into loaves.

moulage /'muːlɑːʒ/ *noun*. E20.
[ORIGIN French = moulding, moulded reproduction, from *mouler* to mould: see -AGE.]
A cast or impression of a (part of a) person or thing; the material used for or the process of making a cast or taking an impression.

mould /məʊld/ *noun*¹. Also ***mold**.
[ORIGIN Old English *molde* = Old Frisian *molde*, Middle Dutch & mod. Dutch *moude*, Old High German *molta*, Old Norse *mold*, Gothic *mulda*, from Germanic base meaning 'pulverize, grind'. Cf. Old English *myl*, Middle Dutch *mul*, *mol* dust, MEAL *noun*¹. Cf. also MOOL *noun*.]
1 Loose, broken, or friable earth; surface soil, esp. as readily broken up. Also in *pl*. (now chiefly *Scot. & dial.*), lumps or clods of earth. OE.
H. MAUNDRELL Vast naked Rocks without the least sign of Mould. J. CLARE In fresh-turn'd moulds which first beheld the sun.
2 The ground regarded as a place of burial. Now only *poet. & dial*. OE.
WORDSWORTH They were not loth To give their bodies to the family mould. A. E. HOUSMAN The bed of mould Where there's neither heat nor cold.
†**3** The ground regarded as a surface or as a solid stratum. OE–E17.
M. DRAYTON Where now it lyes even levell'd with the mold.
4 The world in which humans live; the earth. Also, the land of a particular region. *obsolete* exc. *poet*. OE.
SIR W. SCOTT The fairest knight on Scottish mold.
5 The upper soil of cultivated land, garden soil, esp. if rich in organic matter. Freq. with specifying word. ME.
N. NICHOLLS The loose and fermenting mould of the garden and fields. G. J. ROMANES The amount of mould which worms are able to cast up.
leaf mould etc.
6 (The material of) the human body. *obsolete* exc. *poet*. and in ***man of mould*** below. ME. ▸†**b** The dust (DUST *noun* 2a) to which a human body is regarded as returning after death; a dead person's remains. LME–M17.
COVERDALE *Tobit* 8:6 Thou maydest Adam of the moulde of the earth. MILTON And leprous sin will melt from earthly mould. **b** G. SANDYS Though wormes devoure mee, though I turne to mold.
man of mould a mere mortal.
– COMB.: **mould board**, (long *obsolete* exc. *Scot.*) **mouldbred** the board or metal plate in a plough for turning over the furrow slice.

mould /məʊld/ *noun*². Now *dial*.
[ORIGIN Old English *molda*, *molde* = Middle Dutch *moude* rel. to Sanskrit *mūrdhan* highest point, head.]
The top or dome of the head; a fontanelle in an infant's head.

mould /məʊld/ *noun*³. Also ***mold**. ME.
[ORIGIN App. (with metathesis) from Old French *modle* (mod. *moule*) from Latin MODULUS.]
▸ **I** A pattern by which something is shaped.
1 a A pattern or template used by a mason, bricklayer, etc., as a guide in shaping mouldings etc. ME. ▸**b** Any of various thin flexible pieces of wood used for making a pattern of the frames used in constructing a ship's hull. M18.
J. NICHOLSON To find the moulds necessary for the construction of a semicircular arch.
b ***temple mould***: see TEMPLE *noun*³ 2.
2 a A hollow form or matrix into which fluid material is poured or plastic material is pressed to harden into a required shape. Also, an impressed surface from which a cast can be taken. LME. ▸**b** COOKERY. A hollow vessel used to give a shape to puddings, jelly, etc. Freq. with specifying word. L16.
J. BRONOWSKI The Chinese made the mould for a bronze casting. **b** *Sunday Express* Line a paté mould with the remaining 4oz streaky bacon.
b ***dariole mould***, ***jelly mould***, etc.
3 *transf. & fig*. **a** That which gives an essential shape and form to something. Esp. in ***cast in a heroic mould*** below. M16. ▸†**b** The body regarded as the form within its clothes. E–M17.
a SHAKES. *Coriol*. My wife comes foremost, then the honour'd mould Wherein this trunk was fram'd. J. WESLEY Cast in the Mould of Sin I am. **b** SHAKES. *Macb*. New honours . . Like our strange garments, cleave not to their mould But with the aid of use.
†**4** An object of imitation; a model, a pattern. M16–E17.
W. LAMBARDE Having neither good arte . . nor yet approved patterne or Moald to imitate and follow.
5 A frame or body on or round which a manufactured article is made. M17.
6 A package of leaves of gold-beaters' skin between which gold leaf is placed for beating. E18.
7 In photo-engraving, the gelatin which receives the impression from the negative and from which the copper plate is taken. L19.
▸ **II** Imparted form; result of moulding.
8 The distinctive nature of a person, character, etc., as indicative of origin. ME.
M. PRIOR Hans Carvel . . Married a lass of London mould. B. JOWETT He has a character of a finer mould.
9 ARCHITECTURE. A moulding, a group of mouldings. L15.
10 a The form or shape of something, esp. an animal body. E16. ▸**b** Bodily form, body. Chiefly *poet*. L16.
a SIR W. SCOTT The buff-coat . . Mantles his form's gigantic mould. **b** WORDSWORTH Whom doth she behold? . . His vital presence? his corporeal mould?
11 Orig., plastic material. Later, that which is moulded or fashioned. *rare*. M16.
MILTON The formless Mass, This worlds material mould, came to a heap.
†**12** The form, structural type, or model of a building, ship, etc. L16–L18.
M. MACKENZIE A Vessel . . of such a Mould as to draw little Water.
†**13** Style, fashion, mode. E–M17.
P. HEYLIN The houses of the new mould in London, are just after their fashion.
14 In full ***mould-candle***. A candle made in a mould as distinct from one made by dipping a wick in melted tallow. E19.
T. L. PEACOCK She . . would have burned like a short mould.
15 GEOLOGY. A fossil impression of a convex structure. M19.
16 A pudding, jelly, etc., shaped in a mould. M19.
– PHRASES: **break the mould** *fig*. make impossible the repetition of a certain type of creation. **cast in a heroic mould** etc., of a heroic etc. character. ***running mould***: see RUNNING *adjective*. ***waste mould***: see WASTE *noun*. ***wove mould***: see WOVE *adjective & noun*.
– COMB.: **mould-blowing** GLASS-MAKING the blowing of glass inside a mould to give it the required shape; ***mould-candle***: see sense 14

M

above; **mould loft** SHIPBUILDING & AERONAUTICS a room on the floor of which the plans of a ship etc. are drawn at full size; **mould-made** *adjective* (of paper) made on a type of machine producing sheets resembling sheets of handmade paper; **mould oil** BUILDING an oil applied to formwork to prevent concrete adhering to it; **mould-runner** an operative in a pottery responsible for transferring a completed article to the drying oven.

mould /məʊld/ *noun*[4]. Also ***mold**. LME.
[ORIGIN Prob. from pa. pple of MOUL *verb*[1]. Cf. MOULD *adjective*.]
A woolly, furry, or staining growth of minute fungi, as that which forms on food, textiles, etc., esp. in moist warm air. Also *spec.*, = FEN *noun*[2] 2.

DICKENS Mildew and mould began to lurk in closets. ANTHONY HUXLEY Glistening droplets of fluid such as exude from moulds on decaying matter.

blue mould, ***potato mould***, ***slime mould***, ***sooty mould***, etc.

mould /məʊld/ *noun*[5]. Long *obsolete* exc. in IRON MOULD. Also **mold**. L16.
[ORIGIN Alt.]
= MOLE *noun*[1].

mould /məʊld/ *adjective*. Long *obsolete* exc. *dial.* ME.
[ORIGIN pa. pple of MOUL *verb*[1]. Cf. MOULD *noun*[4].]
Mouldy.

mould /məʊld/ *verb*[1]. Also ***mold**. ME.
[ORIGIN from MOULD *noun*[3].]
1 *verb trans.* Mix or knead (dough); shape (bread) into loaves. ME.
†**2** *verb trans.* Mix (ingredients) to form a paste. LME–M19.
3 *verb trans.* Shape (fluid or plastic material) into a required shape by pouring or pressing into a hollow form or matrix. Also foll. by *into*. Cf. earlier MOUL *verb*[2]. LME.

J. BRONOWSKI To take some clay and mould it into a ball. T. E. HULME I have no material clay to mould to the given shape.

4 *verb trans.* Produce (an object) in a particular form, esp. *out of* or *from* a certain element, *on* or *upon* a certain pattern (*lit.* & *fig.*). LME. ▸†**b** Foll. by *up*: make up, constitute. Only in E17.

ADDISON There is great art in moulding a question. SHELLEY Obscure clouds, moulded by the casual air. **b** SHAKES. *Hen. VIII* All princely graces That mould up such a mighty piece as this is.

M

5 *verb trans.* SHIPBUILDING. Orig., give a particular form or structure to (a vessel). Later, provide a particular pattern for (timbers etc.) using moulds. L16.
6 *verb trans.* Bring (material) into a particular shape or form; shape or model the character, style, or development of. Foll. by *into*, *to*. E17.

MAX-MÜLLER His character was chiefly moulded by his intercourse with men. P. G. WODEHOUSE A weaker spirit whom she could mould to her will.

7 *verb intrans.* & (*rare*) *refl.* Assume a certain form; become shaped. E17.

Ecclesiologist When the Norman man-at-arms had begun to mould into the English country gentleman.

8 *verb trans.* Of a garment: fit close to (the figure). L19.
■ **moulda'bility** *noun* ability to be moulded L19. **mouldable** *adjective* able to be moulded E17. **mouldableness** *noun* (*rare*) L19.

mould /məʊld/ *verb*[2]. Also ***mold**. L15.
[ORIGIN from MOULD *noun*[4] or from MOUL *verb*[1] + -*d*.]
1 *verb trans.* Orig., allow to become mouldy. Later, cause to contract mould. Now *rare*. L15.

E. RAINBOWE Sloth moulding some, anxiety consuming others.

2 *verb intrans.* Become mouldy or covered with mould. M16.

E. FIELD The little toy soldier is red with rust, And his musket moulds in his hands. *fig.*: SPENSER The man that moulds in ydle cell.

mould /məʊld/ *verb*[3]. Also ***mold**. M16.
[ORIGIN from MOULD *noun*[1].]
1 *verb trans.* Bury. Long *obsolete* exc. *Scot.* M16.
2 *verb intrans.* & (*rare*) *trans.* Moulder (*away*), crumble to pieces. Now *rare*. M16.
3 *verb trans.* Cover (the stems and roots of plants) with soil; earth *up*. Now chiefly *US* & *dial.* E17.

moulded /'məʊldɪd/ *adjective*[1]. *rare*. Also ***molded**. M16.
[ORIGIN from MOULD *noun*[4], *verb*[2]: see -ED[2], -ED[1].]
Mouldy.

moulded /'məʊldɪd/ *adjective*[2]. Also ***molded**. M16.
[ORIGIN from MOULD *noun*[3], *verb*[1]: see -ED[2], -ED[1].]
That has been moulded; that has a mould or moulds.
moulded breadth, **moulded width**, etc. the greatest breadth, width, etc., of a vessel.

moulder /'məʊldə/ *noun*. Also ***molder**. ME.
[ORIGIN from MOULD *verb*[1] + -ER[1].]
1 A person who moulds something; a person who moulds dough, clay, etc.; a person who makes loaves, bricks, etc., by moulding. Also, a person employed in making moulds for casting. ME.

Times Mr Sydney Lavington . . an unemployed moulder and caster. M. STOTT The chief moulders of public opinion are commercial interests.

2 An instrument for moulding; a mould. Now *rare* or *obsolete*. E17.

moulder /'məʊldə/ *verb*. Also ***molder**. M16.
[ORIGIN Perh. from MOULD *noun*[1] + -ER[5], but cf. Norwegian dial. *muldra*.]
1 *verb intrans.* Decay to dust; rot *away*; crumble. M16.

E. SHANKS We shall moulder in the plains of France. T. HOOPER [Honey]Combs which have dried out and partly mouldered away. *fig.*: TENNYSON Never man . . So moulder'd in a sinecure as he.

2 *verb trans.* Cause to decay to dust, rot away, or crumble. Now *rare* exc. *dial.* M17.

WORDSWORTH Long after we . . are mouldered in our graves. *fig.*: DONNE How many men have we seene Molder and crumble away great Estates.

3 *verb intrans.* Esp. of an army: be diminished in number; dwindle (*away*). Now *rare* or *obsolete*. L17.

CLARENDON If he had sat still the other great army would have mouldered to nothing.

4 *verb intrans.* Move *off* in an aimless or lifeless manner. *rare*. M20.

E. BOWEN I mouldered off by myself . . to watch the old clock.

■ **mouldery** *adjective* (long *rare* exc. *dial.*) (esp. of soil) crumbly, friable E17.

moulding /'məʊldɪŋ/ *noun*[1]. Also ***molding**. ME.
[ORIGIN from MOULD *verb*[1] + -ING[1].]
1 The action of MOULD *verb*[1]; an instance of this. ME.
2 A moulded object; ARCHITECTURE an ornamental variety of outline in the cornices, capitals, etc., of a building (freq. with specifying word); a similar outline in ornamental woodwork; a strip of wood, metal, plastic, etc., with an ornamental variety of outline. LME.

M. MOORCOCK She noticed the terra-cotta mouldings, depicting monks of olden days. D. LODGE Lifting the heavy-looking mouldings reeking of hot resin, from the machine.

bed moulding, ***bird's beak moulding***, ***dovetail moulding***, ***hood moulding***, ***waste moulding***, etc.
– COMB.: **moulding board** a board used in moulding, *esp.* one on which dough etc. is kneaded; **moulding plane** a plane for shaping mouldings.

moulding /'məʊldɪŋ/ *noun*[2]. Also ***molding**. Now *rare*. M16.
[ORIGIN from MOULD *verb*[2] + -ING[1].]
1 The process of becoming mouldy. M16.
†**2** Mould, mouldy growth. E17–M18.

moulding /'məʊldɪŋ/ *noun*[3]. Also ***molding**. Now *rare* or *obsolete*. L17.
[ORIGIN from MOULD *verb*[3] + -ING[1].]
The action or an act of covering the stems and roots of plants with soil.

mouldwarp /'məʊldwɔːp/ *noun*. Now chiefly *poet.* & *dial.* Also **mouldywarp** /'məʊldɪwɔːp/ & other vars. ME.
[ORIGIN Prob. from Middle Low German *moldewerp* (whence Dutch *muldvarp*) = Old High German *multwurf*, from West Germanic, from Germanic bases of MOULD *noun*[1], WARP *verb*.]
= MOLE *noun*[2].

mouldy /'məʊldi/ *noun*. *military slang*. E20.
[ORIGIN Perh. shortened from *mouldywarp* var. of MOULDWARP.]
A torpedo.

mouldy /'məʊldi/ *adjective*[1]. Also ***moldy**. L15.
[ORIGIN from MOULD *noun*[4] + -Y[1].]
1 Overgrown or covered with mould; decaying, decayed. L15. ▸**b** Of, consisting of, or resembling mould. L16.

K. LETTE Mouldy Big Macs and sweet-and-sour containers were scattered all over the park. J. SULLY The mouldy, dank-looking archway. **b** ADDISON The walls On all sides furr'd with mouldy damps.

2 Stale, out of date; wretched; dull, miserable, boring. *colloq.* L16.

MARGARET KENNEDY Do please come home soon, for it's mouldy without you.

– SPECIAL COLLOCATIONS & COMB.: **mouldy fig** *slang* (**a**) an admirer or performer of traditional jazz (as opp. to other kinds of jazz); (**b**) a very traditional or conservative person.
■ **mouldily** *adverb* (*rare*) M18. **mouldiness** *noun* M16.

mouldy /'məʊldi/ *adjective*[2]. Now chiefly *dial.* Also ***moldy**. L16.
[ORIGIN from MOULD *noun*[1] + -Y[1].]
Of the nature of mould or fine soil.

moule /mul/ *noun*. Pl. pronounced same. M19.
[ORIGIN French.]
COOKERY. A mussel. Usu. in *pl.*
moules bonne femme etc. ***moules à la marinière***, ***moules marinière(s)*** /(a la) marinjɛːr/ [lit. 'in the marinier manner'] mussels served in their shells and cooked in a wine and onion sauce.

Mouli /'muːli/ *noun*. Also **m-**. M20.
[ORIGIN Abbreviation of MOULINETTE.]
(Proprietary name for) a type of kitchen utensil for grinding or puréeing food.

moulin /'muːlɪn, *foreign* mulɛ̃ (*pl. same*)/ *noun*. M19.
[ORIGIN French, lit. 'mill'.]
1 A deep, nearly vertical shaft in a glacier, formed by falling water. Also called ***glacier mill***. M19.
2 A type of kitchen utensil for grinding or puréeing food. M20.

moulinet /muːlɪ'nɛt/ *noun*. E17.
[ORIGIN French, dim. of *moulin* mill: see -ET[1].]
1 A device for winding, hoisting, etc.; a winch. Now *rare* or *obsolete*. E17.
†**2** A kind of turnstile. E18–L19.
3 FENCING. A circular swing of a sword or sabre. M19.

Moulinette /muːlɪ'nɛt/ *noun*. Also **m-**. M20.
[ORIGIN formed as MOULINET: see -ETTE.]
(Proprietary name for) a type of kitchen utensil for grinding or puréeing food.

moult /məʊlt/ *noun*. Also ***molt**. E19.
[ORIGIN from MOULT *verb*.]
The action or an act of moulting. Freq. in ***in the moult***, in a condition of moulting.

Times August, with many birds in the moult. R. F. CHAPMAN A pellet of faecal matter is deposited at the larva-pupa moult.

moult /məʊlt/ *verb*. Also ***molt**. ME.
[ORIGIN Corresp. (with intrusive *l*) to Middle Low German, Middle Dutch *müten*, Old High German *mûzzôn* (German *mause(r)n*), from West Germanic, from Latin *mutare* change: prob. already in Old English (implied in *bimūtian* to exchange).]
1 *verb intrans.* Of hair etc.: fall out. Of feathers: be shed in the process of a bird's changing plumage. Also foll. by *off*. Long *rare*. ME.
2 *verb intrans.* Of a bird: shed feathers in the process of changing plumage. Of an animal: shed a shell, a skin, hair, etc., in the process of acquiring a new growth. LME.

Scientific American Crabs are most vulnerable to attack when they molt. *Cage & Aviary Birds* They begin to moult into adult colour at about five months old. *transf.*: B. BAINBRIDGE He was covered in strands of saffron-coloured fur. She had moulted all over him.

3 *verb trans.* Of a bird: shed (feathers) in the process of changing plumage. Of an animal: shed (a shell, a skin, hair, etc.) in the process of acquiring a new growth. M16.

D. ATTENBOROUGH The feathers on which a bird's life is so dependent are regularly moulted and renewed.

■ **moulted** *ppl adjective* (**a**) that has moulted; deprived of feathers, hair, etc., by moulting; (**b**) shed during moulting: LME. †**moulten** *ppl adjective* = MOULTED (a): only in L16.

moulter /'məʊltə/ *noun*. *rare*. Also ***molter**. LME.
[ORIGIN from MOULT *verb* + -ER[1].]
A moulting bird.

moulter /'məʊltə/ *verb*[1] *trans.* & *intrans.* Long *obsolete* exc. *dial.* Also **molter**. M16.
[ORIGIN Perh. alt. of MOULDER *verb*.]
= MOULDER *verb*.

moulter /'məʊltə/ *verb*[2] *intrans.* & *trans.* Now *dial.* & *W. Indian*. M17.
[ORIGIN Perh. from MOULTER *noun*.]
Moult.

moulvi *noun* var. of MAULVI.

mouly /'məʊli/ *adjective*. Long *obsolete* exc. *dial.* LME.
[ORIGIN from MOUL *verb*[1] + -Y[1].]
Mouldy.

mound /maʊnd/ *noun*[1]. ME.
[ORIGIN Old French & mod. French *monde* from Latin *mundus* world.]
†**1** The world; the earth as the abode of humankind. Only in ME.
2 A globe forming part of royal regalia, usu. of gold and often surmounted by a cross; an orb; HERALDRY this as a charge. M16.

mound /maʊnd/ *noun*[2] & *verb*. L15.
[ORIGIN Unknown.]
▸ **A** *noun*. **1** A hedge or fence, esp. as forming a boundary. Long *obsolete* exc. *dial.* L15.

SPENSER This great gardin, compast with a mound.

2 A fortification consisting of a raised bank of earth or stones (cf. MOUNT *noun*[1] 2); *gen.* an embankment, a dam. Now *rare*. M16.

J. THOMSON The circly Mound That runs around the Hill; the Rampart once Of Iron War. BURKE The mounds and dykes of the low fat Bedford level.

3 An artificially constructed elevation of earth or stones; *esp.* a pile of earth heaped up on a grave, a tumulus. Also *gen.*, a heap, a pile, esp. of objects of the same kind. M17.

P. BOWLES She pushed herself further back into the mound of pillows. P. ROTH The little mounds of pebbles piled there by the pilgrims. W. RAEPER The grass-grown burial mound.

4 A naturally occurring elevation resembling a heap or pile of earth; a small hill. L18.

Cornwall Review St. Agnes Beacon is a great mound rising to 600 feet.

mound of Venus = *mount of* VENUS.

5 *BASEBALL.* The slight elevation on which a pitcher stands. **E20.**

Billings (Montana) Gazette Buddy Welch . . won't be on the mound . . this season, he'll be in the outfield.

▸**B** *verb trans.* **1** Enclose or surround with a mound or mounds. **E16.**

SHELLEY Let hell unlock Its mounded oceans of tempestuous fire. TENNYSON A sand-built ridge Of heaped hills that mound the sea.

2 Heap up in a mound or mounds. **M19.**

C. CONRAN Mound the green beans on top in little pyramids.

– COMB.: **mound ant** *Austral.* = ***meat-ant*** s.v. MEAT *noun*; **mound-bird** a megapode; **mound-builder** (***a***) a member of a prehistoric N. American Indian people whose culture was characterized by the erection of mounds; (***b***) a megapode; **moundsman** *BASEBALL* a pitcher.

■ **moundy** *adjective* covered with mounds **M19.**

mounseer /maʊnˈsɪə/ *noun. joc. & derog. arch.* **M18.**

[ORIGIN Repr. an anglicized pronunc. of MONSIEUR. Cf. MOSSOO.]

A Frenchman.

mount /maʊnt/ *noun*[1]. **OE.**

[ORIGIN Latin *mont-, mons* mountain, reinforced in Middle English by forms from Old French & mod. French *mont*. In sense 6 also infl. by Italian *monte*.]

▸**I 1** Orig., a mountain, a high hill. Later, an approximately conical hill of moderate height rising from a plain; a hillock. Now chiefly *poet.* and in names of particular mountains etc. **OE.**

BROWNING Ye mounts Where I climb to 'scape my fellow.

Mount Everest, St Michael's Mount, the Mount of Olives, etc. ***Sermon on the Mount***: see SERMON *noun*.

2 *MILITARY.* A substantial defensive or protective work of earth etc. Formerly also = CAVALIER *noun* 1. *obsolete* exc. *hist.* **M16.**

AV *Isa.* 29:3 I . . will lay siege against thee with a mount.

†**3** An artificially constructed mound of earth, stones, debris, etc., esp. in a garden. **L16–E19.**

H. COGAN Behind their houses . . were two great Mounts of dead mens bones. S. JOHNSON Digging canals and raising mounts.

▸**II 4** Any of various fleshy prominences on the palm of the hand regarded in palmistry as significant of the degree of influence exercised by a particular planet. **LME.**

mount of Venus.

†**5** A measure of quantity of plaster equal to 30 hundredweight (approx. 1524 kg). **M16–E18.**

†**6** A financial institution; *spec.* a bank. **E17–M18.**

mount of piety [translation] = MONTE DI PIETÀ, MONT DE PIÉTÉ.

mount /maʊnt/ *noun*[2]. **L15.**

[ORIGIN from MOUNT *verb*. Perh. also infl. by French *monte*.]

†**1** = AMOUNT *noun*. **L15–M17.**

2 An act of rising or mounting. **L15.** ▸**b** An act of copulation. Now *ZOOLOGY*. **L19.**

3 A support in or on which something is set or placed or to which something is fixed, esp. for the purpose of display; *spec.* (***a***) a margin surrounding a picture etc., a card or other backing to which a drawing etc. is fastened; (***b***) a glass slide to which an object is secured for viewing by microscope; (***c***) a setting for a gem; (***d***) a stamp hinge or other device for the arrangement and display of stamps in an album etc.; (***e***) the frame or support of a fan made of pieces of wood, ivory, etc.; (***f***) *PHOTOGRAPHY* a fitting to support a camera lens, *esp.* one on a camera with interchangeable lenses; (***g***) in *pl.*, ornamental metal edges, borders, etc., esp. of decorative furniture. **M18.**

g *Antique Collector* A remarkably fine satinwood veneered corner cabinet . . embellished with ormolu mounts.

4 A horse, bicycle, etc., on which a person is mounted; a horse etc. provided for a person's riding. **M19.** ▸**b** An opportunity for riding, esp. as a jockey. **M19.**

E. ELMHIRST Others merely give their mounts a kick in the ribs and gallop onwards. G. HARRIS There was hardly enough fodder for the soldiers' mounts.

5 A stuffed and mounted skin, esp. of a bird. **E20.**

mount /maʊnt/ *verb.* **ME.**

[ORIGIN Old French *munter*, (also mod.) *monter* from Proto-Romance, from Latin *mont-, mons* MOUNT *noun*[1]. Cf. AMOUNT *verb*.]

▸**I** *verb intrans.* **1** Go or move upwards, ascend, (freq. foll. by *up*); (of the blood) rise into the cheeks. Also, extend in an upward direction. **ME.**

C. KINGSLEY A body of gladiators . . planting their scaling-ladders . . mounted to the attack. A. TROLLOPE The blood mounted all over his face. G. GREENE A bank mounted steeply on either side of the train.

2 Get on a horse, bicycle, etc., for the purpose of riding. (Foll. by *on*, †*to*.) **ME.**

F. NORRIS Annixter mounted and rode into Bonneville.

†**3** Amount or be equal *to* a certain number, quantity, etc. **LME–M18.**

POPE Bring then these blessings to a strict account; . . see to what they mount.

4 *fig.* **a** Rise or ascend to a higher level of rank, power, etc.; be or become elevated. **LME.** ▸**b** Go back in time. Foll. by (*up*) *to*. **L18.**

a WORDSWORTH As high as we have mounted in delight In our dejection do we sink as low. **b** J. M. JEPHSON An antiquity which mounts up to the eighth century.

5 Increase in amount or intensity; (of a sound) rise in pitch, grow louder. Freq. foll. by *up*. **LME.**

6 Get up *on* something serving to raise one from a lower to a higher level. **M17.**

7 Orig., ascend a stage, platform, etc.; appear as a performer. Later *spec.*, appear as a witness, give (false) evidence. *arch. slang.* **M18.**

▸**II** *verb trans.* †**8** Cause to ascend or rise; lift up or *up*; erect. **ME–E19.**

J. CLARE Water-lilies mount their snowy buds.

†**9** *fig.* Elevate; raise to a higher level of rank, power, etc. **M16–L18.**

F. QUARLES Who mounts the meeke, and beates the lofty downe.

10 Set or place on an elevation. Now only foll. by *on, upon*. **M16.**

DRYDEN We bear thee on our Backs and mount thee on the Throne. M. KINGSLEY A cluster of outbuildings . . each mounted on poles.

11 a Raise (guns) into position; place in a position ready for firing. Also (now *rare*), raise the muzzle of (a gun); place at a particular angle of elevation. **M16.** ▸**b** Provide (a fort, ship, etc.) *with* guns (usu. in *pass.*). Also, (of a fort, ship, etc.) have (guns) in position. **M17.** ▸**c** Place (a guard, watch, etc.) for the purpose of defence or observation. Now chiefly in ***mount guard*** s.v. GUARD *noun*. **E18.**

a SHAKES. *John* By east and west let France and England mount Their battering cannon, charged to the mouths. *Shooting Life* To mount the gun in a position that might not suit you. **b** H. LATHAM Earthworks mounted with cannon. B. B. SCHOFIELD The German ships . . mounted 10 5.9-inch and 5 5-inch guns.

12 Place (a person) on a horse, bicycle, etc., for the purpose of riding; help into the saddle, provide with a horse for riding; in *pass.*, be seated on horseback. **E17.**

H. BELLOC I don't suppose he rides, but I can't mount him anyhow. A. HARDING Charles, mounted upon the same horse.

13 a Fix in position for a particular purpose; bring into readiness for operation. **E18.** ▸**b** Set or place in or on or fix to a support, esp. for the purpose of display; *spec.* (***a***) surround (a picture etc.) with a margin, fasten (a drawing etc.) on to a card or other backing; (***b***) set (a gem etc.) in gold etc.; (***c***) secure (an object) on a microscope slide; (***d***) prepare (a preserved specimen) for examination and viewing. Also, fit (esp. decorative furniture) with ornamental edges, borders, etc. **E19.**

a *Outing (US)* He mounted his rod, and tried casting in shallow water. **b** G. J. HINDE Spicules . . when mounted in Canada balsam are nearly transparent. G. GREENE Photographs mounted on mauve silk in oval frames.

14 Put on or show oneself as wearing (an article of clothing). *arch.* **E19.**

S. LOVER It was time to . . mount fresh linen and cambric.

15 Stage, present for public viewing or display, (a play, exhibition, etc.). Also, put on, produce, (a radio or television programme). **L19.**

Listener The first town that . . asked us to mount a festival. H. CARPENTER The Group Theatre . . mounted a couple of small-scale productions.

16 Take action to initiate or effect (esp. a military offensive). **M20.**

New York Times Warplanes of the Far East Air Forces mounted 1,283 sorties. *Listener* Governments mount big campaigns to secure an 'incomes policy'.

▸**III** *verb trans.* **17 a** Ascend, climb up, (a hill, slope, stairs, etc.). **L15.** ▸**b** Rise on to (an obstruction etc.) in the course of progression, esp. accidentally. **M20.**

b *Morning Post* He just managed to avoid a crash . . , and in doing so he mounted the footpath.

18 Get on (a horse, bicycle, etc.) for the purpose of riding. **M16.**

19 Esp. of an animal: get on for the purpose of copulation. **L17.**

20 Ascend and take a place in or on; get up on or into. **L17.**

C. THIRLWALL Since he himself had mounted the throne. P. ABRAHAMS He's very sure of himself, Rae thought as he mounted the pulpit. *Times* Sentenced to death for drug trafficking and soon to mount the gallows.

mount the ladder: see LADDER *noun* 1b.

■ **mountable** *adjective* (earlier in UNMOUNTABLE) **L16.** **mounter** *noun* **L16.**

mountain /ˈmaʊntɪn/ *noun.* **ME.**

[ORIGIN Old French *montaigne* (mod. *montagne*), from Proto-Romance fem. sing. or neut. pl. of adjective, from Latin *mont-, mons* MOUNT *noun*[1].]

1 A large natural elevation of the earth's surface, *esp.* one high and steep in form (larger and higher than a hill) and with a summit of relatively small area. Also in *pl.*, such elevations constituting a region characterized by remoteness and inaccessibility. **ME.** ▸†**b** A large artificially constructed hill or tumulus. **M16–M17.**

2 a A large heap or pile; a towering mass. Also, a huge quantity *of*. **LME.** ▸**b** A large surplus stock, esp. of a commodity. Freq. with specifying word. Cf. LAKE *noun*[2] 2b. **M20.**

a S. KAUFFMANN Mountains of . . meaningless, commercial tripe. D. FRANCIS The gaze of both men swept the mountain of paper. *Sunday Times* Try harder . . to overcome the mountain of debt. **b** *Times* A butter mountain of 1,032,000 tonnes and a milk lake of 845,000 tonnes.

b *beef mountain, grain mountain*, etc.

3 More fully ***mountain wine***. A variety of Malaga wine. **E18.**

4 *FRENCH HISTORY.* ***the Mountain***, an extreme party in the National Convention during the French Revolution, led by Robespierre and Danton, so called because its members occupied the most elevated position in the hall; any of several later political groups or parties of extreme views. Cf. PLAIN *noun*[1] 7. **E19.**

5 (**M-**.) A steam locomotive of 4-8-2 wheel arrangement. **L19.**

– PHRASES ETC.: *BURNING* ***mountain***. ***cat o' mountain***, ***cat of the mountain***: see CATAMOUNTAIN. ***make a mountain of a molehill***, ***make a mountain out of a molehill***: see MOLEHILL. †**mountain of ice** an iceberg. **mountains high** (of the sea) in huge waves. ***old man of the mountain***: see OLD MAN *noun phr.* ***snow-on-the-mountains***: see SNOW *noun*[1]. ***the Mountain***: see sense 4 above. ***Welsh mountain (sheep)***: see WELSH *adjective*.

– ATTRIB. & COMB.: In the senses 'of, belonging to, or characteristic of mountains, occurring among mountains', as ***mountain air***, ***mountain road***, ***mountain stream***, etc.; 'that is a native or inhabitant of mountains, originating among mountains', as ***mountain tiger***, ***mountain tribe***, etc. Special combs., as **mountain ash** (***a***) a small European tree of the rose family, *Sorbus aucuparia*, with pinnate leaves, white flowers, and scarlet berries, esp. characteristic of heathy or hilly districts (also called ***rowan***); also, either of two related N. American trees, *S. americana* and *S. decora*; (***b***) *Austral.* any of several tall eucalypts, esp. *Eucalyptus regnans*; ***mountain*** AVENS; **mountain bat** a very small social bat, *Emballonura monticola*, of Borneo, Java, Sumatra, and the Philippines; **mountain beaver** a small burrowing rodent, *Aplodontia rufa*, of forests in the north-western US; also called ***sewellel***; **mountain bike** a rugged lightweight bicycle with deeply treaded tyres; **mountain blackbird** the ring ouzel; **mountain blue** a blue or bluish-copper mineral, *esp.* (***a***) azurite; (***b***) chrysocolla; **mountain bluebird** *N. Amer.* a bluebird of western N. America, *Sialia currucoides*, distinguished by a blue (rather than red) breast; **mountain-building** the formation of mountains, esp. as a result of folding and thrusting of the earth's crust; **mountain cat** any of various wild cats of mountainous regions, as the bobcat, the lynx; **mountain chain** a connected series of mountains; *esp.* an aggregate of ranges of mountains having a common alignment; **mountain chicken** *colloq.* an edible W. Indian frog of the genus *Leptodactylus*, a crapaud; **mountain-climber** a person who climbs mountains, esp. as a sport; **mountain-climbing** the action or activity of climbing mountains, esp. as a sport; **mountain cock** = CAPERCAILLIE; **mountain cranberry** *US* (the fruit of) the cowberry, *Vaccinium vitis-idaea*; **mountain daisy** any of various plants of the genus *Celmisia*, of the composite family, with large daisy-like flowers, mostly confined to the mountains of New Zealand; ***Mountain*** DAMARA; **mountain devil** (***a***) = MOLOCH 2; (***b***) *Austral.* the honey flower, *Lambertia formosa*; **mountain dew** *colloq.* whisky (esp. Scotch whisky), esp. when illicitly distilled; **mountain duck** (***a***) *Austral.* a chestnut-breasted shelduck, *Tadorna tadornoides*; (***b***) *NZ* the blue duck, *Hymenolaimus malacorhynchos* (also called ***whio***); **mountain ebony** (the dark hard wood of) any of several leguminous trees of the genus *Bauhinia*, esp. the Asian *B. variegata* and the Australian *B. hookeri*; **mountain fern** a fern of mountain pastures, *Oreopteris limbosperma*, with lemon-scented fronds; **mountain fever** any of various malarial or typhoid fevers contracted in mountain regions; **mountain finch** (***a***) = BRAMBLING; (***b***) = ***snow finch*** s.v. SNOW *noun*[1]; **mountain flax** (***a***) any of various upland plants; *esp.* a New Zealand plant, *Phormium cookianum*, a smaller relative of the New Zealand flax, *P. tenax*; (***b***) = AMIANTHUS; **mountain-folding** the formation of mountains as a result of folding of the earth's crust; **mountain gazelle** a small gazelle, *Gazella gazella*, now confined to semi-desert and scrub in the Arabian peninsula; **mountain goat** a goat of mountain regions; *esp.* a Rocky Mountain goat, *Oreamnos americanus*; **mountain gorilla**: of a race occurring at higher altitudes in the Congo, Rwanda, and Uganda, with long hair and long teeth; **mountain green** (***a***) glauconite or (formerly) malachite, esp. used as a pigment; the colour of this; (***b***) = ***mountain pride*** below; **mountain hare** a hare, *Lepus timidus*, of northern Eurasia whose coat is brown in summer and white in winter; also called ***Arctic hare***, ***blue hare***; **mountain heath** an evergreen alpine shrub, *Phyllodoce caerulea*, of the heath family; **mountain hemlock** a large coniferous tree, *Tsuga mertensiana*, of western N. America; **mountain-high** *adjective* (*hyperbol.*) very high; **mountain land** *Irish & US* open waste land with poor vegetation, esp. in a hilly or mountainous region; **mountain laurel** a N. American evergreen shrub, *Kalmia latifolia*, of the heath family, with glossy leaves and pink flowers; **mountain limestone** *GEOLOGY* a thick massive Carboniferous limestone; **mountain linnet** = TWITE; ***mountain lion***: see LION *noun*; **mountain mahogany** *N. Amer.* (***a***) sweet birch, *Betula lenta*; (***b***) any of various shrubs of the genus *Cercocarpus*, of the rose family; **mountain man** (***a***) an inhabiter or frequenter of mountains or mountainous country; (***b***) *US* a trapper; a pioneer; **mountain maple** = ***MAPLE bush***; **mountain mint** any of various N. American labiate plants of the genus *Pycnanthemum*, whose leaves smell

M

of mint when crushed; *mountain* NYALA; **mountain oyster** a lamb's testicle, as food; *mountain pansy*: see PANSY *noun* 1; **mountain panther** (*a*) = *snow leopard* s.v. SNOW *noun*[1]; (*b*) = PUMA; **mountain parrot** = KEA; **mountain partridge** = *mountain quail* below; **mountain plover** a small N. American plover, *Charadrius montanus*; **mountain plum** (the fruit of) a small spiny neotropical tree, *Ximenia americana* (family Olacaceae); **mountain pride** a small W. Indian tree, *Spathelia sorbifolia*, of the rue family, producing showy purple flowers at the top of an unbranched stem; also called *mountain green*; **mountain quail** a brown and grey plumed quail, *Oreortyx picta*, of western N. America; **mountain railway** (*a*) a light railway for transport in mountain regions; (*b*) a miniature ascending railway designed for amusement; a scenic railway; a funicular railway; **mountain range** a line or group of mountains connected by elevated ground; **mountain rat** the bushy-tailed woodrat, *Neotoma cinerea*, of the western US; **mountain reedbuck** a small reedbuck, *Redunca fulvorufula*, of montane grassland in southern, eastern, and central Africa; **mountain rescue** an organization for rescuing mountaineers, climbers, etc., in distress; **mountain rice** any of various grasses of the genus *Oryzopsis*, esp. *O. hymenoides*, used as grain by N. American Indians; **mountain ringlet** a satyrid butterfly, *Erebia epiphron*, of upland in northern Britain and parts of Europe; **mountain sheep** a sheep of the mountain regions; *esp.* (*N. Amer.*) a bighorn; **mountain sickness** a malady caused by breathing the rarefied air at a great height, altitude sickness; **mountainside** the sloping surface of a mountain below the summit; **mountain slide** a landslip occurring on a mountainside; **mountain snow** a spurge, *Euphorbia marginata*, of the western US, so called from the broad white border of its bracts; also called *snow-on-the-mountain*; *mountain sorrel*: see SORREL *noun*[1]; *mountain spiderwort*: see *spiderwort* (a) s.v. SPIDER *noun*; **Mountain Standard time**, **Mountain time** *N. Amer.* the standard time of parts of Canada and the US in or near the Rocky Mountains; **mountain system** a group of mountain ranges in a region, assumed to have been formed by the same geological processes; **mountain tea** *N. Amer.* the checkerberry, *Gaultheria procumbens*; a drink made from an infusion of its leaves; **mountain thrush** any of several Old World thrushes found in mountainous areas, esp. *Zoothera mollissima* of the Himalayas and SE Asia and *Turdus abyssinicus* of E. Africa; *Mountain time*: see *Mountain Standard time* above; **mountain tortoise** = *leopard-tortoise* s.v. LEOPARD *noun*; **mountain trout** any of various fishes of mountain streams related to or resembling trout; *esp.* (chiefly *Austral.*) any of various fishes of the family Galaxiidae of the southern hemisphere; *mountain* VISCACHA; *mountain wine*: see sense 3 above; **mountain witch** a brightly coloured Jamaican quail dove, *Geotrygon versicolor*, of forest undergrowth; **mountain zebra** a zebra, *Equus zebra*, which has predominantly black stripes and a white belly, found locally on the mountain grasslands of SW Africa.

■ **mountained** *adjective* (*rare*, chiefly *poet.*) (*a*) situated on a mountain; elevated, lofty; †(*b*) heaped mountain-high; †(*c*) obstructed by mountains; (*d*) containing mountains: E17.

mountainboard /ˈmaʊntɪnˌbɔːd/ *noun*. L20.
[ORIGIN from MOUNTAIN *noun*[1] + BOARD *noun*.]
(Proprietary name for) a board resembling a skateboard that is used for riding down mountainsides.
■ **mountainboarder** *noun* a person who rides on a mountainboard L20. **mountainboarding** *noun* the activity of riding on a mountainboard L20.

mountaineer /maʊntɪˈnɪə/ *noun & verb*. E17.
[ORIGIN from MOUNTAIN + -EER.]
▸ **A** *noun*. **1** A native, inhabitant, or frequenter of mountains. E17. ▸**b** More fully ***Mountaineer Indian***. A member of any of various N. American Indian peoples of mountainous regions of Canada, esp. (formerly) the Montagnais or the Naskapi. *obsolete* exc. *hist.* L18. ▸**c** A poorly educated person from a remote rural area. *US colloq.* (*derog.*). L19.
2 FRENCH HISTORY. A member of the Mountain (see MOUNTAIN 4). E19.
3 A person skilled or occupied in mountaineering. M19.
▸ **B** *verb intrans.* Be a mountain-climber, practise mountain-climbing, esp. as a sport. Chiefly as ***mountaineering*** *verbal noun & ppl adjective*. E19.

mountainer /ˈmaʊntɪnə/ *noun*. *rare*. LME.
[ORIGIN from MOUNTAIN + -ER[1].]
†**1** An adherent of a school of thought etc. with a name associated with mountains, as a Montanist. LME–M18.
2 A native or inhabitant of a mountain region. L16.
†**3** = MONTAGNAIS. Only in E17.

mountainet /maʊntɪˈnɛt/ *noun*. Now chiefly *arch.* & *poet.* Also **-ette**. L16.
[ORIGIN from MOUNTAIN + -ET[1], -ETTE.]
A small mountain; a hillock, a mound.

mountainous /ˈmaʊntɪnəs/ *adjective*. LME.
[ORIGIN from MOUNTAIN + -OUS, partly after French *montagneux*.]
†**1** Situated among mountains. *rare*. LME–M17.
2 Characterized by mountains; having many mountains. E17.

> *Holiday Which?* The . . volcanic landscape of the Auvergne, mountainous but not wild.

3 Resembling a mountain or mountains; huge, enormous. E17.

> J. RUSKIN The white edges of the mountainous clouds. M. WARNER She was almost blind, and mountainous.

†**4** Inhabiting mountains; living in a remote mountain region; uncivilized. E17–E18.
†**5** Derived from or characteristic of mountains. L17–E19.

> A. SEWARD Gales, mountainous and maritime, which blow around you delightful retreat.

■ **mountainously** *adverb* E17. **mountainousness** *noun* E17.

mountainward /ˈmaʊntɪnwəd/ *adverb & adjective*. M19.
[ORIGIN from MOUNTAIN + -WARD.]
▸ **A** *adverb*. In the direction of mountains. M19.
▸ **B** *adjective*. Directed towards mountains. L19.
■ Also **mountainwards** *adverb* L19.

mountainy /ˈmaʊntɪni/ *adjective*. L16.
[ORIGIN from MOUNTAIN + -Y[1].]
1 Belonging to or inhabiting a mountain or mountains. L16.
2 Having mountains, mountainous. L16.

mountant /ˈmaʊnt(ə)nt/ *noun*. L19.
[ORIGIN from MOUNT *verb* + -ANT[1], after French *montant*. Cf. MOUNTANT *adjective*.]
An adhesive substance for mounting photographs etc. Also, a material for securing or embedding specimens for microscopy.

mountant /ˈmaʊnt(ə)nt/ *adjective*. Long *rare* or *obsolete*. E16.
[ORIGIN French *montant* pres. pple of *monter* MOUNT *verb*: see -ANT[1]. Cf. MOUNTANT *noun*.]
Mounting, rising.

mountebank /ˈmaʊntɪbaŋk/ *noun & adjective*. L16.
[ORIGIN Italian *montambanco*, *montimbanco*, from *monta in banco* mount (imper.) on a bench: see BANK *noun*[2].]
▸ **A** *noun*. **1** An itinerant quack, esp. a vendor of medicines, appealing to an audience from a raised platform and using stories, juggling, etc., and often the assistance of a professional clown or fool. *obsolete* exc. *hist.* and as passing into sense 2. L16.
2 A false pretender to skill or knowledge, a charlatan; a person incurring contempt or ridicule through efforts to acquire something, esp. social distinction and glamour. L16.
†**3** = MOUNTEBANKERY. M17–E18.
▸ **B** *attrib.* or as *adjective*. Of, pertaining to, or characteristic of a mountebank. E17.

> GLADSTONE Theatrical, not to say charlatan and mountebank, politics.

■ **mountebankism** *noun* (*rare*) mountebankery M17.

mountebank /ˈmaʊntɪbaŋk/ *verb*. E17.
[ORIGIN from the noun.]
†**1** *verb trans.* Prevail over (a person) by persuasion characteristic of a mountebank. E17–E18.
2 *verb intrans. & trans.* with *it*. Behave as a mountebank, play the mountebank. Chiefly as ***mountebanking*** *verbal noun & ppl adjective*. E17.

mountebankery /ˈmaʊntɪbaŋk(ə)ri/ *noun*. E17.
[ORIGIN formed as MOUNTEBANK *verb* + -ERY.]
1 An act characteristic of a mountebank. E17.
2 Behaviour or practice characteristic of a mountebank. L17.

mounted /ˈmaʊntɪd/ *adjective*. L16.
[ORIGIN from MOUNT *verb* + -ED[1].]
1 *gen.* That has mounted or been mounted. L16.
2 Esp. of a member of a police force, an army, etc.: riding or serving on horseback or bicycle. L16.

Mountie /ˈmaʊnti/ *noun*. *colloq.* E20.
[ORIGIN from MOUNTED + -IE.]
1 A member of the Royal Canadian (formerly North West) Mounted Police. E20.
2 A member of a similar police force outside Canada. M20.

mounting /ˈmaʊntɪŋ/ *noun*. LME.
[ORIGIN from MOUNT *verb* + -ING[1].]
1 The action of MOUNT *verb*. LME.
2 A thing serving as a mount, support, or setting. M16. ***Rowland mounting***, ***Rowland's mounting***: see ROWLAND.
†**3** *sing.* & in *pl.* A soldier's outfit or kit. L17–E18.
4 = MUNTIN. E19.
– COMB.: **mounting block** a block of stone from which to mount on horseback.

mounting /ˈmaʊntɪŋ/ *adjective*. M16.
[ORIGIN from MOUNT *verb* + -ING[2].]
1 That mounts. M16.
†**2** HERALDRY. Of a beast of the chase or a reptile: standing on the left hind foot with the forefeet in the air. L17–M18.

†**mountjack** *noun* see MANJAK.

Mountmellick /maʊntˈmɛlɪk/ *adjective*. L19.
[ORIGIN A town in Ireland where orig. made.]
Designating a type of white-work embroidery characterized by raised surfaces.

†**mounture** *noun*. LME.
[ORIGIN Old French *monteüre* (mod. *monture*), from *monter* MOUNT *verb*: see -URE.]
1 A horse or other animal for riding. LME–E17.
2 A raised surface to mount on; a mound, a hillock. LME–E17.
3 A mount or support. L16–L17.
4 = HARNESS *noun* 7. M–L18.

moup /muːp/ *verb*. *Scot.* Also **moop**. E16.
[ORIGIN Prob. var. of MOP *verb*[1].]
1 *verb trans. & intrans.* Nibble on or eat (small pieces of food). Also foll. by *up*. E16.
2 *verb intrans.* Associate *with*. L18.

mourn /mɔːn/ *noun*. Long *rare* exc. *Scot. & dial.* ME.
[ORIGIN from MOURN *verb*.]
Grief, mourning; a murmuring sound expressing grief.

mourn /mɔːn/ *adjective*. Long *arch. rare*. Also **mourne**. ME.
[ORIGIN Perh. from French *morne*, ult. from Germanic, cogn. with MOURN *verb*.]
Sad, mournful.

mourn /mɔːn/ *verb*.
[ORIGIN Old English *murnan* corresp. to Old Saxon *mornan*, *mornian*, Old High German *mornēn* be anxious, Old Norse *morna* pine away, Gothic *maurnan* be anxious.]
▸ **I** *verb intrans.* **1** Feel or show grief or deep regret; lament a misfortune etc. Freq. foll. by *for*, *over*. OE. ▸**b** *spec.* Feel or show grief for a dead person or a person's death (freq. foll. by *for*); show the conventional signs of grief for a period after a person's death, esp. by wearing mourning garments. ME. ▸**c** Utter lamentations *to*. *rare*. M16. ▸**d** Of an animal: pine. *obsolete* exc. *Scot.* L16.

> W. CONGREVE Some Here are, who seem to mourn at our Success! LYTTON Let us not waste them in mourning over blighted hopes. **c** T. GRAY I fruitless mourn to him that cannot hear.

†**2** Yearn *for*, *after*, *to do*; care *for*. OE–LME.
3 (Of a dove) make its natural low murmuring sound (*literary*); (of a person, esp. an infant) make a plaintive sound similar to this, moan, (long *dial.*). E16.

> SHELLEY The dove mourned in the pine, Sad prophetess of sorrows not her own.

▸ **II** *verb trans.* **4** Feel or show grief or deep regret for (a dead person, a person's death, a misfortune, etc.). LME.

> A. N. WILSON Both mourned a rural . . England which was vanishing forever. V. S. NAIPAUL The Parray woman lived on . . mourning her pundit son. B. GILROY They buried her . . . She had many friends to mourn her.

5 Utter in a mournful manner. E17.

> J. STEINBECK 'Where is our happiness gone?' Pablo mourned.

mourne *adjective* var. of MOURN *adjective*.

mourner /ˈmɔːnə/ *noun*[1]. LME.
[ORIGIN from MOURN *verb* + -ER[1].]
1 A person who mourns; a participant in funeral rites, esp. for a friend or relation. LME. ▸**b** A person employed or hired to attend a funeral or to utter formal lamentations for the dead. L17.
2 A penitent. *US*. M19.

mournful /ˈmɔːnfʊl, -f(ə)l/ *adjective*. LME.
[ORIGIN from MOURN *verb* + -FUL.]
1 Expressing mourning or grief; doleful, sad, dismal. LME.

> OUIDA The scene was bleak and mournful. CONAN DOYLE The dog's mournful eye passed from one . . to the other.

2 Full of or oppressed with grief; grieving. Formerly also, making a show of grief. L16.

> J. WESLEY Thou wilt the mournful Spirit chear.

3 Causing mourning or grief; lamentable. *rare*. L16.

> SHAKES. *1 Hen. VI* The treacherous manner of his mournful death.

– SPECIAL COLLOCATIONS: **mournful widow** = *mourning bride* s.v. MOURNING *ppl adjective*.
■ **mournfully** *adverb* M16. **mournfulness** *noun* M17.

mourning /ˈmɔːnɪŋ/ *noun*[1]. OE.
[ORIGIN from MOURN *verb* + -ING[1].]
†**1** Anxiety, worry, apprehension; an instance of this. OE–L15.
2 The action of MOURN *verb*; the expression of grief for a person's death, esp. formally by the wearing of black clothes. Also, the period during which such clothes are worn. ME. ▸**b** An instance of this; a lament; a formal manifestation of grief for a person's death. Now *rare*. LME. ▸**c** *sing.* & (now *Scot. & N. English*) in *pl.* The (esp. black) clothes worn by a mourner. LME.

> TENNYSON Bury the Great Duke To the noise of the mourning of a mighty nation. H. R. LANDON Theatres . . did not reopen until the official period of mourning ended. **b** AV *Gen.* 50:10 And he made a mourning for his father seuen dayes. **c** B. GUEST Mourning was never worn. Death was not a subject for sorrow.

– PHRASES ETC.: ***close mourning***: see CLOSE *adjective*. ***deep mourning***: see DEEP *adjective*. ***half-mourning***: see HALF-. **in mourning** (*a*) grieving for a person's death, wearing (esp. black) clothes as a token of grief for a person's death; (*b*) *slang* (of an eye) blacked in fighting. ***second mourning***: see SECOND *adjective*.
– ATTRIB. & COMB.: In the sense 'used or worn as a token of grief at a person's death', as ***mourning brooch***, ***mourning envelope***, ***mourning jewellery***, ***mourning ring***, etc. Special combs., as **mourning band** (*a*) a strip of black material worn round the sleeve of a coat or a hat in token of bereavement; (*b*) *slang* a dirty edge to a fingernail; **mourning cloak** †(*a*) a cloak worn by a mourner attending a funeral; (*b*) *N. Amer.* = CAMBERWELL BEAUTY; **mourning coach** (chiefly *hist.*) (*a*) a black coach used by a person in mourning; (*b*) a (usu. black) closed carriage for conveying

mourners at a funeral; **mourning paper** notepaper with a black edge; **mourning piece** *US* a pictorial representation of a tomb etc. intended as a memorial of the dead.

mourning /ˈmɔːnɪŋ/ *noun*[2]. Long *hist.* **E16.**
[**ORIGIN** Alt. of French *mortechien* (of unknown origin), after **MOURNING** *noun*[1].]
mourning of the chine, glanders.

mourning /ˈmɔːnɪŋ/ *ppl adjective*. **OE.**
[**ORIGIN** from **MOURN** *verb* + **-ING**[2].]
That mourns.
mourning bride sweet scabious, *Scabiosa atropurpurea*. **mourning dove** a common grey-brown N. American pigeon, *Zenaida macroura*, with a plaintive call. **mourning iris** a cultivated iris, *Iris susiana*, with patches of purple-black on the flowers. **mourning warbler** a warbler, *Geothlypis philadelphia*, of Canada and the north-eastern US, with a grey head and yellow underparts. **mourning widow** (**a**) any of several cultivated plants with dark or dingy flowers; *esp.* dusky cranesbill, *Geranium phaeum*; (**b**) a widow bird.
■ **mourningly** *adverb* **LME.**

mournival /ˈmɔːnɪv(ə)l/ *noun*. **M16.**
[**ORIGIN** French *mornifle* (now) a slap, a taunt, ult. origin unknown.]
1 **CARDS.** A set of four aces, kings, queens, or jacks, in one hand. *obsolete* exc. *hist.* **M16.**
2 *gen.* Any set of four. Long *arch. rare.* **E17.**

mousaka *noun* var. of **MOUSSAKA**.

mouse /maʊs/ *noun*. Pl. **mice** /mʌɪs/, in sense 4 also **mouses**.
[**ORIGIN** Old English *mūs*, pl. *mȳs* = Old Frisian, Old Saxon, Old High German *mūs* (Dutch *muis*, German *Maus*), Old Norse *mús*, from Germanic from Indo-European base repr. also by Latin *mus*, Greek *mus*.]
▸ **I 1** Any of various small rodents, mostly of the family Muridae, usu. having a pointed snout and relatively large ears and eyes, and typically living on seeds and nuts. Also, any of various animals resembling these, as a shrew, a vole. **OE.**
*a **deer mouse**, **field mouse**, **flying mouse**, **harvest mouse**, **house mouse**, **jumping mouse**, **marsupial mouse**, **pocket mouse**, **waltzing mouse**, **white mouse**, etc.*
2 a A term of endearment esp. for a woman or child: darling, pet. Long *rare.* **E16.** ▸**b** Orig., a person or thing likened to a mouse in being small or insignificant. Now, a quiet, timid, or retiring person. **L16.**
a **DICKENS** Not low this morning I hope? You ought *not* to be, dear Mouse. **b** **DOUGLAS CLARK** He was an uncouth bully, she was a mouse, a nonentity.
3 In full ***mouse-colour***. A shade of grey with a yellowish-brown tint. Also, a light dull brown shade esp. of hair. **E17.**
4 Any of various objects regarded as resembling a mouse in shape or appearance; *spec.* (**a**) **NAUTICAL** a small collar made with yarn round a wire or rope and intended to hold a loop etc. in place; (**b**) **COMPUTING** a small hand-held device moved over a flat surface to produce a corresponding movement of a cursor or arrow on a VDU, usu. having fingertip controls for selecting a function or entering a command. **M18.**
Mini-Micro Systems Using the mouse to . . select, a user can bring a 'page' to the top of the screen.
5 A small humped cowrie, *Cypraea mus*, cream with brown markings. **E19.**
6 A small greyish-brown noctuid moth, *Amphipyra tragopoginis*, which scuttles away when disturbed. Also more fully ***mouse moth***. **E19.**
7 A lump or discoloured bruise, *esp.* one on or near the eye and caused by a blow; a black eye. *slang.* **M19.**
▸ **II 8** A muscle. Long *obsolete* exc. as passing into sense 9. **OE.**
9 *spec.* Any of various muscular parts of meat. Long *dial.* **L16.**
– **PHRASES**: **country mouse** *fig.* a person from a rural area unfamiliar with urban life, as distinguished from ***town mouse*** below. **mouse and man** every living thing. ***play cat and mouse***: see **CAT** *noun*[1]. **quiet as a mouse** very quiet. ***strong enough to trot a mouse on***, ***thick enough to trot a mouse on***: see **TROT** *verb*. **town mouse** an inhabitant of a city familiar with urban life, as distinguished from ***country mouse*** above.
– **COMB.**: **mousebird** any of various long-tailed fruit-eating birds of the African genus *Colius* (and family Coliidae), with soft hairlike plumage; also called ***coly***; ***mouse-colour***: see sense 3 above; **mouse-coloured** *adjective* of mouse-colour; **mouse deer** = **CHEVROTAIN**; **mouse-dun** mouse-colour; **mouse-ear** any of various plants with softly hairy leaves resembling a mouse's ear; *esp.* (**a**) (more fully ***mouse-ear hawkweed***) any of several stoloniferous plants of the genus *Pilosella*, allied to the hawkweeds; spec. *P. officinarum*, common in dry grassland; (**b**) (more fully ***mouse-ear chickweed***) any of various small plants of the genus *Cerastium*, of the pink family, with white flowers resembling chickweed; (**c**) a forget-me-not, esp. *Myosotis scorpioides*; (**d**) (more fully ***mouse-ear cress***) thale cress, *Arabidopsis thaliana*; **mouse-eared** *adjective* having an appendage resembling a mouse's ear; ***mouse-eared bat***, any of numerous bats of the genus *Myotis*, esp. the Eurasian *M. myotis*, brown with greyish-white undersides, a rare visitor to Britain; **mouse-fish** (**a**) = ***SARGASSUM fish***; (**b**) a slim, brightly coloured Indo-Pacific fish, *Gonorhynchus gonorhynchus*, which burrows in sand on the seabed; **mouse-hare** = **PIKA**; **mouse-hawk** a bird of prey that catches mice; *spec.* the short-eared owl, *Asio flammeus*; **mousehole** *noun & verb* (**a**) *noun* a hole used or made by a mouse for habitation or passage; a very small hole; (**b**) *verb trans. & intrans.* make a mousehole (in); make a narrow passage or tunnel (through); **mouse-hunt** *noun*[1] (*obsolete* exc. *dial.*) an animal that hunts mice, *spec.* a weasel; **mouse-hunt** *noun*[2] a hunt for a mouse or mice; **mouse-lemur** any of various small Madagascan lemurs of the family Cheirogaleidae, esp. of the genus *Microcebus*; ***mouse moth***: see sense 6 above; **mouse mat** a piece of rigid or slightly resilient material on which a computer mouse is moved; **mouse opossum** = **MANICOU**; **mouse pad** = ***mouse mat*** above; **mouse potato** [after ***COUCH potato***] *slang* a person who spends large amounts of leisure time using a computer; **mouse pox** **VETERINARY MEDICINE** infectious ectromelia; **mousetail** a plant of damp fields, *Myosurus minimus*, of the buttercup family, with a long spike of tiny flowers.
■ **mousekin** *noun* (*rare*) = **MOUSELING** **M19.** **mouselet** *noun* (*rare*) †(**a**) = ***reed dagger*** s.v. **REED** *noun*[1]; (**b**) = **MOUSELING**: **M19.** **mouselike** *adjective* resembling (that of) a mouse; *esp.* very small, very quiet: **E19.** **mouseling** *noun* a young or small mouse **M19.** **mouseship** *noun* (*rare*) **E18.**

mouse /maʊz, -s/ *verb*. **ME.**
[**ORIGIN** from the noun.]
1 *verb intrans.* Esp. of a cat or owl: hunt for or catch mice. **ME.**
†**2** *verb trans.* Esp. of a cat: claw at, tear, bite, (a mouse etc.). **M16–M17.** ▸**b** Pull (a woman) about good-naturedly but roughly. Chiefly in ***touse and mouse***. Only in **17.**
3 *verb intrans.* Search industriously; prowl *about* (as if) in search of something. Also foll. by *around*, *along*. **L16.** ▸**b** *verb trans.* Foll. by *over*: study (a book) industriously. *US.* **E19.** ▸**c** *verb trans.* Search industriously for. Also foll. by *out*. *US.* **M19.**
4 *verb trans.* **NAUTICAL.** Put a mouse (see **MOUSE** *noun* 4) on (a stay); secure (a hook) with a mouse. **M18.**
5 *verb intrans.* **COMPUTING.** Use a mouse to control applications, browse through data, etc. Usu. with adverb (esp. *over*). **L20.**

mouser /ˈmaʊzə, -s-/ *noun*. **LME.**
[**ORIGIN** from **MOUSE** *noun*, *verb* + **-ER**[1].]
An animal that catches mice; *esp.* a cat, an owl.

mousery /ˈmaʊs(ə)ri/ *noun*. **L19.**
[**ORIGIN** from **MOUSE** *noun* + **-ERY**.]
1 A place where mice abound; a colony of mice. **L19.**
2 A place where mice are bred or kept. **M20.**

mousetrap /ˈmaʊstrap/ *noun & verb*. **LME.**
[**ORIGIN** from **MOUSE** *noun* + **TRAP** *noun*[1].]
▸ **A** *noun*. **1** A trap for catching mice; *fig.* a device for enticing a person to destruction or defeat. **LME.**
T. MIDDLETON Like a mouse-trap baited with bacon. **M. R. D. FOOT** The agents taken in the Villa des Bois mousetrap . . were in the noisome Béleyme prison.
2 More fully ***mousetrap cheese***. Cheese for baiting a mousetrap; poor quality cheese. **M17.**
Times Farm cheddar that will dazzle the tastebuds accustomed to factory mousetrap.
3 A very small house. *joc.* **M19.**
▸ **B** *verb trans.* Infl. **-pp-**. Catch (as) in a mousetrap; entice (a person) to destruction or defeat. **L19.**

mousey *noun*, *adjective* vars. of **MOUSY** *noun*, *adjective*.

mousie *noun* var. of **MOUSY** *noun*.

mousle /ˈmaʊz(ə)l/ *verb trans.* Long *arch. rare.* **M17.**
[**ORIGIN** Frequentative of **MOUSE** *verb*: see **-LE**[3]. Cf. **TOUSLE**.]
Pull about roughly.

mousmé /ˈmuːsmeɪ/ *noun*. *hist.* Also **musume** /ˈmuːsʊmeɪ/. **M19.**
[**ORIGIN** Japanese *musume* daughter, girl, from *musu* to be born, to grow + *me* female.]
An unmarried Japanese girl, *esp.* one who serves tea.

mousquetaire /muːskəˈtɛː/ *noun & adjective*. **E18.**
[**ORIGIN** French, from *mousquet* **MUSKET** *noun*[2] + *-aire* **-EER**. Cf. **MUSKETEER**.]
▸ **A** *noun*. **1** *hist.* A French musketeer. **E18.**
2 = ***mousquetaire glove*** below. **L19.**
▸ **B** *attrib.* or as *adjective*. Of an article of clothing: in the style of that of a French musketeer. **M19.**
mousquetaire glove a glove with a long loose wrist.

moussaka /muːˈsɑːkə, muːsəˈkɑː/ *noun*. Also **mousaka**. **M19.**
[**ORIGIN** Ottoman Turkish *mūsaqa*, Turkish *musakka*, from Arabic *musaqqā*; cf. mod. Greek *mousakas*, Albanian, Bulgarian *musaka*, Romanian *musaca*.]
A Greek and eastern Mediterranean baked dish made with minced beef or lamb, aubergine, etc., with a topping of white sauce.

mousse /muːs/ *noun & verb*. **M19.**
[**ORIGIN** French = moss, froth.]
▸ **A** *noun*. **1** The aggregation of tiny bubbles in sparkling wine, as champagne etc. **M19.**
2 A sweet or savoury dish made from a purée or other base stiffened with whipped cream, gelatin, egg whites, etc., and usu. served chilled. Freq. with specifying word. **L19.** ▸**b** In full ***chocolate mousse***. A brown emulsion of seawater and oil produced by the weathering of oil spills and resistant to dispersal; a mass of this substance. **M20.**
chocolate mousse, ***lemon mousse***, ***salmon mousse***, etc.
3 a A frothy preparation for applying to the hair to facilitate setting or colouring. **L20.** ▸**b** A soap or other cosmetic preparation in the form of a soft, light, or aerated gel. **L20.**
▸ **B** *verb trans.* Apply mousse to (hair); set or colour (hair) using mousse. **L20.**

mousseline /ˈmuːsliːn/ *noun*. **L17.**
[**ORIGIN** French: see **MUSLIN**.]
1 French muslin; a dress of this material. Also = ***mousseline-de-laine*** below. **L17.**
2 In full ***mousseline glass***. (A wine glass of) a very thin blown glassware with ornamentation resembling muslin or lace. **M19.**
3 **COOKERY.** In full ***mousseline sauce***. A rich frothy sauce of seasoned or sweetened eggs or cream. **E20.** ▸**b** Any of various dishes with a light frothy texture and usu. prepared by whipping or beating; a mousse. **E20.**
– **COMB.**: **mousseline-de-laine** /dəˈlɛːn/ [French = of wool] a fine dress material of wool or now esp. wool and cotton; **mousseline-de-soie** /dəˈswɑː/ [French = of silk] a thin silk fabric with a texture like that of muslin; ***mousseline glass***: see sense 2 above; ***mousseline sauce***: see sense 3 above.

mousseron /ˈmuːsərɒn/ *noun*. **M17.**
[**ORIGIN** French: see **MUSHROOM** *noun*.]
An edible agaric, *Clitopilus prunulus*, with a flattish white cap, pink gills, and a mealy smell.

mousseux /musø, muːˈsəː/ *adjective & noun*. **E19.**
[**ORIGIN** French, formed as **MOUSSE**.]
▸ **A** *adjective*. Of wine: sparkling. **E19.**
▸ **B** *noun*. Pl. same. A sparkling wine. **M20.**

Moussorgskian *adjective* var. of **MUSSORGSKIAN**.

moustache /məˈstɑːʃ/ *noun*. Also ***must-**. **L16.**
[**ORIGIN** French from Italian *mostaccio*, *mostacchio*: see **MUSTACHIO**.]
1 A (cultivated) growth of hair above the whole or either half (freq. in *pl.*, esp. in ***pair of moustaches***) of a man's lip or extending from this on either side of the lip; a growth of hair above a woman's lip. Also, an artificial strip of hair worn in imitation of this. **L16.**
G. GREENE The old fellow with the moustaches . . was English. **P. THEROUX** I . . left the stubble on my upper lip for a moustache I planned to grow. *transf.*: **A. UTTLEY** They all sipped the milk, and . . wiped the creamy moustaches from their lips.
handlebar moustache, ***Hitler moustache***, ***Kaiser Bill moustache***, ***pencil-line moustache***, ***Zapata moustache***, etc.
2 A growth of hairs or bristles, or a marking resembling a man's moustache, round the mouth of certain animals or birds. **E17.**
3 In full ***moustache monkey***. A W. African guenon, *Cercopithecus cephus*, with a pronounced white bar below the nose. **L18.**
4 ***old moustache*** [translating French *vieille moustache*], an old soldier. *arch.* **E19.**
– **COMB.**: **moustache cup** a cup with a partial cover to protect a moustache during drinking; **moustache-lifter** a device for lifting one's moustache when drinking, sleeping, etc.; ***moustache monkey***: see sense 3 above; **moustache tern** the whiskered tern, *Chlidonias hybridus*.
■ **moustacheless** *adjective* (*rare*) **L19.**

moustached /məˈstɑːʃt/ *adjective*. Also ***must-**. **M19.**
[**ORIGIN** from **MOUSTACHE** + **-ED**[2].]
Having a moustache.
moustached honeyeater, ***moustached tamarin***, ***moustached warbler***, etc. **moustached guenon**, **moustached monkey** = ***MOUSTACHE monkey***.

moustachial /məˈstɑːʃɪəl/ *adjective*. Also ***must-**. **L19.**
[**ORIGIN** from **MOUSTACHE** + **-IAL**.]
Chiefly **ORNITHOLOGY.** Resembling a moustache; *spec.* designating a streak of colour running back from the sides of a bird's beak.

moustachio *noun*, **moustachioed** *adjective* vars. of **MUSTACHIO**, **MUSTACHIOED**.

Mousterian /muːˈstɪərɪən/ *adjective & noun*. Also (now *rare*) **-stier-**. **L19.**
[**ORIGIN** French *moust(i)érien*, from *Le Moustier* a cave in the department of Dordogne, SW France, where remains were found: see **-IAN**.]
ARCHAEOLOGY. ▸ **A** *adjective*. Designating or pertaining to a Middle Palaeolithic culture following the Acheulian and preceding the Aurignacian, typified by flints worked on one side only. **L19.**
▸ **B** *noun*. (A person of) this culture. **E20.**
■ **ˈMousteroid** *adjective* resembling the Mousterian culture **M20.**

†**moustic** *noun*. *rare*. Also **-tique**. **M17–L19.**
[**ORIGIN** French *moustique* by metathesis from Spanish **MOSQUITO**.]
A mosquito.

Moustierian *adjective & noun* see **MOUSTERIAN**.

Moustiers /ˈmuːstɪə, *foreign* mustje/ *noun & adjective*. **M19.**
[**ORIGIN** *Moustiers*-Sainte-Marie (see below).]
(Designating) a type of faience formerly made at Moustiers-Sainte-Marie, a small town in the department of Basses Alpes, SE France.

mousy /ˈmaʊsi/ *noun*. Also **-ey**, **-ie**. **L17.**
[**ORIGIN** Dim. or pet form of **MOUSE** *noun*: see **-Y**[6], **-IE**.]
A child's word for a mouse.

M

mousy /ˈmaʊsi/ *adjective*. Also **-ey**. E19.
[ORIGIN from MOUSE *noun* + -Y¹.]
1 Of or pertaining to mice, mouselike; of the nature or appearance of a mouse; (esp. of the hair) greyish-brown in colour; *fig.* (of a person) shy, quiet, timid, ineffectual. E19.
D. LIVINGSTONE We inhaled.. the heavy mousy smell. M. WEST A small mousy fellow stood up. L. R. BANKS Thin, pale,.. with this mousy hair.
2 Containing mice, infested with mice. L19.
M. SPARK Mrs. Hogg.. climbing to her mousy room.
■ **mousily** *adverb* E20. **mousiness** *noun* L19.

moutan /ˈmuːt(ə)n/ *noun*. E19.
[ORIGIN Chinese *mǔdan* (Wade–Giles *mu-tan*) from *mǔ* male + *dān* red.]
A tree peony, *Paeonia suffruticosa*, with white pink-blotched flowers, native to China and Tibet and the parent of many garden varieties.

mouth /maʊθ/ *noun*.
[ORIGIN Old English *mūþ* = Old Frisian *mūth*, later *mund*, Old Norse *munnr*, *muðr*, Gothic *munþs*, from Germanic from Indo-European, corresp. to Latin *mentum* chin.]
▸ **I** **1 a** The opening in the head of a person or animal through which food is ingested and vocal sounds emitted, closed by the lips; the cavity immediately behind this, containing the teeth and tongue. Also, the opening through which any animal organism ingests food. OE. ▸**b** A person viewed as a consumer of food. Freq. in ***a mouth to feed*** below. M16. ▸**c** A horse's readiness to feel and obey the pressure of the bit (usu. with qualifying adjective, as *bad*, *good*, *hard*, etc.); a horse's ability to be guided by the bit. E18.
a *Encycl. Brit.* The cavity of the mouth forms the commencement of the alimentary canal. B. SCHULBERG Sammy had his mouth full of.. steak sandwich. **b** P. S. BUCK There was only another mouth coming which must be fed.
2 The flesh surrounding the opening of the mouth, considered as a part of the human face; the lips. OE.
TENNYSON And on her mouth A doubtful smile dwelt. DAY LEWIS A small, thin mouth.. and eyes set well apart.
3 a The mouth as the instrument of speech or voice; a person's voice; a person who is speaking. Formerly also, a person's utterance. Now chiefly *rhet.* exc. in ***out of a person's own mouth***, ***hush one's mouth***, and other phrs. below. OE. ▸**b** The barking or baying of a hound etc. Freq. in ***give mouth*** below. L16. ▸**c** Extravagant, insolent, or boastful talk, a propensity for this, (freq. in ***be all mouth***); empty bragging, impudence. M20.
a ADDISON You don't now thunder in the capitol, With all the mouths of Rome to second you. M. PATTISON Learned.. his faith from the mouth of the Roman priest. **b** SHAKES. *Mids. N. D.* My hounds are.. match'd in mouth like bells.
4 A person who speaks on behalf of another or of others; a spokesman. Now *rare* or *obsolete*. M16.
5 A silly person; a dupe; (now chiefly *Scot.*) a noisy person; a talkative or indiscreet person. *slang*. L17.
▸ **II** **6** The place where a river enters the sea; the entrance to a harbour, valley, etc. OE.
LD MACAULAY The castle.. situated at the mouth of Loch Riddan.
7 The opening for filling or emptying something of containing capacity. ME.
SWIFT Wipe the Mouth of the Bottle.
8 a The surface opening of a pit, well, cave, etc. ME. ▸**b** The crater of a volcano. E17.
a SPENSER His deepe devouring jawes Wyde gaped, like the griesly mouth of hell. E. HEMINGWAY Anselmo came out of the mouth of the cave.
9 The aperture in an artificial structure (esp. a beehive) permitting ingress and egress. LME.
Beekeeping The skep should be placed over.. them, mouth downwards, then the bees encouraged to climb.. into it.
10 The opening out of the end of a tube, passage, vessel, etc. L16.
LONGFELLOW The valley.. opens upon the broad plain.. like the mouth of a trumpet.
11 The muzzle of a gun. L16.
SHAKES. *John* Their battering cannon, charged to the mouths.
12 The opening between the forked jaws of a pair of scissors, pincers, etc. L16.
13 The cutting or working edge of a tool. Now chiefly *Scot.* E17.
14 A mouthpiece. Now *rare* or *obsolete*. E17.
15 a A hole in the stock of a plane admitting the passage of shavings. L17. ▸**b** An aperture in a musical pipe for producing the sound. E18.
16 BOTANY. **a** The orifice of a corolla tube. M18. ▸**b** The opening produced by the dehiscence of the spore capsule of mosses. M19.
17 ZOOLOGY. The aperture of a univalve shell. L18.
– PHRASES ETC.: ***a bone in her mouth***: see BONE *noun*. **a mouth to feed** a dependent, *esp.* a child; a person who consumes food but does no useful work in return. ***bad mouth***, ***bad-mouth***: see BAD *adjective*. ***big mouth***: see BIG *adjective*. ***born with a silver spoon in one's mouth***: see SPOON *noun*. **by word of mouth** by spoken words, orally. ***down in the mouth***: see DOWN *adverb*. ***foot-and-mouth (disease)***: see FOOT *noun*. ***from hand to mouth***: see HAND *noun*. ***from the horse's mouth***: see HORSE *noun*. **give mouth** (of a hound etc.) bark or bay vehemently, give tongue. ***hand to mouth***: see HAND *noun*. ***have one's heart in one's mouth***: see HEART *noun*. ***hoof-and-mouth disease***: see HOOF *noun*. ***hush one's mouth***: see HUSH *verb*¹. **in a person's mouth** when said by a person. **keep one's mouth shut** *colloq.* say nothing, not reveal a secret. ***laugh on the other side of one's mouth***, ***laugh on the wrong side of one's mouth***: see LAUGH *verb*. ***look a gift-horse in the mouth***: see HORSE *noun*. ***look as if butter would not melt in one's mouth***: see BUTTER *noun*¹. ***make a person's mouth water***: see WATER *verb*. **make a poor mouth** plead poverty. **make a wry mouth** grimace in disgust, derision, etc. ***motor mouth***: see MOTOR *noun* & *adjective*. ***not open one's mouth***: see OPEN *verb*. ***one's mouth waters***: see WATER *verb*. **out of a person's own mouth** (with ref. to *Luke* 19:22) using a person's actual words. ***plum-in-the-mouth***: see PLUM *noun*. ***poor mouth***: see POOR *adjective*. ***put one's money where one's mouth is***: see MONEY *noun*. **put words into a person's mouth** (**a**) tell a person what to say; (**b**) represent a person as having uttered words previously stated. ***roof of the mouth***: see ROOF *noun* 2C. ***run off at the mouth***: see RUN *verb*. ***run one's mouth***: see RUN *verb*. ***scabby mouth***. ***shoot off one's mouth***: see SHOOT *verb*. **shut a person's mouth** *slang* prevent a person from revealing something. **shut one's mouth** *slang* stop talking (freq. in *imper.*). **stop a person's mouth** block or obstruct a person's mouth (as) with a gag or muzzle; *fig.* = ***shut a person's mouth*** above. ***take the bread out of a person's mouth***: see BREAD *noun*¹. **take the words out of a person's mouth** say what a person was about to say. ***the lion's mouth***: see LION *noun*. ***wash one's mouth out (with soap)***: see WASH *verb*. **with one mouth** (now *rare*) with one voice or one consent; unanimously. ***with open mouth***: see OPEN *adjective*. ***word of mouth***: see WORD *noun*.
– COMB.: **mouth-breather** *N. Amer. slang* a stupid person; **mouth-breeder**, **mouth-brooder** any of various fishes of the families Cichlidae and Ariidae which protect their eggs, and occas. their offspring, by carrying them in the mouth; **mouthfeel** the way an item of food or drink feels in the mouth, *esp.* a sensation of consistency, richness, etc., produced during tasting; **mouth-filling** *adjective* bombastic; **mouth glue** (now *rare*) (**a**) glue, orig. a preparation of isinglass, used by moistening with the tongue; †(**b**) isinglass; **mouth guard** a guard worn to protect the mouth, esp. by rugby players; **mouth harp**: see HARP *noun* 1C; **mouth music** (**a**) = ***mouth organ*** below; (**b**) singing without distinct utterance of words; **mouth organ** (**a**) a musical instrument operated by the mouth; *spec.* a thin rectangular box containing metal reeds, each tuned to a note, moved along the lips while the air is blown or sucked through; a harmonica; *dial.* a Jew's harp; (**b**) ZOOLOGY an organ associated with the mouth, a mouthpart; **mouthpart** ZOOLOGY any of the (usu. paired) organs surrounding the mouth of an insect or other arthropod, adapted for feeding (usu. in *pl.*); **mouth ring** the ring forming the mouth of a bottle; **mouth root** *US* the plant goldthread, *Coptis trifolia*, with an astringent root reputed to cure sore mouths; **mouth rot** an oral canker which may affect snakes in captivity; **mouth-to-mouth** *adjective* involving the contact of one individual's mouth with another's; *spec.* designating a method of artificial respiration in which a person breathes into a patient's lungs through the mouth; **mouthwash** a liquid antiseptic etc. for use in the mouth; *fig.* nonsense, twaddle; **mouth-watering** *adjective* (of food) so appetizing as to make the mouth run with saliva; *fig.* exciting desire or envy.
■ **mouthless** *adjective* OE.

mouth /maʊð, *in sense 4* maʊθ/ *verb*. ME.
[ORIGIN from the noun.]
▸ **I** *verb trans.* **1** Pronounce, speak (words etc.), esp. pompously or with exaggerated clarity; rant, declaim. Also foll. by *out*. ME. ▸**b** Articulate (words etc.) silently or whisperingly; shape (words etc.) without voicing. Freq. with direct speech as obj. M20.
BYRON Who Taught you to mouth that name of 'villain'? A. BIRRELL The pompous high-placed imbecile mouthing his platitudes. **b** M. WOODHOUSE 'Security patrol,' she mouthed, and pulled my head down next to hers. M. GEE He still kept reading.., frowning and sometimes mouthing a word.
2 Put or take (esp. food) in the mouth; seize with the mouth; touch (a thing) with the mouth. LME.
R. KIPLING A wolf.. can.. mouth an egg without breaking it. TED HUGHES He mouthed her teat. L. ERDRICH Tor mouthed a chewed cigar.
3 Train the mouth of (a horse); accustom (a horse) to the use of the bit. M16.
4 Estimate the age of (a sheep) by examining the teeth. *Austral.* & *NZ*. L19.
▸ **II** *verb intrans.* **5** †**a** Speak, talk, (*together*). Only in LME. ▸**b** Pronounce or speak one's words, esp. pompously or with exaggerated clarity; rant, declaim. E17. ▸**c** Articulate words etc. silently or whisperingly; shape words etc. without voicing. Freq. foll. by *at*. M20.
b ADDISON I'll.. mouth at Caesar 'till I shake the Senate. **c** G. GREENE The sergeant mouthed at him; you didn't mention the word death before a child. I. MCEWAN He was waving and mouthing at the stranger to stand aside or sit down.
b mouth off *colloq.* talk loudly, express one's opinions forcefully (also foll. by *at*).
6 Of a river: emerge or be discharged (*in*, *into*). L16.
F. TROLLOPE The Ohio and Chesapeake canal.. there mouths into the Potomac.
†**7** Join lips (*with*); kiss. *derog.* Only in 17.
SHAKES. *Meas. for M.* The Duke.. would mouth with a beggar though she smelt brown bread and garlic.
8 Grimace; make derisive grimaces and noises with the mouth. L18. ▸**b** Foll. by *off*: talk in a loud and boastful or opinionated way. M20.
R. GOWER Retaining her calm demeanour as the mob shouted and mouthed around her. **b** *Racing Post* They ought to get their facts straight before they start mouthing off.
■ **mouthable** *adjective* E19. **mouther** *noun* a person who mouths; *esp.* a person given to boastful or declamatory speech: M18. **mouthingly** *adverb* in a mouthing manner L17.

mouthed /maʊðd/ *adjective*. ME.
[ORIGIN from MOUTH *noun*, *verb*: see -ED², -ED¹.]
1 Having a mouth (of a specified kind); provided with a mouth. ME.
KEATS I.. sat me down, and took a mouthed shell.
big-mouthed, ***close-mouthed***, ***deep-mouthed***, ***foul-mouthed***, ***open-mouthed***, etc.
†**2** Gaping, having the mouth widely opened. L16–M17.
SHAKES. *Sonn.* The wrinkles.. Of mouthed graves will give thee memory.

mouthful /ˈmaʊθfʊl, -f(ə)l/ *noun*. LME.
[ORIGIN from MOUTH *noun* + -FUL.]
1 A quantity that fills the mouth; as much or as many as a mouth will hold or take in at one time. Also, a small quantity (*of* something). LME.
L. WOOLF Trying to induce her to eat a few mouthfuls. *fig.*: *Sunday Times* We do not want a mouthful of elementary caveman's speech.
give someone a mouthful *colloq.* direct an outburst of abusive language at someone. **say a mouthful** *colloq.* (orig. *US*) make a striking or important statement; say something noteworthy.
2 A long or complicated word or phrase to pronounce. *colloq.* L19.
M. GEE Miranda Buchanan-Couttes-Hughes. What a mouthful.

mouthpiece /ˈmaʊθpiːs/ *noun*. L17.
[ORIGIN from MOUTH *noun* + PIECE *noun*.]
1 A piece placed at or forming the mouth of something; *spec.* the part of a telephone into which one speaks. L17.
Which? Putting your hand over the mouthpiece often doesn't work with modern phones.
2 Something placed in the mouth; *spec.* (**a**) the part of a bit crossing a horse's mouth; (**b**) the part of a musical instrument, breathing apparatus, etc., placed between the lips. E18.
D. DELILLO Murray relighted his pipe, sucking impressively at the mouthpiece.
3 The mouth; something representing this. *rare*. M18.
4 A person, organization, etc., expressing views on behalf of another or others, a spokesman; *slang* a lawyer. E19.
P. B. YUILL The Abreys would get legal aid. The state would fix them up with a good mouthpiece. CLIVE JAMES The paper *Soviet Russia*, mouthpiece of the Central Committee, carried the full text. A. S. DALE Father Brown is Chesterton's Mr Pickwick, a mouthpiece for his own wit and wisdom.
5 A protector for the mouth; a respirator; a gumshield. L19.

mouthy /ˈmaʊði/ *adjective*. L16.
[ORIGIN from MOUTH *noun* + -Y¹.]
1 Railing, ranting, bombastic. L16.
Sun (Baltimore) I was kind of a big mouth. I wasn't a bully, just mouthy. J. C. OATES Brigit was always headstrong and mouthy.
2 Of a hound: giving tongue unnecessarily. M20.
■ **mouthily** *adverb* (*rare*) E20. **mouthiness** *noun* (*rare*) M19.

mouton /ˈmuːtɒn/ *noun*. LME.
[ORIGIN formed as MUTTON.]
1 *hist.* A French gold coin, bearing the figure of the Lamb of God, current in the 14th and 15th cents. LME.
2 A spy quartered with an accused person with a view to obtaining incriminating evidence. *arch.* E19.
3 The dressed skin of a sheep cut and dyed to resemble beaver's or seal's fur. M20.

mouton enragé /mutɔ̃ ɑ̃raʒe/ *noun phr.* Pl. **-s -s** (pronounced same). L19.
[ORIGIN French, lit. 'angry sheep'.]
A normally calm person who has become suddenly enraged or violent.

moutonnée /muːˈtɒneɪ/ *adjective*. Also **-éed**. M19.
[ORIGIN from French *moutonnée*, from *mouton* sheep (see MUTTON) + -ED¹.]
PHYSICAL GEOGRAPHY. Of a rock, hill, etc.: rounded like a sheep's back, esp. by glacial action. Cf. ROCHE MOUTONNÉE.

moutons enragés *noun phr.* pl. of MOUTON ENRAGÉ.

mouvementé /muvmɑ̃te/ *adjective*. E20.
[ORIGIN French.]
Animated, agitated, bustling, full of variety; *spec.* (of music) lively.

movable /ˈmuːvəb(ə)l/ *adjective & noun.* Also (now the usual form in LAW) **moveable**. ME.
[ORIGIN Old French *movable*, from *moveir* MOVE verb: see -ABLE.]
▸ **A** *adjective*. **1** Able to be moved; not fixed in one place or posture; changing from one date to another every year. ME. ▸**b** Of property: admitting of being removed or displaced, personal; *esp*. in SCOTS LAW (now *hist.*) designating property which devolved on an executor for division among the next of kin as opp. to the heir-at-law (opp. ***heritable***). LME.

Independent on Sunday This . . cartilage is found in all movable joints.

†**2** Quick or ready in movement; having a tendency to move. LME–E18.
†**3** Changeable, fickle, inconstant. LME–L17.
movable* DOH. *movable feast: see FEAST noun. ***movable kidney*** = FLOATING ***kidney***. ***movable rib*** = FLOATING ***rib***. ***movable sheva***: see SHEVA 1. **movable type** PRINTING (now chiefly *hist.*) individually cast pieces of metal type.
4 SEMITIC GRAMMAR. Of a letter etc.: pronounced, not silent. Opp. ***quiescent***. M19.
▸ **B** *noun*. †**1** ASTRONOMY. In the Ptolemaic system: each of the nine (or ten) concentric revolving spheres of the heavens. Chiefly in ***first movable***, ***highest movable***, = PRIMUM MOBILE. LME–L17.
2 In *pl.* Personal property; property admitting of being removed or displaced; SCOTS LAW (now *hist.*) moveable as opposed to heritable property. LME.
3 An article of furniture that may be removed from the building in which it is placed. Formerly also, a portable personal object. Now usu. in *pl.* E16.
†**4** A thing able to be moved or set in motion; *spec.* a moving part of a watch. E17–L18.
†**5** A person given to movement or change. E–M17.
■ **mova'bility** *noun* LME. **movableness** *noun* LME. **movably** *adverb* (*rare*) in a movable manner; so as to be movable: L17.

movant /ˈmuːv(ə)nt/ *noun & adjective.* US LAW. L19.
[ORIGIN from MOVE verb + -ANT[1].]
(Designating) a person who applies to or petitions a court of law or a judge with the intention of obtaining a ruling in his or her favour.

move /muːv/ *noun*. LME.
[ORIGIN from the verb.]
†**1** A proposal, a motion. *rare*. Only in LME.
2 a A moving or change of position of a piece in chess, draughts, or some other game; a player's turn to move. M17. ▸**b** An action calculated to secure some end; an action which initiates or advances a process or plan, a step, a proceeding; a play in a game. E19. ▸**c** An act of moving from a stationary position; an act of rising from a seated position; a beginning of movement or departure, a movement. E19. ▸**d** A change of place of habitation, employment, etc. M19.

b W. C. WILLIAMS My first move was to try and get a job on one of the newspapers. M. FOOT Months before David Owen made his formal move to leave the Labour Party. G. NAYLOR It challenged me more than other sports, with its infinite possibility of moves. **c** G. GREENE He said nothing and made no move towards the door. L. CODY Mr. Fourie nodded but made no move to shake hands. **d** M. ANGELOU Why are you going to New York? Is he happy about the move?

3 ***on the move***, in the process of moving from one place to another, travelling, moving about; progressing. L18.
– PHRASES: **get a move on** *colloq.* hurry up, bestir oneself. ***key move***: see KEY *noun*[1].

move /muːv/ *verb*. ME.
[ORIGIN Anglo-Norman *mover* = Old French *moveir* (mod. *mouvoir*) from Latin *movere*.]
▸ **I** *verb trans.* **1** Change the place, position, or posture of; take from one place, position, or situation to another; remove, dislodge, displace; put or keep in motion; shake, stir, disturb. Also foll. by adverb or adverbial phr. ME. ▸**b** Take off or lift (a hat, a cap) from one's head, as a gesture of salutation. Now *rare*. L16. ▸**c** Cause (the bowels) to be evacuated. E19. ▸**d** COMMERCE. Find purchasers for; sell a stock of. E20. ▸**e** CRICKET. Cause (the ball) to swerve. M20.

E. HOYLE When you castle your King, do not move the Pawns before him till forced to it. T. HARDY She moved her lips . . but could not speak. J. GALSWORTHY Sir Laurence Mont . . moved his legs with speed. E. WAUGH The lake was moved by strange tides. J. RULE I must have that phone moved out of the hall. J. FOWLES I . . moved the towel with my foot. R. INGALLS Two policemen walked by and moved a couple of the men. M. WARNOCK The essential characteristic of material objects . . that they can be moved about in space. R. P. JHABVALA The date of . . Founder's Day had been moved forward.

2 Affect with emotion; rouse or excite feeling in (a person); perturb; excite *to* anger, laughter, pity, tears, etc.; *spec.* (*a*) affect with tender or compassionate emotion; †(*b*) provoke to anger. ME. ▸†**b** *refl.* Be perturbed; become excited or angry. ME–M16.

A. WILSON His dismal, little rabbit face might have moved any heart less hard than his wife's. V. BROME Passionate language came naturally to Freud whenever he was deeply moved.

3 a Operate as a motive or influence on the will or belief of (a person); prompt, actuate, or impel *to* an action, *to do*; in *pass.*, have an inward prompting, feel inclined. ME. ▸**b** Urge (a person) *to* an action, *to do*; make a proposal or request, now only in a formal manner, to (a monarch, court, Parliament, etc., formerly any person, *for* a thing, *in* or *of* a matter, *that*). *arch.* LME.

a J. H. NEWMAN God moves us in order to make the beginning of duty easy. J. BARZUN It is not commercial greed . . that moves one government official to butter up another. J. M. COETZEE Money . . to buy your way to Africa or Brazil, as the desire moves you. **b** CLARENDON If he desired any thing . . he would move the King in it. W. TEMPLE He would move the Parliament to have my Statue set up. SWIFT I . . begged him . . that he would move the Captains to take some Pity on us.

†**4** Stir up, initiate (strife, war, etc.). ME–L17.
5 Excite or provoke (laughter, an emotion, appetite, etc.) in or *in* a person. LME.

LD MACAULAY All the prejudices, all the exaggerations of both the great parties in the state, moved his scorn.

†**6** Utter (sound), say. LME–L17.
7 †**a** Put forward as a proposal, request, or complaint; propound (a question etc.), mention (a matter). LME–M18. ▸†**b** *spec.* Plead (a cause or suit) in a court; bring (an action at law). LME–M17. ▸**c** Propose (a question, resolution, etc.) formally in a deliberative assembly; propose (now only, in a formal manner) *that*, *to do*. LME.

b S. KINGSLEY I move to strike out the clause condemning the slave traffic. W. S. CHURCHILL The Resolution . . which I now, Mr. Speaker, have the honour to move. H. MACMILLAN The Opposition chose to move a vote of censure on the Government. D. CAUTE I move that we unlock the door and listen to what they have to say.

8 With cognate obj.: dance, perform (a dance). Now *rare*. M17.
▸ **II** *verb intrans.* **9** Go, advance, proceed; pass or be transferred from one place to another; change place, position, or posture; be in motion; exhibit physical activity, stir. Also foll. by adverb or adverbial phr. ME. ▸**b** Advance in time, make progress, develop; grow. LME. ▸**c** Depart, start off. Now *colloq.* LME. ▸**d** Dance. Now *rare*. L16. ▸**e** Bow in salutation. Now *rare*. L16. ▸**f** Of the bowels: evacuate faeces. L17. ▸**g** Change one's place of residence, transfer to other working premises. E18. ▸**h** Transfer a piece from one position to another in the course of a game of chess, draughts, etc. M18. ▸**i** Of merchandise, a stock of goods, an edition or impression of a book, etc.: find purchasers, be sold (*off*). M18. ▸**j** Go quickly. *colloq.* E20. ▸**k** Dance or play music energetically or with a strong rhythm; be exciting or dynamic. *colloq.* M20.

MILTON Whether Heav'n move or Earth Imports not, if thou reck'n right. SWIFT The Door did not move on Hinges, but up and down like a Sash. S. TOWNSEND The shadows moved round from west to east. I. MURDOCH His hands moved weakly, gesturing the judgment away. W. GOLDING I could hear my mother moving about in the kitchen. *Shetland Times* The birds . . have not yet begun to move south. I. MCEWAN They were moving again, picking up speed. **b** *Spectator* The story moves far too slowly, and the long conversations . . are tiresome. G. VIDAL Events moved rapidly. J. GARDAM He says things are going to start moving again here soon. **g** H. E. BATES In the first week of May that year we moved into another house. DAY LEWIS After my mother's death we had moved from Ealing to Notting Hill. L. HELLMAN Dash and I moved to Hollywood for four or five months.

†**10** Speak, treat, or argue *of*. ME–E16.
11 Exist, live; operate; be socially active *in* a particular sphere, *with* particular people etc. LME.

SCOTT FITZGERALD They moved with a fast crowd, all of them young and rich and wild. W. RAEPER MacDonald did not move in the most glittering circles of the day.

12 Take action, act, proceed, (*in*, *against*). LME.

J. LUBBOCK I would urge parents to move in the matter. *Scientific American* Your legal counsel can take care of registration when preparing to move against an infringer.

†**13** Be excited, be stirred up, be initiated. LME–L16.
†**14** Proceed, emanate, originate *from*. LME–L17.
†**15** Incline, tend *to*, *to do*; incline *toward* (a proposal). LME–L17.
16 Be a motive or influence. Now *rare*. L16.
17 Make a request, proposal, or application *for*. M17.
– PHRASES: ***move a peg***: see PEG *noun*[1]. ***move heaven and earth***: see HEAVEN *noun*. **move house** change one's place of residence. **move it** *colloq.* hurry up, bestir oneself, (usu. in *imper.*). **move with the times** be up to date in one's way of thinking or living.
– WITH ADVERBS & PREPOSITIONS IN SPECIALIZED SENSES: **move about** keep changing one's place of residence. **move in** (*a*) take possession of a new place of residence, occupy new premises; begin a new job etc.; take up residence *with*, begin to live *with*; help (a person) to do this; (*b*) ***move in on***, take up residence with (someone), esp. so as to cause inconvenience or annoyance; attach oneself to, put pressure on (a person); become involved in, take control of (a project etc.). **move into** become involved in, take control of; begin investing in. **move on** (*a*) go to a new place; advance, progress; *spec.* move from a place where one is considered by a police officer to have stood too long and to be causing an obstruction; (*b*) (of a police officer) cause or order (a pedestrian) to move on. **move out** leave a place of residence to live elsewhere, end one's occupancy of premises; help (a person) to do this. **move over** adjust one's position in a horizontal direction to make room for another (*lit.* & *fig.*). **move up** adjust one's position in an upward direction to make room for another (*lit.* & *fig.*).
– COMB.: **move-in** the action or an act of moving into a new place of residence or new premises.

moveable *adjective & noun* see MOVABLE.

moveless /ˈmuːvlɪs/ *adjective*. L16.
[ORIGIN from MOVE verb or noun + -LESS.]
Having no movement or motion, not moving, motionless; immovable, fixed.
■ **movelessly** *adverb* E19. **movelessness** *noun* M17.

movement /ˈmuːvm(ə)nt/ *noun*. LME.
[ORIGIN Old French (mod. *mouvement*) from medieval Latin *movimentum*, from Latin *movere* MOVE verb: see -MENT.]
1 The action or process of moving; change of place, position, or posture; passage from one place or situation to another; activity. Also, an instance or kind of this; a particular act or manner of moving. LME. ▸**b** *spec.* A change of position of a military force, *esp.* a change in the disposition of troops etc. for reasons of tactics or strategy. L18. ▸**c** In *pl.* The actions or activities and whereabouts of a person or body of people. M19. ▸**d** The conveying of cattle from one district to another, esp. as prohibited or restricted during an epidemic of cattle disease. M19. ▸**e** The departure or arrival of an aircraft, public transport vehicle, etc. M20.

T. H. HUXLEY Movements of the land . . brought about by the comparatively sudden action of subterranean forces. A. ARONSON Delilah . . cutting off his hair with quick, nervous movements.

b ***pincer movement*** etc.
2 A mental impulse, an act of will. Now *rare*. LME.
3 The moving (as distinguished from the stationary) parts of a mechanism, esp. of a watch or clock; a particular part or group of parts in a mechanism serving some special purpose. L17.
4 a The impression of motion in a work of art; harmonious variety in the lines and ornamentation of a building. L18. ▸**b** Progression of incidents or development of plot in a poem or narrative; the literary quality of giving a sense of progression through abundance of incident etc. or of carrying the interest of a reader through the course of a work. M19.
5 a The manner of transition from note to note or passage to passage in a piece of music; the manner of melodic progression, tempo; rhythmical or accentual character in music or prosody. L18. ▸**b** A principal division of a longer musical work having a distinctive structure of its own and usu. ending with the players ceasing to play. L18.

b *Musical Quarterly* The second movement of Beethoven's Piano Sonata, op. 14, no. 2.

6 a A course or series of actions and endeavours on the part of a body of people towards some special end; a body engaged in such a course. Freq. with specifying word. E19. ▸**b** The way in which events or conditions are moving at a particular time or in a particular sphere; a tendency, a trend. M19.

a ROSEMARY MANNING Two of the most fruitful movements of this century . . : the anti-nuclear movement and feminism. **b** M. ESSLIN The Theatre of the Absurd is thus part of the 'anti-literary' movement of our time.

a ***the Labour movement***, ***the Oxford Movement***, etc.
7 COMMERCE. Activity in the market for some commodity; a rise or fall in price. L19.
8 A motion of the bowels. L19.
– PHRASES: **in the movement** in the direction or according to the tendency prevalent at a particular period or in a particular sphere. **the Movement** (the characteristics of) a group of English poets in the 1950s.
– NOTE: Rare before 18: not in Shakes., AV, or Milton's poetry.

†**movent** *adjective & noun*. M17–M19.
[ORIGIN Latin *movent-* pres. ppl stem of *movere* MOVE verb: see -ENT.]
(A thing) that moves or is moved.

mover /ˈmuːvə/ *noun*. LME.
[ORIGIN from MOVE verb + -ER[1]. In sense 6 from MOVE noun.]
1 A person who or thing which sets or keeps something in motion; a machine or mechanical agency which imparts motion. LME. ▸†**b** A cause (*of*). *rare*. Only in E17.

C. G. WOLFF There is no throughgoing sense of a malevolent God or an indifferent cosmic mover. P. MONETTE He was tireless and unfailing, a mover of mountains.

2 a A person who incites or instigates to action; a promoter or originator of an action etc.; *colloq.* an enterprising person, a person who gets things done. LME. ▸**b** *spec.* A person who moves a proposition or proposal in a deliberative assembly. E17.

a C. THIRLWALL The chief movers of the rebellion made their escape.

3 A person who or thing which moves or is in motion; now chiefly with adjective, an animal which moves in the specified manner or at the specified speed. L16.

M

Horse & Rider He should be a good straight mover.

4 A person who moves from place to place; *spec.* a person migrating westwards. *US.* **E19.**
5 A remover of furniture and other household goods. *N. Amer.* **M19.**

L. EDEL The movers arrive to take her things to the new apartment.

6 *CHESS.* With prefixed numeral: a problem in which the king is to be mated in the specified number of moves. **L19.**

– PHRASES: **first mover** (***a***) = PRIME MOVER 1, 2; (***b***) = PRIMUM MOBILE 1. ***mover and*** *SHAKER*. PRIME MOVER.

movie /ˈmuːvi/ *noun*. Orig. *US.* **E20.**
[ORIGIN Abbreviation of ***moving picture*** s.v. MOVING *adjective*: see -IE.]
1 A motion picture, a film; a showing of a motion picture. **E20.** **2** ***the movies***, motion pictures as an industry, an art form, or a form of entertainment. **E20.** **3** A cinema. *US.* **E20.**
– COMB.: **movie camera** a cine camera; **moviegoer** a frequenter of the cinema, a filmgoer; **movie house** a cinema; **moviemaker** a person who directs or produces cinema films; **movie palace** a (palatial) cinema; **movie star** a celebrated cinema actor or actress, a film star; **Movietone** (proprietary name for) an early system employed in the making of sound films.
■ **moviedom** *noun* = FILMDOM **E20.**

movieola *noun* var. of MOVIOLA.

moving /ˈmuːvɪŋ/ *noun*. **ME.**
[ORIGIN from MOVE *verb* + -ING[1].]
The action of MOVE *verb*; an instance of this; *spec.* (***a***) a change of place, position, or posture; movement; †(***b***) power or faculty of motion; †(***c***) a bodily movement or gesture; (***d***) an inward prompting, an impulse.
– COMB.: **moving day** (***a***) a day of a move to a new residence or new premises; (***b***) *MILITARY* a day on which a regiment or troops are on the march; **moving man** *N. Amer.* = MOVER 5.

moving /ˈmuːvɪŋ/ *adjective*. **LME.**
[ORIGIN from MOVE *verb* + -ING[2].]
1 That moves; that passes from one place, position, or posture to another; capable of moving, able to be moved; not fixed or stationary, in motion. **LME.** ▸**b** *fig.* Unstable, changeful. Now *rare.* **M16.**

E. FITZGERALD The Moving Finger writes; and, having writ, Moves on. R. CROMPTON They leapt on to a moving train. G. LORD In the moving light of the yellow fire. **b** POPE The moving Toyshop of their heart.

2 That moves something or someone; that causes or produces motion; that originates, causes, instigates, or actuates something. **L15.** ▸**b** *spec.* That touches or has power to touch the feelings; affecting. **L16.**

A. PRYCE-JONES He was also the moving spirit of the Shakespeare Society. **b** J. AGATE He was . . in the death scene immensely moving. A. C. BOULT He made a moving speech of thanks to the orchestra.

– SPECIAL COLLOCATIONS & COMB.: **moving average** a succession of averages derived from successive segments (usu. of constant size and overlapping) of a series of values. **moving-coil** *adjective* designating electrical instruments and apparatus in which a coil of wire is suspended in a magnetic field, so that either the coil moves when a current flows through it or else a current is generated when the coil is caused to move. **moving-iron** *adjective* designating electrical instruments and apparatus in which a current in a fixed coil of wire causes the movement of a piece of iron within the coil. **moving map** a map carried in a ship, aircraft, etc., which is displayed so that as the craft moves its position always corresponds to a fixed point in the middle of the map. **moving pavement** a footway arranged as a conveyor belt for the carrying of passengers. **moving picture** †(***a***) a painting, drawing, etc., in which objects move or appear to move; (***b***) a continuous picture of events obtained by projecting a sequence of photographs taken at very short intervals, a motion picture, a cinematographic film. **moving plant** = ***telegraph plant*** s.v. TELEGRAPH *noun*. **moving sidewalk** *N. Amer.* = ***moving pavement*** above. **moving stair**, **moving staircase** an escalator. **moving-target** *adjective* designating radar apparatus or techniques that indicate only those objects which are moving relative to the transmitter.
■ **movingly** *adverb* in a moving, touching, or affecting manner **L16.** **movingness** *noun* the quality of being moving, touching, or affecting **M17.**

Moviola /muːvɪˈəʊlə/ *noun*. Also **movieola**. **E20.**
[ORIGIN from MOVIE + -OLA.]
(Proprietary name for) a device whereby the picture and sound of a cinematographic film are reproduced on a small scale so that the film may be edited or checked.

mow /maʊ/ *noun*[1]. Now chiefly *N. Amer. & dial.*
[ORIGIN Old English *mūga*, *mūha*, *mūwa* corresp. to Old Norse *múgi* swathe, (also *múgr*) crowd, of unknown origin.]
1 A stack of hay, corn, beans, peas, etc.; a heap of grain or hay in a barn. **OE.**
†**2** A heap, a pile; a mound, a hillock. **LME–L17.**
3 A place in a barn where hay or corn is heaped up. **M18.**
– COMB.: **mowburn** *verb intrans.* become mowburnt; **mowburnt** *adjective* (of hay, corn, etc.) spoilt by being stacked damp or too green; **mowhay** *dial.* a rickyard.

mow /məʊ, maʊ/ *noun*[2]. **ME.**
[ORIGIN Prob. from Old French *moe*, (also mod.) *moue*) pouting, †mouth, †lip, or Middle Dutch *mouwe* (perh. the source of the French).]
1 A grimace; *esp.* a derisive grimace. Now *arch. & literary.* **ME.** ***mops and mows***.
2 A jest. Long only *pred.* & after prepositions in *pl.*, jest (as opp. to earnest), a laughing matter, (usu. in neg. contexts). *Scot.* **LME.**

mow /məʊ/ *noun*[3]. **E19.**
[ORIGIN from MOW *verb*[1].]
†**1** A sweeping stroke of a scythe. Only in **E19.**
2 *CRICKET.* A sweeping stroke to leg. **E20.**
3 An act or instance of mowing something, esp. a lawn. **L20.**

mow /məʊ/ *verb*[1]. Pa. pple **mowed**, **mown** /məʊn/.
[ORIGIN Old English *māwan* (strong) corresp. to (weak) Old Frisian *mēa*, Middle Dutch *maeien* (Dutch *maaien*), Old High German *māen* (German *mähen*), from Germanic base also of MEAD *noun*[2], MEADOW.]
1 *verb trans. & intrans.* Cut down (grass, corn, etc.) with a scythe or (now) a machine (also foll. by *down*); cut down the produce of (a field etc.) in this way. **OE.**

T. F. POWYS A field of rich clover ready to be mown. J. GARDAM We'll mow all day and if need be through the night. M. ANGELOU Neighbours spoke to each other as they mowed their lawns.

2 *transf. & fig.* **a** *verb trans. & (rare) intrans.* Cut with a sweeping stroke like that of a scythe; destroy or kill indiscriminately or in great numbers. Also, defeat comprehensively. Now usu. foll. by *down*. **ME.** ▸**b** *verb trans.* Create (a passage), make (one's way), by indiscriminate killing. **M17.** ▸**c** *verb trans.* Shave. *joc.* Now *rare.* **M17.** ▸**d** *verb trans. & intrans. CRICKET.* Hit (the ball) to leg with a sweeping stroke. **M19.**

a POPE 'Tis not in me . . To mow whole Troops, and make whole Armies fly. *Daily Mirror* S.S. troops waited to mow them down with machine-guns. *Independent* A suspected gang member . . was himself mown down by two gunmen.

■ **mowable** *adjective* (now *rare*) **E17.**

mow /maʊ/ *verb*[2] *trans.* Now *dial.* **ME.**
[ORIGIN from MOW *noun*[1].]
Put (hay, corn, etc.) in stacks or heaps. Also foll. by *up*.

mow /məʊ, maʊ/ *verb*[3] *intrans.* Now *arch. & literary.* **ME.**
[ORIGIN from MOW *noun*[2].]
Make mouths, grimace. Freq. in collocation with *mock*, *mop*.

M. LOWRY Yvonne Griffaton's father . . came to mock and mow at her. W. H. AUDEN Mopped and mowed at, as their train worms through a tunnel.

mower /ˈməʊə/ *noun*. **ME.**
[ORIGIN from MOW *verb*[1] + -ER[1].]
1 A person who mows grass etc. **ME.**
mower's mite a harvest mite.
2 A mowing machine; a lawnmower. **M19.**

mowing /ˈməʊɪŋ/ *noun*. **LME.**
[ORIGIN from MOW *verb*[1] + -ING[1].]
1 The action of MOW *verb*[1]. **LME.**
2 The quantity of grass etc. cut at one time; in *pl.*, grass etc. removed by mowing. **M18.**
3 Land on which grass is grown for hay; a hayfield. *US.* **M18.**
– COMB.: **mowing machine** an agricultural machine for mowing grass etc.; ***mowing-machine bird***, the grasshopper warbler, *Locustella naevia*.

mown *verb pa. pple*: see MOW *verb*[1].

MOX /mɒks/ *abbreviation*.
Mixed oxide (denoting a type of nuclear fuel used in breeder reactors, consisting of uranium and plutonium oxides).

moxa /ˈmɒksə/ *noun*[1]. **L17.**
[ORIGIN Japanese *mogusa* (disyllabic) contr. of *moe kusa* burning herb.]
1 A soft wool prepared from down from the young leaves of any of various Asiatic plants, as *Artemisia indica* or *Crossostephium artemisioides*, used esp. in Eastern medicine in the form of a cone or cylinder for burning next to the skin as a counterirritant, cauterizing agent, etc. Also, a plant so used. **L17.**
2 Any substance prepared for moxibustion. **M19.**
■ **moxiˈbustion** *noun* [blend with COMBUSTION] the therapeutic use of burning moxa or another substance next to the skin **M19.**

†**Moxa** *adjective & noun*[2] var. of MOCHICA.

moxie /ˈmɒksi/ *noun*. *N. Amer. slang.* **M20.**
[ORIGIN *Moxie*, proprietary name for a soft drink.]
Courage, force of character; energy; ingenuity, wit.

moya /mɔɪˈɑː/ *interjection*. *Irish.* Also **mauryah** /mɔːˈjɑː/ & other vars. **E20.**
[ORIGIN Irish *mar dh'eadh* as if it were so.]
Expr. deep scepticism.

moyen /ˈmɔɪən/ *noun*[1]. Long *obsolete* exc. *Scot.* **LME.**
[ORIGIN Old French *moien* (mod. *moyen*) use as noun of adjective: see MEAN *adjective*[2]. Cf. MEAN *noun*[1].]
†**1** A mediator, an intermediary. **LME–E17.**
†**2** A means, an agency; *sing.* & in *pl.*, means, resources. **LME–L17.**
3 *sing.* & in *pl.* Mediation, intercession; exercise of influence. **LME.**
†**4** Instrumentality. **LME–E18.**
†**5** A middle condition or quality; a mean. **L15–L16.**

†**moyen** *noun*[2]. **E16–E19.**
[ORIGIN Old French *moienne* use as noun of fem. of *moien*: see MOYEN *noun*[1].]
A kind of cannon of middle size.

moyen-âge /mwɑːjənˈɑːʒ/ *adjective*. Also **moyen-age** & with cap. initials. **M19.**
[ORIGIN French = the Middle Ages.]
Of or pertaining to the Middle Ages, medieval.

Moygashel /ˈmɔɪɡəʃ(ə)l/ *noun*. **M20.**
[ORIGIN A village in Co. Tyrone, N. Ireland.]
(Proprietary name for) a type of Irish linen.

moz *noun & verb* var. of MOZZ.

Mozambican /məʊzamˈbiːk(ə)n/ *adjective & noun*. Also **-quan**. **L19.**
[ORIGIN from *Mozambique* (see below) + -AN.]
▸ **A** *adjective*. Of or pertaining to Mozambique, a country on the east coast of Africa (formerly a Portuguese colony). **L19.**
▸ **B** *noun*. A native or inhabitant of Mozambique. **L20.**
■ **Mozambiquer** *noun* (now *rare*) = MOZAMBICAN *noun* **E19.**

Mozarab /məʊˈzarəb/ *noun*. **E17.**
[ORIGIN Spanish *mozárabe* from Arabic *mustaʻrib* lit. 'making oneself an Arab'.]
In Muslim Spain: a person allowed to practise Christianity (on condition of owning allegiance to the Moorish king).

Mozarabic /məʊˈzarəbɪk/ *adjective*. **E17.**
[ORIGIN formed as MOZARAB + -IC.]
Of or pertaining to the Mozarabs, or Christianity in Muslim Spain.

Mozartian /məʊtˈsɑːtɪən/ *adjective & noun*. Also **-ean**. **M19.**
[ORIGIN from *Mozart* (see below) + -IAN, -EAN.]
▸ **A** *adjective*. Of, pertaining to, or characteristic of the Austrian composer Wolfgang Amadeus Mozart (1756–91) or his music. **M19.**
▸ **B** *noun*. An interpreter, student, or admirer of Mozart or his music. **M20.**
■ **Mozartianly** *adverb* in the manner or style of or appropriate to Mozart's music **E20.**

moze /məʊz/ *verb trans.* Now *rare* or *obsolete*. **E16.**
[ORIGIN Perh. from MOSS *noun*.]
= GIG *verb*[1].

mozetta *noun* var. of MOZZETTA.

mozo /ˈmoθo, ˈməʊzəʊ/ *noun*. Pl. **-os** /-ɒs, -əʊz/. **E19.**
[ORIGIN Spanish, lit. 'boy'.]
In Spain and Spanish-speaking countries: a male servant or attendant, a groom, a labourer; *spec.* a bullfighter's attendant.

mozz /mɒz/ *noun & verb*. *Austral. colloq.* Also **moz**. **E20.**
[ORIGIN Abbreviation of MOZZLE.]
▸ **A** *noun*. An inconvenience, a jinx, a malign influence. Chiefly in ***put the mozz on***, = sense B. below. **E20.**
▸ **B** *verb trans.* Inconvenience, jinx, deter. **M20.**

mozzarella /mɒtsəˈrɛlə/ *noun*. **E20.**
[ORIGIN Italian, dim. of *mozza* a kind of cheese, from *mozzare* cut off: see + -ELLA.]
More fully ***mozzarella cheese***. A white Italian cheese originally made in the Naples area from buffalo milk.

mozzetta /məʊˈzɛtə, -ˈtsɛtə/ *noun*. Also **mozetta**. **E17.**
[ORIGIN Italian, aphet. from *almozzetta*, from medieval Latin *almucia* AMICE *noun*[1] + *-etta* -ET[1].]
ROMAN CATHOLIC CHURCH. A short cape with a hood, worn by the Pope, cardinals, and some other ecclesiastics.

mozzie *noun* var. of MOSSIE *noun*[2].

mozzle /ˈmɒz(ə)l/ *noun*. *Austral. colloq.* **L19.**
[ORIGIN Hebrew *mazzāl* star, luck.]
Luck, fortune.

MP *abbreviation*[1].
1 Megapixel(s).
2 Member of Parliament.
3 Military police(man).

mp *abbreviation*[2].
MUSIC. Mezzo piano.

m.p. *abbreviation*.
Melting point.

MPC *abbreviation*.
Multimedia personal computer.

MPD *abbreviation*.
Multiple personality disorder

MPEG /ˈɛmpɛɡ/ *abbreviation*.
COMPUTING. Motion Picture Experts Group, denoting an international standard for encoding and compressing video images.

m.p.g. *abbreviation.*
Miles per gallon.

mph *abbreviation.* Also **m.p.h.**
Miles per hour.

mph /(ə)mh/ *interjection.* **L19.**
[ORIGIN Natural exclam. Cf. UMPH *interjection.*]
Expr. disapproval, doubt, or qualified approval.

M.Phil. *abbreviation.*
Master of Philosophy.

mpingo /(ə)mˈpɪŋɡəʊ/ *noun.* Pl. **-os.** **E20.**
[ORIGIN Kiswahili.]
An E. African leguminous tree, *Dalbergia melanoxylon*, whose dense black wood is used for carving and in making musical (esp. woodwind) instruments; the wood of this tree. Also called ***African blackwood***.

Mpongwe /(ə)mˈpɒŋɡweɪ/ *noun & adjective.* **M19.**
[ORIGIN Bantu.]
▸ **A** *noun.* Pl. **-s**, same. A member of a people living in Gabon, esp. in the region of the Gabon estuary; the Bantu language of this people. **M19.**
▸ **B** *attrib.* or as *adjective.* Of or pertaining to the Mpongwe or their language. **M19.**

MPS *abbreviation.*
hist. Member of the Pharmaceutical Society.

MP3 *abbreviation.*
[ORIGIN from *MPEG-1 Audio Layer-3* (full name of the format).]
COMPUTING. A format for compressing digital audio files.

MPV *abbreviation.*
Multi-purpose vehicle, a large van-like car.

MR *abbreviation.*
Master of the Rolls.

Mr /ˈmɪstə/ *noun.* Also **Mr.** (point). Pl. served by MESSRS. **LME.**
[ORIGIN Abbreviation of MASTER *noun*[1], (now) MISTER *noun*[2].]
1 Used as a title preceding the name of any man without a higher or honorific or professional title (formerly below the rank of knight and above some undefined level of social status, the limit of which has been continually lowered) or preceding any of various designations of office. **LME.** ▸**b** Used with following adjective or noun to form a name for a man who is an exemplar or type of the class or quality specified or who is closely associated with the thing specified. **E19.** ▸**c** A person addressed as 'Mr'; the word 'Mr' as a title (in correspondence). **E19.**

> *Times* Mr. Justice Foster had agreed to resume the hearing of the case. *Guardian* Mr Heath . . made his reputation at the Board of Trade. M. FOOT A reply given by the new Speaker, Mr Speaker Weatherill. **b** *Health & Strength* In that first contest there was only one Mr Universe title to win. *Listener* In 1953, Ford, Mr Industry himself, commissioned the first geodesic dome. J. WAMBAUGH I been too nice to you . . . Well, no more Mr. Nice Guy!

Mr Chairman, ***Mr Mayor***, ***Mr President***, etc.
†**2** *gen.* = MASTER *noun*[1]. **M16–L17.**
– COMB.: **Mr Big** the head of an organization of criminals; any important man; ***Mr Chad***: see CHAD *noun*[1]; **Mr Charley**, **Mr Charlie** *derog.* a black man; **Mr Clean** an honourable or incorruptible politician; ***Mr Fixit***: see FIXIT 1; ***Mr Lo***: see LO *noun*; ***Mr Next-Door***: see ***next door*** s.v. NEXT *adjective*; **Mr Right** the man who would make the ideal husband for a particular person, one's destined husband; ***Mr Speaker***: see SPEAKER 2a.

MRA *abbreviation.*
Moral Re-Armament.

MRBM *abbreviation.*
Medium-range ballistic missile.

MRC *abbreviation.*
Medical Research Council.

MRCA *abbreviation.*
Multi-role combat aircraft.

MRE *abbreviation.*
Meal ready to eat (a precooked and prepackaged meal used by US military personnel).

MRI *abbreviation.*
Magnetic resonance imaging.

mridangam /mrɪˈdaŋəm/ *noun.* Also **-ga** /-ɡə/. **L19.**
[ORIGIN Tamil *mṛdaṅgam* and Sanskrit *mṛdaṅga*.]
A double-headed barrel-shaped drum, once made of clay, now usually of wood, with one head larger than the other, used in southern Indian music. Cf. MADAL.

MRM *abbreviation.*
Mechanically recovered meat.

mRNA *abbreviation.*
BIOCHEMISTRY. Messenger RNA.

Mrs /ˈmɪsɪz, -s/ *noun.* Also **Mrs.** (point). Pl. same (also served by MESDAMES). **L15.**
[ORIGIN Abbreviation of MISTRESS *noun*. Cf. MISSUS.]
1 Used as a title preceding the surname of a married woman without a higher or honorific or professional title, sometimes with the forename(s) of herself or (now less frequently) her husband intervening (formerly distinctive of gentlewomen); a woman so designated. **L15.** ▸**b** Used as a title preceding the name of an unmarried lady or girl, Miss. *obsolete* exc. *hist.* **M16.** ▸**c** *ellipt.* The wife of the person speaking, addressed, or referred to; a person's wife; freq. as ***the Mrs.*** *colloq.* **L16.**

> R. H. BARHAM Mrs. John Ingoldsby at the table. *Daily Telegraph* Mrs. Anne Kerr, Labour M.P. for Rochester and Chatham. *Church Times* Cakes Mrs Beeton would have been proud of. **c** R. BROOKE He passed through Fiji lately . . Mrs, I gather, is not with him. F. ASTAIRE I walked back with him to his box, where his Mrs. was waiting. E. BULLINS I'll have the Mrs. call the doctor as soon as I get home.

†**2** *gen.* = MISTRESS *noun.* **E16–L17.**
– COMB.: ***Mrs Grundy***; ***Mrs Justice***: see JUSTICE *noun*; ***Mrs Lo***: see LO *noun*; **Mrs Mop(p)** (a nickname for) a charwoman; the typical charwoman; ***Mrs Next-Door***: see ***next door*** s.v. NEXT *adjective*; **Mrs Thing**: used in place of a married woman's name of which the speaker is uncertain.

MRSA *abbreviation.*
Methicillin-resistant *Staphylococcus aureus*, a strain of bacterium resistant to antibiotics.

MS *abbreviation.*
1 Manuscript.
2 Master of Science.
3 Master of Surgery.
4 Mississippi.
5 Motor ship.
6 Multiple sclerosis.

Ms /mɪz/ *noun.* Also **Ms.** (point). Pl. **Mses**, **Mss**, /ˈmɪzɪz/. **E20.**
[ORIGIN Contr. of MRS, MISS *noun*[2]. Cf. MIZ 2.]
Used as a title preceding the surname of any woman regardless of her marital status, sometimes with her forename(s) intervening; a woman so designated.

msasa /(ə)mˈsɑːsə/ *noun.* **E20.**
[ORIGIN Shona *musasa*.]
A leguminous tree, *Brachystegia spiciformis*, of central Africa (esp. Zimbabwe), with fragrant white flowers and pinnate leaves which are crimson and bronze in spring.

MSB *abbreviation.*
COMPUTING. Most significant bit.

MSC *abbreviation.*
Manpower Services Commission.

M.Sc. *abbreviation.*
Master of Science.

MS-DOS /ɛmɛsˈdɒs/ *abbreviation.*
COMPUTING. Microsoft disk operating system (a proprietary name).

Mses, **Mss** *nouns pl.* see Ms.

MSF *abbreviation.*
Manufacturing, Science, and Finance (Union).

MSG *abbreviation.*
Monosodium glutamate.

Msgr *abbreviation.*
French *Monseigneur* Monsignor.

MSH *abbreviation.*
Melanocyte-stimulating hormone.

MSP *abbreviation.*
Member of the Scottish Parliament.

MSS /ɛmˈɛsɪz/ *abbreviation.*
Manuscripts.

MST *abbreviation. N. Amer.*
Mountain Standard Time.

M.St. *abbreviation.*
Master of Studies.

Mswahili *noun sing.* see SWAHILI.

MSY *abbreviation.*
Maximum sustainable yield.

MT *abbreviation*[1].
1 Machine translation.
2 Mechanical transport.
3 Montana.
4 Motor transport.

Mt *abbreviation*[2].
Mount.

Mt *symbol.*
CHEMISTRY. Meitnerium.

MTB *abbreviation.*
1 Motor torpedo boat.
2 Mountain bike.

MTBF *abbreviation.*
Mean time between failures, a measure of the reliability of a device or system.

M.Tech. *abbreviation.*
Master of Technology.

mtepe /(ə)mˈteɪpeɪ/ *noun.* **E19.**
[ORIGIN Kiswahili.]
A sailing craft characterized by a square matting sail, used on the east coast of Africa.

M-theory /ˈɛmθɪəri/ *noun.* **L20.**
[ORIGIN from M, M (app. representing MEMBRANE) + THEORY.]
PARTICLE PHYSICS. A unified theory involving branes that subsumes eleven-dimensional supergravity and the five ten-dimensional superstring theories.

MTV *abbreviation.*
Music Television, a proprietary name for a cable and satellite television channel broadcasting popular music and promotional videos.

mu /mjuː/ *noun*[1]. **ME.**
[ORIGIN Greek.]
1 The twelfth letter (M, μ) of the Greek alphabet. **ME.**
2 Pl. same. One micrometre (micron). Usu. denoted by μ. **L19.**
3 ELECTRONICS. The amplification factor of a valve. **E20.**
– COMB. **mu-meson** (*obsolete* exc. *hist.*) = MUON.

mu *noun*[2] var. of MOU.

†**mucaginous** *adjective.* **M17–E19.**
[ORIGIN from medieval Latin *mucagin-*, *mucago*, formed as MUCUS, + -OUS.]
= MUCILAGINOUS.

mucate /ˈmjuːkeɪt/ *noun.* **E19.**
[ORIGIN from MUCIC + -ATE[1].]
CHEMISTRY. A salt or ester of mucic acid.

mucedinous /mjuːˈsiːdɪnəs/ *adjective.* **M19.**
[ORIGIN from mod. Latin *mucedin-*, *mucedo* mould (from *mucere* be mouldy) + -OUS.]
BOTANY. Of the nature of or resembling mould.

much /mʌtʃ/ *adjective* (in mod. usage also classed as a *determiner*), *pronoun, noun, & adverb.* Compar. served by MORE *adjective* etc., superl. by MOST. **ME.**
[ORIGIN Abbreviation of reflex of Old English *mićel*: see MUCKLE.]
▸ **A** *adjective.* **1** Great in size, bulk, amount, or degree. Long *obsolete* exc. in names of English villages, as ***Much Wenlock***. **ME.**

> SWIFT I have heard them say, 'Much talkers, little walkers'.

2 A great quantity or amount of, existing or present in great quantity. (Preceding the noun without the indef. article *a(n)*; *arch.* after the def. article *the*). **ME.** ▸†**b** A great number of. **ME–E17.** ▸**c** Many. Now chiefly *US dial.* **M16.**

> R. KIPLING A pale yellow sun . . showed the much dirt of the place. A. P. HERBERT There wasn't much rain here—only a drizzle. W. RAEPER Edward Lear's first *Book of Nonsense* had been published, with much acclaim. *iron.*: *Observer* They went on in the same way . . . Much good did it do them. **b** AV *Num.* 20:20 And Edom came out against him with much people.

▸ **B** *pronoun & noun.* A great deal, a great quantity, (*of*); *pred.* something or someone great or important. **ME.**

> D. EDEN I won't say you've got Dietrich's legs, ducky, but they don't miss by much. K. AMIS There may not be much to be said for Charlie-boy here. G. CHARLES Though he dazzled me at the beginning, I knew after a time that he wasn't much really. C. SAGAN We know rather much about the past and almost nothing about the future. R. ELLMANN Much of his time went into reading in other fields.

▸ **C** *adverb.* **1** In a great degree; to a great extent; greatly. (Qualifying a verb or the whole predication; comparatives or words implying comparison; occas. with the intervention of *the* before a comparative; (*obsolete* exc. *US dial.*) positive or uncompared adjectives and adverbs.) **ME.**

> J. CONRAD His mother wept very much after his disappearance. C. P. SNOW I suppose he was much the better trained. W. FAULKNER 'Been much busy?' Earl says. 'Not much,' I says. J. STEINBECK I know this land ain't much good. B. PYM This shabby part of London, so very much the 'wrong' side of Victoria Station. A. S. BYATT She thought Julia much changed. P. KAVANAGH Her daughter . . cut off the woman's disquisition on actors much to Patrick's delight. S. HASTINGS With two best-sellers in . . four years, Nancy was much in demand. *comb.*: SOUTHEY This so much-to-be-admired eternal Providence. *Irish Times* This highly exclusive, much-sought-after . . cul-de-sac. A. BROOKNER I am getting some much needed exercise.

2 Very nearly, approximately. Chiefly qualifying expressions denoting similarity. **M16.**

> MILTON The Booke . . which came out . . much about the time. M. KEANE Sylvester returned to his party which he found much as when he had left it. C. MCCULLOUGH He and his sister were much of a height.

3 For a large part of one's time. **L18.**

> C. DARWIN I have not been much away from home of late.

– PHRASES: ***a bit much***: see BIT *noun*[2]. ***as much***: see AS *adverb* etc. ***as much as the traffic will bear***, ***as much as the traffic will stand***: see TRAFFIC *noun* 1. **by much** by a great deal. ***how much***: see HOW *adverb*. ***know too much***: see KNOW *verb*. ***leave much to be desired***: see LEAVE *verb*[1]. ***make much of***: see MAKE *verb*. **much as** even though, however much. ***much cry and little wool***: see CRY *noun*. ***much less***: see LESS *adjective* etc. ***much obliged***: see OBLIGE *verb*. **much of a —** (in neg. contexts) a great —, a — of any noteworthy quality, a — in any great degree. ***much of a*** MUCHNESS. ***much the same***: see SAME *adjective*. ***much to seek***: see SEEK *verb*. **not come to much** have little success. **not much** *colloq.* certainly not, far from it; *iron.* certainly, very much. ***not much in it***: see IN *preposition*. **not much on** *colloq.* not useful or effective for (a purpose); no good at (something). **not much to look at** of insignificant or unattractive appearance. ***not much wiser***: see WISE *adjective & noun*[2]. **not up to much** *colloq.* not very good, of a low standard. ***pretty much***: see

PRETTY *adverb*. **say much for**: see SAY *verb*[1]. **see much of**: see SEE *verb*. **set much by**: see SET *verb*[1]. **so much**: see SO *adverb* etc. **think it much**, **think much** *arch.* regard as important or onerous (*to do*). **think much of**: see THINK *verb*[2]. **THIS much**. **TOO much**. **without so much as a by your leave**: see LEAVE *noun*[1].
– COMB.: †**muchwhat** *adverb* greatly; nearly, almost; to a considerable degree.

muchacha /mʊˈtʃɑːtʃə/ *noun*. E19.
[ORIGIN Spanish: fem. of MUCHACHO.]
In Spain and Spanish-speaking countries: a girl, a young woman; a female servant.

muchacho /mʊˈtʃɑːtʃəʊ/ *noun*. Pl. **-os**. L16.
[ORIGIN Spanish.]
In Spain and Spanish-speaking countries: a boy, a young man; a male servant.

muchi /ˈmuːtʃi/ *noun*. Also **moocha** /ˈmuːtʃə/. L19.
[ORIGIN Zulu *umutsha*.]
A loincloth made of hide or animal tails worn as traditional dress in South Africa.

muchly /ˈmʌtʃli/ *adverb*. Now *joc.* E17.
[ORIGIN from MUCH *adjective* + -LY[2].]
Much, exceedingly.

muchness /ˈmʌtʃnɪs/ *noun*. LME.
[ORIGIN from MUCH *adjective* + -NESS.]
†**1** Large size or bulk. Also, size, magnitude (large or small). LME–M17.
2 Greatness in quantity, number, or degree. LME. ▸**b** An instance of this. Now *rare*. L17.
– PHRASES: **much of a muchness** *colloq.* much of the same importance or value; very much the same or alike.

mucho /ˈmʊtʃəʊ, ˈmʌ-/ *adjective (determiner) & adverb*. *joc. & colloq.* L19.
[ORIGIN Spanish = much, many.]
▸ **A** *adjective*. Much, many. L19.

H. MASTERS That caused me mucho problems later on.

▸ **B** *adverb*. Very. L19.

www.fictionpress.com The way the book explains it is mucho confusing.

muci- /ˈmjuːsi/ *combining form* of MUCUS: see -I-. Cf. MUCO-.
■ **muciˈcarmine** *noun* (HISTOLOGY) a specific stain for mucin, consisting of carmine and aluminium chloride in water L19. **muˈciferous** *adjective* secreting or conveying mucus M19. **mucigel** *noun* (BIOCHEMISTRY) a mucilaginous gel secreted by plant roots and usu. associated with large numbers of bacteria M20. **mucigen** *noun* the substance in a mucus-secreting cell from which mucin is derived L19. **muˈcigenous** *adjective* (*a*) producing or secreting mucus; (*b*) of the nature of mucigen: L19. **muˈciparous** *adjective* = MUCIGENOUS (a) E19.

mucic /ˈmjuːsɪk/ *adjective*. E19.
[ORIGIN French *mucique*, formed as MUCUS: see -IC.]
CHEMISTRY. **mucic acid**, a crystalline carboxylic acid obtained by oxidation of lactose or various plant gums, and used in the synthesis of pyrroles; 2,3,4,5tetrahydroxyhexanedioic acid, $HOOC(CHOH)_4COOH$.

mucid /ˈmjuːsɪd/ *adjective*. *rare*. M17.
[ORIGIN Latin *mucidus*, from *mucere* be mouldy: see -ID[1].]
Mouldy, musty, slimy.

mucification /ˌmjuːsɪfɪˈkeɪʃ(ə)n/ *noun*. M20.
[ORIGIN from MUCI- + -FICATION.]
PHYSIOLOGY. Transformation of epithelial cells into mucus-secreting cells.
■ ˈ**mucify** *verb intrans. & trans.* (cause to) undergo mucification M20.

mucilage /ˈmjuːsɪlɪdʒ/ *noun*. LME.
[ORIGIN Old French & mod. French from late Latin *mucilago* musty juice, formed as MUCUS: see -AGE.]
1 A polysaccharide substance extractable as a viscous or gelatinous solution in water from roots, seeds, and other parts of certain plants, and used in medicines and adhesives. LME. ▸**b** *transf.* A viscous mass, a pulp. L17. ▸**c** An aqueous solution of a gum etc. used as an adhesive; glue, gum. Chiefly *N. Amer.* M19.
2 A viscous secretion or bodily fluid (as mucus, synovia). LME.

mucilaginous /mjuːsɪˈladʒɪnəs/ *adjective*. LME.
[ORIGIN from medieval Latin *mucilaginosus*, from late Latin *mucilagin-*, *-ago*: see MUCILAGE, -OUS. Cf. Old French & mod. French *mucilagineux*.]
1 Having the nature or properties of mucilage; of a soft, moist, and viscous quality or appearance. Also, pertaining to or characteristic of mucilage. LME.
2 Containing or secreting mucilage. L17.
■ **mucilaginously** *adverb* M19.

mucin /ˈmjuːsɪn/ *noun*. M19.
[ORIGIN from MUCUS + -IN[1].]
BIOLOGY. Orig., mucus. Now, any of various glycoproteins forming the main constituents of mucus.

mucinous /ˈmjuːsɪnəs/ *adjective*. M19.
[ORIGIN from MUCIN + -OUS.]
MEDICINE. Mucous; mucoid.

muck /mʌk/ *noun*[1]. ME.
[ORIGIN Prob. of Scandinavian origin: cf. Old Norse *myki*, *mykr* dung, Danish *møg*, *mug*, *mog*, *møk*, Norwegian *myk*, from Germanic word meaning 'soft'.]
1 Mud, dirt, filth; *spec.* the dung of cattle, usu. mixed with decomposing vegetable refuse, used for manure; farmyard manure. ME. ▸**b** SOIL SCIENCE. Soil material consisting of decayed plant remains, distinguished from peat as being more thoroughly decomposed and having a higher mineral content. Orig. *US*. M19. ▸**c** Waste material removed during mining or civil engineering operations; *spec.* (*US*), surface material overlying a placer deposit. L19.

B. GILROY A window that had accumulated years of grime and muck.

2 a *fig.* Worldly wealth, money. Now *rare*. ME. ▸**b** Anything regarded as disgusting or worthless. *colloq.* L19. ▸**c** Bad weather; rain, snow. *slang & dial.* M20. ▸**d** Hostile anti-aircraft fire. *Air Force slang*. M20.

b J. OSBORNE A nice drop of gin—some of the muck they give you nowadays—tastes like cheap scent. I. MURDOCH Do you want pornographic muck to circulate?

3 An untidy or dirty state, a mess. *colloq.* M18.
– PHRASES: ***Lady Muck***: see LADY *noun & adjective*. ***Lord Muck***: see LORD *noun*. **make a muck of** *colloq.* do (something) badly; spoil, bungle, (an undertaking etc.).
– COMB.: **muck-heap**, **muckhill** a manure heap, a midden; **muck soil** = sense 1b above; **muck-spreader** a machine for spreading dung; **muck-spreading** the action of distributing dung over a field; **muck sweat** *colloq.* a profuse sweat; **muckworm** a worm or grub that lives in muck; *fig.* a miser; a guttersnipe.

†**muck** *noun*[2]. L17–L19.
[ORIGIN The 2nd syll. of AMOK taken erron. as a noun.]
A murderous frenzy, a rampage. Chiefly in ***run a muck***, run amok.

muck /mʌk/ *verb*. LME.
[ORIGIN from MUCK *noun*[1]. Cf. Old Norse *moka* shovel (manure).]
1 *verb trans.* Free from muck; remove muck from (a stable, pigpen, or other shelter for an animal). Now usu. foll. by *out*. LME. ▸**b** *verb trans.* Remove muck from the shelter of (an animal). Usu. foll. by *out*. M20. ▸**c** *verb intrans.* Foll. by *out*: remove muck from a stable, pigpen, etc. M20.

J. BETJEMAN She can muck out the stables and clean Her snaffle. **b** *Times* She did manual work . . toiling in the fields, mucking out the chickens. **c** C. WATSON Used to stand work and willing to muck out.

2 *verb trans.* Cover with muck, manure. LME.
3 *verb trans.* **a** = MESS *verb* 7a. Usu. foll. by *up*. M19. ▸**b** = MESS *verb* 7b. Usu. foll. by *about*, *around*. L19.

a J. TEY You don't want that dazzling outfit of yours to be mucked up. **b** N. BAWDEN I don't like to see him muck his life up.

4 *verb intrans.* Foll. by *about*, *around*: behave in a silly or aimless way, mess about. M19.

JACQUELINE WILSON I love mucking about, doing daft things and being a bit cheeky.

5 *verb intrans.* Foll. by *in*: share food, facilities, etc.; eat; share tasks, cooperate, participate, consort *with*. E20.

Daily Telegraph He mucked in with the rest of us.

6 *verb intrans. euphem.* = FUCK *verb* 1. Chiefly in imprecations (see FUCK *verb* 3). E20.
– COMB.: **muck-about** *colloq.* a person who mucks about; an act of mucking about; **muck-up** *colloq.* a blunder, a fiasco; a mess, a muddle.
■ **mucking** *ppl adjective & adverb* (*euphem.*) = FUCKING E20.

muck-a-muck /ˈmʌkəmʌk/ *noun*. *N. Amer.* M19.
[ORIGIN Chinook Jargon, perh. from Nootka *ma·ḥo·ma(q-)* choice whale meat. Cf. MUCKY-MUCK.]
1 Among Indians of western N. America: food. M19.
2 = HIGH-MUCK-A-MUCK. *colloq.* E20.

mucka-mucka *noun* var. of MOCO-MOCO.

muckender /ˈmʌkəndə/ *noun*. *obsolete* exc. *dial.* LME.
[ORIGIN Prob. from French *mouchoir*, from *moucher* clear the nose from popular Latin: cf. mod. Provençal *moucadour*, Spanish *mocador*, *-dero*. For the intrusive *n* cf. *colander*. See also MOCKET.]
A handkerchief. Formerly also, a table napkin, a bib.

mucker /ˈmʌkə/ *noun*[1]. ME.
[ORIGIN from MUCK *verb* + -ER[1].]
1 A person who or machine which removes or spreads manure. ME.
†**2** A scavenger. L15–L18.
3 A miser. *obsolete* exc. *dial.* M16.
4 *euphem.* = FUCKER. E20.
5 ***mucker-in***, a person who mucks in. M20.
6 A friend, a companion, a mate. *slang*. M20.

A. JUDD Mucker of mine from Sandhurst was killed there.

mucker /ˈmʌkə/ *noun*[2]. M19.
[ORIGIN from MUCK *noun*[1] + -ER[1].]
1 A heavy fall. Chiefly in ***come a mucker***, ***go a mucker***, fall, come to grief. *slang*. M19.
2 A person who or machine which removes mining waste. L19.

mucker /ˈmʌkə/ *noun*[3]. *slang* (orig. *US*). L19.
[ORIGIN Prob. from German *Mucker* a sulky person.]
A fanatic, a hypocrite; a coarse rough person.
■ **muckerish** *adjective* E20.

mucker /ˈmʌkə/ *verb*[1] *trans. obsolete* exc. *dial.* LME.
[ORIGIN Perh. from MUCK *noun*[1] + -ER[5].]
Hoard (money or goods). Also foll. by *up*.
■ †**muckerer** *noun* (*rare*) ME–M18.

mucker /ˈmʌkə/ *verb*[2]. *slang*. M19.
[ORIGIN from MUCKER *noun*[2].]
1 *verb intrans.* Come to grief, fail. M19.
2 *verb trans.* Ruin, spoil; squander, throw *away*. M19.

muckle /ˈmʌk(ə)l/ *adjective* (in mod. usage also classed as a *determiner*), *pronoun*, *noun*, & *adverb*. Now *Scot. & dial.* Also **mickle** /ˈmɪk(ə)l/.
[ORIGIN Old English *micel*, superseded in Middle English by forms from cognate Old Norse *mikeli*, from Germanic. Cf. MUCH.]
▸ **A** *adjective*. **1** Great; considerable in size, bulk, number, importance, or (passing into sense A.2) amount or degree. OE.
2 A great quantity or amount of; much. OE.
– COMB.: **muckle-mouthed** *adjective* (of a person) disfigured by a disproportionately large mouth; **muckle wheel** the large wheel of a spinning wheel.
▸ **B** *pronoun & noun*. **1** A great quantity or amount; much. OE.
†**2** Great or eminent people. Only in ME.
†**3** Size, stature; bigness. LME–E17.
4 a A large sum or amount. Chiefly in ***many a little makes a muckle***, ***many a pickle makes a muckle***. L16. ▸**b** (*mickle*.) [By confusion.] A small amount. Chiefly in ***many a mickle makes a muckle***. L18.
– PHRASES: **make muckle of** make much of, cherish. ***so muckle***: see SO *adverb* etc.
▸ **C** *adverb*. To a great extent or degree. OE.
– NOTE: The original proverb *many a little makes a mickle* was misquoted in L18 as *many a mickle makes a muckle*, leading to the widespread misapprehension that *mickle* means 'a small amount' and *muckle* means 'a large amount'.
■ **muckleness** *noun* greatness, largeness; size: ME.

muckluck *noun* var. of MUKLUK.

muckna /ˈmʌknə/ *noun*. L18.
[ORIGIN Hindi *makunā*, *makhnā* from Tamil *mokka* blunt.]
In the Indian subcontinent: a male elephant without tusks, or having only rudimentary tusks.

muckrake /ˈmʌkreɪk/ *noun & verb*. LME.
[ORIGIN from MUCK *noun*[1] + RAKE *noun*[1].]
▸ **A** *noun*. A rake for collecting or sifting through muck (*lit. & fig.*). LME.
▸ **B** *verb*. **1** *verb intrans.* Rake refuse together. Chiefly *fig.*, search for evidence of corruption or scandal in order to expose it, esp. among powerful or well-known people or institutions. L19.

Investors Chronicle It was a commendable bit of muck-raking, a sordid story of local government graft.

2 *verb trans.* Subject (a person or institution) to muckraking. *US*. E20.
■ **muckraker** *noun* †(*a*) a miser; (*b*) a person who seeks out and exposes scandals etc. about prominent people; (*c*) a prurient inquirer into private morals: E17.

mucky /ˈmʌki/ *adjective & verb*. M16.
[ORIGIN from MUCK *noun*[1] + -Y[1].]
▸ **A** *adjective*. **1** Covered with muck, dirty, muddy; involving muck. M16. ▸**b** Consisting of or resembling muck. L16. ▸**c** Grimy, grubby; unpleasant, corrupt, sordid, *colloq.* L19. ▸**d** Indecent, mildly pornographic or obscene. *colloq.* L20.

Sunday Express A mucky job in the garden. **c** D. ROWE I can't stand going to my friend's house—she lets it get so mucky. **d** B. REID Good vulgarity is marvellous—it's just when it's a bit mucky I don't like it.

mucky pup *joc.* a dirty or messy person, esp. a child.
†**2** Of money: filthy, corrupting. Of a person: miserly. M16–M17.
3 Of weather: bad, foul. Chiefly *dial.* E19.
▸ **B** *verb trans.* Make dirty. *dial.* E19.
■ **muckiness** *noun* L17.

mucky-muck /ˈmʌkɪmʌk/ *noun*. *N. Amer. slang*. E20.
[ORIGIN Redupl. of MUCKY, after MUCK-A-MUCK.]
= HIGH-MUCK-A-MUCK.

muco- /ˈmjuːkəʊ/ *combining form* of MUCUS or (in BIOCHEMISTRY) MUCOID *noun*, *adjective*, MUCIN: see -O-. Cf. MUCI-.
■ **mucocele**, **-coele** *noun* (MEDICINE) a distended structure containing mucus, as produced by the blockage of secretory ducts, the appendix, etc. E19. **mucoˈciliary** *adjective* (ANATOMY) designating or pertaining to a system of cilia and mucous glands lining the respiratory passages and serving to expel extraneous particles M20. **mucocuˈtaneous** *adjective* involving or pertaining to a mucous membrane and the skin L19. **mucoˈlytic** *noun & adjective* (MEDICINE) (an agent) able to disperse or break down mucus or its constituents M20. **mucoˈmembranous** *adjective* (ANATOMY) of or pertaining to a mucous membrane, mucosal L19. **mucoˈpeptide** *noun* (BIOCHEMISTRY) = MUREIN M20. **mucoperiˈosteum** *noun* (ANATOMY) a periosteum closely associated or continuous with a mucous membrane E20. **mucoˈprotein** *noun* (BIOCHEMISTRY) = PROTEOGLYCAN

M

E20. **muco'purulent** *adjective* (MEDICINE) designating or characterized by mingled pus and mucus E19. **mucopus** *noun* (MEDICINE) pus mingled with mucus M19. **mucovisci'dosis** *noun* (MEDICINE) = *cystic fibrosis* M20.

mucoid /ˈmjuːkɔɪd/ *noun*. L19.
[ORIGIN from MUCIN + -OID.]
BIOCHEMISTRY. A substance resembling mucin, esp. a proteoglycan.

mucoid /ˈmjuːkɔɪd/ *adjective*. M19.
[ORIGIN from MUCUS + -OID.]
Resembling, involving, or of the nature of mucus.
■ Also **mu'coidal** *adjective* (*rare*) M19.

mucoitin /mjuːˈkəʊɪtɪn/ *noun*. E20.
[ORIGIN from MUCO- after *chondroitin*.]
BIOCHEMISTRY. A mixture of partly sulphated glycosaminoglycans extracted from various mucins.

mucopolysaccharide /ˌmjuːkəʊpɒlɪˈsakərʌɪd/ *noun*. M20.
[ORIGIN from MUCO- + POLYSACCHARIDE.]
Chiefly MEDICINE & BIOLOGY. = GLYCOSAMINOGLYCAN.
■ **mucopolysacchari'dosis** *noun*, pl. **-doses** /-ˈdəʊsiːz/, any of various congenital disorders of mucopolysaccharide metabolism characterized by mental disability, skeletal abnormalities, and other symptoms M20.

mucor /ˈmjuːkɔː/ *noun*. M17.
[ORIGIN Latin (in sense 2 as mod. Latin genus name), from *mucere* be mouldy.]
†**1** Mouldiness, mustiness; mould. M17–M19.
2 Orig., any mould fungus. Now *spec.* a mould of the genus *Mucor* or the order Mucorales, found on decaying organic matter and occasionally pathogenic in humans. E19.
■ **muco'raceous** *adjective* of, pertaining to, or characteristic of the order Mucorales or (esp.) the family Mucoraceae of moulds M19.

mucormycosis /ˌmjuːkɔːmʌɪˈkəʊsɪs/ *noun*. Pl. **-coses** /-ˈkəʊsiːz/. E20.
[ORIGIN from MUCOR + MYCOSIS.]
MEDICINE & VETERINARY MEDICINE. Phycomycosis; *esp.* infection with fungus of the genus *Mucor*, affecting the skin, ears, paranasal sinuses, and respiratory passages.

mucosa /mjuːˈkəʊsə/ *noun*. Pl. **-sae** /-siː/ M19.
[ORIGIN mod. Latin (*membrana*) *mucosa*, fem. of Latin *mucosus* MUCOUS.]
ANATOMY. A mucous membrane.
■ **mucosal** *adjective* of or pertaining to a mucosa L19.

mucose /ˈmjuːkəʊs/ *adjective*. M18.
[ORIGIN Latin *mucosus*: see MUCOUS, -OSE¹.]
Slimy; covered with mucus.

mucosity /mjuːˈkɒsɪti/ *noun*. Now *rare*. L17.
[ORIGIN French *mucosité*, formed as MUCOSE: see -ITY.]
A mucous secretion, a slimy covering.

mucous /ˈmjuːkəs/ *adjective*. L16.
[ORIGIN from Latin *mucosus* slimy, mucous formed as MUCUS: see -OUS.]
Containing, secreting, consisting of, or resembling mucus; covered with mucus; characterized by the presence of mucus. Formerly also *gen.*, slimy.
mucous membrane a mucus-secreting membrane which lines the gut, respiratory passages, and other cavities in the body.
■ †**mucousness** *noun* L17–M18.

mucro /ˈmjuːkrəʊ/ *noun*. Pl. **mucrones** /mjuːˈkrəʊniːz/, **mucros**. M17.
[ORIGIN Latin *mucro(n-)* point.]
A pointed part or organ; *esp.* (ZOOLOGY & BOTANY) a short, sharp terminal point, process, or apex.

mucronate /ˈmjuːkrənеɪt/ *adjective*. L18.
[ORIGIN Latin *mucronatus*, formed as MUCRO: see -ATE².]
Terminating in a point; *esp.* (BOTANY) abruptly terminated by a hard short point.
■ Also **mucronated** *adjective* (now *rare* or *obsolete*) M17.

mucrones *noun pl.* see MUCRO.

mucronulate /mjuːˈkrɒnjʊlət/ *adjective*. E19.
[ORIGIN mod. Latin *mucronulatus*, from *mucronula* dim. of MUCRO: see -ULE, -ATE².]
BOTANY. Having a small mucro.

muculent /ˈmjuːkjʊl(ə)nt/ *adjective*. M17.
[ORIGIN Late Latin *muculentus*, formed as MUCUS: see -ULENT.]
Slimy; mucous.

mucuna /mjuːˈkjuːnə/ *noun*.
[ORIGIN mod. Latin, from Portuguese *mucunã* from Tupi *mucuná*.]
A tropical climbing bean plant of the genus *Mucuna*, *esp.* the velvet bean.

mucus /ˈmjuːkəs/ *noun*. L16.
[ORIGIN Latin, cogn. with Greek *mussesthai* blow the nose (cf. Latin *emungere*), *mukter* nose, nostril.]
A viscid or slimy substance not miscible with water, containing mucin and other glycoproteins and secreted by the mucous glands and membranes of animals for protection, lubrication, etc. Also, a viscid substance secreted by or present in plants.

MUD /mʌd/ *abbreviation*.
Multi-user dungeon (or dimension), a computer-based text or virtual reality game for several players, who interact with each other as well as with characters controlled by the computer.

mud /mʌd/ *noun*¹. LME.
[ORIGIN Prob. from Middle Low German *mudde* (Low German *mudde, mod, möde, müde*: cf. Dutch *modden* dabble in mud), Middle High German *mot* (German dial. *Mott*) bog, peat.]
1 Soft wet soil, sand, dust, or other earthy matter; mire, sludge. Also, hard ground produced by the drying of an area of this; *colloq.* soil. LME. ▸**b** In *pl.* Tracts of mud on the margin of a tidal river. L19. ▸**c** *spec.* in GEOLOGY. A semi-liquid or soft and plastic mixture of finely comminuted rock particles with water; a kind of this. L19. ▸**d** A liquid (freq. a suspension of clay etc. in water) that is pumped down inside a drill pipe and up outside it during the drilling of an oil or gas well, to remove drill cuttings, cool and lubricate the bit, and prevent the collapse of the sides of the hole or leakage through them. E20.

> **c** T. H. HUXLEY Herculaneum was sealed up by a crust of volcanic mud.

2 *fig.* **a** Something regarded as worthless or polluting. M16. ▸†**b** The lowest or worst part of anything; the dregs. L16–M19. ▸**c** Coffee, esp. when strong and bitter; *US* opium. *slang*. E20.

– PHRASES: ***as clear as mud***: see CLEAR *adjective*. ***drag through the mud***: see DRAG *verb*. **drilling mud** = sense 1d above. **fling mud** = *sling mud* below. **here's mud in your eye!** cheers! good health! **mud and stud** posts and laths filled in with mud, as a building material for walls of cottages etc. **mud in your eye!** = *here's mud in your eye!* above. **one's name is mud** one is in disgrace or temporarily unpopular. ***red mud***: see RED *adjective*. **sling mud** make disparaging or slanderous allegations, criticize someone maliciously. ***stick in the mud***: see STICK *verb*¹. **throw mud** = *sling mud* above.

– COMB.: **mud balance**: for measuring the density of drilling mud; **mudbank** a bank of mud in the bed of a river or on the bottom of the sea; **mud-bath** (*a*) a medicinal bath of heated mud, used esp. to relieve rheumatism etc.; (*b*) a muddy place or occasion; **mud box** NAUTICAL a box containing a coarse filter used to trap sediment in bilge water; **mud-brick** brick made with mud; **mudbug** *N. Amer.* a freshwater crayfish; **mudcat** *US* (*a*) any of several N. American catfish of muddy rivers, esp. in the Mississippi valley; †(*b*) *colloq.* a native or inhabitant of Mississippi; **mud crab** *Austral.* a large edible swimming crab, *Scylla serrata*, of Indo-Pacific mangrove swamps; **mud dab** *N. Amer.* (*a*) = *winter flounder* s.v. WINTER *noun*; (*b*) = YELLOWFIN *sole*; **mud-dauber** (*a*) any of various sphecid wasps that deposit their eggs, together with live prey, in cells made of mud; (*b*) *US* = CLIFF *swallow* (cf. *mud swallow* below); *fig.* a travelling workman; **mud eel** an elongate creature of muddy water; *esp.* (*a*) a larval lamprey; (*b*) a salamander, *Siren lacertina*, of the south-eastern US; **mud engineer** a person responsible for the quality and supply of drilling mud; **mud fever** VETERINARY MEDICINE erythema of a horse's feet; **mudflap** a piece of rubber, metal, etc., hung behind a vehicle wheel to prevent mud, stones, etc., thrown up from the road from hitting the bodywork; **mudflat** (*a*) a stretch of muddy land left uncovered at low tide; (*b*) a mudbank in a non-tidal river; **mud-flinger**, **mud-flinging** = *mud-slinger*, *mud-slinging* below; **mud-flow** a fluid or hardened stream or avalanche of mud; the flow or motion of such a stream; **mud fluid** = sense 1d above; **mud flush** a flow of drilling mud; **mudguard** a curved strip or cover over a cycle or other vehicle wheel to reduce the splashing of mud etc. from the ground; **mudguarded** *adjective* fitted with mudguards; **mudhead** (*a*) *slang* a stupid person; (*b*) a ceremonial clown among the Zuni and Hopi peoples who wears a mud-daubed mask; **mud-hen** (chiefly *N. Amer.*) any of various rails or coots; **mud hog** = *mud pump* below; **mudhole** (*a*) a hole containing mud, esp. as forming a defect in a road; a waterhole dried so as to become mud; (*b*) a hole at the base of a boiler, condenser, etc., through which sediment can be removed; **mudhook** *slang* (*a*) an anchor; (*b*) a foot; a hand; **mud-hopper** = *mudskipper* below; **mud-laden** *adjective* laden with mud; ***mud-laden fluid***, = sense 1d above; **mud-lava** volcanic mud; **mud-line** the limit of wave action on a coastal seabed below which mud will settle permanently on the bottom; **mud-logger** an engineer who monitors drilling by mud-logging; **mud-logging** examination of the drilling mud coming out of a borehole for signs of oil or gas or other indications of the strata being drilled; **mud-lump** *US* a mound or cone of mud or silt formed in a river delta; **mud-mask** = *mud-pack* below; **mud minnow** a small carnivorous fish of muddy water in N. America; **mud-pack** a facepack containing fuller's earth or some similar material; **mud pie** (*a*) a mass of mud formed into the shape of a pie, esp. by a child; (*b*) a rich mousse-like chocolate cake; **mud pilot** a pilot who works in shallow water; **mudpout** *N. Amer.* = *mudcat* (a) above; **mud pump**: for circulating mud fluid; **mud puppy** *US* any of various large neotenous aquatic salamanders, esp. of the genus *Necturus*; an axolotl, a hellbender; **mud room** *N. Amer.* a cloakroom, *spec.* one in which wet or muddy footwear may be left; **mud shark** (*a*) *US dial.* the burbot, *Lota lota*; (*b*) *N. Amer.* any of various benthic sharks, esp. of the family Hexanchidae; **mud-sill** (*a*) the lowest sill of a structure, usu. embedded in soil; (*b*) *US* the lowest class of society; a person of this class; **mudskipper** any of various small gobies of the genus *Periophthalmus* and related genera, of tropical Asian, Australasian, and African coasts, which are able to scramble over mud, along tree roots, etc., by means of stout pectoral fins; **mudslide** an avalanche of mud, rock, etc.; earthy material deposited by such an avalanche; **mud-slinger** a person given to abuse, slander, or malevolent criticism; **mud-slinging** (the employment of) abuse, slander, or malevolent criticism; **mud snail** either of two European pond snails of the genus *Lymnaea*, the slender-shelled *L. glabra* and (occas.) *L. truncatula*; **mud snake** a non-venomous black and red colubrid snake of the southern US, *Farancia abacura*; also called ***hoop-snake***, ***horn-snake***; **mudstone** GEOLOGY any clayey or silty rock, usu. formed by hardening of mud, *esp.* a mixed clay and silt rock lacking the laminations of shale; **mud-sucker** an American goby, *Gillichthys mirabilis*, often used as bait; **mud swallow** *US* = CLIFF *swallow*; **mud-thrower** = *mud-slinger* above; **mud-throwing** = *mud-slinging* above; **mud trout** = *brook trout* (b) s.v. BROOK *noun*; **mud-turtle** any small turtle of the American family Kinosternidae, of mud or muddy water; **mud volcano** (*a*) a crack or fissure discharging mud and freq. forming a hardened mound or cone; (*b*) = *mud-lump* above; **mud wall** a wall built of earth or clay or having clay as a substitute for mortar; **mud wasp** *US* = *mud dauber* (a) above; **mud wing** a mudguard, a mudflap; **mud-worm** a worm that lives in mud; *fig.* a contemptible person; **mudwort** any of several dwarf creeping plants of the genus *Limosella*, of the figwort family, esp. *L. aquatica*, growing in mud at the edge of ponds; **mud-wrestler** an exponent of mud-wrestling; **mud-wrestling** a kind of entertainment in which usu. female contestants wrestle in a mud-filled ring.
■ **muddish** *adjective* somewhat muddy M17. **mudless** *adjective* E17.

†**mud** *noun*² see MUID *noun*².

mud /mʌd/ *verb*. Now *rare*. Infl. **-dd-**. L16.
[ORIGIN from MUD *noun*¹.]
1 *verb trans.* Cloud (liquid) by stirring up mud or sediment. L16.
2 *verb trans.* †**a** Bury in mud. *rare* (Shakes.). Only in E17. ▸**b** In *pass.* Become stuck in mud. M19.
3 *verb trans.* Cover or plaster with mud. M17. ▸**b** Seal (porous strata) by depositing a layer of mud on the sides of a borehole. (Foll. by *off*, *up*.) E20.
4 *verb intrans.* Esp. of a fish: lie dormant, burrow, or hide in mud. M17.

mudalali /mʊdəˈlɑːli/ *noun*. M19.
[ORIGIN Sinhalese *mudalāli*, Tamil *mutalāḷi*, from *mutal* property.]
In India and Sri Lanka: a proprietor, a businessman, a rich trader.

mudaliyar /mʊˈdəljɑː, ˈmʊdəlɪə/ *noun*. Also (earlier) **modeliar**. M17.
[ORIGIN Tamil *mutaliyār* pl. of *mutali* a chief from *mutal* best.]
In Sri Lanka: a headman, a chief; a chief military officer.

mudar /məˈdɑː/ *noun*. Also **madar**. E19.
[ORIGIN Hindi *madār* from Sanskrit *mandāra*.]
Any of several shrubs of the genus *Calotropis* (family Asclepiadaceae), of tropical Asia and Africa; esp. *C. procera* and *C. gigantea*, whose bark yields a fibre and whose seed floss is used like kapok. Also, a preparation of the root of any of these trees.

mudder /ˈmʌdə/ *noun*. *slang* (chiefly *US*). E20.
[ORIGIN from MUD *noun*¹ + -ER¹.]
A racehorse which runs well in wet or muddy conditions; a sportsman or sportswoman or a team able to perform well in wet or muddy conditions.

muddie /ˈmʌdi/ *noun*. *Austral. colloq.* Also **muddy**. M20.
[ORIGIN from MUD *noun*¹ + -IE, -Y⁶.]
A mud-crab.

muddied /ˈmʌdɪd/ *adjective*. M17.
[ORIGIN from MUDDY *verb* + -ED¹.]
Covered with mud; made muddy; (of water) turbid.

> R. KIPLING The flannelled fools at the wicket or the muddied oafs at the goals.

muddify /ˈmʌdɪfʌɪ/ *verb trans*. M18.
[ORIGIN from MUDDY *adjective* + -FY.]
1 Make muddy. M18.
2 Make unclear, muddle. L18.

muddle /ˈmʌd(ə)l/ *noun*. E19.
[ORIGIN from the verb.]
1 A muddled condition; confusion, disorder; mental confusion, bewilderment. Also, a result of muddling, a bungle, a mess. E19.

> *Jazz Monthly* A muddle unparalleled in the history of jazz record issues. P. AUSTER The brain is in a muddle.

2 A confused assemblage, a jumble. M19.

> K. ISHIGURO Wedged in between was a dense muddle of roofs.

– PHRASES: **make a muddle of** mishandle (an undertaking etc.); disorder (objects etc.).
■ **muddledom** *noun* (*rare*) the condition of muddle L19.

muddle /ˈmʌd(ə)l/ *verb*. ME.
[ORIGIN Perh. from Middle Dutch *moddelen* frequentative of *modden* dabble in mud (cf. MUD *noun*¹): see -LE³.]
1 *verb intrans.* **a** Bathe or wallow in mud or muddy water. *arch.* ME. ▸**b** Grub or root in soil; (of a bird) dabble in water. Now *rare* exc. *Scot. dial.* E17.
2 *verb trans.* **a** Make muddy or turbid, cloud. Now *rare*. L16. ▸**b** Crush and mix (ingredients) to make a drink. *US*. L19.
3 *verb trans.* Confuse, bewilder; fuddle or stupefy, esp. with alcoholic drink. L17.
4 *verb intrans.* **a** Foll. by *along*, *on*: progress or live life in a haphazard way. E18. ▸**b** Busy oneself in a confused, unmethodical, and ineffective manner. (Foll. by *with*, *at*.) M19. ▸**c** Foll. by *through*: attain one's end haphazardly and despite a lack of skill or foresight. M19.

> **a** M. MOORCOCK I expect she's muddling along like the rest of us. **c** *Village Voice* In the absence of a national program, America muddles through to produce its energy.

5 *verb trans.* Foll. by *away*: squander or fritter away (money, time, etc.) without purpose or result. E19.
6 *verb trans.* **a** Fail to distinguish correctly, confuse *together*, mix *up*. M19. ▸**b** Bungle, mismanage (an undertaking etc.); bring into disorder. (Foll. by *up*.) L19.

a P. GROSSKURTH She muddled up her Latin conjugations.

■ **muddled** *adjective* †(**a**) made muddy or turbid, clouded; (**b**) confused, disorganized, disordered: E17. **muddledly** *adverb* E20. **muddlement** *noun* muddle, confusion, bewilderment M19. **muddler** *noun* (**a**) a person or thing which muddles; (**b**) *spec.* (*US*) a small stick for crushing and mixing the ingredients for a drink; (**c**) (more fully ***muddler minnow***) a type of fly used in trout-fishing: M19. **muddlingly** *adverb* in a muddling manner M19.

muddle-headed /mʌd(ə)l'hɛdɪd/ *adjective. colloq.* M18.
[ORIGIN from MUDDLE *noun, verb* + HEAD *noun* + -ED².]
Having an unclear mind; stupid, confused.
■ '**muddle-head** *noun* (**a**) a confused or stupid person, a block-head; (**b**) a disorganized vague mind: M19. **muddleheadedly** *adverb* E20. **muddle-headedness** *noun* M19.

muddly /'mʌd(ə)li/ *adjective.* M19.
[ORIGIN from MUDDLE *noun* + -Y¹.]
Confused, muddled; confusing, bewildering.
■ **muddliness** *noun* L19.

muddy *noun*¹ var. of MUDDIE.

muddy /'mʌdi/ *adjective & noun*². ME.
[ORIGIN from MUD *noun*¹ + -Y¹.]
▸ **A** *adjective* **1 a** Containing much mud; turbid or clouded with mud; covered or spattered with mud. ME. ▸**b** Of the nature of mud, resembling mud. E17.

a M. ROBERTS The lane is muddy and soft after the storms. B. MOORE Oh, look at your coat, it's all muddy.

2 Morally corrupt, base; carnal. Now *rare.* LME.
3 Living or growing in mud. L16.
4 Not clear or pure; clouded, opaque, turbid; dull, dim. L16. ▸**b** Of a musical sound: blurred, undefined. M20.

J. CARLYLE We breakfasted . . on muddy coffee and scorched toast. M. HUGHES It makes your eyes look green instead of that funny muddy shade.

5 Gloomy; sullen. Now *rare.* L16.
6 Not clear in mind, confused, muddled; (of literary style, thought, etc.) obscure, vague. E17. ▸**b** Partly intoxicated. Now *rare* or *obsolete.* L18.
▸ **B** *noun. The* Missouri River (also ***the Big Muddy***); *the* Mississippi River. *US.* E19.
■ **muddily** *adverb* M17. **muddiness** *noun* M17.

muddy /'mʌdi/ *verb.* E17.
[ORIGIN from the adjective.]
1 *verb trans.* Make muddy; *fig.* make confused or obscure; taint. E17.

C. G. LELAND I only muddied the palms of my gloves, on which I fell. GROVER SMITH In the original play there is no such muddying of the facts. M. SCAMMELL Came a new misunderstanding to muddy their relationship.

muddy the waters make an issue or situation more confusing and harder to understand by introducing complications.
2 *verb intrans.* Become muddy or turbid. M19.

Mudéjar /mu:'deɪhɑ:/ *adjective & noun.* Also **Mudejar**, **m-**. Pl. of noun **-res** /-rɛs/. M19.
[ORIGIN Spanish from Arabic *mudajjan* pass. pple of *dajjana* allow to stay.]
(Of, pertaining to, or characteristic of) a subject Muslim during the reconquest of the Iberian peninsula from the Moors who was allowed to retain Islamic laws and religion in return for owing allegiance and paying tribute to a Christian monarch; *spec.* (designating) a partly Islamic, partly Gothic style of architecture and decorative art of the 12th to the 15th cents.

mudfish /'mʌdfɪʃ/ *noun.* Pl. **-es** /-ɪz/, (usu.) same. E16.
[ORIGIN from MUD *noun*¹ + FISH *noun*¹.]
Any of various fishes which live in marine, estuarine, or freshwater mud; *esp.* (**a**) a bowfin; (**b**) a lungfish; (**c**) a mud minnow; (**d**) a mud-sucker; (**e**) a mummichog; (**f**) a burrowing fish of New Zealand, *Neochanna apoda.*

mudim /'mu:dɪm/ *noun.* Also **-in** /-ɪn/. E17.
[ORIGIN Malay (now *mudin, modin*), from Arabic *mu'aḏḏin* muezzin.]
A junior Muslim official in Malaysia or Indonesia, *spec.* a person who performs the operation of circumcision.

mudir /mu:'dɪə/ *noun.* M19.
[ORIGIN Ottoman Turkish *müdir*, Turkish *müdür* director, administrator, from Arabic *mudir* active pple of *adāra* direct, manage.]
In Turkey: the governor of a subdistrict. In Egypt and Sudan: the governor of a province.
■ ***mudirate*** *noun* = MUDIRIEH L19.

mudirieh /mu:dɪ'rɪə/ *noun.* L19.
[ORIGIN Arabic *mudīriyya*, formed as MUDIR.]
In Egypt: the territory or province of a mudir; the official headquarters of a mudir.

Mudjur /'mʊdʒʊə/ *noun.* Also **Mujur**. E20.
[ORIGIN See below.]
(Designating) a type of prayer rug made in or associated with Mudjur, a small town in Turkey, usu. with a deep border and an arch motif.

mudlark /'mʌdlɑ:k/ *noun & verb.* L18.
[ORIGIN from MUD *noun*¹ + LARK *noun*¹.]
▸ **A** *noun.* †**1** A hog. *slang.* L18–E20.
2 A person who scavenges for usable debris in the mud of a river or harbour. Also, a street urchin; *joc.* a messy person, esp. a child. *colloq.* L18.
3 A magpie lark. *Austral.* L19.
4 = MUDDER. *slang.* E20.
▸ **B** *verb intrans.* Carry on the occupation of a mudlark. Also, play in mud. M19.
■ **mudlarker** *noun* = MUDLARK *noun* 2 E19.

mudra /'mʌdrə, 'mu:-/ *noun.* E19.
[ORIGIN Sanskrit *mudrā* seal, sign, token.]
Any of a large number of symbolic hand gestures used in Hindu religious ceremonies and in Indian dance. Also, a movement or pose in yoga.

muduga oil /'mu:dʊgə, mʊ'du:gə/ *noun.* M19.
[ORIGIN Telugu *mōdugu*.]
Oil from the seeds of the dhak tree, used as an anthelmintic.

Mudville /'mʌdvɪl/ *noun.* M20.
[ORIGIN The name of a fictional town in E. L. Thayer's poem 'Casey at the Bat' (1888), which features the defeat of its baseball team.]
Used allusively to designate the world of baseball, usu. with ref. to fans' feelings of disappointment or happiness after a loss or victory. Freq. in ***no joy in Mudville***

muesli /'mu:zli, 'mju:zli/ *noun.* M20.
[ORIGIN Swiss German.]
A dish, originating in Switzerland, consisting of a cereal (usu. oats), fruit, nuts, etc., eaten with milk or cream, esp. for breakfast.
– COMB.: **muesli belt** *joc.* a region supposed to be densely populated by (prosperous middle-class) health-food faddists.

muezzin /mu:'ɛzɪn/ *noun.* L16.
[ORIGIN Arabic *mu'aḏḏin* active pple of *aḏḏana* call to prayer.]
A Muslim crier who proclaims the hours of prayer from a minaret or the roof of a mosque.

muff /mʌf/ *noun*¹. M16.
[ORIGIN Dutch *mof* abbreviation of Middle Dutch *moffel, muffel* (corresp. to French *moufle*, Italian *mufla*) from medieval Latin *muff(u)la* glove, of unknown origin.]
1 A covering, usu. of cylindrical shape, into which both hands may be inserted from opposite ends to keep them warm. M16. ▸**b** Any of various warming or protective coverings resembling a muff for the hands. L18.
b ***earmuff, foot muff***, etc.
2 The female external genitals. *slang.* L17. ▸**b** A woman, a girl, *esp.* a promiscuous one; a prostitute. *slang* (orig. *US*). E20.
3 FOUNDING. Any of various devices for controlling heat in a furnace. Cf. MUFFLE *noun*⁴. L17.
4 A tuft of feathers on the head, neck, or legs of a bird. M19.
– COMB.: **muff cock** *Scot.* a woodcock; **muff coupling** a cylindrical shaft coupling to fit over the abutting ends of shafts; **muff diver** *slang* a person who performs cunnilingus; **muff pistol** a small 19th-cent. pocket pistol.

muff /mʌf/ *noun*². Long *obsolete* exc. *dial.* M17.
[ORIGIN Imit. of an inarticulate sound.]
An utterance, a sound. Usu. in neg. contexts, as ***not say muff***.

muff /mʌf/ *noun*³. *colloq.* E19.
[ORIGIN Uncertain: rel. to MUFF *verb*².]
1 A person without skill or aptitude for something, orig. *spec.* some sport; a person lacking in practical sense. E19.
2 A failure; anything done clumsily or bungled, esp. in a ball game. M19.
■ **muffish** *adjective* M19. **muffishness** *noun* M19.

muff /mʌf/ *adjective.* M19.
[ORIGIN from MUFF *verb*³.]
Of glass: frosted.

muff /mʌf/ *verb*¹ *intrans.* Chiefly *dial. rare.* L15.
[ORIGIN from MUFF *noun*².]
Utter a word or sound. Usu. in neg. contexts.

muff /mʌf/ *verb*² *trans. colloq.* E19.
[ORIGIN Uncertain: rel. to MUFF *noun*³.]
Do or handle (something) badly or clumsily, make a mess of, bungle; *spec.* (**a**) miss (a ball) in a ball game; (**b**) fail (an examination); (**c**) THEATRICAL confuse or forget (one's lines).

R. COBB I might have done very well, or I might have completely muffed it, got everything wrong. R. THOMAS 'That must make a change', Cass said, carefully, not wanting to muff her line. *Cricketer International* Archie . . muffs a hard hit shot and allows the day's first boundary.

muff /mʌf/ *verb*³ *trans.* M19.
[ORIGIN Uncertain: cf. MUFFLE *verb*.]
= MUFFLE *verb* 5. Chiefly as ***muffed*** *ppl adjective.* Cf. MUFF *adjective.*

muffed /mʌft/ *adjective.* M18.
[ORIGIN from MUFF *noun*¹ + -ED².]
Provided with or having a muff; *spec.* (of a bird) having a tuft of feathers on the head, neck, or legs.

muffetee /mʌfɪ'ti:/ *noun.* E18.
[ORIGIN App. irreg. from MUFF *noun*¹.]
1 A muffler worn round the neck. *obsolete* exc. *dial.* E18.
2 A wristlet worn for warmth. M18.

muffin /'mʌfɪn/ *noun.* E18.
[ORIGIN Perh. from Low German *muffe* little cake; cf. also Old French *moflet, mouflet* a kind of bread.]
1 **a** Orig. (now *dial.*), a cake of any of various kinds of (esp. sweet) bread. Now, a flat circular spongy bread roll made from yeast dough and eaten split, toasted, and buttered. In N. America more fully ***English muffin***. E18. ▸**b** A small domed spongy cake made with eggs and baking powder. Orig. *N. Amer.* M19.
2 A kind of earthenware or china plate. Now *rare.* E19.
3 A person who muffs catches etc. *arch. US slang.* M19.
4 A young woman, *esp.* one who regularly partners a particular man at social occasions. *Canad. slang.* M19.
– COMB.: **muffin-face** *slang* an expressionless countenance; **muffin-fight** *colloq.* = ***muffin-worry*** below; **muffin man** *hist.* a seller of muffins; **muffin-worry** *arch. slang* a tea party.
■ **muffi'neer** *noun* (**a**) a small caster with a perforated top for sprinkling salt or sugar on muffins; (**b**) *rare* a covered dish to keep toasted muffins hot: L18.

muffle /'mʌf(ə)l/ *noun*¹. M16.
[ORIGIN App. from MUFFLE *verb*.]
1 Something that muffles or covers the face or neck; a muffler. *rare.* M16.
2 A device for muffling or deadening sound. M18.
3 Muffling effect; muffled sound. L19.

muffle /'mʌf(ə)l/ *noun*². L16.
[ORIGIN French *moufle*. Cf. MUFFLE *noun*⁴, MUFFLE *verb*.]
1 = MITTEN *noun* 1, MITT 1. L16.
†2 A boxing glove; = MUFFLER 2a. M18–M19.
3 A pulley containing several sheaves. E19.

muffle /'mʌf(ə)l/ *noun*³. E17.
[ORIGIN French *mufle*, of unknown origin.]
Orig. (*rare*), a proboscis. Now, the mobile part of the upper lip and nose of a rodent, ruminant, or other mammal.

muffle /'mʌf(ə)l/ *noun*⁴. M17.
[ORIGIN French *moufle*, perh. transf. use of *moufle* mitten, thick glove. Cf. MUFFLE *noun*², MUFFLE *verb*.]
A receptacle in which a substance can be heated in a furnace without coming in contact with combustion products; an inner chamber in a kiln in which pottery etc. can be fired at a low temperature without contact with the heat source.
– COMB.: **muffle kiln**: containing a muffle.

muffle /'mʌf(ə)l/ *verb trans.* LME.
[ORIGIN Perh. aphet. from Old French *enmoufler*, formed as EN-¹ + MUFFLE *noun*².]
1 Wrap, cover up, or enfold, esp. so as to conceal, subdue, or provide protection from the weather. Freq. foll. by *up*. LME. ▸**b** *gen.* Cover, conceal, obscure; stifle, suppress. L16.

S. LEACOCK I was muffled up, to avoid recognition, in a long overcoat with the collar turned up. G. SWIFT They came every morning . . muffled in the winter in little anoraks and scarves. **b** R. ELLIS Mystical emblems, Emblems muffled darkly. D. MACDONALD Reviewers had their doubts. But they adopted various strategies for muffling them.

†2 Cover (the eyes) to prevent seeing; cover the eyes of; blindfold. Usu. in *pass.* M16–E18.
3 = GAG *verb*¹ 2. L16.
4 Wrap up (a thing) so as to deaden its sound. M18. ▸**b** Limit the audibility of, deaden (a sound). Usu. in *pass.* M19.

b E. L. DOCTOROW All the sounds of the city were muffled by the snow.

5 Make (glass) semi-opaque by giving it a crinkled surface; frost. Cf. MUFF *verb*³. E20.
■ **muffledly** *adverb* in a muffled manner E20.

muffler /'mʌflə/ *noun.* M16.
[ORIGIN from MUFFLE *verb* + -ER¹.]
1 **a** *hist.* A sort of kerchief or scarf worn by women in the 16th and 17th cents. to cover part of the face and the neck. M16. ▸†**b** A bandage for blindfolding a person. L16–E17. ▸**c** A wrap or scarf worn round the neck or throat for warmth; *gen.* anything used to wrap a part of the body. L16.

c V. NABOKOV Shovelling the snow in my shirt-sleeves, a voluminous black and white muffler around my neck.

2 **a** A boxing glove; = MUFFLE *noun*² 2. M18. ▸**b** A glove, a mitten. Cf. MUFFLE *noun*² 1. E19. ▸**c** *hist.* A leather muff used to bind the hands of a mentally disordered person. M19.
3 Something that deadens sound; *spec.* (**a**) in a piano, a pad of felt inserted between the hammers and the strings; (**b**) in a steam engine, a device for silencing the escape of steam. Also (chiefly *N. Amer.*), a silencer on a vehicle's exhaust system. M19.

G. E. EVANS Attaching . . *mufflers*—leather pads—to the striking side of the clappers. S. BRILL The day before the tail pipe and muffler had broken off.

muffling /ˈmʌflɪŋ/ *noun*. M16.
[ORIGIN from MUFFLE *verb* + -ING[1].]
1 The action of MUFFLE *verb*. M16.
2 (An item of) clothing worn for warmth. L18.
– COMB.: **muffling box** a device for silencing the escape of steam from a steam engine.

mufti /ˈmʌfti/ *noun*[1]. L16.
[ORIGIN Arabic *muftī* active pple of *aftā* decide a point of law, from *fatā*: see FATWA. Cf. MUFTI *noun*[2].]
A Muslim cleric or legal expert empowered to give rulings on religious matters; in the Ottoman Empire, a chief legal authority, esp. of a large city (also ***Grand Mufti***).

mufti /ˈmʌfti/ *noun*[2]. E19.
[ORIGIN Perh. joc. use of MUFTI *noun*[1].]
1 Plain clothes worn by a person having the right to wear a uniform, esp. a military uniform. Freq. in ***in mufti***. E19.
E. P. THOMPSON The soldiers . . were allowed to don mufti. A. GUINNESS He was dressed in mufti but introduced himself as an Anglican priest.
2 A civilian; a person wearing mufti. *rare*. M19.

mug /mʌg/ *noun*[1]. LME.
[ORIGIN Prob. of Scandinavian origin (cf. Norwegian *mugge*, Swedish *mugg* pitcher with a handle), ult. origin unknown. See also MUG *noun*[3].]
†**1** A dry measure for salt etc. Only in LME.
2 A (large) earthenware vessel or bowl; a pot, a jug, a ewer. *Scot. & N. English*. E16.
3 A large cup, usu. cylindrical and with a handle and used without a saucer. M17. ▸**b** A mug with the drink it contains; the contents of a mug, a mugful. L17.
M. M. R. KHAN A mug with a handle . . for morning coffee. **b** J. HOWKER He hadn't touched the mug of tea I'd made for him.
– COMB.: **mug-house** (**a**) *arch.* a public house; ***mug-house club*** (*hist.*), any of various political clubs of Hanoverian sympathies meeting at public houses; (**b**) *dial.* a pottery.
■ **mugful** *noun* the contents of a mug; as much as a mug will hold: M19.

mug /mʌg/ *noun*[2]. Chiefly *Scot. & N. English*. L16.
[ORIGIN Unknown.]
(An animal of) a breed of sheep with the face covered in wool, *esp.* (a) Wensleydale.

mug /mʌg/ *noun*[3]. *slang*. E18.
[ORIGIN Perh. a use of MUG *noun*[1], from the practice of representing faces on mugs. See also MUG *noun*[6].]
1 The face, the mouth. Also, a grimace. E18. ▸**b** A photograph or other likeness of a person's face, esp. in police or other official records. Cf. ***mug shot*** below. Orig. *US*. L19.
M. LEITCH Not once had a flicker of amusement . . crossed that suffering mug. **b** L. CODY We've been showing them the books . . and some women picked out a mug.
2 The action of throttling or strangling a person. Chiefly in ***put the mug on***. M19.
– COMB.: **mug book** *US* a book containing photographs of people's faces, esp. in police records; **mug shot** (orig. *US*) a photograph of a person's face, esp. in police or other official records (cf. sense 1b above).

Mug /mʌg/ *noun*[4] & *adjective*[1]. *Indian*. Now *rare*. M18.
[ORIGIN Bengali *Mag(h)*, of unknown origin.]
▸ **A** *noun*. = ARAKANESE *noun*. Also, a native or inhabitant of Chittagong on the Bay of Bengal. M18.
▸ **B** *attrib.* or as *adjective*. = ARAKANESE *adjective*. L19.

mug /mʌg/ *noun*[5]. *Scot. & dial.* L18.
[ORIGIN from MUG *verb*[1].]
Fog, mist; light rain, drizzle.

mug /mʌg/ *noun*[6] & *adjective*[2]. *slang*. M19.
[ORIGIN Perh. a use of MUG *noun*[3].]
▸ **A** *noun*. **1** A stupid or incompetent person, a fool, a simpleton; a gullible person. M19.
R. C. HUTCHINSON I'm not such a mug as to think that. P. BARKER He's got one mug working to keep him. He doesn't need two.
mug's game a thankless task; a useless, foolish, or unprofitable activity.
2 A person, a fellow; *spec.* a person on the opposite side of the law to oneself; (chiefly *US*) a hoodlum, a thug. L19.
Observer There were recognised . . putters up of jobs, what the mugs called master minds.
▸ **B** *attrib.* or as *adjective*. Of a person: stupid, incompetent; gullible. E20.
L. GRIFFITHS I despise mug punters, the kind of people who bet on every race.

mug /mʌg/ *noun*[7]. *arch. slang*. M19.
[ORIGIN from MUG *verb*[5].]
1 An examination. *rare*. M19.
2 A person who learns a subject by concentrated study. L19.

mug /mʌg/ *verb*[1] *intrans.* Long *obsolete* exc. *Scot. & dial.* Infl. **-gg-**. LME.
[ORIGIN Prob. of Scandinavian origin: cf. Old Norse *mugga* mist, drizzle, Norwegian, Swedish dial. *mugg* mould, mildew, prob. rel. to MUCUS. See also MUG *verb*[2].]
Drizzle, rain lightly.

mug /mʌg/ *verb*[2] *intrans. slang & dial.* Infl. **-gg-**. M18.
[ORIGIN Perh. a use of MUG *verb*[1].]
Pout, grow sullen; mope.

mug /mʌg/ *verb*[3]. Infl. **-gg-**. E19.
[ORIGIN from MUG *noun*[3].]
1 *verb trans.* Strike in the face; thrash; assault; strangle. Also (now the usual sense), rob with violence, esp. in a public place. E19.
V. S. PRITCHETT He took the affair as if his person had been assaulted, as if he had been mugged. W. MCILVANNEY An old woman could be mugged in a park.
2 *verb intrans.* Pull a face, esp. in front of an audience, a camera, etc.; grimace. *slang*. M19.
J. HELLER I mug and gesticulate right along with the people on the screen.
3 *verb trans.* Photograph the face of, esp. for police or other official records. *US slang*. L19.
G. V. HIGGINS We brought him up to the marshal's office and mugged him and printed him.
4 *verb trans.* Kiss, fondle. *slang* (chiefly *Austral. & NZ*). E20.
■ **mugging** *noun* the action or an act of the verb; *spec.* (an instance of) the robbing of a person with violence, esp. in a public place: M19.

mug /mʌg/ *verb*[4] *trans. slang & dial.* Infl. **-gg-**. M19.
[ORIGIN from MUG *noun*[1].]
Bribe with alcoholic drink; buy a drink for (a person).

mug /mʌg/ *verb*[5]. *slang*. Infl. **-gg-**. M19.
[ORIGIN Uncertain: perh. rel to MUG *verb*[2].]
1 *verb intrans.* Read or study in a concentrated manner. Freq. foll. by *up*. M19.
W. H. AUDEN You need not mug up on dates.
2 *verb trans.* Learn (a subject) by concentrated study. Freq. foll. by *up*. L19.
P. SCOTT I suspect that he mugged it up before he came to Tradura.

mug /mʌg/ *verb*[6] *intrans. slang* (chiefly *Canad.* & NAUTICAL). Infl. **-gg-**. M19.
[ORIGIN Prob. from MUG *noun*[1].]
Foll. by *up*: eat heartily; also, have a snack, meal, or hot drink.
– COMB.: **mug-up** a snack, meal, or hot drink.

muga /ˈmuːgə/ *noun*. Also **moonga** /ˈmuːŋgə/. E17.
[ORIGIN Assamese *mugā*.]
A wild silk obtained from the cocoon of an Assamese saturniid silk moth, *Antheraea assamensis*.
attrib.: ***muga silk***, ***muga worm***, etc.

Muganda /mʊˈgandə/ *noun & adjective*. M19.
[ORIGIN Bantu, from *mu* sing. prefix + *ganda*. Cf. BAGANDA, LUGANDA.]
▸ **A** *noun*. Pl. BAGANDA *noun*. A member of the Baganda people; a native or inhabitant of the former kingdom of Buganda, now part of Uganda. M19.
▸ **B** *attrib.* or as *adjective*. Of or pertaining to a Muganda or the Baganda. M19.

mugearite /ˈmʌgɪərʌɪt/ *noun*. E20.
[ORIGIN from *Mugeary*, a village on the Isle of Skye, Scotland + -ITE[1].]
PETROGRAPHY. A dark fine-grained trachyte which has oligoclase as the main feldspar and also contains olivine, orthoclase, and apatite.
■ **mugearitic** /mʌgɪəˈrɪtɪk/ *adjective* E20.

muggee /mʌˈgiː/ *noun*. L20.
[ORIGIN from MUG *verb*[3] + -EE[1].]
The victim of a mugging; a person who is robbed with violence, esp. in a public place.

mugger /ˈmʌgə/ *noun*[1]. *dial.* M18.
[ORIGIN from MUG *noun*[1] + -ER[1].]
A hawker of earthenware.

mugger /ˈmʌgə/ *noun*[2]. M19.
[ORIGIN Hindi *magar* from Sanskrit *makara* MAKARA.]
A broad-nosed Indian crocodile, *Crocodylus palustris*, venerated by many Hindus.

mugger /ˈmʌgə/ *noun*[3]. M19.
[ORIGIN from MUG *verb*[3] + -ER[1].]
1 A person who mugs another; *spec.* a person who robs someone with violence, esp. in a public place. M19.
2 A person who pulls a face or grimaces, esp. in front of an audience, a camera, etc. *slang*. L19.

mugger /ˈmʌgə/ *noun*[4]. *slang*. L19.
[ORIGIN from MUG *verb*[5] + -ER[1].]
A person who studies in a concentrated manner.

mugger /ˈmʌgə/ *noun*[5]. M20.
[ORIGIN Unknown.]
A nail, usu. of wrought iron, used for protecting the inner soles of mountaineering boots.

mugger /ˈmʌgə/ *noun*[6] & *verb*. *slang*. M20.
[ORIGIN Alt. of BUGGER *noun*[1], *verb*.]
▸ **A** *noun*. An unpleasant or undesirable person or thing, a person, a chap. Also, a negligible amount. M20.
▸ **B** *verb*. **1** *verb trans.* Curse, damn. Chiefly in imprecations in optative form. M20.
2 *verb intrans.* Foll. by *off*: go away. M20.

mugget /ˈmʌgɪt/ *noun*. *obsolete* exc. *dial.* L15.
[ORIGIN Unknown.]
The intestines of a calf or sheep, esp. when cooked as food. Formerly also (*rare*), a dish made from this.

muggins /ˈmʌgɪnz/ *noun*. Pl. same, **-inses**. E18.
[ORIGIN Perh. the surname *Muggins*, with allus. to MUG *noun*[6]. Cf. JUGGINS.]
1 A fool, a simpleton; a dupe, a person who is outwitted. Now usu. (a name for) a person who has acted foolishly, esp. oneself. *colloq.* E18.
Daily Telegraph The letter bomb was not meant for me personally. I was just the muggins who opened it. *Undercurrents* I didn't . . put a copyright on it, . . and Muggins has not received a penny in payment.
2 **a** A card game resembling snap. M19. ▸**b** A game of dominoes in which the players count by fives or multiples of five. M19.

muggish /ˈmʌgɪʃ/ *adjective*. Long *rare* or *obsolete*. M17.
[ORIGIN Prob. from MUG *noun*[5] + -ISH[1]. Cf. MUG *verb*[1].]
Damp, musty.

muggle /ˈmʌg(ə)l/ *noun*[1]. *slang* (orig. *US*). E20.
[ORIGIN Unknown.]
1 *sing.* & (usu.) in *pl.*, treated as *sing.* or *pl.* Marijuana. E20.
2 A marijuana cigarette. E20.
■ **muggler** *noun* a marijuana addict M20.

muggle /ˈmʌg(ə)l/ *noun*[2]. *colloq.* L20.
[ORIGIN Invented by J. K. Rowling, the Brit. writer of the *Harry Potter* books, and used by her to mean 'a person without magical powers'.]
A person who is not conversant with a particular activity or skill.

Muggletonian /mʌg(ə)lˈtəʊnɪən/ *adjective & noun*. M17.
[ORIGIN from *Muggleton* (see below) + -IAN.]
▸ **A** *noun*. A member of a Christian sect founded in England *c* 1651 by Lodowicke Muggleton (d. 1691) and John Reeve, who claimed to be the two witnesses of *Revelation* 11:3–6; a believer in the personal inspiration of Muggleton and Reeve. M17.
▸ **B** *adjective*. Of or pertaining to this sect. L17.
■ **Muggletonianism** *noun* (adherence to) the doctrines of this sect L19.

muggy /ˈmʌgi/ *adjective*. E18.
[ORIGIN from MUG *noun*[5] or *verb*[1] + -Y[1].]
1 Of air, atmosphere, etc.: oppressively damp, close, and warm. Also, (of a room) close and stuffy through lack of ventilation. E18.
R. GITTINGS London was warm and muggy.
2 Mouldy, moist, damp, wet. *obsolete* exc. *dial.* M18.

Mughal *noun & adjective* see MOGUL *noun*[1] & *adjective*.

mugient /ˈmjuːdʒɪənt/ *adjective*. *rare*. M17.
[ORIGIN Latin *mugient-* pres. ppl stem of *mugire* to bellow: see -ENT.]
Lowing, bellowing.

mugo /ˈmuːgəʊ/ *noun*. Pl. **-os**. M18.
[ORIGIN French *mugho*, Italian *mugo*.]
In full ***mugo pine***. A dwarf pine, *Pinus mugo*, of the mountains of central and southern Europe.

muguet /mygɛ/ *noun*. L16.
[ORIGIN French from medieval Latin *muscatum* musk-scented, from *muscus* MUSK *noun*. Cf. MUGWORT.]
†**1** Any of certain fragrant plants; *spec.* woodruff, *Galium odoratum*. L16–M17.
2 Lily of the valley, *Convallaria majalis*; a scent made from or resembling it. L16.
– NOTE: Formerly naturalized.

mugwort /ˈmʌgwəːt/ *noun*. OE.
[ORIGIN from base of MIDGE + WORT *noun*[1]. In sense 2 perh. alt. of MUGUET.]
1 An aromatic hedge plant, *Artemisia vulgaris*, of the composite family, with small flower heads in leafy panicles and pinnatifid leaves. Also, any of various other plants of this genus. OE.
2 Crosswort, *Cruciata laevipes*. *rare*. L18.

mugwump /ˈmʌgwʌmp/ *noun & adjective*. Chiefly *N. Amer.* M19.
[ORIGIN Massachusett *mugquomp* war leader.]
▸ **A** *noun*. **1** A great man, a boss. Chiefly *joc.* M19.
2 A person who holds aloof from party politics; *spec.* in *US* HISTORY a Republican who in 1884 refused to support the Republican nominee for president. Also, a person who remains neutral or non-committal. L19.
▸ **B** *attrib.* or as *adjective*. That is a mugwump; of or pertaining to mugwumps. L19.
■ **mugwumpery** *noun* behaviour or qualities characteristic of a mugwump L19. **mugwumpish** *adjective* L19. **mugwumpism** *noun* behaviour characteristic of a mugwump; the principles or practice of mugwumps: L19.

muhajir /məˈhɑːdʒɪə, mʊ-/ *noun*. L17.
[ORIGIN Arabic *muhājir* emigrant, from *hajara*: see HEGIRA.]
1 A person who accompanied Muhammad in his emigration from Mecca to Medina in 622. L17.

M

2 (A descendant of) a Muslim emigrant who left India for Pakistan at the time of partition in 1947 or subsequently. **M20.**

Muhammad /mʊˈhaməd/ *noun*. Also **Mohammed** /məʊˈhaməd/. **E17.**
[ORIGIN Arabic *Muḥammad*. See also MAHOMET.]
(The name of) the Arabian prophet of Islam (*c* 570–632), whose revelations constitute the Koran, regarded by Muslims as the final messenger sent by God to warn humankind against the consequences of rebelliousness against the divinely ordered way.
■ **Muhammadism** *noun* (*arch.*) the Muslim religion, Islam (regarded as *offensive* by Muslims) **E17.**

Muhammadan /mʊˈhaməd(ə)n/ *adjective & noun*. *arch.* Also **Mohammedan** /məʊˈhaməd(ə)n/. **M17.**
[ORIGIN from MUHAMMAD + -AN.]
▶ **A** *adjective*. Of or pertaining to the prophet Muhammad; Muslim. **M17.**
Muhammadan blue a cobalt blue used as an underglaze colour on Chinese porcelain of the Ming dynasty.
▶ **B** *noun*. A follower or adherent of Muhammad; a Muslim. **L17.**
■ **Muhammadanism** *noun* (*arch.*) the Muslim religion, Islam **E19.**
– NOTE: *Muhammadan* and *Muhammadanism*, with their vars. *Mohammedan* and *Mohammedanism*, are regarded as offensive by some Muslims and should be avoided.

Muharram /məˈhʌrəm/ *noun*. Also **Mo-**. **L18.**
[ORIGIN Arabic *muḥarram* inviolable.]
The first month of the year in the Islamic calendar; an annual celebration in this month commemorating the deaths of the grandsons of Muhammad.

muhimbi /muːˈhɪmbi, muːˈwɪmbi/ *noun*. **E20.**
[ORIGIN Luo.]
An evergreen leguminous tree, *Cynometra alexandri*, of central and eastern Africa; the hard heavy timber of this tree.

muid /ˈmuːɪd, *foreign* mɥi/ *noun*[1]. Long *obsolete* exc. *hist.* **LME.**
[ORIGIN Old French *mui* (mod. *muid*) from Latin *modium* neut. of MODIUS. Cf. MUID *noun*[2].]
A former French dry unit of capacity equivalent to several bushels, varying widely among localities and commodities. Formerly also, a liquid measure of varying capacity; a cask holding this.

muid /ˈmuːɪd/ *noun*[2]. Now chiefly *S. Afr.* Also (earlier) †**mud**. **L15.**
[ORIGIN Dutch *mud(de)* = Old Saxon *muddi*, Old High German *mutti*, German *Mutt*, from West Germanic from Latin MODIUS. Cf. MUID *noun*[1].]
A Dutch or (now esp.) South African dry measure of capacity equal to approx. 117 litres (3.22 bushels).

M

muishond /ˈməʊshɒnt/ *noun*. *S. Afr.* Pl. **-honds**, same, **-honde** /-hɒndə/. **L18.**
[ORIGIN Afrikaans from Dutch dial., or directly from Middle Dutch *muushont* weasel (lit. 'mouse-dog').]
A mongoose, a polecat, a skunk; *spec.* the zorilla, *Ictonyx striatus*.

muisvoël /ˈməʊsfəʊəl/ *noun*. *S. Afr.* Also **-vogel** /-fəʊg(ə)l/. **E19.**
[ORIGIN Afrikaans, from *muis* mouse + *voël* bird.]
= *mousebird* s.v. MOUSE *noun*.

mujahideen /ˌmʊdʒɑːhɪˈdiːn/ *noun pl.* Also **-hidin**, **-hedin**. **L19.**
[ORIGIN Persian, Arabic *mujāhidīn* colloq. pl. of *mujāhid* a person who fights a jihad.]
Guerrilla fighters in an Islamic country, esp. those supporting the cause of Islam.

mujtahid /mʊdʒˈtɑːhɪd/ *noun*. **E19.**
[ORIGIN Persian from Arabic, active pple of *ijtahada* strive.]
Esp. in Iran: a person accepted in Shiism as an authority on the interpretation of Islamic law.

Mujur *noun* var. of MUDJUR.

mukhtar /ˈmʊktɑː/ *noun*. **E19.**
[ORIGIN (Turkish *muhtar* from) Arabic *muḵtār* pass. pple of *iḵtāra* choose, elect.]
1 Formerly in India: an authorized agent; an attorney or solicitor. **E19.**
2 In Turkey and some Arab countries: the head of the local government of a town or village; a minor provincial official. **L19.**

mukim /ˈmuːkɪm/ *noun*. Pl. same, **-s**. **E19.**
[ORIGIN Malay, from Arabic *muqīm* remaining, resident.]
In Malaysia and Indonesia: the smallest administrative district.

mukluk /ˈmʌklʌk/ *noun*. Also **muckluck**. **M19.**
[ORIGIN Yupik *maklak* bearded seal.]
A high boot made of sealskin, or now also of canvas or some other material, as worn by Eskimos.

mukti /ˈmʌkti, ˈmʊkti/ *noun*. **L18.**
[ORIGIN Sanskrit = release, from *muc* set free, release.]
HINDUISM & JAINISM. = MOKSHA.

muktuk /ˈmʌktʌk/ *noun*. **M19.**
[ORIGIN Inupiaq *maktak*.]
The skin and outer blubber of a whale, used as food by Eskimos.

mulatta /mjuːˈlatə/ *noun*. *arch.*, *offensive*. **E17.**
[ORIGIN Spanish *mulata* fem. of *mulato* MULATTO.]
A woman with one white and one black parent.

mulatto /mjuːˈlatəʊ/ *noun & adjective*. *arch.*, *offensive*. Pl. **-o(e)s**. **L16.**
[ORIGIN Spanish & Portuguese *mulato* young mule, mulatto, irreg. from *mulo* MULE *noun*[1].]
▶ **A** *noun*. A person having one white and one black parent; a person of mixed white and black parentage. **L16.**
▶ **B** *adjective*. **1** Having brown skin; tawny. **E17.**
2 Designating a kind of mid-brown fertile soil. *US*. **M18.**

mulattress /mjuːˈlatrɪs/ *noun*. *arch.*, *offensive*. **E19.**
[ORIGIN French *mulâtresse* fem. of *mulâtre* MULATTO: see -ESS[1].]
A woman with one white and one black parent.

mulberry /ˈmʌlb(ə)ri/ *noun & adjective*.
[ORIGIN Old English *mōrberie*, corresp. to Dutch *moerbezie*, Old High German *mōrberi*, *murb-* (Middle High German *mülber*, German *Maulbeere*), from Latin *morum* mulberry, *morus* mulberry tree + BERRY *noun*[1], with dissimilation of *r* . . *r* to *l* . . *r*.]
▶ **A** *noun*. **1** Any of various trees of the genus *Morus* (family Moraceae), *esp.* (**a**) (more fully ***black mulberry***) *Morus nigra*, grown for its purple, succulent fruit; (**b**) (more fully ***white mulberry***) *Morus alba*, which has white insipid fruit and whose leaves are used to feed silkworms; the berry-like multiple fruit of these trees. Also, (the similar fruit of) any of various other plants, esp. (*dial.* & *US*) a blackberry or raspberry. **OE.**
2 In full ***mulberry colour***. The dark red or purple colour of a mulberry. **E19.**
3 In full ***Mulberry harbour***. A man-made usu. prefabricated harbour, orig. and esp. as used under this code name in the Allied invasion of Europe in 1944. **M20.**
– COMB.: **mulberry-bird** *Austral.* the southern figbird, *Sphecotheres vieilloti*; ***mulberry colour***: see sense 2 above; **mulberry molar** MEDICINE a first molar with a small, nodular, pitted crown resulting from congenital syphilis; **mulberry tree** a tree which bears mulberries.
▶ **B** *adjective*. Of the colour of a mulberry. **E19.**

mulch /mʌl(t)ʃ/ *noun & verb*. **M17.**
[ORIGIN Prob. from use as noun of MULSH.]
▶ **A** *noun*. Partly rotted straw; a mixture of wet straw, leaves, etc., spread around (the roots of) a plant to enrich or insulate the soil. **M17.**
▶ **B** *verb trans.* Treat or cover with mulch. **E18.**
■ **mulching** *noun* (**a**) the action of the verb; (**b**) a mulch: **E18.**

mulct /mʌlkt/ *noun*. *arch.* **L16.**
[ORIGIN Latin *mulcta*, *multa*: see MULCT *verb*. Cf. French †*mulcte*, †*multe*.]
A fine imposed for an offence; a penalty of any kind.

T. L. PEACOCK Imposed a heavy mulct on every one of his servants. I. ZANGWILL Nor was this the only mulct which Providence exacted.

mulct /mʌlkt/ *verb trans.* *literary*. Pa. t. & pple **mulct**, **mulcted**. **L15.**
[ORIGIN French †*mul(c)ter* from Latin *mul(c)tare*, from *mul(c)ta* fine, amercement.]
1 Punish (a person) by a fine; extract money from (a person) by fine or taxation. Formerly also, subject to a penalty of any kind. **L15.**

G. M. TREVELYAN No government dared to propose to mulct the taxpayer for such a purpose. C. P. SNOW The Revenue might mulct him with largish fines.

2 Deprive (a person) *of* money, goods, etc., esp. by duress or fraudulent means; swindle. Usu. in *pass.* **M18.**

Contemporary Review Each tree is mulcted of her spreading boughs.

3 Obtain by swindling. **M20.**

P. GALLICO A rapacious old moneybag who would never miss the few dollars mulcted of her.

mulctuary /ˈmʌlktjʊəri/ *adjective*. *rare*. **E17.**
[ORIGIN from MULCT *noun* after *tumultuary*.]
That punishes by a fine. Formerly also, punishable by a fine.

mule /mjuːl/ *noun*[1] & *adjective*.
[ORIGIN Old English *mūl* prob. from Germanic from Latin, reinforced in Middle English by Old French *mul(e)* from Latin *mulus*, *mula*.]
▶ **A** *noun*. **1** An animal born of a mating between a male ass and a mare or *loosely* between a female ass and a stallion (= HINNY *noun*[1]), used esp. as a draught animal and for bearing loads, and proverbially regarded as the epitome of obstinacy. **OE.** ▸**b** A person considered to resemble a mule; *esp.* a stupid or obstinate person. **LME.** ▸**c** A person acting as a courier for illicit drugs. *slang*. **M20.**

W. VAN T. CLARK A good mule can work two horses into the ground. J. WYNDHAM Obstinate as a mule over that, he was. **c** L. D. ESTLEMAN He was just another mule running kilos for the big boys.

2 A hybrid animal or plant. **E18.**
3 Any of various devices combining the characteristics of two distinct types; *spec.* (**a**) *hist.* a kind of spinning machine producing yarn on spindles, intermediate between earlier types; (**b**) a coin with obverse and reverse produced by dies not originally intended for use on the same coin; (**c**) (now *dial.*) a boat combining the characteristics of a coble and a fishing boat; (**d**) a small tractor or locomotive for towing canal boats, moving trailers, etc. **L18.**
4 NAUTICAL. A large triangular sail sometimes used on a ketch. **M20.**
▶ **B** *attrib.* or as *adjective*. Hybrid. **M18.**
– COMB. & SPECIAL COLLOCATIONS: **mule-bird**, **mule canary** a cross between a canary and another finch, esp. a goldfinch; **mule chest** a chest with a drawer or drawers; **mule deer** a black-tailed deer of western N. America, *Odocoileus hemionus*, with long ears; **mule-driver** a person who drives a mule, or a team or train of mules; **mule-driving** the occupation or activity of a mule-driver; **mule-ear rabbit**, **mule-eared rabbit** = JACKRABBIT; **mule-headed** *adjective* stubborn; **mule-killer** *US* (**a**) a kind of small cart drawn by a mule or mules; (**b**) a scorpion; **mule rabbit** *US* = ***mule-ear rabbit*** above; **mule-skinner** *N. Amer.* a mule-driver, esp. on the prairies; **mule-skinning** *N. Amer.* mule-driving, esp. on the prairies; **mule-whacker** *US* a mule-driver.

mule /mjuːl/ *noun*[2]. **LME.**
[ORIGIN French *mule* (fem.) slipper, *mules* (pl.) chilblains.]
1 A chilblain, esp. on the heel; a sore on a horse's pastern. Long *obsolete* exc. *Scot.* **LME.**
2 A kind of (esp. backless) slipper or light shoe. **M16.**

M. WESLEY Pink feathered mules on her feet.

muled /mjuːld/ *adjective*. **E20.**
[ORIGIN from MULE *noun*[1] + -ED[2].]
NUMISMATICS. Of a coin: having obverse and reverse produced by dies not originally intended for use on the same coin.

Mules /mjuːlz/ *noun*. Chiefly *Austral.* **M20.**
[ORIGIN J. H. W. *Mules* (d. 1946), Austral. sheep-farmer.]
Used ***attrib.*** and in ***possess.*** to designate an operation developed by Mules to reduce blowfly strike in sheep by removing the folds of skin in the crotch most likely to be affected.
■ **mulesed** /mjuːlzd/ *adjective* (of a sheep) treated by the Mules operation **M20.** **mulesing** *noun* the application of the Mules operation **M20.**

muleta /məˈleɪtə/ *noun*. **L18.**
[ORIGIN Spanish.]
BULLFIGHTING. A red cloth fixed to a stick used by a matador during the *faena*.

muleteer /mjuːlɪˈtɪə/ *noun*. **M16.**
[ORIGIN French *muletier*, from *mulet* dim. of Old French *mul(e)* MULE *noun*[1]: see -ET[1], -EER.]
A mule-driver.

muley /ˈmjuːli/ *noun & adjective*[1]. Now chiefly *US*. Also **mooley** /ˈmuːli/, (earlier) **mulley** /ˈmʌli/. **L16.**
[ORIGIN Perh. formed as MOILEY. Cf. MULL *noun*[3].]
▶ **A** *noun*. **1** A cow, *esp.* a hornless one. Also ***muley cow***. **L16.**
2 A long saw that is guided by carriages and operates with a rapid vertical reciprocating motion. Also ***muley saw***. *US*. **M19.**
▶ **B** *adjective*. Of cattle: hornless. **M19.**

muley /ˈmjuːli/ *adjective*[2]. Long *obsolete* exc. *Scot.* **E17.**
[ORIGIN from MULE *noun*[2] + -Y[1].]
Having chilblains, esp. on the heel.

muley /ˈmjuːli/ *adjective*[3]. **L19.**
[ORIGIN from MULE *noun*[1] + -Y[1].]
Mulish, stubborn; sulky.

mulga /ˈmʌlgə/ *noun*. *Austral.* **M19.**
[ORIGIN Kamilaroi *malga*.]
1 Any of several small acacia, esp. *Acacia aneura*, forming dense scrub in dry inland areas and sometimes used for fodder (also ***mulga tree***); *the* land covered with such vegetation, (colloq.) *the* outback. **M19.**
red mulga: see RED *adjective*.
2 A thing made of the wood of a mulga tree, *esp.* a club or shield. **M19.**
3 In full ***mulga wire***. A rumour, a message, a (false) report; *the* grapevine. *slang*. **L19.**
– COMB.: **mulga parrot** a multicoloured parrot, *Psephotus varius*, of southern Australia; ***mulga tree***: see sense 1 above; ***mulga wire***: see sense 3 above.

mulgara /məlˈgɑːrə/ *noun*. **M20.**
[ORIGIN Prob. from Wangganguru (an Australian Aboriginal language of northern South Australia) *mardagura*.]
A rat-sized carnivorous marsupial, *Dasycercus cristicauda* (family Dasyuridae), with a pointed snout, native to central Australia.

muli *noun* var. of MOOLI.

muliebral /mjuːlɪˈiːbr(ə)l/ *adjective*. *rare*. **M17.**
[ORIGIN from Latin *muliebris* (see MULIEBRITY) + -AL[1].]
Of or pertaining to woman or womanhood.

muliebrity /mjuːlɪˈɛbrɪti/ *noun*. *literary*. **L16.**
[ORIGIN Late Latin *muliebritas*, from Latin *muliebris*, from *mulier* woman: see -ITY.]
Womanhood; the characteristics or qualities of a woman (opp. ***virility***); softness, effeminacy.

mulier /ˈmjuːlɪə/ *adjective & noun*. Long *rare* or *obsolete*. LME.
[ORIGIN Repr. Anglo-Norman *mulieré* (Anglo-Latin *mulieratus*), from *mulier*, Old French *moiller* wife from Latin *mulier* woman.]
LAW. ▸**A** *adjective*. Of a child: born in wedlock, legitimate; legitimated by the subsequent marriage of the parents. LME.
▸**B** *noun*. A legitimate child; a child born in wedlock. LME.

mulierose /ˈmjuːlɪərəʊs/ *adjective*. *rare*. E18.
[ORIGIN Latin *mulierosus*, from *mulier* woman: see -OSE[1].]
Fond of women.

mulierosity /ˌmjuːlɪəˈrɒsɪti/ *noun*. *rare*. E17.
[ORIGIN Latin *mulierositas*, formed as MULIEROSE: see -OSITY.]
(Excessive) fondness for women.

mulish /ˈmjuːlɪʃ/ *adjective*. E18.
[ORIGIN from MULE *noun*[1] + -ISH[1].]
Characteristic of a mule; resembling a mule; stubborn, sulky.

Times The attitude of the exchange staff . . is often off-hand, uncomprehending and mulish. N. MARSH 'Come, sir,' he said as Warrender still looked mulish.

■ **mulishly** *adverb* L18. **mulishness** *noun* M18.

mull /mʌl/ *noun*[1]. ME.
[ORIGIN Middle Dutch & mod. Dutch *mul*, *mol* cogn. with Old English *myl* dust, Old Norse *moli* crumb, *mylja* crush, from Germanic base also of MEAL *noun*[1]. Cf. MOULD *noun*[1], MULL *noun*[7].]
1 Something reduced to small particles; dust, ashes, rubbish. *obsolete* exc. *dial.* ME.
2 *SCIENCE*. A suspension of a finely ground solid in a liquid, esp. as used in recording the infrared spectrum of the solid. M20.

mull /mʌl/ *noun*[2]. *Scot*. ME.
[ORIGIN Rel. to Gaelic *maol*, Old Irish *mael* (mod. *maol*), Old Norse *múli* (perh. identical with *múli* snout) = Old High German *mūl* (German *Maul*) snout.]
A promontory, a headland. Freq. in place names.
Mull of Kintyre etc.

mull /mʌl, mʊl/ *noun*[3]. Long *obsolete* exc. *dial.* M17.
[ORIGIN Perh. formed as MOIL *noun*[3]. Cf. MULEY *noun*.]
A heifer, a cow.

mull /mʌl/ *noun*[4]. L17.
[ORIGIN Abbreviation of MULMUL.]
More fully ***mull muslin***. A thin soft plain muslin, freq. used in bookbinding. Cf. SUPER *noun*[2]

mull /mʌl/ *noun*[5]. *Scot*. M18.
[ORIGIN Var. of MILL *noun*[1].]
A snuffbox, orig. one having a grinder.

†**mull** *noun*[6]. *colloq.* E–L19.
[ORIGIN Uncertain: perh. from MULL *verb*[1].]
A muddle, a mess. Chiefly in ***make a mull of***.

mull /mʌl/ *noun*[7]. E20.
[ORIGIN Danish *muld* MOULD *noun*[1], rel. to MULL *noun*[1].]
SOIL SCIENCE. Humus which does not form a distinct top layer but is admixed with the underlying mineral soil, characteristic of grassland and hardwood forest and usu. not very acidic. Cf. MOR.

mull /mʌl/ *noun*[8]. E20.
[ORIGIN from MULL *verb*[2].]
Mulled wine.

mull /mʌl/ *verb*[1]. LME.
[ORIGIN from MULL *noun*[1].]
†**1** *verb intrans*. Become wet or liquid. Also, rain lightly, drizzle. Only in LME.
2 *verb trans*. **a** Grind to powder, pulverize; crumble. *obsolete* exc. *dial.* LME. ▸**b** Convert (solid material) into a mull (MULL *noun*[1] 2). M20.
†**3** *verb trans*. Make mild; soften; thaw. E–L17.

mull /mʌl/ *verb*[2] *trans*. E17.
[ORIGIN Unknown.]
Make (wine, beer, etc.) into a hot drink with sugar, spices, etc. Chiefly as ***mulled*** *ppl adjective*.

mull /mʌl/ *verb*[3] *trans*. *colloq.* M19.
[ORIGIN from MULL *noun*[6].]
Bungle, miss, or mishandle (a catch, ball, etc.).

mull /mʌl/ *verb*[4] *trans*. M19.
[ORIGIN Uncertain: cf. MILL *verb*[1] II.]
1 †**a** *verb intrans*. Of a thought etc.: develop without active consideration. *US colloq.* Only in M19. ▸**b** *verb trans*. Consider, ponder upon. *US*. L19.

b *Science* The Germans . . were mulling a public recommendation from their safety advisory committee.

2 *verb trans*. Foll. by *over*. Turn over in one's mind; reflect upon, think over. L19.

J. WAINWRIGHT I . . stared into the darkness and mulled over what had been said.

mull /mʌl/ *verb*[5]. M20.
[ORIGIN Unknown.]
1 *verb trans*. Moisten (leather) during manufacture to increase suppleness. M20.
2 *verb intrans*. Of leather: become more supple through being moistened. M20.

mullah /ˈmʌlə, ˈmʊlə/ *noun*. E17.
[ORIGIN Persian & Urdu *mullā*, Turkish *molla* from Arabic *mawlā* lord, master.]
(A title given to) a Muslim learned in Islamic theology and sacred law.

mullein /ˈmʌlɪn/ *noun*. Also ***mullen**. LME.
[ORIGIN Old French *moleine* (mod. *molène*) from a Gaulish base corresp. to Breton *melen*, Cornish & Welsh *melyn* yellow.]
1 Any of various tall plants of the genus *Verbascum*, of the figwort family, with long spiky racemes of usu. yellow flowers and often with densely woolly leaves; *esp.* (in full ***great mullein***), *V. thapsus*. LME.
†**2** Any of several plants resembling these in foliage; *esp.* Jerusalem sage, *Phlomis fruticosa*. L16–M18.
3 = ***mullein moth*** below. E19.
– COMB.: **mullein moth** a pale brown and grey noctuid moth, *Cucullia verbasci*, whose larvae feed on mullein; **mullein pink** the rose campion, *Lychnis coronaria*; **mullein shark** = ***mullein moth*** above; **mullein tea** an infusion of mullein leaves, used medicinally; **mullein wave** a white geometrid moth with pale grey markings, *Scopula marginepunctata*.

mullen /ˈmʌlən/ *noun*[1]. Long *obsolete* exc. *dial.* Also (earlier) †**molan**. LME.
[ORIGIN Unknown.]
A horse's headstall or bridle.

mullen *noun*[2] see MULLEIN.

muller /ˈmʌlə/ *noun*[1]. LME.
[ORIGIN Perh. from Anglo-Norman (cf. Old French *moloir* adjective), from *moldre* grind: cf. -ER[2].]
1 A stone, or piece of a similar substance, with a flat base or grinding surface used for grinding powders on a slab. LME.
2 Any of various mechanical contrivances for grinding or crushing. E19.

muller /ˈmʌlə/ *noun*[2]. M19.
[ORIGIN from MULL *verb*[2] + -ER[1].]
A person who or thing which mulls wine etc.; *spec.* a vessel in which wine etc. may be mulled.

Muller /ˈmʊlə/ *noun*[3]. E20.
[ORIGIN See below.]
Used ***attrib.*** and in ***possess.*** to designate a set of bodily exercises published and promoted by the 19th-cent. Danish physical educationalist J. P. Muller.

Muller *noun*[4] var. of MÜLLER *noun*[1].

muller /ˈmʌlə/ *verb trans*. *slang*. L20.
[ORIGIN Unknown. Cf. MULLERED.]
1 Wreck, ruin, destroy. L20.
2 Of a sports player, team, etc.: comprehensively beat or outplay. L20.

Daily Mirror We absolutely mullered Huddersfield in the second half.

Müller /ˈmʊlə/ *noun*[1]. Also **Muller**. L18.
[ORIGIN A German surname, app. that of its discoverer.]
MINERALOGY. ***Müller glass***, ***Müller's glass***, = HYALITE.

Müller /ˈmʊlə/ *noun*[2]. M19.
[ORIGIN Heinrich *Müller* (1820–64), German anatomist.]
ANATOMY. Used **attrib.**, in **possess.**, and with *of* to designate various structures of the eye described by Müller, esp. (***a***) any of the fibroid glial cells which form the supportive tissue of the retina; (***b***) any of certain involuntary muscles of the eye.

mullered /ˈmʌləd/ *adjective*. *slang*. L20.
[ORIGIN Prob. from MULLER *verb* + -ED[1].]
Extremely drunk.

Müllerian /mʊˈlɪərɪən/ *adjective*[1]. L19.
[ORIGIN from J. *Müller* (1801–58), German physiologist + -IAN.]
ANATOMY. ***Müllerian duct***, either of a pair of ducts in a vertebrate embryo which, in the female, form the Fallopian tubes and other reproductive structures. Also called ***paramesonephric duct***.

Müllerian /mʊˈlɪərɪən/ *adjective*[2]. Also **Mu-**. L19.
[ORIGIN from J. F. T. *Müller* (1821–97), German zoologist + -IAN.]
ZOOLOGY. **1** ***Müllerian mimicry***, a form of mimicry in which two or more noxious species develop similar patterns of coloration etc. as a protective device. L19.
2 ***Müllerian mimic***, an animal exhibiting this. M20.

Müller-Lyer illusion /mʊləˈlʌɪər ɪˌl(j)uːʒ(ə)n/ *noun phr*. L19.
[ORIGIN F. C. *Müller-Lyer* (1857–1916), German sociologist and philosopher.]
An optical illusion in which a line with an arrowhead pointing outwards at each end appears shorter than one of equal length with the arrowheads pointing inwards.

Müller-Thurgau /mʊləˈtʊəgaʊ/ *noun*. M20.
[ORIGIN H. *Müller-Thurgau* (1850–1927), Swiss viniculturist.]
(The vine bearing) a white grape from a cross between Riesling and Sylvaner vines; fruity white wine made from these grapes.

mullet /ˈmʌlɪt/ *noun*[1]. Pl. same, **-s**. LME.
[ORIGIN Old French *mulet*, from Latin *mullus* red mullet from Greek *mullos* rel. to *melos* black: see -ET[1].]
Any of various edible, mainly marine fishes, esp. of the families Mullidae and Mugilidae; *US* a grey mullet.
grey mullet: see GREY *adjective*. **red mullet** a mullet of the family Mullidae; *spec.* a red or reddish-brown food fish, *Mullus surmuletus*, of the Mediterranean and NE Atlantic.
– COMB.: **mullet-head** *US colloq.* (***a***) a freshwater fish with a large flat head; (***b***) a stupid person; **mullet-headed** *adjective* (*US colloq.*) stupid.

mullet /ˈmʌlɪt/ *noun*[2]. LME.
[ORIGIN Anglo-Norman *molet*, Old French *molette* rowel, dim. of *meule* millstone from Latin *mola* grindstone: see -ET[1].]
HERALDRY. A star with five (or more) straight points, as a charge or as a cadency mark for a third son.

mullet /ˈmʌlɪt/ *noun*[3]. L20.
[ORIGIN Uncertain: popularized (and perh. coined) by the US hip-hop group the Beastie Boys (1994).]
A hairstyle, worn esp. by men, in which the hair is cut short at the front and sides and left long at the back.

mulley *noun & adjective* see MULEY *noun & adjective*[1].

mulligan /ˈmʌlɪg(ə)n/ *noun*. *N. Amer. colloq.* In sense 2 also **M-**. L19.
[ORIGIN App. from the surname *Mulligan*.]
1 A stew made from odds and ends of food. L19.
2 *GOLF*. An extra stroke awarded after a poor shot, not counted on the scorecard. M20.

mulligatawny /ˌmʌlɪgəˈtɔːni/ *noun*. L18.
[ORIGIN Tamil *milaku-taṇṇi* lit. 'pepper-water'.]
More fully ***mulligatawny soup***. A highly seasoned soup orig. from India.

mulligrubs /ˈmʌlɪgrʌbz/ *noun pl*. Now *dial.* L16.
[ORIGIN Uncertain: perh rel. to MULLYGRUB.]
1 A state of depression; a fit of low spirits. L16.
2 Stomach ache, colic. E17.

mullion /ˈmʌljən/ *noun*. M16.
[ORIGIN Metath. var. of MONIAL: cf. MUNNION.]
1 *ARCHITECTURE*. A vertical bar dividing the lights in a window, esp. in Gothic architecture. M16.
2 *GEOLOGY*. Each of a series of ribs or columns on a rock face, usu. formed by folding. L19.
mullion structure.
■ **mullioned** *adjective* having mullions; constructed with mullions: M18.

mullipuff /ˈmʌlɪpʌf/ *noun*. Long *obsolete* exc. *dial.* E17.
[ORIGIN from MULLY *adjective* + PUFF *noun*.]
A puffball fungus; *fig.* a contemptible person.

mullite /ˈmʌlʌɪt/ *noun*. E20.
[ORIGIN from the island of *Mull*, Scotland + -ITE[1].]
MINERALOGY. A colourless orthorhombic aluminium silicate formed naturally or artificially from other aluminium silicates at high temperatures and used in heat-resistant porcelains and bricks.

mullock /ˈmʌlək/ *noun & verb*. LME.
[ORIGIN from MULL *noun*[1] + -OCK.]
▸**A** *noun*. **1** Rubbish, refuse. Now *Austral., NZ, & dial.* LME.
2 Rock which does not contain gold or from which gold has been extracted. *Austral. & NZ*. M19.
3 *fig.* Worthless information, nonsense. *Austral. & NZ*. M19.
– PHRASES: **poke mullock (at)** *Austral. & NZ* deride, ridicule, poke fun (at).
▸**B** *verb*. **1** *verb trans*. Litter (a place), esp. with refuse from gold-mining. *Austral. & NZ*. M19.
2 *verb intrans*. Work quickly and carelessly. Usu. foll. by *over*. *Austral.* L19.
■ **mullocky** *adjective* of the nature of mullock M19.

mulloway /ˈmʌləweɪ/ *noun*. Also (earlier) †**mallowe**. M19.
[ORIGIN Yaralde (an Australian Aboriginal language of South Australia) *malowe*.]
A large sciaenid food and game fish, *Argyrosomos hololepidotus*, of Australian coastal waters. Also called ***jewfish***.

mully /ˈmʌli/ *adjective*. Long *obsolete* exc. *dial.* L16.
[ORIGIN from MULL *noun*[1] + -Y[1].]
Dusty, powdery.

mullygrub /ˈmʌlɪgrʌb/ *noun*. Now *Austral.* M18.
[ORIGIN Prob. from MULLY + GRUB *noun*.]
A grub or caterpillar; now *esp.* a witchetty grub.

mulmul /ˈmʌlmʌl/ *noun*. E17.
[ORIGIN Hindi *malmal*, perh. ult. from Sanskrit *mala* dirt, inferior.]
A thin variety of muslin. Cf. MULL *noun*[4].

Mulozi *noun sing*. see LOZI.

Mulready /mʌlˈriːdi/ *noun*. Pl. **-dys**, **-dies**. M19.
[ORIGIN See below.]
In full ***Mulready envelope***. A postal envelope with a design by the Irish painter William Mulready (1786–1863), the designer of the first penny postage envelope (1840).

mulsh /mʌlʃ/ *adjective*. Long *dial.* *rare*. LME.
[ORIGIN Prob. rel. to MELSH.]
Soft.

mult- *combining form* see MULTI-.

†**multangle** *noun*. L16–L18.
[ORIGIN mod. Latin *multangulum* neut. sing. of *multangulus*, from Latin MULTI- + *angulus* ANGLE *noun*[3].]
A polygon.

M

multangular /mʌlˈtaŋɡjʊlə/ *adjective. rare.* E17.
[ORIGIN mod. Latin *multangularis*, from Latin MULTI- + *angulus* ANGLE *noun*[1]: see -AR[1]. Cf. MULTI-ANGULAR.]
Having many angles; polygonal.

†**multarticulate** *adjective.* L17–E19.
[ORIGIN from MULT(I- + ARTICULATE *adjective*.]
= MULTI-ARTICULATE.

multeity /mʌlˈtiːɪti/ *noun.* E19.
[ORIGIN from MULT(I- after *aseity*.]
1 The quality or condition of being many or of consisting of many individual parts. E19.
2 A thing consisting of many individual parts. M19.

multi- /ˈmʌlti/ *combining form.* Before a vowel also **mult-**.
[ORIGIN Latin, from *multus* much, many: see -I-.]
Many; more than one.
■ **multi-ˈaccess** *adjective* pertaining to or involving the simultaneous use of a computer by operators at a number of terminals M20. **multi-ˈangular** *adjective* = MULTANGULAR *adjective* M19. **multi-arˈticular** *adjective* (MEDICINE) affecting more than one joint L19. **multi-arˈticulate** *adjective* (chiefly ZOOLOGY) having many joints or articulations E19. **multiˈaxial** *adjective* involving several or many axes M19. **multibillioˈnaire** *noun* a person whose assets are worth several or many billions of dollars, pounds, etc. E20. **multibuy** *noun* a purchase of two or more articles at a special discount compared to the price when bought separately L20. **multicast** *verb & noun* (*a*) *verb trans.* send (data) across a computer network to several users at the same time; (*b*) *noun* a set of data sent across a computer network to many users at the same time: L20. **multiˈcellular** *adjective* having, consisting of, or involving several or many cells M19. **multicelluˈlarity** *noun* the state of being multicellular E20. **multiˈcentral** *adjective* = MULTICENTRIC (a) M19. **multiˈcentric** *adjective* (*a*) pertaining to, arising from, or having several or many centres; (*b*) CYTOLOGY having more than two centromeres: E20. **multiˈchannel** *adjective* employing or possessing several or many communication or television channels M20. **multiˈcircuit** *adjective* supplying or containing several or many electric circuits E20. **multicollineˈarity** *noun* (STATISTICS) the existence of a perfect or nearly perfect linear correlation between a set of variables when the regression of some dependent variable on them is being investigated M20. **multicolour** *noun & adjective* (*a*) *noun* the condition of being of several or many colours; in *pl.*, several or many colours; (*b*) *adjective* = MULTICOLOURED: M19. **multicoloured** *adjective* being of several or many colours M19. **multicore** *adjective* (esp. of an electric cable) having several or many cores E20. **multiˈcostate** *adjective* (BOTANY) having more than one rib M19. **multiˈcuspid**, **multiˈcuspidate** *adjectives* having more than two cusps M19. **multiˈcyclic** *adjective* (GEOLOGY) produced by or having undergone several cycles of erosion and deposition M20. **multiˈdentate** *adjective* (*a*) having many teeth; (*b*) CHEMISTRY (of a ligand) having more than one point of attachment to a central atom; polydentate: E19. **multidiaˈlectal** *adjective* fluent in the use of several dialects of the same language M20. **multidiaˈlectalism** *noun* the condition of being multidialectal; facility in using, the use of, several dialects of the same language: L20. **multidiˈmensional** *adjective* having or pertaining to more than three dimensions L19. **multidimensioˈnality** *noun* the property of being multidimensional E20. **multidiˈmensionally** *adverb* in a manner that involves or requires more than three dimensions M20. **multidisciˈplinary** *adjective* combining or involving several or many separate academic disciplines M20. **multiˈdisciplined** *adjective* concerned with several or many separate academic disciplines M20. **multi-eˈlectrode** *adjective* possessing or involving several electrodes; *spec.* (of a valve) having two or more sets of electrodes, associated with separate electron beams, within a single envelope E20. **multi-ˈethnic** *adjective* composed of or involving several ethnic groups M20. **multiˈfaceted** *adjective* having several or many facets (chiefly *fig.*) L19. **multifactor** *adjective* = MULTIFACTORIAL E20. **multifacˈtorial** *adjective* involving or dependent on a number of factors (esp. genes) or causes E20. **multifacˈtorially** *adverb* in a multifactorial manner M20. **multi-faith** *adjective* involving or characterized by several religions M20. **multiˈfilament** *adjective* containing or composed of several or many filaments; *spec.* (of yarn) made up of many fine threads: M20. **multiflash** *adjective* (*a*) PHOTOGRAPHY made with two or more flashbulbs which are operated in rapid succession; (*b*) designating or pertaining to a process or apparatus for desalinating seawater by repeated sudden boiling at successively lower pressures: M20. **multiˈfocal** *adjective & noun* (*a*) *adjective* having or pertaining to several foci, or a range of focal lengths; (*b*) *noun* a multifocal lens; usu. in *pl.*, spectacles with multifocal lenses: L19. **multifeˈtation** *noun* (*a*) pregnancy with more than one fetus; (*b*) pregnancy with more than two fetuses: M19. **multiˈfoliate** *adjective* (BOTANY) having many (more than 7 or 9) leaflets M19. **multifont** *adjective* (COMPUTING) pertaining to or having the ability to read or print characters of several different fonts M20. **multifunction** *adjective* = MULTIFUNCTIONAL M20. **multiˈfunctional** *adjective* having or fulfilling several or many functions M20. **multifunctioˈnality** *noun* the state of being multifunctional M20. **multigene** *adjective* (GENETICS) designating or pertaining to a group of genes which act together to produce a gene product or phenotypic effect M20. **multigenerˈational** *adjective* of or relating to several generations M20. **multigeˈneric** *adjective* (BIOLOGY) derived from or involving more than one genus E20. **multigerm** *adjective* (AGRICULTURE) designating or pertaining to varieties of sugar beet in which each seed ball contains several fruits and so gives rise to several seedlings M20. **multigrade** *adjective & noun* (*a*) *adjective* (of engine oil) meeting the requirements of several standard grades; (*b*) *noun* (proprietary name for) a kind of photographic paper made with two emulsions of different sensitivities, from which prints with different levels of contrast can be made using colour filters: M20. **multigrain** *adjective* involving more than one grain; *spec.* (of bread) made from more than one kind of grain: M20. **multigym** *noun* (*a*) a piece of exercise equipment which can be used in several ways or by several people at once; (*b*) a room containing several pieces of exercise equipment: L20. **multijugate** /mʌlˈtɪdʒʊɡət, mʌltɪˈdʒuːɡət/ *adjective* [Latin *jugum* yoke, pair] BOTANY having many pairs of leaflets M19. **multilaˈmellar** *adjective* having or consisting of several or many lamellae L19. **multilaˈmellate**, **multilaˈmellous** *adjectives* = MULTILAMELLAR M19. **multiˈlaminar**, **multiˈlaminate** *adjectives* having or consisting of several or many laminae or layers L19. **multilayer** *adjective & noun* (*a*) *adjective* composed of or occurring in several or many layers; (*b*) *noun* a structure or film composed of several or many layers, *spec.* of more than one monolayer: E20. **multiˈlayered** *adjective* having several or many layers, multilayer E20. **multiˈlevel** *adjective* having, involving, or operating on several or many levels; *spec.* designating a method of direct selling in which buyers at each level of a hierarchy secure the participation of further buyers at a level below them: E20. **multiˈlevelled** *adjective* having several or many levels, multilevel M20. **multiˈlineal** *adjective* having several or many lines; *spec.* designating a kinship system including relationships derived from the parents, grandparents, etc., of both father and mother: L18. **multiˈlinear** *adjective* having, consisting of, or involving several or many lines L19. **multiˈlobate**, **multiˈlobed** *adjectives* having or consisting of several or many lobes M19. **multiˈlobular** *adjective* having, consisting of, or affecting more than one lobule L19. **multiloˈcation** *noun* the fact of being or power to be in several or many places simultaneously M19. **multiˈlocular** *adjective* having, consisting of, or characterized by several or many cells or chambers E19. **multiˈmammate** *adjective* having several pairs of mammae; *multimammate rat*, a tropical African rodent, *Mastomys natalensis*, freq. destructive to crops: E20. **multiˈmedia** *adjective* designating or pertaining to a form of artistic, educational, etc., communication using more than one medium M20. **multimillioˈnaire** *noun* a person whose assets are worth several or many millions of dollars etc. M19. **multi-ˈnegative** *noun* an array of similar images in negative form for printing small items several at a time by photolithography E20. **multiˈnuclear**, **multiˈnucleate** *adjectives* having more than one nucleus M19. **multi-occuˈpation** *noun* occupation, esp. tenancy, of a house by more than one family with shared cooking, washing, etc., facilities M20. **multi-ˈoccupy** *verb trans.* occupy, esp. tenant, (a house) with one or more other families and with shared cooking, washing, etc., facilities; house (people, esp. tenants) in such accommodation: M20. **multiˈovulate** *adjective* (BOTANY) containing several or many ovules M19. **multipack** *noun* a package containing a number of similar or identical products sold at a discount compared to the price when bought separately M20. **multi-ˈpartism** *noun* (belief in or advocacy of) a multi-party system M20. **multi-ˈpartist** *adjective* of or pertaining to multipartism M20. **multi-ˈparty** *adjective* comprising (members of) several political parties; designating or pertaining to an electoral system in which the interests of the electorate are represented by three or more political parties: E20. **multi-ˈpartyism** *noun* = MULTI-PARTISM M20. **multipath** *adjective* (TELECOMMUNICATIONS) involving (radio) signals that have travelled from a single source by several paths M20. **multiˈpersonal** *adjective* comprising several or many personalities E19. **multiphase** *adjective* having or producing two or more phases; multiphased; ELECTRICITY polyphase: L19. **multiphased** *adjective* occurring in several stages M20. **multiˈphasic** *adjective* designating a form of test or investigation designed to reveal various phases or aspects of personality, health, etc. (MINNESOTA *Multiphasic Personality Inventory*) M20. **multiˈpinnate** *adjective* (BOTANY) several or many times pinnate L19. **multiˈplanar** *adjective* consisting of or pertaining to a number of planes M19. **multiplane** *noun & adjective* (*a*) *noun* an aeroplane or glider having two or more sets of wings, one above the other; (*b*) *adjective* involving or occupying several or many distinct planes or layers; CINEMATOGRAPHY designating a technique used to give an enhanced impression of perspective: E20. **multiplaned** *adjective* having or occupying several or many planes E20. **multi-ˈplatinum** *adjective* designating or pertaining to a musical recording or artist that has sold more than two million copies L20. **multiplayer** *noun &. adjective* (*a*) *noun* a compact disc player which can play a number of discs in succession; (*b*) *adjective* designed for or involving several players: L20. **multi-ply** *noun & adjective* (*a*) *noun* plywood consisting of more than three layers; (*b*) *adjective* consisting of more than three strands, layers, or thicknesses: M20. **multipoint** *adjective* having or serving several or many points; *spec.* (of a water heater) serving a number of hot-water taps: E20. **multi-poˈsition** *adjective* able to be used or placed in several or many positions M20. **multi-ˈpositive** *noun* an array of similar images in positive form for printing small items several at a time by photolithography M20. **multipoˈtential** *adjective* (BIOLOGY & MEDICINE) = PLURIPOTENTIAL E20. **multiˈprocessing** *noun* (COMPUTING) processing by a number of processors sharing a common memory and common peripherals M20. **multiˈprocessor** *noun* a computer capable of performing multiprocessing M20. **multiˈprogram** *adjective* (COMPUTING) designed for or pertaining to multiprogramming M20. **multiˈprogrammed** *adjective* = MULTIPROGRAM M20. **multiˈprogramming** *noun* (COMPUTING) the execution of two or more independent programs concurrently M20. **multi-ˈpurpose** *adjective* serving several or many purposes M20. **multiˈradiate** *adjective* having several or many rays M19. **multiˈsection** *noun* (*rare*) division into several or many parts M19. **multiˈseptate** *adjective* (BOTANY) having several or many septa or partitions M19. **multiˈserial** *adjective* arranged in several or many series or rows M19. **multiˈserially** *adverb* in a multiserial manner L19. **multiˈsided** *adjective* having several or many sides, many-sided E20. **multiˈsonant** *adjective* (*rare*) producing many sounds M17. **multiˈsonous** *adjective* (*rare*) = MULTISONANT E20. **multiˈspectral** *adjective* operating in or involving several regions of the electromagnetic spectrum M20. **multiˈspiral** *adjective* having several or many spiral coils or convolutions M19. **multistaˈbility** *noun* the property or state of being multistable M20. **multiˈstable** *adjective* (of a system) composed of a number of interconnected subsystems each of which can achieve stability independently of the others M20. **multistage** *adjective* (*a*) consisting of, occurring in, or involving several or many stages; (*b*) STATISTICS designating sampling carried out in a number of stages, the sample obtained at each stage being divided into smaller units and taken as the population for the next stage of sampling: E20. **multistage** *verb trans.* make multistage E20. **multiˈstorey** *adjective & noun* (a building, esp. a car park) having several or many storeys E20. **multi-ˈtask** *adjective* (COMPUTING) involving multitasking; capable of multi-tasking: M20. **multi-ˈtask** *verb intrans.* (*a*) (of a computer) execute more than one program or task simultaneously; (*b*) (of a person) deal with more than one task at the same time: M20. **multi-ˈthreaded** *adjective* (COMPUTING) employing multi-threading L20. **multi-ˈthreading** *noun* (COMPUTING) the execution of different parts of a program concurrently by the use of multiple processors; a technique whereby several processors can operate on the same data concurrently without interference: L20. **multi-ˈtier**, **multi-ˈtiered** *adjectives* having or comprising several or many tiers or layers M20. **multi-ˈuse** *adjective* serving several or many uses M20. **multi-ˈuser** *adjective* having several or many users; (of a computer system) able to be used by more than one person and accessed from more than one terminal concurrently: M20. **multi-uˈtility** *noun* a privatized utility which offers its customers several services L20. **multiˈvariant** *adjective* influenced by or taking account of several variables; STATISTICS multivariate: E20. **multiˈvariate** *adjective* (STATISTICS) involving or having two or more variates or random variables E20. **multiˈvarious** *adjective* (now *rare*) manifold and diverse E17. **multivendor** *adjective* (of computer services, hardware, etc.) provided by more than one supplier L20. **multiˈvitamin** *adjective & noun* (a tablet or preparation) containing a combination of vitamins M20. **multiˈvoltine** *adjective* (ENTOMOLOGY) producing several generations in a year L19. **multiwall** *adjective* having several or many walls; *spec.* (of a large bag etc.) made of several layers of strong paper usu. attached to one another along the bottom and the side folds: M20.

multiculti /ˌmʌltɪˈkʌlti/ *adjective & noun. US slang.* L20.
[ORIGIN Rhyming alt. of MULTICULTURAL.]
▸ **A** *adjective.* Multicultural; of or relating to multiculturalism or multiculturalists. L20.
▸ **B** *noun.* **1** Multiculturalism. L20.
2 A multiculturalist. L20.

multicultural /mʌltɪˈkʌltʃ(ə)r(ə)l/ *adjective.* M20.
[ORIGIN from MULTI- + CULTURAL.]
Designating or pertaining to a society consisting of several or many culturally distinct groups.

> *Times* This multicultural, multi-lingual society . . is one of the most cosmopolitan in the world.

■ **multiculturalism** *noun* the characteristics of a multicultural society; a policy advocating the establishment of a multicultural society: M20. **multiculturalist** *noun & adjective* L20. **multiculturally** *adverb* L20.

multifarious /mʌltɪˈfɛːrɪəs/ *adjective & noun.* L16.
[ORIGIN from Latin *multifarius* varied, diverse (formed as MULTI-) + -OUS.]
▸ **A** *adjective.* **1** Having great variety or diversity; (with *noun pl.*) many and various. L16.

> A. J. CRONIN The whole range of his multifarious duties found Llewellyn blandly expert and prepared. CLIVE JAMES The place is too multifarious to be captured by the pen.

2 LAW (now *hist.*). Of a bill: that inappropriately or confusingly embraces two or more distinct matters. E19.
▸ **B** *noun.* KANTIAN PHILOSOPHY. A manifold (see MANIFOLD *noun* 2). L18.
■ **multifariously** *adverb* M17. **multifariousness** *noun* L17.

multifid /ˈmʌltɪfɪd/ *adjective.* M18.
[ORIGIN from MULTI- + -FID. Cf. Latin *multifidus*.]
BOTANY & ZOOLOGY. Divided into several or many parts by deep clefts or notches.
■ **multifidly** *adverb* M19.

†**multifidous** *adjective.* M17–M19.
[ORIGIN formed as MULTIFID + -OUS.]
ZOOLOGY. Multifid; (of an animal) having multifid feet.

multiflora /mʌltɪˈflɔːrə/ *noun.* E19.
[ORIGIN Late Latin, fem. of *multiflorus* MULTIFLOROUS.]
In full ***multiflora rose***. A rose, *Rosa multiflora*, of eastern Asia, with clusters of small white or pink flowers; any of the cultivated varieties developed from this.

multiflorous /mʌltɪˈflɔːrəs/ *adjective.* M18.
[ORIGIN from late Latin *multiflorus*, formed as MULTI- + *flor-*, *flos* flower: see -OUS.]
BOTANY. Of a stalk: bearing more than three flowers.
■ Also **multifloral** *adjective* M19.

multifold /ˈmʌltɪfəʊld/ *adjective.* E19.
[ORIGIN from MULTI- + -FOLD, after *manifold*.]
Manifold.

multiform /ˈmʌltɪfɔːm/ *adjective & noun.* E17.
[ORIGIN French *multiforme* or Latin *multiformis*, formed as MULTI- + -FORM.]
▸ **A** *adjective.* Having several or many forms; highly diversified in form; of many and various forms or kinds. E17.

> T. DWIGHT The multiform brogue, which salutes the ears of a traveller in . . New-York. *Wireless World* Produced by progressive tooling and multiform methods.

▸ **B** *noun.* A multiform object; something exhibiting many and various forms. Also, multiform character, multiformity. M19.
■ **multiˈformity** *noun* the condition or character of being multiform; diversity or variety of form: L16. **multiˈformous** *adjective* (*rare*) multiform M17.

multigraph /ˈmʌltɪɡrɑːf/ *noun.* L19.
[ORIGIN from MULTI- + -GRAPH.]
1 A small printing machine using specially cast type fitted into grooves on a rotating cylinder. *hist.* L19.
2 MATH. A graph in which two vertices may be connected by more than one edge. M20.

M

multigravida /mʌltɪˈɡravɪdə/ *noun*. Pl. **-das**, **-dae** /-diː/. L19.
[ORIGIN from MULTI- after PRIMIGRAVIDA.]
MEDICINE & ZOOLOGY. A female pregnant for at least the second time. Formerly also, a female who has been pregnant more than once. Cf. PRIMIGRAVIDA, SECUNDIGRAVIDA.
■ ˈ**multigravid** *adjective & noun* (*a*) *adjective* pregnant for at least the second time; (*b*) *noun* = MULTIGRAVIDA: M20.

multihull /ˈmʌltɪhʌl/ *noun & adjective*. M20.
[ORIGIN from MULTI- + HULL *noun*[2].]
(Designating) a boat having more than one hull or float.
■ **multiˈhulled** *adjective* (of a boat) having more than one hull or float M20.

multilateral /mʌltɪˈlat(ə)r(ə)l/ *adjective*. E17.
[ORIGIN from late Latin *multilaterus* + -AL[1], or from medieval Latin *multilateralis*, formed as MULTI- + LATERAL.]
1 (Of a figure) having more than four sides; many-sided (*lit. & fig.*). E17.
J. F. CLARKE The whole poem represents the multilateral character of Hinduism.
2 Orig. (*LAW*), made or entered on by two or more parties. Now, involving three or more states as parties to an agreement, esp. in respect of trade and finance, or of possession of weapons; not unilateral. E19.
Times The . . first effective system of multilateral arms control the world had ever known. A. J. AUGARDE The only way . . is for each nation unilaterally to disarm itself. It is unrealistic to wait for multilateral disarmament.
3 Chiefly *hist.* Of a school: offering two or more distinct curricula for secondary education. M20.
■ **multilateralism** *noun* the quality of being multilateral; adherence to multilateral principles and practice, esp. in respect of (*spec.* nuclear) disarmament: E20. **multilateralist** *noun & adjective* (*a*) *noun* an adherent or advocate of multilateralism; (*b*) *adjective* of, pertaining to, or characteristic of multilateralism or multilateralists: M20. **multilateraliˈzation** *noun* the action or result of multilateralizing something M20. **multilateralize** *verb trans.* make multilateral M20. **multilaterally** *adverb* M19. **multilateralness** *noun* (long *rare*) M18.

multilingual /mʌltɪˈlɪŋɡw(ə)l/ *adjective & noun*. M19.
[ORIGIN from MULTI- + Latin *lingua* tongue + -AL[1].]
▸ **A** *adjective*. Involving several or many languages; written, spoken, etc., in several or many languages; having several or many languages; speaking several or many languages fluently. M19.
A. S. DALE His family was multilingual, well-read and very eccentric.
▸ **B** *noun*. A multilingual person. M20.
■ **multilingualism** *noun* the ability to speak several or many languages; the use of several or many languages: M20. **multilinguist** *noun* a multilingual person E20. **multilingually** *adverb* M20.

Multilith /ˈmʌltɪlɪθ/ *noun*. Also **m-**. M20.
[ORIGIN from MULTI- + LITH(OGRAPH *noun*.]
(Proprietary name for) a small offset-lithographic printing machine.
■ **multilithed** *adjective* printed by a machine of this kind M20.

multiloquent /mʌlˈtɪləkwənt/ *adjective*. *rare*. M17.
[ORIGIN Late Latin *multiloquentia*, formed as MULTI- + LOQUENT.]
Using many words, esp. habitually; characterized by the use of many words; talkative.
■ **multiloquence** *noun* the (habitual) use of many words, talkativeness M18.

multimer /ˈmʌltɪmə/ *noun*. M20.
[ORIGIN from MULTI- + -MER.]
CHEMISTRY. An aggregate of molecules held together by relatively weak bonds, such as hydrogen bonds.
■ **multiˈmeric** *adjective* M20.

multimeter /ˈmʌltɪmiːtə/ *noun*. E20.
[ORIGIN from MULTI- + -METER.]
ELECTRICITY. An instrument designed to measure voltage, current, and usu. resistance, often over several different ranges of value.

multimodal /mʌltɪˈməʊd(ə)l/ *adjective*. L19.
[ORIGIN from MULTI- + MODAL.]
1 *STATISTICS*. (Of a frequency curve or distribution) having several modes or maxima; (of a property) occurring with such a distribution. L19.
2 Characterized by several different modes of occurrence or activity. E20.
■ **multimodalism** (*rare*), **multimoˈdality** *nouns* the property or quality of being multimodal E20.

multinational /mʌltɪˈnaʃ(ə)n(ə)l/ *adjective & noun*. E20.
[ORIGIN from MULTI- + NATIONAL *adjective*.]
▸ **A** *adjective*. **1** Comprising or pertaining to several nationalities or ethnic groups. E20.
2 Of a company or other organization: operating in several or many countries. M20.
▸ **B** *noun*. A multinational company or organization. M20.
■ **multinationally** *adverb* E20.

multinomial /mʌltɪˈnəʊmɪəl/ *adjective & noun*. E17.
[ORIGIN from MULTI- after *binomial*.]
MATH. ▸ **A** *adjective*. = POLYNOMIAL *adjective*. E17.
▸ **B** *noun*. = POLYNOMIAL *noun*. L17.

multinominal /mʌltɪˈnɒmɪn(ə)l/ *adjective*. M17.
[ORIGIN from Latin *multinominis* (formed as MULTI- + Latin *nomin-*, *nomen* name) + -AL[1].]
Having several or many names; polyonymous.

multip /mʌlˈtɪp/ *noun*. *slang*. M20.
[ORIGIN Abbreviation.]
MEDICINE. = MULTIPARA.

multipara /mʌlˈtɪp(ə)rə/ *noun*. Pl. **-ras**, **-rae** /-riː/. M19.
[ORIGIN mod. Latin, fem. of *multiparus*: see MULTIPAROUS.]
MEDICINE & ZOOLOGY. A female who has had more than one pregnancy resulting in viable offspring; a pregnant female with at least one previous delivery. Cf. PRIMIPARA.

multiparous /mʌlˈtɪp(ə)rəs/ *adjective*. M17.
[ORIGIN from mod. Latin *multiparus*, formed as MULTI- + -PAROUS: see -OUS.]
1 *ZOOLOGY*. Pertaining to or characterized by giving birth to more than one young at a single birth. M17.
2 *MEDICINE & ZOOLOGY*. Of, pertaining to, or designating a female who is a multipara. M19.
3 *BOTANY*. Of a cyme: that has many axes. L19.
■ **multiˈparity** *noun* the condition of being multiparous M19.

multipartite /mʌltɪˈpɑːtʌɪt/ *adjective*. M17.
[ORIGIN Latin *multipartitus*, formed as MULTI- + PARTITE.]
Divided into several or many parts; having several or many divisions.

multiped /ˈmʌltɪpɛd/ *noun & adjective*. Now *rare*. Also **-pede** /-piːd/. E17.
[ORIGIN Latin *multipeda*, formed as MULTI- + *ped-*, *pes* foot.]
▸ **A** *noun*. A creature with many feet. Formerly *spec.*, a woodlouse. E17.
▸ **B** *adjective*. Having many feet. M18.
■ **multipedous** /mʌlˈtɪpɪdəs/ *adjective* pertaining to or characteristic of many-footed animals E18.

multiple /ˈmʌltɪp(ə)l/ *noun, adjective, & verb*. L16.
[ORIGIN French from late Latin *multiplus* alt. of classical Latin MULTIPLEX.]
▸ **A** *noun*. †**1** A multitude, a great number. Only in L16.
2 *MATH*. A quantity which is a product of a given quantity and some other, *esp.* one which results from multiplication of that quantity by an integer. L17.
least common multiple, **lowest common multiple** the smallest quantity that has two or more given quantities (and no others) as its factors.
3 *TELEPHONY*. Each of the sections of a multiple switchboard, containing one jack for each subscriber. Also, a circuit in which the same connection may be made at different points. Now *rare*. E20.
in multiple (connected) between the same pairs of wires, so forming such a circuit.
4 A shop or store with many branches, a chain store. M20.
5 An inexpensive work of art that is able to be mass-produced. M20.
P. DICKINSON A bronze . . paperweight . . had the look of one of a large issue of multiples.
▸ **B** *adjective*. **1** Consisting of or characterized by several or many parts, elements, or individual components; having several or many origins, results, actions, etc.; manifold. M17. ▸**b** *MEDICINE*. Of a disease or symptom: affecting several parts, organs, etc. M19.
P. AUSTER The Agents perform a multiple function—part junk dealer, part manufacturer, part shopkeeper.
2 With *noun pl.* Many and various. M17.
P. CUTTING She had multiple cuts on her hands and legs. B. CHATWIN Dr Frankfurter unwrapped the object from its multiple layers of tissue paper.
3 *MATH*. That is a multiple (see sense B.1 above). Formerly also, that is some multiple *of*. E18.
– SPECIAL COLLOCATIONS & COMB.: **multiple-access** *adjective* = MULTI-ACCESS. **multiple allele**, **multiple allelomorph** *GENETICS*: located at a genetic locus known to have three or more alleles. **multiple-aspect** *adjective* designating a colour-light railway signal able to display at least three aspects. **multiple birth** *MEDICINE* the birth of more than one child after a multiple pregnancy. **multiple-choice** *adjective* designating (a question in) an examination etc. presenting the candidate with several possible answers from which one is to be selected as correct. **multiple-disc** *adjective* designating a kind of friction clutch consisting of a row of coaxial discs fixed alternately to the driving and the driven parts. **multiple exposure** *PHOTOGRAPHY* the exposure of the same frame of a film more than once; a multiple image resulting from this. **multiple factors** genes which interact to control the expression of a character. **multiple fission** *BIOLOGY* division of a cell into more than two daughter cells. **multiple image** a composite image consisting of two or more superimposed or adjacent images, e.g. resulting from the combination of reflected light rays, television signals, etc., that have travelled by different paths, or the simultaneous use of several projectors in a cinema. *multiple MYELOMA*. **multiple personality** *PSYCHOLOGY* a dissociative condition in which an individual's personality is apparently split into two or more distinct sub-personalities, each of which may become dominant at different times. **multiplepoinding** *SCOTS LAW* an action by the holder of personal property claimed by several people, causing the claimants to interplead. **multiple pregnancy** *MEDICINE* a single pregnancy in which more than one fetus develops. **multiple proportion** the proportion existing between a quantity and some multiple of it, or between several multiples of it; ***law of multiple proportions*** (*CHEMISTRY*), the tendency of chemical elements to combine in integral proportions. **multiple ratio** the ratio existing between a quantity and some multiple of it, or between several multiples of it. **multiple resistance** *PHARMACOLOGY*: of a micro-organism to the action of more than one antibiotic. **multiple-resistant** *adjective* (*PHARMACOLOGY*) exhibiting multiple resistance. **multiple sclerosis** a chronic progressive demyelinating disease, chiefly affecting young adults, in which sclerosis occurs in patches in the brain and spinal cord and usu. characterized by successive remissions and relapses leading to tremor, paresis, ataxia, and disturbed sight and speech; also called ***disseminated sclerosis***. **multiple shift** a double or treble shift of work. **multiple shop**, **multiple store** any of several or many shops selling the same type of goods and owned by one firm; a shop having branches in various places. **multiple star** *ASTRONOMY* a group of three or more associated stars rotating around a common centre. ***multiple store***: see ***multiple shop*** above. ***multiple superparticular***: see SUPERPARTICULAR *adjective*. **multiple switchboard** *TELEPHONY* (now *hist.*): in which each subscriber's circuit is accessible to each operator. **multiple twin** *CRYSTALLOGRAPHY* a twinned crystal composed of three or more components whose relative orientations are all governed by the same twin law. **multiple-twin** *adjective* (*TELEPHONY*) designating a cable with a number of cores each of which consists of four wires arranged as two twisted pairs twisted together. **multiple-unit** *adjective & noun* (designating or pertaining to) a train with a number of coaches provided with motors controllable by a single driver. **multiple-use** *adjective* = MULTI-USE *adjective*.
▸ **C** *verb trans*. *TELEPHONY*. Make (a circuit) accessible to operators at more than one point; provide or employ duplicates of (a device) for this purpose. E20.

multiplet /ˈmʌltɪplət/ *noun*. M19.
[ORIGIN from MULTIPLE *adjective* + -ET[1], after *doublet*, *triplet*, etc.]
1 A set of more than three or four similar things. M19.
2 *PHYSICS*. **a** A closely spaced group of related spectral lines in a spectrum; a group of related atomic states or energy levels with slightly different energies. E20. ▸**b** A group of subatomic particles that differ only in charge. Also, a series of such groups, each characterized by a different value of hypercharge (or strangeness) but having the same spin and parity. M20.

multiplex /ˈmʌltɪplɛks/ *adjective, noun, & verb*. LME.
[ORIGIN Latin, formed as MULTI- + -PLEX[1].]
▸ **A** *adjective*. †**1** *MATH*. = MULTIPLE *adjective* 3. LME–L18.
2 Manifold; of many elements, having many interrelated features; multiple. E17.
T. L. PEACOCK The whole complex and multiplex detail of the noble science of dinner. F. W. FARRAR Brief and scattered letters out of the multiplex correspondence of a varied life.
3 *TELECOMMUNICATIONS*. Designating or pertaining to the transmission of two or more independent signals or programmes (to be later separated and recovered) simultaneously over a single wire or channel. L19.
4 *MEDICINE*. = MULTIPLE *adjective* 1b. L19.
5 Designating a cinema complex incorporating two or more cinemas on a single site. L20.
▸ **B** *noun*. †**1** *MATH*. = MULTIPLE *noun* 2. L16–L17.
2 *TELECOMMUNICATIONS*. A multiplex system or signal. M20.
3 An object, system, etc., comprising many aspects, parts, or features. M20.
4 A complex of two or more cinemas on a single site. L20.
▸ **C** *verb trans*. *TELECOMMUNICATIONS*. Incorporate into a multiplex signal or system. E20.
■ **multiplexer**, **multiplexor** *nouns* a device which multiplexes something M20. **multiˈplexity** *noun* the quality or condition of being multiplex, multiplex nature or structure; an instance of this: M20.

multipliable /ˈmʌltɪplʌɪəb(ə)l/ *adjective*. E17.
[ORIGIN from MULTIPLY *verb* + -ABLE.]
Able to be multiplied.

multiplicable /ˈmʌltɪplɪkəb(ə)l/ *adjective*. M16.
[ORIGIN Old French, or medieval Latin *multiplicabilis*, from Latin *multiplicare* MULTIPLY *verb*: see -ABLE.]
Able to be multiplied; multipliable.
■ **multiplicaˈbility** *noun* (*rare*) L17.

multiplicand /ˌmʌltɪplɪˈkand, ˈmʌltɪplɪkand/ *noun*. L16.
[ORIGIN medieval Latin *multiplicandus* (sc. *numerus* number) gerundive of Latin *multiplicare* MULTIPLY *verb*: see -AND.]
MATH. A quantity to be multiplied by another (the multiplier).

multiplicate /ˈmʌltɪplɪkət, mʌlˈtɪplɪkət/ *adjective & noun*. Now *rare*. L15.
[ORIGIN Latin *multiplicatus* pa. pple of *multiplicare* MULTIPLY *verb*: see -ATE[2]. As noun from MULTI- after *duplicate* etc.]
▸ **A** *adjective*. Orig., multiplied, increased. Later, manifold, of many elements or parts, multiplex. L15.
▸ **B** *noun*. Any of several or many exactly corresponding copies of a document etc. M19.
in multiplicate in several or many exactly corresponding copies.

multiplication /ˌmʌltɪplɪˈkeɪʃ(ə)n/ *noun*. LME.
[ORIGIN Old French, or Latin *multiplicatio(n-)*, from *multiplicat-* pa. ppl stem of *multiplicare* MULTIPLY *verb*: see -ATION.]
1 The action or an act of multiplying something; the condition of being multiplied. Now chiefly as passing into sense 3. LME.
2 Reproduction of people or animals; propagation of plants. LME.
3 *MATH*. **a** The action or process of multiplying quantities; the process of finding the quantity produced by repeatedly adding one quantity as many times as there are units in a second quantity, or (in the case of fractions) of

M

finding the same fraction of one quantity as a second quantity is of unity. LME. ▸**b** The successive application of an operator; generation of a product. M19.
b ***logical multiplication***: see LOGICAL *adjective*.
†**4** *ALCHEMY*. The action of transmuting metals into gold or silver. LME–L17.
5 *BOTANY*. Abnormal increase in the number of whorls or of organs in a whorl. M19.
– COMB.: **multiplication constant**, **multiplication factor** *NUCLEAR PHYSICS* in nuclear fission, the ratio by which the number of neutrons increases during a period equal to the lifetime of a neutron; **multiplication sign** the sign × placed between two quantities which are to be multiplied together; **multiplication table** a list (written or recited) of products of two factors (esp. the integers 1 to 12) taken in pairs.
▪ **multiplicational** *adjective* (*rare*) M19.

multiplicative /ˈmʌltɪplɪkətɪv/ *adjective & noun*. M17.
[ORIGIN Late Latin *multiplicativus*, from Latin *multiplicat-*: see MULTIPLICATION, -ATIVE.]
▸ **A** *adjective*. Tending to multiply; having the quality or function of multiplying. M17.
▸ **B** *noun*. A numeral expressing a factor of multiplication, as ***duplex***, ***fourfold***, etc. M18.
▪ **multiplicatively** *adverb* L19.

multiplicator /ˈmʌltɪplɪkeɪtə/ *noun*. M16.
[ORIGIN Late Latin, from Latin *multiplicat-*: see MULTIPLICATION, -ATOR.]
1 *MATH*. = MULTIPLIER 3a. Now *rare* or *obsolete*. M16.
2 *PHYSICS*. = MULTIPLIER 4. E19.

multiplicious /mʌltɪˈplɪʃəs/ *adjective*. Long *rare*. E17.
[ORIGIN App. from Latin *multiplic-*: see MULTIPLY *verb*, -IOUS.]
Multiplex.

multiplicity /mʌltɪˈplɪsɪti/ *noun*. LME.
[ORIGIN Late Latin *multiplicitas*, from Latin *multiplic-*, MULTIPLEX: see -ICITY.]
1 The quality or condition of being multiplex or manifold; manifold variety; an instance of this. LME.

> A. STORR One of the major obstacles . . is his multiplicity of ill-formulated definitions for the same thing. ISAIAH BERLIN Tolstoy . . saw the manifold objects and situations on earth in their full multiplicity.

2 A large number *of*; *collect.* large numbers *of*; a variety of kinds *of*. L16.

> L. CODY No chin visible under a multiplicity of woolly scarves and collars. W. RAEPER One symbol can have a multiplicity of meanings.

3 *PHYSICS*. The number of components in a multiplet (that of a spectral line or energy level which is not split being counted as 1). E20.
4 *MEDICINE*. In full ***multiplicity of infection***. The ratio of the number of infective virus particles to the number of susceptible cells. M20.

multiplier /ˈmʌltɪplʌɪə/ *noun*. LME.
[ORIGIN from MULTIPLY *verb* + -ER[1].]
†**1** A person who transmutes base metals into gold or silver (as) by alchemy. Also, a maker of counterfeit coins, a coiner. LME–M16.
2 A person who or thing which multiplies or causes something to increase. LME.
3 **a** *MATH*. A quantity by which another is to be multiplied. M16. ▸**b** *ECONOMICS*. A factor by which an increase in income, employment, etc., is a multiple of the change in investment or government expenditure producing it. M20.
4 *PHYSICS*. An instrument used for multiplying or increasing by repetitive reinforcement the intensity of a force, current, etc., to an appreciable or measurable value. L18.
5 *ANGLING*. A kind of reel in which a mechanism causes the barrel to revolve several times to a single revolution of the handle. M19.
6 A calculating instrument for use in multiplication. L19.
– COMB.: **multiplier effect**: able to be assessed in terms of the economic multiplier.

multiply /ˈmʌltɪplʌɪ/ *verb*. ME.
[ORIGIN Old French & mod. French *multiplier* from Latin *multiplicare*, from *multiplic-*, MULTIPLEX: see -Y[2].]
1 *verb trans.* Cause to become of great(er) number or quantity; increase or augment by accumulation or repetition. Now chiefly as passing into sense 5. ME. ▸**b** Use or utter a great many (words etc.). *arch.* ME. ▸†**c** Increase the intensity of; magnify. LME–E19. ▸**d** Adduce a large number of (instances etc.). E18.

> ADDISON Till into seven it multiplies its stream. GIBBON The activity of the emperor seemed to multiply his presence. TENNYSON Thus truth was multiplied on truth. **b** SWIFT They avoid nothing more than multiplying unnecessary Words. **c** J. CLEVELAND An Optique Glasse contracts the sight At one end, but when turn'd doth multiply 't. **d** ADDISON 'Tis unnecessary to multiply Instances of this nature.

†**2** *verb trans.* Increase (a family etc.) by reproduction or procreation; cause (the earth) to increase in population. ME–L18. ▸**b** Breed (animals); propagate (plants). L15–M19.

> W. COWPER When man was multiplied and spread abroad In tribes and clans. **b** E. BALFOUR A large Mango multiplied at Mergui.

3 *verb intrans.* Become of great(er) number or quantity; be increased or augmented by accumulation or repetition. ME.

> H. E. MANNING As sin has multiplied in its extent, so it would seem also to have become more intense. G. SWIFT Stars which seemed to multiply as we looked at them.

4 *verb intrans.* Increase in number by reproduction or procreation. ME.

> DEFOE As for my Cats, they multiply'd.

5 *MATH*. **a** *verb trans.* Operate on (a given quantity) with another so as to find a product having the same ratio to the first quantity as the second has to unity; combine (two quantities, expressions, etc.) *together* by multiplication. (Foll. by *by*, †*in*, †*into* the second quantity.) LME. ▸**b** *verb trans. & intrans.* Of a quantity: operate on (another quantity) as a multiplier. LME. ▸**c** *verb intrans.* Perform the process of multiplication. L16. ▸**d** *verb trans.* Perform an operation on (two or more quantities, vectors, etc.) analogous to multiplication, to give a product. E18.

> **a** *Journal of Zoology* Sink speed equals the glide angle multiplied by flight velocity. **c** D. LARDNER If we require the area, we have only to multiply by 3.14.

†**6** *verb trans. & intrans.* *ALCHEMY*. Transmute base metals into (gold or silver); cause (gold or silver) to increase. LME–L17.
– COMB.: **multiplying glass** †(*a*) a magnifying glass; (*b*) (chiefly *hist.*) a toy consisting of a faceted concave glass or lens giving numerous reflections of an observed object.

multiply /ˈmʌltɪpli/ *adverb*. L19.
[ORIGIN from MULTIPLE *adjective* + -LY[2].]
In a multiple manner; in more than one way; more than once.

> J. BERMAN Mental functioning is always multiply determined. S. BELLOW We were doubly, multiply, interlinked.

multipolar /mʌltɪˈpəʊlə/ *adjective*. M19.
[ORIGIN from MULTI- + POLAR *adjective*.]
1 Having or pertaining to many poles; *spec.* (**a**) *ANATOMY* (of a nerve cell) having several or many processes; (**b**) *ELECTRICITY* having more than one pair of magnetic poles in a system of field magnets; (**c**) *CYTOLOGY* having or involving more than two spindle poles. M19.
2 Consisting of or divided into more than two (esp. political) alliances, parties, etc. M20.

> *Times* A multipolar world, where major powers could compete and co-operate simultaneously.

multipolarity /ˌmʌltɪpəˈlarɪti/ *noun*. M20.
[ORIGIN from MULTIPOLAR + -ITY.]
1 Multipolar quality or condition. M20.
2 *PHYSICS*. The highest order of multipole associated with a state or phenomenon. M20.

multipole /ˈmʌltɪpəʊl/ *noun & adjective*. E20.
[ORIGIN from MULTI- + POLE *noun*[2].]
▸ **A** *noun*. *PHYSICS*. A system of 2^l monopoles (where the order $l = 1, 2, 3, \ldots$) with no net charge or pole strength and no moment of a lower order than l. Also, a quadrupole ($l = 2$) or higher order system, the dipole ($l = 1$) being treated as a special case. E20.
▸ **B** *attrib.* or as *adjective*. **1** *PHYSICS*. Designating or pertaining to a multipole; *esp.* designating electromagnetic radiation of the kind produced by an electric multipole with a moment varying sinusoidally in magnitude. E20.
2 Of a switch: designed to close or open several circuits simultaneously. E20.

multipotent /mʌlˈtɪpət(ə)nt/ *adjective*. E17.
[ORIGIN Latin *multipotent-*, formed as MULTI- + POTENT *adjective*[2].]
Having much power; very powerful. Chiefly *BIOLOGY & MEDICINE* = MULTIPOTENTIAL.

multipresence /ˈmʌltɪprɛz(ə)ns/ *noun*. E17.
[ORIGIN from MULTI- + PRESENCE.]
The fact of being or power to be present in several or many places simultaneously.

multiracial /mʌltɪˈreɪʃ(ə)l/ *adjective*. E20.
[ORIGIN from MULTI- + RACIAL *adjective*.]
Of, pertaining to, or comprising several or many racially differentiated peoples; *esp.* (of a state, society, etc.) comprising such peoples in more or less equal membership.

> *Economist* He triumphantly created the first multiracial government in Africa. *Times Lit. Suppl.* The pleasant relief of a man living a multi-racial life away from the colour bar.

▪ **multiracialism** *noun* multiracial condition or quality; the principles or practice of a multiracial state, society, etc.: M20. **multiracialist** *noun* an adherent or advocate of multiracialism M20. **multiracially** *adverb* M20.

multitrack /ˈmʌltɪtrak/ *adjective, noun, & verb*. M20.
[ORIGIN from MULTI- + TRACK *noun*.]
AUDIO. ▸**A** *adjective*. Designating, pertaining to, or resulting from the separate recording of several (usu. between two and twenty-four) tracks of sound for subsequent mixing. M20.
▸ **B** *noun*. (A) multitrack recording. L20.
▸ **C** *verb trans.* Record as or mix from separate soundtracks. Freq. as ***multitracked*** *ppl adjective*, ***multitracking*** *verbal noun*. L20.
▪ **multitracker** *noun* a multitrack recording device L20.

multituberculate /ˌmʌltɪtjuːˈbəːkjʊlət/ *adjective & noun*. L19.
[ORIGIN from mod. Latin *Multituberculata* (see below), formed as MULTI- + TUBERCULATE *adjective*.]
▸ **A** *adjective*. (Of a tooth) bearing several cusps arranged in two or three rows; designating, of, or pertaining to the order Multituberculata. L19.
▸ **B** *noun*. Any of various mammals of the extinct order Multituberculata, having multituberculate molar teeth. L19.

multitude /ˈmʌltɪtjuːd/ *noun*. ME.
[ORIGIN Old French & mod. French from Latin *multitudo*, *-din-*, from *multus* many: see -TUDE.]
1 The quality or state of being numerous. ME.
2 A large number *of* people or things; in *pl.*, large numbers *of*. ME. ▸†**b** A great quantity *of*. LME–L18.

> C. BAX The sun is a glowing speck in a dazzling multitude of stars. B. PYM One of those ubiquitous tea-shops which cater for the multitudes of office-workers. M. FOOT Jennie, like a multitude of other Labour candidates, went down to defeat. **b** EARL OF CHATHAM All this disgraceful danger, this multitude of misery.

3 A large gathering of people; a mass of people collected in one place; a throng. LME.

> R. WHATELY A skilful orator's being able to rouse . . the passions of a multitude. J. BALDWIN A long-awaited conqueror . . before whom multitudes cried, Hosanna!

4 *The* populace, *the* common people. M16.

multitudinous /mʌltɪˈtjuːdɪnəs/ *adjective*. E17.
[ORIGIN from Latin *multitudin-*, *-tudo* MULTITUDE + -OUS.]
1 **a** Existing in great numbers; very numerous; consisting of many individuals or elements. E17. ▸**b** Existing in or exhibiting many forms; having many elements or features; arising from or involving a great number. M17.

> **a** H. AINSWORTH When this multitudinous and confused assemblage had nearly filled the inclosure. C. AIKEN Cloud-palaces and kingdoms . . And multitudinous cities. **b** C. KINGSLEY The multitudinous moan and wail of the lost spirits.

2 Of an ocean etc.: vast. *literary*. E17.

> SHAKES. *Macb.* This my hand will rather The multitudinous seas incarnadine.

3 Of or pertaining to the populace, or common people. *rare*. E17.

> SHAKES. *Coriol.* Pluck out The multitudinous tongue; let them not lick The sweet which is their poison.

4 Thronged or crowded (*with*). *poet.* E19.

> SHELLEY Regard this Earth Made multitudinous with thy slaves.

▪ **multitudinism** *noun* (now *rare*) the (esp. religious) principle placing the interests of a large number before those of individuals M19. **multitudinosity** /-ˈnɒsɪti/ *noun* multitudinousness M19. **multitudinously** *adverb* M19. **multitudinousness** *noun* the state or quality of being multitudinous M17.

multivalent /mʌltɪˈveɪl(ə)nt, *esp.* *CYTOLOGY* mʌlˈtɪvəl(ə)nt/ *adjective & noun*. M19.
[ORIGIN from MULTI- + -VALENT.]
▸ **A** *adjective* **1** **a** *CHEMISTRY*. = POLYVALENT 1a. M19. ▸**b** *IMMUNOLOGY*. Of an antigen or antibody: having several sites at which attachment to an antibody or antigen can occur. M20.
2 *CYTOLOGY*. That is (part of) a multivalent. E20.
3 Chiefly *LINGUISTICS & LITERARY CRITICISM*. Having or susceptible of many applications, interpretations, meanings, or values. M20.
▸ **B** *noun*. *CYTOLOGY*. An association of three or more completely or partly homologous chromosomes during the first division of meiosis. E20.
▪ **multivalence**, **multivalency** *nouns* the state or condition of being multivalent L19.

multivallate /mʌltɪˈvaleɪt, -lət/ *adjective*. M20.
[ORIGIN from MULTI- + VALLATE *adjective*.]
Chiefly *ARCHAEOLOGY*. Surrounded by more than one rampart.
▪ **multivaˈllation** *noun* multivallate fortification M20.

multivalve /ˈmʌltɪvalv/ *adjective & noun*. M18.
[ORIGIN from MULTI- + VALVE *noun*.]
▸ **A** *adjective*. **1** *BIOLOGY*. Esp. of a shell or shelled animal: having several or many valves. M18.
2 *ELECTRONICS*. Having several or many thermionic valves. E20.
3 Of an internal-combustion engine: having more than two valves per cylinder, typically four (two inlet and two exhaust). L20.
▸ **B** *noun*. A multivalve shell; an animal, esp. a mollusc, having such a shell. M18.
▪ **multivalved**, **multiˈvalvular** *adjectives* = MULTIVALVE *adjective* 1 M18.

multiverse /ˈmʌltɪvəːs/ *noun*. L19.
[ORIGIN from MULTI- + UNI)VERSE.]
1 The universe considered as lacking order or a single ruling and guiding power. L19.
2 A hypothetical space or realm consisting of a number of universes, of which our own universe is only one. M20.

M

multiversity /mʌltɪˈvəːsɪti/ *noun*. Chiefly *US*. **M20**.
[ORIGIN from MULTI- + UNI)VERSITY.]
A very large university comprising many different departments and activities.

multivibrator /ˌmʌltɪvʌɪˈbreɪtə/ *noun*. **E20**.
[ORIGIN from MULTI- + VIBRATOR.]
ELECTRONICS. A device consisting of two amplifying valves or transistors, each with its output connected to the input of the other, which produces an oscillatory signal rich in harmonics.

multivious /mʌlˈtɪvɪəs/ *adjective*. **M17**.
[ORIGIN from Latin *multivius*, formed as MULTI- + *via* way: see -IOUS.]
Having many ways; going or leading in many directions.

multivocal /mʌlˈtɪvək(ə)l/ *adjective*. **M19**.
[ORIGIN from MULTI- + Latin *vocare* to call + -AL[1], after *univocal*, *equivocal*.]
Susceptible of many interpretations or meanings.
■ **multivoˈcality** *noun* multivocal condition or quality **M20**.

multocular /mʌlˈtɒkjʊlə/ *adjective*. **E18**.
[ORIGIN from MULT(I- + Latin *oculus* eye + -AR[1], after *monocular*.]
Having many eyes; (of a device) adapted for more than one eye.

multum /ˈmʌltəm/ *noun*. *obsolete* exc. *hist*. **E19**.
[ORIGIN Perh. a use of Latin *multum* much.]
A preparation of opium, cocculus indicus, or other plant extracts, added to beer etc. to increase the intoxicating effect.

multum in parvo /mʌltəm ɪn ˈpɑːvəʊ/ *noun phr*. **M17**.
[ORIGIN Latin = much in little.]
A great deal in a small space.

multungulate /mʌlˈtʌŋgjʊlət/ *adjective & noun*. *rare*. **M19**.
[ORIGIN mod. Latin *multungulatus*, formed as MULTI- + UNGULATE.]
ZOOLOGY. (An ungulate animal) having more than two separate toes on each foot.

multure /ˈmʌltʃə/ *noun*. Chiefly *Scot*. *obsolete* exc. *hist*. **ME**.
[ORIGIN Old French *mo(u)lture* (mod. *mouture*) from medieval Latin *molitura*, from *molit-* pa. ppl stem of *molere* grind: see MILL *noun*[1], -URE.]
A toll of grain or flour payable to the proprietor or tenant of a mill in return for grinding corn. Also, the right to exact this toll.
OUTSUCKEN ***multure***.
■ **multurer** *noun* a person who pays multure **ME**.

mum /mʌm/ *noun*[1], *interjection*, *adjective*, & *adverb*. **LME**.
[ORIGIN Imit.]
▸ **A** *noun*. **1** An inarticulate sound made with closed lips, esp. as an indication of inability or unwillingness to speak; a word. Now usu. in neg. contexts. Long *obsolete* exc. *Scot*. **LME**.
2 Refusal to speak, silence. Now chiefly in ***mum's the word***, enjoining silence or secrecy. *colloq*. **M16**.
†**3** A silent person. **M17–E19**.
▸ **B** *interjection*. Hush! Silence! Not a word! **L15**.
▸ **C** *adjective & adverb*. Strictly silent(ly) or secret(ly), not saying a word. *colloq*. **M16**.

R. BRIDGES Don't stand there mum. P. GREGORY Keep mum and it'll blow over and we can have our tea in a bit of peace.

– COMB.: **mumbudget** *noun*, *interjection*, *adjective*, *adverb*, & *verb* †(**a**) = MUM *noun*[1], *interjection*, *adjective*, & *adverb*; (**b**) *verb intrans*. (*dial*.) be silent, come silently or secretly, (chiefly in ***come mumbudgeting***).

mum /mʌm/ *noun*[2]. **E17**.
[ORIGIN German *Mumme*.]
Chiefly *hist*. A kind of beer originally brewed in Brunswick.

mum /mʌm/ *noun*[3]. *colloq*. **L16**.
[ORIGIN Partly var. of MAM, partly abbreviation of MUMMY *noun*[2]. Cf. MOM.]
Mother. Freq. as a form of address or reference.

News on Sunday The pre-school children of the young mums were taking part in a nursery. B. OKRI Mum had to rustle up some food.

be mum = ***be mother*** s.v. MOTHER *noun*[1].

mum /mʌm/ *noun*[4]. *colloq. & dial*. **M19**.
[ORIGIN Repr. a pronunc.]
= MA'AM *noun*.

mum /mʌm/ *noun*[5]. **L19**.
[ORIGIN Abbreviation.]
A chrysanthemum.

mum /mʌm/ *verb*. Infl. **-mm-**. **LME**.
[ORIGIN Imit. Cf. Middle Low German *mummen*, Dutch *mommen*.]
†**1** *verb trans*. Silence; cause to be silent. **LME–M17**.
†**2** *verb intrans*. Make an inarticulate sound with closed lips, esp. indicating inability or unwillingness to speak; whisper; keep silence. **LME–M17**.
3 *verb intrans*. Act in a mime or dumbshow; play as a mummer. **LME**.

mumble /ˈmʌmb(ə)l/ *verb & noun*. **ME**.
[ORIGIN from MUM *verb* + -LE[3]. Cf. Low German *mummelen*, Dutch *mommelen*, *mumm-*.]
▸ **A** *verb*. **1** *verb intrans*. Eat in a slow ineffective manner; chew or bite softly, (as) with toothless gums. **ME**.

F. MARRYAT The calf with gilded horns, who . . mumbles with the flowers of the garland.

2 *verb intrans*. Speak indistinctly or with the lips partly closed; mutter. **ME**.

G. LORD He was . . mumbling with pain. R. FRAME My father spoke quietly . . , he mumbled almost.

3 *verb trans*. Say in subdued or indistinct tones. **ME**.

P. G. WODEHOUSE She eyed the speaker sternly . . . 'Yes, Ma'am,' he mumbled sheepishly. F. TUOHY My brother mumbled something about a holiday, but he did not explain further.

4 *verb trans*. Bite or chew (as) with toothless gums; eat without making much use of the teeth. **L16**. ▸**b** *transf*. Fondle with the lips. **M17**.

P. V. WHITE He mumbled it on his tongue . . before attempting to swallow it.

†**5** *verb trans*. Maul; handle roughly or clumsily. **E17–M18**.
▸ **B** *noun*. A mumbled indistinct utterance or sound. **M17**.

R. C. HUTCHINSON The distant mumble of a congregation at prayer. F. RAPHAEL They heard the mumble of thunder.

■ **mumblement** *noun* (*rare*) mumbling; a mumbled or muttered statement: **L16**. **mumbler** *noun* **M16**. **mumblingly** *adverb* in a mumbling manner **M17**.

mumble-the-peg /ˈmʌmb(ə)lðəpɛg/ *noun*. Now *US*. Also **mumbledypeg** /ˈmʌmb(ə)ldɪpɛg/, **-ty-** /-tɪ-/, & other vars. **E17**.
[ORIGIN from the requirement that an unsuccessful player draw a peg out of the ground with the teeth.]
A game in which each player in turn throws a knife from a series of positions, continuing until the blade fails to stick in the ground. Also called ***knifey***.

mumbo-jumbo /mʌmbəʊˈdʒʌmbəʊ/ *noun*. In sense 1 **Mumbo Jumbo**. Pl. **-os**. **M18**.
[ORIGIN Perh. from Mande *mama dyumbo*.]
1 (A representation of) a grotesque idol said to have been worshipped by certain W. African peoples. **M18**.
2 *transf*. **a** An object of unintelligent veneration. **M19**. ▸**b** Obscure or meaningless talk or writing; nonsense; meaningless or ignorant ritual. **L19**.
■ **mumbo-jumboism** *noun* worship of a Mumbo Jumbo **L19**.

mumchance /ˈmʌmtʃɑːns/ *noun*, *adjective*, & *adverb*. Now *arch*., *dial*., & *literary*. **E16**.
[ORIGIN Middle Low German *mummenschanze*, *-scanze*, *-kanze* game of dice, masked serenade, from *mummen* mask, disguise + *schanz* from Old French & mod. French *chéance* CHANCE *noun*.]
▸ **A** *noun*. †**1** A dicing game resembling hazard. **E16–M17**.
†**2** Masquerade; mumming. **M–L16**.
3 A person who acts in dumbshow; a person who has nothing to say. *obsolete* exc. *dial*. **L17**.
▸ **B** *adjective & adverb*. Silent(ly); tongue-tied. **L17**.

Mumetal /ˈmjuːmɛt(ə)l/ *noun*. Also **m-**. **E20**.
[ORIGIN from MU *noun*[1] (after μ, symbol for permeability) + METAL *noun*.]
(Proprietary name for) an alloy of nickel containing approx. 17 per cent iron, 5 per cent copper, and 2 per cent chromium by weight, which has high magnetic permeability and is used esp. in transformer cores and magnetic shields.

mummer /ˈmʌmə/ *noun & verb*. **LME**.
[ORIGIN Old French *momeur*, from *momer* act in dumbshow, rel. to *momon* mask, Spanish *momo* grimace, perh. of Germanic origin. Partly from MUM *verb* + -ER[1].]
▸ **A** *noun*. **1** A person who mutters or murmurs. *rare*. **LME**.
2 An actor in a (traditional) masked mime or dumbshow; a participant in a mumming. **LME**. ▸**b** A (poor) actor, a play-actor. *arch. slang*. **L18**.
▸ **B** *verb intrans*. Take part in a mumming. Chiefly as ***mummering*** *verbal noun*. **L19**.

Mummerset /ˈmʌməsɛt/ *noun*. **M20**.
[ORIGIN Prob. from MUMMER after *Somerset*.]
An imaginary rustic county in the West of England; its dialect, a pseudo-rustic dialect used by actors.

mummery /ˈmʌm(ə)ri/ *noun*. **LME**.
[ORIGIN Old French & mod. French *momerie*, from *momer*: see MUMMER, -ERY.]
1 Participation in a mummers' play; a performance by mummers. *hist*. **LME**.
2 Ridiculous ceremonial; religious ritual regarded as silly or hypocritical. **M16**.

mummia /ˈmʌmɪə/ *noun*. **LME**.
[ORIGIN medieval Latin *mumia* MUMMY *noun*[1].]
1 = MUMMY *noun*[1] 1. Long *hist*. **LME**.
†**2** = MUMMY *noun*[1] 2. **E18–L19**.

mummichog /ˈmʌmɪtʃɒg/ *noun*. *US*. Also **mummy-**. **L18**.
[ORIGIN Narragansett *moamitteaûg* (pl.).]
A killifish; *esp*. the black and silver killifish, *Fundulus heteroclitus*.

mummied /ˈmʌmɪd/ *adjective*. **E17**.
[ORIGIN from MUMMY *verb*, *noun*[1]: see -ED[1], -ED[2].]
Mummified.

mummification /ˌmʌmɪfɪˈkeɪʃ(ə)n/ *noun*. **E19**.
[ORIGIN from MUMMIFY + -FICATION.]
1 The process of mummifying; the condition of being mummified. **E19**.
2 *MEDICINE*. Drying and shrivelling of tissues. **M19**.

mummified /ˈmʌmɪfʌɪd/ *adjective*. **E19**.
[ORIGIN from MUMMIFY + -ED[1].]
1 That has been mummified. **E19**.
2 *MEDICINE*. Of tissue, an organ: shrivelled or dried up. **L19**.
3 Of a fruit: brown and dry due to brown rot disease. **E20**.

mummiform /ˈmʌmɪfɔːm/ *adjective*. **M19**.
[ORIGIN from MUMMY *noun*[1] + -I- + -FORM.]
Resembling or shaped like a mummy.

mummify /ˈmʌmɪfʌɪ/ *verb trans*. **E17**.
[ORIGIN from MUMMY *noun*[1] + -FY, after French *momifier*.]
Make into a mummy; preserve (a body) by embalming and drying.

mumming /ˈmʌmɪŋ/ *noun*. **LME**.
[ORIGIN from MUM *verb* + -ING[1].]
†**1** Inarticulate murmuring; indistinct speech. **LME–L16**.
2 The action of disguising oneself, esp. during festivities; participation in a mummers' play; a performance of a (traditional) masked mime or dumbshow. **LME**.
3 = MUMMERY 2. **E16**.

mum-mumble /mʌmˈmʌmb(ə)l/ *verb intrans. & trans*. **E20**.
[ORIGIN Redupl. of MUMBLE *verb*, perh. after MUM *verb*.]
Mumble, mutter.

mummy /ˈmʌmi/ *noun*[1] & *verb*. **LME**.
[ORIGIN Old French *mumie*, (also mod.) *momie* from medieval Latin *mumia* from Arabic *mūmiyā* pissasphalt, resinous substance used medicinally.]
▸ **A** *noun* **I 1** A medicinal preparation (supposed to have been) extracted from mummified remains. *obsolete* exc. *hist*. **LME**.
2 *ALCHEMY*. A sovereign remedy. Also, a vital essence (cf. BALSAM *noun* 4). **L16–E18**.
3 (A) pulpy substance or mass, pulp. Chiefly in ***beat to a mummy*** & similar phrs. Formerly also, dead flesh. **L16**.
4 A semi-liquid bituminous substance used as a brown pigment and (formerly) as a medicine (cf. PISSASPHALT). Also, a mixture of wax and pitch formerly used in the transplanting and grafting of trees. **E17**.
▸ **II 5** The body of a human being or animal embalmed (as in the ancient Egyptian fashion) as a preparation for burial. **E17**.

B. BAINBRIDGE Wrapped in strips of cloth like an Egyptian mummy. *fig*.: L. STEPHEN The old theological dogmas had become mummies.

6 A human or animal body desiccated by exposure to sun or air. Also, an animal carcass embedded in prehistoric ice. **E18**.
7 An apple, plum, or other fruit made brown and desiccated by brown rot disease. **E20**.
– COMB.: **mummy bag** a sleeping bag covering the head and body; **mummy brown** (of) a shade of brown resembling that of the pigment mummy; **mummy-case** a case of wood or papier mâché (usually decorated with hieroglyphics) enclosing an Egyptian mummy; **mummy-cloth** a cloth wrapping an Egyptian mummy; **mummy disease** a disease of mushrooms of uncertain cause, characterized by atrophy or distortion and hardening of the fruiting body; **mummy-pits** *arch*. catacombs in which Egyptian mummies were interred.
▸ **B** *verb trans*. Mummify; make into a mummy. **E17**.

mummy /ˈmʌmi/ *noun*[2]. *colloq*. **M18**.
[ORIGIN Repr. a pronunc. of MAMMY *noun*[1]. Cf. MOMMY.]
Mother. Freq. as a form of address or reference.

M. SPUFFORD It's all right. Mummy's here. *Viz* Mummy, I've brought you these flowers.

mummy's boy = ***mother's boy*** s.v. MOTHER *noun*[1].

mummychog *noun* var. of MUMMICHOG.

mump /mʌmp/ *noun*. Now *dial*. See also MUMPS. **L16**.
[ORIGIN Symbolic of the movements of the mouth in grimacing. Cf. MUMP *verb*[1].]
†**1** A grimace. **L16–L18**.
2 a A lump or protuberance; a gnarled piece of wood. **L18**. ▸**b** A block of peat. **L19**.

mump /mʌmp/ *verb*[1]. **L16**.
[ORIGIN formed as MUMP *noun* Cf. Icelandic *mumpa* take into the mouth, *mumpaskælur* grimace, Dutch *mompen*, *-elen* mumble in speaking, German *mumpfeln*, *-en* mumble in eating.]
1 *verb trans*. Say indistinctly; mumble, mutter. *obsolete* exc. *Scot*. **L16**.
2 *verb intrans*. †**a** Grimace; grin. **L16–M18**. ▸**b** Assume a demure, sanctimonious, or miserable expression; be silent and sullen; sulk, mope. Now *arch*. exc. *Scot*. **E17**.
3 *verb intrans. & trans*. Mumble with the gums; turn (food) over and over in the mouth; munch, nibble. *obsolete* exc. *Scot. & dial*. **L16**.

mump /mʌmp/ *verb*[2]. *dial. & slang*. **M17**.
[ORIGIN Prob. from Dutch *mompen* cheat.]
†**1** *verb trans*. Overreach, cheat, (*of*, *out of*). **M17–L19**.
2 *verb intrans*. Beg, go about begging; sponge (*on*). **L17**. ▸**b** Of a police officer: accept small gifts or bribes from tradespeople. Chiefly as ***mumping*** *verbal noun*. *slang*. **L20**.

3 *verb trans.* Obtain by begging or sponging. **L17.**
■ **mumper** *noun* **M17.**

mumpish /ˈmʌmpɪʃ/ *adjective. colloq.* **E18.**
[ORIGIN from MUMP *noun* or *verb*¹ + -ISH¹.]
Sullenly angry; sulky; depressed in spirits.

mumps /mʌmps/ *noun pl.* (usu. treated as *sing.*). **L16.**
[ORIGIN Pl. of MUMP *noun*.]
1 An acute contagious viral disease mainly of children, characterized by swelling of the parotid salivary glands and fever; infectious parotitis. Also foll. by *the*. **L16.**
2 A fit of melancholy or ill humour; *the* sulks. **L16.**

mumpsimus /ˈmʌmpsɪməs/ *noun*. Now *literary*. **M16.**
[ORIGIN Erron. for Latin *sumpsimus* in *quod in ore sumpsimus* 'which we have taken into the mouth' (in the Eucharist), in a story of an illiterate priest who, when corrected, replied 'I will not change my old mumpsimus for your new sumpsimus'.]
1 An obstinate adherent of old ways, in spite of clear evidence of their error; an ignorant and bigoted opponent of reform. Formerly also *loosely*, an old fogey. **M16.**
2 A traditional custom or notion obstinately adhered to although shown to be unreasonable. **M16.**

mums /mʌmz/ *noun. colloq.* **E20.**
[ORIGIN Abbreviation of MUMSY *noun*.]
Mother.

mumsy /ˈmʌmzi/ *noun & adjective. colloq.* Also **-sey**, **-sie**. **L19.**
[ORIGIN from MUM *noun*³ + -SY.]
▸ **A** *noun*. Mother. **L19.**
▸ **B** *adjective*. Motherly, maternal. Also, homely, dowdy, or unfashionable. **M20.**

mu-mu *noun* var. of MUU-MUU.

mun *noun* var. of MON *noun*³.

mun /mʌn/ *aux. verb. dial.* **ME.**
[ORIGIN Old Norse *muna*, from Germanic base of MIND *noun*¹. Cf. MAUN *verb*.]
= MUST *verb*¹ II, III, IV.

munch /mʌn(t)ʃ/ *verb & noun*. **LME.**
[ORIGIN App. imit.: cf. *crunch*, *scrunch*.]
▸ **A** *verb trans. & intrans.* Eat (food or fodder) with continuous and noticeable action of the jaws; eat audibly, esp. with evident enjoyment. **LME.**

R. C. HUTCHINSON A sheep stopped munching the close grass. C. P. SNOW Aunt Milly munched away impassively. R. DAHL Children taking bars of creamy chocolate out of their pockets and munching them greedily.

munch out *US slang* indulge in snacks.
▸ **B** *noun*. **1** Something to eat; a meal. *dial. & joc.* **E19.**
2 An act of munching. **L19.**
■ **muncher** *noun* **M18.**

Munchausen /ˈmʌn(t)ʃaʊz(ə)n, mʌnˈtʃɔːz(ə)n/ *noun & verb.* **E19.**
[ORIGIN Baron *Munchausen* (in German form *Münchhausen*), hero of a pseudo-autobiographical narrative of impossible adventures, written in English by the German Rudolf Eric Raspe (1785).]
▸ **A** *noun*. **1** A narrator of an extravagantly untruthful story of marvellous adventure (also ***Baron Munchausen***); such a story. **E19.**
2 ***Munchausen syndrome***, ***Munchausen's syndrome***, a mental illness in which the patient repeatedly feigns a dramatic or severe illness so as to obtain hospital treatment. **M20.**
▸ **B** *verb intrans.* Tell extravagantly untruthful stories of marvellous adventure. Chiefly as ***Munchausening*** *verbal noun*. **M19.**
■ **Munchausenism** *noun* = MUNCHAUSEN *noun* 1 **M19.**

muncheel /mʌnˈtʃiːl/ *noun*. **E19.**
[ORIGIN Tamil *mañcil* stage, Malayalam *mañjal* stage, day's journey, muncheel.]
A kind of litter resembling a hammock, formerly used in SW India. Cf. MACHILA.

Munchi /ˈmʊn(t)ʃi/ *noun & adjective*. Also **-shi** /-ʃi/. Pl. of noun **-s**, same. **E20.**
[ORIGIN Hausa.]
= TIV.

munchie /ˈmʌn(t)ʃi/ *noun. slang.* **E20.**
[ORIGIN from MUNCH *verb* + -IE.]
1 Food; a snack (usu. in *pl.*). **E20.**

T. CLANCY How about some munchies before my next appointment.

2 ***the munchies***, a sudden strong desire for food. **L20.**

I. BANKS The munchies struck again an hour or so after we'd polished off the last of the sausage rolls.

munchkin /ˈmʌn(t)ʃkɪn/ *noun. N. Amer. colloq.* **L20.**
[ORIGIN from the *Munchkins*, a race of small childlike creatures in L. Frank Baum's *The Wonderful Wizard of Oz* (1900).]
1 A small and endearing person, *esp.* a child. Freq. as a term of endearment. **L20.**

Quarry Magazine He told her he missed her, his little munchkin. T. CLANCY Another father in to pick up his munchkin.

2 A minor public official. **L20.**

New Republic Buchanan has fired two campaign munchkins.

Munda /ˈmʊndə/ *noun & adjective*. **E19.**
[ORIGIN Munda *Muṇḍā*.]
▸ **A** *noun*. Pl. **-s**, same.
1 A member of an ancient Indian people of pre-Aryan origin surviving in NE India. **E19.**
2 The language group including the dialects of the Mundas, belonging to the Austro-Asiatic family. **L19.**
▸ **B** *attrib.* or as *adjective*. Of or pertaining to the Mundas or their language. **M19.**

mundane /ˈmʌndeɪn, mʌnˈdeɪn/ *adjective*. **L15.**
[ORIGIN Old French & mod. French *mondain* from late Latin *mondanus*, from Latin *mundus* world: see -ANE.]
1 Of or pertaining to this world, as contrasted with heaven; worldly; earthly. **L15.**

W. SEWEL By a singular and very strange turn of mundane affairs.

2 Of or pertaining to the cosmos or universe; cosmic. **M17.**

J. B. MOZLEY The idea of God as the Supreme Mundane Being.

mundane egg in Indian and other cosmogonies: a primordial egg from which the world was hatched.
3 ASTROLOGY. Of or pertaining to the horizon as opp. to the ecliptic or zodiac. **L17.**
mundane house: see HOUSE *noun*¹ 9a.
4 Of or pertaining to everyday life; dull, ordinary, routine. **M19.**

RACHEL ANDERSON We all went . . off to fight our war, leaving behind our families to get on with their mundane lives. *Vanity Fair* Talking about something as mundane as the weather.

■ **mundanely** *adverb* **E19.** **mundaneness** *noun* **E18.**

mundanity /mʌnˈdanɪti/ *noun*. **E16.**
[ORIGIN French *mondanité*, formed as MUNDANE: see -ITY.]
1 A mundane concern or event. Usu. in *pl.* **E16.**

Times Lit. Suppl. The glittering mundanities of her parents' circle. J. UGLOW A literalism in art and a commitment to describing the mundanities of life.

2 The quality or fact of being mundane; worldliness. **M17.**

mundatory /ˈmʌndət(ə)ri/ *noun & adjective. rare.* **L17.**
[ORIGIN Late Latin *mundatorius*, from Latin *mundare* cleanse, from *mundus* clean: see -ORY¹.]
▸ **A** *noun*. ECCLESIASTICAL. A purificator. **L17.**
▸ **B** *adjective*. Having the property or quality of cleansing. **E18.**

mundify /ˈmʌndɪfʌɪ/ *verb trans.* **LME.**
[ORIGIN Old French & mod. French *mondifier* or late Latin *mundificare*, from *mundus* clean: see -FY.]
1 Cleanse, purify, (*lit. & fig.*). Now *rare*. **LME.**
†**2** MEDICINE. Free (the body, a wound, etc.) from pus or noxious matter; cleanse. **LME–M19.**
■ †**mundification** *noun* the action of cleansing an ulcer, a wound, etc.; the state of being cleansed: **LME–M19.** **mundificative** *adjective & noun* (**a**) *adjective* (*arch.*) having the power to cleanse (an ulcer, a wound, etc.); †(**b**) *noun* a cleansing medicament: **LME.** †**mundifier** *noun* **L15–E18.**

mundivagant /mʌnˈdɪvəg(ə)nt/ *adjective. rare.* **M17.**
[ORIGIN from Latin *mundus* world + -I- + *vagant-* pres. ppl stem of *vagare* roam: see -ANT¹.]
Roaming, wandering round the world.

mundungus /mʌnˈdʌŋgəs/ *noun*. Now *rare*. Also †**-go**. **M17.**
[ORIGIN Alt. of Spanish MONDONGO.]
†**1** Offal, refuse. **M17–M19.**
2 Bad-smelling tobacco. **M17.**

mung /mʌŋ, muːŋ/ *noun*¹. **E17.**
[ORIGIN Hindi *mūg* from Sanskrit *mudga*.]
(The seed of) either of two widely cultivated tropical Asian legumes: (**a**) (more fully ***mung bean***) the green gram, *Vigna radiata*; (**b**) the black gram, *V. mungo*.

mung *noun*² var. of MONG *noun*¹.

munga /ˈmʌŋgə/ *noun. Austral., NZ, & military slang.* **E20.**
[ORIGIN App. from French *manger* eat.]
Food; a meal.

mungo /ˈmʌŋgəʊ/ *noun*¹. Also †**-os**. Pl. **-os**. **M18.**
[ORIGIN Var. of MONGOOSE.]
†**1** = MONGOOSE 1. **M18–M19.**
2 In full ***mungo root***. A plant of the madder family, *Ophiorrhiza mungos*, regarded as an antidote to snakebites in India and elsewhere. **M18.**

†**mungo** *noun*². Also **M-**. Pl. **-o(e)s**. **M18–M19.**
[ORIGIN A black character in Bickerstaffe's *The Paddock* (1768).]
(A name for) a black slave; a black person.

mungo /ˈmʌŋgəʊ/ *noun*³. **M19.**
[ORIGIN Perh. from Scot. male forename *Mungo* (in parts of NE England often applied to dogs), with allus. to *mung* MONG *noun*¹.]
Fibre made from old woven or felted material that has been shredded; inferior cloth made with such fibre.

†**mungoose** *noun* var. of MONGOOSE.

mungy /ˈmʌŋgi/ *adjective*. Long *obsolete* exc. *dial.* **M17.**
[ORIGIN Perh. alt. of MUGGY *adjective*, but recorded earlier.]
†**1** Dark, gloomy. Only in **M17.**
2 Mouldy, moist, = MUGGY *adjective* 1. **M17.**
3 Of weather etc.: muggy. **E19.**

muni /ˈmʊni/ *noun*¹. **L18.**
[ORIGIN Sanskrit *muni* lit. 'silent', cogn. with Armenian *mownj* dumb.]
HINDUISM & JAINISM. An inspired or holy man; a sage; an ascetic, a hermit.

muni /ˈmjuːni/ *noun*². *US colloq.* **L20.**
[ORIGIN Abbreviation of MUNICIPAL.]
A municipal bond.

munia /ˈmuːnɪə/ *noun*. **L19.**
[ORIGIN Hindi *muniyā*.]
Any of various South Asian waxbills, esp. a mannikin or an avadavat.

Munich /ˈmjuːnɪk/ *noun*. **M20.**
[ORIGIN English name of *München* capital of Bavaria, southern Germany.]
An example of misjudged or dishonourable appeasement such as or comparable to the ceding to Germany of the Sudetenland of northern Czechoslovakia, agreed by Germany, Great Britain, France, and Italy in Munich on 29 September 1938 (the Munich Agreement).
■ **Municheer**, **Munichite** *nouns* an advocate of such an appeasement policy **M20.**

municipal /mjʊˈnɪsɪp(ə)l/ *adjective & noun*. **M16.**
[ORIGIN Latin *municipalis*, from MUNICIPIUM, from *municip-*, *-ceps*, from *munia* civic offices + *capere* take: see -AL¹.]
▸ **A** *adjective*. **1** Of or pertaining to the internal affairs of a state as distinguished from its foreign relations. Orig. & chiefly in ***municipal law***. **M16.** ▸**b** *transf.* Belonging to one place only; having narrow limits. *rare*. **M17.**
2 Of or pertaining to the local self-government or corporate government of a city or town; having such government; conducted by a municipality. **E17.**
municipal bond (chiefly *US*) a security issued by a local authority or its agent, orig. to finance local projects. ***municipal corporation***: see CORPORATION 2.
3 ROMAN HISTORY. Of or pertaining to a municipium; *derog.* provincial. **E17.**
▸ **B** *noun*. †**1** In *pl.* Municipal laws. Only in **L16.**
2 ROMAN HISTORY. An inhabitant of a municipium. **E18.**
3 A municipal bond. Usu. in *pl. US colloq.* **E20.**
■ **municipalism** *noun* (**a**) devotion to one's municipality; municipal or local loyalty (as opp. to national patriotism); (**b**) preference for municipal as opp. to centralized action or control in government: **M19.** **municipalist** *noun* an advocate of the extension of the range of municipal action or control **M19.** **municipaliˈzation** *noun* the action of municipalizing something **L19.** **municipalize** *verb trans.* bring under municipal ownership or control; grant local self-government to: **E19.** **municipalizer** *noun* = MUNICIPALIST **E20.** **municipally** *adverb* **E19.**

municipality /mjʊˌnɪsɪˈpalɪti/ *noun*. **L18.**
[ORIGIN French *municipalité*, from *municipal*, formed as MUNICIPAL: see -ITY.]
1 A town, city, or district having local self-government; the community of such a town etc. **L18.**
2 The governing body of a town, city, or district having local self-government. **L18.**
3 ROMAN HISTORY. A municipium. **E19.**

municipia *noun* pl. of MUNICIPIUM.

municipio /mjuːnɪˈsɪpɪəʊ, -ˈtʃɪp-/ *noun*. Pl. **-os**. **L19.**
[ORIGIN Spanish & Italian, from Latin *municipium*: see MUNICIPAL.]
A Spanish, Latin American, or Italian municipality.

municipium /mjuːnɪˈsɪpɪəm/ *noun*. Pl. **-pia** /-pɪə/. **E18.**
[ORIGIN Latin: see MUNICIPAL.]
ROMAN HISTORY. A provincial city whose citizens had the privileges of Roman citizens.

†**municipy** *noun. rare.* **L16–L19.**
[ORIGIN formed as MUNICIPIUM.]
A municipality.

munificence /mjʊˈnɪfɪs(ə)ns/ *noun*. **LME.**
[ORIGIN French, or Latin *munificentia*, formed as MUNIFICENT: see -ENCE.]
The quality of being munificent; splendid liberality in giving; great generosity.

munificent /mjʊˈnɪfɪs(ə)nt/ *adjective*. **M16.**
[ORIGIN Latin *munificent-*, from *munificus* adjective, from *munus* gift: see -FIC, -ENT.]
Splendidly generous, bountiful.

E. WAUGH: MGM were consistently munificent and we left . . in effortless luxury. R. THOMAS She was awed by the munificent beauty of the gift.

■ **munificently** *adverb* **L16.**

muniment /ˈmjuːnɪm(ə)nt/ *noun*. **LME.**
[ORIGIN Old French & mod. French from Latin *munimentum* fortification, (in medieval Latin) title deed, from *munire* fortify, secure: see -MENT.]
1 A document (as a title deed, charter, etc.) preserved as evidence of rights or privileges (usu. in *pl.*). In *pl.* also, archives. **LME.**
†**2** In *pl.* Things with which a person or place is provided; furnishings. **L15–M19.**
3 Anything serving as a defence or protection. Now *rare*. **M16.**
– COMB.: **muniment deed** a title deed.

muninga /mʊˈnɪŋgə/ *noun*. L19.
[ORIGIN Kiswahili *mninga*.]
= KIAAT.

munition /mjʊˈnɪʃ(ə)n/ *noun & verb*. LME.
[ORIGIN Old French & mod. French from Latin *munitio(n-)*, from *munit-* pa. ppl stem of *munire* fortify, secure: see -ION.]
▸ **A** *noun*. †**1** A granted right or privilege. Only in LME.
†**2** An apparatus. Only in L15.
3 *sing*. (now chiefly when *attrib*.) & in *pl*. Military weapons, ammunition, equipment, and stores; *colloq*. the production of these. Also more fully ***munitions of war***. E16.
†**4** The action of fortifying or defending; (a) fortification (*lit. & fig.*). M16–E19.
▸ **B** *verb trans*. Supply with munitions. L16.
■ **munitioˈneer** *noun* (now *rare*) a worker in a munition factory E20. **munitioner** *noun* (*rare*) a supplier or maker of munitions M17. **munitioˈnette** *noun* (*arch. colloq.*) a female worker in a munition factory E20. **munitionment** *noun* (*a*) provision with or supply of munitions; (*b*) munitions collectively: E20.

munity /ˈmjuːnɪti/ *noun*. Long *rare*. LME.
[ORIGIN medieval Latin *munitas* back-form. from *immunitas* IMMUNITY.]
A granted right or privilege.

munj /ˈmuːn(d)ʒ, ˈmʌn-/ *noun*. M19.
[ORIGIN Hindi *munj*, Sanskrit *muñja*.]
A grass of the Indian subcontinent, *Saccharum munja*, whose leaves provide fibre for ropes etc.

munjeet /mʌnˈdʒiːt/ *noun*. E19.
[ORIGIN Hindi *mañjīṭ(h)* from Sanskrit *mañjiṣṭha* (see MUNJISTIN).]
A plant of the madder family, *Rubia cordifolia*, native to the Indian subcontinent; the roots of this plant, used to make a red dye.

munjistin /mʌnˈdʒɪstɪn/ *noun*. M19.
[ORIGIN from mod. Latin *Munjista* (former genus name of MUNJEET) + -IN¹.]
CHEMISTRY. A crystalline orange dye present in munjeet, madder, and other plants; 1, 3-dihydroxyanthraquinone-2-carboxylic acid.

munnion /ˈmʌnjən/ *noun*. L16.
[ORIGIN Var. of MONIAL with assim. of *l* to preceding *n*: cf. MULLION.]
ARCHITECTURE. A mullion.

Munro /mʌnˈrəʊ/ *noun*. Pl. **-os**. E20.
[ORIGIN Sir H. T. *Munro*, who published a list of all such peaks in the Journal of the Scottish Mountaineering Club for 1891.]
MOUNTAINEERING. A Scottish mountain of at least 3000 feet (approx. 914 metres); any such mountain in the British Isles.

Munsee /ˈmʌnsi/ *noun & adjective*. M18.
[ORIGIN Munsee *mə́n'si:w* person of Minisink Island (in the upper Delaware river).]
▸ **A** *noun*. Pl. **-s**, same.
1 A member of an American Indian people formerly inhabiting the upper Delaware river area in the north-eastern US. M18.
2 The Algonquian language of this people. E19.
▸ **B** *attrib*. or as *adjective*. Of or pertaining to the Munsee or their language. E19.

Munsell /ˈmʌns(ə)l/ *noun*. E20.
[ORIGIN Albert H. *Munsell* (1858–1918), US painter.]
Used *attrib*. with ref. to Munsell's system of classifying colours by means of numerical values for three properties, hue, value (lightness or brightness), and chroma.

munshi /ˈmuːnʃiː/ *noun*¹. E17.
[ORIGIN Persian & Urdu *munšī* from Arabic *munšī'* writer, author, active pple of *'anša'a* write (a book).]
In the Indian subcontinent: a secretary; a language teacher.

Munshi *noun*² *& adjective* var. of MUNCHI.

munsif /ˈmuːnsɪf/ *noun*. L18.
[ORIGIN Persian & Urdu *munṣif*, from Arabic *munṣif* just, honest, from Arabic *'anṣafa* treat justly.]
hist. In the Indian subcontinent: a judge.

Munster /ˈmʊnstə, ˈmʌnstə/ *noun*. M19.
[ORIGIN A town in eastern France.]
A strongly flavoured, semi-soft cheese made in the region around Munster.

Munsterlander /ˈmʊnstəlandə, ˈmʌn-/ *noun*. M20.
[ORIGIN German *Münsterländer*, from *Münsterland*, the region of Germany where the breeds originated: see -ER¹.]
(An animal of) either of two similar German breeds of gun dog, one black and white (more fully ***large Munsterlander***), the other smaller and usu. brown and white (more fully ***small Munsterlander***, ***Munsterlander spaniel***).

munt /mʊnt/ *noun*. *S. Afr. slang. offensive*. M20.
[ORIGIN Bantu *umuntu* person, sing. of *abantu* (see BANTU).]
A black African.

muntin /ˈmʌntɪn/ *noun*. ME.
[ORIGIN Var. of MONTANT with loss of *t*.]
An upright post or bar. Now *spec*. a central vertical piece between two panes of glass or two panels of a door.

muntjac /ˈmʌntdʒak/ *noun*. Also **-jak**. L18.
[ORIGIN Sundanese *minchek*.]
Any of several small deer with short antlers of the Asian genus *Muntiacus*; esp. *M. reevesi*, which has been introduced into Britain and Europe. Also called ***barking deer***.

Muntz metal /ˈmʌnts ˈmɛt(ə)l/ *noun phr*. M19.
[ORIGIN from George Frederick *Muntz* (1794–1857), English metallurgist.]
Brass containing about 55 to 64 per cent of copper (often with 1 per cent or more of lead), used in casting and extrusion and formerly esp. in sheathing ships' hulls.

munyeroo /mʌnjəˈruː/ *noun*. *Austral*. L19.
[ORIGIN Diyari (an Australian Aboriginal language of South Australia) *manyurra*.]
Either of two small succulent plants of the purslane family, *Calandrinia balonensis* and *Portulaca oleracea*; a paste made from the ground seeds of either plant, formerly used as food by Aborigines.

muon /ˈmjuːɒn/ *noun*. M20.
[ORIGIN Contr. of *mu-meson*: see MU *noun*¹, -ON.]
PARTICLE PHYSICS. An unstable lepton similar to the electron but with a mass about 207 times greater, which is the chief constituent of cosmic radiation at the earth's surface.
– COMB.: **muon number** a quantum number that is ±1 for muons and their neutrinos and 0 for other particles and is conserved in all known interactions.
■ **muˈonic** *adjective* of, pertaining to, or involving a muon; (of an atom) having a negative muon orbiting the nucleus: M20.

muonium /mjuːˈəʊnɪəm/ *noun*. M20.
[ORIGIN from MUON + -IUM, after *positronium*.]
PARTICLE PHYSICS. A short-lived neutral system, analogous to an atom, consisting of a positive muon and an electron.

muppet /ˈmʌpɪt/ *noun*. L20.
[ORIGIN App. invented by the American puppeteer Jim Henson (1936–90); later rationalized as a blend of MARIONETTE and PUPPET.]
1 (Proprietary name for) any of a number of puppets and marionettes created for the children's television programmes *Sesame Street* and *The Muppet Show*. L20.
2 An incompetent or foolish person. *slang*. L20.

> *Sunday Times* I should have done something, but I just stood there like a muppet.

muqaddam /mʊˈkadəm/ *noun*. L16.
[ORIGIN Persian & Urdu, from Arabic *muqaddam*, pass. pple of *qaddama* to place in front.]
In the Indian subcontinent: a headman, a local chief.

mura /ˈmjʊərə/ *noun*. Pl. same. L19.
[ORIGIN Japanese.]
A Japanese village or hamlet, esp. as an administrative unit.

muraena /mjʊˈriːnə/ *noun*. Also **murena**. M16.
[ORIGIN Latin *muraena*, *murena* sea eel, lamprey from Greek *muraina*, from *muros* sea eel.]
An eel-like fish. Now chiefly as mod. Latin genus name of the moray eel.

murage /ˈmjʊərɪdʒ/ *noun*. LME.
[ORIGIN Old French, in medieval Latin *muragium*, from French *mur* wall: see MURE *noun*, -AGE.]
1 *hist*. A tax levied for building or repairing the walls of a town; the right granted to a town for the levying of such a tax. LME.
†**2** The building of walls; a system of defensive walls. *rare*. LME–E17.

†**murager** *noun* see MURENGER.

mural /ˈmjʊər(ə)l/ *noun*. L15.
[ORIGIN Old French & mod. French *muraille* from Proto-Romance, repr. Latin *muralia* neut. pl. of *muralis* (see MURAL *adjective*) taken as fem. sing.: see -AL¹. In senses 2, 3 from MURAL *adjective*.]
†**1** A wall. L15–M16.
†**2** A fruit tree growing against and fastened to a wall. Only in L17.
3 A painting executed directly on a wall or (occas.) ceiling, esp. as part of a scheme of decoration. E20.
■ **muralist** *noun* a painter of murals; *spec*. a member of a Mexican school of mural painting active in the first half of the 20th cent.: E20.

mural /ˈmjʊər(ə)l/ *adjective*. LME.
[ORIGIN Old French & mod. French from Latin *muralis*, from *murus* wall: see -AL¹.]
1 *ROMAN ANTIQUITIES*. Designating a crown, garland, etc., awarded to the first soldier to scale the wall of a besieged town. Cf. VALLAR. LME.

> *transf.*: S. JOHNSON He toils without the hope of mural or civick garlands.

2 Placed or executed on a wall; fixed to a wall. M16.

> K. CLARK A large mural painting in the church of St Sulpice.

3 *gen*. Of or pertaining to a wall; resembling a wall. L16.

> G. HARTWIG Bold mural coasts, rising precipitously from the deep sea.

4 *ASTRONOMY*. Designating or pertaining to a wall or walled arch set exactly in the plane of the meridian for the alignment of a large instrument. *obsolete* exc. *hist*. E18.

5 *ANATOMY & MEDICINE*. Of or pertaining to the wall of a body cavity or vessel. L19.
■ **murally** *adverb* (*rare*) (*a*) with a mural crown, garland, etc.; (*b*) by means of a wall or walls; (*c*) on or from a wall or walls: M19.

muralled /ˈmjʊər(ə)ld/ *adjective*. E18.
[ORIGIN from MURAL *adjective*, *noun* + -ED².]
1 Used for or made into a mural crown. *rare*. E18.

> J. P. PHILIPS Ardent to deck his brows with mural'd gold, Or civic wreath of oak.

2 Decorated with murals. M20.

> A. WEST Stella watched the shadows . . as they bobbed on the muralled wall.

muramic /mjʊˈramɪk/ *adjective*. M20.
[ORIGIN from Latin *murus* wall + AM(INE + -IC.]
BIOCHEMISTRY. ***muramic acid***, an amino-sugar, $C_9H_{17}NO_7$, present in the cell walls of bacteria and in bacterial spores.

Murano /mjʊˈrɑːnəʊ/ *noun*. M19.
[ORIGIN See below.]
Used *attrib*. to designate Venetian glass or other articles from or associated with the island of Murano near Venice.
■ **Muraˈnese** *adjective* of or pertaining to Murano L19.

Muratorian /mjʊərəˈtɔːrɪən/ *adjective*. M19.
[ORIGIN from *Muratori* (see below) + -AN.]
Designating (in ***Muratorian fragment***, ***Muratorian canon***) the earliest Western canon of the New Testament, *c* 170, edited by the Italian scholar L. A. Muratori (1672–1750).

murchana /ˈmʊətʃənɑː/ *noun*. L19.
[ORIGIN Sanskrit *mūrchanā* modulation.]
Each of a set of fourteen octave scales in Indian music that start on one of the seven notes of one or other grama.

murder /ˈməːdə/ *noun*. Also (now *arch. & dial.*) **murther** /ˈməːðə/.
[ORIGIN Old English *morþor* = Gothic *maurþr*, from Germanic from Indo-European base also of Old English, Old Saxon *morþ*, Old Norse *morð*, Old & mod. High German *mord*, Dutch *moord*, reinforced in Middle English by Old French *murdre* (mod. *meurtre*), from Germanic.]
1 (An instance of) the unlawful premeditated killing of one human being by another, (a) criminal homicide with malice aforethought. OE. ▸**b** (An instance of) non-criminal homicide of a particularly reprehensible kind; *fig*. (a) mortal sin, (a) great wickedness. L15.

> A. CHRISTIE If I'd committed a murder, I wouldn't go . . and give myself up. *USA Today* He was acquitted of attempted murder. *Daily Telegraph* The detective who solves a murder by deducing the series of events that led to the crime. *Proverb*: Murder will out. *personified*: SHELLEY I met Murder on the way—He had a mask like Castlereagh.

†**2** Terrible slaughter, destruction of life. ME–L16.
3 As *interjection*. Expr. the fear that oneself or another is in danger of murder; *joc*. expr. shock, dismay, etc. LME.

> R. CROMPTON Police! Help! Murder! Robbers!

4 (An instance of) destruction or spoliation tantamount to murder; something extremely unpleasant or undesirable to experience. Freq. *hyperbol*. M19. ▸**b** Something or someone excellent or marvellous. *US slang*. M20.

> A. J. LERNER She should be taken out and hung For the cold-blooded murder of the English tongue! ALAN ROSS An old hip injury . . . Not so bad when I'm just walking . . but murder climbing stairs. **b** M. SHULMAN A Benny Goodman record started to play. 'Oh, B.G.!' cried Noblesse . . 'Man, he's murder, Jack.'

5 A game for a number of participants, involving a mock murder hunt in which one player in the role of detective has to discover the identity of another player taking the role of murderer. M20.
– PHRASES: ***blue murder***: see BLUE *adjective*. ***first-degree murder***, ***second-degree murder***: see DEGREE *noun*. ***get away with murder***: see GET *verb*. ***judicial murder***: see JUDICIAL *adjective*.
– COMB.: **murder bag**: containing equipment for a detailed examination at the scene of a murder; **murder book**, **murder file**: for recording details of a police investigation of a murder; **murder game** = sense 5 above; **murder inquiry**, **murder investigation** a police investigation of a murder; **murder log**: recording details of a police investigation of a murder; **murdermonger** (*a*) a person who commits murder as a profession; (*b*) a writer of murder stories; **murder mystery** (*a*) a mysterious murder; (*b*) a novel, play, etc., about a murder in which the murderer's identity is concealed until the denouement; **murder one**, **murder two** *US colloq*. first-degree (or second-degree) murder; **murder room** a room used as a centre for directing a police investigation into a murder; **murder squad** a division of a police force appointed to investigate murders.
■ **murderish** *adjective* (*rare*) murderous M16.

murder /ˈməːdə/ *verb*. Also (now *arch. & dial.*) **murther** /ˈməːðə/.
[ORIGIN Old English *ā-*, *for-*, *of)myrþrian* = Old High German *murdran*, Gothic *maurþrjan*, from Germanic; superseded in Middle English by a new formation on the noun.]

M

▶ **I** *verb trans.* **1** Kill (a human being) unlawfully, esp. wickedly or inhumanly; *spec.* kill (a human being) with a premeditated motive, kill with malice aforethought. **OE.** ▸**b** *refl.* Commit suicide. *arch.* **LME.**

I. McEwan He was going to find his daughter and murder her abductor.

2 Put an end to or destroy in an act tantamount to murder (chiefly *hyperbol.*); spoil by bad execution, representation, etc. **ME.**

G. Greene A really dreadful woman singer murders the . . charm of 'You're the Top'. D. Caute In the Roundhouse . . they now murder language and with it reason. M. Gee You . . ate red kidney beans and raw garlic while a pianist murdered Gershwin.

3 Slaughter in a terrible manner, massacre. **LME.**

Tennyson They turn on the pursuer . . They murder all that follow. J. Steinbeck Killer whales attacked the sea-lions . . and murdered a great number of them.

4 Consume or spend (time) unprofitably. *arch.* **E18.**
5 Conclusively defeat (an opponent etc.), esp. at a game or sport. *slang.* **M20.**

Observer If the passing had got much worse, a team of corporals' grandmothers would have murdered them.

6 Consume (food or drink) greedily or with relish. *colloq.* **M20.**

L. R. Banks Hey, I could murder an ice cream.

▶ **II** *verb intrans.* **7** Perform the act of murder; commit murder. **M16.**

J. Hyde These men will fight, lie, rob, murder for Mormonism if commanded. A. Storr A measure of sympathy is generally extended to . . the lover who murders from jealousy.

†**murdering piece** = MURDERER 2.

■ **murderable** *adjective* able to be murdered; provoking or inviting murder: **E20.** **murde'ree** *noun* (**a**) a person who is murdered; (**b**) a person who provokes or invites murder: **M19.** **murderess** *noun* a female murderer **LME.**

murderer /ˈmɜːd(ə)rə/ *noun.* Also (now *arch. & dial.*) **murth-** /ˈmɜːð-/. **ME.**
[ORIGIN Partly from MURDER *verb*, partly from Anglo-Norman *mordreour, mur-*, from *mordrer* MURDER *verb*: see -ER[1].]
1 A person who commits murder. **ME.**
†**2** A small anti-personnel cannon or mortar used esp. on board ship. **L15–E18.**

M

murderous /ˈmɜːd(ə)rəs/ *adjective.* Also (now *arch. & dial.*) **murth-** /ˈmɜːð-/. **M16.**
[ORIGIN from MURDER *noun* + -OUS.]
Orig. (now *rare*), guilty of murder. Now, capable of or intending murder; of the nature of murder; characteristic of or involving murder.

D. Hewett The little semis . . defending their privacy . . with rows of murderous iron spikes. H. Macmillan To fall a victim to the murderous attack of a fanatical monk. D. Rowe A terrible rage . . drove us to a murderous fury with our gods.

■ **murderously** *adverb* (**a**) in a murderous manner; (**b**) *colloq.* extremely: **M16.** **murderousness** *noun* **M17.**

†**mure** *noun.* **OE–M17.**
[ORIGIN Latin *murus* wall, later prob. from Old French & mod. French *mur*.]
A wall.

mure /mjʊə/ *verb trans. arch.* **LME.**
[ORIGIN Old French & mod. French *murer*, formed as MURE *noun*.]
†**1** = IMMURE *verb* 1. **LME–L18.**

T. Urquhart All other Abbies are strongly walled and mured about. U. von Troil This bath . . is mured in with a wall of basalt.

2 Block up (a door, gate, etc.). Usu. foll. by *up*. **LME.** ▸**b** Wall up the doors of; stop (*up*) the means of access to. **M16.**

S. Parker Mure up your school doors.

3 = IMMURE *verb* 2. Also foll. by *up*. **E17.**

F. Marryat Not a little tired of being mured up in the cottage.

murein /ˈmjʊəriːn/ *noun.* **M20.**
[ORIGIN from Latin *murus* wall + *-ein*, after PROTEIN.]
BIOCHEMISTRY. A structural polymer forming the cell walls of many bacteria, consisting of glycosaminoglycan chains interlinked with short peptides. Cf. MUCOPEPTIDE, PEPTIDOGLYCAN.

murena *noun* var. of MURAENA.

murenger /ˈmjʊərɪndʒə/ *noun.* Long *obsolete* exc. *hist.* Also (earlier) †**murager**, **muringer**. **ME.**
[ORIGIN Anglo-Latin *muragiarius*, from medieval Latin *muragium* MURAGE: see -ER[2]. For the intrusive *n* cf. *harbinger, messenger*, etc.]
An officer responsible for keeping the walls of a city in repair.

murex /ˈmjʊərɛks/ *noun.* Pl. **murices** /ˈmjʊərɪsiːz/, **murexes**. **L16.**
[ORIGIN Latin, perh. rel. to Greek *muax* sea-mussel.]
Any of various spiny-shelled predatory gastropod molluscs of the genus *Murex* and related genera, of tropical and temperate seas, from some of which the dye Tyrian purple was formerly obtained. Also ***murex shell***.

murexide /mjʊˈrɛksʌɪd/ *noun.* Also **-id** /-ɪd/. **M19.**
[ORIGIN from MUREX + -IDE.]
CHEMISTRY. Ammonium purpurate, used as an indicator.

murgh /mʊəg, mʊrg/ *noun.*
[ORIGIN Urdu *murġ* from Persian *murġ* bird, fowl.]
In Indian cookery: chicken.

Muria /ˈmjʊərɪə, ˈmʊə-/ *noun & adjective.* **M19.**
[ORIGIN Gond.]
▶ **A** *noun.* A member of a Gond hill people of Bastar in India. **M19.**
▶ **B** *adjective.* Of or pertaining to this people. **M19.**

muriate /ˈmjʊərɪət, -eɪt/ *noun. arch.* **L18.**
[ORIGIN French, from *muriatique* MURIATIC: see -ATE[1].]
CHEMISTRY. = CHLORIDE.

muriate /ˈmjʊərɪeɪt/ *verb trans. arch.* **L17.**
[ORIGIN from Latin *muria* brine + -ATE[3].]
Pickle in brine; impregnate with a chloride or chlorides. Formerly also, combine with chlorine. Freq. as ***muriated*** *ppl adjective.*

muriatic /mjʊərɪˈatɪk/ *adjective. arch.* **L17.**
[ORIGIN Latin *muriaticus* pickled in brine, from *muria* brine: see -ATIC.]
†**1** Pertaining to, of the nature of, or containing brine or salt. **L17–M19.**
2 Obtainable from seawater; *CHEMISTRY* of chlorine; ***muriatic acid***, hydrochloric acid. **L17.**

muricate /ˈmjʊərɪkət/ *adjective.* **M17.**
[ORIGIN Latin *muricatus* shaped like a murex, from *muric-*, MUREX: see -ATE[2].]
BOTANY & ZOOLOGY. Having sharp points, studded with short rough projections. Formerly also, ending in a long sharp point, like the murex.
■ Also **muricated** *adjective* **E18.**

murices *noun pl.* see MUREX.

muriculate /mjʊˈrɪkjʊlət/ *adjective.* **M19.**
[ORIGIN mod. Latin *muriculatus*, from *muriculus* small murex, from *muric-*, MUREX: see -CULE, -ATE[2].]
BOTANY. Minutely muricate.

murid /mjʊˈriːd, mʊ-/ *noun*[1]. **E19.**
[ORIGIN Arabic *murīd* person who strives after (spiritual enlightenment), active pple of *arāda* to desire, strive after.]
A follower of a Muslim saint, esp. a disciple in a Sufi order.

murid /ˈmjʊərɪd/ *adjective & noun*[2]. **L19.**
[ORIGIN from mod. Latin *Muridae* (see below), from Latin *mus, mur-* mouse: see -ID[3].]
ZOOLOGY. ▶**A** *adjective.* Of or relating to the mammalian family Muridae, which includes most kinds of rats, mice, and voles. **L19.**
▶ **B** *noun.* A rodent of this family. **E20.**

Muridism /mjʊˈriːdɪz(ə)m, mʊ-/ *noun.* **M19.**
[ORIGIN from MURID *noun*[1] + -ISM.]
An Islamic revival movement in the Caucasus in the 19th cent. advocating the rising of Muslims against their religious and political opponents, the Russians.

muriform /ˈmjʊərɪfɔːm/ *adjective.* **M19.**
[ORIGIN from Latin *murus* wall + -I- + -FORM.]
BOTANY. **1** Having cells regularly arranged like the courses of bricks in a wall. **M19.**
2 Of fungus spores: having both longitudinal and transverse septa. **L19.**

muri gallici *noun phr.* pl. of MURUS GALLICUS.

murine /ˈmjʊərʌɪn, -rɪn/ *adjective & noun.* **E17.**
[ORIGIN Latin *murinus*, from *mur-, mus* mouse: see -INE[1].]
▶ **A** *adjective.* **1** Of, resembling, or characteristic of a mouse; *ZOOLOGY* of or pertaining to the family Muridae or the subfamily Murinae of Old World rodents, usu. having a long hairless tail, and including the rats and mice. **E17.**
2 *VETERINARY MEDICINE.* Affecting mice or rats. **M20.**
murine typhus a mild form of typhus transmissible to humans by rat fleas.
▶ **B** *noun.* A murine animal, a mouse, a rat. **L19.**

†**muring** *noun.* **E17–E18.**
[ORIGIN from MURE *noun* + -ING[1].]
Wall-building; the structure of a wall.

muringer *noun* var. of MURENGER.

muriqui /mjʊˈriːkwi/ *noun.* **M20.**
[ORIGIN Portuguese from Tupi *mbiri'ki*.]
The woolly spider monkey, *Brachyteles arachnoides*, a large spider monkey with a protruding belly, native to SE Brazil.

murk /mɜːk/ *noun*[1]. Also *arch.* **mirk**.
[ORIGIN Old English *mirce, myrce* from Germanic, reinforced in Middle English from Scandinavian (Old Norse *myrkr* noun & adjective = Old Saxon *mirki* adjective). Cf. MURK *adjective*.]
Darkness, gloom, (*lit. & fig.*); air obscured by fog, dense vapour, etc.

Carlyle Aloft from the murk of commonplace rise glancings of a starry splendour. W. de la Mare I still in the thin clear murk of dawn Descry her gliding streams. B. Geldof On foggy days Hoath Head looked like a huge ship looming out of the murk.

■ **murksome** *adjective* (*rare*) dark, obscure **L16.**

†**murk** *noun*[2]. **L17–M19.**
[ORIGIN Perh. var. of MARC.]
= MARC 1.

murk /mɜːk/ *adjective.* Now chiefly *Scot. & literary.* Also *arch.* **mirk**.
[ORIGIN Old English *mirce, myrce*, reinforced in Middle English; of Scandinavian origin (Old Norse *myrkr*: see MURK *noun*[1]).]
Dark, gloomy; murky; indistinct, dim; hard to understand; depressing; unenlightened.

Allan Ramsay Murk despair Made me think life was little worth. Hartley Coleridge Clothes thee in weed of penance, murk and dun. J. R. Lowell The chimes peal muffled with sea-mists murk.

■ **murkness** *noun* (**a**) (now only *Scot.*) darkness (*lit. & fig.*); (**b**) *rare* obscurity of air caused by fog etc., mist: **ME.**

murk /mɜːk/ *verb.* Also **mirk**. **ME.**
[ORIGIN from MURK *adjective* Perh. partly from Old Norse *myrkva* grow dark.]
1 *verb intrans.* Grow or appear dark or gloomy. Long *rare* or *obsolete*. **ME.**
2 *verb trans.* Darken, obscure, (*lit. & fig.*). Now chiefly *Scot. & literary*. **ME.**

murky /ˈmɜːki/ *adjective.* Also *arch.* **mirky**. **L16.**
[ORIGIN from MURK *noun*[1] + -Y[1].]
1 Dark, gloomy; obscured by fog, dense vapour, etc.; grimy; not clear to the sight, indistinct, dim. **L16.** ▸**b** Of liquid: cloudy on account of suspended matter. **M19.**

Sir W. Scott The path was altogether indiscernible in the murky darkness which surrounded them. P. Pullman Murky London air laden with fumes and soot. **b** Conan Doyle A . . bridge, with the murky river flowing sluggishly beneath.

2 *fig.* **a** Sinister, suspiciously obscure; morally suspect. **L18.** ▸**b** Not easy to understand; indistinct; confused. **L18.**

a Dickens One good deed in a murky life of guilt. **b** D. DeLillo Relatives were a sensitive issue, part of the murky and complex past. J. Wilcox This was where . . memory failed him, or at least where it became murky.

■ **murkily** *adverb* **M19.** **murkiness** *noun* **E19.**

murl /mɜːl/ *verb intrans. & trans. Scot. & N. English.* Also **mirl**. **E16.**
[ORIGIN Unknown.]
Crumble; (cause to) decay.

murly /ˈmɜːli/ *adjective. rare.* **E17.**
[ORIGIN from MURL + -Y[1].]
Of earth: crumbly, friable.

Murmi /ˈmɜːmi/ *noun & adjective.* **E19.**
[ORIGIN Prob. from Tibetan, lit. 'people of the frontier', from *mur* at the frontier + *mi* man.]
▶ **A** *noun.* Pl. **-s**, same. = TAMANG *noun*. **E19.**
▶ **B** *attrib.* or as *adjective*. = TAMANG *adjective*. **L19.**

murmur /ˈmɜːmə/ *noun.* **LME.**
[ORIGIN Old French & mod. French *murmure* or Latin *murmur* rel. to *murmurare*: see MURMUR *verb*.]
1 a A subdued continuous sound, as made by waves, a stream, etc. **LME.** ▸**b** *MEDICINE.* A (normal or abnormal) rushing sound heard over the heart, blood vessels, or other organ during auscultation. **M19.** ▸**c** A condition in which the heart produces or is apt to produce such a sound. *colloq.* **E20.**

a E. Bowen The continuous murmur inside the whorls of a shell. F. Wyndham The continual murmur of moving water around and below me.

2 A subdued expression of discontent or anger; a muttered or indistinct complaint. Formerly also, discontent or anger expressed in a subdued or indistinct way. **LME.**

W. Stubbs The murmurs of the people reached the king in Normandy. B. Chatwin People . . wouldn't raise a murmur against the Party or State.

without a murmur without protest or complaint.
†**3** Rumour. **E16–M18.**

Shakes. *Twel. N.* 'Twas fresh in murmur . . That he did seek the love of fair Olivia.

4 A softly spoken word or sentence; subdued or nearly inarticulate speech. **L17.**

Goldsmith What billing, exchanging stolen glances, and broken murmurs?

– COMB.: **murmur diphthong** *PHONETICS* a diphthong ending with a glide or semivowel; **murmur vowel** *PHONETICS* a glide or semivowel, a schwa.

■ **murmurish** *adjective* (*rare*) **M19.** **murmurous** *adjective* (**a**) characterized by a murmur or murmurs, full of murmurs; †(**b**) complaining: **E16.** **murmurously** *adverb* **M19.** **murmurousness** *noun* **E20.**

murmur /ˈmɜːmə/ *verb.* **ME.**
[ORIGIN Old French & mod. French *murmurer* from Latin *murmurare* corresp. to Greek *mormurein*, Sanskrit *marmara* rustling (noun & adjective), (with variation) Old High German *murmurōn, -ulōn* (German *murmeln*), Dutch *murmelen* babble.]
1 *verb intrans.* Complain in low tones; give vent to a muttered or indistinct complaint; grumble (*at, against*). **ME.**

Goldsmith Those veteran legions . . began to murmur, for not having received the rewards which they had expected.

2 *verb intrans.* Make, produce, or emit a subdued continuous sound. **LME.**

I. MURDOCH The waterfall distinctly murmured.

3 *verb trans.* Complain or grumble about, criticize the actions of; accuse. *Scot.* Long *rare.* L15.
4 *verb intrans. & trans.* Utter (sounds, words) in a low voice and indistinctly. E16.

SCOTT FITZGERALD The butler . . murmured something close to Tom's ear. V. WOOLF 'Kreemo,' murmured Mrs. Bletchley, like a sleep-walker. W. GOLDING The assembly murmured in subdued agreement.

■ **murmurer** *noun* a person who murmurs; *esp.* a person who complains about constituted authority: E16. **murmuring** *noun* the action of the verb; an instance of this, a subdued or indistinct expression of discontent or anger: LME. **murmuringly** *adverb* in a murmuring manner E17.

murmuration /mɜːmjʊˈreɪʃ(ə)n/ *noun.* LME.
[ORIGIN French from Latin *murmuratio(n-)*, from *murmurat-* pa. ppl stem of *murmurare* MURMUR *verb*: see -ATION.]
1 The action of murmuring; an instance of this, a murmur. Now chiefly *Scot. & literary.* LME.

Westminster Gazette Murmurations . . for the grievances which they clamoured to have redressed. G. M. BROWN I hear through the tall school window the murmuration of many voices.

2 A company of starlings. L15.
— NOTE: In isolated use in sense 2 in L15, revived M20.

murnong /ˈmɜːnɒŋ/ *noun. Austral.* Also **murrnong** & other vars. M19.
[ORIGIN Wathawurung and Wuywurung *mirnang*.]
A yellow-flowered plant similar to a dandelion, *Microseris scapigera*, of the composite family, with clusters of small tuberous roots, formerly eaten by Aborigines.

Murphy /ˈmɜːfi/ *noun*[1]. *joc. & colloq.* M18.
[ORIGIN Alt.]
= MORPHEUS.

murphy /ˈmɜːfi/ *noun*[2]. Also (esp. in senses 2, 3) **M-**. E19.
[ORIGIN *Murphy*, an Irish surname.]
1 A potato. *slang.* E19.
2 More fully ***Murphy game***. A confidence trick in which the victim is duped by unfulfilled promises of money, sex, etc. *US slang.* M20.
3 ***Murphy's law***, any of various aphoristic expressions of the apparent perverseness and unreasonableness of things. Also called ***Sod's law***. *joc.* M20.

murphy /ˈmɜːfi/ *verb trans. US slang.* Also **M-**. M20.
[ORIGIN from MURPHY *noun*[2].]
Dupe or swindle by a confidence trick giving unfulfilled promises of money, sex, etc.

Murphy bed /ˈmɜːfi bɛd/ *noun phr. N. Amer.* E20.
[ORIGIN from *Murphy* (see below) + BED *noun*.]
Any of various types of folding bed, developed from an original design by the American manufacturer William Lawrence Murphy (1876–1959).

†**murr** *noun.* LME–M18.
[ORIGIN Perh. imit.]
A severe form of catarrh; an attack of this.

murr /mɜː/ *verb intrans. obsolete* exc. *dial.* M17.
[ORIGIN Imit.]
Make a harsh noise; *Scot.* purr.

murra /ˈmʌrə/ *noun.* Now *rare.* Also **-rrha** L16.
[ORIGIN Latin = Greek *morria*.]
A substance, possibly fluorite, used in ancient Rome for making valuable vases, cups, etc.

murrain /ˈmʌrɪn/ *noun & adjective.* ME.
[ORIGIN Anglo-Norman *moryn*, Old French & mod. French *morine*, †*moraine*, from stem of *mourir*, †*morir*, from Proto-Romance alt. of Latin *mori* die.]
▸ **A** *noun.* **1** (A) plague, (a) pestilence, *esp.* the potato blight during the Irish famine in the mid 19th cent. Formerly freq. in imprecations and exclamations. *arch.* ME.

O. NASH A murrain on every bridesmaid and every usher!

2 An infectious disease of livestock; *spec.* babesiosis. LME.
†**3** Flesh of animals killed by disease; dead flesh, carrion. LME–E17.
†**4** Death, mortality, esp. by plague or pestilence. Also (*rare*), slaughter. LME–M17.
▸ †**B** *adjective.* Ill-conditioned; contemptible; excessive. L16–E18.
■ **murrained** *adjective* killed by murrain; infected with murrain: E19.

murram /ˈmʌrəm/ *noun.* E20.
[ORIGIN African name.]
A hard dry lateritic soil found in tropical Africa and used locally as road metal.

Murray /ˈmʌri/ *noun*[1]. M19.
[ORIGIN John *Murray* (1808–92), Brit. publisher.]
Any of a series of guidebooks or railway timetables published by John Murray or his successors.

Murray /ˈmʌri/ *noun*[2]. M19.
[ORIGIN A river and large river system of SE Australia.]
1 Used *attrib.* to designate plants or animals associated with the region of the Murray river system. L19.
Murray cod a large carnivorous serranid food fish, *Maccullochella macquariensis*. **Murray lily** the Darling lily, *Crinum flaccidum*. **Murray pine** any of several cypress pines, esp. (**a**) *Callitris preissii* subsp. *murrayensis*; (**b**) the white pine, *C. columellaris*.
2 MEDICINE. ***Murray Valley encephalitis***, ***Murray Valley fever***, a severe form of epidemic encephalitis caused by a mosquito-borne virus. M20.

murre /mɜː/ *noun.* Now chiefly *N. Amer.* L16.
[ORIGIN Uncertain: prob. imitative of the guillemot's call.]
A guillemot, razorbill, or other auk.
common murre *N. Amer.* the common guillemot, *Uria aalge*. **thick-billed murre** *N. Amer.* Brünnich's guillemot, *U. lomvia*.

murrelet /ˈmɜːlɪt/ *noun.* L19.
[ORIGIN from MURRE + -LET.]
Any of several small auks of the N. Pacific of the genera *Brachyramphus* and *Synthliboramphus*.

murrey /ˈmʌri/ *noun & adjective. arch.* ME.
[ORIGIN Old French *moré* adjective & noun, *morée* noun, from medieval Latin *moratus*, *morata*, from Latin *morum* mulberry: see -Y[5].]
▸ **A** *noun.* The colour of a mulberry, a purple-red, (also ***murrey colour***). Also, cloth of this colour. ME.
▸ **B** *adjective.* Of the colour of a mulberry, purple-red. ME.

murrha *noun* var. of MURRA.

murrhine /ˈmʌrɪn, -rʌɪn/ *adjective & noun.* L16.
[ORIGIN Latin *murr(h)inus*, formed as MURRA: see -INE[1].]
▸ **A** *adjective.* Made of or pertaining to murra. L16.
murrhine glass modern delicate glassware from the East with coloured metal particles embedded in it.
▸ **B** *noun.* A murrhine vase. L18.

Murri /ˈmʌri/ *noun. Austral.* Pl. same, **-s**. L19.
[ORIGIN Kamilaroi (and other Aboriginal languages of Queensland) *mari* person.]
In Queensland and northern New South Wales: an Aborigine (used by Aborigines to refer to themselves).

murrnong *noun* var. of MURNONG.

murther *noun, verb,* **murtherer** *noun,* **murtherous** *adjective* see MURDER *noun* etc.

muru /ˈmʊruː/ *noun.* M19.
[ORIGIN Maori.]
NZ HISTORY. Raiding and plundering by Maori, esp. in reprisal for an offence.

murumuru /ˌmuːruːˈmuːruː, ˈmuːruːˌmuːruː/ *noun.* M19.
[ORIGIN Portuguese from Tupi from Carib.]
An Amazonian palm, *Astrocaryum murumuru*, whose stem is covered with black spines.

murus gallicus /mjʊərəs ˈgalɪkəs/ *noun phr.* Pl. ***-ri -ci*** /-riː -kiː/. M20.
[ORIGIN Latin, from *murus* wall + *gallicus* Gallic.]
ARCHAEOLOGY. A type of late Iron Age Celtic fort having stone walls bound by horizontally placed timber frames.

Murut /ˈmuːrət/ *noun.* M19.
[ORIGIN Bajau *belud* hill.]
▸ **A** *noun.* Pl. same, **-s**. A member of a Dayak people originally inhabiting the hill country in the interior of N. Borneo, although now more widely spread; the language of this people. M19.
▸ **B** *attrib.* or as*adjective*. Of or pertaining to the Murut or their language. M19.

musa /ˈmjuːzə/ *noun*[1]. Pl. **musae** /ˈmjuːziː/, **musas**. L16.
[ORIGIN mod. Latin (see below), from Arabic *mawz(a)*.]
Orig., a banana plant. Now, any plant of the genus *Musa* (family Musaceae), which includes the tropical plantain, *M. paradisiaca*, and bananas.
■ **muˈsaceous** *adjective* of or pertaining to the family Musaceae M19.

musa /ˈmjuːzə/ *noun*[2]. Also **MUSA**. M20.
[ORIGIN Acronym, from multiple unit steerable antenna.]
A radio aerial consisting of an array of elements giving a beam which can be varied in direction by varying the phase relations between the elements.

musae *noun pl.* see MUSA *noun*[1].

†**musaeum** *noun* var. of MUSEUM.

musang /mjʊˈsaŋ/ *noun.* L18.
[ORIGIN Malay = wild cat.]
A palm civet of the Asian genus *Paradoxurus*; esp. the common palm civet or toddy cat, *P. hermaphroditus*.

Mus.B. *abbreviation.* Also **Mus. Bac.**
Latin *Musicae Baccalaureus* Bachelor of Music.

Musca /ˈmʌskə/ *noun.* L18.
[ORIGIN Latin *musca* fly.]
(The name of) a small constellation of the southern hemisphere, lying in the Milky Way between the Southern Cross and the South Pole; the Fly.

muscadel *noun* var. of MUSCATEL.

Muscadelle /mʌskəˈdɛl/ *noun.* L19.
[ORIGIN French, var. of MUSCATEL.]
A variety of white grape mainly grown for sweet white wines in Bordeaux and Australia.

Muscadet /ˈmʌskədeɪ, ˈmʊsk-/ *noun.* E19.
[ORIGIN French, from *muscade* nutmeg, from *musc* MUSK *noun*: see -ET[1].]
A white wine made in the Loire valley near Nantes, France; the variety of grape from which this wine is made.

muscadin /myskadɛ̃ (*pl. same*); ˈmʊskədɪn, ˈmʌsk-/ *noun.* L18.
[ORIGIN French, lit. 'musk-comfit', a sweet.]
hist. A (Parisian) dandy; *derog.* a member of a moderate party in the early years of the French Revolution, composed chiefly of young men of the upper middle class.

muscadine /ˈmʌskədɪn, -ʌɪn/ *noun.* M16.
[ORIGIN Prob. alt. of *muscadel*, MUSCATEL: see -INE[4].]
1 In full ***muscadine wine***. = MUSCATEL 1. *obsolete* exc. *hist.* M16.
2 In full ***muscadine grape***. = MUSCAT 2. Also, (the musky-flavoured grape of) a wild N. American vine, *Vitis rotundifolia*. L16.

muscae /ˈmʌskiː, ˈmʌssiː/ *noun pl.* M18.
[ORIGIN Latin, pl. of *musca* fly.]
Chiefly MEDICINE. In full ***muscae volitantes*** /vɒlɪˈtantiːz/ [pres. pple of *volitare* fly about]. Specks which appear to float before the eyes, freq. due to particles in the vitreous humour of the eye.

muscardine /mʌˈskɑːdiːn/ *noun.* M19.
[ORIGIN French (from the fungus's resemblance to the sweet confection *musca(r)din*: see MUSCADIN).]
Any of various fungal diseases of insects (esp. silkworms); a fungus causing any of these.
■ **muscardined** *adjective* affected with muscardine L19.

muscari /mʌˈskɑːri, -ˈskɛːri/ *noun.* L16.
[ORIGIN mod. Latin (see below), perh. repr. dim. of Greek *moskos* musk, from the musky smell of the flowers.]
Any of various small bulbous plants of the genus *Muscari*, of the lily family; *spec.* = ***grape*** HYACINTH.

muscarine /ˈmʌskəriːn, -ɪn/ *noun.* Also **-in** /-ɪn/. M19.
[ORIGIN from mod. Latin *muscaria* specific epithet of fly agaric (see below), from Latin *muscarius*, from *musca* fly: see -INE[5], -IN[1].]
BIOCHEMISTRY. A poisonous alkaloid, $C_9H_{21}NO_3$, found in fly agaric, *Amanita muscaria*, and other fungi.
■ **muscarinic** /mʌskəˈrɪnɪk/ *adjective* resembling muscarine or its physiological actions; (of a receptor) capable of responding to muscarine: M20.

muscat /ˈmʌskat/ *noun.* M16.
[ORIGIN Old French & mod. French from Provençal (= Italian MOSCATO), from *musc* MUSK *noun*: see -AT[1].]
1 In full ***muscat wine***. = MUSCATEL 1. M16.
2 In full ***muscat grape***. Any of several varieties of grape with a musky taste or smell; a vine bearing a variety of such a grape. M17.
†**3** A kind of peach or pear with a musky taste or smell. M17–M18.

muscatel /mʌskəˈtɛl/ *noun.* Also **-del** /-dɛl/. LME.
[ORIGIN Old French *muscadel*, *-tel* (= Italian MOSCATELLO) from Provençal dim. of *muscat*: see MUSCAT, -EL[2].]
1 A strong sweet wine made from the muscat or similar grape. LME.
2 In full ***muscatel grape***. = MUSCAT 2. E16.
†**3** A variety of pear with a musky taste or smell. M16–M18.
4 In full ***muscatel raisin***. A raisin from the muscatel grape. Usu. in *pl.* M17.

Muschelkalk /ˈmʊʃ(ə)lkalk/ *noun.* E19.
[ORIGIN German, lit. 'shelly limestone', from *Muschel* MUSSEL + *Kalk* CHALK *noun*.]
GEOLOGY. (The limestone of) the Middle Triassic in Europe, esp. Germany.

muscicapine /mʌˈsɪkəpʌɪn/ *adjective.* L19.
[ORIGIN from mod. Latin *Muscicapa* (see below), from Latin *musca* fly + *capere* catch: see -INE[1].]
ORNITHOLOGY. Of, pertaining to, or designating the family Muscicapidae or the genus *Muscicapa* of Old World flycatchers.

muscicole /ˈmʌsɪkəʊl/ *adjective & noun.* L19.
[ORIGIN from Latin *muscus* moss + -I- + -COLE.]
ECOLOGY. ▸**A** *adjective.* Living among or in association with mosses. L19.
▸ **B** *noun.* A muscicole organism. M20.
■ **muˈscicolous** *adjective* = MUSCICOLE *adjective* M19.

muscid /ˈmʌskɪd, ˈmʌsɪd/ *adjective & noun.* M19.
[ORIGIN mod. Latin *Muscidae* (see below), from Latin *musca* fly: see -ID[3].]
▸ **A** *adjective.* Of, pertaining to, or designating the dipteran family Muscidae, which includes houseflies. M19.
▸ **B** *noun.* A fly of this family. M19.

muscimol /ˈmʌskɪmɒl/ *noun.* M20.
[ORIGIN formed as MUSCARINE + IM(INE + -OL.]
BIOCHEMISTRY. A narcotic and hallucinogenic alkaloid found in fly agaric, *Amanita muscaria*, and other fungi; 3-hydroxy-5-aminomethylisoxazole, $C_4H_6N_2O_2$.

muscle /ˈmʌs(ə)l/ *noun*[1]. Also †**-cule**. LME.
[ORIGIN French from Latin *musculus*, from *mus* mouse (from the fancied mouselike form of some muscles): see -CULE.]
1 ANATOMY & PHYSIOLOGY. Any of the fibrous bands or bundles of contractile tissue which act to produce movement in

M

or maintain the position of parts of the human or animal body. LME.
adductor muscle, ciliary muscle, flexor muscle, pectoral muscle, etc. ***flex one's muscles***: see FLEX verb 1. **not move a muscle** be perfectly motionless.
2 The part of the body consisting of muscles; muscular tissue; the substance of which muscles are composed. L18.
SKELETAL ***muscle. smooth muscle***: see SMOOTH *adjective & adverb*. STRIATED ***muscle***. STRIPED ***muscle***.
3 (Muscular) power, strength; influence; force, violence; intimidation; manpower to exert muscular power; *slang* a person employed to use or threaten violence. E19.

S. BRILL The Fund had used its financial muscle for investments that were radically different. B. CALLAGHAN There was heavy-jowled Lambchops.. who hired himself out as muscle to the after-hours clubs.

— COMB.: **muscle-bound** *adjective* having the muscles stiff and enlarged, esp. as a result of too much exercise or training; lacking flexibility; **muscle car** *N. Amer. slang* a powerful car, *spec.* = ***hot rod*** (a) s.v. HOT *adjective*; **muscle cell** each of the elongated contractile cells, containing ordered actin and myosin filaments, of which muscular tissue is composed; **muscle current** the flow of electrical current which occurs on connecting different points of a muscle; **muscle curve** a curve indicating amount of muscular contraction as recorded by a myograph; **muscle fibre** = ***muscle cell*** above; **muscle-flexing** *adjective* demonstrating aggression or strength; **muscle force** the force or power of human agency; **muscle-man** *colloq.* (*a*) a person who employs or threatens violence on behalf of a professional criminal; (*b*) a person with well-developed muscles; **muscle Mary** *slang* a homosexual man with well-developed muscles; **muscle power** = sense 3 above; **muscle pull** *N. Amer.* a pulled muscle; **muscle scar** a marking on a bone, shell, etc., indicating a point of attachment of a muscle; **muscle sense** kinaesthetic sense; **muscle shirt** *N. Amer.* a man's tight-fitting T-shirt; **muscle spindle** any of numerous small sensory organs within muscle which respond to extension and contraction of the muscle and aid coordination.
■ **muscled** *adjective* endowed with muscle (chiefly with qualifying adjective or adverb, as ***full-muscled, well-muscled***, etc.) E17. **muscleless** /-l-l-/ *adjective* M19. **muscling** *noun* muscular structure or development, muscles, formerly *spec.* as delineated or represented in art L17. **muscly** *adjective* composed of muscle; exhibiting great muscular development: M16.

muscle *noun*[2] see MUSSEL *noun*.

muscle /ˈmʌs(ə)l/ *verb*. E19.
[ORIGIN from MUSCLE *noun*[1].]
1 *verb trans.* Coerce by violence or by economic or political pressure. *slang*. E19.

M

New Republic U.S. companies.. don't usually use pricing to muscle their competitors.

2 a *verb trans.* Move (something) by the exercise of (muscular) power. *colloq.* E20. ▸**b** *verb intrans.* Make one's way by the exercise of (muscular) power. M20.

a J. DICKEY We muscled the canoe laboriously cross-river to land.

3 *verb intrans.* Foll. by *in* (*on*), *into*: intrude into the business or activities of another or others by force or fraud; enter forcibly or uninvited. *colloq.* E20.

E. WAUGH You're muscling in on my territory. *Guardian* Visa is planning to muscle into the fledgling electronic cash business in the UK.

muscology /mʌˈskɒlədʒi/ *noun*. E19.
[ORIGIN from Latin *muscus* moss + -OLOGY.]
The branch of biology that deals with bryophytes, esp. mosses; the mosses or bryophytes of a district.
■ **muscologist** *noun* E19.

muscose /ˈmʌskəʊs/ *adjective*. *rare*. E18.
[ORIGIN Latin *muscosus*, from *muscus* moss: see -OSE[1].]
Mosslike.

muscous /ˈmʌskəs/ *adjective*. *rare*. M17.
[ORIGIN formed as MUSCOSE + -OUS.]
Mossy.

muscovado /mʌskəˈvɑːdəʊ/ *noun*. Pl. **-os**. L16.
[ORIGIN Portuguese *mascabado* (Spanish *menoscabado*) use as noun (sc. *açúcar*, Spanish *azúcar* sugar) of pa. pple of *mascabar* make badly: see -ADO.]
More fully ***muscovado sugar***. Raw or unrefined sugar obtained from the juice of the sugar cane by evaporation and draining off the molasses; an example or type of this.

Muscovite /ˈmʌskəvʌɪt/ *noun*[1] *& adjective*. M16.
[ORIGIN mod. Latin *Muscovita*, from *Muscovia*: see MUSCOVY, -ITE[1].]
▸**A** *noun*. A native or inhabitant of Moscow, now the capital of Russia, formerly of the principality of Muscovy; *hist.* a native or inhabitant of Muscovy; *arch.* a Russian. M16.
▸**B** *adjective*. Of or pertaining to Moscow or (*hist.*) Muscovy; *arch.* Russian. L16.

muscovite /ˈmʌskəvʌɪt/ *noun*[2]. M19.
[ORIGIN from *Muscovy glass* (see MUSCOVY) + -ITE[1].]
MINERALOGY. A colourless, silver-grey, or yellowish potassium-containing mica which is a component of many types of rock and is used esp. in electrical insulation. Also called ***common mica, white mica***.
■ **muscoviti'zation** *noun* conversion into muscovite E20. **muscovitized** *adjective* converted into muscovite L19.

Muscovy /ˈmʌskəvi/ *noun*. Also **m-**. L16.
[ORIGIN French †*Muscovie* (now *Mos-*) from mod. Latin *Moscovia*, from Russian *Moskva* Moscow: see -Y[3]. Sense 2 by assoc. with MUSK *noun*.]
1 ***Muscovy glass***, †***Muscovy talc***, common mica, muscovite. L16.
2 In full ***Muscovy duck***. A large duck, *Cairina moschata*, native to Central and S. America but widely domesticated, with variable black or white plumage and (in the male) a red caruncle on the bill and face (also called ***musk duck***). Also = ***musk duck*** (b) s.v. MUSK *noun*. M17.

muscular /ˈmʌskjʊlə/ *adjective*. L17.
[ORIGIN from MUSCULOUS by substitution of -AR[1].]
1 Of or pertaining to muscle or the muscles; (of a disease etc.) affecting the muscles. L17.

J. MANN A chronic condition.. characterized by muscular weakness during exertion.

2 Composed of, containing, or of the nature of muscle. Also, forming a constituent of muscle. L17.
3 Of a body, a limb, etc.: characterized by muscle, having well-developed muscles. M18.

Life He has a fetish about keeping his muscular body at an absolute peak.

— SPECIAL COLLOCATIONS: **muscular Christian** a person believing in or living a life of muscular Christianity. **muscular Christianity** Christian life characterized by cheerful physical activity or robust good works, *spec.* as described in the writings of Charles Kingsley; Christianity without asceticism. ***muscular*** DYSTROPHY. **muscular feeling**, **muscular sensation**, **muscular sense** = ***muscle sense*** s.v. MUSCLE *noun*[1]. **muscular stomach** the gizzard of a bird etc.
■ **muscu'larity** *noun* the quality or state of being muscular; the fact of consisting of muscle or having well-developed muscles; muscular strength or vigour: L17. **muscularize** *verb intrans. & trans.* become or make muscular E19. **muscularly** *adverb* M18.

muscularis /mʌskjʊˈlɑːrɪs/ *noun*. L19.
[ORIGIN mod. Latin, use as noun (perh. sc. *lamina* layer) of *muscularis*, from Latin *musculus* MUSCLE *noun*[1] + *-aris* -ARY[2].]
ANATOMY. A thin layer of smooth muscle fibres in various organs, as the stomach, the ureter; *spec.* (in full ***muscularis mucosae*** /mjuːˈkəʊsiː/), that associated with a mucous membrane, esp. in the gut.

musculation /mʌskjʊˈleɪʃ(ə)n/ *noun*. *rare*. M19.
[ORIGIN French, from Latin *musculus* MUSCLE *noun*[1]: see -ATION.]
1 The function of muscular movement. M19.
2 The disposition or arrangement of muscles. L19.

musculature /ˈmʌskjʊlətʃə/ *noun*. L19.
[ORIGIN French, from Latin *musculus* MUSCLE *noun*[1] + *-atus* -ATE[2]: see -URE.]
(The arrangement of) the muscular system of a body; the arrangement of muscles in an organ or limb.

†**muscule** *noun* var. of MUSCLE *noun*[1].

†**musculite** *noun*. Also (earlier) in mod. Latin form **-ites**. L17–E19.
[ORIGIN mod. Latin *musculites*, from *musculus* MUSSEL *noun*: see -ITE[1].]
PALAEONTOLOGY. A fossil mussel shell.

musculo- /ˈmʌskjʊləʊ/ *combining form*.
[ORIGIN Latin, from *musculus* MUSCLE *noun*[1]: see -O-.]
Chiefly ANATOMY & PHYSIOLOGY. Forming adjectives with the senses 'pertaining to or composed of muscle and —', 'pertaining to the muscular system and —', as ***musculo-membranous, musculoskeletal, musculotendinous***, etc.
■ **musculo'fascial** *adjective* of or pertaining to a muscle and its associated fasciae M20.

†**musculous** *adjective*. LME–L18.
[ORIGIN from Old French & mod. French *musculeux* or Latin *musculosus*, from *musculus* MUSCLE *noun*[1]: see -ULOUS.]
Of or pertaining to muscles; having well-developed muscles; muscular.

Mus.D. *abbreviation*. Also **Mus. Doc.**
Latin *Musicae Doctor* Doctor of Music.

muse /mjuːz/ *noun*[1]. Also (esp. in sense 1) **M-**. LME.
[ORIGIN Old French & mod. French, or Latin *musa* from Greek *mousa*.]
1 CLASSICAL MYTHOLOGY. Each of nine (occas. more) goddesses, the daughters of Zeus and Mnemosyne (Memory), regarded as the inspirers of learning and the arts, esp. of poetry and music; a representation of one of the Muses, usu. as a beautiful young woman. Usu. in *pl.* LME. ▸**b** *The* Muse appropriate to the work in question (as if only one were recognized), *the* source of poetic inspiration. *poet.* E17.
2 The inspiring goddess or adored woman of a particular poet; a poet's particular genius, the character of a particular poet's style. LME.

L. GORDON Emily replaced Vivienne as Eliot's muse in *Ash Wednesday*.

†**3** A poem, a song. LME–E16.
4 A person inspired by a Muse, a poet. E17.
5 A type of poetry or music; ***the Muse***, poetry; ***the Muses***, the liberal arts. *literary*. L17.
— PHRASES: **tenth Muse** a muse of inspiration imagined as added to the nine of classical mythology.

muse /mjuːz/ *noun*[2]. *arch*. L15.
[ORIGIN from MUSE *verb*[2].]
An act or (formerly) the action of musing; a state or fit of abstraction.

muse *noun*[3] *& verb*[1] var. of MEUSE.

muse /mjuːz/ *verb*[2]. Now *literary*. ME.
[ORIGIN Old French & mod. French *muser* †meditate, waste time, perh. ult. from medieval Latin *musum* muzzle.]
▸**I** *verb intrans.* **1** Be absorbed in thought; meditate continuously in silence; ponder. ME.

L. M. MONTGOMERY In school I can look at her and muse over days departed. R. MACAULAY She mused, her chin resting on one strong hand. P. FITZGERALD He appeared to be musing on what had passed between them.

2 Be affected with astonishment or surprise; wonder, marvel, (*at*). Now *poet. rare*. ME.

TENNYSON Then came the fine Gawain and wonder'd at her, And Lancelot later came and mused at her.

3 Gaze meditatively; look thoughtfully or intently. LME.

J. H. NEWMAN He began to eye and muse upon the great bishop. K. TYNAN He hopes to be amused by his bully companions, but the eyes constantly muse beyond them.

†**4** Murmur; grumble, complain. LME–L16.
▸**II** *verb trans.* **5** Ponder over, reflect on; contemplate, meditate; think to oneself; ask oneself meditatively (*how, what*, etc.); say or murmur meditatively. Now only with clause or direct speech as obj. LME.

M. ARNOLD Ah me, I muse what this young fox may mean! R. K. NARAYAN Ramani stood over him, musing indignantly: 'Fast asleep at eight o'clock.' D. WELCH 'I wonder what sort of letters you write?' she mused.

†**6** Marvel at (a thing, *how* etc.); be surprised *that*. E16–M17.
■ **muser** *noun* LME. **musing** *noun* (*a*) the action of the verb; thoughtful abstraction; (*b*) a fit of thoughtful abstraction, a meditation: ME. **musingly** *adverb* in a musing manner E17.

†**musea** *noun pl.* see MUSEUM.

museau /myzo/ *noun*. Pl. **-eaux** /-o/. E19.
[ORIGIN French colloq., lit. 'muzzle, snout'.]
A person's face.

musée /myze (*pl. same*), ˈmjuːzeɪ/ *noun*. M19.
[ORIGIN French formed as MUSEUM.]
a (French) museum.
musée imaginaire /imaʒinɛːr, ɪmadʒɪˈnɛː/ an imaginary collection of all the works of human artifice.

museful /ˈmjuːzfʊl, -f(ə)l/ *adjective*. *arch*. E17.
[ORIGIN from MUSE *noun*[2] + -FUL.]
Absorbed in thought; thoughtful, pensive.
■ **musefully** *adverb* E19.

museless /ˈmjuːzlɪs/ *adjective*. *literary*. M17.
[ORIGIN from MUSE *noun*[1] + -LESS, after Greek *amousos*.]
Without learning; uncultured. Also, uninspired.

musellim /mʊˈsɛlɪm/ *noun*. L17.
[ORIGIN Turkish *müsellim* deputy governor, tax officer from Arabic *mutasallim* active pple of *tasallama* receive.]
In the Ottoman Empire: a deputy provincial governor or military commander.

museography /mjuːzɪˈɒgrəfi/ *noun*. L19.
[ORIGIN from MUSEUM: see -OGRAPHY.]
The systematic description of the contents of museums. Also = MUSEOLOGY.
■ **museographer** *noun* = MUSEOGRAPHIST L19. **museo'graphical** *adjective* M20. **museographist** *noun* L18.

museology /mjuːzɪˈɒlədʒi/ *noun*. L19.
[ORIGIN from MUSEUM: see -OLOGY.]
The science or practice of organizing and managing museums.
■ **museo'logical** *adjective* M20. **museologist** *noun* L19.

muset /ˈmjuːzɪt/ *noun*. Long *obsolete* exc. *dial.* L16.
[ORIGIN Old French *mucette, muss-* hiding place, dim. of *muce, musse* MEUSE *noun*: see -ET[1].]
= MEUSE *noun* 1, 2.

musette /mjuːˈzɛt/ *noun*. LME.
[ORIGIN Old French & mod. French, dim. of *muse* bagpipe: see -ETTE.]
1 A kind of small bagpipe, *esp.* a small French bagpipe of the 18th cent. with a soft tone. LME.
2 A soft pastoral air imitating the sound of the musette; a dance performed to such music. E18.
3 A reed stop in an organ producing a soft tone resembling that of the musette. E19.
4 A small and simple variety of oboe without a reed cap. L19.
5 More fully ***musette bag***. A type of lightweight knapsack used esp. by the military and by racing cyclists. E20.

museum /mjuːˈzɪəm/ *noun*. Also †**musaeum**. Pl. **-eums**, †**-ea**. E17.
[ORIGIN Latin = library, study from Greek *mouseion* seat of the Muses, use as noun of neut. of *mouseios*, from *mousa* MUSE *noun*[1].]
1 a ANCIENT HISTORY. A university building, *spec.* (**M-**) that erected at Alexandria by Ptolemy Soter. E17. ▸†**b** *gen.* A building or apartment dedicated to the pursuit of learning or the arts; a scholar's study. M17–M18.

2 A building or portion of a building used for the storing, preservation, and exhibition of objects considered to be of lasting value or interest, as objects illustrative of antiquities, natural history, fine and industrial art, etc.; an institution responsible for such a building or collection. Also, a collection of objects in such a building. M17.

Daily Telegraph The Reading Room of the British Museum . . , that immense rotunda. C. FRONDEL Curator of Minerals and Gems in the American Museum of Natural History. *Village Voice* The Museum of Modern Art has been running a Will Rogers Retrospective. U. LE GUIN The palace, preserved as a museum of the ancient times of royalty. *New Society* One of those painted wagons . . that gypsies donate to folk museums.

3 *transf. & fig.* A thing resembling a museum, a repository of (esp. historical) information; a collection. M18.

THACKERAY Miss Blanche . . had quite a little museum of locks of hair in her treasure-chest. G. S. FRASER He served . . as a kind of living museum of the older Scots folk-song tradition.

– COMB.: **museum piece** an object suitable for exhibition in a museum; *derog.* an old-fashioned or quaint person, machine, etc.
■ **museumish** *adjective* (*colloq.*) resembling a museum or exhibits in a museum E20.

mush /mʌʃ/ *noun*[1]. In sense 3 also **moosh** /mʊʃ, muːʃ/. L17.
[ORIGIN App. var. of MASH *noun*[1].]
1 Porridge; *spec.* maize porridge, maize meal boiled in water until it thickens (freq. in ***mush and milk***). Chiefly *N. Amer.* L17.
2 *gen.* A soft pulpy or formless mass; soft pulp; slush. Also (*dial.*), something reduced to or resembling a mass of powder. E19. ▸**b** Feeble sentimentality, (sentimental) nonsense. M19.

W. H. AUDEN My mind works abominably slowly, in a vague mush of tepid ideas. F. HOYLE The ice was hard-frozen not a mere pile of mush. J. DAVIS Oh no! My legs are turning to jelly! My mind is turning to mush. P. D. JAMES She trudged through the mush of fallen leaves.

3 The mouth, the face. *slang.* M19.
4 RADIO. Noise or distortion in the form of a hissing or rushing sound, esp. as a result of interference between transmitters. E20.
5 SURFING. The foam produced when a wave breaks. M20.
– COMB.: **mush-head** *slang* a person lacking in firmness, a feebly sentimental person; **mush ice** partly frozen water, ice mixed with water.

mush /mʌʃ/ *noun*[2]. *slang.* E19.
[ORIGIN Abbreviation of MUSHROOM *noun*.]
1 An umbrella. Chiefly in ***mush-faker***, = ***mushroom-faker*** s.v. MUSHROOM *noun*. *arch.* E19.
2 An owner-driver of a cab; a cab-driver who owns one, two, or three cabs. L19.

mush /mʌʃ/ *noun*[3]. *N. Amer.* E20.
[ORIGIN from MUSH *verb*[2].]
A journey made through snow with a dog sledge.

mush /mʌʃ, mʊʃ/ *noun*[4]. *military slang.* Also **moosh** /mʊʃ, muːʃ/. E20.
[ORIGIN Perh. from MUSH *verb*[1].]
A guardroom, a cell; a military prison.

mush /mʌʃ, mʊʃ/ *noun*[5]. *slang.* Also **moosh** /mʊʃ, muːʃ/. M20.
[ORIGIN Uncertain: perh. a use of MUSH *noun*[1] 3.]
A man, a fellow. Also used as a form of address.

mush /mʌʃ/ *noun*[6]. *slang.* M20.
[ORIGIN Contr.]
= MOUSTACHE.

mush /mʌʃ/ *verb*[1]. L18.
[ORIGIN App. orig. var. of MASH *verb*[2]. Later directly from MUSH *noun*[1].]
1 *verb trans. & intrans.* Crush, pulverize, crumble; (now usu.) reduce to soft pulp. Chiefly *dial.* L18.
2 *verb intrans.* Of an aircraft: fly sluggishly, almost stalling or stalling repeatedly; lose or maintain altitude when a gain is expected. M20.
3 *verb intrans.* Sink *in* or *into* a soft surface. *colloq.* M20.
4 *verb trans. & intrans.* Kiss, esp. in public. *slang.* M20.

mush /mʌʃ/ *verb*[2]. *N. Amer.* M19.
[ORIGIN Alt. of French *marchez* (imper.) or *marchons* (3rd person pl. subjunct.), forms of *marcher* MARCH *verb*[2].]
1 *verb intrans.* Travel through snow with a dog sledge; (of dogs) pull a sledge. M19.
2 *verb intrans.* In *imper.* Keep moving! go *on*! (a command to dogs pulling a sledge). L19.
3 *verb intrans.* Travel on foot through snow or ice. L19.
4 *verb trans.* Urge on or drive (dogs) through snow. E20.
5 *verb trans.* Transport by dog sledge. M20.

musha /ˈmʌʃə/ *interjection. Irish.* M18.
[ORIGIN Irish *muise* var. of *maiseadh*, i.e. *má* if, *is* is, *eadh* it, or alt. of *Muire* Mary (i.e. the Virgin Mary): cf. WISHA.]
Expr. surprise or disbelief.

musher /ˈmʌʃə/ *noun*[1]. *slang.* L19.
[ORIGIN from MUSH *noun*[2] + -ER[1].]
= MUSH *noun*[2] 2.

musher /ˈmʌʃə/ *noun*[2]. *N. Amer.* L19.
[ORIGIN from MUSH *verb*[2] + -ER[1].]
A person who travels through snow on foot; a driver of a dog sledge.

mushie /ˈmʌʃi/ *noun. Austral. colloq.* Also **mushy**. M20.
[ORIGIN Abbreviation: see -IE.]
A mushroom.

mushla(w) *nouns* vars. of MISHLA.

mushrat /ˈmʌʃrat/ *noun. N. Amer.* M19.
[ORIGIN formed as MUSKRAT.]
= MUSKRAT.

mushroom /ˈmʌʃruːm, -rʊm/ *noun & adjective.* Also †**-rump**. LME.
[ORIGIN Old French & mod. French MOUSSERON from late Latin *mussirio(n-)*.]
▸ **A** *noun.* **1** Orig., any fungus having a fleshy fruiting body, usu. rounded or caplike, on a stalk growing from the ground, freq. regarded as the type of rapid growth. Now usu., either of two edible agarics, *Agaricus campestris* (in full ***field mushroom***), and *A. bisporus*, which is cultivated for eating; *gen.* any (esp. edible) fungus resembling these in general appearance. Cf. TOADSTOOL *noun* 1. LME.
horse mushroom, ***parasol mushroom***, ***St George's mushroom***, etc.
2 *fig.* A person or family that has suddenly sprung into notice; an upstart; a city, an institution, etc., that is of sudden growth. L16. ▸†**b** A contemptible person. L16–M18.

C. MARLOWE A night growne mushrump, Such a one as my Lord of Cornewall is. S. BRETT He was one of those showbiz mushrooms who spring up overnight.

3 *transf.* A thing shaped like a mushroom; *spec.* (***a***) *arch. slang* an umbrella; (***b***) *arch. colloq.* = ***mushroom hat*** below; (***c***) ARCHITECTURE a reinforced concrete pillar broadening out towards the top, with reinforcing rods passing into a slab forming part of the floor above; (***d***) a cloud (of smoke, fire, etc.) that spreads upwards and outwards; (***e***) a mushroom-shaped implement over which material is stretched in darning, embroidery, etc. E18.
4 A pale pinkish- or greyish-brown colour resembling that of a mushroom. L19.
▸ **B** *attrib.* or as *adjective.* Resembling a mushroom; *spec.* (***a***) of rapid growth; of short duration; *arch.* upstart; (***b***) mushroom-coloured, pale pinkish- or greyish-brown. E17.
– SPECIAL COLLOCATIONS & COMB.: **mushroom anchor** an anchor having a saucer-shaped head on a central shaft. **mushroom cloud** a cloud of smoke shaped like a mushroom, *spec.* such as forms above a nuclear explosion. **mushroom colour** = sense A.4 above. **mushroom-coloured** *adjective* of mushroom colour. **mushroom coral** any of various stony corals which resemble mushrooms or other fungi. **mushroom-faker** *arch. slang* an itinerant umbrella-mender. **mushroom growth** rapid growth like that of a mushroom; a thing that has grown up rapidly. **mushroom hat** a low-crowned circular hat, *esp.* such a lady's hat with a down-curving brim. ***mushroom loaf***: see LOAF *noun*[1]. **mushroom ring** a fairy ring. **mushroom spawn** *colloq.* the mycelium of a mushroom. **mushroom-stone** a (fossil) mushroom coral. **mushroom valve** a lift valve whose moving element somewhat resembles a mushroom in shape.
■ **mushroomy** *adjective* (*colloq.*) resembling a mushroom M19.

mushroom /ˈmʌʃruːm/ *verb.* M18.
[ORIGIN from the noun.]
▸ **I** †**1** *verb trans.* Elevate (a person) in social position with great suddenness. *rare.* Only in M18.
2 *verb intrans.* Esp. of a bullet: expand and flatten like a mushroom. Occas. foll. by *out*. L19.
3 *verb intrans.* Rise like a mushroom; expand or spring up rapidly; increase rapidly. Also foll. by *up*, *out*. E20.

J. KOSINSKI A cloud of dust mushroomed above. S. KITZINGER Clubs mushroomed where swinging couples could go and find new partners. C. MCCULLOUGH Both the younger brothers had mushroomed in self-confidence. *Scotsman* Prices . . are mushrooming by more than 50 per cent a year.

▸ **II 4** *verb intrans.* Gather mushrooms. Chiefly as ***mushrooming*** *verbal noun & ppl adjective.* M19.
■ **mushroomer** *noun* a person who gathers mushrooms L19.

†**mushrump** *noun & adjective* var. of MUSHROOM *noun & adjective.*

mushy *noun* var. of MUSHIE.

mushy /ˈmʌʃi/ *adjective. colloq.* M19.
[ORIGIN from MUSH *noun*[1] + -Y[1].]
1 Soft and slushy; pulpy; formless; lacking firmness or distinctiveness. M19.
mushy peas cooked (esp. processed) peas prepared in a semi-liquid state.
2 Feebly sentimental, insipid. *colloq.* L19.
3 SURFING. Of a wave: breaking slowly; foamy. M20.
4 Of the steering or brakes of a vehicle etc.: lacking firmness, spongy. M20.
■ **mushily** *adverb* L19. **mushiness** *noun* M19.

music /ˈmjuːzɪk/ *noun.* ME.
[ORIGIN Old French & mod. French *musique* from Latin *musica* from Greek *mousikē* use as noun (sc. *tekhnē* art) of fem. of *mousikos* of a Muse or the Muses, of the arts, from *mousa* MUSE *noun*[1]: see -IC.]
1 The art or science of combining vocal or instrumental sounds with a view to beauty or coherence of form and expression of emotion. ME.
2 a Melodic or harmonic vocal or instrumental sound; an example or kind of such sound. LME. ▸**b** Pleasing sound produced by an agent or agency specified or understood, as the song of a bird, the murmur of running water, the cry of hounds on seeing the chase; something which it is a delight to hear; an example or kind of such sound. L16. ▸**c** Melodic or harmonic vocal or instrumental sound as devised by a composer; musical composition. E17.

a R. INGALLS The music came from a portable phonograph. *New Yorker* An overextended . . sequence of procedures from traditional black and modern white musics. W. TREVOR The music of the accordion floated up to my window. **b** G. FLETCHER My love lay sleeping, where birdes musicke made. W. DAVENANT I shall now be kil'd, Even with the musick of her voice. *Hounds* Hounds hunted hard all day . . and the music was enjoyed by a large mounted field.

a ***baroque music***, ***classical music***, ***country music***, ***dance music***, ***early music***, ***incidental music***, ***Indian music***, ***light music***, ***orchestral music***, ***piano music***, ***pop music***, ***programme music***, ***rock music***, ***soul music***, ***violin music***, ***vocal music***, etc.

3 A piece of music composed or performed; a performance of music, a concert. Long *rare.* L16.

Scrutiny To compose *Pomp and Circumstance* and the other occasional musics that so alarm the purists.

4 A company of musicians, a band. *obsolete* exc. MILITARY, now chiefly in ***Master of the King's Music***, ***Master of the Queen's Music***, (the title of) an officer appointed to supervise and conduct military music for the monarch. L16.
5 *collect.* & in †*pl.* Musical instruments. *obsolete* exc. *dial.* E17.
6 The written or printed score of a musical composition; such scores collectively; the graphic representation of musical composition. M17.

E. TAYLOR Charles played the piano . . without music. *Listener* He plays the piano with panache, but cannot read music.

sheet music: see SHEET *noun*[1].
– PHRASES: ***absolute music***: see ABSOLUTE *adjective* 5. ***face the music***: see FACE *verb* 2b. **make music (together)**, **make beautiful music (together)**, **make sweet music (together)** *slang* have sexual intercourse, have a sexual relationship. ***music of the spheres***: see SPHERE *noun* 2. **music to one's ears** something very pleasant to hear. **music while you work** continuous light music played to workers, esp. in factories. ***rough music***: see ROUGH *adjective.* ***set to music***: see SET *verb*[1] 44. ***sweet music***: see SWEET *adjective & adverb.* ***Turkish music***: see TURKISH *adjective.*
– COMB.: **music book** a book containing written or printed music scores; **music box** †(***a***) a barrel organ; (***b***) *N. Amer.* = ***musical box*** s.v. MUSICAL *adjective*; **music case** (***a***) PRINTING (chiefly *hist.*) a case for a font of music type; (***b***) a case for sheet music; **music cassette** a tape cassette of pre-recorded music; abbreviation *MC*; **music centre** a stereophonic system combining disc-player, radio, and cassette tape recorder in a single unit, usu. with separate loudspeakers; **music drama** opera without formal arias etc. and governed by dramatic considerations; **music gallery** a gallery in a church or hall for the accommodation of musicians; **music-grinder** *arch.* an itinerant street musician; **music hall** a public hall or theatre used for musical performances, *spec.* for variety entertainment as singing, dancing, and novelty acts, of a type popular in the late 19th and early 20th cents.; the type of entertainment provided at such halls; **music-hallish**, **music-hally** *adjectives* suggestive of (a) music hall; †**music-house** (***a***) a room in a theatre etc. in which musicians sat to perform; (***b***) a public hall or room for musical performances; **music licence** a magistrates' licence to give vocal and instrumental entertainments in a public building or apartment; **music paper** paper ruled for writing music on, manuscript paper; **music roll** (***a***) a container for rolled-up sheet music; (***b***) a roll, usually of perforated paper, used in a player-piano or similar instrument; **music room** a room in which music is performed; formerly *spec.*, a room at the side of a theatre stage in which musicians sat to perform; **music shell** any of various gastropods, esp. *Voluta musica*, characterized by lines and dots on the shell resembling written music; the shell of such a gastropod; **music stand** a rest or frame to support sheet music or a score; **music stool** a stool for a pianist etc., usu. with adjustable height; **music theatre** the combination of elements from music and drama in new forms distinct from traditional opera, esp. as designed for small casts; **music therapy** performing or listening to music as a form of therapy; **music type** PRINTING (chiefly *hist.*) a font of type used for the typographic printing of music, as distinguished from printing from intaglio plates or lithographically; **music volute** = ***music shell*** above; **music-wire** steel wire such as is used for some stringed musical instruments.
■ **musicless** *adjective* (***a***) lacking taste or ability in music; unmusical; (***b***) without music: E17.

music /ˈmjuːzɪk/ *verb.* Infl. **-ck-**, **-c-**. M17.
[ORIGIN from the noun.]
1 *verb intrans.* Produce music; entertain oneself with music. M17.
†**2** *verb trans.* Influence by music; train in music. E18–M19.
3 *verb trans.* Set to music, describe musically. L19.

musica /ˈmjuːzɪkə/ *noun.* M18.
[ORIGIN Latin = MUSIC *noun*.]
The Latin for 'music' occurring in various phrases used in English, esp. with reference to early music.
■ ***musica ficta*** /ˈfɪktə/ [lit. 'feigned'] (early contrapuntal music characterized by) the introduction by a singer of conventional chromatically altered tones to avoid unacceptable intervals L18. ***musica figurata*** /fɪgjʊˈrɑːtə/ [lit. 'figured'] (***a***) contrapuntal music in which the different melodic strands move more or less independently; (***b***) plainsong with decorated melody: M18. ***musica plana*** /ˈplɑːnə/ [= plain] plainsong, canto fermo M20. ***musica reservata*** /rezəˈvɑːtə/ [lit. 'reserved'] early music characterized by clarity, balance, restraint, and expressiveness M20.

M

musical /ˈmjuːzɪk(ə)l/ *adjective & noun*. LME.
[ORIGIN Old French & mod. French from medieval Latin *musicalis*, formed as MUSICA: see -AL[1].]
▸ **A** *adjective*. **1** Of or pertaining to music. LME.

A. ARONSON Repeatedly Shakespeare uses musical images to distinguish sanity from insanity. E. FEINSTEIN She had genuine musical talent; a light voice, .. but true.

2 Having the nature or characteristics of music; tuneful, melodious, harmonious; pleasing in sound, euphonious. LME.

J. CONRAD The musical clink of broad silver pieces. D. H. LAWRENCE 'Tea is ready, mother,' she said in a musical, quiet voice.

3 Fond of or skilled in music. LME.

V. CRONIN Ivan Rimsky-Korsakov .. too was musical, singing well and playing the violin.

†**4** *MATH.* = HARMONIC *adjective* 4a. L16–E19.
5 Set to or accompanied by music; including music; that plays music. L17.
6 Amusing; ridiculous. *US colloq.* E19.
– SPECIAL COLLOCATIONS: **musical bow** a simple musical instrument consisting of a string stretched across the ends of a curved stick, the string being tapped or plucked, often using the mouth cavity or a gourd etc. as a resonator. **musical box** a mechanical musical instrument consisting of a revolving toothed cylinder working on a resonant comblike metal plate. **musical bumps** a (usu. indoor) game to music in which players must sit down on the floor or ground whenever the music stops, the last to sit being eliminated from the game. **musical chairs** a (usu. indoor) game to music in which players must sit down on a chair whenever the music stops, the one who finds none (there always being fewer chairs than players) being eliminated from the game; *fig.* a series of changes of roles, esp. of little significance. **musical chime** a set of bells arranged to play a tune, a carillon. **musical clock** a clock which produces short tunes at regular intervals. **musical comedy** a light drama on stage or film, consisting of dialogue, songs, and dancing, connected by a slight plot. **musical director** *spec.* the conductor of the orchestra of a theatre. **musical dramatist** a composer of music dramas. **musical drive** an exhibition by a military unit in which horses pull along military equipment to the accompaniment of music. **musical glasses** (*a*) a set of glasses containing different amounts of liquid, played by finger pressure on the moistened rims; (*b*) the glass harmonica. ***musical instrument***: see INSTRUMENT *noun* 2. **musical ride** an exhibition of riding to music by a military unit. **musical saw** a bent handsaw played with a violin bow.
▸ **B** *noun*. †**1** A musical instrument. LME–L15.
†**2** Melody, sweet music. Only in L16.
3 A musical party. Now *rare*. E19.
4 A film or a theatrical piece (not opera or operetta) of which music is an essential element; a musical comedy. M20.
■ **musiˈcality** *noun* the quality or character of being musical M19. **musicaliˈzation** *noun* the action or process of musicalizing something E20. **musicalize** *verb trans.* set (a novel, play, or poem) to music; express or render (an art other than music) in the style or manner of music: E20. **musically** *adverb* (*a*) in a musical manner; (*b*) as regards music: LME. **musicalness** *noun* musicality L17.

musicale /mjuːzɪˈkɑːl/ *noun*. *US*. L19.
[ORIGIN French (*soirée*) *musicale* musical evening.]
A musical party; a concert, esp. at a private address.

musicassette /ˌmjuːzɪkəˈsɛt/ *noun*. M20.
[ORIGIN from MUSIC *noun* + CASSETTE.]
= ***music cassette*** s.v. MUSIC *noun*.

musician /mjuːˈzɪʃ(ə)n/ *noun*. LME.
[ORIGIN Old French & mod. French *musicien*, formed as MUSIC *noun*: see -IAN.]
A person skilled in the science or practice of music; a composer or professional performer of music, esp. of instrumental music.
■ **musicianer** *noun* (now *dial.*) = MUSICIAN M16. **musicianly** *adjective* (*a*) characteristic or worthy of a skilled musician; (*b*) skilled in music: M19. **musicianship** *noun* skilled as a musician M19.

musicker /ˈmjuːzɪkə/ *noun*. Long *dial. & slang*. Also **musiker**. LME.
[ORIGIN from MUSIC *noun* + -ER[1].]
= MUSICIAN.

musico /ˈmuːzɪkəʊ/ *noun*. *rare*. Pl. **-os**. E18.
[ORIGIN Italian from Latin *musicus*, from *musica* MUSIC *noun*.]
A musician.

musico- /ˈmjuːzɪkəʊ/ *combining form*.
[ORIGIN Latin, from *musicus*, from *musica* MUSIC *noun*: see -O-.]
Involving music and (another art or science), musical and —; of or pertaining to music.
■ **musico-draˈmatic** *adjective* of or pertaining to music and drama combined, or of pertaining to music drama L18. **musicoˈgenic** *adjective* (*MEDICINE*) (of an epileptic attack) precipitated by hearing music; (of epilepsy) characterized by such attacks: M20. **musiˈcography** *noun* the science or art of writing music; musical notation: M19. **musico-ˈmania** *noun* an excessive fondness for music M19. **musicophile** *noun* a lover of music M20. **musico-ˈphobia** *noun* hatred of music E20.

musicology /mjuːzɪˈkɒlədʒi/ *noun*. E20.
[ORIGIN French *musicologie*, or directly from MUSIC *noun* + -OLOGY.]
The branch of knowledge that deals with music as a subject of study rather than as a skill or performing art; *esp.* academic research in music.
■ **musicoˈlogical** *adjective* of or pertaining to musicology E20. **musicoˈlogically** *adverb* M20. **musicologist** *noun* L19.

musiker *noun* var. of MUSICKER.

†**musimon** *noun* var. of MUSMON.

musion /ˈmjuːsɪɒn/ *noun*. *obsolete* exc. *hist.* L16.
[ORIGIN Uncertain: perh. arbitrarily from Latin *mus* mouse.]
HERALDRY. A wild cat.

musique concrète /myzik kɔ̃krɛt, mjuːˈziːk kɒnˈkrɛt/ *noun phr.* M20.
[ORIGIN French = concrete music.]
Electronic music constructed by the rearrangement of recorded natural sounds.

musive /ˈmjuːsɪv/ *adjective & noun*. Now *rare* or *obsolete*. E16.
[ORIGIN French *musif*, -ive from late Latin *musivus* (in *opus musivum* mosaic work) from late Greek *mouseion*, *mousion*: see MUSEUM, -IVE.]
▸ **A** *adjective*. = MOSAIC *adjective*[1] 1. E16.
▸ †**B** *noun*. **1** = MOSAIC *noun* 1. E–M17.
2 A Eurasian noctuid moth, *Ochropleura musiva*. Only in M19.

musk /mʌsk/ *noun*. LME.
[ORIGIN Late Latin *muscus* from Persian *mušk*, *mišk* perh. from Sanskrit *muṣka* scrotum (with ref. to the shape of the musk deer's musk-bag).]
1 A reddish-brown glandular secretion of the male musk deer, with a strong, persistent odour, used in perfumery. Also, any of various similar odorous substances secreted by other animals, esp. for scent marking. LME. ▸**b** A substance designed to imitate musk. M17. ▸**c** An aromatic odour resembling that of musk. M19.
2 An animal which secretes musk, as a civet; *spec.* a musk deer. L15.
3 Any of various plants smelling of musk; *esp.* (*a*) = ***musk plant*** below; (*b*) = ***musk storksbill*** s.v. STORK *noun*; (*c*) *Austral.* = ***musk tree*** below. Formerly also, any of certain varieties of apple, pear, etc., with a musky smell. E18.
– COMB.: **musk-bag** the bag or gland in which musk is stored in the musk deer and other animals; **musk-ball** †(*a*) a receptacle for musk; (*b*) *hist.* a ball of soap scented with musk; **musk beetle** a large green longhorn beetle, *Aromia moschata*, having a musky scent; †**musk-cat** (*a*) an animal which secretes musk, *esp.* a civet; (*b*) a fop; (*c*) a courtesan; †**musk-cod** (*a*) = ***musk-bag*** above; (*b*) a fop smelling of perfume; **musk deer** (*a*) any of several small hornless ruminants of forests in eastern Asia, of the family Moschidae, the males of which secrete the scent musk; *esp.* the Siberian *Moschus moschiferus*; (*b*) *occas.* a chevrotain, a mouse deer; **musk duck** (*a*) = ***Muscovy duck*** s.v. MUSCOVY 2; (*b*) a duck, *Biziura lobata*, of southern Australia, the male of which has a musky odour and a pendulous lobe below the bill; **musk kangaroo** a very small arboreal rat-kangaroo, *Hypsiprymnodon moschatus*; **musk lorikeet** a small Australian parrot, *Glossopsitta concinna*, green with red markings; **musk mallow** a mallow of dry grassland, *Malva moschata*, with rose-purple flowers and palmately divided leaves; **musk melon** the fruit of the melon, *Cucumis melo*, *esp.* a variety with netted rind and aromatic flesh; the plant producing this; **musk orchid** an orchid of chalk grassland, *Herminium monorchis*, with small green flowers; **musk ox** a large, shaggy, horned ruminant, *Ovibos moschatus*, of the tundra, esp. in Canada and Greenland, the male of which emits a strong odour during rutting; †**musk parrakeet** = ***musk lorikeet*** above; **musk plant** a yellow-flowered mimulus, *Mimulus moschatus*, formerly grown for the musky smell of its leaves (not perceptible in modern varieties); **musk-rose** a rambling rose, *Rosa moschata*, with large fragrant white flowers; **musk shrew** any of various shrews of the genus *Crocidura*; ***musk storksbill***: see STORK *noun*; **musk thistle** a thistle, *Carduus nutans*, with drooping sweet-scented heads; **musk tortoise** = ***musk turtle*** below; **musk tree** any of several Australian trees or shrubs with musk-scented leaves or timber; esp. *Olearia argyrophylla*, of the composite family; **musk turtle** any of several small N. American freshwater turtles of the genus *Sternotherus*, which emit a musky scent when disturbed; also called ***stinkpot***, ***stinkpot terrapin***, ***stinkpot turtle***; **musk-wood** (*a*) (the wood of) either of two musky-scented W. Indian trees of the family Meliaceae, *Guarea trichilioides* and *Trichilia moschata*; (*b*) *Austral.* (the wood of) the musk tree, *Olearia argyrophylla*.
■ †**muskish** *adjective* somewhat musky E17–L19. **musklike** *adjective* resembling (that of) musk E18.

musk /mʌsk/ *verb*. M17.
[ORIGIN from the noun Cf. earlier MUSKED.]
1 *verb trans.* Perfume (as) with musk. Now *rare*. M17.
2 *verb intrans. & trans.* Of an animal: deposit musk (on). E20.

musked /mʌskt/ *adjective*. Now *rare*. L16.
[ORIGIN from MUSK *noun*, *verb*: see -ED[2], -ED[1].]
Flavoured or perfumed with musk; tasting or smelling like musk.

muskeg /ˈmʌskɛg/ *noun*. *Canad.* E19.
[ORIGIN Cree *maske:k*.]
A swamp or bog consisting of a mixture of water and partly dead vegetation, freq. covered by a layer of sphagnum or other mosses; terrain characterized by such swamps.
■ **muskeggy** *adjective* characterized by muskeg L19.

muskellunge *noun* var. of MASKINONGE.

musket /ˈmʌskɪt/ *noun*[1]. Long *obsolete* exc. *hist.* LME.
[ORIGIN Old Northern French *musket*, *mousquet*, Old French *mou(s)chet*, *moschet* (mod. *émouchet*), of unknown origin.]
The male of the sparrowhawk.

musket /ˈmʌskɪt/ *noun*[2]. Also †**musquet**. L16.
[ORIGIN French *mousquet*, †-*ette* from Italian *moschetto*, -*etta* (formerly) bolt from a crossbow, from *mosca* fly from Latin *musca*: see -ET[1].]
hist. A gun (orig. a matchlock) of the kind used by infantry soldiers, usu. smooth-bored and fired from shoulder level.
– COMB.: **musket-arrow** a short arrow discharged from an early type of musket; **musket ball** a ball used as ammunition for a musket; **musket powder** the kind of gunpowder used for small arms; **musketproof** *adjective* not readily penetrated by musket balls; **musket shot** (*a*) shot fired from a musket; a musket ball; (*b*) the range of a musket.
■ **musketade** *noun* a continued discharge of muskets; an attack with muskets: M17.

musketeer /mʌskɪˈtɪə/ *noun*. Also †**musquet-**. L16.
[ORIGIN from MUSKET *noun*[2] + -EER, after French MOUSQUETAIRE etc.]
hist. A soldier armed with a musket. Also, a member of either of two bodies forming part of the household troops of the French king in the 17th and 18th cents.
– PHRASES: **three musketeers** [from translation of French *les trois mousquetaires* by Alexandre Dumas père] three close associates, three inseparable friends.
– COMB.: **musketeer gauntlet**, **musketeer glove** = ***MOUSQUETAIRE glove***.

musketoon /mʌskɪˈtuːn/ *noun*. Also †**musquet-**. M17.
[ORIGIN French *mousqueton* from Italian *moschettone*, from *mouschetto* MUSKET *noun*[2]: see -OON.]
hist. A kind of short musket with a large bore.

musketry /ˈmʌskɪtri/ *noun*. Also †**musquet-**. E17.
[ORIGIN French *mousqueterie*, formed as MUSKET *noun*[2]: see -RY.]
1 The fire of muskets. E17.
2 Muskets collectively. M17.
3 *collect.* Troops armed with muskets. L18.
4 The art or technique of manipulating small arms. M19.

Muskhogean, **Muskhogee** *nouns & adjectives* vars. of MUSKOGEAN, MUSKOGEE.

muskie *noun* var. of MUSKY *noun*.

Muskogean /mʌskəˈgiːən, mʌˈskəʊgɪən/ *noun & adjective*. Also **-kh-**. L19.
[ORIGIN from MUSKOGEE + -AN.]
(Of or pertaining to) a N. American Indian language family of the south-eastern US, including Creek, Seminole, Apalachee, Choctaw, and Chickasaw. Also, designating or pertaining to (any of) the peoples speaking a Muskogean language.

Muskogee /mʌˈskəʊgiː/ *noun & adjective*. Also **-kh-**. L18.
[ORIGIN Creek *ma:skó:ki*.]
▸ **A** *noun*. Pl. **-s**, same. A member of a N. American Indian people forming part of the Creek Indian confederacy; the Muskogean language of this people. L18.
▸ **B** *attrib.* or as *adjective*. Of or pertaining to the Muskogees or their language. L18.

muskrat /ˈmʌskrat/ *noun*. Pl. **-s**, same. E17.
[ORIGIN from Algonquian, assim. to MUSK *noun* and RAT *noun*[1] (cf. MUSHRAT, MUSQUASH). In sense 2 from MUSK *noun* + RAT *noun*[1].]
1 a A large semi-aquatic N. American rodent, *Ondatra zibethicus*, resembling a beaver; also (in full ***round-tailed muskrat***), a similar animal, *Neofiber alleni*, found in Florida. Also called ***musquash***. E17. ▸**b** An inhabitant of a low-lying district, esp. of the St Clair Flats in Michigan. *US colloq.* M19. ▸**c** The skin or thick brown fur of a muskrat. L19.
2 Any of various somewhat ratlike animals having a musky odour, e.g. a musk shrew, a desman, a pilori, or a musk kangaroo. L17.
– COMB.: **muskrat house** the winter dwelling of a muskrat, built from plant stems etc.

muskwa /ˈmʌskwɔː/ *noun*. *N. Amer.* Also **musquaw**. M19.
[ORIGIN Cree *maskwa*.]
The American black bear.

musky /ˈmʌski/ *noun*. *N. Amer.* Also **muskie**. L19.
[ORIGIN Abbreviation of *muskellunge* var. of MASKINONGE: see -Y[6], -IE.]
= MASKINONGE.

musky /ˈmʌski/ *adjective*. L16.
[ORIGIN from MUSK *noun* + -Y[1].]
Smelling or tasting of musk; having a taste or smell like that of musk, suggestive of musk; perfumed with musk.
■ **muskiness** *noun* the quality of being musky; a musky odour or taste: E18.

Muslim /ˈmʊslɪm, ˈmʌs-, -z-/ *noun & adjective*. Also **Moslem**. Pl. **-s**, (chiefly *collect.*) same. E17.
[ORIGIN Arabic *muslim* active pple of *aslama* submit oneself to the will of God: see ISLAM.]
▸ **A** *noun*. A follower of the religion of Islam. E17.
black Muslim: see BLACK *adjective*.
▸ **B** *adjective*. Of or pertaining to the Muslims or their religion. L18.
Muslim League a political organization founded in India in 1906 whose demands in 1940 for an independent Muslim state led to the establishment of Pakistan.
– NOTE: ***Muslim*** is the preferred spelling, although the form ***Moslem*** is also used. The archaic term ***Muhammadan*** (or ***Mohammedan***) is not favoured by Muslims and should be avoided.

M

■ **Muslimism** *noun* the religious system of the Muslims, Islam L18.

Muslimah /ˈmʊzlɪmə, ˈmʌz-, -s-/ *noun*. M19.
[ORIGIN Arabic *muslima*, fem. of *muslim* MUSLIM *noun*.]
Esp. among Muslims: a Muslim woman.

Muslimin /ˈmʊzlɪmɪn, ˈmʌz-, -s-/ *noun & adjective*. Now *rare* or *obsolete*. Also **Moslemin** /ˈmɒzlɪmɪn, ˈmɒz-/. E19.
[ORIGIN Old pl. (from Arabic *muslimīn*) of MUSLIM taken as sing.]
▸ **A** *noun*. A Muslim. E19.
▸ **B** *attrib.* or as *adjective*. Muslim. M19.

muslin /ˈmʌzlɪn/ *noun & adjective*. E17.
[ORIGIN French MOUSSELINE from Italian *mussolina*, *-ino*, from *Mussolo* Mosul in Iraq, where formerly made: see -INE[1].]
▸ **A** *noun*. **1** Fine delicately woven cotton fabric; an example of this. E17. ▸**b** A dress or skirt made of this. L18. ***butter muslin***, ***mull muslin***, ***Swiss muslin***, etc.
2 Sails collectively. *nautical slang*. E19.
3 In full ***muslin moth***. A small European moth, *Diaphora mendica*, of the family Arctiidae, the male usu. being blackish and the female white with black markings. E19.
4 Fine cotton cloth of a plain weave. *US*. M19.
– PHRASES: ***bit of muslin***: see BIT *noun*[2] 6.
▸ **B** *attrib.* or as *adjective*. Made of muslin. L17.
■ **muslined** *adjective* draped with or dressed in muslin E19. **musliˈnet** *noun & adjective* (of) a fabric resembling muslin L18.

†**musmon** *noun*. Also †**musi-**. E17–L19.
[ORIGIN Latin *musimo(n-)*, late Greek *mousmōn*.]
= MOUFLON.

musnud /ˈmʌsnʌd/ *noun*. M18.
[ORIGIN Persian & Urdu *masnad* from Arabic *masnad* cushion, from *sanada* lean against.]
A seat made of cushions, *esp.* one used as a throne by an Indian prince.

muso /ˈmjuːzəʊ/ *noun*. *colloq.* (orig. *Austral.*). Pl. **-os**. M20.
[ORIGIN Abbreviation of MUSICIAN: see -O.]
A musician; *esp.* a professional musician.

musquash /ˈmʌskwɒʃ/ *noun*. *N. Amer.* E17.
[ORIGIN Western Abnaki *mòskwas*, perh. lit. 'the one whose head bobs above the water'.]
A muskrat. Also, the fur of the muskrat.
– COMB.: **musquash root** a N. American cowbane, *Cicuta maculata*; **musquash sealskin** imitation sealskin made from musquash.

musquaw *noun* var. of MUSKWA.

†**musquet**, **musqueteer** *nouns* etc., vars. of MUSKET *noun*[2] etc.

†**musrol** *noun*. M16–M19.
[ORIGIN French *muserolle* from Italian *museruola*, from *muso* muzzle.]
The noseband of a bridle.

†**muss** *noun*[1]. L16–E19.
[ORIGIN Middle French *mousche*, transferred use of *mouche* a fly: see MOUCHE.]
A game in which small objects are thrown down to be scrambled for; a scramble.

muss /mʌs/ *noun*[2] *& verb*. *dial.* & *N. Amer. colloq.* M19.
[ORIGIN App. alt. of MESS *noun*. Sense A.1 perh. same word as MUSS *noun*[1].]
▸ **A** *noun*. **1** A disturbance, a row. M19.
2 A state of untidiness; a muddle, a mess. M19.
▸ **B** *verb trans.* Make untidy; crumple, ruffle; smear, mess; entangle, confuse. Also foll. by *up*. M19.

mussal /mʌˈsɑːl/ *noun*. L17.
[ORIGIN Urdu *maš'al* from Persian *maš'al* from Arabic *maš'al* from *ša'ala* light a fire.]
In the Indian subcontinent: a torch.

mussalchee /mʌˈsɑːltʃiː/ *noun*. Also ***masalchi***. E17.
[ORIGIN Persian & Urdu *maš'alčī*, from *maš'al* MUSSAL, + *-čī* agent-suffix (from Turkish *-çi*).]
In the Indian subcontinent: a torch-bearer; a menial servant.

mussel /ˈmʌs(ə)l/ *noun*. Also (now *rare*) **muscle**.
[ORIGIN Old English *muscle*, *muxle*, *musle*, superseded by forms from corresp. Middle Low German *mussel*, Middle Dutch *mosscele* (Dutch *mossel*) = Old High German *muscula* (German *Muschel*), all from Proto-Romance alt. of Latin *musculus*: see MUSCLE *noun*[1].]
Any of various bivalve molluscs belonging chiefly to the marine superfamily Mytilacea or to the freshwater superfamily Unionacea; *esp.* the common edible marine bivalve, *Mytilus edulis*, which has a dark grey, slightly elongated shell and adheres by a byssus, freq. in large aggregations.
horse mussel, ***pearl mussel***, ***swan mussel***, etc.
– COMB.: **mussel-bank**, **mussel-bed** a large aggregation of mussels, esp. on intertidal rocks; **mussel crab** a pea crab, *Pinnotheres maculatus*, which lives as a commensal in the shell of the edible mussel; **mussel-cracker** (chiefly *S. Afr.*) any of several fishes with powerful jaws, *esp.* (more fully ***white mussel-cracker***) *Cymatoceps nasutus* and (more fully ***black mussel-cracker***, ***blue mussel-cracker***) *Sparodon durbanensis*, both of the family Sparidae; **mussel-crusher** (chiefly *S. Afr.*) = ***mussel-cracker*** above (***white mussel-crusher*** = ***white mussel-cracker***; ***black mussel-crusher***, ***blue mussel-crusher*** = ***black mussel-cracker***); **mussel digger** *US* (**a**) a grey whale; (**b**) a machine for digging mussel mud; **mussel duck** *dial.* a duck which feeds on mussels; *esp.* a scaup; †**mussel man** a person who gathers mussels for a living; **mussel mud**: containing many mussel shells; **mussel picker** *dial.* an oystercatcher; **mussel plum** a dark purple variety of plum; **mussel rake**: used for gathering mussels; **mussel scalp**, **mussel scaup** a mussel-bed; **mussel shell** (**a**) the shell of a mussel; †(**b**) *rare* a person who gapes like a mussel shell.
■ **musselled** *adjective* poisoned by eating mussels M19.

†**mussitate** *verb intrans.* E17–E18.
[ORIGIN Latin *mussitat-* pa. ppl stem of *mussitare* frequentative of *mussare* mutter: see -ATE[3].]
Mutter.

mussitation /mʌsɪˈteɪʃ(ə)n/ *noun*. Now *rare*. M17.
[ORIGIN Late Latin *mussitatio(n-)*, formed as MUSSITATE: see -ATION.]
Muttering, murmuring; MEDICINE movement of the lips without vocal sound.

Mussolini /mʊsəˈliːniː, mʌs-/ *noun*. E20.
[ORIGIN Benito *Mussolini* (1883–1945), prime minister of Italy and leader of the Fascist Party in Italy.]
A dictator, a tyrant; a fascist.
■ **Mussolinian** *adjective* of, pertaining to, or characteristic of Mussolini E20. **Mussolinism** *noun* the political principles or policy of Mussolini or of the Fascist Party in Italy E20.

Mussorgskian /mʊˈsɔːgskɪən/ *adjective*. Also **Mouss-**. M20.
[ORIGIN from *M(o)ussorgsky* (see below) + -AN.]
Of, pertaining to, or characteristic of the Russian composer Modest Petrovich Mussorgsky (1839–81) or his music.

mussuck /ˈmʌsək/ *noun*. E17.
[ORIGIN Urdu *mašk* from Persian.]
In the Indian subcontinent: a leather water bag.

Mussulman /ˈmʌs(ə)lmən/ *noun & adjective*. L16.
[ORIGIN Persian *musulmān*, ult. from Arabic *muslim* MUSLIM. In sense A.2 from German *Muselmann*.]
▸ **A** *noun*. Pl. **-mans**, **-men**.
1 A Muslim. *arch.* L16.
2 Under the Third Reich, an inhabitant of a concentration camp or extermination camp exhausted to the point of fatalism and loss of initiative. *slang*. M20.
▸ **B** *adjective*. Muslim. *arch.* E17.
■ **Mussulmanic** /mʌs(ə)lˈmanɪk/ *adjective* (*arch.*) Muslim E19. **Mussulmanism** *noun* (*rare*) Islam M18. **Mussulwoman** *noun* (*rare*) a female Muslim L17.

mussurana /mʊsəˈrɑːnə/ *noun*. E20.
[ORIGIN Portuguese *muçurana* from Tupi *moçu'rana* from *moçu* kind of eel-like fish + *-rana* resembling.]
A non-venomous tropical American colubrid snake, *Clelia clelia*, usu. black in colour, which feeds on other snakes, being immune to their venom.

mussy /ˈmʌsi/ *adjective*. *dial.* & *N. Amer. colloq.* M19.
[ORIGIN from MUSS *noun*[2] + -Y[1].]
Untidy, rumpled, tousled.
■ **mussiness** *noun* M19.

must /mʌst/ *noun*[1].
[ORIGIN Old English *must* = Old & mod. High German *most* from Latin *mustum* use as noun of neut. of *mustus* new, fresh.]
1 New wine; grape juice before or during fermentation; an example of this. OE.
†**2 a** Any juice or liquor undergoing or prepared for undergoing alcoholic fermentation. LME–E18. ▸**b** The pulp of apples or pears after the juice has been pressed out in making cider or perry. *dial.* L17–L19.
†**3** A variety of cider apple. M17–M18.

†**must** *noun*[2]. *Scot.* L15–M19.
[ORIGIN Old French, var. of *musc* MUSK *noun*.]
Musk.

must /mʌst/ *noun*[3]. E17.
[ORIGIN Back-form. from MUSTY *adjective*[2].]
Mustiness; mould.

must /mʌst/ *noun*[4] *& adjective*[1]. L16.
[ORIGIN from MUST *verb*[1].]
▸ **A** *noun*. **1** A use of the verb *must* to convey command, obligation, necessity, etc.; an obligation or duty. L16.
2 A thing that cannot or should not be overlooked or missed; a necessity. *colloq.* L19.

> J. WYNDHAM We had finished adding our own secondary wants to the list of musts. S. BELLOW Daddy—you have to read it. A must!

▸ **B** *attrib.* or as *adjective*. Essential, mandatory, obligatory. *colloq.* E20.

> *New Yorker* The Planning Commission . . has yet to act on either of these two must items.

must /mʌst/ *adjective*[2] *& noun*[5]. Also **-th**. L19.
[ORIGIN Persian & Urdu *mast* intoxicated, raving mad.]
▸ **A** *adjective*. Of a male elephant or camel: in a state of dangerous frenzy (associated with the rutting season). L19.
▸ **B** *noun*. The condition or state of being in such a state or frenzy. L19.

must /mʌst/ *aux. verb*[1]. Pres. & pa. (all persons) **must**. Neg. **must not**, (*colloq.*) **mustn't** /ˈmʌs(ə)nt/. No other parts used.
[ORIGIN Old English *mōste* pa. t. of *mōt* MOTE *verb*[1] = Old Frisian *mōt*, Old Saxon *mōt*, *muot* (Dutch *moet*), Old High German *muoz* find room or opportunity, may, must (German *muss*), Gothic *gamōtan* find room, rel. to Middle Low German *mōte*, Old High German *muoza* (German *Musse*) leisure, from Germanic.]
▸ †**I** As pa. t. of MOTE *verb*[1].
1 Expr. permission or possibility, or a wish: might, could. OE–LME.
2 Expr. necessity or obligation: had to, was (were) obliged to, it was necessary that (I, you, he, it, etc.) should. OE–L15.
▸ **II** As pres. t. (indic. & subjunct.), often *ellipt.* with verb understood or supplied from the context.
3 Expr. necessity: am (is, are) obliged or required to; have (has) to; it is necessary that (I, you, he, it, etc.) should; am (is, are) commanded, requested insistently, or recommended to. Also *ellipt.* (*arch.*), must go. ME. ▸**b** Expr. a fixed or certain futurity: am (is, are) fated or certain to (*be* or *do*), shall certainly or inevitably (*be* or *do*). LME. ▸**c** Say (says) or feel (feels) that one has to. LME.

> TENNYSON Seeing he must to Westminster and crown Young Henry there. A. S. NEILL I must get estimates from the printers. J. BUCHAN Haraldsen is an invalid, . . and must keep quiet. P. ROTH Doing as I wished, not as I must. I. MURDOCH You must both have a sip of sherry. J. TROLLOPE Must you look so utterly suburban? **b** DRYDEN Crowds of dead, that never must return. A. LURIE What must it be like in the winter! **c** WORDSWORTH He is not content with a ring . . , but he must have rings in the ears, rings on the nose—rings everywhere.

4 Expr. the inferred or presumed certainty of a fact: certainly am (is, are) or do (does); it cannot be otherwise than that (I, you, he, it, etc.) am (are, is) or do (does). M17.

> *Poetry Nation Review* What he is thinking, because he must be thinking. / I cannot tell. ANTHONY SMITH There must be few who have not been depressed.

▸ **III 5** ***must have done***, (**a**) should necessarily have done; (**b**) should have had to do, should have been obliged to do; (**c**) certainly did, it is to be concluded that I (you, he, it, etc.) did. LME.

> SWIFT Had this point been steadily pursued . . there must probably have been an end of faction. E. BOWEN In the woodwork . . was a hook from which a bird-cage must have hung. J. FOWLES There must have been about a dozen.

▸ **IV** As pa. t. of branch II.
6 Was obliged, had to; it was necessary that (I, he, it, etc.) should; (now *colloq.*) it foolishly happened that (I, he, it, etc.) did. Now only in indirect narration or virtual indirect narration reporting a reflection made at the time, and in conditional clauses. L17.

> W. CATHER The Doctor had said the house must be absolutely quiet. R. P. JHABVALA In order to find . . spiritual enrichment . . they must set off for India.

– PHRASES: **if you must know**: used to introduce information provided against the judgement or inclination of the speaker. ***I must love you and leave you***: see LOVE *verb* 1. **I must say** I cannot refrain from saying. ***must needs***, ***needs must***: see NEEDS *adverb*. **must not** am (is, are) not allowed to, am (is, are) obliged not to. ***the show must go on***: see SHOW *noun*[1]. **you must know**, **you must understand** you ought to be informed, I would have you know.

must /mʌst/ *verb*[2]. *obsolete* exc. *dial.* M16.
[ORIGIN Back-form. from MUSTY *adjective*[2].]
1 *verb intrans.* Become mouldy or musty. M16.
2 *verb trans.* Make mouldy or musty. *rare*. E18.

†**must** *verb*[3] *trans.* *Scot.* M18–E19.
[ORIGIN from MUST *noun*[2].]
Powder with must or hair powder.

must- /ˈmʌst/ *combining form*.
[ORIGIN from MUST *verb*[1].]
Forming nouns and adjectives denoting things that are essential, inevitable, or highly recommended.
■ **must-be** *noun* the inevitable, what is fated to happen M19. **must-have** *noun & adjective* (**a**) *noun* an essential or highly desirable item; (**b**) *adjective* essential or highly desirable: M19. **must-see** *noun & adjective* (**a**) *noun* a place, event, or entertainment which is recommended as worth seeing; (**b**) *adjective* that is a must-see; that is compelling viewing: L20.

mustache *noun*, **mustached** *adjective*, **mustachial** *adjective* see MOUSTACHE etc.

mustachio /məˈstɑːʃɪəʊ, -ʃəʊ/ *noun*. Now chiefly *arch.* & *joc.* Also **mous-**, †**-cho(e)**. Pl. **-os**. M16.
[ORIGIN (Spanish *mostacho* from) Italian *mostaccio* (cf. medieval Latin *mustacia*) based ult. on Greek *mustax*, *mustak-* upper lip, moustache.]
1 A moustache, now *esp.* a large one. M16.
†**2** In *pl.* Hairs or bristles around the mouth of an animal; a cat's whiskers. Also, the awn or bristles of certain grasses; = BEARD *noun* 3. L16–L18.
■ **mustachioed** *adjective* having a (large) moustache E19.

mustafina /mʌstəˈfiːnə/ *noun*. E19.
[ORIGIN App. from MUSTEE + Spanish *fino*, *fina* FINE *adjective*.]
A person with one parent a mustee and the other a white person.

mustang /ˈmʌstaŋ/ *noun & adjective*. E19.
[ORIGIN App. blending of Spanish *mestengo* (now *mesteño*) and *mostrenco* (both meaning) wild or masterless cattle; *mestengo* from *mesta* (from Latin *mixta* use as noun of fem. pa. pple of *miscere* mix) association of graziers who appropriated wild cattle.]
▸ **A** *noun*. **1** The wild or half-wild horse of American plains, esp. of Mexico and California, descended from stock introduced by the Spanish. E19.
2 = ***mustang grape*** below. M19.

M

3 An officer in the US services who has been promoted from the ranks. Also occas., a volunteer officer as distinct from a regular-army officer. *slang*. **M19**.

▸ **B** *attrib.* or as *adjective*. That is a mustang; of or pertaining to a mustang or mustangs. **E19**.

mustang grape (the fruit of) a native vine, *Vitis candicans*, of the south-western US, bearing small red grapes.

■ **mustanger** *noun* (*US*) a person who catches or entraps mustangs **M19**.

mustard /ˈmʌstəd/ *noun & adjective*. **ME**.

[**ORIGIN** Old French *mo(u)starde* (mod. *moutarde*) = Provençal, Catalan, Portuguese, Italian *mostarda* Romanian *muştar*, from Proto-Romance, from Latin *mustum* **MUST** *noun*[1] (orig. the condiment prepared with grape must).]

▸ **A** *noun*. **1** Powder made from the crushed seeds of certain plants (see sense A.2 below); paste made from this, used as a pungent condiment and (esp. formerly) in making poultices or plasters; an example or type of this paste. **ME**.

(as) keen as mustard very keen, acute, or enthusiastic. ***Dijon mustard***, ***Tewkesbury mustard***, etc. **cut the mustard** *slang* (chiefly *N. Amer.*) succeed; come up to expectations, meet requirements. ***Durham mustard***. **English mustard** *esp.* coarse-grained mustard. **French mustard** *esp.* mustard made with vinegar. ***keen as mustard***: see ***as keen as mustard*** above.

2 Any of the cruciferous plants used to make this; spec. *Sinapis alba* (in full ***white mustard***), *Brassica nigra* (in full ***black mustard***), and (in US) *B. juncea* (in full ***brown mustard***). Also (with specifying word): any of various other (chiefly cruciferous) plants, resembling these in appearance, pungency, etc. **ME**.

mustard and cress seedlings of cress, *Lepidium sativum*, and white mustard, used as a relish in salads. ***garlic mustard***, ***hedge mustard***, ***tower mustard***, ***wild mustard***, etc.

3 The brownish-yellow colour of the condiment mustard. **L19**.

4 A thing providing piquancy or zest. *US slang*. **E20**.

5 *ellipt.* = ***mustard gas*** below; *CHEMISTRY* any of a group of compounds with alkylating properties, having a structure typified by that of mustard gas. **E20**.

NITROGEN mustard.

– **COMB.**: †**mustard-bowl** a wooden bowl in which mustard seed was pounded, proverbially referred to as the instrument for producing stage thunder; **mustard bush** *Austral.* an almost leafless shrub, *Apophyllum anomalum*, of the caper family, with yellow flowers and shoots which taste of mustard; **mustard colour** = sense A.3 above; **mustard-coloured** *adjective* of mustard colour; **mustard gas** a colourless oily liquid, dichlorodiethylsulphide, $(ClCH_2CH_2)_2S$, which is a powerful poison and vesicant, acting directly on the skin, used in chemical warfare; **mustard greens** the leaves of the mustard plant, used in salads; **mustard oil** an oil obtained from mustard seed; **mustard plaster** a poultice or plaster made with mustard; **mustard-pot** a pot or cruet for mustard for the table; **mustard seed** (*a*) the seed of mustard; ***grain of mustard seed***, a small thing capable of vast development [from the great height attained by black mustard in Palestine (*Matthew* 13:31)]; †(*b*) a mustard plant; (*c*) *US* very fine shot used for shooting birds with not much injury to the plumage; **mustard weevil** a weevil, *Ceutorhyncus contractus*, which damages the white mustard plant.

▸ **B** *attrib.* or as *adjective*. **1** Of the nature of mustard, pungent; prepared with mustard. **L16**.

2 Of the brownish-yellow colour of the condiment mustard. **M19**.

3 Very good, keen, enthusiastic; thorough. *slang*. **E20**.

> *Daily Express* The Russians and the East Germans are mustard on the theory of numbers.

■ **mustarder** *noun* (*hist.*) a maker of or dealer in mustard **LME**. **mustardy** *adjective* resembling mustard; covered with mustard; containing mustard, tasting of mustard: **M19**.

mustee /mʌˈstiː/ *noun*. Also **mestee** /mɛˈstiː/. **L17**.

[**ORIGIN** Abbreviation of Spanish **MESTIZO**.]

A person with one parent a white person and the other a quadroon; an octoroon; *loosely* a person with parents of different races.

mustelid /ˈmʌstɪlɪd, mʌˈstɛlɪd/ *noun & adjective*. **L19**.

[**ORIGIN** mod. Latin *Mustelidae* (see below), from *Mustela* genus name, from Latin *mustela* weasel: see **-ID**[3].]

▸ **A** *noun*. Any of various carnivorous mammals of the family Mustelidae, which includes weasels, stoats, badgers, mink, skunks, martens, and otters. Cf. **MUSTELINE**. **L19**.

▸ **B** *adjective*. Of, pertaining to, or designating this family. **M20**.

musteline /ˈmʌstɪlɪn, -ʌɪn/ *adjective & noun*. **M17**.

[**ORIGIN** Latin *mustelinus*, from *mustela* weasel.]

▸ **A** *adjective*. Of or like a weasel; *spec.* designating or pertaining to the mustelid subfamily Mustelinae, which includes the weasels, stoats, mink, and martens. **M17**.

▸ **B** *noun*. A musteline animal. **L19**.

muster /ˈmʌstə/ *noun*. **LME**.

[**ORIGIN** Old French *moustre* (later Latinized, mod. *montre*) from Proto-Romance noun from Latin *monstrare* show.]

1 A number of persons or things mustered or assembled on a particular occasion; an assembly, a collection. **LME**.

2 An act of mustering soldiers, sailors, etc.; an assembling of people for inspection, verification of numbers, etc.; a roll-call. **LME**. ▸**b** A muster roll. Formerly also, a census report. **M16**. ▸**c** An act of mustering cattle, sheep, etc., a round-up of stock. *Austral. & NZ*. **M19**. ▸**d** Foll. by *out*: (a) discharge from service. *US*. **L19**.

3 A pattern, a specimen, a sample, latterly only of certain commercial items. **LME**.

†**4** The action or an act of showing something; manifestation; exhibition, display. **LME–M17**.

5 A flock of peacocks. *rare*. **LME**.

– **PHRASES**: **false muster** (chiefly *hist.*) a fraudulent presentation at a muster, or a fraudulent inclusion in a muster roll, of men who are not available for service. **in muster** mustered, assembled for inspection. **pass muster**, (earlier) **pass musters**, †**pass the musters** (orig. *MILITARY*) undergo muster or review without censure; bear examination or inspection, come up to the required standard, be accepted (*as* the possessor of certain qualities).

– **COMB.**: **muster book** a book in which military forces are registered; a book containing the names of the crew of a warship; †**muster file** a muster roll; **muster master** an officer responsible for (the accuracy of) a muster roll, esp. of some portion of an army; **muster roll** (*a*) an official list of the soldiers in an army or the sailors in a ship's company; a register; (*b*) *NAUTICAL* the reading of a muster roll; a roll-call.

muster /ˈmʌstə/ *verb*. **ME**.

[**ORIGIN** Old French *mo(u)strer* (later Latinized, mod. *montrer*) from Latin *monstrare* show.]

†**1** **a** *verb trans.* Show, display, exhibit; show up, report, tell, explain. **ME–E17**. ▸**b** *verb intrans.* Show, appear, be displayed; make a good, bad, etc. appearance. **LME–L16**.

2 **a** *verb trans. & intrans.* Collect or assemble (*spec.* soldiers) for ascertainment or verification of numbers, inspection as to condition and equipment, exercise, display, introduction into service, or (also foll. by *up*) for battle. **LME**. ▸**b** *verb trans. gen.* Collect, get together; *esp.* bring forward from one's own stores, raise (a number or amount); *fig.* summon, gather up, marshal, (one's thoughts, courage, strength, etc.). Also foll. by *up*. **L16**. ▸**c** *verb trans. & intrans.* Collect together or round up (stock, as cattle, sheep, etc.) for counting, shearing, drafting, branding, etc. Also, round up stock from (a place). *Austral. & NZ*. **E19**.

> **a** C. MARLOWE Ile muster vp an army secretly. R. SUTCLIFF Muster the squadron and hold them in readiness. R. K. NARAYAN They were mustering themselves to attack the other group. J. A. MICHENER The Babylonians began to muster the Hebrews for the long march to slavery. **b** E. BOWEN Mrs. Heccomb . . began to muster her parcels. K. CROSSLEY-HOLLAND Mustering his vast strength he dragged the whole quaking mound up the slope. V. GLENDINNING It would be equally easy to muster evidence for a negative view. B. BAINBRIDGE She doubted whether she could muster up the tears expected at such a moment. C. ACHEBE I simply couldn't muster anything you could call enthusiasm. **c** P. V. WHITE I will have all cattle . . that we are taking with us, mustered. K. S. PRICHARD They had been mustering all day on the wide plains of Murndoo station.

3 *verb intrans.* (Of an army etc.) come together for inspection, exercise, or preparation for service; assemble, gather together in a body. **LME**.

> J. R. GREEN The royal army had already mustered in great force. R. HUGHES The children mustered for their soup and biscuit. *fig.*: R. L. STEVENSON The fogs that will begin to muster about sundown.

4 *verb trans.* **a** Enlist, enrol. Foll. by *in*, *into* (service). *obsolete* exc. *US*. **LME**. ▸**b** Foll. by *out*: discharge from service. *US*. **M19**.

5 *verb trans.* †**a** Take a census of. **M16–M17**. ▸**b** Now chiefly *NAUTICAL*. Call the roll of. **L17**.

6 *verb trans.* Of an army etc.: comprise, number. **M19**.

■ **musterer** *noun* **LME**.

musth *adjective & noun* var. of **MUST** *adjective*[2] *& noun*[5].

mustine /ˈmʌstiːn/ *noun*. **M20**.

[**ORIGIN** from **MUSTARD** *noun* + **-INE**[5].]

PHARMACOLOGY. A strongly cytotoxic nitrogen mustard, bis(2-chloroethyl)methylamine $(ClCH_2CH_2)_2NCH_3$, used to treat certain neoplasms, esp. Hodgkin's disease.

†**musty** *adjective*[1]. *rare*. **LME–E19**.

[**ORIGIN** from **MUST** *noun*[1] + **-Y**[1].]

Of or pertaining to must or new wine; not yet fermented, undergoing fermentation.

musty /ˈmʌsti/ *adjective*[2] *& verb*. **L15**.

[**ORIGIN** Perh. alt. of **MOISTY** after **MUST** *noun*[1].]

▸ **A** *adjective*. **1** Mouldy; having a smell or taste indicative or suggestive of mouldiness or decay; stale-smelling, fusty. **L15**.

> DICKENS Unsavoury smells of musty hay. A. CARTER The dining room . . never lost a musty and unused smell. D. LEAVITT Her room was musty from the closed windows.

2 Having lost newness, interest, or liveliness; antiquated, disused, old-fashioned. **L16**.

> HENRY FIELDING None but a musty moralist . . would have condemned such behaviour. CHARLES CHURCHILL Read musty lectures on Benevolence.

3 Bad-tempered, peevish, sullen. *obsolete* exc. *dial.* **E17**.

▸ †**B** *verb intrans. & trans.* Become or make musty. **M17–E18**.

■ **mustily** *adverb* **E17**. **mustiness** *noun* **E16**.

muta /ˈmjuːtə/ *verb intrans.* (*imper.*). **L19**.

[**ORIGIN** Italian, imper. of *mutare* change.]

MUSIC. A direction: change instrument or tuning.

mutable /ˈmjuːtəb(ə)l/ *adjective & noun*. **LME**.

[**ORIGIN** Latin *mutabilis*, from *mutare* change: see **-ABLE**.]

▸ **A** *adjective*. **1** Liable or subject to change or alteration. **LME**. ▸**b** *GRAMMAR*. Of a consonant sound in a Celtic language: subject to mutation. **E18**.

> W. S. MAUGHAM The contemplation of the . . stars . . stimulated him to contempt of all mutable things.

2 Changeable in mind or disposition; fickle, variable. **LME**.

> H. CARPENTER She is mutable: in fact she is faithless.

3 *BIOLOGY*. Able to undergo mutation; liable to undergo frequent mutation. **E20**.

▸ **B** *noun*. **1** A thing able to be changed. *rare*. **M17**.

2 *GRAMMAR*. A mutable consonant. **M18**.

■ **mutaˈbility** *noun* **LME**. **mutableness** *noun* (now *rare*) mutability **L15**. **mutably** *adverb* **E17**.

mutagen /ˈmjuːtədʒ(ə)n/ *noun*. **M20**.

[**ORIGIN** from **MUTA(TION** + **-GEN**.]

BIOLOGY. An agent that causes mutation.

mutagenesis /mjuːtəˈdʒɛnɪsɪs/ *noun*. **M20**.

[**ORIGIN** from **MUTA(TION** + **-GENESIS**.]

BIOLOGY. The production or origination of mutations.

mutagenic /mjuːtəˈdʒɛnɪk/ *adjective*. **M20**.

[**ORIGIN** from **MUTA(TION** + **-GENIC**.]

BIOLOGY. Causing or capable of causing mutation.

■ **mutagenicity** /-dʒəˈnɪsɪti/ *noun* the property of being mutagenic **M20**.

mutagenize /ˈmjuːtədʒənʌɪz/ *verb trans.* Also **-ise**. **M20**.

[**ORIGIN** from **MUTAGEN** + **-IZE**.]

BIOLOGY. Treat (cells or organisms) with mutagenic agents.

mutant /ˈmjuːt(ə)nt/ *noun & adjective*. **E20**.

[**ORIGIN** Latin *mutant-* pres. ppl stem of *mutare* change: see **-ANT**[1].]

BIOLOGY. ▸**A** *noun*. An individual, gene, or (formerly) population which has arisen by or undergone mutation; *esp.* in *SCIENCE FICTION*, an individual with freak or grossly abnormal anatomy, abilities, etc. **E20**.

▸ **B** *adjective*. Having the attributes of a mutant; produced by mutation. **E20**.

mutarotation /mjuːtərəʊˈteɪʃ(ə)n/ *noun*. **L19**.

[**ORIGIN** from Latin *mutare* change + **ROTATION**.]

CHEMISTRY. (A) change of optical activity with time, as exhibited by freshly prepared solutions of some compounds, esp. sugars.

■ **mutarotate** *verb intrans.* exhibit mutarotation **M20**. **mutarotational** *adjective* **M20**.

mutase /ˈmjuːteɪz/ *noun*. **E20**.

[**ORIGIN** from Latin *mutare* change + **-ASE**.]

BIOCHEMISTRY. **1** An enzyme which catalyses a dismutation reaction. **E20**.

2 An enzyme which catalyses the transfer of a phosphate group from one carbon atom to another in a molecule. **M20**.

mutassarif /muːtəˈsɑːriːf/ *noun*. Also **mute-**. **L19**.

[**ORIGIN** (Ottoman) Turkish, from Arabic *mutaṣarrif*, active pple of *taṣarrafa* act without restriction.]

In the Ottoman Empire and certain successor states: a governor of a province or sanjak.

mutate /ˈmjuːteɪt/ *adjective & noun*. **M19**.

[**ORIGIN** Latin *mutatus* pa. pple of *mutare* change: see **-ATE**[2].]

▸ **A** *adjective*. *BOTANY*. Changed. *rare*. **M19**.

▸ **B** *noun*. **1** *GRAMMAR*. A form having a mutated vowel. *rare*. **L19**.

2 *CHESS*. A problem in which White's playing of the key replaces one block by another. **E20**.

mutate /mjuːˈteɪt/ *verb*. **L18**.

[**ORIGIN** Back-form. from **MUTATION**.]

1 *verb trans.* Orig., change, transform. Now, cause to undergo (esp. genetic) mutation. **L18**.

2 *verb intrans.* Undergo change, be transmuted; undergo (esp. genetic) mutation. **E19**. ▸**b** *GRAMMAR*. Undergo mutation. **L20**.

> W. H. AUDEN We had the luck to see/. . old Russia suddenly mutate / into a proletarian state. EDMOND HAMILTON I think they were human once—human colonists who mutated under radioactive influence.

mutation /mjuːˈteɪʃ(ə)n/ *noun*. **LME**.

[**ORIGIN** Latin *mutatio(n-)*, from *mutat-* pa. ppl stem of *mutare* change: see **-ATION**.]

1 The action or process of changing; an alteration, a change. **LME**. ▸†**b** Change in government, revolution. **LME–M18**.

> J. DIDION I had never thought of him having dinner with his family . . but time brings odd mutations.

2 *MUSIC*. In medieval solmization, the change from one hexachord to another involving a change of the syllable applied to a given note. **L16**.

3 *GRAMMAR*. **a** In a Celtic language, a change of initial consonant caused (historically) by the preceding word. **M19**. ▸**b** = **UMLAUT** *noun* 1. **L19**.

4 *BIOLOGY*. **a** A change in genetic material, esp. one which gives rise to heritable variations in offspring; the process by which such changes arise. L19. ▸**b** A distinct form produced by genetic change; a mutant. E20.

– COMB.: **mutation mink** a mink of a mutant strain with a fur colour different from the normal; fur or a garment made from the skin of such a mink; **mutation pressure** GENETICS a tendency for recurring mutation (rather than selection) to alter the frequency of a particular allele within a population; **mutation rank** MUSIC = *mutation stop* below; **mutation rate** GENETICS the rate at which mutations occur in the genes of a given population, or in a given gene; **mutation stop** MUSIC a stop whose pipes produce a tone other than the proper pitch or an octave of the key struck; **mutation theory** (BIOLOGY, now *hist.*) the theory that new species arise by sudden divergence from a parent type, rather than gradually (as by natural selection).

■ **mutational** *adjective* (chiefly BIOLOGY) E20. **mutationally** *adverb* as a result of mutation M20. **mutationist** *noun* (BIOLOGY, now *hist.*) an advocate of mutation theory (opp. *selectionist*) E20.

mutatis mutandis /mjuː,tɑːtɪs mjuːˈtandɪs, muː-, -iːs/ *adverbial phr.* E16.
[ORIGIN Latin, lit. 'things being changed that have to be changed'.]
Making the necessary changes; with due alteration of details.

J. BAYLEY Both gifts he shares, *mutatis mutandis*, with the American poets.

mutative /ˈmjuːtətɪv/ *adjective.* E18.
[ORIGIN medieval Latin *mutativus*, from *mutat-*: see MUTATION, -IVE.]
1 Of or pertaining to change or mutation. E18.
2 GRAMMAR. Designating a verb form or tense which denotes or describes a change of state. M19.

mutato nomine /mjuː,tɑːtəʊ ˈnəʊmɪneɪ, muː-, nɒ-/ *adverbial phr.* E17.
[ORIGIN Latin.]
The name being changed, with a change of name or names.

J. B. FRASER The words of Burns, *mutato nomine*, describe their country exactly.

mutator /mjuːˈteɪtə/ *noun.* M17.
[ORIGIN from MUTATE *verb* + -OR.]
†**1** A person who changes something. *rare.* Only in M17.
2 BIOLOGY. In full ***mutator gene***. A gene which increases the mutation rate of other genes. M20.

mutawwa /muːˈtɑːwə, mʊˈtɑːwə/ *noun.* L19.
[ORIGIN Arabic *muṭṭawwi'* a volunteer, from *taṭawwa'a* perform good deeds beyond those prescribed by Islamic law.]
1 A zealous follower of the Wahhabi sect of Islam. L19.
2 In Saudi Arabia: a member of the religious police. L20.

mutch /mʌtʃ/ *noun.* LME.
[ORIGIN Middle Dutch *mutse* (Dutch *muts*) corresp. to Middle & mod. High German *mütze*, shortened by-forms of Middle Dutch *a(l)mutse* from medieval Latin *almucia* AMICE *noun*².]
†**1** A covering for the head during the night, a nightcap. *Scot.* LME–M19.
2 A cap or coif of linen etc. worn by (esp. old) women and young children. *Scot. & dial.* L16.

mutchkin /ˈmʌtʃkɪn/ *noun. Scot.* LME.
[ORIGIN Early mod. Dutch *mudseken* (now *mutsje*) dim. of *mudde*: see MUD *noun*¹, -KIN.]
A unit of capacity for liquids or dry substances equal to a quarter of the old Scots pint or approx. three-quarters of an imperial pint (0.43 litres).

mute /mjuːt/ *noun*¹. *arch.* LME.
[ORIGIN Old French *muete*, (also mod.) *meute* from popular Latin from Latin *movere* MOVE *verb*.]
1 A pack of hounds. LME.
†**2** The baying of a pack of hounds. Only in LME.

mute /mjuːt/ *adjective & noun*². ME.
[ORIGIN Old French & mod. French *muet* dim. of Old French *mu* from Latin *mutus*. Orig. two syllables.]
▸ **A** *adjective*. **1** Of a person: lacking the faculty of speech. ME. ▸**b** Of an animal: naturally lacking the power of articulate speech. M17.
DEAF MUTE.
2 Refraining from or temporarily deprived of speech, not emitting articulate sound. LME. ▸**b** Characterized by an absence of sound; quiet, still; not expressed or accompanied by speech or vocal utterance. E16.

C. BOWEN Mute with wonder I stood. M. WARNER Mamma had tried to talk to Rosa . . but she'd stayed mute. **b** F. BURNEY Fixed in mute wonder, . . her eyes almost bursting from their sockets. *Daily News* The mute agonies of the suffocating lobster.

stand mute LAW, *hist.* not plead (***stand mute of malice***, refuse to plead; ***stand mute by visitation of God***, be unable to plead).
3 GRAMMAR & PHONETICS. **a** Of a consonant: produced by an entire interruption of the passage of breath or by the complete closure of the organs of the mouth; stopped, plosive. Now *rare.* L16. ▸**b** Of a letter: not pronounced, silent. M17.
4 ASTROLOGY. Of a sign of the zodiac: symbolized by a voiceless creature (viz. Cancer, Scorpio, Pisces). M17.
5 Of a hound: not giving tongue while hunting. L17.
run mute follow the chase without giving tongue.
6 Of a metal or mineral: that does not ring when struck. E19.
7 CINEMATOGRAPHY. Designating a positive or negative film print having no synchronous soundtrack. M20.

– COMB.: **mute button** a device on a telephone etc. that temporarily prevents a caller hearing anything said at the receiver's end; **mute swan** a common Eurasian swan, *Cygnus olor*, with white plumage and an orange-red and black bill.
▸ **B** *noun*. **1** PHONETICS. A mute or stopped consonant, a plosive. M16.
2 A person prevented by nature, mutilation, or employment from speaking; *spec.* (**a**) an actor in a mime; (**b**) *hist.* a servant in an Eastern country deprived usu. deliberately of the power of speech; †(**c**) LAW a person refusing to plead to an indictment; (**d**) a professional attendant or mourner at a funeral. L16.
DEAF MUTE.
3 MUSIC. **a** A clip placed over the bridge of a violin etc. to deaden the resonance without affecting the vibration of the strings. E19. ▸**b** A pad or cone inserted into the bell of a wind instrument to soften the sound. M19.
b ***Harmon mute***, ***straight mute***, etc.
4 CINEMATOGRAPHY. A mute film print. M20.
– NOTE: Use in sense 'lacking the faculty of speech' is now dated and offensive; *speech-impaired* is preferred.
■ **mutely** *adverb* L16. **muteness** *noun* L16.

mute /mjuːt/ *verb*¹ & *noun*³. *arch.* L15.
[ORIGIN Old French *meutir*, later *mutir* aphet. from *esmeutir*, earlier *esmeltir* (mod. *émeutir*), perh. from Frankish verb meaning 'smelt'. Cf. Middle Dutch *smelt* bird's faeces.]
▸ **A** *verb intrans. & trans.* Of a bird, esp. a hawk: discharge (faeces). L15.
▸ **B** *noun*. The action of defecating by a bird, esp. a hawk; *sing.* & in *pl.* (a deposit of) faeces, droppings. L15.
■ **muting** *noun*¹ (**a**) the action of the verb; (**b**) *sing.* & (usu.) in *pl.*, faeces, droppings: L15.

mute /mjuːt/ *verb*². L17.
[ORIGIN from MUTE *adjective*.]
†**1** *verb intrans.* Of a pack of hounds: run without giving tongue. Only in L17.
2 *verb trans.* Deaden or soften the sound of (a thing or person); *spec.* muffle the sound of (a musical instrument); *fig.* tone down, reduce in intensity, subdue. L19. ▸**b** Silence (a thing or person); *spec.* suppress the volume of (a loudspeaker) or the output of (an amplifier or other circuit component). L19.

M. PEMBERTON A heavy Indian carpet muted the footsteps of the Emperor. A. BROOKNER Fierce colour . . muted by the surrounding greyness.

■ **muting** *noun*² (**a**) the action of the verb; (**b**) ELECTRICITY the automatic suppression of the output of an amplifier when the input signal falls below some predetermined level: L19.

muted /ˈmjuːtɪd/ *adjective.* M19.
[ORIGIN from MUTE *verb*² + -ED¹.]
Made mute, silent; muffled, quiet; understated; (of a musical instrument) having a muffled tone, employing a mute; (of colour or lighting) subdued.

Publishers Weekly The muted inner dignity of these deeply religious black people. B. BREYTENBACH He hears the muted rumbling of the city. *Patches* Spring greens are muted and delicate.

■ **mutedly** *adverb* L19.

mutessarif *noun* var. of MUTASSARIF.

mutha /ˈmʌðə/ *noun. non-standard. US.* L20.
[ORIGIN Repr. pronunc.]
= MOTHER *noun*¹, esp. sense 4.
– COMB.: **muthafucka**, **muthafucking** *adjective* (*coarse slang*) = ***motherfucker***, ***motherfucking*** s.v. MOTHER *noun*¹.

muti /ˈmuːti/ *noun. S. Afr.* M19.
[ORIGIN Zulu *umuthi* tree, plant, medicine.]
Traditional African medicine; a medicinal or healing charm, healing magic.

mutic /ˈmjuːtɪk/ *adjective.* L18.
[ORIGIN Latin *muticus*: see MUTICOUS.]
1 BOTANY. = MUTICOUS. Now *rare* or *obsolete*. L18.
2 ENTOMOLOGY. Lacking spines. M19.

muticous /ˈmjuːtɪkəs/ *adjective.* M19.
[ORIGIN from Latin *muticus* awnless + -OUS.]
BOTANY. Having no point or awn.

mutilate /ˈmjuːtɪleɪt/ *adjective & noun.* E16.
[ORIGIN Latin *mutilatus* pa. pple, formed as MUTILATE *verb*: see -ATE².]
▸ **A** *adjective*. **1** Mutilated. *obsolete* exc. *poet.* E16.
†**2** BIOLOGY. Of an animal or plant: having some part common to related forms either absent or present only in an imperfect or modified state. M18–L19.
▸ †**B** *noun*. BIOLOGY. A mutilate organism; *spec.* a cetacean or sirenian as lacking fully developed limbs. M–L19.

mutilate /ˈmjuːtɪleɪt/ *verb trans.* M16.
[ORIGIN Latin *mutilat-* pa. ppl stem of *mutilare*, from *mutilus* maimed: see -ATE³. Cf. MUTILATE *adjective & noun* (earlier).]
1 Deprive (a person or animal) of a limb or bodily organ; cut off, severely wound, (a limb or organ); maim, mangle. M16.

C. THIRLWALL He was condemned to be mutilated, . . in his nose and ears. R. K. NARAYAN Two fellows . . were mutilated—one fellow lost an arm.

2 Make (a thing, esp. a document, book, etc.) imperfect by removing or severely damaging a part. M16.
■ **mutilative** *adjective* (*rare*) causing mutilation L19. **mutilator**, †**mutilater** *noun* M17.

mutilation /mjuːtɪˈleɪʃ(ə)n/ *noun.* E16.
[ORIGIN Late Latin *mutilatio(n-)*, formed as MUTILATE *verb*: see -ATION. Cf. Old French & mod. French *mutilation*.]
1 The action of mutilating a person or animal; the excision or maiming of a limb or bodily organ; an instance of this. E16.
2 The action of mutilating a thing; an instance of this. M17.

M. SPARK Angry authors' letters about the mutilation of their books.

mutillid /mjuːˈtɪlɪd/ *noun & adjective.* L19.
[ORIGIN from mod. Latin *Mutilla* genus name: see -ID³.]
▸ **A** *noun*. Any wasp of the family Mutillidae, which includes the velvet ants and other solitary fossorial parasitic species. L19.
▸ **B** *adjective*. Of, pertaining to, or designating this family. L19.

†**mutilous** *adjective.* M17–E18.
[ORIGIN from Latin *mutilus* maimed + -OUS.]
Of a thing: mutilated, imperfect.

†**mutine** *noun & adjective.* M16.
[ORIGIN Old French & mod. French *mutin*, from *muete* (mod. *meute*) from Proto-Romance: see MUTE *noun*¹, -INE⁴.]
▸ **A** *noun*. **1** Popular disturbance or revolt, rebellion, mutiny. M16–E17.
2 A rebellious person, a mutineer. L16–E17.
▸ **B** *adjective*. Mutinous, rebellious, unsubmissive. L16–L19.

†**mutine** *verb.* M16.
[ORIGIN French *mutiner*, formed as MUTINE *noun & adjective*.]
1 *verb intrans.* Rebel, mutiny. M16–L18.
2 *verb trans.* Incite to revolt. L16–E17.

mutineer /mjuːtɪˈnɪə/ *noun & verb.* E17.
[ORIGIN French *mutinier*, formed as MUTINE *noun*: see -EER.]
▸ **A** *noun*. A person who mutinies. E17.
▸ **B** *verb intrans.* Mutiny, rebel. L17.

mutinize /ˈmjuːtɪnʌɪz/ *verb. arch.* Also **-ise**. E17.
[ORIGIN from MUTINE *noun* + -IZE.]
1 *verb intrans.* Mutiny. E17.
2 *verb trans.* Cause mutiny in. M17.

mutinous /ˈmjuːtɪnəs/ *adjective.* L16.
[ORIGIN from MUTINE *noun* + -OUS.]
1 Of a person: tending to mutiny, rebellious; rebelling, insurgent. L16. ▸†**b** Turbulent, contentious. L16–E17. ▸**c** *transf.* & *fig.* Ungovernable, stormy; wilful, unsubmissive. E17.

I. MURDOCH Titus and Gilbert had been in a state of subdued revolt, they were mutinous. **c** R. G. PRESTON The mutinous Passions of Grief, Anger, and Sadness do . . distract thee.

2 Of the nature of or proceeding from mutiny; characterized by or expressing mutiny. L16.

O. MANNING The sense of mutinous anger had gone.

■ **mutinously** *adverb* L16. **mutinousness** *noun* E17.

mutiny /ˈmjuːtɪni/ *noun.* M16.
[ORIGIN from MUTINE *verb* or *noun* + -Y³.]
†**1** Discord, strife; a dispute, a quarrel. M16–M17.
2 Open revolt against constituted authority, now *spec.* on the part of a military body against its officers or leaders; an instance of this, a mutinous rebellion. L16.

C. FRANCIS He would have to take action to prevent discontent developing into mutiny.

Indian Mutiny, **Sepoy Mutiny** *hist.* revolt of Indian (esp. Bengali) troops against the British in 1857–8.

mutiny /ˈmjuːtɪni/ *verb intrans.* L16.
[ORIGIN from the noun.]
1 Engage in mutiny; revolt *against*; refuse to obey orders of a superior, esp. in the military and naval services. L16.

Argosy The men mutinied and turned us adrift in the boat. JASON ELLIOT Afghan officers refused to lay down artillery on civilians, and mutinied.

†**2** Contend or strive *with*, quarrel. L16–E17.

mutism /ˈmjuːtɪz(ə)m/ *noun.* E19.
[ORIGIN French *mutisme*, from Latin *mutus*: see MUTE *adjective*, -ISM.]
The state or condition of being mute; inability or unwillingness to speak, esp. (PSYCHOLOGY) for psychological rather than physiological reasons.

muton /ˈmjuːtɒn/ *noun.* M20.
[ORIGIN from MUT(ATION + -ON.]
BIOLOGY. The smallest element of genetic material which can undergo a distinct mutation, usu. identified as a single pair of nucleotides. Cf. RECON *noun*².

mutoscope /ˈmjuːtəskəʊp/ *noun.* L19.
[ORIGIN from Latin *mutare* change + -O- + -SCOPE.]
hist. An apparatus in which a series of photographs of a scene in motion may be viewed by looking through an aperture and turning a handle at the side of the instrument.

mutt /mʌt/ *noun. slang* (orig. *US*). L19.
[ORIGIN Abbreviation of *mutton-head* s.v. MUTTON.]
1 A stupid, awkward, or incompetent person; *gen.* a person, a fellow. L19.

M

Mutt and Jeff [from two cartoon characters, one tall and one short, created by H. C. Fisher (1884–1954)] (***a***) a stupid or ill-matched pair of men; (***b***) *rhyming slang* deaf.

2 A dog, *esp.* a mongrel. *derog.* or *joc.* **E20.**

> A. LURIE A medium-sized dirty-white long-haired mutt, mainly Welsh terrier.

mutter /ˈmʌtə/ *noun.* **M17.**
[ORIGIN from the verb.]
An act of muttering; a low indistinct utterance.

mutter /ˈmʌtə/ *verb.* **ME.**
[ORIGIN from base repr. also by **MUTE** *adjective*: see **-ER**[5]. Cf. German dial. *muttern*.]
1 *verb intrans.* Speak in low and barely audible tones with the mouth nearly closed. **ME.** ▸**b** Speak covertly *against*, complain *at*, grumble. **M16.** ▸**c** *transf.* Make a low rumbling sound. **L18.**

> J. CONRAD Muttering cautiously with downcast eyes. **b** DEFOE Our men muttered a little at this; but I pacified them. **c** D. H. LAWRENCE Thunder muttered in different places.

2 *verb trans.* Utter or say (a thing, *that*) indistinctly in a low tone; *fig.* express or say in secret, complain (*that*). **LME.**

> J. B. PRIESTLEY Mrs. Mounder . . muttered something that nobody could catch. *Times* Politicians . . began to mutter that the partnership was getting . . too cosy.

mutter over recite (words) in low indistinct tones, mumble.
■ **mutterer** *noun* **M16.** **muttering** *noun* (***a***) the action of the verb; (***b***) something muttered; a rumour: **L15.** **mutteringly** *adverb* in a muttering manner **L17.**

Mutti /ˈmʊti/ *noun. colloq.* **E20.**
[ORIGIN German, from *Mutter* mother.]
Among German-speaking people: mother.

> M. A. VON ARNIM Mutti, she's a witch!

mutton /ˈmʌt(ə)n/ *noun.* **ME.**
[ORIGIN Old French *moton* (mod. *mouton*) from medieval Latin *multo(n-)*, prob. of Gaulish origin: cf. Old Irish & mod. Irish *molt* castrated ram, Gaelic *mult*, Welsh *mollt*, Cornish *mols* wether, Breton *maout* sheep.]
1 The flesh of sheep used as food. **ME.**
2 a A sheep, *esp.* one intended to be eaten. Now only *joc.* **ME.** ▸**b** The carcass of a sheep. *arch.* **E17.**
3 The genitals of a woman; copulation; *collect.* prostitutes. *slang. obsolete* exc. in ***hawk one's mutton*** below. **E16.**
4 In full ***mutton candle***. A candle made of mutton fat. *obsolete* exc. *hist.* **M19.**
5 *TYPOGRAPHY.* In full ***mutton quad***, ***mutton quadrat***. = ***EM quad***. **L19.**
– PHRASES: ***dead as mutton***: see **DEAD** *adjective*. **hawk one's mutton** *slang* (of a woman) look for a lover; solicit. ***LACED* mutton**. **mutton dressed as lamb** *colloq.* an ageing or unattractive woman dressed or made up as if younger or more attractive. ***POOR MAN* of mutton**. **return to one's muttons** *joc.* [after French *revenons à nos moutons*] return to the matter in hand. ***underground mutton***: see **UNDERGROUND** *adjective*.
– COMB.: ***mutton-candle***: see sense 4 above; **mutton chop** (***a***) a piece of mutton, *spec.* including the rib and half vertebra to which it is attached; (***b***) (in full ***mutton chop whisker***) a side whisker shaped like this, narrow at the top and broad and rounded at the bottom; **mutton-fat** *adjective* (***a***) made of mutton fat; (***b***) designating a creamy white type of jade valued highly by connoisseurs; **mutton-fisted** *adjective* (*colloq.*) clumsy, heavy-handed, ham-fisted; **mutton-head** *colloq.* (orig. *US*) a dull stupid person; **mutton-headed** *adjective* (*colloq.*, orig. *US*) dull, stupid; **mutton-leg sleeve** = ***leg-of-mutton sleeve*** s.v. **LEG** *noun*; ***mutton quad***, ***mutton quadrat***: see sense 5 above; **mutton snapper** a large snapper fish, *Lutjanus analis*, of the Caribbean and W. Atlantic.
■ **muttoned** *adjective* (of a sheep) having flesh (of a specified quality), covered with flesh **M19.** **muttony** *adjective* having the quality of or resembling mutton **M19.**

mutton bird /ˈmʌt(ə)nbəːd/ *noun.* **L18.**
[ORIGIN from **MUTTON** + **BIRD** *noun*.]
1 Any of various seabirds of southern oceans whose cooked flesh is said to resemble mutton in flavour: (***a***) *NZ* the sooty shearwater, *Puffinus griseus*; (***b***) *Austral.* the short-tailed shearwater, *P. tenuirostris*; (***c***) an Antarctic petrel of the genus *Pterodroma*. **L18.**
2 ***mutton-bird scrub***, a shrub or small tree, *Senecio reinoldii*, of the composite family, with round leathery leaves and small yellow flowers. *NZ.* **L19.**
■ **mutton-birder** *noun* (*Austral.* & *NZ*) a person who catches mutton birds for food or sport **L19.**

mutton-fish /ˈmʌt(ə)nfɪʃ/ *noun.* Pl. **-es** /-ɪz/, (usu.) same. **M18.**
[ORIGIN from **MUTTON** + **FISH** *noun*[1].]
1 Any of various marine fishes of the Caribbean and W. Atlantic whose flesh is said to resemble mutton, *esp.* an eelpout. **M18.**
2 (The flesh of) an edible mollusc of the genus *Haliotis*, esp. *H. ruber*; an abalone, a paua. *Austral.* & *NZ.* **M19.**

mutual /ˈmjuːtʃʊəl, -tjʊəl/ *adjective & noun.* **E16.**
[ORIGIN Old French & mod. French *mutuel*, from Latin *mutuus* borrowed, mutual, cogn. with *mutare* to change: see **-AL**[1].]
▸ **A** *adjective.* **1** Of a feeling, action, etc.: experienced, expressed, or performed by each of the parties concerned towards or with regard to the other(s); reciprocal. **E16.** ▸**b** Having the same feelings for each other; standing in a reciprocal relation to another. **M16.** ▸**c** Pertaining to or characterized by some (implied) mutual action or relation; *spec.* designating a building society, insurance company, etc., owned by its members and dividing some or all of its profits between them. **L18.** ▸**d** *ELECTRICITY.* Of a quantity, property, etc.: dependent equally and symmetrically on two circuits or circuit elements, and representing an effect on either of a certain kind of change in the other. **M19.**

> J. S. HUXLEY Mutual aid . . establishes minimum waste. V. BRITTAIN The mutual devotion between herself and Roland was very pleasant to see. P. DICKINSON Can't stand the sight of her . . . Feeling's mutual.

2 Respective, belonging to each respectively. **M16.**
3 Held in common or shared between two or more parties. **E17.**

> P. MONETTE We met . . at a mutual friend's apartment.

†**4** Of a relationship etc.: intimate. **E17–M18.**
†**5** Responsive. **M17–M19.**
– SPECIAL COLLOCATIONS: **mutual admiration society** a group of people prone to overestimate each other's merits. **mutual assured destruction** a US military scenario in which nuclear war is deterred by each side knowing that the other is capable of inflicting unacceptable damage if attacked; abbreviation ***MAD***. **mutual characteristic** *ELECTRONICS* a characteristic curve representing the variation of anode current with grid voltage at constant anode voltage. **mutual conductance** *ELECTRONICS* the ratio of the change in the anode current of a valve to the change of grid voltage causing it, the anode voltage being constant. **mutual fund** *N. Amer.* a unit trust. **mutual inductance** *ELECTRICITY* the property of two circuits or devices by virtue of which a variation in the current flowing through one induces an electromotive force in the other; also called ***transconductance***.
▸ **B** *ellipt.* as *noun.* **1** A mutual fund, society, etc. **M19.**
2 A mutual friend. *rare.* **E20.**
– NOTE: Sense A.3 is sometimes regarded as incorrect, although it was first recorded in Shakespeare and is now generally accepted as part of standard English.
■ **mutualness** *noun* **E17.**

mutualise *verb* var. of **MUTUALIZE**.

mutualism /ˈmjuːtʃʊəlɪz(ə)m, -tjʊə-/ *noun.* **M19.**
[ORIGIN from **MUTUAL** + **-ISM**.]
1 The doctrine that individual and collective well-being is attainable only by mutual dependence; a system based on this, *spec.* one involving non-profit credit and voluntary association for the exchange of services. **M19.**
2 *BIOLOGY.* A condition of (obligate or facultative) symbiosis in which two organisms contribute mutually to the well-being of each other. **L19.**

mutualist /ˈmjuːtʃʊəlɪst, -tjʊə-/ *noun & adjective.* **E19.**
[ORIGIN from **MUTUAL** + **-IST**.]
▸ **A** *noun.* **1** An advocate of mutualism. **E19.**
2 *BIOLOGY.* An organism which lives in a condition of mutualism with another. **L19.**
▸ **B** *attrib.* or as *adjective.* Of or pertaining to mutualists or mutualism. **L19.**
■ **mutuaˈlistic** *adjective* exhibiting or characteristic of mutualism **L19.** **mutuaˈlistically** *adverb* **E20.**

mutuality /mjuːtʃʊˈalɪti, -tjʊ-/ *noun.* **L16.**
[ORIGIN from **MUTUAL** + **-ITY**.]
1 The quality or condition of being mutual; reciprocity. **L16.** ▸**b** *LAW.* A situation in which two parties are mutually bound to perform certain reciprocal duties. **M19.** ▸**c** A system of organizing conditions of work by agreement between the worker involved and the employer. **M20.**
2 An interchange of acts of goodwill; an intimacy. **E17.**

mutualize /ˈmjuːtʃʊəlʌɪz, -tjʊə-/ *verb trans.* Also **-ise**. **E19.**
[ORIGIN from **MUTUAL** + **-IZE**.]
†**1** Give and receive in return; exchange. *rare.* Only in **E19.**
2 Organize (a company etc.) on cooperative or mutual principles. **E20.**
■ **mutualiˈzation** *noun* **E20.**

mutually /ˈmjuːtʃʊəli, -tjʊə-/ *adverb.* **M16.**
[ORIGIN from **MUTUAL** + **-LY**[2].]
1 With mutual action or feeling; in a mutual relation; reciprocally. Freq. in ***mutually exclusive***. **M16.** ▸†**b** In return; as one side of a reciprocal action. **L16–E18.**

> D. H. LAWRENCE They began mutually to mistrust each other. A. T. ELLIS My mother . . thought the two qualities went together and Lili said they . . were mutually exclusive.

mutually assured destruction = ***mutual assured destruction*** s.v. **MUTUAL** *adjective*.
2 In cooperation or companionship; by mutual agreement; jointly, in common. **L16.**

mutuary /ˈmjuːtʃʊəri, -tjʊə-/ *noun.* **M19.**
[ORIGIN Latin *mutuarius*, from *mutuus* borrowed: see **MUTUAL**, **-ARY**[1].]
LAW. A borrower of a thing which is to be consumed and therefore is to be returned in kind.

†**mutuate** *verb trans.* **M16–E18.**
[ORIGIN Latin *mutuat-* pa. ppl stem of *mutuari* borrow, from *mutuus* borrowed: see **MUTUAL**, **-ATE**[3].]
Borrow.

†**mutuation** *noun.* **E17–E19.**
[ORIGIN formed as **MUTUATE** + **-ATION**.]
An act of lending or borrowing.

†**mutuatitious** *adjective.* **E17–E19.**
[ORIGIN from Latin *mutuatitius*, formed as **MUTUATE**: see **-ITIOUS**[1].]
Borrowed, taken from some other.

mutuel /ˈmjuːtʃʊəl, -tjʊəl; *foreign* mytɥɛl (*pl. same*)/ *noun.* Chiefly *N. Amer.* **L19.**
[ORIGIN Abbreviation of **PARI-MUTUEL**.]
A totalizator, a pari-mutuel.

mutule /ˈmjuːtjuːl/ *noun.* **M17.**
[ORIGIN French from Latin *mutulus*.]
ARCHITECTURE. A block projecting under a cornice in the Doric order.
■ Earlier †**mutulo** *noun*, pl. **-li**, [Italian]: only in **M16.**

mutuum /ˈmjuːtʃʊəm, -tjʊəm/ *noun. obsolete* exc. *Scot.* & *US.* **L15.**
[ORIGIN Latin = loan, use as noun of neut. of *mutuus* borrowed: see **MUTUAL**.]
LAW. A contract under which a thing is lent which is to be consumed and therefore is to be returned in kind.

muu-muu /ˈmuːmuː/ *noun.* Also **mu-mu**. **L19.**
[ORIGIN Hawaiian *mu'u mu'u* lit. 'cut off' from the original absence of a yoke.]
A woman's usu. brightly coloured and patterned loose-fitting dress, (as) worn in Hawaii.

muvule /mʊˈvuːli/ *noun.* Also **mvule** /(ə)mˈvuːli/ & other vars. **M19.**
[ORIGIN Luganda *muvule*, Kiswahili *mvule*.]
In E. Africa: (the timber of) an iroko.

muvver /ˈmʌvə/ *noun. dial.* **L19.**
[ORIGIN Repr. a pronunc.]
Mother.

mux /mʌks/ *noun & verb. dial.* (chiefly *US*). **M18.**
[ORIGIN Uncertain: cf. **MUSS** *verb*, **MUCK** *verb*.]
▸ **A** *noun.* Mud, dirt, mire. **M18.**
▸ **B** *verb trans.* Make dirty, mess up. **E19.**

Muzak /ˈmjuːzak/ *noun.* Also **m-**. **M20.**
[ORIGIN Alt. of **MUSIC** *noun*. Cf. **KODAK**.]
(Proprietary name for) a system for transmitting background music by wire for playing in a public place; recorded light background music generally; *transf.* bland undemanding music.

> *attrib.*: *Arena* Muzak versions of 'Walk on By' . . are piped around the restaurants.

■ **Muzaked** *adjective* (***a***) supplied with Muzak; (***b***) played in a style resembling that of Muzak: **M20.**

muzhik /muːˈʒɪk/ *noun.* Also **moujik**. **M16.**
[ORIGIN Russian.]
hist. A Russian peasant.

muzz /mʌz/ *verb & noun.* **M18.**
[ORIGIN Uncertain: cf. **MUG** *verb*[5], **MUZZLE** *verb*[2], **MUZZY**.]
▸ **A** *verb.* **1** *verb intrans.* Study intently, work hard *over* a book etc. *slang.* **M18.**
2 *verb trans.* Make confused or muzzy, fuddle. *colloq.* **L18.**

> G. BLACK Drugs don't seem to have muzzed you.

▸ **B** *noun.* **1** A person who studies intently. *slang.* **L18.**
2 A state of mental confusion; muddle, blur. *colloq.* **M19.**
■ **muzzed** *adjective* (*colloq.*) fuddled; *spec.* drunk, intoxicated: **L18.**

muzzle /ˈmʌz(ə)l/ *noun.* **LME.**
[ORIGIN Old French *musel* (mod. *museau*) from Proto-Gallo-Romance dim. of medieval Latin *musum*, of unknown origin.]
▸ **I 1** The projecting part of an animal's face, including the nose and mouth. **LME.** ▸**b** The part of the human face including the nose and chin. *joc.* **LME.**

> R. SUTCLIFF One of the hounds poked a friendly muzzle into her face.

2 The open end of the barrel of a firearm. **M16.**

> P. CAMPBELL I have looked down the muzzle of a gun.

3 A piece of metal on the end of a plough beam to which the draught tackle is attached; a clevis. Now *Scot.* **M16.**
▸ **II 4** A guard usu. consisting of straps or wires, put over an animal's nose and mouth to prevent it biting or eating. **LME.** ▸**b** *hist.* An ornamental piece of armour covering a horse's nose. **M19.**

> R. CROMPTON They ought to wear muzzles; they've got rabies.

– COMB.: **muzzle-loader** a firearm loaded through the muzzle; **muzzle-loading** *adjective* loaded through the muzzle; **muzzle velocity** the velocity at which a projectile leaves the muzzle of a firearm.

†**muzzle** *adjective.* **L17–E19.**
[ORIGIN Old French *meslé*: see **MUZZLED** *adjective*[2].]
= **MUZZLED** *adjective*[2].

muzzle /ˈmʌz(ə)l/ *verb*[1]. **LME.**
[ORIGIN from the noun.]
▸ **I** *verb trans.* **1** Put a muzzle on (an animal, an animal's mouth); prevent by means of a muzzle from biting etc. **LME.**
2 †**a** Muffle, veil, mask, (the face). *Scot.* **LME–L16.** ▸**b** Muffle the sound of (a musical instrument or bell). Now *dial.* **M17.**
3 Restrain from speaking, impose silence on. Now *spec.* censor, deprive of freedom of speech, (an institution or person, esp. the press). **M16.**

P. HOWARD He tried to frighten the British Government into muzzling *The Times*. A. N. WILSON The only voice . . the Russian Government did not dare to muzzle.

4 a Bring the muzzle or snout close to; *slang* kiss (a person), caress with the mouth. L16. ▸†**b** Root about or amongst. E17–M18.
5 NAUTICAL. Take in (a sail). L17.
6 Hit (a person) on the mouth; beat up, thrash. *slang*. M19.
▸ **II** *verb intrans.* **7** Thrust out the muzzle or nose; feel, smell, or root about with the muzzle. L15.

muzzle /ˈmʌz(ə)l/ *verb²*. *dial.* L18.
[ORIGIN App. connected with MUZZ *verb* & MUZZY.]
1 *verb trans.* Make muzzy or confused, fuddle. L18.
2 *verb intrans.* Drink to excess. E19.

muzzled /ˈmʌz(ə)ld/ *adjective¹*. L15.
[ORIGIN from MUZZLE *noun*, *verb¹*: see -ED², -ED¹.]
Having a muzzle (of a specified kind); wearing a muzzle.

†**muzzled** *adjective²*. M17–M19.
[ORIGIN Prob. from Old French *meslé* pa. pple of *mesler* mingle, mix (see MEDDLE) + -ED². Cf. MUZZLE *adjective*.]
Brindled, dappled, flecked.

muzzler /ˈmʌzlə/ *noun*. M17.
[ORIGIN from MUZZLE *noun*, *verb¹* + -ER¹.]
1 A person who muzzles an animal. M17.
2 A blow on the mouth. *slang*. E19.
3 A muzzle-loading gun. L19.
4 NAUTICAL. A headwind. L19.

muzzy /ˈmʌzi/ *adjective*. *colloq.* E18.
[ORIGIN Uncertain: cf. MUZZ, MUZZLE *verb²*, FUZZY 3.]
1 a Dull, spiritless; mentally hazy or confused; dazed, fuddled, esp. through drinking alcohol. E18. ▸**b** Blurred, indistinct. L18.

a M. KEANE A bit muzzy probably after all that port and brandy. **b** *Daily Telegraph* The muzzy pictures reaching our screens from the moon.

2 Of a place or occasion: tedious, gloomy. E18.
■ **muzzily** *adverb* E20. **muzziness** *noun* E19.

MV *abbreviation*.
1 Megavolt(s).
2 Motor vessel.
3 Muzzle velocity.

MVO *abbreviation*.
Member of the Royal Victorian Order.

MVP *abbreviation*.
Most valuable player.

mvule *noun* var. of MUVULE.

MW *abbreviation¹*.
1 Medium wave.
2 Megawatt(s).

mW *abbreviation²*.
Milliwatt(s).

Mwami /ˈmwɑːmi/ *noun*. M19.
[ORIGIN Rwanda *umwami* chief.]
(The royal title of) any of the former kings of Ruanda and Urundi (now Rwanda and Burundi) in central Africa.

M-way *abbreviation*.
Motorway.

Mx *abbreviation*.
1 Maxwell(s).
2 Middlesex.

MY *abbreviation*.
Motor yacht.

my /mʌɪ, *unstressed* mɪ/ *possess. adjective* (in mod. usage also classed as a **determiner**), **1** *sing.* Also (informal) **m'**, (now repr. non-standard speech) **mi** /mɪ/. ME.
[ORIGIN Reduced form of MINE *adjective* (orig. before consonants except *h*). Cf. ME *adjective*. See also MAH.]
1 Of me; of myself; which belongs or pertains to me. ME. ▸**b** (Before a title) that has the specified social status or relationship with regard to me; (before a personal name) that has a familial relationship with me. ME.

SCOTT FITZGERALD My name is Judy Jones. D. BARNES Oh God, when I think back to my past. E. O'NEILL My saying what I'm telling you now proves it. *Listener* I knew that I did not look my best in my mackintosh. I. MURDOCH I call it my office, but it was more like their office. C. RAYNER You are a very remarkable surgeon, sir . . to have saved my brother from bleeding to death. **b** C. M. YONGE A little pair of socks . . for my Johnnie.

my eye!, ***my foot!***, ***my goodness!***, ***my hat!***, ***my heavens!***, ***my word!***, etc. ***my own***: see OWN *adjective* & *pronoun*. ***my watch***: see WATCH *noun*. **b** ***my lady***: see LADY *noun*. ***my lord***: see LORD *noun*.

2 *voc.* Used affectionately before terms of endearment or (chiefly *literary*) relationship, and affectionately, compassionately, familiarly, or patronizingly before certain designations otherwise rarely used vocatively, as ***my man***, ***my girl***, ***my good woman***, ***my poor man***. ME.

J. STEINBECK These cheap white girls are vicious, my friend. M. KEANE Muriel, my dear, you may take Cynthia up to her room.

3 As *interjection*. Expr. surprise or admiration. Also redupl. (***my, my!***) and ***oh, my!*** E19.

M. DE LA ROCHE My, you boys can play . . . I'd sooner dance to your music than any of the big orchestras. R. DAHL Oh my, it's perfect! It's beautiful. *New Yorker* My my and here I am out where I can't even get a case of Scotch to celebrate.

– COMB.: **my-dear** *verb trans.* address as 'my dear'; **my-lady** *verb trans.* address as 'my lady'; **my-lord** *verb trans.* address as 'my lord'.

mya /ˈmʌɪə/ *noun*. Pl. **myae** /ˈmʌiiː/, **myas**. L18.
[ORIGIN mod. Latin (see below), prob. alt. of Greek *mus* mussel.]
ZOOLOGY. A soft-shelled burrowing bivalve of the genus *Mya*; a gaper. Now chiefly as mod. Latin genus name.

myal /ˈmʌɪəl/ *noun* & *attrib. adjective*. L18.
[ORIGIN Perh. from Hausa *maye* sorcerer.]
(Of or pertaining to) myalism.

myalgia /mʌɪˈaldʒə/ *noun*. M19.
[ORIGIN from MYO- + -ALGIA.]
MEDICINE. Muscular pain.
■ **myalgic** *adjective* pertaining to, involving, or affected with myalgia; ***myalgic encephalomyelitis***, a prolonged form of encephalomyelitis usu. occurring after a viral infection, characterized by headaches, fever, localized muscular pain, and weakness (abbreviation ***ME***; also called ***chronic fatigue syndrome***, ***myalgic encephalopathy***, ***postviral fatigue syndrome***, ***postviral syndrome***): M19.

myalism /ˈmʌɪəlɪz(ə)m/ *noun*. M19.
[ORIGIN from MYAL + -ISM.]
A kind of sorcery or witchcraft similar to obeah, practised in the W. Indies and some other countries.
■ **myalist** *noun* a person who practises myalism M19.

myall /ˈmʌɪəl/ *noun¹* & *adjective*. *Austral.* E19.
[ORIGIN Dharuk *maiyal* stranger, person from another tribe.]
▸ **A** *noun*. **1** Among Australian Aborigines: a stranger. E19.
2 In non-Aboriginal usage: an Aborigine living in a traditional manner. Cf. WARRIGAL *noun* 2. M19.
▸ **B** *attrib.* or as *adjective*. **1** In non-Aboriginal usage: retaining a traditional Aboriginal lifestyle. E19.
2 Of an animal or plant: wild. M19.

myall /ˈmʌɪəl/ *noun²*. M19.
[ORIGIN Uncertain, perh. transf. use of source of MYALL *noun¹* & *adjective*.]
Any of several Australian acacias, *esp.* (more fully ***weeping myall***) *Acacia pendula*, with a hard scented wood; the wood of these trees, used as fencing timber etc.

myasthenia /mʌɪəsˈθiːnɪə/ *noun*. M19.
[ORIGIN from MYO- + ASTHENIA.]
MEDICINE. Abnormal muscular weakness; *spec.* = ***myasthenia gravis*** below.
myasthenia gravis /ˈɡrɑːvɪs, ˈɡravɪs/ [Latin = severe, grave] a rare chronic autoimmune disease, commoner in adolescents and young women, characterized by muscular weakness without atrophy and caused by a defect in the action of acetylcholine at neuromuscular junctions.
■ **myasthenic** /-ˈθɛnɪk/ *adjective* pertaining to, involving, or affected with myasthenia M19.

myatonia *noun* var. of MYOTONIA.

mycelium /mʌɪˈsiːlɪəm/ *noun*. Pl. **-ia** /-ɪə/. M19.
[ORIGIN from Greek *mukēs* fungus + *-elium*, after *epithelium*.]
BOTANY. The vegetative part of the thallus of a fungus, usu. consisting of a network of fine white filaments (hyphae); tissue of this kind.
■ **mycelial** *adjective* consisting of, pertaining to, or characterized by mycelium M19. **mycelioid** *adjective* = MYCELIAL M19.

Mycenaean /mʌɪsɪˈniːən/ *noun* & *adjective*. L15.
[ORIGIN from Latin *Mycenaeus*, from *Mycenae* Mycenae (see below) + -AN.]
▸ **A** *noun*. **1** A native or inhabitant of Mycenae, an ancient Greek city in the Argive plain; a member of a Bronze Age culture centred on Mycenae. L15.
2 The Greek dialect used when Mycenae flourished. M20.
▸ **B** *adjective*. Of or pertaining to Mycenae; *esp.* designating or pertaining to the Bronze Age civilization of which it was the centre. L16.

myceto- /mʌɪˈsiːtəʊ/ *combining form* of Greek *mukēt-*, *mukēs* fungus: see -O-. Cf. MYCO-.
■ **mycetocyte** *noun* (ENTOMOLOGY) any of the large cells found in some insects, sometimes aggregated into a mycetome, which contain yeasts or other symbiotic micro-organisms E20. **mycetophagous** /mʌɪsɪˈtɒfəɡəs/ *adjective* feeding on fungi or mushrooms, fungivorous L19. **mycetophilid** *adjective* & *noun* (**a**) *adjective* designating or pertaining to the dipteran family Mycetophilidae of fungus gnats or midges; (**b**) *noun* a mycetophilid fly: L19. **myceto'zoan** *noun* a myxomycete, a slime mould, *spec.* as considered to belong to the animal kingdom and placed in the class Mycetozoa L19.

mycetoma /mʌɪsɪˈtəʊmə/ *noun*. Pl. **-mas**, **-mata** /-mətə/. M19.
[ORIGIN from MYCETO- + -OMA.]
MEDICINE. Any of various conditions due to fungal infection; *spec.* the tropical disease Madura foot.
■ **mycetomatous** *adjective* affected with mycetoma L19.

mycetome /ˈmʌɪsɪtəʊm/ *noun*. E20.
[ORIGIN from MYCETO- + -OME.]
ENTOMOLOGY. An organ consisting of an aggregation of mycetocytes, present in some insects.

-mycin /ˈmʌɪsɪn/ *suffix*.
[ORIGIN from MYCO- + -IN¹.]
Forming the names of antibiotic compounds derived from fungi, the first elem. usu. being part of a Latin binomial name, as ***actinomycin***, ***erythromycin***, ***streptomycin***, etc.

myco- /ˈmʌɪkəʊ/ *combining form*.
[ORIGIN Irreg. from Greek *mukēs* fungus + -O-. Cf. MYCETO-.]
Forming chiefly scientific words relating to fungi, as ***mycology***, ***mycoplasma***, ***mycosis***, etc.
■ **myco'biont** *noun* [-BIONT] the fungal component of a lichen (cf. PHYCOBIONT) M20. **myco'herbicide** *noun* a fungus, or a substance derived from one, used to destroy weeds L20. **mycophile** *noun* an enthusiast for fungi, esp. edible ones L19. **myco'philic** *adjective* fond of or feeding on wild mushrooms and toadstools M20. **mycoprotein** *noun* †(**a**) the supposed principal constituent of cytoplasm; (**b**) a protein of fungal origin, *esp.* one produced for human consumption: L19. **mycotoxi'cosis** *noun*, pl. **-coses** /-ˈkəʊsiːz/, a pathological condition caused by a mycotoxin M20. **mycotoxin** *noun* a toxic substance produced by a fungus M20.

mycobacterium /ˌmʌɪkə(ʊ)bakˈtɪərɪəm/ *noun*. Pl. **-ia** /-ɪə/. E20.
[ORIGIN mod. Latin (see below), formed as MYCO- + BACTERIUM.]
MEDICINE & BIOLOGY. Any of various Gram-positive, aerobic, filament-forming bacteria of the genus *Mycobacterium* or the family Mycobacteriaceae, including the causative agents of tuberculosis and leprosy.
■ **mycobacterial** *adjective* of, pertaining to, or caused by mycobacteria M20.

mycology /mʌɪˈkɒlədʒi/ *noun*. M19.
[ORIGIN from MYCO- + -LOGY.]
The scientific study of fungi. Also, the fungi of a district or region.
■ **myco'logic**, **myco'logical** *adjectives* of or pertaining to mycology or fungi M19. **myco'logically** *adverb* L19. **mycologist** *noun* M19.

mycophagy /mʌɪˈkɒfədʒi/ *noun*. M19.
[ORIGIN from MYCO- + -PHAGY.]
The eating of fungi, esp. (by a person) of those species usually neglected or avoided.
■ **'mycophage** *noun* = MYCOPHAGIST M20. **mycophagist** *noun* a person who practises mycophagy; an animal that eats fungi: M19. **mycophagous** *adjective* fungus-eating, mycetophagous E20.

mycoplasma /mʌɪkə(ʊ)ˈplazmə/ *noun*. Pl. **-mas**, **-mata** /-mətə/. L19.
[ORIGIN mod. Latin *Mycoplasma* genus name, formed as MYCO- + PLASMA.]
BIOLOGY. Any of a group of pleomorphic, Gram-negative, chiefly parasitic micro-organisms without a cell wall, which are smaller than bacteria but, unlike viruses, capable of growth in artificial media. Also called ***pleuropneumonia-like organism***.
■ **mycoplasmal** *adjective* of, pertaining to, or caused by mycoplasmas M20. **mycoplas'mosis** *noun*, pl. **-moses** /-ˈməʊsiːz/, a disease, esp. one of animals, caused by mycoplasma M20.

mycorrhiza /mʌɪkə(ʊ)ˈrʌɪzə/ *noun*. Also **mycorhiza**. Pl. **-zae** /-ziː/, **-zas**. L19.
[ORIGIN from MYCO- + Greek *rhiza* root.]
BOTANY. A symbiotic or slightly pathogenic fungus growing in association with the roots of a plant, either on the surface or within the cortex.
■ **mycorrhizal** *adjective* E20.

mycosis /mʌɪˈkəʊsɪs/ *noun*. Pl. **-coses** /-ˈkəʊsiːz/. M19.
[ORIGIN from MYCO- + -OSIS.]
MEDICINE. **1** A disease caused by fungal infection, as ringworm. M19.
2 ***mycosis fungoides*** /fʌŋˈɡɔɪdiːz/ [mod. Latin = fungoid], a malignant, usu. protracted lymphoma mainly confined to the skin and resulting in dome-shaped tumours. L19.
■ **mycotic** /mʌɪˈkɒtɪk/ *adjective* pertaining to or of the nature of mycosis; ***mycotic aneurysm***, aneurysm due to fungal or (usu.) bacterial infection: L19.

mycotrophy /mʌɪˈkɒtrəfi/ *noun*. E20.
[ORIGIN from MYCO- + -TROPHY.]
BOTANY. The association of the roots of certain plants with mycorrhizae which apparently aid the uptake of nutrients.
■ **mycotrophic** /-ˈtrəʊfɪk, -ˈtrɒfɪk/ *adjective* of, pertaining to, or characterized by mycotrophy E20.

mycterism /ˈmɪktərɪz(ə)m/ *noun*. *rare*. Also (earlier) in Latin form †**-ismus**. L16.
[ORIGIN Greek *muktērismos*, from *muktērizein* sneer at, from *muktēr* nose: see -ISM.]
A jibe, a scoff; scoffing.

myctophid /ˈmɪktəfɪd/ *noun* & *adjective*. M20.
[ORIGIN mod. Latin *Myctophidae* (see below), from *Myctophum* genus name from Greek *muktēr* nose + *ophis* snake: see -ID³.]
ZOOLOGY. ▸**A** *noun*. Any member of the family Myctophidae of deep-water marine fishes, having luminous organs along their sides. Also called ***lanternfish***. M20.
▸ **B** *adjective*. Of, pertaining to, or designating this family. M20.

mydas fly /ˈmʌɪdəs flʌɪ/ *noun phr.* Also (earlier) **midas fly**. L19.
[ORIGIN from mod. Latin *Mydas* genus name.]
Any of various large insectivorous dipteran flies of the family Mydidae (Mydaidae).

M

mydriasis /mɪdrɪˈeɪsɪs/ *noun*. L17.
[ORIGIN Latin from Greek *mudriasis*: see -IASIS.]
OPHTHALMOLOGY. Excessive dilatation of the pupil of the eye.
■ **mydriatic** /mɪdrɪˈatɪk/ *adjective & noun* (*a*) *adjective* of, pertaining to, or causing mydriasis; (*b*) *noun* a drug that causes mydriasis: M19.

myel- *combining form* see MYELO-.

myelencephalon /mʌɪəlɛnˈsɛf(ə)lɒn, -ˈkɛf-/ *noun*. M19.
[ORIGIN from MYELO- + ENCEPHALON.]
ANATOMY. **1** The cerebrospinal axis or system. Now *rare* or *obsolete*. M19.
2 The medulla oblongata. L19.
■ **myelenceˈphalic**, **myelencephalous** *adjectives* of or pertaining to the myelencephalon M19.

myelin /ˈmʌɪəlɪn/ *noun*. Also †**-ine**. M19.
[ORIGIN from MYELO- + -IN[1], -INE[5].]
†**1** *CHEMISTRY.* A phospholipid substance extracted from various animal and some plant tissues. M–L19.
2 A complex mixture of proteins and phospholipids which forms an insulating sheath around certain nerve fibres. L19.
– COMB.: **myelin sheath** the insulating layer of myelin laid down, usu. spirally, around the axons of certain nerve fibres by Schwann cells, which increases the rapidity of impulse conduction.
■ **myelinated** *adjective* (of a nerve fibre) enclosed in a myelin sheath L19. **myeliˈnation** *noun* the process of becoming myelinated; the state of being myelinated: L19.

myelitis /mʌɪəˈlʌɪtɪs/ *noun*. M19.
[ORIGIN from MYELO- + -ITIS.]
MEDICINE. **1** Inflammation of the spinal cord. M19. ***transverse myelitis***: see TRANSVERSE *adjective*.
2 Inflammation of the bone marrow, osteomyelitis. *rare*. E20.
■ **myelitic** /mʌɪəˈlɪtɪk/ *adjective* M19.

myelo- /ˈmʌɪələʊ/ *combining form* of Greek *muelos*, *-on* marrow, spinal cord: see -O-. Before a vowel also **myel-**.
■ **myeloˈgenesis** *noun* (*PHYSIOLOGY*) the formation of myelin, myelination E20. **myeloˈgenic** *adjective* (*MEDICINE*) originating in the bone marrow L19. **myeˈlogenous** *adjective* (*MEDICINE*) = MYELOGENIC; *spec.* designating a form of leukaemia: L19. **myelogram** *noun* (*MEDICINE*) (*a*) a radiograph obtained by myelography; (*b*) (a list of) the relative numbers of the various cells in a sample of bone marrow: M20. **myeloˈgraphic** *adjective* of or pertaining to myelography E20. **myeloˈgraphically** *adverb* by myelography M20. **myeˈlography** *noun* (*MEDICINE*) radiography of the spinal cord after injection of a contrast medium or air into the subarachnoid space M20. **myelomonoˈcytic** *adjective* (*MEDICINE*) (of leukaemia) characterized by the presence in the blood of monocytes and their myeloid precursor cells M20. **myeˈlopathy** *noun* (*MEDICINE*) disease of the spinal cord L19. **myelopeˈroxidase** *noun* (*BIOCHEMISTRY*) a greenish peroxidase occurring in granules in myelocytes and neutrophils M20. **myeloproˈliferative** *adjective* (*MEDICINE*) characterized by or pertaining to the proliferation of cells of or derived from the bone marrow M20. **myeˈlosis** *noun*, pl. **-loses** /-ˈləʊsiːz/, *MEDICINE* (*a*) *rare* (the formation of) a tumour of the spinal cord; (*b*) the proliferation of blood-cell precursors in the bone marrow: M19.

M

myeloblast /ˈmʌɪələ(ʊ)blast/ *noun*. E20.
[ORIGIN from MYELO- + -BLAST.]
PHYSIOLOGY. An immature bone-marrow cell, the precursor of a myelocyte, appearing in the blood in certain diseases.
■ **myeloˈblastic** *adjective* of, pertaining to, or involving myeloblasts E20. **myeloblaˈstosis** *noun* the presence of abnormally large numbers of myeloblasts in the bone marrow and blood M20.

myelocele /ˈmʌɪələ(ʊ)siːl/ *noun*[1]. Also **-coele**. L19.
[ORIGIN from MYELO- + -CELE.]
MEDICINE. Spina bifida in which the spinal cord is exposed over part of its length, usu. without protrusion as a swelling; an area of neural tissue so exposed. Cf. MYELOMENINGOCELE.

myelocele *noun*[2] var. of MYELOCOELE *noun*[1].

myelocoele /ˈmʌɪələ(ʊ)siːl/ *noun*[1]. Also **-cele**. L19.
[ORIGIN from MYELO- + Greek *koilos* hollow, cavity.]
ANATOMY. The central canal of the spinal cord.

myelocoele *noun*[2] var. of MYELOCELE *noun*[1].

myelocyte /ˈmʌɪələ(ʊ)sʌɪt/ *noun*. M19.
[ORIGIN from MYELO- + -CYTE.]
†**1** The nucleus of a ganglionic nerve cell. M–L19.
2 *PHYSIOLOGY.* An immature bone-marrow cell derived from and smaller than a myeloblast, which gives rise to granulocytes and appears in the blood in certain diseases. L19.
■ **myelocytic** /mʌɪələ(ʊ)ˈsɪtɪk/ *adjective* of or pertaining to a myelocyte or myelocytes; involving myelocytes: L19.

myeloid /ˈmʌɪəlɔɪd/ *adjective*. M19.
[ORIGIN from MYELO- + -OID.]
Chiefly *MEDICINE.* Of, pertaining to, involving, or resembling (the cells of) bone marrow.

myeloma /mʌɪəˈləʊmə/ *noun*. Pl. **-mas**, **-mata** /-mətə/. M19.
[ORIGIN from MYELO- + -OMA.]
MEDICINE. A malignant tumour of bone-marrow cells. Also (more fully ***multiple myeloma***), myelomatosis.

myelomatosis /ˌmʌɪələ(ʊ)məˈtəʊsɪs/ *noun*. Pl. **-toses** /-ˈtəʊsiːz/. E20.
[ORIGIN from MYELOMA + -OSIS.]
MEDICINE. A malignant proliferation of plasma cells, which accumulate in the bone marrow, often associated with abnormal proteins in the blood and urine.

myelomeningocele /ˌmʌɪələ(ʊ)mɪˈnɪŋgəsiːl, -ndʒ-/ *noun*. L19.
[ORIGIN from MYELO- + MENINGO- + -CELE.]
MEDICINE. Spina bifida in which the spinal cord and its meninges protrude through the cleft, forming a rounded swelling; the tissue so protruding. Also called ***meningomyelocele***. Cf. MYELOCELE *noun*[1].

myelon /ˈmʌɪəlɒn/ *noun*. Now *rare* or *obsolete*. M19.
[ORIGIN formed as MYELO-.]
ANATOMY. The spinal cord.

myenteric /mʌɪɛnˈtɛrɪk/ *adjective*. L19.
[ORIGIN from MYO- + ENTERIC.]
ANATOMY. Designating or pertaining to a plexus of sympathetic and parasympathetic nerves situated between and supplying the two layers of muscle in the small intestine.
myenteric reflex an involuntary reaction of these muscles to stimulus, characterized by contraction of the intestine before the point of stimulation and relaxation after it.

mygale /ˈmɪgəli/ *noun*. LME.
[ORIGIN Late Latin from Greek *mugalē*.]
1 A shrew. Long *rare*. LME.
2 *ZOOLOGY.* A very large hairy mygalomorph spider of the American genus *Mygale*. M19.

mygalomorph /ˈmɪg(ə)ləmɔːf/ *adjective & noun*. E20.
[ORIGIN mod. Latin *Mygalomorphae* (see below), formed as MYGALE: see -O-, -MORPH.]
ZOOLOGY. ▶**A** *adjective.* Of or pertaining to the suborder Orthognatha (formerly Mygalomorphae) of (mainly large) spiders, including bird spiders, American tarantulas, funnel-web spiders, and trapdoor spiders. E20.
▶**B** *noun.* A mygalomorph spider. M20.

myiasis /mʌɪˈeɪsɪs, ˈmʌɪəsɪs/ *noun*. Pl. **-ases** /-ˈeɪsiːz, -əsiːz/. M19.
[ORIGIN from Greek *muia* fly + -IASIS.]
MEDICINE. Infestation with maggots; (a) disease caused by this.

Mylar /ˈmʌɪlɑː/ *noun*. Also **m-**. M20.
[ORIGIN Arbitrary.]
(Proprietary name for) a polyester made by the condensation of ethylene glycol and terephthalic acid and used to make strong heat-resistant films.

mylodon /ˈmʌɪləd(ə)n/ *noun*. M19.
[ORIGIN mod. Latin *Mylodon* (see below), from Greek *mulē*, *mulos* molar (lit. 'millstone') + -ODON.]
A gigantic extinct ground sloth of the genus *Mylodon*, with more or less cylindrical teeth, found in deposits from the Pleistocene epoch in S. America.
■ **mylodont** *adjective & noun* (pertaining to or characteristic of) a mylodon L19.

mylohyoid /mʌɪləʊˈhʌɪɔɪd/ *adjective & noun*. Also (earlier) in mod. Latin form **-hyoideus** /-hʌɪˈɔɪdɪəs/. L17.
[ORIGIN mod. Latin, from Greek *mulē*, *mulos*: see MYLODON, HYOID.]
ANATOMY. ▶**A** *adjective.* Connected with the lower jaw and the hyoid bone. Chiefly in ***mylohyoid muscle***, a flat triangular muscle in the floor of the mouth. M19.
▶**B** *noun.* The mylohyoid muscle. M19.
■ **mylohyoiˈdean** *adjective* = MYLOHYOID *adjective* M19.

mylonite /ˈmʌɪlənʌɪt/ *noun*. L19.
[ORIGIN from Greek *mulōn* mill + -ITE[1].]
PETROGRAPHY. A schist, esp. a banded one, resulting from the grinding or crushing of rocks.
■ **mylonitic** /mʌɪləˈnɪtɪk/ *adjective* pertaining to or of the nature of a mylonite L19. **myloniˈtization** *noun* = MYLONIZATION E20. **mylonitize** *verb trans.* = MYLONIZE E20. **myloniˈzation** *noun* the formation of mylonite E20. **mylonize** *verb trans.* convert into mylonite (chiefly as ***mylonized*** *ppl adjective*.) E20.

mynah /ˈmʌɪnə/ *noun*. Also **myna**, (earlier) **mina**. E17.
[ORIGIN Hindi *mainā* from Sanskrit *madana*, short for *madana-śārikā*, lit. 'love bird', from *madana* love + *śārikā* starling.]
Any of various birds of SE Asia and the Indian subcontinent that are related to starlings, some of which can mimic the human voice; *esp.* (***a***) *Acridotheres tristis* (introduced in southern Africa, Australia, and elsewhere); (***b***) *Gracula religiosa* (more fully ***hill mynah***); also (*Austral.*) = MINER 4. Also ***mynah bird***.

mynheer /mʌɪnˈhɛː, -ˈhɪə; məˈnɛː, -ˈnɪə/ *noun*. Also **mijn-**, (*S. Afr.*) **meneer** /məˈnɪə/. E17.
[ORIGIN Dutch *mijnheer* (Afrikaans *meneer*), from *mijn* my + *heer* lord, master.]
1 As a courteous form of address to or a title of a Dutch or Afrikaans man: sir, Mr. E17.
2 A Dutch or Afrikaans man, esp. a gentleman. E18.

myo- /ˈmʌɪəʊ/ *combining form* of Greek *mus* (genit. *muos*) muscle: see -O-. Before a vowel also **my-**.
■ **myoball** *noun* (*BIOLOGY*) a spheroidal syncytium cultured artificially from muscle cells, myotubes, or myoblasts L20. **myoblast** *noun* (*EMBRYOLOGY*) a cell which with other similar cells gives rise to a muscle fibre L19. **myoˈblastic** *adjective* (*EMBRYOLOGY*) of or pertaining to myoblasts L19. **myoˈchemistry** *noun* the biochemistry of muscular action M20. **myoˈclonic** *adjective* pertaining to, affected with, or of the nature of myoclonus L19. **myoˈclonus** *noun* (*MEDICINE*) spasmodic jerky contraction of groups of muscles, esp. in the limbs L19. **myocoel** *noun* [Greek *koilos* hollow] *EMBRYOLOGY* the cavity in the centre of an early embryonic myotome L19. **myocyte** *noun* (*ZOOLOGY*) a muscle cell; *esp.* (in some sponges) a contractile cell not part of an organized muscle: L19. **myoeˈlastic** *adjective* (*ANATOMY & PHONETICS*) pertaining to or involving both muscular and elastic tissue E20. **myoeˈlectric** *adjective* designating, pertaining to, or (esp. of a prosthetic limb) operated by the electric currents associated with muscular action M20. **myoeˈlectrically** *adverb* by means of myoelectric currents M20. **myoepiˈthelial** *adjective* (*ANATOMY & ZOOLOGY*) designating or pertaining to an epithelial cell containing contractile fibres, esp. in the body wall of coelenterates, and in the ducts of some mammalian glands L19. **myoepiˈthelium** *noun*, pl. **-ia**, *ANATOMY & ZOOLOGY* (a) tissue composed of myoepithelial cells L19. **myofiˈbroma** *noun*, pl. **-mas**, **-mata** /-mətə/, *MEDICINE* = MYOMA L19. **myofilament** *noun* (*ANATOMY & ZOOLOGY*) any of the ultramicroscopic thread-like aggregates of protein molecules, thick filaments of myosin and thin filaments of actin, present in contractile cells, esp. in the myofibrils of striated muscle M20. **myoˈgenesis** *noun* (*EMBRYOLOGY*) the formation of muscular tissue L19. **myoˈgenic** *adjective* produced by or arising in muscle tissue M19. **myogram** *noun* a chart or record made by a myograph L19. **myograph** *noun* an instrument for displaying or recording muscular contractions and relaxations; (now usu.) an electromyograph: M19. **myoˈgraphic** *adjective* of or pertaining to a myograph M19. **myohaemoˈglobin** *noun* (*BIOCHEMISTRY*, now *rare*) = MYOGLOBIN E20. **myo-iˈnositol** *noun* (*BIOCHEMISTRY*) an isomer of inositol which is present in animal and plant tissue and is a member of the vitamin B complex (also called ***meso-inositol***) M20. **myoˈkymia** *noun* [Greek *kuma* wave] *MEDICINE* any of several benign disorders associated with fasciculation of muscle fibres E20. **myomere** *noun* (*EMBRYOLOGY*) = MYOTOME M19. **myoˈmeric** *adjective* (*EMBRYOLOGY*) of or pertaining to myomeres L19. **myoneme** *noun* [Greek *nēma* thread] *ZOOLOGY* any of the contractile filaments in the cytoplasm of many protozoans L19. **myoˈneural** *adjective* = NEUROMUSCULAR E20. **myoˈpathic** *adjective* (*MEDICINE*) of, pertaining to, or of the nature of myopathy M19. **myˈopathy** *noun* (*MEDICINE*) (a) disease of muscle tissue M19. **myoplasm** *noun* (*ANATOMY*) = SARCOPLASM E20. **myoˈplasmic** *adjective* = SARCOPLASMIC M20. **myosarˈcoma** *noun*, pl. **-mas**, **-mata** /-mətə/, *MEDICINE* a malignant tumour of muscular tissue M19. **myoˈseptum** *noun*, pl. **-ta**, *ZOOLOGY* a membrane which separates adjacent myomeres in lower vertebrates and the embryos of higher vertebrates L19. **myotatic** /-ˈtatɪk/ *adjective* [Greek *tatikos* exerting tension] *PHYSIOLOGY* (of a muscular contraction, esp. a reflex) caused by stretching of the muscle L19. **myotube** *noun* (*EMBRYOLOGY*) a cylindrical syncytial cell formed during the development of a muscle fibre from myoblasts M20.

MYOB *abbreviation*.
Mind your own business.

myocardium /mʌɪə(ʊ)ˈkɑːdɪəm/ *noun*. L19.
[ORIGIN from MYO-, after *pericardium*.]
ANATOMY. The muscular tissue of the heart.
■ **myocardiac** *adjective* = MYOCARDIAL E20. **myocardial** *adjective* of or pertaining to the myocardium L19. **myocarˈditis** *noun* inflammation of the myocardium M19.

Myochrysine *noun* see MYOCRISIN.

myocomma /mʌɪə(ʊ)ˈkɒmə/ *noun*. Pl. **-mmas**, **-mmata** /-mətə/. M19.
[ORIGIN from MYO- + Greek *komma* segment, COMMA.]
EMBRYOLOGY. Orig. = MYOTOME. Now = MYOSEPTUM.

Myocrisin /mʌɪə(ʊ)ˈkrʌɪsɪn/ *noun*. Also ***-chrysine**. M20.
[ORIGIN French *Myochrysine*, formed as MYO- + CHRYSO- + -INE[5].]
PHARMACOLOGY. (Proprietary name for) sodium aurothiomalate, a gold-containing salt given intramuscularly to treat some cases of rheumatoid arthritis.

myofibril /mʌɪə(ʊ)ˈfʌɪbrɪl/ *noun*. Also in Latin form **-fibrilla** /-fʌɪˈbrɪlə/, pl. **-llae** /-liː/. L19.
[ORIGIN from MYO- + FIBRIL.]
ANATOMY & ZOOLOGY. Any of the numerous long cylindrical bundles of contractile myofilaments arranged in parallel in a striated muscle fibre.
■ **myofiˈbrillar** *adjective* E20.

myogen /ˈmʌɪədʒ(ə)n/ *noun*. L19.
[ORIGIN from MYO(SIN + -O- + -GEN.]
BIOCHEMISTRY. A mixture of albumins extracted from skeletal muscle plasma.

myoglobin /mʌɪə(ʊ)ˈgləʊbɪn/ *noun*. E20.
[ORIGIN from MYO- + GLOBIN, after *haemoglobin*.]
BIOCHEMISTRY. A red iron-containing protein which carries and stores oxygen in muscle cells, and resembles a subunit of haemoglobin in structure.

myology /mʌɪˈɒlədʒi/ *noun*. M17.
[ORIGIN from MYO- + -LOGY.]
1 The scientific study of muscles, esp. of their anatomical arrangement. M17.
2 (A description of) the muscular anatomy of a particular animal or part of the body. L17.
■ **myoˈlogical** *adjective* M19. **myologist** *noun* E19.

myoma /mʌɪˈəʊmə/ *noun*. Pl. **-mas**, **-mata** /-mətə/. L19.
[ORIGIN from MYO- + -OMA.]
MEDICINE. A benign tumour composed of muscular tissue.
■ **myomatous** *adjective* pertaining to or of the nature of a myoma L19. **myoˈmectomy** *noun* (an instance of) surgical removal of a myoma, esp. from the uterus L19.

myometrium /mʌɪə(ʊ)ˈmiːtrɪəm/ *noun*. E20.
[ORIGIN from MYO- + Greek *mētra* womb + -IUM.]
ANATOMY. The muscular layer which forms the bulk of the wall of the uterus.
■ **myometrial** *adjective* E20.

myomorph /ˈmʌɪə(ʊ)mɔːf/ *noun & adjective*. L19.
[ORIGIN mod. Latin *Myomorpha* (see below), from Greek *muo-*, *mus* mouse + -MORPH.]
ZOOLOGY. ▸**A** *noun*. A rodent of the suborder Myomorpha, which includes the ratlike rodents (rats, most mice, voles, hamsters, dormice, jerboas, etc.). L19.
▸**B** *adjective*. Pertaining to or designating this suborder. L19.
■ **myoˈmorphic** *adjective* L19.

myope /ˈmʌɪəʊp/ *noun & adjective*. M18.
[ORIGIN French, from Latin *myop-*, *myops* from Greek *muōps*: see MYOPIA.]
▸**A** *noun*. A short-sighted person. M18.
▸**B** *adjective*. Myopic, short-sighted. L19.

myopia /mʌɪˈəʊpɪə/ *noun*. E18.
[ORIGIN mod. Latin from late Greek *muōpia*, from Greek *muōps* short-sighted, from *muein* blink, shut (an eye): see -OPIA.]
A condition in which distant objects appear blurred because their image is focused in front of the retina; short-sightedness (*lit. & fig.*), near-sightedness.
■ Also **myopism** *noun* E19. **myopy** *noun* (now *rare*) M19.

myopic /mʌɪˈɒpɪk/ *adjective & noun*. E19.
[ORIGIN from MYOPIA + -IC.]
▸**A** *adjective*. Of, pertaining to, or affected with myopia; short-sighted, near-sighted. E19.

A. PRYCE-JONES She was very fair, with huge myopic blue eyes. M. WEST Eyes scarcely visible behind thick myopic lenses. *fig.*: G. DURRELL They had been very myopic about the whole thing.

▸**B** *noun*. = MYOPE *noun*. L19.
■ **myopical** *adjective* (*rare*) = MYOPIC *adjective* M18. **myopically** *adverb* E20.

myosin /ˈmʌɪə(ʊ)sɪn/ *noun*. M19.
[ORIGIN from MYO- + -OSE[2] + -IN[1].]
BIOCHEMISTRY. A protein which with actin forms the contractile filaments of muscle fibres.

myosis *noun* see MIOSIS.

myositis /mʌɪə(ʊ)ˈsʌɪtɪs/ *noun*. E19.
[ORIGIN Irreg. from Greek *muos* genit. of *mus* muscle + -ITIS.]
MEDICINE. (A condition characterized by) inflammation and degeneration of muscle tissue.

myosotis /mʌɪə(ʊ)ˈsəʊtɪs/ *noun*. E17.
[ORIGIN Latin (see below) from Greek *muosōtis*, from *muos* genit. of *mus* mouse + *ōt-*, *ous* ear.]
A plant of the genus *Myosotis*; a forget-me-not. Formerly also, mouse-ear hawkweed, *Pilosella officinarum*.
■ Also ˈ**myosote** *noun* L19.

myotic *adjective* see MIOTIC.

myotome /ˈmʌɪətəʊm/ *noun*. M19.
[ORIGIN from MYO- + -TOME.]
EMBRYOLOGY & ZOOLOGY. (Each segment of) a part of the embryonic mesoderm which gives rise to the skeletal muscles; esp. in fish and amphibians, each of a series of muscle blocks either side of the spine.

myotomy /mʌɪˈɒtəmi/ *noun*. *rare*. L17.
[ORIGIN from MYO- + -TOMY.]
†**1** (An anatomical treatise on) the dissection of muscles. L17–M18.
2 Surgical division of a muscle; an instance of this. L19.
■ **myoˈtomic** *adjective* M19.

myotonia /mʌɪə(ʊ)ˈtəʊnɪə/ *noun*. Also **mya-**. L19.
[ORIGIN from MYO- + Greek *tonos* TONE *noun* + -IA[1].]
MEDICINE. (A condition characterized by) an apparent inability to relax voluntary muscles after vigorous effort. **myotonia atrophica** /əˈtrɒfɪkə/ [Latin = atrophic] = *DYSTROPHIA myotonica*. **myotonia congenita** /kənˈdʒɛnɪtə/ [Latin = congenital] a rare hereditary disease appearing in young children, characterized by myotonia without muscular wasting or other symptoms; also called ***Thomsen's disease***.
■ **myotonic** /-ˈtɒnɪk/ *adjective* of, pertaining to, or affected by myotonia L19.

myrcene /ˈməːsiːn/ *noun*. L19.
[ORIGIN from mod. Latin *Myrcia* former genus name of bayberry + -ENE.]
CHEMISTRY. An oily liquid terpene found in essential oils of bayberry, hop, and other plants; 2-methyl-6-methylene-2,7-octadiene, $C_{10}H_{16}$.

myria- /ˈmɪrɪə/ *combining form*. Also (*rare*) **myrio-** /ˈmɪrɪəʊ/; before a vowel **myri-**. E19.
[ORIGIN from Greek *murias*, *murios*, or *murioi*: see MYRIAD.]
1 With the sense 'very numerous', as ***myriapod***.
2 Used (not now in standard scientific use) in names of units of measurement to denote a factor of ten thousand (10^4), as ***myriagram***, ***myriametre***.
■ **myriaˈmetric** *adjective* (ASTRONOMY) consisting of or designating radio waves with a wavelength between 10 and 100 kilometres M20.

myriad /ˈmɪrɪəd/ *noun & adjective*. M16.
[ORIGIN Late Latin *myriad-*, *-as* from Greek *muriad-*, *-as*, from *murios* countless, innumerable, pl. *murioi* ten thousand: see -AD[1].]
▸**A** *noun*. **1** Chiefly CLASSICAL HISTORY. A unit of ten thousand. M16.
2 a In *pl.* Countless numbers, hosts, (*of*). M16. ▸**b** A countless number, a host, (*of*). E18.

a C. CHAPLIN Broadway . . began to light up with myriads of coloured electric bulbs. A. C. CLARKE Yet though myriads sought forgetfulness, even more found satisfaction. **b** F. W. ROBERTSON A myriad of different universes.

▸**B** *adjective*. **1** With pl. noun: existing in myriads; of indefinitely great number; countless, innumerable. With sing. noun: consisting of myriads; having countless phases or aspects. Chiefly *literary*. M18.

Chambers's Journal For the trespasser, the dangers were myriad. S. J. PERELMAN The myriad twinkling lights of Los Angeles. R. C. ZAEHNER The myriad sum-total of ever-reincarnating souls.

2 Chiefly CLASSICAL HISTORY. Ten thousand. *rare*. L19.
■ **myriadfold** *adjective & noun* (*literary*) (**a**) *noun* an infinitely large amount (used *adverbially*); (**b**) *adjective* countless, innumerable; having innumerable aspects or features: E18. **myriadth** *adjective* (chiefly *literary*) that is a very minute part of a whole E19.

myriapod /ˈmɪrɪəpɒd/ *adjective & noun*. E19.
[ORIGIN mod. Latin *Myriapoda* (see below), formed as MYRIA- + -POD.]
ZOOLOGY. ▸**A** *noun*. An arthropod of the class Myriapoda, which comprises the centipedes and millipedes. E19.
▸**B** *adjective*. Having very many feet; *spec.* pertaining to or of the nature of a myriapod. E19.
■ **myriˈapodal**, **myriˈapodan** *adjectives* = MYRIAPOD *adjective* L19. **myriˈapodous** *adjective* = MYRIAPOD *adjective* M19.

myrica /mɪˈrʌɪkə/ *noun*. M16.
[ORIGIN Latin from Greek *murikē*]
†**1** A tamarisk. M16–M19.
2 Any of various shrubs of the genus *Myrica* (family Myricaceae), with fragrant leaves, *esp.* bog myrtle, *M. gale*, and (in the US) a bayberry, esp. *M. pennsylvanica*. L18.

myricin /mɪˈrʌɪsɪn, ˈmʌɪrɪsɪn, ˈmɪ-/ *noun*. E19.
[ORIGIN from mod. Latin *Myrica* (*cerifera*) wax myrtle (a source of myricin): see MYRICA, -IN[1].]
CHEMISTRY. A wax ester, myricyl palmitate, found in beeswax and some plant waxes.

myricyl /mɪˈrʌɪsʌɪl, -sɪl, ˈmʌɪrɪs-, ˈmɪ-/ *noun*. M19.
[ORIGIN formed as MYRICIN + -YL.]
CHEMISTRY. = MELISSYL.
– COMB.: **myricyl alcohol** = *MELISSYL alcohol*; **myricyl palmitate** = MYRICIN.

myringo- /mɪˈrɪndʒəʊ, -ŋg-/ *combining form* of mod. Latin *myringa* eardrum: see -O-. Before a vowel **myring-**. Cf. TYMPANO-.
■ **myrinˈgitis** /-dʒ-/ *noun* inflammation of the eardrum M19. **myringoplasty** *noun* (an instance of) surgical repair of the eardrum, esp. by grafting L19. **myringotome** *noun* a surgical instrument for perforating the eardrum L19. **myrinˈgotomy** *noun* (an instance of) surgical incision into the eardrum to relieve pressure or drain fluid, esp. as a treatment for otitis media L19.

myrio- *combining form* see MYRIA-.

myriologue /ˈmɪrɪəlɒg/ *noun*. E19.
[ORIGIN mod. Greek *muriologion* alt. of *moirologion*, from classical Greek *moira* fate: see -LOGUE.]
An extemporaneous Greek or Turkish lament or funeral song, composed and sung by a woman.
■ **myriologist** /mɪrɪˈɒlədʒɪst/ *noun* a singer or composer of a myriologue M19.

myriorama /mɪrɪəˈrɑːmə/ *noun*. E19.
[ORIGIN from *myrio-* var. of MYRIA-, after *panorama*.]
A picture made of a number of separate sections able to be combined in numerous ways to form different scenes.

myristic /mʌɪˈrɪstɪk, mɪ-/ *adjective*. L16.
[ORIGIN from mod. Latin *Myristica* genus name, from medieval Latin (*nux*) *myristica* nutmeg, from Greek *murizein* anoint: see -IC.]
†**1** Pertaining to or derived from nutmegs. Only in L16.
2 CHEMISTRY. ***myristic acid***, a straight-chain fatty acid found in oil of nutmeg and other vegetable and animal fats; tetradecanoic acid, $CH_3(CH_2)_{12}COOH$. M19.
■ **myristate** *noun* a salt or ester of myristic acid M19. **myristicin** *noun* a toxic terpene obtained from volatile oils of nutmeg and mace M19. **myristin** *noun* a naturally occurring triglyceride, glyceryl trimyristate M19. **myristyl** *noun* a radical derived from myristic acid, either $C_{14}H_{29}\cdot$ (tetradecyl) or $C_{13}H_{27}CO\cdot$ M19.

myrmeco- /ˈməːmɪkəʊ, məːmiːˈkəʊ/ *combining form* of Greek *murmēk-*, *murmēx* ant (freq. taken to include termites).
■ **myrmecochore** *noun* [Greek *khōrein* spread] BOTANY an oily seed adapted to facilitate dispersal by ants; a plant with such seeds: E20. **myrmecoˈchorous** *adjective* (BOTANY) that is a myrmecochore; pertaining to myrmecochores: E20. **myrmecoˈlogical** *adjective* of or pertaining to myrmecology L19. **myrmeˈcologist** *noun* an expert in or student of myrmecology L19. **myrmeˈcology** *noun* the scientific study of ants L19. **myrmeˈcophagid** *noun & adjective* (ZOOLOGY) (**a**) *noun* an anteater of the family Myrmecophagidae; (**b**) *adjective* pertaining to or designating this family: L19. **myrmeˈcophagous** *adjective* that eats ants, characterized by feeding on ants M19. **myrmecophile** *noun* a myrmecophilous insect L19. **myrmeˈcophilous** *adjective* (BOTANY & ZOOLOGY) pertaining to or exhibiting myrmecophily M19. **myrmeˈcophily** *noun* (BOTANY & ZOOLOGY) the condition of living in association with ants, esp. (in an insect) of living in an ant colony or (in a plant) of being specially adapted to feed or shelter ants L19. **myrmecophyte** *noun* a myrmecophilous plant, an ant plant L19.

myrmecobius /məːmɪˈkəʊbɪəs/ *noun*. Also **M-**. M19.
[ORIGIN mod. Latin, from Greek *murmēkobios* lit. 'living like an ant', formed as MYRMECO- + *bioun* live.]
= NUMBAT. Now chiefly as mod. Latin genus name.

myrmecoid /ˈməːmɪkɔɪd/ *adjective*. *rare*. M19.
[ORIGIN from MYRMECO- + -OID.]
Antlike.

myrmekite /ˈməːmɪkʌɪt/ *noun*. E20.
[ORIGIN from Greek *murmēkia* anthill, wart + -ITE[1].]
PETROGRAPHY. Plagioclase intergrown with drops or wormlike forms of quartz.
■ **myrmeˈkitic** *adjective* of the nature of or containing myrmekite E20. **myrmekitiˈzation** *noun* formation of or conversion into myrmekite E20.

myrmeleon /məːˈmiːlɪən/ *noun*. M18.
[ORIGIN mod. Latin, contr. of medieval Latin *mirmicoleon* from Greek *murmēkoleōn*, from *murmēk-*, *murmēx* ant + *leōn* lion.]
= ***ant lion*** s.v. ANT *noun*. Now *rare* or *obsolete* exc. as mod. Latin genus name.

myrmicine /ˈməːmɪsʌɪn/ *adjective*. L19.
[ORIGIN from mod. Latin *Myrmicinae* (see below), from *Myrmica* genus name, from Greek *murmēk-*, *murmēx* ant: see -INE[1].]
ENTOMOLOGY. Designating or pertaining to the subfamily Myrmicinae of stinging ants.

myrmidon /ˈməːmɪd(ə)n/ *noun*. Also (esp. in sense 1) **M-**. LME.
[ORIGIN Latin *Myrmidones* (pl.) from Greek *Murmidones* (as according to legend orig. created from *murmēkes* ants).]
1 A member of a warlike people of ancient Thessaly, whom, according to a Homeric story, Achilles led to the siege of Troy. LME.
†**2** A bodyguard; a faithful follower or servant. E17–E19.
3 An unscrupulously faithful follower or hireling; a hired thug. M17.
myrmidon of the law, **myrmidon of justice** *arch.* (*derog.*) a police officer, bailiff, or other low-ranking administrative officer of the law.
■ **Myrmidonian** /məːmɪˈdəʊnɪən/ *adjective* (now *rare*) designating or pertaining to the Myrmidons L16.

myrnyong *noun* var. of MIRRNYONG.

M

myrobalan /mʌɪˈrɒbələn/ *noun*. LME.
[ORIGIN Old French & mod. French *myrobolan* or its source Latin *myrobalanum* from Greek *murobalanon*, from *muron* balsam, unguent + *balanos* acorn, date, ben nut.]
1 The astringent plumlike fruit of any of various tropical trees of the genus *Terminalia* (family Combretaceae), esp. *T. chebula* and *T. bellirica*, used in tanning and dyeing; a tree bearing such a fruit. LME.
BELLERIC ***myrobalan***. CHEBULE ***myrobalan***.
2 In full ***myrobalan plum***. The fruit of the cherry plum, *Prunus cerasifera*. M17.

myronic /mʌɪˈrɒnɪk/ *adjective*. M19.
[ORIGIN from Greek *muron* unguent, perfume + -IC.]
CHEMISTRY. ***myronic acid***, a sulphur-containing acidic glycoside of which sinigrin, obtained from black mustard, is the potassium salt.
■ ˈ**myronate** *noun* a salt or ester of myronic acid; ***potassium myronate*** = SINIGRIN: M19.

myrosin /ˈmɪrəsɪn/ *noun*. M19.
[ORIGIN from MYRONIC + -*s*- + -IN[1].]
BIOCHEMISTRY. An enzyme which catalyses the hydrolysis of sinigrin and other sulphur-containing glycosides.

myrrh /məː/ *noun*[1].
[ORIGIN Old English *myrra*, *myrre*, corresp. to Old Saxon *myrra* (Dutch *mirre*), Old High German *myrra* (German *Myrrhe*), Old Norse *mirra*, from Germanic = Latin *myrrha* from Greek *murra*, of Semitic origin (cf. Arabic *murr* bitter, Aramaic *mōrā*, Hebrew *mōr*, Akkadian *murru*).]
1 A bitter aromatic resinous exudate from the stem of various Arabian and African trees of the genus *Commiphora* (family Burseraceae), esp. *C. abyssinica* and *C. myrrha*, formerly important in perfumery and as an ingredient of incense; PHARMACOLOGY a tincture made from this. OE.
†**2** = ***myrrh tree*** below. LME–M17.
– COMB.: **myrrh tree** a tree that yields myrrh.
■ **myrrhed** *adjective* (*rare*) mixed or sprinkled with myrrh L15. **myrrhy** *adjective* smelling like or redolent of myrrh L17.

myrrh /məː/ *noun*[2]. L16.
[ORIGIN Latin *myrris* from Greek *murris*.]
= ***sweet*** CICELY.

myrrhophore /ˈməːrəfɔː, ˈmɪr-/ *noun*. M19.
[ORIGIN from Greek *murra* MYRRH *noun*[1] + -O- + -PHORE.]
A woman carrying spices to the sepulchre of Christ, as represented in art.

myrtaceous /məːˈteɪʃəs/ *adjective*. M19.
[ORIGIN from mod. Latin *Myrtaceae* (see below) fem. pl. of Latin *myrtaceus*, from *myrtus*: see MYRTLE, -ACEOUS.]
BOTANY. Of or pertaining to the family Myrtaceae, of which the myrtle is the type.

myrtle /ˈməːt(ə)l/ *noun*. LME.
[ORIGIN medieval Latin *myrtilla*, *-illus* (whence Old French *myrtille*, *-il*), dim. of Latin *myrtus*, *-ta* from Greek *murtos*.]
†**1** The fruit or berry of the shrub *Myrtus communis* (see below). LME–M18.
2 Any of various evergreen shrubs of the genus *Myrtus* (family Myrtaceae), esp. *M. communis*, of southern Europe, with white sweet-scented flowers, used in perfumery. LME. ▸**b** Any of various plants of this and other families resembling myrtle in appearance, fragrance, etc.; *spec.* (*US*) periwinkle, *Vinca minor*. Usu. with specifying word. L16.
b ***bog myrtle***, ***candleberry myrtle***, ***crape myrtle***, ***honey myrtle***, ***wax-myrtle***, etc.
3 *ellipt.* = ***myrtle-green*** below. L19.
– COMB.: **myrtle-berry** (*a*) the fruit of a myrtle; (*b*) [cf. French *myrtille*] the fruit of the bilberry, *Vaccinium myrtillus*; **myrtle bird** = ***myrtle warbler*** below; **myrtle green** a shade of deep green like that of myrtle leaves; **myrtle-of-the-river** a large evergreen shrub of the myrtle family, *Calyptranthes zuzygium*, of tropical America; **myrtle warbler** a warbler found in eastern N. America, now considered to be a race of the yellow-rumped warbler, *Dendroica coronata*; **myrtle wine** wine made from myrtle berries.

myself /mʌɪˈsɛlf, mɪˈsɛlf/ *pronoun*. Orig. (now *non-standard*) **meself** /mɪˈsɛlf/. OE.
[ORIGIN from ME *pronoun* + SELF *adjective* (but long interpreted as MY *adjective* + SELF *noun*).]
▸ **I** Orig. *emphatic*.
1 In apposition to the subjective pronoun *I* or (less commonly) *me*: in my own person; for my part. OE.

J. STEINBECK If I keep oiling my rifle, I myself may be an officer one day. J. C. POWYS I can tell you myself of one person. G. GREENE Myself I don't care to go fifty yards from the waterfront. R. P. JHABVALA I had . . hoisted my trunk and bedding on to my shoulders and carried them up myself.

2 (Not appositional.) ▸**a** Subjective: I myself (in emphatic use now *arch.* & *rhet.*); (pred. after *be* & after *than*, *as*) I. ME. ▸**b** Objective: me personally (*arch.* in emphatic use). ME.

a S. RICHARDSON Enough to make a better man than myself . . run into madness. E. FITZGERALD Myself when young did eagerly frequent Doctor and Saint. J. CONRAD Being myself a quiet individual I take it that what all men are really after is . . peace. **b** G. BORROW Several of the ultra-popish bishops . . had denounced the Bible, the Bible Society, and myself. T. HARDY As for Steve and myself, we were deeply moved. J. BUCHAN My earliest recollections are not of myself, but of my environment. I. MURDOCH Crystal was . . like myself, unmarried.

▸ **II** *refl*. **3** Refl. (direct, indirect, & after prepositions) corresp. to the subjective pronoun *I*: (to, for, etc.) me personally, me. OE.

M. AMIS I wrapped myself in a sheet and climbed the stairs like a ghost. J. SIMMS I found myself wondering whether I should not try to talk to her.

– PHRASES: **be myself** (*a*) act in my normal unconstrained manner; (*b*) feel as well as I usually do (usu. in neg. contexts). **by myself** on my own.

Mysian /ˈmɪsɪən/ *noun* & *adjective*. L16.
[ORIGIN from Latin *Mysia*, Greek *Musia* Mysia (see below) + -AN.]
▸ **A** *noun*. **1** A native or inhabitant of ancient Mysia in NW Asia Minor. L16.
2 The language of ancient Mysia. M20.
▸ **B** *adjective*. Of or pertaining to ancient Mysia or its language. E17.

mysid /ˈmʌɪsɪd/ *noun* & *adjective*. L19.
[ORIGIN from MYSIS + -ID[3].]
ZOOLOGY. ▸**A** *noun*. A small shrimplike usu. marine crustacean of the family Mysidae or the suborder Mysidacea; an opossum shrimp. L19.
▸ **B** *adjective*. Of, pertaining to, or designating this family or suborder. L19.

mysis /ˈmʌɪsɪs/ *noun*. E19.
[ORIGIN mod. Latin *Mysis* (see below), of unknown origin.]
ZOOLOGY. **1** A mysid shrimp of the genus *Mysis*. Now chiefly as mod. Latin genus name. E19.
2 ***mysis phase***, ***mysis stage***, a stage in the life cycle of certain decapods in which they resemble a shrimp of the genus *Mysis*. M19.

Mysoline /ˈmʌɪsəliːn/ *noun*. M20.
[ORIGIN Unknown.]
PHARMACOLOGY. (Proprietary name for) primidone.

mysophobia /mʌɪsəˈfəʊbɪə/ *noun*. L19.
[ORIGIN from Greek *musos* uncleanness + -PHOBIA.]
Irrational fear of dirt or defilement.

Mysore /mʌɪˈsɔː, ˈmʌɪsɔː/ *noun*. E20.
[ORIGIN See below.]
Coffee grown in or around Karnataka (formerly called Mysore), a state in southern India.

Mysorean /mʌɪsəˈriːən/ *noun* & *adjective*. *hist*. M18.
[ORIGIN from *Mysore* (see below) + -AN.]
▸**A** *noun*. A native or inhabitant of Mysore (now Karnataka) in southern India. M18.
▸ **B** *adjective*. Of or pertaining to Mysore. M19.

mysost /ˈmʌɪsɒst/ *noun*. M19.
[ORIGIN Norwegian, from *myse* whey + *ost* cheese.]
A Norwegian whey cheese, orig. made from goat's milk.

†**myst** *noun*. L17–M19.
[ORIGIN Latin *mysta*, *mystes* from Greek *mustēs*: see MYSTIC.]
= MYSTES.

mystacial /mɪˈsteɪʃ(ə)l/ *adjective*. L18.
[ORIGIN from Greek *mustax*, *-tak-* (see MUSTACHIO) + -IAL.]
Resembling or in the position of a moustache; moustachial.

mystae *noun* pl. of MYSTES.

mystagogic /mɪstəˈgɒdʒɪk/ *adjective*. M17.
[ORIGIN Late Latin *mystagogicus*, Greek *mustagōgikos*, from *mustagōgos*: see MYSTAGOGUE, -IC.]
Of or pertaining to a mystagogue or mystagogy; relating to instruction in mysteries.
■ **mystagogical** *adjective* E17. **mystagogically** *adverb* M19.

mystagogue /ˈmɪstəgɒg/ *noun*. M16.
[ORIGIN French, or Latin *mystagogus* from Greek *mustagōgos*, from *mustēs* (see MYSTIC) + *agōgos* leading, from *agein* to lead.]
In ancient Greece, a person who gave preparatory instruction to candidates for initiation into the Eleusinian or other mysteries; *gen*. a person who introduces others to religious mysteries, a teacher of mystical doctrines, a creator or disseminator of mystical doctrines.
■ **mystaˈgoguery** *noun* the doctrines or practices of a mystagogue E20.

mystagogy /ˈmɪstəgɒdʒi/ *noun*. L16.
[ORIGIN Latin *mystagogia* from Greek *mustagōgia*, from *mustagōgos*: see MYSTAGOGUE, -Y[3].]
(An) initiation into mysteries; instruction preparatory to initiation into mysteries; the doctrines or practices of a mystagogue.

mysterial /mɪˈstɪərɪəl/ *adjective*. Now *rare*. LME.
[ORIGIN Late Latin *mysterialis*, from *mysterium* MYSTERY *noun*[1]: see -IAL.]
Mysterious. Formerly also, mystical.

mysteriarch /mɪˈstɪərɪɑːk/ *noun*. M17.
[ORIGIN ecclesiastical Latin *mysteriarches* from Greek *mustēriarkhes*, from *mustērion* MYSTERY *noun*[1]: see -ARCH.]
A person who presides over mysteries.

mysterioso /mɪˌstɪərɪˈəʊzəʊ/ *adjective*. M20.
[ORIGIN Italian = mysterious.]
MUSIC. Executed in a mysterious manner.

mysteriosophy /mɪˌstɪərɪˈɒsəfi/ *noun*. L19.
[ORIGIN from Greek *mustērion* MYSTERY *noun*[1] + *sophia* wisdom: see -Y[3].]
A system of doctrine concerning mysteries.

mysterious /mɪˈstɪərɪəs/ *adjective*. L15.
[ORIGIN from French *mystérieux*, from *mystère* MYSTERY *noun*[1]: see -IOUS.]
1 Difficult or impossible to understand, explain, or identify; of obscure origin, nature, or purpose. L15. ▸**b** Of a person: delighting in mystery, deliberately enigmatic; elusive, secretive. M17.

W. COWPER God moves in a mysterious way His wonders to perform. J. STEINBECK The communications system on Cannery Row is mysterious to the point of magic. A. MILLER The mysterious deaths . . of the explorers who had broken into his tomb. **b** A. GRAY He wanted to seem mysterious to these boys, someone ageless with strange powers.

†**2** Dealing with or versed in mysteries; using occult arts. L16–L18.
3 That is due to a mystery. *rare*. M17.
■ **mysteriously** *adverb* L15. **mysteriousness** *noun* M17.

†**mysterise** *verb* var. of MYSTERIZE.

mysterium tremendum /mɪˌstɪərɪəm trɪˈmɛndəm/ *noun phr*. E20.
[ORIGIN Latin = tremendous mystery.]
A great or overwhelming mystery, *esp*. the great or overwhelming mystery of God or of existence.

†**mysterize** *verb*. Also **-ise**. M17.
[ORIGIN from MYSTERY *noun*[1] + -IZE.]
1 *verb trans*. Interpret mystically. Only in M17.
2 *verb intrans*. Make mysteries of things. E–M19.

mystery /ˈmɪst(ə)ri/ *noun*[1]. ME.
[ORIGIN Anglo-Norman equiv. of Old French *mistere* (mod. *mystère*), or immed. from the source Latin *mysterium* from Greek *mustērion* secret thing or ceremony, from base also of *mustikos* secret, MYSTIC.]
†**1** Mystic presence; hidden or mystic meaning; hidden religious symbolism. ME–L17.
2 A religious belief based on divine revelation, *esp*. a doctrine of faith involving difficulties which human reason is incapable of solving. Also *gen*., a hidden or secret thing; a thing beyond human knowledge or comprehension; a riddle, an enigma, a puzzle; a person or thing not understood. LME.

SWIFT The Mysteries of the Christian Religion. M. ANGELOU He remained a mystery in my childhood. N. CHOMSKY The neurophysiology of language remains almost a total mystery. B. CHATWIN Or debate with learned rabbis the mysteries of the Cabbala.

make a mystery of treat as a secret; keep (a thing) secret in order to make an impression.
3 A religious ordinance or rite, *esp*. a Christian sacrament; in *pl*., the Eucharist. LME.
4 a A secret rite of an ancient religion or other occult society to which only the initiated are admitted. Usu. in *pl*. L15. ▸**b** A secret of Freemasonry. Usu. in *pl*. M18.
5 †**a** A personal secret. E16–E17. ▸**b** An action or practice shrouded in secrecy; a technical operation in a trade or art, now esp. a trivial one. Cf. MYSTERY *noun*[2]. L16. ▸**c** A political or diplomatic secret; a secret of state. Usu. more fully ***mystery of state***. Now *rare* or *obsolete*. E17.

b HANNAH MORE No man is allowed to set up in an ordinary trade till he has served a long apprenticeship to its mysteries. DISRAELI Harassed with all the mysteries of packing.

6 a The condition or property of being secret or obscure; mysteriousness. Also, mysteries collectively, mysterious matter. E17. ▸**b** The behaviour or attitude of mind of a person who makes a secret of (esp. intrinsically unimportant) things. L17.

a HENRY MILLER The world was full of wonder and mystery. T. O. ECHEWA Sun-glasses for mystery—eyes that saw without being seen.

a bag of mystery: see BAG *noun*.
7 CHRISTIAN CHURCH. An incident in the life of Jesus or of a saint regarded as an object of commemoration or as having a mystical significance; *spec*. each of the events in the life of Jesus contemplated with the use of a rosary, a division of a rosary corresponding to such an event. M17.
8 A miracle play. M18.
9 A girl newly arrived in a town or city; a girl with no fixed address; a young or inexperienced prostitute. *slang*. M20.
10 A mystery story; a mystery novel etc. M20.
– COMB.: **mystery-bag** = ***bag of mystery*** s.v. BAG *noun*; **mystery man** (*a*) a conjuror, a medicine man; (*b*) a man about whom little is known; **mystery novel** a novel about the detection of a crime etc., a novel in which a mystery is unravelled; **mystery play** (*a*) = sense 8 above; (*b*) a play about the detection of a crime etc., a play in which a mystery is unravelled; **mystery religion** an ancient religion based on secret rites; **mystery ship** an armed and camouflaged merchantman used in the First World War as a decoy or to destroy submarines; **mystery shopper** a person employed to visit a shop or restaurant incognito in order to assess the quality of the goods or services; **mystery story** a detective or crime story, a story in which a mystery is unravelled; **mystery tour**, **mystery trip** a pleasure trip for which there is no advance announcement of the place(s) to be visited; **mystery woman** a woman about whom little is known; **mystery writer** a writer of mystery stories.

mystery /ˈmɪst(ə)ri/ *noun*[2]. Also **mistery**. LME.
[ORIGIN medieval Latin *misterium* (cf. MISTER *noun*[1]) contr. of Latin *ministerium* MINISTRY by assoc. with *mysterium*: see MYSTERY *noun*[1].]
†**1 a** An occupation; an office rendered. LME–M16. ▸†**b** A helpful thing. Only in L16.
2 a A handicraft; a craft, an art; one's trade, profession, or calling. *arch*. LME. ▸†**b** Skill, art. E–M17.
a art and mystery: a formula employed in indentures binding apprentices to a trade.
3 A trade guild or company. Now *arch*. or *hist*. L15.

mystes /ˈmɪstiːz/ *noun*. Pl. ***mystae*** /ˈmɪstiː/. L17.
[ORIGIN Latin from Greek *mustēs*: see MYSTIC. Cf. MYST.]
A person initiated into mysteries.

mystic /ˈmɪstɪk/ *noun* & *adjective*. ME.
[ORIGIN Old French & mod. French *mystique* or Latin *mysticus* adjectives from Greek *mustikos*, from *mustēs* initiated person, from *muein* close (the eyes, lips), initiate: see -IC. Cf. MYSTICAL.]
▸ **A** *noun*. †**1** Mystical meaning; mystical representation. Only in ME.
2 Chiefly CHRISTIAN CHURCH. Orig., an exponent of mystical theology, a person who maintains the validity and the supreme importance of mystical theology. Later, a person who seeks by contemplation and self-surrender to obtain union with or absorption into God, or who believes in the possibility of the spiritual apprehension of knowledge inaccessible to the intellect. L17.
3 = MYSTES. *rare*. M19.
▸ **B** *adjective* **1 a** Chiefly CHRISTIAN CHURCH. Spiritually allegorical or symbolical; of the nature of, or characteristic of, a sacred mystery; pertaining to religious mysteries; (now *rhet.*) having direct spiritual significance, transcending human understanding. LME. ▸**b** *spec*. Designating or pertaining to the branch of theology relating to direct communion of the soul with God. Now *rare*. M17.
2 Of or pertaining to ancient religious mysteries or other occult rites or practices; occult, esoteric. E17.
†**3** Secret, concealed. Only in 17.
4 Of hidden meaning or nature; enigmatic, mysterious. M17.
5 Inspiring an awed sense of mystery. M19.
■ **mysticly** *adverb* (*rare*) L15.

mystical /ˈmɪstɪk(ə)l/ *adjective*. E16.
[ORIGIN formed as MYSTIC: see -ICAL. Cf. MYSTIC.]
1 Having an unseen, unknown, or mysterious origin, character, or influence; of hidden or esoteric meaning. E16. ▸†**b** Of a person: obscure in speech or in style. E–L17.

LYTTON Mystical presentiments of the evil days that were to fall on England.

2 a Chiefly CHRISTIAN CHURCH. Having a spiritual character or significance that transcends human understanding. E16.

▸**b** Designating or pertaining to the branch of theology relating to direct communion of the soul with God. Also, of, pertaining to, or characteristic of mystics; relating to or of the nature of mysticism. **M16.**

> **a** R. COKE These two individual persons . . are made one mystical person. E. B. PUSEY Jerome gives here the mystical meaning. **b** M. IGNATIEFF Paul . . retained a mystical reverence for the office of Tsar. A. STORR A mystical experience of unity with the universe.

3 Of or pertaining to mysterious or occult rites or practices. **L16.**

> P. BENSON Americans came to explore the mystical sights of Somerset.

†**4** Secret, concealed. Only in **17.**
■ **mysti'cality** *noun* (*rare*) **M19.** **mystically** *adverb* **E16.** **mysticalness** *noun* (*rare*) **E17.**

mysticete /ˈmɪstɪsiːt/ *noun.* Formerly also in Latin form †**-cetus. L18.**
[ORIGIN mod. Latin *Mysticeti* (see below) from Greek *mustikētos* (in old editions of Aristotle), for *ho mus to kētos* 'the mouse, the whale so called'.]
ZOOLOGY. A whale of the suborder Mysticeti of baleen or whalebone whales; *spec.* the Greenland right whale or bowhead, *Balaena mysticetus.*

mysticise *verb* var. of MYSTICIZE.

mysticism /ˈmɪstɪsɪz(ə)m/ *noun.* **E18.**
[ORIGIN from MYSTIC + -ISM.]
1 Religious belief characterized by vague or confused thought; belief based on the assumption of occult qualities or mysterious agencies. **E18.**
2 The beliefs characteristic of mystics; belief in or reliance on the possibility of spiritual apprehension of knowledge inaccessible to the intellect. **M18.**

mysticity /mɪˈstɪsɪti/ *noun.* Now *rare.* **M18.**
[ORIGIN from MYSTIC + -ITY, after French *mysticité.*]
The quality of being mystic or mystical.

mysticize /ˈmɪstɪsʌɪz/ *verb trans.* Also **-ise. L17.**
[ORIGIN from MYSTIC *adjective* + -IZE.]
Make mystical; introduce a mystical element into, give a mystic meaning to.

mystico- /ˈmɪstɪkəʊ/ *combining form.* **M19.**
[ORIGIN from MYSTIC + -O-.]
Forming adjectives with the senses 'mystical and —', 'mystically —', as ***mystico-allegoric***, ***mystico-religious***.

mystification /ˌmɪstɪfɪˈkeɪʃ(ə)n/ *noun.* **E19.**
[ORIGIN French, formed as MYSTIFY: see -FICATION.]
1 The action of mystifying a person; an instance of this. **E19.**
2 The condition or fact of being mystified. **E19.**

mystificator /ˈmɪstɪfɪˌkeɪtə/ *noun. rare.* **E19.**
[ORIGIN French *mystificateur*, formed as MYSTIFY: see -FIC, -ATOR.]
A mystifier.

mystificatory /ˌmɪstɪfɪˈkeɪt(ə)ri/ *adjective.* **M19.**
[ORIGIN from (the same root as) MYSTIFICATOR: see -ORY².]
Mystifying.

†**mystified** *noun* var. of MISTIFIED.

mystified /ˈmɪstɪfʌɪd/ *adjective.* **E19.**
[ORIGIN from MYSTIFY + -ED¹.]
†**1** Mysterious, confusing. Only in **E19.**
2 Bewildered, puzzled, perplexed. **M19.**

mystifier /ˈmɪstɪfʌɪə/ *noun.* **E19.**
[ORIGIN from MYSTIFY + -ER¹.]
A person who mystifies another or others; a person who or thing which causes perplexity or bewilderment.

mystify /ˈmɪstɪfʌɪ/ *verb trans.* **E19.**
[ORIGIN French *mystifier*, irreg. from *mystère* MYSTERY *noun*¹ or *mystique* MYSTIC: see -FY.]
1 Bewilder, perplex; play on the credulity of; hoax. **E19.**
2 Wrap up or involve in mystery; make mystical; interpret mystically. **E19.**
3 Involve in obscurity; obscure the meaning or character of. **E19.**
■ **mystifyingly** *adverb* in a mystifying manner **M20.**

mystique /mɪˈstiːk/ *noun.* **L19.**
[ORIGIN French: see MYSTIC.]
The atmosphere of mystery and veneration investing some doctrines, arts, professions, or people; a mysterious attraction; any professional skill or technique designed or able to mystify and impress the lay person.

> G. ORWELL All the beliefs . . that characterize our time are really designed to sustain the mystique of the Party. *Times* There is a mystique about violins, especially old violins. J. GATHORNE-HARDY Nannies had their own mystique—their medical and superstitious lore.

PARTICIPATION ***mystique***.

myth /mɪθ/ *noun.* **M19.**
[ORIGIN mod. Latin *mythus*, late Latin *mythos* from Greek *muthos*. Cf. MYTHOS, MYTHUS.]
1 A traditional story, either wholly or partially fictitious, providing an explanation for or embodying a popular idea concerning some natural or social phenomenon or some religious belief or ritual; *spec.* one involving supernatural persons, actions, or events; a similar newly created story. **M19.**

> A. H. SAYCE An attempt . . to extract a pseudo-history from the Greek myths. J. D. CRICHTON At the heart of the ritual action, was the myth. M. HUGHES The heroes and heroines of the old myths and sagas.

solar myth: see SOLAR *adjective*¹ & *noun*².
2 A widely held (esp. untrue or discredited popular) story or belief; a misconception; a misrepresentation of the truth; an exaggerated or idealized conception of a person, institution, etc.; a person, institution, etc., widely idealized or misrepresented. **M19.**

> GEO. ELIOT Many silly myths are already afloat about me, in addition to the truth. J. W. FULBRIGHT The master myth of the cold war is that the Communist bloc is a monolith. B. EMECHETA One of the myths she had been brought up to believe: that the white man never lied.

3 Myths collectively or as a genre; the technique or habit of creating myths. **M19.**

> J. PLAMENATZ Themes as old as poetry and as myth.

■ **mytheme** *noun* [-EME] an element of a myth regarded as a unit of structure **M20.** **mythless** *adjective* **L19.**

mythi *noun* pl. of MYTHUS.

mythic /ˈmɪθɪk/ *adjective.* **M17.**
[ORIGIN Late Latin *mythicus* from Greek *muthikos*, from *muthos* MYTH: see -IC.]
Mythical; widely idealized or misrepresented; fantastic, bizarre.

> T. WRIGHT The names of the different mythic beings and of their habitation and worship. P. LOMAS When we speak of the mysteries of life we may resort to imaginative, poetic or mythic language. J. UGLOW In its forbidden quality . . , their love has a mythic resonance. *Washington Times* A computer crash of mythic proportions.

mythical /ˈmɪθɪk(ə)l/ *adjective.* **L17.**
[ORIGIN formed as MYTHIC + -AL¹.]
1 Of the nature of, consisting of, or based on a myth or myths; of, pertaining to, or characteristic of myth; having no foundation in fact, fictitious. **L17.**

> GLADSTONE A tradition, perhaps true, perhaps mythical, grew up, of Homer's blindness. P. B. CLARKE Rastas seem to prefer to ground themselves in a mythical interpretation of that past. *Daily Telegraph* What mystifies me is the mythical number of people we are told will be living in a certain area in the next 10 years.

2 Belonging to a period of which the accounts handed down are of the nature of myths; existing only in myth. **L17.**

> J. R. SEELEY As mythical as Hercules. V. S. NAIPAUL It was a time beyond recall, mythical.

■ **mythically** *adverb* in a mythical manner; by means of myths: **E19.**

mythicise *verb* var. of MYTHICIZE.

mythicism /ˈmɪθɪsɪz(ə)m/ *noun. rare.* **M19.**
[ORIGIN from MYTHIC + -ISM.]
The principle of attributing an origin in myth to narratives of supernatural events. Also, the tendency to create myths.

mythicist /ˈmɪθɪsɪst/ *noun.* **L19.**
[ORIGIN from MYTHIC + -IST.]
An adherent or student of mythicism; a student, interpreter, or creator of myths.

mythicize /ˈmɪθɪsʌɪz/ *verb trans.* Also **-ise. M19.**
[ORIGIN from MYTHIC + -IZE.]
Turn into myth or a myth; interpret mythically.

> *New Statesman* Accepting that imperialism itself is a lost cause, we are mythicising its administrators. D. CUPITT Jesus had been mythicised by the religious imagination of the early Christians.

■ **mythici'zation** *noun* **M20.** **mythicizer** *noun* **M19.**

mythico- /ˈmɪθɪkəʊ/ *combining form.* **M19.**
[ORIGIN from MYTHIC + -O-.]
Forming adjectives with the sense 'mythical and —', as ***mythico-historical***.

mythify /ˈmɪθɪfʌɪ/ *verb trans. rare.* **L19.**
[ORIGIN from MYTH + -I- + -FY.]
Construct a myth or myths about.
■ **mythifi'cation** *noun* **M19.**

mythist /ˈmɪθɪst/ *noun.* **M19.**
[ORIGIN from MYTH + -IST.]
= MYTHICIST.

mytho- /ˈmɪθəʊ/ *combining form.*
[ORIGIN from Greek *muthos* or directly from MYTH: see -O-.]
Of or pertaining to myth or myths.
■ **mythoclast** *noun* a person who destroys or discredits myths or a myth **L19.** **mytho'clastic** *adjective* destroying or discrediting myths or a myth **L19.** **mytho'genesis** *noun* the creation of myths **L19.** **mytho'genic** *adjective* of or pertaining to the creation of myths **M20.** **mythohe'roic** *adjective* concerned with mythical heroes **M19.** **mythomane** *noun* = MYTHOMANIAC **M20.** **mythomania** *noun* the condition or tendencies of a mythomaniac **E20.** **mythomaniac** *noun* (**a**) a person who is exceedingly interested in myths; a person with a tendency to create or disseminate myths; (**b**) a person who has an abnormal or pathological tendency to lie or exaggerate: **M19.** **mytho-the'ology** *noun* theology based on myth **E20.**

mythographer /mɪˈθɒgrəfə/ *noun.* **M17.**
[ORIGIN from Greek *muthographos*, formed as MYTHO-: see -GRAPHER.]
A writer, narrator, or collector of myths.

mythography /mɪˈθɒgrəfi/ *noun.* **M19.**
[ORIGIN Greek *muthographia*, formed as MYTHO-: see -GRAPHY.]
1 The representation or expression of mythical subjects in art, literature, etc. **M19.**
2 The collecting of myths; analysis of myths. Also, a collection of myths. **L19.**
3 The creation of a myth or myths. **E20.**
■ **mytho'graphic** *adjective* of or pertaining to mythography **L19.** **mytho'graphical** *adjective* = MYTHOGRAPHIC **E20.**

mythoi *noun* pl. of MYTHOS.

mythologem /mɪθəˈləʊdʒ(ə)m/ *noun.* **L19.**
[ORIGIN Greek *muthologēma*, from *muthologein* narrate myths, formed as MYTHO- + *logein* tell.]
A mythical story; a fundamental theme or motif of myth.

mythologer /mɪˈθɒlədʒə/ *noun.* **E17.**
[ORIGIN from French *mythologue* from Greek *muthologos*, formed as MYTHO- + -LOGUE: see -ER¹.]
A mythologist.

mythologian /mɪθəˈləʊdʒɪən, -dʒ(ə)n/ *noun. rare.* **L16.**
[ORIGIN from Latin *mythologus* from Greek *muthologos*: see MYTHOLOGER, -LOGY, -IAN.]
A mythologist.

mythologic /mɪθəˈlɒdʒɪk/ *adjective.* **M17.**
[ORIGIN Late Latin *mythologicus* from Greek *mythologikos*, from *muthologia* MYTHOLOGY: see -IC.]
Mythological.

mythological /mɪθəˈlɒdʒɪk(ə)l/ *adjective.* **E17.**
[ORIGIN formed as MYTHOLOGIC: see -ICAL.]
1 Of or pertaining to mythology; based on or of the nature of mythology or mythical narrative; having reference to a myth or to myths. **E17.**
2 Treated of or celebrated in mythology; found only in myths; fictitious, mythical. **E19.**
■ **mythologically** *adverb* in a mythological manner; in relation to or according to mythology; by means of a myth or myths: **M17.**

mythologise *verb* var. of MYTHOLOGIZE.

mythologist /mɪˈθɒlədʒɪst/ *noun.* **E17.**
[ORIGIN from MYTHOLOGY + -IST.]
1 A writer or creator of myths. **E17.**
2 An expert in or student of myths or mythology. **M17.**

mythologize /mɪˈθɒlədʒʌɪz/ *verb.* Also **-ise. E17.**
[ORIGIN French *mythologiser*, formed as MYTHOLOGY: see -IZE.]
▸ **I** *verb trans.* †**1** Interpret (a story or fable) with regard to mythological features; expound the symbolism of. **E17–E18.**
2 Represent or express mythologically. *rare.* **L17.**
3 Relate in a myth or myths; relate fictitiously. *rare.* **M18.**
4 Make mythical; convert into myth or mythology; make the subject of a myth, mythicize. **M19.**

> W. MCILVANNEY They had mythologised his past and falsified his present.

▸ **II** *verb intrans.* **5** Relate a myth or myths; construct a mythology. **E17.**
■ **mythologi'zation** *noun* **L19.** **mythologizer** *noun* **M17.**

mythology /mɪˈθɒlədʒi/ *noun.* **LME.**
[ORIGIN French *mythologie* or late Latin *mythologia* from Greek *muthologia*, formed as MYTHO- + -LOGY.]
†**1** **a** The exposition of myths; the interpretation of a fable. **LME–M17.** ▸†**b** A symbolical meaning (of a fable etc.). **E17–M18.**
2 A mythical story, a myth. Formerly also, a parable, an allegory. **E17.**

> P. B. CLARKE Biblical references . . underlay the development of Ethiopianism as a dynamic mythology.

3 Mythical stories or traditional beliefs collectively, myth. **M17.**

> W. H. PRESCOTT Mythology may be regarded as the poetry of religion. *Economist* The coal industry is something special . . in British labour practice and mythology.

4 A body or collection of myths, esp. relating to a particular person or subject, or belonging to a particular religious or cultural tradition; a set of beliefs. **L18.**

> A. G. GARDINER The goddess Aphrodite, according to ancient mythology, rose out of the foam of the sea. T. HILLERMAN He told her how the Navajo mythology dealt with it, how Monster Slayer and Child born of Water . . decided to spare one kind of death. D. JOHNSON 'Poets who live in Hell go to Heaven' . . . 'An interesting mythology begins to emerge.'

5 The branch of knowledge that deals with myths. **M19.**

mythopoeia /mɪθə(ʊ)ˈpiːə/ *noun.* **M20.**
[ORIGIN Greek *muthopoiia*, formed as MYTHO- + *poiein* make: see -IA¹.]
The creation of a myth or myths.
■ **mythopoeism** *noun* = MYTHOPOEIA **L19.** **mythopoeist** *noun* a creator of a myth or myths **L19.**

mythopoeic /mɪθə(ʊ)ˈpiːɪk/ *adjective*. M19.
[ORIGIN from Greek *muthopoios*, formed as MYTHO- + *poiein* make: see -IC.]
Creating a myth or myths; productive of myths; of or pertaining to the creation of a myth or myths.

mythopoesis /ˌmɪθəʊpəʊˈiːsɪs/ *noun*. L19.
[ORIGIN Greek *muthopoiēsis*, formed as MYTHO- + *poiēsis* making, from *po(i)ein* make, create.]
= MYTHOPOEIA.
■ **mythopoetic** *adjective* (**a**) = MYTHOPOEIC; (**b**) relating to or denoting a movement for men that uses activities such as story-telling and poetry reading as a means of self-understanding: L19. **mythopoetical** *adjective* = MYTHOPOEIC E20.

mythos /ˈmʌɪθɒs/ *noun*. Pl. **mythoi** /ˈmʌɪθɔɪ/. M18.
[ORIGIN Greek *muthos* MYTH. Cf. MYTHUS.]
1 = MYTH 1; a body of myths. *literary*. M18.
2 A traditional or recurrent narrative theme or pattern; a standard plot in literature. M20.

mythus /ˈmʌɪθəs/ *noun*. *literary*. Pl. **mythi** /ˈmʌɪθʌɪ/. E19.
[ORIGIN formed as MYTH. Cf. MYTHOS.]
= MYTH 1.

Mytilenaean /mɪtɪlɪˈniːən/ *noun* & *adjective*. Also **Mytilenean** /*also* mɪtɪˈliːnɪən/, **Mytilenian** /mɪtɪˈliːnɪən/. M16.
[ORIGIN from Latin *Mytilenaeus*, Greek *Mutilēnaios* of Mytilene (see below) + -AN.]
Of or pertaining to, a native or inhabitant of, the Aegean island of Lesbos (formerly Mytilene), the ancient city of Mytilene, on Lesbos, or modern Mytiline (Mitiline, Mitilíni), the capital of Lesbos.

myxa /ˈmɪksə/ *noun*. Now *rare* or *obsolete*. M16.
[ORIGIN Latin.]
The fruit of the Asian sebesten, *Cordia myxa*; the tree itself.

myxamoeba /mɪksəˈmiːbə/ *noun*. Also ***-meb-**. Pl. **-bae** /-biː/. L19.
[ORIGIN from MYX(O- + AMOEBA.]
MYCOLOGY. In certain slime moulds, a motile feeding cell lacking flagella but capable of amoeboid movement.
■ **myxamoeboid** *adjective* E20.

myxedema *noun* see MYXOEDEMA.

Myxine /mɪkˈsʌɪni, ˈmɪksiːn/ *noun*. E19.
[ORIGIN mod. Latin genus name from Greek *muxinos* slime fish, from *muxa* slime.]
A hagfish; *spec*. the Atlantic hagfish, *Myxine glutinosa*. Now chiefly as mod. Latin genus name.

myxinoid /ˈmɪksɪnɔɪd/ *adjective* & *noun*. M19.
[ORIGIN from MYXINE + -OID.]
ZOOLOGY. ▸**A** *adjective*. Of, pertaining to, or characteristic of the agnathan family Myxinidae, which comprises the hagfishes. M19.
▸**B** *noun*. A myxinoid fish, a hagfish. M19.

myxo /ˈmɪksəʊ/ *noun*. *Austral. colloq*. M20.
[ORIGIN Abbreviation: see -O. Cf. MYXY.]
Myxomatosis.

myxo- /ˈmɪksəʊ/ *combining form* of Greek *muxa* slime, mucus: see -O-. Before a vowel **myx-**.
■ **myxofiˈbroma** *noun*, pl. **-mas**, **-mata** /-mətə/, *MEDICINE* a fibroma containing myxomatous elements L19. **myxosarˈcoma** *noun*, pl. **-mas**, **-mata** /-mətə/, *MEDICINE* a sarcoma containing mucoid material E19.

myxobacterium /ˌmɪksəʊbakˈtɪərɪəm/ *noun*. Pl. **-ia** /-ɪə/. L19.
[ORIGIN from MYXO- + BACTERIUM.]
MICROBIOLOGY. A bacterium of the order Myxobacterales, which includes predominantly saprophytic Gram-negative bacteria having a vegetative state in which unicellular rods are embedded in slime, and forming spores often in distinct fruiting bodies. Also called ***slime bacterium***.
■ **myxobacterial** *adjective* M20.

myxococcus /mɪksəˈkɒkəs/ *noun*. Pl. **-cocci** /-ˈkɒk(s)ʌɪ, -ˈkɒk(s)iː/. L19.
[ORIGIN from MYXO- + COCCUS.]
MICROBIOLOGY. A myxobacterium of the genus *Myxococcus*.
■ **myxococcal** *adjective* M20.

myxoedema /mɪksɪˈdiːmə/ *noun*. Also ***myxed-**. L19.
[ORIGIN from MYX(O- + OEDEMA.]
MEDICINE. A syndrome caused by underactivity of the thyroid in adults, involving mental slowness, intolerance of cold, coarsening of the skin, and other symptoms. Also, a firm waxlike subcutaneous swelling associated with this.
■ **myxoedematous**, **myxoedemic** *adjectives* L19.

myxoid /ˈmɪksɔɪd/ *adjective*. L19.
[ORIGIN from MYXO- + -OID.]
MEDICINE. Resembling mucus, mucoid; containing or producing a lot of mucus.

myxoma /mɪkˈsəʊmə/ *noun*. Pl. **-mas**, **-mata** /-mətə/. M19.
[ORIGIN from MYXO- + -OMA.]
MEDICINE. A benign tumour of connective tissue, containing mucous or gelatinous material.
■ **myxomatous** *adjective* L19.

myxomatosis /mɪksəməˈtəʊsɪs/ *noun*. Pl. **-toses** /-ˈtəʊsiːz/. E20.
[ORIGIN from *myxomat-* (taken as stem of MYXOMA) + -OSIS.]
A highly infectious viral disease of rabbits characterized by fever, swelling of the mucous membranes, and the presence of myxomata.
■ ˈ**myxomatized** *adjective* infected with myxomatosis M20.

myxomycete /mɪksə(ʊ)ˈmʌɪsiːt/ *noun*. Pl. **-mycetes** /-ˈmʌɪsiːts, -mʌɪˈsiːtiːz/. L19.
[ORIGIN mod. Latin *Myxomycetes* (see below), formed as MYXO- + Greek *mukētes* pl. of *mukēs* fungus.]
MYCOLOGY. A slime mould; *spec*. an acellular slime mould of the class Myxomycetes, whose vegetative stage is a multinucleate plasmodium.
■ **myxomyˈcetan**, **myxomyˈcetous** *adjectives* L19.

myxophycean /mɪksə(ʊ)ˈfʌɪsɪən/ *adjective*. E20.
[ORIGIN from mod. Latin *Myxophyceae* (see below), formed as MYXO- + Greek *phukos* seaweed: see -AN.]
BIOLOGY. Of or pertaining to the class Myxophyceae (now Cyanophyceae), which comprises the cyanobacteria (or blue-green algae) when these are classified as plants.

myxospore /ˈmɪksəspɔː/ *noun*. M19.
[ORIGIN from MYXO- + SPORE.]
†**1** *BIOLOGY*. The spore of a myxomycete. Only in M19.
2 *MICROBIOLOGY*. A resting cell formed in response to adverse conditions by a myxobacterium. L20.

myxovirus /ˈmɪksə(ʊ)vʌɪrəs/ *noun*. M20.
[ORIGIN from MYXO- + VIRUS.]
BIOLOGY. Any of a group of related RNA viruses that includes the influenza virus. Orig. also, a paramyxovirus.

myxy /ˈmɪksi/ *noun* & *adjective*. *colloq*. M20.
[ORIGIN Abbreviation. Cf. MYXO.]
▸**A** *noun*. Myxomatosis. M20.
▸**B** *attrib*. or as *adjective*. Suffering from myxomatosis. M20.

myzont /ˈmʌɪzɒnt/ *noun*. *rare*. M19.
[ORIGIN from Greek *muzont-* pres. ppl stem of *muzein* suck.]
ZOOLOGY. = CYCLOSTOME.

myzostomid /mʌɪzə(ʊ)ˈstəʊmɪd/ *noun*. E20.
[ORIGIN from mod. Latin *Myzostomida*, from *Myzostomum* (see below), from Greek *muzein* suck + *stoma* mouth: see -ID[3].]
ZOOLOGY. Any of various small polychaete worms belonging to the genus *Myzostoma* and related genera, which have discoidal bodies with suckers and are ectoparasites of echinoderms, esp. crinoids.
■ Also ˈ**myzostome** *noun* (now *rare* or *obsolete*) L19.

mzee /(ə)mˈzeɪ/ *noun*. L19.
[ORIGIN Kiswahili = ancestor, parent, old person.]
In E. Africa: an older person, an elder. Also as a title of respect.

mzungu /(ə)mˈzʊŋgʊ/ *noun* & *adjective*. *E. Afr*. M19.
[ORIGIN Swahili, from *m-* class prefix + *-zungu* 'European'.]
▸**A** *noun*. A European, a white person. M19.
▸**B** *adjective*. Of or designating a white person; European. M19.

M